THE WORLD ALMANAC™

AND BOOK OF FACTS

2021

WORLD ALMANAC BOOKS

THE WORLD ALMANAC AND BOOK OF FACTS 2021

Executive Editor: Sarah Janssen
Index Editor: Nan Badgett
Contributors: Emily J. Dolbear, Robert Famighetti, Marshall Gerometta, Rebecca Godan, Jacqueline Laks Gorman, Richard Hantula, Andrew Hitchings, M. L. Liu, Laurence A. Marschall, John Mastroberardino, Lisa Mastropasqua, William A. McGeveran Jr., Janet M. Olson, John Rosenthal, Stevonnie Ross, Peter J. Schmidtke, George W. Smith IV, Edward A. Thomas, Lori P. Wiesenfeld

Production: Newgen North America
Design and Production, Year in Pictures: Chris Schultz, Skyhorse Publishing
Design, Cover: Takeshi Takahashi
Photo Research: Edward A. Thomas

The World Almanac™
An imprint of Skyhorse Publishing
www.skyhorsepublishing.com

Hardcover	Ebook	Paperback
ISBN-13: 978-1-5107-6138-4	ISBN-13: 978-1-5107-6140-7	ISBN-13: 978-1-5107-6139-1
ISBN-10: 1-5107-6138-1	ISBN-10: 1-5107-6140-3	ISBN-10: 1-5107-6139-X

International Standard Serial Number
0084-1382

The World Almanac™ and Book of Facts 2021
Book printed and bound by Bang Printing, Brainerd, MN
Date printed: November 2020
Printed in the United States of America
10 9 8 7 6 5 4 3 2 1

On Dec. 22, Pres. Trump signed a **tax-reform** measure reducing corporate and personal income tax rates. It also permitted oil drilling in Alaska's **Arctic National Wildlife Refuge** and repealed Obamacare's individual mandate.

The Dow Jones industrial average closed 2017 up 25% over the close of 2016.

2018 Michigan State Univ. sports physician **Larry Nasser** sentenced to up to 175 years, Jan. 24, after pleading guilty to decades of **sexual abuse** of young athletes; MSU later agreed to pay $500 mil to settle suits by 332 women and girls. In a mass shooting Feb. 14 at **Marjory Stoneman Douglas High School**, in Parkland, FL, 17 were killed and 17 wounded; an expelled student was arrested. Students protesting gun violence led **March for Our Lives** events, Mar. 24, in Washington, DC, and elsewhere.

Mueller probe led to indictment, Feb. 16, of Russian nationals on charges related to cyberattacks and interference in the 2016 U.S. election. Pres. Trump, Mar. 13, announced firing of Sec. of State **Rex Tillerson**; CIA Dir. **Mike Pompeo** was confirmed to succeed him. On Mar. 22 Trump ousted his national security adviser, Lt. Gen. **H. R. McMaster**, to be replaced by former UN Ambassador **John Bolton**, himself replaced in Sept. 2019.

Uber suspended its self-driving cars from four North American test cities after pedestrian fatality in Tempe, AZ, Mar. 18. Blaming **China** for intellectual property theft, U.S. Mar. 22 announced planned tariffs on some $50 bil of Chinese exports, heating up a U.S.-China **trade war**. Facebook CEO **Mark Zuckerberg** apologized before Congress, Apr. 10-11, after revelations that British consulting firm **Cambridge Analytica** had gained access to data from Facebook users allegedly provided to Trump's and other political campaigns.

In response to a reported **chemical weapons attack** by Syria's Assad regime, U.S., UK, and France launched airstrikes against suspected weapons production sites, Apr. 14. Federal regulators announced $1 bil in fines Apr. 20 against **Wells Fargo** for financial improprieties. A Pennsylvania jury found comedian **Bill Cosby** guilty Apr. 26 of aggravated indecent assault; sentenced to 3-10 years in prison.

U.S.-led coalition against **ISIS** Apr. 30 closed its land forces command headquarters in Iraq. Pres. Trump declared May 8 he was withdrawing U.S. from the **2015 Iran nuclear deal**, and later reimposed related economic sanctions. On May 18, eight students and two teachers were killed in shooting at a high school in **Santa Fe, TX**; a student was arrested and charged. **NFL** team owners May 23 announced players must either stand during national anthem or remain in locker room. Pres. Trump met with North Korean leader Kim Jong Un in Singapore June 12.

Following widespread criticism, Trump June 20 signed an executive order on end separation of **undocumented children** at the Mexican border. Former Roman Catholic archbishop **Theodore McCarrick** was removed from public ministry June 20, amid allegations of **sexual abuse**; he later resigned as a cardinal, and was laicized. A gunman arrested at the scene killed five employees and injured two at **Capital Gazette** offices in Annapolis, MD, June 28.

EPA administrator **Scott Pruitt** resigned July 5, amid multiple investigations into alleged financial improprieties. Justice Dept. charged 12 **Russian intelligence officers** July 13 with hacking the Clinton campaign and Democratic National Committee and leaking emails and data prior to the 2016 presidential election. Pres. Trump and Russian Pres. **Vladimir Putin** held summit in Helsinki, Finland, July 16.

A Pennsylvania grand jury Aug. 14 released report detailing seven decades of **clerical sexual abuse** and cover-up in

six Roman Catholic dioceses. Former Trump campaign chair **Paul Manafort**, found guilty Aug. 21 of **financial crimes**, including laundering $30 mil earned consulting for pro-Russian Ukrainian political party. Trump's former attorney **Michael Cohen** pleaded guilty Aug. 21 to campaign finance violations for **hush money** he said he paid to cover up Trump extramarital affairs. He also pleaded guilty Nov. 29 to lying to a Senate committee about timing of efforts to build a **Trump Tower** in Moscow.

Sen. **John McCain** (R, AZ) died Aug. 25 from brain cancer. On Oct. 2, Saudi dissident and journalist **Jamal Khashoggi**, a U.S. resident, entered the Saudi consulate in Istanbul, where he was apparently killed and dismembered; in response Trump administration imposed sanctions on 17 Saudi officials. A white Chicago police officer was convicted of second-degree murder, Oct. 5, in the 2014 shooting of Black teenager **Laquan McDonald**.

U.S. Senate, 50-48, Oct. 6 confirmed nomination of Judge **Brett Kavanaugh** to the U.S. Supreme Court, after volatile hearings in which psychology professor **Christine Blasey Ford** testified he had sexually assaulted her at a party when both were teenagers. **Sears** filed for bankruptcy Oct. 15. Authorities intercepted **package bombs** addressed to prominent Democrats and CNN, and, Oct. 26, arrested the suspected would-be bomber. A heavily armed man opened fire in **Tree of Life Congregation synagogue** in Pittsburgh, PA, Oct. 27, killing 11 people; the alleged gunman was arrested and charged.

On Oct. 29, Trump ordered 5,200 troops to the southern border to halt a caravan of **Central American migrants** and, Nov. 9, issued an order to deny asylum to migrants who crossed that border (enforcement suspended under court order). In Nov. 6 elections Democrats took control of the **U.S. House** Pres. Trump dismissed Attorney Gen. **Jeff Sessions** Nov. 7; **William Barr** confirmed to replace him.

An ex-Marine fatally shot 12 people at a bar in **Thousand Oaks**, CA, Nov. 7, then killed himself. **California's deadliest wildfire** yet, starting on Nov. 8, wiped out the town of **Paradise**; 85 people died, with losses put at $16.5 bil.

NASA's robotic *InSight* lander touched down on Mars, Nov. 26. **General Motors** Nov. 26 announced it would halt production at four U.S. plants. **Taliban** claimed responsibility for a Nov. 27 bomb in **Afghanistan** that killed three U.S. service members; a U.S. airstrike there that day reportedly caused about 30 Afghan civilian deaths. Hotel giant **Marriott** announced Nov. 30 that hackers had gained access to personal info of up to 500 mil guests.

Former Pres. **George H. W. Bush** died Nov. 30 at age 94. Pres. Trump announced Dec. 8 that White House chief of staff **John Kelly** would leave by year's end. Interior Sec. **Ryan Zinke** resigned Dec. 15 amid conflict of interest probe. Justice Dept. Dec. 18 banned **bump-fire stocks**, designed to allow faster firing of semiautomatic weapons.

On Dec. 19 Trump ordered withdrawal of some 2,000 U.S. troops in **Syria**, claiming victory over ISIS there (order later modified allowing some to remain). The next day, Defense Sec. **Jim Mattis**, in disagreement, announced he would resign; hours later plans were announced to withdraw some 7,000 U.S. troops, about half of the total, from **Afghanistan**.

Trump, Dec. 21, signed a bipartisan **criminal justice reform** bill reducing or eliminating mandatory minimum sentences for many drug-related federal crimes. An impasse over border-wall funding led to a partial federal government **shutdown**, Dec. 22, lasting a record 35 days.

2019 Trump administration, Feb. 1, announced it was suspending U.S. obligations under the 1987 Intermediate-Range Nuclear Forces **(INF) Treaty**. A U.S. federal jury, Feb. 12, convicted Mexican drug kingpin Joaquín **"El Chapo"** Guzmán of participation in murder conspiracies. NASA announced the end of its **Mars** *Opportunity* rover mission Feb. 13, after 15 years.

Pres. Trump Feb. 15 declared national state of emergency allowing reallocation of federal funds to construction of **border wall** with Mexico; U.S. Supreme Court, July 26, dismissed a legal challenge to that approach, but other litigation continued.

Among some two dozen candidates for the 2020 Democratic presidential nomination, Sen. **Bernie Sanders** (VT) announced his candidacy on Feb. 19, and former Vice Pres. **Joe Biden** on Apr. 28. Pres. **Trump** formally launched reelection campaign June 18.

Justice Dept. Mar. 12, charged some 50 people, including several celebrities, of involvement in **college admissions cheating schemes**.

2018: Pres. Donald Trump continued to call for construction of a new wall on the southern U.S. border.

2019: Former U.S. ambassador to Ukraine Marie Yovanovitch is among witnesses testifying in the House hearings on the impeachment of Pres. Donald Trump.

Reversing itself, the FAA Mar. 13 grounded **Boeing's 737 Max** aircraft, involved in fatal crashes in Ethiopia and Indonesia. The U.S.-backed **Syrian Democratic Forces** declared victory over ISIS in Syria, Mar. 23. Trump signed a proclamation Mar. 25 endorsing Israeli sovereignty over the disputed **Golan Heights.**

Disney Mar. 20 completed $71.3-bil acquisition of most of **21st Century Fox's** film and TV assets. **OxyContin** maker **Purdue Pharma** and its owners, the Sackler family, Mar. 26 agreed to pay $270 mil to settle suit brought by the state of Oklahoma for allegedly minimizing the drug's addictive potential. The company declared bankruptcy Sept. 15. **Apple** agreed Apr. 16 to pay wireless chipmaker **Qualcomm** at least $4.5 bil to settle a dispute over technology used in Apple iPhones.

Trump administration, Apr. 15, designated Iran's **Islamic Revolutionary Guard Corps** as a foreign terrorist organization. Trump Apr. 16 vetoed a congressional resolution, passed with some GOP support, to end U.S. involvement in a devastating civil war in **Yemen**, where a **Saudi Arabia**-led coalition defended the government against **Iran**-backed **Houthi** rebels.

Redacted version of special counsel Mueller's report on **Russian election interference**, released Apr. 18, found the Russian government had "worked to secure" Trump's election but not that the Trump campaign had conspired with it; the report detailed actions of Trump that could constitute obstruction of justice, while neither accusing him of a prosecutable crime nor exonerating him.

Pres. Trump May 10 increased **tariffs** on Chinese products; China reciprocated. Trump May 23 unveiled **bailout** package to aid U.S. farmers affected by tariffs.

Non-essential staff were evacuated May 15 from U.S. diplomatic facilities in **Iraq** over perceived threats from **Iran**, allegedly involved in attacks on oil tankers, a Saudi oil pipeline, and Baghdad's Green Zone. Trump, May 24, ordered more troops to the Mideast and declared tensions with Iran a national security emergency, allowing U.S. to complete **arms sales** to Saudi Arabia, United Arab Emirates, and Jordan.

On May 23 Justice Dept. announced charges against Australian **WikiLeaks** founder **Julian Assange**, arrested Apr. 11 at the Ecuadorian embassy in London after his asylum there was lifted. A disgruntled city employee shot and killed 12 people, in **Virginia Beach**, VA, May 31; he died in gun battle with police. The EPA, June 19, repealed Obama's signature **Clean Power Plan**, replacing it with weaker regulations for green house gas emissions from power plants. On June 20, Pres. Trump, after being warned of likely heavy civilian casualties, canceled airstrikes he had ordered against **Iran** following its downing of an unmanned U.S. drone.

In a book excerpt published June 21, writer E. Jean Carroll accused Trump of **sexual assault** in the 1990s.

In two 5-4 rulings, June 27, U.S. Supreme Court blocked plans to add a **citizenship question** to the 2020 census short form and barred a judicial role in limiting partisan **gerrymandering.**

Pres. Trump met June 30 with North Korean leader **Kim Jong Un** at the Demilitarized Zone (DMZ), and became the first sitting U.S. president to set foot inside **North Korea.** Trump July 1 signed a $4.6-bil package to help U.S. agencies deal with migrant surge at **U.S.-Mexican border.** He had threatened to veto an earlier version with stronger protections for **migrant children**, reportedly suffering from overcrowding and squalid conditions at border facilities.

U.S. **women's national soccer team** won a record fourth FIFA women's **World Cup** title July 7. Financier **Jeffrey**

Epstein was indicted, July 8, on federal charges of **sexual abuse** involving dozens of girls; he died Aug. 10 while in custody, in apparent suicide. Labor Sec. **Alexander Acosta** stepped down July 19 amid fallout over a 2008 plea deal he had negotiated with Epstein. **Mark Esper** was confirmed as defense sec., July 23, replacing **James Mattis**, who left office at the end of 2018.

Pres. Trump July 29 signed a measure overwhelmingly passed by Congress, extending benefits through 2092 for survivors and first responders of 9/11 terrorist attacks. Citing signs of global economic cooling, the Fed July 31 cut interest rates for the first time since 2008; two other cuts followed in Sept. and Oct.

On Aug. 3 a gunman reportedly targeting Mexicans fatally shot 23 people in all and injured over 20 at an **El Paso, TX, Walmart**, before surrendering. On Aug. 4 a gunman rapidly killed 9 people and injured 27 on a **Dayton, OH**, street before being fatally shot by police. Walmart said, Sept. 3, it would discontinue selling some ammunition and prohibit open carrying of guns.

As U.S.-China **trade war** heated up, Dow Jones industrial average, Aug. 5, fell 767 points; recession fears contributed to 800-point drop on Aug. 14. On Aug. 7 federal immigration authorities raided seven **chicken processing plants** in Mississippi, arresting 680 undocumented workers, in largest such single-state action.

Amid threats by Turkish Pres. **Recep Tayyip Erdogan** to strike **Kurdish militias** in Syria, U.S. and Turkish defense officials agreed Aug. 7 to create a safe zone in NE **Syria** as buffer to Turkey's southern border.

House Speaker **Nancy Pelosi** (D, CA) announced Sept. 24 that the House would launch a formal **impeachment inquiry** against Pres. Trump, following allegations from a whistleblower that he had used his office to pressure Ukraine Pres. **Volodymyr Zelensky** to investigate former Vice Pres. **Joe Biden**, a rival candidate for president, and the business dealings of Biden's son, **Hunter Biden**, in Ukraine. White House Sept. 25 released rough transcript of a July 25 phone call, in which Trump asked Zelensky to investigate the Bidens soon after the U.S. had withheld $400 mil in **aid to Ukraine**. A number of officials testified before House committees behind closed doors, and on Oct. 31 the House, with no GOP support, voted, 232-196, to formalize the inquiry, with procedures for **public hearings.**

Pres. Trump Sept. 7 announced cancellation of **peace talks** with the Afghan **Taliban**, after a bombing in which a U.S. soldier was killed. Talks resumed Dec. 7.

U.S. unemployment for Sept., reported Oct. 4, fell to 3.5%, **lowest unemployment rate** since 1969. In interim "phase-one" deal, Oct. 11, Trump relaxed some **tariffs** on imports from **China**, with China agreeing to buy some U.S. agricultural products. **Chicago public school teachers** went on strike Oct. 17; schools reopened Nov. 1 after tentative agreement. **United Auto Workers** members approved new contract with General Motors Oct. 25, ending a nearly six-week strike.

White House, Oct. 6, announced withdrawal of some U.S. troops from **N Syria** in the face of an imminent Turkish assault against **Kurdish** forces, which were allied with the U.S. against ISIS. U.S. House, in 354-60 vote, condemned the withdrawal. **ISIS** leader **Abu Bakr al-Baghdadi** killed during U.S. military raid on his compound in N Syria, Oct. 26.

On Nov. 17 a gunman shot ten people, killing four, in a **Fresno, CA**, backyard; several alleged gang members arrested. A **Saudi Arabian** military officer in flight training fatally shot three trainees Dec. 7 at U.S. naval base in **Pensacola, FL**; he was killed in gun battle.

Trump, Nov. 25, cleared three members of the armed services accused or convicted of **war crimes**, overruling military leaders. Justice Dept. **watchdog report**, released Dec. 6, found significant procedural errors in the FBI probe into **Russian election interference** but no political bias or evidence of conspiracy against Trump. Pres. Trump and the Chinese government, Dec. 13, confirmed a "phase one" deal aimed at easing U.S.-China **trade war.**

House Judiciary Committee, voting along party lines, Dec. 13, approved **articles of impeachment** against Pres. Trump for **abuse of power** and for **obstruction of Congress.** On Dec. 18 the full House, with no Republican support, passed the first article, 230-197, and the second 229-198.

The Dow Jones industrial average closed the year up 22.3%. U.S. Centers for Disease for Control reported 1,282 cases of **measles** for 2019, largest number in the U.S. since 1992.

U.S. HISTORY: DOCUMENTS, SPEECHES, AND SYMBOLS

Patrick Henry's Speech to the Virginia Convention

The following is an excerpt from Patrick Henry's speech to the Virginia Convention, which met at St. John's Church in Richmond, on Mar. 23, 1775, to react to British oppression.

Gentlemen may cry, Peace, Peace—but there is no peace. The war is actually begun! The next gale that sweeps from the north will bring to our ears the clash of resounding arms! Our brethren are already in the field! Why stand we here idle? What is it that gentlemen wish? What would they have? Is life so dear, or peace so sweet, as to be purchased at the price of chains and slavery? Forbid it, Almighty God! I know not what course others may take; but as for me, give me liberty, or give me death!

Adoption of the Declaration of Independence

On June 7, 1776, Richard Henry Lee, who had issued the first call for a congress of the colonies, introduced in the Continental Congress at Philadelphia a resolution declaring "that these United Colonies are, and of right ought to be, free and independent states, that they are absolved from all allegiance to the British Crown, and that all political connection between them and the state of Great Britain is, and ought to be, totally dissolved."

The resolution, seconded by John Adams on behalf of the Massachusetts delegation, came up again June 11 when a committee of five chaired by Thomas Jefferson (VA) was appointed to express the purpose of the resolution in a declaration of independence. The other four were John Adams, Benjamin Franklin (PA), Robert R. Livingston (NY), and Roger Sherman (CT).

Drafting the Declaration was assigned to Jefferson, who worked on a portable desk of his own construction in a room at Market and 7th St. The committee reported the result on June 28, 1776. The members of the Congress suggested a number of changes, which Jefferson called "deplorable." They did not approve Jefferson's arraignment of the British people and King George III for encouraging and fostering the slave trade, which Jefferson called "an execrable commerce." They eliminated 630 words and added 146, leaving 1,322 words in the final draft. In its final form, capitalization was erratic. Jefferson had written that men were endowed with "inalienable" rights; in the final copy it came out as "unalienable."

The Lee-Adams resolution of independence was adopted by 12 yeas on July 2—the actual date of the act of independence. The Declaration, which explains the act, was adopted July 4.

After the Declaration was adopted, July 4, 1776, it was turned over to printer John Dunlap to be printed on broadsides. The original copy was lost and one of his broadsides was attached to a page in the journal of the Congress. It was read aloud July 8 in Philadelphia; Easton, PA; and Trenton, NJ. On July 9, it was read by order of Gen. George Washington to the troops assembled on the Common in New York City (now City Hall Park).

The Continental Congress of July 19, 1776, adopted the following resolution:

"Resolved, That the Declaration passed on the 4th, be fairly engrossed on parchment with the title and stile of 'The Unanimous Declaration of the thirteen United States of America' and that the same, when engrossed, be signed by every member of Congress." (Engrossing meant clearly writing out an official document.)

Not all delegates who signed the engrossed Declaration had been present on July 4. Among them were Robert Morris (PA), William Williams (CT), and Samuel Chase (MD), who signed on Aug. 2. Oliver Wolcott (CT), George Wythe (VA), Richard Henry Lee (VA), and Elbridge Gerry (MA) signed in Aug. and Sept.; Matthew Thornton (NH) joined the Congress Nov. 4 and signed later. Thomas McKean (DE) rejoined Washington's army before signing and said later that he signed in 1781.

Charles Carroll of Carrollton was appointed a delegate by Maryland on July 4, 1776, presented his credentials July 18, and signed the engrossed Declaration on Aug. 2. Born Sept. 19, 1737, he was 95 years old and the last surviving signer when he died Nov. 14, 1832.

Two Pennsylvania delegates who did not support the Declaration July 4, 1776, were replaced. The four New York delegates did not have authority from their state to vote on July 4. On July 9, the New York state convention authorized its delegates to approve the Declaration, and the Congress was so notified on July 15, 1776. The four signed the Declaration on Aug. 2.

Declaration of Independence

The Declaration of Independence was adopted by the Continental Congress in Philadelphia on July 4, 1776. John Hancock was president of the Congress, and Charles Thomson was secretary. A copy of the Declaration, engrossed (i.e., written in a clear hand) on parchment, was signed by members of Congress on and after Aug. 2, 1776. On Jan. 18, 1777, Congress ordered that "an authenticated copy, with the names of the members of Congress subscribing the same, be sent to each of the United States, and that they be desired to have the same put on record." Authenticated copies were printed in broadside form in Baltimore, where the Continental Congress was then in session. The following text is that of the original printed by John Dunlap in Philadelphia for the Continental Congress. The original is on display at the National Archives in Washington, DC.

In CONGRESS, July 4, 1776.
A DECLARATION
By the REPRESENTATIVES of the
UNITED STATES OF AMERICA,
In GENERAL CONGRESS assembled.

When in the Course of human Events, it becomes necessary for one People to dissolve the Political Bands which have connected them with another, and to assume among the Powers of the Earth, the separate and equal Station to which the Laws of Nature and of Nature's God entitle them, a decent Respect to the Opinions of Mankind requires that they should declare the causes which impel them to the Separation.

We hold these Truths to be self-evident, that all Men are created equal, that they are endowed by their Creator with certain unalienable Rights, that among these are Life, Liberty, and the Pursuit of Happiness—That to secure these Rights, Governments are instituted among Men, deriving their just Powers from the Consent of the Governed, that whenever any Form of Government becomes destructive of these Ends, it is the Right of the People to alter or to abolish it, and to institute new Government, laying its Foundation on such Principles, and organizing its Powers in such Form, as to them shall seem most likely to effect their Safety and Happiness. Prudence, indeed, will dictate that Governments long established should not be changed for light and transient Causes; and accordingly all Experience hath shewn, that Mankind are more disposed to suffer, while Evils are sufferable, than to right themselves by abolishing the Forms to which they are accustomed. But when a long Train of Abuses and Usurpations, pursuing invariably the same Object, evinces a Design to reduce them under absolute Despotism, it is their Right, it is their Duty, to throw off such Government, and to provide new Guards for their future Security. Such has been the patient Sufferance of these Colonies; and such is now the Necessity which constrains them to alter their former Systems of Government. The History of the present King of Great-Britain is a History of repeated Injuries and Usurpations, all having in direct Object the Establishment of an absolute Tyranny over these States. To prove this, let Facts be submitted to a candid World.

He has refused his Assent to Laws, the most wholesome and necessary for the public Good.

He has forbidden his Governors to pass Laws of immediate and pressing Importance, unless suspended in their Operation till his Assent should be obtained; and when so suspended, he has utterly neglected to attend to them.

He has refused to pass other Laws for the Accommodation of large Districts of People, unless those People would relinquish the Right of Representation in the Legislature, a Right inestimable to them, and formidable to Tyrants only.

He has called together Legislative Bodies at Places unusual, uncomfortable, and distant from the Depository of their Public Records, for the sole Purpose of fatiguing them into Compliance with his Measures.

He has dissolved Representative Houses repeatedly, for opposing with manly Firmness his Invasions on the Rights of the People.

He has refused for a long Time, after such Dissolutions, to cause others to be elected; whereby the Legislative Powers, incapable of Annihilation, have returned to the People at large for their exercise; the State remaining in the mean time exposed to all the Dangers of Invasion from without, and Convulsions within.

He has endeavoured to prevent the Population of these States; for that Purpose obstructing the Laws for Naturalization of Foreigners; refusing to pass others to encourage their Migrations hither, and raising the Conditions of new Appropriations of Lands.

He has obstructed the Administration of Justice, by refusing his Assent to Laws for establishing Judiciary Powers.

He has made Judges dependent on his Will alone, for the Tenure of their Offices, and the Amount and Payment of their Salaries.

He has erected a Multitude of new Offices, and sent hither Swarms of Officers to harrass our People, and eat out their Substance.

He has kept among us, in Times of Peace, Standing Armies, without the consent of our Legislatures.

He has affected to render the Military independent of and superior to the Civil Power.

He has combined with others to subject us to a Jurisdiction foreign to our Constitution, and unacknowledged by our Laws; giving his Assent to their Acts of pretended Legislation:

For quartering large Bodies of Armed Troops among us:

For protecting them, by a mock Trial, from Punishment for any Murders which they should commit on the Inhabitants of these States:

For cutting off our Trade with all Parts of the World:

For imposing Taxes on us without our Consent:

For depriving us, in many Cases, of the Benefits of Trial by Jury:

For transporting us beyond Seas to be tried for pretended Offences:

For abolishing the free System of English Laws in a neighbouring Province, establishing therein an arbitrary Government, and enlarging its Boundaries, so as to render it at once an Example and fit Instrument for introducing the same absolute Rule into these Colonies:

For taking away our Charters, abolishing our most valuable Laws, and altering fundamentally the Forms of our Governments:

For suspending our own Legislatures, and declaring themselves invested with Power to legislate for us in all Cases whatsoever.

He has abdicated Government here, by declaring us out of his Protection and waging War against us.

He has plundered our Seas, ravaged our Coasts, burnt our Towns, and destroyed the Lives of our People.

He is, at this Time, transporting large Armies of foreign Mercenaries to compleat the Works of Death, Desolation, and Tyranny, already begun with circumstances of Cruelty

and Perfidy, scarcely paralleled in the most barbarous Ages, and totally unworthy the Head of a civilized Nation.

He has constrained our fellow Citizens taken Captive on the high Seas to bear Arms against their Country, to become the Executioners of their Friends and Brethren, or to fall themselves by their Hands.

He has excited domestic Insurrections amongst us, and has endeavoured to bring on the Inhabitants of our Frontiers, the merciless Indian Savages, whose known Rule of Warfare, is an undistinguished Destruction, of all Ages, Sexes and Conditions.

In every stage of these Oppressions we have Petitioned for Redress in the most humble Terms: Our repeated Petitions have been answered only by repeated Injury. A Prince, whose Character is thus marked by every act which may define a Tyrant, is unfit to be the Ruler of a free People.

Nor have we been wanting in Attentions to our British Brethren. We have warned them from Time to Time of Attempts by their Legislature to extend an unwarrantable Jurisdiction over us. We have reminded them of the Circumstances of our Emigration and Settlement here. We have appealed to their native Justice and Magnanimity, and we have conjured them by the Ties of our common Kindred to disavow these Usurpations, which, would inevitably interrupt our Connections and Correspondence. They too have been deaf to the Voice of Justice and of Consanguinity. We must, therefore, acquiesce in the Necessity, which denounces our Separation, and hold them, as we hold the rest of Mankind, Enemies in War, in Peace, Friends.

We, therefore, the Representatives of the UNITED STATES OF AMERICA, in General Congress, Assembled, appealing to the Supreme Judge of the World for the Rectitude of our Intentions, do, in the Name, and by Authority of the good People of these Colonies, solemnly Publish and Declare, That these United Colonies are, and of Right ought to be, Free and Independent States; that they are absolved from all Allegiance to the British Crown, and that all political Connection between them and the State of Great-Britain, is and ought to be totally dissolved; and that as Free and Independent States, they have full Power to levy War, conclude Peace, contract Alliances, establish Commerce, and to do all other Acts and Things which Independent States may of right do. And for the support of this Declaration, with a firm Reliance on the Protection of divine Providence, we mutually pledge to each other our Lives, our Fortunes, and our sacred Honor.

JOHN HANCOCK, President.

Attest.

CHARLES THOMSON, Secretary.

Signers of the Declaration of Independence

Delegate (state)	Occupation	Birthplace	Born	Died
Adams, John (MA)	Lawyer	Braintree (Quincy), MA	Oct. 30, 1735	July 4, 1826
Adams, Samuel (MA)	Merchant, brewer	Boston, MA	Sept. 27, 1722	Oct. 2, 1803
Bartlett, Josiah (NH)	Physician, judge	Amesbury, MA	Nov. 21, 1729	May 19, 1795
Braxton, Carter (VA)	Plantation owner	Newington Plantation, VA	Sept. 10, 1736	Oct. 10, 1797
Carroll, Charles, of Carrollton (MD)	Plantation owner	Annapolis, MD	Sept. 19, 1737	Nov. 14, 1832
Chase, Samuel (MD)	Lawyer, judge	Princess Anne, MD	Apr. 17, 1741	June 19, 1811
Clark, Abraham (NJ)	Surveyor	Elizabethtown, NJ	Feb. 15, 1726	Sept. 15, 1794
Clymer, George (PA)	Merchant	Philadelphia, PA	Mar. 16, 1739	Jan. 23, 1813
Ellery, William (RI)	Lawyer	Newport, RI	Dec. 22, 1727	Feb. 15, 1820
Floyd, William (NY)	Plantation owner, soldier	Brookhaven, NY	Dec. 17, 1734	Aug. 4, 1821
Franklin, Benjamin (PA)	Printer, inventor	Boston, MA	Jan. 17, 1706	Apr. 17, 1790
Gerry, Elbridge (MA)	Merchant	Marblehead, MA	July 17, 1744	Nov. 23, 1814
Gwinnett, Button (GA)	Merchant	Gloucester, England	c. 1735	May 19, 1777
Hall, Lyman (GA)	Physician	Wallingford, CT	Apr. 12, 1724	Oct. 19, 1790
Hancock, John (MA)	Merchant	Braintree (Quincy), MA	Jan. 12, 1737	Oct. 8, 1793
Harrison, Benjamin (VA)	Plantation owner	Charles City County, VA	Apr. 5, 1726	Apr. 24, 1791
Hart, John (NJ)	Plantation owner	Stonington, CT	c. 1713	May 11, 1779
Hewes, Joseph (NC)	Merchant	Kingston, NJ	Jan. 23, 1730	Nov. 10, 1779
Heyward, Thomas, Jr. (SC)	Lawyer, plantation owner	St. Luke's Parish, SC	July 28, 1746	Mar. 6, 1809
Hooper, William (NC)	Lawyer	Boston, MA	June 17, 1742	Oct. 14, 1790
Hopkins, Stephen (RI)	Judge, merchant	Providence, RI	Mar. 7, 1707	July 13, 1785
Hopkinson, Francis (NJ)	Composer, lawyer	Philadelphia, PA	Oct. 2, 1737	May 9, 1791
Huntington, Samuel (CT)	Lawyer, judge	Windham, CT	July 3, 1731	Jan. 5, 1796
Jefferson, Thomas (VA)	Lawyer, plantation owner	Shadwell, VA	Apr. 13, 1743	July 4, 1826
Lee, Francis Lightfoot (VA)	Plantation owner	Westmoreland County, VA	Oct. 14, 1734	Jan. 11, 1797
Lee, Richard Henry (VA)	Plantation owner	Westmoreland County, VA	Jan. 20, 1732	June 19, 1794
Lewis, Francis (NY)	Merchant	Llandaff, Wales	Mar. 21, 1713	Dec. 31, 1802
Livingston, Philip (NY)	Merchant	Albany, NY	Jan. 15, 1716	June 12, 1778
Lynch, Thomas, Jr. (SC)	Plantation owner	Winyah, SC	Aug. 5, 1749	(at sea) 1779
McKean, Thomas (DE)	Lawyer	New London, PA	Mar. 19, 1734	June 24, 1817
Middleton, Arthur (SC)	Plantation owner	Charleston, SC	June 26, 1742	Jan. 1, 1787
Morris, Lewis (NY)	Farmer, judge	Morrisania (Bronx County), NY	Apr. 8, 1726	Jan. 22, 1798
Morris, Robert (PA)	Merchant	Liverpool, England	Jan. 31, 1734	May 8, 1806
Morton, John (PA)	Surveyor	Ridley, PA	c. 1724	Apr. 1777
Nelson, Thomas, Jr. (VA)	Merchant	Yorktown, VA	Dec. 26, 1738	Jan. 4, 1789
Paca, William (MD)	Lawyer, judge	Abingdon, MD	Oct. 31, 1740	Oct. 23, 1799
Paine, Robert Treat (MA)	Lawyer, judge	Boston, MA	Mar. 11, 1731	May 11, 1814
Penn, John (NC)	Lawyer	Caroline County, VA	May 17, 1741	Sept. 14, 1788
Read, George (DE)	Lawyer, judge	Cecil County, MD	Sept. 18, 1733	Sept. 21, 1798
Rodney, Caesar (DE)	Farmer, judge	Dover, DE	Oct. 7, 1728	June 26, 1784
Ross, George (PA)	Lawyer, judge	New Castle, DE	May 10, 1730	July 14, 1779
Rush, Benjamin (PA)	Physician	Byberry Twp. (Philadelphia), PA	Jan. 4, 1746	Apr. 19, 1813
Rutledge, Edward (SC)	Lawyer, plantation owner	Charleston, SC	Nov. 23, 1749	Jan. 23, 1800
Sherman, Roger (CT)	Lawyer, judge	Newton, MA	Apr. 19, 1721	July 23, 1793
Smith, James (PA)	Lawyer	Ireland	c. 1719	July 11, 1806
Stockton, Richard (NJ)	Lawyer	Princeton, NJ	Oct. 1, 1730	Feb. 28, 1781
Stone, Thomas (MD)	Lawyer	Charles County, MD	c. 1743	Oct. 5, 1787
Taylor, George (PA)	Iron mfr., judge	Ireland	c. 1716	Feb. 23, 1781
Thornton, Matthew (NH)	Physician	Ireland	c. 1714	June 24, 1803
Walton, George (GA)	Lawyer, judge	Cumberland County, VA	c. 1749	Feb. 2, 1804
Whipple, William (NH)	Merchant, judge	Kittery, ME	Jan. 14, 1730	Nov. 28, 1785
Williams, William (CT)	Merchant	Lebanon, CT	c. 1731	Aug. 2, 1811
Wilson, James (PA)	Lawyer	Carskerdo, Scotland	Sept. 14, 1742	Aug. 21, 1798
Witherspoon, John (NJ)	Clergyman, educator	Gifford, Scotland	Feb. 5, 1723	Nov. 15, 1794
Wolcott, Oliver (CT)	Lawyer, judge	Windsor, CT	Nov. 20, 1726	Dec. 1, 1797
Wythe, George (VA)	Lawyer	Elizabeth City County, VA	c. 1726	June 8, 1806

Origin of the Constitution

The War of Independence was conducted by delegates from the original 13 states, who composed the Congress of the United States of America, known as the Continental Congress. In 1777 the Congress submitted to the legislatures of the states the Articles of Confederation and Perpetual Union, which were ratified by New Hampshire, Massachusetts, Rhode Island, Connecticut, New York, New Jersey, Pennsylvania, Delaware, Virginia, North Carolina, South Carolina, Georgia, and finally, in 1781, Maryland.

The first article read: "The stile of this confederacy shall be the United States of America." This did not signify a sovereign nation, because the states delegated only those powers they could not handle individually, such as to wage war, make treaties, and contract debts for general expenses (e.g., paying the army). Taxes for payment of such debts were levied by the individual states. The president signed himself "President of the United States in Congress assembled," but here the United States were considered in the plural, a cooperating group.

When the war was over, it became evident that a stronger federal union was needed. The Congress left the initiative to the legislatures. Virginia in Jan. 1786 appointed commissioners to meet with representatives of other states; delegates from Virginia, Delaware, New York, New Jersey, and Pennsylvania met at Annapolis. Alexander Hamilton prepared their call asking delegates from all states to meet in Philadelphia in May 1787 "to render the Constitution of the federal government adequate to the exigencies of the union." Congress endorsed the plan on Feb. 21, 1787. Delegates were appointed by all states except Rhode Island.

The convention was called for May 14, 1787, but a quorum was not present until May 25. George Washington was chosen president (presiding officer). The states certified 65 delegates, but 10 did not attend. The work was done by 55, not all of whom were present at all sessions. Of the 55 attending delegates, 39 signed Sept. 17, 1787, some with reservations, and 16 failed to sign. Some historians have said 74 delegates (nine more than the 65 actually certified) were named, and 19 failed to attend. These additional persons refused the appointment, were never delegates, and were never counted as absentees. Washington sent the Constitution to Congress, and that body, Sept. 28, 1787, ordered it sent to the legislatures, "in order to be submitted to a convention of delegates chosen in each state by the people thereof."

The Constitution was ratified by the votes of each state's convention as follows: Delaware, Dec. 7, 1787, unanimous; Pennsylvania, Dec. 12, 1787, 46 to 23; New Jersey, Dec. 18, 1787, unanimous; Georgia, Jan. 2, 1788, unanimous; Connecticut, Jan. 9, 1788, 128 to 40; Massachusetts, Feb. 6, 1788, 187 to 168; Maryland, Apr. 28, 1788, 63 to 11; South Carolina, May 23, 1788, 149 to 73; New Hampshire, June 21, 1788, 57 to 46; Virginia, June 25, 1788, 89 to 79; New York, July 26, 1788, 30 to 27. Nine states were needed to establish the operation of the Constitution "between the states so ratifying the same," and New Hampshire was the ninth state. The government did not declare the Constitution in effect until the first Wednesday in Mar. 1789, which was Mar. 4. After that, North Carolina ratified it on Nov. 21, 1789, 194 to 77; and Rhode Island, May 29, 1790, 34 to 32. Vermont in convention ratified it on Jan. 10, 1791, and by act of Congress approved on Feb. 18, 1791, was admitted into the Union as the 14th state, Mar. 4, 1791.

Constitution of the United States

The text of the Constitution given here is from the centennial edition of *The Constitution of the United States of America: Analysis and Interpretation*, prepared by the Library of Congress and issued by the U.S. Government Printing Office. Aug. 26, 2017. Text in brackets indicates that an item has been superseded or amended, or provides background information. **Boldface text** preceding an article, section, or amendment is a brief summary, added by *The World Almanac*.

The Original Seven Articles

PREAMBLE

We the People of the United States, in Order to form a more perfect Union, establish Justice, insure domestic Tranquility, provide for the common defence, promote the general Welfare, and secure the Blessings of Liberty to ourselves and our Posterity, do ordain and establish this Constitution for the United States of America.

ARTICLE I.

Section 1—Legislative powers, in whom vested.

All legislative Powers herein granted shall be vested in a Congress of the United States, which shall consist of a Senate and House of Representatives.

Section 2—House of Representatives, how and by whom chosen. Qualifications of a Representative. Representatives and direct taxes, how apportioned and enumerated. Vacancies to be filled. Choosing of officers and power of impeachment.

The House of Representatives shall be composed of Members chosen every second Year by the People of the several States, and the Electors in each State shall have the Qualifications requisite for Electors of the most numerous Branch of the State Legislature.

No Person shall be a Representative who shall not have attained to the Age of twenty five Years, and been seven Years a Citizen of the United States, and who shall not, when elected, be an Inhabitant of that State in which he shall be chosen.

[Representatives and direct Taxes shall be apportioned among the several States which may be included within this Union, according to their respective Numbers, which shall be determined by adding to the whole Number of free Persons, including those bound to Service for a Term of Years, and excluding Indians not taxed, three fifths of all other Persons.] *[The part of the previous sentence regarding apportionment of representatives among the states was changed by Amendment XIV, section 2, and apportionment of taxes by Amendment XVI.]* The actual Enumeration shall be made within three Years after the first Meeting of the Congress of the United States, and within every subsequent Term of ten Years, in such Manner as they shall by Law direct. The Number of Representatives shall not exceed one for every thirty Thousand, but each State shall have at Least one Representative; and until such enumeration shall be made, the State of New Hampshire shall be entitled to chuse three, Massachusetts eight, Rhode-Island and Providence Plantations one, Connecticut five, New York six, New Jersey four, Pennsylvania eight, Delaware one, Maryland six, Virginia ten, North Carolina five, South Carolina five, and Georgia three.

When vacancies happen in the Representation from any State, the Executive Authority thereof shall issue Writs of Election to fill such Vacancies.

The House of Representatives shall chuse their Speaker and other Officers; and shall have the sole Power of Impeachment.

Section 3—Senators, how and by whom chosen. How assembled. Qualifications of a Senator. President of the Senate. President pro tempore and other officers of the Senate, how chosen. Power to try impeachments. Judgment in cases of impeachment.

The Senate of the United States shall be composed of two Senators from each State, [chosen by the Legislature] *[The preceding words were superseded by Amendment XVII.]* thereof, for six Years; and each Senator shall have one Vote.

Immediately after they shall be assembled in Consequence of the first Election, they shall be divided as equally as may be into three Classes. The Seats of the Senators of the first Class shall be vacated at the Expiration of the second Year, of the second Class at the Expiration of the fourth Year, and of the third Class at the Expiration of the sixth Year, so that one third may be chosen every second Year; [and if Vacancies happen by Resignation, or otherwise, during the Recess of the Legislature of any State, the Executive thereof may make temporary Appointments until the next Meeting of the Legislature, which shall then fill such Vacancies.] *[The words in brackets were superseded by Amendment XVII.]*

No Person shall be a Senator who shall not have attained to the Age of thirty Years, and been nine Years a Citizen of the United States, and who shall not, when elected, be an Inhabitant of that State for which he shall be chosen.

The Vice President of the United States shall be President of the Senate, but shall have no Vote, unless they be equally divided.

The Senate shall chuse their other Officers, and also a President pro tempore, in the Absence of the Vice President, or when he shall exercise the Office of President of the United States.

The Senate shall have the sole Power to try all Impeachments. When sitting for that Purpose, they shall be on Oath or Affirmation. When the President of the United States is tried, the Chief Justice shall preside: And no Person shall be convicted without the Concurrence of two thirds of the Members present.

Judgment in Cases of Impeachment shall not extend further than to removal from Office, and disqualification to hold and enjoy any Office of honor, Trust or Profit under the United States: but the Party convicted shall nevertheless be liable and subject to Indictment, Trial, Judgment and Punishment, according to Law.

Section 4—Times, places, manner of elections. Time of assembly.

The Times, Places and Manner of holding Elections for Senators and Representatives, shall be prescribed in each State by the Legislature thereof; but the Congress may at any time by Law make or alter such Regulations, except as to the Places of chusing Senators.

The Congress shall assemble at least once in every Year, and such Meeting shall be [on the first Monday in December], *[The words in brackets were superseded by Amendment XX, section 2.]* unless they shall by Law appoint a different Day.

Section 5—Membership, quorums, adjournments. Rules of proceedings. Journal of proceedings. Time of adjournments.

Each House shall be the Judge of the Elections, Returns and Qualifications of its own Members, and a Majority of each shall constitute a Quorum to do Business; but a smaller Number may adjourn from day to day, and may be authorized to compel the Attendance of absent Members, in such Manner, and under such Penalties as each House may provide.

Each House may determine the Rules of its Proceedings, punish its Members for disorderly Behaviour, and, with the Concurrence of two thirds, expel a Member.

Each House shall keep a Journal of its Proceedings, and from time to time publish the same, excepting such Parts as may in their Judgment require Secrecy; and the Yeas and Nays of the Members of either House on any question shall, at the Desire of one fifth of those Present, be entered on the Journal.

Neither House, during the Session of Congress, shall, without the Consent of the other, adjourn for more than three days, nor to any other Place than that in which the two Houses shall be sitting.

Section 6—Compensation, privileges. Incompatible offices.

The Senators and Representatives shall receive a Compensation for their Services, to be ascertained by Law, and paid out of the Treasury of the United States. They shall in all Cases, except Treason, Felony and Breach of the Peace, be privileged from Arrest during their Attendance at the Session of their respective Houses, and in going to and returning from the same; and for any Speech or Debate in either House, they shall not be questioned in any other Place.

No Senator or Representative shall, during the Time for which he was elected, be appointed to any civil Office under the Authority of the United States, which shall have been created, or the Emoluments whereof shall have been encreased during such time; and no Person holding any Office under the United States, shall be a Member of either House during his Continuance in Office.

Section 7—House to originate revenue bills. Legislative process; bill presented to the President before becoming law. Passing of bill over objections of President, veto.

All Bills for raising Revenue shall originate in the House of Representatives; but the Senate may propose or concur with Amendments as on other Bills.

Every Bill which shall have passed the House of Representatives and the Senate, shall, before it become a Law, be presented to the President of the United States; If he approve he shall sign it, but if not he shall return it, with his Objections to that House in which it shall have originated, who shall enter the Objections at large on their Journal, and proceed to reconsider it. If after such Reconsideration two thirds of that House shall agree to pass the Bill, it shall be sent, together with the Objections, to the other House, by which it shall likewise be reconsidered, and if approved by two thirds of that House, it shall become a Law. But in all such Cases the Votes of both Houses shall be determined by Yeas and Nays, and the Names of the Persons voting for and against the Bill shall be entered on the Journal of each House respectively. If any Bill shall not be returned by the President within ten Days (Sundays excepted) after it shall have been presented to him, the Same shall be a Law, in like Manner as if he had signed it, unless the Congress by their Adjournment prevent its Return, in which Case it shall not be a Law.

Every Order, Resolution, or Vote to which the Concurrence of the Senate and House of Representatives may be necessary (except on a question of Adjournment) shall be presented to the President of the United States; and before the Same shall take Effect, shall be approved by him, or being disapproved by him, shall be repassed by two thirds of the Senate and House of Representatives, according to the Rules and Limitations prescribed in the Case of a Bill.

Section 8—Powers of Congress.

The Congress shall have Power To lay and collect Taxes, Duties, Imposts and Excises, to pay the Debts and provide for the common Defence and general Welfare of the United States; but all Duties, Imposts and Excises shall be uniform throughout the United States;

To borrow Money on the credit of the United States;

To regulate Commerce with foreign Nations, and among the several States, and with the Indian Tribes;

To establish an uniform Rule of Naturalization, and uniform Laws on the subject of Bankruptcies throughout the United States;

To coin Money, regulate the Value thereof, and of foreign Coin, and fix the Standard of Weights and Measures;

To provide for the Punishment of counterfeiting the Securities and current Coin of the United States;

To establish Post Offices and post Roads;

To promote the Progress of Science and useful Arts, by securing for limited Times to Authors and Inventors the exclusive Right to their respective Writings and Discoveries;

To constitute Tribunals inferior to the supreme Court;

To define and punish Piracies and Felonies committed on the high Seas, and Offences against the Law of Nations;

To declare War, grant Letters of Marque and Reprisal, and make Rules concerning Captures on Land and Water;

To raise and support Armies, but no Appropriation of Money to that Use shall be for a longer Term than two Years;

To provide and maintain a Navy;

To make Rules for the Government and Regulation of the land and naval Forces;

To provide for calling forth the Militia to execute the Laws of the Union, suppress Insurrections and repel Invasions;

To provide for organizing, arming, and disciplining, the Militia, and for governing such Part of them as may be employed in the Service of the United States, reserving to the States respectively, the Appointment of the Officers, and the Authority of training the Militia according to the discipline prescribed by Congress;

To exercise exclusive Legislation in all Cases whatsoever, over such District (not exceeding ten Miles square) as may, by Cession of particular States, and the Acceptance of Congress, become the Seat of the Government of the United States, and to exercise like Authority over all Places purchased by the Consent of the Legislature of the State in which the Same shall be, for the Erection of Forts, Magazines, Arsenals, dock-Yards, and other needful Buildings;—And

To make all Laws which shall be necessary and proper for carrying into Execution the foregoing Powers, and all other Powers vested by this Constitution in the Government of the United States, or in any Department or Officer thereof.

Section 9—Powers denied to Congress: Importation of slaves. Habeas corpus. Bills of attainder. Taxes, how apportioned. Export duty. Preference to ports. Money, how drawn from Treasury. Titles of nobility.

The Migration or Importation of such Persons as any of the States now existing shall think proper to admit, shall not be prohibited by the Congress prior to the Year one thousand eight hundred and eight, but a Tax or duty may be imposed on such Importation, not exceeding ten dollars for each Person.

The Privilege of the Writ of Habeas Corpus shall not be suspended, unless when in Cases of Rebellion or Invasion the public Safety may require it.

No Bill of Attainder or ex post facto Law shall be passed.

No Capitation, or other direct, Tax shall be laid, unless in Proportion to the Census or Enumeration herein before directed to be taken.

No Tax or Duty shall be laid on Articles exported from any State.

No Preference shall be given by any Regulation of Commerce or Revenue to the Ports of one State over those of another: nor shall Vessels bound to, or from, one State, be obliged to enter, clear, or pay Duties in another.

No Money shall be drawn from the Treasury, but in Consequence of Appropriations made by Law; and a regular Statement and Account of the Receipts and Expenditures of all public Money shall be published from time to time.

No Title of Nobility shall be granted by the United States: And no Person holding any Office of Profit or Trust under them, shall, without the Consent of the Congress, accept of any present, Emolument, Office, or Title, of any kind whatever, from any King, Prince, or foreign State.

Section 10—States prohibited from the exercise of certain powers.

No State shall enter into any Treaty, Alliance, or Confederation; grant Letters of Marque and Reprisal; coin Money; emit Bills of Credit; make any Thing but gold and silver Coin a Tender in Payment of Debts; pass any Bill of Attainder, ex post facto Law, or Law impairing the Obligation of Contracts, or grant any Title of Nobility.

No State shall, without the Consent of the Congress, lay any Imposts or Duties on Imports or Exports, except what may be absolutely necessary for executing it's inspection Laws: and the net Produce of all Duties and Imposts, laid by any State on Imports or Exports, shall be for the Use of the Treasury of the United States; and all such Laws shall be subject to the Revision and Controul of the Congress.

No State shall, without the Consent of Congress, lay any Duty of Tonnage, keep Troops, or Ships of War in time of Peace, enter into any Agreement or Compact with another State, or with a foreign Power, or engage in War, unless actually invaded, or in such imminent Danger as will not admit of delay.

ARTICLE II.

Section 1—President, powers and term of office. Electors, number and how appointed. Electors to vote for President. Qualifications of President. On whom duties devolve in case of removal, death, etc., of President. President's compensation. Oath of office.

The executive Power shall be vested in a President of the United States of America. He shall hold his Office during the Term of four Years, and, together with the Vice President, chosen for the same Term, be elected, as follows:

Each State shall appoint, in such Manner as the Legislature thereof may direct, a Number of Electors, equal to the whole Number of Senators and Representatives to which the State may be entitled in the Congress: but no Senator or Representative, or Person holding an Office of Trust or Profit under the United States, shall be appointed an Elector.

[The Electors shall meet in their respective States, and vote by Ballot for two Persons, of whom one at least shall not be an Inhabitant of the same State with themselves. And they shall make a List of all the Persons voted for, and of the Number of Votes for each; which List they shall sign and certify, and transmit sealed to the Seat of the Government of the United States, directed to the President of the Senate. The President of the Senate shall, in the Presence of the Senate and House of Representatives, open all the Certificates, and the Votes shall then be counted. The Person having the greatest Number of Votes shall be the President, if such Number be a Majority of the whole Number of Electors appointed; and if there be more than one who have such Majority, and have an equal Number of Votes, then the House of Representatives shall immediately chuse by Ballot one of them for President; and if no Person have a Majority, then from the five highest on the List the said House shall in like Manner chuse the President. But in chusing the President, the Votes shall be taken by States, the Representation from each State having one Vote; A quorum for this Purpose shall consist of a Member or Members from two thirds of the States, and a Majority of all the States shall be necessary to a Choice. In every Case, after the Choice of the President, the Person having the greatest Number of Votes of the Electors shall be the Vice President. But if there should remain two or more who have equal Votes, the Senate shall chuse from them by Ballot the Vice President.] *[This clause was superseded by Amendment XII.]*

The Congress may determine the Time of chusing the Electors, and the Day on which they shall give their Votes; which Day shall be the same throughout the United States.

No Person except a natural born Citizen, or a Citizen of the United States, at the time of the Adoption of this Constitution, shall be eligible to the Office of President; neither shall any Person be eligible to that Office who shall not have attained to the Age of thirty five Years, and been fourteen Years a Resident within the United States. *[For qualification of the Vice President, see Amendment XII.]*

[In Case of the Removal of the President from Office, or of his Death, Resignation, or Inability to discharge the Powers and Duties of the said Office, the Same shall devolve on the Vice President, and the Congress may by Law provide for the Case of Removal, Death, Resignation or Inability, both of the President and Vice President, declaring what Officer shall then act as President, and such Officer shall act accordingly, until the Disability be removed, or a President shall be elected.] *[This clause was superseded by Amendment XXV.]*

The President shall, at stated Times, receive for his Services, a Compensation, which shall neither be encreased nor diminished during the Period for which he shall have been elected, and he shall not receive within that Period any other Emolument from the United States, or any of them.

Before he enter on the Execution of his Office, he shall take the following Oath or Affirmation:—

"I do solemnly swear (or affirm) that I will faithfully execute the Office of President of the United States, and will to the best of my Ability, preserve, protect and defend the Constitution of the United States."

Section 2—President to be Commander in Chief. Power to make treaties; nominations for, appointments to certain offices. Power to fill vacancies during Senate recess.

The President shall be Commander in Chief of the Army and Navy of the United States, and of the Militia of the several States, when called into the actual Service of the United States; he may require the Opinion, in writing, of the principal Officer in each of the executive Departments, upon any Subject relating to the Duties of their respective Offices, and he shall have Power to Grant Reprieves and Pardons for Offences against the United States, except in Cases of Impeachment.

He shall have Power, by and with the Advice and Consent of the Senate, to make Treaties, provided two thirds of the Senators present concur; and he shall nominate, and by and with the Advice and Consent of the Senate, shall appoint Ambassadors, other public Ministers and Consuls, Judges of the supreme Court, and all other Officers of the United States, whose Appointments are not herein otherwise provided for, and which shall be established by Law: but the Congress may by Law vest the Appointment of such inferior Officers, as they think proper, in the President alone, in the Courts of Law, or in the Heads of Departments.

The President shall have Power to fill up all Vacancies that may happen during the Recess of the Senate, by granting Commissions which shall expire at the End of their next Session.

Section 3—President shall communicate to, may convene and adjourn Congress; shall receive ambassadors, execute laws, and commission officers.

He shall from time to time give to the Congress Information on the State of the Union, and recommend to their Consideration such Measures as he shall judge necessary and expedient; he may, on extraordinary Occasions, convene both Houses, or either of them, and in Case of Disagreement between them, with Respect to the Time of Adjournment, he may adjourn them to such Time as he shall think proper; he shall receive Ambassadors and other public Ministers; he shall take Care that the Laws be faithfully executed, and shall Commission all the Officers of the United States.

Section 4—All civil offices forfeited for certain crimes.

The President, Vice President and all civil Officers of the United States, shall be removed from Office on Impeachment for, and Conviction of, Treason, Bribery, or other high Crimes and Misdemeanors.

ARTICLE III.

Section 1—Judicial powers, tenure, compensation.

The judicial Power of the United States, shall be vested in one supreme Court, and in such inferior Courts as the Congress may from time to time ordain and establish. The Judges, both of the supreme and inferior Courts, shall hold their Offices during good Behaviour, and shall, at stated Times, receive for their Services, a Compensation, which shall not be diminished during their Continuance in Office.

Section 2—Judicial power, cases to which it extends. Jurisdiction of Supreme Court. Trial by jury; where held.

The judicial Power shall extend to all Cases, in Law and Equity, arising under this Constitution, the Laws of the United States, and Treaties made, or which shall be made, under their Authority;—to all Cases affecting Ambassadors, other public Ministers and Consuls;—to all Cases of admiralty and maritime Jurisdiction;—to Controversies to which the United States shall be a Party;—to Controversies between two or more States;—[between a State and Citizens of another State;]—between Citizens of different States;—between Citizens of the same State claiming Lands under Grants of different States, [and between a State, or the Citizens thereof, and foreign States, Citizens or Subjects.] *[This section was modified by Amendment XI.]*

In all Cases affecting Ambassadors, other public Ministers and Consuls, and those in which a State shall be Party, the supreme Court shall have original Jurisdiction. In all the other Cases before mentioned, the supreme Court shall have appellate Jurisdiction, both as to Law and Fact, with such Exceptions, and under such Regulations as the Congress shall make.

The Trial of all Crimes, except in Cases of Impeachment, shall be by Jury; and such Trial shall be held in the State where the said Crimes shall have been committed; but when not committed within any State, the Trial shall be at such Place or Places as the Congress may by Law have directed.

Section 3—Treason defined. Punishment of.

Treason against the United States, shall consist only in levying War against them, or in adhering to their Enemies, giving them Aid and Comfort. No Person shall be convicted of Treason unless on the Testimony of two Witnesses to the same overt Act, or on Confession in open Court.

The Congress shall have Power to declare the Punishment of Treason, but no Attainder of Treason shall work Corruption of Blood, or Forfeiture except during the Life of the Person attainted.

ARTICLE IV.

Section 1—Each State to give credit to the public acts, etc., of every other State.

Full Faith and Credit shall be given in each State to the public Acts, Records, and judicial Proceedings of every other State. And the Congress may by general Laws prescribe the Manner in which such Acts, Records and Proceedings shall be proved, and the Effect thereof.

Section 2—Privileges of citizens of each State. Fugitives from justice to be delivered up. Fugitives from service or labor, to be delivered up.

The Citizens of each State shall be entitled to all Privileges and Immunities of Citizens in the several States.

A Person charged in any State with Treason, Felony, or other Crime, who shall flee from Justice, and be found in another State, shall on Demand of the executive Authority of the State from which he fled, be delivered up, to be removed to the State having Jurisdiction of the Crime.

[No Person held to Service or Labour in one State, under the Laws thereof, escaping into another, shall, in Consequence of any Law or Regulation therein, be discharged from such Service or Labour, but shall be delivered up on Claim of the Party to whom such Service or Labour may be due.] *[This clause was superseded by Amendment XIII.]*

Section 3—Admission of new States. Power of Congress over territory and other property.

New States may be admitted by the Congress into this Union; but no new State shall be formed or erected within the Jurisdiction of any other State; nor any State be formed by the Junction of two or more States, or Parts of States, without the Consent of the Legislatures of the States concerned as well as of the Congress.

The Congress shall have Power to dispose of and make all needful Rules and Regulations respecting the Territory or other Property belonging to the United States; and nothing in this Constitution shall be so construed as to Prejudice any Claims of the United States, or of any particular State.

Section 4—Republican form of government guaranteed; each State to be protected.

The United States shall guarantee to every State in this Union a Republican Form of Government, and shall protect each of them against Invasion; and on Application of the Legislature, or of the Executive (when the Legislature cannot be convened) against domestic Violence.

ARTICLE V.

Constitution, how amended; proviso.

The Congress, whenever two thirds of both Houses shall deem it necessary, shall propose Amendments to this Constitution, or, on the Application of the Legislatures of two thirds of the several States, shall call a Convention for proposing Amendments, which, in either Case, shall be valid to all Intents and Purposes, as Part of this Constitution, when ratified by the Legislatures of three fourths of the several States, or by Conventions in three fourths thereof, as the one or the other Mode of Ratification may be proposed by the Congress; Provided that no Amendment which may be made prior to the Year One thousand eight hundred and eight shall in any Manner affect the first and fourth Clauses in the Ninth Section of the first Article; and that no State, without its Consent, shall be deprived of its equal Suffrage in the Senate.

ARTICLE VI.

Certain debts and engagements shall be valid. Constitution, laws and treaties made, shall be supreme law of the United States. Oath to support Constitution, by whom taken; no religious test shall be required.

All Debts contracted and Engagements entered into, before the Adoption of this Constitution, shall be as valid against the United States under this Constitution, as under the Confederation.

This Constitution, and the Laws of the United States which shall be made in Pursuance thereof; and all Treaties made, or which shall be made, under the Authority of the United States, shall be the supreme Law of the Land; and the Judges in every State shall be bound thereby, any Thing in the Constitution or Laws of any State to the Contrary notwithstanding.

The Senators and Representatives before mentioned, and the Members of the several State Legislatures, and all executive and judicial Officers, both of the United States and of the several States, shall be bound by Oath or Affirmation, to support this Constitution; but no religious Test shall ever be required as a Qualification to any Office or public Trust under the United States.

ARTICLE VII.

Ratification to establish the Constitution.

The Ratification of the Conventions of nine States, shall be sufficient for the Establishment of this Constitution between the States so ratifying the Same.

done in Convention by the Unanimous Consent of the States present the Seventeenth Day of September in the Year of our Lord one thousand seven hundred and Eighty seven and of the Independance of the United States of America the Twelfth. In witness whereof We have hereunto subscribed our Names,

G⁰. Washington, Presid^t. and deputy from Virginia

New Hampshire—John Langdon, Nicholas Gilman

Massachusetts—Nathaniel Gorham, Rufus King

Connecticut—W^m. Saml. Johnson, Roger Sherman

New York—Alexander Hamilton

New Jersey—Wil: Livingston, David Brearley, W^m. Paterson, Jona: Dayton

Pennsylvania—B Franklin, Thomas Mifflin, Robt. Morris, Geo. Clymer, Thos. FitzSimons, Jared Ingersoll, James Wilson, Gouv Morris

Delaware—Geo: Read, Gunning Bedford jun, John Dickinson, Richard Bassett, Jaco: Broom

Maryland—James McHenry, Dan of St Thos. Jenifer, Danl Carroll

Virginia—John Blair, James Madison Jr.

North Carolina—W^m. Blount, Rich^d. Dobbs Spaight, Hu Williamson

South Carolina—J. Rutledge, Charles Cotesworth Pinckney, Charles Pinckney, Pierce Butler

Georgia—William Few, Abr Baldwin

[George Washington was first to sign the Constitution on Sept. 17, 1787, followed by state delegates in order of geography, from north to south. In total, 38 delegates signed the Constitution, although Delaware delegate George Reed signed for absent delegate John Dickinson, bringing the total signatures to 39. Three delegates abstained from signing in protest of the absent Bill of Rights.]

Origin of the Bill of Rights

Congress, at its first session in New York, NY, submitted to the states 12 amendments Sept. 25, 1789, to clarify certain individual and state rights not named in the Constitution. They are generally called the Bill of Rights.

Influential in framing these amendments was the Declaration of Rights of Virginia, written by George Mason (1725-92) in 1776. Mason, a Virginia delegate to the Constitutional Convention, did not sign the Constitution and opposed its ratification on the ground that it did not sufficiently oppose slavery or safeguard individual rights.

In the preamble to the resolution offering the proposed amendments, Congress said: "The Conventions of a number of the States, having at the time of their adopting the Constitution, expressed a desire, in order to prevent misconstruction or abuse of its powers, that further declaratory and restrictive clauses should be added: And as extending the ground of public confidence in the Government, will best insure the beneficent ends of its institution."

Ten of these amendments, originally three to 12 inclusive, were ratified by the states as follows: New Jersey, Nov. 20, 1789; Maryland, Dec. 19, 1789; North Carolina, Dec. 22, 1789; South Carolina, Jan. 19, 1790; New Hampshire, Jan. 25, 1790; Delaware, Jan. 28, 1790; New York, Feb. 27, 1790; Pennsylvania, Mar. 10, 1790; Rhode Island, June 7, 1790; Vermont, Nov. 3, 1791; Virginia, Dec. 15, 1791; Massachusetts, Mar. 2, 1939; Georgia, Mar. 18, 1939; Connecticut, Apr. 19, 1939. These original 10 ratified amendments follow as Amendments I to X inclusive.

Of the two original proposed amendments that were not ratified promptly by the necessary number of states, the first related to apportionment of Representatives; the second, relating to compensation of members of Congress, was ratified in 1992 and became Amendment XXVII.

The Bill of Rights
In force Dec. 15, 1791

AMENDMENT I.

Religious establishment prohibited. Freedom of speech and of press; right to assemble and to petition.

Congress shall make no law respecting an establishment of religion, or prohibiting the free exercise thereof; or abridging the freedom of speech, or of the press; or the right of the people peaceably to assemble, and to petition the Government for a redress of grievances.

AMENDMENT II.

Right to keep and bear arms.

A well regulated Militia, being necessary to the security of a free State, the right of the people to keep and bear Arms shall not be infringed.

AMENDMENT III.

Conditions for quartering of soldiers.

No Soldier shall, in time of peace be quartered in any house, without the consent of the Owner, nor in time of war, but in a manner to be prescribed by law.

AMENDMENT IV.

Protection from unreasonable search and seizure.

The right of the people to be secure in their persons, houses, papers, and effects, against unreasonable searches and seizures, shall not be violated, and no Warrants shall issue but upon probable cause, supported by Oath or affirmation, and particularly describing the place to be searched, and the persons or things to be seized.

AMENDMENT V.

Provisions concerning prosecution and due process of law. Compensation of private property taken for public use.

No person shall be held to answer for a capital, or otherwise infamous crime, unless on a presentment or indictment of a Grand Jury, except in cases arising in the land or naval forces, or in the Militia, when in actual service in time of War or public danger; nor shall any person be subject for the same offence to be twice put in jeopardy of life or limb; nor shall be compelled in any criminal case to be a witness against himself, nor be deprived of life, liberty, or property, without due process of law; nor shall private property be taken for public use, without just compensation.

AMENDMENT VI.

Rights of accused in criminal prosecutions.

In all criminal prosecutions, the accused shall enjoy the right to a speedy and public trial, by an impartial jury of the State and district wherein the crime shall have been committed, which district shall have been previously ascertained by law, and to be informed of the nature and cause of the accusation; to be confronted with the witnesses against him; to have compulsory process for obtaining witnesses in his favor, and to have the Assistance of Counsel for his defense.

AMENDMENT VII.

Right of trial by jury in civil cases.

In Suits at common law, where the value in controversy shall exceed twenty dollars, the right of trial by jury shall be preserved, and no fact tried by a jury, shall be otherwise reexamined in any Court of the United States, than according to the rules of the common law.

AMENDMENT VIII.

Excessive bail or fines; cruel and unusual punishment.

Excessive bail shall not be required, nor excessive fines imposed, nor cruel and unusual punishments inflicted.

AMENDMENT IX.

Unenumerated rights.

The enumeration in the Constitution, of certain rights, shall not be construed to deny or disparage others retained by the people.

AMENDMENT X.

Rights reserved to States.

The powers not delegated to the United States by the Constitution, nor prohibited by it to the States, are reserved to the States respectively, or to the people.

Amendments Since the Bill of Rights

AMENDMENT XI.

Judicial powers construed.

[Proposed by Congress Mar. 4, 1794. Ratification complete Feb. 7, 1795, though official announcement of ratification not made until Jan. 8, 1798.]

The Judicial power of the United States shall not be construed to extend to any suit in law or equity, commenced or prosecuted against one of the United States by Citizens of another State, or by Citizens or Subjects of any Foreign State.

AMENDMENT XII.

Election of President and Vice-President.

[Proposed by Congress Dec. 9, 1803; ratified June 15, 1804.]

The Electors shall meet in their respective states and vote by ballot for President and Vice-President, one of whom, at least, shall not be an inhabitant of the same state with themselves; they shall name in their ballots the person voted for as President, and in distinct ballots the person voted for as Vice-President, and they shall make distinct lists of all persons voted for as President, and of all persons voted for as Vice-President, and of the number of votes for each, which lists they shall sign and certify, and transmit sealed to the seat of the government of the United States, directed to the President of the Senate;—The President of the Senate shall, in the presence of the Senate and House of Representatives, open all the certificates and the votes shall then be counted;—The person having the greatest number of votes for President, shall be the President, if such number be a majority of the whole number of Electors appointed; and if no person have such majority, then from the persons having the highest numbers not exceeding three on the list of those voted for as President, the House of Representatives shall choose immediately, by ballot, the President. But in choosing the President, the votes shall be taken by states, the representation from each state having one vote; a quorum for this purpose shall consist of a member or members from two-thirds of the states, and a majority of all the states shall be necessary to a choice. [And if the House of Representatives shall not choose a President whenever the right of choice shall devolve upon them, before the fourth day of March next following, then the Vice-President shall act as President, as in the case of the death or other constitutional disability of the President.] *[The words in brackets were superseded by Amendment XX, section 3.]* The person having the greatest number of votes as Vice-President, shall be the Vice-President, if such number be a majority of the whole number of Electors appointed, and if no person have a majority, then from the two highest numbers on the list, the Senate shall choose the Vice-President; a quorum for the purpose shall consist of two-thirds of the whole number of Senators, and a majority of the whole number shall be necessary to a choice. But no person constitutionally ineligible to the office of President shall be eligible to that of Vice-President of the United States.

THE RECONSTRUCTION AMENDMENTS

[Amendments XIII, XIV, and XV are commonly known as the Reconstruction Amendments inasmuch as they followed the Civil War and were drafted by Republicans who wanted to impose their own policy of reconstruction on the South. Southern postbellum legislatures in states including Mississippi, South Carolina, and Georgia had set up laws that effectively perpetuated slavery under other names.]

AMENDMENT XIII.

Slavery abolished.

[Proposed by Congress Jan. 31, 1865; ratified Dec. 6, 1865.]

Section 1. Neither slavery nor involuntary servitude, except as a punishment for crime whereof the party shall have been duly convicted, shall exist within the United States, or any place subject to their jurisdiction.

Section 2. Congress shall have power to enforce this article by appropriate legislation.

AMENDMENT XIV.

Citizenship rights not to be abridged.

[Proposed by Congress June 13, 1866, ratified July 9, 1868, and declared to have been ratified in a proclamation by the Secretary of State, July 28, 1868.]

Section 1. All persons born or naturalized in the United States, and subject to the jurisdiction thereof, are citizens of the United States and of the State wherein they reside. No State shall make or enforce any law which shall abridge the privileges or immunities of citizens of the United States; nor shall any State deprive any person of life, liberty, or property, without due process of law; nor deny to any person within its jurisdiction the equal protection of the laws.

Section 2. Representatives shall be apportioned among the several States according to their respective numbers, counting the whole number of persons in each State, excluding Indians not taxed. But when the right to vote at any election for the choice of electors for President and Vice-President of the United States, Representatives in Congress, the Executive and Judicial officers of a State, or the members of the Legislature thereof, is denied to any of the male inhabitants of such State, being [twenty-one] *[The words in brackets were changed by Amendment XXVI.]* years of age, and citizens of the United States, or in any way abridged, except for participation in rebellion, or other crime, the basis of representation therein shall be reduced in the proportion which the number of such male citizens shall bear to the whole number of male citizens twenty-one years of age in such State.

Section 3. No person shall be a Senator or Representative in Congress, or elector of President and Vice-President, or hold any office, civil or military, under the United States, or under any State, who, having previously taken an oath, as a member of Congress, or as an officer of the United States, or as a member of any State legislature, or as an executive or judicial officer of any State, to support the Constitution of the United States, shall have engaged in insurrection or rebellion against the same, or given aid or comfort to the enemies thereof. But Congress may by a vote of two-thirds of each House, remove such disability.

Section 4. The validity of the public debt of the United States, authorized by law, including debts incurred for payment of pensions and bounties for services in suppressing insurrection or rebellion, shall not be questioned. But neither the United States nor any State shall assume or pay any debt or obligation incurred in aid of insurrection or rebellion against the United States, or any claim for the loss or emancipation of any slave; but all such debts, obligations and claims shall be held illegal and void.

Section 5. The Congress shall have power to enforce, by appropriate legislation, the provisions of this article.

AMENDMENT XV.

Race no bar to voting rights.

[Proposed by Congress Feb. 26, 1869; ratified Feb. 3, 1870.]

Section 1. The right of citizens of the United States to vote shall not be denied or abridged by the United States or by any State on account of race, color, or previous condition of servitude.

Section 2. The Congress shall have power to enforce this article by appropriate legislation.

AMENDMENT XVI.

Taxes on income.

[Proposed by Congress July 12, 1909; ratified Feb. 3, 1913.]

The Congress shall have power to lay and collect taxes on incomes, from whatever source derived, without apportionment among the several States, and without regard to any census or enumeration.

AMENDMENT XVII.

Popular election of Senators.

[Proposed by Congress May 13, 1912; ratified Apr. 8, 1913.]

The Senate of the United States shall be composed of two Senators from each State, elected by the people thereof, for six years; and each Senator shall have one vote. The electors in each State shall have the qualifications requisite for electors of the most numerous branch of the State legislatures.

When vacancies happen in the representation of any State in the Senate, the executive authority of such State shall issue writs of election to fill such vacancies: Provided, That the legislature of any State may empower the executive thereof to make temporary appointments until the people fill the vacancies by election as the legislature may direct.

This amendment shall not be so construed as to affect the election or term of any Senator chosen before it becomes valid as part of the Constitution.

AMENDMENT XVIII.

Liquor prohibition amendment.

[Proposed by Congress Dec. 18, 1917; ratified Jan. 16, 1919. Repealed by Amendment XXI, effective Dec. 5, 1933.]
Section 1. After one year from the ratification of this article the manufacture, sale, or transportation of intoxicating liquors within, the importation thereof into, or the exportation thereof from the United States and all territory subject to the jurisdiction thereof for beverage purposes is hereby prohibited.

Section 2. The Congress and the several States shall have concurrent power to enforce this article by appropriate legislation.

Section 3. This article shall be inoperative unless it shall have been ratified as an amendment to the Constitution by the legislatures of the several States, as provided in the Constitution, within seven years from the date of the submission hereof to the States by the Congress.

AMENDMENT XIX.

Nationwide suffrage to women.

[Proposed by Congress June 4, 1919; ratified Aug. 18, 1920.]
The right of citizens of the United States to vote shall not be denied or abridged by the United States or by any State on account of sex.

Congress shall have power to enforce this article by appropriate legislation.

AMENDMENT XX.

Commencement of terms of office.

[Proposed by Congress Mar. 2, 1932; ratified Jan. 23, 1933.]
Section 1. The terms of the President and Vice President shall end at noon on the 20th day of January, and the terms of Senators and Representatives at noon on the 3d day of January, of the years in which such terms would have ended if this article had not been ratified; and the terms of their successors shall then begin.

Section 2. The Congress shall assemble at least once in every year, and such meeting shall begin at noon on the 3d day of January, unless they shall by law appoint a different day.

Section 3. If, at the time fixed for the beginning of the term of the President, the President elect shall have died, the Vice President elect shall become President. If a President shall not have been chosen before the time fixed for the beginning of his term, or if the President elect shall have failed to qualify, then the Vice President elect shall act as President until a President shall have qualified; and the Congress may by law provide for the case wherein neither a President elect nor a Vice President elect shall have qualified, declaring who shall then act as President, or the manner in which one who is to act shall be selected, and such person shall act accordingly until a President or Vice President shall have qualified.

Section 4. The Congress may by law provide for the case of the death of any of the persons from whom the House of Representatives may choose a President whenever the right of choice shall have devolved upon them, and for the case of the death of any of the persons from whom the Senate may choose a Vice President whenever the right of choice shall have devolved upon them.

Section 5. Sections 1 and 2 shall take effect on the 15th day of October following the ratification of this article.

Section 6. This article shall be inoperative unless it shall have been ratified as an amendment to the Constitution by the legislatures of three-fourths of the several States within seven years from the date of its submission.

AMENDMENT XXI.

Repeal of Amendment XVIII.

[Proposed by Congress Feb. 20, 1933; ratified Dec. 5, 1933.]
Section 1. The eighteenth article of amendment to the Constitution of the United States is hereby repealed.

Section 2. The transportation or importation into any State, Territory, or possession of the United States for delivery or use therein of intoxicating liquors, in violation of the laws thereof, is hereby prohibited.

Section 3. This article shall be inoperative unless it shall have been ratified as an amendment to the Constitution by conventions in the several States, as provided in the Constitution, within seven years from the date of the submission hereof to the States by the Congress.

AMENDMENT XXII.

Limit on presidential terms of office.

[Proposed by Congress Mar. 24, 1947; ratified Feb. 27, 1951.]
Section 1. No person shall be elected to the office of the President more than twice, and no person who has held the office of President, or acted as President, for more than two years of a term to which some other person was elected President shall be elected to the office of the President more than once. But this Article shall not apply to any person holding the office of President when this Article was proposed by Congress, and shall not prevent any person who may be holding the office of President, or acting as President, during the term within which this Article becomes operative from holding the office of President or acting as President during the remainder of such term.

Section 2. This Article shall be inoperative unless it shall have been ratified as an amendment to the Constitution by the legislatures of three-fourths of the several States within seven years from the date of its submission to the States by the Congress.

AMENDMENT XXIII.

Presidential vote for District of Columbia.

[Proposed by Congress June 16, 1960; ratified Mar. 29, 1961.]
Section 1. The District constituting the seat of Government of the United States shall appoint in such manner as the Congress may direct:

A number of electors of President and Vice President equal to the whole number of Senators and Representatives in Congress to which the District would be entitled if it were a State, but in no event more than the least populous State; they shall be in addition to those appointed by the States, but they shall be considered, for the purposes of the election of President and Vice President, to be electors appointed by a State; and they shall meet in the District and perform such duties as provided by the twelfth article of amendment.

Section 2. The Congress shall have power to enforce this article by appropriate legislation.

AMENDMENT XXIV.

Poll tax barred in federal elections.

[Proposed by Congress Sept. 14, 1962; ratified Jan. 23, 1964.]
Section 1. The right of citizens of the United States to vote in any primary or other election for President or Vice President, for electors for President or Vice President, or for Senator or Representative in Congress, shall not be denied or abridged by the United States or any State by reason of failure to pay any poll tax or other tax.

Section 2. The Congress shall have power to enforce this article by appropriate legislation.

AMENDMENT XXV.

Presidential vacancy, inability, and succession.

[Proposed by Congress July 6, 1965; ratified Feb. 10, 1967.]

Section 1. In case of the removal of the President from office or of his death or resignation, the Vice President shall become President.

Section 2. Whenever there is a vacancy in the office of the Vice President, the President shall nominate a Vice President who shall take office upon confirmation by a majority vote of both Houses of Congress.

Section 3. Whenever the President transmits to the President pro tempore of the Senate and the Speaker of the House of Representatives his written declaration that he is unable to discharge the powers and duties of his office, and until he transmits to them a written declaration to the contrary, such powers and duties shall be discharged by the Vice President as Acting President.

Section 4. Whenever the Vice President and a majority of either the principal officers of the executive departments or of such other body as Congress may by law provide, transmit to the President pro tempore of the Senate and the Speaker of the House of Representatives their written declaration that the President is unable to discharge the powers and duties of his office, the Vice President shall immediately assume the powers and duties of the office as Acting President.

Thereafter, when the President transmits to the President pro tempore of the Senate and the Speaker of the House of Representatives his written declaration that no inability exists, he shall resume the powers and duties of his office unless the Vice President and a majority of either the principal officers of the executive department or of such other body

as Congress may by law provide, transmit within four days to the President pro tempore of the Senate and the Speaker of the House of Representatives their written declaration that the President is unable to discharge the powers and duties of his office. Thereupon Congress shall decide the issue, assembling within forty-eight hours for that purpose if not in session. If the Congress, within twenty-one days after receipt of the latter written declaration, or, if Congress is not in session, within twenty-one days after Congress is required to assemble, determines by two-thirds vote of both Houses that the President is unable to discharge the powers and duties of his office, the Vice President shall continue to discharge the same as Acting President; otherwise, the President shall resume the powers and duties of his office.

AMENDMENT XXVI.

Voting age lowered to 18 years.

[Proposed by Congress Mar. 23, 1971; ratified July 1, 1971.]

Section 1. The right of citizens of the United States, who are eighteen years of age or older, to vote shall not be denied or abridged by the United States or by any State on account of age.

Section 2. The Congress shall have power to enforce this article by appropriate legislation.

AMENDMENT XXVII.

Congressional pay.

[Proposed by Congress Sept. 25, 1789; ratified May 7, 1992.]

No law, varying the compensation for the services of the Senators and Representatives, shall take effect, until an election of Representatives shall have intervened.

How a Bill Becomes a Law

A senator or representative introduces a bill in Congress by sending it to the clerk of the Senate or the House, who assigns it a number and title. This procedure is termed the first reading. The clerk then refers the bill to the appropriate committee of the Senate or House.

If the committee does not wish to consider the bill, it will table it. Otherwise, the committee holds hearings to gather information, such as by inviting experts and other members of the public to testify. The committee then debates the bill and may offer amendments. A vote is taken, and if favorable, the bill is sent back to the clerk of the Senate or House.

The clerk reads the bill to the house—the second reading. Members may then debate the bill and suggest amendments.

After debate and any amendments, the bill is given a third reading, simply of the title, and put to a voice or roll-call vote. If the bill passes, it goes to the other house, where it may be defeated or passed, with or without amendments. If defeated, the bill dies. If passed with amendments, a conference committee made up of members of both houses works out the differences between the two bills and arrives at a compromise.

After passage of the final version by both houses, the bill is sent to the president. If the president signs it, the bill becomes a law. The president may instead veto the bill by refusing to sign it and sending it back to the house where it originated, with reasons for the veto.

The president's objections are then read and debated, and a roll-call vote is taken. If the bill receives less than a two-thirds majority, it is defeated. If it receives at least two-thirds, it is sent to the other house. If that house also passes it by at least a two-thirds majority, the president's veto is overridden, and the bill becomes a law.

If the president neither signs nor vetoes the bill within 10 days—not including Sundays—it automatically becomes a law even without the president's signature. However, if Congress adjourns within those 10 days, the bill is automatically killed; this indirect rejection is termed a pocket veto.

Under the Line Item Veto Act, effective Jan. 1, 1997, the president was authorized, under certain circumstances, to veto a bill in part. The legislation was found unconstitutional by the Supreme Court, June 25, 1998.

Presidential Oath of Office

The Constitution (Article II, Section 1) directs that the president-elect shall take the following oath to be inaugurated: "I do solemnly swear [affirm] that I will faithfully execute the office of President of the United States, and will, to the best of my ability, preserve, protect, and defend the Constitution of the United States."

Custom decrees the addition of the words "So help me God" at the end of the oath when taken by the president-elect, with the left hand on the Bible for the duration of the oath, and the right hand slightly raised. However, the use of a Bible, or any other religious book, is not required.

Presidential Succession

If, by reason of death, resignation, removal from office, inability, or failure to qualify, there is neither a president nor vice president to discharge the powers and duties of the office of president, then the speaker of the House of

Representatives shall, upon his resignation as speaker and as representative, act as president. The same rule shall apply in the case of the death, resignation, removal from office, or inability of an individual acting as president.

If, at the time when a speaker is to begin the discharge of the powers and duties of the office of president, there is no speaker, or the speaker fails to qualify as acting president, then the president pro tempore of the Senate, upon his resignation as president pro tempore and as senator, shall act as president.

An individual acting as president shall continue to act until the expiration of the then current presidential term, except that (1) if his discharge of the powers and duties of the office is founded in whole or in part in the failure of both the president-elect and the vice president-elect to qualify, then he shall act only until a president or vice president qualifies, and (2) if his discharge of the powers and duties of the office is founded in whole or in part on the inability of the president or vice president, then he shall act only until the removal of the disability of one of such individuals.

If, by reason of death, resignation, removal from office, or failure to qualify, there is no president pro tempore to act as president, then the officer of the United States who is highest on the following list, and who is not under any disability to discharge the powers and duties of president shall act as president: the secretaries of state, treasury, and defense; the attorney general; the secretaries of interior, agriculture, commerce, labor, health and human services, housing and urban development, transportation, energy, education, veterans affairs, and homeland security.

Legislation approved July 18, 1947; amended Sept. 9, 1965, Oct. 15, 1966, Aug. 4, 1977, Sept. 27, 1979, and Mar. 9, 2006. See also Constitutional Amendment XXV.

Confederate States: Secession and Government

The American Civil War (1861-65) grew out of sectional disputes over the continued existence of slavery in the South. Southern legislators contended that the states retained the right to enslave Black people and the right to secede.

The war was not fought by state against state but by one federal regime against another. A Confederate government in Richmond, VA, assumed control over the economic, political, and military life of the seceding states, under protest from Georgia and South Carolina.

South Carolina voted unanimously in convention to secede from the Union, repealing its 1788 ratification of the U.S. Constitution on Dec. 20, 1860, to take effect on Dec. 24. Other states seceded in 1861. Their votes in conventions were Mississippi, Jan. 9, 84-15; Florida, Jan. 10, 62-7; Alabama, Jan. 11, 61-39; Georgia, Jan. 19, 208-89; Louisiana, Jan. 26, 113-17; Texas, Feb. 1, 166-7, ratified by popular vote (34,794 to 11,325) Feb. 23; Virginia, Apr. 17, 88-55, ratified by popular vote (128,884 to 32,134) May 23; Arkansas, May 6, 69-1; Tennessee, May 7, ratified by popular vote (104,019 to 47,238) June 8; and North Carolina, unanimous, May 20.

Missouri Unionists stopped secession in conventions Feb. 28 and Mar. 9, 1861. Under the protection of Confederate troops, secessionist members of the legislature adopted a resolution of secession at Neosho, Oct. 31. The Confederate Congress seated the secessionists' representatives.

Kentucky did not secede, and its government remained Unionist. In a part of the state occupied by Confederate troops, Kentuckians approved secession, and the Confederate Congress admitted their representatives.

The Maryland legislature voted against secession Apr. 27, 1861, 53-13. Delaware did not secede. Pro-Union residents of western Virginia held conventions at Wheeling and, on June 17, 1861, formed the Restored Government of Virginia. It was admitted to the Union as West Virginia on June 20, 1863. Its constitution provided for gradual abolition of slavery.

Forty-two delegates from South Carolina, Georgia, Alabama, Mississippi, Louisiana, and Florida met in convention in Montgomery, AL, on Feb. 4, 1861. They adopted a provisional constitution of the Confederate States of America and elected Jefferson Davis (MS) as provisional president and Alexander H. Stephens (GA) as provisional vice president.

A permanent constitution was adopted Mar. 11. It banned the African slave trade but did not bar interstate commerce in slaves. On July 20 the Congress moved to Richmond. Davis was elected president in Nov. 1861 and was inaugurated Feb. 22, 1862.

The Confederate Congress adopted a flag ("The Stars and Bars") consisting of one white stripe and two red stripes and a blue canton with a circle of white stars. The Confederate battle flag, carried by the Army of Northern Virginia, was more popularly known. It has blue diagonal crossbars with 13 white stars, for the 11 states in the Confederacy plus Kentucky and Missouri, against a red field.

The Gettysburg Address

Delivered by Pres. Abraham Lincoln at the dedication of the Soldiers' National Cemetery in Gettysburg, PA, on Nov. 19, 1863. Five handwritten copies of the Gettysburg Address as made by Lincoln are known to exist. The text differs slightly between copies. The Bliss copy, made for Alexander Bliss, is shown here. The copy is kept on display in the White House.

Four score and seven years ago our fathers brought forth on this continent, a new nation, conceived in Liberty, and dedicated to the proposition that all men are created equal.

Now we are engaged in a great civil war, testing whether that nation, or any nation so conceived and so dedicated, can long endure. We are met on a great battle-field of that war. We have come to dedicate a portion of that field, as a final resting place for those who here gave their lives that that nation might live. It is altogether fitting and proper that we should do this.

But, in a larger sense, we can not dedicate—we can not consecrate—we can not hallow—this ground. The brave men, living and dead, who struggled here, have consecrated it, far above our poor power to add or detract. The world will little note, nor long remember what we say here, but it can never forget what they did here.

It is for us the living, rather, to be dedicated here to the unfinished work which they who fought here have thus far so nobly advanced. It is rather for us to be here dedicated to the great task remaining before us—that from these honored dead we take increased devotion to that cause for which they gave the last full measure of devotion—that we here highly resolve that these dead shall not have died in vain—that this nation, under God, shall have a new birth of freedom—and that government of the people, by the people, for the people, shall not perish from the earth.

Origin of the United States National Motto

In God We Trust, designated as the U.S. National Motto by Congress in 1956, originated during the Civil War as an inscription for U.S. coins. On Nov. 13, 1861, the Rev. M. R. Watkinson, of Ridleyville, PA, wrote to Treasury Sec. Salmon P. Chase requesting "recognition of the Almighty God in some form on our coins." Chase ordered designs prepared with the inscription *In God We Trust* and backed coinage legislation that authorized use of this slogan. The motto first appeared on some U.S. coins in 1864 and sporadically thereafter until 1938, after which all U.S. coins bear the inscription. A joint resolution passed by the 84th Congress and signed by Pres. Dwight D. Eisenhower July 30, 1956, declared *In God We Trust* the national motto of the United States.

Great Seal of the U.S.

On July 4, 1776, the Continental Congress appointed a committee consisting of Benjamin Franklin, John Adams, and Thomas Jefferson "to bring in a device for a seal of the United States of America." The designs submitted by this and a subsequent committee were considered unacceptable. After many delays, a third committee, appointed early in 1782, presented a design prepared by lawyer William Barton. Charles Thomson, the secretary of Congress, suggested certain changes, and Congress finally approved the design on June 20, 1782. The obverse of the seal shows a bald eagle. In the eagle's mouth is a ribbon bearing the motto *E Pluribus Unum* (out of many, one). In the eagle's talons are 13 arrows of war and an olive branch of peace. The reverse shows an unfinished pyramid with an eye (Eye of Providence) above it.

The Flag of the U.S.—The Stars and Stripes

The 50-star flag of the United States was raised for the first time officially at 12:01 AM on July 4, 1960, at Ft. McHenry National Monument in Baltimore, MD. The 50th star had been added for Hawaii; just a year earlier, the 49th star was added for Alaska.

There are so many myths and legends surrounding the history of the Stars and Stripes that the facts are difficult, and in some cases impossible, to establish. For example, it is not certain who designed the Stars and Stripes, who made the first such flag, or even whether it ever flew during any battle of the American Revolution.

Historians agree, however, that the Stars and Stripes originated as the result of a resolution offered by the Marine Committee of the Second Continental Congress at Philadelphia and adopted on June 14, 1777. It read:

"Resolved: that the flag of the United States be thirteen stripes, alternate red and white; that the union be thirteen stars, white in a blue field, representing a new constellation."

Congress gave no hint as to the designer of the flag, no instructions as to the arrangement of the stars, and no information on its appropriate uses.

The resolution establishing the flag was not published until Sept. 2, 1777. Despite repeated requests, George Washington did not get the flags until 1783, after the war was over. And there is no certainty that they were the Stars and Stripes.

Early Flags

Many historians consider the first flag of the U.S. to have been the Grand Union (sometimes called Great Union) flag, although the Continental Congress never officially adopted it. This flag was a modification of the British Meteor flag, which had the red cross of St. George and the white cross of St. Andrew combined in the blue canton. For the Grand Union flag, six horizontal stripes were imposed on the red field, dividing it into 13 alternating red and white stripes. On Jan. 1, 1776, when the Continental Army came into formal existence, this flag was unfurled on Prospect Hill, Somerville, MA. Washington wrote that "we hoisted the Union Flag in compliment to the United Colonies."

One of several flags about which controversy has raged is in Easton, PA. Containing the devices of the national flag in reversed order, this flag has been in the public library in Easton for more than 150 years. Some contend that this flag was actually the first Stars and Stripes, first displayed on July 8, 1776. This flag has 13 red and white stripes in the canton and 13 white stars centered in a blue field.

A flag was hastily improvised from garments by the defenders of Ft. Schuyler at Rome, NY, Aug. 3-22, 1777. Historians believe it was the Grand Union Flag.

The Sons of Liberty had a flag of nine red and white stripes, to signify nine colonies, when they met in New York in 1765 to oppose the Stamp Tax. By 1775, the flag had grown to 13 red and white stripes, with a rattlesnake on it.

At Concord, MA, Apr. 19, 1775, the minutemen from Bedford, MA, are said to have carried a flag having a silver arm with sword on a red field. At Cambridge, MA, the Sons of Liberty used a plain red flag with a green pine tree on it.

In June 1775, Washington went from Philadelphia to Boston to take command of the army. He was escorted to New York by the Philadelphia Light Horse Troop, which carried a yellow flag that had an elaborate coat of arms—the shield charged with 13 knots, the motto "For These We Strive"—and a canton of 13 blue and silver stripes.

In Feb. 1776, Col. Christopher Gadsden, a member of the Continental Congress, gave the South Carolina Provincial Congress a flag "such as is to be used by the commander-in-chief of the American Navy." It had a yellow field, with a rattlesnake about to strike and the words "Don't Tread on Me."

At the Battle of Bennington, Aug. 16, 1777, patriots used a flag of seven white and six red stripes with a blue canton extending down nine stripes. Eleven white stars arch over the figure 76 in the canton; a star appears in each of the canton's upper corners. The stars are seven-pointed. This flag is preserved in a museum in Bennington, VT.

At the Battle of Cowpens, Jan. 17, 1781, the 3rd Maryland Regiment is said to have carried a flag of 13 red and white stripes, with a blue canton containing 12 stars in a circle around one star.

Who Designed the Flag? No one knows for certain. Francis Hopkinson, designer of a naval flag, declared he had designed the flag and in 1781 asked Congress to reimburse him for his services. Congress did not do so.

Who Called the Flag "Old Glory"? The flag is said to have been named Old Glory by William Driver, a sea captain of Salem, MA. One legend has it that he did so when he raised the flag on his brig in 1824. But his daughter said he named it at his 21st birthday celebration on Mar. 17, 1824, when his mother presented the homemade flag to him.

The Betsy Ross Legend. The widely publicized legend that Betsy Ross made the first Stars and Stripes in June 1776, at the request of a committee composed of George Washington, Robert Morris, and George Ross, an uncle, was first made public in 1870, by a grandson of Ross. Historians have been unable to find a historical record of such a meeting or committee.

Adding New Stars

On the admission of Vermont and Kentucky to the Union, Congress designated that after May 1, 1795, the flag should have 15 stripes, alternating red and white, and 15 white stars on a blue field.

When more new states were admitted, it became evident that the flag would become burdened with stars. Congress ordered that after July 4, 1818, the flag should have 13 stripes, symbolizing 13 original states; that the union should have 20 stars; and that whenever a new state was admitted a new star should be added on the July 4 following admission.

No law designates the permanent arrangement of the stars. However, since 1912, when a new state has been admitted, the new design has been announced by executive order. No star is specifically identified with any state.

Pledge of Allegiance to the Flag

I pledge allegiance to the flag of the United States of America, and to the republic for which it stands, one nation under God, indivisible, with liberty and justice for all.

This, the current official version of the Pledge of Allegiance, developed from a pledge first published in the Sept. 8, 1892, issue of *Youth's Companion*, a weekly magazine. The original pledge contained the phrase "my flag," which was changed more than 30 years later to "flag of the United States of America." A 1954 act of Congress added the words "under God." (In 2002, the 9th Circuit U.S. Court of Appeals ruled that recitation of the pledge in public schools could not include that phrase. In 2004, however, the U.S. Supreme Court voted to decline to decide the case on a technicality. The lower court's decision was thus overturned.)

The authorship of the pledge was in dispute for many years. *Youth's Companion* stated in 1917 that the original draft was written by James B. Upham, an executive of the magazine who died in 1910. A leaflet circulated by the magazine later named Upham as the originator of the first draft.

Francis Bellamy, a former member of the *Youth's Companion* editorial staff, publicly claimed authorship of the pledge in 1923. In 1939, the United States Flag Association, acting on the advice of a committee named to study the controversy, upheld the claim by Bellamy, who had died eight years earlier. In 1957 the Library of Congress issued a report attributing the authorship to Bellamy.

According to the federal Flag Code, the pledge should be given while standing at attention facing the flag with the right hand over the heart. Those not in military uniform should remove any non-religious head coverings with their right hand and hold it at the left shoulder, the hand being over the heart. Those in uniform should remain silent, face the flag, and render a military salute. Members and veterans of the Armed Forces not in uniform may also render the military salute in the manner provided for persons in uniform.

History of the U.S. National Anthem

"The Star-Spangled Banner" was formally designated the national anthem by Act of Congress, Mar. 3, 1931. The words were written by Francis Scott Key, of Georgetown, in DC, marking the bombardment of Ft. McHenry in Baltimore, MD, Sept. 13-14, 1814. Key was a lawyer, a graduate of St. John's College in Annapolis, MD, and a volunteer in a light artillery company. When a friend, Dr. William Beanes, a Maryland physician, was arrested by the British for interfering with British deserters and straggling ground troops, Key and U.S. Col. John Skinner, with permission from Pres. Madison, went to the fleet under a flag of truce to ask for Beanes's release. The British consented, but as the fleet was about to sail up the Patapsco River to bombard Ft. McHenry, Key was detained for the duration of the battle.

The bombardment of Ft. McHenry began at 7 AM, Sept. 13, and lasted 25 hours. The British fired more than 1,500 shells. They were unable to approach closely because the U.S. had sunk 22 vessels to form a barrier. Only four Americans were killed and 24 wounded. A British bomb ship was disabled.

The morning after the shelling, Sept. 14, inspired by the flag still flying above the garrison, Key began to draft the poem. Released from British custody in Baltimore Sept. 16, Key revised the poem and gave it to his brother-in-law, Joseph Nicholson, who encouraged its printing on handbills. The first versions were titled "The Defence of Fort McHenry" and included a note suggesting use of the tune "Anacreon in Heaven" (attributed to British composer John Stafford Smith). The poem appeared in several newspapers within days and spread quickly.

The garrison flag that Key saw the morning after the bombardment is preserved at the Smithsonian Institution's National Museum of American History in Washington, DC. Major George Armistead, the commander of the militia unit stationed at Fort McHenry, had ordered a flag "so large that the British will have no difficulty seeing it from a distance." A government contract paid Baltimore flagmaker Mary Pickersgill $405.90 in 1813 for the garrison flag and $168.54 for a smaller storm flag (which was flown during the battle itself). The garrison flag originally measured 30 by 42 ft and had 15 alternating red and white stripes and 15 stars, for the original 13 states plus Kentucky and Vermont. The preserved flag measures 30 by 34 ft and is missing one star. Before the flag was placed in a museum, the family holding the flag would give clippings of it away as souvenirs.

The Star-Spangled Banner

I

Oh, say can you see by the dawn's early light
What so proudly we hailed at the twilight's last gleaming?
Whose broad stripes and bright stars through the perilous fight,
O'er the ramparts we watched were so gallantly streaming?
And the rockets' red glare, the bombs bursting in air,
Gave proof through the night that our flag was still there.
Oh, say does that star-spangled banner yet wave
O'er the land of the free and the home of the brave?

II

On the shore, dimly seen through the mists of the deep,
Where the foe's haughty host in dread silence reposes,
What is that which the breeze, o'er the towering steep,
As it fitfully blows, half conceals, half discloses?
Now it catches the gleam of the morning's first beam,
In full glory reflected now shines in the stream:
'Tis the star-spangled banner! Oh long may it wave
O'er the land of the free and the home of the brave!

III

And where is that band who so vauntingly swore
That the havoc of war and the battle's confusion,
A home and a country should leave us no more!
Their blood has washed out their foul footsteps' pollution.
No refuge could save the hireling and slave
From the terror of flight, or the gloom of the grave:
And the star-spangled banner in triumph doth wave
O'er the land of the free and the home of the brave!

IV

Oh! thus be it ever, when freemen shall stand
Between their loved home and the war's desolation!
Blest with victory and peace, may the heav'n rescued land
Praise the Power that hath made and preserved us a nation.
Then conquer we must, when our cause it is just,
And this be our motto: "In God is our trust."
And the star-spangled banner in triumph shall wave
O'er the land of the free and the home of the brave!

Statue of Liberty National Monument

Since 1886, the Statue of Liberty, formally known as "Liberty Enlightening the World," has stood as a symbol of freedom in New York Harbor. A gift from the people of France to the people of the U.S., it initially was conceived by legal philosopher Édouard de Laboulaye and intended to celebrate the U.S. centennial and commemorate the abolition of slavery. It was designed by French sculptor Frédéric Auguste Bartholdi (1834-1904).

On Feb. 22, 1877, Congress approved the use of a site on Bedloe's Island suggested by Bartholdi. This island of 12 acres had been owned in the 17th cent. by a colonist named Isaac Bedloe. (On Aug. 3, 1956, Pres. Dwight Eisenhower approved a measure changing the name to Liberty Island.)

The statue was finished on May 21, 1884, and presented to the U.S. minister to France, Levi Parsons Morton, July 4, 1884, by French diplomat Ferdinand de Lesseps.

On Aug. 5, 1884, the cornerstone for the granite pedestal—designed by architect Richard Morris Hunt—was laid on the foundations of Fort Wood, erected by the government in 1811. The American Committee for the Statue of Liberty had raised an inadequate $125,000, and *New York World* newspaper owner Joseph Pulitzer appealed Mar. 16, 1885, for general donations. By Aug. 11, 1885, he had raised $100,000. The statue itself arrived dismantled, in 214 packing cases, from Rouen, France, in June 1885. The last rivet of the statue was driven on Oct. 28, 1886, when Pres. Grover Cleveland dedicated the monument.

The Statue of Liberty National Monument was designated as such in 1924. It is administered by the National Park Service. A $2.5-mil building housing the American Museum of Immigration was opened by Pres. Richard Nixon on Sept. 26, 1972, at the base of the statue. It houses a permanent exhibition tracing the history of American immigration.

Four years of restoration work funded and led by the Statue of Liberty-Ellis Island Foundation were completed before the statue's 1986 centennial. The $87-mil project included the replacement of the 1,600 wrought iron bands that hold the statue's copper skin to its frame, replacement of the torch, and installation of an elevator. A four-day extravaganza of concerts, tall ships, cultural and heritage festivals, and fireworks, July 3-6, 1986, celebrated the 100th anniversary. U.S. Supreme Court Chief Justice Warren E. Burger swore in 5,000 new citizens on Ellis Island, while 20,000 others across the country were sworn in through a satellite telecast. Other ceremonies followed on Oct. 28, 1986, the statue's exact 100th birthday.

After the Sept. 11, 2001, terrorist attacks, Liberty Island was closed to visitors. The secretary of the interior reopened the island in Dec. 2001 after installing security screening facilities at passenger embarkation areas at Battery Park in Manhattan and Liberty State Park in New Jersey.

The federal government increased security throughout the park before reopening the statue. In addition to federally funded security upgrades, significant building safety improvements were made. Public access to the statue pedestal was restored on Aug. 3, 2004, and the crown reopened July 4, 2009.

Following the 125th anniversary celebration Oct. 28, 2011, the statue was closed. A $30-mil renovation brought the statue up to contemporary safety standards and allowed for increased visitor access. The statue interior reopened Oct. 28, 2012, but damages caused by Hurricane Sandy forced all of Liberty Island to close again within days. The island and the statue officially reopened to visitors July 4, 2013. A new, 26,000-sq-ft, freestanding Statue of Liberty Museum opened May 16, 2019.

Liberty Island was temporarily closed Mar. 16, 2020, in response to the COVID-19 outbreak, with schedule for reopening to be determined.

Advance reservations are recommended for visiting the statue pedestal and are required for the crown. When the facilities are open, reservations can be made at www.statuecruises.com or by calling 1-877-LADY-TIX. As of early 2020, fees started at $19.25 for adults ($9 child/$14 senior), with an additional $3 fee for crown visits. Visitors to the statue's interior must follow a number of guidelines including age and height restrictions. Park rangers conduct English-language tours throughout the day. Standard self-guided audio tours and a family-friendly audio tour (aimed at children ages 6-10) are available in the following 12 languages: English, Spanish, Arabic, French, German, Hindi, Italian, Japanese, Korean, Mandarin, Portuguese, and Russian.

Statue Statistics

The statue weighs 450,000 lbs, or 225 tons. The copper sheeting weighs 200,000 lbs. There are 377 steps from the main lobby to the crown platform. There are 146 steps from the top of the pedestal (the statue's feet) to the crown platform.

Statue feature	Measurement	
	Ft	In.
Height from base to torch tip	151	1
Foundation of pedestal to torch tip	305	1
Heel to top of head	111	1
Hand, length	16	5
Index finger, length	8	0
Fingernail size		13x10
Head from chin to cranium	17	3
Head thickness, ear to ear	10	0
Nose, length	4	6
Right arm, length	42	0
Right arm, max. thickness	12	0
Waist, thickness	35	0
Mouth, width	3	0
Tablet, length	23	7
Tablet, width	13	7

Ellis Island

Ellis Island was the gateway to America for over 12 mil immigrants between 1892 and 1924. In the late 18th cent., Samuel Ellis, a New York City merchant, purchased the island. From Ellis, it passed to New York state before the U.S. government bought it in 1808. On Jan. 1, 1892, the government opened the first federal immigration center in the U.S. there. The 27.5-acre site eventually supported over 35 buildings, including the Main Building with its Great Hall, designed to process 5,000 people a day. In Ellis Island's peak year, 1907, it received 1,004,756 immigrants; on its peak day (Apr. 17, 1907), 11,747 immigrants were processed.

Closed as an immigration station in 1954, Ellis Island was proclaimed part of the Statue of Liberty National Monument in 1965 by Pres. Lyndon B. Johnson. After a six-year, $170-mil restoration project funded by the Statue of Liberty-Ellis Island Foundation, Ellis Island was reopened as a museum in 1990, now called the Ellis Island National Museum of Immigration. Artifacts, historic photographs and documents, oral histories, and ethnic music depicting 400 years of American immigration are housed in the museum.

In 1998, the U.S. Supreme Court ruled that nearly 90% of the island (the 24.2 acres that are landfill) lies in New Jersey, while the original 3.3 acres, on which the museum is located, are in New York. (The decision settled the issue of jurisdiction over potential development.)

The American Family Immigration History Center opened in Apr. 2001. Visitors can access arrival records on over 51 mil individuals who entered through the Port of New York and Ellis Island from 1892 to 1957. The searchable digitized archives include ships' images and manifests and passenger information such as age, ethnicity, and port of departure. **Website:** www.libertyellisfoundation.org

Damage caused by storm surges from Hurricane Sandy in late Oct. 2012 forced Ellis Island to close for repairs. It reopened Oct. 28, 2013, and new galleries focusing on post-Ellis Island-era immigration opened May 20, 2015.

Ellis Island was closed Mar. 16, 2020, in response to the COVID-19 outbreak, with schedule for re-opening to be determined. For further information and updates on reopening see www.nps.gov/elis.

PRESIDENTS OF THE UNITED STATES

U.S. Presidents

	Name	Politics	Born	Birthplace	Inaug.	Age at inaug.	Died	Age at death
1.	George Washington	Fed.	1732, Feb. 22	VA	1789	57	1799, Dec. 14	67
2.	John Adams	Fed.	1735, Oct. 30	MA	1797	61	1826, July 4	90
3.	Thomas Jefferson	Dem.-Rep.	1743, Apr. 13	VA	1801	57	1826, July 4	83
4.	James Madison	Dem.-Rep.	1751, Mar. 16	VA	1809	57	1836, June 28	85
5.	James Monroe	Dem.-Rep.	1758, Apr. 28	VA	1817	58	1831, July 4	73
6.	John Quincy Adams	Dem.-Rep.	1767, July 11	MA	1825	57	1848, Feb. 23	80
7.	Andrew Jackson	Dem.	1767, Mar. 15	SC	1829	61	1845, June 8	78
8.	Martin Van Buren	Dem.	1782, Dec. 5	NY	1837	54	1862, July 24	79
9.	William Henry Harrison	Whig	1773, Feb. 9	VA	1841	68	1841, Apr. 4	68
10.	John Tyler	Whig	1790, Mar. 29	VA	1841	51	1862, Jan. 18	71
11.	James Knox Polk	Dem.	1795, Nov. 2	NC	1845	49	1849, June 15	53
12.	Zachary Taylor	Whig	1784, Nov. 24	VA	1849	64	1850, July 9	65
13.	Millard Fillmore	Whig	1800, Jan. 7	NY	1850	50	1874, Mar. 8	74
14.	Franklin Pierce	Dem.	1804, Nov. 23	NH	1853	48	1869, Oct. 8	64
15.	James Buchanan	Dem.	1791, Apr. 23	PA	1857	65	1868, June 1	77
16.	Abraham Lincoln	Rep.	1809, Feb. 12	KY	1861	52	1865, Apr. 15	56
17.	Andrew Johnson	Dem.[1]	1808, Dec. 29	NC	1865	56	1875, July 31	66
18.	Ulysses S. Grant	Rep.	1822, Apr. 27	OH	1869	46	1885, July 23	63
19.	Rutherford Birchard Hayes	Rep.	1822, Oct. 4	OH	1877	54	1893, Jan. 17	70
20.	James Abram Garfield	Rep.	1831, Nov. 19	OH	1881	49	1881, Sept. 19	49
21.	Chester Alan Arthur	Rep.	1829, Oct. 5	VT	1881	51	1886, Nov. 18	57
22.	(Stephen) Grover Cleveland	Dem.	1837, Mar. 18	NJ	1885	47	1908, June 24	71
23.	Benjamin Harrison	Rep.	1833, Aug. 20	OH	1889	55	1901, Mar. 13	67
24.	(Stephen) Grover Cleveland	Dem.	1837, Mar. 18	NJ	1893	55	1908, June 24	71
25.	William McKinley	Rep.	1843, Jan. 29	OH	1897	54	1901, Sept. 14	58
26.	Theodore Roosevelt	Rep.	1858, Oct. 27	NY	1901	42	1919, Jan. 6	60
27.	William Howard Taft	Rep.	1857, Sept. 15	OH	1909	51	1930, Mar. 8	72
28.	(Thomas) Woodrow Wilson	Dem.	1856, Dec. 28	VA	1913	56	1924, Feb. 3	67
29.	Warren Gamaliel Harding	Rep.	1865, Nov. 2	OH	1921	55	1923, Aug. 2	57
30.	(John) Calvin Coolidge	Rep.	1872, July 4	VT	1923	51	1933, Jan. 5	60
31.	Herbert Clark Hoover	Rep.	1874, Aug. 10	IA	1929	54	1964, Oct. 20	90
32.	Franklin Delano Roosevelt	Dem.	1882, Jan. 30	NY	1933	51	1945, Apr. 12	63
33.	Harry S. Truman	Dem.	1884, May 8	MO	1945	60	1972, Dec. 26	88
34.	Dwight David Eisenhower	Rep.	1890, Oct. 14	TX	1953	62	1969, Mar. 28	78
35.	John Fitzgerald Kennedy	Dem.	1917, May 29	MA	1961	43	1963, Nov. 22	46
36.	Lyndon Baines Johnson	Dem.	1908, Aug. 27	TX	1963	55	1973, Jan. 22	64
37.	Richard Milhous Nixon[2]	Rep.	1913, Jan. 9	CA	1969	56	1994, Apr. 22	81
38.	Gerald Rudolph Ford	Rep.	1913, July 14	NE	1974	61	2006, Dec. 26	93
39.	James Earl (Jimmy) Carter	Dem.	1924, Oct. 1	GA	1977	52		
40.	Ronald Wilson Reagan	Rep.	1911, Feb. 6	IL	1981	69	2004, June 5	93
41.	George Herbert Walker Bush	Rep.	1924, June 12	MA	1989	64	2018, Nov. 30	94
42.	Wm. Jefferson (Bill) Clinton	Dem.	1946, Aug. 19	AR	1993	46		
43.	George Walker Bush	Rep.	1946, July 6	CT	2001	54		
44.	Barack Hussein Obama	Dem.	1961, Aug. 4	HI	2009	47		
45.	Donald John Trump	Rep.	1946, June 14	NY	2017	70		

(1) Andrew Johnson, a Democrat, had been nominated vice president by Republicans and elected with Lincoln on National Union ticket. (2) Resigned Aug. 9, 1974.

U.S. Presidents, Vice Presidents, Congresses

	President	Service		Vice President	Congresses
1.	George Washington	Apr. 30, 1789-Mar. 3, 1797	1.	John Adams	1, 2, 3, 4
2.	John Adams	Mar. 4, 1797-Mar. 3, 1801	2.	Thomas Jefferson	5, 6
3.	Thomas Jefferson	Mar. 4, 1801-Mar. 3, 1805	3.	Aaron Burr	7, 8
		Mar. 4, 1805-Mar. 3, 1809	4.	George Clinton	9, 10
4.	James Madison	Mar. 4, 1809-Mar. 3, 1813		George Clinton[1]	11, 12
		Mar. 4, 1813-Mar. 3, 1817	5.	Elbridge Gerry[2]	13, 14
5.	James Monroe	Mar. 4, 1817-Mar. 3, 1825	6.	Daniel D. Tompkins	15, 16, 17, 18
6.	John Quincy Adams	Mar. 4, 1825-Mar. 3, 1829	7.	John C. Calhoun	19, 20
7.	Andrew Jackson	Mar. 4, 1829-Mar. 3, 1833		John C. Calhoun[3]	21, 22
		Mar. 4, 1833-Mar. 3, 1837	8.	Martin Van Buren	23, 24
8.	Martin Van Buren	Mar. 4, 1837-Mar. 3, 1841	9.	Richard M. Johnson	25, 26
9.	William Henry Harrison[4]	Mar. 4, 1841-Apr. 4, 1841	10.	John Tyler	27
10.	John Tyler	Apr. 6, 1841-Mar. 3, 1845		(None)	27, 28
11.	James K. Polk	Mar. 4, 1845-Mar. 3, 1849	11.	George M. Dallas	29, 30
12.	Zachary Taylor[4]	Mar. 5, 1849-July 9, 1850	12.	Millard Fillmore	31
13.	Millard Fillmore	July 10, 1850-Mar. 3, 1853		(None)	31, 32
14.	Franklin Pierce	Mar. 4, 1853-Mar. 3, 1857	13.	William R. King[5]	33, 34
15.	James Buchanan	Mar. 4, 1857-Mar. 3, 1861	14.	John C. Breckinridge	35, 36
16.	Abraham Lincoln[4]	Mar. 4, 1861-Mar. 3, 1865	15.	Hannibal Hamlin	37, 38
		Mar. 4, 1865-Apr. 15, 1865	16.	Andrew Johnson	39
17.	Andrew Johnson	Apr. 15, 1865-Mar. 3, 1869		(None)	39, 40
18.	Ulysses S. Grant	Mar. 4, 1869-Mar. 3, 1873	17.	Schuyler Colfax	41, 42
		Mar. 4, 1873-Mar. 3, 1877	18.	Henry Wilson[6]	43, 44
19.	Rutherford B. Hayes	Mar. 4, 1877-Mar. 3, 1881	19.	William A. Wheeler	45, 46
20.	James A. Garfield[4]	Mar. 4, 1881-Sept. 19, 1881	20.	Chester A. Arthur	47
21.	Chester A. Arthur	Sept. 20, 1881-Mar. 3, 1885		(None)	47, 48
22.	Grover Cleveland[7]	Mar. 4, 1885-Mar. 3, 1889	21.	Thomas A. Hendricks[8]	49, 50
23.	Benjamin Harrison	Mar. 4, 1889-Mar. 3, 1893	22.	Levi P. Morton	51, 52
24.	Grover Cleveland[7]	Mar. 4, 1893-Mar. 3, 1897	23.	Adlai E. Stevenson	53, 54
25.	William McKinley[4]	Mar. 4, 1897-Mar. 3, 1901	24.	Garret A. Hobart[9]	55, 56
		Mar. 4, 1901-Sept. 14, 1901	25.	Theodore Roosevelt	57
26.	Theodore Roosevelt	Sept. 14, 1901-Mar. 3, 1905		(None)	57, 58
		Mar. 4, 1905-Mar. 3, 1909	26.	Charles W. Fairbanks	59, 60
27.	William H. Taft	Mar. 4, 1909-Mar. 3, 1913	27.	James S. Sherman[10]	61, 62

President	Service	Vice President	Congresses
28. Woodrow Wilson	Mar. 4, 1913-Mar. 3, 1921	28. Thomas R. Marshall	63, 64, 65, 66
29. Warren G. Harding[4]	Mar. 4, 1921-Aug. 2, 1923	29. Calvin Coolidge	67
30. Calvin Coolidge	Aug. 3, 1923-Mar. 3, 1925	(None)	68
	Mar. 4, 1925-Mar. 3, 1929	30. Charles G. Dawes	69, 70
31. Herbert C. Hoover	Mar. 4, 1929-Mar. 3, 1933	31. Charles Curtis	71, 72
32. Franklin D. Roosevelt[4,11]	Mar. 4, 1933-Jan. 20, 1941	32. John N. Garner	73, 74, 75, 76, 77
	Jan. 20, 1941-Jan. 20, 1945	33. Henry A. Wallace	77, 78, 79
	Jan. 20, 1945-Apr. 12, 1945	34. Harry S. Truman	79
33. Harry S. Truman	Apr. 12, 1945-Jan. 20, 1949	(None)	79, 80, 81
	Jan. 20, 1949-Jan. 20, 1953	35. Alben W. Barkley	81, 82, 83
34. Dwight D. Eisenhower	Jan. 20, 1953-Jan. 20, 1961	36. Richard M. Nixon	83, 84, 85, 86, 87
35. John F. Kennedy[4]	Jan. 20, 1961-Nov. 22, 1963	37. Lyndon B. Johnson	87, 88
36. Lyndon B. Johnson	Nov. 22, 1963-Jan. 20, 1965	(None)	88, 89
	Jan. 20, 1965-Jan. 20, 1969	38. Hubert H. Humphrey	89, 90, 91
37. Richard M. Nixon[13]	Jan. 20, 1969-Jan. 20, 1973	39. Spiro T. Agnew[12]	91, 92, 93
	Jan. 20, 1973-Aug. 9, 1974	40. Gerald R. Ford[14]	93
38. Gerald R. Ford[15]	Aug. 9, 1974-Jan. 20, 1977	41. Nelson A. Rockefeller[16]	93, 94, 95
39. Jimmy Carter	Jan. 20, 1977-Jan. 20, 1981	42. Walter F. Mondale	95, 96, 97
40. Ronald W. Reagan	Jan. 20, 1981-Jan. 20, 1989	43. George H. W. Bush	97, 98, 99, 100, 101
41. George H. W. Bush	Jan. 20, 1989-Jan. 20, 1993	44. Dan Quayle	101, 102, 103
42. Bill Clinton	Jan. 20, 1993-Jan. 20, 2001	45. Al Gore	103, 104, 105, 106, 107
43. George W. Bush	Jan. 20, 2001-Jan. 20, 2009	46. Dick Cheney	107, 108, 109, 110, 111
44. Barack H. Obama	Jan. 20, 2009-Jan. 20, 2017	47. Joe Biden	111, 112, 113, 114, 115
45. Donald J. Trump	Jan. 20, 2017-	48. Mike Pence	115, 116

(1) Died Apr. 20, 1812. (2) Died Nov. 23, 1814. (3) Resigned Dec. 28, 1832, to become U.S. senator. (4) Died in office. (5) Died Apr. 18, 1853. (6) Died Nov. 22, 1875. (7) Terms not consecutive. (8) Died Nov. 25, 1885. (9) Died Nov. 21, 1899. (10) Died Oct. 30, 1912. (11) First president to be inaugurated under 20th Amendment, Jan. 20, 1937. (12) Resigned Oct. 10, 1973, after pleading no contest to a charge of tax evasion. (13) Resigned Aug. 9, 1974. (14) First nonelected vice president, chosen under 25th Amendment procedure. (15) First president never elected president or vice president. (16) Second nonelected vice president, chosen under 25th Amendment. Confirmed Dec. 19, 1974.

Vice Presidents of the U.S.

The numerals given vice presidents do not coincide with those given presidents because some presidents (Tyler, Fillmore, A. Johnson, Arthur) had none, and some had more than one.

Name	Birthplace	Born	Home	Inaug.	Politics/party	Place of death	Died	Age at death
1. John Adams	Quincy, MA	1735	MA	1789	Fed.	Quincy, MA	1826	90
2. Thomas Jefferson	Shadwell, VA	1743	VA	1797	Dem.-Rep.	Monticello, VA	1826	83
3. Aaron Burr	Newark, NJ	1756	NY	1801	Dem.-Rep.	Staten Island, NY	1836	80
4. George Clinton	Little Britain, NY	1739	NY	1805	Dem.-Rep.	Washington, DC	1812	73
5. Elbridge Gerry	Marblehead, MA	1744	MA	1813	Dem.-Rep.	Washington, DC	1814	70
6. Daniel D. Tompkins	Scarsdale, NY	1774	NY	1817	Dem.-Rep.	Staten Island, NY	1825	51
7. John C. Calhoun[1]	Abbeville, SC	1782	SC	1825	Dem.-Rep.	Washington, DC	1850	68
8. Martin Van Buren	Kinderhook, NY	1782	NY	1833	Dem.	Kinderhook, NY	1862	79
9. Richard M. Johnson[2]	Louisville, KY	1780	KY	1837	Dem.	Frankfort, KY	1850	70
10. John Tyler	Greenway, VA	1790	VA	1841	Whig	Richmond, VA	1862	71
11. George M. Dallas	Philadelphia, PA	1792	PA	1845	Dem.	Philadelphia, PA	1864	72
12. Millard Fillmore	Cayuga Co., NY	1800	NY	1849	Whig	Buffalo, NY	1874	74
13. William R. King	Sampson Co., NC	1786	AL	1853	Dem.	Cahaba, AL	1853	67
14. John C. Breckinridge	Lexington, KY	1821	KY	1857	Dem.	Lexington, KY	1875	54
15. Hannibal Hamlin	Paris, ME	1809	ME	1861	Rep.	Bangor, ME	1891	81
16. Andrew Johnson	Raleigh, NC	1808	TN	1865	Dem.[3]	Carter Co., TN	1875	66
17. Schuyler Colfax	New York, NY	1823	IN	1869	Rep.	Mankato, MN	1885	62
18. Henry Wilson	Farmington, NH	1812	MA	1873	Rep.	Washington, DC	1875	63
19. William A. Wheeler	Malone, NY	1819	NY	1877	Rep.	Malone, NY	1887	68
20. Chester A. Arthur	Fairfield, VT	1829	NY	1881	Rep.	New York, NY	1886	57
21. Thomas A. Hendricks	Zanesville, OH	1819	IN	1885	Dem.	Indianapolis, IN	1885	66
22. Levi P. Morton	Shoreham, VT	1824	NY	1889	Rep.	Rhinebeck, NY	1920	96
23. Adlai E. Stevenson[4]	Christian Co., KY	1835	IL	1893	Dem.	Chicago, IL	1914	78
24. Garret A. Hobart	Long Branch, NJ	1844	NJ	1897	Rep.	Paterson, NJ	1899	55
25. Theodore Roosevelt	New York, NY	1858	NY	1901	Rep.	Oyster Bay, NY	1919	60
26. Charles W. Fairbanks	Unionville Centre, OH	1852	IN	1905	Rep.	Indianapolis, IN	1918	66
27. James S. Sherman	Utica, NY	1855	NY	1909	Rep.	Utica, NY	1912	57
28. Thomas R. Marshall	N. Manchester, IN	1854	IN	1913	Dem.	Washington, DC	1925	71
29. Calvin Coolidge	Plymouth Notch, VT	1872	MA	1921	Rep.	Northampton, MA	1933	60
30. Charles G. Dawes	Marietta, OH	1865	IL	1925	Rep.	Evanston, IL	1951	85
31. Charles Curtis	Topeka, KS	1860	KS	1929	Rep.	Washington, DC	1936	76
32. John Nance Garner	Red River Co., TX	1868	TX	1933	Dem.	Uvalde, TX	1967	98
33. Henry A. Wallace	Adair County, IA	1888	IA	1941	Dem.	Danbury, CT	1965	77
34. Harry S. Truman	Lamar, MO	1884	MO	1945	Dem.	Kansas City, MO	1972	88
35. Alben W. Barkley	Graves Co., KY	1877	KY	1949	Dem.	Lexington, VA	1956	78
36. Richard M. Nixon	Yorba Linda, CA	1913	CA	1953	Rep.	New York, NY	1994	81
37. Lyndon B. Johnson	Stonewall, TX	1908	TX	1961	Dem.	San Antonio, TX	1973	64
38. Hubert H. Humphrey	Wallace, SD	1911	MN	1965	Dem.	Waverly, MN	1978	66
39. Spiro T. Agnew[5]	Baltimore, MD	1918	MD	1969	Rep.	Berlin, MD	1996	77
40. Gerald R. Ford[6]	Omaha, NE	1913	MI	1973	Rep.	Rancho Mirage, CA	2006	93
41. Nelson A. Rockefeller[7]	Bar Harbor, ME	1908	NY	1974	Rep.	New York, NY	1979	70
42. Walter F. Mondale	Ceylon, MN	1928	MN	1977	Dem.			
43. George H. W. Bush	Milton, MA	1924	TX	1981	Rep.	Houston, TX	2018	94
44. James Danforth (Dan) Quayle Jr.	Indianapolis, IN	1947	IN	1989	Rep.			
45. Albert A. Gore	Washington, DC	1948	TN	1993	Dem.			
46. Richard B. Cheney	Lincoln, NE	1941	WY	2001	Rep.			
47. Joseph R. Biden Jr.	Scranton, PA	1942	DE	2009	Dem.			
48. Michael R. Pence	Columbus, IN	1959	IN	2017	Rep.			

(1) Resigned Dec. 28, 1832, having been elected to the Senate to fill a vacancy. (2) Richard M. Johnson was the only vice president to be chosen by the Senate because of a tied vote in the Electoral College. (3) Democrat Andrew Johnson was nominated vice president by Republicans and elected with Lincoln on the National Union ticket. (4) Grandfather of Democratic candidate for president in 1952 and 1956. (5) Resigned Oct. 10, 1973, after pleading no contest to a charge of tax evasion. (6) First nonelected vice president, chosen under 25th Amendment procedure. (7) Second nonelected vice president, chosen under 25th Amendment.

Biographies of the Presidents

George Washington (1789-97), first president, Federalist, was born on Feb. 22, 1732, in Wakefield on Pope's Creek, Westmoreland Co., VA, the son of Augustine and Mary Ball Washington. He spent his early childhood on a farm near Fredericksburg. His father died when Washington was 11. He studied mathematics and surveying, and at 16, he went to live with his elder half brother, Lawrence, who built and named Mount Vernon in Virginia. Washington surveyed the lands of Thomas Fairfax in the Shenandoah Valley. He accompanied Lawrence to Barbados, West Indies, where he contracted smallpox and was deeply scarred. Lawrence died in 1752, and Washington inherited his property. He valued land, and when he died, he was a slaveholder who owned 70,000 acres in Virginia and 40,000 acres in what is now West Virginia.

Washington's military service began in 1753, when Lt. Gov. Robert Dinwiddie of Virginia sent him on missions deep into Ohio country. He clashed with the French and had to surrender Fort Necessity on July 3, 1754. He was an aide to the British general Edward Braddock and was at his side when the army was ambushed and defeated (July 9, 1755) on a march to Fort Duquesne. He helped take Fort Duquesne from the French in 1758.

After Washington's marriage to Martha Dandridge Custis, a widow, in 1759, he managed his family estate at Mount Vernon. Although not in favor of independence initially, he opposed the repressive measures of the British crown and took charge of the Virginia troops before war broke out. He was made commander of the newly created Continental Army by the Continental Congress on June 15, 1775.

The American victory was due largely to Washington's leadership. He was resourceful, a disciplinarian, and a dependable force for unity. Washington favored a federal government. He became chairman of the Constitutional Convention of 1787 and helped get the Constitution ratified. Unanimously elected president by the Electoral College, he was inaugurated Apr. 30, 1789, on the balcony of New York's Federal Hall. He was reelected in 1792. Washington made an effort to avoid partisan politics as president.

Refusing to consider a third term, Washington retired to Mount Vernon in Mar. 1797. A ride in snow and rain around his estate led to what present-day doctors believe to have been an attack of acute epiglottitis. Doctors were unsuccessful in treating the inflammation in his throat, and Washington died Dec. 14, 1799.

John Adams (1797-1801), second president, Federalist, was born on Oct. 30, 1735, in Braintree (now Quincy), MA, the son of John and Susanna Boylston Adams. He was a great-grandson of Henry Adams, who came from England in 1636. He graduated from Harvard in 1755, then taught school and studied law. He married Abigail Smith in 1764. In 1770, he successfully defended in court the British soldiers who fired on civilians in the Boston Massacre. He was a delegate to the Continental Congress and a signer of the Declaration of Independence. In 1778, Congress sent Adams and John Jay to join Benjamin Franklin as diplomatic representatives in Europe. Because he ran second to Washington in Electoral College balloting in Feb. 1789, Adams became the nation's first vice president, a post he characterized as highly insignificant; he was reelected in 1792.

In 1796 Adams was chosen president by the electors. His administration was marked by growing conflict with fellow Federalist Alexander Hamilton and with those in his cabinet who shared Hamilton's anti-French position. Adams avoided a declared war with France but became unpopular, especially after securing passage of the Alien and Sedition Acts, which restricted speech critical of the government, in 1798. His foreign policy contributed significantly to the election of Thomas Jefferson in 1800.

Adams lived for a quarter century after he left office, during which time he wrote extensively. He died July 4, 1826, on the same day as his rival Thomas Jefferson (the 50th anniversary of the Declaration of Independence).

Thomas Jefferson (1801-09), third president, Democratic-Republican, was born on Apr. 13, 1743, in Shadwell in Goochland (now Albemarle) Co., VA, the son of Peter and Jane Randolph Jefferson. His father died when Jefferson was 14, leaving him 2,750 acres and his slaves. Jefferson attended (1760-62) the College of William and Mary, read Greek and Latin classics, and played the violin. In 1769 he was elected to the Virginia House of Burgesses. In 1770 he began building his home, Monticello, and in 1772 he married Martha Wayles Skelton, a wealthy widow. Jefferson helped establish the Virginia Committee of Correspondence. As a member of the Second Continental Congress he drafted the Declaration of Independence. He also was a member of the Virginia House of Delegates (1776-79) and was elected governor of Virginia in 1779. He resigned in 1781, after British troops invaded Virginia. During his term he wrote the Virginia Statute of Religious Freedom. After his wife's death in 1782, Jefferson again became a delegate to the Congress, and in 1784 he drafted the report that was the basis for the Ordinances of 1784, 1785, and 1787. He was minister to France from 1785 to 1789, when George Washington appointed him secretary of state.

Jefferson's strong faith in the consent of the governed conflicted with the emphasis on executive control, favored by Sec. of the Treasury Alexander Hamilton, and Jefferson resigned as secretary of state on Dec. 31, 1793. In the 1796 election Jefferson was the Democratic-Republican candidate for president; John Adams won the election, and Jefferson became vice president. In 1800, Jefferson and Aaron Burr received equal numbers of Electoral College votes; the House of Representatives elected Jefferson president. Jefferson was a strong advocate of westward expansion; major events of his first term were the Louisiana Purchase (1803) and the Lewis and Clark expedition. His second term saw the passage of the Embargo Act, barring U.S. ships from setting sail to foreign ports and forbidding foreign ships from loading cargo in U.S. ports. Jefferson established the Univ. of Virginia and designed its buildings. He died July 4, 1826, on the same day as John Adams (the 50th anniversary of the Declaration of Independence).

Jefferson called slavery a "moral depravity" and violation of natural rights, but he profited from it as a slaveholder. He advocated gradual emancipation through voting, in conjunction with deportation. Based partly on DNA taken from descendants of Jefferson and of Sally Hemings, an enslaved woman who lived at Monticello from a young age, many historians conclude that Jefferson fathered one or more of her six children.

James Madison (1809-17), fourth president, Democratic-Republican, was born on Mar. 16, 1751, in Port Conway, King George Co., VA, the son of James and Eleanor Rose Conway Madison. Madison graduated from the College of New Jersey in 1771. He served in the Virginia Constitutional Convention (1776), and, in 1780, became a delegate to the Seond Continental Congress. He was chief recorder of the Constitutional Convention in 1787 and supported ratification in the *Federalist Papers*, written with Alexander Hamilton and John Jay. In 1789, Madison was elected to the House of Representatives, where he helped frame the Bill of Rights and fought against passage of the Alien and Sedition Acts. In the 1790s, he helped found the Democratic-Republican Party, which ultimately became the Democratic Party. He became Jefferson's secretary of state in 1801.

Madison was elected president in 1808. His first term was marked by tensions with Great Britain, and his conduct of foreign policy was criticized by the Federalists and by his own party. Nevertheless, he was reelected in 1812, the year war was declared on Great Britain. The war that many considered a second American revolution ended with a treaty that did not settle any of the issues. Madison's most important action after the war was demilitarizing the U.S.-Canadian border.

In 1817, Madison retired to his Virginia plantation, Montpelier, which made use of slave labor. He edited his famous papers on the Constitutional Convention and helped found the Univ. of Virginia, of which he became rector in 1826. He died June 28, 1836.

James Monroe (1817-25), fifth president, Democratic-Republican, was born on Apr. 28, 1758, in Westmoreland Co., VA, the son of Spence and Elizabeth Jones Monroe. He entered the College of William and Mary in 1774 but left to serve in the Third Virginia Regiment during the American Revolution. After the war, he studied law with Thomas Jefferson. In 1782 he was elected to the Virginia House of Delegates, and he served (1783-86) as a delegate to the Continental Congress. He opposed ratification of the Constitution because it lacked a bill of rights. Monroe was elected to the U.S. Senate in 1790. In 1794, Pres. Washington appointed Monroe minister to France. He was again minister to France (1803) under Pres. Jefferson as well as minister to Great Britain (1803-07). He served twice as governor of Virginia (1799-1802, 1811).

In 1816 Monroe was elected president; he was reelected in 1820 with all but one Electoral College vote. His administration became known as the Era of Good Feeling. He obtained Florida from Spain, settled boundary disputes with Britain over Canada, and eliminated border forts. Though a slaveholder himself, he supported the anti-slavery position that led to the Missouri Compromise. His most significant contribution was the Monroe Doctrine, which opposed European intervention in the Western Hemisphere and became a cornerstone of U.S. foreign policy.

Although Monroe retired to Oak Hill, VA, financial problems forced him to sell his property and move to New York City. He died there on July 4, 1831.

John Quincy Adams (1825-29), sixth president, independent Federalist, later Democratic-Republican, was born on July 11, 1767, in Braintree (now Quincy), MA, the son of John and Abigail Adams. His father was the second president. He studied abroad and at Harvard College, from which he graduated in 1787. In 1803, he was elected to the U.S. Senate. President Monroe chose him as his secretary of state in 1817. In this capacity he negotiated the cession of Florida from Spain, supported exclusion of slavery in the Missouri Compromise, and helped formulate the Monroe Doctrine.

After no candidate won an Electoral College majority in 1824, the presidential election was decided by the House of Representatives. Adams won with support from rival Henry Clay, whom he named secretary of state, fueling accusations of a "corrupt bargain." His expansion of executive powers was strongly opposed, and in the 1828 election he lost to Andrew Jackson. In 1831 he entered the House of Representatives and served 17 years. He opposed slavery, the annexation of Texas, and the Mexican War. He helped establish the Smithsonian Institution.

Adams suffered a stroke in the House and died in the Speaker's Room on Feb. 23, 1848.

Andrew Jackson (1829-37), seventh president, Democratic-Republican, later a Democrat, was born on Mar. 15, 1767, in the Waxhaw district, on the border of North and South Carolina, the son of Andrew and Elizabeth Hutchinson Jackson. At the age of 13, he joined the militia to fight in the American Revolution and was captured. Orphaned at age 14, Jackson was raised by an uncle. By age 20, he was practicing law, and he later served as prosecuting attorney in Nashville, TN. In 1796 he helped draft the constitution of Tennessee, and for a year he occupied its one seat in the House of Representatives. The next year he served in the U.S. Senate.

In the War of 1812, Jackson crushed the Creek Indians at Horseshoe Bend, AL (1814), and, with a greatly outnumbered army consisting chiefly of militia members, privateers, Choctaw Indians, and other volunteer fighters, defeated Gen. Edward Pakenham's British troops at the Battle of New Orleans (1815). Nicknamed "Old Hickory" for his toughness, he emerged a national hero.

In 1818 Jackson briefly invaded Spanish Florida to quell Seminoles and outlaws who harassed frontier settlements. He ran for president against John Quincy Adams in 1824, but did not achieve a majority despite winning the most popular and electoral votes. The House of Representatives decided the election and chose Adams. In the 1828 election, however, Jackson, a slaveholder, defeated Adams by carrying the West and the South.

As president, Jackson introduced what became known as the spoils system—rewarding party members with government posts. A self-professed champion of the common man, he also viewed the Second Bank of the U.S. as a bastion of privilege and made it a major issue in the election of 1832, the first where candidates were chosen at national conventions rather than in congressional caucuses. Defeating Henry Clay, Jackson increasingly diverted funds from the national bank into so-called pet banks run by members of his own party. When South Carolina refused to collect imports under a federal tariff, which it declared null and void, Jackson won passage of legislation confirming his right to use military force to obtain compliance; eventually the tariff rate was reduced and the nullifiers backed down. After leaving office in 1837, he retired to the Hermitage, his estate outside Nashville, where he died on June 8, 1845.

Martin Van Buren (1837-41), eighth president, Democrat, was born on Dec. 5, 1782, in Kinderhook, NY, the son of Abraham and Maria Hoes Van Buren. After attending local schools, he studied law and became a lawyer at the age of 20. A consummate politician, Van Buren began his career in the New York state senate and then served as state attorney general (1816-19). He was elected to the U.S. Senate in 1821. He helped swing Eastern support to Andrew Jackson in the 1828 election and served as Jackson's secretary of state from 1829 to 1831. In 1832 he was elected vice president. Known as the "Little Magician," Van Buren was extremely influential in Jackson's administration.

In 1836, Van Buren defeated William Henry Harrison for president and took office as the financial panic of 1837 initiated a nationwide depression. Although he instituted the independent treasury system, his refusal to spend land revenues led to his defeat by William Henry Harrison in 1840. In 1844 he lost the Democratic nomination to James K. Polk. In 1848 he again ran for president on the Free Soil ticket but lost. He died in Kinderhook on July 24, 1862.

William Henry Harrison (1841), ninth president, Whig, who served only 31 days, was born on Feb. 9, 1773, in Berkeley, Charles City Co., VA, the son of Benjamin Harrison—a signer of the Declaration of Independence—and of Elizabeth Bassett Harrison. He attended Hampden-Sydney College. Harrison served as secretary of the Northwest Territory in 1798 and was its delegate to the House of Representatives in 1799. He was the first governor of Indiana Territory and served as superintendent of Indian affairs. Leading some 950 troops, he repelled an attack by Shawnee Indians at Tippecanoe, IN, on Nov. 7, 1811. A generation later, in 1840, he waged a rousing presidential campaign using the slogan "Tippecanoe and Tyler Too." The Tyler of the slogan was his running mate, John Tyler.

Although born to one of the wealthiest, most prestigious, and most influential families in Virginia, Harrison also campaigned with the slogan "Log Cabin and Hard Cider." He died Apr. 4, 1841, after only one month in office, of what doctors now believe was typhoid fever.

John Tyler (1841-45), 10th president, independent Whig, was born on Mar. 29, 1790, in Greenway, Charles City Co., VA, the son of John and Mary Armistead Tyler. His father was governor of Virginia (1808-11). Tyler graduated from the College of William and Mary in 1807 and in 1811 was elected to the Virginia legislature. In 1816 he was chosen for the U.S. House of Representatives. He served in the Virginia legislature again from 1823 to 1825, when he was elected governor of Virginia. After a stint in the U.S. Senate (1827-36), he was elected vice president (1840).

When William Henry Harrison died only a month after taking office, Tyler succeeded him. Because he was the first person to occupy the presidency without having been elected to that office, he was referred to as "His Accidency." He gained passage of the Preemption Act of 1841, which gave squatters on government land the right to buy 160 acres at the minimum auction price. His last act as president was to sign a resolution annexing Texas. Tyler accepted renomination in 1844 from some Democrats but withdrew in favor of the official party candidate, James K. Polk. A slaveholder who consistently supported the expansion of slavery, he served briefly in the Confederate House of Representatives before he died in Richmond, VA, on Jan. 18, 1862.

James Knox Polk (1845-49), 11th president, Democrat, was born on Nov. 2, 1795, in Mecklenburg Co., NC, the son of Samuel and Jane Knox Polk. He graduated from the Univ. of North Carolina in 1818 and served in the Tennessee state legislature from 1823 to 1825. He served in the U.S. House of Representatives from 1825 to 1839, the last four years as Speaker. He was governor of Tennessee from 1839 to 1841. In 1844, after the Democratic National Convention became deadlocked, it nominated Polk, who became the first "dark horse" candidate for president. He was nominated primarily because he favored annexation of Texas and tolerated slavery.

As president, Polk reestablished the independent treasury system originated by Van Buren. He was so intent on acquiring California from Mexico that he sent troops to the Mexican border and declared a state of war after Mexicans attacked. The Mexican War ended with the annexation of California and much of the Southwest as part of America's "manifest destiny." Polk compromised on the Oregon boundary ("54-40 or fight!") by accepting the 49th parallel and yielding Vancouver Island to the British. Polk died in Nashville, TN, on June 15, 1849, a few months after leaving office.

Zachary Taylor (1849-50), 12th president, Whig, who served only 16 months, was born on Nov. 24, 1784, in Orange Co., VA, the son of Richard and Sarah Strother Taylor. He grew up on his father's plantation near Louisville, KY, where the work was done by enslaved persons and he was educated by private tutors. In 1808 Taylor joined the regular army and was commissioned first lieutenant. He fought in the War of 1812, the Black Hawk War (1832), and the second Seminole War (beginning in 1837). He was called "Old Rough and Ready" for his military prowess. In 1846 Pres. Polk sent him with an army to the Rio Grande. When the Mexicans attacked him, Polk declared war. Outnumbered four to one, Taylor defeated Antonio López de Santa Anna at Buena Vista (1847).

A national hero, Taylor received the Whig nomination in 1848 and was elected president, even though he had never bothered to vote. He resumed the spoils system and, though a slaveholder, worked to admit California as a free state. He fell ill, likely from a case of acute gastroenteritis, and died in office on July 9, 1850.

Millard Fillmore (1850-53), 13th president, Whig, was born on Jan. 7, 1800, in Cayuga Co., NY, the son of Nathaniel and Phoebe Millard Fillmore. Although he had little schooling, he became a law clerk at the age of 22 and was admitted to the bar a year later. He was elected to the New York state assembly in 1828 and served until 1831. From 1833 until 1835 and again from 1837 to 1843, he represented his district in the U.S. House of Representatives. He opposed the entrance of Texas as a slave state and voted for a protective tariff. In 1844 he was defeated for governor of New York.

In 1848, he was elected vice president; he became president after Taylor's death. Fillmore favored the Compromise of 1850 and signed the Fugitive Slave Law. His policies pleased neither expansionists nor slaveholders, and he was not renominated in 1852. In 1856 he was nominated by the American (Know-Nothing) Party, but despite the support of the Whigs, he was defeated by James Buchanan. He died in Buffalo, NY, on Mar. 8, 1874.

Franklin Pierce (1853-57), 14th president, Democrat, was born on Nov. 23, 1804, in Hillsboro, NH, the son of Benjamin Pierce, Revolutionary War general and governor of New Hampshire, and Anna Kendrick. He graduated from Bowdoin College in 1824 and was admitted to the bar in 1827. He was elected to the New Hampshire state legislature in 1829 and was chosen Speaker in 1831. He went to the U.S. House in 1833 and was elected a U.S. senator in 1837. He enlisted in the Mexican War and became brigadier general under Gen. Winfield Scott.

In 1852 Pierce was nominated as the Democratic presidential candidate on the 49th ballot. He decisively defeated Gen. Scott, his Whig opponent, in the election. Although he was against slavery, Pierce was influenced by proslavery Southerners. He supported the controversial Kansas-Nebraska Act, which left the question of slavery in the new territories of Kansas and Nebraska to popular vote. Pierce signed a reciprocity treaty with Canada and approved the Gadsden Purchase, from Mexico, of a border area on a proposed railroad route. Denied renomination, he spent most of his remaining years in Concord, NH, where he died on Oct. 8, 1869.

James Buchanan (1857-61), 15th president, Federalist, later Democrat, was born on Apr. 23, 1791, near Mercersburg, PA, the son of James and Elizabeth Speer Buchanan. He graduated from Dickinson College in 1809 and was admitted to the bar in 1812. He fought in the War of 1812 as a volunteer. He was twice elected to the Pennsylvania general assembly, and in 1821 he entered the U.S. House of Representatives. After briefly serving (1832-33) as minister to Russia, he was elected U.S. senator from Pennsylvania. As Polk's secretary of state (1845-49), he ended the Oregon dispute with Britain and supported the Mexican War and annexation of Texas. As minister to Great Britain, he signed the Ostend Manifesto (1854), declaring a U.S. right to take Cuba by force should efforts to purchase it fail.

Nominated by Democrats, Buchanan was elected president in 1856. On slavery he favored popular sovereignty and choice by state constitutions but did not consistently uphold this position. He denied the right of states to secede but opposed coercion and attempted to keep peace by not provoking secessionists. Buchanan left office having failed to deal decisively with the situation. He died at Wheatland, his estate, near Lancaster, PA, on June 1, 1868.

Abraham Lincoln (1861-65), 16th president, Whig, then Republican, was born on Feb. 12, 1809, in a log cabin on a farm in Hardin (now Larue) Co., KY, the son of Thomas and Nancy Hanks Lincoln. The Lincolns moved to Spencer Co., IN, near Gentryville, when Lincoln was 7. After Lincoln's mother died, his father married Mrs. Sarah Bush Johnston in 1819. In 1830 the family moved to Macon Co., IL.

Defeated in 1832 in a race for the state legislature, Lincoln was elected on the Whig ticket two years later and served in the lower house from 1834 to 1842. In 1837 Lincoln was admitted to the bar and became partner in a Springfield, IL, law office. In 1846, he was elected to Congress, where he attracted attention during a single term for his opposition to the Mexican War and his position on slavery. In 1856 he campaigned for the newly founded Republican Party, and in 1858 he became its senatorial candidate against Stephen A. Douglas. Although he lost the election, Lincoln gained national recognition from his debates with Douglas.

In 1860, Lincoln was nominated for president by the Republican Party on a platform of restricting slavery. He ran against Douglas, a northern Democrat; John C. Breckinridge, a Southern proslavery Democrat; and John Bell, of the Constitutional Union Party. In response to Lincoln's victory, South Carolina seceded from the Union on Dec. 20, 1860, soon followed by six other Southern states.

The Civil War erupted when South Carolina's Fort Sumter, which Lincoln decided to resupply, was attacked by Confederate forces on Apr. 12, 1861. Lincoln called for recruits from the North, and four more Southern states seceded. Hundreds of thousands of Union and Confederate soldiers were killed or wounded in four years of battle that followed. On Sept. 22, 1862, five days after the Battle of Antietam, Lincoln announced that those who were enslaved in territory then in rebellion would be free Jan. 1, 1863, under his Emancipation Proclamation. His speeches, including his Gettysburg and inaugural addresses, are remembered for their eloquence.

Lincoln was reelected, in 1864, over Gen. George B. McClellan, a Democrat. Confederate Gen. Robert E. Lee surrendered on Apr. 9, 1865. On Apr. 14, Lincoln was shot by actor John Wilkes Booth in Ford's Theater, in Washington, DC. He died the next day.

Andrew Johnson (1865-69), 17th president, Democrat, was born on Dec. 29, 1808, in Raleigh, NC, the son of Jacob and Mary McDonough Johnson. He was apprenticed to a tailor as a youth but ran away after two years and eventually settled in Greeneville, TN, where he was elected councilman and later mayor. In 1835 he was sent to the state general assembly. In 1843 he was elected to the U.S. House of Representatives, where he served for 10 years. Johnson was also governor of Tennessee from 1853 to 1857, when he was elected to the U.S. Senate.

Although Johnson had himself exploited enslaved labor, he opposed secession and tried to prevent Tennessee from seceding. In Mar. 1862, Lincoln appointed him military governor of occupied Tennessee.

In 1864, in order to balance Lincoln's ticket with a Southern Democrat, the Republicans nominated Johnson for vice president. He was elected vice president with Lincoln and succeeded to the presidency upon Lincoln's death. Soon afterward, in conflict with Congress over the president's power over the South, he proclaimed an amnesty to all Confederates, except certain leaders, if they would ratify the 13th Amendment abolishing slavery. States doing so added anti-Negro provisions that enraged Republicans, which restored military control over the South. When Johnson removed Sec. of War Edwin M. Stanton without notifying the Senate, the House impeached him in Feb. 1868 on the charge of violating the Tenure of Office Act. In reality, the House was responding to his opposition to harsh congressional Reconstruction, expressed in repeated vetoes. He was acquitted in the Senate by one-vote margins on each of two counts.

Johnson was denied renomination but remained politically active. He was reelected to the Senate in 1874. Johnson died July 31, 1875, at Carter Station, TN.

Ulysses S. Grant (1869-77), 18th president, Republican, was born on Apr. 27, 1822, in Point Pleasant, OH, the son of Jesse R. and Hannah Simpson Grant. The next year the family moved to Georgetown, OH. Grant was named Hiram Ulysses. Upon entering West Point in 1839, he found his name had been put down as Ulysses S. Grant, with his middle name first and his mother's maiden name as his middle name. He eventually adopted it as his true name but maintained the "S" did not stand for anything. Grant graduated in 1843.

During the Mexican War, Grant served under both Gen. Zachary Taylor and Gen. Winfield Scott. In 1854, he resigned his commission because of loneliness and drinking problems, and in the following years he engaged in generally unsuccessful farming and business ventures. With the start of the Civil War, he was named colonel and then brigadier general of the Illinois Volunteers. He took Forts Henry and Donelson and fought at Shiloh. His brilliant campaign against Vicksburg and his victory at Chattanooga made him so prominent that Lincoln placed him in command of all Union armies. Grant accepted Confederate Gen. Robert E. Lee's surrender at Appomattox Court House on Apr. 9, 1865.

Grant was nominated for president by the Republicans in 1868 and elected over Democrat Horatio Seymour. The 15th Amendment, the amnesty bill, and peaceful settlement of disputes with Great Britain were events of his administration. The Liberal Republicans and Democrats opposed him with Horace Greeley in the 1872 election, but Grant was reelected. His second administration was marked by scandals, including the Crédit Mobilier affair, the Whiskey Ring, in which high-ranked officials conspired to defraud the government of taxes, and the impeachment of his secretary of war. An attempt by the Stalwarts (Old Guard Republicans) to nominate him in 1880 failed. Left penniless by the 1884 collapse of an investment firm in which he was a partner, he wrote his well-regarded memoirs while suffering from cancer to provide income for his family. He died at Mt. McGregor, NY, on July 23, 1885.

Rutherford Birchard Hayes (1877-81), 19th president, Republican, was born on Oct. 4, 1822, in Delaware, OH, the son of Rutherford and Sophia Birchard Hayes. He was reared by his uncle, Sardis Birchard. Hayes graduated from Kenyon College in 1842 and from Harvard Law School in 1845. He practiced law in Lower Sandusky (now Fremont), OH, and was city solicitor of Cincinnati from 1858 to 1861. During the Civil War, he was major of the 23rd Ohio Volunteers. He was wounded several times, and by the end of the war he had risen to the rank of brevet major general. While serving (1865-67) in the U.S. House of Representatives, Hayes supported Reconstruction and Johnson's impeachment. He was twice elected governor of Ohio (1867, 1869). After losing a race for the U.S. House in 1872, he was reelected governor of Ohio in 1875.

In 1876, Hayes was nominated for president. He believed he had lost the election to Democrat Samuel J. Tilden. But a few Southern states submitted two sets of electoral votes, and the result was in dispute. An electoral commission, consisting of 8 Republicans and 7 Democrats, awarded all disputed votes to Hayes, allowing him to become president by one electoral vote. Hayes, keeping a promise to Southerners, withdrew troops from areas still occupied in the South, ending the era of Reconstruction. He proposed civil service reforms, alienating those favoring the spoils system, and advocated repeal of the Tenure of Office Act restricting presidential power to dismiss officials. He supported sound money and specie payments.

Hayes died in Fremont, OH, on Jan. 17, 1893.

James Abram Garfield (1881), 20th president, Republican, was born on Nov. 19, 1831, in Orange, Cuyahoga Co., OH, the son of Abram and Eliza Ballou Garfield. His father died in 1833, and he was reared in poverty by his mother. He worked as a canal bargeman, a farmer, and a carpenter. He attended Western Reserve Eclectic Institute and graduated from Williams College in 1856. He returned to Western Reserve to teach and in 1857, at age 25, he became the school's president. In 1859 he was elected to the Ohio legislature. Anti-slavery and anti-secession, he volunteered for military service in the Civil War, becoming colonel of the 42nd Ohio Infantry and brigadier in 1862. He fought at Shiloh, TN, was chief of staff for Gen. William Starke Rosecrans, and was made major general for gallantry at Chickamauga, GA. He entered Congress as a radical Republican in 1863, calling for execution or exile of Confederate leaders, but he moderated his views after the Civil War. On the electoral commission in 1877 he voted for Hayes against Tilden on strict party lines.

Garfield was a senator-elect in 1880 when he became the Republican nominee for president. He was chosen as a compromise over Gen. Grant, James G. Blaine, and John Sherman, and won election despite some bitterness among Grant's supporters. For much of his brief tenure as president, Garfield was concerned with a fight with New York Sen. Roscoe Conkling, who opposed two major appointments made by Garfield. On July 2, 1881, Garfield was shot and seriously wounded by a mentally disturbed office seeker, Charles J. Guiteau, while entering a railroad station in Washington, DC. He died on Sept. 19, 1881, in Elberon, NJ.

Chester Alan Arthur (1881-85), 21st president, Republican, was born on Oct. 5, 1829, in Fairfield, VT, to William and Malvina Stone Arthur. He graduated from Union College in 1848, taught school in Vermont, then studied law and practiced in New York City. In 1853, he argued that fugitives from enslaved labor transported through New York State were thereby freed. In 1871, he was appointed collector of the Port of New York. Pres. Hayes, an opponent of the spoils system, forced him to resign in 1878. This made the New York machine enemies of Hayes. Arthur and the Stalwarts (Old Guard Republicans) tried to nominate Grant for a third term as president in 1880. When Garfield was nominated, Arthur was nominated for vice president in the interests of harmony.

Upon Garfield's assassination, Arthur became president. Despite his past connections, he signed major civil service reform legislation. Arthur tried to dissuade Congress from enacting the high protective tariff of 1883. He was defeated for renomination in 1884 by James G. Blaine. He died in New York City on Nov. 18, 1886.

(Stephen) Grover Cleveland (1885-89; 1893-97) *(According to a State Dept. ruling, Grover Cleveland should be counted as both the 22nd and the 24th president because his two terms were not consecutive)*, Democrat, was born Stephen Grover Cleveland on Mar. 18, 1837, in Caldwell, NJ, the son of Richard F. and Ann Neal Cleveland. When he was a small boy, his family moved to New York. Prevented by his father's death from attending college, he studied on his own and was admitted to the bar in Buffalo, NY, in 1859. In succession he became assistant district attorney (1863), sheriff (1871), mayor (1881), and governor of New York (1882). He was an independent, honest administrator who hated corruption. Cleveland was nominated for president over opposition from New York City's Democratic party machine Tammany Hall in 1884 and defeated Republican James G. Blaine.

As president, he enlarged the civil service and vetoed many pension raids on the Treasury. In the 1888 election he was defeated by Benjamin Harrison, although his popular vote was larger. Reelected over Harrison in 1892, he faced a money crisis brought about by a lowered gold reserve, circulation of paper, and exorbitant silver purchases under the Sherman Silver Purchase Act. He obtained a repeal of the Sherman Act but was unable to secure effective tariff reform. A severe economic depression and labor troubles racked his administration, but he refused to interfere in business matters and rejected business owner Jacob Coxey's demand for unemployment relief. In 1894, he broke the Pullman railroad workers' strike. Cleveland was not renominated in 1896. He died in Princeton, NJ, on June 24, 1908.

Benjamin Harrison (1889-93), 23rd president, Republican, was born on Aug. 20, 1833, in North Bend, OH, the son of John Scott and Elizabeth Irwin Harrison. His great-grandfather, Benjamin Harrison, was a signer of the Declaration of Independence; his grandfather, William Henry Harrison, was the ninth president; his father was a member of Congress. He attended school on his father's farm and graduated from Miami Univ. in Oxford, OH, in 1852. He was admitted to the bar in 1854 and practiced in Indianapolis, IN. During the Civil War, he rose to the rank of brevet brigadier general and fought at Kennesaw Mountain, Peachtree Creek, Nashville, and in the Atlanta campaign. He lost the 1876 gubernatorial election in Indiana but succeeded in becoming a U.S. senator in 1881.

In 1888 he defeated Cleveland for president despite receiving fewer popular votes. As president, he expanded the pension list and signed the McKinley high tariff bill, the Sherman Antitrust Act, and the Sherman Silver Purchase Act. During his administration, six states were admitted to the Union. He was defeated for reelection in 1892. He died in Indianapolis, IN, on Mar. 13, 1901.

William McKinley (1897-1901), 25th president, Republican, was born on Jan. 29, 1843, in Niles, OH, the son of William and Nancy Allison McKinley. McKinley briefly attended Allegheny College in Pennsylvania. When the Civil War broke out in 1861, he enlisted and served for the duration. He rose to captain and in 1865 was made brevet major. After studying law in Albany, NY, he opened a law office in Canton, OH (1867). He served twice in the U.S. House (1877-83; 1885-91) and led the fight there for the McKinley Tariff, passed in 1890; he was not reelected to the House as a result. He served two terms (1892-96) as governor of Ohio.

In 1896 he was elected president as a proponent of a protective tariff and sound money (gold standard) over William Jennings Bryan, the Democrat and a proponent of free silver. McKinley was reluctant to intervene in Cuba, but the loss of the battleship *Maine* at Havana, blamed on Spain, crystallized opinion. He demanded Spain's withdrawal from Cuba; Spain made some concessions, but Congress announced a state of war as of Apr. 21, 1898. He was reelected in the 1900 campaign, defeating Bryan's anti-imperialist arguments with the promise of a "full dinner pail." He waged known for a conservative stance on business issues. On Sept. 6, 1901, at the Pan-American Exposition, in Buffalo, NY, he was shot by Leon Czolgosz, an anarchist. He died Sept. 14.

Theodore Roosevelt (1901-09), 26th president, Republican, was born on Oct. 27, 1858, in New York City, the son of Theodore and Martha Bulloch Roosevelt. He was a fifth cousin of Franklin D. Roosevelt and an uncle of Eleanor Roosevelt. Roosevelt graduated from Harvard Univ. in 1880. He attended Columbia Law School briefly but abandoned law to enter politics. He was elected to the New York State Assembly in 1881 and served until 1884. He spent the next two years ranching and hunting in the Dakota Territory. In 1886, he ran unsuccessfully for mayor of New York City. He was civil service commissioner in Washington, DC, from 1889 to 1895. From 1895 to 1897, he served as New York City's police commissioner. He was assistant secretary of the Navy under McKinley. The Spanish-American War made him nationally known. He organized the First U.S. Volunteer Cavalry (Rough Riders) and, as lieutenant colonel, led the charge up Kettle Hill in San Juan, Cuba. Elected New York governor in 1898, he fought the spoils system and achieved taxation of corporation franchises.

Nominated for vice president in 1900, Roosevelt became the nation's youngest president at the age of 42 when McKinley was assassinated. He was reelected in 1904. As president he fought corruption of politics by big business, dissolved the Northern Securities Co. and others for violating antitrust laws, intervened in the 1902 coal strike on behalf of the public, obtained the Elkins Law (1903) forbidding rebates to favored corporations, and helped pass the Hepburn Railway Rate Act of 1906 (extending jurisdiction of the Interstate Commerce Commission). He helped obtain passage of the Pure Food and Drug Act (1906) and of employers' liability laws. Roosevelt vigorously organized conservation efforts. He mediated the peace between Japan and Russia in 1905, for which he won the Nobel Peace Prize. He abetted the 1903 revolution in Panama that led to U.S. acquisition of territory for the Panama Canal.

In 1908 Roosevelt obtained the nomination of William H. Taft, who was elected. Feeling that Taft had abandoned his policies, he unsuccessfully sought the nomination in 1912. He then ran on the Progressive "Bull Moose" ticket against Taft and Woodrow Wilson, splitting the Republicans and ensuring Wilson's election. During the campaign he was shot by a mentally deranged man but was not seriously wounded. In 1916, after unsuccessfully seeking the presidential nomination, he supported the Republican candidate, Charles E. Hughes. He strongly promoted U.S. intervention in World War I.

Roosevelt was a voracious reader and wrote some 40 books, including *The Winning of the West*. He died Jan. 6, 1919, at Sagamore Hill, his home in Oyster Bay, NY.

William Howard Taft (1909-13), 27th president, Republican, and 10th chief justice of the U.S., was born on Sept. 15, 1857, in Cincinnati, OH, the son of Alphonso and Louisa Maria Torrey Taft. His father was secretary of war and attorney general in Grant's cabinet and minister to Austria and Russia under Arthur. Taft graduated from Yale in 1878 and from Cincinnati Law School in 1880. After working as a law reporter for Cincinnati newspapers, he served as assistant prosecuting attorney (1881-82), assistant county solicitor (1885), superior court judge (1887), U.S. solicitor-general (1890), and federal circuit judge (1892). In 1900 he became head of the U.S. Philippines Commission and was the first civil governor of the Philippines (1901-04). In 1904 he served as secretary of war, and in 1906 he was sent to Cuba to help avert a threatened revolution.

Taft was groomed for the presidency by Theodore Roosevelt and elected over William Jennings Bryan in 1908. Taft vigorously continued Roosevelt's trust-busting, instituted the Dept. of Labor, and drafted amendments calling for direct election of senators and an income tax. However, his tariff and conservation policies angered progressives. Although renominated in 1912, he was opposed by Roosevelt, who ran on the Progressive party ticket; the result was Wilson's election.

Taft, with reservations, supported the League of Nations. He became a professor of constitutional law at Yale (1913-21) and was appointed by Pres. Harding to serve as chief justice of the U.S. (1921-30). Taft was the only person to have been both president and chief justice. He died in Washington, DC, on Mar. 8, 1930.

(Thomas) Woodrow Wilson (1913-21), 28th president, Democrat, was born on Dec. 28, 1856, in Staunton, VA, the son of Joseph Ruggles and Janet (Jessie) Woodrow Wilson. He grew up in Georgia and South Carolina. He attended Davidson College in North Carolina before graduating from Princeton Univ. in 1879. He studied law at the Univ. of Virginia and political science at Johns Hopkins Univ., where he received his PhD in 1886. He taught at Bryn Mawr (1885-88) and at Wesleyan (1888-90) before joining the faculty at Princeton. He was president of Princeton from 1902 until 1910, when he was elected governor of New Jersey. In 1912 he was nominated for president with the aid of William Jennings Bryan, who sought to block James "Champ" Clark and New York City's Democratic party machine Tammany Hall. Wilson won because Theodore Roosevelt, running as a "Bull Moose" Progressive, siphoned votes away from Republican candidate Taft.

As president, Wilson protected American interests in revolutionary Mexico and fought for American rights on the high seas. He oversaw the creation of the Federal Reserve system, cut the tariff, and developed a reputation as a reformer. His sharp warnings to Germany led to the resignation of his secretary of state, Bryan, a pacifist. In 1916 he was reelected by a slim margin with the slogan "He kept us out of war," although his attempts to mediate in the war failed. After several American ships were sunk by the Germans, he secured a declaration of war against Germany on Apr. 6, 1917.

Wilson outlined his peace program on Jan. 8, 1918, in the Fourteen Points, a state paper that enunciated a doctrine of self-determination for the settlement of territorial disputes. The Germans accepted his terms and an armistice on Nov. 11, 1918. Wilson went to Paris to help negotiate the peace treaty, the crux of which he considered the League of Nations. The Senate demanded reservations that would not make the U.S. subordinate to the votes of other nations in case of war. Wilson refused and toured the country to get support. After he suffered a severe stroke in Oct. 1919, his wife, Edith Wilson, concealed the extent of his infirmity, controlled access to him, and in effect largely acted in his place.

Wilson was awarded the 1919 Nobel Peace Prize, but the treaty embodying the League of Nations was ultimately rejected by the Senate in 1920. He left the White House in Mar. 1921. He died in Washington, DC, on Feb. 3, 1924.

Warren Gamaliel Harding (1921-23), 29th president, Republican, was born on Nov. 2, 1865, near Corsica (now Blooming Grove), OH, the son of George Tyron and Phoebe Elizabeth Dickerson Harding. He attended Ohio Central College, studied law, and became editor and publisher of a county newspaper. He entered the political arena as state senator (1901-04) and then served as lieutenant governor (1904-06). In 1910 he ran unsuccessfully for governor of Ohio; in 1914 he was elected to the U.S. Senate. In the Senate he voted for anti-strike legislation, women's suffrage, and the Volstead Prohibition Enforcement Act over Pres. Wilson's veto. He opposed the League of Nations.

In 1920 he was nominated for president and defeated James M. Cox in the election. The Republicans capitalized on war weariness and fear that Wilson's League of Nations would curtail U.S. sovereignty. Harding stressed a return to "normalcy" and worked for tariff revision and the repeal of excess profits law and high income taxes. In the so-called Teapot Dome scandal, his secretary of the interior, Albert B. Fall, resigned and was later convicted of accepting bribes in the leasing of government-owned oil reserves to private companies.

As rumors began to circulate about the corruption in his administration, Harding fell ill after a trip to Alaska, and he died suddenly of a likely heart attack in San Francisco on Aug. 2,

1923. Harding's letters to a longtime mistress were made public by the Library of Congress in 2014, and DNA evidence in 2015 confirmed another mistress's claim that he had fathered her daughter.

(John) Calvin Coolidge (1923-29), 30th president, Republican, was born on July 4, 1872, in Plymouth Notch, VT, the son of John Calvin and Victoria J. Moor Coolidge. Coolidge graduated from Amherst College in 1895. He entered Republican state politics and served as mayor of Northampton, MA, as state senator, as lieutenant governor, and, in 1919, as governor. In Sept. 1919, Coolidge attained national prominence by calling out the state guard in the Boston police strike. He declared, "There is no right to strike against the public safety by anybody, anywhere, anytime." This brought his name before the Republican convention of 1920, where he was nominated for vice president.

Coolidge succeeded to the presidency on Harding's death. As president, he opposed the League of Nations and the soldiers' bonus bill, which was passed over his veto. In 1924 he was elected to the presidency by a huge majority. He substantially reduced the national debt. He twice vetoed legislation to aid financially hard-pressed farmers.

With Republicans eager to renominate him, Coolidge simply announced on Aug. 2, 1927, "I do not choose to run for president in 1928." He died in Northampton, MA, on Jan. 5, 1933.

Herbert Clark Hoover (1929-33), 31st president, Republican, was born on Aug. 10, 1874, in West Branch, IA, the son of Jesse Clark and Hulda Randall Minthorn Hoover. Hoover grew up in Indian Territory (now Oklahoma) and Oregon and graduated from Stanford Univ. with a degree in geology in 1895. He worked briefly with the U.S. Geological Survey and then managed mines in Australia, Asia, Europe, and Africa. While chief engineer of imperial mines in China, he directed food relief for victims of the Boxer Rebellion. He gained a reputation not only as an engineer but as a humanitarian as he directed the American Relief Committee, London (1914-15) and the U.S. Commission for Relief in Belgium (1915-19). He was U.S. Food Administrator (1917-19), American Relief Administrator (1918-23), and in charge of Russian Relief (1918-23). He served as secretary of commerce under both Harding and Coolidge.

In 1928 Hoover was elected president over Alfred E. Smith. In 1929 the stock market crashed, and the economy collapsed. During the Great Depression, Hoover inaugurated some government assistance programs, but he was opposed to administration of aid through a federal bureaucracy. As the effects of the Depression continued, he was defeated in the 1932 election by Franklin D. Roosevelt. Hoover remained active after leaving office. Pres. Truman named him coordinator of the European Food Program (1946) and chairman of the Commission on Organization of the Executive Branch (1947-49); he was later appointed by Pres. Eisenhower to serve in the same role (1953-55).

Hoover died in New York City on Oct. 20, 1964.

Franklin Delano Roosevelt (1933-45), 32nd president, Democrat, was born on Jan. 30, 1882, in Hyde Park, NY, the son of James and Sara Delano Roosevelt, and a fifth cousin of former Pres. Theodore Roosevelt. He graduated from Harvard Univ. in 1903. He attended Columbia University Law School without taking a degree and was admitted to the New York State bar in 1907. His political career began when he was elected to the New York State senate in 1910. In 1913 Pres. Wilson appointed him assistant secretary of the navy, a post he held during World War I.

In 1920 Roosevelt ran for vice president with James Cox and was defeated. From 1921 to 1928 he worked in his New York law office and was also vice president of a bank. In Aug. 1921, he was stricken with poliomyelitis, which left his legs paralyzed. As a result of therapy, he was able to stand and walk a few steps with the aid of leg braces.

Roosevelt served two terms as governor of New York (1929-33). In 1932, Democratic convention delegate W. G. McAdoo, pledged to nominee John N. Garner, threw his votes to Roosevelt, who was nominated for president. The Depression and the promise to repeal Prohibition ensured his election. He asked for emergency powers, proclaimed the New Deal, and put into effect a vast number of administrative changes. Foremost was the use of public funds for relief and public works, resulting in deficit financing. He greatly expanded the federal government's regulation of business and by an excess profits tax and progressive income taxes produced a redistribution of earnings on an unprecedented scale. He also promoted legislation establishing the Social Security system. He was the last president inaugurated on Mar. 4 (1933) and the first inaugurated on Jan. 20 (1937).

Roosevelt was the first president to use radio for "fireside chats." When the Supreme Court nullified some New Deal laws, he sought power to "pack" the Court with additional justices, but Congress refused to give him the authority. He was the first president to break the no-third-term tradition (1940) and was elected to a fourth term in 1944 despite failing health.

Roosevelt was openly hostile to fascist governments before World War II and launched a lend-lease program on behalf of the Allies. With British Prime Min. Winston Churchill he wrote a declaration of principles to be followed after Nazi defeat (the Atlantic Charter of Aug. 14, 1941) and urged the Four Freedoms (freedom of speech, of worship, from want, from fear) Jan. 6, 1941. After Japan attacked Pearl Harbor on Dec. 7, 1941, the U.S. entered the war. Roosevelt guided the nation through the war and conferred with allied heads of state but did not live to see the end of the war. He died of a cerebral hemorrhage in Warm Springs, GA, on Apr. 12, 1945.

Harry S. Truman (1945-53), 33rd president, Democrat, was born on May 8, 1884, in Lamar, MO, the son of John Anderson and Martha Ellen Young Truman. A family disagreement over whether his middle name should be Shipp or Solomon, after his two grandfathers, resulted in his using only the middle initial S. After graduating from high school (1901) in Independence, MO, he worked in the mailroom of the *Kansas City Star*, as a railroad timekeeper, and as a clerk in Kansas City banks until about 1905. He ran his family's farm from 1906 to 1917, then served in France during World War I. After the war he opened a haberdashery, was a judge on the Jackson Co. Court (1922-24), and attended Kansas City School of Law (1923-25).

Truman was elected to the U.S. Senate in 1934 and reelected in 1940. In 1944, with Roosevelt's backing, he was nominated for vice president and elected. On Roosevelt's death in 1945, Truman became president. In 1948, in a famous upset victory, he defeated Republican Thomas E. Dewey to win a new term.

Truman authorized the first uses of the atomic bomb (Hiroshima and Nagasaki, Aug. 6 and 9, 1945), bringing World War II to a rapid end. He was responsible for what came to be called the Truman Doctrine to aid nations such as Greece and Turkey threatened by Communist takeover, and his strong commitment to NATO and to the Marshall Plan helped bring the two about. In 1948-49, he broke a Soviet blockade of West Berlin with a massive airlift. When Communist North Korea invaded South Korea (June 1950), he won UN approval for a "police action" and, without prior congressional consent, sent in forces under Gen. Douglas MacArthur. When MacArthur opposed his policy of limited objectives, Truman removed him.

He died in Kansas City, MO, on Dec. 26, 1972.

Dwight David Eisenhower (1953-61), 34th president, Republican, was born on Oct. 14, 1890, in Denison, TX, the son of David Jacob and Ida Elizabeth Stover Eisenhower, as David Dwight Eisenhower. He grew up on a small farm in Abilene, KS, and graduated from West Point in 1915. He was on the staff of Gen. Douglas MacArthur in the Philippines from 1935 to 1939. In 1942, he was made commander of Allied forces landing in North Africa; the next year he was made full general. He became supreme Allied commander in Europe that same year and led the Normandy invasion (June 6, 1944). He was subsequently given the rank of general of the Army.

On May 7, 1945, Eisenhower received the surrender of Germany at Rheims, France. He returned to the U.S. to serve as chief of staff (1945-48). His memoir, *Crusade in Europe* (1948), was a best-seller. In 1948 he became president of Columbia Univ.; in 1950 he became commander of NATO forces.

Eisenhower was nominated for president by the Republicans in 1952. He defeated Illinois Gov. Adlai E. Stevenson in the 1952 election and defeated Stevenson in 1956 to win reelection. Eisenhower called himself a moderate, favored the "free market system" versus government price and wage controls, kept government out of labor disputes, reorganized the defense establishment, and promoted missile programs. He continued foreign aid, helped negotiate a cease-fire truce in the Korean War, endorsed Taiwan and SE Asia defense treaties, backed the UN in condemning the Anglo-French raid on Egypt, and advocated the "open skies" policy of mutual inspection with the USSR. He sent U.S. troops into Little Rock, AR, in Sept. 1957, to enforce school integration.

Eisenhower died on Mar. 28, 1969, in Washington, DC.

John Fitzgerald Kennedy (1961-63), 35th president, Democrat, was born on May 29, 1917, in Brookline, MA, the son of Rose Fitzgerald Kennedy and Joseph P. Kennedy, a wealthy businessman, investor, and onetime U.S. ambassador to Britain. After graduating from Harvard (1940), Kennedy served in the Navy (1941-45), winning a medal for heroism as commander of a PT (patrol torpedo) boat in the Pacific. He served in the U.S. House, 1947-53, and was elected to the Senate in 1952 and 1958. In 1956, after spinal surgery, he published *Profiles in Courage*, which won a Pulitzer Prize.

In 1960, Kennedy narrowly defeated Vice Pres. Richard Nixon (R) for the presidency. He was the first Catholic and, at 43, the youngest person ever elected to that office. Despite his image of youth and vigor, Kennedy suffered from serious medical problems, including Addison's disease and severe back pain that required him to wear a back brace. The extent of these problems was concealed from the public, as were his frequent sexual liaisons.

In Apr. 1961, the new Kennedy administration was stung by the defeat of an invasion force of anti-Communist Cuban exiles, trained and directed by the CIA, at Cuba's Bay of Pigs. But he successfully demanded, in Oct.1962, that the Soviet Union dismantle its missile bases in Cuba. He also defied Soviet attempts to force the Allies out of Berlin. Kennedy established the Peace Corps, spurred space exploration, especially the program to land humans on the Moon, and won passage of other "New Frontier" legislation. But Congress balked at other initiatives, such as medical coverage for the aged. He eventually introduced major civil rights legislation but did not live to see it passed.

On Nov. 22, 1963, Kennedy was assassinated while riding in a motorcade in Dallas, TX. A commission chaired by Chief Justice Earl Warren concluded in Sept. 1964 that the sole assassin had been Lee Harvey Oswald, an ex-Marine and ardent Marxist. Oswald was captured shortly after the assassination but was shot dead by nightclub owner Jack Ruby while being moved to a county jail.

Lyndon Baines Johnson (1963-69), 36th president, Democrat, was born on Aug. 27, 1908, near Stonewall, TX, the son of Rebekah Baines Johnson and Sam Ealy Johnson, a state legislator. He graduated from Southwest Texas State Teachers College in 1930, with formative experience as a student teacher of underprivileged Mexican-American students in a segregated school, and briefly attended Georgetown Univ. Law School. He served as secretary to a congressman and in 1935 became director of the Texas branch of the New Deal National Youth Administration. In 1937 he won an election to fill a vacancy in Congress; he was subsequently elected to five full terms. During 1941-42 he also served in the Navy.

Johnson won a U.S. Senate seat after a close 1948 primary widely regarded as marred by fraud. He rose quickly in the ranks and, after reelection in 1954, served as a skillful Senate majority leader. He was elected vice president in 1960 on the ticket headed by Sen. John Kennedy, and succeeded to the presidency when Kennedy was assassinated. He was elected to a full term in 1964, defeating Sen. Barry Goldwater (R, AZ) in a landslide.

As president Johnson won passage of landmark civil rights, anti-poverty, education (Head Start), and health care (Medicare, Medicaid) legislation—the "Great Society" program. However, in the face of increasing division in the nation and his own party over his escalation of the Vietnam war, he declined to seek another term. Johnson died on Jan. 22, 1973, at his ranch in Stonewall, TX.

Richard Milhous Nixon (1969-74), 37th president, Republican, was born on Jan. 9, 1913, in Yorba Linda, CA, the son of Francis Anthony and Hannah Milhous Nixon. He graduated from Whittier College in 1934 and from Duke Univ. Law School in 1937. After practicing law and working in the Office of Price Administration he joined the Navy, serving in the Pacific. Elected to the U.S. House in 1946 and 1948, he played a central role in spearheading the prosecution of suspected Communist spy Alger Hiss. Nixon was elected to the Senate in 1950 and served as vice president under Dwight Eisenhower (1953-61). He first ran for president in 1960, narrowly losing to John F. Kennedy, and ran unsuccessfully for governor of California in 1962. In 1968 he was elected president, defeating Vice Pres. Hubert Humphrey (D).

As president, Nixon appointed four Supreme Court justices, including the chief justice, moving the court to the right. As a New Federalist, he sought to shift greater responsibility to state and local governments. At the same time, he championed consequential federal initiatives, including creation of the Office of Management and Budget and the Environmental Protection Agency. The economy suffered periods of high unemployment and inflation, and he imposed wage and price controls in 1971.

In foreign affairs, Nixon dramatically altered relations with China, which he visited in 1972—the first U.S. president to do so. With adviser Henry Kissinger, he pursued détente with the Soviet Union, signing major arms limitation and other treaties and increasing trade. He began a gradual withdrawal from Vietnam, but U.S. troops remained there through his first term. He ordered an incursion into Cambodia (1970) and the bombing of Hanoi and mining of Haiphong Harbor (1972). Reelected by a large majority in Nov. 1972, he secured a Vietnam cease-fire in Jan. 1973.

Nixon's second term was cut short by scandal, after disclosures relating to a June 1972 burglary of Democratic Party headquarters in the Watergate office complex in Washington, DC. The courts and Congress sought tapes of Nixon's office conversations; Nixon claimed executive privilege, but the Supreme Court ruled against him. In July 1974, the House Judiciary Committee recommended adoption of impeachment articles charging obstruction of justice, abuse of power, and contempt of Congress. On Aug. 5, he released transcripts of conversations that linked him to cover-up activities. Nixon resigned on Aug. 9, becoming the first president ever to do so.

In later years, Nixon emerged as an elder statesman. He died Apr. 22, 1994, in New York City.

Gerald Rudolph Ford (1974-77), 38th president, Republican, was born on July 14, 1913, in Omaha, NE, the son of Leslie and Dorothy Gardner King, and was named Leslie Lynch King Jr. His parents divorced in Dec. 1913, and in 1917 his mother married Grand Rapids, MI, businessman Gerald R. Ford, whose name the future president ultimately took. He graduated from Univ. of Michigan in 1935 and Yale Law School in 1941. In 1942, he joined the Navy, serving in the Pacific. He won election in 1948 to the U.S. House, where he served for 25 years, eight of them as Republican leader.

On Oct. 12, 1973, after Vice Pres. Spiro Agnew resigned in a corruption scandal, Pres. Nixon nominated Ford to replace him, in the first use of procedures set out in the 25th Amendment (ratified 1967). When Nixon resigned, in Aug. 1974, Ford succeeded him; he was the only president never elected either to the presidency or to the vice presidency.

Ford was widely credited with helping rebuild morale after the Nixon presidency, though his pardoning of Nixon for any federal crimes in office was controversial. He vetoed 48 bills in his first 21 months in office, mostly in the interest of fighting high inflation; he was less successful in curbing high unemployment. In foreign policy, he continued to pursue détente. Ford was narrowly defeated in the 1976 election. He died Dec. 26, 2006, at home in Rancho Mirage, CA.

James Earl (Jimmy) Carter (1977-81), 39th president, Democrat, was the first president from the Deep South since before the Civil War. He was born on Oct. 1, 1924, in Plains, GA, the son of James and Lillian Gordy Carter. Carter graduated from the U.S. Naval Academy in 1946 and in 1952 entered the Navy's nuclear submarine program as an aide to Capt. (later

Adm.) Hyman Rickover. Carter left the Navy to take over the family peanut farming businesses after his father's death in 1953. He served in the Georgia state senate (1963-67) and as governor of Georgia (1971-75). In 1976, he won the Democratic presidential nomination and defeated Pres. Gerald Ford to win the presidency.

On taking office, Carter pardoned Vietnam draft evaders. He played a major role in negotiations leading to the 1979 peace treaty between Israel and Egypt and reached treaties with Panama ending U.S. control of the Panama Canal, effective in 2000. Carter was widely blamed, however, for the poor state of the economy and viewed by some as weak in handling foreign policy. In Nov. 1979, Iranian student militants attacked the U.S. embassy in Tehran and held 52 members of the embassy staff as hostages; efforts to obtain their release became a major preoccupation of the administration. He responded to the Soviet invasion of Afghanistan (Dec. 1979) by imposing a grain embargo and boycotting the 1980 Moscow Olympics.

Carter was defeated by Ronald Reagan in the 1980 election. The hostages in Iran were finally released on inauguration day, 1981, just after Reagan officially became president. After leaving office, Carter played an active role in diplomatic and humanitarian efforts around the world, especially through the Carter Center, which he founded with his wife, Rosalynn, in 1982. He was awarded the Nobel Peace Prize in 2002.

Ronald Wilson Reagan (1981-89), 40th president, Republican, was born on Feb. 6, 1911, in Tampico, IL, the son of John Edward and Nellie Wilson Reagan. Reagan graduated from Eureka College in 1932, after which he worked as a sports announcer in Des Moines, IA. In 1937 he began a career as a Hollywood movie actor, and he served in the Army Air Force during World War II, making training films. He became president of the Screen Actors Guild and served two terms as California governor (1967-75). In 1980, Reagan won a landslide victory over Pres. Carter. He was shot and seriously wounded in 1981 by John Hinckley Jr., who was found not guilty by reason of insanity. Reagan was easily reelected in 1984.

As president Reagan forged a bipartisan coalition in Congress, which led to enactment of his program of large-scale tax cuts, cutbacks in government programs, and a major increase in defense spending. He also won passage of a Social Security reform bill. In 1982, the U.S. joined in maintaining a peacekeeping force in Beirut, Lebanon; the next year Reagan sent a task force to invade Grenada after two Marxist coups on the island. Reagan ordered airstrikes on Libyan military installations in 1986, ten days after Libyan agents bombed a nightclub in West Berlin, Germany.

Reagan held four summit meetings with Soviet leader Mikhail Gorbachev and signed a major arms-reduction treaty with the Soviet Union in 1987. He also strongly supported anti-Communist governments and forces around the world. In 1986, it was revealed that the U.S. had secretly sold weapons to Iran in exchange for the release of U.S. hostages held in Lebanon and that some of the proceeds had been illegally diverted to anti-Communist contras in Nicaragua. The scandal led to the resignation of leading White House aides, but no proof was found that Reagan himself was involved. As Reagan left office in Jan. 1989, the nation was experiencing its sixth consecutive year of GDP growth, while also piling up large budget deficits.

In 1994, Reagan revealed that he was suffering from Alzheimer's disease. He died on June 5, 2004, in Los Angeles, CA, from complications of the disease.

George Herbert Walker Bush (1989-93), 41st president, Republican, was born June 12, 1924, in Milton, MA, the son of U.S. Sen. Prescott Bush (R, CT, 1952-63) and Dorothy Walker Bush. He was shot down over the Pacific as a Navy pilot in World War II and was awarded the Distinguished Flying Cross. After graduating from Yale Univ. in 1948, he settled in Texas, where he helped found an oil company. He lost a 1964 U.S. Senate race but was elected to two U.S. House terms, in 1966 and 1968. After losing a second Senate race, he served as U.S. ambassador to the UN, head of the U.S. Liaison Office in Beijing, and director of the CIA. Following an unsuccessful bid for the 1980 GOP presidential nomination, Bush became Ronald Reagan's running mate, and served two terms as vice president (1981-89).

In 1988, Bush defeated Gov. Michael Dukakis (D, MA) to win the presidency. He faced severe budget deficits, struggled with military cutbacks, and vetoed abortion-rights legislation. In 1990 he agreed to a deficit-reduction plan that included tax hikes, despite a campaign promise to the contrary. He successfully appointed two justices to the U.S. Supreme Court, David Souter and Clarence Thomas; the latter was confirmed (1991) after hearings in which he was accused of sexual harassment.

Abroad, Bush supported Soviet reforms, Eastern Europe democratization, and good relations with Beijing. In Dec. 1989, he sent troops to Panama, where they overthrew the government and captured dictator Manuel Noriega. Reacting to Iraq's Aug. 1990 invasion of Kuwait, Bush assembled a broad U.S.-led, UN-backed Allied force which retook Kuwait (Feb. 1991) after a month-long air war and four-day ground assault. But the coalition did not seek to drive Iraqi leader Saddam Hussein from power. The quick victory, with extremely light U.S. casualties, gave Bush then-record-high approval ratings, but his popularity plummeted as the economy slipped into recession. He was defeated by Bill Clinton in the 1992 election.

Bush saw his son George W. Bush inaugurated as the 43rd president in 2001. He died Nov. 30, 2018, at home in Houston, TX.

William Jefferson (Bill) Clinton (1993-2001), 42nd president, Democrat, was born Aug. 19, 1946, in Hope, AR, son of William Blythe and Virginia Cassidy Blythe, and was named William Jefferson Blythe IV. Blythe died in an auto accident before his son was born; his widow married Roger Clinton, whose last name Bill Clinton took. Clinton earned his undergraduate degree from Georgetown Univ. in 1968. While attending Oxford Univ. as a Rhodes scholar, he legally avoided the draft and possible service in Vietnam, according to some critics by misleading his draft board. Clinton worked on George McGovern's 1972 presidential campaign and earned a degree from Yale Law School in 1973. He taught at the Univ. of Arkansas law school until 1976, when he was elected state attorney general. In 1978 he was elected governor, becoming the nation's youngest at the time. Though defeated for reelection in 1980, he was returned to office several times thereafter. He married law school classmate Hillary Rodham in 1975; their daughter Chelsea was born in 1980.

Positioning himself as a centrist "New Democrat" in a crowded field, he won the party's 1992 presidential nomination and was elected president, defeating Pres. George H. W. Bush and independent Ross Perot. In 1993, he won passage of a deficit reduction measure and congressional approval of the North American Free Trade Agreement. In 1994 he won passage of a stringent anti-crime bill, which became controversial over time because it allegedly accelerated large-scale incarceration. His administration's plan for major health care reform legislation died in Congress. After 1994 midterm elections, Clinton faced Republican majorities in both houses of Congress. He followed a centrist course at home, sent troops to Bosnia to help implement a peace settlement, and cultivated relations with Russia and China.

Buoyed by a strong economy, Clinton won reelection in 1996, easily defeating Sen. Bob Dole (R, KS), with Reform Party candidate Ross Perot trailing behind. He achieved federal budget surpluses in several years. Clinton was ultimately cleared of involvement in improprieties by associates in the Whitewater land-development venture, but investigation into the matter turned up evidence of a sexual relationship between Clinton and White House intern Monica Lewinsky. In 1998, he was impeached by the House of Representatives, charged with perjury and obstruction of justice in an attempted cover-up of the affair. He was acquitted in a Senate trial, but later in a separate proceeding he agreed to a fine and temporary suspension of his Arkansas law license. In 1999 the U.S. joined other NATO nations in an aerial bombing campaign that induced Serbia to withdraw troops from Kosovo, where they had been terrorizing ethnic Albanians.

After leaving office, Clinton actively supported the political career of senator (D, NY), secretary of state, and presidential candidate Hillary Clinton. He also founded what became the Bill, Hillary and Chelsea Clinton Foundation.

George Walker Bush (2001-09), 43rd president, Republican, was born on July 6, 1946, in New Haven, CT. He was the oldest of six children born to the 41st president, George Herbert Walker Bush, and the former Barbara Pierce. He became the first son of a former president to take office as president since John Quincy Adams in 1825.

Bush grew up in Midland and Houston, TX. He attended Phillips Academy in Andover, MA, and graduated from Yale Univ. in 1968. After serving with the Texas Air National Guard and earning an MBA from Harvard, he returned to Midland, where he went into the oil business. In 1977 he married Laura Welch, a librarian; they had twin daughters, Barbara and Jenna, in 1981. After aiding his father's winning 1988 presidential campaign, he became managing partner of the Texas Rangers baseball team. He was elected governor of Texas in 1994 and reelected in 1998. In 2000, Bush and running mate Dick Cheney defeated the Democratic ticket led by Vice Pres. Al Gore, in one of the closest-ever U.S. presidential elections. The result was not settled until a mid-Dec. Supreme Court ruling left Florida's crucial electoral votes in Bush's column.

Pres. Bush called his governing philosophy "compassionate conservatism." During his first term he won passage of two major tax cuts, the No Child Left Behind education bill, and a Medicare reform bill addressing prescription drug coverage, and he pioneered a major U.S. initiative to fight the AIDS epidemic, especially targeting Africa. He also signed a measure banning so-called partial birth abortions and barred federal funding for research on new human embryonic stem cell lines.

But Bush's first term was dominated by the Sept. 11, 2001, terrorist attack on the U.S. and the nation's response. In Oct. 2001, he signed the controversial USA Patriot Act, greatly expanding surveillance powers of the federal government, and created what became the U.S. Dept. of Homeland Security. Abroad, the U.S. military, aided by allied nations, deposed Afghanistan's Taliban regime, which was sheltering al-Qaeda terrorists. But an operation to capture al-Qaeda leader Osama bin Laden, architect of the Sept. 11 attack, failed when he escaped to Pakistan. In 2003 the U.S., aided mainly by UK forces, launched an air and ground war against Iraq and deposed its autocratic leader, Saddam Hussein. However, no evidence was found that Hussein's regime had developed weapons of mass destruction, the key rationale for the war. A new Iraqi government was formed in June 2004, but insurgent violence and U.S. troop casualties continued.

Reelected in 2004, Bush pressed unsuccessfully for Social Security and immigration reforms, and his administration drew criticism for its response to Hurricane Katrina in 2005. He won Senate confirmation for John Roberts (2005) as Supreme Court chief justice and Samuel Alito (2006) as associate justice. After Democrats won majorities in 2006 midterm elections, Bush accepted the resignation of Defense Sec. Donald Rumsfeld, a target of widespread criticism over the Iraq war. Two months later, Bush announced a "surge" in U.S. troop strength in Iraq; a sharp drop in casualties ensued, aided by a shift in alliances. In 2008, the administration reached an agreement with Iraq allowing U.S. troops to remain there through 2011. But the Taliban was gaining strength in Afghanistan, and the Bush administration was damaged by revelations of prisoner abuse and extreme interrogation methods.

The U.S. economy fell into recession in Dec. 2007; Bush and congressional leaders responded with a $168-bil stimulus plan. Problems in home finance and credit markets triggered a deep economic crisis by Sept. 2008. The Treasury Dept. bailed out mortgage finance firms Fannie Mae and Freddie Mac, investment bank Lehman Bros. filed for bankruptcy, and the Federal Reserve rescued insurance giant AIG with a line of credit reaching $144 bil. An administration-backed plan to buy up to $700 bil in devalued mortgage-related assets cleared Congress in Oct., after a severe stock market plunge bolstered support. The crisis contributed to the GOP's losses in the 2008 election.

In retirement Bush published a memoir, a biography of his father, and a volume featuring his own paintings of U.S. war veterans.

Barack Hussein Obama (2009-17), 44th president, Democrat, was born Aug. 4, 1961, in Honolulu, HI, son of Barack Obama Sr., a Black Kenyan, and Stanley Ann Dunham, a white American. They divorced and, after his mother remarried, the family moved to Indonesia. Obama lived with his maternal grandparents in Hawaii while attending high school. He graduated from Columbia Univ. (1983) and, after working as a community organizer in Chicago, earned a law degree from Harvard Univ. (1991), where he was president of the law review. Obama practiced civil rights law in Chicago and taught at the Univ. of Chicago Law School. In 1992, he married attorney Michelle Robinson; they have two daughters, Malia (b. 1998) and Sasha (b. 2001).

Obama served eight years (1997-2004) in the Illinois state senate. Known for his 1995 memoir *Dreams From My Father*, he gained wider attention with his keynote address at the 2004 Democratic National Convention and was easily elected to the U.S. Senate in Nov. Stressing his opposition to the Iraq war and a message of "hope and change," he won the 2008 Democratic presidential nomination, defeating expected front-runner Sen. Hillary Clinton (NY), and outpolled Sen. John McCain (R, AZ) to become the nation's first Black president.

Pres. Obama was awarded the 2009 Nobel Peace Prize for "efforts to strengthen international diplomacy and cooperation between peoples." He gradually pulled U.S. troops from Iraq, though as sectarian strife heightened they were reintroduced, in what were called noncombat roles. He began force reductions in Afghanistan, but stepped up drone strikes against Islamist militants abroad and authorized a 2011 raid that killed al-Qaeda leader Osama bin Laden. Under Obama the U.S. joined in NATO airstrikes leading to the overthrow of Libyan dictator Muammar al-Qaddafi, but rival militias refused to disarm and the U.S. ambassador and three other Americans were killed in a 2012 attack by Islamist radicals on a U.S. consulate in Benghazi.

The administration won passage of a $787-bil economic stimulus package early in 2009, and the U.S. pulled out of recession, though growth was slow. In Mar. 2010, Obama won passage of his signature health care reform bill ("Obamacare"), aimed at extending coverage to the uninsured. But Democrats lost their House majority in Nov. 2010 elections, limiting Obama's legislative agenda. In 2012, he signed an executive order suspending deportations for most young undocumented immigrants ("dreamers") who came to the U.S. as children. The administration also finalized regulations greatly tightening fuel emission standards for motor vehicles.

After Obama was reelected in Nov. 2012, a compromise in Congress averted a year-end "fiscal cliff" by making expiring Bush tax cuts permanent for most people, while postponing a "sequester" (later implemented) involving equal across-the-board cuts. Battles over the federal budget, debt ceiling, and Obamacare funding continued. The administration was criticized over allegations that the Internal Revenue Service had discriminated against Tea Party groups; further criticism was aimed at technical glitches in the rollout of Obamacare and at revelations of mismanagement at the Dept. of Veterans Affairs. Disclosures of classified information indicating extensive U.S. surveillance by the Natl. Security Agency drew calls for reform. Terrorism remained a threat within the U.S. (as in the Boston Marathon bombing, 2013).

Abroad, Russian forces annexed the Crimean region of Ukraine (Mar. 2014), and pro-Russian separatists, reportedly bolstered by Russian forces, fought the government in eastern Ukraine; Obama joined Europe in imposing economic sanctions. Obama called for an end to the repressive regime of Syria's Bashar al-Assad, pitted against rebel factions in a bloody civil war, but when Assad forces appeared to have launched a chemical weapons attack on civilians, crossing what Obama had called a "red line," he agreed to a Russian-brokered disarmament pact with the regime. After the Sunni militant group Islamic State in Iraq and Syria (ISIS) took over large areas of both countries, proclaiming an Islamic "caliphate" (June 2014) and persecuting religious minorities, Obama sent military advisers into Iraq. He also authorized U.S. airstrikes against ISIS and eventually provided arms to moderate Syrian rebels.

After 2014 midterm elections, which left Republicans controlling both houses of Congress, Obama issued an executive order expanding protection of undocumented immigrants from deportation, but it was blocked in court. His administration unveiled a Clean Power Plan, aimed especially at cutting carbon emissions from coal-fired power plants, and Obama signed onto the Paris agreement aimed at global reductions in greenhouse gas emissions linked to climate change. Under Obama, the U.S. in 2015 restored relations with Cuba, severed since 1961, and entered a multination accord with Iran intended to curb Iranian nuclear weapons development for a time, in return for ending economic sanctions. The administration also participated in negotiations for a 12-nation Trans-Pacific Partnership, but it was not ratified by Congress.

Responding to the mass shooting of children at Sandy Hook Elementary School in Newtown, CT (2012), Obama called for federal gun control legislation, to no avail. He also confronted racial violence (as in the 2015 massacre in a Black Charleston, SC, church) and racial tensions over the deaths of Black people in encounters with police (as in Ferguson, MO, 2014). In Mar. 2016 he nominated U.S. Appeals Court Judge Merrick Garland to the Supreme Court, but the Republican-controlled Senate refused to consider the nomination.

Obama left office with an approval rating close to 60%.

Donald John Trump (2017-), 45th president, Republican, was born June 14, 1946, in Queens, NY, the son of Frederick C. Trump, a wealthy real estate developer, and Mary Anne MacLeod Trump, a Scottish immigrant. At age 13 he was sent to a military boarding school. He earned a bachelor's degree from the Wharton School of Finance in 1968 and eventually rose to control of his father's enterprise. A suit against the company for alleged racial discrimination in housing was settled in 1975. Aided by city tax breaks, Trump spearheaded a successful expansion from New York City's outer boroughs into Manhattan and developed casinos in Atlantic City, NJ, though those eventually failed. He coauthored several business-advice books and hosted two reality TV series (2008-15). He also licensed his name to the now-defunct Trump Univ., an entrepreneurial training program. (A fraud suit against it was settled in 2018 for $25 mil.) Trump's net worth was estimated by *Forbes* at $3.3 bil in Mar. 2020.

After two marriages that ended in divorce, Trump married Melania Knauss in 2005. Their son Barron was born in 2006. He also had two sons, Donald Jr. (b. 1977) and Eric (b. 1984), and a daughter, Ivanka (b. 1981), from his first marriage, and a daughter, Tiffany (b. 1993), from his second. As president he surrendered control, but not ownership, of the Trump Organization to his elder sons.

During Obama's presidency Trump emerged as an outspoken "birther," questioning whether Obama was born in the U.S. In June 2015 Trump announced his candidacy for the Republican presidential nomination, blaming illegal immigration for many ills, and portraying himself as an outsider who would "make America great again." His often provocative rhetoric at rallies and in offhand tweets—which he continued in the White House, to much criticism—energized supporters, and he forged ahead to win the nomination. Multiple accusations of sexual misconduct, and revelation of crude remarks about women, dogged but did not derail his fall campaign. He defeated former senator and Sec. of State Hillary Clinton (D), though she won the popular vote.

Promptly after being inaugurated Pres. Trump issued a slew of executive orders, including orders to minimize any "unwarranted" burdens imposed under Obamacare, deny federal funding to so-called sanctuary cities for undocumented immigrants (blocked in court), ban immigration from seven Muslim-majority nations (later modified; upheld by the Supreme Court), and plan for a wall along the Mexican border (tied up by delays in funding). The administration also sought to end the Obama-era Deferred Action for Childhood Arrivals (DACA) program, which protected many undocumented immigrants who arrived in the U.S. as minors (blocked by court decisions) and took a hard line toward influxes of Central American migrants seeking asylum at, or illegally crossing, the U.S.-Mexico border ("zero tolerance" policy, Apr. 2018). Reports of inhumane conditions at overcrowded detention centers, and especially of children separated from parents, generated widespread criticism, and the administration announced an end to new family separations, though the practice did not end entirely. Trump was also denounced for what many considered racist sympathies, especially when he appeared to blame "both sides" for violence at a white nationalist rally in Charlottesville, VA (Aug. 2017).

Citing protectionist concerns, Trump withdrew the U.S. from the unratified Trans-Pacific Partnership, Obama's signature trade agreement, though he later signed a revised version of the North American Free Trade Agreement between the U.S., Canada, and Mexico. Starting in 2018 the administration imposed tariffs on various imports, leading to tariffs against U.S. products by European allies and an escalating trade war with China.

In mid-2017 the U.S. began a long process of withdrawal from the Paris Agreement on climate change, in effect since 2016. The administration also began a process to roll back fuel efficiency mandates for vehicles, and later repealed and replaced Obama's Clean Power Plan (subject to legal challenge), while making many other changes in environmental regulations.

By June 2020, Trump successfully appointed over 200 conservative-leaning judges to federal courts, and he won confirmation of Neil Gorsuch (2017) and Brett Kavanaugh (2018) to the Supreme Court—the latter after a contentious Senate hearing in which Kavanaugh was accused of sexual assault.

While Trump's son-in-law Jared Kushner became a trusted member of his inner circle, a number of other top aides and officials quit or were pushed out early in his tenure, including former alt-right media executive Steve Bannon as senior adviser; former GOP chair Reince Priebus as chief of staff; former Exxon Mobil CEO Rex Tillerson as secretary of state, replaced by CIA director Mike Pompeo; and retired Gen. James Mattis, who resigned as defense secretary over policy differences. A few others resigned amid scandals or controversies.

Investigations into Russian interference in the 2016 presidential election led to some of these changes. In Feb. 2017, National Security Adviser Michael Flynn resigned after FBI surveillance found he had lied about a conversation with the Russian ambassador. In May 2017, Trump controversially fired FBI director James Comey, who had led the FBI's Russia probe. After Attorney Gen. Jeff Sessions recused himself (he was later fired, replaced by William Barr), the deputy attorney general appointed former FBI director Robert Mueller to oversee the probe, which Trump dismissed as a "witch hunt." As offshoots of the probe, onetime Trump campaign chief Paul Manafort was indicted and convicted of (unrelated) financial crimes, while Trump attorney Michael Cohen pleaded guilty to campaign finance violations and other charges, and implicated Trump in directing hush money payments in 2016 to two women alleging sexual liaisons. Political operative and Trump loyalist Roger Stone was convicted of obstruction of justice and other felonies, but his sentence was commuted by Trump in 2020.

Abroad, Trump cultivated ties with Russian Pres. Vladimir Putin, with whom he met several times. In 2019, however, he suspended participation in a 1987 nuclear arms reduction treaty with Russia, having accused Russia of breaches. After threats and counterthreats between the U.S. and North Korea, Trump met personally with North Korea's leader, Kim Jong Un, in June 2018; this and later meetings apparently did not stem the growth of nuclear weaponry in North Korea.

Trump intensified U.S. support for Israel to the extent of controversially recognizing Jerusalem as Israel's capital in 2017. In 2018 Trump announced U.S. withdrawal from a 2015 multination nuclear deal with Iran and imposed heavy U.S. sanctions the deal had removed. As a counterweight to Iran, Trump strongly supported Saudi Arabia, downplaying the government-sanctioned 2018 murder of a dissident Saudi journalist. Trump later vetoed a Senate attempt to block military assistance to the Saudis in their intervention, with heavy civilian casualties, in the Yemen civil war.

Trump lost ground in the 2018 midterm elections, with Democrats gaining control of the House, though the GOP retained its Senate majority. In Dec. 2018, in a bipartisan effort, Congress passed and Trump signed a major criminal justice reform bill. In Aug. 2019 he signed a two-year federal budget bill, negotiated with Democrats, that set high levels for discretionary spending and raised the debt ceiling. Through 2019, unemployment was holding near 50-year lows, stocks did well, and GDP growth continued, though the budget deficit was on the rise.

Abroad, the White House, in Oct. 2019, announced troop withdrawals from Syria, giving way to an imminent assault by Turkish troops against Kurdish forces, which were allied with the U.S. against ISIS. The move drew a bipartisan rebuke from the U.S. House, in a 354-60 vote. Peace talks with the Taliban in Afghanistan stalled after a partial agreement in Feb. 2020. In early 2020 the Trump administration released an Arab-Israeli peace plan considered weighted toward Israeli concerns. The administration later helped achieve an agreement restoring relations between Israel and the UAE.

The Trump presidency, in 2019 and especially 2020, came up against fundamental challenges that overshadowed other developments.

The first of these started from the Mueller probe. In Apr. 2019, after a 22-month investigation, Mueller released a long report exposing Russian actions to influence the 2016 election and links between Russians and Trump campaign personnel, along with evidence of efforts by Trump to derail the probe. The report made no conclusion as to whether Trump was guilty of criminal action. But support for impeachment increased, especially after a whistleblower's complaint that Trump had pressured the Ukrainian government to discredit former Vice Pres. Joe Biden, whose son Hunter was a board member of a Ukrainian energy company. In Sept. 2019 the White House released the rough transcript of a July phone call in which Trump asked Ukraine's president to investigate the Bidens, soon after the U.S. had withheld $400 mil in aid to Ukraine. Trump allies defended the call, claiming he was being railroaded, and had been concerned over corruption but done nothing impeachable. After congressional hearings at which officials alleged an illicit quid pro quo, the House Judiciary Committee approved articles of impeachment against Trump for abuse of power and obstruction of justice. On Dec. 18 the full House, with no Republican support, passed the first article, 230-197, and the second 229-198. On Feb. 5, 2020, after a trial, the GOP-controlled Senate voted against the two articles, 52-48 and 53-47.

A second challenge was the coronavirus pandemic, which by late summer 2020 had sickened more than 6 mil Americans and caused some 200,000 U.S. deaths, besides leading to widespread unemployment, amid the largest economic contraction ever documented. Although the Trump administration barred entry, in early Feb., to most foreign nationals from China, where the disease originated, arrivals from heavily impacted European countries were not at first addressed. The virus easily spread without adequate testing or tracing of contacts, overwhelming hospitals and supply chains in some areas. Trump created a coronavirus task force and held public briefings at times, at which health experts were able to convey information. But he often downplayed the pandemic and the importance of preventive measures such as wearing masks in public, and he was accused of lacking a coherent strategy. He encouraged efforts to reopen the economy, disparaging advice by public health experts he portrayed as overcautious.

The death in May 2020 of a Black man, George Floyd, attributed to homicidal violence by a white Minneapolis police officer, gave rise to continuing wide-scale protests against systemic racist police brutality and racial oppression, sometimes diverging into looting and vandalism, with incidents of violence. Accused of racist attitudes by his critics, Trump disputed or downplayed protesters' grievances while promoting aggressive action to preserve law and order.

Among several critical books about Trump, tell-all best-sellers by his fired hardline National Security Adviser John Bolton (*The Room Where It Happened*) and by his niece Mary Trump (*Too Much and Never Enough: How My Family Created the World's Most Dangerous Man*) appeared in 2020.

Presidential Rankings, 2017

Source: © 2017 C-SPAN

As assessed by historians and other professional observers of the presidency, 91 of whom participated in the 2017 survey. Participants rated each president on 10 qualities of presidential leadership; rankings here reflect overall score.

Rank	President	2009 rank	2000 rank	Rank	President	2009 rank	2000 rank	Rank	President	2009 rank	2000 rank
1.	Lincoln	1	1	16.	McKinley	16	15	30.	B. Harrison	30	31
2.	Washington	2	3	17.	Madison	20	18	31.	Taylor	29	28
3.	F. D. Roosevelt	3	2	18.	Jackson	13	13	32.	Hayes	33	26
4.	T. Roosevelt	4	4	19.	J. Adams	17	16	33.	G. W. Bush	36	NA
5.	Eisenhower	8	9	20.	G. H. W. Bush	18	20	34.	Van Buren	31	30
6.	Truman	5	5	21.	J. Q. Adams	19	19	35.	Arthur	32	32
7.	Jefferson	7	7	22.	Grant	23	33	36.	Hoover	34	34
8.	Kennedy	6	8	23.	Cleveland	21	17	37.	Fillmore	37	35
9.	Reagan	10	11	24.	Taft	24	24	38.	W. H. Harrison	39	37
10.	L. B. Johnson	11	10	25.	Ford	22	23	39.	Tyler	35	36
11.	Wilson	9	6	26.	Carter	25	22	40.	Harding	38	38
12.	Obama	NA	NA	27.	Coolidge	26	27	41.	Pierce	40	39
13.	Monroe	14	14	28.	Nixon	27	25	42.	A. Johnson	41	40
14.	Polk	12	12	29.	Garfield	28	29	43.	Buchanan	42	41
15.	Clinton	15	21								

NA = Not applicable.

Presidential Facts

Oldest president: Ronald Reagan, who was 77 when he left office

Oldest person elected to first term as president: Donald J. Trump, who was 70 when elected in 2016

Longest-living president: Jimmy Carter, who on Mar. 22, 2019, was 94 years and 172 days old, surpassing George H. W. Bush, who died at the age of 94 years, 171 days.

Youngest president: Theodore Roosevelt, who was 42 when sworn in after McKinley's death

Youngest person elected president: John F. Kennedy, who was 43 when elected in 1960

Tallest president: Abraham Lincoln, who was 6 feet, 4 inches

Shortest president: James Madison, who was 5 feet, 4 inches

Heaviest president: William Howard Taft, who was 332 pounds in 1911

First president to live in the White House: John Adams, who moved there in 1800

First president whose parents were immigrants: Andrew Jackson; his parents emigrated from Ireland in 1765

First president born a U.S. citizen: Martin Van Buren, in Kinderhook, NY, 1782

First president born outside the original colonies: Abraham Lincoln, in Kentucky, 1809

First president born west of the Mississippi: Herbert Hoover, in West Branch, IA, 1874

Most common presidential home state: Virginia, with 8 presidents

First president born in a hospital: Jimmy Carter, in Plains, GA, 1924

First president to have a telephone in the White House: Rutherford B. Hayes, in 1879

First president to travel outside U.S. while in office: Theodore Roosevelt visited Panama Canal site, 1906

First president to address the nation on radio: Warren G. Harding, in 1922

First president to appear on TV: Franklin D. Roosevelt, at opening ceremonies for the 1939 World's Fair

First president to give a live, televised news conference: John F. Kennedy, in 1961

First president to hold an internet chat: Bill Clinton, in 1999

Presidents who lost the popular vote while winning election: John Quincy Adams, in 1824 (elected by the House after general election failed to produce a majority); Rutherford B. Hayes, in 1876; Benjamin Harrison, in 1888; George W. Bush, in 2000; Donald J. Trump, in 2016. (Popular vote totals before 1824 are unknown.)

Only presidents chosen by the House of Representatives: Thomas Jefferson (1st term) and John Quincy Adams

Only president never elected either president or vice president: Gerald Ford; named vice president when Spiro Agnew resigned (1973), became president when Nixon resigned (1974)

Only president who never previously held government or military office: Donald J. Trump

Left-handed presidents: James Garfield, Herbert Hoover, Harry Truman, Gerald Ford, Ronald Reagan, George H. W. Bush, Bill Clinton, and Barack Obama

Only Catholic president: John F. Kennedy; the most common religious affiliations have been Episcopalian (11) and Presbyterian (9)

Only bachelor presidents: James Buchanan, who never married, and Grover Cleveland, who married Frances Folsom in the White House in 1886

First divorced president: Ronald Reagan; divorced from Jane Wyman in 1948, married Nancy Davis in 1952

Presidents who died on July 4: John Adams and Thomas Jefferson (both 1826) and James Monroe (1831)

Presidential Libraries

Presidential libraries are coordinated by the National Archives and Records Administration (www.archives.gov/presidential-libraries/). Materials for presidents before Herbert Hoover are held by private institutions. NARA's Barack Obama Presidential Library (www.obamalibrary.gov) will be a fully digital library. The Obama Presidential Center (www.obama.org/the-center), expected to open in 2021 in Chicago, will be a privately operated, non-governmental organization. Under the Presidential Records Act, material is available through Freedom of Information Act requests starting five years after a president has left office.

Herbert Hoover Library and Museum
210 Parkside Dr.
West Branch, IA 52358
Phone: (319) 643-5301
Email: hoover.library@nara.gov
Website: hoover.archives.gov

Franklin D. Roosevelt Library and Museum
4079 Albany Post Rd.
Hyde Park, NY 12538-1990
Phone: (800) FDR-VISIT
Email: roosevelt.library@nara.gov
Website: www.fdrlibrary.marist.edu

Harry S. Truman Library and Museum
500 West U.S. Hwy. 24
Independence, MO 64050-2481
Phone: (800) 833-1225
Email: truman.library@nara.gov
Website: www.trumanlibrary.org

Dwight D. Eisenhower Library
200 SE 4th St.
Abilene, KS 67410-2900
Phone: (877) RING-IKE
Email: eisenhower.library@nara.gov
Website: eisenhower.archives.gov

John F. Kennedy Library and Museum
Columbia Pt.
Boston, MA 02125-3312

Phone: (866) JFK-1960
Email: kennedy.library@nara.gov
Website: www.jfklibrary.org

Lyndon Baines Johnson Library and Museum
2313 Red River St.
Austin, TX 78705-5737
Phone: (512) 721-0200
Email: johnson.library@nara.gov
Website: www.lbjlibrary.org

Richard Nixon Library and Museum
18001 Yorba Linda Blvd.
Yorba Linda, CA 92886-3903
Phone: (714) 983-9120
Email: nixon@nara.gov
Website: www.nixonlibrary.gov

Gerald R. Ford Library and Museum
Library: 1000 Beal Ave.
Ann Arbor, MI 48109-2109
Phone: (734) 205-0555
Museum: 303 Pearl St. NW
Grand Rapids, MI 49504-5353
Phone: (616) 254-0400
Email: ford.library@nara.gov
Website: www.fordlibrarymuseum.gov

Jimmy Carter Library and Museum
441 Freedom Pkwy.
Atlanta, GA 30307-1498
Phone: (404) 865-7100

Email: carter.library@nara.gov
Website: www.jimmycarterlibrary.gov

Ronald Reagan Library and Museum
40 Presidential Dr.
Simi Valley, CA 93065-0600
Phone: (800) 410-8354
Email: reagan.library@nara.gov
Website: reaganlibrary.gov

George H. W. Bush Library and Museum
1000 George Bush Dr. West
College Station, TX 77845
Phone: (979) 691-4000
Email: library.bush@nara.gov
Website: www.bush41.org

William J. Clinton Library and Museum
1200 President Clinton Ave.
Little Rock, AR 72201
Phone: (501) 374-4242
Email: clinton.library@nara.gov
Website: www.clintonlibrary.gov

George W. Bush Library and Museum
2943 SMU Blvd.
Dallas, TX 75205
Phone: (214) 346-1650
Email: gwbush.library@nara.gov
Website: www.bushcenter.org

Presidential Impeachment in U.S. History

The U.S. Constitution provides for impeachment and removal from office of federal officials on grounds of "Treason, Bribery, or other high Crimes and Misdemeanors" (Article II, Sect. 4). Impeachment is the bringing of charges by the House of Representatives, whose members can adopt impeachment articles on a simple majority vote. It is followed by a Senate trial; a two-thirds majority vote of Senators present is needed for conviction and removal from office.

In 1868, **Andrew Johnson** became the first president impeached by the House, for his removal of Sec. of War Edwin M. Stanton without first notifying the Senate. He was tried but not convicted. In 1974, impeachment articles against Pres. **Richard Nixon**, in connection with the Watergate scandal, were adopted by the House Judiciary Committee. He resigned Aug. 9, and the House accepted the committee report without taking further action. In 1998, Pres. **Bill Clinton** was impeached by the House in connection with his cover-up of a sexual relationship with former White House intern Monica Lewinsky. He was tried in the Senate in 1999 and acquitted. Pres. **Donald Trump** was impeached in 2019 on charges related to allegations that he used his office to pressure the president of Ukraine to investigate a political rival; he was acquitted by the Senate in 2020.

Spouses and Children of the Presidents

Name (born-died; married)	Birth-place	Sons/daughters	Name (born-died; married)	Birth-place	Sons/daughters
Martha Dandridge Custis Washington (1731-1802; 1759)	VA	None	Mary Scott Lord Dimmick Harrison (1858-1948; 1896)	PA	0/1
Abigail Smith Adams (1744-1818; 1764)	MA	3/2	Ida Saxton McKinley (1847-1907; 1871)	OH	0/2
Martha Wayles Skelton Jefferson (1748-82; 1772)	VA	1/5	Alice Hathaway Lee Roosevelt (1861-84; 1880)	MA	0/1
Dolley Payne Todd Madison (1768-1849; 1794)	NC	None	Edith Kermit Carow Roosevelt (1861-1948; 1886)	CT	4/1
Elizabeth Kortright Monroe (1768-1830; 1786)	NY	1/2	Helen Herron Taft (1861-1943; 1886)	OH	2/1
Louisa Catherine Johnson Adams (1775-1852; 1797)	Eng.[1]	3/1	Ellen Louise Axson Wilson (1860-1914; 1885)	GA	0/3
Rachel Donelson Robards Jackson (1767-1828; 1791)	VA	1/0[2]	Edith Bolling Galt Wilson (1872-1961; 1915)	VA	None
Hannah Hoes Van Buren (1783-1819; 1807)	NY	4/0	Florence Kling De Wolfe Harding (1860-1924; 1891)	OH	None
Anna Tuthill Symmes Harrison (1775-1864; 1795)	NJ	6/4	Grace Anna Goodhue Coolidge (1879-1957; 1905)	VT	2/0
Letitia Christian Tyler (1790-1842; 1813)	VA	3/5	Lou Henry Hoover (1875-1944; 1899)	IA	2/0
Julia Gardiner Tyler (1820-89; 1844)	NY	5/2	Anna Eleanor Roosevelt (1884-1962; 1905)	NY	5/1
Sarah Childress Polk (1803-91; 1824)	TN	None	Elizabeth Virginia (Bess) Wallace Truman (1885-1982; 1919)	MO	0/1
Margaret (Peggy) Mackall Smith Taylor (1788-1852; 1810)	MD	1/5	Mamie Geneva Doud Eisenhower (1896-1979; 1916)	IA	2/0
Abigail Powers Fillmore (1798-1853; 1826)	NY	1/1	Jacqueline Lee Bouvier Kennedy (1929-94; 1953)	NY	2/1
Caroline Carmichael McIntosh Fillmore (1813-81; 1858)	NJ	None	Claudia (Lady Bird) Alta Taylor Johnson (1912-2007; 1934)	TX	0/2
Jane Means Appleton Pierce (1806-63; 1834)	NH	3/0	Thelma Catherine Patricia Ryan Nixon (1912-93; 1940)	NV	0/2
Mary Todd Lincoln (1818-82; 1842)	KY	4/0	Elizabeth (Betty) Bloomer Warren Ford (1918-2011; 1948)	IL	3/1
Eliza McCardle Johnson (1810-76; 1827)	TN	3/2	Eleanor Rosalynn Smith Carter (1927- ; 1946)	GA	3/1
Julia Boggs Dent Grant (1826-1902; 1848)	MO	3/1	Anne Frances (Nancy) Robbins Davis Reagan (1921-2016; 1952)	NY	1/1[3]
Lucy Ware Webb Hayes (1831-89; 1852)	OH	7/1	Barbara Pierce Bush (1925-2018; 1945)	NY	4/2
Lucretia Rudolph Garfield (1832-1918; 1858)	OH	5/2	Hillary Diane Rodham Clinton (1947- ; 1975)	IL	0/1
Ellen Lewis Herndon Arthur (1837-80; 1859)	VA	2/1	Laura Lane Welch Bush (1946- ; 1977)	TX	0/2
Frances Folsom Cleveland (1864-1947; 1886)	NY	2/3	Michelle LaVaughn Robinson Obama (1964- ; 1992)	IL	0/2
Caroline Lavinia Scott Harrison (1832-92; 1853)	OH	1/1	Melania Knauss Trump (1970- ; 2005)	Slovenia	1/0[4]

Note: Pres. Buchanan was unmarried. Children not born to the marriages shown are not listed unless otherwise noted. (1) Born in London, father a MD citizen. (2) Adopted son. (3) Pres. Reagan's first wife, whom he later divorced, was Jane Wyman (m. 1940-48). They had two daughters, one of whom died in infancy, and an adopted son. (4) Pres. Trump had four children from two previous marriages: two sons (Donald Jr., Eric) and one daughter (Ivanka) with Ivana Marie Zelníčková Trump (m. 1977-92) and one daughter (Tiffany) with Marla Maples (m. 1993-99).

First Lady Melania Trump

Melania Trump was born Melanija Knavs (later Germanized to Melania Knauss) on Apr. 26, 1970, in Novo Mesto, Slovenia (then part of Yugoslavia). She matriculated at Univ. of Ljubljana in Slovenia but moved to New York City in 1996 to further a modeling career. She and Donald Trump were married in Jan. 2005; their son Barron was born in Mar. 2006, the same year Melania Trump became a U.S. citizen. She was the second first lady born outside of the U.S. (The first was English-born Louisa Adams, wife of John Quincy Adams.) She was the first Catholic first lady since Jacqueline Kennedy. In May 2018, Melania Trump launched the "Be Best" initiative directed at youth, focusing especially on avoidance of cyberbullying and drug abuse.

Burial Places of the Presidents

President	Burial place	President	Burial place	President	Burial place
Washington	Mt. Vernon, VA	Pierce	Concord, NH	Wilson	Wash. Natl. Cathedral, DC
J. Adams	Quincy, MA	Buchanan	Lancaster, PA	Harding	Marion, OH
Jefferson	Charlottesville, VA	Lincoln	Springfield, IL	Coolidge	Plymouth Notch, VT
Madison	Montpelier Station, VA	A. Johnson	Greeneville, TN	Hoover	West Branch, IA
Monroe	Richmond, VA	Grant	New York, NY	F. Roosevelt	Hyde Park, NY
J. Q. Adams	Quincy, MA	Hayes	Fremont, OH	Truman	Independence, MO
Jackson	Nashville, TN	Garfield	Cleveland, OH	Eisenhower	Abilene, KS
Van Buren	Kinderhook, NY	Arthur	Albany, NY	Kennedy	Arlington Natl. Cem., VA
W. H. Harrison	North Bend, OH	Cleveland	Princeton, NJ	L. B. Johnson	Stonewall, TX
Tyler	Richmond, VA	B. Harrison	Indianapolis, IN	Nixon	Yorba Linda, CA
Polk	Nashville, TN	McKinley	Canton, OH	Ford	Grand Rapids, MI
Taylor	Louisville, KY	T. Roosevelt	Oyster Bay, NY	Reagan	Simi Valley, CA
Fillmore	Buffalo, NY	Taft	Arlington Natl. Cem., VA	G. H. W. Bush	College Station, TX

PRESIDENTIAL ELECTIONS

Note: Historical election statistics as of Sept. 2020. For information about the 2020 election, see pp. 14-50.

Popular and Electoral Vote for President, 1789-2016

(D) Democrat; (DR) Democratic Republican; (F) Federalist; (LB) Libertarian; (LR) Liberal Republican; (NR) National Republican; (P) People's/Populist; (PR) Progressive; (R) Republican; (W) Whig; * = See notes below table.

Year	President elected	Popular	Elec.	Major losing candidate(s)	Popular	Elec.
1789	George Washington	Unknown	69	No major opposition	—	—
1792	George Washington	Unknown	132	No major opposition	—	—
1796	John Adams (F)	Unknown	71	Thomas Jefferson (DR)	Unknown	68
1800*	Thomas Jefferson (DR)	Unknown	73	Aaron Burr (DR)	Unknown	73
				John Adams (F)	Unknown	65
1804	Thomas Jefferson (DR)	Unknown	162	Charles Pinckney (F)	Unknown	14
1808	James Madison (DR)	Unknown	122	Charles Pinckney (F)	Unknown	47
1812	James Madison (DR)	Unknown	128	DeWitt Clinton (F)	Unknown	89
1816	James Monroe (DR)	Unknown	183	Rufus King (F)	Unknown	34
1820	James Monroe (DR)	Unknown	231	John Quincy Adams (DR)	Unknown	1
1824*	John Quincy Adams (DR)	113,122	84	Andrew Jackson (DR)	151,271	99
				Henry Clay (DR)	46,587	37
				William H. Crawford (DR)	44,282	41
1828	Andrew Jackson (D)	642,553	178	John Quincy Adams (NR)	500,897	83
1832	Andrew Jackson (D)	701,780	219	Henry Clay (NR)	484,205	49
1836	Martin Van Buren (D)	764,176	170	William H. Harrison (W)	550,816	73
1840	William H. Harrison (W)	1,275,390	234	Martin Van Buren (D)	1,128,854	60
1844	James K. Polk (D)	1,339,494	170	Henry Clay (W)	1,300,004	105
1848	Zachary Taylor (W)	1,361,393	163	Lewis Cass (D)	1,223,460	127
				Martin Van Buren (Free Soil)	291,501	—
1852	Franklin Pierce (D)	1,607,510	254	Winfield Scott (W)	1,386,942	42
1856	James Buchanan (D)	1,836,072	174	John C. Frémont (R)	1,342,345	114
				Millard Fillmore (American/Know-Nothing)	873,053	8
1860 .	Abraham Lincoln (R)	1,865,908	180	Stephen A. Douglas (D)	848,019	12
				John C. Breckinridge (D)	845,763	72
				John Bell (Constitutional Union)	589,581	39
1864	Abraham Lincoln (R)	2,218,388	212	George McClellan (D)	1,812,807	21
1868	Ulysses S. Grant (R)	3,013,650	214	Horatio Seymour (D)	2,708,744	80
1872*	Ulysses S. Grant (R)	3,598,235	286	Horace Greeley (D-LR)	2,834,671	—
1876*	Rutherford B. Hayes (R)	4,034,311	185	Samuel J. Tilden (D)	4,288,546	184
1880	James A. Garfield (R)	4,446,158	214	Winfield S. Hancock (D)	4,444,260	155
1884	Grover Cleveland (D)	4,874,621	219	James G. Blaine (R)	4,848,936	182
1888	Benjamin Harrison (R)	5,443,892	233	Grover Cleveland (D)	5,534,488	168
1892	Grover Cleveland (D)	5,551,883	277	Benjamin Harrison (R)	5,179,244	145
				James Weaver (P)	1,027,329	22
1896	William McKinley (R)	7,108,480	271	William J. Bryan (D-P)	6,511,495	176
1900	William McKinley (R)	7,218,039	292	William J. Bryan (D)	6,358,345	155
1904	Theodore Roosevelt (R)	7,626,593	336	Alton B. Parker (D)	5,082,898	140
1908	William H. Taft (R)	7,676,258	321	William J. Bryan (D)	6,406,801	162
1912	Woodrow Wilson (D)	6,293,152	435	Theodore Roosevelt (PR)	4,119,207	88
				William H. Taft (R)	3,483,922	8
1916	Woodrow Wilson (D)	9,126,300	277	Charles E. Hughes (R)	8,546,789	254
1920	Warren G. Harding (R)	16,153,115	404	James M. Cox (D)	9,133,092	127
1924	Calvin Coolidge (R)	15,719,921	382	John W. Davis (D)	8,386,704	136
				Robert M. La Follette (PR)	4,822,856	13
1928	Herbert Hoover (R)	21,437,277	444	Alfred E. Smith (D)	15,007,698	87
1932	Franklin D. Roosevelt (D)	22,829,501	472	Herbert Hoover (R)	15,760,684	59
1936	Franklin D. Roosevelt (D)	27,757,333	523	Alfred Landon (R)	16,684,231	8
1940	Franklin D. Roosevelt (D)	27,313,041	449	Wendell Willkie (R)	22,348,480	82
1944	Franklin D. Roosevelt (D)	25,612,610	432	Thomas E. Dewey (R)	22,117,617	99
1948	Harry S. Truman (D)	24,179,345	303	Thomas E. Dewey (R)	21,991,291	189
				Strom Thurmond (States' Rights)	1,169,021	39
				Henry A. Wallace (PR)	1,157,172	—
1952	Dwight D. Eisenhower (R)	33,936,234	442	Adlai E. Stevenson (D)	27,314,992	89
1956*	Dwight D. Eisenhower (R)	35,590,472	457	Adlai E. Stevenson (D)	26,022,752	73
1960*	John F. Kennedy (D)	34,226,731	303	Richard M. Nixon (R)	34,108,157	219
1964	Lyndon B. Johnson (D)	43,129,566	486	Barry M. Goldwater (R)	27,178,188	52
1968	Richard M. Nixon (R)	31,785,480	301	Hubert H. Humphrey (D)	31,275,166	191
				George C. Wallace (Amer. Indep.)	9,906,473	46
1972*	Richard M. Nixon (R)	47,169,911	520	George S. McGovern (D)	29,170,383	17
1976*	Jimmy Carter (D)	40,830,763	297	Gerald R. Ford (R)	39,147,793	240
1980	Ronald Reagan (R)	43,904,153	489	Jimmy Carter (D)	35,483,883	49
				John B. Anderson (independent)	5,719,437	—
1984	Ronald Reagan (R)	54,455,075	525	Walter F. Mondale (D)	37,577,185	13
1988*	George H. W. Bush (R)	48,886,097	426	Michael S. Dukakis (D)	41,809,074	111
1992	Bill Clinton (D)	44,909,889	370	George H. W. Bush (R)	39,104,545	168
				H. Ross Perot (independent)	19,742,267	—
1996	Bill Clinton (D)	47,402,357	379	Bob Dole (R)	39,198,755	159
				H. Ross Perot (Reform)	8,085,402	—
2000*	George W. Bush (R)	50,456,002	271	Al Gore (D)	50,999,897	266
				Ralph Nader (Green)	2,882,955	—
2004*	George W. Bush (R)	62,040,610	286	John Kerry (D)	59,028,444	251
2008	Barack H. Obama (D)	69,498,516	365	John McCain (R)	59,948,283	173
2012	Barack H. Obama (D)	65,915,795	332	Mitt Romney (R)	60,933,504	206
2016*	Donald J. Trump (R)	62,984,828	304	Hillary Clinton (D)	65,853,514	227

Note: Not all candidates who received electoral votes are shown. ***1800**—Elected by House of Representatives because of tied electoral vote. **1824**—Elected by House of Representatives because no candidate polled a majority. By 1824, the Democratic Republicans had become a loose coalition of competing political groups. By 1828, Andrew Jackson supporters were known as Democrats and John Q. Adams and Henry Clay supporters as National Republicans. **1872**—Greeley died Nov. 29, 1872. His electoral votes were split among four individuals. **1876**—FL, LA, OR, and SC election returns were disputed. Congress in joint session (Mar. 2, 1877) declared Hayes and Wheeler elected president and vice president. **1956**—Democrats elected 74 electors, but one from AL refused to vote for Stevenson. **1960**—Sen. Harry F. Byrd (D, VA) received 15 electoral votes. **1972**—John Hospers of CA received a vote from an elector of VA. **1976**—Ronald Reagan of CA received a vote from an elector of WA. **1988**—Sen. Lloyd Bentsen (D, TX) received a vote from an elector of WV. **2000**—One Gore elector from Washington, DC, abstained. Nader was listed as "independent" on the ballot in some states; he was not on the ballot in all states. **2004**—One MN elector voted for VP candidate John Edwards for both president and vice president. **2016**—Seven electors from three states (HI, TX, WA) did not vote for the candidate to whom they were pledged (two Trump electors defected, as did five pledged to Clinton).

Presidential Popular Vote, 2016

Source: Federal Election Commission; as of Dec. 2017

Candidate (party)	Vote total	Percent of vote	Candidate (party)	Vote total	Percent of vote
Hillary Clinton (Democrat)	65,853,514	48.18%	Tom Hoefling (America's Party)	4,779	<0.01%
Donald J. Trump (Republican)	62,984,828	46.09	Monica Moorehead (Workers World)	4,317	<0.01
Gary Johnson (Libertarian)	4,489,341	3.28	Laurence Kotlikoff (Independent)	3,581	<0.01
Jill Stein (Green)	1,457,218	1.07	Peter Skewes (American)	3,250	<0.01
Evan McMullin (Independent/ no party affiliation)	731,991	0.54	Rocky Giordani (Independent American)	2,752	<0.01
Darrell L. Castle (Constitution)	203,090	0.15	Emidio Soltysik (Natural Law/Socialist)	2,691	<0.01
Gloria La Riva (Peace and Freedom/			Scott Copeland (Constitution)	2,356	<0.01
Socialism and Liberation)	74,401	0.05	Kyle Kopitke (Independent American)	1,096	<0.01
Rocky De La Fuente (Reform/			Joseph Allen Maldonado (Independent)	962	<0.01
American Delta)	33,136	0.02	Ryan Alan Scott (Unaffiliated)	754	<0.01
Richard Duncan (Nonpartisan)	24,307	0.02	Rod Silva (Nutrition)	751	<0.01
Dan R. Vacek (Legal Marijuana Now)	13,537	0.01	Princess Jacob (Independent)	749	<0.01
Alyson Kennedy (Socialist Workers)	12,467	0.01	Jerry White (Socialism Equality Anti-War)	475	<0.01
Mike Smith (Independent)	9,338	0.01	Bradford Lyttle		
Chris Keniston (Veterans)	7,211	0.01	(Nonviolent Resistance/Pacifist)	382	<0.01
Michael A. Maturen (American Solidarity)	6,462	<0.01	Frank Atwood (Approval Voting)	337	<0.01
Lynn S. Kahn (Independent)	5,733	<0.01	Write-in votes (other/miscellaneous)	698,990	0.51
Jim Hedges (Independent/Prohibition)	5,617	<0.01	None of these candidates (Nevada)	28,863	0.02
			Total	136,669,276	

Note: Party designations vary from one state to another; party label listed may not necessarily represent a political party organization. Vote totals for the candidates listed above include any write-in votes.

The Electoral College

The president and the vice president are the only elective federal officials not chosen by direct vote of the people. They are elected by the members of the Electoral College, an institution provided for in the U.S. Constitution.

On presidential election day, the first Tuesday after the first Monday in Nov. of every fourth year, each state chooses as many electors as it has senators and representatives in Congress. In 1964, for the first time, as provided by the 23rd Amendment to the Constitution, the District of Columbia voted for three electors. Thus, with 100 senators and 435 representatives, there are 538 members of the Electoral College, with a majority of 270 electoral votes needed to elect the president and vice president.

Political parties were not part of the Founding Fathers' original plan. But today, each political party chooses its electors, by nomination at a state convention or by vote of the party central committee in each state. An elector cannot be a member of Congress or federal office holder. In some states, electors' names may be printed below the names of the presidential and vice presidential candidates on the Nov. ballot. In any case, the electors of the party receiving the highest vote count are elected under a winner-take-all system. Two states, Maine and Nebraska, allow for proportional allocation.

The electors meet on the first Monday after the second Wednesday in Dec. in their respective state capitals or in some other place prescribed by state legislatures. By long-established custom, they vote for their party nominees, although this is not required by federal law. They may be bound to do so by state law or party pledge.

The Constitution requires electors to cast a ballot for at least one person who is not an inhabitant of that elector's home state. This ensures that presidential and vice presidential candidates from the same party will not be from the same state.

Certified and sealed lists of the votes of the electors in each state are sent to the president of the U.S. Senate. He or she then opens them in the presence of members of the Senate and House of Representatives in a joint session held in early Jan. The electoral votes of all the states are then officially counted.

If no candidate for president has a majority, the House of Representatives chooses a president from the top three candidates, with all representatives from each state combining to cast one vote for that state. The House decided the outcomes of the 1800 and 1824 presidential elections. If no candidate for vice president has a majority, the Senate chooses from the top two, with the senators voting as individuals. The Senate chose the vice president following the 1836 election.

Under the electoral college system, a candidate who fails to be the top vote-getter in the popular vote still may win a majority of electoral votes. This happened in the elections of 1876, 1888, 2000, and 2016.

Voter Turnout in Presidential Elections, 1932-2016

Source: U.S. Census Bureau, U.S. Dept. of Commerce; Office of the Clerk, U.S. House of Representatives

		Voter participation				Voter participation	
		% of voting-age citizen pop.	% of voting-age pop.			% of voting-age citizen pop.	% of voting-age pop.
Year	Candidates			Year	Candidates		
1932	F. D. Roosevelt-Hoover	NA	52.6%	1976	Carter-Ford	NA	59.2%
1936	F. D. Roosevelt-Landon	NA	56.9	1980	Reagan-Carter	64.0%	59.3
1940	F. D. Roosevelt-Willkie	NA	58.8	1984	Reagan-Mondale	64.9	59.9
1944	F. D. Roosevelt-Dewey	NA	56.1	1988	G. H. W. Bush-Dukakis	62.2	57.4
1948	Truman-Dewey	NA	51.1	1992	Clinton-G. H. W. Bush-Perot	67.7	61.3
1952	Eisenhower-Stevenson	NA	61.6	1996	Clinton-Dole-Perot	58.4	54.2
1956	Eisenhower-Stevenson	NA	59.3	2000	G. W. Bush-Gore	59.5	54.7
1960	Kennedy-Nixon	NA	62.8	2004	G. W. Bush-Kerry	63.8	58.3
1964	L. B. Johnson-Goldwater	NA	69.3	2008	Obama-McCain	63.6	58.2
1968	Nixon-Humphrey	NA	67.8	2012	Obama-Romney	61.8	56.5
1972	Nixon-McGovern	NA	63.0	2016	Trump-Clinton	61.4	56.0

NA = Not available. **Note:** Data prior to 1964 is from a legacy source and may not be directly comparable to more recent data. The 1972 presidential election was the first for which eligible voters included 18- to 20-year-olds. The voting-age citizen pop. includes those who are ineligible to vote due to imprisonment or prior felony convictions. The voting-age pop. comprises the former group as well as residents who are ineligible to vote because they are not U.S. citizens.

Major-Party Nominees for President and Vice President, 1856-2016

Asterisk (*) denotes winning ticket.

	Democratic			Republican	
Year	President	Vice President	Year	President	Vice President
1856	James Buchanan*	John Breckinridge	1856	John Frémont	William Dayton
1860	Stephen A. Douglas[1]	Herschel V. Johnson	1860	Abraham Lincoln*	Hannibal Hamlin
1864	George McClellan	G. H. Pendleton	1864	Abraham Lincoln*	Andrew Johnson
1868	Horatio Seymour	Francis Blair	1868	Ulysses S. Grant*	Schuyler Colfax
1872	Horace Greeley	B. Gratz Brown	1872	Ulysses S. Grant*	Henry Wilson
1876	Samuel J. Tilden	Thomas Hendricks	1876	Rutherford B. Hayes*	William Wheeler
1880	Winfield Hancock	William English	1880	James A. Garfield*	Chester A. Arthur
1884	Grover Cleveland*	Thomas Hendricks	1884	James G. Blaine	John Logan
1888	Grover Cleveland	A. G. Thurman	1888	Benjamin Harrison*	Levi Morton
1892	Grover Cleveland*	Adlai Stevenson	1892	Benjamin Harrison	Whitelaw Reid
1896	William J. Bryan	Arthur Sewall	1896	William McKinley*	Garret Hobart
1900	William J. Bryan	Adlai Stevenson	1900	William McKinley*	Theodore Roosevelt
1904	Alton Parker	Henry Davis	1904	Theodore Roosevelt*	Charles Fairbanks
1908	William J. Bryan	John Kern	1908	William H. Taft*	James Sherman
1912	Woodrow Wilson*	Thomas Marshall	1912	William H. Taft	James Sherman[2]
1916	Woodrow Wilson*	Thomas Marshall	1916	Charles E. Hughes	Charles Fairbanks
1920	James M. Cox	Franklin D. Roosevelt	1920	Warren G. Harding*	Calvin Coolidge
1924	John W. Davis	Charles W. Bryan	1924	Calvin Coolidge*	Charles G. Dawes
1928	Alfred E. Smith	Joseph T. Robinson	1928	Herbert Hoover*	Charles Curtis
1932	Franklin D. Roosevelt*	John N. Garner	1932	Herbert Hoover	Charles Curtis
1936	Franklin D. Roosevelt*	John N. Garner	1936	Alfred M. Landon	Frank Knox
1940	Franklin D. Roosevelt*	Henry A. Wallace	1940	Wendell L. Willkie	Charles McNary
1944	Franklin D. Roosevelt*	Harry S. Truman	1944	Thomas E. Dewey	John W. Bricker
1948	Harry S. Truman*	Alben W. Barkley	1948	Thomas E. Dewey	Earl Warren
1952	Adlai E. Stevenson	John J. Sparkman	1952	Dwight D. Eisenhower*	Richard M. Nixon
1956	Adlai E. Stevenson	Estes Kefauver	1956	Dwight D. Eisenhower*	Richard M. Nixon
1960	John F. Kennedy*	Lyndon B. Johnson	1960	Richard M. Nixon	Henry Cabot Lodge
1964	Lyndon B. Johnson*	Hubert H. Humphrey	1964	Barry M. Goldwater	William E. Miller
1968	Hubert H. Humphrey	Edmund S. Muskie	1968	Richard M. Nixon*	Spiro T. Agnew
1972	George S. McGovern	R. Sargent Shriver Jr.[3]	1972	Richard M. Nixon*	Spiro T. Agnew
1976	Jimmy Carter*	Walter F. Mondale	1976	Gerald R. Ford	Bob Dole
1980	Jimmy Carter	Walter F. Mondale	1980	Ronald Reagan*	George H. W. Bush
1984	Walter F. Mondale	Geraldine Ferraro	1984	Ronald Reagan*	George H. W. Bush
1988	Michael S. Dukakis	Lloyd Bentsen	1988	George H. W. Bush*	Dan Quayle
1992	Bill Clinton*	Al Gore	1992	George H. W. Bush	Dan Quayle
1996	Bill Clinton*	Al Gore	1996	Bob Dole	Jack Kemp
2000	Al Gore	Joseph Lieberman	2000	George W. Bush*	Richard Cheney
2004	John Kerry	John Edwards	2004	George W. Bush*	Richard Cheney
2008	Barack Obama*	Joe Biden	2008	John McCain	Sarah Palin
2012	Barack Obama*	Joe Biden	2012	Mitt Romney	Paul Ryan
2016	Hillary Clinton	Tim Kaine	2016	Donald J. Trump*	Mike Pence

(1) Douglas and Johnson were nominated at the Baltimore convention. An earlier convention in Charleston, SC, failed to reach a consensus and resulted in a split in the party. The Southern faction of the Democrats nominated John Breckinridge for president and Joseph Lane for vice president. (2) Died Oct. 30; replaced on ballot by Nicholas Butler. (3) Chosen by Democratic National Committee after Thomas Eagleton withdrew because of controversy over past treatments for depression.

Third-Party and Independent Presidential Candidates

In most elections since 1860, fewer than one vote in 20 has been cast for a third-party candidate. Still, independent and third-party candidates often bring attention to prominent issues and can affect the outcome between major-party candidates.

Major vote-getters among third-party and independent candidates include James B. Weaver (People's Party), 1892; former Pres. Theodore Roosevelt (Progressive Party), 1912; Robert M. La Follette (Progressive Party), 1924; George C. Wallace (American Independent Party), 1968; and H. Ross Perot, as an independent in 1992 and with the Reform Party in 1996. In these six elections, non-major-party candidates combined polled at least 10% of the vote.

Roosevelt outpolled the Republican candidate, William Howard Taft, in 1912, capturing 28% of the popular vote and 88 electoral votes. In 1948, Strom Thurmond (States' Rights [Dixiecrat]) won 39 electoral votes from five Southern states; however, third-party candidates received only 5.75% of the popular vote. George Wallace's popularity in the same region in 1968 allowed him to get 46 electoral votes and 13.5% of the popular vote.

In 1992, Ross Perot captured 19% of the popular vote but failed to win a single electoral vote. In 1996, Perot won 8% of the popular vote; all third-party candidates combined won just over 10%. In 2000, Ralph Nader (Green, independent) won about 3% of the vote. Gary Johnson (Libertarian) won about 3% in 2016.

Notable Third-Party and Independent Campaigns by Year

Party	Presidential nominee	Year	Issues	Strength in
Anti-Masonic	William Wirt	1832	Against secret societies and oaths	PA, VT
Liberty	James G. Birney	1844	Anti-slavery	North
Free Soil	Martin Van Buren	1848	Anti-slavery	NY, OH
American (Know-Nothing)	Millard Fillmore	1856	Anti-immigrant	Northeast, South
Greenback	Peter Cooper	1876	For "cheap money," labor rights	National
Greenback	James B. Weaver	1880	For "cheap money," labor rights	National
Prohibition	John P. St. John	1884	Anti-liquor	National
People's (Populist)	James B. Weaver	1892	For "cheap money," end of national banks	South, West
Socialist	Eugene V. Debs	1900-12; 1920	For public ownership	National
Progressive (Bull Moose)	Theodore Roosevelt	1912	Against high tariffs	Midwest, West
Progressive	Robert M. La Follette	1924	For farmer and labor rights	Midwest, West
Socialist	Norman Thomas	1928-48	For liberal reforms	National
Union	William Lemke	1936	Anti-New Deal	National
States' Rights (Dixiecrat)	Strom Thurmond	1948	For states' rights	South
Progressive	Henry A. Wallace	1948	Anti-Cold War	NY, CA
American Independent	George C. Wallace	1968	For states' rights	South
American	John G. Schmitz	1972	For "law and order"	West, OH, LA
None (independent)	John B. Anderson	1980	A third choice	National
None (independent)	H. Ross Perot	1992	Federal budget deficit	National
Reform	H. Ross Perot	1996	Deficit, campaign finance	National
Green, independent	Ralph Nader	2000-08	Corporate power, domestic priorities	National
Libertarian	Gary Johnson	2012-16	Public debt, civil liberties	National

Presidential Election Results by State, 1960-2016

Source: Federal Election Commission (FEC); local secretaries of state and state elections offices. Some candidates who did not appear on ballots are omitted from historical results.

Alabama Vote Since 1960

2016: Trump, R, 1,318,255; Clinton, D, 729,547; Johnson, Ind., 44,467; Stein, Ind., 9,391.

2012: Romney, R, 1,255,925; Obama, D, 795,696; Johnson, Ind., 12,328; Stein, Ind., 3,397; Goode, Ind., 2,981.

2008: McCain, R, 1,266,546; Obama, D, 813,479; Nader, Ind., 6,788; Barr, Ind., 4,991; Baldwin, Ind., 4,310.

2004: Bush, R, 1,176,394; Kerry, D, 693,933; Nader, Ind., 6,701; Badnarik, Ind., 3,529; Peroutka, Ind., 1,994.

2000: Bush, R, 941,173; Gore, D, 692,611; Nader, Ind., 18,323; Buchanan, Ind., 6,351; Browne, LB, 5,893; Phillips, Ind., 775; Hagelin, Ind., 447.

1996: Dole, R, 769,044; Clinton, D, 662,165; Perot, RF, 92,149; Browne, LB, 5,290; Phillips, Ind., 2,365; Hagelin, Natural Law, 1,697; Harris, Ind., 516.

1992: Bush, R, 804,283; Clinton, D, 690,080; Perot, Ind., 183,109; Marrou, LB, 5,737; Fulani, New Alliance, 2,161.

1988: Bush, R, 815,576; Dukakis, D, 549,506; Paul, LB, 8,460; Fulani, Ind., 3,311.

1984: Reagan, R, 872,849; Mondale, D, 551,899; Bergland, LB, 9,504.

1980: Reagan, R, 654,192; Carter, D, 636,730; Anderson, Ind., 16,481; Rarick, Amer. Ind., 15,010; Clark, LB, 13,318; Bubar, Statesman, 1,743; Hall, Comm., 1,629; DeBerry, Soc. Workers, 1,303; McReynolds, Soc., 1,006; Commoner, Citizens, 517.

1976: Carter, D, 659,170; Ford, R, 504,070; Maddox, Amer. Ind., 9,198; Bubar, Prohib., 6,669; Hall, Comm., 1,954; MacBride, LB, 1,481.

1972: Nixon, R, 728,701; McGovern, D, 219,108 plus Natl. Dem. Party of AL, 37,815; Schmitz, Conservative, 11,918; Munn, Prohib., 8,551.

1968: Wallace, 3rd party, 691,425; Humphrey, D, 196,579; Nixon, R, 146,923; Munn, Prohib., 4,022.

1964: Goldwater, R, 479,085; D (electors unpledged), 209,848; scattered, 105.

1960: Kennedy, D, 324,050; Nixon, R, 237,981; Faubus, States' Rights, 4,367; Decker, Prohib., 2,106; King, Afro-Americans, 1,485; scattered, 236.

Alaska Vote Since 1960

2016: Trump, R, 163,387; Clinton, D, 116,454; Johnson, LB, 18,725; Stein, Green, 5,735; Castle, Const., 3,866; De La Fuente, unaff., 1,240.

2012: Romney, R, 164,676; Obama, D, 122,640; Johnson, LB, 7,392; Stein, Green, 2,917.

2008: McCain, R, 193,841; Obama, D, 123,594; Nader, Ind., 3,783; Baldwin, AK Ind., 1,660; Barr, LB, 1,589.

2004: Bush, R, 190,889; Kerry, D, 111,025; Nader, Populist, 5,069; Peroutka, AK Ind., 2,092; Badnarik, LB, 1,675; Cobb, Green, 1,058.

2000: Bush, R, 167,398; Gore, D, 79,004; Nader, Green, 28,747; Buchanan, RF, 5,192; Browne, LB, 2,636; Hagelin, Natural Law, 919; Phillips, Const., 596.

1996: Dole, R, 122,746; Clinton, D, 80,380; Perot, RF, 26,333; Nader, Green, 7,597; Browne, LB, 2,276; Phillips, U.S. Taxpayers, 925; Hagelin, Natural Law, 729.

1992: Bush, R, 102,000; Clinton, D, 78,294; Perot, Ind., 73,481; Gritz, Populist/America First, 1,379; Marrou, LB, 1,378.

1988: Bush, R, 119,251; Dukakis, D, 72,584; Paul, LB, 5,484; Fulani, New Alliance, 1,024.

1984: Reagan, R, 138,377; Mondale, D, 62,007; Bergland, LB, 6,378.

1980: Reagan, R, 86,112; Carter, D, 41,842; Clark, LB, 18,479; Anderson, Ind., 11,155; write-in, 857.

1976: Ford, R, 71,555; Carter, D, 44,058; MacBride, LB, 6,785.

1972: Nixon, R, 55,349; McGovern, D, 32,967; Schmitz, Amer., 6,903.

1968: Nixon, R, 37,600; Humphrey, D, 35,411; Wallace, 3rd party, 10,024.

1964: Johnson, D, 44,329; Goldwater, R, 22,930.

1960: Nixon, R, 30,953; Kennedy, D, 29,809.

Arizona Vote Since 1960

2016: Trump, R, 1,252,401; Clinton, D, 1,161,167; Johnson, LB, 106,327; Stein, Green, 34,345; McMullin, Ind., 17,449; Castle, Const., 1,058.

2012: Romney, R, 1,233,654; Obama, D, 1,025,232; Johnson, LB, 32,100; Stein, Green, 7,816.

2008: McCain, R, 1,230,111; Obama, D, 1,034,707; Barr, LB, 12,555; Nader, New Prog., 11,301; McKinney, Green, 3,406.

2004: Bush, R, 1,104,294; Kerry, D, 893,524; Badnarik, LB, 11,856.

2000: Bush, R, 781,652; Gore, D, 685,341; Nader, Green, 45,645; Buchanan, RF, 12,373; Smith, LB, 5,775; Hagelin, Natural Law, 1,120.

1996: Clinton, D, 653,288; Dole, R, 622,073; Perot, RF, 112,072; Browne, LB, 14,358.

1992: Bush, R, 572,086; Clinton, D, 543,050; Perot, Ind., 353,741; Gritz, Populist/America First, 8,141; Marrou, LB, 6,759; Hagelin, Natural Law, 2,267.

1988: Bush, R, 702,541; Dukakis, D, 454,029; Paul, LB, 13,351; Fulani, New Alliance, 1,662.

1984: Reagan, R, 681,416; Mondale, D, 333,854; Bergland, LB, 10,585.

1980: Reagan, R, 529,688; Carter, D, 246,843; Anderson, Ind., 76,952; Clark, LB, 18,784; DeBerry, Soc. Workers, 1,100; Commoner, Citizens, 551; Hall, Comm., 25; Griswold, Workers World, 2.

1976: Ford, R, 418,642; Carter, D, 295,602; McCarthy, Ind., 19,229; MacBride, LB, 7,647; Camejo, Soc. Workers, 928; Anderson, Amer., 564; Maddox, Amer. Ind., 85.

1972: Nixon, R, 402,812; McGovern, D, 198,540; Jenness, Soc. Workers, 30,945; Schmitz, Amer. Ind., 21,208.

1968: Nixon, R, 266,721; Humphrey, D, 170,514; Wallace, 3rd party, 46,573; McCarthy, New Party, 2,751; Cleaver, Peace/Freedom, 217; Halstead, Soc. Workers, 85; Blomen, Soc. Labor, 75.

1964: Goldwater, R, 242,535; Johnson, D, 237,753; Hass, Soc. Labor, 482.

1960: Nixon, R, 221,241; Kennedy, D, 176,781; Hass, Soc. Labor, 469.

Arkansas Vote Since 1960

2016: Trump, R, 684,872; Clinton, D, 380,494; Johnson, LB, 29,949; McMullin, Better For America, 13,176; Stein, Green, 9,473; Hedges, Ind., 4,709; Castle, Const., 4,613; Kahn, Ind., 3,390.

2012: Romney, R, 647,744; Obama, D, 394,409; Johnson, LB, 16,276; Stein, Green, 9,305; Lindsay, Socialism/Liberation, 1,734.

2008: McCain, R, 638,017; Obama, D, 422,310; Nader, Ind., 12,882; Barr, LB, 4,776; Baldwin, Const., 4,023; McKinney, Green, 3,470; La Riva, Socialism/Liberation, 1,139.

2004: Bush, R, 572,898; Kerry, D, 469,953; Nader, Populist, 6,171; Badnarik, LB, 2,352; Peroutka, Const., 2,083; Cobb, Green, 1,488.

2000: Bush, R, 472,940; Gore, D, 422,768; Nader, Green, 13,421; Buchanan, RF, 7,358; Browne, LB, 2,781; Phillips, Const., 1,415; Hagelin, Natural Law, 1,098.

1996: Clinton, D, 475,171; Dole, R, 325,416; Perot, RF, 69,884; Nader, Ind., 3,649; Browne, Ind., 3,076; Phillips, Ind., 2,065; Forbes, Ind., 932; Collins, Ind., 823; Masters, Ind., 749; Moorehead, Ind., 747; Hagelin, Ind., 729; Hollis, Ind., 538; Dodge, Ind., 483.

1992: Clinton, D, 505,823; Bush, R, 337,324; Perot, Ind., 99,132; Phillips, U.S. Taxpayers, 1,437; Marrou, LB, 1,261; Fulani, New Alliance, 1,022.

1988: Bush, R, 466,578; Dukakis, D, 349,237; Duke, Populist, 5,146; Paul, LB, 3,297.

1984: Reagan, R, 534,774; Mondale, D, 338,646; Bergland, LB, 2,220.

1980: Reagan, R, 403,164; Carter, D, 398,041; Anderson, Ind., 22,468; Clark, LB, 8,970; Commoner, Citizens, 2,345; Bubar, Statesman, 1,350; Hall, Comm., 1,244.

1976: Carter, D, 498,604; Ford, R, 267,903; McCarthy, Ind., 639; Anderson, Amer. Ind., 389.

1972: Nixon, R, 445,751; McGovern, D, 198,899; Schmitz, Amer. Ind., 3,016.

1968: Wallace, 3rd party, 235,627; Nixon, R, 189,062; Humphrey, D, 184,901.

1964: Johnson, D, 314,197; Goldwater, R, 243,264; Kasper, Natl. States' Rights, 2,965.

1960: Kennedy, D, 215,049; Nixon, R, 184,508; Faubus, Natl. States' Rights, 28,952.

California Vote Since 1960

2016: Clinton, D, 8,753,792; Trump, R, 4,483,814; Johnson, LB, 478,500; Stein, Green, 278,658; Sanders, Ind., 79,341; La Riva, Peace/Freedom, 66,101; McMullin, Ind., 39,596.

2012: Obama, D, 7,854,285; Romney, R, 4,839,958; Johnson, LB, 143,221; Stein, Green, 85,638; Barr, Peace/Freedom, 53,824; Hoefling, Amer. Ind., 38,372.

2008: Obama, D, 8,274,473; McCain, R, 5,011,781; Nader, Peace/Freedom, 108,381; Barr, LB, 67,582; Alan Keyes, Amer. Ind., 40,673; McKinney, Green, 38,774.

2004: Kerry, D, 6,745,485; Bush, R, 5,509,826; Badnarik, LB, 50,165; Cobb, Green, 40,771; Peltier, Peace/Freedom, 27,607; Peroutka, Amer. Ind., 26,645.

2000: Gore, D, 5,861,203; Bush, R, 4,567,429; Nader, Green, 418,707; Browne, LB, 45,520; Buchanan, RF, 44,987; Phillips, Amer. Ind., 17,042; Hagelin, Natural Law, 10,934.

1996: Clinton, D, 5,119,835; Dole, R, 3,828,380; Perot, RF, 697,847; Nader, Green, 237,016; Browne, LB, 73,600; Feinland, Peace/Freedom, 25,332; Phillips, Amer. Ind., 21,202; Hagelin, Natural Law, 15,403.

1992: Clinton, D, 5,121,325; Bush, R, 3,630,575; Perot, Ind., 2,296,006; Marrou, LB, 48,139; Daniels, Ind., 18,597; Phillips, U.S. Taxpayers, 12,711.

1988: Bush, R, 5,054,917; Dukakis, D, 4,702,233; Paul, LB, 70,105; Fulani, Ind., 31,181.

1984: Reagan, R, 5,305,410; Mondale, D, 3,815,947; Bergland, LB, 48,400.

1980: Reagan, R, 4,524,858; Carter, D, 3,083,661; Anderson, Ind., 739,833; Clark, LB, 148,434; Commoner, Ind., 61,063; Smith, Peace/Freedom, 18,116; Rarick, Amer. Ind., 9,856.

1976: Ford, R, 3,882,244; Carter, D, 3,742,284; McCarthy, write-in, 58,412; MacBride, LB, 56,388; Maddox, Amer. Ind., 51,098; Wright, People's, 41,731; Camejo, Soc. Workers, 17,259; Hall, Comm., 12,766; write-in, 4,935.

1972: Nixon, R, 4,602,096; McGovern, D, 3,475,847; Schmitz, Amer. Ind., 232,554; Spock, Peace/Freedom, 55,167; Hospers, LB, 980; Jenness, Soc. Workers, 574; Hall, Comm., 373; Fisher, Soc. Labor, 197; Munn, Prohib., 53; Green, Universal, 21.

1968: Nixon, R, 3,467,664; Humphrey, D, 3,244,318; Wallace, 3rd party, 487,270; Peace/Freedom, 27,707; McCarthy, Alternative, 20,721; Gregory, write-in, 3,230; Blomen, Soc. Labor, 341; Mitchell, Comm., 260; Munn, Prohib., 59; Soeters, Defense, 17.

1964: Johnson, D, 4,171,877; Goldwater, R, 2,879,108; Hass, Soc. Labor, 489; DeBerry, Soc. Workers, 378; Munn, Prohib., 305; Hensley, Universal, 19.

1960: Nixon, R, 3,259,722; Kennedy, D, 3,224,099; Decker, Prohib., 21,706; Hass, Soc. Labor, 1,051.

Colorado Vote Since 1960

2016: Clinton, D, 1,338,870; Trump, R, 1,202,484; Johnson, LB, 144,121; Stein, Green, 38,437; McMullin, unaff., 28,917; Castle, Const., 11,699; Keniston, Veterans, 5,028; Smith, unaff., 1,819; De La Fuente, Amer. Delta, 1,255; Kopitke, Independent Amer., 1,096; Maldonado, Ind., 872; Maturen, Amer. Solidarity, 862; Silva, Nutrition, 751; Scott, unaff., 749; Hoefling, America's Party, 710; La Riva, Socialism/Liberation, 531; Kennedy, Soc. Workers, 452; Kotlikoff, Ind., 392; Lyttle, Nonviolent/Pacifist, 382; Atwood, Approval Voting, 337; Soltysik, Soc. USA, 271; Hedges, Prohib., 185.

2012: Obama, D, 1,323,102; Romney, R, 1,185,243; Johnson, LB, 35,545; Stein, Green, 7,508; Goode, Const., 6,234; Barr, Peace/Freedom, 5,059; Reed, unaff., 2,589; Anderson, Justice, 1,260; Tittle, We the People, 792; Hoefling, Amer. Ind., 679; La Riva, Socialism/Liberation, 317; Alexander, Soc. USA, 308; Miller, A3P, 266; Stevens, Objectivist, 235; Harris, Soc. Workers, 192; White, Soc. Equality, 189.

2008: Obama, D, 1,288,633; McCain, R, 1,073,629; Nader, unaff., 13,352; Barr, LB, 10,898; Baldwin, Const., 6,233; Alan Keyes, Amer. Ind., 3,051; McKinney, Green, 2,822; McEnulty, unaff., 829; Jay, Boston Tea, 598; Allen, HeartQuake '08, 348; Stevens, Objectivist, 336; Moore, Soc. USA, 226; La Riva, Socialism/Liberation, 158; Harris, Soc. Workers, 154; Lyttle, U.S. Pacifist, 110; Amondson, Prohib., 85.

2004: Bush, R, 1,101,255; Kerry, D, 1,001,732; Nader, RF, 12,718; Badnarik, LB, 7,664; Peroutka, Amer. Const., 2,562; Cobb, Green, 1,591; Andress, Ind., 804; Amondson, Concerns of People, 378; Van Auken, Soc. Equal., 329; Harris, Soc. Workers, 241; Brown, Soc., 216; Dodge, Prohib., 140.

2000: Bush, R, 883,748; Gore, D, 738,227; Nader, Green, 91,434; Browne, LB, 12,799; Buchanan, RF, 10,465; Hagelin, RF, 2,240; Phillips, Amer. Const., 1,319; McReynolds, Soc., 712; Harris, Soc. Workers, 216; Dodge, Prohib., 208.

1996: Dole, R, 691,848; Clinton, D, 671,152; Perot, RF, 99,629; Nader, Green, 25,070; Browne, LB, 12,392; Phillips, Amer. Const., 2,813; Collins, Ind., 2,809; Hagelin, Natural Law, 2,547; Hollis, Soc., 669; Moorehead, Workers World, 599; Templin, Amer., 557; Dodge, Prohib., 375; Harris, Soc. Workers, 244.

1992: Clinton, D, 629,681; Bush, R, 562,850; Perot, Ind., 366,010; Marrou, LB, 8,669; Fulani, New Alliance, 1,608.

1988: Bush, R, 728,177; Dukakis, D, 621,453; Paul, LB, 15,482; Dodge, Prohib., 4,604.

1984: Reagan, R, 821,817; Mondale, D, 454,975; Bergland, LB, 11,257.

1980: Reagan, R, 652,264; Carter, D, 367,973; Anderson, Ind., 130,633; Clark, LB, 25,744; Commoner, Citizens, 5,614; Bubar, Statesman, 1,180; Pulley, Soc., 520; Hall, Comm., 487.

1976: Ford, R, 584,367; Carter, D, 460,353; McCarthy, Ind., 26,107; MacBride, LB, 5,330; Bubar, Prohib., 2,882.

1972: Nixon, R, 597,189; McGovern, D, 329,980; Schmitz, Amer., 17,269; Fisher, Soc. Labor, 4,361; Spock, People's, 2,403; Hospers, LB, 1,111; Jenness, Soc. Workers, 555; Munn, Prohib., 467; Hall, Comm., 432.

1968: Nixon, R, 409,345; Humphrey, D, 335,174; Wallace, 3rd party, 60,813; Blomen, Soc. Labor, 3,016; Gregory, New Party, 1,393; Munn, Prohib., 275; Halstead, Soc. Workers, 235.

1964: Johnson, D, 476,024; Goldwater, R, 296,767; DeBerry, Soc. Workers, 2,537; Munn, Prohib., 1,356; Hass, Soc. Labor, 302.

1960: Nixon, R, 402,242; Kennedy, D, 330,629; Hass, Soc. Labor, 2,803; Dobbs, Soc. Workers, 572.

Connecticut Vote Since 1960

2016: Clinton, D, 897,572; Trump, R, 673,215; Johnson, LB, 48,676; Stein, Green, 22,841; McMullin, Ind., 2,108.

2012: Obama, D, 905,083; Romney, R, 634,892; Johnson, LB, 12,580; Anderson, Ind., 5,487.

2008: Obama, D, 997,772; McCain, R, 629,428; Nader, Ind., 19,162.

2004: Kerry, D, 857,488; Bush, R, 693,826; Nader, petitioning cand., 12,969; Cobb, Green, 9,564; Badnarik, LB, 3,367; Peroutka, Concerned Citizens, 1,543.

2000: Gore, D, 816,015; Bush, R, 561,094; Nader, Green, 64,452; Phillips, Concerned Citizens, 9,695; Buchanan, RF, 4,731; Browne, LB, 3,484.

1996: Clinton, D, 735,740; Dole, R, 483,109; Perot, RF, 139,523; Nader, Green, 24,321; Browne, LB, 5,788; Phillips, Concerned Citizens, 2,425; Hagelin, Natural Law, 1,703.

1992: Clinton, D, 682,318; Bush, R, 578,313; Perot, Ind., 348,771; Marrou, LB, 5,391; Fulani, New Alliance, 1,363.

1988: Bush, R, 750,241; Dukakis, D, 676,584; Paul, LB, 14,071; Fulani, New Alliance, 2,491.

1984: Reagan, R, 890,877; Mondale, D, 569,597.

1980: Reagan, R, 677,210; Carter, D, 541,732; Anderson, Ind., 171,807; Clark, LB, 8,570; Commoner, Citizens, 6,130; scattered, 836.

1976: Ford, R, 719,261; Carter, D, 647,895; Maddox, George Wallace Party, 7,101; LaRouche, U.S. Labor, 1,789.

1972: Nixon, R, 810,763; McGovern, D, 555,498; Schmitz, Amer., 17,239; scattered, 777.

1968: Humphrey, D, 621,561; Nixon, R, 556,721; Wallace, 3rd party, 76,650; scattered, 1,300.

1964: Johnson, D, 826,269; Goldwater, R, 390,996; scattered, 1,313.

1960: Kennedy, D, 657,055; Nixon, R, 565,813.

Delaware Vote Since 1960

2016: Clinton, D, 235,603; Trump, R, 185,127; Johnson, LB, 14,757; Stein, Green, 6,103; McMullin, Ind., 706.

2012: Obama, D, 242,584; Romney, R, 165,484; Johnson, LB, 3,882; Stein, Green, 1,940.

2008: Obama, D, 255,459; McCain, R, 152,374; Nader, Ind. (DE), 2,401; Barr, LB, 1,109; Baldwin, Const., 626; McKinney, Green, 385; Calero, Soc. Workers, 58.

2004: Kerry, D, 200,152; Bush, R, 171,660; Nader, Ind., 2,153; Badnarik, LB, 586; Peroutka, Const., 289; Cobb, Green, 250; Brown, Natural Law, 100.

2000: Gore, D, 180,068; Bush, R, 137,288; Nader, Green, 8,307; Buchanan, RF, 777; Browne, LB, 774; Phillips, Const., 208; Hagelin, Natural Law, 107.
1996: Clinton, D, 140,355; Dole, R, 99,062; Perot, RF, 28,719; Browne, LB, 2,052; Phillips, U.S. Taxpayers, 348; Hagelin, Natural Law, 274.
1992: Clinton, D, 126,054; Bush, R, 102,313; Perot, Ind., 59,213; Fulani, New Alliance, 1,105.
1988: Bush, R, 139,639; Dukakis, D, 108,647; Paul, LB, 1,162; Fulani, New Alliance, 443.
1984: Reagan, R, 152,190; Mondale, D, 101,656; Bergland, LB, 268.
1980: Reagan, R, 111,252; Carter, D, 105,754; Anderson, Ind., 16,288; Clark, LB, 1,974; Greaves, Amer., 400.
1976: Carter, D, 122,596; Ford, R, 109,831; McCarthy, nonpartisan, 2,437; Anderson, Amer., 645; LaRouche, U.S. Labor, 136; Bubar, Prohib., 103; Levin, Soc. Labor, 86.
1972: Nixon, R, 140,357; McGovern, D, 92,283; Schmitz, Amer., 2,638; Munn, Prohib., 238.
1968: Nixon, R, 96,714; Humphrey, D, 89,194; Wallace, 3rd party, 28,459.
1964: Johnson, D, 122,704; Goldwater, R, 78,078; Munn, Prohib., 425; Hass, Soc. Labor, 113.
1960: Kennedy, D, 99,590; Nixon, R, 96,373; Faubus, States' Rights, 354; Decker, Prohib., 284; Hass, Soc. Labor, 82.

District of Columbia Vote Since 1964

2016: Clinton, D, 282,830; Trump, R, 12,723; Johnson, LB, 4,906; Stein, Green, 4,258.
2012: Obama, D, 267,070; Romney, R, 21,381; Stein, DC Statehood Green, 2,458; Johnson, LB, 2,083.
2008: Obama, D, 245,800; McCain, R, 17,367; Nader, Ind., 958; McKinney, Green, 590.
2004: Kerry, D, 202,970; Bush, R, 21,256; Nader, Ind., 1,485; Cobb, DC Statehood Green, 737; Badnarik, LB, 502; Harris, Soc. Workers, 130.
2000: Gore, D, 171,923; Bush, R, 18,073; Nader, Green, 10,576; Browne, LB, 669; Harris, Soc. Workers, 114.
1996: Clinton, D, 158,220; Dole, R, 17,339; Nader, Green, 4,780; Perot, RF, 3,611; Browne, LB, 588; Hagelin, Natural Law, 283; Harris, Soc. Workers, 257.
1992: Clinton, D, 192,619; Bush, R, 20,698; Perot, Ind., 9,681; Fulani, New Alliance, 1,459; Daniels, Ind., 1,186.
1988: Dukakis, D, 159,407; Bush, R, 27,590; Fulani, New Alliance, 2,901; Paul, LB, 554.
1984: Mondale, D, 180,408; Reagan, R, 29,009; Bergland, LB, 279.
1980: Carter, D, 130,231; Reagan, R, 23,313; Anderson, Ind., 16,131; Commoner, Citizens, 1,826; Clark, LB, 1,104; Hall, Comm., 369; DeBerry, Soc. Workers, 173; Griswold, Workers World, 52; write-in, 690.
1976: Carter, D, 137,818; Ford, R, 27,873; Camejo, Soc. Workers, 545; MacBride, LB, 274; Hall, Comm., 219; LaRouche, U.S. Labor, 157.
1972: McGovern, D, 127,627; Nixon, R, 35,226; Reed, Soc. Workers, 316; Hall, Comm., 252.
1968: Humphrey, D, 139, 566; Nixon, R, 31,012.
1964: Johnson, D, 169,796; Goldwater, R, 28,801.

Florida Vote Since 1960

2016: Trump, R, 4,617,886; Clinton, D, 4,504,975; Johnson, LB, 207,043; Stein, Green, 64,399; Castle, Const., 16,475; De La Fuente, RF, 9,108.
2012: Obama, D, 4,237,756; Romney, R, 4,163,447; Johnson, LB, 44,726; Stein, Green, 8,947; Barr, Peace/Freedom, 8,154; Stevens, Objectivist, 3,856; Goode, Const., 2,607; Anderson, Justice, 1,754; Hoefling, Amer. Ind., 946; Barnett, RF, 820; Alexander, Soc., 799; Lindsay, Socialism/Liberation, 322.
2008: Obama, D, 4,282,074; McCain, R, 4,045,624; Nader, Ecology (FL), 28,124; Barr, LB, 17,218; Baldwin, Const., 7,915; McKinney, Green, 2,887; Keyes, Amer. Ind., 2,550; La Riva, Socialism/Liberation, 1,516; Jay, Boston Tea, 795; Harris, Soc. Workers, 533; Stevens, Objectivist, 419; Moore, Soc. USA, 405; Amondson, Prohib., 293.
2004: Bush, R, 3,964,522; Kerry, D, 3,583,544; Nader, RF, 32,971; Badnarik, LB, 11,996; Peroutka, Const., 6,626; Cobb, Green, 3,917; Brown, Soc., 3,502; Harris, Soc. Workers, 2,732.
2000: Bush, R, 2,912,790; Gore, D, 2,912,253; Nader, Green, 97,488; Buchanan, RF, 17,484; Browne, LB, 16,415; Hagelin, Natural Law, 2,281; Moorehead, Workers World, 1,804;

Phillips, Const., 1,371; McReynolds, Soc., 622; Harris, Soc. Workers, 562.
1996: Clinton, D, 2,545,968; Dole, R, 2,243,324; Perot, RF, 483,776; Browne, LB, 23,312.
1992: Bush, R, 2,171,781; Clinton, D, 2,071,651; Perot, Ind., 1,052,481; Marrou, LB, 15,068.
1988: Bush, R, 2,616,597; Dukakis, D, 1,655,851; Paul, LB, 19,796, Fulani, New Alliance, 6,655.
1984: Reagan, R, 2,728,775; Mondale, D, 1,448,344.
1980: Reagan, R, 2,046,951; Carter, D, 1,419,475; Anderson, Ind., 189,692; Clark, LB, 30,524; write-in, 285.
1976: Carter, D, 1,636,000; Ford, R, 1,469,531; McCarthy, Ind., 23,643; Anderson, Amer., 21,325.
1972: Nixon, R, 1,857,759; McGovern, D, 718,117; scattered, 7,407.
1968: Nixon, R, 886,804; Humphrey, D, 676,794; Wallace, 3rd party, 624,207.
1964: Johnson, D, 948,540; Goldwater, R, 905,941.
1960: Nixon, R, 795,476; Kennedy, D, 748,700.

Georgia Vote Since 1960

2016: Trump, R, 2,089,104; Clinton, D, 1,877,963 Johnson, LB, 125,306; McMullin, Ind., 13,017; Stein, Ind., 7,674; Castle, Ind., 1,110.
2012: Romney, R, 2,078,688; Obama, D, 1,773,827; Johnson, LB, 45,324.
2008: McCain, R, 2,048,759; Obama, D, 1,844,123; Barr, LB, 28,731.
2004: Bush, R, 1,914,254; Kerry, D, 1,366,149; Badnarik, LB, 18,387.
2000: Bush, R, 1,419,720; Gore, D, 1,116,230; Browne, LB, 36,332; Buchanan, Ind., 10,926.
1996: Dole, R, 1,080,843; Clinton, D, 1,053,849; Perot, RF, 146,337; Browne, LB, 17,870.
1992: Clinton, D, 1,008,966; Bush, R, 995,252; Perot, Ind., 309,657; Marrou, LB, 7,110.
1988: Bush, R, 1,081,331; Dukakis, D, 714,792; Paul, LB, 8,435; Fulani, New Alliance, 5,099.
1984: Reagan, R, 1,068,722; Mondale, D, 706,628.
1980: Carter, D, 890,955; Reagan, R, 654,168; Anderson, Ind., 36,055; Clark, LB, 15,627.
1976: Carter, D, 979,409; Ford, R, 483,743; write-in, 4,306.
1972: Nixon, R, 881,496; McGovern, D, 289,529; Schmitz, Amer., 812; scattered, 2,935.
1968: Wallace, 3rd party, 535,550; Nixon, R, 380,111; Humphrey, D, 334,440; write-in, 162.
1964: Goldwater, R, 616,600; Johnson, D, 522,557.
1960: Kennedy, D, 458,638; Nixon, R, 274,472; write-in, 239.

Hawaii Vote Since 1960

2016: Clinton, D, 266,891; Trump, R, 128,847; Johnson, LB, 15,594; Stein, Green, 12,737; Castle, Const., 4,508.
2012: Obama, D, 306,658; Romney, R, 121,015; Johnson, LB, 3,840; Stein, Green, 3,184.
2008: Obama, D, 325,871; McCain, R, 120,566; Nader, Ind. (HI), 3,825; Barr, LB, 1,314; Baldwin, Const., 1,013; McKinney, Green, 979.
2004: Kerry, D, 231,708; Bush, R, 194,191; Cobb, Green, 1,737; Badnarik, LB, 1,377.
2000: Gore, D, 205,286; Bush, R, 137,845; Nader, Green, 21,623; Browne, LB, 1,477; Buchanan, RF, 1,071; Phillips, Const., 343; Hagelin, Natural Law, 306.
1996: Clinton, D, 205,012; Dole, R, 113,943; Perot, RF, 27,358; Nader, Green, 10,386; Browne, LB, 2,493; Hagelin, Natural Law, 570; Phillips, Taxpayers, 358.
1992: Clinton, D, 179,310; Bush, R, 136,822; Perot, Ind., 53,003; Gritz, Populist/America First, 1,452; Marrou, LB, 1,119.
1988: Dukakis, D, 192,364; Bush, R, 158,625; Paul, LB, 1,999; Fulani, New Alliance, 1,003.
1984: Reagan, R, 184,934; Mondale, D, 147,098; Bergland, LB, 2,167.
1980: Carter, D, 135,879; Reagan, R, 130,112; Anderson, Ind., 32,021; Clark, LB, 3,269; Commoner, Citizens, 1,548; Hall, Comm., 458.
1976: Carter, D, 147,375; Ford, R, 140,003; MacBride, LB, 3,923.
1972: Nixon, R, 168,865; McGovern, D, 101,409.
1968: Humphrey, D, 141,324; Nixon, R, 91,425; Wallace, 3rd party, 3,469.
1964: Johnson, D, 163,249; Goldwater, R, 44,022.
1960: Kennedy, D, 92,410; Nixon, R, 92,295.

Idaho Vote Since 1960

2016: Trump, R, 409,055; Clinton, D, 189,765; McMullin, Ind., 46,476; Johnson, LB, 28,331; Stein, Ind., 8,496; Castle, Ind., 4,403; Copeland, Const., 2,356; De La Fuente, Ind., 1,373.

2012: Romney, R, 420,911; Obama, D, 212,787; Johnson, LB, 9,453; Stein, Ind., 4,402; Anderson, Ind., 2,499; Goode, Const., 2,222.

2008: McCain, R, 403,012; Obama, D, 236,440; Nader, Ind., 7,175; Baldwin, Const., 4,747; Barr, LB, 3,658.

2004: Bush, R, 409,235; Kerry, D, 181,098; Badnarik, LB, 3,844; Peroutka, Const., 3,084.

2000: Bush, R, 336,937; Gore, D, 138,637; Buchanan, RF, 7,615; Browne, LB, 3,488; Phillips, Const., 1,469; Hagelin, Natural Law, 1,177.

1996: Dole, R, 256,595; Clinton, D, 165,443; Perot, RF, 62,518; Browne, LB, 3,325; Phillips, U.S. Taxpayers, 2,230; Hagelin, Natural Law, 1,600.

1992: Bush, R, 202,645; Clinton, D, 137,013; Perot, Ind., 130,395; Gritz, Populist/America First, 10,281; Marrou, LB, 1,167.

1988: Bush, R, 253,881; Dukakis, D, 147,272; Paul, LB, 5,313; Fulani, Ind., 2,502.

1984: Reagan, R, 297,523; Mondale, D, 108,510; Bergland, LB, 2,823.

1980: Reagan, R, 290,699; Carter, D, 110,192; Anderson, Ind., 27,058; Clark, LB, 8,425; Rarick, Amer., 1,057.

1976: Ford, R, 204,151; Carter, D, 126,549; Maddox, Amer., 5,935; MacBride, LB, 3,558; LaRouche, U.S. Labor, 739.

1972: Nixon, R, 199,384; McGovern, D, 80,826; Schmitz, Amer., 28,869; Spock, People's, 903.

1968: Nixon, R, 165,369; Humphrey, D, 89,273; Wallace, 3rd party, 36,541.

1964: Johnson, D, 148,920; Goldwater, R, 143,557.

1960: Nixon, R, 161,597; Kennedy, D, 138,853.

Illinois Vote Since 1960

2016: Clinton, D, 3,090,729; Trump, R, 2,146,015; Johnson, LB, 209,596; Stein, Green, 76,802; McMullin, Ind., 11,655; Castle, Const., 1,138.

2012: Obama, D, 3,019,512; Romney, R, 2,135,216; Johnson, LB, 56,229; Stein, Green, 30,222.

2008: Obama, D, 3,419,348; McCain, R, 2,031,179; Nader, Ind., 30,948; Barr, LB, 19,642; McKinney, Green, 11,838; Baldwin, Const., 8,256; Polachek, New Party, 1,149.

2004: Kerry, D, 2,891,550; Bush, R, 2,345,946; Badnarik, LB, 32,442.

2000: Gore, D, 2,589,026; Bush, R, 2,019,421; Nader, Green, 103,759; Buchanan, Ind., 16,106; Browne, LB, 11,623; Hagelin, RF, 2,127.

1996: Clinton, D, 2,341,744; Dole, R, 1,587,021; Perot, RF, 346,408; Browne, LB, 22,548; Phillips, U.S. Taxpayers, 7,606; Hagelin, Natural Law, 4,606.

1992: Clinton, D, 2,453,350; Bush, R, 1,734,096; Perot, Ind., 840,515; Marrou, LB, 9,218; Fulani, New Alliance, 5,267; Gritz, Populist/America First, 3,577; Hagelin, Natural Law, 2,751; Warren, Soc. Workers, 1,361.

1988: Bush, R, 2,310,939; Dukakis, D, 2,215,940; Paul, LB, 14,944; Fulani, Solidarity, 10,276.

1984: Reagan, R, 2,707,103; Mondale, D, 2,086,499; Bergland, LB, 10,086.

1980: Reagan, R, 2,358,049; Carter, D, 1,981,413; Anderson, Ind., 346,754; Clark, LB, 38,939; Commoner, Citizens, 10,692; Hall, Comm., 9,711; Criswold, Workers World, 2,257; DeBerry, Soc. Workers, 1,302; write-in, 604.

1976: Ford, R, 2,364,269; Carter, D, 2,271,295; McCarthy, Ind., 55,939; Hall, Comm., 9,250; MacBride, LB, 8,057; Camejo, Soc. Workers, 3,615; Levin, Soc. Labor, 2,422; LaRouche, U.S. Labor, 2,018; write-in, 1,968.

1972: Nixon, R, 2,788,179; McGovern, D, 1,913,472; Fisher, Soc. Labor, 12,344; Hall, Comm., 4,541; Schmitz, Amer., 2,471; others, 2,229.

1968: Nixon, R, 2,174,774; Humphrey, D, 2,039,814; Wallace, 3rd party, 390,958; Blomen, Soc. Labor, 13,878; write-in, 325.

1964: Johnson, D, 2,796,833; Goldwater, R, 1,905,946; write-in, 62.

1960: Kennedy, D, 2,377,846; Nixon, R, 2,368,988; Hass, Soc. Labor, 10,560; write-in, 15.

Indiana Vote Since 1960

2016: Trump, R, 1,557,286; Clinton, D, 1,033,126; Johnson, LB, 133,993; Stein, Green, 7,841; Castle, Const., 1,937.

2012: Romney, R, 1,420,543; Obama, D, 1,152,887; Johnson, LB, 50,111.

2008: Obama, D, 1,374,039; McCain, R, 1,345,648; Barr, LB, 29,257.

2004: Bush, R, 1,479,438; Kerry, D, 969,011; Badnarik, LB, 18,058.

2000: Bush, R, 1,245,836; Gore, D, 901,980; Buchanan, Ind., 16,959; Browne, LB, 15,530.

1996: Dole, R, 1,006,693; Clinton, D, 887,424; Perot, RF, 224,299; Browne, LB, 15,632.

1992: Bush, R, 989,375; Clinton, D, 848,420; Perot, Ind., 455,934; Marrou, LB, 7,936; Fulani, New Alliance, 2,583.

1988: Bush, R, 1,297,763; Dukakis, D, 860,643; Fulani, New Alliance, 10,215.

1984: Reagan, R, 1,377,230; Mondale, D, 841,481; Bergland, LB, 6,741.

1980: Reagan, R, 1,255,656; Carter, D, 844,197; Anderson, Ind., 111,639; Clark, LB, 19,627; Commoner, Citizens, 4,852; Greaves, Amer., 4,750; Hall, Comm., 702; DeBerry, Soc., 610.

1976: Ford, R, 1,185,958; Carter, D, 1,014,714; Anderson, Amer., 14,048; Camejo, Soc. Workers, 5,695; LaRouche, U.S. Labor, 1,947.

1972: Nixon, R, 1,405,154; McGovern, D, 708,568; Reed, Soc. Workers, 5,575; Spock, Peace/Freedom, 4,544; Fisher, Soc. Labor, 1,688.

1968: Nixon, R, 1,067,885; Humphrey, D, 806,659; Wallace, 3rd party, 243,108; Munn, Prohib., 4,616; Halstead, Soc. Workers, 1,293; Gregory, write-in, 36.

1964: Johnson, D, 1,170,848; Goldwater, R, 911,118; Munn, Prohib., 8,266; Hass, Soc. Labor, 1,374.

1960: Nixon, R, 1,175,120; Kennedy, D, 952,358; Decker, Prohib., 6,746; Hass, Soc. Labor, 1,136.

Iowa Vote Since 1960

2016: Trump, R, 800,983; Clinton, D, 653,669; Johnson, LB, 59,186; McMullin, petitioning cand., 12,366; Stein, Green, 11,479; Castle, Const., 5,335; Kahn, New Independent, 2,247; Vacek, Legal Marijuana, 2,246; De La Fuente, petitioning cand., 451; La Riva, Socialism/Liberation, 323.

2012: Obama, D, 822,544; Romney, R, 730,617; Johnson, LB, 12,926; Stein, Green, 3,769; Goode, Const., 3,038; Litzel, Ind., 1,027; Harris, Soc. Workers, 445; La Riva, Socialism/Liberation, 372.

2008: Obama, D, 828,940; McCain, R, 682,379; Nader, Peace/Freedom, 8,014; Barr, LB, 4,590; Baldwin, Const., 4,445; McKinney, Green, 1,423; Harris, Soc. Workers, 292; Moore, Soc. USA, 182; La Riva, Socialism/Liberation, 121.

2004: Bush, R, 751,957; Kerry, D, 741,898; Nader, petitioning cand., 5,973; Badnarik, LB, 2,992; Peroutka, Const., 1,304; Cobb, Green, 1,141; Harris, Soc. Workers, 373; Van Auken, petitioning cand., 176.

2000: Gore, D, 638,517; Bush, R, 634,373; Nader, Green, 29,374; Buchanan, RF, 5,731; Browne, LB, 3,209; Hagelin, Ind., 2,281; Phillips, Const., 613; Harris, Soc. Workers, 190; McReynolds, Soc., 107.

1996: Clinton, D, 620,258; Dole, R, 492,644; Perot, RF, 105,159; Nader, Green, 6,550; Hagelin, Natural Law, 3,349; Browne, LB, 2,315; Phillips, Taxpayers, 2,229; Harris, Soc. Workers, 331.

1992: Clinton, D, 586,353; Bush, R, 504,891; Perot, Ind., 253,468; Hagelin, Natural Law, 3,079; Gritz, Populist/America First, 1,177; Marrou, LB, 1,076.

1988: Dukakis, D, 670,557; Bush, R, 545,355; LaRouche, Ind., 3,526; Paul, LB, 2,494.

1984: Reagan, R, 703,088; Mondale, D, 605,620; Bergland, LB, 1,844.

1980: Reagan, R, 676,026; Carter, D, 508,672; Anderson, Ind., 115,633; Clark, LB, 13,123; Commoner, Citizens, 2,273; McReynolds, Soc., 534; Hall, Comm., 298; DeBerry, Soc. Workers, 244; Greaves, Amer., 189; Bubar, Statesman, 150; scattered, 519.

1976: Ford, R, 632,863; Carter, D, 619,931; McCarthy, Ind., 20,051; Anderson, Amer., 3,040; MacBride, LB, 1,452.

1972: Nixon, R, 706,207; McGovern, D, 496,206; Schmitz, Amer., 22,056; Jenness, Soc. Workers, 488; Hall, Comm., 272; Green, Universal, 199; Fisher, Soc. Labor, 195; scattered, 321.

1968: Nixon, R, 619,106; Humphrey, D, 476,699; Wallace, 3rd party, 66,422; Halstead, Soc. Workers, 3,377; Cleaver, Peace/Freedom, 1,332; Munn, Prohib., 362; Blomen, Soc. Labor, 241.

1964: Johnson, D, 733,030; Goldwater, R, 449,148; Munn, Prohib., 1,902; Hass, Soc. Labor, 182; DeBerry, Soc. Workers, 159.

1960: Nixon, R, 722,381; Kennedy, D, 550,565; Hass, Soc. Labor, 230; write-in, 634.

Kansas Vote Since 1960

2016: Trump, R, 671,018; Clinton, D, 427,005; Johnson, LB, 55,406; Stein, Ind., 23,506; McMullin, Ind., 6,520.

2012: Romney, R, 692,634; Obama, D, 440,726; Johnson, LB, 20,456; Baldwin, RF, 5,017.

2008: McCain, R, 699,655; Obama, D, 514,765; Nader, Ind., 10,527; Barr, LB, 6,706; Baldwin, RF, 4,148.

2004: Bush, R, 736,456; Kerry, D, 434,993; Nader, RF, 9,348; Badnarik, LB, 4,013; Peroutka, Ind., 2,899.

2000: Bush, R, 622,332; Gore, D, 399,276; Nader, Ind., 36,086; Buchanan, RF, 7,370; Browne, LB, 4,525; Hagelin, Ind., 1,373; Phillips, Const., 1,254.

1996: Dole, R, 583,245; Clinton, D, 387,659; Perot, RF, 92,639; Browne, LB, 4,557; Phillips, Ind., 3,519; Hagelin, Ind., 1,655.

1992: Bush, R, 449,951; Clinton, D, 390,434; Perot, Ind., 312,358; Marrou, LB, 4,314.

1988: Bush, R, 554,049; Dukakis, D, 422,636; Paul, Ind., 12,553; Fulani, Ind., 3,806.

1984: Reagan, R, 674,646; Mondale, D, 332,471; Bergland, LB, 3,585.

1980: Reagan, R, 566,812; Carter, D, 326,150; Anderson, Ind., 68,231; Clark, LB, 14,470; Shelton, Amer., 1,555; Hall, Comm., 967; Bubar, Statesman, 821; Rarick, Conservative, 789.

1976: Ford, R, 502,752; Carter, D, 430,421; McCarthy, Ind., 13,185; Anderson, Amer., 4,724; MacBride, LB, 3,242; Maddox, Conservative, 2,118; Bubar, Prohib., 1,403.

1972: Nixon, R, 619,812; McGovern, D, 270,287; Schmitz, Conservative, 21,808; Munn, Prohib., 4,188.

1968: Nixon, R, 478,674; Humphrey, D, 302,996; Wallace, 3rd party, 88,921; Munn, Prohib., 2,192.

1964: Johnson, D, 464,028; Goldwater, R, 386,579; Munn, Prohib., 5,393; Hass, Soc. Labor, 1,901.

1960: Nixon, R, 561,474; Kennedy, D, 363,213; Decker, Prohib., 4,138.

Kentucky Vote Since 1960

2016: Trump, R, 1,202,971; Clinton, D, 628,854; Johnson, LB, 53,752; McMullin, Ind., 22,780; Stein, Green, 13,913; De La Fuente, American Delta, 1,128.

2012: Romney, R, 1,087,190; Obama, D, 679,370; Johnson, LB, 17,063; Terry, Ind., 6,872; Stein, Green, 6,337.

2008: McCain, R, 1,048,462; Obama, D, 751,985; Nader, Ind., 15,378; Barr, LB, 5,989; Baldwin, Const., 4,694.

2004: Bush, R, 1,069,439; Kerry, D, 712,733; Nader, Ind., 8,856; Badnarik, LB, 2,619; Peroutka, Const., 2,213.

2000: Bush, R, 872,520; Gore, D, 638,923; Nader, Green, 23,118; Buchanan, RF, 4,152; Browne, LB, 2,885; Hagelin, Natural Law, 1,513; Phillips, Const., 915.

1996: Clinton, D, 636,614; Dole, R, 623,283; Perot, RF, 120,396; Browne, LB, 4,009; Phillips, U.S. Taxpayers, 2,204; Hagelin, Natural Law, 1,493.

1992: Clinton, D, 665,104; Bush, R, 617,178; Perot, Ind., 203,944; Marrou, LB, 4,513.

1988: Bush, R, 734,281; Dukakis, D, 580,368; Duke, Populist, 4,494; Paul, LB, 2,118.

1984: Reagan, R, 815,345; Mondale, D, 536,756.

1980: Reagan, R, 635,274; Carter, D, 616,417; Anderson, Ind., 31,127; Clark, LB, 5,531; McCormack, Respect for Life, 4,233; Commoner, Citizens, 1,304; Pulley, Soc., 393; Hall, Comm., 348.

1976: Carter, D, 615,717; Ford, R, 531,852; Anderson, Amer., 8,308; McCarthy, Ind., 6,837; Maddox, Amer. Ind., 2,328; MacBride, LB, 814.

1972: Nixon, R, 676,446; McGovern, D, 371,159; Schmitz, Amer., 17,627; Spock, People's, 1,118; Jenness, Soc. Workers, 685; Hall, Comm., 464.

1968: Nixon, R, 462,411; Humphrey, D, 397,547; Wallace, 3rd party, 193,098; Halstead, Soc. Workers, 2,843.

1964: Johnson, D, 669,659; Goldwater, R, 372,977; Kasper, Natl. States' Rights, 3,469.

1960: Nixon, R, 602,607; Kennedy, D, 521,855.

Louisiana Vote Since 1960

2016: Trump, R, 1,178,638; Clinton, D, 780,154; Johnson, LB, 37,978; Stein, Green, 14,031; McMullin, Courage/Char./Serv., 8,547; Castle, Const., 3,129; Keniston, Veterans, 1,881; Hoefling, Life/Fam./Const., 1,581; Kotlikoff, It's Our Children, 1,048; Jacob, Loyal/Trust., 957; Kennedy, Soc. Workers, 480; La Riva, Socialism/Liberation, 446; White, Soc./Eq./Anti-War, 370.

2012: Romney, R, 1,152,262; Obama, D, 809,141; Johnson, LB, 18,157; Stein, Green, 6,978; Goode, Const., 2,508; Tittle, We

the People, 1,767; Anderson, Justice, 1,368; Lindsay, Socialism/Liberation, 622; Fellure, Prohib., 518; Harris, Soc. Workers, 389; White, Soc. Equality, 355.

2008: McCain, R, 1,148,275; Obama, D, 782,989; Paul, LA Taxpayers, 9,368; McKinney, Green, 9,187; Nader, Ind., 6,997; Baldwin, Const., 2,581; Harris, Soc. Workers, 735; La Riva, Socialism/Liberation, 354; Amondson, Prohib., 275.

2004: Bush, R, 1,102,169; Kerry, D, 820,299; Nader, Better Life, 7,032; Peroutka, Const., 5,203; Badnarik, LB, 2,781; Brown, Protect Working Families, 1,795; Amondson, Prohib., 1,566; Cobb, Green, 1,276; Harris, Soc. Workers, 985.

2000: Bush, R, 927,871; Gore, D, 792,344; Nader, Green, 20,473; Buchanan, RF, 14,356; Phillips, Const., 5,483; Browne, LB, 2,951; Harris, Soc. Workers, 1,103; Hagelin, Natural Law, 1,075.

1996: Clinton, D, 927,837; Dole, R, 712,586; Perot, RF, 123,293; Browne, LB, 7,499; Nader, Liberty, Ecology, Community, 4,719; Phillips, U.S. Taxpayers, 3,366; Hagelin, Natural Law, 2,981; Moorehead, Workers World, 1,678.

1992: Clinton, D, 815,971; Bush, R, 733,386; Perot, Ind., 211,478; Gritz, Populist/America First, 18,545; Marrou, LB, 3,155; Daniels, Ind., 1,663; Phillips, U.S. Taxpayers, 1,552; Fulani, New Alliance, 1,434; LaRouche, Ind., 1,136.

1988: Bush, R, 883,702; Dukakis, D, 717,460; Duke, Populist, 18,612; Paul, LB, 4,115.

1984: Reagan, R, 1,037,299; Mondale, D, 651,586; Bergland, LB, 1,876.

1980: Reagan, R, 792,853; Carter, D, 708,453; Anderson, Ind., 26,345; Rarick, Amer. Ind., 10,333; Clark, LB, 8,240; Commoner, Citizens, 1,584; DeBerry, Soc. Workers, 783.

1976: Carter, D, 661,365; Ford, R, 587,446; Maddox, Amer., 10,058; Hall, Comm., 7,417; McCarthy, Ind., 6,588; MacBride, LB, 3,325.

1972: Nixon, R, 686,852; McGovern, D, 298,142; Schmitz, Amer., 52,099; Jenness, Soc. Workers, 14,398.

1968: Wallace, 3rd party, 530,300; Humphrey, D, 309,615; Nixon, R, 257,535.

1964: Goldwater, R, 509,225; Johnson, D, 387,068.

1960: Kennedy, D, 407,339; Nixon, R, 230,890; States' Rights (unpledged), 169,572.

Maine Vote Since 1960

2016: Clinton, D, 357,735; Trump, R, 335,593; Johnson, LB, 38,105; Stein, Green, 14,251; McMullin, Ind., 1,887; Castle, Const., 333.

2012: Obama, D, 401,306; Romney, R, 292,276; Johnson, LB, 9,352; Stein, Green, 8,119.

2008: Obama, D, 421,923; McCain, R, 295,273; Nader, Ind., 10,636; McKinney, Green, 2,900.

2004: Kerry, D, 396,842; Bush, R, 330,201; Nader, Better Life, 8,069; Cobb, Green, 2,936; Badnarik, LB, 1,965; Peroutka, Const., 735.

2000: Gore, D, 319,951; Bush, R, 286,616; Nader, Green, 37,127; Buchanan, RF, 4,443; Browne, LB, 3,074; Phillips, Const., 579.

1996: Clinton, D, 312,788; Dole, R, 186,378; Perot, RF, 85,970; Nader, Green, 15,279; Browne, LB, 2,996; Phillips, Taxpayers, 1,517; Hagelin, Natural Law, 825.

1992: Clinton, D, 263,420; Perot, Ind., 206,820; Bush, R, 206,504; Marrou, LB, 1,681.

1988: Bush, R, 307,131; Dukakis, D, 243,569; Paul, LB, 2,700; Fulani, New Alliance, 1,405.

1984: Reagan, R, 336,500; Mondale, D, 214,515.

1980: Reagan, R, 238,522; Carter, D, 220,974; Anderson, Ind., 53,327; Clark, LB, 5,119; Commoner, Citizens, 4,394; Hall, Comm., 591; write-in, 84.

1976: Ford, R, 236,320; Carter, D, 232,279; McCarthy, Ind., 10,874; Bubar, Prohib., 3,495.

1972: Nixon, R, 256,458; McGovern, D, 160,584; scattered, 229.

1968: Humphrey, D, 217,312; Nixon, R, 169,254; Wallace, 3rd party, 6,370.

1964: Johnson, D, 262,264; Goldwater, R, 118,701.

1960: Nixon, R, 240,608; Kennedy, D, 181,159.

Maryland Vote Since 1960

2016: Clinton, D, 1,677,928; Trump, R, 943,169; Johnson, LB, 79,605; Stein, Green, 35,945; McMullin, Ind., 9,630; Castle, Const., 566; Maturen, Ind., 504.

2012: Obama, D, 1,677,844; Romney, R, 971,869; Johnson, LB, 30,195; Stein, Green, 17,110.

2008: Obama, D, 1,629,467; McCain, R, 959,862; Nader, MD Ind., 14,713; Barr, LB, 9,842; McKinney, Green, 4,747; Baldwin, RF, 3,760.
2004: Kerry, D, 1,334,493; Bush, R, 1,024,703; Nader, Populist, 11,854; Badnarik, LB, 6,094; Cobb, Green, 3,632; Peroutka, Const., 3,421.
2000: Gore, D, 1,144,008; Bush, R, 813,827; Nader, Green, 53,768; Browne, LB, 5,310; Buchanan, RF, 4,248; Phillips, Const., 918.
1996: Clinton, D, 966,207; Dole, R, 681,530; Perot, RF, 115,812; Browne, LB, 8,765; Phillips, Taxpayers, 3,402; Hagelin, Natural Law, 2,517.
1992: Clinton, D, 988,571; Bush, R, 707,094; Perot, Ind., 281,414; Marrou, LB, 4,715; Fulani, New Alliance, 2,786.
1988: Bush, R, 876,167; Dukakis, D, 826,304; Paul, LB, 6,748; Fulani, New Alliance, 5,115.
1984: Reagan, R, 879,918; Mondale, D, 787,935; Bergland, LB, 5,721.
1980: Carter, D, 726,161; Reagan, R, 680,606; Anderson, Ind., 119,537; Clark, LB, 14,192.
1976: Carter, D, 759,612; Ford, R, 672,661.
1972: Nixon, R, 829,305; McGovern, D, 505,781; Schmitz, Amer., 18,726.
1968: Humphrey, D, 538,310; Nixon, R, 517,995; Wallace, 3rd party, 178,734.
1964: Johnson, D, 730,912; Goldwater, R, 385,495; write-in, 50.
1960: Kennedy, D, 565,800; Nixon, R, 489,538.

Massachusetts Vote Since 1960

2016: Clinton, D, 1,995,196; Trump, R, 1,090,893; Johnson, LB, 138,018; Stein, Green, 47,661; McMullin, Ind., 2,719.
2012: Obama, D, 1,921,290; Romney, R, 1,188,314; Johnson, LB, 30,920; Stein, Green, 20,691.
2008: Obama, D, 1,904,097; McCain, R, 1,108,854; Nader, Ind., 28,841; Barr, LB, 13,189; McKinney, Green, 6,550; Baldwin, RF, 4,971.
2004: Kerry, D, 1,803,800; Bush, R, 1,071,109; Badnarik, LB, 15,022; Cobb, Green, 10,623.
2000: Gore, D, 1,616,487; Bush, R, 878,502; Nader, Green, 173,564; Browne, LB, 16,366; Buchanan, RF, 11,149; Hagelin, Natural Law, 2,884.
1996: Clinton, D, 1,571,509; Dole, R, 718,058; Perot, RF, 227,206; Browne, LB, 20,424; Hagelin, Natural Law, 5,183; Moorehead, Workers World, 3,276.
1992: Clinton, D, 1,318,639; Bush, R, 805,039; Perot, Ind., 630,731; Marrou, LB, 9,021; Fulani, New Alliance, 3,172; Phillips, U.S. Taxpayers, 2,218; Hagelin, Natural Law, 1,812; LaRouche, Ind., 1,027.
1988: Dukakis, D, 1,401,415; Bush, R, 1,194,635; Paul, LB, 24,251; Fulani, New Alliance, 9,561.
1984: Reagan, R, 1,310,936; Mondale, D, 1,239,606.
1980: Reagan, R, 1,057,631; Carter, D, 1,053,802; Anderson, Ind., 382,539; Clark, LB, 22,038; DeBerry, Soc. Workers, 3,735; Commoner, Citizens, 2,056; McReynolds, Soc., 62; Bubar, Statesman, 34; Griswold, Workers World, 19; scattered, 2,382.
1976: Carter, D, 1,429,475; Ford, R, 1,030,276; McCarthy, Ind., 65,637; Camejo, Soc. Workers, 8,138; Anderson, Amer., 7,555; LaRouche, U.S. Labor, 4,922; MacBride, LB, 135.
1972: McGovern, D, 1,332,540; Nixon, R, 1,112,078; Jenness, Soc. Workers, 10,600; Schmitz, Amer., 2,077; Fiohor, Soc. Labor, 129; Spock, People's, 101; Hall, Comm., 46; Hospers, LB, 43; scattered, 342.
1968: Humphrey, D, 1,469,218; Nixon, R, 766,844; Wallace, 3rd party, 87,088; Blomen, Soc. Labor, 6,180; Munn, Prohib., 2,369; scattered, 53; blank, 25,394.
1964: Johnson, D, 1,786,422; Goldwater, R, 549,727; Hass, Soc. Labor, 4,755; Munn, Prohib., 3,735; scattered, 159; blank, 48,104.
1960: Kennedy, D, 1,487,174; Nixon, R, 976,750; Hass, Soc. Labor, 3,892; Decker, Prohib., 1,633; others, 31; blank and void, 26,024.

Michigan Vote Since 1960

2016: Trump, R, 2,279,543; Clinton, D, 2,268,839; Johnson, LB, 172,136; Stein, Green, 51,463; Castle, U.S. Taxpayers, 16,139; McMullin, Ind., 8,177; Soltysik, Natural Law, 2,209.
2012: Obama, D, 2,564,569; Romney, R, 2,115,256; Stein, Green, 21,897; Goode, U.S. Taxpayers, 16,119; Johnson, Ind., 7,774, Anderson, Natural Law, 5,147;

2008: Obama, D, 2,872,579; McCain, R, 2,048,639; Nader, Natural Law, 33,085; Barr, LB, 23,716; Baldwin, U.S. Taxpayers, 14,685; McKinney, Green, 8,892.
2004: Kerry, D, 2,479,183; Bush, R, 2,313,746; Nader, Ind., 24,035; Badnarik, LB, 10,552; Cobb, Green, 5,325; Peroutka, U.S. Taxpayers, 4,980; Brown, Natural Law, 1,431.
2000: Gore, D, 2,170,418; Bush, R, 1,953,139; Nader, Green, 84,165; Browne, LB, 16,711; Phillips, U.S. Taxpayers, 3,791; Hagelin, Natural Law, 2,426.
1996: Clinton, D, 1,989,653; Dole, R, 1,481,212; Perot, RF, 336,670; Browne, LB, 27,670; Hagelin, Natural Law, 4,254; Moorehead, Workers World, 3,153; White, Soc. Equality, 1,554.
1992: Clinton, D, 1,871,182; Bush, R, 1,554,940; Perot, Ind., 824,813; Marrou, LB, 10,175; Phillips, U.S. Taxpayers, 8,263; Hagelin, Natural Law, 2,954.
1988: Bush, R, 1,965,486; Dukakis, D, 1,675,783; Paul, LB, 18,336; Fulani, Ind., 2,513.
1984: Reagan, R, 2,251,571; Mondale, D, 1,529,638; Bergland, LB, 10,055.
1980: Reagan, R, 1,915,225; Carter, D, 1,661,532; Anderson, Ind., 275,223; Clark, LB, 41,597; Commoner, Citizens, 11,930; Hall, Comm., 3,262; Griswold, Workers World, 30; Greaves, Amer., 21; Bubar, Statesman, 9.
1976: Ford, R, 1,893,742; Carter, D, 1,696,714; McCarthy, Ind., 47,905; MacBride, LB, 5,406; Wright, People's, 3,504; Camejo, Soc. Workers, 1,804; LaRouche, U.S. Labor, 1,366; Levin, Soc. Labor, 1,148; scattered, 2,160.
1972: Nixon, R, 1,961,721; McGovern, D, 1,459,435; Schmitz, Amer., 63,321; Fisher, Soc. Labor, 2,437; Jenness, Soc. Workers, 1,603; Hall, Comm., 1,210.
1968: Humphrey, D, 1,593,082; Nixon, R, 1,370,665; Wallace, 3rd party, 331,968; Halstead, Soc. Workers, 4,099; Blomen, Soc. Labor, 1,762; Cleaver, New Politics, 4,585; Munn, Prohib., 60; scattered, 29.
1964: Johnson, D, 2,136,615; Goldwater, R, 1,060,152; DeBerry, Soc. Workers, 3,817; Hass, Soc. Labor, 1,704; Prohib. (no candidate listed), 699; scattered, 145.
1960: Kennedy, D, 1,687,269; Nixon, R, 1,620,428; Dobbs, Soc. Workers, 4,347; Decker, Prohib., 2,029; Daly, Tax Cut, 1,767; Hass, Soc. Labor, 1,718; Ind. Amer. (unpledged), 539.

Minnesota Vote Since 1960

2016: Clinton, D, 1,367,716; Trump, R, 1,322,951; Johnson, LB, 112,972; McMullin, Ind., 53,076; Stein, Green, 36,985; Vacek, Legal Marijuana, 11,291; Castle, Const., 9,456; Kennedy, Soc. Workers, 1,672; De La Fuente, Amer. Delta, 1,431.
2012: Obama, D, 1,546,167; Romney, R, 1,320,225; Johnson, LB, 35,098; Stein, Green, 13,023; Goode, Const., 3,722; Carlson, Grassroots, 3,149; Anderson, Justice, 1,996; Morstad, Constitutional, 1,092; Harris, Soc. Workers, 1,051; Lindsay, Socialism/Liberation, 397.
2008: Obama, D, 1,573,354; McCain, R, 1,275,409; Nader, Ind., 30,152; Barr, LB, 9,174; Baldwin, Const., 6,787; McKinney, Green, 5,174; Calero, Soc. Workers, 790.
2004: Kerry, D, 1,445,014; Bush, R, 1,346,695; Nader, Better Life, 18,683; Badnarik, LB, 4,639; Cobb, Green, 4,408; Peroutka, Const., 3,074; Harens, other, 2,387; Van Auken, Soc. Equal., 539; Calero, Soc. Workers, 416.
2000: Gore, D, 1,168,266; Bush, R, 1,109,659; Nader, Green, 126,696; Buchanan, RF MN, 22,166; Browne, LB, 5,282; Phillips, Const., 3,272; Hagelin, RF, 2,294; Harris, Soc. Workers, 1,022.
1996: Clinton, D, 1,120,438; Dole, R, 766,476; Perot, RF, 257,704; Nader, Green, 24,908; Browne, LB, 8,271; Peron, Grass Roots, 4,898; Phillips, U.S. Taxpayers, 3,416; Hagelin, Natural Law, 1,808; Birrenbach, Ind. Grass Roots, 787; Harris, Soc. Workers, 684; White, Soc. Equality, 347.
1992: Clinton, D, 1,020,997; Bush, R, 747,841; Perot, Ind., 562,506; Marrou, LB, 3,373; Gritz, Populist/America First, 3,363; Hagelin, Natural Law, 1,406.
1988: Dukakis, D, 1,109,471; Bush, R, 962,337; McCarthy, MN Prog., 5,403; Paul, LB, 5,109.
1984: Mondale, D, 1,036,364; Reagan, R, 1,032,603; Bergland, LB, 2,996.
1980: Carter, D, 954,173; Reagan, R, 873,268; Anderson, Ind., 174,997; Clark, LB, 31,593; Commoner, Citizens, 8,406; Hall, Comm., 1,117; DeBerry, Soc. Workers, 711; Griswold, Workers World, 698; McReynolds, Soc., 536; write-in, 281.
1976: Carter, D, 1,070,440; Ford, R, 819,395; McCarthy, Ind., 35,490; Anderson, Amer., 13,592; Camejo, Soc. Workers, 4,149; MacBride, LB, 3,529; Hall, Comm., 1,092.

1972: Nixon, R, 898,269; McGovern, D, 802,346; Schmitz, Amer., 31,407; Fisher, Soc. Labor, 4,261; Spock, People's, 2,805; Jenness, Soc. Workers, 940; Hall, Comm., 662; scattered, 962.
1968: Humphrey, D, 857,738; Nixon, R, 658,643; Wallace, 3rd party, 68,931; Cleaver, Peace/Freedom, 935; Halstead, Soc. Workers, 808; McCarthy, write-in, 585; Mitchell, Comm., 415; Blomen, Industrial Govt., 285; scattered, 2,613.
1964: Johnson, D, 991,117; Goldwater, R, 559,624; Hass, Industrial Govt., 2,544; DeBerry, Soc. Workers, 1,177.
1960: Kennedy, D, 779,933; Nixon, R, 757,915; Dobbs, Soc. Workers, 3,077; Hass, Industrial Govt., 962.

Mississippi Vote Since 1960

2016: Trump, R, 700,714; Clinton, D, 485,131; Johnson, LB, 14,435; Castle, Const., 3,987; Stein, Green, 3,731; Hedges, Prohib., 715; De La Fuente, Amer. Delta, 644.
2012: Romney, R, 710,746; Obama, D, 562,949; Johnson, LB, 6,676; Goode, Const., 2,609; Stein, Green, 1,588; Washer, RF, 1,016.
2008: McCain, R, 724,597; Obama, D, 554,662; Nader, Ind., 4,011; Baldwin, Const., 2,551; Barr, LB, 2,529; McKinney, Green, 1,034; Weill, RF, 481.
2004: Bush, R, 684,981; Kerry, D, 458,094; Nader, RF, 3,177; Badnarik, LB, 1,793; Peroutka, Const., 1,759; Harris, Ind., 1,268; Cobb, Green, 1,073.
2000: Bush, R, 572,844; Gore, D, 404,614; Nader, Ind., 8,122; Phillips, Const., 3,267; Buchanan, RF, 2,265; Browne, LB, 2,009; Harris, Ind., 613; Hagelin, Natural Law, 450.
1996: Dole, R, 439,838; Clinton, D, 394,022; Perot, RF, 52,222; Browne, LB, 2,809; Phillips, U.S. Taxpayers, 2,314; Hagelin, Natural Law, 1,447; Collins, Ind., 1,205.
1992: Bush, R, 487,793; Clinton, D, 400,258; Perot, Ind., 85,626; Fulani, New Alliance, 2,625; Marrou, LB, 2,154; Phillips, U.S. Taxpayers, 1,652; Hagelin, Natural Law, 1,140.
1988: Bush, R, 557,890; Dukakis, D, 363,921; Duke, Ind., 4,232; Paul, LB, 3,329.
1984: Reagan, R, 582,377; Mondale, D, 352,192; Bergland, LB, 2,336.
1980: Reagan, R, 441,089; Carter, D, 429,281; Anderson, Ind., 12,036; Clark, LB, 5,465; Griswold, Workers World, 2,402; Pulley, Soc. Workers, 2,347.
1976: Carter, D, 381,309; Ford, R, 366,846; Anderson, Amer., 6,678; McCarthy, Ind., 4,074; Maddox, Ind., 4,049; Camejo, Soc. Workers, 2,805; MacBride, LB, 2,609.
1972: Nixon, R, 505,125; McGovern, D, 126,782; Schmitz, Amer., 11,598; Jenness, Soc. Workers, 2,458.
1968: Wallace, 3rd party, 415,349; Humphrey, D, 150,644; Nixon, R, 88,516.
1964: Goldwater, R, 356,528; Johnson, D, 52,618.
1960: D. (electors unpledged), 116,248; Kennedy, D, 108,362; Nixon, R, 73,561. Mississippi's victorious slate of 8 unpledged Dem. electors cast their votes for Sen. Harry F. Byrd (D, VA).

Missouri Vote Since 1960

2016: Trump, R, 1,594,511; Clinton, D, 1,071,068; Johnson, LB, 97,359; Stein, Green, 25,419; Castle, Const., 13,092; McMullin, Ind., 7,071.
2012: Romney, R, 1,482,440; Obama, D, 1,223,796; Johnson, LB, 43,151; Goode, Const., 7,936.
2008: McCain, R, 1,445,814; Obama, D, 1,441,911; Nader, Ind., 17,813; Barr, LB, 11,386; Baldwin, Const., 8,201.
2004: Bush, R, 1,455,713; Kerry, D, 1,259,171; Badnarik, LB, 9,831; Peroutka, Const., 5,355.
2000: Bush, R, 1,189,924; Gore, D, 1,111,138; Nader, Green, 38,515; Buchanan, RF, 9,818; Browne, LB, 7,436; Phillips, Const., 1,957; Hagelin, Natural Law, 1,104.
1996: Clinton, D, 1,025,935; Dole, R, 890,016; Perot, RF, 217,188; Phillips, U.S. Taxpayers, 11,521; Browne, LB, 10,522; Hagelin, Natural Law, 2,287.
1992: Clinton, D, 1,053,873; Bush, R, 811,159; Perot, Ind., 518,741; Marrou, LB, 7,497.
1988: Bush, R, 1,084,953; Dukakis, D, 1,001,619; Fulani, New Alliance, 6,656; Paul, write-in, 434.
1984: Reagan, R, 1,274,188; Mondale, D, 848,583.
1980: Reagan, R, 1,074,181; Carter, D, 931,182; Anderson, Ind., 77,920; Clark, LB, 14,422; DeBerry, Soc. Workers, 1,515; Commoner, Citizens, 573; write-in, 31.
1976: Carter, D, 999,163; Ford, R, 928,808; McCarthy, Ind., 24,329.

1972: Nixon, R, 1,154,058; McGovern, D, 698,531.
1968: Nixon, R, 811,932; Humphrey, D, 791,444; Wallace, 3rd party, 206,126.
1964: Johnson, D, 1,164,344; Goldwater, R, 653,535.
1960: Kennedy, D, 972,201; Nixon, R, 962,221.

Montana Vote Since 1960

2016: Trump, R, 279,240; Clinton, D, 177,709; Johnson, LB, 28,037; Stein, Green, 7,970; McMullin, Ind., 2,297; De La Fuente, Amer. Delta, 1,570.
2012: Romney, R, 267,928; Obama, D, 201,839; Johnson, LB, 14,165.
2008: McCain, R, 242,763; Obama, D, 231,667; Paul, Const., 10,638; Nader, Ind., 3,686; Barr, LB, 1,355.
2004: Bush, R, 266,063; Kerry, D, 173,710; Nader, Ind., 6,168; Peroutka, Const., 1,764; Badnarik, LB, 1,733; Cobb, Green, 996.
2000: Bush, R, 240,178; Gore, D, 137,126; Nader, Green, 24,437; Buchanan, RF, 5,697; Browne, LB, 1,718; Phillips, Const., 1,155; Hagelin, Natural Law, 675.
1996: Dole, R, 179,652; Clinton, D, 167,922; Perot, RF, 55,229; Browne, LB, 2,526; Hagelin, Natural Law, 1,754.
1992: Clinton, D, 154,507; Bush, R, 144,207; Perot, Ind., 107,225; Gritz, Populist/America First, 3,658.
1988: Bush, R, 190,412; Dukakis, D, 168,936; Paul, LB, 5,047; Fulani, New Alliance, 1,279.
1984: Reagan, R, 232,450; Mondale, D, 146,742; Bergland, LB, 5,185.
1980: Reagan, R, 206,814; Carter, D, 118,032; Anderson, Ind., 29,281; Clark, LB, 9,825.
1976: Ford, R, 173,703; Carter, D, 149,259; Anderson, Amer., 5,772.
1972: Nixon, R, 183,976; McGovern, D, 120,197; Schmitz, Amer., 13,430.
1968: Nixon, R, 138,835; Humphrey, D, 114,117; Wallace, 3rd party, 20,015; Munn, Prohib., 510; Caton, New RF, 470; Halstead, Soc. Workers, 457.
1964: Johnson, D, 164,246; Goldwater, R, 113,032; Kasper, Natl. States' Rights, 519; Munn, Prohib., 499; DeBerry, Soc. Workers, 332.
1960: Nixon, R, 141,841; Kennedy, D, 134,891; Decker, Prohib., 456; Dobbs, Soc. Workers, 391.

Nebraska Vote Since 1960

2016: Trump, R, 495,961; Clinton, D, 284,494; Johnson, LB, 38,946; Stein, petitioning cand., 8,775.
2012: Romney, R, 475,064; Obama, D, 302,081; Johnson, LB, 11,109; Terry, petitioning cand., 2,408.
2008: McCain, R, 452,979; Obama, D, 333,319; Nader, petitioning cand., 5,406; Baldwin, Nebraska, 2,972; Barr, LB, 2,740; McKinney, Green, 1,028.
2004: Bush, R, 512,814; Kerry, D, 254,328; Nader, petitioning cand., 5,698; Badnarik, LB, 2,041; Peroutka, Nebraska, 1,314; Cobb, Green, 978; Calero, petitioning cand., 82.
2000: Bush, R, 433,862; Gore, D, 231,780; Nader, Green, 24,540; Buchanan, Ind., 3,646; Browne, LB, 2,245; Hagelin, Natural Law, 478; Phillips, Ind., 468.
1996: Dole, R, 363,467; Clinton, D, 236,761; Perot, RF, 71,278; Browne, LB, 2,792; Phillips, Ind., 1,928; Hagelin, Natural Law, 1,189.
1992: Bush, R, 343,678; Clinton, D, 216,864; Perot, Ind., 174,104; Marrou, LB, 1,340.
1988: Bush, R, 397,956; Dukakis, D, 259,235; Paul, LB, 2,534; Fulani, New Alliance, 1,740.
1984: Reagan, R, 459,135; Mondale, D, 187,475; Bergland, LB, 2,075.
1980: Reagan, R, 419,214; Carter, D, 166,424; Anderson, Ind., 44,854; Clark, LB, 9,041.
1976: Ford, R, 359,219; Carter, D, 233,287; McCarthy, Ind., 9,383; Maddox, Amer. Ind., 3,378; MacBride, LB, 1,476.
1972: Nixon, R, 406,298; McGovern, D, 169,991; scattered, 817.
1968: Nixon, R, 321,163; Humphrey, D, 170,784; Wallace, 3rd party, 44,904.
1964: Johnson, D, 307,307; Goldwater, R, 276,847.
1960: Nixon, R, 380,553; Kennedy, D, 232,542.

Nevada Vote Since 1960

2016: Clinton, D, 539,260; Trump, R, 512,058; Johnson, LB, 37,384; None of These Candidates, 28,863; Castle, Ind. Amer., 5,268; De La Fuente, unaff., 2,552.

2012: Obama, D, 531,373; Romney, R, 463,567; Johnson, LB, 10,968; None of These Candidates, 5,770; Goode, Ind. Amer., 3,240.

2008: Obama, D, 533,736; McCain, R, 412,827; None of These Candidates, 6,267; Nader, Ind., 6,150; Barr, LB, 4,263; Baldwin, Const., 3,194; McKinney, Green, 1,411.

2004: Bush, R, 418,690; Kerry, D, 397,190; Nader, Ind., 4,838; None of These Candidates, 3,688; Badnarik, LB, 3,176; Peroutka, Ind. Amer., 1,152; Cobb, Green, 853.

2000: Bush, R, 301,575; Gore, D, 279,978; Nader, Green, 15,008; Buchanan, Citizens First, 4,747; None of These Candidates, 3,315; Browne, LB, 3,311; Phillips, Ind. Amer., 621; Hagelin, Natural Law, 415.

1996: Clinton, D, 203,974; Dole, R, 199,244; Perot, RF, 43,986; None of These Candidates, 5,608; Nader, Green, 4,730; Browne, LB, 4,460; Phillips, Ind. Amer., 1,732; Hagelin, Natural Law, 545.

1992: Clinton, D, 189,148; Bush, R, 175,828; Perot, Ind., 132,580; Gritz, Populist/America First, 2,892; Marrou, LB, 1,835.

1988: Bush, R, 206,040; Dukakis, D, 132,738; Paul, LB, 3,520; Fulani, New Alliance, 835.

1984: Reagan, R, 188,770; Mondale, D, 91,655; Bergland, LB, 2,292.

1980: Reagan, R, 155,017; Carter, D, 66,666; Anderson, Ind., 17,651; Clark, LB, 4,358.

1976: Ford, R, 101,273; Carter, D, 92,479; MacBride, LB, 1,519; Maddox, Amer. Ind., 1,497; scattered, 5,108.

1972: Nixon, R, 115,750; McGovern, D, 66,016.

1968: Nixon, R, 73,188; Humphrey, D, 60,598; Wallace, 3rd party, 20,432.

1964: Johnson, D, 79,339; Goldwater, R, 56,094.

1960: Kennedy, D, 54,880; Nixon, R, 52,387.

New Hampshire Vote Since 1960

2016: Clinton, D, 348,526; Trump, R, 345,790; Johnson, LB, 30,777; Stein, Green, 6,496; De La Fuente, Amer. Delta, 678.

2012: Obama, D, 369,561; Romney, R, 329,918; Johnson, LB, 8,212; Goode, Const., 708.

2008: Obama, D, 384,826; McCain, R, 316,534; Nader, Ind., 3,503; Barr, LB, 2,217; Phillies, LB, 531.

2004: Kerry, D, 340,511; Bush, R, 331,237; Nader, Ind., 4,479.

2000: Bush, R, 273,559; Gore, D, 266,348; Nader, Green, 22,198; Browne, LB, 2,757; Buchanan, Independence, 2,615; Phillips, Const., 328.

1996: Clinton, D, 246,166; Dole, R, 196,486; Perot, RF, 48,387; Browne, LB, 4,214; Phillips, Taxpayers, 1,344.

1992: Clinton, D, 209,040; Bush, R, 202,484; Perot, Ind., 121,337; Marrou, LB, 3,548.

1988: Bush, R, 281,537; Dukakis, D, 163,696; Paul, LB, 4,502; Fulani, New Alliance, 790.

1984: Reagan, R, 267,051; Mondale, D, 120,377; Bergland, LB, 735.

1980: Reagan, R, 221,705; Carter, D, 108,864; Anderson, Ind., 49,693; Clark, LB, 2,067; Commoner, Citizens, 1,325; Hall, Comm., 129; Griswold, Workers World, 76; DeBerry, Soc. Workers, 72; scattered, 68.

1976: Ford, R, 185,935; Carter, D, 147,645; McCarthy, Ind., 4,095; MacBride, LB, 936; Reagan, write-in, 388; LaRouche, U.S. Labor, 186; Camejo, Soc. Workers, 161; Levin, Soc. Labor, 66; scattered, 215.

1972: Nixon, R, 213,724; McGovern, D, 116,435; Schmitz, Amer., 3,386; Jenness, Soc. Workers, 368; scattered, 142.

1968: Nixon, R, 154,903; Humphrey, D, 130,589; Wallace, 3rd party, 11,173; New Party, 421; Halstead, Soc. Workers, 104.

1964: Johnson, D, 182,065; Goldwater, R, 104,029.

1960: Nixon, R, 157,989; Kennedy, D, 137,772.

New Jersey Vote Since 1960

2016: Clinton, D, 2,148,278; Trump, R, 1,601,933; Johnson, LB, 72,477; Stein, Green, 37,772; Castle, Const., 6,161; Kennedy, Soc. Workers, 2,156; De La Fuente, Amer. Delta, 1,838; Moorehead, Workers World, 1,749; La Riva, Socialism/Liberation, 1,682.

2012: Obama, D, 2,125,101; Romney, R, 1,477,568; Johnson, LB, 21,045; Stein, Green, 9,888; Goode, Const., 2,064; Anderson, Justice, 1,724; Boss, Ind., 1,007; Harris, Soc. Workers, 710; Miller, A3P, 664; Lindsay, Socialism/Liberation, 521.

2008: Obama, D, 2,215,422; McCain, R, 1,613,207; Nader, Ind., 21,298; Barr, Ind., 8,441; Baldwin, Ind., 3,956; McKinney, Ind., 3,636; Moore, Ind., 699; Boss, Ind., 639; Calero, Ind., 523; La Riva, Ind., 416.

2004: Kerry, D, 1,911,430; Bush, R, 1,670,003; Nader, Ind., 19,418; Badnarik, Ind., 4,514; Peroutka, Ind., 2,750; Cobb, Ind., 1,807; Brown, Ind., 664; Van Auken, Ind., 575; Calero, Ind., 530.

2000: Gore, D, 1,788,850; Bush, R, 1,284,173; Nader, Ind., 94,554; Buchanan, Ind., 6,989; Browne, Ind., 6,312; Hagelin, Ind., 2,215; McReynolds, Ind., 1,880; Phillips, Ind., 1,409; Harris, Ind., 844.

1996: Clinton, D, 1,652,361; Dole, R, 1,103,099; Perot, RF, 262,134; Nader, Green, 32,465; Browne, LB, 14,763; Hagelin, Natural Law, 3,887; Phillips, U.S. Taxpayers, 3,440; Harris, Soc. Workers, 1,837; Moorehead, Workers World, 1,337; White, Soc. Equality, 537.

1992: Clinton, D, 1,436,206; Bush, R, 1,356,865; Perot, Ind., 521,829; Marrou, LB, 6,822; Fulani, New Alliance, 3,513; Phillips, U.S. Taxpayers, 2,670; LaRouche, Ind., 2,095; Warren, Soc. Workers, 2,011; Daniels, Ind., 1,996; Gritz, Populist/America First, 1,867; Hagelin, Natural Law, 1,353.

1988: Bush, R, 1,740,604; Dukakis, D, 1,317,541; Lewin, Peace/Freedom, 9,953; Paul, LB, 8,421.

1984: Reagan, R, 1,933,630; Mondale, D, 1,261,323; Bergland, LB, 6,416.

1980: Reagan, R, 1,546,557; Carter, D, 1,147,364; Anderson, Ind., 234,632; Clark, LB, 20,652; Commoner, Citizens, 8,203; McCormack, Right to Life, 3,927; Lynen, Middle Class, 3,694; Hall, Comm., 2,555; Pulley, Soc. Workers, 2,198; McReynolds, Soc., 1,973; Gahres, Down With Lawyers, 1,718; Griswold, Workers World, 1,288; Wendelken, Ind., 923.

1976: Ford, R, 1,509,688; Carter, D, 1,444,653; McCarthy, Ind., 32,717; MacBride, LB, 9,449; Maddox, Amer., 7,716; Levin, Soc. Labor, 3,686; Hall, Comm., 1,662; LaRouche, U.S. Labor, 1,650; Camejo, Soc. Workers, 1,184; Wright, People's, 1,044; Bubar, Prohib., 554; Zeidler, Soc., 469.

1972: Nixon, R, 1,845,502; McGovern, D, 1,102,211; Schmitz, Amer., 34,378; Spock, People's, 5,355; Fisher, Soc. Labor, 4,544; Jenness, Soc. Workers, 2,233; Mahalchik, America First, 1,743; Hall, Comm., 1,263.

1968: Nixon, R, 1,325,467; Humphrey, D, 1,264,206; Wallace, 3rd party, 262,187; Halstead, Soc. Workers, 8,667; Gregory, Peace/Freedom, 8,084; Blomen, Soc. Labor, 6,784.

1964: Johnson, D, 1,867,671; Goldwater, R, 963,843; DeBerry, Soc. Workers, 8,181; Hass, Soc. Labor, 7,075.

1960: Kennedy, D, 1,385,415; Nixon, R, 1,363,324; Dobbs, Soc. Workers, 11,402; Lee, Conservative, 8,708; Hass, Soc. Labor, 4,262.

New Mexico Vote Since 1960

2016: Clinton, D, 385,234; Trump, R, 319,667; Johnson, LB, 74,541; Stein, Green, 9,879; McMullin, Better for Amer., 5,825; Castle, Const., 1,514; La Riva, Socialism/Liberation, 1,184; De La Fuente, Amer. Delta, 475.

2012: Obama, D, 415,335; Romney, R, 335,788; Johnson, LB, 27,788; Stein, Green, 2,691; Anderson, Ind., 1,174; Goode, Const., 982.

2008: Obama, D, 472,422; McCain, R, 346,832; Nader, Ind., 6,327; Barr, LB, 2,428; Baldwin, Const., 1,597; McKinney, Green, 1,552.

2004: Bush, R, 376,930; Kerry, D, 370,942; Nader, Ind., 4,053; Badnarik, LB, 2,382; Cobb, Green, 1,226; Peroutka, Const., 771.

2000: Gore, D, 286,783; Bush, R, 286,417; Nader, Green, 21,251; Browne, LB, 2,058; Buchanan, RF, 1,392; Hagelin, Natural Law, 361; Phillips, Const., 343.

1996: Clinton, D, 273,495; Dole, R, 232,751; Perot, RF, 32,257; Nader, Green, 13,218; Browne, LB, 2,996; Phillips, Taxpayers, 713; Hagelin, Natural Law, 644.

1992: Clinton, D, 261,617; Bush, R, 212,824; Perot, Ind., 91,895; Marrou, LB, 1,615.

1988: Bush, R, 270,341; Dukakis, D, 244,497; Paul, LB, 3,268; Fulani, New Alliance, 2,237.

1984: Reagan, R, 307,101; Mondale, D, 201,769; Bergland, LB, 4,459.

1980: Reagan, R, 250,779; Carter, D, 167,826; Anderson, Ind., 29,459; Clark, LB, 4,365; Commoner, Citizens, 2,202; Bubar, Statesman, 1,281; Pulley, Soc. Workers, 325.

1976: Ford, R, 211,419; Carter, D, 201,148; Camejo, Soc. Workers, 2,462; MacBride, LB, 1,110; Zeidler, Soc., 240; Bubar, Prohib., 211.

1972: Nixon, R, 235,606; McGovern, D, 141,084; Schmitz, Amer., 8,767; Jenness, Soc. Workers, 474.

1968: Nixon, R, 169,692; Humphrey, D, 130,081; Wallace, 3rd party, 25,737; Chavez, 1,519; Halstead, Soc. Workers, 252.

1964: Johnson, D, 194,017; Goldwater, R, 131,838; Hass, Soc. Labor, 1,217; Munn, Prohib., 543.

1960: Kennedy, D, 156,027; Nixon, R, 153,733; Decker, Prohib., 777; Hass, Soc. Labor, 570.

New York Vote Since 1960

2016: Clinton, D, 4,556,118; Trump, R, 2,819,533; Johnson, LB, 176,598; Stein, Green, 107,935; McMullin, Ind., 10,397.

2012: Obama, D, 4,485,741; Romney, R, 2,490,431; Johnson, LB, 47,256; Stein, Green, 39,982; Goode, Const., 6,274; Lindsay, Socialism/Liberation, 2,050.

2008: Obama, D, 4,804,945; McCain, R, 2,752,771; Nader, Populist, 41,249; Barr, LB, 19,596; McKinney, Green, 12,801; Calero, Soc. Workers, 3,615; La Riva, Socialism/Liberation, 1,639.

2004: Kerry, D, 4,314,280; Bush, R, 2,962,567; Nader, Ind., 99,873; Badnarik, LB, 11,607; Calero, Soc. Workers, 2,405.

2000: Gore, D, 4,112,965; Bush, R, 2,405,570; Nader, Green, 244,360; Buchanan, RF, 31,554; Hagelin, Independence, 24,369; Browne, LB, 7,664; Harris, Soc. Workers, 1,790; Phillips, Const., 1,503.

1996: Clinton, D, 3,756,177; Dole, R, 1,933,492; Perot, RF, 503,458; Nader, Green, 75,956; Phillips, Right to Life, 23,580; Browne, LB, 12,220; Hagelin, Natural Law, 5,011; Moorehead, Workers World, 3,473; Harris, Soc. Workers, 2,762.

1992: Clinton, D, 3,444,450; Bush, R, 2,346,649; Perot, Ind., 1,090,721; Warren, Soc. Workers, 15,472; Marrou, LB, 13,451; Fulani, New Alliance, 11,318; Hagelin, Natural Law, 4,420.

1988: Dukakis, D, 3,347,882; Bush, R, 3,081,871; Marra, Right to Life, 20,497; Fulani, New Alliance, 15,845.

1984: Reagan, R, 3,664,763; Mondale, D, 3,119,609; Bergland, LB, 11,949.

1980: Reagan, R, 2,893,831; Carter, D, 2,728,372; Anderson, Liberal, 467,801; Clark, LB, 52,648; McCormack, Right to Life, 24,159; Commoner, Citizens, 23,186; Hall, Comm., 7,414; DeBerry, Soc. Workers, 2,068; Griswold, Workers World, 1,416; scattered, 1,064.

1976: Carter, D, 3,389,558; Ford, R, 3,100,791; MacBride, LB, 12,197; Hall, Comm., 10,270; Camejo, Soc. Workers, 6,996; LaRouche, U.S. Labor, 5,413; blank, void, and scattered, 143,037.

1972: Nixon, R, 3,824,642; McGovern, D, 2,767,956 and Liberal, 183,128 (total, 2,951,084); Reed, Soc. Workers, 7,797; Fisher, Soc. Labor, 4,530; Hall, Comm., 5,641; blank, void, and scattered, 161,641.

1968: Humphrey, D, 3,378,470; Nixon, R, 3,007,932; Wallace, 3rd party, 358,864; Gregory, Peace/Freedom, 24,517; Halstead, Soc. Workers, 11,851; Blomen, Soc. Labor, 8,432; blank, void, and scattered, 171,624.

1964: Johnson, D, 4,913,156; Goldwater, R, 2,243,559; Hass, Soc. Labor, 6,085; DeBerry, Soc. Workers, 3,215; scattered, 188; blank and void, 151,383.

1960: Kennedy, D, 3,423,909 and Liberal, 406,176 (total, 3,830,085); Nixon, R, 3,446,419; Dobbs, Soc. Workers, 14,319; scattered, 256; blank and void, 88,896.

North Carolina Vote Since 1960

2016: Trump, R, 2,362,631; Clinton, D, 2,189,316; Johnson, LB, 130,126; Stein, Ind., 12,105.

2012: Romney, R, 2,270,395; Obama, D, 2,178,391; Johnson, LB, 44,515.

2008: Obama, D, 2,142,651; McCain, R, 2,128,474; Barr, LB, 25,722.

2004: Bush, R, 1,961,166; Kerry, D, 1,525,849; Badnarik, LB, 11,731.

2000: Bush, R, 1,631,163; Gore, D, 1,257,692; Browne, LB, 13,691; Buchanan, RF, 8,874.

1996: Dole, R, 1,225,938; Clinton, D, 1,107,849; Perot, RF, 168,059; Browne, LB, 8,740; Hagelin, Natural Law, 2,771.

1992: Bush, R, 1,134,661; Clinton, D, 1,114,042; Perot, Ind., 357,864; Marrou, LB, 5,171.

1988: Bush, R, 1,237,258; Dukakis, D, 890,167; Fulani, New Alliance, 5,682; Paul, write-in, 1,263.

1984: Reagan, R, 1,346,481; Mondale, D, 824,287; Bergland, LB, 3,794.

1980: Reagan, R, 915,018; Carter, D, 875,635; Anderson, Ind., 52,800; Clark, LB, 9,677; Commoner, Citizens, 2,287; DeBerry, Soc. Workers, 416.

1976: Carter, D, 927,365; Ford, R, 741,960; Anderson, Amer., 5,607; MacBride, LB, 2,219; LaRouche, U.S. Labor, 755.

1972: Nixon, R, 1,054,889; McGovern, D, 438,705; Schmitz, Amer., 25,018.

1968: Nixon, R, 627,192; Wallace, 3rd party, 496,188; Humphrey, D, 464,113.

1964: Johnson, D, 800,139; Goldwater, R, 624,844.

1960: Kennedy, D, 713,136; Nixon, R, 655,420.

North Dakota Vote Since 1960

2016: Trump, R, 216,794; Clinton, D, 93,758; Johnson, LB, 21,434; Stein, Green, 3,780; Castle, Const., 1,833; De La Fuente, Amer. Delta, 364.

2012: Romney, R, 188,163; Obama, D, 124,827; Johnson, LB, 5,231; Stein, Green, 1,361; Goode, Const., 1,185.

2008: McCain, R, 168,601; Obama, D, 141,278; Nader, Ind., 4,189; Barr, LB, 1,354; Baldwin, Const., 1,199.

2004: Bush, R, 196,651; Kerry, D, 111,052; Nader, Ind., 3,756; Badnarik, LB, 851; Peroutka, Const., 514.

2000: Bush, R, 174,852; Gore, D, 95,284; Nader, Ind., 9,486; Buchanan, RF, 7,288; Browne, Ind., 660; Phillips, Const., 373; Hagelin, Ind., 313.

1996: Dole, R, 125,050; Clinton, D, 106,905; Perot, RF, 32,515; Browne, LB, 847; Phillips, Ind., 745; Hagelin, Natural Law, 349.

1992: Bush, R, 136,244; Clinton, D, 99,168; Perot, Ind., 71,084.

1988: Bush, R, 166,559; Dukakis, D, 127,739; Paul, LB, 1,315; LaRouche, Natl. Econ. Recovery, 905.

1984: Reagan, R, 200,336; Mondale, D, 104,429; Bergland, LB, 703.

1980: Reagan, R, 193,695; Carter, D, 79,189; Anderson, Ind., 23,640; Clark, LB, 3,743; Commoner, LB, 429; McLain, Natl. People's League, 296; Greaves, Amer., 235; Hall, Comm., 93; DeBerry, Soc. Workers, 89; McReynolds, Soc., 82; Bubar, Statesman, 54.

1976: Ford, R, 153,470; Carter, D, 136,078; Anderson, Amer., 3,698; McCarthy, Ind., 2,952; Maddox, Amer. Ind., 269; MacBride, LB, 256; scattered, 371.

1972: Nixon, R, 174,109; McGovern, D, 100,384; Schmitz, Amer., 5,646; Jenness, Soc. Workers, 288; Hall, Comm., 87.

1968: Nixon, R, 138,669; Humphrey, D, 94,769; Wallace, 3rd party, 14,244; Halstead, Soc. Workers, 128; Munn, Prohib., 38; Troxell, Ind., 34.

1964: Johnson, D, 149,784; Goldwater, R, 108,207; DeBerry, Soc. Workers, 224; Munn, Prohib., 174.

1960: Nixon, R, 154,310; Kennedy, D, 123,963; Dobbs, Soc. Workers, 158.

Ohio Vote Since 1960

2016: Trump, R, 2,841,005; Clinton, D, 2,394,164; Johnson, LB, 174,498; Stein, Green, 46,271; Duncan, Ind., 24,235; McMullin, Ind., 12,574; Castle, Const., 1,887.

2012: Obama, D, 2,827,709; Romney, R, 2,661,437; Johnson, LB, 49,493; Stein, Green, 18,573; Duncan, Ind., 12,502; Goode, Const., 8,152; Alexander, Soc., 2,944.

2008: Obama, D, 2,940,044; McCain, R, 2,677,820; Nader, Ind., 42,337; Barr, LB, 19,917; Baldwin, Const., 12,565; McKinney, Green, 8,518; Duncan, Ind., 3,905; Moore, Soc., 2,735.

2004: Bush, R, 2,859,768; Kerry, D, 2,741,167; Badnarik, nonpartisan, 14,676; Peroutka, nonpartisan, 939.

2000: Bush, R, 2,351,209; Gore, D, 2,186,190; Nader, Ind., 117,857; Buchanan, Ind., 26,724; Browne, LB, 13,475; Hagelin, Natural Law, 6,169; Phillips, Ind., 3,823.

1996: Clinton, D, 2,148,222; Dole, R, 1,859,883; Perot, RF, 483,207; Browne, Ind., 12,851; Moorehead, Ind., 10,813; Hagelin, Natural Law, 9,120; Phillips, Ind., 7,361.

1992: Clinton, D, 1,984,942; Bush, R, 1,894,310; Perot, Ind., 1,036,426; Marrou, LB, 7,252; Fulani, New Alliance, 6,413;

Gritz, Populist/America First, 4,699; Hagelin, Natural Law, 3,437; LaRouche, Ind., 2,446.

1988: Bush, R, 2,416,549; Dukakis, D, 1,939,629; Fulani, Ind., 12,017; Paul, Ind., 11,926.

1984: Reagan, R, 2,678,559; Mondale, D, 1,825,440; Bergland, LB, 5,886.

1980: Reagan, R, 2,206,545; Carter, D, 1,752,414; Anderson, Ind., 254,472; Clark, LB, 49,033; Commoner, Citizens, 8,564; Hall, Comm., 4,729; Congress, Ind., 4,029; Griswold, Workers World, 3,790; Bubar, Statesman, 27.

1976: Carter, D, 2,011,621; Ford, R, 2,000,505; McCarthy, Ind., 58,258; Maddox, Amer. Ind., 15,529; MacBride, LB, 8,961; Hall, Comm., 7,817; Camejo, Soc. Workers, 4,717; LaRouche, U.S. Labor, 4,335; scattered, 130.

1972: Nixon, R, 2,441,827; McGovern, D, 1,558,889; Schmitz, Amer., 80,067; Fisher, Soc. Labor, 7,107; Hall, Comm., 6,437; Wallace, Ind., 460.

1968: Nixon, R, 1,791,014; Humphrey, D, 1,700,586; Wallace, 3rd party, 467,495; Gregory, 372; Blomen, Soc. Labor, 120; Halstead, Soc. Workers, 69; Mitchell, Comm., 23; Munn, Prohib., 19.

1964: Johnson, D, 2,498,331; Goldwater, R, 1,470,865.

1960: Nixon, R, 2,217,611; Kennedy, D, 1,944,248.

Oklahoma Vote Since 1960

2016: Trump, R, 949,136; Clinton, D, 420,375; Johnson, LB, 83,481.

2012: Romney, R, 891,325; Obama, D, 443,547.

2008: McCain, R, 960,165; Obama, D, 502,496.

2004: Bush, R, 959,792; Kerry, D, 503,966.

2000: Bush, R, 744,337; Gore, D, 474,276; Buchanan, RF, 9,014; Browne, LB, 6,602.

1996: Dole, R, 582,315; Clinton, D, 488,105; Perot, RF, 130,788; Browne, LB, 5,505.

1992: Bush, R, 592,929; Clinton, D, 473,066; Perot, Ind., 319,878; Marrou, LB, 4,486.

1988: Bush, R, 678,367; Dukakis, D, 483,423; Paul, LB, 6,261; Fulani, New Alliance, 2,985.

1984: Reagan, R, 861,530; Mondale, D, 385,080; Bergland, LB, 9,066.

1980: Reagan, R, 695,570; Carter, D, 402,026; Anderson, Ind., 38,284; Clark, LB, 13,828.

1976: Ford, R, 545,708; Carter, D, 532,442; McCarthy, Ind., 14,101.

1972: Nixon, R, 759,025; McGovern, D, 247,147; Schmitz, Amer., 23,728.

1968: Nixon, R, 449,697; Humphrey, D, 301,658; Wallace, 3rd party, 191,731.

1964: Johnson, D, 519,834; Goldwater, R, 412,665.

1960: Nixon, R, 533,039; Kennedy, D, 370,111.

Oregon Vote Since 1960

2016: Clinton, D, 1,002,106; Trump, R, 782,403; Johnson, LB, 94,231; Stein, Pacific Green, 50,002.

2012: Obama, D, 970,488; Romney, R, 754,175; Johnson, LB, 24,089; Stein, Pacific Green, 19,427; Christensen, Const., 4,432; Anderson, OR Prog., 3,384.

2008: Obama, D, 1,037,291; McCain, R, 738,475; Nader, Peace Party of OR, 18,614; Baldwin, Const., 7,693; Barr, LB, 7,635; McKinney, Pacific Green, 4,543.

2004: Kerry, D, 943,163, Bush, R, 800,831; Badnarik, LD, 7,260; Cobb, Pacific Green, 5,315; Peroutka, Const., 5,257.

2000: Gore, D, 720,342; Bush, R, 713,577; Nader, Green, 77,357; Browne, LB, 7,447; Buchanan, Ind., 7,063; Hagelin, RF, 2,574; Phillips, Const., 2,189.

1996: Clinton, D, 649,641; Dole, R, 538,152; Perot, RF, 121,221; Nader, Pacific, 49,415; Browne, LB, 8,903; Phillips, Taxpayers, 3,379; Hagelin, Natural Law, 2,798; Hollis, Soc., 1,922.

1992: Clinton, D, 621,314; Bush, R, 475,757; Perot, Ind., 354,091; Marrou, LB, 4,277; Fulani, New Alliance, 3,030.

1988: Dukakis, D, 616,206; Bush, R, 560,126; Paul, LB, 14,811; Fulani, Ind., 6,487.

1984: Reagan, R, 658,700; Mondale, D, 536,479.

1980: Reagan, R, 571,044; Carter, D, 456,890; Anderson, Ind., 112,389; Clark, LB, 25,838; Commoner, Citizens, 13,642; scattered, 1,713.

1976: Ford, R, 492,120; Carter, D, 490,407; McCarthy, Ind., 40,207; write-in, 7,142.

1972: Nixon, R, 486,686; McGovern, D, 392,760; Schmitz, Amer., 46,211; write-in, 2,289.

1968: Nixon, R, 408,433; Humphrey, D, 358,866; Wallace, 3rd party, 49,683; write-ins: McCarthy, 1,496; N. Rockefeller, 69; others, 1,075.

1964: Johnson, D, 501,017; Goldwater, R, 282,779; write-in, 2,509.

1960: Nixon, R, 408,060; Kennedy, D, 367,402.

Pennsylvania Vote Since 1960

2016: Trump, R, 2,970,733; Clinton, D, 2,926,441; Johnson, LB, 146,715; Stein, Green, 49,941; Castle, Const., 21,572.

2012: Obama, D, 2,990,274; Romney, R, 2,680,434; Johnson, LB, 49,991; Stein, Green, 21,341.

2008: Obama, D, 3,276,363; McCain, R, 2,655,885; Nader, Ind., 42,977; Barr, LB, 19,912.

2004: Kerry, D, 2,938,095; Bush, R, 2,793,847; Badnarik, LB, 21,185; Cobb, Green, 6,319; Peroutka, Const., 6,318.

2000: Gore, D, 2,485,967; Bush, R, 2,281,127; Nader, Green, 103,392; Buchanan, RF, 16,023; Phillips, Const., 14,428; Browne, LB, 11,248.

1996: Clinton, D, 2,215,819; Dole, R, 1,801,169; Perot, RF, 430,984; Browne, LB, 28,000; Phillips, Const., 19,552; Hagelin, Natural Law, 5,783.

1992: Clinton, D, 2,239,164; Bush, R, 1,791,841; Perot, Ind., 902,667; Marrou, LB, 21,477; Fulani, New Alliance, 4,661.

1988: Bush, R, 2,300,087; Dukakis, D, 2,194,944; McCarthy, Consumer, 19,158; Paul, LB, 12,051.

1984: Reagan, R, 2,584,323; Mondale, D, 2,228,131; Bergland, LB, 6,982.

1980: Reagan, R, 2,261,872; Carter, D, 1,937,540; Anderson, Ind., 292,921; Clark, LB, 33,263; DeBerry, Soc. Workers, 20,291; Commoner, Consumer, 10,430; Hall, Comm., 5,184.

1976: Carter, D, 2,328,677; Ford, R, 2,205,604; McCarthy, Ind., 50,584; Maddox, Const., 25,344; Camejo, Soc. Workers, 3,009; LaRouche, U.S. Labor, 2,744; Hall, Comm., 1,891; others, 2,934.

1972: Nixon, R, 2,714,521; McGovern, D, 1,796,951; Schmitz, Amer., 70,593; Jenness, Soc. Workers, 4,639; Hall, Comm., 2,686; others, 2,715.

1968: Humphrey, D, 2,259,405; Nixon, R, 2,090,017; Wallace, 3rd party, 378,582; Gregory, Peace/Freedom, 7,821; Blomen, Soc. Labor, 4,977; Halstead, Soc. Workers, 4,862; others, 2,264.

1964: Johnson, D, 3,130,954; Goldwater, R, 1,673,657; DeBerry, Soc. Workers, 10,456; Hass, Soc. Labor, 5,092; scattered, 2,531.

1960: Kennedy, D, 2,556,282; Nixon, R, 2,439,956; Hass, Soc. Labor, 7,185; Dobbs, Soc. Workers, 2,678; scattered, 440.

Rhode Island Vote Since 1960

2016: Clinton, D, 252,525; Trump, R, 180,543; Johnson, LB, 14,746; Stein, Green, 6,220; De La Fuente, Amer. Delta, 671.

2012: Obama, D, 279,677; Romney, R, 157,204; Johnson, LB, 4,388; Stein, Green, 2,421; Goode, Const., 430; Anderson, Justice, 416; Lindsay, Socialism/Liberation, 132.

2008: Obama, D, 296,571; McCain, R, 165,391; Nader, Ind., 4,829; Barr, LB, 1,382; McKinney, Green, 797; Baldwin, Const., 675; La Riva, Socialism/Liberation, 122.

2004: Kerry, D, 259,765; Bush, R, 169,046; Nader, RF, 4,651; Cobb, Green, 1,333; Badnarik, LB, 907; Peroutka, Const., 339; Parker, Workers World, 253.

2000: Gore, D, 249,508; Bush, R, 130,555; Nader, Ind., 25,052; Buchanan, RF, 2,273; Browne, Ind., 742; Hagelin, Ind., 271; Moorehead, Ind., 199; Phillips, Ind., 97; McReynolds, Ind., 52; Harris, Ind., 34.

1996: Clinton, D, 233,050; Dole, R, 104,683; Perot, RF, 43,723; Nader, Green, 6,040; Browne, LB, 1,109; Phillips, U.S. Taxpayers, 1,021; Hagelin, Natural Law, 435; Moorehead, Workers World, 186.

1992: Clinton, D, 213,299; Bush, R, 131,601; Perot, Ind., 105,045; Fulani, New Alliance, 1,878.

1988: Dukakis, D, 225,123; Bush, R, 177,761; Paul, LB, 825; Fulani, New Alliance, 280.

1984: Reagan, R, 212,080; Mondale, D, 197,106; Bergland, LB, 277.

1980: Carter, D, 198,342; Reagan, R, 154,793; Anderson, Ind., 59,819; Clark, LB, 2,458; Hall, Comm., 218; McReynolds, Soc., 170; DeBerry, Soc. Workers, 90; Griswold, Workers World, 77.

1976: Carter, D, 227,636; Ford, R, 181,249; MacBride, LB, 715; Camejo, Soc. Workers, 462; Hall, Comm., 334; Levin, Soc. Labor, 188.
1972: Nixon, R, 220,383; McGovern, D, 194,645; Jenness, Soc. Workers, 729.
1968: Humphrey, D, 246,518; Nixon, R, 122,359; Wallace, 3rd party, 15,678; Halstead, Soc. Workers, 383.
1964: Johnson, D, 315,463; Goldwater, R, 74,615.
1960: Kennedy, D, 258,032; Nixon, R, 147,502.

South Carolina Vote Since 1960

2016: Trump, R, 1,155,389; Clinton, D, 855,373; Johnson, LB, 49,204; McMullin, Ind., 21,016; Stein, Green, 13,034; Castle, Const., 5,765; Skewes, American, 3,246.
2012: Romney, R, 1,071,645; Obama, D, 865,941; Johnson, LB, 16,321; Stein, Green, 5,446; Goode, Const., 4,765.
2008: McCain, R, 1,034,896; Obama, D, 862,449; Barr, LB, 7,283; Baldwin, Const., 6,827; Nader, petitioning cand., 5,053; McKinney, Green, 4,461.
2004: Bush, R, 937,974; Kerry, D, 661,699; Nader, Ind., 5,520; Peroutka, Const., 5,317; Badnarik, LB, 3,608; Brown, United Citizens, 2,124; Cobb, Green, 1,488.
2000: Bush, R, 786,892; Gore, D, 566,039; Nader, United Citizens, 20,279; Browne, LB, 4,898; Buchanan, RF, 3,309; Phillips, Const., 1,682; Hagelin, Natural Law, 943.
1996: Dole, R, 573,458; Clinton, D, 506,283; Perot, RF/Patriot, 64,386; Browne, LB, 4,271; Phillips, U.S. Taxpayers, 2,043; Hagelin, Natural Law, 1,248.
1992: Bush, R, 577,507; Clinton, D, 479,514; Perot, Ind., 138,872; Marrou, LB, 2,719; Phillips, U.S. Taxpayers, 2,680; Fulani, New Alliance, 1,235.
1988: Bush, R, 606,443; Dukakis, D, 370,554; Paul, LB, 4,935; Fulani, United Citizens, 4,077.
1984: Reagan, R, 615,539; Mondale, D, 344,459; Bergland, LB, 4,359.
1980: Reagan, R, 439,277; Carter, D, 428,220; Anderson, Ind., 13,868; Clark, LB, 4,807; Rarick, Amer. Ind., 2,086.
1976: Carter, D, 450,807; Ford, R, 346,149; Anderson, Amer., 2,996; Maddox, Amer. Ind., 1,950; write-in, 681.
1972: Nixon, R, 477,044; McGovern, D, 184,559, and United Citizens, 2,265 (total, 186,824); Schmitz, Amer., 10,075; write-in, 17.
1968: Nixon, R, 254,062; Wallace, 3rd party, 215,430; Humphrey, D, 197,486.
1964: Goldwater, R, 309,048; Johnson, D, 215,700; write-ins: Wallace, 5; Nixon, 1; Powell, 1; Thurmond, 1.
1960: Kennedy, D, 198,129; Nixon, R, 188,558; write-in, 1.

South Dakota Vote Since 1960

2016: Trump, R, 227,721; Clinton, D, 117,458; Johnson, LB, 20,850; Castle, Const., 4,064.
2012: Romney, R, 210,610; Obama, D, 145,039; Johnson, LB, 5,795; Goode, Const., 2,371.
2008: McCain, R, 203,054; Obama, D, 170,924; Nader, Ind., 4,267; Baldwin, Const., 1,895; Barr, Ind., 1,835.
2004: Bush, R, 232,584; Kerry, D, 149,244; Nader, Ind., 4,320; Peroutka, Const., 1,103; Badnarik, LB, 964.
2000: Bush, R, 190,700; Gore, D, 118,804; Buchanan, RF, 3,322; Phillips, Ind., 1,781; Browne, LB, 1,662.
1996: Dole, R, 150,543; Clinton, D, 139,333; Perot, RF, 31,250; Browne, LB, 1,472; Phillips, Taxpayers, 912; Hagelin, Natural Law, 316.
1992: Bush, R, 136,718; Clinton, D, 124,888; Perot, Ind., 73,295.
1988: Bush, R, 165,415; Dukakis, D, 145,560; Paul, LB, 1,060; Fulani, New Alliance, 730.
1984: Reagan, R, 200,267; Mondale, D, 116,113.
1980: Reagan, R, 198,343; Carter, D, 103,855; Anderson, Ind., 21,431; Clark, LB, 3,824; Pulley, Soc. Workers, 250.
1976: Ford, R, 151,505; Carter, D, 147,068; MacBride, LB, 1,619; Hall, Comm., 318; Camejo, Soc. Workers, 168.
1972: Nixon, R, 166,476; McGovern, D, 139,945; Jenness, Soc. Workers, 994.
1968: Nixon, R, 149,841; Humphrey, D, 118,023; Wallace, 3rd party, 13,400.

1964: Johnson, D, 163,010; Goldwater, R, 130,108.
1960: Nixon, R, 178,417; Kennedy, D, 128,070.

Tennessee Vote Since 1960

2016: Trump, R, 1,522,925; Clinton, D, 870,695; Johnson, Ind., 70,397; Stein, Green, 15,993; McMullin, Ind., 11,991; Smith, Ind., 7,276; De La Fuente, Ind., 4,075; Kennedy, Ind., 2,877; Castle, Ind., 1,584.
2012: Romney, R, 1,462,330; Obama, D, 960,709; Johnson, Ind., 18,623; Stein, Green, 6,515; Goode, Const., 6,022; Anderson, Ind., 2,639, Miller, Ind., 1,739.
2008: McCain, R, 1,479,178; Obama, D, 1,087,437; Nader, Ind., 11,560; Barr, Ind., 8,547; Baldwin, Ind., 8,191; McKinney, Ind., 2,499; Moore, Ind., 1,326; Jay, Ind., 1,011.
2004: Bush, R, 1,384,375; Kerry, D, 1,036,477; Nader, Ind., 8,992; Badnarik, Ind., 4,866; Peroutka, Ind., 2,570.
2000: Bush, R, 1,061,949; Gore, D, 981,720; Nader, Green, 19,781; Browne, LB, 4,284; Buchanan, RF, 4,250; Brown, Ind., 1,606; Phillips, Ind., 1,015; Hagelin, RF, 613; Venson, Ind., 535.
1996: Clinton, D, 909,146; Dole, R, 863,530; Perot, RF, 105,918; Nader, Ind., 6,427; Browne, Ind., 5,020; Phillips, Ind., 1,818; Collins, Ind., 688; Hagelin, Ind., 636; Michael, Ind., 408; Dodge, Ind., 324.
1992: Clinton, D, 933,521; Bush, R, 841,300; Perot, Ind., 199,968; Marrou, LB, 1,847.
1988: Bush, R, 947,233; Dukakis, D, 679,794; Paul, Ind., 2,041; Duke, Ind., 1,807.
1984: Reagan, R, 990,212; Mondale, D, 711,714; Bergland, LB, 3,072.
1980: Reagan, R, 787,761; Carter, D, 783,051; Anderson, Ind., 35,991; Clark, LB, 7,116; Commoner, Citizens, 1,112; Bubar, Statesman, 521; McReynolds, Soc., 519; Hall, Comm., 503; DeBerry, Soc. Workers, 490; Griswold, Workers World, 400; write-in, 152.
1976: Carter, D, 825,879; Ford, R, 633,969; Anderson, Amer., 5,769; McCarthy, Ind., 5,004; Maddox, Amer. Ind., 2,303; MacBride, LB, 1,375; Hall, Comm., 547; LaRouche, U.S. Labor, 512; Bubar, Prohib., 442; Miller, Ind., 316; write-in, 230.
1972: Nixon, R, 813,147; McGovern, D, 357,293; Schmitz, Amer., 30,373; write-in, 369.
1968: Nixon, R, 472,592; Wallace, 3rd party, 424,792; Humphrey, D, 351,233.
1964: Johnson, D, 635,047; Goldwater, R, 508,965; write-in, 34.
1960: Nixon, R, 556,577; Kennedy, D, 481,453; Faubus, States' Rights, 11,304; Decker, Prohib., 2,458.

Texas Vote Since 1960

2016: Trump, R, 4,685,047; Clinton, D, 3,877,868; Johnson, LB, 283,492; Stein, Green, 71,558; McMullin, Ind., 42,366.
2012: Romney, R, 4,569,843; Obama, D, 3,308,124; Johnson, LB, 88,580; Stein, Green, 24,657.
2008: McCain, R, 4,479,328; Obama, D, 3,528,633 Barr, LB, 56,116.
2004: Bush, R, 4,526,917; Kerry, D, 2,832,704; Badnarik, LB, 38,787.
2000: Bush, R, 3,799,639; Gore, D, 2,433,746; Nader, Green, 137,994; Browne, LB, 23,160; Buchanan, Ind., 12,394.
1996: Dole, R, 2,736,167; Clinton, D, 2,459,683; Perot, RF, 378,537; Browne, LB, 20,256; Phillips, U.S. Taxpayers, 7,472; Hagelin, Natural Law, 4,422.
1992: Bush, R, 2,496,071; Clinton, D, 2,281,815; Perot, Ind., 1,354,781; Marrou, LB, 19,699.
1988: Bush, R, 3,036,829; Dukakis, D, 2,352,748; Paul, LB, 30,355; Fulani, New Alliance, 7,208.
1984: Reagan, R, 3,433,428; Mondale, D, 1,949,276.
1980: Reagan, R, 2,510,705; Carter, D, 1,881,147; Anderson, Ind., 111,613; Clark, LB, 37,643; write-in, 528.
1976: Carter, D, 2,082,319; Ford, R, 1,953,300; McCarthy, Ind., 20,118; Anderson, Amer., 11,442; Camejo, Soc. Workers, 1,723; write-in, 2,982.
1972: Nixon, R, 2,298,896; McGovern, D, 1,154,289; Jenness, Soc. Workers, 8,664; Schmitz, Amer., 6,039; others, 3,393.
1968: Humphrey, D, 1,266,804; Nixon, R, 1,227,844; Wallace, 3rd party, 584,269; write-in, 489.

1964: Johnson, D, 1,663,185; Goldwater, R, 958,566; Lightburn, Const., 5,060.

1960: Kennedy, D, 1,167,932; Nixon, R, 1,121,699; Sullivan, Const., 18,169; Decker, Prohib., 3,870; write-in, 15.

Utah Vote Since 1960

2016: Trump, R, 515,231; Clinton, D, 310,676; McMullin, unaff., 243,690; Johnson, LB, 39,608; Stein, Green, 9,438; Castle, Const., 8,032; Giordani, Ind. Ameri., 2,752; De La Fuente, unaff., 883; Moorehead, unaff., 544; Kennedy, unaff., 521.

2012: Romney, R, 740,600; Obama, D, 251,813; Johnson, LB, 12,572; Anderson, Justice, 5,335; Stein, Green, 3,817; Goode, Const., 2,871; La Riva, unaff., 393.

2008: McCain, R, 596,030; Obama, D, 327,670; Baldwin, Const., 12,012; Nader, unaff., 8,416; Barr, LB, 6,966; McKinney, unaff., 982; La Riva, unaff., 262.

2004: Bush, R, 663,742; Kerry, D, 241,199; Nader, Ind., 11,305; Peroutka, Const., 6,841; Badnarik, LB, 3,375; Jay, Personal Choice, 946; Harris, Soc. Workers, 393.

2000: Bush, R, 515,096; Gore, D, 203,053; Nader, Green, 35,850; Buchanan, RF, 9,319; Browne, LB, 3,616; Phillips, Ind. American, 2,709; Hagelin, Natural Law, 763; Harris, Soc. Workers, 186; Youngkeit, Ind., 161.

1996: Dole, R, 361,911; Clinton, D, 221,633; Perot, RF, 66,461; Nader, Green, 4,615; Browne, LB, 4,129; Phillips, Taxpayers, 2,601; Templin, Ind. American, 1,290; Crane, Ind., 1,101; Hagelin, Natural Law, 1,085; Moorehead, Workers World, 298; Harris, Soc. Workers, 235; Dodge, Prohib., 111.

1992: Bush, R, 322,632; Perot, Ind., 203,400; Clinton, D, 183,429; Gritz, Populist/America First, 28,602; Marrou, LB, 1,900; Hagelin, Natural Law, 1,319; LaRouche, Ind., 1,089.

1988: Bush, R, 428,442; Dukakis, D, 207,352; Paul, LB, 7,473; Dennis, Amer., 2,158.

1984: Reagan, R, 469,105; Mondale, D, 155,369; Bergland, LB, 2,447.

1980: Reagan, R, 439,687; Carter, D, 124,266; Anderson, Ind., 30,284; Clark, LB, 7,226; Commoner, Citizens, 1,009; Greaves, Amer., 965; Rarick, Amer. Ind., 522; Hall, Comm., 139; DeBerry, Soc. Workers, 124.

1976: Ford, R, 337,908; Carter, D, 182,110; Anderson, Amer., 13,304; McCarthy, Ind., 3,907; MacBride, LB, 2,438; Maddox, Amer. Ind., 1,162; Camejo, Soc. Workers, 268; Hall, Comm., 121.

1972: Nixon, R, 323,643; McGovern, D, 126,284; Schmitz, Amer., 28,549.

1968: Nixon, R, 238,728; Humphrey, D, 156,665; Wallace, 3rd party, 26,906; Peace/Freedom, 180; Halstead, Soc. Workers, 89.

1964: Johnson, D, 219,628; Goldwater, R, 181,785.

1960: Nixon, R, 205,361; Kennedy, D, 169,248; Dobbs, Soc. Workers, 100.

Vermont Vote Since 1960

2016: Clinton, D, 178,573; Trump, R, 95,369; Sanders, write-in, 18,218; Johnson, LB, 10,078; Stein, Green, 6,758; De La Fuente, Ind., 1,063; La Riva, Liberty Union, 327.

2012: Obama, D, 199,239; Romney, R, 92,698; Johnson, LB, 3,487; Anderson, Justice, 1,128; Lindsay, Socialism/Liberation, 695.

2008: Obama, D, 219,262; McCain, R, 98,974; Nader, Ind., 3,339; Barr, LB, 1,067; Baldwin, Const., 500; Calero, Soc. Workers, 150; La Riva, Socialism/Liberation, 149; Moore, Liberty Union, 141.

2004: Kerry, D, 184,067; Bush, R, 121,180; Nader, Ind., 4,494; Badnarik, LB, 1,102; Parker, Liberty Union, 265; Calero, Soc. Workers, 244.

2000: Gore, D, 149,022; Bush, R, 119,775; Nader, Green, 20,374; Buchanan, RF, 2,192; Lane, Grass Roots, 1,044; Browne, LB, 784; Hagelin, Natural Law, 219; McReynolds, Liberty Union, 161; Phillips, Const., 153; Harris, Soc. Workers, 70.

1996: Clinton, D, 137,894; Dole, R, 80,352; Perot, RF, 31,024; Nader, Green, 5,585; Browne, LB, 1,183; Hagelin, Natural Law, 498; Peron, Grass Roots, 480; Phillips, Taxpayers, 382; Hollis, Liberty Union, 292; Harris, Soc. Workers, 199.

1992: Clinton, D, 133,590; Bush, R, 88,122; Perot, Ind., 65,985.

1988: Bush, R, 124,331; Dukakis, D, 115,775; Paul, LB, 1,000; LaRouche, Ind., 275.

1984: Reagan, R, 135,865; Mondale, D, 95,730; Bergland, LB, 1,002.

1980: Reagan, R, 94,598; Carter, D, 81,891; Anderson, Ind., 31,760; Commoner, Citizens, 2,316; Clark, LB, 1,900; McReynolds, Liberty Union, 136; Hall, Comm., 118; DeBerry, Soc. Workers, 75; scattered, 413.

1976: Ford, R, 100,387; Carter, D, 77,798 and Ind. Vermonters, 991 (total, 79,789); McCarthy, Ind., 4,001; Camejo, Soc. Workers, 430; LaRouche, U.S. Labor, 196; scattered, 99.

1972: Nixon, R, 117,149; McGovern, D, 68,174; Spock, Liberty Union, 1,010; Jenness, Soc. Workers, 296; scattered, 318.

1968: Nixon, R, 85,142; Humphrey, D, 70,255; Wallace, 3rd party, 5,104; Gregory, New Party, 579; Halstead, Soc. Workers, 295.

1964: Johnson, D, 107,674; Goldwater, R, 54,868.

1960: Nixon, R, 98,131; Kennedy, D, 69,186.

Virginia Vote Since 1960

2016: Clinton, D, 1,981,473; Trump, R, 1,769,443; Johnson, LB, 118,274; McMullin, Ind., 54,054; Stein, Green, 27,638.

2012: Obama, D, 1,971,820; Romney, R, 1,822,522; Johnson, LB, 31,216; Goode, Const., 13,058; Stein, Green, 8,627.

2008: Obama, D, 1,959,532; McCain, R, 1,725,005; Nader, Ind., 11,483; Barr, LB, 11,067; Baldwin, Ind. Green, 7,474; McKinney, Green, 2,344.

2004: Bush, R, 1,716,959; Kerry, D, 1,454,742; Badnarik, LB, 11,032; Peroutka, Const., 10,161.

2000: Bush, R, 1,437,490; Gore, D, 1,217,290; Nader, Green, 59,398; Browne, LB, 15,198; Buchanan, RF, 5,455; Phillips, Const., 1,809.

1996: Dole, R, 1,138,350; Clinton, D, 1,091,060; Perot, RF, 159,861; Phillips, Taxpayers, 13,687; Browne, LB, 9,174; Hagelin, Natural Law, 4,510.

1992: Bush, R, 1,150,517; Clinton, D, 1,038,650; Perot, Ind., 348,639; LaRouche, Ind., 11,937; Marrou, LB, 5,730; Fulani, New Alliance, 3,192.

1988: Bush, R, 1,309,162; Dukakis, D, 859,799; Fulani, Ind., 14,312; Paul, LB, 8,336.

1984: Reagan, R, 1,337,078; Mondale, D, 796,250.

1980: Reagan, R, 989,609; Carter, D, 752,174; Anderson, Ind., 95,418; Commoner, Citizens, 14,024; Clark, LB, 12,821; DeBerry, Soc. Workers, 1,986.

1976: Ford, R, 836,554; Carter, D, 813,896; Camejo, Soc. Workers, 17,802; Anderson, Amer., 16,686; LaRouche, U.S. Labor, 7,508; MacBride, LB, 4,648.

1972: Nixon, R, 988,493; McGovern, D, 438,887; Schmitz, Amer., 19,721; Fisher, Soc. Labor, 9,918.

1968: Nixon, R, 590,319; Humphrey, D, 442,387; Wallace, 3rd party, 320,272*; Blomen, Soc. Labor, 4,671; Gregory, Peace/Freedom, 1,680; Munn, Prohib., 601. *10,561 votes for Wallace were omitted in the count.

1964: Johnson, D, 558,038; Goldwater, R, 481,334; Hass, Soc. Labor, 2,895.

1960: Nixon, R, 404,521; Kennedy, D, 362,327; Coiner, Conservative, 4,204; Hass, Soc. Labor, 397.

Washington Vote Since 1960

2016: Clinton, D, 1,742,718; Trump, R, 1,221,747; Johnson, LB, 160,879; Stein, Green, 58,417; Castle, Const., 17,623; Kennedy, Soc. Workers, 4,307; La Riva, Socialism/Liberation, 3,523.

2012: Obama, D, 1,755,396; Romney, R, 1,290,670; Johnson, LB, 42,202; Stein, Green, 20,928; Goode, Const., 8,851; Anderson, Justice, 4,946; Lindsay, Socialism/Liberation, 1,318; Harris, Soc. Workers, 1,205.

2008: Obama, D, 1,750,848; McCain, R, 1,229,216; Nader, Ind., 29,489; Barr, LB, 12,728; Baldwin, Const., 9,432; McKinney, Green, 3,819; La Riva, Socialism/Liberation, 705; Harris, Soc. Workers, 641.

2004: Kerry, D, 1,510,201; Bush, R, 1,304,894; Nader, Ind., 23,283; Badnarik, LB, 11,955; Peroutka, Const., 3,922; Cobb, Green, 2,974; Parker, Workers World, 1,077; Harris, Soc. Workers, 547; Van Auken, Soc. Equality, 231.

2000: Gore, D, 1,247,652; Bush, R, 1,108,864; Nader, Green, 103,002; Browne, LB, 13,135; Buchanan, Freedom, 7,171; Hagelin, Natural Law, 2,927; Phillips, Const., 1,989; Moorehead, Workers World, 1,729; McReynolds, Soc., 660; Harris, Soc. Workers, 304.

1996: Clinton, D, 1,123,323; Dole, R, 840,712; Perot, RF, 201,003; Nader, Ind., 60,322; Browne, LB, 12,522; Hagelin, Natural Law, 6,076; Phillips, U.S. Taxpayers, 4,578; Collins, Ind., 2,374; Moorehead, Workers World, 2,189; Harris, Soc. Workers, 738.

1992: Clinton, D, 993,037; Bush, R, 731,234; Perot, Ind., 541,780; Marrou, LB, 7,533; Gritz, Populist/America First, 4,854; Hagelin, Natural Law, 2,456; Phillips, U.S. Taxpayers, 2,354; Fulani, New Alliance, 1,776; Daniels, Ind., 1,171.

1988: Dukakis, D, 933,516; Bush, R, 903,835; Paul, LB, 17,240; LaRouche, Ind., 4,412.

1984: Reagan, R, 1,051,670; Mondale, D, 798,352; Bergland, LB, 8,844.

1980: Reagan, R, 865,244; Carter, D, 650,193; Anderson, Ind., 185,073; Clark, LB, 29,213; Commoner, Citizens, 9,403; DeBerry, Soc. Workers, 1,137; McReynolds, Soc., 956; Hall, Comm., 834; Griswold, Workers World, 341.

1976: Ford, R, 777,732; Carter, D, 717,323; McCarthy, Ind., 36,986; Maddox, Amer. Ind., 8,585; Anderson, Amer., 5,046; MacBride, LB, 5,042; Wright, People's, 1,124; Camejo, Soc. Workers, 905; LaRouche, U.S. Labor, 903; Hall, Comm., 817; Levin, Soc. Labor, 713; Zeidler, Soc., 358.

1972: Nixon, R, 837,135; McGovern, D, 568,334; Schmitz, Amer., 58,906; Spock, Ind., 2,644; Hospers, LB, 1,537; Fisher, Soc. Labor, 1,102; Jenness, Soc. Workers, 623; Hall, Comm., 566.

1968: Humphrey, D, 616,037; Nixon, R, 588,510; Wallace, 3rd party, 96,990; Cleaver, Peace/Freedom, 1,609; Blomen, Soc. Labor, 488; Mitchell, Free Ballot, 377; Halstead, Soc. Workers, 270.

1964: Johnson, D, 779,699; Goldwater, R, 470,366; Hass, Soc. Labor, 7,772; DeBerry, Freedom Soc., 537.

1960: Nixon, R, 629,273; Kennedy, D, 599,298; Hass, Soc. Labor, 10,895; Curtis, Const., 1,401; Dobbs, Soc. Workers, 705.

West Virginia Vote Since 1960

2016: Trump, R, 489,371; Clinton, D, 188,794; Johnson, LB, 23,004; Stein, Mountain, 8,075; Castle, Const., 3,807.

2012: Romney, R, 417,655; Obama, D, 238,269; Johnson, LB, 6,302; Stein, Mountain, 4,406; Terry, NPA, 3,806.

2008: McCain, R, 397,466; Obama, D, 303,857; Nader, unaff., 7,219; Baldwin, Const., 2,465; McKinney, Mountain, 2,355.

2004: Bush, R, 423,778; Kerry, D, 326,541; Nader, Ind., 4,063; Badnarik, LB, 1,405.

2000: Bush, R, 336,475; Gore, D, 295,497; Nader, Green, 10,680; Buchanan, RF, 3,169; Browne, LB, 1,912; Hagelin, Natural Law, 367.

1996: Clinton, D, 327,812; Dole, R, 233,946; Perot, RF, 71,639; Browne, LB, 3,062.

1992: Clinton, D, 331,001; Bush, R, 241,974; Perot, Ind., 108,829; Marrou, LB, 1,873.

1988: Dukakis, D, 341,016; Bush, R, 310,065; Fulani, New Alliance, 2,230.

1984: Reagan, R, 405,483; Mondale, D, 328,125.

1980: Carter, D, 367,462; Reagan, R, 334,206; Anderson, Ind., 31,691; Clark, LB, 4,356.

1976: Carter, D, 435,864; Ford, R, 314,726.

1972: Nixon, R, 484,964; McGovern, D, 277,435.

1968: Humphrey, D, 374,091; Nixon, R, 307,555; Wallace, 3rd party, 72,560.

1964: Johnson, D, 538,087; Goldwater, R, 253,953.

1960: Kennedy, D, 441,786; Nixon, R, 395,995.

Wisconsin Vote Since 1960

2016: Trump, R, 1,405,284; Clinton, D, 1,382,536; Johnson, LB, 106,674; Stein, WI Green, 31,072; Castle, Const., 12,162; McMullin, Ind., 11,855; Moorehead, Ind., 1,770; De La Fuente, Ind., 1,502.

2012: Obama, D, 1,620,985; Romney, R, 1,407,966; Johnson, LB, 20,439; Stein, Green, 7,665; White, Soc. Equality, 553; La Riva, Socialism/Liberation, 526.

2008: Obama, D, 1,677,211; McCain, R, 1,262,393; Nader, Ind., 17,605; Barr, LB, 8,858; Baldwin, Ind., 5,072; McKinney, Green, 4,216; Wamboldt, Ind., 764; Moore, Ind., 540; La Riva, Ind., 237.

2004: Kerry, D, 1,489,504; Bush, R, 1,478,120; Nader, Ind., 16,390; Badnarik, LB, 6,464; Cobb, Green, 2,661; Brown, Ind., 471; Harris, Ind., 411.

2000: Gore, D, 1,242,987; Bush, R, 1,237,279; Nader, Green, 94,070; Buchanan, RF, 11,446; Browne, LB, 6,640; Phillips, Const., 2,042; Moorehead, Workers World, 1,063; Hagelin, RF, 878; Harris, Soc. Workers, 306.

1996: Clinton, D, 1,071,971; Dole, R, 845,029; Perot, RF, 227,339; Nader, Green, 28,723; Phillips, U.S. Taxpayers, 8,811; Browne, LB, 7,929; Hagelin, Natural Law, 1,379; Moorehead, Workers World, 1,333; Hollis, Soc., 848; Harris, Soc. Workers, 483.

1992: Clinton, D, 1,041,066; Bush, R, 930,855; Perot, Ind., 544,479; Marrou, LB, 2,877; Gritz, Populist/America First, 2,311; Daniels, Ind., 1,883; Phillips, U.S. Taxpayers, 1,772; Hagelin, Natural Law, 1,070.

1988: Dukakis, D, 1,126,794; Bush, R, 1,047,499; Paul, LB, 5,157; Duke, Populist, 3,056.

1984: Reagan, R, 1,198,584; Mondale, D, 995,740; Bergland, LB, 4,883.

1980: Reagan, R, 1,088,845; Carter, D, 981,584; Anderson, Ind., 160,657; Clark, LB, 29,135; Commoner, Citizens, 7,767; Rarick, Const., 1,519; McReynolds, Soc., 808; Hall, Comm., 772; Griswold, Workers World, 414; DeBerry, Soc. Workers, 383; scattered, 1,337.

1976: Carter, D, 1,040,232; Ford, R, 1,004,987; McCarthy, Ind., 34,943; Maddox, Amer. Ind., 8,552; Zeidler, Soc., 4,298; MacBride, LB, 3,814; Camejo, Soc. Workers, 1,691; Wright, People's, 943; Hall, Comm., 749; LaRouche, U.S. Labor, 738; Levin, Soc. Labor, 389; scattered, 2,839.

1972: Nixon, R, 989,430; McGovern, D, 810,174; Schmitz, Amer., 47,525; Spock, Ind., 2,701; Fisher, Soc. Labor, 998; Hall, Comm., 663; Reed, Ind., 506; scattered, 893.

1968: Nixon, R, 809,997; Humphrey, D, 748,804; Wallace, 3rd party, 127,835; Blomen, Soc. Labor, 1,338; Halstead, Soc. Workers, 1,222; scattered, 2,342.

1964: Johnson, D, 1,050,424; Goldwater, R, 638,495; DeBerry, Soc. Workers, 1,692; Hass, Soc. Labor, 1,204.

1960: Nixon, R, 895,175; Kennedy, D, 830,805; Dobbs, Soc. Workers, 1,792; Hass, Soc. Labor, 1,310.

Wyoming Vote Since 1960

2016: Trump, R, 174,419; Clinton, D, 55,973; Johnson, LB, 13,287; Stein, Ind., 2,515; Castle, Const., 2,042; De La Fuente, Ind., 709.

2012: Romney, R, 170,962; Obama, D, 69,286; Johnson, LB, 5,326; Goode, Const., 1,452.

2008: McCain, R, 164,958; Obama, D, 82,868; Nader, Ind., 2,525; Barr, LB, 1,594; Baldwin, Ind., 1,192.

2004: Bush, R, 167,629; Kerry, D, 70,776; Nader, Ind., 2,741; Badnarik, Ind., 1,171; Peroutka, Ind., 631.

2000: Bush, R, 147,947; Gore, D, 60,481; Buchanan, RF, 2,724; Browne, LB, 1,443; Phillips, Ind., 720; Hagelin, Natural Law, 411.

1996: Dole, R, 105,388; Clinton, D, 77,934; Perot, RF, 25,928; Browne, LB, 1,739; Hagelin, Natural Law, 582.

1992: Bush, R, 79,347; Clinton, D, 68,160; Perot, Ind., 51,263.

1988: Bush, R, 106,867; Dukakis, D, 67,113; Paul, LB, 2,026; Fulani, New Alliance, 545.

1984: Reagan, R, 133,241; Mondale, D, 53,370; Bergland, LB, 2,357.

1980: Reagan, R, 110,700; Carter, D, 49,427; Anderson, Ind., 12,072; Clark, LB, 4,514.

1976: Ford, R, 92,717; Carter, D, 62,239; McCarthy, Ind., 624; Reagan, Ind., 307; Anderson, Amer., 290; MacBride, LB, 89; Brown, Ind., 47; Maddox, Amer. Ind., 30.

1972: Nixon, R, 100,464; McGovern, D, 44,358; Schmitz, Amer., 748.

1968: Nixon, R, 70,927; Humphrey, D, 45,173; Wallace, 3rd party, 11,105.

1964: Johnson, D, 80,718; Goldwater, R, 61,998.

1960: Nixon, R, 77,451; Kennedy, D, 63,331.

UNITED STATES GOVERNMENT

EXECUTIVE BRANCH	LEGISLATIVE BRANCH	JUDICIAL BRANCH
President **Vice President** **Executive Office of the President** Council of Economic Advisers Council on Environmental Quality Executive Residence National Security Council Office of Administration Office of Management and Budget Office of National Drug Control Policy Office of Science and Technology Policy Office of the U.S. Trade Representative Office of the Vice President White House Office*	**CONGRESS** **Senate/House of Representatives** Architect of the Capitol Congressional Budget Office Government Accountability Office Government Publishing Office Library of Congress Medicare Payment Advisory Commission Stennis Center for Public Service U.S. Botanic Garden	**Supreme Court of the United States** Courts of Appeals District Courts Territorial Courts Court of International Trade Court of Federal Claims Bankruptcy Courts Tax Court Court of Appeals for the Armed Forces Court of Appeals for Veterans Claims Administrative Office of the Courts Federal Judicial Center Sentencing Commission Judicial Panel on Multidistrict Litigation

*Includes Domestic Policy Council, National Security Advisor, National Economic Council, Office of Cabinet Affairs, Office of the Chief of Staff, Office of Communications, Office of Digital Strategy, Office of the First Lady, Office of Legislative Affairs, Office of Management and Administration, Oval Office Operations, Office of Presidential Personnel, Office of Public Engagement and Intergovernmental Affairs, Office of Scheduling and Advance, Office of the Staff Secretary, and Office of the White House Counsel.

Trump Administration

1600 Pennsylvania Ave. NW, 20500; www.whitehouse.gov
As of Sept. 2020. Mailing addresses are for Washington, DC, except where otherwise noted.
Terms of office of the president and vice president: Jan. 20, 2017, to Jan. 20, 2021.

President: By law, Pres. Donald J. Trump received an annual salary of $400,000 (taxable) and an annual expense allowance of $50,000 (nontaxable) for costs resulting from official duties. This does not include amounts available for expenditures within the Executive Office of the President, including $3,850,000 for necessary expenses for the White House, up to $100,000 a year for travel expenses, and up to $19,000 for official entertainment.
Website: www.whitehouse.gov/people/donald-j-trump/
Vice President: By law, Vice Pres. Michael R. Pence received an annual salary of $253,300 (taxable) and an annual expense allowance of $20,000 for costs resulting from official duties, plus $90,000 for official entertainment expenses (nontaxable).
Website: www.whitehouse.gov/people/mike-pence/

White House Staff

Assistants to the President:
Chief of Staff: Mark Meadows
Deputy Chief of Staff for Operations: Anthony M. Ornato
Deputy Chief of Staff for Communications: Dan Scavino
Senior Adviser: Jared Kushner
Senior Adviser for Policy: Stephen Miller
Adviser to the President: Ivanka Trump
Counselor to the President: Hope Hicks, Derek S. Lyons
Counsel to the President: Pasquale A. "Pat" Cipollone
Press Secretary: Kayleigh McEnany
National Security Adviser: Robert O'Brien
Deputy National Security Adviser: Matthew F. Pottinger
Deputy Counsel for National Security Affairs: John A. Eisenberg
Acting Director of Domestic Policy Council: Brooke L. Rollins
Director of National Economic Council: Lawrence Kudlow
Acting Director of Legislative Affairs: Amy H. Swonger
Director of Oval Office Operations: Nicholas F. Luna
Director of Presidential Personnel: John D. McEntee II
Director of Strategic Communications: Alyssa A. Farah
Special Rep. for Disaster Recovery: Peter J. Brown
Special Rep. for International Negotiations: Avrahm J. Berkowitz
Trade and Manufacturing Policy: Peter Navarro
Cabinet Secretary: Kristan K. Nevins
Chief of Staff to the First Lady: Stephanie Grisham
Deputy Chief of Staff for Policy to the First Lady: Emma K. Doyle

Deputy Assistants to the President:
Domestic Policy: Jennifer Lichter
Director of Intergovernmental Affairs: Douglas Hoelscher
Director of Office of Public Liaison: Timothy Pataki
Director of Office of Administration: Monica J. Block
Director of Political Affairs: Brian Jack
Director of Presidential Advance: Robert Peede Jr.
Director of Records Management: Philip C. Droege
Director of White House Information Technology: Roger L. Stone
Principal Deputy Press Secretary: J. Hogan Gidley
Social Secretary: Anna Cristina "Rickie" Niceta

Executive Offices

Council of Economic Advisers: Tyler Goodspeed, acting chair; www.whitehouse.gov/cea/
Council on Environmental Quality: Mary B. Neumayr, chair; www.whitehouse.gov/ceq/
Office of Management and Budget: Russ Vought, dir.; www.whitehouse.gov/omb/
Office of Natl. Drug Control Policy: Jim Carroll, dir.; www.whitehouse.gov/ondcp/
Office of Science and Technology Policy: Kelvin K. Droegemeier, dir.; www.whitehouse.gov/ostp/
Office of the U.S. Trade Representative: Robert E. Lighthizer, amb.; www.ustr.gov
Office of the Director of National Intelligence (not formally an executive office): John Ratcliffe, dir.; www.dni.gov

The Cabinet

The heads of major executive departments of the federal government constitute the Cabinet. This institution, not provided for in the U.S. Constitution, developed as an advisory body out of the desire of presidents to consult on policy matters. Aside from its advisory role, the Cabinet as a body has no formal function and wields no executive authority. Individual members exercise authority as heads of their departments, reporting to the president. The Cabinet meets at times set by the president. In addition, the Cabinet commonly includes other officials designated by the president as being of Cabinet rank.

The officials so designated by Pres. Donald Trump include Vice Pres. Mike Pence, White House Chief of Staff Mark Meadows, Environmental Protection Agency Administrator Andrew Wheeler, Office of Management and Budget Director Russ Vought, Director of National Intelligence John Ratcliffe, U.S. Trade Representative Ambassador Robert Lighthizer, Central Intelligence Agency Director Gina Haspel, and Small Business Administration Administrator Jovita Carranza. The White House announced that U.S. ambassador to the United Nations would no longer be a cabinet-rank position in Dec. 2018.

Cabinet Department Heads

(As of Sept. 2020. Salary: $219,200 per year)

Secretary of State: Mike Pompeo
Secretary of the Treasury: Steven T. Mnuchin
Secretary of Defense: Mark T. Esper
Attorney General (Dept. of Justice): William P. Barr
Secretary of the Interior: David Bernhardt
Secretary of Agriculture: Sonny Perdue
Secretary of Commerce: Wilbur L. Ross Jr.
Secretary of Labor: Eugene Scalia

Secretary of Health and Human Services: Alex Azar
Secretary of Housing and Urban Development: Ben Carson
Secretary of Transportation: Elaine L. Chao
Secretary of Energy: Dan Brouillette
Secretary of Education: Betsy DeVos
Secretary of Veterans Affairs: Robert Wilkie
Secretary of Homeland Security: vacant (Chad Wolf, acting)

Cabinet-Level Departments

Department mailing address applies to subordinate bureaus/agencies unless otherwise noted. Mailing addresses are for Washington, DC, except where otherwise noted.

Department of State

2201 C St. NW, 20520; www.state.gov

The Dept. of Foreign Affairs was created by act of Congress on July 27, 1789, and the name changed to Dept. of State on Sept. 15, 1789. Conducts U.S. foreign policy. The Foreign Service protects American citizens and interests through embassies in some 180 countries. Maintains contact with foreign governments, negotiates agreements and treaties, and supports U.S. foreign trade. Promotes democracy, international security, human rights—including issues related to AIDS, human trafficking, war crimes, and migration—and arms and narcotics control. Represents the nation in international organizations. Issues passports to U.S. citizens and visas to foreigners. **Budget:** $27.1 bil (2017); $26.4 bil (2018); $28.0 bil (2019); $32.2 bil (2020 est.); $26.5 bil (2021 est.). Budget for other intl. programs: $18.9 bil (2017); $21.6 bil (2018); $23.6 bil (2019); $25.7 bil (2020 est.); $34.7 bil (2021 est.).

Secretaries of State

President	Secretary	Home	Sworn in
Washington	Thomas Jefferson	VA	1789
	Edmund J. Randolph	VA	1794
	Timothy Pickering	PA	1795
Adams, J.	Timothy Pickering	PA	1797
	John Marshall	VA	1800
Jefferson	James Madison	VA	1801
Madison	Robert Smith	MD	1809
	James Monroe	VA	1811
Monroe	John Quincy Adams	MA	1817
Adams, J. Q.	Henry Clay	KY	1825
Jackson	Martin Van Buren	NY	1829
	Edward Livingston	LA	1831
	Louis McLane	DE	1833
	John Forsyth	GA	1834
Van Buren	John Forsyth	GA	1837
Harrison, W. H.	Daniel Webster	MA	1841
Tyler	Daniel Webster	MA	1841
	Abel P. Upshur	VA	1843
	John C. Calhoun	SC	1844
Polk	John C. Calhoun	SC	1845
	James Buchanan	PA	1845
Taylor	James Buchanan	PA	1849
	John M. Clayton	DE	1849
Fillmore	John M. Clayton	DE	1850
	Daniel Webster	MA	1850
	Edward Everett	MA	1852
Pierce	William L. Marcy	NY	1853
Buchanan	William L. Marcy	NY	1857
	Lewis Cass	MI	1857
	Jeremiah S. Black	PA	1860
Lincoln	Jeremiah S. Black	PA	1861
	William H. Seward	NY	1861
Johnson, A.	William H. Seward	NY	1865
Grant	Elihu B. Washburne	IL	1869
	Hamilton Fish	NY	1869
Hayes	Hamilton Fish	NY	1877
	William M. Evarts	NY	1877
Garfield	William M. Evarts	NY	1881
	James G. Blaine	ME	1881
Arthur	James G. Blaine	ME	1881
	F. T. Frelinghuysen	NJ	1881
Cleveland	F. T. Frelinghuysen	NJ	1885
	Thomas F. Bayard	DE	1885
Harrison, B.	Thomas F. Bayard	DE	1889
	James G. Blaine	ME	1889
	John W. Foster	IN	1892
Cleveland	Walter Q. Gresham	IN	1893
	Richard Olney	MA	1895
McKinley	Richard Olney	MA	1897
	John Sherman	OH	1897
	William R. Day	OH	1898
	John M. Hay	DC	1898
Roosevelt, T.	John M. Hay	DC	1901
	Elihu Root	NY	1905
	Robert Bacon	NY	1909
Taft	Robert Bacon	NY	1909
	Philander C. Knox	PA	1909

President	Secretary	Home	Sworn in
Wilson	Philander C. Knox	PA	1913
	William J. Bryan	NE	1913
	Robert Lansing	NY	1915
	Bainbridge Colby	NY	1920
Harding	Charles E. Hughes	NY	1921
Coolidge	Charles E. Hughes	NY	1923
	Frank B. Kellogg	MN	1925
Hoover	Frank B. Kellogg	MN	1929
	Henry L. Stimson	NY	1929
Roosevelt, F. D.	Cordell Hull	TN	1933
	Edward R. Stettinius Jr.	VA	1944
Truman	Edward R. Stettinius Jr.	VA	1945
	James F. Byrnes	SC	1945
	George C. Marshall	PA	1947
	Dean G. Acheson	CT	1949
Eisenhower	John Foster Dulles	NY	1953
	Christian A. Herter	MA	1959
Kennedy	D. Dean Rusk	GA	1961
Johnson, L. B.	D. Dean Rusk	GA	1963
Nixon	William P. Rogers	NY	1969
	Henry A. Kissinger	DC	1973
Ford	Henry A. Kissinger	DC	1974
Carter	Cyrus R. Vance	NY	1977
	Edmund S. Muskie	ME	1980
Reagan	Alexander M. Haig Jr.	CT	1981
	George P. Shultz	CA	1982
Bush, G. H. W.	James A. Baker III	TX	1989
	Lawrence S. Eagleburger	MI	1992
Clinton	Warren M. Christopher	CA	1993
	Madeleine K. Albright	DC	1997
Bush, G. W.	Colin L. Powell	NY	2001
	Condoleezza Rice	AL	2005
Obama	Hillary Rodham Clinton	NY	2009
	John Kerry	MA	2013
Trump	Rex W. Tillerson	TX	2017
	Mike Pompeo	KS	2018

Department of the Treasury

1500 Pennsylvania Ave. NW, 20220; www.treasury.gov

Organized by act of Congress on Sept. 2, 1789. Responsible for the fiscal affairs of the U.S. Serves as the government's financial agent; collects, borrows, and disburses funds for the federal government. Monitors the nation's financial infrastructure and economic development; recommends domestic and international financial, monetary, economic, trade, and tax policies. Manufactures currency and coins. Carries out monetary and tax law enforcement activities, sanctions, embargoes, and fights illicit finance—counterfeiting, money laundering, narcotics trafficking, terrorist financing. **Budget** (including interest on the public debt): $546.4 bil (2017); $629.5 bil (2018); $689.5 bil (2019); $701.0 bil (2020 est.); $690.7 bil (2021 est.).

- Alcohol and Tobacco Tax and Trade Bureau (1310 G St. NW, Box 12, 20005); www.ttb.gov
- Bureau of Engraving and Printing (14th and C Sts. SW, 20228); www.moneyfactory.gov
- Bureau of the Fiscal Service (401 14th St. SW, 20227); www.fiscal.treasury.gov
- Financial Crimes Enforcement Network; www.fincen.gov
- Internal Revenue Service (1111 Constitution Ave. NW, 20224); www.irs.gov
- U.S. Mint (801 9th St. NW, 20220); www.usmint.gov

Secretaries of the Treasury

President	Secretary	Home	Sworn in
Washington	Alexander Hamilton	NY	1789
	Oliver Wolcott Jr.	CT	1795
Adams, J.	Oliver Wolcott Jr.	CT	1797
	Samuel Dexter	MA	1801
Jefferson	Samuel Dexter	MA	1801
	Albert Gallatin	PA	1801
Madison	Albert Gallatin	PA	1809
	George W. Campbell	TN	1814
	Alexander J. Dallas	PA	1814
	William H. Crawford	GA	1816
Monroe	William H. Crawford	GA	1817
Adams, J. Q.	Richard Rush	PA	1825

President	Secretary	Home	Sworn in
Jackson	Samuel D. Ingham	PA	1829
	Louis McLane	DE	1831
	William J. Duane	PA	1833
	Roger B. Taney	MD	1833
	Levi Woodbury	NH	1834
Van Buren	Levi Woodbury	NH	1837
Harrison, W. H.	Thomas Ewing	OH	1841
Tyler	Thomas Ewing	OH	1841
	Walter Forward	PA	1841
	John C. Spencer	NY	1843
	George M. Bibb	KY	1844
Polk	Robert J. Walker	MS	1845
Taylor	William M. Meredith	PA	1849
Fillmore	Thomas Corwin	OH	1850
Pierce	James Guthrie	KY	1853
Buchanan	Howell Cobb	GA	1857
	Phillip F. Thomas	MD	1860
	John A. Dix	NY	1861
Lincoln	Salmon P. Chase	OH	1861
	William P. Fessenden	ME	1864
	Hugh McCulloch	IN	1865
Johnson, A.	Hugh McCulloch	IN	1865
Grant	George S. Boutwell	MA	1869
	William A. Richardson	MA	1873
	Benjamin H. Bristow	KY	1874
	Lot M. Morrill	ME	1876
Hayes	John Sherman	OH	1877
Garfield	William Windom	MN	1881
Arthur	Charles J. Folger	NY	1881
	Walter Q. Gresham	IN	1884
	Hugh McCulloch	IN	1884
Cleveland	Daniel Manning	NY	1885
	Charles S. Fairchild	NY	1887
Harrison, B.	William Windom	MN	1889
	Charles Foster	OH	1891
Cleveland	John G. Carlisle	KY	1893
McKinley	Lyman J. Gage	IL	1897
Roosevelt, T.	Lyman J. Gage	IL	1901
	Leslie M. Shaw	IA	1902
	George B. Cortelyou	NY	1907
Taft	Franklin MacVeagh	IL	1909
Wilson	William G. McAdoo	NY	1913
	Carter Glass	VA	1918
	David F. Houston	MO	1920
Harding	Andrew W. Mellon	PA	1921
Coolidge	Andrew W. Mellon	PA	1923
Hoover	Andrew W. Mellon	PA	1929
	Ogden L. Mills	NY	1932
Roosevelt, F. D.	William H. Woodin	NY	1933
	Henry Morgenthau Jr.	NY	1934
Truman	Fred M. Vinson	KY	1945
	John W. Snyder	MO	1946
Eisenhower	George M. Humphrey	OH	1953
	Robert B. Anderson	CT	1957
Kennedy	C. Douglas Dillon	NJ	1961
Johnson, L. B.	C. Douglas Dillon	NJ	1963
	Henry H. Fowler	VA	1965
	Joseph W. Barr	IN	1968
Nixon	David M. Kennedy	IL	1969
	John B. Connally	TX	1971
	George P. Shultz	IL	1972
	William E. Simon	NJ	1974
Ford	William E. Simon	NJ	1974
Carter	W. Michael Blumenthal	MI	1977
	G. William Miller	RI	1979
Reagan	Donald T. Rogan	NY	1981
	James A. Baker III	TX	1985
	Nicholas F. Brady	NJ	1988
Bush, G. H. W.	Nicholas F. Brady	NJ	1989
Clinton	Lloyd M. Bentsen	TX	1993
	Robert E. Rubin	NY	1995
	Lawrence H. Summers	CT	1999
Bush, G. W.	Paul H. O'Neill	MO	2001
	John W. Snow	OH	2003
	Henry M. Paulson Jr.	FL	2006
Obama	Timothy F. Geithner	NY	2009
	Jack Lew	NY	2013
Trump	Steven T. Mnuchin	NY	2017

Department of Defense

1400 Defense Pentagon, 20301; www.defense.gov

The Dept. of Defense, originally designated the National Military Establishment, was created on Sept. 18, 1947. Directs and controls the armed forces and assists the president in protecting the nation's security. Military departments of the Army, Navy, and Air Force are each separately organized under its own secretary but all function under the command of the secretary of defense. They conduct military operations as unified commands. The chairman of the Joint Chiefs of Staff is the principal military adviser to the president. Undersecretaries supervise acquisition, technology, and logistics; intelligence; personnel and readiness; and policy. **Budget** for military programs: $568.9 bil (2017); $600.7 bil (2018); $654.0 bil (2019); $689.6 bil (2020 est.); $729.3 bil (2021 est.). **Budget** for civil programs: $65.1 bil (2017); $60.4 bil (2018); $67.4 bil (2019); $70.1 bil (2020 est.); $70.9 bil (2021 est.).

- Def. Advanced Research Projects Agency (675 N. Randolph St., Arlington, VA 22203); www.darpa.mil
- Def. Intelligence Agency (200 MacDill Blvd., 20340); www.dia.mil
- Def. Security Cooperation Agency (201 Twelfth St. South, Ste. 203, Arlington, VA 22202); www.dsca.mil
- Missile Def. Agency (5700 18th St., Bldg. 245, Fort Belvoir, VA 22060); www.mda.mil
- Natl. Geospatial-Intelligence Agency (7500 GEOINT Dr., MS N73-OCCAE, Springfield, VA 22150); www.nga.mil
- Natl. Security Agency/Central Security Service (Ft. Meade, MD 20755); www.nsa.gov

Secretaries of Defense

President	Secretary	Home	Sworn in
Truman	James V. Forrestal	NY	1947
	Louis A. Johnson	WV	1949
	George C. Marshall	PA	1950
	Robert A. Lovett	NY	1951
Eisenhower	Charles E. Wilson	MI	1953
	Neil H. McElroy	OH	1957
	Thomas S. Gates Jr.	PA	1959
Kennedy	Robert S. McNamara	MI	1961
Johnson, L. B.	Robert S. McNamara	MI	1963
	Clark M. Clifford	MD	1968
Nixon	Melvin R. Laird	WI	1969
	Elliot L. Richardson	MA	1973
	James R. Schlesinger	VA	1973
Ford	James R. Schlesinger	VA	1974
	Donald H. Rumsfeld	IL	1975
Carter	Harold Brown	CA	1977
Reagan	Caspar W. Weinberger	CA	1981
	Frank C. Carlucci	PA	1987
Bush, G. H. W.	Richard B. Cheney	WY	1989
Clinton	Les Aspin	WI	1993
	William J. Perry	CA	1994
	William S. Cohen	ME	1997
Bush, G. W.	Donald H. Rumsfeld	IL	2001
	Robert M. Gates	TX	2006
Obama	Robert M. Gates	TX	2009
	Leon E. Panetta	CA	2011
	Chuck Hagel	NE	2013
	Ashton Carter	PA	2015
Trump	James Mattis	WA	2017
	Mark T. Esper	PA	2019

Secretaries of War

The War Dept. (which included jurisdiction over the Navy until 1798) was created by act of Congress on Aug. 7, 1789.

President	Secretary	Home	Sworn in
Washington	Henry Knox	MA	1789
	Timothy Pickering	PA	1795
	James McHenry	MD	1796
Adams, J.	James McHenry	MD	1797
	Samuel Dexter	MA	1800
Jefferson	Henry Dearborn	MA	1801
Madison	William Eustis	MA	1809
	John Armstrong	NY	1813
	James Monroe	VA	1814
	William H. Crawford	GA	1815
Monroe	John C. Calhoun	SC	1817
Adams, J. Q.	James Barbour	VA	1825
	Peter B. Porter	NY	1828
Jackson	John H. Eaton	TN	1829
	Lewis Cass	MI	1831
	Benjamin F. Butler	NY	1837
Van Buren	Joel R. Poinsett	SC	1837
Harrison, W. H.	John Bell	TN	1841
Tyler	John Bell	TN	1841
	John C. Spencer	NY	1841
	James M. Porter	PA	1843
	William Wilkins	PA	1844
Polk	William L. Marcy	NY	1845
Taylor	George W. Crawford	GA	1849
Fillmore	Charles M. Conrad	LA	1850

President	Secretary	Home	Sworn in
Pierce	Jefferson Davis	MS	1853
Buchanan	John B. Floyd	VA	1857
	Joseph Holt	KY	1861
Lincoln	Simon Cameron	PA	1861
	Edwin M. Stanton	PA	1862
Johnson, A.	Edwin M. Stanton	PA	1865
	John M. Schofield	IL	1868
Grant	John A. Rawlins	IL	1869
	William T. Sherman	OH	1869
	William W. Belknap	IA	1869
	Alphonso Taft	OH	1876
	James D. Cameron	PA	1876
Hayes	George W. McCrary	IA	1877
	Alexander Ramsey	MN	1879
Garfield	Robert T. Lincoln	IL	1881
Arthur	Robert T. Lincoln	IL	1881
Cleveland	William C. Endicott	MA	1885
Harrison, B.	Redfield Proctor	VT	1889
	Stephen B. Elkins	WV	1891
Cleveland	Daniel S. Lamont	NY	1893
McKinley	Russell A. Alger	MI	1897
	Elihu Root	NY	1899
Roosevelt, T.	Elihu Root	NY	1901
	William H. Taft	OH	1904
	Luke E. Wright	TN	1908
Taft	Jacob M. Dickinson	TN	1909
	Henry L. Stimson	NY	1911
Wilson	Lindley M. Garrison	NJ	1913
	Newton D. Baker	OH	1916
Harding	John W. Weeks	MA	1921
Coolidge	John W. Weeks	MA	1923
	Dwight F. Davis	MO	1925
Hoover	James W. Good	IL	1929
	Patrick J. Hurley	OK	1929
Roosevelt, F. D.	George H. Dern	UT	1933
	Harry H. Woodring	KS	1937
	Henry L. Stimson	NY	1940
Truman	Robert P. Patterson	NY	1945
	Kenneth C. Royall[1]	NC	1947

(1) Last member of Cabinet with this title. The War Dept. became the Dept. of the Army with the creation of the Defense Dept. in 1947, though the Army secretary maintained Cabinet-level status until 1949.

Secretaries of the Navy

The Navy Dept. was created by act of Congress on Apr. 30, 1798. The Marine Corps is part of this department.

President	Secretary	Home	Sworn in
Adams, J.	Benjamin Stoddert	MD	1798
Jefferson	Benjamin Stoddert	MD	1801
	Robert Smith	MD	1801
Madison	Paul Hamilton	SC	1809
	William Jones	PA	1813
	Benjamin W. Crowninshield	MA	1814
Monroe	Benjamin W. Crowninshield	MA	1817
	Smith Thompson	NY	1818
	Samuel L. Southard	NJ	1823
Adams, J. Q.	Samuel L. Southard	NJ	1825
Jackson	John Branch	NC	1829
	Levi Woodbury	NH	1831
	Mahlon Dickerson	NJ	1834
Van Buren	Mahlon Dickerson	NJ	1837
	James K. Paulding	NY	1838
Harrison, W. H.	George E. Badger	NC	1841
Tyler	George E. Badger	NC	1841
	Abel P. Upshur	VA	1841
	David Henshaw	MA	1843
	Thomas W. Gilmer	VA	1844
	John Y. Mason	VA	1844
Polk	George Bancroft	MA	1845
	John Y. Mason	VA	1846
Taylor	William B. Preston	VA	1849
Fillmore	William A. Graham	NC	1850
	John P. Kennedy	MD	1852
Pierce	James C. Dobbin	NC	1853
Buchanan	Isaac Toucey	CT	1857
Lincoln	Gideon Welles	CT	1861
Johnson, A.	Gideon Welles	CT	1865
Grant	Adolph E. Borie	PA	1869
	George M. Robeson	NJ	1869
Hayes	Richard W. Thompson	IN	1877
	Nathan Goff Jr.	WV	1881
Garfield	William H. Hunt	LA	1881
Arthur	William E. Chandler	NH	1882

President	Secretary	Home	Sworn in
Cleveland	William C. Whitney	NY	1885
Harrison, B.	Benjamin F. Tracy	NY	1889
Cleveland	Hilary A. Herbert	AL	1893
McKinley	John D. Long	MA	1897
Roosevelt, T.	John D. Long	MA	1901
	William H. Moody	MA	1902
	Paul Morton	IL	1904
	Charles J. Bonaparte	MD	1905
	Victor H. Metcalf	CA	1906
	Truman H. Newberry	MI	1908
Taft	George von L. Meyer	MA	1909
Wilson	Josephus Daniels	NC	1913
Harding	Edwin Denby	MI	1921
Coolidge	Edwin Denby	MI	1923
	Curtis D. Wilbur	CA	1924
Hoover	Charles Francis Adams	MA	1929
Roosevelt, F. D.	Claude A. Swanson	VA	1933
	Charles Edison	NJ	1940
	Frank Knox	IL	1940
	James V. Forrestal	NY	1944
Truman	James V. Forrestal[1]	NY	1945

(1) Last member of Cabinet with this title. The Navy Dept. became a branch of the Dept. of Defense when the latter was created in 1947, though the Navy secretary maintained Cabinet-level status until 1949.

Department of Justice

950 Pennsylvania Ave. NW, 20530; www.justice.gov

The Office of Attorney General was established by act of Congress on Sept. 24, 1789. It officially reached Cabinet rank in Mar. 1792, when the first attorney general, Edmund Randolph, attended his initial Cabinet meeting. The Dept. of Justice, headed by the attorney general, was created June 22, 1870. Provides for the enforcement of federal laws and investigation of violations; furnishes legal counsel in cases involving the federal government and interprets laws relating to the activities of other federal departments; supervises federal penal institutions. The attorney general and Office of Legal Counsel render legal advice, upon request, to the president and department heads. The solicitor general conducts all suits brought before the U.S. Supreme Court in which the federal government is concerned. The Civil Division represents the U.S. government in many civil or criminal matters. The 93 U.S. attorneys (for 94 federal districts) are the principal litigators in the U.S. and its territories. **Budget:** $31.0 bil (2017); $34.5 bil (2018); $35.1 bil (2019); $45.3 bil (2020 est.); $41.1 bil (2021 est.).

- Bureau of Alcohol, Tobacco, Firearms and Explosives (99 New York Ave. NE, 20226); www.atf.gov
- Drug Enforcement Admin. (8701 Morrissette Dr., Springfield, VA 22152); www.dea.gov
- Executive Office for Immigration Review (5107 Leesburg Pike, Ste. 1902, Falls Church, VA 22041); www.usdoj.gov/eoir
- Federal Bureau of Investigation (935 Pennsylvania Ave. NW, 20535); www.fbi.gov
- Federal Bureau of Prisons (320 First St. NW, 20534); www.bop.gov
- Foreign Claims Settlement Commission (441 G St. NW, Rm. 6330, 20579); www.justice.gov/fcsc
- INTERPOL Washington (U.S. Natl. Central Bureau) (20530); www.justice.gov/interpol-washington
- Office of Community Oriented Policing Services (935 N. St. NE, 20530); www.cops.usdoj.gov
- Office of Justice Programs (810 Seventh St. NW, 20531); www.ojp.gov
- Office on Violence Against Women (145 N St. NE, Ste. 10W-121, 20530); www.justice.gov/ovw
- U.S. Marshals Service (20530); www.usmarshals.gov
- U.S. Parole Commission (90 K St. NE, 3rd Fl., 20530); www.justice.gov/uspc

Attorneys General

President	Attorney General	Home	Sworn in
Washington	Edmund J. Randolph	VA	1789
	William Bradford	PA	1794
	Charles Lee	VA	1795
Adams, J.	Charles Lee	VA	1797
Jefferson	Levi Lincoln	MA	1801
	John Breckenridge	KY	1805
	Caesar A. Rodney	DE	1807
Madison	Caesar A. Rodney	DE	1807
	William Pinkney	MD	1811
	Richard Rush	PA	1814

President	Attorney General	Home	Sworn in
Monroe	Richard Rush	PA	1817
	William Wirt	VA	1817
Adams, J. Q.	William Wirt	VA	1825
Jackson	John M. Berrien	GA	1829
	Roger B. Taney	MD	1831
	Benjamin F. Butler	NY	1833
Van Buren	Benjamin F. Butler	NY	1837
	Felix Grundy	TN	1838
	Henry D. Gilpin	PA	1840
Harrison, W. H.	John J. Crittenden	KY	1841
Tyler	John J. Crittenden	KY	1841
	Hugh S. Legaré	SC	1841
	John Nelson	MD	1843
Polk	John Y. Mason	VA	1845
	Nathan Clifford	ME	1846
	Isaac Toucey	CT	1848
Taylor	Reverdy Johnson	MD	1849
Fillmore	John J. Crittenden	KY	1850
Pierce	Caleb Cushing	MA	1853
Buchanan	Jeremiah S. Black	PA	1857
	Edwin M. Stanton	PA	1860
Lincoln	Edward Bates	MO	1861
	James Speed	KY	1864
Johnson, A.	James Speed	KY	1865
	Henry Stanbery	OH	1866
	William M. Evarts	NY	1868
Grant	Ebenezer R. Hoar	MA	1869
	Amos T. Akerman	GA	1870
	George H. Williams	OR	1871
	Edwards Pierrepont	NY	1875
	Alphonso Taft	OH	1876
Hayes	Charles Devens	MA	1877
Garfield	I. Wayne MacVeagh	PA	1881
Arthur	Benjamin H. Brewster	PA	1882
Cleveland	Augustus H. Garland	AR	1885
Harrison, B.	William H. H. Miller	IN	1889
Cleveland	Richard Olney	MA	1893
	Judson Harmon	OH	1895
McKinley	Joseph McKenna	CA	1897
	John W. Griggs	NJ	1898
	Philander C. Knox	PA	1901
Roosevelt, T.	Philander C. Knox	PA	1901
	William H. Moody	MA	1904
	Charles J. Bonaparte	MD	1906
Taft	George W. Wickersham	NY	1909
Wilson	James C. McReynolds	TN	1913
	Thomas W. Gregory	TX	1914
	A. Mitchell Palmer	PA	1919
Harding	Harry M. Daugherty	OH	1921
Coolidge	Harry M. Daugherty	OH	1923
	Harlan F. Stone	NY	1924
	John G. Sargent	VT	1925
Hoover	William D. Mitchell	MN	1929
Roosevelt, F. D.	Homer S. Cummings	CT	1933
	Frank Murphy	MI	1939
	Robert H. Jackson	NY	1940
	Francis Biddle	PA	1941
Truman	Thomas C. Clark	TX	1945
	J. Howard McGrath	RI	1949
	James P. McGranery	PA	1952
Eisenhower	Herbert Brownell Jr.	NY	1953
	William P. Rogers	MD	1957
Kennedy	Robert F. Kennedy	MA	1961
Johnson, L. B.	Robert F. Kennedy	MA	1963
	Nicholas Katzenbach	IL	1964
	W. Ramsey Clark	TX	1967
Nixon	John N. Mitchell	NY	1969
	Richard G. Kleindienst	AZ	1972
	Elliot L. Richardson	MA	1973
	William B. Saxbe	OH	1974
Ford	William B. Saxbe	OH	1974
	Edward H. Levi	IL	1975
Carter	Griffin B. Bell	GA	1977
	Benjamin R. Civiletti	MD	1979
Reagan	William French Smith	CA	1981
	Edwin Meese III	CA	1985
	Richard L. Thornburgh	PA	1988
Bush, G. H. W.	Richard L. Thornburgh	PA	1989
	William P. Barr	NY	1991
Clinton	Janet Reno	FL	1993
Bush, G. W.	John Ashcroft	MO	2001
	Alberto R. Gonzales	TX	2005
	Michael B. Mukasey	NY	2007
Obama	Eric H. Holder Jr.	DC	2009
	Loretta E. Lynch	NY	2015
Trump	Jeff Sessions	AL	2017
	William P. Barr	NY	2019

Department of the Interior

1849 C St. NW, 20240; www.doi.gov

Created by act of Congress on Mar. 3, 1849. Custodian of natural resources. Has the responsibility of protecting and conserving the country's land, water, minerals, fish, and wildlife; of promoting the wise use of all these natural resources; of maintaining national parks and recreation areas; and of preserving historic places. It also provides for the welfare of American Indian reservation communities and of inhabitants of island territories under U.S. administration. **Budget:** $12.2 bil (2017); $13.2 bil (2018); $13.9 bil (2019); $17.5 bil (2020 est.); $16.2 bil (2021 est.).

- Bureau of Indian Affairs; www.bia.gov
- Bureau of Indian Education; www.bie.edu
- Bureau of Land Management; www.blm.gov
- Bureau of Ocean Energy Management; www.boem.gov
- Bureau of Reclamation; www.usbr.gov
- Bureau of Safety and Environmental Enforcement; www.bsee.gov
- National Park Service; www.nps.gov
- Office of Surface Mining Reclamation and Enforcement (1849 C St. NW, 20240); www.osmre.gov
- U.S. Fish and Wildlife Service; www.fws.gov
- U.S. Geological Survey (12201 Sunrise Valley Dr., Reston, VA 20192); www.usgs.gov

Secretaries of the Interior

President	Secretary	Home	Sworn in
Taylor	Thomas Ewing	OH	1849
Fillmore	Thomas M. T. McKennan	PA	1850
	Alex H. H. Stuart	VA	1850
Pierce	Robert McClelland	MI	1853
Buchanan	Jacob Thompson	MS	1857
Lincoln	Caleb B. Smith	IN	1861
	John P. Usher	IN	1863
Johnson, A.	John P. Usher	IN	1865
	James Harlan	IA	1865
	Orville H. Browning	IL	1866
Grant	Jacob D. Cox	OH	1869
	Columbus Delano	OH	1870
	Zachariah Chandler	MI	1875
Hayes	Carl Schurz	MO	1877
Garfield	Samuel J. Kirkwood	IA	1881
Arthur	Henry M. Teller	CO	1882
Cleveland	Lucius Q. C. Lamar	MS	1885
	William F. Vilas	WI	1888
Harrison, B.	John W. Noble	MO	1889
Cleveland	M. Hoke Smith	GA	1893
	David R. Francis	MO	1896
McKinley	Cornelius N. Bliss	NY	1897
	Ethan A. Hitchcock	MO	1898
Roosevelt, T.	Ethan A. Hitchcock	MO	1901
	James R. Garfield	OH	1907
Taft	Richard A. Ballinger	WA	1909
	Walter L. Fisher	IL	1911
Wilson	Franklin K. Lane	CA	1913
	John B. Payne	IL	1920
Harding	Albert B. Fall	NM	1921
	Hubert Work	CO	1923
Coolidge	Hubert Work	CO	1923
	Roy O. West	IL	1929
Hoover	Ray Lyman Wilbur	CA	1929
Roosevelt, F. D.	Harold L. Ickes	IL	1933
Truman	Harold L. Ickes	IL	1945
	Julius A. Krug	WI	1946
	Oscar L. Chapman	CO	1949
Eisenhower	Douglas McKay	OR	1953
	Fred A. Seaton	NE	1956
Kennedy	Stewart L. Udall	AZ	1961
Johnson, L. B.	Stewart L. Udall	AZ	1963
Nixon	Walter J. Hickel	AK	1969
	Rogers C. B. Morton	MD	1971
Ford	Rogers C. B. Morton	MD	1971
	Stanley K. Hathaway	WY	1975
	Thomas S. Kleppe	ND	1975
Carter	Cecil D. Andrus	ID	1977
Reagan	James G. Watt	CO	1981
	William P. Clark	CA	1983
	Donald P. Hodel	OR	1985
Bush, G. H. W.	Manuel Lujan	NM	1989
Clinton	Bruce Babbitt	AZ	1993
Bush, G. W.	Gale Norton	CO	2001
	Dirk Kempthorne	ID	2006
Obama	Kenneth L. Salazar	CO	2009
	Sally Jewell	WA	2013
Trump	Ryan Zinke	MT	2017
	David Bernhardt	CO	2019

Department of Agriculture

1400 Independence Ave. SW, 20250; www.usda.gov

Created by act of Congress on May 15, 1862. On Feb. 8, 1889, its commissioner was renamed secretary of agriculture and became a member of the Cabinet. Provides leadership on food, agriculture, and natural resources; supports scientific research and education for agriculture, nutrition, and food safety. Develops nutrition assistance programs, promotes healthy eating, supplies food stamps, grades and inspects the commercial supply of food. Responsible for the health of the land through sustainable management and conservation, manages public lands in national forests and grasslands; safeguards against invasive pests and diseases; ensures the health and care of animals and plants. Oversees assistance and conservation programs for farmers and ranchers and programs to improve the rural economy and quality of life. Facilitates domestic and international marketing of U.S. agricultural products. **Budget:** $127.6 bil (2017); $136.7 bil (2018); $150.1 bil (2019); $154.6 bil (2020 est.); $129.2 bil (2021 est.).

- Agricultural Research Service; www.ars.usda.gov
- Economic Research Service; www.ers.usda.gov
- Food and Nutrition Service (1320 Braddock Pl., Alexandria, VA 22314); www.fns.usda.gov
- Food Safety and Inspection Service; www.fsis.usda.gov
- Foreign Agricultural Service; www.fas.usda.gov
- Natl. Agricultural Statistics Service; www.nass.usda.gov
- Natural Resources Conservation Service; www.nrcs.usda.gov
- U.S. Forest Service; www.fs.usda.gov

Secretaries of Agriculture

President	Secretary	Home	Sworn in
Cleveland	Norman J. Colman	MO	1889
Harrison, B.	Jeremiah M. Rusk	WI	1889
Cleveland	J. Sterling Morton	NE	1893
McKinley	James Wilson	IA	1897
Roosevelt, T.	James Wilson	IA	1901
Taft	James Wilson	IA	1909
Wilson	David F. Houston	MO	1913
	Edwin T. Meredith	IA	1920
Harding	Henry C. Wallace	IA	1921
Coolidge	Henry C. Wallace	IA	1923
	Howard M. Gore	WV	1924
	William M. Jardine	KS	1925
Hoover	Arthur M. Hyde	MO	1929
Roosevelt, F. D.	Henry A. Wallace	IA	1933
	Claude R. Wickard	IN	1940
Truman	Clinton P. Anderson	NM	1945
	Charles F. Brannan	CO	1948
Eisenhower	Ezra Taft Benson	UT	1953
Kennedy	Orville L. Freeman	MN	1961
Johnson, L. B.	Orville L. Freeman	MN	1963
Nixon	Clifford M. Hardin	IN	1969
	Earl L. Butz	IN	1971
Ford	Earl L. Butz	IN	1974
	John A. Knebel	VA	1976
Carter	Bob Bergland	MN	1977
Reagan	John R. Block	IL	1981
	Richard E. Lyng	CA	1986
Bush, G. H. W.	Clayton K. Yeutter	NE	1989
	Edward Madigan	IL	1991
Clinton	Mike Espy	MS	1993
	Dan Glickman	KS	1995
Bush, G. W.	Ann M. Veneman	CA	2001
	Mike Johanns	NE	2005
	Ed Schafer	ND	2008
Obama	Thomas J. Vilsack	IA	2009
Trump	Sonny Perdue	GA	2017

Department of Commerce

1401 Constitution Ave. NW, 20230; www.commerce.gov

The Dept. of Commerce was formed by Congress Mar. 4, 1913, when it divided the Dept. of Commerce and Labor into two departments. Fosters, serves, and promotes the nation's economic development and technological advancement; supports the comprehension and use of the environment and its oceanic life; assists states, communities, and individuals with economic progress; promotes trade abroad and ensures an effective export control and treaty compliance system. Issues trademarks and patents, maintains measurement standards, and manages the federal telecommunications spectrum. Collects, analyzes, and distributes statistics regarding the nation and the economy through the Bureaus of the Census and of Economic Analysis. NOAA explores, monitors, and conserves oceans and coasts, tracks weather and other environmental data. **Budget:** $10.3 bil (2017); $8.6 bil (2018); $11.3 bil (2019); $17.1 bil (2020 est.); $12.2 bil (2021 est.).

- Bureau of Economic Analysis (4600 Silver Hill Rd., Suitland, MD 20746); www.bea.gov
- Minority Business Development Agency; www.mbda.gov
- Natl. Institute of Standards and Technology (100 Bureau Dr., Gaithersburg, MD 20899); www.nist.gov
- Natl. Oceanic and Atmospheric Admin.; www.noaa.gov
- Natl. Technical Information Service (5301 Shawnee Rd., Alexandria, VA 22312); www.ntis.gov
- Natl. Telecommunications and Information Admin.; www.ntia.doc.gov
- U.S. Census Bureau (4600 Silver Hill Rd., 20233); www.census.gov
- U.S. Patent and Trademark Office (600 Dulany St., Alexandria, VA 22314); www.uspto.gov

Secretaries of Commerce

President	Secretary	Home	Sworn in
Wilson	William C. Redfield	NY	1913
	Joshua W. Alexander	MO	1919
Harding	Herbert C. Hoover	CA	1921
Coolidge	Herbert C. Hoover	CA	1923
	William F. Whiting	MA	1928
Hoover	Robert P. Lamont	IL	1929
	Roy D. Chapin	MI	1932
Roosevelt, F. D.	Daniel C. Roper	SC	1933
	Harry L. Hopkins	NY	1939
	Jesse H. Jones	TX	1940
	Henry A. Wallace	IA	1945
Truman	Henry A. Wallace	IA	1945
	W. Averell Harriman	NY	1947
	Charles W. Sawyer	OH	1948
Eisenhower	Sinclair Weeks	MA	1953
	Lewis L. Strauss	NY	1958
	Frederick H. Mueller	MI	1959
Kennedy	Luther H. Hodges	NC	1961
Johnson, L. B.	Luther H. Hodges	NC	1963
	John T. Connor	NJ	1965
	Alex B. Trowbridge	NJ	1967
	Cyrus R. Smith	NY	1968
Nixon	Maurice H. Stans	MN	1969
	Peter G. Peterson	IL	1972
	Frederick B. Dent	SC	1973
Ford	Frederick B. Dent	SC	1974
	Rogers C. B. Morton	MD	1975
	Elliot L. Richardson	MA	1975
Carter	Juanita M. Kreps	NC	1977
	Philip M. Klutznick	IL	1979
Reagan	Malcolm Baldrige	CT	1981
	C. William Verity Jr.	OH	1987
Bush, G. H. W.	Robert A. Mosbacher	TX	1989
	Barbara H. Franklin	PA	1992
Clinton	Ronald H. Brown	DC	1993
	Mickey Kantor	CA	1996
	William M. Daley	IL	1997
	Norman Y. Mineta	CA	2000
Bush, G. W.	Donald L. Evans	TX	2001
	Carlos M. Gutierrez	MI	2005
Obama	Gary F. Locke	WA	2009
	John Bryson	CA	2011
	Penny Pritzker	IL	2013
Trump	Wilbur L. Ross Jr.	NJ	2017

Secretaries of Commerce and Labor

The Dept. of Commerce and Labor was created by Congress on Feb. 14, 1903.

President	Secretary	Home	Sworn in
Roosevelt, T.	George B. Cortelyou	NY	1903
	Victor H. Metcalf	CA	1904
	Oscar S. Straus	NY	1906
Taft	Charles Nagel	MO	1909

Department of Labor

200 Constitution Ave. NW, 20210; www.dol.gov

The Dept. of Labor was formed by Congress Mar. 4, 1913, when it divided the Dept. of Commerce and Labor into two departments. Administers federal labor laws to foster, promote, and develop the welfare of job seekers, wage earners, and retirees of the U.S.; to improve working conditions; and to advance opportunities for profitable employment. Administers standards for wages and overtime pay, safety and health conditions, workers' compensation. Tracks changes in employment, prices, and other national economic measurements. Regulates pension and welfare benefit plans, the hiring and employment of migrant and seasonal workers, and requirements pertaining to the mining, construction, and transportation industries. Monitors labor unions and their funds. **Budget:** $40.1 bil (2017); $39.6 bil (2018); $35.8 bil (2019); $36.4 bil (2020 est.); $38.3 bil (2021 est.).

- Bureau of Labor Statistics (2 Massachusetts Ave. NE, 20212); www.bls.gov
- Employment and Training Admin.; www.doleta.gov
- Mine Safety and Health Admin. (201 12th St. S, Ste. 401, Arlington, VA 22202); www.msha.gov
- Occupational Safety and Health Admin.; www.osha.gov
- Office of Federal Contract Compliance Programs; www.dol.gov/ofccp
- Office of Labor-Management Standards; www.dol.gov/olms
- Office of Workers' Compensation Programs; www.dol.gov/owcp
- Wage and Hour Div.; www.dol.gov/whd

Secretaries of Labor

President	Secretary	Home	Sworn in
Wilson	William B. Wilson	PA	1913
Harding	James J. Davis	PA	1921
Coolidge	James J. Davis	PA	1923
Hoover	James J. Davis	PA	1929
	William N. Doak	VA	1930
Roosevelt, F. D.	Frances Perkins	NY	1933
Truman	L. B. Schwellenbach	WA	1945
	Maurice J. Tobin	MA	1949
Eisenhower	Martin P. Durkin	IL	1953
	James P. Mitchell	NJ	1953
Kennedy	Arthur J. Goldberg	IL	1961
	W. Willard Wirtz	IL	1962
Johnson, L. B.	W. Willard Wirtz	IL	1963
Nixon	George P. Shultz	IL	1969
	James D. Hodgson	CA	1970
	Peter J. Brennan	NY	1973
Ford	Peter J. Brennan	NY	1974
	John T. Dunlop	CA	1975
	W. J. Usery Jr.	GA	1976
Carter	F. Ray Marshall	TX	1977
Reagan	Raymond J. Donovan	NJ	1981
	William E. Brock	TN	1985
	Ann D. McLaughlin	DC	1987
Bush, G. H. W.	Elizabeth H. Dole	NC	1989
	Lynn Martin	IL	1991
Clinton	Robert B. Reich	MA	1993
	Alexis M. Herman	AL	1997
Bush, G. W.	Elaine L. Chao	KY	2001
Obama	Hilda L. Solis	CA	2009
	Thomas E. Perez	MD	2013
Trump	R. Alexander Acosta	FL	2017
	Eugene Scalia	DC	2019

Department of Housing and Urban Development

451 7th St. SW, 20410; www.hud.gov

Created by act of Congress on Sept. 9, 1965. Responsible for housing needs and the improvement and development of urban areas. Supports affordable housing, provides grants for community development and redevelopment. Enforces fair and safe housing standards. Provides funds to assist homeless individuals and families with emergency and transitional shelters. The Federal Housing Administration provides mortgage insurance on loans made by approved lenders. **Budget:** $55.6 bil (2017); $54.7 bil (2018); $29.2 bil (2019); $36.0 bil (2020 est.); $52.4 bil (2021 est.).

- Fannie Mae (Federal Natl. Mortgage Association) (1100 15th St. NW, 20005); www.fanniemae.com
- Federal Housing Admin.; www.hud.gov/federal_housing_administration
- Freddie Mac (Federal Home Loan Mortgage Corporation) (8200 Jones Branch Dr., McLean, VA 22102); www.freddiemac.com
- Ginnie Mae (Government Natl. Mortgage Association) (425 3rd St. SW, Ste. 500, 20024); www.ginniemae.gov

Note: Fannie Mae and Freddie Mac are government-sponsored enterprises (GSEs).

Secretaries of Housing and Urban Development

President	Secretary	Home	Sworn in
Johnson, L. B.	Robert C. Weaver	WA	1966
	Robert C. Wood	MA	1969
Nixon	George W. Romney	MI	1969
	James T. Lynn	OH	1973
Ford	James T. Lynn	OH	1974
	Carla Anderson Hills	CA	1975
Carter	Patricia Roberts Harris	DC	1977
	Moon Landrieu	LA	1979
Reagan	Samuel R. Pierce Jr.	NY	1981
Bush, G. H. W.	Jack F. Kemp	NY	1989
Clinton	Henry G. Cisneros	TX	1993
	Andrew M. Cuomo	NY	1997
Bush, G. W.	Mel Martinez	FL	2001
	Alphonso Jackson	TX	2004
	Steve Preston	VA	2008
Obama	Shaun L. S. Donovan	NY	2009
	Julián Castro	TX	2014
Trump	Ben Carson	MD	2017

Department of Transportation

1200 New Jersey Ave. SE, 20590; www.transportation.gov

Created by act of Congress on Oct. 15, 1966. Promotes and develops rapid, safe, efficient, and convenient transportation in the U.S.; monitors and administers assistance to transportation industries; negotiates and implements international transportation agreements. Manages airspace, commercial space transportation, and the movement of hazardous materials. Resolves railroad rate and service disputes and reviews proposed railroad mergers. Analyzes and shares research and statistics to develop and improve transportation. Develops and enforces regulations on the nation's pipeline transportation system. The Maritime Administration maintains a fleet of cargo ships in reserve for war or national emergencies and commissions officers of the Merchant Marine. Operates the U.S. portion of the St. Lawrence Seaway between Montréal and Lake Erie. **Budget:** $79.4 bil (2017); $78.5 bil (2018); $80.7 bil (2019); $84.7 bil (2020 est.); $88.7 bil (2021 est.).

- Federal Aviation Admin. (800 Independence Ave. SW, 20591); www.faa.gov
- Federal Highway Admin.; www.fhwa.dot.gov
- Federal Motor Carrier Safety Admin.; www.fmcsa.dot.gov
- Federal Railroad Admin. (1200 New Jersey Ave. SE, West Bldg., 20590); www.fra.dot.gov
- Federal Transit Admin. (1200 New Jersey Ave. SE, East Bldg., 20590); www.transit.dot.gov
- Maritime Admin.; www.maritime.dot.gov
- Natl. Highway Traffic Safety Admin.; www.nhtsa.gov
- Pipeline and Hazardous Materials Safety Admin.; www.phmsa.dot.gov
- St. Lawrence Seaway Development Corp.; www.seaway.dot.gov

Secretaries of Transportation

President	Secretary	Home	Sworn in
Johnson, L. B.	Alan S. Boyd	FL	1966
Nixon	John A. Volpe	MA	1969
	Claude S. Brinegar	CA	1973
Ford	Claude S. Brinegar	CA	1974
	William T. Coleman Jr.	PA	1975
Carter	Brock Adams	WA	1977
	Neil E. Goldschmidt	OR	1979
Reagan	Andrew L. Lewis Jr.	PA	1981
	Elizabeth H. Dole	NC	1983
	James H. Burnley	NC	1987
Bush, G. H. W.	Samuel K. Skinner	IL	1989
	Andrew H. Card Jr.	MA	1992
Clinton	Federico F. Peña	CO	1993
	Rodney E. Slater	AR	1997
Bush, G. W.	Norman Y. Mineta	CA	2001
	Mary E. Peters	AZ	2006
Obama	Raymond L. LaHood	IL	2009
	Anthony Foxx	NC	2013
Trump	Elaine L. Chao	KY	2017

Department of Energy

1000 Independence Ave. SW, 20585; www.energy.gov

Created by federal law on Aug. 4, 1977. Secures the nation's energy and promotes scientific and technological innovation. Oversees the national energy supply and electric grid. Investigates and promotes clean and reliable energy. Manages and cleans up nuclear and other radioactive material, including nuclear weapons. The Office of Scientific and Technical Information supports much of America's scientific research through program offices, education initiatives, national laboratories, and technology centers. Four power marketing administrations sell power from federal hydroelectric projects across the West and Southeast. **Budget:** $25.8 bil (2017); $26.5 bil (2018); $28.9 bil (2019); $34.4 bil (2020 est.); $35.5 bil (2021 est.).

* Federal Energy Regulatory Commission (independent regulatory agency) (888 1st St. NE, 20426); www.ferc.gov
* Natl. Nuclear Security Admin.; www.energy.gov/nnsa/national-nuclear-security-administration
* Office of Scientific and Technical Information (P.O. Box 62, Oak Ridge, TN 37831); www.osti.gov
* U.S. Energy Information Admin.; www.eia.gov

Secretaries of Energy

President	Secretary	Home	Sworn in
Carter	James R. Schlesinger	VA	1977
	Charles W. Duncan Jr.	WY	1979
Reagan	James B. Edwards	SC	1981
	Donald P. Hodel	OR	1982
	John S. Herrington	CA	1985
Bush, G. H. W.	James D. Watkins	CA	1989
Clinton	Hazel R. O'Leary	MN	1993
	Federico F. Peña	CO	1997
	Bill Richardson	NM	1998
Bush, G. W.	Spencer Abraham	MI	2001
	Samuel W. Bodman	MA	2005
Obama	Steven Chu	CA	2009
	Ernest Moniz	MA	2013
Trump	Rick Perry	TX	2017
	Dan Brouillette	TX	2019

Department of Health and Human Services

200 Independence Ave. SW, 20201; www.hhs.gov

The Dept. of Health, Education, and Welfare was created by Congress on Apr. 11, 1953. On Sept. 27, 1979, Congress approved creation of a separate Dept. of Education. The existing department was renamed the Dept. of Health and Human Services. Administers a wide range of programs in the fields of health care and social services that affect nearly all Americans. Medicare and Medicaid provide health care insurance for one in four Americans. The HRSA improves health care services for people who are uninsured, isolated, or medically vulnerable; oversees organ, tissue, and blood cell donations. The FDA assures the safety of food, drugs, cosmetics, biological products, and medical devices. The CDC monitors and safeguards against disease outbreaks. The NIH supports research projects nationwide and 27 health institutes and centers. The surgeon general is the nation's chief health educator and leads the U.S. Public Health Service Commissioned Corps. **Budget:** $1.12 tril (2017); $1.12 tril (2018); $1.21 tril (2019); $1.32 tril (2020 est.); $1.37 tril (2021 est.).

* Admin. for Children and Families (330 C St. SW, 20201); www.acf.hhs.gov
* Admin. for Community Living (330 C St. SW, 20201); www.acl.gov
* Agency for Healthcare Research and Quality (5600 Fishers Ln., Rockville, MD 20857); www.ahrq.gov
* Centers for Disease Control and Prevention (1600 Clifton Rd., Atlanta, GA 30333); www.cdc.gov
* Centers for Medicare and Medicaid Services (7500 Security Blvd., Baltimore, MD 21244); www.cms.gov
* Food and Drug Admin. (10903 New Hampshire Ave., Silver Spring, MD 20993); www.fda.gov
* Health Resources and Services Admin. (5600 Fishers Ln., Rockville, MD 20857); www.hrsa.gov
* Indian Health Service (5600 Fishers Ln., Rockville, MD 20857); www.ihs.gov
* Natl. Institutes of Health (1 Center Dr., Bethesda, MD 20892); www.nih.gov
* Substance Abuse and Mental Health Services Admin. (5600 Fishers Ln., Rockville, MD 20857); www.samhsa.gov

Secretaries of Health and Human Services

President	Secretary	Home	Sworn in
Carter	Patricia Roberts Harris	DC	1979
Reagan	Richard S. Schweiker	PA	1981
	Margaret M. Heckler	MA	1983
Reagan	Otis R. Bowen	IN	1985
Bush, G. H. W.	Louis W. Sullivan	GA	1989
Clinton	Donna E. Shalala	WI	1993
Bush, G. W.	Tommy Thompson	WI	2001
	Michael O. Leavitt	UT	2005
Obama	Kathleen Sebelius	KS	2009
	Sylvia Mathews Burwell	WV	2014
Trump	Thomas E. Price	GA	2017
	Alex Azar	IN	2018

Secretaries of Health, Education, and Welfare

President	Secretary	Home	Sworn in
Eisenhower	Oveta Culp Hobby	TX	1953
	Marion B. Folsom	NY	1955
	Arthur S. Flemming	OH	1958
Kennedy	Abraham A. Ribicoff	CT	1961
	Anthony J. Celebrezze	OH	1962
Johnson, L. B.	Anthony J. Celebrezze	OH	1963
	John W. Gardner	NY	1965
	Wilbur J. Cohen	MI	1968
Nixon	Robert H. Finch	CA	1969
	Elliot L. Richardson	MA	1970
	Caspar W. Weinberger	CA	1973
Ford	Caspar W. Weinberger	CA	1974
	Forrest D. Mathews	AL	1975
Carter	Joseph A. Califano Jr.	DC	1977
	Patricia Roberts Harris	DC	1979

Department of Education

400 Maryland Ave. SW, 20202; www.ed.gov

The Dept. of Health, Education, and Welfare was created by Congress on Apr. 11, 1953. On Sept. 27, 1979, Congress approved creation of a separate Dept. of Education. Works with state agencies and local systems to ensure equal access to all levels of education and seeks to improve the quality of that education through federal support, research programs, and information sharing. Oversees a variety of financial aid distributed through competition, need-based requests, or a set formula. Sets policy goals and initiatives. Conducts research and gathers educational information to disseminate to educators and the general public. **Budget:** $111.7 bil (2017); $63.7 bil (2018); $104.4 bil (2019); $159.3 bil (2020 est.); $79.0 bil (2021 est.).

Secretaries of Education

President	Secretary	Home	Sworn in
Carter	Shirley Hufstedler	CA	1979
Reagan	Terrel H. Bell	UT	1981
	William J. Bennett	NY	1985
	Lauro F. Cavazos	TX	1988
Bush, G. H. W.	Lauro F. Cavazos	TX	1989
	Lamar Alexander	TN	1991
Clinton	Richard W. Riley	SC	1993
Bush, G. W.	Roderick R. Paige	TX	2001
	Margaret Spellings	TX	2005
Obama	Arne Duncan	IL	2009
	John King	NY	2016
Trump	Betsy DeVos	MI	2017

Department of Veterans Affairs

810 Vermont Ave. NW, 20420; www.va.gov

Pres. Ronald Reagan signed a bill in 1988 granting Cabinet-level status to the Veterans Administration. The agency became the Dept. of Veterans Affairs on Mar. 15, 1989. Supports veterans and their families with nationwide programs for health care, financial assistance, and burial benefits. Compensates for disabilities incurred during wartime. Provides pensions for veterans with low incomes, education assistance, loan guaranty, and life insurance. Manages America's largest medical education and health professions training program, which includes hospitals, clinics, nursing homes, veterans centers, rehabilitation treatment, readjustment counseling, and home-care programs. Also funds medical research pertaining to veterans issues. Manages 143 national cemeteries; provides headstones and markers. **Budget:** $176.1 bil (2017); $178.5 bil (2018); $199.6 bil (2019); $214.3 bil (2020 est.); $235.3 bil (2021 est.).

Secretaries of Veterans Affairs

President	Secretary	Home	Sworn in
Bush, G. H. W.	Edward J. Derwinski	IL	1989
Clinton	Jesse Brown	IL	1993
	Togo D. West Jr.	NC	1998
Bush, G. W.	Anthony J. Principi	CA	2001
	R. James Nicholson	CO	2005
	James B. Peake	MO	2007
Obama	Eric K. Shinseki	VA	2009
	Robert A. McDonald	OH	2014
Trump	David J. Shulkin	PA	2017
	Robert Wilkie	NC	2018

Department of Homeland Security

20528 (requires no street address); www.dhs.gov

Created by act of Congress on Nov. 25, 2002. Provides a unified core for the national network of organizations and institutions involved in efforts to secure the U.S., its borders, infrastructure, and major events. Provides funding, intelligence, and training for law enforcement and disaster relief. Leads and coordinates response teams to natural and manmade emergencies. Identifies threats, administers the Natl. Terrorism Advisory

System. **Budget:** $50.5 bil (2017); $68.4 bil (2018); $57.7 bil (2019); $62.2 bil (2020 est.); $60.3 bil (2021 est.).
- Fed. Emergency Management Agency (500 C St. SW, 20472); www.fema.gov
- Transportation Security Admin.; www.tsa.gov
- U.S. Citizenship and Immigration Services (111 Massachusetts Ave. NW, MS 2260, 20529); www.uscis.gov
- U.S. Coast Guard (2703 Martin Luther King Jr. Ave. SE, 20593); www.uscg.mil
- U.S. Customs and Border Protection (1300 Pennsylvania Ave. NW, 20229); www.cbp.gov
- U.S. Fire Admin. (16825 S. Seton Ave., Emmitsburg, MD 21727); www.usfa.fema.gov

- U.S. Immigration and Customs Enforcement (500 12th St. SW, 20536); www.ice.gov
- U.S. Secret Service (245 Murray Ln. SW - Bldg. T-5, 20223); www.secretservice.gov

Secretaries of Homeland Security

President	Secretary	Home	Sworn in
Bush, G. W.	Thomas Ridge	PA	2003
	Michael Chertoff	NJ	2005
Obama	Janet A. Napolitano	AZ	2009
	Jeh Johnson	NY	2014
Trump	John F. Kelly	MA	2017
	Kirstjen M. Nielsen	FL	2017

Other Notable U.S. Government Agencies

Source: *The U.S. Government Manual*; National Archives and Records Administration; World Almanac research
All addresses are for Washington, DC, unless otherwise noted; as of Sept. 2020.

Administrative Conference of the U.S.: Matthew L. Wiener, acting chair (1120 20th St. NW, Ste. 706S, 20036); www.acus.gov
African Development Foundation: C. D. Glin, pres. and CEO (1400 I St. NW, 20005); www.usadf.gov
AMTRAK: William J. Flynn, pres. and CEO (1 Massachusetts Ave. NW, 20001); www.amtrak.com
Central Intelligence Agency: Gina Haspel, dir. (20505); www.cia.gov
Commodity Futures Trading Commission: Heath Tarbert, chair (1155 21st St. NW, 20581); www.cftc.gov
Consumer Financial Protection Bureau: Kathy Kraninger, dir. (1700 G St. NW, 20552); www.consumerfinance.gov
Consumer Product Safety Commission: Robert S. Adler, acting chair (4330 East-West Hwy., Bethesda, MD 20814); www.cpsc.gov
Corp. for Natl. and Community Service: Barbara Stewart, CEO (250 E St. SW, 20024); www.nationalservice.gov
Defense Nuclear Facilities Safety Board: Bruce Hamilton, chair (625 Indiana Ave. NW, Ste. 700, 20004); www.dnfsb.gov
Election Assistance Commission: Benjamin Hovland, chair (1335 East-West Hwy., Ste. 4300, Silver Spring, MD 20910); www.eac.gov
Environmental Protection Agency: Andrew Wheeler, admin. (Cabinet rank) (1200 Pennsylvania Ave. NW, 20460); www.epa.gov
Equal Employment Opportunity Commission: Janet Dhillon, chair (131 M St. NE, 20507); www.eeoc.gov
Export-Import Bank of the U.S.: Kimberly A. Reed, pres. and chair (811 Vermont Ave. NW, 20571); www.exim.gov
Farm Credit Admin.: Glen R. Smith, chair and CEO (1501 Farm Credit Dr., McLean, VA 22102); www.fca.gov
Federal Communications Commission: Ajit Pai, chair (445 12th St. SW, 20554); www.fcc.gov
Federal Deposit Insurance Corp.: Jelena McWilliams, chair (550 17th St. NW, 20429); www.fdic.gov
Federal Election Commission: James E. Trainor III, chair (1050 1st St. NE, 20463); www.fec.gov
Federal Housing Finance Agency: Mark A. Calabria, dir. (400 7th St. SW, 20219); www.fhfa.gov
Federal Labor Relations Authority: Colleen Duffy Kiko, chair (1400 K St. NW, 20424); www.flra.gov
Federal Maritime Commission: Michael A. Khouri, chair (800 N. Capitol St. NW, 20573); www.fmc.gov
Federal Mediation and Conciliation Service: Richard Giacolone, dir. (250 E St. SW, 20427); www.fmcs.gov
Federal Mine Safety and Health Review Commission: Marco M. Rajkovich Jr., chair (1331 Pennsylvania Ave. NW, Ste. 520N, 20004); www.fmshrc.gov
Federal Reserve System: Jerome H. Powell, chair (20th St. and Constitution Ave. NW, 20551); www.federalreserve.gov
Federal Retirement Thrift Investment Board: Michael Kennedy, chair (77 K St. NE, Ste. 1000, 20002); www.frtib.gov
Federal Trade Commission: Joseph J. Simons, chair (600 Pennsylvania Ave. NW, 20580); www.ftc.gov
General Services Admin.: Emily W. Murphy, admin. (1800 F St. NW, 20405); www.gsa.gov
Institute of Museum and Library Services: Crosby Kemper III, dir. (955 L'Enfant Plaza North SW, Ste. 4000, 20024); www.imls.gov
Inter-American Foundation: Paloma Adams-Allen, pres. and CEO (1331 Pennsylvania Ave. NW, Ste. 1200N, 20004); www.iaf.gov
Merit Systems Protection Board: chair vacant (1615 M St. NW, 5th Fl., 20419); www.mspb.gov
Natl. Aeronautics and Space Admin.: Jim Bridenstine, admin. (300 E St. SW, Ste. 5R30, 20546); www.nasa.gov
Natl. Archives and Records Admin.: David S. Ferriero, archivist (8601 Adelphi Rd., College Park, MD 20740); www.archives.gov
Natl. Capital Planning Commission: Thomas M. Gallas, vice chair (401 9th St. NW, Ste. 500N, 20004); www.ncpc.gov

Natl. Council on Disability: Neil Romano, chair (1331 F St. NW, Ste. 850, 20004); www.ncd.gov
Natl. Credit Union Admin.: Rodney E. Hood, chair (1775 Duke St., Alexandria, VA 22314); www.ncua.gov
Natl. Endowment for the Arts: Mary Anne Carter, chair (400 7th St. SW, 20506); www.arts.gov
Natl. Endowment for the Humanities: Jon Parrish Peede, chair (400 7th St. SW, 20506); www.neh.gov
Natl. Indian Gaming Commission: E. Sequoyah Simermeyer, chair (1849 C St. NW, Mail Stop 1621, 20240); www.nigc.gov
Natl. Labor Relations Board: John F. Ring, chair (1015 Half St. SE, 20570); www.nlrb.gov
Natl. Mediation Board: Linda A. Puchala, chair (1301 K St. NW, Ste. 250E, 20005); www.nmb.gov
Natl. Science Foundation: Sethuraman Panchanathan, dir. (2415 Eisenhower Ave., Arlington, VA 22314); www.nsf.gov
Natl. Transportation Safety Board: Robert L. Sumwalt, chair (490 L'Enfant Plaza SW, 20594); www.ntsb.gov
Nuclear Regulatory Commission: Kristine L. Svinicki, chair (20555); www.nrc.gov
Nuclear Waste Technical Review Board: Jean M. Bahr, chair (2300 Clarendon Blvd., Ste. 1300, Arlington, VA 22201); www.nwtrb.gov
Occupational Safety and Health Review Commission: James J. Sullivan Jr., chair (1120 20th St. NW, 9th Fl., 20036); www.oshrc.gov
Office of the Dir. of Natl. Intelligence: John Ratcliffe, dir. (20511); www.dni.gov
Office of Government Ethics: Emory A. Rounds III, dir. (1201 New York Ave. NW, Ste. 500, 20005); www.oge.gov
Office of Personnel Management: Michael Rigas, acting dir. (1900 E St. NW, 20415); www.opm.gov
Office of Special Counsel: Henry Kerner, spec. counsel (1730 M St. NW, Ste. 218, 20036); osc.gov
Peace Corps: Josephine Olsen, dir. (1111 20th St. NW, 20526); www.peacecorps.gov
Pension Benefit Guaranty Corp.: Gordon Hartogensis, dir. (1200 K St. NW, 20005); www.pbgc.gov
Postal Regulatory Commission: Robert G. Taub, chair (901 New York Ave. NW, Ste. 200, 20268); www.prc.gov
Railroad Retirement Board: Erhard R. Chorlé, chair (844 N. Rush St., Chicago, IL 60611); www.rrb.gov
Securities and Exchange Commission: Jay Clayton, chair (100 F St. NE, 20549); www.sec.gov
Selective Service System: Donald M. Benton, dir. (Natl. Headquarters, Arlington, VA 22209); www.sss.gov
Small Business Admin.: Jovita Carranza, admin. (Cabinet rank) (409 3rd St. SW, 20416); www.sba.gov
Social Security Admin.: Andrew Saul, comm. (1100 West High Rise, 6401 Security Blvd., Baltimore, MD 21235); www.ssa.gov
Tennessee Valley Authority: James "Skip" Thompson, chair (400 W. Summit Hill Dr., Knoxville, TN 37902); www.tva.gov
U.S. Agency for Global Media (fmr. Broadcasting Board of Governors): Michael Pack, chair and CEO (330 Independence Ave. SW, 20237); www.usagm.gov
U.S. Agency for Intl. Development: John Barsa, acting admin. (Ronald Reagan Bldg., 20523); www.usaid.gov
U.S. Commission on Civil Rights: Catherine E. Lhamon, chair (1331 Pennsylvania Ave. NW, Ste. 1150, 20425); www.usccr.gov
U.S. Intl. Development Finance Corp. (fmr. Overseas Private Investment Corp.): Adam Boehler, CEO (1100 New York Ave. NW, 20527); www.dfc.gov
U.S. Intl. Trade Commission: Jason E. Kearns, chair (500 E St. SW, 20436); www.usitc.gov
U.S. Postal Service: Louis DeJoy, postmaster general and CEO (475 L'Enfant Plaza SW, 20260); www.usps.com
U.S. Trade and Development Agency: dir. vacant (1101 Wilson Blvd., Ste. 1100, Arlington, VA 22209); www.ustda.gov

CONGRESS

Floor Leaders in the U.S. Senate, 1920-2020

MAJORITY LEADERS				MINORITY LEADERS			
Name	Party	State	Tenure	Name	Party	State	Tenure
Charles Curtis[1]	Rep.	KS	1925-1929	Oscar W. Underwood[2]	Dem.	AL	1920-1923
James E. Watson	Rep.	IN	1929-1933	Joseph T. Robinson	Dem.	AR	1923-1933
Joseph T. Robinson	Dem.	AR	1933-1937	Charles L. McNary	Rep.	OR	1933-1944
Alben W. Barkley	Dem.	KY	1937-1947	Wallace H. White	Rep.	ME	1944-1947
Wallace H. White	Rep.	ME	1947-1949	Alben W. Barkley	Dem.	KY	1947-1949
Scott W. Lucas	Dem.	IL	1949-1951	Kenneth S. Wherry	Rep.	NE	1949-1951
Ernest W. McFarland	Dem.	AZ	1951-1953	Henry Styles Bridges	Rep.	NH	1952-1953
Robert A. Taft	Rep.	OH	1953	Lyndon B. Johnson	Dem.	TX	1953-1955
William F. Knowland	Rep.	CA	1953-1955	William F. Knowland	Rep.	CA	1955-1959
Lyndon B. Johnson	Dem.	TX	1955-1961	Everett M. Dirksen	Rep.	IL	1959-1969
Mike Mansfield	Dem.	MT	1961-1977	Hugh D. Scott	Rep.	PA	1969-1977
Robert C. Byrd	Dem.	WV	1977-1981	Howard H. Baker Jr.	Rep.	TN	1977-1981
Howard H. Baker Jr.	Rep.	TN	1981-1985	Robert C. Byrd	Dem.	WV	1981-1987
Robert J. Dole	Rep.	KS	1985-1987	Robert J. Dole	Rep.	KS	1987-1995
Robert C. Byrd	Dem.	WV	1987-1989	Thomas A. Daschle	Dem.	SD	1995-2001[3]
George J. Mitchell	Dem.	ME	1989-1995	Trent Lott	Rep.	MS	2001-2002[3,4]
Robert J. Dole	Rep.	KS	1995-1996	Thomas A. Daschle	Dem.	SD	2003-2005
Trent Lott	Rep.	MS	1996-2001[3]	Harry M. Reid	Dem.	NV	2005-2007
Thomas A. Daschle	Dem.	SD	2001-2003[3]	Mitch McConnell	Rep.	KY	2007-2015
William Frist	Rep.	TN	2003-2007[4]	Harry M. Reid	Dem.	NV	2015-2017
Harry M. Reid	Dem.	NV	2007-2015	Charles E. Schumer	Dem.	NY	2017-
Mitch McConnell	Rep.	KY	2015-				

Note: The offices of party (majority and minority) leaders in the Senate did not evolve until the 20th century. (1) First Republican to be formally designated floor leader. Henry Cabot Lodge (MA) served as unofficial party leader prior to Curtis's election. (2) First Democrat to be designated floor leader. (3) Democrats held the majority Jan. 3, 2001, until Dick Cheney (R) was installed as vice pres., Jan. 20. Republicans subsequently lost the majority when Jim Jeffords (VT) switched his affiliation from Republican to Independent, June 6, 2001. (4) Trent Lott resigned from Republican leadership Dec. 20, 2002. William Frist was elected Republican leader Dec. 23, 2002, and began service Jan. 7, 2003, as majority leader.

Speakers of the U.S. House of Representatives, 1789-2020

Name	Party	State	Tenure	Name	Party	State	Tenure
Frederick A. C. Muhlenberg	Federalist	PA	1789-1791	Samuel J. Randall	Dem.	PA	1876-1881
Jonathan Trumbull	Federalist	CT	1791-1793	J. Warren Keifer	Rep.	OH	1881-1883
Frederick A. C. Muhlenberg	Federalist	PA	1793-1795	John G. Carlisle	Dem.	KY	1883-1889
Jonathan Dayton	Federalist	NJ	1795-1799	Thomas B. Reed	Rep.	ME	1889-1891
Theodore Sedgwick	Federalist	MA	1799-1801	Charles F. Crisp	Dem.	GA	1891-1895
Nathaniel Macon	Dem.-Rep.	NC	1801-1807	Thomas B. Reed	Rep.	ME	1895-1899
Joseph B. Varnum	Dem.-Rep.	MA	1807-1811	David B. Henderson	Rep.	IA	1899-1903
Henry Clay	Dem.-Rep.	KY	1811-1814	Joseph G. Cannon	Rep.	IL	1903-1911
Langdon Cheves	Dem.-Rep.	SC	1814-1815	Champ Clark	Dem.	MO	1911-1919
Henry Clay	Dem.-Rep.	KY	1815-1820	Frederick H. Gillett	Rep.	MA	1919-1925
John W. Taylor	Dem.-Rep.	NY	1820-1821	Nicholas Longworth	Rep.	OH	1925-1931
Philip P. Barbour	Dem.-Rep.	VA	1821-1823	John N. Garner	Dem.	TX	1931-1933
Henry Clay	Dem.-Rep.	KY	1823-1825	Henry T. Rainey	Dem.	IL	1933-1934
John W. Taylor	Dem.	NY	1825-1827	Joseph W. Byrns	Dem.	TN	1935-1936
Andrew Stevenson	Dem.	VA	1827-1834	William B. Bankhead	Dem.	AL	1936-1940
John Bell	Dem.	TN	1834-1835	Sam Rayburn	Dem.	TX	1940-1947
James K. Polk	Dem.	TN	1835-1839	Joseph W. Martin Jr.	Rep.	MA	1947-1949
Robert M. T. Hunter	Dem.	VA	1839-1841	Sam Rayburn	Dem.	TX	1949-1953
John White	Whig	KY	1841-1843	Joseph W. Martin Jr.	Rep.	MA	1953-1955
John W. Jones	Dem.	VA	1843-1845	Sam Rayburn	Dem.	TX	1955-1961
John W. Davis	Dem.	IN	1845-1847	John W. McCormack	Dem.	MA	1962-1971
Robert C. Winthrop	Whig	MA	1847-1849	Carl B. Albert	Dem.	OK	1971-1977
Howell Cobb	Dem.	GA	1849-1851	Thomas P. O'Neill Jr.	Dem.	MA	1977-1987
Linn Boyd	Dem.	KY	1851-1855	James C. Wright Jr.	Dem.	TX	1987-1989
Nathaniel P. Banks	American	MA	1856-1857	Thomas S. Foley	Dem.	WA	1989-1995
James L. Orr	Dem.	SC	1857-1859	Newt Gingrich	Rep.	GA	1995-1999
William Pennington	Rep.	NJ	1860-1861	J. Dennis Hastert	Rep.	IL	1999-2007
Galusha A. Grow	Rep.	PA	1861-1863	Nancy Pelosi	Dem.	CA	2007-2011
Schuyler Colfax	Rep.	IN	1863-1869	John Boehner	Rep.	OH	2011-2015
Theodore M. Pomeroy	Rep.	NY	1869	Paul Ryan	Rep.	WI	2015-2019
James G. Blaine	Rep.	ME	1869-1875	Nancy Pelosi	Dem.	CA	2019-
Michael C. Kerr	Dem.	IN	1875-1876				

Political Divisions of Congress, 1901-2020

Source: Office of the Clerk, U.S. House of Representatives; Congressional Research Service, Library of Congress

All figures reflect post-election party breakdown except where noted; **boldface** denotes party in majority immediately after election.

		SENATE					HOUSE OF REPRESENTATIVES				
Congress	Years	Total members	Dem.	Rep.	Other parties	Vacant	Total members	Dem.	Rep.	Other parties	Vacant
57th	1901-1903	90	29	**56**	3	2	357	153	**198**	5	1
58th	1903-1905	90	32	**58**			386	178	**207**		1
59th	1905-1907	90	32	**58**			386	136	**250**		
60th	1907-1909	92	29	**61**		2	386	164	**222**		
61st	1909-1911	92	32	**59**		1	391	172	**219**		
62nd	1911-1913	92	42	**49**		1	391	**228**	162	1	
63rd	1913-1915	96	**51**	44	1		435	**290**	127	18	
64th	1915-1917	96	**56**	39	1		435	**231**	193	8	3
65th	1917-1919	96	**53**	42	1		435	210[1]	216	9	
66th	1919-1921	96	47	**48**	1		435	191	**237**	7	
67th	1921-1923	96	37	**59**			435	132	**300**	1	2
68th	1923-1925	96	43	**51**	2		435	207	**225**	3	

		SENATE					HOUSE OF REPRESENTATIVES				
Congress	Years	Total members	Dem.	Rep.	Other parties	Vacant	Total members	Dem.	Rep.	Other parties	Vacant
69th	1925-1927	96	40	54	1	1	435	183	247	5	
70th	1927-1929	96	47	48	1		435	195	237	3	
71st	1929-1931	96	39	56	1		435	163	267	1	4
72nd	1931-1933	96	47	48	1		435	216[2]	218	1	
73rd	1933-1935	96	59	36	1		435	313	117	5	
74th	1935-1937	96	69	25	2		435	322	103	10	
75th	1937-1939	96	75	17	4		435	333	89	13	
76th	1939-1941	96	69	23	4		435	262	169	4	
77th	1941-1943	96	66	28	2		435	267	162	6	
78th	1943-1945	96	57	38	1		435	222	209	4	
79th	1945-1947	96	57	38	1		435	243	190	2	
80th	1947-1949	96	45	51			435	188	246	1	
81st	1949-1951	96	54	42			435	263	171	1	
82nd	1951-1953	96	48	47	1		435	234	199	2	
83rd	1953-1955	96	46	48	2		435	213	221	1	
84th	1955-1957	96	48	47	1		435	232	203		
85th	1957-1959	96	49	47			435	234	201		
86th	1959-1961	98	64	34			436[3]	283	153		
87th	1961-1963	100	64	36			437[3]	262	175		
88th	1963-1965	100	67	33			435	258	176		1
89th	1965-1967	100	68	32			435	295	140		
90th	1967-1969	100	64	36			435	248	187		
91st	1969-1971	100	58	42			435	243	192		
92nd	1971-1973	100	54	44	2		435	255	180		
93rd	1973-1975	100	56	42	2		435	242	192	1	
94th	1975-1977	100	61	37	2		435	291	144		
95th	1977-1979	100	61	38	1		435	292	143		
96th	1979-1981	100	58	41	1		435	277	158		
97th	1981-1983	100	46	53	1		435	242	192	1	
98th	1983-1985	100	46	54			435	269	166		
99th	1985-1987	100	47	53			435	253	182		
100th	1987-1989	100	55	45			435	258	177		
101st	1989-1991	100	55	45			435	260	175		
102nd	1991-1993	100	56	44			435	267	167	1	
103rd	1993-1995	100	57	43			435	258	176	1	
104th	1995-1997	100	48	52			435	204	230	1	
105th	1997-1999	100	45	55			435	207	226	2	
106th	1999-2001	100	45	55			435	211	223	1	
107th	2001-2003	100	50	50[4]			435	212	221	2	
108th	2003-2005	100	48	51	1		435	204	229	1	1
109th	2005-2007	100	44	55	1		435	202	232	1	
110th	2007-2009	100	49	49	2[5]		435	233	202		
111th	2009-2011	100	55	41	2[5]	2	435	256	178		1
112th	2011-2013	100	51	47	2[5]		435	193	242		
113th	2013-2015	100	53	45	2[5]		435	200	234		1
114th	2015-2017	100	44	54	2[5]		435	188	247		
115th	2017-2019	100	46	52	2[5]		435	194	241		
116th	2019-	100	45	53	2[5]		435	235	199		1

(1) Democrats organized the House with help of other parties. (2) Democrats organized the House because of Republican deaths. (3) Number of House seats was increased temporarily when proclamations were issued declaring Alaska (Jan. 3, 1959) and Hawaii (Aug. 21, 1959) new states. (4) While the Senate was split 50-50, control was held by whichever party had an incumbent vice president. Republican Sen. Jim Jeffords (VT) changed his party designation to Independent on June 6, 2001, switching control of the Senate to Democrats. (5) Both Independent senators chose to caucus with the Democrats.

Congressional Bills Vetoed, 1789-2020

Source: Virtual Reference Desk, U.S. Senate; as of Sept. 2020

The president has 10 days (excluding Sundays) to consider a bill or joint resolution passed by Congress. The president can sign it into law or exercise a veto. Only a two-thirds vote in both the Senate and the House can override a regular veto. (A pocket veto cannot be overridden as it takes effect when Congress is adjourned.)

President	Regular vetoes	Pocket vetoes	Total vetoes	Vetoes overridden	President	Regular vetoes	Pocket vetoes	Total vetoes	Vetoes overridden
Washington	2	—	2	—	Cleveland[2]	42	128	170	5
J. Adams	—	—	—	—	McKinley	6	36	42	—
Jefferson	—	—	—	—	T. Roosevelt	42	40	82	1
Madison	5	2	7	—	Taft	30	9	39	1
Monroe	1	—	1	—	Wilson	33	11	44	6
J. Q. Adams	—	—	—	—	Harding	5	1	6	—
Jackson	5	7	12	—	Coolidge	20	30	50	4
Van Buren	—	1	1	—	Hoover	21	16	37	3
W. H. Harrison	—	—	—	—	F. D. Roosevelt	372	263	635	9
Tyler	6	4	10	1	Truman	180	70	250	12
Polk	2	1	3	—	Eisenhower	73	108	181	2
Taylor	—	—	—	—	Kennedy	12	9	21	—
Fillmore	—	—	—	—	L. Johnson	16	14	30	—
Pierce	9	—	9	5	Nixon	26	17	43	7
Buchanan	4	3	7	—	Ford	48	18	66	12
Lincoln	2	5	7	—	Carter	13	18	31	2
A. Johnson	21	8	29	15	Reagan	39	39	78	9
Grant	45	48	93	4	G. H. W. Bush[3]	29	15	44	1
Hayes	12	1	13	1	Clinton[4]	36	1	37	2
Garfield	—	—	—	—	G. W. Bush	12	—	12	4
Arthur	4	8	12	1	Obama	12	—	12	1
Cleveland[1]	304	110	414	2	Trump	8	—	8	—
B. Harrison	19	25	44	1	Total[3,4]	1,516	1,066	2,582	111

— = 0. (1) First term only. (2) Second term only. (3) Excluded from the figures are two bills that Pres. George H. W. Bush claimed were pocket vetoed but which Congress considered to be enacted because the president had failed to return them during a Congressional recess. (4) Does not include line-item vetoes, which were ruled unconstitutional by the U.S. Supreme Court on June 25, 1998.

Congressional Firsts and Milestones

House of Representatives

First House meeting: Mar. 4, 1789, at Federal Hall in New York, NY. A quorum of 30 representatives was not reached until Apr. 1, 1789.

First House meeting in its current Capitol Building chamber: Dec. 16, 1857.

First former president to serve as representative: John Quincy Adams (MA, 1831-48); president, 1825-29.

First woman representative: Jeannette Rankin (R, MT, 1917-19, 1941-43).

First woman House speaker: Nancy Pelosi (D, CA), on Jan. 4, 2007.

First Black representative: Joseph Rainey (R, SC, 1870-79).

First Black woman representative: Shirley Chisholm (D, NY, 1969-83).

First American Indian women representatives: Deb Haaland (Laguna Pueblo) (D, NM, 2019-) and Sharice Davids (Ho-Chunk) (D, KS, 2019-).

First Asian-Pacific American representative: India-born Dalip Saund (D, CA, 1957-63).

First elected Hispanic-American representative: Romualdo Pacheco (R, CA, 1877-83); Pacheco was born in California when it was Mexican territory.

First Jewish representative: Lewis Charles Levin (PA, 1845-51).

First Muslim representative: Keith Ellison (D, MN, 2007-19).

First Muslim women representatives: Ilhan Omar (D, MN, 2019-) and Rashida Tlaib (D, MI, 2019-). Omar was also the first Somali-American member of Congress and the first member to wear a hijab, or headscarf.

First representative to give birth in office: Yvonne Brathwaite Burke (D, CA, 1973-79), on Nov. 23, 1973.

Longest-serving representative: John Dingell Jr. (D, MI, 1955-2015), with more than 59 years of service.

Longest-serving House speaker: Sam Rayburn (D, TX, 1913-61) speaker for 17 years, 2 months, 2 days (non-consecutive).

Oldest representative: Ralph Hall (D-R, TX, 1981-2015); retired at age 91.

Youngest representative: William Charles Cole Claiborne (TN), who was elected at 22 years of age and began service Nov. 23, 1797.

First live-TV broadcast of House proceedings: Mar. 19, 1979, by public television and C-SPAN. Al Gore Jr. (D, TN) was the first representative to give a speech before cameras that day.

First declaration of war made by the House: June 4, 1812, against Great Britain and Ireland.

Senate

First Senate meeting: Mar. 4, 1789, at Federal Hall in New York, NY. A quorum of senators (12) was not reached until Apr. 6, 1789.

First Senate meeting in its current chamber in the Capitol Building: Jan. 4, 1859.

First woman senator: Rebecca Felton (D, GA, 1922). Appointed to a seat left vacant by a death, 87-year-old Felton served only 24 hours after being sworn in Nov. 21. (Felton was also the oldest freshman senator and the last senator to have been a slave owner.)

First elected woman senator: Hattie Caraway (D, AR, 1931-45). Appointed in 1931 to fill the vacancy left by the death of her husband, Thaddeus H. Caraway, she was elected in 1932.

First Black senator: Hiram R. Revels (R, MS, 1870-71).

First Black woman senator: Carol Moseley-Braun (D, IL, 1993-99).

First American Indian senators: Charles Curtis (Kaw) (R, KS, 1907-13, 1915-29) and Robert Owen (Cherokee) (D, OK, 1907-25).

First Hispanic American senator: Mexico-born Octaviano Larrazolo (R, NM, 1928-29).

First Asian American senator: Hiram L. Fong (R, HI, 1959-77).

First Jewish senator: David Levy Yulee (D, FL, 1845-51, 1855-61).

First senator to give birth in office: Tammy Duckworth (D, IL, 2017-), on Apr. 9, 2018.

Longest-serving senator: Robert C. Byrd (D, WV, 1959-2010) died while in office, having served 51 years, 5 months, and 26 days.

Oldest senator: Strom Thurmond (R, SC), who turned 100 years of age on Dec. 5, 2002, one month before he retired from office.

Youngest senator: John H. Eaton (TN), who was 28 years, 5 months old when he was sworn in Nov. 16, 1818.

Longest speech by a senator (since 1900): 24 hours, 18 minutes, by Strom Thurmond (D, SC) in his filibuster against the 1957 Civil Rights Act, Aug. 28-29, 1957.

Number of Senate impeachment trials: 20, resulting in 8 acquittals, 8 convictions, 3 dismissals, and 1 resignation with no further action.

First regular live-TV broadcast from the Senate chamber: June 2, 1986, by the C-SPAN network.

Number of senators who have received the Nobel Peace Prize: 5 (Elihu Root, Frank Kellogg, Cordell Hull, Al Gore, Barack Obama). Root is the only one of the five to receive the award while serving as senator.

Number of senators who have changed party affiliation during their Senate service (since 1890): 21.

Congressional Activity, 1947-2020

Source: *Congressional Record*, U.S. Govt. Publishing Office; Library of Congress

Congress in recent years has been widely perceived as being less productive than in previous sessions. The data below shows the number of public laws and measures passed in every session of Congress since 1947.

Congress (years)	Public laws passed	Measures passed	Congress (years)	Public laws passed	Measures passed
80th (1947-48)	906	4,132	99th (1985-86)	664	2,698
81st (1949-50)	921	5,764	100th (1987-88)	713	2,932
82nd (1951-52)	594	4,593	101st (1989-90)	650	2,691
83rd (1953-54)	781	5,201	102nd (1991-92)	590	2,615
84th (1955-56)	1,028	5,713	103rd (1993-94)	465	2,054
85th (1957-58)	936	5,126	104th (1995-96)	333	1,834
86th (1959-60)	800	4,165	105th (1997-98)	394	2,077
87th (1961-62)	885	4,769	106th (1999-2000)	580	2,779
88th (1963-64)	666	3,425	107th (2001-02)	377	2,163
89th (1965-66)	810	4,116	108th (2003-04)	498	2,674
90th (1967-68)	640	3,390	109th (2005-06)	482	2,684
91st (1969-70)	695	3,318	110th (2007-08)	460	3,336
92nd (1971-72)	607	2,840	111th (2009-10)	383	2,939
93rd (1973-74)	649	3,088	112th (2011-12)	283	1,744
94th (1975-76)	588	3,176	113th (2013-14)	296	1,788
95th (1977-78)	633	3,211	114th (2015-16)	329	2,110
96th (1979-80)	613	2,960	115th (2017-18)	338	2,563
97th (1981-82)	473	2,267	116th (2019-20)	150*	1,547*
98th (1983-84)	623	2,670			

* = As of July 31, 2020. Incomplete congressional session; should not be compared to earlier years. **Note:** Public laws are bills or joint resolutions that have been enacted. Measures passed refers to bills, joint resolutions, concurrent resolutions, or simple resolutions approved by the House or Senate.

U.S. SUPREME COURT

Justices of the U.S. Supreme Court

The Supreme Court comprises the chief justice of the U.S. and eight associate justices, all appointed for life by the president with advice and consent of the U.S. Senate. Names of chief justices are in **boldface**. Terms of service begin with the year each justice took the judicial oath. Service years are the number of complete years served by a justice. 2020 salaries: chief justice, $277,700; associate justice, $265,600. The U.S. Supreme Court Building is at 1 First St. NE, Washington, DC 20543.

Website: www.supremecourt.gov

Name, appointed from	Service Term	Yrs.	Born	Died
John Jay, NY	1789-1795	5	1745	1829
John Rutledge, SC[1]	1790-1791	1	1739	1800
William Cushing, MA	1790-1810*	20	1732	1810
James Wilson, PA	1789-1798	8	1742	1798
John Blair, VA	1790-1795*	5	1732	1800
James Iredell, NC	1790-1799	9	1751	1799
Thomas Johnson, MD	1792-1793	<1	1732	1819
William Paterson, NJ	1793-1806	13	1745	1806
John Rutledge, SC[2,3]	1795	<1	1739	1800
Samuel Chase, MD	1796-1811	15	1741	1811
Oliver Ellsworth, CT	1796-1800	4	1745	1807
Bushrod Washington, VA	1799-1829*	30	1762	1829
Alfred Moore, NC	1800-1804	3	1755	1810
John Marshall, VA	1801-1835	34	1755	1835
William Johnson, SC	1804-1834	30	1771	1834
Henry B. Livingston, NY	1807-1823	16	1757	1823
Thomas Todd, KY	1807-1826	18	1765	1826
Gabriel Duvall, MD	1811-1835	23	1752	1844
Joseph Story, MA	1812-1845*	33	1779	1845
Smith Thompson, NY	1823-1843	20	1768	1843
Robert Trimble, KY	1826-1828	2	1777	1828
John McLean, OH	1830-1861*	31	1785	1861
Henry Baldwin, PA	1830-1844	14	1780	1844
James M. Wayne, GA	1835-1867	32	1790	1867
Roger B. Taney, MD	1836-1864	28	1777	1864
Philip P. Barbour, VA	1836-1841	4	1783	1841
John Catron, TN	1837-1865	28	1786	1865
John McKinley, AL	1838-1852*	14	1780	1852
Peter V. Daniel, VA	1842-1860*	18	1784	1860
Samuel Nelson, NY	1845-1872	27	1792	1873
Levi Woodbury, NH	1845-1851	5	1789	1851
Robert C. Grier, PA	1846-1870	23	1794	1870
Benjamin R. Curtis, MA	1851-1857	5	1809	1874
John A. Campbell, AL	1853-1861*	8	1811	1889
Nathan Clifford, ME	1858-1881	23	1803	1881
Noah H. Swayne, OH	1862-1881	18	1804	1884
Samuel F. Miller, IA	1862-1890	28	1816	1890
David Davis, IL	1862-1877	14	1815	1886
Stephen J. Field, CA	1863-1897	33	1816	1899
Salmon P. Chase, OH	1864-1873	8	1808	1873
William Strong, PA	1870-1880	10	1808	1895
Joseph P. Bradley, NJ	1870-1892	21	1813	1892
Ward Hunt, NY	1873-1882	9	1810	1886
Morrison R. Waite, OH	1874-1888	14	1816	1888
John M. Harlan, KY	1877-1911	33	1833	1911
William B. Woods, GA	1881-1887	6	1824	1887
Stanley Matthews, OH	1881-1889	7	1824	1889
Horace Gray, MA	1882-1902	20	1828	1902
Samuel Blatchford, NY	1882-1893	11	1820	1893
Lucius Q. C. Lamar, MS	1888-1893	5	1825	1893
Melville W. Fuller, IL	1888-1910	21	1833	1910
David J. Brewer, KS	1890-1910	20	1837	1910
Henry B. Brown, MI	1891-1906	15	1836	1913
George Shiras Jr., PA	1892-1903	10	1832	1924
Howell E. Jackson, TN	1893-1895	2	1832	1895
Edward D. White, LA[1]	1894-1910	16	1845	1921
Rufus W. Peckham, NY	1896-1909	13	1838	1909
Joseph McKenna, CA	1898-1925	26	1843	1926
Oliver W. Holmes, MA	1902-1932	29	1841	1935
William R. Day, OH	1903-1922	19	1849	1923

Name, appointed from	Service Term	Yrs.	Born	Died
William H. Moody, MA	1906-1910	3	1853	1917
Horace H. Lurton, TN	1910-1914	4	1844	1914
Charles E. Hughes, NY[1]	1910-1916	5	1862	1948
Willis Van Devanter, WY	1911-1937	26	1859	1941
Joseph R. Lamar, GA	1911-1916	5	1857	1916
Edward D. White, LA[2]	1910-1921	10	1845	1921
Mahlon Pitney, NJ	1912-1922	10	1858	1924
James C. McReynolds, TN	1914-1941	26	1862	1946
Louis D. Brandeis, MA	1916-1939	22	1856	1941
John H. Clarke, OH	1916-1922	5	1857	1945
William H. Taft, CT	1921-1930	8	1857	1930
George Sutherland, UT	1922-1938	15	1862	1942
Pierce Butler, MN	1923-1939	16	1866	1939
Edward T. Sanford, TN	1923-1930	7	1865	1930
Harlan F. Stone, NY[1]	1925-1941	16	1872	1946
Charles E. Hughes, NY[2]	1930-1941	11	1862	1948
Owen J. Roberts, PA	1930-1945	15	1875	1955
Benjamin N. Cardozo, NY	1932-1938	6	1870	1938
Hugo L. Black, AL	1937-1971	34	1886	1971
Stanley F. Reed, KY	1938-1957	19	1884	1980
Felix Frankfurter, MA	1939-1962	23	1882	1965
William O. Douglas, CT	1939-1975	36[4]	1898	1980
Frank Murphy, MI	1940-1949	9	1890	1949
Harlan F. Stone, NY[2]	1941-1946	4	1872	1946
James F. Byrnes, SC	1941-1942	1	1879	1972
Robert H. Jackson, NY	1941-1954	13	1892	1954
Wiley B. Rutledge, IA	1943-1949	6	1894	1949
Harold H. Burton, OH	1945-1958	13	1888	1964
Fred M. Vinson, KY	1946-1953	7	1890	1953
Tom C. Clark, TX	1949-1967	17	1899	1977
Sherman Minton, IN	1949-1956	7	1890	1965
Earl Warren, CA	1953-1969	15	1891	1974
John Marshall Harlan, NY	1955-1971	16	1899	1971
William J. Brennan Jr., NJ	1956-1990	33	1906	1997
Charles E. Whittaker, MO	1957-1962	5	1901	1973
Potter Stewart, OH	1958-1981	22	1915	1985
Byron R. White, CO	1962-1993	31	1917	2002
Arthur J. Goldberg, IL	1962-1965	2	1908	1990
Abe Fortas, TN	1965-1969	3	1910	1982
Thurgood Marshall, NY	1967-1991	24	1908	1993
Warren E. Burger, VA	1969-1986	17	1907	1995
Harry A. Blackmun, MN	1970-1994	24	1908	1999
Lewis F. Powell Jr., VA	1972-1987	15	1907	1998
William H. Rehnquist, AZ[1]	1972-1986	14	1924	2005
John Paul Stevens, IL	1975-2010	34	1920	2019
Sandra Day O'Connor, AZ	1981-2006	24	1930	
William H. Rehnquist, VA[2]	1986-2005	18	1924	2005
Antonin Scalia, VA	1986-2016	29	1936	2016
Anthony M. Kennedy, CA	1988-2018	30	1936	
David H. Souter, NH	1990-2009	18	1939	
Clarence Thomas, GA	1991-		1948	
Ruth Bader Ginsburg, NY	1993-2020	27	1933	2020
Stephen G. Breyer, MA	1994-		1938	
John G. Roberts Jr., MD	2005-		1955	
Samuel A. Alito Jr., NJ	2006-		1950	
Sonia Sotomayor, NY	2009-		1954	
Elena Kagan, MA	2010-		1960	
Neil M. Gorsuch, CO	2017-		1967	
Brett Kavanaugh, DC	2018-		1965	

* = Because of inadequate government record keeping, date of oath is estimated. (1) Later, chief justice, as listed. (2) Formerly associate justice. (3) Named acting chief justice; confirmation rejected by the Senate. (4) Longest term of service.

Supreme Court History and Notable Firsts

The U.S. Supreme Court first convened Feb. 1, 1790, in New York, NY. Acting on the authority of Congress as outlined in the Judiciary Act of 1789, the court consisted of Chief Justice John Jay and five associate justices who held sessions for a few weeks in Feb. and Aug. The justices also served twice a year in each of the nation's then-13 judicial districts, a requirement known as riding circuit. Since it was established, 113 justices have served on the court for an average of 16 years.

The Court's first major legal decision, *Chisholm v. Georgia* (1793), ruled that federal courts held jurisdiction over disputes between individual states and citizens of other states. (The 11th Amendment, which the states ratified in 1795, removed that jurisdiction.) The Court over time has expanded its impact on the nation's affairs. Since 1803 it has declared unconstitutional more than 180 acts of Congress and over 1,000 state, territorial, and municipal laws and statutes. The Court usually hears oral arguments in about 70-80 cases per term. The Supreme Court announced Mar. 12, 2020, that its building would be closed indefinitely to the general public because of the COVID-19 pandemic. Oral arguments were postponed for the first time since the 1918 flu pandemic. On May 4, 2020, the Court held oral arguments by telephone and offered a livestream audio broadcast of the session, both for the first time ever.

Of 162 nominations to the Court (including chief justice nominations), the Senate has voted to reject just 12, most recently Robert Bork in 1987. George W. Bush-nominee Harriet Miers withdrew her nomination before the Senate considered it, in 2005. The Senate did not hold hearings on Obama-nominated appellate court judge Merrick Garland in 2016.

Justices may be removed from the Court by impeachment. In 1804, the House of Representatives, in the control of Jeffersonian Republicans, impeached Samuel Chase, a Federalist; he was acquitted by the Senate in 1805.

First fully vested justice: James Wilson, who took the Constitutional Oath of the Court Oct. 5, 1789
First Jewish justice: Louis D. Brandeis (1916-39)
First and only person to serve as both U.S. president and chief justice: William Howard Taft (president, 1909-13; chief justice, 1921-30)

First justice to take an oath at the White House: Frank Murphy, Jan. 18, 1940
First Black justice: Thurgood Marshall (1967-91)
First woman justice: Sandra Day O'Connor (1981-2006)
First Hispanic justice: Sonia Sotomayor (2009-)

U.S. Supreme Court Decisions by Issue and Leadership Era, 1946-2019

Source: Supreme Court Database, supremecourtdatabase.org

Decisions through the end of the 2018-19 term. Figures are the number of cases decided in each issue category (number of 5-4 decisions in parentheses). The Court begins its term the first Monday in Oct. and typically recesses in late June.

Issue	Number of decisions under Chief Justice—				
	Vinson (1946-53)	Warren (1953-69)	Burger (1969-86)	Rehnquist (1986-2005)	Roberts (2005-)
Attorneys[1]	2 (0)	12 (1)	37 (5)	31 (7)	20 (3)
Civil rights	74 (7)	316 (30)	555 (79)	326 (68)	179 (36)
Criminal procedure	123 (29)	462 (72)	627 (110)	509 (139)	308 (69)
Due process	47 (6)	40 (5)	144 (19)	86 (23)	31 (8)
Economic activity	224 (38)	493 (53)	452 (52)	347 (40)	227 (23)
Federal taxation	49 (2)	118 (6)	75 (7)	56 (3)	14 (3)
Federalism	33 (1)	94 (3)	107 (6)	124 (26)	48 (8)
First amendment	44 (8)	206 (47)	236 (57)	140 (37)	54 (15)
Interstate relations	12 (2)	14 (0)	40 (0)	23 (1)	10 (2)
Judicial power	135 (18)	299 (21)	366 (35)	286 (28)	146 (28)
Miscellaneous[2]	1 (0)	1 (0)	4 (0)	10 (0)	8 (1)
Privacy	4 (0)	2 (0)	48 (10)	42 (7)	20 (2)
Private action[3]	0 (0)	0 (0)	0 (0)	0 (0)	4 (1)
Unions	41 (4)	131 (8)	109 (24)	55 (11)	25 (8)
Total	789 (115)	2,188 (246)	2,800 (404)	2,035 (390)	1,094 (207)

Note: Decision types include orally argued judgments, per curiams, and opinions; per curiams without oral arguments; equally divided votes; and decrees. (1) Includes cases on commercial fees, attorneys' fees, admission to state or federal bar, attorney discipline, and disbarment. (2) Includes cases that could not be classified. (3) Includes cases on civil procedures, commercial transactions, contracts, evidence, personal and real property, torts, and wills and trusts.

Selected Landmark Decisions of the U.S. Supreme Court

1803: *Marbury v. Madison.* The Court ruled that Congress exceeded its power in the Judiciary Act of 1789. The Court thus established its power to review acts of Congress and to declare invalid those it found to be in conflict with the Constitution.

1819: *Trustees of Dartmouth College v. Woodward.* The Court ruled that a state could not arbitrarily alter the terms of a college's contract. The Court later used a similar principle to limit the states' ability to interfere with business contracts.

1819: *McCulloch v. Maryland.* The Court ruled that Congress had the authority to charter a national bank, under the Constitution's granting of power to enact all laws "necessary and proper" to responsibilities of government.

1824: *Gibbons v. Ogden.* The Court ruled that New York state had overstepped its authority in granting a monopoly to two steamboat operators. According to the ruling, Congress's power to regulate interstate commerce included transportation.

1857: *Dred Scott v. Sandford.* The Court declared unconstitutional the already-repealed Missouri Compromise of 1820 because it deprived a person of "property"—an enslaved person—without due process of law. The Court also ruled that enslaved individuals were not citizens of any state nor of the U.S. The latter part of the decision was overturned by ratification of the 14th Amendment in 1868.

1880: *Strauder v. West Virginia.* The Court struck down a state law mandating that jurors must be white, ruling it a

violation of the right to equal protection under the 14th Amendment.

1896: *Plessy v. Ferguson.* The Court ruled that a state law requiring federal railroad trains to provide "equal but separate" facilities for Black and white passengers neither infringed upon federal authority to regulate interstate commerce nor violated the 13th and 14th Amendments. What became known as the "separate but equal" doctrine remained in effect until the 1954 *Brown v. Board of Education* decision.

1904: *Northern Securities Co. v. U.S.* The Court ruled that a holding company formed solely to eliminate competition between two railroad lines was a combination in restraint of trade, violating the 1890 federal Sherman Antitrust Act.

1908: *Muller v. Oregon.* The Court upheld a state law limiting the working hours of women. (Louis D. Brandeis, counsel for the state, in what is known as the "Brandeis brief," cited evidence from social workers, physicians, and factory inspectors that long work hours were harmful to women.)

1911: *Standard Oil Co. of New Jersey v. U.S.* The Court ruled that the Standard Oil Trust must be dissolved because of its unreasonable restraint of trade.

1919: *Schenck v. U.S.* The Court sustained the Espionage Act of 1917, maintaining that freedom of speech and press could be constrained if "the words used ... create a clear and present danger."

1925: Gitlow v. New York. The Court ruled that the 1st Amendment prohibition against government abridgment of the freedom of speech applied to the states as well as to the federal government. The decision was the first of a number of rulings holding that the 14th Amendment extended the guarantees of the Bill of Rights to state action.

1935: Schechter Poultry Corp. v. U.S. The Court ruled that Congress exceeded its authority to delegate legislative powers and to regulate interstate commerce when it enacted the National Industrial Recovery Act (1933), which afforded the U.S. president too much discretionary power.

1944: Korematsu v. U.S. The Court upheld the constitutionality of an order barring all persons of Japanese ancestry, including U.S. citizens, from much of the West Coast, forcing them into internment camps, ruling that the need to prevent espionage outweighed the petitioner's civil rights. The ruling, never officially overturned, followed **Hirabayashi v. U.S.** (1943), in which the Court upheld the imposition of curfews on minority populations perceived to be a potential wartime threat.

1951: Dennis v. U.S. The Court upheld convictions under the Smith Act of 1940 for invoking Communist theory advocating the forcible overthrow of the government. In **Yates v. U.S.** (1957), the Court moderated this ruling by allowing such advocacy in the abstract, if not connected to action to achieve the goal.

1952: Youngstown Sheet & Tube Co. v. Sawyer. The Court ruled that the president had exceeded his wartime power in ordering the seizure of private steel mills during a nationwide steelworkers' strike. The Court held that neither the Constitution nor the role of commander in chief gave the president the authority to interfere in labor issues.

1954: Brown v. Board of Education of Topeka. The Court ruled that separate public schools for Black and white students were inherently unequal, so state-sanctioned segregation in public schools violated the equal protection guarantee of the 14th Amendment. The Court decided **Bolling v. Sharpe** the same year, ruling that the congressionally mandated segregated public school system in the District of Columbia violated the 5th Amendment's due process guarantee of personal liberty. In **Brown II** (1955), the Court ordered the integration of schools with "all deliberate speed." The Brown rulings also led to abolition of state-sponsored segregation in other public facilities.

1957: Roth v. U.S.; Alberts v. California. The Court ruled obscene material—defined as appealing primarily to "prurient interest" in the view of "the average person, applying contemporary community standards"—was not protected by 1st Amendment guarantees of freedom of speech and press, being "utterly without redeeming social importance." This definition was modified in later decisions, including **Miller v. California** (1973).

1958: Cooper v. Aaron. The Court held that Arkansas could not nullify **Brown v. Board of Education** (1954) through the passage of legislation or constitutional amendments barring integration. The opinion of the Court affirmed its reading of the Constitution as the "supreme law of the land."

1961: Mapp v. Ohio. The Court ruled that evidence obtained in violation of the 4th Amendment guarantee against unreasonable search and seizure must be excluded from use in state as well as federal trials.

1962: Baker v. Carr. The Court held that constitutional challenges to the unequal distribution of voters among legislative districts could be resolved by federal courts.

1962: Engel v. Vitale. The Court held that government bodies could not encourage the recitation of a state-composed prayer in public schools, even if nondenominational, because that would be an unconstitutional attempt to establish religion.

1963: Gideon v. Wainwright. The Court ruled that indigent defendants, even in state cases, have a right to legal counsel as guaranteed by the 6th Amendment.

1964: New York Times Co. v. Sullivan. The Court ruled that the 1st Amendment protected the press from libel suits for defamatory reports about public officials unless an injured party could prove that a defamatory report was made out of "actual malice," with "reckless disregard" for the truth.

1964: Heart of Atlanta Motel v. U.S. The Court upheld the constitutionality of Title II of the 1964 Civil Rights Act banning racial discrimination in motels/hotels engaged in interstate commerce (by accommodating travelers from other states). The Court in **Katzenbach v. McClung** (1964) held that Title II also applied to restaurants and businesses that purchased a substantial percentage of food or goods from other states.

1965: Griswold v. Connecticut. The Court ruled that a state unconstitutionally interfered with privacy in a marriage when it prohibited all persons, including married couples, from using contraceptives.

1966: Miranda v. Arizona. The Court ruled that, under the guarantee of due process, suspects in custody, before being questioned, must be informed that they have the right to remain silent, that anything they say may be used against them, and that they have the right to counsel.

1967: Loving v. Virginia. The Court unanimously struck down all state laws banning interracial marriage.

1968: Terry v. Ohio. The Court ruled that a "stop and frisk" performed without a warrant or probable cause was not a violation of 4th Amendment rights, provided that the law enforcement officer had a reasonable suspicion that the subject was armed and dangerous, or had committed or was about to commit a crime.

1969: Brandenburg v. Ohio. The Court held that government cannot restrict inflammatory speech unless it is "directed to inciting or producing imminent lawless action AND is likely to incite or produce such action." The so-called Brandenburg test refined the "clear and present danger" outlined in **Schenck v. U.S.** (1927) and overturned the holding in **Whitney v. California** (1927) that speech advocating violence could be prohibited.

1973: Roe v. Wade; Doe v. Bolton. The Court ruled that the fetus was not a "person" with constitutional rights and that a right to privacy inherent in the 14th Amendment's due process guarantee of personal liberty protected a woman's decision to have an abortion. During the first trimester of pregnancy, the Court maintained, the decision should be left entirely to a woman and her physician. Some regulation of abortion procedures was allowed in the second trimester and some restriction of abortion in the third.

1974: U.S. v. Nixon. The Court ruled that neither the separation of powers nor the need to preserve the confidentiality of presidential communications could alone justify an absolute executive privilege of immunity from judicial demands for evidence to be used in a criminal trial.

1976: Gregg v. Georgia; Proffitt v. Florida; Jurek v. Texas. The Court held that death, as a punishment for persons convicted of first-degree murder, was not in and of itself cruel and unusual punishment in violation of the 8th Amendment. But the Court ruled that the sentencing judge and jury must consider the character of the offender and the circumstances of the particular crime.

1978: Regents of the Univ. of Calif. v. Bakke. The Court ruled that an admissions program for a state medical school, under which a set number of places were reserved for minorities, violated the 1964 Civil Rights Act, which forbids the exclusion of anyone from a federally funded program based on race. However, the Court ruled that race could be considered as one of a complex of factors.

1985: New Jersey v. T.L.O. The Court ruled that officials who carry out searches on school grounds do not violate students' 4th Amendment rights because students' privacy rights may be outweighed by schools' need to maintain learning environments. The ruling put in place less stringent standards of required "reasonableness" for such searches.

1986: Batson v. Kentucky. The Court ruled that a peremptory challenge cannot be used in a criminal case to exclude a juror solely because of race.

1986: Bowers v. Hardwick. The Court refused to extend any right of privacy to homosexual activity, upholding a Georgia anti-sodomy law that in effect made such activity a crime. Georgia's supreme court struck down the law in 1998, and in **Lawrence v. Texas** (2003), the U.S. Supreme Court struck down all state antisodomy laws as violations of liberty prohibited in the 14th Amendment's due process clause. In **Romer v. Evans** (1996), the Court struck down a Colorado constitutional provision that barred homosexuals from recognition as a protected class, ruling that it violated the 14th Amendment's Equal Protection clause.

1989: Texas v. Johnson. The Court held the actions of a political activist who burned an American flag outside of the 1984 Republican National Convention were expressive and therefore protected by the 1st Amendment. The ruling invalidated laws in 48 states prohibiting flag desecration.

1990: Cruzan v. Missouri. The Court ruled that while a person had the right to refuse life-sustaining medical treatment, a state could require evidence that a comatose patient would not have wanted to live before withholding treatment. In two 1997 rulings, **Washington v. Glucksberg** and **Vacco v. Quill**, the Court ruled that states could ban doctor-assisted suicide.

1995: U.S. Term Limits, Inc. v. Thornton. The Court ruled that neither states nor Congress could limit terms of members of Congress because the Constitution reserves to the people the right to choose federal lawmakers.

1995: Adarand Constructors, Inc. v. Peña. The Court held that federal programs that classify people by race, unless "narrowly tailored" to further a "compelling governmental interest," may violate the right to equal protection and are thus subject to strict scrutiny.

1997: *Clinton v. Jones.* Rejecting an appeal by Pres. Clinton in a sexual harassment suit, the Court ruled that a sitting president did not have temporary immunity from a lawsuit for actions outside the realm of official duties.

1997: *City of Boerne v. Flores.* The Court overturned the portion of a 1993 law banning enforcement of state laws that "substantially burden" religious practice unless there is a "compelling governmental interest" to do so. The Court held that the act was an unwarranted intrusion by Congress on states' prerogatives and an infringement of the judiciary's role.

1997: *Reno v. ACLU.* Citing the right to free expression, the Court overturned a provision making it a crime to display or distribute "obscene or indecent" or "patently offensive" material on the Internet. The Court ruled, however, in *NEA v. Finley* (1998) that "general standards of decency" may be used as a criterion in federal arts funding.

1998: *Clinton v. City of New York.* The Court struck down the Line-Item Veto Act (1996), holding that it unconstitutionally gave the president "the unilateral power to change the text of duly enacted statutes."

1998: *Faragher v. City of Boca Raton; Burlington Industries, Inc. v. Ellerth.* The Court issued new guidelines for workplace sexual harassment suits, holding employers responsible for misconduct by supervisory employees. And in *Oncale v. Sundowner Offshore Services, Inc.* the same year, the Court ruled that the law against discrimination based on sex applies even if the harasser and harassed are the same sex.

1999: *Dept. of Commerce v. U.S. House of Representatives.* Upholding a challenge to plans for the 2000 census, the Court prohibited statistical sampling, favored by Democrats, in apportioning seats in the U.S. House.

1999: *Alden v. Maine; Florida Prepaid v. College Savings Bank; College Savings Bank v. Florida Prepaid.* In a series of rulings, the Court applied the principle of sovereign immunity to shield states in large part from being sued under federal law.

2000: *Boy Scouts of America v. Dale.* The Court ruled that the Boy Scouts could dismiss a troop leader after learning he was gay, holding that the right to freedom of association outweighed a New Jersey antidiscrimination statute.

2000: *Bush v. Gore.* The Court ruled that manual recounts in Florida of ballots cast in the 2000 presidential election could not proceed because inconsistent evaluation standards violated the equal protection clause. In effect, the ruling meant the existing official results would stand, making George W. Bush the narrow winner of the election.

2001: *Good News Club v. Milford Central School.* The justices found that a private religious organization could not be denied equal access to a public school facility for after-school meetings because that would violate free speech rights.

2002: *Federal Maritime Commission v. South Carolina State Ports Authority.* The Court ruled that the 11th Amendment gave states immunity from private lawsuits involving federal agencies.

2002: *Atkins v. Virginia.* The Court ruled that the execution of mentally retarded criminals violated the 8th Amendment ban on cruel and unusual punishment. The Court ruled in *Roper v. Simmons* (2005) that executions of convicts who committed their crimes before age 18 were also prohibited on the same grounds.

2002: *Zelman v. Simmons-Harris.* The Court ruled that publicly funded tuition vouchers could be used at religious schools without violating the separation of church and state.

2003: *Grutter v. Bollinger; Gratz v. Bollinger.* The Court upheld the use of race as a factor in the Univ. of Michigan Law School's admissions policies because of the school's interest in a diverse student body. But the Court ruled against a strict point system based on racial and ethnic backgrounds as used in the university's undergraduate admissions process.

2004: *Tennessee v. Lane.* The Court ruled that disabled individuals could sue states under the Americans With Disabilities Act (1990) for failing to provide adequate access to state courthouses, despite states' usual immunity from private lawsuits in federal court under the 11th Amendment, which the Court ruled on in *Federal Maritime Commission v. South Carolina State Ports Authority* (2002).

2004: *Locke v. Davey.* The justices decided that a scholarship program provided by the state of Washington did not violate the right to free exercise of religion in denying aid to students preparing for the clergy.

2004: *Ashcroft v. ACLU.* The Court struck down federal legislation passed in 1998 to restrict online access to pornography by minors, as violating the right of free speech.

2005: *Kelo v. City of New London.* The Court ruled that local governments could force property owners to sell their land in order to facilitate private development projects deemed to be economically beneficial to the community.

2006: *Garcetti v. Ceballos.* The Court ruled that the 1st Amendment guarantee of free speech did not protect statements made by public employees in the course of their official duties.

2006: *Hamdan v. Rumsfeld.* The Court ruled that Pres. George W. Bush's system for trying terrorism detainees at the U.S. military base in Guantánamo Bay, Cuba, was unauthorized under federal law and the international Geneva Conventions. The Court furthermore ruled in *Boumediene v. Bush* (2008) that detainees had a right to challenge their detention in federal court by applying for a writ of habeas corpus.

2007: *Gonzales v. Carhart; Gonzales v. Planned Parenthood Federation of America.* The Court upheld a 2003 federal law prohibiting the abortion procedure known as intact dilation and extraction, or "partial-birth" abortion.

2007: *Parents Involved in Community Schools v. Seattle School District No. 1; Meredith v. Jefferson County Board of Education.* The Court ruled that two school districts could not, to encourage diversity, use "racial classifications in making school assignments."

2008: *Crawford v. Marion County Election Board.* The Court upheld the constitutionality of an Indiana law requiring in-person voters to present valid government photo identification.

2008: *District of Columbia v. Heller.* The Court overturned DC's handgun ban, ruling that the 2nd Amendment protected an individual's right to own guns for personal use.

2010: *Citizens United v. Federal Election Commission.* The Court ruled that a federal law barring corporations from using general funds to finance campaign advertisements was unconstitutional. The decision cast doubt on many laws restricting political spending by corporations and unions.

2011: *Snyder v. Phelps.* The justices found that an antigay church whose members protested at the funeral of a Marine could not be held liable for intrusion or emotional distress because the protests were protected by the 1st Amendment.

2012: *U.S. v. Jones.* The Court ruled that attaching a GPS tracking device to a suspect's car and monitoring its movements requires a search warrant, as the 4th Amendment prohibition against unreasonable search and seizure applies.

2012: *Miller v. Alabama.* The Court ruled that mandatory life sentences of juveniles without the possibility of parole constitute cruel and unusual punishment, barred by the 8th Amendment. The decision extended *Graham v. Florida,* a 2010 case holding that juveniles may not receive life sentences for nonhomicide crimes.

2012: *Natl. Federation of Independent Business v. Sebelius.* The Court ruled Congress acted within its powers of taxation in enacting the individual-mandate provision of the Patient Protection and Affordable Care Act (ACA). But the Court ruled unconstitutional the provision of the act's Medicaid expansion that threatened non-compliant states with loss of funding.

2013: *Shelby County v. Holder.* The justices struck down a key provision of the 1965 Voting Rights Act, meant to prevent discriminatory voting regulations, because it relied on outdated information to identify jurisdictions for additional scrutiny.

2013: *U.S. v. Windsor.* The Court struck down the central provision of the 1996 federal Defense of Marriage Act (DOMA), which prohibited federal recognition of same-sex marriages. A separate decision the same year, in *Hollingsworth v. Perry,* had the effect of legalizing same-sex marriage in California.

2014: *Riley v. California; U.S. v. Wurie.* The Court decided that police generally could not search the mobile telephones of arrested individuals without a search warrant.

2014: *Burwell v. Hobby Lobby Stores; Conestoga Wood Specialties Corp. v. Burwell.* The justices ruled that some closely held corporations could claim an exemption—based on their owners' religious beliefs and the 1993 Religious Freedom Restoration Act—from a 2010 ACA mandate requiring many businesses to provide health insurance that covers contraception.

2015: *Obergefell v. Hodges.* The Court ruled that state bans on same-sex marriage violated same-sex couples' rights under the due process and equal protection clauses of the 14th Amendment.

2016: *Whole Woman's Health v. Hellerstedt.* The justices ruled that a Texas law that included stringent regulations on abortion providers did not pass the "undue burden" standard the Court established in 1992's *Planned Parenthood v. Casey.*

2018: *Janus v. American Federation of State, County and Municipal Employees (AFSCME).* The Court struck down rules compelling public employees who opted not to join a union to pay fees in support of its collective-bargaining efforts.

2019: *Rucho v. Common Cause; Lamone v. Benisek.* The Court found that federal courts have no constitutional basis for intervening to block partisan gerrymandering.

See also Year in Review: Notable Supreme Court Decisions.

STATES AND OTHER AREAS OF THE U.S.

Sources: Population: Decennial Censuses and Population Estimates Program, U.S. Census Bureau, U.S. Dept. of Commerce; population as of July 1, 2019, unless otherwise noted. Pop. density is for land area only. **Racial distribution** categories are abbreviated; their full forms are white, Black or African American, Asian, American Indian and Alaska Native, Native Hawaiian and other Pacific Islander, two or more races. Categories may not add up to 100% due to rounding. **Hispanic** or Latino persons may be of any race. **Area:** Geography Division, U.S. Census Bureau, U.S. Dept. of Commerce. **Acres forested:** U.S. Forest Service, U.S. Dept. of Agriculture; source year may vary. **Chief airports:** Federal Aviation Admin., U.S. Dept. of Transportation. Chief airports had 500,000+ boardings in 2019; not all states had airports meeting this threshold. All **Economy** data as of 2019 unless otherwise noted. **Chief manuf. goods:** Manufacturing and Construction Division, U.S. Census Bureau, U.S. Dept. of Commerce. **Chief crops:** Natl. Agricultural Statistics Service, U.S. Dept. of Agriculture. **Farm income:** Economic Research Service, U.S. Dept. of Agriculture; 2018 cash receipts. **Nonfuel minerals:** Office of Mineral Information, U.S. Dept. of Interior; estimated 2019 data. Some states exclude small amounts to avoid disclosing proprietary data. **Commercial fishing:** Natl. Marine Fisheries Service, U.S. Dept. of Commerce; 2018 value. **Gross state product** and **Per cap. pers. income:** Bureau of Economic Analysis, U.S. Dept. of Commerce; as of Dec. 2019. **Sales tax:** Federation of Tax Administrators; as of Jan. 1, 2020. **Gasoline tax:** American Petroleum Institute; as of Jan. 1, 2020; incl. state excise tax, federal excise tax (18.4 cents per gallon), and other state fees. **Employment distrib.** and **Unemployment:** Bureau of Labor Statistics, U.S. Dept. of Labor; distribution is for non-farm jobs as of May 2020; annual unemployment rate for 2019. **Min. wage/hr.:** U.S. Dept. of Labor; as of July 1, 2020. If a state has no minimum wage, or the state minimum wage is lower than the federal minimum wage, the federal rate of $7.25 applies. Small businesses may have lower minimum wages. Some municipalities may have different minimum wages. **New private housing:** Manufacturing and Construction Division, U.S. Census Bureau, U.S. Dept. of Commerce. Figures are building permits issued and est. value of the construction. **Broadband internet:** Industry Analysis and Tech. Division, Fed. Communications Commission; Natl. Telecommunications and Information Administration, U.S. Dept. of Commerce. Broadband connections have minimum speeds of at least 3 megabits per second (Mbps) downstream and 200 kilobits per second (kbps) upstream as of Dec. 2017; figure given is broadband as a percentage of total internet connections. **Commercial banks** and **Savings institutions:** Federal Deposit Insurance Corp., as of June 30, 2019; FDIC-insured institutions only. **Lottery:** North American Assn. of State and Provincial Lotteries, FY 2019. Data may be unaudited and in some cases were gathered by third party; profit is amount of total funds transferred to public beneficiaries, after prizes to players/retailers and administrative costs. **Fed. civ. employees:** Office of Personnel Mgmt., U.S. Dept. of Labor; as of June 2019. **Education:** Natl. Ctr. for Education Statistics; high school graduation rates as of 2017-18 school year; number of colleges/univ. as of 2018-19. Data for 4-yr. private institutions does not include for-profit colleges/universities. **Energy:** Energy Information Admin., U.S. Dept. of Energy; average per capita monthly electricity consumption and cost for residential customers in 2018. **Tourism:** U.S. Travel Assn.; tourist spending in 2018. Other information from sources in individual states. NA = Not available; AFB = Air Force base; JRB = joint reserve base; NAS = naval air station.

    Famous persons lists may include non-natives associated with the state as well as persons born there. **Websites** are subject to change and are not endorsed by *The World Almanac.*

Alabama (AL)

Heart of Dixie, Camellia State

People. Population: 4,903,185; rank: 24. **Pop. change** (2010-19): 2.6%. **Pop. density:** 96.8 per sq mi. **Racial distribution:** 69.1% white; 26.8% Black; 1.5% Asian; 0.7% Amer. Ind.; 0.1% Hawaiian/Pacific Islander; 2 or more races, 1.8%. **Hispanic pop.:** 4.6%.

    Geography. Total area: 52,420 sq mi; rank: 30. **Land area:** 50,645 sq mi; rank: 28. **Acres forested:** 23.1 mil. **Location:** East South Central state extending N-S from Tennessee to the Gulf of Mexico; E of the Mississippi R. **Climate:** long, hot summers; mild winters; generally abundant rain. **Topography:** coastal plains, including Prairie Black Belt, give way to hills, broken terrain; highest elevation 2,413 ft. **Capital:** Montgomery. **Chief airports:** Birmingham, Huntsville.

    Economy. Chief industries: chemicals, electronics, apparel, primary metals, lumber and wood products, food processing, fabricated metals, automotive tires, oil and gas exploration. **Chief manuf. goods:** poultry processing, paper and paperboard, iron and steel, petroleum, automotive tires, aerospace, aluminum, auto body and parts. **Chief crops:** cotton, greenhouse and nursery, hay, peanuts, corn, soybeans. **Farm income:** Crops: $1.25 bil. Livestock: $4.54 bil. **Nonfuel minerals:** $1.7 bil; cement (portland), lime, sand and gravel (construction), sand and gravel (industrial), stone (crushed). **Commercial fishing:** $67.7 mil. **Chief port:** Mobile. **Gross state product:** $231.0 bil. **Sales tax:** 4.0%. **Gasoline tax:** 45.61 cents/gal. **Employment distrib.:** 19.8% govt.; 19.4% trade/trans./util.; 13.2% mfg.; 12.0% ed./health; 11.6% prof./bus. serv.; 7.8% leisure/hosp.; 5.0% finance; 5.4% constr./mining/log.; 1.0% info.; 4.8% other serv. **Unemployment:** 3.0%. **Min. wage/hr.:** none. **Per cap. pers. income:** $43,880. **New private housing:** 17,748 units/$3.5 bil. **Broadband internet:** 94.9%. **Commercial banks:** 146; deposits: $107.2 bil. **Savings institutions:** /; deposits: $425.0 mil.

    Federal govt. Fed. civ. employees: 38,764; **avg. salary:** $85,021. **Notable fed. facilities:** Redstone Arsenal; Ft. Rucker; Marshall Space Flight Ctr., Huntsville; Anniston Army Depot; Maxwell AFB and Gunter Annex; Army Corps of Engineers, Mobile District.

    Education. High school grad. rate: 90.0%. **4-yr. public coll./univ.:** 14; **2-yr. public:** 24; **4-yr. private:** 20.

    Energy. Electricity use/cost: 1,236 kWh, $150.54.

    State data. Motto: Audemus Jura Nostra Defendere (We dare defend our rights). **Flower:** Camellia. **Bird:** Northern flicker (yellowhammer is local nickname). **Tree:** Southern longleaf pine. **Song:** "Alabama." **Entered union:** Dec. 14, 1819; rank: 22nd.

    Tourism. Tourist spending: $11.5 bil. **Attractions:** First White House of the Confederacy, Civil Rights Memorial, Alabama Shakespeare Festival, Legacy Museum, National Memorial for Peace and Justice, in Montgomery; Ivy Green (Helen Keller birthplace), Tuscumbia; Barber Vintage Motorsports Museum, Civil Rights Institute, Vulcan Park and Museum (world's largest cast iron statue), in Birmingham; G. W. Carver Interpretive Museum, Tuskegee; W. C. Handy Home, Museum, and Library, Frank Lloyd Wright's Rosenbaum House, in Florence; U.S. Space & Rocket Ctr., Huntsville; Moundville Archaeological Park; USS *Alabama* Memorial Park, Mobile; Gulf State Park, Gulf Shores. **Information:** Alabama Tourism Dept., 401 Adams Ave., Ste. 126, P.O. Box 4927, Montgomery, AL 36103; 1-800-ALABAMA, (334) 242-4169; alabama.travel

    History. Alabama was inhabited by the Creek, Cherokee, Chickasaw, Alabama, and Choctaw peoples when Spanish explorers arrived in the early 1500s. The French made the first permanent settlement at Ft. Louis, 1702, and founded Mobile, 1711. France later gave up the entire region to England under the Treaty of Paris, 1763. Spanish forces took control of the Mobile Bay area, 1780, and it remained under Spanish control until seized by U.S. troops, 1813. Most of present-day Alabama was held by the Creeks until Gen. Andrew Jackson broke their power, 1814. When Alabama became a state, 1819, enslaved Black people made up about one-third of the population. The Indian Removal Act of 1830 forced most remaining Creeks east. The state seceded, 1861, and the Confederate states were organized Feb. 4, at Montgomery, the first capital. The state was readmitted, 1868. Birmingham, founded 1871, became a center for iron- and steelmaking. The Montgomery bus boycott, 1955, sparked by Rosa Parks, helped launch the civil rights movement. Other confrontations occurred at Birmingham, 1963, and Selma, 1965. The leading political figure from the 1960s through the '80s, four-term gov. George Wallace, started as a segregationist but later won with Black support. Growth in the auto industry boosted the economy as the 21st cent. began. A string of tornadoes in 2011 killed at least 248. Jefferson County, which includes Birmingham, filed the then-most expensive municipal bankruptcy in 2011. Gov. Robert Bentley pleaded guilty to misdemeanor charges connected with a sex scandal and resigned, 2017. Roy Moore, a former state chief justice, was upset by Doug Jones (D) in a special election for the U.S. Senate in 2017 after several women alleged Moore had a history of sexual misconduct. A tornado in Lee County killed 23 people Mar. 3, 2019. The state in May 2019 passed a law outlawing abortion in nearly all cases, which a judge, Oct. 2019, temporarily blocked from taking effect.

    Famous Alabamians. Hank Aaron, Tallulah Bankhead, Charles Barkley, Hugo L. Black, Paul "Bear" Bryant, George Washington Carver, Nat King Cole, Courteney Cox, William Christopher "W. C." Handy, Polly Holliday, Bo Jackson, Helen Keller, Coretta Scott King, Harper Lee, Joe Louis, Willie Mays, Jim Nabors, Jesse Owens, Terrell Owens, Rosa Parks, Condoleezza Rice, Lionel Richie, Robin Roberts, Octavia Spencer, Channing Tatum, George C. Wallace, Booker T. Washington, Hank Williams.

    Website. www.alabama.gov

Alaska (AK)

The Last Frontier (unofficial)

People. Population: 731,545; rank: 48. **Pop. change** (2010-19): 3.0%. **Pop. density:** 1.3 per sq mi. **Racial**

distribution: 65.3% white; 3.7% Black; 6.5% Asian; 15.6% Amer. Ind.; 1.4% Hawaiian/Pacific Islander; 2 or more races, 7.5%. **Hispanic pop.:** 7.3%.

Geography. Total area: 665,384 sq mi; rank: 1. **Land area:** 570,641 sq mi; rank: 1. **Acres forested:** 12.0 mil. **Location:** NW corner of North America, bordered on E by Canada. **Climate:** SE, SW, and central regions, moist and mild; far N extremely dry. Extended summer days, winter nights throughout. **Topography:** includes Pacific and Arctic mountain systems, central plateau, and Arctic slope. Denali, formerly Mt. McKinley, 20,310 ft, is the highest point in N. America. **Capital:** Juneau. **Chief airports:** Anchorage, Fairbanks.

Economy. Chief industries: petroleum, tourism, fishing, mining, forestry, transportation, aerospace. **Chief manuf. goods:** petroleum, seafood. **Chief crops:** greenhouse products, barley, oats, hay, potatoes, carrots. **Farm income:** Crops: $30.62 mil. Livestock: $8.04 mil. **Nonfuel minerals:** $3.1 bil; gold, lead, sand and gravel (construction), silver, zinc. **Commercial fishing:** $1.8 bil. **Chief ports:** Anchorage, Dutch Harbor, Kodiak, Juneau, Sitka, Valdez. **Gross state product:** $55.4 bil. **Sales tax:** none. **Gasoline tax:** 32.75 cents/gal. **Employment distrib.:** 25.2% govt.; 21.1% trade/trans./util.; 3.0% mfg.; 15.7% ed./health; 9.1% prof./bus. serv.; 7.7% leisure/hosp.; 3.9% finance; 9.4% constr./mining/log.; 1.7% info.; 3.2% other serv. **Unemployment:** 6.1%. **Min. wage/hr.:** $10.19. **Per cap. pers. income:** $62,102. **New private housing:** 1,680 units/$412.9 mil. **Broadband internet:** 92.0%. **Commercial banks:** 6; deposits $11.4 bil. **Savings institutions:** 1; deposits $353.0 mil.

Federal govt. Fed. civ. employees: 11,328; **avg. salary:** $81,814. **Notable fed. facilities:** Joint Base Elmendorf-Richardson; Ft. Wainwright; Eielson AFB; Ft. Greely.

Education. High school grad. rate: 78.5%. **4-yr. public coll./univ.:** 4; **2-yr. public:** 0; **4-yr. private:** 2.

Energy. Electricity use/cost: 572 kWh, $125.57.

State data. Motto: North to the future. **Flower:** Forget-me-not. **Bird:** Willow ptarmigan. **Tree:** Sitka spruce. **Song:** "Alaska's Flag." **Entered union:** Jan. 3, 1959; rank: 49th.

Tourism. Tourist spending: $2.9 bil. **Attractions:** Portage Glacier, in Chugach Natl. Forest; Mendenhall Glacier, in Tongass Natl. Forest; Totem Heritage Ctr., Ketchikan; Glacier Bay Natl. Park and Preserve; Denali (formerly Mt. McKinley, N. America's highest peak), in Denali Natl. Park and Preserve; Mt. Roberts Tramway, Juneau; Alaska Maritime Natl. Wildlife Refuge; St. Michael's Cathedral, Alaska Raptor Ctr., in Sitka; White Pass & Yukon Route railroad, Skagway; Katmai Natl. Park and Preserve; Univ. of Alaska Museum of the North, Fairbanks. **Information:** Alaska Travel Industry Association, 2600 Cordova St., Ste. 201, Anchorage, AK 99503; 1-800-327-9372; www.travelalaska.com

History. Early inhabitants included the Tlingit-Haida and Athabascan peoples. Ancestors of the Aleut and Inuit (Eskimo) probably arrived from Siberia between 10,000 and 6,000 years ago. Vitus Bering, a Dane sailing for Russia, was the first European to land in Alaska, 1741. Russians, pursuing the fur trade, established a permanent settlement on Kodiak Island, 1784. Sec. of State William H. Seward bought Alaska from Russia for $7.2 mil in 1867, a deal some called "Seward's Folly." Discovery of gold in the Klondike region of Canada's Yukon Territory, 1896, triggered an Alaskan gold rush. Alaska became a territory, 1912, and a state, 1959. A huge oil find at Prudhoe Bay, 1968, led to construction of the Trans-Alaska Pipeline, 1974-77. The *Exxon Valdez* supertanker ran aground, 1989, spilling about 11 mil gallons of crude oil; the cleanup cost more than $2.2 bil. Congress included a measure permitting oil and gas drilling in the Arctic National Wildlife Refuge in the tax bill passed in Dec. 2017, ending a four-decade battle. A magnitude 7.0 earthquake centered near Anchorage struck Nov. 30, 2018, causing at least $75 mil in damage.

Famous Alaskans. Tom Bodett, Susan Butcher, Ernest Gruening, Jewel (Kilcher), Tony Knowles, Sydney Laurence, Sarah Palin, Libby Riddles, Curt Schilling, Jefferson "Soapy" Smith.

Website. www.alaska.gov

Arizona (AZ)
Grand Canyon State

People. Population: 7,278,717; rank: 14. **Pop. change** (2010-19): 13.9%. **Pop. density:** 64.1 per sq mi. **Racial distribution:** 82.6% white; 5.2% Black; 3.7% Asian; 5.3% Amer. Ind.; 0.3% Hawaiian/Pacific Islander; 2 or more races, 2.9%. **Hispanic pop.:** 31.7%.

Geography. Total area: 113,990 sq mi; rank: 6. **Land area:** 113,594 sq mi; rank: 6. **Acres forested:** 18.5 mil. **Location:** southwestern U.S. **Climate:** clear and dry in southern regions and northern plateau; high central areas have heavy winter

snows. **Topography:** Colorado Plateau in the N, containing the Grand Canyon; Mexican Highlands run NW to SE; Sonoran Desert in the SW. **Capital:** Phoenix. **Chief airports:** Phoenix, Tucson, Mesa.

Economy. Chief industries: manufacturing, construction, tourism, mining, agriculture. **Chief manuf. goods:** aerospace, semiconductors, navigational instruments, cement, plastics, structural metals, dairy, printing, furniture. **Chief crops:** cotton, grapes, apples, lettuce, hay, potatoes, sorghum, barley, corn, wheat. **Farm income:** Crops: $2.43 bil. Livestock: $1.73 bil. **Nonfuel minerals:** $7.0 bil; cement (portland), copper, molybdenum concentrates, sand and gravel (construction), stone (crushed). **Gross state product:** $366.2 bil. **Sales tax:** 5.6%. **Gasoline tax:** 37.40 cents/gal. **Employment distrib.:** 15.1% govt.; 19.2% trade/trans./util.; 6.1% mfg.; 16.0% ed./health; 14.8% prof./bus. serv.; 8.8% leisure/hosp.; 8.3% finance; 6.7% constr./mining/log.; 1.6% info.; 3.3% other serv. **Unemployment:** 4.7%. **Min. wage/hr.:** $12.00. **Per cap. pers. income:** $46,233. **New private housing:** 46,580 units/$10.9 bil. **Broadband internet:** 97.4%. **Commercial banks:** 61; deposits: $137.4 bil. **Savings institutions:** 7; deposits: $4.5 bil. **Lottery:** total sales: $1.1 bil; profit: $230.4 mil.

Federal govt. Fed. civ. employees: 32,306; **avg. salary:** $72,044. **Notable fed. facilities:** Luke AFB; Davis-Monthan AFB; Ft. Huachuca; Yuma Proving Ground.

Education. High school grad. rate: 78.7%. **4-yr. public coll./univ.:** 9; **2-yr. public:** 20; **4-yr. private:** 12.

Energy. Electricity use/cost: 1,028 kWh, $131.31.

State data. Motto: Ditat Deus (God enriches). **Flower:** Blossom of the saguaro cactus. **Bird:** Cactus wren. **Tree:** Paloverde. **Song:** "Arizona." **Entered union:** Feb. 14, 1912; rank: 48th.

Tourism. Tourist spending: $21.6 bil. **Attractions:** Grand Canyon; Painted Desert, in Grand Canyon and Petrified Forest Natl. Parks; Glen Canyon Natl. Recreation Area; Canyon de Chelly Natl. Monument; Meteor Crater, near Winslow; London Bridge, Lake Havasu City; Biosphere 2, Oracle; Navajo Natl. Monument; Tombstone historic mining town; Tempe Town Lake. **Information:** Arizona Office of Tourism, 1110 W. Washington St., Ste. 155, Phoenix, AZ 85007; 1-866-275-5816; www.visitarizona.com

History. Paleo-Indians hunted large game in the area at least 12,000 years ago. Anasazi, Mogollon, and Hohokam civilizations lived there c. 300 BCE-1300 CE; Navajo and Apache came c. 15th cent. Marcos de Niza, a Spanish Franciscan, and Estevanico, a Moroccan-born enslaved Black man, explored, 1539; explorer Francisco Vásquez de Coronado visited, 1540. Eusebio Francisco Kino, a Jesuit missionary, taught Indians, 1692-1711, and left missions. Tubac, a Spanish fort, became the first European settlement, 1752. Spain ceded Arizona to Mexico, 1821. The U.S. took over, 1848, after the Mexican War. The area below the Gila R. came from Mexico in the Gadsden Purchase, 1853. Arizona became a territory, 1863. Apache wars ended with Geronimo's surrender, 1886. Arizona became a state, 1912, and grew rapidly after 1960 with a fourfold rise in population over the next four decades. Barry Goldwater was a leading conservative voice in the U.S. Senate (1953-65, 1969-87). The border with Mexico is a major gateway for illegal immigration to the U.S. In 2012, the U.S. Supreme Court struck down most provisions of a 2010 state immigration law that allowed police to make warrantless arrests of those reasonably suspected of having immigrated illegally. A statewide teacher walkout in Apr. 2018 demanded increased pay and school funding.

Famous Arizonans. Bruce Babbitt, Cochise, Alice Cooper, Geronimo, Gabrielle Giffords, Barry Goldwater, Zane Grey, Carl Hayden, George W. P. Hunt, Helen Hull Jacobs, Bil Keane, Percival Lowell, John McCain, John J. Rhodes, Linda Ronstadt, Emma Stone, Morris K. Udall, Stewart L. Udall, Frank Lloyd Wright.

Website. www.az.gov

Arkansas (AR)
Natural State, Razorback State

People. Population: 3,017,804; rank: 33. **Pop. change** (2010-19): 3.5%. **Pop. density:** 58.0 per sq mi. **Racial distribution:** 79.0% white; 15.7% Black; 1.7% Asian; 1.0% Amer. Ind.; 0.4% Hawaiian/Pacific Islander; 2 or more races, 2.2%. **Hispanic pop.:** 7.8%.

Geography. Total area: 53,179 sq mi; rank: 29. **Land area:** 52,035 sq mi; rank: 27. **Acres forested:** 18.9 mil. **Location:** West South Central state. **Climate:** long, hot summers, mild winters; generally abundant rainfall. **Topography:** eastern delta and prairie, southern lowland forests, and the northwestern highlands, which include the Ozark Plateaus. **Capital:** Little Rock. **Chief airports:** Little Rock, Bentonville.

Economy. Chief industries: manufacturing, agriculture, tourism, forestry. **Chief manuf. goods:** poultry processing, motor vehicles and parts, iron and steel, paper and paperboard, plastics, preserved fruits and vegetables, aerospace, rubber. **Chief crops:** rice, soybeans, cotton, hay, wheat, corn, sorghum, tomatoes, peaches, watermelons, pecans, blueberries, grapes. **Farm income:** Crops: $3.47 bil. Livestock: $5.57 bil. **Nonfuel minerals:** $901 mil; bromine, cement (portland), sand and gravel (construction), sand and gravel (industrial), stone (crushed). **Chief port:** Helena. **Gross state product:** $133.2 bil. **Sales tax:** 6.5%. **Gasoline tax:** 43.20 cents/gal. **Employment distrib.:** 17.0% govt.; 20.7% trade/trans./util.; 12.0% mfg.; 15.2% ed./health; 11.7% prof./bus. serv.; 7.8% leisure/hosp.; 5.1% finance; 4.9% constr./mining/log.; 0.9% info.; 4.6% other serv. **Unemployment:** 3.5%. **Min. wage/hr.:** $10.00. **Per cap. pers. income:** $44,845. **New private housing:** 12,723 units/$2.2 bil. **Broadband internet:** 94.2%. **Commercial banks:** 115; deposits: $70.8 bil. **Savings institutions:** 2; deposits: $187.0 mil. **Lottery:** total sales: $515.5 mil; profit: $98.4 mil.

Federal govt. Fed. civ. employees: 13,177; **avg. salary:** $69,442. **Notable fed. facilities:** Little Rock AFB; Pine Bluff Arsenal; Natl. Ctr. for Toxicological Research, Jefferson.

Education. High school grad. rate: 89.2%. **4-yr. public coll./univ.:** 11; **2-yr. public:** 22; **4-yr. private:** 14.

Energy. Electricity use/cost: 1,156 kWh, $113.36.

State data. Motto: Regnat Populus (The people rule). **Flower:** Apple blossom. **Bird:** Northern mockingbird. **Tree:** Pine. **Song:** "Arkansas." **Entered union:** June 15, 1836; rank: 25th.

Tourism. Tourist spending: $7.4 bil. **Attractions:** Eureka Springs; Ozark Folk Ctr. State Park, Mountain View; Blanchard Springs Caverns, in Ozark Natl. Forest; Crater of Diamonds State Park, Murfreesboro; Toltec Mounds Archeological State Park, Scott; Buffalo Natl. River; Hot Springs Natl. Park; Pea Ridge Natl. Military Park; William J. Clinton Presidential Library and Museum, Little Rock Central High School Natl. Historic Site, in Little Rock; Crystal Bridges Museum of American Art, Bentonville. **Information:** Arkansas Dept. of Parks & Tourism, 1 Capitol Mall, Little Rock, AR 72201; 1-800-NATURAL; www.arkansas.com

History. Quapaw, Caddo, Osage, Cherokee, and Choctaw peoples lived in the area at the time of European contact. The first European explorers were Hernando de Soto, 1541; Jacques Marquette and Louis Jolliet, 1673; and René-Robert Cavelier, sieur de La Salle, 1682. French fur trader Henri de Tonty founded the first settlement, 1686, at Arkansas Post. In 1762, the area was ceded by France to Spain, then given back, 1800, and was part of the Louisiana Purchase, 1803. It was made a territory, 1819, and entered the Union as a slave state, 1836. Arkansas seceded in 1861, after the Civil War began; it was readmitted, 1868. Pres. Eisenhower sent federal troops, 1957, to keep Gov. Orval Faubus from blocking racial integration at Central High School in Little Rock. Walmart, now the world's leading retailer, opened its first store in Rogers, 1962. Elected five times as governor, Bill Clinton later served two terms as president (1993-2001). His presidential library opened, 2004, in Little Rock. After 12 years without an execution, the state put to death four inmates in eight days in 2017.

Famous Arkansans. Daisy Bates, Dee Brown, Paul "Bear" Bryant, Glen Campbell, Hattie Wyatt Caraway, Johnny Cash, Wesley Clark, Bill Clinton, Jay Hanna "Dizzy" Dean, Orval Faubus, James William Fulbright, Al Green, John Grisham, Levon Helm, John H. Johnson, Douglas MacArthur, John Little McClellan, James E. McDonnell, Scottie Pippen, Dick Powell, Brooks Robinson, Winthrop Rockefeller, Mary Steenburgen, Edward Durell Stone, Billy Bob Thornton, Sam Walton, Archibald Yell.

Website. www.arkansas.gov

California (CA)
Golden State

People. Population: 39,512,223; rank: 1. **Pop. change** (2010-19): 6.1%. **Pop. density:** 253.6 per sq mi. **Racial distribution:** 71.9% white; 6.5% Black; 15.5% Asian; 1.6% Amer. Ind.; 0.5% Hawaiian/Pacific Islander; 2 or more races, 4.0%. **Hispanic pop.:** 39.4%.

Geography. Total area: 163,695 sq mi; rank: 3. **Land area:** 155,779 sq mi; rank: 3. **Acres forested:** 31.7 mil. **Location:** western coast of U.S. **Climate:** moderate temperatures and rainfall along the coast; extremes in the interior. **Topography:** long mountainous coastline; central valley; Sierra Nevada on the E; desert basins in southern interior; rugged mountains in N. **Capital:** Sacramento. **Chief airports:** Los Angeles,

San Francisco, San Diego, San Jose, Oakland, Sacramento, Santa Ana, Burbank, Ontario, Long Beach, Palm Springs, Fresno, Santa Barbara.

Economy. Chief industries: agriculture, tourism, apparel, electronics, telecommunications, entertainment. **Chief manuf. goods:** petroleum, aerospace, precision instruments, semiconductors, telecom and broadcasting equip., pharmaceutical, wineries, plastics, medical equip., preserved fruits and vegetables, printing, dairy, cut and sew apparel, motor vehicles. **Chief crops:** grapes, nursery products, almonds, lettuce, hay, strawberries, floriculture, tomatoes, cotton, oranges, pistachios, walnuts, broccoli, carrots, rice, peaches, lemons. **Farm income:** Crops: $38.08 bil. Livestock: $11.74 bil. **Nonfuel minerals:** $4.5 bil; boron minerals, cement (portland), gold, sand and gravel (construction), stone (crushed). **Commercial fishing:** $182.9 mil. **Chief ports:** Long Beach, Los Angeles, San Diego, Port Hueneme, Richmond, Oakland, San Francisco, Stockton. **Gross state product:** $3.1 tril. **Sales tax:** 7.25%. **Gasoline tax:** 79.00 cents/gal. **Employment distrib.:** 16.4% govt.; 17.5% trade/trans./util.; 7.9% mfg.; 17.0% ed./health; 16.5% prof./bus. serv.; 7.5% leisure/hosp.; 5.4% finance; 5.6% constr./mining/log.; 3.3% info.; 2.8% other serv. **Unemployment:** 4.0%. **Min. wage/hr.:** $12.00. **Per cap. pers. income:** $66,661. **New private housing:** 110,197 units/$26.6 bil. **Broadband internet:** 97.8%. **Commercial banks:** 181; deposits: $1.4 tril. **Savings institutions:** 17; deposits: $18.7 bil. **Lottery:** total sales: $7.4 bil; profit: $1.8 bil.

Federal govt. Fed. civ. employees: 145,125; **avg. salary:** $86,286. **Notable fed. facilities:** USMC Camp Pendleton; Naval Base Coronado; Marine Corps Air Ground Combat Ctr., 29 Palms; Marine Corps Air Station Miramar; Travis AFB; Naval Research Lab, Monterey; Lawrence Livermore Natl. Lab; Lawrence Berkeley Natl. Lab; NASA Jet Propulsion Lab, Pasadena; Edwards AFB (NASA Dryden Flight Research Ctr., AF Test Ctr.); San Francisco Mint.

Education. High school grad. rate: 83.0%. **4-yr. public coll./univ.:** 49; **2-yr. public:** 102; **4-yr. private:** 143.

Energy. Electricity use/cost: 546 kWh, $102.90.

State data. Motto: Eureka (I have found it). **Flower:** Golden poppy. **Bird:** California valley quail. **Tree:** California redwood. **Song:** "I Love You, California." **Entered union:** Sept. 9, 1850; rank: 31st.

Tourism. Tourist spending: $148.4 bil. **Attractions:** Queen Mary, Aquarium of the Pacific, in Long Beach; Palomar Observatory, Palomar Mountain; Disneyland Resort, Anaheim; Getty Center, Universal Studios Hollywood, Griffith Observatory, in Los Angeles; Tournament of Roses and Rose Bowl, Pasadena; The California Museum, California State Railroad Museum, in Sacramento; San Diego Zoo, USS Midway Museum, in San Diego; Yosemite Valley; Lassen Volcanic, Sequoia, and Kings Canyon Natl. Parks; Mojave and Sonoran Deserts; Death Valley; Golden Gate Park, Alcatraz Island, in San Francisco; Napa Valley wine region; Monterey Bay Aquarium, Monterey Peninsula; Ancient Bristlecone Pine Forest (oldest known living trees on Earth), in Inyo Natl. Forest; Redwood Natl. and State Parks; Muir Woods Natl. Monument, Mill Valley. **Information:** California Tourism, P.O. Box 1499, Sacramento, CA 95812-1499; 1-877-225-4367; www.visitcalifornia.com

History. Early inhabitants included more than 100 different Native American tribes with multiple dialects. The first European explorers were Juan Rodríguez Cabrillo, 1542, and Sir Francis Drake, 1579. The first settlement was the Spanish Alta California mission at San Diego, 1769, first in a string founded by Franciscan Father Junípero Serra. California became a province of independent Mexico, 1821. U.S. traders and settlers arrived in the 19th cent. and staged the Bear Flag revolt, 1846, in protest against Mexican rule; later that year U.S. forces occupied California. At the end of the Mexican War, Mexico ceded the territory to the U.S., 1848; that same year gold was discovered, and the famed gold rush began. California became a state, 1850. An economic downturn in the 1870s spurred riots against Chinese immigrants, who had come as laborers in the boom years. An earthquake and related fires devastated San Francisco, 1906. During World War II, Japanese Americans, many of them U.S. citizens, were held in detention camps, 1942-45. Ronald Reagan, a former movie actor, became state governor (1967-75) and U.S. president (1981-89). A budget crisis, 2003, resulted in the recall of Gov. Gray Davis and the election of another actor, Arnold Schwarzenegger. A 6-year-old drought mostly ended in 2017. Wildfires caused 54 deaths in 2017 and destroyed thousands of homes and other structures. The 2018 fire season was the deadliest—at least 85 killed in Nov. 2018 Camp fire alone—and most destructive (1.7 mil acres burned) in state history. Gov. Gavin Newsom in 2019 issued a moratorium on the death penalty. San Francisco in 2019 became the first major U.S. city to ban use of facial recognition technology by law enforcement and government. In Sept. 2019, a dive boat fire off Santa Cruz island killed 34 of 39 people aboard.

Famous Californians. Tom Brady, Edmund G. (Pat) Brown, Jerry Brown, Luther Burbank, Julia Child, Ted Danson, Cameron Diaz, Leonardo DiCaprio, Joe DiMaggio, Landon Donovan, Clint Eastwood, Dianne Feinstein, John C. Fremont, Tom Hanks, Kamala Harris, William Randolph Hearst, Helen Hunt, Steve Jobs, Jimmie Johnson, Angelina Jolie, Jack Kemp, Jason Kidd, Brie Larson, Lisa Leslie, Monica Lewinsky, Jack London, George Lucas, Phil Mickelson, Marilyn Monroe, John Muir, Richard M. Nixon, Gwyneth Paltrow, George S. Patton Jr., Gregory Peck, Nancy Pelosi, Ronald Reagan, Sally K. Ride, William Saroyan, Arnold Schwarzenegger, Junípero Serra, O. J. Simpson, Kevin Spacey, Leland Stanford, Gwen Stefani, John Steinbeck, Shirley Temple, Earl Warren, Serena Williams, Ted Williams, Venus Williams, Tiger Woods.

Website. www.ca.gov

Colorado (CO)
Centennial State

People. Population: 5,758,736; rank: 21. **Pop. change** (2010-19): 14.5%. **Pop. density:** 55.6 per sq mi. **Racial distribution:** 86.9% white; 4.6% Black; 3.5% Asian; 1.6% Amer. Ind.; 0.2% Hawaiian/Pacific Islander; 2 or more races, 3.1%. **Hispanic pop.:** 21.8%.

Geography. Total area: 104,094 sq mi; rank: 8. **Land area:** 103,642 sq mi; rank: 8. **Acres forested:** 22.9 mil. **Location:** W central U.S. **Climate:** low relative humidity, abundant sun, wide daily/seasonal temperature ranges; alpine conditions in the high mountains. **Topography:** eastern dry high plains; hilly to mountainous central plateau; western Rocky Mts. of high ranges with broad valleys, deep, narrow canyons. **Capital:** Denver. **Chief airports:** Denver, Colorado Springs.

Economy. Chief industries: manufacturing, construction, government, tourism, agriculture, aerospace, electronics equip. **Chief manuf. goods:** animal slaughtering, beer, petroleum, pharmaceuticals, aerospace, medical equip., precision instruments, printing, semiconductors. **Chief crops:** hay, corn, potatoes, wheat, onions, dry edible beans, sunflowers, sugar beets, barley, proso millet, cabbage, peaches, lettuce, apples, cantaloupes. **Farm income:** Crops: $2.41 bil. **Livestock:** $4.70 bil. **Nonfuel minerals:** $1.8 bil; cement (portland), gold, molybdenum concentrates, sand and gravel (construction), stone (crushed). **Gross state product:** $390.3 bil. **Sales tax:** 2.9%. **Gasoline tax:** 40.40 cents/gal. **Employment distrib.:** 17.8% govt.; 17.2% trade/trans./util.; 5.7% mfg.; 12.8% ed./health; 17.1% prof./bus. serv.; 8.2% leisure/hosp.; 6.7% finance; 7.7% constr./mining/log.; 2.9% info.; 3.9% other serv. **Unemployment:** 2.8%. **Min. wage/hr.:** $12.00. **Per cap. pers. income:** $61,348. **New private housing:** 38,633 units/$9.6 bil. **Broadband internet:** 96.4%. **Commercial banks:** 115; deposits: $138.2 bil. **Savings institutions:** 16; deposits: $4.4 bil. **Lottery:** total sales: $679.8 mil; profit: $166.5 mil.

Federal govt. Fed. civ. employees: 37,455; **avg. salary:** $85,869. **Notable fed. facilities:** U.S. Air Force Academy; Peterson AFB; Denver Mint; Ft. Carson; Natl. Renewable Energy Lab, Golden; Transportation Tech. Ctr., Pueblo; NORAD and USNORTHCOM Alt. Command Ctr., Cheyenne Mtn. Complex; Denver Fed. Ctr.; Natl. Ctr. for Atmospheric Research, Natl. Inst. of Standards & Technology, NOAA Earth System Research Lab, Boulder; Natl. Wildlife Research Ctr., Fort Collins.

Education. High school grad. rate: 80.8%. **4-yr. public coll./univ.:** 19; **2-yr. public:** 9; **4-yr. private:** 12.

Energy. Electricity use/cost: 691 kWh, $83.90.

State data. Motto: Nil Sine Numine (Nothing without Providence). **Flower:** Rocky Mountain columbine. **Bird:** Lark bunting. **Tree:** Colorado blue spruce. **Songs:** "Where the Columbines Grow"; "Rocky Mountain High." **Entered union:** Aug. 1, 1876; rank: 38th.

Tourism. Tourist spending: $21.6 bil. **Attractions:** Denver Museum of Nature & Science, Denver Botanic Gardens, Denver Zoo; Red Rocks Park and Amphitheatre, Morrison; Natl. Ctr. for Atmospheric Research, Boulder; Rocky Mountain, Black Canyon of the Gunnison, and Mesa Verde (Anasazi cliff dwellings) Natl. Parks; Aspen, Breckenridge, Steamboat, and Vail ski resorts; Garden of the Gods, Colorado Springs; Great Sand Dunes Natl. Park and Preserve; Dinosaur and Colorado Natl. Monuments; Pikes Peak and Mount Evans; Grand Mesa Natl. Forest; historic mining towns of Central City, Silverton, Cripple Creek; Bent's Old Fort Natl. Historic Site, near La Junta; Georgetown Loop Historic Mining and Railroad Park; Durango & Silverton Narrow Gauge Railroad Museum, Durango; Cumbres & Toltec Scenic Railroad, Antonito; gambling in Black Hawk, Central City, Cripple Creek and on tribal land in Ignacio and Towaoc. **Information:** Colorado Tourism Office, 1625 Broadway, Ste. 1700, Denver, CO 80202; 1-800-265-6723; www.colorado.com

History. Paleo-Indians hunted big game in the area at least 11,000 years ago. Anasazi cliff dwellers flourished around Mesa Verde until about 1300 CE; other Native Americans were the Ute, Pueblo, Cheyenne, and Arapaho. The region was claimed by Spain but passed to France, 1800. The U.S. acquired eastern Colorado in the Louisiana Purchase, 1803. Lt. Zebulon M. Pike explored the area, 1806, sighting the peak that bears his name. After the Mexican War, 1846-48, U.S. immigrants settled in the east, former Mexicans in the south. Gold was discovered in 1858, causing a population boom. Congress created Colorado Territory, 1861. Conflict between newcomers and displaced Native Americans led to the Sand Creek Massacre, 1864, in which U.S. soldiers and settlers killed some 150 Cheyenne and Arapaho. U.S. Army troops forced the removal to reservations (mostly in present-day Oklahoma) of most Native Americans in the state, 1867. The 1870s brought statehood, 1876, and rich silver finds that turned Leadville into a boomtown. Federal military and civilian employment in Colorado surged in the 1940s and '50s; since then, tourism and technology have fueled the economy. The state's Hispanic population grew from 5.8% in 1980 to 20.7% in 2010. Colorado became the first state in the U.S. to legalize selling recreational marijuana in 2014. The state raised $302.5 mil in fees and tax revenue from marijuana sales in 2019.

Famous Coloradans. Tim Allen, Chauncey Billups, Frederick Bonfils, Molly Brown, William N. Byers, M. Scott Carpenter, Lon Chaney, Jack Dempsey, Mamie Eisenhower, Douglas Fairbanks, Barney Ford, Neil Gorsuch, Roy Halladay, Ouray, Trey Parker, "Baby Doe" Tabor, Lowell Thomas, Byron R. White, Paul Whiteman.

Website. www.colorado.gov

Connecticut (CT)
Constitution State, Nutmeg State

People. Population: 3,565,287; rank: 29. **Pop. change** (2010-19): –0.2%. **Pop. density:** 736.3 per sq mi. **Racial distribution:** 79.7% white; 12.2% Black; 5.0% Asian; 0.6% Amer. Ind.; 0.1% Hawaiian/Pacific Islander; 2 or more races, 2.5%. **Hispanic pop.:** 16.9%.

Geography. Total area: 5,543 sq mi; rank: 48. **Land area:** 4,842 sq mi; rank: 48. **Acres forested:** 1.8 mil. **Location:** New England state in NE corner of U.S. **Climate:** moderate; winters avg. slightly below freezing; warm, humid summers. **Topography:** western upland, the Berkshires, in the NW, highest elevations; narrow central lowland N-S; hilly eastern upland drained by rivers. **Capital:** Hartford. **Chief airport:** Windsor Locks.

Economy. Chief industries: manufacturing, retail trade, government, services, finances, insurance, real estate. **Chief manuf. goods:** aerospace, chemicals, fabricated metals, precision instruments, toiletries, medical equip., printing, plastics. **Chief crops:** nursery stock, Christmas trees, mushrooms, sweet corn, apples, tobacco, hay. **Farm income:** Crops: $416.66 mil. **Livestock:** $180.13 mil. **Nonfuel minerals:** $191 mil; clay (common clay), sand and gravel (construction), stone (crushed), stone (dimension). **Commercial fishing:** $16.5 mil. **Chief ports:** New Haven, Bridgeport, New London. **Gross state product:** $285.6 bil. **Sales tax:** 6.35%. **Gasoline tax:** 58.53 cents/gal. **Employment distrib.:** 14.7% govt.; 17.1% trade/trans./util.; 10.6% mfg.; 20.8% ed./health; 14.0% prof./bus. serv.; 5.8% leisure/hosp.; 8.2% finance; 3.9% constr./mining/log.; 2.0% info.; 3.1% other serv. **Unemployment:** 3.7%. **Min. wage/hr.:** $11.00. **Per cap. pers. income:** $79,087. **New private housing:** 5,854 units/$1.4 bil. **Broadband internet:** 99.2%. **Commercial banks:** 31; deposits: $117.4 bil. **Savings institutions:** 28; deposits: $22.5 bil. **Lottery:** total sales: $1.3 bil; profit: $372.3 mil.

Federal govt. Fed. civ. employees: 8,053; **avg. salary:** $84,005. **Notable fed. facilities:** U.S. Coast Guard Academy; Naval Sub Base New London.

Education. High school grad. rate: 88.4%. **4-yr. public coll./univ.:** 10; **2-yr. public:** 12; **4-yr. private:** 17.

Energy. Electricity use/cost: 724 kWh, $153.46.

State data. Motto: Qui Transtulit Sustinet (He who transplanted still sustains). **Flower:** Mountain laurel. **Bird:** American robin. **Tree:** White oak. **Song:** "Yankee Doodle." **Fifth** of the 13 original states to ratify the Constitution, Jan. 9, 1788.

Tourism. Tourist spending: $12.2 bil. **Attractions:** Mark Twain House and Museum, Hartford; Yale Univ. Art Gallery, Peabody Museum of Natural History, in New Haven; Mystic

Seaport, Mystic Aquarium; Barnum Museum, Bridgeport; Gillette Castle State Park, East Haddam; USS *Nautilus* (1st nuclear-powered submarine) at Submarine Force Library and Museum, Groton; Mashantucket Pequot Museum and Research Ctr.; Foxwoods Resort Casino, Ledyard; Mohegan Sun, Uncasville; Lake Compounce (est. 1846; oldest continuously operating amusement park in U.S.), Bristol; Philip Johnson Glass House, New Canaan. **Information:** Connecticut Office of Tourism, 450 Columbus Blvd., Ste. 5, Hartford, CT 06103; 1-888-CTVISIT, (860) 256-2800; www.ctvisit.com

History. At the time of European contact, inhabitants of the area were Algonquian peoples, including the Mohegan and Pequot. Dutch explorer Adriaen Block was the first European visitor, 1614. By 1634, English settlers from Plymouth had started colonies along the Connecticut R.; in 1637 they defeated the Pequots. The Colony of Connecticut was chartered by England, 1662; New Haven colony was added, 1665. A Patriot stronghold in the American Revolution, the state actively supported the antislavery movement and the Union cause in the Civil War. The state economy prospered in the 20th cent. from insurance- and defense-related industries. *Nautilus*, the first nuclear-powered submarine, was launched at Groton, 1954. Connecticut Sen. Joseph Lieberman was the Democratic nominee for vice president in 2000. American Indian casinos, starting with Foxwoods in 1992, were an economic boon to the state, but tourism revenues declined sharply with the recession that began in late 2007. Twenty children and six staff members were killed in a mass shooting at Sandy Hook Elementary School in Newtown, Dec. 14, 2012.

Famous "Nutmeggers." Ethan Allen, P. T. Barnum, Michael Bolton, Glenn Close, Samuel Colt, Ann Coulter, Jonathan Edwards, Nathan Hale, Katharine Hepburn, Isaac Hull, Norman Lear, Seth MacFarlane, John Mayer, Robert Mitchum, J. P. Morgan, Ralph Nader, Israel Putnam, Wallace Stevens, Harriet Beecher Stowe, Mark Twain, Noah Webster, Eli Whitney.

Website. www.ct.gov

Delaware (DE)
First State, Diamond State

People. Population: 973,764; rank: 45. **Pop. change** (2010-19): 8.4%. **Pop. density:** 499.6 per sq mi. **Racial distribution:** 69.2% white; 23.2% Black; 4.1% Asian; 0.7% Amer. Ind.; 0.1% Hawaiian/Pacific Islander; 2 or more races, 2.7%. **Hispanic pop.:** 9.6%.

Geography. Total area: 2,489 sq mi; rank: 49. **Land area:** 1,949 sq mi; rank: 49. **Acres forested:** 0.4 mil. **Location:** Delmarva Peninsula on the Atlantic coastal plain. **Climate:** moderate. **Topography:** Piedmont Plateau to the N, sloping to a near sea-level plain. **Capital:** Dover.

Economy. Chief industries: chemicals, agriculture, finance, poultry, shellfish, tourism, auto assembly, food processing, transportation equip. **Chief manuf. goods:** pharmaceuticals, poultry processing, soap and cleaning compounds, precision instruments, basic chemicals, plastics. **Chief crops:** soybeans, corn, greenhouse and nursery, wheat, potatoes, barley, hay, watermelons, lima beans, green peas, pumpkins, mushrooms, cabbage. **Farm income:** Crops: $276.24 mil. Livestock: $1.13 bil. **Nonfuel minerals:** $30 mil: magnesium compounds, sand and gravel (construction), stone (crushed). **Commercial fishing:** $10.6 mil. **Chief port:** Wilmington. **Gross state product:** $75.4 bil. **Sales tax:** none. **Gasoline tax:** 41.40 cents/gal. **Employment distrib.:** 16.4% govt.; 17.4% trade/trans./util.; 6.0% mfg.; 17.6% ed./health; 14.8% prof./bus. serv.; 0.7% leisure/hosp.; 11.0% finance, 5.3% constr./mining/log.; 0.9% info.; 3.3% other serv. **Unemployment:** 3.8%. **Min. wage/hr.:** $9.25. **Per cap. pers. income:** $54,264. **New private housing:** 6,539 units/$849.1 mil. **Broadband internet:** 98.7%. **Commercial banks:** 37; deposits: $373.8 bil. **Savings institutions:** 4; deposits: $5.3 bil. **Lottery:** total sales: $649.7 mil; profit: $215.6 mil.

Federal govt. Fed. civ. employees: 3,150; **avg. salary:** $75,504. **Notable fed. facilities:** Dover AFB; Bombay Hook Natl. Wildlife Refuge.

Education. High school grad. rate: 86.9%. **4-yr. public coll./univ.:** 3; 2-yr. public: 0; 4-yr. private: 3.

Energy. Electricity use/cost: 977 kWh, $122.43.

State data. Motto: Liberty and independence. **Flower:** Peach blossom. **Bird:** Blue hen chicken. **Tree:** American holly. **Song:** "Our Delaware." **First** of original 13 states to ratify the Constitution, Dec. 7, 1787.

Tourism. Tourist spending: $2.3 bil. **Attractions:** Fort Christina (site of founding of colony of New Sweden), Holy Trinity (Old Swedes) Church (erected 1698, oldest church in U.S. still standing as built and in use), Hagley Museum

and Library, Nemours Mansion and Gardens, in Wilmington; Winterthur Museum, Garden, and Library, near Wilmington; New Castle Historic District; John Dickinson "Penman of the Revolution" Plantation, First State Heritage Park, Dover Intl. Speedway, in Dover; Rehoboth Beach. **Information:** Delaware Tourism Office, 99 Kings Hwy., Dover, DE 19901; 1-866-2VISITDE; www.visitdelaware.com

History. The Lenni Lenape (Delaware) people lived in the region at the time of European contact. Henry Hudson located the Delaware R., 1609. In 1610, English explorer Samuel Argall entered Delaware Bay and named the area after Virginia's governor, Lord De La Warr. Dutch, Swedish, and Finnish settlers were followed by the British, who took control in 1664. After 1682, Delaware became part of Pennsylvania, and in 1704 it was granted its own assembly. It adopted a constitution as the state of Delaware, 1776, and was the first state to ratify the federal Constitution, 1787. Although it remained in the Union during the Civil War, Delaware retained slavery until the 13th Amendment abolished it in 1865. The DuPont company, founded as a gunpowder mill in 1802, became an industrial giant in the 20th cent. making nylon, Teflon, and other synthetics. Pro-business laws drew many out-of-state firms to incorporate in Delaware. In 2000, Ruth Ann Minner was elected Delaware's first woman governor. Joe Biden, the state's former U.S. senator, served as U.S. vice president, 2009-17, and ran for president, 2020.

Famous Delawareans. Thomas F. Bayard, Joe Biden, Henry Seidel Canby, E. I. du Pont, John P. Marquand, Aubrey Plaza, Howard Pyle, Caesar Rodney, Susan Stroman.

Website. www.delaware.gov

Florida (FL)
Sunshine State

People. Population: 21,477,737; rank: 3. **Pop. change** (2010-19): 14.2%. **Pop. density:** 400.5 per sq mi. **Racial distribution:** 77.3% white; 16.9% Black; 3.0% Asian; 0.5% Amer. Ind.; 0.1% Hawaiian/Pacific Islander; 2 or more races, 2.2%. **Hispanic pop.:** 26.4%.

Geography. Total area: 65,758 sq mi; rank: 22. **Land area:** 53,625 sq mi; rank: 26. **Acres forested:** 17.0 mil. **Location:** peninsula jutting southward 500 mi between the Atlantic and Gulf of Mexico. **Climate:** subtropical N of Bradenton-Lake Okeechobee-Vero Beach line; tropical S of line. **Topography:** land is flat or rolling; highest point is 345 ft in the NW. **Capital:** Tallahassee. **Chief airports:** Orlando, Miami, Fort Lauderdale, Tampa, Fort Myers, Jacksonville, West Palm Beach, Sanford, Clearwater, Pensacola, Sarasota, Punta Gorda, Valparaiso, Panama City.

Economy. Chief industries: tourism, agriculture, manufacturing, construction, services, international trade. **Chief manuf. goods:** navigational instruments, medical equip., cement, broadcasting equip., beverages, phosphatic fertilizer, preserved fruits and vegetables, structural metal, printing. **Chief crops:** greenhouse and nursery, oranges, sugarcane, tomatoes, green peppers, grapefruit, strawberries, snap beans, sweet corn, potatoes, cucumbers, tangerines. **Farm income:** Crops: $5.72 bil. Livestock: $1.60 bil. **Nonfuel minerals:** $3.4 bil; cement (portland), phosphate rock, sand and gravel (construction), stone (crushed), zirconium mineral concentrates. **Commercial fishing:** $255.9 mil. **Chief ports:** Pensacola, Tampa, Port Manatee, Miami, Port Everglades, Jacksonville, Canaveral. **Gross state product:** $1.1 tril. **Sales tax:** 6.0%. **Gasoline tax:** 60.69 cents/gal. **Employment distrib.:** 13.8% govt.; 20.6% trade/trans./util.; 4.5% mfg.; 15.7% ed./health; 15.8% prof./bus. serv.; 10.2% leisure/hosp.; 7.1% finance; 7.0% constr./mining/log.; 1.6% info.; 3.8% other serv. **Unemployment:** 3.1%. **Min. wage/hr.:** $8.56. **Per cap. pers. income:** $51,989. **New private housing:** 154,302 units/$33.2 bil. **Broadband internet:** 98.1%. **Commercial banks:** 189; deposits: $568.5 bil. **Savings institutions:** 16; deposits: $35.0 bil. **Lottery:** total sales: $7.2 bil; profit: $1.9 bil.

Federal govt. Fed. civ. employees: 81,775; **avg. salary:** $78,456. **Notable fed. facilities:** John F. Kennedy Space Ctr.; Eglin AFB; MacDill AFB; Hurlburt Field; Pensacola NAS; Jacksonville NAS; Mayport Naval Sta.

Education. High school grad. rate: 86.3%. **4-yr. public coll./univ.:** 42; 2-yr. public: 1; 4-yr. private: 58.

Energy. Electricity use/cost: 1,110 kWh, $128.10.

State data. Motto: In God we trust. **Flower:** Orange blossom. **Bird:** Northern mockingbird. **Tree:** Sabal palmetto palm. **Song:** "Old Folks at Home." **Entered union:** Mar. 3, 1845; rank: 27th.

Tourism. Tourist spending: $102.8 bil. **Attractions:** Miami Beach; Castillo de San Marcos Natl. Monument, St. Augustine Lighthouse & Museum, Lightner Museum, in St.

Augustine (oldest permanent European settlement in U.S.); Walt Disney World Resort, SeaWorld Orlando, Universal Studios, Discovery Cove, in Orlando; Kennedy Space Ctr., U.S. Astronaut Hall of Fame; Everglades Natl. Park; Ringling Museum of Art, Ringling Circus Museum, in Sarasota; Cypress Gardens at Legoland Florida, Winter Haven; Busch Gardens, Big Cat Rescue, in Tampa; Florida Caverns State Park, Marianna; Key West. **Information:** Visit Florida, 2540 W. Executive Center Cir., Ste. 200, Tallahassee, FL 32301; 1-888-7FLA-USA; www.visitflorida.com

History. Florida has been inhabited for at least 12,000 years. Timucua, Apalachee, and Calusa peoples were living in the region when the earliest Europeans came; later the Seminole migrated from Georgia to Florida, becoming dominant there in the early 18th cent. The first European to see Florida was Spain's Ponce de León, 1513. France established a colony, Ft. Caroline, on the St. Johns R., 1564. Spain settled St. Augustine, 1565, and Spanish troops massacred most of the French. Britain's Sir Francis Drake burned St. Augustine, 1586. In 1763, Spain ceded Florida to Great Britain, which held the area 20 years before returning it to Spain. Florida was ceded to the U.S. in the Adams-Onís Treaty, 1819. The Seminole War, 1835-42, resulted in the removal of most Native Americans to Indian Territory. Florida joined the Union in 1845, seceded in 1861, and was readmitted in 1868. In the late 19th cent., hotel and railroad builder Henry M. Flagler laid the foundations of the tourism industry. The state experienced phenomenal population growth in the 20th cent., especially after 1950. The first U.S. astronaut was launched into space from Cape Canaveral, 1961. Walt Disney World opened near Orlando, 1971. Hurricane Andrew slammed Florida, 1992, causing at least $25 bil in property damage. A dispute over Florida's presidential vote in 2000 was decided by the U.S. Supreme Court and resulted in George W. Bush's victory. Four hurricanes hit the state in 2004, causing more than $40 bil in damages. In June 2016, a gunman carried out the then-deadliest mass shooting in modern U.S. history when he killed 49 people at a gay nightclub in Orlando. The CDC in 2016 issued its first-ever travel warning for part of the continental U.S. amid reports of the Zika virus in a Miami neighborhood. The Palm Beach private club Mar-a-Lago frequently hosted its owner, Pres. Donald Trump, after he took office in 2017. A Feb. 2018 mass shooting at a Parkland high school killed 17 and galvanized a wave of youth-led activism against gun violence. Hurricane Michael in Oct. 2018 became the first Category 5 storm to hit the U.S. since 1992.

Famous Floridians. Edna Buchanan, Jeb Bush, Marjory Stoneman Douglas, Henry Morrison Flagler, Carl Hiaasen, Perez Hilton, Zora Neale Hurston, James Weldon Johnson, Deacon Jones, MacKinlay Kantor, Osceola, Claude Pepper, Tom Petty, Henry B. Plant, A. Philip Randolph, Marjorie Kinnan Rawlings, Janet Reno, Marco Rubio, Deion Sanders, Emmitt Smith, Joseph W. Stilwell, Amar'e Stoudemire, Charles P. Summerall.

Website. www.myflorida.com

Georgia (GA)
Empire State of the South, Peach State

People. Population: 10,617,423; rank: 8. **Pop. change** (2010-19): 9.6%. **Pop. density:** 184.6 per sq mi. **Racial distribution:** 60.2% white; 32.6% Black; 4.4% Asian; 0.5% Amer. Ind.; 0.1% Hawaiian/Pacific Islander; 2 or more races, 2.2%. **Hispanic pop.:** 9.9%.

Geography. Total area: 59,425 sq mi; rank: 24. **Land area:** 57,513 sq mi; rank: 21. **Acres forested:** 24.5 mil. **Location:** South Atlantic state. **Climate:** maritime tropical air masses dominate in summer; polar air masses in winter; E central area drier. **Topography:** most southerly of the Blue Ridge Mts. cover NE and N central; central Piedmont extends to the fall line of rivers; coastal plain levels to the coast flatlands. **Capital:** Atlanta. **Chief airports:** Atlanta, Savannah.

Economy. Chief industries: services, manufacturing, retail trade. **Chief manuf. goods:** carpet and rugs, animal slaughtering and processing, motor vehicles and parts, plastics, aircrafts, paper, chemicals, food. **Chief crops:** cotton, greenhouse and nursery, peanuts, pecans, corn, tomatoes, cucumbers, onions, watermelons, tobacco, squash, blueberries, hay, cabbage, soybeans, peaches, snap beans, wheat. **Farm income:** Crops: $3.06 bil. Livestock: $6.04 bil. **Nonfuel minerals:** $2.2 bil; cement (portland), clay (kaolin and montmorillonite), sand and gravel (construction), stone (crushed). **Commercial fishing:** $16.7 mil. **Chief ports:** Savannah, Brunswick. **Gross state product:** $616.3 bil. **Sales tax:** 4.0%. **Gasoline tax:** 52.87 cents/gal. **Employment distrib.:** 15.7% govt.; 21.5% trade/trans./util.; 8.8% mfg.; 13.8%

ed./health; 15.5% prof./bus. serv.; 8.1% leisure/hosp.; 5.8% finance; 4.9% constr./mining/log.; 2.4% info.; 3.4% other serv. **Unemployment:** 3.4%. **Min. wage/hr.:** $7.25. **Per cap. pers. income:** $48,199. **New private housing:** 53,823 units/$10.7 bil. **Broadband internet:** 96.5%. **Commercial banks:** 200; deposits: $254.4 bil. **Savings institutions:** 13; deposits: $1.9 bil. **Lottery:** total sales: $4.8 bil; profit: $1.2 bil.

Federal govt. Fed. civ. employees: 73,086; **avg. salary:** $79,936. **Notable fed. facilities:** Ft. Benning; Ft. Stewart; Fed. Law Enforcement Training Ctr., Brunswick; Robins AFB; Ft. Gordon; Naval Sub Base Kings Bay; Moody AFB; Centers for Disease Control, Atlanta; Marine Corps Logistics Base Albany.

Education. High school grad. rate: 81.6%. **4-yr. public coll./univ.:** 27; **2-yr. public:** 23; **4-yr. private:** 33.

Energy. Electricity use/cost: 1,142 kWh, $131.05.

State data. Motto: Wisdom, justice, and moderation. **Flower:** Cherokee rose. **Bird:** Brown thrasher. **Tree:** Southern live oak. **Song:** "Georgia on My Mind." **Fourth** of the 13 original states to ratify the Constitution, Jan. 2, 1788.

Tourism. Tourist spending: $31.1 bil. **Attractions:** Georgia State Capitol, Stone Mountain, Centennial Olympic Park, Six Flags Over Georgia, Martin Luther King Jr. Natl. Historical Park, Jimmy Carter Library and Museum, Atlanta Botanical Garden, Georgia Aquarium (largest in Western Hemisphere), in Atlanta; Kennesaw Mountain Natl. Battlefield Park; Chickamauga and Chattanooga Natl. Military Park; Chattahoochee-Oconee Natl. Forest; Dahlonega, site of earliest U.S. gold rush; Brasstown Bald (highest mtn. in state); Franklin D. Roosevelt's Little White House Historic Site, Warm Springs; Callaway Gardens, Pine Mountain; Andersonville Natl. Historic Site (Confederate military prison); Okefenokee Natl. Wildlife Refuge; Jekyll, St. Simons, and Cumberland barrier islands; Savannah Historic District. **Information:** Dept. of Economic Development, 75 Fifth St., NW, Ste. 1200, Atlanta, GA 30308; 1-800-VISITGA; www.exploregeorgia.org

History. Creek and Cherokee peoples were living in the region when Spaniards founded Santa Catalina mission, 1566, on Saint Catherines Island. Gen. James Oglethorpe established a colony at Savannah, 1733, for the poor and religiously persecuted. Oglethorpe defeated a Spanish army from Florida at Bloody Marsh, 1742. Georgia was a battleground in the American Revolution, with the British finally evacuating Savannah in 1782. When Georgia entered the Union, 1788, its plantation economy relied on enslaving Black workers for rice and cotton growing. The Cherokee were removed to Indian Territory, 1838-39, and thousands died on the long march, known as the Trail of Tears. By 1860 the enslaved population exceeded 462,000 (nearly 44% of the total population). Georgia seceded from the Union, 1861, and was invaded by Union forces, 1864, under Gen. William T. Sherman, who took Atlanta, Sept. 2, and proceeded on his famous "march to the sea," ending in Savannah in Dec. Georgia was readmitted, 1870. Born 1929 in Atlanta, Martin Luther King Jr. made the city his base during the civil rights struggles of the 1960s. Atlanta became the leading city of the "New South," world headquarters of Coca-Cola and CNN, and host of the 1996 Summer Olympic Games. More than 70 tornadoes struck the South in late Jan. 2017, killing 16 people in southern Georgia. With the state offering significant tax breaks and other economic incentives, film and TV production was a $2.9-bil industry in 2019.

Famous Georgians. Kim Basinger, Griffin Bell, James Brown, Erskine Caldwell, Jimmy Carter, Ray Charles, Ty Cobb, James Dickey, Walt Frazier, John C. Fremont, Newt Gingrich, Nancy Grace, Joel Chandler Harris, "Doc" Holliday, Larry Holmes, Holly Hunter, Alan Jackson, Martin Luther King Jr., Gladys Knight, Sidney Lanier, Little Richard, Juliette Gordon Low, Margaret Mitchell, Jessye Norman, Sam Nunn, Flannery O'Connor, Otis Redding, Burt Reynolds, Julia Roberts, Jackie Robinson, Ryan Seacrest, Clarence Thomas, Travis Tritt, Ted Turner, Carl Vinson, Alice Walker, Herschel Walker, Joanne Woodward, Trisha Yearwood, Andrew Young.

Website. www.georgia.gov

Hawai'i (HI)
Aloha State

People. Population: 1,415,872; rank: 40. **Pop. change** (2010-19): 4.1%. **Pop. density:** 220.4 per sq mi. **Racial distribution:** 25.5% white; 2.2% Black; 37.6% Asian; 0.4% Amer. Ind.; 10.1% Hawaiian/Pacific Islander; 2 or more races, 24.2%. **Hispanic pop.:** 10.7%.

Geography. Total area: 10,932 sq mi; rank: 43. **Land area:** 6,423 sq mi; rank: 47. **Acres forested:** 1.5 mil. **Location:** Pacific archipelago of about 132 islands 2,100 mi SW of U.S.

mainland. **Climate:** subtropical, with wide variations in rainfall; Mt. Waialeale, on Kaua'i, wettest spot in U.S. (annual avg. rainfall 422 in., 1912-2015). **Topography:** islands are tops of a chain of submerged volcanic mountains; Mauna Loa, Kilauea are active volcanoes. **Capital:** Honolulu. **Chief airports:** Honolulu, Kahului, Kailua Kona, Lihue, Hilo.

Economy. Chief industries: tourism, defense, sugar, pineapples. **Chief manuf. goods:** concrete, printing, baked goods, sugar, preserved fruits and vegetables, apparel. **Chief crops:** flowers and nursery, pineapples, seed crops, sugarcane, macadamia nuts, coffee, algae, papayas, tomatoes, bananas, basil, ginger. **Farm income:** Crops: $427.52 mil. Livestock: $165.82 mil. **Nonfuel minerals:** $134 mil; sand and gravel (construction), stone (crushed). **Commercial fishing:** $119.2 mil. **Chief ports:** Honolulu, Hilo, Barbers Point, Kahului. **Gross state product:** $97.3 bil. **Sales tax:** 4.0%. **Gasoline tax:** 66.77 cents/gal. **Employment distrib.:** 21.8% govt.; 19.7% trade/trans./util.; 2.2% mfg.; 15.8% ed./health; 12.4% prof./bus. serv.; 9.6% leisure/hosp.; 5.2% finance; 7.1% constr./mining/log.; 1.4% info.; 4.7% other serv. **Unemployment:** 2.7%. **Min. wage/hr.:** $10.10. **Per cap. pers. income:** $57,450. **New private housing:** 4,093 units/$1.3 bil. **Broadband internet:** 99.7%. **Commercial banks:** 9; deposits: $36.8 bil. **Savings institutions:** 4; deposits $8.0 bil.

Federal govt. Fed. civ. employees: 22,998; **avg. salary:** $79,601. **Notable fed. facilities:** Joint Base Pearl Harbor-Hickam; Schofield Barracks; Marine Corps Base Hawaii, Kaneohe Bay; Tripler Army Med. Ctr.; Ft. Shafter; Wheeler Army Airfield; Prince Kuhio Federal Bldg., Honolulu.

Education. High school grad. rate: 84.5%. **4-yr. public coll./univ.:** 4; **2-yr. public:** 6; **4-yr. private:** 5.

Energy. Electricity use/cost: 518 kWh, $168.13.

State data. Motto: Ua mau ke ea o ka aina i ka pono (The life of the land is perpetuated in righteousness). **Flower:** Yellow hibiscus. **Bird:** Hawaiian goose. **Tree:** Kukui (candlenut). **Song:** "Hawai'i Pono'i" (Hawai'i's Own). **Entered union:** Aug. 21, 1959; rank: 50th.

Tourism. Tourist spending: $26.1 bil. **Attractions:** Oahu Isl.: Natl. Memorial Cemetery of the Pacific, Waikiki Beach, Diamond Head, in Honolulu; USS *Arizona* Memorial, Pearl Harbor; Polynesian Cultural Ctr., Laie; Hanauma Bay; Nu'uanu Pali. Kaua'i Isl.: Waimea Canyon. Maui Isl.: Haleakala Natl. Park. Hawai'i Isl.: Hawaii Volcanoes Natl. Park, Wailoa and Wailuku River State Parks. **Information:** Hawaii Visitors and Conventions Bureau, 2270 Kalakaua Ave., Ste. 801, Honolulu, HI 96815; 1-800-GOHAWAII; www.gohawaii.com

History. Polynesians from islands 2,000 mi to the S settled the Hawaiian Islands, probably 300-600 CE. The first European visitor was British captain James Cook, 1778. King Kamehameha I united the islands by 1810. Christian missionaries arrived, 1819, bringing Western culture. Under the reign, 1825-54, of King Kamehameha III, a constitution, legislature, and public school system were instituted. Sugar production began, 1835, and it became the dominant industry. Queen Liliuokalani was deposed, 1893, and a republic was established, 1894, headed by Sanford B. Dole, born in Hawaii to American missionaries. Annexation by the U.S. came in 1898. The Japanese attack on Pearl Harbor, Dec. 7, 1941, brought the U.S. into World War II. Hawai'i attained statehood, 1959. Hurricane Iniki pounded Kaua'i, 1992, causing about $1 bil in damage. In 2006, Pres. George W. Bush designated the Northwestern Hawaiian Islands Natl. Monument, a marine area of 140,000 sq mi. The Kilauea volcano on Hawaii's Big Island started to erupt, May 2018, forcing a series of evacuations.

Famous Islanders. Bernice Pauahi Bishop, Tia Carrere, Alexander Cartwright, St. Damien de Veuster, Don Ho, Daniel K. Inouye, Duke Kahanamoku, King Kamehameha, Nicole Kidman, Brook Mahealani Lee, Jason Scott Lee, Queen Liliuokalani, Bruno Mars, Bette Midler, Barack Obama, Ellison S. Onizuka, Michelle Wie.

Website. portal.ehawaii.gov

Idaho (ID)
Gem State

People. Population: 1,787,065; rank: 39. **Pop. change** (2010-19) 14.0%. **Pop. density:** 21.6 per sq mi. **Racial distribution:** 93.0% white; 0.9% Black; 1.6% Asian; 1.7% Amer. Ind.; 0.2% Hawaiian/Pacific Islander; 2 or more races, 2.6%. **Hispanic pop.:** 12.8%.

Geography. Total area: 83,569 sq mi; rank: 14. **Land area:** 82,643 sq mi; rank: 11. **Acres forested:** 21.7 mil. **Location:** northwestern Mountain state bordering British Columbia, Canada. **Climate:** tempered by Pacific westerly winds; drier, colder, continental climate in SE; altitude an important

factor. **Topography:** Snake R. plains in the S; central region of mountains, canyons, gorges (Hells Canyon, 7,900 ft, deepest in N. America); subalpine northern region. **Capital:** Boise. **Chief airport:** Boise.

Economy. Chief industries: manufacturing, agriculture, tourism, lumber, mining, electronics. **Chief manuf. goods:** computers and electronics, preserved fruits and vegetables, cheese, lumber. **Chief crops:** potatoes, wheat, hay, sugar beets, barley, greenhouse and nursery, onions, dry beans, corn, mint, apples, hops, peaches, lentils, peas, cherries, plums and prunes, oats. **Farm income:** Crops: $3.12 bil. Livestock: $4.33 bil. **Nonfuel minerals:** $185 mil; lead, phosphate rock, sand and gravel (construction), silver, stone (crushed). **Chief port:** Lewiston. **Gross state product:** $80.9 bil. **Sales tax:** 6.0%. **Gasoline tax:** 51.40 cents/gal. **Employment distrib.:** 17.1% govt.; 19.8% trade/trans./util.; 9.4% mfg.; 14.6% ed./health; 13.4% prof./bus. serv.; 8.2% leisure/hosp.; 5.3% finance; 8.2% constr./mining/log.; 1.1% info.; 3.0% other serv. **Unemployment:** 2.9%. **Min. wage/hr.:** $7.25. **Per cap. pers. income:** $45,642. **New private housing:** 17,716 units/$3.4 bil. **Broadband internet:** 95.3%. **Commercial banks:** 28; deposits: $26.3 bil. **Savings institutions:** 1; deposits: $580.0 mil. **Lottery:** total sales: $287.9 mil; profit: $60.0 mil.

Federal govt. Fed. civ. employees: 10,129; **avg. salary:** $65,379. **Notable fed. facilities:** Idaho Natl. Lab, Idaho Falls; Mountain Home AFB.

Education. High school grad. rate: 80.7%. **4-yr. public coll./univ.:** 4; **2-yr. public:** 4; **4-yr. private:** 6.

Energy. Electricity use/cost: 944 kWh, $95.84.

State data. Motto: Esto Perpetua (It is perpetual). **Flower:** Syringa. **Bird:** Mountain bluebird. **Tree:** White pine. **Song:** "Here We Have Idaho." **Entered union:** July 3, 1890; rank: 43rd.

Tourism. Tourist spending: $5.7 bil. **Attractions:** Hells Canyon (deepest river gorge in N. America); World Ctr. for Birds of Prey, Boise Art Museum, in Boise; Craters of the Moon Natl. Monument and Preserve; Sun Valley; Shoshone Falls, near Twin Falls; Lava Hot Springs; Lake Coeur d'Alene; Sawtooth Natl. Recreation Area; Frank Church-River of No Return Wilderness Area; Nez Perce Natl. Historical Park. **Information:** Idaho Division of Tourism Development, 700 W. State St., P.O. Box 83720, Boise, ID 83720; 1-800-VISITID; www.visitidaho.org

History. Paleo-Indian hunters roamed the land over 13,000 years ago; later inhabitants included Shoshone, Northern Paiute, Bannock, and Nez Percé peoples. The Meriwether Lewis and William Clark Expedition took place 1804-06. Next came fur traders, 1809-34, and missionaries, 1830s-50s. Mormons made their first permanent settlement at Franklin, 1860. Idaho's gold rush began the same year and brought thousands of permanent settlers. A series of Indian wars followed, including a campaign by Chief Joseph and the Nez Percé that ended with his surrender in Montana, 1877. Idaho became a territory, 1863, and a state, 1890. In the 20th cent., it emerged as a leader in potato, lumber, and silver output. The Sun Valley ski resort opened in 1936, boosting tourism. Startup of Lewiston's river port, 1975, opened Idaho to oceangoing trade. Fueled by technology job growth, the state's population jumped 21.2% in 2000-10.

Famous Idahoans. William Borah, Frank Church, Lou Dobbs, Fred Dubois, W. Mark Felt, Chief Joseph, Harmon Killebrew, Ezra Pound, Marilynne Robinson, Sacagawea, Picabo Street, Lana Turner.

Website. www.idaho.gov

Illinois (IL)
Prairie State

People. Population: 12,671,821; rank: 6. **Pop. change** (2010-19): −1.2%. **Pop. density:** 228.2 per sq mi. **Racial distribution:** 76.8% white; 14.6% Black; 5.9% Asian; 0.6% Amer. Ind.; 0.1% Hawaiian/Pacific Islander; 2 or more races, 2.1%. **Hispanic pop.:** 17.5%.

Geography. Total area: 57,914 sq mi; rank: 25. **Land area:** 55,519 sq mi; rank: 24. **Acres forested:** 4.9 mil. **Location:** East North Central state; western, southern, and eastern boundaries formed by Mississippi, Ohio, and Wabash Rivers, respectively. **Climate:** temperate; typically cold, snowy winters, hot summers. **Topography:** prairie and fertile plains throughout; open hills in the southern region. **Capital:** Springfield. **Chief airports:** Chicago (2).

Economy. Chief industries: services, manufacturing, travel, wholesale and retail trade, finance, insurance, real estate, construction, health care, agriculture. **Chief manuf. goods:** food, petroleum, plastics, chemicals, agricultural machinery, pharmaceuticals, motor vehicles, printing. **Chief**

crops: corn, soybeans, hay, wheat, greenhouse and nursery, apples, peaches, sorghum. **Farm income:** Crops: $14.48 bil. Livestock: $2.33 bil. **Nonfuel minerals:** $1.5 bil; cement (portland), sand and gravel (construction), sand and gravel (industrial), silica (tripoli), stone (crushed). **Chief port:** Chicago. **Gross state product:** $897.1 bil. **Sales tax:** 6.25%. **Gasoline tax:** 72.05 cents/gal. **Employment distrib.:** 14.6% govt.; 20.3% trade/trans./util.; 9.9% mfg.; 15.9% ed./health; 15.7% prof./bus. serv.; 6.5% leisure/hosp.; 7.4% finance; 4.2% constr./mining/log.; 1.6% info.; 3.9% other serv. **Unemployment:** 4.0%. **Min. wage/hr.:** $10.00. **Per cap. pers. income:** $58,935. **New private housing:** 20,524 units/$3.7 bil. **Broadband internet:** 97.7%. **Commercial banks:** 423; deposits: $478.7 bil. **Savings institutions:** 57; deposits: $20.0 bil. **Lottery:** total sales: $3.0 bil; profit: $735.5 mil.

Federal govt. Fed. civ. employees: 40,228; **avg. salary:** $85,404. **Notable fed. facilities:** Great Lakes Naval Station; Fermi Natl. Accelerator Lab, Batavia; Argonne Natl. Lab, Lemont; Scott AFB; Rock Island Arsenal.

Education. High school grad. rate: 86.5%. **4-yr. public coll./univ.:** 12; **2-yr. public:** 48; **4-yr. private:** 78.

Energy. Electricity use/cost: 744 kWh, $94.98.

State data. Motto: State sovereignty, national union. **Flower:** Native violet. **Bird:** Northern cardinal. **Tree:** White oak. **Song:** "Illinois." **Entered union:** Dec. 3, 1818; rank: 21st.

Tourism. Tourist spending: $41.7 bil. **Attractions:** Art Institute of Chicago, Field Museum of Natural History, Shedd Aquarium, Millennium Park, Navy Pier, in Chicago; Illinois State Museum, Abraham Lincoln Presidential Library and Museum, in Springfield; Cahokia Mounds State Historic Site, Collinsville; Starved Rock State Park; Crab Orchard Natl. Wildlife Refuge; Forts Kaskaskia, de Chartres, Massac; Shawnee Natl. Forest; Dickson Mounds Museum, Lewistown. **Information:** Illinois Bureau of Tourism, 100 W. Randolph St., Ste. 3-400, Chicago, IL 60601; 1-800-226-6632; www.enjoyillinois.com

History. The region has been inhabited for at least 10,000 years; seminomadic Algonquian peoples, including the Peoria, Illinois, Kaskaskia, and Tamaroa, lived there at the time of European contact. Fur traders were the first Europeans in Illinois, followed shortly by Louis Jolliet and Jacques Marquette, 1673, and René-Robert Cavelier, sieur de La Salle, 1680, who built a fort near present-day Peoria. French priests established the first permanent settlements at Cahokia, near present-day St. Louis, 1699, and Kaskaskia, 1703. France ceded the area to Britain, 1763, and in 1778, American Gen. George Rogers Clark took Kaskaskia from the British without a shot. Illinois became a separate territory, 1809, and a state, 1818. Defeat of Native American tribes in the Black Hawk War, 1832, and canal, rail, and road construction brought rapid change. Mormon settlers at Nauvoo, 1839, met with hostility, and a Carthage mob killed Mormon leader Joseph Smith and his brother, 1844. The Great Chicago Fire, 1871, destroyed the city's downtown. Illinois became a center for the labor movement, leading to bitter conflicts such as the Haymarket riot, 1886, and Pullman strike, 1894. Social reformer Jane Addams founded Hull House, 1889, to aid immigrants and the poor. The expansion of manufacturing, 1900-70, drew African Americans from the South in the Great Migration. Chicago police violently suppressed antiwar protests at the 1968 Democratic National Convention. Barack Obama, elected in 2004 to serve in the U.S. Senate, became the 44th U.S. president in 2009. Political corruption and criminality have plagued the state; since 1960, five former governors have been charged with criminal offenses. A U.S. Justice Dept. investigation of the Chicago Police Dept., launched after a 2014 video of a white officer fatally shooting a Black teen sparked protests, found in 2017 that officers used excessive force too often and without repercussions. The officer was found guilty of 2nd-degree murder and sentenced in Jan. 2019 to 6.75 years in prison. A Chicago public school teachers' strike shut down schools for 11 days in Oct. 2019.

Famous Illinoisans. Jane Addams, Saul Bellow, John Belushi, Jack Benny, Ray Bradbury, Gwendolyn Brooks, St. Frances Xavier Cabrini, Al Capone, Hillary Rodham Clinton, Clarence Darrow, John Deere, Stephen A. Douglas, Katherine Dunham, Wyatt Earp, Roger Ebert, James T. Farrell, Marshall Field, Harrison Ford, Betty Friedan, Benny Goodman, Ulysses S. Grant, Dennis Hastert, Hugh Hefner, Ernest Hemingway, Charlton Heston, Jennifer Hudson, Henry J. Hyde, Abraham Lincoln, Vachel Lindsay, David Mamet, Edgar Lee Masters, Oscar Mayer, Cyrus McCormick, Eliot Ness, Bob Newhart, Michelle Obama, Ronald Reagan, Shonda Rhimes, Donald Rumsfeld, Carl Sandburg, Shel Silverstein, Adlai E. Stevenson, James Watson, Frank Lloyd Wright, Philip K. Wrigley.

Website. www.illinois.gov

Indiana (IN)
Hoosier State

People. Population: 6,732,219; rank: 17. **Pop. change** (2010-19): 3.8%. **Pop. density:** 187.9 per sq mi. **Racial distribution:** 84.8% white; 9.9% Black; 2.6% Asian; 0.4% Amer. Ind.; 0.1% Hawaiian/Pacific Islander; 2 or more races, 2.2%. **Hispanic pop.:** 7.3%.

Geography. Total area: 36,420 sq mi; rank: 38. **Land area:** 35,826 sq mi; rank: 38. **Acres forested:** 4.8 mil. **Location:** East North Central state; Lake Michigan on N border. **Climate:** four distinct seasons with temperate climate. **Topography:** hilly southern region; fertile rolling plains of central region; flat, heavily glaciated N; dunes along Lake Michigan shore. **Capital:** Indianapolis. **Chief airport:** Indianapolis.

Economy. Chief industries: manufacturing, services, agriculture, government, wholesale and retail trade, transportation, public utilities. **Chief manuf. goods:** motor vehicles and parts, iron and steel mills, pharmaceuticals, petroleum, plastics, medical equip., printing. **Chief crops:** corn, soybeans, greenhouse and nursery, wheat, hay, tomatoes, watermelons, apples. **Farm income:** Crops: $6.70 bil. Livestock: $3.80 bil. **Nonfuel minerals:** $695 mil; cement (portland), lime, sand and gravel (construction), stone (crushed), stone (dimension). **Chief ports:** Burns Harbor-Portage, Mt. Vernon, Jeffersonville. **Gross state product:** $377.1 bil. **Sales tax:** 7.0%. **Gasoline tax:** 65.02 cents/gal. **Employment distrib.:** 14.4% govt.; 19.8% trade/trans./util.; 16.5% mfg.; 15.5% ed./health; 10.8% prof./bus. serv.; 8.1% leisure/hosp.; 4.8% finance; 5.3% constr./mining/log.; 0.9% info.; 3.9% other serv. **Unemployment:** 3.3%. **Min. wage/hr.:** $7.25. **Per cap. pers. income:** $48,657. **New private housing:** 22,309 units/$5.0 bil. **Broadband internet:** 97.2%. **Commercial banks:** 117; deposits: $132.6 bil. **Savings institutions:** 27; deposits: $5.3 bil. **Lottery:** total sales: $1.3 bil; profit: $312.2 mil.

Federal govt. Fed. civ. employees: 23,797; **avg. salary:** $73,780. **Notable fed. facilities:** Naval Surface Warfare Ctr., Crane Div.; Grissom Air Reserve Base.

Education. High school grad. rate: 88.1%. **4-yr. public coll./univ.:** 15; **2-yr. public:** 1; **4-yr. private:** 42.

Energy. Electricity use/cost: 1,006 kWh, $123.39.

State data. Motto: Crossroads of America. **Flower:** Peony. **Bird:** Northern cardinal. **Tree:** Tulip poplar. **Song:** "On the Banks of the Wabash, Far Away." **Entered union:** Dec. 11, 1816; rank: 19th.

Tourism. Tourist spending: $12.3 bil. **Attractions:** Lincoln Boyhood Natl. Memorial, Lincoln City; George Rogers Clark Natl. Historical Park, Vincennes; Tippecanoe Battlefield Museum and Park, Battle Ground; Benjamin Harrison Presidential Site, Indianapolis Motor Speedway and Hall of Fame Museum, Indianapolis Museum of Art, in Indianapolis; Indiana Dunes Natl. Park, Chesterton; College Football Hall of Fame, Studebaker Natl. Museum, in South Bend; Hoosier Natl. Forest. **Information:** Indiana Office of Tourism Development, 1 North Capital, Ste. 600, Indianapolis, IN 46204; 1-800-677-9800; www.visitindiana.com

History. When the Europeans arrived, Miami, Potawatomi, Kickapoo, Piankashaw, Wea, and Shawnee peoples inhabited the region. René-Robert Cavelier, sieur de La Salle, visited the present South Bend area, 1679 and 1681. The first French fort was built near present-day Lafayette, 1717. A French trading post was established, 1731-32, at Vincennes. France ceded the area to Britain, 1763. During the American Revolution, American Gen. George Rogers Clark captured Vincennes, 1778, and defeated British forces, 1779. Indiana became a territory, 1800, and a state, 1816. The Miami were beaten, 1794, at Fallen Timbers, and Gen. William H. Harrison defeated Tecumseh's Indian confederation, 1811, at Tippecanoe. Manufacturing grew rapidly after the Civil War. U.S. Steel founded Gary, 1906. An automotive test track was the site of the first Indianapolis 500 race, 1911. The auto industry remains key to the state economy; in 2008, Honda opened a $550-mil plant near Greensburg. Heavy rain in June 2008 flooded southwest and central Indiana. Some rights groups and businesses criticized the state's 2015 Religious Freedom Restoration Act as discriminatory to LGBT individuals. Mike Pence, the state's governor, 2013-17, was sworn in as U.S. vice president in Jan. 2017.

Famous "Hoosiers." Larry Bird, Ambrose Burnside, Meg Cabot, Hoagy Carmichael, Jim Davis, James Dean, Eugene V. Debs, John Dillinger, Theodore Dreiser, Paul Dresser, Jeff Gordon, Benjamin Harrison, Gil Hodges, Michael Jackson, David Letterman, Carole Lombard, Marjorie Main, John Mellencamp, Jane Pauley, Cole Porter, Gene Stratton Porter, Ernie Pyle, Dan Quayle, James Whitcomb Riley, Oscar Robertson, Red Skelton, Tony Stewart, Booth Tarkington, Kurt Vonnegut, Lew Wallace, Ryan White, Wendell L. Willkie, Wilbur Wright.

Website. www.in.gov

Iowa (IA)
Hawkeye State

People. Population: 3,155,070; rank: 31. **Pop. change** (2010-19): 3.6%. **Pop. density:** 56.5 per sq mi. **Racial distribution:** 90.6% white; 4.1% Black; 2.7% Asian; 0.5% Amer. Ind.; 0.2% Hawaiian/Pacific Islander; 2 or more races, 2.0%. **Hispanic pop.:** 6.3%.

Geography. Total area: 56,273 sq mi; rank: 26. **Land area:** 55,857 sq mi; rank: 23. **Acres forested:** 2.9 mil. **Location:** West North Central state bordered by Mississippi R. on the E, Missouri R. on the W. **Climate:** humid, continental. **Topography:** watershed from NW to SE; soil especially rich and land level in the N central counties. **Capital:** Des Moines. **Chief airports:** Des Moines, Cedar Rapids.

Economy. Chief industries: agriculture, communications, construction, finance, insurance, trade, services, manufacturing. **Chief manuf. goods:** machinery, vegetable oils, animal slaughtering and processing, laundry equip., plastics, motor vehicles and parts. **Chief crops:** corn, soybeans, hay, greenhouse and nursery, oats. **Farm income:** Crops: $13.18 bil. Livestock: $14.29 bil. **Nonfuel minerals:** $836 mil; cement (portland), lime, sand and gravel (construction), sand and gravel (industrial), stone (crushed). **Gross state product:** $194.8 bil. **Sales tax:** 6.0%. **Gasoline tax:** 48.90 cents/gal. **Employment distrib.:** 16.8% govt.; 20.5% trade/trans./util.; 15.0% mfg.; 15.0% ed./health; 8.8% prof./bus. serv.; 6.2% leisure/hosp.; 7.5% finance; 5.4% constr./mining/log.; 1.4% info.; 3.5% other serv. **Unemployment:** 2.7%. **Min. wage/hr.:** $7.25. **Per cap. pers. income:** $52,636. **New private housing:** 11,870 units/$2.5 bil. **Broadband internet:** 94.4%. **Commercial banks:** 303; deposits: $86.3 bil. **Savings institutions:** 8; deposits: $3.7 bil. **Lottery:** total sales: $390.9 mil; profit: $92.9 mil.

Federal govt. Fed. civ. employees: 8,696; **avg. salary:** $70,739. **Notable fed. facilities:** Ames Lab; Natl. Animal Disease Ctr.

Education. High school grad. rate: 91.4%. **4-yr. public coll./univ.:** 8; **2-yr. public:** 16; **4-yr. private:** 34.

Energy. Electricity use/cost: 892 kWh, $109.27.

State data. Motto: Our liberties we prize, and our rights we will maintain. **Flower:** Wild rose. **Bird:** Eastern goldfinch. **Tree:** Oak. **Song:** "The Song of Iowa." **Entered union:** Dec. 28, 1846; rank: 29th.

Tourism. Tourist spending: $9.2 bil. **Attractions:** Des Moines Art Ctr., Iowa State Fairgrounds, Iowa State Capitol, in Des Moines; Natl. Czech & Slovak Museum & Library, Cedar Rapids; Herbert Hoover Natl. Historic Site, Presidential Library and Museum, in West Branch; Effigy Mounds Natl. Monument, Marquette; Amana Colonies (former communal society); Figge Art Museum, Davenport; Living History Farms, Urbandale; Adventureland, Altoona; Boone & Scenic Valley Railroad and Museum; riverboat cruises and casino gambling, Mississippi and Missouri Rivers; Iowa Great Lakes, Okoboji; American Gothic House, Eldon; *Field of Dreams* movie site, Dyersville; Natl. Mississippi River Museum & Aquarium, Dubuque. **Information:** Iowa Tourism Office, Iowa Dept. of Economic Development, 200 E. Grand Ave., Des Moines, IA 50309; 1-800-345-IOWA; www.traveliowa.com

History. Early inhabitants were Mound Builders who dwelt on Iowa's fertile plains. Later, Iowa and Yankton Sioux lived in the area. The first Europeans, Jacques Marquette and Louis Jolliet, gave France its claim to the area, 1673. In 1762, France ceded the region to Spain, but Napoleon took it back, 1800. It became part of the U.S. through the Louisiana Purchase, 1803. Native American Sauk and Fox tribes moved into the area but relinquished their land in defeat after the 1832 uprising led by Sauk chieftain Black Hawk. Iowa became a territory in 1838 and a free state in 1846, strongly supporting the Union. Fertile land lured farmers from eastern states, 1850-1900, and the population rose rapidly. Growth slowed in the 20th cent., as farming became mechanized. Severe flooding in eastern Iowa in June 2008 caused billions of dollars in damages and forced the evacuation of thousands of residents. The Iowa caucuses have been the first statewide electoral event in the presidential nomination process since 1972. Severe flooding in western Iowa in Mar. 2019, in part from a so-called "bomb cyclone," caused an est. $2 bil in damages.

Famous Iowans. Tom Arnold, Johnny Carson, William F. "Buffalo Bill" Cody, Mamie Dowd Eisenhower, Michael Emerson, Bob Feller, George Gallup, Susan Glaspell, James Norman Hall, Herbert Hoover, Shawn Johnson, Ashton Kutcher, Ann Landers, Cloris Leachman, Glenn Miller, Lillian Russell, Billy Sunday, James A. Van Allen, Abigail Van Buren, Carl Van Vechten, Henry Wallace, Kurt Warner, John Wayne, Meredith Willson, Elijah Wood, Grant Wood.

Website. www.iowa.gov

Kansas (KS)
Sunflower State

People. Population: 2,913,314; rank: 35. **Pop. change** (2010-19): 2.1%. **Pop. density:** 35.6 per sq mi. **Racial distribution:** 86.3% white; 6.1% Black; 3.2% Asian; 1.2% Amer. Ind.; 0.1% Hawaiian/Pacific Islander; 2 or more races, 3.1%. **Hispanic pop.:** 12.2%.

Geography. Total area: 82,278 sq mi; rank: 15. **Land area:** 81,759 sq mi; rank: 13. **Acres forested:** 2.5 mil. **Location:** West North Central state with Missouri R. on E. **Climate:** temperate but continental, with great extremes between summer and winter. **Topography:** hilly Osage Plains in the E; central region level prairie and hills; high plains in the W. **Capital:** Topeka. **Chief airport:** Wichita.

Economy. Chief industries: manufacturing, finance, insurance, real estate, services. **Chief manuf. goods:** animal slaughtering, aerospace, petroleum, plastics, machinery, navigational instruments, printing. **Chief crops:** wheat, corn, soybeans, hay, sorghum, sunflowers, cotton, potatoes. **Farm income:** Crops: $6.51 bil. Livestock: $9.51 bil. **Nonfuel minerals:** $1.1 bil; cement (portland), helium (Grade-A), salt, sand and gravel (construction), stone (crushed). **Chief port:** Kansas City. **Gross state product:** $173.1 bil. **Sales tax:** 6.5%. **Gasoline tax:** 42.43 cents/gal. **Employment distrib.:** 19.1% govt.; 19.5% trade/trans./util.; 12.0% mfg.; 14.2% ed./health; 12.7% prof./bus. serv.; 7.1% leisure/hosp.; 5.7% finance; 5.3% constr./mining/log.; 1.2% info.; 3.2% other serv. **Unemployment:** 3.2%. **Min. wage/hr.:** $7.25. **Per cap. pers. income:** $53,453. **New private housing:** 7,961 units/$1.7 bil. **Broadband internet:** 95.8%. **Commercial banks:** 266; deposits: $68.2 bil. **Savings institutions:** 13; deposits: $8.3 bil. **Lottery:** total sales: $295.3 mil; profit: $74.9 mil.

Federal govt. Fed. civ. employees: 16,414; **avg. salary:** $72,604. **Notable fed. facilities:** Ft. Riley; Leavenworth Fed. Penitentiary, Dwight D. Eisenhower VA Medical Ctr., Leavenworth; McConnell AFB; Colmery-O'Neil VA Medical Ctr., Topeka.

Education. High school grad. rate: 87.2%. **4-yr. public coll./univ.:** 8; **2-yr. public:** 25; **4-yr. private:** 24.

Energy. Electricity use/cost: 934 kWh, $124.68.

State data. Motto: Ad Astra per Aspera (To the stars through difficulties). **Flower:** Native sunflower. **Bird:** Western meadowlark. **Tree:** Cottonwood. **Song:** "Home on the Range." **Entered union:** Jan. 29, 1861; rank: 34th.

Tourism. Tourist spending: $8.1 bil. **Attractions:** Eisenhower Presidential Library and Museum, Abilene; Natl. Agricultural Ctr. and Hall of Fame, Bonner Springs; Boot Hill Museum, Dodge City; Old Cowtown Museum, Wichita; Ft. Scott and Ft. Larned Natl. Historic Sites; Kansas Cosmosphere and Space Ctr., Hutchinson; U.S. Cavalry Museum, Ft. Riley; Tallgrass Prairie Natl. Preserve, Strong City; Kansas Speedway, Kansas City. **Information:** Kansas Dept. of Commerce, Travel and Tourism Div., 1000 SW Jackson St., Ste. 100, Topeka, KS 66612; (785) 296-2009; www.travelks.com

History. Wichita, Pawnee, Kansa, and Osage peoples lived in the area when Spain's Francisco de Coronado explored it in 1541. These Native Americans—hunters who also farmed—were joined on the Plains by the nomadic Cheyenne, Arapaho, Comanche, and Kiowa about 1800. France claimed the region, 1682, ceded its claim to Spain, 1762, then regained control, 1800, before selling it to the U.S. in the Louisiana Purchase, 1803. After 1830, thousands of Native Americans were removed from more eastern states to Kansas. Organized as a territory, 1854, the area witnessed violent clashes between pro- and antislavery settlers and became known as "Bleeding Kansas." It entered the Union as a free state, 1861. After the Civil War, rail construction and huge cattle drives from Texas turned Abilene and Dodge City into cowboy capitals. Russian Mennonite immigrants brought a new strain of winter wheat, 1874, transforming Kansas agriculture. Carry Nation launched her anti-saloon crusade in the 1890s. Part of the Dust Bowl, the state experienced drought and depression in the 1930s. Topeka was the focus of the famous *Brown v. Board of Education* decision, 1954, that led to desegregation of U.S. public schools. Bob Dole represented Kansas in the U.S. Senate (1969-96) but failed in several efforts to win higher office.

Famous Kansans. Kirstie Alley, Roscoe "Fatty" Arbuckle, Ed Asner, John Brown, Walter P. Chrysler, Glenn Cunningham, John Steuart Curry, Robert Joseph "Bob" Dole, Amelia Earhart, Dwight D. Eisenhower, Melissa Etheridge, Ron Evans, Georgia Neese Clark Gray, Maurice Greene, James Butler "Wild Bill" Hickok, Cyrus K. Holliday, Dennis Hopper, William Inge, Don Johnson, Walter Johnson, Nancy Landon Kassebaum, Buster Keaton, Emmett Kelly, Alfred M. "Alf" Landon, Hattie McDaniel, Oscar Micheaux, Carry Nation,

Charlie Parker, Gordon Parks, Jim Ryun, Barry Sanders, Vivian Vance, William Allen White, Jess Willard.
Website. www.kansas.gov

Kentucky (KY)
Bluegrass State

People. Population: 4,467,673; rank: 26. **Pop. change** (2010-19): 3.0%. **Pop. density:** 113.1 per sq mi. **Racial distribution:** 87.5% white; 8.5% Black; 1.6% Asian; 0.3% Amer. Ind.; 0.1% Hawaiian/Pacific Islander; 2 or more races, 2.0%. **Hispanic pop.:** 3.9%.

Geography. Total area: 40,408 sq mi; rank: 37. **Land area:** 39,486 sq mi; rank: 37. **Acres forested:** 12.4 mil. **Location:** East South Central state bordered on N by Illinois, Indiana, Ohio; on E by West Virginia and Virginia; on S by Tennessee; on W by Missouri. **Climate:** moderate, with plentiful rainfall. **Topography:** mountainous in E; rounded hills of the Knobs region in the N; Bluegrass region in heart of state; wooded rocky hillsides of the Pennyroyal Plateau; Western Coal Field; the fertile Jackson Purchase region in the SW. **Capital:** Frankfort. **Chief airports:** Hebron, Louisville, Lexington.

Economy. Chief industries: manufacturing, services, finance, insurance and real estate, retail trade, public utilities. **Chief manuf. goods:** motor vehicles and parts, aluminum, basic chemicals, plastics, iron and steel, rubber, printing. **Chief crops:** hay, corn, soybeans, tobacco, wheat. **Farm income:** Crops: $2.53 bil. Livestock: $3.37 bil. **Nonfuel minerals:** $591 mil; cement (portland), clay (common clay), lime, sand and gravel (construction), stone (crushed). **Chief ports:** Louisville, Hickman-Fulton County. **Gross state product:** $214.7 bil. **Sales tax:** 6.0%. **Gasoline tax:** 44.40 cents/gal. **Employment distrib.:** 17.3% govt.; 21.4% trade/trans./util.; 12.4% mfg.; 15.1% ed./health; 10.5% prof./bus. serv.; 8.4% leisure/hosp.; 5.2% finance; 5.1% constr./mining/log.; 1.0% info.; 3.5% other serv. **Unemployment:** 4.3%. **Min. wage/hr.:** $7.25. **Per cap. pers. income:** $44,017. **New private housing:** 11,811 units/$2.1 bil. **Broadband internet:** 95.1%. **Commercial banks:** 159; deposits: $83.1 bil. **Savings institutions:** 13; deposits: $1.2 bil. **Lottery:** total sales: $1.1 bil; profit: $283.6 mil.

Federal govt. Fed. civ. employees: 21,983; **avg. salary:** $68,555. **Notable fed. facilities:** U.S. Bullion Depository, Ft. Knox; Ft. Campbell; Fed. Medical Ctr., Lexington; Army Corps of Engineers, Louisville District.

Education. High school grad. rate: 90.3%. **4-yr. public coll./univ.:** 8; **2-yr. public:** 16; **4-yr. private:** 25.

Energy. Electricity use/cost: 1,166 kWh, $123.57.

State data. Motto: United we stand, divided we fall. **Flower:** Goldenrod. **Bird:** Northern cardinal. **Tree:** Tulip poplar. **Song:** "My Old Kentucky Home." **Entered union:** June 1, 1792; rank: 15th.

Tourism. Tourist spending: $10.2 bil. **Attractions:** Churchill Downs (Kentucky Derby), Louisville Slugger Museum and Factory, in Louisville; Land Between the Lakes Natl. Recreation Area (Kentucky and Barkley Lakes); Mammoth Cave Natl. Park (world's longest known cave system); Abraham Lincoln Birthplace Natl. Historical Park, Hodgenville; My Old Kentucky Home State Park, Bardstown; Cumberland Gap Natl. Historical Park, Middlesboro; Creation Museum, Petersburg; Kentucky Horse Park, Lexington; Shaker Village of Pleasant Hill, Harrodsburg; Natl. Corvette Museum, Bowling Green. **Information:** Kentucky Dept. of Tourism, 100 Airport Road, 2nd Fl., Frankfort, KY 40601; 1-800-225-8747; www.kentuckytourism.com

History. Paleo-Indians first arrived about 14,000 years ago. Much later, Shawnee, Wyandot, Delaware, and Cherokee peoples used the area mostly for hunting. Explored by Thomas Walker and Christopher Gist, 1750-51, Kentucky was the first area W of the Alleghenies settled by American pioneers. The first permanent settlement was Harrodsburg, 1774. Daniel Boone blazed the Wilderness Trail through the Cumberland Gap and founded Ft. Boonesborough, 1775. Clashes with Native Americans were frequent, 1774-94. Virginia dropped its claims to the region, and Kentucky became a state, 1792. Tobacco growing, horse breeding, coal mining, and bourbon whiskey making were major industries in the 19th cent. A slave state, Kentucky tried to stay neutral in the Civil War, but then opted for the Union; many Kentuckians sided with the Confederacy. The U.S. gold depository at Ft. Knox opened, 1937. Prior to the 2008 economic downturn, auto manufacturing had grown in recent decades. A Rowan County clerk attracted national attention after being jailed in 2015 for refusing to issue marriage licenses to same-sex couples. A statewide teacher walkout in Mar.-Apr. 2018 demanded increased pay and school funding.

Famous Kentuckians. Muhammad Ali, Alben W. Barkley, Ned Beatty, Louis D. Brandeis, John C. Breckinridge, Kit Carson, Albert B. "Happy" Chandler, Henry Clay, George Clooney, Rosemary Clooney, Jefferson Davis, D. W. Griffith, "Casey" Jones, Jennifer Lawrence, Abraham Lincoln, Mary Todd Lincoln, Thomas Hunt Morgan, Carry Nation, Colonel Harland Sanders, Diane Sawyer, Chris Stapleton, Jesse Stuart, Zachary Taylor, Hunter S. Thompson, Robert Penn Warren, Whitney M. Young Jr.
Website. www.kentucky.gov

Louisiana (LA)
Pelican State

People. Population: 4,648,794; rank: 25. **Pop. change** (2010-19): 2.5%. **Pop. density:** 107.6 per sq mi. **Racial distribution:** 62.8% white; 32.8% Black; 1.8% Asian; 0.8% Amer. Ind.; 0.1% Hawaiian/Pacific Islander; 2 or more races, 1.8%. **Hispanic pop.:** 5.3%.

Geography. Total area: 52,378 sq mi; rank: 31. **Land area:** 43,204 sq mi; rank: 33. **Acres forested:** 15.0 mil. **Location:** West South Central state on the Gulf Coast. **Climate:** subtropical, affected by continental weather patterns. **Topography:** lowlands of marshes and Mississippi R. floodplain; Red R. Valley lowlands; upland hills in the Florida Parishes; avg. elevation, 100 ft. **Capital:** Baton Rouge. **Chief airport:** Kenner (New Orleans).

Economy. Chief industries: wholesale and retail trade, tourism, manufacturing, construction, transportation, communication, public utilities, finance, insurance, real estate, mining. **Chief manuf. goods:** petroleum, chemicals, plastics material and resin, pesticides and fertilizers, cleaning prods., paper and paperboard, ships, structural metals. **Chief crops:** sugarcane, cotton, rice, soybeans, corn, sweet potatoes. **Farm income:** Crops: $1.98 bil. Livestock: $1.14 bil. **Nonfuel minerals:** $614 mil; clay (common clay), salt, sand and gravel (construction), sand and gravel (industrial), stone (crushed). **Commercial fishing:** $375.9 mil. **Chief ports:** New Orleans, Baton Rouge, Lake Charles, Port of S. Louisiana (La Place), Shreveport, Plaquemine, St. Bernard, Alexandria. **Gross state product:** $263.9 bil. **Sales tax:** 4.45%. **Gasoline tax:** 38.41 cents/gal. **Employment distrib.:** 18.1% govt.; 19.4% trade/trans./util.; 7.3% mfg.; 16.5% ed./health; 11.3% prof./bus. serv.; 8.7% leisure/hosp.; 5.1% finance; 8.8% constr./mining/log.; 1.1% info.; 3.8% other serv. **Unemployment:** 4.8%. **Min. wage/hr.:** none. **Per cap. pers. income:** $48,008. **New private housing:** 15,793 units/$3.1 bil. **Broadband internet:** 95.4%. **Commercial banks:** 111; deposits: $103.0 bil. **Savings institutions:** 17; deposits: $3.5 bil. **Lottery:** total sales: $524.0 mil; profit: $184.3 mil.

Federal govt. Fed. civ. employees: 18,993; **avg. salary:** $73,529. **Notable federal facilities:** Ft. Polk (Joint Readiness Training Ctr.); Barksdale AFB; Strategic Petroleum Reserve, Michoud Assembly Facility, USDA Southern Regional Research Ctr., New Orleans NAS JRB.

Education. High school grad. rate: 81.4%. **4-yr. public coll./univ.:** 17; **2-yr. public:** 15; **4-yr. private:** 12.

Energy. Electricity use/cost: 1,282 kWh, $122.86.

State data. Motto: Union, justice, and confidence. **Flower:** Magnolia blossom. **Bird:** Eastern brown pelican. **Tree:** Bald cypress. **Song:** "Give Me Louisiana." **Entered union:** Apr. 30, 1812; rank: 18th.

Tourism. Tourist spending: $13.1 bil. **Attractions:** Mardi Gras, French Quarter, Bourbon Street, in New Orleans; Jean Lafitte Natl. Historical Park and Preserve; Longfellow-Evangeline State Historic Site, St. Martinville; Kent Plantation House, Alexandria; Oak Alley Plantation, Vacherie; Whitney Plantation, Wallace; Hodges Gardens State Park, Florien; USS *Kidd* Veterans Memorial, Baton Rouge. **Information:** Louisiana Office of Tourism, P.O. Box 94291, Baton Rouge, LA 70804-9291; 1-800-677-4082; www.louisianatravel.com

History. Caddo, Tunica, Choctaw, Chitimacha, and Chawash peoples lived in the region at the time of European contact. Spanish explorers in the early 16th cent. reached the mouth of the Mississippi. René-Robert Cavelier, sieur de La Salle, 1682, claimed the region for France. Early French and Spanish settlers were the ancestors of Louisiana Creoles. Cajuns descended from the Acadians, French settlers expelled by the British from Nova Scotia, Canada, in 1755. France ceded the Louisiana region to Spain, 1762, took it back, 1800, and sold it to the U.S., 1803, in the Louisiana Purchase. Admitted as a state in 1812, Louisiana witnessed the Battle of New Orleans, 1815. Cotton and sugar plantations relied on the enslaved labor of Black workers, who made up close to 47% of the population in 1860, on the eve of the Civil War. Louisiana seceded, 1861, and was readmitted, 1868. Jazz was born in New Orleans in the early 20th cent. As governor

(1928-32), Huey Long pushed populist programs. Many tropical storms and floods have battered Louisiana, including Hurricane Katrina and subsequent flooding, 2005, which devastated New Orleans. The offshore oil and gas industry developed after World War II. An oil rig explosion off the state's Gulf coast spilled millions of barrels of oil, damaging coastal wetlands and many of the state's marine-dependent industries in 2010. Rain caused severe flooding in and around Baton Rouge and Lafayette in 2016. In May 2017, New Orleans removed several monuments honoring the Confederacy and a racially motivated Reconstruction-era attack.

Famous Louisianans. Louis Armstrong, Pierre Beauregard, Judah P. Benjamin, Braxton Bragg, Kate Chopin, Harry Connick Jr., Ellen DeGeneres, Fats Domino, George "Buddy" Guy, Lillian Hellman, Grace King, Jerry Lee Lewis, Bob Livingston, Huey Long, Eli Manning, Peyton Manning, Wynton Marsalis, Tim McGraw, Leonidas K. Polk, Anne Rice, Bill Russell, Henry Miller Shreve, Britney Spears, Madam C. J. Walker (Sarah Breedlove), Edward Douglass White Jr.

Website. www.louisiana.gov

Maine (ME)
Pine Tree State

People. Population: 1,344,212; rank: 42. **Pop. change** (2010-19): 1.2%. **Pop. density:** 43.6 per sq mi. **Racial distribution:** 94.4% white; 1.7% Black; 1.3% Asian; 0.7% Amer. Ind.; <0.05% Hawaiian/Pacific Islander; 2 or more races, 1.8%. **Hispanic pop.:** 1.8%.

Geography. Total area: 35,380 sq mi; rank: 39. **Land area:** 30,843 sq mi; rank: 39. **Acres forested:** 17.5 mil. **Location:** New England state at northeastern tip of U.S. **Climate:** southern interior and coast influenced by air masses from the S and W; northern clime harsher, avg. over 100 in. snow in winter. **Topography:** Appalachian Mts. extend through state; western borders have rugged terrain; long sand beaches on southern coast; northern coast mainly rocky promontories, peninsulas, fjords. **Capital:** Augusta. **Chief airport:** Portland.

Economy. Chief industries: manufacturing, agriculture, fishing, services, trade, government, finance, insurance, real estate, construction. **Chief manuf. goods:** paper, ships and boats, cardboard, frozen/canned fruits and vegetables, plastics, baked goods. **Chief crops:** potatoes, greenhouse and nursery, wild blueberries, apples, hay, maple syrup. **Farm income:** Crops: $378.98 mil. Livestock: $286.62 mil. **Nonfuel minerals:** $102 mil; cement (portland), peat, sand and gravel (construction), stone (crushed), stone (dimension). **Commercial fishing:** $647.1 mil. **Chief ports:** Searsport, Portland, Eastport. **Gross state product:** $67.5 bil. **Sales tax:** 5.5%. **Gasoline tax:** 48.41 cents/gal. **Employment distrib.:** 17.2% govt.; 19.4% trade/trans./util.; 8.6% mfg.; 20.6% ed./health; 11.6% prof./bus. serv.; 6.4% leisure/hosp.; 5.8% finance; 5.8% constr./mining/log.; 1.0% info.; 3.5% other serv. **Unemployment:** 3.0%. **Min. wage/hr.:** $12.00. **Per cap. pers. income:** $50,950. **New private housing:** 4,760 units/$1.0 bil. **Broadband internet:** 95.4%. **Commercial banks:** 11; deposits: $18.8 bil. **Savings institutions:** 20; deposits: $13.0 bil. **Lottery:** total sales: $299.5 mil; profit: $63.2 mil.

Federal govt. Fed. civ. employees: 11,234; **avg. salary:** $70,490. **Notable fed. facilities:** Portsmouth Naval Shipyard.

Education. High school grad. rate: 86.7%. **4-yr. public coll./univ.:** 10; **2-yr. public:** 7; **4-yr. private:** 12.

Energy. Electricity use/cost: 572 kWh, $96.33.

State data. Motto: Dirigo (I direct). **Flower:** White pine cone and tassel. **Bird:** Black-capped chickadee. **Tree:** Eastern white pine. **Song:** "State of Maine Song." **Entered union:** Mar. 15, 1820; rank: 23rd.

Tourism. Tourist spending: $4.5 bil. **Attractions:** Acadia Natl. Park, Bar Harbor, on Mt. Desert Island; Old Orchard Beach; Old Port historic waterfront, Victoria Mansion, Portland; Portland Head Light, Cape Elizabeth; Maine Maritime Museum, Bath; Baxter State Park; L.L. Bean flagship store and outlet shopping, Freeport. **Information:** Maine Office of Tourism, 59 State House Station, Augusta, ME 04330; 1-888-624-6345; www.visitmaine.com

History. Paleo-Indians arrived about 11,500 years ago. Maine was inhabited by Algonquian peoples including the Abnaki, Penobscot, and Passamaquoddy at the time of European contact. French settled, 1604, at the St. Croix R., the English, c. 1607, on the Kennebec; both settlements failed. A royal charter, 1691, made Maine part of Massachusetts. Maine broke off, 1819, and became a separate state, 1820. Drawing on vast forest resources, the pulp and paper industry developed after the Civil War. Bath Iron Works began building U.S. Navy vessels and other ships in the 1890s. Mail-order and retail giant L.L. Bean was founded, 1912. Women have

fared well in state politics: Margaret Chase Smith became the first woman to serve in both houses of Congress (House, 1940-49; Senate, 1949-73), and Olympia Snowe and Susan Collins represented Maine in the Senate since the mid-1990s (Snowe retired in Jan. 2013).

Famous "Down Easters." Leon Leonwood (L. L.) Bean, James G. Blaine, Patrick Dempsey, Hannibal Hamlin, Sarah Orne Jewett, Stephen King, Henry Wadsworth Longfellow, Sir Hiram and Hudson Maxim, Edna St. Vincent Millay, George J. Mitchell, Edmund Muskie, Judd Nelson, Edwin Arlington Robinson, Joan Benoit Samuelson, Liv Tyler, Kate Douglas Wiggin, Ben Ames Williams.

Website. www.maine.gov

Maryland (MD)
Old Line State, Free State

People. Population: 6,045,680; rank: 19. **Pop. change** (2010-19): 4.7%. **Pop. density:** 622.8 per sq mi. **Racial distribution:** 58.5% white; 31.1% Black; 6.7% Asian; 0.6% Amer. Ind.; 0.1% Hawaiian/Pacific Islander; 2 or more races, 2.9%. **Hispanic pop.:** 10.6%.

Geography. Total area: 12,406 sq mi; rank: 42. **Land area:** 9,707 sq mi; rank: 42. **Acres forested:** 2.4 mil. **Location:** South Atlantic state stretching from the ocean to the Allegheny Mts. **Climate:** continental in W; humid subtropical in the E. **Topography:** coastal plain on Eastern Shore separated by Chesapeake Bay from coastal plain, Piedmont Plateau, and the Blue Ridge. **Capital:** Annapolis. **Chief airport:** Glen Burnie (Baltimore/Washington).

Economy. Chief industries: manufacturing, biotechnology and information technology, services, tourism. **Chief manuf. goods:** navigational instruments, pharmaceutical and medicine, broadcasting equip., plastics, printing, milk and ice cream. **Chief crops:** greenhouse and nursery, corn, soybeans, wheat, hay, tomatoes, watermelons, barley, potatoes, apples. **Farm income:** Crops: $881.44 mil. Livestock: $1.36 bil. **Nonfuel minerals:** $575 mil; cement (masonry and portland), sand and gravel (construction), stone (crushed), stone (dimension). **Commercial fishing:** $71.8 mil. **Chief port:** Baltimore. **Gross state product:** $428.3 bil. **Sales tax:** 6.0%. **Gasoline tax:** 55.10 cents/gal. **Employment distrib.:** 20.1% govt.; 16.8% trade/trans./util.; 4.2% mfg.; 17.4% ed./health; 17.6% prof./bus. serv.; 6.9% leisure/hosp.; 5.6% finance; 6.6% constr./mining/log.; 1.2% info.; 3.6% other serv. **Unemployment:** 3.6%. **Min. wage/hr.:** $11.00. **Per cap. pers. income:** $65,683. **New private housing:** 18,491 units/$3.8 bil. **Broadband internet:** 98.5%. **Commercial banks:** 71; deposits: $146.3 bil. **Savings institutions:** 16; deposits: $3.4 bil. **Lottery:** total sales: $4.0 bil; profit: $1.2 bil.

Federal govt. Fed. civ. employees: 127,783; **avg. salary:** $110,873. **Notable fed. facilities:** U.S. Naval Academy; Beltsville Agriculture Res. Ctr.; Ft. Meade; Aberdeen Proving Ground; Joint Base Andrews; Naval Air Sys. Command; Goddard Space Flight Ctr.; Natl. Inst. of Standards & Technology, Gaithersburg; Food & Drug Admin., Natl. Marine Fisheries Serv., Natl. Oceanic and Atmospheric Admin., Silver Spring; Bureau of the Census, Suitland; Natl. Inst. of Health, Walter Reed Natl. Military Med. Ctr., Bethesda.

Education. High school grad. rate: 87.1%. **4-yr. public coll./univ.:** 14; **2-yr. public:** 16; **4-yr. private:** 20.

Energy. Electricity use/cost: 1,005 kWh, $133.68.

State data. Motto: Fatti Maschii, Parole Femine (Manly deeds, womanly words). **Flower:** Black-eyed Susan. **Bird:** Baltimore oriole. **Tree:** White oak. **Song:** "Maryland, My Maryland." **Seventh** of original 13 states to ratify the Constitution, Apr. 28, 1788.

Tourism. Tourist spending: $18.2 bil. **Attractions:** Ocean City; Ft. McHenry (the defense of which inspired Francis Scott Key to write "The Star-Spangled Banner"), Pimlico Race Course (Preakness Stakes), Edgar Allan Poe House and Museum, Oriole Park at Camden Yards, Natl. Aquarium, Inner Harbor, in Baltimore; Antietam Natl. Battlefield, Sharpsburg; South Mountain State Battlefield, Middletown; U.S. Naval Academy, Maryland State House (oldest in continuous legislative use in U.S.), in Annapolis; Natl. Cryptologic Museum, Ft. Meade. **Information:** Maryland Office of Tourism Development, 401 E. Pratt St., 14th Fl., Baltimore, MD 21202; 1-866-639-3526; www.visitmaryland.org

History. Europeans encountered Algonquian-speaking Nanticoke and Piscataway and Iroquois-speaking Susquehannock when they first visited the area. Italian navigator Giovanni da Verrazzano reached the Chesapeake region in the early 16th cent. English Capt. John Smith explored and mapped the area, 1608. William Claiborne set up a trading post on Kent Island in Chesapeake Bay, 1631. King Charles

I granted land to Cecilius Calvert, Lord Baltimore, 1632; Calvert's brother Leonard, with about 200 settlers, founded St. Mary's, 1634. During the Revolutionary War, Baltimore (1776-77) and Annapolis (1783-84) served as temporary capitals of the U.S. When a British fleet tried to take Ft. McHenry in the War of 1812, Marylander Francis Scott Key wrote "The Star-Spangled Banner," 1814. Born into slavery at Tuckahoe in 1818, Frederick Douglass became a leading abolitionist. Although a slaveholding state, Maryland stayed in the Union during the Civil War and was the site of the battle of Antietam, 1862. Gov. Spiro Agnew, elected U.S. vice pres., 1968 and 1972, pleaded no contest to tax evasion and resigned, 1973. Israeli and Egyptian leaders reached a historic peace accord at the Camp David presidential retreat, 1978. A major effort is under way to clean up pollution in the Chesapeake Bay watershed. The death of a young Black man in police custody touched off sometimes violent protests in Baltimore in 2015. Six law enforcement officers were charged in his death; after three were acquitted, charges against the others were dropped. According to a 2016 Justice Dept. report, Baltimore's police dept. regularly violated the constitutional rights of Black residents. A gunman in June 2018 fatally shot five employees at the office of Annapolis's *Capital Gazette*. Baltimore Mayor Catherine Pugh resigned, May 2019, amid a "self-dealing" corruption scandal.

Famous Marylanders. John Astin, Benjamin Banneker, Tom Clancy, Frederick Douglass, Matthew Henson, Francis Scott Key, Thurgood Marshall, H. L. Mencken, Kweisi Mfume, Ogden Nash, Charles Willson Peale, Michael Phelps, William Pinkney, Edgar Allan Poe, Cal Ripken Jr., Babe Ruth, Upton Sinclair, Roger B. Taney, Harriet Tubman, John Waters, Montel Williams.

Website. www.maryland.gov

Massachusetts (MA)
Bay State, Old Colony

People. Population: 6,892,503; rank: 15. **Pop. change** (2010-19): 5.3%. **Pop. density:** 883.7 per sq mi. **Racial distribution:** 80.6% white; 9.0% Black; 7.2% Asian; 0.5% Amer. Ind.; 0.1% Hawaiian/Pacific Islander; 2 or more races, 2.6%. **Hispanic pop.:** 12.4%.

Geography. Total area: 10,554 sq mi; rank: 44. **Land area:** 7,800 sq mi; rank: 45. **Acres forested:** 3.0 mil. **Location:** New England state on Atlantic seaboard. **Climate:** temperate, with colder, drier clime in western region. **Topography:** jagged indented coast from Rhode Island around Cape Cod; flat land yields to stony upland pastures near central region and gentle hilly country in W; except in W, land is rocky, sandy, and not fertile. **Capital:** Boston. **Chief airport:** Boston.

Economy. Chief industries: services, trade, manufacturing. **Chief manuf. goods:** electronics and instruments, pharmaceuticals, telecom and broadcasting equip., plastics, medical equip., printing. **Chief crops:** greenhouse and nursery, cranberries, tomatoes, sweet corn, apples, hay, tobacco. **Farm income:** Crops: $330.93 mil. Livestock: $101.59 mil. **Nonfuel minerals:** $289 mil; clay (common clay), lime, sand and gravel (construction), stone (crushed), stone (dimension). **Commercial fishing:** $647.7 mil. **Chief ports:** Boston, Fall River. **Gross state product:** $595.6 bil. **Sales tax:** 6.25%. **Gasoline tax:** 44.94 cents/gal. **Employment distrib.:** 14.0% govt.; 14.9% trade/trans./util.; 7.3% mfg.; 23.3% ed./health; 18.2% prof./bus. serv.; 5.2% leisure/hosp.; 7.1% finance; 4.0% constr./mining/log.; 2.9% info.; 3.0% other serv. **Unemployment:** 2.9%. **Min. wage/hr.:** $12.75. **Per cap. pers. income:** $74,967. **New private housing:** 17,365 units/$3.7 bil. **Broadband internet:** 98.6%. **Commercial banks:** 40; deposits: $323.8 bil. **Savings institutions:** 103; deposits: $83.7 bil. **Lottery:** total sales: $5.5 bil; profit: $1.1 bil.

Federal govt. Fed. civ. employees: 24,839; **avg. salary:** $87,632. **Notable fed. facilities:** Thomas P. O'Neill Jr. Fed. Bldg., J.W. McCormack Bldg., JFK Fed. Bldg., Boston; Hanscom AFB; Army Natick Soldier Systems Ctr.

Education. High school grad. rate: 87.8%. **4-yr. public coll./univ.:** 14; **2-yr. public:** 16; **4-yr. private:** 75.

Energy. Electricity use/cost: 607 kWh, $131.20.

State data. Motto: Ense Petit Placidam Sub Libertate Quietem (By the sword we seek peace, but peace only under liberty). **Flower:** Mayflower. **Bird:** Black-capped chickadee. **Tree:** American elm. **Song:** "All Hail to Massachusetts." **Sixth** of original 13 states to ratify the Constitution, Feb. 6, 1788.

Tourism. Tourist spending: $24.2 bil. **Attractions:** Provincetown art colony; Cape Cod; Plymouth Rock, Plimoth Plantation, Mayflower II in Plymouth; Freedom Trail, Museum of Fine Arts, New England Aquarium, Faneuil Hall, Boston Harbor Isls. Natl. Recreation Area, Boston Public Garden, in Boston; Tanglewood, Hancock Shaker Village, Berkshire Scenic Railway Museum, Norman Rockwell Museum, in the Berkshires region; Peabody Essex Museum, House of the Seven Gables, in Salem; Old Sturbridge Village; Historic Deerfield; Walden Pond, Louisa May Alcott's Orchard House, in Concord; Naismith Memorial Basketball Hall of Fame, Springfield. **Information:** Massachusetts Office of Travel & Tourism, 136 Blackstone St., 5th Fl., Boston, MA 02109; 1-800-227-MASS; www.massvacation.com

History. Early inhabitants were Algonquian peoples: Nauset, Wampanoag, Massachuset, Pennacook, Nipmuc, and Pocumtuc. Pilgrims settled in Plymouth, 1620, giving thanks for their survival with a Thanksgiving feast alongside Wampanoag living there, 1621. About 20,000 new settlers arrived, 1630-40. Colonist-Native American relations deteriorated, leading to King Philip's War, 1675-76, which the colonists won. Witch trials at Salem, 1692, led to the execution of 20 people. Demonstrations against British restrictions set off the Boston Massacre, 1770, and the Boston Tea Party, 1773. The first bloodshed of American Revolution was at Lexington, 1775. After statehood, Massachusetts prospered from shipbuilding, seafaring, and the making of textiles, shoes, and metal goods, while artists, writers, and social reformers flourished. The controversial Sacco-Vanzetti case, 1920-27, ended with the execution of two Italian immigrants on murder and robbery charges. After World War II, old industries declined, knowledge-intensive enterprises thrived, and the Kennedys became a dominant political family. The state's highest court ruled, 2003, that same-sex couples could legally marry. Two bombs exploded Apr. 15, 2013, near the finish line of the Boston Marathon, killing three and injuring more than 250. The surviving of two brothers believed to have planted the bombs was convicted on multiple charges in Apr. 2015 and sentenced to death; appellate court overturned sentence, July 2020, ordered a new penalty phase.

Famous "Bay Staters." John Adams, John Quincy Adams, Samuel Adams, Louisa May Alcott, Horatio Alger, Susan B. Anthony, Crispus Attucks, Clara Barton, Michael Bloomberg, George H. W. Bush, Steve Carell, John Cheever, E. E. Cummings, Bette Davis, Emily Dickinson, Charles Eliot, Ralph Waldo Emerson, William Lloyd Garrison, Edward Everett Hale, John Hancock, Nathaniel Hawthorne, Oliver Wendell Holmes Jr., Winslow Homer, Elias Howe, John F. Kennedy, Jack Kerouac, John Kerry, Emeril Lagasse, Jack Lemmon, James Russell Lowell, Cotton Mather, Maria Mitchell, Samuel F. B. Morse, Conan O'Brien, Paul Revere, Norman Rockwell, Dr. Seuss (Theodor Seuss Geisel), Henry David Thoreau, Barbara Walters, James Abbott McNeil Whistler, John Greenleaf Whittier.

Website. www.mass.gov

Michigan (MI)
Great Lakes State, Wolverine State

People. Population: 9,986,857; rank: 10. **Pop. change** (2010-19): 1.0%. **Pop. density:** 176.6 per sq mi. **Racial distribution:** 79.2% white; 14.1% Black; 3.4% Asian; 0.7% Amer. Ind.; <0.05% Hawaiian/Pacific Islander; 2 or more races, 2.5%. **Hispanic pop.:** 5.3%.

Geography. Total area: 96,714 sq mi; rank: 11. **Land area:** 56,539 sq mi; rank: 22. **Acres forested:** 20.2 mil. **Location:** East North Central state bordering four of the Great Lakes, divided into an Upper and Lower Peninsula by the Straits of Mackinac, which link Lakes Michigan and Huron. **Climate:** well-defined seasons tempered by the Great Lakes. **Topography:** low rolling hills give way to northern tableland of hilly belts in Lower Peninsula; Upper Peninsula is level in the E with swampy areas; western region is higher and more rugged. **Capital:** Lansing. **Chief airports:** Detroit, Grand Rapids.

Economy. Chief industries: manufacturing, services, tourism, agriculture, forestry/lumber. **Chief manuf. goods:** motor vehicles and parts, plastics, metalworking machinery, non-wood office furniture, fabricated metals. **Chief crops:** greenhouse and nursery, soybeans, corn, wheat, sugar beets, apples, blueberries, potatoes, dry beans, cherries, hay, cucumbers, tomatoes, grapes. **Farm income:** Crops: $4.19 bil. Livestock: $3.30 bil. **Nonfuel minerals:** $2.8 bil; cement (portland), iron ore, salt, sand and gravel (construction), stone (crushed). **Commercial fishing:** $8.0 mil. **Chief ports:** Detroit, Escanaba, Calcite, Port Inland, Muskegon, Port Huron. **Gross state product:** $541.6 bil. **Sales tax:** 6.0%. **Gasoline tax:** 60.38 cents/gal. **Employment distrib.:** 15.7% govt.; 19.2% trade/trans./util.; 13.2% mfg.; 16.2% ed./health; 15.0% prof./bus. serv.; 5.6% leisure/hosp.; 6.1% finance; 4.4% constr./mining/log.; 1.4% info.; 3.3% other serv. **Unemployment:** 4.1%. **Min. wage/hr.:** $9.65. **Per cap. pers. income:** $50,320. **New private housing:** 20,600 units/$4.6 bil. **Broadband internet:** 97.3%. **Commercial banks:** 108; deposits: $212.4 bil. **Savings institutions:** 10; deposits: $14.9 bil. **Lottery:** total sales: $3.9 bil; profit: $1.1 bil.

Federal govt. Fed. civ. employees: 25,834; **avg. salary:** $83,459. **Notable fed. facilities:** Army TACOM Life Cycle Mgmt., Detroit Arsenal; DLA Logistics Info. Service; Selfridge Air Natl. Guard Base; Hart-Dole-Inouye Fed. Ctr., Battle Creek.

Education. High school grad. rate: 80.6%. **4-yr. public coll./univ.:** 22; **2-yr. public:** 24; **4-yr. private:** 40.

Energy. Electricity use/cost: 671 kWh, $103.59.

State data. Motto: Si Quaeris Peninsulam Amoenam, Circumspice (If you seek a pleasant peninsula, look about you). **Flower:** Apple blossom. **Bird:** American robin. **Tree:** White pine. **Song:** "Michigan, My Michigan." **Entered union:** Jan. 26, 1837; rank: 26th.

Tourism. Tourist spending: $23.3 bil. **Attractions:** Henry Ford Museum and Greenfield Village, Dearborn; Frederik Meijer Gardens and Sculpture Park, Grand Rapids; Tahquamenon Falls (of Longfellow's poem *Song of Hiawatha*); De Zwaan windmill, Tulip Time Festival, in Holland; Soo Locks (bet. Lakes Superior and Huron), Sault Ste. Marie; Air Zoo, Portage; Mackinac Island; Belle Isle Park, Detroit Institute of Arts, Charles H. Wright Museum of African-American History, Motown Historical Museum, in Detroit. **Information:** Michigan Economic Development Corp., 300 N. Washington Sq., Lansing, MI 48913; 1-888-784-7328; www.michigan.org

History. Hunting and fishing peoples lived in the region as early as 11,000 years ago. Ojibwa, Ottawa, Miami, Potawatomi, and Huron inhabited the area at the time of European contact. French fur traders and missionaries arrived in the 17th cent. and established a settlement at Sault Ste. Marie, 1668. British took over, 1763, and crushed a Native American uprising led by Ottawa chieftain Pontiac. The area was ceded to the U.S. by the Treaty of Paris, 1783, but the British remained until 1796. Michigan was organized as a territory, 1805. The British seized Ft. Mackinac and Detroit, 1812, but the U.S. regained control, 1814. The opening of the Erie Canal, 1825, and new land laws and Native American cessions led the way for a flood of settlers. Strongly antislavery, Michigan became a state, 1837, and supplied 90,000 soldiers to the Union army in the Civil War. In the 20th cent., automobile manufacturing was the backbone of the economy. Henry Ford launched the Model T car, 1908; the United Auto Workers union was founded, 1935. Motown music flourished in Detroit in the 1960s, but riots in 1967 dealt the city a heavy blow. As the auto industry faltered, Michigan lost more than 20% of its automotive-related jobs in 2002-07. In 2009, the federal government loaned billions of dollars to GM and Chrysler to keep them solvent. Detroit formally emerged from a 17-month bankruptcy process—the largest in U.S. municipal history—in Dec. 2014, having shed nearly $7 bil in debts. The state closed its last four bottled water distribution centers in Flint in Apr. 2018; state prosecutors dropped all criminal charges against state and local officials over their alleged roles in the lead-contamination crisis that began in 2014 in Flint's municipal water supply system, and signaled they would reinvestigate. Michigan State Univ. in May 2018 agreed to pay $500 mil to settle sexual abuse lawsuits related to claims against former MSU doctor Larry Nassar.

Famous Michiganders. Ralph Bunche, Paul de Kruif, Thomas Edison, Eminem (Marshall Mathers), Edna Ferber, Gerald R. Ford, Henry Ford, Aretha Franklin, Edgar Guest, Lee Iacocca, Magic Johnson, Casey Kasem, Will Kellogg, Ring Lardner, Elmore Leonard, Charles Lindbergh, Joe Louis, Madonna, Malcolm X, Terry McMillan, Michael Moore, Larry Page, Pontiac, Gilda Radner, Mitt Romney, Diana Ross, Tom Selleck, Sinbad (David Adkins), John Smoltz, Lily Tomlin, Serena Williams.

Website. www.michigan.gov

Minnesota (MN)
North Star State, Gopher State

People. Population: 5,639,632; rank: 22. **Pop. change** (2010-19): 6.3%. **Pop. density:** 70.8 per sq mi. **Racial distribution:** 83.8% white; 7.0% Black; 5.2% Asian; 1.4% Amer. Ind.; 0.1% Hawaiian/Pacific Islander; 2 or more races, 2.6%. **Hispanic pop.:** 5.6%.

Geography. Total area: 86,936 sq mi; rank: 12. **Land area:** 79,627 sq mi; rank: 14. **Acres forested:** 17.7 mil. **Location:** West North Central state bounded on the E by Wisconsin and Lake Superior, on the N by Canada, on the W by the Dakotas, and on the S by Iowa. **Climate:** northern part of state lies in the moist Great Lakes storm belt; the western border lies at the edge of the semiarid Great Plains. **Topography:** central

hill and lake region covers approx. half the state; to the NE, rocky ridges and deep lakes; to the NW, flat plain; to the S, rolling plains and deep river valleys. **Capital:** St. Paul. **Chief airport:** Minneapolis.

Economy. Chief industries: agribusiness, forest prods., mining, manufacturing, tourism. **Chief manuf. goods:** petroleum and asphalt, computers and electronics, milk and cheese, printing, animal slaughtering, paper and paper prods., medical equip. **Chief crops:** corn, soybeans, hay, sugar beets, wheat, potatoes, greenhouse and nursery, dry edible beans, green peas, sunflowers. **Farm income:** Crops: $9.78 bil. Livestock: $7.47 bil. **Nonfuel minerals:** $5.3 bil; iron ore, lime, sand and gravel (construction), sand and gravel (industrial), stone (crushed). **Commercial fishing:** $0.2 mil. **Chief ports:** Two Harbors, Silver Bay, Duluth, St. Paul. **Gross state product:** $380.9 bil. **Sales tax:** 6.875%. **Gasoline tax:** 47.00 cents/gal. **Employment distrib.:** 14.8% govt.; 18.8% trade/trans./util.; 11.4% mfg.; 18.8% ed./health; 13.8% prof./bus. serv.; 5.5% leisure/hosp.; 7.1% finance; 5.0% constr./mining/log.; 1.5% info.; 3.3% other serv. **Unemployment:** 3.2%. **Min. wage/hr.:** $10.00. **Per cap. pers. income:** $59,683. **New private housing:** 28,586 units/$6.1 bil. **Broadband internet:** 96.2%. **Commercial banks:** 322; deposits: $230.0 bil. **Savings institutions:** 17; deposits: $6.2 bil. **Lottery:** total sales: $636.8 mil; profit: $153.2 mil.

Federal govt. Fed. civ. employees: 16,663; **avg. salary:** $78,461. **Notable fed. facilities:** Bishop Henry Whipple Fed. Bldg.; Minneapolis-St. Paul Air Reserve Station.

Education. High school grad. rate: 83.2%. **4-yr. public coll./univ.:** 12; **2-yr. public:** 32; **4-yr. private:** 33.

Energy. Electricity use/cost: 786 kWh, $103.34.

State data. Motto: L'Etoile du Nord (The star of the north). **Flower:** Pink and white lady's-slipper. **Bird:** Common loon. **Tree:** Red pine. **Song:** "Hail! Minnesota." **Entered union:** May 11, 1858; rank: 32nd.

Tourism. Tourist spending: $15.4 bil. **Attractions:** Minneapolis Institute of Arts, Walker Art Center, Minneapolis Sculpture Garden, Minnehaha Falls (in Longfellow's poem *Song of Hiawatha*), Guthrie Theater, in Minneapolis; Mall of America, Bloomington; Ordway Ctr. for the Performing Arts, Science Museum of Minnesota, in St. Paul; Voyageurs Natl. Park; Mayo Clinic, Rochester; North Shore (Lake Superior); Lake Minnetonka; Boundary Waters Canoe Area Wilderness; Superior Natl. Forest; Aerial Lift Bridge, Duluth. **Information:** Explore Minnesota Tourism, Metro Square, 121 7th Pl. E., Ste. 360, St. Paul, MN 55101; 1-888-VISITMN; www.exploreminnesota.com

History. Inhabited for at least 10,000 years, the region was home to Dakota Sioux when Europeans arrived. French fur traders Pierre Esprit Radisson and Médard Chouart, sieur des Groseilliers, explored in the mid-17th cent. In 1679, Daniel Greysolon, sieur Duluth, claimed the entire region for France. Ojibwa arrived in the 18th cent. and warred with the Sioux for over 100 years. Britain took the area east of the Mississippi, 1763. The U.S. took over that portion after the American Revolution and gained the western area, 1803, in the Louisiana Purchase. The U.S. built Ft. St. Anthony (now Ft. Snelling), 1819, and bought Native American lands, 1837, spurring an influx of settlers from the east. Minnesota became a territory, 1849, and a state, 1858. The Sioux staged a bloody uprising, the Battle of Wood Lake, 1862, and were driven from the state. Railroad construction after the Civil War spurred the growth of the grain, timber, and iron mining industries. The opening of the St. Lawrence Seaway, 1959, aided the port of Duluth. Elected as a reformer, former pro wrestler Jesse Ventura served as governor, 1999-2003. Sen. Paul Wellstone (D) died when his campaign plane crashed, 2002. The I-35W Mississippi River Bridge in Minneapolis collapsed in 2007, killing 13. Former comedian and two-term Sen. Al Franken (D) resigned in 2018 amid allegations of sexual misconduct. After George Floyd, a Black man, was killed in Minneapolis police custody May 25, 2020, several days of protests/riots damaged about 1,500 businesses in the Twin Cities. The protest movement spread to hundreds of cities, calling for an end to police brutality and other forms of systemic racism.

Famous Minnesotans. Andrews Sisters, Warren E. Burger, Ethan and Joel Coen, Bob Dylan, F. Scott Fitzgerald, Al Franken, Judy Garland, Cass Gilbert, Hubert H. Humphrey, Garrison Keillor, Sister Elizabeth Kenny, Jessica Lange, Sinclair Lewis, Paul Manship, E. G. Marshall, William J. and Charles H. Mayo, Eugene McCarthy, Walter F. Mondale, Prince (Prince Rogers Nelson), Charles M. Schulz, Ann Sothern, Harold Stassen, Thorstein Veblen, Jesse Ventura, Lindsey Vonn, Paul Wellstone.

Website. www.minnesota.gov

Mississippi (MS)
Magnolia State

People. Population: 2,976,149; rank: 34. **Pop. change** (2010-19): 0.3%. **Pop. density:** 63.4 per sq mi. **Racial distribution:** 59.1% white; 37.8% Black; 1.1% Asian; 0.6% Amer. Ind.; 0.1% Hawaiian/Pacific Islander; 2 or more races, 1.3%. **Hispanic pop.:** 3.4%.

Geography. Total area: 48,432 sq mi; rank: 32. **Land area:** 46,923 sq mi; rank: 31. **Acres forested:** 19.2 mil. **Location:** East South Central state bordered on the W by the Mississippi R., on the S by the Gulf of Mexico. **Climate:** semitropical, with abundant rainfall and long growing season. **Topography:** low, fertile delta between the Yazoo and Mississippi Rivers; loess bluffs stretch around delta border; sandy gulf coastal terraces followed by piney woods and prairie; rugged, high sandy hills in extreme NE followed by Prairie Black Belt, Pontotoc Ridge, and flatwoods into the N central highlands. **Capital:** Jackson. **Chief airport:** Jackson.

Economy. Chief industries: warehousing and distribution, services, manufacturing, government, wholesale and retail trade. **Chief manuf. goods:** petroleum, upholstered furniture, poultry processing, motor vehicle parts, plastics, ships and boats, chemicals. **Chief crops:** cotton, soybeans, rice, hay, corn, sweet potatoes. **Farm income:** Crops: $2.07 bil. Livestock: $3.40 bil. **Nonfuel minerals:** $504 mil; clay (ball clay and montmorillonite), sand and gravel (construction), sand and gravel (industrial), stone (crushed). **Commercial fishing:** $18.5 mil. **Chief ports:** Pascagoula, Vicksburg, Gulfport, Biloxi, Greenville. **Gross state product:** $118.8 bil. **Sales tax:** 7.0%. **Gasoline tax:** 37.19 cents/gal. **Employment distrib.:** 21.6% govt.; 20.6% trade/trans./util.; 13.0% mfg.; 12.7% ed./health; 9.1% prof./bus. serv.; 10.0% leisure/hosp.; 4.0% finance; 4.4% constr./mining/log.; 0.9% info.; 3.7% other serv. **Unemployment:** 5.4%. **Min. wage/hr.:** none. **Per cap. pers. income:** $39,368. **New private housing:** 6,952 units/$1.2 bil. **Broadband internet:** 93.0%. **Commercial banks:** 89; deposits: $54.8 bil. **Savings institutions:** 4; deposits: $358.0 mil.

Federal govt. Fed. civ. employees: 18,076; **avg. salary:** $71,681. **Notable fed. facilities:** Keesler AFB; Meridian NAS; Columbus AFB; NASA Stennis Space Ctr.; Army Corps of Eng. Waterways Experiment Sta., Vicksburg; Naval Constr. Battalion Ctr., Gulfport.

Education. High school grad. rate: 84.0%. **4-yr. public coll./univ.:** 8; **2-yr. public:** 15; **4-yr. private:** 9.

Energy. Electricity use/cost: 1,247 kWh, $138.63.

State data. Motto: Virtute et Armis (By valor and arms). **Flower:** Magnolia. **Bird:** Northern mockingbird. **Tree:** Magnolia. **Song:** "Go, Mississippi!" **Entered union:** Dec. 10, 1817; rank: 20th.

Tourism. Tourist spending: $9.1 bil. **Attractions:** Vicksburg Natl. Military Park and Cemetery; Natchez Trace Parkway; antebellum home tours in Natchez and other cities; Tupelo Natl. Battlefield, Elvis Presley Birthplace, in Tupelo; Smith Robertson Museum and Cultural Ctr., Mynelle Gardens, Eudora Welty House, in Jackson; Mardi Gras parades on Gulf Coast; Beauvoir (Jefferson Davis Home and Presidential Library), Biloxi; Gulf Islands Natl. Seashore; Delta Blues Museum, Clarksdale. **Information:** Mississippi Division of Tourism, P.O. Box 849, Jackson, MS 39205; 1-866-SEE-MISS; www.visitmississippi.org

History. Choctaw, Chickasaw, and Natchez peoples were living in the region at the time of European contact. The Spaniard Hernando de Soto explored the area, 1540-41. René-Robert Cavelier, sieur de La Salle, traced the Mississippi R. from Illinois to its mouth and claimed the entire Mississippi Valley for France, 1682. The first settlement was the French Ft. Maurepas, 1699, on Biloxi Bay. The region was ceded to Britain, 1763, and claimed by Spain, 1779-98, then became a U.S. territory, 1798, and a state, 1817. Slavery spread along with cotton plantations dependent on forced Black labor. By 1860, 55% of the population was enslaved. Mississippi seceded, 1861, in the Civil War. Union forces captured Vicksburg, 1863, and caused extensive damage elsewhere. Mississippi reentered the Union, 1870. For the next 100 years, resistance to desegregation and violence against the Black population made the state a battleground for the civil rights movement. Hurricanes Camille, 1969, and Katrina, 2005, caused substantial damage to the Gulf Coast. Since the early 1990s, casino gambling has boosted the economy, but the state's poverty rate remained the highest in the nation 2018. Legislation retiring the state flag, which featured a Confederate battle flag emblem, was signed into law June 30, 2020.

Famous Mississippians. Margaret Walker Alexander, Dana Andrews, Jimmy Buffett, Bo Diddley, Medgar Evers, William Faulkner, Brett Favre, Shelby Foote, Morgan Freeman, John Grisham, Fannie Lou Hamer, Jim Henson, Faith Hill, John Lee Hooker, Robert Johnson, James Earl Jones, B. B. King, L. Q. C. Lamar, Trent Lott, Gerald McRaney, Willie Morris, Walter Payton, Elvis Presley, Leontyne Price, Charley Pride, LeAnn Rimes, Robin Roberts, Muddy Waters, Eudora Welty, Tennessee Williams, Oprah Winfrey, Johnny Winter, Richard Wright, Tammy Wynette.
Website. www.ms.gov

Missouri (MO)
Show Me State

People. Population: 6,137,428; rank: 18. **Pop. change** (2010-19): 2.5%. **Pop. density:** 89.3 per sq mi. **Racial distribution:** 82.9% white; 11.8% Black; 2.2% Asian; 0.6% Amer. Ind.; 0.2% Hawaiian/Pacific Islander; 2 or more races, 2.4%. **Hispanic pop.:** 4.4%.

Geography. Total area: 69,707 sq mi; rank: 21. **Land area:** 68,742 sq mi; rank: 18. **Acres forested:** 15.3 mil. **Location:** West North Central state near the geographic center of the conterminous U.S.; bordered on the E by Mississippi R., on the NW by Missouri R. **Climate:** continental, susceptible to cold Canadian air; moist, warm Gulf air; and drier SW air. **Topography:** rolling hills, open, fertile plains, and well-watered prairie N of the Missouri R.; S of the river, land is rough and hilly with deep, narrow valleys; alluvial plain in the SE; low elevation in the W. **Capital:** Jefferson City. **Chief airports:** St. Louis, Kansas City, Springfield.

Economy. Chief industries: agriculture, manufacturing, aerospace, tourism. **Chief manuf. goods:** motor vehicles and parts, aerospace, pharmaceuticals, plastics, soap, animal slaughtering and processing, printing. **Chief crops:** soybeans, corn, hay, cotton and cottonseed, wheat, rice, sorghum. **Farm income:** Crops: $5.43 bil. Livestock: $4.71 bil. **Nonfuel minerals:** $3.1 bil; cement (portland), lead, lime, sand and gravel (industrial), stone (crushed). **Gross state product:** $332.1 bil. **Sales tax:** 4.225%. **Gasoline tax:** 35.82 cents/gal. **Employment distrib.:** 15.9% govt.; 18.8% trade/trans./util.; 9.5% mfg.; 17.5% ed./health; 13.5% prof./bus. serv.; 7.6% leisure/hosp.; 6.5% finance; 5.0% constr./mining/log.; 1.6% info.; 4.1% other serv. **Unemployment:** 3.3%. **Min. wage/hr.:** $9.45. **Per cap. pers. income:** $49,589. **New private housing:** 17,460 units/$3.4 bil. **Broadband internet:** 95.4%. **Commercial banks:** 293; deposits: $167.7 bil. **Savings institutions:** 12; deposits: $2.7 bil. **Lottery:** total sales: $1.5 bil; profit: $346.7 mil.

Federal govt. Fed. civ. employees: 36,247; **avg. salary:** $69,599. **Notable fed. facilities:** Federal Reserve banks; Ft. Leonard Wood; Jefferson Barracks Natl. Cemetery; Natl. Personnel Records Ctr., St. Louis; Whiteman AFB.

Education. High school grad. rate: 89.2%. **4-yr. public coll./univ.:** 14; **2-yr. public:** 14; **4-yr. private:** 52.

Energy. Electricity use/cost: 1,118 kWh, $126.79.

State data. Motto: Salus Populi Suprema Lex Esto (Let the welfare of the people be the supreme law). **Flower:** Hawthorn. **Bird:** Eastern bluebird. **Tree:** Flowering dogwood. **Song:** "Missouri Waltz." **Entered union:** Aug. 10, 1821; rank: 24th.

Tourism. Tourist spending: $15.2 bil. **Attractions:** Silver Dollar City, Branson; Mark Twain Boyhood Home and Museum, Hannibal; Pony Express Natl. Museum, St. Joseph; Harry S. Truman Library and Museum, Independence; Gateway Arch Natl. Park, Ulysses S. Grant Natl. Historic Site, St. Louis Zoo, in St. Louis; Worlds of Fun amusement park, Kansas City; Lake of the Ozarks; Ozark Natl. Scenic Riverways; Natl. Churchill Museum, Fulton; State Capitol, Jefferson City; Wilson's Creek Natl. Battlefield; George Washington Carver Natl. Monument, Diamond; Bass Pro Shops Outdoor World, Springfield. **Information:** Missouri Division of Tourism, P.O. Box 1055, Jefferson City, MO 65102; 1-800-519-2100; www.visitmo.com

History. In the 17th cent., when French explorers arrived, Algonquian-speaking Sauk, Fox, and Illinois as well as Siouan-speaking Osage, Missouri, Iowa, and Kansa peoples were living in the region; few remained by the 1830s. French hunters and lead miners made the first settlement, c. 1735, at Ste. Genevieve. The territory was ceded to Spain by the French, 1762, then returned to France, 1800, and acquired by the U.S. in the Louisiana Purchase, 1803. Powerful earthquakes rocked New Madrid, 1811-12. Missouri became a territory, 1812, and entered the Union as a slave state, 1821. St. Louis became the gateway for pioneers heading west. Though Missouri stayed with the Union, pro- and antislavery forces battled there during the Civil War. In the late 19th cent. railroad building and the cattle trade made Kansas City a boomtown. The most notable Missourian of the 20th cent., Harry S. Truman, was U.S. president, 1945-53. The state, a political bellwether, voted for the winner in every presidential election from 1960 to 2004. In May 2011, a tornado in Joplin killed about 162. The police-shooting death of Michael Brown in Ferguson in Aug. 2014 touched off major protests that spread nationwide and revived debate over the relationship between law enforcement officers and the communities they serve. With the state legislature considering impeachment, Gov. Eric Greitens resigned his office June 1, 2018, four months after he was indicted on felony charges related to an extramarital affair. In July 2018, an amphibious duckboat sank in Branson, killing 17. More than 200 flood incidents occurred in Mar. 2019; additional flooding affected NE that June and NW in July.

Famous Missourians. Maya Angelou, Robert Altman, John Ashcroft, Burt Bacharach, Josephine Baker, Scott Bakula, Thomas Hart Benton, Yogi Berra, Chuck Berry, George Caleb Bingham, Daniel Boone, Omar Bradley, William S. Burroughs, Kate Capshaw, Dale Carnegie, George Washington Carver, Bob Costas, Walter Cronkite, Sheryl Crow, Walt Disney, T. S. Eliot, Richard "Dick" Gephardt, John Goodman, Betty Grable, Jon Hamm, Edwin Hubble, Jesse James, Rush Limbaugh, Marianne Moore, Reinhold Niebuhr, J. C. Penney, John J. Pershing, Brad Pitt, Joseph Pulitzer, Ginger Rogers, Bess Truman, Harry S. Truman, Kathleen Turner, Tina Turner, Mark Twain, Dick Van Dyke, Tennessee Williams, Lanford Wilson, Shelley Winters, Jane Wyman.

Website. www.mo.gov

Montana (MT)
Treasure State

People. Population: 1,068,778; rank: 43. **Pop. change** (2010-19): 8.0%. **Pop. density:** 7.3 per sq mi. **Racial distribution:** 88.9% white; 0.6% Black; 0.9% Asian; 6.7% Amer. Ind.; 0.1% Hawaiian/Pacific Islander; 2 or more races, 2.8%. **Hispanic pop.:** 4.1%.

Geography. Total area: 147,040 sq mi; rank: 4. **Land area:** 145,546 sq mi; rank: 4. **Acres forested:** 25.9 mil. **Location:** Mountain state bounded on the E by the Dakotas, on the S by Wyoming, on the SSW by Idaho, on the N by Canada. **Climate:** colder, continental with low humidity. **Topography:** Rocky Mts. in western third of state; eastern two-thirds gently rolling northern Great Plains. **Capital:** Helena. **Chief airport:** Bozeman.

Economy. Chief industries: agriculture, timber, mining, tourism, oil and gas. **Chief manuf. goods:** sawmills, softwood veneer and plywood, petroleum. **Chief crops:** wheat, barley, hay, sugar beets, potatoes, dry beans, flaxseed, cherries, corn, oats. **Farm income:** Crops: $1.95 bil. Livestock: $1.61 bil. **Nonfuel minerals:** $1.3 bil; copper, molybdenum concentrates, palladium, platinum, sand and gravel (construction). **Gross state product:** $52.2 bil. **Sales tax:** none. **Gasoline tax:** 51.15 cents/gal. **Employment distrib.:** 19.6% govt.; 20.1% trade/trans./util.; 4.2% mfg.; 16.6% ed./health; 9.4% prof./bus. serv.; 10.9% leisure/hosp.; 5.8% finance; 8.4% constr./mining/log.; 1.2% info.; 3.8% other serv. **Unemployment:** 3.5%. **Min. wage/hr.:** $8.65. **Per cap. pers. income:** $49,074. **New private housing:** 4,776 units/$855.7 mil. **Broadband internet:** 93.1%. **Commercial banks:** 53; deposits: $24.4 bil. **Savings institutions:** 2; deposits: $72.0 mil. **Lottery:** total sales: $61.3 mil; profit: $12.2 mil.

Federal govt. Fed. civ. employees: 10,823; **avg. salary:** $64,063. **Notable fed. facilities:** Malmstrom AFB and missile silos; Ft. Peck, Hungry Horse, Libby, Yellowtail, and other dams.

Education. High school grad. rate: 86.4%. **4-yr. public coll./univ.:** 7; **2-yr. public:** 10; **4-yr. private:** 4.

Energy. Electricity use/cost: 850 kWh, $93.19.

State data. Motto: Oro y Plata (Gold and silver). **Flower:** Bitterroot. **Bird:** Western meadowlark. **Tree:** Ponderosa pine. **Song:** "Montana." **Entered union:** Nov. 8, 1889; rank: 41st.

Tourism. Tourist spending: $4.9 bil. **Attractions:** Glacier and Yellowstone Natl. Parks; Museum of the Rockies, Bozeman; Museum of the Plains Indian, Blackfeet Reservation, in Browning; Custer Natl. Cemetery at Little Bighorn Battlefield Natl. Monument; Lewis and Clark Caverns State Park, Whitehall; Lewis and Clark Natl. Historic Trail Interpretive Ctr., Great Falls. **Information:** Travel Montana, Dept. of Commerce, 301 S. Park Ave., P.O. Box 200533, Helena, MT 59601; 1-800-VIS-ITMT; www.visitmt.com

History. Paleo-Indian hunters reached the area over 12,000 years ago. Cheyenne, Blackfoot, Crow, Assiniboin, Salish (Flatheads), Kootenai, and Kalispel peoples lived in

the region before Europeans arrived. French explorers visited the region, 1742. The U.S. acquired the area partly through the Louisiana Purchase, 1803, partly through the Lewis and Clark Expedition, 1804-06. Fur traders and missionaries established posts in the early 19th cent. Gold was discovered on Grasshopper Creek, 1862, and Montana Territory was established, 1864. Indian uprisings reached their peak with the defeat of Gen. George Custer at the Battle of Little Bighorn, 1876. Chief Joseph and the Nez Percé tribe surrendered in Montana, 1877, after being driven from their lands in Oregon. Mining activity and the coming of the Northern Pacific Railway, 1883, brought population growth. Montana became a state, 1889. Copper wealth from the Butte pits resulted in the turn of the century "War of Copper Kings" as feuding factions contended for "the richest hill on earth." During the first half of the 20th cent., the Anaconda Copper firm wielded enormous political influence. Jeannette Rankin, a suffragist and pacifist, was the first woman elected to Congress, 1916. Mike Mansfield served 34 years in Congress and was Senate Democratic leader, 1961-77. An 18-year hunt for notorious "Unabomber" Theodore Kaczynski ended with his arrest, 1996, at his cabin near Lincoln. Ryan Zinke became the first Montanan in the president's cabinet since statehood when he served as interior secretary, 2017-18.

Famous Montanans. Dana Carvey, Gary Cooper, Marcus Daly, Chet Huntley, Phil Jackson, Will James, Myrna Loy, David Lynch, Mike Mansfield, Brent Musburger, Jeannette Rankin, Charles M. Russell, Lester Thurow.

Website. www.mt.gov

Nebraska (NE)
Cornhusker State

People. Population: 1,934,408; rank: 37. **Pop. change** (2010-19): 5.9%. **Pop. density:** 25.2 per sq mi. **Racial distribution:** 88.1% white; 5.2% Black; 2.7% Asian; 1.5% Amer. Ind.; 0.1% Hawaiian/Pacific Islander; 2 or more races, 2.3%. **Hispanic pop.:** 11.4%.

Geography. Total area: 77,348 sq mi; rank: 16. **Land area:** 76,824 sq mi; rank: 15. **Acres forested:** 1.4 mil. **Location:** West North Central state with the Missouri R. for a border on NE and E. **Climate:** continental semiarid. **Topography:** till plains of the central lowland in the eastern third rises to the Great Plains and hill country of the N central and NW. **Capital:** Lincoln. **Chief airport:** Omaha.

Economy. Chief industries: agriculture, manufacturing. **Chief manuf. goods:** animal slaughtering, grain and oilseed, farm machinery, medical equip., motor vehicle parts, printing, structural metals. **Chief crops:** corn, sorghum, soybeans, hay, wheat, dry beans, oats, potatoes, sugar beets. **Farm income:** Crops: $9.39 bil. Livestock: $11.91 bil. **Nonfuel minerals:** $214 mil; cement (portland), lime, sand and gravel (construction), sand and gravel (industrial), stone (crushed). **Gross state product:** $127.0 bil. **Sales tax:** 5.5%. **Gasoline tax:** 48.60 cents/gal. **Employment distrib.:** 17.0% govt.; 19.5% trade/trans./util.; 10.1% mfg.; 15.8% ed./health; 11.7% prof./bus. serv.; 7.1% leisure/hosp.; 7.8% finance; 5.9% constr./mining/log.; 1.7% info.; 3.4% other serv. **Unemployment:** 3.0%. **Min. wage/hr.:** $9.00. **Per cap. pers. income:** $54,871. **New private housing:** 8,025 units/$1.3 bil. **Broadband internet:** 96.7%. **Commercial banks:** 177; deposits: $61.2 bil. **Savings institutions:** 7; deposits: $5.9 bil. **Lottery:** total sales: $192.2 mil; profit: $46.6 mil.

Federal govt. Fed. civ. employees: 9,838; **avg. salary:** $74,045. **Notable fed. facilities:** Offutt AFB.

Education. High school grad. rate: 88.7%. **4-yr. public coll./univ.:** 9; **2-yr. public:** 9; **4-yr. private:** 16.

Energy. Electricity use/cost: 1,021 kWh, $109.27.

State data. Motto: Equality before the law. **Flower:** Giant goldenrod. **Bird:** Western meadowlark. **Tree:** Cottonwood. **Song:** "Beautiful Nebraska." **Entered union:** Mar. 1, 1867; rank: 37th.

Tourism. Tourist spending: $5.5 bil. **Attractions:** Univ. of Nebraska State Museum at Morrill Hall, Nebraska State Capitol, in Lincoln; Stuhr Museum of the Prairie Pioneer, Grand Island; Boys Town; Omaha's Henry Doorly Zoo and Aquarium, Joslyn Art Museum, The Durham Museum, in Omaha; Ashfall Fossil Beds State Hist. Park, near Royal; Strategic Air and Space Museum, Ashland; Arbor Lodge State Historical Park, Nebraska City; Buffalo Bill Ranch State Historical Park, North Platte; Pioneer Village, Minden; Oregon Trail landmarks, incl. at Scotts Bluff Natl. Monument and Chimney Rock Natl. Historic Site; Great Platte River Road Archway, Museum of Nebraska Art, in Kearney. **Information:** Nebraska Tourism Commission, 301 Centennial Mall S., Lincoln, NE 68508; 1-888-444-1867; www.visitnebraska.com

History. When Europeans arrived, Pawnee, Ponca, Omaha, and Oto peoples lived in the region. Spanish and French explorers and fur traders visited the area prior to its acquisition in the Louisiana Purchase, 1803. Meriwether Lewis and William Clark passed through, 1804-06. The first permanent settlement was Bellevue, near Omaha, 1823. The 1834 Indian Intercourse Act declared Nebraska Indian country and excluded white settlement, but conflicts with settlers eventually forced Native Americans to move to reservations. Nebraska became a territory, 1854, and a state, 1867. Many Civil War veterans settled under free land terms of the 1862 Homestead Act; as agriculture grew, struggles followed between homesteaders and ranchers. Since the mid-1930s, Nebraska has been the only state with a unicameral legislature. A leader in agribusiness, Nebraska has also become a major telemarketing center. Investor Warren Buffett, one of the world's wealthiest men, said in 2006 he would give most of his then-$44-bil fortune to charity. Historic flooding from a so-called "bomb cyclone" Mar. 13-15, 2019, caused nearly $1.4 bil in damage.

Famous Nebraskans. Grover Cleveland Alexander, Fred Astaire, Marlon Brando, Charles W. Bryan, William Jennings Bryan, Warren Buffett, Johnny Carson, Willa Cather, Dick Cavett, Dick Cheney, Loren Eiseley, Father Edward J. Flanagan, Henry Fonda, Bob Gibson, Rollin Kirby, Harold Lloyd, Malcolm X, J. Sterling Morton, John G. Neihardt, Nick Nolte, George W. Norris, Tom Osborne, Roscoe Pound, Red Cloud, Mari Sandoz, Robert Taylor, Darryl F. Zanuck.

Website. www.nebraska.gov

Nevada (NV)
Sagebrush State, Battle Born State, Silver State

People. Population: 3,080,156; rank: 32. **Pop. change** (2010-19): 14.1%. **Pop. density:** 28.1 per sq mi. **Racial distribution:** 73.9% white; 10.3% Black; 8.7% Asian; 1.7% Amer. Ind.; 0.8% Hawaiian/Pacific Islander; 2 or more races, 4.6%. **Hispanic pop.:** 29.2%.

Geography. Total area: 110,572 sq mi; rank: 7. **Land area:** 109,781 sq mi; rank: 7. **Acres forested:** 10.6 mil. **Location:** Mountain state bordered on N by Oregon and Idaho, on E by Utah, on SE by Arizona, and on SW and W by California. **Climate:** semiarid and arid. **Topography:** rugged N-S mountain ranges; highest elevation, Boundary Peak, 13,146 ft; southern area is within the Mojave Desert; lowest elevation, Colorado R., at southern tip of state, 479 ft. **Capital:** Carson City. **Chief airports:** Las Vegas, Reno.

Economy. Chief industries: gaming, tourism, mining, manufacturing, government, retailing, warehousing, trucking. **Chief manuf. goods:** gaming machines, cement and concrete, plastics, printing, architectural and structural metals, electricity instruments. **Chief crops:** hay, onions, potatoes, alfalfa, wheat, garlic, mint, barley. **Farm income:** Crops: $176.07 mil. Livestock: $478.52 mil. **Nonfuel minerals:** $8.2 bil; copper, diatomite, gold, lime, sand and gravel (construction). **Gross state product:** $177.6 bil. **Sales tax:** 6.85%. **Gasoline tax:** 52.18 cents/gal. **Employment distrib.:** 13.7% govt.; 18.6% trade/trans./util.; 4.8% mfg.; 11.0% ed./health; 13.3% prof./bus. serv.; 19.1% leisure/hosp.; 5.8% finance; 9.7% constr./mining/log.; 1.2% info.; 2.9% other serv. **Unemployment:** 3.9%. **Min. wage/hr.:** $8.00-$9.00. **Per cap. pers. income:** $50,883. **New private housing:** 20,143 units/$3.7 bil. **Broadband internet:** 98.4%. **Commercial banks:** 38; deposits: $68.5 bil. **Savings institutions:** 12; deposits: $210.7 bil.

Federal govt. Fed. civ. employees: 11,698; **avg. salary:** $73,180. **Notable fed. facilities:** Nevada Natl. Security Site; Hawthorne Army Depot; Creech AFB; Nellis AFB; Fallon NAS; Natl. Wild Horse & Burro Ctr. at Palomino Valley.

Education. High school grad. rate: 83.2%. **4-yr. public coll./univ.:** 7; **2-yr. public:** 0; **4-yr. private:** 4.

Energy. Electricity use/cost: 947 kWh, $112.18.

State data. Motto: All for our country. **Flower:** Sagebrush. **Bird:** Mountain bluebird. **Trees:** Single-leaf piñon and bristlecone pine. **Song:** "Home Means Nevada." **Entered union:** Oct. 31, 1864; rank: 36th.

Tourism. Tourist spending: $42.5 bil. **Attractions:** Legalized gambling, incl. at Lake Tahoe, Reno, Las Vegas, Laughlin, and Elko; Hoover Dam, Lake Mead Natl. Recreation Area, near Boulder City; Great Basin Natl. Park; Valley of Fire State Park; Red Rock Canyon Natl. Conservation Area; Las Vegas Strip, Fremont St., Natl. Atomic Testing Museum, Pinball Hall of Fame, Las Vegas Motor Speedway, in Las Vegas; Natl. Automobile Museum, Reno. **Information:** Commission on Tourism, 401 N. Carson St., Carson City, NV 89701; 1-800-NEVADA-8; www.travelnevada.com

History. Shoshone, Paiute, Bannock, and Washoe peoples lived in the area at the time of European contact. Nevada was first explored by Spaniards, 1776. In the 1820s, fur traders Peter Skene Ogden, a Canadian, and Jedediah Smith separately explored the area. It was acquired by the U.S., 1848, at the end of the Mexican War. A trading post at Mormon Station, now Genoa, was established, 1850. Discovery of the Comstock Lode, rich in gold and silver, 1859, spurred a population boom. Nevada became a territory, 1861, and a state, 1864. Hoover Dam was built, 1931-36. With gambling legal since 1931, a surge in resort casino construction after World War II turned Las Vegas into one of the nation's most popular tourist destinations. An influx of both native and foreign-born Hispanics and Asians, attracted by the thriving service and construction industries, helped make Nevada the fastest-growing state in the U.S. in 1990-2005. The 2007-09 recession had an equally powerful effect, with high unemployment and foreclosures. In the deadliest mass shooting in modern U.S. history, a gunman killed 58 when he fired indiscriminately from his 32nd floor Las Vegas hotel suite on an outdoor country music festival in Oct. 2017.

Famous Nevadans. Andre Agassi, Kurt Busch, Kyle Busch, Walter Van Tilburg Clark, George W. G. Ferris, Sarah Winnemucca Hopkins, Paul Laxalt, Dat So La Lee, John William Mackay, Anne Henrietta Martin, Pat McCarran, Key Pittman, William Morris Stewart.

Website. www.nv.gov

New Hampshire (NH)
Granite State

People. Population: 1,359,711; rank: 41. **Pop. change** (2010-19): 3.3%. **Pop. density:** 151.9 per sq mi. **Racial distribution:** 93.1% white; 1.8% Black; 3.0% Asian; 0.3% Amer. Ind.; <0.05% Hawaiian/Pacific Islander; 2 or more races, 1.8%. **Hispanic pop.:** 4.0%.

Geography. Total area: 9,349 sq mi; rank: 46. **Land area:** 8,953 sq mi; rank: 44. **Acres forested:** 4.7 mil. **Location:** New England state bounded on S by Massachusetts, on W by Vermont, on N by Canada, on E by Maine and the Atlantic Ocean. **Climate:** highly varied, due to its nearness to high mountains and ocean. **Topography:** low, rolling coast followed by countless hills and mountains rising out of a central plateau. **Capital:** Concord. **Chief airport:** Manchester.

Economy. Chief industries: tourism, manufacturing, agriculture, trade, mining. **Chief manuf. goods:** navigational instruments, circuit boards, electrical equip., fabricated metal, machinery, medical equip., plastics. **Chief crops:** greenhouse and nursery, apples, sweet corn, hay, Christmas trees, berries, maple syrup. **Farm income:** Crops: $115.58 mil. Livestock: $106.98 mil. **Nonfuel minerals:** $156 mil; sand and gravel (construction), stone (crushed), stone (dimension). **Commercial fishing:** $38.5 mil. **Chief port:** Portsmouth. **Gross state product:** $88.6 bil. **Sales tax:** none. **Gasoline tax:** 42.23 cents/gal. **Employment distrib.:** 14.4% govt.; 19.6% trade/trans./util.; 11.2% mfg.; 19.5% ed./health; 12.8% prof./bus. serv.; 6.2% leisure/hosp.; 5.7% finance; 4.7% constr./mining/log.; 2.0% info.; 4.0% other serv. **Unemployment:** 2.5%. **Min. wage/hr.:** $7.25. **Per cap. pers. income:** $63,880. **New private housing:** 4,743 units/$1.1 bil. **Broadband internet:** 96.6%. **Commercial banks:** 15; deposits: $27.5 bil. **Savings institutions:** 25; deposits: $7.9 bil. **Lottery:** total sales: $384.4 mil; profit: $105.6 mil.

Federal govt. Fed. civ. employees: 4,510; **avg. salary:** $88,417. **Notable fed. facilities:** Army Cold Regions Res. and Engineering Lab, Hanover.

Education. High school grad. rate: 88.8%. **4-yr. public coll./univ.:** 6; **2-yr. public:** 7; **4-yr. private:** 11.

Energy. Electricity use/cost: 621 kWh, $122.27.

State data. Motto: Live free or die. **Flower:** Purple lilac. **Bird:** Purple finch. **Tree:** White birch. **Song:** "Old New Hampshire." **Ninth** of original 13 states to ratify the Constitution, June 21, 1788.

Tourism. Tourist spending: $4.4 bil. **Attractions:** Mt. Washington Cog Railway, Mt. Washington (highest peak in Northeast); Lake Winnipesaukee; Crawford, Franconia, Pinkham Notches (mountain passes); Flume Gorge, Cannon Mountain Aerial Tramway, in White Mountains region; Strawbery Banke Museum, Portsmouth; Canterbury Shaker Village; Saint-Gaudens Natl. Historical Park, Cornish; Mt. Monadnock; Santa's Village, Jefferson. **Information:** Division of Travel & Tourism Development, 172 Pembroke Rd., P.O. Box 1856; Concord, NH 03302; 1-800-FUN-IN-NH; www.visitnh.gov

History. The area has been inhabited for about 10,000 years. Algonquian-speaking peoples, including the Pennacook, lived in the region when the Europeans arrived. The first explorers to visit the area were England's Martin Pring, 1603, and France's Samuel de Champlain, 1605. The first settlement was Odiorne's Point (now port of Rye), 1623. Before the American Revolution, New Hampshire residents raided a British fort at Portsmouth, 1774, and drove the royal governor out, 1775. New Hampshire became the first colony to adopt its own constitution, 1776. After statehood, 1788, New Hampshire became a textile manufacturing center. The mill towns declined in the first half of the 20th cent., but tourism and technology industries, lured by low taxes, have revived the economy since the 1960s. A state law requires it to hold the first primary of the presidential campaign season.

Famous New Hampshirites. Dan Brown, Salmon P. Chase, Ralph Adams Cram, Mary Baker Eddy, Daniel Chester French, Robert Frost, Horace Greeley, Sarah Josepha Buell Hale, John Irving, Seth Meyers, Bode Miller, Franklin Pierce, Augustus Saint-Gaudens, Adam Sandler, Alan B. Shepard Jr., Sarah Silverman, David H. Souter, Daniel Webster.

Website. www.nh.gov

New Jersey (NJ)
Garden State

People. Population: 8,882,190; rank: 11. **Pop. change** (2010-19): 1.0%. **Pop. density:** 1,207.8 per sq mi. **Racial distribution:** 71.9% white; 15.1% Black; 10.0% Asian; 0.6% Amer. Ind.; 0.1% Hawaiian/Pacific Islander; 2 or more races, 2.3%. **Hispanic pop.:** 20.9%.

Geography. Total area: 8,723 sq mi; rank: 47. **Land area:** 7,354 sq mi; rank: 46. **Acres forested:** 2.0 mil. **Location:** Middle Atlantic state bounded on N and E by New York and Atlantic Ocean, on S and W by Delaware and Pennsylvania. **Climate:** moderate, with marked difference between NW and SE extremities. **Topography:** Appalachian Valley in NW also has highest elevation, High Pt., 1,803 ft; Appalachian Highlands, flat-topped NE-SW mountain ranges; Piedmont Plateau, low plains broken by high ridges (Palisades) rising 400-500 ft; Coastal Plain, covering three-fifths of state in SE, rises from sea level to gentle slopes. **Capital:** Trenton. **Chief airports:** Newark, Atlantic City.

Economy. Chief industries: pharmaceuticals, telecommunications, biotechnology, printing and publishing. **Chief manuf. goods:** petroleum, pharmaceuticals, toiletries, chemicals, plastics, printing, navigational instruments, medical equip., paper prods. **Chief crops:** greenhouse and nursery, blueberries, peaches, corn, hay, tomatoes, bell peppers, cranberries, soybeans, apples. **Farm income:** Crops: $982.09 mil. **Livestock:** $131.07 mil. **Nonfuel minerals:** $377 mil; peat, sand and gravel (construction), sand and gravel (industrial), stone (crushed). **Commercial fishing:** $169.6 mil. **Chief ports:** Newark-Elizabeth, Camden. **Gross state product:** $644.8 bil. **Sales tax:** 6.625%. **Gasoline tax:** 59.80 cents/gal. **Employment distrib.:** 16.6% govt.; 21.3% trade/trans./util.; 6.7% mfg.; 17.3% ed./health; 17.2% prof./bus. serv.; 5.1% leisure/hosp.; 6.7% finance; 4.0% constr./mining/log.; 1.7% info.; 3.4% other serv. **Unemployment:** 3.6%. **Min. wage/hr.:** $11.00. **Per cap. pers. income:** $70,979. **New private housing:** 36,505 units/$4.5 bil. **Broadband internet:** 98.7%. **Commercial banks:** 84; deposits: $287.3 bil. **Savings institutions:** 42; deposits: $55.6 bil. **Lottery:** total sales: $3.5 bil; profit: $1.1 bil.

Federal govt. Fed. civ. employees: 20,329; **avg. salary:** $95,943. **Notable fed. facilities:** Joint Base McGuire-Dix-Lakehurst; Picatinny Arsenal; FAA William J. Hughes Technical Ctr.

Education. High school grad. rate: 90.9%. **4-yr. public coll./univ.:** 13; 2-yr. public: 19; 4-yr. private: 37.

Energy. Electricity use/cost: 690 kWh, $106.28.

State data. Motto: Liberty and prosperity. **Flower:** Purple violet. **Bird:** Eastern goldfinch. **Tree:** Red oak. **Third** of the original 13 states to ratify the Constitution, Dec. 18, 1787.

Tourism. Tourist spending: $34.1 bil. **Attractions:** 130 mi of beaches, boardwalks on the Jersey Shore at Atlantic City (with gambling), Seaside Heights, Ocean City, Wildwood; Grover Cleveland Birthplace, Caldwell; Cape May Historic District; Thomas Edison Natl. Historical Park, West Orange; Six Flags Great Adventure, Jackson; Liberty State Park, Liberty Science Ctr., in Jersey City; Pine Barrens wilderness; Princeton Univ., Princeton Battlefield State Park, in Princeton; Morristown Natl. Historical Park; Adventure Aquarium, Battleship *New Jersey*, Walt Whitman House, in Camden. **Information:** Dept. of State, Division of Travel and Tourism, P.O. Box 460, Trenton, NJ 08625; 1-800-VISITNJ; www.visitnj.org

History. The Lenni Lenape (Delaware) peoples lived in the region and had mostly peaceful relations with European colonists, who arrived after the explorers Giovanni da Verrazzano, 1524, and Henry Hudson, 1609. The first permanent European settlement was Dutch, at Bergen (now Jersey City), 1660. When the British took New Netherland, 1664, the area between the Delaware and Hudson Rivers was given to Lord John Berkeley and Sir George Carteret. During the American Revolution, New Jersey was the scene of many major battles, including Trenton, 1776; Princeton, 1777; and Monmouth, 1778. New Jersey was the third state to ratify the Constitution, 1787, and the first to approve the Bill of Rights, 1789. In a duel at Weehawken, 1804, Vice Pres. Aaron Burr fatally shot former Treasury Sec. Alexander Hamilton. Canal and railroad building stimulated the growth of cities and industries in the 19th cent. The 20th-cent. arrival of large numbers of African Americans, Italians, Irish, European Jews, Puerto Ricans, South Asians, and other groups made New Jersey one of the most diverse states in the U.S. Construction of resort casinos in Atlantic City from the late 1970s revitalized tourism. Gov. James McGreevey resigned, 2004, after acknowledging an extramarital affair with a man identified as his former homeland security adviser. An estimated 37 people in New Jersey were killed when Hurricane Sandy (by then downgraded to a tropical storm) made landfall in 2012. Two members of Gov. Chris Christie's administration were convicted in 2016 on federal charges related to allegations that officials had created traffic jams to punish a political opponent.

Famous New Jerseyans. Buzz Aldrin, Jason Alexander, Samuel Alito, Count Basie, Judy Blume, Jon Bon Jovi, Bill Bradley, Aaron Burr, Grover Cleveland, Stephen Crane, Danny DeVito, Thomas Edison, Albert Einstein, James Gandolfini, Allen Ginsberg, Alexander Hamilton, Ed Harris, Whitney Houston, Joyce Kilmer, Jack Nicholson, Shaquille O'Neal, Thomas Paine, Bill Parcells, Dorothy Parker, Joe Pesci, Molly Pitcher, Paul Robeson, Philip Roth, Antonin Scalia, Wally Schirra, H. Norman Schwarzkopf, Frank Sinatra, Bruce Springsteen, Martha Stewart, Meryl Streep, Dave Thomas, John Travolta, Walt Whitman, William Carlos Williams, Woodrow Wilson.

Website. www.nj.gov

New Mexico (NM)
Land of Enchantment

People. Population: 2,096,829; rank: 36. **Pop. change** (2010-19): 1.8%. **Pop. density:** 17.3 per sq mi. **Racial distribution:** 81.9% white; 2.6% Black; 1.8% Asian; 11.0% Amer. Ind.; 0.2% Hawaiian/Pacific Islander; 2 or more races, 2.6%. **Hispanic pop.:** 49.3%.

Geography. Total area: 121,590 sq mi; rank: 5. **Land area:** 121,298 sq mi; rank: 5. **Acres forested:** 24.6 mil. **Location:** southwestern state bounded by Colorado on the N; Oklahoma, Texas, and Mexico on the E and S; Arizona on the W. **Climate:** dry, with temperatures rising or falling 5°F with every 1,000 ft elevation. **Topography:** eastern third, Great Plains; central third, Rocky Mts. (85% of the state is over 4,000-ft elevation); western third, high plateau. **Capital:** Santa Fe. **Chief airport:** Albuquerque.

Economy. Chief industries: government, services, trade. **Chief manuf. goods:** semiconductors, medical equip., navigational/measuring/medical/control instruments, aircraft, chemicals, jewelry. **Chief crops:** hay, pecans, corn, greenhouse and nursery, chiles, onions, cotton, wheat, peanuts. **Farm income:** Crops: $708.18 mil. Livestock: $2.22 bil. **Nonfuel minerals:** $1.1 bil; cement (portland), copper, potash, sand and gravel (construction), stone (crushed). **Gross state product:** $104.0 bil. **Sales tax:** 5.125%. **Gasoline tax:** 37.28 cents/gal. **Employment distrib.:** 24.1% govt.; 16.3% trade/trans./util.; 3.1% mfg.; 17.3% ed./health; 13.3% prof./bus. serv.; 8.2% leisure/hosp.; 4.4% finance; 9.0% constr./mining/log.; 1.2% info.; 3.1% other serv. **Unemployment:** 4.9% **Min. wage/hr.:** $9.00. **Per cap. pers. income:** $43,984. **New private housing:** 5,020 units/$1.1 bil. **Broadband internet:** 93.9%. **Commercial banks:** 50; deposits: $31.2 bil. **Savings institutions:** 6; deposits: $1.1 bil. **Lottery:** total sales: $143.6 mil; profit: $43.1 mil.

Federal govt. Fed. civ. employees: 21,863; **avg. salary:** $74,406. **Notable fed. facilities:** Kirtland, Cannon, Holloman AF Bases; Los Alamos Natl. Lab; White Sands Missile Range; Natl. Solar Observatory, Sunspot; Natl. Radio Astronomy Observatory (Very Large Array), Socorro; Sandia Natl. Labs, Albuquerque.

Education. High school grad. rate: 73.9%. **4-yr. public coll./univ.:** 9; 2-yr. public: 19; 4-yr. private: 3.

Energy. Electricity use/cost: 639 kWh, $81.08.

State data. Motto: Crescit Eundo (It grows as it goes). **Flower:** Yucca. **Bird:** Roadrunner. **Tree:** Piñon. **Songs:** "O,

Fair New Mexico"; "Asi Es Nuevo Mexico." **Entered union:** Jan. 6, 1912; rank: 47th.

Tourism.Tourist spending: $7.7 bil. **Attractions:** Carlsbad Caverns Natl. Park (with Lechuguilla Cave, among world's longest caves); Petroglyph Natl. Monument, Sandia Peak Tramway, in Albuquerque; New Mexico History Museum, Museum of Intl. Folk Art, in Santa Fe (oldest U.S. capital); White Sands Natl. Monument (world's largest gypsum dune field); Chaco Culture Natl. Historical Park; Acoma Pueblo, or Sky City, built atop a 367-ft mesa; Taos Art Colony, Taos Ski Valley; Elephant Butte Lake State Park; Shiprock volcanic remnant; Intl. UFO Museum and Research Ctr., Roswell. **Information:** New Mexico Dept. of Tourism, 491 Old Santa Fe Trl., Santa Fe, NM 87501; 1-800-733-6396; www.newmexico.org

History. Inhabited for more than 10,000 years, the region was home to Sandia, Clovis, Folsom, Mogollon, and Anasazi cultures, followed by the Pueblo people, Anasazi descendants; later, nomadic Navajo and Apache came. Spanish Franciscan Marcos de Niza and Estevanico, a Moroccan-born enslaved Black man, explored the area, 1539, seeking gold; Coronado followed, 1540. First settlements were near San Juan Pueblo, 1598, and at Santa Fe, 1610. Settlers alternately traded and fought with the Apache, Comanche, and Navajo. Trade on the Santa Fe Trail to Missouri started, 1821. After the Mexican War began, 1846, Gen. Stephen Kearny took Santa Fe without firing a shot, and declared New Mexico part of the U.S. All Hispanic New Mexicans and Pueblo became U.S. citizens by terms of the 1848 treaty ending the war. New Mexico became a territory, 1850, but did not attain statehood until 1912. Mexican revolutionary leader Pancho Villa raided Columbus, 1916, and U.S. troops were sent to the area. The world's first atomic bomb was exploded at a test site near Alamogordo, 1945. An underground nuclear waste depository opened near Carlsbad, 1999. Spaceport America, a state-owned commercial spaceport, hosted its first test launch in 2006.

Famous New Mexicans. Ben Abruzzo, Maxie Anderson, Jeff Bezos, William Bonney (Billy the Kid), Kit Carson, Bob Foster, Neil Patrick Harris, Tony Hillerman, Peter Hurd, Jean Baptiste Lamy, Nancy Lopez, Bill Mauldin, Georgia O'Keeffe, Bill Richardson, Kim Stanley, Al Unser, Bobby Unser.

Website. www.newmexico.gov

New York (NY)
Empire State

People. Population: 19,453,561; rank: 4. **Pop. change** (2010-19): 0.4%. **Pop. density:** 412.8 per sq mi. **Racial distribution:** 69.6% white; 17.6% Black; 9.0% Asian; 1.0% Amer. Ind.; 0.1% Hawaiian/Pacific Islander; 2 or more races, 2.7%. **Hispanic pop.:** 19.3%.

Geography.Total area: 54,555 sq mi; rank: 27. **Land area:** 47,126 sq mi; rank: 30. **Acres forested:** 18.6 mil. **Location:** Middle Atlantic state bordered by the New England states, Atlantic Ocean on E; New Jersey and Pennsylvania on S; Lakes Ontario and Erie on W; Canada on N. **Climate:** variable; the SE region moderated by the ocean. **Topography:** highest and most rugged mountains in the NE Adirondack upland; St. Lawrence-Champlain lowlands extend from Lake Ontario NE along the Canadian border; Hudson-Mohawk lowland follows rivers N and W, 10-30 mi wide; Atlantic coastal plain in the SE; Appalachian Highlands, covering half the state westward from the Hudson Valley, include the Catskill Mts., Finger Lakes; plateau of Erie-Ontario lowlands. **Capital:** Albany. **Chief airports:** New York (2), Buffalo, Albany, Rochester, Syracuse, White Plains, Islip.

Economy. Chief industries: manufacturing, finance, communications, tourism, transportation, services. **Chief manuf. goods:** pharmaceuticals, photographic chemicals, electronics, automotive parts, toiletries, printing, plastics, apparel. **Chief crops:** greenhouse and nursery, apples, corn, hay, cabbage, onions, soybeans, potatoes, snap beans, grapes, squash, pumpkins, tomatoes, wheat, cucumbers, green peas. **Farm income:** Crops: $1.94 bil. Livestock: $3.08 bil. **Nonfuel minerals:** $1.9 bil; cement (portland), salt, sand and gravel (construction), stone (crushed), zinc. **Commercial fishing:** $48.7 mil. **Chief ports:** New York, Buffalo, Albany. **Gross state product:** $1.7 tril. **Sales tax:** 4.0%. **Gasoline tax:** 63.43 cents/gal. **Employment distrib.:** 17.6% govt.; 15.1% trade/trans./util.; 4.6% mfg.; 23.9% ed./health; 14.7% prof./bus. serv.; 4.7% leisure/hosp.; 8.5% finance; 3.8% constr./mining/log.; 3.2% info.; 3.7% other serv. **Unemployment:** 4.0%. **Min. wage/hr.:** $11.80. **Per cap. pers. income:** $71,440. **New private housing:** 45,219 units/$7.7 bil. **Broadband internet:** 98.7%. **Commercial banks:** 158; deposits: $1.6 tril. **Savings institutions:** 45; deposits: $68.0 bil. **Lottery:** total sales: $10.3 bil; profit: $3.5 bil.

Federal govt. Fed. civ. employees: 51,377; **avg. salary:** $83,053. **Notable fed. facilities:** Ft. Drum; West Point Military Academy; Merchant Marine Academy, Kings Point; NY Fed. Reserve; U.S. Army Watervliet Arsenal; Brookhaven Natl. Lab; U.S. Mission to the United Nations.

Education. High school grad. rate: 82.3%. **4-yr. public coll./univ.:** 43; **2-yr. public:** 36; **4-yr. private:** 169.

Energy. Electricity use/cost: 604 kWh, $111.93.

State data. Motto: Excelsior (Ever upward). **Flower:** Rose. **Bird:** Eastern bluebird. **Tree:** Sugar maple. **Song:** "I Love New York." **Eleventh** of original 13 states to ratify the Constitution, July 26, 1788.

Tourism. Tourist spending: $83.0 bil. **Attractions:** New York City; Adirondack and Catskill Mountains; Watkins Glen State Park; Thousand Islands region; Niagara Falls; Saratoga Race Course, Saratoga Springs; Philipsburg Manor, Old Dutch Church of Sleepy Hollow, in Sleepy Hollow; Washington Irving's Sunnyside, Tarrytown; Corning Museum of Glass; Fenimore Art Museum, Natl. Baseball Hall of Fame and Museum, in Cooperstown; Ft. Ticonderoga; New York State Capitol, Albany; Home of Franklin D. Roosevelt Natl. Historic Site, Hyde Park; Long Island beaches; Sagamore Hill (Theodore Roosevelt's "Summer White House"), Oyster Bay. **Information:** Empire State Development, Travel Information Center, 30 South Pearl St., Albany, NY 12245; 1-800-CALL-NYS; www.iloveny.com

History. When Europeans arrived, Algonquians including the Mahican, Wappinger, and Lenni Lenape inhabited the region, as did the Iroquoian Mohawk, Oneida, Onondaga, Cayuga, and Seneca tribes, who established the League of the Five Nations. Italian Giovanni da Verrazzano entered New York harbor, 1524. In 1609, England's Henry Hudson visited the river later named for him, and France's Samuel de Champlain explored the lake that now bears his name. The first permanent settlement was Dutch, near present-day Albany, 1624. New Amsterdam was settled, 1626, at the southern tip of Manhattan island. A British fleet seized New Netherland, 1664. Key battles of the American Revolution included Saratoga, 1777. In the 19th cent., New York City emerged as one of the world's great metropolitan areas, a center for trade, finance, and arts, and a haven for millions of immigrants. Completion of the Erie Canal, 1825, established the state as a gateway to the West. The first women's rights convention was held in Seneca Falls, 1848. Although the state backed the Union in the Civil War, an 1863 military draft triggered three days of riots in New York City. Industry declined in the 20th cent., and California and Texas passed New York in population. Attica was the scene of a bloody prison revolt, 1971. Two jet aircraft hijacked by terrorists on Sept. 11, 2001, destroyed the World Trade Center in lower Manhattan and killed thousands. An estimated 65 people in New York state were killed when Hurricane Sandy (by then downgraded to a tropical storm) made landfall in Oct. 2012. Citing concerns over health risks, Gov. Andrew Cuomo in 2014 announced a statewide ban on hydraulic fracturing (or "fracking") as a method to access the state's natural gas resources. New York City became an early U.S. epicenter of the coronavirus pandemic beginning in Mar. 2020.

Famous New Yorkers. Woody Allen, Susan B. Anthony, James Baldwin, Lucille Ball, Ann Bancroft, L. Frank Baum, Milton Berle, Humphrey Bogart, Barbara Boxer, Mel Brooks, Benjamin Cardozo, De Witt Clinton, James Fenimore Cooper, Peter Cooper, Aaron Copland, Francis Ford Coppola, Tom Cruise, Robert De Niro, George Eastman, Jimmy Fallon, Millard Fillmore, Lou Gehrig, George and Ira Gershwin, Ruth Bader Ginsburg, Rudolph Giuliani, Jackie Gleason, Stephen Jay Gould, Julia Ward Howe, Charles Evans Hughes, Washington Irving, Henry and William James, John Jay, Edward Koch, Fiorello LaGuardia, Herman Melville, Arthur Miller, Lin-Manuel Miranda, J. Pierpont Morgan Jr., Eddie Murphy, Joyce Carol Oates, Carroll O'Connor, Rosie O'Donnell, Eugene O'Neill, Jerry Orbach, George Pataki, Colin Powell, Nancy Reagan, John Roberts, John D. Rockefeller, Nelson Rockefeller, Richard Rodgers, Ray Romano, Eleanor Roosevelt, Franklin D. Roosevelt, Theodore Roosevelt, J. D. Salinger, Caroline Kennedy Schlossberg, Jerry Seinfeld, Al Sharpton, Paul Simon, Alfred E. Smith, Elizabeth Cady Stanton, Barbra Streisand, Donald Trump, William (Boss) Tweed, Martin Van Buren, Luther Vandross, Gore Vidal, Denzel Washington, Edith Wharton, Walt Whitman, Mark Zuckerberg.

Website. www.ny.gov

North Carolina (NC)
Tar Heel State, Old North State

People. Population: 10,488,084; rank: 9. **Pop. change** (2010-19): 10.0%. **Pop. density:** 215.7 per sq mi. **Racial**

distribution: 70.6% white; 22.2% Black; 3.2% Asian; 1.6% Amer. Ind.; 0.1% Hawaiian/Pacific Islander; 2 or more races, 2.3%. **Hispanic pop.:** 9.8%.

Geography. Total area: 53,819 sq mi; rank: 28. **Land area:** 48,618 sq mi; rank: 29. **Acres forested:** 18.8 mil. **Location:** South Atlantic state bounded on N by Virginia, on S by South Carolina, on SW by Georgia, on W by Tennessee, and on E by Atlantic. **Climate:** subtropical in SE, medium-continental in mountain region; tempered by the Gulf Stream and mountains in W. **Topography:** coastal plain and tidewater in two-fifths of state, extending to the fall line of the rivers; Piedmont Plateau in another two-fifths has gentle to rugged hills; southern Appalachian Mts. contain the Blue Ridge and Great Smoky Mts. **Capital:** Raleigh. **Chief airports:** Charlotte, Raleigh, Greensboro, Asheville, Wilmington.

Economy. Chief industries: manufacturing, agriculture, tourism. **Chief manuf. goods:** transportation, tobacco, pharmaceuticals, toiletries, plastics, animal slaughtering and processing, household furniture, fabric and apparel. **Chief crops:** greenhouse and nursery, tobacco, cotton, soybeans, corn, Christmas trees, sweet potatoes, wheat, peanuts, blueberries, cucumbers, tomatoes, hay, potatoes. **Farm income:** Crops: $3.45 bil. Livestock: $7.63 bil. **Nonfuel minerals:** $1.4 bil; clay (common clay), phosphate rock, sand and gravel (construction), sand and gravel (industrial), stone (crushed). **Commercial fishing:** $78.4 mil. **Chief ports:** Morehead City, Wilmington. **Gross state product:** $587.7 bil. **Sales tax:** 4.75%. **Gasoline tax:** 54.75 cents/gal. **Employment distrib.:** 17.0% govt.; 19.3% trade/trans./util.; 10.5% mfg.; 13.9% ed./health; 14.7% prof./bus. serv.; 7.7% leisure/hosp.; 6.1% finance; 5.5% constr./mining/log.; 1.7% info.; 3.4% other serv. **Unemployment:** 3.9%. **Min. wage/hr.:** $7.25. **Per cap. pers. income:** $47,803. **New private housing:** 71,307 units/$13.8 bil. **Broadband internet:** 96.8%. **Commercial banks:** 66; deposits: $362.7 bil. **Savings institutions:** 18; deposits: $2.2 bil. **Lottery:** total sales: $2.9 bil; profit: $710.2 mil.

Federal govt. Fed. civ. employees: 45,289; **avg. salary:** $75,094. **Notable fed. facilities:** Ft. Bragg; Camp Lejeune Marine Base, Marine Corps Air Station Cherry Point; NOAA Natl. Centers for Environmental Information, Asheville; Natl. Inst. of Environmental Health Sciences, EPA Research and Dev. Labs, all in Research Triangle Park.

Education. High school grad. rate: 86.3%. **4-yr. public coll./univ.:** 17; **2-yr. public:** 58; **4-yr. private:** 48.

Energy. Electricity use/cost: 1,129 kWh, $125.17.

State data. Motto: Esse Quam Videri (To be rather than to seem). **Flower:** Dogwood. **Bird:** Cardinal. **Tree:** Pine. **Song:** "The Old North State." **Twelfth** of the original 13 states to ratify the Constitution, Nov. 21, 1789.

Tourism. Tourist spending: $26.3 bil. **Attractions:** Cape Hatteras and Cape Lookout Natl. Seashores; Great Smoky Mountains Natl. Park; Guilford Courthouse Natl. Military Park; Moore's Creek Natl. Battlefield (1776 victory ended British rule in colony); Bennett Place (site of largest troop surrender of Civil War), Durham; Ft. Raleigh Natl. Historic Site, North Carolina Aquarium, on Roanoke Island; Wright Brothers Natl. Mem., Kill Devil Hills; USS *North Carolina*, Wilmington; North Carolina Zoo, Asheboro; North Carolina Symphony, Marbles Kids Museum, North Carolina Museum of Art, North Carolina Museum of Natural Sciences, in Raleigh; Carl Sandburg Home, Flat Rock; Biltmore House and Gardens, North Carolina Arboretum, in Asheville; U.S. Natl. Whitewater Ctr., Discovery Place, in Charlotte; Fort Macon State Park, Atlantic Beach. **Information:** North Carolina Dept. of Commerce, Tourism Div., 15000 Weston Pkwy., Cary, NC 27513; 1-800-VISIT-NC, (919) 733-8372; www.visitnc.com

History. Algonquian, Siouan, and Iroquoian peoples lived in the region at the time of European contact. Sir Walter Raleigh tried to found a colony, 1584-87; the "Lost Colony" on Roanoke Island, 1587, seemingly disappeared. Permanent settlers came from Virginia in the mid-17th cent. The province's congress was the first to vote for independence, 1776. In the Revolutionary War, Gen. Charles Cornwallis's forces were defeated at Kings Mountain, 1780, and forced out after Guilford Courthouse, 1781. The state ratified the Constitution, 1789, only after Congress passed the Bill of Rights. North Carolina, where one-third of the population was enslaved, seceded from the Union, 1861, and provided more troops to the Confederacy than any other state; it was readmitted, 1868. The Wright brothers made the first powered airplane flight at Kitty Hawk, 1903. Sit-ins at segregated Greensboro lunch counters, 1960, drew national attention to the civil rights movement. Long reliant on tobacco, textiles, and wood products, North Carolina has prospered since the 1960s from advanced technologies in the Raleigh-Durham-Chapel Hill area and banking in Charlotte. The hurricane-prone state

was hit hard by Hazel, 1954, Fran, 1996, and Floyd, 1999. The state drew immediate backlash in 2016 after passing a "bathroom bill" requiring people to use public facilities that correspond with the sex assigned on their birth certificate; a revised bill was passed in 2017. The state's election board Feb. 21, 2019, ordered the 9th U.S. Congressional District to redo its 2018 general election, citing ballot fraud allegedly committed by GOP nominee Mark Harris's campaign.

Famous North Carolinians. David Brinkley, Shirley Caesar, John Coltrane, Stephen Curry, Rick Dees, Elizabeth Hanford Dole, Dale Earnhardt Sr., John Edwards, Ava Gardner, Richard Jordan Gatling, Billy Graham, Andy Griffith, O. Henry, Andrew Jackson, Andrew Johnson, Michael Jordan, William Rufus King, Charles Kuralt, Meadowlark Lemon, Dolley Madison, Thelonious Monk, Edward R. Murrow, Richard Petty, James K. Polk, Charlie Rose, Carl Sandburg, Enos Slaughter, Dean Smith, James Taylor, Thomas Wolfe.

Website. www.nc.gov

North Dakota (ND)
Peace Garden State

People. Population: 762,062; rank: 47. **Pop. change** (2010-19): 13.3%. **Pop. density:** 11.0 per sq mi. **Racial distribution:** 86.9% white; 3.4% Black; 1.7% Asian; 5.6% Amer. Ind.; 0.1% Hawaiian/Pacific Islander; 2 or more races, 2.3%. **Hispanic pop.:** 4.1%.

Geography. Total area: 70,698 sq mi; rank: 19. **Land area:** 69,001 sq mi; rank: 17. **Acres forested:** 0.8 mil. **Location:** West North Central state situated exactly in the middle of North America, bounded on the N by Canada, on the E by Minnesota, on the S by South Dakota, on the W by Montana. **Climate:** continental, with a wide range of temperatures and moderate rainfall. **Topography:** Central Lowland in the E comprises the flat Red R. Valley and the Rolling Drift Prairie; Missouri Plateau of the Great Plains on the W. **Capital:** Bismarck.

Economy. Chief industries: agriculture, mining, tourism, manufacturing, telecommunications, energy, food processing. **Chief manuf. goods:** machinery, wood prods., motor vehicles and parts, furniture, processed foods. **Chief crops:** wheat, soybeans, corn, sugar beets, barley, dry beans, sunflowers, canola, potatoes, flaxseed, hay, dry peas, lentils, oats. **Farm income:** Crops: $6.49 bil. Livestock: $1.26 bil. **Nonfuel minerals:** $58 mil; clay (common clay), lime, sand and gravel (construction), sand and gravel (industrial), stone (crushed). **Gross state product:** $57.0 bil. **Sales tax:** 5.0%. **Gasoline tax:** 41.40 cents/gal. **Employment distrib.:** 19.5% govt.; 21.8% trade/trans./util.; 6.2% mfg.; 16.1% ed./health; 7.9% prof./bus. serv.; 6.7% leisure/hosp.; 6.1% finance; 10.8% constr./mining/log.; 1.4% info.; 3.4% other serv. **Unemployment:** 2.4%. **Min. wage/hr.:** $7.25. **Per cap. pers. income:** $57,501. **New private housing:** 2,495 units/$537.5 mil. **Broadband internet:** 97.6%. **Commercial banks:** 83; deposits: $27.5 bil. **Savings institutions:** 2; deposits: $2.0 bil. **Lottery:** total sales: $35.4 mil; profit: $9.3 mil.

Federal govt. Fed. civ. employees: 5,555; **avg. salary:** $68,827. **Notable fed. facilities:** Minot AFB; Grand Forks AFB; Northern Prairie Wildlife Res. Ctr., Jamestown; Garrison Dam Natl. Fish Hatchery; Grand Forks Human Nutrition Res. Ctr.

Education. High school grad. rate: 88.1%. **4-yr. public coll./univ.:** 9; **2-yr. public:** 5; **4-yr. private:** 5.

Energy. Electricity use/cost: 1,118 kWh, $114.60.

State data. Motto: Liberty and union, now and forever, one and inseparable. **Flower:** Wild prairie rose. **Bird:** Western meadowlark. **Tree:** American elm. **Song:** "North Dakota Hymn." **Entered union:** Nov. 2, 1889; rank: 39th.

Tourism. Tourist spending: $3.1 bil. **Attractions:** North Dakota Heritage Ctr., North Dakota State Capitol, in Bismarck; Bonanzaville, West Fargo; Ft. Union Trading Post Natl. Historic Site; Intl. Peace Garden, Dunseith; Elkhorn Ranch site, in Theodore Roosevelt Natl. Park; Ft. Abraham Lincoln State Park and Museum, Mandan; Dakota Dinosaur Museum, Dickinson; Knife River Indian Villages Natl. Historic Site; Scandinavian Heritage Park, Minden. **Information:** North Dakota Tourism Division, Century Center, 1600 E. Century Ave., Ste. 2, P.O. Box 2057, Bismarck, ND 58502; 1-800-435-5663; www.ndtourism.com

History. Paleo-Indian peoples hunted in the area at least 11,000 years ago. At the time of European contact, the Ojibwa, Yanktonai and Teton Sioux, Mandan, Arikara, and Hidatsa peoples lived in the region. Pierre de Varennes, sieur de La Vérendrye, was the first French fur trader in the area, 1738, followed by the English at the end of the 18th cent. Lewis and Clark built Ft. Mandan, near present-day Washburn, 1804-05, and wintered there. The first permanent settlement was at

Pembina, 1812. Missouri River steamboats reached the area, 1832. Dakota Territory was organized, 1861. The first railroad arrived, 1872. The "bonanza farm" craze of the 1870s-80s led to statehood, 1889. The Nonpartisan League, a farmers' group favoring state ownership of industries, helped elect Lynn Frazier as governor, 1916, but he and others were ousted in a recall vote, 1921. The predominantly agricultural state has one of the nation's lowest unemployment rates, mostly due to increased oil production since late 2008 in the state's Bakken Formation. Construction of the Dakota Access Pipeline drew international attention and vigorous protests in 2016-17, in particular from the Standing Rock Sioux tribe.

Famous North Dakotans. Maxwell Anderson, Angie Dickinson, Josh Duhamel, John Bernard Flannagan, Phil Jackson, Louis L'Amour, Peggy Lee, Roger Maris, Eric Sevareid, Vilhjalmur Stefansson, Lawrence Welk.

Website. www.nd.gov

Ohio (OH)
Buckeye State

People. Population: 11,689,100; rank: 7. **Pop. change** (2010-19): 1.3%. **Pop. density:** 286.1 per sq mi. **Racial distribution:** 81.7% white; 13.1% Black; 2.5% Asian; 0.3% Amer. Ind.; 0.1% Hawaiian/Pacific Islander; 2 or more races, 2.4%. **Hispanic pop.:** 4.0%.

Geography. Total area: 44,826 sq mi; rank: 34. **Land area:** 40,861 sq mi; rank: 35. **Acres forested:** 7.9 mil. **Location:** East North Central state bounded on the N by Michigan and Lake Erie; on the E and S by Pennsylvania, West Virginia, and Kentucky; on the W by Indiana. **Climate:** temperate but variable; weather subject to much precipitation. **Topography:** generally rolling plain; Allegheny Plateau in E; Lake Erie Plains extend southward; central plains in the W. **Capital:** Columbus. **Chief airports:** Cleveland, Columbus, Dayton.

Economy. Chief industries: manufacturing, trade, services. **Chief manuf. goods:** motor vehicles and parts, petroleum, plastics and rubber, iron and steel, aircraft, machinery, fabricated metal, printing. **Chief crops:** corn, soybeans, hay, wheat, grapes, potatoes, tomatoes, apples, strawberries, tobacco. **Farm income:** Crops: $5.50 bil. Livestock: $3.52 bil. **Nonfuel minerals:** $1.4 bil; cement (portland), lime, salt, sand and gravel (construction), stone (crushed). **Commercial fishing:** $3.8 mil. **Chief ports:** Cincinnati, Toledo, Conneaut, Cleveland, Ashtabula. **Gross state product:** $698.5 bil. **Sales tax:** 5.75%. **Gasoline tax:** 56.91 cents/gal. **Employment distrib.:** 14.8% govt.; 19.1% trade/trans./util.; 12.9% mfg.; 17.4% ed./health; 13.3% prof./bus. serv.; 6.8% leisure/hosp.; 6.1% finance; 4.6% constr./mining/log.; 1.3% info.; 3.7% other serv. **Unemployment:** 4.1%. **Min. wage/hr.:** $8.70. **Per cap. pers. income:** $50,546. **New private housing:** 23,047 units/$5.4 bil. **Broadband internet:** 97.3%. **Commercial banks:** 164; deposits: $345.9 bil. **Savings institutions:** 53; deposits: $23.3 bil. **Lottery:** total sales: $4.4 bil; profit: $1.2 bil.

Federal govt. Fed. civ. employees: 50,521; **avg. salary:** $82,769. **Notable fed. facilities:** Wright-Patterson AFB; Defense Supply Ctr., Columbus; NASA Glenn Research Ctr., Cleveland; Joint Systems Manufacturing Ctr., Lima.

Education. High school grad. rate: 82.1%. **4-yr. public coll./univ.:** 36; **2-yr. public:** 24; **4-yr. private:** 68.

Energy. Electricity use/cost: 914 kWh, $114.80.

State data. Motto: With God, all things are possible. **Flower:** Scarlet carnation. **Bird:** Northern cardinal. **Tree:** Ohio buckeye. **Song:** "Beautiful Ohio." **Entered union:** Mar. 1, 1803; rank: 17th.

Tourism. Tourist spending: $31.6 bil. **Attractions:** Hopewell Culture Natl. Historical Park, Chillicothe; Cuyahoga Valley Natl. Park; Armstrong Air and Space Museum, Wapakoneta; Natl. Museum of the U.S. Air Force, near Dayton; Pro Football Hall of Fame, First Ladies Natl. Historic Site, in Canton; Kings Island amusement park, Mason; Lake Erie Islands, Cedar Point amusement park, in Sandusky; birthplaces, homes of, and memorials to presidents W. H. Harrison, Grant, Hayes, Garfield, B. Harrison, McKinley, Taft, and Harding; Amish Country, particularly in Holmes County; German Village historic neighborhood, Franklin Park Conservatory and Botanical Gardens, in Columbus; Rock and Roll Hall of Fame and Museum, West Side Market, Cleveland Metroparks Zoo, in Cleveland; Cincinnati Museum Center at Union Terminal; Toledo Zoo. **Information:** TourismOhio, P.O. Box 1001, Columbus, OH 43216; 1-800-BUCKEYE; www.ohio.org

History. Paleo-Indians hunted in the area about 11,000 years ago; the Adena and Hopewell cultures followed. Wyandot, Delaware, Miami, and Shawnee peoples sparsely occupied the area when the first Europeans arrived. René-Robert Cavelier, sieur de La Salle, visited the region, 1669. France claimed it, 1682, but ceded it to Britain, 1763. After the American Revolution, Ohio became part of the Northwest Territory, 1787. The first permanent settlement was at Marietta, 1788. Cincinnati was also founded, 1788; Cleveland, 1796. Indian warfare abated with the Treaty of Greenville, 1795. Ohio became a state, 1803. In the War of 1812, Oliver Hazard Perry's victory on Lake Erie and William Henry Harrison's invasion of Canada, 1813, ended British incursions. Columbus, founded 1812, became the state capital, 1816. Before the Civil War, some Ohioans aided the Underground Railroad. Agricultural for much of the 19th cent., the state became an industrial powerhouse in the 20th cent. but struggled to replace well-paying manufacturing jobs that began disappearing even before the 2007-09 recession. Cleveland hosted the Republican Natl. Convention in July 2016; no Republican has ever won the presidency without winning Ohio's electoral votes. A mass shooting in Aug. 2019 killed 10 in a Dayton nightlife district.

Famous Ohioans. Berenice Abbott, Sherwood Anderson, Neil Armstrong, George Bellows, Halle Berry, Ambrose Bierce, Erma Bombeck, Drew Carey, Hart Crane, George Custer, Clarence Darrow, Paul Laurence Dunbar, Thomas Edison, Clark Gable, John Glenn, Zane Grey, Bob Hope, William Dean Howells, LeBron James, John Legend, Maya Lin, Toni Morrison, Paul Newman, Jack Nicklaus, Annie Oakley, Jesse Owens, Jack Paar, Pontiac, Eddie Rickenbacker, John D. Rockefeller Sr. and Jr., Roy Rogers, Pete Rose, Arthur Schlesinger Jr., Gen. William Sherman, Steven Spielberg, Gloria Steinem, Harriet Beecher Stowe, Robert A. Taft, William H. Taft, Tecumseh, James Thurber, Orville and Wilbur Wright.

Website. www.ohio.gov

Oklahoma (OK)
Sooner State

People. Population: 3,956,971; rank: 28. **Pop. change** (2010-19): 5.5%. **Pop. density:** 57.7 per sq mi. **Racial distribution:** 74.0% white; 7.8% Black; 2.4% Asian; 9.4% Amer. Ind.; 0.2% Hawaiian/Pacific Islander; 2 or more races, 6.3%. **Hispanic pop.:** 11.1%.

Geography. Total area: 69,899 sq mi; rank: 20. **Land area:** 68,595 sq mi; rank: 19. **Acres forested:** 11.9 mil. **Location:** West South Central state bounded on the N by Colorado and Kansas, on the E by Missouri and Arkansas, on the S and W by Texas and New Mexico. **Climate:** temperate; southern humid belt merging with colder northern continental; humid eastern and dry western zones. **Topography:** high plains predominate in the W, hills and small mountains in the E; the E central region is dominated by the Arkansas R. Basin, and the S by the Red R. Plains. **Capital:** Oklahoma City. **Chief airports:** Oklahoma City, Tulsa.

Economy. Chief industries: manufacturing, mineral and energy exploration and production, agriculture, services. **Chief manuf. goods:** animal slaughtering and processing, petroleum, plastics and rubber, fabricated metals, machinery, motor vehicles and parts. **Chief crops:** wheat, greenhouse and nursery, hay, cotton, corn, soybeans, pecans, sorghum, peanuts. **Farm income:** Crops: $1.46 bil. Livestock: $5.29 bil. **Nonfuel minerals:** $1.1 bil; cement (portland), iodine, sand and gravel (construction), sand and gravel (industrial), stone (crushed). **Chief port:** Catoosa. **Gross state product:** $206.1 bil. **Sales tax:** 4.5%. **Gasoline tax:** 38.40 cents/gal. **Employment distrib.:** 21.6% govt.; 18.2% trade/trans./util.; 8.1% mfg.; 14.4% ed./health; 11.0% prof./bus. serv.; 9.4% leisure/hosp.; 4.9% finance; 7.0% constr./mining/log.; 1.2% info.; 4.2% other serv. **Unemployment:** 3.3%. **Min. wage/hr.:** $7.25. **Per cap. pers. income:** $47,951. **New private housing:** 12,152 units/$2.5 bil. **Broadband internet:** 96.6%. **Commercial banks:** 220; deposits: $85.5 bil. **Savings institutions:** 3; deposits: $7.0 bil. **Lottery:** total sales: $241.7 mil; profit $67.6 mil.

Federal govt. Fed. civ. employees: 39,158; **avg. salary:** $70,730. **Notable fed. facilities:** Tinker AFB; FAA Mike Monroney Aeronautical Ctr., Oklahoma City; Ft. Sill; Altus AFB; McAlester Army Ammunition Plant; Vance AFB; Natl. Severe Storms Lab., Norman.

Education. High school grad. rate: 81.8%. **4-yr. public coll./univ.:** 17; **2-yr. public:** 13; **4-yr. private:** 13.

Energy. Electricity use/cost: 1,139 kWh, $117.28.

State data. Motto: Labor Omnia Vincit (Labor conquers all things). **Flower:** Oklahoma rose. **Bird:** Scissor-tailed flycatcher. **Tree:** Redbud. **Song:** "Oklahoma!" **Entered union:** Nov. 16, 1907; rank: 46th.

Tourism. Tourist spending: $9.3 bil. **Attractions:** Cherokee Heritage Ctr., Tahlequah; Oklahoma City Natl. Memorial and Museum, Natl. Cowboy and Western Heritage Museum, White Water Bay and Frontier City amusement parks, Museum of Osteology, Bricktown neighborhood, in Oklahoma City; Will

Rogers Memorial Museum and Birthplace Ranch, Claremore and Oologah; Gathering Place, Philbrook Museum of Art, Gilcrease Museum, in Tulsa; Wichita Mountains Wildlife Refuge; Woolaroc Museum and Wildlife Preserve, Price Tower Arts Center, in Bartlesville; Sequoyah's Cabin, Sallisaw; Sam Noble Museum of Natural History, Norman. **Information:** Oklahoma Tourism Dept., Travel Promotion Division, 900 N. Stiles Ave., Oklahoma City, OK 73104-3234; 1-800-652-6552; www.travelok.com

History. Few Native Americans inhabited the region when Spanish explorer Coronado arrived, 1541; in the 16th and 17th cent., French traders visited. Part of the Louisiana Purchase, 1803, Oklahoma was known as Indian Country and, from 1834, Indian Territory. It became home to the "Five Civilized Tribes"—Cherokee, Choctaw, Chickasaw, Creek, and Seminole—after the forced removal of Indians from the eastern U.S., 1828-46. The land was also used by Comanche, Osage, and other Plains Indians. As white settlers pressed west, land was opened for homesteading by "runs" and lottery. The first run was in 1889; the most famous run, 1893, was to the Cherokee Outlet. Oklahoma became a state, 1907. In the early 20th cent., oil finds brought wealth to the Tulsa area; Tulsa's Greenwood section, then known as the "Negro Wall Street," was looted and destroyed by a white mob, 1921. Depression and drought drove many "Okies" from the Dust Bowl to California in the 1930s. A truck bomb in Oklahoma City, 1995, destroyed a federal office building, killing 168 people; an anti-government extremist was executed for the crime, 2001. A tornado in Moore killed 23 people May 20, 2013; the widest tornado on record touched down in El Reno May 31, 2013, killing 10 people. Since 2010, Oklahoma has experienced thousands of earthquakes (more than 1,400 greater than 3 magnitude in 2015-16 alone) believed to be connected with the use of disposal wells for wastewater from oil and gas operations. A teacher walkout in Apr. 2018 demanded increased pay and school funding. Purdue Pharma agreed Mar. 26, 2019, to pay Oklahoma $270 mil for allegedly downplaying OxyContin's addictive qualities and overstating its benefits. Flooding caused major damage in 10 eastern counties, May 2019.

Famous Oklahomans. Troy Aikman, Carl Albert, Gene Autry, Johnny Bench, William Boyd (Hopalong Cassidy), Garth Brooks, Lon Chaney, Gordon Cooper, Ralph Ellison, John Hope Franklin, James Garner, Vince Gill, Woody Guthrie, Paul Harvey, Ron Howard, Patrick J. Hurley, Ben Johnson, Jeane Kirkpatrick, Louis L'Amour, Shannon Lucid, Wilma Mankiller, Mickey Mantle, Reba McEntire, Wiley Post, Tony Randall, Oral Roberts, Will Rogers, Barry Switzer, Maria Tallchief, Jim Thorpe, Carrie Underwood, J. C. Watts Jr.

Website. www.ok.gov

Oregon (OR)
Beaver State

People. Population: 4,217,737; rank: 27. **Pop. change** (2010-19): 10.1%. **Pop. density:** 43.9 per sq mi. **Racial distribution:** 86.7% white; 2.2% Black; 4.9% Asian; 1.8% Amer. Ind.; 0.5% Hawaiian/Pacific Islander; 2 or more races, 4.0%. **Hispanic pop.:** 13.4%.

Geography. Total area: 98,379 sq mi; rank: 9. **Land area:** 95,988 sq mi; rank: 10. **Acres forested:** 29.6 mil. **Location:** Pacific shore bounded on N by Washington, on E by Idaho, on S by Nevada and California, on W by the Pacific. **Climate:** mild and humid on coast; continental dryness and extreme temperatures in the interior. **Topography:** Coast Range of rugged mountains; fertile Willamette R. Valley to E and S; Cascade Mt. Range of volcanic peaks E of the valley; plateau E of Cascades, remaining two-thirds of state. **Capital:** Salem. **Chief airports:** Portland, Eugene, Medford.

Economy. Chief industries: manufacturing, services, trade, finance, insurance, real estate, government, construction. **Chief manuf. goods:** wood prods., frozen produce, printing, computers and electronics, transportation equip., industrial machinery. **Chief crops:** greenhouse and nursery, grass seed, hay, wheat, potatoes, Christmas trees, onions, pears, hazelnuts, corn, grapes, cherries, blackberries, blueberries, peppermint, snap beans, apples, hops. **Farm income:** Crops: $3.48 bil. Livestock: $1.44 bil. **Nonfuel minerals:** $499 mil; cement (portland), diatomite, perlite (crude), sand and gravel (construction), stone (crushed). **Commercial fishing:** $172.5 mil. **Chief ports:** Portland, Coos Bay. **Gross state product:** $251.6 bil. **Sales tax:** none. **Gasoline tax:** 55.22 cents/gal. **Employment distrib.:** 16.7% govt.; 19.4% trade/trans./util.; 10.4% mfg.; 16.2% ed./health; 13.6% prof./bus. serv.; 6.6% leisure/hosp.; 5.6% finance; 6.4% constr./mining/log.; 1.8% info.; 3.3% other serv. **Unemployment:** 3.7%. **Min. wage/hr.:** $12.00. **Per cap. pers. income:** $52,937.

New private housing: 22,037 units/$4.4 bil. **Broadband internet:** 96.6%. **Commercial banks:** 39; deposits: $78.9 bil. **Savings institutions:** 4; deposits: $978.0 mil. **Lottery:** total sales: $1.3 bil; profit: $730.1 mil.

Federal govt. Fed. civ. employees: 20,527; **avg. salary:** $74,056. **Notable fed. facilities:** Bonneville Power Admin.

Education. High school grad. rate: 78.7%. **4-yr. public coll./univ.:** 9; **2-yr. public:** 17; **4-yr. private:** 24.

Energy. Electricity use/cost: 901 kWh, $99.00.

State data. Motto: She flies with her own wings. **Flower:** Oregon grape. **Bird:** Western meadowlark. **Tree:** Douglas fir. **Song:** "Oregon, My Oregon." **Entered union:** Feb. 14, 1859; rank: 33rd.

Tourism. Tourist spending: $13.0 bil. **Attractions:** John Day Fossil Beds Natl. Monument; Multnomah Falls, Columbia River Gorge; Timberline Lodge, Mount Hood Natl. Forest; Crater Lake Natl. Park; Oregon Dunes Natl. Rec. Area; Ft. Clatsop (Lewis and Clark Natl. Historical Park), Astoria Column, in Astoria; Oregon Caves Natl. Monument and Preserve; Intl. Rose Test Garden, Lan Su Chinese Garden, Pittock Mansion, Oregon Museum of Science and Industry, in Portland; Oregon Shakespeare Festival, Ashland; High Desert Museum, Bend; "Spruce Goose" (largest aircraft ever built), Evergreen Aviation and Space Museum, McMinnville; Yaquina Head Outstanding Natural Area, Oregon Coast Aquarium, in Newport. **Information:** Travel Oregon, 530 Center St. NE, Ste. 200, Salem, OR 97301; 1-800-547-7842; www.traveloregon.com

History. More than 100 Native American tribes inhabited the area at the time of European contact, including the Chinook, Yakima, Cayuse, Modoc, and Nez Percé. Capt. Robert Gray sighted and sailed into the Columbia R., 1792. Lewis and Clark, traveling overland, wintered at its mouth, 1805-06. Fur traders sent by John Jacob Astor established the Astoria trading post in the Columbia River region, 1811. Settlers arrived in the Willamette Valley, 1834. In 1843, the first large wave of settlers arrived via the Oregon Trail. Oregon became a territory, 1848, and a state, 1859. Early in the 20th cent., the "Oregon System"—political reforms that included initiative, referendum, recall, direct primary, and woman suffrage—was adopted. Originally dominated by forest products, the economy diversified after World War II, with technology firms clustering in the "Silicon Forest" area around Portland. Oregonians were the first in the U.S. to pass measures allowing physician-assisted suicide for terminally ill patients, 1994, and establishing an all-mail voting system, 1998. Gov. John Kitzhaber resigned a month into his unprecedented fourth term in 2015, amidst an ethics scandal. A 41-day armed occupation of Malheur Natl. Wildlife Refuge ended in Feb. 2016. In July 2020, federal Dept. of Homeland Security agents reportedly detained anti-racism protesters in Portland and drew backlash from Gov. Kate Brown.

Famous Oregonians. Ernest Bloch, Bill Bowerman, Ty Burrell, Beverly Cleary, Matt Groening, Ernest Haycox, Chief Joseph, Ken Kesey, Phil Knight, Ursula K. Le Guin, Edwin Markham, Tom McCall, John McLoughlin, Joaquin Miller, Bob Packwood, Linus Pauling, Steve Prefontaine, John "Jack" Reed, Alberto Salazar, Mary Decker Slaney, William Simon U'Ren.

Website. www.oregon.gov

Pennsylvania (PA)
Keystone State

People. Population: 12,801,989; rank: 5. **Pop. change** (2010-19): 0.8%. **Pop. density:** 286.1 per sq mi. **Racial distribution:** 81.6% white; 12.0% Black; 3.8% Asian; 0.4% Amer. Ind.; 0.1% Hawaiian/Pacific Islander; 2 or more races, 2.1%. **Hispanic pop.:** 7.8%.

Geography. Total area: 46,054 sq mi; rank: 33. **Land area:** 44,743 sq mi; rank: 32. **Acres forested:** 16.6 mil. **Location:** Middle Atlantic state bordered on the E by the Delaware R., on the S by the Mason-Dixon Line, on the W by West Virginia and Ohio, on the N/NE by Lake Erie and New York. **Climate:** continental with wide fluctuations in seasonal temperatures. **Topography:** Allegheny Mts. run SW-NE, with Piedmont and Coast Plain in the SE triangle; Allegheny Front a diagonal spine across the state's center; N and W rugged plateau falls to Lake Erie Lowland. **Capital:** Harrisburg. **Chief airports:** Philadelphia, Pittsburgh, Harrisburg.

Economy. Chief industries: agribusiness, advanced manufacturing, health care, travel and tourism, depository institutions, biotechnology, printing and publishing, research and consulting, trucking and warehousing, transportation by air, engineering and management, legal services. **Chief manuf. goods:** petroleum, pharmaceuticals, plastics, iron and steel, printing, paper and paperboard, confectionery and snacks, animal slaughtering and processing. **Chief crops:** greenhouse and nursery, mushrooms, corn, hay, soybeans, apples, tomatoes, wheat, grapes, peaches, potatoes, strawberries, tobacco. **Farm income: Crops:** $2.48 bil. **Livestock:** $4.22 bil. **Nonfuel minerals:** $2.1 bil; cement (portland), lime, sand and gravel (construction), sand and gravel (industrial), stone (crushed). **Commercial fishing:** $0.3 mil. **Chief ports:** Philadelphia, Pittsburgh. **Gross state product:** $813.5 bil. **Sales tax:** 6.0%. **Gasoline tax:** 77.10 cents/gal. **Employment distrib.:** 13.2% govt.; 18.7% trade/trans./util.; 10.1% mfg.; 22.1% ed./health; 14.1% prof./bus. serv.; 5.6% leisure/hosp.; 6.2% finance; 5.0% constr./mining/log.; 1.4% info.; 3.6% other serv. **Unemployment:** 4.4%. **Min. wage/hr.:** $7.25. **Per cap. pers. income:** $58,775. **New private housing:** 23,539 units/$4.7 bil. **Broadband internet:** 97.3%. **Commercial banks:** 126; deposits: $384.2 bil. **Savings institutions:** 56; deposits $31.7 bil. **Lottery:** total sales: $4.9 bil; profit: $1.1 bil.

Federal govt. Fed. civ. employees: 61,360; **avg. salary:** $77,109. **Notable fed. facilities:** Army War College, Carlisle Barracks; Naval Supply Systems Command (NAVSUP), Mechanicsburg; Philadelphia Mint, Defense Supply Ctr., Naval Surface Warfare Ctr., all in Phila.; DLA Distribution Ctr. Susquehanna, New Cumberland, Mechanicsburg; Tobyhanna Army Depot; Letterkenny Army Depot.

Education. High school grad. rate: 85.9%. **4-yr. public coll./univ.:** 45; **2-yr. public:** 18; **4-yr. private:** 105.

Energy. Electricity use/cost: 864 kWh, $120.04.

State data. Motto: Virtue, liberty, and independence. **Flower:** Mountain laurel. **Bird:** Ruffed grouse. **Tree:** Eastern hemlock. **Song:** "Pennsylvania." **Second** of the original 13 states to ratify the Constitution, Dec. 12, 1787.

Tourism. Tourist spending: $37.5 bil. **Attractions:** Liberty Bell Ctr. at Independence Natl. Historical Park, Franklin Institute, Philadelphia Museum of Art, in Philadelphia; Valley Forge Natl. Historical Park, King of Prussia; Gettysburg Natl. Military Park; Pennsylvania Dutch Country, Lancaster County; Hersheypark, Hershey; Duquesne Incline, Carnegie Museums of Pittsburgh, Heinz Hall for the Performing Arts, in Pittsburgh; Pocono Mountains; Pine Creek Gorge (Pennsylvania Grand Canyon), Allegheny Natl. Forest; Fallingwater (house designed by Frank Lloyd Wright), Mill Run; Johnstown Flood Natl. Memorial; Steamtown Natl. Historic Site, Scranton; U.S. Brig *Niagara*, Erie Maritime Museum, Presque Isle State Park, in Erie; Oil Region Natl. Heritage Area; Longwood Gardens, Kennett Square. **Information:** Pennsylvania Tourism Office, Dept. of Community and Economic Development, Commonwealth Keystone Building, 4th Fl., 400 North St., Harrisburg, PA 17120-0225; 1-800-VISITPA; www.visitpa.com

History. When Europeans came, Algonquian-speaking Lenni Lenape (Delaware) and Shawnee and the Iroquoian Susquehannocks, Erie, and Seneca occupied the region. Swedish explorers made the first permanent settlement, 1643, on Tinicum Island. The Dutch seized the settlement, 1655, but lost it to the British, 1664. The region was given by Charles II to William Penn, 1681. Philadelphia ("brotherly love") was the capital of the colonies during most of the American Revolution and of the U.S., 1790-1800; the Declaration of Independence, 1776, and Constitution, 1787, were signed here. Philadelphia was taken by the British, 1777. George Washington's troops encamped at Valley Forge in the bitter winter of 1777-78. Slavery was abolished, 1780. Union victory at the Battle of Gettysburg, July 1-3, 1863, marked a turning point in the Civil War. A dam collapse at Johnstown, 1889, killed at least 2,200 people. From the late 19th to the mid-20th cent., Pittsburgh prospered from coal and steel; later, heavy industry declined, but the city revived as a hub of finance, health care, and research. The Three Mile Island nuclear plant near Harrisburg had a near-meltdown, 1979. One of four hijacked planes on Sept. 11, 2001, crashed near Shanksville; the Flight 93 national memorial was officially dedicated on the site in 2011. A shooting at Pittsburgh's Tree of Life synagogue, Oct. 2018, killed 11; the alleged shooter was arrested.

Famous Pennsylvanians. Marian Anderson, Maxwell Anderson, George Blanda, Kobe Bryant, James Buchanan, Andrew Carnegie, Rachel Carson, Wilt Chamberlain, Noam Chomsky, Perry Como, Bill Cosby, Cyrus H. K. Curtis, Thomas Eakins, Tina Fey, Stephen Foster, Benjamin Franklin, Robert Fulton, Martha Graham, Milton Hershey, Gene Kelly, Grace Kelly (Princess Grace of Monaco), Dan Marino, George C. Marshall, Chris Matthews, John J. McCloy, Margaret Mead, Andrew W. Mellon, Joe Montana, Stan Musial, Joe Namath, John O'Hara, Arnold Palmer, Robert E. Peary, Mike Piazza, Pink (Alecia Beth Moore), Mary Roberts Rinehart, Fred Rogers, Betsy Ross, Will Smith, Jimmy Stewart, Taylor Swift, Jim Thorpe, Johnny Unitas, John Updike, Honus Wagner, Andy Warhol, Benjamin West.

Website. www.pa.gov

Rhode Island (RI)
Little Rhody, Ocean State

People. Population: 1,059,361; rank: 44. **Pop. change** (2010-19): 0.6%. **Pop. density:** 1,024.5 per sq mi. **Racial distribution:** 83.6% white; 8.5% Black; 3.7% Asian; 1.1% Amer. Ind.; 0.2% Hawaiian/Pacific Islander; 2 or more races, 2.9%. **Hispanic pop.:** 16.3%.

Geography. Total area: 1,545 sq mi; rank: 50. **Land area:** 1,034 sq mi; rank: 50. **Acres forested:** 0.4 mil. **Location:** New England state. **Climate:** invigorating and changeable. **Topography:** eastern lowlands of Narragansett Basin; western uplands of flat and rolling hills. **Capital:** Providence. **Chief airport:** Warwick.

Economy. Chief industries: services, manufacturing. **Chief manuf. goods:** plastics, fabricated metals, electrical equip., jewelry. **Chief crops:** greenhouse and nursery, sweet corn, berries, potatoes, apples, hay. **Farm income: Crops:** $43.59 mil. **Livestock:** $29.38 mil. **Nonfuel minerals:** $54 mil; sand and gravel (construction), sand and gravel (industrial), stone (crushed). **Commercial fishing:** $105.1 mil. **Chief ports:** Providence, Davisville, Newport. **Gross state product:** $63.5 bil. **Sales tax:** 7.0%. **Gasoline tax:** 53.40 cents/gal. **Employment distrib.:** 15.3% govt.; 15.6% trade/trans./util.; 8.8% mfg.; 22.0% ed./health; 14.0% prof./bus. serv.; 6.8% leisure/hosp.; 8.1% finance; 4.3% constr./mining/log.; 1.2% info.; 3.8% other serv. **Unemployment:** 3.6%. **Min. wage/hr.:** $10.50. **Per cap. pers. income:** $56,542. **New private housing:** 1,400 units/$280.4 mil. **Broadband internet:** 98.8%. **Commercial banks:** 10; deposits: $27.6 bil. **Savings institutions:** 11; deposits: $3.4 bil. **Lottery:** total sales: $956.3 mil; profit: $397.3 mil.

Federal govt. Fed. civ. employees: 7,585; **avg. salary:** $91,122. **Notable fed. facilities:** Naval War College, Naval Undersea Warfare Ctr., Newport; EPA Atlantic Ecology Div. Lab, Narragansett.

Education. High school grad. rate: 84.0%. **4-yr. public coll./univ.:** 2; **2-yr. public:** 1; **4-yr. private:** 10.

Energy. Electricity use/cost: 589 kWh, $121.05.

State data. Motto: Hope. **Flower:** Common blue violet. **Bird:** Rhode Island red chicken. **Tree:** Red maple. **Song:** "Rhode Island." **Thirteenth** of original 13 states to ratify the Constitution, May 29, 1790.

Tourism. Tourist spending: $2.3 bil. **Attractions:** Block Island; mansions (The Breakers, The Elms, others); Cliff Walk, Intl. Tennis Hall of Fame and Museum, Touro Synagogue (completed 1763, oldest in U.S.), in Newport; First Baptist Church in America, Rhode Island School of Design Museum of Art, WaterFire art installation, in Providence; Slater Mill Historic Site, Pawtucket; Gilbert Stuart Birthplace and Museum, Saunderstown. **Information:** Rhode Island Tourism Division, 315 Iron Horse Way, Ste. 101, Providence, RI 02908; 1-800-556-2484; www.visitrhodeisland.com

History. When Europeans arrived, Narragansett, Niantic, Nipmuc, and Wampanoag peoples lived in the region. Italian Giovanni da Verrazzano visited the area, 1524. The first permanent settlement was founded at Providence, 1636, by Roger Williams, who was exiled from the Massachusetts Bay Colony. Anne Hutchinson, also exiled, settled Portsmouth, 1638. Quaker and Jewish immigrants seeking freedom of worship began arriving, 1650s-60s. The colonists broke the power of the Narragansett in the Great Swamp Fight, 1675, the decisive battle in King Philip's War. The colony was the first to formally renounce all allegiance to King George III, May 4, 1776. Initially opposed to joining the Union, Rhode Island was the last of the 13 colonies to ratify the Constitution, 1790. Trade, textiles, and metal goods dominated the economy in the 19th cent., and Newport became a fashionable resort after the Civil War. The U.S. Navy was the state's largest civilian employer, 1945-73, until the destroyer force was relocated from Newport. A nightclub fire in West Warwick killed 100 people in 2003.

Famous Rhode Islanders. Ambrose Burnside, George M. Cohan, Viola Davis, Nelson Eddy, Jabez Gorham, Nathanael Greene, Elisabeth Hasselbeck, Christopher and Oliver La Farge, Cormac McCarthy, John McLaughlin, Matthew C. and Oliver Hazard Perry, Gilbert Stuart, Meredith Vieira.

Website. www.ri.gov

South Carolina (SC)
Palmetto State

People. Population: 5,148,714; rank: 23. **Pop. change** (2010-19): 11.3%. **Pop. density:** 171.3 per sq mi. **Racial distribution:** 68.6% white; 27.0% Black; 1.8% Asian; 0.5% Amer. Ind.; 0.1% Hawaiian/Pacific Islander; 2 or more races, 2.0%. **Hispanic pop.:** 6.0%.

Geography. Total area: 32,020 sq mi; rank: 40. **Land area:** 30,061 sq mi; rank: 40. **Acres forested:** 12.9 mil. **Location:** South Atlantic state bordered by North Carolina on the N; Georgia on the SW and W; the Atlantic Ocean on the E, SE, and S. **Climate:** humid subtropical. **Topography:** Blue Ridge province in NW has highest peaks; piedmont lies between the mountains and the fall line; coastal plain covers two-thirds of state. **Capital:** Columbia. **Chief airports:** Charleston, Myrtle Beach, Greer, Columbia.

Economy. Chief industries: tourism, agriculture, manufacturing. **Chief manuf. goods:** chemicals and synthetics, motor vehicles and parts, plastics, paper and paper prods., turbines, rubber, textiles. **Chief crops:** greenhouse and nursery, tobacco, soybeans, cotton, corn, peaches, wheat, tomatoes, peanuts. **Farm income:** Crops: $1.12 bil. Livestock: $1.39 bil. **Nonfuel minerals:** $1.1 bil; cement (masonry and portland), gold, sand and gravel (construction), stone (crushed). **Commercial fishing:** $20.7 mil. **Chief ports:** Charleston, Georgetown. **Gross state product:** $246.3 bil. **Sales tax:** 6.0%. **Gasoline tax:** 41.15 cents/gal. **Employment distrib.:** 18.0% govt.; 19.4% trade/trans./util.; 12.2% mfg.; 11.9% ed./health; 13.5% prof./bus. serv.; 9.3% leisure/hosp.; 5.1% finance; 5.6% constr./mining/log.; 1.3% info.; 3.7% other serv. **Unemployment:** 2.8%. **Min. wage/hr.:** none. **Per cap. pers. income:** $45,314. **New private housing:** 36,034 units/$8.0 bil. **Broadband internet:** 96.8%. **Commercial banks:** 62; deposits: $88.1 bil. **Savings institutions:** 14; deposits: $1.3 bil. **Lottery:** total sales: $2.0 bil; profit: $488.1 mil.

Federal govt. Fed. civ. employees: 21,966; **avg. salary:** $74,325. **Notable fed. facilities:** Ft. Jackson; Joint Base Charleston; Marine Corps Recruit Depot Parris Island; Shaw AFB; USMC Air Station Beaufort; Savannah River Site.

Education. High school grad. rate: 81.0%. **4-yr. public coll./univ.:** 13; **2-yr. public:** 20; **4-yr. private:** 22.

Energy. Electricity use/cost: 1,159 kWh, $144.20.

State data. Motto: Dum Spiro Spero (While I breathe, I hope). **Flower:** Yellow jessamine. **Bird:** Carolina wren. **Tree:** Palmetto. **Song:** "Carolina." **Eighth** of the original 13 states to ratify the Constitution, May 23, 1788.

Tourism. Tourist spending: $15.3 bil. **Attractions:** Historic Charleston, Waterfront Park, Charleston Museum (est. 1773, oldest in U.S.), Middleton Place, Magnolia Plantation and Gardens, Drayton Hall, in Charleston; Ft. Sumter Natl. Monument (where first shots of Civil War were fired), in Charleston Harbor; Cypress Gardens, Moncks Corner; Boone Hall Plantation and Gardens, Mt. Pleasant; Brookgreen Gardens, Murrells Inlet; Myrtle Beach; Hilton Head Island; Andrew Jackson State Park, Lancaster; South Carolina State Museum, Riverbanks Zoo, in Columbia. **Information:** SC Dept. of Parks, Recreation, and Tourism, 1205 Pendleton St., Columbia, SC 29201; 1-866-224-9339, (803) 734-1700; discoversouthcarolina.com

History. When Europeans arrived, Cherokee, Catawba, and Muskogean peoples lived in the area. Spanish and French came in the 16th cent. The first English colonists settled near the Ashley R., 1670, and moved to the site of present-day Charleston, 1680. The colonists seized the government, 1775, and the royal governor fled. The British took Charleston, 1780, but were defeated at Kings Mountain that same year and at Cowpens, 1781. In the 1830s, South Carolinians, angered by federal protective tariffs, adopted the Nullification Doctrine, holding that a state can void an act of Congress. Plantation agriculture relied on the enslaved labor of Black workers to cultivate rice and cotton. Enslaved Black people made up 57% of the population in 1860, when South Carolina was the first state to secede from the Union. Confederate troops fired on and forced the surrender of U.S. troops at Ft. Sumter, in Charleston Harbor, 1861, launching the Civil War. The state was readmitted to the Union, 1868. Strom Thurmond, who ran for president as a segregationist in 1948, later served 48 years in the U.S. Senate (1955-2003). Formerly dependent on textiles, the state has attracted new industries by courting foreign investment. The state removed the Confederate flag from its capitol grounds in July 2015 after an alleged white supremacist shot and killed nine Black parishioners at a Charleston church the previous month; the shooter was sentenced to death in 2017.

Famous South Carolinians. Aziz Ansari, Charles F. Bolden Jr., Chadwick Boseman, James F. Byrnes, John C. Calhoun, Stephen Colbert, Marian Wright Edelman, Joe Frazier, DuBose Heyward, Ernest F. Hollings, Andrew Jackson, Jesse Jackson, "Shoeless" Joe Jackson, Jasper Johns, Andie MacDowell, Francis Marion, Ronald E. McNair, Charles Pinckney, John Rutledge, Thomas Sumter, Strom Thurmond, John B. Watson.

Website. www.sc.gov

South Dakota (SD)
Coyote State, Mount Rushmore State

People. Population: 884,659; rank: 46. **Pop. change** (2010-19): 8.7%. **Pop. density:** 11.7 per sq mi. **Racial distribution:** 84.6% white; 2.3% Black; 1.5% Asian; 9.0% Amer. Ind.; 0.1% Hawaiian/Pacific Islander; 2 or more races, 2.5%. **Hispanic pop.:** 4.2%.

Geography. Total area: 77,116 sq mi; rank: 17. **Land area:** 75,811 sq mi; rank: 16. **Acres forested:** 1.9 mil. **Location:** West North Central state bounded on the N by North Dakota, on the E by Minnesota and Iowa, on the S by Nebraska, on the W by Wyoming and Montana. **Climate:** characterized by extremes of temperature, persistent winds, low precipitation and humidity. **Topography:** Prairie Plains in the E; rolling hills of the Great Plains in the W; the Black Hills, rising 3,500 ft, in the SW corner. **Capital:** Pierre. **Chief airport:** Sioux Falls.

Economy. Chief industries: agriculture, services, manufacturing. **Chief manuf. goods:** animal slaughtering, machinery, semiconductors, surgical appliances. **Chief crops:** corn, soybeans, wheat, hay, sunflowers, sorghum, oats, barley. **Farm income:** Crops: $5.04 bil. Livestock: $4.07 bil. **Nonfuel minerals:** $312 mil; cement (portland), gold, lime, sand and gravel (construction), stone (crushed). **Gross state product:** $53.3 bil. **Sales tax:** 4.5%. **Gasoline tax:** 48.40 cents/gal. **Employment distrib.:** 17.8% govt.; 19.6% trade/trans./util.; 10.5% mfg.; 17.0% ed./health; 8.0% prof./bus. serv.; 8.5% leisure/hosp.; 7.1% finance; 6.5% constr./mining/log.; 1.3% info.; 3.6% other serv. **Unemployment:** 3.3%. **Min. wage/hr.:** $9.30. **Per cap. pers. income:** $53,925. **New private housing:** 4,415 units/$836.3 mil. **Broadband internet:** 97.5%. **Commercial banks:** 76; deposits: $686.9 bil. **Savings institutions:** 4; deposits: $5.0 mil. **Lottery:** total sales: $293.2 mil; profit: $129.8 mil.

Federal govt. Fed. civ. employees: 8,515; **avg. salary:** $65,340. **Notable fed. facilities:** Ellsworth AFB.

Education. High school grad. rate: 84.1%. **4-yr. public coll./univ.:** 7; **2-yr. public:** 5; **4-yr. private:** 7.

Energy. Electricity use/cost: 1,045 kWh, $121.16.

State data. Motto: Under God, the people rule. **Flower:** Pasqueflower. **Bird:** Chinese ring-necked pheasant. **Tree:** Black Hills spruce. **Song:** "Hail, South Dakota." **Entered union:** Nov. 2, 1889; rank: 40th.

Tourism. Tourist spending: $3.4 bil. **Attractions:** Mt. Rushmore Natl. Memorial, Keystone; Harney Peak (tallest E of Rockies); Custer State Park; Crazy Horse Memorial (mtn. carving in progress); Wind Cave Natl. Park, near Hot Springs; Black Hills Natl. Forest; Needles Hwy., part of Peter Norbeck Natl. Scenic Byway; Minuteman Missile Natl. Historic Site; Deadwood (1876 gold rush town); Jewel Cave Natl. Monument, near Custer; Badlands Natl. Park; Great Lakes of South Dakota; Great Plains Zoo and Delbridge Museum of Natural History, Sioux Falls; Corn Palace, Mitchell; Reptile Gardens, Chapel in the Hills, Bear Country USA, in Rapid City. **Information:** Dept. of Tourism, Dolly Reed Plaza, 711 E. Wells Ave., c/o 500 E. Capitol Ave., Pierre, SD 57501; 1-800-SDA-KOTA; www.travelsd.com

History. Paleo-Indians hunted in the region at least 11,500 years ago. At the time of first European contact, Mandan, Hidatsa, Arikara, and Sioux lived in the area. The French Vérendrye brothers explored the region, 1742-43. The U.S. acquired the territory in the Louisiana Purchase, 1803, and Meriwether Lewis and William Clark passed through, 1804-06. In 1817 a trading post opened at what would become Ft. Pierre. Dakota Territory was established, 1861. Gold was discovered, 1874, in the Black Hills on Lakota Sioux land; the "Great Dakota Boom" began in 1879. South Dakota became a state, 1889. The massacre of more than 200 Native American men, women, and children at Wounded Knee, 1890, ended Sioux resistance. Armed supporters of the American Indian Movement, a Native American rights group, occupied the area, leading to a 70-day standoff, 1973. Major economic activities include agribusiness and, since the 1980s, credit card services. Republicans scored a key election victory, 2004, with the defeat of three-term U.S. Sen. Tom Daschle, a national Democratic leader. A Smithfield Foods pork processing facility in Sioux Falls in Apr. 2020 became the site of the U.S.'s largest known single-source coronavirus cluster.

Famous South Dakotans. Sparky Anderson, Bob Barker, Black Elk, Tom Brokaw, Crazy Horse, Tom Daschle, Myron Floren, Mary Hart, Cheryl Ladd, Ernest O. Lawrence, George McGovern, Russell Means, Billy Mills, Allen H. Neuharth, Pat O'Brien, Sitting Bull.

Website. www.sd.gov

Tennessee (TN)
Volunteer State

People. Population: 6,829,174; rank: 16. **Pop. change** (2010-19): 7.6%. **Pop. density:** 165.6 per sq mi. **Racial distribution:** 78.4% white; 17.1% Black; 2.0% Asian; 0.5% Amer. Ind.; 0.1% Hawaiian/Pacific Islander; 2 or more races, 2.0%. **Hispanic pop.:** 5.7%.

Geography. Total area: 42,144 sq mi; rank: 36. **Land area:** 41,235 sq mi; rank: 34. **Acres forested:** 13.9 mil. **Location:** East South Central state bounded on the N by Kentucky and Virginia; on the E by North Carolina; on the S by Georgia, Alabama, and Mississippi; on the W by Arkansas and Missouri. **Climate:** humid continental to the N; humid subtropical to the S. **Topography:** rugged country in E; Great Smoky Mts. of the Unaka Range; low ridges of the Appalachian Valley; flat Cumberland Plateau; slightly rolling terrain and knobs of the Interior Low Plateau, the largest region; Eastern Gulf Coastal Plain to the W, laced with streams; Mississippi Alluvial Plain, a narrow strip of swamp and floodplain in extreme W. **Capital:** Nashville. **Chief airports:** Nashville, Memphis, Alcoa, Chattanooga.

Economy. Chief industries: manufacturing, trade, services, tourism, finance, insurance, real estate. **Chief manuf. goods:** motor vehicles and parts, computers and electronics, food, chemicals, plastics, printing, appliances, aluminum. **Chief crops:** greenhouse and nursery, soybeans, cotton, corn, tobacco, hay, tomatoes, wheat. **Farm income:** Crops: $2.10 bil. Livestock: $1.41 bil. **Nonfuel minerals:** $1.4 bil; cement (portland), sand and gravel (construction), sand and gravel (industrial), stone (crushed), zinc. **Chief ports:** Memphis, Nashville, Chattanooga. **Gross state product:** $380.1 bil. **Sales tax:** 7.0%. **Gasoline tax:** 45.80 cents/gal. **Employment distrib.:** 14.8% govt.; 21.5% trade/trans./util.; 10.9% mfg.; 14.6% ed./health; 13.4% prof./bus. serv.; 9.0% leisure/hosp.; 6.0% finance; 4.4% constr./mining/log.; 1.5% info.; 3.7% other serv. **Unemployment:** 3.4%. **Min. wage/hr.:** none. **Per cap. pers. income:** $48,761. **New private housing:** 41,361 units/$7.9 bil. **Broadband internet:** 96.8%. **Commercial banks:** 178; deposits: $157.2 bil. **Savings institutions:** 10; deposits: $3.1 bil. **Lottery:** total sales: $1.8 bil; profit: $447.2 mil.

Federal govt. Fed. civ. employees: 26,713; **avg. salary:** $71,007. **Notable fed. facilities:** Tennessee Valley Authority, Knoxville; Oak Ridge Natl. Lab; Arnold Engineering Development Ctr.; Ft. Campbell; NSA Mid-South, Millington.

Education. High school grad. rate: 90.0%. **4-yr. public coll./univ.:** 10; **2-yr. public:** 13; **4-yr. private:** 43.

Energy. Electricity use/cost: 1,283 kWh, $137.35.

State data. Motto: Agriculture and commerce. **Flower:** (cultivated) iris; (wildflower) passion flower, Tennessee coneflower. **Bird:** Northern mockingbird. **Tree:** Tulip poplar. **Songs:** "My Homeland, Tennessee"; "When It's Iris Time in Tennessee"; "My Tennessee"; "Tennessee Waltz"; "Rocky Top"; "Smoky Mountain Rain." **Entered union:** June 1, 1796; rank: 16th.

Tourism. Tourist spending: $22.0 bil. **Attractions:** Lookout Mountain, Tennessee Aquarium, Ruby Falls, in Chattanooga; Great Smoky Mountains Natl. Park; Lost Sea (largest underground lake in U.S.), Sweetwater; Cherokee Natl. Forest; Cumberland Gap Natl. Historical Park; James K. Polk Ancestral Home, Columbia; American Museum of Science and Energy, Oak Ridge; The Hermitage (home of Pres. Andrew Jackson), Country Music Hall of Fame and Museum, Ryman Auditorium, Belle Meade Plantation, Parthenon replica, Grand Ole Opry, in Nashville; Dollywood theme park, Pigeon Forge; Graceland (home of Elvis Presley), Sun Studio, in Memphis; Alex Haley Museum and Interpretive Ctr., Henning; Casey Jones Village, Jackson; Bristol Motor Speedway. **Information:** Dept. of Tourist Development, Wm. Snodgrass/Tennessee Tower, 312 Rosa L. Parks Ave., 13th Fl., Nashville, TN 37243; 1-800-462-8366; www.tnvacation.com

History. Inhabited for at least 20,000 years, the region was home to Creek and Yuchi peoples when the first Europeans arrived; the Cherokee moved into the region in the early 18th cent. Spanish explorers visited the area, 1540. English traders crossed the Great Smoky Mtns. from the east, while France's Jacques Marquette and Louis Jolliet sailed down the Mississippi on the west, 1673. The first permanent settlement was of Virginians on the Watauga R., 1769. After the American Revolution, in which Tennesseans fought in eastern campaigns, the region became a territory, 1790, and a state, 1796. Slavery was widespread in western Tennessee, where cotton was the main crop, but much less common in the east. The state seceded, 1861, and saw many Civil War engagements; some 187,000 Tennesseans fought for the Confederacy and 51,000 for the Union. Tennessee was readmitted in 1866, the only former Confederate state not to have a postwar military

government. The famous Scopes trial, 1925, questioned the teaching of evolution in public schools. In the 1930s, the Tennessee Valley Authority, a federal program, brought electric power to rural areas. Nashville became the capital of country music while Memphis fostered the blues and, with Elvis Presley in the 1950s, rock 'n' roll. Martin Luther King Jr. was assassinated in Memphis, 1968. Since the 1970s, auto plants have become major employers, as has Federal Express. Al Gore Jr., U.S. vice pres. (1993-2001), lost his 2000 presidential bid partly because he failed to carry his home state of Tennessee. Record amounts of rainfall flooded Nashville in 2010. Wildfires killed 14 in East Tennessee in Nov. 2016. On Mar. 2-3, 2020, tornadoes in central TN killed at least 25 people.

Famous Tennesseans. Roy Acuff, Kenny Chesney, Davy Crockett, David Farragut, Ernie Ford, Aretha Franklin, Bill Frist, Al Gore Jr., Alex Haley, William C. Handy, Sam Houston, Cordell Hull, Andrew Jackson, Andrew Johnson, Casey Jones, Estes Kefauver, Grace Moore, Dolly Parton, Minnie Pearl, James Polk, Elvis Presley, Wilma Rudolph, Dinah Shore, Bessie Smith, Fred Thompson, Justin Timberlake, Tina Turner, Hank Williams Jr., Alvin York.

Website. www.tn.gov

Texas (TX)
Lone Star State

People. Population: 28,995,881; rank: 2. **Pop. change** (2010-19): 15.3%. **Pop. density:** 111.0 per sq mi. **Racial distribution:** 78.7% white; 12.9% Black; 5.2% Asian; 1.0% Amer. Ind.; 0.1% Hawaiian/Pacific Islander; 2 or more races, 2.1%. **Hispanic pop.:** 39.7%.

Geography. Total area: 268,596 sq mi; rank: 2. **Land area:** 261,232 sq mi; rank: 2. **Acres forested:** 62.0 mil. **Location:** southwestern state bounded on the SE by the Gulf of Mexico; on the SW by Mexico, separated by the Rio Grande; surrounding states are Louisiana, Arkansas, Oklahoma, New Mexico. **Climate:** extremely varied; driest region is the Trans-Pecos; wettest is the NE. **Topography:** Gulf Coast Plain in the S and SE; North Central Plains slope upward with some hills; the Great Plains extend over the Panhandle, are broken by low mountains; the Trans-Pecos is the southern extension of the Rockies. **Capital:** Austin. **Chief airports:** Fort Worth, Houston (2), Austin, Dallas, San Antonio, El Paso, Midland, Lubbock.

Economy. Chief industries: manufacturing, trade, oil and gas extraction, services. **Chief manuf. goods:** petroleum, chemicals and resins, computers and electronics, animal slaughtering and processing, plastics, aerospace. **Chief crops:** cotton, greenhouse and nursery, corn, wheat, sorghum, hay, peanuts, onions, rice, pecans, grapefruit. **Farm income:** Crops: $7.54 bil. Livestock: $14.44 bil. **Nonfuel minerals:** $6.5 bil; cement (portland), salt, sand and gravel (construction), sand and gravel (industrial), stone (crushed). **Commercial fishing:** $211.8 mil. **Chief ports:** Houston, Galveston, Brownsville, Beaumont, Port Arthur, Corpus Christi, Texas City, Freeport. **Gross state product:** $1.9 tril. **Sales tax:** 6.25%. **Gasoline tax:** 38.40 cents/gal. **Employment distrib.:** 16.2% govt.; 19.9% trade/trans./util.; 7.3% mfg.; 13.9% ed./health; 14.4% prof./bus. serv.; 8.8% leisure/hosp.; 6.7% finance; 7.9% constr./mining/log.; 1.6% info.; 3.3% other serv. **Unemployment:** 3.5%. **Min. wage/hr.:** $7.25. **Per cap. pers. income:** $52,504. **New private housing:** 209,895 units/$37.4 bil. **Broadband internet:** 97.6%. **Commercial banks:** 474; deposits: $781.4 bil. **Savings institutions:** 36; deposits: $96.7 bil. **Lottery:** total sales: $6.3 bil; profit: $1.6 bil.

Federal govt. Fed. civ. employees: 116,752; **avg. salary:** $77,554. **Notable fed. facilities:** Ft. Hood; Ft. Bliss; Sheppard, Dyess, Goodfellow AF Bases; Joint Base San Antonio; NASA Johnson Space Ctr., Houston; Naval Air Training School, Corpus Christi NAS; Red River Army Depot; Western Currency Facility, Ft. Worth.

Education. High school grad. rate: 90.0%. **4-yr. public coll./univ.:** 49; **2-yr. public:** 60; **4-yr. private:** 65.

Energy. Electricity use/cost: 1,176 kWh, $131.63.

State data. Motto: Friendship. **Flower:** Bluebonnet. **Bird:** Northern mockingbird. **Tree:** Pecan. **Song:** "Texas, Our Texas." **Entered union:** Dec. 29, 1845; rank: 28th.

Tourism. Tourist spending: $76.4 bil. **Attractions:** Big Bend and Guadalupe Mountains Natl. Parks; Fort Davis Natl. Historic Site; Six Flags Over Texas, Arlington; SeaWorld San Antonio, Six Flags Fiesta Texas, The Alamo, San Antonio Missions Natl. Historical Park, San Antonio River Walk, in San Antonio; Natl. Cowgirl Museum and Hall of Fame, Kimbell Art Museum, Ft. Worth Zoo, Bureau of Engraving and Printing, in Ft. Worth; Lyndon B. Johnson Natl. Historical Park, Johnson City; LBJ Presidential Library and Museum, Bullock Texas State History Museum, Austin; George H. W.

Bush Presidential Library and Museum, College Station; Dallas Arboretum and Botanical Garden, Sixth Floor Museum at Dealey Plaza, George W. Bush Presidential Library and Museum, in Dallas; USS *Lexington*, Texas State Aquarium, Padre Island Natl. Seashore, in Corpus Christi. **Information:** Texas Tourism, P.O. Box 141009, Austin, TX 78714; 1-800-452-9292, (512) 486-5876; www.traveltexas.com

History. Humans have lived in the region for at least 12,000 years. Coahuiltecan, Karankawa, Caddo, Jumano, and Tonkawa peoples were in the area when the first Europeans came; later, Apache, Comanche, Cherokee, and Wichita arrived. Early Spanish explorers included Alonso Alvarez de Pineda, who sailed along the Texas coast, 1519; Cabeza de Vaca, shipwrecked near Galveston along with Estevanico, a Moroccan-born enslaved black man, 1528; and Coronado, who crossed the Panhandle, 1541. Spaniards made the first settlement at Ysleta, near El Paso, 1682. Americans moved into the land early in the 19th cent. Mexico, of which Texas was a part, won independence from Spain, 1821. Texans rebelled, 1836, losing to Mexican Gen. Santa Anna at the Alamo but winning decisively under Sam Houston at San Jacinto. With Houston as president, 1836-38 and 1841-44, the Republic of Texas functioned as a nation until admitted to the Union. With an enslaved population of 30%, Texas seceded, 1861; mostly unscathed by the Civil War, it was readmitted, 1870. In 1900 a powerful hurricane lashed Galveston, killing at least 8,000. Cotton and cattle were dominant until 1901, when the Spindletop gusher, near Beaumont, launched the petroleum and petrochemical industries. With wealth and population came political power, notably in the presidencies of Lyndon B. Johnson (1963-69), George H. W. Bush (1989-93), and George W. Bush (2001-09). Amid backlash over police killings of Black men, a Black military veteran in 2016 fatally shot five police officers in Dallas. Hurricane Harvey brought historic rainfall and flooding to Houston and surrounding areas in Aug. 2017, displacing thousands. A shooter killed 26 at a Baptist church in Sutherland Springs in Nov. 2017. A string of bombings, Mar. 2018, unleashed terror in Austin and killed two. A shooter at a Santa Fe (TX) High School killed 10 in May 2018. Mass shootings in El Paso, Aug. 2019, and Odessa, Sept. 2019, killed dozens.

Famous Texans. Lance Armstrong, Stephen F. Austin, Lloyd Bentsen, James Bowie, Drew Brees, Carol Burnett, George H. W. Bush, George W. Bush, Earl Campbell, Joan Crawford, Dwight D. Eisenhower, Morgan Fairchild, Farrah Fawcett, George Foreman, Sam Houston, Howard Hughes, Molly Ivins, Lyndon B. Johnson, Tommy Lee Jones, Janis Joplin, Barbara Jordan, Beyoncé Knowles, Mary Martin, Matthew McConaughey, Chester Nimitz, Sandra Day O'Connor, H. Ross Perot, Katherine Anne Porter, Dan Rather, Sam Rayburn, Ann Richards, Michael Strahan, George Strait, Bob Wills, Babe Didrikson Zaharias.
Website. www.texas.gov

Utah (UT)
Beehive State

People. Population: 3,205,958; rank: 30. **Pop. change** (2010-19): 16.0%. **Pop. density:** 39.0 per sq mi. **Racial distribution:** 90.6% white; 1.5% Black; 2.7% Asian; 1.6% Amer. Ind.; 1.1% Hawaiian/Pacific Islander; 2 or more races, 2.6%. **Hispanic pop.:** 14.4%.

Geography. Total area: 84,897 sq mi; rank: 13. **Land area:** 82,170 sq mi; rank: 12. **Acres forested:** 18.0 mil. **Location:** middle Rocky Mountain state; its SE corner touches Colorado, New Mexico, and Arizona and is the only spot in the U.S. where four states join. **Climate:** arid; ranges from warm desert in SW to alpine in NE. **Topography:** high Colorado Plateau is cut by brilliantly colored canyons of the SE; broad, flat, desertlike Great Basin of the W; the Great Salt Lake and Bonneville Salt Flats to the NW; Middle Rockies in the NE run E-W; valleys and plateaus of the Wasatch Front. **Capital:** Salt Lake City. **Chief airport:** Salt Lake City.

Economy. Chief industries: services, trade, manufacturing, government, transportation, utilities. **Chief manuf. goods:** food, petroleum, nonferrous metal, motor vehicles and parts, aerospace, sporting goods, fabricated metal, computers and electronics. **Chief crops:** hay, greenhouse and nursery, wheat, cherries, onions, apples, barley, peaches, corn. **Farm income:** Crops: $485.59 mil. Livestock: $1.20 bil. **Nonfuel minerals:** $3.3 bil; copper, gold, molybdenum concentrates, salt, sand and gravel (construction). **Gross state product:** $188.5 bil. **Sales tax:** 6.1%. **Gasoline tax:** 49.51 cents/gal. **Employment distrib.:** 16.6% govt.; 19.0% trade/trans./util.; 9.1% mfg.; 13.6% ed./health; 14.5% prof./bus. serv.; 7.4% leisure/hosp.; 6.0% finance; 8.5% constr./mining/log.; 2.6% info.; 2.8% other serv. **Unemployment:** 2.6%. **Min.**

wage/hr.: $7.25. **Per cap. pers. income:** $48,395. **New private housing:** 28,779 units/$6.5 bil. **Broadband internet:** 97.6%. **Commercial banks:** 49; deposits: $506.7 bil. **Savings institutions:** 2; deposits: $68.6 bil.

Federal govt. Fed. civ. employees: 30,365; **avg. salary:** $69,389. **Notable fed. facilities:** Hill AFB; Tooele Army Depot; Army Dugway Proving Ground; NSA Utah Data Ctr.

Education. High school grad. rate: 87.0%. **4-yr. public coll./univ.:** 7; **2-yr. public:** 1; **4-yr. private:** 10.

Energy. Electricity use/cost: 742 kWh, $77.25.

State data. Motto: Industry. **Flower:** Sego lily. **Bird:** (California) sea gull. **Tree:** Blue spruce. **Song:** "Utah, This Is the Place." **Entered union:** Jan. 4, 1896; rank: 45th.

Tourism. Tourist spending: $9.7 bil. **Attractions:** Temple Square (site of Mormon Church headquarters), Salt Lake City; Great Salt Lake; Zion, Canyonlands, Bryce Canyon, Arches, and Capitol Reef Natl. Parks; Dinosaur, Rainbow Bridge, Timpanogos Cave, and Natural Bridges Natl. Monuments; Lake Powell; Flaming Gorge Natl. Recreation Area; Utah Olympic Park, Sundance Film Festival, in Park City. **Information:** Utah Office of Tourism, Council Hall/Capitol Hill, 300 N. State St., Salt Lake City, UT 84114; 1-800-200-1160; visit www.visitutah.com

History. Ute, Gosiute, Southern Paiute, and Navajo peoples lived in the region at the time of European contact. Spanish Franciscans visited the area, 1776; American fur traders followed. Permanent settlement began with the arrival of the Latter-day Saints, or Mormons, 1847, who created a prosperous economy. Organized in 1849, the State of Deseret asked admission to the Union; instead, Congress established Utah Territory, 1850, and appointed Brigham Young governor. The Union Pacific and Central Pacific railroads met near Promontory Point, May 10, 1869, creating the first transcontinental railroad. Statehood was not achieved until 1896, after a long controversy over the Mormon practices of economic isolationism and polygamy (the church renounced the latter in 1890). The 20th cent. brought expansion in mining, defense-related industries, and, more recently, information technologies. More than two-thirds of Utahans are Mormons; the church has its world headquarters in Salt Lake City. Utah experienced 60% population growth, 1990-2010. Environmentalists and tribal groups said they would challenge a Trump administration decision in Dec. 2017 to drastically cut the land area covered by Bears Ears and Grand Staircase-Escalante National Monuments.

Famous Utahans. Maude Adams, Roseanne Barr, Ezra Taft Benson, John Moses Browning, Butch Cassidy, Marriner S. Eccles, Philo T. Farnsworth, David M. Kennedy, J. Willard Marriott, Merlin Olsen, the Osmonds, Ivy Baker Priest, George W. Romney, Wallace Stegner, Brigham Young, Loretta Young.
Website. www.utah.gov

Vermont (VT)
Green Mountain State

People. Population: 623,989; rank: 50. **Pop. change** (2010-19): −0.3%. **Pop. density:** 67.7 per sq mi. **Racial distribution:** 94.2% white; 1.4% Black; 1.9% Asian; 0.4% Amer. Ind.; <0.05% Hawaiian/Pacific Islander; 2 or more races, 2.0%. **Hispanic pop.:** 2.0%.

Geography. Total area: 9,616 sq mi; rank: 45. **Land area:** 9,217 sq mi; rank: 43. **Acres forested:** 4.5 mil. **Location:** northern New England state. **Climate:** temperate, with considerable temperature extremes; heavy snowfall in mountains. **Topography:** Green Mts. N-S backbone 20-36 mi wide; avg. altitude 1,000 ft. **Capital:** Montpelier. **Chief airport:** Burlington.

Economy. Chief industries: manufacturing, tourism, agriculture, trade, finance, insurance, real estate, government. **Chief manuf. goods:** dairy, plastics, printing, wood furniture, sporting goods, metalworking machinery. **Chief crops:** greenhouse and nursery, hay, maple syrup, apples, berries, sweet corn. **Farm income:** Crops: $183.22 mil. Livestock: $549.95 mil. **Nonfuel minerals:** $95 mil; sand and gravel (construction), stone (crushed), stone (dimension), talc (crude). **Gross state product:** $34.8 bil. **Sales tax:** 6.0%. **Gasoline tax:** 49.21 cents/gal. **Employment distrib.:** 20.6% govt.; 17.9% trade/trans./util.; 10.3% mfg.; 22.4% ed./health; 10.1% prof./bus. serv.; 5.3% leisure/hosp.; 4.3% finance; 4.3% constr./mining/log.; 1.5% info.; 3.2% other serv. **Unemployment:** 2.4%. **Min. wage/hr.:** $10.96. **Per cap. pers. income:** $56,691. **New private housing:** 1,801 units/$351.9 mil. **Broadband internet:** 93.9%. **Commercial banks:** 15; deposits: $11.4 bil. **Savings institutions:** 8; deposits: $2.3 bil. **Lottery:** total sales: $139.3 mil; profit: $29.1 mil.

Federal govt. Fed. civ. employees: 3,386; **avg. salary:** $75,213. **Notable fed. facilities:** Law Enforcement Support Ctr., Williston.

Education. High school grad. rate: 85.1%. **4-yr. public coll./univ.:** 4; **2-yr. public:** 1; **4-yr. private:** 16.

Energy. Electricity use/cost: 560 kWh, $100.83.

State data. Motto: Freedom and unity. **Flower:** Red clover. **Bird:** Hermit thrush. **Tree:** Sugar maple. **Song:** "These Green Mountains." **Entered union:** Mar. 4, 1791; rank: 14th.

Tourism. Tourist spending: $2.7 bil. **Attractions:** Shelburne Museum; Shelburne Farms; Vermont Marble Museum, Proctor; Bennington Battle Monument; Pres. Calvin Coolidge Homestead, Plymouth; Ben & Jerry's Factory, Waterbury; Stowe, Killington, and Burke ski resorts: Hildene (Robert Todd Lincoln home), Manchester; Marsh-Billings-Rockefeller Natl. Historical Park, Woodstock. **Information:** Vermont Dept. of Tourism and Marketing, Natl. Life Building, 6th Fl., Montpelier, VT 05620; 1-800-VERMONT, (802) 828-3237; www.vermontvacation.com

History. Inhabited for 10,000 years or more, the region attracted Abenaki and Mahican peoples before Europeans arrived. France's Champlain explored the lake that now bears his name, 1609. The first European settlement was on Isle la Motte in Lake Champlain, 1666. During the American Revolution, Ethan Allen and the Green Mountain Boys captured Ft. Ticonderoga (NY), 1775. Under a constitution that provided for public schools and abolished slavery, settlers declared a republic, 1777. Vermont joined the Union, 1791. Agriculture dominated in the 19th cent. Still mainly rural, the state expanded tourism and manufacturing after World War II, and IBM became the largest private employer. Vermont was the first state to recognize same-sex civil unions (2000) and to enact equal same-sex marriage rights via legislation (2009). Legislation to legalize recreational marijuana went into effect in July 2018.

Famous Vermonters. Ethan Allen, Chester A. Arthur, Calvin Coolidge, Howard Dean, John Deere, George Dewey, John Dewey, Stephen A. Douglas, Dorothy Canfield Fisher, James Fisk, James "Jim" Jeffords, Bernie Sanders, Jody Williams.

Website. www.vermont.gov

Virginia (VA)
Old Dominion

People. Population: 8,535,519; rank: 12. **Pop. change** (2010-19): 6.7%. **Pop. density:** 216.1 per sq mi. **Racial distribution:** 69.4% white; 19.9% Black; 6.9% Asian; 0.5% Amer. Ind.; 0.1% Hawaiian/Pacific Islander; 2 or more races, 3.2%. **Hispanic pop.:** 9.8%.

Geography. Total area: 42,775 sq mi; rank: 35. **Land area:** 39,490 sq mi; rank: 36. **Acres forested:** 16.1 mil. **Location:** South Atlantic state bounded by the Atlantic Ocean on the E and surrounded by North Carolina, Tennessee, Kentucky, West Virginia, and Maryland. **Climate:** mild and equable. **Topography:** mountain and valley region in the W, including the Blue Ridge Mts.; rolling Piedmont Plateau; tidewater, or coastal plain, including the Eastern Shore. **Capital:** Richmond. **Chief airports:** Dulles, Arlington, Highland Springs (Richmond), Norfolk.

Economy. Chief industries: services, trade, government, manufacturing, tourism, agriculture. **Chief manuf. goods:** beverages and tobacco, transportation equip., animal slaughtering and processing, plastics, textiles, paper and paper prods., printing, pharmaceuticals, furniture, chemicals. **Chief crops:** greenhouse and nursery, soybeans, tomatoes, corn, tobacco, hay, cotton, apples, wheat, peanuts, potatoes. **Farm income:** Crops: $1.29 bil. Livestock: $2.23 bil. **Nonfuel minerals:** $1.5 bil; cement (portland), kyanite, lime, sand and gravel (construction), stone (crushed). **Commercial fishing:** $182.2 mil. **Chief ports:** Norfolk Harbor, Newport News, Richmond, Hopewell. **Gross state product:** $554.2 bil. **Sales tax:** 5.3%. **Gasoline tax:** 40.35 cents/gal. **Employment distrib.:** 18.7% govt.; 16.4% trade/trans./util.; 6.2% mfg.; 13.4% ed./health; 20.0% prof./bus. serv.; 7.3% leisure/hosp.; 5.7% finance; 5.7% constr./mining/log.; 1.8% info.; 4.8% other serv. **Unemployment:** 2.8%. **Min. wage/hr.:** $7.25. **Per cap. pers. income:** $60,116. **New private housing:** 32,418 units/$5.8 bil. **Broadband internet:** 97.2%. **Commercial banks:** 115; deposits: $292.3 bil. **Savings institutions:** 6; deposits: $43.0 bil. **Lottery:** total sales: $2.3 bil; profit: $649.7 mil.

Federal govt. Fed. civ. employees: 136,648; **avg. salary:** $96,658. **Notable fed. facilities:** Pentagon; Norfolk Naval Sta., Shipyard, and other Hampton Roads military bases; Ft. Belvoir; Joint Base Langley-Eustis; NASA Langley Res. Ctr.; CIA George Bush Ctr. for Intelligence, Langley; FBI Academy, Quantico USMC Base; Dahlgren Nav. Surface Warfare Ctr. and Lab; USDA Food and Nutrition Serv., Alexandria; U.S. Geological Survey Natl. Ctr., Reston.

Education. High school grad. rate: 87.5%. **4-yr. public coll./univ.:** 17; **2-yr. public:** 24; **4-yr. private:** 40.

Energy. Electricity use/cost: 1,165 kWh, $136.59.

State data. Motto: Sic Semper Tyrannis (Thus always to tyrants). **Flower:** American dogwood. **Bird:** Northern cardinal. **Tree:** American dogwood. **Song emeritus:** "Carry Me Back to Old Virginia." **Tenth** of original 13 states to ratify the Constitution, June 25, 1788.

Tourism. Tourist spending: $26.7 bil. **Attractions:** Colonial Williamsburg, Busch Gardens Williamsburg, Jamestown Settlement, in Williamsburg; Yorktown Victory Ctr.; Wolf Trap Natl. Park for the Performing Arts, near Vienna; Arlington Natl. Cemetery; George Washington's Mount Vernon; Thomas Jefferson's Monticello, Charlottesville; Stratford Hall (Robert E. Lee birthplace); Appomattox Court House Natl. Historical Park; Shenandoah Natl. Park; Blue Ridge Natl. Parkway; Virginia Beach; Kings Dominion amusement park, Doswell. **Information:** Virginia Tourism Corp., 901 E. Cary St., Ste. 900, Richmond, VA 23219; 1-800-VISITVA; www.virginia.org

History. Cherokee and Susquehanna peoples and the Algonquians of the Powhatan Confederacy were in the region when Europeans arrived. English settlers founded Jamestown, 1607. Four of the first five U.S. presidents—Washington, Jefferson, Madison, and Monroe—came from Virginia. The conclusive battle of the American Revolution took place at Yorktown, 1781. The state profited from tobacco, cotton, and the slave trade; in 1860, nearly one-third of the population was enslaved. Virginia seceded from the Union, 1861, and Richmond became the capital of the Confederacy. Western counties, loyal to the Union, split off to become West Virginia, 1863. The war ended with Robert E. Lee's surrender to Ulysses S. Grant at Appomattox, 1865; Virginia was readmitted to the Union, 1870. In the 20th cent., expansion of federal civilian jobs and military facilities transformed the economy. State officials pledged "massive resistance" to racial integration in the mid-1950s but eventually accommodated it. In 1989, L. Douglas Wilder became the first elected Black governor in U.S. history. On Sept. 11, 2001, terrorist hijackers crashed a jet into U.S. defense headquarters at the Pentagon, in Arlington. Seven-term Rep. Eric Cantor became the first House majority leader ever to lose a primary race in 2014. Convicted of murder in state court in Dec. 2018, a driver who steered his car into a crowd of counterprotesters at a 2017 white nationalist rally in Charlottesville pleaded guilty to federal hate crimes charges in Mar. 2019. In 2019, Virginia's top three state officeholders faced calls to resign, over separate blackface and sexual assault scandals.

Famous Virginians. Arthur Ashe, Sandra Bullock, Richard E. Byrd, James B. Cabell, Henry Clay, Katie Couric, Gabby Douglas, Jubal Early, Jerry Falwell, William Henry Harrison, Patrick Henry, A. P. Hill, Thomas Jefferson, Joseph E. Johnston, Robert E. Lee, Meriwether Lewis and William Clark, James Madison, John Marshall, George Mason, James Monroe, Sean Parker, George Pickett, Pocahontas, Edgar Allan Poe, John Randolph, Walter Reed, Rev. Pat Robertson, John Smith, J. E. B. Stuart, William Styron, Zachary Taylor, John Tyler, Maggie Walker, Booker T. Washington, George Washington, L. Douglas Wilder, Woodrow Wilson.

Website. www.virginia.gov

Washington (WA)
Evergreen State

People. Population: 7,614,893; rank: 13. **Pop. change** (2010-19): 13.2%. **Pop. density:** 114.6 per sq mi. **Racial distribution:** 78.5% white; 4.4% Black; 9.6% Asian; 1.9% Amer. Ind.; 0.8% Hawaiian/Pacific Islander; 2 or more races, 4.9%. **Hispanic pop.:** 13.0%.

Geography. Total area: 71,298 sq mi; rank: 18. **Land area:** 66,456 sq mi; rank: 20. **Acres forested:** 22.1 mil. **Location:** Pacific state bordered by Canada on the N, Idaho on the E, Oregon on the S, the Pacific Ocean on the W. **Climate:** mild, dominated by the Pacific Ocean and protected by the Cascades. **Topography:** Olympic Mts. on NW peninsula; open land along coast to Columbia R.; flat terrain of Puget Sound Lowland; high peaks of Cascade Mts. to the E; Columbia Basin in central portion; highlands to the NE; mountains to the SE. **Capital:** Olympia. **Chief airports:** Seattle, Spokane.

Economy. Chief industries: advanced technology, aerospace, biotechnology, intl. trade, forestry, tourism, recycling, agriculture and food processing. **Chief manuf. goods:** aerospace, petroleum, food, paper, milled lumber, plastics, structural metals, computers and electronics. **Chief crops:** apples, potatoes, wheat, hay, cherries, greenhouse and nursery, forest products, pears, grapes, onions, hops, sweet corn, Christmas trees, mint, raspberries. **Farm income:** Crops: $6.99 bil. Livestock: $2.48 bil. **Nonfuel minerals:** $869 mil; cement (portland), diatomite, sand and gravel (construction), stone (crushed), zinc. **Commercial fishing:** $239.9 mil. **Chief ports:** Seattle, Tacoma, Vancouver, Kelso-Longview,

Anacortes. **Gross state product:** $599.6 bil. **Sales tax:** 6.5%. **Gasoline tax:** 67.80 cents/gal. **Employment distrib.:** 18.0% govt.; 19.3% trade/trans./util.; 8.8% mfg.; 14.6% ed./health; 13.6% prof./bus. serv.; 6.3% leisure/hosp.; 5.0% finance; 6.6% constr./mining/log.; 4.6% info.; 3.2% other serv. **Unemployment:** 4.3%. **Min. wage/hr.:** $13.50. **Per cap. pers. income:** $64,898. **New private housing:** 48,424 units/$10.2 bil. **Broadband internet:** 96.9%. **Commercial banks:** 65; deposits: $157.8 bil. **Savings institutions:** 12; deposits: $6.7 bil. **Lottery:** total sales: $803.3 mil; profit: $215.8 mil.

Federal govt. Fed. civ. employees: 55,323; **avg. salary:** $79,327. **Notable fed. facilities:** Bonneville Power Admin.; Lewis-McChord Joint Base; Fairchild AFB; Hanford Site (fmr. nuclear weapons production facility); Naval Base Kitsap (Bremerton and Bangor); Whidbey Island NAS; Pacific Northwest Natl. Lab, Richland.

Education. High school grad. rate: 86.7%. **4-yr. public coll./univ.:** 36; **2-yr. public:** 7; **4-yr. private:** 20.

Energy. Electricity use/cost: 957 kWh, $93.34.

State data. Motto: Alki (By and by). **Flower:** Western rhododendron. **Bird:** Willow goldfinch. **Tree:** Western hemlock. **Song:** "Washington, My Home." **Entered union:** Nov. 11, 1889; rank: 42nd.

Tourism. Tourist spending: $20.3 bil. **Attractions:** Seattle Center, Space Needle, EMP Museum, Museum of Flight, Pike Place Market, Underground Tour, in Seattle; Mount Rainier, Olympic, and North Cascades Natl. Parks; Mount St. Helens Natl. Volcanic Monument; Puget Sound; San Juan Islands; Grand Coulee Dam; Columbia R. Gorge Natl. Scenic Area; Riverfront Park, Spokane; Snoqualmie Falls. **Information:** Washington Tourism Alliance, 506 2nd Ave., 30th Fl., P.O. Box 953, Seattle, WA 98104; 1-800-544-1800; www.experiencewa.com

History. People of the Clovis culture lived in the region 11,000 years ago. At the time of European contact, Native Americans in the area included Nez Percé, Spokane, Yakima, Cayuse, Okanogan, Walla Walla, and Colville peoples in the interior, and Nooksak, Chinook, Nisqually, Clallam, Makah, Quinault, and Puyallup peoples along the coast. Spain's Bruno de Heceta sailed the coast, 1775. In 1792, British naval officer George Vancouver mapped the Puget Sound area, and American Capt. Robert Gray sailed up the Columbia R. Fur traders and missionaries arrived in the first half of the 19th cent. Final agreement on the border of Washington and Canada was made with Britain, 1846. Completion in 1883 of a transcontinental rail link between Puget Sound and the eastern U.S. aided immigration, and Washington became a state in 1889. In the 20th cent., cheap hydroelectric power spurred growth in the aluminum and aircraft industries. Founded in 1975, Microsoft became a computer software giant. Mount St. Helens erupted, 1980. With Starbucks coffee and Amazon.com, Seattle became a national trendsetter in the 1990s. Violent street protests disrupted a World Trade Organization meeting there in 1999. Gary Locke, in office 1997-2005, was the first U.S. governor of Chinese ancestry. A mudslide in Mar. 2014 killed 43 people in a rural area north of Seattle.

Famous Washingtonians. Paul Allen, Glenn Beck, Raymond Carver, Kurt Cobain, Bing Crosby, William O. Douglas, Bill Gates, Jimi Hendrix, Henry M. Jackson, Gary Larson, Mary McCarthy, Robert Motherwell, Edward R. Murrow, Apolo Ohno, Chris Pratt, Theodore Roethke, Ann Rule, Hope Solo, Hilary Swank, Julia Sweeney, Adam West, Marcus Whitman, Minoru Yamasaki.

Website. access.wa.gov

West Virginia (WV)
Mountain State

People. Population: 1,792,147; rank: 38. **Pop. change** (2010-19): -3.3%. **Pop. density:** 74.6 per sq mi. **Racial distribution:** 93.5% white; 3.6% Black; 0.8% Asian; 0.3% Amer. Ind.; <0.05% Hawaiian/Pacific Islander; 2 or more races, 1.8%. **Hispanic pop.:** 1.7%.

Geography. Total area: 24,230 sq mi; rank: 41. **Land area:** 24,038 sq mi; rank: 41. **Acres forested:** 12.0 mil. **Location:** South Atlantic state bounded on the N by Pennsylvania, Maryland; on the S, W, and NW by Virginia, Kentucky, Ohio; on the E by Maryland and Virginia. **Climate:** humid continental except for marine modification in the lower panhandle. **Topography:** hilly to mountainous; Allegheny Plateau in the W covers two-thirds of state; mountains here are the highest in the state, over 4,000 ft. **Capital:** Charleston.

Economy. Chief industries: manufacturing, services, mining, tourism. **Chief manuf. goods:** chemicals, aluminum, motor vehicle parts, lumber and plywood, primary and fabricated metals. **Chief crops:** hay, apples, corn, peaches, soybeans, tobacco, wheat. **Farm income:** Crops: $161.11 mil. Livestock: $523.49 mil. **Nonfuel minerals:** $332 mil; cement

(masonry and portland), lime, sand and gravel (industrial), stone (crushed). **Chief port:** Huntington. **Gross state product:** $78.2 bil. **Sales tax:** 6.0%. **Gasoline tax:** 54.10 cents/gal. **Employment distrib.:** 22.5% govt.; 17.8% trade/trans./util.; 7.1% mfg.; 18.7% ed./health; 9.8% prof./bus. serv.; 7.0% leisure/hosp.; 4.3% finance; 8.3% constr./mining/log.; 1.1% info.; 3.3% other serv. **Unemployment:** 4.9%. **Min. wage/hr.:** $8.75. **Per cap. pers. income:** $42,336. **New private housing:** 3,010 units/$500.1 mil. **Broadband internet:** 97.4%. **Commercial banks:** 67; deposits: $33.4 bil. **Savings institutions:** 4; deposits: $799.0 mil. **Lottery:** total sales: $1.2 bil; profit: $495.1 mil.

Federal govt. Fed. civ. employees: 15,285; **avg. salary:** $76,869. **Notable fed. facilities:** Natl. Radio Astronomy Observatory, Green Bank; Bureau of the Fiscal Service Bldg.; Alderson Fed. Prison Camp; FBI Criminal Justice Information Services.

Education. High school grad. rate: 90.2%. **4-yr. public coll./univ.:** 13; **2-yr. public:** 9; **4-yr. private:** 10.

Energy. Electricity use/cost: 1,133 kWh, $126.70.

State data. Motto: Montani Semper Liberi (Mountaineers are always free). **Flower:** Big rhododendron. **Bird:** Cardinal. **Tree:** Sugar maple. **Songs:** "The West Virginia Hills"; "This Is My West Virginia"; "West Virginia, My Home, Sweet Home." **Entered union:** June 20, 1863; rank: 35th.

Tourism. Tourist spending: $4.3 bil. **Attractions:** Harpers Ferry Natl. Historical Park, Appalachian Trail Conservancy and Visitor Ctr., in Harpers Ferry; Clay Center for the Arts and Sciences and Avampato Discovery Museum, Charleston; The Greenbrier resort, White Sulphur Springs; Berkeley Springs State Park; Seneca Rocks State Park; New River Gorge Natl. River; Beckley Exhibition Coal Mine; Monongahela Natl. Forest; Fenton Art Glass Company, Williamstown; Mountain State Forest Festival, Elkins; Mountain State Art & Craft Fair, Ripley; Green Bank Telescope (world's largest fully steerable radio telescope); Cass Scenic Railroad State Park. **Information:** West Virginia Tourism Office, Bldg. 3, Ste. 100, State Capitol Complex, 1900 Kanawha Blvd. East, Charleston, WV 25305; 1-800-CALLWVA; wvtourism.com

History. Sparsely inhabited at the time of European contact, the area was primarily Native American hunting grounds. British explorers Thomas Batts and Robert Fallam reached the New R., 1671. Coal, discovered in 1742, was mined extensively by the mid-19th cent. White settlement led to conflicts with Native Americans, including a major battle in which settlers defeated an Indian confederacy at Point Pleasant, 1774. The region joined the Union as part of Virginia, 1788. Longstanding tensions between the E and W parts of the state came to a head in 1861, when Virginia seceded. Delegates of western counties, meeting at Wheeling, repudiated the act and created a new state, Kanawha, later renamed West Virginia, which was admitted to the Union in 1863. Poverty has been a problem for much of the state's subsequent history. It continued to rank low in per capita personal income, despite billions of dollars in federal contracts brought to the state by nine-term U.S. Sen. Robert Byrd, who passed away in 2010. Coal mining, though dangerous and challenged by environmental concerns, continues to be a major industry; nearly 30 miners were killed in a mine explosion in 2010. Flash flooding across the state killed at least 23 people in late June 2016. A statewide teacher walkout in Apr. 2018 demanded increased pay and school funding.

Famous West Virginians. George Brett, Pearl S. Buck, Robert C. Byrd, Henry Louis Gates Jr., Stonewall Jackson, Don Knotts, Michael Joseph Owens, Brad Paisley, Mary Lou Retton, Walter Reuther, Cyrus Vance, Jerry West, Charles "Chuck" Yeager.

Website. www.wv.gov

Wisconsin (WI)
Badger State

People. Population: 5,822,434; rank: 20. **Pop. change** (2010-19): 2.4%. **Pop. density:** 107.5 per sq mi. **Racial distribution:** 87.0% white; 6.7% Black; 3.0% Asian; 1.2% Amer. Ind.; 0.1% Hawaiian/Pacific Islander; 2 or more races, 2.0%. **Hispanic pop.:** 7.1%.

Geography. Total area: 65,496 sq mi; rank: 23. **Land area:** 54,158 sq mi; rank: 25. **Acres forested:** 17.0 mil. **Location:** East North Central state bounded on the N by Lake Superior and Upper Michigan, on the E by Lake Michigan, on the S by Illinois, on the W by the St. Croix and Mississippi Rivers. **Climate:** long, cold winters and short, warm summers tempered by the Great Lakes. **Topography:** narrow Lake Superior Lowland plain met by Northern Highland, which slopes gently to the sandy crescent Central Plain; Western Upland in the SW; three broad parallel limestone ridges running N-S are separated by wide and shallow lowlands in the SE. **Capital:** Madison. **Chief airports:** Milwaukee, Madison.

Economy. Chief industries: services, manufacturing, trade, government, agriculture, tourism. **Chief manuf. goods:** transportation, dairy, animal slaughtering and processing, paper, printing, plastics, computers and electronics. **Chief crops:** corn, greenhouse and nursery, soybeans, potatoes, cranberries, hay, wheat, snap beans, apples, peas. **Farm income:** Crops: $3.62 bil. Livestock: $7.34 bil. **Nonfuel minerals:** $2.0 bil; lime, sand and gravel (construction), sand and gravel (industrial), stone (crushed), stone (dimension). **Commercial fishing:** $2.9 mil. **Chief ports:** Superior, Milwaukee, Green Bay. **Gross state product:** $347.3 bil. **Sales tax:** 5.0%. **Gasoline tax:** 51.30 cents/gal. **Employment distrib.:** 13.9% govt.; 18.6% trade/trans./util.; 17.4% mfg.; 16.2% ed./health; 11.1% prof./bus. serv.; 5.9% leisure/hosp.; 5.8% finance; 4.8% constr./mining/log.; 1.5% info.; 4.7% other serv. **Unemployment:** 3.3%. **Min. wage/hr.:** $7.25. **Per cap. pers. income:** $53,583. **New private housing:** 17,480 units/$4.0 bil. **Broadband internet:** 95.9%. **Commercial banks:** 199; deposits: $143.3 bil. **Savings institutions:** 26; deposits: $7.9 bil. **Lottery:** total sales: $713.1 mil; profit: $235.3 mil.

Federal govt. Fed. civ. employees: 15,878; **avg. salary:** $71,459. **Notable fed. facilities:** Ft. McCoy; USDA Forest Products Lab, Madison.

Education. High school grad. rate: 89.7%. **4-yr. public coll./univ.:** 17; **2-yr. public:** 17; **4-yr. private:** 34.

Energy. Electricity use/cost: 693 kWh, $97.09.

State data. Motto: Forward. **Flower:** Wood violet. **Bird:** American robin. **Tree:** Sugar maple. **Song:** "On, Wisconsin!" **Entered union:** May 29, 1848; rank: 30th.

Tourism. Tourist spending: $12.5 bil. **Attractions:** Wade House, Greenbush; Villa Louis, Prairie du Chien; Circus World Museum, Baraboo; Wisconsin Dells; Old World Wisconsin, Eagle; shoreline and state parks of Door County; Chequamegon-Nicolet Natl. Forest; House on the Rock, Taliesin, in Spring Green; Monona Terrace Community and Convention Ctr., Madison; Milwaukee Art Museum, Pabst Mansion, in Milwaukee. **Information:** Wisconsin Dept. of Tourism, 201 W. Washington Ave., P.O. Box 8690, Madison, WI 53703; 1-800-432-TRIP; www.travelwisconsin.com

History. At the time of European contact, Ojibwa, Menominee, Winnebago, Kickapoo, Sauk, Fox, and Potawatomi peoples inhabited the area. French explorer Jean Nicolet reached Green Bay, 1634; French missionaries and fur traders followed. The British took over, 1763. The U.S. won the land after the American Revolution but did not wield control until forts were established at Green Bay and Prairie du Chien, 1816. Native Americans rebelled against the seizure of tribal lands in the Black Hawk War, 1832, but were defeated and relocated to reservations. Wisconsin became a territory, 1836, and a state, 1848. Some 96,000 soldiers served the Union cause during the Civil War. Many immigrants arrived from Germany, Poland, and Scandinavia. Wisconsin agriculture focused on dairy; Milwaukee became a manufacturing center. As governor, 1901-06, Robert La Follette pushed Progressive reforms such as direct primary voting and consumer protection laws. The era of McCarthyism ended when anti-Communist crusader U.S. Sen. Joseph McCarthy of Wisconsin was censured by the Senate, 1954. The state legislature passed controversial measures in 2011 to restrict collective bargaining by some 170,000 public-sector employees and in 2014 became the 25th state to pass a "right-to-work" law. The state offered Taiwan-based tech giant Foxconn a package of subsidies and tax incentives est. in 2017 at $3-$4.5 bil to build a new manufacturing hub in Racine County; the project had changed in scale and scope, and in the number of jobs Foxconn pledged to create, by 2019. The state supreme court in Apr. 2020 blocked a governor's order to halt in-person presidential primary voting amid the coronavirus pandemic, and in May struck down the state's stay-at-home order.

Famous Wisconsinites. Don Ameche, Carrie Chapman Catt, Willem Dafoe, Edna Ferber, Hamlin Garland, King Camp Gillette, Harry Houdini, Robert La Follette, (Vladzio Valentino) Liberace, Alfred Lunt, Pat O'Brien, Georgia O'Keeffe, Danica Patrick, Les Paul, William H. Rehnquist, John Ringling, Donald K. "Deke" Slayton, Spencer Tracy, Orson Welles, Laura Ingalls Wilder, Thornton Wilder, Frank Lloyd Wright. **Website.** www.wisconsin.gov

Wyoming (WY)
Equality State, Cowboy State

People. Population: 578,759; rank: 51. **Pop. change** (2010-19): 2.7%. **Pop. density:** 6.0 per sq mi. **Racial distribution:** 92.5% white; 1.3% Black; 1.1% Asian; 2.7% Amer. Ind.; 0.1% Hawaiian/Pacific Islander; 2 or more races, 2.2%. **Hispanic pop.:** 10.1%.

Geography. Total area: 97,813 sq mi; rank: 10. **Land area:** 97,093 sq mi; rank: 9. **Acres forested:** 10.5 mil. **Location:** Mountain state in the high western plateaus of the Great Plains. **Climate:** semidesert conditions throughout; true desert in the Bighorn and Great Divide Basins. **Topography:** eastern Great Plains rise to the foothills of the Rocky Mts.; the Continental Divide crosses the state from the NW to the SE. **Capital:** Cheyenne.

Economy. Chief industries: mineral extraction, oil, natural gas, tourism and recreation, agriculture. **Chief manuf. goods:** petroleum, chemicals, fabricated metal, beet sugar, lumber. **Chief crops:** hay, sugar beets, barley, dry beans, wheat, corn, greenhouse and nursery, oats. **Farm income:** Crops: $394.45 mil. Livestock: $1.15 bil. **Nonfuel minerals:** $2.6 bil; cement (portland), clay (bentonite), helium (Grade-A), sand and gravel (construction), soda ash. **Gross state product:** $39.6 bil. **Sales tax:** 4.0%. **Gasoline tax:** 42.40 cents/gal. **Employment distrib.:** 25.1% govt.; 19.1% trade/trans./util.; 3.8% mfg.; 10.4% ed./health; 6.7% prof./bus. serv.; 9.8% leisure/hosp.; 4.0% finance; 14.7% constr./mining/log.; 1.1% info.; 5.2% other serv. **Unemployment:** 3.6%. **Min. wage/hr.:** $7.25. **Per cap. pers. income:** $63,316. **New private housing:** 1,708 units/$541.0 mil. **Broadband internet:** 94.0%. **Commercial banks:** 45; deposits: $15.6 bil. **Savings institutions:** 2; deposits: $496.0 mil. **Lottery:** total sales: $36.9 mil; profit: $6.6 mil.

Federal govt. Fed. civ. employees: 6,569; **avg. salary:** $62,861. **Notable fed. facilities:** Warren AFB.

Education. High school grad. rate: 81.7%. **4-yr. public coll./univ.:** 1; **2-yr. public:** 7; **4-yr. private:** 0.

Energy. Electricity use/cost: 841 kWh, $94.90.

State data. Motto: Equal rights. **Flower:** Indian paintbrush. **Bird:** Western meadowlark. **Tree:** Plains cottonwood. **Song:** "Wyoming." **Entered union:** July 10, 1890; rank: 44th.

Tourism. Tourist spending: $3.7 bil. **Attractions:** Yellowstone Natl. Park (est. 1872, first U.S. national park); Grand Teton Natl. Park; Natl. Elk Refuge, Jackson; Devils Tower Natl. Monument; Ft. Laramie Natl. Historic Site; Oregon Trail ruts, Guernsey; Buffalo Bill Historical Ctr., Cody; Cheyenne Frontier Days. **Information:** Wyoming Office of Tourism, 5611 High Plains Rd., Cheyenne, WY 82007; 1-800-225-5996; www.travelwyoming.com

History. Inhabited for at least 12,000 years, the region supported Shoshone, Crow, Cheyenne, Oglala Sioux, and Arapaho peoples when Europeans arrived. France's Vérendrye brothers were the first Europeans to see the region, 1742-43. John Colter, an American, traversed the Yellowstone area, 1807-08. Trappers and fur traders followed in the 1820s. Forts Laramie and Bridger became important stops on trails to the West Coast. Population grew after the Union Pacific railroad crossed the state, 1867-68. Wyoming became a territory, 1868, and the first to extend full voting rights to women, 1869. Statehood was attained, 1890. Disputes between large landowners and small ranchers culminated in the Johnson County Cattle War, 1892; federal troops were called in to restore order. Nellie Tayloe Ross was the first woman governor to take office in the U.S., 1925. Wyoming, the least populous state, has relied on the energy, tourism, and ranching industries in recent decades. Dick Cheney, Wyoming's representative in the U.S. House, 1979-89, served as U.S. vice pres. (2001-09).

Famous Wyomingites. James Bridger, Dick Cheney, William F. "Buffalo Bill" Cody, Curt Gowdy, Esther Hobart Morris, Nellie Tayloe Ross.
Website. www.wyoming.gov

District of Columbia (DC)

People. Population: 705,749; rank: 49. **Pop. change** (2010-19): 17.3%. **Pop. density:** 11,569.7 per sq mi. **Racial distribution:** 46.0% white; 46.0% Black; 4.5% Asian; 0.6% Amer. Ind.; 0.1% Hawaiian/Pacific Islander; 2 or more races, 2.9%. **Hispanic pop.:** 11.3%.

Geography. Total area: 68 sq mi; rank: 51. **Land area:** 61 sq mi; rank: 51. **Acres forested:** N/A. **Location:** at the confluence of the Potomac and Anacostia Rivers, flanked by Maryland on the N, E, and SE and by Virginia on the SW. **Climate:** hot humid summers, mild winters. **Topography:** low hills rise toward the N away from the Potomac R. and slope to the S; highest elevation, 409 ft; lowest on Potomac R., 1 ft.

Economy. Chief industries: government, legal, publishing, medical, service, tourism. **Gross state product:** $146.2 bil. **Sales tax:** 6.0%. **Gasoline tax:** 41.90 cents/gal. **Employment distrib.:** 32.8% govt.; 4.1% trade/trans./util.; 0.2% mfg.; 16.4% ed./health; 22.7% prof./bus. serv.; 4.7% leisure/hosp.; 4.0% finance; 1.9% constr./mining/log.; 2.5% info.; 9.4% other serv. **Unemployment:** 5.5%. **Min. wage/hr.:** $15.00. **Per cap. pers. income:** $84,538. **New private housing:** 5,945 units/$680.5 mil. **Broadband internet:** 98.0%. **Commercial banks:** 29; deposits: $53.3 bil. **Savings institutions:** 1; deposits: $37.0 mil. **Lottery:** total sales: $213.1 mil; profit: $44.5 mil.

Federal govt. Fed. civ. employees: 141,995; **avg. salary:** $122,028.

Education. High school grad. rate: 68.5%. **4-yr. public coll./univ.:** 2; **2-yr. public:** 0; **4-yr. private:** 12.

Energy. Electricity use/cost: 787 kWh, $101.01.

District data. Motto: Justitia omnibus (Justice for all). **Flower:** American beauty rose. **Bird:** Wood thrush. **Tree:** Scarlet oak.

Tourism. Tourist spending: $13.6 bil. **Attractions:** See Attractions in and around Washington, DC, pp. 467-68. **Information:** Destination DC, 901 7th St. NW, 4th Fl., Washington, DC, 20001-3719; 1-800-422-8644; www.washington.org

History. The District of Columbia, coextensive with the city of Washington, is the seat of the U.S. federal government. It lies on the west central edge of Maryland on the Potomac R., opposite Virginia. The Piscataway, an Algonquian-speaking people, were living in the region when Europeans arrived in the 17th cent. Proposals for a "federal town" for the deliberations of the Continental Congress were made in 1783. Authorized by Congress, 1790, Pres. George Washington chose the Potomac site and persuaded landowners to sell their holdings to the government. Its area was originally 100 sq mi taken from the sovereignty of Maryland and Virginia. Virginia's portion south of the Potomac was given back to that state in 1846.

Pres. Washington chose Pierre Charles L'Enfant, a Frenchman, to plan the capital. Surveyor Andrew Ellicott finished the official map and design of the city, assisted by Benjamin Banneker, a Black architect and astronomer. Washington laid the cornerstone of the north wing of the Capitol building, 1793, and Pres. John Adams moved to the new national capital,

1800. The City of Washington was incorporated, 1802. British troops invaded, 1814, setting fire to the Capitol, the President's House (as the White House was then called), and other buildings. Pres. Abraham Lincoln ended slavery in the district, 1862. Many African Americans arrived after the Civil War, but racial segregation remained legal until the mid-20th cent. After federal government expansion spurred population growth, 1930-50, an exodus to the suburbs shrank the city's population, 1950-2005.

The 23rd Amendment (1961) granted residents the right to vote for president and vice president. Congress, which has legislative authority over the District under the Constitution, approved legislation in 1970 giving the District one delegate to the House of Representatives, who could vote in committee but not on the floor. Voters approved, 1974, a congressionally drafted charter giving them the right to elect their own mayor and city council. The district won the right to levy taxes, but Congress retained power to veto council actions and approve the city budget. Security measures were dramatically increased after terrorists attacked the U.S. on Sept. 11, 2001. After a 34-year absence, major league baseball returned to the city in 2005. Former Washington Catholic archbishop Theodore McCarrick was expelled from the priesthood by Pope Francis in Feb. 2019 after McCarrick was found guilty of sex abuse-related charges.

Famous Washingtonians. Edward Albee, Michael Chabon, Frederick Douglass, John Foster Dulles, Kevin Durant, Edward Kennedy, Duke Ellington, Marvin Gaye, Katharine Graham, Goldie Hawn, Taraji P. Henson, J. Edgar Hoover, Bill Nye, Pete Sampras, John Philip Sousa.

Website. www.dc.gov

OUTLYING U.S. AREAS

American Samoa (AS)

People. Population: 49,437. **Pop. change** (2010-20): –11.0%. **Pop. density:** 650.5 per sq mi. **Racial distribution** (2010): 92.6% Hawaiian/Pacific Islander; 3.6% Asian; 1.2% other; 2 or more races, 2.7%. **Languages:** Samoan, English, Tongan.

Geography. Total area: 581 sq mi. **Land area:** 76 sq mi. **Acres forested:** 39,156. **Location:** most southerly of all lands under U.S. sovereignty, about 2,300 mi SW of Honolulu. It is an unincorporated territory consisting of seven islands: Samoan group: **Tutuila** (52.59 sq mi), **Aunu'u** (0.59 sq mi); Manu'a group: **Ta'u** (17.57 sq mi), **Olosega** (2.03 sq mi), **Ofu** (2.83 sq mi); and the atolls **Rose** (0.03 sq mi) and **Swains** (1.38 sq mi). **Climate:** marine tropical, avg. temp 82°F with little seasonal variation; avg. annual rainfall about 36 in. **Topography:** volcanic islands, rugged peaks, and limited coastal plains. About 70% of the land is bush and mountains. **Capital:** Pago Pago, on Tutuila. **Airport:** Pago Pago.

Economy. Chief industries: tuna fishing and processing, trade, services, tourism. **Chief crops:** giant taro, taro, yams, coconuts, breadfruits, bananas, papayas. **Livestock** (2008): 35,709 chickens, 16,904 hogs/pigs. **Nonfuel minerals:** crushed stone, trap rock. **Commercial fishing** (2008): $9.7 mil. **Unemployment** (2010): 9.2%. **Min. wage/hr.:** $4.98-$6.39. **Gross domestic product** (2018 est.): $636.0 mil. **Broadband internet** (Dec. 2013): 96.8%. **Commercial banks:** 2 deposits: $166.0 mil.

Fed. govt. Fed. civ. employees: 103; **avg. salary:** $60,482.

Education. 4-yr. public coll./univ.: 1; **4-yr. public coll./ univ.:** 1; **2-yr. public:** 0; **4-yr. private:** 0.

Energy. Total electricity production (2016 est.): 169 mil kWh.

Misc. data. Motto: Samoa Muamua le Atua (In Samoa, God is first). **Flower:** Paogo (Ula-fala). **Plant:** Ava. **Song:** "Amerika Samoa."

Tourism. Attractions: Natl. Park of American Samoa; Natl. Marine Sanctuary of American Samoa; Jean P. Haydon Museum. **Information:** American Samoa Visitors Bureau, Ground Fl., Fagatogo Sq., Route 001, Fagatogo, AS 96799; (684) 633-9805; www.americansamoa.travel

History. A tripartite agreement between Great Britain, Germany, and the U.S. in 1899 gave the U.S. sovereignty over the eastern islands of the Samoan group; these islands became American Samoa. Local chiefs ceded Tutuila and Aunu'u to the U.S. in 1900 and the Manu'a group and Rose Island in 1904; Swains Island was annexed in 1925. Samoa (Western), comprising the larger islands of the Samoan group, was a New Zealand mandate and UN Trusteeship until it became independent Jan. 1, 1962 (now called Samoa).

From 1900 to 1951, American Samoa was under the jurisdiction of the U.S. Navy. Since 1951, it has been under the Interior Dept. On Jan. 3, 1978, the first popularly elected Samoan governor and lieutenant governor were inaugurated. Previously, the governor was appointed by the Sec. of the

Interior. American Samoa has a bicameral legislature and elects a delegate to the U.S. House of Representatives who has a voice but no vote, except in committees.

Five of the seven islands are volcanoes. Scientists discovered a rapidly growing volcano, Vailulu'u, between Ta'u and Rose in 1975.

The tuna canning industry has been the backbone of the economy since the 1950s, but one of two canneries closed in 2009, and a third cannery closed in 2016 after opening the year before. An 8.1 magnitude earthquake in Sept. 2009 triggered a tsunami that severely damaged Tutuila.

American Samoans are of Polynesian origin. They are nationals of the U.S. As of 2010, 109,637 lived in the U.S., including 18,287 in Hawaii and 40,100 in California.

Website. www.americansamoa.gov

Guam (GU)

People. Population: 168,485. **Pop change** (2010-20): 5.7%. **Pop. density:** 802.3 per sq mi. **Racial/ethnic distribution** (2010 est.): 37.3% Chamorro; 26.3% Filipino; 12.0% other Pac. Isl.; 7.1% white. **Languages:** English, Chamorro, Philippine/other Pacific Island languages.

Geography. Total area: 571 sq mi. **Land area:** 210 sq mi. **Acres forested:** 69,851. **Location:** largest and southernmost of the Mariana Islands in the West Pacific, 3,700 mi W of Hawaii. **Climate:** tropical, with temperatures from 70° to 90°F; rainy July to Nov., avg. annual rainfall about 80-100 in. **Topography:** coralline limestone plateau in the N; southern chain of low volcanic mountains slope gently to the W, more steeply to coastal cliffs on the E; general elevation, 500 ft; highest point, Mt. Lamlam, 1,332 ft. **Capital:** Hagåtña. **Chief airport:** Tamuning.

Economy. Chief industries: U.S. military, tourism, construction, shipping, concrete prods., printing and publishing. **Chief manuf. goods:** textiles, foods. **Chief crops:** watermelons, cucumbers, eggplant, long beans, bananas, corn. **Livestock** (2007): 533 chickens, 112 cattle, 635 hogs/pigs, 124 goats. **Nonfuel minerals** (2008): $3.8 mil; crushed stone. **Commercial fishing** (2008): $499,095. **Chief port:** Apra Harbor. **Gross domestic product** (2018 est.): $5.9 bil. **Employment distrib.** (Mar. 2019): 29.7% serv.; 23.5% govt.; 19.8% trade; 10.4% constr.; 6.7% trans.; 3.9% insur./ real estate/finance; 2.1% mfg.; 0.6% agric. **Unemployment** (Sept. 2019): 3.6%. **Min. wage/hr.:** $8.25. **Per capita income** (2016): $31,961. **Broadband internet** (Dec. 2013): 99.2%. **Commercial banks:** 4; deposits: $2.9 bil. **Savings institutions:** 1; deposits: $89.0 mil.

Federal govt. Fed. civ. employees: 2,534; **avg. salary:** $68,052. **Notable fed. facilities:** Andersen AFB.

Education. 4-yr. public coll./univ.: 1; **2-yr. public:** 1; **4-yr. private:** 1.

Energy. Total electricity production (2016 est.): 1.7 bil kWh.

Misc. data. Motto: Where America's day begins. **Flower:** Puti Tai Nobio (Bougainvillea). **Bird:** Ko'ko (Guam rail). **Tree:** Ifit (Intsia bijuga). **Song:** "Stand Ye Guamanians."

Tourism. Attractions: Ritidian Point, Guam Natl. Wildlife Refuge; War in the Pacific Natl. Historical Park; Chamorro Village; Two Lovers Point. **Information:** Guam Visitors Bureau, 401 Pale San Vitores Rd., Tumon, Guam 96913; (671) 646-5278; www.visitguam.com

History. Guam was probably settled by voyagers from the Indonesian-Philippine archipelago by 3rd cent. BCE. Pottery, rice cultivation, and megalithic technology show strong East Asian cultural influence. Centralized, village clan-based communities engaged in agriculture and offshore fishing. The estimated population by the early 16th cent. was 50,000-75,000. Portuguese explorer Ferdinand Magellan, sailing for Spain, arrived in the Marianas Mar. 6, 1521. They were colonized in 1668 by Spanish missionaries, who named them the Mariana Islands in honor of Maria Anna, queen of Spain. When Spain ceded Guam to the U.S., it sold the other Marianas to Germany. Japan obtained a League of Nations mandate over the German islands in 1919; in Dec. 1941 it seized Guam, which was retaken by the U.S. in July-Aug. 1944.

Guam is a self-governing organized unincorporated U.S. territory. The Organic Act of 1950 provided for a governor, elected to a four-year term, and a 21-member unicameral legislature, elected biennially by the residents, who are American citizens. In 1970, the first governor was elected. In 1972, a U.S. law gave Guam one U.S. House delegate, who has a voice but no vote except in committees.

Guam's quest to change its status to a U.S. commonwealth began in the late 1970s. The Guam Commission on Self-Determination, created in 1984, developed a draft Commonwealth Act. In 1993, legislation proposing a change of status was submitted to the U.S. Congress. In 1994, the U.S. Congress passed legislation transferring 3,200 acres of land on Guam from federal to local control. The Navy approved in 2015 a plan to move 5,000 Marines stationed in Okinawa, Japan, to Guam by 2021. North Korea in Aug. 2017 threatened to target Guam in the wake of new UN sanctions and increasingly heated rhetoric from Pres. Trump.

Website. www.guam.gov

Commonwealth of the Northern Mariana Islands (MP)

People. Population: 51,433. **Pop. change** (2010-20): -4.5%. **Pop. density:** 282.6 per sq mi. **Racial/ethnic distribution** (2010 est.): 50.0% Asian; 34.9% Hawaiian/Pacific Islander; 2.5% other; 2 or more races/ethnicities, 12.7%. **Languages:** Philippine languages, Chinese, Chamorro (official), English (official), other Pacific Island languages.

Geography. Total area: 1,976 sq mi. **Land area:** 182 sq mi. **Acres forested:** 60,207. **Location:** between Guam and the Tropic of Cancer, the 14 islands of the Northern Marianas form a 300-mi-long archipelago. Indigenous population is concentrated on the three largest of the six inhabited islands: **Saipan,** the seat of government and commerce, **Rota,** and **Tinian.** **Climate:** tropical, with avg. temperature around 82°F, moderated by NE trade winds; avg. annual rainfall 80-100 in. **Topography:** limestone southern islands with even terraces, coral reefs; volcanic northern isles. **Capital:** Saipan. **Airport:** Saipan.

Economy. Chief industries: banking, construction, fishing, mining, tourism, apparel manufacturing, retail. **Chief manuf. goods:** apparel, stone, clay and glass prods. **Chief crops:** bananas, cucumbers, sweet potatoes, taro, watermelons. **Livestock** (2007): 9,700 chickens, 1,395 cattle, 1,483 hogs/pigs. **Commercial fishing** (2010 est.): $608,971. **Chief port:** Saipan. **Gross domestic product** (2018): $1.3 bil. **Employment distrib.:** 1.9% agriculture; 10.0% industry; 88.1% serv. **Unemployment** (2016): 13.8%. **Min. wage/hr.:** $7.25. **Per capita income** (2016): $20,968. **Broadband internet** (Dec. 2013): 80.9%. **Commercial banks:** 3; deposits: $883.0 mil. **Savings institutions:** 1; deposits: $8.0 mil.

Federal govt. Fed. civ. employees: 77; **avg. salary:** $59,767.

Education. 4-yr. public coll./univ.: 1; **2-yr. public:** 0; **4-yr. private:** 0.

Energy. Total electricity production (2009): 60,600 kWh.

Misc. data. Flower: Plumeria. **Bird:** Mariana fruit-dove. **Tree:** Flame tree. **Song:** "Gi Talo Gi Halom Tasi" (In the Middle of the Sea).

Tourism. Attractions: House of Taga; American Memorial Park; Banzai Cliff. **Information:** Marianas Visitors Authority, P.O. Box 500861, Saipan, MP 96950; (670) 664-3200; www.mymarianas.com

History. The people of the Northern Marianas are predominantly of Chamorro cultural extraction, although Carolinians and immigrants from other areas of E. Asia and Micronesia have also settled in the islands. English is among the several languages commonly spoken.

The German-controlled Northern Marianas were placed under Japanese control by a League of Nations mandate after World War I. The U.S. captured the islands during World War II. From July 18, 1947, the U.S. administered the Northern Marianas under a trusteeship agreement with the UN Security Council. In 1975, the residents voted to become a U.S. commonwealth.

The Northern Mariana Islands has been self-governing since 1978, when a constitution drafted and adopted by the people became effective and a popularly elected bicameral legislature (two-year term), with offices of governor (four-year term) and lieut. governor, was inaugurated. Pres. Ronald Reagan proclaimed the Northern Marianas a commonwealth, 1986, and the UN formally ended its trusteeship, 1990. In 2008, U.S. law gave the islands one delegate to the U.S. House of Representatives who has a voice but no vote, except in committees.

Under the 1976 Commonwealth Covenant with the U.S., the islands are exempt from federal immigration and import laws, and minimum wage is lower than on the mainland. The garment-making industry, which has since boomed, has drawn accusations of sweatshop conditions from some critics. As mandated by legislation passed in 2007, the minimum wage finally reached the federal rate in Sept. 2018.

Website. gov.mp

Commonwealth of Puerto Rico (PR)
Estado Libre Asociado de Puerto Rico

People. Population: 3,193,694 (about 5 mil additional Puerto Ricans reside in mainland U.S.). **Pop. change** (2010-19): -14.3%. **Pop. density:** 932.7 per sq mi. **Racial distribution** (2019): 67.4% white; 10.8% Black; 0.2% Asian; 0.3% Amer. Ind.; <0.05% Pac. Isl.; 2 or more races, 5.2%. **Hispanic pop.:** 98.9%. **Languages:** Spanish and English are joint official languages.

Geography. Total area: 5,325 sq mi. **Land area:** 3,424 sq mi. **Acres forested:** 1.2 mil. **Location:** island between the Atlantic to the N and the Caribbean to the S; it is easternmost of the West Indies group called the Greater Antilles, of which Cuba, Hispaniola, and Jamaica are the larger islands. **Climate:** mild, with a mean temperature of 77°F. **Topography:** mountainous throughout three-fourths of its rectangular area, surrounded by a broken coastal plain; highest peak, Cerro de Punta, 4,390 ft. **Capital:** San Juan. **Chief airport:** San Juan.

Economy. Chief industries: manufacturing, service, tourism. **Chief manuf. goods:** pharmaceuticals, medical equip., electronics, apparel, food products. **Chief crops:** pumpkins, coffee, watermelons, plantains, yams, oranges, pineapples, sugarcane, bananas. **Livestock** (2012): 10.9 mil chickens, 257,285 cattle, 12,539 sheep, 48,262 hogs/pigs. **Nonfuel minerals** (2013): $66.3 mil; crushed stone, lime, salt, cement (portland), clays (common), cement (masonry). **Commercial fishing** (2008): $3.8 mil. **Chief ports:** San Juan, Ponce, Mayagüez. **Gross domestic product** (2018): $104.3 bil. **Employment distrib.:** 26.0% govt.; 18.6% trade/trans./util.; 9.2% mfg.; 14.6% ed./health; 13.2% prof./bus. serv.; 6.3% leisure/hosp.; 5.5% finance; 2.4% constr./mining/log.; 1.9% info.; 2.1% other serv. **Unemployment** (Feb. 2020): 8.8%. **Min. wage/hr.:** $7.25. **Per capita income** (2018): $12,451. **Broadband internet:** 84.7%. **Commercial banks:** 7; deposits: $74.3 bil. **Lottery** (2009): total sales: $421.2 mil; profit: $146.9 mil.

Federal govt. Fed. civ. employees: 11,365; **avg. salary:** $63,025. **Notable fed. facilities:** PR Natl. Guard Training Area at Camp Santiago; Ft. Buchanan; Intl. Inst. of Tropical Forestry, San Juan; Vieques Natl. Wildlife Refuge; USGS Caribbean Water Science Ctr., Guaynabo.

Education. High school grad. rate: 73.9%. **4-yr. public coll./univ.:** 14; **2-yr. public:** 4; **4-yr. private:** 46.

Energy. Total electricity production (2016 est.): 21.0 bil kWh.

Misc. data. Motto: Joannes Est Nomen Eius (John is his name). **Flower:** Maga. **Bird:** Reinita. **Tree:** Ceiba. **Anthem:** "La Borinqueña."

Tourism. Tourist spending: $5.0 bil. **Tourism. Attractions:** Museo de Arte de Ponce; San Felipe del Morro and San Cristóbal forts, San Juan Natl. Historic Site, Walled City of Old San Juan, Casa Blanca in San Juan; Arecibo Observatory; Cordillera Central mtn. range; El Yunque Natl. Forest (only tropical rain forest in Natl. Forest system); Cathedral of San Juan Bautista; Porta Coeli (Doorway to Heaven) Church and Religious Art Museum, San Germán; Rio Camuy Cave Park, Camuy; Mosquito Bay. **Information:** The Puerto Rico Tourism Company, La Princesa Bldg. #2, Paseo La Princesa, Old San Juan, PR 00902; (800) 981-7575; www.prtourism.com

History. Puerto Rico (or Borinquen, after the original Arawak Indian name, Boriquen) was visited by Christopher

Columbus on his second voyage, Nov. 19, 1493. In 1508, the Spanish arrived.

Sugarcane was introduced, 1515, and enslaved Black laborers three years later. Gold mining petered out, 1570. Spaniards fought off a series of British and Dutch attacks; slavery was abolished, 1873. Under the Treaty of Paris, Puerto Rico was ceded to the U.S. after the Spanish-American War, 1898. In 1952 the people voted in favor of commonwealth status.

The Commonwealth of Puerto Rico is a self-governing part of the U.S. with a primarily Hispanic culture. The island's citizens have virtually the same control over their internal affairs as do the 50 states of the U.S. However, they do not vote in national general elections, only in national primaries.

Puerto Rico is represented in the U.S. House of Representatives by a Resident Commissioner who has a voice but no vote, except in committees.

No federal income tax is collected from residents on income earned from local sources in Puerto Rico. Nevertheless, as part of the U.S. legal system, Puerto Rico is subject to the provisions of the U.S. Constitution; most federal laws apply as they do in the 50 states.

Puerto Rico's "Operation Bootstrap," begun in the late 1940s, succeeded in changing the island from the "Poorhouse of the Caribbean" to an area with the highest per capita income in Latin America. This program encouraged manufacturing and development of the tourist trade by selective tax exemptions, low-interest loans, and other incentives. Despite the marked success of Puerto Rico's development efforts over an extended period of time, per capita income in Puerto Rico is low in comparison to that of the 50 states.

In plebiscites held in 1967, 1993, and 1998, voters chose to retain commonwealth status. In 2012, a half-million ballots were left blank, with 61.1% of those casting votes favoring statehood over free association (33.3%) or independence (5.6%). In a June 2017 referendum, 97% favored statehood, but only 23% of eligible voters participated, rendering the result indecisive. Protests mounted in the late 1990s over the U.S. Navy's use of Vieques Island for live ammunition training; official military exercises there were terminated, 2003. Puerto Rico went into default for the first time in its history Aug. 2015 after it missed a bond payment. Pres. Barack Obama signed contentious debt-relief legislation in 2016. The island in May 2017 officially filed to restructure its debt load of more than $70 bil. Hurricane Maria in Sept. 2017 caused some $90 bil in damages, including widespread devastation of infrastructure. A Harvard study published May 2018 in the *New England Journal of Medicine* estimated at least 4,645 deaths were linked with the hurricane and its aftermath, far greater than the government estimate of 64. A separate analysis, commissioned and accepted by the government, raised the official death toll to 2,975 in Aug. 2018. Gov. Ricardo Rosselló resigned effective Aug. 2, 2019, following weeks of mass protests over corruption allegations and the public leak of offensive private chat messages between the governor and his allies.

Cultural facilities and events. Festival Casals classical music concerts, mid-June; Puerto Rico Symphony Orchestra at Music Conservatory; Botanical Garden and Museum of Anthropology, Art, and History at the Univ. of Puerto Rico; Institute of Puerto Rican Culture, at the Dominican Convent.

Famous Puerto Ricans. Julia de Burgos, Marta Casals Istomin, Pablo Casals, José Celso Barbosa, Orlando Cepeda, Roberto Clemente, José de Diego, José Feliciano, Doña Felisa Rincón de Gautier, Luis A. Ferré, José Ferrer, Commodore Diégo E. Hernández, Miguel Hernández Agosto, Rafael Hernández (El Jibarito), Rafael Hernández Colón, Raúl Juliá, René Marqués, Ricky Martin, Concha Meléndez, Rita Moreno, Luis Muñoz Marín, Luis Palés Matos, Joaquin Phoenix, Adm. Horacio Rivero.

Website. www.pr.gov (in Spanish)

Virgin Islands (VI)
St. John, St. Croix, St. Thomas

People. Population: 106,235. **Pop. change** (2010-20): −0.2%. **Pop. density:** 792.8 per sq mi. **Racial distribution** (2010): 76.0% Black; 15.6% white; 6.2% other race; 2 or more races, 2.1%. **Languages:** English (official), Spanish, Creole.

Geography. Total area: 733 sq mi. **Land area:** 134 sq mi. **Acres forested:** 46,967. **Location:** 3 larger and 50 smaller islands and cays in the S and W of the V.I. group (British V.I. colony to the N and E), which is situated 70 mi E of Puerto Rico; W of Anegada Passage, a major channel connecting the Atlantic Ocean and Caribbean Sea. **Climate:** subtropical; sun tempered by gentle trade winds; humidity is low; avg. temperature 78°F. **Topography:** St. Thomas is mainly a ridge of hills running E-W and has little tillable land; St. Croix rises abruptly in the N, slopes to flatlands and lagoons in the S;

St. John has steep, lofty hills and valleys with little level tillable land. **Capital:** Charlotte Amalie, on St. Thomas. **Chief airport:** Charlotte Amalie.

Economy. Chief industries: retail, petroleum, tourism, prof. consulting. **Chief manuf. goods:** rum, stone, glass and clay products, electronics, textiles. **Chief crops:** cucumbers, coconuts, mangoes, tomatoes, bananas. **Livestock** (2007): 699 chickens, 776 cattle, 2,981 sheep, 1,125 hogs/pigs, 2,331 goats. **Nonfuel minerals:** crushed stone, limestone, trap rock. **Commercial fishing** (2011): $7.1 mil. **Chief port:** Charlotte Amalie. **Gross domestic product** (2018): $4.0 bil. **Employment distrib.:** 30.7% govt.; 17.4% trade/trans./util.; 2.2% mfg.; 5.8% ed./health; 10.2% prof./bus. serv.; 12.2% leisure/hosp.; 5.0% finance; 10.8% constr./mining/log.; 1.4% info.; 4.4% other serv. **Unemployment** (2017 est.): 10.4%. **Min. wage/hr.:** $10.50. **Per capita income** (2012): $19,982. **Broadband internet:** 85.7%. **Commercial banks:** 3; deposits: $2.4 bil. **Savings institutions:** 1; deposits: $246.0 mil.

Federal govt. Fed. civ. employees: 417; **avg. salary:** $67,327.

Education. 4-yr. public coll./univ.: 1; **2-yr. public:** 0; **4-yr. private:** 0.

Energy. Total electricity production (2016 est.): 704.0 mil kWh.

Misc. data. Motto: United in pride and hope. **Flower:** Yellow cedar. **Bird:** Bananaquit (yellow breast). **Song:** "Virgin Islands March."

Tourism. Attractions: St. Croix Isl.: Salt River Bay Natl. Historic Park and Ecological Preserve, Christiansted Natl. Historic Site. St. John and Hassel Isl.: Virgin Islands Natl. Park. St. Thomas Isl.: Blackbeard's Castle, Coral World Ocean Park, Magens Bay, 99 Steps. **Information:** USVI Division of Tourism, P.O. Box 6400, St. Thomas, VI 00804; 1-800-372-USVI; www.visitusvi.com

History. The islands were visited by Columbus in 1493. Spanish forces, 1555, defeated the Caribes and claimed the territory; by 1596 the native population was annihilated. The first permanent settlement in the U.S. territory, 1672, was by the Danes; U.S. purchased the islands, 1917, for defense purposes.

The Virgin Islands has a republican form of government, headed by a governor and lieut. governor elected, since 1970, by popular vote for four-year terms. There is a 15-member unicameral legislature, elected by popular vote for a two-year term. Residents of the V.I. have been U.S. citizens since 1927. Since 1973 they have elected a U.S. House delegate, who has a voice but no vote except in committees. Hurricanes Maria and Irma in Sept. 2017 caused some $5.5 bil in damages, according to Gov. Kenneth Mapp.

Website. www.vi.gov

Other Islands

Navassa lies between Haiti and Jamaica, 100 mi S of Guantánamo Bay, Cuba, in the Caribbean. It covers 1,147 acres and is uninhabited. Claimed 1857, a Coast Guard lighthouse was built 1917, now inoperative. Natl. Wildlife Refuge since 1999. Administered by the Dept. of Interior.

The three coral islands of **Wake Atoll—Wake, Wilkes,** and **Peale**—lie in the Pacific Ocean on a direct route from Hawaii to Hong Kong, about 2,300 mi W of Honolulu and 1,500 mi NE of Guam. The group is 4.5 mi long, 1.5 mi wide. Land area totals 2.5 sq mi. The U.S. annexed Wake Atoll Jan. 17, 1899. Japan occupied Wake 1941-45. Designated a National Historic Landmark in 1985. Wake is owned by the U.S. Air Force, administered by the Dept. of Interior, and used by the Army as a missile launch facility. The population consists of military personnel and contractors. Most infrastructure was damaged by super typhoon Ioke in 2006.

The following mostly uninhabited islands are part of the **Pacific/Remote Islands National Wildlife Refuge Complex,** which along with Wake Atoll are administered by the Dept. of Interior: **Midway Atoll,** acquired in 1867, has three main islands—Sand, Spit, and Eastern—1,250 mi WNW of Honolulu, with an area of about 1,500 acres. Naval activity ended in 1997. Has the world's largest albatross colony (Laysan and black-footed). **Johnston Atoll,** 800 mi WSW of Honolulu, is two natural and two artificial islands across 107 sq mi administered by the Navy. Johnston was a nuclear test site in 1958, 1962; the Army disposed of chemical weapons 1990-2000. Cleanup ended in 2005. **Kingman Reef** is a barren coral atoll 932 mi S of Hawaii, annexed 1922. **Palmyra Atoll** is about 54 islets over 753 sq mi, 1,052 mi S of Hawaii; annexed with Hawaii in 1898. Part privately owned by the Nature Conservancy. **Jarvis Island** covers 1,086 acres, 1,300 mi S of Honolulu near the equator. West of Jarvis are **Howland and Baker Islands,** 36 mi apart and about 1,600 mi SW of Honolulu.

100 MOST POPULOUS U.S. CITIES

Sources: Population: Decennial Census and Population Estimates Program, U.S. Census Bureau, U.S. Dept. of Commerce. Population is as of July 1, 2019; population rank is indicated within parentheses. Pop. density specifies the number of persons per square mile (sq mi) of land area. Unless otherwise noted, all other figures are estimates for 2014-18 by American Community Survey, U.S. Census Bureau. Racial distribution categories are abbreviated; their full forms are white, Black or African American, Asian, American Indian and Alaska Native, Native Hawaiian and Other Pacific Islander, some other race, two or more races. Hispanic or Latino persons may be of any race. Language is what is spoken at home. Employment: Bureau of Labor Statistics, U.S. Dept. of Labor for 2019. Per capita income: Bureau of Economic Analysis, U.S. Dept. of Commerce; figures apply to MSAs for 2018. Educational attainment is the percentage of persons age 25 and up who have graduated high school (HS) and who have a bachelor's degree or higher. Avg. commute is the time it takes for workers 16 years and over to travel from home to work. "Drive" includes only those who drive to work alone. Forms of transport used by less than 10% are omitted. Avg. home: National Association of Realtors®. Figures represent median 2019 sales price of existing single-family homes in the metropolitan area; data not available for all cities. Avg. rent is the median gross rent (rent asked plus est. avg. cost of utilities) per month. Crime rates: Crime in the United States, 2018, Federal Bureau of Investigation, U.S. Dept. of Justice. Rates are per 100,000 in population. Violent crimes include murder, nonnegligent manslaughter, rape, robbery, aggravated assault; property crimes include burglary, larceny-theft, motor vehicle theft. Mayor (or other city leader) and website: World Almanac research as of mid-2020; subject to change. A nonpartisan mayor is one whose party affiliation was not indicated on the ballot.

Included here are the 100 most populous U.S. cities, according to U.S. Census Bureau estimates released in May 2020. Most data are for the city proper; some, where noted, apply to the Metropolitan Statistical Area (MSA). Inc. = incorporated; est. = established; NA = Not available.

Albuquerque, New Mexico

Population: 560,513 (32). Pop. density: 2,994. Pop. change (2010-19): 2.5%. Area: 187.2 sq mi. Racial distribution: 73.5% white; 3.2% Black; 2.8% Asian; 4.6% Amer. Ind.; 0.1% Pac. Isl.; 11.3% other; 2+ races, 4.5%. Hispanic pop. 49.0%. Foreign born: 10.0%. U.S. citizens: 94.3%. Language: 71.3% English only; 22.7% Spanish.
Employment: 268,618 employed; 4.4% unemployment. Per capita income: $42,536; change (2017-18): 4.5%. Below poverty: 15.5%; 13.1% of families. Educational attainment: 89.7% HS; 34.7% bachelor's. Avg. commute: 21.6 min. 80.2% drive. Housing units: 244,382; 91.1% occupied. Home ownership: 59.6%. Avg. home: $225,000; change (2017-19): 14.4%. Avg. rent: $855. Crime rates: violent: 1,365; property: 6,179.
Mayor: Tim Keller, nonpartisan
History: Founded 1706 by the Spanish; inc. 1891.
Website: www.cabq.gov

Anaheim, California

Population: 350,365 (55). Pop. density: 6,963. Pop. change (2010-19): 4.0%. Area: 50.3 sq mi. Racial distribution: 67.3% white; 2.5% Black; 16.7% Asian; 0.4% Amer. Ind.; 0.4% Pac. Isl.; 9.4% other; 2+ races, 3.3%. Hispanic pop. 54.0%. Foreign born: 36.6%. U.S. citizens: 79.9%. Language: 39.2% English only; 43.5% Spanish.
Employment: 166,837 employed; 3.0% unemployment. Per capita income: $63,913; change (2017-18): 5.4%. Below poverty: 12.8%; 11.8% of families. Educational attainment: 77.1% HS; 25.5% bachelor's. Avg. commute: 28.5 min. 77.3% drive, 12.3% carpool. Housing units: 105,286; 95.6% occupied. Home ownership: 45.2%. Avg. home: $825,000; change (2017-19): 5.8%. Avg. rent: $1,569. Crime rates: violent: 336; property: 2,453.
Mayor: Harry Sidhu, nonpartisan
History: Founded 1857; inc. 1876. Home of Disneyland, the Anaheim Ducks, and the Los Angeles Angels.
Website: www.anaheim.net

Anchorage, Alaska

Population: 288,000 (69). Pop. density: 169. Pop. change (2010-19): −1.8%. Area: 1,706.8 sq mi. Racial distribution: 63.0% white; 5.6% Black; 9.6% Asian; 7.4% Amer. Ind.; 2.3% Pac. Isl.; 2.3% other; 2+ races, 9.8%. Hispanic pop. 9.1%. Foreign born: 10.7%. U.S. citizens: 96.0%. Language: 82.3% English only; 4.8% Spanish.
Employment: 139,526 employed; 5.1% unemployment. Per capita income: $60,953; change (2017-18): 4.9%. Below poverty: 7.6%; 6.1% of families. Educational attainment: 93.8% HS; 35.3% bachelor's. Avg. commute: 18.7 min. 76.3% drive, 11.6% carpool. Housing units: 116,493; 91.4% occupied. Home ownership: 60.9%. Avg. rent: $1,306. Crime rates: violent: 1,310; property: 4,928.
Mayor: Ethan Berkowitz, nonpartisan
History: Founded 1914 as a railroad construction port; HQ of Alaska Defense Command, WWII. Severely damaged in earthquake, 1964.
Website: www.muni.org

Arlington, Texas

Population: 398,854 (49). Pop. density: 4,164. Pop. change (2010-19): 9.0%. Area: 95.8 sq mi. Racial distribution: 61.5% white; 22.5% Black; 6.9% Asian; 0.4% Amer. Ind.; 0.1% Pac. Isl.; 5.5% other; 2+ races, 3.1%. Hispanic pop. 29.2%. Foreign born: 20.8%. U.S. citizens: 87.6%. Language: 66.8% English only; 22.4% Spanish.
Employment: 206,864 employed; 3.4% unemployment. Per capita income: $55,886; change (2017-18): 4.7%. Below poverty: 12.9%; 11.9% of families. Educational attainment: 84.8% HS; 29.5% bachelor's. Avg. commute: 27.2 min. 82% drive, 10.7% carpool. Housing units: 146,962; 91.8% occupied. Home ownership: 55.2%. Avg. home: $268,600; change (2017-19): 8.6%. Avg. rent: $997. Crime rates: violent: 445; property: 2,938.
Mayor: Jeff Williams, nonpartisan

Arlington, Virginia

History: Anglo-Americans began to settle in 1840s; inc. 1884.
Website: www.arlingtontx.gov

Atlanta, Georgia

Population: 506,811 (37). Pop. density: 3,734. Pop. change (2010-19): 18.0%. Area: 135.7 sq mi. Racial distribution: 40.3% white; 51.8% Black; 4.2% Asian; 0.2% Amer. Ind.; <0.05% Pac. Isl.; 1.0% other; 2+ races, 2.4%. Hispanic pop. 4.3%. Foreign born: 7.1%. U.S. citizens: 95.6%. Language: 90.8% English only; 3.8% Spanish.
Employment: 252,208 employed; 3.7% unemployment. Per capita income: $52,473; change (2017-18): 4.4%. Below poverty: 18.6%; 16.9% of families. Educational attainment: 90.3% HS; 49.9% bachelor's. Avg. commute: 27.0 min. 67.6% drive, 10.5% public trans. Housing units: 242,421; 82.3% occupied. Home ownership: 43.4%. Avg. home: $233,200; change (2017-19): 17.5%. Avg. rent: $1,099. Crime rates: violent: 769; property: 4,654.
Mayor: Keisha Lance Bottoms, nonpartisan
History: Founded as Terminus, 1837; renamed Atlanta, 1845; inc. 1847. Played major role in Civil War; became state capital, 1868. Birthplace of civil rights movement; host to 1996 Olympic Games.
Website: www.atlantaga.gov

Aurora, Colorado

Population: 379,289 (54). Pop. density: 2,459. Pop. change (2010-19): 16.3%. Area: 154.3 sq mi. Racial distribution: 60.7% white; 16.0% Black; 6.3% Asian; 0.9% Amer. Ind.; 0.3% Pac. Isl.; 10.4% other; 2+ races, 5.4%. Hispanic pop. 28.4%. Foreign born: 19.9%. U.S. citizens: 87.2%. Language: 67.2% English only; 21.3% Spanish.
Employment: 194,981 employed; 2.9% unemployment. Per capita income: $64,287; change (2017-18): 6.1%. Below poverty: 10.2%; 8.8% of families. Educational attainment: 87.1% HS; 29.1% bachelor's. Avg. commute: 29.7 min. 76.7% drive, 10.9% carpool. Housing units: 133,940; 95.7% occupied. Home ownership: 59.0%. Avg. home: $462,100; change (2017-19): 11.4%. Avg. rent: $1,241. Crime rates (2017): violent: 608; property: 3,004.
Mayor: Mike Coffman, nonpartisan
History: Founded as Fletcher, 1891; renamed Aurora, 1907; inc. 1928. Early growth stimulated by military bases; fast-growing trade, technology, and med. science center.
Website: www.auroragov.org

Austin, Texas

Population: 978,908 (11). Pop. density: 3,060. Pop. change (2010-19): 21.4%. Area: 319.9 sq mi. Racial distribution: 73.5% white; 7.8% Black; 7.3% Asian; 0.6% Amer. Ind.; <0.05% Pac. Isl.; 7.5% other; 2+ races, 3.3%. Hispanic pop. 34.3%. Foreign born: 18.5%. U.S. citizens: 87.5%. Language: 67.8% English only; 23.6% Spanish.
Employment: 577,715 employed; 2.5% unemployment. Per capita income: $58,773; change (2017-18): 5.8%. Below poverty: 13.0%; 9.6% of families. Educational attainment: 89.1% HS; 50.4% bachelor's. Avg. commute: 24.3 min. 74.1% drive. Housing units: 404,262; 91.5% occupied. Home ownership: 45.2%. Avg. home: $329,200; change (2017-19): 11.3%. Avg. rent: $1,225. Crime rates: violent: 382; property: 3,458.
Mayor: Steve Adler, nonpartisan
History: First permanent Anglo-American settlement, 1830s; capital of Rep. of Texas, 1839; named after Stephen Austin.
Website: www.austintexas.gov

Bakersfield, California

Population: 384,145 (52). Pop. density: 2,565. Pop. change (2010-19): 10.1%. Area: 149.8 sq mi. Racial distribution: 68.2% white; 7.4% Black; 7.3% Asian; 1.1% Amer. Ind.; 0.2% Pac. Isl.; 11.9% other; 2+ races, 3.9%. Hispanic pop. 49.5%. Foreign born: 18.4%. U.S. citizens: 89.8%. Language: 58.9% English only; 33.6% Spanish.

Employment: 169,511 employed; 5.3% unemployment. **Per capita income:** $39,703; change (2017-18): 3.2%. **Below poverty:** 15.7%; 14.9% of families. **Educational attainment:** 80.4% HS; 21.8% bachelor's. **Avg. commute:** 22.6 min. 81.8% drive, 10.8% carpool. **Housing units:** 124,227; 94.1% occupied. **Home ownership:** 58.7%. **Avg. rent:** $1,078. **Crime rates:** violent: 491; property: 4,174.

Mayor: Karen Goh, nonpartisan

History: Named after Col. Thomas Baker, an early settler; inc. 1898.

Website: www.bakersfieldcity.us

Baltimore, Maryland

Population: 593,490 (30). **Pop. density:** 7,332. **Pop. change (2010-19):** –4.4%. **Area:** 80.9 sq mi. **Racial distribution:** 30.4% white; 62.5% Black; 2.6% Asian; 0.3% Amer. Ind.; <0.05% Pac. Isl.; 1.7% other; 2+ races, 2.5%. **Hispanic pop.:** 5.1%. **Foreign born:** 8.1%. **U.S. citizens:** 95.2%. **Language:** 90.4% English only; 4.1% Spanish.

Employment: 275,911 employed; 5.1% unemployment. **Per capita income:** $62,402; change (2017-18): 4.8%. **Below poverty:** 19.2%; 16.6% of families. **Educational attainment:** 84.9% HS; 31.2% bachelor's. **Avg. commute:** 31.0 min. 60.1% drive, 18% public trans. **Housing units:** 294,522; 81.0% occupied. **Home ownership:** 47.3%. **Avg. home:** $299,400; change (2017-19): 13.9%. **Avg. rent:** $1,051. **Crime rates:** violent: 1,833; property: 4,495.

Mayor: Bernard C. "Jack" Young, Democrat

History: Founded by Maryland legislature, 1729; inc. 1797. British artillery barrage of Ft. McHenry (1814) inspired "Star-Spangled Banner." Birthplace of America's railroads, 1828; rebuilt after fire, 1904. Site of National Aquarium.

Website: www.baltimorecity.gov

Baton Rouge, Louisiana

Population: 220,236 (100). **Pop. density:** 2,548. **Pop. change (2010-19):** –4.0%. **Area:** 86.4 sq mi. **Racial distribution:** 38.7% white; 55.0% Black; 3.2% Asian; 0.2% Amer. Ind.; <0.05% Pac. Isl.; 1.4% other; 2+ races, 1.4%. **Hispanic pop.:** 3.7%. **Foreign born:** 5.2%. **U.S. citizens:** 96.7%. **Language:** 92.0% English only; 3.3% Spanish.

Employment: 106,636 employed; 4.8% unemployment. **Per capita income:** $48,042; change (2017-18): 4.7%. **Below poverty:** 22.5%; 17.1% of families. **Educational attainment:** 88.0% HS; 33.1% bachelor's. **Avg. commute:** 21.3 min. 80% drive, 9.8% carpool. **Housing units:** 101,691; 83.8% occupied. **Home ownership:** 49.1%. **Avg. home:** $216,400; change (2017-19): 9.0%. **Avg. rent:** $860. **Crime rates:** violent: 920; property: 5,323.

Mayor-President: Sharon Weston Broome, Democrat

History: Claimed by Spain at time of Louisiana Purchase, 1803; est. independence by rebellion, 1810; inc. as town, 1817. Became state capital, 1849; Union-held most of Civil War.

Website: www.brla.gov

Boise City, Idaho

Population: 228,959 (98). **Pop. density:** 2,736. **Pop. change (2010-19):** 9.2%. **Area:** 83.7 sq mi. **Racial distribution:** 89.1% white; 2.1% Black; 3.1% Asian; 0.6% Amer. Ind.; 0.2% Pac. Isl.; 1.7% other; 2+ races, 3.3%. **Hispanic pop.:** 9.0%. **Foreign born:** 6.8%. **U.S. citizens:** 96.4%. **Language:** 89.9% English only; 4.7% Spanish.

Employment: 129,118 employed; 2.5% unemployment. **Per capita income:** $45,973; change (2017-18): 4.3%. **Below poverty:** 13.0%; 8.1% of families. **Educational attainment:** 94.9% HS; 41.1% bachelor's. **Avg. commute:** 18.5 min. 80.4% drive. **Housing units:** 95,104; 94.6% occupied. **Home ownership:** 60.2%. **Avg. home:** $294,200; change (2017-19): 29.8%. **Avg. rent:** $910. **Crime rates:** violent: 277; property: 2,018.

Mayor: Lauren McLean, nonpartisan

History: Gold discovered in area, 1862; proclaimed capital of Idaho Terr., 1864; inc. 1866; on Oregon Trail.

Website: www.cityofboise.org

Boston, Massachusetts

Population: 692,600 (21). **Pop. density:** 14,328. **Pop. change (2010-19):** 11.5%. **Area:** 48.3 sq mi. **Racial distribution:** 52.6% white; 25.3% Black; 9.6% Asian; 0.3% Amer. Ind.; <0.05% Pac. Isl.; 7.1% other; 2+ races, 5.1%. **Hispanic pop.:** 19.7%. **Foreign born:** 28.5%. **U.S. citizens:** 85.5%. **Language:** 62.0% English only; 16.9% Spanish.

Employment: 389,042 employed; 2.6% unemployment. **Per capita income:** $78,694; change (2017-18): 5.2%. **Below poverty:** 18.3%; 15.3% of families. **Educational attainment:** 86.4% HS; 48.5% bachelor's. **Avg. commute:** 30.8 min. 38.8% drive, 33.4% public trans. **Housing units:** 289,763; 92.0% occupied. **Home ownership:** 35.2%. **Avg. home:** $491,900; change (2017-19): 8.6%. **Avg. rent:** $1,539. **Crime rates:** violent: 622; property: 2,016.

Mayor: Martin J. Walsh, nonpartisan

History: Settled 1630 by John Winthrop; capital of Mass. Bay Colony; figured strongly in American Revolution; inc. 1822.

Website: www.boston.gov

Buffalo, New York

Population: 255,284 (86). **Pop. density:** 6,322. **Pop. change (2010-19):** –2.3%. **Area:** 40.4 sq mi. **Racial distribution:** 47.4% white; 36.7% Black; 5.6% Asian; 0.5% Amer. Ind.; <0.05% Pac. Isl.; 5.8% other; 2+ races, 4.0%. **Hispanic pop.:** 11.6%. **Foreign born:** 10.0%. **U.S. citizens:** 94.3%. **Language:** 81.8% English only; 8.1% Spanish.

Employment: 102,344 employed; 5.5% unemployment. **Per capita income:** $50,414; change (2017-18): 3.1%. **Below poverty:** 25.6%; 24.6% of families. **Educational attainment:** 83.9% HS; 26.6% bachelor's. **Avg. commute:** 21.1 min. 67.3% drive, 10.9% carpool, 11.6% public trans. **Housing units:** 131,868; 83.9% occupied. **Home ownership:** 40.8%. **Avg. home:** $160,900; change (2017-19): 12.8%. **Avg. rent:** $757. **Crime rates:** violent: 1,043; property: 3,815.

Mayor: Byron W. Brown, Democrat

History: Settled 1780 by Seneca Indians; raided by British in War of 1812; inc. 1832. Served as western terminus for Erie Canal and a center for trade and manufacturing.

Website: www.buffalony.gov

Chandler, Arizona

Population: 261,165 (81). **Pop. density:** 4,010. **Pop. change (2010-19):** 10.5%. **Area:** 65.1 sq mi. **Racial distribution:** 75.7% white; 5.3% Black; 10.3% Asian; 1.6% Amer. Ind.; 0.1% Pac. Isl.; 2.8% other; 2+ races, 4.2%. **Hispanic pop.:** 21.3%. **Foreign born:** 15.4%. **U.S. citizens:** 91.9%. **Language:** 75.4% English only; 13.2% Spanish.

Employment: 148,089 employed; 3.5% unemployment. **Per capita income:** $46,125; change (2017-18): 4.3%. **Below poverty:** 7.6%; 6.1% of families. **Educational attainment:** 92.8% HS; 43.7% bachelor's. **Avg. commute:** 24.1 min. 78.5% drive, 10.1% carpool. **Housing units:** 95,052; 93.6% occupied. **Home ownership:** 62.9%. **Avg. home:** $287,100; change (2017-19): 16.4%. **Avg. rent:** $1,246. **Crime rates** (MSA): violent: 237; property: 2,121.

Mayor: Kevin Hartke, nonpartisan

History: Formed 1912; population doubled in 1990s when marketed as "the high-tech oasis of the Silicon Desert."

Website: www.chandleraz.gov

Charlotte, North Carolina

Population: 885,708 (15). **Pop. density:** 2,883. **Pop. change (2010-19):** 19.9%. **Area:** 307.2 sq mi. **Racial distribution:** 49.5% white; 35.1% Black; 6.5% Asian; 0.4% Amer. Ind.; 0.1% Pac. Isl.; 5.6% other; 2+ races, 2.8%. **Hispanic pop.:** 14.0%. **Foreign born:** 16.5%. **U.S. citizens:** 89.1%. **Language:** 78.5% English only; 12.0% Spanish.

Employment: 480,391 employed; 3.7% unemployment. **Per capita income:** $52,176; change (2017-18): 4.3%. **Below poverty:** 11.9%; 10.4% of families. **Educational attainment:** 88.9% HS; 43.5% bachelor's. **Avg. commute:** 25.7 min. 76.6% drive, 9.8% carpool. **Housing units:** 351,143; 92.2% occupied. **Home ownership:** 52.9%. **Avg. home:** $258,600; change (2017-19): 14.0%. **Avg. rent:** $1,086. **Crime rates:** violent: NA; property: 3,746.

Mayor: Vi Alexander Lyles, Democrat

History: Scotch-Irish immigrants arrived, c. 1750; inc. 1768 and named after Queen Charlotte, wife of King George III. Site of first major U.S. gold discovery, 1799.

Website: charlottenc.gov

Chesapeake, Virginia

Population: 244,835 (91). **Pop. density:** 723. **Pop. change (2010-19):** 9.5%. **Area:** 338.5 sq mi. **Racial distribution:** 61.4% white; 29.9% Black; 3.3% Asian; 0.2% Amer. Ind.; 0.1% Pac. Isl.; 1.6% other; 2+ races, 3.6%. **Hispanic pop.:** 5.9%. **Foreign born:** 5.7%. **U.S. citizens:** 97.9%. **Language:** 92.0% English only; 3.9% Spanish.

Employment: 119,957 employed; 2.9% unemployment. **Per capita income:** $50,619; change (2017-18): 4.4%. **Below poverty:** 6.9%; 7.1% of families. **Educational attainment:** 92.2% HS; 32.5% bachelor's. **Avg. commute:** 26.4 min. 85.4% drive. **Housing units:** 89,882; 93.7% occupied. **Home ownership:** 71.3%. **Avg. home:** $235,000; change (2017-19): 4.4%. **Avg. rent:** $1,235. **Crime rates** (MSA): violent: 307; property: 2,405.

Mayor: Rick West, Republican

History: First English colonies on banks of Elizabeth River, 1620s; home to Dismal Swamp Canal, first envisioned by George Washington in 1763. Battle of Great Bridge, Dec. 1775; inc. 1963.

Website: www.cityofchesapeake.net

Chicago, Illinois

Population: 2,693,976 (3). **Pop. density:** 11,848. **Pop. change (2010-19):** –0.1%. **Area:** 227.4 sq mi. **Racial distribution:** 49.4% white; 30.1% Black; 6.4% Asian; 0.3% Amer. Ind.; <0.05% Pac. Isl.; 10.9% other; 2+ races, 2.7%. **Hispanic pop.:** 29.0%. **Foreign born:** 20.6%. **U.S. citizens:** 88.6%. **Language:** 64.0% English only; 24.4% Spanish.

Employment: 1,286,484 employed; 4.0% unemployment. **Per capita income:** $61,089; change (2017-18): 5.3%. **Below poverty:**

17.0%; 15.5% of families. **Educational attainment:** 84.5% HS; 38.4% bachelor's. **Avg. commute:** 35.0 min. 49% drive, 28.4% public trans. **Housing units:** 1,208,839; 87.4% occupied. **Home ownership:** 45.0%. **Avg. home:** $265,100; change (2017-19): 6.7%. **Avg. rent:** $1,077. **Crime rates:** violent: 1,006; property: 3,182.
Mayor: Lori E. Lightfoot, nonpartisan
History: First nonnative residence established by Point Du Sable, 1780s; Fort Dearborn built, 1803; significant white settlement began with completion of Erie Canal, 1825; inc. 1837. Boomed with arrival of railroads and canal to Mississippi R.; one-third of city destroyed by fire, 1871. Major Great Migration destination, 1910-30.
Website: www.chicago.gov

Chula Vista, California

Population: 274,492 (75). **Pop. density:** 5,530. **Pop. change (2010-19):** 12.2%. **Area:** 49.6 sq mi. **Racial distribution:** 65.6% white; 4.6% Black; 16.0% Asian; 0.3% Amer. Ind.; 0.7% Pac. Isl.; 7.3% other; 2+ races, 5.5%. **Hispanic pop.:** 58.8%. **Foreign born:** 30.7%. **U.S. citizens:** 85.3%. **Language:** 41.1% English only; 47.4% Spanish.
Employment: 119,319 employed; 3.5% unemployment. **Per capita income:** $61,386; change (2017-18): 5.7%. **Below poverty:** 10.0%; 8.8% of families. **Educational attainment:** 82.0% HS; 28.8% bachelor's. **Avg. commute:** 29.7 min. 79.5% drive, 9.5% carpool. **Housing units:** 85,810; 92.0% occupied. **Home ownership:** 58.3%. **Avg. home:** $645,000; change (2017-19): 7.7%. **Avg. rent:** $1,536. **Crime rates** (MSA): violent: 304; property: 1,316.
Mayor: Mary Casillas Salas, nonpartisan
History: Visited by Spanish, 1542; became part of Spanish land grant, 1795; claimed by U.S. in Mexican-American War, 1847; inc. 1911. WWII brought aircraft industry and growth.
Website: www.chulavistaca.gov

Cincinnati, Ohio

Population: 303,940 (64). **Pop. density:** 3,905. **Pop. change (2010-19):** 2.3%. **Area:** 77.8 sq mi. **Racial distribution:** 50.3% white; 42.7% Black; 2.0% Asian; 0.1% Amer. Ind.; 0.1% Pac. Isl.; 1.2% other; 2+ races, 3.6%. **Hispanic pop.:** 3.7%. **Foreign born:** 5.7%. **U.S. citizens:** 96.4%. **Language:** 91.9% English only; 2.9% Spanish.
Employment: 141,117 employed; 4.2% unemployment. **Per capita income:** $54,176; change (2017-18): 4.7%. **Below poverty:** 23.5%; 21.0% of families. **Educational attainment:** 87.6% HS; 36.1% bachelor's. **Avg. commute:** 22.9 min. 71.4% drive. **Housing units:** 162,279; 84.6% occupied. **Home ownership:** 37.8%. **Avg. home:** $185,600; change (2017-19): 14.6%. **Avg. rent:** $709. **Crime rates:** violent: 840; property: 4,540.
Mayor: John Cranley, nonpartisan
History: Founded 1788; named after Society of the Cincinnati, an organization of Revolutionary War officers; chartered as town, 1802; inc. 1819.
Website: www.cincinnati-oh.gov

Cleveland, Ohio

Population: 381,009 (53). **Pop. density:** 4,904. **Pop. change (2010-19):** −3.8%. **Area:** 77.7 sq mi. **Racial distribution:** 39.8% white; 49.6% Black; 2.4% Asian; 0.5% Amer. Ind.; <0.05% Pac. Isl.; 3.4% other; 2+ races, 4.3%. **Hispanic pop.:** 11.6%. **Foreign born:** 5.4%. **U.S. citizens:** 97.0%. **Language:** 86.2% English only; 8.8% Spanish.
Employment: 150,993 employed; 5.2% unemployment. **Per capita income:** $53,738; change (2017-18): 4.5%. **Below poverty:** 29.8%; 30.2% of families. **Educational attainment:** 79.2% HS; 16.6% bachelor's. **Avg. commute:** 24.0 min. 70% drive, 10.2% carpool, 10% public trans. **Housing units:** 212,347; 79.8% occupied. **Home ownership:** 41.3%. **Avg. home:** $164,100; change (2017-19): 16.9%. **Avg. rent:** $700. **Crime rates:** violent: 916; property: 5,588.
Mayor: Frank G. Jackson, nonpartisan
History: Surveyed in 1796; inc. as village, 1814; inc. as city, 1836; annexed Ohio City 1854. Major Great Lakes port and early hub for steel, oil industries.
Website: www.city.cleveland.oh.us

Colorado Springs, Colorado

Population: 478,221 (39). **Pop. density:** 2,452. **Pop. change (2010-19):** 13.7%. **Area:** 195.0 sq mi. **Racial distribution:** 78.3% white; 6.2% Black; 3.0% Asian; 0.7% Amer. Ind.; 0.3% Pac. Isl.; 5.6% other; 2+ races, 6.0%. **Hispanic pop.:** 17.7%. **Foreign born:** 7.5%. **U.S. citizens:** 96.2%. **Language:** 86.9% English only; 8.4% Spanish.
Employment: 230,192 employed; 3.2% unemployment. **Per capita income:** $48,492; change (2017-18): 3.8%. **Below poverty:** 11.1%; 9.0% of families. **Educational attainment:** 93.3% HS; 39.0% bachelor's. **Avg. commute:** 22.3 min. 78.6% drive, 11% carpool. **Housing units:** 189,012; 94.5% occupied. **Home ownership:** 59.1%. **Avg. home:** $320,500; change (2017-19): 13.8%. **Avg. rent:** $1,072. **Crime rates:** violent: 555; property: 3,343.
Mayor: John Suthers, nonpartisan
History: Founded 1871 at the foot of Pikes Peak; inc. 1886.
Website: coloradosprings.gov

Columbus, Ohio

Population: 898,553 (14). **Pop. density:** 4,099. **Pop. change (2010-19):** 13.6%. **Area:** 219.2 sq mi. **Racial distribution:** 59.5% white; 28.5% Black; 5.7% Asian; 0.2% Amer. Ind.; 0.1% Pac. Isl.; 1.8% other; 2+ races, 4.3%. **Hispanic pop.:** 5.9%. **Foreign born:** 12.5%. **U.S. citizens:** 92.9%. **Language:** 84.7% English only; 4.2% Spanish.
Employment: 458,580 employed; 3.6% unemployment. **Per capita income:** $51,165; change (2017-18): 3.7%. **Below poverty:** 17.5%; 15.3% of families. **Educational attainment:** 89.5% HS; 35.7% bachelor's. **Avg. commute:** 21.7 min. 79.8% drive. **Housing units:** 389,820; 90.4% occupied. **Home ownership:** 44.7%. **Avg. home:** $216,600; change (2017-19): 14.1%. **Avg. rent:** $928. **Crime rates:** violent: 495; property: 3,530.
Mayor: Andrew J. Ginther, nonpartisan
History: Laid out as state capital, 1812; inc. 1834.
Website: www.columbus.gov

Corpus Christi, Texas

Population: 326,586 (59). **Pop. density:** 2,045. **Pop. change (2010-19):** 7.0%. **Area:** 159.7 sq mi. **Racial distribution:** 89.3% white; 4.1% Black; 2.2% Asian; 0.4% Amer. Ind.; 0.1% Pac. Isl.; 2.1% other; 2+ races, 1.7%. **Hispanic pop.:** 62.9%. **Foreign born:** 8.9%. **U.S. citizens:** 94.5%. **Language:** 64.5% English only; 33.0% Spanish.
Employment: 145,939 employed; 4.1% unemployment. **Per capita income:** $44,311; change (2017-18): 4.5%. **Below poverty:** 13.7%; 12.0% of families. **Educational attainment:** 83.0% HS; 22.0% bachelor's. **Avg. commute:** 19.2 min. 84% drive. **Housing units:** 131,136; 88.9% occupied. **Home ownership:** 56.6%. **Avg. home:** $201,100; change (2017-19): 7.9%. **Avg. rent:** $996. **Crime rates:** violent: 757; property: 3,644.
Mayor: Joe McComb, nonpartisan
History: Anglo-Americans settled, 1838-39; inc. 1852. One of the largest U.S. ports.
Website: www.cctexas.com

Dallas, Texas

Population: 1,343,573 (9). **Pop. density:** 3,955. **Pop. change (2010-19):** 11.9%. **Area:** 339.7 sq mi. **Racial distribution:** 62.5% white; 24.3% Black; 3.4% Asian; 0.3% Amer. Ind.; <0.05% Pac. Isl.; 7.0% other; 2+ races, 2.5%. **Hispanic pop.:** 41.7%. **Foreign born:** 24.6%. **U.S. citizens:** 81.4%. **Language:** 56.2% English only; 38.2% Spanish.
Employment: 668,242 employed; 3.4% unemployment. **Per capita income:** $55,886; change (2017-18): 4.7%. **Below poverty:** 16.6%; 16.8% of families. **Educational attainment:** 76.5% HS; 32.3% bachelor's. **Avg. commute:** 27.0 min. 76.5% drive, 11.1% carpool. **Housing units:** 563,993; 89.7% occupied. **Home ownership:** 41.2%. **Avg. home:** $268,600; change (2017-19): 8.6%. **Avg. rent:** $987. **Crime rates:** violent: 765; property: 3,249.
Mayor: Eric Johnson, nonpartisan
History: First nonnatives settled, 1841; inc. 1871. Developed as financial and commercial hub; center of TX oil boom from 1930s.
Website: dallascityhall.com

Denver, Colorado

Population: 727,211 (19). **Pop. density:** 4,744. **Pop. change (2010-19):** 20.5%. **Area:** 153.3 sq mi. **Racial distribution:** 76.5% white; 9.4% Black; 3.8% Asian; 1.0% Amer. Ind.; 0.1% Pac. Isl.; 5.7% other; 2+ races, 3.6%. **Hispanic pop.:** 30.3%. **Foreign born:** 15.6%. **U.S. citizens:** 90.1%. **Language:** 73.5% English only; 19.8% Spanish.
Employment: 409,074 employed; 2.7% unemployment. **Per capita income:** $64,287; change (2017-18): 6.1%. **Below poverty:** 12.2%; 10.0% of families. **Educational attainment:** 87.1% HS; 47.9% bachelor's. **Avg. commute:** 25.4 min. 69.6% drive. **Housing units:** 314,045; 93.7% occupied. **Home ownership:** 49.6%. **Avg. home:** $462,100; change (2017-19): 11.4%. **Avg. rent:** $1,217. **Crime rates** (2017): violent: 676; property: 3,667.
Mayor: Michael B. Hancock, nonpartisan
History: Miners arrived, 1858; inc. 1861; became territorial capital, 1867. Growth spurred by gold and silver boom; became financial, industrial, cultural center of Rocky Mtn. region.
Website: www.denvergov.org

Detroit, Michigan

Population: 670,031 (24). **Pop. density:** 4,830. **Pop. change (2010-19):** −5.8%. **Area:** 138.7 sq mi. **Racial distribution:** 14.6% white; 78.6% Black; 1.6% Asian; 0.3% Amer. Ind.; <0.05% Pac. Isl.; 2.9% other; 2+ races, 1.9%. **Hispanic pop.:** 7.6%. **Foreign born:** 6.1%. **U.S. citizens:** 96.2%. **Language:** 88.9% English only; 6.6% Spanish.
Employment: 230,555 employed; 8.8% unemployment. **Per capita income:** $53,086; change (2017-18): 4.6%. **Below poverty:** 31.2%; 31.3% of families. **Educational attainment:** 80.0% HS; 14.6% bachelor's. **Avg. commute:** 26.2 min. 69.2% drive, 13.4% carpool. **Housing units:** 364,089; 71.5% occupied. **Home ownership:** 47.4%. **Avg. home:** $195,800. **Avg. rent:** $798. **Crime rates:** violent: 2,008; property: 4,305.

Mayor: Mike Duggan, nonpartisan
History: Founded by French, 1701; controlled by British, 1760; acquired by U.S., 1796; inc. 1815; capital of state 1837-47. First automobile factory opened, 1899. Major Great Migration destination, 1910-30.
Website: www.detroitmi.gov

Durham, North Carolina

Population: 278,993 (74). **Pop. density:** 2,486. **Pop. change (2010-19):** 20.9%. **Area:** 112.2 sq mi. **Racial distribution:** 48.4% white; 39.3% Black; 5.3% Asian; 0.3% Amer. Ind.; <0.05% Pac. Isl.; 3.7% other; 2+ races, 2.9%. **Hispanic pop.:** 14.1%. **Foreign born:** 14.7%. **U.S. citizens:** 89.6%. **Language:** 80.1% English only; 12.4% Spanish.
Employment: 145,767 employed; 3.4% unemployment. **Per capita income:** $54,036; change (2017-18): 5.6%. **Below poverty:** 14.2%; 12.7% of families. **Educational attainment:** 87.9% HS; 48.7% bachelor's. **Avg. commute:** 22.7 min. 76.3% drive, 10.1% carpool. **Housing units:** 116,651; 92.3% occupied. **Home ownership:** 49.5%. **Avg. home:** $295,900; change (2017-19): 16.2%. **Avg. rent:** $1,005. **Crime rates** (2017): violent: NA; property: 3,826.
Mayor: Steve Schewel, nonpartisan
History: Inc. 1869. Trinity College moved to Durham, 1892, renamed Duke Univ.,1924.
Website: durhamnc.gov

El Paso, Texas

Population: 681,728 (22). **Pop. density:** 2,648. **Pop. change (2010-19):** 4.8%. **Area:** 257.4 sq mi. **Racial distribution:** 80.8% white; 3.8% Black; 1.4% Asian; 0.5% Amer. Ind.; 0.2% Pac. Isl.; 10.7% other; 2+ races, 2.7%. **Hispanic pop.:** 80.9%. **Foreign born:** 23.8%. **U.S. citizens:** 87.5%. **Language:** 30.7% English only; 67.0% Spanish.
Employment: 291,637 employed; 3.7% unemployment. **Per capita income:** $35,836; change (2017-18): 4.7%. **Below poverty:** 16.9%; 16.8% of families. **Educational attainment:** 79.6% HS; 24.7% bachelor's. **Avg. commute:** 22.8 min. 81% drive, 10.7% carpool. **Housing units:** 248,776; 90.5% occupied. **Home ownership:** 59.1%. **Avg. home:** $164,400; change (2017-19): 8.5%. **Avg. rent:** $814. **Crime rates:** violent: 371; property: 1,506.
Mayor: Dee Margo, nonpartisan
History: First nonnatives settled, 1598; inc. 1873; arrival of railroad, 1881, boosted population and industries.
Website: www.elpasotexas.gov

Fort Wayne, Indiana

Population: 270,402 (77). **Pop. density:** 2,444. **Pop. change (2010-19):** 6.4%. **Area:** 110.6 sq mi. **Racial distribution:** 73.8% white; 14.9% Black; 4.6% Asian; 0.2% Amer. Ind.; <0.05% Pac. Isl.; 1.9% other; 2+ races, 4.5%. **Hispanic pop.:** 8.9%. **Foreign born:** 7.9%. **U.S. citizens:** 95.7%. **Language:** 87.9% English only; 6.1% Spanish.
Employment: 125,491 employed; 3.3% unemployment. **Per capita income:** $46,141; change (2017-18): 4.7%. **Below poverty:** 14.0%; 13.1% of families. **Educational attainment:** 88.5% HS; 27.6% bachelor's. **Avg. commute:** 20.9 min. 83.7% drive. **Housing units:** 116,658; 90.2% occupied. **Home ownership:** 61.7%. **Avg. home:** $155,300; change (2017-19): 16.9%. **Avg. rent:** $735.
Crime rates: violent: 383; property: 2,618.
Mayor: Tom Henry, Democrat
History: U.S. fort founded, 1794; inc. 1840 prior to Wabash-Erie Canal completion, 1843.
Website: www.cityoffortwayne.org

Fort Worth, Texas

Population: 909,585 (13). **Pop. density:** 2,632. **Pop. change (2010-19):** 21.5%. **Area:** 345.6 sq mi. **Racial distribution:** 64.1% white; 19.0% Black; 4.2% Asian; 0.5% Amer. Ind.; 0.1% Pac. Isl.; 8.9% other; 2+ races, 3.3%. **Hispanic pop.:** 35.0%. **Foreign born:** 16.8%. **U.S. citizens:** 88.9%. **Language:** 67.1% English only; 27.0% Spanish.
Employment: 424,603 employed; 3.4% unemployment. **Per capita income:** $55,886; change (2017-18): 4.7%. **Below poverty:** 13.6%; 12.5% of families. **Educational attainment:** 81.7% HS; 28.6% bachelor's. **Avg. commute:** 27.2 min. 81.9% drive, 11.1% carpool. **Housing units:** 319,650; 91.3% occupied. **Home ownership:** 57.2%. **Avg. home:** $268,600; change (2017-19): 8.6%. **Avg. rent:** $1,015. **Crime rates:** violent: 501; property: 2,846.
Mayor: Betsy Price, nonpartisan
History: Established as military post, 1849; inc. 1873; oil discovered, 1917.
Website: fortworthtexas.gov

Fremont, California

Population: 241,110 (93). **Pop. density:** 3,113. **Pop. change (2010-19):** 12.4%. **Area:** 77.5 sq mi. **Racial distribution:** 24.1% white; 3.1% Black; 58.4% Asian; 0.4% Amer. Ind.; 0.9% Pac. Isl.; 8.1% other; 2+ races, 4.9%. **Hispanic pop.:** 13.1%. **Foreign born:** 48.2%. **U.S. citizens:** 78.0%. **Language:** 38.6% English only; 8.4% Spanish.
Employment: 117,664 employed; 2.5% unemployment. **Per capita income:** $99,424; change (2017-18): 7.3%. **Below poverty:** 5.2%; 3.0% of families. **Educational attainment:** 93.4% HS; 56.1% bachelor's. **Avg. commute:** 35.0 min. 71.7% drive, 9.6% carpool, 10.1% public trans. **Housing units:** 77,756; 95.7% occupied. **Home ownership:** 61.6%. **Avg. home:** $988,000; change (2017-19): 9.8%. **Avg. rent:** $2,188. **Crime rates** (MSA): violent: 473; property: 3,283.
Mayor: Lily Mei, nonpartisan
History: Spanish mission founded, 1797; inc. 1956 as consolidation of five communities.
Website: fremont.gov

Fresno, California

Population: 531,576 (34). **Pop. density:** 4,633. **Pop. change (2010-19):** 6.8%. **Area:** 114.7 sq mi. **Racial distribution:** 58.2% white; 7.6% Black; 13.7% Asian; 1.2% Amer. Ind.; 0.1% Pac. Isl.; 15.0% other; 2+ races, 4.2%. **Hispanic pop.:** 49.4%. **Foreign born:** 20.6%. **U.S. citizens:** 88.7%. **Language:** 56.4% English only; 30.0% Spanish.
Employment: 221,220 employed; 5.7% unemployment. **Per capita income:** $43,084; change (2017-18): 4.7%. **Below poverty:** 22.5%; 22.0% of families. **Educational attainment:** 76.7% HS; 21.6% bachelor's. **Avg. commute:** 21.8 min. 78% drive, 12% carpool. **Housing units:** 178,081; 93.6% occupied. **Home ownership:** 46.4%. **Avg. home:** $281,600; change (2017-19): 11.3%. **Avg. rent:** $969. **Crime rates:** violent: 555; property: 3,345.
Mayor: Lee Brand, nonpartisan
History: Founded by railroad company, 1872; inc. 1885.
Website: www.fresno.gov

Garland, Texas

Population: 239,928 (94). **Pop. density:** 4,205. **Pop. change (2010-19):** 5.5%. **Area:** 57.1 sq mi. **Racial distribution:** 63.9% white; 14.0% Black; 11.1% Asian; 0.4% Amer. Ind.; <0.05% Pac. Isl.; 7.0% other; 2+ races, 3.5%. **Hispanic pop.:** 42.8%. **Foreign born:** 29.4%. **U.S. citizens:** 82.4%. **Language:** 49.9% English only; 36.5% Spanish.
Employment: 122,935 employed; 3.3% unemployment. **Per capita income:** $55,886; change (2017-18): 4.7%. **Below poverty:** 10.8%; 11.9% of families. **Educational attainment:** 76.3% HS; 22.8% bachelor's. **Avg. commute:** 29.1 min. 79% drive, 12.7% carpool. **Housing units:** 79,520; 94.9% occupied. **Home ownership:** 62.5%. **Avg. home:** $268,600; change (2017-19): 8.6%. **Avg. rent:** $1,078. **Crime rates** (MSA): violent: 351; property: 2,233.
Mayor: Scott LeMay, nonpartisan
History: Settled 1850s; inc. 1891.
Website: www.garlandtx.gov

Gilbert, Arizona

Population: 254,114 (87). **Pop. density:** 3,711. **Pop. change (2010-19):** 21.3%. **Area:** 68.5 sq mi. **Racial distribution:** 82.8% white; 3.6% Black; 6.0% Asian; 1.0% Amer. Ind.; 0.2% Pac. Isl.; 2.5% other; 2+ races, 4.0%. **Hispanic pop.:** 16.9%. **Foreign born:** 9.3%. **U.S. citizens:** 96.8%. **Language:** 86.0% English only; 6.7% Spanish.
Employment: 138,527 employed; 3.4% unemployment. **Per capita income:** $46,125; change (2017-18): 4.3%. **Below poverty:** 5.7%; 4.2% of families. **Educational attainment:** 96.0% HS; 43.7% bachelor's. **Avg. commute:** 27.9 min. 79.1% drive. **Housing units:** 80,626; 93.7% occupied. **Home ownership:** 72.7%. **Avg. home:** $287,100; change (2017-19): 16.4%. **Avg. rent:** $1,429. **Crime rates** (MSA): violent: 446; property: 2,609.
Mayor: Jenn Daniels, nonpartisan
History: Est. 1902; inc. 1920.
Website: www.gilbertaz.gov

Glendale, Arizona

Population: 252,381 (88). **Pop. density:** 4,098. **Pop. change (2010-19):** 11.6%. **Area:** 61.6 sq mi. **Racial distribution:** 76.8% white; 6.8% Black; 4.7% Asian; 1.3% Amer. Ind.; 0.2% Pac. Isl.; 5.8% other; 2+ races, 4.4%. **Hispanic pop.:** 37.2%. **Foreign born:** 17.5%. **U.S. citizens:** 89.7%. **Language:** 67.1% English only; 24.5% Spanish.
Employment: 123,087 employed; 4.2% unemployment. **Per capita income:** $46,125; change (2017-18): 4.3%. **Below poverty:** 15.6%; 14.6% of families. **Educational attainment:** 83.6% HS; 21.4% bachelor's. **Avg. commute:** 28.1 min. 76.5% drive, 12.5% carpool. **Housing units:** 90,600; 91.0% occupied. **Home ownership:** 54.5%. **Avg. home:** $287,100; change (2017-19): 16.4%. **Avg. rent:** $958. **Crime rates** (MSA): violent: 99; property: 1,519.
Mayor: Jerry Weiers, nonpartisan
History: Est. 1892; inc. 1910.
Website: www.glendaleaz.com

Greensboro, North Carolina

Population: 296,710 (67). **Pop. density:** 2,299. **Pop. change (2010-19):** 10.1%. **Area:** 131.1 sq mi. **Racial distribution:** 47.8% white; 41.6% Black; 4.7% Asian; 0.5% Amer. Ind.; 0.1% Pac. Isl.; 2.7% other; 2+ races, 2.6%. **Hispanic pop.:** 7.5%. **Foreign born:** 10.9%. **U.S. citizens:** 93.6%. **Language:** 86.7% English only; 6.0% Spanish.

Employment: 141,482 employed; 4.2% unemployment. **Per capita income:** $43,189; change (2017-18): 3.6%. **Below poverty:** 16.3%; 13.8% of families. **Educational attainment:** 89.8% HS; 37.4% bachelor's. **Avg. commute:** 21.0 min. 82.6% drive. **Housing units:** 130,208; 88.7% occupied. **Home ownership:** 50.4%. **Avg. home:** $176,200; change (2017-19): 12.1%. **Avg. rent:** $846. **Crime rates:** violent: NA; property: 3,352.

Mayor: Nancy Vaughan, nonpartisan

History: Est. c. 1740; site of Revolutionary War conflict, 1781, between namesake Gen. Nathanael Greene and Gen. Cornwallis; inc. 1807. Origin of civil rights sit-in movement.

Website: www.greensboro-nc.gov

Henderson, Nevada

Population: 320,189 (61). **Pop. density:** 3,018. **Pop. change (2010-19):** 24.4%. **Area:** 106.1 sq mi. **Racial distribution:** 76.1% white; 5.7% Black; 7.8% Asian; 0.5% Amer. Ind.; 0.4% Pac. Isl.; 4.6% other; 2+ races, 4.8%. **Hispanic pop.:** 16.4%. **Foreign born:** 12.8%. **U.S. citizens:** 95.8%. **Language:** 82.3% English only; 9.5% Spanish.

Employment: 157,189 employed; 3.7% unemployment. **Per capita income:** $47,090; change (2017-18): 4.4%. **Below poverty:** 7.9%; 5.8% of families. **Educational attainment:** 93.5% HS; 32.5% bachelor's. **Avg. commute:** 22.9 min. 82.8% drive. **Housing units:** 127,559; 89.3% occupied. **Home ownership:** 62.7%. **Avg. home:** $306,000; change (2017-19): 19.3%. **Avg. rent:** $1,226.

Crime rates: violent: 188; property: 1,961.

Mayor: Debra March, nonpartisan

History: Early growth spurred by WWII magnesium mining; inc. 1953.

Website: www.cityofhenderson.com

Hialeah, Florida

Population: 233,339 (96). **Pop. density:** 10,812. **Pop. change (2010-19):** 3.5%. **Area:** 21.6 sq mi. **Racial distribution:** 92.6% white; 2.5% Black; 0.5% Asian; <0.05% Amer. Ind.; <0.05% Pac. Isl.; 3.7% other; 2+ races, 0.6%. **Hispanic pop.:** 96.1%. **Foreign born:** 74.3%. **U.S. citizens:** 65.8%. **Language:** 6.4% English only; 93.0% Spanish.

Employment: 111,288 employed; 2.4% unemployment. **Per capita income:** $57,228; change (2017-18): 5.2%. **Below poverty:** 22.0%; 20.8% of families. **Educational attainment:** 70.7% HS; 14.6% bachelor's. **Avg. commute:** 27.5 min. 77.5% drive. **Housing units:** 75,635; 96.1% occupied. **Home ownership:** 45.8%. **Avg. home:** $360,000; change (2017-19): 9.1%. **Avg. rent:** $1,117. **Crime rates** (MSA): violent: 428; property: 2,781.

Mayor: Carlos Hernandez, nonpartisan

History: Inc. 1925. Industrial and residential city NW of Miami; site of major race track.

Website: www.hialeahfl.gov

Honolulu, Hawaii

Population: 345,064 (56). **Pop. density:** 5,699. **Pop. change (2010-19):** 1.8%. **Area:** 60.5 sq mi. **Racial distribution:** 17.5% white; 1.9% Black; 53.3% Asian; 0.1% Amer. Ind.; 8.2% Pac. Isl.; 0.9% other; 2+ races, 18.2%. **Hispanic pop.:** 7.3%. **Foreign born:** 26.9%. **U.S. citizens:** 87.9%. **Language:** 63.2% English only; 1.4% Spanish.

Employment: 438,936 employed; 2.6% unemployment. **Per capita income:** $59,608; change (2017-18): 4.5%. **Below poverty:** 10.8%; 7.4% of families. **Educational attainment:** 88.8% HS; 36.4% bachelor's. **Avg. commute:** 23.5 min. 56.6% drive, 13.3% carpool, 11.8% public trans. **Housing units:** 151,368; 85.1% occupied. **Home ownership:** 44.4%. **Avg. home:** $802,500; change (2017-19): 6.0%. **Avg. rent:** $1,465. **Crime rates** (MSA): violent: 250; property: 2,941.

Mayor: Kirk Caldwell, nonpartisan

History: Europeans entered harbor, 1794; declared capital of the Hawaii Kingdom by King Kamehameha III, 1850. Pearl Harbor naval base attacked by Japanese, Dec. 7, 1941.

Website: www.honolulu.gov

Houston, Texas

Population: 2,320,268 (4). **Pop. density:** 3,624. **Pop. change (2010-19):** 10.5%. **Area:** 640.2 sq mi. **Racial distribution:** 57.6% white; 22.5% Black; 6.9% Asian; 0.3% Amer. Ind.; 0.1% Pac. Isl.; 10.5% other; 2+ races, 2.1%. **Hispanic pop.:** 44.8%. **Foreign born:** 29.5%. **U.S. citizens:** 79.3%. **Language:** 51.2% English only; 38.8% Spanish.

Employment: 1,115,328 employed; 3.7% unemployment. **Per capita income:** $56,077; change (2017-18): 4.9%. **Below poverty:** 16.6%; 17.5% of families. **Educational attainment:** 78.3% HS; 32.1% bachelor's. **Avg. commute:** 27.4 min. 77.1% drive, 10.9% carpool. **Housing units:** 955,525; 88.8% occupied. **Home ownership:** 42.9%. **Avg. home:** $245,800; change (2017-19): 6.4%. **Avg. rent:** $990. **Crime rates:** violent: 1,026; property: 4,010.

Mayor: Sylvester Turner, Democrat

History: Founded 1836; inc. 1837; capital of Rep. of Texas, 1837-39; developed rapidly after completion of channel to Gulf of Mexico, 1914. World center of oil, natural gas technology.

Website: www.houstontx.gov

Indianapolis, Indiana

Population: 876,384 (17). **Pop. density:** 2,424. **Pop. change (2010-19):** 6.7%. **Area:** 361.6 sq mi. **Racial distribution:** 61.4% white; 28.3% Black; 3.2% Asian; 0.3% Amer. Ind.; 0.1% Pac. Isl.; 3.5% other; 2+ races, 3.2%. **Hispanic pop.:** 10.2%. **Foreign born:** 9.5%. **U.S. citizens:** 93.4%. **Language:** 86.3% English only; 8.5% Spanish.

Employment: 431,941 employed; 3.3% unemployment. **Per capita income:** $54,179; change (2017-18): 3.7%. **Below poverty:** 16.0%; 14.2% of families. **Educational attainment:** 85.5% HS; 30.4% bachelor's. **Avg. commute:** 23.4 min. 82.3% drive. **Housing units:** 384,955; 87.1% occupied. **Home ownership:** 53.3%. **Avg. home:** $200,100; change (2017-19): 16.7%. **Avg. rent:** $865. **Crime rates:** violent: 1,273; property: 4,129.

Mayor: Joe Hogsett, Democrat

History: Founded 1821; became planned state capital, 1825.

Website: www.indy.gov

Irvine, California

Population: 287,401 (72). **Pop. density:** 4,380. **Pop. change (2010-19):** 34.6%. **Area:** 65.6 sq mi. **Racial distribution:** 47.6% white; 1.9% Black; 42.3% Asian; 0.2% Amer. Ind.; 0.2% Pac. Isl.; 2.8% other; 2+ races, 5.2%. **Hispanic pop.:** 10.3%. **Foreign born:** 40.4%. **U.S. citizens:** 80.5%. **Language:** 49.8% English only; 6.2% Spanish.

Employment: 144,446 employed; 2.6% unemployment. **Per capita income:** $63,913; change (2017-18): 5.4%. **Below poverty:** 14.4%; 7.5% of families. **Educational attainment:** 96.4% HS; 68.5% bachelor's. **Avg. commute:** 25.6 min. 76.6% drive. **Housing units:** 101,434; 94.0% occupied. **Home ownership:** 47.3%. **Avg. home:** $825,000; change (2017-19): 5.8%. **Avg. rent:** $2,259. **Crime rates:** violent: 56; property: 1,270.

Mayor: Christina L. Shea, nonpartisan

History: Univ. of CA–Irvine campus announced, 1959; planned city developed around campus; inc. 1971.

Website: www.cityofirvine.org

Irving, Texas

Population: 239,798 (95). **Pop. density:** 3,576. **Pop. change (2010-19):** 10.6%. **Area:** 67.1 sq mi. **Racial distribution:** 51.3% white; 13.2% Black; 18.5% Asian; 0.6% Amer. Ind.; 0.2% Pac. Isl.; 13.4% other; 2+ races, 2.8%. **Hispanic pop.:** 43.2%. **Foreign born:** 37.0%. **U.S. citizens:** 72.2%. **Language:** 41.9% English only; 37.9% Spanish.

Employment: 129,377 employed; 3.2% unemployment. **Per capita income:** $55,886; change (2017-18): 4.7%. **Below poverty:** 11.1%; 11.1% of families. **Educational attainment:** 79.5% HS; 36.3% bachelor's. **Avg. commute:** 24.2 min. 79.2% drive, 11.3% carpool. **Housing units:** 96,670; 93.4% occupied. **Home ownership:** 37.1%. **Avg. home:** $208,500; change (2017-19): 8.6%. **Avg. rent:** $1,086. **Crime rates:** violent: 209; property: 2,361.

Mayor: Rick Stopfer, nonpartisan

History: Founded 1903; inc. 1914; remained small until 1950s.

Website: www.cityofirving.org

Jacksonville, Florida

Population: 911,507 (12). **Pop. density:** 1,219. **Pop. change (2010-19):** 10.7%. **Area:** 747.5 sq mi. **Racial distribution:** 58.7% white; 31.0% Black; 4.8% Asian; 0.2% Amer. Ind.; 0.1% Pac. Isl.; 1.8% other; 2+ races, 3.4%. **Hispanic pop.:** 9.6%. **Foreign born:** 11.1%. **U.S. citizens:** 95.0%. **Language:** 85.2% English only; 6.9% Spanish.

Employment: 449,104 employed; 3.3% unemployment. **Per capita income:** $49,754; change (2017-18): 4.0%. **Below poverty:** 13.4%; 12.1% of families. **Educational attainment:** 89.2% HS; 27.8% bachelor's. **Avg. commute:** 24.9 min. 80% drive, 9.7% carpool. **Housing units:** 379,288; 88.0% occupied. **Home ownership:** 56.0%. **Avg. home:** $225,700; change (2017-19): −1.4%. **Avg. rent:** $1,029. **Crime rates:** violent: 596; property: 3,334.

Mayor: Lenny Curry, Republican

History: Settled as Cow Ford; renamed after Andrew Jackson, 1822; inc. 1832; scene of Civil War conflict, 1864.

Website: www.coj.net

Jersey City, New Jersey

Population: 262,075 (80). **Pop. density:** 17,775. **Pop. change (2010-19):** 5.5%. **Area:** 14.7 sq mi. **Racial distribution:** 35.0% white; 23.9% Black; 25.1% Asian; 0.5% Amer. Ind.; 0.1% Pac. Isl.; 12.1% other; 2+ races, 3.3%. **Hispanic pop.:** 29.1%. **Foreign born:** 41.4%. **U.S. citizens:** 77.8%. **Language:** 46.6% English only; 23.6% Spanish.

Employment: 135,878 employed; 3.5% unemployment. **Per capita income:** $76,681; change (2017-18): 5.1%. **Below poverty:** 16.2%; 14.8% of families. **Educational attainment:** 86.8% HS; 46.1% bachelor's. **Avg. commute:** 37.1 min. 31.2% drive, 48.5% public trans. **Housing units:** 112,480; 89.8% occupied. **Home ownership:** 28.7%. **Avg. home:** $386,500; change (2017-19): 1.0%. **Avg. rent:** $1,334. **Crime rates** (2017): violent: 510; property: 1,807.

Mayor: Steven M. Fulop, nonpartisan

History: Chartered as town by British 1668; scene of Revolutionary War conflict, 1779. Important station on Underground Railroad.
Website: jerseycitynj.gov

Kansas City, Missouri

Population: 495,327 (38). **Pop. density:** 1,573. **Pop. change (2010-19):** 7.5%. **Area:** 314.9 sq mi. **Racial distribution:** 60.1% white; 29.0% Black; 2.7% Asian; 0.4% Amer. Ind.; 0.1% Pac. Isl.; 4.1% other; 2+ races, 3.5%. **Hispanic pop.:** 10.2%. **Foreign born:** 7.7%. **U.S. citizens:** 95.6%. **Language:** 88.2% English only; 6.7% Spanish.
Employment: 251,461 employed; 3.6% unemployment. **Per capita income:** $53,788; change (2017-18): 4.0%. **Below poverty:** 14.0%; 12.0% of families. **Educational attainment:** 89.6% HS; 34.3% bachelor's. **Avg. commute:** 21.9 min. 81% drive. **Housing units:** 230,335; 87.0% occupied. **Home ownership:** 53.4%. **Avg. home:** $219,400; change (2017-19): 12.6%. **Avg. rent:** $899. **Crime rates:** NA.
Mayor: Quinton Lucas, nonpartisan
History: Est. by 1838 at confluence of Missouri and Kansas Rivers; inc. 1850.
Website: www.kcmo.gov

Laredo, Texas

Population: 262,491 (79). **Pop. density:** 2,482. **Pop. change (2010-19):** 10.8%. **Area:** 105.7 sq mi. **Racial distribution:** 95.4% white; 0.4% Black; 0.5% Asian; 0.2% Amer. Ind.; <0.05% Pac. Isl.; 2.9% other; 2+ races, 0.5%. **Hispanic pop.:** 95.4%. **Foreign born:** 26.2%. **U.S. citizens:** 81.3%. **Language:** 9.9% English only; 89.5% Spanish.
Employment: 109,467 employed; 3.7% unemployment. **Per capita income:** $31,635; change (2017-18): 4.9%. **Below poverty:** 24.0%; 25.4% of families. **Educational attainment:** 68.3% HS; 18.9% bachelor's. **Avg. commute:** 21.1 min. 81.3% drive, 12.1% carpool. **Housing units:** 76,283; 91.6% occupied. **Home ownership:** 62.0%. **Avg. rent:** $826. **Crime rates:** violent: 337; property: 2,410.
Mayor: Pete Saenz, nonpartisan
History: Founded by Spanish colonists, 1755; part of U.S. from 1848. Fast growth fueled by immigration; principal port of entry into Mexico.
Website: www.cityoflaredo.com

Las Vegas, Nevada

Population: 651,319 (27). **Pop. density:** 4,594. **Pop. change (2010-19):** 11.4%. **Area:** 141.8 sq mi. **Racial distribution:** 62.2% white; 12.2% Black; 6.6% Asian; 0.9% Amer. Ind.; 0.8% Pac. Isl.; 12.5% other; 2+ races, 4.9%. **Hispanic pop.:** 32.9%. **Foreign born:** 20.8%. **U.S. citizens:** 88.5%. **Language:** 67.0% English only; 25.1% Spanish.
Employment: 301,995 employed; 4.2% unemployment. **Per capita income:** $47,090; change (2017-18): 4.4%. **Below poverty:** 13.6%; 11.8% of families. **Educational attainment:** 84.4% HS; 23.9% bachelor's. **Avg. commute:** 25.7 min. 77.8% drive, 9.9% carpool. **Housing units:** 255,611; 88.6% occupied. **Home ownership:** 52.5%. **Avg. home:** $306,000; change (2017-19): 19.3%. **Avg. rent:** $1,057. **Crime rates:** violent: 605; property: 2,838.
Mayor: Carolyn G. Goodman, nonpartisan
History: Occupied by Mormons 1855-57; bought by railroad 1903; city of Las Vegas inc. 1911; gambling legalized 1931.
Website: www.lasvegasnevada.gov

Lexington-Fayette, Kentucky

Population: 323,152 (60). **Pop. density:** 1,139. **Pop. change (2010-19):** 8.9%. **Area:** 283.6 sq mi. **Racial distribution:** 75.4% white; 14.4% Black; 3.6% Asian; 0.3% Amer. Ind.; 0.1% Pac. Isl.; 2.7% other; 2+ races, 3.6%. **Hispanic pop.:** 7.2%. **Foreign born:** 9.5%. **U.S. citizens:** 93.1%. **Language:** 87.1% English only; 6.3% Spanish.
Employment: 170,028 employed; 3.3% unemployment. **Per capita income:** $47,875; change (2017-18): 3.2%. **Below poverty:** 16.6%; 11.8% of families. **Educational attainment:** 90.9% HS; 42.9% bachelor's. **Avg. commute:** 20.9 min. 78.5% drive. **Housing units:** 140,662; 91.6% occupied. **Home ownership:** 54.5%. **Avg. home:** $180,000; change (2017-19): 10.6%. **Avg. rent:** $864. **Crime rates:** violent: 302; property: 3,173.
Mayor: Linda Gorton, nonpartisan
History: Site founded and named in 1775 after site of the Revolutionary War's opening battle at Lexington, MA; chartered 1782. Merged with Fayette County, 1974.
Website: www.lexingtonky.gov

Lincoln, Nebraska

Population: 289,102 (68). **Pop. density:** 3,004. **Pop. change (2010-19):** 11.4%. **Area:** 96.2 sq mi. **Racial distribution:** 85.2% white; 4.4% Black; 4.7% Asian; 0.6% Amer. Ind.; 0.1% Pac. Isl.; 1.4% other; 2+ races, 3.6%. **Hispanic pop.:** 7.4%. **Foreign born:** 8.4%. **U.S. citizens:** 95.4%. **Language:** 87.9% English only; 4.5% Spanish.
Employment: 155,401 employed; 2.8% unemployment. **Per capita income:** $49,886; change (2017-18): 4.9%. **Below poverty:** 13.8%; 8.9% of families. **Educational attainment:** 93.2%

HS; 38.8% bachelor's. **Avg. commute:** 18.7 min. 81% drive. **Housing units:** 118,258; 94.8% occupied. **Home ownership:** 57.3%. **Avg. home:** $198,400; change (2017-19): 13.1%. **Avg. rent:** $822. **Crime rates:** violent: 362; property: 2,878.
Mayor: Leirion Gaylor Baird, nonpartisan
History: Originally called Lancaster; chosen state capital, 1867, renamed after Abraham Lincoln; inc. 1871.
Website: lincoln.ne.gov

Long Beach, California

Population: 462,628 (43). **Pop. density:** 9,126. **Pop. change (2010-19):** 0.0%. **Area:** 50.7 sq mi. **Racial distribution:** 52.0% white; 12.9% Black; 13.1% Asian; 0.9% Amer. Ind.; 0.8% Pac. Isl.; 15.6% other; 2+ races, 4.7%. **Hispanic pop.:** 42.5%. **Foreign born:** 25.4%. **U.S. citizens:** 87.4%. **Language:** 53.9% English only; 34.0% Spanish.
Employment: 228,873 employed; 4.6% unemployment. **Per capita income:** $63,913; change (2017-18): 5.4%. **Below poverty:** 15.8%; 13.4% of families. **Educational attainment:** 80.2% HS; 30.6% bachelor's. **Avg. commute:** 30.6 min. 75% drive. **Housing units:** 175,235; 95.0% occupied. **Home ownership:** 40.1%. **Avg. home:** $611,200; change (2017-19): 11.0%. **Avg. rent:** $1,252. **Crime rates:** violent: 698; property: 2,534.
Mayor: Robert Garcia, nonpartisan
History: Settled c. 1784 by Spanish; by 1884, developed as harbor; inc. 1888; oil discovered 1921.
Website: www.longbeach.gov

Los Angeles, California

Population: 3,979,576 (2). **Pop. density:** 8,486. **Pop. change (2010-19):** 4.8%. **Area:** 469.0 sq mi. **Racial distribution:** 52.4% white; 8.9% Black; 11.6% Asian; 0.7% Amer. Ind.; 0.2% Pac. Isl.; 22.5% other; 2+ races, 3.6%. **Hispanic pop.:** 48.6%. **Foreign born:** 37.3%. **U.S. citizens:** 80.3%. **Language:** 40.7% English only; 42.4% Spanish.
Employment: 1,988,456 employed; 4.5% unemployment. **Per capita income:** $63,913; change (2017-18): 5.4%. **Below poverty:** 16.8%; 14.8% of families. **Educational attainment:** 77.0% HS; 33.7% bachelor's. **Avg. commute:** 31.4 min. 69.4% drive. **Housing units:** 1,474,043; 93.2% occupied. **Home ownership:** 36.8%. **Avg. home:** $611,200; change (2017-19): 11.0%. **Avg. rent:** $1,376. **Crime rates:** violent: 748; property: 2,513.
Mayor: Eric Garcetti, nonpartisan
History: Est. by Mexicans near Spanish mission, 1781; ceded to U.S., 1848; inc. 1850; grew rapidly after coming of railroads, 1876 and 1885. Film and defense industries drove 20th-century growth.
Website: www.lacity.org

Louisville/Jefferson County, Kentucky

Population: 617,638 (29). **Pop. density:** 2,345. **Pop. change (2010-19):** 3.5%. **Area:** 263.4 sq mi. **Racial distribution:** 69.9% white; 23.5% Black; 2.7% Asian; 0.2% Amer. Ind.; 0.1% Pac. Isl.; 0.9% other; 2+ races, 2.7%. **Hispanic pop.:** 5.4%. **Foreign born:** 7.4%. **U.S. citizens:** 95.9%. **Language:** 90.6% English only; 4.2% Spanish.
Employment: 386,373 employed; 4.0% unemployment. **Per capita income:** $50,101; change (2017-18): 4.0%. **Below poverty:** 14.1%; 11.9% of families. **Educational attainment:** 88.9% HS; 29.2% bachelor's. **Avg. commute:** 22.7 min. 79.8% drive. **Housing units:** 275,493; 89.4% occupied. **Home ownership:** 60.0%. **Avg. home:** $192,700; change (2017-19): 12.3%. **Avg. rent:** $812. **Crime rates:** violent: 647; property: 4,122.
Mayor: Greg Fischer, Democrat
History: Est. 1778; named for Louis XVI of France; inc. 1828; base for Union forces in Civil War.
Website: louisvilleky.gov

Lubbock, Texas

Population: 258,862 (83). **Pop. density:** 1,921. **Pop. change (2010-19):** 12.0%. **Area:** 134.7 sq mi. **Racial distribution:** 80.2% white; 8.1% Black; 2.5% Asian; 1.0% Amer. Ind.; 0.1% Pac. Isl.; 5.2% other; 2+ races, 2.8%. **Hispanic pop.:** 35.2%. **Foreign born:** 6.2%. **U.S. citizens:** 96.1%. **Language:** 77.8% English only; 18.5% Spanish.
Employment: 129,384 employed; 2.8% unemployment. **Per capita income:** $42,181; change (2017-18): 4.4%. **Below poverty:** 19.7%; 12.0% of families. **Educational attainment:** 86.0% HS; 30.3% bachelor's. **Avg. commute:** 16.4 min. 79.5% drive, 13.4% carpool. **Housing units:** 105,296; 89.7% occupied. **Home ownership:** 51.3%. **Avg. rent:** $928. **Crime rates:** violent: 997; property: 4,563.
Mayor: Dan Pope, nonpartisan
History: Became county seat, 1891; inc. 1909.
Website: ci.lubbock.tx.us

Madison, Wisconsin

Population: 259,680 (82). **Pop. density:** 3,273. **Pop. change (2010-19):** 11.1%. **Area:** 79.3 sq mi. **Racial distribution:** 78.4% white; 6.8% Black; 9.0% Asian; 0.4% Amer. Ind.; <0.05% Pac. Isl.; 1.8% other; 2+ races, 3.6%. **Hispanic pop.:** 6.9%. **Foreign born:** 12.0%. **U.S. citizens:** 92.5%. **Language:** 84.3% English only; 5.8% Spanish.

Employment: 153,189 employed; 2.4% unemployment. **Per capita income:** $59,371; change (2017-18): 4.7%. **Below poverty:** 18.4%; 7.4% of families. **Educational attainment:** 95.3% HS; 57.9% bachelor's. **Avg. commute:** 19.4 min. 64.2% drive. **Housing units:** 113,665; 95.5% occupied. **Home ownership:** 47.1%. **Avg. home:** $299,200; change (2017-19): 11.7%. **Avg. rent:** $1,068. **Crime rates:** violent: 404; property: 2,601.

Mayor: Satya Rhodes-Conway, nonpartisan

History: Selected as site for state capital, named for James Madison, 1836; chartered 1856.

Website: www.cityofmadison.com

Memphis, Tennessee

Population: 651,073 (28). **Pop. density:** 2,052. **Pop. change (2010-19):** −0.2%. **Area:** 317.4 sq mi. **Racial distribution:** 29.1% white; 64.2% Black; 1.6% Asian; 0.2% Amer. Ind.; <0.05% Pac. Isl.; 3.4% other; 2+ races, 1.6%. **Hispanic pop.:** 7.2%. **Foreign born:** 6.2%. **U.S. citizens:** 95.6%. **Language:** 90.5% English only; 6.3% Spanish.

Employment: 285,274 employed; 4.4% unemployment. **Per capita income:** $46,620; change (2017-18): 4.4%. **Below poverty:** 21.1%; 21.5% of families. **Educational attainment:** 85.2% HS; 25.7% bachelor's. **Avg. commute:** 21.6 min. 81.6% drive, 10.6% carpool. **Housing units:** 299,132; 83.8% occupied. **Home ownership:** 46.9%. **Avg. home:** $188,700; change (2017-19): 13.2%. **Avg. rent:** $884. **Crime rates:** violent: 1,943; property: 6,406.

Mayor: Jim Strickland, nonpartisan

History: French, Spanish, and U.S. forts by 1797; settled by 1819; inc. 1826; surrendered charter to state 1879 after yellow fever epidemics; rechartered as city 1893.

Website: memphistn.gov

Mesa, Arizona

Population: 518,012 (35). **Pop. density:** 3,751. **Pop. change (2010-19):** 17.5%. **Area:** 138.1 sq mi. **Racial distribution:** 82.8% white; 3.8% Black; 2.0% Asian; 2.3% Amer. Ind.; 0.4% Pac. Isl.; 5.2% other; 2+ races, 3.4%. **Hispanic pop.:** 27.7%. **Foreign born:** 12.0%. **U.S. citizens:** 92.0%. **Language:** 78.6% English only; 17.6% Spanish.

Employment: 251,588 employed; 4.0% unemployment. **Per capita income:** $46,125; change (2017-18): 4.3%. **Below poverty:** 13.2%; 11.6% of families. **Educational attainment:** 88.1% HS; 26.3% bachelor's. **Avg. commute:** 24.8 min. 75.9% drive, 11.8% carpool. **Housing units:** 209,537; 85.1% occupied. **Home ownership:** 60.3%. **Avg. home:** $287,100; change (2017-19): 16.4%. **Avg. rent:** $988. **Crime rates:** violent: 364; property: 1,985.

Mayor: John Giles, nonpartisan

History: Founded by Mormons from Utah and Idaho, 1878; inc. 1883.

Website: www.mesaaz.gov

Miami, Florida

Population: 467,963 (42). **Pop. density:** 13,000. **Pop. change (2010-19):** 16.8%. **Area:** 36.0 sq mi. **Racial distribution:** 75.2% white; 17.7% Black; 1.1% Asian; 0.2% Amer. Ind.; <0.05% Pac. Isl.; 3.9% other; 2+ races, 1.8%. **Hispanic pop.:** 72.5%. **Foreign born:** 58.2%. **U.S. citizens:** 69.8%. **Language:** 23.0% English only; 69.9% Spanish.

Employment: 228,114 employed; 2.3% unemployment. **Per capita income:** $57,228; change (2017-18): 5.2%. **Below poverty:** 22.5%; 20.2% of families. **Educational attainment:** 77.0% HS; 27.9% bachelor's. **Avg. commute:** 29.1 min. 69.7% drive, 10% public trans. **Housing units:** 202,289; 84.6% occupied. **Home ownership:** 29.8%. **Avg. home:** $360,000; change (2017-19): 9.1%. **Avg. rent:** $1,120. **Crime rates:** violent: 630; property: 3,559.

Mayor: Francis Suarez, nonpartisan

History: Site of fort, 1836; inc. 1896. Modern city developed into financial and tourism center. Land speculation in 1920s added to city's growth.

Website: www.miamigov.com

Milwaukee, Wisconsin

Population: 590,157 (31). **Pop. density:** 6,136. **Pop. change (2010-19):** −0.8%. **Area:** 96.2 sq mi. **Racial distribution:** 44.6% white; 38.8% Black; 4.3% Asian; 0.6% Amer. Ind.; <0.05% Pac. Isl.; 7.7% other; 2+ races, 4.0%. **Hispanic pop.:** 18.8%. **Foreign born:** 9.8%. **U.S. citizens:** 93.6%. **Language:** 80.0% English only; 14.1% Spanish.

Employment: 261,737 employed; 4.5% unemployment. **Per capita income:** $57,005; change (2017-18): 5.1%. **Below poverty:** 22.4%; 22.1% of families. **Educational attainment:** 83.4% HS; 24.7% bachelor's. **Avg. commute:** 22.2 min. 72.3% drive, 10.3% carpool. **Housing units:** 257,506; 89.1% occupied. **Home ownership:** 41.8%. **Avg. home:** $268,400; change (2017-19): 12.0%. **Avg. rent:** $842. **Crime rates:** violent: 1,413; property: 2,972.

Mayor: Tom Barrett, Democrat

History: Indian trading post by 1674; inc. 1846. Famous beer industry.

Website: city.milwaukee.gov

Minneapolis, Minnesota

Population: 429,606 (46). **Pop. density:** 7,956. **Pop. change (2010-19):** 12.1%. **Area:** 54.0 sq mi. **Racial distribution:** 63.8% white; 19.4% Black; 6.1% Asian; 1.4% Amer. Ind.; <0.05% Pac. Isl.; 4.7% other; 2+ races, 4.6%. **Hispanic pop.:** 9.6%. **Foreign born:** 15.7%. **U.S. citizens:** 91.3%. **Language:** 77.7% English only; 8.0% Spanish.

Employment: 237,996 employed; 2.8% unemployment. **Per capita income:** $62,889; change (2017-18): 4.5%. **Below poverty:** 18.3%; 12.6% of families. **Educational attainment:** 89.7% HS; 49.4% bachelor's. **Avg. commute:** 23.1 min. 60.7% drive, 13.5% public trans. **Housing units:** 185,260; 93.9% occupied. **Home ownership:** 47.3%. **Avg. home:** $288,600; change (2017-19): 14.5%. **Avg. rent:** $985. **Crime rates:** violent: 793; property: 3,911.

Mayor: Jacob Frey, Democrat (DFL)

History: Visited by French missionary Louis Hennepin, 1680; included in area of military reservations, 1819; inc. 1867.

Website: minneapolismn.gov

Nashville-Davidson, Tennessee

Population: 670,820 (23). **Pop. density:** 1,411. **Pop. change (2010-19):** 11.0%. **Area:** 475.5 sq mi. **Racial distribution:** 63.2% white; 27.9% Black; 3.6% Asian; 0.2% Amer. Ind.; 0.1% Pac. Isl.; 2.5% other; 2+ races, 2.6%. **Hispanic pop.:** 10.4%. **Foreign born:** 13.1%. **U.S. citizens:** 91.4%. **Language:** 82.3% English only; 9.2% Spanish.

Employment: 399,502 employed; 2.5% unemployment. **Per capita income:** $57,953; change (2017-18): 4.6%. **Below poverty:** 13.6%; 12.6% of families. **Educational attainment:** 88.3% HS; 39.7% bachelor's. **Avg. commute:** 24.7 min. 78.6% drive, 10.1% carpool. **Housing units:** 295,259; 90.8% occupied. **Home ownership:** 53.7%. **Avg. home:** $275,000; change (2017-19): 13.8%. **Avg. rent:** $1,033. **Crime rates:** violent: 1,113; property: 4,011.

Mayor: John Cooper, nonpartisan

History: Est. 1779; first chartered, 1806; became permanent state capital 1843. Home of Grand Ole Opry.

Website: www.nashville.gov

New Orleans, Louisiana

Population: 390,144 (50). **Pop. density:** 2,303. **Pop. change (2010-19):** 12.2%. **Area:** 169.4 sq mi. **Racial distribution:** 34.0% white; 59.7% Black; 2.9% Asian; 0.2% Amer. Ind.; <0.05% Pac. Isl.; 1.4% other; 2+ races, 1.8%. **Hispanic pop.:** 5.5%. **Foreign born:** 5.6%. **U.S. citizens:** 96.9%. **Language:** 91.6% English only; 4.2% Spanish.

Employment: 170,121 employed; 4.9% unemployment. **Per capita income:** $52,431; change (2017-18): 5.3%. **Below poverty:** 21.4%; 17.8% of families. **Educational attainment:** 86.2% HS; 36.8% bachelor's. **Avg. commute:** 24.1 min. 68.4% drive. **Housing units:** 191,738; 80.3% occupied. **Home ownership:** 47.4%. **Avg. home:** $222,000; change (2017-19): 11.9%. **Avg. rent:** $973. **Crime rates:** violent: 1,163; property: 4,557.

Mayor: LaToya Cantrell, Democrat

History: Founded by French colonists, 1718; became major seaport on Mississippi R.; acquired by U.S. in Louisiana Purchase, 1803; inc. 1805. Hurricane Katrina, 2005, inflicted major damage and killed 1,450+.

Website: www.nola.gov

New York, New York

Population: 8,336,817 (1). **Pop. density:** 27,754. **Pop. change (2010-19):** 1.8%. **Area:** 300.4 sq mi. **Racial distribution:** 42.7% white; 24.3% Black; 13.9% Asian; 0.4% Amer. Ind.; 0.1% Pac. Isl.; 15.1% other; 2+ races, 3.5%. **Hispanic pop.:** 29.1%. **Foreign born:** 37.0%. **U.S. citizens:** 83.7%. **Language:** 51.3% English only; 24.2% Spanish.

Employment: 3,908,497 employed; 3.9% unemployment. **Per capita income:** $76,681; change (2017-18): 5.1%. **Below poverty:** 16.8%; 15.6% of families. **Educational attainment:** 81.6% HS; 37.4% bachelor's. **Avg. commute:** 41.2 min. 22.3% drive, 56.2% public trans. **Housing units:** 3,472,353; 90.8% occupied. **Home ownership:** 32.7%. **Avg. home:** $386,500; change (2017-19): 1.0%. **Avg. rent:** $1,396. **Crime rates** (2017): violent: 539; property: 1,449.

Mayor: Bill de Blasio, Democrat

History: Trading post est., 1624; British took control from Dutch, 1664, named city New York; U.S. capital, 1785-90. Under new charter, 1898, city expanded to include five boroughs: Bronx, Brooklyn, Queens, and Staten Island, as well as Manhattan. Sept. 11, 2001, terrorist attacks destroyed World Trade Center, killed more than 2,750.

Website: www.nyc.gov

Newark, New Jersey

Population: 282,011 (73). **Pop. density:** 11,680. **Pop. change (2010-19):** 1.7%. **Area:** 24.1 sq mi. **Racial distribution:** 26.1% white; 49.7% Black; 2.1% Asian; 0.5% Amer. Ind.; <0.05% Pac. Isl.; 19.1% other; 2+ races, 2.4%. **Hispanic pop.:** 36.4%. **Foreign**

born: 30.6%. **U.S. citizens:** 82.8%. **Language:** 52.3% English only; 32.5% Spanish.

Employment: 108,613 employed; 6.0% unemployment. **Per capita income:** $76,681; change (2017-18): 5.1%. **Below poverty:** 24.2%; 24.9% of families. **Educational attainment:** 74.9% HS; 14.8% bachelor's. **Avg. commute:** 35.3 min. 51.7% drive, 10.6% carpool, 26.3% public trans. **Housing units:** 112,724; 86.0% occupied. **Home ownership:** 22.7%. **Avg. home:** $397,100; change (2017-19): 4.7%. **Avg. rent:** $1,055. **Crime rates** (2017): violent; 896; property: 2,395.

Mayor: Ras J. Baraka, nonpartisan

History: Est. by Puritans, 1666; inc. as city, 1836. Major industry and shipping hub from mid-19th century.

Website: www.newarknj.gov

Norfolk, Virginia

Population: 242,742 (92). **Pop. density:** 4,556. **Pop. change (2010-19):** –0.1%. **Area:** 53.3 sq mi. **Racial distribution:** 47.0% white; 41.6% Black; 3.7% Asian; 0.4% Amer. Ind.; 0.1% Pac. Isl.; 3.0% other; 2+ races, 4.3%. **Hispanic pop.:** 7.9%. **Foreign born:** 7.4%. **U.S. citizens:** 96.5%. **Language:** 89.5% English only; 4.9% Spanish.

Employment: 108,487 employed; 3.5% unemployment. **Per capita income:** $50,619; change (2017-18): 4.4%. **Below poverty:** 17.1%; 15.0% of families. **Educational attainment:** 87.7% HS; 28.0% bachelor's. **Avg. commute:** 21.3 min. 73.7% drive. **Housing units:** 97,257; 90.6% occupied. **Home ownership:** 43.1%. **Avg. home:** $235,000; change (2017-19): 4.4%. **Avg. rent:** $1,031. **Crime rates:** violent: 464; property: 3,464.

Mayor: Kenneth Cooper Alexander, nonpartisan

History: Founded 1682; burned by colonists to prevent capture by British during Revolutionary War. Inc. as city, 1845. Site of world's largest naval base; major commercial port.

Website: www.norfolk.gov

North Las Vegas, Nevada

Population: 251,974 (89). **Pop. density:** 2,571. **Pop. change (2010-19):** 16.2%. **Area:** 98.0 sq mi. **Racial distribution:** 54.3% white; 20.8% Black; 6.2% Asian; 0.6% Amer. Ind.; 0.6% Pac. Isl.; 11.8% other; 2+ races, 5.7%. **Hispanic pop.:** 41.1%. **Foreign born:** 21.3%. **U.S. citizens:** 87.8%. **Language:** 60.2% English only; 33.5% Spanish.

Employment: 100,021 employed; 4.4% unemployment. **Per capita income:** $47,090; change (2017-18): 4.4%. **Below poverty:** 11.7%; 11.7% of families. **Educational attainment:** 80.7% HS; 16.8% bachelor's. **Avg. commute:** 27.1 min. 81.4% drive, 11% carpool. **Housing units:** 79,551; 91.2% occupied. **Home ownership:** 57.0%. **Avg. home:** $306,000; change (2017-19): 19.3%. **Avg. rent:** $1,168. **Crime rates** (MSA): violent: NA; property: 2,671.

Mayor: John J. Lee, nonpartisan

History: Inc. 1946.

Website: www.cityofnorthlasvegas.com

Oakland, California

Population: 433,031 (45). **Pop. density:** 7,747. **Pop. change (2010-19):** 10.6%. **Area:** 55.9 sq mi. **Racial distribution:** 36.1% white; 23.6% Black; 15.7% Asian; 0.9% Amer. Ind.; 0.6% Pac. Isl.; 16.1% other; 2+ races, 6.8%. **Hispanic pop.:** 26.9%. **Foreign born:** 27.6%. **U.S. citizens:** 85.2%. **Language:** 59.2% English only; 22.1% Spanish.

Employment: 207,758 employed; 3.4% unemployment. **Per capita income:** $99,424; change (2017-18): 7.3%. **Below poverty:** 15.7%; 13.7% of families. **Educational attainment:** 81.6% HS; 42.5% bachelor's. **Avg. commute:** 32.7 min. 51% drive, 11% carpool, 22.4% public trans. **Housing units:** 171,829; 94.0% occupied. **Home ownership:** 40.4%. **Avg. home:** $988,000; change (2017-19): 9.8%. **Avg. rent:** $1,354. **Crime rates:** violent: 1,274; property: 5,390.

Mayor: Libby Schaaf, nonpartisan

History: Area settled by Spanish, 1820; inc. 1854.

Website: www.oaklandca.gov

Oklahoma City, Oklahoma

Population: 655,057 (25). **Pop. density:** 1,080. **Pop. change (2010-19):** 12.5%. **Area:** 606.4 sq mi. **Racial distribution:** 67.5% white; 14.6% Black; 4.6% Asian; 2.8% Amer. Ind.; 0.1% Pac. Isl.; 4.0% other; 2+ races, 6.4%. **Hispanic pop.:** 19.2%. **Foreign born:** 12.0%. **U.S. citizens:** 92.0%. **Language:** 79.7% English only; 14.9% Spanish.

Employment: 311,314 employed; 3.1% unemployment. **Per capita income:** $48,571; change (2017-18): 5.7%. **Below poverty:** 13.8%; 12.6% of families. **Educational attainment:** 86.2% HS; 30.3% bachelor's. **Avg. commute:** 21.4 min. 82% drive, 11% carpool. **Housing units:** 270,236; 89.0% occupied. **Home ownership:** 58.6%. **Avg. home:** $158,900; change (2017-19): 3.0%. **Avg. rent:** $849. **Crime rates:** violent: 867; property: 4,028.

Mayor: David Holt, nonpartisan

History: Settled during land rush, 1889; inc. 1890; became capital, 1910; oil discovered, 1928. Bomb in 1995 destroyed federal office bldg., killed 168 people.

Website: www.okc.gov

Omaha, Nebraska

Population: 478,192 (40). **Pop. density:** 3,392. **Pop. change (2010-19):** 4.0%. **Area:** 141.0 sq mi. **Racial distribution:** 77.8% white; 12.3% Black; 3.7% Asian; 0.7% Amer. Ind.; 0.1% Pac. Isl.; 2.2% other; 2+ races, 3.2%. **Hispanic pop.:** 13.9%. **Foreign born:** 10.5%. **U.S. citizens:** 92.9%. **Language:** 83.6% English only; 10.6% Spanish.

Employment: 235,830 employed; 3.3% unemployment. **Per capita income:** $58,037; change (2017-18): 5.1%. **Below poverty:** 12.4%; 10.0% of families. **Educational attainment:** 88.8% HS; 36.6% bachelor's. **Avg. commute:** 18.8 min. 82.1% drive. **Housing units:** 197,869; 92.6% occupied. **Home ownership:** 58.0%. **Avg. home:** $200,700; change (2017-19): 14.1%. **Avg. rent:** $896. **Crime rates** (2017): violent: 647; property: 3,880.

Mayor: Jean Stothert, nonpartisan

History: Founded 1854; inc. 1857. Large food-processing, telecommunications, information-processing center.

Website: www.cityofomaha.org

Orlando, Florida

Population: 287,442 (71). **Pop. density:** 2,600. **Pop. change (2010-19):** 20.1%. **Area:** 110.6 sq mi. **Racial distribution:** 60.7% white; 25.4% Black; 4.3% Asian; 0.2% Amer. Ind.; <0.05% Pac. Isl.; 6.2% other; 2+ races, 3.2%. **Hispanic pop.:** 31.1%. **Foreign born:** 21.2%. **U.S. citizens:** 87.9%. **Language:** 63.3% English only; 25.3% Spanish.

Employment: 164,439 employed; 2.8% unemployment. **Per capita income:** $43,491; change (2017-18): 4.2%. **Below poverty:** 16.4%; 15.1% of families. **Educational attainment:** 90.2% HS; 36.7% bachelor's. **Avg. commute:** 25.8 min. 78.8% drive. **Housing units:** 130,664; 85.5% occupied. **Home ownership:** 35.1%. **Avg. home:** $276,000; change (2017-19): 12.7%. **Avg. rent:** $1,139. **Crime rates:** violent: 796; property: 4,815.

Mayor: Buddy Dyer, nonpartisan

History: Ft. Gatlin built just south of present-day Orlando, 1838; name changed from Jernigan, 1856; inc. 1875. Walt Disney World opened, 1971.

Website: www.orlando.gov

Philadelphia, Pennsylvania

Population: 1,584,064 (6). **Pop. density:** 11,797. **Pop. change (2010-19):** 3.6%. **Area:** 134.3 sq mi. **Racial distribution:** 41.2% white; 42.3% Black; 7.2% Asian; 0.4% Amer. Ind.; <0.05% Pac. Isl.; 5.9% other; 2+ races, 3.0%. **Hispanic pop.:** 14.5%. **Foreign born:** 13.9%. **U.S. citizens:** 93.1%. **Language:** 76.9% English only; 10.6% Spanish.

Employment: 682,012 employed; 5.5% unemployment. **Per capita income:** $64,440; change (2017-18): 5.5%. **Below poverty:** 21.8%; 19.6% of families. **Educational attainment:** 83.9% HS; 28.6% bachelor's. **Avg. commute:** 33.4 min. 50.9% drive, 25% public trans. **Housing units:** 682,893; 87.1% occupied. **Home ownership:** 53.0%. **Avg. home:** $246,200; change (2017-19): 7.0%. **Avg. rent:** $1,007. **Crime rates:** violent: 909; property: 3,097.

Mayor: Jim F. Kenney, Democrat

History: Named Philadelphia, 1682; chartered 1701. Continental Congresses convened 1774, 1775; Declaration of Independence signed, 1776; U.S. capital, 1790-1800.

Website: www.phila.gov

Phoenix, Arizona

Population: 1,680,992 (5). **Pop. density:** 3,247. **Pop. change (2010-19):** 16.0%. **Area:** 517.7 sq mi. **Racial distribution:** 73% white; 6.0% Black; 3.7% Asian; 2.1% Amer. Ind.; 0.2% Pac. Isl.; 10.9% other; 2+ races, 3.8%. **Hispanic pop.:** 42.6%. **Foreign born:** 19.5%. **U.S. citizens:** 87.0%. **Language:** 62.5% English only; 31.0% Spanish.

Employment: 832,490 employed; 4.1% unemployment. **Per capita income:** $46,125; change (2017-18): 4.3%. **Below poverty:** 16.1%; 15.1% of families. **Educational attainment:** 81.5% HS; 28.2% bachelor's. **Avg. commute:** 25.7 min. 74.5% drive, 12.6% carpool. **Housing units:** 614,870; 90.3% occupied. **Home ownership:** 53.8%. **Avg. home:** $287,100; change (2017-19): 16.4%. **Avg. rent:** $999. **Crime rates:** violent: 733; property: 3,492.

Mayor: Kate Gallego, nonpartisan

History: Founded 1867; inc. 1881; became territorial capital, 1889.

Website: www.phoenix.gov

Pittsburgh, Pennsylvania

Population: 300,286 (66). **Pop. density:** 5,423. **Pop. change (2010-19):** –1.6%. **Area:** 55.4 sq mi. **Racial distribution:** 66.9% white; 23.2% Black; 5.7% Asian; 0.1% Amer. Ind.; <0.05% Pac. Isl.; 0.6% other; 2+ races, 3.5%. **Hispanic pop.:** 3.1%. **Foreign born:** 8.5%. **U.S. citizens:** 94.5%. **Language:** 89.0% English only; 2.2% Spanish.

Employment: 150,791 employed; 4.3% unemployment. **Per capita income:** $58,072; change (2017-18): 6.6%. **Below poverty:** 19.9%; 14.2% of families. **Educational attainment:** 92.4% HS; 42.9% bachelor's. **Avg. commute:** 24.1 min. 55.5% drive, 17.9% public trans. **Housing units:** 156,617; 87.0% occupied. **Home ownership:** 47.8%. **Avg. rent:** $922. **Crime rates:** violent: 579; property: 3,016.

Mayor: William "Bill" Peduto, Democrat

History: Settled around Ft. Pitt, 1758; inc. 1816; became an inland port; a center for iron production by Civil War.

Website: pittsburghpa.gov

Plano, Texas

Population: 287,677 (70). **Pop. density:** 4,013. **Pop. change (2010-19):** 10.1%. **Area:** 71.7 sq mi. **Racial distribution:** 65.6% white; 8.4% Black; 20.4% Asian; 0.5% Amer. Ind.; 0.1% Pac. Isl.; 2.0% other; 2+ races, 3.0%. **Hispanic pop.:** 15.2%. **Foreign born:** 26.6%. **U.S. citizens:** 85.6%. **Language:** 65.4% English only; 12.1% Spanish.

Employment: 158,999 employed; 3.1% unemployment. **Per capita income:** $55,886; change (2017-18): 4.7%. **Below poverty:** 6.3%; 5.0% of families. **Educational attainment:** 93.4% HS; 56.7% bachelor's. **Avg. commute:** 26.9 min. 81.7% drive. **Housing units:** 111,066; 95.0% occupied. **Home ownership:** 60.3%. **Avg. home:** $268,600; change (2017-19): 8.6%. **Avg. rent:** $1,330. **Crime rates:** violent: 139; property: 1,709.

Mayor: Harry LaRosiliere, nonpartisan

History: Settled 1846; inc. 1873.

Website: www.plano.gov

Portland, Oregon

Population: 654,741 (26). **Pop. density:** 4,907. **Pop. change (2010-19):** 11.8%. **Area:** 133.4 sq mi. **Racial distribution:** 77.1% white; 5.8% Black; 8.1% Asian; 0.7% Amer. Ind.; 0.7% Pac. Isl.; 2.1% other; 2+ races, 5.5%. **Hispanic pop.:** 9.7%. **Foreign born:** 13.9%. **U.S. citizens:** 93.0%. **Language:** 80.6% English only; 6.9% Spanish.

Employment: 363,911 employed; 3.2% unemployment. **Per capita income:** $56,991; change (2017-18): 5.5%. **Below poverty:** 14.4%; 9.0% of families. **Educational attainment:** 92.2% HS; 49.0% bachelor's. **Avg. commute:** 26.3 min. 57.8% drive, 12.6% public trans. **Housing units:** 282,139; 93.7% occupied. **Home ownership:** 53.1%. **Avg. home:** $409,300; change (2017-19): 7.2%. **Avg. rent:** $1,187. **Crime rates:** violent: 520; property: 5,460.

Mayor: Ted Wheeler, nonpartisan

History: Est. 1843; developed as trading center, aided by California Gold Rush, 1849; city chartered, 1851.

Website: www.portland.gov

Raleigh, North Carolina

Population: 474,069 (41). **Pop. density:** 3,250. **Pop. change (2010-19):** 16.7%. **Area:** 145.9 sq mi. **Racial distribution:** 58.5% white; 29.0% Black; 4.5% Asian; 0.4% Amer. Ind.; 0.1% Pac. Isl.; 4.7% other; 2+ races, 3.0%. **Hispanic pop.:** 11.0%. **Foreign born:** 13.1%. **U.S. citizens:** 91.9%. **Language:** 82.9% English only; 9.6% Spanish.

Employment: 251,604 employed; 3.6% unemployment. **Per capita income:** $55,045; change (2017-18): 5.4%. **Below poverty:** 12.1%; 9.1% of families. **Educational attainment:** 91.7% HS; 50.4% bachelor's. **Avg. commute:** 23.7 min. 78.5% drive. **Housing units:** 199,214; 90.4% occupied. **Home ownership:** 51.5%. **Avg. home:** $291,500; change (2017-19): 9.3%. **Avg. rent:** $1,074. **Crime rates:** NA.

Mayor: Mary-Ann Baldwin, nonpartisan

History: Named after Sir Walter Raleigh; chosen state capital, 1788; inc. 1795; occupied by Union Gen. Sherman, 1865.

Website: raleighnc.gov

Reno, Nevada

Population: 255,601 (85). **Pop. density:** 2,350. **Pop. change (2010-19):** 13.3%. **Area:** 108.7 sq mi. **Racial distribution:** 76.4% white; 2.7% Black; 6.5% Asian; 1.1% Amer. Ind.; 0.8% Pac. Isl.; 7.7% other; 2+ races, 4.8%. **Hispanic pop.:** 24.7%. **Foreign born:** 16.0%. **U.S. citizens:** 91.1%. **Language:** 74.3% English only; 17.9% Spanish.

Employment: 133,590 employed; 3.2% unemployment. **Per capita income:** $59,639; change (2017-18): 6.3%. **Below poverty:** 13.6%; 8.8% of families. **Educational attainment:** 87.9% HS; 32.9% bachelor's. **Avg. commute:** 19.9 min. 76.2% drive, 11.7% carpool. **Housing units:** 106,663; 92.7% occupied. **Home ownership:** 47.7%. **Avg. home:** $393,900; change (2017-19): 14.1%. **Avg. rent:** $967. **Crime rates:** violent: 648; property: 2,399.

Mayor: Hillary Schieve, nonpartisan

History: Originally named Lake's Crossing; name changed to Reno, after a Union Civil War general, 1868, with arrival of transcontinental railroad.

Website: www.reno.gov

Richmond, Virginia

Population: 230,436 (97). **Pop. density:** 3,846. **Pop. change (2010-19):** 12.8%. **Area:** 59.9 sq mi. **Racial distribution:** 45.4% white; 47.8% Black; 2.1% Asian; 0.4% Amer. Ind.; <0.05% Pac. Isl.; 1.0% other; 2+ races, 3.3%. **Hispanic pop.:** 6.7%. **Foreign born:** 6.7%. **U.S. citizens:** 95.6%. **Language:** 90.7% English only; 5.5% Spanish.

Employment: 115,360 employed; 3.3% unemployment. **Per capita income:** $57,301; change (2017-18): 3.7%. **Below poverty:** 21.1%; 17.7% of families. **Educational attainment:** 85.0% HS; 38.5% bachelor's. **Avg. commute:** 21.6 min. 71.4% drive, 10% carpool. **Housing units:** 100,119; 89.7% occupied. **Home ownership:** 42.2%. **Avg. home:** $264,000; change (2017-19): 5.4%. **Avg. rent:** $979. **Crime rates:** violent: 518; property: 3,830.

Mayor: Levar M. Stoney, nonpartisan

History: First explored, 1607; became capital of Virginia, 1779; attacked by British, 1781; inc. as city, 1782; capital of Confederate States of America, 1861-65.

Website: www.richmondgov.com

Riverside, California

Population: 331,360 (58). **Pop. density:** 4,078. **Pop. change (2010-19):** 8.5%. **Area:** 81.3 sq mi. **Racial distribution:** 60.9% white; 6.2% Black; 7.4% Asian; 0.8% Amer. Ind.; 0.3% Pac. Isl.; 19.6% other; 2+ races, 4.8%. **Hispanic pop.:** 53.3%. **Foreign born:** 22.7%. **U.S. citizens:** 87.9%. **Language:** 56.5% English only; 35.8% Spanish.

Employment: 149,359 employed; 3.6% unemployment. **Per capita income:** $40,486; change (2017-18): 4.3%. **Below poverty:** 14.0%; 10.9% of families. **Educational attainment:** 80.3% HS; 22.6% bachelor's. **Avg. commute:** 30.5 min. 75.3% drive, 13.7% carpool. **Housing units:** 96,797; 93.9% occupied. **Home ownership:** 54.0%. **Avg. home:** $378,500; change (2017-19): 12.6%. **Avg. rent:** $1,308. **Crime rates:** violent: 509; property: 3,089.

Mayor: Rusty Bailey, nonpartisan

History: Founded 1870; inc. 1883. Known for citrus industry; home of the parent navel orange tree.

Website: riversideca.gov

Sacramento, California

Population: 513,624 (36). **Pop. density:** 5,256. **Pop. change (2010-19):** 9.9%. **Area:** 97.7 sq mi. **Racial distribution:** 47.2% white; 13.4% Black; 18.9% Asian; 0.8% Amer. Ind.; 1.7% Pac. Isl.; 11.0% other; 2+ races, 7.0%. **Hispanic pop.:** 28.7%. **Foreign born:** 22.6%. **U.S. citizens:** 89.8%. **Language:** 61.8% English only; 18.6% Spanish.

Employment: 228,309 employed; 3.7% unemployment. **Per capita income:** $56,278; change (2017-18): 4.2%. **Below poverty:** 16.3%; 13.6% of families. **Educational attainment:** 84.7% HS; 32.6% bachelor's. **Avg. commute:** 25.6 min. 74.7% drive, 10.6% carpool. **Housing units:** 195,749; 93.5% occupied. **Home ownership:** 48.0%. **Avg. home:** $380,000; change (2017-19): 11.8%. **Avg. rent:** $1,179. **Crime rates:** violent: 657; property: 3,041.

Mayor: Darrell Steinberg, nonpartisan

History: Est. 1839; important trading center during Gold Rush; became state capital, 1854.

Website: www.cityofsacramento.org

St. Louis, Missouri

Population: 300,576 (65). **Pop. density:** 4,868. **Pop. change (2010-19):** −5.9%. **Area:** 61.7 sq mi. **Racial distribution:** 46.2% white; 46.9% Black; 3.2% Asian; 0.2% Amer. Ind.; 0.1% Pac. Isl.; 1.0% other; 2+ races, 2.3%. **Hispanic pop.:** 4.0%. **Foreign born:** 6.8%. **U.S. citizens:** 96.2%. **Language:** 90.9% English only; 3.0% Spanish.

Employment: 147,111 employed; 3.9% unemployment. **Per capita income:** $55,883; change (2017-18): 5.6%. **Below poverty:** 20.5%; 18.6% of families. **Educational attainment:** 86.9% HS; 35.0% bachelor's. **Avg. commute:** 24.4 min. 72.1% drive. **Housing units:** 176,375; 79.6% occupied. **Home ownership:** 43.4%. **Avg. home:** $187,500; change (2017-19): 10.7%. **Avg. rent:** $810. **Crime rates:** violent: 1,800; property: 5,912.

Mayor: Lyda Krewson, Democrat

History: Founded 1764 as French fur trading post on Mississippi R., near confluence with Missouri R.; acquired by U.S., 1803; chartered as city, 1823.

Website: www.stlouis-mo.gov

St. Paul, Minnesota

Population: 308,096 (63). **Pop. density:** 5,927. **Pop. change (2010-19):** 7.9%. **Area:** 52.0 sq mi. **Racial distribution:** 56.7% white; 16.0% Black; 18.4% Asian; 0.9% Amer. Ind.; <0.05% Pac. Isl.; 2.9% other; 2+ races, 5.0%. **Hispanic pop.:** 9.6%. **Foreign born:** 19.7%. **U.S. citizens:** 90.5%. **Language:** 70.4% English only; 6.7% Spanish.

Employment: 155,321 employed; 3.1% unemployment. **Per capita income:** $62,889; change (2017-18): 4.5%. **Below poverty:**

16.8%; 15.1% of families. **Educational attainment:** 86.3% HS; 40.1% bachelor's. **Avg. commute:** 24.0 min. 67.5% drive, 10.8% carpool, 9.5% public trans. **Housing units:** 119,940; 94.2% occupied. **Home ownership:** 49.8%. **Avg. home:** $288,600; change (2017-19): 14.5%. **Avg. rent:** $935. **Crime rates:** violent: 627; property: 3,255.

Mayor: Melvin Carter, nonpartisan
History: Est. c. 1840 as Pig's Eye Landing; became capital of Minnesota territory, 1849; chartered as St. Paul, 1854.
Website: www.stpaul.gov

St. Petersburg, Florida

Population: 265,351 (78). **Pop. density:** 4,289. **Pop. change (2010-19):** 8.2%. **Area:** 61.9 sq mi. **Racial distribution:** 68.8% white; 22.6% Black; 3.7% Asian; 0.2% Amer. Ind.; 0.1% Pac. Isl.; 1.3% other; 2+ races, 3.3%. **Hispanic pop.:** 7.9%. **Foreign born:** 11.2%. **U.S. citizens:** 95.6%. **Language:** 87.3% English only; 5.1% Spanish.

Employment: 137,718 employed; 2.9% unemployment. **Per capita income:** $47,240; change (2017-18): 4.3%. **Below poverty:** 13.0%; 10.0% of families. **Educational attainment:** 91.0% HS; 34.5% bachelor's. **Avg. commute:** 23.4 min. 78.8% drive. **Housing units:** 132,622; 80.8% occupied. **Home ownership:** 58.8%. **Avg. home:** $245,000; change (2017-19): 11.4%. **Avg. rent:** $1,067. **Crime rates:** violent: 624; property: 3,303.

Mayor: Rick Kriseman, nonpartisan
History: Founded 1888; inc. 1903. Site of Salvador Dali Museum.
Website: www.stpete.org

San Antonio, Texas

Population: 1,547,253 (7). **Pop. density:** 3,189. **Pop. change (2010-19):** 16.1%. **Area:** 485.1 sq mi. **Racial distribution:** 80.5% white; 6.9% Black; 2.8% Asian; 0.8% Amer. Ind.; 0.1% Pac. Isl.; 6.0% other; 2+ races, 2.8%. **Hispanic pop.:** 64.2%. **Foreign born:** 14.3%. **U.S. citizens:** 91.2%. **Language:** 56.6% English only; 39.5% Spanish.

Employment: 709,743 employed; 3.1% unemployment. **Per capita income:** $46,995; change (2017-18): 4.7%. **Below poverty:** 15.6%; 14.6% of families. **Educational attainment:** 82.0% HS; 25.9% bachelor's. **Avg. commute:** 24.4 min. 79% drive, 11.1% carpool. **Housing units:** 543,762; 91.5% occupied. **Home ownership:** 54.4%. **Avg. home:** $236,600; change (2017-19): 8.9%. **Avg. rent:** $958. **Crime rates:** violent: 627; property: 3,994.

Mayor: Ron Nirenberg, nonpartisan
History: First Spanish mission est., 1718; Battle of the Alamo, 1836; city subsequently captured by Texans; inc. 1837.
Website: www.sanantonio.gov

San Diego, California

Population: 1,423,851 (8). **Pop. density:** 4,369. **Pop. change (2010-19):** 9.0%. **Area:** 325.9 sq mi. **Racial distribution:** 64.8% white; 6.5% Black; 16.7% Asian; 0.4% Amer. Ind.; 0.4% Pac. Isl.; 6.0% other; 2+ races, 5.2%. **Hispanic pop.:** 30.1%. **Foreign born:** 26.3%. **U.S. citizens:** 87.7%. **Language:** 59.3% English only; 23.0% Spanish.

Employment: 699,092 employed; 3.0% unemployment. **Per capita income:** $61,386; change (2017-18): 5.7%. **Below poverty:** 12.8%; 9.2% of families. **Educational attainment:** 87.9% HS; 45.3% bachelor's. **Avg. commute:** 24.1 min. 74.8% drive. **Housing units:** 540,644; 93.1% occupied. **Home ownership:** 46.9%. **Avg. home:** $645,000; change (2017-19): 7.7%. **Avg. rent:** $1,611. **Crime rates:** violent: 373; property: 1,909.

Mayor: Kevin L. Faulconer, nonpartisan
History: Claimed by Spanish, 1542; first mission est., 1769; scene of conflict during Mexican-American War, 1846; inc. 1850.
Website: www.sandiego.gov

San Francisco, California

Population: 881,549 (16). **Pop. density:** 18,795. **Pop. change (2010-19):** 9.4%. **Area:** 46.9 sq mi. **Racial distribution:** 46.7% white; 5.2% Black; 34.2% Asian; 0.3% Amer. Ind.; 0.3% Pac. Isl.; 7.7% other; 2+ races, 5.4%. **Hispanic pop.:** 15.2%. **Foreign born:** 34.4%. **U.S. citizens:** 87.2%. **Language:** 56.9% English only; 10.8% Spanish.

Employment: 570,412 employed; 2.2% unemployment. **Per capita income:** $99,424; change (2017-18): 7.3%. **Below poverty:** 10.9%; 5.8% of families. **Educational attainment:** 88.5% HS; 57.1% bachelor's. **Avg. commute:** 33.3 min. 32.9% drive, 34.2% public trans. **Housing units:** 393,975; 91.3% occupied. **Home ownership:** 37.6%. **Avg. home:** $988,000; change (2017-19): 9.8%. **Avg. rent:** $1,805. **Crime rates:** violent: 691; property: 5,534.

Mayor: London N. Breed, nonpartisan
History: Est. by 1776; claimed by U.S., 1846; became major city during Gold Rush, 1849; inc. 1850. Devastated by earthquake, 1906.
Website: sf.gov

San Jose, California

Population: 1,021,795 (10). **Pop. density:** 5,747. **Pop. change (2010-19):** 7.0%. **Area:** 177.8 sq mi. **Racial distribution:** 40.0% white; 3.0% Black; 35.4% Asian; 0.5% Amer. Ind.; 0.5% Pac. Isl.; 15.3% other; 2+ races, 5.2%. **Hispanic pop.:** 32.0%. **Foreign born:** 39.5%. **U.S. citizens:** 82.8%. **Language:** 43.2% English only; 22.7% Spanish.

Employment: 540,954 employed; 2.6% unemployment. **Per capita income:** $106,213; change (2017-18): 7.6%. **Below poverty:** 8.9%; 6.0% of families. **Educational attainment:** 84.2% HS; 42.7% bachelor's. **Avg. commute:** 30.2 min. 76% drive, 11.7% carpool. **Housing units:** 334,350; 96.3% occupied. **Home ownership:** 57.2%. **Avg. home:** $1,265,000; change (2017-19): 7.2%. **Avg. rent:** $1,970. **Crime rates:** violent: 424; property: 2,459.

Mayor: Sam Liccardo, nonpartisan
History: Founded by Spanish, 1777, between San Francisco and Monterey; state capital, 1849-51; inc. 1850.
Website: www.sanjoseca.gov

Santa Ana, California

Population: 332,318 (57). **Pop. density:** 12,146. **Pop. change (2010-19):** 2.1%. **Area:** 27.4 sq mi. **Racial distribution:** 44.2% white; 1.1% Black; 11.8% Asian; 0.6% Amer. Ind.; 0.2% Pac. Isl.; 40.1% other; 2+ races, 1.9%. **Hispanic pop.:** 76.8%. **Foreign born:** 44.5%. **U.S. citizens:** 72.2%. **Language:** 19.4% English only; 69.1% Spanish.

Employment: 153,834 employed; 2.9% unemployment. **Per capita income:** $63,913; change (2017-18): 5.4%. **Below poverty:** 14.4%; 15.3% of families. **Educational attainment:** 58.1% HS; 14.0% bachelor's. **Avg. commute:** 25.3 min. 73.9% drive, 14.5% carpool. **Housing units:** 78,597; 97.4% occupied. **Home ownership:** 46.2%. **Avg. home:** $825,000; change (2017-19): 5.8%. **Avg. rent:** $1,488. **Crime rates:** violent: 468; property: 1,905.

Mayor: Miguel Pulido, nonpartisan
History: Founded by Spanish, 1769; inc. 1886.
Website: www.santa-ana.org

Scottsdale, Arizona

Population: 258,069 (84). **Pop. density:** 1,403. **Pop. change (2010-19):** 18.6%. **Area:** 184.0 sq mi. **Racial distribution:** 87.9% white; 1.8% Black; 4.9% Asian; 0.8% Amer. Ind.; 0.1% Pac. Isl.; 2.2% other; 2+ races, 2.3%. **Hispanic pop.:** 10.4%. **Foreign born:** 12.2%. **U.S. citizens:** 94.6%. **Language:** 86.3% English only; 6.2% Spanish.

Employment: 145,677 employed; 3.4% unemployment. **Per capita income:** $46,125; change (2017-18): 4.3%. **Below poverty:** 7.5%; 5.0% of families. **Educational attainment:** 96.5% HS; 57.2% bachelor's. **Avg. commute:** 22.1 min. 77.5% drive. **Housing units:** 135,092; 82.3% occupied. **Home ownership:** 65.9%. **Avg. home:** $287,100; change (2017-19): 16.4%. **Avg. rent:** $1,284. **Crime rates:** violent: 166; property: 2,229.

Mayor: W. J. "Jim" Lane, nonpartisan
History: Founded 1888 by namesake Army Chaplain Winfield Scott; inc. 1951.
Website: www.scottsdaleaz.gov

Seattle, Washington

Population: 753,675 (18). **Pop. density:** 8,987. **Pop. change (2010-19):** 23.4%. **Area:** 83.9 sq mi. **Racial distribution:** 68.0% white; 7.0% Black; 15.1% Asian; 0.6% Amer. Ind.; 0.3% Pac. Isl.; 2.3% other; 2+ races, 6.8%. **Hispanic pop.:** 6.6%. **Foreign born:** 18.5%. **U.S. citizens:** 90.7%. **Language:** 78.8% English only; 4.0% Spanish.

Employment: 464,346 employed; 2.5% unemployment. **Per capita income:** $74,620; change (2017-18): 6.7%. **Below poverty:** 11.7%; 6.0% of families. **Educational attainment:** 94.6% HS; 62.8% bachelor's. **Avg. commute:** 27.8 min. 47.6% drive, 21.8% public trans. **Housing units:** 344,503; 93.9% occupied. **Home ownership:** 46.1%. **Avg. home:** $524,700; change (2017-19): 12.6%. **Avg. rent:** $1,496. **Crime rates:** violent: 680; property: 5,149.

Mayor: Jenny A. Durkan, nonpartisan
History: Settled 1851; inc. 1869. Suffered severe fire, 1889; played prominent role in Alaska Gold Rush, 1897; growth followed opening of Panama Canal 1914. Center of aircraft industry during WWII.
Website: www.seattle.gov

Spokane, Washington

Population: 222,081 (99). **Pop. density:** 3,230. **Pop. change (2010-19):** 6.0%. **Area:** 68.8 sq mi. **Racial distribution:** 85.1% white; 2.2% Black; 2.6% Asian; 1.9% Amer. Ind.; 0.8% Pac. Isl.; 1.6% other; 2+ races, 5.9%. **Hispanic pop.:** 6.5%. **Foreign born:** 6.0%. **U.S. citizens:** 97.1%. **Language:** 92.0% English only; 2.4% Spanish.

Employment: 102,975 employed; 5.5% unemployment. **Per capita income:** $45,903; change (2017-18): 4.3%. **Below poverty:** 16.9%; 12.0% of families. **Educational attainment:** 92.9% HS; 30.4% bachelor's. **Avg. commute:** 20.2 min. 75.5% drive,

9.8% carpool. **Housing units:** 97,825; 91.6% occupied. **Home ownership:** 55.2%. **Avg. home:** $265,300; change (2017-19): 18.8%. **Avg. rent:** $842. **Crime rates:** violent: 798; property: 7,075.
Mayor: Nadine Woodward, nonpartisan
History: Founded 1872; inc. as village of Spokane Falls 1881; destroyed in fire 1889; re-inc. as city of Spokane 1891.
Website: my.spokanecity.org

Stockton, California

Population: 312,697 (62). **Pop. density:** 5,030. **Pop. change (2010-19):** 6.8%. **Area:** 62.2 sq mi. **Racial distribution:** 44.7% white; 11.8% Black; 21.6% Asian; 0.7% Amer. Ind.; 0.8% Pac. Isl.; 9.5% other; 2+ races, 10.8%. **Hispanic pop.:** 42.1%. **Foreign born:** 25.9%. **U.S. citizens:** 87.0%. **Language:** 54.1% English only; 26.7% Spanish.
Employment: 121,714 employed; 6.8% unemployment. **Per capita income:** $44,995; change (2017-18): 6.1%. **Below poverty:** 17.7%; 17.1% of families. **Educational attainment:** 76.4% HS; 17.7% bachelor's. **Avg. commute:** 30.3 min. 78% drive, 14.6% carpool. **Housing units:** 102,490; 92.9% occupied. **Home ownership:** 47.5%. **Avg. rent:** $1,059. **Crime rates:** violent: 1,400; property: 3,768.
Mayor: Michael Tubbs, nonpartisan
History: Est. 1849 to serve gold miners; inc. 1850.
Website: www.stocktonca.gov

Tampa, Florida

Population: 399,700 (48). **Pop. density:** 3,506. **Pop. change (2010-19):** 18.6%. **Area:** 114.0 sq mi. **Racial distribution:** 64.9% white; 24.2% Black; 4.2% Asian; 0.3% Amer. Ind.; 0.1% Pac. Isl.; 2.6% other; 2+ races, 3.8%. **Hispanic pop.:** 25.7%. **Foreign born:** 16.5%. **U.S. citizens:** 91.4%. **Language:** 72.6% English only; 20.0% Spanish.
Employment: 197,252 employed; 3.2% unemployment. **Per capita income:** $47,240; change (2017-18): 4.3%. **Below poverty:** 17.2%; 14.5% of families. **Educational attainment:** 87.3% HS; 37.3% bachelor's. **Avg. commute:** 24.5 min. 77.3% drive. **Housing units:** 167,950; 88.9% occupied. **Home ownership:** 47.8%. **Avg. home:** $245,000; change (2017-19): 11.4%. **Avg. rent:** $1,082. **Crime rates:** violent: 407; property: 1,674.
Mayor: Jane Castor, nonpartisan
History: U.S. army fort on site, 1824; inc. 1855.
Website: www.tampagov.net

Toledo, Ohio

Population: 272,779 (76). **Pop. density:** 3,389. **Pop. change (2010-19):** –5.0%. **Area:** 80.5 sq mi. **Racial distribution:** 62.8% white; 27.0% Black; 1.5% Asian; 0.3% Amer. Ind.; <0.05% Pac. Isl.; 2.8% other; 2+ races, 5.6%. **Hispanic pop.:** 8.6%. **Foreign born:** 3.7%. **U.S. citizens:** 98.1%. **Language:** 92.7% English only; 3.2% Spanish.
Employment: 121,442 employed; 5.2% unemployment. **Per capita income:** $46,868; change (2017-18): 4.9%. **Below poverty:** 22.1%; 20.9% of families. **Educational attainment:** 87.3% HS; 18.7% bachelor's. **Avg. commute:** 20.2 min. 82.6% drive. **Housing units:** 138,107; 85.3% occupied. **Home ownership:** 51.3%. **Avg. home:** $131,000; change (2017-19): 10.8%. **Avg. rent:** $700. **Crime rates:** violent: 848; property: 3,717.
Mayor: Wade Kapszukiewicz, nonpartisan
History: Site of Ft. Industry, 1800; figured in Toledo War between OH and MI over borders, 1835-36; inc. 1837.
Website: toledo.oh.gov

Tucson, Arizona

Population: 548,073 (33). **Pop. density:** 2,303. **Pop. change (2010-19):** 4.0%. **Area:** 238.0 sq mi. **Racial distribution:** 72.4% white; 5.1% Black; 3.2% Asian; 3.5% Amer. Ind.; 0.2% Pac. Isl.; 10.4% other; 2+ races, 5.1%. **Hispanic pop.:** 43.2%. **Foreign born:** 15.2%. **U.S. citizens:** 91.3%. **Language:** 66.3% English only; 28.3% Spanish.
Employment: 255,701 employed; 4.6% unemployment. **Per capita income:** $44,028; change (2017-18): 4.5%. **Below poverty:** 21.2%; 17.2% of families. **Educational attainment:** 84.9% HS; 26.8% bachelor's. **Avg. commute:** 22.4 min. 74.3% drive, 10.7% carpool. **Housing units:** 238,177; 88.5% occupied. **Home ownership:** 50.0%. **Avg. home:** $238,900; change (2017-19): 13.6%. **Avg. rent:** $825. **Crime rates:** violent: 737; property: 4,954.
Mayor: Regina Romero, Democrat
History: Est. 1775 by Spanish as a presidio; acquired by U.S. in Gadsden Purchase, 1854; inc. 1877.
Website: www.tucsonaz.gov

Tulsa, Oklahoma

Population: 401,190 (47). **Pop. density:** 2,032. **Pop. change (2010-19):** 2.2%. **Area:** 197.5 sq mi. **Racial distribution:** 64.0% white; 15.3% Black; 3.3% Asian; 4.4% Amer. Ind.; 0.1% Pac. Isl.; 5.3% other; 2+ races, 7.6%. **Hispanic pop.:** 16.3%. **Foreign born:** 11.1%. **U.S. citizens:** 91.9%. **Language:** 81.9% English only; 13.6% Spanish.

Employment: 190,077 employed; 3.4% unemployment. **Per capita income:** $54,866; change (2017-18): 7.3%. **Below poverty:** 16.2%; 15.4% of families. **Educational attainment:** 87.0% HS; 30.8% bachelor's. **Avg. commute:** 18.6 min. 80.2% drive, 10.7% carpool. **Housing units:** 187,701; 87.5% occupied. **Home ownership:** 50.8%. **Avg. home:** $173,200; change (2017-19): 8.1%. **Avg. rent:** $810. **Crime rates:** violent: 1,065; property: 5,431.
Mayor: G.T. Bynum, nonpartisan
History: Settled in 1836 by Creek Indians; modern town founded 1882; inc. 1898; oil discovered early 20th century.
Website: www.cityoftulsa.org

Virginia Beach, Virginia

Population: 449,974 (44). **Pop. density:** 1,839. **Pop. change (2010-19):** 2.5%. **Area:** 244.7 sq mi. **Racial distribution:** 66.7% white; 19.0% Black; 6.6% Asian; 0.3% Amer. Ind.; 0.1% Pac. Isl.; 2.0% other; 2+ races, 5.3%. **Hispanic pop.:** 8.0%. **Foreign born:** 9.3%. **U.S. citizens:** 96.5%. **Language:** 87.9% English only; 4.7% Spanish.
Employment: 228,266 employed; 2.7% unemployment. **Per capita income:** $50,619; change (2017-18): 4.4%. **Below poverty:** 6.8%; 5.5% of families. **Educational attainment:** 93.2% HS; 35.2% bachelor's. **Avg. commute:** 23.7 min. 82.1% drive. **Housing units:** 183,906; 92.1% occupied. **Home ownership:** 64.1%. **Avg. home:** $235,000; change (2017-19): 4.4%. **Avg. rent:** $1,339. **Crime rates:** violent: 117; property: 1,723.
Mayor: Bobby Dyer, nonpartisan
History: Settlement by Capt. John Smith, 1607; formed by merger with Princess Anne Co., 1963.
Website: www.vbgov.com

Washington, District of Columbia

Population: 705,749 (20). **Pop. density:** 11,544. **Pop. change (2010-19):** 16.6%. **Area:** 61.1 sq mi. **Racial distribution:** 41.0% white; 46.9% Black; 3.9% Asian; 0.3% Amer. Ind.; <0.05% Pac. Isl.; 4.9% other; 2+ races, 2.9%. **Hispanic pop.:** 10.9%. **Foreign born:** 14.0%. **U.S. citizens:** 91.8%. **Language:** 82.6% English only; 9.0% Spanish.
Employment: 387,482 employed; 5.5% unemployment. **Per capita income:** $72,483; change (2017-18): 4.6%. **Below poverty:** 15.0%; 12.9% of families. **Educational attainment:** 90.6% HS; 57.6% bachelor's. **Avg. commute:** 30.3 min. 34.3% drive, 34.8% public trans. **Housing units:** 311,545; 90.3% occupied. **Home ownership:** 41.8%. **Avg. home:** $440,900; change (2017-19): 8.4%. **Avg. rent:** $1,487. **Crime rates:** violent: 941; property: 4,270.
Mayor: Muriel Bowser, Democrat
History: U.S. capital; planned site on Potomac R. chosen by George Washington, 1790, on land ceded from VA and MD (portion S of Potomac returned to VA, 1846). Congress first met there, 1800; inc. 1802; sacked by British, War of 1812.
Website: dc.gov

Wichita, Kansas

Population: 389,938 (51). **Pop. density:** 2,412. **Pop. change (2010-19):** 1.9%. **Area:** 161.7 sq mi. **Racial distribution:** 74.6% white; 11.1% Black; 5.0% Asian; 1.0% Amer. Ind.; 0.1% Pac. Isl.; 4.0% other; 2+ races, 4.3%. **Hispanic pop.:** 17.0%. **Foreign born:** 10.1%. **U.S. citizens:** 94.4%. **Language:** 82.9% English only; 11.4% Spanish.
Employment: 182,731 employed; 3.6% unemployment. **Per capita income:** $51,854; change (2017-18): 6.2%. **Below poverty:** 14.2%; 11.7% of families. **Educational attainment:** 87.9% HS; 30.0% bachelor's. **Avg. commute:** 18.4 min. 83.4% drive, 9.5% carpool. **Housing units:** 171,175; 88.9% occupied. **Home ownership:** 59.4%. **Avg. home:** $158,200; change (2017-19): 19.0%. **Avg. rent:** $789. **Crime rates:** violent: 1,180; property: 5,619.
Mayor: Brandon Whipple, nonpartisan
History: Founded 1864; inc. 1871.
Website: www.wichita.gov

Winston-Salem, North Carolina

Population: 247,945 (90). **Pop. density:** 1,870. **Pop. change (2010-19):** 7.8%. **Area:** 132.6 sq mi. **Racial distribution:** 56.3% white; 34.8% Black; 2.4% Asian; 0.2% Amer. Ind.; 0.1% Pac. Isl.; 3.5% other; 2+ races, 2.8%. **Hispanic pop.:** 14.6%. **Foreign born:** 9.9%. **U.S. citizens:** 93.3%. **Language:** 83.0% English only; 13.2% Spanish.
Employment: 115,276 employed; 4.0% unemployment. **Per capita income:** $44,850; change (2017-18): 3.6%. **Below poverty:** 18.2%; 15.7% of families. **Educational attainment:** 87.5% HS; 34.2% bachelor's. **Avg. commute:** 20.8 min. 82.6% drive. **Housing units:** 107,116; 88.6% occupied. **Home ownership:** 53.6%. **Avg. home:** $177,300; change (2017-19): 14.4%. **Avg. rent:** $782. **Crime rates:** NA.
Mayor: Allen Joines, Democrat
History: Salem founded, 1766; Winston founded, 1849; became Winston-Salem, 1913. Reynolds Building, completed 1929, used as model for Empire State Building (designed by same architects).
Website: www.cityofws.org

UNITED STATES POPULATION

Census Origins and Methods

A census is conducted in the U.S. every 10 years. The primary purpose is to apportion seats in the House of Representatives. Census data is also used to determine the boundaries of state legislative districts and the distribution of federal funds to local, state, and tribal governments.

The first U.S. census, mandated by the Constitution, was conducted in 1790, a little more than a year after George Washington became president. It counted the numbers of free white males ages 16 and over (as a measure of available workers and military personnel), free white males under 16, free white females, all other free persons, and enslaved persons. The data was collected over 18 months, at a cost of about $44,000, or $1.2 million in current dollars. (The 2020 census was expected to cost an est. $15.6 billion in total.) The 1790 census counted a total of 3.9 million people, resulting in an increase from 65 to 105 U.S. House seats.

As the nation grew, so did the scope of the census. The first inquiries on manufacturing were made in 1810. Questions on "the pursuits, industry, education, and resources of the country" were added to the 1840 census. It took a full 10 years to publish the results of the 1880 and 1890 censuses due to the number of questions asked. Because of those delays, Congress limited the 1900 census to questions on population, mortality, agriculture, and manufacturing.

Today, the secretary of commerce and the Census Bureau are directed by law to collect data on population, housing, employment, trade, construction, transportation, and governments, among other things, at stated intervals. They also conduct smaller-scale surveys on behalf of other federal agencies. After the World Health Organization declared COVID-19 a pandemic on Mar. 11, 2020, the Census Bureau launched the experimental 90-day Household Pulse Survey to measure the pandemic's social and economic impact.

U.S. marshals administered the earliest decennial censuses by visiting each household and reporting to the president (1790), to the secretary of state (1800-40), or to the secretary of the interior (1850-70). Trained census-takers were hired for the 1880 census and thereafter. In 1902, Congress authorized a permanent Census Office within the Interior Department. In 1903, the agency was transferred to the new Department of Commerce and Labor and remained with the Commerce Department when a separate labor department was created in 1913.

The 1790 through 1820 decennial censuses were officially enumerated the first Monday in Aug. The 1830-1900 censuses were as of June 1, though the 1890 census was not started until June 2 (June 1 was a Sunday). The 1910 census was as of Apr. 15, the 1920 census as of Jan. 1, and every census since 1930 has been for Apr. 1.

The Census Bureau began using statistical sampling techniques in the 1940s, the first modern computer in the 1950s, and enumeration by mail in the 1960s. These innovations allowed the Bureau to publish data more quickly and affordably. Any personally identifiable information gathered is withheld from the public for 72 years, after which records are made available through the National Archives. The 1940 census records, the most recent set to be released, can be accessed at 1940census.archives.gov.

In 1970 through 2000, about five in six households responded to a short-form census while one in six households answered a long-form questionnaire, which asked about details such as ancestry, marital status, and citizenship status. The American Community Survey (ACS)—conducted yearly on a random sample of the population—was implemented in 2005 to replace the long-form questionnaire.

In response to the COVID-19 pandemic, the Census Bureau temporarily suspended its field operations. As of July 1, 2020, 61.9% of U.S. households had responded to the 2020 Census. Census takers will need to visit an estimated 56 million addresses to collect responses in person. As of mid-2020, the Census Bureau was seeking Congressional approval to delay delivery of House seat apportionment data to the president and redistricting data to the states.

U.S. Population by State and Region, 2000, 2019

Source: Population Estimates Program and Decennial Census, U.S. Census Bureau, U.S. Dept. of Commerce
(ranked by 2019 resident population)

Rank	State	2019[1]	2000[2]	% change, 2000-19	Rank	State	2019[1]	2000[2]	% change, 2000-19
1.	California	39,512,223	33,871,653	16.7%	29.	Connecticut	3,565,287	3,405,602	4.7%
2.	Texas	28,995,881	20,851,790	39.1	30.	Utah	3,205,958	2,233,198	43.6
3.	Florida	21,477,737	15,982,824	34.4	31.	Iowa	3,155,070	2,926,382	7.8
4.	New York	19,453,561	18,976,821	2.5	32.	Nevada	3,080,156	1,998,257	54.1
5.	Pennsylvania	12,801,989	12,281,054	4.2	33.	Arkansas	3,017,804	2,673,400	12.9
6.	Illinois	12,671,821	12,419,647	2.0	34.	Mississippi	2,976,149	2,844,656	4.6
7.	Ohio	11,689,100	11,353,145	3.0	35.	Kansas	2,913,314	2,688,824	8.3
8.	Georgia	10,617,423	8,186,816	29.7	36.	New Mexico	2,096,829	1,819,046	15.3
9.	North Carolina	10,488,084	8,046,485	30.3	37.	Nebraska	1,934,408	1,711,265	13.0
10.	Michigan	9,986,857	9,938,480	0.5	38.	West Virginia	1,792,147	1,808,350	-0.9
11.	New Jersey	8,882,190	8,414,347	5.6	39.	Idaho	1,787,065	1,293,956	38.1
12.	Virginia	8,535,519	7,079,030	20.6	40.	Hawaii	1,415,872	1,211,537	16.9
13.	Washington	7,614,893	5,894,141	29.2	41.	New Hampshire	1,359,711	1,235,786	10.0
14.	Arizona	7,278,717	5,130,632	41.9	42.	Maine	1,344,212	1,274,923	5.4
15.	Massachusetts	6,892,503	6,349,105	8.6	43.	Montana	1,068,778	902,195	18.5
16.	Tennessee	6,829,174	5,689,267	20.0	44.	Rhode Island	1,059,361	1,048,319	1.1
17.	Indiana	6,732,219	6,080,517	10.7	45.	Delaware	973,764	783,600	24.3
18.	Missouri	6,137,428	5,596,683	9.7	46.	South Dakota	884,659	754,844	17.2
19.	Maryland	6,045,680	5,296,507	14.1	47.	North Dakota	762,062	642,200	18.7
20.	Wisconsin	5,822,434	5,363,715	8.6	48.	Alaska	731,545	626,931	16.7
21.	Colorado	5,758,736	4,302,015	33.9	49.	Dist. of Columbia	705,749	572,059	23.4
22.	Minnesota	5,639,632	4,919,492	14.6	50.	Vermont	623,989	608,827	2.5
23.	South Carolina	5,148,714	4,011,816	28.3	51.	Wyoming	578,759	493,782	17.2
24.	Alabama	4,903,185	4,447,351	10.2		**United States**	**328,239,523**	**281,421,906**	**16.6**
25.	Louisiana	4,648,794	4,468,958	4.0		Northeast[3]	55,982,803	53,594,378	4.5
26.	Kentucky	4,467,673	4,042,285	10.5		Midwest[4]	68,329,004	64,392,776	6.1
27.	Oregon	4,217,737	3,421,436	23.3		South[5]	125,580,448	100,236,820	25.3
28.	Oklahoma	3,956,971	3,450,652	14.7		West[6]	78,347,268	63,197,932	24.0

Note: The U.S. resident population consists of individuals whose usual residence, or where they live and sleep most of the time, is in one of the 50 states or DC. It excludes overseas U.S. military personnel and civilian U.S. citizens living abroad. (1) Estimates are as of July 1. (2) Figures are for Apr. 1 of decennial census year. Population figures may reflect revisions/corrections to initial tabulated census counts. (3) Incl. the states of the New England (Connecticut, Maine, Massachusetts, New Hampshire, Rhode Island, Vermont) and Middle Atlantic (New Jersey, New York, Pennsylvania) divisions. (4) Incl. the states of the East North Central (Illinois, Indiana, Michigan, Ohio, Wisconsin) and West North Central (Iowa, Kansas, Minnesota, Missouri, Nebraska, North Dakota, South Dakota) divisions. (5) Incl. the states of the South Atlantic (Delaware, DC, Florida, Georgia, Maryland, North Carolina, South Carolina, Virginia, West Virginia), East South Central (Alabama, Kentucky, Mississippi, Tennessee), and West South Central (Arkansas, Louisiana, Oklahoma, Texas) divisions. (6) Incl. the states of the Mountain (Arizona, Colorado, Idaho, Montana, Nevada, New Mexico, Utah, Wyoming) and Pacific (Alaska, California, Hawaii, Oregon, Washington) divisions.

Density of U.S. Population by State, 1930-2010

Source: Decennial Censuses, U.S. Census Bureau, U.S. Dept. of Commerce

(per square mile of land area, as measured for the 2010 census)

State	1930	1950	1970	1990	2010	State	1930	1950	1970	1990	2010
AL......	52.3	60.5	68.0	79.8	94.4	MT	3.7	4.1	4.8	5.5	6.8
AK......	0.1	0.2	0.5	1.0	1.2	NE.......	17.9	17.3	19.3	20.5	23.8
AZ.......	3.8	6.6	15.6	32.3	56.3	NV.......	0.8	1.5	4.5	10.9	24.6
AR......	35.6	36.7	37.0	45.2	56.0	NH	52.0	59.6	82.4	123.9	147.0
CA......	36.4	68.0	128.1	191.0	239.1	NJ......	549.5	657.5	974.7	1,051.1	1,195.5
CO	10.0	12.8	21.3	31.8	48.5	NM	3.5	5.6	8.4	12.5	17.0
CT......	331.8	414.5	626.1	678.8	738.1	NY.......	267.1	314.7	387.0	381.7	411.2
DE.......	122.3	163.2	281.3	341.9	460.8	NC	65.2	83.5	104.5	136.3	196.1
DC 7,975.1		13,140.0	12,392.0	9,941.3	9,856.5	ND	9.9	9.0	9.0	9.3	9.7
FL.......	27.4	51.7	126.6	241.3	350.6	OH	162.7	194.5	260.7	265.5	282.3
GA	50.6	59.9	79.8	112.6	168.4	OK	34.9	32.6	37.3	45.9	54.7
HI	57.3	77.8	119.7	172.6	211.8	OR	9.9	15.8	21.8	29.6	39.9
ID	5.4	7.1	8.6	12.2	19.0	PA......	215.3	234.6	263.6	265.6	283.9
IL.......	137.4	156.9	200.2	205.9	231.1	RI	665.0	766.0	915.8	970.6	1,018.1
IN	90.4	109.8	145.0	154.8	181.0	SC.......	57.8	70.4	86.2	116.0	153.9
IA	44.2	46.9	50.6	49.7	54.5	SD.......	9.1	8.6	8.8	9.2	10.7
KS......	23.0	23.3	27.5	30.3	34.9	TN.......	63.5	79.8	95.2	118.3	153.9
KY.......	66.2	74.6	81.5	93.3	109.9	TX.......	22.3	29.5	42.9	65.0	96.3
LA......	48.6	62.1	84.3	97.7	104.9	UT.......	6.2	8.4	12.9	21.0	33.6
ME......	25.9	29.6	32.2	39.8	43.1	VT.......	39.0	41.0	48.2	61.1	67.9
MD	168.1	241.4	404.1	492.6	594.8	VA	61.3	84.0	117.7	156.7	202.6
MA	544.8	601.3	729.4	771.3	839.4	WA	23.5	35.8	51.3	73.2	101.2
MI	85.6	112.7	157.0	164.4	174.8	WV.......	71.9	83.4	72.6	74.6	77.1
MN	32.2	37.5	47.8	54.9	66.6	WI.......	54.3	63.4	81.6	90.3	105.0
MS	42.8	46.4	47.2	54.8	63.2	WY......	2.3	3.0	3.4	4.7	5.8
MO	52.8	57.5	68.0	74.4	87.1	U.S.	34.7	42.6	57.5	70.4	87.4

Note: For the sake of comparison, the densities of Alaska and Hawaii in 1930 and 1950 are included though they were not yet states.

U.S. Area and Population, 1790-2010

Source: Decennial Censuses, U.S. Census Bureau, U.S. Dept. of Commerce

	AREA (square miles)			RESIDENT POPULATION			
						Increase over preceding census	
Census date	Total area[1]	Land area	Water area[1]	Number	Per sq mi of land	Number	%
1790 (Aug. 2)	891,364	864,746	24,065	3,929,214	4.5	—	—
1800 (Aug. 4)	891,364	864,746	24,065	5,308,483	6.1	1,379,269	35.1%
1810 (Aug. 6)	1,722,685	1,681,828	34,175	7,239,881	4.3	1,931,398	36.4
1820 (Aug. 7)	1,792,552	1,749,462	38,544	9,638,453	5.5	2,398,572	33.1
1830 (June 1)	1,792,552	1,749,462	38,544	12,860,702	7.4	3,222,249	33.4
1840 (June 1)	1,792,552	1,749,462	38,544	17,063,453	9.8	4,203,751	32.7
1850 (June 1)	2,991,655	2,940,042	52,705	23,191,876	7.9	6,128,423	35.9
1860 (June 1)	3,021,295	2,969,640	52,747	31,443,321	10.6	8,251,445	35.6
1870 (June 1)	3,612,299	3,540,705	68,082	38,558,371	10.9	7,115,050	22.6
1880 (June 1)	3,612,299	3,540,705	68,082	50,189,209	14.2	11,630,838	30.2
1890 (June 1)	3,612,299	3,540,705	68,082	62,979,766	17.8	12,790,557	25.5
1900 (June 1)	3,618,770	3,547,314	67,901	76,212,168	21.5	13,232,402	21.0
1910 (Apr. 15)	3,618,770	3,547,045	68,170	92,228,496	26.0	16,016,328	21.0
1920 (Jan. 1)	3,618,770	3,546,931	68,284	106,021,537	29.9	13,793,041	15.0
1930 (Apr. 1)	3,618,770	3,554,608	60,607	123,202,624	34.7	17,181,087	16.2
1940 (Apr. 1)	3,618,770	3,554,608	60,607	132,164,569	37.2	8,961,945	7.3
1950 (Apr. 1)	3,618,770	3,552,206	63,005	151,325,798	42.6	19,161,229	14.5
1960 (Apr. 1)	3,618,770	3,540,911	74,212	179,323,175	50.6	27,997,377	18.5
1970 (Apr. 1)	3,618,770	3,536,855	78,444	203,302,031	57.5	23,978,856	13.4
1980 (Apr. 1)	3,618,770	3,539,289	79,481	226,542,199	64.0	23,240,168	11.4
1990 (Apr. 1)	3,717,796	3,536,278	181,518	248,718,302	70.3	22,176,103	9.8
2000 (Apr. 1)	3,794,083	3,537,438	256,645	281,424,603	79.6	32,706,301	13.1
2010 (Apr. 1)	3,796,742	3,531,905	264,837	308,746,065	87.4	27,321,462	9.7

Note: Area and population density figures represent the area within the boundaries of the U.S. under its jurisdiction on the date in question including, in some cases, considerable areas not organized or settled and not covered by the census. Beginning in 1870, area data include Alaska; from 1900 on, data include Hawaii. Population figures may reflect revisions/corrections to initial tabulated census counts. (1) Figures for 1790-1980 cover inland water only. Figures for 1990 include inland, coastal, and Great Lakes water. Figures for 2000-10 include additional territorial water.

U.S. Population by Official

Source: Decennial Censuses, U.S. Census Bureau,
(population figures for 1790-1860,

State	1790	1800	1810	1820	1830	1840	1850	1860	1870	1880	1890	1900	1910	1920
AL	—	1	9	128	310	591	772	964	996,992	1,262,505	1,513,401	1,828,697	2,138,093	2,348,174
AK	—	—	—	—	—	—	—	—	—	33,426	32,052	63,592	64,356	55,036
AZ	—	—	—	—	—	—	—	—	9,658	40,440	88,243	122,931	204,354	334,162
AR	—	—	1	14	30	98	210	435	484,471	802,525	1,128,211	1,311,564	1,574,449	1,752,204
CA	—	—	—	—	—	—	93	380	560,247	864,694	1,213,398	1,485,053	2,377,549	3,426,861
CO	—	—	—	—	—	—	—	34	39,864	194,327	413,249	539,700	799,024	939,629
CT	238	251	262	275	298	310	371	460	537,454	622,700	746,258	908,420	1,114,756	1,380,631
DE	59	64	73	73	77	78	92	112	125,015	146,608	168,493	184,735	202,322	223,003
DC[1]	—	8	15	23	30	34	52	75	131,700	177,624	230,392	278,718	331,069	437,571
FL	—	—	—	—	35	54	87	140	187,748	269,493	391,422	528,542	752,619	968,470
GA	83	163	251	341	517	691	906	1,057	1,184,109	1,542,180	1,837,353	2,216,331	2,609,121	2,895,832
HI	—	—	—	—	—	—	—	—	—	—	—	154,001	191,874	255,881
ID	—	—	—	—	—	—	—	—	14,999	32,610	88,548	161,772	325,594	431,866
IL	—	—	12	55	157	476	851	1,712	2,539,891	3,077,871	3,826,352	4,821,550	5,638,591	6,485,280
IN	—	6	25	147	343	686	988	1,350	1,680,637	1,978,301	2,192,404	2,516,462	2,700,876	2,930,390
IA	—	—	—	—	—	43	192	675	1,194,020	1,624,615	1,912,297	2,231,853	2,224,771	2,404,021
KS	—	—	—	—	—	—	—	107	364,399	996,096	1,428,108	1,470,495	1,690,949	1,769,257
KY[1]	74	221	407	564	688	780	982	1,156	1,321,011	1,648,690	1,858,635	2,147,174	2,289,905	2,416,630
LA	—	—	77	153	216	352	518	708	726,915	939,946	1,118,588	1,381,625	1,656,388	1,798,509
ME[2]	97	152	229	298	399	502	583	628	626,915	648,936	661,086	694,466	742,371	768,014
MD	320	342	381	407	447	470	583	687	780,894	934,943	1,042,390	1,188,044	1,295,346	1,449,661
MA[2]	379	423	472	523	610	738	995	1,231	1,457,351	1,783,085	2,238,947	2,805,346	3,366,416	3,852,356
MI	—	—	5	7	28	212	398	749	1,184,059	1,636,937	2,093,890	2,420,982	2,810,173	3,668,412
MN	—	—	—	—	—	—	6	172	439,706	780,773	1,310,283	1,751,394	2,075,708	2,387,125
MS	—	8	31	75	137	376	607	791	827,922	1,131,597	1,289,600	1,551,270	1,797,114	1,790,618
MO	—	—	20	67	140	384	682	1,182	1,721,295	2,168,380	2,679,185	3,106,665	3,293,335	3,404,055
MT	—	—	—	—	—	—	—	—	20,595	39,159	142,924	243,329	376,053	548,889
NE	—	—	—	—	—	—	—	29	122,993	452,402	1,062,656	1,066,300	1,192,214	1,296,372
NV	—	—	—	—	—	—	—	7	42,491	62,266	47,355	42,335	81,875	77,407
NH	142	184	214	244	269	285	318	326	318,300	346,991	376,530	411,588	430,572	443,083
NJ	184	211	246	278	321	373	490	672	906,096	1,131,116	1,444,933	1,883,669	2,537,167	3,155,900
NM	—	—	—	—	—	—	62	94	91,874	119,565	160,282	195,310	327,301	360,350
NY	340	589	959	1,373	1,919	2,429	3,097	3,881	4,382,759	5,082,871	6,003,174	7,268,894	9,113,614	10,385,227
NC	394	478	557	639	738	753	869	993	1,071,361	1,399,750	1,617,949	1,893,810	2,206,287	2,559,123
ND[3]	—	—	—	—	—	—	—	—	2,405	36,909	190,983	319,146	577,056	646,872
OH	—	42	231	581	938	1,519	1,980	2,340	2,665,260	3,198,062	3,672,329	4,157,545	4,767,121	5,759,394
OK[4]	—	—	—	—	—	—	—	—	—	—	258,657	790,391	1,657,155	2,028,283
OR	—	—	—	—	—	—	12	52	90,923	174,768	317,704	413,536	672,765	783,389
PA	434	602	810	1,049	1,348	1,724	2,312	2,906	3,521,951	4,282,891	5,258,113	6,302,115	7,665,111	8,720,017
RI	69	69	77	83	97	109	148	175	217,353	276,531	345,506	428,556	542,610	604,397
SC	249	346	415	503	581	594	669	704	705,606	995,577	1,151,149	1,340,316	1,515,400	1,683,724
SD[3]	—	—	—	—	—	—	—	5	11,776	98,268	348,600	401,570	583,888	636,547
TN	36	106	262	423	682	829	1,003	1,110	1,258,520	1,542,359	1,767,518	2,020,616	2,184,789	2,337,885
TX	—	—	—	—	—	—	213	604	818,579	1,591,749	2,235,527	3,048,710	3,896,542	4,663,228
UT	—	—	—	—	—	—	11	40	86,336	143,963	210,779	276,749	373,351	449,396
VT	85	154	218	236	281	292	314	315	330,551	332,286	332,422	343,641	355,956	352,428
VA[1]	692	808	878	938	1,044	1,025	1,119	1,220	1,225,163	1,512,565	1,655,980	1,854,184	2,061,612	2,309,187
WA	—	—	—	—	—	—	1	12	23,955	75,116	357,232	518,103	1,141,990	1,356,621
WV[1]	56	79	105	137	177	225	302	377	442,014	618,457	762,794	958,800	1,221,119	1,463,701
WI	—	—	—	—	—	31	305	776	1,054,670	1,315,497	1,693,330	2,069,042	2,333,860	2,632,067
WY	—	—	—	—	—	—	—	—	9,118	20,789	62,555	92,531	145,965	194,402
U.S.[5]	3,929	5,308	7,240	9,638	12,861	17,063	23,192	31,443	38,558,371	50,189,209	62,979,766	76,212,168	92,228,496	106,021,537

Note: With some exceptions, pop. shown is number of residents in a state (or territory of the same name) at the time of each decennial census. Figures may differ from originally published census data because of revisions. Excl. overseas U.S. military personnel and civilian U.S. citizens living abroad. (1) 1790-1860 VA figures are for present-day boundaries. That is, they incl. pop. in areas then part of DC (1800-40) and excl. pop. of areas that went to KY (1790) and WV (1790-1860). (2) 1790-1810 figures for MA do not incl. district taken to form state of ME in 1820. (3) 1860 SD figure is for area reported as "unorganized Dakota"; 1870-80 figures are for present-day ND and SD. (4) 1890-1900 figures incl. pop. for Indian Terr. (5) 1830-40 totals excl. persons (5,318 in 1830; 6,100 in 1840) on public ships in service of the U.S. not credited to any state. 1890 total incl. Indian Terr. and Indian Reservations pop. (325,464) specially enumerated.

Estimated Population of American Colonies, 1630-1780

Source: U.S. Census Bureau, U.S. Dept. of Commerce
(numbers in thousands)

Colony	1630	1650	1670	1690	1710	1720	1740	1750	1760	1770	1780
Total	4.6	50.4	111.9	210.4	250.9	466.2	905.6	1,170.8	1,593.6	2,148.1	2,780.4
Connecticut	—	4.1	12.6	21.6	26.0	58.8	89.6	111.3	142.5	183.9	206.7
Delaware	—	0.2	0.7	1.5	2.5	5.4	19.9	28.7	33.3	35.5	45.4
Georgia	—	—	—	—	—	—	2.0	5.2	9.6	23.4	56.1
Kentucky[1]	—	—	—	—	—	—	—	—	—	15.7	45.0
Maine (counties)[2]	0.4	1.0	—	—	—	—	—	—	20.0	31.3	49.1
Maryland	—	4.5	13.2	24.0	29.6	66.1	116.1	141.1	162.3	202.6	245.5
Massachusetts and Plymouth[2,3]	0.9	15.6	35.3	56.9	55.9	91.0	151.6	188.0	202.6	235.3	268.6
New Hampshire	0.5	1.3	1.8	4.2	5.0	9.4	23.3	27.5	39.1	62.4	87.8
New Jersey	—	—	1.0	8.0	14.0	29.8	51.4	71.4	93.8	117.4	139.6
New York	0.4	4.1	5.8	13.9	19.1	36.9	63.7	76.7	117.1	162.9	210.5
North Carolina	—	—	3.9	7.6	10.7	21.3	51.8	73.0	110.4	197.2	270.1
Pennsylvania	—	—	—	11.4	18.0	31.0	85.6	119.7	183.7	240.1	327.3
Rhode Island	—	0.8	2.2	4.2	5.9	11.7	25.3	33.2	45.5	58.2	52.9
South Carolina	—	—	0.2	3.9	5.7	17.0	45.0	64.0	94.1	124.2	180.0
Tennessee[4]	—	—	—	—	—	—	—	—	—	—	10.0
Vermont[5]	—	—	—	—	—	—	—	—	—	10.0	47.6
Virginia	2.5	18.7	35.3	53.0	58.6	87.8	180.4	231.0	339.7	447.0	538.0

Note: With the exception of KY, ME, Plymouth, TN, and VT, colonies shown are the original 13 states (ratified the Constitution 1787-90). (1) Admitted as state 1792. (2) For 1660-1750, the pop. of ME counties are included with MA. ME was annexed by MA in the 1650s but became a separate state in 1820. (3) Plymouth became part of Prov. of Massachusetts in 1691. (4) Admitted as state 1796. (5) Admitted as state 1791.

Census, 1790-2010

U.S. Dept. of Commerce
only are in thousands)

1930	1940	1950	1960	1970	1980	1990	2000	2010	State
2,646,248	2,832,961	3,061,743	3,266,740	3,444,354	3,894,025	4,040,389	4,447,351	4,779,753	AL
59,278	72,524	128,643	226,167	302,583	401,851	550,043	626,931	710,235	AK
435,573	499,261	749,587	1,302,161	1,775,399	2,716,546	3,665,339	5,130,632	6,392,017	AZ
1,854,482	1,949,387	1,909,511	1,786,272	1,923,322	2,286,357	2,350,624	2,673,400	2,915,919	AR
5,677,251	6,907,387	10,586,223	15,717,204	19,971,069	23,667,764	29,758,213	33,871,653	37,253,956	CA
1,035,791	1,123,296	1,325,089	1,753,947	2,209,596	2,889,735	3,294,473	4,302,015	5,029,196	CO
1,606,903	1,709,242	2,007,280	2,535,234	3,032,217	3,107,564	3,287,116	3,405,602	3,574,097	CT
238,380	266,505	318,085	446,292	548,104	594,338	666,168	783,600	897,934	DE
486,869	663,091	802,178	763,956	756,668	638,432	606,900	572,059	601,767	DC
1,468,211	1,897,414	2,771,305	4,951,560	6,791,414	9,746,961	12,938,071	15,982,824	18,801,332	FL
2,908,506	3,123,723	3,444,578	3,943,116	4,587,930	5,462,982	6,478,149	8,186,816	9,687,850	GA
368,300	422,770	499,794	632,772	769,913	964,691	1,108,229	1,211,537	1,360,301	HI
445,032	524,873	588,637	667,191	713,015	944,127	1,006,734	1,293,956	1,567,652	ID
7,630,654	7,897,241	8,712,176	10,081,158	11,110,285	11,427,409	11,430,602	12,419,647	12,830,632	IL
3,238,503	3,427,796	3,934,224	4,662,498	5,195,392	5,490,210	5,544,156	6,080,517	6,483,802	IN
2,470,939	2,538,268	2,621,073	2,757,537	2,825,368	2,913,808	2,776,831	2,926,382	3,046,355	IA
1,880,999	1,801,028	1,905,299	2,178,611	2,249,071	2,364,236	2,477,588	2,688,824	2,853,118	KS
2,614,589	2,845,627	2,944,806	3,038,156	3,220,711	3,660,324	3,686,892	4,042,285	4,339,367	KY
2,101,593	2,363,880	2,683,516	3,257,022	3,644,637	4,206,116	4,220,164	4,468,958	4,533,372	LA
797,423	847,226	913,774	969,265	993,722	1,125,043	1,227,928	1,274,923	1,328,361	ME
1,631,526	1,821,244	2,343,001	3,100,689	3,923,897	4,216,933	4,780,753	5,296,507	5,773,626	MD
4,249,614	4,316,721	4,690,514	5,148,578	5,689,170	5,737,093	6,016,425	6,349,105	6,547,629	MA
4,842,325	5,256,106	6,371,766	7,823,194	8,881,826	9,262,044	9,295,287	9,938,480	9,883,706	MI
2,563,953	2,792,300	2,982,483	3,413,864	3,806,103	4,075,970	4,375,665	4,919,492	5,303,925	MN
2,009,821	2,183,796	2,178,914	2,178,141	2,216,994	2,520,770	2,575,475	2,844,656	2,967,297	MS
3,629,367	3,784,664	3,954,653	4,319,813	4,677,623	4,916,766	5,116,901	5,596,683	5,988,927	MO
537,606	559,456	591,024	674,767	694,409	786,690	799,065	902,195	989,415	MT
1,377,963	1,315,834	1,325,510	1,411,330	1,485,333	1,569,825	1,578,417	1,711,265	1,826,341	NE
91,058	110,247	160,083	285,278	488,738	800,508	1,201,675	1,998,257	2,700,551	NV
465,293	491,524	533,242	606,921	737,681	920,610	1,109,252	1,235,786	1,316,470	NH
4,041,334	4,160,165	4,835,329	6,066,782	7,171,112	7,365,011	7,730,188	8,414,347	8,791,909	NJ
423,317	531,818	681,187	951,023	1,017,055	1,303,302	1,515,069	1,819,046	2,059,181	NM
12,588,066	13,479,142	14,830,192	16,782,304	18,241,391	17,558,165	17,990,778	18,976,821	19,378,102	NY
3,170,276	3,571,623	4,061,929	4,556,155	5,084,411	5,880,095	6,632,448	8,046,485	9,535,483	NC
680,845	641,935	619,636	632,446	617,792	652,717	638,800	642,200	672,591	ND
6,646,697	6,907,612	7,946,627	9,706,397	10,657,423	10,797,603	10,847,115	11,353,145	11,536,504	OH
2,396,040	2,336,434	2,233,351	2,328,284	2,559,463	3,025,481	3,145,576	3,450,652	3,751,351	OK
953,786	1,089,684	1,521,341	1,768,687	2,091,533	2,633,156	2,842,337	3,421,436	3,831,074	OR
9,631,350	9,900,180	10,498,012	11,319,366	11,800,766	11,864,720	11,882,842	12,281,054	12,702,379	PA
687,497	713,346	791,896	859,488	949,723	947,154	1,003,464	1,048,319	1,052,567	RI
1,738,765	1,899,804	2,117,027	2,382,594	2,590,713	3,120,729	3,486,310	4,011,816	4,625,364	SC
692,849	642,961	652,740	680,514	666,257	690,768	696,004	754,844	814,191	SD
2,616,556	2,915,841	3,291,718	3,567,089	3,926,018	4,591,023	4,877,203	5,689,267	6,346,105	TN
5,824,715	6,414,824	7,711,194	9,579,677	11,198,655	14,225,513	16,986,335	20,851,790	25,145,565	TX
507,847	550,310	688,862	890,627	1,059,273	1,461,037	1,722,850	2,233,198	2,763,885	UT
359,611	359,231	377,747	389,881	444,732	511,456	562,758	608,827	625,741	VT
2,421,851	2,677,773	3,318,680	3,966,949	4,651,448	5,346,797	6,189,197	7,079,030	8,001,024	VA
1,563,396	1,736,191	2,378,963	2,853,214	3,413,244	4,132,353	4,866,669	5,894,141	6,724,540	WA
1,729,205	1,901,974	2,005,552	1,860,421	1,744,237	1,950,186	1,793,477	1,808,350	1,852,994	WV
2,939,006	3,137,587	3,434,575	3,951,777	4,417,821	4,705,642	4,891,769	5,363,715	5,686,986	WI
225,565	250,742	290,529	330,066	332,416	469,557	453,589	493,782	563,626	WY
123,202,624	132,164,569	151,325,798	179,323,175	203,302,031	226,542,199	248,718,302	281,424,603	308,746,065	U.S.

U.S. Center of Population, 1790-2010

Source: Decennial Censuses, Geography Division, U.S. Census Bureau, U.S. Dept. of Commerce

The country's (**mean**) **center of population** is the center of population gravity. In other words, it is the point upon which the U.S. would balance if the country were a rigid, weightless plane and its population was distributed thereon, with each individual assuming an equal weight.

Census year	N Latitude °	'	"	W Longitude °	'	"	Approximate location
1790	39	16	30	76	11	12	Kent Co., MD, 23 miles east of Baltimore
1800	39	16	6	76	56	30	Howard Co., MD, 18 miles west of Baltimore
1810	39	11	30	77	37	12	Loudoun Co., VA, 40 miles northwest by west of Washington, DC
1820	39	5	42	78	33	0	Hardy Co., WV[1], 16 miles east of Moorefield
1830	38	57	54	79	16	54	Grant Co., WV[1], 19 miles west-southwest of Moorefield
1840	39	2	0	80	18	0	Upshur Co., WV[1], 16 miles south of Clarksburg
1850	38	59	0	81	19	0	Wirt Co., WV[1], 23 miles southeast of Parkersburg
1860	39	0	24	82	48	48	Pike Co., OH, 20 miles south by east of Chillicothe
1870	39	12	0	83	35	42	Highland Co., OH, 48 miles east by north of Cincinnati
1880	39	4	8	84	39	40	Boone Co., KY, 8 miles by south of Cincinnati, OH
1890	39	11	56	85	32	53	Decatur Co., IN, 20 miles east of Columbus
1900	39	9	36	85	48	54	Bartholomew Co., IN, 6 miles southeast of Columbus
1910	39	10	12	86	32	20	Monroe Co., IN, in the city of Bloomington
1920	39	10	21	86	43	15	Owen Co., IN, 8 miles south-southeast of Spencer
1930	39	3	45	87	8	6	Greene Co., IN, 3 miles northeast of Linton
1940	38	56	54	87	22	35	Sullivan Co., IN, 2 miles southeast by east of Carlisle
1950	38	50	21	88	9	33	Richland Co., IL, 8 miles north-northwest of Olney
1950[2]	38	48	15	88	22	8	Clay Co., IL, 3 miles northeast of Louisville
1960[2]	38	35	58	89	12	35	Clinton Co., IL, 6.5 miles northwest of Centralia
1970[2]	38	27	47	89	42	22	St. Clair Co., IL, 5 miles east-southeast of Mascoutah
1980[2]	38	8	13	90	34	26	Jefferson Co., MO, 0.25 mile west of DeSoto
1990[2]	37	52	20	91	12	55	Crawford Co., MO, 9.7 miles southeast of Steelville
2000[2]	37	41	49	91	48	34	Phelps Co., MO, 2.8 miles east of Edgar Springs
2010[2]	37	31	3	92	10	23	Texas Co., MO, 2.7 miles northeast of Plato

(1) Pres. Lincoln signed a bill Dec. 31, 1862, approving statehood for West Virginia (made up of former Virginia counties). It was admitted to the Union June 20, 1863. (2) Incl. Alaska and Hawaii.

U.S. Congressional Apportionment by Census Year, 1850-2010
Source: Decennial Censuses, U.S. Census Bureau, U.S. Dept. of Commerce

The U.S. Constitution, in Article 1, Section 2, mandates that the population be counted every 10 years so that the number of U.S. representatives can be apportioned among the states. Every state is entitled to at least one House seat. The size of a state's resident population, both citizens and noncitizens, determines if it may send additional representatives to Congress. A congressional apportionment has been made after every decennial census except for that of 1920. Prior to 1870, enslaved persons were counted as being only three-fifths of a person in the apportionment population. Since the 1970 census (excluding 1980), overseas military personnel and federal civilian employees as well as their dependents have been allocated to a home state for apportionment purposes. Residents of the District of Columbia, Puerto Rico, and U.S. island areas are not included in the apportionment population as they lack voting seats in the U.S. House.

Under a law approved in 1941, House seats are allocated using the Huntington-Hill, or equal proportions, method. It allows for the least possible variation in the average number of people each House member represents.

The first House of Representatives, in 1789, had 65 members as provided by the Constitution. As the nation's population grew, the number of representatives was increased. A 1911 act fixed the total House membership at 435. (Alaska and Hawaii each gained one House seat when they became states, temporarily raising the total to 437 representatives until after the 1960 census was conducted.) Because of the coronavirus pandemic, the Census Bureau requested congressional approval to delay delivery of final apportionment data based on the 2020 census.

State	2010	2000	1990	1970	1950	1900	1850	State	2010	2000	1990	1970	1950	1900	1850
AL....	7	7	7	7	9	9	7	NE.....	3	3	3	3	4	6	NA
AK....	1	1	1	1	1	NA	NA	NV.....	4	3	2	1	1	1	NA
AZ....	9	8	6	4	2	NA	NA	NH	2	2	2	2	2	2	3
AR....	4	4	4	4	6	7	2	NJ.....	12	13	13	15	14	10	5
CA....	53	53	52	43	30	8	2	NM	3	3	3	2	2	NA	NA
CO	7	7	6	5	4	3	NA	NY....	27	29	31	39	43	37	33
CT....	5	5	6	6	6	5	4	NC	13	13	12	11	12	10	8
DE....	1	1	1	1	1	1	1	ND	1	1	1	1	2	2	NA
FL....	27	25	23	15	8	3	1	OH	16	18	19	23	23	21	21
GA	14	13	11	10	10	11	8	OK	5	5	6	6	6	5	NA
HI	2	2	2	2	1	NA	NA	OR	5	5	5	4	4	2	1
ID	2	2	2	2	2	1	NA	PA.....	18	19	21	25	30	32	25
IL.....	18	19	20	24	25	25	9	RI	2	2	2	2	2	2	2
IN	9	9	10	11	11	13	11	SC....	7	6	6	6	6	7	6
IA	4	5	5	6	8	11	2	SD....	1	1	2	2	2	2	NA
KS....	4	4	4	5	6	8	NA	TN....	9	9	9	8	9	10	10
KY....	6	6	6	7	8	11	10	TX.....	36	32	30	24	22	16	2
LA....	6	7	7	8	8	7	4	UT....	4	3	3	2	2	1	NA
ME....	2	2	2	2	3	4	6	VT....	1	1	1	1	1	2	3
MD	8	8	8	8	7	6	6	VA.....	11	11	11	10	10	10	13
MA	9	10	10	12	14	14	11	WA	10	9	9	7	7	3	NA
MI....	14	15	16	19	18	12	4	WV	3	3	3	4	6	5	NA
MN ...	8	8	8	8	9	9	2	WI.....	8	8	9	9	10	11	3
MS ...	4	4	5	5	6	8	5	WY	1	1	1	1	1	1	NA
MO ...	8	9	9	10	11	16	7								
MT ...	1	1	1	2	2	1	NA	**Total...**	**435**	**435**	**435**	**435**	**437**	**391**	**237**

NA = Not applicable.

U.S. Enslaved and "Free Colored" Population, 1790, 1820, 1860
Source: Decennial Censuses, U.S. Census Bureau, U.S. Dept. of Commerce

	1790			1820			1860		
	Enslaved	% enslaved[1]	Free colored	Enslaved	% enslaved[1]	Free colored	Enslaved	% enslaved[1]	Free colored
Northern states[2]	40,354	2.1%	27,070	19,108	0.4%	99,307	18	0.0%	225,224
Connecticut	2,764	1.2	2,808	97	0.0	7,870	0	0.0	8,627
New Jersey	11,423	6.2	2,762	7,557	2.7	12,460	18	0.0	25,318
New York	21,324	6.3	4,654	10,088	0.7	29,279	0	0.0	49,005
Pennsylvania	3,737	0.9	6,537	211	0.0	30,202	0	0.0	56,949
Border/disputed states ..	124,353	27.5	12,056	248,860	22.4	55,794	429,403	13.2	118,652
Delaware	8,887	15.0	3,899	4,509	6.2	12,958	1,798	1.6	19,829
Kansas	—	—	—	—	—	—	2	0.0	625
Kentucky............	12,430	16.9	114	126,732	20.5	2,759	225,483	19.5	10,684
Maryland............	103,036	32.2	8,043	107,397	26.4	39,730	87,189	12.7	83,942
Missouri	—	—	—	10,222	15.4	347	114,931	9.7	3,572
Southern states	532,974	35.3	20,401	1,265,534	37.8	75,775	3,521,110	38.7	132,760
Alabama	—	—	—	41,879	32.7	571	435,080	45.1	2,690
Arkansas	—	—	—	1,617	11.3	59	111,115	25.5	144
Florida	—	—	—	—	—	—	61,745	44.0	932
Georgia.............	29,264	35.5	398	149,656	43.9	1,763	462,198	43.7	3,500
Louisiana	—	—	—	69,064	45.0	10,476	331,726	46.9	18,647
Mississippi	—	—	—	32,814	43.5	458	436,631	55.2	773
North Carolina	100,572	25.5	4,975	204,917	32.1	14,712	331,059	33.4	30,463
South Carolina	107,094	43.0	1,801	258,475	51.4	6,826	402,406	57.2	9,914
Tennessee	3,417	9.6	361	80,107	18.9	2,737	275,719	24.8	7,300
Texas	—	—	—	—	—	—	182,566	30.2	355
Virginia	292,627	39.1	12,866	427,005	39.7	38,173	490,865	30.7	58,042
Total territories[3]	—	—	—	4,520	19.4	2,758	3,229	1.1	11,434
Total states and territories	**697,681**	**17.8**	**59,527**	**1,538,022**	**16.0**	**233,634**	**3,953,760**	**12.6**	**488,070**

Note: "Free colored" was an official Census Bureau designation in these decades. States are grouped roughly by allegiance in the Civil War. (1) Percentage of total pop., all races. (2) The following states are not listed separately but are included in totals for Northern states (relevant census years in parentheses): CA (1860), IL (1820, 1860), IN (1820, 1860), ME (1790, 1820, 1860), MA (1790, 1820, 1860), MI (1820, 1860), MN (1860), NH (1790, 1820, 1860), OH (1820, 1860), OR (1860), RI (1790, 1820, 1860), VT (1790, 1820, 1860), WI (1820, 1860). (3) Incl. AZ (1860), CO (1860), Dakota (1860), DC (1820, 1860), NE (1860), NV (1860), NM (1860), UT (1860), WA (1860).

U.S. Population by Sex, Race, Residence, and Median Age, 1790-2010

Source: Decennial Censuses, U.S. Census Bureau, U.S. Dept. of Commerce

(numbers in thousands, unless otherwise noted)

Census date	SEX Male	SEX Female	RACE[2] White	RACE[2] Black Number	RACE[2] Black % tot. pop.	RACE[2] Other	RESIDENCE Urban[3]	RESIDENCE Rural	MEDIAN AGE (years) All races	MEDIAN AGE (years) White[2]	MEDIAN AGE (years) Black[2]
Conterminous U.S.[1]											
1790 (Aug. 2)	NA	NA	3,172	757	19.3%	NA	202	3,728	NA	NA	NA
1800 (Aug. 4)	NA	NA	4,306	1,002	18.9	NA	322	4,986	NA	NA	NA
1810 (Aug. 6)	NA	NA	5,862	1,378	19.0	NA	525	6,714	NA	16.0	NA
1820 (Aug. 7)	4,897	4,742	7,867	1,772	18.4	NA	693	8,945	16.7	16.6	17.2
1830 (June 1)	6,532	6,334	10,537	2,329	18.1	NA	1,127	11,733	17.2	17.3	17.2
1840 (June 1)	8,689	8,381	14,196	2,874	16.8	NA	1,845	15,218	17.8	17.9	17.6
1850 (June 1)	11,838	11,354	19,553	3,639	15.7	NA	3,574	19,617	18.9	19.2	17.4
1860 (June 1)	16,085	15,358	26,923	4,442	14.1	79	6,217	25,227	19.4	19.7	17.5
1870 (June 1)	19,494	19,065	33,589	4,880	12.7	89	9,902	28,656	20.2	20.4	18.5
1880 (June 1)	25,519	24,637	43,403	6,581	13.1	172	14,130	36,059	20.9	21.4	18.0
1890 (June 1)	32,237	30,711	55,101	7,489	11.9	358	22,106	40,874	22.0	22.5	17.8
1900 (June 1)	38,816	37,178	66,809	8,834	11.6	351	30,215	45,997	22.9	23.4	19.4
1910 (Apr. 15).	47,332	44,640	81,732	9,828	10.7	413	42,064	50,164	24.1	24.5	20.8
1920 (Jan. 1)	53,900	51,810	94,821	10,463	9.9	427	54,253	51,768	25.3	25.5	22.3
1930 (Apr. 1).	62,137	60,638	110,287	11,891	9.7	597	69,161	54,042	26.5	26.9	23.5
1940 (Apr. 1).	66,062	65,608	118,215	12,866	9.8	589	74,705	57,459	29.0	29.5	25.3
United States											
1950 (Apr. 1).	74,833	75,864	135,150	15,045	10.0	713	96,847	54,479	30.2	30.8	26.1
1960 (Apr. 1).	88,331	90,992	158,832	18,872	10.5	1,620	125,269	54,054	29.5	30.3	23.5
1970 (Apr. 1).	98,926	104,309	178,098	22,581	11.1	2,557	149,647	53,565	28.1	28.9	22.4
1980 (Apr. 1).	110,053	116,493	194,713	26,683	11.8	5,150	167,051	59,495	30.0	30.9	24.9
1990 (Apr. 1).	121,284	127,507	208,741	30,517	12.3	9,533	187,053	61,656	32.8	33.7	27.9
2000 (Apr. 1).	138,054	143,368	194,553	34,658	12.3	13,118	222,361	59,061	35.3	38.6	30.2
2010 (Apr. 1).	151,781	156,964	196,818	38,929	12.6	18,147	249,253	59,492	37.2	42.0	32.4

NA = Not available. **Note:** Population figures may reflect revisions/corrections to initial tabulated census counts. (1) Excludes Alaska and Hawaii. (2) New race categories were introduced in the 2000 census. Race data for 2000 and on are for people who reported being of one race alone. "White" does not include people who reported being of Hispanic or Latino origin. "Other" comprises Asians, Native Hawaiians and other Pacific Islanders, American Indians and Alaska Natives. Because of these changes, race data from 2000 on are not comparable to figures from previous years. (3) The Census Bureau's definition of "urban" has changed over time. Figures for 2000 and 2010 include residents of urbanized areas (50,000 or more inhabitants) and urban clusters (at least 2,500 but fewer than 50,000 inhabitants).

U.S. Population by Race and Hispanic Origin, 2000-10

Source: Decennial Censuses, U.S. Census Bureau, U.S. Dept. of Commerce

	2010 One race alone	2010 One or more races[1]	2000 One race alone	2000 One or more races[1]	% change, 2000-10[2] One race alone	% change, 2000-10[2] One or more races
Total population	299,736,465	308,746,065	274,595,678	281,421,906	9.2%	9.7%
Race						
White	223,553,265	231,040,398	211,460,626	216,930,975	5.7	6.5
Black or African American	38,929,319	42,020,743	34,658,190	36,419,434	12.3	15.4
Asian	14,674,252	17,320,856	10,242,998	11,898,828	43.3	45.6
American Indian and Alaska Native . . .	2,932,248	5,220,579	2,475,956	4,119,301	18.4	26.7
Native Hawaiian and other Pac. Isl. . . .	540,013	1,225,195	398,835	874,414	35.4	40.1
Some other race	19,107,368	21,748,084	15,359,073	18,521,486	24.4	17.4
Hispanic origin and race						
Hispanic or Latino, any race	47,435,002	50,477,594	33,081,736	35,305,818	43.4	43.0
Not Hispanic or Latino	252,301,463	258,267,944	241,513,942	246,116,088	4.5	4.9
White	196,817,552	201,856,108	194,552,774	198,177,900	1.2	1.9
Black or African American	37,685,848	40,123,525	33,947,837	35,383,751	11.0	13.4
Asian	14,465,124	16,722,710	10,123,169	11,579,494	42.9	44.4
American Indian and Alaska Native . .	2,247,098	4,029,675	2,068,883	3,444,700	8.6	17.0
Native Hawaiian and other Pac. Isl.	481,576	1,014,888	353,509	748,149	36.2	35.7
Some other race	604,265	1,033,866	467,770	1,770,645	29.2	−41.6

Note: Population figures may reflect revisions/corrections to initial tabulated census counts. (1) Alone or in combination with one or more of the other races listed. Numbers do not add up to totals because of individuals reporting more than one race. (2) An error in data processing resulted in the overstatement in the 2000 census of the number of people reporting more than one race, in particular race combinations involving some other race. Percent change in multiple-race populations between 2000 and 2010 should ideally be calculated with specific race combinations (e.g., White and Black or White and Asian).

U.S. Population Growth by Race and Hispanic Origin, 1970-2030

Source: Decennial Censuses and Population Projections Program, U.S. Census Bureau, U.S. Dept. of Commerce
(numbers in millions)

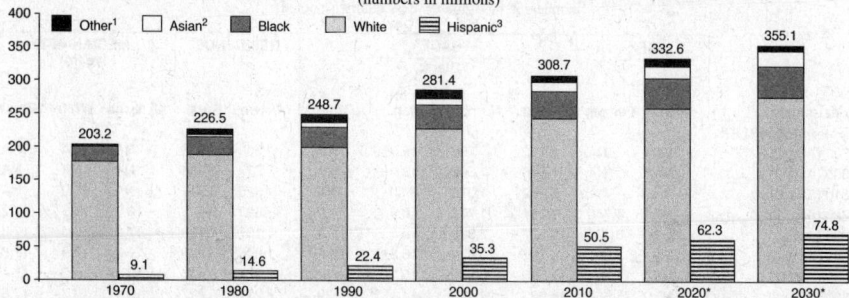

*Projected. **Note:** Because of changes in census questions and methods, data on race and Hispanic origin are not wholly comparable over time. Population figures may reflect revisions/corrections to initial tabulated census counts. (1) Includes American Indians and Alaska Natives as well as other races not shown. For 2000 and on, this category also includes Native Hawaiians and other Pacific Islanders along with persons reporting two or more races. (2) Figures for 1970-90 include Pacific Islanders. (3) May be of any race. 1970 figure is based on sample of households.

State Population by Race and Hispanic Origin, 2010

Source: Decennial Census, U.S. Census Bureau, U.S. Dept. of Commerce
(percentage of state or country's total population)

State	One race alone[1]						Two or more races[1]	Hispanic or Latino, any race
	White	Black or African American	Asian	American Indian and Alaska Native	Native Hawaiian and other Pacific Islander	Some other race		
Alabama	67.0%	26.0%	1.1%	0.5%	0.04%	0.08%	1.3%	3.9%
Alaska	64.1	3.1	5.3	14.4	1.02	0.16	6.4	5.5
Arizona	57.8	3.7	2.7	4.0	0.17	0.13	1.8	29.6
Arkansas	74.5	15.3	1.2	0.7	0.19	0.07	1.6	6.4
California	40.1	5.8	12.8	0.4	0.35	0.23	2.6	37.6
Colorado	70.0	3.8	2.7	0.6	0.11	0.15	2.0	20.7
Connecticut	71.2	9.4	3.8	0.2	0.03	0.34	1.7	13.4
Delaware	65.3	20.8	3.2	0.3	0.03	0.17	2.0	8.2
District of Columbia	34.8	50.0	3.5	0.2	0.04	0.24	2.1	9.1
Florida	57.9	15.2	2.4	0.3	0.05	0.26	1.5	22.5
Georgia	55.9	30.0	3.2	0.2	0.05	0.20	1.6	8.8
Hawaii	22.7	1.5	37.7	0.2	9.43	0.14	19.4	8.9
Idaho	84.0	0.6	1.2	1.1	0.14	0.10	1.7	11.2
Illinois	63.7	14.3	4.5	0.1	0.02	0.12	1.4	15.8
Indiana	81.5	9.0	1.6	0.2	0.03	0.13	1.5	6.0
Iowa	88.7	2.9	1.7	0.3	0.06	0.07	1.4	5.0
Kansas	78.2	5.7	2.3	0.8	0.07	0.10	2.3	10.5
Kentucky	86.3	7.7	1.1	0.2	0.05	0.11	1.5	3.1
Louisiana	60.3	31.8	1.5	0.6	0.03	0.15	1.3	4.2
Maine	94.4	1.1	1.0	0.6	0.02	0.08	1.4	1.3
Maryland	54.7	29.0	5.5	0.2	0.04	0.21	2.2	8.2
Massachusetts	76.1	6.0	5.3	0.2	0.02	0.94	1.9	9.6
Michigan	76.6	14.0	2.4	0.6	0.02	0.10	1.9	4.4
Minnesota	83.1	5.1	4.0	1.0	0.04	0.11	1.9	4.7
Mississippi	58.0	36.9	0.9	0.5	0.03	0.06	0.9	2.7
Missouri	81.0	11.5	1.6	0.4	0.10	0.09	1.8	3.5
Montana	87.8	0.4	0.6	6.1	0.06	0.05	2.2	2.9
Nebraska	82.1	4.4	1.7	0.8	0.05	0.12	1.6	9.2
Nevada	54.1	7.7	7.1	0.9	0.57	0.18	2.9	26.5
New Hampshire	92.3	1.0	2.1	0.2	0.02	0.14	1.4	2.8
New Jersey	59.3	12.8	8.2	0.1	0.02	0.31	1.5	17.7
New Mexico	40.5	1.7	1.3	8.5	0.06	0.18	1.4	46.3
New York	58.3	14.4	7.3	0.3	0.03	0.42	1.7	17.6
North Carolina	65.3	21.2	2.2	1.1	0.06	0.16	1.6	8.4
North Dakota	88.9	1.1	1.0	5.3	0.04	0.05	1.5	2.0
Ohio	81.1	12.0	1.7	0.2	0.03	0.13	1.8	3.1
Oklahoma	68.7	7.3	1.7	8.2	0.11	0.08	5.1	8.9
Oregon	78.5	1.7	3.6	1.1	0.33	0.14	2.9	11.7
Pennsylvania	79.5	10.4	2.7	0.1	0.02	0.13	1.4	5.7
Rhode Island	76.4	4.9	2.8	0.4	0.03	0.84	2.2	12.4
South Carolina	64.1	27.7	1.3	0.4	0.05	0.12	1.4	5.1
South Dakota	84.7	1.2	0.9	8.5	0.04	0.06	1.8	2.7
Tennessee	75.6	16.5	1.4	0.3	0.04	0.10	1.4	4.6
Texas	45.3	11.5	3.8	0.3	0.07	0.14	1.3	37.6
Utah	80.4	0.9	2.0	1.0	0.87	0.13	1.8	13.0
Vermont	94.3	0.9	1.3	0.3	0.02	0.09	1.6	1.5
Virginia	64.8	19.0	5.5	0.3	0.06	0.19	2.3	7.9
Washington	72.5	3.4	7.1	1.3	0.58	0.18	3.7	11.2
West Virginia	93.2	3.4	0.7	0.2	0.02	0.06	1.3	1.2
Wisconsin	83.3	6.2	2.3	0.9	0.03	0.07	1.4	5.9
Wyoming	85.9	0.8	0.8	2.1	0.06	0.08	1.5	8.9
United States	**63.7**	**12.2**	**4.7**	**0.7**	**0.16**	**0.20**	**1.9**	**16.3**

Note: Population figures may reflect revisions/corrections to initial tabulated census counts. (1) Not Hispanic or Latino.

American Indian and Alaska Native Population by State, 2010

Source: Decennial Census, U.S. Census Bureau, U.S. Dept. of Commerce
(ranked by one race alone)

Rank	State	One race alone[1]	More than one race[2]	Rank	State	One race alone[1]	More than one race[2]
1.	California	362,801	360,424	27.	Kansas	28,150	30,980
2.	Oklahoma	321,687	161,073	28.	Missouri	27,376	45,000
3.	Arizona	296,529	56,857	29.	Pennsylvania	26,843	54,249
4.	New Mexico	193,222	26,290	30.	Ohio	25,292	64,832
5.	Texas	170,972	144,292	31.	Arkansas	22,248	25,340
6.	North Carolina	122,110	61,972	32.	Idaho	21,441	14,944
7.	New York	106,906	114,152	33.	Maryland	20,420	38,237
8.	Alaska	104,871	33,441	34.	Tennessee	19,994	34,880
9.	Washington	103,869	95,129	35.	South Carolina	19,524	22,647
10.	South Dakota	71,817	10,256	36.	Massachusetts	18,850	31,855
11.	Florida	71,458	91,104	37.	Indiana	18,462	31,276
12.	Montana	62,555	16,046	38.	Nebraska	18,427	11,389
13.	Michigan	62,007	77,088	39.	Mississippi	15,030	10,880
14.	Minnesota	60,916	40,984	40.	Wyoming	13,336	5,260
15.	Colorado	56,010	51,822	41.	Connecticut	11,256	19,884
16.	Wisconsin	54,526	31,702	42.	Iowa	11,084	13,427
17.	Oregon	53,203	56,020	43.	Kentucky	10,120	21,235
18.	Illinois	43,963	57,488	44.	Maine	8,568	9,914
19.	North Dakota	36,591	6,405	45.	Rhode Island	6,058	8,336
20.	Utah	32,927	17,137	46.	Delaware	4,181	5,718
21.	Georgia	32,151	51,873	47.	Hawaii	4,164	29,306
22.	Nevada	32,062	23,883	48.	West Virginia	3,787	9,527
23.	Louisiana	30,579	24,500	49.	New Hampshire	3,150	7,374
24.	Virginia	29,225	51,699	50.	Vermont	2,207	5,172
25.	New Jersey	29,026	41,690	51.	District of Columbia	2,079	4,442
26.	Alabama	28,218	28,900		United States	2,932,248	2,288,331

(1) Respondents who self-identified as American Indian and Alaska Native (AIAN) alone. (2) Respondents who self-identified as AIAN in combination with one or more other races.

American Indian and Alaska Native Population by Selected Tribal Groupings, 2010

Source: Decennial Census, U.S. Census Bureau, U.S. Dept. of Commerce
(ranked by American Indian and Alaska Native [AIAN] alone, one tribal grouping alone)

Tribal grouping	AIAN alone — One tribal grouping alone[1]	AIAN alone — One or more tribal groupings[2]	AIAN alone or in combination — One or more tribal groupings[3]	Tribal grouping	AIAN alone — One tribal grouping alone[1]	AIAN alone — One or more tribal groupings[2]	AIAN alone or in combination — One or more tribal groupings[3]
Total	2,879,638	2,932,248	5,220,579	Crow	10,332	10,860	15,203
AIAN tribes, not specified	693,709	693,709	1,545,963	Kiowa	9,437	10,355	13,787
Amer. Ind. tribes, specified	1,935,363	2,032,133	3,397,251	Paiute	9,340	10,205	13,767
Navajo	286,731	295,016	332,129	Osage	8,938	10,063	18,576
Cherokee	284,247	300,463	819,105	Yakama	8,786	9,096	11,527
Mexican Amer. Ind.	121,221	123,550	175,494	Menominee	8,374	8,627	11,133
Chippewa	112,757	115,402	170,742	Houma	8,169	8,240	10,768
Sioux	112,176	116,477	170,110	Colville	8,114	8,314	10,549
Choctaw	103,910	110,308	195,764	Arapaho	8,014	8,402	10,861
Apache	63,193	69,694	111,810	Shoshone	7,852	8,462	13,002
Lumbee	62,306	62,957	73,691	Delaware	7,843	8,215	18,264
Pueblo	49,695	52,026	62,540	Yuman	7,727	8,278	10,089
Creek	48,352	52,948	88,332	Ute	7,435	8,220	11,491
Iroquois	40,570	42,461	81,002	Ottawa	7,272	8,048	13,033
Chickasaw	27,973	30,206	52,278	Canadian/French Amer. Ind.	6,433	7,051	14,822
Blackfeet	27,279	31,798	105,304	Cree	2,211	2,950	7,983
Pima	22,040	23,205	26,655	All other Amer. Ind. tribes	270,141	282,747	429,629
Yaqui	21,679	23,195	32,595	Amer. Ind. tribes, not specified	131,943	132,060	234,320
S. Amer. Ind.	20,901	21,380	47,233	AK Native tribes, specified	98,892	103,086	138,850
Potawatomi	20,412	20,874	33,771	Yup'ik	28,927	29,618	33,889
Tohono O'Odham	19,522	20,247	23,478	Inupiat[4]	24,859	25,736	33,360
Central Amer. Ind.	15,882	16,454	27,844	Alaskan Athabascan	15,623	16,427	22,484
Puget Sound Salish	14,320	14,535	20,260	Tlingit-Haida	15,256	16,115	26,080
Seminole	14,080	16,448	31,971	Aleut	11,920	12,643	19,282
Spanish Amer. Ind.	13,460	13,758	19,951	Tsimshian	2,307	2,547	3,755
Hopi	12,580	14,634	18,327	AK Native tribes, not specified	19,731	19,904	29,933
Comanche	12,284	13,471	23,330				
Cheyenne	11,375	12,493	19,051				

Note: This table measures the number of responses, not respondents. Respondents who self-identified with multiple tribal groupings are counted more than once. A tribal grouping refers to combined individual tribes (e.g., Fort Sill Apache and San Carlos Apache as Apache or King Salmon Tribe and Native Village of Kanatak as Aleut). (1) The example, Navajo or Alaskan Athabascan. (2) As in footnote 1 or in combination with other tribal groupings (e.g., Yakama and Aleut). (3) As in footnotes 1 or 2 or in combination with another race (e.g., Apache, Navajo, and white; or Inupiat, white, and Black). (4) Eskimo in previous censuses.

Largest U.S. Cities by Population, 1850-2019

Source: Population Estimates Program and Decennial Censuses, U.S. Census Bureau, U.S. Dept. of Commerce
(ranked by 2019 population)

Rank City	2019	2000	1990	1980	1970	1950	1900	1850
1. New York, NY	8,336,817	8,008,654	7,322,564	7,071,639	7,895,563	7,891,957	3,437,202	515,547
2. Los Angeles, CA	3,979,576	3,694,742	3,485,557	2,968,528	2,811,801	1,970,358	102,479	1,610
3. Chicago, IL	2,693,976	2,896,016	2,783,726	3,005,072	3,369,537	3,620,962	1,698,575	29,963
4. Houston, TX	2,320,268	1,953,631	1,630,864	1,595,138	1,233,535	596,163	44,633	2,396
5. Phoenix, AZ	1,680,992	1,321,045	983,392	789,704	584,303	106,818	5,544	—
6. Philadelphia, PA	1,584,064	1,517,550	1,585,577	1,688,210	1,949,996	2,071,605	1,293,697	121,376
7. San Antonio, TX	1,547,253	1,144,646	935,393	785,940	654,153	408,442	53,321	3,488
8. San Diego, CA	1,423,851	1,223,400	1,110,623	875,538	697,471	334,387	17,700	—
9. Dallas, TX	1,343,573	1,188,580	1,007,618	904,599	844,401	434,462	42,638	—
10. San Jose, CA	1,021,795	894,943	782,224	629,400	459,913	95,280	21,500	—
11. Austin, TX	978,908	656,562	465,648	345,890	253,539	132,459	22,258	629
12. Jacksonville, FL[1]	911,507	735,617	635,230	540,920	504,265	204,517	28,429	1,045
13. Fort Worth, TX	909,585	534,694	447,619	385,164	393,455	278,778	26,688	—
14. Columbus, OH	898,553	711,470	632,945	565,021	540,025	375,901	125,560	17,882
15. Charlotte, NC	885,708	540,167	395,934	315,474	241,420	134,042	18,091	1,065
16. San Francisco, CA[2]	881,549	776,733	723,959	678,974	715,674	775,357	342,782	34,776
17. Indianapolis, IN[1]	876,384	791,926	741,915	710,868	746,992	427,173	169,164	8,091
18. Seattle, WA	753,675	563,376	516,259	493,846	530,831	467,591	80,671	—
19. Denver, CO	727,211	553,693	467,610	492,686	514,678	415,786	133,859	—
20. Washington, DC	705,749	572,059	606,900	638,432	756,668	802,178	278,718	40,001
21. Boston, MA	692,600	589,141	574,283	562,994	641,071	801,444	560,892	136,881
22. El Paso, TX	681,728	563,662	515,342	425,259	322,261	130,485	15,906	—
23. Nashville-Davidson, TN[1]	670,820	569,892	510,786	477,811	447,877	174,307	80,865	10,165
24. Detroit, MI	670,031	951,270	1,027,974	1,203,368	1,514,063	1,849,568	285,704	21,019
25. Oklahoma City, OK	655,057	506,132	444,724	404,014	368,164	243,504	10,037	—
26. Portland, OR	654,741	529,121	438,802	368,148	379,967	373,628	90,426	—
27. Las Vegas, NV	651,319	479,137	258,204	164,674	125,787	24,624	—	—
28. Memphis, TN	651,073	650,100	610,337	646,174	623,988	396,000	102,320	8,841
29. Louisville/Jefferson Co., KY[1]	617,638	256,231	269,555	298,694	361,706	369,129	204,731	43,194
30. Baltimore, MD	593,490	651,154	736,014	786,741	905,787	949,708	508,957	169,054
31. Milwaukee, WI	590,157	596,974	628,088	636,297	717,372	637,392	285,315	20,061
32. Albuquerque, NM	560,513	448,607	384,619	332,920	244,501	96,815	6,238	—
33. Tucson, AZ	548,073	486,699	405,371	330,537	262,933	45,454	7,531	—
34. Fresno, CA	531,576	427,652	354,091	217,491	165,655	91,669	12,470	—
35. Mesa, AZ	518,012	396,375	288,104	152,404	63,049	16,790	722	—
36. Sacramento, CA	513,624	407,018	369,365	275,741	257,105	137,572	29,282	6,820
37. Atlanta, GA	506,811	416,267	393,929	425,022	495,039	331,314	89,872	2,572
38. Kansas City, MO	495,327	441,545	434,829	448,028	507,330	456,622	163,752	—
39. Colorado Springs, CO	478,221	360,890	280,430	215,105	135,517	45,472	21,085	—
40. Omaha, NE	478,192	390,007	335,719	313,939	346,929	251,117	102,555	—
41. Raleigh, NC	474,069	276,094	212,092	150,255	122,830	65,679	13,643	4,518
42. Miami, FL	467,963	362,470	358,648	346,681	334,859	249,276	1,681	—
43. Long Beach, CA	462,628	461,522	429,321	361,498	358,879	250,767	2,252	—
44. Virginia Beach, VA	449,974	425,257	393,089	262,199	172,106	5,390	—	—
45. Oakland, CA	433,031	399,484	372,242	339,337	361,561	384,575	66,960	—
46. Minneapolis, MN	429,606	382,747	368,383	370,951	434,400	521,718	202,718	—
47. Tulsa, OK	401,190	393,049	367,302	360,919	330,350	182,740	1,390	—
48. Tampa, FL	399,700	303,447	280,015	271,577	277,714	124,681	15,839	—
49. Arlington, TX	398,854	332,969	261,717	160,113	90,229	7,692	1,079	—
50. New Orleans, LA	390,144	484,674	496,938	557,927	593,471	570,445	287,104	116,375
51. Wichita, KS	389,938	346,753	304,017	279,838	276,554	168,279	24,671	—
52. Bakersfield, CA	384,145	246,889	174,978	105,611	69,515	34,784	4,836	—
53. Cleveland, OH	381,009	477,459	505,616	573,822	750,879	914,808	381,768	17,034
54. Aurora, CO	379,289	275,921	222,103	158,588	74,974	11,421	202	—
55. Anaheim, CA	350,365	328,014	266,406	219,494	166,408	14,556	1,456	—
56. Urban Honolulu, HI[3]	345,064	371,657	365,272	365,048	324,871	248,034	39,306	—
57. Santa Ana, CA	332,318	337,977	293,827	204,023	155,710	45,533	4,933	—
58. Riverside, CA	331,360	255,166	226,546	170,591	140,089	46,764	7,973	—
59. Corpus Christi, TX	326,586	277,454	257,453	232,134	204,525	108,287	4,703	—
60. Lexington-Fayette, KY[1]	323,152	260,512	225,366	204,165	108,137	55,534	26,369	8,159
61. Henderson, NV	320,189	175,381	64,948	24,363	16,395	—	—	—
62. Stockton, CA	312,697	243,771	210,943	148,283	109,963	70,853	17,506	—
63. St. Paul, MN	308,096	286,840	272,235	270,230	309,866	311,349	163,065	1,112
64. Cincinnati, OH	303,940	331,285	364,114	385,409	453,514	503,998	325,902	115,435
65. St. Louis, MO	300,576	348,189	396,685	452,801	622,236	856,796	575,238	77,860
66. Pittsburgh, PA	300,286	334,563	369,879	423,959	520,089	676,806	321,616	46,601
67. Greensboro, NC	296,710	223,891	183,894	155,642	144,076	74,389	10,035	—
68. Lincoln, NE	289,102	225,581	191,972	171,932	149,518	98,884	40,169	—
69. Anchorage, AK	288,000	260,283	226,338	174,431	48,081	11,254	—	—
70. Plano, TX	287,677	222,030	127,885	72,331	17,872	2,126	1,304	—
71. Orlando, FL	287,442	185,951	164,674	128,291	99,006	52,367	2,481	—
72. Irvine, CA	287,401	143,072	110,330	62,134	—	—	—	—
73. Newark, NJ	282,011	272,537	275,221	329,248	381,930	438,776	246,070	38,894
74. Durham, NC	278,993	187,035	136,612	101,149	95,438	71,311	6,679	—
75. Chula Vista, CA	274,492	173,556	135,160	83,927	67,901	15,927	—	—
76. Toledo, OH	272,779	313,782	332,943	354,635	383,062	303,616	131,822	3,829
77. Fort Wayne, IN	270,402	205,727	172,971	172,391	178,269	133,607	45,115	4,282
78. St. Petersburg, FL	265,351	248,232	240,318	238,647	216,159	96,738	1,575	—
79. Laredo, TX	262,491	176,576	122,899	91,449	69,024	51,910	13,429	—
80. Jersey City, NJ	262,075	240,055	228,517	223,532	260,350	299,017	206,433	6,856
81. Chandler, AZ	261,165	176,581	89,862	29,673	13,763	3,799	—	—
82. Madison, WI	259,680	208,054	190,766	170,616	171,809	96,056	19,164	1,525
83. Lubbock, TX	258,862	199,564	186,206	174,361	149,101	71,747	—	—
84. Scottsdale, AZ	258,069	202,705	130,075	88,622	67,823	—	—	—
85. Reno, NV	255,601	180,480	133,850	100,756	72,863	32,497	4,500	—

Rank City	2019	2000	1990	1980	1970	1950	1900	1850
86. Buffalo, NY	255,284	292,648	328,175	357,870	462,768	580,132	352,387	42,261
87. Gilbert, AZ	254,114	109,697	29,122	5,717	1,971	1,114	—	—
88. Glendale, AZ	252,381	218,812	147,864	97,172	36,228	8,179	—	—
89. North Las Vegas, NV	251,974	115,488	47,849	42,739	46,067	—	—	—
90. Winston-Salem, NC	247,945	185,776	143,485	131,885	133,683	87,811	13,650	—
91. Chesapeake, VA	244,835	199,184	151,982	114,486	89,580	—	—	—
92. Norfolk, VA	242,742	234,403	261,250	266,979	307,951	213,513	46,624	14,326
93. Fremont, CA	241,110	203,413	173,339	131,945	100,869	—	—	—
94. Garland, TX	239,928	215,768	180,635	138,857	81,437	10,571	819	—
95. Irving, TX	239,798	191,615	155,037	109,943	97,260	2,621	—	—
96. Hialeah, FL	233,339	226,419	188,008	145,254	102,452	19,676	—	—
97. Richmond, VA	230,436	197,790	202,798	219,214	249,332	230,310	85,050	27,570
98. Boise City, ID	228,959	185,787	125,551	102,249	74,990	34,393	5,957	—
99. Spokane, WA	222,081	195,629	177,165	171,300	170,516	161,721	36,848	—
100. Baton Rouge, LA	220,236	227,818	219,531	220,394	165,291	125,629	11,269	3,905

— = Not available. **Note:** 2019 population estimates are as of July 1. Decennial census figures for 1950-2000 are for Apr. 1; 1850 and 1900 are for June 1. Figures may reflect revisions/corrections to initial tabulated census counts. Cities are incorporated places unless otherwise noted. (1) Consolidated city-county government. For years predating consolidation, city population figures are shown. (2) 1850 figure is for 1852, from state census. 1850 census results were destroyed by fire. (3) Census designated place (CDP). Figures for years prior to 2019 are for Honolulu CDP and are not directly comparable.

Population Change in Largest U.S. Cities, 2010-19

Source: Population Estimates Program and Decennial Census, U.S. Census Bureau, U.S. Dept. of Commerce

(ranked by % change, 2010-19; 2019 estimates are as of July 1; 2010 decennial census figures are for Apr. 1)

Cities With Most Growth

Rank City	Population 2019	Population 2010	% change, 2010-19
1. Irvine, CA	287,401	212,375	35.3%
2. Henderson, NV	320,189	257,729	24.2
3. Austin, TX	978,908	790,390	23.9
4. Seattle, WA	753,675	608,660	23.8
5. Fort Worth, TX	909,585	741,206	22.7
6. Durham, NC	278,993	228,330	22.2
7. Gilbert, AZ	254,114	208,453	21.9
8. Denver, CO	727,211	600,158	21.2
9. Charlotte, NC	885,708	731,424	21.1
10. Atlanta, GA	506,811	420,003	20.7
11. Orlando, FL	287,442	238,300	20.6
12. Tampa, FL	399,700	335,709	19.1
13. Scottsdale, AZ	258,069	217,385	18.7
14. Mesa, AZ	518,012	439,041	18.0
15. Raleigh, NC	474,069	403,892	17.4
16. Washington, DC	705,749	601,723	17.3
17. Miami, FL	467,963	399,457	17.1
18. Omaha, NE	478,192	408,958	16.9
19. Aurora, CO	379,289	325,078	16.7
20. San Antonio, TX	1,547,253	1,327,407	16.6

Cities With Least Growth

Rank City	Population 2019	Population 2010	% change, 2010-19
1. Detroit, MI	670,031	713,777	−6.1%
2. St. Louis, MO	300,576	319,294	−5.9
3. Toledo, OH	272,779	287,208	−5.0
4. Baltimore, MD	593,490	620,961	−4.4
5. Baton Rouge, LA	220,236	229,493	−4.0
6. Cleveland, OH	381,009	396,815	−4.0
7. Buffalo, NY	255,284	261,310	−2.3
8. Pittsburgh, PA	300,286	305,704	−1.8
9. Anchorage, AK	288,000	291,826	−1.3
10. Milwaukee, WI	590,157	594,833	−0.8
11. Chicago, IL	2,693,976	2,695,598	−0.1
12. Norfolk, VA	242,742	242,803	0.0
13. Long Beach, CA	462,628	462,257	0.1
14. Memphis, TN	651,073	646,889	0.6
15. Newark, NJ	282,011	277,140	1.8
16. New York, NY	8,336,817	8,175,133	2.0
17. Wichita, KS	389,938	382,368	2.0
18. Urban Honolulu, HI	345,064	337,256	2.3
19. Cincinnati, OH	303,940	296,943	2.4
20. Tulsa, OK	401,190	391,906	2.4

Note: This table shows which of the 100 largest U.S. cities by 2019 population size experienced the most and least population growth since 2010. Figures may reflect revisions/corrections to initial tabulated census counts. Cities are typically incorporated places.

Largest U.S. Counties by Population, 2000, 2019

Source: Population Estimates Program and Decennial Census, U.S. Census Bureau, U.S. Dept. of Commerce

(ranked by 2019 population, estimated as of July 1; 2000 decennial census figures are for Apr. 1)

Rank County	2019	2000	% change, 2000-19
1. Los Angeles Co., CA	10,039,107	9,519,338	5.5%
2. Cook Co., IL	5,150,233	5,376,815	−4.2
3. Harris Co., TX	4,713,325	3,400,578	38.6
4. Maricopa Co., AZ	4,485,414	3,072,149	46.0
5. San Diego Co., CA	3,338,330	2,813,833	18.6
6. Orange Co., CA	3,175,692	2,846,289	11.6
7. Miami-Dade Co., FL	2,716,940	2,253,779	20.6
8. Dallas Co., TX	2,635,516	2,218,774	18.8
9. Kings Co., NY	2,559,903	2,465,525	3.8
10. Riverside Co., CA	2,470,546	1,545,387	59.9
11. Clark Co., NV	2,266,715	1,375,765	64.8
12. Queens Co., NY	2,253,858	2,229,379	1.1
13. King Co., WA	2,252,782	1,737,044	29.7
14. San Bernardino Co., CA	2,180,085	1,709,434	27.5
15. Tarrant Co., TX	2,102,515	1,446,219	45.4
16. Bexar Co., TX	2,003,554	1,392,931	43.8
17. Broward Co., FL	1,952,778	1,623,018	20.3
18. Santa Clara Co., CA	1,927,852	1,682,585	14.6
19. Wayne Co., MI	1,749,343	2,061,162	−15.1
20. Alameda Co., CA	1,671,329	1,443,741	15.8
21. New York Co., NY	1,628,706	1,537,372	5.9
22. Middlesex Co., MA	1,611,699	1,466,394	9.9
23. Philadelphia Co., PA	1,584,064	1,517,550	4.4
24. Sacramento Co., CA	1,552,058	1,223,499	26.9
25. Palm Beach Co., FL	1,496,770	1,131,191	32.3%
26. Suffolk Co., NY	1,476,601	1,419,369	4.0
27. Hillsborough Co., FL	1,471,968	998,948	47.4
28. Bronx Co., NY	1,418,207	1,332,650	6.4
29. Orange Co., FL	1,393,452	896,344	55.5
30. Nassau Co., NY	1,356,924	1,334,544	1.7
31. Franklin Co., OH	1,316,756	1,068,869	23.2
32. Travis Co., TX	1,273,954	812,280	56.8
33. Hennepin Co., MN	1,265,843	1,116,039	13.4
34. Oakland Co., MI	1,257,584	1,194,156	5.3
35. Cuyahoga Co., OH	1,235,072	1,393,845	−11.4
36. Allegheny Co., PA	1,216,045	1,281,666	−5.1
37. Salt Lake Co., UT	1,160,437	898,412	29.2
38. Contra Costa Co., CA	1,153,526	948,816	21.6
39. Fairfax Co., VA	1,147,532	969,749	18.3
40. Wake Co., NC	1,111,761	627,846	77.1
41. Mecklenburg Co., NC	1,110,356	695,370	59.7
42. Fulton Co., GA	1,063,937	815,806	30.4
43. Montgomery Co., MD	1,050,688	873,341	20.3
44. Pima Co., AZ	1,047,279	843,746	24.1
45. Collin Co., TX	1,034,730	491,774	110.4
46. Fresno Co., CA	999,101	799,407	25.0
47. St. Louis Co., MO	994,205	1,016,300	−2.2
48. Pinellas Co., FL	974,996	921,495	5.8

Note: Decennial pop. figures may reflect revisions/corrections to initial tabulated census counts. The 10 smallest counties or county equivalents by estimated 2019 population: (1) Kalawao Co., HI (pop. 86); (2) Loving Co., TX (169); (3) King Co., TX (272); (4) Kenedy Co., TX (404); (5) Arthur Co., NE (463); (6) Blaine Co., NE (465); (7) Petroleum Co., MT (487); (8) McPherson Co., NE (494); (9) Yakutat City, AK (579); and (10) Grant Co., NE (623).

Largest U.S. Metropolitan Areas by Population, 2000-19

Source: Population Estimates Program and Decennial Censuses, U.S. Census Bureau, U.S. Dept. of Commerce

Metropolitan Statistical Areas (MSAs) are defined, or delineated geographically, for federal statistical use by the Office of Management and Budget (OMB) with technical assistance from the Census Bureau. An MSA consists of at least one urbanized area of 50,000 or more inhabitants, plus adjacent territory closely integrated socially and economically with the core as measured by commuting ties. The Census Bureau's 2019 population estimates are for delineations issued by the OMB in Mar. 2020, which designated 384 MSAs in the U.S. About 85.8% of the resident population lived in an MSA in 2019.

(ranked by 2019 population, estimated as of July 1; 2000 and 2010 decennial census figures are for Apr. 1)

Rank	Metropolitan Statistical Area	Population 2019	Population 2010	Population 2000	Percent change 2010-19	Percent change 2000-19
1.	New York-Newark-Jersey City, NY-NJ-PA	19,216,182	18,897,109	18,944,519	1.7%	1.4%
2.	Los Angeles-Long Beach-Anaheim, CA	13,214,799	12,828,837	12,365,627	3.0	6.9
3.	Chicago-Naperville-Elgin, IL-IN-WI	9,458,539	9,461,105	9,098,316	0.0	4.0
4.	Dallas-Fort Worth-Arlington, TX	7,573,136	6,366,542	5,204,126	19.0	45.5
5.	Houston-The Woodlands-Sugar Land, TX	7,066,141	5,920,416	4,693,161	19.4	50.6
6.	Washington-Arlington-Alexandria, DC-VA-MD-WV	6,280,487	5,649,540	4,837,428	11.2	29.8
7.	Miami-Fort Lauderdale-Pompano Beach, FL	6,166,488	5,564,635	5,007,564	10.8	23.1
8.	Philadelphia-Camden-Wilmington, PA-NJ-DE-MD	6,102,434	5,965,343	5,687,147	2.3	7.3
9.	Atlanta-Sandy Springs-Alpharetta, GA	6,020,364	5,286,728	4,263,438	13.9	41.2
10.	Phoenix-Mesa-Chandler, AZ	4,948,203	4,192,887	3,251,876	18.0	52.2
11.	Boston-Cambridge-Newton, MA-NH	4,873,019	4,552,402	4,391,344	7.0	11.0
12.	San Francisco-Oakland-Berkeley, CA	4,731,803	4,335,391	4,123,740	9.1	14.7
13.	Riverside-San Bernardino-Ontario, CA	4,650,631	4,224,851	3,254,821	10.1	42.9
14.	Detroit-Warren-Dearborn, MI	4,319,629	4,296,250	4,452,557	0.5	-3.0
15.	Seattle-Tacoma-Bellevue, WA	3,979,845	3,439,809	3,043,878	15.7	30.7
16.	Minneapolis-St. Paul-Bloomington, MN-WI	3,640,043	3,333,633	3,031,918	9.2	20.1
17.	San Diego-Chula Vista-Carlsbad, CA	3,338,330	3,095,313	2,813,833	7.9	18.6
18.	Tampa-St. Petersburg-Clearwater, FL	3,194,831	2,783,243	2,395,997	14.8	33.3
19.	Denver-Aurora-Lakewood, CO	2,967,239	2,543,482	2,179,240	16.7	36.2
20.	St. Louis, MO-IL	2,803,228	2,787,701	2,675,343	0.6	4.8
21.	Baltimore-Columbia-Towson, MD	2,800,053	2,710,489	2,552,994	3.3	9.7
22.	Charlotte-Concord-Gastonia, NC-SC	2,636,883	2,243,960	1,717,372	17.5	53.5
23.	Orlando-Kissimmee-Sanford, FL	2,608,147	2,134,411	1,644,561	22.2	58.6
24.	San Antonio-New Braunfels, TX	2,550,960	2,142,508	1,711,703	19.1	49.0
25.	Portland-Vancouver-Hillsboro, OR-WA	2,492,412	2,226,009	1,927,881	12.0	29.3
26.	Sacramento-Roseville-Folsom, CA	2,363,730	2,149,127	1,796,857	10.0	31.5
27.	Pittsburgh, PA	2,317,600	2,356,285	2,431,087	-1.6	-4.7
28.	Las Vegas-Henderson-Paradise, NV	2,266,715	1,951,269	1,375,765	16.2	64.8
29.	Austin-Round Rock-Georgetown, TX	2,227,083	1,716,289	1,249,763	29.8	78.2
30.	Cincinnati, OH-KY-IN	2,221,208	2,137,667	1,994,830	3.9	11.3
31.	Kansas City, MO-KS	2,157,990	2,009,342	1,811,254	7.4	19.1
32.	Columbus, OH	2,122,271	1,901,974	1,675,013	11.6	26.7
33.	Indianapolis-Carmel-Anderson, IN	2,074,537	1,887,877	1,658,462	9.9	25.1
34.	Cleveland-Elyria, OH	2,048,449	2,077,240	2,148,143	-1.4	-4.6
35.	San Jose-Sunnyvale-Santa Clara, CA	1,990,660	1,836,911	1,735,819	8.4	14.7
36.	Nashville-Davidson—Murfreesboro—Franklin, TN	1,934,317	1,646,200	1,381,287	17.5	40.0
37.	Virginia Beach-Norfolk-Newport News, VA-NC	1,768,901	1,713,954	1,580,057	3.2	12.0
38.	Providence-Warwick, RI-MA	1,624,578	1,600,852	1,582,997	1.5	2.6
39.	Milwaukee-Waukesha, WI	1,575,179	1,555,908	1,500,741	1.2	5.0
40.	Jacksonville, FL	1,559,514	1,345,596	1,122,750	15.9	38.9
41.	Oklahoma City, OK	1,408,950	1,252,987	1,095,421	12.4	28.6
42.	Raleigh-Cary, NC	1,390,785	1,130,490	797,071	23.0	74.5
43.	Memphis, TN-MS-AR	1,346,045	1,316,100	1,213,230	2.3	10.9
44.	Richmond, VA	1,291,900	1,186,501	1,055,683	8.9	22.4
45.	New Orleans-Metairie, LA	1,270,530	1,189,866	1,337,726	6.8	-5.0
46.	Louisville/Jefferson County, KY-IN	1,265,108	1,202,718	1,121,109	5.2	12.8
47.	Salt Lake City, UT	1,232,696	1,087,873	939,122	13.3	31.3
48.	Hartford-East Hartford-Middletown, CT	1,204,877	1,212,381	1,148,618	-0.6	4.9
49.	Buffalo-Cheektowaga, NY	1,127,983	1,135,509	1,170,111	-0.7	-3.6
50.	Birmingham-Hoover, AL	1,090,435	1,061,024	1,052,238	2.8	3.6
51.	Grand Rapids-Kentwood, MI	1,077,370	993,670	930,670	8.4	15.8
52.	Rochester, NY	1,069,644	1,079,671	1,062,452	-0.9	0.7
53.	Tucson, AZ	1,047,279	980,263	843,746	6.8	24.1

Population by Urban and Rural Residency, 1790-2010

Source: Decennial Censuses, U.S. Census Bureau, U.S. Dept. of Commerce

The Census Bureau currently defines an area as urban if it has at least 2,500 people (at least 1,500 of whom do not reside in institutional group quarters, such as a correctional facility). All other areas are rural. Prior to 1950, the definition of urban was limited to incorporated places and other areas meeting certain criteria.

Year	Total pop.	No. of places of 2,500 or more	% of total pop. Urban	% of total pop. Rural	Year	Total pop.	No. of places of 2,500 or more	% of total pop. Urban	% of total pop. Rural
Pre-1950 urban definition					1930	123,202,624	3,183	56.1%	43.9%
1790	3,929,214	24	5.1%	94.9%	1940	132,164,569	3,485	56.5	43.5
1800	5,308,483	33	6.1	93.9	1950	151,325,798	4,077	59.6	40.4
1810	7,239,881	46	7.3	92.7	1960	179,323,175	5,023	63.1	36.9
1820	9,638,453	61	7.2	92.8	1950-90 urban definition				
1830	12,860,702	90	8.8	91.2	1950	151,325,798	4,307	64.0	36.0
1840	17,063,353	131	10.8	89.2	1960	179,323,175	5,445	69.9	30.1
1850	23,191,876	237	15.4	84.6	1970	203,302,031	6,433	73.6	26.3
1860	31,443,321	392	19.8	80.2	1980	226,542,199	7,749	73.7	26.3
1870	38,558,371	663	25.7	74.3	1990	248,718,302	8,510	75.2	24.8
1880	50,189,209	939	28.2	71.8	Current urban definition				
1890	62,979,766	1,348	35.1	64.9	1990	248,718,302	8,510	78.0	22.0
1900	76,212,168	1,740	39.6	60.4	2000	281,424,603	9,063	79.0	21.0
1910	92,228,496	2,266	45.6	54.4	2010	308,746,065	9,644	80.7	19.3
1920	106,021,537	2,725	51.2	48.8					

Note: Figures may not add up to 100 due to rounding.

Mobility of U.S. Population by Selected Characteristics, 2018-19

Source: Annual Social and Economic Supplement, Current Population Survey (CPS), U.S. Census Bureau, U.S. Dept. of Commerce
(numbers in thousands)

	Total movers	Location of previous residence					Total movers	Location of previous residence			
		Same county	Diff. county, same state	Diff. state	Abroad			Same county	Diff. county, same state	Diff. state	Abroad
Age						**Marital status[1]**					
1 to 14 years.........	6,231	3,914	1,258	841	218	Married, spouse present	8,994	5,175	1,874	1,580	366
15 years and older	25,141	14,920	5,405	3,897	919	Married, spouse absent	563	274	95	104	90
25 years and older	18,979	11,093	4,170	3,011	711	Widowed............	831	473	209	127	22
65 years and older	2,026	1,182	464	342	41	Divorced...........	2,459	1,511	570	347	31
85 years and older	262	154	72	37	—	Separated..........	648	421	174	43	11
Income[1]						Never married....	11,644	7,066	2,482	1,696	399
Without income.......	3,256	1,895	567	429	365	**Educational attainment[2]**					
Under $10,000 or loss	3,180	1,886	669	513	112	Not a HS graduate	1,790	1,211	347	155	76
$10,000-$19,999	3,382	2,081	727	481	94	High school graduate ..	5,056	3,108	1,060	700	189
$20,000-$29,999	3,288	2,028	678	519	63	Some college or					
$30,000-$39,999	2,856	1,808	642	360	45	associate's degree ..	4,798	2,767	1,123	827	81
$40,000-$59,999	3,899	2,321	932	559	87	Bachelor's degree.....	4,614	2,627	1,045	750	192
$60,000-$74,999	1,774	966	390	351	68	Prof. or grad. degree ...	2,723	1,379	594	579	171
$75,000-$99,999	1,484	847	332	278	27	**Tenure**					
$100,000 and over	2,021	1,089	467	407	59	In owner-occupied unit	10,434	6,231	2,548	1,441	214
						In renter-occupied unit	20,937	12,602	4,115	3,296	924
						Total movers	31,371	18,833	6,663	4,738	1,137

— = Represents zero or rounds to zero. **Note:** Total movers consist of persons ages 1 and older whose place or residence changed since the survey was administered one year earlier. Figures may not add up to totals due to rounding. (1) Ages 15 and older. (2) Ages 25 and older.

Mobility of U.S. Population, 1948-2019

Source: Annual Social and Economic Supplement, Current Population Survey (CPS), U.S. Census Bureau, U.S. Dept. of Commerce
(numbers in thousands unless otherwise noted)

Mobility period	Total movers		Location of previous residence							
			Same county		Diff. county, same state		Diff. state		Abroad	
	No.	% of pop.	No.	% distrib.	No.	% distrib.	No.	% distrib.	No.	% distrib.
1947-48	28,672	20.2%	19,202	67.0%	4,638	16.2%	4,370	15.2%	462	1.6%
1950-51	31,464	21.2	20,694	65.8	5,276	16.8	5,188	16.5	306	1.0
1955-56	34,040	21.1	22,186	65.2	5,859	17.2	5,053	14.8	942	2.8
1960-61	36,533	20.6	24,289	66.5	5,493	15.0	5,753	15.7	998	2.7
1965-66	37,586	19.8	24,165	64.3	6,275	16.7	6,263	16.7	883	2.3
1970-71	37,705	18.7	23,018	61.0	6,197	16.4	6,946	18.4	1,544	4.1
1975-76	36,793	17.7	22,399	60.9	7,106	19.3	6,140	16.7	1,148	3.1
1980-81	38,200	17.2	23,097	60.5	7,614	19.9	6,175	16.2	1,313	3.4
1985-86	43,237	18.6	26,401	61.1	8,665	20.0	6,971	16.1	1,200	2.8
1990-91	41,539	17.0	25,151	60.5	7,881	19.0	7,122	17.1	1,385	3.3
1995-96	42,537	16.3	26,696	62.8	8,009	18.8	6,471	15.2	1,361	3.2
2000-01	39,007	14.2	21,918	56.2	7,550	19.4	7,783	20.0	1,756	4.5
2005-06	39,837	13.7	24,851	62.4	8,010	20.1	5,679	14.3	1,296	3.3
2010-11	35,038	11.6	23,330	66.6	5,868	16.7	4,756	13.6	1,084	3.1
2015-16	35,138	11.2	21,588	61.4	7,501	21.3	4,768	13.6	1,281	3.6
2018-19	31,371	9.8	18,833	60.0	6,663	21.2	4,738	15.1	1,137	3.6

Note: Total movers consists of persons ages 1 and older whose place of residence changed since the survey was administered one year earlier. Figures may not add up to totals due to rounding. Because of changes in survey processing, numbers may not be comparable over time.

U.S. Households by Size, 1900-2010

Source: Decennial Censuses, U.S. Census Bureau, U.S. Dept. of Commerce

The household population does not include those living in group quarters (either institutionalized like a correctional facility or noninstitutionalized like a college dormitory). Data on households by size not available for 1910, 1920, or 1930; 1960 figures are based on a sample of the population. Average household size is shown above each bar.

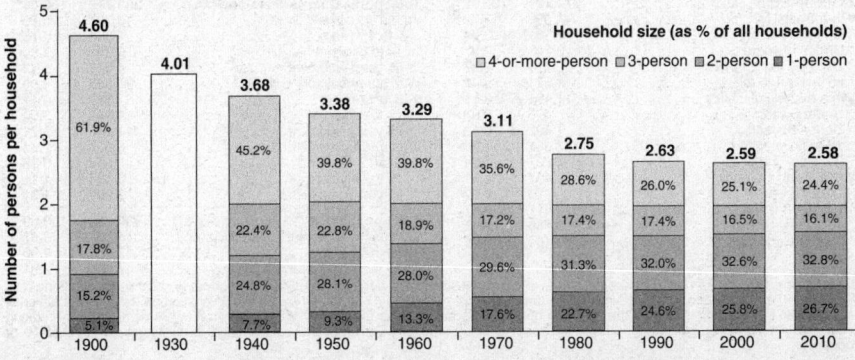

U.S. Population by Age, Sex, and Household, 2019
Source: American Community Survey (ACS), U.S. Census Bureau, U.S. Dept. of Commerce

	Number	% of tot.		Number	% of tot.
Total population[1]	328,239,523	100.0%	**Sex**		
Age			Male	161,588,973	49.2%
Under 5 years	19,404,835	5.9	Female	166,650,550	50.8
5 to 14 years	41,113,916	12.5	**Total households[2]**	**122,802,852**	**100.0%**
15 to 17 years	12,449,034	3.8	Family households	79,594,270	64.8
18 years and over	255,271,738	77.8	2-person household	35,153,927	28.6
Male	124,267,346	48.7	3-person household	17,836,939	14.5
Female	131,004,392	51.3	4-person household	14,946,880	12.2
18 to 24 years	30,373,170	9.3	5-or-more-person household	11,656,524	9.5
25 to 34 years	45,578,475	13.9	Married-couple family household	58,370,842	47.5
35 to 44 years	41,914,845	12.8	Male HH, no spouse present	6,167,908	5.0
45 to 54 years	40,863,107	12.4	Female HH, no spouse present	15,055,520	12.3
55 to 64 years	42,468,113	12.9	Nonfamily households	43,208,582	35.2
65 years and over	54,074,028	16.5	1-person household, or HH living alone	34,752,631	28.3
75 years and over	22,498,467	6.9	HH 65 years and over	13,983,306	11.4
85 years and over	6,358,229	1.9	2-person household	6,941,337	5.7
Median age (years)	38.5	NA	3-or-more-person household	1,514,714	1.2
			Average household size	2.61	NA

NA = Not applicable. HH = Householder, or person in whose name a home is owned or rented. **Note:** Data based on sample and subject to sampling variability. (1) Includes population living in group quarters (institutional and noninstitutional, e.g., correctional facilities, university housing). (2) Number of occupied housing units, not household members. Group quarters are not considered households.

Elderly U.S. Population, 1900-2060
Source: Decennial Censuses and Population Projections Program, U.S. Census Bureau, U.S. Dept. of Commerce
(numbers of resident population in thousands)

Year	65 and over Number	65 and over % tot. pop.	85 and over Number	85 and over % tot. pop.	Year	65 and over Number	65 and over % tot. pop.	85 and over Number	85 and over % tot. pop.
1900[1]	3,080	4.1%	122	0.2%	2010	40,268	13.0%	5,493	1.8%
1920[1]	4,933	4.7	210	0.2	2020	56,052	16.9	6,701	2.0
1940[1]	9,019	6.8	365	0.3	2030	73,138	20.6	9,074	2.6
1960	16,560	9.2	929	0.5	2040	80,827	21.6	14,430	3.9
1980	25,549	11.3	2,240	1.0	2050	85,675	22.0	18,561	4.8
2000	34,992	12.4	4,240	1.5	2060	94,676	23.4	19,019	4.7

Note: 1900 figures are for June 1; 1920 figures are for Jan. 1; and 1940-2010 figures are for Apr. 1. 2020-60 projections are as of July 1. (1) Excludes Alaska and Hawaii.

U.S. Population Projections by Age, 2020-60
Source: Population Projections Program, U.S. Census Bureau, U.S. Dept. of Commerce
(numbers of resident population in thousands)

Age	2020 No.	2020 % distrib.	2030 No.	2030 % distrib.	2040 No.	2040 % distrib.	2050 No.	2050 % distrib.	2060 No.	2060 % distrib.
Total	332,639	100.0%	355,101	100.0%	373,528	100.0%	388,922	100.0%	404,483	100.0%
Under 5 years	20,439	6.1	20,976	5.9	21,106	5.7	21,610	5.6	22,144	5.5
5 to 13 years	36,780	11.1	38,051	10.7	38,568	10.3	39,049	10.0	40,090	9.9
14 to 17 years	16,748	5.0	16,625	4.7	17,457	4.7	17,566	4.5	17,903	4.4
18 to 24 years	30,380	9.1	30,612	8.6	31,369	8.4	32,126	8.3	32,467	8.0
25 to 44 years	88,843	26.7	94,370	26.6	95,067	25.5	97,459	25.1	100,230	24.8
45 to 64 years	83,398	25.1	81,329	22.9	89,135	23.9	95,437	24.5	96,973	24.0
65 years and over	56,052	16.9	73,138	20.6	80,827	21.6	85,675	22.0	94,676	23.4
85 years and over	6,701	2.0	9,074	2.6	14,430	3.9	18,561	4.8	19,019	4.7
100 years and over	92	0.03	140	0.04	196	0.05	386	0.10	589	0.15

Note: Projections are as of July 1 of given year. They are based on assumptions about future births, deaths, and net international migration.

Disability Status of U.S. Population by Age, 2019
Source: American Community Survey (ACS), U.S. Census Bureau, U.S. Dept. of Commerce
(numbers in thousands, by difficulty type)

Characteristic	Number	% of pop.	Characteristic	Number	% of pop.
Total population (all ages)	323,121	100.00%	**Total population (5 years and over)**	303,719	100.00%
With a disability[1]	41,090	12.72	With a cognitive difficulty[2]	15,797	5.20
Under 5 years	139	0.04	5 to 17 years	2,354	0.78
Under 18 years	3,145	0.97	18 to 64 years	9,085	2.99
18 to 64 years	20,274	6.27	65 years and over	4,358	1.43
65 years and over	17,671	5.47	With an ambulatory difficulty[3]	20,843	6.86
With a hearing disability	11,495	3.56	5 to 17 years	330	0.11
Under 5 years	95	0.03	18 to 64 years	9,246	3.04
Under 18 years	402	0.12	65 years and over	11,268	3.71
18 to 64 years	3,867	1.20	With a self-care difficulty[4]	8,004	2.64
65 years and over	7,227	2.24	5 to 17 years	557	0.18
With a vision disability	7,467	2.31	18 to 64 years	3,464	1.14
Under 5 years	76	0.02	65 years and over	3,983	1.31
Under 18 years	547	0.17			
18 to 64 years	3,756	1.16	**Total population (18 years and over)**	250,286	100.00%
65 years and over	3,164	0.98	With an independent living difficulty[5]	14,691	5.87
			18 to 64 years	7,399	2.96
			65 years and over	7,291	2.91

Note: Data based on sample and subject to sampling variability. Does not include military personnel and civilian institutionalized population (i.e., those under formal supervision or custody in a facility). (1) Identified by the ACS as persons "who report difficulty with specific functions and may, in the absence of accommodation, have a disability." (2) Concentrating, remembering, or making decisions. (3) Walking or climbing stairs. (4) Dressing or bathing. (5) Doing errands alone such as visiting a doctor's office or shopping.

Marital Status of the U.S. Population, 1960-2019

Source: Annual Social and Economic Supplements, Current Population Surveys (CPS), U.S. Census Bureau, U.S. Dept. of Commerce
(numbers in millions; data based on sample of occupied households in civilian noninstitutional pop.)

Marital status	Both sexes 2019	2000	1980	1960	Male 2019	2000	1980	1960	Female 2019	2000	1980	1960
Total	263.5	213.8	171.9	124.9	127.9	103.1	81.9	60.3	135.6	110.7	89.9	64.6
Married[1]	137.8	120.2	104.8	84.4	68.5	59.7	51.8	41.8	69.3	60.5	53.0	42.6
Never married	85.4	60.0	44.5	27.5	45.3	32.3	24.2	15.3	40.1	27.8	20.2	12.3
Divorced	25.5	19.9	9.9	2.8	10.7	8.6	3.9	1.1	14.8	11.3	6.0	1.7
Widowed	14.9	13.7	12.7	10.2	3.5	2.6	2.0	2.1	11.4	11.1	10.8	8.1
% of total or subset pops.												
Married[1]	52.3%	56.2%	61.0%	67.6%	53.6%	57.9%	63.2%	69.3%	51.1%	54.7%	58.9%	65.9%
Never married	32.4	28.1	25.9	22.0	35.4	31.3	29.6	25.3	29.6	25.1	22.5	19.0
Divorced	9.7	9.3	5.8	2.3	8.3	8.3	4.8	1.8	10.9	10.2	6.6	2.6
Widowed	5.6	6.4	7.4	8.1	2.7	2.5	2.4	3.5	8.4	10.0	12.0	12.5

Note: Total pop. for 1980, 2000, and 2019 is persons ages 15 and older and for 1960, persons ages 14 and older. Figures may not add up to totals due to rounding. (1) Comprises subcategories Married, spouse present; Married, spouse absent; and Separated.

Household Characteristics of Couples in the U.S., 2018

Source: American Community Survey (ACS), U.S. Census Bureau, U.S. Dept. of Commerce
(as percent of all households with same couple relationship type, unless otherwise noted)

Household characteristics	Opposite-sex couples Married	Unmarried	Same-sex couples Married Total couples	Male couple	Female couple	Unmarried Total couples	Male couple	Female couple
Total number of households (thous.)	57,581.9	7,411.9	592.6	285.0	307.6	402.9	200.1	202.8
Age of householder								
15 to 24 years	1.1%	11.0%	1.7%	1.1%	2.4%	7.7%	5.0%	10.3%
25 to 34 years	12.7	35.1	15.6	13.2	17.9	28.9	26.3	31.6
35 to 44 years	19.7	20.9	19.7	17.1	22.2	18.3	19.3	17.3
45 to 54 years	20.9	15.3	22.6	25.0	20.5	18.6	22.1	15.2
55 to 64 years	21.3	10.8	21.2	23.3	19.3	16.3	17.4	15.2
65 years and over	24.2	6.9	19.1	20.4	17.9	10.2	10.0	10.5
Average age of householder (years)	52.6	39.7	50.6	52.1	49.3	43.5	44.7	42.4
Household income								
Less than $35,000	11.9%	19.1%	11.3%	9.3%	13.2%	13.2%	10.2%	16.2%
$35,000 to $49,999	9.8	13.8	8.7	7.6	9.6	10.9	8.9	12.9
$50,000 to $74,999	17.4	22.2	14.7	13.2	16.2	18.7	15.8	21.7
$75,000 to $99,999	15.7	16.1	14.9	13.8	15.9	15.8	15.8	16.1
$100,000 or more	45.3	28.8	50.3	56.1	45.1	41.3	49.6	33.1
Median household income (dollars)	$91,678	$68,501	$100,489	$111,762	$91,806	$85,183	$99,161	$73,892
Children in household[1]	38.6%	37.6%	19.2%	12.4%	25.5%	12.2%	4.9%	19.3%

Note: Data based on sample and subject to sampling variability. Householder is person in whose name a home is owned or rented. (1) Includes own children and nonrelatives of the householder under 18 years.

Same-Sex Couple Households in the U.S., 2008-18

Source: American Community Survey (ACS), U.S. Census Bureau, U.S. Dept. of Commerce
(in thousands; data based on sample and subject to sampling variability)

Year	Total same-sex couples Total	Male couple	Female couple	Same-sex married couples Total	Male couple	Female couple	Same-sex unmarried partner couples Total	Male couple	Female couple
2008	539.2	257.9	281.3	142.5	62.2	80.3	396.7	195.8	201.0
2009	581.3	280.4	300.9	152.1	66.3	85.8	429.2	214.1	215.0
2010	593.3	287.7	305.6	152.3	68.5	83.8	441.0	219.2	221.8
2011	605.5	284.3	321.2	168.1	69.5	98.6	437.4	214.8	222.6
2012	639.4	305.8	333.6	181.9	80.7	101.2	457.5	225.1	232.5
2013	726.6	352.6	374.0	251.7	117.5	134.2	474.9	235.1	239.8
2014	783.1	377.9	405.2	334.8	163.2	171.6	448.3	214.7	233.6
2015	858.9	412.0	446.9	425.4	201.8	223.6	433.5	210.2	223.3
2016	887.5	435.9	451.6	487.0	235.2	251.8	400.5	200.7	199.8
2017	935.2	451.5	483.7	555.5	262.3	293.2	379.7	189.2	190.6
2018	995.4	485.1	510.4	592.6	285.0	307.6	402.9	200.1	202.8

Children in the U.S. by Selected Characteristics, 2019

Source: Annual Social and Economic Supplement, Current Population Survey (CPS), U.S. Census Bureau, U.S. Dept. of Commerce
(numbers in thousands; data based on sample of occupied households in civilian noninstitutional pop.)

Characteristic	Number	% of tot.	Characteristic	Number	% of tot.
All children	73,525	100.0%	**Nativity of child/parent(s) in household**		
Age of child			Native-born child and parent	51,079	69.5%
Under 1 year	3,687	5.0	Native-born child and foreign-born parent	16,926	23.0
1-2 years	7,957	10.8	Foreign-born child and parent	2,386	3.2
3-5 years	12,078	16.4	All other combinations	3,134	4.3
6-8 years	12,141	16.5	**Labor force status of parent(s) in household**		
9-11 years	12,359	16.8	Father in labor force, mother not in labor		
12-14 years	12,525	17.0	force	15,584	21.2
15-17 years	12,777	17.4	Mother and father in labor force	31,907	43.4
Race/ethnicity of child			Mother in labor force, father not present	12,309	16.7
White alone, non-Hispanic	36,800	50.1	Mother not in labor force, father not		
Black alone	11,101	15.1	present	3,455	4.7
Asian alone	3,993	5.4	No parents present or parents are		
Hispanic (any race)	18,757	25.5	same-sex	3,157	4.3
			All other combinations	7,113	9.7

Note: Children are defined as all persons under 18 years of age excluding those who are a family reference person or spouse.

Persons Granted Lawful Permanent Resident Status by State, 2018

Source: Office of Immigration Statistics, U.S. Dept. of Homeland Security

(ranked by fiscal year 2018 number)

State/territory	Number	State/territory	Number	State/territory	Number	State/territory	Number
Total	1,096,611	Michigan	19,850	Oklahoma	5,938	New Hampshire	2,200
California	200,897	Ohio	18,809	Utah	5,723	Delaware	1,831
New York	134,839	Arizona	18,335	Kansas	5,630	Maine	1,749
Florida	130,405	Minnesota	16,721	Iowa	5,484	North Dakota	1,674
Texas	104,515	Colorado	13,913	Hawaii	5,430	Mississippi	1,643
New Jersey	54,424	Connecticut	11,629	South Carolina	5,078	Alaska	1,375
Illinois	38,287	Nevada	10,851	Louisiana	4,889	Guam	1,231
Massachusetts	33,174	Indiana	9,741	Rhode Island	4,336	South Dakota	1,132
Virginia	27,426	Oregon	9,679	New Mexico	4,296	Vermont	824
Georgia	26,725	Tennessee	9,590	Alabama	3,737	West Virginia	675
Pennsylvania	26,078	Kentucky	8,734	Puerto Rico	3,062	Montana	565
Washington	26,029	Missouri	7,638	Arkansas	3,000	Wyoming	409
Maryland	24,301	Wisconsin	7,433	Dist. of Columbia	2,775	Other[1]	1,212
North Carolina	20,838	Nebraska	6,500	Idaho	2,728	Unknown	624

Note: Applicants for lawful permanent resident (LPR) status, or "green cards," may already live in the U.S. They include refugees and asylees, temp. workers, foreign students, family members of U.S. citizens, and unauthorized immigrants. Applicants from outside the U.S. are granted LPR status upon entry with a visa. (1) Incl. Amer. Samoa, Northern Mariana Isls., U.S. Virgin Isls., and armed forces posts.

Persons Granted Lawful Permanent Resident Status by Top Areas of Residence, 2018

Source: Office of Immigration Statistics, U.S. Dept. of Homeland Security

(ranked by fiscal year 2018 number)

Area of residence[1]	Number	% of total	Area of residence[1]	Number	% of total
Total	1,096,611	100.0%	Tampa-Saint Petersburg-Clearwater, FL	14,399	1.3%
New York-Newark-Jersey City, NY-NJ-PA	168,931	15.4	Minneapolis-Saint Paul-Bloomington, MN-WI	12,859	1.2
Miami-Fort Lauderdale-Pompano Beach, FL	80,341	7.3	Orlando-Kissimmee-Sanford, FL	12,730	1.2
Los Angeles-Long Beach-Anaheim, CA	74,032	6.8	Phoenix-Mesa-Chandler, AZ	12,707	1.2
Washington-Arlington-Alexandria,			Detroit-Warren-Dearborn, MI	12,454	1.1
DC-VA-MD-WV	37,796	3.4	Sacramento-Roseville-Folsom, CA	11,646	1.1
Houston-The Woodlands-Sugar Land, TX	36,263	3.3	Austin-Round Rock-Georgetown, TX	9,366	0.9
Chicago-Naperville-Elgin, IL-IN-WI	35,045	3.2	Denver-Aurora-Lakewood, CO	9,285	0.8
San Francisco-Oakland-Berkeley, CA	31,918	2.9	Las Vegas-Henderson-Paradise, NV	9,181	0.8
Dallas-Fort Worth-Arlington, TX	28,915	2.6	Portland-Vancouver-Hillsboro, OR-WA	8,299	0.8
Boston-Cambridge-Newton, MA-NH	26,411	2.4	Baltimore-Columbia-Towson, MD	8,244	0.8
Atlanta-Sandy Springs-Alpharetta, GA	21,334	1.9	Columbus, OH	7,184	0.7
San Jose-Sunnyvale-Santa Clara, CA	19,906	1.8	San Antonio-New Braunfels, TX	7,155	0.7
Seattle-Tacoma-Bellevue, WA	19,553	1.8	Charlotte-Concord-Gastonia, NC-SC	6,892	0.6
San Diego-Chula Vista-Carlsbad, CA	19,381	1.8	Louisville/Jefferson County, KY-IN	5,538	0.5
Philadelphia-Camden-Wilmington,			Other CBSAs	301,780	27.5
PA-NJ-DE-MD	17,705	1.6	Non-CBSA or unknown	14,361	1.3
Riverside-San Bernardino-Ontario, CA	15,000	1.4			

Note: Applicants for lawful permanent resident (LPR) status, or "green cards," may already live in the U.S. They include refugees and asylees, temporary workers, foreign students, family members of U.S. citizens, and unauthorized immigrants. Applicants from outside the U.S. are granted LPR status upon entry with a visa. (1) Residence by Core Based Statistical Areas, or CBSAs, which refer collectively to metropolitan and micropolitan statistical areas. These areas are defined for federal statistical use by the Office of Management and Budget with Census Bureau assistance.

Unauthorized Immigrant Population in the U.S., 1990-2017

Source: Pew Research Center

The unauthorized immigrant population had been increasing steadily since 1990 before it peaked in 2007 with the beginning of the recession. In 2017, about 14.3% of the unauthorized immigrant population were covered by the Deferred Action for Childhood Arrivals (DACA) program or the Temporary Protected Status program for people from countries where war, natural disaster, or disease make return dangerous.

(ranked by 2017 est. population; numbers in thousands)

	Country of Birth					State of Residence			
	Est. population			% change,		Est. population			% change,
Country	2017	2007	1990	2007-17	State	2017	2007	1990	2007-17
All countries	10,500	12,200	3,500	−13.9%	All states	10,500	12,200	3,500	−13.9%
Mexico	4,950	6,950	2,050	−28.8	California	2,000	2,800	1,450	−28.6
El Salvador	750	600	300	25.0	Texas	1,600	1,550	450	3.2
Guatemala	600	400	120	50.0	Florida	825	1,050	240	−21.4
India	525	325	30	61.5	New York	650	1,000	350	−35.0
Honduras	400	300	40	33.3	New Jersey	450	550	95	−18.2
China[1]	375	325	80	15.4	Illinois	425	550	200	−22.7
Dominican Rep.	240	200	50	20.0	Georgia	375	425	35	−11.8
Brazil	160	180	20	−11.1	North Carolina	325	325	25	0.0
Philippines	160	190	70	−15.8	Arizona	275	500	90	−45.0
Korea[2]	150	180	25	−16.7	Massachusetts	275	220	55	25.0
Colombia	140	180	50	−22.2	Virginia	275	250	50	10.0
Venezuela	130	55	10	136.4	Maryland	250	220	35	13.6
Ecuador	120	150	35	−20.0	Washington	250	250	40	0.0
Haiti	100	110	65	−9.1	Nevada	210	240	25	−12.5
Peru	100	150	25	−33.3	Pennsylvania	190	150	25	26.7

Note: Unauthorized immigrant pop. ests. are made using the residual method. The estimated number of immigrants residing legally in the country is subtracted from the total foreign-born pop. Numbers are rounded independently and may not add up to totals. Incl. asylum seekers waiting for their applications to be processed. (1) Incl. Hong Kong and Taiwan. (2) Incl. North and South Korea.

Active U.S. DACA Population by Birth Country, 2020

Source: U.S. Citizenship and Immigration Services, U.S. Dept. of Homeland Security

The Deferred Action for Childhood Arrivals (DACA) program grants (1) temporary protection from deportation and (2) permission to legally work to undocumented individuals living in the U.S. who were brought to the country as children.

(number of valid DACA recipients as of Mar. 31, 2020, ranked by country of birth)

Country of birth	Number	Country of birth	Number	Country of birth	Number
Total	643,560	Ecuador	4,780	Uruguay	1,700
Mexico	517,460	Colombia	4,240	Trinidad and Tobago	1,500
El Salvador	24,830	Argentina	3,360	Bolivia	1,430
Guatemala	16,840	Philippines	3,270	Costa Rica	1,340
Honduras	15,450	Jamaica	2,250	Nicaragua	1,270
Peru	6,250	India	2,220	Chile	1,190
South Korea	6,210	Venezuela	2,100	Poland	1,150
Brazil	5,060	Dominican Republic	1,990	Pakistan	1,150

Note: Numbers are approximate and rounded and may not add up to total. Countries with fewer than 1,000 valid DACA recipients are not shown here. Does not include individuals who have obtained lawful permanent resident status or U.S. citizenship.

Refugee Arrivals in the U.S. by Region and Nationality, 2001-19

Source: Refugee Processing Center, Bureau of Population, Refugees, and Migration, U.S. Dept. of State

Under the Refugee Act of 1980, the president in consultation with Congress establishes a refugee admissions ceiling and regional allocations before each fiscal year (Oct. 1-Sept. 30). Applicants for refugee status are outside of the U.S. whereas applicants seeking asylum are in the U.S. or at a U.S. port of entry.

(countries ranked by nationality of most refugee arrivals in fiscal year 2019)

Region/country of nationality	2019	2016	2014	2012	2010	2008	2006	2004	2002	2001
Total ceiling	30,000	85,000	70,000	76,000	80,000	80,000	70,000	70,000	70,000	80,000
Total refugee arrivals	30,000	84,994	69,987	58,238	73,311	60,191	41,223	52,873	27,131	69,886
COUNTRY										
Congo, Dem. Rep. of	12,958	16,370	4,540	1,863	3,174	727	405	569	107	264
Myanmar (Burma)	4,932	12,347	14,598	14,160	16,693	18,139	1,612	1,056	128	544
Ukraine	4,451	2,543	490	372	449	1,022	2,483	3,482	5,217	7,313
Eritrea	1,757	1,949	1,488	1,346	2,570	251	538	128	13	114
Afghanistan	1,198	2,737	753	481	515	576	651	959	1,683	2,930
Syria	563	12,587	105	31	25	24	27	0	4	8
Iraq	465	9,880	19,769	12,163	18,016	13,822	202	66	466	2,465
Sudan	382	1,458	1,315	1,077	558	375	1,848	3,500	897	5,944
El Salvador	311	364	0	0	0	0	0	0	0	0
Colombia	298	529	252	126	123	94	115	577	8	0
Pakistan	264	545	240	274	59	104	20	11	0	3
Ethiopia	247	1,131	728	620	668	299	1,271	2,689	330	1,457
Central African Republic	244	401	25	136	45	56	23	24	0	1
Somalia	231	9,020	9,000	4,911	4,884	2,523	10,357	13,331	237	4,946
Iran	199	3,750	2,846	1,758	3,543	5,270	2,792	1,786	1,535	6,461
Burundi	196	694	68	186	530	2,889	466	276	62	109
Russia	184	462	139	197	327	426	6,003	1,446	2,105	4,596
Moldova	120	465	142	255	356	487	721	1,711	1,022	1,199
Guatemala	118	8	0	0	0	0	0	0	0	0
Belarus	96	185	46	83	103	111	350	659	680	984
All other countries	786	7,569	13,443	18,199	20,673	12,996	11,339	20,603	12,637	30,548
REGION										
Africa	16,366	31,624	17,476	10,608	13,305	8,935	18,126	29,104	2,551	19,020
East Asia	5,030	12,518	14,784	14,366	17,716	19,489	5,659	8,084	3,512	4,163
Europe	4,994	3,957	959	1,129	1,526	2,343	10,456	9,254	5,459	15,794
Former Soviet Union[1]	—	—	—	—	—	—	—	—	9,969	15,978
Latin America/Caribbean	809	1,340	4,318	2,078	4,982	4,277	3,264	3,577	1,934	2,975
Near East/South Asia	2,801	35,555	32,450	30,057	35,782	25,147	3,718	2,854	3,706	11,956

— = Not applicable. **Note:** Includes Amerasian immigrants (children born in Cambodia, Korea, Laos, Thailand, or Vietnam in 1950-82 and fathered by a U.S. citizen). (1) Former Soviet Union countries are grouped under Europe from 2004 and on.

Persons Granted Asylum and Refugee Arrivals in the U.S., 1980-2019

Source: U.S. Dept. of Homeland Security; U.S. Dept. of Justice; Refugee Processing Center, Bureau of Population, Refugees, and Migration, U.S. Dept. of State

Individuals apply for asylum from within the U.S. or at a U.S. port of entry. Applicants for refugee status are outside of the U.S.

Year	Number granted asylum	Number of refugee arrivals	Year	Number granted asylum	Number of refugee arrivals	Year	Number granted asylum	Number of refugee arrivals
1980	—	207,116	1994	—	13,826	2007	25,334	48,218
1981	—	159,252	1995	20,697	111,680	2008	23,026	60,107
1982	—	98,096	1996	23,525	98,973	2009	22,314	74,602
1983	—	61,218	1997	22,933	75,421	2010	19,772	73,293
1984	—	70,393	1998	20,520	69,653	2011	23,572	56,384
1985	—	67,704	1999	26,578	76,712	2012	27,951	58,179
1986	—	62,146	2000	32,542	85,285	2013	25,014	69,909
1987	—	64,528	2001	39,179	72,165	2014	23,371	69,975
1988	—	76,483	2002	36,977	68,920	2015	26,015	69,920
1989	—	107,070	2003	28,791	26,785	2016	20,362	84,989
1990	8,472	122,066	2004	27,426	28,286	2017	26,509	53,691
1991	5,035	113,389	2005	25,349	52,840	2018	38,687	22,405
1992	6,307	115,548	2006	26,398	53,738	2019	—	30,000
1993	9,540	114,181			41,094			

— = Not available. **Note:** Fiscal year (Oct. 1-Sept. 30) data. Excludes Amerasians (children born in Cambodia, Korea, Laos, Thailand, or Vietnam after Dec. 31, 1950, and before Oct. 22, 1982, and fathered by a U.S. citizen) except in fiscal years 1989-91 and 2019.

U.S. Foreign-Born Population

Source: Decennial Censuses and Annual Social and Economic Supplements, Current Population Surveys (CPS), U.S. Census Bureau, U.S. Dept. of Commerce

Foreign-Born as a Percentage of U.S. Population, 1900-2019

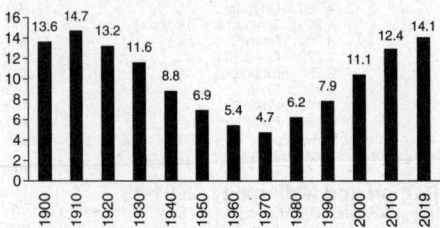

Foreign-Born Population by Region of Birth, 1995-2019

(numbers in thousands)

Region	2019[1] No.	%	2000	1995
Asia.............	13,864	30.3%	7,916	6,121
Under 18......	797	28.9	696	767
Europe	4,522	9.9	4,382	3,937
Under 18.....	218	7.9	247	232
Latin America	23,718	51.8	15,323	11,777
Under 18.....	1,242	45.1	1,786	1,451
Other[2]..........	3,716	8.1	2,364	2,658
Under 18.....	498	18.1	249	275
All regions	**45,820**	**100.0**	**29,985**	**24,493**
Under 18	**2,754**	**100.0**	**2,977**	**2,726**

(1) Figures are percentage of total foreign-born pop. or of all foreign-born under 18 years of age. (2) Incl. those born at sea.

U.S. Foreign-Born Population: Top Countries of Origin, 1880-2019

Source: Decennial Censuses and American Community Survey (ACS), U.S. Census Bureau, U.S. Dept. of Commerce

(numbers in thousands; percentage is of all foreign-born excluding population born at sea)

1880 Country	No.	%	1920 Country	No.	%	1960 Country	No.	%	2000 Country	No.	%	2019[4] Country	No.	%
Germany	1,967	29.4	Germany	1,686	12.1	Italy	1,257	12.9	Mexico	9,177	29.5	Mexico	10,932	24.3
Ireland	1,855	27.8	Italy	1,610	11.6	Germany	990	10.2	China[2]	1,519	4.9	China[2]	2,854	6.4
UK	918	13.7	USSR	1,400	10.1	Canada	953	9.8	Philippines	1,369	4.4	India	2,688	6.0
Canada	717	10.7	Poland	1,140	8.2	UK	765	7.9	India	1,023	3.3	Philippines	2,045	4.6
Sweden	194	2.9	Canada	1,138	8.2	Poland	748	7.7	Vietnam	988	3.2	El Salvador	1,412	3.1
Norway	182	2.7	UK	1,135	8.2	USSR	691	7.1	Cuba	873	2.8	Vietnam	1,384	3.1
France	107	1.6	Ireland	1,037	7.5	Mexico	576	5.9	Korea[3]	864	2.8	Cuba	1,360	3.0
China[1]	104	1.6	Sweden	626	4.5	Ireland	339	3.5	Canada	821	2.6	Dominican Republic	1,169	2.6
Switzerland	89	1.3	Austria	576	4.1	Austria	305	3.1	El Salvador	817	2.6	Guatemala	1,111	2.5
Czech.	85	1.3	Mexico	486	3.5	Hungary	245	2.5	Germany	707	2.3	Korea[3]	1,039	2.3
Total	**6,680**	**100.0**	**Total**	**13,921**	**100.0**	**Total**	**9,738**	**100.0**	**Total**	**31,108**	**100.0**	**Total**	**44,933**	**100.0**

(1) Incl. Taiwan. (2) Incl. Hong Kong and Taiwan. (3) North and South Korea. (4) Data based on sample and subject to sampling variability. The Census Bureau collects data from residents regardless of immigration status, so the foreign-born population implicitly includes unauthorized migrants.

Language Spoken at Home by the U.S. Population, 2019

Source: American Community Survey (ACS), U.S. Census Bureau, U.S. Dept. of Commerce

(number of speakers 5 years of age and over by language or language group most often used)

Language	Number (thous.)	% of tot. pop.	% English inability[1]
Total population	308,834.7	100.00%	8.2%
Speak only English........	241,032.3	78.05	NA
Speak another language ...	67,802.3	21.95	37.6
Spanish			
Spanish..................	41,757.4	13.52	38.6
Other Indo-European languages			
Armenian	236.9	0.08	40.5
Bengali	369.1	0.12	41.1
French (incl. Cajun).......	1,171.8	0.38	20.5
German	895.3	0.29	15.0
Greek	264.1	0.09	22.8
Gujarati.................	455.3	0.15	31.7
Haitian	924.8	0.30	35.0
Hindi	892.6	0.29	17.7
Italian	539.5	0.17	24.6
Malayalam, Kannada, other Dravidian	266.3	0.09	19.8
Nepali, Marathi, other Indic...	417.5	0.14	37.5
Persian (incl. Farsi, Dari).....	457.1	0.15	35.3
Polish	510.4	0.17	36.2
Portuguese	845.8	0.27	36.2
Punjabi	322.4	0.10	38.5
Russian.................	941.5	0.30	41.2
Serbo-Croatian	243.2	0.08	32.8
Tamil	293.9	0.10	15.7
Telugu..................	419.8	0.14	19.0
Ukrainian, other Slavic	321.9	0.10	36.1
Urdu	519.9	0.17	26.7

Language	Number (thous.)	% of tot. pop.	% English inability[1]
Yiddish, Penn. Dutch, other West Germanic	560.2	0.18%	28.9%
Other Indo-European languages	576.2	0.19	28.2
Asian and Pacific Island languages			
Chinese (incl. Mandarin, Cantonese)	3,494.5	1.13	52.0
Hmong..................	230.3	0.07	36.8
Ilocano, Samoan, Hawaiian, other Austronesian	485.9	0.16	33.3
Japanese	455.0	0.15	38.5
Khmer..................	193.1	0.06	48.2
Korean	1,075.2	0.35	51.0
Tagalog (incl. Filipino)	1,763.6	0.57	29.6
Thai, Lao, other Tai-Kadai....	315.5	0.10	51.0
Vietnamese..............	1,570.5	0.51	56.9
Other Asian languages......	409.7	0.13	50.4
All other languages			
Amharic, Somali, other Afro-Asiatic	589.6	0.19	39.4
Arabic..................	1,260.4	0.41	35.0
Hebrew.................	210.8	0.07	11.7
Navajo..................	171.3	0.06	25.5
Swahili, other Central/ Eastern/Southern Africa	299.2	0.10	33.3
Yoruba, Twi, Igbo, other Western Africa...........	588.6	0.19	20.9
Other Native North American	197.6	0.06	12.3
Other and unspecified	288.6	0.09	27.3

NA = Not applicable. **Note:** Data based on sample and subject to sampling variability. (1) Percent of respondents who speak the language at left who indicated that they spoke English less than "very well." For example, 40.5% of respondents who use Armenian at home do not speak English very well.

U.S. Population by Ancestry Reported, 2019

Source: American Community Survey (ACS), U.S. Census Bureau, U.S. Dept. of Commerce
(numbers in thousands; ranked by number)

Ancestry	Number	% of total	Ancestry	Number	% of total	Ancestry	Number	% of total
Total population	328,240	100.0%	Norwegian	4,296	1.3%	French Canadian	1,995	0.6%
German	40,364	12.3	Subsaharan African[1]	4,018	1.2	Welsh	1,956	0.6
Irish	30,353	9.2	Dutch	3,578	1.1	Portuguese	1,371	0.4
English	23,593	7.2	Swedish	3,536	1.1	Hungarian	1,323	0.4
American	20,071	6.1	West Indian (excl.			Czech	1,295	0.4
Italian	16,147	4.9	Hispanic groups)[2]	3,067	0.9	Greek	1,247	0.4
Polish	8,970	2.7	Scotch-Irish	2,925	0.9	Other ancestry not		
French (excl. Basque)	7,116	2.2	British	2,458	0.7	shown here	139,101	42.4
European	6,918	2.1	Russian	2,433	0.7	Unclassified or not		
Scottish	5,131	1.6	Arab[3]	2,098	0.6	reported	64,936	19.8

Note: Data based on sample and subject to sampling variability. Because respondents could self-identify with more than one ancestry, numbers do not add up to total. (1) Incl. Cabo Verdean, Ethiopian, Ghanian, Kenyan, Liberian, Nigerian, Senegalese, Sierra Leonean, Somali, South African, Sudanese, Ugandan, Zimbabwean, African, and other Subsaharan African. (2) Incl. Bahamian, Barbadian, Belizean, Bermudan, British or Dutch West Indian, Haitian, Jamaican, Trinidadian and Tobagonian, U.S. Virgin Islander, West Indian, and other West Indian. (3) Incl. Egyptian, Iraqi, Jordanian, Lebanese, Moroccan, Palestinian, Syrian, Arab, and other Arab.

U.S. Population by Race, Hispanic Origin, and Age, 2019

Source: American Community Survey (ACS), U.S. Census Bureau, U.S. Dept. of Commerce

Race and origin/age	Number	% of group	Race and origin/age	Number	% of group
White (not Hispanic or Latino)	196,789,401	100.0%	Native Hawaiian and other		
Under 5 years	9,626,516	4.9	Pacific Islander	628,683	100.0%
Under 18 years	36,507,254	18.6	Under 5 years	43,785	7.0
18 to 64 years	119,158,881	60.6	Under 18 years	159,875	25.4
65 years and over	41,123,266	20.9	18 to 64 years	409,248	65.1
85 years and over	5,031,987	2.6	65 years and over	59,560	9.5
Black or African American	41,989,671	100.0	85 years and over	5,263	0.8
Under 5 years	2,661,009	6.3	Some other race	16,352,553	100.0
Under 18 years	10,209,668	24.3	Under 5 years	1,210,493	7.4
18 to 64 years	26,685,370	63.6	Under 18 years	4,709,896	28.8
65 years and over	5,094,633	12.1	18 to 64 years	10,615,544	64.9
85 years and over	499,685	1.2	65 years and over	1,027,113	6.3
Asian	18,636,984	100.0	85 years and over	93,390	0.6
Under 5 years	894,211	4.8	Two or more races	11,308,895	100.0
Under 18 years	3,533,847	19.0	Under 5 years	1,556,087	13.8
18 to 64 years	12,618,281	67.7	Under 18 years	5,038,860	44.6
65 years and over	2,484,856	13.3	18 to 64 years	5,662,666	50.1
85 years and over	281,983	1.5	65 years and over	607,369	5.4
American Indian and Alaska Native	2,847,336	100.0	85 years and over	54,939	0.5
Under 5 years	178,770	6.3	Hispanic or Latino (any race)	60,481,746	100.0
Under 18 years	736,723	25.9	Under 5 years	5,029,471	8.3
18 to 64 years	1,791,988	62.9	Under 18 years	18,624,877	30.8
65 years and over	318,625	11.2	18 to 64 years	37,218,036	61.5
85 years and over	22,360	0.8	65 years and over	4,638,833	7.7
			85 years and over	489,880	0.8

Note: Data based on sample and subject to sampling variability. Categories are for one race alone, not in combination with any other race, unless otherwise noted.

Educational Attainment of the U.S. Population, 2019

Source: American Community Survey (ACS), U.S. Census Bureau, U.S. Dept. of Commerce
(numbers in thousands; population 25 years of age and over)

Race and origin/highest ed. completed	Number	% of group	Race and origin/highest ed. completed	Number	% of group
White (not Hispanic or Latino)	144,203	100.0%	Native Hawaiian and other		
Less than HS diploma	9,647	6.7	Pacific Islander	395	100.0%
HS diploma or equiv. credential	38,699	26.8	Less than HS diploma	54	13.7
Some college or associate's degree	42,695	29.6	HS diploma or equiv. credential	140	35.5
Bachelor's degree or higher	53,162	36.9	Some college or associate's degree	129	32.7
Black or African American	27,337	100.0	Bachelor's degree or higher	72	18.1
Less than HS diploma	3,537	12.9	Some other race	9,753	100.0
HS diploma or equiv. credential	8,733	31.9	Less than HS diploma	3,469	35.6
Some college or associate's degree	8,903	32.6	HS diploma or equiv. credential	2,842	29.1
Bachelor's degree or higher	6,164	22.5	Some college or associate's degree	2,147	22.0
Asian	13,381	100.0	Bachelor's degree or higher	1,294	13.3
Less than HS diploma	1,634	12.2	Two or more races	4,896	100.0
HS diploma or equiv. credential	1,932	14.4	Less than HS diploma	531	10.8
Some college or associate's degree	2,381	17.8	HS diploma or equiv. credential	1,100	22.5
Bachelor's degree or higher	7,435	55.6	Some college or associate's degree	1,632	33.3
American Indian and Alaska Native	1,802	100.0	Bachelor's degree or higher	1,633	33.4
Less than HS diploma	333	18.5	Hispanic or Latino (any race)	34,949	100.0
HS diploma or equiv. credential	568	31.5	Less than HS diploma	10,325	29.5
Some college or associate's degree	612	34.0	HS diploma or equiv. credential	9,854	28.2
Bachelor's degree or higher	290	16.1	Some college or associate's degree	8,606	24.6
			Bachelor's degree or higher	6,164	17.6

HS = High school. Note: Data based on sample and subject to sampling variability. Categories are for one race alone, not in combination with any other race, unless otherwise noted.

Populations, ZIP, and Area Codes for U.S. Places of 10,000 or More

Source: Decennial Census and Population Estimates Program, U.S. Census Bureau, U.S. Dept. of Commerce; NeuStar Inc.; www.usps.com

The following is a list of places of 10,000 or more residents according to the Census Bureau's 2019 population estimates and 2010 census results. Included are **places incorporated** under state law as cities, towns, villages, or boroughs, and **Census designated places (CDPs)**, marked with a (c). This list also includes, in italics, **minor civil divisions (MCDs)** in Connecticut, Maine, Massachusetts, New Hampshire, Rhode Island, and Vermont. **Townships are not included.** The Census Bureau delineates CDPs as statistical counterparts to incorporated places but does not typically include CDPs in its estimates program. MCDs, which are also not incorporated, are often the primary political or administrative divisions of a county. (Balance) indicates the given population is for a consolidated area minus the residents of any separately incorporated places within its boundaries.

An asterisk (*) denotes a **ZIP code** for general delivery; mail routes and/or P.O. boxes within the place may use a different one. Telephone **area codes** are given in parentheses. New phone numbers may be assigned a different area code from that of existing phone numbers. These areas of overlay are noted. When two or more area codes are listed for one place, consult local operators for assistance. Area codes based on latest information as of mid-2020. — = Not available.

Alabama
Area code 659 overlays area code 205; 938 overlays 256.

ZIP	Place	Area code	2010 population	2019 estimate
*35007	Alabaster	(205)	30,352	33,487
*35950	Albertville	(256)	21,160	21,711
*35010	Alexander City	(256)	14,875	14,317
*36201	Anniston	(256)	23,106	21,287
*35611	Athens	(256)	21,897	27,366
*36830	Auburn	(334)	53,380	66,259
*35020	Bessemer	(205)	27,456	26,472
*35203	Birmingham	(205)	212,237	209,403
35040	Calera	(205)	11,620	14,717
*35215	Center Point	(205)	16,921	16,110
35043	Chelsea	(205)	10,183	14,126
*35055	Cullman	(256)	14,775	16,034
*36526	Daphne	(251)	21,570	26,869
*35601	Decatur	(256)	55,683	54,445
*36301	Dothan	(334)	65,496	68,941
*36330	Enterprise	(334)	26,562	28,376
36027	Eufaula	(334)	13,137	11,709
35064	Fairfield	(205)	11,117	10,568
*36532	Fairhope	(251)	15,326	22,677
*35630	Florence	(256)	39,319	40,797
*36535	Foley	(251)	14,618	20,391
35214	Forestdale (c)	(205)	10,162	—
*35967	Fort Payne	(256)	14,012	14,074
*35901	Gadsden	(256)	36,856	35,000
35071	Gardendale	(205)	13,893	14,177
*36542	Gulf Shores	(251)	9,741	12,757
*35640	Hartselle	(256)	14,255	14,466
*35080	Helena	(205)	16,793	19,925
*35209	Homewood	(205)	25,167	25,377
*35216	Hoover	(205)	81,619	85,768
*35023	Hueytown	(205)	16,105	15,322
*35801	Huntsville	(256)	180,105	200,574
35210	Irondale	(205)	12,349	12,893
36265	Jacksonville	(256)	12,548	12,544
*35501	Jasper	(205)	14,352	13,431
35094	Leeds	(205)	11,773	12,040
*35758	Madison	(256)	42,938	51,593
36054	Millbrook	(334)	14,640	15,896
*36602	Mobile	(251)	195,111	188,720
*36104	Montgomery	(334)	205,764	198,525
35004	Moody	(205)	11,726	13,065
*35223	Mountain Brook	(205)	20,413	20,297
*35661	Muscle Shoals	(256)	13,146	14,575
*35476	Northport	(205)	23,330	26,115
*36801	Opelika	(334)	26,477	30,908
36203	Oxford	(256)	21,348	21,225
*36360	Ozark	(334)	14,907	14,284
35124	Pelham	(205)	21,352	23,911
*35125	Pell City	(205)	12,695	14,045
*36007	Phenix City	(334)	32,822	36,487
36064	Pike Road	(334)	5,406	10,159
*36066	Prattville	(334)	33,960	35,957
*36610	Prichard	(251)	22,659	21,428
36206	Saks (c)	(256)	10,744	—
36571	Saraland	(251)	13,405	14,649
*35768	Scottsboro	(256)	14,770	14,436
*36701	Selma	(334)	20,756	17,231
*35150	Sylacauga	(256)	12,749	12,034
*35160	Talladega	(256)	15,676	15,457
36619	Tillman's Corner (c)	(251)	17,398	—
*36081	Troy	(334)	18,033	18,957
35173	Trussville	(205)	19,933	22,635
*35401	Tuscaloosa	(205)	90,468	101,129
*35216	Vestavia Hills	(205)	34,033	34,413

Alaska
Area code 907 applies to the entire state.

ZIP	Place	2010 population	2019 estimate
*99501	Anchorage	291,826	288,000
99711	Badger (c)	19,482	—
*99708	College (c)	12,964	—
*99701	Fairbanks	31,535	30,917
*99801	Juneau	31,275	31,974
99654	Knik-Fairview (c)	14,923	—
*99623	Wasilla	7,831	10,838

Arizona

ZIP	Place	Area code	2010 population	2019 estimate
85086	Anthem (c)	(623)	21,700	—
*85119	Apache Junction	(480)	35,840	42,571
85123	Arizona City (c)	(520)	10,475	—
*85323	Avondale	(623)	76,238	87,931
*85326	Buckeye	(623)	50,876	79,620
*86442	Bullhead City	(928)	39,540	40,884
86322	Camp Verde	(928)	10,873	11,187
*85122	Casa Grande	(520)	48,571	58,632
85740	Casas Adobes (c)	(520)	66,795	—
85718	Catalina Foothills (c)	(520)	50,796	—
*85225	Chandler	(480)	236,123	261,165
86323	Chino Valley	(928)	10,817	12,375
85128	Coolidge	(520)	11,825	13,130
86326	Cottonwood	(928)	11,265	12,253
*85607	Douglas	(520)	17,378	16,193
*85746	Drexel Heights (c)	(520)	27,749	—
85335	El Mirage	(623)	31,797	35,753
85131	Eloy	(520)	16,631	19,625
*86001	Flagstaff	(928)	65,870	75,038
85132	Florence	(520)	25,536	27,422
85705	Flowing Wells (c)	(520)	16,419	—
*86426	Fort Mohave (c)	(928)	14,364	—
85367	Fortuna Foothills (c)	(928)	26,265	—
*85268	Fountain Hills	(480)	22,489	25,200
*85234	Gilbert	(480)	208,453	254,114
*85301	Glendale	(623)	226,721	252,381
85118	Gold Canyon (c)	(480)	10,159	—
*85338	Goodyear	(623)	65,275	86,840
*85622	Green Valley (c)	(520)	21,391	—
*86401	Kingman	(928)	28,068	31,013
*86403	Lake Havasu City	(928)	52,527	55,865
*85653	Marana	(520)	34,961	49,030
*85138	Maricopa	(520)	43,482	52,127
*85201	Mesa	(480)	439,041	518,012
86401	New Kingman-Butler (c)	(928)	12,134	—
85087	New River (c)	(623)	14,952	—
*85621	Nogales	(520)	20,837	20,103
*85737	Oro Valley	(520)	41,011	46,044
85253	Paradise Valley	(480)	12,820	14,637
*85541	Payson	(928)	15,301	15,813
*85345	Peoria	(623)	154,065	175,961
*85003	Phoenix	(480)/(602)/(623)	1,445,632	1,680,992
*86301	Prescott	(028)	39,040	44,299
*86314	Prescott Valley	(928)	38,822	46,515
*85142	Queen Creek	(480)	26,361	50,890
85648	Rio Rico (c)	(520)	18,962	—
85629	Sahuarita	(520)	25,259	31,421
85349	San Luis	(928)	25,505	34,778
*85142	San Tan Valley (c)	(480)	81,321	—
*85251	Scottsdale	(480)	217,385	258,069
*86336	Sedona	(928)	10,031	10,339
*85901	Show Low	(928)	10,660	11,442
*85635	Sierra Vista	(520)	43,888	43,045
85650	Sierra Vista Southeast (c)	(520)	14,797	—
85350	Somerton	(928)	14,287	16,554
*85351	Sun City (c)	(623)	37,499	—
*85375	Sun City West (c)	(623)	24,535	—
85248	Sun Lakes (c)	(480)	13,975	—
*85374	Surprise	(623)	117,517	141,664
85749	Tanque Verde (c)	(520)	16,901	—
*85281	Tempe	(480)	161,719	195,805
*85701	Tucson	(520)	520,116	548,073
85735	Tucson Estates (c)	(520)	12,192	—
85641	Vail (c)	(520)	10,208	—
86326	Verde Village (c)	(928)	11,605	—
*85364	Yuma	(928)	93,064	98,285

Arkansas

ZIP	Place	Area code	2010 population	2019 estimate
*71923	Arkadelphia	(870)	10,714	10,726
*72501	Batesville	(870)	10,248	10,878
*72714	Bella Vista	(479)	26,461	28,872
*72015	Benton	(501)	30,681	36,820
*72712	Bentonville	(479)	35,301	54,909
*72315	Blytheville	(870)	15,620	13,455
*72022	Bryant	(501)	16,688	20,968
*72023	Cabot	(501)	23,776	26,352
*71701	Camden	(870)	12,183	10,749
*72719	Centerton	(479)	9,515	16,244
*72032	Conway	(501)	58,908	67,638
*71730	El Dorado	(870)	18,884	17,651
*72701	Fayetteville	(479)	73,580	87,590
*72335	Forrest City	(870)	15,371	13,820
*72901	Fort Smith	(479)	86,209	87,891
*72601	Harrison	(870)	12,943	13,080
*72342	Helena-West Helena	(870)	12,282	10,299
*71901	Hot Springs	(501)	35,193	38,797
*71909	Hot Springs Village (c)	(501)	12,807	—
*72076	Jacksonville	(501)	28,364	28,235
*72401	Jonesboro	(870)	67,263	78,394
*72201	Little Rock	(501)	193,524	197,312
*71753	Magnolia	(870)	11,577	11,467
72104	Malvern	(501)	10,318	10,931
72364	Marion	(870)	12,345	12,310
72113	Maumelle	(501)	17,163	18,199
*72653	Mountain Home	(870)	12,448	12,569
*72113	North Little Rock	(501)	62,304	65,903
*72450	Paragould	(870)	26,113	28,986
*71601	Pine Bluff	(870)	49,083	41,474
*72756	Rogers	(479)	55,964	68,669
*72801	Russellville	(479)	27,920	29,115
*72143	Searcy	(501)	22,858	23,660
*72120	Sherwood	(501)	29,523	31,436
72761	Siloam Springs	(479)	15,039	17,101
*72764	Springdale	(479)	69,797	81,125
71854	Texarkana	(870)	29,919	29,657
*72956	Van Buren	(479)	22,791	23,683
*72301	West Memphis	(870)	26,245	24,402

California

Area code 279 overlays area code 916; 323 overlays 213; 341 overlays 510; 424 overlays 310; 442 overlays 760; 628 overlays 415; 657 overlays 714; 669 overlays 408; 747 overlays 818; 820 overlays 805; 840 overlays 909 effective May 23, 2021.

ZIP	Place	Area code	2010 population	2019 estimate
92301	Adelanto	(760)	31,765	34,049
*91301	Agoura Hills	(818)	20,330	20,222
*94501	Alameda	(510)	73,812	77,624
94507	Alamo (c)	(925)	14,570	—
*94706	Albany	(510)	18,539	19,696
*91801	Alhambra	(626)	83,089	83,750
*92656	Aliso Viejo	(949)	47,823	50,887
*91901	Alpine (c)	(619)	14,236	—
*91001	Altadena (c)	(626)	42,777	—
95127	Alum Rock (c)	(408)	15,536	—
*94503	American Canyon	(707)	19,454	20,475
*92805	Anaheim	(714)	336,265	350,365
96007	Anderson	(530)	9,932	10,630
95843	Antelope (c)	(916)	45,770	—
94509	Antioch	(925)	102,372	111,502
*92307	Apple Valley	(760)	69,135	73,453
*91006	Arcadia	(626)	56,364	57,939
*95521	Arcata	(707)	17,231	18,431
*95825	Arden-Arcade (c)	(916)	92,186	—
*93420	Arroyo Grande	(805)	17,252	17,976
*90701	Artesia	(562)	16,522	16,601
93203	Arvin	(661)	19,304	21,851
94541	Ashland (c)	(510)	21,925	—
*93422	Atascadero	(805)	28,310	30,075
95301	Atwater	(209)	28,168	29,559
*95603	Auburn	(530)	13,330	14,195
93204	Avenal	(559)	15,505	13,496
91746	Avocado Heights (c)	(626)	15,411	—
91702	Azusa	(626)	46,361	49,974
*93301	Bakersfield	(661)	347,483	384,145
91706	Baldwin Park	(626)	75,390	75,251
92220	Banning	(951)	29,603	31,221
*92310	Barstow	(760)	22,639	23,915
94565	Bay Point (c)	(925)	21,349	—
92223	Beaumont	(951)	36,877	51,063
*90201	Bell	(323)	35,477	35,521
*90201	Bell Gardens	(213)/(562)	42,072	42,012
*90706	Bellflower	(562)	76,616	76,435
94002	Belmont	(650)	25,835	26,941
94510	Benicia	(707)	26,997	28,240
*94704	Berkeley	(510)	112,580	121,363
*90210	Beverly Hills	(310)	34,109	33,792
*92314	Big Bear City (c)	(909)	12,304	—
92316	Bloomington (c)	(909)	23,851	—
*92225	Blythe	(760)	20,817	19,682
*91902	Bonita (c)	(619)	12,538	—
92021	Bostonia (c)	(619)	15,379	—
92227	Brawley	(760)	24,953	26,227
*92821	Brea	(714)	39,282	43,255
94513	Brentwood	(925)	51,481	64,474
*90620	Buena Park	(714)	80,530	81,788
*91502	Burbank	(818)	103,340	102,511
*94010	Burlingame	(650)	28,806	30,889
*91301	Calabasas	(747)	23,058	23,853
*92231	Calexico	(760)	38,572	39,825
*93505	California City	(760)	14,120	14,198
*93010	Camarillo	(805)	65,201	69,888
95682	Cameron Park (c)	(530)	18,228	—
*92058	Camp Pendleton South (c)	(760)	10,616	—
*95008	Campbell	(408)	39,349	41,793
92587	Canyon Lake	(951)	10,561	11,280
95010	Capitola	(831)	9,918	10,010
*92008	Carlsbad	(760)	105,328	115,382
*95608	Carmichael (c)	(916)	61,762	—
93013	Carpinteria	(805)	13,040	13,385
*90745	Carson	(310)	91,714	91,394
*91941	Casa de Oro-Mt. Helix (c)	(619)	18,762	—
*91384	Castaic (c)	(661)	19,015	—
*94546	Castro Valley (c)	(510)	61,388	—
*92234	Cathedral City	(760)	51,200	55,007
95307	Ceres	(209)	45,417	48,706
90703	Cerritos	(562)	49,041	49,859
*94541	Cherryland (c)	(510)	14,728	—
*95926	Chico	(530)	86,187	103,301
*91708	Chino	(909)	77,983	94,371
91709	Chino Hills	(909)	74,799	83,853
93610	Chowchilla	(559)	18,720	18,310
*91910	Chula Vista	(619)	243,916	274,492
91702	Citrus (c)	(626)	10,866	—
*95610	Citrus Heights	(916)	83,301	87,796
91711	Claremont	(909)	34,926	36,266
94517	Clayton	(925)	10,897	12,265
95422	Clearlake	(707)	15,250	15,267
*93612	Clovis	(559)	95,631	114,584
92236	Coachella	(760)	40,704	45,743
93210	Coalinga	(559)	13,380	17,179
92324	Colton	(909)	52,154	54,824
*90040	Commerce	(323)	12,823	12,661
*90220	Compton	(310)	96,455	95,605
*94520	Concord	(925)	122,067	129,295
*93212	Corcoran	(559)	24,813	21,960
*92882	Corona	(951)	152,374	169,868
92118	Coronado	(619)	18,912	23,731
*92626	Costa Mesa	(714)/(949)	109,960	113,003
92679	Coto de Caza (c)	(949)	14,866	—
*91722	Covina	(626)	47,796	47,450
92325	Crestline (c)	(909)	10,770	—
90201	Cudahy	(213)	23,805	23,569
*90230	Culver City	(310)	38,883	39,185
*90630	Cypress	(714)	47,802	49,006
*94015	Daly City	(415)/(650)	101,123	106,280
92629	Dana Point	(949)	33,351	33,577
*94526	Danville	(925)	42,039	44,510
*95616	Davis	(530)	65,622	69,413
90250	Del Aire (c)	(310)/(323)	10,001	—
*93215	Delano	(661)	53,041	53,573
95315	Delhi (c)	(209)	10,755	—
*92240	Desert Hot Springs	(760)	25,938	28,878
*91765	Diamond Bar	(909)	55,544	55,720
95619	Diamond Springs (c)	(530)	11,037	—
93618	Dinuba	(559)	21,453	24,461
*94514	Discovery Bay (c)	(925)	13,352	—
95620	Dixon	(707)	18,351	20,698
*90240	Downey	(562)	111,772	111,126
*91008	Duarte	(626)	21,321	21,271
94568	Dublin	(925)	46,036	64,826
92544	East Hemet (c)	(951)	17,418	—
90022	East Los Angeles (c)	(213)	126,496	—
94303	East Palo Alto	(650)	28,155	29,314
90221	East Rancho Dominguez (c)	(310)/(323)	15,135	—
91775	East San Gabriel (c)	(626)	14,874	—
*91752	Eastvale[1]	(909)/(951)	53,712	64,157
*92020	El Cajon	(619)	99,478	102,708
*92243	El Centro	(760)	42,598	44,079
94530	El Cerrito	(510)	23,549	25,508
95762	El Dorado Hills (c)	(916)	42,108	—
*91731	El Monte	(626)	113,475	115,487

ZIP	Place	Area code	2010 population	2019 estimate
*93446	El Paso de Robles (Paso Robles)	(805)	29,793	32,153
90245	El Segundo	(310)	16,654	16,610
*94803	El Sobrante (c) (Contra Costa Co.)	(510)	12,669	—
92503	El Sobrante (c) (Riverside Co.)	(714)/(909)	12,723	—
*95624	Elk Grove	(916)	153,015	174,775
*94608	Emeryville	(510)	10,080	12,086
*92024	Encinitas	(760)	59,518	62,709
*92025	Escondido	(760)	143,911	151,625
*95501	Eureka	(707)	27,191	26,710
93221	Exeter (c)	(559)	10,334	10,485
95628	Fair Oaks (c)	(916)	30,912	—
*94533	Fairfield	(707)	105,321	117,133
94541	Fairview (c)	(510)	10,003	—
*92028	Fallbrook (c)	(760)	30,534	—
93223	Farmersville	(559)	10,588	10,703
*93015	Fillmore	(805)	15,002	15,870
90001	Florence-Graham (c)	(213)	63,387	—
95828	Florin (c)	(916)	47,513	—
*95630	Folsom	(916)	72,203	81,328
*92335	Fontana	(909)	196,069	214,547
95841	Foothill Farms (c)	(916)	33,121	—
95540	Fortuna	(707)	11,926	12,259
94404	Foster City	(650)	30,567	33,901
*92704	Fountain Valley	(714)	55,313	55,357
*94538	Fremont	(510)	214,089	241,110
92596	French Valley (c)	(951)	23,067	—
*93721	Fresno	(559)	494,665	531,576
*92831	Fullerton	(714)	135,161	138,632
95632	Galt	(209)	23,647	26,536
95215	Garden Acres (c)	(209)	10,648	—
*92840	Garden Grove	(714)	170,883	171,644
*90247	Gardena	(310)	58,829	59,329
*95020	Gilroy	(408)	48,821	59,032
*91201	Glendale	(818)	191,719	199,303
*91741	Glendora	(626)	50,073	51,544
*93117	Goleta	(805)	29,888	30,911
*92313	Grand Terrace	(951)	12,040	12,584
*95746	Granite Bay (c)	(916)	20,402	—
*95945	Grass Valley	(530)	12,860	12,817
93927	Greenfield	(831)	16,330	17,516
*93433	Grover Beach	(805)	13,156	13,459
91745	Hacienda Heights (c)	(626)	54,038	—
94019	Half Moon Bay	(650)	11,324	12,932
*93230	Hanford	(559)	53,967	57,703
90716	Hawaiian Gardens	(562)	14,254	14,159
*90250	Hawthorne	(310)	84,293	86,068
*94541	Hayward	(510)	144,186	159,203
95448	Healdsburg	(707)	11,254	11,845
*92543	Hemet	(951)	78,657	85,334
94547	Hercules	(510)	24,060	26,276
90254	Hermosa Beach	(310)	19,506	19,320
*92344	Hesperia	(760)	90,173	95,750
92346	Highland	(909)	53,104	55,417
94010	Hillsborough	(650)	10,825	11,387
*95023	Hollister	(831)	34,928	40,740
92879	Home Gardens (c)	(909)	11,570	—
*92647	Huntington Beach	(714)	189,992	199,223
90255	Huntington Park	(323)	58,114	57,509
92251	Imperial	(760)	14,758	18,120
*91932	Imperial Beach	(619)	26,324	27,440
*92201	Indio	(760)	76,036	91,765
*90301	Inglewood	(310)	109,673	108,151
*92602	Irvine	(949)	212,375	287,401
93117	Isla Vista (c)	(805)	23,096	—
*91752	Jurupa Valley[1]	(951)	94,986	109,527
93630	Kerman	(559)	13,544	15,282
93930	King City	(831)	12,874	14,077
93631	Kingsburg	(559)	11,382	12,108
*91011	La Cañada Flintridge	(818)	20,246	20,009
*91214	La Crescenta-Montrose (c)	(818)	19,653	—
*90631	La Habra	(562)	60,239	60,513
*91941	La Mesa	(619)	57,065	59,249
*90638	La Mirada	(562)/(714)	48,527	48,183
90623	La Palma	(714)	15,568	15,428
91977	La Presa (c)	(619)	34,169	—
*91744	La Puente	(626)	39,816	39,614
*92253	La Quinta	(760)	37,467	41,748
95401	La Riviera (c)	(916)	10,802	—
91750	La Verne	(909)	31,063	31,974
92694	Ladera Ranch (c)	(949)	22,980	—
94549	Lafayette	(925)	23,893	26,638
*92651	Laguna Beach	(949)	22,723	22,827
92653	Laguna Hills	(949)	30,344	31,207
*92677	Laguna Niguel	(949)	62,979	66,385
*92637	Laguna Woods	(949)	16,192	15,850
92352	Lake Arrowhead (c)	(909)	12,424	—
*92530	Lake Elsinore	(951)	51,821	69,283
*92630	Lake Forest	(949)	77,264	85,531
*93535	Lake Los Angeles (c)	(661)	12,328	—
92530	Lakeland Village (c)	(909)/(951)	11,541	—
92040	Lakeside (c)	(619)	20,648	—
*90712	Lakewood	(562)	80,048	79,307
93241	Lamont (c)	(661)	15,120	—
*93534	Lancaster	(661)	156,633	157,601
*94939	Larkspur	(415)	11,926	12,254
95330	Lathrop	(209)	18,023	24,483
*90260	Lawndale	(310)	32,769	32,389
*91945	Lemon Grove	(619)	25,320	26,811
95824	Lemon Hill (c)	(916)	13,729	—
*93245	Lemoore	(559)	24,531	26,725
90304	Lennox (c)	(310)	22,753	—
95648	Lincoln	(916)	42,819	48,275
95901	Linda (c)	(530)	17,773	—
93247	Lindsay	(559)	11,768	13,463
95953	Live Oak (c)	(530)	17,158	—
*94550	Livermore	(925)	80,968	90,189
95334	Livingston	(209)	13,058	14,896
*95240	Lodi	(209)	62,134	67,586
*92354	Loma Linda	(909)	23,261	24,482
90717	Lomita	(310)	20,256	20,320
*93436	Lompoc	(805)	42,434	42,853
*90802	Long Beach	(562)	462,257	462,628
*90720	Los Alamitos	(562)	11,449	11,399
*94022	Los Altos	(650)	28,976	30,089
*90012	Los Angeles	(213)	3,792,621	3,979,576
93635	Los Banos	(209)	35,972	41,036
*95030	Los Gatos	(408)	29,413	30,222
*93402	Los Osos (c)	(805)	14,276	—
90262	Lynwood	(310)	69,772	69,887
*93638	Madera	(559)	61,416	65,860
95954	Magalia (c)	(530)	11,310	—
*90265	Malibu	(310)	12,645	11,820
*90266	Manhattan Beach	(310)	35,135	35,183
*95336	Manteca	(209)	67,096	83,028
93933	Marina	(831)	19,718	22,781
94553	Martinez	(925)	35,824	38,297
95901	Marysville	(530)	12,072	12,476
90270	Maywood	(323)	27,395	26,973
93250	McFarland	(661)	12,707	15,506
*95521	McKinleyville (c)	(707)	15,177	—
92570	Mead Valley (c)	(951)	18,510	—
93640	Mendota	(559)	11,014	11,511
*92586	Menifee	(951)	77,519	94,756
*94025	Menlo Park	(650)	32,026	34,698
*95340	Merced	(209)	78,958	83,676
94941	Mill Valley	(415)	13,903	14,259
94030	Millbrae	(650)	21,532	22,394
*95035	Milpitas	(408)	66,790	84,196
91752	Mira Loma (c)	(951)	21,930	—
*92691	Mission Viejo	(949)	93,305	94,381
*95350	Modesto	(209)	201,165	215,196
91016	Monrovia	(626)	36,590	36,331
*91763	Montclair	(909)	36,664	40,083
90640	Montebello	(323)	62,500	61,954
*93940	Monterey	(831)	27,810	28,178
*91754	Monterey Park	(323)/(626)	60,269	59,669
*93021	Moorpark	(805)	34,421	36,375
*94556	Moraga	(925)	16,016	17,783
*92551	Moreno Valley	(951)	193,365	213,055
*95037	Morgan Hill	(408)	37,882	45,952
*93442	Morro Bay	(805)	10,234	10,543
*94041	Mountain View	(650)	74,066	82,739
*92562	Murrieta	(951)	103,466	116,223
92407	Muscoy (c)	(909)	10,644	—
*94558	Napa	(707)	76,915	78,130
*91950	National City	(619)	58,582	61,394
94560	Newark	(510)	42,573	49,149
95360	Newman	(209)	10,224	11,784
*92657	Newport Beach	(949)	85,186	84,534
93444	Nipomo (c)	(805)	16,714	—
92860	Norco	(951)	27,063	26,604
95603	North Auburn (c)	(530)	13,022	—
94025	North Fair Oaks (c)	(650)	14,687	—
95660	North Highlands (c)	(916)	42,694	—
92705	North Tustin (c)	(714)	24,917	—
*90650	Norwalk	(562)	105,549	103,949
*94947	Novato	(415)	51,904	55,516
*91377	Oak Park (c)	(805)/(818)	13,811	—
95361	Oakdale	(209)	20,675	23,596
*94601	Oakland	(510)	390,724	433,031
94561	Oakley	(925)	35,432	42,543
*92054	Oceanside	(760)	167,086	175,742
93308	Oildale (c)	(661)	32,684	—
95961	Olivehurst (c)	(530)	13,656	—
*91761	Ontario	(909)	163,924	185,010
*92866	Orange	(714)	136,416	138,669

ZIP	Place	Area code	2010 population	2019 estimate
*93646	Orange Cove	(559)	9,078	10,273
95662	Orangevale (c)	(916)	33,960	—
*93455	Orcutt (c)	(805)	28,905	—
94563	Orinda	(925)	17,643	19,926
*95965	Oroville	(530)	15,546	20,737
*93030	Oxnard	(805)	197,899	208,881
93950	Pacific Grove	(831)	15,041	15,413
94044	Pacifica	(650)	37,234	38,546
*92260	Palm Desert	(760)	48,445	53,275
*92262	Palm Springs	(760)	44,552	48,518
*93550	Palmdale	(661)	152,750	155,079
*94303	Palo Alto	(650)	64,403	65,364
*90274	Palos Verdes Estates	(310)	13,438	13,273
*95969	Paradise	(530)	26,218	4,476[2]
90723	Paramount	(562)	54,098	53,955
95823	Parkway (c)	(916)	14,670	—
93648	Parlier	(559)	14,494	15,618
*91101	Pasadena	(323)/(626)	137,122	141,029
	Paso Robles. *See* El Paso de Robles			
95363	Patterson	(209)	20,413	22,524
92509	Pedley (c)	(951)	12,672	—
*92570	Perris	(951)	68,386	79,291
*94952	Petaluma	(707)	57,941	60,520
*92371	Phelan (c)	(760)	14,304	—
*90660	Pico Rivera	(562)	62,942	62,027
*94611	Piedmont	(510)	10,667	11,135
94564	Pinole	(510)	18,390	19,250
94565	Pittsburg	(925)	63,264	72,588
*92870	Placentia	(714)	50,533	51,233
95667	Placerville	(530)	10,389	11,175
94523	Pleasant Hill	(925)	33,152	34,839
*94566	Pleasanton	(925)	70,285	81,777
*91765	Pomona	(909)	149,058	151,691
*93041	Port Hueneme	(805)	21,723	21,926
*93257	Porterville	(559)	54,165	59,599
*92064	Poway	(858)	47,811	49,323
93907	Prunedale (c)	(831)	17,560	—
*93536	Quartz Hill (c)	(661)	10,912	—
92065	Ramona (c)	(760)	20,292	—
*95670	Rancho Cordova	(916)	64,776	75,087
*91730	Rancho Cucamonga	(909)	165,269	177,603
92270	Rancho Mirage	(760)	17,218	18,528
90275	Rancho Palos Verdes	(310)	41,643	41,530
*92019	Rancho San Diego (c)	(619)	21,208	—
92688	Rancho Santa Margarita	(949)	47,853	47,896
96080	Red Bluff	(530)	14,076	14,539
*96001	Redding	(530)	89,861	92,590
*92373	Redlands	(909)	68,747	71,513
*90277	Redondo Beach	(310)	66,748	66,749
*94063	Redwood City	(650)	76,815	85,925
93654	Reedley	(559)	24,194	25,658
*92376	Rialto	(909)	99,171	103,526
*94801	Richmond	(510)	103,701	110,567
*93555	Ridgecrest	(760)	27,616	28,973
95673	Rio Linda (c)	(916)	15,106	—
95366	Ripon	(209)	14,297	16,386
95367	Riverbank	(209)	22,678	24,881
*92501	Riverside	(951)	303,871	331,360
*95677	Rocklin	(916)	56,974	68,823
*94928	Rohnert Park	(707)	40,971	43,291
93560	Rosamond (c)	(661)	18,150	—
93314	Rosedale (c)	(661)	14,058	—
*91770	Rosemead	(626)	53,764	54,058
95826	Rosemont (c)	(916)	22,681	—
*95678	Roseville	(916)	118,788	141,500
90720	Rossmoor (c)	(714)	10,244	—
91748	Rowland Heights (c)	(626)	48,993	—
92509	Rubidoux (c)	(951)	34,280	—
*95814	Sacramento	(916)	466,488	513,624
95368	Salida (c)	(209)	13,722	—
*93901	Salinas	(831)	150,441	155,465
*94960	San Anselmo	(415)	12,336	12,476
*92401	San Bernardino	(909)	209,924	215,784
94066	San Bruno	(650)	41,114	42,807
*93001	San Buenaventura (Ventura)	(805)	106,433	109,106
94070	San Carlos	(650)	28,406	30,185
92672	San Clemente	(949)	63,522	64,558
*92101	San Diego	(619)/(858)	1,307,402	1,423,851
92065	San Diego Country Estates (c)	(760)	10,109	—
91773	San Dimas	(909)	33,371	33,621
*91340	San Fernando	(818)	23,645	24,322
*94102	San Francisco	(415)	805,235	881,549
*91775	San Gabriel	(626)	39,718	39,899
*92582	San Jacinto	(951)	44,199	49,215
*95113	San Jose	(408)	945,942	1,021,795
*92675	San Juan Capistrano	(949)	34,593	35,911
*94577	San Leandro	(510)	84,950	88,815
94580	San Lorenzo (c)	(510)	23,452	—
*93401	San Luis Obispo	(805)	45,119	47,459
*92069	San Marcos	(760)	83,781	96,664
*91108	San Marino	(626)	13,147	13,048
*94403	San Mateo	(650)	97,207	104,430
*94806	San Pablo	(510)	29,139	30,990
*94901	San Rafael	(415)	57,713	58,440
*94583	San Ramon	(925)	72,148	75,995
93657	Sanger	(559)	24,270	25,339
*92701	Santa Ana	(714)/(949)	324,528	332,318
*93101	Santa Barbara	(805)	88,410	91,364
95050	Santa Clara	(408)	116,468	130,365
*91355	Santa Clarita	(661)	176,320	212,979
*95060	Santa Cruz	(831)	59,946	64,608
90670	Santa Fe Springs	(562)	16,223	17,630
*93454	Santa Maria	(805)	99,553	107,263
*90401	Santa Monica	(310)	89,736	90,401
*93060	Santa Paula	(805)	29,321	29,806
*95401	Santa Rosa	(707)	167,815	176,753
*92071	Santee	(619)	53,413	58,081
*95070	Saratoga	(408)	29,926	30,153
*95066	Scotts Valley	(831)	11,580	11,757
90740	Seal Beach	(562)	24,168	23,896
*93955	Seaside	(831)	33,025	33,748
93662	Selma	(559)	23,219	24,825
93263	Shafter	(661)	16,988	20,401
*96019	Shasta Lake	(916)	10,164	10,413
*91024	Sierra Madre	(626)	10,917	10,793
90755	Signal Hill	(562)	11,016	11,421
*93065	Simi Valley	(805)	124,237	125,613
92075	Solana Beach	(858)	12,867	13,296
93960	Soledad	(831)	25,738	25,999
95476	Sonoma	(707)	10,648	11,024
91733	South El Monte	(626)	20,116	20,574
90280	South Gate	(323)	94,396	93,444
96150	South Lake Tahoe	(530)	21,403	22,197
*91030	South Pasadena	(323)/(626)	25,619	25,329
*94080	South San Francisco	(650)	63,632	67,789
91744	South San Jose Hills (c)	(626)	20,551	—
90605	South Whittier (c)	(562)	57,156	—
*91977	Spring Valley (c) (San Diego Co.)	(619)	28,205	—
*94305	Stanford (c)	(650)	13,809	—
90680	Stanton	(714)	38,186	38,139
91381	Stevenson Ranch (c)	(661)	17,557	—
*95202	Stockton	(209)	291,707	312,697
*94585	Suisun City	(707)	28,111	29,663
93543	Sun Village (c)	(661)	11,565	—
*94086	Sunnyvale	(408)	140,081	152,703
*96130	Susanville	(530)	17,947	15,010
94941	Tamalpais-Homestead Valley (c)	(415)	10,735	—
*93561	Tehachapi	(661)	14,414	13,011
*92590	Temecula	(951)	100,097	114,761
92883	Temescal Valley (c)	(951)	22,535	—
91780	Temple City	(626)	35,558	35,811
*91360	Thousand Oaks	(805)	126,683	126,813
*90053	Torrance	(310)	145,438	143,592
*95376	Tracy	(209)	82,922	94,740
*96161	Truckee	(530)	16,180	16,735
*93274	Tulare	(559)	59,278	65,496
*95380	Turlock	(209)	68,549	73,631
*92780	Tustin	(714)/(949)	75,540	79,348
*92277	Twentynine Palms	(760)	25,048	26,073
95482	Ukiah	(707)	16,075	15,995
94587	Union City	(510)	69,516	74,107
*91784	Upland	(909)	73,732	77,140
*95687	Vacaville	(707)	92,428	100,670
91744	Valinda (c)	(626)	22,822	—
92343	Valle Vista (c)	(951)	14,578	—
*94590	Vallejo	(707)	115,942	121,692
	Ventura. *See* San Buenaventura			
*92392	Victorville	(760)	115,903	122,385
*90043	View Park-Windsor Hills (c)	(213)	11,075	—
91722	Vincent (c)	(925)	15,922	—
95829	Vineyard (c)	(916)	24,836	—
*93277	Visalia	(559)	124,442	134,605
92084	Vista	(760)	93,834	101,638
*91789	Walnut	(909)	29,172	29,685
*94596	Walnut Creek	(925)	64,173	70,166
90255	Walnut Park (c)	(213)	15,966	—
93280	Wasco	(661)	25,545	28,710
*95076	Watsonville	(831)	51,199	53,856
90502	West Carson (c)	(310)	21,699	—
*91790	West Covina	(626)	106,098	105,101
*90069	West Hollywood	(310)/(323)	34,399	36,475
91746	West Puente Valley (c)	(626)	22,636	—
*95591	West Sacramento	(916)	48,744	53,519
*90606	West Whittier-Los Nietos (c)	(562)	25,540	—
*92683	Westminster	(714)	89,701	90,643
*90047	Westmont (c)	(213)	31,853	—
*90602	Whittier	(562)	85,331	85,098
92595	Wildomar	(951)	32,176	37,229

ZIP	Place	Area code	2010 population	2019 estimate
*90222	Willowbrook (c)	(323)	35,983	—
95492	Windsor	(707)	26,801	27,128
92040	Winter Gardens (c)	(619)	20,631	—
95388	Winton (c)	(209)	10,613	—
92504	Woodcrest (c)	(909)/(951)	14,347	—
*95695	Woodland	(530)	55,468	60,548
*92886	Yorba Linda	(714)	64,234	67,644
*95991	Yuba City	(530)	64,925	67,010
92399	Yucaipa	(909)	51,367	53,921
*92284	Yucca Valley	(760)	20,700	21,777

(1) Incorporated after 2010 Census; 2010 figure is Census Bureau est. (2) Pop. decline due to 2018 wildfire disaster.

Colorado
Area code 720 overlays area code 303.

ZIP	Place	Area code	2010 population	2019 estimate
*80004	Arvada	(303)	106,433	121,272
*80010	Aurora	(303)	325,078	379,289
80221	Berkley (c)	(970)	11,207	—
*80908	Black Forest (c)	(719)	13,116	—
*80302	Boulder	(303)	97,385	105,673
*80601	Brighton	(303)	33,352	41,554
*80020	Broomfield	(303)	55,889	70,465
*81212	Cañon City	(719)	16,400	16,725
80108	Castle Pines[1]	(303)	10,333	10,763
*80104	Castle Rock	(303)	48,231	68,484
*80015	Centennial	(303)	100,377	110,937
80206	Cherry Creek (c)	(303)	11,120	—
80915	Cimarron Hills (c)	(719)	16,161	—
81520	Clifton (c)	(970)	19,889	—
*80903	Colorado Springs	(719)	416,427	478,221
*80128	Columbine (c)	(303)	24,280	—
*80022	Commerce City	(303)	45,913	60,336
80127	Dakota Ridge (c)	(303)	32,005	—
*80202	Denver	(303)	600,158	727,211
*81301	Durango	(970)	16,887	18,973
81632	Edwards (c)	(970)	10,266	—
*80110	Englewood	(303)	30,255	34,917
*80516	Erie	(303)	18,135	27,003
*80620	Evans	(970)	18,537	21,205
*80260	Federal Heights	(303)	11,467	12,827
*80504	Firestone	(303)	10,147	16,177
*80913	Fort Carson (c)	(719)	13,813	—
*80521	Fort Collins	(970)	143,986	170,243
*80701	Fort Morgan	(970)	11,315	11,463
80817	Fountain	(719)	25,846	30,735
*80530	Frederick	(303)	8,679	13,960
81521	Fruita	(970)	12,646	13,478
*80401	Golden	(303)	18,867	20,767
*81501	Grand Junction	(970)	58,566	63,597
*80631	Greeley	(970)	92,889	108,649
*80111	Greenwood Village	(303)	13,925	15,735
*80126	Highlands Ranch (c)	(303)	96,713	—
80534	Johnstown	(970)	9,887	15,198
*80127	Ken Caryl (c)	(303)	32,438	—
80026	Lafayette	(303)	24,453	30,687
*80226	Lakewood	(303)	142,980	157,935
*80120	Littleton	(303)	41,737	48,065
*80124	Lone Tree	(303)	10,218	13,082
*80501	Longmont	(303)	86,270	97,261
80027	Louisville	(303)	18,376	20,816
*80537	Loveland	(970)	66,859	78,877
*81401	Montrose	(970)	19,132	19,782
*80233	Northglenn	(303)	35,789	38,819
*80134	Parker	(303)	45,297	57,706
*81003	Pueblo	(719)	106,595	-112,361
81007	Pueblo West (c)	(719)	29,637	—
80911	Security-Widefield (c)	(719)	32,882	—
80221	Sherrelwood (c)	(303)	18,287	—
*80487	Steamboat Springs	(970)	12,088	13,214
80751	Sterling	(970)	14,777	14,495
80027	Superior	(303)	12,483	13,087
80134	The Pinery (c)	(303)	10,517	—
*80229	Thornton	(303)	118,772	141,464
80229	Welby (c)	(303)	14,846	—
80549	Wellington	(970)	6,289	10,437
*80031	Westminster	(303)	106,114	113,166
*80033	Wheat Ridge	(303)	30,166	31,324
*80550	Windsor	(970)	18,644	30,477

(1) Incorporated after 2010 Census; 2010 figure is Census Bureau est.

Connecticut
Area code 475 overlays area code 203; 959 overlays 860. See introductory note.

ZIP	Place	Area code	2010 population	2019 estimate
06401	Ansonia	(203)	19,249	18,654
06001	Avon	(860)	18,098	18,276
06037	Berlin	(860)	19,866	20,436
06801	Bethel	(203)	18,584	19,800
06002	Bloomfield	(860)	20,486	21,211
06405	Branford	(203)	28,026	27,900
*06604	Bridgeport	(203)	144,229	144,399
*06010	Bristol	(860)	60,477	59,947
06804	Brookfield	(203)	16,452	16,973
06019	Canton	(860)	10,292	10,254
*06410	Cheshire	(203)	29,261	28,937
06413	Clinton	(203)	13,260	12,925
*06415	Colchester	(860)	16,068	15,809
06238	Coventry	(860)	12,435	12,407
06416	Cromwell	(860)	14,005	13,839
*06810	Danbury	(203)	80,893	84,694
06820	Darien	(203)	20,732	21,728
06418	Derby	(203)	12,902	12,339
*06424	East Hampton	(860)	12,959	12,800
*06108	East Hartford	(860)	51,252	49,872
*06512	East Haven	(203)	29,257	28,569
06333	East Lyme	(860)	19,159	18,462
06088	East Windsor	(860)	11,162	11,668
06029	Ellington	(860)	15,602	16,467
*06082	Enfield	(860)	44,654	43,659
*06824	Fairfield	(203)	59,404	62,045
*06032	Farmington	(860)	25,340	25,497
06033	Glastonbury	(860)	34,427	34,482
06035	Granby	(860)	11,282	11,507
*06830	Greenwich	(203)	61,171	62,840
*06830	Greenwich (c)	(203)	12,942	—
06351	Griswold	(860)	11,951	11,534
*06340	Groton	(860)	40,115	38,436
06437	Guilford	(203)	22,375	22,133
*06514	Hamden	(203)	60,960	60,556
*06103	Hartford	(860)	124,775	122,105
*06239	Killingly	(860)	17,370	17,336
06443	Madison	(203)	18,269	18,030
*06040	Manchester	(860)	58,241	57,584
*06040	Manchester (c)	(860)	30,577	—
*06250	Mansfield	(860)	26,543	25,487
*06450	Meriden	(203)	60,868	59,395
*06457	Middletown	(860)	47,648	46,258
*06460	Milford (balance)	(203)	51,271	53,195
*06460	Milford	(203)	52,759	54,747
06468	Monroe	(203)	19,479	19,434
06353	Montville	(860)	19,571	18,508
06770	Naugatuck	(203)	31,862	31,108
*06051	New Britain	(860)	73,206	72,495
06840	New Canaan	(203)	19,738	20,233
06812	New Fairfield	(203)	13,881	13,878
*06511	New Haven	(203)	129,779	130,250
06320	New London	(860)	27,620	26,858
06776	New Milford	(860)	28,142	26,805
*06111	Newington	(860)	30,562	30,014
06470	Newtown	(203)	27,560	27,891
06471	North Branford	(203)	14,407	14,146
06473	North Haven	(203)	24,093	23,683
*06850	Norwalk	(203)	85,603	88,816
*06360	Norwich	(860)	40,493	38,768
06475	Old Saybrook	(860)	10,242	10,061
06477	Orange	(203)	13,956	13,926
06478	Oxford	(203)	12,683	13,255
06374	Plainfield	(860)	15,405	15,125
06062	Plainville	(860)	17,716	17,534
06782	Plymouth	(860)	12,243	11,598
*06877	Ridgefield	(203)	24,638	24,959
06067	Rocky Hill	(860)	19,709	20,115
*06483	Seymour	(203)	16,540	16,437
06484	Shelton	(203)	39,559	41,129
06070	Simsbury	(860)	23,511	25,395
06071	Somers	(860)	11,444	10,784
06074	South Windsor	(860)	25,709	26,162
06488	Southbury	(203)	19,904	19,571
06489	Southington	(860)	43,069	43,834
*06075	Stafford	(860)	12,087	11,893
*06901	Stamford	(203)	122,643	129,638
06378	Stonington	(860)	18,545	18,559
*06268	Storrs (c)	(860)	15,344	—
*06614	Stratford	(203)	51,384	51,849
*06078	Suffield	(860)	15,735	15,814
06084	Tolland	(860)	15,052	14,618
*06790	Torrington	(860)	36,383	34,044
*06611	Trumbull	(203)	36,018	35,673
06066	Vernon	(860)	29,179	29,359
*06492	Wallingford	(203)	45,135	44,326
*06492	Wallingford Center (c)	(203)	18,209	—
*06702	Waterbury	(203)	110,366	107,568
06385	Waterford	(860)	19,517	18,746
*06795	Watertown	(860)	22,514	21,578
*06105	West Hartford	(860)	63,268	62,965

ZIP	Place	Area code	2010 population	2019 estimate
06516	West Haven	(203)	55,564	54,620
06883	Weston	(203)	10,179	10,252
*06880	Westport	(203)	26,391	28,491
*06109	Wethersfield	(860)	26,668	26,008
06226	Willimantic (c)	(860)	17,737	—
06897	Wilton	(203)	18,062	18,343
*06098	Winchester	(860)	11,242	10,604
06280	Windham	(860)	25,268	24,561
*06095	Windsor	(860)	29,044	28,733
06096	Windsor Locks	(860)	12,498	12,854
*06716	Wolcott	(203)	16,680	16,587

Delaware

Area code 302 applies to the entire state.

ZIP	Place	2010 population	2019 estimate
19701	Bear (c)	19,371	—
19713	Brookside (c)	14,353	—
*19901	Dover	36,047	38,166
19702	Glasgow (c)	14,303	—
19707	Hockessin (c)	13,527	—
19709	Middletown	18,871	22,900
19963	Milford	9,559	11,732
*19711	Newark	31,454	33,515
19808	Pike Creek Valley (c)	11,217	—
19977	Smyrna	10,023	11,813
*19801	Wilmington	70,851	70,166

District of Columbia

Area code 202 applies to the entire district.

ZIP	Place	2010 population	2019 estimate
*20001	Washington	601,723	705,749

Florida

Part of area code 321 overlays area code 407; 448 overlays 850 effective Mar. 30, 2021; 689 overlays 407; 754 overlays 954; 786 overlays 305.

ZIP	Place	Area code	2010 population	2019 estimate
*32828	Alafaya (c)	(407)	78,113	—
*32701	Altamonte Springs	(407)	41,496	44,143
33572	Apollo Beach (c)	(813)	14,055	—
*32712	Apopka	(407)	41,542	53,447
32233	Atlantic Beach	(904)	12,655	13,872
33823	Auburndale	(863)	13,507	16,650
*33180	Aventura	(305)	35,762	36,987
*33825	Avon Park	(863)	8,836	10,689
32807	Azalea Park (c)	(407)	12,556	—
*33830	Bartow	(863)	17,298	20,147
34667	Bayonet Point (c)	(727)	23,467	—
34207	Bayshore Gardens (c)	(941)	16,323	—
32073	Bellair-Meadowbrook Terrace (c)	(904)	13,343	—
33430	Belle Glade	(561)	17,467	20,134
32526	Bellview (c)	(850)	23,355	—
*33509	Bloomingdale (c)	(813)	22,711	—
*33431	Boca Raton	(561)	84,392	99,805
34135	Bonita Springs	(239)	43,914	59,637
*33436	Boynton Beach	(561)	68,217	78,679
*34201	Bradenton	(941)	49,546	59,439
*33510	Brandon (c)	(813)	103,483	—
32503	Brent (c)	(850)	21,804	—
33142	Brownsville (c)	(305)	15,313	—
34743	Buenaventura Lakes (c)	(407)	26,079	—
32404	Callaway	(850)	14,405	14,060
32920	Cape Canaveral	(321)	9,912	10,470
*33990	Cape Coral	(239)	154,305	194,495
*33618	Carrollwood (c)	(813)	33,365	—
*32707	Casselberry	(407)	26,241	28,757
33558	Cheval (c)	(813)	10,702	—
33625	Citrus Park (c)	(813)	24,252	—
*33755	Clearwater	(727)	107,685	116,946
*34711	Clermont	(352)	28,742	38,654
32922	Cocoa	(321)	17,140	18,603
*32931	Cocoa Beach	(321)	11,231	11,705
*33063	Coconut Creek	(954)	52,909	61,248
32809	Conway (c)	(407)	13,467	—
*33328	Cooper City	(954)	28,547	35,800
*33134	Coral Gables	(305)	46,780	49,700
*33065	Coral Springs	(954)	121,096	133,759
33155	Coral Terrace (c)	(305)	24,376	—
33015	Country Club (c)	(305)	47,105	—
33196	Country Walk (c)	(305)	15,997	—
*32536	Crestview	(850)	20,978	25,274
*33189	Cutler Bay (c)	(305)	40,286	43,718
33919	Cypress Lake (c)	(239)	11,846	—
*33004	Dania Beach	(954)	29,639	32,271
*33314	Davie	(954)	91,992	106,306
*32114	Daytona Beach	(386)	61,005	69,186
*32713	DeBary	(386)	19,320	21,305
*33441	Deerfield Beach	(954)	75,018	81,066
*32720	DeLand	(386)	27,031	34,851
*33444	Delray Beach	(561)	60,522	69,451
*32738	Deltona	(386)	85,182	92,757
32541	Destin	(850)	12,305	14,247
*32819	Doctor Phillips (c)	(407)	10,981	—
33166	Doral	(305)	45,704	65,741
*34698	Dunedin	(727)	35,321	36,537
*34685	East Lake (c)	(727)	30,962	—
33619	East Lake-Orient Park (c)	(813)	22,753	—
32583	East Milton (c)	(850)	11,074	—
*32132	Edgewater	(386)	20,750	23,918
33614	Egypt Lake-Leto (c)	(813)	35,282	—
34680	Elfers (c)	(727)	13,986	—
*34223	Englewood (c)	(941)	14,863	—
32534	Ensley (c)	(850)	20,602	—
*33928	Estero[1]	(239)	27,991	33,871
*32726	Eustis	(352)	18,558	21,303
32804	Fairview Shores (c)	(305)	10,239	—
*32034	Fernandina Beach	(904)	11,487	13,169
32514	Ferry Pass (c)	(850)	28,921	—
33547	Fish Hawk (c)	(813)	14,087	—
*32003	Fleming Island (c)	(904)	27,126	—
33034	Florida City	(305)	11,245	11,771
32960	Florida Ridge (c)	(772)	18,164	—
32714	Forest City (c)	(407)	13,854	—
*33301	Fort Lauderdale	(954)	165,521	182,437
*33901	Fort Myers	(239)	62,298	87,103
*34950	Fort Pierce	(772)	41,590	46,103
*32548	Fort Walton Beach	(850)	19,507	22,521
33172	Fountainebleau (c)	(305)	59,764	—
34747	Four Corners (c)	(863)	26,116	—
32259	Fruit Cove (c)	(904)	29,362	—
34731	Fruitland Park	(352)	4,078	10,730
34232	Fruitville (c)	(941)	13,224	—
*32601	Gainesville	(352)	124,354	133,997
33534	Gibsonton (c)	(813)	14,234	—
33138	Gladeview (c)	(954)	11,535	—
33143	Glenvar Heights (c)	(305)	16,898	—
34116	Golden Gate (c)	(239)	23,961	—
*33161	Golden Glades (c)	(305)	33,145	—
32733	Goldenrod (c)	(407)	12,039	—
32560	Gonzalez (c)	(850)	13,273	—
33170	Goulds (c)	(305)	10,103	—
*33463	Greenacres	(561)	37,573	41,117
*34736	Groveland	(352)	8,729	16,423
33581	Gulf Gate Estates (c)	(941)	10,911	—
*33707	Gulfport	(727)	12,029	12,342
*33844	Haines City	(863)	20,535	26,009
*33009	Hallandale Beach	(954)	37,113	39,847
*33010	Hialeah	(305)	224,669	233,339
33016	Hialeah Gardens	(305)	21,744	23,474
33846	Highland City (c)	(863)	10,834	—
*33455	Hobe Sound (c)	(772)	11,521	—
*34690	Holiday (c)	(727)	22,403	—
*33117	Holly Hill	(386)	11,659	12,357
*33019	Hollywood	(954)	140,768	154,817
*33030	Homestead	(305)	60,512	69,523
34446	Homosassa Springs (c)	(352)	13,791	—
34787	Horizon West (c)	(352)	14,000	—
*34667	Hudson (c)	(727)	12,158	—
32837	Hunters Creek (c)	(407)	14,321	—
34142	Immokalee (c)	(239)	24,154	—
33908	Iona (c)	(239)	15,369	—
33162	Ives Estates (c)	(305)	19,525	—
*32202	Jacksonville	(904)	821,784	911,507
*32250	Jacksonville Beach	(904)	21,362	23,628
33568	Jasmine Estates (c)	(727)	18,989	—
*34957	Jensen Beach (c)	(772)	11,707	—
*33458	Jupiter	(561)	55,156	65,791
33478	Jupiter Farms (c)	(561)	11,994	—
33183	Kendale Lakes (c)	(305)	56,148	—
*33156	Kendall (c)	(305)	75,371	—
33193	Kendall West (c)	(305)	36,154	—
33149	Key Biscayne	(305)	12,344	12,846
33037	Key Largo (c)	(305)	10,433	—
*33040	Key West	(305)	24,649	24,118
33556	Keystone (c)	(813)	24,039	—
*34741	Kissimmee	(407)	59,682	72,717
*32159	Lady Lake (c)	(352)	13,926	16,020
32054	Lake Butler (c)	(386)	15,400	—
32055	Lake City	(386)	12,046	12,352
33612	Lake Magdalene (c)	(813)	28,509	—
32746	Lake Mary	(407)	13,822	17,479
*33853	Lake Wales	(863)	14,225	16,759
*33460	Lake Worth	(561)	34,910	38,526
*33801	Lakeland	(863)	97,422	112,136

ZIP	Place	Area code	2010 population	2019 estimate
33801	Lakeland Highlands (c)...	(863)	11,056	—
32073	Lakeside (c)..........	(904)	30,943	—
34951	Lakewood Park (c)......	(772)	11,323	—
*34639	Land O' Lakes (c)......	(813)	31,996	—
*33462	Lantana.............	(561)	10,423	12,581
*33770	Largo...............	(727)	77,648	84,948
*33319	Lauderdale Lakes.......	(954)	32,593	36,194
*33313	Lauderhill...........	(954)	66,887	71,868
*33702	Lealman (c)...........	(727)	19,879	—
*34748	Leesburg............	(352)	20,117	23,671
*33936	Lehigh Acres (c)......	(239)	86,784	—
*33030	Leisure City (c).......	(305)	22,655	—
*33064	Lighthouse Point.......	(954)	10,344	11,270
32810	Lockhart (c)..........	(407)	13,060	—
*32750	Longwood............	(407)	13,657	15,561
*33549	Lutz (c)............	(813)	19,344	—
32444	Lynn Haven...........	(850)	18,493	20,525
*32751	Maitland............	(407)	15,751	17,652
33550	Mango (c)...........	(813)	11,313	—
*34145	Marco Island.........	(239)	16,413	17,947
*33063	Margate.............	(954)	53,284	58,796
32824	Meadow Woods (c)......	(407)	25,558	—
*32901	Melbourne...........	(321)	76,068	83,029
*32953	Merritt Island (c)......	(321)	34,743	—
*33125	Miami..............	(305)	399,457	467,963
*33140	Miami Beach..........	(305)	87,779	88,885
*33014	Miami Gardens........	(305)	107,167	110,001
*33014	Miami Lakes..........	(305)	29,361	31,367
*33138	Miami Shores.........	(305)	10,493	10,365
*33166	Miami Springs.........	(305)	13,809	13,917
*32068	Middleburg (c)........	(904)	13,008	—
32563	Midway (c) (Santa Rosa Co.)	(850)	16,115	—
*32570	Milton.............	(850)	8,826	10,523
34715	Minneola............	(352)	9,403	12,595
*33023	Miramar............	(305)	122,041	141,191
*32757	Mount Dora..........	(352)	12,370	14,516
32526	Myrtle Grove (c)......	(850)	15,870	—
*34102	Naples.............	(239)	19,537	22,088
32566	Navarre (c)..........	(850)	31,378	—
*34653	New Port Richey.......	(727)	14,911	16,737
34653	New Port Richey East (c)..	(727)	10,036	—
*32168	New Smyrna Beach......	(386)	22,464	27,843
*32578	Niceville...........	(850)	12,749	15,972
*33917	North Fort Myers (c)....	(239)	39,407	—
*33068	North Lauderdale.......	(954)	41,023	44,262
*33161	North Miami..........	(305)	58,786	62,822
*33160	North Miami Beach......	(305)	41,523	43,041
*33408	North Palm Beach......	(561)	12,015	13,127
*34286	North Port...........	(941)	57,357	70,724
*33624	Northdale (c).........	(813)	22,079	—
33860	Oak Ridge (c)........	(407)	22,685	—
*33334	Oakland Park.........	(954)	41,363	45,202
32065	Oakleaf Plantation (c)...	(904)	20,315	—
*34470	Ocala..............	(352)	56,315	60,786
34761	Ocoee..............	(407)	35,579	48,263
33163	Ojus (c)............	(305)	18,036	—
34677	Oldsmar............	(813)	13,591	15,061
*33265	Olympia Heights (c)....	(305)	13,488	—
*33054	Opa-locka...........	(305)	15,219	15,887
*32763	Orange City..........	(386)	10,599	12,335
*32801	Orlando............	(407)	238,300	287,442
*32174	Ormond Beach........	(386)	38,137	43,759
*32765	Oviedo.............	(407)	33,342	41,860
32571	Pace (c)............	(850)	20,039	—
*32177	Palatka............	(386)	10,558	10,451
*32905	Palm Bay............	(321)	103,190	115,552
*33410	Palm Beach Gardens.....	(561)	48,452	57,704
*34990	Palm City (c).........	(772)	23,120	—
*32137	Palm Coast...........	(386)	75,180	89,800
*34683	Palm Harbor (c).......	(727)	57,439	—
*33601	Palm River-Clair Mel (c)..	(813)	21,024	—
*33406	Palm Springs.........	(561)	18,928	25,216
32082	Palm Valley (c).......	(407)	20,019	—
*34221	Palmetto............	(941)	12,606	13,748
*33157	Palmetto Bay.........	(305)	23,410	24,523
33157	Palmetto Estates (c)....	(305)	13,535	—
*32401	Panama City..........	(850)	36,484	34,667
*32413	Panama City Beach......	(850)	12,018	12,583
*33067	Parkland............	(954)	23,962	34,170
*33026	Pembroke Pines........	(954)	154,750	173,591
*32502	Pensacola...........	(850)	51,923	52,975
*32809	Pine Castle (c).......	(407)	10,805	—
*32808	Pine Hills (c)........	(407)	60,076	—
*33156	Pinecrest...........	(305)	18,223	19,155
*33781	Pinellas Park.........	(727)	49,079	53,637
33168	Pinewood (c).........	(305)	16,520	—
*33566	Plant City...........	(813)	34,721	39,744
*33311	Plantation...........	(954)	84,955	94,580
*34758	Poinciana (c).........	(407)	53,193	—
*33060	Pompano Beach........	(954)	99,845	112,118
*33952	Port Charlotte (c).....	(941)	54,392	—

ZIP	Place	Area code	2010 population	2019 estimate
*32129	Port Orange..........	(386)	56,048	64,842
32927	Port St. John (c)......	(321)	12,267	—
*34953	Port St. Lucie........	(772)	164,603	201,846
34992	Port Salerno (c).......	(772)	10,091	—
*33032	Princeton (c).........	(305)	22,038	—
*33950	Punta Gorda..........	(941)	16,641	20,369
*33177	Richmond West (c).....	(305)	31,973	—
*33569	Riverview (c).........	(813)	71,050	—
*33404	Riviera Beach.........	(561)	32,488	35,463
*32955	Rockledge...........	(321)	24,926	28,227
*33411	Royal Palm Beach......	(561)	34,140	40,396
*33570	Ruskin (c)...........	(813)	17,208	—
34695	Safety Harbor........	(727)	16,884	18,016
*32084	Saint Augustine.......	(904)	12,975	15,415
*34769	Saint Cloud..........	(407)	35,183	54,579
*33701	Saint Petersburg......	(727)	244,769	265,351
33912	San Carlos Park (c)....	(239)	16,824	—
*32771	Sanford............	(407)	53,570	61,448
*34231	Sarasota............	(941)	51,917	58,285
33577	Sarasota Springs (c)...	(941)	14,395	—
*32937	Satellite Beach.......	(321)	10,109	11,130
*32958	Sebastian...........	(772)	21,929	26,118
*33870	Sebring............	(863)	10,491	10,600
*33772	Seminole............	(727)	17,233	18,838
34610	Shady Hills (c).......	(727)	11,523	—
*34207	South Bradenton (c)....	(941)	22,178	—
*32119	South Daytona........	(386)	12,252	13,080
*33143	South Miami..........	(305)	11,657	11,911
33157	South Miami Heights (c)..	(305)	35,696	—
33595	South Venice (c)......	(941)	13,949	—
32824	Southchase (c).......	(407)	15,921	—
*34604	Spring Hill (c).......	(352)	98,621	—
*34994	Stuart.............	(772)	15,593	16,237
*33573	Sun City Center (c)....	(813)	19,258	—
33160	Sunny Isles Beach.....	(305)	20,832	21,804
*33325	Sunrise............	(954)	84,439	95,166
*33283	Sunset (c)...........	(305)	16,389	—
*33144	Sweetwater..........	(305)	13,499	20,994
*32301	Tallahassee..........	(850)	181,376	194,500
*33321	Tamarac............	(954)	60,427	66,721
33184	Tamiami (c)..........	(305)	55,271	—
*33602	Tampa.............	(813)	335,709	399,700
*34689	Tarpon Springs.......	(727)	23,484	25,577
32778	Tavares............	(352)	13,951	17,749
*33617	Temple Terrace.......	(813)	24,541	26,639
*33412	The Acreage (c).......	(561)	38,704	—
33186	The Crossings (c)......	(305)	22,758	—
33196	The Hammocks (c).....	(305)	51,003	—
*32162	The Villages (c)......	(352)	51,442	—
33592	Thonotosassa (c)......	(813)	13,014	—
33186	Three Lakes (c).......	(305)	15,047	—
*32780	Titusville...........	(321)	43,761	46,580
33615	Town 'n' Country (c)	(813)	78,442	—
34655	Trinity (c)..........	(727)	10,907	—
33613	University (c) (Hillsborough Co.)....	(813)	41,163	—
32826	University (c) (Orange Co.)	(407)	31,084	—
34201	University Park (c).....	(941)	26,995	—
32401	Upper Grand Lagoon (c)..	(850)	13,963	—
*33594	Valrico (c)..........	(813)	35,545	—
*34285	Venice.............	(941)	20,748	23,985
*32960	Vero Beach..........	(772)	15,220	17,503
*32960	Vero Beach South (c)...	(772)	23,092	—
32955	Viera East (c)........	(321)	10,757	—
33901	Villas (c)...........	(239)	11,569	—
32507	Warrington (c)........	(850)	14,531	—
32779	Wekiwa Springs (c).....	(407)	21,998	—
*33414	Wellington..........	(561)	56,508	65,398
*33544	Wesley Chapel (c).....	(813)	44,092	—
33714	West Lealman (c)......	(727)	15,651	—
33147	West Little River (c)....	(305)	34,699	—
*32904	West Melbourne.......	(321)	18,355	24,259
*33401	West Palm Beach......	(561)	99,919	111,955
33023	West Park...........	(954)	14,156	15,089
32505	West Pensacola (c).....	(850)	21,339	—
33626	Westchase (c)........	(813)	21,747	—
33165	Westchester (c).......	(305)	29,862	—
*33326	Weston............	(954)	65,333	71,166
33165	Westwood Lakes (c)....	(305)	11,838	—
*33305	Wilton Manors........	(954)	11,632	12,756
*34787	Winter Garden........	(407)	34,568	46,051
*33880	Winter Haven........	(863)	33,874	44,955
*32789	Winter Park..........	(407)	27,852	30,825
*32708	Winter Springs.......	(407)	33,282	37,312
32092	World Golf Village (c)	(904)	12,310	—
32547	Wright (c)..........	(850)	23,127	—
*32097	Yulee (c)............	(904)	11,491	—
*33540	Zephyrhills..........	(813)	13,288	16,456

(1) Incorporated after 2010 Census; 2010 figure is Census Bureau est.

Georgia

Area codes 470/678/770 overlay area code 404; 762 overlays 706.

ZIP	Place	Area code	2010 population	2019 estimate
*30101	Acworth.	(770)	20,425	22,818
*30701	Albany.	(229)	77,434	72,130
*30004	Alpharetta	(770)	57,551	67,213
*30709	Americus	(229)	17,041	15,108
*30601	Athens-Clarke Co. (balance).	(706)	115,452	126,913
*30303	Atlanta	(404)	420,003	506,811
*30901	Augusta-Richmond Co. (balance).	(706)	195,844	197,888
*39817	Bainbridge	(229)	12,697	12,081
30032	Belvedere Park (c)	(404)	15,152	—
30517	Braselton	(706)	7,511	12,961
*30319	Brookhaven[1]	(404)	49,640	55,554
*31520	Brunswick	(912)	15,383	16,256
*30518	Buford	(404)	12,225	15,522
*30701	Calhoun	(706)	15,650	17,271
30032	Candler-McAfee (c)	(404)	23,025	—
*30114	Canton	(770)	22,958	30,528
*30117	Carrollton	(770)	24,388	27,259
*30120	Cartersville	(770)	19,731	21,760
*30341	Chamblee	(770)	9,892	30,307
30021	Clarkston	(404)	7,554	12,637
*30337	College Park	(404)	13,942	15,159
*31901	Columbus	(706)	189,885	195,769
*30013	Conyers	(404)	15,195	16,256
*31015	Cordele	(229)	11,147	10,521
*30014	Covington	(770)	13,118	14,206
31805	Cusseta-Chattahoochee Co.	(706)	11,267	10,907
*30132	Dallas	(770)	11,544	13,981
*30720	Dalton	(706)	33,128	33,665
*30030	Decatur	(404)	19,335	25,696
*30340	Doraville	(770)	8,330	10,265
*31533	Douglas	(912)	11,589	11,695
*30134	Douglasville	(770)	30,961	33,992
30333	Druid Hills (c)	(404)	14,568	—
*31021	Dublin	(478)	16,201	15,881
*30096	Duluth	(770)	26,600	29,609
*30338	Dunwoody	(770)	46,267	49,356
*30344	East Point	(404)	33,712	34,875
30809	Evans (c)	(706)	29,011	—
30213	Fairburn	(770)	12,950	16,768
*30214	Fayetteville	(770)	15,945	17,991
*30297	Forest Park	(404)	18,468	20,020
*30501	Gainesville	(770)	33,804	43,232
39854	Georgetown (c)	(912)	11,823	—
*30223	Griffin	(770)	23,643	22,813
30813	Grovetown	(706)	11,216	15,152
*31313	Hinesville	(912)	33,437	33,273
*30114	Holly Springs	(770)	9,189	15,442
30549	Jefferson	(706)	9,432	12,032
*30097	Johns Creek	(404)	76,728	84,579
*30144	Kennesaw	(770)	29,783	34,077
31548	Kingsland	(912)	15,946	17,949
*30240	LaGrange	(706)	29,588	30,305
*30045	Lawrenceville	(770)	28,546	30,834
*30047	Lilburn	(404)	11,596	12,810
30122	Lithia Springs (c).	(770)	15,491	—
30052	Loganville	(770)	10,458	12,880
30126	Mableton (c)	(770)	37,115	—
*31201	Macon-Bibb Co.[1]	(478)	155,783	153,159
*30060	Marietta	(404)	56,579	60,867
30907	Martinez (c)	(706)	35,795	—
*30253	McDonough	(770)	22,084	26,768
*31061	Milledgeville	(478)	17,715	18,704
*30004	Milton	(770)	32,661	39,587
*30655	Monroe	(770)	13,234	13,673
*31768	Moultrie	(229)	14,268	14,211
30075	Mountain Park (c)	(770)	11,554	—
*30263	Newnan	(770)	33,039	41,581
*30071	Norcross	(770)	9,116	16,592
30319	North Atlanta (c)	(404)	40,456	—
30033	North Decatur (c)	(404)	16,698	—
30033	North Druid Hills (c)	(404)	18,947	—
*30269	Peachtree City	(770)	34,364	36,223
*30092	Peachtree Corners[1]	(678)	38,014	43,905
31069	Perry	(478)	13,839	17,894
31322	Pooler	(912)	19,140	25,694
30127	Powder Springs	(770)	13,940	15,758
30074	Redan (c)	(770)	33,015	—
31324	Richmond Hill	(912)	9,281	13,839
31326	Rincon	(912)	8,836	10,361
*30274	Riverdale	(770)	15,134	15,594
*30161	Rome	(706)	36,303	36,716
*30075	Roswell	(404)	88,346	94,763
31558	Saint Marys	(912)	17,121	18,567
31522	Saint Simons (c)	(912)	12,743	—
*30350	Sandy Springs	(404)	93,853	109,452
*31401	Savannah	(912)	136,286	144,464
30079	Scottdale (c)	(404)	10,631	—
*30080	Smyrna	(770)	51,271	56,666
*30078	Snellville	(770)	18,242	20,077
*30336	South Fulton[1]	(470)	85,589	99,155
*30458	Statesboro	(912)	28,422	32,954
30281	Stockbridge	(770)	25,636	29,904
*30038	Stonecrest[1]	(770)	50,207	54,903
30518	Sugar Hill	(770)	18,522	24,617
30024	Suwanee	(770)	15,355	20,907
*31792	Thomasville	(229)	18,413	18,518
*31794	Tifton	(229)	16,350	16,838
*30084	Tucker[1]	(678)	33,380	36,395
30291	Union City	(770)	19,456	22,399
*31601	Valdosta	(229)	54,518	56,457
30474	Vidalia	(912)	10,473	10,402
30180	Villa Rica	(770)	13,956	16,058
*31088	Warner Robins	(478)	66,588	77,617
*31501	Waycross	(912)	14,649	13,480
31410	Wilmington Island (c)	(912)	15,138	—
30680	Winder	(770)	14,099	17,937
*30188	Woodstock	(770)	23,896	33,039

(1) Incorporated after 2010 Census; 2010 figure is Census Bureau est.

Hawaii

Area code 808 applies to the entire state.

ZIP	Place	2000 population	2010 population
96821	East Honolulu (c)	—	49,914
96706	Ewa Beach (c)	14,650	14,955
96706	Ewa Gentry (c)	4,939	22,690
96701	Halawa (c)	13,891	14,014
96749	Hawaiian Paradise Park (c)	7,051	11,404
*96720	Hilo (c)	40,759	43,263
*96813	Honolulu, urban (c)	371,657	337,256[1]
*96732	Kahului (c)	20,146	26,337
96740	Kailua (c) (Hawaii Co.)	9,870	11,975
96734	Kailua (c) (Honolulu Co.)	36,513	38,635
96744	Kaneohe (c)	34,970	34,597
96746	Kapaa (c)	9,472	10,699
*96707	Kapolei (c)	—	15,186
96753	Kihei (c)	16,749	20,881
*96761	Lahaina (c)	9,118	11,704
96707	Makakilo (c)	13,156	18,248
96789	Mililani Mauka (c)	—	21,039
96789	Mililani Town (c)	28,608	27,629
96792	Nanakuli (c)	10,814	12,666
96782	Pearl City (c)	30,976	47,698
96797	Royal Kunia (c)	—	14,525
96857	Schofield Barracks (c)	14,428	16,370
96786	Wahiawa (c)	16,151	17,821
96792	Waianae (c)	10,506	13,177
96793	Wailuku (c)	12,296	15,313
96701	Waimalu (c)	29,371	13,730
96797	Waipahu (c)	33,108	38,216
96797	Waipio (c)	11,672	11,674

(1) 2019 est. pop. was 345,064.

Idaho

Area code 986 overlays 208, which applies to the entire state.

ZIP	Place	2010 population	2019 estimate
*83401	Ammon	13,816	17,115
83221	Blackfoot	11,899	12,034
*83702	Boise	205,671	228,959
83318	Burley	10,345	10,582
*83605	Caldwell	46,237	58,481
83202	Chubbuck	13,922	15,588
*83814	Coeur d'Alene	44,137	52,414
*83616	Eagle	19,908	29,796
*83714	Garden City	10,972	11,969
83835	Hayden	13,294	15,434
*83402	Idaho Falls	56,813	62,888
83338	Jerome	10,890	11,994
*83634	Kuna	15,210	22,257
83501	Lewiston	31,894	32,788
*83642	Meridian	75,092	114,161
*83843	Moscow	23,800	25,702
83647	Mountain Home	14,206	14,562
*83651	Nampa	81,557	99,277
*83201	Pocatello	54,255	56,637
*83854	Post Falls	27,574	36,250
*83440	Rexburg	25,484	29,400
83669	Star	5,793	10,532
*83301	Twin Falls	44,125	50,197

Illinois

Area code 224 overlays area code 847; 331 overlays 630; 447 overlays 217 effective Mar. 27, 2021; 779 overlays 815; 872 overlays 312/773.

ZIP	Place	Area code	2010 population	2019 estimate
60101	Addison	(630)	36,942	36,482
*60102	Algonquin	(847)	30,046	30,897
60803	Alsip	(708)	19,277	18,709
62002	Alton	(618)	27,865	26,208
60002	Antioch	(847)	14,430	14,175
*60005	Arlington Heights	(847)	75,101	74,760
*60505	Aurora	(630)	197,899	197,757
*60010	Barrington	(847)	10,327	10,217
*60103	Bartlett	(630)	41,208	40,647
*60510	Batavia	(630)	26,045	26,420
*60099	Beach Park	(847)	13,638	13,701
*62220	Belleville	(618)	44,478	40,897
60104	Bellwood	(708)	19,071	18,672
61008	Belvidere	(815)	25,585	25,143
*60106	Bensenville	(630)	18,352	18,044
60402	Berwyn	(708)	56,657	54,391
*60108	Bloomingdale	(630)	22,018	21,779
*61701	Bloomington	(309)	76,610	77,330
60406	Blue Island	(708)	23,706	22,899
*60440	Bolingbrook	(630)	73,366	74,545
60914	Bourbonnais	(815)	18,631	19,462
60915	Bradley	(815)	15,895	15,314
60455	Bridgeview	(708)	16,446	16,096
60513	Brookfield	(708)	18,978	18,310
60089	Buffalo Grove	(847)	41,496	40,494
60459	Burbank	(708)	28,925	28,289
60527	Burr Ridge	(630)	10,559	10,758
62206	Cahokia	(618)	15,241	13,880
60409	Calumet City	(708)	37,042	35,913
*60175	Campton Hills	(630)/(847)	11,131	11,091
61520	Canton	(309)	14,704	13,506
*62901	Carbondale	(618)	25,902	25,083
*60188	Carol Stream	(630)	39,711	39,203
60110	Carpentersville	(847)	37,691	37,254
60013	Cary	(847)	18,271	18,067
62801	Centralia	(618)	13,032	12,210
*61820	Champaign	(217)	81,055	88,909
60410	Channahon	(815)	12,560	13,239
61920	Charleston	(217)	21,838	20,117
62629	Chatham	(217)	11,500	13,008
*60602	Chicago	(312)/(773)	2,695,598	2,693,976
*60411	Chicago Heights	(708)	30,276	29,322
60415	Chicago Ridge	(708)	14,305	13,928
60804	Cicero	(708)	83,891	80,796
62234	Collinsville	(618)	25,579	24,395
62236	Columbia	(618)	9,707	10,513
60478	Country Club Hills	(708)	16,541	16,482
*60403	Crest Hill	(815)	20,837	20,376
*60418	Crestwood	(708)	10,950	10,706
*60014	Crystal Lake	(815)	40,743	39,829
*61832	Danville	(217)	33,027	30,479
60561	Darien	(630)	22,086	21,628
*62521	Decatur	(217)	76,122	70,746
60015	Deerfield	(847)	18,225	18,646
60115	DeKalb	(815)	43,862	42,847
*60018	Des Plaines	(847)	58,364	58,899
61021	Dixon	(815)	15,733	15,115
60419	Dolton	(708)	23,153	22,348
*60515	Downers Grove	(630)	47,833	49,057
61244	East Moline	(309)	21,302	20,645
*61611	East Peoria	(309)	23,402	22,546
*62201	East St. Louis	(618)	27,006	26,047
*62025	Edwardsville	(618)	24,293	25,233
62401	Effingham	(217)	12,328	12,511
*60120	Elgin	(847)	108,188	110,849
*60007	Elk Grove Village	(847)	33,127	32,400
60126	Elmhurst	(630)	44,121	46,746
60707	Elmwood Park	(708)	24,883	24,098
*60201	Evanston	(847)	74,486	73,473
60805	Evergreen Park	(708)	19,852	19,147
62208	Fairview Heights	(618)	17,078	16,303
60130	Forest Park	(708)	14,167	13,704
60020	Fox Lake	(847)	10,579	10,451
60423	Frankfort	(815)	17,782	19,973
60131	Franklin Park	(847)	18,333	17,627
61032	Freeport	(815)	25,638	23,775
60030	Gages Lake (c)	(847)	10,198	—
*61401	Galesburg	(309)	32,195	30,197
60134	Geneva	(630)	21,495	21,809
62034	Glen Carbon	(618)	12,934	12,850
60137	Glen Ellyn	(630)	27,450	27,714
*60139	Glendale Heights	(630)	34,208	33,617
*60025	Glenview	(847)	44,692	47,308
62035	Godfrey	(618)	17,982	17,400
62040	Granite City	(618)	29,849	28,158
60030	Grayslake	(847)	20,957	20,725
60031	Gurnee	(847)	31,295	30,378
60133	Hanover Park	(630)	37,973	37,426
*60426	Harvey	(708)	25,282	24,408
60429	Hazel Crest	(708)	14,100	13,565
62948	Herrin	(618)	12,501	12,687
60457	Hickory Hills	(708)	14,049	13,710
*60035	Highland Park	(847)	29,763	29,515
*60521	Hinsdale	(630)	16,816	17,637
60195	Hoffman Estates	(847)	51,895	50,932
*60491	Homer Glen	(708)	24,220	24,472
*60430	Homewood	(708)	19,323	18,703
60142	Huntley	(847)	24,291	27,228
*62650	Jacksonville	(217)	19,446	18,603
*60436	Joliet	(815)	147,433	147,344
60458	Justice	(708)	12,926	12,608
60901	Kankakee	(815)	27,537	26,024
61443	Kewanee	(309)	12,916	12,339
*60525	La Grange	(708)	15,550	15,322
60526	La Grange Park	(708)	13,579	13,178
60045	Lake Forest	(847)	19,375	19,446
*60102	Lake in the Hills	(847)	28,965	28,634
60047	Lake Zurich	(847)	19,631	19,877
60438	Lansing	(708)	28,331	27,402
60439	Lemont	(630)	16,000	17,291
60048	Libertyville	(847)	20,315	20,205
62656	Lincoln	(217)	14,504	13,524
*60712	Lincolnwood	(847)	12,590	12,245
60046	Lindenhurst	(847)	14,462	14,216
60532	Lisle	(630)	22,390	23,270
*60441	Lockport	(815)	24,839	25,615
60148	Lombard	(630)	43,165	44,303
*61111	Loves Park	(815)	23,996	23,371
60534	Lyons	(708)	10,729	10,372
*61115	Machesney Park	(815)	23,499	22,677
61455	Macomb	(309)	19,288	17,413
62959	Marion	(618)	17,193	17,520
*60428	Markham	(708)	12,508	12,314
60443	Matteson	(708)	19,009	19,448
61938	Mattoon	(217)	18,555	17,615
*60153	Maywood	(708)	24,090	23,158
*60050	McHenry	(815)	26,992	27,061
*60160	Melrose Park	(708)	25,411	24,703
60445	Midlothian	(708)	14,819	14,346
60447	Minooka	(815)	10,924	11,397
60448	Mokena	(708)	18,740	20,159
*61265	Moline	(309)	43,483	41,356
60538	Montgomery	(630)	18,438	19,638
60450	Morris	(815)	13,636	15,053
61550	Morton	(309)	16,267	16,277
60053	Morton Grove	(847)	23,270	22,796
60056	Mount Prospect	(847)	54,167	53,719
62864	Mount Vernon	(618)	15,277	14,723
60060	Mundelein	(847)	31,064	31,051
*60540	Naperville	(630)	141,853	148,449
60451	New Lenox	(815)	24,394	26,926
60714	Niles	(847)	29,803	28,938
*61761	Normal	(309)	52,497	54,469
*60706	Norridge	(708)	14,572	14,152
60542	North Aurora	(630)	16,760	18,057
*60064	North Chicago	(847)	32,574	29,615
*60062	Northbrook	(847)	33,170	32,958
60164	Northlake	(708)	12,323	12,161
60452	Oak Forest	(708)	27,962	27,173
*60453	Oak Lawn	(708)	56,690	55,022
*60301	Oak Park	(708)	51,878	52,381
62269	O'Fallon	(618)	28,281	29,583
60462	Orland Park	(708)	56,767	57,857
60543	Oswego	(630)	30,355	36,252
61350	Ottawa	(815)	18,768	18,063
*60067	Palatine	(847)	68,557	67,482
60463	Palos Heights	(708)	12,515	12,520
60465	Palos Hills	(708)	17,484	17,060
*60466	Park Forest	(708)	21,975	21,210
60068	Park Ridge	(847)	37,480	36,950
*61554	Pekin	(309)	34,094	32,045
*61602	Peoria	(309)	115,007	110,417
*60544	Plainfield	(815)	39,581	44,308
60545	Plano	(630)	10,856	11,665
61764	Pontiac	(815)	11,931	11,253
60070	Prospect Heights	(847)	16,256	15,887
*62301	Quincy	(217)	40,633	39,949
61866	Rantoul	(217)	12,941	12,493
60471	Richton Park	(708)	13,646	13,292
60305	River Forest	(708)	11,172	10,816
60827	Riverdale	(708)	13,549	13,077
*61201	Rock Island	(309)	39,018	37,176
*61101	Rockford	(815)	152,871	145,609
60008	Rolling Meadows	(847)	24,099	23,532
60446	Romeoville	(815)	39,680	39,746
61073	Roscoe	(815)	10,785	10,510
60172	Roselle	(630)	22,763	22,463

ZIP	Place	Area code	2010 population	2019 estimate
60073	Round Lake	(847)	18,289	18,100
60073	Round Lake Beach	(847)	28,175	27,100
*60174	Saint Charles	(630)	32,974	32,887
60411	Sauk Village	(708)	10,506	10,246
*60193	Schaumburg	(847)	74,227	72,887
*60176	Schiller Park	(847)	11,793	11,403
*62269	Shiloh	(618)	12,651	13,586
*60404	Shorewood	(815)	15,615	17,509
*60077	Skokie	(847)	64,784	62,700
60177	South Elgin	(847)	21,985	24,755
60473	South Holland	(708)	22,030	21,296
*62701	Springfield	(217)	116,250	114,230
61081	Sterling	(815)	15,370	14,463
60107	Streamwood	(630)	39,858	39,228
*61364	Streator	(815)	13,710	13,113
60501	Summit	(708)	11,054	11,116
*62226	Swansea	(618)	13,430	13,350
60178	Sycamore	(815)	17,519	18,322
62568	Taylorville	(217)	11,246	10,360
*60477	Tinley Park	(708)	56,703	55,773
62294	Troy	(618)	9,888	10,375
*61801	Urbana	(217)	41,250	42,214
60061	Vernon Hills	(847)	25,113	26,521
60181	Villa Park	(630)	21,904	21,483
60555	Warrenville	(630)	13,140	13,174
61571	Washington	(309)	15,134	16,516
62298	Waterloo	(618)	9,811	10,578
60084	Wauconda	(847)	13,603	13,504
*60085	Waukegan	(847)	89,078	86,075
*60185	West Chicago	(630)	27,086	26,816
60154	Westchester	(708)	16,718	16,117
60558	Western Springs	(708)	12,975	13,359
60559	Westmont	(630)	24,685	24,443
*60187	Wheaton	(630)	52,894	52,745
60090	Wheeling	(847)	37,648	38,646
60091	Wilmette	(847)	27,087	27,089
60093	Winnetka	(847)	12,187	12,316
*60191	Wood Dale	(630)	13,770	13,607
62095	Wood River	(618)	10,657	10,051
60517	Woodridge	(630)	32,971	33,432
60098	Woodstock	(815)	24,770	25,240
60482	Worth	(708)	10,789	10,466
60560	Yorkville	(630)	16,921	20,613
60099	Zion	(847)	24,413	23,487

Indiana

Area code 463 overlays area code 317; 930 overlays 812.

ZIP	Place	Area code	2010 population	2019 estimate
*46011	Anderson	(765)	56,129	54,755
46706	Auburn	(260)	12,731	13,484
46123	Avon	(317)	12,446	18,706
47421	Bedford	(812)	13,413	13,212
46107	Beech Grove	(317)	14,192	14,937
*47408	Bloomington	(812)	80,405	85,755
46714	Bluffton	(260)	9,897	10,147
46112	Brownsburg	(317)	21,285	27,001
*46032	Carmel	(317)	79,191	101,068
46303	Cedar Lake	(219)	11,560	13,183
46304	Chesterton	(219)	13,068	14,088
*47129	Clarksville	(812)	21,724	21,558
*47201	Columbus	(812)	44,061	48,046
47331	Connersville	(765)	13,481	12,796
47933	Crawfordsville	(765)	15,915	16,118
*46307	Crown Point	(219)	27,317	30,488
46122	Danville	(317)	9,001	10,126
*46311	Dyer	(219)	16,390	15,976
46312	East Chicago	(219)	29,698	27,817
*46514	Elkhart	(574)	50,949	52,358
*47708	Evansville	(812)	117,429	117,979
*46038	Fishers	(317)	76,794	95,310
*46802	Fort Wayne	(260)	253,691	270,402
*46041	Frankfort	(765)	16,422	15,884
46131	Franklin	(317)	23,712	25,608
*46402	Gary	(219)	80,294	74,879
*46526	Goshen	(574)	31,719	34,217
46530	Granger (c)	(574)	30,465	—
46135	Greencastle	(765)	10,326	10,270
46140	Greenfield	(317)	20,602	23,006
47240	Greensburg	(812)	11,492	11,891
*46142	Greenwood	(317)	49,791	59,458
46319	Griffith	(219)	16,893	16,060
*46320	Hammond	(219)	80,830	75,522
*46322	Highland	(219)	23,727	22,316
46342	Hobart	(219)	29,059	27,939
46750	Huntington	(260)	17,391	17,138
*46201	Indianapolis (balance)	(317)	820,445	876,384
*47546	Jasper	(812)	15,038	15,724
*47130	Jeffersonville	(812)	44,953	48,126

ZIP	Place	Area code	2010 population	2019 estimate
*46902	Kokomo	(765)	45,468	58,020
*46350	La Porte	(219)	22,053	21,569
*47901	Lafayette	(765)	67,140	71,721
46405	Lake Station	(219)	12,572	11,845
46226	Lawrence	(317)	46,001	49,462
46052	Lebanon	(765)	15,792	16,065
46947	Logansport	(574)	18,396	17,584
47250	Madison	(812)	11,967	11,861
*46952	Marion	(765)	29,948	27,930
46151	Martinsville	(765)	11,828	11,669
*46410	Merrillville	(219)	35,246	34,792
*46360	Michigan City	(219)	31,479	31,015
*46544	Mishawaka	(574)	48,252	50,363
*47302	Muncie	(765)	70,085	67,999
46321	Munster	(219)	23,603	22,476
*47150	New Albany	(812)	36,372	36,843
47362	New Castle	(765)	18,114	17,113
46774	New Haven	(260)	14,794	15,922
*46060	Noblesville	(317)	51,969	64,668
*46970	Peru	(765)	11,417	11,023
*46168	Plainfield	(317)	27,631	35,287
46368	Portage	(219)	36,828	36,988
*47374	Richmond	(765)	36,812	35,342
46373	Saint John	(219)	14,850	18,796
46375	Schererville	(219)	29,243	28,527
47274	Seymour	(812)	17,503	19,959
46176	Shelbyville	(765)	19,191	19,407
*46601	South Bend	(574)	101,168	102,026
46224	Speedway	(317)	11,812	12,193
*47802	Terre Haute	(812)	60,785	60,622
*46383	Valparaiso	(219)	31,730	33,897
47591	Vincennes	(812)	18,423	16,862
*46580	Warsaw	(574)	13,559	15,150
*47501	Washington	(812)	11,509	12,528
*47906	West Lafayette	(765)	29,596	50,996
*46074	Westfield	(317)	30,068	43,649
47396	Yorktown	(765)	9,405	11,111
46077	Zionsville	(317)	14,160	28,357

Iowa

ZIP	Place	Area code	2010 population	2019 estimate
50009	Altoona	(515)	14,541	19,221
*50010	Ames	(515)	58,965	66,258
*50021	Ankeny	(515)	45,582	67,355
52722	Bettendorf	(563)	33,217	36,543
*50036	Boone	(515)	12,661	12,384
52601	Burlington	(319)	25,663	24,713
*50613	Cedar Falls	(319)	39,260	40,536
*52401	Cedar Rapids	(319)	126,326	133,562
*52732	Clinton	(563)	26,885	25,093
*50325	Clive	(515)	15,447	17,242
52241	Coralville	(319)	18,907	22,290
*51501	Council Bluffs	(712)	62,230	62,166
*52801	Davenport	(563)	99,685	101,590
*50309	Des Moines	(515)	203,433	214,237
*52001	Dubuque	(563)	57,637	57,882
*52556	Fairfield	(641)	9,464	10,425
50501	Fort Dodge	(515)	25,206	23,888
52627	Fort Madison	(319)	11,051	10,321
50111	Grimes	(515)	8,246	14,804
50125	Indianola	(515)	14,782	16,015
*52240	Iowa City	(319)	67,862	75,130
50131	Johnston	(515)	17,278	22,582
52632	Keokuk	(319)	10,780	10,157
51031	Le Mars	(712)	9,826	10,081
52302	Marion	(319)	34,768	40,359
50158	Marshalltown	(641)	27,552	26,666
*50401	Mason City	(641)	28,079	26,931
52761	Muscatine	(563)	22,886	23,631
50208	Newton	(641)	15,254	15,182
52317	North Liberty	(319)	13,374	19,501
50211	Norwalk	(515)	8,945	11,938
52577	Oskaloosa	(641)	11,463	11,506
52501	Ottumwa	(641)	25,023	24,368
50219	Pella	(641)	10,352	10,237
*50327	Pleasant Hill	(515)	8,785	10,019
*51101	Sioux City	(712)	82,684	82,651
51301	Spencer	(712)	11,233	10,952
50588	Storm Lake	(712)	10,600	10,322
*50322	Urbandale	(515)	39,463	44,379
*50701	Waterloo	(319)	68,406	67,328
50263	Waukee	(515)	13,790	24,089
50677	Waverly	(319)	9,874	10,198
*50265	West Des Moines	(515)	56,609	67,899

Kansas

ZIP	Place	Area code	2010 population	2019 estimate
67002	Andover	(316)	11,791	13,405
67005	Arkansas City	(620)	12,415	11,669

ZIP	Place	Area code	2010 population	2019 estimate
66002	Atchison	(913)	11,021	10,476
67037	Derby	(316)	22,158	24,943
*67801	Dodge City	(620)	27,340	27,104
67042	El Dorado	(316)	13,021	12,954
66801	Emporia	(620)	24,916	24,598
*67846	Garden City	(620)	26,658	26,408
66030	Gardner	(913)	19,123	22,031
67530	Great Bend	(620)	15,995	14,974
*67601	Hays	(785)	20,510	20,744
67060	Haysville	(316)	10,826	11,338
*67501	Hutchinson	(620)	42,080	40,383
*66441	Junction City	(785)	23,353	21,482
*66101	Kansas City	(913)	145,786	152,960
66043	Lansing	(913)	11,265	11,949
*66044	Lawrence	(785)	87,643	98,193
*66048	Leavenworth	(913)	35,251	35,957
*66211	Leawood	(913)	31,867	34,727
*66215	Lenexa	(913)	48,190	55,625
*67901	Liberal	(620)	20,525	19,774
*66502	Manhattan	(785)	52,281	54,604
67460	McPherson	(620)	13,155	13,061
*66202	Merriam	(913)	11,003	11,081
*67114	Newton	(316)	19,132	18,861
*66061	Olathe	(913)	125,872	140,545
66067	Ottawa	(785)	12,649	12,254
*66212	Overland Park	(913)	173,372	195,494
*66762	Pittsburg	(620)	20,233	20,050
*66208	Prairie Village	(913)	21,447	22,295
*67401	Salina	(785)	47,707	46,550
*66203	Shawnee	(913)	62,209	65,807
*66603	Topeka	(785)	127,473	125,310
*67202	Wichita	(316)	382,368	389,938
67156	Winfield	(620)	12,301	11,943

Kentucky
Area code 364 overlays area code 270.

ZIP	Place	Area code	2010 population	2019 estimate
*41101	Ashland	(606)	21,684	20,146
40004	Bardstown	(502)	11,700	13,253
*40403	Berea	(859)	13,561	16,026
*42101	Bowling Green	(270)	58,067	70,543
41005	Burlington (c)	(859)	15,926	—
*42718	Campbellsville	(270)	9,108	11,482
*41011	Covington	(859)	40,640	40,341
*40422	Danville	(859)	16,218	16,769
*42701	Elizabethtown	(270)	28,531	30,289
*41018	Erlanger	(859)	18,082	19,246
*41042	Florence	(859)	29,951	33,004
42223	Fort Campbell North (c)	(270)	13,685	—
40121	Fort Knox (c)	(270)	10,124	—
41075	Fort Thomas	(859)	16,325	16,263
*40601	Frankfort	(502)	25,527	27,755
40324	Georgetown	(502)	29,098	34,992
42141	Glasgow	(270)	14,028	14,485
*42420	Henderson	(270)	28,757	28,207
*42240	Hopkinsville	(270)	31,577	30,680
41051	Independence	(859)	24,757	28,521
*40299	Jeffersontown	(502)	26,595	27,715
40342	Lawrenceburg	(502)	10,505	11,509
*40507	Lexington-Fayette	(859)	295,803	323,152
*40202	Louisville-Jefferson Co. (balance)	(502)	597,337	617,638
*40222	Lyndon	(502)	11,002	11,423
42431	Madisonville	(270)	19,591	18,621
40047	Mount Washington	(502)	9,117	14,817
42071	Murray	(270)	17,741	19,327
*41071	Newport	(859)	15,273	14,932
*40356	Nicholasville	(859)	28,015	30,865
*42301	Owensboro	(270)	57,265	60,131
*42003	Paducah	(270)	25,024	24,865
*40160	Radcliff	(270)	21,688	22,914
*40475	Richmond	(859)	31,364	36,157
*40207	Saint Matthews	(502)	17,472	18,105
*40066	Shelbyville	(502)	14,045	16,585
40165	Shepherdsville	(502)	11,222	12,442
*40216	Shively	(502)	15,264	15,689
*42501	Somerset	(606)	11,196	11,585
*40391	Winchester	(859)	18,368	18,548

Louisiana

ZIP	Place	Area code	2010 population	2019 estimate
*70510	Abbeville	(337)	12,257	12,038
*71301	Alexandria	(318)	47,723	46,180
70714	Baker	(225)	13,895	13,194
71220	Bastrop	(318)	11,365	10,023
*70801	Baton Rouge	(225)	229,493	220,236
70360	Bayou Blue (c)	(985)	12,352	—
*70364	Bayou Cane (c)	(985)	19,355	—
*70037	Belle Chasse (c)	(504)	12,679	—
*70427	Bogalusa	(985)	12,232	11,504
*71111	Bossier City	(318)	61,315	68,159
70518	Broussard	(337)	8,197	12,700
70837	Central	(225)	26,864	29,357
*70043	Chalmette (c)	(504)	16,751	—
70433	Claiborne (c)	(985)	11,507	—
*70433	Covington	(985)	8,765	10,564
*70526	Crowley	(337)	13,265	12,588
70634	DeRidder	(337)	10,578	10,588
*70047	Destrehan (c)	(985)	11,535	—
*70072	Estelle (c)	(504)	16,377	—
*70810	Gardere (c)	(225)	10,580	—
*70737	Gonzales	(225)	9,781	10,957
*70053	Gretna	(504)	17,736	17,647
*70401	Hammond	(985)	20,019	21,437
*70058	Harvey (c)	(504)	20,348	—
*70360	Houma	(985)	33,727	32,696
70121	Jefferson (c)	(504)	11,193	—
*70062	Kenner	(504)	66,702	66,340
*70501	Lafayette	(337)	120,623	126,185
*70601	Lake Charles	(337)	71,993	78,396
*70068	LaPlace (c)	(985)	29,872	—
70070	Luling (c)	(985)	12,119	—
*70448	Mandeville	(985)	11,560	12,475
*70072	Marrero (c)	(504)	33,141	—
*70001	Metairie (c)	(504)	138,481	—
*71055	Minden	(318)	13,082	11,840
*71201	Monroe	(318)	48,815	47,294
*70380	Morgan City	(985)	12,404	10,742
70611	Moss Bluff (c)	(337)	11,557	—
*71457	Natchitoches	(318)	18,323	17,485
*70560	New Iberia	(337)	30,617	28,454
*70112	New Orleans	(504)	343,829	390,144
*70570	Opelousas	(337)	16,634	15,911
*71360	Pineville	(318)	14,555	14,122
70769	Prairieville (c)	(225)	26,895	—
*70394	Raceland (c)	(985)	10,193	—
70123	River Ridge (c)	(504)	13,494	—
*71270	Ruston	(318)	21,859	21,854
70817	Shenandoah (c)	(225)	18,399	—
*71101	Shreveport	(318)	199,311	187,112
*70458	Slidell	(985)	27,068	27,633
*70663	Sulphur	(337)	20,410	20,065
70056	Terrytown (c)	(504)	23,319	—
*70301	Thibodaux	(985)	14,566	14,425
70056	Timberlane (c)	(504)	10,243	—
70094	Waggaman (c)	(504)	10,015	—
*71291	West Monroe	(318)	13,065	12,227
70058	Woodmere (c)	(504)	12,080	—
*70592	Youngsville	(337)	8,105	14,704
*70791	Zachary	(225)	14,960	17,949

Maine
Area code 207 applies to the entire state. See introductory note.

ZIP	Place	2010 population	2019 estimate
*04210	Auburn	23,055	23,414
*04330	Augusta	19,136	18,697
*04401	Bangor	33,039	32,262
*04005	Biddeford	21,277	21,504
04011	Brunswick	20,278	20,535
04011	Brunswick (c)	15,175	—
04105	Falmouth	11,185	12,312
04038	Gorham	16,381	17,978
04043	Kennebunk	10,798	11,625
*04240	Lewiston	36,592	30,225
*04473	Orono	10,362	10,799
*04101	Portland	66,194	66,215
04072	Saco	18,482	19,964
04073	Sanford[1]	20,793	21,223
*04074	Scarborough	18,919	20,991
*04106	South Portland	25,002	25,532
04084	Standish	9,874	10,099
*04901	Waterville	15,722	16,558
04090	Wells	9,589	10,675
*04092	Westbrook	17,494	19,074
*04062	Windham	17,001	18,540
03909	York	12,529	13,290

(1) Incorporated after 2010 Census; 2010 figure is Census Bureau est.

Maryland
Area code 240 overlays area code 301; 443/667 overlay 410.

ZIP	Place	Area code	2010 population	2019 estimate
21001	Aberdeen	(410)	14,959	16,019
20607	Accokeek (c)	(301)	10,573	—
20783	Adelphi (c)	(301)	15,086	—

ZIP	Place	Area code	2010 population	2019 estimate
*21401	Annapolis	(410)	38,394	39,223
21403	Annapolis Neck (c)	(410)	10,950	—
21227	Arbutus (c)	(410)	20,483	—
21012	Arnold (c)	(410)	23,106	—
*20906	Aspen Hill (c)	(301)	48,759	—
21220	Ballenger Creek (c)	(301)	18,274	—
*21202	Baltimore	(410)	620,961	593,490
*21014	Bel Air	(410)	10,120	10,119
21050	Bel Air North (c)	(410)	30,568	—
*21015	Bel Air South (c)	(410)	47,709	—
*20705	Beltsville (c)	(301)	16,772	—
20603	Bensville (c)	(301)	11,923	—
*20814	Bethesda (c)	(301)	60,858	—
*20715	Bowie	(301)	54,727	58,643
21225	Brooklyn Park (c)	(410)	14,373	—
20619	California (c)	(301)	11,857	—
20705	Calverton (c)	(301)	17,724	—
21613	Cambridge	(410)	12,326	12,260
*20748	Camp Springs (c)	(301)	19,096	—
21234	Carney (c)	(410)	29,941	—
21228	Catonsville (c)	(410)	41,567	—
20657	Chesapeake Ranch Estates (c)	(301)	10,519	—
20782	Chillum (c)	(301)	33,513	—
20871	Clarksburg (c)	(301)	13,766	—
20735	Clinton (c)	(301)	35,970	—
20904	Cloverly (c)	(301)	15,126	—
21030	Cockeysville (c)	(410)	20,776	—
*20904	Colesville (c)	(301)	14,647	—
*20740	College Park	(301)	30,413	32,163
*21044	Columbia (c)	(410)	99,615	—
21114	Crofton (c)	(410)	27,348	—
*21502	Cumberland	(301)	20,859	19,284
20872	Damascus (c)	(301)	15,257	—
21222	Dundalk (c)	(410)	63,597	—
20737	East Riverdale (c)	(301)	15,509	—
21601	Easton	(410)	15,945	16,671
21040	Edgewood (c)	(410)	25,562	—
21784	Eldersburg (c)	(410)	30,531	—
21075	Elkridge (c)	(410)	15,593	—
*21921	Elkton	(410)	15,443	15,622
*21043	Ellicott City (c)	(410)	65,834	—
21221	Essex (c)	(410)	39,262	—
20904	Fairland (c)	(301)	23,681	—
21061	Ferndale (c)	(410)	16,746	—
*20747	Forestville (c)	(301)	12,353	—
*20744	Fort Washington (c)	(301)	23,717	—
*21701	Frederick	(301)	65,239	72,244
*20877	Gaithersburg	(301)	59,933	67,985
*20874	Germantown (c)	(301)	86,395	—
20745	Glassmanor (c)	(301)	17,295	—
*21061	Glen Burnie (c)	(410)	67,639	—
20906	Glenmont (c)	(301)	13,529	—
20769	Glenn Dale (c)	(301)	13,466	—
*20770	Greenbelt	(301)	23,068	23,224
*21740	Hagerstown	(301)	39,662	40,100
21740	Halfway (c)	(301)	10,701	—
21078	Havre de Grace	(410)	12,952	14,018
20748	Hillcrest Heights (c)	(301)	16,469	—
*20781	Hyattsville (c)	(301)	17,557	18,230
21043	Ilchester (c)	(410)	23,476	—
21085	Joppatowne (c)	(410)	12,616	—
20902	Kemp Mill (c)	(301)	12,564	—
*20774	Kettering (c)	(301)	12,790	—
*21122	Lake Shore (c)	(410)	19,477	—
20785	Landover (c)	(301)	23,078	—
*20787	Langley Park (c)	(301)	18,755	—
*20706	Lanham (c)	(301)	10,157	—
*20774	Largo (c)	(301)	10,709	—
*20707	Laurel	(301)	25,115	25,631
20653	Lexington Park (c)	(410)	11,626	—
21090	Linthicum (c)	(410)	10,324	—
21207	Lochearn (c)	(410)	25,333	—
20724	Maryland City (c)	(301)	16,093	—
21093	Mays Chapel (c)	(410)	11,420	—
21220	Middle River (c)	(410)	25,191	—
*21244	Milford Mill (c)	(410)	29,042	—
*20716	Mitchellville (c)	(301)	10,967	—
*20886	Montgomery Village (c)	(301)	32,032	—
20784	New Carrollton (c)	(301)	12,135	12,928
*20852	North Bethesda (c)	(301)	43,828	—
20878	North Potomac (c)	(301)	24,410	—
21811	Ocean Pines (c)	(410)	11,710	—
21113	Odenton (c)	(410)	37,132	—
*20832	Olney (c)	(301)	33,844	—
21236	Overlea (c)	(410)	12,275	—
21117	Owings Mills (c)	(410)	30,622	—
*20745	Oxon Hill (c)	(301)	17,722	—
21234	Parkville (c)	(410)	30,734	—
21401	Parole (c)	(410)	15,922	—
*21122	Pasadena (c)	(410)	24,287	—

ZIP	Place	Area code	2010 population	2019 estimate
21128	Perry Hall (c)	(410)	28,474	—
*21207	Pikesville (c)	(410)	30,764	—
*20850	Potomac (c)	(301)	44,965	—
21133	Randallstown (c)	(410)	32,430	—
20855	Redland (c)	(301)	17,242	—
*21136	Reisterstown (c)	(410)	25,968	—
*21122	Riviera Beach (c)	(410)	12,677	—
*20850	Rockville	(301)	61,209	68,079
20772	Rosaryville (c)	(301)	10,697	—
21237	Rosedale (c)	(410)	19,257	—
21221	Rossville (c)	(410)	15,147	—
*21801	Salisbury	(410)	30,343	32,935
20723	Scaggsville (c)	(301)	24,333	—
*20706	Seabrook (c)	(301)	17,287	—
21144	Severn (c)	(410)	44,231	—
21146	Severna Park (c)	(410)	37,634	—
*20901	Silver Spring (c)	(301)	71,452	—
20707	South Laurel (c)	(301)	26,112	—
*20746	Suitland (c)	(301)	25,825	—
21842	Summerfield (c)	(410)	10,898	—
*20912	Takoma Park	(301)	16,715	17,725
*21204	Towson (c)	(410)	55,197	—
20854	Travilah (c)	(301)	12,159	—
*20602	Waldorf (c)	(301)	67,752	—
20743	Walker Mill (c)	(301)	11,302	—
*21157	Westminster	(410)	18,590	18,640
*20902	Wheaton (c)	(301)	48,284	—
20904	White Oak (c)	(301)	17,403	—
21207	Woodlawn (c) (Balt. Co.)	(410)	37,879	—

Massachusetts

Area code 339 overlays area code 781; 351 overlays 978; 774 overlays 508; 857 overlays 617. See introductory note.

ZIP	Place	Area code	2010 population	2019 estimate
02351	Abington	(781)	15,985	16,668
*01720	Acton	(978)	21,924	23,662
*02743	Acushnet	(508)	10,303	10,625
01001	Agawam	(413)	28,438	28,613
01913	Amesbury	(978)	16,283	17,532
*01002	Amherst	(413)	37,819	39,924
*01002	Amherst Center (c)	(413)	19,065	—
*01810	Andover	(978)	33,201	36,356
01721	Ashland	(508)	16,593	17,807
01331	Athol	(978)	11,584	11,732
01501	Auburn	(508)	16,188	16,766
02630	Barnstable	(508)	45,193	44,477
*01730	Bedford	(781)	13,320	14,123
01007	Belchertown	(413)	14,649	15,098
02019	Bellingham	(508)	16,332	17,270
02478	Belmont	(617)	24,729	26,116
01915	Beverly	(978)	39,502	42,174
*01821	Billerica	(978)	40,243	43,367
*02108	Boston	(617)	617,594	692,600
*02532	Bourne	(508)	19,754	19,762
*02184	Braintree	(781)	35,744	37,190
*02324	Bridgewater	(508)	26,563	27,619
*02301	Brockton	(508)	93,810	95,708
*02446	Brookline	(617)	58,732	59,121
*01803	Burlington	(781)	24,498	28,627
*02139	Cambridge	(617)	105,162	118,927
02021	Canton	(781)	21,561	23,805
*02330	Carver	(508)	11,509	11,767
01507	Charlton	(508)	12,981	13,713
01824	Chelmsford	(978)	33,802	35,391
02150	Chelsea	(617)	35,177	39,690
*01020	Chicopee	(413)	55,298	55,126
01510	Clinton	(978)	13,606	14,000
01742	Concord	(978)	17,668	18,918
01923	Danvers	(978)	26,493	27,549
*02747	Dartmouth	(508)	34,032	34,188
*02026	Dedham	(781)	24,729	25,219
02638	Dennis	(508)	14,207	13,871
01826	Dracut	(978)	29,457	31,634
01571	Dudley	(508)	11,390	11,773
*02332	Duxbury	(781)	15,059	15,921
02333	East Bridgewater	(508)	13,794	14,526
*01028	East Longmeadow	(413)	15,720	16,192
01027	Easthampton	(413)	16,053	15,829
*02356	Easton	(508)	23,112	25,105
02149	Everett	(617)	41,667	46,451
02719	Fairhaven	(508)	15,873	16,078
*02720	Fall River	(508)	88,857	89,541
*02540	Falmouth	(508)	31,531	30,993
01420	Fitchburg	(978)	40,318	40,638
02035	Foxborough	(508)	16,865	18,399
*01701	Framingham	(508)	68,323	74,416
02038	Franklin	(508)	31,635	34,087
01440	Gardner	(978)	20,228	20,683

ZIP	Place	Area code	2010 population	2019 estimate
*01930	Gloucester	(978)	28,789	30,430
01519	Grafton	(508)	17,765	18,883
*01301	Greenfield	(413)	17,456	17,258
*01450	Groton	(978)	10,646	11,325
02339	Hanover	(781)	13,879	14,570
*02341	Hanson	(781)	10,209	10,914
02645	Harwich	(508)	12,243	12,142
*01830	Haverhill	(978)	60,879	64,014
*02043	Hingham	(781)	22,157	24,679
02343	Holbrook	(781)	10,791	11,033
01520	Holden	(508)	17,346	19,303
01746	Holliston	(508)	13,547	14,912
*01040	Holyoke	(413)	39,880	40,117
01748	Hopkinton	(508)	14,925	18,470
01749	Hudson	(978)	19,063	19,864
01749	Hudson (c)	(978)	14,907	—
02045	Hull	(781)	10,293	10,475
01938	Ipswich	(978)	13,175	14,074
02364	Kingston	(781)	12,629	13,863
02347	Lakeville	(508)	10,602	11,561
*01840	Lawrence	(978)	76,377	80,028
01524	Leicester	(508)	10,970	11,341
01453	Leominster	(978)	40,759	41,716
*02420	Lexington	(781)	31,394	33,132
01460	Littleton	(978)	8,924	10,227
*01028	Longmeadow	(413)	15,784	15,705
*01850	Lowell	(978)	106,519	110,997
01056	Ludlow	(413)	21,103	21,233
*01462	Lunenburg	(978)	10,086	11,736
*01901	Lynn	(781)	90,329	94,299
01940	Lynnfield	(781)	11,596	12,999
02148	Malden	(781)	59,450	60,470
02048	Mansfield	(508)	23,184	24,470
01945	Marblehead	(781)	19,808	20,555
01752	Marlborough	(508)	38,499	39,597
*02050	Marshfield	(781)	25,132	25,967
02649	Mashpee	(508)	14,006	14,229
01754	Maynard	(978)	10,106	11,336
02052	Medfield	(508)	12,024	12,955
*02155	Medford	(781)	56,173	57,341
02053	Medway	(508)	12,752	13,479
02176	Melrose	(781)	26,983	28,016
01844	Methuen	(978)	47,255	50,706
*02346	Middleborough	(508)	23,116	25,463
01949	Middleton	(978)	8,987	10,110
01757	Milford	(508)	27,999	29,101
01757	Milford (c)	(508)	25,055	—
*01527	Millbury	(508)	13,261	13,947
02186	Milton	(617)	27,003	27,593
*02584	Nantucket	(508)	10,172	11,399
01760	Natick	(508)	33,006	36,050
*02494	Needham	(781)	28,886	31,388
*02740	New Bedford	(508)	95,072	95,363
*01950	Newburyport	(978)	17,416	18,289
*02456	Newton	(617)	85,146	88,414
02056	Norfolk	(508)	11,227	12,003
01247	North Adams	(413)	13,708	12,730
01845	North Andover	(978)	28,352	31,188
*02760	North Attleborough	(508)	28,712	29,364
*01864	North Reading	(978)	14,892	15,865
*01060	Northampton	(413)	28,549	28,451
01532	Northborough	(508)	14,155	15,109
01534	Northbridge	(508)	15,707	16,679
02766	Norton	(508)	19,031	19,948
02061	Norwell	(781)	10,506	11,153
02062	Norwood	(781)	28,602	29,725
01540	Oxford	(508)	13,709	14,009
01069	Palmer	(413)	12,140	12,232
*01960	Peabody	(978)	51,251	53,070
02359	Pembroke	(781)	17,837	18,509
01463	Pepperell	(978)	11,497	12,114
*01201	Pittsfield	(413)	44,737	42,142
*02360	Plymouth	(508)	56,468	61,528
*02169	Quincy	(617)	92,271	94,470
02368	Randolph	(781)	32,112	34,362
*02767	Raynham	(508)	13,383	14,470
01867	Reading	(781)	24,747	25,400
02769	Rehoboth	(508)	11,608	12,385
02151	Revere	(781)	51,755	53,073
02370	Rockland	(781)	17,489	17,986
*01970	Salem	(978)	41,340	43,226
02563	Sandwich	(508)	20,675	20,169
01906	Saugus	(781)	26,628	28,361
*02066	Scituate	(781)	18,133	18,924
02771	Seekonk	(508)	13,722	15,770
02067	Sharon	(781)	17,612	18,895
*01545	Shrewsbury	(508)	35,608	38,526
*02725	Somerset	(508)	18,165	18,129
*02143	Somerville	(617)	75,754	81,360
01075	South Hadley	(413)	17,514	17,625
02664	South Yarmouth (c)	(508)	11,092	—

ZIP	Place	Area code	2010 population	2019 estimate
*01745	Southborough	(508)	9,767	10,208
01550	Southbridge	(508)	16,719	16,878
01562	Spencer	(508)	11,688	11,935
*01103	Springfield	(413)	153,060	153,606
02180	Stoneham	(781)	21,437	24,126
02072	Stoughton	(781)	26,962	28,915
01776	Sudbury	(978)	17,659	19,655
01907	Swampscott	(781)	13,787	15,298
02777	Swansea	(508)	15,865	16,834
*02780	Taunton	(508)	55,874	57,464
01876	Tewksbury	(978)	28,961	31,178
01879	Tyngsborough	(978)	11,292	12,527
01569	Uxbridge	(508)	13,457	14,195
01880	Wakefield	(781)	24,932	27,045
02081	Walpole	(508)	24,070	25,200
*02451	Waltham	(781)	60,632	62,495
02571	Wareham	(508)	21,822	22,745
*02742	Watertown	(617)	31,915	35,939
01778	Wayland	(508)	12,994	13,835
01570	Webster	(508)	16,767	16,949
01570	Webster (c)	(508)	11,412	—
*02457	Wellesley	(781)	27,982	28,670
*01089	West Springfield	(413)	28,391	28,517
*01581	Westborough	(508)	18,272	19,144
*01085	Westfield	(413)	41,094	41,204
01886	Westford	(978)	21,951	24,817
02493	Weston	(781)	11,261	12,124
02790	Westport	(508)	15,532	16,034
02090	Westwood	(781)	14,618	16,400
*02188	Weymouth	(781)	53,743	57,746
02382	Whitman	(781)	14,489	15,216
01095	Wilbraham	(413)	14,219	14,689
01887	Wilmington	(978)	22,325	23,445
01475	Winchendon	(978)	10,300	10,905
01890	Winchester	(781)	21,374	22,799
02152	Winthrop	(617)	17,497	18,544
*01801	Woburn	(781)	38,120	40,228
*01602	Worcester	(508)	181,045	185,428
*02093	Wrentham	(508)	10,955	12,023
*02664	Yarmouth	(508)	23,793	23,203

Michigan

Area code 947 overlays area code 248.

ZIP	Place	Area code	2010 population	2019 estimate
49221	Adrian	(517)	21,133	20,600
48101	Allen Park	(313)	28,210	26,940
49401	Allendale (c)	(616)	17,579	—
*48103	Ann Arbor	(734)	113,934	119,980
*48326	Auburn Hills	(248)	21,412	24,748
*49014	Battle Creek	(269)	52,347	51,093
*48708	Bay City	(989)	34,932	32,717
48505	Beecher (c)	(810)	10,232	—
48072	Berkley	(248)	14,970	15,366
48025	Beverly Hills	(248)	10,267	10,352
49307	Big Rapids	(231)	10,601	10,363
*48009	Birmingham	(248)	20,103	21,389
*48509	Burton	(810)	29,999	28,574
49601	Cadillac	(231)	10,355	10,497
48017	Clawson	(248)	11,825	11,845
49036	Coldwater	(517)	10,945	12,215
49321	Comstock Park (c)	(616)	10,088	—
*49508	Cutlerville (c)	(616)	14,370	—
*48120	Dearborn	(313)	98,153	93,932
*48127	Dearborn Heights	(313)	57,774	55,353
*48201	Detroit	(313)	713,777	670,031
*48606	East Grand Rapids	(616)	10,694	11,956
*48823	East Lansing	(517)	48,579	48,145
48021	Eastpointe	(586)	32,442	32,081
49829	Escanaba	(906)	12,616	12,160
*48335	Farmington	(248)	10,372	10,491
*48331	Farmington Hills	(248)	79,740	80,612
48430	Fenton	(810)	11,756	11,403
48220	Ferndale	(248)	19,900	20,033
48134	Flat Rock	(734)	9,878	10,004
*48502	Flint	(810)	102,434	95,538
49506	Forest Hills (c)	(616)	25,867	—
48026	Fraser	(586)	14,480	14,480
*48135	Garden City	(734)	27,692	26,408
49417	Grand Haven	(616)	10,412	11,047
*49503	Grand Rapids	(616)	188,040	201,013
*49418	Grandville	(616)	15,378	15,858
*48230	Grosse Pointe Park	(313)	11,555	11,050
48236	Grosse Pointe Woods	(313)	16,135	15,332
*48212	Hamtramck	(313)	22,423	21,599
48225	Harper Woods	(313)	14,236	13,746
48840	Haslett (c)	(517)	19,220	—
48030	Hazel Park	(248)	16,422	16,347
*48203	Highland Park	(313)	11,776	10,775
*49423	Holland	(616)	33,051	33,216

ZIP	Place	Area code	2010 population	2019 estimate
48842	Holt (c)	(517)	23,973	—
48141	Inkster	(313)/(734)	25,369	24,284
48846	Ionia	(616)	11,394	11,168
*49201	Jackson	(517)	33,534	32,440
*49428	Jenison (c)	(616)	6,538	—
*49001	Kalamazoo	(269)	.262	76,200
*49508	Kentwood	(616)	.,707	51,898
*48915	Lansing	(517)	11-,297	118,210
48146	Lincoln Park	(313)	38,144	36,321
*48150	Livonia	(734)	96,942	93,665
48071	Madison Heights	(248)	29,694	29,886
49855	Marquette	(906)	21,355	20,995
48122	Melvindale	(313)	10,715	10,248
*48640	Midland	(989)	41,863	41,701
*48161	Monroe	(734)	20,733	19,552
*48043	Mount Clemens	(586)	16,314	16,163
*48858	Mount Pleasant	(989)	26,016	24,797
*49440	Muskegon	(231)	38,401	36,565
49444	Muskegon Heights	(231)	10,856	10,736
*48047	New Baltimore	(586)	12,084	12,347
49120	Niles	(269)	11,600	11,149
49505	Northview (c)	(616)	14,541	—
*49441	Norton Shores	(231)	23,994	24,664
*48374	Novi	(248)	55,224	60,896
48237	Oak Park	(248)	29,319	29,431
*48864	Okemos (c)	(517)	21,369	—
*48867	Owosso	(989)	15,194	14,441
*48340	Pontiac	(248)	59,515	59,884
*48060	Port Huron	(810)	30,184	28,749
49024	Portage	(269)	46,292	49,445
*48193	Riverview	(734)	12,486	12,032
*48307	Rochester	(248)	12,711	13,296
*48306	Rochester Hills	(248)	70,995	74,516
48174	Romulus	(313)/(734)	23,989	23,573
48066	Roseville	(586)	47,299	47,018
*48067	Royal Oak	(248)	57,236	59,277
*48601	Saginaw	(989)	51,508	48,115
*48080	Saint Clair Shores	(586)	59,715	58,984
*49783	Sault Ste. Marie	(906)	14,144	13,420
48178	South Lyon	(248)	11,327	11,821
*48033	Southfield	(248)	71,739	72,689
48195	Southgate	(734)	30,047	28,959
*48310	Sterling Heights	(586)	129,699	132,438
49091	Sturgis	(269)	10,994	10,861
*48180	Taylor	(313)/(734)	63,131	60,922
*49684	Traverse City	(231)	14,674	15,738
48183	Trenton	(734)	18,853	18,157
*48083	Troy	(248)	80,980	84,092
*49534	Walker	(616)	23,537	24,869
*48088	Warren	(586)	134,056	133,943
48917	Waverly (c)	(517)	23,925	—
48184	Wayne	(734)	17,593	16,814
*48185	Westland	(734)	84,094	81,511
48393	Wixom	(248)	13,498	14,049
48183	Woodhaven	(734)	12,875	12,469
*48192	Wyandotte	(734)	25,883	24,859
*49509	Wyoming	(616)	72,125	75,667
*48197	Ypsilanti	(734)	19,435	20,171

Minnesota

ZIP	Place	Area code	2010 population	2019 estimate
56007	Albert Lea	(507)	18,016	17,656
56308	Alexandria	(320)	11,070	13,822
*55304	Andover	(763)	30,598	33,140
*55303	Anoka	(763)	17,142	17,549
55124	Apple Valley	(952)	49,084	55,135
*55112	Arden Hills	(651)	9,552	10,281
55912	Austin	(507)	24,718	25,233
*56601	Bemidji	(218)	13,431	15,434
55309	Big Lake	(763)	10,060	11,226
*55014	Blaine	(763)	57,186	65,607
*55420	Bloomington	(952)	82,893	84,943
*56401	Brainerd	(218)	13,590	13,434
*55430	Brooklyn Center	(763)	30,104	30,690
*55443	Brooklyn Park	(763)	75,781	80,389
55313	Buffalo	(763)	15,453	16,442
*55337	Burnsville	(952)	60,306	61,339
55316	Champlin	(763)	23,089	25,268
55317	Chanhassen	(952)	22,952	26,389
55318	Chaska	(952)	23,770	26,989
55720	Cloquet	(218)	12,124	12,009
55421	Columbia Heights	(763)	19,496	20,427
*55553	Coon Rapids	(763)	61,476	62,998
*55016	Cottage Grove	(651)	34,589	37,604
*55422	Crystal	(763)	22,151	22,899
*55802	Duluth	(218)	86,265	85,618
*55121	Eagan	(651)	64,206	66,372
*55011	East Bethel	(763)	11,626	12,038
*55344	Eden Prairie	(952)	60,797	64,893

ZIP	Place	Area code	2010 population	2019 estimate
*55424	Edina	(952)	47,941	52,857
55330	Elk River	(763)	22,974	25,213
*56031	Fairmont	(507)	10,666	10,030
55021	Faribault	(507)	23,352	23,897
55024	Farmington	(651)	21,086	23,091
*56537	Fergus Falls	(218)	13,138	13,794
55025	Forest Lake	(651)	18,375	20,933
*55432	Fridley	(763)	27,208	27,826
*55427	Golden Valley	(763)	20,371	21,886
*55744	Grand Rapids	(218)	10,869	11,214
55304	Ham Lake	(763)	15,296	16,783
55033	Hastings	(651)	22,172	22,886
*55746	Hibbing	(218)	16,361	15,855
*55343	Hopkins	(952)	17,591	18,468
55038	Hugo	(651)	13,332	15,267
*55350	Hutchinson	(320)	14,178	13,983
*55076	Inver Grove Heights	(651)	33,880	35,672
55044	Lakeville	(952)	55,954	67,317
*55014	Lino Lakes	(651)	20,216	22,119
*55117	Little Canada	(651)	9,773	10,501
*56001	Mankato	(507)	39,309	42,931
*55311	Maple Grove	(763)	61,567	72,622
*55109	Maplewood	(651)	38,018	40,885
56258	Marshall	(507)	13,680	13,487
*55118	Mendota Heights	(651)	11,071	11,343
*55401	Minneapolis	(612)	382,578	429,606
*55345	Minnetonka	(952)	49,734	54,064
55362	Monticello	(763)	12,759	13,824
*56560	Moorhead	(218)	38,065	43,652
55112	Mounds View	(763)	12,155	13,324
55112	New Brighton	(651)	21,456	22,753
*54427	New Hope	(763)	20,339	20,907
56073	New Ulm	(507)	13,522	13,212
55056	North Branch	(651)	10,125	10,767
*56002	North Mankato	(507)	13,394	13,948
55109	North St. Paul	(651)	11,460	12,506
55057	Northfield	(507)	20,007	20,742
*55128	Oakdale	(651)	27,378	27,933
*55330	Otsego	(763)	13,571	18,113
55060	Owatonna	(507)	25,599	25,704
*55446	Plymouth	(763)	70,576	79,768
*55372	Prior Lake	(952)	22,796	27,241
*55303	Ramsey	(763)	23,668	27,721
55066	Red Wing	(651)	16,459	16,320
55423	Richfield	(612)	35,228	36,354
*55422	Robbinsdale	(763)	13,953	14,389
*55901	Rochester	(507)	106,769	118,935
*55374	Rogers	(763)	8,597	13,490
55068	Rosemount	(651)	21,874	25,207
*55113	Roseville	(651)	33,660	36,457
*56301	Saint Cloud	(320)	65,842	68,462
*55416	Saint Louis Park	(952)	45,250	48,662
*55376	Saint Michael	(763)	16,399	18,204
*55101	Saint Paul	(651)	285,068	308,096
56082	Saint Peter	(507)	11,196	11,953
56377	Sartell	(320)	15,876	18,926
56379	Sauk Rapids	(320)	12,773	14,146
55378	Savage	(952)	26,911	32,362
*55379	Shakopee	(952)	37,076	41,570
55126	Shoreview	(651)	25,043	27,130
*55075	South St. Paul	(651)	20,160	20,060
*55082	Stillwater	(651)	18,225	19,627
*55127	Vadnais Heights	(651)	12,302	13,607
*55318	Victoria	(952)	7,345	10,206
*55387	Waconia	(952)	10,697	12,370
*55118	West St. Paul	(651)	19,540	19,961
*55110	White Bear Lake	(651)	23,797	25,875
56201	Willmar	(320)	19,610	19,869
*55987	Winona	(507)	27,592	26,594
*55125	Woodbury	(651)	61,961	72,828
56187	Worthington	(507)	12,764	13,099

Mississippi

Area code 769 overlays area code 601.

ZIP	Place	Area code	2010 population	2019 estimate
*39520	Bay St. Louis	(228)	9,260	14,034
*39530	Biloxi	(228)	44,054	46,212
*39042	Brandon	(601)	21,705	24,289
*39601	Brookhaven	(601)	12,513	11,947
*39272	Byram	(601)	11,489	11,428
39046	Canton	(601)	13,189	12,094
*38614	Clarksdale	(662)	17,962	14,894
*38732	Cleveland	(662)	12,334	11,073
*39056	Clinton	(601)	25,216	24,440
*39701	Columbus	(662)	23,640	23,573
*38834	Corinth	(662)	14,573	14,472
39540	D'Iberville	(228)	9,486	14,012
39553	Gautier	(228)	18,572	18,490
*38701	Greenville	(662)	34,400	29,085

ZIP	Place	Area code	2010 population	2019 estimate
*38930	Greenwood	(662)	15,205	13,561
*38901	Grenada	(662)	13,092	12,219
*39501	Gulfport	(228)	67,793	71,705
*39401	Hattiesburg	(601)	45,989	45,863
38632	Hernando	(662)	14,090	16,399
38637	Horn Lake	(662)	26,066	27,272
*39201	Jackson	(601)	173,514	160,628
*39440	Laurel	(601)	18,540	18,338
39560	Long Beach	(228)	14,792	16,023
*39110	Madison	(601)	24,149	25,661
*39648	McComb	(601)	12,790	13,013
*39301	Meridian	(601)	41,148	36,347
*39563	Moss Point	(228)	13,704	13,350
*39120	Natchez	(601)	15,792	14,615
*39564	Ocean Springs	(228)	17,442	17,862
38654	Olive Branch	(662)	33,484	38,924
*38655	Oxford	(662)	18,916	28,122
*39567	Pascagoula	(228)	22,392	21,699
*39208	Pearl	(601)	25,092	26,510
39465	Petal	(601)	10,454	10,632
39466	Picayune	(601)	10,878	10,904
*39157	Ridgeland	(601)	24,047	24,104
*38671	Southaven	(662)	48,982	55,780
*39759	Starkville	(662)	23,888	25,653
*38801	Tupelo	(662)	34,546	38,312
*39180	Vicksburg	(601)	23,856	21,653
39773	West Point	(662)	11,307	10,404
*39194	Yazoo City	(662)	11,403	10,869

Missouri

ZIP	Place	Area code	2010 population	2019 estimate
63123	Affton (c)	(314)	20,307	—
63010	Arnold	(636)	20,808	21,091
*63011	Ballwin	(636)	30,404	30,082
63137	Bellefontaine Neighbors	(314)	10,860	10,397
64012	Belton	(816)	23,116	23,642
*64015	Blue Springs	(816)	52,575	55,829
*65613	Bolivar	(417)	10,325	11,067
*65616	Branson	(417)	10,520	11,630
63044	Bridgeton	(314)	11,550	11,520
*63701	Cape Girardeau	(573)	37,941	40,559
64836	Carthage	(417)	14,378	14,746
*63017	Chesterfield	(636)	47,484	47,538
*63105	Clayton	(314)	15,939	16,747
*65201	Columbia	(573)	108,500	123,195
*63128	Concord (c)	(314)	16,421	—
63126	Crestwood	(314)	11,912	11,834
63141	Creve Coeur	(314)	17,833	18,622
*63366	Dardenne Prairie	(636)	11,494	13,348
63025	Eureka	(636)	10,189	10,946
64024	Excelsior Springs	(816)	11,084	11,731
63640	Farmington	(573)	16,240	19,113
63135	Ferguson	(314)	21,203	20,525
63028	Festus	(636)	11,602	12,036
*63031	Florissant	(314)	52,158	50,952
65473	Fort Leonard Wood (c)	(573)	15,061	—
65251	Fulton	(573)	12,790	12,596
*64118	Gladstone	(816)	25,410	27,489
64029	Grain Valley	(816)	12,854	14,526
64030	Grandview	(816)	24,475	24,856
63401	Hannibal	(573)	17,916	17,346
64701	Harrisonville	(816)	10,019	10,078
*63042	Hazelwood	(314)	25,703	25,117
*64050	Independence	(816)	116,830	116,672
63755	Jackson	(573)	13,758	14,836
*65101	Jefferson City	(573)	43,079	42,708
63136	Jennings	(314)	14,712	14,575
*64801	Joplin	(417)	50,150	50,925
*64106	Kansas City	(816)	459,787	495,327
64060	Kearney	(816)	8,381	10,858
63857	Kennett	(573)	10,932	10,094
63501	Kirksville	(660)	17,505	17,602
63122	Kirkwood	(314)	27,540	27,807
63367	Lake St. Louis	(636)	14,545	16,864
65536	Lebanon	(417)	14,474	14,798
*64063	Lee's Summit	(816)	91,364	99,357
63125	Lemay (c)	(314)	16,645	—
*64068	Liberty	(816)	29,149	32,100
*63011	Manchester	(636)	18,094	18,073
65340	Marshall	(660)	13,065	12,841
63043	Maryland Heights	(314)	27,472	26,956
64468	Maryville	(660)	11,972	11,599
63129	Mehlville (c)	(314)	28,380	—
65265	Mexico	(573)	11,543	11,517
65270	Moberly	(660)	13,974	13,615
*64850	Neosho	(417)	11,835	12,054
65714	Nixa	(417)	19,022	22,515
63129	Oakville (c)	(314)	36,143	—
*63366	O'Fallon	(636)	79,329	88,673
63034	Old Jamestown (c)	(314)	19,184	—

ZIP	Place	Area code	2010 population	2019 estimate
63114	Overland	(314)	16,062	15,551
65721	Ozark	(417)	17,820	20,482
*63901	Poplar Bluff	(573)	17,023	16,937
*64083	Raymore	(816)	19,206	22,194
*64133	Raytown	(816)	29,526	28,991
65738	Republic	(417)	14,751	16,938
*65401	Rolla	(573)	19,559	20,431
63074	Saint Ann	(314)	13,020	12,629
*63301	Saint Charles	(636)	65,794	71,028
*64501	Saint Joseph	(816)	76,780	74,875
*63101	Saint Louis	(314)	319,294	300,576
*63376	Saint Peters	(636)	52,575	58,212
*65301	Sedalia	(660)	21,387	21,629
*63801	Sikeston	(573)	16,318	16,023
64089	Smithville	(816)	8,425	10,795
63138	Spanish Lake (c)	(314)	19,650	—
*65802	Springfield	(417)	159,498	167,882
63017	Town and Country	(314)	10,815	11,109
63379	Troy	(314)	10,540	12,820
63084	Union	(636)	10,204	11,990
63130	University City	(314)	35,371	34,165
64093	Warrensburg	(660)	18,838	20,418
63090	Washington	(636)	13,982	14,081
64870	Webb City	(417)	10,996	12,134
63119	Webster Groves	(314)	22,995	22,819
63385	Wentzville	(636)	29,070	41,784
65775	West Plains	(417)	11,986	12,304
*63040	Wildwood	(636)	35,517	35,432

Montana
Area code 406 applies to the entire state.

ZIP	Place	2010 population	2019 estimate
*59101	Billings	104,170	109,577
*59715	Bozeman	37,280	49,831
*59701	Butte-Silver Bow (balance)	33,525	34,207
*59401	Great Falls	58,505	58,434
*59601	Helena	28,190	33,124
*59901	Kalispell	19,927	24,565
*59801	Missoula	66,788	75,516

Nebraska
Area code 531 overlays area code 402.

ZIP	Place	Area code	2010 population	2019 estimate
68310	Beatrice	(402)	12,459	12,279
*68005	Bellevue	(402)	50,137	53,544
68138	Chalco (c)	(402)	10,994	—
*68601	Columbus	(402)	22,111	23,468
*68025	Fremont	(402)	26,397	26,383
*68801	Grand Island	(308)	48,520	51,267
*68901	Hastings	(402)	24,907	24,692
*68847	Kearney	(308)	30,787	33,867
*68128	La Vista	(402)	15,758	17,170
68850	Lexington	(308)	10,230	10,115
*68502	Lincoln	(402)	258,379	289,102
*68701	Norfolk	(402)	24,210	24,449
*69101	North Platte	(308)	24,733	23,639
*68102	Omaha	(402)	408,958	478,192
*68046	Papillion	(402)	18,894	20,471
*69361	Scottsbluff	(308)	15,039	14,556
68776	South Sioux City	(402)	13,353	12,809

Nevada
Area code 725 overlays area code 702.

ZIP	Place	Area code	2010 population	2019 estimate
*89005	Boulder City	(702)	15,023	16,207
*89701	Carson City	(775)	55,274	55,916
*89801	Elko	(775)	18,297	20,452
89124	Enterprise (c)	(702)	108,481	—
89408	Fernley	(775)	19,368	21,476
*89410	Gardnerville Ranchos (c)	(775)	11,312	—
*89015	Henderson	(702)	257,729	320,189
*89101	Las Vegas	(702)	583,756	651,319
*89027	Mesquite	(702)	15,276	19,726
*89030	North Las Vegas	(702)	216,961	251,974
*89048	Pahrump (c)	(775)	36,441	—
*89121	Paradise (c)	(702)	223,167	—
*89501	Reno	(775)	225,221	255,601
*89436	Spanish Springs (c)	(775)	15,064	—
*89431	Sparks	(775)	90,264	105,006
89815	Spring Creek (c)	(775)	12,361	—
*89117	Spring Valley (c)	(702)	178,395	—
89135	Summerlin South (c)	(702)	24,085	—
89433	Sun Valley (c)	(775)	19,299	—
*89110	Sunrise Manor (c)	(702)	189,372	—
89122	Whitney (c)	(702)	38,585	—
*89121	Winchester (c)	(702)	27,978	—

New Hampshire

Area code 603 applies to the entire state. See introductory note.

ZIP	Place	2010 population	2019 estimate
03031	Amherst	11,201	11,393
03110	Bedford	21,203	22,628
03570	Berlin	10,051	10,122
03743	Claremont	13,355	12,932
*03301	Concord	42,695	43,627
03818	Conway	10,115	10,252
03038	Derry	33,109	33,485
03038	Derry (c)	22,015	—
*03820	Dover	29,987	32,191
03824	Durham	14,638	16,293
03824	Durham (c)	10,345	—
03833	Exeter	14,306	15,313
03045	Goffstown	17,651	18,053
*03842	Hampton	15,430	15,495
03755	Hanover	11,260	11,473
03106	Hooksett	13,451	14,542
03051	Hudson	24,467	25,619
*03431	Keene	23,409	22,786
*03246	Laconia	15,951	16,581
*03766	Lebanon	13,151	13,651
*03053	Londonderry	24,129	26,490
*03053	Londonderry (c)	11,037	—
*03101	Manchester	109,565	112,673
03054	Merrimack	25,494	26,490
03055	Milford	15,115	16,411
*03060	Nashua	86,494	89,355
03076	Pelham	12,897	14,220
*03801	Portsmouth	20,779	21,927
03077	Raymond	10,138	10,529
*03867	Rochester	29,752	31,526
03079	Salem	28,776	29,791
03878	Somersworth	11,766	11,968
03087	Windham	13,592	14,853

New Jersey

Area code 551 overlays area code 201; 640 overlays 609; 848 overlays 732; 862 overlays 973.

ZIP	Place	Area code	2010 population	2019 estimate
07712	Asbury Park	(732)	16,116	15,408
*08401	Atlantic City	(609)	39,558	37,743
07001	Avenel (c)	(732)	17,011	—
07002	Bayonne	(201)	63,024	64,897
08722	Beachwood	(732)	11,045	11,312
*08031	Bellmawr	(856)	11,583	11,359
07621	Bergenfield	(201)	26,764	27,327
08805	Bound Brook	(732)	10,402	10,180
08807	Bradley Gardens (c)	(908)	14,206	—
08302	Bridgeton	(856)	25,349	24,160
08015	Browns Mills (c)	(609)	11,223	—
*08102	Camden	(856)	77,344	73,562
07008	Carteret	(732)	22,844	23,408
08002	Cherry Hill Mall (c)	(856)	14,171	—
07010	Cliffside Park	(201)	23,594	26,133
*07013	Clifton	(973)	84,136	85,052
*08108	Collingswood	(856)	13,926	13,884
07067	Colonia (c)	(732)	17,795	—
*07801	Dover	(973)	18,157	17,725
07628	Dumont	(201)	17,479	17,516
*07018	East Orange	(973)	64,270	64,367
*07724	Eatontown	(732)	12,709	12,157
08043	Echelon (c)	(856)	10,743	—
07020	Edgewater	(201)	11,513	13,364
*07201	Elizabeth	(908)	124,969	129,216
07407	Elmwood Park	(201)	19,403	19,966
*07631	Englewood	(201)	27,147	28,402
07410	Fair Lawn	(201)	32,457	32,896
07022	Fairview	(201)	13,835	14,189
07932	Florham Park	(973)	11,696	11,496
08863	Fords (c)	(732)	15,187	—
07024	Fort Lee	(201)	35,345	38,605
07417	Franklin Lakes	(201)	10,590	11,119
08823	Franklin Park (c)	(732)	13,295	—
07728	Freehold	(732)	12,052	11,682
07026	Garfield	(973)	30,487	31,802
08028	Glassboro	(856)	18,579	20,288
07452	Glen Rock	(201)	11,601	11,707
08030	Gloucester City	(856)	11,456	11,219
*08053	Greentree (c)	(856)	11,367	—
07093	Guttenberg	(201)	11,176	11,121
*07601	Hackensack	(201)	43,010	44,188
08033	Haddonfield	(856)	11,593	11,317
08690	Hamilton Square (c)	(609)	12,784	—
08037	Hammonton	(609)	14,791	13,934
07029	Harrison	(973)	13,620	20,061
07604	Hasbrouck Heights	(201)	11,842	11,992
*07506	Hawthorne	(973)	18,791	18,753
08904	Highland Park	(732)	13,982	13,711
07642	Hillsdale	(201)	10,219	10,307
07030	Hoboken	(201)	50,005	52,677
*08753	Holiday City-Berkeley (c)	(732)	12,831	—
07843	Hopatcong	(973)	15,147	14,186
08830	Iselin (c)	(732)	18,695	—
*07302	Jersey City	(201)	247,597	262,075
*07032	Kearny	(201)/(973)	40,684	41,058
08701	Lakewood (c)	(732)	53,805	—
07035	Lincoln Park	(973)	10,521	10,111
07036	Linden	(732)/(908)	40,499	42,361
08021	Lindenwold	(856)	17,613	17,263
07643	Little Ferry	(201)	10,626	10,739
07644	Lodi	(973)	24,136	24,347
07740	Long Branch	(732)	30,719	30,241
07940	Madison	(973)	15,845	17,654
08835	Manville	(908)	10,344	10,121
08053	Marlton (c)	(856)	10,133	—
08836	Martinsville (c)	(908)	11,980	—
08619	Mercerville (c)	(609)	13,230	—
08840	Metuchen	(732)	13,574	14,543
08846	Middlesex	(732)	13,635	13,679
08332	Millville	(856)	28,400	27,391
08057	Moorestown-Lenola (c)	(856)	14,217	—
*07960	Morristown	(973)	18,411	19,261
*08901	New Brunswick	(732)	55,181	55,676
07646	New Milford	(201)	16,341	16,429
07974	New Providence	(908)	12,171	13,595
*07102	Newark	(973)	277,140	282,011
07031	North Arlington	(201)	15,392	15,683
*07060	North Plainfield	(908)	21,936	21,289
07436	Oakland	(201)	12,754	12,926
*08050	Ocean Acres (c)	(609)	16,142	—
08226	Ocean City	(609)	11,701	10,971
08857	Old Bridge (c)	(732)	23,753	—
07650	Palisades Park	(201)	19,622	20,715
*07652	Paramus	(201)	26,342	26,264
07055	Passaic	(973)	69,781	69,703
*07505	Paterson	(973)	146,199	145,233
08070	Pennsville (c)	(856)	11,888	—
*08861	Perth Amboy	(732)	50,814	51,390
08865	Phillipsburg	(908)	14,950	14,212
08021	Pine Hill	(856)	10,233	10,417
*07060	Plainfield	(908)	49,808	50,317
08232	Pleasantville	(609)	20,249	20,149
08742	Point Pleasant	(732)	18,392	18,772
07442	Pompton Lakes	(973)	11,097	10,986
*08540	Princeton	(609)	12,307	31,187
08536	Princeton Meadows (c)	(609)	13,834	—
07065	Rahway	(732)	27,346	29,895
07446	Ramsey	(201)	14,473	14,884
*07701	Red Bank	(732)	12,206	11,966
07657	Ridgefield	(201)	11,032	11,171
07660	Ridgefield Park	(201)	12,729	12,901
07450	Ridgewood	(201)	24,958	25,056
07456	Ringwood	(973)	12,228	12,198
07661	River Edge	(201)	11,340	11,435
07751	Robertsville (c)	(732)	11,297	—
07203	Roselle	(908)	21,085	21,811
07204	Roselle Park	(908)	13,297	13,588
07070	Rutherford	(201)	18,061	18,303
*08872	Sayreville	(732)	42,704	44,173
*07094	Secaucus	(201)	16,264	21,893
07078	Short Hills (c)	(973)	13,165	—
08244	Somers Point	(609)	10,795	10,174
*08873	Somerset (c)	(732)	22,083	—
08876	Somerville	(908)	12,098	12,063
07080	South Plainfield	(732)/(908)	23,385	24,052
08882	South River	(732)	16,008	15,779
08003	Springdale (c)	(856)	14,518	—
*07901	Summit	(908)	21,457	21,897
07670	Tenafly	(201)	14,488	14,453
*07724	Tinton Falls	(732)	17,892	17,451
08753	Toms River (c)	(732)	88,791	—
*07512	Totowa	(973)	10,804	10,792
*08608	Trenton	(609)	84,913	83,203
07087	Union City	(201)	66,455	67,982
07043	Upper Montclair (c)	(973)	11,565	—
*08360	Vineland	(856)	60,724	59,439
07463	Waldwick	(201)	9,625	10,108
07057	Wallington	(201)/(973)	11,335	11,495
07465	Wanaque	(201)/(973)	11,116	11,762
07728	West Freehold (c)	(908)	13,613	—
07093	West New York	(201)	49,708	52,723
*07090	Westfield	(908)	30,316	29,512
*07675	Westwood	(201)	10,908	11,078
08094	Williamstown (c)	(609)/(856)	15,567	—
07095	Woodbridge (c)	(732)	19,265	—
07424	Woodland Park	(973)	11,819	12,581

New Mexico

ZIP	Place	Area code	2010 population	2019 estimate
*88310	Alamogordo	(575)	30,403	31,980
*87102	Albuquerque	(505)	545,852	560,513
*88210	Artesia	(575)	11,301	12,356

ZIP	Place	Area code	2010 population	2019 estimate
87004	Bernalillo..............	(505)	8,320	10,477
*88220	Carlsbad.............	(575)	26,138	29,810
*88021	Chaparral (c).........	(575)	14,631	—
*88101	Clovis..............	(575)	37,775	38,319
*88030	Deming.............	(575)	14,855	13,880
*87532	Española.............	(505)	10,224	10,044
*87401	Farmington...........	(505)	45,877	44,372
*87301	Gallup..............	(505)	21,678	21,493
*88240	Hobbs..............	(575)	34,122	39,141
*88001	Las Cruces...........	(575)	97,618	103,432
*87701	Las Vegas............	(505)	13,753	12,919
*87544	Los Alamos (c)........	(505)	12,019	—
88031	Los Lunas............	(505)	14,835	16,061
88260	Lovington............	(575)	11,009	11,489
87107	North Valley (c)........	(505)	11,333	—
*88130	Portales.............	(575)	12,280	11,610
*87124	Rio Rancho...........	(505)	87,521	99,178
*88201	Roswell.............	(575)	48,366	47,551
*87501	Santa Fe.............	(505)	67,947	84,683
87105	South Valley (c)........	(505)	40,976	—
*88063	Sunland Park..........	(575)	14,106	17,978

New York

Area codes 347/929 overlay area code 718; 332/646/917 overlay 212; 680 overlays 315; 838 overlays 518; 934 overlays 631.

ZIP	Place	Area code	2010 population	2019 estimate
*12202	Albany..............	(518)	97,856	96,460
12010	Amsterdam...........	(518)	18,620	17,766
*13021	Auburn.............	(315)	27,687	26,173
*11702	Babylon.............	(631)	12,166	11,992
11510	Baldwin (c)..........	(516)	24,033	—
*14020	Batavia.............	(585)	15,465	14,379
11706	Bay Shore (c).........	(631)	26,337	—
12508	Beacon.............	(845)	15,541	13,968
11710	Bellmore (c)..........	(516)	16,218	—
11714	Bethpage (c)..........	(516)	16,429	—
*13901	Binghamton..........	(607)	47,376	44,399
11716	Bohemia (c)..........	(631)	10,180	—
11717	Brentwood (c).........	(631)	60,664	—
*14610	Brighton (c)..........	(585)	36,609	—
*14201	Buffalo.............	(716)	261,310	255,284
*14424	Canandaigua.........	(585)	10,545	10,156
11720	Centereach (c)........	(631)	31,578	—
*11722	Central Islip (c).......	(631)	34,450	—
*14227	Cheektowaga (c).......	(716)	75,178	—
12047	Cohoes.............	(518)	16,168	16,687
11725	Commack (c).........	(631)	36,124	—
11726	Copiague (c).........	(631)	22,993	—
11727	Coram (c)...........	(631)	39,113	—
*14830	Corning.............	(607)	11,183	10,538
13045	Cortland............	(607)	19,204	18,670
11729	Deer Park (c).........	(631)	27,745	—
14043	Depew.............	(716)	15,303	15,011
*11746	Dix Hills (c)..........	(631)	26,892	—
10522	Dobbs Ferry..........	(914)	10,875	11,027
*14048	Dunkirk.............	(716)	12,563	11,756
11730	East Islip (c).........	(631)	14,475	—
11758	East Massapequa (c)....	(516)	19,069	—
11554	East Meadow (c).......	(516)	38,132	—
11731	East Northport (c)......	(631)	20,217	—
11772	East Patchogue (c).....	(631)	22,469	—
*10709	Eastchester (c)........	(914)	19,554	—
14226	Eggertsville (c)........	(716)	15,019	—
*14901	Elmira..............	(607)	29,200	27,054
11003	Elmont (c)...........	(516)	33,198	—
11731	Elwood (c)...........	(631)	11,177	—
*13760	Endicott.............	(607)	13,392	12,532
13762	Endwell (c)...........	(607)	11,446	—
13219	Fairmount (c).........	(315)	10,224	—
11738	Farmingville (c)........	(631)	15,481	—
*11001	Floral Park...........	(516)	15,863	15,844
*13602	Fort Drum (c).........	(315)	12,955	—
11768	Fort Salonga (c).......	(631)	10,008	—
11010	Franklin Square (c).....	(516)	29,320	—
14063	Fredonia............	(716)	11,230	10,303
11520	Freeport............	(516)	42,860	42,956
13069	Fulton.............	(315)	11,896	11,102
*11530	Garden City..........	(516)	22,371	22,454
14456	Geneva.............	(315)	13,261	12,631
11542	Glen Cove...........	(516)	26,964	27,166
*12801	Glens Falls..........	(518)	14,700	14,262
12078	Gloversville..........	(518)	15,665	14,747
*11023	Great Neck..........	(516)	9,989	10,209
14616	Greece (c)..........	(585)	14,519	—
11740	Greenlawn (c)........	(631)	13,742	—
11946	Hampton Bays (c)......	(631)	13,603	—
10528	Harrison............	(914)	27,472	28,943
*11788	Hauppauge (c)........	(631)	20,882	—
10927	Haverstraw..........	(845)	11,910	12,045
*11550	Hempstead..........	(516)	53,891	55,113

ZIP	Place	Area code	2010 population	2019 estimate
*11801	Hicksville (c).........	(516)	41,547	—
11741	Holbrook (c).........	(631)	27,195	—
*11742	Holtsville (c).........	(631)	19,714	—
11743	Huntington (c)........	(631)	18,046	—
*11746	Huntington Station (c)....	(631)	33,029	—
*14617	Irondequoit (c).......	(585)	51,692	—
11751	Islip (c)............	(631)	18,689	—
*14850	Ithaca.............	(607)	30,014	30,837
*14701	Jamestown..........	(716)	31,146	29,058
*10535	Jefferson Valley-Yorktown (c)	(914)	14,142	—
11753	Jericho (c)..........	(516)	13,567	—
13790	Johnson City.........	(607)	15,174	14,161
*14217	Kenmore............	(716)	15,423	15,020
11754	Kings Park (c)........	(631)	17,282	—
*12401	Kingston............	(845)	23,893	22,793
10950	Kiryas Joel..........	(845)	20,175	26,813
14218	Lackawanna..........	(716)	18,141	17,720
11755	Lake Grove..........	(631)	11,163	11,056
11779	Lake Ronkonkoma (c)....	(631)	20,155	—
14086	Lancaster...........	(716)	10,352	10,109
11756	Levittown (c).........	(516)	51,881	—
11757	Lindenhurst..........	(631)	27,253	26,801
*14094	Lockport............	(716)	21,165	20,305
11561	Long Beach..........	(516)	33,275	33,454
11563	Lynbrook............	(516)	19,427	19,448
10543	Mamaroneck.........	(914)	18,929	19,131
11949	Manorville (c)........	(631)	14,314	—
11758	Massapequa (c).......	(516)	21,685	—
11762	Massapequa Park......	(516)	17,008	17,143
13662	Massena............	(315)	10,936	10,200
11950	Mastic (c)..........	(631)	15,481	—
11951	Mastic Beach (c)......	(631)	12,930	—
11763	Medford (c)..........	(631)	24,142	—
*11747	Melville (c)..........	(631)	18,985	—
11566	Merrick (c)..........	(516)	22,097	—
11953	Middle Island (c)......	(631)	10,483	—
*10940	Middletown..........	(845)	28,086	28,189
11764	Miller Place (c).......	(631)	12,339	—
11501	Mineola............	(516)	18,799	19,207
10952	Monsey (c)..........	(845)	18,412	—
10549	Mount Kisco.........	(914)	10,877	10,795
11766	Mount Sinai (c).......	(631)	12,118	—
*10550	Mount Vernon........	(914)	67,292	67,345
10954	Nanuet (c)..........	(845)	17,882	—
11767	Nesconset (c)........	(631)	13,387	—
11590	New Cassel (c).......	(516)	14,059	—
10956	New City (c).........	(845)	33,559	—
*10801	New Rochelle........	(914)	77,062	78,557
*10001	New York........	(212)/(718)	8,175,133	8,336,817
*12550	Newburgh..........	(845)	28,866	28,177
*14301	Niagara Falls........	(716)	50,193	47,720
11701	North Amityville (c)....	(631)	17,862	—
11703	North Babylon (c).....	(631)	17,509	—
11706	North Bay Shore (c)....	(631)	18,944	—
11710	North Bellmore (c).....	(516)	19,941	—
11713	North Bellport (c).....	(631)	11,545	—
11757	North Lindenhurst (c)...	(631)	11,652	—
11758	North Massapequa (c)...	(516)	17,886	—
11566	North Merrick (c)......	(516)	12,272	—
11040	North New Hyde Park (c)	(516)	14,899	—
14120	North Tonawanda......	(716)	31,568	30,245
11580	North Valley Stream (c)..	(516)	16,628	—
11793	North Wantagh (c).....	(516)	11,960	—
11572	Oceanside (c)........	(516)	32,109	—
13669	Ogdensburg.........	(315)	11,128	10,436
14760	Olean............	(585)/(716)	14,452	13,437
13421	Oneida.............	(315)	11,393	10,894
13820	Oneonta............	(007)	13,901	13,907
10562	Ossining............	(914)	25,060	24,812
13126	Oswego.............	(315)	18,142	17,236
11772	Patchogue...........	(631)	11,798	12,321
10965	Pearl River (c)........	(845)	15,876	—
10566	Peekskill............	(914)	23,583	24,295
11803	Plainview (c).........	(516)	26,217	—
*12901	Plattsburgh..........	(518)	19,989	19,515
*10573	Port Chester.........	(914)	28,967	29,163
*11050	Port Washington (c)....	(516)	15,846	—
12601	Poughkeepsie........	(845)	32,736	30,515
11961	Ridge (c)...........	(631)	13,336	—
11901	Riverhead (c)........	(631)	13,299	—
*14604	Rochester...........	(585)	210,565	205,695
*11570	Rockville Centre.......	(516)	24,023	24,550
11778	Rocky Point (c).......	(631)	14,014	—
*13440	Rome.............	(315)	33,725	32,148
11779	Ronkonkoma (c).......	(631)	19,082	—
11575	Roosevelt (c).........	(516)	16,258	—
12306	Rotterdam (c)........	(518)	20,652	—
10580	Rye..............	(914)	15,720	15,695
*11780	Saint James (c).......	(631)	13,338	—
13454	Salisbury (c).........	(315)	12,093	—
12866	Saratoga Springs......	(518)	26,586	28,212

ZIP	Place	Area code	2010 population	2019 estimate
11782	Sayville (c)	(631)	16,853	—
*10583	Scarsdale	(914)	17,166	17,871
*12305	Schenectady	(518)	66,135	65,273
11783	Seaford (c)	(516)	15,294	—
11784	Selden (c)	(631)	19,851	—
11733	Setauket-East Setauket (c)	(631)	15,477	—
11967	Shirley (c)	(631)	27,854	—
10591	Sleepy Hollow	(914)	9,870	10,046
*11787	Smithtown (c)	(631)	26,470	—
11735	South Farmingdale (c)	(516)	14,486	—
10977	Spring Valley	(845)	31,347	32,261
*11790	Stony Brook (c)	(631)	13,740	—
10980	Stony Point (c)	(845)	12,147	—
10901	Suffern	(845)	10,723	11,007
*11791	Syosset (c)	(516)	18,829	—
*13202	Syracuse	(315)	145,170	142,327
10591	Tarrytown	(914)	11,277	11,370
11776	Terryville (c)	(631)	11,849	—
*14150	Tonawanda	(716)	15,130	14,745
*14150	Tonawanda (c)	(716)	58,144	—
*12180	Troy	(518)	50,129	49,154
*11553	Uniondale (c)	(516)	24,759	—
*13501	Utica	(315)	62,235	59,750
*11580	Valley Stream	(516)	37,511	37,431
11793	Wantagh (c)	(516)	18,871	—
*13601	Watertown	(315)	27,023	24,838
*11704	West Babylon (c)	(631)	43,213	—
10993	West Haverstraw	(845)	10,165	10,189
*11552	West Hempstead (c)	(516)	18,862	—
11795	West Islip (c)	(631)	28,335	—
*14224	West Seneca (c)	(716)	44,711	—
*11590	Westbury	(516)	15,146	15,351
*10601	White Plains	(914)	56,853	58,109
11797	Woodbury	(845)	10,686	11,089
11598	Woodmere (c)	(516)	17,121	—
11798	Wyandanch (c)	(631)	11,647	—
*10701	Yonkers	(914)	195,976	200,370

North Carolina

Area code 743 overlays area code 336; 980 overlays 704; 984 overlays 919.

ZIP	Place	Area code	2010 population	2019 estimate
*28001	Albemarle	(704)	15,903	16,246
*27502	Apex	(919)	37,476	59,300
27263	Archdale	(336)	11,415	11,513
*27203	Asheboro	(336)	25,012	25,940
*28801	Asheville	(828)	83,393	92,870
28012	Belmont	(704)	10,076	12,558
28607	Boone	(828)	17,122	19,667
*27215	Burlington	(336)	49,963	54,606
27510	Carrboro	(919)	19,582	21,190
*27511	Cary	(919)	135,234	170,282
*27514	Chapel Hill	(919)	57,233	64,051
*28202	Charlotte	(704)	731,424	885,708
*27520	Clayton	(919)	16,116	24,887
27012	Clemmons	(336)	18,627	20,867
*28025	Concord	(704)	79,066	96,341
28031	Cornelius	(704)	24,866	30,257
28036	Davidson	(704)	10,944	13,054
*27701	Durham	(919)	228,330	278,993
*27288	Eden	(336)	15,527	14,886
*27909	Elizabeth City	(252)	18,683	17,751
27244	Elon	(336)	9,419	12,232
*28301	Fayetteville	(910)	200,564	211,657
27526	Fuquay-Varina	(919)	17,937	30,324
27529	Garner	(919)	25,745	31,407
*28052	Gastonia	(704)	71,741	77,273
*27530	Goldsboro	(919)	36,437	34,186
27253	Graham	(336)	14,153	15,646
*27401	Greensboro	(336)	269,666	296,710
*27834	Greenville	(252)	84,554	93,400
28075	Harrisburg	(704)	11,526	16,576
*28532	Havelock	(252)	20,735	19,854
*27536	Henderson	(252)	15,368	14,911
*28792	Hendersonville	(828)	13,137	14,157
*28601	Hickory	(828)	40,010	41,171
*27260	High Point	(336)	104,371	112,791
27540	Holly Springs	(919)	24,661	37,812
28348	Hope Mills	(910)	15,176	15,849
*28078	Huntersville	(704)	46,773	58,098
28079	Indian Trail	(704)	33,518	40,252
*28540	Jacksonville	(910)	70,145	72,436
28081	Kannapolis	(704)	42,625	50,841
*27284	Kernersville	(336)	23,123	24,660
28086	Kings Mountain	(704)	10,296	10,982
*28501	Kinston	(252)	21,677	20,041
27545	Knightdale	(919)	11,401	17,843
*28352	Laurinburg	(910)	15,962	15,002
28451	Leland	(910)	13,527	23,544
*28645	Lenoir	(828)	18,228	17,913
27023	Lewisville	(336)	12,639	14,228
*27292	Lexington	(336)	18,931	18,933
*28092	Lincolnton	(704)	10,486	11,200
*28358	Lumberton	(910)	21,542	20,484
*28105	Matthews	(704)	27,198	33,138
27302	Mebane	(919)	11,393	16,262
28227	Mint Hill	(704)	22,722	27,617
*28110	Monroe	(704)	32,797	35,540
*28115	Mooresville	(704)	32,711	39,132
28655	Morganton	(828)	16,918	16,577
27560	Morrisville	(919)	18,576	28,846
*27030	Mount Airy	(336)	10,388	10,208
28120	Mount Holly	(704)	13,656	16,257
28411	Murraysville (c)	(910)	14,215	—
*28560	New Bern	(252)	29,524	29,994
28658	Newton	(828)	12,968	13,177
*28374	Pinehurst	(910)	13,124	16,620
28399	Piney Green (c)	(910)	13,293	—
*27601	Raleigh	(919)	403,892	474,069
*27320	Reidsville	(336)	14,520	13,987
27870	Roanoke Rapids	(252)	15,754	14,320
*27801	Rocky Mount	(252)	57,477	53,922
*28144	Salisbury	(704)	33,662	33,988
*27330	Sanford	(919)	28,094	30,085
*28150	Shelby	(704)	20,323	20,026
27577	Smithfield	(919)	10,966	12,985
*28387	Southern Pines	(910)	12,334	14,657
28390	Spring Lake	(910)	11,964	12,005
28104	Stallings	(704)	13,831	16,145
*28677	Statesville	(704)	24,532	27,528
27358	Summerfield	(336)	10,232	11,376
27886	Tarboro	(252)	11,415	10,715
*27360	Thomasville	(336)	26,757	26,649
*27587	Wake Forest	(919)	30,117	45,629
28173	Waxhaw	(704)	9,859	17,147
*28785	Waynesville	(828)	9,869	10,141
28104	Weddington	(704)	9,459	11,182
*28401	Wilmington	(910)	106,476	123,744
*27893	Wilson	(252)	49,167	49,459
*27101	Winston-Salem	(336)	229,617	247,945

North Dakota

Area code 701 applies to the entire state.

ZIP	Place	2010 population	2019 estimate
*58501	Bismarck	61,272	73,529
*58601	Dickinson	17,787	23,133
*58102	Fargo	105,549	124,662
*58201	Grand Forks	52,838	55,839
*58401	Jamestown	15,427	15,084
58554	Mandan	18,331	22,752
*58701	Minot	40,888	47,382
58078	West Fargo	25,830	37,058
*58801	Williston	14,716	29,033

Ohio

Area code 220 overlays area code 740; 234 overlays 330; 326 overlays 937; 380 overlays 614; 567 overlays 419.

ZIP	Place	Area code	2010 population	2019 estimate
*44301	Akron	(330)	199,110	197,597
44601	Alliance	(330)	22,322	21,446
44001	Amherst	(440)	12,021	12,219
44805	Ashland	(419)	20,362	20,275
*44004	Ashtabula	(440)	19,124	18,017
45701	Athens	(740)	23,832	24,536
44202	Aurora	(330)	15,548	16,338
44515	Austintown (c)	(330)	29,677	—
44011	Avon	(440)	21,193	23,399
44012	Avon Lake	(440)	22,581	24,504
44203	Barberton	(330)	26,550	25,953
44140	Bay Village	(440)	15,651	15,194
44122	Beachwood	(216)	11,953	11,590
*45432	Beavercreek	(937)	45,193	47,741
44146	Bedford	(216)/(440)	13,074	12,457
*44146	Bedford Heights	(216)/(440)	10,751	10,460
43311	Bellefontaine	(937)	13,370	13,249
44017	Berea	(440)	19,093	18,609
43209	Bexley	(614)	13,057	13,770
*45242	Blue Ash	(513)	12,114	12,372
*44512	Boardman (c)	(330)	35,376	—
*43402	Bowling Green	(419)	30,028	31,504
44141	Brecksville	(440)	13,656	13,604
45211	Bridgetown (c)	(513)	14,407	—
44147	Broadview Heights	(440)	19,400	19,102
44142	Brook Park	(216)/(440)	19,212	18,382
44144	Brooklyn	(216)	11,169	10,646
44212	Brunswick	(330)	34,255	34,880
44820	Bucyrus	(419)	12,362	11,764
*43725	Cambridge	(740)	10,635	10,289

ZIP	Place	Area code	2010 population	2019 estimate
*44702	Canton	(330)	73,007	70,447
*45822	Celina	(419)	10,400	10,425
*45458	Centerville	(937)	23,999	23,703
45601	Chillicothe	(740)	21,901	21,722
*45202	Cincinnati	(513)	296,943	303,940
43113	Circleville	(740)	13,314	14,050
45315	Clayton	(937)	13,209	13,222
*44102	Cleveland	(216)	396,815	381,009
*44118	Cleveland Heights	(216)	46,121	43,992
*43201	Columbus	(614)	787,033	898,553
44030	Conneaut	(440)	12,841	12,530
43812	Coshocton	(740)	11,216	11,051
*44221	Cuyahoga Falls	(330)	49,652	49,106
*45402	Dayton	(937)	141,527	140,407
43512	Defiance	(419)	16,494	16,634
43015	Delaware	(740)	34,753	41,283
*45247	Dent (c)	(513)	10,497	—
44622	Dover	(330)	12,826	12,723
*43016	Dublin	(614)	41,751	49,037
*44112	East Cleveland	(216)	17,843	16,964
43920	East Liverpool	(330)	11,195	10,603
*44095	Eastlake	(440)	18,577	18,042
*44035	Elyria	(440)	54,533	53,757
45322	Englewood	(937)	13,465	13,435
*44117	Euclid	(216)	48,920	46,550
45324	Fairborn	(937)	32,352	33,876
*45011	Fairfield	(513)	42,510	42,558
44126	Fairview Park	(440)	16,826	16,161
*45840	Findlay	(419)	41,202	41,225
*45224	Finneytown (c)	(513)	12,741	—
45240	Forest Park	(513)	18,720	18,583
45230	Forestville (c)	(513)	10,532	—
44830	Fostoria	(419)	13,441	13,225
45005	Franklin	(513)	11,771	11,612
43420	Fremont	(419)	16,734	15,917
43230	Gahanna	(614)	33,248	35,483
*44125	Garfield Heights	(216)	28,849	27,448
44232	Green	(330)	25,699	25,752
45331	Greenville	(937)	13,227	12,615
43123	Grove City	(614)	35,575	41,820
*45011	Hamilton	(513)	62,477	62,082
45030	Harrison	(513)	9,897	11,896
43056	Heath	(740)	10,310	10,942
43026	Hilliard	(614)	28,435	36,534
45424	Huber Heights	(937)	38,101	38,154
*44236	Hudson	(330)	22,262	22,237
45638	Ironton	(740)	11,129	10,532
*44240	Kent	(330)	28,904	29,646
*45429	Kettering	(937)	56,163	54,955
44107	Lakewood	(216)	52,131	49,678
43130	Lancaster	(740)	38,780	40,505
45036	Lebanon	(513)	20,033	20,659
*45801	Lima	(419)	38,771	36,659
43140	London	(740)	9,904	10,328
*44052	Lorain	(440)	64,097	63,855
*45140	Loveland	(513)	12,081	13,145
44124	Lyndhurst	(216)/(440)	14,001	13,366
*44056	Macedonia	(330)	11,188	12,000
*45248	Mack (c)	(513)	11,585	—
*44902	Mansfield	(419)	47,821	46,599
44137	Maple Heights	(216)	23,138	22,078
45750	Marietta	(740)	14,085	13,354
*43302	Marion	(740)	36,837	35,883
*43040	Marysville	(937)	22,094	24,667
*45036	Mason	(513)	30,712	33,870
*44646	Massillon	(330)	32,149	32,584
43537	Maumee	(419)	14,286	13,669
44124	Mayfield Heights	(440)	19,155	18,487
*44256	Medina	(330)	26,678	25,956
*44060	Mentor	(440)	47,159	47,262
*45343	Miamisburg	(937)	20,181	20,143
44130	Middleburg Heights	(216)/(440)	15,946	15,432
*45042	Middletown	(513)	48,694	48,807
*45247	Monfort Heights (c)	(513)	11,948	—
*45050	Monroe	(513)	12,442	14,015
45242	Montgomery	(513)	10,251	10,872
43050	Mount Vernon	(740)	16,990	16,769
43054	New Albany	(614)	7,724	10,933
*44216	New Franklin	(330)	14,227	14,133
44663	New Philadelphia	(330)	17,288	17,410
*43055	Newark	(740)	47,573	50,315
44446	Niles	(330)	19,266	18,176
*44720	North Canton	(330)	17,488	17,716
44070	North Olmsted	(440)	32,718	31,341
*44039	North Ridgeville	(440)	29,465	34,392
44133	North Royalton	(440)	30,444	30,068
*45251	Northbrook (c)	(513)	10,668	—
44203	Norton	(330)	12,085	11,966
44857	Norwalk	(419)	17,012	16,867
45212	Norwood	(513)	19,207	19,776
*43616	Oregon	(419)	20,291	20,055
45056	Oxford	(513)	21,371	23,110
44077	Painesville	(440)	19,563	19,886
*44129	Parma	(216)/(440)	81,601	78,103
44130	Parma Heights	(440)	20,718	19,790
*43062	Pataskala	(740)	14,962	15,883
*43551	Perrysburg	(419)	20,623	21,626
43147	Pickerington	(614)/(740)	18,291	22,158
*45356	Piqua	(937)	20,522	21,332
*45662	Portsmouth	(740)	20,226	20,158
43065	Powell	(614)	11,500	13,375
44266	Ravenna	(330)	11,724	11,361
*45215	Reading	(513)	10,385	10,296
*43008	Reynoldsburg	(614)	35,893	38,327
44143	Richmond Heights	(216)/(440)	10,546	10,342
45431	Riverside	(937)	25,201	25,133
44116	Rocky River	(216)/(440)	20,213	19,986
*44460	Salem	(330)	12,303	11,612
*44870	Sandusky	(419)	25,793	24,564
44131	Seven Hills	(216)/(440)	11,804	11,590
*44120	Shaker Heights	(216)	28,448	27,027
45241	Sharonville	(513)	13,560	13,684
*45365	Sidney	(937)	21,229	20,449
44139	Solon	(440)	23,348	22,779
*44121	South Euclid	(216)/(440)	22,295	21,297
45066	Springboro	(937)	17,409	18,931
45246	Springdale	(513)	11,223	11,166
*45502	Springfield	(937)	60,608	58,877
*43952	Steubenville	(740)	18,659	17,753
44224	Stow	(330)	34,837	34,785
44241	Streetsboro	(330)	16,028	16,478
*44136	Strongsville	(440)	44,750	44,660
44471	Struthers	(330)	10,713	10,111
43560	Sylvania	(419)	18,965	19,311
44278	Tallmadge	(330)	17,537	17,519
44883	Tiffin	(419)	17,963	17,582
45371	Tipp City	(937)	9,689	10,115
*43604	Toledo	(419)	287,208	272,779
45067	Trenton	(513)	11,869	13,141
*45426	Trotwood	(937)	24,431	24,403
*45373	Troy	(937)	25,058	26,281
44087	Twinsburg	(330)	18,795	18,856
*44122	University Heights	(216)	13,539	12,797
*43221	Upper Arlington	(614)	33,771	35,366
43078	Urbana	(937)	11,793	11,404
45891	Van Wert	(419)	10,846	10,676
45377	Vandalia	(937)	15,246	14,997
*44089	Vermilion	(440)	10,594	10,394
*44281	Wadsworth	(330)	21,567	24,046
*44481	Warren	(330)	41,557	38,752
*44122	Warrensville Heights	(216)	13,542	13,108
43160	Washington Court House	(740)	14,192	14,091
*45449	West Carrollton	(937)	13,143	12,864
*43081	Westerville	(614)	36,120	41,103
44145	Westlake	(440)	32,729	32,032
*45239	White Oak (c)	(513)	19,167	—
43213	Whitehall	(614)	18,062	18,926
44092	Wickliffe	(440)	12,750	12,744
*44094	Willoughby	(440)	22,268	22,977
44095	Willowick	(440)	14,171	14,105
45177	Wilmington	(937)	12,520	12,366
*44691	Wooster	(330)	26,119	26,394
43085	Worthington	(614)	13,575	14,692
45385	Xenia	(937)	25,719	26,947
*44503	Youngstown	(330)	66,982	65,469
*43701	Zanesville	(740)	25,487	25,158

Oklahoma

Area code 539 overlays area code 918; 572 overlays 405 effective May 24, 2021.

ZIP	Place	Area code	2010 population	2019 estimate
*74820	Ada	(580)	16,810	17,235
*73521	Altus	(580)	19,813	18,338
*73401	Ardmore	(580)	24,283	24,698
*74003	Bartlesville	(918)	35,750	36,144
73008	Bethany	(405)	19,051	19,221
73008	Bixby	(918)	20,884	27,944
*74012	Broken Arrow	(918)	98,850	110,198
*73018	Chickasha	(405)	16,036	16,431
73020	Choctaw	(405)	11,146	12,674
74017	Claremore	(918)	18,581	18,743
74429	Coweta	(918)	9,943	10,032
*73115	Del City	(405)	21,332	21,712
*73533	Duncan	(580)	23,431	22,344
*74701	Durant	(580)	15,856	18,673
*73034	Edmond	(405)	81,405	94,054
73036	El Reno	(405)	16,749	19,965
*73644	Elk City	(580)	11,693	11,577
*73701	Enid	(580)	49,379	49,688
74033	Glenpool	(918)	10,808	13,936
73044	Guthrie	(405)	10,191	11,661

ZIP	Place	Area code	2010 population	2019 estimate
73942	Guymon	(580)	11,442	10,996
74037	Jenks	(918)	16,924	23,767
*73501	Lawton	(580)	96,867	93,025
*74501	McAlester	(918)	18,383	17,814
*74354	Miami	(918)	13,570	13,088
*73110	Midwest City	(405)	54,371	57,407
*73160	Moore	(405)	55,081	62,055
*74401	Muskogee	(918)	39,223	37,113
73064	Mustang	(405)	17,395	22,959
73065	Newcastle	(405)	7,685	10,655
*73069	Norman	(405)	110,925	124,880
*73102	Oklahoma City	(405)	579,999	655,057
74447	Okmulgee	(918)	12,321	11,711
74055	Owasso	(918)	28,915	36,957
*74601	Ponca City	(580)	25,387	23,660
74063	Sand Springs	(918)	18,906	19,905
*74066	Sapulpa	(918)	20,544	21,278
*74801	Shawnee	(405)	29,857	31,436
*74074	Stillwater	(405)	45,688	50,299
*74464	Tahlequah	(918)	15,753	16,819
*74103	Tulsa	(918)	391,906	401,190
*73122	Warr Acres	(405)	10,043	10,118
73096	Weatherford	(580)	10,833	12,017
*73801	Woodward	(580)	12,051	12,121
*73099	Yukon	(405)	22,709	28,084

Oregon

Area code 458 overlays area code 541; 971 overlays 503.

ZIP	Place	Area code	2010 population	2019 estimate
*97321	Albany	(541)	50,158	55,338
*97006	Aloha (c)	(503)	49,425	—
97603	Altamont (c)	(541)	19,257	—
97520	Ashland	(541)	20,078	21,281
97103	Astoria	(503)	9,477	10,015
*97005	Beaverton	(503)	89,803	99,037
*97701	Bend	(541)	76,639	100,421
97229	Bethany (c)	(503)	20,646	—
97013	Canby	(503)	15,829	17,932
97291	Cedar Mill (c)	(503)	14,546	—
97502	Central Point	(541)	17,169	18,848
97420	Coos Bay	(541)	15,967	16,361
*97113	Cornelius	(503)	11,869	12,822
*97330	Corvallis	(541)	54,462	58,856
97424	Cottage Grove	(541)	9,686	10,465
97338	Dallas	(503)	14,583	16,979
*97401	Eugene	(541)	156,185	172,622
97116	Forest Grove	(503)	21,083	25,553
97301	Four Corners (c)	(503)	15,947	—
97027	Gladstone	(503)	11,497	12,324
*97526	Grants Pass	(541)	34,533	38,170
97030	Gresham	(503)	105,594	109,381
*97015	Happy Valley	(503)	13,903	22,553
97303	Hayesville (c)	(503)	19,936	—
97838	Hermiston	(541)	16,745	17,782
*97123	Hillsboro	(503)	91,611	109,128
97351	Independence	(503)	8,590	10,272
*97303	Keizer	(503)	36,478	39,713
*97601	Klamath Falls	(541)	20,840	21,753
*97850	La Grande	(541)	13,082	13,614
*97034	Lake Oswego	(503)	36,619	39,822
97355	Lebanon	(541)	15,518	17,417
97128	McMinnville	(503)	32,187	34,743
*97501	Medford	(541)	74,907	83,072
*97222	Milwaukie	(503)	20,291	20,990
97361	Monmouth	(503)	9,534	10,586
97132	Newberg	(503)	22,068	23,886
*97365	Newport	(541)	9,989	10,853
*97222	Oak Grove (c)	(503)	16,629	—
97006	Oak Hills (c)	(503)	11,333	—
97267	Oatfield (c)	(503)	13,415	—
97914	Ontario	(541)	11,366	10,994
97045	Oregon City	(503)	31,859	37,339
97801	Pendleton	(541)	16,612	16,789
*97201	Portland	(503)	583,776	654,741
97754	Prineville	(541)	9,253	10,734
97756	Redmond	(541)	26,215	32,421
*97470	Roseburg	(541)	21,181	23,479
97051	Saint Helens	(503)	12,883	13,739
*97301	Salem	(503)	154,637	174,365
97055	Sandy	(503)	9,570	11,387
97140	Sherwood	(503)	18,194	19,879
97381	Silverton	(503)	9,222	10,618
*97477	Springfield	(541)	59,403	63,230
97058	The Dalles	(541)	13,620	15,761
*97223	Tigard	(503)	48,035	55,514
97060	Troutdale	(503)	15,962	16,183
97062	Tualatin	(503)	26,054	27,837
97068	West Linn	(503)	25,109	26,736
97070	Wilsonville	(503)	19,509	24,918
97071	Woodburn	(503)	24,080	26,273

Pennsylvania

Area code 223 overlays area code 717; 267/445 overlay 215; 272 overlays 570; 484 overlays 610; 878 overlays 412/724.

ZIP	Place	Area code	2010 population	2019 estimate
*18101	Allentown	(610)	118,032	121,442
15101	Allison Park (c)	(412)/(724)	21,552	—
*16601	Altoona	(814)	46,320	43,364
19003	Ardmore (c)	(610)	12,455	—
15234	Baldwin	(412)	19,767	19,554
15102	Bethel Park	(412)	32,313	32,345
*18016	Bethlehem	(610)	74,982	75,815
17815	Bloomsburg	(570)	14,855	13,811
19008	Broomall (c)	(610)	10,789	—
*16001	Butler	(724)	13,757	12,885
*17013	Carlisle	(717)	18,682	19,198
15108	Carnot-Moon (c)	(412)	11,372	—
*17201	Chambersburg	(717)	20,268	21,143
*19013	Chester	(610)	33,972	34,000
19320	Coatesville	(610)	13,100	13,069
17109	Colonial Park (c)	(717)	13,229	—
17512	Columbia	(717)	10,400	10,355
19023	Darby	(610)	10,687	10,702
19026	Drexel Hill (c)	(610)	28,043	—
18512	Dunmore	(570)	14,057	12,954
*18301	East Stroudsburg	(570)	9,840	10,433
*18042	Easton	(610)	26,800	27,189
17022	Elizabethtown	(717)	11,545	11,445
*18049	Emmaus	(610)	11,211	11,467
17522	Ephrata	(717)	13,394	13,862
*16501	Erie	(814)	101,786	95,508
16063	Fernway (c)	(724)	12,414	—
15237	Franklin Park	(412)	13,470	14,885
18052	Fullerton (c)	(610)	14,925	—
*15601	Greensburg	(724)	14,892	14,113
*17331	Hanover	(717)	15,289	15,719
*17101	Harrisburg	(717)	49,528	49,271
*18201	Hazleton	(570)	25,340	24,794
16148	Hermitage	(724)	16,220	15,471
17033	Hershey (c)	(717)	14,257	—
19044	Horsham (c)	(215)	14,842	—
*15701	Indiana	(724)	13,975	13,167
15025	Jefferson Hills	(412)	10,619	11,101
*15901	Johnstown	(814)	20,978	19,195
*19406	King of Prussia (c)	(610)	19,936	—
18704	Kingston	(570)	13,182	12,812
*17601	Lancaster	(717)	59,322	59,265
19446	Lansdale	(215)	16,269	17,083
19050	Lansdowne	(610)	10,620	10,647
17042	Lebanon	(717)	25,477	25,879
*19055	Levittown (c)	(215)	52,983	—
15068	Lower Burrell	(724)	11,761	11,078
*15132	McKeesport	(412)	19,731	19,009
*16335	Meadville	(814)	13,388	12,655
*15146	Monroeville	(412)/(724)	28,386	27,380
18936	Montgomeryville (c)	(215)	12,624	—
18707	Mountain Top (c)	(570)	10,982	—
15120	Munhall	(412)	11,406	11,006
*15668	Murrysville	(412)/(724)	20,079	19,590
18634	Nanticoke	(570)	10,465	10,312
*16101	New Castle	(724)	23,273	21,618
15068	New Kensington	(724)	13,116	12,292
*19401	Norristown	(610)	34,324	34,341
*19107	Philadelphia	(215)	1,526,006	1,584,064
*19460	Phoenixville	(610)	16,440	16,968
*15201	Pittsburgh	(412)	305,704	300,286
15239	Plum	(412)	27,126	27,087
*19464	Pottstown	(610)	22,377	22,600
17901	Pottsville	(570)	14,324	13,475
*19601	Reading	(610)	88,082	88,375
15857	Saint Marys	(814)	13,070	12,260
*18503	Scranton	(570)	76,089	76,653
*16146	Sharon	(724)	14,038	12,933
17404	Shiloh (c)	(717)	11,218	—
*16801	State College	(814)	42,034	42,160
15241	Upper St. Clair (c)	(412)	19,229	—
15301	Washington	(724)	13,663	13,433
17268	Waynesboro	(717)	10,568	10,886
17315	Weigelstown (c)	(717)	12,875	—
*19380	West Chester	(610)	18,461	20,029
*15122	West Mifflin	(412)	20,313	19,699
18052	Whitehall	(610)	13,944	13,393
*18701	Wilkes-Barre	(570)	41,498	40,766
15221	Wilkinsburg	(412)	15,930	15,292
*17701	Williamsport	(570)	29,381	28,186
19090	Willow Grove (c)	(215)	15,726	—
19610	Wyomissing	(610)	10,461	10,635
19050	Yeadon	(610)	11,443	11,496
*17401	York	(717)	43,718	43,932

Rhode Island
Area code 401 applies to the entire state. See introductory note.

ZIP	Place	2010 population	2019 estimate
02806	Barrington	16,310	16,053
02809	Bristol	22,954	21,915
*02830	Burrillville	15,955	16,854
02863	Central Falls	19,376	19,568
*02816	Coventry	35,014	34,819
*02910	Cranston	80,387	81,456
02864	Cumberland	33,506	35,263
02818	East Greenwich	13,146	13,120
02914	East Providence	47,037	47,618
*02814	Glocester	9,746	10,323
02919	Johnston	28,769	29,471
*02865	Lincoln	21,105	21,987
02842	Middletown	16,150	15,888
*02882	Narragansett	15,868	15,349
*02840	Newport	24,672	24,334
02842	Newport East (c)	11,769	—
02852	North Kingstown	26,486	26,323
*02908	North Providence	32,078	32,686
02896	North Smithfield	11,967	12,582
*02860	Pawtucket	71,148	72,117
02871	Portsmouth	17,389	17,226
*02903	Providence	178,042	179,883
*02857	Scituate	10,329	10,730
*02917	Smithfield	21,430	21,897
*02879	South Kingstown	30,639	30,348
02878	Tiverton	15,780	15,662
02864	Valley Falls (c)	11,547	—
02885	Warren	10,611	10,511
*02886	Warwick	82,672	81,004
02893	West Warwick	29,191	28,962
02891	Westerly	22,787	22,381
02891	Westerly (c)	17,936	—
02895	Woonsocket	41,186	41,751

South Carolina
Area code 839 overlays area code 803; 854 overlays 843.

ZIP	Place	Area code	2010 population	2019 estimate
*29801	Aiken	(803)	29,524	30,869
*29621	Anderson	(864)	26,686	27,676
*29902	Beaufort	(843)	12,361	13,436
29611	Berea (c)	(864)	14,295	—
*29910	Bluffton	(843)	12,530	25,557
*29033	Cayce	(803)	12,528	14,009
*29401	Charleston	(843)	120,083	137,566
*29631	Clemson	(864)	13,905	17,501
*29201	Columbia	(803)	129,272	131,674
*29526	Conway	(843)	17,103	25,956
29204	Dentsville (c)	(803)	14,062	—
*29640	Easley	(864)	19,993	21,364
29681	Five Forks (c)	(864)	14,140	—
*29501	Florence	(843)	37,056	38,531
29206	Forest Acres	(803)	10,361	10,298
*29715	Fort Mill	(803)	10,811	22,284
29644	Fountain Inn	(864)	7,799	10,441
*29341	Gaffney	(864)	12,414	12,609
29605	Gantt (c)	(864)	14,229	—
29445	Goose Creek	(843)	35,938	43,665
*29601	Greenville	(864)	58,409	70,635
*29646	Greenwood	(864)	23,222	23,403
*29650	Greer	(864)	25,515	33,373
29410	Hanahan	(843)	17,997	26,917
*29928	Hilton Head Island	(843)	37,099	39,861
29063	Irmo	(803)	11,097	12,483
29412	James Island[1]	(843)	11,218	12,109
*29456	Ladson (c)	(843)	13,790	—
*29072	Lexington	(803)	17,870	22,157
29662	Mauldin	(864)	22,889	25,409
29461	Moncks Corner	(843)	7,885	11,986
*29464	Mount Pleasant	(843)	67,843	91,684
*29572	Myrtle Beach	(843)	27,109	34,695
29108	Newberry	(803)	10,277	10,199
*29841	North Augusta	(803)	21,348	23,845
*29410	North Charleston	(843)	97,471	115,382
*29582	North Myrtle Beach	(843)	13,752	16,819
29073	Oak Grove (c)	(803)	10,291	—
*29115	Orangeburg	(803)	13,964	12,654
29611	Parker (c)	(864)	11,431	—
29935	Port Royal	(843)	10,678	13,235
*29920	Red Hill (c)	(843)	13,223	—
*29730	Rock Hill	(803)	66,154	75,048
29407	Saint Andrews (c)	(843)	20,493	—
29210	Seven Oaks (c)	(803)	15,144	—
*29681	Simpsonville	(864)	18,238	24,221
29577	Socastee (c)	(843)	19,952	—
*29306	Spartanburg	(864)	37,013	37,399
*29483	Summerville	(843)	43,392	52,549
*29150	Sumter	(803)	40,524	39,642

ZIP	Place	Area code	2010 population	2019 estimate
29687	Taylors (c)	(864)	21,617	—
29708	Tega Cay	(803)	7,620	11,335
*29607	Wade Hampton (c)	(864)	20,622	—
*29169	West Columbia	(803)	14,988	17,998

(1) Incorporated after 2010 Census; 2010 figure is Census Bureau est.

South Dakota
Area code 605 applies to the entire state.

ZIP	Place	2010 population	2019 estimate
*57401	Aberdeen	26,091	28,257
57719	Box Elder	7,800	10,119
57005	Brandon	8,785	10,074
*57006	Brookings	22,056	24,415
*57350	Huron	12,592	13,380
57301	Mitchell	15,254	15,679
57501	Pierre	13,646	13,867
*57701	Rapid City	67,956	77,503
*57103	Sioux Falls	153,888	183,793
*57783	Spearfish	10,494	11,756
57069	Vermillion	10,571	10,926
57201	Watertown	21,482	22,174
57078	Yankton	14,454	14,687

Tennessee
Area code 629 overlays area code 615.

ZIP	Place	Area code	2010 population	2019 estimate
38002	Arlington	(901)	11,517	11,743
*37303	Athens	(423)	13,458	14,020
*38133	Bartlett	(901)	54,613	59,440
*37027	Brentwood	(615)	37,060	42,783
*37620	Bristol	(423)	26,702	26,987
*37402	Chattanooga	(423)	167,674	182,799
*37311	Cleveland	(423)	41,285	45,504
*37716	Clinton	(865)	9,841	10,075
37315	Collegedale	(423)	8,282	11,378
*38017	Collierville	(901)	43,965	51,040
*38401	Columbia	(931)	34,681	40,335
*38501	Cookeville	(931)	30,435	34,706
*38555	Crossville	(931)	10,795	11,779
*37055	Dickson	(615)	14,538	15,575
*38024	Dyersburg	(731)	17,145	16,314
37412	East Ridge	(423)	20,979	21,182
*37643	Elizabethton	(423)	14,176	13,509
*37922	Farragut	(865)	20,676	23,778
*37064	Franklin	(615)	62,487	83,097
37066	Gallatin	(615)	30,278	42,918
*38138	Germantown	(901)	38,844	39,225
*37072	Goodlettsville	(615)	15,921	16,798
*37743	Greeneville	(423)	15,062	14,891
37074	Hartsville/Trousdale Co.		7,870	11,284
*37075	Hendersonville	(615)	51,372	58,113
*38301	Jackson	(731)	65,211	67,191
*37601	Johnson City	(423)	63,152	66,906
*37660	Kingsport	(423)	48,205	54,127
*37902	Knoxville	(865)	178,874	187,603
*37086	La Vergne	(615)	32,588	35,716
38002	Lakeland	(901)	12,430	12,642
38464	Lawrenceburg	(931)	10,428	11,035
*37087	Lebanon	(615)	26,190	36,479
37091	Lewisburg	(931)	11,100	12,368
*37355	Manchester	(931)	10,102	11,038
*38237	Martin	(731)	11,473	10,484
*37801	Maryville	(865)	27,465	29,742
*37110	McMinnville	(931)	13,605	13,769
*38103	Memphis	(901)	646,889	651,073
37343	Middle Valley (c)	(423)	12,684	—
*38053	Millington	(901)	10,176	10,641
*37813	Morristown	(423)	29,137	30,193
*37122	Mount Juliet	(615)	23,671	37,029
37130	Murfreesboro	(615)	108,755	146,900
*37201	Nashville-Davidson (bal.)	(615)	601,222	670,820
37135	Nolensville	(615)	5,861	10,062
*37830	Oak Ridge	(865)	29,330	29,156
38242	Paris	(731)	10,156	10,056
37148	Portland	(615)	11,480	13,030
37415	Red Bank	(423)	11,651	11,840
*37862	Sevierville	(865)	14,807	17,117
37865	Seymour (c)	(865)	10,919	—
*37160	Shelbyville	(931)	20,335	22,101
37167	Smyrna	(615)	39,974	51,586
*37379	Soddy-Daisy	(423)	12,714	13,619
37174	Spring Hill	(931)	29,036	43,769
37172	Springfield	(615)	16,440	17,277
*37388	Tullahoma	(931)	18,655	19,555
*38261	Union City	(731)	10,895	10,325
37188	White House	(615)	10,255	12,638

Texas

Area code 346 overlays area codes 281/713/832; 430 overlays 903; 469/972 overlay 214; 682 overlays 817; 726 overlays 210; 737 overlays 512.

ZIP	Place	Area code	2010 population	2019 estimate
*79601	Abilene	(325)	117,063	123,420
75001	Addison	(972)	13,056	16,263
78516	Alamo	(956)	18,353	19,910
77039	Aldine (c)	(281)	15,869	—
*78332	Alice	(361)	19,104	18,682
*75002	Allen	(214)	84,246	105,623
78573	Alton	(956)	12,341	18,105
*77511	Alvin	(281)	24,236	26,723
*79101	Amarillo	(806)	190,695	199,371
79714	Andrews	(432)	11,088	14,109
*77515	Angleton	(979)	18,862	19,431
75409	Anna	(972)	8,249	15,000
*76001	Arlington	(817)	365,438	398,854
77346	Atascocita (c)	(281)	65,844	—
*75751	Athens	(903)	12,710	12,753
*78701	Austin	(512)	790,390	978,908
*76020	Azle	(817)	10,947	13,351
*75180	Balch Springs	(214)	23,728	25,007
*77414	Bay City	(979)	17,614	17,535
*77520	Baytown	(281)/(832)	71,802	77,192
*77701	Beaumont	(409)	118,296	116,825
*76021	Bedford	(817)	46,979	49,049
*78102	Beeville	(361)	12,863	12,793
*77401	Bellaire	(713)	16,855	18,971
*76704	Bellmead	(254)	9,901	10,744
76513	Belton	(254)	18,216	22,885
*76126	Benbrook	(817)	21,234	23,502
*79720	Big Spring	(432)	27,282	28,187
*78006	Boerne	(830)	10,471	18,232
75418	Bonham	(903)	10,127	10,386
*79007	Borger	(806)	13,251	12,415
*77833	Brenham	(979)	15,716	17,863
78520	Brownsville	(956)	175,023	182,781
*76801	Brownwood	(325)	19,288	18,455
78717	Brushy Creek (c)	(512)	21,764	—
*77801	Bryan	(979)	76,201	86,276
78610	Buda	(512)	7,295	16,906
76354	Burkburnett	(940)	10,811	11,270
*76028	Burleson	(817)	36,690	48,225
*79015	Canyon	(806)	13,303	15,945
*78130	Canyon Lake (c)	(830)	21,262	—
*75006	Carrollton	(214)	119,097	139,248
*75104	Cedar Hill	(214)	45,028	47,930
*78613	Cedar Park	(512)	48,937	79,462
75009	Celina	(972)	6,028	16,299
77530	Channelview (c)	(281)	38,289	—
78108	Cibolo	(210)	15,349	31,281
*77494	Cinco Ranch (c)	(281)	18,274	—
*76031	Cleburne	(817)	29,337	31,295
77015	Cloverleaf (c)	(713)	22,942	—
77531	Clute	(979)	11,211	11,690
*77840	College Station	(979)	93,857	117,911
76034	Colleyville	(817)	22,807	27,091
*77301	Conroe	(936)	56,207	91,079
78109	Converse	(210)	18,198	28,171
*75019	Coppell	(214)	38,659	41,421
76522	Copperas Cove	(254)	32,032	33,235
76208	Corinth	(940)	19,935	22,099
*78401	Corpus Christi	(361)	305,215	326,586
*75110	Corsicana	(903)	23,770	23,906
76036	Crowley	(817)	12,838	16,840
*75201	Dallas	(214)	1,197,816	1,343,573
77536	Deer Park	(281)	32,010	33,474
*78840	Del Rio	(830)	35,591	35,760
*75020	Denison	(903)	22,682	25,529
76201	Denton	(940)	113,383	141,541
*75115	DeSoto	(214)	49,047	52,988
77539	Dickinson	(281)	18,680	21,129
78537	Donna	(956)	15,798	16,338
79029	Dumas	(806)	14,691	13,827
*75116	Duncanville	(214)	38,524	38,751
*78852	Eagle Pass	(830)	26,248	29,684
*78539	Edinburg	(956)	77,100	101,170
77437	El Campo	(979)	11,602	11,539
*79901	El Paso	(915)	649,121	681,728
78621	Elgin	(512)	8,135	10,314
*75119	Ennis	(214)	18,513	20,357
*76039	Euless	(817)	51,277	57,197
*78015	Fair Oaks Ranch	(210)	5,986	10,042
*75234	Farmers Branch	(214)	28,616	48,158
75087	Fate	(214)	6,357	15,603
*75022	Flower Mound	(214)	64,669	79,135
76119	Forest Hill	(817)	12,355	12,988
75126	Forney	(214)	14,661	27,236
76544	Fort Hood (c)	(254)	29,589	—
*76102	Fort Worth	(817)	741,206	909,585
77498	Four Corners (c)	(281)	12,382	—
78624	Fredericksburg	(830)	10,530	11,496

ZIP	Place	Area code	2010 population	2019 estimate
*77541	Freeport	(979)	12,049	12,136
77545	Fresno (c)	(281)	19,069	—
*77546	Friendswood	(281)	35,805	40,290
*75034	Frisco	(214)	116,989	200,490
*77441	Fulshear	(281)/(713)	1,134	13,914
*76240	Gainesville	(940)	16,002	16,886
77547	Galena Park	(713)	10,887	10,757
*77550	Galveston	(409)	47,743	50,446
*75040	Garland	(214)	226,876	239,928
*76528	Gatesville	(254)	15,751	12,401
*78626	Georgetown	(512)	47,400	79,604
75154	Glenn Heights	(972)	11,278	13,377
*76048	Granbury	(817)	7,978	10,730
*75051	Grand Prairie	(214)	175,396	194,543
*76051	Grapevine	(817)	46,334	55,281
77479	Greatwood (c)	(281)	11,538	—
75401	Greenville	(903)	25,557	28,827
77619	Groves	(409)	16,144	15,480
*76117	Haltom City	(817)	42,409	43,874
76548	Harker Heights	(254)	26,700	32,421
*78550	Harlingen	(956)	64,849	65,022
*75652	Henderson	(903)	13,712	13,154
79045	Hereford	(806)	15,370	14,622
76643	Hewitt	(254)	13,549	14,937
78557	Hidalgo	(956)	11,198	14,183
75077	Highland Village	(214)	15,056	16,668
*79927	Horizon City	(915)	16,735	19,642
*77002	Houston	(281)/(713)/(832)	2,099,451	2,320,268
*77338	Humble	(281)	15,133	15,824
*77340	Huntsville	(936)	38,548	42,241
*76053	Hurst	(817)	37,337	38,655
78634	Hutto	(512)	14,698	27,947
78362	Ingleside	(361)	9,387	10,192
*75060	Irving	(214)	216,290	239,798
77029	Jacinto City	(713)	10,553	10,466
75766	Jacksonville	(903)	14,544	14,815
78729	Jollyville (c)	(512)	16,151	—
*77449	Katy	(281)/(713)	14,102	21,729
*76248	Keller	(817)	39,627	47,213
*78028	Kerrville	(830)	22,347	23,754
*75662	Kilgore	(903)	12,975	14,852
*76541	Killeen	(254)	127,921	151,666
*78363	Kingsville	(361)	26,213	25,315
78640	Kyle	(512)	28,016	48,393
78572	La Homa (c)	(956)	11,985	—
77568	La Marque	(409)	14,509	17,319
*77571	La Porte	(281)/(832)	33,800	34,976
*77566	Lake Jackson	(979)	26,849	27,220
*78734	Lakeway	(512)	11,391	15,981
*75146	Lancaster	(214)	36,361	39,228
*78040	Laredo	(956)	236,091	262,491
*77573	League City	(281)	83,560	107,536
78641	Leander	(512)	26,521	62,608
*78238	Leon Valley	(210)	10,151	12,306
*79336	Levelland	(806)	13,542	13,502
75057	Lewisville	(214)	95,290	109,212
75068	Little Elm	(214)	25,898	53,126
*78233	Live Oak	(210)	13,131	16,499
78644	Lockhart	(512)	12,698	14,133
*75601	Longview	(903)	80,455	81,631
*79401	Lubbock	(806)	229,573	258,862
75901	Lufkin	(936)	35,067	35,021
77657	Lumberton	(409)	11,943	13,073
78653	Manor	(512)	5,037	13,866
76063	Mansfield	(817)	56,368	72,419
77578	Manvel	(281)	5,179	12,671
*75670	Marshall	(903)	23,523	22,831
*78501	McAllen	(956)	129,877	143,268
*75070	McKinney	(214)	131,117	199,177
75454	Melissa	(972)	4,695	12,117
78570	Mercedes	(956)	15,570	16,604
*75149	Mesquite	(214)	139,824	140,937
*79701	Midland	(432)	111,147	146,038
76065	Midlothian	(214)	18,037	33,532
*76067	Mineral Wells	(940)	16,788	15,213
*76063	Mission	(956)	77,058	84,331
*77083	Mission Bend (c)	(281)	36,501	—
*77489	Missouri City	(281)	67,358	75,457
*75455	Mount Pleasant	(903)	15,564	15,978
*75094	Murphy	(214)	17,708	20,500
*75961	Nacogdoches	(936)	32,996	32,877
77627	Nederland	(409)	17,547	17,371
*78130	New Braunfels	(830)	57,740	90,209
77479	New Territory (c)	(281)	15,186	—
76117	North Richland Hills	(817)	63,343	70,670
*79761	Odessa	(432)	99,940	123,334
*77630	Orange	(409)	18,595	18,118
*75801	Palestine	(903)	18,712	17,730
79065	Pampa	(806)	17,994	17,068
*75460	Paris	(903)	25,171	24,847
*77502	Pasadena	(281)/(713)/(832)	149,043	151,227
*77581	Pearland	(281)/(713)/(832)	91,252	122,460

ZIP	Place	Area code	2010 population	2019 estimate
78061	Pearsall	(830)	9,146	10,609
*77406	Pecan Grove (c)	(281)	15,963	—
79772	Pecos	(432)	8,780	10,461
*78660	Pflugerville	(512)	46,936	65,380
78577	Pharr	(956)	70,400	79,112
*79072	Plainview	(806)	22,194	20,143
*75074	Plano	(214)	259,841	287,677
78064	Pleasanton	(830)	8,934	10,855
*77640	Port Arthur	(409)	53,818	54,280
77979	Port Lavaca	(361)	12,248	11,854
77651	Port Neches	(409)	13,040	12,655
78374	Portland	(361)	15,099	17,268
75407	Princeton	(214)	6,807	13,894
75078	Prosper	(214)	9,423	24,579
*78580	Raymondville	(956)	11,284	10,880
75154	Red Oak	(214)	10,769	13,464
76140	Rendon (c)	(817)	12,552	—
*75080	Richardson	(214)	99,223	121,323
*77469	Richmond .... (281)/(832)		11,679	12,578
78582	Rio Grande City	(956)	13,834	14,511
76706	Robinson	(254)	10,509	11,926
78380	Robstown	(361)	11,487	11,261
*78382	Rockport	(361)	8,766	10,604
75087	Rockwall	(214)	37,490	45,888
78584	Roma	(956)	9,765	11,490
*77471	Rosenberg	(832)	30,618	38,307
*78681	Round Rock	(512)	99,887	133,372
*75088	Rowlett	(214)	56,199	67,339
75189	Royse City	(214)	9,349	14,702
75048	Sachse	(214)	20,329	26,046
*76179	Saginaw	(817)	19,806	24,310
*76901	San Angelo	(325)	93,200	101,004
*78201	San Antonio	(210)	1,327,407	1,547,253
78586	San Benito	(956)	24,250	24,243
79849	San Elizario (c)	(915)	13,603	—
78589	San Juan	(956)	33,856	37,008
*78666	San Marcos	(512)	44,894	64,776
*77510	Santa Fe	(409)	12,222	13,449
*78154	Schertz	(210)	31,465	42,042
77586	Seabrook	(281)	11,952	14,149
75159	Seagoville	(214)	14,835	16,861
*78155	Seguin	(830)	25,175	29,992
78154	Selma	(214)	5,540	11,132
*75090	Sherman	(903)	38,521	44,002
77459	Sienna Plantation (c)	(281)	13,721	—
*79549	Snyder	(325)	11,202	11,023
*79927	Socorro	(915)	32,013	34,370
77587	South Houston	(713)	16,983	17,438
76092	Southlake	(817)	26,575	32,376
*77373	Spring (c) ..... (281)/(713)/(832)		54,298	—
*77477	Stafford	(281)	17,693	17,362
*76401	Stephenville	(254)	17,123	21,247
*77478	Sugar Land.... (281)/(713)/(832)		78,817	118,488
*75482	Sulphur Springs	(903)	15,449	16,234
79556	Sweetwater	(325)	10,906	10,469
76574	Taylor	(512)	15,191	17,383
*76501	Temple	(254)	66,102	78,439
*75160	Terrell	(214)	15,816	18,869
*75501	Texarkana	(903)	36,411	36,317
*77510	Texas City	(409)	45,099	50,094
75056	The Colony	(214)	36,328	44,438
*77381	The Woodlands (c)	(281)	93,847	—
78260	Timberwood Park (c)	(830)	13,447	—
*77375	Tomball	(281)	10,753	11,778
76262	Trophy Club	(817)	8,024	12,451
*75702	Tyler	(903)	96,900	106,985
*78148	Universal City	(210)	18,530	20,890
75205	University Park	(214)	23,068	24,985
*78801	Uvalde	(830)	15,751	16,001
*76384	Vernon	(940)	11,002	10,323
*77901	Victoria	(361)	62,592	66,916
*77662	Vidor	(409)	10,579	10,403
*76701	Waco	(254)	124,805	139,236
*76148	Watauga	(817)	23,497	24,481
75165	Waxahachie	(214)	29,621	41,068
*76086	Weatherford	(817)	25,250	33,547
77598	Webster	(281)	10,400	11,451
78728	Wells Branch (c)	(512)	12,120	—
*78596	Weslaco	(956)	35,670	41,629
79764	West Odessa (c)	(432)	22,707	—
77005	West University Place	(713)	14,787	15,585
76108	White Settlement	(817)	16,116	17,851
*76301	Wichita Falls	(940)	104,553	104,683
75098	Wylie	(214)	41,427	53,067

Utah
Area code 385 overlays area code 801.

ZIP	Place	Area code	2010 population	2019 estimate
84004	Alpine	(801)	9,555	10,498
84003	American Fork	(801)	26,263	33,161
84065	Bluffdale	(801)	7,598	16,358

ZIP	Place	Area code	2010 population	2019 estimate
*84010	Bountiful	(801)	42,552	43,981
84302	Brigham City	(435)	17,899	19,601
*84720	Cedar City	(435)	28,857	34,764
84062	Cedar Hills	(801)	9,796	10,083
84014	Centerville	(801)	15,335	17,587
*84015	Clearfield	(801)	30,112	32,118
84015	Clinton	(801)	20,426	22,499
*84047	Cottonwood Heights	(801)	33,433	33,843
84020	Draper	(801)	42,274	48,587
*84005	Eagle Mountain	(801)	21,415	38,391
84025	Farmington	(801)	18,275	25,339
*84029	Grantsville	(435)	8,893	12,064
*84032	Heber City	(435)	11,362	17,082
*84096	Herriman	(801)	21,785	51,348
84003	Highland	(801)	15,523	19,175
*84117	Holladay	(801)	26,472	30,325
84737	Hurricane	(435)	13,748	19,074
84037	Kaysville	(801)	27,300	32,390
84118	Kearns (c)	(801)	35,731	—
*84041	Layton	(801)	67,311	78,014
84043	Lehi	(801)	47,407	69,724
84042	Lindon	(801)	10,070	11,100
*84321	Logan	(435)	48,174	51,542
84044	Magna (c)	(801)	26,505	—
84664	Mapleton	(801)	7,979	10,731
84047	Midvale	(801)	27,964	34,124
*84106	Millcreek[1]	(801)	58,750	61,450
*84107	Murray	(801)	46,746	48,917
84341	North Logan	(435)	8,269	11,237
84404	North Ogden	(801)	17,357	20,582
84054	North Salt Lake	(801)	16,322	20,948
*84401	Ogden	(801)	82,825	87,773
84057	Orem	(801)	88,328	97,828
84651	Payson	(801)	18,294	20,303
*84062	Pleasant Grove	(801)	33,509	38,258
*84414	Pleasant View	(801)	7,979	10,839
*84601	Provo	(801)	112,488	116,618
84065	Riverton	(801)	38,753	44,440
*84067	Roy	(801)	36,884	39,613
*84770	Saint George	(435)	72,897	89,587
*84101	Salt Lake City	(801)	186,440	200,567
84070	Sandy	(801)	87,461	96,380
84655	Santaquin	(801)	9,128	12,865
*84043	Saratoga Springs	(801)	17,781	33,282
84335	Smithfield	(435)	9,495	12,025
*84095	South Jordan	(801)	50,418	76,598
*84403	South Ogden	(801)	16,532	17,199
*84115	South Salt Lake	(801)	23,617	25,582
84660	Spanish Fork	(801)	34,691	40,913
*84663	Springville	(801)	29,466	33,310
84075	Syracuse	(801)	24,331	31,458
*84118	Taylorsville	(801)	58,652	59,805
84074	Tooele	(435)	31,605	36,015
*84078	Vernal	(435)	9,089	10,438
*84058	Vineyard	(801)	139	11,866
84780	Washington	(435)	18,761	29,174
84401	West Haven	(801)	10,272	16,109
*84084	West Jordan	(801)	103,712	116,480
84015	West Point	(801)	9,511	10,957
*84119	West Valley City	(801)	129,480	135,248
*84087	Woods Cross	(801)	9,761	11,431

(1) Incorporated after 2010 Census; 2010 figure is Census Bureau est.

Vermont
Area code 802 applies to the entire state. See introductory note.

ZIP	Place	2010 population	2019 estimate
05201	Bennington	15,764	14,964
*05301	Brattleboro	12,046	11,332
*05401	Burlington	42,417	42,019
05446	Colchester	17,067	17,127
*05452	Essex	19,587	21,890
*05452	Essex Junction	9,271	10,852
05468	Milton	10,352	10,829
*05701	Rutland	16,495	15,074
*05403	South Burlington	17,904	19,509
05495	Williston	8,698	10,081

Virginia
Area code 571 overlays area code 703.

ZIP	Place	Area code	2010 population	2019 estimate
*22314	Alexandria	(703)	139,966	159,428
22003	Annandale (c)	(703)	41,008	—
*22201	Arlington (c)	(703)	207,627	—
*20147	Ashburn (c)	(703)	43,511	—
22041	Bailey's Crossroads (c)	(703)	23,643	—
*24060	Blacksburg	(540)	42,620	44,233
23235	Bon Air (c)	(804)	16,366	—
23112	Brandermill (c)	(804)	13,173	—
*24201	Bristol	(276)	17,835	16,762

ZIP	Place	Area code	2010 population	2019 estimate
20148	Broadlands (c)	(703)	12,313	—
20111	Buckhall (c)	(703)	16,293	—
20109	Bull Run (c)	(703)	14,983	—
*22015	Burke (c)	(703)	41,055	—
22015	Burke Centre (c)	(703)	17,326	—
24069	Cascades (c)	(703)	11,912	—
24018	Cave Spring (c)	(540)	24,922	—
*20120	Centreville (c)	(703)	71,135	—
*20151	Chantilly (c)	(703)	23,039	—
*22901	Charlottesville	(434)	43,475	47,266
22026	Cherry Hill (c)	(703)	16,000	—
*23320	Chesapeake	(757)	222,209	244,835
*23831	Chester (c)	(804)	20,987	—
*24073	Christiansburg	(540)	21,041	22,473
23834	Colonial Heights	(804)	17,411	17,370
20165	Countryside (c)	(703)	10,072	—
22701	Culpeper	(540)	16,379	18,873
22193	Dale City (c)	(703)	65,969	—
*24541	Danville	(434)	43,055	40,044
20170	Dranesville (c)	(703)	11,921	—
23222	East Highland Park (c)	(804)	14,796	—
22033	Fair Oaks (c)	(703)	30,223	—
*22030	Fairfax	(703)	22,565	24,019
22039	Fairfax Station (c)	(703)	12,030	—
*22046	Falls Church	(703)	12,332	14,617
22308	Fort Hunt (c)	(703)	16,045	—
22310	Franconia (c)	(703)	18,245	—
20171	Franklin Farm (c)	(703)	19,288	—
*22401	Fredericksburg	(540)	24,286	29,036
22630	Front Royal (c)	(540)	14,440	15,278
*20155	Gainesville (c)	(703)	11,481	—
*23059	Glen Allen (c)	(804)	14,774	—
22066	Great Falls (c)	(703)	15,427	—
22306	Groveton (c)	(703)	14,598	—
*23669	Hampton	(757)	137,436	134,510
*22801	Harrisonburg	(540)	48,914	53,016
*20170	Herndon	(703)	23,292	24,601
23075	Highland Springs (c)	(804)	15,711	—
24019	Hollins (c)	(540)	14,673	—
*23860	Hopewell	(804)	22,591	22,529
22303	Huntington (c)	(703)	11,267	—
22306	Hybla Valley (c)	(703)	15,801	—
22043	Idylwood (c)	(703)	17,288	—
22038	Kings Park West (c)	(703)	13,390	—
22315	Kingstowne (c)	(703)	15,556	—
22192	Lake Ridge (c)	(703)	41,058	—
23228	Lakeside (c)	(804)	11,849	—
20176	Lansdowne (c)	(703)	11,253	—
23228	Laurel (c)	(804)	16,713	—
*20175	Leesburg (c)	(703)	42,616	53,727
22312	Lincolnia (c)	(703)	22,855	—
20136	Linton Hall (c)	(703)	35,725	—
22079	Lorton (c)	(703)	18,610	—
20165	Lowes Island (c)	(703)	10,756	—
*24501	Lynchburg	(434)	75,568	82,168
24572	Madison Heights (c)	(434)	11,285	—
*20110	Manassas	(703)	37,821	41,085
*20111	Manassas Park (c)	(703)	14,273	17,478
23235	Manchester (c)	(804)	10,804	—
24112	Martinsville	(276)	13,821	12,554
22191	Marumsco (c)	(703)	35,036	—
*22101	McLean (c)	(703)	48,115	—
20171	McNair (c)	(703)	17,513	—
23234	Meadowbrook (c)	(804)	18,312	—
*23111	Mechanicsville (c)	(804)	36,348	—
*22081	Merrifield (c)	(703)	15,212	—
22025	Montclair (c)	(703)	19,570	—
22121	Mount Vernon (c)	(703)	12,416	—
22191	Neabsco (c)	(703)	12,068	—
22122	Newington (c)	(703)	12,943	—
22153	Newington Forest (c)	(703)	12,442	—
*23607	Newport News	(757)	180,719	179,225
*23502	Norfolk	(757)	242,803	242,742
*22124	Oakton (c)	(703)	34,166	—
*23704	Petersburg	(804)	32,420	31,346
23662	Poquoson	(757)	12,150	12,271
*23704	Portsmouth	(757)	95,535	94,398
*20132	Purcellville	(540)	7,727	10,178
*24141	Radford	(540)	16,408	18,249
*20190	Reston (c)	(703)	58,404	—
*23219	Richmond	(276)/(804)	204,214	230,436
*24011	Roanoke	(540)	97,032	99,143
24281	Rose Hill (c) (Fairfax Co.)	(276)	20,226	—
24153	Salem	(540)	24,802	25,301
23233	Short Pump (c)	(804)	24,729	—
20152	South Riding (c)	(703)	24,256	—
22150	Springfield (c)	(703)	30,484	—
*24401	Staunton	(540)	23,746	24,932
*20164	Sterling (c)	(703)	27,822	—
20109	Sudley (c)	(703)	16,203	—
*23434	Suffolk	(757)	84,585	92,108
20164	Sugarland Run (c)	(703)	11,799	—

ZIP	Place	Area code	2010 population	2019 estimate
24502	Timberlake (c)	(434)	12,183	—
23229	Tuckahoe (c)	(804)	44,990	—
*22102	Tysons Corner (c)	(703)	19,627	—
*22180	Vienna	(703)	15,687	16,485
*23451	Virginia Beach	(757)	437,994	449,974
23888	Wakefield (c)	(757)	11,275	—
*20186	Warrenton	(540)	9,611	10,027
22980	Waynesboro	(540)	21,006	22,630
*22042	West Falls Church (c)	(703)	29,207	—
22152	West Springfield (c)	(703)	22,460	—
*23185	Williamsburg	(757)	14,068	14,954
*22601	Winchester	(540)	26,203	28,078
*22182	Wolf Trap (c)	(703)	16,131	—
24381	Woodlawn (c) (Fairfax Co.)	(276)	20,804	—

Washington
Area code 564 overlays area code 360.

ZIP	Place	Area code	2010 population	2019 estimate
98520	Aberdeen	(360)	16,896	16,756
*98221	Anacortes	(360)	15,778	17,527
98223	Arlington	(360)	17,926	20,523
98335	Artondale (c)	(253)	12,653	—
*98001	Auburn	(253)	70,180	81,464
98110	Bainbridge Island	(206)	23,025	25,298
98604	Battle Ground	(360)	17,571	21,252
*98004	Bellevue	(425)	122,363	148,164
*98225	Bellingham	(360)	80,885	92,314
98391	Bonney Lake	(253)	17,374	21,148
*98011	Bothell	(425)	33,505	47,415
98036	Bothell West (c)	(425)	16,607	—
*98337	Bremerton	(360)	37,729	41,405
98178	Bryn Mawr-Skyway (c)	(206)	15,645	—
*98166	Burien	(206)	33,313	51,500
98607	Camas	(360)	19,355	24,418
98531	Centralia	(360)	16,336	17,745
99004	Cheney	(509)	10,590	12,522
98072	Cottage Lake (c)	(425)	22,494	—
*98042	Covington	(253)	17,575	21,175
*98198	Des Moines	(206)	29,673	32,348
*98011	East Hill-Meridian (c)	(253)	29,878	—
98056	East Renton Highlands (c)	(425)	11,140	—
98802	East Wenatchee	(509)	13,190	14,219
98204	Eastmont (c)	(425)	20,101	—
*98872	Edgewood	(253)	9,387	13,053
*98020	Edmonds	(425)	39,709	42,605
98387	Elk Plain (c)	(253)	14,205	—
*98926	Ellensburg	(509)	18,174	21,111
98022	Enumclaw	(360)	10,669	12,190
*98201	Everett	(425)	103,019	111,475
98058	Fairwood (c) (King Co.)	(425)	19,102	—
*98001	Federal Way	(253)	89,306	96,289
98248	Ferndale	(360)	11,415	14,897
98424	Fife	(253)	9,173	10,184
98597	Five Corners (c)	(360)	18,159	—
98433	Fort Lewis (c)	(253)	11,046	—
98375	Frederickson (c)	(253)	18,719	—
*98329	Gig Harbor	(253)	7,126	10,717
98338	Graham (c)	(253)	23,491	—
98930	Grandview	(509)	10,862	11,078
98665	Hazel Dell (c)	(360)	19,435	—
*98011	Inglewood-Finn Hill (c)	(425)	22,707	—
*98027	Issaquah	(425)	30,434	39,509
98626	Kelso	(360)	11,925	12,417
98028	Kenmore	(425)	20,460	23,097
*99336	Kennewick	(509)	73,917	84,347
*98031	Kent	(253)/(425)	92,411	132,319
*98033	Kirkland	(425)	48,787	93,010
98029	Klahanie (c)	(425)	10,674	—
*98503	Lacey	(360)	42,393	52,592
98155	Lake Forest Park	(206)	12,598	13,504
98042	Lake Morton-Berrydale (c)	(253)/(425)	10,160	—
98258	Lake Stevens	(425)	28,069	33,911
98391	Lake Tapps (c)	(253)	11,859	—
98002	Lakeland North (c)	(253)	12,942	—
*98002	Lakeland South (c)	(253)	11,574	—
*98498	Lakewood	(253)	58,163	61,037
*99016	Liberty Lake	(509)	7,591	10,956
98632	Longview	(360)	36,648	38,440
98264	Lynden	(360)	11,951	15,223
*98036	Lynnwood	(425)	35,836	39,141
98290	Maltby (c)	(360)/(425)	10,830	—
98038	Maple Valley	(425)	22,684	27,202
98012	Martha Lake (c)	(425)	15,473	—
*98270	Marysville	(360)	60,020	70,298
98040	Mercer Island	(206)	22,699	25,894
*98012	Mill Creek	(425)	18,244	20,897
98012	Mill Creek East (c)	(425)	15,709	—
98272	Monroe	(360)	17,304	19,776
98837	Moses Lake	(509)	20,366	24,086

ZIP	Place	Area code	2010 population	2019 estimate
*98273	Mount Vernon	(360)	31,743	36,006
98043	Mountlake Terrace	(425)	19,909	21,338
98275	Mukilteo	(425)	20,254	21,441
*98056	Newcastle	(425)	10,380	12,292
98037	North Lynnwood (c)	(425)	16,574	—
*98277	Oak Harbor	(360)	22,075	23,565
*98501	Olympia	(360)	46,478	52,882
98662	Orchards (c)	(360)	19,556	—
*98444	Parkland (c)	(253)	35,803	—
*99301	Pasco	(509)	59,781	75,432
*98362	Port Angeles	(360)	19,038	20,229
*98366	Port Orchard	(360)	11,144	14,597
*98370	Poulsbo	(360)	9,200	11,168
98391	Prairie Ridge (c)	(253)	11,464	—
*99163	Pullman	(509)	29,799	34,506
*98371	Puyallup	(253)	37,022	42,361
*98052	Redmond	(425)	54,144	71,929
*98057	Renton	(425)	90,927	101,751
*99352	Richland	(509)	48,058	58,225
*98685	Salmon Creek (c)	(360)	19,686	—
*98074	Sammamish	(425)	45,780	65,892
*98148	SeaTac	(206)	26,909	29,044
*98101	Seattle	(206)/(425)	608,660	753,675
98284	Sedro-Woolley	(360)	10,540	12,072
98584	Shelton	(360)	9,834	10,655
*98133	Shoreline	(206)	53,007	57,027
98208	Silver Firs (c)	(425)	20,891	—
*98315	Silverdale (c)	(360)	19,204	—
*98290	Snohomish	(360)	9,098	10,154
98065	Snoqualmie	(425)	10,670	13,622
*98373	South Hill (c)	(253)	52,431	—
*98387	Spanaway (c)	(253)	27,227	—
*99201	Spokane	(509)	208,916	222,081
*99206	Spokane Valley	(509)	89,755	101,060
*98390	Sumner	(253)	9,451	10,427
98944	Sunnyside	(509)	15,858	16,796
*98402	Tacoma	(253)	198,397	217,827
*98188	Tukwila	(206)	19,107	20,347
*98501	Tumwater	(360)	17,371	24,024
98053	Union Hill-Novelty Hill (c)	(425)	18,805	—
*98466	University Place	(253)	31,144	34,001
*98660	Vancouver	(360)	161,791	184,463
*98070	Vashon (c)	(206)	10,624	—
99362	Walla Walla	(509)	31,731	32,900
98671	Washougal	(360)	14,095	16,107
*98801	Wenatchee	(509)	31,925	34,360
*99353	West Richland	(509)	11,811	15,075
*98106	White Center (c)	(206)	13,495	—
*98072	Woodinville	(425)	10,938	13,263
*98901	Yakima	(509)	91,067	93,637

West Virginia

Area code 681 overlays area code 304; both apply to the entire state.

ZIP	Place	2010 population	2019 estimate
*25801	Beckley	17,614	15,940
*25301	Charleston	51,400	46,536
*26301	Clarksburg	16,578	15,225
*26554	Fairmont	18,704	18,388
*25701	Huntington	49,138	45,110
25401	Martinsburg	17,227	17,454
*26505	Morgantown	29,660	30,549
26101	Parkersburg	31,492	29,306
*25303	South Charleston	13,450	12,047
*25526	Teays Valley (c)	13,175	—
26105	Vienna	10,749	10,124
26062	Weirton	19,746	18,266
26003	Wheeling	28,486	26,430

Wisconsin

Area code 534 overlays area code 715.

ZIP	Place	Area code	2010 population	2019 estimate
54301	Allouez	(920)	13,975	13,894
*54911	Appleton	(920)	72,623	74,098
*54304	Ashwaubenon	(920)	16,963	17,161
53913	Baraboo	(608)	12,048	12,165
53916	Beaver Dam	(920)	16,214	16,403
54311	Bellevue	(920)	14,570	15,944
*53511	Beloit	(608)	36,966	36,926
*53045	Brookfield	(262)	37,920	39,115
*53223	Brown Deer	(414)	11,999	11,839
53105	Burlington	(262)	10,464	10,980
53108	Caledonia	(262)	24,705	25,277
53012	Cedarburg	(262)	11,412	11,603
*54729	Chippewa Falls	(715)	13,661	14,366
53110	Cudahy	(414)	18,267	18,104
54115	De Pere	(920)	23,800	24,970
53532	DeForest	(608)	8,936	10,691
*54701	Eau Claire	(715)	65,883	68,802
53121	Elkhorn	(262)	10,084	10,019

ZIP	Place	Area code	2010 population	2019 estimate
*53711	Fitchburg	(608)	25,260	30,792
*54935	Fond du Lac	(920)	43,021	43,263
53538	Fort Atkinson	(920)	12,368	12,422
*54956	Fox Crossing[1]	(920)	18,227	19,012
53132	Franklin	(414)	35,451	35,811
53022	Germantown	(262)	19,749	20,116
*53209	Glendale	(414)	12,872	12,768
53024	Grafton	(262)	11,459	11,715
*54301	Green Bay	(920)	104,057	104,578
53129	Greendale	(414)	14,046	14,143
*53220	Greenfield	(414)	36,720	37,221
54952	Harrison[1]	(920)	10,841	12,358
53027	Hartford	(262)	14,223	15,445
*54155	Hobart	(920)	6,182	10,082
54636	Holmen	(608)	9,005	10,034
*54303	Howard	(920)	17,399	20,177
54016	Hudson	(715)	12,719	14,103
*53545	Janesville	(608)	63,575	64,575
*54130	Kaukauna	(920)	15,462	16,270
*53140	Kenosha	(262)	99,218	99,944
*54601	La Crosse	(608)	51,320	51,227
*54140	Little Chute	(920)	10,449	12,081
*53703	Madison	(608)	233,209	259,680
*54220	Manitowoc	(920)	33,736	32,579
54143	Marinette	(715)	10,968	10,539
*54449	Marshfield	(715)	19,118	18,471
54952	Menasha	(920)	17,353	17,873
*53051	Menomonee Falls	(262)	35,626	38,014
54751	Menomonie	(715)	16,264	16,551
*53092	Mequon	(262)	23,132	24,382
*53562	Middleton	(608)	17,442	20,034
*53202	Milwaukee	(414)	594,833	590,157
53566	Monroe	(608)	10,827	10,565
*53406	Mount Pleasant	(262)	26,197	27,082
53150	Muskego	(262)	24,135	25,127
*54956	Neenah	(920)	25,501	26,300
53151	New Berlin	(262)	39,584	39,691
53154	Oak Creek	(414)	34,451	36,325
53066	Oconomowoc	(262)	15,759	16,981
54650	Onalaska	(608)	17,736	18,943
53575	Oregon	(608)	9,231	10,571
*54901	Oshkosh	(920)	66,083	67,004
53072	Pewaukee	(262)	13,195	14,631
53818	Platteville	(608)	11,224	12,087
53158	Pleasant Prairie	(262)	19,719	21,034
54467	Plover	(715)	12,123	13,099
53074	Port Washington	(262)	11,250	11,911
53901	Portage	(608)	10,324	10,399
*53402	Racine	(262)	78,860	76,760
*53076	Richfield	(262)	11,300	11,854
54022	River Falls	(715)	15,000	16,027
53168	Salem Lakes[1]	(262)	14,520	14,852
*53081	Sheboygan	(920)	49,288	47,965
53211	Shorewood	(414)	13,162	13,145
53172	South Milwaukee	(414)	21,156	20,696
*54481	Stevens Point	(715)	26,717	25,880
53589	Stoughton	(608)	12,611	13,114
*54313	Suamico	(920)	11,346	13,052
*53590	Sun Prairie	(608)	29,364	34,661
54880	Superior	(715)	27,244	25,977
53089	Sussex	(262)	10,518	10,981
54241	Two Rivers	(920)	11,712	11,041
53593	Verona	(608)	10,619	13,233
*53094	Watertown	(920)	23,861	23,479
*53186	Waukesha	(262)	70,718	72,299
53597	Waunakee	(608)	12,097	14,052
53963	Waupun	(920)	11,340	11,199
*54403	Wausau	(715)	39,106	38,561
*53213	Wauwatosa	(414)	46,396	48,118
*53214	West Allis	(414)	60,411	59,890
*53095	West Bend	(262)	31,078	31,563
*54476	Weston	(715)	14,868	15,167
*53217	Whitefish Bay	(414)	14,110	13,783
53190	Whitewater	(262)	14,390	14,895
*54494	Wisconsin Rapids	(715)	18,367	17,610

(1) Incorporated after 2010 Census; 2010 figure is Census Bureau est.

Wyoming

Area code 307 applies to the entire state.

ZIP	Place	2010 population	2019 estimate
*82601	Casper	55,316	57,931
*82001	Cheyenne	59,466	64,235
*82930	Evanston	12,359	11,641
*82716	Gillette	29,087	32,030
*82935	Green River	12,515	11,759
83001	Jackson	9,577	10,559
*82070	Laramie	30,816	32,711
82501	Riverton	10,615	10,772
*82901	Rock Springs	23,036	22,653
82801	Sheridan	17,444	17,940

WORLD HISTORY

Chronology of World History

Note: In this section, the notation BCE (before the common era) is applied to years dating to the traditional BC (before Christ) era, and CE (common era) is applied to AD (anno domini) dates. This notation is now preferred in many scientific and academic publications. The traditional Gregorian calendar system and its dates and years are unaltered except by these labels.

Other abbreviations used in this chapter include the following: KYA = thousand years ago, MYA = million years ago, c. = circa, fl. = flourished, r. = ruled, b. = born, d. = died.

Prehistory: Our Ancestors Emerge

Reviewed by Marc Kissel, Ph.D., Univ. of Notre Dame, 2016; other updates per World Almanac research.

Evidence of the origins of *Homo sapiens*, the genus and species to which all living humans belong, comes from an ever increasing number of fossils and DNA studies, and from the archaeological record. Put together, the latest evidence suggests that humans evolved from an ape-like ancestor that lived in eastern and central Africa 8 to 5 million years ago.

Current theories trace the first hominin[1] (primates more closely related to humans than to any other living primate) to Africa, where several distinct genera appear in the fossil record 6-4 MYA. Skeletally, hominins are defined by signs of bipedalism (walking on two legs). They lived in a variety of environments, including swampy forest margins, woodlands, and open savannas (usually near lakes or springs).

Claims of the earliest hominin are inherently controversial. The earliest currently proposed species are *Sahelanthropus tchadensis* (c. 7 MYA, Chad) and *Orrorin tugenensis* (c. 6 MYA, Kenya). The recently described species *Ardipithecus ramidus* (4.4 MYA, Ethiopia) had a chimp-sized brain and a fairly primitive body plan but was bipedal.

Although all humans living today are members of a single species, the fossil record confirms that our ancestors coexisted with a number of similar species throughout our evolutionary history. Starting around 4 MYA one of these earliest hominins gave rise to the australopithecines, a genus of early hominins referred to as "bipedal apes." Scientists divided these into two groups, "gracile" and "robust," each containing a number of species.

The robust australopithecines were characterized by larger molar and premolar teeth; they probably went extinct around 1 MYA. Members of this species adapted a new dietary niche of eating hard foods such as nuts and tubers and have been found in both E and S Africa.

The gracile lineage most likely led to modern humans. *Australopithecus sediba* (2 MYA, South Africa) shows a mosaic of both Australopithecus and early *Homo* traits, leading some to suggest that this is the predecessor to our genus; the morphology of its hand is very suggestive of tool-use. However, while originally believed to arise solely within the genus *Homo*, recent work at the sites of Dikika (3.3 MYA, Etiopia) and Lomekwi (3.3 MYA, Kenya) suggest that earlier hominins were making stone tools.

Our genus, *Homo*, arose 3-2 MYA, with fossils showing early members of our genus being fully bipedal, having larger brains, and hands well-adapted to tool use. The Oldowan tools first appear 2.6 MYA and were used to cut and scrape meat. It is not known whether these early hominins had the ability to speak, but they were social primates, had campsites, and subsisted by gathering plants and small animals, and by scavenging other kills, as well as perhaps hunting.

Homo ergaster appeared in E Africa around 1.9 MYA and was the first to leave the continent, spreading throughout Eurasia by c. 1.8 MYA. *H. ergaster* is sometimes grouped with *H. erectus*, a species first identified on the Indonesian island of Java. It was capable of hunting large and medium-sized animals, such as antelopes and horses, learned to make and control fire, and produced bifacially-flaked tools (sharpened on both sides).

The ability to control fire enormously expanded the human food niche as well as creating new opportunities in the social world. Fire-making possibly began as early as 1 MYA in Africa and is clearly documented throughout Eurasia after c. 500 KYA. Hearths were found in northern Israel by c. 750 KYA, and by 465 KYA in southwestern France.

After about 800 KYA, Europe provides a particularly rich set of fossil evidence usually assigned to *H. erectus*, *H. antecessor*, or *H. heidelbergensis*. This population gave rise to the Neanderthals, who appeared c. 350 KYA. While originally portrayed as savage and unhuman-like, recent research suggests they could probably speak, were proficient hunters of large game, had sophisticated tools and weapons, had ornamentation and other forms of symbolic expression, and a well-developed social organization. On the island of Flores, Indonesia, remains of a species known as *Homo floresiensis*, a 1.1-m (3.5-ft) tall hominin, date from c. 100-60 KYA. Its small stature may be due to limited food and few predators on the small island.

The remains of *Homo naledi*, dating to c. 335-236 KYA, raised questions about a possible overlap in existence and behaviors with early humans. It has a human-like foot and lower limbs, but other aspects of the skeleton, such as the pelvis and shoulder, are more primitive looking. They seem to have been deliberately deposited into a cave system, suggesting an early form of burial.

Improved dating techniques call into question the age of modern humans. The oldest modern human fossils (*Homo sapiens*) were dated to c. 300 KYA and were found at the Jebel Irhoud site in Morocco. Until that 2017 analysis, the oldest, found in Omo Kibish, Ethiopia, were believed to date to c. 195 KYA. Fossils considered some of the oldest modern humans were also found at the Herto site in Ethiopia's Middle Awash Valley. The species spread out of Africa, reaching Israel by c. 100 KYA, and Romania by c. 35 KYA. Migration from Asia to Australia took place as early as 60 KYA. What happened when they met other hominins is a subject of intense research. Genetic evidence in the form of ancient DNA suggests that Neanderthals interbred with modern humans. Genetic data also provide information about the Denisovans, a population of early humans dated to perhaps c. 200 KYA. Some modern populations retain Denisovan DNA, suggesting a complex web of interactions between these populations.

First confirmation for the crossing from Asia to the Americas by the Bering land bridge dates to the end of the last Ice Age, at 14 KYA. Their arrival was rapidly followed by the extinction of the indigenous Pleistocene megafauna (e.g., mammoths, mastodons) due either to overexploitation by humans, climate change, or a combination of both.

Wooden throwing spears about 3 m (10 ft) long were fashioned by big-game hunters 300 KYA at Schöningen, Germany. Scraping tools, dated after 750 KYA in Europe, N Africa, the Middle East, and Central Asia, suggest the preparation of hides for clothing. Some of the oldest evidence of personal adornment date to around 300 KYA in the form of ochre, while various sites around 100 KYA from South Africa, Morocco, and Israel show the use of perforated shell beads, suggestive of symbolic expression. Although they were probably invented much earlier, impressions in burnt clay from the Czech Republic document the ability to weave cloth baskets and nets by 28 KYA.

Some of the earliest well-dated cave paintings come from the island of Sulawesi, Indonesia, where they date to around the same time as the earliest cave paintings in Europe. The painted caves of Cosquer and Chauvet in southern France have (contested) radiocarbon dates of c. 32 KYA. Painting, engraving, and bodily decoration flourished in Europe 15 KYA, along with stone and ivory sculpture. More than 200 western European caves show remarkable examples of naturalistic wall painting. A few musical instruments—bone flutes with precisely bored holes—have been found in sites dated after 40 KYA.

Skeletal data suggests that after 60-30 KYA the number of people who survived to become grandparents increased. With more adults available to provide child care, humans began to develop more complex, multigenerational social systems. In general, as human cognitive capacities slowly expanded over the Pleistocene, a variety of behavioral modes—in toolmaking,

Cave paintings in Lascaux, France, discovered in 1940, have been carbon-dated to 11,000 to 30,000 years before the present.

diet, shelter, social arrangements, and spiritual expression—arose as humans adapted to different geographic and climatic zones. By about 13,000 years ago, sites from all over the world show seasonal migration patterns and efficient exploitation of a wide range of plant and animal foods, some of which were eventually domesticated.

Shortly after 12 KYA, among widely separated foraging communities in both hemispheres, a series of dramatic technological and social changes occurred, marking the Neolithic, or New Stone Age. As the world climate became drier and warmer, population/resource imbalances ensued, creating the conditions that allowed for increased human interference in the life cycles of certain plants and animals. This interference ultimately resulted in the appearance of domestication, initially in the northern Middle East.

Domesticated plants and animals encouraged population growth and the appearance of permanent settlements. Agricultural economies increasingly replaced or assimilated hunting and gathering. Reliance upon domesticated plants and animals, coupled with technological advances like pottery-making, precipitated a dramatic increase in world population and social complexity. Genetic research suggests that mutations related to traits currently found in some human populations, such as Europeans' ability to process lactose, arose after this time.

Sites in the Americas, SE Europe, and the Middle East show roughly contemporaneous (12-6 KYA) evidence of Neolithic domestication economies; similar evidence of E and S Asian, W European, and sub-Saharan African Neolithic adaptations dates to 10-7 KYA. From W Asian sources, farming and the herding of sheep and goats spread rapidly throughout the Mediterranean Basin, perhaps in as short a time interval as 100-200 years. The variety of crops—wheat, barley, rice, maize, squash, beans, and tubers—and a mix of other characteristics suggest that this adaptation occurred independently in as many as 12 or 13 places in both hemispheres.

Evidence for fermented beverages likewise coincides with the early Neolithic settled farming lifestyle. Northern Chinese farmers concocted a wine-like drink from rice, honey, and fruit between 9 and 8 KYA. In highland W Asia, in what is today Iran, vintners were fermenting grapes and making wine by c. 7.4 KYA. The plants and animals associated with the Neolithic Revolution provided the basis for all subsequent social and cultural evolution worldwide.

(1) Although "hominid" was standard usage several decades ago, "hominin" is now more commonly used in reference to human ancestors because of developments in the interpretation of primate evolution.

Earliest Civilizations: 4000-1000 BCE

Mesopotamia. Recorded history began with writing in Mesopotamia in the Tigris-Euphrates river valley. The Sumerians used clay tablets with pictographs to keep records after 4000 BCE. A **cuneiform** (wedge-shaped) script, evolved by 3000 BCE as a full syllabic alphabet. Neighboring peoples adapted the script for their own use.

Sumerian life centered, from 4000 BCE, on large cities (Eridu, Ur, Uruk, Nippur, Kish, and Lagash) organized around temples and priestly bureaucracies, with surrounding plains watered by vast irrigation works and worked with traction plows. Sailboats, wheeled vehicles, potter's wheels, and kilns were used. Copper was smelted and tempered from c. 4000 BCE; bronze was produced not long after. Ores, as well as precious stones and metals, were obtained through long-distance ship and caravan trade. Iron was used from c. 2000 BCE. Improved ironworking, developed partly by the Hittites, became widespread by 1200 BCE.

Sumerian political primacy passed among cities and their kingly dynasties. Semitic-speaking peoples, with cultures derived from the Sumerian, founded a succession of dynasties that ruled in Mesopotamia and neighboring areas for most of 1,800 years. Among them were the **Akkadians** (first under Sargon I, c. 2350 BCE), the Amorites (whose laws, codified by **Hammurabi**, c. 1792-1750 BCE, have biblical parallels), and the Assyrians, with interludes of rule by the Hittites, Kassites, and Mitanni.

Mesopotamian learning, preserved in vast libraries, was practically oriented. Scribes maintained lists of astronomical phenomena, plants, animals, and stones. Medical texts listed ailments and herbal cures. The Sumerians worshipped anthropomorphic gods representing natural forces. Sacrifices were made at **ziggurats**, or huge stepped temples.

The Syria-Palestine area, site of some of the earliest urban remains (Jericho, 7000 BCE) and of the **Ebla** civilization (fl. 2500 BCE), experienced Egyptian cultural and political influence along with Mesopotamian. The **Phoenician** coast was an active commercial center. A phonetic alphabet was invented here before 1600 BCE. It became the ancestor of many other alphabets.

Egypt. Agricultural villages along the Nile R. were united by around 3300 BCE into two kingdoms, Upper and Lower Egypt. They were unified (c. 3100 BCE) under the pharaoh Menes, as detailed on the Narmer Palate. A bureaucracy supervised construction of canals and monuments (**pyramids** starting 2700 BCE). Control over Nubia to the S was asserted from 2600 BCE.

Brilliant **Old Kingdom** period achievements in architecture, sculpture, and painting reached their height during the 3rd and 4th dynasties. **Hieroglyphic writing** appeared by 3200 BCE, recording a sophisticated literature that included religious writings, philosophy, history, and science. An ordered hierarchy of gods, including totemistic animal elements, was served by a powerful priesthood in Memphis. The pharaoh was identified with the falcon god Horus. Other trends included belief in an afterlife and short-lived quasi-monotheistic reforms introduced by the pharaoh **Akhenaton** (c. 1379-1362 BCE), who was married to Nefertiti.

After a period of dominance by Semitic Hyksos from Asia (c. 1700-1550 BCE), the **New Kingdom** established an empire in Syria. Egypt became increasingly embroiled in Asiatic wars and diplomacy. Conquered by Persia in 525 BCE, it eventually faded away as an independent culture.

South Asia. The Bronze Age Indus Civilization spanned more than a million square kilometers in Pakistan and Northwestern India with many sites that expanded beyond the fertile core area of the Indus river system. The civilization independently grew out of local traditions developing complex trade networks and technologies during the Regionalization Era (5500-2600 BCE). The fully urban Harappan 2600-1900 BCE phase featured a standardized system of weights, uniform bricks, stamp seals featuring animals and unicorns, well laid out streets, and water management systems. Long distance trade with Mesopotamia and complex technologies were important. The writing system is one of the last to not be fully deciphered.

The major urban centers such as Dholavira, Harappa, and **Mohenjo-daro** were independent states. The civilization gradually changed due to environmental and cultural changes during the Localization Era (1900-1300 BCE). Post-Indus cultural complexes include the Gandara Grave culture (Swat, c. 1500-500 BCE) and the Painted Grey Ware (1200-800 BCE) culture, which some have associated with Vedic chiefdoms of the **Rig Veda**.

Europe. On Crete, the Bronze Age **Minoan civilization** emerged c. 2500 BCE. A prosperous economy and richly decorative art was supported by seaborne commerce. Mycenae and other cities in mainland Greece and Asia Minor (e.g., **Troy**) preserved elements of the culture until c. 1200 BCE. Cretan Linear A script (c. 2000-1700 BCE) remains undeciphered; Linear B script (c. 1300-1200 BCE) records an early Greek dialect. The possible connection between Mycenaean monumental stonework and

Sumerian clay tablets have some of the earliest known forms of written language, dating as far back as 4000 BCE.

the megalithic monuments of Western Europe, Iberia, and Malta (c. 4000-1500 BCE) is unclear.

China. Proto-Chinese Neolithic cultures had long covered N and SE China when the first large political state was organized in the N by the **Shang dynasty** (c. 1523 BCE). Shang kings called themselves the Sons of Heaven, and they presided over a cult of human and animal sacrifice to ancestors and nature gods. The Zhou dynasty, starting c. 1027 BCE, expanded the area of the Sons of Heaven's dominion, but feudal states exercised most temporal power.

A writing system with 2,000 characters was already in use under the Shang, with **pictographs** later supplemented by phonetic characters. Many of its principles and symbols, despite changes in spoken Chinese, were preserved in later writing systems. Technical advances allowed urban specialists to create fine ceramic and jade products, and bronze casting after 1500 BCE was the most advanced in the world. Bronze artifacts discovered in northern Thailand date from 3600 BCE, hundreds of years before similar Middle Eastern finds.

Americas. Olmecs settled (1500 BCE) on the Gulf coast of Mexico and developed the first known civilization in the Western Hemisphere. Temple cities and huge stone sculptures date from 1200 BCE. A rudimentary calendar and writing system existed. Olmec religion—centered on a jaguar god—and art forms influenced later Mesoamerican cultures.

Formation of Classical Societies: 1000-400 BCE

Greece. After a period of decline during the Dorian Greek invasions (1200-1000 BCE), the Aegean area developed a unique civilization. Drawing on Mycenaean traditions, Mesopotamian learning (weights and measures, lunisolar calendar, astronomy, musical scales), the Phoenician alphabet (modified for Greek), and Egyptian art, **Greek city-states** saw a rich elaboration of intellectual life. The two great epic poems attributed to **Homer**, the *Iliad* and the *Odyssey*, were probably composed around the 8th cent. BCE. Long-range commerce was aided by metal coinage (introduced by the Lydians in Asia Minor before 700 BCE). Colonies were founded around the Mediterranean (Cumae in Italy in 760 BCE; Massalia in France c. 600 BCE) and Black Sea shores.

Philosophy, starting with Ionian speculation on the nature of matter (Thales, c. 634-546 BCE), continued by other "Pre-Socratics" (e.g., Heraclitus, c. 540-480 BCE; Parmenides, b. c. 515 BCE), reached a high point in Athens in the rationalist idealism of **Plato** (c. 428-347 BCE), a disciple of **Socrates** (c. 469-399 BCE; executed for alleged impiety), and in **Aristotle** (384-322 BCE), a pioneer in many fields, from natural sciences to logic, ethics, and metaphysics. The arts were highly valued. Architecture culminated in the **Parthenon** (438 BCE) by Phidias (fl. 490-430 BCE). Poetry (Sappho, c. 610-580 BCE; Pindar, c. 518-438 BCE) and drama (Aeschylus, 525-456 BCE; Sophocles, c. 496-406 BCE; Euripides, c. 484-406 BCE) thrived. Male beauty and strength, a chief artistic theme, were celebrated at the national games at Olympia.

Ruled by local tyrants or **oligarchies**, the Greeks were not politically united but managed to resist inclusion in the Persian Empire. Persian king Darius was defeated at Marathon (490 BCE), his son Xerxes at Salamis (480 BCE), and the Persian army at Plataea (479 BCE). Democracy sprouted in Athens as statesman Pericles (495-429 BCE) sought participation in government from all citizens. Local warfare was common; the **Peloponnesian Wars** (431-404 BCE) ended in Sparta's victory over Athens. Greek political power subsequently waned, but Greek cultural forms spread far and wide.

Hebrews. Nomadic Hebrew tribes entered Canaan before 1200 BCE, settling among other Semitic peoples speaking the same language. They brought from the desert a **monotheistic** faith said to have been revealed to Abraham in Canaan c. 1800 BCE and Moses at Mt. Sinai c. 1250 BCE, after the Hebrews' escape from bondage in Egypt. David (r. 1000-961 BCE) and Solomon (r. 961-922 BCE) united them in a kingdom that briefly dominated the area. **Phoenicians** to the N founded Mediterranean colonies (Carthage, c. 814 BCE) and sailed into the Atlantic.

A temple in Jerusalem became the national religious center, with sacrifices performed by a hereditary priesthood. Polytheistic influences, especially of the fertility cult of Baal, were opposed by **prophets** (Elijah, Amos, Isaiah).

Divided into **two kingdoms** after Solomon, the Hebrews were unable to resist the revived Assyrian empire, which conquered **Israel**, the northern kingdom, in 722 BCE. **Judah**, the southern kingdom, was conquered in 586 BCE by the Babylonians under Nebuchadnezzar II. With the fixing of most of the biblical canon by the mid-4th cent. BCE and the emergence of rabbis, Judaism successfully survived the loss of Hebrew autonomy. A Jewish kingdom was revived under the Hasmoneans (168-42 BCE).

China. During the **Eastern Zhou** dynasty (770-256 BCE), Chinese culture spread E to the sea and S to the Yangtze R. Large feudal states on the periphery of the empire contended for preeminence but continued to recognize the Son of Heaven (king), who retained a purely ritual role enriched with courtly music and dance. In the Age of Warring States (403-221 BCE), when the first sections of the **Great Wall** were built, the Qin state in the W gained supremacy and finally united all of China.

Iron tools entered China c. 500 BCE. Casting techniques were advanced, aiding agriculture. Peasants owned their land and owed civil and military service to nobles. China's cities grew in number and size; barter remained the chief trade medium.

Intellectual ferment among noble scribes and officials produced a classical age of Chinese literature and philosophy. **Confucius** (551-479 BCE) urged a restoration of a supposedly harmonious social order of the past through proper conduct in accordance with one's station and through filial and ceremonial piety. The *Analects* attributed to him are revered throughout E Asia.

Among other thinkers, **Mencius** (d. 289 BCE) added the view that the Mandate of Heaven can be removed from an unjust dynasty. The Legalists sought to curb the supposed natural wickedness of people through new institutions and harsh laws. The Naturalists sought the balance of opposites—yin, yang—in the world. Daoists sought mystical knowledge through meditation and disengagement.

India. The political and cultural center of India shifted from the Indus to the Ganges River Valley. Buddhism, Jainism, and mystical revisions of orthodox Vedism all developed c. 500-300 BCE. The *Upanishads*, last part of the *Veda*, urged escape from the cycle of rebirth into the physical world. Vedism remained the preserve of the Brahman caste.

In contrast, **Buddhism**, founded by Siddhartha Gautama (c. 563-c. 483 BCE)—Buddha ("Enlightened One")—appealed to merchants in the urban centers and took hold at first (and most lastingly) on the geographic fringes of Indian civilization. The classic Indian epics were composed in this era: the *Ramayana* perhaps c. 300 BCE, the *Mahabharata* over a period starting around 400 BCE.

Northern India was divided into a large number of monarchies and aristocratic republics, probably derived from tribal groupings, when the Magadha kingdom was formed in Bihar c. 542 BCE. It soon became the dominant power. The **Maurya** dynasty, founded by Chandragupta c. 321 BCE, expanded the kingdom, uniting most of Northern India in a centralized bureaucratic empire. The third Mauryan king, **Asoka** (r. c. 274-236 BCE), conquered most of the subcontinent. He converted to Buddhism, inscribed its tenets on pillars throughout India, and downplayed the caste system.

Before its final decline in India, Buddhism developed into a popular worship of heavenly Bodhisattvas ("enlightened beings"), and it produced a refined architecture (the Great Stupa [shrine] at Sanchi, 100 CE) and sculpture (Gandhara reliefs, 1-400 CE).

Persia. Aryan peoples (Persians, Medes) dominated the area of present Iran by the beginning of the 1st millennium BCE. The prophet **Zoroaster** (b. c. 628 BCE) introduced a dualistic religion in which the forces of good (Ahura Mazda, "Lord of Wisdom") and evil (Ahriman) battle for dominance; individuals are judged by their actions and earn damnation or salvation. Zoroaster's hymns (*Gathas*) are included in the *Avesta*, the Zoroastrian scriptures. A version of this faith became the established religion of the Persian Empire.

Africa. Nubia, periodically occupied by Egypt since about 2600 BCE, ruled Egypt c. 750-661 BCE and survived as an independent Egyptianized kingdom (**Kush**; capital Meroe) for 1,000 years. The Iron Age Nok culture flourished c. 500 BCE-200 CE on the Benue Plateau of **Nigeria**.

Americas. The Chavin culture controlled Northern Peru c. 900 BCE to 200 BCE. Its ceremonial centers, featuring the jaguar god, survived long after. Its architecture, ceramics, and textiles had influenced other Peruvian cultures. **Mayan civilization** began to develop in Central America as early as 1500 BCE.

Great Empires Unite the Classical World: 400 BCE-400 CE

Persia and the Mediterranean. Cyrus, ruler of a small kingdom in Persia from 559 BCE, united the Persians and Medes within 10 years and conquered Asia Minor and Babylonia in another 10. His son Cambyses, followed by **Darius** (r. 522-486 BCE), added vast lands to the E and N as far as the Indus Valley and Central Asia, as well as Egypt and Thrace. The whole empire was ruled by an international bureaucracy and army, with Persians holding the chief positions. The resources and styles of all the subject civilizations were exploited to create a rich syncretic art.

The kingdom of Macedon, which under Philip II dominated the Greek world and Egypt, was passed on to Philip's son **Alexander** in 336 BCE. Within 13 years, Alexander had conquered all the Persian dominions. Imbued by his tutor Aristotle with Greek ideals, Alexander encouraged colonization, and Greek-style cities were founded. After his death in 323 BCE, wars of succession divided the empire into three significant dynasties—the **Antigonids** in Asia Minor and Macedon, the **Ptolemies** in Egypt, and the **Seleucids** in Mesopotamia. In the ensuing 300 years (the **Hellenistic Era**), a cosmopolitan Greek-oriented culture permeated the ancient world from Western Europe to the borders of India, absorbing native elites everywhere.

Hellenistic philosophy stressed the private individual's search for happiness. The Cynics followed Diogenes (c. 400-c. 325 BCE), who stressed self-sufficiency and restriction of desires and expressed contempt for luxury and social convention. Zeno (c. 335-c. 263 BCE) and the **Stoics** exalted reason, identified it with virtue, and counseled an ascetic disregard for misfortune. The **Epicureans** tried to build lives of moderate pleasure without political or emotional involvement. Hellenistic arts imitated life realistically, especially in sculpture and literature (comedies of Menander, 342-292 BCE).

The sciences thrived, especially at Alexandria, where the Ptolemies financed a great library and museum. Fields of study included mathematics (**Euclid**'s geometry, c. 300 BCE); astronomy (heliocentric theory of Aristarchus, 310-230 BCE; Julian calendar, 45 BCE; **Ptolemy**'s *Almagest*, c. 150 CE); geography (world map of Eratosthenes, 276-194 BCE); hydraulics (**Archimedes**, 287-212 BCE); medicine (Galen, 130-200 CE); and chemistry. Inventors refined uses for siphons, valves, gears, springs, screws, levers, cams, and pulleys.

A restored Persian empire under the **Parthians** (northern Iranian tribespeople) controlled the eastern Hellenistic world from 250 BCE to 229 CE. The Parthians and the succeeding **Sassanian dynasty** (c. 224-651 CE) fought with Rome periodically. The Sassanians revived Zoroastrianism as a state religion and patronized a nationalistic artistic and scholarly renaissance.

Rome. The city of Rome was founded, according to legend, by Romulus in 753 BCE. Through military expansion and colonization, and by granting citizenship to leading members of conquered tribes, the city annexed all of Italy S of the Po R. in the 100-year period before 268 BCE. The Latin and other Italic tribes were annexed first, followed by the **Etruscans** (founders of a great civilization N of Rome) and Greek colonies in the S. With a large standing army and reserve forces of several hundred thousand, Rome was able to defeat **Carthage** in the three

Punic Wars (264-241 BCE, 218-201 BCE, 149-146 BCE), despite the invasion of Italy by **Hannibal** (218 BCE), thus gaining Sicily and territory in Spain and N Africa.

Rome exploited local disputes to conquer Greece and Asia Minor in the 2nd cent. BCE and Egypt in the 1st (after the defeat and suicide of **Antony and Cleopatra**, 30 BCE). The Mediterranean civilized world, up to the disputed Parthian border, was now Roman and remained so for 500 years. Less civilized regions were added to the Empire: Gaul (conquered by **Julius Caesar**, 58-51 BCE), Britain (43 CE), and Dacia NE of the Danube (107 CE).

The original aristocratic republican government, with democratic features added in the 5th and 4th cent. BCE, deteriorated under the pressures of empire and class conflict (**Gracchus** brothers, social reformers, murdered in 133 BCE and 121 BCE; slave revolts in 135 BCE and 73 BCE). After a series of civil wars (Marius vs. Sulla, 88-82 BCE; Caesar vs. **Pompey**, 49-45 BCE; triumvirate vs. Caesar's assassins, 44-43 BCE; Antony vs. Octavian, 32-30 BCE), the empire came under the rule of a deified monarch (first emperor, **Augustus**, 27 BCE-14 CE).

Provincials (nearly all granted citizenship by Caracalla, 212 CE) came to dominate the army and civil service. Traditional **Roman law**, systematized and interpreted by independent jurists, and local self-rule in provincial cities were supplanted by a vast tax-collecting bureaucracy in the 3rd and 4th cent. The legal rights of women, children, and slaves were strengthened.

Roman innovations in **civil engineering** included water mills, windmills, and rotary mills and the use of cement that hardened under water. Monumental architecture (baths, theaters, temples) relied on the arch and the dome. A network of roads (some still standing) stretched 53,000 mi, passing through mountain tunnels as long as 3.5 mi. Aqueducts brought water to cities; underground sewers removed waste.

Roman art and literature were derivative of Greek models. Innovations were made in sculpture (naturalistic busts, equestrian statues), decorative wall painting (as at Pompeii), satire (**Juvenal**, 60-127 CE), history (**Tacitus**, 56-120 CE), and prose romance (**Petronius**, d. 66 CE). Gladiatorial contests dominated public amusements, which were supported by the state.

India. The **Gupta** monarchs reunited Northern India c. 320 CE. Their peaceful and prosperous reign saw a revival of Hindu religious thought and Brahman power. The old Vedic traditions were combined with devotion to many indigenous deities (who were seen as manifestations of Vedic gods). Caste lines were reinforced, and Buddhist practices gradually disappeared or were integrated with **Hindu** traditions. The art (often erotic), architecture, and literature of the period, patronized by the Gupta court, are considered among India's finest achievements (Kalidasa, poet and dramatist, fl. c. 400 CE). Mathematical innovations included the use of zero and decimal numbers. Invasions by White Huns from the NW led to the empire's destruction c. 550 CE. Rich cultures also developed in Southern India during this period. Emotional Tamil religious poetry contributed to the Hindu revival. The Pallava kingdom controlled much of Southern India c. 350-880 CE and helped to spread Indian civilization to SE Asia.

China. The Qin ruler Shi Huang (r. 221-210 BCE), known as the First Emperor, centralized political authority; standardized the written language, laws, weights, measures, and coinage; and conducted a census. But he tried to destroy most philosophical texts. The **Han** dynasty (202 BCE-220 CE) instituted the Mandarin bureaucracy, which lasted 2,000 years. Local officials were selected by examination in Confucian classics and trained at the imperial university and provincial schools.

The invention of **paper** facilitated this bureaucratic system. Agriculture was promoted, but peasants bore most of the tax burden. Irrigation was improved, water clocks and sundials were used, astronomy and mathematics thrived, and landscape painting was perfected.

With the expansion S and W (to nearly the present borders of today's China), trade was opened with India, SE Asia, and the Middle East over sea and caravan routes. Indian missionaries brought Mahayana Buddhism to China by the 1st cent. CE and spawned a variety of sects. Daoism was revived and merged with popular superstitions. **Daoist and Buddhist monasteries** and convents multiplied in the turbulent centuries after the collapse of the Han dynasty in 220 CE.

China's Great Wall, first built during the Age of Warring States (403-221 BCE), was rebuilt, extended, and modified over thousands of years to protect China from invaders.

Monotheism Spreads: 1-750 CE

Roman Empire. Polytheism was practiced in the Roman Empire, and religions indigenous to particular Middle Eastern nations became international. Roman citizens worshiped **Isis** of Egypt, **Mithras** of Persia, **Demeter** of Greece, and the great mother **Cybele** of Phrygia. Their cults centered on mysteries (secret ceremonies) and the promise of an afterlife, symbolized by the death and rebirth of the god. The Jews of the empire preserved their monotheistic religion, Judaism, the world's oldest (c. 1300 BCE) continuous religion. Its teachings are contained in the Bible (the Old Testament). 1st-cent. CE Judaism embraced several sects, including the **Sadducees**, mostly drawn from the Temple priesthood, who were culturally Hellenized; the **Pharisees**, who upheld the full range of traditional customs and practices of equal weight to literal scriptural law and elaborated synagogue worship; and the **Essenes**, an ascetic, millenarian sect. Messianic fervor led to repeated, unsuccessful rebellions against Rome (66-70, 135 CE). As a result, the Temple in Jerusalem was destroyed and the population decimated; this event marked the beginning of the Diaspora (living in exile). To preserve the faith, codification of law was begun at the academy of Yavneh. The work continued for some 500 years in Palestine and in Babylonia, ending in the final redaction (c. 600) of the **Talmud**, a huge collection of legal and moral debates, rulings, liturgy, biblical exegesis, and legendary materials.

Christianity. Emerging as a distinct sect by the second half of the 1st cent. CE, Christianity is based on the teachings of **Jesus**, whom believers considered the Savior (Messiah or Christ) and son of God. Missionary activities of the Apostles and such early leaders as **Paul of Tarsus** spread the faith. Intermittent persecution, as in Rome under Nero in 64 CE, on grounds of suspected disloyalty, failed to disrupt Christian communities. Each congregation, generally urban and of plebeian character, was tightly organized under a leader (bishop), elders (presbyters or priests), and assistants (deacons). The four **Gospels** (accounts of the life and teachings of Jesus) and the Acts of the Apostles were written down in the late 1st and early 2nd cent. and circulated along with letters of Paul and other Christian leaders. An authoritative canon of these writings was not fixed until the 4th cent.

A school for priests was established at Alexandria in the 2nd cent. Its teachers (**Origen**, c. 182-251) helped define doctrine and promote the faith in Greek-style philosophical works. Neoplatonism underwent Christian coloration in the writings of Church Fathers such as **Augustine** (354-430). Christian hermits began to associate in monasteries, first in Egypt (St. Pachomius, c. 290-345), then in other eastern lands, then in the W (**St. Benedict's rule**, 529). Devotion to saints, especially Mary, mother of Jesus, spread. Under **Constantine** (r. 306-37), Christianity became in effect the established religion of the Empire. Pagan temples were expropriated, state funds were used to build churches and support the hierarchy, and laws were adjusted in accordance with Christian ideas. Pagan worship was banned by the end of the 4th cent., and severe restrictions were placed on Judaism.

The newly established church was rocked by doctrinal disputes, often exacerbated by regional rivalries. Chief heresies (as defined by church councils, backed by imperial authority) were **Arianism**, which denied the divinity of Jesus; **Monophysitism**, denying the human nature of Christ; **Donatism**, which regarded as invalid any sacraments administered by sinful clergy; and **Pelagianism**, which denied the necessity of unmerited divine aid (grace) for salvation.

Islam. The earliest Arab civilization emerged by the end of the 2nd millennium BCE in the watered highlands of Yemen. Seaborne and caravan trade in frankincense and myrrh connected the area with the Nile and Fertile Crescent. The Minaean, Sabean (Sheba), and Himyarite states successively held sway. By Muhammad's time (7th cent. CE), the region was a province of Sassanian Persia. In the N, the Nabataean kingdom at Petra and the kingdom of Palmyra were Aramaicized, Romanized, and finally absorbed, as neighboring Judea had been, into the Roman Empire. Nomads shared the central region with a few trading towns and oases. Wars between tribes and raids on communities were common and were celebrated in a poetic tradition that by the 6th cent. helped establish a classic literary Arabic.

About 610, **Muhammad**, a 40-year-old Arab man of Mecca, emerged as a prophet. He proclaimed a revelation from the one true God, calling on contemporaries to abandon idolatry and restore the faith of Abraham. He introduced his religion as **Islam**, meaning "submission" to the one God, Allah, as a continuation of the biblical faith of Abraham, Moses, and Jesus, all respected as prophets in this system. His teachings, recorded in the Quran, in many ways were inclusive of Abrahamic monotheistic ideas known to the Jews and Christians in Arabia. A key aspect of the Abrahamic connection was insistence on justice in society, which led to severe opposition among the aristocrats in Mecca. As conditions worsened for Muhammad and his followers, he decided in 622 to make a *hegira* (flight) to Medina, 200 mi to the N. This event marks the beginning of the Muslim lunar calendar. Hostilities between Mecca and Medina increased, and in 629 Muhammad conquered Mecca. By the time he died in 632, nearly all the Arabian peninsula accepted his political and religious leadership.

After his death the majority of Muslims (later known as **Sunni** Muslims) recognized the leadership of the **caliph** (successor) Abu Bakr (632-34), followed by Umar (634-44), Uthman (644-56), and Ali (656-60). A minority, the **Shiites**, insisted instead on the leadership of Ali, Muhammad's cousin and son-in-law. By 644, **Muslim rule** over Arabia was confirmed. Muslim armies had threatened the Byzantine and Persian empires, which were weakened by wars and disaffection among subject peoples (including Coptic and Syriac Christians opposed to the Byzantine Orthodox establishment). Syria, Palestine, Egypt, Iraq, and Persia fell to Muslim armies. The new administration assimilated existing systems in the region; hence the conquered peoples participated in running the empire. The Quran recognized the so-called Peoples of the Book, i.e., Christians, Jews, and Zoroastrians, as tolerated monotheists, and Muslim policy was relatively tolerant to minorities living as "protected" peoples. An expanded tax system, based on conquests of the Persian and Byzantine empires, provided revenue to organize campaigns against neighboring non-Muslim regions.

Under the **Umayyads** (661-750) and **Abbasids** (750-1256), territorial expansion led Muslim armies across N Africa and into Spain (711). Muslim armies in the W were stopped at Tours, France, in 732 by the Frankish ruler **Charles Martel**. Asia Minor, the Indus Valley, and Transoxiana were conquered in the E. The conversion of conquered peoples to Islam was gradual. In many places the official Arabic language supplanted the local tongues. But in the eastern regions the Arab rulers and their armies adopted Persian cultures and language as part of their Muslim identity.

Disputes over succession and pious opposition to injustices in society led to a number of oppositional movements, which led to the factionalization of Muslim community. The **Shiites** supported leadership candidates descended from Muhammad, believing them to be carriers of some kind of divine authority. The **Kharijites** supported an egalitarian system derived from the Quran, opposing and even engaging in battle against those who did not agree with them.

The now-typical use of a minaret as the location for the Muslim call to prayer began at the Mosque of Uqba, or Great Mosque of Kairouan, built from 670 CE in present-day Tunisia.

New Peoples Enter World History: 400-900 CE

Barbarian invasions and fall of Rome. Germanic tribes infiltrated S and E from their Baltic homeland during the 1st millennium BCE, reaching southern Germany by 100 BCE and the Black Sea by 214 CE. Organized into large federated tribes under elected kings, most resisted Roman domination and raided the empire in times of civil war (Goths took Dacia in 214, raided Thrace in 251-69). Germanic troops and commanders dominated the Roman armies by the end of the 4th cent. **Huns,** invaders from Asia, entered Europe in 372, driving more Germans into the empire. Emperor Valens allowed Visigoths to cross the Danube in 376. Huns under Attila (d. 453) raided Gaul, Italy, and the Balkans.

The western empire, weakened by overtaxation and social stagnation, was overrun in the 5th cent. Gaul was effectively lost in 406-07, Spain in 409, Britain in 410, and Africa in 429-39. Rome was sacked in 410 by Visigoths under Alaric and in 455 by Vandals. The **last western emperor,** Romulus Augustulus, was deposed in 476 by the Germanic chief Odoacer.

Celts. Celtic cultures, which in pre-Roman times covered most of W Europe, were confined almost entirely to the British Isles after the Germanic invasions. **St. Patrick** completed (c. 457-92) the conversion of Ireland and a strong monastic tradition took hold. Irish monastic missionaries in Scotland, England, and on the continent (Columba, c. 521-97; Columbanus, c. 543-615) helped restore Christianity after the Germanic invasions. **Monasteries** became centers of classic and Christian learning and presided over the recording of a Christianized Celtic mythology, elaborated by secular writers and bards. An intricate decorative art style developed, especially in book illumination (Lindisfarne Gospels, c. 700; Book of Kells, 8th cent.).

Successor states. The Visigothic kingdom in Spain (from 419) and much of France (to 507) saw continuation of Roman administration, language, and law (Breviary of Alaric, 506) until its destruction by Muslim forces from North Africa (711). The Vandal kingdom in Africa (from 429) was conquered by the Byzantines in 533. Italy was ruled successively by an Ostrogothic kingdom under Byzantine suzerainty (489-554), direct Byzantine government, and German Lombards (568-774). The Lombards divided the peninsula with the Byzantines and papacy under the dynamic reformer **Pope Gregory the Great** (590-604) and successors.

King Clovis (r. 481-511) united the Franks on both sides of the Rhine and, after his conversion to Christianity, defeated the Arian heretics, Burgundians (after 500), and Visigoths (507) with the support of native clergy and the papacy. Under the **Merovingian** kings, a feudal system emerged: power was fragmented among hierarchies of military landowners. Social stratification, which in late Roman times had acquired legal, hereditary sanction, was reinforced.

The Carolingians (747-987) expanded the kingdom and restored central power. **Charlemagne** (r. 768-814) conquered nearly all the Germanic lands, including Lombard Italy. He was crowned emperor by Pope Leo III in Rome in 800. A centuries-long decline in commerce and arts was reversed under Charlemagne's patronage. He welcomed Jews to his kingdom, which became a center of Jewish learning (Rashi, 1040-1105). He sponsored the Carolingian Renaissance of learning under the Anglo-Latin scholar Alcuin (c. 732-804), who reformed church liturgy.

The pyramid of Kukulkan (El Castillo) at Chichen Itza is one of the existing examples of Mayan architecture in present-day Mexico.

Byzantine Empire. Under **Diocletian** (r. 284-305) the Roman empire had been divided into two parts to facilitate administration and defense. **Constantine** founded (330) **Constantinople** (at old Byzantium) as a fully Christian city. Commerce and taxation financed a sumptuous, orientalized court, a class of hereditary bureaucratic families, and magnificent urban construction (Hagia Sophia, 532-37). The city's fortifications and naval innovations repelled assaults by Goths, Huns, Slavs, Bulgars, Avars, Arabs, and Scandinavians. Greek replaced Latin as the official language by c. 700. **Byzantine art,** a solemn, sacral, and stylized variation of late classical styles (mosaics at the Church of San Vitale, Ravenna, Italy, 526-48), was a starting point for medieval art in Eastern and Western Europe.

Justinian (r. 527-65) briefly reconquered parts of Spain, N Africa, and Italy, codified **Roman law** (Codex Justinianus [529] was medieval Europe's chief legal text), closed the Platonic Academy at Athens, and ordered all pagans to convert. Lombards in Italy and Arabs in Africa retook most of his conquests. The Isaurian dynasty from Anatolia (from 717) and the Macedonian dynasty (867-1054) restored military and commercial power. The Iconoclast controversy (726-843) over the permissibility of images helped alienate the Eastern Church from the papacy.

Abbasid Empire. Baghdad (established 762) became seat of the **Abbasid dynasty** (established 750), while Umayyads continued to rule in Spain. A brilliant cosmopolitan civilization emerged, inaugurating a Muslim-Arab golden age. Arabic was the lingua franca of the empire; intellectual sources from Persian, Sanskrit, Greek, and Syriac were rendered into Arabic. Christians and Jews equally participated in this translation movement, which also involved interaction between Jewish legal thought and Islamic law, as much as between Christian theology and Muslim scholasticism. Persian-style court life, with art and music, flourished at the court of **Harun al-Rashid** (786-809), celebrated in the masterpiece known to English readers as *The Arabian Nights.* The sciences, medicine, and mathematics were pursued at Baghdad, Cordova, and Cairo (c. 969). The culmination of this intellectual synthesis in Islamic civilization came with the scientific and philosophical works of **Avicenna** (Ibn Sina, 980-1037), **Averroes** (Ibn Rushd, 1126-98), and **Maimonides** (1135-1204), a Jew who wrote in Arabic. This intellectual tradition was translated into Latin and opened a new period in Christian thought.

The decentralization of the Abbasid empire, from 874, led to the establishment of various Muslim dynasties under different ethnic groups. Persians, Berbers, and Turks ruled different regions, retaining connection with the Abbasid caliph at the religious level. The Abbasid period also saw various religious movements against the orthodox position held by governing authorities. This situation in Islam led to the establishment of different legal, theological, and mystical schools of thought. The most influential mass movement was **Sufism,** which aimed at the reaching out of the average individual in quest of a spiritual path. Al-Ghazali (1058-1111) is credited with reconciling personal Sufism with orthodox Sunni tradition.

Africa. Immigrants from Saba in S Arabia helped set up the **Axum** kingdom in Ethiopia in the 1st cent. (their language, Ge'ez, is preserved by the Ethiopian Church). In the 3rd cent., when the kingdom became Christianized, it defeated Kushite Meroe and expanded its influence into Yemen. Axum was the center of a vast ivory trade and controlled the Red Sea coast until c. 1100. Arab conquest in Egypt cut Axum's political and economic ties with Byzantium.

The Iron Age entered W Africa by the end of the 1st millennium BCE. **Ghana,** the first known sub-Saharan state, ruled in the upper Senegal-Niger region c. 400-1240, controlling the trade of gold from mines in the S to trans-Sahara caravan routes to the N. The **Bantu** peoples, probably of W African origin, began to spread E and S perhaps 2,000 years ago, displacing the Pygmies and Bushmen of central and southern Africa during a 1,500-year period.

Japan. The advanced Neolithic Yayoi period, when irrigation, rice farming, and iron and bronze casting techniques were introduced from China or Korea, persisted to c. 400 CE. The myriad Japanese states were then united by the **Yamato** clan, under an emperor who acted as chief priest of the animistic Shinto cult. Japanese political and military intervention by the 6th cent. in Korea, then under strong Chinese influence, quickened a Chinese cultural invasion of Japan, bringing Buddhism, the Chinese language (which long remained a literary and governmental medium), Chinese ideographs, and Buddhist styles in painting, sculpture, literature, and architecture (7th cent., Horyuji temple at Nara). The Taika Reforms (646) tried unsuccessfully to centralize Japan according to Chinese bureaucratic and Buddhist philosophical values.

A nativist reaction against the Buddhist **Nara** period (710-94) ushered in the **Heian** period (794-1185) centered at the new capital, Kyoto. Japanese elegance and simplicity modified Chinese styles in architecture, scroll painting, and literature; the writing system was also simplified. The courtly novel *Tale of Genji* (1010-20) testifies to the enhanced role of women in medieval Japanese literature and culture.

Southeast Asia. The historic peoples of SE Asia began arriving some 2,500 years ago from China and Tibet, displacing scattered aborigines. Their agriculture relied on rice and yams. Indian cultural influences were strongest; literacy and Hindu and Buddhist ideas followed the S India-China trade route. From the southern tip of Indochina, the kingdom of **Funan** (1st-7th cent.) traded as far W as Persia. It was absorbed by Chenla, itself conquered by the **Khmer** empire (800-1300). The Khmers, under Hindu god-kings (Suryavarman II, 1113-c. 1150), built the monumental Angkor Wat temple center for the royal phallic cult. The **Nam-Viet** kingdom in Annam, dominated by China and Chinese culture for 1,000 years, emerged in the 10th cent., growing at the expense of the Khmers, who also lost ground in the NW to the new, highly organized **Thai** kingdom. On Sumatra, the **Srivijaya** empire controlled vital sea lanes (7th-10th cent.). A Buddhist dynasty, the Sailendras, ruled central **Java**

(8th-9th cent.), building at Borobudur one of the largest stupas (dome-shaped Buddhist shrines) in the world.

China. The Sui dynasty (581-618) ushered in a period of commercial, artistic, and scientific achievement in China, which continued under the **Tang** dynasty (618-906). Inventions like the magnetic compass, gunpowder, the abacus, and printing were introduced or perfected. Medical innovations included cataract surgery. The state, from its cosmopolitan capital, Chang-an, supervised foreign trade, which exchanged Chinese silks, porcelains, and art for spices and ivory over Central Asian caravan routes and sea routes reaching Africa. A golden age of poetry bequeathed valuable works to later generations (Tu Fu, 712-70; Li Po, 701-62). Landscape painting flourished.

Commercial and industrial expansion continued under the **Northern Song** (960-1126), facilitated by paper money and credit notes. But commerce never achieved full respectability; government monopolies expropriated successful merchants. The population, long stable at 50 million, doubled in 200 years with the introduction of early-ripening rice and the double harvest. In art, native Chinese styles were revived.

Americas. From 300 to 600, a Native American empire stretched from the Valley of Mexico to Guatemala, centering on the huge city **Teotihuacán** (founded 100 BCE). To the S, in Guatemala, a high **Mayan** civilization developed (150-900) around hundreds of rural ceremonial centers. The Mayans improved on Olmec writing and the calendar and pursued astronomy and mathematics. In South America, a widespread pre-Inca culture grew from **Tiahuanacu**, Bolivia, near Lake Titicaca (Gateway of the Sun doorway, c. 700).

Christian Europe Regroups and Expands: 900-1300

Scandinavia. Pagan Danish and Norse (Viking) adventurers, traders, and pirates raided the coasts of the British Isles (Dublin, c. 831), France, and even the Mediterranean for over 200 years beginning in the late 8th cent. Inland settlement in the W was limited to Great Britain (King Canute, 994-1035) and Normandy, settled (911) under Rollo, as a fief of France. Vikings also reached Iceland (874), Greenland (c. 986), and North America (**Leif Ericson** and others, c. 1000). Norse traders (**Varangians**) developed Russian river commerce from the 8th to the 11th cent. and helped set up a state at Kiev in the late 9th cent. Conversion to Christianity occurred in the 10th cent., reaching Sweden 100 years later. In the 11th cent. Norman bands conquered Southern Italy and Sicily, and Duke **William of Normandy** conquered (1066) England, bringing feudal government and the French language, essential elements in later English civilization.

Central and East Europe. Slavs began to expand from about 150 CE in all directions in Europe. By the 7th cent. they reached as far S as the Adriatic and Aegean seas. In the Balkan Peninsula they dislocated Romanized local populations or assimilated newcomers (Bulgarians, a Turkic people). The first **Slavic** states were Moravia (628) in Central Europe and the Bulgarian state (680) in the Balkans. Byzantine missions of St. Methodius and Cyril (whose Greek-based cyrillic alphabet is still used by some Southern and Eastern Slavs) converted (863) Moravia.

The Eastern Slavs, part-civilized under the overlordship of the Turkish-Jewish **Khazar** trading empire (7th-10th cent.), gravitated toward Constantinople by the 9th cent. The **Kievan** state adopted (989) Eastern Christianity under Prince Vladimir. King Boleslav I (992-1025) began **Poland**'s long history of conquest. The Magyars (**Hungarians**), in present-day Hungary since 896, accepted (1001) Latin Christianity.

Germany. The German kingdom that emerged after the breakup of Charlemagne's Western Empire remained a confederation of largely autonomous states. Otto I, a Saxon who was king from 936, established the **Holy Roman Empire**—a union of Germany and Northern Italy—in alliance with Pope John XII, who crowned (962) him emperor; he defeated (955) the Magyars. Imperial power was greatest under the **Hohenstaufens** (1138-1254), despite the growing opposition of the papacy, which ruled central Italy, and the Lombard League cities. Frederick II (1194-1250) improved administration and patronized the arts. After his death, German influence was removed from Italy.

Christian Spain. From its northern mountain redoubts, Christian rule slowly migrated S through the 11th cent., when Muslim unity collapsed. After the capture (1085) of **Toledo**, the kingdoms of Portugal, Castile, and Aragon undertook repeated crusades of reconquest, finally completed in 1492. Elements of Islamic civilization persisted in recaptured areas, influencing all Western Europe.

Crusades. Pope **Urban II** called for a crusade (1095) to restore Asia Minor to Byzantium and the Holy Land to Christendom. This first crusade captured Jerusalem and led to the foundation of four Frankish states in the Levant. The defeat inflicted upon crusaders at the Battle of Hattin (1187) by **Saladin** (c. 1137-93), the Kurdish ruler of Egypt and Syria, effectively negated territorial gains. Many crusades followed until 1291. The 4th crusade sacked Constantinople (1204). Other crusades were launched against Christian heretics (Albigensian Crusade, 1229), pagans, and enemies of the papacy.

Economy. The agricultural base of European life benefited from improvements in **plow design** (c. 1000) and by the draining of lowlands and clearing of forests, leading to a rural population increase. Towns grew in Northern Italy, Flanders, and Northern Germany (Hanseatic League). Improvements in **loom design** permitted factory textile production. Guilds dominated urban trades from the 12th cent. Banking (centered in Italy, 12th-15th cent.) facilitated long-distance trade.

Christianity. The split between the Eastern and Western churches was formalized in 1054. Western and Central Europe was divided into 500 bishoprics under one united hierarchy, but conflicts between secular and church authorities were frequent (German **Investiture Controversy**, 1075-1122). Clerical power was first strengthened through the international monastic reform begun at Cluny in 910. Popular religious enthusiasm often expressed itself in heretical movements (Waldensians from 1173), but was channeled by the **Dominican** (1215) and **Franciscan** (1223) friars into the religious mainstream.

Arts. Romanesque architecture (9th to mid-12th cent.) expanded on late Roman models, using the rounded arch and massed stone to support enlarged basilicas. Painting and sculpture followed Byzantine models. The literature of chivalry was exemplified by the epic (*Chanson de Roland*, c. 1100) and by courtly love poems of the troubadours of Provence and minnesingers of Germany. **Gothic** architecture emerged in France (choir of St. Denis, c. 1140) and spread along with French cultural influence. Rib vaulting and pointed arches were used to combine soaring heights with delicacy, and they freed walls for display of stained glass. Exteriors were covered with painted relief sculpture and embellished with elaborate architectural detail.

Learning. Law, medicine, and philosophy were advanced at independent **universities** (Bologna, Paris, 12th cent.), originally corporations of students and masters. Twelfth-cent. translations of Greek classics, especially by Aristotle, encouraged an analytic approach. Scholastic philosophy, from Anselm (1033-1109) to **Aquinas** (1225-74), attempted to understand revelation through reason.

Apogee of Central Asian Power and the Spread of Islam: 1250-1500

Turks. Turkic peoples, of Central Asian ancestry, were a military threat to the Byzantine and Persian Empires from the 6th cent. After several waves of invasions, during which most of the Turks adopted Islam, the **Seljuk Turks** took (1055) Baghdad. They ruled Persia, Iraq, and, after 1071, Asia Minor, where massive numbers of Turks settled. The empire was divided in the 12th cent. into smaller states ruled by Seljuks, Kurds, and Mamluks (a military caste of former Turk, Kurd, and Circassian slaves), which governed Egypt and the Middle East until the Ottoman era (c. 1290-1922).

Osman I (r. c. 1290-1326) and succeeding sultans united Anatolian Turkish warriors in a militaristic state that waged holy war against Byzantium and Balkan Christians. Most of the Balkans had been subdued and Anatolia united when Constantinople fell (1453). By the mid-16th cent., Hungary, the Middle East, and N Africa had been conquered. The Turkish advance was stopped at Vienna (1529) and at the naval battle of Lepanto (1571) by Spain, Venice, and the papacy.

The **Ottoman state** was governed in accordance with orthodox Muslim law. Greek, Armenian, and Jewish communities were segregated and were ruled by religious leaders responsible for taxation; they dominated trade. Many state offices and most army ranks were filled by slaves, in part through a system of child conscription among Christians.

India. Mahmud of Ghazni (971-1030) led repeated Turkish raids into N India. Turkish power was consolidated in 1206 with the start of the **Sultanate at Delhi**. Centralization of state power under the early Delhi sultans went far beyond traditional Indian practice. Muslim rule of much of the subcontinent lasted until the British conquest 600 years later, though Hinduism remained the majority religion.

Mongols. Genghis Khan (c. 1167-1227) first united the feuding Mongol tribes and built their armies into an effective offensive force around a core of highly mobile cavalry. He and his immediate successors created the largest land empire in history; by 1279 it stretched from the E coast of Asia to the Danube and from the Siberian steppes to the Arabian Sea. East-West trade and contacts were facilitated (Marco Polo, c. 1254-1324). The western Mongols were Islamized by 1295; successor states soon lost their Mongol character by assimilation. They were briefly reunited under the Turk Tamerlane (1336-1405).

Kublai Khan ruled China from his new capital Beijing (established c. 1264). Naval campaigns against Japan (1274, 1281) and Java (1293) were defeated, the latter by the Hindu-Buddhist maritime kingdom of Majapahit. The **Yuan** dynasty used Mongols and other foreigners (including Europeans) in official posts and tolerated the return of Nestorian Christianity

(suppressed 841-45) and the spread of Islam in the S and W. A native reaction expelled the Mongols in 1367-68.

Russia. The Kievan state in Russia, weakened by the decline of Byzantium and the rise of the Catholic Polish-Lithuanian state, was overrun (1238-40) by the Mongols. Only the northern trading republic of Novgorod remained independent. The grand dukes of Moscow emerged as leaders of a coalition of princes that eventually (by 1481) defeated the Mongols. After the fall of Constantinople in 1453, the **Tsars** (Caesars) at Moscow (from Ivan III, r. 1462-1505) set up an independent Russian Orthodox Church. Commerce failed to revive. The isolated Russian state remained agrarian with the peasant class falling into serfdom.

Persia. A revival of Persian literature, making use of the Arab alphabet and literary forms, began in the 10th cent. (epic of Firdausi, 935-1020). An art revival, influenced by Chinese styles introduced after the Mongols came to power in Iran, began in the 13th cent. Persian cultural and political forms, and often the Persian language, were used for centuries by Turkish and Mongol elites from the Balkans to India. Persian mystics from Rumi (1207-73) to Jami (1414-92) promoted **Sufism** in their poetry.

Africa. Two militant Islamic Berber dynasties emerged from the Sahara to carve out empires from the Sahel to central Spain—the **Almoravids** (c. 1050-1140) and the fanatical **Almohads** (c. 1125-1269). The Ghanaian empire was replaced in the upper Niger by Mali (c. 1230-1340), whose Muslim rulers imported Egyptians to help make **Timbuktu** a center of commerce (in gold, leather, and slaves) and learning. The Songhay empire (to 1590) replaced Mali. To the S, forest kingdoms produced refined artworks (Ife terra cotta, **Benin** bronzes).

Other **Muslim states** in Nigeria (Hausas) and Chad originated in the 11th cent. and continued in some form until the 19th-cent. European conquest. Less-developed Bantu kingdoms existed across central Africa.

Some 40 Muslim Arab-Persian trading colonies and city-states were established all along the E African coast from the 10th cent. (Kilwa, Mogadishu). The interchange with Bantu peoples produced the **Swahili** language and culture. Gold, palm oil, and people to enslave were brought from the interior, stimulating the growth of the Monamatapa kingdom of the Zambezi (15th cent.). The Christian Ethiopian empire (from 13th cent.) continued the traditions of Axum.

Southeast Asia. Islam was introduced into Malaya and the Indonesian islands by Arab, Persian, and Indian traders. Coastal Muslim cities and states (starting before 1300) soon dominated the interior. Chief among these was the **Malacca** state (c. 1400-1511), on the Malay peninsula.

Arts and Statecraft Thrive in Europe; New Asian Empires Rise: 1350-1600

Italy. Distinctive Italian achievements in literature and fine arts during the late Middle Ages (**Dante**, 1265-1321; Giotto, 1276-1337) led to the vigorous new styles of the Renaissance (14th-16th cent.). Patronized by the rulers of the quarreling petty states of Italy (**Medicis** in Florence and the papacy, c. 1400-1737), the plastic arts perfected realistic techniques, including **perspective** (Masaccio, 1401-28; Leonardo **da Vinci**, 1452-1519). Classical motifs were used in architecture, and increased talent and expense were put into secular buildings. The Florentine dialect was refined as a national literary language (**Petrarch**, 1304-74). Greek refugees from the E strengthened the respect of humanist scholars for the classic sources. Soon an international movement aided by the spread of **printing** (Gutenberg, c. 1397-1468), **humanism** was optimistic about the power of human reason (Erasmus of Rotterdam, 1466-1536, **More**'s *Utopia*, 1516) and valued individual effort in the arts and in politics (**Machiavelli**, 1469-1527).

France. The French monarchy, strengthened in its repeated struggles with powerful nobles (Burgundy, Flanders, Aquitaine) by alliances with the growing commercial towns, consolidated bureaucratic control under Philip IV (r. 1285-1314) and extended French influence into Germany and Italy (popes at Avignon, France, 1309-1417). The **Hundred Years War** (1337-1453) ended English dynastic claims in France (battles of Crécy, 1346, and Poitiers, 1356; Joan of Arc executed, 1431). A French Renaissance, dating from royal invasions (1494, 1499)

of Italy, was encouraged at the court of Francis I (r. 1515-47), who centralized taxation and law. French vernacular literature consciously asserted its independence (La Pléiade, 1549).

England. The evolution of England's political institutions began with the **Magna Carta** (1215), by which King John guaranteed the privileges of nobles and church against the monarchy and assured jury trial. After the **Wars of the Roses** (1455-85), the **Tudor** dynasty reasserted royal prerogatives (Henry VIII, r. 1509-47), but the trend toward independent departments and ministerial government also continued. English trade (wool exports from c. 1340) was protected by the nation's growing maritime power (**Spanish Armada** destroyed, 1588).

English replaced French and Latin in the late 14th cent. in law and literature (**Chaucer**, c. 1340-1400), and English translation of the Bible began (Wycliffe, 1380s). **Elizabeth I** (r. 1558-1603) presided over the development of poetry (Spenser, 1552-99), drama (**Shakespeare**, 1564-1616), and music.

German Empire. From among a welter of minor feudal states, church lands, and independent cities, the **Habsburgs** assembled a far-flung territorial domain, based in Austria from 1276. Family members held the title of Holy Roman Emperor from 1438 to the Empire's dissolution in 1806 but failed to centralize its domains, leaving Germany disunited for centuries. Resistance to Turkish expansion brought Hungary under Austrian control from the 16th cent. The Netherlands, Luxembourg, and Burgundy were added in 1477, curbing French expansion.

The Flemish painting tradition of naturalism, technical proficiency, and bourgeois subject matter began in the 15th cent. (Jan van Eyck, c. 1390-1441), the earliest northern manifestation of the Renaissance. Albrecht **Dürer** (1471-1528) typified the merging of late Gothic and Italian trends in 16th-cent. German art. Imposing civic architecture flourished in the prosperous commercial cities.

Black Death. The bubonic plague reached Europe from the E in 1348, killing up to half the population by 1350 (and recurring periodically in most areas until the early 18th cent.). Labor scarcity forced wages to rise and brought greater freedom to the peasantry, making possible **peasant uprisings** (Jacquerie in France, 1358; Wat Tyler's rebellion in England, 1381).

Spain. Despite the unification of Castile and Aragon in 1479, the two countries retained separate governments, and the nobility, especially in Aragon and Catalonia, retained many privileges. Spanish lands in Italy (Naples, Sicily) and the Netherlands entangled the country in European wars through the mid-17th cent., while explorers, traders, and conquerors built up a Spanish empire in the Americas and the Philippines.

From the late 15th cent., a **golden age** of literature and art produced works of social satire (plays of Lope de Vega, 1562-1635; **Cervantes**, 1547-1616), as well as spiritual intensity (**El Greco**, 1541-1614; **Velázquez**, 1599-1660).

Explorations. Organized European maritime exploration began, seeking to evade the Venice-Ottoman monopoly of eastern trade and to promote Christianity. A key goal was to satisfy a growing taste for Asian goods. Beginning in 1418, expeditions from Portugal explored the W coast of Africa, until Vasco da Gama rounded the Cape of Good Hope in 1497 and reached India. A Portuguese trading empire was consolidated by the seizure of Goa (1510) and Malacca (1551). Japan was reached in 1542. The voyages of Christopher **Columbus** (1492-1504) uncovered a world new to Europeans, which Spain hastened to subdue. Navigation schools in Spain and Portugal, the development of large sailing ships (carracks) mounted with cannons, and the invention (c. 1475) of the rifle aided European penetration.

Mughals and Safavids. E of the Ottoman Empire, two Muslim dynasties ruled unchallenged in the 16th and 17th cent. The Mughal dynasty of India, founded by Persianized Turkish invaders from the NW under Babur, dates from their 1526 conquest of the Delhi Sultanate. The dynasty ruled most of India for more than 200 years, surviving nominally until 1857. **Akbar** (r. 1556-1605) consolidated administration at his glorious court, where the Urdu language (Persian-influenced Hindi) developed. Trade relations with Europe increased. Under Shah Jahan (1629-58), a secularized art fusing Hindu and Muslim elements flourished in miniature painting and in architecture (**Taj Mahal**). **Sikhism** (founded late 15th cent.) combined elements of both faiths. Suppression of Hindus and Shiite Muslims in S India in the late 17th cent. weakened the empire.

Intense devotion to the Shiite sect characterized the Safavids (1502-1736) of Persia and led to hostilities with the Sunni Ottomans for more than a century. The prosperity and the strength of the empire are evidenced by the mosques at its

The population of Western Europe was so reduced by the bubonic plague, or "Black Death," that it would not reach pre-plague levels again until the early 16th century.

capital city, **Isfahan**. The Safavids enhanced Iranian national consciousness.

China. The **Ming** emperors (1368-1644), the last native dynasty in China, wielded strong personal power. European trade (Portuguese monopoly through **Macau** from 1557) was strictly controlled. Jesuit scholars and scientists (Matteo Ricci, 1552-1610) introduced some Western science; their writings familiarized the West with China. The arts thrived, especially in the areas of painting and ceramics. Chinese manufacturing boomed, bringing in new profits from world trade.

Japan. After the decline of the first hereditary *shogunate* (chief generalship) at **Kamakura** (1185-1333), fragmentation of power accelerated, as did the consequent social mobility. Under Kamakura and the Ashikaga shogunate (1338-1573), the *daimyos* (lords) and *samurai* (warriors) grew more powerful and promoted a martial ideology. Japanese pirates and traders plied the China coast. Popular Buddhist movements included the nationalist Nichiren sect (from c. 1250) and **Zen** (brought from China, 1191), which stressed meditation and a disciplined aesthetic (tea ceremony, gardening, martial arts, *No* drama).

Change and Development in Europe: 1500-1700

Reformation. Theological debate and protests against real and perceived clerical corruption existed in the medieval Christian world, expressed by such dissenters as John Wycliffe (c. 1320-84) and his followers (the Lollards) in England, and **Huss** (burned as a heretic, 1415) in Bohemia.

Martin **Luther** (1483-1546) preached that faith alone, without the mediation of clergy or good works, leads to salvation. He attacked the authority of the pope, rejected priestly celibacy, and recommended individual study of the Bible (which he translated into German c. 1525). His 95 Theses (1517) led to his excommunication (1521). John **Calvin** (1509-64) said that God's elect were predestined for salvation and all others for damnation; good conduct and success were signs of election. Calvin in Geneva and John **Knox** (1505-72) in Scotland established theocratic states.

Henry VIII asserted English national authority and secular power by breaking away (1534) from the Catholic Church, creating what would become the Anglican Church. Monastic property was confiscated, and some Protestant doctrines given official sanction.

Religious wars. A century and a half of religious wars began with a southern German peasant uprising (1524),

repressed with Luther's support. Radical sects—democratic, pacifist, millenarian—arose (Anabaptists ruled Münster, 1534-35) and were suppressed violently. Civil war in France from 1562 between **Huguenots** (Protestant nobles and merchants) and Catholics ended with the 1598 **Edict of Nantes**, tolerating Protestants (revoked 1685). Habsburg attempts to restore Catholicism in Germany were resisted in 25 years of fighting. The 1555 Peace of Augsburg guarantee of religious independence to local princes and cities was confirmed only after the **Thirty Years' War** (1618-48), when much of Germany was devastated by local and foreign armies (Sweden, France).

A Catholic Reformation, or **Counter-Reformation**, met the Protestant challenge, defining an official theology at the Council of Trent (1545-63). The **Jesuit** order (Society of Jesus), founded in 1534 by Ignatius Loyola (1491-1556), helped reconvert large areas of Poland, Hungary, and S Germany and sent missionaries to the New World, India, and China. The **Inquisition** suppressed heresy in Catholic countries. A revival of religious fervor appeared in devotional literature (Teresa of Avila, 1515-82) and in grandiose **Baroque** art (Bernini, 1598-1680).

Scientific Revolution. The late nominalist thinkers (Ockham, c. 1300-49) of Paris and Oxford challenged Aristotelian orthodoxy, allowing for a freer scientific approach. At the same time, metaphysical values, such as the Neoplatonic faith in an orderly, mathematical cosmos, still motivated and directed inquiry. Nicolaus **Copernicus** (1473-1543) promoted the heliocentric theory, which was confirmed when Johannes **Kepler** (1571-1630) discovered the mathematical laws describing the elliptical orbits of the planets. The traditional Christian-Aristotelian belief that the heavens and the Earth were fundamentally different collapsed when **Galileo Galilei** (1564-1642) discovered moving sunspots, irregular moon topography, and moons around Jupiter, but he faced religious opposition (Galileo's retraction, 1633). He and Sir Isaac **Newton** (1642-1727) developed a mechanics that unified cosmic and earthly phenomena. Newton and Gottfried von **Leibniz** (1646-1716) invented calculus. René **Descartes** (1596-1650), best known for his influential philosophy, also invented analytic geometry.

An explosion of **observational science** included the discovery of blood circulation (Harvey, 1578-1657) and microscopic life (Leeuwenhoek, 1632-1723) and advances in anatomy (Vesalius, 1514-64, dissected corpses) and chemistry (Boyle, 1627-91). Scientific research institutes were founded in Florence (1657), London (**Royal Society**, 1660), and Paris (1666). Inventions proliferated (Savery's steam engine, 1698).

Arts. Mannerist trends of the High Renaissance (**Michelangelo**, 1475-1564) exploited virtuosity, grace, novelty, and exotic subjects and poses. The notion of artistic genius was promoted. Private connoisseurs entered the art market. These trends were elaborated in the 17th cent. **Baroque** era on a grander scale. Dynamic movement in painting and sculpture was emphasized by sharp lighting effects, rich materials (colored marble, gilt), and realistic details. Curved facades, broken lines, rich detail, and ceiling decoration characterized Baroque architecture. Monarchs, princes, and prelates, usually Catholic, used Baroque art to enhance and embellish their authority, as in royal portraits (Velázquez, 1599-1660; Van Dyck, 1599-1641).

National styles emerged. In France, a taste for rectilinear order and serenity (Poussin, 1594-1665), linked to the new rational philosophy, was expressed in classical forms. The influence of **classical values** in French literature (tragedies of **Racine**, 1639-99) gave rise to the "battle of the Ancients and Moderns." New forms included the essay (**Montaigne**, 1533-92) and novel (*Princesse de Clèves*, La Fayette, 1678).

Dutch painting of the 17th cent. was unique in its wide social distribution. The Flemish tradition of undemonstrative realism reached its peak in **Rembrandt** (1606-69) and Jan Vermeer (1632-75).

Economy. European economic expansion, known as the **commercial revolution**, was stimulated by new trade with the East, by New World gold and silver, and by a doubling of population (50 million in 1450, 100 million in 1600). **New business and financial techniques** were developed and refined, such as joint-stock companies, insurance, and letters of credit and exchange. The Bank of Amsterdam (1609) and the Bank of England (1694) broke the old monopoly of private banking families. The rise of a business mentality was typified by the spread of clock towers in cities in the 14th cent. By the mid-15th cent., portable clocks were available; the first watch was invented in 1502.

By 1650, most governments had adopted the **mercantile system**, in which they sought to amass metallic wealth by protecting merchants' foreign and colonial trade monopolies. The rise in prices and the new coin-based economy undermined craft guild and feudal manorial systems. Expanding industries (clothweaving, mining) benefited from technical advances. Coal began to replace wood as the chief fuel; it was used to fuel new 16th-cent. blast furnaces making cast iron.

New World. The **Aztecs** united much of the Mesoamerican area in a militarist empire by 1519 from their capital, Tenochtitlán (pop. 300,000), which was the center of a cult requiring ritual human sacrifice. Most of the civilized areas of South America were ruled by the centralized Inca Empire (1476-1534), stretching 2,000 mi from Ecuador to NW Argentina. Lavish and sophisticated traditions in pottery, weaving, sculpture, and architecture were maintained in both regions.

These empires, beset by revolts, fell in two short campaigns to gold-seeking Spanish forces based in the Antilles and Panama. Hernán **Cortés** took Mexico (1519-21); Francisco **Pizarro**,

The exact purpose of the Incan city of Machu Picchu, built in the 15th century and abandoned less than 150 years later, is unknown; one theory is that it served as a royal retreat.

Peru (1532-35). From these centers, land and sea expeditions claimed most of North and South America for Spain. The indigenous high cultures did not survive the impact of **Christian missionaries** and the new upper class of whites. Although the Spanish administration intermittently concerned itself with their welfare, the population was devastated by European diseases and remained impoverished at most levels. New World silver and such native products as potatoes, tobacco, corn, peanuts, chocolate, and rubber exercised a major economic influence on Europe.

Brazil, which the Portuguese reached in 1500 and settled after 1530, and the Caribbean colonies of several European nations developed a plantation economy where sugarcane, tobacco, cotton, coffee, rice, indigo, and lumber were grown by enslaved people. From the early 16th to late 19th cent., 10 million Africans were transported to slavery in the Americas and Caribbean islands.

Netherlands. The urban, Calvinist northern provinces of the Netherlands rebelled (1568) against Habsburg Spain and founded an oligarchic mercantile republic. Their control of the Baltic grain market enabled them to exploit Mediterranean food shortages. Religious refugees—French and Belgian Protestants, Iberian Jews—added to the commercial talent pool. After Spain absorbed Portugal (1580), the Dutch seized Portuguese possessions and created a vast commercial empire ultimately centered in parts of the Caribbean and in Indonesia. The Dutch also challenged or supplanted Portuguese traders in China and Japan. Revolution in 1640 restored Portuguese independence.

England. Anglicanism became firmly established under **Elizabeth I** after a brief Catholic interlude under "Bloody" Mary I (1553-58). But religious and political conflicts led to a rebellion (1642) by Parliament. Forces of the Roundheads (Puritans) defeated the Cavaliers (Royalists); Charles I was beheaded (1649). The new Commonwealth was ruled as a military dictatorship by Oliver **Cromwell**, who also brutally crushed (1649-51) an Irish rebellion. Conflicts within the Puritan camp (democratic Levelers defeated, 1649) aided the Stuart restoration (1660), but Parliament was strengthened and the peaceful **"Glorious Revolution"** (1688) advanced political and religious liberties (writings of **Locke**, 1632-1704). British privateers (Drake, 1540-96) challenged Spanish control of the New World and penetrated Asian trade routes (Madras taken, 1639). North American colonies (Jamestown, 1607; Plymouth, 1620) provided an outlet for private enterprise and religious dissenters from Europe. The British East India Co. gained growing sway in 18th-cent. India, as Mughal power declined.

France. Emerging from the religious civil wars in 1628, France regained military and commercial great power status (under the ministries of **Richelieu**, Mazarin, and Colbert). Under **Louis XIV** (r. 1643-1715), royal absolutism triumphed over nobles and local *parlements* (defeat of Fronde, 1648-53). Durable colonies were founded in Canada (1608), the Caribbean (1626), and India (1674).

Sweden. Sweden seceded from the Scandinavian Union in 1523. The thinly populated agrarian state (with copper, iron, and timber exports) was united by the Vasa kings, whose conquests by the mid-17th cent. made Sweden the dominant Baltic power. The empire collapsed in the Great Northern War (1700-21).

Poland. After the union with Lithuania in 1447, Poland ruled vast territories from the Baltic to the Black Sea, resisting German and Turkish incursions. Catholic nobles failed to gain the loyalty of their Orthodox Christian subjects in the E; commerce and trades were practiced by German and Jewish immigrants. The bloody 1648-49 Cossack uprising began the kingdom's dismemberment.

Russia. Growing authority of the tsars continued with advancing serfdom. Around 1700, **Peter the Great** imported new Western styles and technologies. Steady territorial expansion created a vast territory touching China, the Ottoman Empire, and east-central Europe.

China. A new dynasty, the **Manchus**, invaded from the NE, seized power in 1644, and expanded Chinese control to its greatest extent in Central and SE Asia. Trade and diplomatic contact with Europe grew, carefully controlled by China. New crops (sweet potato, maize, peanut) allowed economic and population growth (pop. 300 million, in 1800). Traditional arts and literature were pursued with increased sophistication (*Dream of the Red Chamber*, novel, mid-18th cent.).

Japan. Tokugawa Ieyasu, shogun from 1603, finally unified and pacified feudal Japan. Hereditary nobles (daimyos and samurai) monopolized government office and the professions. An urban merchant class grew, literacy spread, and a cultural renaissance occurred (**haiku**, a verse innovation of the poet Basho, 1644-94). Fear of European domination led to persecution of Christian converts from 1597 and to substantial isolation from outside contact from 1640.

Philosophy, Industry, and Revolution: 1700-1800

Science and reason. Greater faith in reason and empirical observation, instead of tradition and religious beliefs, espoused since the Renaissance (Francis Bacon, 1561-1626), was bolstered by scientific discoveries. René Descartes (1596-1650) used a rationalistic approach modeled on geometry and introspection to discover "self-evident" truths as a foundation of knowledge. Sir Isaac Newton emphasized induction from experimental observation. Baruch de Spinoza (1632-77), who called for political and intellectual freedom, developed a systematic rationalistic philosophy in his classic work *Ethics*.

French philosophers assumed leadership of the **Enlightenment** in the 18th cent. Montesquieu (1689-1755) used British history to support his notions of limited government. **Voltaire's** (1694-1778) diaries and novels of exotic travel illustrated the intellectual trends toward secular ethics and relativism. Jean-Jacques **Rousseau's** (1712-78) radical concepts of the **social contract** and of the inherent goodness of the common man gave impetus to antimonarchical republicanism. The *Encyclopedia* (1751-72, edited by Diderot and d'Alembert), designed as a monument to reason, was largely devoted to practical technology.

In England, ideals of liberty were connected with empiricist philosophy and science in the followers of John **Locke**. But British empiricism, especially as developed by the skeptical David **Hume** (1711-76), radically reduced the role of reason in philosophy, as did the evolutionary approach to law and politics of Edmund Burke (1729-97) and the utilitarian ethics of Jeremy Bentham (1748-1832). Adam Smith (1723-90) and other economists called for a rationalization of economic activity by removing artificial barriers to a supposedly natural free exchange of goods known as **laissez-faire**.

German writers participated in the new philosophical trends popularized by Christian von Wolff (1679-1754). Immanuel **Kant's** (1724-1804) transcendental idealism, unifying an empirical epistemology with a priori moral and logical concepts, directed German thought away from skepticism. Italian contributions included work on electricity (Galvani, 1737-98; Volta, 1745-1827), the pioneer historiography of Vico (1668-1744), and writings on penal reform (Beccaria, 1738-94).

Benjamin Franklin (1706-90) was celebrated in Europe for his varied achievements.

The growth of the **press** (*Spectator*, 1711-12) and the wide distribution of sentimental **novels** attested to the increase of a large bourgeois public.

Arts. Rococo art, characterized by extravagant decorative effects, asymmetries copied from organic models, and artificial pastoral subjects, was favored by the continental aristocracy for most of the century (Watteau, 1684-1721) and had musical analogies in the ornamentalized polyphony of late Baroque. The **Neoclassical** art after 1750, associated with the new scientific archaeology, was more streamlined and was infused with the supposed moral and geometric rectitude of the Roman Republic (David, 1748-1825). In England, **town planning** on a grand scale began.

Industrial Revolution in England. Agricultural improvements, such as the sowing drill (1701) and livestock breeding, were implemented on the large fields provided by enclosure of common lands by private owners. Profits from agriculture and from colonial and foreign trade (1800 volume, £54 million) were channeled through hundreds of banks and the **Stock Exchange** (est. 1773) into new industrial processes.

The Newcomen steam pump (1712) aided coal mining. Coal fueled the new efficient steam engines patented by James Watt in 1769, and coke-smelting produced cheap, sturdy iron for machinery by the 1730s. The **flying shuttle** (1733) and **spinning jenny** (c. 1764) were used in the large new cotton textile factories, where women and children were much of the workforce. Goods were transported cheaply over **canals** (2,000 mi; built 1760-1800). By the early 19th cent., industrialization spread in Western Europe and North America.

American Revolution. The British colonies in North America attracted a mass immigration of religious dissenters and poor people throughout the 17th and 18th cent., coming from the British Isles, Germany, the Netherlands, and other countries, along with Africans to serve as enslaved labor. The population reached 3 million non-natives by the 1770s. The Indigenous population was greatly reduced by European diseases and by wars with the various colonies. British attempts to control colonial trade and to tax the colonists to pay for the costs of colonial administration and defense clashed with local self-government and eventually provoked the colonies to a successful rebellion.

Central and East Europe. The monarchs of the three states that dominated E Europe—Austria, Prussia, and Russia—expanded royal power and centralized institutions in their kingdoms, which were enlarged by the division (1772-95) of Poland.

Under **Frederick II** (the Great) (r. 1740-86), Prussia, with its efficient modern army, doubled in size. State monopolies and tariff protection fostered industry, and some legal reforms were introduced. Austria's heterogeneous realms were unified under **Maria Theresa** (r. 1740-80) and **Joseph II** (r. 1765-90). Reforms in education, law, and religion were enacted, and the Austrian serfs were freed (1781). With its defeat in the Seven Years' War in 1763, Austria failed to regain Silesia, which had been seized by Prussia, but it was compensated by expansion to the E and S (Hungary, Slavonia, 1699; Galicia, 1772).

Russia, whose borders continued to expand, adopted some Western bureaucratic and economic policies under **Peter I** (r. 1682-1725) and **Catherine II** (r. 1762-96). Trade and

Between the 16th and 19th centuries, an estimated 10-12 million people were transported from Africa in deplorable conditions to serve as enslaved labor in the Americas.

cultural contacts with the West multiplied from the new Baltic Sea capital, **St. Petersburg** (est. 1703).

French Revolution. The growing French middle class lacked political power and resented aristocratic tax privileges, especially in light of the successful American Revolution. Peasants lacked adequate land and were burdened with feudal obligations to nobles. War with Britain led to the loss of French Canada and drained the treasury, finally forcing the king to call the **Estates-General** in 1789 for the first time since 1614, in an atmosphere of food riots (poor crop in 1788).

Aristocratic resistance to absolutism was soon overshadowed by the reformist Third Estate (middle class), which proclaimed itself the **National Constituent Assembly** June 17 and took the "Tennis Court Oath" on June 20 to secure a constitution. The storming of the **Bastille** fortress/prison on July 14, 1789, by Parisian artisans was followed by looting and the seizure of aristocratic property throughout France. Assembly reforms included abolition of class and regional privileges, a Declaration of Rights, suffrage by taxpayers (75% of male population), and the **Civil Constitution of the Clergy** providing for election and loyalty oaths for priests. A republic was declared Sept. 22, 1792, in spite of royalist pressure from Austria and Prussia, which had declared war in Apr. (joined by Britain the next year). Louis XVI was beheaded Jan. 21, 1793, and Queen Marie Antoinette was beheaded Oct. 16, 1793.

Royalist uprisings in La Vendée and military reverses led to institution of a **reign of terror** in which tens of thousands of opponents of the Revolution and criminals were executed. Radical reforms in the **Convention** period (Sept. 1793-Oct. 1795) included the abolition of colonial slavery, economic measures to aid the poor, support of public education, and a short-lived de-Christianization.

Division among radicals (execution of Hebert, Danton, and Robespierre, 1794) aided the ascendancy of a moderate **Directory**, which consolidated military victories. **Napoleon Bonaparte** (1769-1821), a popular young general, exploited political divisions and participated in a coup Nov. 9, 1799, making himself first consul (dictator).

India. Sikh and Hindu rebels (Rajputs, Marathas) and Afghans destroyed the power of the Mughals during the 18th cent. After France's defeat (1763) in the Seven Years' War, Britain was the primary European trade power in India. Its control of inland **Bengal** and **Bihar** was recognized (1765) by the Mughal shah, who granted the **British East India Co.** (under Clive, 1725-74) the right to collect land revenue there. Despite objections from Parliament (1784 India Act), the company's involvement in local wars and politics led to repeated acquisitions of new territory. The company exported Indian textiles, sugar, and indigo, but industry was discouraged to promote British imports.

Nationalism Gathers Momentum: 1800-40

French ideals and empire spread. Inspired by the ideals of the French Revolution, and supported by the expanding French armies, new republican regimes arose near France: the **Batavian** Republic in the Netherlands (1795-1806), the **Helvetic** Republic in Switzerland (1798-1803), the **Cisalpine** Republic in Northern Italy (1797-1805), the **Ligurian** Republic in Genoa (1797-1805), and the **Parthenopean** Republic in Southern Italy (1799). A Roman Republic existed briefly in 1798 after Pope Pius VI was arrested by French troops. In Italy and Germany, new nationalist sentiments were stimulated both in imitation of and in reaction to developments in France (anti-French and anti-Jacobin peasant uprisings in Italy, 1796-99).

From 1804, when Napoleon declared himself emperor, to 1812, a succession of military victories (Austerlitz, 1805; Jena, 1806) extended his control over most of Europe through puppet states (**Confederation of the Rhine** united W German states for the first time and **Grand Duchy of Warsaw** revived Polish national hopes), expansion of the empire, and alliances.

Among the lasting reforms initiated under Napoleon's absolutist reign were establishment of the Bank of France, centralization of tax collection, codification of law along Roman models (Code Napoléon), and reform and extension of secondary and university education. In an 1801 concordat, the papacy recognized the effective autonomy of the French Catholic Church.

Napoleon's continental successes were offset by a British victory under Adm. Horatio Nelson in the **Battle of Trafalgar** (1805). Some 400,000 French soldiers were killed in the Napoleonic Wars, along with about 600,000 foreign troops.

Last gasp of old regimes. The disastrous 1812 invasion of Russia exposed Napoleon's overextension. After Napoleon's 1814 exile to Elba, his armies were defeated (1815) at **Waterloo** by British and Prussian troops.

At the **Congress of Vienna**, the monarchs and princes of Europe redrew their boundaries, to the advantage of Prussia (in Saxony and the Ruhr), Austria (in Illyria and Venetia), and Russia (in Poland and Finland). British conquest of Dutch and French colonies (S Africa, Ceylon, Mauritius) was recognized. France, under the restored Bourbons, retained its expanded 1792 borders. The settlement brought 50 years of international peace to Europe.

But the Congress was unable to check the advance of liberal ideals and of nationalism among the smaller European nations. The 1825 **Decembrist** uprising by liberal officers in Russia was easily suppressed. But an independence movement in **Greece**, stirred by commercial prosperity and a cultural revival, succeeded in expelling Ottoman rule by 1831, with the aid of Britain, France, and Russia.

A constitutional monarchy was secured in France by the **1830 Revolution**; Louis Philippe became king. The revolutionary contagion spread to **Belgium**, which gained its independence (1830) from the Dutch monarchy, to **Poland**, whose rebellion was defeated (1830-31) by Russia, and to Germany.

Romanticism. A new style in intellectual and artistic life replaced Neoclassicism and Rococo after the mid-18th cent. By the early 19th cent., Romanticism prevailed in Europe.

Rousseau had begun the reaction against rationalism; in education (*Émile*, 1762) he stressed subjective spontaneity over regularized instruction. German writers (Lessing, 1729-81; Herder, 1744-1803) favorably compared the German folk song to classical forms and began a cult of Shakespeare, whose passion and "natural" wisdom was a model for the romantic *Sturm und Drang* (Storm and Stress) movement. **Goethe**'s *Sorrows of Young Werther* (1774) set the model for the tragic, passionate genius.

A new interest in **Gothic architecture** in England after 1760 (Walpole, 1717-97) spread through Europe, associated with an aesthetic Christian and mystic revival (**Blake**, 1757-1827). Celtic, Norse, and German mythology and folk tales were revived or imitated (Grimm's Fairy Tales, 1812-22). The medieval revival (Scott's *Ivanhoe*, 1819) led to a new interest in history, stressing national differences and organic growth (**Carlyle**, 1795-1881; Michelet, 1798-1874), corresponding to theories of natural evolution (Lamarck's *Philosophie Zoologique*, 1809; Lyell's *Geology*, 1830-33). A reaction against classicism characterized the English **romantic poets** (beginning with **Wordsworth**, 1770-1850). Revolution and war fed an emphasis on freedom and conflict, expressed by both poets (**Byron**, 1788-1824; **Hugo**, 1802-85) and philosophers (**Hegel**, 1770-1831).

Wild gardens replaced the formal French variety, and painters favored rural, stormy, and mountainous landscapes (**Turner**, 1775-1851; **Constable**, 1776-1837). Clothing became freer, with wigs, hoops, and ruffles discarded. Originality and genius were expected in the life and work of inspired artists (Murger's *Scenes From Bohemian Life*, 1847-49). Exotic locales and themes (as in Gothic horror stories) were used in art and literature (Delacroix, 1798-1863; **Poe**, 1809-49). Music exhibited the new dramatic style and a breakdown of classical forms (**Beethoven**, 1770-1827). The use of folk melodies and modes aided the growth of distinct national traditions (Glinka in Russia, 1804-57).

Latin America. François **Toussaint L'Ouverture** led a successful slave revolt in Haiti, which subsequently became the first Caribbean state to achieve independence (1804). The mainland Spanish colonies won their independence (1810-24) under such leaders as Simón **Bolívar** (1783-1830). Brazil became an independent empire (1822) under the Portuguese prince regent. A new class of military officers divided power with large landholders and the church.

United States. Territory under U.S. control nearly doubled in size with the **Louisiana Purchase** (1803). Heavy immigration and exploitation of ample natural resources fueled rapid economic growth. The spread of the franchise, public education, and antislavery sentiment were signs of a widespread democratic ethic.

China. Failure to keep pace with Western arms technology exposed China to greater European influence and hampered efforts to bar imports of opium, which had damaged Chinese society and drained wealth overseas. In the **Opium War** (1839-42), Britain forced China to expand trade opportunities and to cede Hong Kong.

New Complexities: Reforms and Imperialism: 1840-80

Idea of progress. As a result of the cumulative scientific, economic, and political changes of the preceding eras, the idea took hold among literate people in the West that continuing growth and improvement constituted the usual state of human and natural life.

Charles **Darwin**'s statement of the **theory of evolution** and survival of the fittest (*On the Origin of Species*, 1859), defended by intellectuals and scientists against theological objections, was taken as confirmation that progress was the natural direction of life. The controversy helped define popular ideas of the dedicated scientist and of science's increasing control over the world (Foucault's demonstration of Earth's rotation, 1851; **Pasteur**'s germ theory, 1861).

Liberals following Ricardo (1772-1823) in their faith that unrestrained competition would bring continuous economic expansion sought to adjust political life to new social realities and believed that unregulated competition of ideas would yield truth (**Mill**, 1806-73). In England, successive reform bills (1832, 1867, 1884) gave representation to the new industrial towns and extended the franchise to the middle and lower classes and to Catholics, Dissenters, and Jews. On both sides of the Atlantic, reformists tried to improve conditions for the mentally ill (**Dix**, 1802-87), women (Anthony, 1820-1906), and prisoners. Slavery was barred in the British Empire (1833), the U.S. (1865), and Brazil (1888).

Socialist theories based on ideas of human perfectibility or progress were widely disseminated. Utopian socialists such as Saint-Simon (1760-1825) envisaged an orderly, just society directed by a technocratic elite. A model factory town, New Lanark, Scotland, was set up by utopian Robert Owen (1771-1858), and communal experiments were tried in the U.S. (Brook Farm, MA, 1841-47). Bakunin's (1814-76) anarchism represented the opposite extreme of total freedom. Karl **Marx** (1818-83) posited the inevitable triumph of socialism in industrial countries through a dialectical process of class conflict. Effective development of oceanic steamship lines (Cunard Lines, 1840s) and the opening of the **Suez Canal** accelerated shipping and commerce. Telegraph lines (Australia-Europe, 1871) sped communication. International organizations included the General (later Universal) Postal Union (1874) and conferences to limit epidemics like cholera. The initial **Geneva Convention** (1864) regulated treatment of prisoners of war.

Spread of industry. The technical processes and managerial innovations of the English industrial revolution spread to Europe (especially Germany) and the U.S., causing an explosion of industrial production, demand for raw materials, and competition for markets. Inventors, both trained and self-taught, provided means for larger-scale production (Bessemer steel, 1856; sewing machine, 1846). Many inventions were shown at the universal prosperity-themed 1851 London Great Exhibition at the **Crystal Palace**.

Local specialization and long-distance trade were aided by a revolution in transportation and communication. Railroads were first introduced in the 1820s in England and the U.S. Over 150,000 mi of track had been laid worldwide by 1880, with another 100,000 mi laid in the next decade. Steamships were improved (*Savannah* crossed Atlantic, 1819). The **telegraph**, perfected by 1844 (Morse), connected the Old and New Worlds by cable in 1866 and quickened the pace of international commerce and politics. The first commercial **telephone** exchange went into operation in the U.S. in 1878.

The new class of industrial workers, uprooted from their rural homes, lacked job security and suffered from dangerous overcrowding at work and at home. Many responded by organizing **trade unions** (legalized in England, 1824; France, 1884). The U.S. Knights of Labor had 700,000 members by 1886. The First International (1864-76) tried to unite workers worldwide around a Marxist program. The quasi-Socialist Paris Commune uprising (1871) was violently suppressed. Acts to reduce child labor and regulate conditions were passed (1833-50 in England). Social security measures were introduced by the Bismarck regime (1883-89) in Germany.

Revolutions of 1848. Among the causes of the continent-wide revolutions were an international collapse of credit and resulting unemployment, bad harvests in 1845-47, and a cholera epidemic. The new urban proletariat and expanding bourgeoisie demanded greater political roles. Republics were proclaimed in France, Rome, and Venice. Nationalist feelings reached fever pitch in the Habsburg empire, as Hungary declared independence under Kossuth, a Slav Congress demanded equality, and Piedmont tried to drive Austria from Lombardy. A national liberal assembly at Frankfurt called for German unification.

But riots fueled bourgeois fear of socialism (**Marx and Engels**, *Communist Manifesto*, 1848), and peasants remained conservative. The old establishment—the Papacy, the Habsburgs with the help of the Tsarist Russian army—was able to rout the revolutionaries by 1849. The French Republic succumbed to a renewed monarchy by 1852 (Emperor Napoleon III).

Great nations unified. Using the "blood and iron" tactics of Bismarck from 1862, Prussia controlled N Germany by 1867 (war with Denmark, 1864; Austria, 1866). After defeating France in 1870 (annexation of Alsace-Lorraine), it won the allegiance of S German states. A new **German Empire** was proclaimed (1871). **Italy**, inspired by Giuseppe Mazzini (1805-72) and Giuseppe Garibaldi (1807-82), was unified by the reformed Piedmont kingdom through uprisings, plebiscites, and war.

The **United States** expanded its area after the 1846-48 Mexican War and defeated (1861-65) a secession attempt by Southern states in the **Civil War**. Canadian provinces were united in an autonomous **Dominion of Canada** (1867). Control in **India** was removed from the East India Co. and centralized under British administration after the 1857-58 Sepoy rebellion, laying the groundwork for the modern Indian state. Queen Victoria was named Empress of India (1876).

Europe dominates Asia. The Ottoman Empire began to weaken in the face of Balkan nationalisms and European imperial incursions in N Africa (**Suez Canal**, 1869). The Ottomans had lost control of most of both regions by 1882. Russia completed its expansion S by 1884 (despite the temporary setback of the **Crimean War** with Turkey, Britain, and France, 1853-56), taking Turkestan, all the Caucasus, and Chinese areas in the E and sponsoring Balkan Slavs against the Turks. A succession of reformist and reactionary regimes presided over a slow modernization (serfs freed, 1861). Persian independence suffered as Russia and British India competed for influence.

China was forced to sign a series of unequal treaties with European powers and Japan. Overpopulation and an inefficient dynasty brought misery and caused rebellions (Taiping, Muslims) leaving tens of millions dead. **Japan** was forced by the U.S. (Commodore Perry's visits, 1853-54) and Europe to end its isolation. The Meiji restoration (1868) gave power to a Westernizing oligarchy, abolishing feudalism and expanding education. Intensified empire-building gave Burma to Britain (1824-85) and Indochina to France (1862-95). Christian missionary activity followed imperial and trade expansion in Asia.

Arts. The official **Beaux Arts** school in Paris set an international style of imposing public buildings (Paris Opera, 1861-74; Vienna Opera, 1861-69) and uplifting statues (Bartholdi's Statue of Liberty, 1884). Realist painting, influenced by photography

The opening of the Suez Canal, which connected the Mediterranean and Red Seas in 1869, provided a more direct sea route for international trade between the Atlantic and Indian Oceans.

(Daguerre, 1837), appealed to a new mass audience with social or historical narrative (Wilkie, 1785-1841; Poynter, 1836-1919) or with serious religious, moral, or social messages (pre-Raphaelites, Millet's *Angelus*, 1858), often drawn from ordinary life. The **Impressionists** (Monet, 1840-1926; Pissarro, 1830-1903; Renoir, 1841-1919) rejected the formalism, sentimentality, and precise techniques of academic art in favor of a spontaneous,

undetailed rendering of the world through careful representation of the effect of natural light on objects. They were strongly influenced by Asian and African styles.

Realistic **novelists** presented the full panorama of social classes and personalities but retained sentimentality and moral judgment (**Dickens**, 1812-70; **Eliot**, 1819-80; **Tolstoy**, 1828-1910; **Balzac**, 1799-1850).

Veneer of Stability: 1880-1900

Imperialism triumphant. The vast **African** interior, visited by European explorers (Barth, 1821-65; Livingstone, 1813-73), was conquered by the European powers in rapid, competitive thrusts from their coastal bases after 1880, mostly for domestic political and international strategic reasons. W African Muslim kingdoms (Fulani), Arab slave traders (Zanzibar), and Bantu military confederations (Zulu) were alike subdued. Only Christian Ethiopia (defeat of Italy, 1896) and Liberia resisted successfully. France (W Africa) and Britain ("Cape to Cairo," **Boer War**, 1899-1902) were the major beneficiaries. The ideology of "the white man's burden" (Kipling, *Barrack Room Ballads*, 1892) justified the conquests, which in fact reflected Europe's weapons superiority.

W European foreign capital investment soared to nearly $40 billion by 1914, but most was in E Europe (France, Germany), the Americas (Britain), and Europe's colonies. The foundation of the modern interdependent world economy was laid, with cartels dominating raw material trade. Global developments included a new agreement on international patents (1883), the modern Olympics (1896), and the worldwide spread of department stores.

An industrious world. Industrial and technological proficiency characterized the two new great powers—Germany and the U.S. Coal and iron deposits enabled Germany to reach second- or third-place status in iron, steel, and shipbuilding by the 1900s. German electrical and chemical industries were world leaders. The U.S. post-Civil War boom (interrupted by financial panics—1873, 1884, and 1893) was shaped by massive immigration from S and E Europe from 1880, government subsidy of railroads, and huge private monopolies (Standard Oil, 1870; U.S. Steel, 1901). The **Spanish-American War**, 1898 (Philippine Insurrection, 1899-1902), and the **Open Door policy** in China (1899) made the U.S. a world power.

England led in **urbanization**, with London the world capital of finance, insurance, and shipping. Sewer systems (Paris, 1850s), electric subways (London, 1890), parks, and bargain department stores helped improve living standards for most of the urban population of the industrial world. Birthrates declined in the West while infant mortality rates plunged (demographic transition, 1880-1920).

Upheavals in Asia. Asian reaction to European economic, military, and religious incursions took the form of imitation of Western techniques and adoption of Western ideas of progress and freedom. The Chinese "self-strengthening" movement of the 1860s and 1870s included rail, port, and arsenal improvements and metal and textile mills. Reformers such as **K'ang** Yu-wei (1858-1927) won liberalizing reforms

in 1898, right after the European and Japanese "scramble for concessions."

A universal education system in Japan and importation of foreign industrial, scientific, and military experts aided Japan's rapid modernization after 1868 under the authoritarian Meiji regime. Japan's victory in the **Sino-Japanese War** (1894-95) put Formosa and Korea in its power. Industrialization began in earnest by 1890.

In India, the British alliance with the remaining princely states masked reform sentiment among the Westernized urban elite; higher education had been conducted largely in English for 50 years. The **Indian National Congress**, founded in 1885, demanded a larger government role for Indians.

Fin-de-siècle sophistication. **Naturalist** writers pushed realism to its extreme limits, adopting a quasi-scientific attitude and writing about formerly taboo subjects such as sex, crime, extreme poverty, and corruption (Flaubert, 1821-80; Zola, 1840-1902; Hardy, 1840-1928). Unseen or repressed psychological motivations were explored in the clinical and theoretical works of Sigmund **Freud** (1856-1939) and in works of fiction (**Dostoyevsky**, 1821-81; Henry James, 1843-1916; Schnitzler, 1862-1931).

A contempt for bourgeois life or a desire to shock a complacent audience was shared by the French **symbolist** poets (Verlaine, 1844-96; Rimbaud, 1854-91), by neopagan English writers (Swinburne, 1837-1909), by continental dramatists (**Ibsen**, 1828-1906), and by satirists (**Wilde**, 1854-1900). The German philosopher Friedrich **Nietzsche** (1844-1900) was influential in his elitism and pessimism.

Postimpressionist art neglected long-cherished conventions of representation (**Cézanne**, 1839-1906) and showed a willingness to learn from primitive and non-European art (**Gauguin**, 1848-1903; Japanese prints).

Racism. Gobineau (1816-82) gave a pseudobiological foundation to modern racist theories, which spread in Europe in the latter 19th cent., along with **Social Darwinism**, the belief that societies are and should be organized as a struggle for survival of the fittest. The medieval period was interpreted as an era of natural Germanic rule (Chamberlain, 1855-1927), and notions of racial superiority were associated with German national aspirations (Treitschke, 1834-96). **Anti-Semitism**, with a new racist rationale, became a significant political force in Germany (Anti-Semitic Petition, 1880), Austria (Lueger, 1844-1910), and France (**Dreyfus affair**, 1894-1906).

Imperialism's High Point: 1900-09

Alliances. While the peace of Europe (and its dependencies) continued to hold (1907 **Hague Conference** extended the rules of war and international arbitration procedures), imperial rivalries, protectionist trade practices (in Germany and France), and the escalating arms race (British *Dreadnought* battleship launched; Germany widens Kiel canal, 1906) exacerbated minor disputes (German-French Moroccan "crises," 1905, 1911).

Security was sought through balance-of-power alliances: **Triple Alliance** (Germany, Austria-Hungary, Italy; renewed in 1902 and 1907); Anglo-Japanese Alliance (1902), Franco-Russian Alliance (1899), **Entente Cordiale** (Britain, France, 1904), Anglo-Russian Treaty (1907), German-Ottoman friendship. Global developments included the establishment of an international court in The Hague, the first transatlantic radio transmission (1901), and the creation of the first international association for European football (1904).

Ottomans decline. The Ottoman government was unable to resist further loss of territory, and earlier reform efforts gave way to greater authoritarianism. Nearly all European lands were lost in 1912 to Serbia, Greece, Montenegro, and Bulgaria. Italy took Libya and the Dodecanese islands the same year. Britain took Kuwait (1899) and the Sinai (1906). The **Young Turk** revolution in 1908 forced the sultan to restore a constitution, and it introduced some social reform and secularization.

British Empire. British trade and cultural influence remained dominant in the empire, but constitutional reforms presaged its eventual dissolution. The colonies of **Australia** were united in 1901 under a self-governing commonwealth. **New Zealand** acquired dominion status in 1907. The old Boer republics joined Cape Colony and Natal in the self-governing Union of **South Africa** in 1910.

The 1909 Indian Councils Act enhanced the role of elected province legislatures in **India**. The Muslim League (founded 1906) sought separate communal representation.

East Asia. Japan exploited its growing industrial power to expand its empire. Victory in the 1904-05 war against Russia (naval battle of Tsushima, 1905) assured Japan's domination of **Korea** (annexed 1910) and Manchuria (Port Arthur taken, 1905).

In China, central authority began to crumble (empress died, 1908). Reforms (Confucian exam system ended 1905, modernization of the army, building of railroads) were inadequate, and secret societies of reformers and nationalists, inspired by the Westernized **Sun** Yat-sen (1866-1925), fomented periodic uprisings in the S.

Siam, whose independence had been guaranteed by Britain and France in 1896, was split into spheres of influence by those countries in 1907.

Russia. The population of the Russian Empire approached 150 million in 1900. Reforms in education, in law, and in local institutions (*zemstvos*) and an industrial boom starting in the 1880s (oil, railroads) created the beginnings of a modern society, despite the autocratic tsarist regime. Liberals (1903 Union of Liberation), Socialists (Social Democrats founded 1898, Bolsheviks split off 1903), and populists (Social Revolutionaries founded 1901) were periodically repressed, and national minorities were persecuted (anti-Jewish pogroms, 1903, 1905-06).

An industrial crisis after 1900 and harvest failures aggravated poverty among urban workers, and the 1904-05 defeat by Japan (which checked Russia's Asian expansion) sparked the **Revolution of 1905-06.** A **Duma** (parliament) was created under Tsar Nicholas II. Agricultural reform (under Stolypin, prime minister, 1906-11) created a large class of land-owning peasants (*kulaks*).

The world shrinks. Developments in transportation and communication and mass population movements helped create an awareness of an interdependent world. Early **automobiles** (Daimler, Benz, 1885) were experimental or were designed as luxuries. Assembly-line mass production (Ford Motor Co., 1903) made the invention practical, and by 1910 nearly 500,000 motor vehicles were registered in the U.S. alone. **Heavier-than-air flights** began in 1903 in the U.S. (Wright brothers' *Flyer*), preceded by glider, balloon, and model plane advances in several countries. Trade was advanced by improvements in **ship design** (gyrocompass, 1910), speed (*Lusitania* crossed Atlantic in five days, 1907), and reach (Panama Canal begun, 1904).

The first transatlantic **radio** telegraphic transmission occurred in 1901, six years after Marconi discovered radio. Radio transmission of human speech had been made in 1900. Telegraphic transmission of photos was achieved in 1904, lending immediacy to news reports. **Phonographs**, popularized by Caruso's recordings (starting 1902), made for quick international spread of musical styles (ragtime). **Motion pictures**, perfected in the 1890s (Dickson, Lumière brothers), became a popular and artistic medium after 1900; newsreels appeared in 1909.

Emigration from crowded European centers soared in the decade: 9 million migrated to the U.S., and millions more went to Siberia, Canada, Argentina, Australia, South Africa, and Algeria. Some 70 million Europeans emigrated in the century before 1914. Several million Chinese, Indians, and Japanese migrated to SE Asia, where their urban skills often enabled them to take a predominant economic role.

Social reform. The social and economic problems of the poor were kept in the public eye by realist fiction writers (Dreiser's *Sister Carrie*, 1900; Gorky's *Lower Depths*, 1902; Sinclair's *The Jungle*, 1906), journalists (U.S. **muckrakers**—Steffens, Tarbell), and artists (Ashcan school). Frequent labor strikes and occasional assassinations by anarchists or radicals (Empress Elizabeth of Austria, 1898; King Umberto I of Italy, 1900; U.S. Pres. McKinley, 1901; Russian Interior Min. Plehve, 1904; Portugal's King Carlos, 1908) added to social

Emigration from densely populated European countries to the Americas soared in the early 20th century; many landed on Ellis Island, in New York Harbor, en route to U.S. cities.

tension and fear of revolution. Feminist agitators for the vote surfaced in several countries.

But democratic reformism responded in part. In Germany, Bernstein's (1850-1932) **revisionist Marxism**, downgrading revolution, was accepted by the powerful Social Democrats and trade unions. The British Fabian Society (the Webbs, Shaw) and the Labour Party (founded 1906) worked for reforms such as social security and union rights (1906), while woman suffragists grew more militant. U.S. **progressives** fought big business (Pure Food and Drug Act, 1906). In France, the 10-hour workday (1904) and separation of church and state (1905) were reform victories, as was universal suffrage in Austria (1907).

Arts. An unprecedented period of experimentation, centered in France, produced several new **painting styles**: Fauvism exploited bold color areas (Matisse, *Woman With Hat*, 1905); expressionism reflected powerful inner emotions (Brücke group, 1905); Cubism combined several views of an object on one flat surface (Picasso, *Demoiselles*, 1906-07); futurism tried to depict speed and motion (Italian Futurist Manifesto, 1910). **Architects** explored new uses of steel structures, with facades either neoclassical (Adler and Sullivan in U.S.), curvilinear Art Nouveau (Gaudi's Casa Mila, 1905-10), or functionally streamlined (Wright's Robie House, 1909).

Music and dance shared the experimental spirit. Ruth St. Denis (1877-1968) and Isadora Duncan (1878-1927) pioneered modern dance, while Sergei Diaghilev in Paris revitalized classic ballet from 1909. Composers explored atonal music (Debussy, 1862-1918) and dissonance (Schoenberg, 1874-1951) or revolutionized classical forms (Stravinsky, 1882-1971), often showing jazz or folk music influences.

War and Revolution: 1910-19

War threatens. Germany under Wilhelm II sought a political and imperial role consonant with its industrial strength, challenging Britain's world supremacy and threatening France, which was still resenting the loss (1871) of Alsace-Lorraine. Austria wanted to curb an expanded Serbia (after 1912) and the threat it posed to its own Slav lands. Russia feared Austrian and German political and economic aims in the Balkans and Turkey.

An accelerated arms race resulted from these circumstances. The German standing army rose to more than 2 million men by 1914. Russia and France had more than a million each, and Austria and the British Empire nearly a million each. Dozens of enormous battleships were built by the powers after 1906.

The **assassination of Austrian Archduke Franz Ferdinand** by a Serbian nationalist, June 28, 1914, was the trigger for war. The system of alliances made the conflict Europe-wide; Germany's invasion of Belgium to outflank France forced Britain to enter the war. Patriotic fervor was nearly unanimous among all classes in most countries.

World War I. German forces were stopped in France in one month. The rival armies dug **trench networks**. Artillery and improved machine guns prevented either side from any lasting advance despite repeated assaults (600,000 dead at **Verdun**, Feb.-July 1916). German deployment of poisonous chlorine gas (Ypres, 1915) was first major use of lethal **chemical weapons**. The entrance of more than 1 million U.S. troops tipped the

balance after mid-1917, forcing Germany to sue for peace the next year. The formal armistice was signed on Nov. 11, 1918, and the German emperor abdicated.

In the E, the Russian armies were thrown back (battle of **Tannenberg**, Aug. 20, 1914), and the war grew unpopular in Russia. An allied attempt to relieve Russia through Turkey failed (**Gallipoli**, 1915). The **Russian Revolution** (1917) abolished the monarchy. The new Bolshevik regime signed the capitulatory Brest-Litovsk peace in Mar. 1918. Italy entered the war on the allied side in May 1915 but was pushed back by Oct. 1917. A renewed offensive with Allied aid in Oct.-Nov. 1918 forced Austria to surrender.

The British Navy successfully blockaded Germany, which responded with submarine U-boat attacks; **unrestricted submarine warfare** against neutrals after Jan. 1917 helped bring the U.S. into the war. Other battlefields included Palestine and Mesopotamia, both of which Britain wrested from the Turks in 1917, and the African and Pacific colonies of Germany, most of which fell to Britain, France, Australia, Japan, and South Africa.

Settlement. At the **Paris Peace Conference** (Jan.-June 1919), concluded by the **Treaty of Versailles**, and in subsequent negotiations and local wars (Russian-Polish War, 1920), the **map of Europe** was redrawn with a nod to U.S. Pres. Woodrow Wilson's principle of self-determination. Austria and Hungary were separated, and much of their land was given to Yugoslavia

Both sides in World War I developed elaborate networks of dug-in trenches from which to fight.

(formerly Serbia), Romania, Italy, and the newly independent Poland and Czechoslovakia. Germany lost territory in the W, N, and E, while Finland and the Baltic states were detached from Russia. The Ottoman Empire ended (1922) and most of its Arab lands went to British-sponsored Arab states or to direct French and British rule. Belgium's sovereignty was recognized.

From 1916, the civilian populations and economies of both sides were mobilized to an unprecedented degree. Hardships intensified among fighting nations in 1917 (French mutiny crushed in May). More than 10 million soldiers died in the war.

A huge **reparations** burden and partial demilitarization were imposed on Germany. Pres. Wilson proposed a League of Nations, but the U.S. Senate voted against U.S. involvement.

Russian revolution. Military defeats and high casualties caused a contagious lack of confidence in Tsar Nicholas, who was forced to abdicate Mar. 1917. A liberal provisional government failed to end the war, and massive desertions, riots, and fighting between factions followed. A moderate socialist government under Aleksandr Kerensky was overthrown (Nov. 1917) in a violent coup by the **Bolsheviks** in Petrograd under **Lenin**, who later disbanded the elected Constituent Assembly.

The Bolsheviks brutally suppressed all opposition and ended the war with Germany in Mar. 1918. **Civil war** broke out in the summer between the Red Army (the Bolsheviks and their supporters), and monarchists, anarchists, minority nationalities (Ukrainians, Georgians, Poles), and others. Small U.S., British, French, and Japanese units also opposed the Bolsheviks (1918-19; Japan

in Vladivostok to 1922). The civil war, anarchy, and pogroms devastated the country until the 1920 Red Army victory. The **Communist Party** leadership retained absolute power.

Other European revolutions. An unpopular monarchy in **Portugal** was overthrown in 1910. The new republic took severe anticlerical measures in 1911.

After a century of Home Rule agitation, during which **Ireland** was devastated by famine (1 million dead, 1846-47) and emigration, republican militants staged an unsuccessful uprising in Dublin during **Easter 1916**. The execution of the leaders and mass arrests by the British won popular support for the rebels. The **Irish Free State**, comprising all but the six northern counties, achieved dominion status in 1922.

In the aftermath of the world war, radical revolutions were attempted in Germany (**Spartacist** uprising, Jan. 1919), **Hungary** (Kun regime, 1919), and elsewhere. All were suppressed or failed for lack of support.

Chinese revolution. The Qinq, or Manchu, Dynasty was overthrown and a republic proclaimed, 1911-12. Revolutionary leader Sun Yat-sen, who organized the nationalist **Kuomintang** party and led a provisional republican government in Nanjing, resigned in a unification compromise with former imperial viceroy Yuan Shikai. Yuan became president upon the abdication of the emperor in Feb. 1912.

Students launched protests on May 4, 1919, against League of Nations concessions in China to Japan. Nationalist, liberal, and socialist ideas and political groups spread. The **Chinese Communist Party** was founded in 1921. A Communist regime took power in Mongolia with Soviet support in 1921.

India restive. Indian objections to British rule erupted in nationalist riots as well as in the nonviolent tactics of Mahatma **Gandhi** (1869-1948). Nearly 400 unarmed demonstrators were shot at **Amritsar** in Apr. 1919. Britain approved limited self-rule that year.

Mexican revolution. Under the long Díaz dictatorship (1877-1911) the economy advanced, but Indian and mestizo lands were confiscated, and concessions to foreigners (mostly U.S.) damaged the middle class. A revolution in 1910 led to civil wars and U.S. intervention (1914, 1916-17). Land reform and a more democratic constitution (1917) were achieved.

Sciences. Scientific specialization prevailed by the 20th cent. Advances in knowledge and technological aptitude increased with the geometric rise in the number of practitioners. Physicists challenged common-sense views of causality, observation, and a mechanistic universe, putting science further beyond popular grasp (**Einstein**'s general theory of relativity, 1915-16; Bohr's quantum mechanics, 1913; Heisenberg's uncertainty principle, 1927).

Aftermath of War: 1920-29

U.S. Easy credit, technological ingenuity, and war-related industrial decline in Europe caused a long economic boom, in which ownership of new products—**autos**, **phones**, **radios**—became more democratized. **Prosperity**, an increase in women workers, women's suffrage (19th Amendment ratified, 1920), and drastic change in fashion (**flappers**, mannish bob for women, clean-shaven men) created a wide perception of social change despite prohibition of alcoholic beverages (1919-33). Union membership and strikes increased. Fear of radicals led to Palmer raids (1919-20) and the Sacco-Vanzetti case (1921-27).

Europe sorts itself out. Germany's liberal **Weimar constitution** (1919) could not guarantee a stable government in the face of rightist violence (Foreign Min. Rathenau assassinated, 1922) and Communist refusal to cooperate with Socialists. Reparations and Allied occupation of the Rhineland caused staggering inflation that destroyed middle-class savings, but economic expansion resumed after mid-decade, aided by U.S. loans. A sophisticated, **innovative culture** developed in architecture and design (Bauhaus, 1919-28), film (Lang, *M*, 1931), painting (Grosz), music (Weill, *Threepenny Opera*, 1928), theater (Brecht, *A Man's a Man*, 1926), criticism (Benjamin), philosophy (Jung), and fashion. This culture was considered decadent and socially disruptive by rightists.

England elected its first Labour governments (Jan. 1924, June 1929). A 10-day general strike in support of coal miners failed in May 1926. In **Italy**, strikes, political chaos, and violence by small Fascist bands culminated in the Oct. 1922 Fascist March on Rome, which established **Mussolini**'s dictatorship. Strikes were outlawed (1926), and Italian influence was pressed in the Balkans (Albania made a protectorate, 1926). A conservative dictatorship was also established in **Portugal** in a 1926 military coup.

Czechoslovakia, the only stable democracy to emerge from the war in Central or E Europe, faced opposition from Germans (in the Sudetenland), Ruthenians, and some Slovaks. As the industrial heartland of the old Habsburg empire, it remained fairly prosperous. With French backing, it formed the Little Entente with Yugoslavia (1920) and **Romania** (1921) to block Austrian or Hungarian irredentism. Croats and Slovenes in **Yugoslavia** demanded a federal state until King Alexander I proclaimed (1929) a royal dictatorship. Poland faced internal nationality problems as well (Germans, Ukrainians, Jews); Pilsudski ruled as dictator from 1926. The Baltic states were threatened by traditionally dominant ethnic Germans and by Soviet-supported Communists.

An economic collapse and famine in **Russia** (1921-22) claimed 5 million lives. The New Economic Policy (1921) allowed land ownership by peasants and some private commerce and industry. **Stalin** was absolute ruler within four years of Lenin's death (1924). He inaugurated a brutal collectivization program (1929-32) and used foreign Communist parties for Soviet state advantage. Industrialization advanced rapidly.

Internationalism. Revulsion against World War I led to pacifist agitation, to the Kellogg-Briand Pact renouncing aggressive war (1928), and to **naval disarmament** pacts (Washington, 1922; London, 1930). But the League of Nations was able to arbitrate only minor disputes (Greece-Bulgaria, 1925). A number of countries pulled back from global contacts, as with American isolationism and Russia's separation from international capitalism.

Middle East. Mustafa Kemal (**Ataturk**) led **Turkish** nationalists in resisting Italian, French, and Greek military advances (1919-23). The sultanate was abolished (1922), and elaborate reforms were passed, including secularization of law and adoption of the Latin alphabet. Ethnic conflict led to persecution of **Armenians** (more than 1 million dead in 1915, 1 million expelled), Greeks (forced Greek-Turk population exchange, 1923), and Kurds (1925 uprising).

With evacuation of the Turks from **Arab** lands, the puritanical Wahabi dynasty of E Arabia conquered (1919-25) what is now Saudi Arabia. British, French, and Arab dynastic and nationalist maneuvering resulted in the creation of two more Arab monarchies in 1921—Iraq and Transjordan (both under British control)—and two French mandates—Syria and Lebanon. Jewish immigration into British-mandated **Palestine**, inspired by the Zionist movement, was resisted by Arabs, at times violently (1921, 1929 riots).

Reza Khan ruled **Persia** after his 1921 coup (shah from 1925), centralized control, and created the trappings of a modern secular state.

In 1922, English archaeologist Howard Carter discovered the tomb of the boy pharaoh **Tutankhamun** in the Valley of the Kings in Egypt.

China. The Kuomintang under **Chiang Kai-shek** (1887-1975) subdued the warlords by 1928. The Communists were brutally suppressed after their alliance with the Kuomintang was broken in 1927. Relative peace thereafter allowed for industrial and financial improvements, with some Russian, British, and U.S. cooperation.

Arts. Nearly all bounds of subject matter, style, and attitude were broken in the arts of the period. **Abstract** art first took inspiration from natural forms or narrative themes (Kandinsky from 1911) and then worked free of any representational aims (Malevich's suprematism, 1915-19; Mondrian's geometric style from 1917). The **Dada** movement (from 1916) mocked artistic pretension with absurd collages and constructions. Paradox, illusion, and psychological taboos were exploited by **surrealists** by the late 1920s (Dali, Magritte). Architectural schools celebrated industrial values, whether vigorous abstract constructivism (Tatlin, *Monument to the Third International*, 1919) or the machined, streamlined **Bauhaus** style, which was extended to many design fields (Helvetica typeface).

Prose writers explored revolutionary narrative modes related to dreams (Kafka's *Trial*, 1925), internal monologue (Joyce's *Ulysses*, 1922), and word play (Stein's *Making of Americans*, 1925). Poets and novelists wrote of modern alienation (Eliot's *Waste Land*, 1922) and aimlessness ("The Lost Generation").

Rise of Totalitarians: 1930-39

Depression. A worldwide financial panic and economic depression began with the Oct. 1929 U.S. stock market crash and the May 1931 failure of the Austrian Credit-Anstalt. A credit crunch caused international bankruptcies and **unemployment:** 12 million jobless by 1932 in the U.S., 5.6 million in Germany, 2.7 million in England. Governments responded with **tariff restrictions** (Smoot-Hawley Act, 1930; Ottawa Imperial Conference, 1932), which dried up world trade. Government public works programs were vitiated by deflationary budget balancing.

Germany. As **Nazi Party** leader, **Adolf Hitler** built up a mass movement (feeding on economic hardship, ideas of racial superiority, fear of leftist influence). With a plurality in the Reichstag, he persuaded Pres. **Hindenburg** to name him chancellor (Jan. 1933); Hindenburg further granted him emergency powers after the Reichstag fire in Feb. Other parties and most forms of opposition, including strikes, were banned, and the media and most aspects of life fell under Nazi control. Severe persecution of Jews began (**Nuremberg Laws**, Sept. 1935). Many Jews, political opponents, and others were sent to concentration camps (Dachau, 1933), where thousands died or were killed. Public works, renewed conscription (1935), arms production, and a four-year plan (1936) all but ended unemployment.

Hitler's expansionism started with reincorporation of the Saar (1935), occupation of the **Rhineland** (Mar. 1936), and annexation of Austria (Mar. 1938). At **Munich** (Sept. 1938) Britain and France attempted to appease Hitler and avoid war by successfully encouraging Czechoslovakia's surrender of the Sudetenland territory.

Russia. Rapid industrialization was achieved through successive **five-year plans** starting in 1928, using severe labor discipline and mass forced labor. Industry was financed by exploitation of agriculture, which was almost totally collectivized by the early 1930s. Millions perished in a series of manufactured disasters: extermination (1929-34) of kulaks (peasant landowners), severe famine (1932-33), party purges and show trials (Great Purge, 1936-38), suppression of nationalities, and poor conditions in labor camps. Purges also increased Stalin's power in the Communist party.

Spain. An industrial revolution during World War I created an urban proletariat, which was attracted to socialism and anarchism; Catalan nationalists challenged central authority. The five years after King Alfonso left Spain in Apr. 1931

were dominated by tension between intermittent leftist and anticlerical governments and clericals, monarchists, and other rightists. Anarchist and Communist rebellions were crushed, but a July 1936 extreme right rebellion led by Gen. Francisco **Franco** and aided by Nazi Germany and Fascist Italy succeeded after a three-year **civil war** (more than 1 million dead in battles and atrocities). The war polarized international public opinion.

Italy. Despite propaganda for the ideal of the Corporate State, few domestic reforms were attempted. An entente with Hungary and Austria (Mar. 1934), a pact with Germany and Japan (Nov. 1937), and intervention by 50,000-75,000 troops in Spain (1936-39) sealed Italy's identification with the fascist bloc (anti-Semitic laws after Mar. 1938). Ethiopia was conquered (1935-36) and Albania annexed (Jan. 1939) in conscious imitation of ancient Rome.

Eastern Europe. Repressive regimes fought for power against an active opposition (liberals, socialists, Communists, peasants, Nazis). Minority groups and Jews were restricted

Mahatma Gandhi (right) led efforts for Indian autonomy and independence for more than 25 years.

within national boundaries that did not coincide with ethnic population patterns. In the destruction of **Czechoslovakia**, Hungary occupied S Slovakia (Nov. 1938) and Ruthenia (Mar. 1939), and a pro-Nazi regime took power in the rest of Slovakia. Other boundary disputes (e.g., Poland-Lithuania, Yugoslavia-Bulgaria, and Romania-Hungary) doomed attempts to build joint fronts against Germany or Russia. Economic depression was severe.

East Asia. After a period of liberalism in **Japan**, nativist militarists dominated the government with peasant support. Manchuria was seized (Sept. 1931-Feb. 1932), and a puppet state was set up (Manchukuo). Adjacent Jehol (Inner Mongolia) was occupied in 1933. **China** proper was invaded in July 1937; large areas were conquered by Oct. 1938. Hundreds of thousands of rapes, murders, and other atrocities were attributed to the Japanese.

Communist forces left Kuomintang-besieged strongholds in the S of China in a Long March (1934-35) to the N. The Kuomintang-Communist civil war was suspended in Jan. 1937 in the face of threatening Japan.

Democracies. The Franklin Roosevelt administration, in office Mar. 1933, embarked on an extensive program of **New Deal** social reform and economic stimulation, including protection for labor unions (heavy industries organized), Social Security, public works, wage-and-hour laws, and assistance to farmers. Isolationist sentiment (1937 Neutrality Act) prevented U.S. intervention in Europe, but military expenditures were increased in 1939.

French political instability and polarization prevented resolution of economic and international security questions. The **Popular Front** government under Léon Blum (June 1936-Apr. 1938) passed social reforms (40-hour work week) and raised arms spending. National coalition governments, which ruled Britain from Aug. 1931, brought economic recovery but failed to define a consistent international policy until Chamberlain's government (from May 1937), which practiced **appeasement** of Germany and Italy.

India. Twenty years of agitation for autonomy and then for independence (Gandhi's **salt march**, 1930) achieved some constitutional reform (extended provincial powers, 1935) despite Muslim-Hindu strife. Social issues assumed prominence with peasant uprisings (1921), strikes (1928), Gandhi's efforts for untouchables (1932 "fast unto death"), and social and agrarian reform by the provinces after 1937.

Arts. The streamlined, geometric design motifs of Art Deco (from 1925) prevailed through the 1930s. **Abstract art** flourished (Moore sculptures from 1931) alongside a new **realism** related to social and political concerns (Socialist Realism, the official Soviet style from 1934; Mexican muralist Rivera, 1886-1957; Orozco, 1883-1949), which were also expressed in fiction and poetry (Steinbeck's *Grapes of Wrath*, 1939; Sandburg's *The People, Yes*, 1936). Modern architecture (International Style, 1932) was unchallenged in its use of artificial materials (concrete, glass), lack of decoration, and monumentality (Rockefeller Center, 1929-40). Larger-than-life U.S.-made films captured a worldwide audience *(Gone With the Wind, The Wizard of Oz*, both 1939).

War, Hot and Cold: 1940-49

War in Asia-Pacific. Japan occupied Indochina in Sept. 1940, dominated Thailand in Dec. 1941, and attacked Hawaii (**Pearl Harbor**), the Philippines, Hong Kong, and Malaya on Dec. 7, 1941 (precipitating U.S. entrance into the war). Indonesia was attacked in Jan. 1942, and Burma was conquered in Mar. 1942. The Battle of **Midway** (June 1942) turned back the Japanese advance. "Island-hopping" battles (**Guadalcanal**, Aug. 1942-Jan. 1943; **Leyte Gulf**, Oct. 1944; **Iwo Jima**, Feb.-Mar. 1945; **Okinawa**, Apr. 1945) and massive bombing raids on Japan from June 1944 wore out Japanese defenses. U.S. atom bombs, dropped Aug. 6 and 9 on **Hiroshima** and **Nagasaki**, forced Japan to agree, on Aug. 14, to surrender; formal surrender was on Sept. 2, 1945.

The U.S. bombing of Hiroshima and Nagasaki, Japan, in 1945 demonstrated the deadly, destructive power of atomic weapons.

War in Europe. The **Nazi-Soviet nonaggression** pact (Aug. 1939) freed Germany to attack Poland (Sept. 1939). Britain and France, which had guaranteed Polish independence, declared war on Germany. Russia seized E Poland (Sept. 1939), attacked Finland (Nov. 1939), and took the Baltic states (July 1940). Mobile German forces staged *blitzkrieg* attacks during Apr.-June 1940, conquering neutral Belgium, Denmark, Luxembourg, Netherlands, and Norway and defeating France; 350,000 British and French troops were evacuated at **Dunkirk**, France (May). The **Battle of Britain** (June-Dec. 1940) denied Germany air superiority. German-Italian campaigns won the Balkans by Apr. 1941. Three million Axis troops **invaded Russia** in June 1941, marching through Ukraine to the Caucasus, and through White Russia and the Baltic republics to Moscow and Leningrad.

Russian winter counterthrusts (1941-42 and 1942-43) stopped the German advance (**Stalingrad**, Sept. 1942-Feb. 1943). Sustaining great casualties, the Russians drove the Axis from all E Europe and the Balkans in the next two years. Invasions of N Africa (Nov. 1942), Italy (Sept. 1943), and **Normandy** (launched on D-Day, June 6, 1944) brought U.S., British, Free French, and allied troops to Germany by spring 1945. In Feb. 1945, the three Allied leaders, Winston **Churchill** (Britain), Joseph **Stalin** (USSR), and Franklin D. **Roosevelt** (U.S.), met in **Yalta** to discuss strategy and resolve political issues, including the postwar Allied occupation of Germany. Germany surrendered May 7, 1945.

Atrocities. The war brought 20th-cent. cruelty to its peak. The Nazi regime systematically killed an estimated 5-6 million Jews, including some 3 million who died in death camps (e.g., **Auschwitz**). The Nazis also killed Roma (also known as Gypsies), political opponents, people with mental or physical disabilities, homosexuals, others deemed undesirable, and vast numbers of Slavs.

German bombs killed 70,000 British civilians. More than 100,000 Chinese civilians were killed by Japanese forces in the capture and occupation of Nanking. Severe retaliation by the Soviet army, E European partisans, Free French, and others took a heavy toll. U.S. and British bombing of Germany killed hundreds of thousands, as did U.S. bombing of Japan (80,000-200,000 at Hiroshima alone). Some 45 million people died in the war.

Settlement. The **United Nations** charter was signed in San Francisco on June 26, 1945, by 50 nations. The International Tribunal at **Nuremberg** convicted 22 German leaders for war crimes in Sept. 1946; 23 Japanese leaders were convicted in Nov. 1948. Postwar border changes included large gains in territory for the USSR, losses for Germany, a shift to the W in Polish borders, and minor losses for Italy. Communist regimes, supported by Soviet troops, took power in most of Eastern Europe, including Soviet-occupied Germany (GDR, a.k.a. East Germany, proclaimed Oct. 1949). Japan lost all overseas lands. Global developments involved establishing new economic coordinating bodies like the International Monetary Fund (1944) and the Universal Declaration of Human Rights (1948).

Recovery. Basic political and social changes were imposed on Japan and W Germany by the Western allies (Japan constitution adopted, Nov. 1946; W German basic law, May 1949). U.S. **Marshall Plan** aid ($12 billion, 1947-51) spurred W European economic recovery after a period of severe inflation and strikes in Europe and the U.S. The British Labour Party introduced a national health service and nationalized basic industries in 1946.

Cold War. Western fears of further Soviet advances (Cominform formed in Oct. 1947; Czechoslovakia coup, Feb. 1948; Berlin blockade, Apr. 1948-Sept. 1949) led to the formation of **NATO**. Civil war in Greece and Soviet pressure on Turkey led to U.S. aid under the **Truman Doctrine** (Mar. 1947). Other anti-Communist security pacts were the Organization of American States (Apr. 1948) and the SE Asia Treaty Organization (Sept. 1954). A new wave of **Soviet purges** and repression intensified in the last years of Stalin's rule, extending to E Europe (Slansky trial in Czechoslovakia, 1951). Only Yugoslavia resisted Soviet control (expelled by Cominform, June 1948; U.S. aid, June 1949).

China, Korea. Communist forces emerged from World War II strengthened by the Soviet takeover of industrial Manchuria. In four years of fighting, the Kuomintang was driven from the mainland; the People's Republic of China was proclaimed Oct. 1, 1949. Korea was divided by USSR and U.S. occupation forces. Separate republics were proclaimed in the two zones in Aug.-Sept. 1948.

India. India and Pakistan became independent dominions on Aug. 15, 1947. Millions of Hindu and Muslim refugees were created by the partition. Riots (1946-47) took hundreds of thousands of lives. Mahatma **Gandhi** was assassinated in Jan. 1948. Burma became completely independent in Jan. 1948; Ceylon (later Sri Lanka) took dominion status in Feb.

Middle East. The UN approved partition of Palestine into Jewish and Arab states. **Israel** was proclaimed a state, May 14, 1948. Arabs rejected partition, but failed to defeat Israel in war (May 1948-July 1949). Immigration from Europe and the Middle East swelled Israel's Jewish population. British and French forces left Lebanon and Syria in 1946. Transjordan occupied most of Arab Palestine.

Southeast Asia. Communists and others fought against restoration of French rule in **Indochina** from 1946; a non-Communist government was recognized by France in Mar. 1949, but fighting continued. Both Indonesia and the Philippines became independent; the former in 1949 after four years of war with the Netherlands, the latter in 1946. Philippine economic and military ties with the U.S. remained strong; a Communist-led peasant rising was checked in 1948.

Arts. New York City became the center of the world art market; **abstract expressionism** was the chief mode (Pollock from 1943, de Kooning from 1947). Literature and philosophy explored **existentialism** (Camus's The Stranger, 1942; Sartre's Being and Nothingness, 1943). Non-Western attempts to revive or create regional styles (Senghor's Négritude, Mishima's novels) were responses to global cultural influences. Radio and phonograph records spread American popular music (swing, bebop) around the world.

The Cold War Decade: 1950-59

Decolonization. The relatively peaceful decline of European political and military power in Asia and Africa accelerated in the 1950s. Nearly all of N Africa was freed by 1956, but France fought bitterly to retain Algeria, with its large European minority, until 1962. **Ghana**, independent in 1957, led a parade of new self-led African nations (more than two dozen by 1962), which altered the political character of the UN. Ethnic, political, and other factional disputes often exploded in the new nations after decolonization (UN troops in Cyprus, 1964; **Nigerian civil war**, 1967-70). Leaders of the new states, mostly sharing socialist ideologies, tried to create an Afro-Asian bloc (Bandung Conference, 1955), but Western economic influence and U.S. political ties remained strong (Baghdad Pact, 1955).

Trade. World trade volume soared, in an atmosphere of monetary stability assured by international accords (**Bretton Woods**, 1944). In Europe, economic integration advanced (**European Economic Community**, 1957; European Free Trade Association, 1960). Comecon (1949) coordinated the economies of Soviet-bloc countries. Global developments included transcontinental jet travel (first South Africa to Britain flight, 1952; introduction of term "jet lag," 1965) and the increasing spread of English in global business, sports, and transportation.

U.S. Economic growth produced an abundance of consumer goods (9.3 million motor vehicles sold, 1955). Suburban housing changed life patterns for middle and working classes (Levittown, NY, 1947-51). Pres. Dwight **Eisenhower's** landslide election victories (1952, 1956) reflected consensus politics. A system of alliances and military bases bolstered U.S. influence on all continents. Trade and payments surpluses were balanced by overseas investments and foreign aid ($50 billion, 1950-59).

USSR. In the "thaw" after Stalin's death in 1953, relations with the West improved (evacuation of Vienna, Geneva summit conference, both 1955). Repression of scientific and cultural life eased, and many prisoners were freed culminating in de-Stalinization (1956). Nikita **Khrushchev's** leadership aimed at consumer sector growth, but farm production lagged, despite the virgin lands program (from 1954). Soviet crushing of the 1956 Hungarian revolution, the 1960 U-2 spy plane episode, and other incidents renewed E-W tension and domestic curbs.

Eastern Europe. Resentment of Russian domination and Stalinist repression combined with nationalist, economic, and religious factors to produce periodic violence. E Berlin workers rioted (1953), Polish workers rioted in Poznan (June 1956), and a broad-based **revolution** broke out in **Hungary** (Oct. 1956). All were suppressed by de Soviet force or threats (at least 7,000 dead in Hungary), but Poland was allowed to restore private ownership of farms, and a degree of personal and economic freedom returned to Hungary. Yugoslavia experimented with worker self-management and a market economy.

Korea. The 1945 division of Korea along the 38th parallel left industry in the N, which was organized into a militant regime and armed by the USSR. The S was politically disunited. More than 60,000 N Korean troops invaded the S on June 25, 1950. The U.S., backed by the UN Security Council, sent troops. UN troops reached the Chinese border in Nov. Some 200,000 Chinese troops crossed the Yalu R. and drove back UN forces. By spring 1951, battle lines had become stabilized near the original 38th parallel border, but heavy fighting continued. Finally, an armistice was signed on July 27, 1953. U.S. troops remained in the S, and U.S. economic and military aid continued. The war stimulated rapid economic recovery in Japan.

China. Starting in 1952, industry, agriculture, and social institutions were forcibly collectivized. In a massive purge, as many as several million people were executed as Kuomintang supporters or as class and political enemies. The **Great Leap Forward** (1958-60) unsuccessfully tried to force the pace of development by substituting labor for investment.

Southeast Asia. Ho Chi Minh's forces, aided by the USSR and the new Chinese Communist government, fought French and pro-French Vietnamese forces to a standstill and captured the strategic **Dien Bien Phu** camp on May 1954. The Geneva Agreements divided Vietnam in half pending elections (never held) and recognized Laos and Cambodia as independent. The U.S. aided the anti-Communist Republic of Vietnam in the S.

Middle East. Arab revolutions placed leftist, militantly nationalist regimes in power in Egypt (1952) and Iraq (1958). But Arab unity attempts failed (United Arab Republic joined Egypt, Syria, Yemen, 1958-61). Arab refusal to recognize Israel (Arab League economic blockade began Sept. 1951) led to a permanent **state of war**, with repeated incidents (Gaza, 1955). Israel occupied Sinai, and Britain and France took (Oct. 1956) the Suez Canal, but were replaced by the UN Emergency Force. The Mossadegh government in Iran nationalized (May 1951) the British-owned oil industry in May, but was overthrown (Aug. 1953) in a U.S.-aided coup.

Latin America. Argentinian dictator Juan Perón, in office 1946, crushed opposition and enforced land reform, some nationalization, welfare state measures, and curbs on the Roman Catholic Church. A Sept. 1955 coup deposed Perón. The 1952 revolution in Bolivia brought land reform, nationalization of tin mines, and improvement in the status of the Indigenous population, who nevertheless remained poor. The Batista regime in Cuba was overthrown (Jan. 1959) by Fidel **Castro**, who imposed a Communist dictatorship, aligned Cuba with the USSR, and improved education and health care. A U.S.-backed anti-Castro invasion (**Bay of Pigs**, Apr. 1961) was crushed. Self-government advanced in the British Caribbean.

Technology. Large outlays on research and development in the U.S. and the USSR focused on military applications (H-bomb in U.S., 1952; USSR, 1953; Britain, 1957; intercontinental missiles, late 1950s). Soviet launching of the **Sputnik** satellite (Oct. 4, 1957) spurred increases in U.S. science education funds (National Defense Education Act).

Literature and film. Alienation from social and literary conventions reached an extreme in the theater of the absurd (Beckett's *Waiting for Godot*, 1952), the "new novel" (Robbe-Grillet's *Voyeur*, 1955), and avant-garde film (Antonioni's *L'Avventura*, 1960). U.S. beatniks (Kerouac's *On the Road*, 1957) and others rejected the supposed conformism of Americans (Riesman's *The Lonely Crowd*, 1950).

Rising Expectations and New Protests: 1960-69

Global economy. The longest sustained economic boom on record spanned almost the entire decade in the capitalist world; the closely watched GNP figure doubled (1960-70) in the U.S., fueled by **Vietnam War**-related budget deficits. The **General Agreement on Tariffs and Trade** (1967) stimulated Western European prosperity, which spread to peripheral areas (Spain, Italy, E Germany). Japan became a top economic power. Foreign investment aided the industrialization of Brazil. There were limited Soviet economic reform attempts. Outside the Soviet zone the global economy was marked by the growing role of multinational corporations (3,000 in 1914; 6,000 in 1970). International nongovernmental organizations (NGOs) also multiplied rapidly (Amnesty International, 1961).

Reform and radicalization. Pres. John F. **Kennedy**, inaugurated 1961, emphasized youthful idealism and vigor; his assassination Nov. 22, 1963, was a national trauma. Political and social reform movements took root in U.S. and other countries. Blacks demonstrated nonviolently and with partial success against segregation and poverty (1963 March on Washington; 1964 **Civil Rights Act**), but some urban areas erupted in riots (Watts, 1965; Detroit, 1967; more than 100 cities following **Martin Luther King Jr.** assassination, Apr. 4, 1968). New concern for the poor (Harrington's *Other America*, 1963) helped lead to Pres. Lyndon Johnson's **"Great Society"** programs (Medicare, Water Quality Act, Higher Education Act, all 1965). Concern for the **environment** surged (Carson's *Silent Spring*, 1962).

Feminism revived as a cultural and political movement (Friedan's *Feminine Mystique*, 1963; National Organization for Women founded, 1966), and a movement for homosexual rights emerged (Stonewall riot in NYC, 1969). Pope John XXIII called the **Second Vatican Council** (1962-65), which liberalized Roman Catholic liturgy and some other aspects of Catholicism. Opposition to U.S. involvement in Vietnam, especially among university students (**Moratorium** protest, Nov. 1969), turned violent (Weatherman Chicago riots, Oct. 1969). **New Left** and Marxist theories became popular, and membership in radical groups (Students for a Democratic Society, Black Panthers) increased. Maoist groups, especially in Europe, called for total transformation of society. In France, students sparked a nationwide strike affecting 10 million workers in May-June 1968.

China. China's revolutionary militancy under **Mao** Zedong led to border disputes and other conflict with the USSR under "revisionist" Khrushchev, starting in 1960. The **"Great Proletarian Cultural Revolution"** tried to impose a utopian egalitarian program in China and spread revolution abroad; political struggle, often violent, convulsed China in 1965-68.

Southeast Asia. Communist-led guerrillas aided by N Vietnam fought from 1960 against the S Vietnam government of Ngo Dinh Diem (killed 1963). The U.S. military role increased after the 1964 **Tonkin Gulf** incident. Laotian and Cambodian neutrality were threatened by Communist insurgencies, with N Vietnamese aid, and U.S. intrigues.

Developing world. A bloc of authoritarian leftist regimes among the newly independent nations came to dominate the conference of nonaligned nations (Belgrade, 1961; Cairo, 1964; Lusaka, 1970). Soviet political ties and military bases were established in Cuba, Egypt, Algeria, Guinea, and other countries. Some leaders were ousted in coups by pro-Western groups—Dem. Rep. of the Congo's Patrice Lumumba (killed 1961), Ghana's Kwame Nkrumah (exiled 1966), and Indonesia's Sukarno (effectively ousted in 1965 after a Communist coup failed).

Middle East. Arab-Israeli tension erupted into a brief war June 1967. Israel emerged from the war as a major regional power. Military shipments before and after the war increased Soviet influence in much of the Arab world. Most Arab states broke U.S. diplomatic ties, while Communist commitments cut their ties to Israel. Intra-Arab disputes continued: Egypt and Saudi Arabia supported rival factions in a bloody Yemen civil war 1962-70; Lebanese troops fought Palestinian commandos 1969.

Eastern Europe. To stop the large-scale exodus of citizens, E German authorities built (Aug. 1961) a fortified **wall across Berlin** that enclosed West Berlin. Soviet sway in the Balkans was weakened by Albania's realignment with China (USSR broke ties with Albania in Dec. 1961) and Romania's assertion (1964) of limited autonomy. Liberalization (spring 1968) in **Czechoslovakia** was crushed with massive force by troops of five Warsaw Pact countries. W German treaties (1970) with the USSR and Poland facilitated transfer of German technology and confirmed postwar boundaries.

Arts and styles. The boundary between fine and popular arts was blurred to some extent by Pop Art (Warhol) and rock musicals (*Hair*, 1968). Informality and exaggeration prevailed in fashion (beards, miniskirts). A nonpolitical "counterculture" developed, rejecting traditional bourgeois life goals and personal habits, and use of marijuana and hallucinogens spread (**Woodstock** festival, Aug. 1969). **The Beatles** brought unprecedented sophistication to rock music.

Science. Achievements in space (**humans on the moon**, July 1969) and electronics (lasers, integrated circuits) encouraged a faith in scientific solutions to problems in agriculture ("green revolution"), medicine (heart transplants, 1967), and other areas. Harmful technology, it was believed, could be controlled (1963 Limited Test Ban Treaty, 1968 Nuclear Nonproliferation Treaty).

East Germany in 1961 began construction on a barrier to slow the exodus of its population to West Berlin.

New Global Balances and Religious Revivals: 1970-79

U.S. trends. A sluggish economy, energy shortages, and environmental problems contributed to a **"limits to growth"** philosophy. Communist forces' takeover of **South Vietnam** (evacuation of U.S. civilians, Apr. 1975), revelations of **CIA** misdeeds (Rockefeller Commission report, June 1975), and **Watergate** scandal (Nixon resignation, Aug. 1974) reduced faith in U.S. influence and leadership. Social issues spurred controversy—school busing and racial quotas were challenged (**Bakke** case decided by Supreme Court, June 1978), and proposed **Equal Rights Amendment**, sent to states for approval in Mar. 1972, fell short of ratification. **Three Mile Island** nuclear reactor accident (Mar. 1979) reinforced fears of nuclear energy.

Economic woes. The 1960s boom faltered in the 1970s; a severe **recession** in U.S. and Europe (1974-75) followed a huge oil price hike (Dec. 1973). Monetary instability (U.S. cut ties to gold, 1971), decline of the dollar, and protectionist moves by industrial countries (1977-78) threatened trade. Business investment declined. Severe **inflation** plagued many countries (25% in Britain, 1975; 18% in U.S., 1979).

China readjusts. After the 1976 deaths of **Mao** Zedong and **Zhou** Enlai, relative pragmatists won the struggle for leadership. Orthodox Maoists were purged; Mao's widow and other members of the so-called **Gang of Four** were among those arrested. New leaders freed many political prisoners and reduced official adulation of Mao. Political and trade ties to Japan, Europe, and the U.S. (Nixon visit, 1972) expanded, as relations with the USSR, Cuba, and Vietnam eventually worsened (four-week invasion by China, 1979). Ideological guidelines were reversed (bonuses to workers, exams for college entrance, 1977); some restrictions on cultural expression were eased.

Europe. European unity (**EEC-EFTA** trade accord, 1972) faltered as economic problems developed (Britain floated pound, 1972; France floated franc, 1974). Germany and Switzerland curbed guest workers from S Europe, while Greece and Turkey quarreled over Cyprus and Aegean oil rights. **Democratic rule** expanded: the conservative, colonialist regime in **Portugal** was overthrown (Apr. 1974), **Greece**'s seven-year military dictatorship yielded power (July 1974), and **Spain** held free elections (June 1977) after Francisco Franco's death.

Britain's Labour government imposed (1975) wage curbs and suspended nationalization schemes. Terrorism in **Germany** (1972 **Munich Olympics** killings) led to laws curbing some civil liberties. **France**'s Socialist-Communist coalition lost 1978 election bid.

Religion and politics. With the political situation improved in **Muslim** countries (except in Central Asia under Soviet and Chinese rule) and the growth of Arab oil wealth, there was a resurgence of religiously motivated activism. Libyan dictator Muammar al-**Qaddafi** mixed Islamic laws with socialism. The illegal **Muslim Brotherhood** in Egypt was accused of violence, while extreme groups bombed (1977) theaters to protest Western and secular values. In **Turkey**, the National Salvation Party became the first Islamic group to win a share in power (1974) since secularization in the 1920s. In **Iran**, Ayatollah Ruhollah **Khomeini** led a revolution that deposed the secular shah (Jan. 1979) and created an Islamic republic. A religiously motivated insurrection in **Saudi Arabia** briefly seized (1979) the Grand Mosque in Mecca. Muslim puritan opposition to **Pakistan** Pres. Zulfikar Ali-**Bhutto** contributed to his overthrow (July 1977). Muslim solidarity, however, could not prevent Pakistan's eastern province (**Bangladesh**) from declaring (Dec. 1971) independence after a bloody civil war.

Muslim and Hindu opposition to coerced sterilization in **India** helped defeat the Indira **Gandhi** government, to be replaced (Mar. 1977) by a coalition including Hindu religious parties.

Muslims in the S **Philippines**, aided by Libya, rebelled against central rule from 1973. The **Buddhist** Soka Gakkai movement launched (1964) the Komeito party in **Japan**, a major opposition party in 1972 and 1976 elections. Israel's secularist **Israeli** Labor party was ousted in 1977 by conservatives led by Menachem Begin; religious militants founded settlements on the disputed **West Bank**, part of biblically promised Israel.

Religious wars raged in **Northern Ireland** (Catholic vs. Protestant, 1969-97) and **Lebanon** (Christian vs. Muslim, 1975-90), while religious militancy complicated the Israel-Arab dispute (1973 Israel-Arab war). The **Camp David Accords**, negotiated in 1978 by Egyptian Pres. Anwar al-**Sadat**, Israeli Prime Min. Menachem **Begin**, and U.S. Pres. Jimmy **Carter**, facilitated landmark 1979 **Egypt-Israel peace treaty**, but increased militancy on the West Bank impeded further progress. **Evangelical Protestant** groups grew in the U.S. Reform **Judaism** in U.S. expanded and revived many traditional practices; ordained first woman rabbi (1972).

Latin America. Repressive conservative forces strengthened their hold, with a violent coup against the elected (Sept. 1973) leftist **Allende** government in **Chile**, a military coup in **Argentina** (1976), and coups against reformist regimes in **Bolivia** (1971, 1979) and **Peru** (1976). In Central America, increasing liberal and leftist militancy led to ouster (1979) of the **Somoza** regime of **Nicaragua** and to civil conflict in **El Salvador**.

Southeast Asia. Communist victories in Vietnam, Cambodia, and Laos by May 1975 led to new turmoil. **Pol Pot**'s **Khmer Rouge** regime in **Cambodia** ordered millions to resettle in rural areas, in a program of forced labor and terrorism that cost more than 1 million lives (1975-79) and caused hundreds of thousands to flee. The Vietnamese invasion of Cambodia (1979) swelled the refugee population and contributed to widespread starvation.

Russian expansion. Soviet influence, checked in some countries (troops ousted by **Egypt**, 1972), was projected farther afield (**Angola**, 1975-89; **Ethiopia**, 1977-88). Détente with the West—1972 Berlin pact, 1972 strategic arms pact (**SALT**)—gave way to a more antagonistic relationship in the late 1970s, exacerbated by revelations of Soviet atrocities (Solzhenitsyn's *Gulag Archipelago*, 1974) and the 1979 Soviet invasion of **Afghanistan**.

Africa. The last European colonies won independence (**Spanish Sahara**, 1976; **Djibouti**, 1977), and, after 10 years of civil war, a Black government took over (1979) in **Zimbabwe** (Rhodesia); white domination remained in **South Africa**. Ethnic or tribal conflicts were widespread, with European intervention in local wars (France in **Chad**, **Zaire**, **Mauritania**) and heavy involvement of Cuban troops.

The Vietnam War, in which an estimated 2 million Vietnamese and 58,000 Americans died, also engulfed Laos and Cambodia in deadly violence.

End of the Cold War and Demand for Democracy: 1980-89

Global developments. International contacts accelerated thanks to **new openness** in China (1978) and USSR (1985); **global consumerism** was symbolized by rapid spread of McDonald's restaurants (Japan, 1971; Russia, 1990). New forms of home media proliferated (VCRs, personal computers, video gaming systems). HIV/AIDS is identified; WHO estimates 400,000 cases worldwide by 1989.

USSR, Eastern Europe. The late 1980s saw the remaking of the Soviet state and the beginning of the disintegration of the Soviet empire. After the deaths of Gen. Sec. Leonid **Brezhnev** (1982) and two successors, the harsh treatment of dissent and restriction of emigration, and the Soviet invasion (Dec. 1979) of Afghanistan, Gen. Sec. Mikhail **Gorbachev** (in office 1985-91) promoted **glasnost** and **perestroika**—economic, political, and social reform. Four Reagan-Gorbachev **summits** (1985-88) yielded the INF disarmament treaty (1987). Military withdrawal from **Afghanistan** was completed in Feb. 1989, and the Soviet people chose (Mar. 1989) part of the new Congress of People's Deputies from competing candidates. By decade's end the **Cold War** appeared to be fading away.

In **Poland,** Solidarity, the labor union founded (1980) by Lech **Walesa,** was outlawed in 1982 but legalized in 1988, after years of unrest. Poland's first free election since the Communist takeover brought **Solidarity** victory (June 1989); Tadeusz **Mazowiecki,** a Walesa adviser, became prime minister in a government with the Communists. In fall 1989 the failure of Marxist economies in **Hungary, East Germany, Czechoslovakia, Bulgaria,** and **Romania** brought the collapse of the Communist monopoly and a demand for democracy. In a historic step, the **Berlin Wall** was opened in Nov. 1989.

U.S. The **"Reagan Years"** (1981-88) featured new economic policies via budget and tax cuts, deregulation, "junk bond" financing, leveraged buyouts, and mergers. However, there was a stock market crash (Oct. 1987), and federal budget deficits and the trade deficit increased. Even as Soviet reforms took place, U.S. foreign policy showed a **strong anti-Communist stance,** via increased defense spending, aid to anti-Communists in Central America, invasion of Cuba-threatened **Grenada,** and championing of the **"Star Wars"** missile defense program. The **Iran-Contra affair** (Oliver North testimony, July 1987) was a major political scandal.

Middle East. The Middle East remained militarily unstable, with sharp divisions along economic, political, racial, and religious lines. The 1979 Islamic revolution in **Iran** led to increasing antagonism toward U.S. and the West (hostage crisis, Nov. 1979-Jan. 1981; first U.S. sanctions imposed). In Sept. 1980, **Iraq** repudiated its border agreement with Iran and hostilities led to an eight-year war, in which hundreds of thousands died. **Libya's** support for terrorism induced U.S. to close (May 1981) its diplomatic mission there and embargo (1982) Libyan oil. Following an attack on a West Berlin disco frequented by U.S. military (Apr. 1986, 3 killed), U.S. bombed targets in Libya. **Israel** affirmed (July 1980) all **Jerusalem** as its capital, destroyed (June 1981) an **Iraqi atomic reactor,** and invaded **Lebanon,** citing terrorism from the Palestine Liberation Organization; PLO withdrew from Lebanon after cease-fire.

A **Palestinian uprising** began (Dec. 1987) in Israeli-occupied Gaza and spread to the West Bank; troops responded with force, killing 300 by the end of 1988, with 6,000 in detention camps. Israel began (Feb. 1985) withdrawal from war-torn Lebanon; artillery duels, Mar.-Apr. 1989, between Christian East Beirut and Muslim West Beirut left 200 dead.

Latin America. In Nicaragua, the leftist **Sandinista** National Liberation Front, in power after the 1979 civil war, gave military aid to guerrillas in El Salvador, while U.S. provided aid to anti-Sandinista **contras,** utilizing profits from secret arms sales to Iran, and the **CIA** directed the mining of Nicaraguan ports. In **El Salvador,** a military coup (Oct. 1979) failed to halt a leftist insurgency armed by Cuba and Nicaragua. Salvadoran Archbishop Oscar **Romero,** advocate for poor, was assassinated Mar. 1980; right-wing death squads killed thousands in ensuing decade of civil war. In **Chile,** Gen. Augusto **Pinochet**—in power since 1973, imposing harsh measures against leftists and dissidents—yielded the presidency after elections (Dec. 1989) but remained head of the army. In **Panama,** U.S. troops overthrew dictator Manuel **Noriega** (Dec. 1989); later convicted on drug and human rights charges, he served time in the U.S., France, and Panama.

Africa. The 1980s saw continuing economic decline in virtually all African countries, a result of accelerating desertification, the world economic recession, heavy indebtedness to overseas creditors, rapid population growth, and political instability. Some 60 million Africans faced prolonged hunger in 1981. Much of Africa suffered one of the worst **droughts** ever in 1983; by year's end, one-third of the population, or about 150 million, were near **famine.** Live Aid, a marathon rock concert (July 1985) raised relief funds, and Western nations sent aid. Wars in **Ethiopia** and **Sudan** and military strife in several other nations continued.

Anti-apartheid sentiment gathered force in **South Africa,** with demonstrations meeting violent police response. White voters approved (Nov. 1983) the first constitution to give people of mixed-race backgrounds and Asians a voice, while still excluding the Black majority. Twelve nations imposed economic **sanctions** in Aug.-Sept. 1985. Pres. P. W. **Botha** was succeeded (Sept. 1989) by F. W. **de Klerk,** who promised negotiation with the Black population.

Asia and Pacific. Benazir **Bhutto** became the first woman to lead a majority-Muslim nation as prime minister of **Pakistan** (Dec. 1988). The "people power" revolt in the **Philippines** ousted Ferdinand **Marcos** (Feb. 1986) after two decades as president; he was replaced by Corazon **Aquino.** Trade imbalances favoring **Japan** dominated the nation's foreign relations. During the 1980s **China's** Communist government and paramount leader **Deng** Xiaoping expanded commercial and technical ties to the West and the role of market forces. In Apr. 1989 student demonstrators camped out in **Tiananmen Square,** Beijing, in a peaceful call for political reform. Some 100,000 students and workers marched; at least 20 other cities saw protests. Army troops crushed the demonstration in and around Tiananmen Square on June 3-4; an estimated 500-7,000 killed, up to 10,000 arrested, 31 tried and executed. The conciliatory Communist Party chief was ousted; the Politburo adopted (1989) reforms against official corruption.

Europe. With the addition of Greece, Portugal, and Spain, the **European Community** became a common market of more than 300 million people. Conservative Margaret **Thatcher** became the first British prime minister in the 20th century to win a third consecutive term (1987). **France** elected (1981) its first socialist president, François **Mitterrand** (reelected, 1988). Elections in 1983 brought **Italy** its first socialist premier, Bettino **Craxi.**

International terrorism. With the 1979 overthrow of the shah of **Iran** and instability in the **Middle East,** terrorism became a prominent tactic. In 1979-81, Iranian militants held 52 **U.S. hostages** in Iran for 444 days. In Oct. 1983, in **Lebanon,** truck bombs exploded at U.S. Marine headquarters, killing 241 Americans, and at a French paratrooper barracks, killing 58. The **Achille Lauro** cruise ship was hijacked in Oct. 1985, and an American passenger killed. **Assassinated leaders** included Egypt's Pres. Anwar al-**Sadat** (1981), India's Prime Min. Indira **Gandhi** (1984), and Lebanese Prem. Rashid **Karami** (1987).

A series of summits between USSR Gen. Sec. Mikhail Gorbachev and U.S. Pres. Ronald Reagan produced the 1987 INF disarmament treaty.

New Regional Tensions in a Post-Cold War World: 1990-99

Soviet Empire collapse. Breakup of the Soviet Union into 15 independent states began with declarations of independence by **Lithuania, Latvia,** and **Estonia** during abortive coup against Mikhail **Gorbachev** (Aug. 1991). Other republics followed. In Dec. 1991, **Russia, Ukraine,** and **Belarus** declared the Soviet Union dead; Gorbachev resigned. The **Warsaw Pact** and Council for Mutual Economic Assistance (**Comecon**) disbanded. Most former Soviet republics joined in loose confederation (**Commonwealth of Independent States**). Hardship ensued as Russia, under Pres. Boris **Yeltsin,** moved to reboot the economy under a free-market system.

When the Muslim-majority Russian republic of **Chechnya** declared independence (Dec. 1994), Russian forces invaded (Dec. 1994), withdrawing after 1996 cease-fire. In 1999, Russia forcibly suppressed Muslim insurgents in Russian republic of Dagestan and entered Chechnya, again fighting separatists. Yeltsin resigned presidency, Dec. 1999, with Prime Min. Vladimir **Putin** becoming acting president.

Europe. Yugoslavia broke apart, and hostilities ensued along ethnic and religious lines. **Croatia, Slovenia,** and **Macedonia** declared independence (1991), followed by **Bosnia-Herzegovina** (1992). **Serbia** and **Montenegro** remained as the republic of Yugoslavia. Bitter fighting followed, especially in Bosnia, where Serbs engaged in **ethnic cleansing** of the Muslim population; peace plan (**Dayton accord,** 1995) was brokered by the U.S., with **NATO** policing its implementation. In spring 1999, NATO conducted a bombing campaign aimed at stopping Yugoslavia from driving ethnic Albanians from the **Kosovo** region; a June accord brought in NATO peacekeepers.

The **two Germanys were reunited** after 45 years (Oct. 1990). Czechoslovakia broke apart (Jan. 1993) into the **Czech Republic** and **Slovakia.** Labor leader Lech **Walesa** was elected president of Poland (Dec. 1991). In Jan. 1994, NATO approved the **Partnership for Peace,** coordinating defense of E and Central European countries; Russia later joined. NATO signed cooperation pact with **Russia** (May 1997) allowing for NATO expansion into former Soviet-bloc countries. Czech Republic, **Hungary,** and **Poland** joined NATO in Jan. 1999. Efforts toward European unity continued with adoption of a single market (Jan. 1993) and conversion of the European Community to the **European Union** as the **Maastricht Treaty** took effect (Nov. 1993). The **euro** was launched as common currency for non-cash uses, Jan. 1999, and as cash, Jan. 2002, in the then-12 Eurozone countries.

An intraparty revolt forced Margaret **Thatcher** out as UK prime minister, to be succeeded by John **Major** (Nov. 1990); Labour took power under Tony **Blair** (May 1997). Prince **Charles** and **Diana** divorced (Aug. 1996); Diana died in car crash a year later. Talks on **Northern Ireland** led to peace plan, approved in all-Ireland vote (May 1998). In Dec. 1999, Northern Ireland was granted home rule. Voters in **Scotland** (overwhelmingly) and **Wales** (narrowly) approved creation of regional legislatures (1997). In **France,** socialist Pres. François Mitterrand declined to run for a third term and conservative Jacques **Chirac** was elected (May 1995) to the office.

Middle East. In Aug. 1990, **Iraq**'s Saddam Hussein ordered troops to invade **Kuwait.** A UN-approved international force, led by U.S., bombed Iraq (Jan. 1991) and launched a land attack, crushing the invasion; cease-fire agreed to, Apr. 1991. The UN extended sanctions on Iraq for failure to abide by cease-fire terms. Iraq's reported failure to cooperate with UN inspectors seeking to eliminate **weapons of mass destruction** led to airstrikes by U.S. and Britain (1998).

Israel and the **PLO** signed **peace accord** (Sept. 1993) providing for Palestinian self-government in **West Bank** and **Gaza** Strip; Prime Min. Yitzhak **Rabin** and Foreign Min. Shimon **Peres** of Israel and Yasir **Arafat** of the PLO shared 1994 Nobel Peace Prize. Six Arab nations relaxed boycott against Israel (1994), and Israel and **Jordan** signed peace treaty (Oct. 1994). Rabin was assassinated (Nov. 1995) by an Israeli extremist; Benjamin **Netanyahu** became prime minister (May 1996). Arafat was elected president of the Palestinian Authority (Jan. 1996).

Asia and Pacific. Longtime **North Korean** dictator Kim Il Sung died (July 1994), to be succeeded by son Kim Jong Il. In Oct. 1994 North Korea signed agreement with U.S. setting timetable for ending **nuclear weapons** program (deal collapsed in 2002). Well over 200,000 (and perhaps more than 2 million) North Koreans died in the 1990s from **famine** conditions. **Palau** achieved independence, Oct. 1994. **Hong Kong** was returned to **China** (July 1997), after 156 years as a British colony, and **Macau** reverted to China (Dec. 1999) after over 400 years of Portuguese rule. Jiang Zemin, general secretary of the Chinese Communist Party, also became China's president (Mar. 1993). China released several well-known dissidents but continued to jail and execute many. U.S. and China signed trade pact (Nov. 1999). In **Japan** members of a religious cult released the nerve gas sarin on **Tokyo subway,** killing 12 and injuring more than 5,500 (Mar. 1995).

After years of growing prosperity, **Thailand, Indonesia,** and **South Korea** in 1997 began to suffer economic reverses, with worldwide ripple effect, and received IMF **bailout** packages. In South Korea, former dissident **Kim** Dae-jung was elected president (Dec. 1997). In Indonesia, protests over mismanagement led to the resignation of Pres. **Suharto** (May 1998) after 32 years of rule. In a referendum (Aug. 1999), **East Timorese** voted for independence; pro-Indonesian militias rampaged, but a multinational peacekeeping force helped restore order (Sept. 1999).

In **Afghanistan** the radical Islamist **Taliban** gained control of Kabul (Sept. 1996) and, eventually, most of the country. **Indian** forces repeatedly clashed with pro-independence demonstrators in the disputed majority-Muslim region of **Kashmir,** exacerbating relations with **Pakistan.** India and Pakistan both conducted **nuclear tests** in 1998. Conflict between government and the military led to a **bloodless coup** in Pakistan (Oct. 1999).

Africa. South Africa's Pres. F. W. de Klerk released dissident Black leader Nelson **Mandela** from prison (Feb. 1990) after 27 years, and the white minority government repealed **apartheid** laws (1990, 1991); also dismantled its nuclear weapons program. The African National Congress won in multiracial elections (Apr. 1994), making Mandela president, and a new constitution became law (Dec. 1996). **Namibia** became independent in Mar. 1990, after almost 20 years under UN trusteeship. **Eritrea** achieved independence from **Ethiopia,** July 1993, after over 30 years of war. **Mobutu** Sese Seko, longtime ruler of **Zaire,** was deposed (May 1997) by rebel forces under Laurent **Kabila,** who changed country's name back to **Democratic Republic of the Congo.** In **Nigeria,** former Gen. Olusegun **Obasanjo** was elected (Feb. 1999) as the nation's first civilian leader in 15 years.

Civil war broke out in **Liberia** (Dec. 1989) and lasted, with interruptions, through the 1990s and beyond, leaving hundreds of thousands dead. Factional fighting erupted in **Somalia** (Jan. 1991); a U.S.-led UN peacekeeping force failed to restore order and left (Mar. 1995). In **Algeria,** the army canceled parliamentary elections (Jan. 1992) after the Islamic party won a first round. Ensuing civil war left more than 150,000 dead; a peace and amnesty plan was approved in a Sept. 1999 referendum. Assassination of **Burundi**'s president (June 1993) renewed ethnic violence between **Hutus** and **Tutsis** there. A suspicious plane crash that killed the presidents of Burundi and Rwanda

South Africa abandoned apartheid and transitioned to a non-racial democratic government, with Nelson Mandela (pictured, with U.S. Pres. Bill Clinton) elected president in 1994.

(Apr. 1994) led to genocide in **Rwanda**; some 800,000 died, mostly Tutsis massacred by Hutu militias.

North America. U.S. Pres. Bill **Clinton** (D) (elected 1992, 1996) presided over growing economy, promoted free trade, intervened in Bosnia. Impeached by House (Dec. 1998) on charges stemming from affair with intern, he was acquitted by the Senate. In **Canada**, Liberal Jean **Chrétien** became prime minister (Nov. 1993; reelected 1997). The Canadian territory of **Nunavut** was created, Apr. 1999, carved from Northwest Territories. In **Mexico**, Ernesto **Zedillo** of the ruling PRI party was elected president (July 1994) after PRI's first candidate was assassinated. The country weathered a **monetary crisis** with the help of a 1995 U.S. bailout. The North American Free Trade Agreement (**NAFTA**), liberalizing trade between U.S., Canada, and Mexico, took effect Jan. 1994. Globalization trends drew protests from radical activists (**World Trade Org.** meeting, Nov.-Dec. 1999).

Central America and Caribbean. In **Haiti**, Jean-Bertrand **Aristide** was elected president (Dec. 1990); ousted in Sept. 1991 military coup, but restored to office (Oct. 1994) through U.S.-led negotiations. In Feb. 1990 elections in **Nicaragua** the opposition won a surprise victory over **Sandinista** Pres. Daniel **Ortega**. A 12-year civil war in **El Salvador** ended with **peace treaty**, Jan. 1992, between government and leftist rebels. In Dec. 1999, Panama assumed full control of the **Panama Canal**, in accord with 1977 treaty with U.S.

South America. Alberto **Fujimori** was elected president of **Peru** in June 1990; condemned for human rights abuses but popular for reducing terrorism; reelected in 1995. Leftist guerrillas took hostages in Lima (Dec. 1996); one hostage killed during rescue operation (Apr. 1997). Peronist Pres. Carlos Saúl **Menem** was **Argentina**'s president for much of the decade, imposing economic austerity. Former **Chilean** Pres. Augusto

Pinochet was arrested in London (Oct. 1998) and charged with human-rights violations but judged unfit for trial. In **Brazil**, Fernando Henrique **Cardoso** was elected president (Oct. 1994) and reelected in 1998 despite economic slump; the IMF announced a $42-billion aid package (Nov. 1998). In **Venezuela** two coups were thwarted (1992), but leftist coup leader Hugo **Chávez** was elected president, Dec. 1998.

Terrorism. A bomb exploded in garage beneath New York City's **World Trade Center**, killing six (Feb. 1993); six Islamic fundamentalists were convicted. Bombs outside U.S. embassies in **Kenya** and **Tanzania** killed over 220 (Aug. 1998); U.S. retaliated with airstrikes in Afghanistan and Sudan. Anti-government U.S. radicals bombed a federal building in **Oklahoma City**, OK (Apr. 1995), killing 168.

Science, technology, and environment. The powerful **Hubble Space Telescope** was launched in Apr. 1990. U.S. space shuttle *Atlantis* docked with the orbiting Russian space station *Mir* (June 1995) in first of several joint missions. In Nov. 1998 the first component for a new **International Space Station** was launched into space from Kazakhstan. Scottish scientists announced (Feb. 1997) **cloning** of a sheep—first mammal successfully cloned from a cell from an adult animal. Tim **Berners-Lee** launched first **World Wide Web** server (1990); user-friendly graphical browsers (Mosaic, 1993; Netscape, 1994) and internet service providers followed, beginning a global transformation of communications and information access. Efforts to limit **global climate change** intensified with tentative agreements adopted in **Kyoto**, Japan (Dec. 1997). In 1999, World Health Org. announced 33 million people were living with **HIV**, and **AIDS** was fourth leading cause of death worldwide (No. 1 cause in Africa), with an estimated 14 million deaths since the epidemic began.

Globalization and Global Realignments: 2000-09

Terrorism. In Oct. 2000, 17 U.S. Navy sailors were killed aboard the USS *Cole* in Aden, **Yemen**, in suicide bombing tied to **al-Qaeda** terrorist network, based in Afghanistan. Hijackers on Sept. 11, 2001, crashed two jetliners into the twin towers of

The attacks of Sept. 11, 2001, killed more than 2,750 people in New York.

the **World Trade Center** in New York City and another into the **Pentagon** outside Washington, DC, with a fourth crashing in a Pennsylvania field. The attacks, linked to al-Qaeda and its leader, **Osama bin Laden**, killed nearly 3,000 and destroyed both towers.

Islamic radicals also planted a car bomb on the Indonesian island of **Bali** (Oct. 2002; over 200 killed) and bombed mass transit systems in **Madrid** (Mar. 2004; some 200 killed), **London** (July 2005; 56 killed), and **Mumbai** (July 2006; over 180 killed). Jihadists in Mumbai attacked sites frequented by foreigners in Nov. 2008 (over 160 died). **Chechen** separatist guerrillas were implicated in an attack on a **Moscow** movie theater (Oct. 2002; at least 120 hostages died) and takeover of a school in Beslan (Sept. 2004; over 330 killed). Bombing attacks on **Yazidi** towns in **Iraq** (Aug. 2007) killed at least 500.

Economic crisis. Rapid economic growth in **China** and other developing countries contrasted with sluggish rates in traditional economic powers. A global **recession**, beginning in late 2007, combined with **financial meltdown** (Sept. 2008). **Iceland**'s banking system collapsed (Oct. 2008); rescued by loans and austerity. **Dubai**'s state-controlled investment company was bailed out (Dec. 2009) by neighboring emirate Abu Dhabi. Soaring food and fuel prices sparked unrest in **Egypt** and **Haiti** (Apr. 2008). **Austerity** measures spurred protests in Europe,

War in Iraq and Afghanistan. The U.S., with the UK, invaded **Iraq** (Mar. 2003) to oust the regime of Saddam **Hussein**. U.S. Pres. George W. **Bush** declared major combat ended by May, but insurgents caused continuing casualties. Though cited as grounds for the invasion, **weapons of mass destruction** were not found. Hussein was captured by U.S. troops (Dec. 2003) and executed by Iraq (2006) for crimes against humanity. Iraqi **elections** led to a **Shiite coalition government** under Prime Min. Nouri al-**Maliki** (May 2006). With **insurgent** violence intensifying, Bush announced (Jan. 2007) a **"surge"** of additional U.S. troops; casualties fell sharply, aided by changing sectarian aims. In **Afghanistan**, a U.S.-led military coalition ousted the **Taliban** regime. A transitional government was installed (Dec. 2001), and NATO assumed control of multinational forces (Aug. 2003). Afghans elected Hamid **Karzai** president (Nov. 2004). From 2007, Taliban and other Islamist militants stepped up attacks, often operating from safe havens inside **Pakistan**.

Middle East. Palestinian **suicide bombings** continued, and **Israel** mounted a major offensive (Mar. 2002), reoccupying much of the **West Bank**. The U.S., Russia, UN, and EU introduced (Apr. 2003) **"road map"** for peace negotiations but made little progress. After Palestinian leader Yasir **Arafat** died (Nov. 2004), Mahmoud **Abbas** was elected in his place; in Jan. 2006 the militant Palestinian party **Hamas** won a parliamentary majority. Israel launched attacks on **Lebanon** (July 2006) after a raid by Lebanon-based **Hezbollah** guerrillas, and in reaction to **Hamas** launched an offensive in the **Gaza Strip** (Dec. 2008), with heavy Palestinian casualties. Feb. 2009 elections in Israel led to a coalition government headed by conservative former Prime Min. Benjamin **Netanyahu**. In **Yemen**, U.S. used drones to kill suspected **al-Qaeda** terrorists (Nov. 2002), and the government, from 2004 onward, battled a growing insurgency from **Shiite Houthi** rebels, believed aided by Iran.

Asia and Pacific. Gen. Pervez **Musharraf**, brought to power in a 1999 coup, assumed **Pakistan**'s presidency (June 2001); former Prime Min. Benazir **Bhutto** was assassinated, Dec. 2007. Riots in the mostly Hindu state of Gujarat, **India**, (Feb.-Apr. 2002) left more than 1,200 dead, mostly Muslims. Pakistan and **India** restored ties (May 2003) and declared ceasefire in disputed **Kashmir** (Nov. 2003); relations remained tense.

East Timor **(Timor-Leste)** achieved independence (May 2002). Leaders of **North** and **South Korea** met (June 2000) in first-ever postwar summit. North Korea agreed, Feb. 2007, to end **nuclear weapons** development in exchange for aid, but reneged in 2009. In **China**, **Hu** Jintao succeeded **Jiang** Zemin as party chief (Nov. 2002) and president (Mar. 2003). The UN Intl. Atomic Energy Agency (IAEA) censured **Iran** (Dec. 2003) for covering up aspects of its nuclear program; UN sanctions imposed, Dec. 2006, after Iran continued enriching uranium. Hardline Pres. Mahmoud **Ahmadinejad** was declared landslide winner in June 2009 Iranian elections widely perceived as rigged; massive protests were crushed, with dozens killed, hundreds jailed, some tortured. In **Kyrgyzstan**, protests (Mar. 2005) against election fraud brought down Pres. Askar **Akayev** in **"tulip revolution."** **Myanmar**'s military junta cracked down on hundreds of thousands of protesters (Sept. 2007). In **Australia** the center-left Labor Party won landslide victory in Nov. 2007 elections. **Tamil** guerrillas in **Sri Lanka**, soundly defeated in bloody battles against government forces, ended their rebellion (May 2009), which in 26 years had claimed at least 80,000 lives.

In Dec. 2004 a **tsunami** devastated Indian Ocean nations, leaving some 228,000 dead. **Earthquakes** struck the Indian subcontinent (Oct. 2005; nearly 80,000 died) and China's Sichuan province (May 2008; nearly 70,000 died). Over 80,000 died in a May 2008 **cyclone** in Myanmar.

Europe. The **European Union** admitted 12 E European nations by Jan. 2007. Voters in France and Netherlands rejected treaty to establish a new EU constitution (May-June 2005); modified plan **(Treaty of Lisbon)** came into force Dec. 2009. **Yugoslav** strongman Slobodan **Milosevic** yielded power in Oct. 2000 and died, Mar. 2006, while on trial for **war crimes**. **Serbia** and **Montenegro** separated into two independent nations, May-June 2006. **Kosovo** declared independence, Feb. 2008.

Vladimir **Putin**, elected Mar. 2000, began long tenure as Russian president, interrupted (2008-12) when his protégé, Dmitri **Medvedev**, held that office. Russians captured capital of **Chechnya** (Feb. 2000) and established direct rule, but the insurgency continued. In **Ukraine**, a tainted presidential runoff election (Nov. 2004) led to the country's **"orange revolution"**; recount gave power to nationalist Viktor **Yushchenko**.

British Labour Prime Min. Tony **Blair** won reelection twice (2001, 2005); Angela **Merkel** began (Nov. 2005) long tenure as German chancellor. Riots broke out in **France**'s immigrant communities, Nov. 2005. French voters elected conservative Nicolas **Sarkozy** president (May 2007), and France rejoined **NATO** military command (Apr. 2009) after more than 40 years. **Netherlands** became first country to legalize **same-sex marriage**, effective Apr. 2001.

Africa. **Ethiopia** and **Eritrea** signed peace treaty (Dec. 2000), ending two-year border war, but clashes continued. Laurent **Kabila**, president of Dem. Rep. of the Congo **(DRC)**, was assassinated, Jan. 2001. A peace agreement in DRC (Apr. 2003) did not end violence there. Pres. Charles **Taylor** went into exile (Aug. 2003) in deal to end 14-year civil war in **Liberia**; other accords aimed at ending civil wars in **Angola** (Apr. 2002) and **Côte d'Ivoire** (Jan. 2003). In **Sudan** the Muslim-led government and rebels from the Christian south signed power-sharing agreement, Jan. 2005. Rebellion in the **Darfur** area of western

One of the deadliest natural disasters in recorded history, a 2004 tsunami killed more than 200,000 people in African and Asian countries.

Sudan led to large-scale violence, especially by Arab militias **(janjaweed)**, reportedly backed by the government; over 2 million people were displaced and 300,000 killed by the end of 2009. The Intl. Criminal Court issued an arrest warrant for Sudanese Pres. Omar al-**Bashir** for war crimes (Mar. 2009), to no avail. Disputed elections sparked violence in **Kenya** (Jan. 2008) and **Zimbabwe** (Apr. 2008). Under longtime Pres. Robert **Mugabe**, Zimbabwe sustained soaring unemployment and hyperinflation. **Guinea-Bissau**'s defense chief and president were assassinated, Mar. 2009.

Americas and the Caribbean. George W. **Bush** (R) served as U.S. president, 2001-09, after close election. He pursued wars in Afghanistan and Iraq following Sept. 2001 terror attack. Barack **Obama** (D), first-ever Black U.S. president, elected in 2008, pledged to end Afghanistan and Iraq conflicts. The long-supreme Institutional Revolutionary Party **(PRI)** lost power in **Mexico** with election of center-right presidents Vicente **Fox** (2000) and Felipe **Calderón** (2006); drug violence claimed over 30,000 lives. After 12 years in power, **Canada**'s Liberal Party was defeated in Jan. 2006 elections.

Leftists held power in **Chile** under Ricardo **Lagos** Escobar (from 2000) and Michelle **Bachelet** (from 2006), in **Brazil** under Luiz Inácio **Lula** da Silva (elected 2002; reelected 2006), and in **Bolivia** under Evo **Morales** (elected 2005). In **Venezuela**, leftist populist Pres. Hugo **Chávez** regained power after a failed coup (2002). Peronist Néstor **Kirchner** was elected president of **Argentina** (Apr. 2003); his wife **Cristina** was elected (2007) to succeed him. In **Honduras**, leftist leader Manuel **Zelaya** was elected president (Nov. 2005) but was ousted by the military (June 2009). In **Nicaragua** Sandinista leader Daniel **Ortega** won back the presidency, Nov. 2006, and strengthened ties with Cuba and Iran.

In **Peru**, right-wing Pres. Alberto **Fujimori** was reelected (May 2000) but fled the country; he was extradited (2007) and convicted on human rights and corruption charges. **Haiti** was wracked by antigovernment protests, leading to resignation of Jean-Bertrand **Aristide** in Feb. 2004; a UN peacekeeping mission was brought in. Ailing Pres. **Fidel Castro**, **Cuba**'s strongman leader since 1959, ceded powers (July 2006) to his brother, **Raúl.**

Religion. **John Paul II** died, Apr. 2005, after 26 years as pope; German Cardinal Joseph Ratzinger succeeded him, under the name **Benedict XVI**. The Catholic Church was shaken by **sexual abuse scandal**.

Science and technology. The U.S. **space shuttle** *Columbia* broke up on reentering Earth's atmosphere (Feb. 2003), killing seven crewmembers. NASA landed two rovers, *Spirit* and *Opportunity*, on **Mars** (Jan. 2004); observations verified presence of water. **China** launched its first manned space flight, Oct. 2003. **Internet** penetration and access to technology expanded exponentially; online commerce, use of **social media** (Facebook, 2004; Twitter, 2006), mobile computing (iPhone, 2007), and file-sharing services became common.

Environment and health. Under the **Kyoto Protocol** (effective Feb. 2005), most industrialized nations agreed to specific reductions in emissions of **greenhouse gases** linked to global warming. Worldwide **AIDS** estimates showed (Nov. 2007) new infections had peaked in the late 1990s. A pandemic of **swine flu**, or influenza A (H1N1), broke out in **Mexico** (Apr. 2009) and spread, killing more than 150,000.

Searching for Resolutions: 2010-19

Middle East. UN General Assembly granted observer-state status to **Palestine** (Nov. 2012). Arab-Israeli **peace talks** foundered as **Fatah** and militant **Hamas** factions agreed (Apr. 2014) to aim for unification. **Israel** launched airstrikes on **Gaza** (July-Aug. 2014) after rocket attacks by Hamas-affiliated groups; at least 2,000 Palestinians and 60 Israeli soldiers killed. Sometimes violent protests at the border (starting Mar. 2018) were met with Israeli gunfire, leading to further Palestinian casualties. Conservative Israeli Prime Min. Benjamin **Netanyahu**, in office continuously since 2009, remained as prime minister into 2020, despite indecisive elections (Apr., Sept. 2019) and his Nov. 2019 indictment on corruption charges.

Poverty, religious and ethnic conflict, and government corruption and repression fueled revolts against entrenched regimes. In **Tunisia**, protests forced ouster of Pres. Zine al-Abidine **Ben Ali** (Jan. 2011); elections followed and a new constitution (Jan. 2014) recognized civil liberties. But the so-called **Arab Spring** also backfired. In **Egypt**, after mass demonstrations led to overthrow of longtime Pres. Hosni **Mubarak** (Feb. 2011), an elected **Muslim Brotherhood**-dominated government, led by Mohammed **Morsi**, fell in a military coup (July 2013); raids (over 600 killed) and mass arrests followed. Coup leader Abdel Fattah al-**Sisi** was elected president, May 2014; Morsi died during trial, June 2019. In **Libya**, insurgents backed by NATO overthrew Muammar al-**Qaddafi**, who was killed (Oct. 2011), but Libya became a chaotic battleground for rival Islamist factions (U.S. consulate attacked in **Benghazi**, Sept. 2012) and a hub for extralegal migration to Europe. In **Yemen**, Pres. Ali Abdullah **Saleh** yielded power, Feb. 2012, after protests; **Houthi** rebels, backed by Iran, continued their insurgency, deposing Saleh's successor and taking over the capital, Sept. 2014. A **Saudi**-led coalition of Arab states (Mar. 2015) launched bombings against Houthi; war continued through 2019, with massive casualties, including many civilians.

In Oct. 2018 Saudi dissident journalist Jamal **Khashoggi** was killed and dismembered inside Saudi consulate in Istanbul; eight Saudis were convicted in the crime, Dec. 2019, but higher-level Saudi involvement was suspected.

In **Iraq**, the last U.S. combat unit withdrew, Aug. 2010; U.S. military left, Dec. 2011. Death toll, 2003-11: about 4,500 U.S. service members, 300 from allied countries, with Iraqi civilian deaths estimated at over 100,000. But **sectarian violence** accelerated, with government forces and Shia militia fighting insurgents, including the Sunni extremist Islamic State in Iraq and Syria (**ISIS**). U.S. and allies conducted airstrikes against ISIS and sent in advisers. Separatist **Kurds** controlled part of Iraq and fought ISIS on the ground. After taking **Fallujah** and **Mosul**, ISIS declared a caliphate (June 2014) and seized **Ramadi**, May 2015. ISIS imposed strict Islamic law, murdered minorities and resisters, and promoted terrorism in Iraq and beyond (over 300 killed in ISIS bombings in **Baghdad**, July 2016). Iraqi troops seized Kurdish-held **Kirkuk** (Oct. 2017) and by Dec. 2017 had routed ISIS from virtually all its territory in Iraq. Anger over the economy and alleged corruption stirred political instability and mass protests (at least 400 killed by security forces, Oct.-Dec. 2019).

In **Afghanistan**, U.S. and NATO-led troops reached about 140,000 by mid-2011, when drawdown began; combat operations ended Dec. 2014, but thousands of troops remained in support roles. Coalition death toll, 2001-14: close to 3,500. Fighting continued, with nearly half of all districts in **Taliban** hands or contested as of Jan. 2019. Taliban insurgents bombed civilian areas (150 killed in truck bomb, May 2017; over 100 in ambulance bombing, Jan. 2018; some 80 in wedding party bombing, Aug. 2019; all in **Kabul**). Civilian deaths, 2010-19: more than 30,000. In **Syria**, Pres. Bashar al-**Assad**, Mar. 2011, launched offensive against protesters, giving rise to **civil war**. After about 1,400 people were killed in **chemical attacks**, mostly attributed to the regime, the government, Sept. 2013, agreed to a Russian-backed plan for surrender of chemical weapons. Despite sporadic cease-fires, fighting continued (death toll through 2019 put at 380,000 by Syrian Observatory for Human Rights) and the regime allegedly continued sporadic chemical attacks. In Dec. 2016, after years-long siege, Syrian government forces, supported by Russia and Iran, gained control of **Aleppo**. U.S.-backed rebels took the **ISIS** capital of **Raqqa**, Oct. 2017, and conquered last remnant of ISIS territory in Syria, Mar. 2019.

Iran, July 2015, accepted multinational agreement to cut back **nuclear weapon** capability in return for lifting of sanctions and release of over $100 billion in frozen assets; U.S. withdrew from agreement, May 2018. Iran was shaken by strikes and **protests** over poor economy, corruption, and political leadership (thousands arrested, many allegedly tortured); in major demonstrations, Nov. 2019, 300-1,500 protesters were killed by security forces. **U.S.-Iran tensions** increased in 2019, amid stepped-up U.S. economic sanctions, attacks on oil tankers in Gulf of Oman, and a shot-down U.S. drone.

Crime and terrorism. Despite killing of **al-Qaeda** leader Osama **bin Laden**, in U.S. raid in **Pakistan** (May 2011), al-Qaeda remained entrenched along Afghan-Pakistan border, while **ISIS** and al-Qaeda affiliates were both active on a wide scale. Al-**Shabab** militants linked to al-Qaeda were behind Oct. 2017 bombings in Mogadishu, **Somalia** (Oct. 2017, over 350 killed; Dec. 2019, about 90 killed) and repeated attacks in **Kenya** (Sept. 2013 shootings at Nairobi shopping mall, close to 70 died; Apr. 2015 massacre at college in Garissa, nearly 150 killed). In **Yemen**, al-Qaeda in the Arabian Peninsula (**AQAP**) attacked military parade rehearsal (May 2012; over 100 killed). **Boko Haram** jihadists abducted over 200 schoolgirls in **Nigeria** (Apr. 2014). **Taliban** gunmen in **Pakistan** killed some 150 at a Peshawar school (Dec. 2014).

Attackers possibly linked to AQAP killed 17 in and around **Paris**, Jan. 2015, most at offices of a satirical magazine. Jihadists linked to ISIS murdered 130 in or near Paris, Nov. 2015, and 36 in and around **Brussels**, Mar. 2016. Islamists also launched attacks in **Tunisia** (Mar., June 2015; about 60 killed) and **Turkey** (over 100 killed at peace rally, Oct. 2015; over 40 at airport, June 2016; 39 at nightclub, Jan. 2017). A **Russian airliner** exploded over **Egypt** (Oct. 2015, killing 224). ISIS-inspired shooter killed 49 (June 2016) at **gay nightclub** in Orlando, FL; ISIS also claimed responsibility for truck attack killing 86 (July 2016) in **Nice**, France.

In **Egypt**, ISIS-affiliated terrorists attacked Coptic Christian churches (Apr.-May 2017; about 75 killed) and a non-Sunni mosque (Nov. 2017; over 300 died). Suicide bombing at pop music concert in **Manchester**, England (May 2017), killed 22. Three radicalized families launched suicide attacks in Surabaya, **Indonesia** (May 2018; 25 died in all). Jihadist targets also included churches and hotels in **Sri Lanka** (Easter Sunday, 2019; over 250 killed), as well as sites in **London**, a Christmas market in **Berlin**, a subway in **St. Petersburg**, and a cathedral in the **Philippines**.

An anti-Muslim extremist killed 77 people in **Norway**, July 2011; another killed six in a **Québec City** mosque, June 2017; and over 50 died in mass shooting at two mosques in Christchurch, **New Zealand**, Mar. 2019. In Oct. 2017 a shooter killed 58 at a **Las Vegas** music festival, before killing himself. Van driver killed 10 pedestrians in **Toronto** (Apr. 2018); 9 family members were killed in ambush near **U.S.-Mexico border** (Nov. 2019), attributed to drug cartel.

Europe. The EU, with IMF help, provided loans to bail out **Greece** (beginning May 2010). Also receiving **bailouts** were **Ireland** (2010), **Portugal** (2011), **Spain** (2013), and **Cyprus** (2013). **Croatia** became 28th EU member, July 2013; **Lithuania**

Fleeing violence, overcrowded camps, or poverty in Northern Africa, the Middle East, and Afghanistan, millions of refugees and migrants sought refuge in Europe in a wave that peaked 2014-16.

became 19th nation to adopt the **euro**, Jan. 2015. Millions of **migrants**, mostly from Middle East and Africa, sought asylum in Europe, 2014-19; thousands drowned attempting to cross the Mediterranean. EU, Sept. 2015, approved plan aimed at redistributing many migrants from heavily impacted **Greece** and **Italy**. Migrant influx fueled anti-EU sentiment and support for right-wing populist parties.

In Apr. 2010 elections, **Hungary**'s center-right Fidesz party outpolled socialists, bringing former Prime Min. Viktor **Orbán** back into office (reelected 2014 and 2018). Conservatives returned to power in **UK**, under David **Cameron**, May 2010, but were split over EU membership. In June 2016 UK voted to leave the EU ("**Brexit**"); EU supporter Cameron resigned, and new Conservative leader Theresa **May** became prime minister. After June 2017 elections she formed a minority government; unable to win support for her negotiated Brexit terms, she resigned, and Boris **Johnson** won leadership election, July 2019. In snap general election, Dec. 2019, Conservatives won a big majority; Parliament approved Johnson's Brexit agreement and UK left the EU in Jan. 2020, for transition period with negotiations pending.

In **France**, socialist François **Hollande** defeated conservative Nicolas **Sarkozy** to become president (May 2012). He was succeeded by pro-EU centrist Emmanuel **Macron**, elected May 2017, despite challenge from rising far-right nationalist Marine **LePen**. French government faced **"yellow-vest"** mass protests (beginning Nov. 2018), initially targeting fuel-tax hike. Notre-Dame Cathedral, in Paris, was severely damaged in fire, Apr. 2019. In **Italy**, center-left Prime Min. Matteo **Renzi** resigned, Dec. 2017, leading to a populist coalition government. In **Turkey** conservative Recep Tayyip **Erdogan**, prime minister since 2003, was elected president, Aug. 2014; he cracked down on opponents and journalists, following July 2016 **coup** attempt (160,000 jailed), and launched offensives against Kurds in N Syria, including a major invasion in Oct. 2019, in advance of which the U.S. pulled out troops. He was reelected June 2018, with expanded powers. **Spain**, in Oct. 2017, imposed direct rule over **Catalonia**, where lawmakers had declared independence following a referendum. In May 2018, **ETA**, the Basque separatist group responsible for over 800 deaths in Spain over some 40 years, announced its dissolution. Spain's socialists took power in June 2018, after a conservative government corruption scandal.

After interregnum as prime minister, Vladimir **Putin** was elected again as **Russia**'s president (Mar. 2012, 2018). Claiming danger to ethnic Russians, he sent troops to annex Ukrainian territory of **Crimea**, Mar. 2014, resulting in international sanctions. Russia also intervened in **Syrian** civil war and interfered in 2016 **U.S. elections**. Hundreds were arrested in anti-corruption **protests**, June 2017. After Mar. 2018 **poisoning** in London of a Russian former spy and his daughter, several Western countries expelled Russian diplomats.

Pro-Russian Viktor **Yanukovych**, elected president of **Ukraine** in Feb. 2010, fled in Feb. 2014 after mass protests. **Civil war** soon broke out in E Ukraine between Ukrainian forces and pro-Russian separatists, aided by Russia. The government pursued westernization under Pres. Petro **Poroshenko** (elected May 2014) and Volodymyr **Zelenskiy** (elected Apr. 2019). Malaysia Airlines passenger jet crashed over E Ukraine, allegedly shot down by Russian missile (July 2014; 298 killed). In **Moldova**, following the 2014 disappearance of $1 billion from banks, the election of Pavel **Filip** as prime minister (Jan. 2016) stirred anticorruption protests. Over 20 years after the **Srebrenica massacre** in Bosnia, former Bosnian Serb leader Radovan **Karadzic** (Mar. 2016) and commander Ratko **Mladic** (Nov. 2017) were convicted of war crimes.

Traditionally Catholic **Ireland** became first country to legalize **same-sex marriage** by popular vote, May 2015, and voted, May 2018, to repeal constitutional ban on **abortion**. So-called **Panama Papers**, leaked Apr. 2016, showed how politicians concealed assets abroad; implicated were leaders in **Russia**, **Ukraine**, **UK**, and **Iceland**.

Asia and Pacific. A UN-backed tribunal that opened in 2006, ruling on war crimes in **Cambodia** during the **Khmer Rouge** regime, issued convictions against a prison guard (July 2010) and two high officials (for crimes against humanity, Aug. 2014, and genocide, Nov. 2018).

An **earthquake and tsunami** (Mar. 2011) struck **Japan**, killing more than 16,000 and leading to meltdowns at nuclear reactors. Over 8,500 were killed in two earthquakes in **Nepal** (Apr.-May 2015); over 2,000 in **Indonesia** quake and tsunami (Sept. 2018). A **Malaysian airliner** with 239 aboard vanished en route to Beijing (Mar. 2014).

Kyrgyzstan's president was ousted, Apr. 2010, after clashes with protesters left at least 85 dead; up to 2,000 killed in ethnic violence, June 2010; in Dec. 2016 voters approved constitutional changes strengthening executive power. In **Kazakhstan** autocratic Pres. Nursultan **Nazarbayev**, in office since 1990, resigned Mar. 2019, but retained some powers; new president elected June 2019, with token opposition.

North Korean dictator **Kim Jong Il** died, Dec. 2011; succeeded by son **Kim Jong Un**, who resumed nuclear and ballistic missile tests, leading to international sanctions. In **South Korea**, Pres. **Park** Geun-hye was removed, Mar. 2017 (convicted of corruption, Apr. 2018); replaced by center-left **Moon** Jae-in. Moon and Kim met in historic summits Apr.-Sept. 2018. Kim and U.S. Pres. **Trump** met in **Singapore**, June 2018, agreed to aim at "denuclearization of the Korean peninsula." **Myanmar**'s military-backed party lost Nov. 2015 election to party of dissident leader Aung San **Suu Kyi**. However, sectarian and government violence against Myanmar's **Rohingya** Muslim minority surged; thousands of Rohingya were killed, while hundreds of thousands fled.

In **China**, **Xi** Jinping succeeded **Hu** Jintao as Communist party chief, Nov. 2012, and president, Mar. 2013. In Mar. 2018, party reelected Xi and supported constitutional changes eliminating term limits. Mass demonstrations in **Hong Kong** protested anti-democratic policies with "umbrella" protests, 2014. New demonstrations spread after introduction (Apr. 2019) of extradition law, not eased by its withdrawal in Sept.; thousands arrested. **U.S.-China trade war**, initiated by U.S. in Mar. 2018, led to tariffs on both sides; "phase-one" trade deal, signed Jan. 2020, reduced some tariffs.

In **Australia**, a center-right coalition came to power after Sept. 2013 elections; returned in May 2019 elections. **Hindu nationalists** won majority in May 2014 elections in **India**; Narendra **Modi** became prime minister (won new term, May 2019). In Muslim-majority territory of **Kashmir** hundreds died in clashes with security forces (beginning July 2016), and a suicide bomb (Feb. 2019) killed more than 40 Indian paramilitary troops. Anti-crime hardliner Rodrigo **Duterte** was elected **Philippines** president, May 2016; thousands of alleged drug dealers and users were killed in government's **anti-drug campaign**. In **Sri Lanka**, Gotabaya **Rajapaksa**, former defense minister accused of brutal tactics in crushing Tamil rebellion, elected president, Nov. 2019.

Thailand's King **Bhumibol** Adulyadej died Oct. 2016, ending 70-year reign; new king **Vajiralongkorn** signed army-drafted constitution, Apr. 2017. In **Malaysian** elections, May 2018, the ruling coalition since independence fell to the opposition; 92-year-old former leader **Mahathir** Mohamad became prime minister. In **Indonesia** protests followed the May 2019 reelection of Pres. Joko **Widodo**. In **Japan**, Prince **Naruhito** acceded to the throne, May 2019, following abdication of Emperor **Akihito** after 30-year reign.

Trans-Pacific Partnership (TPP), trade pact covering 12 Pacific nations, was signed Feb. 2016; after new U.S. administration repudiated it, remaining nations signed replacement, Mar. 2018.

Africa. Coups ousted **Niger**'s president (Feb. 2010) and ended elections in **Guinea-Bissau** (Apr. 2012); in both cases, civilian rule returned following new elections. In a referendum, southern Sudanese (mostly Christian or indigenous religion) voted overwhelmingly for separation from the north (mostly Arab Muslim), and **South Sudan** was granted independence as

Leaders of North Korea and South Korea, two nations still technically at war, held summits in Apr., May, and Sept. 2018.

After a gunman killed 51 at two Christchurch-area mosques in Mar. 2019, New Zealand Prime Min. Jacinda Ardern called for reforms; Parliament the next month outlawed many weapons and launched a gun buyback program.

of July 2011. An ethnic-based leadership struggle led to **civil war** in South Sudan, beginning Dec. 2013, with thousands killed, famine conditions, millions displaced; peace deal signed Sept. 2018. After a coup in **Mali** (Mar. 2012), junta ceded power to civilians, but Islamic rebels seized control in the north. French and West African forces intervened; a peace deal (June 2013) proved fragile. Armed attackers killed over 130 mostly Islamic villagers in central Mali, Mar. 2019; ISIS attacks on military posts in Mali and Niger, Sept.-Dec. 2019, killed close to 200 soldiers. Former **Liberian** Pres. Charles **Taylor** was convicted of war crimes, Apr. 2012. The Muslim Seleka coalition overran **Central African Republic**'s capital and seized power (Mar. 2013), precipitating civil war; UN peacekeepers were brought in; new president elected, Feb. 2016.

In **Burkina Faso**, longtime Pres. Blaise **Campaoré** fled amid protests (Oct. 2014); elections in Dec. 2015 brought in new government. In **Nigeria**, former dictator Muhammadu **Buhari** was elected president, Mar. 2015; reelected 2019 amid ethnic violence. During the decade, thousands of Nigerians were killed in attacks by **Boko Haram** jihadists and in land-use conflicts between mostly Christian farmers and mostly Muslim herders. In **Burundi** hundreds died and thousands were displaced in violent antigovernment clashes (starting Apr. 2015) and their repression.

An African Union court, June 2016, convicted Hissène **Habré** of crimes against humanity while ruler of **Chad** in the 1980s. In **Gambia** longtime Pres. Yahya **Jammeh** reluctantly yielded power, Jan. 2017, after election defeat. In **Zimbabwe** Pres. Robert **Mugabe**, in power since 1980, resigned, Nov. 2017, after house arrest by military and impeachment threat. In **South Africa**, Jacob **Zuma**, president since 2009, resigned Feb. 2018, amid corruption charges. **Ethiopia** and **Eritrea** opened their common border for the first time in 20 years (Sept. 2018). Ailing **Algerian** Pres. Abdelaziz **Bouteflika** stepped down, Apr. 2019, following protests over his plans to seek fifth term. After months of demonstrations, Omar al-**Bashir**, president of **Sudan** since a 1989 coup, was deposed in Apr. 2019 and imprisoned; protests demanding civilian rule were repressed (over 100 protesters killed); a power sharing agreement, July 2019, led to transitional government pending elections. Bashir was convicted of money laundering and corruption, Dec. 2019.

An **Ebola** epidemic in W Africa (2014-15) caused over 11,000 deaths, mostly in Guinea, Liberia, and Sierra Leone.

Americas and the Caribbean.
In **Haiti** an earthquake (Jan. 2010) killed over 200,000; lingering **cholera** epidemic introduced by aid workers left thousands more dead.

Poverty and violence fueled by drug cartels spurred **migration** to the U.S. from **Mexico, El Salvador, Honduras,** and **Guatemala.** In the **U.S.,** Pres. Barack **Obama** was reelected, Nov. 2012. Real estate magnate Donald **Trump** staged an upset to win election, Nov. 2016, as U.S. president, after populist campaign that made treatment of **illegal immigration** a focus. Trump was impeached on charges of abuse of power and obstruction of justice, Dec. 2019, but acquitted (Feb. 2020) by the Senate.

U.S., under Pres. Obama, restored relations with **Cuba,** July 2015. Miguel **Díaz-Canel** succeeded Raúl Castro as Cuba's president, Apr. 2018. With Trump administration opposing

NAFTA, the U.S., Canada, and Mexico signed revised trade agreement (**USMCA**), Nov. 2018.

In **Canada,** Conservatives, under Prime Min. Stephen **Harper,** won a majority in May 2011 elections. Liberals came back to win decisively in Oct. 2015 under charismatic party leader Justin **Trudeau;** weakened by political scandal, he formed a minority government after losses in Oct. 2019 elections. In **Mexico,** leftist candidate Andrés Manuel **López Obrador** was elected president, July 2018, following a campaign in which over 100 politicians were murdered.

Several leftist regimes suffered setbacks. In **Chile,** Pres. Michelle **Bachelet** was replaced by billionaire conservative Sebastián **Piñera** following Jan. 2010 election; after she returned for second term, Piñera was returned to office, Dec. 2017. In **Nicaragua** leftist Pres. Daniel **Ortega** twice won reelections challenged as flawed (Nov. 2011, 2016); protests, beginning Apr. 2018, were violently suppressed (over 300 killed, hundreds jailed, some tortured). In **Venezuela,** Pres. Hugo **Chávez** died Mar. 2013. Under his ally and elected successor Nicolás **Maduro** Moros, the economy collapsed into chaos; millions fled. Results of a legislative election (Dec. 2015) won by the opposition were cast aside; mass protests saw heavy casualties. Maduro was installed for new term, Jan. 2019, after reelection denounced as fraudulent. In **Brazil,** with a declining economy and leftist presidents **Lula** da Silva and Dilma **Rousseff** damaged by corruption scandals, far-right populist Jair **Bolsonaro** was elected president, Oct. 2018. In **Bolivia** leftist Pres. Evo **Morales** resigned, Nov. 2019, after widespread unrest; an interim right-wing president was appointed, pending elections. **Peru**'s voters elected a conservative, Pedro Pablo **Kuczynski,** as president (June 2016), but he resigned, Mar. 2018, in corruption scandal. **Argentine** voters ended 12 years of Peronist rule, choosing center-right candidate Mauricio **Macri** as president (Nov. 2015). After over 50 years of fighting, the **Colombian** government signed peace accord (Nov. 2016) with Revolutionary Army of Colombia (**FARC**) guerrillas, but conflict continued.

Uruguay (Dec. 2013) and **Canada** (June 2018) became first countries to fully legalize **marijuana.** Extradited Mexican drug kingpin known as **"El Chapo"** was convicted on drug trafficking and other charges by U.S. jury, Feb. 2019.

Religion.
Pope Benedict XVI resigned, Feb. 2013; Argentinean Cardinal Jorge Mario Bergoglio was elected to succeed him, taking the name **Francis.** He stressed poverty, environment, and migrant rights as issues, convened summit in Rome (Feb. 2019) on **clerical sex abuse.** Australian Cardinal George **Pell** was convicted on sex abuse charges, Dec. 2018; conviction overturned Apr. 2020.

U.S. State Dept., Dec. 2018, cited 10 countries as of "particular concern" for violations of **religious freedom:** China, Eritrea, Iran, Myanmar (Burma), North Korea, Pakistan, Saudi Arabia, Sudan, Tajikistan, and Turkmenistan. The advisory U.S. Commission on Intl. Religious Freedom added six more, Apr. 2019: Central African Republic, Nigeria, Russia, Syria, Uzbekistan, and Vietnam.

Science, technology, environment.
After 30 years, NASA's **space shuttle** program ended with return of *Atlantis* to Earth (July 2011). NASA's rover *Curiosity* landed on **Mars,** Aug. 2012; **China** landed unmanned *Yulu* rover on moon, Dec. 2013, and space probe on moon's far side, Dec. 2018. NASA's Kepler/K2 missions ended, Oct. 2018, having found over 2,600 exoplanets. **Ransomware** emerged as increasing global threat with launch of CryptoLocker (Sept. 2013) and other cyberattacks. Scientists, Feb. 2016, reported direct observation of **gravitational waves,** confirming Einstein prediction. Two new **Boeing 737 Max 8 jets** with automated anti-stall system crashed after takeoff (Oct. 2018, Mar. 2019; 346 died); model was grounded pending probes. Rogue scientist in **China** announced (Nov. 2018) first **genetically altered** human babies.

Representatives of 195 nations, meeting in Paris (Dec. 2015), committed to individual plans for reductions in greenhouse gas emissions linked to **climate change;** the U.S., however, initiated formal process, Nov. 2019, to withdraw. **Global Climate Strike** protests (Sept. 2019), inspired by Swedish teen activist Greta **Thunberg,** drew millions of participants around the world. Average **global temperatures** for the decade were the highest recorded, with 2016 at the top, followed by 2019.

A European **heat wave** (summer 2019) brought temperature records to locations in France, Spain, Germany, Switzerland, and Austria. **Flooding** in Venice (Nov. 2019) reached its highest level since 1966.

HISTORICAL FIGURES

Note: Information accurate as of Sept. 2020.

Ancient Greeks and Romans

Greeks

Aeschines, orator, 389-314 BCE
Aeschylus, dramatist, 525-456 BCE
Aesop, fableist, c. 620-c. 5 60 BCE
Alcibiades, politician, 450-404 BCE
Anacreon, poet, c. 582-c. 485 BCE
Anaxagoras, philosopher, c. 500-428 BCE
Anaximander, philosopher, 611-546 BCE
Anaximenes, philosopher, c. 570-500 BCE
Antiphon, speechwriter, c. 480-411 BCE
Apollonius, mathematician, c. 265-170 BCE
Archimedes, mathematician, 287-212 BCE
Aristophanes, dramatist, c. 448-380 BCE
Aristotle, philosopher, 384-322 BCE
Athenaeus, scholar, fl. c. 200
Callicrates, architect, fl. 5th cent. BCE
Callimachus, poet, c. 305-240 BCE
Cratinus, comic dramatist, 520-421 BCE
Democritus, philosopher, c. 460-370 BCE
Demosthenes, orator, 384-322 BCE
Diodorus, historian, fl. 20 BCE
Diogenes, philosopher, c. 400-c. 325 BCE
Dionysius, historian, d. c. 7 BCE
Empedocles, philosopher, c. 490-430 BCE
Epicharmus, dramatist, c. 530-440 BCE
Epictetus, philosopher, c. 55-c. 135
Epicurus, philosopher, 341-270 BCE
Eratosthenes, scientist, 276-194 BCE
Euclid, mathematician, fl. c. 300 BCE
Euripides, dramatist, c. 484-406 BCE
Galen, physician, 129-200
Heraclitus, philosopher, c. 540-c. 480 BCE
Herodotus, historian, c. 484-420 BCE

Hesiod, poet, 8th cent. BCE
Hippocrates, physician, c. 460-377 BCE
Homer, poet, fl. c. 8th cent. BCE
Isocrates, orator, 436-338 BCE
Menander, dramatist, 342-292 BCE
Parmenides, philosopher, c. 515-440 BCE
Pericles, statesman, c. 495-429 BCE
Phidias, sculptor, fl. 490-430 BCE
Pindar, poet, c. 518-c. 438 BCE
Plato, philosopher, c. 428-347 BCE
Plutarch, biographer, c. 46-120
Polybius, historian, c. 200-c. 118 BCE
Praxiteles, sculptor, 400-330 BCE
Pythagoras, phil., math., c. 580-c. 500 BCE
Sappho, poet, c. 610-c. 580 BCE
Simonides, poet, 556-c. 468 BCE
Socrates, philosopher, 469-399 BCE
Solon, statesman, 640-560 BCE
Sophocles, dramatist, c. 496-406 BCE
Strabo, geographer, c. 63 BCE-24 CE
Thales, philosopher, c. 634-546 BCE
Themistocles, politician, c. 524-c. 460 BCE
Theocritus, poet, c. 310-250 BCE
Theophrastus, phil., c. 372-c. 287 BCE
Thucydides, historian, fl. 5th cent. BCE
Timon, philosopher, c. 320-c. 230 BCE
Xenophon, historian, c. 434-c. 355 BCE
Zeno, philosopher, c. 335-c. 263 BCE

Romans

Ammianus, historian, c. 330-395
Apuleius, satirist, c. 124-c. 170
Boethius, scholar, c. 480-524
Caesar, Julius, leader, 100-44 BCE

Catiline, politician, c. 108-62 BCE
Cato (Elder), statesman, 234-149 BCE
Catullus, poet, c. 84-54 BCE
Cicero, orator, 106-43 BCE
Claudian, poet, c. 370-c. 404
Ennius, poet, 239-170 BCE
Gellius, author, c. 130-c. 165
Horace, poet, 65-8 BCE
Juvenal, satirist, 60-127
Livy, historian, 59 BCE-17 CE
Lucan, poet, 39-65
Lucilius, poet, c. 180-c.102 BCE
Lucretius, poet, c. 99-c. 55 BCE
Martial, epigrammatist, c. 38-c. 103
Nepos, historian, c. 100-c. 25 BCE
Ovid, poet, 43 BCE-17 CE
Persius, satirist, 34-62
Plautus, dramatist, c. 254-c. 184 BCE
Pliny the Elder, scholar, 23-79
Pliny the Younger, author, 62-113
Quintilian, rhetorician, c. 35-c. 97
Sallust, historian, 86-34 BCE
Seneca, philosopher, 4 BCE-65 CE
Silius, poet, c. 25-101
Statius, poet, c. 45-c. 96
Suetonius, biographer, c. 69-c. 122
Tacitus, historian, 56-120
Terence, dramatist, 195/185-c. 159 BCE
Tibullus, poet, c. 55-c. 19 BCE
Virgil (or Vergil), poet, 70-19 BCE
Vitruvius, architect, fl. late 1st cent. BCE

Roman Rulers

From Romulus to the end of the Empire in the West (Rome). Rulers in the East sat in Constantinople and, for a brief period, in Nicaea, until the capture of Constantinople by the Turks in 1453, when Byzantium was succeeded by the Ottoman Empire.

The Kingdom

BCE
753 Romulus (Quirinus)
715 Numa Pompilius
673 Tullus Hostilius
641 Ancus Marcius
616 L. Tarquinius Priscus
579 Servius Tullius
534 L. Tarquinius Superbus

The Republic

509 Consulate established;
    Quaestorship instituted
498 Dictatorship introduced
494 Plebeian Tribunate created;
    Plebeian Aedileship created
444 Consular Tribunate organized
435 Censorship instituted
366 Praetorship established;
    Curule Aedileship created
362 Military Tribunate elected
326 Proconsulate introduced
311 Naval Duumvirate elected
217 Dictatorship of Fabius Maximus
133 Tribunate of Tiberius Gracchus
123 Tribunate of Gaius Gracchus
82 Dictatorship of Sulla
60 First Triumvirate formed
    (Caesar, Pompeius, Crassus)
47 Dictatorship of Caesar
43 Second Triumvirate formed
    (Octavianus, Antonius, Lepidus)

The Empire

27 Augustus (or Octavian)
CE
14 Tiberius
37 Caligula
41 Claudius
54 Nero
68 Galba
69 Otho; Vitellius; Vespasian,
    established Flavian Dynasty
79 Titus
81 Domitian, end of Flavian Dynasty

96 Nerva
98 Trajan
117 Hadrian
138 Antoninus Pius
161 Marcus Aurelius and Lucius Verus
169 Marcus Aurelius (alone)
177 Marcus Aurelius and Commodus
180 Commodus
193 Pertinax
193 Didius Julianus
193 Septimius Severus, founded
    Severan Dynasty
211 Caracalla and Geta
212 Caracalla (alone)
217 Macrinus
218 Elagabalus (or Heliogabalus)
222 Alexander Severus, end of dynasty
235 Maximinus (the Thracian)
238 Gordian I and Gordian II
238 Pupienus and Balbinus
238 Gordian III
244 Philip (the Arabian)
249 Decius
251 Gallus and Volusianus
253 Aemilian
253 Valerian and Gallienus
258 Gallienus (alone)
268 Claudius II (or Claudius Gothicus)
270 Quintillus
270 Aurelian
275 Tacitus
276 Florian
276 Probus
282 Carus
283 Carinus and Numerian
284 Diocletian
286 Diocletian and Maximian
305 Galerius and Constantius I
306 Galerius, Maximinus (or
    Maximinus Daia), Severus
307 Galerius, Maximinus (Daia),
    Constantine I, Licinius, Maxentius
311 Maximinus (Daia), Constantine I,
    Licinius, Maxentius

314 Constantine I, Licinius
324 Constantine I (the Great), first
    Christian emperor
337 Constantine II, Constans I,
    Constantius II
340 Constantius II and Constans I
353 Constantius II (alone)
361 Julian (the Apostate)
363 Jovian

West (Rome) and East (Constantinople)

364 Valentinian I (West),
    Valens (East)
367 Valentinian I with Gratian (W),
    Valens (E)
375 Gratian with Valentinian II (W),
    Valens (E)
379 Gratian with Valentinian II (W),
    Theodosius I (E)
383 Magnus Maximus and
    Valentinian II (W),
    Theodosius I (E)
388 Valentinian II (W), Theodosius I (E)
392 Eugenius (W), Theodosius I (E)
394 Theodosius I (the Great)
395 Honorius (W), Arcadius (E)
408 Honorius (W), Theodosius II (E)
423 Valentinian III (W),
    Theodosius II (E)
450 Valentinian III (W), Marcian (E)
455 Petronius Maximus (W),
    Marcian (E)
455 Avitus (W), Marcian (E)
457 Majorian (W), Leo I (E)
461 Libius Severus (W), Leo I (E)
467 Anthemius (W), Leo I (E)
472 Olybrius (W), Leo I (E)
473 Glycerius (W), Leo I (E)
474 Julius Nepos (W), Leo II (E)
475 Romulus Augustulus (W), Zeno (E)
476 End of Empire in W when Romulus
    Augustulus deposed by Germanic
    chief Odoacer, who was later
    murdered by King Theodoric of
    Ostrogoths, 493

Rulers of England and the United Kingdom

Reign began	England: Saxons and Danes	Age at death[1]
829	Egbert, king of Wessex, won allegiance of all English	NA
839	Ethelwulf, son, king of Wessex, Sussex, Kent, Essex	NA
858	Ethelbald, eldest son, displaced father in Wessex	NA
860	Ethelbert, 2nd son of Ethelwulf, united Kent and Wessex	NA
866	Ethelred I, 3rd son of Ethelwulf, king of Wessex, fought Danes	NA
871	Alfred (the Great), 4th son of Ethelwulf, defeated Danes, fortified London	52
899	Edward (the Elder), son, united English, claimed Scotland	55
924	Athelstan (the Glorious), eldest son, king of Mercia, Wessex	45
940	Edmund, 3rd son of Edward, king of Wessex, Mercia	25
946	Edred, 4th son of Edward	32
955	Edwy (the Fair), eldest son of Edmund, king of Wessex	18
959	Edgar (the Peaceful), 2nd son of Edmund, ruled all English	32
975	Edward (the Martyr), eldest son, murdered by stepmother	17
978; 1014[2]	Ethelred II (the Unready), 2nd son of Edgar, married Emma of Normandy	48
1016	Edmund II (Ironside), son, king of London	27
1016	Canute (the Dane), son of Sweyn, who conquered English territory; gave Wessex to Edmund II; married Emma, Ethelred II's widow	40
1035	Harold I (Harefoot), illegitimate son	NA
1040	Hardecanute, son of Canute by Emma, also king of Denmark	24
1042	Edward (the Confessor), son of Ethelred II, canonized 1161	62
1066	Harold II, brother-in-law, last Saxon king	44

	England: House of Normandy	
1066	William I (the Conqueror), son of Duke Robert I of Normandy, defeated Harold II at Hastings	60
1087	William II (Rufus), 3rd son, killed by arrow while hunting in possible assassination	43
1100	Henry I (Beauclerc), youngest son of William I	67

	England: House of Blois	
1135	Stephen, son of Adela, daughter of William I, and Count of Blois	50

	England: House of Plantagenet	
1154	Henry II, son of Geoffrey Plantagenet (Angevin) by Matilda, daughter of Henry I	56
1189	Richard I (Coeur de Lion), son, crusader	42
1199	John (Lackland), son of Henry II, approved Magna Carta, 1215	50
1216	Henry III, son, acceded at 9, under regency until 1227	65
1272	Edward I (Longshanks), son	68
1307	Edward II, son, deposed by Parliament	43
1327	Edward III (of Windsor), son	65
1377	Richard II, grandson of Edward III, deposed	30

	England: House of Lancaster	
1399	Henry IV (of Bolingbroke), son of John of Gaunt, duke of Lancaster, son of Edward III	47
1413	Henry V, son, victor over French at Agincourt	34
1422; 1470	Henry VI, son, overthrown by Edward IV in 1461 but was returned to throne in 1470. Deposed, died in Tower of London, 1471	49

	England: House of York	
1461; 1471	Edward IV, great-great-grandson of Edward III, son of duke of York. Acclaimed king by Parliament, 1461. Driven into exile in 1470 but regained throne, 1471	40
1483	Edward V, son, murdered in Tower of London	13
1483	Richard III, brother of Edward IV, fell in battle at Bosworth Field against Henry Tudor	32

Reign began	England: House of Tudor	Age at death[1]
1485	Henry VII, son of Edmund Tudor, earl of Richmond, whose father had married Henry V's widow. Descended from Edward III through mother, Margaret Beaufort, via John of Gaunt. Married Elizabeth of York, eldest daughter of Edward IV, to unite Lancaster and York.	53
1509	Henry VIII, 2nd son, by Elizabeth	56
1547	Edward VI, son, by Jane Seymour, his 3rd queen. Was persuaded by John Dudley to name Lady Jane Grey, his cousin and Dudley's daughter-in-law, his successor. Council of State proclaimed her queen, July 10, 1553, but she ruled only nine days before Mary Tudor overthrew her	16
1553	Mary I, daughter of Henry VIII, by his 1st wife, Catherine of Aragon	43
1558	Elizabeth I, daughter of Henry VIII, by his 2nd wife, Anne Boleyn	69

	Great Britain: House of Stuart	
1603	James I (James VI of Scotland), son of Mary, Queen of Scots. First to call self king of Great Britain; this became official with Acts of Union, 1707	59
1625	Charles I, only surviving son of James I	48

	Great Britain: Commonwealth	
1649	Declared upon execution of Charles I	NA

	Great Britain: Protectorate	
1653	Oliver Cromwell, served on Council of State, executive body of Commonwealth, following overthrow of monarchy. Named Lord Protector upon creation of Protectorate by 1653 Instrument of Government	59
1658	Richard Cromwell, 3rd son, resigned as Lord Protector amid civil war, 1659	86

	Great Britain: House of Stuart (restored)	
1660	Charles II, eldest son of Charles I, acceded to throne by Restoration, died without issue	55
1685	James II, 2nd son of Charles I, deposed 1688	68
1689	William III, son of William, Prince of Orange, by Mary, daughter of Charles I. Offered joint rule of throne with wife by Parliament	51
1689	Mary II, eldest daughter of James II and wife of William III, died 1694	33
1702	Anne, 2nd daughter of James II, assumed throne on William's death	49

	United Kingdom of Great Britain[3]: House of Hanover	
1714	George I, son of Elector of Hanover by Sophia, granddaughter of James I	67
1727	George II, only son, married Caroline of Brandenburg	77
1760	George III, grandson, married Charlotte of Mecklenburg	81
1820	George IV, eldest son, prince regent from Feb. 1811	67
1830	William IV, 3rd son of George III, married Adelaide of Saxe Meiningen	71
1837	Victoria, daughter of Edward, 4th son of George III; married Prince Albert of Saxe-Coburg and Gotha, 1840	81

	United Kingdom of Great Britain[3]: House of Saxe-Coburg-Gotha	
1901	Edward VII, eldest son, married Alexandra, Princess of Denmark	68

	United Kingdom of Great Britain[3]: House of Windsor[4]	
1910	George V, 2nd son, married Princess Mary of Teck	70
1936	Edward VIII, eldest son, acceded Jan. 20, abdicated Dec. 11	77
1936	George VI, 2nd son of George V, married Lady Elizabeth Bowes-Lyon	56
1952	Elizabeth II, elder daughter, acceded Feb. 6	NA

NA = Age/birthdate not certain or not applicable. (1) Except where noted, year of death is the same year the next ruler's reign began. (2) King Sweyn I of Denmark invaded England in 1013 and declared himself king. Ethelred II reclaimed the throne upon Sweyn's death in 1014. (3) Officially the United Kingdom of Great Britain and Ireland after Act of Union 1801 and the United Kingdom of Great Britain and Northern Ireland after Anglo-Irish Treaty of 1921 (name formalized 1927). (4) Name adopted by proclamation of George V, July 17, 1917, because of anti-German feeling during World War I.

Rulers of Scotland

Reign began	Name	Reign began	Name
846	Kenneth I, first Scot to rule both Scots and Picts	1306	Robert I (the Bruce), victor at Bannockburn, 1314. Treaty with England and secured throne, 1328
1005	Malcolm II, son of Kenneth II	1329	David II, only surviving son
1034	Duncan I, grandson, first general ruler	1371	Robert II (the Steward), son of Robert I's daughter Marjorie and Walter, steward of Scotland. First of Stewart line
1040	Macbeth, seized kingdom, slain by Malcolm Canmore	1390	Robert III, son
1057	Malcolm III (Canmore), eldest son of Duncan I	1406	James I, son, assassinated
1093	Donald III (the Fair), younger brother	1437	James II, son
1094	Duncan II, eldest son of Malcolm III by first wife	1460	James III, eldest son, possibly assassinated
1095	Donald III (restored)	1488	James IV, eldest son
1097	Edgar, 4th son of Malcolm III and Queen Margaret	1513	James V, eldest son, died at Battle of Flodden
1107	Alexander I, brother	1542	Mary (Queen of Scots), daughter, became queen before she was 1 week old. Married Francis II (d. 1560), son of King Henry II of France, 1558. Married her cousin, Henry Stewart, Lord Darnley (d. 1567), 1565. Married James Hepburn, Earl of Bothwell, 1567. Imprisoned by her cousin Elizabeth I of England, 1568; beheaded, 1587
1124	David I, brother		
1153	Malcolm IV (the Maiden), grandson		
1165	William (the Lion), brother		
1214	Alexander II, son		
1249	Alexander III, son		
1286	Margaret (Maid of Norway), granddaughter; died 1290 at age 8. (Interregnum, 1290-92)	1567	James VI, son of Mary and Lord Darnley, became James I, king of England, on Elizabeth's death, 1603. (Legislative union of Scotland and England as United Kingdom of Great Britain not official until Acts of Union, 1707)
1292	John Balliol, proclaimed king of Scotland by Edward I of England. (Interregnum, 1296-1306[1])		

Note: Not all rulers before 1005 are shown. (1) Edward I decreed annexation of Scotland to England, 1296, after defeating Balliol in battle. William Wallace led resistance, 1297-1305.

Prime Ministers of the United Kingdom

Titles are given on first mention only. C = Conservative; La. = Labour; Li. = Liberal; P = Peelite; T = Tory; W = Whig.

Entered office	Name (party)	Entered office	Name (party)	Entered office	Name (party)
1721	Sir Robert Walpole (W)[1]	1827	George Canning (T)	1894	Archibald Primrose, 5th Earl of Rosebery (Li.)
1742	Spencer Compton, 1st Earl of Wilmington (W)	1827	Frederick John Robinson, Viscount Goderich (T)	1895	Robert Gascoyne-Cecil (C)
1743	Henry Pelham (W)	1828	Arthur Wellesley, 1st Duke of Wellington (T)	1902	Arthur James Balfour (C)
1754	Thomas Pelham-Holles, 1st Duke of Newcastle (W)	1830	Charles Grey, 2nd Earl Grey (W)	1905	Sir Henry Campbell-Bannerman (Li.)
1756	William Cavendish, 4th Duke of Devonshire (W)	1834	William Lamb, 2nd Viscount Melbourne (W)	1908	Herbert Henry Asquith (Li.[2])
1757	Thomas Pelham-Holles (W)	1834	Arthur Wellesley (T)	1916	David Lloyd George (Li.[2])
1762	John Stuart, 3rd Earl of Bute (T)	1834	Sir Robert Peel, 2nd Baronet (C)	1922	Andrew Bonar Law (C)
1763	George Grenville (W)	1835	William Lamb (W)	1923	Stanley Baldwin (C)
1765	Charles Watson-Wentworth, 2nd Marquess of Rockingham (W)	1841	Sir Robert Peel (C)	1924	Ramsay MacDonald (La.)
1766	William Pitt the Elder, 1st Earl of Chatham (W)	1846	John Russell, 1st Earl Russell (W)	1924	Stanley Baldwin (C)
1768	Augustus Henry Fitzroy, 3rd Duke of Grafton (W)	1852	Edward Stanley, 14th Earl of Derby (T)	1929	Ramsay MacDonald (La.[2])
1770	Lord Frederick North (T)	1852	George Hamilton Gordon, 4th Earl of Aberdeen (P[2])	1935	Stanley Baldwin (C[2])
1782	Charles Watson-Wentworth (W)	1855	Henry John Temple, 3rd Viscount Palmerston (W-Li.)	1937	Neville Chamberlain (C[2])
1782	William Petty, 2nd Earl of Shelburne (W)	1858	Edward Stanley (T)	1940	Winston Churchill (C[2])
1783	William Cavendish-Bentinck, 3rd Duke of Portland (W[2])	1859	Henry John Temple (W-Li.)	1945	Clement Attlee (La.)
1783	William Pitt the Younger (T)	1865	John Russell (Li.)	1951	Winston Churchill (C)
1801	Henry Addington (T)	1866	Edward Stanley (C)	1955	Anthony Eden (C)
1804	William Pitt the Younger (T)	1868	Benjamin Disraeli (C)	1957	Harold Macmillan (C)
1806	William Wyndham Grenville, 1st Baron Grenville (W)	1868	William E. Gladstone (Li.)	1963	Alec Douglas-Home (C)
1807	William Cavendish-Bentinck (T)	1874	Benjamin Disraeli (C)	1964	Harold Wilson (La.)
1809	Spencer Perceval (T)	1880	William E. Gladstone (Li.)	1970	Edward Heath (C)
1812	Robert Banks Jenkinson, 2nd Earl of Liverpool (T)	1885	Robert Gascoyne-Cecil, 3rd Marquess of Salisbury (C)	1974	Harold Wilson (La.)
		1886	William E. Gladstone (Li.)	1976	James Callaghan (La.)
		1886	Robert Gascoyne-Cecil (C)	1979	Margaret Thatcher (C)
		1892	William E. Gladstone (Li.)	1990	John Major (C)
				1997	Tony Blair (La.)
				2007	Gordon Brown (La.)
				2010	David Cameron (C[2])
				2016	Theresa May (C)
				2019	Boris Johnson (C)

Note: Prime ministers prior to 1801 are for Great Britain. The Conservative Party was formed in 1834, an outgrowth of the Tory party. (1) Walpole is traditionally regarded as the first prime minister of Britain though the title was not commonly used then and did not become official until 1905. (2) Led a coalition government for all or part of time in office.

Prime Ministers of Canada

C = Conservative; Lib. = Liberal; PC = Progressive Conservative; U = Unionist

Entered office	Name (party)	Entered office	Name (party)	Entered office	Name (party)
1867	John A. Macdonald (C)	1921	W. L. Mackenzie King (Lib.)	1979	Joe Clark (PC)
1873	Alexander Mackenzie (Lib.)	1926[3]	Arthur Meighen (C)	1980	Pierre Trudeau (Lib.)
1878	John A. Macdonald (C)	1926	W. L. Mackenzie King (Lib.)	1984[3]	John Turner (Lib.)
1891	John Abbott (C)	1930	Richard Bedford Bennett (C)	1984	Brian Mulroney (PC)
1892	John Thompson (C)	1935	W. L. Mackenzie King (Lib.)	1993[4]	Kim Campbell (PC)
1894	Mackenzie Bowell (C)	1948	Louis St. Laurent (Lib.)	1993	Jean Chrétien (Lib.)
1896[1]	Charles Tupper (C)	1957	John G. Diefenbaker (PC)	2003	Paul Martin (Lib.)
1896	Wilfrid Laurier (Lib.)	1963	Lester B. Pearson (Lib.)	2006	Stephen Harper (C)
1911	Robert Borden (C/U)[2]	1968	Pierre Trudeau (Lib.)	2015	Justin Trudeau (Lib.)
1920	Arthur Meighen (U)				

(1) May-July. (2) Conservative 1911-17, Unionist 1917-20. (3) June-Sept. (4) June-Nov.

Rulers of France

Caesar to Charlemagne

Julius Caesar subdued the Gauls, native tribes of Gaul (France), 58 to 51 BCE. The Romans ruled 500 years. The Franks, a Teutonic tribe, reached the Somme from the east c. 250 CE. By the 5th cent., the Merovingian Franks ousted the Romans. In 451, with the help of Visigoths, Burgundians, and others, they defeated Attila and the Huns at Châlons-sur-Marne.

Childeric I became leader of the Merovingians, 458. After son Clovis I (crowned 481) defeated the Alemanni (Germans), 496, he was baptized a Christian and made Paris his capital. Line ended when Childeric III was deposed, 751.

The West Merovingians were called Neustrians, the eastern Austrasians. Pepin of Herstal (687-714), major domus (head of the palace) of Austrasia, took over Neustria as dux (leader) of the Franks. Pepin's son, Charles, called Martel (the Hammer), defeated the Saracens at Tours-Poitiers, 732; was succeeded in 741 by his sons, Pepin the Short and Carloman (abdicated 747). Pepin deposed Childeric III and ruled as king until 768.

His son, Charlemagne, or Charles the Great (742-814), became king of the Franks, 768, with his brother Carloman (751-71). Charlemagne ruled France, Germany, parts of Italy, Spain, and Austria, and enforced Christianity. Crowned Emperor of the Romans by Pope Leo III in Rome, 800. Succeeded by son, Louis I (the Pious), 814. At death, 840, Louis left empire to sons Lothair (Roman emperor), Pepin I (king of Aquitaine), Louis II (the German), and Charles II (the Bald, of France). They quarreled and, by the Treaty of Verdun, 843, divided the empire.

The date preceding each entry is year of accession.

Carolingian Dynasty

843 Charles II (the Bald), Roman emperor, 875
877 Louis II (the Stammerer), son
879 Louis III (d. 882), son, and brother Carloman
885 Charles III (the Fat), son of Louis the German, Roman emperor, 881
888 Eudes (Odo), son of Robert the Strong, elected by nobles
898 Charles III (the Simple), son of Louis II the Stammerer, deposed
922 Robert I, brother of Eudes, defeated forces of Charles III but died in battle
923 Rudolph (Raoul), Robert I's son-in-law, duke of Burgundy
936 Louis IV, son of Charles III (the Simple); struggled with Hugh the Great, son of Robert I
954 Lothair, son, dominated by Hugh the Great
986 Louis V (the Sluggard), left no heirs

House of Capet

987 Hugh Capet, son of Hugh the Great
996 Robert II (the Pious), son
1031 Henry I, son
1060 Philip I (the Fair), son
1108 Louis VI (the Fat), son
1137 Louis VII (the Younger), son
1180 Philip II Augustus, son, crowned at Reims
1223 Louis VIII (the Lion), son
1226 Louis IX, son, arbitrated disputes with English King Henry III; led crusades, 1248 (captured in Egypt, 1250) and 1270, when he died of plague in Tunis. Canonized as St. Louis, 1297
1270 Philip III (the Bold), son
1285 Philip IV (the Fair), son, king at 17
1314 Louis X (the Headstrong), son. His posthumous son, John I, lived and reigned only five days.
1316 Philip V (the Tall), brother of Louis X
1322 Charles IV (the Fair), brother of Louis X

House of Valois

1328 Philip VI (of Valois), grandson of Philip III
1350 John II (the Good), son, retired to England
1364 Charles V (the Wise), son
1380 Charles VI (the Beloved), son
1422 Charles VII (the Victorious), son. In 1429, Joan of Arc defeated English at Orleans and Patay and had Charles crowned at Reims. Joan was captured, 1430, and executed, 1431, at Rouen for heresy.
1461 Louis XI (the Cruel), son, civil reformer
1483 Charles VIII (the Affable), son
1498 Louis XII, great-grandson of Charles V
1515 Francis I, of Angouleme, nephew, son-in-law. Fought four major wars, was patron of the arts
1547 Henry II, son, killed at joust. Husband of Catherine (daughter of Lorenzo) de Médicis and lover of Diane de Poitiers. By marriage to Henry II, Catherine became the mother of Francis II, Charles IX, Henry III, and Queen Margaret (Reine Margot), wife of Henry IV (of Navarre).
1559 Francis II, son. Betrothed in 1548 at age 4 to Mary, Queen of Scots, aged 6; they were married 1558. Francis died 1560, aged 16. Mary returned to rule Scotland, 1561.

1560 Charles IX, brother
1574 Henry III, brother, assassinated

House of Bourbon

1589 Henry IV (of Navarre), grandson of Queen Margaret of Navarre. Made enemies when he gave tolerance to Protestants by Edict of Nantes, 1598. Married Margaret of Valois, daughter of Henry II and Catherine de Médicis; was divorced. Married Marie de Médicis, 1600. She became regent upon Henry's assassination, 1610-17, for her son, Louis XIII; she was exiled by Richelieu, 1631.
1610 Louis XIII (the Just), son, married Anne of Austria. His chief minister (1622-42), Cardinal Richelieu, determined his policies.
1643 Louis XIV (the Sun King); son; was king 72 years. Until 1661, Anne of Austria was regent with Cardinal Mazarin as chief minister; Louis then ruled absolutely. Known for lavish court and arts patronage, he exhausted the economy with wars for territory.
1715 Louis XV (the Beloved), great-grandson. Married a Polish princess, lost Canada to England. Favorite mistresses Mme. de Pompadour and Mme. Du Barry influenced policies. Pompadour's saying "Après moi, le déluge" (After me, the deluge) is often incorrectly attributed to Louis XV.
1774 Louis XVI, grandson, married Marie Antoinette, daughter of Empress Maria Therese of Austria. Couple executed by guillotine in French Revolution, 1793. Louis XVII, son, never ruled and died in prison.

First Republic

1792 National Convention of the French Revolution
1795 Directory, under Viscount of Barras and others
1799 Consulate, Napoleon Bonaparte, first consul. Elected consul for life, 1802

First Empire

1804 Napoleon I (Napoleon Bonaparte), emperor. Josephine (de Beauharnais), empress, 1804-09; Marie Louise, empress, 1810-14. Son, Napoleon II (1811-32), titular king of Rome, later duke of Reichstadt, never ruled. Napoleon I abdicated 1814; died in exile, 1821.

House of Bourbon (restored)

1814 Louis XVIII, brother of Louis XVI, king
1824 Charles X, brother, reactionary, deposed by the July Revolution, 1830

House of Orleans

1830 Louis-Philippe (the Citizen King)

Second Republic

1848 Louis Napoleon Bonaparte, nephew of Napoleon I, president

Second Empire

1852 Napoleon III (Louis Napoleon Bonaparte), emperor; Eugenie (de Montijo) (d. 1920), empress. Lost Franco-Prussian war, deposed 1870. Son, Prince Imperial (1856-79), died in Zulu War.

Third Republic

1871 Adolphe Thiers (1797-1877), president
1873 Patrice de Mac-Mahon (1808-93)
1879 Jules Grévy (1807-91)
1887 Sadi Carnot (1837-94), assassinated
1894 Jean Casimir-Périer (1847-1907)
1895 Félix Faure (1841-99)
1899 Émile Loubet (1838-1929)
1906 Armand Fallières (1841-1931)
1913 Raymond Poincaré (1860-1934)
1920 Paul Deschanel (1855-1922)
1920 Alexandre Millerand (1859-1943)
1924 Gaston Doumergue (1863-1937)
1931 Paul Doumer (1857-1932), assassinated
1932 Albert Lebrun (1871-1950), resigned 1940

Vichy Regime

1940 Philippe Pétain (1856-1951), chief of state, 1940-44, under German armistice

Provisional Government

1944 Charles de Gaulle (1890-1970)
1946 Félix Gouin (1884-1977)
1946 Georges Bidault (1899-1983)

Fourth Republic

1947 Vincent Auriol (1884-1966), president
1954 René Coty (1882-1962)

Fifth Republic

1959 Charles de Gaulle (1890-1970), president; resigned 1969. Alain Poher (1909-96), interim pres., Apr.-June 1969
1969 Georges Pompidou (1911-74); Poher, interim pres., Apr.-May 1974
1974 Valéry Giscard d'Estaing (1926-)
1981 François Mitterrand (1916-96)
1995 Jacques Chirac (1932-2019)
2007 Nicolas Sarkozy (1955-)
2012 François Hollande (1954-)
2017 Emmanuel Macron (1977-)

Rulers of Middle Europe and Germany

Carolingian Dynasty

Charles I (the Great), or Charlemagne, made Roman emperor by pope in Rome, 800. Ruled France, Italy, and Middle Europe; established Ostmark (later Austria). Died 814.

Louis I (Ludwig) (the Pious), son, crowned co-emperor by Charlemagne, 813. Divided empire among sons. Died 840; sons fought for control.

Louis II (the German), son, succeeded to East Francia (Germany), 843-76, with Treaty of Verdun.

Charles III (the Fat), son, inherited Swabia, 876. With brothers' deaths, acquired East Francia and West Francia (France), reuniting empire. Crowned emperor by pope, 881; deposed 887.

Arnulf, nephew, 887-99, took over East Francia; partition of empire.

Louis IV (the Child), son, 900-11, last direct descendant of Charlemagne.

Conrad I, duke of Franconia, first elected German king, 911-18.

Saxon Dynasty; First Reich

Henry I (the Fowler), duke of Saxony, elected king 919-36.

Otto I (the Great), son, 936-73, crowned Holy Roman Emperor by pope, 962.

Otto II, son, 961-83, ruled with Otto I as king, then emperor, 967.

Otto III, son, 983-1002, crowned Holy Roman Emperor, 996.

Henry II (the Saint), great-grandson of Otto the Great, duke of Bavaria, 1002-24. Crowned emperor, 1014.

Salian Dynasty

Conrad II, 1024-39, elected king of Germany.

Henry III (the Black), son, 1039-56, deposed three popes; annexed Burgundy.

Henry IV, son, 1056-1106, with mother, Agnes of Poitou, as regent in early years. He and Pope Gregory VII tried to depose each other. Civil war lasted about 20 years.

Henry V, son, 1106-25, last of Salian Dynasty.

Lothair, duke of Saxony, elected king 1125-37. Crowned emperor in Rome, 1133.

Hohenstaufen Dynasty

Conrad III, duke of Franconia, 1138-52, in Second Crusade.

Frederick I (Barbarossa, Italian for "Redbeard"), nephew, 1152-90.

Henry VI, son, 1190-97, gained kingdom of Sicily through marriage.

Philip of Swabia, brother, 1197-1208. Otto IV, nephew of King Richard I of England, 1198-1215, was elected rival king. Philip's murder, in 1208, led to Otto's win in new election same year. Civil war followed before Otto was deposed, 1215.

Frederick II, son of Henry VI, elected 1212-50. Had earlier succeeded father as king of Sicily; crowned himself king of Jerusalem, 1229, in Sixth Crusade.

Conrad IV, son, 1250-54. Conquered Naples.

(Interregnum, 1254-73. Conradin, son of Conrad IV and last legitimate Hohenstaufen, defeated by Charles of Anjou—brother of King Louis IX of France—and executed, 1268. Rise of electors of German monarch.)

Transition

Rudolf I, of Habsburg, 1273-91, defeated King Ottocar II of Bohemia, 1278. Bequeathed duchies of Austria and Styria to sons.

Adolf of Nassau, 1292-98, killed in war with Albert I.

Albert I, elder son of Rudolf I, 1298-1308, assassinated.

Henry VII, of Luxemburg, 1308-13. Gained Bohemia, 1310; crowned Holy Roman Emperor, 1312.

Louis IV, of Wittelsbach, 1314-46. Also elected was a son of Albert I, Frederick of Austria, whom Louis defeated in 1322. Rejected need for papal confirmation of elected German king.

Charles IV, of Luxemburg, grandson of Henry VII, 1346-78. Took Brandenburg.

Wenceslaus, son, 1378-1400; deposed.

Rupert, of Wittelsbach, elector palatine, 1400-10.

Sigismund, brother of Wenceslaus, 1410-37.

Habsburg Dynasty

Albert II, duke of Austria, son-in-law of Sigismund, elected German king, 1438-39; king of Hungary and Holy Roman Emperor.

Frederick III, cousin, 1440-93, fought Turks.

Maximilian I, son, 1493-1519, archduke of Austria.

Charles V, grandson, 1519-58. King of Spain; assumed title of Holy Roman Emperor. Martin Luther, who had been excommunicated by pope, appeared at Diet of Worms, 1521. Charles attempted church reform and conciliation between Catholicism and Protestantism; abdicated.

Ferdinand I, brother, 1558-64; king of Hungary and Bohemia, 1526 (successive leaders through Maria Theresa will rule these lands as well).

Maximilian II, son, 1564-76.

Rudolf II, son, 1576-1612.

Matthias, brother, 1612-19.

Ferdinand II, grandson of Ferdinand I, 1619-37. Bohemian Protestants, unhappy with Ferdinand's support of Catholic Counter-Reformation, crowned Frederick V, elector palatine. Frederick became known as "Winter King" with defeat in battle, 1620; start of Thirty Years' War.

Ferdinand III, son, 1637-57. Treaties signed, 1648, in Peace of Westphalia ended war.

Leopold I, son, 1658-1705.

Joseph I, son, 1705-11.

Charles VI, brother, 1711-40; died without male heir.

Maria Theresa, daughter, 1740-80. Appointed husband, Francis Stephen of Lorraine, co-regent. Dispute over her inheritance led to War of the Austrian Succession. Charles VII, also known as Charles Albert, elected in opposition to Francis, 1742-45. After Charles's death, Maria Theresa obtained election of her husband as Holy Roman Emperor Francis I, 1745-65. Fought Seven Years' War with Frederick II of Prussia.

Habsburg-Lorraine Dynasty

Joseph II, son, 1765-90, reformer. Ruled jointly with Maria Theresa until her death. Participated in first partition of Poland, with Prussia and Russia.

Leopold II, brother, 1790-92; king of Hungary and Bohemia.

Francis II, son, 1792-1806; king of Hungary and Bohemia. Proclaimed first emperor of Austria, 1804-35. Unsuccessfully fought against Napoleon; forced to abdicate, 1806, as Holy Roman Emperor, last use of title.

Ferdinand, son, 1835-48, emperor of Austria; king of Hungary and Bohemia. Abdicated in favor of nephew after revolution broke out in Vienna.

Austro-Hungarian Monarchy

Francis Joseph I, nephew, 1848-1916, emperor of Austria and king of Hungary. Defeated in Austro-Prussian War, 1866. Formed dual monarchy of Austria-Hungary, 1867. After Serbian nationalist assassinated Francis Joseph's nephew and heir, Archduke Francis Ferdinand, June 28, 1914, Austrian diplomacy precipitated World War I.

Charles I, grandnephew, 1916-18, last emperor of Austria and king of Hungary. Abdicated Nov. 1918; died in exile, 1922.

Second and Third Reichs

William I, brother of Frederick William IV, 1861-88, king of Prussia. Appointed Otto von Bismarck chancellor, 1862. Franco-Prussian War, also known as Franco-German War, 1870-71, unified German states. William proclaimed German emperor, 1871; beginning of Second Reich.

Frederick III, son, 1888.

William II, son, 1888-1918, led Germany into World War I. Abdicated Nov. 1918; died in exile in the Netherlands, 1941.

Germany adopted constitution at Weimar, July 1, 1919, setting up Weimar Republic. Presidents included Friedrich Ebert, 1919-25, and Paul von Hindenburg, 1925-34, field marshal in World War I. Hindenburg appointed Adolf Hitler chancellor, 1933, at beginning of Third Reich. Following Hindenburg's death, Hitler succeeded as Führer and chancellor, 1934-45, with dictatorial powers. Annexed Austria, 1938. Precipitated World War II, 1939-45. Hitler committed suicide, 1945.

Germany After 1945

After World War II, Germany was split between democratic West German and Soviet-dominated East. West German chancellors: Konrad Adenauer, 1949-63; Ludwig Erhard, 1963-66; Kurt Georg Kiesinger, 1966-69; Willy Brandt, 1969-74; Helmut Schmidt, 1974-82; Helmut Kohl, 1982-90. East German Communist party leaders: Walter Ulbricht, 1950-71; Erich Honecker, 1971-89; Egon Krenz, 1989. (Berlin Wall fell, Nov. 1989.)

Germany reunited Oct. 3, 1990. Post-reunification chancellors: Helmut Kohl, 1990-98; Gerhard Schröder, 1998-2005; Angela Merkel, 2005- .

Rulers of Hungary

The first king of Hungary was Stephen I, of the Arpad Dynasty, 1000-38. Feuds followed his death.

Charles I, also known as Charles Robert, became king, 1308-42.

Louis I (the Great), son, 1342-82. Succeeded uncle Casimir III as ruler of Poland, 1370.

Mary, elder daughter, 1382-95, ruled with husband, Sigismund of Luxemburg, 1387-1437, who also became king of Bohemia, Germany and Holy Roman Emperor. Hedwig (Jadwiga), younger daughter of Louis I, became queen of Poland. (See **Rulers of Poland**.)

Albert II, duke of Austria, son-in-law of Sigismund, 1438-39. Also king of Germany and Holy Roman Emperor.

Vladislaus I, 1440-44, king of Poland.

Ladislaus V, posthumous son of Albert II, 1444-57, not crowned until 1453. Janos Hunyadi acted as governor under young king, 1446-52; fought Turks.

Matthias I (Corvinus), son of Janos Hunyadi, 1458-90. Shared title of king of Bohemia. Captured Vienna, 1485; annexed Styria, Carinthia.

Vladislaus II, 1490-1516, king of Bohemia.

Louis II, son, 1516-26. Died in Battle of Mohács against Suleiman (the Magnificent), head of Ottoman Empire.

Ferdinand I, of Austria, brother-in-law, and John I, also known as John Zapolya of Transylvania, elected rival kings. Suleiman claimed part of Hungary for Ottoman Empire. Hungary partitioned. (Refer to **Habsburg Dynasty** for continuation.)

Rulers of Prussia

Nucleus of Prussia was the margravate of Brandenburg, an electorate of the Holy Roman Empire. Frederick VI, burgrave of Nuremberg, was made elector of Brandenburg, 1415. Rise of Hohenzollern Dynasty in territory that included Brandenburg and duchy of Prussia.

Frederick William (the Great Elector), 1640-88, elector of Brandenburg.

Frederick III, son, 1688-1713, elector of Brandenburg. Crowned Frederick I, king in Prussia, 1701.

Frederick William I, son, 1713-40.

Frederick II (the Great), son, 1740-86; military strategist who expanded Prussia's holdings.

Frederick William II, nephew, 1786-97.

Frederick William III, son, 1797-1840; Napoleonic Wars.

Frederick William IV, son, 1840-61. Revolution of 1848; constitution adopted, 1850. (Refer to **Second and Third Reichs** for continuation.)

Rulers of Poland

House of Piast

Mieszko I, c. 963-92, duke of Poland; Poland Christianized, 966. Expansion under three with name Boleslaus (reigns not consecutive): Boleslaus I (the Brave), son, 992-1025, crowned first king of Poland, 1025; Boleslaus II (the Bold), great-grandson, 1058-79, exiled after killing bishop of Krakow, Stanislaus (who became a patron saint of Poland); Boleslaus III (the Wry-Mouthed), nephew, 1102-38, divided Poland among four sons with oldest also in control of crown. Period of feudal division followed.

A Polish duke, Conrad of Masovia, asked the Teutonic Knights—a German military religious order—to crusade against Prussia, 1226. Teutonic Knights conquered lands; thereafter warred with Poland. Mongols/Tatars invaded Poland, 1241.

Vladislaus I, 1306-33, reunited most Polish territories; crowned king, 1320. Casimir III (the Great), son, 1333-70, developed economy, cultural life, foreign policy. No male heir. Succeeded by Louis I, nephew, 1370-82, who was also Louis I (the Great) of Hungary.

Jadwiga, daughter, 1384-99.

House of Jagiello

Vladislaus Jagiello, grand duke of Lithuania, married Jadwiga, 1386, and ruled jointly as Vladislaus II, 1386-1434. Poland and Lithuania united; Lithuania converted to Christianity. Defeated Teutonic Knights at Grunwald (Tannenberg), 1410.

Vladislaus III, son, 1434-44, also king of Hungary. Fought Turks; killed in Battle of Varna, 1444.

Casimir IV, brother, 1447-92, put son Vladislaus on throne of Bohemia and Hungary. Victorious over Teutonic Knights; signed treaty, 1466, after 13-year war.

John I, son, 1492-1501.

Alexander I, brother, 1501-05.

Sigismund I, brother, 1506-48, patronized sciences and arts; his and son's reign were golden age. Grand Master of Teutonic Order, Albert Hohenzollern, converted to Protestantism; secularized his state and made first duke of Prussia by Sigismund, 1525.

Sigismund II, son, 1548-72; Union of Lublin, 1569, established dual state of Poland and Lithuania. No male heir.

Elective Kings

Henry of Valois, 1573-74, first king elected by nobility. Left Poland to assume crown of France after brother's death. Interregnum.

Stephen Bathory, 1576-86, prince of Transylvania, married Anna, sister of Sigismund II. Fought Russians.

Sigismund III Vasa, nephew of Sigismund II and son of king of Sweden, 1587-1632. Fought to reclaim Swedish crown, which he'd lost because of his Catholicism; battled Russians and Turks.

Vladislaus IV Vasa, son, 1632-48.

John II Casimir Vasa, brother, 1648-68. Fought Cossacks, Swedish, Russians, Turks, Tatars; period of invasions known as "the Deluge."

Michael Korybut Wisniowiecki, 1669-73.

John III Sobieski, 1674-96, freed Vienna from besieging Turks, 1683.

Augustus II (the Strong), 1697-1733, elector of Saxony.

Augustus III, son, 1733-63, elector of Saxony.

Stanislaus II, 1764-95, last king. Encouraged reforms; first modern constitution in Europe, 1791. Poland lost territory to Russia, Austria, and Prussia in three partitions (1772, 1793, 1795). Thaddeus Kosciusko, American-Polish general, attempted unsuccessful insurrection, 1794.

Poland Under Foreign Rule

Grand duchy of Warsaw created by Napoleon I out of Prussian (formerly Polish) territory. Frederick Augustus I, king of Saxony, ruled grand duchy, 1807-15. Defeat of Napoleon led to Congress of Vienna, 1814-15; part of Poland claimed as kingdom by Russia. Polish uprisings against Russia (1830, 1863) and Austria (1846) repressed. Poland regained independence following World War I.

Second Republic

Jozef Pilsudski, 1918-22, head of state. Presidents: Gabriel Narutowicz, 1922, assassinated by extremist; Stanislaus Wojciechowski, 1922-26, resigned after coup d'état by Pilsudski; Ignacy Moscicki, 1926-39, ruled with Pilsudski (d. 1935) and Pilsudski's military colleagues as virtual dictator during what came to be known as Sanacja (meaning "cleansing" or "healing") regime.

Poland Under Foreign Occupation, Influence

After Hitler and Stalin signed nonaggression pact, Germany invaded Poland Sept. 1, 1939; Russia invaded Sept. 17. Polish government-in-exile formed in France, then England. Vladislaus Raczkiewicz, 1939-47, president; Gen. Vladislaus Sikorski, 1939-43, and Stanislaus Mikolajczyk, 1943-44, prime ministers. Polish residents were sent to German concentration camps and Soviet labor camps; about 3 million Jewish Poles were killed in the Holocaust. Thousands of Polish prisoners of war, mostly military officers, massacred in Katyn Forest by Soviet secret police, 1940. Soviet-sponsored Polish Committee of National Liberation took formative role in new government, 1945, renamed Polish People's Republic in 1952. Communist Polish United Workers' Party ruled the country. Brief period of liberalization followed Stalin's death in 1953. Vladislaus Gomulka, 1956-70, and Edward Gierek, 1970-80, led country as first secretary of Polish United Workers' Party.

Election of Cardinal Karol Wojtyla, archbishop of Krakow, as pope (John Paul II) inspired Poles, 1978. Strikes in 1980 prompted creation of Solidarity, an independent trade union headed by Lech Walesa. Solidarity gained control of government in partly free elections, 1985.

Third Republic

Presidents: Lech Walesa, 1990-95; Aleksander Kwasniewski, 1995-2005; Lech Kaczynski, 2005, died in plane crash; Bronislaus Komorowski and Grzegorz Schetyna, acting, 2010; Komorowski, 2010-15; Andrzej Duda, 2015- .

Rulers of Denmark, Sweden, Norway

Denmark

Canute (the Great) ruled area that included England, Denmark, and Norway, 1016-35. Valdemar IV Atterdag reunited Denmark, 1361. Margaret I, daughter, married to Haakon VI, king of Norway, 1363. After Valdemar's death, Olaf, Margaret's infant son, made king of Denmark, 1375. He was also crowned king of Norway after death of Haakon, 1380. Following Olaf's death, 1387, Margaret served as regent of Denmark, Norway, and Sweden. She effected the Union of Kalmar of the three kingdoms, 1397. She had her grandnephew, Eric of Pomerania, crowned (she held actual power until her death, 1412).

Succeeding rulers were unable to enforce their claims on Sweden until Christian II, 1512-23, conquered the country, 1520. He was soon deposed; accession of Gustavus I as king of Sweden, 1523, ended Kalmar Union. Denmark continued to dominate Norway until the Napoleonic Wars when Frederick VI, 1808-39, allied with Napoleon I after Danish fleet was attacked by Britain, 1807. By 1814 treaty, Denmark was forced to cede Norway to Sweden.

Succession: House of Oldenborg (began with Christian I, 1448): Christian VIII, 1839-48; Frederick VII, son, 1848-63. House of Glücksburg: Christian IX, 1863-1906; Frederick VIII, son, 1906-12; Christian X, son, 1912-47; Frederick IX, son, 1947-72; Margrethe II, daughter, 1972- .

Sweden

Under King Magnus Ladulas, hereditary nobility established around 1280. Swedish nobles opposed to Albert of Mecklenburg accepted Margaret I, regent of Denmark, as ruler, 1389. Sweden joined Kalmar Union, 1397. After internal unrest, Sweden was conquered anew by Denmark's Christian II, 1520. Execution of Christian's opponents in "Stockholm Bloodbath" led to uprising under Gustavus Vasa, who was elected Swedish king, 1523-60. Gustavus established an independent kingdom with centralized power, state church, and hereditary throne.

Gustavus II Adolphus (Lion of the North), 1611-32, fought Russia, Poland, Germany; died in battle.

Later rulers: Christina, daughter, 1632-54, abdicated; Charles X Gustavus, cousin, 1654-60; Charles XI, son, 1660-97; Charles XII, son, 1697-1718; Ulrika Eleonora, sister, 1718-20, abdicated; Frederick I, of Hesse, husband, 1720-51; Adolphus Frederick, 1751-71; Gustavus III, son, 1771-92; Gustavus IV Adolphus, son, 1792-1809, deposed; Charles XIII, uncle, 1809-18. Charles XIV John (born Jean Baptiste Bernadotte, a general under Napoleon I), 1818-44, founded House of Bernadotte.

Succession: Oscar I, son, 1844-59; Charles XV, son, 1859-72; Oscar II, brother, 1872-1907; Gustavus V, son, 1907-50; Gustavus VI Adolf, son, 1950-73; Carl XVI Gustavus, grandson, 1973- .

Norway

Harald I (Fairhair) overcame rivals to become first king of Norway, c. 885-c. 933. Olaf II Haraldsson, 1015-28, Christianized country; became patron saint of Norway. Haakon V Magnusson, 1299-1319, died without male heir. His daughter Ingeborg was married to Erik, a son of the Norwegian king; their son Magnus VII Eriksson became ruler of Norway, 1319-55, and Sweden, 1319-63. Haakon VI Magnusson, son, 1355-80, married Margaret of Denmark. Olaf IV, son, became king of Norway, 1380-87, and Denmark, 1375-87, with mother as regent. Margaret took over rule upon his death, 1387. Union of Kalmar, 1397, united Norway, Denmark, and Sweden.

After Napoleonic Wars, Denmark ceded Norway to Sweden, 1814. A strong nationalist movement forced Norway to recognize Norway as an independent kingdom under the Swedish kings. Norwegian constitution, adopted 1814, allowed for creation of the Storting (Norwegian parliament), which governed country domestically. In 1905, the union was dissolved. Prince Charles of Denmark elected king of Norway as Haakon VII, 1905-57; founded House of Glücksburg. Succession: Olav V, son, 1957-91; Harald V, son, 1991- .

Rulers of the Netherlands and Belgium

The Netherlands

William I, son of Prince William V of Orange, came to power after French rule ended in the Netherlands, 1813; crowned king with approval of Congress of Vienna, 1815. Started House of Orange-Nassau. Northern Netherlands was known as Holland. Belgians, in southern Netherlands, rebelled against the Dutch and seceded, Oct. 4, 1830. Dutch formally recognized Belgian independence, Apr. 19, 1839. William I abdicated, 1840.

Succession: William II, son, 1840-49; William III, son, 1849-90; Wilhelmina, daughter, 1890-1948; Juliana, daughter, 1948-80; Beatrix, daughter, 1980-2013; Willem-Alexander, son, 2013- .

Belgium

A national congress elected Prince Leopold of Saxe-Coburg as king. He took the throne July 21, 1831, as Leopold I.

Succession: Leopold II, son, 1865-1909; Albert I, nephew, 1909-34; Leopold III, son, 1934-51, in exile after Germany invaded Belgium, later abdicated; Prince Charles, brother, acted as regent 1944-50; Baudouin I, son of Leopold III, 1951-93; Albert II, brother, 1993-2013; Philippe, son, 2013- .

Rulers of Modern Italy

After the fall of Napoleon, the Congress of Vienna, 1814-15, restored Italy as a political patchwork, comprising the Kingdom of the Two Sicilies (Naples and Sicily), the Papal States, and smaller units. King Victor Emmanuel I of Savoy ruled Sardinia, Piedmont, and Genoa.

Victor Emmanuel I abdicated 1821. Charles Felix, brother, 1821-31, died without issue. Succeeded by Charles Albert, 1831-49; he abdicated upon defeat by the Austrians. Succeeded by Victor Emmanuel II, son, 1849-61. United Italy emerged under Camillo Benso di Cavour, prime minister of the Kingdom of Sardinia, 1852-61. Giuseppe Mazzini and Giuseppe Garibaldi were also figures in Risorgimento ("resurgence") period before Italy's unification.

In 1859, France forced Austria to cede Lombardy to Sardinia. In 1860, Garibaldi led more than 1,000 volunteers in a campaign against King Francis II of the Two Sicilies, taking Sicily and Naples. The House of Savoy subsequently annexed the Two Sicilies, Tuscany, Parma, Modena, Romagna, the Marches, and Umbria. Victor Emmanuel II assumed leadership of a united Kingdom of Italy, Mar. 17, 1861.

In 1866, Victor Emmanuel II allied with Prussia in the Austro-Prussian War and, with Prussia's victory, received Venetia. On Sept. 20, 1870, Italian troops entered Rome, ending the temporal power of the Roman Catholic Church. (The 1929 Lateran Treaty established papal sovereignty in Vatican City.)

Succession: Umberto I, son, 1878-1900, assassinated; Victor Emmanuel III, son, 1900-46; Umberto II, son, 1946, ruled only one month before voters in a referendum chose to establish a republic. In 1919, Benito Mussolini helped found the nationalist Fasci di Combattimento (Fighting Leagues), or Fascists. After Mussolini organized March on Rome, 1922, Victor Emmanuel III agreed to a coalition government. Mussolini eventually became dictator (Il Duce). He entered World War II as an ally of Hitler, 1940. He was dismissed by the king, 1943; captured and executed by partisans, 1945.

At a plebiscite, 1946, voters approved a republic. Prime minister Alcide de Gasperi was chief of state, 1945-53; Enrico de Nicola was provisional president. Successive presidents: Luigi Einaudi, 1948-55; Giovanni Gronchi, 1955-62; Antonio Segni, 1962-64; Giuseppe Saragat, 1964-71; Giovanni Leone, 1971-78; Alessandro Pertini, 1978-85; Francesco Cossiga, 1985-92; Oscar Luigi Scalfaro, 1992-99; Carlo Azeglio Ciampi, 1999-2006; Giorgio Napolitano, 2006-15; Sergio Mattarella, 2015- .

Rulers of Spain

From 8th to 11th centuries, Spain was dominated by the Moors (Muslims from North Africa of Arab and Berber origin). A number of small kingdoms—Aragon, Asturias, Castile, Catalonia, Leon, Navarre, and Valencia—undertook a Christian reconquest. In 1474, Isabella I became Queen of Castile and Leon. By the Catholic Monarchs' request, Pope Sixtus IV authorized the Inquisition, 1478. Isabella's husband, Ferdinand V, acceded to the throne of Aragon, 1479. Last Moorish kingdom, Granada, seized 1492. Spain sponsored Christopher Columbus, who led European exploration of New World, 1492. Isabella was succeeded by daughter, Joanna (the Mad), but Ferdinand acted as regent until his death, 1516.

Charles I, son of Joanna and grandson of Habsburg Emperor Maximilian I, became Holy Roman Emperor as Charles V, 1520;

abdicated 1556. Philip II, son, 1556-98, inherited only part of empire. He conquered Portugal, fought against Ottoman Empire, sent Armada in unsuccessful invasion of England. Succession: Philip III, son, 1598-1621; Philip IV, son, 1621-65; Charles II, son, 1665-1700, no issue, left Spain to Philip of Anjou, grandson of Louis XIV of France. As Philip V, he was first of Bourbon dynasty in Spain, 1700-46 (his son Louis ruled briefly in 1724); Ferdinand VI, son, 1746-59; Charles III, brother, 1759-88; Charles IV, son, 1788-1808, abdicated.

Joseph Bonaparte made king of Spain, 1808-13, by his brother Napoleon. Ferdinand VII, son of Charles IV, 1808, 1814-33, lost American colonies except Cuba, Puerto Rico. Maria Christina of the Two Sicilies, wife, was regent until 1843 for Isabella II, daughter, who was driven into exile by revolution, 1868. Amadeo of Savoy elected king by the Cortes (parliament), 1870-73. First

Republic, 1873-74. Alfonso XII, son of Isabella II, 1875-85; Alfonso XIII, posthumous son, 1901-31, with mother Maria Christina as regent before he assumed throne. Spain ceded territory after loss in Spanish-American War, 1898. Primo de Rivera ruled as dictator, 1923-30, after military coup but was forced to resign after losing support. Alfonso agreed to exile without formal abdication. Monarchy abolished; Second Republic established with socialist backing. Presidents: Niceto Alcala Zamora, 1931-36; Manuel Azaña, 1936-39.

Revolt by military started Spanish Civil War, 1936-39. Gen. Francisco Franco ruled as head of Nationalist regime, 1939-73. Monarchy restored after 1947 referendum. Juan Carlos, grandson of Alfonso XIII, acceded to throne after Franco's death in 1975; abdicated, 2014. Felipe VI, son, 2014- .

Leaders in the South American Wars of Liberation

Francisco de Miranda, José de San Martín, and Simón Bolívar led early 19th-cent. struggles of South American nations to free themselves from Spain.

Miranda (1750-1816), a Venezuelan, served as an officer in the Spanish army. After a dispute with the army, he fled to the U.S., 1783, where he met leaders of the American Revolution. He traveled seeking support for South American independence from other world leaders. Miranda unsuccessfully attempted a revolt in Venezuela, 1806. Napoleon's invasion of Spain, 1808, prompted the start of a revolution in Venezuela. Miranda returned, 1810, and headed the revolution with dictatorial powers. Venezuela declared independence, 1811. Overcome by royalist forces, 1812, Miranda surrendered and was arrested; he died in a Spanish prison.

San Martín (1778-1850) was born in present-day Argentina. He served in Spanish campaigns in Europe until 1811. He returned to Argentina and joined the independence movement, 1812. In 1817, he invaded Chile through the Andean mountain passes. He and Bernardo O'Higgins defeated the Spanish at Chacabuco, 1817. Chile gained independence, 1819; O'Higgins became first director of Chile, 1817-23. In 1821, San Martín entered Lima and took the port of Callao; he became protector of an independent Peru.

Bolívar (1783-1830) was born into an aristocratic family in Venezuela. He served under Miranda until Miranda's surrender

in 1812. Bolívar continued to fight; he captured Caracas and was named Liberator, 1813. But he was forced to flee by royalist forces, 1814. In 1817, Bolívar again fought for control of Venezuela. With Francisco de Paula Santander and José Antonio Páez, he defeated the Spanish at the Battle of Boyacá, 1819, freeing New Granada (present-day Colombia). New Granada, Venezuela, and the area that is now Panama and Ecuador were joined as the Republic of Colombia, or Gran Colombia, with Bolívar as president later that same year, though parts of the republic remained under Spanish control. He decisively defeated the Spanish in the Battle of Carabobo in Venezuela, 1821.

Antonio José de Sucre, Bolívar's chief lieutenant, overcame Spanish forces at the Battle of Pichincha in Ecuador, 1822. Bolívar convinced San Martín to resign as protector of Peru. Peru was declared independent after Bolívar and Sucre won the Battle of Junín, Aug. 1824, and Sucre triumphed at the Battle of Ayacucho, Dec. 1824.

Sucre organized Upper Peru as Republica Bolívar (now Bolivia), 1825, and acted as president in place of Bolívar, who wrote its constitution.

Civil strife caused the Colombian federation to break apart. Bolívar gave up the presidency, 1830.

Rulers of Russia; Leaders of the USSR and Russian Federation

The Varangian (Viking) prince Rurik is considered to be the first leader of the Russians; he established himself at Novgorod, c. 862 CE. His successor, Oleg, and those who followed Oleg ruled as princes of Kiev. Vladimir I, or Saint Vladimir, married sister of Byzantine emperor and converted to Christianity, 988. Yaroslav I (the Wise), brother, 1019-54, was important organizer and lawgiver; his daughters married kings of Norway, Hungary, and France. In 1169, Andrew Bogolyubsky conquered Kiev and began the line of Vladimir.

Daniel, a son of grand prince of Vladimir, Alexander Nevsky, was first to be called prince of Muscovy (Moscow), 1263-1303. Dmitri Ivanovich (Donskoi), prince of Moscow, defeated the Tatars at the Battle of Kulikovo, 1380. His successors were grand princes of Moscow. Ivan III (the Great), 1462-1505, achieved considerable territorial expansion.

Ivan III married Sofia Palaeologus, niece of the last Byzantine emperor. Succession: Vasily III, son. Ivan IV (the Terrible), son, crowned 1547 as Tsar of Russia. Fyodor I, son, reigned 1584-98, but his brother-in-law Boris Godunov had real control before becoming tsar himself, 1598-1605. After years of internal strife ("Time of Troubles"), the Russians united under 16-year-old Michael Romanov, distantly related to Ivan IV's first wife. He ruled 1613-45, establishing the Romanov line.

Tsars, or emperors, of Russia (Romanovs): Peter I (the Great), 1682-1725, with Ivan V, brother, as co-ruler, 1682-96. Catherine I, his widow, 1725-27. Peter II, grandson of Peter I, 1727-30. Anna, daughter of Ivan V and niece of Peter I, 1730-40. Ivan VI, nephew, 1740-41; deposed by Elizabeth, daughter of Peter I, 1741-62. Peter III, nephew, 1762; deposed by his wife, Catherine II (the Great), former princess of Anhalt Zerbst (Germany), 1762-96. Paul I, son, 1796-1801, assassinated. Alexander I, son, 1801-25, defeated Napoleon. Nicholas I, brother, 1825-55. Alexander II, son, 1855-81, assassinated. Alexander III, son, 1881-94. Nicholas II, son, 1894-1917, last tsar of Russia, was forced to abdicate by revolutionaries following losses to Germany in WWI. The tsar, empress, tsarevich (crown prince), and tsar's four daughters were murdered by the Bolsheviks, July 1918.

Premiers of provisional government: Prince Georgi Lvov, followed by Alexander Kerensky, 1917.

Union of Soviet Socialist Republics

Bolshevik Revolution, Nov. 7, 1917, (also known as the October Revolution, based on Russia's then use of the Julian calendar) removed Kerensky from power. Council of People's Commissars formed with Lenin (Vladimir Ilyich Ulyanov) as chair (or premier), 1917-24. Aleksei Rykov (executed 1938) and Vyacheslav M. Molotov held the office, but effective ruler was Joseph Stalin (Joseph Vissarionovich Dzhugashvili), general secretary of the Communist Party. Stalin was chair of the Council of People's Commissars from 1941 until his death in 1953. Succeeded by Georgi M. Malenkov, who also briefly served as general secretary of the Communist Party before being ousted from the position by Nikita S. Khrushchev. Malenkov was forced to resign as premier, 1955, and was expelled from the Communist Party, 1961. Nikolai A. Bulganin was premier, 1955-58, until his replacement by Khrushchev, 1958-64.

Leonid I. Brezhnev ousted Khrushchev as general secretary of the party, a post he held until his death in 1982. Aleksei N. Kosygin was premier, 1964-80. The Central Committee elected former KGB (state security) head Yuri V. Andropov general secretary, 1982-84. After Andropov's death, Konstantin U. Chernenko was chosen for the position, 1984-85. Upon Chernenko's death, he was succeeded by Mikhail Gorbachev. Gorbachev assumed the newly created position of president of the Soviet Union, 1990. Boris Yeltsin was sworn in July 1991 as the Russian Republic's first elected president. Under Yeltsin, Russia became a founding member of the Commonwealth of Independent States. Gorbachev resigned the presidency, Dec. 25, 1991, and the Soviet Union officially disbanded Dec. 31. Each of the 15 former Soviet constituent republics became independent.

Post-Soviet Russia

Presidents of the Russian Federation: Boris Yeltsin, 1991-99; Vladimir Putin, 2000-08; Dmitry Medvedev, 2008-12; Putin, 2012- .

Rulers of China

Where dynastic dates overlap, the rulers or events referred to appeared in different areas of China.

Years in power	Dynasty/ruler(s)
c. 1994-c. 1766 BCE	Xia dynasty, first hereditary Chinese dynasty
c. 1766-c. 1045 BCE	Shang dynasty, first Chinese dynasty with historical records
c. 1045-771 BCE	Western Zhou dynasty, capital near present-day Xi'an
770-256 BCE	Eastern Zhou dynasty, new capital established at Luoyang. During Chunqiu (Spring and Autumn) period (722-481 BCE), Zhou began to lose authority. Period of the Warring States (403-221 BCE) involved major powers of Qi, Chu, Yan, Han, Zhao, Wei, and Qin
221-207 BCE	Qin dynasty, quasi-feudal states unified for first time under self-proclaimed Shi Huang Di, or First Emperor. Prefectures/counties organized under central govt., uniform laws; written language, weights standardized
206 BCE-9 CE	Earlier, or Western Han dynasty, founded by rebel leader Liu Bang. Expansion under Emperor Wudi (born Liu Che), 140-87 BCE; civil service system established
9-23	Xin dynasty, established by Wang Mang, who deposed infant emperor for whom he was regent
25-220	Later, or Eastern Han dynasty
220-265[1]	Wei dynasty, established by son of Han general Cao Cao
221-263[1]	Shu Han dynasty in SW China
222-280[1]	Wu dynasty in SE China
265-317	Western Jin dynasty, established by Sima Yan, Wei dynasty general
317-420	Eastern Jin dynasty, established by prince of Sima family
420-589	Southern dynasties, four short-lived dynasties with capital at Jiankang (present-day Nanjing)
581-618	Sui dynasty, reunified China; established by Emperor Wendi (born Yang Jian), military appointee who usurped throne of non-Chinese Northern Zhou, 581
618-906	Tang dynasty, founded by Li Yuan (known as Emperor Gaozu of Tang), who led rebellion against the Sui. Notable rulers include former imperial concubine Empress Wu, 683-705; Xuanzong, 712-56
907-960	Five Dynasties. Period of disunion with short-lived dynasties in N; Ten Kingdoms (states) in S and W
907-1125	Liao dynasty, of Khitan Mongols, capital at Yanjing (present-day Beijing)
960-1126	Northern Song dynasty, established by military leader Zhao Kuangyin (Emperor Taizu), capital at Kaifeng
1122-1234	Jin dynasty, of Juchen people of Manchuria; drove Song out of N China
1127-1279	Southern Song dynasty, capital at Lin'an (present-day Hangzhou)
1279-1368	Yuan, or Mongol dynasty; Kublai Khan, grandson of Genghis Khan, high point of Mongol power
1368-1644	Ming dynasty, founded by Buddhist monk turned rebel general Zhu Yuanzhang. Country again under Chinese rule; capital in present-day Nanjing, then Beijing after Mongolian tribes' defeat
1644-1912	Qing, or Manchu dynasty, under rule of Manchu people. Last imperial dynasty; Emperor Xuantong, or Puyi, last emperor. Sun Yat-sen organized Kuomintang (Nationalist party) and led provisional republican government in Nanjing, 1911-12. Sun resigned in unification compromise with former imperial viceroy Yuan Shikai, who became president upon emperor's abdication in Feb. 1912
1912-1949	Rep. of China, power passed to provincial warlords upon Yuan's death, 1916. Gen. Chiang Kai-shek sought to reunify China under Kuomintang with new government at Nanjing, 1928. War with Japan, then civil war, led to Nationalist authority collapse, Communist declaration of People's Rep. of China, 1949

(1) Also known as the period of the Three Kingdoms because of warfare between the Wei, Shu Han, and Wu dynasties.

Leaders of People's Republic of China

Name	Title/position, years in power
Mao Zedong	People's Rep. of China (PRC) Chairman, 1949-59; Chinese Communist Party (CCP) Chairman, 1949-76
Zhou Enlai	Premier, 1949-76
Liu Shaoqi	PRC Chairman, 1959-68; one-time Mao successor removed from power during Cultural Revolution (1966-76)
Lin Biao	Red Army cmdr. designated Mao's successor, 1966; govt. reported his death in plane crash, 1971, after coup attempt
Hua Guofeng	Premier, 1976-80; CCP Chairman, 1976-81
Deng Xiaoping	"Paramount leader," 1977-97
Hu Yaobang	CCP General Secretary, 1980-87; CCP Chairman, 1981-82[1]
Zhao Ziyang	Premier, 1980-87; CCP General Secretary, 1987-89
Li Xiannian	President, 1983-88
Yang Shangkun	President, 1988-93
Li Peng	Premier, 1988-98
Jiang Zemin	CCP General Secretary, 1989-2002; President, 1993-2003
Zhu Rongji	Premier, 1998-2003
Hu Jintao	CCP General Secretary, 2002-12; President, 2003-13
Wen Jiabao	Premier, 2003-13
Xi Jinping	CCP General Secretary, 2012- ; President, 2013-
Li Keqiang	Premier, 2013-

(1) Position of CCP chairman was abolished in 1982, making the CCP general secretary the party's highest-ranking official.

Historical Periods of Japan

Years in power	Period	Founding event
c. 300-592	Yamato	The Yamato clan united various Japanese states. Also called Tumulus, or Tomb, period for its large burial mounds
593-710	Asuka	Accession of Empress Suiko, with her nephew Prince Shotoku as regent. The Taika reforms (from 645) established a centralized government under the emperor; capital moved to Asuka
710-794	Nara	Capital moved to Nara
794-1185	Heian	Capital moved to Heian (present-day Kyoto) by Emperor Kammu
858-1160	Fujiwara	Fujiwara no Yoshifusa became regent for his grandson
1160-1185	Taira	Taira no Kiyomoro assumed control; Minamoto no Yoritomo defeated Taira, 1185
1192-1333	Kamakura	Yoritomo became shogun, head of military government, with the emperor as titular leader
1334-1392	Namboku	Emperor Go-Daigo returned to power in Kemmu Restoration; 1336 revolt drove him from Kyoto to establish Southern Court at Yoshino
1392-1573	Muromachi	Unification of Southern and Northern Courts; Ashikaga family dominates
1467-1600	Sengoku	Onin War began; also known as Warring States period
1573-1603	Momoyama	Oda Nobunaga entered Kyoto, 1568, deposed last Ashikaga shogun, 1573. Tokugawa Ieyasu victor at Battle of Sekigahara, 1600
1603-1867	Edo	Ieyasu established Tokugawa shogunate, became shogun
1868-1912	Meiji	Meiji Restoration of imperial power, with Meiji (reign name of Mutsuhito) ascending throne; Charter Oath, 1868, led to Westernization
1912-1926	Taisho	Accession of Emperor Taisho (reign name of Yoshihito)
1926-1989	Showa	Accession of Emperor Hirohito (posthumous name Showa)
1989-2019	Heisei	Accession of Emperor Akihito[1]
2019-	Reiwa	Accession of Emperor Naruhito[1]

(1) A 2017 law allowed Akihito to abdicate, the first Japanese emperor to do so in about 200 years, on Apr. 30, 2019, and assume the title of emperor emeritus. His eldest son acceded to the throne the next day.

WORLD EXPLORATION AND GEOGRAPHY

Early Explorers of the Western Hemisphere

Genetic evidence suggests that beginning around 15,000 years before the present (BP), humans reached the Americas by sailing along the Pacific coast or by crossing the Bering Land Bridge between Siberia and Alaska. Extant remains known as Anzick-1 (c. 12,600 BP), a male infant of the Clovis people found buried in present-day Montana; Xach'itee'aanenh T'eede Gaay (Sunrise Girl-Child) (c. 11,500 BP) of the Ancient Beringians, in Alaska; Luzia Woman (11,500 BP) in Brazil; and Kennewick Man (8,500 BP), in Washington State, belonged to some of these early arrivals. Modern Native Americans appear to be descended from peoples indigenous to N and Central Asia who split into two Native American populations—Northern and Southern—as they dispersed across the continents.

The Americas were populated mostly by hunter-gatherers and small-scale horticulturalists, but complex chiefdoms and state-level societies appeared in a few areas (SE U.S., Mesoamerica, coastal Chile). The earliest known state in the Americas spanned 700 sq mi across river valleys in coastal Peru between 3,500 and 500 BP.

The Norse, led by Leif Ericson, are usually credited as being the first Europeans to reach America, with at least five voyages occurring about 1000 CE to areas they called Helluland, Markland, and Vinland—possibly present-day Baffin Island,

Labrador, and either Newfoundland or New England. L'Anse aux Meadows, Newfoundland, is the only documented settlement, with evidence of a village dating to c. 1000 CE.

Sustained contact between the hemispheres began with Christopher Columbus (born Cristoforo Colombo, c. 1451, near Genoa, Italy), who made four voyages to the Americas with funding from the Spanish monarchs and private investors. He left Spain, Aug. 3, 1492, with 88 men and a fleet of three vessels—the Niña, Pinta, and Santa María—and landed on the island of San Salvador in present-day Bahamas on Oct. 12, 1492. He also visited Cuba, Hispaniola, and many smaller Caribbean islands, then populated by the Taíno. A second expedition, in 1493, reached the island of Dominica in the Lesser Antilles; a third, in 1498, took Columbus to Trinidad and the adjacent S American coast. A fourth voyage reached Mexico, Honduras, Panama, and what he christened Santiago (the present-day island of Jamaica) in 1502.

In 1497 and 1499, Amerigo Vespucci (for whom the Americas are named), an Italian sailing for Spain, passed along the N and E coasts of S America. He was the first to claim these lands were previously unknown and not part of Asia. Some early explorations are listed below.

Year	Explorer	Nationality (sponsor, if different)	Area reached or explored
1497	John Cabot	Italian (English)	Newfoundland, possibly Nova Scotia
1497-98	Vasco da Gama	Portuguese	Cape of Good Hope (Africa), India
1499	Alonso de Ojeda	Spanish	Northern S Amer. coast, Venezuela
1500	Vicente Yañez Pinzón	Spanish	S American coast, Amazon R.
1500	Pedro Álvarez Cabral	Portuguese	Brazil
1501	Rodrigo de Bastidas	Spanish	Central America
1513	Vasco Núñez de Balboa	Spanish	Panama, Pacific Ocean
1513	Juan Ponce de León	Spanish	Florida, Yucatán Peninsula
1515	Juan de Solis	Spanish	Río de la Plata
1519	Alonso de Pineda	Spanish	Mouth of Mississippi R.
1519	Hernán Cortés	Spanish	Mexico
1519-20	Ferdinand Magellan	Portuguese (Spanish)	Straits of Magellan, Tierra del Fuego
1524	Giovanni da Verrazano	Italian (French)	Atlantic coast, incl. New York Harbor
1528	Álvar Núñez Cabeza de Vaca	Spanish	Texas coast and interior
1532	Francisco Pizarro	Spanish	Peru
1534	Jacques Cartier	French	Canada, Gulf of St. Lawrence
1536	Pedro de Mendoza	Spanish	Up Río de la Plata, Buenos Aires
1539	Francisco de Ulloa	Spanish	California coast
1539	Marcos de Niza	Italian (Spanish)	SW United States
1539-41	Hernando de Soto	Spanish	Mississippi R., near Memphis, TN
1540	Francisco de Coronado	Spanish	SW United States
1540	Hernando de Alarcón	Spanish	Colorado R.
1540	Garcia Lopez de Cárdenas	Spanish	Colorado, Grand Canyon
1541	Francisco de Orellana	Spanish	Amazon R.
1542	Juan Rodriguez Cabrillo	Portuguese (Spanish)	Western Mexico, San Diego Harbor
1565	Pedro Menéndez de Avilés	Spanish	St. Augustine, FL
1576	Sir Martin Frobisher	English	Frobisher Bay, Canada
1577-80	Sir Francis Drake	English	CA coast, on voyage around world
1582	Antonio de Espejo	Spanish	SW U.S. (New Mexico)
1584	Philip Amadas and Arthur Barlowe (for Raleigh)	English	Virginia, Roanoke Isl.
1585-87	Sir Walter Raleigh's men	English	Roanoke Isl., NC
1595	Sir Walter Raleigh	English	Orinoco R., Venezuela
1603-09	Samuel de Champlain	French	Canadian interior, Lake Champlain
1607	John Smith	English	Atlantic coast
1609-10	Henry Hudson	English (Dutch)	Hudson R., Hudson Bay
1634	Jean Nicolet	French	Lake Michigan, Wisconsin
1673	Jacques Marquette and Louis Jolliet	French	Mississippi R., south to Arkansas
1682	René-Robert Cavelier, sieur de La Salle	French	Mississippi R., south to Gulf of Mexico
1727-29	Vitus Bering	Danish (Russian)	Bering Strait, Alaska
1789	Sir Alexander Mackenzie	Canadian	NW Canada
1804-06	Meriwether Lewis and William Clark	American	Missouri R., Rocky Mts., Columbia R.

Arctic Exploration

1596-97: Willem Barents (Dutch) touched Spitsbergen, 79°49′N, and rounded Novaya Zemlya, where he and crew were forced to winter ashore, first W Europeans to successfully do so in the Arctic.

1610: Henry Hudson (Eng.) explored Hudson Strait, Hudson Bay on search for Northwest Passage. After winter ashore, crew mutinied, 1611, and set him, his son, and some others adrift on small boat.

1733-43: Great Northern Expedition (Russ.), led by Vitus Bering (Dan./Russ.), surveyed Siberian Arctic coast. Bering had sailed through what would become known as Bering Strait,

1728, but this second expedition proved that Asia and North America were separate.

1827: William Edward Parry (Eng.), attempting to reach North Pole, made it to 82°45′N via sledge, setting record for farthest north.

1831: James Clark Ross (Eng.) was first to north magnetic pole.

1878-79: Baron Adolf Erik Nordenskiöld (Swed.) was first to navigate Northeast Passage—ocean route connecting Europe's North Sea to Pacific O.

1881-84: Adolphus Greely led 25-person U.S. expedition to Ellesmere Isl. as part of first Intl. Polar Year (1882-83). Only he and five others survived scurvy and starvation after relief ships failed to reach them.

1893-96: Fridtjof Nansen (Nor.) deliberately allowed *Fram* to become icebound and drift from New Siberian Isls. Leaving others in charge of ship, he tried polar dash in 1895 but only reached 86°14´N.

1903-06: Roald Amundsen (Nor.) was first to sail length of Northwest Passage—route linking Atlantic and Pacific via Canada's marine waterways.

1909: Robert E. Peary (U.S.) began dash for North Pole, Mar. 1, from Ellesmere Isl. Reportedly reached the pole, 90°N, Apr. 6, with Matthew Henson and four Inuit. Research suggests he may have fallen short of goal by c. 30-60 mi. (Dr. Frederick Cook [U.S.] claimed to have reached the North Pole in 1908.)

1926: Richard E. Byrd and Floyd Bennett (both U.S.) reputedly flew over North Pole, May 9. Amundsen, Lincoln Ellsworth

(U.S.), and Umberto Nobile (Ital.) flew over North Pole May 12 in dirigible *Norge.*

1958: Nuclear-powered submarine USS *Nautilus* crossed the North Pole beneath the ice.

1968: Ralph Plaisted (U.S.) and three amateur explorers on snowmobiles became first independently confirmed surface expedition to reach North Pole.

1978: Naomi Uemura (Jpn.) became first person to reach the North Pole alone, traveling by dog sled in 54-day, 600-mi trek.

1982: Ranulph Fiennes (Eng.) and Charles Burton (S. Afr.-UK) reached the North Pole and became first to circle the Earth from pole to pole. They had reached the South Pole 16 months earlier. The 52,000-mi trek took three years at an est. cost of $18 mil.

1995: Richard Weber (Can.) and Mikhail Malakhov (Russ.) became first to North Pole and back without any mechanical assistance. The 940-mi trip on skis took 121 days.

Antarctic Exploration

Explorers have approached Antarctica since 1773-75, when Capt. James Cook (Eng.) reached 71°10´S. Fabian von Bellingshausen (Russ.) mapped the region on an expedition sponsored by Tsar Alexander I, 1819-21. In 1823, James Weddell (Brit.) reached 74°15´S and found the Weddell Sea.

First to announce existence of the continent of Antarctica was Charles Wilkes (U.S.), who followed the coast for 1,500 mi, 1840. Ross Ice Shelf was found by James Clark Ross (Brit.), 1841-42.

1895: Leonard Kristensen (Nor.) landed a party on Victoria Land, first ashore on main continental mass. C. E. Borchgrevink, a member of that party, returned in 1899 with a Brit. expedition, first to winter on Antarctica.

1901-04: Robert Falcon Scott (Eng.), commander of Brit. Natl. Antarctic Expedition, crossed Ross Ice Shelf to 82°17´S, farthest south then reached.

1911: Roald Amundsen (Nor.) with four men and dog teams were first to reach South Pole, Dec. 14. Scott and four companions reached South Pole on Jan. 17, 1912; they died on return trip.

1929: Richard E. Byrd (U.S.) crossed South Pole, Nov. 29, with three others on 1,600-mi airplane flight.

1934-35: Byrd led second expedition to Little America base camp, explored 450,000 sq mi, wintered alone at 80°08´S.

1935: Lincoln Ellsworth (U.S.) made first transcontinental crossing by air, flying south along E coast of Palmer Peninsula then across to Little America.

1946-48: Ronne Antarctic Research Expedition Cmdr. Finn Ronne determined Antarctic to be one continent with no strait between Weddell and Ross Seas.

1955-57: Supporting U.S. scientific efforts for Intl. Geophysical Year (IGY), the U.S. Navy's Operation Deep Freeze, led by Byrd, established five coastal stations and three interior stations; explored more than 1 mil sq mi in Wilkes Land.

1957-58: During the IGY, scientists from 12 countries conducted research within network of some 60 stations on Antarctica. Vivian E. Fuchs (Eng.) led 12-person Trans-Antarctic Expedition on first land crossing of Antarctica; completed in Mar. 1958 after traveling 2,158 mi in 99 days.

1959: Argentina, Australia, Belgium, Chile, France, Japan, New Zealand, Norway, South Africa, USSR, UK, and U.S. signed a treaty (in force 1961) affirming the use of Antarctica (specifically the area south of 60°S) "for peaceful purposes only." Territorial claims suspended.

1961-62: Scientists discovered Bentley Trench, running from Ross Ice Shelf into Marie Byrd Land, near the end of the Ellsworth Mts., toward Weddell Sea.

1985: Ocean Drilling Project finds that E Antarctic Ice Sheet is 37 mil years old, W Antarctic Ice Sheet 8 mil years old.

1991: Protocol to the Antarctic Treaty on Environmental Protection, or Madrid Protocol, adopted (in force 1998); it banned activities—except for scientific research—related to mineral resources.

1995: After 1994 solo expedition to North Pole, Borge Ousland (Nor.) reached South Pole on skis, becoming first to reach both poles alone. He later became the first to traverse both Antarctica (1996-97) and the Arctic (2001) solo.

2018: Colin O'Brady (U.S.) makes first solo Antarctic crossing without assistance or wind aid (54 days). UK Army Cpt. Louis Rudd completed the same feat a little over two days later (56 days).

Volcanoes

Source: *Volcanoes of the World,* Geoscience Press; Global Volcanism Program, Smithsonian Institution, volcano.si.edu

Eruptions have been confirmed in some 563 volcanoes. More than half to three-quarters of historically active volcanoes can be found on the so-called **Ring of Fire,** which runs along the W coast of the Americas from the southern tip of Chile to Alaska, down the E coast of Asia from Kamchatka to Indonesia, and continues from New Guinea to New Zealand. The Ring of Fire marks boundaries between tectonic plates underlying the Pacific Ocean and the surrounding continents. Volcanic activity also occurs along rift zones like Iceland, where plates pull apart, or over hot spots such as Hawaii, where molten material rises from the mantle to Earth's crust. The majority of Earth's volcanism takes place at submarine rift zones, on the seafloor.

Notable Volcanic Eruptions

In approximately 5,700 BC, Mount Mazama, in southern Oregon, erupted violently, ejecting large amounts of ash and pumice and sending out pyroclastic flows (mixture of volcanic debris and gases). The top of the mountain collapsed, leaving a caldera about 6 mi across and 1 mi deep. This depression filled with water from rain and snow to form Crater Lake.

Date	Volcano	Est. deaths	Date	Volcano	Est. deaths
Aug. 24, 79 CE	Vesuvius, Italy	16,000[1]	Jan. 30, 1911	Taal, Philippines	1,400
1586	Kelut, Java, Indon.	10,000	June 6-8, 1912	Novarupta, AK, U.S.[5]	1
Dec. 15, 1631	Vesuvius, Italy	4,000	May 19, 1919	Kelut, Java, Indon.	5,000
Aug. 12, 1772	Papandayan, Java, Indon.	3,000	Jan. 17-21, 1951	Lamington, Papua New Guinea	3,000
June 8, 1783	Laki, Iceland	9,350	May 18, 1980	St. Helens, WA, U.S.	57
May 21, 1792	Unzen, Japan	14,500	Mar. 28, 1982	El Chichón, Mexico	1,880
Apr. 10-12, 1815	Tambora, Sumbawa, Indon.	92,000[2]	Nov. 13, 1985	Nevado del Ruiz, Colombia	23,000
Aug. 26-27, 1883	Krakatau, Indon.	36,000[3]	Aug. 21, 1986	Lake Nyos, Cameroon	1,700[6]
Apr. 24, 1902	Santa María, Guatemala	1,000[4]	June 15, 1991	Pinatubo, Luzon, Philippines	800[7]
May 8, 1902	Pelée, Martinique	28,000			

(1) Heated mud and ash engulfed Pompeii, Herculaneum, and Stabiae with debris more than 60 ft deep. About 10% of the three towns' pop. were killed. (2) Of these, about 10,000 were directly related to the eruption. Released gases and particles altered the global climate, leading to additional deaths from starvation and disease when crops failed. (3) At least 2,000 died in pyroclastic flows, Aug. 26. Collapse of volcano, Aug. 27, sank most of island, killing over 3,000. Resulting tsunamis were responsible for the majority of deaths, in Java and Sumatra. (4) An additional 3,000 deaths due to a malaria outbreak are sometimes attributed to the eruption. (5) Biggest eruption of 20th cent. by volume. (6) Caused by release of massive amount of carbon dioxide from crater lake. (7) Of these, about 500 were associated with post-eruption lahars (volcanic mudflows).

Notable Active Volcanoes

Source: Global Volcanism Program, Smithsonian Inst.; Volcano Hazards Program, U.S. Geological Survey, U.S. Dept. of the Interior
Active volcanoes display a wide range of activity, including the production of ash plumes and seismic swarms. An eruption may involve the explosive ejection of fragmental material and escape of liquid lava. Year of a volcano's last known or confirmed eruption, as of May 2020, is given. Volcanoes are listed by elevation, which does not reflect eruptive magnitude. Submarine volcanoes are not included.

Volcano (last eruption)	Location	Elev. (ft)
Africa		
Cameroon (2000)	Cameroon	13,435
Nyiragongo (2020)	Dem. Rep. of the Congo	11,385
Nyamuragira (2020)	Dem. Rep. of the Congo	10,033
Ol Doinyo Lengai (2020)	Tanzania	9,718
Fogo (2015)	Cape Verde Isls.	9,281
Piton de la Fournaise (2020)	Réunion Isl. (Fr.), Indian O.	8,635
Karthala (2007)	Comoros	7,746
Nabro (2012)	Eritrea	7,277
Antarctica		
Erebus (2020)	Ross Isl.	12,448
Melbourne (1892)	Victoria Land	8,963
Asia and Oceania		
Ararat (1840)	Turkey	16,946
Klyuchevskoy (2020)	Kamchatka, Russia	15,597
Kerinci (2020)	Sumatra, Indon.	12,467
Fuji (1708)	Honshu, Japan	12,388
Rinjani (2016)	Lombok, Indon.	12,224
Semeru (2020)	Java, Indon.	11,998
Tolbachik (2013)	Kamchatka, Russia	11,847
Koryaksky (2009)	Kamchatka, Russia	11,253
Slamet (2014)	Java, Indon.	11,247
Shiveluch (Sheveluch) (2020)	Kamchatka, Russia	10,771
Raung (2015)	Java, Indon.	10,696
Dempo (2017)	Sumatra, Indon.	10,308
Ontake (2014)	Honshu, Japan	10,062
Agung (2019)	Bali, Indon.	9,833
Merapi (2020)	Java, Indon.	9,547
Zhupanovsky (2016)	Kamchatka, Russia	9,511
Marapi (2018)	Sumatra, Indon.	9,465
Bezymianny (2020)	Kamchatka, Russia	9,455
Ruapehu (2007)	North Isl., New Zealand	9,177
Heard (2020)	Heard Isl., Australia	9,006
Changbaishan (1903)	China-North Korea	9,003
Avachinsky (2001)	Kamchatka, Russia	8,914
Papandayan (2002)	Java, Indon.	8,743
Talang (2007)	Sumatra, Indon.	8,448
Asama (2019)	Honshu, Japan	8,425
Dieng Volcanic Complex (2018)	Java, Indon.	8,415
Mayon (2019)	Luzon, Philippines	8,077
Sinabung (2019)	Sumatra, Indon.	8,071
Kanlaon (2017)	Negros, Philippines	7,989
Niigata-Yakeyama (1998)	Honshu, Japan	7,874
Kizimen (2013)	Kamchatka, Russia	7,657
Ulawun (2019)	Papua New Guinea	7,657
Tengger Caldera (2019)	Java, Indon.	7,641
Alaid (2018)	Kuril Isls., Russia	7,497
Chokai (1974)	Honshu, Japan	7,336
Galunggung (1984)	Java, Indon.	7,113
Kusatsu-Shirane (2018)	Honshu, Japan	7,103
Sorikmarapi (1986)	Sumatra Isl., Indon.	7,037
Kambalny (2017)	Kamchatka, Russia	6,942
Tangkubanparahu (2019)	Java, Indon.	6,837
Tongariro (2012)	North Isl., New Zealand	6,490
Azuma (1977)	Honshu, Japan	6,394
Kaba (2000)	Sumatra Isl., Indon.	6,365
Nasu (1963)	Honshu, Japan	6,283
Sangeang Api (2020)	Lesser Sunda Isls., Indon.	6,273
Bagana (2020)	Papua New Guinea	6,086
Karkar (2014)	Papua New Guinea	6,033
Chachadake (Tiatia) (1981)	Kunashir Isl., Japan-admin. by Russia.	5,978
Bandai (1888)	Honshu, Japan	5,958
Manam (2020)	Papua New Guinea	5,928
Gorely (2010)	Kamchatka, Russia	5,902
Karangetang (Api Siau) (2020)	Siau Isl., Indon.	5,896
Kuju (1996)	Kyushu, Japan	5,876
Soputan (2020)	Sulawesi, Indon.	5,856
Chikurachki (2016)	Kuril Isls., Russia	5,843
Kelut (2014)	Java, Indon.	5,679
Adatara (1996)	Honshu, Japan	5,669
Batur (2000)	Bali, Indon.	5,633
Gamalama (2018)	Ternate, Indon.	5,627
Lewotobi (2003)	Flores Isl., Indon.	5,587
Kirishima (2018)	Kyushu, Japan	5,577
Egon (2008)	Flores, Indon.	5,449
Gamkonora (2007)	Halmahera, Indon.	5,364
Aso (2020)	Kyushu, Japan	5,223
Lokon-Empung (2015)	Sulawesi, Indon.	5,184
Bulusan (2017)	Luzon, Philippines.	5,036
Karymsky (2020)	Kamchatka, Russia	4,964
Akan (2008)	Hokkaido, Japan	4,918
Pinatubo (1993)	Luzon, Philippines	4,875
Central America and West Indies		
Tacaná (1986)	Mexico-Guatemala	13,333
Acatenango (1972)	Guatemala	13,045
Fuego (2020)	Guatemala	12,346
Santa María (2020)	Guatemala	12,287
Irazú (1994)	Costa Rica	11,260
Turrialba (2019)	Costa Rica	10,958
Poás (2019)	Costa Rica	8,885
Pacaya (2020)	Guatemala	8,428
Santa Ana (2005)	El Salvador	7,812
San Miguel (2020)	El Salvador	6,988
Rincón de la Vieja (2020)	Costa Rica	6,286
San Cristóbal (2019)	Nicaragua	5,725
Concepción (2011)	Nicaragua	5,577
Arenal (2010)	Costa Rica	5,479
Soufrière Guadeloupe (1977)	Guadeloupe (France)	4,813
Pelée (1932)	Martinique (France)	4,573
Momotombo (2016)	Nicaragua	4,167
North America		
Pico de Orizaba (1846)	Mexico	18,255
Popocatépetl (2020)	Mexico	17,694
Rainier (1450)	Washington	14,409
Shasta (1250)	California	14,163
Wrangell (1912)	Alaska	14,035
Colima (2019)	Mexico	12,631
Hood (1866)	Oregon	11,240
Spurr (1992)	Alaska	11,070
Lassen Peak (1917)	California	10,456
Redoubt (2009)	Alaska	10,197
Iliamna (1876)	Alaska	10,016
Shishaldin (2020)	Unimak Isl., Aleutians, AK	9,373
St. Helens (2008)	Washington	8,363
Veniaminof (2018)	Alaska	8,225
Pavlof (2016)	Alaska	8,179
Fourpeaked (2006)	Alaska	6,906
Katmai (1912)	Alaska	6,716
Makushin (1995)	Unalaska Isl., Aleutians, AK	5,906
Great Sitkin (2019)	Great Sitkin Isl., Aleutians, AK	5,709
Cleveland (2020)	Chuginadak Isl., Aleutians, AK	5,676
South America		
Llullaillaco (1877)	Chile-Argentina	22,110
San Pedro-San Pablo (1960)	Chile	20,151
Guallatiri (1960)	Chile	19,918
San José (1960)	Chile-Argentina	19,915
Sabancaya (2020)	Peru	19,554
Cotopaxi (2016)	Ecuador	19,393
El Misti (1985)	Peru	19,101
Ubinas (2019)	Peru	18,609
Tupungato (1987)	Chile-Argentina	18,570
Láscar (2017)	Chile	18,346
Nevado del Huila (2012)	Colombia	17,598
Sangay (2020)	Ecuador	17,343
Nevado del Ruiz (2020)	Colombia	17,320
Irruputuncu (1995)	Chile-Bolivia	16,939
Tungurahua (2016)	Ecuador	16,480
Guagua Pichincha (2002)	Ecuador	15,696
Puracé (1977)	Colombia	15,256
Galeras (2010)	Colombia	14,029
Planchón-Peteroa (2019)	Chile	13,048
Lautaro (1979)	Chile	11,834
Reventador (2020)	Ecuador	11,686
Nevados de Chillán (2020)	Chile	10,433
Llaima (2009)	Chile	10,253
Europe		
Etna (2019)	Italy	10,810
Vesuvius (1944)	Italy	4,203
Stromboli (2020)	Italy	3,031
Mid-Atlantic		
La Palma (1971)	Canary Isls. (Spain)	7,959
Beerenberg (1985)	Jan Mayen (Norway)	7,208
Bardarbunga (2015)	Iceland	6,562
Grímsvötn (2011)	Iceland	5,640
Eyjafjallajökull (2010)	Iceland	5,417
Hekla (2000)	Iceland	4,888
Mid-Pacific		
Mauna Loa (1984)	Hawaii, HI	13,681
Haleakala (1750)	Maui, HI	10,023
Kilauea (2018)	Hawaii, HI	4,009

Mountains
North America

Source: U.S. Geological Survey, U.S. Dept. of the Interior; National Geodetic Survey, NOAA, U.S. Dept. of Commerce; Natural Resources Canada. Survey dates and elevation sources may differ.

Peak, state/prov., country	Height (ft)	Peak, state/prov., country	Height (ft)	Peak, state/prov., country	Height (ft)
Denali (fmr. McKinley), AK	20,310	La Malinche (Matlalcuéyetl),		Wilson, CO	14,246
Logan, Yukon, Canada	19,551	Mexico	14,636	Cameron, CO	14,238
Pico de Orizaba, Mexico	18,619	Hunter, AK	14,573	Shavano, CO	14,231
St. Elias, AK-YT, U.S.-Can.	18,009	Browne Tower, AK	14,530	Princeton, CO	14,204
Popocatépetl, Mexico	17,802	Whitney, CA	14,505	Belford, CO	14,203
Foraker, AK	17,400	Alverstone, AK-YT, U.S.-Can.	14,500	Yale, CO	14,200
Iztaccíhuatl, Mexico	17,159	University Peak, AK	14,470	Crestone Needle, CO	14,197
Lucania, YT, Canada	17,146	Elbert, CO	14,440	Bross, CO	14,172
King Peak, YT, Canada	16,972	Massive, CO	14,421	Kit Carson, CO	14,165
Steele, YT, Canada	16,624	Harvard, CO	14,421	Point Success, WA	14,164
Bona, AK	16,500	Rainier, WA	14,410	Shasta, CA	14,163
Blackburn, AK	16,390	Williamson, CA	14,376	Wrangell, AK	14,163
Sanford, AK	16,237	Blanca Peak, CO	14,345	Maroon Peak, CO	14,163
South Buttress, AK	15,885	La Plata Peak, CO	14,336	Tabeguache, CO	14,162
Wood, YT, Canada	15,873	Uncompahgre Peak, CO	14,321	Oxford, CO	14,160
Vancouver, AK-YT, U.S.-Can.	15,699	Crestone Peak, CO	14,294	El Diente Peak, CO	14,159
Churchill, AK	15,638	Lincoln, CO	14,293	Sill, CA	14,159
Nevado de Toluca (Xinantécatl),		Castle Peak, CO	14,279	Democrat, CO	14,155
Mexico	15,354	Grays Peak, CO	14,278	Sneffels, CO	14,150
Fairweather, AK-BC, U.S.-Can.	15,299	Antero, CO	14,276	Capitol Peak, CO	14,130
Macaulay, YT, Canada	15,299	Torreys Peak, CO	14,275	Liberty Cap, WA	14,118
Slaggard, YT, Canada	15,299	Quandary Peak, CO	14,271	Pikes Peak, CO	14,115
Hubbard, AK-YT, U.S.-Can.	15,016	Evans, CO	14,265	Snowmass, CO	14,099
Bear, AK	14,831	Longs Peak, CO	14,259	Russell, CA	14,094
Walsh, YT, Canada	14,780	McArthur, YT, Canada	14,253	Eolus, CO	14,083
East Buttress, AK	14,700	White Mountain Peak, CA	14,252	Windom, CO	14,082
		North Palisade, CA	14,248	Challenger Point, CO	14,081

Note: The highest point in the West Indies is Pico Duarte (10,417 ft), in the Dominican Republic.

Other Notable U.S. Mountains

Peak, state	Height (ft)	Peak, state	Height (ft)	Peak, state	Height (ft)
Gannett, WY	13,810	Adams, WA	12,281	Mitchell, NC	6,683
Grand Teton, WY	13,775	San Gorgonio, CA	11,503	Clingmans Dome, NC-TN	6,644
Kings, UT	13,518	Hood, OR	11,247	Washington, NH	6,289
Cloud, WY	13,171	Cleveland, MT	10,466	Rogers, VA	5,729
Wheeler, NM	13,167	Lassen, CA	10,461	Marcy, NY	5,343
Boundary, NV	13,146	Granite, CA	10,325	Katahdin, ME	5,269
Granite, MT	12,807	Guadalupe, TX	8,751	Spruce Knob, WV	4,863
Borah, ID	12,668	Olympus, WA	7,973	Mansfield, VT	4,395
Humphreys, AZ	12,637	Harney, SD	7,244	Black Mountain, KY	4,139

South America

Peak, country	Height (ft)	Peak, country	Height (ft)	Peak, country	Height (ft)
Aconcagua, Argentina	22,831	Coropuna, Peru	21,083	Solo, Argentina	20,492
Ojos del Salado, Arg.-Chile	22,569	Laudo, Argentina	20,997	Polleras, Argentina	20,456
Bonete, Argentina	22,546	Ancohuma, Bolivia	20,958	Pular, Chile	20,423
Tupungato, Argentina-Chile	22,310	Ausangate, Peru	20,945	Chani, Argentina	20,341
Pissis, Argentina	22,241	Toro, Argentina-Chile	20,932	Aucanquilcha, Chile	20,295
Mercedario, Argentina	22,211	Illampu, Bolivia	20,873	Juncal, Argentina-Chile	20,276
Huascarán, Peru	22,205	Tres Cruces, Argentina-Chile	20,853	Negro, Argentina	20,184
Llullaillaco, Argentina-Chile	22,110	Huandoy, Peru	20,852	Quela, Argentina	20,128
El Libertador, Argentina	22,047	Parinacota, Bolivia-Chile	20,768	Condoriri, Bolivia	20,095
Cachi, Argentina	22,047	Tortolas, Argentina-Chile	20,745	Palermo, Argentina	20,079
Yerupajá, Peru	21,765	Ampato, Peru	20,702	Solimana, Peru	20,068
Incahuasi, Argentina-Chile	21,720	El Condor, Argentina	20,669	San Juan, Argentina-Chile	20,049
Galan, Argentina	21,654	Salcantay, Peru	20,574	Sierra Nevada, Argentina-Chile	20,023
Nevado Sajama, Bolivia	21,463	Chimborazo, Ecuador	20,564	Antofalla, Argentina	20,013
El Muerto, Argentina-Chile	21,457	Huancarhuas, Peru	20,531	Marmolejo, Argentina-Chile	20,013
Nacimiento, Argentina	21,302	Famatina, Argentina	20,505	Chachani, Peru	19,931
Illimani, Bolivia	21,201	Pumasillo, Peru	20,492		

Africa

Peak, country	Height (ft)	Peak, country	Height (ft)	Peak, country	Height (ft)
Kilimanjaro, Tanzania	19,341	Karisimbi, Congo-Rwanda	14,787	Guna, Ethiopia	13,881
Kenya, Kenya	17,057	Tullu Dimtu, Ethiopia	14,360	Gughe, Ethiopia	13,780
Margherita Pk., Uganda-Congo	16,765	Elgon, Kenya-Uganda	14,178	Jebel Toubkal, Morocco	13,665
Meru, Tanzania	14,977	Batu, Ethiopia	14,131	Cameroon, Cameroon	13,435
Ras Dashen, Ethiopia	14,872				

Australia, New Zealand, SE Asian Islands

Peak, country	Height (ft)	Peak, country	Height (ft)	Peak, country	Height (ft)
Jaya, New Guinea, Indon.	16,024	Wilhelm, Papua New Guinea	14,793	Aoraki/Cook, New Zealand	12,218
Trikora, New Guinea, Indon.	15,585	Kinabalu, Malaysia	13,436	Semeru, Java, Indon.	12,060
Mandala, New Guinea, Indon.	15,420	Kerinci, Sumatra, Indon.	12,467	Kosciusko, Australia	7,310

Height of Mount Everest

Mt. Everest, the world's highest mountain, was considered 29,002 ft when Edmund Hillary and Tenzing Norgay became the first to scale it, in 1953. In 1954, the Surveyor General of the Republic of India set the height at 29,028 ft, plus or minus 10 ft because of snow. In 1999, a team of climbers sponsored by Boston's Museum of Science and the National Geographic Society measured the height at the summit using satellite-based technology. The new measurement, of 29,035 ft, was accepted by other authorities, including the U.S. National Imagery and Mapping Agency, but not by Nepal. In May 2019, Nepal government surveyors successfully ascended Everest in order to determine a new official height; a similar Chinese effort was launched in May 2020, taking advantage of the canceled commercial climbing season.

Climbers typically ascend Everest on its north (Tibet) or south face (Nepal). By the end of the 2019 climbing season, which runs from April through May, a total of about 5,780 different climbers had made successful ascents while around 306 climbers had died in the attempt, among them 16 Sherpas killed in 2014 when falling ice set off an avalanche. A 7.8 magnitude earthquake hit Nepal Apr. 25, 2015, triggering avalanches that swept through Everest Base Camp on the south side, killing 19. The 2015 season was subsequently canceled, making it the first year since 1974 that no one reached the top of Everest. The 2019 climbing season included 11 deaths, raising concerns about overcrowding and the number of permits issued to inexperienced climbers.

Europe

Peak, country	Height (ft)	Peak, country	Height (ft)	Peak, country	Height (ft)
Alps		Dent D'Herens, Switzerland	13,686	Schalihorn, Switzerland	13,040
		Breithorn, It.-Switzerland	13,665	Scerscen, Switzerland	13,028
Mont Blanc, France-Italy	15,781	Bishorn, Switzerland	13,645	Eiger, Switzerland	13,025
Dufourspitze (highest of Monte		Jungfrau, Switzerland	13,642	Jagerhorn, Switzerland	13,024
Rosa group), Switzerland	15,203	Ecrins, France	13,461	Rottalhorn, Switzerland	13,022
Dom, Switzerland	14,911	Monch, Switzerland	13,448		
Liskamm, It.-Switzerland	14,852	Pollux, Switzerland	13,422	**Pyrenees**	
Weisshorn, Switzerland	14,780	Schreckhorn, Switzerland	13,379	Aneto, Spain	11,168
Taschhorn, Switzerland	14,733	Ober Gabelhorn, Switzerland	13,330	Posets, Spain	11,073
Matterhorn, It.-Switzerland	14,692	Gran Paradiso, Italy	13,323	Perdido, Spain	11,007
Dent Blanche, Switzerland	14,293	Bernina, It.-Switzerland	13,284	Vignemale, France-Spain	10,820
Nadelhorn, Switzerland	14,196	Fiescherhorn, Switzerland	13,283	Long, Spain	10,479
Grand Combin, Switzerland	14,154	Grunhorn, Switzerland	13,266	Estats, Spain	10,304
Lenzpitze, Switzerland	14,088	Lauteraarhorn, Switzerland	13,261	Montcalm, Spain	10,105
Finsteraarhorn, Switzerland	14,022	Durrenhorn, Switzerland	13,238		
Castor, Switzerland	13,865	Allalinhorn, Switzerland	13,213	**Caucasus (Europe-Asia)**	
Zinalrothorn, Switzerland	13,849	Weissmies, Switzerland	13,199	Elbrus, Russia	18,510
Hohberghom, Switzerland	13,842	Lagginhorn, Switzerland	13,156	Shkhara, Georgia	17,064
Alphubel, Switzerland	13,799	Zupo, Switzerland	13,120	Dykh Tau, Russia	17,054
Rimpfischhorn, Switzerland	13,776	Fletschhorn, Switzerland	13,110	Kashtan Tau, Russia	16,877
Aletschhorn, Switzerland	13,763	Adlerhorn, Switzerland	13,081	Janqi, Georgia	16,565
Strahlhorn, Switzerland	13,747	Gletscherhorn, Switzerland	13,068	Kazbek, Georgia	16,558

Asia (Mainland)

Peak, country/region	Height (ft)	Peak, country/region	Height (ft)	Peak, country/region	Height (ft)
Everest, Nepal-Tibet	29,035	Minya Konka, China	24,900	Nunkun, Kashmir	23,410
K2 (Godwin Austen), Kashmir	28,251	Annapurna III, Nepal	24,786	Lenin Peak, Tajikistan	23,406
Kanchenjunga, India-Nepal	28,169	Kula Gangri, Bhutan-Tibet	24,784	Pyramid, India-Nepal	23,400
Lhotse I (Everest), Nepal-Tibet	27,923	Changtse (Everest), Nepal-Tibet	24,780	Api, Nepal	23,399
Makalu I, Nepal-Tibet	27,824	Muztagh Ata, Xinjiang, China	24,757	Pauhunri, India-Tibet	23,385
Lhotse II (Everest), Nepal-Tibet	27,560	Skyang Kangri, Kashmir	24,750	Trisul, India	23,360
Dhaulagiri, Nepal	26,795	Annapurna IV, Nepal	24,688	Kangto, India-Tibet	23,260
Manaslu I, Nepal	26,781	Ismail Samani Peak, Tajikistan	24,590	Nyenchen Thanglha, Tibet	23,255
Cho Oyu, Nepal-Tibet	26,750	Noshaq, Afghanistan	24,580	Trisuli, India	23,210
Nanga Parbat, Kashmir	26,660	Jongsong Peak,		Pumori, Nepal-Tibet	23,190
Annapurna I, Nepal	26,545	India-Nepal-China	24,472	Dunagiri, India	23,184
Annapurna II, Nepal	26,545	Jengish Chokusu, Xinjiang,		Lombo Kangra, Tibet	23,165
Gasherbrum, Kashmir	26,470	China-Kyrgyzstan	24,406	Saipal, Nepal	23,100
Broad, Kashmir	26,400	Sia Kangri, Kashmir	24,350	Macha Pucchare, Nepal	22,958
Gosainthan, Nepal-Tibet	26,287	Haramosh Peak, Pakistan	24,270	Khan Tengri, Kazakhstan-	
Gyachung Kang, Nepal-Tibet	25,910	Istoro Nal, Pakistan	24,240	Kyrgyzstan-Xinjiang, China	22,949
Disteghil Sar, Kashmir	25,868	Kirat Chuli, India-Nepal	24,165	Ulugh Muztagh, Xinjiang,	
Himalchuli, Nepal	25,801	Chomo Lhari, Bhutan-Tibet	24,040	China-Tibet	22,877
Nuptse (Everest), Nepal-Tibet	25,726	Chamlang, Nepal	24,012	Numbar, Nepal	22,817
Masherbrum, Kashmir	25,660	Kabru, India-Nepal	24,002	Kanjiroba, Nepal	22,580
Nanda Devi, India	25,645	Alung Gangri, Tibet	24,000	Ama Dablam, Nepal	22,350
Rakaposhi, Kashmir	25,550	Baltoro Kangri, Kashmir	23,990	Cho Polu, Nepal	22,093
Kamet, India-Tibet	25,447	Mana, India	23,860	Lingtren, Nepal-Tibet	21,972
Namcha Barwa, Tibet	25,445	Baruntse, Nepal	23,688	Khumbutse, Nepal-Tibet	21,785
Gurla Mandhata, Tibet	25,355	Nepal Peak, India-Nepal	23,500	Hlako Gangri, Tibet	21,266
Kungur, Xinjiang, China	25,325	Amne Machin, China	23,490	Grosvenor, China	21,190
Tirich Mir, Pakistan	25,230	Gauri Sankar, Nepal-Tibet	23,440	Damavand, Iran	18,406
Makalu II, Nepal-Tibet	25,120	Badrinath, India	23,420	Ararat, Turkey	16,854

Antarctica

Peak	Height (ft)	Peak	Height (ft)	Peak	Height (ft)
Vinson Massif	16,066	Sidley	13,720	Donaldson	12,894
Tyree	15,919	Ostenso	13,710	Ray	12,808
Shinn	15,750	Minto	13,668	Sellery	12,779
Gardner	15,375	Miller	13,650	Waterman	12,730
Epperly	15,100	Long Gables	13,620	Anne	12,703
Kirkpatrick	14,855	Dickerson	13,517	Press	12,566
Elizabeth	14,698	Giovinetto	13,412	Falla	12,549
Markham	14,290	Wade	13,400	Rucker	12,520
Bell	14,117	Fisher	13,386	Goldthwait	12,510
Mackellar	14,098	Fridtjof Nansen	13,350	Morris	12,500
Anderson	13,957	Wexler	13,202	Erebus	12,448
Bentley	13,934	Lister	13,200	Campbell	12,434
Kaplan	13,878	Shear	13,100	Don Pedro Christophersen	12,355
Andrew Jackson	13,750	Odishaw	13,008	Lysaght	12,326

Notable Islands and Their Areas

Figures are for total area in square miles. Boldface figures in parentheses show rank among the world's 10 largest individual islands. Only the largest islands in an island group are shown. Table does not include islands smaller than 10 sq mi in area. Canada's Manitoulin Island (1,068 sq mi), in Lake Huron, is the world's largest island in a freshwater lake.

Antarctica

Adelaide	1,400
Alexander	16,700
Berkner	18,500
Roosevelt	2,900

Arctic Ocean

Amund Ringnes, NU, Can.	2,029
Axel Heiberg, NU, Can.	16,671
Baffin, NU, Can. **(5)**	195,928
Banks, NT, Can.	27,038
Bathurst, NU, Can.	6,194
Bolshoy Lyakhovsky, Russia	1,776
Borden, NT-NU, Can.	1,079
Bylot, NU, Can.	4,273
Coats, NU, Can.	2,123
Cornwallis, NU, Can.	2,701
Devon, NU, Can.	21,331
Disko, Greenland, Denmark	3,312
Ellef Ringnes, NU, Can.	4,361
Ellesmere, NU, Can. **(10)**	75,767
Faddayevskiy, Russia.	1,930
Franz Josef Land, Russia	8,000
Iturup (Etorofu), Russia	2,596
King William, NU, Can.	5,062
Kotelny, Russia.	4,504
Mackenzie King, NT, Can.	1,949
Melville, NT-NU, Can.	16,274
Milne Land, Greenland, Den.	1,400
New Siberian Isls., Russia	14,500
Novaya Zemlya, Russia (2 isls.)	31,730
Prince Charles, NT, Can.	3,676
Prince Patrick, NT, Can.	6,119
Prince of Wales, NU, Can.	12,872
Severnaya Zemlya, Russia (tot. group)	14,175
Bol'shevik	4,368
Komsomolets	3,477
Oktyabr'skoy Revolyutsii.	5,471
Somerset, NU, Can.	9,570
Southampton, NU, Can.	15,913
Svalbard, Norway (tot. group).	23,561
Nordaustlandet	5,576
Spitsbergen	14,546
Traill, Greenland, Denmark	1,300
Victoria, NT-NU, Can. **(8)**	83,897
Wrangel, Russia	2,937

Atlantic Ocean

Anticosti, QC, Can.	3,066
Ascension, UK	35
Azores, Portugal (tot. group)	868
Faial	67
San Miguel	291
Bahama Isls. (tot. group)	5,382
Andros	2,300
Bermuda Isls., UK (tot. group)	21
Bioko Isl., Equatorial Guinea	785
Block Island, RI, U.S.	21
Cabo Verde	1,557
Canary Isls., Spain (tot. group).	2,807
Fuerteventura	688
Gran Canaria	592
Tenerife	795
Cape Breton, NS, Can.	3,981
Caviana, Pará, Brazil	1,918
Channel Isls., UK (tot. group)	75
Guernsey	24
Jersey	45
Falkland Isls., UK (tot. group)	4,700
East Falkland	2,550
West Falkland	1,750
Faroe Isls., Denmark	538
Great Britain, UK **(9)**	80,823
Greenland, Denmark **(1)**	836,330
Gurupá, Pará, Brazil.	1,878
Hebrides, Scotland, UK	2,744
Iceland	39,958
Ireland, Ireland-UK	32,589
Isle of Man, UK.	221
Isle of Wight, England, UK	147
Long Island, NY, U.S.	1,320
Madeira Isls., Portugal	306
Marajó, Brazil	15,444
Martha's Vineyard, MA, U.S.	89

Atlantic Ocean

Mount Desert, ME, U.S.	104
Nantucket, MA, U.S.	45
Newfoundland, Canada	42,031
Orkney Isls., Scotland, UK	383
Prince Edward Isl. (main), Can.	2,170
St. Helena, UK	47
Shetland Isls., Scotland, UK	555
Skye, Scotland, UK.	647
South Georgia, UK	1,450
Tierra del Fuego, Chile-Arg.	18,800
Tristan da Cunha, UK	38

Baltic Sea

Aland Isls., Finland	610
Bornholm, Denmark	227
Funen, Denmark	1,154
Gotland, Sweden	1,159
Zealand, Denmark	2,722

Caribbean Sea

Antigua	108
Aruba, Netherlands.	69
Barbados	166
Cayman Isls., UK (tot. group)	102
Cuba	40,285
Isle of Youth	934
Curaçao, Netherlands.	171
Dominica	290
Guadeloupe, France.	687
Hispaniola (Haiti and Dominican Rep.)	29,389
Jamaica	4,244
Martinique, France	436
Montserrat, UK	39
Nevis.	36
Puerto Rico, U.S.	3,425
St. Kitts	65
St. Lucia	238
St. Vincent	133
Tobago	116
Trinidad	1,864
Virgin Isls., UK	59
Virgin Isls., U.S.	134

East Indies

Bali, Indonesia	2,171
Bangka, Indonesia	4,375
Borneo, Indonesia-Malaysia-Brunei **(3)**	290,321
Bougainville, Papua New Guinea	3,880
Buru, Indonesia	3,670
Flores, Indonesia	5,500
Halmahera, Indonesia	6,865
Java (Jawa), Indonesia.	48,900
Madura, Indonesia	2,113
Moluccas, Indonesia.	32,307
New Britain, PNG	14,093
New Guinea, Indon.-PNG **(2)**	303,381
New Ireland, PNG.	3,707
Seram, Indonesia	6,621
Sulawesi (Celebes), Indonesia	69,000
Sumatra, Indonesia **(6)**	182,543
Sumba, Indonesia.	4,306
Sumbawa, Indonesia	5,965
Timor, Indon.–Timor-Leste	13,094
Yos Sudarsa, Indonesia	4,500

Indian Ocean

Andaman Isls., India	2,500
Kerguelen, France	2,247
Madagascar **(4)**	226,917
Mauritius	720
Pemba, Tanzania	380
Réunion, France	970
Seychelles	176
Sri Lanka	25,332
Zanzibar, Tanzania	640

Mediterranean Sea

Balearic Isls., Spain	1,927
Corfu, Greece	229
Corsica, France	3,369
Crete, Greece	3,189
Cyprus	3,572
Elba, Italy	86
Euboea, Greece	1,411

Mediterranean Sea

Malta	95
Rhodes, Greece	540
Sardinia, Italy	9,301
Sicily, Italy.	9,926

Pacific Ocean

Admiralty, AK, U.S.	1,709
Aleutian Isls., AK, U.S. (tot. group)	6,912
Adak	275
Attu	350
Tanaga	195
Umnak	686
Unalaska.	1,051
Unimak	1,571
Baranof, AK, U.S.	1,636
Chichagof, AK, U.S.	2,062
Chiloe, Chile	3,241
Easter Isl. (Rapa Nui), Chile	63
Fiji (tot. group)	7,056
Vanua Levu	2,242
Viti Levu	4,109
Galapagos Isls., Ecuador	3,043
Graham Isl., BC, Can.	2,456
Guadalcanal, Solomon Isls.	2,180
Guam, U.S.	210
Hainan, China	13,000
Hawaiian Isls., HI, U.S. (tot. group)	6,428
Hawaii	4,028
Oahu	597
Hong Kong, China	31
Hoste, Chile	1,590
Japan (tot. group)	145,936
Hokkaido	32,210
Honshu **(7)**	89,240
Kyushu	16,305
Okinawa	881
Shikoku	7,254
Kangaroo, South Australia	1,705
Kiritimati (Christmas), Kiribati	150
Kodiak, AK, U.S.	3,485
Kupreanof, AK, U.S.	1,084
Marquesas Isls., France	492
Marshall Islands	70
Melville, Northern Terr., Australia	2,234
Micronesia	271
New Caledonia, France	6,530
New Zealand (tot. group)	103,362
Chatham Isls.	372
North.	44,075
South	58,076
Stewart	649
Northern Mariana Isls., U.S.	179
Nunivak, AK, U.S.	1,600
Palau	188
Philippines (tot. group)	115,831
Leyte.	2,787
Luzon	40,680
Mindanao	36,775
Mindoro.	3,690
Negros	4,907
Palawan	4,554
Panay	4,446
Samar.	5,050
Prince of Wales, AK, U.S.	2,770
Revillagigedo, AK, U.S.	1,134
Riesco, Chile	1,973
St. Lawrence, AK, U.S.	1,780
Sakhalin, Russia.	29,500
Samoa Isls. (tot. group)	1,177
American Samoa, U.S.	77
Savaii, Samoa	659
Tutuila, U.S.	55
Upolu, Samoa.	432
Santa Catalina, CA, U.S.	75
Santa Ines, Chile	1,407
Tahiti, France	402
Taiwan (tot. group)	13,892
Jinmen Dao (Quemoy)	56
Tasmania, Australia	26,178
Tonga	288
Vancouver Isl., BC, Can.	12,079
Vanuatu	4,707
Wellington, Chile	2,549

Persian Gulf

Bahrain	295

Notable Deserts of the World

Deserts are defined as regions of the Earth receiving less than 10 in. of precipitation annually, usually in combination with an evaporation rate exceeding precipitation.

In addition to areas listed below, the continent of Antarctica, with an area of about 5.48 mil sq mi (of which 110,039 sq mi are ice free), is generally considered a desert. Average annual precipitation for the continent as a whole is 2-6 in., with most precipitation falling along the coast; there is little evaporation.

Arabian, 899,618 sq mi, spanning almost all of Arabian Peninsula
Atacama, 600-mi-long area rich in nitrate and copper deposits in northern Chile
Chihuahuan, 139,769 sq mi in TX, NM, AZ, and Mexico
Dasht-e Kavir, approx. 500 mi long by 200 mi wide in north-central Iran
Dasht-e Lut, approx. 300 mi long by 200 mi wide in south-central Iran
Death Valley, 3,300 sq mi in CA and NV
Eastern (Arabian), 86,000 sq mi in Egypt between the Nile R. and Red Sea, extending south into Sudan
Gibson, 60,232 sq mi in the interior of western Australia
Gobi, 500,002 sq mi in Mongolia and China
Great Sandy, 103,186 sq mi in western Australia
Great Victoria, 134,653 sq mi in southwestern Australia
Kalahari, 347,492 sq mi in southern Africa
Karakum, 135,136 sq mi in Turkmenistan
Kyzyl Kum, 115,000 sq mi in Kazakhstan and Uzbekistan
Libyan, 425,000 sq mi in the Sahara, extending from Libya through southwestern Egypt into Sudan

Mojave, 15,000 sq mi in southern CA
Namib, long narrow area (varies 30-100 mi wide) extending 800 mi along SW coast of Africa
Nubian, 157,000 sq mi in the Sahara in northeastern Sudan
Painted Desert, section of high plateau in northern AZ extending 200 mi southeast from Grand Canyon
Patagonia, 259,847 sq mi in southern Argentina
Rub al-Khali (Empty Quarter), 250,000 sq mi in the S Arabian Peninsula
Sahara, 3,552,140 sq mi in N Africa, extending west to the Atlantic. Largest desert in the world
Sonoran, 120,000 sq mi in southwestern AZ and southeastern CA extending into NW Mexico
Syrian, 193,051 sq mi over much of northern Saudi Arabia, eastern Jordan, southern Syria, and western Iraq
Taklamakan, 130,000 sq mi in Xinjiang Prov., China
Tanami, 71,236 sq mi in northern Australia
Thar (Great Indian), 100,000-sq-mi area extending 400 mi along India-Pakistan border

Areas and Average Depths of Oceans, Seas, and Gulfs

Geographers and mapmakers recognize at least four major bodies of water: the Pacific, Atlantic, Indian, and Arctic Oceans. The Atlantic and Pacific Oceans are considered divided at the equator into N and S. The Arctic Ocean is the name for waters north of the continental landmasses in the region of the Arctic Circle. The International Hydrographic Organization delimited a fifth world ocean in 2000. The Southern Ocean extends from the coast of Antarctica north to 60°S latitude, encompassing portions of the Atlantic, Indian, and Pacific Oceans. A Woods Hole Oceanographic Institution study published in 2010 calculated a mean depth of 12,081 ft for the world's oceans.

Body of water	Area (sq mi)	Avg. depth (ft)	Body of water	Area (sq mi)	Avg. depth (ft)
Pacific Ocean	60,060,893	14,040	Sea of Japan	391,100	5,468
Atlantic Ocean	29,637,974	11,810	Hudson Bay	281,900	305
Indian Ocean	26,469,620	12,800	East China Sea	256,600	620
Southern Ocean	7,848,299	14,450	Andaman Sea	218,100	3,667
Arctic Ocean	5,427,052	4,300	Black Sea	196,100	3,906
South China Sea	2,688,429	4,802	Red Sea	174,900	1,764
Caribbean Sea	971,400	8,448	North Sea	164,900	308
Mediterranean Sea	969,100	4,926	Baltic Sea	147,500	180
Bering Sea	873,000	4,893	Yellow Sea	113,500	121
Gulf of Mexico	582,100	5,297	Persian Gulf	88,800	328
Sea of Okhotsk	537,500	3,192	Gulf of California	59,100	2,375

Principal Ocean Depths

Source: Intl. Hydrographic Org. (IHO); Intergovernmental Oceanographic Commission (IOC) of UNESCO; National Geospatial-Intelligence Agency, U.S. Dept. of Defense

Body of water	Location (lat.)	(long.)	Depth (meters)	(fathoms)	(feet)
Pacific Ocean					
Mariana Trench	11°22′ N	142°36′ E	10,994	6,012	36,069
Tonga Trench	23°16′ S	174°44′ W	10,800	5,906	35,433
Philippine Trench	10°38′ N	126°36′ E	10,057	5,499	32,995
Kermadec Trench	31°53′ S	177°21′ W	10,047	5,494	32,963
Bonin Trench	24°30′ N	143°24′ E	9,994	5,464	32,788
Kuril Trench	44°15′ N	150°34′ E	9,750	5,331	31,988
Izu Trench	31°05′ N	142°10′ E	9,695	5,301	31,808
New Britain Trench	06°19′ S	153°45′ E	8,940	4,888	29,331
Yap Trench	08°33′ N	138°02′ E	8,527	4,663	27,976
Japan Trench	36°08′ N	142°43′ E	8,412	4,600	27,599
Peru-Chile Trench	23°18′ S	71°14′ W	8,064	4,409	26,457
Palau Trench	07°52′ N	134°56′ E	8,054	4,404	26,424
Aleutian Trench	50°51′ N	177°11′ E	7,679	4,199	25,194
New Hebrides Trench	20°36′ S	168°37′ E	7,570	4,139	24,836
North Ryukyu Trench	24°00′ N	126°48′ E	7,181	3,927	23,560
Middle America Trench	14°02′ N	93°39′ W	6,662	3,643	21,857
Atlantic Ocean					
Puerto Rico Trench	19°55′ N	65°27′ W	8,605	4,705	28,232
South Sandwich Trench	55°42′ S	25°56′ W	8,325	4,552	27,313
Romanche Gap	0°13′ S	18°26′ W	7,728	4,226	25,354
Cayman Trench	19°12′ N	80°00′ W	7,535	4,120	24,721
Brazil Basin	09°10′ S	23°02′ W	6,119	3,346	20,076
Indian Ocean					
Java Trench	10°19′ S	109°58′ E	7,125	3,896	23,376
Ob' Trench	09°45′ S	67°18′ E	6,874	3,759	22,553
Diamantina Trench	35°50′ S	105°14′ E	6,602	3,610	21,660
Vema Trench	09°08′ S	67°15′ E	6,402	3,501	21,004
Agulhas Basin	45°20′ S	26°50′ E	6,195	3,387	20,325
Arctic Ocean					
Eurasia Basin	82°23′ N	19°31′ E	5,450	2,980	17,881
Mediterranean Sea					
Ionian Basin	36°32′ N	21°06′ E	5,150	2,816	16,896

Note: Greater depths have been reported in some areas but have not been officially confirmed by research vessels.

Major World Rivers

North American rivers are listed in a separate table.

River	Source or upper limit of length	Outflow	Length (mi)
Africa			
Chari	Bamingui-Bangoran region, Central African Republic	Lake Chad	650
Congo	Junction of Lualaba and Luvua Rivers, Dem. Rep. of Congo	Atlantic Ocean	2,720
Cubango (fmr. Okavango)	Central Angola	Okavango Delta	1,000
Gambia	Fouta Djallon Highlands, Guinea	Atlantic Ocean	700
Kasai	Central Angola	Congo River	1,100
Limpopo	Junction of Marico and Ngotwane Rivers, South Africa	Indian Ocean	1,100
Lualaba	Southeastern Dem. Rep. of Congo	Congo River	1,100
Niger	Fouta Djallon Highlands, Guinea	Gulf of Guinea	2,600
Nile	Luvironza River, Burundi	Mediterranean Sea	4,160
Orange	Maluti Mountains, northern Lesotho	Atlantic Ocean	1,300
Sénégal	Junction of Bafing and Bakoy Rivers, Mali	Atlantic Ocean	1,000
Ubangi	Junction of Uele and Bomu Rivers, Dem. Rep. of Congo	Congo River	700
Zambezi	Northwestern Zambia	Indian Ocean	1,700
Asia			
Amu Darya	Junction of Vakhsh and Panj Rivers, Afghanistan-Tajikistan	Aral Sea	1,660
Amur	Junction of Shilka and Argun Rivers, China-Russia	Tartar Strait	1,780
Angara	Lake Baikal, Russia	Yenisei River	1,150
Ayeyarwady (fmr. Irrawaddy)	Junction of Mali and Nmai Rivers, Myanmar	Andaman Sea	1,000
Brahmaputra	Kailas Range, Himalayas, southwestern Tibet	Bay of Bengal	1,800
Chang-Jiang	Tibetan Plateau, southwestern Qinghai, China	East China Sea	3,450
Euphrates	Junction of Kara (Sarasu) and Murat Rivers, Turkey	Shatt al-Arab	1,700
Ganges	Gangotri glacier, Himalayas, India	Bay of Bengal	1,560
Godavari	Western Ghats, Maharashtra, India	Bay of Bengal	900
Hsi (see Xi He)			
Huang-He	Kunlun Mountains, Qinghai, China	Yellow Sea	3,000
Indus	Kailas Range, Himalayas, Tibet	Arabian Sea	1,900
Irtysh	Kazakhstan-Russia	Ob River	2,650
Jordan	Junction of Dan, Banias, and Hazbani streams, Israel	Dead Sea	200
Kolyma	Kolyma and Cherskogo Ranges, Russia	Arctic Ocean	1,500
Krishna	Western Ghats, Maharashtra, India	Bay of Bengal	800
Kura	Northeastern Turkey	Caspian Sea	950
Lena	Western Baikal Range, Russia	Laptev Sea	2,648
Mekong	Eastern Tibetan Plateau, China	South China Sea	2,700
Narmada	Madhya Pradesh, India	Arabian Sea	775
Ob	Junction of Biya and Katun Rivers, Russia	Gulf of Ob	2,300
Salween	Eastern Tibet, China	Gulf of Martaban	1,750
Songhua Jiang	Changbai Mountains, Jilin, China	Amur River	1,150
Sungari (see Songhua Jiang)			
Sutlej	Kailas Range, Himalayas, Tibet	Indus River	900
Syr	Junction of Naryn and Kara Darya Rivers, Uzbekistan	Aral Sea	1,380
Tarim	Junction of Kashi and Yarkant Rivers, China	Lop Nor	1,300
Tigris	Taurus Mountains, Turkey	Shatt al-Arab	1,150
Xi He	Eastern Yunnan, China	South China Sea	1,250
Yamuna	Yamnotri glacier, Uttarakhand, India	Ganges River	850
Yangtze (see Chang-Jiang)			
Yellow (see Huang-He)			
Yenisei	Kyzyl, Tuva Republic, Russia	Kara Sea	2,500
Australia			
Darling	Eastern Highlands, NE New South Wales/SE Queensland	Murray River	1,703
Murray	Australian Alps, SE New South Wales	Southern Ocean	1,558
Murrumbidgee	Australian Alps, SE New South Wales	Murray River	923
Europe			
Buh, Southern	Podolian Upland, Ukraine	Black Sea	532
Buh, Western	Western Ukraine	Vistula River	500
Danube	Brege and Brigach Rivers, Black Forest, southwestern Germany	Black Sea	1,770
Dnieper	Valdai Hills, western Russia	Black Sea	1,420
Dniester	Carpathian Mountains, Ukraine	Black Sea	850
Don	SE of Tula, Russia	Sea of Azov	1,200
Drava	Carnic Alps, northern Italy	Danube River	450
Dvina, North	Near Veliki Ustyug, Vologda, Russia	White Sea	465
Dvina, West	Valdai Hills, Russia	Gulf of Riga	635
Ebro	Cantabrian Mountains, northern Spain	Mediterranean Sea	575
Elbe	Giant Mountains, northwestern Czech Republic	North Sea	725
Garonne	Central Pyrenees, Spain	Bay of Biscay	402
Kama	Ural Mountains, N of Kuliga, Russia	Volga River	1,260
Loire	Mt. Gerbier-de-Jonc, Vivrais Mountains, France	Atlantic Ocean	630
Marne	Langres Plateau, northeastern France	Seine River	325
Meuse	Langres Plateau, northeastern France	North Sea	560
Oder	Sudetes Mountains, northeastern Czech Republic	Baltic Sea	562
Oka	S of Orël, Russia	Volga River	925
Pechora	Northern Ural Mountains, Russia	Barents Sea	1,120
Po	Cottian Alps, Piedmont, northwestern Italy	Adriatic Sea	405
Rhine	Swiss Alps	North Sea	766

River	Source or upper limit of length	Outflow	Length (mi)
Rhône	Rhône glacier, northeastern Valais, Switzerland	Mediterranean Sea	505
Seine	Langres Plateau, northern Burgundy, France	English Channel	480
Shannon	Near Cuilcagh Mountain, northwestern Cavan County, Ireland	Atlantic Ocean	240
Tagus	E of Madrid, Spain	Atlantic Ocean	585
Thames	4 headstreams in the Cotswold Hills, Gloucestershire, England, UK	North Sea	215
Tiber	Etruscan Apennines, Italy	Tyrrhenian Sea	251
Tisza	N of Rakhiv, western Ukraine	Danube River	700
Ural	Southern Ural Mountains, northeastern Bashkortostan, Russia	Caspian Sea	1,580
Vistula (Wisla)	W Beskid range, Carpathian Mountains, southwestern Poland	Gulf of Gdansk	665
Volga	Valdai Hills, Smolensk, Russia	Caspian Sea	2,290
Weser	Junction of Fulda and Werra Rivers, Germany	North Sea	273

South America

River	Source or upper limit of length	Outflow	Length (mi)
Amazon	Junction of Ucayali and Marañón Rivers, Andes Mountains, Peru	Atlantic Ocean	3,900
Araguaía	Serra das Araras, Goiás-Mato Grosso, Brazil	Tocantins River	1,100
Beni	Cordillera Real, La Paz, Bolivia	Madeira River	1,000
Caquetá-Japura	Andes Mountains, southwestern Colombia	Amazon River	1,750
Juruá	Cerros de Canchyuaya, eastern Peru	Amazon River	1,500
Madeira	Junction of Beni and Mamoré Rivers, Bolivia	Amazon River	2,100
Magdalena	Cordillera Central, southwestern Colombia	Caribbean Sea	1,000
Negro	Southeastern Colombia	Amazon River	1,400
Orinoco	Near Mt. Delgado Chalbaud, Guiana Highlands, S Venezuela	Atlantic Ocean	1,600
Paraguay	Central Mato Grosso highlands, Brazil	Paraná River	1,584
Paraná	Junction of Paranaíba and Rio Grande Rivers, SE Brazil	Río de la Plata	2,485
Pilcomayo	E of Lake Poopó, Bolivia	Paraguay River	1,000
Purus	Andes Mountains, eastern Peru	Amazon River	2,100
Putumayo	Andes Mountains, southern Colombia	Amazon River	1,000
Río de la Plata	Estuary of Paraná and Uruguay Rivers, Argentina-Uruguay	Atlantic Ocean	170
São Francisco	Serra de Canastra, southwestern Minas Gerais, Brazil	Atlantic Ocean	1,800
Tocantins	South-central Goiás, Brazil	Para River	1,640
Ucayali	Junction of Apurímac and Urubamba Rivers, eastern Peru	Marañón River	1,000
Uruguay	Southern Brazil	Río de la Plata	1,000
Xingu	Central Mato Grosso, Brazil	Amazon River	1,230

Major Rivers in North America

River	Source or upper limit of length	Outflow	Length (mi)
Alabama	Gilmer County, GA	Mobile River	729
Albany	Lake St. Joseph, ON, Can.	James Bay	610
Allegheny	Potter County, PA.	Ohio River, Pittsburgh, PA.	325
Altamaha-Ocmulgee	Junction of Yellow and South Rivers, Newton Co., GA	Atlantic Ocean	392
Apalachicola-Chattahoochee	Towns County, GA	Gulf of Mexico	524
Arkansas	Lake County, CO	Mississippi River	1,459
Assiniboine	Eastern Saskatchewan, Can.	Red River	450
Athabasca	Columbia Icefield, AB, Can.	Lake Athabasca	765
Attawapiskat	Attawapiskat, ON, Can.	James Bay	465
Back (NT)	Contwoyto Lake, NT, Can.	Chantrey Inlet, Arctic Ocean	605
Big Black	Webster County, MS	Mississippi River	330
Brazos	Junction of Salt and Double Mountain Forks, Stonewall Co., TX	Gulf of Mexico	1,280
Canadian	Las Animas County, CO	Arkansas River	906
Cedar (IA)	Dodge County, MN	Iowa River	329
Cheyenne	Junction of Antelope Creek and Dry Fork, Converse Co., WY	Missouri River	290
Churchill, Labrador	Lake Ashuanipi, NL, Can.	Atlantic Ocean	532
Churchill, Manitoba	Methy Lake, SK, Can.	Hudson Bay	1,000
Cimarron	Colfax County, NM	Arkansas River	600
Colorado (AZ)	Rocky Mountain Natl. Park, CO	Gulf of California	1,450
Colorado (TX)	Dawson County, TX	Matagorda Bay	862
Columbia	Columbia Lake, BC, Can.	Pacific Ocean, Astoria, OR	1,243
Columbia, Upper	Columbia Lake, BC, Can.	Mouth of Snake River	890
Connecticut	Third Connecticut Lake, NH	Long Island Sound, CT	407
Coppermine	Lac de Gras, NT, Can.	Coronation Gulf, Arctic Ocean	525
Cumberland	Letcher County, KY	Ohio River	720
Delaware	Schoharie County, NY	Liston Point, Delaware Bay	390
Fraser	Near Mount Robson (on Continental Divide)	Strait of Georgia	851
Gila	Catron County, NM	Colorado River	649
Green (UT-WY)	Junction of Wells and Trail Creeks, Sublette County, WY	Colorado River	730
Hudson	Henderson Lake, Essex County, NY	Upper New York Bay	306
Illinois	St. Joseph County, IN.	Mississippi River	420
James (ND-SD)	Wells County, ND	Missouri River	710
James (VA)	Junction of Jackson and Cowpasture Rivers, Botetourt Co., VA	Hampton Roads	340
Kanawha-New	Junction of North and South Forks of New River, NC	Ohio River	352
Kentucky	Junction of North and Middle Forks, Lee County, KY	Ohio River	259
Klamath	Lake Ewauna, Klamath Falls, OR	Pacific O., Klamath, CA	250

River	Source or upper limit of length	Outflow	Length (mi)
Kootenay (Kootenai)	Rocky Mountains, BC, Can.	Columbia River	485
Koyukuk	Endicott Mountains, AK	Yukon River	470
Kuskokwim	Alaska Range	Kuskokwim Bay	724
Liard	Southern Yukon, AK.	Mackenzie River	693
Little Missouri	Crook County, WY	Missouri River	560
Mackenzie	Great Slave Lake, NT, Can.	Arctic Ocean	2,635
Milk	Junction of North and South Forks, AB, Can.	Missouri River	624
Minnesota	Big Stone Lake, MN	Mississippi River	332
Mississippi	Lake Itasca, Clearwater County, MN	Gulf of Mexico	2,340
Mississippi-Missouri-Red Rock	Source of Red Rock, Beaverhead County, MT	Gulf of Mexico	3,710
Missouri	Junction of Jefferson, Madison, and Gallatin Rivers, Gallatin County, MT	Mississippi River	2,315
Missouri-Red Rock	Source of Red Rock, Beaverhead County, MT	Mississippi River	2,540
Mobile-Alabama-Coosa	Gilmer County, GA	Mobile Bay	774
Nelson	Lake Winnipeg, MB, Can.	Hudson Bay	400
Neosho	Morris County, KS	Arkansas River, OK	460
Niobrara	Niobrara County, WY	Missouri River, NE	431
North Canadian	Union County, NM	Canadian River, OK	800
North Platte	Junction of Grizzly and Little Grizzly Creeks, Jackson Co., CO	Platte River, NE	618
Ohio	Junction of Allegheny and Monongahela Rivers, Pittsburgh, PA	Mississippi River, Cairo, IL	981
Osage	East-central Kansas	Missouri River	500
Ottawa	Lake Capimitchigama, QC, Can.	St. Lawrence River	790
Ouachita	Polk County, AR	Black River	605
Peace	Junction of Finlay and Parsnip Rivers, BC, Can.	Slave River	1,195
Pearl	Neshoba County, MS	Gulf of Mexico	411
Pecos	Mora County, NM	Rio Grande	926
Pee Dee-Yadkin	Watauga County, NC	Winyah Bay	435
Pend Oreille-Clark Fork	Near Butte, MT	Columbia River	531
Platte	Junction of North Platte and South Platte Rivers, NE.	Missouri River	990
Porcupine	West-central Yukon, Can.	Yukon River, AK	569
Potomac	Garrett County, MD	Chesapeake Bay	383
Powder	Junction of South and Middle Forks, WY	Yellowstone River	375
Red (River of the South)	Curry County, NM.	Atchafalaya River, LA	1,290
Red River of the North	Junction of Otter Tail and Bois de Sioux Rivers, Wilkin Co., MN	Lake Winnipeg	545
Republican	Junction of North Fork and Arikaree Rivers, NE.	Kansas River	445
Rio Grande (Rio Bravo)	San Juan County, CO.	Gulf of Mexico	1,900
Roanoke	Junction of North and South Forks, Montgomery Co., VA	Albemarle Sound	380
Rock (IL-WI)	Dodge County, WI	Mississippi River	300
Sabine	Junction of South and Caddo Forks, Hunt Co., TX	Sabine Lake	380
Sacramento	Siskiyou County, CA.	Suisun Bay	377
Saguenay	Lake St. John, QC, Can.	St. Lawrence River	434
St. Francis	Iron County, MO.	Mississippi River	425
St. John	Northwestern Maine	Bay of Fundy	418
St. Lawrence	Lake Ontario, NY-ON, Can.	Gulf of St. Lawrence, Atlantic Ocean	800
Salmon (ID)	Custer County, ID.	Snake River	420
San Joaquin	Junction of South and Middle Forks, Madera Co., CA	Suisun Bay	350
San Juan	Silver Lake, Archuleta County, CO.	Colorado River	360
Santee-Wateree-Catawba	McDowell County, NC	Atlantic Ocean	538
Saskatchewan, North	Rocky Mountains, AB, Can.	Saskatchewan R.	800
Saskatchewan, South	Rocky Mountains, AB, Can.	Saskatchewan R.	865
Savannah	Junction of Seneca and Tugaloo Rivers, Anderson Co., SC	Atlantic Ocean, GA-SC	314
Severn (ON)	Sandy Lake, ON, Can.	Hudson Bay	610
Smoky Hill	Cheyenne County, CO	Kansas River, KS	540
Snake	Teton County, WY	Columbia River, WA	1,038
South Platte	Junction of South and Middle Forks, Park County, CO	Platte River	424
Susitna	Alaska Range	Cook Inlet	313
Susquehanna	Otsego Lake, Otsego County, NY	Chesapeake Bay	447
Tallahatchie	Tippah County, MS.	Yazoo River	301
Tanana	Wrangell Mountains, AK.	Yukon River	659
Tennessee	Junction of French Broad and Holston Rivers, TN	Ohio River	652
Tennessee-French Broad	Courthouse Creek, Transylvania County, NC	Ohio River	886
Tombigbee	Prentiss County, MS.	Mobile River	525
Trinity	N of Dallas, TX	Galveston Bay	360
Usumacinta	Junction of Pasión and Chixoy Rivers, Guatemala	Bay of Campeche, Mex.	600
Wabash	Darke County, OH	Ohio River	512
Washita	Hemphill County, TX.	Red River, OK	500
White (AR-MO)	Madison County, AR.	Mississippi River	722
Willamette	Douglas County, OR.	Columbia River	309
Wind-Bighorn	Junction of Wind and Little Wind Rivers, Fremont Co., WY (source of Wind R. is Togwotee Pass, Teton Co., WY)	Yellowstone River	338
Wisconsin	Lac Vieux Desert, Vilas County, WI	Mississippi River	430
Yellowstone	Park County, WY	Missouri River	682
Yukon	McNeil River, YT, Can.	Bering Sea	1,979

Major Natural Lakes of the World

Source: U.S. Geological Survey, U.S. Dept. of the Interior; Natural Resources Canada

A lake is generally defined as a body of water surrounded by land. By this definition some bodies of water that are called seas, such as the Caspian Sea and the Aral Sea, are really lakes. In the following table, the word "lake" is omitted when it is part of the name.

Name	Continent	Area (sq mi)	Length (mi)	Maximum depth (ft)	Elevation (ft)
Caspian Sea[1]	Asia-Europe	143,244	760	3,363	−92
Superior	North America	31,700	350	1,333	601
Victoria	Africa	26,828	209	270	3,720
Huron	North America	23,000	206	750	578
Michigan	North America	22,300	307	923	578
Tanganyika	Africa	12,700	420	4,823	2,534
Baikal	Asia	12,162	395	5,315	1,493
Great Bear	North America	12,096	192	1,463	512
Nyasa (Malawi)	Africa	11,150	360	2,280	1,550
Great Slave	North America	11,030	298	2,014	512
Erie	North America	9,910	241	210	569
Winnipeg	North America	9,416	266	200	712
Ontario	North America	7,340	193	802	243
Balkhash[1]	Asia	7,115	376	85	1,115
Ladoga	Europe	6,835	124	738	13
Maracaibo	South America	5,217	133	115	sea level
Aral Sea[1,2]	Asia	4,040	260	180	175
Onega	Europe	3,710	145	328	108
Eyre[1]	Australia	3,600[3]	90	4	−49
Titicaca	South America	3,200	122	922	12,500
Nicaragua	North America	3,100	102	230	102
Athabasca	North America	3,064	208	407	699
Reindeer	North America	2,568	143	720	1,106
Tonle Sap	Asia	2,500[3]	70	45	NA
Turkana (Rudolf)	Africa	2,473	154	240	1,230
Issyk Kul[1]	Asia	2,355	115	2,303	5,279
Torrens[1]	Australia	2,230[3]	130	NA[3]	92
Vänern	Europe	2,181	91	328	144
Nettilling	North America	2,140	67	NA[3]	98
Winnipegosis	North America	2,075	141	38	833
Albert	Africa	2,075	100	168	2,030
Nipigon	North America	1,872	72	540	853
Gairdner[1]	Australia	1,840[3]	90	NA[3]	112
Manitoba	North America	1,799	140	21	813
Urmia[1]	Asia	888	90	49	4,177
Chad	Africa	521[4]	175	24	787

NA = Not available. (1) Salt lake. (2) The diversion of its two feeder rivers since the 1960s has devastated the Aral—once the world's fourth-largest lake (26,000 sq mi) with length, max. depth, and elevation shown. By 2000, the Aral had effectively become three lakes, with the total area shown. (3) Subject to great seasonal variation. (4) Once fourth-largest lake in Africa (about 10,000 sq mi in the 1960s), Chad had shrunk to around 5% of its original size by 2006 as a result of irrigation and long-term drought.

The Great Lakes

Source: National Ocean Service, National Oceanic and Atmospheric Administration, U.S. Dept. of Commerce

The Great Lakes form the world's **largest freshwater body** (in surface area) and with their connecting waterways are the largest inland water transportation unit. Draining the north-central basin of the U.S., they enable shipping to get to the Atlantic via their outlet, the St. Lawrence R.; the Gulf of Mexico can be reached via the Illinois Waterway, between Lake Michigan and the Mississippi R. A third outlet connects with the Hudson R. and then the Atlantic via the New York State Barge Canal System. Illinois Waterway and NYS Barge Canal System traffic is limited to recreational boating and small shipping vessels.

Only Lake Michigan is wholly in the U.S.; the other lakes are shared with Canada. Ships move from the shores of Lake Superior to Whitefish Bay in the east, then through the Soo Locks in Sault Ste. Marie, MI, onto St. Mary's R. and into Lake Huron. To reach the Port of Indiana-Burns Harbor and South Chicago, IL, ships travel west from Lake Huron to Lake Michigan through the Straits of Mackinac. Low water datum is based on the International Great Lakes Datum (1985), with Rimouski, Quebec, as the reference zero point. The distance between Duluth, MN, and Lake Ontario's east end is 1,156 mi.

	Superior	Michigan	Huron	Erie	Ontario
Length (mi)	350	307	206	241	193
Breadth (mi)	160	118	183	57	53
Deepest soundings (ft)	1,333	923	750	210	802
Volume of water (cu mi)	2,935	1,180	850	116	393
Area (sq mi) water surface—U.S.	20,600	22,300	9,100	4,980	3,460
Canada	11,100	NA	13,900	4,930	3,880
Area (sq mi) entire drainage basin—U.S.	16,900	45,600	16,200	18,000	15,200
Canada	32,400	NA	35,500	4,720	12,100
Total area (sq mi), U.S. and Canada	81,000	67,900	74,700	32,630	34,850
Low water datum above mean water level at Rimouski, QC, avg. level (ft)	601.10	577.50	577.50	569.20	243.30
Latitude, N	46°25′	41°37′	43°00′	41°23′	43°11′
	49°00′	46°06′	46°17′	42°52′	44°15′
Longitude, W	84°22′	84°45′	79°43′	78°51′	76°03′
	92°06′	88°02′	84°45′	83°29′	79°53′
National boundary line (mi)	282.8	NA	260.8	251.5	174.6
U.S. shoreline (mainland only) (mi)	863	1,400	580	431	300

NA = Not applicable.

Notable Waterfalls

The magnitude of a waterfall is determined not only by height but also by volume and steadiness of flow, crest width, the angle of a drop, and the number of leaps it may make. A series of low falls over a considerable distance is known as a cascade. Waterfalls are highly variable and few authoritative figures exist. For more information and some alternative measurements, see the World Waterfall Database at www.worldwaterfalldatabase.com.

Estimated mean annual flow (ft³/sec): Niagara, 205,000; Paulo Afonso, 100,000; Iguazú, 61,000; Victoria, 35,400.

Height is total drop in feet in one or more leaps. If river name is not shown, it is the same as the waterfall. # = more than one leap; * = diminishes greatly seasonally; ** = reduces to a trickle or is dry for part of each year; R. = river; (C) = cascade.

Name, location	Height (ft)	Name, location	Height (ft)	Name, location	Height (ft)
Africa		**Switzerland**		**Maryland**	
Angola-Namibia		Giessbach (C)	984	Great, Potomac R. (C)*	76
Ruacana, Cunene R.	352	Reichenbach#	394	**Minnesota**	
Lesotho		Staubbach	974	Minnehaha**	53
Maletsunyane*	630	Trümmelbach#	950	**New Jersey**	
South Africa		**United Kingdom**		Great, Passaic R.	70
Augrabies, Orange R.*	480	Glomach, Scotland	370	**New York**	
Tugela#	2,800	Pistyll Rhaeadr, Wales	240	Kaaterskill, Lake Creek*	231
Tanzania-Zambia		**North America**		Niagara (American)	120
Kalambo*	704	**Canada**		Taughannock*	215
Zimbabwe-Zambia		**Alberta**		**Oregon**	
Victoria, Zambezi R.*	343	Panther, Nigel Creek	600	Multnomah#	620
Asia and Oceania		**British Columbia**		**Tennessee**	
Australia		Della#	1,444	Fall Creek	256
New South Wales		Takakkaw, Daly Glacier#	992	**Washington**	
Wentworth	614	**Ontario**		Colonial Creek	2,568
Wollomombi	722	Niagara (Horseshoe)	167	Sluiskin, Paradise R.	300
Queensland		**Québec**		Snoqualmie**	268
Tully**	984	Montmorency	276	**Wisconsin**	
Wallaman, Stony Creek	879	**United States**		Big Manitou, Black R. (C)*	165
India		**Alabama**		**Wyoming**	
Jog, Sharavati R.*	829	Noccalula Falls	90	Tower	132
Sivasamudram	320	**California**		Yellowstone (lower)*	308
Japan		Feather*	640	Yellowstone (upper)*	109
Kegon, Lake Chuzenji*	350	**Yosemite National Park**		**South America**	
New Zealand		Bridalveil*	620	**Argentina-Brazil**	
Helena	722	Nevada, Merced R.*	594	Iguazú	269
Sutherland, Arthur R.#	1,904	Ribbon**	1,612	**Brazil**	
Europe		Silver Strand,		Cachoeira da Fumaça*	1,312
Austria		Meadow Brook**	574	Paulo Afonso, São Francisco R.	275
Gastein#	487	Vernal, Merced R.*	317	**Colombia**	
Krimml#	1,246	Wapama	1,310	Tequendama, Bogota R.*	482
France		Yosemite#**	2,425	**Ecuador**	
Gavarnie*	1,385	**Colorado**		Agoyan, Pastaza R.*	200
Italy		Seven Falls,		**Guyana**	
Toce (C)	470	S. Cheyenne Creek#	300	Kaieteur, Potaro R.	741
Norway		**Hawaii**		King George VI, Kamarang R.	1,600
Mardalsfossen#**	2,154	Akaka, Kolekole Stream	420	Marina, Ipobe R.#	500
Skykje**	984	**Idaho**		**Venezuela**	
Vetti, Morka-Koldedola R.	900	Shoshone, Snake R.**	212	Angel (Kerepakupai Merú),	
Sweden		**Kentucky**		Churún#*	3,212
Handol#	345	Cumberland	68	Cuquenan	2,000

Latitude and Longitude of World Cities

Source: National Geospatial-Intelligence Agency, U.S. Dept. of Defense

	Lat.		Long.			Lat.		Long.	
	°	´	°	´		°	´	°	´
City, country					**City, country**				
Athens, Greece	37	59 N	23	44 E	Manila, Philippines	14	35 N	121	0 E
Bangkok, Thailand	13	45 N	100	31 E	Mexico City, Mexico	19	26 N	99	8 W
Beijing, China	39	55 N	116	23 E	Moscow, Russia	55	45 N	37	36 E
Berlin, Germany	52	31 N	13	24 E	Mumbai (Bombay), India	18	59 N	72	50 E
Bogotá, Colombia	4	38 N	74	3 W	New Delhi, India	28	36 N	77	12 E
Buenos Aires, Argentina	34	35 S	58	40 W	Paris, France	48	52 N	2	20 E
Cairo, Egypt	30	4 N	31	17 E	Rio de Janeiro, Brazil	22	52 S	43	16 W
Jakarta, Indonesia	6	10 S	106	49 E	Rome, Italy	41	54 N	12	29 E
Jerusalem, Israel	31	45 N	35	0 E	Santiago, Chile	33	27 S	70	40 W
Johannesburg, South Africa	26	12 S	28	2 E	Seoul, South Korea	37	35 N	127	0 E
Kiev, Ukraine	50	26 N	30	31 E	Sydney, Australia	33	51 S	151	12 E
Lagos, Nigeria	6	35 N	3	45 E	Tehran, Iran	35	40 N	51	25 E
London, UK (Greenwich)	51	28 N	0	0	Tokyo, Japan	35	41 N	139	45 E

Highest and Lowest Continental Elevations

Continent	Highest point	Elev. (ft)	Continent	Lowest point	Ft below sea level
Asia	Everest, Nepal-Tibet	29,035	Antarctica	Bentley Subglacial Trench	8,333
South America	Aconcagua, Argentina	22,831	Asia	Dead Sea, Israel-Jordan	1,414
North America	Denali (fmr. McKinley), Alaska, U.S.	20,310	Africa	Lake Assal, Djibouti	509
Africa	Kilimanjaro, Tanzania	19,341	South America	Laguna del Carbón, Argentina	344
Europe	Elbrus, Russia	18,510	North America	Death Valley, California, U.S.	282
Antarctica	Vinson Massif	16,066	Europe	Caspian Sea, Azer.-Kazakh.-Russ.	92
Australia	Kosciusko, New South Wales	7,310	Australia	Lake Eyre, South Australia	49

(1) Estimated level of the continental floor. Lower points that have yet to be discovered may exist beneath the ice.

Latitude, Longitude, and Elevation of U.S. and Canadian Cities

Source: U.S. geographic positions and altitudes provided by U.S. Geological Survey, U.S. Dept. of the Interior. Canadian geographic positions and altitudes provided by Natural Resources Canada.

City, state/province	Lat. N °	′	″	Long. W °	′	″	Elev. (ft)
Albany, NY	42	39	9	73	45	22	149
Albuquerque, NM	35	5	4	106	39	4	4,956
Anchorage, AK	61	13	5	149	54	1	104
Annapolis, MD	38	58	42	76	29	32	43
Atlanta, GA	33	44	56	84	23	17	1,050
Augusta, GA	33	28	15	81	58	29	141
Augusta, ME	44	18	38	69	46	46	123
Austin, TX	30	16	2	97	44	35	489
Baltimore, MD	39	17	25	76	36	44	36
Baton Rouge, LA	30	27	3	91	9	16	46
Billings, MT	45	47	0	108	30	2	3,124
Birmingham, AL	33	31	14	86	48	9	610
Bismarck, ND	46	48	30	100	47	1	1,695
Boise, ID	43	36	49	116	12	12	2,699
Boston, MA	42	21	30	71	3	35	45
Buffalo, NY	42	53	11	78	52	42	600
Burlington, VT	44	28	33	73	12	43	196
Calgary, AB	51	2	45	114	3	27	3,557
Carson City, NV	39	9	50	119	46	3	4,681
Casper, WY	42	52	0	106	18	47	5,105
Cedar Rapids, IA	42	0	30	91	38	39	808
Charleston, SC	32	46	36	79	55	51	11
Charleston, WV	38	20	59	81	37	57	596
Charlotte, NC	35	13	38	80	50	35	762
Charlottetown, PE	46	14	25	63	8	5	160
Cheyenne, WY	41	8	24	104	49	13	6,087
Chicago, IL	41	51	0	87	39	0	586
Churchill, MB	58	46	51	94	11	13	94
Cleveland, OH	41	29	58	81	41	43	653
Colorado Springs, CO	38	50	2	104	49	17	6,010
Columbia, SC	34	0	3	81	2	5	300
Columbus, OH	39	57	40	82	59	56	780
Concord, NH	43	12	29	71	32	15	273
Corpus Christi, TX	27	48	2	97	23	47	7
Dallas, TX	32	46	59	96	48	24	421
Denver, CO	39	44	21	104	59	5	5,277
Des Moines, IA	41	36	2	93	36	33	873
Detroit, MI	42	19	53	83	2	45	598
Dover, DE	39	9	29	75	31	27	28
Durham, NC	35	59	39	78	53	55	400
Edmonton, AB	53	32	4	113	29	25	2,200
El Paso, TX	31	45	31	106	29	13	3,717
Eugene, OR	44	3	7	123	5	12	430
Evansville, IN	37	58	29	87	33	21	388
Fairbanks, AK	64	50	16	147	42	59	445
Fargo, ND	46	52	38	96	47	23	902
Ft. Smith, AR	35	23	9	94	23	55	440
Ft. Wayne, IN	41	7	50	85	7	44	810
Ft. Worth, TX	32	43	31	97	19	15	653
Frankfort, KY	38	12	3	84	52	24	507
Fredericton, NB	45	56	43	66	40	0	67
Greensboro, NC	36	4	21	79	47	31	827
Greenville, SC	34	51	9	82	23	38	984
Gulfport, MS	30	22	3	89	5	34	21
Halifax, NS	44	52	0	63	42	58	477
Hamilton, ON	43	14	34	79	59	22	780
Harrisburg, PA	40	16	25	76	53	4	332
Hartford, CT	41	45	49	72	41	6	29
Helena, MT	46	35	34	112	2	10	4,047
Hilo, HI	19	43	47	155	5	24	59
Honolulu, HI	21	18	25	157	51	30	17
Houston, TX	29	45	48	95	21	48	37
Idaho Falls, ID	43	28	0	112	2	3	4,705
Indianapolis, IN	39	46	6	86	9	29	720
Iqaluit, NU	63	45	0	68	31	0	112
Jackson, MS	32	17	56	90	11	5	280
Jacksonville, FL	30	19	56	81	39	20	15
Jefferson City, MO	38	34	36	92	10	25	630
Jersey City, NJ	40	43	41	74	4	40	34
Juneau, AK	58	18	7	134	25	11	33
Kansas City, MO	39	5	59	94	34	43	898
Knoxville, TN	35	57	38	83	55	15	904
Lansing, MI	42	43	57	84	33	20	853
Laredo, TX	27	30	23	99	30	20	415
Las Vegas, NV	36	10	30	115	8	14	2,001
Lexington, KY	37	59	19	84	28	40	968

City, state/province	Lat. N °	′	″	Long. W °	′	″	Elev. (ft)
Lincoln, NE	40	48	0	96	40	0	1,200
Little Rock, AR	34	44	47	92	17	23	333
Los Angeles, CA	34	3	8	118	14	37	291
Louisville, KY	38	15	15	85	45	34	466
Madison, WI	43	4	23	89	24	4	873
Manchester, NH	42	59	44	71	27	17	258
Memphis, TN	35	8	58	90	2	56	260
Miami, FL	25	46	27	80	11	37	8
Milwaukee, WI	43	2	20	87	54	23	615
Minneapolis, MN	44	58	48	93	15	50	830
Mobile, AL	30	41	40	88	2	35	10
Montgomery, AL	32	22	0	86	18	0	238
Montpelier, VT	44	15	36	72	34	31	526
Montréal, QC	45	31	0	73	39	0	221
Nashville, TN	36	9	57	86	47	4	567
New Orleans, LA	29	57	17	90	4	30	1
New York, NY	40	42	51	74	0	22	35
Newark, NJ	40	44	8	74	10	21	32
Nome, AK	64	30	4	165	24	23	37
Oklahoma City, OK	35	28	3	97	30	59	1,198
Olympia, WA	47	2	16	122	54	3	93
Omaha, NE	41	15	31	95	56	16	1,059
Ottawa, ON	45	20	0	75	35	3	382
Overland Park, KS	38	58	56	94	40	15	1,084
Philadelphia, PA	39	57	8	75	9	50	45
Phoenix, AZ	33	26	54	112	4	27	1,085
Pierre, SD	44	22	6	100	21	3	1,479
Pittsburgh, PA	40	26	26	79	59	45	766
Portland, OR	45	31	24	122	40	34	33
Providence, RI	41	49	26	71	24	46	9
Provo, UT	40	14	2	111	39	31	4,551
Québec, QC	46	49	0	71	13	0	244
Raleigh, NC	35	46	20	78	38	19	315
Rapid City, SD	44	4	50	103	13	52	3,243
Regina, SK	50	27	17	104	36	24	1,894
Reno, NV	39	31	47	119	48	50	4,505
Richmond, VA	37	33	14	77	27	37	213
Rochester, NY	43	9	17	77	36	56	504
Sacramento, CA	38	34	54	121	29	40	27
St. John's, NL	47	28	56	52	47	49	461
St. Louis, MO	38	37	38	90	11	52	464
St. Paul, MN	44	56	34	93	5	36	789
Salem, OR	44	56	35	123	2	6	157
Salt Lake City, UT	40	45	39	111	53	28	4,265
San Antonio, TX	29	25	27	98	29	37	649
San Diego, CA	32	42	55	117	9	26	63
San Francisco, CA	37	46	30	122	25	10	54
San Jose, CA	37	20	22	121	53	42	82
San Juan, PR	18	27	59	66	6	21	26
Santa Fe, NM	35	41	13	105	56	16	6,995
Saskatoon, SK	52	8	23	106	41	10	1,653
Savannah, GA	32	5	1	81	5	59	20
Seattle, WA	47	36	22	122	19	55	177
Shreveport, LA	32	31	31	93	45	1	151
Sioux City, IA	42	30	0	96	24	1	1,201
Sioux Falls, SD	43	33	0	96	42	1	1,473
Spokane, WA	47	39	35	117	25	45	1,732
Springfield, IL	39	48	6	89	38	37	600
Tacoma, WA	47	15	10	122	26	39	250
Tampa, FL	27	56	51	82	27	30	15
Topeka, KS	39	2	54	95	40	41	948
Toronto, ON	43	44	30	79	22	24	251
Trenton, NJ	40	13	1	74	44	35	61
Tucson, AZ	32	13	18	110	55	35	2,490
Tulsa, OK	36	9	14	95	59	34	721
Vancouver, BC	49	15	40	123	6	50	14
Victoria, BC	48	25	42	123	21	53	63
Virginia Beach, VA	36	51	11	75	58	41	11
Washington, DC	38	53	42	77	2	11	24
Whitehorse, YT	60	41	46	135	4	51	2,305
Wichita, KS	37	41	32	97	20	15	1,302
Wilmington, DE	39	44	45	75	32	48	91
Wilmington, NC	34	13	33	77	56	41	36
Winnipeg, MB	49	53	4	97	8	47	783
Yakima, WA	46	36	7	120	30	21	1,068
Yellowknife, NT	62	27	13	114	22	12	675

RELIGION

Religious Affiliation in the U.S., 2021

Source: Todd M. Johnson and Brian J. Grim, eds., *World Religion Database* (Leiden/Boston: Brill, July 2020)

Affiliation	2021 pop.	Percent	Affiliation	2021 pop.	Percent	Affiliation	2021 pop.	Percent
Agnostics	56,441,000	16.9%	Christians	245,264,000	73.5%	Muslims	5,003,000	1.5%
Atheists	10,883,000	3.3	Daoists	13,000	—	New religionists	1,786,000	0.5
Baha'is	592,000	0.2	Ethnic religionists	1,123,000	0.3	Shintoists	66,300	—
Buddhists	4,438,000	1.3	Hindus	1,674,000	0.5	Sikhs	411,000	0.1
Chinese			Jains	98,200	—	Spiritists	261,000	0.1
folk-religionists	116,000	—	Jews	5,596,000	1.7	Zoroastrians	18,000	—

— = Less than 0.05%.

Religious Group Membership in the U.S., 2015

Source: Todd M. Johnson and Gina A. Zurlo, eds., *World Christian Database* (Leiden/Boston: Brill, July 2020)

Figures generally are based on collected reports made by each denomination as of 2015 and include only persons affiliated with a congregation of the denomination. Reporting practices vary from one denomination to another but generally include all members, not only full communicants. Denominations with fewer than 28,000 members not generally shown. Broad religious groups are indicated in **boldface**.

Group (congregations)	Members
African Methodist Episcopal Church (9,000)	2,800,000
African Methodist Episcopal Zion Church (3,400)	1,750,000
Agnosticism	**51,178,000**
Albanian Orthodox Archdiocese in America (15)	35,000
American Baptist Assn. (1,500)	100,000
American Baptist Churches in the USA (5,100)	1,469,000
Antiochian Orthodox Christian (270)	480,000
Apostolic Assemblies of Christ Intl. (260)	50,000
Apostolic Assembly of the Faith in Christ Jesus (760)	89,700
Armenian Apostolic Church of America (37)	360,000
Armenian Church of North America (100)	370,000
Armenian Evangelical Union of Churches (60)	40,000
Assemblies of God USA (13,700)	3,522,000
Assemblies of the Lord Jesus Christ (440)	62,000
Assembly of Christian Churches (140)	28,000
Assn. of Free Lutheran Congregations (280)	48,000
Assn. of Intl. Gospel Assemblies (260)	270,000
Associate Reformed Presbyterian Church (290)	50,000
Assyrian Church of the East (23)	115,000
Atheism	**9,287,000**
Baha'i Faith	**540,000**
Baptist Bible Fellowship Intl. (4,500)	1,730,000
Baptist General Conference (1,300)	399,000
Baptist Missionary Assn. of America (1,300)	230,000
Bible Way Churches of Our Lord Jesus Christ World-Wide (750)	150,000
Buddhism	**4,156,000**
Calvary Chapels Intl. (1,200)	525,000
Catholic Church in the USA[1] (18,000)	72,798,000
Charis Fellowship (260)	36,500
Chinese folk-religions[2]	**112,000**
Christian and Missionary Alliance (2,100)	653,000
Christian Brethren (Open) (1,300)	112,000
Christian Church (Disciples of Christ) (3,600)	786,000
Christian Churches and Churches of Christ (4,800)	1,150,000
Christian Congregation (1,600)	130,000
Christian International Ministries (150)	36,000
Christian Methodist Episcopal Church (3,900)	1,000,000
Christian Reformed Church in N. America (1,100)	236,000
Christianity	**239,495,000**
Church of Christ, Scientist (1,200)	140,000
Church of God (Anderson, IN) (2,000)	277,000
Church of God (Cleveland, OH) (6,500)	1,454,000
Church of God (Huntsville, AL) (1,600)	83,000
Church of God in Christ (24,000)	8,046,000
Church of God of Prophecy (1,700)	108,000
Church of Jesus Christ (400)	100,000
Church of Jesus Christ of Latter-day Saints (14,200)	6,642,000
Church of Our Lord Jesus Christ of Apostolic Faith (550)	670,000
Church of the Brethren (970)	138,000
Church of the Living God (170)	42,000
Church of the Nazarene (4,500)	773,000
Churches of Christ (Non-Instrumental) (12,200)	1,510,000
Churches of God General Conference (330)	39,000
Churches of God (Holiness) (30)	30,000
Churches on the Rock Intl. (100)	100,000
Community of Christ (900)	170,000
Conservative Baptist Assn. of America (1,100)	186,000
Conservative Congregational Christian Conference (320)	40,000
Coptic Orthodox Church (250)	500,000
Covenant Ministries Intl. (35)	95,000
Crenshaw Christian Center (2)	28,000

Group (congregations)	Members
Cumberland Presbyterian Church (920)	70,800
Czechoslovak Hussite Church (20)	50,000
Daoism	**12,800**
Defenders of the Christian Faith (90)	30,000
Elim Assemblies Fellowship (260)	40,000
Episcopal Church in the USA (4,800)	1,917,000
Ethiopian Orthodox Church in the USA (80)	85,000
Ethnic religions[2]	**1,118,000**
Evangelical Covenant Church of America (900)	160,000
Evangelical Fellowship Intl. (300)	90,000
Evangelical Free Church of America (1,500)	375,000
Evangelical Lutheran Church in America (10,500)	4,300,000
Evangelical Presbyterian Church (600)	145,000
Evangelistic Messengers Assn. (650)	65,000
Faith Christian Fellowship Intl. (150)	75,000
Fellowship of Christian Believers (70)	30,000
Free Methodist Church of North America (1,100)	76,000
Friends General Conference (600)	28,000
Friends United Meeting (600)	40,000
Full Gospel Baptist Church Fellowship (600)	180,000
Full Gospel Fellowship of Churches and Ministers (800)	450,000
General Assn. of General Baptists (820)	59,200
General Assn. of Regular Baptist Churches (1,200)	200,000
Global Christian Ministry Forum (75)	37,500
Global Network of Christian Ministries (280)	45,000
Grace Communion International (130)	30,000
Grace Intl. (110)	130,000
Greater Emmanuel Intl. Fellowship (50)	50,000
Greek Orthodox Archdiocese of America (540)	1,500,000
Gulf States Pastors & Churches Fellowship (360)	28,000
Hinduism	**1,549,000**
Independent Assemblies Fellowship (500)	80,000
Independent Assemblies of God Intl. (310)	122,000
Independent Fundamental Churches of America (620)	58,000
Intl. Church of the Foursquare Gospel (1,900)	327,000
Intl. Churches of Christ (170)	52,100
Intl. Convention of Faith Ministries (420)	105,000
Intl. Council of Community Churches (130)	66,000
Intl. Pentecostal Holiness Church (1,700)	265,000
Islam[3]	**4,411,000**
Jainism	**91,200**
Jehovah's Witnesses (13,600)	2,834,000
Judaism[4]	**5,616,000**
Korean American Presbyterian Church (670)	72,000
Korean Full Gospel Churches of America (850)	260,000
Korean Presbyterian Church in America (310)	60,000
Korean Presbyterian Church of America (1,900)	600,000
Latin American Council of Christian Churches (200)	36,000
Lutheran Church-Missouri Synod (6,100)	2,061,000
Malankara Orthodox Syrian Church of the East (100)	50,000
Mennonite Church USA (850)	130,000
Ministers Fellowship Intl. (210)	55,000
Missionary Church (400)	50,000
Moravian Church in America (170)	40,000
Native American Church of North America (400)	200,000
Natl. Assn. of Free Will Baptists (2,100)	178,000
Natl. Baptist Convention of America (12,500)	4,250,000
Natl. Baptist Convention, USA (40,000)	9,200,000
Natl. Missionary Baptist Conv. of America (270)	440,000
Natl. Primitive Baptist Convention (1,600)	600,000
New Apostolic Church USA (220)	38,400
New Religions[2]	**1,645,000**

Group (congregations)	Members	Group (congregations)	Members
North American Baptist Conference (380)	61,900	Southern Baptist Convention (47,300)	18,836,000
North American Old Roman Catholic Church (140)	66,000	**Spiritism**	**232,000**
Old Order Amish Mennonite Church (1,000)	126,000	Syriac Orthodox Church of Antioch (33)	31,000
Old Order & Wisler Mennonite Church (64)	28,000	Unitarian Universalist Assn. (1,000)	216,000
Open Bible Churches (320)	42,000	United Baptist churches (400)	55,000
Orthodox Church in America (530)	2,900,000	United Brethren in Christ (200)	37,000
Orthodox Presbyterian Church (270)	32,000	United Church of Christ (5,000)	880,000
Pentecostal Assemblies of the World (1,600)	1,300,000	United Church of Jesus Christ (Apostolic) (120)	36,000
Pentecostal Church of God (1,100)	100,000	United Free Will Baptist Church (700)	100,000
Pentecostal Churches of the Apostolic Faith (350)	75,000	United House of Prayer for All People (140)	1,700,000
Potter's House (10)	35,000	United Methodist Church (33,000)	7,067,000
Presbyterian Church in America (1,900)	372,000	United Pentecostal Church Intl. (4,500)	875,000
Presbyterian Church (USA) (9,600)	1,705,000	Unity School of Christianity (680)	140,000
Primitive Baptists (3,000)	135,000	Universal Fellowship of MCCs (220)	40,000
Progressive Natl. Baptist Convention (1,200)	1,857,000	U.S. Conference of Mennonite Brethren	
Redeemed Christian Church of God (700)	35,000	Churches (200)	45,000
Reformed Church in America (890)	214,000	Vineyard Churches (USA) (590)	180,000
Rhema Bible Churches (600)	180,000	Way of the Cross Church of Christ (75)	80,000
Romanian Orthodox Episcopate of America (100)	110,000	Wesleyan Church (1,600)	135,000
Salvation Army (1,100)	400,000	Willow Creek Assn. of Churches (2,200)	440,000
Serbian Orthodox Church in N. and S. Amer. (120)	68,000	Wisconsin Evangelical Lutheran Synod (1,300)	367,000
Seventh-day Adventist Church (5,000)	1,309,000	World Council of Independent Christian Chs. (240)	40,000
Shintoism	**64,600**	World Harvest Ministerial Alliance (140)	40,000
Sikhism	**403,000**	Zoroastrianism	18,200

(1) According to the U.S. Center for Applied Research in the Apostolate, there were 75.4 mil self-identified Catholics in the U.S. in 2015 and 72.4 mil in 2019. (2) **Chinese folk-religionists** include followers of traditional Chinese religion; it may involve worship of local deities, ancestor veneration, Confucian ethics, divination, and Buddhist or Taoist elements, among other beliefs and practices. **Ethnic religionists** include followers of local, tribal, animistic, or shamanistic religions, generally belonging to a single ethnic group. **New religionists** include followers of Asian new religions, neoreligious movements, radical new crisis religions, and syncretistic mass religions. (3) Other sources vary. In 2017, the Council on American-Islamic Relations estimated a total of 2,000 mosques and 6-7 mil Muslims in the U.S., and a Pew Research Center report in Jan. 2018 estimated the U.S. Muslim pop. at 3.45 mil. (4) Includes Jewish Reconstructionist Communities (about 90), Union of Orthodox Jewish Congregations of America (500), Other Orthodox congregations (1,200), Chabad (over 2,000), Union for Reform Judaism (850), and United Synagogue of Conservative Judaism (580). Among Jewish adherents in the U.S., about 35% classify themselves as Reform, 18% as Conservative, 10% as Orthodox, 2% as Reconstructionist, the rest as "just Jewish." Source: Ira M. Sheskin and Arnold Dashefsky, "United States Jewish Population, 2019," in *The American Jewish Year Book* (Dordrecht: Springer, 2019). (This source estimates the total American Jewish population at 6.7 mil.)

World Adherents of Religions by Continental Area, 2021

Source: Todd M. Johnson and Brian J. Grim, eds., *World Religion Database* (Leiden/Boston: Brill, July 2020). All adherents figures are midyear estimates, in thous.

Religion (no. of countries/territories)	Africa	Asia	Europe	Latin America	Northern America	Oceania	World	% of world pop.
Baha'is (224)	2,787	3,885	170	1,043	647	138	8,671	0.1%
Buddhists (152)	376	541,094	2,026	856	5,105	1,036	550,493	7.0
Chinese folk-religionists (120)	249	468,873	685	216	885	195	471,103	6.0
Christians (234)	684,931	382,829	563,906	617,295	268,822	27,796	2,545,579	32.3
Catholics (234)	242,820	151,466	247,592	510,520	88,225	9,695	1,250,319	15.9
Protestants (231)	263,882	107,793	86,817	64,450	57,539	13,180	593,660	7.5
Independents (231)	131,714	126,525	11,900	59,362	65,351	2,139	396,991	5.0
Orthodox (142)	58,954	18,801	204,881	1,383	8,448	1,132	293,599	3.7
Confucianists (17)	37	8,486	17	1	—	70	8,610	0.1
Ethnoreligionists (148)	108,443	154,725	1,163	3,927	1,267	424	269,949	3.4
Hindus (144)	3,762	1,064,609	1,398	806	2,208	835	1,073,619	13.6
Jains (20)	122	5,889	24	2	116	8	6,160	0.1
Jews (148)	92	6,987	1,299	393	5,956	111	14,838	0.2
Muslims (217)	575,416	1,286,741	54,758	1,818	6,451	933	1,926,115	24.5
Sunnis (214)	569,712	1,088,746	52,060	1,330	4,489	711	1,717,048	21.8
Shiites (149)	994	186,921	2,658	474	1,249	218	192,513	2.4
New religionists (121)	148	60,962	392	1,909	1,886	143	65,441	0.8
Shintoists (9)	—	2,698	—	9	66	—	2,774	—
Sikhs (64)	95	26,551	742	8	947	195	28,538	0.4
Spiritists (59)	3	2	152	14,485	280	9	14,932	0.2
Daoists (7)	—	9,120	—	—	13	14	9,147	0.1
Zoroastrians (29)	1	146	6	—	25	3	181	—
All religious adherents (234)	**1,376,461**	**4,023,596**	**626,741**	**642,767**	**294,674**	**31,911**	**6,996,150**	**88.8**
Nonreligious (233)	9,194	637,442	116,755	27,744	77,157	11,023	879,315	11.2
Agnostics (233)	8,487	523,523	101,216	24,212	65,197	9,070	731,705	9.3
Atheists (223)	707	113,919	15,539	3,532	11,960	1,952	147,609	1.9

— = Less than 500 adherents or 0.05% of world pop. **Note:** Figures may not add up to totals due to rounding. Continental areas are as per UN demographic terminology; "Asia" is defined to include the former Soviet Central Asian states, while "Europe" includes all of Russia, extending to the Pacific coast. Figures in parentheses indicate the number of countries/territories where the religion or type of belief has a significant following. **Buddhists** include Mahayana (72%), Theravada or Hinayana (25%), and Tantrayana (incl. Lamaists, Tibetans) (3%). **Chinese folk-religionists** are followers of traditional Chinese religion; it may involve worship of local deities, ancestor veneration, Confucian ethics, divination, and Buddhist or Daoist elements, among other beliefs and practices. **Christians** are usually baptized members of a church belonging to one of the major Christian traditions shown here. Those characterized as Independents belong to groups that consider themselves independent of historical mainstream institutionalized Christianity; these include groups such as Unitarians, Church of Jesus Christ of Latter-day Saints, and Jehovah's Witnesses. **Confucianists** are followers of Confucius, mostly living in China or elsewhere in East/Southeast Asia. **Ethnic religionists** are followers of local, tribal, animistic, or shamanistic religions, generally belonging to a single ethnic group. **Hindus** include Vaishnavites (38%); Shaivites (36%); and Shaktas, neo-Hindi, and reformed Hindi (26%). **New religionists** include followers of Asian new religions, neoreligious movements, radical new crisis religions, and syncretistic mass religions.

Episcopal Church Liturgical Colors and Calendar, 2020-24

The most common liturgical colors in the Episcopal Church are as follows: **White**—Christmas Day through first Sunday after Epiphany; Maundy Thursday (as an alternative to crimson at the Eucharist); from the Vigil of Easter to the Day of Pentecost (Whitsunday); Trinity Sunday; Feasts of the Lord (except Holy Cross Day); the Confession of St. Peter; the Conversion of St. Paul; St. Joseph; St. Mary Magdalene; St. Mary the Virgin; St. Michael and All Angels; All Saints' Day; St. John the Evangelist; memorials of other saints who were not martyred; Independence Day and Thanksgiving Day; weddings and funerals. **Red**—the Day of Pentecost; Holy Cross Day; feasts of apostles and evangelists (except those previously mentioned); feasts and memorials of martyrs (including Holy Innocents' Day). **Violet**—Advent and Lent. **Crimson** or oxblood (dark red)—Holy Week. **Green**—the seasons after Epiphany and after Pentecost. **Black**—optional alternative for funerals and Good Friday.

The days of fasting are Ash Wednesday and Good Friday. Other days of special devotion (penitence) include the 40 days of Lent. Ember days are days of prayer for the church's ministry. They fall on the Wednesday, Friday, and Saturday after the first Sunday in Lent, the Day of Pentecost, Holy Cross Day, and Dec. 13. Rogation Days, the three days before Ascension Day, are days of prayer for God's blessing on the crops, on commerce and industry, and for conservation of the Earth's resources.

Holy days and other variables	2020	2021	2022	2023	2024
Golden Number	7	8	9	10	11
Sunday Letter	E/D	C	B	A	G/F
Sundays after Epiphany	7	6	8	7	6
Ash Wednesday	Feb. 26	Feb. 17	Mar. 2	Feb. 22	Feb. 14
First Sunday in Lent	Mar. 1	Feb. 21	Mar. 6	Feb. 26	Feb. 18
Passion/Palm Sunday	Apr. 5	Mar. 28	Apr. 10	Apr. 2	Mar. 24
Good Friday	Apr. 10	Apr. 2	Apr. 15	Apr. 7	Mar. 29
Easter Day	Apr. 12	Apr. 4	Apr. 17	Apr. 9	Mar. 31
Ascension Day	May 21	May 13	May 26	May 18	May 9
Day of Pentecost	May 31	May 23	June 5	May 28	May 19
Trinity Sunday	June 7	May 30	June 12	June 4	May 26
Numbered Proper of 2 Pentecost	#6	#5	#7	#5	#4
First Sunday of Advent	Nov. 29	Nov. 28	Nov. 27	Dec. 3	Dec. 1

Greek Orthodox Movable Ecclesiastical Dates, 2020-24

Feast days and fasting days are determined annually on the basis of the date of Holy Pascha (Easter). Western Easter dates are also included for reference. This ecclesiastical cycle begins with the first day of the Triodion and ends with the Sunday of All Saints, a total of 18 weeks. In years where Pascha falls on or after May 3, Fast of Holy Apostles lasts zero days.

Holy days and observances	2020	2021	2022	2023	2024
Triodion begins	Feb. 9	Feb. 21	Feb. 13	Feb. 5	Feb. 25
1st Saturday of Souls	Feb. 22	Mar. 6	Feb. 26	Feb. 18	Mar. 9
Meat-Fare Sunday	Feb. 23	Mar. 7	Feb. 27	Feb. 19	Mar. 10
2nd Saturday of Souls	Feb. 29	Mar. 13	Mar. 5	Feb. 25	Mar. 16
Lent begins	Mar. 2	Mar. 15	Mar. 7	Feb. 27	Mar. 18
St. Theodore—3rd Saturday of Souls	Mar. 7	Mar. 20	Mar. 12	Mar. 4	Mar. 23
Sunday of Orthodoxy	Mar. 8	Mar. 21	Mar. 13	Mar. 5	Mar. 24
Saturday of Lazarus	Apr. 11	Apr. 24	Apr. 16	Apr. 8	Apr. 27
Palm Sunday	Apr. 12	Apr. 25	Apr. 17	Apr. 9	Apr. 28
Holy (Good) Friday	Apr. 17	Apr. 30	Apr. 22	Apr. 14	May 3
Western Easter	Apr. 12	Apr. 4	Apr. 17	Apr. 9	Mar. 31
Orthodox Pascha (Easter)	Apr. 19	May 2	Apr. 24	Apr. 16	May 5
Ascension	May 28	June 10	June 2	May 25	June 13
Saturday of Souls	June 6	June 19	June 11	June 3	June 22
Pentecost	June 7	June 20	June 12	June 4	June 23
All Saints	June 14	June 27	June 19	June 11	June 30
Fast of Holy Apostles (first day)	June 15	June 28	June 20	June 12	NA
Fast of Holy Apostles lasts	14 days	1 day	9 days	15 days	0 days

Jewish Holy Days, 5780-5784 (2019-24)

The Jewish calendar consists of 12 lunar months, alternating between 29 and 30 days. It is lunisolar and adjusts for the solar cycle by adding an extra month (Adar II) in the 3rd, 6th, 8th, 11th, 14th, 17th, and 19th years of a 19-year cycle. The calendar starts on the day of Creation, reckoned in the 2nd-3rd cent. BCE as Tishrei 1, 3,761 years before the common era.

The religious calendar begins with the month Nisan, from which all other months are counted, and the civil calendar with Tishrei. The months are 1) Nisan, 2) Iyar, 3) Sivan, 4) Tammuz, 5) Av (also Abh), 6) Elul, 7) Tishrei, 8) Cheshvan (also Marcheshvan), 9) Kislev, 10) Tevet (also Tebeth), 11) Shevat (also Shebhat), 12) Adar, and 12a) Adar Sheni (II), added in leap years.

All holidays listed below begin at sunset of the previous day and end at nightfall on the last day shown.

Holiday	Date on Jewish cal.	5780 (2019-20)		5781 (2020-21)		5782 (2021-22)		5783 (2022-23)		5784 (2023-24)	
Rosh Hashanah (New Year)	Tishrei 1	Sept. 30	Mon.	Sept. 19	Sat.	Sept. 7	Tue.	Sept. 26	Mon.	Sept. 16	Sat.
	Tishrei 2	Oct. 1	Tue.	Sept. 20	Sun.	Sept. 8	Wed.	Sept. 27	Tue.	Sept. 17	Sun.
Yom Kippur (Day of Atonement)	Tishrei 10	Oct. 9	Wed	Sept. 28	Mon.	Sept. 16	Thu.	Oct. 5	Wed.	Sept. 25	Mon.
Sukkot	Tishrei 15	Oct. 14	Mon.	Oct. 3	Sat.	Sept. 21	Tue.	Oct. 10	Mon.	Sept. 30	Sat.
	Tishrei 20	Oct. 20	Sun.	Oct. 9	Fri.	Sept. 27	Mon.	Oct. 16	Sun.	Oct. 6	Fri.
Shemini Atzeret	Tishrei 22	Oct. 21	Mon.	Oct. 10	Sat.	Sept. 28	Tue.	Oct. 17	Mon.	Oct. 7	Sat.
Simchat Torah	Tishrei 23	Oct. 22	Tue.	Oct. 11	Sun.	Sept. 29	Wed.	Oct. 18	Tue.	Oct. 8	Sun.
Hanukkah	Kislev 25	Dec. 23	Mon.	Dec. 11	Fri.	Nov. 29	Mon.	Dec. 19	Mon.	Dec. 8	Fri.
	Tevet 2 or 3	Dec. 30	Mon.	Dec. 18	Fri.	Dec. 6	Mon.	Dec. 26	Mon.	Dec. 15	Fri.
Purim	Adar 14	Mar. 10	Tue.	Feb. 26	Fri.	Mar. 17	Thu.	Mar. 7	Tue.	Mar. 24	Sun.
Pesach (Passover)	Nisan 15	Apr. 9	Thu.	Mar. 28	Sun.	Apr. 16	Sat.	Apr. 6	Thu.	Apr. 23	Tue.
	Nisan 22	Apr. 16	Thu.	Apr. 4	Sun.	Apr. 23	Sat.	Apr. 13	Thu.	Apr. 30	Tue.
Shavuot	Sivan 6	May 29	Fri.	May 17	Mon.	June 5	Sun.	May 26	Fri.	June 12	Wed.
	Sivan 7	May 30	Sat.	May 18	Tue.	June 6	Mon.	May 27	Sat.	June 13	Thu.
Fast of the 9th of Av	Av 9	July 30	Thu.	July 18	Sun.	Aug. 7	Sun.	July 27	Thu.	Aug. 13	Tue.

Hindu Festivals, 2020-24

There are various traditional lunisolar Hindu calendars. Most have similar names for the 12 lunar months, with days beginning at dawn or sunrise, but they differ in various ways, including the numbering of years and the starting point of months. The Indian civil (Saka) calendar, adopted in 1957, is solar-based, and begins Mar. 22 (Mar. 21 in leap years). The year 1942 on the Saka calendar begins Mar. 9, 2020. There are many Hindu holidays and festivals; some are observed only in certain regions. Below are three of the most widely observed.

Festival	2020	2021	2022	2023	2024
Maha Shivaratri (Night of Shiva)[1]	Feb. 21	Mar. 11	Feb. 28	Feb. 18	Mar. 8
Holi (Festival of Color)	Mar. 9	Mar. 28	Mar. 18	Mar. 7	Mar. 25
Diwali (Festival of Lights)	Nov. 14	Nov. 4	Oct. 24	Nov. 12	Oct. 31

(1) Begins the night of the previous day.

Islamic Holy Days, 1441-1445 AH (late 2019-24)

The Islamic calendar is a strict lunar calendar reckoned from the year of the Hijra—Muhammad's flight from Mecca to Medina, in 622 CE. Each year consists of 12 lunar months of 29 or 30 days beginning and ending with each new moon's visible crescent. Common years have 354 days; leap years have 355 days. Some Muslim countries employ a conventionalized calendar with the leap day added to the last month, Dhu'l-Hijja, but for religious purposes the leap date is taken into account by tracking each new moon sighting.

Holy days begin at sunset of the day previous to the day cited. The actual dates may vary slightly from what is shown below, depending on the locality and the times of actual moon sightings as determined by different authorities.

Holy day (date)	1441 (2019-20)	1442 (2020-21)	1443 (2021-22)	1444 (2022-23)	1445 (2023-24)
New Year's Day (Muharram 1)	Aug. 31, 2019	Aug. 20, 2020	Aug. 9, 2021	July 30, 2022	July 19, 2023
Ashura (Muharram 10)	Sept. 9, 2019	Aug. 29, 2020	Aug. 18, 2021	July 8, 2022	July 28, 2023
Mawlid (Rabi' I 12)	Nov. 10, 2019	Oct. 29, 2020	Oct. 19, 2021	Oct. 8, 2022	Sept. 27, 2023
Ramadan begins (Ramadan 1)	Apr. 24, 2020	Apr. 13, 2021	Apr. 3, 2022	Mar. 23, 2023	Mar. 11, 2024
Eid al-Fitr (Shawwal 1)	May 24, 2020	May 13, 2021	May 3, 2022	Apr. 22, 2023	Apr. 10, 2024
Eid al-Adha (Dhu'l-Hijja 10)	July 31, 2020	July 20, 2021	July 10, 2022	June 29, 2023	June 17, 2024

Ash Wednesday and Easter Sunday (Western Churches), 2001-2100

Year	Ash Wed.	Easter Sunday	Year	Ash Wed.	Easter Sunday	Year	Ash Wed.	Easter Sunday	Year	Ash Wed.	Easter Sunday	Year	Ash Wed.	Easter Sunday
2001	Feb. 28	Apr. 15	2021	Feb. 17	Apr. 4	2041	Mar. 6	Apr. 21	2061	Feb. 23	Apr. 10	2081	Feb. 12	Mar. 30
2002	Feb. 13	Mar. 31	2022	Mar. 2	Apr. 17	2042	Feb. 19	Apr. 6	2062	Feb. 8	Mar. 26	2082	Mar. 4	Apr. 19
2003	Mar. 5	Apr. 20	2023	Feb. 22	Apr. 9	2043	Feb. 11	Mar. 29	2063	Feb. 28	Apr. 15	2083	Feb. 17	Apr. 4
2004	Feb. 25	Apr. 11	2024	Feb. 14	Mar. 31	2044	Mar. 2	Apr. 17	2064	Feb. 20	Apr. 6	2084	Feb. 9	Mar. 26
2005	Feb. 9	Mar. 27	2025	Mar. 5	Apr. 20	2045	Feb. 22	Apr. 9	2065	Feb. 11	Mar. 29	2085	Feb. 28	Apr. 15
2006	Mar. 1	Apr. 16	2026	Feb. 18	Apr. 5	2046	Feb. 7	Mar. 25	2066	Feb. 24	Apr. 11	2086	Feb. 13	Mar. 31
2007	Feb. 21	Apr. 8	2027	Feb. 10	Mar. 28	2047	Feb. 27	Apr. 14	2067	Feb. 16	Apr. 3	2087	Mar. 5	Apr. 20
2008	Feb. 6	Mar. 23	2028	Mar. 1	Apr. 16	2048	Feb. 19	Apr. 5	2068	Mar. 7	Apr. 22	2088	Feb. 25	Apr. 11
2009	Feb. 25	Apr. 12	2029	Feb. 14	Apr. 1	2049	Mar. 3	Apr. 18	2069	Feb. 27	Apr. 14	2089	Feb. 16	Apr. 3
2010	Feb. 17	Apr. 4	2030	Mar. 6	Apr. 21	2050	Feb. 23	Apr. 10	2070	Feb. 12	Mar. 30	2090	Mar. 1	Apr. 16
2011	Mar. 9	Apr. 24	2031	Feb. 26	Apr. 13	2051	Feb. 15	Apr. 2	2071	Mar. 4	Apr. 19	2091	Feb. 21	Apr. 8
2012	Feb. 22	Apr. 8	2032	Feb. 11	Mar. 28	2052	Mar. 6	Apr. 21	2072	Feb. 24	Apr. 10	2092	Feb. 13	Mar. 30
2013	Feb. 13	Mar. 31	2033	Mar. 2	Apr. 17	2053	Feb. 19	Apr. 6	2073	Feb. 8	Mar. 26	2093	Feb. 25	Apr. 12
2014	Mar. 5	Apr. 20	2034	Feb. 22	Apr. 9	2054	Feb. 11	Mar. 29	2074	Feb. 28	Apr. 15	2094	Feb. 17	Apr. 4
2015	Feb. 18	Apr. 5	2035	Feb. 7	Mar. 25	2055	Mar. 3	Apr. 18	2075	Feb. 20	Apr. 7	2095	Mar. 9	Apr. 24
2016	Feb. 10	Mar. 27	2036	Feb. 27	Apr. 13	2056	Feb. 16	Apr. 2	2076	Mar. 4	Apr. 19	2096	Feb. 29	Apr. 15
2017	Mar. 1	Apr. 16	2037	Feb. 18	Apr. 5	2057	Mar. 7	Apr. 22	2077	Feb. 24	Apr. 11	2097	Feb. 13	Mar. 31
2018	Feb. 14	Apr. 1	2038	Mar. 10	Apr. 25	2058	Feb. 27	Apr. 14	2078	Feb. 16	Apr. 3	2098	Mar. 5	Apr. 20
2019	Mar. 6	Apr. 21	2039	Feb. 23	Apr. 10	2059	Feb. 12	Mar. 30	2079	Mar. 8	Apr. 23	2099	Feb. 25	Apr. 12
2020	Feb. 26	Apr. 12	2040	Feb. 15	Apr. 1	2060	Mar. 3	Apr. 18	2080	Feb. 21	Apr. 7	2100	Feb. 10	Mar. 28

Roman Catholic Church Hierarchy

The Roman Catholic Church is headed by the pope, or bishop of Rome. He is assisted and advised by members of the College of Cardinals. The church is governed through a central administrative body, the Roman Curia. Dioceses around the world are headed by bishops appointed by the pope; collectively they also play a part in leadership of the church as a whole.

The Papacy

Roman Catholics consider Peter the Apostle to have been the first bishop of Rome and first in a line of popes extending to the present. He is said to have arrived in Rome c. 42 CE and to have been martyred there c. 67; he was later canonized as a saint. Popes through history have had both religious and secular roles. The pope today is the head of state of Vatican City as well as leader of the church.

German-born Pope **Benedict XVI**, formerly Cardinal Joseph Ratzinger, who was elected in Apr. 2005, resigned effective Feb. 28, 2013, citing his age (85) and declining health. Assuming the title of supreme pontiff emeritus, he took up residence in a restored convent near the Vatican.

At a papal conclave in Mar. 2013, 115 cardinals from 48 countries chose Argentinean Cardinal Jorge Mario Bergoglio as pope. He took the name **Francis**, after St. Francis of Assisi (1182-1226), known for his life of poverty and devotion to the poor. Pope Francis was the first member of the Society of Jesus (Jesuits), a Roman Catholic order, to become pope, and the first born outside Europe since Syrian-born Gregory III, who died in 741.

Chronological List of Popes

Source: *Annuario Pontificio*

Table lists year of accession of each pope. * = antipope, an illegitimate claimant to the papal throne.

Year	Pope	Year	Pope	Year	Pope	Year	Pope	Year	Pope
NA	St. Peter	530	Boniface II	884	St. Adrian III	1102	Albert*	1431	Eugene IV
67	St. Linus	530	Dioscorus*	885	Stephen V (VI)	1105	Sylvester IV*	1439	Felix V*
76	St. Anacletus, or Cletus	533	John II	891	Formosus	1118	Gelasius II	1447	Nicholas V
		535	St. Agapitus I	896	Boniface VI	1118	Gregory III*	1455	Callistus III
88	St. Clement I	536	St. Silverius, Martyr	896	Stephen VI (VII)	1119	Callistus II	1458	Pius II
97	St. Evaristus	537	Vigilius	897	Romanus	1124	Honorius II	1464	Paul II
105	St. Alexander I	556	Pelagius I	897	Theodore II	1124	Celestine II*	1471	Sixtus IV
115	St. Sixtus I	561	John III	898	John IX	1130	Innocent II	1484	Innocent VIII
125	St. Telesphorus	575	Benedict I	900	Benedict IV	1130	Anacletus II*	1492	Alexander VI
136	St. Hyginus	579	Pelagius II	903	Leo V	1138	Victor IV*	1503	Pius III
140	St. Pius I	590	St. Gregory I	903	Christopher*	1143	Celestine II	1503	Julius II
155	St. Anicetus	604	Sabinian	904	Sergius III	1144	Lucius II	1513	Leo X
166	St. Soter	607	Boniface III	911	Anastasius III	1145	Bl. Eugene III	1522	Adrian VI
175	St. Eleutherius	608	St. Boniface IV	913	Landus	1153	Anastasius IV	1523	Clement VII
189	St. Victor I	615	St. Deusdedit, or Adeodatus	914	John X	1154	Adrian IV	1534	Paul III
199	St. Zephyrinus			928	Leo VI	1159	Alexander III	1550	Julius III
217	St. Callistus I	619	Boniface V	928	Stephen VII (VIII)	1159	Victor IV*	1555	Marcellus II
217	St. Hippolytus*	625	Honorius I	931	John XI	1164	Paschal III*	1555	Paul IV
222	St. Urban I	640	Severinus	936	Leo VII	1168	Callistus III*	1559	Pius IV
230	St. Pontian	640	John IV	939	Stephen VIII (IX)	1179	Innocent III*	1566	St. Pius V
235	St. Anterus	642	Theodore I	942	Marinus II	1181	Lucius III	1572	Gregory XIII
236	St. Fabian	649	St. Martin I, Martyr	946	Agapitus II	1185	Urban III	1585	Sixtus V
251	St. Cornelius	654	St. Eugene I	955	John XII	1187	Clement III	1590	Urban VII
251	Novatian*	657	St. Vitalian	963	Leo VIII	1187	Gregory VIII	1590	Gregory XIV
253	St. Lucius I	672	Adeodatus II	964	Benedict V	1191	Celestine III	1591	Innocent IX
254	St. Stephen I	676	Donus	965	John XIII	1198	Innocent III	1592	Clement VIII
257	St. Sixtus II	678	St. Agatho	973	Benedict VI	1216	Honorius III	1605	Leo XI
259	St. Dionysius	682	St. Leo II	974	Boniface VII*	1227	Gregory IX	1605	Paul V
269	St. Felix I	684	St. Benedict II	974	Benedict VII	1241	Celestine IV	1621	Gregory XV
275	St. Eutychian	685	John V	983	John XIV	1243	Innocent IV	1623	Urban VIII
283	St. Caius	686	Conon	984	Boniface VII*	1254	Alexander IV	1644	Innocent X
296	St. Marcellinus	687	Theodore*	985	John XV	1261	Urban IV	1655	Alexander VII
308	St. Marcellus I	687	Paschal*	996	Gregory V	1265	Clement IV	1667	Clement IX
309	St. Eusebius	687	St. Sergius I	997	John XVI*	1271	Bl. Gregory X	1670	Clement X
311	St. Melchiades	701	John VI	999	Sylvester II	1276	Bl. Innocent V	1676	Bl. Innocent XI
314	St. Sylvester I	705	John VII	1003	John XVII	1276	Adrian V	1689	Alexander VIII
336	St. Marcus	708	Sisinnius	1004	John XVIII	1276	John XXI	1691	Innocent XII
337	St. Julius I	708	Constantine	1009	Sergius IV	1277	Nicholas III	1700	Clement XI
352	Liberius	715	St. Gregory II	1012	Benedict VIII	1281	Martin IV	1721	Innocent XIII
355	Felix II*	731	St. Gregory III	1012	Gregory*	1285	Honorius IV	1724	Benedict XIII
366	St. Damasus I	741	St. Zachary	1024	John XIX	1288	Nicholas IV	1730	Clement XII
366	Ursinus*	752	Stephen II (III)[1]	1032	Benedict IX	1294	St. Celestine V	1740	Benedict XIV
384	St. Siricius	757	St. Paul I	1045	Sylvester III	1294	Boniface VIII	1758	Clement XIII
399	St. Anastasius I	767	Constantine*	1045	Benedict IX	1303	Bl. Benedict XI	1769	Clement XIV
401	St. Innocent I	768	Philip*	1045	Gregory VI	1305	Clement V	1775	Pius VI
417	St. Zosimus	768	Stephen III (IV)	1046	Clement II	1316	John XXII	1800	Pius VII
418	St. Boniface I	772	Adrian I	1047	Benedict IX	1328	Nicholas V*	1823	Leo XII
418	Eulalius*	795	St. Leo III	1048	Damasus II	1334	Benedict XII	1829	Pius VIII
422	St. Celestine I	816	Stephen IV (V)	1049	St. Leo IX	1342	Clement VI	1831	Gregory XVI
432	St. Sixtus III	817	St. Paschal I	1055	Victor II	1352	Innocent VI	1846	Pius IX
440	St. Leo I	824	Eugene II	1057	Stephen IX (X)	1362	Bl. Urban V	1878	Leo XIII
461	St. Hilary	827	Valentine	1058	Benedict X*	1370	Gregory XI	1903	St. Pius X
468	St. Simplicius	827	Gregory IV	1059	Nicholas II	1378	Urban VI	1914	Benedict XV
483	St. Felix III (II)	844	John*	1061	Alexander II	1378	Clement VII*	1922	Pius XI
492	St. Gelasius I	844	Sergius II	1061	Honorius II*	1389	Boniface IX	1939	Pius XII
496	Anastasius II	847	St. Leo IV	1073	St. Gregory VII	1394	Benedict XIII*	1958	St. John XXIII
498	St. Symmachus	855	Benedict III	1080	Clement III*	1404	Innocent VII	1963	Paul VI
498	Lawrence* (also in 501-505)	855	Anastasius*	1086	Bl. Victor III	1406	Gregory XII	1978	John Paul I
		858	St. Nicholas I	1088	Bl. Urban II	1409	Alexander V*	1978	St. John Paul II
514	St. Hormisdas	867	Adrian II	1099	Paschal II	1410	John XXIII*	2005	Benedict XVI
523	St. John I, Martyr	872	John VIII	1100	Theodoric*	1417	Martin V	2013	Francis
526	St. Felix IV (III)	882	Marinus I						

NA = Not available. Bl. = Blessed. (1) A Roman priest named Stephen was elected but died before assuming the papacy. Another Stephen was then elected to succeed St. Zachary, as Stephen II. He is sometimes listed as Stephen III.

Pope Francis

Pope Francis was born Jorge Mario Bergoglio in Buenos Aires, Argentina, Dec. 17, 1936; his parents were Italian immigrants. He joined the Jesuits in 1958 and was ordained a priest in 1969. Bergoglio served as a parish priest, theology professor, and college administrator. Ordained a bishop in 1992, he was named archbishop of Buenos Aires in 1998 and made a cardinal in 2001.

Soon after his election in 2013, Francis approved measures for reform of the scandal-ridden Vatican Bank and established a commission on clerical sex abuse. In 2015, Francis released an encyclical focusing on consumerism and the environment, and the next year addressed family life, divorce, and inclusion. A 2018 publication offered guidance on holy behavior, including the need to care for poor, sick, and migrant populations. Francis convened a summit on clergy sex abuse in Rome in Feb. 2019 and in May 2019 issued guidance mandating that church officials worldwide report clergy sexual abuse and cover-ups to their church superiors.

College of Cardinals

Members of the Sacred College of Cardinals are chosen by the pope to be his chief assistants and advisers in the administration of the church. Among their duties is the election of the pope.

In its present form, the College of Cardinals dates from the 12th century. The first cardinals, from about the 6th century, were deacons and priests of the leading churches of Rome and were bishops of neighboring dioceses. The title of cardinal was limited to members of the college in 1567. The number of cardinals was set at 70 in 1586. Pope John XXIII began to increase the number in 1959; however, the number eligible to participate in papal elections was limited to 120. Previous limitations were set aside by Pope John Paul II when he created new cardinals. In 1918, the Code of Canon Law specified that all cardinals must be priests. Pope John XXIII in 1962 ruled that cardinals must ordinarily be bishops. In 1971, Pope Paul VI decreed that at age 80, cardinals must retire from curial departments and offices and cannot be summoned to participate in papal elections.

As of Sept. 2020, there were 219 cardinals from 89 countries, of whom 122 from 67 countries remained eligible to vote.

North American Cardinals

Name	Office	Born	Named cardinal
Carlos Aguiar Retes	Archbishop of Mexico City	1950	2016
Raymond L. Burke	Archbishop emeritus of St. Louis	1948	2010
Thomas C. Collins[1]	Archbishop of Toronto, Canada	1947	2012
Blase J. Cupich	Archbishop of Chicago	1949	2016
Michael Czerny	Undersecretary of Migrant and Refugee Section, Dicastery for Promoting Integral Human Development	1946	2019
Daniel N. DiNardo[2]	Archbishop of Galveston-Houston	1949	2007
Timothy M. Dolan	Archbishop of New York	1950	2012
Kevin J. Farrell	Prefect, Dicastery for Laity, Family, and Life; bishop emer. of Dallas	1947	2016
James M. Harvey	Archpriest of St. Paul Outside-the-Walls	1949	2012
Gérald Cyprien Lacroix	Archbishop of Québec, Canada	1957	2014
Javier Lozano Barragán[3]	Bishop emeritus of Zacatecas, Mexico	1933	2003
Roger Mahony[3]	Archbishop emeritus of Los Angeles	1936	1991
Adam Joseph Maida[3]	Archbishop emeritus of Detroit	1930	1994
Edwin F. O'Brien[3]	Archbishop emeritus of Baltimore	1939	2012
Sean O'Malley[4]	Archbishop emeritus of Boston	1944	2006
Marc Ouellet	Prefect, Congregation for Bishops; pres., Pontifical Commission for Latin America	1944	2003
Justin F. Rigali[3]	Archbishop emeritus of Philadelphia	1935	2003
Norberto Rivera Carrera[2]	Archbishop emeritus of Mexico City, Mexico	1942	1998
José Francisco Robles Ortega	Archbishop emeritus of Guadalajara, Mexico	1949	2007
Juan Sandoval Íñiguez[3]	Archbishop emeritus of Guadalajara, Mexico	1933	1994
James F. Stafford[3]	Archbishop emeritus of Denver	1932	1998
Alberto Suárez Inda[3]	Archbishop emeritus of Morelia, Mexico	1939	2015
Joseph W. Tobin	Archbishop of Newark	1952	2016
Donald W. Wuerl[5]	Archbishop emeritus of Washington, DC	1940	2010

Note: (1) Member, Commission of Cardinals Overseeing the Institute for Works of Religion (Vatican Bank). (2) Member, Council for the Economy. (3) Ineligible to vote in a papal conclave because of age. (4) Member, Council of Cardinals and Pres., Pontifical Commission for the Protection of Minors. (5) Resigned as archbishop in Oct. 2018 after allegations he concealed clergy sexual abuse.

The Ten Commandments

In the Hebrew Bible (Old Testament) the Ten Commandments (also called the Decalogue, from the Greek meaning "ten words") were revealed by God to Moses on Mt. Sinai. They form the covenant between God and the Israelites and the moral code that is the basis for the Jewish and Christian religions. The Ten Commandments appear in two places in the Old Testament—Exodus 20:1-17 and Deuteronomy 5:6-21.

Most Protestant, Anglican, and Orthodox Christians follow Jewish tradition, as shown here, which considers the introduction ("I am the Lord ...") the first commandment and makes the prohibition against idolatry the second. Roman Catholic and Lutheran traditions combine I and II and split the last commandment into two that separately prohibit coveting of a neighbor's wife and of a neighbor's goods. This arrangement alters the numbering of the other commandments by one.

Following is the text as it appears in Exodus 20:1-17 in the King James version of the Bible [Roman numerals added]:

And God spake all these words, saying,

I. I *am* the LORD thy God, which have brought thee out of the land of Egypt, out of the house of bondage. Thou shalt have no other gods before me.

II. Thou shalt not make unto thee any graven image, or any likeness of *any thing* that *is* in heaven above, or that *is* in the earth beneath, or that *is* in the water under the earth. Thou shalt not bow down thyself to them, nor serve them: for I the LORD thy God *am* a jealous God, visiting the iniquity of the fathers upon the children unto the third and fourth *generation* of them that hate me; and shewing mercy unto thousands of them that love me, and keep my commandments.

III. Thou shalt not take the name of the LORD thy God in vain: for the LORD will not hold him guiltless that taketh his name in vain.

IV. Remember the sabbath day, to keep it holy. Six days shalt thou labour, and do all thy work: but the seventh day *is* the sabbath of the LORD thy God: *in it* thou shalt not do any

work, thou, nor thy son, nor thy daughter, thy manservant, nor thy maidservant, nor thy cattle, nor thy stranger that *is* within thy gates: for *in* six days the LORD made heaven and earth, the sea, and all that in them *is*, and rested the seventh day: wherefore the LORD blessed the sabbath day, and hallowed it.

V. Honour thy father and thy mother: that thy days may be long upon the land which the LORD thy God giveth thee.

VI. Thou shalt not kill.

VII. Thou shalt not commit adultery.

VIII. Thou shalt not steal.

IX. Thou shalt not bear false witness against thy neighbour.

X. Thou shalt not covet thy neighbour's house, thou shalt not covet thy neighbour's wife, nor his manservant, nor his maidservant, nor his ox, nor his ass, nor any thing that *is* thy neighbour's.

Books of the Bible

Old Testament—Standard Protestant List

Genesis	I Kings	Ecclesiastes	Obadiah
Exodus	II Kings	Song of Solomon	Jonah
Leviticus	I Chronicles	Isaiah	Micah
Numbers	II Chronicles	Jeremiah	Nahum
Deuteronomy	Ezra	Lamentations	Habakkuk
Joshua	Nehemiah	Ezekiel	Zephaniah
Judges	Esther	Daniel	Haggai
Ruth	Job	Hosea	Zechariah
I Samuel	Psalms	Joel	Malachi
II Samuel	Proverbs	Amos	

New Testament List

Matthew	Ephesians	Hebrews
Mark	Philippians	James
Luke	Colossians	I Peter
John	I Thessalonians	II Peter
Acts	II Thessalonians	I John
Romans	I Timothy	II John
I Corinthians	II Timothy	III John
II Corinthians	Titus	Jude
Galatians	Philemon	Revelation

The standard Protestant Old Testament consists of the same 39 books as in the Bible of Judaism, but the latter is organized differently. The Old Testament used by Roman Catholics has 7 additional deuterocanonical books, plus some additional parts of books. The 7 are **Tobit, Judith, Wisdom, Sirach (Ecclesiasticus), Baruch, I Maccabees,** and **II Maccabees.** Both Catholic and Protestant versions of the New Testament have 27 books with the same names.

Figures in the Hebrew Bible (Old Testament)

Aaron: First of Hebrew high priests; brother of Moses and Miriam.

Abel: Second son of Adam and Eve; slain by Cain.

Abraham: Founder of monotheism; patriarch; also called Abram.

Adam: First human according to Genesis.

Amos: Herdsman; prophesized against social injustice and oppression of the poor.

Bathsheba: Seduced by King David; mother of King Solomon.

Cain: First son of Adam and Eve; killed his brother Abel.

Cyrus: Persian ruler; sent Jews home to Jerusalem from exile.

Daniel: Cast into lion's den for violating decree of King Darius; saved.

David: Israel's greatest king; shepherd, warrior, musician, psalmist.

Deborah: Prophet and judge; ruled over Israel.

Elijah: Great prophet; was victorious over the priests of the Phoenician god Baal.

Elisha: Prophet; successor to Elijah.

Esther: Jewish wife of the king of Persia; saved Jews from annihilation.

Eve: First woman according to Genesis.

Ezekiel: Visionary; prophesized hope to exiled Jews in Babylon.

Ezra: Great Jewish leader; rededicated worship and Torah law after exile.

Goliath: Giant Philistine warrior; slain by David.

Hannah: Childless; promised child to God; mother to the prophet Samuel.

Hosea: Enacted prophecy; asked God's forgiveness for Israel's unfaithfulness.

Isaac: Son of Abraham and Sarah; saved from sacrificial altar.

Isaiah: Highly educated prophet; avoided war with Assyria; Israel destroyed; Jerusalem survived.

Jacob: Son of Isaac; father of the Twelve Tribes; renamed "Israel" by angel.

Jeremiah: Confronted leaders and urged surrender to Babylon.

Jezebel: Phoenician queen of King Ahab of Israel; had Israelite prophets killed.

Job: "Blameless" man; allowed by God to lose family, health, and possessions in a test of his faith.

Jonah: Swallowed by a great fish; prophesied destruction of the city of Nineveh, averted when the people repented.

Jonathan: Son of King Saul; friend of David.

Joseph: Favorite of Jacob; interpreted Pharaoh's dreams; brought Hebrews to Egypt.

Joshua: Successor of Moses; led Hebrews into Canaan.

Josiah: Reformist king; repaired Solomon's Temple; restored worship; reintroduced Passover.

Leah: Matriarch; older sister of Rachel; Jacob's wife.

Micah: Prophet; predicted the end of war and beginning of peace.

Miriam: Prophet and great leader of the Hebrews; sister to Moses and Aaron.

Moses: Most important Hebrew prophet; leader of the Israelites; received the Torah.

Nathan: Prophet; confronted King David over his seduction of the married Bathsheba.

Nebuchadnezzar: Babylonian king; destroyed Jerusalem.

Nehemiah: Led Jews back to Jerusalem from Babylonian exile.

Noah: Man of great faith who, according to Genesis, saved his family and two of every living thing on Earth from a great flood.

Rachel: Matriarch; younger sister of Leah; Jacob's wife; Joseph's mother.

Rebecca: Matriarch; wife of Isaac; mother of Jacob.

Ruth: Moabite convert; ancestor of David.

Samson: Judge and military leader of Israel; possessed super-human strength.

Samuel: Prophet; anointed Saul king of Israel and later anointed David to succeed him.

Sarah: First matriarch of Israel; wife of Abraham; mother of Isaac.

Saul: First king of Israel; father of Jonathan.

Solomon: King of Israel at its zenith; known for great wisdom.

Zechariah: Prophet; encouraged rebuilding of Solomon's Temple, which had been destroyed by Babylonians.

Figures in the New Testament

Andrew: One of the Twelve Apostles; brother of Peter and former fisherman; one of the earlier disciples.

Barabbas: Imprisoned with Jesus; set free by Pilate on Passover.

Barnabas: Disciple of Jesus; closely connected with Paul.

Bartholomew: A lesser-known member of the Twelve Apostles; cheerful and prayed often.

Cornelius: Roman convert; defended by Peter, allowing Gentiles to become Christians.

Elizabeth: Mother of John the Baptist; relation of the Virgin Mary.

Gabriel: Archangel; appeared to the Virgin Mary to announce that she was to give birth to the Messiah.

Herod: May refer to Herod the Great, who ordered the death of children after Jesus's birth, or to his son, Herod, who had John the Baptist beheaded.

James: May refer to either of two apostles: James, son of Zebedee, brother of John the Apostle, or the lesser-known James, son of Alphaeus.

Jesus: Central figure of the Gospels; believed to be the Messiah and son of God; crucified by the Romans.

John (Apostle): Beloved disciple of Jesus; one of the Twelve Apostles; possible author of fourth Gospel; brother of James.

John (Baptist): Known as John the Baptist; important prophet and forerunner to Jesus; relation of the Virgin Mary.

Joseph: Husband of the Virgin Mary; descendant of King David.

Judas Iscariot: Betrayer of Jesus; prominent member of the Apostles; committed suicide.

Judas Thaddeus: One of the Twelve Apostles; also called Jude to distinguish him from Judas Iscariot.

Lazarus: Brother of the disciples Martha and Mary of Bethany; raised from the dead by Jesus at their request; possibly the same Lazarus who appears in Jesus's parable of the rich man.

Luke: Traditional author of the Gospel of Luke; possibly a follower of Paul.

Mark: Traditional author of the Gospel of Mark; possibly a disciple of Peter.

Mary, the mother of Jesus: Traditionally believed to be a virgin who conceived without sin; wife of Joseph.

Mary Magdalene: Important female disciple of Jesus; witness to his death and resurrection.

Matthew: One of the Twelve Apostles; possible author of the Gospel of Matthew; former tax collector.

Matthias: Often included on lists of the Twelve Apostles as the apostle who replaced Judas Iscariot after his betrayal.

Paul (Saul): Writer of nearly a quarter of the New Testament; a former persecutor of Christians, converted after a vision; played a significant role in spreading Christianity.

Peter: Considered the foremost of the Twelve Apostles; traditionally the first pope and "rock" of the Christian church; author of epistles; also called Simon and Simon Peter.

Philip: One of the Twelve; considered pragmatic and sensible.

Pilate, Pontius: A Roman prefect; played large role in the trial and crucifixion of Jesus.

Simon: One of the Twelve Apostles; known as "the Zealot" to distinguish from Simon Peter.

Stephen: Fervently preached that Jesus was the Messiah; stoned to death by angry mob, including Saul (Paul); important figure in Saul's conversion.

Thomas: One of the Twelve Apostles; known as "Doubting Thomas" because he did not believe Jesus was risen until he could touch him.

Timothy: A disciple closely connected with Paul; recipient of epistles.

Zacharias: Father of John the Baptist; husband of Elizabeth; struck dumb when he doubted his barren wife could become pregnant.

Major Christian Denominations:

Brackets indicate some features that tend to

Denomination	Origins	Organization	Authority	Special rites
Baptists	In radical Reformation, objections to infant baptism, demands for church and state separation; John Smyth, English Separatist, in 1609; Roger Williams, 1638, Providence, RI.	Congregational; each local church is autonomous.	Scripture; some Baptists, particularly in the South, interpret the Bible literally.	[Baptism, usually early teen years and after, by total immersion]; Lord's Supper.
Church of Christ (Disciples)	Among evangelical Presbyterians in KY (1804) and PA (1809), in distress over Protestant factionalism and decline of fervor; organized in 1832.	Congregational.	["Where the Scriptures speak, we speak; where the Scriptures are silent, we are silent."]	Adult baptism; Lord's Supper (weekly).
Episcopalians	Henry VIII separated English Catholic Church from Rome, 1534, for political reasons; Protestant Episcopal Church in U.S. founded in 1789.	[Diocesan bishops, in apostolic succession, are elected by parish representatives; the national Church is headed by General Convention and Presiding Bishop; part of the Anglican Communion.]	Scripture as interpreted by tradition, especially 39 Articles (1563); tri-annual convention of bishops, priests, and lay people.	Infant baptism, Eucharist, and other sacraments; sacrament taken to be symbolic, but as having real spiritual effect.
Jehovah's Witnesses	Founded in 1870 in PA by Charles Taze Russell; incorporated as Watch Tower Bible and Tract Society of PA, 1884; name Jehovah's Witnesses adopted in 1931.	A governing body located in NY coordinates worldwide activities; each congregation cared for by a body of elders; each Witness considered a minister.	The Bible.	Baptism by immersion; annual Lord's Meal ceremony.
Latter-day Saints (Mormons)	In a vision of the Father and the Son reported by Joseph Smith (1820s) in NY; Smith also reported receiving new scripture on golden tablets: the Book of Mormon.	Theocratic; 1st Presidency (church president, two counselors), 12 Apostles preside over international church; local congregations headed by lay priesthood leaders.	Revelation to living prophet (church president). The Bible, Book of Mormon, and other revelations to Smith and his successors.	Baptism at age 8; laying on of hands (which confers the gift of the Holy Ghost); Lord's Supper; temple rites: baptism for the dead, marriage for eternity, others.
Lutherans	Begun by Martin Luther in Wittenberg, Germany, in 1517; objection to Catholic doctrine of salvation and sale of indulgences; break complete, 1519.	Varies from congregational to episcopal; in U.S., a combination of regional synods and congregational polities is most common.	Scripture alone; the Book of Concord (1580), which includes the three Ecumenical Creeds, is subscribed to as a correct exposition of Scripture.	Infant baptism; Lord's Supper; Christ's true body and blood present "in, with, and under the bread and wine."
Methodists	Rev. John Wesley began movement in 1738, within Church of England; first U.S. denomination in Baltimore (1784).	Conference and superintendent system; [in United Methodist Church, general superintendents are bishops—not a priestly order, only an office—who are elected for life].	Scripture as interpreted by tradition, reason, and experience.	Baptism of infants or adults; Lord's Supper commanded; other rites: marriage, ordination, solemnization of personal commitments.
Orthodox	Developed in original Christian proselytizing; broke with Rome in 1054 after centuries of doctrinal disputes and diverging traditions.	Synods of bishops in autonomous, usually national, churches elect a patriarch, archbishop, or metropolitan; these men, as a group, are the heads of the church.	Scripture, tradition, and the first seven church councils up to Nicaea II in 787; bishops in council have authority in doctrine and policy.	Seven sacraments: infant baptism and anointing, Eucharist, ordination, penance, marriage, and anointing of the sick.
Pentecostal	In Topeka, KS (1901) and Los Angeles (1906), in reaction to perceived loss of evangelical fervor among Methodists and others.	Originally a movement, not a formal organization, Pentecostalism now has a variety of organized forms and continues also as a movement.	Scripture; individual charismatic leaders, the teachings of the Holy Spirit.	[Spirit baptism, especially as shown in "speaking in tongues"; faith healing; sometimes exorcism]; adult baptism; Lord's Supper.
Presbyterians	In 16th-cent. Calvinist reformation; differed with Lutherans over sacraments, church government; John Knox founded Scotch Presbyterian church about 1560.	[Highly structured representational system of ministers and lay persons (presbyters) in local, regional, and national bodies (synods).]	Scripture.	Infant baptism; Lord's Supper; bread and wine symbolize Christ's spiritual presence.
Roman Catholics	Traditionally, founded by Jesus who named St. Peter the first vicar; developed in early Christian proselytizing, especially after the conversion of imperial Rome in the 4th cent.	[Hierarchy with supreme power vested in pope elected by cardinals]; councils of bishops advise on matters of doctrine and policy.	[The pope, when speaking for the whole church in matters of faith and morals, and tradition (which is expressed in church councils and in part contained in Scripture.)]	Mass; seven sacraments: baptism, reconciliation, Eucharist, confirmation, marriage, ordination, and anointing of the sick (unction).
United Church of Christ	By ecumenical union, in 1957, of Congregationalists and Evangelical and Reformed, representing both Calvinist and Lutheran traditions.	Congregational; a General Synod, representative of all congregations, sets general policy.	Scripture.	Infant baptism; Lord's Supper.

How Do They Differ?

distinguish a denomination sharply from others.

Practice	Ethics	Doctrine	Other	Denomination
Worship style varies from staid to evangelistic; extensive missionary activity.	Usually opposed to alcohol and tobacco; some tendency toward a perfectionist ethical standard.	[No creed; true church is of believers only, who are all equal.]	Believing no authority can stand between the believer and God, the Baptists are strong supporters of church and state separation.	**Baptists**
Tries to avoid any rite not considered part of the 1st-cent. church; some congregations may reject instrumental music.	Some tendency toward perfectionism; increasing interest in social action programs.	Simple New Testament faith; avoids any elaboration not firmly based on Scripture.	Highly tolerant in doctrinal and religious matters; strongly supportive of scholarly education.	**Church of Christ (Disciples)**
Formal, based on Book of Common Prayer, updated 1979; services range from austerely simple to highly liturgical.	Tolerant, sometimes permissive; some social action programs.	Scripture; the "historic creeds," which include the Apostles, Nicene, and Athanasian, and the Book of Common Prayer; ranges from Anglo-Catholic to low church, with Calvinist influences.	Strongly ecumenical, holding talks with many branches of Christendom.	**Episcopalians**
Meetings are held in Kingdom Halls and members' homes for study and worship; [extensive door-to-door visitations.]	High moral code; stress on marital fidelity and family values; avoidance of tobacco and blood transfusions.	[God, by his first creation, Christ, will soon destroy all wickedness; 144,000 faithful ones will rule in heaven with Christ over others on a paradise earth.]	Total allegiance proclaimed only to God's kingdom or heavenly government by Christ; main periodical, The Watchtower, is available in over 250 languages.	**Jehovah's Witnesses**
Simple service with prayers, hymns, sermon; private temple ceremonies may be more elaborate.	Temperance; strict moral code; [tithing]; a strong work ethic with communal self-reliance; [strong missionary activity]; family emphasis.	Jesus Christ is the Son of God, the Eternal Father. Jesus's atonement saves all humans; those who are obedient to God's laws may become joint-heirs with Christ in God's kingdom.	Mormons believe theirs is the true church of Jesus Christ, restored by God through Joseph Smith. Official name: The Church of Jesus Christ of Latter-day Saints.	**Latter-day Saints (Mormons)**
Relatively simple, formal liturgy with emphasis on the sermon.	Generally conservative in personal and social ethics; doctrine of "two kingdoms" (worldly and holy) supports conservatism in secular affairs.	Salvation by grace alone through faith; Lutheranism has made major contributions to Protestant theology.	Though still somewhat divided along ethnic lines (German, Swedish, etc.), main divisions are between fundamentalists and liberals.	**Lutherans**
Worship style varies widely by denomination, local church, geography.	Originally pietist and perfectionist; always strong social activist elements.	No distinctive theological development; 25 articles abridged from Church of England's 39, not binding.	In 1968, The United Methodist Church was formed by the union of The Methodist Church and The Evangelical United Brethren Church.	**Methodists**
Elaborate liturgy, usually in the vernacular, though extremely traditional; the liturgy is the essence of Orthodoxy; veneration of icons.	Tolerant; little stress on social action; divorce, remarriage permitted in some cases; bishops are celibate; priests need not be.	Emphasis on Christ's resurrection, rather than crucifixion; the Holy Spirit proceeds from God the Father only.	Orthodox Church in America originally under Patriarch of Moscow, was granted autonomy in 1970; Greek Orthodox do not recognize this autonomy.	**Orthodox**
Loosely structured service with rousing hymns and sermons, culminating in spirit baptism.	Usually, emphasis on perfectionism, with varying degrees of tolerance.	Simple traditional beliefs, usually Protestant, with emphasis on the immediate presence of God in the Holy Spirit.	Once appealed mostly to lower classes; formation of charismatic fellowships in mainline churches expanded reach.	**Pentecostal**
A simple, sober service in which the sermon is central.	Traditionally, a tendency toward strictness, with firm church- and self-discipline; otherwise tolerant.	Emphasizes the sovereignty and justice of God; no longer dogmatic.	Although traces of belief in predestination (that God has foreordained salvation for the "elect") remain, this idea is no longer a central element in Presbyterianism.	**Presbyterians**
Relatively elaborate ritual centered on the Mass; also rosary recitation, novenas.	Traditionally strict but increasingly tolerant in practice; divorce and remarriage not accepted, but annulments sometimes granted; celibate clergy, except in Eastern rite.	Highly elaborated; salvation by merit gained through grace; dogmatic; special veneration of Mary, the mother of Jesus.	Relatively rapid changes followed Vatican Council II (1962-65). Mass held in vernacular instead of Latin; more stress on social action, tolerance, ecumenism.	**Roman Catholics**
Usually simple service with emphasis on the sermon.	Tolerant; some social action emphasis.	Standard Protestant; Statement of Faith (1959) is not binding.	Two main churches in the 1957 union represented earlier unions with small groups of almost every Protestant denomination.	**United Church of Christ**

Major Religions

Islam

Founded: Muhammad received his first revelation in 610 CE.

Founder: Muhammad (c. 570-632 CE), the Prophet.

Sacred texts: Two texts constitute the Muslim sacred canon, the *Quran* (Koran) and the *Hadith*. The Quran provides the foundation for Islamic religion and culture. It is regarded as the final, perfect, and complete word of God as revealed to Muhammad over the course of his life. Received by Muhammad in the Arabic language, it is memorized in Arabic by adherents regardless of their native language. It is divided into 114 chapters of unequal length, the shortest containing only 3 verses, and the longest containing 286 verses. The Quran is the ultimate source of everything Islamic, from metaphysics to theology to sacred history, to ethics and law, to art. The Hadith, which describes Muhammad's actions, attitudes, and teachings, complements the Quran. Due to its long history of oral transmission, the Hadith's lessons are seen as somewhat vulnerable to human error. It is not said to contain God's unadulterated voice as is the Quran but functions as a powerful spiritual and behavioral code nonetheless.

Organization: Muhammad was both the last prophet and a statesman. Muslim leaders have often assumed both civil and moral functions within Islamic states. Within the larger community, there are cultural and national groups, held together by a common religious law, the *Sharia*. Muslims believe that God is the ultimate lawgiver and that human beings cannot devise laws that oppose divine laws. Still, the Sharia is approached differently in different parts of the Islamic world. Over the centuries, Sunnis have developed four major schools of law: the Hanafi, the Shafi'i, the Hanbali, and the Maliki. The Ja'fari is the most important and well-known Shiite school. Before the 20th century, religious scholars known as the *ulama* held much legal power. Judges (*qadis*) and law-interpreters (*muftis*) are people learned in religious law who lead congregational prayers in mosques and perform other religious duties.

Practice: Five duties (of both men and women), known as the Pillars of Islam, are regarded as cardinal in Islam and as central to the life of the Islamic community. In accordance with Islam's absolute commitment to monotheism, the first duty is the profession of faith (the *Shahadah*): "There is no God but Allah and Muhammad is His Prophet." A Muslim must profess this belief publicly at least once in his or her lifetime; it defines the membership of an individual in the Islamic community. The second duty is that of five daily prayers organized in intervals throughout the day: sunrise, early afternoon, late afternoon, immediately after sunset, and before midnight. During prayer, Muslims face the Kaaba, a small, cube-shaped structure in the courtyard of al-Haram (the "inviolate place"), at the Grand Mosque of Mecca in Saudi Arabia. All five prayers in Islam are congregational and are to be offered in a mosque, but they may be offered individually if one cannot be present with a congregation. Congregational prayer is required only at the early afternoon prayer on Friday for men. The third cardinal duty of a Muslim is to pay alms, or *zakat*, which should be 2.5% of one's total wealth. This was originally the tax levied by Muhammad on the wealthy members of the community, primarily to help the poor. Only when zakat has been paid is the rest of a Muslim's property considered purified and legitimate. The fourth duty is the fast of the lunar month of Ramadan. During the fasting month, one must abstain from eating, drinking, smoking, impure thoughts, and sexual intercourse from dawn until sunset, and feed at least one poor person, if able. The fifth duty is the pilgrimage to the Kaaba, known as the hajj, which a Muslim must undertake, with exceptions for poverty and ill health, at least once during his or her lifetime.

Divisions: There are two major groups: the majority Sunni (85%-90% of the worldwide Muslim population) and the minority Shiites. Sects first appeared in Islam at the time of Muhammad's death. The group that came to be known as Sunni accepted Abu Bakr, an early convert, as his successor (caliph), while a smaller number, which became the Shia, believed that Ali ibn Abi Talib, the son-in-law and first cousin of the prophet, should have become his successor (Imam). Imams are believed to interpret the Quran infallibly. **Shiites** fall into three major branches: Fivers, Seveners, and Twelvers, reflecting the number of Imams they recognize. Twelvers believe that the 12th Imam has lived an invisible existence since 874, and will return as the Mahdi (a messiah figure) who will usher in a 1,000-year reign of peace and justice. **Sufism** (mystical dimension of Islam) emphasizes personal relation to God and obedience informed by love of God; it is prevalent among both Sunni and Shiites.

Location: W Africa to Philippines, across a band including E Africa, Central Asia and western China, India, Malaysia, Indonesia. Islam has several million adherents in North America and about 30 mil in Europe.

Beliefs: Strictly monotheistic. God is creator of the universe, omnipotent, omniscient, just, forgiving, and merciful. God revealed the Quran to Muhammad to guide humanity to truth and justice. Those who sincerely "submit" (literal meaning of "Islam") to God attain salvation.

World's Largest Muslim Populations, 2021

Source: *World Christian Database* and *World Religion Database* (Leiden/Boston: Brill, July 2020)

Rank	Country	Muslim population	% of country's pop.
1.	Indonesia	218,754,000	79.6%
2.	Pakistan	204,547,000	96.4
3.	India	202,265,000	14.5
4.	Bangladesh	152,837,000	89.1
5.	Nigeria	97,954,000	46.3
6.	Egypt	94,478,000	90.2
7.	Iran	83,101,000	98.6
8.	Turkey	83,072,000	98.3
9.	Algeria	43,185,000	98.2
10.	Iraq	41,649,000	97.7
11.	Sudan	40,969,000	91.9
12.	Ethiopia	39,747,000	34.4
13.	Afghanistan	38,864,000	99.9
14.	Morocco	37,380,000	99.7
15.	Uzbekistan	32,415,000	96.3
16.	Saudi Arabia	31,945,000	90.6
17.	Yemen	30,663,000	99.2
18.	China	25,987,000	1.8
19.	Niger	24,162,000	96.6
20.	Tanzania	20,044,000	31.0
21.	Malaysia	19,222,000	57.7
22.	Mali	18,565,000	88.9
23.	Syria	18,544,000	94.7
24.	Russia	18,219,000	12.7
25.	Somalia	16,505,000	99.9

Baha'i

Founded: Mid-19th century.

Founder: Mirza Husayn-Ali Nuri (1817-92), later known as Baha'u'llah (Arabic for "Glory of God").

Sacred texts: The writings of Baha'u'llah and of his herald the Bab (Siyyid Ali-Muhammad, 1819-50). The primary text is *Kitab-i-Aqdas* (Most Holy Book).

Organization: The Baha'i administrative system consists of elected nine-member councils at the local, national, and international levels. There are also more than 180 National Spiritual Assemblies and an elected, international governing body known as the Universal House of Justice.

Practice: Prayer, meditation, and fasting are key components of the Baha'i Faith. Work performed in a spirit of service to humanity is considered an important form of worship. The Baha'i Faith has no clergy and minimal ritual and congregational worship.

Divisions: In a religion in which unity is perhaps the central spiritual value, the Baha'i Faith has avoided separating into sects with differentiated theologies and practices.

Location: Worldwide.

Beliefs: God has progressively revealed His will and purpose through a series of Divine manifestations including Jesus, Buddha, Muhammad, Zoroaster, and Baha'u'llah. Baha'u'llah's teachings include the oneness of humanity, the equality of men and women, the harmony of science and religion, and the need to abandon all forms of prejudice and eliminate extremes of poverty and wealth.

Buddhism

Founded: About 525 BCE, reportedly near Benares, India.

Founder: Gautama Siddhartha (c. 563-483 BCE), the Buddha, who achieved enlightenment through intense meditation.

Sacred texts: The *Tripitaka*, a collection of the Buddha's teachings, rules of monastic life, and philosophical commentaries on the teachings; also a vast body of Buddhist teachings and commentaries, many of which are called *sutras*.

Organization: The basic institution is the *sangha*, or monastic order, through which traditions are passed down. Monastic life tends to be democratic and antiauthoritarian.

Practice: Varies widely according to the sect and ranges from austere meditation to magical chanting and elaborate temple rites. Many practices, such as exorcism of devils, reflect pre-Buddhist beliefs.

Divisions: A variety of sects grouped into three primary branches: Theravada, which emphasizes the importance of pure thought and deed; Mahayana (includes Zen and Sokagakkai), which ranges from philosophical schools to belief in the saving grace of higher beings or ritual practices and to practical meditative disciplines; and Vajrayana, or Tantrism, a combination of belief in ritual magic and sophisticated philosophy.

Location: Mainly in Asia, from Sri Lanka to Japan.

Beliefs: Life is suffering, and there is no ultimate reality behind it. The cycle of birth and rebirth continues because of desire and attachment to the unreal "self." Meditation and deeds will end the cycle and achieve Nirvana (nothingness, enlightenment).

Hinduism

Founded: About 1500 BCE to 300 CE as a religion and *dharma* (way of life); a diverse synthesis of primarily Indian traditions, practices, and beliefs.

Sacred texts: The *Vedas* (Rig, Sama, Yajur, Atharva); the *Upanishads*, a collection of rituals and commentaries; a vast number of epic stories about gods, heroes, and saints, including the *Puranas*, *Ramayana*, and *Mahabharata*; the *Bhagavad Gita*; and the *Agamas*.

Organization: None, strictly speaking. No single founder, establishment date, authoritative scripture, or central religious organization exist.

Practice: *Sanskara*, or rites of passage (e.g., initiation, marriage, death), and devotionals (*bhakti*). Bhakti may be practiced privately, as at a household shrine, or in a group.

Divisions: There is no concept of orthodoxy in Hinduism, which presents a variety of sects. Three major traditions are those devoted to the gods Vishnu and Shiva and to the goddess Shakti, but others believe in *brahman* (the All) as a more impersonal but infinite spiritual core. Numerous beliefs and practices, often in amalgamation, exist side by side with various philosophical schools.

Location: Mainly India, Nepal, Malaysia, Mauritius, Guyana, Suriname, and Sri Lanka.

Beliefs: Two basic tenets of Hinduism include a belief in the unity of existence as well as in the process of transmigration and rebirth (*samsara*) with no clear beginning or end. Life in all its forms is an aspect or manifestation of the divine or of divine qualities.

Judaism

Founded: About 2000 BCE.

Founder: Abraham is regarded as the founding patriarch.

Sacred texts: The five books of Moses (the Torah), the basic source of teachings.

Organization: Originally theocratic, Judaism has evolved into a congregational polity. The basic institution is the local synagogue or temple, operated by the congregation and led by a rabbi of their choice. Chief rabbis in France and Great Britain have authority only over those who accept it; in Israel, the two chief rabbis (one each from the Sephardic Jewish and Ashkenazi Jewish communities) have civil authority in family law.

Practice: Among traditional practitioners, almost all areas of life are governed by strict discipline. Sabbath and holidays are marked by observances, and attendance at public worship is considered especially important. Chief annual observances are Passover, celebrating liberation of the Israelites from Egypt and marked by the Seder meal in homes, and the 10 days from Rosh Hashanah (New Year) to Yom Kippur (Day of Atonement), a period of penitence.

Divisions: Judaism is an unbroken spectrum from ultraconservative to ultraliberal, largely reflecting different points of view regarding the binding character of the prohibitions and duties—particularly the dietary and Sabbath observations—traditionally prescribed for the daily life of the Jew.

Location: Mainly in Israel and the U.S.

Beliefs: Strictly monotheistic. God is the creator and ruler of the universe. God established a particular relationship with the Hebrew people: by obeying a divine law God gave them, they would be a special witness to God's mercy and justice. Judaism stresses ethical behavior (and, among the traditional, careful ritual obedience) as true worship of God.

Sikhism

Founded: Late 15th century in South Asia.

Founder: Guru Nanak Dev ji, Sikhism's first Guru.

Sacred texts: The *Guru Granth Sahib* was compiled by the Sikh Gurus and contains their experiences of the Divine. It also contains writings by other saintly figures of different faiths.

Organization: Each Sikh must make her or his own spiritual journey and not depend on clergy. Congregational prayer led by both men and women takes place in local *Gurdwaras* ("doorway to the Guru"). Harmandir Sahib in Amritsar, Punjab (northern India), is the central place of worship.

Practice: Prayers are required in the morning, evening, and before sleeping. The most important mode of congregational prayer is the singing of hymns from the Guru Granth Sahib. The "Five Ks" are five articles of faith required of all Sikhs: *Kes* (uncut hair), *Kangha* (comb), *Kara* (steel bracelet), *Kirpan* (sword), and *Kaccha* (short pants).

Divisions: The last living Guru, Guru Gobind Singh (1666-1708), crystallized the practices and beliefs of the faith and determined that no future living Guru was needed. Today the religion is guided by joint sovereignty of Guru Granth and Guru Panth. Guru Granth is the Sikh scripture, as the spiritual manifestation of the Guru, while the Guru Panth is the collectivity of all initiated Sikhs worldwide, as the physical manifestation of the Guru.

Location: Many Sikhs have Punjabi backgrounds. The Punjab region was divided between India and Pakistan with the end of British rule.

Beliefs: Sikhism preaches a message of devotion, remembrance of God at all times, truthful living, equality between all human beings, and social justice, while denouncing what is considered superstition and blind ritualism. Sikhism is a monotheistic religion based on revelation.

LANGUAGE

New Words in English

The following new words and definitions were provided by Merriam-Webster Inc., publishers of *Merriam-Webster's Collegiate Dictionary*, and other language references. The words are among those added in 2020 by Merriam-Webster's editors to the digital version of the dictionary, available as the *Merriam-Webster Dictionary* app and at www.merriam-webster.com.

athleisure: casual clothing designed to be worn both for exercising and for general use

biophilia: a hypothetical human tendency to interact or be closely associated with other forms of life in nature: a desire or tendency to commune with nature

body shaming: the act or practice of subjecting someone to criticism or mockery for supposed bodily faults or imperfections

bomb cyclone: a powerful, rapidly intensifying storm associated with a sudden and significant drop in atmospheric pressure

COVID-19: a mild to severe respiratory illness that is caused by a coronavirus, is transmitted chiefly by contact with infectious material (such as respiratory droplets) or with objects or surfaces contaminated by the causative virus, and is characterized especially by fever, cough, and shortness of breath and may progress to pneumonia and respiratory failure

crab rangoon: a dish consisting of deep-fried wontons filled with a mixture of crab meat and cream cheese

cryosphere: the part of the earth's surface characterized by the presence of frozen water

dad joke *informal:* a wholesome joke of the type said to be told by fathers with a punchline that is often an obvious or predictable pun or play on words and usually judged to be endearingly corny or unfunny

deepfake: an image or recording that has been convincingly altered and manipulated to misrepresent someone as doing or saying something that was not actually done or said

escape room: a game in which participants confined to a room or other enclosed setting (such as a prison cell) are given a set amount of time to find a way to escape (as by discovering hidden clues and solving a series of riddles or puzzles)

fast-casual: of, relating to, or being a restaurant that combines elements of fast-food service (such as counter ordering) with other elements (such as made-to-order food) that are typical of a full-service restaurant

fatberg: a large mass of fat and solid waste that collects in a sewer system

FOMO *informal:* fear of missing out: fear of not being included in something (such as an interesting or enjoyable activity) that others are experiencing

free solo *rock climbing:* a climb in which a climber uses no artificial aids for support and has no rope or other safety equipment for protection in case of a fall

Friendsgiving *U.S., informal:* a celebration or meal shared among friends on or near Thanksgiving Day

intensivist: a physician who specializes in the care and treatment of patients in intensive care

jegging: a legging that is made of stretchable fabric and that resembles tight fitting denim jean

ketogenic diet: a diet that supplies large amounts of fats, moderate amounts of proteins, and minimal amounts of carbohydrates and that is undertaken for weight loss or to control seizures in treatment-resistant epilepsy

melissophobia: intense fear or dislike of bees

name-check: to mention or acknowledge (someone or something) specifically and publicly by name

patient zero: a person identified as the first to become infected with an illness or disease in an outbreak; *especially:* a person documented as being the first known case of a communicable disease in a particular population or region

pickleball: an indoor or outdoor game that is played on a level court with short-handled paddles and a perforated plastic ball volleyed over a low net by two players or pairs of players

pitmaster: a person who oversees the cooking done in a barbecue pit: a professional or skilled barbecuer

red flag law *U.S.:* a law allowing courts to prevent people who show signs of being a danger to themselves or to others from having access to firearms (as by ordering the seizure of weapons)

roid rage *or* **'roid rage:** an outburst of anger, aggression, or violence attributed to the use of anabolic steroids

slow-walk: to delay or prevent the progress of (something) by acting in a deliberately slow manner

super-spreader: an individual who is highly contagious and capable of transmitting a communicable disease to an unusually large number of uninfected individuals

trendspotter: a person who identifies and makes predictions about developing trends in the culture at large or in a particular field (such as fashion)

tres leches cake: a sponge cake soaked in a mixture of condensed milk, evaporated milk, and cream

truthiness: a truthful or seemingly truthful quality that is claimed for something not because of supporting facts or evidence but because of a feeling that it is true or a desire for it to be true

upsell: to try to convince (a customer) to purchase something additional or at a higher cost

upskill: to provide (someone, such as an employee) with more advanced skills through additional education and training

virtual private network: a private computer network that functions over a public network (such as the internet) and usually utilizes data encryption to provide secure access to something (such as an internal business server or private network)

National Spelling Bee

The Scripps National Spelling Bee, conducted each year since 1925, allows students under age 16 in 8th grade or lower to compete for a chance to advance to national championship finals in Washington, DC. After announcing it was running out of challenging words, the competition named eight spellers co-champions in 2019; the 2020 Bee was canceled due to the COVID-19 outbreak.

Here are the last words given and spelled correctly at the National Spelling Bee in recent years:

Year	Word	Year	Word	Year	Word	Year	Word	Year	Word
1982	psoriasis	1991	antipyretic	2000	demarche	2009	Laodicean	2016	Feldenkrais
1983	purim	1992	lyceum	2001	succedaneum	2010	stromuhr		gesellschaft
1984	luge	1993	kamikaze	2002	prospicience	2011	cymotrichous	2017	marocain
1985	milieu	1994	antediluvian	2003	pococurante	2012	guetapens	2018	koinonia
1986	odontalgia	1995	xanthosis	2004	autochthonous	2013	knaidel	2019	auslaut, erysipelas,
1987	staphylococci	1996	vivisepulture	2005	appoggiatura	2014	feuilleton		palama, aiguillette,
1988	elegiacal	1997	euonym	2006	Ursprache		stichomythia		odylic, cernuous,
1989	spoliator	1998	chiaroscurist	2007	serrefine	2015	scherenschnitte		pendeloque,
1990	fibranne	1999	logorrhea	2008	guerdon		nunatak		bougainvillea

Non-English Words and Phrases Commonly Used by English Speakers

A = Arabic; F = French; Ger = German; Gr = Greek; I = Italian; J = Japanese; L = Latin; R = Russian; S = Spanish; Y = Yiddish

ad hoc (L; ad-HOK): for the end or purpose at hand; impromptu

ad hominem (L; ad-HOH-mee-nem): argument that criticizes an opponent, often unfairly, rather than addressing an issue directly

al fresco (I; ahl-FRAYS-koh): outdoors

anime (J; A-nuh-may): Japanese-style animation

apparatchik (R: ap-per-AT-chik): functionary; blindly devoted official or working member of a party/other organization

au courant (F; oh-koo-RAHN): up-to-date, fashionable

belles lettres (F; bel-LET-truh): writing aspiring to artistic merit

bête noire (F; bet-NWAHR): literally, black beast; a thing or person viewed with particular dislike or fear

bildungsroman (Ger; BIL-doongs-roh-mahn): novel embodying coming-of-age story

bodega (S; boh-DAY-gah): grocery store

bon vivant (F; bon-vee-VAHN): a person with refined tastes, esp. for food and drink

bonhomie (F; boh-noh-MEE): friendliness

bourgeois (F; boo-ZHWAH): middle-class; materialistic

carte blanche (F; kahrt-BLANSH): full discretionary power

cause célèbre (F; kawz-suh-LEB): a notorious incident

chutzpah (Y, HUHTS-pah): audacity, nerve

coup de grâce (F; kooh-duh-GRAHS): the decisive final blow

cum laude/magna cum laude/summa cum laude (L; kuhm-LOU-day; MAG-na … ; SOO-ma …): with praise or honor/with great praise or honor/with the highest praise or honor

de facto (L; day-FAK-toh): in fact, if not by law

de jure (L; dee-JOOR-ee, day-YOOR-ay): by right or by law

de rigueur (F; duh-ree-GUR): required by convention or etiquette

détente (F; day-TAHNT): an easing of strained relations

deus ex machina (L; DAY-uhs-eks-MAH-keh-nah): person/event that provides a solution unexpectedly or suddenly, esp. (in literature) a contrived solution to a problem

doppelgänger (Ger; DAH-pul-gang-ur): a double or ghostly counterpart of a person

double entendre (F; DOO-blahn-TAHN-druh): expression with a double meaning, one meaning of which is often risqué

e pluribus unum (L; eh-PLOO-ree-boos-OO-noom): out of many, one (U.S. motto)

éminence grise (F; ay-meh-nahns-GREEZ): one who wields power behind the scenes

ennui (F; ah-NOOEE): boredom; world-weariness; annoyance

ersatz (Ger; EHR-zats): artificial; being a (usually inferior) substitute

ex post facto (L; eks-pohst-FAK-toh): retroactive(ly)

fait accompli (F; fayt-uh-kom-PLEE): an accomplished fact

fatwa (A; FAHT-wah): in Islam, a legal or religious decree

faux pas (F; foh-PAH): false step; breach of etiquette

habeas corpus (L; HAY-bee-ahs-KOR-pus): an order for a prisoner to be brought to court to challenge his or her detention

hoi polloi (Gr; hoy-puh-LOY): the masses

impresario (I; im-prah-SAH-ri-oh): manager, promoter, or sponsor of a musical or theatrical program or company

imprimatur (L; im-prah-MAH-toor): approval or official permission to print, esp. by the Roman Catholic church

in loco parentis (L; in-LOH-koh-puh-REN-tis): in place of a parent

in medias res (L; in-MAY-dee-oos-rays): into the middle of things

intelligentsia (R; in-te-luh-JEN-see-uh): elite social class made up of intellectuals and educated people

ipso facto (L; ip-soh-FAK-toh): by that fact itself

je ne sais quoi (F; zhuh-nuh-say-KWAH): literally, "I don't know what"; the little something that eludes description

jihad (A; jih-HAHD): Islamic holy war; struggle in devotion to Islam

joie de vivre (F; zhwah-duh-VEEV-ruh): zest for life

kvetch (Y; Kuh-VETCH): complain, gripe

leitmotif (Ger; lyt-moh-TEEF): the central theme or idea, particularly in art and literature

mano a mano (S; MAH-noh-ah-MAH-noh): hand to hand; in direct combat

mea culpa (L; MAY-uh-CUL-puh): through my fault

mensch (Y; MENTSCH): an upright, noble, admirable person

modus operandi (L; MOH-duhs-op-uh-RAN-dee): method of operation

mujahedeen (A; moo-jah-ha-DEEN): Islamic holy warrior

noblesse oblige (F; noh-BLES-oh-BLEEZH): the obligation of nobility to help the less fortunate

nolo contendere (L; NOH-loh-kohn-TEN-duh-ree): a plea of no contest to charges, without admitting guilt

non compos mentis (L; non-KOM-puhs-MEN-tis): not of sound mind

non sequitur (L; non-SEH-kwi-tour): a conclusion that does not logically follow from what preceded it

nouveau riche (F; noo-voh-REESH): a newly rich person, esp. one who spends money conspicuously

ombudsman (Swedish; AHM-budz-muhn): person who receives, investigates, and settles complaints

pariah (Tamil; par-EYE-ah): an outcast; member of low caste in India

persona non grata (L; per-SOH-nah-non-GRAH-tah): unwelcome person

pièce de résistance (F; pee-es-duh-ray-ZEES-tonz): the outstanding item in a series or group

prima facie (L; pry-muh-FAY-shee-ee; pry-muh-FAY-shuh): true at first glance; presumptively valid

pro bono (L; proh-BOH-noh): (work) donated for the public good

quid pro quo (L; kwid-proh-KWOH): something given or received for something else

raison d'être (F; RAY-zohnn-DET-ruh): reason for being

savoir faire (F; sav-wahr-FAIR): dexterity in social affairs

schadenfreude (Ger; SHAH-duhn-froy-deh): joy at another's misfortune

semper fidelis (L; SEM-puhr-fee-DAY-lis): always faithful

sobriquet (F; SOH-bri-kay): nickname or informal descriptive name for someone

sotto voce (I; sah-toh-VOH-chee); in a low voice

sui generis (L; soo-ee-JEN-er-is): unique; one of a kind

terra firma (L; TER-uh-FUR-muh): solid ground

verboten (Ger; ver-BOH-ten): forbidden

vis-à-vis (F; vee-zuh-VEE): compared with; with regard to

voir dire (F; vwar-DEER): examination by lawyers or judge to determine the suitability of a witness or a prospective juror

zeitgeist (Ger; ZITE-gyste): the general intellectual, moral, and cultural climate of an era

Names for Animal Young

calf: cattle, elephant, hippo, camel, others

cheeper: grouse, partridge, quail

chick: chicken, penguin, other birds

cockerel: rooster

codling, sprag: codfish

colt: horse, zebra (male)

cria: llama, alpaca

cub: lion, bear, shark, fox, others

cygnet: swan

duckling: duck

elver: eel

ephyra: jellyfish

eyas: hawk, other birds

fawn: deer, antelope

filly: horse, zebra (female)

fingerling, fry: fish generally

fledgling, nestling: birds generally

foal: horse, zebra, others

gosling: goose

heifer: cow

hoglet: hedgehog

joey: kangaroo, opossum, wombat

kid: goat

kit: beaver, rabbit, ferret, others

kitten: cat, other small mammals

lamb: sheep

larva: frog, sea urchin, insects generally

parr, smolt, grilse: salmon

piglet, shoat, farrow, suckling: pig

polliwog, tadpole: frog

poult: turkey

pullet: hen

pup: dog, fox, seal, rat, others

spat: oyster, other bivalves

spiderling: spider

spike, blinker, tinker: mackerel

squab: pigeon

whelp: dog, tiger, other carnivores

yearling: cattle, sheep, horse, others

Names for Animal Collectives

alligators: congregation

ants: army, colony, swarm

apes: shrewdness, troop

bears: sleuth, sloth

bees: colony, swarm, hive

birds: flight, volery

buffalo: gang, obstinacy

butterflies: flutter

buzzards: wake

camels: caravan, flock, train

cats: clowder, cluster, pounce

cattle: drove

cheetahs: coalition

cockroaches: intrusion

cranes: sedge, siege

crocodiles: bask, nest, float

crows: murder, horde

dolphins: pod

doves: dule, pitying

ducks: brace, team

eagles: convocation, aerie

ferrets: business

finches: charm

fish: school, shoal

flamingos: stand, flamboyance

foxes: skulk

geese: flock, gaggle, skein

giraffes: corps, herd, tower

goats: tribe, trip

gorillas: band, troop, whoop

grasshoppers: cloud

hawks: cast, kettle

hedgehogs: array, prickle

hippopotamuses: bloat

horses: pair, team

hounds: cry, mute, pack

hyenas: cackle

iguanas: mess

jellyfish: smack

kangaroos: mob, troop

larks: exaltation

leopards: leap

lions: pride

locusts: plague, swarm

mice, rats: mischief

moles: labor

monkeys: troop

mules: barren, span

nightingales: watch

otters: romp

owls: parliament

oxen: yoke

peacocks: muster

pheasants: nest, nide, bouquet

ponies: string

raccoons: gaze

ravens: unkindness

rhinoceroses: crash

seals: pod

sheep: flock, drove, hurtle

snakes: nest

squirrels: dray, scurry

starlings: flock, murmuration

swans: bevy

tigers: streak

toads: knot

trout: hover

turkeys: rafter

turtles: bale

vultures: committee

whales: gam, herd, pod

woodchucks: fall

woodpeckers: descent

zebras: herd, zeal

Some Common Abbreviations

(See also Abbreviations in the General Index.) Abbreviations include acronyms, pronounceable words formed from first letters, or syllables, of other words, e.g., AIDS. Some acronyms are words coined as abbreviations and written in lowercase (e.g., sonar). Italicized words below are Latin unless otherwise noted.

A: ampere

AA: Alcoholics Anonymous

ABA: American Bar Association

AC: alternating current; air-conditioning

ACA: Affordable Care Act

ACLU: American Civil Liberties Union

AD: *anno Domini* (in the year of the Lord)

AD(H)D: attention deficit (hyperactivity) disorder

AFL-CIO: American Federation of Labor-Congress of Industrial Organizations

AFSCME: American Federation of State, County, and Municipal Employees

AFT: American Federation of Teachers

AI: artificial intelligence

AIDS: acquired immune deficiency syndrome

ALA: American Library Association

a.m. or **AM:** *ante meridiem* (before noon)

AP: Associated Press

APO: army post office

APR: annual percentage rate

AQAP: al-Qaeda in the Arabian Peninsula

ARM: adjustable rate mortgage

ASAP: as soon as possible

ASCAP: American Society of Composers, Authors, and Publishers

ASCII: American Standard Code for Information Interchange

ATM: automated teller machine

Ave.: Avenue

AWOL: absent without leave

BA: Bachelor of Arts

bbl: barrel(s)

BC: before Christ

BCE: before Common, or Christian, Era

Benelux: Belgium, Netherlands, Luxembourg

bpd or **b/d:** barrels per day

BRB: be right back

Brexit: British exit (from the EU)

BS: Bachelor of Science

Btu: British thermal unit(s)

BTW: by the way

B2B: business-to-business (company)

bu: bushel(s)
BYOB: bring your own bottle
C: Celsius, centigrade
c.: *circa* (about); copyright
C(A)T: computerized (axial) tomography
CD: compact disc
CDC: Centers for Disease Control and Prevention; Community Development Corporation
CE: Common Era; Christian Era
CEO: chief executive officer
cf.: *confer* (compare)
CFO: chief financial officer
CIA: Central Intelligence Agency
COBRA: Consolidated Omnibus Budget Reconciliation Act (health insurance continuation)
COD: cash (or collect) on delivery
COL or Col.: Colonel
COLA: cost of living adjustment
COO: chief operating officer
CPA: certified public accountant
CPI: consumer price index
CPL or Cpl.: Corporal
CPR: cardiopulmonary resuscitation
CPU: central processing unit
CST: central standard time
CV: curriculum vitae
DA: district attorney
DACA: Deferred Action for Childhood Arrivals
DC: direct current
DD: Doctor of Divinity
DDS: Doctor of Dental Surgery
DEA: Drug Enforcement Administration
DHS: Department of Homeland Security
DJ or deejay: disc jockey
DM: direct message
DMD: Doctor of Dental Medicine
DMZ: demilitarized zone
DNA: deoxyribonucleic acid
DNC: Democratic National Committee
DNR: do not resuscitate
DOA: dead on arrival
DOB: date of birth
DoD: Department of Defense
dpi: dots per inch
DPT: diphtheria, pertussis, tetanus
DUI: driving under the influence
DVD: digital video disc
DVM: Doctor of Veterinary Medicine
DWI: driving while intoxicated
ECB: European Central Bank
ed.: edited; edition; editor
EEG: electroencephalogram
e.g.: *exempli gratia* (for example)
EKG or ECG: electrocardiogram
EMT: emergency medical technician
EOE: equal opportunity employer
EP: extended play
EPA: Environmental Protection Agency
ERA: Equal Rights Amendment; earned run average
ESL: English as a second language
ESP: extrasensory perception
Esq.: Esquire
EST: eastern standard time
et al.: *et alii* (and others)
etc.: *et cetera* (and so forth)
EU: European Union
F: Fahrenheit
Fannie Mae: Federal National Mortgage Association
FAQ: frequently asked questions
FBI: Federal Bureau of Investigation
FDA: Food and Drug Administration
FDIC: Federal Deposit Insurance Corporation
FEC: Federal Election Commission

FEMA: Federal Emergency Management Agency
ff.: and those following
FICA: Federal Insurance Contributions Act (Social Security)
FIFA: Fédération Internationale de Football Association
fl.: *floruit* (flourished), used for historical figures when life dates uncertain
FLOTUS: First Lady of the United States
FOMO: Fear of missing out
Freddie Mac: Federal Home Loan Mortgage Corporation
FTP: file transfer protocol
FWIW: for what it's worth
FY: fiscal year
FYI: for your information
GB: gigabyte(s)
GDP: gross domestic product
GED: general equivalency diploma
GMO: genetically modified organism
GMT: Greenwich mean time
GOP: Grand Old Party (Republican Party)
GPS: Global Positioning System
GTG: got to go
GUI: graphical user interface
ha: hectare
hazmat: HAZardous MATerial
HDTV: high-definition television
HIV: human immunodeficiency virus
HMO: health maintenance organization
HMS: His/Her Majesty's Ship (UK)
Hon.: the Honorable
HOV: high-occupancy vehicle
HRH: Her (His) Royal Highness (UK)
HTML: hypertext markup language
HTTP: hypertext transfer protocol
HUD: Department of Housing and Urban Development
HVAC: heating, ventilating, and air-conditioning
Hz: hertz
ibid.: *ibidem* (in the same place)
ICE: Immigration and Customs Enforcement (agency)
ICU: intensive care unit
i.e.: *id est* (that is)
IM: instant messaging
IMF: International Monetary Fund
IM(H)O: in my (humble) opinion
INS: Immigration and Naturalization Service
IPO: initial public offering
IQ: intelligence quotient
IRA: individual retirement account; Irish Republican Army
IRS: Internal Revenue Service
ISBN: International Standard Book Number
ISIL or ISIS: Islamic State of Iraq in the Levant, or of Iraq and Syria
ISP: Internet service provider
IVF: in vitro fertilization
JD: *Juris Doctor* (Doctor of Law)
k: karat; **K:** Kelvin
kWh: kilowatt-hour(s)
laser: Light Amplification by Stimulated Emission of Radiation
lb: pound
LGBT(QIA): lesbian, gay, bisexual, transgender (queer/questioning, intersex, asexual)
LLP: limited liability partnership
loc. cit.: *loco citato* (in the place cited)
LOL: laughing out loud
LSAT: Law School Admission Test
LT or Lt.: Lieutenant
MA: Master of Arts
MB: megabyte(s)
MBA: Master of Business Administration
MCAT: Medical College Admission Test

MD: *Medicinae Doctor* (Doctor of Medicine)
MIA: missing in action
modem: MOdulator-DEModulator
MP: member of Parliament (UK)
mph: miles per hour
MRI: magnetic resonance imaging
ms, mss: manuscript(s)
MS: Master of Science; multiple sclerosis
MSG: monosodium glutamate
MST: mountain standard time
MVP: most valuable player
MYOB: mind your own business
NA: not applicable; not available
NAACP: National Association for the Advancement of Colored People
NAFTA: North American Free Trade Agreement
NASA: National Aeronautics and Space Administration
NATO: North Atlantic Treaty Organization
NB or n.b.: *nota bene* (note carefully)
NCAA: National Collegiate Athletic Association
NEA: National Education Association; National Endowment for the Arts
NIH: National Institutes of Health
NIMBY: not in my backyard
NOW: National Organization for Women
NPR: National Public Radio
NRA: National Rifle Association
NSA: National Security Agency
NSC: National Security Council
obs.: obsolete
OECD: Organization for Economic Cooperation and Development
OED: Oxford English Dictionary
OMB: Office of Management and Budget
OMG: Oh my goodness/gosh/God!
op., opp.: *opus* (work[s])
OPEC: Organization of Petroleum Exporting Countries
OTC: over-the-counter
oz: ounce
p., pp.: page(s)
PA: public address
PAC: political action committee
PC: personal computer; politically correct
PDA: personal digital assistant
PET: positron emission tomography
PETA: People for the Ethical Treatment of Animals
PhD: *Philosophiae Doctor* (Doctor of Philosophy)
PIN: personal identification number
p.m. or PM: post meridiem (after noon)
PM: private message; prime minister
POTUS: President of the United States
PPO: preferred provider organization, a type of health-care provider network
PS: *post scriptum* (postscript)
PST: Pacific standard time
pt: part(s); pint(s); point(s)
PT: physical therapy/training
PTSD: post-traumatic stress disorder
PVT or Pvt.: Private
QC: Queen's Council (UK)
QED: *quod erat demonstrandum* (which was to be demonstrated)
radar: RAdio Detecting And Ranging
RAM: random access memory
RC: Roman Catholic
RCMP: Royal Canadian Mounted Police
REM: rapid eye movement
Rev.: Reverend
rev.: revised; reviewed
RIP: *requiescat in pace* (may he/she rest in peace)
RN: registered nurse
RNA: ribonucleic acid
RNC: Republican National Committee

ROFL: rolling on the floor laughing
ROM: read only memory
ROTC: Reserve Officers' Training Corps
rpm: revolutions per minute
RSVP: *répondez s'il vous plaît* (Fr.) (please reply)
SARS: severe acute respiratory syndrome
SCOTUS: Supreme Court of the United States
scuba: self-contained underwater breathing apparatus
SEC: Securities and Exchange Commission
SEO: search engine optimization
SETI: Search for Extraterrestrial Intelligence
SGT or Sgt.: Sergeant
SIDS: sudden infant death syndrome
SJ: Society of Jesus (Jesuits)
SMH: shaking my head
sonar: SOund NAvigation and Ranging
SOTU: State of the Union
SPCA: Society for the Prevention of Cruelty to Animals

SSI: Supplementary Security Income
St.: Saint; Street
STEM: science, technology, engineering, math
TB: tuberculosis; terabyte(s)
TBA/TBD: to be announced/determined
tbsp: tablespoon
TBT: Throwback Thursday
TEFL: teaching English as a foreign language
TIA: transient ischemic attack
TMI: too much information
TPP: Trans-Pacific Partnership (trade agreement)
TSA: Transportation Security Administration
tsp: teaspoon
UFO: unidentified flying object
UPC: Universal Product Code
URL: Universal Resource Locator
USDA: United States Department of Agriculture

USS: United States ship
UTC: coordinated universal time
VA: Department of Veterans Affairs
VAT: value-added tax
VCR: videocassette recorder
viz: *videlicet* (namely)
VP: vice president
W: watt(s)
WHO: World Health Organization
WMD: weapon of mass destruction
WPM: words per minute
WTF: what the f--- [expletive]
WTO: World Trade Organization
WWW: World Wide Web
YMCA/YWCA: Young Men's/Women's Christian Association
YOLO: you only live once
YTD: year to date
yuppie: young urban professional
ZIP: zone improvement plan (U.S. Postal Service)

Most Popular U.S. First Names by Decade or Year of Birth

Source: U.S. Social Security Administration

All names are from Social Security card applications for births that occurred in the United States after 1879. Rankings are based on one spelling of the name; variant spellings and similar sounding names are considered separate names.

BOYS

1880-1889	John, William, James, George, Charles, Frank, Joseph, Henry, Robert, Thomas
1890-1899	John, William, James, George, Charles, Joseph, Frank, Robert, Edward, Henry
1900-1909	John, William, James, George, Charles, Robert, Joseph, Frank, Edward, Thomas
1910-1919	John, William, James, Robert, Joseph, George, Charles, Edward, Frank, Thomas
1920-1929	Robert, John, James, William, Charles, George, Joseph, Richard, Edward, Donald
1930-1939	Robert, James, John, William, Richard, Charles, Donald, George, Thomas, Joseph
1940-1949	James, Robert, John, William, Richard, David, Charles, Thomas, Michael, Ronald
1950-1959	Michael, David, James, John, Robert, Mark, William, Richard, Thomas, Jeffrey
1960-1969	Michael, David, John, James, Robert, Mark, William, Richard, Thomas, Jeffrey
1970-1979	Michael, Christopher, Jason, David, James, John, Robert, Brian, William, Matthew
1980-1989	Michael, Christopher, Matthew, Joshua, David, James, Daniel, Robert, John, Joseph
1990-1999	Michael, Christopher, Matthew, Joshua, Jacob, Nicholas, Andrew, Daniel, Tyler, Joseph
2000-2009	Jacob, Michael, Joshua, Matthew, Daniel, Christopher, Andrew, Ethan, Joseph, William
2010-19.	Noah, Liam, Jacob, William, Mason, Michael, Alexander, James, Elijah
2019	Liam, Noah, Oliver, William, Elijah, James, Benjamin, Lucas, Mason, Ethan

GIRLS

1880-1889	Mary, Anna, Emma, Elizabeth, Margaret, Minnie, Ida, Bertha, Clara, Alice
1890-1899	Mary, Anna, Margaret, Helen, Elizabeth, Ruth, Florence, Ethel, Emma, Marie
1900-1909	Mary, Helen, Margaret, Anna, Ruth, Elizabeth, Dorothy, Marie, Florence, Mildred
1910-1919	Mary, Helen, Dorothy, Margaret, Ruth, Mildred, Anna, Elizabeth, Frances, Virginia
1920-1929	Mary, Dorothy, Helen, Betty, Margaret, Ruth, Virginia, Doris, Mildred, Frances
1930-1939	Mary, Betty, Barbara, Shirley, Patricia, Dorothy, Joan, Margaret, Nancy, Helen
1940-1949	Mary, Linda, Barbara, Patricia, Carol, Sandra, Nancy, Sharon, Judith, Susan
1950-1959	Mary, Linda, Patricia, Susan, Deborah, Barbara, Debra, Karen, Nancy, Donna
1960-1969	Lisa, Mary, Susan, Karen, Kimberly, Patricia, Linda, Donna, Michelle, Cynthia
1970-1979	Jennifer, Amy, Melissa, Michelle, Kimberly, Lisa, Angela, Heather, Stephanie, Nicole
1980-1989	Jessica, Jennifer, Amanda, Ashley, Sarah, Stephanie, Melissa, Nicole, Elizabeth, Heather
1990-1999	Jessica, Ashley, Emily, Sarah, Samantha, Amanda, Brittany, Elizabeth, Taylor, Megan
2000-2009	Emily, Madison, Emma, Olivia, Hannah, Abigail, Isabella, Samantha, Elizabeth, Ashley
2010-19	Emma, Olivia, Sophia, Isabella, Ava, Mia, Emily, Abigail, Charlotte, Madison
2019	Olivia, Emma, Ava, Sophia, Isabella, Charlotte, Amelia, Mia, Harper, Evelyn

Words and Expressions in Common Languages

English	Arabic	Chinese[1]	French	German	Hebrew	Russian	Spanish
Hello/hi	Salam	Ni hao	Bonjour	Hallo	Shalom	Privet (informal)	Hola
Good morning	Sabah el kheer	Zao shang hao	Bonjour	Guten Morgen	Boker tov	Dobraye utra	Buenos días
Good night	Tosbeho 'ala khair	Wan an	Bonne nuit	Gute Nacht	Layla tov	Spakoynay noci	Buenas noches
Goodbye	Ma'a salama	Zai jian	Au revoir	Auf wiedersehen	Lehitraot	Da svidan'ya	Adiós
Please	Men fadlek	Qing	S'il vous plaît	Bitte	Bevakasha	Pazhalusta	Por favor
Thank you very much	Shokran jazeelan	Xie xie	Merci beaucoup	Danke schön	Toda raba	Spasiba	Muchas gracias
You're welcome	Al' afw	Huan ying	De rien/pas de quoi	Bitte schön	Bevakasha	Pazhalusta	De nada
How are you?	Kaifa haloka?	Ni hao?	Comment allez-vous?	Wie geht's dir/Ihnen?	Ma shelomkha?	Kak dela?	¿Cómo estás?
I'm fine	Ana bekhair	Hen hao	Je vais bien	Mir geht's gut	Tov	Harasho	Estoy bien
I'm sorry	Aasef	Bao qian	Je suis désolé	Entschuldigung	Ani mamash mitstaer	Prastite	Lo siento
Excuse me	Alma'derah	Bao qian	Pardon	Darf ich mal vorbei?	Selikha	Izvinite	Perdone
yes	na'am	shi [it is so]	oui	ja	ken	da	sí
no	laa	bu [not]	non	nein	lo	nyet	no
one	wahed	yi	un	eins	ekhad	adin	uno
two	ithnaan	er	deux	zwei	shenayim	dva	dos
three	thalatha	san	trois	drei	shelosha	tri	tres
four	arba'a	si	quatre	vier	arbaa	chityri	cuatro
five	khamsa	wu	cinq	fünf	khamisha	p'at	cinco

Note: Actual form or usage of some words and expressions may vary depending on dialect, grammar, or circumstances. Transliterations for languages not in Latin alphabet vary. (1) Mandarin.

Principal Languages of the World

Source: Used by permission. © 2020 SIL International, from *Ethnologue: Languages of the World, 23rd Edition*

Languages shown in italics are macrolanguages, or language groups that are equivalent in some ways to individual languages. Each language group consists of a number of variants, which may be mutually unintelligible; these variants, when they have 2.5 mil speakers or more, appear in the larger table below, and occasionally have the same name as the macrolanguage. Numbers are estimates and count only speakers for whom the language is a first language, or mother tongue.

Languages Spoken by the Most People

Language	Speakers (mil)	Language	Speakers (mil)	Language	Speakers (mil)
Chinese	1,321.0	Marathi	83.1	Javanese	68.3
Spanish	463.0	Telugu	82.4	*Persian*	65.0
English	369.7	*Malay*	81.5	Italian	64.6
Hindi	342.0	Turkish	79.5	*Pushto*	53.1
Arabic	338.5	Korean	79.4	Gujarati	56.5
Bengali	228.5	Tamil	77.8	Bhojpuri	52.2
Portuguese	227.9	French	77.3	Hausa	47.7
Russian	153.6	Vietnamese	76.0	Kannada	43.6
Japanese	126.2	German	75.5	Yoruba	40.5
Lahnda	117.1	Urdu	69.0	Polish	40.0

Languages With at Least 2.5 Million Speakers

Primary country is country of origin, not necessarily the country where the most speakers reside (e.g., Portugal is the primary country for Portuguese, but more Portuguese speakers live in Brazil). Number of speakers is worldwide total for each language.

Primary country	Language	Countries	Speakers (mil)	Primary country	Language	Countries	Speakers (mil)
Afghanistan	Pashto, Southern	4	16.9	Ethiopia (cont.)	Amharic	2	32.3
	Dari	3	10.2		Oromo, West Central	1	19.2
	Uzbek, Southern	2	4.6		Tigrigna	3	9.7
	Hazaragi	3	3.6		Oromo, Eastern	1	9.7
Albania	*Albanian*	21	5.9		Oromo, Borana-Arsi-Guji	3	8.1
	Albanian, Gheg	6	3.9		Sidamo	1	4.3
Algeria	Arabic, Algerian Spoken	2	29.6	Finland	Finnish	5	5.2
	Kabyle	1	5.6	France	French	75	77.3
Angola	Umbundu	1	7.0	Georgia	Georgian	4	3.9
Armenia	Armenian	4	3.8	Germany	German, Standard	37	75.5
Austria	Bavarian	4	14.4	Ghana	Akan	1	8.3
Azerbaijan	Azerbaijani, North	4	9.2		Ghanaian Pidgin English	1	5.0
Bangladesh	Bengali	4	228.5		Ewé	2	5.0
	Chittagonian	1	13.0	Greece	Greek	9	13.1
	Rangpuri	2	10.5	Guinea	*Mandingo*	7	8.4
	Sylheti	2	9.8		Pular	5	5.4
Belarus	Belarusian	4	2.6		Maninkakan, Eastern	3	3.6
Bosnia and				Haiti	Haitian Creole	3	7.6
Herzegovina	Bosnian	6	2.7	Hungary	Hungarian	9	12.5
Botswana	Setswana	4	5.8	India	Hindi	5	342.0
Brazil	Hunsrik	1	3.0		Marathi	1	83.1
Bulgaria	Bulgarian	8	8.1		Telugu	2	82.4
Burkina Faso	Mòoré	4	8.0		Tamil	7	77.8
Burundi	Rundi	1	11.2		Gujarati	7	56.5
Cambodia	Khmer	2	16.6		Bhojpuri	3	52.2
China	*Chinese*	46	1,321.0		Kannada	1	43.6
	Chinese, Mandarin	15	921.5		Malayalam	2	37.2
	Chinese, Yue	14	84.5		Maithili	2	33.9
	Chinese, Wu	1	81.7		Punjabi, Eastern	3	33.5
	Chinese, Min Nan	10	48.2		Magahi	2	20.7
	Chinese, Jinyu	1	47.1		*Marwari*	3	20.6
	Chinese, Hakka	13	43.0		Chhattisgarhi	1	16.3
	Chinese, Xiang	1	37.4		*Rajasthani*	3	16.1
	Chinese, Gan	1	22.2		Assamese	1	15.3
	Zhuang	2	14.9		Deccan	1	12.8
	Chinese, Min Bei	2	11.1		Haryanvi	1	9.8
	Chinese, Min Dong	6	10.8		Indian Sign Language	2	8.1
	Uyghur	4	10.4		Marwari	2	7.9
	Hmong	9	7.7		Santhali	3	7.6
	Chinese, Huizhou	1	5.4		Varhadi-Nagpuri	1	7.0
	Chinese, Min Zhong	1	3.6		Kashmiri	2	6.9
	Mongolian, Peripheral	2	3.4		Kanauji	1	6.0
	Chinese, Pu-Xian	3	3.2		Konkani	5	5.8
	Bouyei	3	2.7		Bundeli	1	5.6
Congo, Dem.					Malvi	1	5.4
Rep. of	*Kongo*	3	6.9		Sadri	2	5.1
	Luba-Kasai	2	6.4		Lambadi	1	5.1
	Koongo	3	6.2		Awadhi	2	4.4
	Kituba	1	4.2		Mewari	1	4.2
Côte d'Ivoire	Baoulé	1	4.7		Merwari	1	3.9
Croatia	Croatian	9	5.5		*Dogri*	1	3.7
Czechia	Czech	8	10.7		Konkani, Goan	2	3.7
Denmark	Danish	5	5.6		Wagdi	1	3.4
Egypt	Arabic, Egyptian Spoken	2	67.8		Bhili	1	3.3
	Arabic, Sa'idi Spoken	4	23.5		Shekhawati	1	3.0
Ethiopia	*Oromo*	4	37.1		Godwari	1	3.0

Primary country	Language	Countries	Speakers (mil)
India (cont.)	Haroti	1	2.9
	Bagheli	1	2.7
	Dogri	1	2.6
Indonesia	Javanese	3	68.3
	Indonesian	1	43.6
	Sunda	1	32.4
	Madura	2	7.8
	Betawi	1	5.0
	Minangkabau	1	4.2
	Bugis	2	3.9
	Banjar	2	3.7
	Aceh	1	3.5
	Bali	1	3.3
	Musi	1	3.1
Iran	Persian	33	65.0
	Persian, Iranian	7	55.0
	Azerbaijani	21	23.1
	Azerbaijani, South	5	13.9
	Kurdish, Southern	2	3.7
Iraq	Kurdish	29	22.8
	Arabic, Mesopotamian Spoken	4	15.9
	Arabic, North Mesopotamian Spoken	4	8.8
	Kurdish, Central	2	4.6
Israel	Hebrew	2	6.0
Italy	Italian	17	64.6
	Venetian	5	7.9
	Napoletano-Calabrese	1	5.7
	Sicilian	1	4.7
	Lombard	2	3.9
Jamaica	Jamaican Creole English	3	3.0
Japan	Japanese	3	126.2
Jordan	Arabic, South Levantine Spoken	4	11.9
Kazakhstan	Kazakh	6	13.2
Kenya	Gikuyu	1	6.6
	Oluluyia	3	5.3
	Kalenjin	3	4.8
	Dholuo	2	4.2
	Kamba	2	3.9
Korea, South	Korean	7	79.4
Kuwait	Arabic, Gulf Spoken	10	10.4
Kyrgyzstan	Kyrgyz	5	5.0
Laos	Lao	3	3.7
Lesotho	Sotho, Southern	2	5.6
Libya	Arabic, Libyan Spoken	3	5.0
Lithuania	Lithuanian	2	3.0
Madagascar	Malagasy	5	18.1
	Malagasy, Plateau	2	7.5
Malawi	Chichewa	5	9.7
	Yao	4	2.6
Malaysia	Malay	24	81.5
	Malay	3	16.1
	Malay, Kedah	2	2.6
Mali	Bamanankan	3	4.1
Mauritania	Hassaniyya	7	9.5
Mongolia	Mongolian	9	6.0
	Mongolian, Halh	2	2.7
Morocco	Arabic, Moroccan Spoken	3	27.9
	Tachelhit	3	7.2
	Tamazight, Central Atlas	1	4.7
	Tarifit	2	4.4
Mozambique	Makhuwa	2	3.6
Myanmar	Burmese	1	32.9
	Shan	3	4.7
	Rohingya	2	2.5
Nepal	Nepali	13	16.6
	Nepali	3	15.9
Netherlands	Dutch	7	22.8
Niger	Zarma	4	4.0
Nigeria	Hausa	9	47.7
	Yoruba	3	40.5
	Igbo	1	29.0
	Fulfulde, Nigerian	3	15.6
	Kanuri	6	8.4
	Kanuri, Yerwa	5	7.9
	Ibibio	1	5.9
	Tiv	2	4.3
	Anaang	1	2.7
Norway	Norwegian	1	5.3
Oman	Arabic, Omani Spoken	4	2.7
Pakistan	Lahnda	6	117.1
	Punjabi, Western	2	82.8
	Urdu	7	69.0
	Pushto	14	53.1
	Sindhi	4	32.9
	Pashto, Northern	4	27.8
	Saraiki	2	26.0
	Baluchi	10	8.8
	Pashto, Central	1	8.5
	Balochi, Southern	4	3.6
	Hindko, Northern	1	3.6
	Pahari-Potwari	2	3.5
	Balochi, Eastern	2	2.9
	Brahui	3	2.9
Paraguay	Guaraní	5	6.2
	Guaraní, Paraguayan	1	6.1
Peru	Quechua	6	7.7
Philippines	Tagalog	4	25.0
	Cebuano	1	15.9
	Ilocano	1	6.5
	Hiligaynon	1	6.2
	Waray-Waray	1	2.6
Poland	Polish	10	40.0
Portugal	Portuguese	16	227.9
Romania	Romanian	6	24.5
Russian Federation	Russian	21	153.6
	Tatar	4	5.3
Rwanda	Kinyarwanda	3	13.1
Saudi Arabia	Arabic	66	338.5
	Arabic, Najdi Spoken	4	17.9
	Arabic, Hijazi Spoken	3	10.7
Senegal	Fulah	20	33.0
	Wolof	2	5.9
	Pulaar	6	5.4
Serbia	Serbo-Croatian	28	17.2
	Serbian	11	8.8
Slovakia	Slovak	8	5.2
Somalia	Somali	4	18.5
South Africa	Zulu	5	12.1
	Xhosa	2	8.2
	Afrikaans	6	7.2
	Tsonga	4	5.5
	Sotho, Northern	1	4.6
Spain	Spanish	40	463.0
	Catalan	4	4.1
	Galician	3	3.1
Sri Lanka	Sinhala	2	15.9
Sudan	Arabic, Sudanese Spoken	5	33.2
Sweden	Swedish	4	9.7
Switzerland	German, Swiss	5	5.7
Syria	Arabic, North Levantine Spoken	5	24.5
Tajikistan	Tajik	5	8.1
Tanzania	Swahili	21	18.2
	Swahili	8	16.2
	Sukuma	1	8.1
Thailand	Thai	2	20.7
	Thai, Northeastern	1	15.0
	Thai, Northern	1	6.0
	Thai, Southern	1	4.5
Tunisia	Arabic, Tunisian Spoken	1	11.6
Turkey	Turkish	9	79.5
	Kurdish, Northern	9	14.6
Turkmenistan	Turkmen	7	7.0
Uganda	Ganda	1	5.6
	Nyankore	2	3.4
	Soga	1	3.0
	Teso	2	2.7
Ukraine	Ukrainian	9	27.3
United Kingdom	English	158	369.7
Uzbekistan	Uzbek	13	31.4
Uzbekistan	Uzbek, Northern	6	26.8
Vietnam	Vietnamese	5	76.0
Yemen	Arabic, Sanaani Spoken	1	12.2
	Arabic, Ta'izzi-Adeni Spoken	2	11.3
	Arabic, Hadrami Spoken	1	4.9
Zambia	Bemba	2	4.1
Zimbabwe	Shona	3	7.2

BUILDINGS, BRIDGES, AND TUNNELS

100 Tallest Buildings in the World

Source: Phorio, phorio.com; Council on Tall Buildings and Urban Habitat (CTBUH), www.ctbuh.org

Only buildings that are completed or under construction and topped out as of Oct. 2020, are shown here. Structures under construction and topped out architecturally are denoted by an asterisk (*). Year in parentheses is date of completion or projected completion. Height is generally measured from the lowest significant open-air pedestrian entrance to the architectural top, including spires and other decorative features that are an integral part of the design, but not including flagpoles and antennae. Stories generally counted from street level. NA = Not available.

Building	Ht. (ft)	Stories
Burj Khalifa, Dubai, United Arab Emirates (2010)	2,717	163
Shanghai Tower, Shanghai, China (2015)	2,074	128
Makkah Royal Clock Tower Hotel, Mecca, Saudi Arabia (2013)	1,972	120
Ping An Finance Center, Shenzhen, China (2016)	1,965	115
*Goldin Finance 117, Tianjin, China (2022)	1,957	128
Lotte World Tower, Seoul, South Korea (2017)	1,819	123
One World Trade Center, New York, NY, U.S. (2014)	1,782	94
CTF Finance Centre, Guangzhou, China (2016)	1,739	111
Chow Tai Fook Binhai Center, Tianjin, China (2019)	1,739	97
Citic Tower, Beijing, China (2018)	1,732	108
Taipei 101, Taipei, Taiwan (2004)	1,667	101
Shanghai World Financial Center, Shanghai, China (2008)	1,614	101
International Commerce Centre, Hong Kong, China (2010)	1,588	108
*Wuhan Greenland Center, Wuhan, China (2022)	1,560	97
*Central Park Tower, New York, NY, U.S. (2020)	1,550	95
Lakhta Center, St. Petersburg, Russia (2019)	1,516	87
Vincom Landmark 81, Ho Chi Minh City, Vietnam (2018)	1,513	81
The Exchange 106, Kuala Lumpur, Malaysia (2019)	1,488	97
Changsha IFS Tower T1, Changsha, China (2018)	1,483	94
Petronas Tower I, Kuala Lumpur, Malaysia (1998)	1,483	88
Petronas Tower II, Kuala Lumpur, Malaysia (1998)	1,483	88
Suzhou IFS, Suzhou, China (2019)	1,476	95
Zifeng Tower, Nanjing, China (2010)	1,476	66
Willis (fmr. Sears) Twr., Chicago, IL, U.S. (1974)	1,451	108
KK100, Shenzhen, China (2011)	1,449	100
Guangzhou International Finance Center, Guangzhou, China (2010)	1,439	103
Wuhan Center, Wuhan, China (2019)	1,437	88
*111 West 57th St., New York, NY, U.S. (2020)	1,428	82
*Dongguan International Trade Center 1, Dongguan, China (2020)	1,401	88
*One Vanderbilt Place, New York, NY, U.S. (2021)	1,401	58
432 Park Avenue, New York, NY, U.S. (2015)	1,397	85
Marina 101, Dubai, UAE (2017)	1,394	101
Trump Intl. Hotel & Tower, Chicago, IL, U.S. (2009)	1,389	98
Jin Mao Tower, Shanghai, China (1999)	1,380	88
Princess Tower, Dubai, UAE (2012)	1,356	101
Al Hamra Tower, Kuwait City, Kuwait (2011)	1,354	80
Two International Finance Centre, Hong Kong, China (2003)	1,352	88
*LCT Landmark Tower, Busan, South Korea (2020)	1,350	101
*China Resources Tower, Nanning, China (2020)	1,321	86
Guiyang Financial Center Tower 1, Guiyang, China (2020)	1,316	79
China Resources Headquarters, Shenzhen, China (2018)	1,288	66
23 Marina, Dubai, UAE (2012)	1,287	88
CITIC Plaza, Guangzhou, China (1997)	1,280	80
*Sum Yip Upperhills Twr. 1, Shenzhen, China (2020)	1,273	80
30 Hudson Yards, New York, NY (2019)	1,268	73
*PIF Tower, Riyadh, Saudi Arabia (2020)	1,260	76
Shun Hing Square, Shenzhen, China (1996)	1,260	69
Eton Place Dalian Tower 1, Dalian, China (2016)	1,257	80
*Thamrin Nine Tower 1, Jakarta, Indonesia (2021)	1,256	75
Logan Century Center 1, Nanning, China (2019)	1,251	82
Burj Mohammed Bin Rashid Tower, Abu Dhabi, UAE (2014)	1,251	88
Empire State Building, New York, NY, U.S. (1931)	1,250	102
Elite Residence, Dubai, UAE (2012)	1,248	87
*Shenzhen Center, Shenzhen, China (2020)	1,232	74
Central Plaza, Hong Kong, China (1992)	1,227	78
Vostok, Moscow, Russia (2017)	1,226	93
Dalian Intl. Trade Center, Dalian, China (2019)	1,214	86
*Hai Tian Center Tower 2, Qingdao, China (2021)	1,211	72
*Golden Eagle Tiandi Tower A, Nanjing, China (2019)	1,207	76
Address Boulevard, Dubai, UAE (2017)	1,207	72
Bank of China Tower, Hong Kong, China (1989)	1,205	72
Bank of America Twr., New York, NY, U.S. (2009)	1,200	55
*Vista Tower, Chicago, IL, U.S. (2021)	1,191	101
Almas Tower, Dubai, UAE (2008)	1,181	68
Huiyin Center, Shenzhen, China (2022)	1,178	80
*Greenland Group Suzhou Center, Suzhou, China (2021)	1,175	77
Gevora Hotel, Dubai, UAE (2017)	1,169	76
JW Marriott Marquis Hotel Dubai Tower 2, Dubai, UAE (2013)	1,166	82
JW Marriott Marquis Hotel Dubai Tower 1, Dubai, UAE (2012)	1,166	82
*Chongqing Raffles City T4N, Chongqing, China (2019)	1,163	81
*Chongqing Raffles City T3N, Chongqing, China (2019)	1,163	81
Emirates Office Tower, Dubai, UAE (2000)	1,163	54
OKO South Tower, Moscow, Russia (2015)	1,162	90
The Torch, Dubai, UAE (2011)	1,155	86
Forum 66 Tower 1, Shenyang, China (2015)	1,150	67
The Pinnacle, Guangzhou, China (2012)	1,149	60
*Glory-Xi'an Intl. Finance Ctr., Xi'an, China (2020)	1,148	75
Hanking Center, Shenzhen, China (2018)	1,148	65
Spring City 66, Kunming, China (2019)	1,145	61
Tuntex Sky Tower, Kaohsiung, Taiwan (1998)	1,140	85
*Shimao Hunan Center, Changsha, China (2020)	1,138	76
Aon Center, Chicago, IL, U.S. (1973)	1,136	83
The Center, Hong Kong, China (1998)	1,135	73
*Neva Towers 2, Moscow, Russia (2020)	1,132	79
*Xiamen Cross-Strait Financial Centre, Xiamen, China (2020)	1,128	68
875 N. Michigan Ave. (fmr. John Hancock Center), Chicago, IL, U.S. (1969)	1,128	100
Four Seasons Place, Kuala Lumpur, Malay. (2018)	1,124	65
ADNOC Headquarters, Abu Dhabi, UAE (2015)	1,122	65
Comcast Technology Ctr., Phila., PA, U.S. (2018)	1,121	59
One Shenzhen Bay Tower 7, Shenzhen, China (2018)	1,120	71
*LCT Residential Twr. A, Busan, S. Korea (2020)	1,113	85
Chongqing World Financial Center, Chongqing, China (2015)	1,112	72
Mercury City Tower, Moscow, Russia (2013)	1,112	75
Wuxi Intl. Finance Square, Wuxi, China (2014)	1,112	68
Heartland 66 Main Tower, Wuhan, Chinan (2020)	1,112	60
Suning Plaza Tower 1, Zhenjiang, China (2018)	1,109	75
*Parc1 Tower A, Seoul, South Korea (2020)	1,109	68
Tianjin Modern City Office Tower, Tianjin, China (2016)	1,109	65
Tianjin World Financial Center, Tianjin, China (2011)	1,105	75
*Hengqin IFC, Zhuhai, China (2020)	1,105	69

Tallest Free-Standing Towers in the World

Source: Phorio, phorio.com; Council on Tall Buildings and Urban Habitat (CTBUH), www.ctbuh.org
Year is date of completion or projected completion. As of Oct. 2020.

Tower	Ht. (ft)	Year
Tokyo Sky Tree, Tokyo, Japan	2,080	2012
Canton Tower, Guangzhou, China	1,969	2010
CN Tower, Toronto, ON, Canada	1,815	1976
Ostankino Tower, Moscow, Russia	1,772	1967
Oriental Pearl Television Tower, Shanghai, China	1,535	1995
Milad Tower, Tehran, Iran	1,427	2008
Manara Kuala Lumpur, Kuala Lumpur, Malaysia	1,379	1996
Tianjin Radio & TV Tower, Tianjin, China	1,362	1991
Central Radio & TV Tower, Beijing, China	1,347	1992
Henan Province Radio & Television Emission Tower, Zhengzhou, China	1,273	2010
Kiev TV Tower, Kiev, Ukraine	1,263	1974
Tashkent Tower, Tashkent, Uzbekistan	1,230	1985
Liberation Tower, Kuwait City, Kuwait	1,220	1996
Alma-Ata Tower, Almaty, Kazakhstan	1,217	1982
Camlica TV Tower, Istanbul, Turkey	1,211	2019
TV Tower, Riga, Latvia	1,208	1987
Berliner Fernsehturm, Berlin, Germany	1,207	1969
Stratosphere Tower, Las Vegas, NV, U.S.	1,149	1996
Lotus Tower, Colombo, Sri Lanka	1,148	2019
West Pearl Tower, Chengdu, China	1,112	2004
Macau Tower, Macau, China	1,109	2001

Tall Buildings in Selected North American Cities

Source: Phorio, phorio.com; Council on Tall Buildings and Urban Habitat (CTBUH), www.ctbuh.org

List includes freestanding towers and other structures that do not have stories and are not technically considered buildings. Structures still under construction as of Oct. 2020 are denoted by an asterisk (*). Year in parentheses is date of completion or projected completion. Height is generally measured from the lowest significant open-air pedestrian entrance to the architectural top, including penthouses, spires, and other decorative features that are an integral part of the design, but not including flagpoles and antennae. Stories generally counted from street level. NA = Not applicable/available.

Building/structure	Ht. (ft)	Stories
Atlanta, GA		
Bank of America Plaza (incl. spire),		
600 Peachtree St. NE (1992)	1,023	55
SunTrust Plaza, 303 Peachtree St. NE[1] (1993)	867	60
One Atlantic Center, 1201 W. Peachtree St. (1987) . .	820	50
191 Peachtree Tower (1991)	770	50
*No2 Opus Place, 98 14th St. NE (2021)	730	53
Westin Peachtree Plaza, 210 Peachtree St. NW[2]		
(1976)	723	73
Georgia Pacific Tower, 133 Peachtree St. NE (1981) . .	697	51
Promenade II (incl. spire), 1230 Peachtree St. NE		
(1989)	691	40
AT&T Bldg., 675 W. Peachtree St. (1980)	677	47
Sovereign, 3344 Peachtree (2008)	665	48
1180 Peachtree (2006)	657	41
GLG Grand/Four Seasons Hotel, 75 14th St. NE		
(1992)	609	53
The Mansion on Peachtree, 3376 Peachtree Rd. NE		
(2008)	580	42
Atlantic, 270 17th St. NW (2009)	577	46
State of Georgia Bldg., 2 Peachtree St. NW[3] (1967)	556	44
Marriott Marquis, 265 Peachtree Center Ave NE		
(1985)	554	52
(1) 902 ft incl. antenna. (2) 883 ft incl. antenna. (3) 599 ft incl. antenna.		
Austin, TX		
*6 X Guadalupe, 400 W. 6th St. (2022)	847	66
The Independent, 301 West Ave. (2019)	694	58
Austonian, 200 Congress Ave. (2010)	683	56
Fairmont Austin (incl. spire), 101 Red River St.		
(2018)	591	36
*601 West 2nd Street (2022)	589	35
360 Condominiums (incl. spire), 360 Nueces St.		
(2008)	581	45
*Indeed Tower, 200 W. 6th St. (2021)	542	36
Baltimore, MD		
Transamerica Tower, 100 Light St. (1973)	529	40
Boston, MA		
200 Clarendon (1976)	790	62
Prudential Tower, 800 Boylston St.[1] (1964)	750	52
Four Seasons Hotel and Private Residences		
One Dalton Street (2019)	746	61
*115 Winthrop Square (2022)	691	48
Millennium Tower, 426 Washington St. (2016)	681	54
*South Station Tower (2024)	678	51
Federal Reserve Bldg., 600 Atlantic Ave. (1978)	604	32
BNY Mellon Center at One Boston Place,		
201 Washington St. (1970)	602	41
One International Place, 100 Oliver St. (1987)	600	46
100 Federal St. (1971)	591	37
One Financial Center, 10 Dewey Square (1984)	590	46
111 Huntington Ave. (2002)	564	36
Two International Place (1993)	538	35
One Post Office Square (1981)	525	40
(1) 920 ft incl. antenna.		
Burnaby, BC, Canada		
Solo District-Altus (2017)	616	49
Brentwood One (2019)	611	53
Brentwood Two (2019)	611	53
*Brentwood Three (2020)	597	55
*Highline, 6511 Sussex Ave. (2023)	581	53
*6000 McKay (2021)	564	52
4670 Assembly Way (2018)	535	48
Calgary, AB, Canada		
Brookfield Place Tower One, 225 6th Ave. (2017)	810	56
The Bow, 510 Centre St. (2012)	779	57
Telus Sky (2019)	729	59
Petro Canada Centre West Tower,		
150 6th Ave. SW (1984)	705	53
Eighth Avenue Place East Tower,		
8th Ave. & 5th St. SW (2011)	696	49
Bankers Hall East Tower, 855 2nd St. SW (1989)	645	50
Bankers Hall West Tower, 888 3rd St. SW (2000)	645	50
Calgary Tower, 101 9th Ave. SW (1967)	626	NA
Centennial Place 1 (incl. spire), 520 3rd Ave. SW		
(2010)	599	40
TransCanada Tower, 450 1st St. SW (2001)	581	38
Canterra Tower, 400 3rd Ave. SW (1988)	580	46
Eighth Avenue Place West Tower,		
8th Ave. & 5th St. SW (2014)	580	40
Jamieson Place (incl. spires), 302 4th Ave. SW (2009)	568	38

Building/structure	Ht. (ft)	Stories
First Canadian Centre, 350 7th Ave. SW (1982)	547	41
Western Canadian Place-N. Tower,		
707 6th St. SW (1983)	538	41
Canada Trust, Calgary Eatons Centre,		
421 7th Ave. SW (1991)	530	40
Charlotte, NC		
Bank of America Corporate Center, 100 N. Tryon St.		
(1992)	871	60
Duke Energy Center, 534 S. Tryon St. (2010)	786	48
Hearst Tower, 214 N. Tryon St. (2002)	659	47
Bank of America Tower, 620 Tryon St. (2019)	632	33
*Charlotte Metro, S. Tryon St. (2022)	629	40
One Wells Fargo Center, 301 S. College St. (1988) . .	588	42
The Vue, 400 W. 5th St. (2010)	574	50
Chicago, IL		
Willis (fmr. Sears) Tower, 233 S. Wacker Dr.[1] (1974)	1,451	108
Trump International Hotel & Tower (incl. spire),		
401 N. Wabash Ave. (2009)	1,389	98
*Vista Tower, 381 E. Wacker Dr. (2021)	1,191	101
Aon Center, 200 E. Randolph St. (1973)	1,136	83
875 N. Michigan Ave. (fmr. John Hancock Ctr.)[2] (1969)	1,128	100
Franklin Center-North Tower (incl. spires),		
227 W. Monroe St. (1989)	1,007	60
Two Prudential Plaza (incl. spire), 180 N. Stetson		
Ave. (1990)	978	64
*One Chicago Square East Tower, 733 N. Dearborn		
St. (2022)	969	76
311 S. Wacker Drive (1990)	961	65
NEMA Chicago, 1200 S. Indiana Ave. (2019)	896	81
900 N. Michigan Ave. (1989)	871	66
Chase Tower, 21 S. Clark St. (1969)	868	61
Aqua at Lakeshore East, 225 N. Columbus Dr. (2009)	859	86
Water Tower Place, 845 N. Michigan Ave. (1976)	859	74
Park Tower, 800 N. Michigan Ave. (2000)	844	68
One Bennett Park, 451 E. Grand Ave. (2018)	837	67
*Salesforce Tower, 333 Wolf Point Plaza (2023)	835	60
*1000M, 1000 South Michigan Ave. (2022)	832	74
The Legacy at Millennium Park, 21-39 S. Wabash		
(2010)	818	73
110 N. Wacker Dr. (2020)	817	56
300 N. La Salle (2009)	785	60
3 First National Plaza, 70 W. Madison St. (1981)	767	57
Grant Thornton Tower, 161 N. Clark St. (1992)	756	50
Blue Cross Headquarters, 300 E. Randolph St. (2010)	744	54
River Point, 444 W. Lake St. (2017)	732	52
Olympia Centre, 737 N. Michigan Ave. (1986)	731	63
*BMO Tower, 310 S. Canal St. (2022)	727	50
One Museum Park, 1215 S. Prairie Ave. (2009)	726	62
150 North Riverside (2017)	725	53
AMA Plaza, 330 N. Wabash Ave. (1973)	695	52
Waldorf Astoria Chicago, 940 N. Rush St. (2009)	686	60
111 S. Wacker Dr. (2005)	681	51
181 W. Madison St. (1990)	680	50
71 S. Wacker (2005)	679	48
One Magnificent Mile, 980 N. Michigan Ave. (1983) . .	673	57
340 on the Park, 340 E. Randolph St. (2007)	672	64
Wolf Point East Tower, 350 N. Orleans St. (2020)	668	60
United Bldg., 77 W. Wacker Dr. (1992)	668	49
UBS Tower, 1 N. Wacker Dr. (2001)	652	50
Daley Center, 55 W. Washington St. (1965)	648	31
55 E. Erie St. (2004)	647	56
Lake Point Tower, 505 N. Lake Shore Dr. (1968)	645	70
River East Center , 350 E. Illinois St. (2001)	644	58
Grand Plaza I (incl. spire), 540 N. State St. (2003) . . .	641	57
155 N. Wacker Dr. (2009)	638	45
Leo Burnett Bldg., 35 W. Wacker Dr. (1989)	635	46
The Heritage at Millennium Park, 125 N. Wabash		
Ave. (2005)	631	57
NBC Tower (incl. spire), 455 N. Cityfront Plaza Dr.		
(1989)	627	37
353 N. Clark (2009)	623	44
Essex on the Park, 812 S. Michigan Ave. (2019)	620	57
OneEleven, 111 West Wacker (2014)	616	58
Millennium Centre , 33 W. Ontario St. (2003)	610	58
Board of Trade (incl. statue), 141 W. Jackson Blvd.		
(1930)	609	44
Chicago Place, 700 N. Michigan Ave. (1991)	608	49
CNA Plaza, 325 S. Wabash St. (1972)	601	44
One Prudential Plaza, 130 E. Randolph St. (1955)[3] . .	601	41
500 W. Monroe St. (1992)	600	45
One Madison Plaza, 200 W. Madison St. (1982)	599	44
The Grant, 201 E. Roosevelt Rd. (2010)	595	54
1000 Lake Shore Plaza (1964)	590	55

Building/structure	Ht. (ft)	Stories
The Clare at Water Tower, 55 East Pearson St. (2008)	589	52
Marina City I, 300 N. State St. (1964)	588	61
Marina City II, 301 N. Dearborn St. (1964)	588	61
Accenture Tower, 500 W. Madison St. (1987)	588	42
Optima Signature, 220 E. Illinois St. (2017)	587	57
The Park Monroe, 65 E. Monroe St. (1972)	583	49
Crain Communications Bldg., 150 N. Michigan Ave. (1983)	582	41
North Pier Apts., 474 N. Lake Shore Dr. (1990)	581	61
Citadel Center, 131 S. Dearborn St. (2003)	580	39
The Fordham, 25 E. Superior St. (2003)	574	52
*One Chicago Square West Tower, 733 N. Dearborn St. (2022)	574	49
190 S. LaSalle St. (1987)	573	40
One S. Dearborn (2005)	571	39
Onterie Center, 446 E. Ontario St. (1986)	570	58
Loews Chicago Hotel, 455 North Park Dr. (2015)	569	52
Chicago Temple, 77 W. Washington St. (1924)	568	23
Palmolive Bldg. (incl. beacon), 919 N. Michigan Ave. (1929)	565	37
Kluczynski Federal Bldg., 230 S. Dearborn St. (1974)	562	42
Huron Plaza Apts., 30 E. Huron St. (1983)	560	56
Boeing International Headquarters, 100 N. Riverside Plaza (1990)	560	36
*Cirrus, 211 N. Harbor Dr. (2021)	559	47
The Parkshore, 195 N. Harbor Dr. (1991)	556	56
North Harbor Tower, 175 N. Harbor Dr. (1988)	556	55
Civic Opera Bldg., 20 N. Wacker Dr. (1929)	555	45
Streeter Place, 351 E. Ohio St. (2009)	554	55
Harbor Point, 155 N. Harbor Dr. (1975)	554	54
Newberry Plaza, 1000 N. State St. (1974)	553	53
Michigan Plaza South, 205 N. Michigan Ave. (1985)	553	46
30 N. LaSalle St. (1975)	553	44
Pittsfield Bldg., 55 E. Washington St. (1927)	551	38
One S. Wacker Dr. (1982)	550	40
Park Millennium, 222 N. Columbus Dr. (2002)	544	57
AMLI River North, 401 N. Clark St. (2013)	543	49
Franklin Center-South Tower, 125 S. Franklin St. (1992)	538	35
The Pinnacle, 21 E. Huron St. (2004)	535	48
LaSalle National Bank, 135 S. LaSalle St. (1934)	535	45
Park Place Tower, 655 W. Irving Park Rd. (1971)	531	56
One N. LaSalle St. (1930)	530	48
The Elysees, 111 E. Chestnut St. (1973)	529	56
465 North Park Drive (2018)	525	48

(1) 1,729 ft incl. antenna. (2) 1,499 incl. ft antenna. (3) 912 ft incl. antenna.

Cleveland, OH

Building/structure	Ht. (ft)	Stories
Key Tower (incl. spire), 127 Public Sq. (1991)	947	57
Terminal Tower, 50 Public Sq. (1928)[1]	708	52
200 Public Sq. (1985)	658	46
Tower at Erieview, 1301 E. 9th St. (1964)	529	40

(1) 771 ft incl. flagpole.

Columbus, OH

Building/structure	Ht. (ft)	Stories
James A. Rhodes State Office Tower, 30 E. Broad St. (1973)	624	41
Leveque-Lincoln Tower, 50 W. Broad St. (1927)	555	47
William Green Building, 30 W. Spring St. (1990)	530	33

Dallas, TX

Building/structure	Ht. (ft)	Stories
Bank of America Plaza, 901 Main St. (1985)	921	72
Renaissance Tower (incl. spire), 1201 Elm St. (1974)	886	56
Comerica Bank Tower, 1717 Main St. (1987)	787	60
JP Morgan Chase Tower, 2200 Ross Ave. (1987)	738	55
Fountain Place, 1445 Ross Ave. (1986)	720	58
Trammel Crow Center, 2001 Ross Ave. (1984)	686	50
1700 Pacific Ave. (1983)	655	50
Thanksgiving Tower, 1600 Pacific Ave. (1982)	645	50
Energy Plaza, 1601 Bryan St. (1983)	629	49
The Drever, 1401 Elm St. (1965)	628	52
Gables Republic Tower (incl. spire), 300 N. Ervay (1954)	602	36
Republic Center Tower II, 325 N. St. Paul (1964)	598	50
One AT&T Plaza, 208 S. Akard St. (1984)	580	37
Ross Tower, N. 500 Akard St. (1984)	579	45
AMLI Fountain Place, 1800 N. Field St. (2020)	562	46
Tower at Cityplace, 2711 N. Haskell Ave. (1989)	560	42
Museum Tower, 2112 Flora St. (2013)	560	42
Reunion Tower, 300 Reunion Blvd. (1976)	560	NA
Sheraton Dallas Hotel Center Tower, 400 Olive St. (1959)	550	42

Denver, CO

Building/structure	Ht. (ft)	Stories
Republic Plaza, 330 17th St. (1984)	714	56
1801 California Street (1982)	709	52
Wells Fargo Center, 1700 Lincoln Ave. (1983)	698	50
Four Seasons Hotel & Private Residences, 1111 14th St. (2010)	639	45
1144 Fifteenth (2018)	602	42
1999 Broadway (1985)	544	43

Detroit, MI

Building/structure	Ht. (ft)	Stories
Marriott Hotel, Renaissance Center I[1] (1977)	727	70
*Hudsons Tower, 1246 Woodward Ave. (2023)	680	49
One Detroit Center, 500 Woodward Ave. (1991)	619	43
Penobscot Bldg., 633 Griswold Ave.[2] (1928)	565	47

(1) 755 ft incl. antenna. (2) 665 ft incl. antenna.

Fort Worth, TX

Building/structure	Ht. (ft)	Stories
Burnett Plaza, 801 Cherry St. (1983)	567	40
D.R. Horton Tower, 301 Commerce St. (1984)	547	38

Hartford, CT

Building/structure	Ht. (ft)	Stories
City Place I, 185 Asylum St. (1980)	535	38
Travelers Tower, 26 Grove St. (1919)	527	24

Houston, TX

Building/structure	Ht. (ft)	Stories
600 Travis St. (1982)	1,002	75
Wells Fargo Plaza, 1000 Louisiana St. (1983)	992	71
Williams Tower, 2800 Post Oak Blvd. (1982)	901	64
Bank of America Center, 700 Louisiana St. (1983)	780	56
Texaco Heritage Plaza, 1111 Bagby St. (1987)	762	53
Enterprise Plaza, 1100 Louisiana St.[1] (1980)	756	55
609 Main at Texas (2017)	755	48
Centerpoint Energy Plaza, 1111 Louisiana St. (1996)	741	53
*Texas Tower, 801 Texas Ave. (2021)	735	47
1600 Smith St. (1984)	732	55
Fulbright Tower, 1301 McKinney St. (1982)	725	52
One Shell Plaza, 900 Louisiana St.[2] (1970)	714	50
1400 Smith St. (1983)	691	50
3 Allen Center, 333 Clay St. (1980)	685	50
LyondellBassell Tower, 1221 McKinney St. (1978)	678	47
First City Tower, 1001 Fannin St. (1984)	662	47
BG Group Place, 811 Main St. (2011)	632	46
San Felipe Plaza, 5847 San Felipe Blvd. (1984)	625	45
ExxonMobil Bldg., 800 Bell Ave. (1962)	606	44
1500 Louisiana St. (2002)	600	40
America General Center, 2929 Allen Parkway (1983)	590	42
Two Houston Center, 909 Fannin St. (1974)	579	40
San Jacinto Monument, La Porte (1939)	570	NA
Marathon Oil Tower, 5555 San Felipe Blvd. (1983)	562	41
1415 Louisiana (1983)	550	44
KBR Tower, 601 Jefferson St. (1973)	550	40
Memorial Hermann Tower, 929 Gessner Rd. (incl. spires) (2009)	542	35
2929 Weslayan (2015)	533	40
Bank of America Tower, 800 Capitol St. (2019)	532	35

(1) 782 ft incl. antenna. (2) 999 ft incl. antenna.

Indianapolis, IN

Building/structure	Ht. (ft)	Stories
Salesforce Tower, 111 Monument Circle[1] (1990)	701	49
One America Tower, 200 N. Illinois St. (1982)	533	38

(1) 811 ft incl. antenna.

Jersey City, NJ

Building/structure	Ht. (ft)	Stories
99 Hudson St. (2020)	889	76
30 Hudson St. (2004)	781	42
*J1, 601 Pavonia Ave. (2024)	759	72
URL Harborside Tower 1 (2016)	700	70
*The Charlotte, 25 Columbus Dr. (2022)	626	57
J3, 615 Pavonia Ave. (2016)	574	53
101 Hudson St. (1992)	548	42
Trump Plaza I, 88 Morgan St. (2008)	532	55
Newport Tower, 525 Washington Blvd. (1990)	531	37
70 Columbus (2015)	529	50
90 Columbus (2018)	529	50

Las Vegas, NV

Building/structure	Ht. (ft)	Stories
Stratosphere Tower, 2000 Las Vegas Blvd. S. (1996)	1,149	NA
*The Drew Las Vegas, 2755 Las Vegas Blvd. S. (2022)	735	63
*Resorts World Las Vegas Tower I (2021)	674	57
The Palazzo, 3339 Las Vegas Blvd. S. (2007)	642	53
Encore at Wynn Las Vegas, 3145 Las Vegas Blvd. S. (2008)	631	52
Trump International Hotel and Tower 1, 3128 Las Vegas Blvd. S. (2008)	622	64
Wynn Las Vegas, 3145 Las Vegas Blvd. S. (2005)	613	45
Cosmopolitan Casino Spa Tower, Las Vegas Blvd. and Harmon Ave. (2010)	603	52
Cosmopolitan Beach Resort Tower, Las Vegas Blvd. and Harmon Ave. (2010)	603	50
Aria Resort & Casino (2009)	600	60
Planet Hollywood Towers, 3667 Las Vegas Blvd. S. (2009)	597	50
VDARA, 2551 W. Harmon Ave. (2009)	556	55
Eiffel Tower, Paris Hotel and Casino, 3645 Las Vegas Blvd. S. (1998)	540	NA
Mandarin Oriental Hotel Las Vegas, 3750 Las Vegas Blvd. S. (2009)	539	47
New York, New York Hotel & Casino, 3790 Las Vegas Blvd. S. (1997)	529	48

Los Angeles, CA

Building/structure	Ht. (ft)	Stories
Wilshire Grand Center (2017)	1,100	62
US Bank Tower, 633 W. 5th St. (1990)	1,018	72
Aon Center, 707 Wilshire Blvd. (1974)	858	62
Two California Plaza, 350 S. Grand Ave. (1992)	750	52

Building/structure	Ht. (ft)	Stories
Gas Company Tower, 555 W. 5th St. (1991)	749	52
Wells Fargo Tower, 333 S. Grand Ave. (1983)	740	54
Bank of America Plaza, 333 South Hope St. (1975)	735	55
777 Tower, 777 S. Figueroa St. (1991)	725	53
Figueroa at Wilshire, 601 S. Figueroa St. (1989)	717	52
Paul Hastings Tower, 515 S. Flower St. (1971)	699	52
City National Tower, 555 S. Flower St. (1971)	699	52
*960 W. 7th St. (2022)	695	64
*Oceanwide Plaza Tower I (2020)	677	53
Ritz Carlton/Marriott Marquis Los Angeles, 900 W. Olympic Blvd. (2010)	667	54
Thea at Metropolis Tower D (2019)	647	56
FourFortyFour South Flower (1982)	625	48
611 Place, 611 W. 6th St. (1969)	620	42
KPMG Tower, 355 S. Grand Ave. (1984)	606	45
One California Plaza, 300 S. Grand Ave. (1985)	578	42
Century Plaza Tower 1, 2029 Century Park East (1973)	571	44
Century Plaza Tower 2, 2049 Century Park East (1973)	571	44
825 S. Hill (2019)	563	53
*Century Plaza N. Tower, 2025 Ave. of the Stars (2021)	537	46
*Century Plaza S. Tower, 2025 Ave. of the Stars (2021)	537	46
Ernst & Young, LLP Plaza, 725 S. Figueroa St. (1986)	534	41
AIG-SunAmerica Center, 1999 Ave. of the Stars (1989)	533	39

Mexico City, Mexico

Building/structure	Ht. (ft)	Stories
*Torre Mitikah Residencial, Rio Churubusco 601 (2021)	876	62
Torre Reforma, Paseo de la Reforma 483 (2016)	807	57
Chapultepec Uno, Reforma 509 (2019)	789	59
Torre BBVA Bancomer, Paseo de la Reforma 506 (2015)	771	50
Torre Mayor, Paseo de la Reforma 505 (2003)	738	55
Torre Ejecutiva Pemex, Marina Nacional 329 Col. Huasteca (1984)	693	51
*Downtown & Be Grand Reforma, La Fragura 7 (2022)	653	50
*The University Tower, Paseo de la Reforma 150 (2022)	645	57
Torre Paradox, Av. Santa Fe 562 (2018)	644	60
Altus, Paseo de los Laureles 416 (1999)	640	44
Torre Reforma Latino, Paseo de la Reforma 296 (2016)	607	46
*Iqono Interlomas Torre 2, Circuito Empresarial 83, Huixquilucan (2022)	604	48
Torre Cuarzo, Paseo de la Reforma 26 (2017)	591	40
*Iqono Interlomas Torre 1, Circuito Empresarial 83, Huixquilucan (NA)	599	47
Miyana Torre Chapulin, Av. Ejecito Nacional (2020)	577	48
Torre M, Rio Churubusco 601 (2019)	577	35
Peninsula Santa Fe T 300, Santa Fe 528 (2019)	571	53
Sofitel Hotel Mexico City, Paseo de la Reforma 297 (2019)	561	41
World Trade Center, Montecito 38 Col. Napoles (1972)	565	50
Siroco Elite Residences, Av. Santa Fe 482 (2015)	561	43
Torre Latino Americana, Eje Central Lazaro Cardenas 2[1] (1956)	545	44
Peninsula Tower, Av. Santa Fe 1240 (2014)	539	50
Torre Punta Reforma, Paseo de la Reforma 180 (2015)	537	37
Arcos Torre I, Paseo de los Tamarindos 400 (1997)	529	35
Arcos Torre II West, Paeo de los Tamarindos 400 (2008)	529	35
Arcos Torre II East, Paeo de los Tamarindos 400 (2008)	529	35
(1) 595 ft incl. antenna		

Miami, FL

Building/structure	Ht. (ft)	Stories
Panorama Tower, 1101 Brickell Ave. (2018)	828	81
*Aston Martin Residences, 300 Biscayne Blvd. Way (2022)	817	66
Four Seasons Hotel & Tower, 1441 Brickell Ave (2003)	789	64
Wachovia Financial Center, 200 S. Biscayne Blvd. (1983)	764	55
Brickell Flatiron, 1001 S. Miami Ave. (2019)	736	64
*888 Brickell Plaza, 830 SE 1st Ave. (2022)	732	52
Paramount Miami Worldcenter, 129 NE 8th St. (2019)	706	57
Marquis, 1100 Biscayne Blvd. (2009)	702	63
One Thousand Museum, 1000 Biscayne Blvd. (2019)	699	60
Met 2 Office Tower, 200 SE 3rd St. (2010)	655	47
900 Biscayne Bay, 900 Biscayne Blvd. (2008)	650	63
*Missoni Baia, 700 NE 26th Terrace (2021)	646	57
*Elysee, 700 NE 23rd St. (2020)	644	57
Echo Brickell, 1451 Brickell Ave. (2017)	637	57
Mint at Riverfront, 90 SW 3rd St. (2009)	631	55
Infinity at Brickell, 60 W. 13th St. (2008)	630	52
Miami Tower, 100 S.E. Second St. (1987)	625	47
Marinablue, 888 Biscayne Blvd. (2007)	615	57
Plaza on Brickell Tower I, 901 Brickell Ave. (2007)	610	56
Epic Residences & Hotel, 300 Biscayne Blvd. Way (2009)	601	54
One Paraiso, 620 NE 31st St. (2018)	601	53
SLS Brickell, 1300 S. Miami Ave. (2016)	599	52
SLS Lux Brickell, 801 S. Miami Ave. (2018)	595	57
Icon Brickell North Tower, 495 Brickell Ave. (2008)	586	58
Icon Brickell South Tower, 495 Brickell Ave. (2008)	586	58
*400 Biscayne (2021)	573	49
Paramount at Edgewater Square, 2066 N. Bayshore Dr. (2009)	555	47
50 Biscayne Blvd. (2007)	554	55
Quantum on the Bay South Tower, 1900 N. Bayshore Dr. (2008)	554	51
Biscayne Beach, 701 NE 29th St. (2017)	550	51
Solitair Brickell, 80 SW 8th St. (2018)	550	49
Brickell Heights North Tower, 850 S. Miami Ave. (2017)	549	52
GranParaiso, 600 NE 31st St. (2018)	548	55
ParaisoBay, 600 NE 31st St. (2017)	548	55
1010 Brickell (2017)	548	50
Opera Tower, 1750 N. Bayshore Dr. (2007)	543	56
Viceroy, 495 Brickell Ave. (2009)	542	50
Vizcayne North Tower, 244 Biscayne Blvd. (2008)	538	49
Vizcayne South Tower, 244 Biscayne Blvd. (2008)	538	49
Avant at Met Square, 340 SE 3rd St. (2018)	538	46
Quantum on the Bay North Tower, 1900 N. Bayshore Dr. (2008)	536	44
Aria on the Bay, 1770 N. Bayshore Dr. (2018)	535	53
Ten Museum Park, 1040 Biscayne Blvd. (2007)	530	50
Brickell Heights South Tower, 850 S. Miami Ave. (2017)	529	52
Jade at Brickell Bay, 1331 Brickell Bay Dr. (2004)	528	49
Plaza on Brickell Tower II, 901 Brickell Ave. (2007)	525	48

Minneapolis, MN

Building/structure	Ht. (ft)	Stories
IDS Center, 80 8th St. South (1973)[1]	792	55
Capella Tower, 225 South Sixth (1992)	776	56
Wells Fargo Center, 90 7th St. South (1988)	775	56
33 South 6th St. (1983)	668	52
Campbell Mithun Tower, 222 9th St. South (1985)	582	42
US Bank Plaza I, 200 6th St. South (1981)	561	40
*Eleven, 1111 West River Parkway (2021)	547	44
RBC Plaza, 60 6th St. South (1992)	539	40
(1) 910 ft incl. antenna		

Monterrey, Mexico

Building/structure	Ht. (ft)	Stories
T.Op Torre 1 (2020)	1,000	61
Torre Koi, San Pedro Garza Garcia (2017)	916	65
*Sohl, Constitucion 999 (2023)	879	62
Hotel Safi Metropolitan, San Pedro Garza Garcia (2020)	764	56
Pabellon M (2015)	674	47
Santa Maria Business Campus Torre 6 (2020)	620	45
*Lola! (2021)	604	40
Metropolitan Center Torre II, San Pedro Garza Garcia (2017)	594	52
Centro de Gobierno Plaza Civica (2010)	591	36
LIU East, San Pedro Garza Garcia (2013)	564	39
Sofitel Hotel Mexico City, Paseo de la Reforma 297 (2019)	561	41
Torre Avalanz, San Pedro Garza Garcia (2000)	548	41

Montréal, QC, Canada

Building/structure	Ht. (ft)	Stories
1250 Boulevard Rene Levesque (incl. spire) (1992)	743	47
1000 Rue de la Gauchetiere (1992)	673	51
*Victoria Sur le Parc, 700 Rue Saint James (2023)	656	58
*National Bank Headquarters, 800 Rue Saint James (2022)	656	46
Maestra Tour B (2023)	651	58
Tour de la Bourse, 800 Place Victoria (1964)	624	47
1 Place Villa Marie (1962)	616	43
Maestra Tour A (2023)	606	55
L'Avenue, 1175 Avenue des Canadiens (2017)	605	51
La Tour CIBC, 1155 Rene Levesque Blvd.[1] (1962)	604	45
Montreal Tower (1987)	574	NA
Tour des Canadiens 2, 1150 Rue Saint-Antoine Ouest (2019)	551	53
*Tour des Canadiens 3, 1250 Rue Saint-Antoine Ouest (2021)	551	53
Tour des Canadiens, 1288 Avenue des Canadiens (2016)	548	50
(1) 740 ft incl. antenna		

New Orleans, LA

Building/structure	Ht. (ft)	Stories
Hancock Whitney Center, 701 Poydras St. (1972)	697	51
CapitalOne Center, 201 St. Charles Ave. (1985)	645	53
Plaza Tower, 1001 Howard Ave. (1968)	531	45
Energy Centre, 1100 Poydras St. (1984)	530	39

New York, NY

Building/structure	Ht. (ft)	Stories
One World Trade Center (incl. spire) (2014)	1,782	94
*Central Park Tower, 217 West 57th Street (2020)	1,550	98
*111 W. 57th St. (2020)	1,428	82
*One Vanderbilt Place, 51 E. 42nd St. (2021)	1,401	58
432 Park Avenue (2015)	1,397	85
30 Hudson Yards (2019)	1,268	73
Empire State Building, 350 5th Ave.[1] (1931)	1,250	102
Bank of America Tower (incl. spire), One Bryant Park (2009)	1,200	55

Building/structure	Ht. (ft)	Stories
*9 DeKalb (2022)	1,099	73
Three World Trade Center, 175 Greenwich St. (2018)	1,079	69
53 West 53rd (2019)	1,050	77
Chrysler Building. (incl. spire), 405 Lexington Ave. (1930)	1,046	77
New York Times Tower (incl. spire), 620 8th Ave. (2007)	1,046	52
*The Spiral, 435 10th Ave. (2021)	1,041	66
*50 Hudson Yards, 504 W. 34th St. (2022)	1,011	58
35 Hudson Yards (2019)	1,010	71
One57, 157 W. 57th St. (2014)	1,005	75
One Manhattan West, 401 9th Ave. (2019)	995	67
*3 Hudson Boulevard, 555 W. 34th St. (2023)	987	56
4 World Trade Center, 150 Greenwich St. (2014)	977	65
220 Central Park South (2019)	952	70
70 Pine (incl. spire) (1932)	952	67
*Two Manhattan West (2022)	935	58
The Trump Bldg., 40 Wall St. (1930)	927	71
30 Park Place, 99 Church St. (2016)	926	67
Citigroup Center, 153 E. 53rd St. (1977)	915	63
15 Hudson Yards (2019)	914	70
*125 Greenwich St. (2020)	912	72
10 Hudson Yards (2016)	878	50
New York by Gehry at Eight Spruce Street (2011)	870	76
Trump World Tower, 845 UN Plaza (2001)	861	72
*425 Park Avenue (2020)	860	44
Comcast Bldg., 30 Rockefeller Center (1933)	850	70
One Manhattan Square, 250 South St. (2019)	847	72
*Sutton 58, 428-432 East 58th St. (2021)	847	65
Cityspire Center, 150 W. 56th St. (1987)	814	75
28 Liberty (1961)	813	60
56 Leonard St. (2016)	813	57
4 Times Square[2] (1999)	809	48
MetLife Bldg., 200 Park Ave. (1963)	808	59
Bloomberg Tower, 731 Lexington Ave.[3] (2005)	806	54
*Madison House, 126 Madison Ave. (2021)	805	56
The Centrale, 138 E. 50th St. (2019)	803	64
Woolworth Building, 233 Broadway (1913)	792	58
111 Murray St. (2019)	788	60
520 Park Avenue (2018)	781	52
50 West, 50 West St. (2018)	779	64
*Skyline Tower, 23-15 44th Dr., Queens (2021)	778	67
Madison Square Park Tower, 41 East 22nd Street (2017)	778	61
55 Hudson Yards (2019)	778	51
1 Worldwide Plaza, 935 8th Ave. (1989)	778	47
*50 W. 66th St. (2022)	775	52
19 Dutch St. (2018)	758	63
Carnegie Hall Tower, 152 W. 57th St. (1991)	757	60
*Sven, 29-55 Northern Blvd., Queens (2021)	755	67
The Wall Street Tower, 130 William St. (2020)	755	61
383 Madison Ave. (2001)	755	47
1717 Broadway (2013)	753	67
AXA Center, 787 7th Ave. (1985)	752	51
One Penn Plaza, 250 W. 34th St. (1972)	750	57
1251 Ave. of Americas (1971)	750	54
Time Warner Center South Tower, 10 Columbus Circle (2004)	749	55
Time Warner Center North Tower, 10 Columbus Circle (2004)	749	55
Goldman Sachs HQ, 200 Murray St. (2010)	749	44
60 Wall Street (1989)	745	55
One Astor Plaza, 1515 Broadway (1972)	745	54
One Liberty Plaza, 165 Broadway (1972)	743	54
7 World Trade Center, 250 Greenwich St. (2006)	743	49
Twenty Exchange, 20 Exchange Place (1931)	741	57
Three World Financial Center, 200 Vesey St. (1986)	739	51
ARO, 242 W. 53rd St. (2018)	738	62
1540 Broadway (incl. spire) (1990)	732	42
Times Square Tower, 1459 Broadway (2004)	726	47
Metropolitan Tower, 142 W. 57th St. (1985)	716	68
252 E. 57th St. (2016)	715	59
100 East 53rd Street (2018)	711	61
General Motors Bldg., 767 5th Ave. (1968)	705	50
The Eugene, 401 W. 31st St. (2017)	702	64
25 Park Row (2020)	702	54
Metropolitan Life Tower, 1 Madison Ave. (1909)	700	50
500 5th Ave. (1931)	697	59
*Brooklyn Point, 138 Willoughby St., Brooklyn (2020)	696	57
*Block 675 Tower A, 601 W. 29th St. (2021)	695	62
Americas Tower, 1177 Ave. of the Americas (1992)	692	48
Solow Bldg. 9 W. 57th St. (1974)	689	49
Marine Midland Bldg., 140 Broadway (1967)	688	52
55 Water St. (1972)	687	53
277 Park Ave. (1963)	687	50
The Beekman Hotel & Residences, 5 Beekman St. (2017)	687	47
1585 Broadway (1989)	685	42
Random House/Park Imperial, 1739 Broadway (2003)	684	52
Four Seasons Hotel, 57 E. 57th St. (1993)	682	52
Sky, 605 W. 42nd St (2015)	676	61
McGraw-Hill Bldg., 1221 Ave. of the Americas (1972)	674	51
Barclay Tower, 10 Barclay St. (2007)	673	56
One Grand Central Place, 60 E. 42nd St. (1930)	673	53
277 5th Ave. (2019)	673	52
One Court Square, Queens (1990)	673	50
*One Seaport, 161 Maiden Lane (2021)	670	60
Paramount Plaza, 1633 Broadway (1970)	670	48
*200 Amsterdam Ave. (2020)	668	55
*45 Park Place (2020)	667	43
Trump Tower, 725 5th Ave. (1982)	664	58
Bank of New York Bldg., 1 Wall St. (1932)	654	50
Silver Towers East, 600 W. 42nd St. (2009)	653	58
Silver Towers West, 600 W. 42nd St. (2009)	653	58
599 Lexington Ave. (1986)	653	51
712 5th Ave. (1990)	650	53
Chanin Bldg., 122 E. 42nd St. (1929)	649	56
245 Park Avenue (1967)	648	47
550 Madison Ave. (1983)	647	37
Two World Financial Center, 225 Liberty St. (1986)	645	44
1095 Ave. of Americas (1974)	645	43
570 Lexington Ave. (1931)	642	50
1 New York Plaza, 1 Water St. (1969)	640	50
*Rose Hill, 30 E. 29th St. (2021)	639	45
1 MiMA Tower, 440 W. 42nd St. (2011)	638	63
Tower 28, 42-12 28th St., Queens (2017)	638	58
1 Dag Hammarskjold Plaza, 885 2nd Ave. (1972)	637	48
345 Park Ave. (1968)	634	44
Langham Place, 400 5th Ave. (2010)	632	58
Mercantile Bldg., 10 E. 40th St. (1929)	632	48
W New York Downtown Hotel & Residences, 123 Washington St. (2010)	631	57
Grace Plaza, 1114 Ave. of Amer. (1972)	630	50
Home Insurance Bldg., 59 Maiden Ln. (1966)	630	44
101 Park Ave. (1982)	629	49
Central Park Place, 301 W. 57th St. (1988)	628	56
888 7th Ave. (1971)	628	46
11 Hoyt St., Brooklyn (2020)	626	51
Burlington House, 1345 Ave. of Americas (1969)	625	50
Waldorf Astoria New York, 301 Park Ave. (1931)	625	47
Avalon Willoughby West, 100 Willoughby St., Brooklyn (2015)	624	57
Trump Palace, 200 E. 69th St. (1991)	623	54
One Madison Park, 20 E. 23rd St. (2010)	621	51
Olympic Tower, 645 5th Ave. (1976)	620	51
425 5th Ave. (2003)	618	55
The Epic, 125 W. 31st St. (2007)	615	61
919 3rd Ave. (1970)	615	47
Tower 49, 12 E. 49th St. (1985)	615	44
750 7th Ave. (incl. spire) (1989)	615	35
New York Life, 51 Madison Ave. (1928)	615	33
835 6th Ave. (2010)	614	53
551 10th Ave. (2016)	612	52
Baccarat Hotel & Residences, 20 West 53rd St. (2014)	610	46
Credit Lyonnais Bldg., 1301 Ave. of Amer. (1964)	609	46
The Orion, 350 W. 42nd St. (2006)	604	58
590 Madison Ave. (1983)	603	41
The Hub, 333 Schermerhorn St., Brooklyn (2017)	602	54
250 W. 55th St. (2013)	602	40
Eleven Times Square, 644 8th Ave. (2011)	601	40
1166 Avenue of the Americas (1974)	600	44
Eagle Lofts, 43-22 Queens St., Queens (2018)	598	55
Hawthorn Park, 160 W. 62nd St. (2014)	598	54
Hearst Magazine Tower, 959 8th Ave. (2006)	597	46
3 Lincoln Center, 160 W. 66th St. (1993)	595	60
Celanese Bldg., 1211 Ave. of Amer. (1973)	592	45
The London NYC, 151 W. 54th St. (1990)	590	54
388 Bridge St., Brooklyn (2014)	590	51
Thurgood Marshall U.S. Courthouse, 505 Pearl St. (1936)	590	37
Museum Tower Apts. 21 W. 53rd St. (1985)	589	52
The Millennium Hilton Hotel, 55 Church St. (1992)	588	58
Sky House, 11 E. 29th St. (2008)	588	55
*52-03 Center Blvd., Queens (2022)	587	56
Time-Life Bldg., 1271 Ave. of Amer. (1959)	587	48
Jacob K. Javits Federal Bldg., 26 Federal Plaza (1967)	587	41
W Times Square, 1567 Broadway (2000)	584	53
Trump International Hotel & Tower, 15 Columbus Circle (1970)	583	44
3 Jackson Park, 28-30 Jackson Ave., Queens (2018)	581	54
Stevens Tower, 1185 Ave. of Amer. (1971)	580	42
*1185 Broadway (2021)	580	40
Municipal Bldg., 1 Centre St. (1914)	580	34
520 Madison Ave. (1981)	577	43
One World Financial Center, 200 Liberty St. (1985)	577	37
Merchandise Mart, 41 Madison Ave. (1973)	576	42
Park Ave. Plaza, 55 E. 52nd St. (1981)	575	44
Lehman Bldg., 745 7th Ave. (2001)	575	38
300 Madison Ave. (2003)	575	38
32 Old Slip (1987)	575	37
Marriott Marquis Times Square, 1531 Broadway (1985)	574	50
299 Park Ave. (1967)	574	42
5 Times Square, 590 7th Ave. (2002)	574	40
Socony Mobil Bldg., 150 E. 42nd St. (1956)	572	42
1290 Ave. of the Americas (1963)	571	43

Building/structure	Ht. (ft)	Stories
780 3rd Ave. (1983)	570	49
600 3rd Ave. (1971)	570	42
The Ashland, 590 Fulton St., Brooklyn (2016)	568	51
450 Lexington Ave. (1991)	568	38
Paramount Tower, 240 E. 39th St. (1998)	567	51
230 Park Ave. (1928)	565	35
New York Palace Hotel, 455 Madison Ave. (1980)	563	51
Continental Bank Bldg., 30 Broad St. (1932)	562	48
Park Ave. Tower, 65 E. 55th St. (1986)	561	36
*Turkevi Center, 821 UN Plaza (2021)	561	36
Nelson Tower, 450 7th Ave. (1931)	560	46
Sherry-Netherland, 781 5th Ave. (1927)	560	40
623 5th Ave. (1990)	560	36
South Park Tower, 124 W. 60th St. (1986)	558	51
100 UN Plaza, 327 E. 48th St. (1986)	557	52
Continental Can, 633 3rd Ave. (1962)	557	39
3 Park Ave. (1975)	556	42
Summit New York, 222 E. 44th St. (2018)	556	42
Continental Center, 180 Maiden Lane (1983)	555	41
330 Madison Ave. (1964)	555	41
Equitable Bldg., 120 Broadway (1915)	555	38
Reuters Bldg., 3 Times Square[4] (2001)	555	30
Instrada Nomad, 10 E. 29th St. (1999)	554	48
Tower 111, 885 6th Ave. (2011)	554	48
Inmont Bldg., 1133 Ave. of Amer. (1970)	552	45
Downtown by Philippe Starck, 15 Broad St. (1927)	551	42
*Strata Tower, 8 W. 30th St. (2022)	551	34
Hyatt Times Square, 135 W. 45th St. (2013)	550	53
Biltmore Tower, 267 W. 47th St. (2003)	550	51
Unisys Bldg., 605 3rd Ave. (1963)	550	44
2 Grand Central Tower, 140 E. 45th St. (1982)	550	43
The Tower at 15 Central Park West (2008)	550	35
AT&T Long Lines Bldg., 33 Thomas St. (1974)	550	29
50 UN Plaza, 345 E. 46th St. (2015)	548	44
Bankers Trust, 33 E. 48th St. (1971)	547	41
The Corinthian, 330 E. 38th St. (1988)	546	55
Transportation Bldg., 225 Broadway (1928)	546	44
MillenniumTower, 101 W. 67th St. (1995)	545	54
The Galleria, 117 E. 57th St. (1975)	544	56
2 Gold St. (2005)	543	51
220 Riverside Blvd. at Trump Place (2003)	542	49
17 State St. (1988)	542	41
The Downtown Club, 19 West St. (1930)	542	39
Grand Central Plaza, 622 3rd Ave. (1973)	542	38
American Copper Buildings West Tower, 626 1st Ave. (2017)	540	47
New York Telephone, 375 Pearl St. (1976)	540	42
1285 Ave. of the Americas (1960)	540	42
Ritz Tower, 109 E. 57th St. (1925)	540	41
14 Wall (1912)	540	29
Tribeca Tower, 105 Duane St. (1990)	537	53
Lefcourt Colonial Bldg., 295 Madison Ave. (1929)	537	45
*540 Fulton St., Brooklyn (2020)	535	43
The Encore, 175 W. 60th St. (2016)	533	48
1700 Broadway (1969)	533	41
*18 Sixth Ave., Brooklyn (2023)	532	49
Westin Hotel New York, 43rd and 8th Ave. (2002)	532	45
515 Park Ave. (1999)	532	43
Du Mont Bldg., 515 Madison Ave. (1931)	532	42
The Brooklyner, 111 Lawrence St., Brooklyn (2010)	531	52
One East River Place, 525 E. 72nd St. (1989)	530	49
21 West End Ave. (2016)	529	45
The Metropolis, 150 E. 44th St. (2001)	528	53
William Beaver House, 15 William St. (2010)	528	47
North American Plywood, 800 3rd Ave. (1972)	526	41
City Point Tower II, 336 Flatbush Ext., Brooklyn (2016)	525	46
The Pierre, 2 E. 61st. St. (1930)	525	44
767 3rd Ave. (1980)	525	39

(1) 1,455 ft incl. antenna. (2) 1,118 ft incl. antenna. (3) 941 ft incl. antenna. (4) 659 ft incl. antenna.

Philadelphia, PA

Building/structure	Ht. (ft)	Stories
Comcast Technology Center, 1800 Arch St. (2018)	1,121	59
Comcast Center, 1701 JFK Blvd. (2008)	974	57
One Liberty Place (incl. spire), 1650 Market St. (1987)	945	61
Two Liberty Place (incl. spire), 1601 Chestnut St. (1989)	848	58
BNY Mellon Bank Center, 1735 Market St. (1990)	792	54
Three Logan, 1717 Arch St. (1991)	739	55
FMC Tower at Cira Centre South (2017)	730	49
G. Fred DiBona Jr. Bldg., 1901 Market St. (1990)	625	45
The W Philadelphia and Element, 1441 Chestnut St. (2019)	617	51
*The Laurel, 1911 Walnut St. (2021)	599	50
Commerce Square #1, 2005 Market St. (1990)	572	40
Commerce Square #2, 2001 Market St. (1992)	572	40
City Hall (incl. statue) (1901)	548	7
*Arthaus, 309 S. Broad St. (2021)	528	47

Pittsburgh, PA

Building/structure	Ht. (ft)	Stories
US Steel Tower, 600 Grant St. (1970)	841	64
BNY Mellon Center, 500 Grant St. (1983)	725	54
One PPG Place (1984)	635	40
Fifth Ave. Place, 120 5th Ave. (1987)	616	32
One Oxford Centre, 301 Grant St. (1982)	615	46
Gulf Tower, 707 Grant St. (1932)	582	44
The Tower at PNC Plaza (2015)	545	33
University of Pittsburgh Cathedral of Learning, 4200 5th Ave. (1936)	535	42

Portland, OR

Building/structure	Ht. (ft)	Stories
Wells Fargo Center, 1300 SW 5th Ave. (1973)	546	40
Park Avenue West, 728 SW 9th Ave. (incl. spire) (2016)	537	30
U.S. Bancorp Tower, 111 SW 5th Ave. (1983)	536	42

Puebla, Mexico

Building/structure	Ht. (ft)	Stories
*Oak 58 High Living (2022)	761	58
*Torre JV Angelopolis (2021)	722	46
*Torre NVBOLA (2020)	650	40

St. Louis, MO

Building/structure	Ht. (ft)	Stories
Gateway Arch, 11 N. 4th St. (1965)	630	NA
Metropolitan Square Tower, 211 N. Broadway (1988)	593	42
900 Pine St. (1986)	588	44
Thomas F. Eagleton Federal Courthouse, 111 S. 10th St. (2000)	557	29

San Francisco, CA

Building/structure	Ht. (ft)	Stories
Salesforce Tower, 415 Mission St. (2018)	1,070	61
Sutro Tower (1972)	977	NA
*Oceanwide Center Tower 1 (2021)	910	61
Transamerica Pyramid, 600 Montgomery St. (1972)	853	48
181 Fremont (2018)	810	56
555 California St. (1969)	779	52
345 California Center (1986)	695	48
Millennium Tower, 301 Mission St. (2009)	645	58
*Oceanwide Center Tower 2 (2021)	625	54
The Avery, 400 Folsom St. (2019)	618	56
One Rincon Hill South Tower, 425 First St. (2008)	605	54
Park Tower at Transbay (2018)	605	43
101 California St. (1982)	600	48
50 Fremont Center (1985)	600	43
575 Market St. (1975)	573	40
Four Embarcadero Center, 55 Clay St. (1984)	570	45
One Embarcadero Center, 355 Clay St. (1970)	569	45
44 Montgomery St. (1967)	565	43
Spear Tower, 1 Market St. (1976)	565	42
One Sansome Street (1984)	550	43
One Rincon Hill North Tower, 425 First St. (2014)	541	45
Shaklee Terrace Bldg., 444 Market St. (1982)	537	38
McKesson Plaza, 1 Post St. (1969)	529	38
First Market Tower, 525 Market St. (1972)	529	38

Seattle, WA

Building/structure	Ht. (ft)	Stories
Columbia Center, 701 5th Ave. (1985)	933	76
*Rainier Square Tower, 1301 5th Ave. (2020)	850	58
1201 Third Avenue Tower, 1201 3rd Ave. (1988)	772	55
Two Union Square, 601 Union St. (1989)	740	56
Seattle Municipal Tower, 700 5th Ave. (1990)	722	57
The Mark, 811 5th Ave. (2017)	660	44
Safeco Plaza, 1001 4th Ave. (1969)	630	50
City Centre, 1420 5th Ave. (1989)	606	44
Space Needle, 203 6th Ave. (1962)	605	NA
Russell Investments Center, 1301 2nd Ave. (2006)	598	42
Wells Fargo Center, 999 3rd Ave. (1983)	574	47
Madison Centre, 505 Madison St. (2017)	560	36
Bank of America Fifth Avenue Plaza, 800 Fifth Ave. (1981)	543	42
901 5th Ave. (1973)	536	41

Sunny Isles Beach, FL

Building/structure	Ht. (ft)	Stories
Armani Residences, 18975 Collins Ave. (2019)	649	60
*Turnberry Ocean Club, 18501 Collins Ave. (2020)	649	52
Muse, 17141 Collins Ave. (2018)	649	47
Porsche Design Tower, 18555 Collins Ave. (2016)	644	58
*Estates at Acqualina 1, 17901 Collins Ave (2020)	643	50
*Estates at Acqualina 2, 17901 Collins Ave (2021)	643	50
Mansions at Acqualina, 17749 Collins Ave. (2015)	643	46
The Ritz-Carlton Residences, 15701 Collins Ave. (2020)	642	52
Jade Signature, 16901 Collins Ave. (2017)	636	57
Jade on the Beach Condominiums, 17001 Collins Ave. (2008)	574	51
Trump Palace, 18101 Collins Ave. (2005)	551	43
Trump Royale, 18201 Collins Ave. (2008)	551	43
Acqualina Resort & Spa, 17875 Collins Ave. (2004)	550	51
Jade Ocean, 17121 Collins Ave. (2009)	543	51

Tampa, FL

Building/structure	Ht. (ft)	Stories
Regions Bldg, 100 N. Tampa St. (1992)	579	42
Bank of America Plaza, 101 E. Kennedy Blvd. (1986)	577	42
One Tampa City Center, 201 N. Franklin St. (1981)	537	39
Suntrust Financial Center, 401 E. Jackson St. (1992)	525	36

Building/structure	Ht. (ft)	Stories
Toronto, ON, Canada		
CN Tower, 310 Front St. West (1976)	1,815	NA
*The One, 1 Bloor St. West (2022)	1,005	83
First Canadian Place, 100 King St. West[1] (1975)	978	72
The St. Regis Toronto (incl. spire), 325 Bay St. (2012)	908	63
Scotia Tower, 40 King St. West (1989)	902	68
Aura at College Park, 388 Yonge St. (2014)	892	78
Brookfield Place (incl. spire), 161 Bay St. (1990)	856	53
Number One Bloor, 1 Bloor St. East (2017)	844	75
*CIBC Square I, 81 Bay St. (2020)	792	52
*160 Front (2022)	787	46
Commerce Court West, 199 Bay St.[2] (1973)	784	57
Ice Condos at York Centre 2, 16 York St. (2015)	768	67
Harbour Plaza Residences East, 90 Harbour St. (2017)	764	71
*Canada House 1, 23 Spadina Ave. (2022)	759	69
*Sugar Wharf Tower D, 95 Lakeshore East (2022)	755	70
Eau de Soleil Sky Tower, 2183 Lake Shore Blvd. West, Etobicoke (2019)	747	67
Ten York (2018)	735	65
Harbour Plaza Residences West, 90 Harbour St. (2017)	735	67
TD Centre - Toronto Dominion Bank Tower, 66 Wellington St. West (1967)	730	56
*Sugar Wharf Tower E, 95 Lakeshore East (2022)	717	65
*The Prestige at Pinnacle One Yonge (2022)	709	65
Bay-Adelaide Center West Tower, 335 Bay St. (2010)	704	52
Living Shangri-La Toronto, 180 University Ave. (2012)	702	65
Ritz-Carlton Hotel and Residences, 185 Wellington St. West (2011)	687	54
Massey Tower, 199 Yonge St. (2019)	683	60
The Residences of 488 University Avenue (2019)	679	55
BCE Place, Bay-Wellington Tower, 181 Bay St. (1991)	679	49
L Tower. 1 Front St. (2014)	673	59
88 Scott St. (2017)	669	58
Four Seasons Private Residences West, 48 Yorkville Ave. (2012)	669	55
YC Condos, 460 Yonge St. (2018)	664	60
*Canada House 2, 23 Spadina Ave. (2022)	663	59
Ice Condos at York Centre 1, 16 York St. (2014)	663	57
Bay-Adelaide Center East Tower, 40 Adelaide St. (2016)	643	44
E Condos South, 8 Eglinton Ave. (2019)	642	58
Wellesley on the Park, 11 Wellesley St. West (2020)	637	60
*22|21 Yonge, 2221 Yonge St. (2020)	632	58
EY Tower, 100 Adelaide St. West (2017)	617	40
*19 Duncan St. (2022)	612	58
RBC Centre, 155 Wellington St. West (2009)	607	42
CASA II, 42 Charles St. East (2020)	605	57
U Condominiums East Tower, 50 St. Joseph St. (2016)	604	55
*One Yorkville (2020)	601	58
TD North Tower, 77 King St. West (1969)	600	46
Maple Leaf Square North Tower, 65 Bremner Blvd. (2010)	595	54
Eau de Soleil Water Tower, 2183 Lake Shore Blvd. West, Etobicoke (2019)	593	49
CASA III, 50 Charles St. East (2018)	589	55
*Rosedale on Bloor, 403 Bloor St. East (2021)	587	52
INDX Condominiums, 70 Temperance St. (2016)	585	54
*Vita on the Lake, 2165 Lake Shore Blvd. West, Etobicoke (2021)	581	53
1 King West (2005)	578	51
*The Well Office Tower, 410 Front St. West (2020)	571	36
Success Tower 2, 33 Bay St. (2010)	567	41
Royal Bank Plaza - South Tower, 200 Bay St. (1976)	567	41
Maple Leaf Square South Tower, 55 Bremner Blvd. (2010)	562	50
The Selby Condominiums, 592 Shelbourne St. (2019)	560	51
*Teahouse Condominiums South, 501 Yonge St. (2020)	558	52
*Eight Cumberland, 826 Yonge St. (2021)	557	51
Hullmark Centre I, 4789 Yonge St. (2017)	557	45
Lago at the Waterfront, 2151 Lake Shore Blvd. West, Etobicoke (2016)	550	49
44 Charles St. West (1974)	545	51
Karma, 9 Grenville St. (2016)	544	50
*Social, 229 Church St. (2021)	541	52
Quantum 2, 2195 Yonge St. (2008)	541	51
Theatre Park, 224 King St. West (2015)	541	47
Residences @ College Park I, 763 Bay St. (2006)	535	51

Building/structure	Ht. (ft)	Stories
Burano, 832 Bay St. (2012)	535	50
Success Tower 1, 18 Harbour St. (2011)	531	52
*E2 at E Place, 41 Roehampton Ave. (2022)	531	48
*Pinnacle Etobicoke 2A (NA)	531	48
X2, 580 Jarvis St. (2015)	529	44
FIVE, 606 Yonge St. (2016)	528	48
(1) 1,116 ft incl. antenna. (2) 942 ft incl. antenna.		
Tulsa, OK		
BOK Tower 1, E. 2nd St. (1975)	667	52
Cityplex Central Tower, 2448 E 81st St. (1979)	648	60
Vancouver, BC, Canada		
Shangri-La Vancouver, 1120 W. Georgia St. (2009)	659	59
1153 W. Georgia (2016)	616	58
*The Butterfly, 969 Burrard St. (2023)	586	57
*One Burrard Place (2020)	551	54
Telus Garden Residential Tower, 777 Richards St. (2016)	550	53
*The Stack, 1133 Melville St. (2022)	533	38

Other Tall Buildings in North America

Building/structure	City	Ht. (ft)	Stories
Devon Energy Center (2012)	Oklahoma City, OK	844	52
Stantec Tower (2019)	Edmonton, Alberta	816	66
RSA Battle House Tower (incl. spire) (2007)	Mobile, AL	745	35
Hotel Riu Plaza Guadalajara (incl. spire) (2011)	Guadalajara, Mexico	669	42
Great American Tower at Queen City Square (2011)	Cincinnati, OH	665	40
*M City Tower 2 (2022)	Mississauga, ON, Can.	659	62
*M City Tower 1 (2022)	Mississauga, ON, Can.	650	61
The Tower at First National Center (2002)	Omaha, NE	634	45
*CG Tower (2023)	Vaughan, ON, Can.	634	60
801 Grand (1991)	Des Moines, IA	630	44
JW Marriott-Legends Private Residences (2019)	Edmonton, Alberta	627	56
One Kansas City Place (incl. spire) (1988)	Kansas City, MO	623	42
Tower of the Americas (1968)	San Antonio, TX	622	NA
Bank of America Tower (1990)	Jacksonville, FL	617	42
AT&T Building (1994)	Nashville TN	617	33
U.S. Bank Center (1973)	Milwaukee, WI	601	42
Town Pavilion (1986)	Kansas City, MO	591	38
Erastus Corning II Tower (1973)	Albany, NY	589	44
*Transit City Condos 3 (2022)	Vaughan, ON, Can.	587	55
*Pier West 1, 660 Quayside Dr. (2023)	New Westminster, BC, Can.	584	53
Niagara Falls Hilton (2009)	Niagara Falls, ON, Can.	581	58
Absolute World 56 (2012)	Mississauga, ON, Can.	576	56
*Transit City Condos 1 (2021)	Vaughan, ON, Can.	575	55
*Transit City Condos 2 (2021)	Vaughan, ON, Can.	575	55
Carew Tower[1] (1931)	Cincinnati, OH	574	49
*TC4 (2023)	Vaughan, ON, Can.	572	50
Concourse Corporate Center V (incl. spire) (1988)	Sandy Springs, GA	570	34
Hyatt Regency Andares (2017)	Zapopan, Mex.	568	41
Torre Aura Altitude (2008)	Zapopan, Mex.	563	44
Blue Diamond Tower (2000)	Miami Beach, FL	559	44
Green Diamond Tower (2000)	Miami Beach, FL	559	44
Washington Monument (1884)	Washington, DC	555	NA
Concourse Corporate Center VI (incl. spire) (1991)	Sandy Springs, GA	553	34
Northwestern Mutual Tower (2017)	Milwaukee, WI	550	33
400 West Market (1992)	Louisville, KY	549	35
Simmons Tower (1986)	Little Rock, AK	546	40
Marriott Rivercenter (incl. spire) (1988)	San Antonio, TX	546	38
PNC Plaza (incl. spire) (2008)	Raleigh, NC	538	32
Modis Tower (1975)	Jacksonville, FL	535	37
*567 Clarke + Como (2020)	Coquitlam, BC, Can.	532	49
Corporativo Bansi (2019)	Guadalajara, Mexico	532	32
*Torre 40 Residencial Gran Jardin (2020)	León, Mexico	531	44
Seneca One (1970)	Buffalo, NY	529	38
(1) 623 ft incl. antenna.			

Selected Bridge Styles

Bridges support weight through tension (pulling), compression (pushing), or a combination of both. **Suspension** and **cable-stayed** bridges are characterized by cables under tension. While the deck of a suspension bridge hangs from suspenders, that of a cable-stayed bridge ties directly to a bridge tower. The elements of a **truss** form triangles, which distribute the forces of tension and compression. Truss bridges can thus carry more weight than beam bridges. Steel plates can be welded or bolted together to make a **plate girder**, a kind of beam. A common form is the **box girder**.

A bridge can have a **simple** configuration, whereby its load is supported at both ends. If a bridge is **continuous**, its load extends across multiple supports. In a **cantilever** configuration, structural elements (e.g., trusses or girders) supported at one end project out, or cantilever, to carry a span.

Notable North American Bridges

Source: World Almanac research; Office of Bridge Technology, Federal Highway Administration, U.S. Dept. of Transportation
Asterisk (*) designates a bridge that carries railroads only. All other bridges carry roads or roads and rail unless otherwise noted.
Year is date of completion or projected completion. Span of bridge is the distance between its main supports. As of mid-2019.

Year Bridge	Location	Main span (ft)
Suspension		
1964 Verrazano-Narrows	New York, NY	4,260
1937 Golden Gate	San Francisco Bay, CA	4,200
1957 Mackinac	Straits of Mackinac, MI	3,800
1931 George Washington	New York, NY-Fort Lee, NJ	3,500
1950/		
2007 Tacoma Narrows (twin)	Tacoma, WA	2,800
2003 Al Zampa Mem. (New Carquinez) (westbound)	Carquinez Strait, CA	2,388
1936 San Francisco-Oakland Bay (West Span)[1]	San Francisco-Yerba Buena Isl., CA	2,310
1939 Bronx-Whitestone	East R., New York, NY	2,300
1970 Pierre Laporte	Quebec City, QC, Can.	2,190
1951/Delaware Mem. (twin) 68	Pennsville, NJ-New Castle, DE	2,150
1957 Walt Whitman	Philadelphia, PA-NJ	2,000
1929 Ambassador	Detroit, MI-Windsor, ON, Can.	1,850
1961 Throgs Neck	New York, NY	1,801
1926 Benjamin Franklin	Phila., PA-Camden, NJ	1,750
1924 Bear Mountain	Hudson R., Peekskill, NY	1,632
1969 Claiborne Pell/Newport	Narragansett Bay, RI	1,600
1952/William Preston Lane Jr. 73 Memorial (twin)	Sandy Point, MD	1,600
1903 Williamsburg	East R., New York, NY	1,600
1883 Brooklyn	East R., New York, NY	1,596
1938 Lions Gate	Vancouver, BC, Can.	1,549
1963 Vincent Thomas	L.A. Harbor, CA	1,500
1930 Mid-Hudson	Poughkeepsie, NY	1,495
1909 Manhattan	East R., New York, NY	1,470
1955 Angus L. Macdonald	Halifax, NS, Can.	1,447
1970 A. Murray MacKay	Halifax, NS, Can.	1,400
1936 Triborough (Harlem R. Lift/Bronx Crossing/ East R. Suspension)	East R., New York, NY	1,380
2013 San Francisco-Oakland Bay (SAS)[2]	San Francisco Bay, CA	1,263
Cantilever		
1917 Quebec	Quebec City, QC, Can.	1,800
1974 Commodore Barry	Chester, PA-Bridgeport, NJ	1,644
1958/Crescent City Connection 88 (twin)	Mississippi R., New Orleans, LA	1,575
1995 Veterans Memorial	Gramercy, LA	1,460
1968 Baton Rouge	Mississippi R., LA	1,235
1930 Lewis and Clark	Longview, WA-Rainier, OR	1,200
1909 Queensboro	East R., New York, NY	1,182
1958 Carquinez (eastbound)	San Francisco Bay, CA	1,100
1930 Jacques Cartier	Montreal, QC, Can.	1,097
1968 Isaiah D. Hart	Jacksonville, FL	1,088
1956 Richmond-San Rafael (twin)	San Francisco Bay, CA	1,070
1963/ 80 Newburgh-Beacon (twin)	Hudson R., NY	1,000
Truss		
1966 Astoria-Megler (U.S. 101)	Columbia R., OR-WA	1,232
1976 Francis Scott Key	Baltimore, MD	1,200
1981 Ravenswood	Ohio R., Ravenswood, WV	902
1995 Taylor-Southgate, Ohio R.	Cincinnati, OH-Newport, KY	850
1943 Julien Dubuque (U.S. 20)	Mississippi R., IA-IL	845
1966 Charles Braga	Fall River, MA	840
1956 Shawneetown (KY 56) (twin)	Ohio R., IL-KY	825
1953 John E. Mathews	Jacksonville, FL	810
1992 Cooper R.	Charleston, SC	800
1957 Kingston-Rhinecliff	Hudson R., NY	800
1950 Maurice J. Tobin	Boston, MA	800
1940 Gov. Nice Mem.	Newburg, MD-Dahlgren, VA	800
1986 Rochester-Monaca	Rochester-Monaca, PA	780
1973/Atchafalaya R. (U.S. 190) 88 (twin)	Krotz Springs, LA	780
1988 Phil G. McDonald (Glade Creek)	Beckley, WV	784
1917 *Sciotoville RR (twin)	Sciotoville, OH-KY	775
1981 Sewickley	Sewickley, PA	750
1977 Jennings Randolph	Chester, WV-E. Liverpool, OH	750
1974 Carroll C. Cropper (I-275)	Ohio R., IN-KY	750

Year Bridge	Location	Main span (ft)
1940 Glover Cary	Ohio R., Owensboro, KY-IN	750
1984 13th Street	Ohio R., Ashland, KY-OH	740
1959 Monaca-E. Rochester	Monaca-E. Rochester, PA	730
1976 Betsy Ross	Phila., PA-Pennsauken, NJ	729
2013 Milton-Madison (U.S. 421)	Ohio R., KY-IN	727
1967 Matthew E. Welsh	Ohio R., Mauckport, IN-KY	725
1994 Robert C. Byrd	Huntington, WV	720
1971 Atchafalaya R. (LA 1)	Simmesport, LA	720
1962 U.S. 41 Twin	Ohio R., Evansville, IN-Henderson, KY	720
1929 Irvin S. Cobb (U.S. 45)	Ohio R., Brookport, IL-Paducah, KY	716
1970 Vanport	Vanport, PA	715
1973 Girard Point	Philadelphia, PA	700
1963 John F. Kennedy (I-65)	Ohio R., Louisville, KY-Jeffersonville, IN	700
1923 *Mears Mem., Tanana R.	Nenana, AK	700
Plate and Box Girder		
1997 Confederation[3]	Prince Edward Isl.-NB, Can.	820
2010 Kanawha R. (I-64)	S. Charleston-Dunbar, WV	760
1982 Jesse H. Jones Memorial	Houston, TX	750
1977 LA 27, Intracoastal Canal	Gibbstown, LA	750
1976 LA 82, Intracoastal Canal	Forked Isl., LA	750
1967 San Mateo-Hayward	San Francisco Bay, CA	750
1992 Jamestown-Verrazano	Narragansett Bay, RI	674
2002 Vietnam Veterans Mem.	James R., Richmond, VA.	672
1986 Umatilla	Columbia R., OR-WA	660
1969 San Diego-Coronado (twin)	San Diego Bay, CA	660
2007 Benicia-Martinez (new)	Carquinez Strait, CA	659
Cable-Stayed		
2024 Gordie Howe Intl.	Detroit, MI-Windsor, ON, Can.	2,798
2012 Baluarte Bicentennial	Sinaloa-Durango, Mex.	1,706
2023 New Harbor Bridge (U.S. 181)	Corpus Christi Ship Channel, TX	1,661
2011 John James Audubon	St. Francisville, LA	1,583
2005 Arthur Ravenel Jr.	Charleston, SC.	1,546
2012 Port Mann	Vancouver, BC, Can.	1,542
1986 Alex Fraser	Vancouver, BC, Can.	1,526
2014 Stan Musial Veterans Memorial (I-70)	Miss. R., St. Louis, MO-IL	1,500
2010 U.S. 82, Mississippi R.	Greenville, MS-Lake Village, AR	1,378
1994 Clark	Alton, IL-MO	1,360
1989 Dames Point	Jacksonville, FL	1,300
2003 Sidney Lanier	Brunswick, GA	1,250
1995 Fred Hartman	Houston Ship Channel, Baytown, TX	1,250
2007 Veterans' Glass City Skyway	Maumee R., Toledo, OH	1,225
1983 Hale Boggs Memorial	Luling, LA	1,222
2017 Mario Cuomo (I-287) (twin)	Hudson R., Tarrytown-Nyack, NY	1,200
2002 William Natcher, Ohio R.	Owensboro, KY-IN	1,200
1987 Sunshine Skyway (I-275)	Tampa Bay, FL	1,200
2012 Margaret Hunt Hill	Trinity R., Dallas, TX	1,197
1988 Tampico	Panuco R., Mex.	1,181
2006 Penobscot Narrows	Bucksport, ME	1,161
2003 Bill Emerson Memorial	Cape Girardeau, MO-IL	1,150
1988 Skybridge[4]	Vancouver, BC, Can.	1,115
1991 Talmadge Memorial	Savannah, GA	1,100
2000 Maysville (Wm. H. Harsha)	Savannah, GA	1,050
Steel Arch		
1977 New River Gorge	Fayetteville, WV	1,700
1931 Bayonne (Kill Van Kull)	Bayonne, NJ-New York, NY	1,675
1973 Fremont	Portland, OR	1,255
1964 Port Mann	Vancouver, BC, Can.	1,200
1967 Laviolette	Trois-Rivières, QC, Can.	1,100
1990 Roosevelt Lake	Roosevelt Lake, AZ	1,080
1959 Glen Canyon	Page, AZ	1,028
1962 Lewiston-Queenston	NY-ON, Can.	1,001
1976 Perrine	Twin Falls, ID	993
1916 *Hell Gate	East R., New York, NY	978
1941 Rainbow	Niagara Falls, NY-ON, Can.	950
1997 Second Blue Water	Port Huron, MI-ON, Can.	922
1977 Moundsville	Ohio R., WV	912

Year Bridge	Location	Main span (ft)
1983/Jefferson Barracks (I-255)		
92 (twin)...............	Mississippi R., IL-MO.....	910
1973 Hernando DeSoto (I-40)		
(two spans)........	Mississippi R., AR-TN....	900
2008 Blennerhassett (U.S. 50)...	Parkersburg, WV-OH.....	878
1936 Henry Hudson.........	Harlem R., New York, NY	840
2021 Wellsburg, Ohio R.......	WV-Brilliant, OH......	830
1966 Bob Cummings Lincoln Trail	Ohio R., IN-KY..........	825
1978 I-57, Mississippi R........	Cairo, IL..........	821
1980 I-65, Mobile R.........	Mobile, AL.......	800
1961 Sherman Minton (I-64).....	IN-Louisville, KY.....	800
1978 I-470, Ohio R..........	Wheeling, WV......	780
1932 West End.........	Pittsburgh, PA......	780
1971 Piscataqua R.......	Portsmouth, NH-	
(I-95 High Level).......	Kittery, ME......	756
1959 Fort Pitt.........	Pittsburgh, PA......	750

Movable Bridges
Vertical Lift

Year Bridge	Location	Main span (ft)
1959 *Arthur Kill........	New York, NY-Elizabeth, NJ	558
1935 *Cape Cod Canal........	Buzzards Bay, MA......	544
1896 *Delair.........	Pennsauken, NJ-Phila., PA	542

Year Bridge	Location	Main span (ft)
1937 Marine Pkwy. Hodges Mem.	Jamaica Bay, New York, NY	540
1931 Burlington-Bristol........	Delaware R., NJ-PA......	540
1908 *Burlington Northern RR[5]...	Portland, OR......	516
1968 *Second Narrows Railway..	Vancouver, BC, Can.....	499
1911 *Armour-Swift-Burlington..	Missouri R., Kansas City, MO	428

Bascule

Year Bridge	Location	Main span (ft)
1940 Charles Berry Memorial...	Lorain, OH......	333
1917 Market St./Ch. John Ross..	Chattanooga, TN......	310
2003 SW 2nd Avenue.........	Miami, FL......	302

Swing

Year Bridge	Location	Main span (ft)
1927 Fort Madison (Santa Fe)...	Mississippi R., IA......	525
1952 George P. Coleman Mem...	Yorktown, VA......	500
1991 SW Spokane St..........	Seattle, WA......	480
1899 *Illinois Central RR.......	Chicago, IL......	479
1914 *Coos Bay RR.........	Coos Bay, OR......	458
1913 East Haddam (Rt. 82)....	Connecticut R., CT......	458

Floating Pontoon[6]

Year Bridge	Location	Main span (ft)
2016 New SR 520.........	Seattle, WA......	7,709
1993 Lacey V. Murrow (I-90)....	Seattle, WA......	6,620
1961 Hood Canal (SR 104).....	Kitsap-Jefferson Cos., WA	6,521
1989 Homer M. Hadley (I-90)....	Seattle, WA......	5,811

Other Notable North American Bridges

Year Bridge	Type	Location	Tot. length (ft)
1956/			
69 Lake Pontchartrain Causeway[7]	Twin concrete trestle	Metairie-Mandeville, LA	126,055
1979 Manchac Swamp	Twin concrete trestle	Manchac, LA	120,384
1973 Atchafalaya Basin (I-10)	Twin concrete trestle	Baton Rouge, LA	95,040
1982 Seven Mile (Overseas Hwy., U.S. 1)	Segmental concrete	Florida Keys	35,867
2009/			
11 I-10 Twin Spans	Twin concrete trestle	Slidell-New Orleans, LA	29,040
2002 Croatan Sound	Continuous post-tensioned girder	Manteo, NC	27,000
1993 Choctawhatchee Mid-Bay	Segmental concrete	Destin-Niceville, FL	19,265
1962 International	Arch truss	Sault Ste. Marie, MI-ON, Can	9,278
2009 Walkway Over the Hudson[8]	Pedestrian	Poughkeepsie-Highland, NY	6,768
1874 Eads, Mississippi R.[9]	Steel arch	St. Louis, MO-IL	6,442
2013 San Francisco-Oakland Bay (Skyway)	Segmental concrete box girder	San Francisco Bay, CA	6,336
1987 Powder Point	Tropical hardwood	Duxbury, MA	2,200
1969 Silver Memorial, Ohio R.[10]	Cantilever	Pt. Pleasant, WV-OH	1,964
2010 O'Callaghan-Tillman Mem. (U.S. 93)[11]	Concrete arch	Colorado R., AZ-NV	1,900
1994 Natchez Trace Parkway	Concrete arch	Franklin, TN	1,572
1901 Hartland[12]	Covered	St. John R., Hartland, NB, Can	1,282

(1) Two complete bridges each 2,310-ft long, which share an anchor point. (2) Self-Anchored Suspension Bridge. (3) World's longest bridge crossing ice-covered water, with total length of 8 mi. (4) World's longest cable-stayed bridge carrying mass transit only. (5) Vertical lift replaced swing span in 1989. (6) Length listed is of bridge's floating section. (7) World's longest continuous spans over water. (8) Originally opened in 1889 as a railroad bridge. (9) World's first major structure made of alloy steel. (10) Replaced Silver Bridge, the collapse of which in 1967 led to the creation of National Bridge Inspection Standards in the U.S. (11) Longest single-span concrete arch in Western Hemisphere. (12) World's longest covered bridge.

Oldest U.S. Bridges in Continuous Use

Built in 1697, the stone-arch Frankford Ave. Bridge (U.S. 13) crosses Pennypack Creek in Philadelphia, PA. It is 73-ft long and consists of three spans. The bridge was constructed as part of the King's Road, which connected Philadelphia to New York.

The oldest covered bridge, completed in 1829, is the double-span, 256-ft-long Bath-Haverhill Bridge, which spans the Ammonoosuc River between the towns of Bath and Haverhill, NH. The bridge was bypassed in 1999. It has since reopened to pedestrian traffic only.

Notable World Bridges

Source: World Almanac research

Year is date of completion or projected completion. Span of bridge is the distance between its main supports. As of mid-2020. NA = Not available.

Suspension

Year Bridge	Location	Main span (ft)
2022 Çanakkale 1915...............	Turkey.....	6,637
1998 Akashi Kaikyo...............	Japan.....	6,532
2009 Xihoumen.........	China.....	5,413
1998 Storebælt (Great Belt, East Bridge)	Denmark.....	5,328
2016 Osman Gazi (Izmit Bay)....	Turkey.....	5,085
2012 Yi Sun-sin (Gwangyang)	South Korea.....	5,069
2005 Runyang Yangtze R. (south)......	China.....	4,888
2012 Nanjing Fourth Yangtze R......	China.....	4,652
1981 Humber.........	England.....	4,625
2016 Yavuz Sultan Selim		
(Third Bosphorus)...........	Turkey.....	4,619
1999 Jiangyin Yangtze R........	China.....	4,544
1997 Tsing Ma.........	China.....	4,518
2013 Hardanger.........	Norway.....	4,298
2007 Yangluo Yangtze R........	China.....	4,199
1997 Höga Kusten.........	Sweden.....	3,970
2016 Longjian.........	China.....	3,924
2012 Aizhai.........	China.....	3,858
2015 Ulsan Grand.........	South Korea.....	3,773
2018 Halogaland.........	Norway.....	3,756
2008 Huangpu.........	China.....	3,635
1988 Minami Bisan-Seto........	Japan.....	3,609
1988 Fatih Sultan Mehmet (Bosphorus II)	Turkey.....	3,576
2009 Baling R.........	China.....	3,570
2012 Taizhou Yangtze R.[1].........	China.....	3,543

Year Bridge	Location	Main span (ft)
1973 Bosphorus.........	Turkey.....	3,524
1999 Kurushima III.........	Japan.....	3,379
1999 Kurushima II.........	Japan.....	3,346
1966 Ponte 25 de Abril, Tagus R....	Portugal.....	3,323
1964 Forth Road.........	Scotland.....	3,300

Note: Turkey's Çanakkale 1915 bridge across the Dardanelles Strait will have world's longest suspension span (6,637 ft) upon expected completion in 2023. (1) Two consecutive spans of equal length.

Steel Arch

Year Bridge	Location	Main span (ft)
2009 Chaotianmen Yangtze R........	China.....	1,811
2003 Lupu.........	China.....	1,804
2012 Bosideng.........	China.....	1,739
1932 Sydney Harbour.........	Australia.....	1,650
2005 Wushan Yangtze R........	China.....	1,614
2021 Chenab (rail)[1].........	India.....	1,532
2013 Xijiang (rail).........	China.....	1,476
2007 Xinguang.........	China.....	1,404
2007 Caiyuanba.........	China.....	1,378
2010 Daning R.........	China.....	1,312
2007 Lianxiang.........	China.....	1,312
2010 Hiroshima Airport........	Japan.....	1,247
1959 Sloboda.........	Croatia.....	1,224
2007 Maocao Street.........	China.....	1,207
2005 Wanzhou Yangtze R. Railway....	China.....	1,181

Year	Bridge	Location	Main span (ft)
2000	Yajisha	China	1,181
1962	Bridge of the Americas	Panama	1,128

(1) Will be world's highest rail bridge (1,178 ft) upon completion.

Concrete Arch

Year	Bridge	Location	Main span (ft)
2016	Beipanjiang	China	2,362
1997	Wanxian Yangtze R.	China	1,378
2015	Nanpanjiang (rail)	China	1,365
1980	Krk I	Croatia	1,280
2016	Almonte Viaduct	Spain	1,260

Cantilever

Year	Bridge	Location	Main span (ft)
1890	Forth Rail[1]	Scotland	1,710
1974	Minato	Japan	1,673
1943	Rabindra Setu (Howrah)	India	1,500

(1) Two spans of equal length.

Plate and Box Girder

Year	Bridge	Location	Main span (ft)
2006	Shibanpo	China	1,083
1998	Stolmasundet	Norway	988
1974	Pres. Costa e Silva (Rio-Niterói)	Brazil	984
1998	Raftsund	Norway	978

Cable-Stayed

Year	Bridge	Location	Main span (ft)
2012	Russky Island	Russia	3,622
2008	Sutong Yangtze R.	China	3,570
2009	Stonecutters	China	3,340
2009	Edong	China	3,038
1999	Tatara	Japan	2,920
1995	Normandy	France	2,808
2013	Jiujiang Yangtze R. Expressway	China	2,684
2010	Jingyue Yangtze R.	China	2,677
2009	Incheon	South Korea	2,625
2012	Zolotoy Rog	Russia	2,418
2009	Shanghai Yangtze R.	China	2,395
2009	Minpu	China	2,323
2017	Queensferry	Scotland	2,132
2005	Third Nanjing Yangtze R.	China	2,126
2001	Second Nanjing Yangtze R.	China	2,060
2000	Third Wuhan Yangtze R. (Baishazhou)	China	2,028

Year	Bridge	Location	Main span (ft)
2002	Qingzhou Minjiang R.	China	1,985
1993	Yangpu	China	1,975
1998	Meiko Chuo	Japan	1,936
1997	Xupu	China	1,936
2004	Rion-Antirion	Greece	1,837
2015	La Pepa	Spain	1,772
2014	Bukhang	South Korea	1,772
1991	Skarnsund	Norway	1,739
1999	Shantou Queshi	China	1,699
1995	Tsurumi Tsubasa	Japan	1,673
2008	Tianxingzhou Yangtze R.	China	1,654
2012	Mokpo	South Korea	1,640
2007	Kanchanaphisek	Thailand	1,640
2002	Jingsha	China	1,640
2000	Øresund	Denmark-Sweden	1,608
1991	Ikuchi	Japan	1,608

Other Notable World Bridges[1]

Year	Bridge	Location	Main span (ft)
2011	Danyang-Kunshan Grand (rail)[2]	China	538,000
2011	Tianjin Grand (rail)	China	373,824
2008	Weinan Weihe Grand (rail)	China	261,588
2000	Bang Na Expressway[3]	Thailand	180,446
2010	Beijing Grand (rail)	China	157,982
2007	Yangcun (rail)	China	117,493
2007	Hangzhou Bay	China	117,037
2011	Qingdao-Haiwan (Jiaozhou Bay)	China	87,598
2018	Hong Kong-Zhuhai-Macau Main[4]	China	75,131
2013	Jiashao	China	33,136
2018	Maputo-Katembe[5]	Mozambique	9,977
2004	Millau Viaduct[6]	France	8,071
1978	Demerara Harbour (floating)	Guyana	6,074
1991	Ikitsuki[7]	Japan	1,312

(1) Length listed is total length of bridge unless otherwise noted. (2) World's longest bridge. (3) World's longest road bridge. (4) World's longest oversea bridge in aggregate (only length of its multiple bridges given here). Part of HZMB link, which also consists of an underwater tunnel and artificial islands. (5) Longest suspension bridge in Africa. (6) World's tallest bridge, with max. height of 1,125 ft from top of pylon to valley floor. (7) Length listed is of main span, world's longest continuous truss span.

World's Longest Railway Tunnels

Source: World Almanac research
Year is date of opening or projected opening unless otherwise noted. As of mid-2020.

Year	Tunnel	Location	Operating railway	Length (mi)
2028	Brenner Base (twin)	Austria-Italy	Austrian Federal Railways (ÖBB) and Ferrovie dello Stato (FS)	39.8
2016	Gotthard Base (twin)	Switzerland-Italy	Swiss Federal Railways (SBB)	35.4/35.5
1988	Seikan	Japan	Japan Railways Group	33.5
1994	English Channel (Chunnel) (twin)	UK-France	Eurotunnel	31.5
2016	Yulhyeon	South Korea	SR/Korea Railroad Corporation (Korail)	31.2
2016	Songshan Lake	China	Dongguan-Huizhou Intercity Railway	24.0
2007	Lötschberg Base (twin)	Switzerland	BLS Lötschbergbahn AG	21.5
2014	New Guanjiao	China	Qinghai-Tibet Railway Company	20.3
2007	Guadarrama (twin)	Spain	Renfe	17.6
2016	West Qinling	China	Chongqing-Lanzhou Railway	17.5
2009	Taihang (twin)	China	China's Ministry of Railways	17.3
1940	Northern Line	UK	London Underground	17.3
2005	Hakkoda	Japan	Japan Railways Group	16.4
2018	Guangzhou-Shenzhen-Hong Kong Express Rail Link (XRL), Hong Kong section	China	MTR Corporation	16.2
2002	Iwate-Ichinohe	Japan	Japan Railways Group	16.0
2020	Pajares (twin)	Spain	Renfe	15.3
2015	Iiyama	Japan	Japan Railways Group	13.8
1982	Daishimizu	Japan	Japan Railways Group	13.8
2021	Crossrail (twin)	UK	Transport for London	13.0
2008-09	Geumjeong	South Korea	Korea Railroad Corporation (Korail)	12.6
2006	Wushaoling (twin)	China	China's Ministry of Railways	12.5
2021	Follo Line (twin)	Norway	Vy (Norwegian State Railways)	12.1
1906/22	Simplon No. 1 and 2	Switzerland-Italy	BLS Lötschbergbahn AG	12.3
1999	Vereina	Switzerland	Rhätische Bahn (RhB)	11.8
1975	Shin-Kanmon (twin)	Japan	Japan Railways Group	11.6
1934	Apennine	Italy	Ferrovie dello Stato (FS)	11.5
2028	Fehmarn Belt[1]	Denmark-Germany	Rail Net Denmark (Banedanmark)	11.3

NA = Not available. (1) Would be world's longest immersed tunnel for rail and auto.

Underwater U.S. Vehicular Tunnels

Source: National Tunnel Inventory, Federal Highway Administration, U.S. Dept. of Transportation (year is date of opening)

Year	Name	Location	Waterway	Length (ft)
1950	Hugh L. Carey (twin)	Brooklyn-Manhattan, New York, NY	East River	9,137
1927	Holland	New York, NY-Jersey City, NJ	Hudson River	8,556
1937/45/57	Lincoln (center/north/south tubes)	New York, NY-Weehawken, NJ	Hudson River	8,216/7,482/8,006
1958	Baltimore Harbor (twin)	Baltimore, MD	Baltimore Harbor	7,651
1957/1976	Hampton Roads (westbound, eastbound)	Norfolk-Hampton, VA	Hampton Roads Harbor	7,479/7,315
1985	Fort McHenry (twin)	Baltimore, MD	Patapsco River	7,209
1940	Queens Midtown (twin)	Queens-Manhattan, New York, NY	East River	6,272
2004	Silver Line	Boston, MA	Boston Harbor	6,233
1964	Thimble Shoal	Virginia Beach, VA	Chesapeake Bay	5,738
1934	Sumner	Boston, MA	Boston Harbor	5,655
1964	Chesapeake Channel	Northampton Co., VA	Chesapeake Bay	5,424
1930	Detroit-Windsor	Detroit, MI-Windsor, ON, Canada	Detroit River	5,160
1961	Callahan	Boston, MA	Boston Harbor	5,070

Land Vehicular Tunnels in the U.S.

Source: World Almanac research; Federal Highway Administration, U.S. Dept. of Transportation

Name	Location	Length (ft)	Name	Location	Length (ft)
Anton Anderson Memorial[1].	Whittier, AK	13,300	Kittatinny Mountain (twin)...	Franklin Co., PA	4,727
SR99 (Alaskan Way)	Seattle, WA	12,244	Lehigh (twin)	Lehigh Co.-Carbon Co., PA	4,383
Edwin C. Johnson Memorial	I-70, Clear Creek Co.-Summit Co., CO	8,877	Tom Lantos/Devil's Slide (twin)	San Mateo Co., CA	4,342/ 4,265
Eisenhower Memorial	I-70, Clear Creek Co.-Summit Co., CO	8,856	Blue Mountain (twin)	Newburg, PA	4,340
Ted Williams[2]	MA Turnpike, Boston, MA	8,448	Wawona	Yosemite Natl. Pk., CA	4,237
Thomas P. O'Neill Jr.	I-93, Boston, MA	7,920	Big Walker Mountain (twin).	Bland Co., VA	4,228
Tetsuo Harano (twin)	Oahu, HI	6,336	Squirrel Hill (twin)	Pittsburgh, PA	4,225
Allegheny (twin)	Somerset Co., PA	6,069	Hanging Lake (twin)	Glenwood Canyon, CO	4,035/ 3,941
Liberty (twin)	PA Turnpike, Pittsburgh, PA	5,898	Cave Rock (eastbound)	Douglas Co., NV	3,915
East River Mountain (twin)..	I-77, Rocky Gap, VA-Bluefield, WV	5,661	Wabash HOV	Pittsburgh, PA	3,661
Zion-Mount Carmel	Zion Natl. Park, UT	5,613	Caldecott (4 tubes)	Oakland, CA	3,616/3,610/ 3,371/3,399
Tuscarora Mountain (twin)	Franklin Co.-Huntingdon Co., PA	5,324	Fort Pitt (twin)	Pittsburgh, PA	3,614
Cumberland Gap (twin)	U.S. 25E, KY-TN	4,860	Mount Washington Transit...	Pittsburgh, PA	3,549
			I-395 Mall (Third St.)	Washington, DC	3,400

(1) Vehicles and trains take turns using the tunnel's one lane. (2) Total length of tunnel is 8,448 ft, 3,960 ft of which is underwater.

Major U.S. Dams and Reservoirs

Source: 2019 National Inventory of Dams, U.S. Army Corps of Engineers

Highest U.S. Dams

Rank	Dam (year completed)	River	Location	Type	Height (ft)
1.	Oroville (1968)	Feather	California	Embankment earthfill	770
2.	Hoover (1935).	Colorado	Nevada-Arizona	Arch-Gravity	730
3.	Dworshak (1973)	N. Fork Clearwater	Idaho	Gravity	717
4.	Glen Canyon (1963)	Colorado	Arizona	Arch	710
5.	New Bullards Bar (1970).	North Yuba	California	Arch	645
6.	New Melones (1979)	Stanislaus	California	Embankment rockfill	625
7.	Mossyrock (1968)	Cowlitz	Washington	Arch	606
8.	Shasta (1945).	Sacramento	California	Gravity	602
9.	Don Pedro (1971)	Tuolumne	California	Embankment earthfill	585
10.	Hungry Horse (1952)	S. Fork Flathead	Montana	Arch	564

Note: The height of a dam is the vertical distance between the original streambed or excavated foundation and the dam's crest, parapet wall, or maximum design water level. Tailings and other mining dams (i.e., dams built from the waste generated by mining operations) are not included in this list.

Largest U.S. Embankment Dams

Rank	Dam (year completed)	River	Location	Volume in cubic yards (thous.)
1.	Fort Peck (1957)	Missouri	Montana	125,628
2.	Oahe (1966)	Missouri	South Dakota	92,000
3.	Oroville (1968)	Feather	California	80,000
4.	B. F. Sisk (San Luis) (1967)	San Luis Creek	California	77,670
5.	Garrison (1953)	Missouri	North Dakota	66,500
6.	Scotts Flat (1948)	Deer Creek	California	66,300
7.	Cochiti (1975)	Rio Grande	New Mexico	65,000
8.	Herbert Hoover (1965)	Kissimmee River Basin	Florida	54,700
9.	Fort Randall (1954).	Missouri	South Dakota	50,200
10.	Castaic (1973)	Castaic Creek	California	44,000

Note: An embankment dam is any dam constructed with excavated material, including earth, rocks, and mining or other industrial waste. (In contrast, gravity, arch, and buttress dams are generally made out of concrete or masonry.) The majority of the world's dams are embankment dams. All dams in this list are earthfill, or formed primarily out of layers of compacted earth.

Largest-Capacity U.S. Reservoirs

Rank	Dam (year completed)	Reservoir	Location	Maximum capacity (thous. acre-feet)
1.	Hoover (1935).	Lake Mead	Nevada-Arizona	30,237
2.	Glen Canyon (1963)	Lake Powell	Arizona	29,875
3.	Garrison (1953)	Lake Sakakawea	North Dakota	26,000
4.	Oahe (1966)	Lake Oahe	South Dakota	23,600
5.	Fort Peck (1957).	Fort Peck Lake	Montana	19,100
6.	Grand Coulee (1941)	Lake Roosevelt	Washington	9,562
7.	Herbert Hoover (1965)	Lake Okeechobee	Florida	8,519
8.	Kentucky (1944)	Kentucky Lake	Kentucky	7,535
9.	Sam Rayburn (1965)	Sam Rayburn Lake	Texas	6,520
10.	Wright Patman (1954).	Wright Patman Lake	Texas	6,505

Note: A reservoir is a body of water created by a dam for storage. This water may serve a single or multiple purposes, such as irrigation, flood reduction, and electricity generation.

Major Dams and Reservoirs of the World

Source: World Register of Dams, Intl. Commission on Large Dams (ICOLD)
Asterisk (*) designates structure is planned or under construction as of mid-2020.

World's Highest Dams

Rank	Dam	Country	Meters	Feet
1.	*Rogun	Tajikistan	335	1,099
2.	*Shuangjiangkou	China	312	1,023
3.	Jinping 1	China	305	1,001
4.	Nurek	Tajikistan	300	984
5.	*Lianghekou	China	295	968
6.	Xiaowan	China	294	965
7.	Xiluodu	China	286	938
8.	Grande Dixence	Switzerland	285	935
9.	*Baihetan	China	277	909
10.	*Bakhtiyari	Iran	275	902
11.	*Diamer-Bhasha	Pakistan	272	892
12.	Enguri	Georgia	272	892
13.	*Yusufeli	Turkey	270	886
14.	Narsinghpura	India	264	866
15.	Manuel Moreno Torres (Chicoasén)	Mexico	262	860

World's Largest-Capacity Reservoirs

Rank	Dam	Country	Max. capacity (thous. cubic meters)
1.	Robert-Bourassa	Canada	460,702,900
2.	Kariba	Zambia/Zimbabwe	180,600,000
3.	Bratsk	Russia	169,000,000
4.	Akosombo	Ghana	150,000,000
5.	Daniel Johnson	Canada	141,851,350
6.	Guri	Venezuela	135,000,000
7.	High Aswan	Egypt	132,000,000
8.	W.A.C. Bennett	Canada	74,300,000
9.	*Grand Ethiopian Renaissance	Ethiopia	74,000,000
10.	Krasnoyarsk	Russia	73,300,000
11.	Zeya	Russia	68,400,000
12.	La Grande-3	Canada	59,994,000
13.	Ust-Ilimsk	Russia	59,300,000
14.	Cutarm Creek	Canada	58,595,982
15.	Boguchany	Russia	58,200,000

World's Largest-Capacity Hydroelectric Plants

Rank	Dam	Country	Installed capacity (MW)	Energy generated (GWh/year)
1.	Sanxia (Three Gorges)	China	22,500	98,100
2.	*Baihetan	China	16,000	51,500
3.	Itaipu	Brazil/Paraguay	14,000	98,300
4.	Xiluodu	China	13,860	57,120
5.	Belo Monte	Brazil	11,234	NA
6.	Guri	Venezuela	10,235	53,400
7.	Tucurui	Brazil	8,370	41,400
8.	*Ta Sang	Myanmar	7,100	35,446
9.	Grand Coulee	U.S.	6,809	NA
10.	*Grand Ethiopian Renaissance	Ethiopia	6,420	NA
11.	Sayano-Shushenskaya	Russia	6,400	22,800
12.	Xiangjiaba	China	6,400	30,747
13.	Longtan	China	6,300	18,710
14.	Krasnoyarsk	Russia	6,000	20,400
15.	Nuozhadu	China	5,850	23,912

Dams by Purpose, Worldwide

Purpose	Single-purpose dams		Multi-purpose dams	
	Number	Percent of total	Number	Percent of total
Irrigation	13,142	47%	6,180	24%
Flood control	2,536	9	4,911	19
Water supply	3,339	12	4,534	17
Hydropower	6,102	22	4,127	16
Recreation	1,351	5	3,010	12
Fish farming, navigation, tailing, and other	1,744	5	3,318	13

Note: Based on a survey of 28,214 single-purpose dams and 10,207 multi-purpose dams registered with ICOLD. Percentages may not sum to 100 due to rounding.

Timeline of Selected Architectural Styles and Structures

Asterisk (*) denotes part of a UNESCO World Heritage site as of mid-2020.

Style and period	Location; characteristics; significant examples
Mesopotamian c. 3500-539 BCE	City-states of Sumer, Akkad, Babylon, Assyria (modern-day Iraq). Mud-brick rectangular temples on oval platforms with simple corbel vaults, later ziggurats. Painted terra-cotta mosaics and murals; carved reliefs on columns and walls. **Ziggurat of Nanna**, Ur (Muqayyar, Iraq), ordered by Ur-Nammu, c. 2100 BCE **Anu Ziggurat and White Temple**, Uruk (Warka, Iraq), c. 3000 BCE
Egyptian c. 3000-30 BCE	Along Nile R. Mud-brick and limestone tombs and massive, geometric pyramids, post-and-lintel construction. Highly decorative with colorful hieroglyphics, carvings, columns, obelisks, paintings, and sculpture. ***Stepped Pyramid of Pharaoh Djoser** (Saqqara, Egypt), by Imhotep, c. 2737-2717 BCE ***Great Pyramid of Khufu** (Giza, Egypt), c. 2250 BCE ***Great Temple of Amon-Ra** (Karnak, Egypt), c. 1530-300 BCE ***Mortuary Temple of Queen Hatshepsut**, Deir el-Bahari (Thebes, Egypt), by Senenmut, c. 1479-1458 BCE
Three Dynasties c. 2100-221 BCE	China. Single-level mud-brick or mud-smeared timber structures on earthen platforms with thatched roofs. Later, bracketed wooden-framed structures with brick-tiled floors, roofs with overhanging eaves. **City of Erlitou** (Yanshi, China), c. 1900-1500 BCE

Style and period	Location; characteristics; significant examples
Minoan c. 1800-1450 BCE	Crete. Palaces, tombs in monumental style adapted from Mesopotamia and Egypt. Multilevel stone palaces with large central court, no fortifications. Walls made of doors (*polythyron*); stone porticoes and lintels; wooden ceilings and columns; beehive-shaped tombs (*tholi*). **Palace at Knossos** (Heraklion, Crete, Greece), c. 1700 BCE
Mycenaean c. 1600-1100 BCE	Greece. Adapted Minoan style, with large stone masonry, huge walls, and fortified citadels with complex palaces (*megaron*). ***Treasury of Atreus** (Mycenae, Greece), c. 1250 BCE
Olmec c. 1200-400 BCE	Mexico Gulf Coast. Many religious structures, including stone temple-pyramids centered in cities; also large stone sculptures and mosaic pavement with natural and animistic themes. **Great Pyramid** (La Venta, Mexico), c. 800-400 BCE
Mayan c. 900 BCE-900 CE	Central America. Religious structures with plaster-surfaced stone temple-pyramids with stairs containing tombs. Decorative animistic and geometric relief sculptures, lintels, and stone monuments with hieroglyphics. ***Pyramid of the Magician** (Uxmal, Mexico), c. 700-910 CE ***North Acropolis** (Tikal, Guatemala), c. 200 CE
Greek c. 750-323 BCE	Greek peninsula, Asia Minor, North Africa, western Mediterranean. Religious, civic buildings in monumental style, inspired by Egypt, based on strict rules of form and human proportion; many ornamental details. Marble and limestone structures (including rectangular temples) with pediment, colonnaded porticoes in diverse regional styles, defined by orders of architecture like Ionic, Doric, Corinthian. Most early buildings with timber supports; solid stone in later temples. ***Parthenon, Acropolis** (Athens, Greece), by Ictinus and Callicrates, 447-436 BCE ***Temple of Zeus** (Olympia, Greece), by Libon of Elis, mid-5th cent. BCE **Mausoleum of Halicarnassus** (Bodrum, Turkey), by Pythis, c. 353 BCE (destroyed) ***Temple of Apollo Epicurius** (Bassae, Greece), by Ictinus, c. 420 BCE
Achaemenid c. 550-334 BCE	Persian Empire (Eastern Mediterranean to Indus R.). Palatial complexes influenced by cultures absorbed by the empire; limestone and mud-brick complexes on raised stone terraces with ornamental stairways, rectangular pillared audience halls with porticoes and corner towers; pleasure gardens (*bâgh*) as focal point of architecture. ***Pasargadae** (Iran), founded by Cyrus II, after 547 BCE ***Persepolis** (Iran), founded by Darius I, around 518 BCE
Roman c. 500 BCE-400 CE	Roman Empire. Civic and religious structures with grandiose limestone brick and concrete construction in systematic, practical layout. Adapted Greek orders in many structures, including circular temples and large covered halls (basilica), but emphasized movement with rounded arches and domes, geometric vaults. ***Pantheon** (Rome, Italy), ordered by Emperor Hadrian, 118-128 CE ***Colosseum** (Rome, Italy), ordered by Emperor Vespasian, 70-82 CE ***Roman Forum** (Rome, Italy), 500s BCE-608 CE
Qin and Han c. 221 BCE-220 CE	China. Massive public works, palaces, tombs, and planned cities; systematic layout and design determined by divination techniques (geomancy). Multistoried timber palace complexes with gardens, courtyards laid along a long hall with a south-north axis for weather; decorative roof with overhanging eaves. ***The Great Wall** (China), ordered by Qin Shi Huang, 220 BCE-c. 1600 CE ***Mausoleum of the First Qin Emperor** (Xianyang [Xi'an], China), c. 210 BCE
Sassanian 226-651	Iran. Mud-brick, mortared rubble, and stone palaces on platforms. Tall, vaulted entry chambers with one open side (*iwans*). Three-aisled hall chambers covered with rudimentary barrel vaults. Parabolic domes abandoned for square courtyards in later Sassanian period. ***Palace of Ardashir I** (Firuzabad, Iran), c. 224 ***Taq-i Kisra** [Arch of Khosrau] (Ctesiphon, Iraq), c. 260 or c. 550
Byzantine 330-1453	Byzantine Empire, Italy, Russia. Religious structures with masonry construction based on Roman architecture, many salvaged pieces. Centralized cross-in-square layout, with large central dome supported by vaults. Highly decorative, with iconographic frescoes, glass mosaics. ***Hagia Sophia** (Istanbul, Turkey), by Anthemius and Isidorus, 532-37 ***St. Mark's Basilica** (Venice, Italy), ordered by Domenico Contarini, 1063-94
Sui and Tang 581-906	China. Includes influences from other cultures; geomancy used to enhance harmony and social status. Rectangular, multistory modular timber structures with interlinking corridors; single-eaved roofs with exposed beams. **Daming Palace** (Xi'an, China), 634 (destroyed) ***Hall of the Great Buddha**, Foguang Temple (Mount Wutai, China), ordered rebuilt by Xuan Zhong, 857
Early Islamic (Umayyad) 692-c. 1000	Syria, Middle East, North Africa, southern Spain. Mosques in adapted Sassanian style. Austere exteriors; simple columned halls with minarets and mihrabs (prayer niches), walled courtyards and gardens, onion domes. Highly decorative interiors with patterned marble, mosaics. ***Dome of the Rock** [Qubbat al-Sakhra] (Jerusalem), ordered by Abd al-Malik, 692 ***Great Mosque of Córdoba** (Spain), ordered by Abd al-Rahman I, 784-86
Khmer c. 880-1200s	Indochina. Hindu or Buddhist temple complexes, including brick, later sandstone beehive-shaped shrines with arches atop terraced temple "mountains" symbolizing Mount Meru, Hindu and Buddhist center of the universe, where the gods dwell. Concentric layout of structures mimics the cosmos, relating religious narrative in carved reliefs. ***Angkor Wat** (Cambodia), ordered by Suryavarman II, 12th cent.
Romanesque (Norman) c. 900s-1100s	Western Europe. Churches and monasteries in localized Roman style; many reused material from Roman structures. Austere, heavy, simple masonry construction with thick walls, concealed buttresses, small windows, barrel arches, and vaults. Churches like Roman basilica with arched central nave, lower side aisles, apse, transept formed Latin cross. Monumental art and ornaments with Christian narrative throughout, especially on façade and portals. ***Durham Cathedral** (England, UK), ordered by Bishop William de Saint-Calais, 1093-1133 ***Cathedral, Baptistery, and "Leaning" Tower** (Pisa, Italy), by various architects, begun in 1063, tower not completed until 1372
Gothic c. 1100s-1500s	France, Europe. Cathedrals meant to inspire spirituality with design like Roman basilica: pointed arches and spires that reach toward heavens, skeletal masonry, revealed structure like flying buttresses, ribbed vaults to allow better lighting, large stained-glass windows. **Abbey Church of Saint-Denis** (France), ordered by Abbot Suger, 1135-44 ***Cathedral of Notre-Dame** (Paris, France), ordered by Bishop Maurice de Sully, 1163-1351 ***Cologne Cathedral** (Cologne, Germany), ordered by Archbishop Konrad von Hochstaden, 1248-1880 ***St. Vitus Cathedral** (Prague, Czech Republic), by Matthias of Arras, later Peter Parler, 1344-1929
Yuan and Ming 1279-1644	China. Mongol-influenced timber and some brick structures influenced by geomancy. Emphasized monumental mass in low-lying, sprawling structures with simple rectangular pavilions, great halls, elaborate wooden latticework, carved and painted details. ***Forbidden City** (Beijing, China), ordered by Emperor Yongle, 1406-20

Style and period	Location; characteristics; significant examples
Renaissance 1420s-1520s	Italy. The rebirth or rediscovery of ancient Roman design, grounded in a scholarly approach to architecture. Followed rules of proportion in perspective and symmetry, classical orders, and simple but perfected geometric forms; emphasis on human scale. ***Pazzi Chapel** (Florence, Italy), by Filippo Brunelleschi, 1429-61 ***Palazzo Medici-Riccardi** (Florence, Italy), by Michelozzo di Bartolomeo, 1444-60 ***Tempietto San Pietro** (Rome, Italy), by Donato Bramante, 1502-10 ***Villa Almerico Capra, or La Rotonda** (near Vicenza, Italy), by Andrea Palladio, later Vincenzo Scamozzi, 1566-1610
Mughal 1526-1858	India. Monumental palaces and mosques blending Hindu and Islamic architecture. Sandstone with marble inlay; highly decorative, with semiprecious stones, vegetal and Koranic motifs. Formulaic four-part pleasure gardens (*charbâgh*), exemplified by grounds of Taj Mahal. ***Humayun's Tomb** (Delhi, India), by Sayyid Muhammad, 1562-72 ***Taj Mahal** (Agra, India), ordered by Emperor Shah Jahan, 1631-48
Baroque 1630s-1700s	Italy, later Western Europe. Elaborate and theatrical religious and civic structures, focused on dramatic overall effect. Complex geometric shapes and elaborate sculptures meant to be viewed from many angles. **St. Carlo alle Quattro Fontane** (Rome, Italy), by Francesco Borromini, 1638-41 ***Palace of Versailles** (Versailles, France), royal hunting lodge (built 1631-34) expanded under Louis XIV, 1661-1710 **Church of San Lorenzo** (Turin, Italy), by Guarino Guarini, 1666-79 **Church of St. John of Nepomuk, or Asamkirche** (Munich, Germany), by Cosmas Damian and Egid Quirin Asam, 1733-46
Rococo 1690s-1700s	Europe. Mostly interior, simplified but still fanciful Baroque designs; ornate with natural motifs, gold trim, light and creamy colors, asymmetrical designs, and unusual materials. ***Sanssouci Palace** (Potsdam, Germany), by Georg Wenzeslaus von Knobelsdorff, 1745-47
Neoclassicism 1750-1830	Europe, Americas. Civic, commercial, and religious structures; chaste, non-decorative designs in reaction to Baroque excess. Grounded in Enlightenment-era principles and simple, strict adherence to classic (Greek, Roman, Renaissance) forms and details. Palladian style in England, Federal style in U.S. **Chiswick House** (Chiswick, England, UK), by Richard Boyle, 1725-29 ***Monticello** (Charlottesville, VA), by Thomas Jefferson, 1768-1809
Neo-Gothic 1837-1900s	Britain, U.S. Civic, commercial, and religious structures utilizing Gothic forms in new commercial enterprises like railway stations and hotels. Traditional masonry façade disguised modern structural material like iron and glass. ***Westminster Palace** (London, England, UK), by Charles Barry and A.W.N. Pugin, 1840-47 **Hotel fronting St. Pancras Railway Station** (London, England, UK), by George Gilbert Scott, 1865-71
Arts and Crafts 1850s-1930s	England, U.S. Residential structures made of brick and other indigenous materials with pastoral and traditional elements like gabled roofs. Conceived as a reaction against homogenization of style following the Industrial Revolution. **Red House** (Bexley Heath, England, UK), by Philip Webb, 1859 **Tigbourne Court** (Surrey, England, UK), by Edwin Lutyens, 1898
Beaux-Arts 1870s-1930s	France, U.S. Grandiose, highly decorative style, using a mix of classical forms taught at the École des Beaux-Arts (School of Fine Arts) in Paris: columns, wall projections, elaborate rooftops, high-relief decoration. **Boston Public Library** (Boston, MA), by McKim, Mead, and White, 1888-95 **Grand Central Terminal** (New York, NY), Reed & Stem and Warren & Wetmore, 1903-13
Art Nouveau 1884-1905	Europe (esp. Brussels, Belgium; France). Civic and residential structures using industrial products like metal and glass to mimic natural forms; airy, fluid, and ornate. ***Hôtel Tassel** (Brussels, Belgium), by Victor Horta, 1892-93 **Entrances to Métro (subway)** (Paris, France), by Hector Guimard, 1900
Prairie 1893-1917	U.S. Mostly residences, some civic buildings in adapted Arts and Crafts style. Inspired by American Midwest and small-town values. Frank Lloyd Wright most notable architect of the style. Buildings centered on chimney, with overhanging eaves and horizontal emphasis, long bands of windows. ***Robie House** (Chicago, IL), by Frank Lloyd Wright, 1908-10 **National Farmer's Bank** (Owatonna, MN), by Louis Sullivan, 1906-08
Futurism 1913-14	Italy. Purely theoretical style that produced no actual structures. Emphasized concrete, glass, and steel construction; pure geometric and straight lines; and exposed structure and utilities. **La Città Nuova (The New City)** (sketches), by Antonio Sant'Elia, 1913
Constructivism 1914-20s	Russia, Europe. Public buildings based on socialist philosophies. Purely utilitarian industrial design, modern materials. **Rusakov Club** (Moscow, Russia), by Konstantin Melnikov, 1927-28
De Stijl 1917-31	Netherlands. Building and fixtures designed as a complete, sculpture-like piece of art; emphasis on primary colors, simple but asymmetrical geometry. Name is Dutch for "The Style." ***Schröder House** (Utrecht, Netherlands), by Gerrit Thomas Rietveld, 1924
Bauhaus 1919-33	Weimar Republic Germany. Art and design school founded by Walter Gropius with philosophy that the machine is the modern medium. Concrete, glass, and steel construction that united industrial crafts and fine arts with simple geometric forms and colors. ***Bauhaus** (Dessau, Germany), by Walter Gropius, 1925-26
International Style 1920s-70s	Asia, Europe, North America. Reinforced concrete and steel structures, mostly commercial buildings with some residences and civic structures. Post-and-slab construction meant walls no longer supported weight so façades could be continuous strip (ribbon) glass "curtain-walls" with modular interiors. Emphasis on simple forms; glass, marble, and stainless steel; minimal decoration. **Philadelphia Savings Fund Society Building** (Philadelphia, PA), by George Howe and William Lescaze, 1926-32 **Villa Savoye** (Poissy, France), by Le Corbusier, 1928-31 **Seagram Building** (New York, NY), by Ludwig Mies Van Der Rohe with Philip Johnson, 1954-58
Art Deco 1925-30s	Europe, U.S. Traditional, symmetric, elegant construction like Beaux-Arts whimsically mixed with modern styles like geometric forms and steel or chrome features. **Chrysler Building** (New York, NY), by William van Alen, 1928-30 **Empire State Building** (New York, NY), by Shreve, Lamb & Harmon, 1930-31
Postmodernism 1970s-present	Asia, Europe, North America. Playful reaction against generic, mainstream "orthodox modern architecture," according to Robert Venturi. Token references to traditional architectural elements like pediments or gables on houses; aim to present, Venturi wrote, "old clichés in new settings." **Vanna Venturi House** (Philadelphia, PA), by Robert Venturi, 1962 **Public Service Building** (Portland, OR), by Michael Graves, 1980-82

INTERNATIONAL STATISTICS

World Population Growth

The global population in ancient times can only be very roughly estimated, but there were perhaps 50 mil people in the world in 1000 BCE. The United Nations (UN) Population Division estimates a figure of 300 mil for 1 CE. This diagram shows estimated population growth since then.

Although different sources may provide varying estimates, they agree that the world's population began growing more rapidly in the 18th and 19th centuries and increased at an even greater rate in the 20th century. According to the UN, the total population reached 1 bil in 1804; rose to 2 bil 123 years later, in 1927; to 3 bil 33 years after that, in 1960; to 4 bil in 1974; to 5 bil in 1987; to 6 bil in 1999; and to 7 bil in 2011.

The UN put the world population in mid-2020 at 7.8 bil. It projects that the population will reach 8 bil by 2023. The UN expects that between 2019 and 2050, nine countries will account for more than half the increase in the world population (in descending order): India, Nigeria, Pakistan, Dem. Rep. of the Congo, Ethiopia, Tanzania, Indonesia, Egypt, and the U.S.

```
2023  8 bil
2011  7 bil
1999  6 bil
1987  5 bil
1974  4 bil
1960  3 bil
1927  2 bil
1804  1 bil
```

```
1 CE              1250        1500
300 mil          400 mil    500 mil
```

Area and Population of the World by Continent, 1950-2025

Source: International Data Base, International Programs Center, U.S. Census Bureau, U.S. Dept. of Commerce; *The World Factbook*, Central Intelligence Agency (CIA)

Continent/ region	Land area (sq mi)	(sq km)	% of Earth's land	Population (midyear) 1950	1975	2000	2020	% of world total, 2020	2025[1]
Asia	11,922,585	30,879,354	21.1	1,437,565,483	2,412,701,231	3,681,745,306	4,539,569,435	59.1	4,716,433,901
Africa	11,532,127	29,868,071	20.5	229,058,740	417,203,164	807,045,083	1,339,491,577	17.4	1,511,880,060
Europe[2]	8,559,255	22,168,368	15.2	547,140,324	678,635,710	730,793,541	749,332,680	9.8	749,411,116
N. America	7,880,082	20,409,318	14.0	165,945,185	238,783,486	313,388,332	370,467,900	4.8	383,464,627
Latin America[3]	7,723,205	20,003,010	13.7	165,442,794	320,617,049	518,597,668	644,336,252	8.4	672,176,767
Oceania	3,277,072	8,487,578	5.8	12,476,128	21,114,852	30,203,373	41,094,539	0.5	43,640,368
Antarctica[4]	5,482,651	14,200,000	9.7	NA	NA	NA	NA	NA	NA
World	56,376,976	146,015,698	100.0	2,557,628,654	4,089,055,492	6,081,773,303	7,684,292,383	100.0	8,077,006,839

NA = Not applicable. **Note:** Composition of geographical (continental) regions are as defined by the United Nations. Figures may not add up to totals due to rounding. (1) Projected. (2) Includes all of Russia. (3) Includes the Caribbean. (4) Antarctica has no indigenous inhabitants, though people are present at permanent and seasonal research stations. Only an est. 110,039 sq mi are ice free.

Population of the World's Largest Urban Areas, 1975-2035

Source: *World Urbanization Prospects: The 2018 Revision*, Dept. of Economic and Social Affairs, UN Population Division

Population figures are midyear estimates or projections for urban agglomerations, i.e., whole metropolitan areas comprising an urban center and surrounding settlements of lower density. In 2020, 56.2% of the world's population lived in an urban area. That proportion is expected to increase as the population grows to an est. 62.5% in 2035. Data may differ from figures elsewhere in *The World Almanac*. MMA = Major Metropolitan Area.

(ranked by mid-2020 population)

Rank	Urban area, country	Population (thous.) 1975	2000	2020	2035	Rate of change (%) 1975-2000	2000-20	2020-35	Pop. of urban area as % of country's 2020 pop.
1.	Tokyo, Japan	26,615	34,450	37,393	36,014	29.4%	8.5%	-3.7%	29.6%
2.	Delhi, India	4,436	15,692	30,291	43,345	253.7	93.0	43.1	2.2
3.	Shanghai, China	5,658	14,247	27,058	34,341	151.8	89.9	26.9	1.9
4.	São Paulo, Brazil	9,614	17,014	22,043	24,490	77.0	29.6	11.1	10.3
5.	Mexico City, Mexico	10,734	18,457	21,782	25,415	72.0	18.0	16.7	16.3
6.	Dhaka, Bangladesh	2,221	10,285	21,006	31,234	363.1	104.2	48.7	12.4
7.	Cairo, Egypt	6,450	13,626	20,901	28,504	111.3	53.4	36.4	20.3
8.	Beijing, China	4,828	10,285	20,463	25,366	113.0	99.0	24.0	1.4
9.	Mumbai (Bombay), India	7,685	16,147	20,411	27,343	110.1	26.4	34.0	1.5
10.	Kinki MMA (Osaka), Japan	16,298	18,660	19,165	18,346	14.5	2.7	-4.3	15.2
11.	New York, NY-Newark, NJ, U.S.	15,880	17,813	18,804	20,817	12.2	5.6	10.7	5.7
12.	Karachi, Pakistan	3,989	9,825	16,094	23,128	146.3	63.8	43.7	7.7
13.	Chongqing, China	2,545	7,863	15,872	20,531	209.0	101.9	29.4	1.1
14.	Istanbul, Turkey	3,600	8,744	15,190	17,986	142.9	73.7	18.4	18.1
15.	Buenos Aires, Argentina	9,143	12,504	15,154	17,128	36.8	21.2	13.0	33.3
16.	Kolkata (Calcutta), India	8,166	13,097	14,850	19,564	60.4	13.4	31.7	1.1
17.	Lagos, Nigeria	1,890	7,281	14,368	24,419	285.3	97.3	69.9	7.0
18.	Kinshasa, Dem. Rep. of Congo	1,482	6,140	14,342	26,682	314.4	133.6	86.0	16.0
19.	Manila, Philippines	4,999	9,958	13,923	18,649	99.2	39.8	33.9	12.7
20.	Tianjin, China	3,527	6,989	13,589	16,446	98.1	94.4	21.0	1.0
21.	Rio de Janeiro, Brazil	7,733	11,307	13,458	14,810	46.2	19.0	10.0	6.3
22.	Guangzhou, Guangdong, China	1,698	7,812	13,302	16,741	360.0	70.3	25.9	0.9
23.	Lahore, Pakistan	2,399	5,576	12,642	19,117	132.5	126.7	51.2	6.1
24.	Moscow, Russia	7,623	10,005	12,538	12,823	31.2	25.3	2.3	8.7
25.	Los Angeles-Long Beach-Santa Ana, CA, U.S.	8,926	11,798	12,447	13,778	32.2	5.5	10.7	3.8
26.	Shenzhen, China	36	6,550	12,357	15,185	18,327.5	88.6	22.9	0.9
27.	Bangalore, India	2,111	5,581	12,327	18,066	164.4	120.9	46.6	0.9
28.	Paris, France	8,558	9,737	11,017	12,065	13.8	13.2	9.5	16.8
29.	Bogotá, Colombia	3,040	6,329	10,978	12,753	108.2	73.5	16.2	21.9
30.	Chennai (Madras), India	3,594	6,593	10,971	15,376	83.5	66.4	40.1	0.8

National Rankings by Population, Area, Population Density, 2020

Source: International Data Base, International Programs Center, U.S. Census Bureau, U.S. Dept. of Commerce; *The World Factbook*, Central Intelligence Agency (CIA)

Population figures are for midyear. In mid-2020, the world had an estimated population of close to 7.7 bil, of which China represented nearly one-fifth. Population density is calculated using land area, which does not include inland water.

Largest Populations

Rank	Country	Population
1.	China[1]	1,394,015,977
2.	India	1,326,093,247
3.	United States	332,639,102
4.	Indonesia	267,026,366
5.	Pakistan	233,500,636
6.	Nigeria	214,028,302
7.	Brazil	211,715,973
8.	Bangladesh	162,650,853
9.	Russia	141,722,205
10.	Mexico	128,649,565

Smallest Populations

Rank	Country	Population
1.	Vatican City[2]	1,000
2.	Nauru	9,785
3.	Tuvalu	11,342
4.	Palau	21,685
5.	Monaco	30,940
6.	San Marino	34,232
7.	Liechtenstein	39,137
8.	Saint Kitts and Nevis	53,821
9.	Dominica	74,243
10.	Marshall Islands	77,917

Largest Land Areas

Rank	Country	Area (sq mi)	Area (sq km)
1.	Russia	6,323,482	16,377,742
2.	China	3,600,947	9,326,410
3.	United States	3,532,315	9,148,655
4.	Canada	3,511,023	9,093,507
5.	Brazil	3,227,096	8,358,140
6.	Australia	2,966,153	7,682,300
7.	India	1,147,956	2,973,193
8.	Argentina	1,056,642	2,736,690
9.	Kazakhstan	1,042,360	2,699,700
10.	Algeria	919,595	2,381,741

Smallest Land Areas

Rank	Country	Area (sq mi)	Area (sq km)
1.	Vatican City	0.17	0.44
2.	Monaco	0.77	2
3.	Nauru	8	21
4.	Tuvalu	10	26
5.	San Marino	24	61
6.	Liechtenstein	62	160
7.	Marshall Islands	70	181
8.	Saint Kitts and Nevis	101	261
9.	Maldives	115	298
10.	Malta	122	316

Most Densely Populated

Rank	Country	Persons per sq mi	Persons per sq km
1.	Monaco	40,067.1	15,470.0
2.	Singapore	22,684.0	8,758.3
3.	Vatican City[2]	5,886.3	2,272.7
4.	Bahrain	5,128.9	1,980.3
5.	Malta	3,747.8	1,447.0
6.	Maldives	3,406.1	1,315.1
7.	Bangladesh	3,236.3	1,249.5
8.	Taiwan	1,895.0	731.7
9.	Barbados	1,774.2	685.0
10.	Mauritius	1,759.9	679.5

Least Densely Populated

Rank	Country	Persons per sq mi	Persons per sq km
1.	Mongolia	5.3	2.0
2.	Namibia	8.3	3.2
3.	Australia	8.6	3.3
4.	Iceland	9.1	3.5
5.	Guyana	9.9	3.8
6.	Mauritania	10.1	3.9
7.	Suriname	10.1	3.9
8.	Libya	10.1	3.9
9.	Botswana	10.6	4.1
10.	Canada	10.7	4.1

(1) Does not include mid-2020 population of Hong Kong (7,249,907) and Macau (614,458). (2) Population is for mid-2019.

Current Population and Projections for Countries and Other Areas

Source: International Data Base, International Programs Center, U.S. Census Bureau, U.S. Dept. of Commerce; *The World Factbook*, Central Intelligence Agency (CIA)

(midyear figures)

Country/area	2020	2025	2050
Afghanistan	36,643,815	41,117,073	63,795,418
Albania	3,074,579	3,104,932	2,824,012
Algeria	42,972,878	45,841,317	55,444,735
American Samoa	49,437	45,973	29,167
Andorra	85,635	85,112	74,765
Angola	32,522,339	38,467,070	82,179,028
Anguilla	18,090	19,749	26,980
Antigua and Barbuda	98,179	103,830	122,930
Argentina	45,479,118	47,333,842	54,115,246
Armenia	3,021,324	2,961,175	2,468,311
Aruba	119,428	126,130	150,730
Australia	25,466,459	27,026,047	32,531,358
Austria	8,859,449	8,987,330	9,107,912
Azerbaijan	10,205,810	10,533,598	11,209,644
Bahamas, The	337,721	349,116	371,219
Bahrain	1,505,003	1,579,899	1,847,072
Bangladesh	162,650,853	170,280,989	193,092,763
Barbados	294,560	297,015	282,041
Belarus	9,477,918	9,325,020	8,339,664
Belgium	11,720,716	12,037,746	12,772,233
Belize	399,598	433,389	590,608
Benin	12,864,634	15,202,077	32,206,548
Bermuda	71,750	72,851	69,874
Bhutan	782,318	820,143	951,873
Bolivia	11,639,909	12,463,434	16,003,638
Bosnia and Herzegovina	3,835,586	3,787,402	3,216,039
Botswana	2,317,233	2,483,999	3,201,058
Brazil	211,715,973	218,259,140	232,304,177
Brunei	464,478	498,756	638,157
Bulgaria	6,966,899	6,728,056	5,531,820
Burkina Faso	20,835,401	23,599,713	37,009,374
Burundi	11,865,821	14,026,457	25,504,480
Cabo Verde	583,255	619,168	741,842
Cambodia	16,926,984	18,037,946	22,338,891
Cameroon	27,744,989	31,815,705	57,359,252
Canada	37,694,085	39,095,195	43,035,661
Cayman Islands	61,944	67,661	91,118
Central African Republic	5,990,855	6,637,613	10,338,863
Chad	16,877,357	19,676,074	37,468,757
Chile	18,186,770	18,764,737	19,688,474
China	1,394,015,977	1,407,006,788	1,301,627,048
Colombia	49,084,841	51,194,904	56,227,630
Comoros	846,281	905,545	1,169,893
Congo, Dem. Rep. of	101,780,263	119,065,765	240,992,203
Congo Republic	5,293,070	5,947,999	10,201,971
Cook Islands	8,574	7,621	5,460
Costa Rica	5,097,988	5,353,218	6,065,989
Côte d'Ivoire	27,481,086	30,639,091	47,023,289
Croatia	4,227,746	4,125,465	3,538,821
Cuba	11,059,062	10,938,159	9,829,024
Curaçao	151,345	153,501	150,128
Cyprus	1,266,676	1,329,908	1,392,078
Czechia	10,702,498	10,696,842	10,209,638
Denmark	5,869,410	5,994,785	6,266,278
Djibouti	921,804	1,016,919	1,395,810
Dominica	74,243	74,374	64,772
Dominican Republic	10,499,707	10,978,295	12,542,490
Ecuador	16,904,867	17,867,616	21,102,550
Egypt	104,124,440	115,502,146	168,937,974
El Salvador	6,481,102	6,646,948	6,139,315
Equatorial Guinea	836,178	935,553	1,428,139
Eritrea	6,081,196	6,411,164	8,935,060

Country/area	2020	2025	2050
Estonia	1,228,624	1,182,920	923,335
Eswatini (Swaziland)	1,104,479	1,142,871	1,268,089
Ethiopia	108,113,150	122,146,055	196,219,076
Faroe Islands	51,628	53,200	57,112
Fiji	935,974	956,003	1,013,636
Finland	5,571,665	5,630,882	5,475,753
France	67,848,156	68,860,292	69,484,481
French Polynesia	295,121	305,484	324,712
Gabon	2,230,908	2,515,181	4,088,698
Gambia, The	2,173,999	2,369,298	3,210,223
Gaza Strip	1,918,221	2,120,751	3,053,554
Georgia	4,930,030	4,929,789	4,714,548
Germany	80,159,662	79,226,209	71,541,906
Ghana	29,340,248	32,610,058	52,415,526
Gibraltar	29,581	29,753	28,423
Greece	10,607,051	10,418,496	9,215,660
Greenland	57,616	57,174	49,356
Grenada	113,094	114,741	114,205
Guam	168,485	169,588	157,176
Guatemala	17,153,288	18,550,664	24,400,094
Guernsey	67,052	67,710	66,521
Guinea	12,527,440	14,375,261	27,531,955
Guinea-Bissau	1,927,104	2,187,466	4,038,893
Guyana	750,204	781,231	878,028
Haiti	11,067,777	11,749,583	14,542,914
Honduras	9,235,340	9,796,816	11,844,749
Hong Kong	7,249,907	7,296,877	6,623,263
Hungary	9,771,827	9,615,020	8,489,811
Iceland	350,734	366,578	406,766
India	1,326,093,247	1,396,046,308	1,656,553,632
Indonesia	267,026,366	276,746,433	300,183,166
Iran	84,923,314	88,968,954	98,601,804
Iraq	38,872,655	42,970,570	62,966,921
Ireland	5,176,569	5,417,947	6,333,836
Isle of Man	90,499	92,606	92,840
Israel	8,675,475	9,305,235	12,364,874
Italy	62,402,659	62,591,055	61,415,852
Jamaica	2,808,570	2,790,919	2,319,218
Japan	125,507,472	123,385,521	107,209,536
Jersey	101,073	104,140	107,581
Jordan	10,820,644	11,310,890	15,600,166
Kazakhstan	19,091,949	19,809,426	22,237,156
Kenya	53,527,936	59,465,978	89,732,268
Kiribati	111,796	117,779	139,738
Korea, North	25,643,466	26,242,210	26,969,396
Korea, South	51,835,110	52,565,679	47,731,321
Kosovo	1,932,774	1,999,461	2,222,619
Kuwait	2,993,706	3,169,497	3,863,453
Kyrgyzstan	5,964,897	6,218,713	7,063,351
Laos	7,447,396	7,971,675	10,068,995
Latvia	1,881,232	1,772,796	1,249,812
Lebanon	5,469,612	5,396,843	5,621,049
Lesotho	1,969,334	1,970,540	1,920,225
Liberia	5,073,296	5,811,539	10,569,823
Libya	6,890,535	7,462,016	9,616,633
Liechtenstein	39,137	40,505	43,610
Lithuania	2,731,464	2,573,431	1,801,002
Luxembourg	628,381	680,527	864,238
Macau	614,458	630,434	620,184
Madagascar	26,955,737	30,182,920	45,807,534
Malawi	21,196,629	24,957,849	51,780,996
Malaysia	32,652,083	34,683,300	42,928,546
Maldives	391,904	388,681	444,429
Mali	19,553,397	22,636,934	41,656,105
Malta	457,267	471,365	475,293
Marshall Islands	77,917	83,203	103,092
Mauritania	4,005,475	4,425,089	6,536,272
Mauritius	1,379,365	1,412,384	1,441,100
Mexico	128,649,565	134,828,700	150,567,503
Micronesia	102,436	98,948	74,483
Moldova	3,364,406	3,176,863	2,261,208
Monaco	30,940	31,706	29,810
Mongolia	3,168,026	3,301,176	3,669,264
Montenegro	609,859	596,968	484,207
Montserrat	5,373	5,529	5,707
Morocco	35,561,654	37,136,957	42,001,773
Mozambique	30,098,197	34,208,893	63,427,357
Myanmar (Burma)	56,590,071	58,786,637	64,503,165
Namibia	2,630,073	2,879,366	4,156,634
Nauru	9,785	10,008	11,995
Nepal	30,327,877	31,565,692	33,265,760
Netherlands	17,280,397	17,572,113	17,906,594
New Caledonia	290,009	307,452	370,511
New Zealand	4,925,477	5,203,717	5,867,546
Nicaragua	6,203,441	6,493,913	7,233,620
Niger	22,772,361	27,360,330	62,414,745
Nigeria	214,028,302	242,556,503	416,996,080
North Macedonia	2,125,971	2,137,317	2,033,994
Northern Mariana Islands	51,433	49,909	38,616

Country/area	2020	2025	2050
Norway	5,467,439	5,682,068	6,364,008
Oman	3,634,689	3,981,057	5,401,957
Pakistan	233,500,636	257,222,083	367,580,587
Palau	21,685	22,102	22,894
Panama	3,894,082	4,117,882	4,859,334
Papua New Guinea	7,259,456	7,823,210	10,110,027
Paraguay	7,191,685	7,602,853	8,840,105
Peru	31,914,989	33,283,408	36,943,693
Philippines	109,180,815	117,445,897	155,380,252
Poland	38,282,325	37,753,766	32,738,308
Portugal	10,302,674	10,201,334	9,463,025
Puerto Rico	3,189,068	2,980,352	2,089,492
Qatar	2,444,174	2,562,764	2,558,854
Romania	21,302,893	20,872,127	18,060,354
Russia	141,722,205	140,139,049	129,908,086
Rwanda	12,712,431	13,851,378	19,169,209
Saint Barthélemy	7,122	7,056	6,527
Saint Helena, Ascension, and Tristan da Cunha	7,862	7,888	7,296
Saint Kitts and Nevis	53,821	55,405	56,362
Saint Lucia	166,487	168,519	162,356
Saint Martin	32,556	33,048	34,601
Saint Pierre and Miquelon	5,347	5,030	3,516
Saint Vincent and the Grenadines	101,390	100,409	93,507
Samoa	203,774	210,369	245,010
San Marino	34,232	35,203	35,178
São Tomé and Príncipe	211,122	227,395	309,457
Saudi Arabia	34,173,498	37,038,252	46,923,312
Senegal	15,736,368	17,580,816	27,244,158
Serbia	7,012,165	6,845,638	5,869,146
Seychelles	95,981	98,843	100,391
Sierra Leone	6,624,933	7,500,140	13,593,862
Singapore	6,209,660	6,732,999	8,609,518
Sint Maarten	43,847	46,560	53,001
Slovakia	5,440,602	5,405,646	4,850,540
Slovenia	2,102,678	2,093,610	1,922,216
Solomon Islands	685,097	747,001	1,015,731
Somalia	11,757,124	13,274,251	22,626,120
South Africa	56,463,617	59,108,375	68,528,850
South Sudan	10,561,244	13,301,507	23,624,573
Spain	50,015,792	51,415,437	52,490,640
Sri Lanka	22,889,201	23,563,343	25,166,733
Sudan	45,561,556	51,818,208	89,327,551
Suriname	609,569	636,782	717,936
Sweden	10,202,491	10,587,441	12,011,256
Switzerland	8,403,994	8,665,531	9,539,097
Syria	19,398,448	24,271,054	33,171,702
Taiwan	23,603,049	23,642,264	20,834,040
Tajikistan	8,873,669	9,510,130	12,132,365
Tanzania	58,552,845	66,904,889	118,586,412
Thailand	68,977,400	69,588,429	66,063,997
Timor-Leste	1,383,723	1,539,173	2,191,749
Togo	8,608,444	9,741,450	16,583,950
Tonga	106,095	104,648	78,995
Trinidad and Tobago	1,208,789	1,183,838	1,023,741
Tunisia	11,721,177	12,114,586	12,679,219
Turkey	82,017,514	84,544,177	89,290,126
Turkmenistan	5,528,627	5,800,391	6,607,083
Turks and Caicos Islands	55,926	61,293	84,240
Tuvalu	11,342	11,819	13,423
Uganda	43,252,966	50,871,987	97,113,476
Ukraine	43,922,939	42,887,003	37,148,031
United Arab Emirates	9,992,083	10,756,080	13,280,643
United Kingdom	65,761,117	67,243,723	71,153,797
United States	332,639,102	344,234,377	388,922,201
Uruguay	3,387,605	3,431,610	3,495,238
Uzbekistan	30,565,411	31,823,964	35,116,374
Vanuatu	298,333	323,464	432,658
Vatican City[1]	1,000	NA	NA
Venezuela	28,644,603	31,785,735	36,228,137
Vietnam	98,721,275	102,458,828	111,173,583
Virgin Islands, British	37,381	41,324	59,618
Virgin Islands, U.S.	106,235	103,539	79,884
Wallis and Futuna	15,854	16,023	15,598
West Bank	2,900,034	3,153,234	4,213,540
Western Sahara	652,271	735,697	1,173,350
Yemen	29,884,405	32,822,216	46,080,625
Zambia	17,426,623	20,104,997	38,992,619
Zimbabwe	14,546,314	16,030,790	25,552,730
World[2]	7,684,292,383	8,077,006,839	9,665,309,763

NA = Not available. **Note:** Figures for countries do not include the population of any dependencies listed separately in this table. For example, China's population estimate and projections do not include Hong Kong or Macau. (1) Current pop. is as of 2019. (2) Total projected populations do not include countries for which projections were not available.

Countries Ranked by Gross Domestic Product and Per Capita GDP, 2019

Source: The World Bank

Estimates of gross domestic product (GDP)—the value of all final goods and services that a country produced in a year—were made based on purchasing power parity exchange rates. Per capita GDP is calculated using the estimated population size as of July 1 in a given year. GDP figures are 2019 ests. unless otherwise noted.

GDP (in mil)				Per capita GDP			
Highest		**Lowest**		**Highest**		**Lowest**	
1. China[1]	$23,460,170	1. Tuvalu	$52	1. Luxembourg	$121,293	1. Burundi	$783
2. U.S.	21,427,700	2. Nauru	152	2. Singapore	101,376	2. Central African Republic	984
3. India	9,611,679	3. Marshall Islands[2]	233	3. Qatar	96,491	3. Malawi	1,104
4. Japan	5,459,155	4. Kiribati	279	4. Ireland	88,241	4. Congo, Dem. Rep. of	1,143
5. Germany	4,659,795	5. Palau[2]	331	5. Switzerland	70,989	5. Niger	1,270
6. Russia	4,281,807	6. Micronesia[2]	400	6. United Arab Emirates	69,901	6. Mozambique	1,334
7. Indonesia	3,329,169	7. Tonga[2]	662	7. Norway	66,832	7. Liberia	1,487
8. France	3,315,118	8. São Tomé and Príncipe	888	8. U.S.	65,281	8. Chad	1,645
9. UK	3,255,484	9. Dominica	909	9. Brunei	64,673	9. Togo	1,662
10. Brazil	3,220,373	10. Vanuatu	982	10. San Marino[2]	60,750	10. Madagascar	1,714
11. Italy	2,664,946	11. Samoa	1,338	11. Iceland	60,061	11. Sierra Leone	1,790
12. Mexico	2,603,907	12. St. Vincent and the Grenadines	1,436	12. Denmark	59,830	12. Haiti	1,801
13. Turkey	2,325,617	13. St. Kitts and Nevis	1,450	13. Netherlands	59,687	13. Guinea-Bissau	2,072
14. South Korea	2,224,985	14. Solomon Islands	1,651	14. Austria	59,111	14. Uganda	2,272
15. Spain	1,987,305	15. Grenada	2,011	15. Germany	56,052	15. Burkina Faso	2,280
16. Canada	1,929,897	16. San Marino[2]	2,052	16. Sweden	55,815	16. Afghanistan	2,294
17. Saudi Arabia	1,676,022	17. Antigua and Barbuda	2,216	17. Belgium	54,545	17. The Gambia	2,298
18. Australia	1,352,432	18. Comoros	2,731	18. Australia	53,320	18. Ethiopia	2,312
19. Thailand	1,338,781	19. Belize	2,848	19. Kuwait	51,912	19. Rwanda	2,318
20. Poland	1,299,277	20. St. Lucia	2,941	20. Canada	51,342	20. Kiribati	2,369

(1) Does not include Hong Kong ($468.3 bil GDP) or Macau ($82.7 bil GDP). (2) 2018 est.

Budget Deficits as Percent of GDP in Selected Countries, 1995-2020

Source: *OECD Economic Outlook*, Organisation for Economic Co-operation and Development (OECD); as of June 4, 2020

Country	1995	2000	2005	2010	2014	2016	2018	2019	2020[1]	2020[2]
Australia	-1.7%	1.0%	2.3%	-4.2%	-1.8%	-1.7%	0.1%	0.0%	-10.2%	-12.2%
Austria	-6.1	-2.4	-2.5	-4.4	-2.7	-1.5	0.2	0.7	-7.3	-9.8
Belgium	-4.5	-0.1	-2.7	-4.1	-3.1	-2.4	-0.8	-1.9	-8.6	-11.0
Brazil*	NA	-3.3	-3.5	-2.4	-6.0	-9.0	-7.1	-5.9	-14.5	-15.1
Bulgaria*	-5.5	-0.5	1.0	-3.1	-5.4	0.1	2.0	2.1	-3.3	-3.4
Canada	-5.5	2.6	1.6	-4.7	0.2	-0.5	-0.4	-0.3	-7.5	-9.2
China*	-1.0	-2.6	-0.6	-0.4	-0.3	-3.0	-3.1	-3.7	-7.2	-7.6
Colombia	NA	-5.6	-3.4	-2.2	-3.1	-4.9	-4.7	-2.7[3]	-5.1	-6.1
Czechia	-12.4	-3.6	-3.0	-4.2	-2.1	0.7	0.9	0.3	-6.5	-8.3
Denmark	-3.6	1.9	5.0	-2.7	1.1	-0.1	0.5	3.7	-7.6	-9.1
Estonia	1.0	-0.1	1.1	0.2	0.7	-0.5	-0.6	-0.3	-7.9	-9.3
Finland	-5.9	6.9	2.7	-2.5	-3.0	-1.7	-0.9	-1.1	-7.6	-8.4
France	-5.1	-1.3	-3.4	-6.9	-3.9	-3.6	-2.3	-3.0	-10.4	-12.0
Germany	-9.4	-1.6	-3.3	-4.4	0.6	1.2	1.9	1.4	-7.1	-9.1
Greece	-8.7	-4.0	-6.2	-11.2	-3.6	0.5	1.0	1.5	-7.7	-8.8
Hungary	-8.6	-3.0	-7.8	-4.5	-2.8	-1.8	-2.1	-2.0	-8.8	-9.9
Iceland	-3.0	1.2	4.4	-9.5	-0.1	12.4	0.8	-1.0	-9.5	-9.8
India*	-6.5	-9.4	-6.6	-7.0	-6.7	-6.9	-6.2	-6.1	-8.2	-8.9
Indonesia*	NA	NA	NA	-0.3	-1.9	-2.3	-2.2	-1.9	-6.7	-6.9
Ireland	-2.1	4.8	1.6	-32.1	-3.6	-0.7	0.1	0.4	-8.4	-9.7
Israel	NA	-0.9	-2.7	-3.5	-2.3	-1.4	-3.6	-4.0	-11.1	-12.1
Italy	-7.2	-2.4	-4.1	-4.2	-3.0	-2.4	-2.2	-2.2	-11.2	-12.8
Japan	-4.3	-7.4	-4.4	-9.1	-5.4	-3.5	-2.3	-2.6	-11.6	-12.9
Korea, South	2.8	4.2	1.4	0.9	1.2	2.2	3.0	0.9	-2.9	-3.2
Latvia	-1.4	-2.7	-0.5	-8.7	-1.6	0.2	-0.8	-0.2	-5.9	-7.0
Lithuania	-1.5	-3.2	-0.3	-6.9	-0.6	0.2	0.6	0.3	-9.8	-11.3
Luxembourg	2.6	5.5	-0.2	-0.4	1.3	1.8	3.1	2.2	-5.8	-6.7
Netherlands	-8.7	1.2	-0.4	-5.2	-2.2	0.0	1.4	1.7	-11.5	-12.6
New Zealand	2.4	1.7	4.8	-6.8	0.3	1.3	1.2	-3.6	-10.0	-10.6
Norway	3.1	15.1	14.8	10.9	8.6	4.1	7.8	6.4	-1.4	-2.4
Poland	-4.3	-3.0	-4.0	-7.4	-3.6	-2.4	-0.2	-0.7	-9.4	-11.3
Portugal	-5.2	-3.2	-6.1	-11.4	-7.4	-1.9	-0.4	0.2	-7.9	-9.5
Romania*	-2.0	-4.6	-0.8	-6.9	-1.2	-2.6	-2.9	-4.3	-8.0	-9.1
Russia*	NA	NA	5.0	-1.0	-2.3	-2.6	3.0	2.7	-2.5	-2.6
Slovakia	-3.5	-12.6	-2.9	-7.5	-3.1	-2.5	-1.0	-1.3	-9.3	-10.5
Slovenia	-8.1	-3.6	-1.3	-5.6	-5.5	-1.9	0.7	0.5	-8.0	-8.8
South Africa*	-5.9	-4.1	-2.4	-3.3	-3.8	-3.4	-3.4	-6.5	-9.0	-10.0
Spain	-6.8	-1.2	1.2	-9.5	-5.9	-4.3	-2.5	-2.8	-10.3	-12.5
Sweden	-7.0	3.1	1.8	0.0	-1.5	1.0	0.8	0.5	-8.0	-8.8
Switzerland	-1.9	0.4	-0.7	0.4	-0.2	0.3	1.4	1.2	-6.1	-7.1
United Kingdom	-5.0	1.4	-3.0	-9.3	-5.5	-3.2	-2.2	-2.1	-12.4	-14.2
United States	-4.7	0.3	-4.5	-12.6	-5.4	-5.5	-6.7	-7.3	-15.0	-16.8
OECD countries	-5.2	-0.9	-2.9	-8.2	-3.7	-3.0	-2.9	-3.3	-11.1	-12.7

* = Not an OECD member nation; excluded from OECD country total. NA = Not available. **Note:** The OECD made two economic projections—one in which a second outbreak of COVID-19 occurs towards the end of 2020 (double-hit) and one in which a second outbreak is avoided (single-hit). (1) Single-hit scenario. (2) Double-hit scenario. (3) Single-hit scenario; double-hit scenario is -2.8%.

Gold Reserves of Selected Central Banks and Governments, 1975-2019

Source: *International Financial Statistics*, International Monetary Fund (IMF)

(in mil fine troy ounces)

Year end	All countries[1]	China[2]	France	Germany[3]	India	Italy	Japan	Nether-lands	Russia	Saudi Arabia	Switzer-land	Turkey	U.S.
1975	1,179.8	NA	100.9	117.6	7.0	82.5	21.1	54.3	NA	3.1	83.2	3.6	274.7
1980	1,152.9	12.8	81.9	95.2	8.6	66.7	24.2	43.9	NA	4.6	83.3	3.8	264.3
1985	1,146.7	12.7	81.9	95.2	9.4	66.7	24.2	43.9	NA	4.6	83.3	3.9	262.7
1990	1,144.2	12.7	81.9	95.2	10.7	66.7	24.2	43.9	NA	4.6	83.3	4.1	261.9
1995	1,114.7	12.7	81.9	95.2	12.8	66.7	24.2	34.8	9.4	4.6	83.3	3.7	261.7
2000	1,067.8	12.7	97.2	111.5	11.5	78.8	24.5	29.3	12.4	4.6	77.8	3.7	261.6
2005	992.9	19.3	90.9	110.2	11.5	78.8	24.6	22.3	12.4	4.6	41.5	3.7	261.6
2007	965.0	19.3	83.7	109.9	11.5	78.8	24.6	20.0	14.5	4.6	36.8	3.7	261.5
2009	981.5	33.9	78.3	109.5	17.9	78.8	24.6	19.7	20.9	10.4	33.4	3.7	261.5
2010	991.8	33.9	78.3	109.3	17.9	78.8	24.6	19.7	25.4	10.4	33.4	3.7	261.5
2011	1,003.6	33.9	78.3	109.2	17.9	78.8	24.6	19.7	28.4	10.4	33.4	6.3	261.5
2012	1,018.8	33.9	78.3	109.0	17.9	78.8	24.6	19.7	30.8	10.4	33.4	11.6	261.5
2013	1,030.0	33.9	78.3	108.9	17.9	78.8	24.6	19.7	33.3	10.4	33.4	16.7	261.5
2014	1,037.5	33.9	78.3	108.8	17.9	78.8	24.6	19.7	38.8	10.4	33.4	17.0	261.5
2015	1,061.6	56.7	78.3	108.7	17.9	78.8	24.6	19.7	45.5	10.4	33.4	16.6	261.5
2016	1,080.1	59.2	78.3	108.6	17.9	78.8	24.6	19.7	51.9	10.4	33.4	12.1	261.5
2017	1,093.1	59.2	78.3	108.5	17.9	78.8	24.6	19.7	59.1	10.4	33.4	18.2	261.5
2018	1,100.6	59.6	78.3	108.3	19.3	78.8	24.6	19.7	67.9	10.4	33.4	15.7	261.5
2019	1,117.3	62.6	78.3	108.2	20.4	78.8	24.6	19.7	73.0	10.4	33.4	16.8	261.5

NA = Not available. (1) Includes countries not shown here. (2) Figures are for mainland China only and do not include Hong Kong (0.07 mil oz t in 2019) or Macau. (3) West Germany prior to 1991.

Unemployment Rates in Selected Countries, 1960-2020

Source: *OECD Economic Outlook*, Organisation for Economic Co-operation and Development (OECD); data as of June 4, 2020

Year	Australia	Canada	France	Germany	Greece	Italy	Japan	South Korea	Sweden	Turkey	UK	U.S.
1960	NA	6.9%	1.2%	NA	NA	3.9%	1.6%	NA	2.2%	8.8%	2.8%	5.6%
1965	1.3%	3.9	1.3	NA	NA	3.8	1.2	7.3%	1.5	9.1	2.7	4.5
1970	1.6	5.7	2.1	NA	NA	3.8	1.2	4.4	2.0	5.7	3.5	5.0
1975	4.9	6.9	3.4	NA	NA	4.1	1.9	4.1	2.1	6.9	4.5	8.5
1980	6.1	7.5	5.3	NA	NA	5.3	2.0	5.2	2.6	7.5	6.8	7.2
1985	8.3	10.6	8.8	NA	NA	8.2	2.6	4.0	3.6	6.6	11.4	7.2
1990	6.9	8.2	7.9	NA	NA	8.7	2.1	2.4	2.1	7.5	7.1	5.6
1995	8.5	9.5	10.0	8.2%	9.7%	11.2	3.1	2.1	10.5	7.1	8.6	5.6
2000	6.3	6.8	8.5	7.9	11.6	10.0	4.7	4.4	6.7	6.0	5.5	4.0
2005	5.0	6.8	8.8	11.0	10.0	7.7	4.4	3.7	7.7	9.5	4.8	5.1
2008	4.2	6.1	7.4	7.4	7.8	6.7	4.0	3.2	6.2	10.0	5.7	5.8
2010	5.2	8.0	9.2	7.0	12.7	8.3	5.0	3.7	8.6	11.1	7.9	9.6
2012	5.2	7.3	9.8	5.4	24.4	10.7	4.3	3.2	8.0	8.4	8.0	8.1
2014	6.1	6.9	10.3	5.0	26.5	12.6	3.6	3.5	7.9	9.9	6.2	6.2
2015	6.1	6.9	10.3	4.6	24.9	11.9	3.4	3.6	7.4	10.3	5.4	5.3
2016	5.7	7.0	10.0	4.2	23.5	11.7	3.1	3.7	6.9	10.9	4.9	4.9
2017	5.6	6.3	9.4	3.8	21.5	11.3	2.8	3.7	6.7	10.9	4.4	4.4
2018	5.3	5.8	9.0	3.4	19.3	10.6	2.4	3.9	6.3	11.0	4.1	3.9
2019	5.2	5.7	8.4	3.2	17.3	9.9	2.4	3.8	6.8	13.7	3.8	3.7
2020[1]	7.4	8.9	11.0	4.5	19.4	10.1	3.2	4.5	10.0	15.6	9.1	11.3
2020[2]	7.6	9.4	11.3	4.6	19.6	10.1	3.4	4.6	10.6	16.8	10.4	12.9

NA = Not available. **Note:** Labor market data are subject to differences in definitions across countries. Because of changes in methodology, some data may not be fully comparable over time. (1) Projection in which a second outbreak of COVID-19 is avoided. (2) Projection in which a second COVID-19 outbreak occurs in late 2020.

Personal Tax Rates in Selected Countries, 2019

Source: *Taxing Wages*, Organisation for Economic Co-operation and Development (OECD)

Rates are averages for a single person without children at the income level of the average full-time worker.

(as % of total gross wage earnings before taxes in U.S. dollars with equal purchasing power; ranked by total payment rate)

Country	Total payment rate[1]	Income tax	Employee soc. sec. contribs.	Gross wage earnings	Country	Total payment rate[1]	Income tax	Employee soc. sec. contribs.	Gross wage earnings
Germany	39.3%	19.2%	20.1%	$70,355	Poland	25.0%	7.2%	17.8%	$33,447
Belgium	39.3	25.3	14.0	64,505	Czechia	25.0	14.0	11.0	32,532
Lithuania	36.1	16.6	19.5	31,736	Sweden	24.7	17.7	7.0	51,785
Denmark	35.6	35.6	0.0	63,426	Slovakia	24.2	10.8	13.4	25,924
Slovenia	34.5	12.4	22.1	35,830	United States	24.0	16.4	7.7	57,055
Hungary	33.5	15.0	18.5	31,406	Australia	23.6	23.6	0.0	59,680
Austria	33.2	15.2	18.0	63,204	United Kingdom	23.3	13.9	9.5	59,211
Italy	31.6	22.1	9.5	46,842	Canada	23.2	15.8	7.4	45,813
Finland	30.0	20.2	9.8	52,615	Japan	22.4	7.9	14.5	50,582
Luxembourg	29.9	17.6	12.3	71,102	Spain	21.4	15.0	6.4	43,491
Netherlands	29.7	16.5	13.2	67,518	New Zealand	18.8	18.8	0.0	42,757
Iceland	28.7	28.4	0.3	68,443	Israel	18.3	10.3	8.0	42,577
Latvia	28.7	17.7	11.0	26,198	Switzerland	17.4	11.2	6.2	79,038
Turkey	28.5	13.5	15.0	32,000	Estonia	16.0	14.4	1.6	31,111
France	27.3	16.0	11.3	48,465	South Korea	15.3	6.7	8.7	58,514
Norway	27.3	19.1	8.2	64,066	Mexico	10.8	9.5	1.4	14,187
Portugal	26.9	15.9	11.0	32,702	Chile	7.0	0.0	7.0	24,160
Greece	26.1	10.2	15.9	38,086	OECD[2]	25.9	15.9	10.0	47,855
Ireland	25.9	21.9	4.0	62,430					

(1) Figures may not add up to totals due to rounding. (2) The 36 countries shown here.

Consumer Price Changes in Selected Countries, 1975-2019

Source: *International Financial Statistics*, International Monetary Fund (IMF)

(annual average % change)

Country	1975-80	1980-85	1985-90	1990-95	1995-2000	2000-05	2005-10	2010-12	2012-14	2014-15	2015-16	2016-17	2017-18	2018-19
Canada	8.8%	7.5%	4.5%	2.3%	1.7%	2.3%	1.7%	2.2%	1.4%	1.1%	1.4%	1.6%	2.3%	1.9%
China[1]	NA	NA	9.5	13.1	1.9	1.3	3.0	4.1	2.3	1.4	2.0	1.6	2.1	2.9
France	10.5	9.7	3.0	2.2	1.2	1.9	1.5	2.0	0.7	0.04	0.2	1.0	1.9	1.1
Germany	4.0	3.9	1.4	3.6	1.3	1.5	1.6	2.0	1.2	0.5	0.5	1.5	1.7	1.4
Italy	16.3	13.8	5.7	5.1	2.4	2.4	1.9	2.9	0.7	0.04	-0.1	1.2	1.1	0.6
Japan	6.6	2.8	1.4	1.4	0.3	-0.4	-0.1	-0.2	1.6	0.8	-0.1	0.5	1.0	0.5
Spain	18.6	12.2	6.5	5.2	2.6	3.2	2.4	2.8	0.6	-0.5	-0.2	2.0	1.7	0.7
Sweden	10.5	9.0	6.2	4.2	0.5	1.5	1.5	1.9	-0.1	-0.05	1.0	1.8	2.0	1.8
Switzerland	2.3	4.3	2.5	3.2	0.7	0.8	0.9	-0.2	-0.1	-1.1	-0.4	0.5	0.9	0.4
United Kingdom	14.4	7.2	5.1	3.9	2.0	1.6	2.6	3.2	1.9	0.4	1.0	2.6	2.3	1.7
United States	8.9	5.5	4.0	3.1	2.5	2.6	2.2	2.6	1.5	0.1	1.3	2.1	2.4	1.8
All countries	NA	NA	NA	NA	NA	NA	NA	4.6	4.0	3.5	3.4	3.8	5.1	NA

NA = Not available. (1) Figures for mainland China only and do not include Hong Kong (2.9% in 2018-19) or Macau (3.0% in 2017-18).

Number of Days Off Work Per Year in Selected Countries

Source: Organisation for Economic Co-operation and Development; Center for Economic and Policy Research

Entitlements are generally for full-time, full-year private-sector employees working a five-day week who have been with their current employer for at least one year. The U.S. is the only OECD country without a national statute that entitles workers to a minimum number of days off per year.

Country	Paid days off[1]	Public holidays[2]	Total minimum days off	Country	Paid days off[1]	Public holidays[2]	Total minimum days off	Country	Paid days off[1]	Public holidays[2]	Total minimum days off
Australia	20	8	28	Germany	20	10-13	30-33	Netherlands	20	9	29
Austria	25	13	38	Greece	20	11	31	New Zealand	20	11	31
Belgium	20	10	30	Hungary	20	11	31	Norway	21	10	31
Bulgaria	20	12	32	Iceland	24	12	36	Poland	20	12	32
Canada	10	9	19	Ireland	20	9	29	Portugal	22	12	34
Chile	15	15	30	Israel	12	9	21	Romania	20	13	33
Costa Rica	10	11	21	Italy	20	12	32	Slovakia	20	15	35
Croatia	20	13	33	Japan	10	19	29	Slovenia	20	12	32
Cyprus	20	14-17	34-37	Korea, South	15	15	30	Spain	22	14	36
Czechia	20	13	33	Latvia	20	12	32	Sweden	25	11	36
Denmark	25	11	36	Lithuania	20	12	32	Switzerland	20	9	29
Estonia	20	11	31	Luxembourg	26	11	37	Turkey	12	14	26
Finland	25	11	36	Malta	24	14	38	UK	28	8	36
France	25	11	36	Mexico	6	7	13	U.S.	0	NA[3]	0

NA = Not applicable. (1) Statutory minimum. (2) Generally set at the national or federal level. May vary at the state level. In some countries, including the U.S., public holidays do not have to be given as paid leave. (3) The government designates 10 federal holidays per year, though private-sector employers decide how much paid leave to offer.

International Migrants by Destination and Origin, 2000, 2019

Source: *International Migrant Stock: The 2019 Revision*, Dept. of Economic and Social Affairs, UN Population Division

(numbers in thousands)

	Places hosting the most international migrants				Places of origin with the largest diaspora populations			
	2019		**2000**		**2019**		**2000**	
	Country/terr.	Migrants	Country/terr.	Migrants	Country/terr.	Population	Country/terr.	Population
1.	U.S.	50,661.1	U.S.	34,814.1	India	17,510.9	Russia	10,721.4
2.	Germany	13,132.1	Russia	11,900.3	Mexico	11,796.2	Mexico	9,562.9
3.	Saudi Arabia	13,122.3	Germany	8,992.6	China[1]	10,732.3	India	7,932.4
4.	Russia	11,640.6	India	6,411.3	Russia	10,491.7	China[1]	5,885.0
5.	UK	9,552.1	France	6,278.7	Syria	8,225.5	Ukraine	5,596.9
6.	UAE	8,587.3	Ukraine	5,527.1	Bangladesh	7,835.2	Bangladesh	5,442.7
7.	France	8,334.9	Canada	5,511.9	Pakistan	6,303.3	Afghanistan	4,606.4
8.	Canada	7,960.7	Saudi Arabia	5,263.4	Ukraine	5,901.1	UK	3,866.2
9.	Australia	7,549.3	UK	4,730.2	Philippines	5,377.3	Kazakhstan	3,554.5
10.	Italy	6,273.7	Australia	4,386.3	Afghanistan	5,120.8	Pakistan	3,401.3
11.	Spain	6,104.2	Pakistan	4,181.9	Indonesia	4,533.0	Germany	3,235.4
12.	Turkey	5,876.8	Kazakhstan	2,874.2	Poland	4,447.0	Philippines	3,092.3
13.	India	5,154.7	Iran	2,803.8	UK	4,275.0	Italy	3,067.6
14.	Ukraine	4,964.3	Hong Kong	2,669.1	Germany	4,014.2	Turkey	2,891.9
15.	South Africa	4,224.3	UAE	2,447.0	Kazakhstan	4,005.6	Palestine	2,768.0
16.	Kazakhstan	3,705.6	Côte d'Ivoire	2,163.6	Palestine	3,890.7	Indonesia	2,431.5
17.	Thailand	3,635.1	Italy	2,121.7	Myanmar	3,699.5	Morocco	2,077.2
18.	Malaysia	3,430.4	Jordan	1,927.8	Romania	3,572.8	Poland	2,048.4
19.	Jordan	3,346.7	Israel	1,851.3	Egypt	3,547.6	Portugal	1,995.4
20.	Pakistan	3,258.0	Japan	1,686.4	Turkey	3,493.1	U.S.	1,991.8
21.	Kuwait	3,034.8	Spain	1,657.3	U.S.	3,167.1	South Korea	1,952.2
22.	Hong Kong	2,942.3	Switzerland	1,570.8	Morocco	3,136.1	Vietnam	1,885.1
23.	Iran	2,682.2	Netherlands	1,556.3	Italy	3,077.8	Egypt	1,708.5
24.	Switzerland	2,572.0	Argentina	1,540.2	Colombia	2,869.0	Belarus	1,685.7
25.	Côte d'Ivoire	2,549.1	Malaysia	1,463.6	Vietnam	2,684.0	Azerbaijan	1,628.5
26.	Japan	2,498.9	Uzbekistan	1,406.5	Portugal	2,631.6	Puerto Rico	1,600.8
27.	Oman	2,286.2	Singapore	1,351.7	South Sudan	2,608.2	Uzbekistan	1,576.0
28.	Netherlands	2,282.8	Turkey	1,281.0	Venezuela	2,519.8	France	1,555.6
29.	Qatar	2,229.7	Belgium	1,268.4	France	2,296.5	Bosnia and Herzegovina	1,496.7
30.	Argentina	2,212.9	Thailand	1,257.8	Nepal	2,285.4	Colombia	1,436.4
	World	**271,642.1**	**World**	**173,588.4**	**World**	**271,642.1**	**World**	**173,588.4**

(1) Not incl. Hong Kong or Macau.

Refugees and Other Populations of Concern, 2010-19

Source: *UNHCR Global Trends*, United Nations High Commissioner for Refugees (UNHCR)

Refugees are persons recognized under the 1951 UN Refugee Convention/1967 Protocol or the 1969 OAU (Org. of African Unity) Refugee Convention, those recognized in accordance with the UNHCR Statute, and persons granted or receiving protection. The UNHCR also extends assistance to internally displaced persons (IDPs), although they legally remain under their home country's protection. Stateless persons are not considered nationals under any state under the operation of its laws. Others of concern comprises persons who do not necessarily belong in any one category. Population as of year-end.

Category	2010	2012	2014	2016	2017	2018	2019	% change 2018-19
Refugees	10,549,700	10,498,000	14,380,100	17,187,500	19,941,300	20,360,600	20,445,900	0.4%
Asylum-seekers (pending cases)	837,500	942,800	1,796,200	2,826,500	3,090,900	3,503,300	4,149,900	18.5
Returned refugees[1]	197,700	525,900	126,900	552,200	667,400	593,800	317,200	–46.6
IDPs	14,697,900	17,670,400	32,274,600	36,627,100	39,118,500	41,425,100	43,503,400	5.0
Returned IDPs[1]	2,923,300	1,545,400	1,822,700	6,511,100	4,229,000	2,312,900	5,343,800	131.0
Stateless persons	3,463,000	3,335,800	3,492,100	3,242,200	2,796,200	2,820,300	4,162,000	47.6
Others of concern	1,255,600	1,329,700	1,052,800	803,100	1,596,200	1,182,900	6,140,700	419.1
Venezuelans displaced abroad[2]	NA	NA	NA	NA	NA	2,592,900	3,582,200	38.2
Total	**33,924,700**	**35,848,000**	**54,945,400**	**67,749,800**	**71,439,500**	**74,791,900**	**86,531,700**	**15.7**

NA = Not available. (1) Persons who have returned to their place of origin in that year. (2) Persons who have left Venezuela but who have not applied for asylum. Prior to 2018, this pop. was included in "Others of concern."

Refugees and People in a Refugee-Like Situation, 2019

Source: *UNHCR Global Trends*, United Nations High Commissioner for Refugees (UNHCR)

Refugees are persons recognized under the 1951 UN Refugee Convention/1967 Protocol or the 1969 OAU (Org. of African Unity) Refugee Convention, the refugee definition in the 1984 Cartagena Declaration as incorporated into national laws, those recognized in accordance with the UNHCR Statute, and persons granted or receiving protection. Persons in a refugee-like situation have not yet had their refugee status ascertained. Only countries hosting 50,000 or more refugees and people in a refugee-like situation are shown; of those countries, only places hosting 5,000 or more persons are given, in decreasing order. As of year-end.

Place of asylum	Origin of most refugees (excl. asylum-seekers with pending cases)	Number
Africa		**6,803,799**
Algeria	Western Sahara, Syria	98,604
Burundi	Dem. Rep. of the Congo	78,473
Cameroon	Central African Republic, Nigeria	406,260
Chad	Sudan, Central African Republic, Nigeria	442,672
Dem. Rep. of the Congo	Rwanda, Central African Republic, South Sudan, Burundi	523,734
Egypt	Syria, Palestinian[1], Sudan, South Sudan, Eritrea	258,401
Ethiopia	South Sudan, Somalia, Eritrea, Sudan	733,125
Kenya	Somalia, South Sudan, Dem. Rep. of the Congo, Ethiopia, Burundi	438,901
Mauritania	Mali, Western Sahara	84,909
Niger	Nigeria, Mali	180,006
Nigeria	Cameroon	54,166
Rwanda	Dem. Rep. of the Congo, Burundi	145,057
South Africa	Somalia, Dem. Rep. of the Congo, Ethiopia, Congo Republic	89,285
South Sudan	Sudan, Dem. Rep. of the Congo	298,313
Sudan	South Sudan, Eritrea, Syria, Central African Republic, Ethiopia	1,055,489
Tanzania	Burundi, Dem. Rep. of the Congo	242,171
Uganda	South Sudan, Dem. Rep. of the Congo, Burundi, Somalia, Rwanda, Eritrea	1,359,464
Zambia	Dem. Rep. of the Congo, Burundi	57,521
Asia		**9,892,341**
Afghanistan	Pakistan	72,228
Bangladesh	Myanmar (Burma)	854,782
China	Vietnam	303,381
India	China, Sri Lanka, stateless[2], Afghanistan	195,105
Iran	Afghanistan, Iraq	979,435
Iraq	Syria, Turkey, Palestinian[1], Iran	273,992
Jordan	Syria, Iraq	693,684
Lebanon	Syria	916,156
Malaysia	Myanmar (Burma)	129,095
Pakistan	Afghanistan	1,419,606
Thailand	Myanmar (Burma)	97,571
Turkey	Syria	3,579,531
Yemen	Somalia, Ethiopia	268,511
Europe		**2,958,113**
Austria	Syria, Afghanistan, Russia, Iraq, Somalia, Iran	135,955
Belgium	Syria, various/unknown, Iraq, Afghanistan	61,677
France	Various/unknown, Afghanistan, Sri Lanka, Sudan, Syria, Dem. Rep. of the Congo, Russia, Serbia-Kosovo, Turkey, Guinea, Cambodia, Iraq, Vietnam, China, Laos, Eritrea, Bangladesh, Albania, Mauritania, Côte d'Ivoire, Mali	407,923
Germany	Syria, Iraq, Afghanistan, Eritrea, Iran, various/unknown, Turkey, Somalia, stateless[2], Russia, Serbia-Kosovo, Nigeria	1,146,685
Greece	Syria, Afghanistan, various/unknown, Iraq	80,468
Italy	Nigeria, Pakistan, Afghanistan, Mali, Somalia, The Gambia, Bangladesh, Senegal, Côte d'Ivoire, Eritrea, Iraq, Ukraine, Ghana	207,619
Netherlands	Syria, Eritrea, Somalia, Iraq, Afghanistan	94,430
Norway	Syria, Eritrea, Somalia, Afghanistan	53,888
Spain	Venezuela, Syria	57,761
Sweden	Syria, Afghanistan, Eritrea, stateless[2], Somalia, Iraq, Iran	253,794
Switzerland	Eritrea, Syria, Afghanistan, Sri Lanka	110,168
United Kingdom	Iran, Eritrea, Sudan, Syria, Afghanistan, Pakistan, various/unknown, Iraq, Sri Lanka	133,094
Latin America		**255,501**
Ecuador	Colombia	104,574
Venezuela	Colombia	67,755
North America and the Caribbean		**446,151**
Canada	Nigeria, Haiti, China, Turkey, Pakistan	101,760
United States	China, El Salvador, Guatemala, Venezuela, Haiti, Honduras, Egypt, Mexico, Ethiopia, Syria, India, Nepal, Russia, various/unknown, Eritrea, Iran, Iraq, Cameroon	341,711
Oceania		**89,994**
Australia	Iraq, Afghanistan, Iran, Pakistan	76,764
Total		**20,445,899**

(1) Number includes Palestinians under the UNHCR mandate only. (2) Persons not considered nationals under any state under the operation of its laws.

Internally Displaced Persons, 2019

Source: Internal Displacement Monitoring Centre, Norwegian Refugee Council

Internally displaced persons (IDPs) are people who have been forced to move due to conflict or disasters (e.g., earthquakes) but who have not crossed into another country. As such, they are not protected by international refugee law and legally remain under the protection of their home country. Estimates shown are of those displaced by conflict and violence only as of year-end 2019; they may comprise only registered IDPs or those displaced from a certain area of a country.

Country	Number	Country	Number	Country	Number
Afghanistan	2,993,000	Haiti	2,100	Papua New Guinea	14,000
Azerbaijan	351,000	Honduras	247,000	Peru	60,000
Bangladesh	427,000	India	470,000	Philippines	182,000
Benin	3,700	Indonesia	40,000	Russia	1,800
Bolivia	31	Iraq	1,555,000	Senegal	8,400
Bosnia and Herzegovina	99,000	Kenya	162,000	Sierra Leone	5,500
Burkina Faso	560,000	Kosovo	16,000	Somalia	2,648,000
Burundi	23,000	Lebanon	7,000	South Africa	250
Cameroon	969,000	Libya	451,000	South Sudan[2]	1,352,000
Central African Republic	592,000	Madagascar	3,000	Sri Lanka	27,000
Chad	176,000	Malawi	150	Sudan[2]	2,134,000
Colombia	5,576,000	Mali	208,000	Syria	6,495,000
Congo, Dem. Rep. of.	5,512,000	Mexico	345,000	Thailand	41,000
Congo Republic	134,000	Mozambique	110,000	Togo	2,000
Côte d'Ivoire	303,000	Myanmar (Burma)	457,000	Tunisia	4
Cyprus	228,000	Niger	195,000	Turkey	1,099,000
Egypt	65,000	Nigeria	2,583,000	Uganda	32,000
Ethiopia	1,414,000	North Macedonia	140	Ukraine	730,000
Georgia	301,000	Pakistan	106,000	Yemen	3,635,000
Ghana	230	Palestine[1]	243,000	**Total**	**45.7 mil**
Guatemala	242,000				

(1) Populations in the West Bank, East Jerusalem, and Gaza. (2) Number does not incl. an est. 31,000 IDPs from Abyei Area, disputed territory between Sudan and South Sudan.

Countries With Highest Mortality Rates by Selected Causes of Death

Source: *World Health Statistics 2020*, World Health Organization (WHO)

(per 100,000 live births or 100,000 population)

Rank	Country	Maternal mortality ratio, 2017	Rank	Country	Suicide mortality rate, 2016	Rank	Country	Mortality rate due to homicide, 2017
1.	South Sudan	1,150	1.	Lithuania	31.9	1.	El Salvador	82.3
2.	Chad	1,140	2.	Russia	31.0	2.	Venezuela	62.0
3.	Sierra Leone	1,120	3.	Guyana	29.2	3.	Honduras	57.8
4.	Nigeria	917	4.	Korea, South	26.9	4.	Jamaica	57.4
5.	Central African Rep.	829	5.	Belarus	26.2	5.	Lesotho	46.2
6.	Somalia	829	6.	Suriname	22.8	6.	Colombia	41.7
7.	Mauritania	766	7.	Kazakhstan	22.5	7.	South Africa	39.7
8.	Guinea-Bissau	667	8.	Ukraine	22.4	8.	Belize	36.7
9.	Liberia	661	9.	Lesotho	21.2	9.	Trinidad and Tobago	36.2
10.	Afghanistan	638		Latvia	21.2	10.	Brazil	33.3
11.	Côte d'Ivoire	617	11.	Belgium	20.7	11.	The Bahamas	32.2
12.	The Gambia	597	12.	Hungary	19.1	12.	St. Vincent and the Grenadines	28.3
13.	Guinea	576	13.	Slovenia	18.6	13.	Mexico	25.7
14.	Mali	562	14.	Japan	18.5	14.	Guatemala	24.7
15.	Burundi	548	15.	Uruguay	18.4	15.	St. Lucia	23.3
16.	Lesotho	544	16.	Estonia	17.8	16.	Central African Republic	22.9
17.	Cameroon	529	17.	France	17.7	17.	Haiti	19.9
18.	Tanzania	524	18.	Switzerland	17.2	18.	Guyana	18.6
19.	Niger	509	19.	Croatia	16.5	19.	Namibia	18.4
20.	Eritrea	480	20.	Equatorial Guinea	16.4	20.	Eswatini	18.1
	Global	**211**		**Global**	**10.6**		**Global**	**6.3**

Note: 2016 rankings did not include countries with a population of less than 90,000.

Global HIV/AIDS Status, 2019

Source: HIV Justice Network, Joint United Nations Programme on HIV/AIDS (UNAIDS)

Between 2004—when the number of AIDS-related deaths reached a peak of 1.7 million—and 2019, there was an approximate 59.4% drop in annual deaths due to AIDS. And while the number of new infections each year has also decreased, from a high of 2.8 million in 1998, the year-on-year declines have gotten smaller, offset by increases in new infections in Eastern Europe and Central Asia, the Middle East and North Africa, and Latin America. The risk of HIV infection remained high for certain groups, including sex workers, people who inject drugs, men who have sex with men, and transgender persons (particularly transgender women). These key populations and their sexual partners accounted for more than 60% of new infections in 2019. Tuberculosis remained the leading cause of death for those with HIV. In 2019, about 67% of all people living with HIV had access to treatment. Laws allowing specifically for HIV criminalization existed in 75 countries as of year-end 2018 and 32 U.S. states as of July 2020.

An estimated $562.6 billion was spent on the HIV/AIDS epidemic in 2000-15 according to a study published in *The Lancet* in 2018. At year-end 2019, some $18.6 billion (in constant 2016 dollars) was available to low- and middle-income countries in responding to AIDS.

Current and New HIV/AIDS Cases and Deaths by Region, 2019

Source: Joint United Nations Programme on HIV/AIDS (UNAIDS)

Region	Number living with HIV	Percent of world total[1]	New HIV infections	AIDS-related deaths
Eastern and Southern Africa	20,700,000	54.5%	730,000	300,000
Asia and the Pacific	5,800,000	15.3	300,000	160,000
Western and Central Africa	4,900,000	12.9	240,000	140,000
Western and Central Europe and North America	2,200,000	5.8	65,000	12,000
Latin America	2,100,000	5.5	120,000	37,000
Eastern Europe and Central Asia	1,700,000	4.5	170,000	35,000
Caribbean	330,000	0.9	13,000	6,900
Middle East and North Africa	240,000	0.6	20,000	8,000
World[2]	**38,000,000**	**100.0**	**1,700,000**	**690,000**

(1) Population within a region living with HIV as a percentage of population worldwide living with HIV. (2) Figures may not add up to totals because of rounding.

Drinking Water, Sanitation, and Hygiene, 2017

Source: World Health Organization (WHO) and United Nations Children's Fund (UNICEF)

In 2017, an estimated 90% of the world's population had access to at least basic drinking water services, up from 82% in 2000. A gap remained, however, between coverage in urban (97%) and rural areas (81%). Having basic drinking water service means access to an off-premise improved water source, collecting water from which takes up to 30 min. roundtrip. As of the same year, 74% of people worldwide, compared to 56% in 2000, used at least basic sanitation services; 18% of the rural population and 1% of the urban population still practiced open defecation. Those without access to improved sanitation facilities, which are designed to prevent contact with human waste, are at increased risk of contracting a variety of infectious and parasitic diseases such as diarrhea, malaria, and hepatitis A.

The G7 countries had near-universal (99% or greater) access to at least basic water and sanitation services in 2017. In comparison, while 97% of Russia's population had access to at least basic drinking water services, only 90% had access to at least basic sanitation services. In China, the figures were 93% and 85%, respectively.

In 2017, only 60% of the world population met the WHO and UNICEF's sustainable development goal of having home access to a basic handwashing facility with soap and water available.

Lowest Access to Basic Drinking Water Services, 2017

Source: World Health Organization (WHO) and United Nations Children's Fund (UNICEF)

A person who spends up to 30 min. roundtrip collecting water from an off-premise improved water source is said to have basic access to drinking water. Improved water sources protect from outside contamination and include piped water, boreholes or tube-wells, dug wells, rainwater, and packaged or delivered water.

(ranked by % of total pop. with at least basic access)

Rank	Country/area	Total	Urban	Rural	Rank	Country/area	Total	Urban	Rural
1.	Chad	38.7%	69.8%	29.5%	16.	Zambia	60.0%	83.9%	42.0%
2.	South Sudan	40.7	64.8	34.9	17.	Sudan	60.3	73.8	53.2
3.	Ethiopia	41.1	80.3	31.1	18.	Cameroon	60.4	77.3	39.0
4.	Papua New Guinea	41.3	85.8	34.6	19.	Sierra Leone	60.8	75.8	50.1
5.	Congo, Dem. Rep. of	43.2	69.3	22.8	20.	Burundi	60.8	89.8	56.6
6.	Burkina Faso	47.9	79.9	35.0		Australia and New Zealand	>99	>99	>99
7.	Uganda	49.1	75.1	41.3		Central and Southern Asia	93	96	91
8.	Niger	50.3	84.3	43.6		Eastern and South-Eastern Asia	93	98	86
9.	Somalia	52.4	82.9	28.1		Europe and Northern America	99	>99	98
10.	Madagascar	54.4	85.8	36.3		Latin America and the Caribbean	97	99	88
11.	Mozambique	55.7	84.3	40.0		Northern Africa and Western Asia	92	97	84
12.	Angola	55.8	71.2	27.4		Oceania	55	92	44
13.	Tanzania	56.7	85.5	42.5		Sub-Saharan Africa	61	84	45
14.	Rwanda	57.7	82.2	52.6		**World**	**90**	**97**	**81**
15.	Kenya	58.9	84.6	49.6					

Lowest Access to Basic Sanitation Services, 2017

Source: World Health Organization (WHO) and United Nations Children's Fund (UNICEF)

Improved sanitation facilities are those designed to hygienically prevent human contact with feces and urine, including sewer or septic system connections, ventilated improved pit latrines, and composting toilets, and are not shared with other households. If human waste is not safely managed on- or off-site, then access to sanitation services is considered basic.

(ranked by % of total pop. with at least basic access)

Rank	Country/area	Total	Urban	Rural	Rank	Country/area	Total	Urban	Rural
1.	Ethiopia	7.3%	19.6%	4.2%	16.	Guinea-Bissau	20.5%	36.9%	8.2%
2.	Chad	8.3	30.1	1.9	17.	Guinea	22.7	33.8	16.6
3.	Madagascar	10.5	17.8	6.3	18.	Malawi	26.2	34.1	24.7
4.	South Sudan	11.3	36.9	5.2	19.	Zambia	26.4	36.2	18.9
5.	Papua New Guinea	12.9	47.8	7.7	20.	Kenya	29.1	34.7	27.0
6.	Niger	13.6	43.8	7.7		Australia and New Zealand	>99	NA	NA
7.	Sierra Leone	15.7	25.7	8.5		Central and Southern Asia	61	74	55
8.	Togo	16.1	28.6	7.4		Eastern and South-Eastern Asia	84	91	75
9.	Benin	16.5	26.5	7.6		Europe and Northern America	98	99	94
10.	Liberia	17.0	27.7	5.9		Latin America and the Caribbean	87	91	70
11.	Ghana	18.5	23.7	11.9		Northern Africa and Western Asia	88	95	76
12.	Uganda	18.5	26.1	16.2		Oceania	30	70	18
13.	Burkina Faso	19.4	39.4	11.3		Sub-Saharan Africa	31	44	22
14.	Congo	20.2	27.2	6.3		**World**	**74**	**85**	**59**
15.	Dem. Rep. of the Congo	20.5	23.4	18.2					

NA = Not available.

Foreign Development Aid Donors, 2017-19

Source: Development Assistance Committee (DAC), Organisation for Economic Co-operation and Development (OECD)
The amount of official development assistance (ODA), in the form of grants or loans, each DAC member country disbursed to developing countries is given here. Numbers are net flows, or amounts disbursed less repayments on earlier loans. The OECD uses the ODA grant equivalent to better reflect donor effort, with more generous loans having a higher ODA value.

(ranked by size of ODA grant equivalent as % of 2019 gross national income [GNI]; 2019 figures are prelim.)

Rank	Donor	ODA as % of GNI 2019	ODA in mil of current U.S. dollars			Rank	Donor	ODA as % of GNI 2019	ODA in mil of current U.S. dollars		
			2017	2018	2019				2017	2018	2019
1.	Luxembourg ..	1.05%	$424.2	$473.4	$474.4	18.	Italy	0.24%	$5,858.0	$5,098.3	$4,732.9
2.	Norway	1.02	4,125.0	4,257.6	4,292.0	19.	Australia	0.22	3,036.0	3,149.0	2,949.3
3.	Sweden.	0.99	5,563.3	6,000.0	5,396.0	20.	Hungary	0.22	148.7	284.9	316.7
4.	Denmark.	0.71	2,448.0	2,576.8	2,534.1	21.	Spain	0.21	2,560.3	2,589.6	2,661.7
5.	UK.	0.70	18,103.4	19,462.2	19,342.7	22.	Slovenia	0.16	75.8	83.5	86.1
6.	Germany.	0.60	25,005.1	25,670.4	23,729.2	23.	United States	0.16	34,732.0	33,787.1	33,889.1
7.	Netherlands . .	0.59	4,958.5	5,616.6	5,292.0	24.	Portugal	0.16	380.7	387.8	344.2
8.	Switzerland. . .	0.44	3,146.6	3,097.1	3,089.3	25.	South Korea . .	0.15	2,201.4	2,423.4	2,574.9
9.	France.	0.44	11,330.9	12,839.7	11,979.8	26.	Greece	0.14	313.6	290.4	308.1
10.	Belgium.	0.42	2,196.2	2,348.0	2,210.7	27.	Czechia.	0.13	304.1	305.4	306.1
11.	Finland	0.42	1,083.8	984.0	1,144.0	28.	Slovakia	0.12	119.2	137.7	128.7
12.	Ireland	0.31	838.0	934.3	934.5	29.	Poland.	0.12	679.5	759.2	668.9
13.	Japan	0.29	11,462.7	10,064.3	11,639.2		**Total DAC countries**	**0.30**	**147,168.8**	**150,058.5**	**147,373.5**
14.	New Zealand . .	0.28	449.8	556.0	558.8		**G7 countries[1]** . . .	**0.29**	**110,796.9**	**111,562.5**	**109,827.2**
15.	Iceland	0.27	68.3	74.2	67.4		**EU institutions**	**NA**	**16,440.4**	**17,116.3**	**15,153.6**
16.	Canada.	0.27	4,304.9	4,640.5	4,514.3		**Total non-DAC**				
17.	Austria	0.27	1,251.3	1,167.2	1,208.3		**countries[2]**	**NA**	**17,201.4**	**20,132.8**	**18,818.3**

NA = Not applicable/available. (1) Canada, France, Germany, Italy, Japan, the UK, and the U.S. (2) Countries not shown here.

Recipients of U.S. Official Development Assistance, 2017-18

Source: Development Assistance Committee (DAC), Organisation for Economic Co-operation and Development (OECD)
(net flows of official development assistance, in mil of current U.S. dollars; ranked by 2018 numbers)

Rank	Country	2017	2018	Rank	Country	2017	2018
1.	Jordan.	$894.96	$1,134.97	12.	Iraq.	$412.06	$555.46
2.	Afghanistan.	1,215.11	914.37	13.	Mozambique.	503.53	519.64
3.	Nigeria	726.78	841.76	14.	Zambia	495.15	479.14
4.	Kenya	855.41	829.23	15.	Dem. Rep. of the Congo	442.08	464.98
5.	Ethiopia.	1,026.68	821.32	16.	Pakistan	492.24	464.35
6.	Syria	627.38	694.53	17.	Malawi	446.90	442.08
7.	South Sudan.	886.04	678.65	18.	Somalia.	332.04	382.14
8.	Tanzania	597.02	658.67	19.	Colombia	304.53	339.21
9.	Uganda	639.98	611.41	20.	Haiti	416.79	334.05
10.	Yemen	439.42	598.67		**Total developing countries**	**30,006.21**	**29,934.72**
11.	South Africa	596.05	575.65				

Nuclear Powers of the World

As of Sept. 2020, eight countries were acknowledged nuclear weapons states: the **U.S., UK, France, China, India, Pakistan, Russia, North Korea. Israel** was presumed to have an arsenal.

All of the more than 40 nations with the knowledge or technology to produce nuclear weapons have signed the Nuclear Non-Proliferation Treaty (NPT) with the exception of Israel, India, and Pakistan. After expelling Intl. Atomic Energy Agency (IAEA) inspectors in Dec. 2002, North Korea announced on Jan. 10, 2003, its withdrawal from the NPT effective the following day.

Iran argued for the right to pursue the peaceful application of nuclear technology, but the IAEA maintained the country had violated the NPT. In 2015, the so-called P5+1 (the five permanent members of the UN Security Council plus Germany) signed a Joint Comprehensive Plan of Action (JCPOA) with Iran, which agreed to curb its ability to enrich uranium as well as reduce its current stockpile of the material. Nuclear-related sanctions on Iran were lifted on Jan. 16, 2016, after the IAEA certified the country had implemented key measures. The U.S.,

under Pres. Donald Trump, pulled out of the JCPOA on May 8, 2018, and reimposed sanctions Nov. 5. The other JCPOA states maintained their commitment. In July 2019, Iran resumed enriching uranium, increasing its stockpile beyond what the deal allowed. Even while the U.S. in Aug. 2020 sought a reimposition of all UN sanctions on Iran, Iran and the remaining parties held out hope of a deal being salvaged.

North Korea conducted six nuclear tests between 2006 and Sept. 2017. In July 2017, it held two intercontinental ballistic missile tests, which appeared to indicate North Korean missiles were capable of reaching the U.S. In response, the UN Security Council unanimously approved new sanctions on North Korea. The country resumed missile testing in May 2019. Although Trump and North Korean leader Kim Jong Un met in June 2018 and in Feb. and June 2019, no formal agreement on denuclearization was reached. An interim UN report Aug. 2020 indicated that several countries believed North Korea had "probably developed miniaturized nuclear devices," as reported by Reuters.

Estimated Numbers of Nuclear Weapons by Country, 1945-2020

Source: *Bulletin of the Atomic Scientists*; Carnegie Endowment for International Peace; Federation of American Scientists (FAS); Natural Resources Defense Council (NRDC); Nuclear Threat Initiative (NTI); Stockholm Intl. Peace Research Inst. (SIPRI)

Year	United States	USSR/Russia	United Kingdom	France	China	Israel[1]	India	Pakistan	Total[2]
1945	6	—	—	—	—	—	—	—	6
1950	369	5	—	—	—	—	—	—	374
1960	20,434	1,605	30	—	—	—	—	—	22,069
1970	26,662	11,643	280	36	75	8	—	—	38,696
1980	24,304	30,062	350	250	280	31	—	—	55,246
1990	21,004	37,000	300	505	430	53	—	—	59,239
2000	10,577	21,000	185	470	400	72	—	—	32,632
2010	9,400	12,300	225	300	240	60-80	60-80	70-90	22,400
2020[3]	5,800	6,372	195	290	320	90	160	160	13,410

(1) Israel is widely presumed to have a nuclear stockpile although it has never confirmed nor denied its nuclear status. (2) Numbers may not add up to totals due to rounding and include deployed warheads, those in reserve or in a military stockpile, and retired warheads awaiting dismantlement. (3) As of Apr. North Korea was estimated to have produced sufficient material for about 35 warheads, although how many were assembled or deployed was difficult to assess.

Nuclear Arms Treaties and Negotiations: A Historical Overview

Aug. 5, 1963: Partial (Limited) Test Ban Treaty signed by the UK, U.S., and USSR, went into effect Oct. 10, 1963. Prohibits parties from testing or participating in the testing of nuclear weapons in the atmosphere, in outer space, and under water.

July 1, 1968: Nuclear Non-Proliferation Treaty (NPT) opened to signatures, went into effect Mar. 5, 1970. With the UK, U.S., and USSR as major signers, the parties agree not to help non-nuclear nations get or make nuclear weapons, though such nations can pursue the peaceful application of nuclear energy.

On May 11, 1995, parties to the treaty voted to extend it indefinitely. As of Sept. 2020, 191 states were party to the treaty, not including North Korea, which withdrew in 2003. Israel, India, and Pakistan were not signatories.

May 26, 1972: The Strategic Arms Limitation Talks (SALT I) led to the signing of two agreements by the U.S. and USSR: the **Treaty on the Limitation of Anti-Ballistic Missile Systems** (or **ABM Treaty**) and an interim agreement. These agreements cap the numbers of intercontinental ballistic missile (ICBM) launchers and submarine-launched ballistic missile (SLBM) launchers.

July 3, 1974: Treaty on the Limitation of Underground Nuclear Weapon Tests (or **Threshold Test Ban Treaty**) signed by the U.S. and USSR. Limits underground testing of nuclear weapons to yields of 150 kilotons or less. On May 28, 1976, U.S. and Russia signed the **Peaceful Nuclear Explosions Treaty**, governing explosions outside weapons test sites. Both treaties entered into force Dec. 11, 1990.

June 18, 1979: Strategic Offensive Arms Limitation Treaty (or **SALT II**) signed by the U.S. and USSR. Limited each side to 2,400 missile launchers and heavy bombers; ceiling to apply until Jan. 1, 1985. Never ratified; superseded by START I.

Dec. 8, 1987: Intermediate-Range Nuclear Forces (INF) Treaty signed by the U.S. and USSR. Eliminated all U.S. and Soviet intermediate- and shorter-range nuclear missiles, the first time a treaty banned an entire category of nuclear weapons and established a comprehensive verification system. Entered into force June 1, 1988. The treaty lapsed Aug. 2, 2019, after the U.S., citing Russian "noncompliance," gave formal notice of its withdrawal from the treaty, Feb. 2, 2019, and Russia responded by suspending its participation.

July 31, 1991: Strategic Arms Reduction Treaty (START I) signed by the USSR and U.S. to reduce long-range nuclear forces

no later than seven years after the treaty entered into force. This was the first treaty to mandate reductions in so-called strategic nuclear weapons by the superpowers.

With the Soviet Union breakup in Dec. 1991, four former republics became independent nations with strategic nuclear arms: Russia, Ukraine, Kazakhstan, and Belarus. Under the **Lisbon Protocol** of May 1992, Ukraine, Kazakhstan, and Belarus agreed to accede to the NPT as non-nuclear-weapon states, to destroy or transfer their nuclear weapons to Russia, and to ratify START I. START I expired on Dec. 5, 2009.

Jan. 3, 1993: START II signed by the U.S. and Russia, ratified by the two on Jan. 26, 1996, and Apr. 14, 2000, respectively. Called for further reductions in their long-range nuclear arsenals. Both sides withdrew before the treaty went into force.

Sept. 24, 1996: Comprehensive Nuclear-Test-Ban Treaty (CTBT) signed by 71 countries, including the five nuclear-weapons states (China, France, Russia, UK, U.S.). The CTBT bans all nuclear explosions. It is intended to prevent the nuclear powers from developing more advanced weapons while limiting the ability of other states to acquire such devices. As of Sept. 2020, the CTBT had been signed by 184 nations and ratified by 168 of them. It will enter into force only after all Annex 2 states—the 44 states with nuclear capabilities at the time of the treaty's final negotiations—have signed and ratified it. Only 36 have done so to date. Of the remaining Annex 2 countries, five have yet to ratify the CTBT (China, Egypt, Iran, Israel, the U.S.), and three have yet to sign it (India, North Korea, Pakistan).

Dec. 13, 2001: The U.S. announced its intention to withdraw from the ABM Treaty in 180 days, arguing that it hindered the government in protecting itself from "future terrorist or rogue state missile attacks." Russia responded by withdrawing from START II, stating that U.S. withdrawal from the ABM Treaty effectively invalidated START II.

May 24, 2002: Strategic Offensive Reductions Treaty (SORT or **Moscow Treaty)** signed by the U.S. and Russia, entered into force June 1, 2003. Committed both countries to cutting nuclear arsenals to 1,700-2,200 warheads each by Dec. 31, 2012. SORT lapsed upon entry into force of the New START Treaty.

Apr. 8, 2010: New START Treaty signed by the U.S. and Russia, entered into force Feb. 5, 2011. It limits each country's arsenal of deployed strategic nuclear warheads to 1,550. The treaty was set to expire Feb. 2021.

Major International Organizations

African Union (AU), inaugurated July 9, 2002, in Durban, South Africa, following disbanding of the Organization of African Unity (OAU). Africa's 55 countries make up its members. (Morocco withdrew in 1984 after the OAU admitted Western Sahara [Sahrawi Arab Dem. Rep.], a territory it claimed, but Morocco rejoined in 2017.) The AU is focused on achieving greater socioeconomic integration and unity among its member states. Its founding document authorized the organization to intervene to stop genocide, war crimes, or human rights abuses within individual member nations. **Headquarters:** Addis Ababa, Ethiopia. **Website:** au.int

Asia-Pacific Economic Cooperation (APEC), founded Nov. 1989 as a forum to further cooperation on trade and investment. Its 21 member economies are Australia, Brunei, Canada, Chile, China, Hong Kong, Indonesia, Japan, Malaysia, Mexico, New Zealand, Papua New Guinea, Peru, Philippines, Russia, Singapore, South Korea, Taiwan, Thailand, the U.S., and Vietnam. **Secretariat:** Singapore. **Website:** www.apec.org

Association of Southeast Asian Nations (ASEAN), formed Aug. 8, 1967, to promote economic, social, and cultural collaboration and development among the states of Southeast Asia. Its 10 members are Brunei, Cambodia, Indonesia, Laos, Malaysia, Myanmar, Philippines, Singapore, Thailand, and Vietnam. **Secretariat:** Jakarta, Indonesia. **Website:** asean.org

Caribbean Community (CARICOM), established Aug. 1, 1973, to coordinate economic integration, foreign policy, social

development, and security. Its 15 members are Antigua and Barbuda, The Bahamas, Barbados, Belize, Dominica, Grenada, Guyana, Haiti, Jamaica, Montserrat, St. Kitts and Nevis, St. Lucia, St. Vincent and the Grenadines, Suriname, and Trinidad and Tobago. Anguilla, Bermuda, British Virgin Islands, Cayman Islands, and Turks and Caicos Islands are associate members. **Secretariat:** Georgetown, Guyana. **Website:** www.caricom.org

The Commonwealth, originally called the British Commonwealth of Nations, then the Commonwealth of Nations, in 1949, is an association of nations and dependencies, most part of the former British Empire. Queen Elizabeth II, the current British monarch, is the symbolic head of the Commonwealth. (The secretary-general is chosen by Commonwealth leaders.)

There are 54 independent, sovereign nations in the Commonwealth as of Sept. 2020. Among them are the UK and 15 other nations, known as Commonwealth Realms, that recognize the British monarch as their head of state. **Secretariat:** London, UK. **Website:** thecommonwealth.org

Commonwealth of Independent States (CIS), established in Dec. 1991 as an alliance of former Soviet constituent republics. Its members are Armenia, Azerbaijan, Belarus, Kazakhstan, Kyrgyzstan, Moldova, Russia, Tajikistan, and Uzbekistan; Turkmenistan is an associate member. Georgia and Ukraine withdrew from the organization following fighting with Russia over disputed territory. Policy is set through coordinating bodies such as the Council of the Heads of States and Council of the Heads of Governments. **Headquarters:** Minsk, Belarus. **Website:** www.cis.minsk.by or www.cisstat.com/eng/

European Free Trade Association (EFTA), created May 3, 1960, to promote free trade and economic integration. The European Economic Area (EEA) agreement, in force since 1994, set up a single market, with free flow of goods, services, capital, and labor, among EU nations and Iceland, Liechtenstein, and Norway, the EFTA members party to the EEA. Switzerland, the fourth EFTA member, has bilateral agreements with the EU. **Headquarters:** Geneva, Switzerland. **Website:** www.efta.int

European Union (EU), known as the European Community (EC) until 1993, aims to integrate economies, coordinate social developments, and foster political partnerships between member states. As of Jan. 1, 1993, there has been a single market, with no restrictions on the movement of people, goods, services, and money, within the EU.

The EU has its origins in such organizations as the European Coal and Steel Community (ECSC), established by the 1951 Treaty of Paris, and the European Economic Community (EEC, or Common Market) and European Atomic Energy Community (Euratom), created by the 1957 Treaties of Rome. A merger of the three communities' executives went into effect in 1967. As of Sept. 2020, there were 27 EU members: 11 of the 12 original members (Belgium, Denmark, France, Germany, Greece, Ireland, Italy, Luxembourg, Netherlands, Portugal, Spain); 3 that joined in 1995 (Austria, Finland, Sweden); 10 in 2004 (Cyprus, Czechia, Estonia, Hungary, Latvia, Lithuania, Malta, Poland, Slovakia, Slovenia); 2 in 2007 (Bulgaria, Romania); and 1 in 2013 (Croatia). Albania, Montenegro, North Macedonia, Serbia, and Turkey were candidate countries. The UK, one of the original EU members, withdrew from the organization on Jan. 31, 2020, after UK citizens voted in favor of Brexit in 2016. All 79 member-states of the Africa, Caribbean, and Pacific (ACP) group of states with the exception of Cuba are affiliated with the EU under the Cotonou Agreement (for the 20-year period ending in Dec. 2020). **De facto capital:** Brussels, Belgium. **Website:** europa.eu

Leaders of the then-12 member nations signed the Treaty on European Union, also known as the Maastricht Treaty, on Feb. 7, 1992. It went into effect in 1993, committing the organization to launching a common currency, to establishing common foreign policies, and to taking a lead on social policy among other issues. The European Central Bank was established in 1998. In 1999, 11 of the then-15 EU countries began using the euro. By 2002, national currencies in those 11 countries and Greece were removed from circulation, leaving the euro as the only currency of legal tender. EU peacekeeping forces replaced NATO troops in Macedonia, 2003, the first such mission for the organization. A Treaty Establishing a Constitution for Europe was signed in 2004 by EU members but was never ratified.

Group of Seven (G7), forum of major industrialized countries. France, Germany, Italy, Japan, the UK, and the U.S. first met in 1975 as the Group of Six. Canada joined in 1976; Russia in 1998. In 2014, group members boycotted a planned G8 summit in Russia in condemnation of its annexation of Crimea. Since that year, they have met as the Group of Seven. The EU is represented at summits. The **Group of Twenty (G20)**, which first gathered in 1999, comprises 19 countries and the EU. Together, they account for around 80% of global economic output.

International Criminal Police Organization (INTERPOL), created 1923 as the International Criminal Police Commission before changing its name in 1956, is the world's largest international police organization. There were 194 member nations as of Sept. 2020. **General Secretariat:** Lyon, France. **Website:** www.interpol.int

League of Arab States (Arab League), created Mar. 22, 1945. The League promotes economic, social, political, and military cooperation, mediates disputes, and represents Arab states in certain international negotiations. Its members are Algeria, Bahrain, Comoros, Djibouti, Egypt, Iraq, Jordan, Kuwait, Lebanon, Libya, Mauritania, Morocco, Oman, Palestine (considered an independent state by the League), Qatar, Saudi Arabia, Somalia, Sudan, Syria (membership suspended since 2011), Tunisia, United Arab Emirates, and Yemen. **Headquarters:** Cairo, Egypt. **Website:** www.lasportal.org

North Atlantic Treaty Organization (NATO), created with the signing of what is popularly known as the Washington Treaty Apr. 4, 1949 (in effect Aug. 24, 1949). Its 30 members as of Sept.

2010 are Albania, Belgium, Bulgaria, Canada, Croatia, Czechia, Denmark, Estonia, France, Germany, Greece, Hungary, Iceland, Italy, Latvia, Lithuania, Luxembourg, Montenegro, Netherlands, North Macedonia, Norway, Poland, Portugal, Romania, Slovakia, Slovenia, Spain, Turkey, UK, and U.S.

Members agree to settle disputes by peaceful means, to develop their capacity to resist armed attack, to regard an attack on one as an attack on all, and to take necessary action to repel an attack under Article 51 of the UN Charter. **Headquarters:** Brussels, Belgium. **Website:** www.nato.int

NATO's military representatives include the Military Committee; International Military Staff, the committee's executive body; and the military command structure (Allied Command Operations and Allied Command Transformation). The North Atlantic Council is NATO's main political decision-making body.

With the end of the Cold War in the early 1990s, members put greater stress on political action and on creating a force that could rapidly deploy to local crises. By the mid-1990s, Russia and other former Soviet republics, among other countries, had joined with NATO in the so-called Partnership for Peace program, which provides for limited joint military exercises and peacekeeping missions. (NATO suspended cooperation with Russia, Apr. 2014, in response to Russia's conflict with Ukraine.) NATO also engages with countries through its Mediterranean Dialogue and Istanbul Cooperation Initiative.

A NATO-led multinational force was deployed to help keep the peace in Bosnia and Herzegovina in 1995. In 1999, a force was deployed in Kosovo. Following the Sept. 2001 terrorist attacks on the U.S., the NATO Council agreed to invoke for the first time Article 5 of the treaty, which stipulates mutual defense of alliance members. NATO assumed control of the International Security Assistance Force in Afghanistan (ISAF), Aug. 2003, marking the first time NATO led a mission outside Europe.

Organization of American States (OAS), which describes itself as the world's oldest regional organization, was officially formed by the signing of a charter on Apr. 30, 1948. Its four main pillars are democracy, human rights, security, and development.

The OAS's 35 members are Antigua and Barbuda, Argentina, The Bahamas, Barbados, Belize, Bolivia, Brazil, Canada, Chile, Colombia, Costa Rica, Cuba, Dominica, Dominican Republic, Ecuador, El Salvador, Grenada, Guatemala, Guyana, Haiti, Honduras, Jamaica, Mexico, Nicaragua, Panama, Paraguay, Peru, St. Kitts and Nevis, St. Lucia, St. Vincent and the Grenadines, Suriname, Trinidad and Tobago, U.S., Uruguay, and Venezuela. **Headquarters:** Washington, DC. **Website:** www.oas.org

Organization for Economic Cooperation and Development (OECD), established Dec. 14, 1960, to promote the economic and social welfare of member countries and to stimulate efforts for developing nations. Its 37 members, as of Sept. 2020, are Australia, Austria, Belgium, Canada, Chile, Colombia, Czechia, Denmark, Estonia, Finland, France, Germany, Greece, Hungary, Iceland, Ireland, Israel, Italy, Japan, Latvia, Lithuania, Luxembourg, Mexico, Netherlands, New Zealand, Norway, Poland, Portugal, Slovakia, Slovenia, South Korea, Spain, Sweden, Switzerland, Turkey, UK, and the U.S. **Headquarters:** Paris, France. **Website:** www.oecd.org

Organization of the Petroleum Exporting Countries (OPEC), created Sept. 14, 1960, by Iran, Iraq, Kuwait, Saudi Arabia, and Venezuela. This group made up of most major petroleum exporting nations seeks to stabilize the oil market and set world oil prices by controlling production. In addition to the founding countries, members as of Sept. 2020 include Algeria, Angola, Congo Republic, Equatorial Guinea, Gabon, Libya, Nigeria, and United Arab Emirates. Indonesia suspended its membership in 2016. Qatar terminated its membership Jan. 2019. Ecuador withdrew from OPEC in Jan. 2020. **Secretariat/headquarters:** Vienna, Austria. **Website:** www.opec.org

Organization for Security and Cooperation in Europe (OSCE), established in 1972 as the Conference on Security and Cooperation in Europe; current name adopted 1995. The group, formed by NATO and Warsaw Pact members, seeks improved East-West relations through a commitment to nonaggression and human rights, and cooperation in economics, science and technology, cultural exchange, and environmental protection. There were 57 member states as of Sept. 2020, making it the world's largest regional security organization. **Secretariat:** Vienna, Austria. **Website:** www.osce.org

United Nations

The 75th regular session of the UN General Assembly opened, largely remotely due to the coronavirus pandemic, on Sept. 15, 2020, attended by delegates from 193 member states. The UN headquarters is located on 18 acres, considered international territory, in New York, NY.

Proposals to establish an organization for maintenance of world peace led to the convening of the United Nations Conference on International Organization in San Francisco, Apr. 25-June 26, 1945, where the UN charter was drawn. It was signed June 26 by 50 nations and on Oct. 15 by Poland. It went into effect Oct. 24, 1945, upon ratification by the permanent members of the Security Council and a majority of the other signatories.

Purposes. To maintain international peace and security; to promote sustained economic growth and sustainable development; to achieve international cooperation in solving economic, social, cultural, and humanitarian problems; to protect human rights; and to advance justice and international law.

Visitors to the UN. Normally, the UN headquarters is open every day except New Year's Day, Good Friday, Memorial Day, Eid al-Fitr, Independence Day, Eid al-Adha, Labor Day, Thanksgiving, and Christmas. It is typically closed to the public during the UN general debate and for meetings of heads of state and government. Because of the COVID-19 pandemic, the UN closed its headquarters (including the Visitor Center) to the public and temporarily suspended guided tours in Mar. 2020.

As of Sept. 2020, the UN was offering a one-hour virtual tour with a live guide to groups of up to 20-30 people. In addition, groups could book a 30- to 60-min. online briefing with a UN expert. Normally, the UN conducts guided tours lasting 45-60 min. and children's tours, aimed at 5- to 10-year-olds, on weekdays. Children under 5 years of age are not admitted on tours. Guided tours at the UN's other headquarters—in Geneva, Switzerland; Vienna, Austria; and Nairobi, Kenya—were similarly suspended because of the pandemic. For updates, visit the UN website. **Website:** visit.un.org

Six Main Organs of the United Nations

General Assembly. The General Assembly comprises representatives from all member nations. Each nation is entitled to one vote. The General Assembly meets in Sept. for an annual session; the Security Council or a majority of UN members can convoke a special session. Decisions on important issues, such as security, require a two-thirds majority of the General Assembly; a simple majority can decide other issues.

The General Assembly must approve the UN budget and apportion expenses among members. A member in arrears can lose its vote if the amount of arrears equals or exceeds the amount of the contributions due for the preceding two full years. **Website:** www.un.org/en/ga/

Security Council. The Security Council has primary responsibility within the UN for maintaining peace and security. It consists of 15 members, five of whom (China, France, Russia, United Kingdom, U.S.) have permanent seats. Ten are elected for two-year terms by the General Assembly. Nonpermanent members with terms expiring Dec. 31, 2020, are Belgium, Dominican Republic, Germany, Indonesia, and South Africa; those with terms expiring Dec. 31, 2021, are Estonia, Niger, Saint Vincent and the Grenadines, Tunisia, and Vietnam. India, Ireland, Kenya, Mexico, and Norway have been elected to two-year terms starting on Jan. 1, 2021.

Any UN member may participate in Council discussions at its invitation. Decisions on procedural questions are made by an affirmative vote of nine members. On all other matters the affirmative vote of nine members must include the concurring votes of all permanent members (giving them veto power). The Security Council directs the various peacekeeping forces deployed throughout the world. **Website:** www.un.org/securitycouncil/

Secretariat. The Secretariat is responsible for the UN's day-to-day operations. It is headed by the secretary-general, who is appointed by the General Assembly, on the recommendation of the Security Council, for a five-year, renewable term. The secretary-general reports to the General Assembly and may bring to the attention of the Security Council any matter that threatens international peace. The Secretariat maintained an international staff of 37,505 as of Dec. 31, 2018. **Website:** www.un.org/en/sections/about-un/secretariat/

United Nations Secretaries General

Took office	Secretary, nation
1946	Trygve Lie, Norway
1953	Dag Hammarskjöld, Sweden
1961	U Thant, Burma (Myanmar)
1972	Kurt Waldheim, Austria
1982	Javier Pérez de Cuéllar, Peru
1992	Boutros Boutros-Ghali, Egypt
1997	Kofi Annan, Ghana
2007	Ban Ki-moon, South Korea
2017	António Guterres, Portugal

Economic and Social Council. ECOSOC consists of 54 members elected by the General Assembly to overlapping three-year terms. The council is responsible for economic, social, and environmental issues in relation to sustainable development. It meets with academics, non-governmental organizations, and private-sector representatives throughout the year. A multi-week substantive session is held each July in New York or Geneva, Switzerland. **Website:** www.un.org/ecosoc/

International Court of Justice (World Court). The International Court of Justice is the principal judicial organ of the UN. The Court has jurisdiction over cases that UN members or parties to the court's statute submit to it. In addition to rendering judgments, the Court issues advisory opinions.

The court's 15 judges are elected to nine-year terms by the General Assembly and the Security Council. No two judges may come from the same nation, and they should represent the world's principal legal systems. Once elected, the judges no longer act as representatives of a government. The Court remains permanently in session, except during vacations. All questions are decided by a majority. The International Court of Justice sits in The Hague, Netherlands. **Website:** www.icj-cij.org

Trusteeship Council. The Trusteeship Council, made up of the five permanent Security Council members, supervised the administration of UN trust territories. All 11 trust territories have since attained their right to self-determination. The Council formally suspended its work on Nov. 1, 1994, with Palau's independence.

The text of the **UN Charter** is online at www.un.org/en/charter-united-nations/

Selected UN Programs and Funds, Specialized Agencies, and Related Organizations

UN programs and funds operate with voluntary funding. UN specialized agencies and related organizations are autonomous groups that have a functional relationship or working agreement with the UN. Their financing comes from voluntary and assessed contributions. The location in parentheses is the primary office or headquarters.

Food and Agriculture Org. (FAO) works to achieve food security, eliminate malnutrition, and increase the productivity and sustainability of farms, forests, and fisheries. (Rome, Italy) **Website:** www.fao.org

International Atomic Energy Agency (IAEA) promotes safe, peaceful uses of atomic energy. (Vienna, Austria) **Website:** www.iaea.org

International Civil Aviation Org. (ICAO) sets international civil aviation standards and regulations. (Montréal, Quebec, Canada) **Website:** www.icao.int

International Fund for Agricultural Development (IFAD) seeks to alleviate poverty in rural areas of developing countries. (Rome, Italy) **Website:** www.ifad.org

International Labor Org. (ILO) promotes decent and productive employment standards, the improvement of labor conditions and worker protections, and vocational training. (Geneva, Switzerland) **Website:** www.ilo.org

International Maritime Org. (IMO) seeks cooperation on technical matters affecting international shipping. (London, England, UK) **Website:** www.imo.org

International Monetary Fund (IMF) promotes international monetary cooperation, currency stabilization, and the expansion of international trade. (Washington, DC) **Website:** www.imf.org

International Telecommunication Union (ITU) regulates all aspects of global communication, including setting standards for radio and phone, and allocating the radio-frequency spectrum and satellite orbits. (Geneva, Switzerland) **Website:** www.itu.int

Office of the United Nations High Commissioner for Refugees (UNHCR) safeguards the rights of and provides essential assistance to refugees. (Geneva, Switzerland) **Website:** www.unhcr.org

United Nations Children's Fund (UNICEF) provides financial aid and development assistance to programs for children and mothers in developing countries. (New York, NY) **Website:** www.unicef.org

United Nations Educational, Scientific, and Cultural Org. (UNESCO) works to improve education around the world and to preserve historical and cultural sites. (Paris, France) **Website:** www.unesco.org

United Nations Industrial Development Org. (UNIDO) helps developing and transitional nations pursue sustainable industrial development while promoting international industrial cooperation. (Vienna, Austria) **Website:** www.unido.org

Universal Postal Union (UPU) facilitates international collaboration among postal service providers. (Berne, Switzerland) **Website:** www.upu.int

World Bank Group is focused on ending extreme poverty and promoting the sharing of prosperity worldwide. It encompasses five institutions. The **International Bank for Reconstruction and Development (IBRD)** provides loans and technical assistance for projects in developing member countries. The **International Development Assn. (IDA)** provides funds for development projects on concessionary terms to the poorest countries. The IBRD and IDA make up the World Bank. The **International Finance Corp. (IFC)** promotes private-sector growth in developing countries; encourages the development of local capital markets; and stimulates the international flow of private capital. The **Multilateral Investment Guarantee Agency (MIGA)** promotes foreign direct investment in developing countries by guaranteeing investments from noncommercial political risks. The **International Center for Settlement of Investment Disputes (ICSID)** provides conciliation and arbitration services for disputes between foreign investors and host governments that arise out of an investment. (Washington, DC) **Website:** www.worldbank.org, www.ifc.org, www.miga.org

World Health Org. (WHO) responds to public-health emergencies and works to eradicate life-threatening diseases. (Geneva, Switzerland) **Website:** www.who.int

World Intellectual Property Org. (WIPO) protects literary, industrial, scientific, and artistic works through international cooperation. (Geneva, Switzerland) **Website:** www.wipo.int

World Meteorological Org. (WMO) coordinates the free exchange of world meteorological data. (Geneva, Switzerland) **Website:** public.wmo.int

World Tourism Org. (UNWTO) advocates for responsible, sustainable, and universally accessible tourism. (Madrid, Spain) **Website:** www.unwto.org

World Trade Org. (WTO) administers trade agreements and treaties between nations, attempts to settle disputes, and keeps track of trade measures and statistics. (Geneva, Switzerland) **Website:** www.wto.org

Ongoing UN Peacekeeping Missions, 2020

Source: Dept. of Peacekeeping Operations (DPKO), Dept. of Field Support, Dept. of Management; United Nations Secretariat

Unless otherwise noted, numbers are for peacekeeping operations only (not including political and peacebuilding missions), as of June 30, 2020, unless otherwise noted. Year given in graphic is the year each mission started.

Uniformed personnel (troops, police, military observers, and staff officers)	80,979	Total personnel serving in 13 current peacekeeping operations	94,875
Countries contributing uniformed personnel	121	Approved budget for July 1, 2020-June 30, 2021	$6.6 bil
Civilian personnel (as of May 31, 2018):		Peacekeeping operations since 1948	71
International	4,386	Total fatalities in all peace operations since 1948	3,964
Local	8,221	Est. total cost of operations, 1948 to June 30, 2010	$69 bil

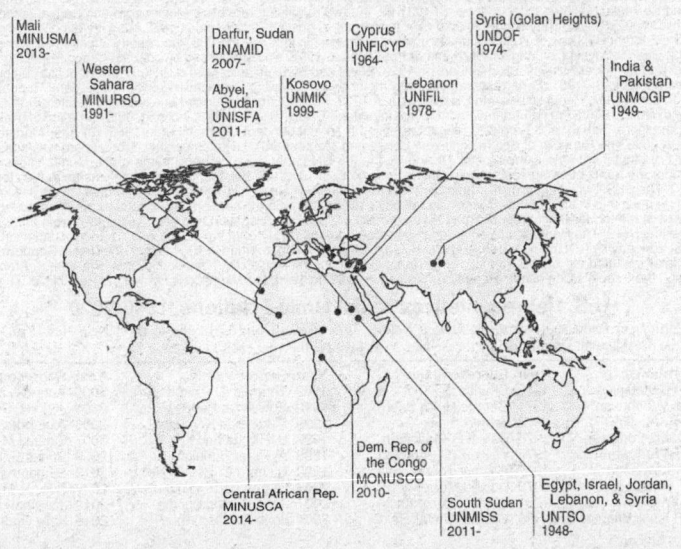

Mali
MINUSMA
2013-

Western
Sahara
MINURSO
1991-

Darfur, Sudan
UNAMID
2007-

Abyei,
Sudan
UNISFA
2011-

Kosovo
UNMIK
1999-

Cyprus
UNFICYP
1964-

Lebanon
UNIFIL
1978-

Syria (Golan Heights)
UNDOF
1974-

India &
Pakistan
UNMOGIP
1949-

Dem. Rep. of
the Congo
MONUSCO
2010-

Central African Rep.
MINUSCA
2014-

South Sudan
UNMISS
2011-

Egypt, Israel, Jordan,
Lebanon, & Syria
UNTSO
1948-

Roster of the United Nations

Listed below are the 193 members of the United Nations, with the years in which they were admitted (as of Sept. 2020). Vatican City (Holy See), Kosovo, and China (Taiwan)[1] are not members. Taiwan's repeated bids for UN membership have so far been unsuccessful. Palestine and Vatican City are non-member states of the UN with permanent observer status.

Member	Year	Member	Year	Member	Year	Member	Year
Afghanistan	1946	Dominica	1978	Libya	1955	Saint Vincent and the	
Albania	1955	Dominican Republic	1945	Liechtenstein	1990	Grenadines	1980
Algeria	1962	Ecuador	1945	Lithuania	1991	Samoa	1976
Andorra	1993	Egypt[4]	1945	Luxembourg	1945	San Marino	1992
Angola	1976	El Salvador	1945	Madagascar	1960	São Tomé and Príncipe	1975
Antigua and Barbuda	1981	Equatorial Guinea	1968	Malawi	1964	Saudi Arabia	1945
Argentina	1945	Eritrea	1993	Malaysia[7]	1957	Senegal	1960
Armenia	1992	Estonia	1991	Maldives	1965	Serbia[2,9]	2000
Australia	1945	Ethiopia	1945	Mali	1960	Seychelles	1976
Austria	1955	Fiji	1970	Malta	1964	Sierra Leone	1961
Azerbaijan	1992	Finland	1955	Marshall Islands	1991	Singapore[8]	1965
Bahamas, The	1973	France	1945	Mauritania	1961	Slovakia[3]	1993
Bahrain	1971	Gabon	1960	Mauritius	1968	Slovenia[2]	1992
Bangladesh	1974	Gambia, The	1965	Mexico	1945	Solomon Islands	1978
Barbados	1966	Georgia	1992	Micronesia	1991	Somalia	1960
Belarus	1945	Germany[5]	1973	Moldova	1992	South Africa[11]	1945
Belgium	1945	Ghana	1957	Monaco	1993	South Sudan[12]	2011
Belize	1981	Greece	1945	Mongolia	1961	Spain	1955
Benin	1960	Grenada	1974	Montenegro[2,8]	2006	Sri Lanka	1955
Bhutan	1971	Guatemala	1945	Morocco	1956	Sudan[12]	1956
Bolivia	1945	Guinea	1958	Mozambique	1975	Suriname	1975
Bosnia and		Guinea-Bissau	1974	Myanmar (Burma)	1948	Swaziland	1968
Herzegovina[2]	1992	Guyana	1966	Namibia	1990	Sweden	1946
Botswana	1966	Haiti	1945	Nauru	1999	Switzerland	2002
Brazil	1945	Honduras	1945	Nepal	1955	Syria[3]	1945
Brunei	1984	Hungary	1955	Netherlands	1945	Tajikistan	1992
Bulgaria	1955	Iceland	1946	New Zealand	1945	Tanzania[13]	1961
Burkina Faso	1960	India	1945	Nicaragua	1945	Thailand	1946
Burundi	1962	Indonesia[6]	1950	Niger	1960	Timor-Leste	2002
Cabo Verde	1975	Iran	1945	Nigeria	1960	Togo	1960
Cambodia	1955	Iraq	1945	North Macedonia[2,9]	1993	Tonga	1999
Cameroon	1960	Ireland	1955	Norway	1945	Trinidad and Tobago	1962
Canada	1945	Israel	1949	Oman	1971	Tunisia	1956
Central African Rep.	1960	Italy	1955	Pakistan	1947	Turkey	1945
Chad	1960	Jamaica	1962	Palau	1994	Turkmenistan	1992
Chile	1945	Japan	1956	Panama	1945	Tuvalu	2000
China[1]	1945	Jordan	1955	Papua New Guinea	1975	Uganda	1962
Colombia	1945	Kazakhstan	1992	Paraguay	1945	Ukraine	1945
Comoros	1975	Kenya	1963	Peru	1945	United Arab Emirates	1971
Congo, Dem. Rep. of	1960	Kiribati	1999	Philippines	1945	United Kingdom	1945
Congo Republic	1960	Korea, North	1991	Poland	1945	United States	1945
Costa Rica	1945	Korea, South	1991	Portugal	1955	Uruguay	1945
Côte d'Ivoire	1960	Kuwait	1963	Qatar	1971	Uzbekistan	1992
Croatia[2]	1992	Kyrgyzstan	1992	Romania	1955	Vanuatu	1981
Cuba	1945	Laos	1955	Russia[10]	1945	Venezuela	1945
Cyprus	1960	Latvia	1991	Rwanda	1962	Vietnam	1977
Czechia[3]	1993	Lebanon	1945	Saint Kitts and Nevis	1983	Yemen[14]	1947
Denmark	1945	Lesotho	1966	Saint Lucia	1979	Zambia	1964
Djibouti	1977	Liberia	1945			Zimbabwe	1980

(1) The General Assembly (GA) voted in 1971 to expel the Chinese government in Taiwan and admit the government in Beijing. (2) The Socialist Federal Republic of Yugoslavia was an original UN member. After four of its six republics (Bosnia and Herzegovina, Croatia, Macedonia, and Slovenia) declared independence in 1991-92, the two remaining republics, Montenegro and Serbia, reconstituted as the Federal Republic of Yugoslavia. They sought to take over the former Yugoslavia's UN seat in 1992 but were expelled a few months later by GA vote. The Federal Republic of Yugoslavia was granted membership in 2000. In 2003, the country changed its name to Serbia and Montenegro. (3) Czechoslovakia, an original UN member from 1945 to 1992, was succeeded by both the Czech Republic and Slovakia in 1993. (4) Egypt and Syria were original UN members. In 1958, Egypt and Syria established the United Arab Republic and continued under a single UN membership. In 1961, Syria resumed separate membership following independence. (5) The Federal Republic of Germany and the German Democratic Republic became UN members in 1973. In 1990, the two formed one sovereign state. (6) Withdrew from the UN in 1965; rejoined in 1966. (7) The Federation of Malaya joined the UN in 1957. In 1963, it changed its name to Malaysia following the accession of Singapore, Sabah, and Sarawak. Singapore became an independent UN member in 1965. (8) After Montenegro declared independence in 2006, the Republic of Serbia continued Serbia and Montenegro's UN membership. Montenegro was admitted to the UN as the Republic of Montenegro the same month. (9) Admitted to the UN under the provisional name of the former Yugoslav Republic of Macedonia. Under the terms of an agreement with Greece in force Feb. 12, 2019, the country changed its name to the Republic of North Macedonia. (10) The USSR was an original UN member. After the USSR's dissolution in 1991, Russia informed the UN it would continue the Soviet Union's membership in the Security Council and all other UN organs with the support of the Commonwealth of Independent States (comprising most of the former Soviet republics). (11) Readmitted in 1994. Its delegation had been suspended from participation in 1974 because of apartheid. (12) The Republic of South Sudan seceded from the Republic of the Sudan in 2011 and was admitted to the UN the same year. (13) Tanganyika (UN member from 1961) and Zanzibar (from 1963), merged in 1964 to form the United Republic of Tanganyika and Zanzibar, later renamed the United Republic of Tanzania. It continued a single UN membership. (14) The Yemen Arab Republic was admitted in 1947; the People's Democratic Republic of Yemen in 1967. In 1990, the two nations formed the Republic of Yemen.

U.S. Representatives to the United Nations, 1946-2020

The U.S. Permanent Representative to the United Nations is head of the U.S. Mission to the UN in New York. He or she is appointed by the president and confirmed by the Senate. Year given is the year each took office.

Year	Representative	Year	Representative	Year	Representative	Year	Representative
1946	Edward R. Stettinius Jr.	1969	Charles W. Yost	1989	Thomas R. Pickering	2005	Anne W. Patterson[1]
1946	Herschel V. Johnson[1]	1971	George H. W. Bush	1992	Edward J. Perkins	2005	John R. Bolton
1947	Warren R. Austin	1973	John A. Scali	1993	Madeleine K. Albright	2006	Alejandro D. Wolff[1]
1953	Henry Cabot Lodge Jr.	1975	Daniel P. Moynihan	1997	Bill Richardson	2007	Zalmay M. Khalilzad
1960	James J. Wadsworth	1976	William W. Scranton	1998	A. Peter Burleigh[1]	2009	Susan E. Rice
1961	Adlai E. Stevenson	1977	Andrew Young	1999	Richard C. Holbrooke	2013	Samantha Power
1965	Arthur J. Goldberg	1979	Donald McHenry	2001	James B. Cunningham[1]	2017	Nikki R. Haley
1968	George W. Ball	1981	Jeane J. Kirkpatrick	2001	John D. Negroponte	2019	Jonathan R. Cohen[1]
1968	James Russell Wiggins	1985	Vernon A. Walters	2004	John C. Danforth	2019	Kelly Craft

(1) Acting.

International Criminal Court

The International Criminal Court (ICC) was created when 120 nations signed the Rome Statute on July 17, 1998. Its mission is to try individuals accused of genocide, war crimes, and crimes against humanity, which was undertaken in the past by temporary tribunals. The statute came into force on July 1, 2002. As of Sept. 2020, 123 nations were state parties to the Rome Statute of the ICC. China, Russia, and the U.S. are among those countries that have not yet signed or ratified the treaty.

The ICC, unlike the International Court of Justice (or World Court), is not part of the UN. It is an independent international agency with its own administration and budget, which is made up of funds from member states and voluntary contributions by other institutions, international groups, individuals, and corporations. It consists of 18 judges elected by state parties to nine-year, non-renewable terms. An absolute majority of these 18 judges elect three from among themselves to serve as president and first and second vice presidents. A Registry handles the nonjudicial aspects of administration. The Office of the Prosecutor

reviews, investigates, and prosecutes cases referred to it by a state or by the UN Security Council.

As of Sept. 2020, 28 cases had been brought before the ICC. The Office of the Prosecutor was investigating situations in Afghanistan, Bangladesh/Myanmar (Burma), Burundi, Central African Republic, Côte d'Ivoire, Dem. Rep. of the Congo, Georgia, Kenya, Libya, Mali, Sudan (Darfur), and Uganda. It was conducting preliminary examinations in Colombia, Guinea, Iraq (involving UK nationals), Nigeria, Palestine, the Philippines, Ukraine, and Venezuela. The court issued its first-ever conviction in 2012, when it found the warlord Thomas Lubanga Dyilo guilty of war crimes for his use of child soldiers in the Dem. Rep. of the Congo.

Though jurisdiction is limited to member nations, the ICC is a court of last resort. It may also initiate cases involving non-member nations if it deems the country's authorities have not taken steps to investigate or prosecute a case. The ICC is headquartered in The Hague, Netherlands, though it may sit elsewhere.

Website: www.icc-cpi.int

Geneva Conventions

The Geneva Conventions are four international treaties governing the protection of civilians and medical and religious personnel in times of war, the treatment of prisoners of war, and the care of the wounded and sick in the armed forces. The first convention, covering the sick and wounded in war, was concluded in Geneva, Switzerland, in 1864, at a conference convened by the Swiss government at the urging of the International Committee of the Red Cross. The convention was amended and expanded in 1906. In 1929, two more conventions covering the wounded and prisoners of war were signed. Outrage at the treatment of prisoners and civilians during WWII by some belligerents, notably Germany and Japan, prompted the conclusion, on Aug. 12, 1949, of four new conventions. Three of these restated and strengthened the previous conventions.

The fourth Geneva Convention of 1949 codified general principles of international law governing the treatment of civil-

ians in wartime, with special safeguards for wounded persons, children under 15 years of age, pregnant women, and the elderly. Discrimination on racial, religious, national, or political grounds was forbidden. Torture, collective punishment, unwarranted destruction of property, and forced use of civilians for an occupier's armed forces were prohibited. Also included was a pledge for the humane treatment, adequate feeding, and delivery of supplies to prisoners. Two additional protocols, adopted in June 1977, increased protections for victims of international and non-international armed conflicts (e.g., civil wars). (A third protocol, adopted in 2005, created the Red Crystal emblem for use along with the Red Cross and Red Crescent.)

Nearly all countries have formally accepted all or most international humanitarian law as binding. However, there is no permanent international machinery in place to enforce these treaties.

Genocide

Source: Convention on the Prevention and Punishment of the Crime of Genocide, United Nations Treaty Series 277; Rome Statute of the International Criminal Court (ICC)

The term "genocide" (which combines Greek and Latin roots to mean "murder of a race") was coined by Polish-Jewish lawyer Raphael Lemkin in 1944 to describe the intentional or attempted destruction of a national, ethnic, racial, or religious group. Genocide is defined as killing members of a group, causing serious bodily harm to members of a group, or otherwise attempting to bring about a group's destruction, including efforts to prevent births or transfer children away from a group. Although the legal definition of genocide does not extend to political groups, the term is often used colloquially to refer to large-scale political violence.

The prohibition against genocide is part of customary international law and is codified in the Convention on the Prevention and Punishment of the Crime of Genocide, which entered into force on Jan. 12, 1951. As of Sept. 2020, 152 nations, including the U.S., were parties to it. Genocide is also prohibited by the domestic laws of many nations.

The first modern trials for genocide were conducted by the Allies after WWII. Although the charter of the Nuremberg Tribunal— the international court set up to try Nazi war criminals—did not

use the term genocide, its definition of "crimes against humanity" included persecution on racial or religious grounds. More recently, the UN Security Council created ad hoc tribunals to try those responsible for genocide and other serious crimes in former Yugoslavia and in Rwanda. The ICC also has jurisdiction to try perpetrators. Sudanese Pres. Omar Hassan al-Bashir is the first person the ICC has charged with the crime of genocide, for the violence in Darfur against the Fur, Masalit, and Zaghawa people. Bashir was deposed in Apr. 2019 and remained detained in Sudan. He was indicted on corruption charges in Aug. 2019 but faced more charges in 2020 for his role in the 1989 coup that enabled him to take office.

UN investigators recommended, Aug. 2018, that Myanmar's top military leaders be tried on charges including genocide of the country's Rohingya population. At least 6,700 Rohingya are estimated to have been killed by armed government forces in Aug.-Sept. 2017. In Jan. 2020, the International Criminal Court ruled that Myanmar must prevent genocidal acts against the Rohingya.

Examples of Genocides Since 1900

Year	Event	Location	Est. deaths
1915	Extermination of Armenians by the nationalist Young Turks	Turkey/Ottoman Empire	1,000,000+
1930s	Intentional infliction of famine on Ukraine	Soviet Union (Ukraine)	6,000,000-7,000,000
1933-45	Attempted destruction of European Jewry (Holocaust)	Europe	6,000,000
1975-79	Khmer Rouge campaign of extermination under Pol Pot[1]	Cambodia	1,500,000-2,000,000
1981-83	Army and paramilitary killings of indigenous Mayan during civil war	Guatemala	200,000+
1988	Anfal Campaign (named by the Iraqi government) against Iraqi Kurds	Iraq	100,000-200,000
1992-95	Ethnic killings during the breakup of Yugoslavia, chiefly Serbs against Bosnian Muslims (known as Bosniaks)	Bosnia-Herzegovina, Serbia, Croatia	200,000
1994	Hutu massacre of Tutsis	Rwanda	800,000
2003-present	Govt. forces and govt.-backed Arab militia (Janjaweed) attacks on non-Arab southern tribes, mainly Fur, Masalit, Zaghawa[2]	Darfur region, Sudan	300,000-600,000
2014-19	Self-proclaimed Islamic State (ISIS) against Yazidi, Christian, and Shia Muslim population	Iraq, Syria	3,100+

Note: Ests. based on historical evidence. The legal definition of "genocide" does not include politically motivated mass killings. Therefore, instances of mass violence against political or class enemies, such as Josef Stalin's purges of some 20 mil Soviets in the 1930s, and Mao Zedong's Cultural Revolution, which killed several million Chinese, are not included. (1) Though many of the murders committed by the Khmer Rouge regime were politically or class motivated, Nov. 2018, found two senior officials guilty of genocide of Vietnamese in Cambodia and the Cham ethnic group. (2) In 2005, a UN commission concluded that although the "international offenses … that have been committed in Darfur may be no less serious and heinous than genocide," it did not term the situation a genocide.

NATIONS OF THE WORLD

As of mid-2020, there were **196 nations** in the world. This number includes three nations that are not United Nations (UN) members—Kosovo, Taiwan, and Vatican City (Holy See). Certain regions and territories can be found under the entry for their governing nation. **Sources:** FAOSTAT and AQUASTAT, Food and Agric. Org. of the UN (FAO); Global Health Observatory, World Health Organization (WHO); Intl. Data Base, U.S. Census Bureau; International Energy Statistics, Energy Information Admin., U.S. Dept. of Energy; *International Financial Statistics*, Intl. Monetary Fund (IMF); Joint UN Programme on HIV/AIDS (UNAIDS); *Key Indicators of the Labour Market*, International Labour Organization; *The Military Balance*, Intl. Inst. for Strategic Studies; *Oil & Gas Journal*, PennWell Corp.; *Trends in International Migrant Stock* and *World Urbanization Prospects*, Population Div., UN Dept. of Economic and Social Affairs; UN Educational, Scientific, and Cultural Org. (UNESCO); *UNWTO World Tourism Barometer* © World Tourism Org.; U.S. Dept. of State; Wards Intelligence, a div. of Informa; The World Bank; *The World Factbook*, Central Intelligence Agency (CIA); Todd M. Johnson and Brian J. Grim, eds., *World Religion Database* (Leiden/Boston: Brill, July 2020) and Todd M. Johnson and Gina A. Zurlo, eds., *World Christian Database* (Leiden/Boston: Brill, Aug. 2020); World Telecommunication/ICT Indicators Database, Intl. Telecommunication Union.

Note: Because of rounding or incomplete enumeration, percentages may not add up to 100%. FY = Fiscal year. NA = Not available/applicable. Figures are for years noted below unless otherwise indicated within a country's profile. **Population, age distrib.,** and **pop. density** are mid-2020 ests. **Growth** gives the avg. annual percent change in the pop. resulting from **births** and **deaths** at midyear 2020 as well as the flow of migrants into and out of a country. International **migrants**, including foreign-born citizens and refugees, as a percent of the total pop. is for mid-2019. Percent of total pop. living in **urban** areas, as defined by each country, are projections for mid-2020. **Ethnic groups** are given in descending order of size; data are most recent available. **Languages** are ranked with those most widely spoken listed first. **Arable land** is given as percentage of country's land area. Pop. of **capitals** and **cities** are projected ests. for urban agglomerations as of mid-2019 or mid-2020. **Defense budget** is for 2019, **active troops** for 2019. Selected **industries** are ranked by descending value of annual output. Selected **chief agric.** products are listed in descending order of importance. Total renewable **water** resources per inhabitant is for 2017. **Crude oil reserves** are as of Jan. 1, 2020; countries without this entry lack reserves. **Electricity prod.** indicates net, not gross, generated in 2018. **Labor force** percentages are latest available; **unemployment** (percentage of total labor force age 15 and older currently available for and seeking work) are 2020 ests. **Monetary unit** exchange rate is as of Sept. 2020. **GDP** and **per capita GDP**, 2019 ests., are based on purchasing power parity exchange rates; **GDP growth** is annual. Value of **imports** and **exports**, calculated on an exchange rate basis, are from 2017 (unless noted); 2017 trade partners are listed in descending order of importance by percentage of total dollar value. **Tourism** is 2018 or 2019 provisional receipts from intl. visitors; data not available for all countries. **Budget** calculated on an exchange rate basis, not purchasing power parity terms, is 2017 expenditures. **Inflation** is measured by the percent change in the consumer price index (or avg. consumer cost for certain goods and services) between 2018 and 2019. Total length of a country's **railway** network is the latest available. **Motor vehicle** statistics, for cars and comm. vehicles in operation based on registrations, are for 2019. The number of **airports** with paved, usable runways are latest available. Number of fixed-**telephone** subscriptions and **mobile**-cellular telephone subscriptions offering voice communications are for 2018. Percentage of pop. accessing the **internet**, regardless of device used, and active mobile-**broadband** subscriptions are for 2017. Current health **expend.** (both government and private) is given as a percentage of GDP in 2017. **Life expect.** is in avg. number of years at birth for persons born in 2020. **Infant mortality** measures the probability of a child dying between birth and exact age 1 in 2020. **Undernourished**, or the prevalence of undernourishment, is the estimated proportion of the population in 2017-19 that lacks enough dietary energy for a healthy, active life. **HIV** prevalence is the percentage of a country's pop. of 15- to 49-year-olds living with HIV in 2019. **Education** and **literacy** rate ests. are latest available. Literacy measures the percent of the pop. age 15 and older able to read and write simple statements; some countries define as literate those who have completed certain schooling. **Embassy** addresses are for Wash., DC, area code (202). Current events as of Oct. 1, 2020; COVID-19 cases and deaths per the World Health Org. (WHO) unless otherwise cited.

See pages 489-504 for full-color maps and flags of all nations.

Afghanistan
Islamic Republic of Afghanistan

People: Population: 36,643,815 (39). **Age distrib.:** <15: 40.6%; 65+: 2.7%. **Growth:** 2.4%. **Migrants:** 0.4%. **Pop. density:** 145.5 per sq mi, 56.2 per sq km. **Urban:** 26.0%. **Ethnic groups:** Pashtun, Tajik, Hazara, Uzbek, smaller numbers of 10 other constitutionally recognized ethnic groups; Kyrghyz. **Languages:** Afghan Persian or Dari, Pashto (both official); Uzbek, English, Turkmen, Urdu. **Religions:** Muslim 99.9% (Sunni [official] 89%, Shia 11%).

Geography: Total area: 251,827 sq mi, 652,230 sq km (40). **Land area:** 251,827 sq mi, 652,230 sq km. **Location:** SW Asia, NW of Indian subcontinent. Pakistan on E, S; Iran on W; Turkmenistan, Uzbekistan, Tajikistan on N. NE tip touches China. **Topography:** Landlocked and mountainous, much of it over 4,000 ft above sea level. The Hindu Kush Mts. tower 16,000 ft above Kabul and reach a height of 25,000 ft to the E. Dry climate with extreme temperatures; large desert regions. **Arable land:** 11.8%. **Capital:** Kabul, 4,221,532.

Government: Type: Presidential Islamic republic. **Head of state and govt.:** Pres. Ashraf Ghani Ahmadzai; b. 1949; in office: Sept. 29, 2014; and Chief Exec. Abdullah Abdullah; b. 1960; in office: Sept. 29, 2014. **Local divisions:** 34 provinces. **Defense budget:** $1.9 bil. **Active troops:** 180,900.

Economy: Industries: small-scale prod. of bricks, textiles, soap, furniture, shoes, fertilizer, apparel, food prods. **Chief agric.:** opium, wheat, fruits, nuts; wool, mutton. **Natural resources:** nat. gas, petroleum, coal, copper, chromite, talc, barites, sulfur, lead, zinc, iron ore, salt, prec./semiprec. stones. **Water:** 1,839 cu m per capita. **Electricity prod.:** 1.3 bil kWh. **Labor force:** agric. 42.4%, industry 18.3%, services 39.4%. **Unemployment:** 11.2%.

Finance: Monetary unit: Afghani (AFN) (76.56 = $1 U.S.). **GDP:** $87.3 bil; **per capita GDP:** $2,294; **GDP growth:** 2.9%. **Imports:** $7.6 bil; China 21%, Iran 20.5%, Pakistan 11.8%, Kazakhstan 11%, Uzbekistan 6.8%, Malaysia 5.3%. **Exports:** $784 mil (not incl. illicit trade); India 56.5%, Pakistan 29.6%. **Tourism:** $72 mil. **Budget:** $5.3 bil. **Inflation:** 2.3%.

Transport: Motor vehicles: 46.6 per 1,000 pop. **Airports:** 29. **Communications: Telephone:** 0.3 per 100 pop. **Mobile:** 59.1 per 100 pop. **Broadband:** 16 per 100 pop. **Internet:** 13.5%.

Health: Expend.: 11.8%. **Life expect.:** 51.4 male; 54.4 female. **Births:** 36.7 per 1,000 pop. **Deaths:** 12.7 per 1,000 pop. **Infant mortality:** 104.3 per 1,000 live births. **Undernourished:** 29.9%. **HIV:** <0.1%.

Education: Compulsory: ages 7-15. **Literacy:** 65.4%.
Embassy: 2341 Wyoming Ave. NW 20008; 483-6410.
Website: president.gov.af/en/

Afghanistan, occupying a favored invasion route since antiquity, has been variously known as Ariana or Bactria (in ancient times) and Khorasan (in the Middle Ages). Foreign empires alternated rule with local emirs and kings until the 18th cent., when a unified kingdom was established. In 1973, a military coup ushered in a republic.

Pro-Soviet leftists took power in a bloody 1978 coup. In Dec. 1979 the USSR began a massive airlift into Kabul and backed a new coup, leading to the installation of a more pro-Soviet leader. Soviet forces fanned out over Afghanistan and waged a protracted guerrilla war against Muslim rebels (aided by the U.S.); some 15,000 Soviet troops reportedly died.

A UN-mediated agreement was signed Apr. 14, 1988, providing for withdrawal of Soviet troops, a neutral Afghan state, and repatriation of refugees. Afghan rebels rejected the pact. The Soviets completed their troop withdrawal Feb. 15, 1989; fighting between Afghan rebels and government forces ensued. Communist Pres. Najibullah resigned Apr. 16, 1992, as competing guerilla forces advanced on Kabul. The rebels achieved power Apr. 28. More than 2 mil Afghans had been killed, and 6 mil had left the country since 1979.

Clashes between moderates and Islamic fundamentalist forces followed the rebel victory. The Taliban, an insurgent radical-Islamist faction, captured Kabul in Sept. 1996 and empowered religious police to enforce strict Islamic codes of dress and behavior.

Victories in the northern cities of Mazar-e Sharif, Aug. 8, 1998, and Taloqan, Aug. 8-11, essentially gave the Taliban control over the entire country. On Aug. 20, U.S. cruise missiles struck SE of Kabul, hitting facilities the U.S. said were terrorist training camps run by Osama bin Laden. The UN imposed sanctions Nov. 14, 1999, when Afghanistan refused to turn over bin Laden to the U.S. for prosecution.

After the Sept. 11, 2001, attacks on the World Trade Center and Pentagon, the U.S., blaming bin Laden, demanded that the Taliban surrender him and shut down his al-Qaeda terrorist network. When the Taliban refused, the U.S., with British assistance, began bombing Afghanistan Oct. 7, and sent in ground troops as part of Operation Enduring Freedom (OEF).

Supported by the U.S., the opposition Northern Alliance recaptured Mazar-e Sharif Nov. 9 and took Kabul 4 days later; Taliban forces abandoned Kandahar, their last stronghold, to southern tribal fighters Dec. 7. A power-sharing agreement signed by four anti-Taliban factions, including the Northern Alliance, provided for an interim government headed by Hamid Karzai, a Pashtun tribal leader. The UN authorized a multinational security force Dec. 20, 2001.

Meeting June 13, 2002, in Kabul, a traditional council (*loya jirga*) chose Karzai to head a new transitional government. A new constitution, approved in Jan. 2004, included protections for women's rights denied under Taliban rule. Karzai won the Oct. 9, 2004, presidential election.

Although the U.S. announced the end of major combat operations in Afghanistan, May 1, 2003, resistance continued. NATO officially assumed control of peacekeeping forces—the Intl. Security Assistance Force (ISAF)—Aug. 11, 2003.

The most intense fighting in more than 4 years erupted Mar. 2006 with a new wave of attacks and other strikes by Taliban insurgents. Operating from sanctuaries in Pakistan, Islamist suicide bombers and Taliban insurgents stepped up their activities, 2007-11. Violence escalated in the run-up to the first-round presidential election Aug. 20, 2009. After a Nov. runoff election was canceled when Karzai's lone opponent dropped out, Karzai was sworn in for a second term Nov. 19.

Ending a decade-long manhunt, U.S. commandos killed bin Laden shortly after midnight May 2, 2011, in Abbottabad, Pakistan.

Between Jan. 2009 and June 2011, the number of U.S. troops in Afghanistan rose from about 36,000 to 101,000, while the number of allied foreign forces under ISAF increased from nearly 32,000 to more than 42,000. The U.S., June 22, 2011, outlined a timetable for drawing down troops and ending their combat role, with a residual force focusing on combating Islamic extremists and training and advising Afghan troops. OEF and ISAF officially ended Dec. 28, 2014; since Oct. 2001, 2,215 U.S. and 1,270 allied troops had been killed. The NATO-led Resolute Support Mission (RSM) to aid Afghan forces began Jan. 1, 2015.

The first round of elections for a new president was held Apr. 5, 2014. A June 14 runoff between the two top vote-getters—former Foreign Min. Abdullah Abdullah and former Finance Min. Ashraf Ghani Ahmadzai—was marred by allegations of electoral fraud. Ghani was declared the winner Sept. 21. Under a U.S.-brokered power-sharing agreement, he appointed Abdullah chief executive of the government. Fighting between government and Taliban forces continued.

The government announced, July 29, 2015, that longtime Taliban leader Mohammad Omar had died in 2013. A U.S. drone strike in Pakistan, May 21, 2016, killed Omar's successor, Akhtar Muhammad Mansour; Haibatullah Akhundzada succeeded Mansour. Beginning in 2014, an affiliate of the Sunni extremist group ISIS was active in eastern Afghanistan. The U.S. special inspector general for Afghanistan reconstruction estimated that, in late 2018, the government effectively controlled about 54% of the country's districts; insurgent groups controlled about 12% and contested 34%. U.S. intelligence officials concluded, by early 2020, that Russia had paid bounties to Taliban-linked forces to kill U.S. and allied troops.

Combat, including airstrikes, and terrorist attacks caused high civilian casualties. The UN reported 21,389 conflict-related civilian deaths, 2014-19, and a further 1,282, Jan.-June 2020. Conflict in 2020 had internally displaced about 115,000 people by Aug. About 2.5 mil refugees from decades of Afghanistan violence were in Pakistan as of 2016. Hundreds of thousands subsequently returned, amid accusations that Pakistan forced many of them; about 1.4 mil remained in Pakistan in 2020.

On Feb. 18, 2020, Ghani was officially declared the winner over Abdullah in a Sept. 28, 2019, presidential election.

U.S.-Taliban direct talks in Qatar produced a bilateral agreement signed Feb. 29, 2020. The Taliban pledged that Afghanistan would not be a base for anti-U.S. terrorism. The U.S. pledged a reduction of U.S. and allied troops, as well as a complete withdrawal of such troops contingent on the Taliban's abiding by the agreement. By mid-2020, there were about 8,600 U.S. troops in Afghanistan (down from 12,000 in Feb., with further reductions planned by Nov.) and about 8,000 non-U.S. RSM troops. The agreement also called for direct Taliban-Afghan government talks, which began in Qatar, Sept. 12, 2020.

Afghanistan was impacted by the 2020 COVID-19 pandemic, with more than 39,000 cases and over 1,450 deaths by Sept. 30.

Albania
Republic of Albania

People: Population: 3,074,579 (134). **Age distrib.:** <15: 17.6%; 65+: 13.0%. **Growth:** 0.3%. **Migrants:** 1.7%. **Pop. density:** 290.6 per sq mi, 112.2 per sq km. **Urban:** 62.1%. **Ethnic groups:** Albanian 82.6%. **Languages:** Albanian (official). **Religions:** Muslim 63.1% (Sunni 59%, Shia 5%), Christian 33.7% (Orthodox 16.5%, Catholic 16%).

Geography: Total area: 11,100 sq mi, 28,748 sq km (141); **Land area:** 10,578 sq mi, 27,398 sq km. **Location:** SE Europe, on SE coast of Adriatic Sea. Greece on S; Montenegro, Kosovo on N; Macedonia on E. **Topography:** Narrow coastal plain; hills and mountains covered with scrub forest, cut by small E-W rivers. **Arable land:** 22.1%. **Capital:** Tirana, 493,712.

Government: Type: Parliamentary republic. **Head of state:** Pres. Ilir Meta; b. 1969; in office: July 24, 2017. **Head of govt.:** Prime Min. Edi Rama; b. 1964; in office: Sept. 15, 2013. **Local divisions:** 12 counties. **Defense budget:** $142 mil. **Active troops:** 8,000.

Economy: Industries: food, footwear, apparel, clothing, lumber. **Chief agric.:** wheat, corn, potatoes, vegetables, fruits, olives and olive oil, grapes; meat, dairy prods. **Natural resources:** petroleum, nat. gas, coal, bauxite, chromite, copper, iron ore, nickel, salt, timber, hydropower. **Water:** 10,307 cu m per capita. **Crude oil reserves:** 150 mil bbls. **Electricity prod.:** 4.5 bil kWh. **Labor force:** agric. 36.1%, industry 20.2%, services 43.7%. **Unemployment:** 12.8%.

Finance: Monetary unit: Lek (ALL) (104.88 = $1 U.S.). **GDP:** $41.4 bil; **per capita GDP:** $14,495; **GDP growth:** 2.2%. **Imports:** $4.1 bil; Italy 28.5%, Turkey 8.1%, Germany 8%, Greece 8%, China 7.9%. **Exports:** $900.7 mil; Italy 53.4%, Kosovo 7.7%, Spain 5.6%. **Tourism:** $2.3 bil. **Budget:** $3.9 bil. **Inflation:** 1.4%.

Transport: Railways: 421 mi. **Airports:** 3.

Communications: Telephone: 8.6 per 100 pop. **Mobile:** 94.2 per 100 pop. **Broadband:** 69.3 per 100 pop. **Internet:** 71.8%.

Health: Expend. (2016): 6.7%. **Life expect.:** 76.3 male; 81.9 female. **Births:** 13 per 1,000 pop. **Deaths:** 7.1 per 1,000 pop. **Infant mortality:** 10.8 per 1,000 live births. **Undernourished:** 3.6%. **HIV:** <0.1%.

Education: Compulsory: ages 6-14. **Literacy:** 99.3%.

Embassy: 2100 S St. NW 20008; 223-4942.

Website: www.kryeministria.al

Ancient Illyria was conquered by Romans, Slavs, and Turks (15th cent.); the Turks Islamized the population. Independent Albania was proclaimed in 1912. Italy invaded in 1939.

Communist partisans took over in 1944 and allied themselves with the USSR but broke with the USSR in 1960 over de-Stalinization. Billions of dollars in Chinese financial assistance was cut off in 1978 when Albania attacked China's policies. Large-scale purges of officials occurred during the 1970s.

Enver Hoxha, the nation's ruler for four decades, died Apr. 11, 1985. The new regime introduced some liberalization.

Albania's former Communists were routed in elections Mar. 1992, amid economic collapse and social unrest. Sali Berisha was elected as the first non-Communist president since WWII. Berisha's party claimed a landslide victory in disputed parliamentary elections, May 26 and June 2, 1996. Public protests over the collapse of fraudulent investment schemes in Jan. 1997 led to armed rebellion. The UN Security Council, Mar. 28, authorized a 7,000-member force to restore order. Socialists and their allies won parliamentary elections, June 29 and July 6, and international peacekeepers pulled out by Aug. 11, 1997.

During NATO's air war against Yugoslavia, Mar.-June 1999, Albania hosted some 465,000 Kosovar refugees. A pro-Berisha coalition victory in July 3, 2005, elections ended eight years of Socialist rule. Albania became a full member of NATO Apr. 1, 2009. Socialists won June 23, 2013, parliamentary elections, and Edi Rama became prime min. The EU granted Albania official candidate status June 27, 2014. The Socialists won June 25, 2017, elections; in the campaign, Rama pledged to reduce organized crime and political corruption, key issues for EU membership. The EU, Mar. 26, 2020, approved beginning membership negotiations.

The 2020 COVID-19 pandemic caused about 13,400 cases and 380 deaths in Albania as of Sept. 30.

Algeria
People's Democratic Republic of Algeria

People: Population: 42,972,878 (35). **Age distrib.:** <15: 29.6%; 65+: 6.2%. **Growth:** 1.5%. **Migrants:** 0.6%. **Pop. density:** 46.7 per sq mi, 18.0 per sq km. **Urban:** 73.7%. **Ethnic groups:** Arab-Berber 99%. **Languages:** Arabic (official), French (lingua franca), Berber or Tamazight (official), Berber dialects. **Religions:** Muslim 98.2% (Sunni [official]).

Geography: Total area: 919,595 sq mi, 2,381,740 sq km (10); **Land area:** 919,595 sq mi, 2,381,740 sq km. **Location:** NW Africa, from Medit. Sea into Sahara. Morocco, Western Sahara on W; Mauritania, Mali, Niger on S; Libya, Tunisia on E. **Topography:** The Tell, on the coast, comprises fertile plains 50-100 mi wide with a moderate climate and adequate rain. Two major chains of Atlas Mts., running roughly E-W and reaching 7,000 ft, enclose a dry plateau region. The Sahara lies below. **Arable land:** 3.1%. **Capital:** Algiers, 2,767,661. **Cities:** Oran, 899,182.

Government: Type: Presidential republic. **Head of state:** Pres. Abdelmadjid Tebboune; b. 1945; in office: Dec. 12, 2019. **Head of govt.:** Prime Min. Abdelaziz Djerad; b. 1954; in office: Dec. 28, 2019. **Local divisions:** 48 provinces. **Defense budget:** $10.4 bil. **Active troops:** 130,000.

Economy: Industries: petroleum, nat. gas, light industries, mining, electrical, petrochemical, food proc. **Chief agric.:** wheat, barley, oats, grapes, olives, citrus, fruits; sheep, cattle. **Natural resources:** petroleum, nat. gas, iron ore, phosphates, uranium, lead, zinc. **Water:** 282 cu m per capita. **Crude oil reserves:** 12.2 bil bbls. **Electricity prod.:** 71.5 bil kWh. **Labor force:** agric. 9.7%, industry 30.7%, services 59.6%. **Unemployment:** 11.5%.

Finance: Monetary unit: Dinar (DZD) (128.32 = $1 U.S.). **GDP:** $508.9 bil; **per capita GDP:** $11,820; **GDP growth:** 0.8%. **Imports:** $48.5 bil; China 18.2%, France 9.1%, Italy 8%, Germany 7%, Spain 6.9%. **Exports:** $34.4 bil; Italy 17.4%, Spain 13%, France 11.9%, U.S. 9.4%, Brazil 6.2%, Netherlands 5.5%. **Tourism** (2017): $141 mil. **Budget:** $70.2 bil. **Inflation:** 2.0%.

Transport: Railways: 2,469 mi. **Motor vehicles:** 139.4 per 1,000 pop. **Airports:** 67.

Communications: Telephone: 9.8 per 100 pop. **Mobile:** 121.9 per 100 pop. **Broadband:** 78.4 per 100 pop. **Internet** (2018): 59.6%.

Health: Expend.: 6.4%. **Life expect.:** 76.1 male; 79.1 female. **Births:** 20 per 1,000 pop. **Deaths:** 4.4 per 1,000 pop. **Infant**

mortality: 17.6 per 1,000 live births. **Undernourished:** 2.8%. **HIV:** <0.1%.

Education: Compulsory: ages 6-15. **Literacy:** 97.4%.

Embassy: 2118 Kalorama Rd. NW 20008; 265-2800.

Website: www.algerianembassy.org or www.premier-ministre. gov.dz

Earliest known inhabitants were ancestors of Berbers, followed by Phoenicians, Romans, Vandals, and Arabs. Turkey ruled 1518-1830, when France took control. Large-scale European immigration followed. Arab nationalists launched a guerrilla war, 1954, that more than 400,000 French troops were unable to suppress. After French Pres. Charles de Gaulle came to power, 1958, colonial rule ended, nearly all Europeans left, and Algeria declared independence July 5, 1962. Ahmed Ben Bella ruled until 1965, when an army coup installed Col. Houari Boumedienne, a former guerrilla leader who held power until his death in 1978.

Hundreds died in anti-government riots protesting economic hardship, Oct. 1988. The government canceled the Jan. 1992 elections and banned all nonreligious activities at Algeria's 10,000 mosques. Pres. Mohammed Boudiaf was assassinated June 29, 1992. Over the next seven years, Muslim fundamentalists attacked high-ranking officials, security forces, and foreigners; pro-government death squads were active.

Liamine Zeroual won the Nov. 16, 1995, presidential election. A new constitution banning Islamic political parties and increasing the president's powers passed in a Nov. 1996 referendum. Abdelaziz Bouteflika, who became president after a flawed Apr. 15, 1999, election, reconciled with rebels and won approval for an amnesty plan in a referendum, Sept. 16. Bouteflika was reelected Apr. 8, 2004, though opponents charged fraud.

Under a reconciliation plan approved by referendum Sept. 2005, the government in Mar. 2006 began freeing Islamists jailed for their role in the 1990s civil war, which left up to 200,000 people dead and 8,000 "disappeared."

Radical Islamists bombed police stations in Oct. 2006 and Feb. 2007. A group known as al-Qaeda in the Islamic Maghreb (AQIM) carried out terrorist attacks, 2007-08, that killed more than 200 people.

Bouteflika claimed more than 90% of the vote in a 2009 election denounced as fraudulent by opposition parties. During Arab Spring uprisings in early 2011, Bouteflika's government suppressed street protests in Algiers, Feb. 12. The country's governing party, the Natl. Liberation Front (FLN), strengthened its hold on power in May 10, 2012, parliamentary elections that opposition groups called fraudulent.

AQIM members seized the In Amenas gas facility Jan. 16, 2013, holding about 40 foreign workers hostage for 4 days and demanding the release of about 100 Islamist prisoners; 38 hostages died, as well as some 29 militants, as Algerian special forces attempted to liberate the facility.

The 77-year-old Bouteflika, who had suffered a stroke in 2013, won a fourth term as president with 81.5% of the vote in the Apr. 17, 2014, election. The FLN won May 4, 2017, parliamentary elections.

Large-scale protests following the Feb. 2019 announcement that Bouteflika would seek a fifth term led to his forced resignation Apr. 2, 2019. Pro-democracy protests continued. In a Dec. 12, 2019, presidential election, boycotted by many government opponents, FLN candidate Abdelmadjid Tebboune won with 58% of the vote.

The government instituted travel restrictions and lockdown measures in 2020 to combat the COVID-19 pandemic. As of Sept. 30, Algeria had more than 51,000 cases and over 1,700 deaths.

Andorra
Principality of Andorra

People: Population: 85,635 (186). **Age distrib.:** <15: 13.4%; 65+: 17.4%. **Growth:** −0.1%. **Migrants:** 58.5%. **Pop. density:** 473.9 per sq mi, 183.0 per sq km. **Urban:** 87.9%. **Ethnic groups:** Andorran 48.8%, Spanish 25.1%, Portuguese 12%, French 4.4%. **Languages:** Catalan (official), French, Castilian, Portuguese. **Religions:** Christian 89.7% (Catholic [official] 88.7%), agnostic 6.9%.

Geography: Total area: 181 sq mi, 468 sq km (180). **Land area:** 181 sq mi, 468 sq km. **Location:** SW Europe, in Pyrenees Mts. Spain on S, France on N. **Topography:** High mountains and narrow valleys across country. **Arable land:** 1.7%. **Capital:** Andorra la Vella, 22,614.

Government: Type: Parliamentary democracy. **Heads of state:** President of France and Bishop of Urgell (Spain), as co-princes. **Head of govt.:** Xavier Espot Zamora; in office: May 16, 2019. **Local divisions:** 7 parishes. **Defense budget/active troops:** NA.

Economy: Industries: tourism (skiing), banking, timber, furniture. **Chief agric.:** rye, wheat, barley, oats, vegetables, tobacco; sheep, cattle. **Natural resources:** hydropower, mineral water, timber, iron ore, lead. **Water:** 4,101 cu m per capita. **Labor force:** agric. 0.5%, industry 4.4%, services 95.1%. **Unemployment:** NA.

Finance: Monetary unit: Euro (EUR) (0.84 = $1 U.S.). **GDP:** NA; **per capita GDP:** NA; **GDP growth:** 1.8%. **Imports** (2015): $1.3 bil; Spain 63.6%, France 15.8%. **Exports** (2015): $78.7 mil; Spain 52.6%, France 18.7%. **Budget** (2016): $2.1 bil. **Inflation** (2014-15): −0.9%.

Transport: NA.

Communications: Telephone: 51.1 per 100 pop. **Mobile:** 107.3 per 100 pop. **Broadband:** 55.6 per 100 pop. **Internet:** 91.6%.

Health: Expend.: 10.3%. **Life expect.:** 80.8 male; 85.4 female. **Births:** 7 per 1,000 pop. **Deaths:** 7.7 per 1,000 pop. **Infant mortality:** 3.5 per 1,000 live births. **Undernourished:** NA. **HIV:** NA.

Education: Compulsory: ages 6-15. **Literacy:** 100%.

Embassy: 2 UN Plz., 27th Fl., New York, NY 10017; (212) 750-8064.

Website: www.govern.ad

France and the bishop of Urgell held joint sovereignty over Andorra from 1278 to 1993. Voters chose to adopt a parliamentary system Mar. 14, 1993, although co-princes remain heads of state. Tourism, especially skiing, and banking are economic mainstays. For years, Andorra served as a tax haven, but it began reforms in 2008 and was removed by the OECD from its list of uncooperative tax havens, May 27, 2009. In Mar. 2015, the government seized control of Banca Privada d'Andorra (BPA) and arrested its chief executive after money laundering accusations. The parliament approved, Nov. 30, 2016, a measure to end, in stages, banking secrecy for foreigners' accounts. The 2020 COVID-19 pandemic caused almost 2,000 cases and over 50 deaths as of Sept. 30.

Angola
Republic of Angola

People: Population: 32,522,339 (43). **Age distrib.:** <15: 47.8%; 65+: 2.3%. **Growth:** 3.4%. **Migrants:** 2.1%. **Pop. density:** 67.6 per sq mi, 26.1 per sq km. **Urban:** 66.8%. **Ethnic groups:** Ovimbundu 37%, Kimbundu 25%, Bakongo 13%, mestico (mixed European/native African) 2%. **Languages:** Portuguese (official), Umbundu, Kikongo, Kimbundu, Chokwe. **Religions:** Christian 93.3% (Catholic 57.4%, Protestant 29.2%, independent 6.7%), ethnic religionist 4.7%.

Geography: Total area: 481,354 sq mi, 1,246,700 sq km (22). **Land area:** 481,354 sq mi, 1,246,700 sq km. **Location:** SW Africa on Atlantic coast. Namibia on S, Zambia on E, Dem. Rep. of the Congo on N; Cabinda, an exclave separated from rest of country by short Atlantic coast of Dem. Rep. of the Congo, borders Congo Rep. **Topography:** Mostly plateau 3,000-5,000 ft above sea level, rising from a narrow coastal strip. Temperate highland area in the W-central region, a desert in S, and a tropical rain forest in Cabinda. **Arable land:** 3.9%. **Capital:** Luanda, 8,329,798.

Government: Type: Presidential republic. **Head of state and govt.:** João Lourenço; b. 1954; in office: Sept. 26, 2017. **Local divisions:** 18 provinces. **Defense budget:** $1.7 bil. **Active troops:** 107,000.

Economy: Industries: petroleum, diamonds, cement, metal prods., fish/food proc. **Chief agric.:** bananas, sugarcane, coffee, sisal, corn, cotton, cassava, tobacco; livestock; fish. **Natural resources:** petroleum, diamonds, iron ore, phosphates, copper, feldspar, gold, bauxite, uranium. **Water:** 4,983 cu m per capita. **Crude oil reserves:** 8.2 bil bbls. **Electricity prod.:** 10.7 bil kWh. **Labor force:** agric. 50.2%, industry 8.1%, services 41.7%. **Unemployment:** 6.8%.

Finance: Monetary unit: Kwanza (AOA) (621.86 = $1 U.S.). **GDP:** $220.5 bil; **per capita GDP:** $6,930; **GDP growth:** −0.9%. **Imports:** $19.5 bil; Portugal 17.8%, China 13.5%, U.S. 7.4%, South Africa 6.2%, Brazil 6.1%. **Exports:** $33.1 bil; China 61.2%, India 13%. **Tourism:** $384 mil. **Budget:** $45.4 bil. **Inflation** (2016-17): 25.7%.

Transport: Railways: 1,772 mi. **Motor vehicles:** 5.4 per 1,000 pop. **Airports:** 32.

Communications: Telephone: 0.6 per 100 pop. **Mobile:** 43.1 per 100 pop. **Broadband:** 14.6 per 100 pop. **Internet:** 14.3%.

Health: Expend.: 2.8%. **Life expect.:** 59.3 male; 63.4 female. **Births:** 42.7 per 1,000 pop. **Deaths:** 8.5 per 1,000 pop. **Infant mortality:** 62.3 per 1,000 live births. **Undernourished:** 18.6%. **HIV:** 1.9%.

Education: Compulsory: ages 6-11. **Literacy:** 77.4%.

Embassy: 2100-2108 16th St NW 20009; 785-1156.

Website: www.angola.gov.ao

From the early centuries ce to 1500, Bantu tribes penetrated most of the region. Portuguese came in 1583, allied with the Bakongo kingdom in the north, and developed the slave trade. Large-scale colonization began in the 20th cent., when 400,000 Portuguese immigrated.

A guerrilla war, 1961-75, ended when Portugal granted Angola independence. Fighting then erupted among rival rebel groups, including the Soviet-backed Popular Movement for the Liberation of Angola (MPLA) and the National Union for the Total Independence of Angola (UNITA), aided by the U.S. and South Africa. Cuban troops helped the MPLA win control of most of the country by 1976, although fighting continued. MPLA-UNITA peace accords in 1991 and 1994 failed to hold. The UN estimated that the civil war had claimed down some 1 mil lives and left another 2.5 mil people homeless by mid-2001. Government troops killed rebel leader Jonas Savimbi Feb. 22, 2002. UNITA agreed to a truce Apr. 4, 2002. Separatist rebels in oil-rich Cabinda agreed to a cease-fire July 2006.

With proven petroleum reserves estimated at about 8 bil barrels, Angola is among Africa's leading oil producers. Wealth is extremely unevenly distributed and corruption has been wide-spread. The ruling MPLA claimed victory in voting Sept. 2008, in Angola's first parliamentary elections in 16 years. Parliament approved Jan. 21, 2010, a new constitution augmenting the power of MPLA leader José Eduardo dos Santos, Angola's president since 1979. The MPLA won flawed elections, Aug 31, 2012, giving dos Santos another 5-year term. The MPLA won disputed Aug. 23, 2017, elections, and João Lourenço took office as president, Sept. 26. On Nov. 15, Lourenço dismissed as head of the state oil company dos Santos's daughter, Isabel dos Santos, suspected of misappropriating government funds. On Jan. 11, 2018, Lourenço removed as head of the country's sovereign wealth fund dos Santos's son, José Filomeno dos Santos; he was sentenced, Aug. 2020, to 5 years in prison for embezzlement.

A new penal code, approved Jan. 23, 2019, decriminalized same-sex relationships and prohibited discrimination based on sexual orientation. The 2020 COVID-19 pandemic caused about 4,800 cases and 176 deaths in Angola by Sept. 30.

Antigua and Barbuda

People: Population: 98,179 (184). **Age distrib.:** <15: 22.5%; 65+: 8.9%. **Growth:** 1.2%. **Migrants:** 30.1%. **Pop. density:** 574.5 per sq mi, 221.8 per sq km. **Urban:** 24.4%. **Ethnic groups:** African descent 87.3%, mixed 4.7%, Hispanic 2.7%. **Languages:** English (official), Antiguan creole. **Religions:** Christian 93.3% (Protestant 78.8%, Catholic 10.3%), Spiritist 3.4%.

Geography: Total area: 171 sq mi, 443 sq km (Antigua, 108 sq mi, 280 sq km; Barbuda, 62 sq mi, 161 sq km) (183); **Land area:** 171 sq mi, 443 sq km. **Location:** E Caribbean. St. Kitts and Nevis to W, Guadeloupe (Fr.) to S. **Topography:** Mostly low-lying and limestone coral islands. Antigua is mostly hilly with an indented coast; Barbuda is a flat island with a large lagoon on W. **Arable land:** 9.1%. **Capital:** St. John's, 20,764.

Government: Type: Parliamentary democracy under constitutional monarchy. **Head of state:** Queen Elizabeth II, rep. by Gov.-Gen. Rodney Williams; b. 1947; in office: Aug. 14, 2014. **Head of govt.:** Prime Min. Gaston Browne; b. 1967; in office: June 13, 2014. **Local divisions:** 6 parishes, 2 dependencies. **Defense budget:** $7 mil. **Active troops:** 180.

Economy: Industries: tourism, constr., light mfg. **Chief agric.:** cotton, fruits, vegetables, bananas, coconuts; livestock. **Natural resources:** negligible. **Water:** 510 cu m per capita. **Electricity prod.:** 331 mil kWh. **Labor force:** NA. **Unemployment:** NA.

Finance: Monetary unit: East Caribbean Dollar (XCD) (2.70 = $1 U.S.). **GDP:** $2.2 bil; **per capita GDP:** $22,816; **GDP growth:** 4.7%. **Imports:** $560 mil; U.S. 48%. **Exports:** $86.7 mil; Poland 62.2%, Cameroon 9.5%, U.S. 5.1%. **Tourism:** $733 mil. **Budget:** $334.0 mil. **Inflation** (2017-18): 1.2%.

Transport: Airports: 2.

Communications: Telephone (2017): 25.2 per 100 pop. **Mobile** (2017): 192.8 per 100 pop. **Broadband:** 47.1 per 100 pop. **Internet:** 76%.

Health: Expend.: 4.5%. **Life expect.:** 75.1 male; 79.6 female. **Births:** 15.4 per 1,000 pop. **Deaths:** 5.8 per 1,000 pop. **Infant mortality:** 11.1 per 1,000 live births. **Undernourished:** NA. **HIV** (2018): 1.1%.

Education: Compulsory: ages 5-15. **Literacy:** 99%.
Embassy: 3216 New Mexico Ave. NW 20016; 362-5122.
Website: ab.gov.ag

Christopher Columbus landed on Antigua in 1493. The British colonized it in 1632. The British-associated state of Antigua achieved independence as Antigua and Barbuda on Nov. 1, 1981. Tourism accounts for almost 60% of GDP. The worldwide recession caused the economy to shrink in 2009-11. With the economy still weak, the opposition Antigua and Barbuda Labour Party (ABLP) won June 12, 2014, parliamentary elections. ABLP leader Gaston Browne became prime minister and supported economic development projects opposed by environmental groups and others. The ABLP retained power in Mar. 21, 2018, elections.

Hurricane Irma caused massive damage on Barbuda, Sept. 5-6, 2017. Travel restrictions and lockdown measures in 2020 to prevent COVID-19 spread hurt the tourism industry.

Argentina
Argentine Republic

People: Population: 45,479,118 (32). **Age distrib.:** <15: 24.0%; 65+: 12.1%. **Growth:** 0.9%. **Migrants:** 4.9%. **Pop. density:** 43.0 per sq mi, 16.6 per sq km. **Urban:** 92.1%. **Ethnic groups:** European (mostly Spanish and Italian) and mestizo (mixed European/Amerindian) 97.2%, Amerindian 2.4%. **Languages:** Spanish (official), Italian, English, German, French, Indigenous (Mapudungun, Quechua). **Religions:** Christian 88.7% (Catholic [official] 77.2%), agnostic 6.9%.

Geography: Total area: 1,073,518 sq mi, 2,780,400 sq km (8); **Land area:** 1,056,642 sq mi, 2,736,690 sq km. **Location:** Occupies most of southern S America. Chile on W; Bolivia, Paraguay on N; Brazil, Uruguay on NE. **Topography:** Andean, Central, Misiones, and Southern mountain ranges in W. Aconcagua (22,831

ft) is highest peak in Western Hemisphere. Heavily wooded plains called the Gran Chaco are E of Andes in the N; fertile, treeless Pampas in the central region. Patagonia, in S, is bleak and arid. Rio de la Plata, an estuary in NE, 170 by 140 mi, is mostly freshwater, from 2,485-mi Parana and 1,000-mi Uruguay Rivers. **Arable land:** 14.3%. **Capital:** Buenos Aires, 15,153,729. **Cities:** Córdoba, 1,571,944; Rosario, 1,532,128; Mendoza, 1,172,619.

Government: Type: Presidential republic. **Head of state and govt.:** Pres. Alberto Ángel Fernández; b. 1956; in office: Dec. 10, 2019. **Local divisions:** 23 provinces, 1 autonomous city. **Defense budget:** $3.3 bil. **Active troops:** 74,200.

Economy: Industries: food proc., motor vehicles, consumer durables, textiles, chemicals and petrochemicals. **Chief agric.:** sunflower seeds, lemons, soybeans, grapes, corn, tobacco; livestock. **Natural resources:** lead, zinc, tin, copper, iron ore, manganese, petroleum, uranium. **Water:** 19,792 cu m per capita. **Crude oil reserves:** 2.4 bil bbls. **Electricity prod.:** 138.4 bil kWh. **Labor force:** agric. 0.1%, industry 21.0%, services 78.9%. **Unemployment:** 10.4%.

Finance: Monetary unit: Peso (ARS) (74.44 = $1 U.S.). **GDP:** $1.0 tril; **per capita GDP:** $22,947; **GDP growth:** −2.2%. **Imports:** $64 bil; Brazil 26.9%, China 18.5%, U.S. 11.3%. **Exports:** $58.5 bil; Brazil 16.1%, U.S. 7.9%, China 7.5%. **Tourism:** $5.2 bil. **Budget:** $158.6 bil. **Inflation** (2016-17): 25.7%.

Transport: Railways: 22,939 mi. **Motor vehicles:** 322.4 per 1,000 pop. **Airports:** 161.

Communications: Telephone: 21.9 per 100 pop. **Mobile:** 132.1 per 100 pop. **Broadband:** 80 per 100 pop. **Internet:** 74.3%.

Health: Expend.: 9.1%. **Life expect.:** 74.7 male; 81.1 female. **Births:** 16 per 1,000 pop. **Deaths:** 7.4 per 1,000 pop. **Infant mortality:** 9.0 per 1,000 live births. **Undernourished:** 3.8%. **HIV:** 0.4%.

Education: Compulsory: ages 4-17. **Literacy:** 99.5%.
Embassy: 1600 New Hampshire Ave. NW 20009; 238-6400.
Website: www.argentina.gob.ar

Nomadic Indians roamed the Pampas when Spaniards arrived, 1515-16, led by Juan Díaz de Solís. Nearly all the Indians were killed by the late 19th cent. The colonists won independence, 1816. A long period of disorder ended in a strong centralized government.

Large-scale Italian, German, and Spanish immigration in the decades after 1880 spurred modernization. Social reforms were enacted in the 1920s, but military coups prevailed, 1930-46, until Gen. Juan Perón was elected president.

Perón, with his wife, Eva Duarte (d. 1952), introduced labor reforms but suppressed speech and press freedoms, closed religious schools, and ran the country into debt. A 1955 coup exiled Perón. A series of military and civilian regimes followed. Perón returned in 1973 and was again elected president. He died 10 months later. His wife and vice president, Isabel, succeeded him.

A military junta ousted Isabel Perón in 1976 amid charges of corruption. Under a continuing state of siege, the army conducted a "dirty war" against guerrillas and leftists. An estimated 30,000 people "disappeared."

Argentine troops seized control of the British-held Falkland Islands (Islas Malvinas) on Apr. 2, 1982. The British imposed an air and sea blockade around the Falklands. Fighting began May 1. British troops landed on East Falkland May 21. Argentine troops surrendered, June 14.

Democratic rule returned in 1983. On Dec. 9, 1985, five former junta members were found guilty of murder and human rights abuses during the "dirty war" period. Buenos Aires Mayor Fernando de la Rúa won the presidential election Oct. 24, 1999, but resigned in 2001 after a prolonged recession resulted in debt of more than $130 bil. Congress, Jan. 1, 2002, chose a Peronist, Eduardo Alberto Duhalde, to finish de la Rúa's term. Further economic decline and renewed protests led Duhalde, July 2, to schedule an early presidential election for Mar. 2003; another Peronist, Néstor Kirchner, took office May 25, 2003. A new IMF aid deal, approved Sept. 10, 2003, rescued Argentina from default.

The Supreme Court, June 14, 2005, overturned amnesty laws that had barred prosecution for "dirty war" crimes committed while the military ruled Argentina. In July 2010, Argentina became the first Latin American country to extend full marriage rights to same-sex couples.

Cristina Fernández de Kirchner ran as the Peronist candidate after her husband and was elected president Oct. 28, 2007. She was reelected Oct. 23, 2011. In 2013, Argentine special prosecutor Alberto Nisman accused Fernández de Kirchner of interfering with his investigation of Iranian involvement in a 1994 Jewish community center bombing in Buenos Aires that killed 85 people. Nisman was found dead in his home from a gunshot to the head Jan. 18, 2015. Contradicting earlier police reports, a border police investigation concluded, Nov. 2017, that Nisman had been murdered. On Mar. 5, 2018, Fernández de Kirchner was ordered to stand trial on charges of covering up Iranian involvement in the Jewish center bombing. She had been indicted, May 13, 2016, for allegedly manipulating the value of the Argentine peso while president. She was also indicted, 2016-18, on financial corruption and bribery charges.

Buenos Aires Archbishop Jorge Mario Bergoglio was elected pope Mar. 13, 2013; he was the first pope from the Americas. He took the name Francis.

Former Pres. Carlos Saúl Menem (1989-99) was convicted, Dec. 1, 2015, of embezzlement of public funds.

Defeating Peronist candidate Daniel Scioli in a runoff, Mauricio Macri of the center-right Republican Proposal Party was elected president Nov. 22, 2015. Pres. Macri, Sept. 3, 2018, announced austerity measures to stem a budget deficit and a sharp drop in the value of the peso. With economic problems continuing, Peronist Alberto Fernández defeated Macri in the Oct. 27, 2019, presidential election; Cristina Fernández de Kirchner was elected vice president. COVID-19 and lockdown measures to slow spread of the disease further hurt the economy in 2020. By Sept. 30, Argentina had more than 723,000 COVID-19 cases and over 16,000 deaths.

Armenia
Republic of Armenia

People: Population: 3,021,324 (135). **Age distrib.:** <15: 18.6%; 65+: 12.6%. **Growth:** −0.3%. **Migrants:** 6.4%. **Pop. density:** 277.5 per sq mi, 107.1 per sq km. **Urban:** 63.3%. **Ethnic groups:** Armenian 98.1%, Yezidi (Kurd) 1.2%. **Languages:** Armenian (official), Kurdish. **Religions:** Christian 94.4% (Orthodox [official] 81.6%, Catholic 8.3%), agnostic 3.1%.

Geography: Total area: 11,484 sq mi, 29,743 sq km (139); **Land area:** 10,889 sq mi, 28,203 sq km. **Location:** SW Asia. Georgia on N, Azerbaijan on E, Iran on S, Turkey on W. **Topography:** Mountainous with many peaks above 10,000 ft. **Arable land:** 15.7%. **Capital:** Yerevan, 1,086,275.

Government: Type: Parliamentary democracy. **Head of state:** Pres. Armen Sarkissian; b. 1953; in office: Apr. 9, 2018. **Head of govt.:** Prime Min. Nikol Pashinyan; b. 1975; in office: May 8, 2018. **Local divisions:** 11 provinces. **Defense budget:** $644 mil. **Active troops:** 44,800.

Economy: Industries: brandy, mining, diamond proc., metal-cutting machine tools, forging/pressing machines, elec. motors, knitted wear. **Chief agric.:** fruit (espec. grapes, apricots), vegetables; livestock. **Natural resources:** gold, copper, molybdenum, zinc, bauxite. **Water:** 2,652 cu m per capita. **Electricity prod.:** 7.4 bil kWh. **Labor force:** agric. 28.9%, industry 17.5%, services 53.6%. **Unemployment:** 16.6%.

Finance: Monetary unit: Dram (AMD) (481.62 = $1 U.S.). **GDP:** $42.1 bil; **per capita GDP:** $14,220; **GDP growth:** 7.6%. **Imports:** $3.8 bil; Russia 28%, China 11.5%, Turkey 5.5%. **Exports:** $2.4 bil; Russia 24.2%, Bulgaria 12.8%, Switzerland 12%, Georgia 6.9%, Germany 5.9%, China 5.5%, Iraq 5.4%. **Tourism:** $1.5 bil. **Budget:** $3.2 bil. **Inflation:** 1.4%.

Transport: Railways: 485 mi (only partly operational). **Airports:** 10.

Communications: Telephone: 16.1 per 100 pop. **Mobile:** 121.3 per 100 pop. **Broadband:** 66.8 per 100 pop. **Internet:** 64.7%.

Health: Expend.: 10.4%. **Life expect.:** 72.3 male; 79.2 female. **Births:** 11.9 per 1,000 pop. **Deaths:** 9.5 per 1,000 pop. **Infant mortality:** 11.5 per 1,000 live births. **Undernourished:** 2.6%. **HIV:** 0.2%.

Education: Compulsory: ages 6-17. **Literacy:** 99.8%.
Embassy: 2225 R St. NW 20008; 319-1976.
Website: www.gov.am

Ancient Armenia extended into parts of what are now Turkey and Iran. Present-day Armenia was set up as a Soviet republic Apr. 2, 1921. It joined Georgian and Azerbaijan SSRs Mar. 12, 1922, to form the Transcaucasian SFSR, which became part of the USSR Dec. 30, 1922. Armenia became a constituent republic of the USSR Dec. 5, 1936. An earthquake struck Armenia Dec. 7, 1988; approximately 25,000 were killed.

Armenia declared independence Sept. 23, 1991, and became an independent state when the USSR disbanded Dec. 26, 1991. Nagorno-Karabakh, an enclave in Azerbaijan with an ethnic Armenian majority, seceded from Azerbaijan in 1988. A 1992-94 war that cost 30,000 lives ended in a cease-fire with Armenian forces in control. Voters in the breakaway region approved a pro-independence constitution Dec. 10, 2006. Deadly clashes between Armenian and Azerbaijani forces occurred in 2015-16 in and near Nagorno-Karabakh. New fighting broke out in July 2020 and again beginning in Sept. 2020.

Voters approved, July 5, 1995, a new constitution increasing presidential powers. Pres. Levon Ter-Petrosian won reelection Sept. 22, 1996, amid claims of fraud. He resigned Feb. 3, 1998, and Robert Kocharian, a nationalist born in Nagorno-Karabakh, won the presidency Mar. 30, 1998. Gunmen stormed Parliament Oct. 27, 1999, killing Prime Min. Vazgen Sarkissian and 7 others. Kocharian won a second term Mar. 5, 2003.

Prime Min. Serzh Sargsyan defeated Ter-Petrosian in a Feb. 19, 2008, presidential election and won reelection Feb. 18, 2013. Constitutional revisions transitioned the government to a parliamentary system as of 2018, with presidential powers reduced. Sargsyan's party won Apr. 2, 2017, parliamentary elections. Sargsyan became prime min., Apr. 17, 2018, but large-scale protests led to his resignation Apr. 23. Opposition leader Nikol Pashinyan was elected prime min. by parliament May 8. Pashinyan's party won a landslide victory in Dec. 9, 2018, parliamentary elections.

Armenia did not ratify an Oct. 2009 treaty it had approved with Turkey over the 1915-18 killing of more than 1 mil Armenians by Ottoman Turks, due to renewed friction between the countries in 2010. On Jan. 2, 2015, Armenia joined the new Russian-led Eurasian Economic Union. Affected by the 2020 COVID-19 pandemic, Armenia had about 50,000 cases and almost 1,000 deaths by Sept. 30.

Australia
Commonwealth of Australia

People: Population: 25,466,459 (55). **Age distrib.:** <15: 18.7%; 65+: 15.9%. **Growth:** 1.4%. **Migrants:** 30.0%. **Pop. density:** 8.6 per sq mi, 3.3 per sq km. **Urban:** 86.2%. **Ethnic groups:** English 25.9%, Australian 25.4%, Irish 7.5%, Scottish 6.4%, Italian 3.3%, German 3.2%, Chinese 3.1%. **Languages:** English, Chinese, Arabic, Vietnamese, Italian. **Religions:** Christian 53.4% (Catholic 23%, Protestant 22.9%), agnostic 28.2%, atheist 7.3%, Buddhist 3.2%, Muslim 3.1% (Sunni 2%).

Geography: Total area: 2,988,902 sq mi, 7,741,220 sq km (6); **Land area:** 2,966,153 sq mi, 7,682,300 sq km. **Location:** SE of Asia. Surrounded by Indian O. on W and S, Pacific O. (Coral, Tasman Seas) in E. Tasmania lies 150 mi S of Victoria state, across Bass Strait. Nearest are Indonesia, Papua New Guinea on N; Solomons, Fiji, and New Zealand on E. **Topography:** An island continent. The Great Dividing Range along the E coast has Mt. Kosciusko (7,310 ft). The Western Plateau rises to 2,000 ft, with arid areas in the Great Sandy and Great Victoria Deserts. The NW part of Western Australia and Northern Terr. are arid and hot. The NE has heavy rainfall. Jungles in Cape York Peninsula. **Arable land:** 4.0%. **Capital:** Canberra, 457,330. **Cities:** Melbourne, 4,967,733; Sydney, 4,925,987; Brisbane, 2,406,182; Perth, 2,041,959; Adelaide, 1,336,403.

Government: Type: Parliamentary democracy under constitutional monarchy. **Head of state:** Queen Elizabeth II, rep. by Gov.-Gen. David Hurley; b. 1953; in office: July 1, 2019. **Head of govt.:** Prime Min. Scott Morrison; b. 1968; in office: Aug. 24, 2018. **Local divisions:** 6 states, 2 territories. **Defense budget:** $25.5 bil. **Active troops:** 57,200.

Economy: Industries: mining, industrial and transp. equip., food proc., chemicals, steel. **Chief agric.:** wheat, barley, sugarcane, fruits; cattle, sheep, poultry. **Natural resources:** bauxite, coal, iron ore, copper, tin, gold, silver, uranium, nickel, tungsten, rare earth elements, mineral sands, lead, zinc, diamonds, nat. gas, petroleum. **Water:** 20,123 cu m per capita. **Crude oil reserves:** 2.4 bil bbls. **Electricity prod.** (2018): 248.8 bil kWh. **Labor force:** agric. 2.5%, industry 19.8%, services 77.7%. **Unemployment:** 5.3%.

Finance: Monetary unit: Dollar (AUD) (1.37 = $1 U.S.). **GDP:** $1.4 tril; **per capita GDP:** $53,320; **GDP growth:** 1.9%. **Imports:** $221 bil; China 22.9%, U.S. 10.8%, Japan 7.5%, Thailand 5.1%. **Exports:** $231.6 bil; China 33.5%, Japan 14.6%, South Korea 6.6%, India 5%. **Tourism:** $45.7 bil. **Budget:** $496.9 bil. **Inflation:** 1.6%.

Transport: Railways: 20,718 mi. **Motor vehicles:** 794 per 1,000 pop. **Airports:** 349.

Communications: Telephone: 32.5 per 100 pop. **Mobile:** 113.6 per 100 pop. **Broadband:** 134.9 per 100 pop. **Internet** 86.5%.

Health: Expend.: 9.2%. **Life expect.:** 80.5 male; 85.0 female. **Births:** 12.4 per 1,000 pop. **Deaths:** 6.9 per 1,000 pop. **Infant mortality:** 3.1 per 1,000 live births. **Undernourished:** <2.5%. **HIV:** 0.1%.
Education: Compulsory: ages 6-15. **Literacy:** 99%.
Embassy: 1601 Massachusetts Ave. NW 20036; 797-3000. Temp. location during construction (beg. Dec. 2019): 1145 17th St. NW.
Website: www.australia.gov.au

Australia harbors many plant and animal species not found elsewhere, including kangaroos, koalas, platypuses, dingoes (wild dogs), Tasmanian devils, wombats, and barking and frilled lizards.

Capt. James Cook explored the eastern coast in 1770, when the continent and offshore islands were inhabited by Indigenous peoples. The first European settlers, beginning in 1788, were mostly convicts, soldiers, and government officials. By 1830, Britain had claimed the entire continent, and the immigration of free settlers accelerated. The Commonwealth was proclaimed Jan. 1, 1901. Northern Terr. was granted limited self-rule July 1, 1978.

State/territory, capital	Tot. area (sq mi)	Population (2019 est.)
New South Wales, Sydney	309,326	8,128,984
Victoria, Melbourne	87,817	6,651,074
Queensland, Brisbane	667,857	5,129,996
Western Australia, Perth	975,685	2,639,080
South Australia, Adelaide	380,048	1,759,184
Tasmania, Hobart	26,410	537,012
Australian Capital Terr., Canberra	910	427,419
Northern Terr., Darwin	520,385	244,761

Note: Preliminary pop. est. as of Dec. 31. (Source: Australian Bureau of Statistics.)

In a 1967 referendum, Australians voted to change parts of the country's constitution that discriminated against Aboriginal

Australians. Racially discriminatory immigration policies ended in 1973, after 3 mil Europeans (half British) had entered since 1945.

Australia is among the top exporters of lamb, wool, and wheat. Major mineral deposits, including coal, have been developed, largely for export. Slumping commodity prices and sluggish exports to China impacted the economy beginning in 2016. By 2019, the government instituted various economic stimulus measures to boost sagging GDP growth.

In a referendum Nov. 6, 1999, voters rejected a proposal that would have made Australia a republic.

Australian troops fought in U.S.-led military operations in Afghanistan (since 2001) and Iraq (beginning 2003); about 200 Australian troops were in Afghanistan in mid-2020. Some 2,000 Australian peacekeepers began arriving in the Solomon Isls., July 24, 2003; nearly all were withdrawn by mid-2005. In race riots in Sydney suburbs, Dec. 11-12, 2005, thousands of youths assaulted people of Middle Eastern ancestry, who then retaliated. Australian troops were dispatched, 2006, to suppress disorder in the Solomon Isls. in Apr. and Timor in May. The last Australian troops in Timor returned home on Mar. 27, 2013. Australian warplanes, Oct. 1, 2014, joined the U.S.-led air campaign in Iraq against the Sunni extremist group ISIS. Beginning in late 2014, Australia sent military advisers (about 160 as of 2020) to train and assist Iraqi armed forces. In Sept. 2015, Australia joined the U.S.-led air campaign against ISIS in Syria. Australia ended air combat missions in Iraq and Syria in Jan. 2018.

The Labor Party's Julia Gillard became, June 24, 2010, Australia's first female prime minister. Downpours from Cyclone Tasha and other storms caused severe flooding in Queensland, Dec. 2010-Jan. 2011. Prime Min. Gillard, Mar. 20, 2013, officially apologized for Australia's forced adoption policy (in effect late 1950s-70s), in which the state took the babies of single, teenage, or "unfit" mothers, often under duress. Labor's Kevin Rudd replaced Gillard June 26, 2013.

The conservatives returned to power after Sept. 7, 2013, elections. Prime Min. Tony Abbott announced, Sept. 9, 2015, that Australia would accept, in a special program, 12,000 refugees from the conflicts in Syria and Iraq; a total of about 23,000 Syrian and Iraqi refugees arrived in Australia 2015-17. Malcolm Turnbull replaced Abbott as prime min., Sept. 15, 2015, after defeating him in a vote for Liberal Party leader. Turnbull's Liberal/National Party coalition won a narrow victory in July 2, 2016, elections. Liberal Scott Morrison replaced Turnbull as prime min., Aug. 24, 2018.

Bushfires in New South Wales and other areas beginning in Sept. 2019 burned at least 12 mil acres and caused more than 30 deaths by early 2020. National and state governments instituted travel restrictions and lockdown measures in 2020 to combat the COVID-19 pandemic; as of Sept. 30, Australia had about 27,000 cases and almost 900 deaths.

Australian External Territories

Norfolk Isl., area 14 sq mi, pop. (2018 est.) 1,756, was taken over, 1914. The soil is very fertile, suitable for citrus, bananas, and coffee. Many of the inhabitants are descended from Pitcairn Islanders who moved to Norfolk in 1856 after the British abandoned an attempted penal colony. Australia offered the island limited home rule in 1979 but revoked its autonomy in 2015. The island's legislative assembly was replaced by an elected regional council in 2016. **Website:** www.norfolkisland.gov.nf

The only inhabitants of **Coral Sea Isls.**, area <1.2 sq mi, are meteorological staff on Willis Isl.

Ashmore and Cartier Isls., area 1.9 sq mi, in the Indian O., came under Australian authority in 1934. **Heard Isl. and McDonald Isls.**, area 159 sq mi, are administered by the Australian Antarctic Division.

Cocos (Keeling) Isls. are 27 coral islands in the Indian O. about 1,833 mi NW of Australia. Area 5.4 sq mi; pop. (2018 est.) 538. The residents voted to become part of Australia, Apr. 1984. **Website:** www.shire.cc

Christmas Isl., area 52 sq mi, pop. (2018 est.) 1,928; 230 mi S of Java, was transferred by Britain in 1958. Phosphate mining is the main economic activity, though high-grade phosphate deposits are nearly depleted. **Website:** www.shire.gov.cx

Australian Antarctic Territory was claimed by the UK and then transferred to Australian sovereignty in 1933. It comprises some 2.2 mil sq mi of territory S of 60th parallel S lat. between 45°E and 160°E (not incl. France's Adelie Coast) and between 136°E and 142°E.

Austria
Republic of Austria

People: Population: 8,859,449 (97). **Age distrib.:** <15: 14.0%; 65+: 19.9%. **Growth:** 0.3%. **Migrants:** 19.9%. **Pop. density:** 278.3 per sq mi, 107.5 per sq km. **Urban:** 58.7%. **Ethnic groups** (by birth country): Austrian 80.8%, German 2.6%. **Languages:** German (official), Turkish, Serbian, Croatian (official in one state). **Religions:** Christian 71.2% (Catholic 63.4%), agnostic 18.3%, Muslim 7.5%.

Geography: Total area: 32,383 sq mi, 83,871 sq km (112); **Land area:** 31,832 sq mi, 82,445 sq km. **Location:** S Central Europe. Switzerland, Liechtenstein on W; Germany, Czech Rep. on N; Slovakia, Hungary on E; Slovenia, Italy on S. **Topography:** Primarily mountainous, with the Alps and foothills covering the western and southern provinces. The eastern provinces and Vienna are located in the Danube River Basin. **Arable land:** 16.1%. **Capital:** Vienna, 1,929,944.

Government: Type: Federal parliamentary republic. **Head of state:** Pres. Alexander Van der Bellen; b. 1944; in office: Jan. 26, 2017. **Head of govt.:** Chancellor Sebastian Kurz; b. 1986; in office: Jan. 2, 2020. **Local divisions:** 9 states. **Defense budget:** $3.2 bil. **Active troops:** 22,850.

Economy: Industries: constr., machinery, vehicles and parts, food, metals, chemicals, lumber and paper, electronics, tourism. **Chief agric.:** grains, potatoes, wine, fruit; dairy prods., cattle, pigs. **Natural resources:** oil, coal, lignite, timber, iron ore, copper, zinc, antimony, magnesite, tungsten, graphite, salt, hydropower. **Water:** 8,895 cu m per capita. **Crude oil reserves:** 37 mil bbls. **Electricity prod.** (2018): 61.1 bil kWh. **Labor force:** agric. 3.5%, industry 25.0%, services 71.5%. **Unemployment:** 4.8%.

Finance: Monetary unit: Euro (EUR) (0.84 = $1 U.S.). **GDP:** $524.7 bil; **per capita GDP:** $59,111; **GDP growth:** 1.6%. **Imports:** $158.1 bil; Germany 41.8%, Italy 5.8%, Switzerland 5.5%. **Exports:** $156.7 bil; Germany 29.4%, U.S. 6.3%, Italy 6.2%, Switzerland 5.1%. **Tourism:** $22.9 bil. **Budget:** $204.6 bil. **Inflation:** 1.5%.

Transport: Railways: 3,604 mi. **Motor vehicles:** 623.7 per 1,000 pop. **Airports:** 24.

Communications: Telephone: 42.4 per 100 pop. **Mobile:** 123.5 per 100 pop. **Broadband:** 86.2 per 100 pop. **Internet** (2018): 87.7%.

Health: Expend.: 10.4%. **Life expect.:** 79.2 male; 84.7 female. **Births:** 9.5 per 1,000 pop. **Deaths:** 9.8 per 1,000 pop. **Infant mortality:** 3.3 per 1,000 live births. **Undernourished:** <2.5%. **HIV:** NA.

Education: Compulsory: ages 5-17. **Literacy:** 98%. **Embassy:** 3524 International Ct. NW 20008; 895-6700. **Website:** www.bundeskanzleramt.gv.at

Rome conquered Austrian lands from Celtic tribes around 15 BCE. In 788 the territory was incorporated into Charlemagne's empire. By 1300, the House of Habsburg had gained control; it added vast territories in all parts of Europe to the realm in the next few hundred years.

Austrian dominance of Germany was undermined in the 18th cent. and ended by Prussia by 1866. But the Congress of Vienna, 1815, confirmed Austrian control of a large empire in SE Europe consisting of Germans, Hungarians, Slavs, Italians, and others. The dual Austro-Hungarian monarchy was established in 1867, giving autonomy to Hungary and almost 50 years of peace.

World War I, which started after the June 28, 1914, assassination of Archduke Franz Ferdinand, the Habsburg heir, by a Serbian nationalist, destroyed the empire. By 1918 Austria was reduced to a small republic, with the borders it has today.

Nazi Germany, ruled by the Austrian-born Adolf Hitler, annexed Austria Mar. 13, 1938. The republic was reestablished in 1945, under Allied occupation. Full independence and neutrality were restored in 1955. Austria joined the EU Jan. 1, 1995.

The right-wing, anti-immigrant Austrian Freedom Party (FPO) challenged the dominance of the Social Democratic Party (SPO) beginning in the late 1990s. However, the SPO won parliamentary elections in 2006, 2008, and 2013. Former Green Party leader Alexander Van der Bellen defeated FPO candidate Norbert Hofer in a Dec. 4, 2016, presidential runoff election. The conservative Austrian People's Party (OVP) won Oct. 15, 2017, parliamentary elections; after forming a coalition with the FPO, OVP leader Sebastian Kurz became chancellor Dec. 18. The OVP/FPO coalition collapsed, May 2019. After the OVP won Sept. 29, 2019, elections, Kurz formed a new coalition with the Green Party and again became chancellor Jan. 7, 2020, governing with Austria's first female-majority cabinet.

Hundreds of thousands of migrants fleeing war and hardship in Syria and elsewhere entered Austria in 2015, many en route to N Europe. About 125,000 migrants applied for asylum in Austria in 2015-16. Government actions in 2016 sharply limited future asylum claims. Affected by the 2020 COVID-19 pandemic, Austria recorded about 44,000 cases by Sept. 30 and almost 800 deaths.

Azerbaijan
Republic of Azerbaijan

People: Population: 10,205,810 (90). **Age distrib.:** <15: 22.8%; 65+: 7.3%. **Growth:** 0.7%. **Migrants:** 2.5%. **Pop. density:** 319.9 per sq mi, 123.5 per sq km. **Urban:** 56.4%. **Ethnic groups:** Azerbaijani 91.6%, Lezghin 2%. **Languages:** Azerbaijani (Azeri) (official), Russian, Armenian. **Religions:** Muslim 96.3% (Shia 66%, Sunni 30%), Christian 2.4%.

Geography: Total area: 33,436 sq mi, 86,600 sq km (111); **Land area:** 31,903 sq mi, 82,629 sq km. **Location:** SW Asia. Russia, Georgia on N; Iran on S; Armenia on W; Caspian Sea on E. **Topography:** The Great Caucasus Mts. in N, Karabakh Upland in W border the Kur-Araz lowland. Arid climate except in subtropical SE. **Arable land:** 25.3%. **Capital:** Baku, 2,341,443.

Government: Type: Presidential republic. **Head of state:** Pres. Ilham Aliyev; b. 1961; in office: Oct. 31, 2003. **Head of govt.:** Prime

Min. Ali Asadov; b. 1956; in office: Oct. 8, 2019. **Local divisions:** 66 rayons, 11 cities. **Defense budget:** $1.8 bil. **Active troops:** 66,950.

Economy: Industries: petroleum/petroleum prods., nat. gas, oil field equip.; steel, iron ore; cement. **Chief agric.:** fruit, vegetables, grain, rice; cattle, pigs, sheep, goats. **Natural resources:** petroleum, nat. gas, iron ore, nonferrous metals, bauxite. **Water:** 3,529 cu m per capita. **Crude oil reserves:** 7 bil bbls. **Electricity prod.** (2018): 23.8 bil kWh. **Labor force:** agric. 35.5%, industry 15.0%, services 49.5%. **Unemployment:** 6.0%.

Finance: Monetary unit: Manat (AZN) (1.70 = $1 U.S.). **GDP:** $150.4 bil; **per capita GDP:** $15,001; **GDP growth:** 2.2%. **Imports:** $9 bil; Russia 17.7%, Turkey 14.8%, China 9.9%, U.S. 8.3%, Ukraine 5.3%, Germany 5.1%. **Exports:** $15.2 bil; Italy 23.2%, Turkey 13.6%, Israel 6.1%, Russia 5.4%, Germany 5%. **Tourism:** $2.6 bil. **Budget:** $10.2 bil. **Inflation:** 2.6%.

Transport: Railways: 1,830 mi. **Motor vehicles:** 173.7 per 1,000 pop. **Airports:** 30.

Communications: Telephone: 16.9 per 100 pop. **Mobile:** 103.9 per 100 pop. **Broadband:** 56.8 per 100 pop. **Internet** (2018): 79.8%.

Health: Expend.: 6.7%. **Life expect.:** 70.5 male; 76.9 female. **Births:** 14.5 per 1,000 pop. **Deaths:** 7 per 1,000 pop. **Infant mortality:** 21.3 per 1,000 live births. **Undernourished:** <2.5%. **HIV:** 0.1%.

Education: Compulsory: ages 5-14. **Literacy:** 99.9%.
Embassy: 2741 34th St. NW 20008; 337-3500.
Website: www.president.az

Azerbaijan was home to Scythian tribes and part of the Roman Empire. Overrun by Turks in the 11th cent. and conquered by Russia in 1806 and 1813, it joined the USSR Dec. 30, 1922, and became a constituent republic in 1936. Azerbaijan gained independence when the Soviet Union disbanded Dec. 26, 1991.

Nagorno-Karabakh, an enclave with a majority population of ethnic Armenians, seceded from Azerbaijan in 1988, triggering a war between mostly Muslim Azerbaijan and mostly Christian Armenia, 1992-94, in which 30,000 lives were lost.

Voters approved a new constitution expanding presidential powers, Nov. 12, 1995. Pres. Haydar Aliyev, a pro-Russian former Communist, was reelected Oct. 11, 1998, but international monitors called the vote seriously flawed. The dying Pres. Aliyev named his son Ilham prime min. Aug. 4, 2003. The younger Aliyev won a flawed Oct. 15, 2003, presidential election. He responded to violent protests Oct. 16 by arresting hundreds of opposition leaders and their supporters. The opening May 25, 2005, of the Baku-Tbilisi-Ceyhan pipeline, providing an outlet for Azerbaijan's vast Caspian oil reserves, transformed the nation's economy. Construction began in 2014 on new pipelines to carry natural gas from Caspian Sea deposits in Azerbaijan to Georgia, Turkey, and Europe.

Pres. Ilham Aliyev won a second term Oct. 15, 2008; term limits were abolished in 2009. In OSCE-criticized elections, Aliyev won a third term Oct. 9, 2013, and a fourth term Apr. 11, 2018.

The European Parliament voted, Sept. 2017, to investigate a so-called Azerbaijani Laundromat scheme, in which almost $3 bil was reportedly sent out of Azerbaijan, including money allegedly paid to European officials to influence policy toward Azerbaijan.

Azerbaijan adopted travel restrictions and lockdown measures to combat the 2020 COVID-19 pandemic; as of Sept. 30, there were about 40,000 Azerbaijani cases and almost 600 deaths.

The Bahamas
Commonwealth of The Bahamas

People: Population: 337,721 (173). **Age distrib.:** <15: 22.0%; 65+: 8.7%. **Growth:** 0.7%. **Migrants:** 16.2%. **Pop. density:** 87.4 per sq mi, 33.7 per sq km. **Urban:** 83.2%. **Ethnic groups:** Black 90.6%, white 4.7%, Black and white 2.1%. **Languages:** English (official), Creole (among Haitian immigrants). **Religions:** Christian (official) 92.9% (Protestant 72.2%, Catholic 13.2%), agnostic 4.3%.

Geography: Total area: 5,359 sq mi, 13,880 sq km (156); **Land area:** 3,865 sq mi, 10,010 sq km. **Location:** In Atlantic O., SE of Florida. U.S. is on W, Cuba to SW. **Topography:** Nearly 700 islands (30 inhabited) and over 2,000 cays in the W Atlantic O. extend 760 mi NW to SE. **Arable land:** 0.8%. **Capital:** Nassau, 279,568.

Government: Type: Parliamentary democracy under constitutional monarchy. **Head of state:** Queen Elizabeth II, rep. by Gov.-Gen. Cornelius A. Smith; b. 1937; in office: June 28, 2019. **Head of govt.:** Prime Min. Hubert Minnis; b. 1954; in office: May 11, 2017. **Local divisions:** 31 districts. **Defense budget:** $92 mil. **Active troops:** 1,300.

Economy: Industries: tourism, banking, oil bunkering, maritime, transshipment, salt, aragonite, pharmaceuticals. **Chief agric.:** citrus, vegetables; poultry; seafood. **Natural resources:** salt, aragonite, timber. **Water:** 1,770 cu m per capita. **Electricity prod.:** 1.7 bil kWh. **Labor force:** agric. 2.1%, industry 14.0%, services 83.9%. **Unemployment:** 11.3%.

Finance: Monetary unit: Dollar (BSD) (1.00 = $1 U.S.). **GDP:** $14.5 bil; **per capita GDP:** $37,266; **GDP growth:** 1.8%. **Imports:** $3.2 bil; U.S. 83.2%. **Exports:** $550 mil; U.S. 63.9%, Namibia 19.3%. **Tourism:** $3.6 bil. **Budget:** $2.5 bil. **Inflation:** 2.5%.

Transport: Motor vehicles: 430.5 per 1,000 pop. **Airports:** 24.
Communications: Telephone: 29.4 per 100 pop. **Mobile:** 99 per 100 pop. **Broadband:** 81.6 per 100 pop. **Internet:** 85%.
Health: Expend.: 5.8%. **Life expect.:** 70.8 male; 75.8 female. **Births:** 14.8 per 1,000 pop. **Deaths:** 7.4 per 1,000 pop. **Infant mortality:** 10.6 per 1,000 live births. **Undernourished:** NA. **HIV** (2018): 1.8%.

Education: Compulsory: ages 5-16. **Literacy:** 95%+.
Embassy: 2220 Massachusetts Ave. NW 20008; 319-2660.
Website: www.bahamas.gov.bs

Christopher Columbus likely first set foot in the Americas on San Salvador (Watling Isl.) in 1492, when Arawak Indians inhabited the islands. British settlement began in 1647; the islands became a British colony in 1783. Independence was attained July 10, 1973. International finance and tourism are major industries. Hurricane Dorian, Sept. 1-3, 2019, devastated the northern Bahamas; the official death toll was 74, and many others were missing and not accounted for. The COVID-19 pandemic hurt tourism in 2020; international commercial flights were barred, Mar. 24-June 30. About 3,900 Bahamas cases and over 90 deaths had occurred by Sept. 30.

Bahrain
Kingdom of Bahrain

People: Population: 1,505,003 (150). **Age distrib.:** <15: 18.5%; 65+: 3.4%. **Growth:** 2.1%. **Migrants:** 45.2%. **Pop. density:** 5,128.9 per sq mi, 1,980.3 per sq km. **Urban:** 89.5%. **Ethnic groups:** Bahraini 46%, Asian 45.5%, other Arab 4.7%. **Languages:** Arabic (official), English, Farsi, Urdu. **Religions:** Muslim (official) 82.3% (Shia 53%, Sunni 29%), Christian 11.2%, Hindu 5.6%.

Geography: Total area: 293 sq mi, 760 sq km (174); **Land area:** 293 sq mi, 760 sq km. **Location:** SW Asia, in Persian Gulf. Saudi Arabia on W, Qatar on E. **Topography:** Bahrain Island and several adjacent, smaller islands, are flat, hot, and humid with little rain. **Arable land:** 2.1%. **Capital:** Manama, 634,508.

Government: Type: Constitutional monarchy. **Head of state:** King Hamad bin Isa al-Khalifa; b. 1950; in office: as emir Mar. 6, 1999; as king Feb. 14, 2002. **Head of govt.:** Prime Min. Khalifa bin Salman al-Khalifa; b. 1936; in office: 1971. **Local divisions:** 4 governorates. **Defense budget:** $1.5 bil. **Active troops:** 8,200.

Economy: Industries: petroleum proc. and refining, aluminum smelting, iron pelletization, fertilizers, Islamic and offshore banking, insurance. **Chief agric.:** fruit, vegetables; poultry; shrimp, fish. **Natural resources:** oil, nat. gas, fish, pearls. **Water:** 78 cu m per capita. **Crude oil reserves:** 95 mil bbls. **Electricity prod.:** 27.5 bil kWh. **Labor force:** agric. 1.0%, industry 35.1%, services 64.0%. **Unemployment:** 0.8%.

Finance: Monetary unit: Dinar (BHD) (0.38 = $1 U.S.). **GDP:** $77.0 bil; **per capita GDP:** $46,892; **GDP growth:** 1.8%. **Imports:** $16.1 bil; China 8.8%, UAE 7.2%, U.S. 7.1%, Australia 5.3%. **Exports:** $15.4 bil; UAE 19.6%, Saudi Arabia 11.7%, U.S. 10.8%, Oman 8.1%, China 6.5%, Qatar 5.7%. **Tourism:** $3.7 bil. **Budget:** $9.4 bil. **Inflation** (2017-18): 2.1%.

Transport: Motor vehicles: 565.1 per 1,000 pop. **Airports:** 4.
Communications: Telephone: 18.4 per 100 pop. **Mobile:** 133.3 per 100 pop. **Broadband:** 147.3 per 100 pop. **Internet** (2018): 98.6%.

Health: Expend.: 4.7%. **Life expect.:** 77.1 male; 81.8 female. **Births:** 12.7 per 1,000 pop. **Deaths:** 2.8 per 1,000 pop. **Infant mortality:** 8.3 per 1,000 live births. **Undernourished:** NA. **HIV:** NA.

Education: Compulsory: ages 6-14. **Literacy:** 97%.
Embassy: 3502 International Dr. NW 20008; 342-0741.
Website: www.bahrain.bh

Long ruled by the Khalifa family, Bahrain was a British protectorate from 1861 to Aug. 15, 1971, when it regained independence. Oil was discovered in 1932. Natural gas output has more than doubled since 1990. Low oil prices hurt the economy beginning in 2015. A major offshore oil and gas field discovery was announced in Apr. 2018.

Emir Hamad bin Isa al-Khalifa proclaimed himself king Feb. 14, 2002. Local elections in May 2002 marked the first time Bahraini women were allowed to vote and run for office. The monarchy suppressed Arab Spring demonstrations Feb.-Mar. 2011, aided by a Saudi-led Gulf Cooperation Council force. Protests, however, continued, largely by members of the country's Shiite majority against the mostly Sunni ruling elite. A Nov. 2015 Human Rights Watch report accused the government of torturing detained dissidents. Forced labor and sexual exploitation of Asian and African immigrants also gained international attention. Court rulings July 17, 2016, and May 31, 2017, ordered the dissolution of leading Shiite and secular opposition groups.

Bahrain was one of a Saudi-led group of nations that June 5, 2017, broke diplomatic relations with Qatar, alleging Qatari support for terrorist and sectarian groups. Bahrain and Israel signed an agreement, Sept. 15, 2020, to establish diplomatic relations.

Bahrain was impacted by the 2020 COVID-19 pandemic, with foreign workers living in crowded dormitories at especially high risk; as of Sept. 30, Bahrain had over 70,000 cases and almost 250 deaths.

Bangladesh
People's Republic of Bangladesh

People: Population: 162,650,853 (8). **Age distrib.:** <15: 26.5%; 65+: 6.8%. **Growth:** 1.0%. **Migrants:** 1.3%. **Pop. density:** 3,236.3 per sq mi, 1,249.5 per sq km. **Urban:** 38.2%. **Ethnic groups:** Bengali 98%+. **Languages:** Bangla or Bengali (official). **Religions:** Muslim (official) 89.1% (Sunni), Hindu 9.1%.

Geography: Total area: 57,321 sq mi, 148,460 sq km (92); **Land area:** 50,259 sq mi, 130,170 sq km. **Location:** S Asia, on N bend of Bay of Bengal. India nearly surrounds country on W, N, E; Myanmar on SE. **Topography:** Mostly a low plain cut by the Ganges and Brahmaputra R. and their delta. Alluvial and marshy along the coast. Hilly only in the extreme SE and NE. Its tropical monsoon climate makes country among the rainiest in the world. **Arable land:** 59.1%. **Capital:** Dhaka, 21,005,860. **Cities:** Chittagong, 5,019,824.

Government: Type: Parliamentary republic. **Head of state:** Pres. Abdul Hamid; b. 1944; in office: Apr. 24, 2013. **Head of govt.:** Prime Min. Sheikh Hasina; b. 1947; in office: Jan. 6, 2009. **Local divisions:** 8 divisions. **Defense budget:** $3.5 bil. **Active troops:** 163,050.

Economy: Industries: jute, cotton, garments, paper, leather, fertilizer, iron and steel, cement, petroleum prods., tobacco, pharmaceuticals. **Chief agric.:** rice, jute, tea, wheat, sugarcane, potatoes, tobacco, pulses, oilseeds, spices; beef, milk, poultry. **Natural resources:** nat. gas, timber, coal. **Water:** 7,451 cu m per capita. **Crude oil reserves:** 28 mil bbls. **Electricity prod.:** 68.8 bil kWh. **Labor force:** agric. 37.8%, industry 21.6%, services 40.6%. **Unemployment:** 4.2%.

Finance: Monetary unit: Taka (BDT) (84.76 = $1 U.S.). **GDP:** $807.2 bil; **per capita GDP:** $4,951; **GDP growth:** 8.2%. **Imports:** $47.6 bil; China 21.9%, India 15.3%, Singapore 5.7%. **Exports:** $35.3 bil; Germany 12.9%, U.S. 12.2%, UK 8.7%, Spain 5.3%, France 5.1%. **Tourism:** $388 mil. **Budget:** $33.5 bil. **Inflation:** 5.6%.

Transport: Railways: 1,529 mi. **Motor vehicles:** 2.7 per 1,000 pop. **Airports:** 16.

Communications: Telephone: 0.4 per 100 pop. **Mobile:** 97.3 per 100 pop. **Broadband:** 30 per 100 pop. **Internet:** 15%.

Health: Expend.: 2.3%. **Life expect.:** 72.0 male; 76.5 female. **Births:** 18.1 per 1,000 pop. **Deaths:** 5.5 per 1,000 pop. **Infant mortality:** 28.3 per 1,000 live births. **Undernourished:** 13.0%. **HIV** (2018): <0.1%.

Education: Compulsory: ages 6-10. **Literacy:** 93.3%.

Embassy: 3510 International Dr. NW 20008; 244-0183.

Website: bangladesh.gov.bd

Muslim invaders conquered the formerly Hindu area in the 12th cent. British rule lasted from the 18th cent. to 1947, when East Bengal became part of Pakistan.

Opposing domination by West Pakistan, the Awami League, based in the East, won control of the National Assembly in 1971. Assembly sessions were postponed; riots broke out. Pakistani troops attacked, Mar. 25; Bangladesh independence was proclaimed the next day. In the ensuing civil war, 1 mil died and 10 mil fled to India. War between India and Pakistan broke out Dec. 3, 1971. Pakistan surrendered in the East on Dec. 16. Mujibur Rahman, known as Sheikh Mujib, became prime min.; he was killed in a coup Aug. 15, 1975.

Army rivals killed Pres. Ziaur Rahman in an unsuccessful coup attempt, May 1981. Vice Pres. Abdus Sattar assumed the presidency but was ousted in a coup led by army chief of staff Gen. H. M. Ershad, Mar. 1982. A parliamentary system of government was adopted in 1991. A cyclone, Apr. 1991, killed over 131,000 people.

Political turmoil led to the resignation, Mar. 1996, of Prime Min. Khaleda Zia, Ziaur Rahman's widow. Sheikh Mujib's daughter, known as Sheikh Hasina, led the country after the June 1996 election. Khaleda Zia returned to power following parliamentary elections, Oct. 1, 2001. Militant Islamists set off more than 400 small bombs in more than 50 cities and towns, Aug. 17, 2005, killing 3. Another wave of jihadist bombings killed 22, Nov. 29-Dec. 8, 2005. Bangladeshi economist Muhammad Yunus won the 2006 Nobel Peace Prize for using very small loans (microcredit) to help alleviate the nation's severe poverty.

Amid escalating political violence, Pres. Iajuddin Ahmed declared a state of emergency, Jan. 11, 2007, and a military-backed caretaker government took office. Cyclone Sidr struck Nov. 15, 2007, damaging more than 1.5 mil homes and leaving about 3,400 dead.

The Awami League triumphed in parliamentary elections Dec. 2008, and Sheikh Hasina returned as prime min. Jan. 6, 2009, ending two years of emergency rule. She remained in office when her party won 2014 and 2018 elections. Her political rival, Khaleda Zia, was convicted, Feb. and Oct. 2018, on embezzlement charges Zia claimed were politically motivated; she was sentenced to a total of 17 years in prison.

A garment factory fire Nov. 24, 2012, near Dhaka killed 112 workers. Rana Plaza, a nearby tower that housed garment factories, collapsed Apr. 24, 2013, killing more than 1,100 workers in the deadliest garment-industry disaster in world history. The owner of Rana Plaza, Sohel Rana, was among 38 people formally charged, July 18, 2016, with murder in connection with the disaster. With the murder case still pending, Sohel Rana was convicted, Aug. 29, 2017, and sentenced to 3 years in prison on corruption charges.

Security forces in Dhaka, July 1-2, 2015, arrested 12 people said to be affiliated with al-Qaeda. Assassinations of non-Muslims attributed to al-Qaeda or ISIS escalated in 2016. In an attack in Dhaka, July 1-2, 2016, for which ISIS claimed responsibility, 20 people, mostly foreigners, held hostage inside a restaurant were killed, as well as 2 police officers and 5 terrorist gunmen.

Beginning in late 2016, recurrent military and vigilante attacks in neighboring Myanmar caused much of the Rohingya population to seek refuge in Bangladesh. Anti-Rohingya violence in Myanmar peaked in Aug.-Sept. 2017, leading hundreds of thousands to flee. As of July 31, 2020, about 860,000 Rohingya refugees were in Bangladesh. Crowded, unsanitary conditions in refugee camps were a concern as the 2020 COVID-19 pandemic reached Bangladesh; as of Sept. 30, the country had about 362,000 cases and over 5,200 deaths.

Barbados

People: Population: 294,560 (175). **Age distrib.:** <15: 17.5%; 65+: 13.6%. **Growth:** 0.2%. **Migrants:** 12.1%. **Pop. density:** 1,774.2 per sq mi, 685.0 per sq km. **Urban:** 31.2%. **Ethnic groups:** African descent 92.4%, mixed 3.1%, white 2.7%. **Languages:** English (official), Bajan (English-based Creole). **Religions:** Christian (official) 94.6% (Protestant 79.1%, independent 10.2%, Catholic 5.1%).

Geography: Total area: 166 sq mi, 430 sq km (184); **Land area:** 166 sq mi, 430 sq km. **Location:** In Atlantic O., farthest E of West Indies. Nearest neighbors are St. Lucia and St. Vincent and the Grenadines to the W. **Topography:** Almost completely surrounded by coral reefs. Highest point is Mt. Hillaby (1,102 ft). **Arable land:** 16.3%. **Capital:** Bridgetown, 89,201.

Government: Type: Parliamentary democracy under constitutional monarchy. **Head of state:** Queen Elizabeth II, rep. by Gov.-Gen. Sandra Mason; b. 1965; in office: Jan. 8, 2018. **Head of govt.:** Prime Min. Mia Mottley; b. 1965; in office: May 25, 2018. **Local divisions:** 11 parishes, 1 city. **Defense budget:** $38 mil. **Active troops:** 610.

Economy: Industries: tourism, sugar, light mfg., component assembly for export. **Chief agric.:** sugarcane, vegetables, cotton. **Natural resources:** petroleum, fish, nat. gas. **Water:** 280 cu m per capita. **Crude oil reserves:** 2 mil bbls. **Electricity prod.:** 1.0 bil kWh. **Labor force:** agric. 2.6%, industry 18.9%, services 78.5%. **Unemployment:** 10.9%.

Finance: Monetary unit: Dollar (BBD) (2.00 = $1 U.S.). **GDP:** $4.7 bil; **per capita GDP:** $16,287; **GDP growth:** –0.1%. **Imports:** $1.5 bil; U.S. 38.5%, Trinidad and Tobago 14.6%, China 7.1%. **Exports:** $485.4 mil; U.S. 38%, Trinidad and Tobago 10.2%, Guyana 5.5%, Jamaica 5%. **Tourism:** $1.3 bil. **Budget:** $1.7 bil. **Inflation:** 4.1%.

Transport: Motor vehicles: 404.9 per 1,000 pop. **Airports:** 1.

Communications: Telephone: 44.4 per 100 pop. **Mobile:** 122.6 per 100 pop. **Broadband:** 50.6 per 100 pop. **Internet:** 81.8%.

Health: Expend.: 6.8%. **Life expect.:** 73.6 male; 78.4 female. **Births:** 11.3 per 1,000 pop. **Deaths:** 8.8 per 1,000 pop. **Infant mortality:** 9.6 per 1,000 live births. **Undernourished:** 4.3%. **HIV:** 0.8%.

Education: Compulsory: ages 5-15. **Literacy:** 99.7%.

Embassy: 2144 Wyoming Ave. NW 20008; 939-9200.

Website: www.gov.bb

Barbados was probably named by Portuguese sailors in reference to bearded fig trees. An English ship visited in 1605, and British settled on the uninhabited island in 1627. Slaves worked the sugarcane plantations until slavery was abolished in 1834. Barbados became independent Nov. 30, 1966. Tourism, banking, and manufacturing have surpassed sugarcane in economic importance since the 1990s. Barbados's slow recovery from the 2008-09 global recession hurt the ruling Democratic Labor Party in the May 24, 2018, elections. The opposition Barbados Labour Party won all 30 House of Assembly seats, making Mia Mottley the country's first female prime min.

A Zika virus outbreak in the Americas affected Barbados from late 2015 to early 2017, with more than 850 confirmed or suspected cases reported.

Belarus
Republic of Belarus

People: Population: 9,477,918 (94). **Age distrib.:** <15: 16.1%; 65+: 15.9%. **Growth:** –0.3%. **Migrants:** 11.3%. **Pop. density:** 121.0 per sq mi, 46.7 per sq km. **Urban:** 79.5%. **Ethnic groups:** Belarusian 83.7%, Russian 8.3%, Polish 3.1%. **Languages:** Russian, Belarusian (both official). **Religions:** Christian 79.1% (Orthodox 64.1%, Catholic 11.7%), agnostic 18.5%.

Geography: Total area: 80,155 sq mi, 207,600 sq km (84); **Land area:** 78,340 sq mi, 202,900 sq km. **Location:** Eastern Europe. Poland on W; Latvia, Lithuania on N; Russia on E; Ukraine on S. **Topography:** Landlocked country consisting mostly of hilly lowland with significant marsh areas in S. **Arable land:** 28.2%. **Capital:** Minsk, 2,028,104.

Government: Type: Presidential republic in name; in fact a dictatorship. **Head of state:** Pres. Aleksandr Lukashenko; b. 1954; in office: July 20, 1994. **Head of govt.:** Prime Min. Roman Golovchenko; b. 1973; in office: June 4, 2020. **Local divisions:** 6 provinces, 1 municipality. **Defense budget:** $650 mil. **Active troops:** 45,350.

Economy: Industries: metal-cutting machine tools, tractors, trucks, earthmovers. **Chief agric.:** grain, potatoes, vegetables, sugar beets, flax; beef, milk. **Natural resources:** timber, peat, oil, nat. gas, granite, dolomitic limestone, marl, chalk, sand, gravel, clay. **Water:** 6,115 cu m per capita. **Crude oil reserves:** 198 mil bbls. **Electricity prod.** (2018): 36.4 bil kWh. **Labor force:** agric. 10.8%, industry 30.2%, services 59.0%. **Unemployment:** 4.6%.

Finance: Monetary unit: Ruble (BYN) (2.64 = $1 U.S.). **GDP:** $188.8 bil; **per capita GDP:** $19,943; **GDP growth:** 1.2%. **Imports:** $31.6 bil; Russia 57.2%, China 8%, Germany 5.1%. **Exports:** $28.7 bil; Russia 41.9%, Ukraine 11.5%, UK 8.2%. **Tourism:** $905 mil. **Budget:** $20.6 bil. **Inflation:** 5.6%.

Transport: Railways: 3,435 mi. **Motor vehicles:** 379.5 per 1,000 pop. **Airports:** 33.

Communications: Telephone: 47.5 per 100 pop. **Mobile:** 122.9 per 100 pop. **Broadband:** 76.2 per 100 pop. **Internet** (2018): 79.1%.

Health: Expend.: 5.9%. **Life expect.:** 68.3 male; 79.5 female. **Births:** 9.5 per 1,000 pop. **Deaths:** 13.1 per 1,000 pop. **Infant mortality:** 3.5 per 1,000 live births. **Undernourished:** <2.5%. **HIV:** 0.5%.

Education: Compulsory: ages 6-14. **Literacy:** 99.9%.
Embassy: 1619 New Hampshire Ave. NW 20009; 986-1604.
Website: www.belarus.by

Belarus became a constituent republic of the USSR in 1922. Overrun by German armies in 1941, Belarus was recaptured by Soviet troops in 1944. Following WWII, Belarus increased in area through Soviet annexation of part of NE Poland. Belarus declared independence Aug. 25, 1991, and became independent when the Soviet Union disbanded Dec. 26, 1991.

Russia and Belarus signed a pact, Apr. 2, 1996, linking their political and economic systems. An authoritarian constitution enacted in Nov. gave Pres. Aleksandr Lukashenko (elected 1994) vast new powers. He retained office in flawed 2001, 2006, 2010, and 2015 elections. Lukashenko crushed 2010 post-election protests. Belarus joined Russia and three other nations, 2015, in the Eurasian Economic Union. Early-2017 protests against a weak economy were suppressed. Lukashenko disparaged concerns about the 2020 COVID-19 pandemic, but as of Sept. 30, the WHO reported about 78,000 cases in Belarus and over 800 deaths. Weeks of large-scale protests—sometimes met with a brutal government response, as well as arrests and expulsions—followed flawed Aug. 9, 2020, elections, in which official results gave Lukashenko 80% of the vote.

Belgium
Kingdom of Belgium

People: Population: 11,720,716 (80). **Age distrib.:** <15: 17.2%; 65+: 19.2%. **Growth:** 0.6%. **Migrants:** 17.2%. **Pop. density:** 1,002.6 per sq mi, 387.1 per sq km. **Urban:** 98.1%. **Ethnic groups:** Belgian 75.2%, Italian 4.1%, Moroccan 3.7%, French 2.4%, Turkish 2%, Dutch 2%. **Languages:** Dutch, French, German (all official). **Religions:** Christian 62.2% (Catholic 59.4%), agnostic 25.8%, Muslim 8.7%.

Geography: Total area: 11,787 sq mi, 30,528 sq km (137); **Land area:** 11,690 sq mi, 30,278 sq km. **Location:** Western Europe, on North Sea. France on W and S, Luxembourg on SE, Germany on E, Netherlands on N. **Topography:** Mostly flat; trisected by the Scheldt and Meuse, major commercial rivers. The land becomes hilly and forested in the Ardennes region to the SE. **Arable land:** 27.6%. **Capital:** Bruxelles-Brussel, 2,080,788. **Cities:** Antwerpen, 1,042,471.

Government: Type: Federal parliamentary democracy under constitutional monarchy. **Head of state:** King Philippe; b. 1960; in office: July 21, 2013. **Head of govt.:** Prime Min. Sophie Wilmès; b. 1975; in office: Oct. 26, 2019. **Local divisions:** 3 regions. **Defense budget:** $4.8 bil. **Active troops:** 26,300.

Economy: Industries: engineering and metal prods., motor vehicle assembly, transp. equip., scientific instruments, processed food and beverages. **Chief agric.:** sugar beets, vegetables, fruits, grain, tobacco; beef, veal. **Natural resources:** constr. materials, silica sand, carbonates. **Water:** 1,601 cu m per capita. **Electricity prod.** (2018): 69.4 bil kWh. **Labor force:** agric. 0.9%, industry 20.6%, services 78.4%. **Unemployment:** 5.7%.

Finance: Monetary unit: Euro (EUR) (0.84 = $1 U.S.). **GDP:** $626.4 bil; **per capita GDP:** $54,545; **GDP growth:** 1.4%. **Imports:** $300.4 bil; Netherlands 17.3%, Germany 13.8%, France 9.5%, U.S. 7.1%. **Exports:** $300.8 bil; Germany 16.6%, France 14.9%, Netherlands 12%, UK 8.4%. **Tourism:** $8.9 bil. **Budget:** $258.6 bil. **Inflation:** 1.4%.

Transport: Railways: 2,232 mi. **Motor vehicles:** 575.9 per 1,000 pop. **Airports:** 26.

Communications: Telephone: 35.8 per 100 pop. **Mobile:** 103.4 per 100 pop. **Broadband:** 75.1 per 100 pop. **Internet** (2018): 88.7%.

Health: Expend.: 10.3%. **Life expect.:** 78.8 male; 84.2 female. **Births:** 11.1 per 1,000 pop. **Deaths:** 9.8 per 1,000 pop. **Infant mortality:** 3.3 per 1,000 live births. **Undernourished:** <2.5%. **HIV:** NA.

Education: Compulsory: ages 6-17. **Literacy:** 99%.
Embassy: 3330 Garfield St. NW 20008; 333-6900.
Website: www.belgium.be

Belgium derives its name from the Belgae, the first recorded inhabitants, probably Celts. The land was ruled for 1,800 years by conquerors, including Rome, the Franks, Burgundy, Spain, Austria, and France. After 1815, Belgium was made a part of the Netherlands but became an independent constitutional monarchy in 1830.

King Leopold III surrendered to Germany, May 28, 1940. After WWII, he was forced to abdicate in favor of his son, King Baudouin. Baudouin was succeeded by his brother, Albert II, Aug. 9, 1993. Albert's son Philippe became king July 21, 2013.

The Flemings of northern Belgium speak Dutch, while the Walloons in the south speak French. The language difference is a source of controversy between the two groups. Parliament has passed measures transferring power from the central government to three regions—Wallonia, Flanders, and Brussels. Constitutional changes in 1993 made Belgium a federal state. After elections June 2007, rivalries between Flemings and Walloons created a 9-month political stalemate. June 2010 elections led to a political deadlock that lasted until Dec. 2011. After May 25, 2014, elections, Charles Michel was sworn in as prime min. Oct. 11, heading a center-right coalition government.

Evidence emerged in Nov. 2015 that Islamist extremists living in Belgium planned and took part in terrorist attacks in France, Nov. 13, that killed 130. In Mar. 22, 2016, attacks for which the Sunni extremist group ISIS claimed responsibility, 3 suicide bombers killed 32 others in a Brussels subway station and at the city's airport.

Michel's coalition collapsed, Dec. 2018, over immigration policy; he continued as caretaker prime min. After inconclusive May 26, 2019, elections, Sophie Wilmès became caretaker prime min., Oct. 27—Belgium's first female head of government. Rival parties agreed, Mar. 2020, to give her temporary special powers to deal with the COVID-19 pandemic. Hard-hit by the pandemic in Mar.-Apr., with a spike in cases July-Sept., Belgium had about 115,000 cases and 10,000 deaths as of Sept. 30.

Belize

People: Population: 399,598 (170). **Age distrib.:** <15: 32.6%; 65+: 4.5%. **Growth:** 1.7%. **Migrants:** 15.4%. **Pop. density:** 45.4 per sq mi, 17.5 per sq km. **Urban:** 46.0%. **Ethnic groups:** mestizo 52.9%, Creole 25.9%, Maya 11.3%, Garifuna 6.1%, East Indian 3.9%, Mennonite 3.6%. **Languages:** English (official), Spanish, Creole, Maya, German, Garifuna. **Religions:** Christian 92.7% (Catholic 61%, Protestant 26.3%), Baha'i 2.3%.

Geography: Total area: 8,867 sq mi, 22,966 sq km (148); **Land area:** 8,805 sq mi, 22,806 sq km. **Location:** Eastern coast of Central America. Mexico on N, Guatemala on W and S. **Topography:** Swampy lowlands in N, Maya Mts. in S, coral reefs and cays near coast. Tropical climate. **Arable land:** 3.9%. **Capital:** Belmopan, 22,964.

Government: Type: Parliamentary democracy under constitutional monarchy. **Head of state:** Queen Elizabeth II, rep. by Gov.-Gen. Colville Young; b. 1932; in office: Nov. 17, 1993. **Head of govt.:** Prime Min. Dean Barrow; b. 1951; in office: Feb. 8, 2008. **Local divisions:** 6 districts. **Defense budget:** $23 mil. **Active troops:** 1,500.

Economy: Industries: garment prod., food proc., tourism, constr. **Chief agric.:** bananas, cacao, citrus, sugar; fish, cultured shrimp. **Natural resources:** timber, fish, hydropower. **Water:** 57,993 cu m per capita. **Crude oil reserves:** 7 mil bbls. **Electricity prod.:** 409 mil kWh. **Labor force:** agric. 16.6%, industry 15.7%, services 67%. **Unemployment:** 6.4%.

Finance: Monetary unit: Dollar (BZD) (2.01 = $1 U.S.). **GDP:** $2.8 bil; **per capita GDP:** $7,295; **GDP growth:** 0.3%. **Imports:** $845.9 mil; U.S. 35.6%, China 11.2%, Mexico 11.2%, Guatemala 6.9%. **Exports:** $457.5 mil; UK 33.9%, U.S. 22%, Jamaica 6.7%, Italy 6.4%, Barbados 5.9%, Ireland 5.5%. **Tourism:** $510 mil. **Budget:** $572.0 mil. **Inflation** (2016-17): 1.1%.

Transport: Motor vehicles: 113 per 1,000 pop. **Airports:** 6.
Communications: Telephone: 5.4 per 100 pop. **Mobile:** 85.5 per 100 pop. **Broadband:** 14.1 per 100 pop. **Internet:** 47.1%.

Health: Expend.: 5.6%. **Life expect.:** 73.7 male; 77.0 female. **Births:** 22 per 1,000 pop. **Deaths:** 4.1 per 1,000 pop. **Infant mortality:** 11.2 per 1,000 live births. **Undernourished:** 7.6%. **HIV** (2018): 1.9%.

Education: Compulsory: ages 5-12. **Literacy:** 79.7%.
Embassy: 2535 Massachusetts Ave. NW 20008; 332-9636.
Website: www.belize.gov.bz

Belize (formerly British Honduras) gained independence from Great Britain Sept. 21, 1981. Belize has become a center for drug trafficking between Colombia and the U.S. Beginning in 2016, thousands of people fleeing violence in El Salvador, Honduras, and Guatemala sought refuge in Belize. The COVID-19 pandemic caused almost 1,900 cases and 24 deaths in Belize as of Sept. 30, 2020.

Benin
Republic of Benin

People: Population: 12,864,634 (74). **Age distrib.:** <15: 45.6%; 65+: 2.4%. **Growth:** 3.4%. **Migrants:** 3.3%. **Pop. density:** 301.2 per sq mi, 116.3 per sq km. **Urban:** 48.4%. **Ethnic groups:** Fon and related 38.4%, Adja/related 15.1%, Yoruba/related 12%, Bariba/related 9.6%, Fulani/related 8.6%, Ottamari/related 6.1%, Yoa-Lokpa/related 4.3%, Dendi/related 2.9%. **Languages:** French (official), Fon, Yoruba, tribal langs. **Religions:** Christian 46.9% (Catholic 24.6%, independent 12%, Protestant 10.3%), Muslim 28.2% (Sunni), ethnic religionist 24.6%.

Geography: Total area: 43,484 sq mi, 112,622 sq km (100); **Land area:** 42,711 sq mi, 110,622 sq km. **Location:** W Africa on Gulf of Guinea. Togo on W; Burkina Faso, Niger on N; Nigeria on E. **Topography:** Mostly flat and covered with dense vegetation. The coast is hot, humid, and rainy. **Arable land:** 24.8%. **Capital:** Cotonou (seat), 691,949; Porto-Novo (constitutional), 285,328.

Government: Type: Presidential republic. **Head of state and govt.:** Pres. Patrice Talon; b. 1958; in office: Apr. 6, 2016. **Local divisions:** 12 departments. **Defense budget:** $68 mil. **Active troops:** 7,250.

Economy: Industries: textiles, food proc., constr. materials, cement. **Chief agric.:** cotton, corn, cassava, yams, beans, palm oil. **Natural resources:** offshore oil, limestone, marble, timber. **Water:** 2,361 cu m per capita. **Crude oil reserves:** 8 mil bbls. **Electricity prod.:** 312 mil kWh. **Labor force:** agric. 38.0%, industry 19.1%, services 42.9%. **Unemployment:** 2.0%.

Finance: Monetary unit: CFA Franc (XOF) (553.52 = $1 U.S.). **GDP:** $40.4 bil; **per capita GDP:** $3,424; **GDP growth:** 6.9%. **Imports:** $2.8 bil; Thailand 18.1%, India 15.9%, France 8.5%, China 7.5%, Togo 5.9%. **Exports:** $2 bil; Bangladesh 18.1%, India 10.7%, Ukraine 9%, Niger 8.1%, China 7.7%, Nigeria 7.2%. **Tourism:** $162 mil. **Budget:** $2.2 bil. **Inflation:** –0.9%.

Transport: Railways: 272 mi. **Motor vehicles:** 3.6 per 1,000 pop. **Airports:** 1.

Communications: Telephone: 0.4 per 100 pop. **Mobile:** 82.4 per 100 pop. **Broadband:** 12 per 100 pop. **Internet:** 20%.

Health: Expend.: 3.7%. **Life expect.:** 59.6 male; 63.3 female. **Births:** 42.1 per 1,000 pop. **Deaths:** 8.4 per 1,000 pop. **Infant mortality:** 58.7 per 1,000 live births. **Undernourished:** 7.4%. **HIV:** 1.0%.

Education: Compulsory: ages 6-11. **Literacy:** 60.9%.
Embassy: 2124 Kalorama Rd. NW 20008; 232-6656.
Website: www.gouv.bj

The Kingdom of Abomey, rising to power in the 17th cent., came under French domination in the late 19th cent. and was incorporated into French West Africa by 1904. Under the name Dahomey, the country gained independence Aug. 1, 1960; it became Benin in 1975. In the fifth coup since independence, Mathieu (Ahmed) Kérékou took power in 1972; he ruled until 1991, when democracy was restored, and served as elected president 1996-2006.

Patrice Talon won a presidential runoff election Mar. 20, 2016. Rule changes to help Talon loyalists in Apr. 28, 2019, legislative elections, as well as a crackdown on dissent, led to violent protests.

Beginning Nov. 2017, Benin troops joined a multinational force to fight the Nigeria-based Islamist extremist group Boko Haram. Seeking to prevent Islamist terrorists infiltrating from Burkina Faso, Benin stationed troops on its northern border in 2019.

Impacted by the 2020 COVID-19 pandemic, Benin had 2,340 cases and 40 deaths as of Sept. 30.

Bhutan
Kingdom of Bhutan

People: Population: 782,318 (161). **Age distrib.:** <15: 24.5%; 65+: 6.6%. **Growth:** 1.0%. **Migrants:** 7.0%. **Pop. density:** 52.8 per sq mi, 20.4 per sq km. **Urban:** 42.3%. **Ethnic groups:** Ngalop or Bhote 50%, ethnic Nepalese (incl. Lhotsampa) 35%, Indigenous or migrant tribes 15%. **Languages:** Sharchhopka, Dzongkha (official), Lhotshamkha. **Religions:** Buddhist (official) 82.6%, Hindu 11.4%, ethnic religionist 3.4%.

Geography: Total area: 14,824 sq mi, 38,394 sq km (133); **Land area:** 14,824 sq mi, 38,394 sq km. **Location:** S Asia, in eastern Himalayan Mts. India (Sikkim state) on W and S, China on N. **Topography:** Very high mountains in the N, fertile valleys in the center, and thick forests in the Duar Plain in the S. **Arable land:** 2.6%. **Capital:** Thimphu, 203,297.

Government: Type: Constitutional monarchy. **Head of state:** King Jigme Khesar Namgyel Wangchuck; b. 1980; in office: Dec. 14, 2006. **Head of govt.:** Prime Min. Lotay Tshering; in office: Nov. 7, 2018. **Local divisions:** 20 districts. **Defense budget/active troops:** NA.

Economy: Industries: cement, wood prods., processed fruits, alcoholic beverages, calcium carbide, tourism. **Chief agric.:** rice, corn, root crops, citrus; dairy prods. **Natural resources:** timber,

hydropower, gypsum, calcium carbonate. **Water:** 96,582 cu m per capita. **Electricity prod.:** 7.7 bil kWh. **Labor force:** agric. 54.6%, industry 11.1%, services 34.3%. **Unemployment:** 2.4%.

Finance: Monetary unit: Ngultrum (BTN) (73.26 = $1 U.S.). **GDP** (2018): $8.8 bil; **per capita GDP** (2018): $11,613; **GDP growth** (2018): 3.0%. **Imports:** $1 bil; India 89.5%. **Exports:** $554.6 mil; India 95.3%. **Tourism:** $103 mil. **Budget:** $737.4 mil (nearly one-quarter financed by India's govt.). **Inflation:** 2.7%.

Transport: Airports: 2.

Communications: Telephone: 2.9 per 100 pop. **Mobile:** 93.3 per 100 pop. **Broadband:** 87.4 per 100 pop. **Internet:** 48.1%.

Health: Expend.: 5.2%. **Life expect.:** 71.0 male; 73.2 female. **Births:** 16.3 per 1,000 pop. **Deaths:** 6.3 per 1,000 pop. **Infant mortality:** 27.0 per 1,000 live births. **Undernourished:** NA. **HIV** (2018): 0.3%.

Education: Compulsory: NA. **Literacy:** 93.1%.
Permanent UN mission: 343 E. 43rd St., New York, NY 10017; (212) 682-2268.
Website: www.bhutan.gov.bt

The region came under Tibetan rule in the 16th cent. British influence grew in the 19th cent. A Buddhist monarchy was set up in 1907. After a 1910 treaty, Britain guided Bhutan's external affairs, while the country remained internally self-governing. Upon independence the treaty was revised, 1949, to allow India to assume Britain's role.

Isolated for much of its history, Bhutan has taken steps toward modernization. King Jigme Singye Wangchuck, in power since 1972, stepped down Dec. 14, 2006, in favor of his son, Jigme Khesar Namgyel Wangchuck. Multiparty parliamentary elections took place Mar. 24, 2008. A new constitution, ratified July 18, made Bhutan a democratic constitutional monarchy. Tashi Chhozom became the first woman appointed to the country's Supreme Court, Aug. 3, 2012. The People's Democratic Party won July 13, 2013, parliamentary elections. After the United Party of Bhutan won Oct. 18, 2018, elections, surgeon Lotay Tshering became prime min.

Bolivia
Plurinational State of Bolivia

People: Population: 11,639,909 (81). **Age distrib.:** <15: 30.3%; 65+: 5.7%. **Growth:** 1.4%. **Migrants:** 1.4%. **Pop. density:** 27.8 per sq mi, 10.7 per sq km. **Urban:** 70.1%. **Ethnic groups:** mestizo (mixed white/Amerindian) 68%, Indigenous 20%, white 5%, cholo/chola 2%. **Languages:** Spanish, Quechua, Aymara, Guarani (all official). **Religions:** Christian 92.7% (Catholic 78.8%, Protestant 9.4%).

Geography: Total area: 424,164 sq mi, 1,098,581 sq km (27); **Land area:** 418,265 sq mi, 1,083,301 sq km. **Location:** W central South America, in the Andes Mts. One of two landlocked countries in S America. Peru, Chile on W; Argentina, Paraguay on S; Brazil on E and N. **Topography:** The great central plateau, more than 500 mi long at an elevation of 12,000 ft, lies between two cordilleras having three of the highest peaks in S America. Lake Titicaca, on Peruvian border, is world's highest lake (12,500 ft) navigable by large boats. The E central region has semitropical forests; the llanos, or Amazon-Chaco lowlands, are in E. **Arable land:** 3.9%. **Capital:** La Paz (admin.), 1,857,797; Sucre (legis./judicial), 277,910. **Cities:** Santa Cruz, 1,712,688; Cochabamba, 1,303,907.

Government: Type: Presidential republic. **Head of state and govt.:** Interim Pres. Jeanine Áñez Chávez; b. 1967; in office: Nov. 12, 2019. **Local divisions:** 9 departments. **Defense budget:** $479 mil. **Active troops:** 34,100.

Economy: Industries: mining, smelting, electricity, petroleum, food/beverages, handicrafts, clothing, jewelry. **Chief agric.:** soybeans, quinoa, Brazil nuts, sugarcane, coffee, corn, rice, potatoes. **Natural resources:** tin, nat. gas, petroleum, zinc, tungsten, antimony, silver, iron, lead, gold, timber, hydropower. **Water:** 51,936 cu m per capita. **Crude oil reserves:** 240.9 mil bbls. **Electricity prod.:** 9.5 bil kWh. **Labor force:** agric. 30.4%, industry 19.4%, services 50.3%. **Unemployment:** 3.5%.

Finance: Monetary unit: Boliviano (BOB) (6.90 = $1 U.S.). **GDP:** $104.6 bil; **per capita GDP:** $9,086; **GDP growth:** 2.2%. **Imports:** $8.6 bil; China 21.7%, Brazil 16.8%, Argentina 12.6%, U.S. 8.4%, Peru 6.5%. **Exports:** $7.7 bil; Brazil 17.9%, Argentina 16%, U.S. 7.8%, Japan 7.3%, India 6.6%, South Korea 6.3%, Colombia 5.8%, China 5.1%. **Tourism:** $797 mil. **Budget:** $18.0 bil. **Inflation:** 1.8%.

Transport: Railways: 2,461 mi. **Motor vehicles:** 78.5 per 1,000 pop. **Airports:** 21.

Communications: Telephone: 6.3 per 100 pop. **Mobile:** 100.8 per 100 pop. **Broadband:** 76.5 per 100 pop. **Internet:** 43.8%.

Health: Expend.: 6.4%. **Life expect.:** 67.6 male; 73.4 female. **Births:** 20.8 per 1,000 pop. **Deaths:** 6.3 per 1,000 pop. **Infant mortality:** 32.2 per 1,000 live births. **Undernourished:** 15.5%. **HIV:** 0.2%.

Education: Compulsory: ages 4-17. **Literacy:** 99.4%.
Embassy: 3014 Massachusetts Ave. NW 20008; 483-4410.
Website: www.bolivia.gob.bo

The Incas conquered the region's earlier Indian inhabitants in the 13th cent. Spanish colonial rule began in the 1530s and lasted until Aug. 6, 1825. The country is named after independence fighter Simón Bolívar. In a series of wars, Bolivia lost its Pacific coast to Chile, the oil-bearing Chaco to Paraguay, and rubber-growing areas to Brazil, 1879-1935.

Economic unrest, especially among militant mine workers, led to continuing political instability. A reformist government under Victor Paz Estenssoro, 1951-64, nationalized tin mines and attempted to improve conditions for the Indian majority but was overthrown by a military junta. A series of coups and countercoups continued until constitutional government was restored in 1982.

U.S. pressure on the government to reduce production of coca, the raw material for cocaine, led to clashes between police and growers. Gen. Hugo Banzer Suárez, who ruled as a dictator, 1971-78, later governed as president, 1997-2001.

Leftist Juan Evo Morales Ayma won the presidential election, Dec. 2005. Bolivia's first Indigenous president, he nationalized the hydrocarbon sector and launched a land-redistribution program. Voters, Jan. 25, 2009, approved a new constitution strengthening the rights of Bolivia's Indigenous majority and increasing federal control over the country's natural resources. Morales won a second term Dec. 6, 2009. His government nationalized major utility companies in 2012. Morales won reelection Oct. 12, 2014.

After Morales appeared to narrowly win a fourth term in Oct. 20, 2019, elections, large-scale protests and allegations of fraud forced his resignation, Nov. 10; second Senate Vice Pres. Jeanine Áñez Chavez became acting president, Nov. 12. A new election scheduled for May 3, 2020, was postponed because of the COVID-19 pandemic—prompting massive protests. Severely affected by the pandemic, Bolivia had more than 134,000 COVID-19 cases (including Áñez) and 7,900 deaths by Sept. 30, according to WHO data (other estimates of the death toll were significantly higher).

Bosnia and Herzegovina

People: Population: 3,835,586 (129). **Age distrib.:** <15: 13.2%; 65+: 16.2%. **Growth:** −0.2%. **Migrants:** 1.1%. **Pop. density:** 194.1 per sq mi, 74.9 per sq km. **Urban:** 49.0%. **Ethnic groups:** Bosniak 50.1%, Serb 30.8%, Croat 15.4%. **Languages:** Bosnian, Serbian, Croatian (all official). **Religions:** Christian 48.7% (Orthodox 36.8%, Catholic 11.7%), Muslim 48.1% (Sunni).

Geography: Total area: 19,767 sq mi, 51,197 sq km (125); **Land area:** 19,763 sq mi, 51,187 sq km. **Location:** Balkan Peninsula in SE Europe. Serbia, Montenegro on E and SE; Croatia on N and W. **Topography:** Hilly with some mountains. **Arable land:** 20.7%. **Capital:** Sarajevo, 343,089.

Government: Type: Parliamentary republic. **Heads of state:** Collective presidency with rotating leadership every 8 months. **Head of govt.:** Chairman of the Council of Ministers Zoran Tegeltija b. 1961; in office: Dec. 5, 2019. **Local divisions:** 3 first-order admin. divisions. **Defense budget:** $167 mil. **Active troops:** 10,500.

Economy: Industries: steel, coal, iron ore, lead, zinc, manganese, bauxite, aluminum, motor vehicle assembly, textiles, tobacco prods. **Chief agric.:** wheat, corn, fruits, vegetables; livestock. **Natural resources:** coal, iron ore, bauxite, copper, lead, zinc, chromite, cobalt, manganese, nickel, clay, gypsum, salt, sand, timber, hydropower. **Water:** 10,693 cu m per capita. **Electricity prod.:** 15.7 bil kwH. **Labor force:** agric. 15.1%, industry 32.3%; services 52.6%. **Unemployment:** 18.4%.

Finance: Monetary unit: Convertible Marka (BAM) (1.65 = $1 U.S.). **GDP:** $52.1 bil; **per capita GDP:** $15,792; **GDP growth:** 2.6%. **Imports:** $9.5 bil; Germany 11.6%, Italy 11.3%, Serbia 11.1%, Croatia 10.1%, China 6.5%, Slovenia 5%. **Exports:** $5.2 bil; Germany 14.7%, Croatia 11.8%, Italy 11.1%, Serbia 10%, Slovenia 9%, Austria 8.3%. **Tourism:** $1.1 bil. **Budget:** $7.6 bil. **Inflation:** 0.6%.

Transport: Railways: 600 mi. **Airports:** 7.

Communications: Telephone: 19.6 per 100 pop. **Mobile:** 104.1 per 100 pop. **Broadband:** 43.4 per 100 pop. **Internet** (2018): 70.1%.

Health: Expend.: 8.9%. **Life expect.:** 74.5 male; 80.7 female. **Births:** 8.6 per 1,000 pop. **Deaths:** 10.2 per 1,000 pop. **Infant mortality:** 5.2 per 1,000 live births. **Undernourished:** <2.5%. **HIV** (2018): <0.1%.

Education: Compulsory: ages 0-14. **Literacy:** 99.7%.

Embassy: 2109 E St. NW 20037; 337-1500.

Website: www.fbihvlada.gov.ba

Bosnia was ruled by Croatian kings c. 958 CE, and by Hungary 1000-1200. It became organized c. 1200 and later took control of Herzegovina. The kingdom disintegrated after 1391, with the southern part becoming the independent duchy of Herzegovina. It was conquered by Turks in 1463 and made a Turkish province. The area was placed under control of Austria-Hungary in 1878 and made part of the province of Bosnia and Herzegovina, which was formally annexed to Austria-Hungary, 1908. Bosnia became a province of Yugoslavia in 1918. It was reunited with Herzegovina as a federated republic under the 1946 Yugoslav constitution.

Bosnia and Herzegovina declared sovereignty Oct. 15, 1991. A referendum for independence was passed Feb. 29, 1992. Ethnic Serbs' opposition to the referendum spurred violent clashes and bombings. The U.S. and EU recognized the republic Apr. 7. Fierce three-way fighting continued between Bosnia's Serbs, Muslims, and Croats. Serb forces engaged in ethnic cleansing, killing thousands of Bosnian Muslims (Bosniaks) and expelling Muslims and other non-Serbs from areas under Bosnian Serb control. Muslims and Croats

in Bosnia began a cease-fire Feb. 23, 1994, and signed an accord, Mar. 18, to create a Muslim-Croat confederation in Bosnia. However, by mid-1994, Bosnian Serbs controlled over 70% of the country.

As fighting continued in 1995, the balance of power shifted toward the Muslim-Croat alliance. Massive NATO airstrikes on Bosnian Serb targets beginning Aug. 30 triggered a new round of peace talks. These talks produced an agreement to create autonomous regions within Bosnia, with the Serb region (Republika Srpska) constituting 49% of the country.

A 1995 peace agreement was signed in Paris, Dec. 14, 1995, by leaders of Bosnia, Croatia, and Serbia. Some 60,000 NATO troops (about 20,000 from the U.S.) moved in to police the accord. Meanwhile, a UN tribunal—the International Criminal Tribunal for the Former Yugoslavia (ICTY), established in 1993 at The Hague, Netherlands—began bringing charges against suspected war criminals. Elections were held Sept. 14, 1996, for a 3-person collective presidency, for seats in a federal parliament, and for regional offices. In Dec. a revamped NATO Stabilization Force (SFOR) of over 30,000 members (more than 8,000 from the U.S.) received an 18-month mandate, which was later extended.

The ICTY found Radislav Krstic, a Bosnian Serb general, guilty in 2001, in connection with the genocide of thousands of Muslims at Srebrenica in 1995. An EU peacekeeping force (EUFOR), initially with 7,000 members, assumed responsibility from SFOR, Dec. 2, 2004. Accused of complicity in the Srebrenica and other atrocities, former Bosnian Serb leader Radovan Karadzic was convicted, Mar. 24, 2016, by the ICTY of genocide, war crimes, and crimes against humanity; he was ultimately sentenced to life in prison. Gen. Ratko Mladic, the former Bosnian Serb military commander accused of directing the Srebrenica massacre, was convicted by the ICTY, Nov. 22, 2017, of genocide, war crimes, and crimes against humanity and sentenced to life in prison. Mladic's close associate Zdravko Tolimir had been convicted of genocide on Dec. 12, 2012, and sentenced to life in prison, where he died in 2016. The ICTY concluded its work in Dec. 2017. EUFOR strength in Bosnia was about 600 in 2020.

Affected by the 2020 COVID-19 pandemic, Bosnia had about 27,000 cases and over 800 deaths as of Sept. 30.

Botswana
Republic of Botswana

People: Population: 2,317,233 (141). **Age distrib.:** <15: 30.5%; 65+: 5.6%. **Growth:** 1.5%. **Migrants:** 4.8%. **Pop. density:** 10.6 per sq mi, 4.1 per sq km. **Urban:** 70.9%. **Ethnic groups:** Tswana or Setswana 79%, Kalanga 11%, Basarwa 3%, other (incl. Kgalagadi, white) 7%. **Languages:** Setswana, Sekalanga, Shekgalagadi, English (official). **Religions:** Christian 71.9% (independent 47.3%, Protestant 17.1%, Catholic 7.4%), ethnic religionist 26.7%.

Geography: Total area: 224,607 sq mi, 581,730 sq km (47); **Land area:** 218,816 sq mi, 566,730 sq km. **Location:** Southern Africa. Namibia on N and W, Zambia on N, Zimbabwe on NE, South Africa on S. **Topography:** The Kalahari Desert, supporting nomadic peoples and wildlife, spreads over SW. Swamplands and farming areas in N; rolling plains in E where livestock are grazed. **Arable land:** 0.5%. **Capital:** Gaborone, 269,338.

Government: Type: Parliamentary republic. **Head of state and govt.:** Pres. Mokgweetsi Masisi; b. 1962; in office: Apr. 1, 2018. **Local divisions:** 10 districts, 6 town councils. **Defense budget:** $537 mil. **Active troops:** 9,000.

Economy: Industries: diamonds, copper, nickel, salt, soda ash, potash, coal, iron ore, silver. **Chief agric.:** livestock; sorghum, maize, millet, beans, sunflowers, groundnuts. **Natural resources:** diamonds, copper, nickel, salt, soda ash, potash, coal, iron ore, silver. **Water:** 5,340 cu m per capita. **Electricity prod.:** 2.8 bil kwH. **Labor force:** agric. 20.4%, industry 18.1%, services 61.5%. **Unemployment:** 18.7%.

Finance: Monetary unit: Pula (BWP) (11.48 = $1 U.S.). **GDP:** $42.6 bil; **per capita GDP:** $18,503; **GDP growth:** 3.0%. **Imports:** $5 bil; South Africa 66.1%, Canada 8.3%, Israel 5.3%. **Exports:** $5.9 bil; Belgium 20.3%, India 12.6%, UAE 12.4%, South Africa 11.9%, Singapore 8.7%, Israel 7%. **Tourism:** $574 mil. **Budget:** $5.5 bil. **Inflation:** 2.8%.

Transport: Railways: 552 mi. **Motor vehicles:** 223.3 per 1,000 pop. **Airports:** 10.

Communications: Telephone: 6.3 per 100 pop. **Mobile:** 150 per 100 pop. **Broadband:** 66.9 per 100 pop. **Internet:** 47%.

Health: Expend.: 6.1%. **Life expect.:** 62.8 male; 66.9 female. **Births:** 20.9 per 1,000 pop. **Deaths:** 9.2 per 1,000 pop. **Infant mortality:** 26.8 per 1,000 live births. **Undernourished:** 24.1%. **HIV:** 20.7%.

Education: Free primary and junior secondary; not compulsory. **Literacy:** 97.5%.

Embassy: 1531-1533 New Hampshire Ave. NW 20036; 244-4990.

Website: www.gov.bw

First inhabited by San people, then Bantus, the region became the British protectorate of Bechuanaland in 1886. The country became fully independent Sept. 30, 1966. Mining, especially of diamonds, has contributed to economic growth. Pres. Festus Mogae transferred power Apr. 1, 2008, to Seretse Khama Ian Khama, son of Botswana's independence leader and first president (1966-80), Sir Seretse Khama. Mokgweetsi Eric Masisi became president, Apr. 1, 2018. In power since independence, the Botswana Democratic Party won Oct. 23, 2019, legislative elections—keeping the BDP's Masisi in office.

The High Court, June 11, 2019, struck down 1965 penal code provisions criminalizing same-sex relationships. The 2020 COVID-19 pandemic caused almost 3,200 cases and 16 deaths in Botswana as of Sept. 30.

Brazil
Federative Republic of Brazil

People: Population: 211,715,973 (7). **Age distrib.:** <15: 21.1%; 65+: 9.2%. **Growth:** 0.7%. **Migrants:** 0.4%. **Pop. density:** 65.6 per sq mi, 25.3 per sq km. **Urban:** 87.1%. **Ethnic groups:** white 47.7%, mulatto (mixed white/Black) 43.1%, Black 7.6%. **Languages:** Portuguese (official). **Religions:** Christian 90.6% (Catholic 65%, Protestant 14%, independent 11.5%), Spiritist 4.8%.

Geography: Total area: 3,287,957 sq mi, 8,515,770 sq km (5); **Land area:** 3,227,096 sq mi, 8,358,140 sq km. **Location:** Occupies E half of South America. French Guiana, Suriname, Guyana, Venezuela on N; Colombia, Peru, Bolivia, Paraguay, on W; Argentina, Uruguay on S. **Topography:** Atlantic coastline stretches 4,603 mi. Heavily wooded Amazon basin covers N half of country. Vast network of navigable rivers. The Amazon itself flows 2,093 mi in Brazil. The NE region is semiarid scrubland, heavily settled and poor. Almost half of pop. resides in S central region. Most major cities are in the narrow coastal belt. Almost the entire country has a tropical or semitropical climate. **Arable land:** 6.6%. **Capital:** Brasília, 4,645,843. **Cities:** São Paulo, 22,043,028; Rio de Janeiro, 13,458,075; Belo Horizonte, 6,084,430.

Government: Type: Federal presidential republic. **Head of state and govt.:** Pres. Jair Bolsonaro; b. 1955; in office: Jan. 1, 2019. **Local divisions:** 26 states, 1 federal district. **Defense budget:** $27.5 bil. **Active troops:** 366,500.

Economy: Industries: textiles, shoes, chemicals, cement, lumber, iron ore, tin, steel, aircraft, motor vehicles and parts. **Chief agric.:** coffee, soybeans, wheat, rice, corn, sugarcane, cocoa, citrus; beef. **Natural resources:** bauxite, gold, iron ore, manganese, nickel, phosphates, platinum, tin, rare earth elements, uranium, petroleum, hydropower, timber. **Water:** 41,316 cu m per capita. **Crude oil reserves:** 13.2 bil bbls. **Electricity prod.** (2018): 591.6 bil kWh. **Labor force:** agric. 9.1%, industry 19.6%, services 71.3%. **Unemployment:** 12.0%.

Finance: Monetary unit: Real (BRL) (5.30 = $1 U.S.). **GDP:** $3.2 tril; **per capita GDP:** $15,259; **GDP growth:** 1.1%. **Imports:** $153.2 bil; China 18.1%, U.S. 16.7%, Argentina 6.3%, Germany 6.1%. **Exports:** $217.2 bil; China 21.8%, U.S. 12.5%, Argentina 8.1%. **Tourism:** $5.9 bil. **Budget:** $756.3 bil. **Inflation:** 3.7%.

Transport: Railways: 18,548 mi. **Motor vehicles:** 212.8 per 1,000 pop. **Airports:** 698.

Communications: Telephone: 18.3 per 100 pop. **Mobile:** 98.8 per 100 pop. **Broadband:** 90.2 per 100 pop. **Internet:** 67.5%.

Health: Expend.: 9.5%. **Life expect.:** 71.2 male; 78.4 female. **Births:** 13.6 per 1,000 pop. **Deaths:** 6.9 per 1,000 pop. **Infant mortality:** 15.9 per 1,000 live births. **Undernourished:** <2.5%. **HIV:** 0.5%.

Education: Compulsory: ages 4-17. **Literacy:** 99.2%.

Embassy: 3006 Massachusetts Ave. NW 20008; 238-2700.

Website: www.brasil.gov.br

Pedro Álvares Cabral, a Portuguese navigator, is generally credited as the first European to reach Brazil, in 1500. The country was thinly settled by various Indigenous groups. Only a few survive today, mostly in the Amazon Basin.

In the next centuries, Portuguese colonists gradually pushed inland, bringing along large numbers of African slaves. (Slavery was not abolished until 1888.) The king of Portugal, fleeing Napoleon's army, moved the seat of government to Brazil in 1808. Brazil thereupon became a kingdom under Dom Joao VI. After Joao VI returned to Portugal, his son Pedro proclaimed Brazil's independence, Sept. 7, 1822, and was crowned emperor. The second emperor, Dom Pedro II, was deposed in 1889, and a republic proclaimed.

A military junta took control in 1930; Getulio Vargas assumed dictatorial power. The military forced him out in 1945. A democratic regime prevailed 1945-64, during which time the capital was moved from Rio de Janeiro to Brasília. Military-backed governments ruled Brazil for the next 20 years. Censorship was imposed, and the opposition was suppressed. Democratic presidential elections held in 1985 brought back civilian rule.

By the 1990s, Brazil had one of the world's largest economies (8th-largest in 2018). Income is unevenly distributed, however, and poverty widespread. Development has destroyed much of the Amazon ecosystem.

A new civil code guaranteeing legal equality for women was enacted Aug. 15, 2001. Luiz Inácio Lula da Silva, a union leader and reformer, won a presidential runoff, Oct. 2002. Brazil's space program launched its first rocket into space Oct. 23, 2004.

Despite political corruption scandals, Lula won a second presidential term, Oct. 2006. The nation reported huge offshore oil finds in 2007-08. Lula's former chief of staff, Dilma Rousseff, won a runoff election Oct. 31, 2010, to become Brazil's first woman president. She narrowly won reelection in an Oct. 26, 2014, runoff.

Responding to a Zika virus outbreak and related cases of microcephaly, Brazil declared a public health emergency, Nov. 11, 2015. The emergency was ended May 11, 2017, although some additional cases occurred. Through the end of 2017, health officials recorded 2,952 confirmed microcephaly cases and 369,013 confirmed or suspected Zika infections.

A $3-bil bribery and corruption scandal involving Petrobras (the national oil company), Pres. Rousseff's Workers' Party, and high-level government officials led to the resignations of Petrobras's top executives in Feb. 2015 and to arrests, in Nov. 2014 and June 2015, of business executives at Petrobras subcontractors. The Workers' Party's former treasurer was convicted of bribery and sentenced, Sept. 21, 2015, to more than 15 years in prison, while José Dirceu, Lula's former chief of staff, was sentenced, May 18, 2016, to 23 years in prison for money laundering and other Petrobras-related offenses. Former Pres. Lula was convicted, July 12, 2017, of bribery and money laundering in connection with the Petrobras scandal. Imprisoned in Apr. 2018, he was released Nov. 8, 2019, following a Supreme Court decision allowing his freedom pending appeals.

As Brazil suffered an economic downturn, the lower house of Congress, Apr. 17, 2016, charged Pres. Rousseff with illegally manipulating the federal budget to conceal the size of the deficit. Her Senate impeachment trial, Aug. 25-31, ended with her conviction and removal from office. Vice Pres. Michel Temer, a centrist and political rival, succeeded Rousseff. Former lower house speaker Eduardo Cunha was sentenced, Mar. 30, 2017, to more than 15 years in prison following his conviction on Petrobras-related corruption and bribery charges. Pres. Temer was twice charged with corruption in 2017, but the lower house of Congress voted not to send him to trial. Temer faced prosecution after leaving office, Jan. 1, 2019.

Campaigning against corruption, pledging to boost the economy (including through further Amazon development), and promising harsh action against violent crime and an alleged leftist threat, far-right candidate Jair Bolsonaro won an Oct. 28, 2018, presidential runoff election. Amazon deforestation accelerated beginning in 2019.

As Bolsonaro belittled the threat of COVID-19, Brazil was hard hit by the COVID-19 pandemic in 2020. As of Sept. 30, Brazil had more than 4,745,000 cases (3rd-highest in the world) and over 142,000 deaths (2nd-highest). Bolsonaro tested positive in July for the coronavirus that causes COVID-19.

Brunei
Brunei Darussalam

People: Population: 464,478 (168). **Age distrib.:** <15: 22.4%; 65+: 5.9%. **Growth:** 1.5%. **Migrants:** 25.5%. **Pop. density:** 228.5 per sq mi, 88.2 per sq km. **Urban:** 78.3%. **Ethnic groups:** Malay 65.7%, Chinese 10.3%. **Languages:** Malay (Bahasa Melayu) (official), English, Chinese dialects. **Religions:** Muslim 58.7% (Sunni [official]), Christian 11.7%, ethnic religionist 10.1%, Buddhist 9.4%, Chinese folk-religionist 5.6%.

Geography: Total area: 2,226 sq mi, 5,765 sq km (165); **Land area:** 2,033 sq mi, 5,265 sq km. **Location:** SE Asia, on the N coast of the island of Borneo. It is surrounded on its landward side by the Malaysian state of Sarawak. **Topography:** Narrow coastal plain with mountains in E, hilly lowlands in W. Swamps in W and NE. Tropical climate. **Arable land:** 0.9%. **Capital:** Bandar Seri Begawan, 40,781.

Government: Type: Absolute monarchy or sultanate. **Head of state and govt.:** Sultan and Prime Min. Sir Hassanal Bolkiah Mu'izzaddin Waddaulah; b. 1946; in office: Jan. 1, 1984 (sultan since Oct. 5, 1967). **Local divisions:** 4 districts. **Defense budget:** $435 mil. **Active troops:** 7,200.

Economy: Industries: petroleum, petroleum refining, liquefied nat. gas, constr. **Chief agric.:** rice, vegetables, fruits; chickens, water buffalo. **Natural resources:** petroleum, nat. gas, timber. **Water:** 19,827 cu m per capita. **Crude oil reserves:** 1.1 bil bbls. **Electricity prod.:** 3.9 bil kWh. **Labor force:** agric. 1.4%, industry 15.8%, services 82.8%. **Unemployment:** 9.0%.

Finance: Monetary unit: Dollar (BND) (1.36 = $1 U.S.). **GDP:** $28.0 bil; **per capita GDP:** $64,673; **GDP growth:** 3.9%. **Imports:** $3 bil; China 19.6%, Singapore 19%, Malaysia 18.8%, U.S. 9.2%, Germany 5.9%. **Exports:** $5.9 bil; Japan 27.8%, South Korea 12.4%, Thailand 11.5%, Malaysia 11.3%, India 9.3%, Singapore 7.7%, Switzerland 5%. **Tourism:** $217 mil. **Budget:** $4.3 bil. **Inflation:** –0.4%.

Transport: Motor vehicles: 986.8 per 1,000 pop. **Airports:** 1.

Communications: Telephone: 18.3 per 100 pop. **Mobile:** 131.9 per 100 pop. **Broadband:** 126.6 per 100 pop. **Internet:** 94.6%.

Health: Expend.: 2.4%. **Life expect.:** 75.5 male; 80.4 female. **Births:** 16.5 per 1,000 pop. **Deaths:** 3.8 per 1,000 pop. **Infant mortality:** 8.8 per 1,000 live births. **Undernourished:** <2.5%. **HIV:** NA.

Education: Compulsory: ages 6-14. **Literacy:** 99.7%.

Embassy: 3520 International Ct. NW 20008; 237-1838.

Website: www.gov.bn

The Sultanate of Brunei was a powerful state in the early 16th cent., with authority over all of the island of Borneo as well as parts of the Sulu Islands and the Philippines. In 1888, a treaty placed the state under the protection of Great Britain.

Brunei became a fully sovereign and independent state on Jan. 1, 1984. The country fielded female athletes for the first time at the 2012 Summer Olympics. A new penal code based on Islamic law, implemented in stages 2014-19, imposed harsh physical punishments for crimes such as theft, as well as for adultery and gay sex. Brunei outlawed public Christmas celebrations and displays in 2015.

Oil and natural gas account for 65% of GDP and 95% of exports. Brunei's GDP per capita is among the world's highest.

Bulgaria
Republic of Bulgaria

People: Population: 6,966,899 (105). **Age distrib.:** <15: 14.5%; 65+: 20.1%. **Growth:** –0.7%. **Migrants:** 2.4%. **Pop. density:** 166.3 per sq mi, 64.2 per sq km. **Urban:** 75.7%. **Ethnic groups:** Bulgarian 76.9%, Turkish 8%, Romani 4.4%. **Languages:** Bulgarian (official), Turkish, Romani. **Religions:** Christian 82.8% (Orthodox 79%), Muslim 13.7% (Sunni 13%, Shia 1%).

Geography: Total area: 42,811 sq mi, 110,879 sq km (103); **Land area:** 41,888 sq mi, 108,489 sq km. **Location:** SE Europe, in E Balkan Peninsula on Black Sea. Romania on N; Serbia, Macedonia on W; Greece, Turkey on S. **Topography:** The Stara Planina (Balkan) Mts. stretch E-W across the center of country, with the Danubian plain on N, the Rhodope Mts. on SW, and Thracian Plain on SE. **Arable land:** 32.1%. **Capital:** Sofia, 1,280,968.

Government: Type: Parliamentary republic. **Head of state:** Pres. Rumen Radev; b. 1963; in office: Jan. 22, 2017. **Head of govt.:** Prime Min. Boyko Borisov; b. 1959; in office: May 4, 2017. **Local divisions:** 28 provinces. **Defense budget:** $2.1 bil. **Active troops:** 36,950.

Economy: Industries: electricity, gas, water; food, beverages, tobacco; machinery and equip. **Chief agric.:** vegetables, fruits, tobacco, wine, wheat, barley, sunflowers, sugar beets; livestock. **Natural resources:** bauxite, copper, lead, zinc, coal, timber. **Water:** 3,006 cu m per capita. **Crude oil reserves:** 15 mil bbls. **Electricity prod.:** (2018): 43.4 bil kWh. **Labor force:** agric. 6.3%, industry 30.1%, services 63.7%. **Unemployment:** 3.9%.

Finance: Monetary unit: Lev (BGN) (1.65 = $1 U.S.). **GDP:** $171.3 bil; **per capita GDP:** $24,561; **GDP growth:** 3.4%. **Imports:** $31.4 bil; Germany 12.3%, Russia 10.3%, Italy 7.3%, Romania 7.1%, Turkey 6.2%, Spain 5.3%. **Exports:** $29.1 bil; Germany 13.5%, Italy 8.3%, Romania 8.2%, Turkey 7.7%, Greece 6.5%. **Tourism:** $4.3 bil. **Budget:** $19.4 bil. **Inflation:** 3.1%.

Transport: Railways: 3,178 mi. **Motor vehicles:** 479.4 per 1,000 pop. **Airports:** 57.

Communications: Telephone: 15.9 per 100 pop. **Mobile:** 118.1 per 100 pop. **Broadband:** 91.6 per 100 pop. **Internet** (2018): 64.8%.

Health: Expend.: 8.1%. **Life expect.:** 71.8 male; 78.5 female. **Births:** 8.3 per 1,000 pop. **Deaths:** 14.6 per 1,000 pop. **Infant mortality:** 8.1 per 1,000 live births. **Undernourished:** 3.0%. **HIV:** <0.1%.

Education: Compulsory: ages 5-15. **Literacy:** 98.4%.
Embassy: 1621 22nd St. NW 20008; 387-0174.
Website: www.gob.bg

Bulgaria was settled by Slavs in the 6th cent. Turkic Bulgars arrived in the 7th cent., merged with the Slavs, became Christians by the 9th cent., and set up powerful empires in the 10th and 12th cents. Ottomans took over in 1396 and ruled for nearly 500 years.

An 1876 revolt led to an independent kingdom in 1908. Bulgaria expanded after the first Balkan War but lost its Aegean coastline in WWI, when it sided with Germany. Bulgaria joined the Axis in WWII but withdrew in 1944. Communists took power with Soviet aid; the monarchy was abolished Sept. 8, 1946.

On Nov. 10, 1989, Communist Party leader and head of state Todor Zhivkov resigned after 35 years. In Jan. 1990, Parliament voted to revoke the constitutionally guaranteed dominant role of the Communist Party. A new constitution took effect July 13, 1991.

Bulgaria became a full member of NATO, Apr. 2, 2004, and entered the EU, Jan. 1, 2007.

A terrorist blew up a bus carrying Israeli tourists, July 18, 2012, leaving 5 Israelis, the Bulgarian bus driver, and the bomber dead. An investigation ending Feb. 5, 2013, blamed the Muslim militant group Hezbollah, which denied involvement.

Worsening economic conditions in 2012-13 inspired protests that led center-right, pro-EU Prime Min. Boyko Borisov to submit his government's resignation Feb. 20, 2013. No clear winner emerged from May 12 elections. Parliament elected Plamen Oresharski, with no party affiliation, prime min. May 29. Amid a banking crisis, Oresharski resigned July 23, 2014. After Oct. 5 elections, Borisov again became prime min., Nov. 7, 2014. Construction began in 2015 on the second phase of a security fence along the Turkish border, intended to stop Middle Eastern, SW Asian, and African migrants from entering Bulgaria; about 30,000 entered in 2015. Socialist-backed, pro-Moscow candidate Rumen Radev won

Bulgaria's presidential runoff election Nov. 13, 2016. Borisov resigned but returned as prime min. after his party won Mar. 26, 2017, parliamentary elections. Anti-corruption protests beginning July 2020 led Borisov to propose, Aug. 14, constitutional changes, but protests continued.

The 2020 COVID-19 pandemic caused more than 20,000 cases and over 800 deaths in Bulgaria as of Sept. 30.

Burkina Faso

People: Population: 20,835,401 (61). **Age distrib.:** <15: 43.6%; 65+: 3.2%. **Growth:** 2.6%. **Migrants:** 3.5%. **Pop. density:** 197.1 per sq mi, 76.1 per sq km. **Urban:** 30.6%. **Ethnic groups:** Mossi 52%, Fulani 8.4%, Gurma 7%, Bobo 4.9%, Gurunsi 4.6%, Senufo 4.5%, Bissa 3.7%, Lobi 2.4%, Dagara 2.4%. **Languages:** French (official), native African Sudanic-family langs. **Religions:** Muslim 55.9% (Sunni), Christian 23.8% (Catholic 15.3%), ethnic religionist 19.7%.

Geography: Total area: 105,869 sq mi, 274,200 sq km (74); **Land area:** 105,715 sq mi, 273,800 sq km. **Location:** W Africa, S of the Sahara. Mali on NW; Niger on NE; Benin, Togo, Ghana, Côte d'Ivoire on S. **Topography:** Landlocked in the savanna region of W Africa. The N is arid, hot, and thinly populated. **Arable land:** 21.9%. **Capital:** Ouagadougou, 2,780,331.

Government: Type: Presidential republic. **Head of state:** Pres. Roch Marc Christian Kaboré; b. 1957; in office: Dec. 29, 2015. **Head of govt.:** Prime Min. Christophe Dabiré; in office: Jan. 24, 2019. **Local divisions:** 13 regions. **Defense budget:** $361 mil. **Active troops:** 11,200.

Economy: Industries: cotton lint, beverages, agric. proc., soap, cigarettes, textiles. **Chief agric.:** cotton, peanuts, shea nuts, sesame, sorghum, millet, corn, rice. **Natural resources:** manganese, limestone, marble, gold, phosphates, pumice, salt. **Water:** 703 cu m per capita. **Electricity prod.:** 1.1 bil kWh. **Labor force:** agric. 24.7%, industry 33.9%, services 41.4%. **Unemployment:** 6.4%.

Finance: Monetary unit: CFA Franc (XOF) (553.52 = $1 U.S.). **GDP:** $46.3 bil; **per capita GDP:** $2,280; **GDP growth:** 5.7%. **Imports:** $3.3 bil; China 13.2%, Côte d'Ivoire 9.5%, U.S. 8.2%, Thailand 8.1%, France 6.5%. **Exports:** $3.1 bil; Switzerland 44.9%, India 15.6%, South Africa 11.3%. **Tourism:** $121 mil. **Budget:** $3.7 bil. **Inflation:** –3.2%.

Transport: Railways: 386 mi. **Motor vehicles:** 17.4 per 1,000 pop. **Airports:** 2.

Communications: Telephone: 0.4 per 100 pop. **Mobile:** 97.9 per 100 pop. **Broadband:** 28.8 per 100 pop. **Internet:** 16%.

Health: Expend.: 6.9%. **Life expect.:** 60.9 male; 64.5 female. **Births:** 35.1 per 1,000 pop. **Deaths:** 8.2 per 1,000 pop. **Infant mortality:** 52.0 per 1,000 live births. **Undernourished:** 19.2%. **HIV:** 0.7%.

Education: Compulsory: ages 6-15. **Literacy:** 58.3%.
Embassy: 2340 Massachusetts Ave. NW 20008; 332-5577.
Website: www.gouvernement.gov.bf or burkina-usa.org

The Mossi people entered Burkina Faso in the 11th-13th cents. Their kingdoms ruled until they were defeated by the Mali and Songhai empires. French control came by 1896, but Upper Volta (renamed Burkina Faso on Aug. 4, 1984) was not established as a separate territory until 1947. Independence came Aug. 5, 1960. The military seized power in 1980. After a 1987 coup, Blaise Compaoré became sole ruler by 1989. Violent protests in 2014 against economic hardship and Pres. Compaoré's plan to run for reelection again led to his resignation Oct. 31. Civilian Michel Kafando became interim president Nov. 18, 2014. Forces loyal to Compaoré ousted Kafando, Sept. 16, 2015. An ECOWAS-negotiated agreement restored Kafando, Sept. 23, and provided for Nov. 29, 2015, elections; former center-left Prime Min. Roch Marc Christian Kaboré was elected president.

Islamist extremists attacked a café and hotel in Ouagadougou Jan. 15-16, 2016, leaving 30 victims dead. Terrorist gunmen killed at least 19 at an Ouagadougou restaurant, Aug. 13-14, 2017. By mid-2019, insurgents allied with Islamist extremists controlled parts of northern and eastern Burkina Faso, and violence escalated in late 2019 and 2020. About 1 mil people were internally displaced by Sept. 2020.

As of Sept. 30, 2020, the COVID-19 pandemic had caused more than 1,900 cases and 56 deaths in Burkina Faso.

Burma
See Myanmar.

Burundi
Republic of Burundi

People: Population: 11,865,821 (77). **Age distrib.:** <15: 43.8%; 65+: 3.1%. **Growth:** 2.9%. **Migrants:** 2.8%. **Pop. density:** 1,196.7 per sq mi, 462.1 per sq km. **Urban:** 13.7%. **Ethnic groups:** Hutu 85%, Tutsi 14%. **Languages:** Kirundi, French (both official).

Religions: Christian 94.1% (Catholic 64%, Protestant 26.9%), ethnic religionist 3.5%.

Geography: Total area: 10,745 sq mi, 27,830 sq km (143); **Land area:** 9,915 sq mi, 25,680 sq km. **Location:** Central Africa. Rwanda on N, Dem. Rep. of the Congo on W, Tanzania on E and S. **Topography:** Mostly grassy highland, with mountains reaching 8,900 ft. The southernmost source of the White Nile is located in Burundi. Lake Tanganyika is the world's second deepest lake (max. depth 4,823 ft). **Arable land:** 46.7%. **Capital:** Bujumbura, 1,012,996.

Government: Type: Presidential republic. **Head of state and govt.:** Pres. Evariste Ndayishimiye b. 1968; in office: June 18, 2020. **Local divisions:** 18 provinces. **Defense budget:** $62 mil. **Active troops:** 30,050.

Economy: Industries: light consumer goods, assembly of imported components, public works constr., food proc. (fruits). **Chief agric.:** coffee, cotton, tea, corn, beans, sorghum, sweet potatoes, bananas, cassava; beef. **Natural resources:** nickel, uranium, rare earth oxides, peat, cobalt, copper, platinum, vanadium, hydropower, niobium, tantalum, gold, tin, tungsten, kaolin, limestone. **Water:** 1,154 cu m per capita. **Electricity prod.:** 220 mil kWh. **Labor force:** agric. 92.0%, industry 1.4%, services 6.5%. **Unemployment:** 1.4%.

Finance: Monetary unit: Franc (BIF) (1,936.09 = $1 U.S.). **GDP:** $9.0 bil; **per capita GDP:** $783; **GDP growth:** 1.8%. **Imports:** $603.8 mil; India 18.5%, China 13%, Kenya 7.9%, UAE 6.8%, Saudi Arabia 6.8%, Uganda 6%, Tanzania 5.4%. **Exports:** $119 mil; Dem. Rep. of the Congo 25.5%, Switzerland 18.4%, UAE 14.9%, Belgium 6%. **Tourism:** $4 mil. **Budget:** $729.6 mil. **Inflation:** –0.7%.

Transport: Motor vehicles: 6.6 per 1,000 pop. **Airports:** 1.

Communications: Telephone: 0.2 per 100 pop. **Mobile:** 56.5 per 100 pop. **Broadband:** 17.2 per 100 pop. **Internet:** 2.7%.

Health: Expend.: 7.5%. **Life expect.:** 64.6 male; 68.8 female. **Births:** 36.5 per 1,000 pop. **Deaths:** 6.2 per 1,000 pop. **Infant mortality:** 40.1 per 1,000 live births. **Undernourished:** NA. **HIV:** 1.0%.

Education: Compulsory: NA. **Literacy:** 88.2%.

Embassy: 2233 Wisconsin Ave. NW, Ste. 408, 20007; 342-2574.

Website: presidence.gov.bi or www.burundiembassydc.usa.com
The pygmy Twa were the first inhabitants, followed by Bantu Hutus, who were conquered in the 16th cent. by the Tutsi (Watusi), probably from Ethiopia. Germany gained control in 1899. Belgium took over in 1916, successively exercising a League of Nations mandate and UN trusteeship over Ruanda-Urundi (now the two countries of Rwanda and Burundi). Burundi became independent July 1, 1962.

An unsuccessful Hutu rebellion in 1972-73 left 10,000 Tutsi and 150,000 Hutu dead. Over 100,000 Hutu fled to Tanzania and Zaire (now Dem. Rep. of the Congo). In the 1980s, Burundi's Tutsi-dominated regime pledged itself to ethnic reconciliation and democratic reform. In the nation's first democratic presidential election, June 1993, a Hutu, Melchior Ndadaye, was elected. He was killed in an attempted coup, Oct. 21, 1993. At least 150,000 Burundians died in ethnic conflicts over the next three years. Pres. Cyprien Ntaryamira, elected Jan. 1994, and the president of Rwanda were killed when missiles shot down their plane, Apr. 6. The incident sparked massive carnage in Rwanda; violence in Burundi, initially far more limited, intensified in 1995. Ethnic strife continued after a military coup, July 25, 1996. Most warring groups signed a draft peace treaty, Aug. 2000. A power-sharing government headed by Pierre Buyoya was sworn in Nov. 1, 2001, but clashes with rebels continued.

Domitien Ndayizeye, a Hutu, became president Apr. 2003. The UN Security Council authorized, May 2004, a peacekeeping force (ONUB) for Burundi. Approval of a power-sharing constitution by referendum, Feb. 28, 2005, paved the way for local and parliamentary elections. Chosen by parliament, Pierre Nkurunziza, former leader of a Hutu rebel group, became president Aug. 2005. ONUB was succeeded by the UN Integrated Office in Burundi (BINUB), 2007-10, and by the UN Office in Burundi (BNUB), 2011-14, both intended to assist with political transition. Under a reconciliation accord reached Dec. 4, 2008, remaining Hutu rebels began to demobilize. Candidates opposing Nkurunziza dropped out of the June 2010 presidential election, claiming the vote was rigged. The government was accused of ordering extrajudicial killings, 2010-11.

Violent protests began after Nkurunziza's Apr. 2015 decision to seek a constitutionally dubious third term, which he won, July 21, despite a coup attempt. Political violence and harsh government repression continued in Nkurunziza's third term, leading hundreds of thousands to flee the country. Widely criticized constitutional changes approved in a May 17, 2018, referendum could have facilitated Nkurunziza's staying in power, but he stated, June 7, that he would not seek reelection in 2020. Evariste Ndayishimiye, of Nkurunziza's ruling party, won the May 20, 2020, election, which the opposition claimed was rigged. Nkurunziza died June 8, before the end of his term.

Cabo Verde
Republic of Cabo Verde

People: Population: 583,255 (167). **Age distrib.:** <15: 28.0%; 65+: 5.5%. **Growth:** 1.3%. **Migrants:** 2.8%. **Pop. density:** 374.6 per sq mi, 144.6 per sq km. **Urban:** 66.7%. **Ethnic groups:** Creole (mulatto) 71%, African 28%. **Languages:** Portuguese (offi-

cial), Krioulo (Portuguese/West African blend). **Religions:** Christian 95% (Catholic 84.5%), Muslim 2.8% (Sunni).

Geography: Total area: 1,557 sq mi, 4,033 sq km (167); **Land area:** 1,557 sq mi, 4,033 sq km. **Location:** In Atlantic O., off W tip of Africa. Nearest neighbors are Mauritania, Senegal to E. **Topography:** 15 Cabo Verde islands, volcanic in origin (active crater on Fogo). Landscape is eroded and stark, with vegetation mostly in interior valleys. **Arable land:** 12.4%. **Capital:** Praia, 167,504.

Government: Type: Parliamentary republic. **Head of state:** Pres. Jorge Carlos Fonseca; b. 1950; in office: Sept. 9, 2011. **Head of govt.:** Prime Min. José Ulisses Correia e Silva; b. 1962; in office: Apr. 22, 2016. **Local divisions:** 22 municipalities. **Defense budget:** $11 mil. **Active troops:** 1,200.

Economy: Industries: food and beverages, fish proc., shoes and garments, salt mining, ship repair. **Chief agric.:** bananas, corn, beans, sweet potatoes, sugarcane, coffee, peanuts; fish. **Natural resources:** salt, basalt rock, limestone, kaolin, fish, clay, gypsum. **Water:** 549 cu m per capita. **Electricity prod.:** 448 mil kWh. **Labor force:** agric. 11.1%, industry 22.1%, services 66.8%. **Unemployment:** 12.3%.

Finance: Monetary unit: Escudo (CVE) (93.05 = $1 U.S.). **GDP:** $4.1 bil; **per capita GDP:** $7,469; **GDP growth:** 5.7%. **Imports:** $836.1 mil; Portugal 43.9%, Spain 11.6%, Netherlands 6.1%, China 6.1%. **Exports:** $189 mil; Spain 45.3%, Portugal 40.3%, Netherlands 8.1%. **Tourism:** $484 mil. **Budget:** $546.7 mil. **Inflation:** 1.1%.

Transport: Airports: 9.

Communications: Telephone: 11.5 per 100 pop. **Mobile:** 112.2 per 100 pop. **Broadband:** 69.9 per 100 pop. **Internet (2018):** 58.2%.

Health: Expend.: 5.2%. **Life expect.:** 70.8 male; 75.6 female. **Births:** 19.1 per 1,000 pop. **Deaths:** 5.9 per 1,000 pop. **Infant mortality:** 19.7 per 1,000 live births. **Undernourished:** 18.5%. **HIV:** 0.6%.

Education: Compulsory: ages 6-15. **Literacy:** 98.1%.

Embassy: 3415 Massachusetts Ave. NW 20007; 965-6820.

Website: www.governo.cv
The first Portuguese colonists landed in 1462; African slaves were brought soon after, and most Cabo Verdeans descend from both groups. Independence for Cabo Verde (known as Cape Verde until Oct. 2013) came July 5, 1975. Remittances from Cabo Verdean emigrants are a major source of income.

The nation's first free presidential election was held Feb. 17, 1991. Jorge Carlos Fonseca won a presidential runoff election Aug. 21, 2011; he was reelected, Oct. 2, 2016.

In 2020, Cabo Verde was affected by the COVID-19 pandemic, with more than 5,800 cases and 59 deaths as of Sept. 30.

Cambodia
Kingdom of Cambodia

People: Population: 16,926,984 (69). **Age distrib.:** <15: 30.2%; 65+: 4.6%. **Growth:** 1.4%. **Migrants:** 0.5%. **Pop. density:** 248.4 per sq mi, 95.9 per sq km. **Urban:** 24.2%. **Ethnic groups:** Khmer 97.6%. **Languages:** Khmer (official). **Religions:** Buddhist 85.2%, ethnic religionist 4.3%, Christian 2.9%, Chinese folk-religionist 2.4%.

Geography: Total area: 69,898 sq mi, 181,035 sq km (88); **Land area:** 68,153 sq mi, 176,515 sq km. **Location:** SE Asia, on Indochina Peninsula. Thailand on W and N, Laos on NE, Vietnam on E. **Topography:** The central area, formed by the Mekong R. basin and Tonle Sap Lake, is level. Hills and mountains in SE; long escarpment in NW separates the country from Thailand. **Arable land:** 22.2%. **Capital:** Phnom Penh, 2,077,757.

Government: Type: Parliamentary constitutional monarchy. **Head of state:** King Norodom Sihamoni; b. 1953; in office: Oct. 29, 2004. **Head of govt.:** Prime Min. Hun Sen; b. 1952; in office: Jan. 14, 1985. **Local divisions:** 24 provinces, 1 municipality. **Defense budget:** $1 bil. **Active troops:** 124,300.

Economy: Industries: tourism, garments, constr., rice milling, fishing, wood and wood prods., rubber, cement, gem mining, textiles. **Chief agric.:** rice, rubber, corn, vegetables, cashews, cassava, silk. **Natural resources:** oil and gas, timber, gemstones, iron ore, manganese, phosphates. **Water:** 29,747 cu m per capita. **Electricity prod.:** 6.7 bil kWh. **Labor force:** agric. 31.2%, industry 29.6%, services 39.2%. **Unemployment:** 0.7%.

Finance: Monetary unit: Riel (KHR) (4,104.59 = $1 U.S.). **GDP:** $75.4 bil; **per capita GDP:** $4,571; **GDP growth:** 7.1%. **Imports:** $14.4 bil; China 34.1%, Singapore 12.8%, Thailand 12.4%, Vietnam 10.1%. **Exports:** $11.4 bil; U.S. 21.5%, UK 9%, Germany 8.6%, Japan 7.6%, China 6.9%, Canada 6.7%. **Tourism:** $4.8 bil. **Budget:** $4.4 bil. **Inflation** (2017-18): 2.5%.

Transport: Railways: 399 mi (under restoration). **Airports:** 6.

Communications: Telephone: 0.5 per 100 pop. **Mobile:** 119.5 per 100 pop. **Broadband:** 66.9 per 100 pop. **Internet (2018):** 40%.

Health: Expend.: 5.9%. **Life expect.:** 63.4 male; 68.6 female. **Births:** 21.3 per 1,000 pop. **Deaths:** 7.3 per 1,000 pop. **Infant mortality:** 43.7 per 1,000 live births. **Undernourished:** 14.5%. **HIV:** 0.5%.

Education: Compulsory: NA. **Literacy:** 80.5%.

Embassy: 4530 16th St. NW 20011; 726-7742.

Website: cnv.org.kh

Early kingdoms dating from that of Funan in the 1st cent. CE culminated in the great Khmer empire that flourished from the 9th cent. to the 13th, encompassing present-day Thailand, Cambodia, Laos, and southern Vietnam. The peripheral areas were lost to invading Siamese and Vietnamese. France established a protectorate in 1863. Independence came in 1953.

Prince Norodom Sihanouk, king (1941-55) and head of state from 1960, tried to maintain neutrality during the Vietnam War. The U.S. bombed Cambodia, 1969-73, targeting suspected border sanctuaries of Vietnamese insurgents.

In 1970, pro-U.S. Prem. Lon Nol seized power, demanded removal of 40,000 North Vietnamese troops, and abolished the monarchy. Open war began between Lon Nol's government and Communist Khmer Rouge guerrillas, led by Pol Pot and supported by Vietnam and China. The U.S. provided Lon Nol with military and economic aid.

Khmer Rouge forces captured Phnom Penh Apr. 17, 1975. Cities were depopulated with the stated goal of making Cambodia a classless agrarian society; Cambodians were executed or forced to work on cooperative farms. An estimated 1.7 mil people died in "killing fields" or from other hardships under Khmer Rouge rule, 1975-79.

Border fighting in 1978 developed into a full-fledged Vietnamese invasion. Formation of a Vietnamese-backed government was announced, Jan. 8, 1979, one day after Phnom Penh was seized. Thousands of refugees fled to Thailand; widespread starvation was reported. Vietnamese troops remained in Cambodia until Sept. 1989 to combat resistance from Khmer Rouge guerrillas. Following 1993 UN-sponsored elections, two leading parties agreed to share power in an interim government. On Sept. 21, the National Assembly adopted a constitution reestablishing a monarchy with Sihanouk as king. The Khmer Rouge insurgency weakened and splintered by 1996.

Co-Prime Min. Hun Sen staged a coup July 5, 1997, ousting his rival, Prince Norodom Ranariddh. Pol Pot was denounced by his former comrades at a show trial, July 25, 1997, and sentenced to house arrest; he died Apr. 15, 1998. Sihanouk abdicated because of poor health and was succeeded, Oct. 2004, by his son Norodom Sihamoni. A UN-backed war crimes tribunal convicted a former prison warden known as Duch July 2010 for overseeing the killing and torture of more than 14,000 inmates under the Khmer Rouge. Two high-level Khmer Rouge leaders were convicted of crimes against humanity, Aug. 7, 2014, and of genocide, Nov. 16, 2018.

Hun Sen's party retained power through a series of flawed elections, most recently on July 29, 2018, and repressive policies. Opposition leader Kem Sokha's political party was dissolved in Nov. 2017, and several media outlets were shut down by the government. A trial of Kem Sokha for treason began Jan. 15, 2020. Apr. 2020 state-of-emergency legislation, passed during the COVID-19 pandemic, broadened Hun Sen's powers. As of Sept. 30, the WHO reported 277 Cambodian cases.

In recent years, Chinese investment, military and other aid, and tourism have increased sharply.

Cameroon
Republic of Cameroon

People: Population: 27,744,989 (51). **Age distrib.:** <15: 42.3%; 65+: 3.1%. **Growth:** 2.8%. **Migrants:** 2.0%. **Pop. density:** 152.0 per sq mi, 58.7 per sq km. **Urban:** 57.6%. **Ethnic groups:** Bamileke-Bamu 24.3%, Beti/Bassa, Mbam 21.6%, Biu-Mandara 14.6%, Arab-Choa/Hausa/Kanuri 11%, Adamawa-Ubangi 9.8%, Grassfields 7.7%, Kako, Meka/Pygmy 3.3%, Cotier/Ngoe/Oroko 2.7%, Southwestern Bantu 0.7%, foreign/other ethnic group 4.5%. **Languages:** English, French (both official); 24 major African languages. **Religions:** Christian 61.8% (Catholic 29.7%, Protestant 25.2%), Muslim 20.6% (Sunni), ethnic religionist 16.6%.

Geography: Total area: 183,568 sq mi, 475,440 sq km (53). **Land area:** 182,514 sq mi, 472,710 sq km. **Location:** Between W and central Africa. Nigeria on NW; Chad, Central African Republic on E; Congo Rep., Gabon, Equatorial Guinea on S. **Topography:** Low coastal plain with rain forests in S; plateaus in center lead to forested mountains in W, including Mt. Cameroon (13,435 ft). Grasslands in N, marshes around Lake Chad. **Arable land:** 13.1%. **Capital:** Yaoundé 3,992,411. **Cities:** Douala, 3,663,227.

Government: Type: Presidential republic. **Head of state:** Pres. Paul Biya; b. 1933; in office: Nov. 6, 1982. **Head of govt.:** Prime Min. Joseph Dion Ngute; b. 1954; in office: Jan. 4, 2019. **Local divisions:** 10 regions. **Defense budget:** $424 mil. **Active troops:** 25,400.

Economy: Industries: petroleum prod./refining, aluminum prod., food proc., light consumer goods, textiles, lumber, ship repair. **Chief agric.:** coffee, cocoa, cotton, rubber, bananas, oilseed, grains, cassava; livestock. **Natural resources:** petroleum, bauxite, iron ore, timber, hydropower. **Water:** 11,769 cu m per capita. **Crude oil reserves:** 200 mil bbls. **Electricity prod.:** 8.3 bil kWh. **Labor force:** agric. 42.9%, industry 15.1%, services 42.1%. **Unemployment:** 3.4%.

Finance: Monetary unit: Central African CFA Franc (XAF) (553.52 = $1 U.S.). **GDP:** $98.4 bil; **per capita GDP:** $3,804; **GDP growth:** 4.0%. **Imports:** $4.8 bil; China 19%, France 10.3%, Thai-

land 7.9%. **Exports:** $4.7 bil; Netherlands 15.6%, France 12.6%, China 11.7%, Belgium 6.8%, Italy 6.3%. **Tourism:** $581 mil. **Budget:** $6.6 bil. **Inflation:** 2.5%.

Transport: Railways: 613 mi. **Motor vehicles:** 16.7 per 1,000 pop. **Airports:** 11.

Communications: Telephone: 2.4 per 100 pop. **Mobile:** 69.1 per 100 pop. **Broadband:** 17.7 per 100 pop. **Internet** 23.2%.

Health: Expend.: 4.7%. **Life expect.:** 60.6 male; 64.0 female. **Births:** 36.3 per 1,000 pop. **Deaths:** 8.1 per 1,000 pop. **Infant mortality:** 51.5 per 1,000 live births. **Undernourished:** 6.3%. **HIV:** 3.1%.

Education: Compulsory: ages 6-11. **Literacy:** 85.1%.

Embassy: 3400 International Dr. NW 20008; 265-8790.

Website: www.spm.gov.cm

Portuguese sailors were the first Europeans to reach Cameroon, in the 15th cent. The European and American slave trade was very active in the area. German control lasted from 1884 to 1916, when France and Britain divided the territory. French Cameroon became independent Jan. 1, 1960; one part of British Cameroon joined Nigeria in 1961 while the other part joined Cameroon. Pres. Paul Biya has retained power since 1982 in a series of elections that were boycotted by opposition parties or disputed as fraudulent.

More than a dozen French citizens were kidnapped during 2013, allegedly in retaliation for France's intervention in Mali, by the Nigerian-based jihadist group Boko Haram. Kidnappings and attacks by Boko Haram in northern Cameroon continued in 2014-20. Beginning in 2015, Cameroon troops fought in Nigeria against Boko Haram forces. A 2017 Amnesty Intl. report accused the Cameroon military of torturing suspected Boko Haram detainees.

Since late 2016, government forces have violently suppressed protesters and fought separatists in Anglophone areas of western Cameroon. Violence in the north and west had caused more than 1 mil people to be internally displaced by Aug. 31, 2020.

The 2020 COVID-19 pandemic caused almost 21,000 cases and over 400 deaths in Cameroon by Sept. 30.

Canada

People: Population: 37,694,085 (38). **Age distrib.:** <15: 16.0%; 65+: 19.0%. **Growth:** 0.8%. **Migrants:** 21.3%. **Pop. density:** 10.7 per sq mi, 4.1 per sq km. **Urban:** 81.6%. **Ethnic groups:** Canadian 32.3%, English 18.3%, Scottish 13.9%, French 13.6%, Irish 13.4%, German 9.6%, Chinese 5.1%, Italian 4.6%, N. Amer. Indian 4.4%, East Indian 4%. **Languages:** English, French (both official). **Religions:** Christian 61.8% (Catholic 43.3%, Protestant 10.6%), agnostic 23.1%, Muslim 3.8% (Sunni 3%), atheist 2.8%, Chinese folk-religionist 2%, Buddhist 1.8%, Sikh 1.4%, Hindu 1.4%.

Geography: Total area: 3,855,103 sq mi, 9,984,670 sq km (2); **Land area:** 3,511,023 sq mi, 9,093,507 sq km. **Location:** Extends 3,426 mi E-W and S from the North Pole to the U.S. **Topography:** Seacoast includes 36,356 mi of mainland and 115,133 mi of islands, including the Arctic islands almost from Greenland to near the Alaskan border. Generally temperate, though varies from freezing winter cold to blistering summer heat. **Arable land:** 4.3%. **Capital:** Ottawa-Gatineau, 1,393,086. **Cities:** Toronto, 6,196,731; Montréal, 4,220,566; Vancouver, 2,581,079; Calgary, 1,547,484; Edmonton, 1,461,182; Québec City, 826,109; Winnipeg, 816,593; Halifax, 412,674; Victoria, 385,999.

Government: Type: Federal parliamentary democracy under constitutional monarchy. **Head of state:** Queen Elizabeth II, rep. by Gov.-Gen. Julie Payette; b. 1963; in office: Oct. 2, 2017. **Head of govt.:** Prime Min. Justin Trudeau; b. 1971; in office: Nov. 4, 2015. **Local divisions:** 10 provinces, 3 territories. **Defense budget:** $18.7 bil. **Active troops:** 47,000.

Economy: Industries: transp. equip., chemicals, minerals, food prods., wood and paper prods., fish prods. **Chief agric.:** wheat, barley, oilseed, tobacco, fruits, vegetables; dairy prods.; fish. **Natural resources:** iron ore, nickel, zinc, copper, gold, lead, rare earth elements, molybdenum, potash, diamonds, silver, fish, timber, wildlife, coal, petroleum, nat. gas, hydropower. **Water:** 79,238 cu m per capita. **Crude oil reserves:** 167.9 bil bbls. **Electricity prod.:** (2018): 633.2 bil kWh. **Labor force:** agric. 1.4%, industry 19.4%, services 79.2%. **Unemployment:** 5.4%.

Finance: Monetary unit: Dollar (CAD) (1.31 = $1 U.S.). **GDP:** $1.9 tril; **per capita GDP:** $51,342; **GDP growth:** 1.7%. **Imports:** $442.1 bil; U.S. 51.5%, China 12.6%, Mexico 6.3%. **Exports:** $423.5 bil; U.S. 76.4%. **Tourism:** $27 bil. **Budget:** $665.7 bil. **Inflation:** 1.9%.

Transport: Railways: 48,425 mi. **Motor vehicles:** 678.1 per 1,000 pop. **Airports:** 523.

Communications: Telephone: 37.5 per 100 pop. **Mobile:** 89.2 per 100 pop. **Broadband:** 72.5 per 100 pop. **Internet:** 91%.

Health: Expend.: 10.6%. **Life expect.:** 81.1 male; 85.9 female. **Births:** 10.2 per 1,000 pop. **Deaths:** 7.9 per 1,000 pop. **Infant mortality:** 4.3 per 1,000 live births. **Undernourished:** <2.5%. **HIV:** NA.

Education: Compulsory: ages 6-15. **Literacy:** 99%.

Embassy: 501 Pennsylvania Ave. NW 20001; 682-1740.

Website: www.canada.ca

Indigenous people have lived in Canada for at least 12,000 years. Vikings reached and briefly settled in part of Newfoundland in the 10th cent. Italian seaman Giovanni Caboto (a.k.a. John Cabot) claimed parts of the Atlantic coast for England in 1497 and 1498.

Canada's Provinces and Territories

Province/territory	Joined confed.	Tot. area (sq mi)	Population (2019 est.)	Capital	Premier	Party	In office
Alberta	1905	255,541	4,371,316	Edmonton	Jason Kenney	United Cons.	2019
British Columbia	1871	364,764	5,071,336	Victoria	John Horgan	New Democratic	2017
Manitoba	1870	250,116	1,369,465	Winnipeg	Brian Pallister	Prog. Cons.	2016
New Brunswick	1867	28,150	776,827	Fredericton	Blaine Higgs	Prog. Cons.	2018
Newfoundland and Labrador	1949	156,453	521,542	St. John's	Andrew Furey	Liberal	2020
Nova Scotia	1867	21,345	971,395	Halifax	Stephen McNeil	Liberal	2013
Ontario	1867	415,598	14,566,547	Toronto	Doug Ford	Prog. Cons.	2018
Prince Edward Island	1873	2,185	156,947	Charlottetown	Dennis King	Prog. Cons.	2019
Québec	1867	595,391	8,484,965	Québec	François Legault	Coalition Avenir Québec	2018
Saskatchewan	1905	251,366	1,174,462	Regina	Scott Moe	Saskatchewan	2018
Northwest Territories[1]	1871	519,734	44,826	Yellowknife	Caroline Cochrane	Nonpartisan	2019
Nunavut[1,2]	1999	808,185	38,780	Iqaluit	Joe Savikataaq	Nonpartisan	2018
Yukon[1]	1898	186,272	40,854	Whitehorse	Sandy Silver	Liberal	2016

Note: Pop. est. as of July 1. (Source: Statistics Canada.) (1) Territories also have federally appointed commissioners to represent federal interests. (2) Territory created in 1999 from eastern portion of Northwest Territories.

After French explorer Jacques Cartier reached the Gulf of St. Lawrence in 1534, France pioneered Canadian settlement by Western Europeans, establishing Québec City (1608) and Montréal (1642) and declaring New France a colony in 1663.

Britain acquired Acadia (later Nova Scotia) in 1717 and defeated French forces in Canada to gain control of all of New France by 1763. The French, through the Quebec Act of 1774, retained rights to their language, religion, and civil law. During the American Revolution, many colonials, calling themselves United Empire Loyalists, moved north to Canada. Fur traders and explorers led Canadians of European origin westward across the continent. Sir Alexander Mackenzie reached the Pacific in 1793 and scrawled on a rock, "From Canada by land."

In Upper and Lower Canada (later called Ontario and Quebec) and in the Maritimes, legislative assemblies were formed in the 18th cent. Upper Canada was involved in the War of 1812 between Great Britain and the U.S.

In 1837 political agitation for a more democratic government culminated in rebellions in Upper and Lower Canada and the union of the two into the colony of Canada in 1839. The union lasted until the 1867 British North America Act (now known as the Constitution Act, 1867) launched the Dominion of Canada, consisting of Ontario, Quebec, and the former colonies of Nova Scotia and New Brunswick.

The British North America Act, which was the basis for the country's written constitution, established a federal system of government modeled on the British parliament and cabinet structure under the crown. Canada was proclaimed a self-governing dominion within the British Empire in 1931. The Constitution Act, 1982, gave Canada the right to amend its constitution, thereby severing its last legislative link with Britain.

Failure in 1990 of the so-called Meech Lake Accord, which would have assured constitutional protection for Quebec's efforts to preserve its French language and culture, sparked a separatist revival in Quebec. The Charlottetown agreement, calling for constitutional changes, such as recognition of Quebec as a "distinct society" within the Canadian confederation, was defeated by a national referendum Oct. 1992. A Quebec referendum on secession, Oct. 1995, also failed.

On Jan. 7, 1998, the government apologized to Indigenous peoples for 150 years of mistreatment. Nunavut ("Our Land"), carved from the Northwest Territories as a homeland for the Inuit, was established Apr. 1, 1999.

Canada sent troops and warships to aid the U.S.-led coalition in Afghanistan beginning Oct. 2001; 157 Canadian troops had been killed in Afghanistan by the time Canada's combat mission ended July 7, 2011.

Same-sex marriage (already permitted in 8 provinces) became legal throughout the country July 2005. Marijuana was legalized nationally for medical purposes in 2001 and for recreational use in 2018.

Twelve years of Liberal Party rule ended when the Conservatives won parliamentary elections, Jan. 23, 2006. Elections Oct. 19, 2015, returned Liberals to power, and Justin Trudeau, son of former Prime Min. Pierre Trudeau, became prime min. The Liberals won the most seats, but lost their majority, in Oct. 21, 2019, elections; Justin Trudeau continued as prime minister.

Improved technology has facilitated extracting oil from Alberta's tar sands. The Canadian government approved, Nov. 29, 2016, a major expansion of the Trans Mountain pipeline to transport oil from Alberta to British Columbia; construction proceeded in 2020, after court challenges to the project failed. Building the Keystone XL pipeline, to carry Alberta oil through the central U.S. to the Gulf of Mexico, was approved by Pres. Donald Trump, Mar. 24, 2017; some construction occurred in 2020, but U.S. legal challenges continued.

On Oct. 22, 2014, a terrorist gunman in Ottawa, apparently inspired by the Islamist extremist group ISIS, killed a soldier at the Canadian War Memorial and opened fire in the Parliament building before being shot to death. Two days earlier in Montréal, a terrorist with apparently similar motivation ran down two soldiers with his car, killing one, before being fatally shot. Canada joined the U.S.-led campaign of airstrikes against ISIS forces in Iraq (2014-16) and Syria (2015-16). Canada began, Nov. 2015, a resettlement program for tens of thousands of Syrian refugees.

The North American Free Trade Agreement (NAFTA) among Canada, Mexico, and the U.S. went into effect Jan. 1, 1994. Negotiations to revise NAFTA, called for by the U.S., began Aug. 16, 2017. A revised agreement—renamed the U.S.-Mexico-Canada Agreement (USMCA)—was signed Nov. 30, 2018, including auto industry changes and increased U.S. access to the Canadian dairy market. After some modifications to win U.S. congressional approval, the USMCA went into effect July 1, 2020.

A Canada-EU trade agreement eliminating almost all tariffs was signed Oct. 30, 2016. Canada signed, Mar. 8, 2018, the 11-nation Comprehensive and Progressive Agreement for Trans-Pacific Partnership; that trade-liberalization agreement replaced a proposed 12-nation pact that the U.S. withdrew from in 2017.

The COVID-19 pandemic reached Canada by early 2020, with new cases peaking in Apr.-May and trending upward again in Sept. By Sept. 30, Canada had recorded more than 155,000 total cases and almost 9,300 deaths.

Central African Republic

People: Population: 5,990,855 (112). **Age distrib.:** <15: 39.5%; 65+: 3.4%. **Growth:** 2.1%. **Migrants:** 1.9%. **Pop. density:** 24.9 per sq mi, 9.6 per sq km. **Urban:** 42.2%. **Ethnic groups:** Baya 28.8%, Banda 22.9%, Mandjia 9.9%, Sara 7.9%, M'Baka-Bantu 7.9%, Arab-Fulani (Peul) 6%, Mbum 6%, Ngbanki 5.5%, Zande-Nzakara 3%, other Central African Republic ethnic groups 2%. **Languages:** French (official), Sangho (lingua franca and national lang.), tribal langs. **Religions:** Christian 75.4% (Catholic 39.3%, independent 18.13%, Protestant 17.8%), Muslim 13.1% (Sunni), ethnic religionist 10.5%.

Geography: Total area: 240,535 sq mi, 622,984 sq km (44); **Land area:** 240,535 sq mi, 622,984 sq km. **Location:** Central Africa. Chad on N, Cameroon on W, Congo Republic and Dem. Rep. of the Congo on S, South Sudan and Sudan on E. **Topography:** Mostly rolling plateau, avg. elevation 2,000 ft, with rivers draining S to the Congo and N to Lake Chad. Open, well-watered savanna covers most of area, with an arid area in NE and tropical rain forest in SW. **Arable land:** 2.9%. **Capital:** Bangui, 889,231.

Government: Type: Presidential republic. **Head of state:** Pres. Faustin-Archange Touadéra; b. 1957; in office: Mar. 30, 2016. **Head of govt.:** Prime Min. Firmin Ngrébada; b. 1968; in office: Feb. 25, 2019. **Local divisions:** 14 prefectures, 2 economic prefectures, 1 commune. **Defense budget:** $33 mil. **Active troops:** 9,150.

Economy: Industries: gold, diamond mining; logging; brewing; sugar refining. **Chief agric.:** cotton, coffee, tobacco, cassava, yams, millet, corn, bananas. **Natural resources:** diamonds, uranium, timber, gold, oil, hydropower. **Water:** 30,264 cu m per capita. **Electricity prod.:** 151 mil kWH. **Labor force:** agric. 77.1%, industry 5.4%, services 17.5%. **Unemployment:** 3.7%.

Finance: Monetary unit: Central African CFA Franc (XAF) (553.52 = $1 U.S.). **GDP:** $4.7 bil; **per capita GDP:** $984; **GDP growth:** 3.0%. **Imports:** $393.1 mil; France 17.1%, U.S. 12.3%, India 11.5%, China 8.2%, South Africa 7.4%, Japan 5.8%, Italy 5.1%. **Exports:** $113.7 mil; France 31.2%, Burundi 16.2%, China 12.5%, Cameroon 9.6%, Austria 7.8%. **Tourism** (2010): $11 mil. **Budget:** $300.1 mil. **Inflation** (2015-16): −0.6%.

Transport: Motor vehicles: 1 per 1,000 pop. **Airports:** 1. **Communications: Telephone:** 0.05 per 100 pop. **Mobile:** 27.7 per 100 pop. **Broadband:** 4.7 per 100 pop. **Internet:** 4.3%.

Health: Expend.: 5.8%. **Life expect.:** 52.7 male; 55.7 female. **Births:** 33.2 per 1,000 pop. **Deaths:** 12.3 per 1,000 pop. **Infant mortality:** 80.6 per 1,000 live births. **Undernourished:** NA. **HIV:** 3.5%.

Education: Compulsory: ages 6-15. **Literacy:** 38.3%.
Embassy: 2704 Ontario Rd. NW 20009; 483-7800.
Website: rcawashington.org

Various Bantu peoples migrated through the region for centuries before French control was asserted in the late 19th cent., when the region was named Ubangi-Shari. Independence was attained Aug. 13, 1960.

Pres. Jean-Bedel Bokassa, who seized power in a 1965 military coup, proclaimed himself emperor Dec. 1976. Bokassa's rule was characterized by ruthless authoritarianism. He was ousted in a bloodless coup aided by France, Sept. 20, 1979. In 1981, Gen. André Kolingba became head of state in another bloodless coup. Elections in Aug. and Sept. 1993 led to civilian rule under Pres. Ange-Félix Patassé.

Patassé was ousted Mar. 15, 2003, by rebels under former army chief François Bozizé. Bozizé won a presidential runoff election May 8, 2005, but insurgent activity by Patassé loyalists and others continued in the north. A national peace conference, Dec. 8-20, 2008, enabled the installation of a unity government Jan. 19, 2009. Pres. Bozizé won reelection Jan. 23, 2011, but was ousted when the largely Muslim rebel group Seleka, led by Michel Djotodia, seized the capital Mar. 24, 2013. Bozizé supporters and Christian militias clashed with pro-Djotodia and Muslim fighters, resulting in thousands of deaths. A National Transitional Council elected Catherine Samba-Panza interim pres. Jan. 20, 2014. France sent peacekeeping troops (2014-16). A UN peacekeeping force (MINUSCA) was authorized Apr. 10, 2014. UNICEF reported, Mar. 2016, over 100 mostly under-age women alleged sexual abuse by peacekeepers, 2013-15.

Faustin-Archange Touadéra, a Christian, won a UN-supervised presidential runoff election, Feb. 14, 2016. Violence between Muslims and Christians, as well as between rival militias and ethnic groups, continued in 2017-19. The government signed peace agreements with rebel groups Feb. 6 and Apr. 9, 2019. But some violence continued after the accords, and rebels controlled large areas of the country. About 13,000 MINUSCA uniformed personnel were in the CAR in mid-2020. The UNHCR estimated that, as of June 30, 2020, 659,000 people were internally displaced; over 613,000 were refugees as of Aug. 31.

The 2020 COVID-19 pandemic caused 4,825 cases and 62 deaths in the CAR by Sept. 30.

Chad
Republic of Chad

People: Population: 16,877,357 (71). **Age distrib.:** <15: 47.4%; 65+: 2.4%. **Growth:** 3.2%. **Migrants:** 3.2%. **Pop. density:** 34.7 per sq mi, 13.4 per sq km. **Urban:** 23.5%. **Ethnic groups:** Sara (Ngambaye/Sara/Madjingaye/Mbaye) 30.5%, Kanembu/Bornu/Buduma 9.8%, Arab 9.7%, Wadai/Maba/Masalit/Mimi 7%, Gorane 5.8%, Masa/Musseye/Musgum 4.9%, Bulala/Medogo/Kuka 3.7%, Marba/Lele/Mesme 3.5%, Mundang 2.7%, Bidiyo/Migaama/Kenga/Dangleat 2.5%, Dadjo/Kibet/Muro 2.4%, Tupuri/Kera 2%, Gabri/Kabalaye/Nanchere/Somrai 2%. **Languages:** French, Arabic (both official); Sara; 120+ langs. and dialects. **Religions:** Muslim 57.7% (Sunni), Christian 34.8% (Catholic 19.9%), ethnic religionist 6.6%.

Geography: Total area: 495,755 sq mi, 1,284,000 sq km (20). **Land area:** 486,180 sq mi, 1,259,200 sq km. **Location:** Central N Africa. Libya on N; Niger, Nigeria, Cameroon on W; Central African Republic on S; Sudan on E. **Topography:** Wooded savanna, steppe, and desert in the S; part of the Sahara in the N. Southern rivers flow N to Lake Chad, surrounded by marshland. **Arable land:** 4.1%. **Capital:** N'Djaména, 1,422,547.

Government: Type: Presidential republic. **Head of state and govt.:** Pres. Idriss Déby Itno; b. 1952; in office: Dec. 4, 1990. (Prime minister position eliminated under 2018 constitution.) **Local divisions:** 23 regions. **Defense budget:** $206 mil. **Active troops:** 33,250.

Economy: Industries: oil, cotton textiles, brewing, natron (sodium carbonate), soap, cigarettes, constr. materials. **Chief agric.:** cotton, sorghum, millet, peanuts, sesame, corn, rice, potatoes, onions, cassava; cattle, sheep, goats, camels. **Natural resources:** petroleum, uranium, natron, kaolin, fish, gold, limestone, sand and gravel, salt. **Water:** 3,067 cu m per capita. **Crude oil reserves:** 1.5 bil bbls. **Electricity prod.:** 229 mil kWh. **Labor force:** agric. 76.3%, industry 2.1%, services 21.6%. **Unemployment:** 1.9%.

Finance: Monetary unit: Central African CFA Franc (XAF) (553.52 = $1 U.S.). **GDP:** $26.2 bil; **per capita GDP:** $1,645; **GDP growth:** 3.2%. **Imports:** $2.2 bil; China 19.9%, Cameroon 17.2%, France 17%, U.S. 5.4%. **Exports:** $2.5 bil; U.S. 38.7%, China 16.6%, Netherlands 15.7%, UAE 12.2%, India 6.3%. **Budget:** $1.5 bil. **Inflation:** −1.0%.

Transport: Airports: 9.
Communications: Telephone: 0.1 per 100 pop. **Mobile:** 45.1 per 100 pop. **Broadband:** 22.6 per 100 pop. **Internet:** 6.5%.
Health: Expend.: 4.5%. **Life expect.:** 56.5 male; 60.1 female.
Births: 41.7 per 1,000 pop. **Deaths:** 10 per 1,000 pop. **Infant mor-**

tality: 68.6 per 1,000 live births. **Undernourished:** 39.6%. **HIV:** 1.2%.

Education: Compulsory: ages 6-15. **Literacy:** 30.8%.
Embassy: 2401 Massachusetts Ave. NW 20008; 652-1312.
Website: www.gouvernement.td

Chad was the site of Paleolithic and Neolithic cultures before the Sahara Desert formed. A succession of kingdoms and Arab slave traders dominated Chad until France took control around 1900. Independence came Aug. 11, 1960. Northern Muslim rebels fought animist and Christian southern government and French troops from 1966.

Rebel forces led by Hissène Habré captured the capital and forced Pres. Goukouni Oueddei to flee the country in June 1982. In Dec. 1990, a Libyan-supported insurgent group, the Patriotic Salvation Movement, overthrew Habré, who went into exile in Senegal. After approval of a new constitution Mar. 1996, Chad's first multi-party presidential election was held in June and July.

Violence along the Sudan border escalated in 2006, as Sudanese *janjaweed* militias and Chadian rebels attacked civilians, and Darfur rebels preyed on refugee camps. Between 140 and 700 civilians died in N'Djaména, Feb. 2-5, 2008, as more than 2,000 Chadian rebels stormed the capital and clashed with government troops in a failed coup attempt.

On Jan. 15, 2010, Chad and Sudan signed an accord aimed at normalizing relations and suppressing cross-border activities by rebel groups. About 368,000 Sudanese refugees were living in Chad as of Aug. 31, 2020.

Pres. Idriss Déby won reelection for a fifth term, Apr. 10, 2016.

After Islamist groups took over northern Mali and imposed a repressive regime in late 2012, Chad contributed roughly 2,000 soldiers to aid French, Malian, and other African forces in a military intervention. On Apr. 15, 2013, Chad announced it would begin pulling its troops out of Mali. Beginning in 2015, Chad periodically sent troops into Nigeria to fight Boko Haram Islamist extremists. Boko Haram fighters and suicide bombers staged attacks in Chad, including a Mar. 2020 attack that killed more than 90 Chadian troops.

Former Pres. Habré, accused of killing and torturing thousands of opponents in the 1980s, was arrested in Senegal June 30, 2013. The Extraordinary African Chambers (created within Senegal's court system) convicted Habré of crimes against humanity and torture, May 30, 2016, and sentenced him to life in prison.

The 2020 COVID-19 pandemic caused 1,185 cases and 85 deaths in Chad by Sept. 30.

Chile
Republic of Chile

People: Population: 18,186,770 (65). **Age distrib.:** <15: 19.8%; 65+: 11.8%. **Growth:** 0.7%. **Migrants:** 5.0%. **Pop. density:** 63.3 per sq mi, 24.5 per sq km. **Urban:** 87.7%. **Ethnic groups:** white and non-Indigenous 88.9%, Mapuche 9.1%. **Languages:** Spanish (official), English, Indigenous. **Religions:** Christian 87.6% (Catholic 61.1%, independent 22.2%), agnostic 8.8%.

Geography: Total area: 291,933 sq mi, 756,102 sq km (37). **Land area:** 287,187 sq mi, 743,812 sq km. **Location:** W coast of southern S America. Peru on N, Bolivia on NE, Argentina on E. **Topography:** Andes Mts., with some of world's highest peaks, on E border; on W is 2,650-mi Pacific coast. Width varies 100-250 mi. Atacama Desert in N. **Arable land:** 1.7%. **Capital:** Santiago, 6,767,223; Valparaíso (seat of natl. legislature) 983,751.

Government: Type: Presidential republic. **Head of state and govt.:** Pres. Sebastián Piñera Echenique; b. 1949; in office: Mar. 11, 2018. **Local divisions:** 16 regions. **Defense budget:** $4.6 bil. **Active troops:** 77,200.

Economy: Industries: copper, lithium, other minerals; foodstuffs, fish proc.; iron and steel; wood and wood prods.; transp. equip.; cement; textiles. **Chief agric.:** grapes, apples, pears, onions, wheat, corn, oats, peaches, garlic, asparagus, beans; beef, poultry, wool; fish. **Natural resources:** copper, timber, iron ore, nitrates, prec. metals, molybdenum, hydropower. **Water:** 51,127 cu m per capita. **Crude oil reserves:** 150 mil bbls. **Electricity prod. (2018):** 78 bil kWh. **Labor force:** agric. 8.8%, industry 22.0%, services 69.2%. **Unemployment:** 7.1%.

Finance: Monetary unit: Peso (CLP) (770.74 = $1 U.S.). **GDP:** $476.7 bil; **per capita GDP:** $25,155; **GDP growth:** 1.1%. **Imports:** $61.3 bil; China 23.9%, U.S. 18.1%, Brazil 8.6%. **Exports:** $69.2 bil; China 27.5%, U.S. 14.5%, Japan 9.3%, South Korea 6.2%, Brazil 5%. **Tourism:** $2.4 bil. **Budget:** $65.4 bil. **Inflation:** 2.6%.

Transport: Railways: 4,525 mi. **Motor vehicles:** 287.3 per 1,000 pop. **Airports:** 90.

Communications: Telephone: 16 per 100 pop. **Mobile:** 134.4 per 100 pop. **Broadband:** 88.2 per 100 pop. **Internet** 82.3%.
Health: Expend.: 9.0%. **Life expect.:** 76.3 male; 82.5 female.
Births: 13.1 per 1,000 pop. **Deaths:** 6.5 per 1,000 pop. **Infant mortality:** 6.2 per 1,000 live births. **Undernourished:** 3.5%. **HIV:** 0.5%.

Education: Compulsory: ages 6-17. **Literacy:** 99.0%.
Embassy: 1732-1736 Massachusetts Ave. NW 20036; 785-1746.
Website: www.gob.cl

Northern Chile was under Inca rule before the Spanish conquest, 1536-40. The southern Araucanian Indians resisted until the late 19th cent. Independence was gained 1810-18 under José de San Martin and Bernardo O'Higgins; the latter, as supreme director 1817-23, sought social and economic reforms until deposed. Chile defeated Peru and Bolivia in 1836-39 and 1879-84, gaining mineral-rich northern land. Chile is the world's largest producer of copper, responsible for more than 25% of the world total; copper exports are a mainstay of the economy.

In 1970, Salvador Allende Gossens, a Marxist, became president. His government improved conditions for the poor, but property seizures by left-wing extremists, poorly planned socialist economic programs, and a destabilization campaign backed by the U.S. led to political and financial chaos. A U.S.-backed military junta seized power Sept. 11, 1973. With the presidential palace under attack, Allende refused to surrender; a 2011 autopsy confirmed police reports that he killed himself. The junta, headed by Gen. Augusto Pinochet Ugarte, implemented plans to privatize the economy and "exterminate Marxism." Repression continued into the 1980s.

In Dec. 1989 voters elected a civilian president, although Pinochet continued to head the army until Mar. 10, 1998. In Mar. 1994, a Chilean human rights group estimated that more than 3,100 people were killed or "disappeared" during Pinochet's rule.

Ricardo Lagos Escobar, Chile's first Socialist president since the 1973 coup, took office Mar. 11, 2000. Michelle Bachelet Jeria, also a Socialist, won a runoff election Jan. 2006 and took office in Mar. as Chile's first woman president.

Billionaire businessman Sebastián Piñera Echenique, a conservative, won a presidential runoff election Jan. 2010. An earthquake and tsunami, Feb. 27, 2010, killed at least 521 people and caused up to $30 bil in property damage. Despite economic growth, lagging wages sparked protests against the Piñera government. Bachelet returned to the presidency after winning a runoff election Dec. 15, 2013. Chile legalized civil unions between same-sex couples, Oct. 22, 2015, and abortion in very limited circumstances, Aug. 2, 2017.

With the Socialists' popularity hurt by a sluggish economy, Piñera returned as president after winning a Dec. 17, 2017, runoff. After a Vatican investigation, Pope Francis, Apr. 11, 2018, apologized for "grave errors" in the handling by Catholic Church officials in Chile of numerous allegations of child sex abuse by clergy. Months of large-scale demonstrations, beginning Oct. 2019, protested economic inequality. A harsh police response resulted in more than 30 deaths, thousands of injuries, and allegations of torture and sexual abuse of detainees. In 2020, Chile was among the South American countries hardest hit by the COVID-19 pandemic, with 461,300 cases and 12,725 deaths by Sept. 30.

Tierra del Fuego is the largest (18,800 sq mi) island in the archipelago of the same name at the southern tip of S America. It was visited 1520 by Magellan and named Land of Fire because of its many Indian bonfires. Part of the island is in Chile, part in Argentina. Punta Arenas, on a mainland peninsula, is the world's southernmost city; Puerto Williams is the southernmost settlement.

China
People's Republic of China

(Statistical data do not include Hong Kong or Macau.)

People: Population: 1,394,015,977 (1). **Age distrib.:** <15: 17.3%; 65+: 12.3%. **Growth:** 0.3%. **Migrants:** 0.1%. **Pop. density:** 387.1 per sq mi, 149.5 per sq km. **Urban:** 61.4%. **Ethnic groups:** Han Chinese 91.6%, other (incl. Hui, Manchu, Uighur, Miao, Yi, Tujia, Tibetan, Mongol, Dong, Buyei, Yao, Bai, Korean, Hani, Li, Kazakh, Dai) 7.1%. **Languages:** Standard Chinese or Mandarin (official; Putonghua, based on Beijing dialect), Yue (Cantonese), Wu (Shanghainese), Minbei (Fuzhou), Minnan (Hokkien-Taiwanese), Xiang, Gan. **Religions:** agnostic 31.5%, Chinese folk-religionist 30.9%, Buddhist 16.8%, Christian 7.5%, atheist 6.7%, ethnic religionist 4.1%.

Geography: Total area: 3,705,407 sq mi, 9,596,960 sq km (4); **Land area:** 3,600,947 sq mi, 9,326,410 sq km. **Location:** Occupies most of the habitable mainland of E Asia. Mongolia on N; Russia on NE and NW; Kazakhstan, Kyrgyzstan, Tajikistan, Afghanistan, Pakistan on W; India, Nepal, Bhutan, Myanmar, Laos, Vietnam on S; North Korea on NE. **Topography:** Two-thirds of territory is mountainous or desert. The Da Xing'an Ling Mts. in N separate Manchuria and Mongolia. Other ranges incl. the Tien Shan in Xinjiang and the Himalayan and Kunlun Mts. in the SW and in Tibet. Three great river systems—the Chang (Yangtze), Huang (Yellow), and Xi—cross the eastern half of China. **Arable land:** 12.7%. **Capital:** Beijing, 20,462,610. **Cities:** Shanghai, 27,058,479; Chongqing, 15,872,179; Tianjin, 13,589,078; Guangzhou, Guangdong, 13,301,532; Shenzhen, 12,356,820; Chengdu, 9,135,768; Nanjing, Jiangsu, 8,847,372; Wuhan, 8,364,978; Xi'an, Shaanxi, 8,000,965; Hangzhou, 7,642,147; Dongguan, 7,407,852; Foshan, 7,326,852; Shenyang, 7,220,104.;

Government: Type: Communist party-led state. **Head of state:** Pres. Xi Jinping; b. 1953; in office: Mar. 14, 2013 (gen. sec. of Communist Party since Nov. 15, 2012). **Head of govt.:** Prem. Li Keqiang; b. 1955; in office: Mar. 15, 2013. **Local divisions:** 22

provinces (not incl. Taiwan), 5 autonomous regions, 4 municipalities, special admin. regions of Hong Kong (as of July 1, 1997) and Macau (as of Dec. 20, 1999). **Defense budget:** $181.1 bil. **Active troops:** 2,035,000.

Economy: Industries: mining and ore proc., iron, steel, aluminum, other metals, coal; machine building; armaments; textiles and apparel; petroleum; cement; chemicals; fertilizers; consumer prods.; food proc.; transp. equip.; telecom equip.; comm. space launch vehicles, satellites. **Chief agric.:** rice, wheat, potatoes, corn, tobacco, peanuts, tea, apples, cotton; pork, mutton; fish, shrimp. **Natural resources:** coal, iron ore, petroleum, nat. gas, mercury, tin, tungsten, antimony, manganese, molybdenum, vanadium, magnetite, aluminum, lead, zinc, rare earth elements, uranium. **Water:** 1,971 cu m per capita. **Crude oil reserves:** 26.2 bil bbls. **Electricity prod.** (2018): 6.7 tril kwH. **Labor force:** agric. 24.7%, industry 28.2%, services 47.1%. **Unemployment:** 4.4%.

Finance: Monetary unit: Yuan Renminbi (CNY) (6.84 = $1 U.S.). **GDP:** $23.5 tril; **per capita GDP:** $16,785; **GDP growth:** 6.1%. **Imports** (2018): $2.14 tril; South Korea 9.7%, Japan 8.6%, U.S. 7.3%, Germany 5%. **Exports** (2018): $2.49 tril; U.S. 19.2%, Hong Kong 12.2%, Japan 5.9%. **Tourism:** $35.8 bil. **Budget:** $3.0 tril. **Inflation:** 2.9%.

Transport: Railways: 81,400 mi. **Motor vehicles:** 167 per 1,000 pop. **Airports:** 510.

Communications: Telephone: 12.8 per 100 pop. **Mobile:** 115 per 100 pop. **Broadband:** 83.6 per 100 pop. **Internet** 54.3%.

Health: Expend.: 5.2%. **Life expect.:** 74.0 male; 78.4 female. **Births:** 11.6 per 1,000 pop. **Deaths:** 8.2 per 1,000 pop. **Infant mortality:** 11.4 per 1,000 live births. **Undernourished:** <2.5%. **HIV:** NA.

Education: Compulsory: ages 6-14. **Literacy:** 99.8%.

Embassy: 3505 International Pl. NW 20008; 495-2000.

Website: www.gov.cn

Remains of various humanlike creatures who lived as early as several hundred thousand years ago have been found in many parts of China. Neolithic agricultural settlements dotted the Huang (Yellow) R. basin from about 5000 BCE. Their language, religion, and art were the sources of later Chinese civilization.

Bronze metallurgy reached a peak and Chinese pictographic writing, similar to today's, was in use in the more developed culture of the Shang Dynasty (c. 1766 BCE-c. 1045 BCE), which ruled much of North China.

A succession of dynasties and interdynastic warring kingdoms ruled China for the next 3,000 years. They expanded Chinese political and cultural domination to the south and west, and developed a technologically and culturally advanced society that was unaffected by foreign rule (Mongols in the Yuan Dynasty, 1279-1368, and Manchus in the Qing Dynasty, 1644-1912).

Rebellions in the 19th cent. left tens of millions dead. Russia, Japan, Britain, and other powers exercised political and economic control in large parts of the country. China became a republic in 1912, when the Qing emperor Puyi abdicated following the Wuchang Uprising inspired by Dr. Sun Yat-sen, founder of the Kuomintang (Nationalist) party. By 1928, the Kuomintang, led by Chiang Kai-shek, succeeded in nominal reunification of China. About the same time, a bloody purge of Communists from the ranks of the Kuomintang fomented hostilities.

For over 50 years, 1894-1945, China was involved in conflicts with Japan. In 1895, China ceded Korea, Taiwan, and other areas. On Sept. 18, 1931, Japan seized the Northeastern Provinces (Manchuria) and set up a puppet state called Manchukuo. Taking advantage of Chinese dissension, Japan invaded China proper July 7, 1937. On Nov. 20 the retreating Nationalist government moved its capital to Chongqing (Chungking) from Nanjing (Nanking), which Japanese troops then ravaged Dec. 13.

From 1939 the Sino-Japanese War (1937-45) became part of the broader world conflict. After its defeat in World War II, Japan relinquished China. Within China, conflicts involving the Kuomintang, Communists, and other factions resumed. China came under the domination of Communist armies, 1949-50. The Kuomintang government fled to Taiwan, Dec. 8, 1949.

The People's Republic of China was proclaimed in Beijing (Peking) Oct. 1, 1949, under Mao Zedong. China and the USSR signed a 30-year treaty of "friendship, alliance, and mutual assistance," Feb. 15, 1950. The U.S. refused to recognize the new regime. On Nov. 26, 1950, the People's Republic sent armies into Korea against U.S. troops and forced a stalemate in the Korean War.

Frequent drastic changes in policy and violent factionalism 1949-52 interfered with economic development. In 1957, Mao admitted an estimated 800,000 people had been executed 1949-54; opponents claimed much higher figures. The Great Leap Forward, 1958-60, tried to accelerate economic development through intensive labor on huge new rural communes and emphasis on ideological purity. Many resisted, and the program was largely abandoned.

By the 1960s, relations with the USSR deteriorated, and the USSR canceled aid accords. The Great Proletarian Cultural Revolution, 1965, an attempt to instruct a new generation in revolutionary principles, resulted in massive purges. Millions of urban teenagers were relocated to rural areas. By 1968 the movement had run its course; many purged officials returned to office in subsequent years, and several ideological reforms were gradually weakened.

On Oct. 25, 1971, the UN General Assembly ousted the Taiwan government from the UN and seated the People's Republic in its place. U.S. Pres. Richard Nixon visited China Feb. 21-28, 1972. China and the U.S. opened liaison offices in each other's capitals, May-June 1973. The U.S., Dec. 15, 1978, formally recognized the People's Republic of China as the sole legal government of China; diplomatic relations between the two were established, Jan. 1, 1979.

Mao died Sept. 9, 1976. By 1978, Vice Prem. Deng Xiaoping had consolidated power, succeeding Mao as "paramount leader" of China. The new ruling group modified Maoist policies in education, culture, and industry, and sought better ties with non-Communist countries. By the mid-1980s, China had enacted far-reaching economic reforms, including market-oriented incentives, although close government-industry coordination continued.

Some 100,000 students and workers marched in Beijing to demand political reforms, May 4, 1989. As the unrest spread, martial law was imposed, May 20. Troops entered Beijing, June 3-4, and crushed the pro-democracy protests, as tanks and armored personnel carriers rolled through Tiananmen Square. It is estimated that hundreds died and thousands were injured, and hundreds of students and workers were arrested.

Deng Xiaoping died Feb. 19, 1997. Hong Kong reverted to Chinese sovereignty July 1, 1997. Portugal returned Macau to China Dec. 20, 1999.

With the successful launch and recovery, Oct. 15-16, 2003, of the Shenzhou 5 spacecraft, China became the third nation (after the U.S. and USSR) to send a person into space. In Dec. 2013, China became the third nation to reach the moon with a spacecraft that made a soft landing. China became, Jan. 2019, the first country to land a craft on the far side of the moon.

China's industries, exports, and energy demand have increased rapidly since the 1980s. China became the world's largest producer and consumer of coal. In part to diversify energy production, China completed construction in 2006 of the world's largest hydroelectric dam, the Three Gorges Dam on the Yangtze R. However, the burning of fossil fuels has caused severe air pollution. China announced, Sept. 3, 2016, that it had ratified the 195-nation agreement to limit climate change negotiated in Paris in Dec. 2015.

An earthquake in Sichuan prov. May 12, 2008, left 69,226 dead and 17,923 missing. The Nobel Peace Prize was awarded Oct. 8, 2010, to Liu Xiaobo, an incarcerated human rights activist; Liu died of cancer in government custody, July 13, 2017. Xi Jinping was chosen Communist Party general secretary, Nov. 15, 2012. In Mar. 2013, the National People's Congress (NPC) elected Xi as president of China and Li Keqiang as premier. They were reelected Mar. 2018 by the NPC, which also amended the constitution to eliminate presidential term limits.

Western experts Jan.-Feb. 2010 blamed hackers in China for cyberattacks on Google and other firms. Hackers in China were suspected in two attacks on U.S. government computer systems in 2015.

After double-digit gains for many years since the 1980s, China's GDP growth slowed beginning in 2012; it was 6.1% in 2019. However, by 2014, China's GDP (measured by purchasing power parity) was the largest in the world. Since 2010, China has been the world's largest exporter. Since 2013, partly under the $1-tril Belt and Road Initiative, China has been financing and building infrastructure projects in Asia, Africa, the Pacific, Latin America, and Eastern Europe.

The U.S. accused China in 2017 of unfair trade practices. The U.S. implemented tariffs on Chinese solar panels, Jan. 2018, and steel and aluminum Mar. 2018. It imposed tariffs on a total of about $250 bil worth of Chinese products July 6, Aug. 23, and Sept. 24; China retaliated with tariffs on U.S. goods. Both countries raised many tariff rates and added new tariffs, May 10-Sept. 1, 2019. The U.S. trade in goods deficit with China fell from $419 bil in 2018 to $345 bil in 2019. In a "phase 1" trade agreement signed Jan. 15, 2020, the U.S. reduced some tariffs and delayed new tariffs in exchange for Chinese pledges to increase purchases of some U.S. products and take steps to protect U.S. technology and intellectual property.

China has occupied the Paracel Isls., in the South China Sea, since 1974. Taiwan and Vietnam also claim the resource-rich islands. The Spratly Isls. are similarly in dispute with Taiwan, Vietnam, Malaysia, and the Philippines. The international Permanent Court of Arbitration in The Hague, July 12, 2016, rejected China's claim to most of the South China Sea as territorial waters and ruled that China's building of artificial islands—in some cases militarized—in disputed areas violated international law. After a two-decade shipbuilding program, China had the world's largest navy by 2017.

A new coronavirus, causing the disease COVID-19, emerged in late 2019 in Wuhan (its severity may have been initially concealed, especially by local officials). By the end of Feb. 2020, the virus had caused about 80,000 cases in China, prompting strict lockdown measures to slow transmission, and was spreading worldwide. As of Sept. 30, 2020, the COVID-19 pandemic had caused more than 33.4 mil cases globally (over 91,000 in China) and over 1 mil deaths (over 4,700 in China). By Sept., China was reportedly widely using vaccines that had not yet completed clinical trials for safety and effectiveness.

Autonomous Regions

Guangxi Zhuang is in SE China, bounded on the N by Guizhou and Hunan provinces, E and S by Guangdong, on the SW by Vietnam, and on the W by Yunnan. It produces rice and forest products. Pop. (2010): 46,026,629. Capital: Nanning; pop. (2019 est.) 3,743,602.

Inner Mongolia was organized by the People's Republic in 1947. Its boundaries were later expanded, to an area of 454,600 sq mi, allegedly to dilute the minority Mongol population. Han Chinese greatly outnumber Mongols. China began, Sept. 1, 2020, replacing Mongolian- with Mandarin-language instruction in schools. Pop. (2010) 24,706,321. Capital: Hohhot; pop. (2019 est.) 2,085,969.

Ningxia Hui, in N central China, is about 60,000 sq mi. Pop. (2010) 6,301,350. Capital: Yinchuan; pop. (2019 est.) 1,530,944. The climate is mostly semiarid, with desert areas in the N. The Huang (Yellow) R. furnishes water for irrigation. The majority of the population is Han. The Hui, most of whom follow Islam, constitute about one-third of the population; a crackdown on Muslim practices began in the late 2010s.

Xinjiang Uighur, in Central Asia, is 635,900 sq mi, pop. (2010) 21,813,334 (75% Uighurs, a Turkic Muslim group, with a heavy Han Chinese increase in recent years). Capital: Urumqi; pop. (2020 est.) 4,368,865. It is China's richest region in strategic minerals. China has moved to suppress Uighur cultural and religious practices and to crack down on Uighur separatists. A protest march July 5, 2009, by Uighurs in Urumqi led to violent clashes with Han Chinese; at least 197 people (mostly Han) were killed. Unrest and domestic terrorist attacks continued. Violence in Yarkand July 28, 2014, left almost 100 people dead. An apparent separatist attack at a coal mine, Sept. 18, 2015, left about 50 dead. Legislation effective Apr. 1, 2017, placed new restrictions on women wearing face veils in public. Chinese authorities reportedly destroyed mosques, removed children from Uighur families, forced birth control measures on Uighur women, and carried out intensive electronic surveillance of the Uighur population. The number of people sentenced to prison terms began increasing sharply in 2017. In addition, by 2019, an estimated 1-1.5 mil Uighurs had been interned in "re-education" or labor camps; thousands were reportedly sent to other parts of China as forced factory laborers. China alleged that, by the end of 2019, most camps had been closed, but dissidents and others reported that large numbers of Uighurs remained in detention in 2020.

Tibet, 471,700 sq mi, is a thinly populated region of high plateaus and massive mountains, the Himalayas on the S, the Kunluns on the N. Capital: Lhasa. Avg. elevation is 15,000 ft. Jiachan, 15,870 ft, is believed to be the highest inhabited town on Earth. Pop. (2010) 3,002,166 (of whom about 500,000 are Chinese). Millions of Tibetans live in vast adjacent areas that have long been incorporated into China.

China ruled all of Tibet from the 18th cent. Independence came in 1911, but China reasserted control in 1951, and a Communist government was installed in 1953. Serfdom was abolished, but all land remained collectivized. A Tibetan uprising within China in 1956 spread to Lhasa in 1959. The rebellion was crushed by Chinese troops, and Buddhism was almost totally suppressed. The Dalai Lama and 100,000 Tibetans fled to India. Efforts by Chinese authorities to halt peaceful demonstrations by Tibetan monks led to anti-Chinese riots in Lhasa, Mar. 14, 2008—crushed by Chinese government troops. Protests (including more than 150 self-immolations, 2009-19), as well as government repression and coerced assimilation, continued in subsequent years.

Hong Kong

Hong Kong (Xianggang), located at the mouth of the Zhu Jiang (Pearl R.) in SE China, 90 mi S of Guangzhou, was a British dependency from 1842 until July 1, 1997, when it became a Special Administrative Region of China. Its nucleus is Hong Kong Isl., 31 sq mi, occupied by the British in 1841 and formally ceded to them in 1842, on which is located the seat of government. Opposite is Kowloon Peninsula, 3 sq mi, and Stonecutters Isl., added to the territory in 1860. An additional 355 sq mi known as the New Territories, a mainland area and islands, were leased from China, 1898, for 99 years. Area 428 sq mi (total); 414 sq mi (land); pop. (2020 est.) 7,547,652. **Website:** www.gov.hk

Hong Kong is a major trade and banking center. Per capita GDP, $64,488 (2018 est.), is among the highest in the world. Principal industries are textiles and apparel, tourism, banking, shipping, and electronics. A majority of tourists are from mainland China.

Hong Kong harbor was long an important British naval station and one of the world's great transshipment ports. The colony often provided refuge for exiles from mainland China. It was occupied by Japan during WWII.

From 1949 to 1962, Hong Kong absorbed more than 1 mil refugees fleeing Communist China. Starting in the 1950s, cheap labor led to a boom in light manufacturing, while liberal tax policies attracted foreign investment. Hong Kong became one of the wealthiest, most productive areas in the Far East. In recent years, manufacturing has been shifting from Hong Kong to mainland China.

With the end of the 99-year lease on the New Territories drawing near, Britain and China signed an agreement, Dec. 19, 1984, under which all of Hong Kong was to be returned to China in 1997; under this agreement Hong Kong was to be allowed to keep its capitalist system for 50 years. Following the transfer of government, Hong Kong retained its currency, the Hong Kong dollar; in recent years, a growing portion of financial transactions use the Chinese renminbi. Cantonese, English, and Mandarin are official languages.

Leung Chunying, with close ties to China, was elected chief executive Mar. 2012 by a committee of about 1,200 members. Large pro-democracy protests took place July-Dec. 2014, opposing Chinese plans to restrict candidate selection for a proposed direct election of the chief executive in 2017; Hong Kong's Legislative Council, June 18, 2015, rejected China's direct-election plan. Six activists from the 2014 protests won seats on the Legislative Council in Sept. 4, 2016, elections; they were subsequently barred from serving. Pro-Beijing candidate Carrie Lam was chosen chief executive by the election committee, Mar. 26, 2017. China's foreign ministry stated, June 30, 2017, that the 1984 agreement with Britain no longer had binding force.

Large-scale protests (up to 2 mil people) in 2019 opposed proposed legislation authorizing Hong Kong to extradite suspects to mainland China. Police often used tear gas, rubber bullets, batons, and water cannons against sometimes-violent demonstrations. Lam announced, Sept. 4, full withdrawal of the extradition bill. Protests continued, demanding greater democracy and an investigation of police tactics. With demonstrations ongoing in mid-2020, the Chinese government enacted a broad Hong Kong security law. In effect as of June 30, the law was quickly used to crack down on speech, peaceful protests, media outlets, and political activists and groups deemed subversive by authorities. Citing the COVID-19 pandemic, Lam announced, July 31, that Legislative Council elections would be postponed from Sept. 2020 to Sept. 2021.

Macau

Macau, area of 11 sq mi, is a peninsula and two small islands at the mouth of the Xi (Pearl) R. in China. It was established as a Portuguese trading colony in 1557. In 1849, Portugal claimed sovereignty over the territory; this claim was accepted by China in an 1887 treaty. Portugal granted broad autonomy in 1976. Under a 1987 agreement, Macau reverted to China Dec. 20, 1999. The Chinese government guaranteed Macau it would not interfere in its way of life and capitalist system for a period of 50 years. The tourism industry, including casino gambling, is a mainstay of the economy; two-thirds of tourists are from mainland China. Per capita GDP was 122,435 in 2018. Pop. (2020 est.) 651,875. **Website:** www.gov.mo

Colombia
Republic of Colombia

People: Population: 49,084,841 (30). **Age distrib.:** <15: 23.3%; 65+: 8.4%. **Growth:** 0.9%. **Migrants:** 2.3%. **Pop. density:** 122.4 per sq mi, 47.3 per sq km. **Urban:** 81.4%. **Ethnic groups:** mestizo and white 87.6%, Afro-Colombian (incl. mulatto, Raizal, Palenquero) 6.8%, Amerindian 4.3%. **Languages:** Spanish (official). **Religions:** Christian 94.9% (Catholic [official] 86.1%), agnostic 2.9%.

Geography: Total area: 439,736 sq mi, 1,138,910 sq km (25); **Land area:** 401,044 sq mi, 1,038,700 sq km. **Location:** NW corner of S America. Panama on NW, Ecuador and Peru on S, Brazil and Venezuela on E. **Topography:** Three Andes ranges—Western, Central, and Eastern Cordilleras—run N-S. The eastern range consists mostly of high tablelands. The Magdalena R. rises in the Andes, flows N to Caribbean through a rich alluvial plain. Sparsely settled plains in E are drained by Orinoco and Amazon systems. **Arable land:** 1.6%. **Capital:** Bogotá 10,978,360. **Cities:** Medellín, 4,000,263; Cali, 2,781,980; Barranquilla, 2,272,914.

Government: Type: Presidential republic. **Head of state and govt.:** Pres. Iván Duque Marquez; b. 1976; in office: Aug. 7, 2018. **Local divisions:** 32 departments, 1 capital district. **Defense budget:** $10.5 bil. **Active troops:** 293,200.

Economy: Industries: textiles, food proc., oil, clothing and footwear, beverages, chemicals, cement. **Chief agric.:** coffee, cut flowers, bananas, rice, tobacco, corn, sugarcane, cocoa beans, oilseed, vegetables; shrimp. **Natural resources:** petroleum, nat. gas, coal, iron ore, nickel, gold, copper, emeralds, hydropower. **Water:** 48,098 cu m per capita. **Crude oil reserves:** 2 bil bbls. **Electricity prod.:** 73.4 bil kWh. **Labor force:** agric. 16.5%, industry 20.0%, services 63.5%. **Unemployment:** 9.7%.

Finance: Monetary unit: Peso (COP) (3,715.66 = $1 U.S.). **GDP:** $787.5 bil; **per capita GDP:** $15,644; **GDP growth:** 3.3%. **Imports:** $44.2 bil; U.S. 26.3%, China 19.3%, Mexico 7.5%, Brazil 5%. **Exports:** $39.5 bil; U.S. 28.5%, Panama 8.6%, China 5.1%. **Tourism:** $5.7 bil. **Budget:** $91.7 bil. **Inflation:** 3.5%.

Transport: Railways: 1,330 mi. **Motor vehicles:** 133.5 per 1,000 pop. **Airports:** 121.

Communications: Telephone: 14 per 100 pop. **Mobile:** 129.9 per 100 pop. **Broadband:** 48.8 per 100 pop. **Internet:** 62.3%.

Health: Expend.: 7.2%. **Life expect.:** 73.5 male; 80.0 female. **Births:** 15.4 per 1,000 pop. **Deaths:** 5.6 per 1,000 pop. **Infant mortality:** 12.3 per 1,000 live births. **Undernourished:** 5.5%. **HIV:** 0.5%.

Education: Compulsory: ages 5-16. **Literacy:** 98.9%.
Embassy: 1724 Massachusetts Ave. NW 20036; 387-8338.
Website: id.presidencia.gov.co

Spain subdued the local Indian kingdoms (Funza, Tunja) by the 1530s and ruled Colombia and neighboring areas as New Granada for 300 years. Independence was won by 1819. Venezuela and Ecuador broke away in 1829-30, and Panama withdrew in 1903.

In the 20th and early 21st cents., Colombia was plagued by rural and urban violence. "La Violencia" of 1948-58 claimed 200,000 lives. Guerrilla warfare and terrorist attacks by leftist rebels, including the Revolutionary Armed Forces of Colombia (FARC), began in the 1960s. Violence by right-wing paramilitary groups became widespread by the 1980s. Government activity against drug cartels sparked retaliation killings of politicians and judges. The FARC engaged in drug trafficking and kidnappings for ransom to finance its operations.

Álvaro Uribe Vélez, a hardliner, won a presidential election, May 2002, and launched a new government offensive against the FARC. Uribe easily won reelection, May 2006. Key political figures were arrested in 2007 on charges of colluding with paramilitary death squads. Former Defense Min. Juan Manuel Santos Calderón won presidential elections, June 2010 and June 2014. The government signed a peace accord with the FARC, Sept. 26, 2016, providing for FARC disarmament and reintegration into civilian life. In an Oct. 2, 2016, referendum, Colombian voters narrowly rejected the accord, believing it treated FARC members too leniently. A revised agreement went into effect Dec. 1, 2016, one day after gaining final congressional approval. On Oct. 7, 2016, Santos won the Nobel Peace Prize. On June 27, 2017, about 7,000 FARC rebels finished surrendering weapons, but violence by criminal gangs, former FARC members, and other rebels continued. Iván Duque, a conservative, won a June 17, 2018, presidential runoff election. Alleging government violations of the 2016 accord, a former FARC leader, Aug. 29, 2019, urged group members to return to war. At year-end 2019, about 5.6 mil Colombians were internally displaced as a result of violence.

A series of national strikes, Nov.-Dec. 2019, protested government economic policies, failure to fully implement the FARC accord, and killings of Indigenous and other rights activists. More than 100 activists were killed in 2019, and over 100 Jan.-Aug. 2020.

Beginning in 2015, large numbers of Venezuelans fleeing extreme economic hardship and political repression entered Colombia. About 1.7 mil Venezuelans were in the country by 2020.

Hard-hit by the 2020 COVID-19 pandemic, Colombia recorded more than 818,000 cases and over 25,600 deaths by Sept. 30.

Comoros
Union of the Comoros

People: Population: 846,281 (159). **Age distrib.:** <15: 36.7%; 65+: 4.1%. **Growth:** 1.4%. **Migrants:** 1.5%. **Pop. density:** 980.7 per sq mi, 378.6 per sq km. **Urban:** 29.4%. **Ethnic groups:** Antalote, Cafre, Makoa, Oimatsaha, Sakalava. **Languages:** Arabic, French, Shikomoro (Swahili/Arabic blend) (all official). **Religions:** Muslim 98.3% (Sunni [official]).

Geography: Total area: 863 sq mi, 2,235 sq km (170); **Land area:** 863 sq mi, 2,235 sq km. **Location:** 3 islands—Grande Comore (Njazidja), Anjouan (Nzwani), and Moheli (Mwali)—in the Mozambique Channel between NW Madagascar and SE Africa. Nearest neighbor is Mozambique on W. **Topography:** Of volcanic origin; an active volcano on Grande Comore. **Arable land:** 35.5%. **Capital:** Moroni, 62,351.

Government: Type: Federal presidential republic. **Head of state and govt.:** Pres. Azali Assoumani; b. 1959; in office: May 26, 2016. **Local divisions:** 3 islands. **Defense budget/active troops:** NA.

Economy: Industries: fishing, tourism, perfume distillation. **Chief agric.:** vanilla, cloves, ylang-ylang, coconuts, bananas, cassava. **Natural resources:** fish. **Water:** 1,474 cu m per capita. **Electricity prod.:** 40 mil kWh. **Labor force:** agric. 49.9%, industry 13.0%, services 37.0%. **Unemployment:** 4.4%.

Finance: Monetary unit: Franc (KMF) (415.14 = $1 U.S.). **GDP:** $2.7 bil; **per capita GDP:** $3,209; **GDP growth:** 2.7%. **Imports:** $207.8 mil; UAE 32.8%, France 17.3%, China 13.2%, Madagascar 6.1%. **Exports:** $18.9 mil; France 36.5%, India 12.2%, Germany 8.2%, Pakistan 6.3%, Switzerland 5.8%. **Tourism:** $76 mil. **Budget:** $207.3 mil. **Inflation** (2016-17): 1%.

Transport: Airports: 4.

Communications: Telephone: 1.2 per 100 pop. **Mobile:** 59.9 per 100 pop. **Broadband:** 37.8 per 100 pop. **Internet:** 8.5%.

Health: Expend.: 7.4%. **Life expect.:** 63.3 male; 68.1 female. **Births:** 23.6 per 1,000 pop. **Deaths:** 6.9 per 1,000 pop. **Infant mortality:** 55.0 per 1,000 live births. **Undernourished:** 0.0%. **HIV:** <0.1%.

Education: Compulsory: ages 6-11. **Literacy:** 78.3%.
Permanent UN Mission: 866 UN Plz., Ste. 418, New York, NY 10017; (212) 750-1637.
Website: www.gouvernement.km

France acquired the islands from Muslim sultans, 1841-1909. The islands were granted internal autonomy in 1961. In a 1974 referendum, all islands favored independence except Mayotte. The French National Assembly decided to allow each island to decide its own fate. The Comorian government declared independence July 6, 1975, with Ahmed Abdallah as its president. In a 1976 referendum, Mayotte voted to remain French.

A leftist regime that seized power from Abdallah in 1975 was deposed in a pro-French 1978 coup in which he regained the presidency. In Nov. 1989, Pres. Abdallah was assassinated; soon after, a multiparty system was instituted.

Anjouan and Moheli seceded from the Comoros in 1997. Unrest on Grande Comore culminated in a military coup, Apr. 1999. A constitution adopted in a referendum Dec. 2001 that went into effect the following year reunited Anjouan and Moheli with Grande Comore, granting each a semi-autonomous status and its own president.

Irregularities marred the Apr. 2002 runoff election for national president, won by Azali Assoumani, who led the 1999 coup. Ahmed Abdallah Mohamed Sambi won a presidential runoff vote, May 2006. Sambi's Vice Pres. Ikililou Dhoinine won a runoff election for national president Dec. 2010. Assoumani again was elected president in an Apr. 10, 2016, runoff. Assoumani won reelection, Mar. 24, 2019, in voting international observers deemed not credible.

Congo
Democratic Republic of the Congo

(The Democratic Republic of the Congo [formerly Zaire], now commonly called Congo or DRC, is also known as Congo-Kinshasa. The Republic of the Congo, commonly called Congo Republic, is also known as Congo-Brazzaville.)

People: Population: 101,780,263 (15). **Age distrib.:** <15: 46.4%; 65+: 2.5%. **Growth:** 3.2%. **Migrants:** 7.5%. **Pop. density:** 116.3 per sq mi, 44.9 per sq km. **Urban:** 45.6%. **Ethnic groups:** 200+ groups, majority Bantu. Four largest tribes (Mongo, Luba, Kongo [all Bantu], and Mangbetu-Azande [Hamitic]) 45%. **Languages:** French (official), Lingala (lingua franca trade lang.), Kingwana (Kiswahili or Swahili dialect), Kikongo, Tshiluba. **Religions:** Christian 95.1% (Catholic 52%, independent 25.6%, Protestant 17.5%), ethnic religionist 2.4%.

Geography: Total area: 905,355 sq mi, 2,344,858 sq km (11); **Land area:** 875,312 sq mi, 2,267,048 sq km. **Location:** Central Africa. Congo Republic on W; Central African Republic, South Sudan on N; Uganda, Rwanda, Burundi, Tanzania on E; Zambia, Angola on S. **Topography:** Includes the bulk of the Congo R. basin. Central region is a low-lying plateau covered by rain forest. Mountainous terraces in the W, savannas in the S and SE, grasslands toward the N, and Ruwenzori Mts. on the E. A short strip of territory borders the Atlantic O. **Arable land:** 5.2%. **Capital:** Kinshasa, 14,342,439. **Cities:** Mbuji-Mayi, 2,525,263; Lubumbashi, 2,478,262.

Government: Type: Semi-presidential republic. **Head of state:** Pres. Felix Tshisekedi; b. 1963; in office: Jan. 24, 2019. **Head of govt.:** Prime Min. Sylvestre Ilunga Ilunkamba; in office: May 20, 2019. **Local divisions:** 26 provinces. **Defense budget:** $329 mil. **Active troops:** 134,250.

Economy: Industries: mining, mineral proc., consumer prods., metal prods., processed foods and beverages, timber, cement. **Chief agric.:** coffee, sugar, palm oil, rubber, tea, cotton, cocoa, quinine, cassava, bananas, plantains, peanuts, root crops, corn, fruits. **Natural resources:** cobalt, copper, niobium, tantalum, petroleum, diamonds, gold, silver, zinc, manganese, tin, uranium, coal, hydropower, timber. **Water:** 15,773 cu m per capita. **Crude oil reserves:** 180 mil bbls. **Electricity prod.:** 9.4 bil kWh. **Labor force:** agric. 65.1%, industry 9.8%, services 25.1%. **Unemployment:** 4.3%.

Finance: Monetary unit: Franc (CDF) (553.52 = $1 U.S.). **GDP:** $99.2 bil; **per capita GDP:** $1,143; **GDP growth:** 4.4%. **Imports:** $10.8 bil; China 19.9%, South Africa 18%, Zambia 10.4%, Belgium 9.1%. **Exports:** $11 bil; China 41.4%, Zambia 22.7%, South Korea 7.2%, Finland 6.2%. **Tourism:** $61 mil. **Budget:** $5.0 bil. **Inflation** (2015-16): 2.9%.

Transport: Railways: 2,490 mi. **Motor vehicles:** 25.9 per 1,000 pop. **Airports:** 26.

Communications: Telephone (2012): 0.1 per 100 pop. **Mobile:** 43.4 per 100 pop. **Broadband:** 16.2 per 100 pop. **Internet:** 8.6%.

Health: Expend.: 4.0%. **Life expect.:** 59.9 male; 62.7 female. **Births:** 32.6 per 1,000 pop. **Deaths:** 8.7 per 1,000 pop. **Infant mortality:** 50.7 per 1,000 live births. **Undernourished:** NA. **HIV:** 0.8%.

Education: Compulsory: ages 6-11. **Literacy:** 85.0%.

Embassy: 1100 Connecticut Ave. NW, Ste. 725, 20036; 234-7690.

Website: www.presidentrdc.cd

The earliest inhabitants of Congo may have been the pygmies, followed by Bantus from the east and Nilotic people from the north. The large Bantu Bakongo kingdom ruled much of Congo and Angola when Portuguese explorers visited in the 15th cent.

Leopold II, king of the Belgians, formed an international group to exploit the Congo region in 1877. In 1877, British explorer Henry M. Stanley traveled the Congo R, and in 1879, in the service of Leopold II, he returned to help colonize the region. The Conference of Berlin, 1884-85, established the Congo Free State with Leopold as king and chief owner. The colony became known as the Belgian

Congo in 1908 when Leopold sold it to the Belgian government. Millions of Congolese rubber plantation workers were exploited and died under brutal European rule between 1880 and 1920. (On June 30, 2020, Belgium's king expressed "deepest regrets for the wounds of the past.")

Belgian and Congolese leaders agreed Jan. 27, 1960, that Congo would become independent. In May 31 elections, Patrice Lumumba's party won a plurality in the National Assembly. The Republic of the Congo was proclaimed June 30. Europeans and others fled widespread violence. The UN Security Council, Aug. 9, called on Belgium to withdraw its troops and sent a UN contingent. Lumumba was dismissed as premier in Sept. and murdered Jan. 17, 1961. The last UN troops left the Congo June 30, 1964.

In late 1965, Gen. Joseph D. Mobutu was named president. He later changed his name to Mobutu Sese Seko and ruled as a dictator. The country became the Democratic Republic of the Congo (DRC, 1966) and the Republic of Zaire (1971). Under Mobutu, economic decline and government corruption plagued the country.

During 1994, Zaire was inundated with refugees from the massive ethnic bloodshed in Rwanda. Ethnic violence spread to eastern Zaire in 1996. In Oct., militant Hutus, who dominated in the refugee camps, fought rebels (mostly Tutsis) in Zaire, precipitating intervention by government troops. The rebels, led by Gen. Laurent Kabila, moved west across Zaire. On May 17, 1997, Kabila's troops entered Kinshasa, and Mobutu went into exile. The country again became the DRC.

Kabila, who ruled by decree, alienated UN officials, international aid donors, and former allies. Rebels assisted by Rwanda and Uganda threatened Kinshasa in Aug. 1998 but were turned back with help from Angola, Namibia, and Zimbabwe. Rebel groups agreed to a cease-fire, Aug. 31, 1999, but the truce was widely violated. Kabila was assassinated Jan. 16, 2001, and was succeeded by his son Joseph.

The estimated death toll from the civil war and related causes was 3.3 mil through Nov. 2002. By then, Rwanda and Uganda had agreed to pull out their remaining troops. A power-sharing accord signed Apr. 2, 2003, led to the installation of a new Congolese government in July. Under a new constitution in effect as of Feb. 18, 2006, a UN peacekeeping force (MONUC), established in 1999, oversaw July 2006 elections. Kabila defeated former rebel leader Jean-Pierre Bemba in a presidential runoff election, Oct. 2006.

Hundreds reportedly died in Kinshasa, Mar. 22-23, 2007, in clashes between security forces and a militia loyal to Bemba. A peace deal with militia groups in eastern Congo, including one led by Tutsi rebel Gen. Laurent Nkunda, was signed Jan. 23, 2008, but Nkunda launched a new offensive Aug. 28; Rwandan authorities arrested him Jan. 2009.

Kabila was reelected, Nov. 28, 2011. A June 2011 study estimated that more than 1,000 women were raped in Congo every day. The Intl. Criminal Court (ICC) at The Hague convicted Congolese warlord Thomas Lubanga Dyilo Mar. 2012 of war crimes for conscripting child soldiers during the country's civil war. The ICC, May 23, 2014, sentenced rebel leader Germain Katanga to 12 years in prison in connection with a 2003 massacre of more than 200 villagers.

The MONUC peacekeeping mission, reconstituted and renamed MONUSCO as of July 1, 2010, included about 15,000 uniformed personnel in mid-2020. Eleven African nations signed a peace plan Feb. 24, 2013, designed to end the violence in Congo. Rebel leader Bosco Ntaganda surrendered in Rwanda Mar. 18, 2013, to face charges of war crimes and crimes against humanity; he was convicted by the ICC, July 8, 2019. A peace agreement with the M23 militia group was reached in Dec. 2013. About 8,000 rebels laid down their arms, but other fighters remained active. With Kabila legally required to leave office in Dec. 2016, protests occurred, 2016-17, over government delays in scheduling the next presidential election. After a Dec. 30, 2018, election—in which widespread voting irregularities were reported—opposition candidate Félix Tshisekedi was declared the winner; a pro-Kabila bloc retained influence in the government.

Political and ethnic violence continued in eastern Congo, involving dozens of armed rebel groups (including an ISIS affiliate). Nationwide, about 5 mil Congolese were internally displaced as of mid-2020, and more than 920,000 were refugees as of July 31.

A severe Ebola outbreak in eastern Congo began in 2018. By the time the WHO declared the outbreak over, June 25, 2020, there had been 3,470 cases and 2,287 deaths; more than 300,000 people had been vaccinated. The 2020 COVID-19 pandemic caused about 10,600 cases in Congo, as of Sept. 30, and 271 deaths.

Congo Republic
Republic of the Congo

(Congo Republic, officially Republic of the Congo, is also known as Congo-Brazzaville. The Democratic Republic of the Congo [formerly Zaire], now commonly called Congo or DRC, is also known as Congo-Kinshasa.)

People: Population: 5,293,070 (120). **Age distrib.:** <15: 41.6%; 65+: 3.2%. **Growth:** 2.3%. **Migrants:** 1.1%. **Pop. density:** 40.1 per sq mi, 15.5 per sq km. **Urban:** 67.8%. **Ethnic groups:** Kongo 40.5%, Teke 16.9%, Mbochi 13.1%, Sangha 5.6%, Mbere/

Mbeti/Kele 4.4%, Punu 4.3%. **Languages:** French (official); Lingala, Monokutuba (lingua franca trade langs.); many local langs., dialects (Kikongo most widespread). **Religions:** Christian 89.9% (Catholic 66%, Protestant 12.4%, independent 11.5%), ethnic religionist 4.8%, agnostic 3%.

Geography: Total area: 132,047 sq mi, 342,000 sq km (63); **Land area:** 131,854 sq mi, 341,500 sq km. **Location:** W central Africa. Gabon and Cameroon on W, Central African Republic on N, Dem. Rep. of the Congo on E, Angola on SW. **Topography:** Thick forests across much of country. A coastal plain leads to the fertile Niari Valley. The Congo R. basin consists of flood plains in the lower portion and savanna in the upper. **Arable land:** 1.6%. **Capital:** Brazzaville, 2,388,090. **Cities:** Pointe-Noire, 1,214,281.

Government: Type: Presidential republic. **Head of state:** Pres. Denis Sassou-Nguesso; b. 1943; in office: Oct. 25, 1997. **Head of govt.:** Prime Min. Clement Mouamba; in office: Apr. 23, 2016. **Local divisions:** 12 departments. **Defense budget:** $301 mil. **Active troops:** 10,000.

Economy: Industries: petroleum extraction, cement, lumber, brewing, sugar, palm oil, soap. **Chief agric.:** cassava, sugar, rice, corn, peanuts, vegetables, coffee, cocoa. **Natural resources:** petroleum, timber, potash, lead, zinc, uranium, copper, phosphates, gold, magnesium, nat. gas, hydropower. **Water:** 158,145 cu m per capita. **Crude oil reserves:** 3 bil bbls. **Electricity prod.:** 3.3 bil kWh. **Labor force:** agric. 33.8%, industry 21.7%, services 44.5%. **Unemployment:** 9.3%.

Finance: Monetary unit: Central African CFA Franc (XAF) (1,953.79 = $1 U.S.). **GDP:** $18.5 bil; **per capita GDP:** $3,435; **GDP growth:** −0.9%. **Imports:** $2.5 bil; France 15%, China 14%, Belgium 12.2%, Norway 8.1%. **Exports:** $4.2 bil; China 53.8%, Angola 6.2%, Gabon 5.7%, Italy 5.4%, Spain 5.4%. **Tourism** (2010): $27 mil. **Budget:** $2.6 bil. **Inflation:** 2.2%.

Transport: Railways: 317 mi. **Motor vehicles:** 18.4 per 1,000 pop. **Airports:** 8.

Communications: Telephone (2017): 0.3 per 100 pop. **Mobile** (2017): 98.9 per 100 pop. **Broadband:** 5.9 per 100 pop. **Internet:** 8.7%.

Health: Expend.: 2.9%. **Life expect.:** 59.3 male; 62.8 female. **Births:** 41 per 1,000 pop. **Deaths:** 8.4 per 1,000 pop. **Infant mortality:** 64.5 per 1,000 live births. **Undernourished:** 28.0%. **HIV:** 3.1%.

Education: Compulsory: ages 6-15. **Literacy:** 82.1%.
Embassy: 1720 16th St. NW 20009; 726-5500.
Website: www.presidence.cg/president/ or www.ambacongo-us.org

The Loango kingdom flourished in the 15th cent., as did the Anzico kingdom of the Batekes; by the late 17th cent. they had weakened. By 1885, France controlled the region. The Republic of the Congo gained independence Aug. 15, 1960.

After a 1963 coup, the country adopted a Marxist-Leninist stance. However, France remained a dominant trade partner and source of technical assistance, and French-owned private enterprise retained a major economic role. In 1970, the country was renamed People's Republic of the Congo. Since the 1980s, oil has dominated the economy. In June 2018, the country joined OPEC.

In 1990, Marxism was renounced and opposition parties were legalized. In 1991 the country's name was changed back to Rep. of the Congo. A democratically elected government came into office in 1992. Factional fighting broke out in Brazzaville, June 1997. Troops loyal to former Marxist dictator Denis Sassou-Nguesso took control of the city Oct. 15, 1997; he claimed lopsided victories in 2002 and 2009 presidential elections. After 2015 constitutional changes allowed him to run again, Sassou-Nguesso was reelected Mar. 20, 2016; the U.S. and EU criticized the fairness of the election. Violence between government forces and opposition militias erupted in the weeks after voting, and opposition leaders were arrested.

In 2020, COVID-19 caused about 5,000 cases and 89 deaths by Sept. 30.

Costa Rica
Republic of Costa Rica

People: Population: 5,097,988 (122). **Age distrib.:** <15: 22.1%; 65+: 8.8%. **Growth:** 1.1%. **Migrants:** 8.3%. **Pop. density:** 258.6 per sq mi, 99.8 per sq km. **Urban:** 80.8%. **Ethnic groups:** white or mestizo 83.6%, mulatto 6.7%, Indigenous 2.4%. **Languages:** Spanish (official), English. **Religions:** Christian 94.8% (Catholic [official] 75.9%, Protestants 9.9%, Independent 9.1%), agnostic 3.7%.

Geography: Total area: 19,730 sq mi, 51,100 sq km (126); **Land area:** 19,714 sq mi, 51,060 sq km. **Location:** Central America. Nicaragua on N, Panama on S. **Topography:** Tropical lowlands by the Caribbean. The interior plateau, at an elevation of about 4,000 ft, is temperate. **Arable land:** 4.9%. **Capital:** San José 1,399,629.

Government: Type: Presidential republic. **Head of state and govt.:** Pres. Carlos Alvarado Quesada; b. 1980; in office: May 8, 2018. **Local divisions:** 7 provinces. **Defense budget:** $433 mil (paramilitary budget). **Active troops:** No armed forces. 9,800 paramilitary-style police only.

Economy: Industries: medical equip., food proc., textiles and clothing, constr. materials, fertilizer, plastic prods. **Chief agric.:** bananas, pineapples, coffee, melons, ornamental plants, sugar, corn, rice, beans, potatoes; beef, poultry, dairy. **Natural resources:** hydropower. **Water:** 23,033 cu m per capita. **Electricity prod.:** 11.2 bil kWh. **Labor force:** agric. 11.9%, industry 19.8%, services 68.3%. **Unemployment:** 12.7%.

Finance: Monetary unit: Colon (CRC) (595.12 = $1 U.S.). **GDP:** $103.1 bil; **per capita GDP:** $20,434; **GDP growth:** 2.1%. **Imports:** $15.2 bil; U.S. 38.1%, China 13.1%, Mexico 7.3%. **Exports:** $10.8 bil; U.S. 40.9%, Belgium 6.3%, Panama 5.6%, Netherlands 5.6%, Nicaragua 5.1%, Guatemala 5%. **Tourism:** $4 bil. **Budget:** $11.9 bil. **Inflation:** 2.1%.

Transport: Railways: 173 mi (some sections rehabilitated after entire network fell into disrepair). **Motor vehicles:** 247.5 per 1,000 pop. **Airports:** 47.

Communications: Telephone: 15.5 per 100 pop. **Mobile:** 169.9 per 100 pop. **Broadband:** 116.6 per 100 pop. **Internet (2018):** 74.1%.

Health: Expend.: 7.3%. **Life expect.:** 76.5 male; 82.0 female. **Births:** 14.8 per 1,000 pop. **Deaths:** 4.9 per 1,000 pop. **Infant mortality:** 7.5 per 1,000 live births. **Undernourished:** 3.2%. **HIV:** 0.4%.

Education: Compulsory: ages 4-16. **Literacy:** 99.4%.
Embassy: 2114 S St. NW 20008; 499-2991.
Website: presidencia.gob.cr

Guaymi Indians inhabited the area when Spaniards arrived, 1502. Independence came in 1821. Costa Rica seceded from the Central American Federation in 1838. Since the civil war of 1948-49, free political institutions have been preserved.

Nobel Peace Prize-winner Óscar Arias Sánchez, president 1986-90, won a second term in 2006. In 2010, the ruling party's Laura Chinchilla Miranda became the nation's first female president. The opposition Citizen Action Party (PAC) won 2014 and 2018 presidential elections. From 2018 to mid-2020, more than 80,000 Nicaraguan asylum seekers, fleeing political violence and repression, entered Costa Rica.

The economically important tourism industry was hurt in 2020 by travel bans and business closures to combat the COVID-19 pandemic. Costa Rica had more than 73,700 cases and 861 deaths by Sept. 30.

Côte d'Ivoire
Republic of Côte d'Ivoire

People: Population: 27,481,086 (52). **Age distrib.:** <15: 38.5%; 65+: 2.8%. **Growth:** 2.2%. **Migrants:** 9.9%. **Pop. density:** 223.8 per sq mi, 86.4 per sq km. **Urban:** 51.7%. **Ethnic groups:** Akan 28.8%, Voltaique or Gur 16.1%, Northern Mande 14.5%, Kru 8.5%, Southern Mande 6.9%, non-Ivoiran 42.3%. **Languages:** French (official), 60 native dialects (Dioula most widely spoken). **Religions:** Muslim 44% (Sunni), Christian 33.9% (Catholic 17.6%, Protestant 11.7%, independent 4.6%), ethnic religionist 21.5%.

Geography: Total area: 124,504 sq mi, 322,463 sq km (68). **Land area:** 122,782 sq mi, 318,003 sq km. **Location:** S coast of W Africa. Liberia, Guinea on W; Mali, Burkina Faso on N; Ghana on E. **Topography:** Forests cover W half of country. A sparse inland plain leads to low mountains in NW. **Arable land:** 11.0%. **Capital:** Yamoussoukro (official), 231,072; Abidjan (de facto), 5,202,762.

Government: Type: Presidential republic. **Head of state:** Pres. Alassane Ouattara; b. 1942; in office: Apr. 11, 2011 (sworn in Dec. 4, 2010). **Head of govt.:** Prime Min. Hamed Bakayoko; b. 1965; in office: July 30, 2020. **Local divisions:** 12 districts, 2 autonomous districts. **Defense budget:** $898 mil. **Active troops:** 27,400.

Economy: Industries: foodstuffs, beverages, wood prods., oil refining, gold mining, truck and bus assembly, textiles, fertilizer. **Chief agric.:** coffee, cocoa beans, bananas, palm kernels, corn, rice, cassava, sweet potatoes, sugar, cotton, rubber. **Natural resources:** petroleum, nat. gas, diamonds, manganese, iron ore, cobalt, bauxite, copper, gold, nickel, tantalum, silica sand, clay, cocoa beans, coffee, palm oil, hydropower. **Water:** 3,463 cu m per capita. **Crude oil reserves:** 100 mil bbls. **Electricity prod.:** 9.7 bil kWh. **Labor force:** agric. 39.3%, industry 13.4%, services 47.3%. **Unemployment:** 3.4%.

Finance: Monetary unit: CFA Franc (XOF) (553.52 = $1 U.S.). **GDP:** $140.3 bil; **per capita GDP:** $5,455; **GDP growth:** 6.9%. **Imports:** $9.4 bil; Nigeria 15%, France 13.4%, China 11.3%. **Exports:** $11.7 bil; Netherlands 11.8%, U.S. 7.9%, France 6.4%, Belgium 6.4%, Germany 5.8%. **Tourism:** $443 mil. **Budget:** $9.5 bil. **Inflation:** −1.1%.

Transport: Railways: 410 mi. **Motor vehicles:** 26 per 1,000 pop. **Airports:** 7.

Communications: Telephone: 1.2 per 100 pop. **Mobile:** 134.9 per 100 pop. **Broadband:** 53.9 per 100 pop. **Internet (2018):** 46.8%.

Health: Expend.: 4.5%. **Life expect.:** 59.2 male; 63.6 female. **Births:** 29.1 per 1,000 pop. **Deaths:** 7.9 per 1,000 pop. **Infant mortality:** 59.1 per 1,000 live births. **Undernourished:** 19.9%. **HIV:** 2.4%.

Education: Compulsory: ages 6-15. **Literacy:** 58.4%.
Embassy: 2424 Massachusetts Ave. NW 20008; 797-0300.
Website: www.gouv.ci

A French protectorate from 1842, Côte d'Ivoire became independent in 1960. The name was officially changed from Ivory Coast, Oct. 1985.

Students and workers protested, Feb. 1990, demanding the ouster of longtime Pres. Félix Houphouët-Boigny. Côte d'Ivoire held its first multiparty presidential election Oct. 1990, which Houphouët-Boigny won. He died Dec. 7, 1993. His successor, Henri Konan Bédié, was reelected Oct. 1995 but ousted in a military coup Dec. 24, 1999. The coup leader, Robert Guéi, lost a presidential vote Oct. 2000 but claimed victory anyway. After mass protests, he fled, and Laurent Gbagbo became president. Guéi was killed in Abidjan Sept. 19, 2002.

Agreement on power sharing was reached in Mar. 2003, and Gbagbo and former rebel leaders declared an end to their war July 5. The country remained divided, however. Rebels held the north and government forces controlled the south. Under a new accord reached Mar. 2007, rebel leader Guillaume Soro became prime min.

After apparently losing a presidential runoff election, Nov. 28, 2010, to former Prime Min. Alassane Ouattara, Gbagbo clung to power. A violent power struggle followed, claiming several thousand lives and displacing at least 1 mil people. Ouattara loyalists captured Gbagbo in Abidjan, Apr. 2011. After Ouattara took power, Gbagbo supporters were killed and tortured. Ouattara won reelection Oct. 25, 2015. Legislative elections were held and a new constitution approved in 2016.

The ICC, June 12, 2014, ordered Gbagbo to stand trial for crimes against humanity. He was acquitted, Jan. 15, 2019; the verdict was appealed, Sept. 16, 2019. His wife, Simone Gbagbo, was sentenced, Mar. 10, 2015, by a Côte d'Ivoire court to 20 years in prison for her role in the violence that followed the 2010 election. (She was amnestied and released in Aug. 2018.) In attacks, Mar. 13, 2016, for which al-Qaeda in the Islamic Maghreb claimed responsibility, gunmen killed 19 people and wounded more than 30 at three resort hotels in Grand-Bassam.

The 2020 COVID-19 pandemic caused almost 20,000 cases and 120 deaths in Côte d'Ivoire as of Sept. 30.

Croatia
Republic of Croatia

People: Population: 4,227,746 (126). **Age distrib.:** <15: 14.2%; 65+: 21.1%. **Growth:** –0.5%. **Migrants:** 12.5%. **Pop. density:** 195.6 per sq mi, 75.5 per sq km. **Urban:** 57.6%. **Ethnic groups:** Croat 90.4%, Serb 4.4%, other (incl. Bosniak, Hungarian, Slovene, Czech, Romani) 4.4%. **Languages:** Croatian (official), Serbian. **Religions:** Christian 94.6% (Catholic [official] 86.9%), agnostic 2.3%.

Geography: Total area: 21,851 sq mi, 56,594 sq km (124); **Land area:** 21,612 sq mi, 55,974 sq km. **Location:** SE Europe, on the Balkan Peninsula. Slovenia, Hungary on N; Bosnia and Herzegovina, Serbia, Montenegro on E. **Topography:** Flat plains in NE; highlands, low mts. along Adriatic. **Arable land:** 14.4%. **Capital:** Zagreb, 684,878.

Government: Type: Parliamentary republic. **Head of state:** Pres. Zoran Milanovic; b. 1966; in office: Feb. 18, 2020. **Head of govt.:** Prime Min. Andrej Plenkovic; b. 1970; in office: Oct. 19, 2016. **Local divisions:** 20 counties, 1 city with special county status. **Defense budget:** $1 bil. **Active troops:** 15,200.

Economy: Industries: chemicals and plastics, machine tools, fabricated metal, electronics. **Chief agric.:** arable crops (incl. wheat, corn, barley, sugar beets), vegetables, fruits, grapes for wine; cattle, pigs. **Natural resources:** oil, coal, bauxite, iron ore, calcium, gypsum, nat. asphalt, silica, mica, clays, salt, hydropower. **Water:** 25,185 cu m per capita. **Crude oil reserves:** 71 mil bbls. **Electricity prod.** (2018): 13.1 bil kwH. **Labor force:** agric. 5.8%, industry 27.5%, services 66.8%. **Unemployment:** 7.1%.

Finance: Monetary unit: Kuna (HRK) (6.36 = $1 U.S.). **GDP:** $121.0 bil; **per capita GDP:** $29,973; **GDP growth:** 2.9%. **Imports:** $22.3 bil; Germany 15.7%, Italy 12.9%, Slovenia 10.7%, Hungary 7.5%, Austria 7.5%. **Exports:** $13.2 bil; Italy 13.4%, Germany 12.2%, Slovenia 10.6%, Bosnia and Herzegovina 9.8%, Austria 6.2%. **Tourism:** $11.8 bil. **Budget:** $24.8 bil. **Inflation:** 0.8%.

Transport: Railways: 1,691 mi. **Motor vehicles:** 431.2 per 1,000 pop. **Airports:** 24.

Communications: Telephone: 32.6 per 100 pop. **Mobile:** 105.6 per 100 pop. **Broadband:** 79.7 per 100 pop. **Internet** (2018): 72.7%.

Health: Expend.: 6.8%. **Life expect.:** 73.6 male; 80.1 female. **Births:** 8.7 per 1,000 pop. **Deaths:** 12.8 per 1,000 pop. **Infant mortality:** 8.6 per 1,000 live births. **Undernourished:** <2.5%. **HIV:** <0.1%.

Education: Compulsory: ages 7-14. **Literacy:** 99.3%.
Embassy: 2343 Massachusetts Ave. NW 20008; 588-5899.
Website: vlada.gov.hr

From the 7th cent. the area was inhabited by Croats, a south Slavic people. It was formed into a kingdom under Tomislav in 924, and joined with Hungary in 1102. The Croats became westernized and separated from Slavs under Austro-Hungarian influence. Croatia united with other Yugoslav areas to proclaim the Kingdom of Serbs, Croats, and Slovenes in 1918. A nominally independent state between 1941 and 1945, it became a constituent republic of Yugoslavia in the 1946 constitution.

On June 25, 1991, Croatia declared independence from Yugoslavia. Fighting began between ethnic Serbs and Croats. The Serbs gained control of some Croatian territory, but Croatian troops recaptured most of it Aug. 1995. A peace accord was signed in Dec. The last Serb-held enclave, E Slavonia, was returned to Croatia in 1998. Croatia became a full NATO member Apr. 1, 2009, and joined the EU July 1, 2013.

Kolinda Grabar-Kitarovic of the conservative Croatian Democratic Union (HDZ) party won a runoff election, Jan. 11, 2015, to become Croatia's first woman president. Zoran Milanovic of the center-left Social Democratic Party defeated her in a Jan. 5, 2020, presidential runoff.

The HDZ won the most seats in Sept. 11, 2016, parliamentary elections, and party leader Andrej Plenkovic formed a coalition government, Oct. 19. Plenkovic's HDZ increased its number of seats in July 5, 2020, elections.

Beginning Sept. 2015, tens of thousands of Middle Eastern, Asian, and African refugees and other migrants—most trying to reach N Europe—entered Croatia from Serbia. Croatia announced that as of Mar. 9, 2016, it would block virtually all migrants from transiting through the country.

The 2020 COVID-19 pandemic caused 16,245 cases and 272 deaths in Croatia by Sept. 30.

Cuba
Republic of Cuba

People: Population: 11,059,062 (83). **Age distrib.:** <15: 16.3%; 65+: 15.8%. **Growth:** –0.3%. **Migrants:** 0.0%. **Pop. density:** 260.8 per sq mi, 100.7 per sq km. **Urban:** 77.2%. **Ethnic groups:** white 64.1%, mulatto or mixed 26.6%, Black 9.3%. **Languages:** Spanish (official). **Religions:** Christian 61.9% (Catholic 55.1%), agnostic 17.1%, Spiritist 16.6%, atheist 3.8%.

Geography: Total area: 42,803 sq mi, 110,860 sq km (104); **Land area:** 42,402 sq mi, 109,820 sq km. **Location:** In Caribbean, westernmost of West Indies. The Bahamas, U.S. to N; Mexico to W; Jamaica to S; Haiti to E. **Topography:** Coastline is about 2,500 mi. The N coast is steep and rocky, the S coast low and marshy. Low hills and fertile valleys cover more than half the country. Three mountain ranges. **Arable land:** 27.9%. **Capital:** Havana, 2,140,423.

Government: Type: Communist state. **Head of state:** Pres. Miguel Díaz-Canel Bermúdez; b. 1960; in office: Oct. 10, 2019. **Head of govt.:** Prime Min. Manuel Marrero Cruz; b. 1963; in office: Dec. 21, 2019. **Local divisions:** 15 provinces, 1 special municipality. **Defense budget:** NA. **Active troops:** 49,000.

Economy: Industries: petroleum, nickel, cobalt, pharmaceuticals, tobacco, constr., steel, cement, agric. machinery, sugar. **Chief agric.:** sugar, tobacco, citrus, coffee, rice, potatoes, beans. **Natural resources:** cobalt, nickel, iron ore, chromium, copper, salt, timber, silica, petroleum. **Water:** 3,319 cu m per capita. **Crude oil reserves:** 124 mil bbls. **Electricity prod.:** 19.4 bil kwH. **Labor force:** agric. 17.3%, industry 16.8%, services 65.9%. **Unemployment:** 1.6%.

Finance: Monetary unit: Peso (CUP) (26.50 = $1 U.S.). **GDP:** NA; **per capita GDP:** NA; **GDP growth** (2018): 2.2%. **Imports:** $11.1 bil; China 22%, Spain 14%, Russia 5%, Brazil 5%. **Exports:** $2.6 bil; Venezuela 17.8%, Spain 12.2%, Russia 7.9%, Lebanon 6.1%. **Tourism:** $2.9 bil. **Budget:** $64.6 bil. **Inflation** (2016-17): 5.5%.

Transport: Railways: 5,199 mi. **Motor vehicles:** 47.4 per 1,000 pop. **Airports:** 64.

Communications: Telephone: 12.7 per 100 pop. **Mobile:** 47.4 per 100 pop. **Broadband:** NA. **Internet:** 57.1%.

Health: Expend.: 11.7%. **Life expect.:** 76.8 male; 81.7 female. **Births:** 10.4 per 1,000 pop. **Deaths:** 9.1 per 1,000 pop. **Infant mortality:** 4.3 per 1,000 live births. **Undernourished:** <2.5%. **HIV:** 0.4%.

Education: Compulsory: ages 6-14. **Literacy:** 99.8%.
Embassy: 2630 16th St. NW 20009; 797-8518.
Website: www.presidencia.gob.cu

Some 50,000 Indigenous people lived in Cuba when Christopher Columbus reached it in 1492. Except for British occupation of Havana, 1762-63, Cuba remained Spanish until 1898. A slave-based sugar plantation economy developed from the 18th cent. Sugar remains a leading agricultural product. Spain failed to deliver on rights guaranteed in 1878, prompting a full-scale liberation movement under Jose Martí in 1895.

The Spanish-American War began Apr. 1898, following the Feb. sinking of the USS *Maine* in Havana harbor. Spain lost the war and gave up all claims to Cuba. U.S. troops withdrew in 1902, but under 1903 and 1934 agreements, the U.S. continued to lease a site at Guantánamo Bay in the SE as a naval base. U.S. and other foreign investors dominated the economy. In 1952, former Pres. Fulgencio Batista established a dictatorship, which grew increasingly harsh and corrupt. Fidel Castro began a rebellion in 1956.

Batista fled Jan. 1, 1959, and Castro took power, becoming premier Feb. 16.

Government-instituted economic and social changes failed to restore promised liberties. Opponents were imprisoned or executed. Some 700,000 Cubans emigrated in the first years after Castro's takeover, mostly to the U.S. By 1960, all banks and industrial companies had been nationalized, including over $1-bil worth of U.S.-owned properties, mostly without compensation. U.S. economic sanctions became a complete trade embargo under legislation passed by Congress in 1961. The U.S. broke diplomatic relations with Cuba in Jan. 1961.

In Apr. 1961, some 1,400 Cubans, trained and backed by the U.S. Central Intelligence Agency, unsuccessfully tried to overthrow the regime. On Oct. 22, 1962, U.S. Pres. John F. Kennedy ordered a naval blockade around Cuba and demanded that Soviet-installed nuclear missiles be withdrawn. The crisis ended Oct. 28 when Soviet Prem. Nikita S. Khrushchev agreed to withdraw the missiles; the U.S. ended the blockade, pledged not to invade Cuba, and removed its own missiles from Turkey.

In 1978 and 1980, the U.S. agreed to accept political prisoners released by Cuba, some of whom were criminals and mental patients. A 1987 agreement provided for 20,000 Cubans to emigrate to the U.S. each year. Cuba's support for left-wing regimes and liberation movements in Central America, Africa, and the Caribbean contributed to poor relations with the U.S.

Cuba's economy, hobbled by U.S. sanctions and dependent on aid from other Communist countries, was shaken by the collapse of the Communist bloc in the late 1980s. Anti-government demonstrations in Aug. 1994 prompted Castro to loosen emigration restrictions. A new U.S.-Cuba accord in Sept. ended the exodus of "boat people" after more than 30,000 had left Cuba. The U.S. also announced May 1995 it would admit 20,000 Cuban refugees held at Guantánamo but would return additional refugees to Cuba.

On July 31, 2006, the ailing Fidel Castro yielded power to his 75-year-old brother Raúl, who served as acting head of state until formally succeeding Feb. 24, 2008. (Fidel Castro, age 90, died Nov. 25, 2016.) The U.S. in 2009 eased restrictions on remittances and family travel to Cuba. The Cuban government announced, Sept. 2010, economic restructuring plans involving cutting more than 500,000 public jobs. A Communist Party conference, Apr. 2011, approved an expansion of private property rights and private ownership of some small businesses. Legislation to encourage foreign investment was adopted in Mar. 2014.

The U.S., Jan. 11, 2002, began using its naval base at Guantánamo Bay to detain prisoners captured in Afghanistan and other suspected Islamist fighters or terrorists. The indefinite detention, as well as aggressive interrogation of prisoners in the early 2000s, was criticized by human rights groups. After hundreds of prisoner releases to other countries, the detention center held 40 men as of Sept. 2020. The 2020 COVID-19 pandemic delayed pretrial hearings in the planned military-commission trial of five detainees accused of plotting the Sept. 11, 2001, attacks.

Pres. Barack Obama announced, Dec. 17, 2014, that the U.S. would restore full diplomatic relations with Cuba. Following the announcement, some travel and economic restrictions were eased. Relations were formally resumed July 20, 2015. Scheduled U.S. commercial flights to Cuba, suspended since the early 1960s, resumed Aug. 31, 2016. In 2017 and again in 2019, the Trump administration tightened travel regulations and economic sanctions; in 2019, it facilitated lawsuits related to American-owned property confiscated by the Cuban government.

The U.S. announced, Sept. 29, 2017, the withdrawal of nonessential personnel from its Havana embassy, after about two dozen diplomats and family members developed various medical problems; on Oct. 3, the U.S. expelled 15 Cuban diplomats.

Elected by the National Assembly, Miguel Díaz-Canel Bermúdez became head of state Apr. 19, 2018, succeeding Raúl Castro, who remained head of the Communist Party. A new constitution, approved in a Feb. 24, 2019, referendum, established the position president of the republic (with term limits) for head of state and created a new office of prime minister.

Cuba had about 5,500 COVID-19 cases and 122 deaths as of Sept. 30.

Cyprus
Republic of Cyprus

People: Population: 1,266,676 (153). **Age distrib.: <15:** 15.7%; **65+:** 13.0%. **Growth:** 1.2%. **Migrants:** 16.0%. **Pop. density:** 355.0 per sq mi, 137.1 per sq km. **Urban:** 66.8%. **Ethnic groups:** Greek 98.8% (govt.-controlled area only). **Languages:** Greek, Turkish (both official); English; Romanian; Russian; Bulgarian. **Religions:** Christian 70.1% (Orthodox 66.9%), Muslim 23.2% (Sunni), agnostic 3.7%.

Geography: Total area: 3,572 sq mi, 9,251 sq km (164). **Land area:** 3,568 sq mi, 9,241 sq km. **Location:** Eastern Mediterranean Sea, off Turkish coast. **Nearest neighbors** are Turkey to N, Syria and Lebanon to E. **Topography:** Two mountain ranges run E-W, separated by a wide, fertile plain. **Arable land:** 10.3%. **Capital:** Nicosia (Lefkosia), 269,469.

Government: Type: Presidential republic. **Head of state and govt.:** Pres. Nicos Anastasiades; b. 1946; in office: Feb. 28, 2013. **Local divisions:** 6 districts. **Defense budget:** $403 mil. **Active troops:** 15,000.

Economy: Industries: tourism, food and beverage proc., cement and gypsum, ship repair and refurb., textiles, light chemicals, metal prods. **Chief agric.:** citrus, vegetables, barley, grapes, olives, vegetables; poultry, pork, lamb. **Natural resources:** copper, pyrites, asbestos, gypsum, timber, salt, marble, clay earth pigment. **Water:** 661 cu m per capita. **Electricity prod.** (2018): 4.8 bil kWh. **Labor force:** agric. 2.0%, industry 16.3%, services 81.7%. **Unemployment:** 7.2%.

Finance: Monetary unit: Euro (EUR) (0.84 = $1 U.S.). **GDP:** $36.4 bil; **per capita GDP:** $41,254; **GDP growth:** 3.2%. **Imports:** $7.9 bil; Greece 19%, Italy 7.5%, China 7.4%, South Korea 7.3%, Germany 7%, Netherlands 5.1%, UK 5%. **Exports:** $2.8 bil; Libya 9.4%, Greece 7.7%, Norway 6.7%, UK 5.3%. **Tourism:** $3.3 bil. **Budget:** $7.9 bil. **Inflation:** 0.3%.

Transport: Motor vehicles: 694.8 per 1,000 pop. **Airports:** 13. **Communications: Telephone:** 26.2 per 100 pop. **Mobile:** 100.9 per 100 pop. **Broadband:** 106.4 per 100 pop. **Internet** (2018): 84.4%.

Health: Expend.: 6.7%. **Life expect.:** 76.4 male; 82.2 female. **Births:** 10.9 per 1,000 pop. **Deaths:** 7 per 1,000 pop. **Infant mortality:** 7.4 per 1,000 live births. **Undernourished:** 6.8%. **HIV:** NA. **Education:** Compulsory: ages 5-14. **Literacy:** 99.1%. **Embassy:** 2211 R St. NW 20008; 462-5772. **Website:** www.cyprus.gov.cy

The Ottoman Empire held Cyprus, 1571-1878, until it yielded control to Britain. Agitation for enosis (union) with Greece, which the Turkish minority opposed, increased after WWII and led to violence in 1955-56. In 1959, Britain, Greece, Turkey, and Cypriot leaders approved a plan for an independent republic, with constitutional guarantees for the Turkish minority.

Archbishop Makarios III was elected president, and full independence became final Aug. 16, 1960. Strife between Greek Cypriot and Turkish Cypriot communities prompted the UN to send a peacekeeping force (UNFICYP) in 1964; about 850 UNFICYP uniformed personnel were in Cyprus in mid-2020.

The Cypriot National Guard, led by officers from the Greek army, seized the government July 15, 1974. On July 20, Turkey invaded the island, and by Aug. 16, Turkish forces had occupied the northeastern 40%. Turkish troops remained in northern Cyprus in 2020.

Turkish Cyprus opened its border with Greek Cyprus Apr. 23, 2003, for the first time since partition. In separate referendums Apr. 2004, 65% of Turkish Cypriot voters accepted a UN-sponsored reunification plan, but 76% of Greek Cypriots rejected it. Still divided, Cyprus became a full member of the EU on May 1, 2004. Greek Cyprus began using the euro as its currency in 2008. In a runoff election Feb. 24, 2013, the conservative candidate and head of the Democratic Rally party, Nicos Anastasiades, was elected president; he was reelected in a runoff, Feb. 4, 2018.

In part because Cypriot banks held large amounts of Greek bonds, Cyprus suffered a banking crisis in 2013. A bailout package was agreed upon Mar. 5, 2013, by the Intl. Monetary Fund, the European Central Bank, and eurozone countries. In exchange for $13 bil in IMF and EU assistance, Cyprus agreed to stringent banking reforms and economic austerity; large depositors lost some of their money.

Cyprus had about 1,700 COVID-19 cases and 22 deaths as of Sept. 30, 2020.

Turkish Republic of Northern Cyprus

A declaration of independence was announced by Turkish-Cypriot leader Rauf Denktash, Nov. 15, 1983. The state, a parliamentary republic with enhanced presidency, is not internationally recognized but has trade relations with some countries. Political moderate Mustafa Akinci won an Apr. 26, 2015, presidential runoff election. Akinci and Anastasiades met in May, and new UN-sponsored reunification talks began in June 2015. After several rounds of negotiations, the UN announced, July 7, 2017, that talks had failed, although Akinci and Anastasiades continued to meet in 2018-20. Akinci sought a second term in 2020 elections postponed from Apr. to Oct. because of the COVID-19 pandemic. Area 1,295 sq mi; pop. (2011 census) 286,257, nearly all ethnically Turkish. Capital: Nicosia (Lefkosia). Local divisions: 5 districts. Active troops: 3,500. **Website:** www.kktcb.org

Czechia
Czech Republic

(As of May 17, 2016, the country's official short form name in English was Czechia.)

People: Population: 10,702,498 (85). **Age distrib.: <15:** 15.2%; **65+:** 20.2%. **Growth:** 0.1%. **Migrants:** 4.8%. **Pop. density:** 358.8 per sq mi, 138.5 per sq km. **Urban:** 74.1%. **Ethnic groups:** Czech 64.3%, Moravian 5%. **Languages:** Czech (official), Slovak. **Religions:** agnostic 58.2%, Christian (official) 34.7% (Catholic 30.4%), atheist 6.2%.

Geography: Total area: 30,451 sq mi, 78,867 sq km (114); **Land area:** 29,825 sq mi, 77,247 sq km. **Location:** E central Europe. Poland on N, Germany on N and W, Austria on S, Slovakia on E and SE. **Topography:** Bohemia, in W, is a plateau surrounded by mountains; Moravia is hilly. **Arable land:** 32.4%. **Capital:** Prague, 1,305,737.

Government: Type: Parliamentary republic. **Head of state:** Pres. Milos Zeman; b. 1944; in office: Mar. 8, 2013. **Head of govt.:** Prime Min. Andrej Babis; b. 1954; in office: Dec. 13, 2017. **Local divisions:** 13 regions, 1 capital city. **Defense budget:** $2.9 bil. **Active troops:** 21,750.

Economy: Industries: motor vehicles, metallurgy, machinery and equip., glass, armaments. **Chief agric.:** wheat, potatoes, sugar beets, hops, fruit; pigs, poultry. **Natural resources:** coal, kaolin, clay, graphite, timber. **Water:** 1,238 cu m per capita. **Crude oil reserves:** 15 mil bbls. **Electricity prod.** (2018): 81.9 bil kWh. **Labor force:** agric. 2.6%, industry 37.1%, services 60.2%. **Unemployment:** 1.9%.

Finance: Monetary unit: Koruna (CZK) (22.33 = $1 U.S.). **GDP:** $454.3 bil; **per capita GDP:** $42,576; **GDP growth:** 2.6%. **Imports:** $134.7 bil; Germany 29.8%, Poland 9.1%, China 7.4%, Slovakia 5.8%, Netherlands 5.3%. **Exports:** $144.8 bil; Germany 32.8%, Slovakia 7.8%, Poland 6.1%, France 5.1%. **Tourism:** $7.3 bil. **Budget:** $83.9 bil. **Inflation:** 2.8%.

Transport: Railways: 5,846 mi. **Motor vehicles:** 616.3 per 1,000 pop. **Airports:** 41.

Communications: Telephone: 14 per 100 pop. **Mobile:** 119.2 per 100 pop. **Broadband:** 81.9 per 100 pop. **Internet** (2018): 80.7%.

Health: Expend.: 7.2%. **Life expect.:** 76.3 male; 82.4 female. **Births:** 8.9 per 1,000 pop. **Deaths:** 10.7 per 1,000 pop. **Infant mortality:** 2.6 per 1,000 live births. **Undernourished:** <2.5%. **HIV** (2018): <0.1%.

Education: Compulsory: ages 6-14. **Literacy:** 99%.

Embassy: 3900 Spring of Freedom St. NW 20008; 274-9100.

Website: www.czech.cz

Bohemia and Moravia were part of the Great Moravian Empire in the 9th cent. and later became part of the Holy Roman Empire. Under the kings of Bohemia, Prague in the 14th cent. was the cultural center of Central Europe. Bohemia and Hungary became part of Austria-Hungary.

In 1914-18, Thomas G. Masaryk and Eduard Benes formed a provisional government with the support of Slovak leaders, including Milan Stefanik. They proclaimed the Republic of Czechoslovakia Oct. 28, 1918.

By 1938, Nazi Germany had generated disaffection among German-speaking citizens in Sudetenland and demanded its cession. British Prime Min. Neville Chamberlain signed with Adolf Hitler at Munich, Sept. 30, 1938, an agreement to the cession, with a guarantee of peace by Hitler and Italian dictator Benito Mussolini. Germany occupied Sudetenland Oct. 1-2. Hitler on Mar. 15, 1939, dissolved Czechoslovakia, made protectorates of Bohemia and Moravia, and supported the autonomy of Slovakia, proclaimed independent Mar. 14, 1939.

Soviet troops with some Czechoslovak contingents entered eastern Czechoslovakia in 1944 and reached Prague in May 1945; Benes returned as president. In May 1946 elections, the Communist Party won 38% of the votes. In Feb. 1948, the Communists seized power in advance of scheduled elections. The country was renamed the Czechoslovak Socialist Republic. A harsh Stalinist period followed; all opposition was suppressed.

In Jan. 1968 a liberalization movement spread through Czechoslovakia. Long-time Stalinist ruler Antonin Novotny was deposed; the democrat Slovak Alexander Dubcek succeeded him. On Aug. 20, troops from the USSR and 4 Warsaw Pact nations invaded Czechoslovakia. Despite demonstrations and riots by students and workers, press censorship was imposed and liberal leaders were ousted. On Apr. 17, 1969, Dubcek resigned as Communist Party leader and was succeeded by Gustav Husak. Censorship was tightened, and the Communist Party expelled a third of its members.

More than 700 leading Czechoslovak intellectuals and former party leaders signed a human rights manifesto in 1977, called Charter 77, prompting a renewed crackdown by the regime.

The police crushed a massive protest in Prague, Nov. 17, 1989. As protesters demanded free elections, the Communist Party leadership resigned Nov. 24; millions went on strike Nov. 27.

On Dec. 10, 1989, the first cabinet in 41 years without a Communist majority took power; Vaclav Havel, playwright and human rights campaigner, was chosen president, Dec. 29. In Mar. 1990 the country was officially renamed the Czech and Slovak Federal Republic. A Slovak-led coalition blocked Havel's bid to win reelection July 1992.

Slovakia declared sovereignty, July 17, 1992. Czech and Slovak leaders agreed, July 23, on a plan for a peaceful division of Czechoslovakia. It split into two separate states—the Czech Republic and Slovakia—Jan. 1, 1993. Havel was elected president of the Czech Republic on Jan. 26. The country became a full member of NATO in 1999.

Vaclav Klaus replaced the retiring Havel, 2003. The nation became a full EU member May 1, 2004.

Center-right parties made a strong showing in May 2010 parliamentary elections. Conservative Milos Zeman, a former Social Democrat prime min., was elected president, Jan. 26, 2013; running on an anti-immigration, anti-EU platform, Zeman narrowly won reelection, Jan. 2018.

Billionaire Andrej Babis became prime minister, Dec. 13, 2017, after his new, anti-immigration party ANO won the most seats in Oct. elections. Babis lost a no-confidence vote, Jan. 16, 2018, but was reappointed prime minister by Zeman, June 6, after forming a coalition with the Social Democrats. In 2019, Babis resisted calls, amid large protests in Prague, for his resignation over corruption allegations.

The 2020 COVID-19 pandemic caused almost 68,000 cases (over 60% in Sept.) and 636 deaths in Czechia by Sept. 30.

Denmark
Kingdom of Denmark

People: Population: 5,869,410 (114). **Age distrib.:** <15: 16.4%; 65+: 19.9%. **Growth:** 0.4%. **Migrants:** 12.5%. **Pop. density:** 358.2 per sq mi, 138.3 per sq km. **Urban:** 88.1%. **Ethnic groups:** Danish (incl. Greenlandic [predom. Inuit] and Faroese) 86.3%, Turkish 1.1%, other (incl. Polish, Syrian, German, Iraqi, Romanian) 12.6%. **Languages:** Danish, Faroese, Greenlandic, English (predominant second lang.). **Religions:** Christian 79.5% (Protestant 77.3%), agnostic 12.4%, Muslim 5.6% (Sunni).

Geography: Total area: 16,639 sq mi, 43,094 sq km (130); **Land area:** 16,384 sq mi, 42,434 sq km. **Location:** Northern Europe, separating North and Baltic Seas. Germany on S, Norway on NW, Sweden on NE. **Topography:** Consists of the Jutland Peninsula and more than 400 islands; flat and gently rolling plains. **Arable land:** 59.3%. **Capital:** Copenhagen, 1,346,485.

Government: Type: Parliamentary constitutional monarchy. **Head of state:** Queen Margrethe II; b. 1940; in office: Jan. 14, 1972. **Head of govt.:** Prime Min. Mette Frederiksen; b. 1977; in office: June 27, 2019. **Local divisions:** 5 regions. **Defense budget:** $4.6 bil. **Active troops:** 14,500.

Economy: Industries: wind turbines, pharmaceuticals, medical equip., shipbuilding and refurbishment, iron, steel, nonferrous metals, chemicals, food proc., machinery and transp. equip., textiles and clothing, electronics, constr., furniture and other wood prods. **Chief agric.:** barley, wheat, potatoes, sugar beets; pork, dairy prods.; fish. **Natural resources:** petroleum, nat. gas, fish, salt, limestone, chalk, stone, gravel and sand. **Water:** 1,046 cu m per capita. **Crude oil reserves:** 441 mil bbls. **Electricity prod.** (2018): 29.5 bil kWh. **Labor force:** agric. 2.1%, industry 18.3%, services 79.6%. **Unemployment:** 4.9%.

Finance: Monetary unit: Krone (DKK) (6.28 = $1 U.S.). **GDP:** $348.1 bil; **per capita GDP:** $59,830; **GDP growth:** 2.4%. **Imports:** $94.9 bil; Germany 21.3%, Sweden 11.9%, Netherlands 7.8%, China 7.1%, Norway 6.3%. **Exports:** $113.6 bil; Germany 15.5%, Sweden 11.6%, UK 8.2%, U.S. 7.5%, Norway 6%. **Tourism:** $8.8 bil. **Budget:** $168.9 bil. **Inflation:** 0.8%.

Transport: Railways: 2,160 mi. **Motor vehicles:** 523.2 per 1,000 pop. **Airports:** 28.

Communications: Telephone: 19.7 per 100 pop. **Mobile:** 125.1 per 100 pop. **Broadband:** 129 per 100 pop. **Internet** (2018): 97.6%.

Health: Expend.: 10.1%. **Life expect.:** 79.3 male; 83.3 female. **Births:** 11.1 per 1,000 pop. **Deaths:** 9.5 per 1,000 pop. **Infant mortality:** 3.2 per 1,000 live births. **Undernourished:** <2.5%. **HIV** (2018): 0.1%.

Education: Compulsory: ages 6-15. **Literacy:** 99%.

Embassy: 3200 Whitehaven St. NW 20008; 234-4300.

Website: denmark.dk

Most of the Viking raiders in the early Middle Ages were Danes. The Danish kingdom was a major power until the 17th cent., when it lost its land in southern Sweden. Norway was separated in 1815, and Schleswig-Holstein in 1864. Northern Schleswig was returned in 1920. Nazi Germany occupied Denmark, Apr. 1940-May 1945, but Danes helped more than 7,200 Jews escape to safety in Sweden, Sept. 1943.

The Danish newspaper Jyllands-Posten published, Sept. 30, 2005, cartoon images of the prophet Muhammad, offensive to Muslims; the caricatures, republished elsewhere, triggered violent protests and a boycott of Danish products in Islamic countries.

After Sept. 2011 parliamentary elections, Helle Thorning-Schmidt of the center-left Social Democrats became Denmark's first female prime min. A bill granting marriage rights to same-sex couples was voted into law, June 7, 2012. In 2014-16, in part as a result of the Syrian refugee crisis, almost 50,000 migrants sought asylum in Denmark. A center-right coalition returned to power in June 2015 elections in which the anti-immigration Danish People's Party won 21% of the vote. A 2016 law allowed the government to seize the assets of arriving asylum seekers. Asylum applications fell sharply beginning in 2017. May 2018 legislation banned wearing a face-covering garment such as a burqa or niqab in public. Dec. 2018 legislation required preschool education, including "Danish values" lessons, in largely immigrant areas. The Social Democrats won June 5, 2019, elections. Party leader Mette Frederiksen formed a minority government with leftist-party support after agreeing to modify anti-immigration positions and take stronger action to combat climate change.

Denmark instituted lockdown measures, Mar. 11, 2020, to combat the COVID-19 pandemic. Restrictions were eased beginning in Apr. but tightened again in Sept. as new cases spiked. As of Sept. 30, Denmark had about 27,500 COVID-19 cases and 650 deaths.

The **Faroe Islands** in the N Atlantic, about 300 mi NW of the Shetlands, and 850 mi from Denmark proper, 18 inhabited, have an area of 538 sq mi and pop. (2020 est.) of 51,628. They are an administrative division of Denmark, self-governing in most matters. Capital: Tórshavn; pop. (2018 est.) 20,817. Fish is a primary export. **Website:** www.government.fo

Kalaallit Nunaat (Greenland)

Greenland, an island between the North Atlantic and the Arctic Oceans, is separated from the North American continent by Davis Strait and Baffin Bay. Total area is 836,330 sq mi, about 79% of which is ice-capped. Most of the island is a lofty plateau 9,000-10,000 ft in elevation. The average thickness of the cap is 1,000 ft. Scientists point to accelerated melting of Greenland's ice sheet in recent years as evidence of global warming. The pop. (2020 est.) was 57,616. About 88% of the pop. in 2010 were Inuit. Under the 1953 Danish constitution the colony became an integral part of the realm with representatives in the Folketing (Danish legislature). The Danish parliament, 1978, approved home rule for Greenland, effective May 1, 1979. With home rule, Greenlandic place names came into official use. The official name for Greenland is Kalaallit Nunaat. The name for its capital is Nuuk (2018 est. pop., 18,406), rather than Godthab. Voters approved a new Self-Government Act in Nov. 2008. Per capita GDP was $41,800 (2015 est.). The labor force is distributed as follows: agric. 15.9%, industry 10.1%, services 73.9%. Fish and fish products account for over 90% of exports. Other natural resources include coal, iron ore, lead, zinc, molybdenum, diamonds, gold, platinum, uranium, and hydropower. **Website:** naalakkersuisut.gl

Djibouti
Republic of Djibouti

People: Population: 921,804 (158). **Age distrib.:** <15: 30.0%; 65+: 4.0%. **Growth:** 2.1%. **Migrants:** 11.8%. **Pop. density:** 103.0 per sq mi, 39.8 per sq km. **Urban:** 78.1%. **Ethnic groups:** Somali 60%, Afar 35%, other (incl. French, Arab, Ethiopian, Italian) 5%. **Languages:** French, Arabic (both official); Somali; Afar. **Religions:** Muslim (official) 97.4% (Sunni).

Geography: Total area: 8,958 sq mi, 23,200 sq km (147); **Land area:** 8,950 sq mi, 23,180 sq km. **Location:** E coast of Africa, separated from Arabian Peninsula by strategically vital strait of Bab el-Mandeb. Eritrea on NW, Ethiopia on W and SW, Somalia on SE. **Topography:** Low coastal plain with mountains behind and an interior plateau. Arid, sandy, and desolate. Hot and dry climate. **Arable land:** 0.1%. **Capital:** Djibouti, 576,157.

Government: Type: Presidential republic. **Head of state:** Pres. Ismail Omar Guelleh; b. 1947; in office: May 8, 1999. **Head of govt.:** Prime Min. Abdoulkader Kamil Mohamed; b. 1951; in office: Apr. 1, 2013. **Local divisions:** 6 districts. **Defense budget:** NA. **Active troops:** 10,450.

Economy: Industries: constr., agric. proc., shipping. **Chief agric.:** fruits, vegetables; goats, sheep, camels. **Natural resources:** potential geothermal power, gold, clay, granite, limestone, marble, salt, diatomite, gypsum, pumice, petroleum. **Water:** 314 cu m per capita. **Electricity prod.:** 381 mil kwH. **Labor force:** agric. 32.4%, industry 13.3%, services 54.3%. **Unemployment:** 10.3%.

Finance: Monetary unit: Franc (DJF) (177.77 = $1 U.S.). **GDP:** $5.6 bil; **per capita GDP:** $5,748; **GDP growth:** 7.5%. **Imports:** $726.4 mil; UAE 25%, France 15.2%, Saudi Arabia 11%, China 9.6%, Ethiopia 6.8%. **Exports** (2016): $139.9 mil; Ethiopia 38.8%, Somalia 17.1%, Qatar 9.1%, Brazil 8.9%. **Tourism:** $57 mil. **Budget:** $899.2 mil. **Inflation:** 3.3%.

Transport: Railways: 60 mi (Djibouti segment of railway jointly controlled with Ethiopia). **Airports:** 3.

Communications: Telephone: 3.8 per 100 pop. **Mobile:** 41.2 per 100 pop. **Broadband:** 11.7 per 100 pop. **Internet:** 55.7%.

Health: Expend.: 3.3%. **Life expect.:** 62.1 male; 67.4 female. **Births:** 22.7 per 1,000 pop. **Deaths:** 7.3 per 1,000 pop. **Infant mortality:** 41.6 per 1,000 live births. **Undernourished:** NA. **HIV:** 0.8%. **Education:** Compulsory: ages 6-15. **Literacy:** NA. **Embassy:** 1156 15th St. NW, Ste. 515, 20005; 331-0270. **Website:** www.presidence.dj

France gained control of the territory in stages between 1862 and 1900. As French Somaliland, it became an overseas French territory in 1945; in 1967 it was renamed the French Territory of the Afars and the Issas. Ethiopia and Somalia renounced their claims to the area, but each accused the other of trying to gain control. There were clashes between Afars (ethnically related to Ethiopians) and Issas (related to Somalis) in 1976. Immigrants from both countries continued to enter Djibouti until independence on June 27, 1977.

Post-independence economic support has come from France, Arab countries, the U.S., and China. A peace accord Dec. 1994 ended a 3-year Afar rebel uprising. Protests associated with the Arab Spring broke out in late Jan. 2011 demanding the resignation of Pres. Ismail Omar Guelleh. Authorities suppressed the protests. The U.S. announced, May 5, 2014, the signing of a new 20-year lease for its military base in Djibouti, used for operations in the Middle East and Africa. Guelleh won a fourth term in disputed Apr. 8, 2016, elections. A 460-mi Chinese-built railroad linking Addis Ababa, Ethiopia, with Djibouti City began service Oct. 5, 2016. China opened a naval base in Djibouti, Aug. 1, 2017. The 2020 COVID-19 pandemic caused about 5,400 cases and 61 deaths in Djibouti by Sept. 30.

Dominica
Commonwealth of Dominica

People: Population: 74,243 (188). **Age distrib.:** <15: 21.4%; 65+: 12.1%. **Growth:** 0.1%. **Migrants:** 11.5%. **Pop. density:** 256.0 per sq mi, 98.9 per sq km. **Urban:** 71.1%. **Ethnic groups:** African descent 86.6%, mixed 9.1%, Indigenous 2.9%. **Languages:** English (official), French patois. **Religions:** Christian 94.4% (Catholic 50.2%, Protestant 41.2%), Spiritist 2.5%, Baha'i 1.7%.

Geography: Total area: 290 sq mi, 751 sq km (175); **Land area:** 290 sq mi, 751 sq km. **Location:** E Caribbean, most northerly Windward Isl. Guadeloupe to N, Martinique to S (both French terr.). **Topography:** Central ridge runs N-S, terminating in cliffs. Volcanic in origin, with numerous thermal springs. **Arable land:** 8.0%. **Capital:** Roseau, 14,942.

Government: Type: Parliamentary republic. **Head of state:** Pres. Charles A. Savarin; b. 1943; in office: Oct. 2, 2013. **Head of govt.:** Prime Min. Roosevelt Skerrit; b. 1972; in office: Jan. 8, 2004. **Local divisions:** 10 parishes. **Defense budget/active troops:** NA.

Economy: Industries: soap, coconut oil, tourism, copra, furniture, cement blocks, shoes. **Chief agric.:** bananas, citrus, mangoes, root crops, coconuts, cocoa. **Natural resources:** timber, hydropower. **Water:** 2,706 cu m per capita. **Electricity prod.:** 83 mil kwH. **Labor force:** agric. 22.3%, industry 12.6%, services 65.1%. **Unemployment:** NA.

Finance: Monetary unit: East Caribbean Dollar (XCD) (2.70 = $1 U.S.). **GDP:** $909.0 mil; **per capita GDP:** $12,659; **GDP growth:** 5.7%. **Imports:** $206.6 mil; U.S. 61.3%, Trinidad and Tobago 9.8%. **Exports:** $28 mil; Saudi Arabia 42.6%, Trinidad and Tobago 9.3%, Jamaica 8.1%, St. Kitts and Nevis 7.1%, Guyana 6.7%. **Tourism:** $105 mil. **Budget:** $260.4 mil. **Inflation** (2017-18): 1.0%.

Transport: Airports: 2.

Communications: Telephone: 3.7 per 100 pop. **Mobile:** 105.8 per 100 pop. **Broadband:** 39.2 per 100 pop. **Internet:** 69.6%.

Health: Expend.: 5.9%. **Life expect.:** 74.7 male; 80.9 female. **Births:** 14.5 per 1,000 pop. **Deaths:** 8 per 1,000 pop. **Infant mortality:** 9.7 per 1,000 live births. **Undernourished:** NA. **HIV** (2018): 0.6%. **Education:** Compulsory: ages 5-16. **Literacy:** NA. **Embassy:** 3216 New Mexico Ave. NW 20016; 364-6781. **Website:** www.dominica.gov.dm

A British colony since 1805, Dominica was granted self-government in 1967. Independence was achieved Nov. 3, 1978.

Hurricane David struck, Aug. 30, 1979, devastating the island and destroying the banana plantations, Dominica's economic mainstay. Coups were attempted in 1980 and 1981. Prime Min. Pierre Charles died Jan. 6, 2004, and was succeeded by Roosevelt Skerrit. Tropical storm Erika, Aug. 27, 2015, killed 30 and caused widespread damage. Hurricane Maria, Sept. 18, 2017, left more than 30 dead and damaged or destroyed over 90% of buildings.

Dominican Republic

People: Population: 10,499,707 (88). **Age distrib.:** <15: 26.8%; 65+: 6.3%. **Growth:** 0.9%. **Migrants:** 5.3%. **Pop. density:** 562.8 per sq mi, 217.3 per sq km. **Urban:** 82.5%. **Ethnic groups:** mixed 70.4% (mestizo/indio 58%, mulatto 12.4%), Black 15.8%, white 13.5%. **Languages:** Spanish (official). **Religions:** Christian 94.5% (Catholic [official] 81.4%), agnostic 2.6%.

Geography: Total area: 18,792 sq mi, 48,670 sq km (128); **Land area:** 18,656 sq mi, 48,320 sq km. **Location:** W Indies, sharing isl. of Hispaniola with Haiti on W, Puerto Rico (U.S.) to E. **Topography:** The Cordillera Central range crosses center, rising to over 10,000 ft, highest in the Caribbean. Cibao Valley to N. **Arable land:** 16.6%. **Capital:** Santo Domingo, 3,317,784.

Government: Type: Presidential republic. **Head of state and govt.:** Pres. Danilo Medina Sánchez; b. 1951; in office: Aug. 16, 2012. **Local divisions:** 10 regions. **Defense budget:** $621 mil. **Active troops:** 56,050.

Economy: Industries: tourism, sugar proc., gold mining, textiles, cement, tobacco. **Chief agric.:** cocoa, tobacco, sugarcane, coffee, cotton, rice, beans, potatoes, corn, bananas; cattle, pigs. **Natural resources:** nickel, bauxite, gold, silver. **Water:** 2,183 cu m per capita. **Electricity prod.:** 18.0 bil kwH. **Labor force:** agric. 8.8%, industry 19.9%, services 71.3%. **Unemployment:** 5.9%.

Finance: Monetary unit: Peso (DOP) (58.39 = $1 U.S.). **GDP:** $206.0 bil; **per capita GDP:** $19,182; **GDP growth:** 5.1%. **Imports:** $17.7 bil; U.S. 41.4%, China 13.9%. **Exports:** $10.1 bil; U.S. 50.3%,

Haiti 9.1%, Canada 8.2%, India 5.6%. **Tourism:** $7.5 bil. **Budget:** $13.6 bil. **Inflation:** 1.8%.

Transport: Railways: 308 mi. **Motor vehicles:** 183.6 per 1,000 pop. **Airports:** 16.

Communications: Telephone: 12 per 100 pop. **Mobile:** 84.1 per 100 pop. **Broadband:** 55.7 per 100 pop. **Internet** (2018): 74.8%.

Health: Expend.: 6.1%. **Life expect.:** 70.3 male; 73.8 female. **Births:** 18.5 per 1,000 pop. **Deaths:** 6.3 per 1,000 pop. **Infant mortality:** 20.9 per 1,000 live births. **Undernourished:** 5.5%. **HIV:** 0.9%.

Education: Compulsory: ages 3-17. **Literacy:** 98.8%.

Embassy: 1715 22nd St. NW 20008; 332-6280.

Website: www.dominicana.gob.do

Carib and Arawak Indians inhabited the island of Hispaniola when Christopher Columbus landed in 1492. The city of Santo Domingo, founded 1496, is the oldest European settlement in the Western Hemisphere.

France took over the western third of the island (now Haiti) in 1697 and Santo Domingo in 1795. Spain returned intermittently 1803-21, as several native republics came and went. Haiti ruled again, 1822-44; Spanish occupation occurred 1861-63. U.S. Marines occupied the country 1916-24.

In 1930, Gen. Rafael Leonidas Trujillo Molina was elected president. The brutal Trujillo era ended with his assassination in 1961. Pres. Joaquín Balaguer, appointed by Trujillo in 1960, resigned under pressure in 1962.

Juan Bosch, elected president in the first free elections in 38 years, was overthrown in 1963. On Apr. 24, 1965, Bosch's followers and others, including a few Communists, launched a revolt. Four days later U.S. Marines intervened against pro-Bosch forces. A provisional government supervised a June 1966 election in which Balaguer defeated Bosch. Balaguer remained in office for most of the next 28 years, but his May 1994 reelection was widely denounced as fraudulent. He called for new elections but did not run, and Leonel Fernández Reyna was elected June 1996. After a presidential election defeat in 2000, Fernández again won the presidency in 2004 and 2008. Fernández ally Danilo Medina Sánchez, of the center-left Dominican Liberation Party (PLD), was elected in 2012 and 2016. In the 2020 presidential election (delayed from May 17 to July 5 by the COVID-19 pandemic), businessman Luis Rodolfo Abinader defeated the PLD candidate.

The Constitutional Court ruled, Sept. 23, 2013, that people born in the Dominican Rep. after 1929 to undocumented immigrant parents were not entitled to citizenship. The decision affected perhaps 200,000 people, most of Haitian descent. May 2014 legislation provided a complex path to citizenship for such people, which most did not complete. In 2015, the government also required undocumented immigrants—estimated at more than 500,000, most of them Haitian—to register by June 17 or face deportation; about half had not registered by the deadline. By the end of 2017, more than 250,000 Haitians had left the country voluntarily or been deported.

A 2015-16 Zika virus outbreak resulted in about 5,250 confirmed or suspected cases. By Sept. 30, 2020, the Dominican Rep. had 111,900 COVID-19 cases and over 2,100 deaths.

Ecuador
Republic of Ecuador

People: Population: 16,904,867 (70). **Age distrib.:** <15: 25.8%; 65+: 8.1%. **Growth:** 1.2%. **Migrants:** 2.2%. **Pop. density:** 158.2 per sq mi, 61.1 per sq km. **Urban:** 64.2%. **Ethnic groups:** mestizo (mixed Amerindian/white) 71.9%, Montubio 7.4%, Amerindian 7%, white 6.1%, Afroecuadorian 4.3%. **Languages:** Spanish (Castilian) (official), Quechua. **Religions:** Christian 95% (Catholic 83.8%), agnostic 3.7%.

Geography: Total area: 109,484 sq mi, 283,561 sq km (73); **Land area:** 106,889 sq mi, 276,841 sq km. **Location:** NW S America, on Pacific coast, astride the equator. Colombia on N, Peru on E and S. **Topography:** Two Andes ranges run N-S, splitting country into 3 zonoo: hot, humid lowlands on coast; temperate highlands between ranges; and rainy, tropical lowlands to E. **Arable land:** 4.2%. **Capital:** Quito, 1,873,763. **Cities:** Guayaquil, 2,994,218.

Government: Type: Presidential republic. **Head of state and govt.:** Pres. Lenín Moreno; b. 1953; in office: May 24, 2017. **Local divisions:** 24 provinces. **Defense budget:** $1.6 bil. **Active troops:** 40,250.

Economy: Industries: petroleum, food proc., textiles, wood prods., chemicals. **Chief agric.:** bananas, coffee, cocoa, rice, potatoes, cassava, plantains, sugarcane; cattle, sheep, pigs; fish, shrimp. **Natural resources:** petroleum, fish, timber, hydropower. **Water:** 26,611 cu m per capita. **Crude oil reserves:** 8.3 bil bbls. **Electricity prod.:** 28.6 bil kwH. **Labor force:** agric. 29.4%, industry 18.2%, services 52.5%. **Unemployment:** 4.2%.

Finance: Monetary unit: U.S. Dollar (USD) (1.00 = $1 U.S.). **GDP:** $205.8 bil; **per capita GDP:** $11,847; **GDP growth:** 0.1%. **Imports:** $19.3 bil; U.S. 22.8%, China 15.4%, Colombia 8.7%, Panama 4.4%. **Exports:** $19.6 bil; U.S. 31.5%, Vietnam 7.6%, Peru 6.7%, Chile 6.5%. **Tourism:** 3.2 bil. **Budget:** $38.1 bil. **Inflation:** 0.3%.

Transport: Railways: 600 mi. **Motor vehicles:** 105.2 per 1,000 pop. **Airports:** 104.

Communications: Telephone: 13.8 per 100 pop. **Mobile:** 92.3 per 100 pop. **Broadband:** 53 per 100 pop. **Internet:** 57.3%.

Health: Expend.: 8.3%. **Life expect.:** 74.5 male; 80.6 female. **Births:** 17 per 1,000 pop. **Deaths:** 5.2 per 1,000 pop. **Infant mortality:** 15.0 per 1,000 live births. **Undernourished:** 8.8%. **HIV:** 0.4%.

Education: Compulsory: ages 3-17. **Literacy:** 99.3%.

Embassy: 2535 15th St. NW 20009; 234-7200.

Website: www.presidencia.gob.ec

The region, which was the northern Inca empire, was conquered by Spain in 1533. Liberation forces defeated the Spanish May 24, 1822, near Quito. Ecuador became part of the Great Colombia Republic but seceded, May 13, 1830.

Ecuadoran Indigenous peoples, demanding greater rights, staged protests in the 1990s. A border war with Peru flared Jan. 26-Mar. 1, 1995. Elected president, July 1996, Abdalá Bucaram—a populist known as El Loco, or "The Crazy One"—imposed stiff price increases and other austerity measures. His rising unpopularity and erratic behavior led the National Congress, Feb. 1997, to dismiss him for "mental incapacity."

Jamil Mahuad Witt won a presidential runoff election July 1998. Opposed by Indian groups and military leaders, he was ousted Jan. 2000, and succeeded by Vice Pres. Gustavo Noboa Bejarano. Noboa enacted a plan introduced by Mahuad to replace the sucre with the U.S. dollar as Ecuador's currency. Lucio Gutiérrez Borbúa, a leader in the 2000 coup, won a presidential runoff Nov. 2002.

Gutiérrez imposed economic austerity measures, purged opponents from the Supreme Court, Dec. 2004, and then dissolved it, Apr. 2005. Congress ousted Gutiérrez Apr. 20. In May 2006, Ecuador took over oil assets belonging to U.S.-based Occidental Petroleum.

Rafael Correa, a left-wing economist, won a presidential runoff vote Nov. 2006. Early in his term, when oil revenues were high, Correa boosted development spending and aid to poor families; later, as oil prices dropped, he restricted imports to prevent an outflow of dollars and, Dec. 2008, allowed Ecuador to default on part of its $10-bil foreign debt. Correa, reelected Apr. 2009, pressured foreign oil companies in 2010 to renegotiate contracts to increase the government's share of mineral revenues.

Ecuador granted asylum, Aug. 16, 2012, to Julian Assange, the founder of WikiLeaks. Assange was in Ecuador's UK embassy in London, avoiding possible extradition to Sweden for sexual assault charges or to the U.S. in connection with the hacking and publication of classified information. After Ecuador withdrew asylum, Assange was arrested at the embassy, Apr. 11, 2019. A hearing on extradition to the U.S. began in Feb. 2020 and was then delayed by the COVID-19 pandemic.

Correa was reelected Feb. 17, 2013. A 2013 communications law limited press freedom. Beginning in 2013, the government encouraged new exploration for oil and other mineral resources in the Amazon. Lenín Moreno Garces won an Apr. 2, 2017, presidential runoff election. Nearly two weeks of sometimes violent protests against an austerity package including sharp cuts in fuel subsidies ended Oct. 13, 2019, when Moreno agreed to withdraw the package.

Beginning in 2018, hundreds of thousands of Venezuelans fleeing economic hardship and repression entered Ecuador; many continued on to Peru or other nations. About 178,000 had temporary residency status in Ecuador as of mid-Aug. 2020.

Severely impacted by COVID-19, Ecuador had almost 136,000 cases and over 11,300 deaths by Sept. 30, 2020.

The **Galápagos Islands**, pop. (2008 est.) 30,000, about 600 mi to the W, are the home of giant tortoises and other distinctive animals. The oil tanker Jessica ran aground Jan. 16, 2001, off San Cristóbal Isl., spilling some 185,000 gallons of fuel.

Egypt
Arab Republic of Egypt

People: Population: 104,124,440 (14). **Age distrib.:** <15: 33.6%; 65+: 4.4%. **Growth:** 2.3%. **Migrants:** 0.5%. **Pop. density:** 270.9 per sq mi, 104.6 per sq km. **Urban:** 42.8%. **Ethnic groups:** Egyptian 99.7%. **Languages:** Arabic (official), English and French widely understood by educated classes. **Religions:** Muslim 90.2% (Sunni [official]), Christian 9.1% (Orthodox 8.3%).

Geography: Total area: 386,662 sq mi, 1,001,450 sq km (29); **Land area:** 384,345 sq mi, 995,450 sq km. **Location:** NE corner of Africa. Libya on W; Sudan on S; Israel, Gaza Strip on E. **Topography:** Almost entirely desolate and barren with hills and mountains in E and along Nile. Most people live in 550-mi-long Nile Valley. **Arable land:** 2.8%. **Capital:** Cairo, 20,900,604. **Cities:** Alexandria, 5,280,664.

Government: Type: Presidential republic. **Head of state:** Pres. Abdel Fattah al-Sisi; b. 1954; in office: June 8, 2014. **Head of govt.:** Prime Min. Mostafa Madbouly; in office: June 7, 2018. **Local divisions:** 27 governorates. **Defense budget:** $3.4 bil. **Active troops:** 438,500.

Economy: Industries: textiles, food proc., tourism, chemicals, pharmaceuticals, hydrocarbons, constr., cement, metals, light manufactures. **Chief agric.:** cotton, rice, corn, wheat, beans, fruits, vegetables; cattle, water buffalo, sheep, goats. **Natural resources:** petroleum, nat. gas, iron ore, phosphates, manganese, limestone, gypsum, talc, asbestos, lead, rare earth elements, zinc. **Water:** 589

cu m per capita. **Crude oil reserves:** 3.3 bil bbls. **Electricity prod.:** 182.7 bil kWh. **Labor force:** agric. 23.3%, industry 28.2%, services 48.6%. **Unemployment:** 10.1%.

Finance: Monetary unit: Pound (EGP) (15.81 = $1 U.S.). **GDP:** $1.3 tril; **per capita GDP:** $12,251; **GDP growth:** 5.6%. **Imports:** $59.8 bil; China 7.9%, UAE 5.2%. **Exports:** $23.3 bil; UAE 10.9%, Italy 10%, U.S. 7.4%, UK 5.7%. **Tourism:** $13 bil. **Budget:** $62.6 bil. **Inflation** (2017-18): 14.4%.

Transport: Railways: 3,160 mi. **Motor vehicles:** 66.4 per 1,000 pop. **Airports:** 72.

Communications: Telephone: 8 per 100 pop. **Mobile:** 95.3 per 100 pop. **Broadband:** 50.1 per 100 pop. **Internet** (2018): 46.9%.

Health: Expend.: 5.3%. **Life expect.:** 72.3 male; 75.3 female. **Births:** 27.2 per 1,000 pop. **Deaths:** 4.4 per 1,000 pop. **Infant mortality:** 17.1 per 1,000 live births. **Undernourished:** 4.7%. **HIV:** <0.1%.

Education: Compulsory: ages 6-17. **Literacy:** 88.2%.

Embassy: 3521 International Ct. NW 20008; 895-5400.

Website: www.egypt.gov.eg

Archaeological records of ancient Egyptian civilization date back to 4000 BCE. A unified kingdom arose around 3200 BCE and extended south into Nubia and as far north as Syria. A high culture of rulers and priests was built on an economic base of serfdom, fertile soil, and annual flooding of the Nile.

Imperial decline facilitated conquest by Asian invaders (Hyksos, Assyrians). The last native dynasty fell in 341 BCE to the Persians, who were in turn replaced by Greeks (Alexander and the Ptolemies), Romans, Byzantines, and Arabs, who introduced Islam and the Arabic language. The ancient Egyptian language is preserved only in Coptic Christian liturgy.

Egypt was ruled as part of larger Islamic empires for many centuries. Britain intervened in Egypt in 1882 and ruled the country as a protectorate, 1914-22. A 1936 treaty strengthened Egyptian autonomy, but Britain retained bases in Egypt and a condominium (joint rule with Egypt) over Sudan. When the state of Israel was proclaimed in 1948, Egypt joined other Arab nations invading Israel and was defeated. In 1951 Egypt abrogated the 1936 treaty; Sudan became independent in 1956.

A July 1952 uprising overthrew King Farouk and established a republic. Lt. Col. Gamal Abdel Nasser rose to power, becoming premier in 1954 and president in 1956. Nasser pushed construction of Egypt's Aswan High Dam, completed in 1970.

After guerrilla raids across its border, Israel invaded Egypt's Sinai Peninsula, Oct. 29, 1956. Egypt rejected a cease-fire demanded by Britain and France; on Oct. 31 the two nations dropped bombs and on Nov. 5-6 landed forces. Egypt and Israel accepted a UN cease-fire; fighting ended Nov. 7. Full-scale war with Israel broke out again, June 5, 1967; before it ended under a UN cease-fire June 10, Israel had captured Gaza and the Sinai Peninsula and taken control of the E bank of the Suez Canal.

Nasser died Sept. 28, 1970, and was replaced by Vice Pres. Anwar Sadat. In a surprise attack Oct. 6, 1973, Egyptian forces crossed the Suez Canal into the Sinai. (At the same time, Syrian forces attacked Israelis on the Golan Heights.) Israel counterattacked, crossed the canal, and surrounded Suez City. A UN cease-fire took effect Oct. 24. Under an agreement signed Jan. 1974, Israeli forces withdrew from the canal's W bank; limited numbers of Egyptian forces occupied a strip along the E bank. A second accord was signed in 1975, with Israel yielding Sinai oil fields.

Pres. Sadat's surprise visit to Jerusalem, Nov. 1977, opened the prospect of peace with Israel. On Mar. 26, 1979, Egypt and Israel signed a formal peace treaty, ending 30 years of war and establishing diplomatic relations. On Oct. 6, 1981, Muslim extremists within the army assassinated Pres. Sadat, who was succeeded by Hosni Mubarak. Israel returned control of the Sinai to Egypt in Apr. 1982.

Egyptian security forces battled Islamist violence in the 1990s and early 2000s. On Nov. 17, 1997, near Luxor, Muslim extremists killed 58 foreign tourists and 4 Egyptians. Bombs Oct. 7, 2004, in and near Taba, a Sinai tourist site popular with Israelis, killed at least 35 people. Another 88 people were killed in bombings July 23, 2005, at Sharm el Sheikh, a Red Sea resort city. Suicide bombings at the Sinai resort town of Dahab, Apr. 24, 2006, killed at least 18 people; security forces May 9 killed Nasser Khamis al-Mallahi, leader of the group blamed for the Taba, Sharm el Sheikh, and Dahab attacks.

Following 18 days of mass protests in which at least 846 people died in clashes between Arab Spring dissidents and Mubarak loyalists, Mubarak surrendered power Feb. 11, 2011. A transitional military regime prepared for elections and charged Mubarak and associates with corruption and abuse of power. Mubarak was convicted on corruption charges, May 9, 2015, and sentenced to three years in prison. Released, Mar. 24, 2017, from the military hospital where he had been held, Mubarak died Feb. 25, 2020.

Islamist candidate Mohammed Morsi of the Muslim Brotherhood was declared winner of the presidential election, June 2012. Morsi overhauled the military leadership Aug. 12. On Oct. 8, 2012, he pardoned select political prisoners detained during the Arab Spring uprising. Violent clashes between Morsi supporters and opponents erupted Nov. 23 after Morsi announced an edict interpreted as a

power-grab. The proposal of a new Islamist constitution prompted demonstrations throughout Dec.; it passed Dec. 23, 2012.

The military forced Morsi out of office July 3, 2013, and cracked down violently, Aug. 14, on pro-Morsi protesters. More than 600 protesters and at least 40 police officers died in confrontations. The military outlawed the Muslim Brotherhood as a terrorist organization Dec. 25, 2013. Under a new constitution approved in a Jan. 2014 referendum, former Gen. Abdel Fattah al-Sisi, one of the leaders in ousting Morsi, won a May presidential election. Violence between Morsi supporters and security forces continued, causing hundreds of deaths on both sides. Muslim Brotherhood leader Mohamed Badie was sentenced to death June 21, 2014, in connection with July 2013 violence; the sentence was reduced to life in prison Aug. 30, 2014. Morsi was sentenced to 20 years in prison, Apr. 21, 2015, in a trial related to Dec. 2012 street violence. He died, June 17, 2019, after collapsing in court while facing separate espionage charges.

The Sisi government carried out a series of arrests of dissidents and journalists and continually suppressed protests. Sisi won a new term as president in a Mar. 2018 election from which opposition candidates were essentially barred. Constitutional changes approved in an Apr. 2019 referendum extended the president's term to 6 years and increased presidential power over the judiciary.

Beginning in 2013, Islamist militants battled security forces and seized territory in the northern Sinai. Terrorist attacks occurred at major tourist sites in Luxor and Giza in June 2015. A Russian airliner crashed in the Sinai, Oct. 31, 2015, apparently after a bomb onboard exploded, killing all 224 on board; Sinai Province, an ISIS-affiliated Islamist group, claimed responsibility. Egypt announced, Aug. 4, 2016, that it had killed Sinai Province's leader in an airstrike. A suicide bombing, for which ISIS claimed responsibility, killed about 30 people at a Coptic Christian chapel in Cairo, Dec. 11, 2016. About 75 people were killed in three attacks on Coptic Christians, Apr.-May 2017. More than 40 Egyptian soldiers and police were killed in July 7 and Sept. 11, 2017, attacks by Islamist militants in the Sinai; over 50 police officers died in a gun battle with militants SW of Cairo, Oct. 20. An attack on a Sufi mosque in the northern Sinai, Nov. 24, 2017, left more than 300 dead. An Egyptian military offensive, launched Feb. 2018, against Islamist militants in the Sinai and other areas met with some success, but militant attacks continued in 2019-20.

The 2020 COVID-19 pandemic caused about 103,000 cases in Egypt by Sept. 30 and killed about 5,900 Egyptians.

The Suez Canal, 103 mi long, links the Mediterranean and Red Seas. It was built by a French corporation 1859-69, but Britain obtained controlling interest in 1875. On July 26, 1956, Egypt nationalized the canal.

El Salvador
Republic of El Salvador

People: Population: 6,481,102 (108). **Age distrib.:** <15: 25.8%; 65+: 7.6%. **Growth:** 0.8%. **Migrants:** 0.7%. **Pop. density:** 810.1 per sq mi, 312.8 per sq km. **Urban:** 73.4%. **Ethnic groups:** mestizo 86.3%, white 12.7%. **Languages:** Spanish (official), Nawat. **Religions:** Christian 96.3% (Catholic [official] 65.6%, independent 15.6%, Protestant 15.1%).

Geography: Total area: 8,124 sq mi, 21,041 sq km (150); **Land area:** 8,000 sq mi, 20,721 sq km. **Location:** Central America. Guatemala on W, Honduras on N. **Topography:** A hot Pacific coastal plain in S rises to a cooler plateau and valley region, densely populated. The N is mountainous with many volcanoes. **Arable land:** 34.8%. **Capital:** San Salvador, 1,105,766.

Government: Type: Presidential republic. **Head of state and govt.:** Pres. Nayib Bukele; b. 1981; in office: June 1, 2019. **Local divisions:** 14 departments. **Defense budget:** $145 mil. **Active troops:** 24,500.

Economy: Industries: food proc., beverages, petroleum, chemicals, fertilizer, textiles, furniture, light metals. **Chief agric.:** coffee, sugar, corn, rice, beans, oilseed, cotton, sorghum; beef, dairy prods. **Natural resources:** hydropower, geothermal power, petroleum. **Water:** 4,119 cu m per capita. **Electricity prod.:** 5.0 bil kWh. **Labor force:** agric. 16.0%, industry 22.1%, services 62.0%. **Unemployment:** 4.2%.

Finance: Monetary unit: Colon (SVC) (8.75 = $1 U.S.). **GDP:** $59.0 bil; **per capita GDP:** $9,140; **GDP growth:** 2.4%. **Imports:** $9.5 bil; U.S. 36.7%, Guatemala 10.5%, China 8.7%, Mexico 7.4%, Honduras 6.7%. **Exports:** $4.7 bil; U.S. 45.7%, Honduras 13.9%, Guatemala 13.5%, Nicaragua 6.7%. **Tourism:** $1.3 bil. **Budget:** $6.5 bil. **Inflation:** 0.1%.

Transport: Railways: 8 mi. **Motor vehicles:** 49.2 per 1,000 pop. **Airports:** 5.

Communications: Telephone: 13.7 per 100 pop. **Mobile:** 146.9 per 100 pop. **Broadband:** 56.1 per 100 pop. **Internet:** 33.8%.

Health: Expend.: 7.2%. **Life expect.:** 71.3 male; 78.6 female. **Births:** 18.6 per 1,000 pop. **Deaths:** 5.9 per 1,000 pop. **Infant mortality:** 11.8 per 1,000 live births. **Undernourished:** 8.9%. **HIV:** 0.5%. **Education:** Compulsory: ages 1-15. **Literacy:** 98.0%.

Embassy: 1400 16th St. NW, Ste. 100, 20036; 265-9671.

Website: www.presidencia.gob.sv

El Salvador became independent of Spain in 1821 and of the Central American Federation in 1839.

After a military coup in 1979, a military-civilian junta failed to quell a rebellion by leftist insurgents, armed by Cuba and Nicaragua. Right-wing death squads killed thousands of suspected leftists in the 1980s. The U.S. supported the government with military aid. After taking the lives of some 75,000 people (with thousands more "disappeared"), the civil war ended Jan. 16, 1992, as the government and leftist rebels signed a peace treaty.

The right-wing ARENA party held the presidency, 1989-2009. The leftist FMLN won 2009 and 2014 elections. Rejecting both major parties, voters elected Nayib Bukele of the center-right GANA party in the Feb. 3, 2019, presidential election.

Beginning in 2013, tens of thousands of migrants or asylum seekers from El Salvador tried to enter the U.S. from Mexico; many were families or unaccompanied children fleeing widespread gang violence. On Jan. 8, 2018, the Trump administration said it would end temporary residence status for about 263,000 Salvadorans allowed to live in the U.S. following 2001 earthquakes; a court challenge delayed implementation until at least 2021. On Sept. 20, 2019, the U.S. and El Salvador signed an agreement under which asylum seekers from other nations entering El Salvador en route to the U.S. would have to apply for asylum in El Salvador.

A Zika virus outbreak that began in 2015 caused more than 11,800 confirmed or suspected cases through the end of 2017. The 2020 COVID-19 pandemic caused about 29,000 cases and over 800 deaths in El Salvador by Sept. 30.

Equatorial Guinea
Republic of Equatorial Guinea

People: Population: 836,178 (160). **Age distrib.:** <15: 38.7%; 65+: 3.9%. **Growth:** 2.3%. **Migrants:** 16.8%. **Pop. density:** 77.2 per sq mi, 29.8 per sq km. **Urban:** 73.1%. **Ethnic groups:** Fang 85.7%, Bubi 6.5%, Mdowe 3.6%. **Languages:** Spanish, French (both official); Fang; Bubi. **Religions:** Christian (official) 90% (Catholic 84.4%), Muslim 4.1% (Sunni), agnostic 3.5%.

Geography: Total area: 10,831 sq mi, 28,051 sq km (142); **Land area:** 10,831 sq mi, 28,051 sq km. **Location:** Bioko Isl. off W Africa coast in Gulf of Guinea. Rio Muni, mainland enclave, has Gabon on S, Cameroon on E and N. **Topography:** Bioko Isl. consists of 2 volcanic mountains and connecting valley. Rio Muni, with over 90% of area, has coastal plain and low hills. **Arable land:** 4.3%. **Capital:** Malabo, 296,770. New administrative capital of Oyala has been in development. **Cities:** Bata, 415,270.

Government: Type: Presidential republic. **Head of state:** Pres. Teodoro Obiang Nguema Mbasogo; b. 1942; in office: Aug. 3, 1979. **Head of govt.:** Prime Min. Francisco Pascual Eyegue Obama Asue; in office: June 23, 2016. **Local divisions:** 7 provinces. **Defense budget:** NA. **Active troops:** 1,450.

Economy: Industries: petroleum, nat. gas, sawmilling. **Chief agric.:** coffee, cocoa, rice, yams, cassava, bananas, palm oil nuts. **Natural resources:** petroleum, nat. gas, timber, gold, bauxite, diamonds, tantalum, sand and gravel, clay. **Water:** 20,505 cu m per capita. **Crude oil reserves:** 1.1 bil bbls. **Electricity prod.:** 1.7 bil kWH. **Labor force:** agric. 42.5%, industry 18.5%, services 38.9%. **Unemployment:** 6.5%.

Finance: Monetary unit: Central African CFA Franc (XAF) (553.52 = $1 U.S.). **GDP:** $26.2 bil; **per capita GDP:** $19,327; **GDP growth:** –5.6%. **Imports:** $2.6 bil; Spain 20.5%, China 19.4%, U.S. 13%, Côte d'Ivoire 6.2%. **Exports:** $6.1 bil; China 28%, India 11.8%, South Korea 10.3%, Portugal 8.7%, U.S. 6.9%. **Budget:** $2.5 bil. **Inflation:** 1.2%.

Transport: Airports: 6.

Communications: Telephone: 0.8 per 100 pop. **Mobile:** 45.2 per 100 pop. **Broadband:** 1.3 per 100 pop. **Internet:** 26.2%.

Health: Expend.: 3.1%. **Life expect.:** 64.4 male; 66.9 female. **Births:** 30.7 per 1,000 pop. **Deaths:** 7.3 per 1,000 pop. **Infant mortality:** 59.7 per 1,000 live births. **Undernourished:** NA. **HIV:** 7.2%.

Education: Compulsory: ages 7-12. **Literacy:** 95.3%.

Embassy: 2020 16th St. NW 20009; 518-5700.

Website: www.guineaecuatorialpress.com

Fernando Po (now Bioko) Island was reached by Portugal in the late 15th cent. and ceded to Spain in 1778. Independence came Oct. 12, 1968. Anti-Spanish riots erupted in 1969 in Rio Muni province on the mainland.

Masie Nguema Biyogo, a mainlander, became president for life in 1972. His reign, among the most brutal in Africa, left the nation bankrupt; most of the nation's 7,000 Europeans emigrated. He was ousted in a military coup, Aug. 1979. Teodoro Obiang Nguema Mbasogo, leader of the coup, became president. Presidential elections in 1996, 2002, 2009, and 2016 were seriously flawed.

The economy is dependent on oil exports. As a result of government misuse and embezzlement of oil revenue, poverty remains widespread.

Human Rights Watch reported in 2012 that the regime "tortures and arbitrarily detains" dissidents. The seat of government was officially moved, Feb. 2017, from Malabo (on Bioko) to a new capital, Oyala (officially, Ciudad de la Paz), constructed on the mainland.

The 2020 COVID-19 pandemic caused about 5,000 cases and over 80 deaths in Equatorial Guinea by Sept. 30.

Eritrea
State of Eritrea

People: Population: 6,081,196 (111). **Age distrib.:** <15: 38.2%; 65+: 4.0%. **Growth:** 0.9%. **Migrants:** 0.5%. **Pop. density:** 155.9 per sq mi, 60.2 per sq km. **Urban:** 41.3%. **Ethnic groups:** Tigrinya 55%, Tigre 30%, Saho 4%, Kunama 2%, Rashaida 2%, bilen 2%, other (Afar, Beni Amir, Nera) 5%. **Languages:** Tigrinya, Arabic, English (all official); Tigre; Kunama; Afar. **Religions:** Muslim 51.4% (Sunni 50%, Shia 1%), Christian 47% (Orthodox 42.4%).

Geography: Total area: 45,406 sq mi, 117,600 sq km (99); **Land area:** 38,996 sq mi, 101,000 sq km. **Location:** E Africa, on SW coast of Red Sea. Sudan on W, Ethiopia on S, Djibouti on SE. **Topography:** Includes many islands of the Dahlak Archipelago. Low coastal plains in S, mountain range with peaks to 9,000 ft in N. **Arable land:** 6.8%. **Capital:** Asmara, 962,985.

Government: Type: Presidential republic. **Head of state and govt.:** Pres. Isaias Afworki; b. 1946; in office: June 8, 1993. **Local divisions:** 6 regions. **Defense budget:** NA. **Active troops:** 201,750.

Economy: Industries: food proc., beverages, clothing and textiles, light mfg., salt, cement. **Chief agric.:** sorghum, lentils, vegetables, corn, cotton, tobacco, sisal; goats; fish. **Natural resources:** gold, potash, zinc, copper, salt, fish. **Water:** 1,443 cu m per capita. **Electricity prod.:** 403 mil kWH. **Labor force:** agric. 60.8%, industry 8.5%, services 30.7%. **Unemployment:** 5.2%.

Finance: Monetary unit: Nakfa (ERN) (15.00 = $1 U.S.). **GDP:** NA; **per capita GDP:** NA; **GDP growth:** NA. **Imports:** $1.1 bil; UAE 14.5%, China 13.2%, Saudi Arabia 13.2%, Italy 12.9%, Turkey 5.6%. **Exports:** $624.3 mil; China 62%, South Korea 28.3%. **Budget:** $2.6 bil. **Inflation** (2016-17): 9%.

Transport: Railways: 190 mi. **Airports:** 4.

Communications: Telephone (2017): 1.9 per 100 pop. **Mobile** (2017): 20.4 per 100 pop. **Broadband:** NA. **Internet:** 1.3%.

Health: Expend.: 2.9%. **Life expect.:** 63.6 male; 68.8 female. **Births:** 27.9 per 1,000 pop. **Deaths:** 6.9 per 1,000 pop. **Infant mortality:** 43.3 per 1,000 live births. **Undernourished:** NA. **HIV:** 0.6%.

Education: Compulsory: ages 6-13. **Literacy:** 93.3%.

Embassy: 1708 New Hampshire Ave. NW 20009; 319-1991.

Website: www.shabait.com

Eritrea was part of the Ethiopian kingdom of Aksum. It was an Italian colony from 1890 to 1941, when it was captured by the British. Following a period of British and UN supervision, Eritrea was awarded to Ethiopia as part of a federation in 1952. Ethiopia annexed Eritrea as a province in 1962. After a 31-year struggle, Eritrea formally declared its independence May 24, 1993. A constitution was ratified in 1997 but not implemented.

A border war with Ethiopia erupted in June 1998. Although a peace treaty was signed Dec. 12, 2000, border disputes and tensions continued. Agreements signed July 9, 2018, ended the "state of war between Ethiopia and Eritrea" and restored diplomatic relations as well as communications, transportation, and commercial links.

Many thousands have fled repressive conditions and forced labor in Eritrea. A UN report, issued June 8, 2016, concluded that the government was committing widespread human rights violations. Tens of thousands of Eritreans were among migrants reaching or trying to reach Europe, 2014-18. Thousands migrated to Ethiopia after the border reopened in 2018.

Asmara, known for its early-20th-cent. Italian architecture, was named a UNESCO World Heritage Site, July 8, 2017.

UN sanctions against Eritrea, imposed in 2009 over alleged support of Islamic extremists, were lifted, Nov. 14, 2018.

Estonia
Republic of Estonia

People: Population: 1,228,624 (154). **Age distrib.:** <15: 16.2%; 65+: 21.0%. **Growth:** –0.7%. **Migrants:** 14.4%. **Pop. density:** 75.1 per sq mi, 29.0 per sq km. **Urban:** 69.2%. **Ethnic groups:** Estonian 68.7%, Russian 24.8%. **Languages:** Estonian (official), Russian. **Religions:** agnostic 59.2%, Christian 36.1% (Protestant 18.6%, Orthodox 15.6%), atheist 4.1%.

Geography: Total area: 17,463 sq mi, 45,228 sq km (129); **Land area:** 16,366 sq mi, 42,388 sq km. **Location:** Eastern Europe, bordering Baltic Sea and Gulf of Finland. Russia on E, Latvia on S. **Topography:** Marshy lowland with numerous lakes and swamps. Elongated hills show evidence of former glaciation. More than 800 islands on Baltic coast. **Arable land:** 15.7%. **Capital:** Tallinn, 445,259.

Government: Type: Parliamentary republic. **Head of state:** Pres. Kersti Kaljulaid; b. 1969; in office: Oct. 10, 2016. **Head of govt.:** Prime Min. Juri Ratas; b. 1978; in office: Nov. 23, 2016. **Local divisions:** 15 urban municipalities, 64 rural municipalities. **Defense budget:** $691 mil. **Active troops:** 6,700.

Economy: Industries: food, engineering, electronics, wood/wood prods., textiles, information tech., telecom. **Chief agric.:** grain, potatoes, vegetables; livestock, dairy prods.; fish. **Natural**

resources: oil shale, peat, rare earth elements, phosphorite, clay, limestone, sand, dolomite, sea mud. **Water:** 9,779 cu m per capita. **Electricity prod.** (2018): 11.5 bil kWh. **Labor force:** agric. 3.1%, industry 29.4%, services 67.6%. **Unemployment:** 5.4%.

Finance: Monetary unit: Euro (EUR) (0.84 = $1 U.S.). **GDP:** $51.5 bil; **per capita GDP:** $38,811; **GDP growth:** 4.3%. **Imports:** $14.4 bil; Finland 14%, Germany 10.7%, Lithuania 8.9%, Sweden 8.5%, Latvia 8.2%, Poland 7.2%, Russia 6.7%, Netherlands 5.9%. **Exports:** $13.4 bil; Finland 16.2%, Sweden 13.5%, Latvia 9.2%, Russia 7.3%, Germany 6.9%, Lithuania 5.9%. **Tourism:** $1.7 bil. **Budget:** $10.4 bil. **Inflation:** 2.3%.

Transport: Railways: 1,333 mi. **Airports:** 13.

Communications: Telephone: 26.1 per 100 pop. **Mobile:** 145.4 per 100 pop. **Broadband:** 133.4 per 100 pop. **Internet** (2018): 89.4%.

Health: Expend.: 6.4%. **Life expect.:** 72.7 male; 82.3 female. **Births:** 9.3 per 1,000 pop. **Deaths:** 12.9 per 1,000 pop. **Infant mortality:** 3.7 per 1,000 live births. **Undernourished:** <2.5%. **HIV** (2018): 0.9%.

Education: Compulsory: ages 7-15. **Literacy:** 99.8%.

Embassy: 2131 Massachusetts Ave. NW 20008; 588-0101.

Website: www.eesti.ee

Estonia, a province of imperial Russia before World War I, was independent between World Wars I and II. The USSR conquered it in 1940 and incorporated it as the Estonian SSR. Estonia, Aug. 20, 1991, declared independence, which the Soviet Union recognized Sept. 1991. The first free elections in over 50 years were held Sept. 20, 1992. The last occupying Russian troops departed Aug. 31, 1994.

Estonia became a full member of the EU and NATO, 2004, and adopted the euro, 2011. NATO leaders, July 2016, agreed to station troops in Estonia to deter Russian aggression. Parliament elected Kersti Kaljulaid, Oct. 3, 2016, to be Estonia's first woman president. After Reform Party Prime Min. Taavi Rõivas lost a no-confidence vote, Nov. 9, 2016, he was replaced, Nov. 23, by the Center Party's Juri Ratas. The Center Party finished second, after Reform, in Mar. 3, 2019, elections, but Ratas formed a coalition government, Apr. 29, with a conservative and a far-right party.

The 2020 COVID-19 pandemic caused 3,315 cases and 64 deaths in Estonia by Sept. 30.

Eswatini
Kingdom of eSwatini

(King Mswati III announced, Apr. 19, 2018, that he was changing the country's name from Swaziland to "eSwatini" to celebrate the 50th anniversary of its independence.)

People: Population: 1,104,479 (156). **Age distrib.:** <15: 33.6%; 65+: 3.8%. **Growth:** 0.8%. **Migrants:** 2.8%. **Pop. density:** 166.3 per sq mi, 64.2 per sq km. **Urban:** 24.2%. **Ethnic groups:** African 97%, European 3%. **Languages:** English (used in govt.), siSwati (both official). **Religions:** Christian 89.6% (independent 65.4%, Protestant 18.2%), ethnic religionist 8.2%.

Geography: Total area: 6,704 sq mi, 17,364 sq km (154). **Land area:** 6,643 sq mi, 17,204 sq km. **Location:** Southern Africa, near Indian O. coast. South Africa on N, W, S; Mozambique on E. **Topography:** Descends W-E in broad belts, becoming more arid in low veld region, then rising to plateau in E. **Arable land:** 10.2%. **Capital:** Mbabane (admin.), 68,001; Lobamba (legis./royal).

Government: Type: Absolute monarchy. **Head of state:** King Mswati III; b. 1968; in office: Apr. 25, 1986. **Head of govt.:** Prime Min. Ambrose Mandvulo Dlamini; b. 1968; in office: Oct. 27, 2018. **Local divisions:** 4 regions. **Defense budget/active troops:** NA.

Economy: Industries: soft drink concentrates, coal, forestry, sugar proc., textiles, apparel. **Chief agric.:** sugarcane, corn, cotton, citrus, pineapples, cattle, goats. **Natural resources:** asbestos, coal, clay, cassiterite, hydropower, forests, small gold and diamond deposits, quarry stone, talc. **Water:** 3,299 cu m per capita. **Electricity prod.:** 569 mil kWh. **Labor force:** agric. 12.3%, industry 23.5%, services 64.2%. **Unemployment:** 22.0%.

Finance: Monetary unit: Lilangeni (SZL) (16.57 = $1 U.S.). **GDP:** $10.4 bil; **per capita GDP:** $9,048; **GDP growth:** 2.0%. **Imports:** $1.5 bil; South Africa 81.6%, China 5.2%. **Exports:** $1.8 bil; South Africa 94%. **Tourism:** $14 mil. **Budget:** $1.6 bil. **Inflation:** 2.6%.

Transport: Railways: 187 mi. **Airports:** 2.

Communications: Telephone (2017): 3.6 per 100 pop. **Mobile** (2017): 93.5 per 100 pop. **Broadband:** 13.1 per 100 pop. **Internet:** 47%.

Health: Expend.: 6.9%. **Life expect.:** 56.5 male; 60.7 female. **Births:** 24.5 per 1,000 pop. **Deaths:** 10.1 per 1,000 pop. **Infant mortality:** 42.8 per 1,000 live births. **Undernourished:** 16.9%. **HIV:** 27.0%.

Education: Compulsory: ages 6-12. **Literacy:** 95.5%.

Embassy: 1712 New Hampshire Ave. NW 20009; 234-5002.

Website: www.gov.sz

The royal house of Eswatini traces back 400 years. The Zulus drove the Swazis, a Bantu people, from lands to the N, 1820. Britain and Transvaal (later part of South Africa) later guaranteed their autonomy, and Britain assumed control after 1903. Independence came Sept. 6, 1968. In 1973, the king repealed the constitution and assumed full powers.

A new constitution banning political parties took effect Oct. 13, 1978. Under a revised constitution effective Feb. 8, 2006, non-partisan parliamentary elections were permitted. An attempt failed in 2012 to unite pro-democracy groups under the People's United Democratic Movement (PUDEMO), which had been outlawed as a terrorist group in 2008.

In recent decades, Eswatini has suffered from an AIDS epidemic. AIDS-related deaths fell sharply due to antiretroviral therapy, but as of 2018, 27.3% of people ages 15-49 were HIV positive, still the highest rate in the world. The 2020 COVID-19 pandemic caused almost 5,500 cases and over 100 deaths by Sept. 30.

Ethiopia
Federal Democratic Republic of Ethiopia

People: Population: 108,113,150 (13). **Age distrib.:** <15: 39.8%; 65+: 3.4%. **Growth:** 2.6%. **Migrants:** 1.1%. **Pop. density:** 255.4 per sq mi, 98.6 per sq km. **Urban:** 21.7%. **Ethnic groups:** Oromo 34.9%, Amhara (Amara) 27.9%, Tigray (Tigrinya) 7.3%, Sidama 4.1%, Welaita 3%, Gurage 2.8%, Somali (Somalie) 2.7%, Hadiya 2.2%, Afar (Affar).6%, other 12.6%. **Languages:** Oromo (official in one state); Amharic (official nationally); Somali, Tigrigna (both official in one state each); Sidamo; Wolaytta; Gurage. **Religions:** Christian 60% (Orthodox 40.5%, Protestant 16.4%), Muslim 34.4% (Sunni), ethnic religionist 5.5%.

Geography: Total area: 426,373 sq mi, 1,104,300 sq km (26). **Land area:** 423,388 sq mi, 1,096,570 sq km. **Location:** E Africa. Sudan, South Sudan on W; Kenya on S; Somalia, Djibouti on E; Eritrea on N. **Topography:** A central plateau, 6,000-10,000 ft high, rises to mountains near the Great Rift Valley, cutting in from SW. Blue Nile and other rivers cross the plateau, which descends to plains on W and SE. **Arable land:** 16.0%. **Capital:** Addis Ababa, 4,793,699.

Government: Type: Federal parliamentary republic. **Head of state:** Pres. Sahle-Work Zewde; b. 1950; in office: Oct. 25, 2018. **Head of govt.:** Prime Min. Abiy Ahmed; b. 1976; in office: Apr. 2, 2018. **Local divisions:** 9 states (ethnically based), 2 self-governing administrations. **Defense budget:** $518 mil. **Active troops:** 138,000.

Economy: Industries: food proc., beverages, textiles, leather, garments, chemicals, metals proc., cement. **Chief agric.:** cereals, coffee, oilseed, cotton, sugarcane, vegetables, khat, cut flowers; hides, cattle, sheep, goats; fish. **Natural resources:** gold, platinum, copper, potash, nat. gas, hydropower. **Water:** 1,162 cu m per capita. **Crude oil reserves:** 428,000 bbls. **Electricity prod.:** 13.7 bil kWh. **Labor force:** agric. 65.6%, industry 10.4%, services 24.0%. **Unemployment:** 2.1%.

Finance: Monetary unit: Birr (ETB) (36.30 = $1 U.S.). **GDP:** $259.1 bil; **per capita GDP:** $2,312; **GDP growth:** 8.3%. **Imports:** $15.6 bil; China 24.1%, Saudi Arabia 10.1%, India 6.4%, Kuwait 5.3%, France 5.2%. **Exports:** $3.2 bil; Sudan 23.3%, Switzerland 10.2%, China 8.1%, Somalia 6.6%, Netherlands 6.2%. **Tourism:** $773 mil. **Budget:** $13.8 bil. **Inflation** (2016-17): 9.8%.

Transport: Railways: 409 mi (Ethiopian segment of Addis Ababa-Djibouti railroad). **Motor vehicles:** 1.7 per 1,000 pop. **Airports:** 17.

Communications: Telephone (2017): 1.1 per 100 pop. **Mobile** (2017): 37.2 per 100 pop. **Broadband:** 7.1 per 100 pop. **Internet:** 18.6%.

Health: Expend.: 3.5%. **Life expect.:** 65.5 male; 69.7 female. **Births:** 31.6 per 1,000 pop. **Deaths:** 5.9 per 1,000 pop. **Infant mortality:** 35.8 per 1,000 live births. **Undernourished:** 19.7%. **HIV:** 0.9%.

Education: Compulsory: ages 7-14. **Literacy:** 72.8%.

Embassy: 3506 International Dr. NW 20008; 364-1200.

Website: www.ethiopia.gov.et

Ethiopian culture was influenced by Egypt and Greece. Italy invaded the region in 1880, but Ethiopia maintained its independence until the Italian invasion of 1936. British forces freed the country in 1941.

A series of droughts in the 1970s killed hundreds of thousands. An army mutiny, strikes, and student demonstrations led to the 1974 dethronement of Ethiopia's Emperor, Haile Selassie I, ending his 58-year reign; he died a prisoner of the ruling junta, known as the Dergue, 1975. The junta dissolved parliament, abolished the monarchy, established a socialist state, redistributed land, curbed the influence of the Coptic Church, and violently suppressed opposition.

The regime, torn by bloody coups, faced uprisings by tribal and political groups aided in part by Sudan and Somalia. In 1978, Soviet advisers and Cuban troops helped defeat Somali forces. Ethiopia and Somalia signed a peace agreement in 1988. A worldwide relief effort began in 1984, as an extended drought precipitated famine; up to 1 mil people died.

The Ethiopian People's Revolutionary Democratic Front (EPRDF), an umbrella organization of rebel groups, launched a major push against government forces in 1991, prompting Pres. Mengistu Haile Mariam's resignation. The EPRDF set up a transitional government. It won five parliamentary elections, 1995-2015.

Eritrea, a province on the Red Sea, declared its independence May 24, 1993. Fighting along the border with Eritrea, which erupted in 1998, intensified in May 2000. Although a peace treaty was signed Dec. 12, 2000, tensions and border conflicts persisted until a July 9, 2018, accord.

Ethiopian troops joined an African Union peacekeeping force in Somalia in Jan. 2014. About 200,000 refugees from Somalia were in Ethiopia as of Aug. 31, 2020.

Violent protests by members of the Oromo ethnic group claimed hundreds of lives in 2016. Successive droughts caused severe food shortages in 2015-17, affecting about 18 mil people. Amid continuing ethnic violence in eastern Ethiopia and anti-government protests, Prime Min. Hailemariam Desalegn resigned, Feb. 15, 2018. New Prime Min. Abiy Ahmed, the country's first Oromo leader, pledged economic reforms, reduced censorship, freed political prisoners, and allowed political exiles to return. For his domestic policies and 2018 peace accord with Eritrea, Abiy was awarded the Nobel Peace Prize, Oct. 11, 2019.

Elected by parliament, Oct. 25, 2018, Sahle-Work Zewde became Ethiopia's first female president.

Ethnic and political violence, as well as drought and food shortages, continued in 2019-20. More than 1.7 mil Ethiopians were internally displaced in 2020. Hundreds died in violent protests following the late June 2020 murder of popular Oromo singer and activist Hachalu Hundessa.

Ethiopia began construction, Apr. 2, 2011, of Africa's largest dam, the Grand Renaissance Dam across the Blue Nile. The dam raised concerns in Sudan and, especially, in Egypt over loss of water resources. Filling the reservoir behind the dam began in mid-2020.

An Ethiopian Airlines flight crashed near Addis Ababa, Mar. 10, 2019, killing all 157 on board; the crash was apparently related to a malfunctioning system in the Boeing 737 Max 8 aircraft.

Scheduled Aug. 2020 legislative elections were postponed due to the COVID-19 pandemic. As of Sept. 30, Ethiopia had about 74,500 COVID-19 cases and almost 1,200 deaths.

Fiji
Republic of Fiji

People: Population: 935,974 (157). **Age distrib.:** <15: 26.9%; 65+: 7.3%. **Growth:** 0.5%. **Migrants:** 1.6%. **Pop. density:** 132.7 per sq mi, 51.2 per sq km. **Urban:** 57.2%. **Ethnic groups:** iTaukei (predom. Melanesian with Polynesian admixture; name for original, native settlers of Fiji) 56.8%, Indian 37.5%, other (European, part European, other Pac. Islanders, Chinese) 4.5%. **Languages:** English, Fijian (both official); Hindustani. **Religions:** Christian 64.8% (Protestant 41.8%, Catholic 11.6%, independent 11.3%), Hindu 26.9%, Muslim 6.1% (Sunni).

Geography: Total area: 7,056 sq mi, 18,274 sq km (152); **Land area:** 7,056 sq mi, 18,274 sq km. Viti Levu, largest island of group, has over half the total land area. **Location:** Western S Pacific O. Nearest neighbors are Vanuatu to W, Tonga to E. **Topography:** 322 isls. (about 110 inhabited), many mountainous, with tropical forests and large fertile areas. **Arable land:** 9.0%. **Capital:** Suva, 178,339.

Government: Type: Parliamentary republic. **Head of state:** Pres. Jioji "George" Konrote; b. 1947; in office: Nov. 12, 2015. **Head of govt.:** Prime Min. Voreqe "Frank" Bainimarama; b. 1954; in office: Sept. 22, 2014 (acting from Jan. 5, 2007). **Local divisions:** 14 provinces, 1 dependency. **Defense budget:** $56 mil. **Active troops:** 4,040.

Economy: Industries: tourism, sugar proc., clothing, copra. **Chief agric.:** sugarcane, coconuts, cassava, rice, sweet potatoes, bananas; cattle, pigs, horses; fish. **Natural resources:** timber, fish, gold, copper, hydropower. **Water:** 31,530 cu m per capita. **Electricity prod.:** 1.0 bil kWh. **Labor force:** agric. 35.7%, industry 13.3%, services 51.0%. **Unemployment:** 4.1%.

Finance: Monetary unit: Dollar (FJD) (2.12 = $1 U.S.) **GDP:** $12.8 bil; **per capita GDP:** $14,428; **GDP growth:** 1.1%. **Imports:** $1.9 bil; Australia 19.2%, New Zealand 17.2%, Singapore 17%, China 13.8%. **Exports:** $908.2 mil; U.S. 20.8%, Australia 14.9%, New Zealand 7.7%, Tonga 5%. **Tourism:** $963 mil. **Budget:** $1.6 bil. **Inflation:** 1.8%.

Transport: Railways: 371 mi. **Motor vehicles:** 128.9 per 1,000 pop. **Airports:** 4.

Communications: Telephone: 8.7 per 100 pop. **Mobile** (2017): 117.8 per 100 pop. **Broadband:** 55.7 per 100 pop. **Internet:** 50%.

Health: Expend.: 3.5%. **Life expect.:** 71.0 male; 76.6 female. **Births:** 17.4 per 1,000 pop. **Deaths:** 6.3 per 1,000 pop. **Infant mortality:** 8.8 per 1,000 live births. **Undernourished:** 3.9%. **HIV:** 0.2%.

Education: Compulsory: NA. **Literacy:** 99.7%.

Embassy: 1707 L St. NW, Ste. 200, 20036; 466-8320.

Website: www.fiji.gov.fj

A British colony since 1874, Fiji became independent Oct. 10, 1970. Cultural differences between Indo-Fijians (mostly descendants of contract laborers brought to the islands from India in the 19th cent.) and Indigenous Fijians have led to political tensions. More than 100,000 people of Indian descent left Fiji after a 1987 coup deposed an Indian-Fijian-majority government.

The country's first Indo-Fijian prime minister, Mahendra Chaudhry, and other government officials were taken captive May 19, 2000, by Indigenous Fijian gunmen led by George Speight, culminating in a military takeover, May 29, led by Frank Bainimarama. Release of the last remaining hostages in July 2000 coincided with the installation of an interim military-backed government. Speight was convicted of treason and sentenced to life in prison in 2002. Prime Min. Laisenia Qarase headed an elected civilian government, 2001-06,

but was ousted in a military coup Dec. 5, 2006. Bainimarama took office as interim prime min. After a court ruled in 2009 that the 2006 coup was illegal, Fiji's president abrogated the constitution, dissolved the judiciary, and reappointed Bainimarama. He accepted a new draft constitution released Mar. 22, 2013, and he retained office in democratic elections Sept. 17, 2014. The Commonwealth, Sept. 26, 2014, reinstated Fiji's membership, suspended since the 2006 coup; U.S. sanctions were lifted Oct. 2014. A Dec. 2016 Amnesty Intl. report said physical and sexual abuse of detainees by Fiji's police and military was widespread. Bainimarama's party narrowly won Nov. 18, 2018, elections.

Finland
Republic of Finland

People: Population: 5,571,665 (115). **Age distrib.:** <15: 16.4%; 65+: 22.3%. **Growth:** 0.3%. **Migrants:** 6.9%. **Pop. density:** 47.5 per sq mi, 18.3 per sq km. **Urban:** 85.5%. **Ethnic groups:** Finn, Swede, Russian, Estonian, Romani, Sami. **Languages:** Finnish, Swedish (both official). **Religions:** Christian (official) 76.8% (Protestant 74.5%), agnostic 17.6%, Muslim 3.3% (Sunni), atheist 2%.

Geography: Total area: 130,559 sq mi, 338,145 sq km (64); **Land area:** 117,304 sq mi, 303,815 sq km. **Location:** Northern Europe. Norway on N, Sweden on W, Russia on E. **Topography:** Flat with low hills and many lakes in S and center. The N has mountainous areas 3,000-4,000 ft above sea level. **Arable land:** 7.4%. **Capital:** Helsinki, 1,304,851.

Government: Type: Parliamentary republic. **Head of state:** Pres. Sauli Niinistö; b. 1948; in office: Mar. 1, 2012. **Head of govt.:** Prime Min. Sanna Marin; b. 1985; in office: Dec. 10, 2019. **Local divisions:** 19 regions. **Defense budget:** $4 bil. **Active troops:** 21,500.

Economy: Industries: metals and metal prods., electronics, machinery and scientific instruments, shipbuilding, pulp and paper, foodstuffs, chemicals, textiles, clothing. **Chief agric.:** barley, wheat, sugar beets, potatoes; dairy cattle; fish. **Natural resources:** timber, iron ore, copper, lead, zinc, chromite, nickel, gold, silver, limestone. **Water:** 19,917 cu m per capita. **Electricity prod.** (2018): 67.1 bil kWh. **Labor force:** agric. 3.5%, industry 22.0%, services 74.5%. **Unemployment:** 6.7%.

Finance: Monetary unit: Euro (EUR) (0.84 = $1 U.S.). **GDP:** $283.3 bil; **per capita GDP:** $51,324; **GDP growth:** 1.0%. **Imports:** $65.3 bil; Germany 17.7%, Sweden 15.8%, Russia 13.1%, Netherlands 8.7%. **Exports:** $67.7 bil; Germany 14.2%, Sweden 10.1%, U.S. 7%, Netherlands 6.8%, China 5.7%, Russia 5.7%. **Tourism:** $3.7 bil. **Budget:** $135.6 bil (central govt.). **Inflation:** 1.0%.

Transport: Railways: 3,682 mi. **Motor vehicles:** 565.4 per 1,000 pop. **Airports:** 74.

Communications: Telephone: 5.8 per 100 pop. **Mobile:** 132.2 per 100 pop. **Broadband:** 153.8 per 100 pop. **Internet** (2018): 88.9%.

Health: Expend.: 9.2%. **Life expect.:** 78.4 male; 84.4 female. **Births:** 10.6 per 1,000 pop. **Deaths:** 10.3 per 1,000 pop. **Infant mortality:** 2.5 per 1,000 live births. **Undernourished:** <2.5%. **HIV** (2018): 0.1%.

Education: Compulsory: ages 6-15. **Literacy:** 100%.

Embassy: 3301 Massachusetts Ave. NW 20008; 298-5800.

Website: valtioneuvosto.fi

Early Finns may have migrated from the Ural region and other areas about 6,000 years ago. Swedish settlers brought the country into Sweden, 1154 to 1809, when Finland became an autonomous grand duchy of the Russian Empire. On Dec. 6, 1917, Finland declared its independence, and in 1919 it became a republic. On Nov. 30, 1939, the Soviet Union invaded, and Finland was forced to cede 16,173 sq mi of territory. After World War II, further cessions were exacted.

Finland entered the EU Jan. 1, 1995. More than 32,000 migrants applied for asylum in Finland in 2015. The government announced, Jan. 28, 2016, it would deport rejected applicants, and Finland concluded agreements with Russia, Mar. 2016, to reduce border crossings. During 2016, 65% of asylum applications were rejected. A rejected applicant from Morocco, who claimed to be inspired by ISIS, fatally stabbed two and wounded eight in Turku, Aug. 18, 2017.

The Social Democratic Party (SDP) narrowly won Apr. 14, 2019, parliamentary elections; party leader Antti Rinne formed a coalition government, with women holding a majority of cabinet posts. The SDP's Sanna Marin became prime minister, Dec. 10, after Rinne resigned over his handling of a labor dispute. At age 34, she was the world's youngest prime minister when sworn in.

The 2020 COVID-19 pandemic caused about 9,900 cases and 345 deaths in Finland by Sept. 30.

Aland, or Ahvenanmaa, an autonomous, Swedish-speaking province, is a group of small islands, 590 sq mi, in the Gulf of Bothnia, 25 mi from Sweden, 15 mi from Finland. Mariehamn is the chief port and seat of government. **Website:** www.aland.ax

France
French Republic

People: Population: 67,848,156 (21). **Age distrib.:** <15: 18.4%; 65+: 20.5%. **Growth:** 0.3%. **Migrants:** 12.8%. **Pop. density:** 274.4 per sq mi, 105.9 per sq km. **Urban:** 81.0%. **Ethnic groups:** Celtic and Latin with Teutonic, Slavic, North African, Indochinese,

Basque minorities. **Languages:** French (official), declining regional dialects and langs. (Provençal, Breton, Alsatian, Corsican, Catalan, Basque, Flemish). **Religions:** Christian 62.8% (Catholic 58.8%), agnostic 20.9%, Muslim 9.6% (Sunni), atheist 4.4%.

Geography: Total area: 248,573 sq mi, 643,801 sq km (incl. overseas departments) (42); **Land area:** 247,270 sq mi, 640,427 sq km (incl. overseas departments). **Location:** Western Europe, between Atlantic O. and Medit. Sea. Spain, Andorra, Monaco on S; Italy, Switzerland, Germany on E; Luxembourg, Belgium on N. **Topography:** A wide plain covers more than half of the country, in N and W, drained to W by Seine, Loire, Garonne Rivers. The Alps (Mt. Blanc is tallest in W Europe at 15,781 ft), the lower Jura range, and forested Vosges are in E. The Rhone flows from Lake Geneva to Mediterranean. Pyrenees are on SW border. **Arable land:** 33.7%.
Capital: Paris, 11,017,230. **Cities:** Lyon, 1,719,268; Marseille-Aixen-Provence, 1,608,236; Lille, 1,063,085; Toulouse, 1,024,167.

Government: Type: Semi-presidential republic. **Head of state:** Pres. Emmanuel Macron; b. 1977; in office: May 14, 2017. **Head of govt.:** Prime Min. Jean Castex; b. 1965; in office: July 3, 2020. **Local divisions:** 13 metropolitan regions, 5 overseas regions. **Defense budget:** $52.3 bil. **Active troops:** 203,750.

Economy: Industries: machinery, chemicals, automobiles, metallurgy, aircraft, electronics, textiles, food proc., tourism. **Chief agric.:** wheat, cereals, sugar beets, potatoes, wine grapes; beef, dairy prods.; fish. **Natural resources:** coal, iron ore, bauxite, zinc, uranium, antimony, arsenic, potash, feldspar, fluorspar, gypsum, timber, fish. **Water:** 3,247 cu m per capita. **Crude oil reserves:** 56 mil bbls. **Electricity prod.** (2018): 549.8 bil kwH. **Labor force:** agric. 2.4%, industry 19.9%, services 77.7%. **Unemployment:** 8.3%.
Finance: Monetary unit: Euro (EUR) (0.84 = $1 U.S.). **GDP:** $3,315.1 bil; **per capita GDP:** $49,435; **GDP growth:** 1.5%. **Imports:** $601.7 bil; Germany 18.5%, Belgium 10.2%, Netherlands 8.3%, Italy 7.9%, Spain 7.1%, UK 5.3%, U.S. 5.2%, China 5.1%. **Exports:** $549.9 bil; Germany 14.8%, Spain 7.7%, Italy 7.5%, U.S. 7.2%, Belgium 7%, UK 6.7%. **Tourism:** $63.8 bil. **Budget:** $1.5 tril. **Inflation:** 1.1%.
Transport: Railways: 18,417 mi. **Motor vehicles:** 594.5 per 1,000 pop. **Airports:** 294.
Communications: Telephone: 59.4 per 100 pop. **Mobile:** 108.4 per 100 pop. **Broadband:** 87.5 per 100 pop. **Internet** (2018): 82%.
Health: Expend.: 11.3%. **Life expect.:** 79.1 male; 85.4 female. **Births:** 11.9 per 1,000 pop. **Deaths:** 9.6 per 1,000 pop. **Infant mortality:** 3.2 per 1,000 live births. **Undernourished:** <2.5%. **HIV:** 0.3%.
Education: Compulsory: ages 6-15. **Literacy:** 99%.
Embassy: 4101 Reservoir Rd. NW 20007; 944-6000.
Website: www.gouvernement.fr

Julius Caesar conquered Celtic Gaul 58-51 BCE; Romans ruled for 500 years. Under Charlemagne, Frankish rule extended over much of Europe. After his death (in 814), France emerged as one of the successor kingdoms.

The monarchy was overthrown in the French Revolution (1789-93) and succeeded by the First Republic, followed by the First Empire under Napoleon I (1804-15), a monarchy (1814-48), the Second Republic (1848-52), the Second Empire (1852-70), the Third Republic (1871-1946), the Fourth Republic (1946-58), and the Fifth Republic (1958-present).

France suffered severe losses in people and wealth in WWI (1914-18) when it was invaded by Germany. By the Treaty of Versailles, 1919, France exacted return of Alsace and Lorraine, provinces seized by Germany in 1871 after it defeated France in the Franco-Prussian War. During WWII (1939-45), Germany invaded France in May 1940 and signed an armistice with a government based in Vichy. After the Allies liberated France in 1944, Gen. Charles de Gaulle became head of the provisional government, serving until 1946. De Gaulle again became premier in 1958, during a crisis over Algeria, and obtained voter approval for a new constitution, ushering in the Fifth Republic. He then became president.

France withdrew from Indochina in 1954 and from Morocco and Tunisia in 1956. Most of its remaining African territories, including Algeria, were freed 1958-62.

In May 1968, students in Paris and other centers rioted, battled police, and were joined by workers who launched nationwide strikes. De Gaulle resigned from office in Apr. 1969, after losing a nationwide referendum on constitutional reform. Georges Pompidou was elected to succeed him. After Pompidou's death, in 1974, Valery Giscard d'Estaing was elected president; he continued his predecessors' conservative policies.

In 1981, France elected Socialist François Mitterrand president. Under Mitterrand the government nationalized industries and banks. After 1986, however, when rightists won a narrow victory in the National Assembly, France pursued a privatization program, selling many state-owned companies. Mitterrand won a second 7-year term in 1988.

Conservative Jacques Chirac won the presidency in 1995 and was reelected in 2002. A summer 2003 heat wave caused an est. 15,000 deaths. Parliament gave final approval in 2004 to a law barring the wearing of Islamic head scarves and other religious symbols in public schools. A state of emergency was declared Nov. 8, 2005, after 12 days of riots that began in Paris and spread to some 300 French cities and towns; rioters were mainly young immigrants from N and W Africa.

The conservative Nicolas Sarkozy won the 2007 presidential run-off election. Sarkozy responded to the global recession, Dec. 2008,

with a $33-bil economic stimulus plan; following labor protests, aid for lower-income people was increased in 2009. With France's economy still struggling, the Socialist François Hollande won a presidential runoff over Sarkozy in 2012. Hollande, May 18, 2013, signed a bill that legalized same-sex marriage and allowed gay couples to adopt children. After forming a new party, *La République en Marche* (Onward!), in 2016, centrist Emmanuel Macron was elected president, May 7, 2017, defeating Marine Le Pen of the far-right National Front (renamed National Rally in 2018) in a runoff. Macron pledged reforms to improve GDP growth and reduce unemployment. His party won June 2017 parliamentary elections. On Sept. 22, Macron signed decrees (ratified by the National Assembly, Nov. 28) making it easier for many companies to hire, fire, and negotiate terms with workers. Months of "yellow vest" demonstrations—sometimes involving hundreds of thousands of protesters—began Nov. 17, 2018, triggered by a fuel-tax increase and expanding to express discontent with economic conditions. Government responses included rolling back the tax increase and raising the minimum wage.

France participated in military operations that ousted Libyan leader Muammar al-Qaddafi, Aug. 23, 2011. France took part in the U.S.-led campaign of airstrikes against the Sunni extremist group ISIS in Iraq (beginning 2014) and in Syria (beginning 2015). French troops entered the conflict between government forces in Mali and Islamist militants Jan. 11, 2013; they pushed the militants out of most seized territory. France maintained a counterterrorism force in the region, consisting of more than 5,000 troops in 2020.

On Jan. 7, 2015, two French gunmen of Algerian descent attacked the Paris offices of the magazine Charlie Hebdo, which had published satirical images of Muhammad. The gunmen, who claimed affiliation with al-Qaeda in the Arabian Peninsula, killed 12 people. A third gunman, who claimed loyalty to ISIS, fatally shot a police officer Jan. 8 and killed 4 people at a kosher supermarket Jan. 9. On Nov. 13, 2015, in coordinated attacks in and near Paris for which ISIS claimed responsibility, terrorists killed 130, many in Paris's Bataclan concert hall. In a July 14, 2016, attack ISIS claimed to have inspired, a Tunisian-born French resident drove a truck through a Bastille Day fireworks crowd in Nice, killing 86.

France ratified, Dec. 15, 2016, a global agreement to reduce greenhouse gas emissions negotiated at a UN climate conference in Paris, Dec. 2015. A fire, Apr. 15, 2019, heavily damaged Paris's Notre-Dame Cathedral, largely built in the 12th and 13th cents. June and July 2019 heat waves, including the highest temperature ever recorded in France (46°C, or 114.8°F, on June 28), caused about 1,500 deaths.

France was one of the European countries hardest hit by the 2020 COVID-19 pandemic. With cases rising sharply, the government ordered lockdown measures Mar. 16. The lockdown, eased beginning in May as new cases fell, and other impacts of the pandemic caused a steep decline in GDP (down almost 14% in Q2 2020). Cases rose sharply again in Aug. and Sept. By Sept. 30, France had more than 526,000 COVID-19 cases and almost 31,700 deaths.

The pandemic had a severe impact on the economically important tourism industry in mainland France, Corsica, and French islands in the Caribbean, the Pacific, and the Indian Ocean.

The island of **Corsica**, in the Mediterranean W of Italy and N of Sardinia, is a territorial collectivity and region of France comprising two departments. It elects 2 senators and 3 deputies to the French Parliament. Area 3,369 sq mi; pop. (2019 est.) 339,178. The capital is Ajaccio, birthplace of Napoleon I. Violence by Corsican separatist groups was common in the 1980s and 1990s. Corsicans rejected, 51%-49%, a limited autonomy plan in a referendum July 6, 2003.
Website: www.isula.corsica

French Overseas Departments

French Guiana is on the NE coast of South America with Suriname on the W and Brazil on the E and S. Its area is 35,135 sq mi (total), 34,421 sq mi (land); pop. (2020 est.) 290,691. Guiana sends 1 senator and 2 deputies to the French Parliament. Guiana is administered by a prefect and has a Council General of 16 elected members; capital is Cayenne, pop. (2020 est.) 61,645.

The famous penal colony, Devil's Island, was phased out between 1938 and 1951. The European Space Agency helps to maintain a satellite-launching center, established by France in 1964, in the city of Kourou.

Immense forests of rich timber cover much of the land. Fishing (especially shrimp), forestry, and gold mining are the most important industries. Natural resources include petroleum, kaolin, niobium, tantalum, and clay.

Guadeloupe, in the West Indies' Leeward Isls., consists of two large islands, Basse-Terre and Grande-Terre, separated by the Salt R., plus Marie Galante and the Saintes group to the S and Desirade to the N. A French possession since 1635, the department is represented in the French Parliament; administration consists of a prefect (governor) as well as an elected general and regional councils.

Area of the islands is 525 sq mi; pop. (2020 est.) 376,879, mainly descendants of slaves; capital is Basse-Terre (2018 est. pop. 58,397) on Basse-Terre Island. The land is fertile; sugar, rum, and bananas are exported. Tourism is an important industry.

Martinique, the northernmost of the Windward Islands, in the West Indies, has been a possession since 1635, and a department since Mar. 1946. It is represented in the French Parliament by 2 senators and 4 deputies. The island was the birthplace of Napoleon's first wife, Empress Josephine.

It has an area of 425 sq mi (total), 409 sq mi (land); pop. (2020 est.) 358,749, mostly descendants of enslaved laborers. The capital is Fort-de-France; pop. (2018 est.) 79,361. It is a popular tourist destination. The chief exports are rum, bananas, and petroleum products. **Website:** www.collectivitedemartinique.mq

Mayotte, claimed by Comoros and administered by France, voted in 1976 to become a territorial collectivity of France. An island NW of Madagascar, area is 144 sq mi, pop. (2020 est.) 279,471. The capital is Mamoudzou; pop. (2018 est.) 6,180. In a Mar. 29, 2009, referendum, 95% of voters endorsed a plan under which Mayotte became an overseas department of France as of Mar. 31, 2011.

Réunion is a volcanic island in the Indian O. about 420 mi E of Madagascar, and has belonged to France since 1665. Area, 972 sq mi (total), 968 sq mi (land); pop. (2020 est.) 859,959. Capital: Saint-Denis; pop. (2018 est.) 147,209. The chief export is sugar. Tourism contributes to the economy. Réunion elects 5 deputies, 3 senators to the French Parliament. **Website:** www.regionreunion.com

French Overseas Territorial Collectivities

French Polynesia, comprises 130 islands widely scattered among 5 archipelagos in the S Pacific; administered by a Council of Ministers (headed by a president). Territorial Assembly and the Council have headquarters at Papeete, on Tahiti, one of the Society Islands (which include the Windward Isls. and Leeward Isls.). Two deputies and a senator are elected to the French Parliament.

Other groups are the Marquesas Isls.; the Tuamotu Archipelago; the Gambier Isls.; and the Austral, or Tubuai, Isls.

Total area of the islands administered from Tahiti is 1,609 sq mi (total), 1,478 sq mi (land); pop. (2020 est.) 295,121. Tahiti is mountainous with a productive coastline bearing coconuts, citrus, pineapples, and vanilla. Tourism is the largest industry.

Tahiti was visited by Capt. James Cook in 1769 and by Capt. Bligh in the *Bounty*, 1788-89. Its beauty impressed Herman Melville, Paul Gauguin, and Charles Darwin. A UN General Assembly resolution May 17, 2013, called on France to grant French Polynesia independence, but anti-independence parties won general elections May 5, 2013, and May 6, 2018. A 2013-14 Zika virus outbreak affected about 28,000 people.

St. Pierre and Miquelon became a territorial collectivity in 1985. It consists of two groups of rocky islands near the SW coast of Newfoundland. Fish products are the chief export. The St. Pierre group has an area of 10 sq mi; Miquelon, 83 sq mi. Total pop. (2020 est.) 5,347. Capital: Saint-Pierre. Both Mayotte and St. Pierre and Miquelon elect a deputy and a senator to the French Parliament.

St. Barthélemy and **St. Martin**, both formerly part of Guadeloupe, voted for secession in 2003 and became overseas territorial collectivities in 2007. Both suffered severe damage from Hurricane Irma, Sept. 6, 2017, which caused at least 11 deaths. Total area 10 sq mi and 21 sq mi; total pop. (2020 est.) 7,122 and 32,556 respectively.

The territorial collectivity of **Wallis and Futuna** comprises two island groups in the SW Pacific S of Tuvalu, N of Fiji, and W of Samoa. It became an overseas territory July 29, 1961. The islands have a total area of 55 sq mi and pop. (2020 est.) 15,854. Alofi, attached to Futuna, is uninhabited. Capital: Mata-Utu; pop. (2018 est.) 1,025. Chief exports are copra, chemicals, and construction materials. A senator and a deputy are elected to the French Parliament.

Overseas Territory and Special Collectivity

The territory of the **French Southern and Antarctic Lands** comprises island groups in the Indian O. Area: 2,991 sq mi (total), 2,960 sq mi (land).

The U.S. does not recognize French claim to Adelie Land, an area of about 193,051 sq mi on Antarctica. Adelie, reached 1840, has a 185-mi coastline and tapers 1,240 mi inland to the S Pole. It has a research station. The area includes the Ninnis and Mertz glaciers.

The Indian O. groups are as follows: Kerguelen Archipelago, visited 1772, consists of one large and 300 small Islands. The chief is 87 mi long, 74 mi wide, and has Mt. Ross (6,429 ft). Principal research station is Port-aux-Français. There are seals, blue whales, coal, peat, semiprecious stones. Crozet Archipelago, reached 1772, covers 136 sq mi. Eastern Island rises to 6,560 ft. Volcanic Saint Paul, in southern Indian O., has warm springs. Amsterdam Island is nearby; both produce cod and rock lobster. Military garrisons and meteorological stations are located on the Scattered Isls.

The special collectivity of **New Caledonia** and Dependencies is a group of islands in the Pacific O. about 1,115 mi E of Australia and approx. the same distance NW of New Zealand. Dependencies are the Loyalty Isls., Isle of Pines, Belep Archipelago, and Huon Isls.

The largest island, New Caledonia, is 6,530 sq mi. Total area of the territory is 7,172 sq mi, 7,056 sq mi (land); pop. (2020 est.) 290,009. The group was acquired by France in 1853.

The territory is administered by a High Commissioner. There is a popularly elected Territorial Congress. Two deputies and two senators are elected to the French Parliament. Capital: Nouméa; pop. (2018 est.) 197,787.

Mining is a key industry. New Caledonia is one of the world's largest nickel producers. Chrome, iron, cobalt, manganese, silver, gold, lead, and copper are also found. Tourism is an important industry.

In 1987, New Caledonian voters chose by referendum to remain within France. French and Melanesians (Kanaks) clashed in 1988. An agreement (the Nouméa Accord) signed May 5, 1998, between France and rival New Caledonian factions specified a 20-year period of shared sovereignty and up to three referenda on independence, 2018-22. On Nov. 4, 2018, voters rejected independence. Parties favoring remaining part of France won a slim majority in May 12, 2019, Territorial Congress elections. A second referendum was scheduled for Oct. 2020.

Website: www.gouv.nc

Gabon
Gabonese Republic

People: Population: 2,230,908 (142). **Age distrib.:** <15: 36.5%; 65+: 4.0%. **Growth:** 2.4%. **Migrants:** 18.9%. **Pop. density:** 22.4 per sq mi, 8.7 per sq km. **Urban:** 90.1%. **Ethnic groups:** Gabonese-born 80.1% (incl. Fang, Shira-Punu/Vili, Nzabi-Duma, Mbede-Teke, Myene, Kota-Kele, Okande-Tsogo, Pygmy), Cameroonian 4.6%, Malian 2.4%, Beninese 2.1%, other (incl. Congolese [Kinshasa], Equatorial Guinean, Nigerian) 5.5%. **Languages:** French (official), Fang, Myene, Nzebi, Bapounou/Eschira, Bandjabi. **Religions:** Christian 85.9% (Catholic 57.3%, independent 16.1%, Protestant 12.6%), Muslim 9.4% (Sunni), ethnic religionist 2.9%.

Geography: Total area: 103,347 sq mi, 267,667 sq km (76). **Land area:** 99,486 sq mi, 257,667 sq km. **Location:** Atlantic coast of W central Africa. Equatorial Guinea, Cameroon on N; Congo Republic on E and S. **Topography:** Heavily forested, consisting of coastal lowlands; plateaus in N, E, and S; mountains in N, SE, and center. The Ogooue R. system covers most of Gabon. **Arable land:** 1.3%. **Capital:** Libreville, 834,204.

Government: Type: Presidential republic. **Head of state:** Pres. Ali Bongo Ondimba; b. 1959; in office: Oct. 16, 2009. **Head of govt.:** Prime Min. Rose Christiane Ossouka Raponda; b. 1964; in office: July 16, 2020. **Local divisions:** 9 provinces. **Defense budget:** $269 mil. **Active troops:** 4,700.

Economy: Industries: petroleum extraction and refining; manganese, gold; chemicals, ship repair, food and beverages, textiles. **Chief agric.:** cocoa, coffee, sugar, palm oil, rubber; cattle; fish. **Natural resources:** petroleum, nat. gas, diamonds, niobium, manganese, uranium, gold, timber, iron ore, hydropower. **Water:** 81,975 cu m per capita. **Crude oil reserves:** 2 bil bbls. **Electricity prod.:** 2.2 bil kWh. **Labor force:** agric. 32.4%, industry 10.8%, services 56.9%. **Unemployment:** 20.2%.

Finance: Monetary unit: Central African CFA Franc (XAF) (553.52 = $1 U.S.). **GDP:** $33.6 bil; **per capita GDP:** $15,486; **GDP growth:** 3.4%. **Imports:** $2.8 bil; France 23.6%, Belgium 19.6%, China 15.2%. **Exports:** $5.6 bil; China 36.4%, U.S. 10%, Ireland 8.5%, Netherlands 6.3%, South Korea 5.1%, Australia 5%. **Tourism** (2010): $86 mil. **Budget:** $2.9 bil. **Inflation:** 2.5%.

Transport: Railways: 403 mi. **Airports:** 14.

Communications: Telephone: 1 per 100 pop. **Mobile:** 138.3 per 100 pop. **Broadband:** 84.1 per 100 pop. **Internet:** 62%.

Health: Expend.: 2.8%. **Life expect.:** 67.3 male; 70.8 female. **Births:** 26.3 per 1,000 pop. **Deaths:** 5.9 per 1,000 pop. **Infant mortality:** 30.4 per 1,000 live births. **Undernourished:** 16.6%. **HIV:** 3.5%. **Education:** Compulsory: ages 6-15. **Literacy:** 89.8%.

Embassy: 2034 20th St. NW 20009; 797-1000.
Website: www.gouvernement.ga

France established control over the region in the second half of the 19th cent. Gabon became independent Aug. 17, 1960. Backed by France, Pres. Albert-Bernard Bongo (later Omar Bongo Ondimba) ruled the country 1967-2009, greatly enriching himself and his family. After he died June 8, 2009, his son Ali Bongo Ondimba claimed victory in a disputed 2009 presidential election. He claimed a disputed reelection victory in 2016. With Bongo out of the country since Oct. 2018 for medical treatment, government forces put down a Jan. 7, 2019, attempted coup. On July 16, 2020, Bongo named Rose Christiane Ossouka Raponda as Gabon's first female prime minister.

Gabon has abundant natural resources (including oil) and is one of the most prosperous African countries, although there is extreme income inequality.

The 2020 COVID-19 pandemic caused about 8,750 cases and over 50 deaths in Gabon by Sept. 30.

The Gambia
Republic of The Gambia

People: Population: 2,173,999 (143). **Age distrib.:** <15: 36.0%; 65+: 3.7%. **Growth:** 1.9%. **Migrants:** 9.2%. **Pop. density:** 556.4 per sq mi, 214.8 per sq km. **Urban:** 62.6%. **Ethnic groups:** Mandinka/Jahanka 34%, Fulani/Tukulur/Lorobo 22.4%, Wolof 12.6%, Jola/Karoninka 10.7%, Serahuleh 6.6%, Serer 3.2%, Manjago 2.1%. **Languages:** English (official), Mandinka, Wolof, Fula, other indigenous vernaculars. **Religions:** Muslim 89.2% (Sunni), Christian 4.7%, ethnic religionist 4.7%.

Geography: Total area: 4,363 sq mi, 11,300 sq km (160); **Land area:** 3,907 sq mi, 10,120 sq km. **Location:** Atlantic coast near W tip of Africa. Surrounded on 3 sides by Senegal. **Topography:** Narrow strip of land on each side of lower Gambia R. **Arable land:** 43.5%. **Capital:** Banjul, 450,689.

Government: Type: Presidential republic. **Head of state and govt.:** Pres. Adama Barrow; b. 1965; in office: Jan. 19, 2017. **Local divisions:** 5 regions, 1 city, 1 municipality. **Defense budget:** NA. **Active troops:** 4,100.

Economy: Industries: peanuts, fish, hides, tourism, beverages, agric. machinery assembly. **Chief agric.:** rice, millet, sorghum, peanuts, corn, sesame, cassava, palm kernels; cattle, sheep, goats. **Natural resources:** fish, clay, silica sand, titanium, tin, zircon. **Water:** 3,808 cu m per capita. **Electricity prod.:** 303 mil kWh. **Labor force:** agric. 26.6%, industry 15.8%, services 57.7%. **Unemployment:** 9.1%.

Finance: Monetary unit: Dalasi (GMD) (51.83 = $1 U.S.). **GDP:** $5.4 bil; **per capita GDP:** $2,298; **GDP growth:** 6.0%. **Imports:** $376.9 mil; Côte d'Ivoire 11.5%, Brazil 10.6%, Spain 10.2%, China 7.8%, Russia 6.4%, Netherlands 5.3%, India 5%. **Exports:** $72.9 mil; Guinea-Bissau 51.9%, Vietnam 14.6%, Senegal 8.8%, Mali 7.2%. **Tourism:** $154 mil. **Budget:** $339.0 mil. **Inflation:** 7.1%.

Transport: Airports: 1.

Communications: Telephone: 1.9 per 100 pop. **Mobile:** 139.5 per 100 pop. **Broadband:** 27 per 100 pop. **Internet:** 19.8%.

Health: Expend.: 3.3%. **Life expect.:** 63.5 male; 68.3 female. **Births:** 27 per 1,000 pop. **Deaths:** 6.7 per 1,000 pop. **Infant mortality:** 54.9 per 1,000 live births. **Undernourished:** 11.9%. **HIV:** 1.9%.

Education: Compulsory: ages 7-15. **Literacy:** 67.2%.

Embassy: 5630 16th St. NW 20011; 785-1379.

Website: www.statehouse.gm

The peoples of The Gambia were at one time associated with the West African empires of Ghana, Mali, and Songhai. The area became Britain's first African possession in 1588.

Independence came Feb. 18, 1965; republic status within the Commonwealth was achieved in 1970. The country suffered from severe famine in the 1970s. Senegambia, a confederation with Senegal, lasted from 1982 to 1989.

On July 22, 1994, after 24 years in power, Pres. Dawda K. Jawara was deposed in a bloodless coup by a military officer, Yahya Jammeh. Jammeh barred political activity, detained opponents, and governed by decree. There was a nominal return to constitutional government in 1996. Jammeh won a fourth 5-year term in 2011. After businessman Adama Barrow defeated Jammeh in the Dec. 1, 2016, presidential election, Jammeh rejected the results. Barrow was sworn in, Jan. 19, 2017, in Senegal. Under pressure from ECOWAS and the UN, Jammeh left the country Jan. 21, 2017.

The 2020 COVID-19 pandemic caused almost 3,600 cases and 112 deaths in The Gambia by Sept. 30.

Georgia

People: Population: 4,930,030 (124). **Age distrib.:** <15: 18.4%; 65+: 16.8%. **Growth:** 0.1%. **Migrants:** 2.0%. **Pop. density:** 183.2 per sq mi, 70.7 per sq km. **Urban:** 59.5%. **Ethnic groups:** Georgian 86.8%, Azeri 6.3%, Armenian 4.5%. **Languages:** Georgian (official), Azeri, Armenian, Abkhaz (official in Abkhazia). **Religions:** Christian 86% (Orthodox [official] 83%), Muslim 11% (Shia 6%, Sunni 5%), agnostic 2.5%.

Geography: Total area: 26,911 sq mi, 69,700 sq km (119). (About 18% is occupied by Russia.) **Land area:** 26,911 sq mi, 69,700 sq km. **Location:** SW Asia, on E coast of Black Sea. Russia on N and NE, Turkey and Armenia on S, Azerbaijan on SE. **Topography:** Main range of Caucasus Mts. in NE separates country from Russia. **Arable land:** 4.7%. **Capital:** Tbilisi, 1,077,833.

Government: Type: Semi-presidential republic. **Head of state:** Pres. Salome Zourabichvili; b. 1952; in office: Dec. 16, 2018. **Head of govt.:** Prime Min. Giorgi Gakharia; b. 1975; in office: Sept. 8, 2019. **Local divisions:** 9 regions, 1 city, 2 autonomous republics. **Defense budget:** $311 mil. **Active troops:** 20,650.

Economy: Industries: steel, machine tools, elec. appliances, mining, chemicals, wood prods., wine. **Chief agric.:** citrus, grapes, tea, hazelnuts, vegetables. **Natural resources:** timber, hydropower, manganese, iron ore, copper, minor coal and oil deposits. **Water:** 16,189 cu m per capita. **Crude oil reserves:** 35 mil bbls. **Electricity prod.:** 11.3 bil kWh. **Labor force:** agric. 41.3%, industry 14.2%, services 44.5%. **Unemployment:** 14.7%.

Finance: Monetary unit: Lari (GEL) (3.08 = $1 U.S.). **GDP:** $58.2 bil; **per capita GDP:** $15,637; **GDP growth:** 5.1%. **Imports:** $7.4 bil; Turkey 17.2%, Russia 9.9%, China 9.2%, Azerbaijan 7.6%, Ukraine 5.6%, Germany 5.4%. **Exports:** $3.6 bil; Russia 14.5%, Azerbaijan 10%, Turkey 7.9%, Armenia 7.7%, China 7.6%, Bulgaria 6.6%. **Tourism:** $3.3 bil. **Budget:** $4.9 bil. **Inflation:** 4.9%.

Transport: Railways: 847 mi. **Airports:** 18.

Communications: Telephone: 14.5 per 100 pop. **Mobile:** 133.4 per 100 pop. **Broadband:** 66.6 per 100 pop. **Internet** (2018): 64%.

Health: Expend.: 7.6%. **Life expect.:** 72.9 male; 81.3 female. **Births:** 11.6 per 1,000 pop. **Deaths:** 11 per 1,000 pop. **Infant mortality:** 13.8 per 1,000 live births. **Undernourished:** 8.2%. **HIV:** 0.4%.

Education: Compulsory: ages 6-14. **Literacy:** 99.6%.

Embassy: 1824-1826 R St. NW 20009; 387-2390.

Website: www.gov.ge

The region, which contained the ancient kingdoms of Colchis and Iberia, was Christianized in the 4th cent. and conquered by Arabs in the 8th cent. Annexed by Russia in 1801, Georgia was forcibly incorporated into the USSR in 1922.

Georgia declared independence Apr. 9, 1991, and became an independent country when the Soviet Union disbanded Dec. 26. After a power struggle, former Soviet Foreign Min. Eduard A. Shevardnadze became president. He survived several coup attempts and won reelection in 1995 and 2000. Parliamentary elections Nov. 2, 2003, denounced as fraudulent sparked massive anti-government protests, causing Shevardnadze to resign Nov. 23. Opposition leader Mikhail Saakashvili won the 2004 presidential election. He survived an apparent assassination attempt along with U.S. Pres. George W. Bush in Tbilisi May 10, 2005. He suppressed an alleged coup plot, Sept. 6, 2006, and cracked down violently on anti-government protests, Nov. 2007. He called early elections, Jan. 2008, which he won. Barred by term limits from seeking reelection in 2013, he left the country. In Jan. and June 2018, he was sentenced to prison terms after convictions in absentia for abuse of power.

Giorgi Margvelashvili of the recently formed Georgian Dream coalition, which won 2012 parliamentary elections, was elected president Oct. 27, 2013. Constitutional changes that went into effect in 2013 greatly increased the powers of the prime minister. Georgian Dream won Oct. 2016 parliamentary elections. Independent Salome Zurabishvili, backed by Georgian Dream, won a disputed Nov. 28, 2018, presidential election, becoming Georgia's first female president. Giorgi Gakharia of Georgian Dream became prime minister, Sept. 8, 2019, after his predecessor resigned.

Georgia has close economic ties with the EU under a 2014 cooperation agreement. In 2020, Georgia had about 6,200 COVID-19 cases by Sept. 30; 36 people had died.

After independence, secessionist movements in South Ossetia and Abkhazia, supported by Russia, rejected the Tbilisi government. Open warfare between Georgia and Russia erupted when Saakashvili sent troops, Aug. 7, 2008, to suppress insurgent activity in Tskhinvali, the South Ossetian capital. Russia, Aug. 8-9, dispatched forces to South Ossetia and Abkhazia and attacked key Georgian cities. After a cease-fire signed Aug. 15-16, thousands of Russian troops remained in the breakaway regions. Russia, Aug. 2008, formally recognized South Ossetia and Abkhazia's independence; almost all other nations have not. Abkhazia signed a cooperation agreement with Russia, Nov. 24, 2014. South Ossetia signed a military cooperation treaty with Russia, Mar. 18, 2015.

Germany
Federal Republic of Germany

People: Population: 80,313,272 (19). **Age distrib.:** <15: 12.9%; 65+: 23.0%. **Growth:** –0.2%. **Migrants:** 15.7%. **Pop. density:** 595.4 per sq mi, 229.9 per sq km. **Urban:** 77.5%. **Ethnic groups:** German 87.2%, Turkish 1.8%, Polish 1%, Syrian 1%. **Languages:** German (official); Danish, Frisian, Sorbian, Romany (all official minority langs.). **Religions:** Christian 65.6% (Protestant 31.2%, Catholic 30%), agnostic 24.4%, Muslim 6.6% (Sunni), atheist 2.8%.

Geography: Total area: 137,847 sq mi, 357,022 sq km (62). **Land area:** 134,623 sq mi, 348,672 sq km. **Location:** Central Europe. Denmark on N; Netherlands, Belgium, Luxembourg, France on W; Switzerland, Austria on S; Czech Rep., Poland on E. **Topography:** Flat in N, hilly in center and W, and mountainous in Bavaria in the S. Chief rivers are Elbe, Weser, Ems, Rhine, and Main, all flowing toward North Sea, and Danube, flowing toward Black Sea. **Arable land:** 33.7%. **Capital:** Berlin, 3,562,038. **Cities:** Hamburg, 1,789,954; Munich, 1,538,302; Cologne, 1,118,789.

Government: Type: Federal parliamentary republic. **Head of state:** Pres. Frank-Walter Steinmeier; b. 1956; in office: Mar. 22, 2017. **Head of govt.:** Chancellor Angela Merkel; b. 1954; in office: Nov. 22, 2005. **Local divisions:** 16 states. **Defense budget:** $48.5 bil. **Active troops:** 181,400.

Economy: Industries: iron, steel, coal, cement, chemicals, machinery, vehicles, machine tools, electronics, automobiles, food and beverages. **Chief agric.:** potatoes, wheat, barley, sugar beets, fruit, cabbages; milk prods.; cattle, pigs, poultry. **Natural resources:** coal, lignite, nat. gas, iron ore, copper, nickel, uranium, potash, salt, constr. materials, timber. **Water:** 1,875 cu m per capita. **Crude oil reserves:** 102 mil bbls. **Electricity prod.** (2018): 612.2 bil kWh. **Labor force:** agric. 1.2%, industry 26.8%, services 72.1%. **Unemployment:** 3.0%.

Finance: Monetary unit: Euro (EUR) (0.84 = $1 U.S.). **GDP:** $4.7 tril; **per capita GDP:** $56,052; **GDP growth:** 0.6%. **Imports:** $1.1 tril; Netherlands 13.8%, China 7%, France 6.6%, Belgium 5.9%, Italy 5.4%, Poland 5.4%. **Exports:** $1.4 tril; U.S. 8.8%, France 8.2%, China 6.8%, Netherlands 6.7%, UK 6.6%, Italy 5.1%. **Tourism:** $41.6 bil. **Budget:** $1.6 tril. **Inflation:** 1.4%.

Transport: Railways: 20,872 mi. **Motor vehicles:** 632 per 1,000 pop. **Airports:** 318.

Communications: Telephone: 51.7 per 100 pop. **Mobile:** 129.3 per 100 pop. **Broadband:** 79.8 per 100 pop. **Internet** (2018): 89.7%.

Health: Expend.: 11.2%. **Life expect.:** 78.7 male; 83.6 female. **Births:** 8.6 per 1,000 pop. **Deaths:** 12.1 per 1,000 pop. **Infant mortality:** 3.3 per 1,000 live births. **Undernourished:** <2.5%. **HIV** (2018): 0.1%.

Education: Compulsory: ages 6-18. **Literacy:** 99%.
Embassy: 4645 Reservoir Rd. NW, 20007; 298-4000.
Website: www.deutschland.de

Julius Caesar defeated Germanic tribes, 55 and 53 BCE, but Roman expansion north of the Rhine was stopped in 9 CE. Charlemagne, ruler of the Franks, consolidated Saxon, Bavarian, Rhenish, Frankish, and other lands; after him the eastern part became the German Empire. The Thirty Years' War, 1618-48, split Germany into small principalities and kingdoms.

Otto von Bismarck, Prussian chancellor, formed the North German Confederation, 1867. In 1870 Bismarck maneuvered Napoleon III into declaring war. After the quick defeat of France, Bismarck formed the German Empire and on Jan. 18, 1871, in Versailles, proclaimed King Wilhelm I of Prussia the German emperor (Deutscher kaiser).

The German Empire reached its peak before WWI in 1914, with 208,780 sq mi, plus overseas colonies. After losing the war in 1918, Germany ceded Alsace-Lorraine to France, West Prussia and Posen (Poznan) province to Poland, and part of Schleswig to Denmark. It lost all colonies and the ports of Memel and Danzig.

Republic of Germany, 1919-33, adopted the Weimar constitution; met reparation payments and elected Friedrich Ebert and Gen. Paul von Hindenburg presidents.

Third Reich, 1933-45: Adolf Hitler led the National Socialist German Workers' (Nazi) party after WWI. Pres. von Hindenburg named Hitler chancellor in 1933; on Aug. 3, 1934, the day after Hindenburg's death, the cabinet joined the offices of president and chancellor and made Hitler *führer* (leader). Hitler abolished freedom of speech and assembly, and began a long series of persecutions culminating in the murder of millions of Jews and others.

He repudiated the Versailles treaty and reparations agreements, remilitarized the Rhineland (1936), and annexed Austria (Anschluss, 1938). At Munich he made an agreement with British Prime Min. Neville Chamberlain, which permitted Germany to annex part of Czechoslovakia. He declared war on Poland Sept. 1, 1939, precipitating WWII. With total defeat near, Hitler committed suicide in Berlin Apr. 1945. The victorious Allies voided all acts and annexations of Hitler's Reich.

Germany was sectioned into four zones of occupation, administered by the Allied Powers (U.S., USSR, UK, and France). The USSR took control of many E German states. The territory E of the so-called Oder-Neisse line was assigned to, and later annexed by, Poland. The USSR annexed Northern East Prussia (now Kaliningrad). Greater Berlin, within but not part of the Soviet zone, was administered by the four occupying powers under the Allied Command. In 1948 the USSR withdrew, established its single command in East Berlin, and cut off supplies. The Western Allies utilized a gigantic airlift to bring food to West Berlin, 1948-49.

In 1949, two separate German states were established. The zones administered by the Western Allies became West Germany; the Soviet sector became East Germany. West Berlin was considered a West German enclave, a status the Soviet bloc disputed.

East Germany. The German Democratic Republic (East Germany) was proclaimed in the Soviet sector of Berlin Oct. 7, 1949. It was declared fully sovereign in 1954, but Soviet troops remained.

Coincident with the entrance of West Germany into the European defense community in 1952, the East German government decreed a prohibited zone 3 mi deep along its 600-mi border with West Germany. East Germany also erected a fortified wall dividing Berlin in 1961, after over 3 mil East Germans had fled to the West. The oppressive Communist regime maintained control through the state security police, known as the Stasi.

By the early 1970s, the economy of East Germany was highly industrialized, and the nation was credited with the highest standard of living among Warsaw Pact countries. Growth slowed in the late 1970s because of shortages of natural resources and labor and huge debt. Comparison with the lifestyle in the West caused many young people to emigrate.

In the late 1980s the government firmly resisted following the USSR's policy of openness (*glasnost*) but was faced with nationwide demonstrations demanding reform. Pres. Erich Honecker, in office since 1976, was forced to resign Oct. 18, 1989. On Nov. 9, the East German government announced its decision to open the border with the West, signaling the end of the Berlin Wall. On Aug. 23, 1990, the East German parliament agreed to reunite with West Germany.

West Germany. The Federal Republic of Germany (West Germany) was proclaimed May 23, 1949, in Bonn. The occupying powers—the U.S., Britain, and France—restored civil status, Sept. 21. The Western Allies ended the state of war with Germany in 1951, while the USSR did so in 1955. The republic became fully independent May 5, 1955. The U.S. maintained military bases. (On July 29, 2020, the U.S. announced a reduction in its troop strength in Germany from 36,000 to 24,000.)

Dr. Konrad Adenauer, a Christian Democrat, was made chancellor 1949 and was reelected 1953, 1957, and 1961. Willy Brandt, heading a coalition of Social Democrats and Free Democrats, became chancellor 1969 and pursued a policy of *Ostpolitik*, or rapprochement with East Germany and the USSR. Brandt resigned May 1974 after a spy scandal. Terrorist acts on German soil in the 1970s included activities of the Baader-Meinhof gang, also known as the Red Army Faction, and the murder of Israeli athletes by Palestinian commandos at the Olympic Games in Munich, Sept. 5, 1972.

Helmut Kohl became chancellor in 1982 and led the Christian Democratic Union (CDU) and its Bavarian sister party Christian Social Union (CSU) to victory in 1983 and 1987.

Unified Germany. In May 1990, NATO ministers voted to make the united Germany a full member of NATO and barred the new Germany from having its own nuclear, chemical, or biological weapons. The merger of the two Germanys took place Oct. 3, and the first all-German elections since 1932 were held Dec. 2, with Kohl confirmed as leader of the unified nation. Eastern Germany received over $1 tril in public and private funds from western Germany, 1990-95. In 1991, Berlin again became Germany's official capital; the Bundestag (parliament) relocated from Bonn to Berlin in 1999. The Christian Democrats lost parliamentary elections, Sept. 27, 1998, and Gerhard Schröder, of the Social Democratic Party (SPD), became chancellor. The Christian Democrats, led by Angela Merkel, won a razor-thin plurality in 2005 parliamentary elections, and she became chancellor Nov. 22, heading a "grand coalition" that included the SPD.

Responding to the global recession, the government passed a 50-bil euro economic stimulus plan in early 2009. Merkel led a center-right coalition to victory in 2009 national elections. Merkel led the response to the European debt crisis beginning in late 2009; debtor nations were required to adopt stern austerity measures.

Merkel's Christian Democrats won Sept. 22, 2013, parliamentary elections but fell short of a majority. She formed a new coalition, including the SPD, in Dec.

Germany was the destination in 2015-16 for many migrants reaching Europe after fleeing war or hardship in the Middle East, SW Asia, or Africa; it also received, in 2015, large numbers of migrants from the Balkans. More than 1.2 mil migrants applied for asylum, 2015-16. Germany provided temporary care, set up expedited procedures for asylum applicants, and began repatriating migrants judged not to be refugees. About 62% of asylum applications decided in 2016 were approved. Germany played a key role in negotiating a Mar. 2016 EU-Turkey agreement to stem the flow of migrants to Europe. In an attack for which ISIS claimed responsibility, a Tunisian migrant killed 12 when he stole a truck and drove it into a crowded Berlin outdoor market, Dec. 19, 2016.

Legislation legalizing same-sex marriage was signed into law by Germany's president, July 21, 2017.

Merkel's CDU/CSU won a plurality in Sept. 24, 2017, elections; the far-right, anti-immigration Alternative for Germany party won 12.6% of the vote. Merkel reached agreement, Feb. 2018, on a new coalition with the SPD. To prevent a CSU defection from the coalition, Merkel agreed, July 2, to toughen asylum policies. Far-right protests and rioting in Chemnitz in Aug. included attacks on apparent immigrants. On Feb. 19, 2020, a far-right extremist fatally shot 9 people at two bars in Hanau popular with immigrants.

A study commissioned by the German Catholic Church, released Sept. 2018, found evidence that more than 3,600 children had been sexually abused, 1946-2014, by over 1,600 members of the clergy.

Merkel announced, Oct. 29, 2018, she would not seek to remain as chancellor after scheduled 2021 parliamentary elections.

German Defense Min. Ursula von der Leyen became, Dec. 1, 2019, the first woman to head the European Commission.

German cases of COVID-19 increased sharply in Mar. Merkel's government instituted strict lockdown measures, triggering a drop in Germany's GDP, which is Europe's largest. With new cases declining, easing of the lockdown began Apr. 20. New cases rose again July-Sept. Germany had totals of about 289,000 cases and about 9,500 deaths by Sept. 30.

Helgoland, an island of 0.66 sq mi in the North Sea, was taken from Denmark by a British naval force in 1807 and ceded to Germany in 1890. The island was surrendered to the UK, May 23, 1945, and returned to then-West Germany, Mar. 1, 1952.

Ghana
Republic of Ghana

People: Population: 29,340,248 (49). **Age distrib.:** <15: 37.4%; 65+: 4.4%. **Growth:** 2.2%. **Migrants:** 1.5%. **Pop. density:** 334.0 per sq mi, 128.9 per sq km. **Urban:** 57.3%. **Ethnic groups:** Akan 47.5%, Mole-Dagbon 16.6%, Ewe 13.9%, Ga-Dangme 7.4%, Gurma 5.7%, Guan 3.7%, Grusi 2.5%. **Languages:** Asante, Ewe, Fante, Boron, Dagomba, Dangme, Dagarte, Kokomba, Akyem, Ga, English (official). **Religions:** Christian 72.9% (Protestant 33.9%, independent 23.2%, Catholic 15.8%), Muslim 18.1% (Sunni 11%, Islamic schismatic 7%), ethnic religionist 8.5%.

Geography: Total area: 92,098 sq mi, 238,533 sq km (80). **Land area:** 87,851 sq mi, 227,533 sq km. **Location:** S coast of W Africa. Côte d'Ivoire on W, Burkina Faso on N, Togo on E. **Topography:** Mostly low fertile plains and scrubland, cut by rivers and by the artificial Lake Volta. **Arable land:** 20.7%. **Capital:** Accra, 2,514,005. **Cities:** Kumasi, 3,348,062.

Government: Type: Presidential republic. **Head of state and govt.:** Pres. Nana Addo Dankwa Akufo-Addo; b. 1944; in office: Jan. 7, 2017. **Local divisions:** 16 regions. **Defense budget:** $233 mil. **Active troops:** 15,500.

Economy: Industries: mining, lumbering, light mfg., aluminum smelting, food proc., cement, small comm. shipbuilding. **Chief agric.:** cocoa, rice, cassava, peanuts, corn, shea nuts, bananas. **Natural resources:** gold, timber, industrial diamonds, bauxite, manganese, fish, rubber, hydropower, petroleum, silver, salt, limestone. **Water:** 1,949 cu m per capita. **Crude oil reserves:** 660 mil bbls. **Electricity prod.:** 13.5 bil kWh. **Labor force:** agric. 28.5%, industry 22.2%, services 49.4%. **Unemployment:** 4.5%.

Finance: Monetary unit: Cedi (GHS) (5.79 = $1 U.S.). **GDP:** $171.5 bil; **per capita GDP:** $5,637; **GDP growth:** 6.5%. **Imports:** $12.7 bil; China 16.8%, U.S. 8%, UK 6.2%, Belgium 5.9%. **Exports:** $13.8 bil; India 23.8%, UAE 13.4%, China 10.8%, Switzerland 11%, Vietnam 5.2%. **Tourism:** $944 mil. **Budget:** $12.4 bil. **Inflation:** 7.2%.

Transport: Railways: 588 mi. **Motor vehicles:** 6.9 per 1,000 pop. **Airports:** 7.

Communications: Telephone: 0.9 per 100 pop. **Mobile:** 137.5 per 100 pop. **Broadband:** 83.2 per 100 pop. **Internet:** 39%.

Health: Expend.: 3.3%. **Life expect.:** 65.6 male; 70.8 female. **Births:** 29.6 per 1,000 pop. **Deaths:** 6.6 per 1,000 pop. **Infant mortality:** 32.1 per 1,000 live births. **Undernourished:** 6.5%. **HIV:** 1.7%.

Education: Compulsory: ages 4-14. **Literacy:** 92.5%.

Embassy: 3512 International Dr. NW 20008; 686-4520.

Website: www.ghana.gov.gh

Named for an African empire along the Niger R., 400-1240 CE, Ghana was ruled by Britain for 113 years as the Gold Coast. The UN in 1956 approved merger with the British Togoland trust territory. Independence came Mar. 6, 1957, and republic status within the Commonwealth in 1960.

Pres. Kwame Nkrumah built hospitals and schools and promoted development projects but ran the country into debt, jailed opponents, and was accused of corruption. A 1964 referendum gave Nkrumah dictatorial powers and set up a one-party socialist state. A police-army coup overthrew Nkrumah in 1966. Elections were held in 1969, but four further coups occurred in 1972, 1978, 1979, and 1981. A new constitution, allowing multiparty politics, was approved in Apr. 1992. Former coup leader Jerry Rawlings won the 1996 presidential election.

Opposition leader John Agyekum Kufuor won a 2000 runoff vote and was sworn in Jan. 7, 2001, marking Ghana's first peaceful transfer of power from one elected president to another. A major offshore oil and gas find was announced June 2007; production began Dec. 2010. When Pres. John Atta Mills died in 2012, Vice Pres. John Dramani Mahama replaced him and won a full term. With unemployment high, Mahama lost to Nana Addo Dankwa Akufo-Addo in the Dec. 7, 2016, presidential election.

The 2020 COVID-19 pandemic caused about 46,500 cases in Ghana and about 300 deaths by Sept. 30.

Greece
Hellenic Republic

People: Population: 10,607,051 (86). **Age distrib.:** <15: 14.5%; 65+: 22.4%. **Growth:** –0.3%. **Migrants:** 11.6%. **Pop. density:** 210.3 per sq mi, 81.2 per sq km. **Urban:** 79.7%. **Ethnic groups:** Greek 91.6%, Albanian 4.4%. (Greece does not collect ethnicity data.) **Languages:** Greek (official). **Religions:** Christian 88.8% (Orthodox [official] 86.5%), Muslim 6% (Sunni), agnostic 4.4%.

Geography: Total area: 50,949 sq mi, 131,957 sq km (95). **Land area:** 50,443 sq mi, 130,647 sq km. **Location:** S end of Balkan Peninsula in SE Europe. Albania, Macedonia, Bulgaria on N; Turkey on E. **Topography:** About three-quarters is non-arable, with mountains in all areas incl. N-S Pindus Mts. Heavily indented coastline is 9,385 mi long. About 2,000 islands, only 169 inhabited, among them Crete, Rhodes, Milos, Kerkira (Corfu), Chios, Lesbos, Samos, Euboea, Delos, Mykonos. **Arable land:** 16.6%. **Capital:** Athens, 3,153,355. **Cities:** Thessaloniki, 812,166.

Government: Type: Parliamentary republic. **Head of state:** Pres. Katerina Sakellaropoulou; b. 1956; in office: Mar. 13, 2020. **Head of govt.:** Prime Min. Kyriakos Mitsotakis; b. 1968; in office: July 8, 2019. **Local divisions:** 13 regions, 1 autonomous monastic state. **Defense budget:** $4.8 bil. **Active troops:** 143,850.

Economy: Industries: tourism, food and tobacco proc., textiles, chemicals, metal prods. **Chief agric.:** wheat, corn, barley, sugar beets, olives, tomatoes, wine, tobacco, potatoes; beef. **Natural resources:** lignite, petroleum, iron ore, bauxite, lead, zinc, nickel, magnesite, marble, salt. **Water:** 6,129 cu m per capita. **Crude oil reserves:** 10 mil bbls. **Electricity prod.** (2018): 50.2 bil kWh. **Labor force:** agric. 11.7%, industry 15.2%, services 73.1%. **Unemployment:** 15.5%.

Finance: Monetary unit: Euro (EUR) (0.84 = $1 U.S.). **GDP:** $336.5 bil; **per capita GDP:** $31,399; **GDP growth:** 1.9%. **Imports:** $52.3 bil; Germany 10.4%, Italy 8.2%, Russia 6.8%, Iraq 6.3%, South Korea 6.1%, China 5.4%, Netherlands 5.3%. **Exports:** $31.5 bil; Italy 10.6%, Germany 7.1%, Turkey 6.8%, Cyprus 6.5%. **Tourism:** $20.4 bil. **Budget:** $96.4 bil. **Inflation:** 0.3%.

Transport: Railways: 1,583 mi. **Motor vehicles:** 618.2 per 1,000 pop. **Airports:** 68.

Communications: Telephone: 47 per 100 pop. **Mobile:** 115.7 per 100 pop. **Broadband:** 63.4 per 100 pop. **Internet** (2018): 73%.

Health: Expend.: 8.0%. **Life expect.:** 78.5 male; 83.8 female. **Births:** 7.8 per 1,000 pop. **Deaths:** 12 per 1,000 pop. **Infant mortality:** 3.7 per 1,000 live births. **Undernourished:** <2.5%. **HIV:** NA.

Education: Compulsory: ages 5-14. **Literacy:** 99.2%.

Embassy: 2217 Massachusetts Ave. NW 20008; 939-1300.

Website: primeminister.gr

The achievements of ancient Greece in art, architecture, science, mathematics, philosophy, drama, literature, and democracy became legacies for succeeding ages. Greece reached the height of its power, particularly in the Athenian city-state, in the 5th cent. BCE. Greece fell under Roman rule in the 2nd and 1st cents. BCE. In the 4th cent. CE, it became part of the Byzantine Empire and, after the fall of Constantinople to the Turks in 1453, part of the Ottoman Empire.

Greece won its war of independence from Turkey, 1821-29, and became a kingdom. A republic was established 1924; the monarchy was restored, 1935. In Oct. 1940, Greece rejected an ultimatum from Italy, but the country was defeated and occupied by German, Italian, and Bulgarian forces. By the end of 1944 the invaders withdrew. Communist resistance forces were overcome by Royalist and British troops. A plebiscite restored the monarchy.

Communists waged guerrilla war 1947-49 against the government but were defeated with the aid of the U.S. A period of reconstruction and rapid development followed, mainly with conservative governments under Prem. Constantine Karamanlis. The Center Union, led by Georgios Papandreou, won elections in 1963 and 1964, but King Constantine forced Papandreou to resign. A period of political maneuvers ended with Col. George Papadopoulos's military takeover Apr. 1967. King Constantine tried to reverse the consolidation of the harsh dictatorship, Dec. 1967, but failed and fled to Italy. Papadopoulos was ousted Nov. 1973.

Greek army officers serving in the Cyprus National Guard staged a coup on the island July 15, 1974. Turkey invaded Cyprus a week later, precipitating the collapse of the Greek junta. Democratic government returned, and in 1975 the monarchy was abolished.

The 1981 electoral victory of the Panhellenic Socialist Movement (Pasok) of Andreas Papandreou (Georgios's son) substantially changed Greece's internal and external policies. A scandal contributed to the 1989 defeat of the Socialists at the polls. Papandreou, who was acquitted Jan. 1992 of corruption charges, led the Socialists to a comeback victory in 1993 general elections. The Socialists retained power in 1996 and 2000 elections.

The conservative New Democracy (ND) party won 2004 parliamentary elections, and Konstantinos (Costas) Karamanlis became prime min. Beset by scandals and an ailing economy, Karamanlis called early elections for Oct. 4, 2009, won by Pasok under the leadership of the U.S.-born George A. Papandreou (Andreas's son). The IMF and eurozone countries agreed in 2010 on a 110-bil euro loan package to prevent Greece from defaulting on its debt; in return, Greek leaders implemented an austerity plan. As the debt crisis continued, parliament passed, amid violent anti-austerity protests, new austerity measures, Feb. 2012, to obtain a second, 130-bil euro bailout in Mar. The conservative, pro-bailout Antonis Samaras of ND became prime min., June 2012. Recession and austerity measures, 2007-13, caused Greece's GDP to shrink by 26%. In 2014, 36% of people lived below the poverty line.

Campaigning against austerity, the leftist Syriza party won Jan. 25, 2015, elections. Syriza's Alexis Tsipras became prime min. and negotiated for a third bailout needed by mid-2015 to avert default. In a July 5 referendum, Greek voters decisively rejected further austerity. However, negotiations after the referendum produced an 86-bil euro bailout agreement with tough austerity terms—including further tax increases and pension cuts, sales of government assets, and banking system reform. Tsipras called election for Sept. 20, 2015, which Syriza won. As austerity measures were implemented, unemployment was over 20% in 2016 and 2017. After negotiating extended repayment of more than 200 bil euros of eurozone debt, Greece exited the bailout program, Aug. 20, 2018, but was still subject to international supervision of government finances. Hurt by continued austerity, Syriza lost July 7, 2019, elections to ND, and Kyriakos Mitsotakis became prime min. Elected by parliament, Jan. 22, 2020, Ekaterini Sakellaropoulou took office, Mar. 13, as Greece's first woman president.

In 2015, more than 861,000 migrants from the Middle East, SW Asia, and Africa trying to reach the EU arrived in Greece. About 177,000 arrived in 2016, and more than 173,000 from 2017 to Aug. 31, 2020. An EU-Turkey agreement, effective Mar. 20, 2016, reduced the number of undocumented migrants arriving in Greece by boat from Turkey. Most migrants reaching Greece tried to continue to N Europe. However, several countries closed their borders to migrants traveling north or tightened asylum policies, and EU resettlement programs progressed slowly. In 2020, more than 100,000 migrants were in Greece, including tens of thousands living in harsh conditions in crowded Aegean island refugee camps; beginning Sept. 8, fires reportedly set by a few residents destroyed most of the largest camp, on Lesbos.

The 2020 COVID-19 pandemic caused more than 18,000 cases and almost 400 deaths in Greece by Sept. 30.

Grenada

People: Population: 113,094 (179). **Age distrib.:** <15: 23.2%; 65+: 10.9%. **Growth:** 0.4%. **Migrants:** 6.4%. **Pop. density:** 851.5 per sq mi, 328.8 per sq km. **Urban:** 36.5%. **Ethnic groups:** African descent 82.4%, mixed 13.3%, East Indian 2.2%. **Languages:** English (official), French patois. **Religions:** Christian 96.2% (Catholic 49.7%, Protestant 40.2%).

Geography: Total area: 133 sq mi, 344 sq km (186); **Land area:** 133 sq mi, 344 sq km. **Location:** In Caribbean, 90 mi N of Venezuela. Trinidad and Tobago to S, St. Vincent and the Grenadines to N. **Topography:** Main island is mountainous. Country also comprised of Carriacou and Petit Martinique Isls. **Arable land:** 8.8%. **Capital:** St. George's, 39,297.

Government: Type: Parliamentary democracy under constitutional monarchy. **Head of state:** Queen Elizabeth II, rep. by Gov.-Gen. Cecile La Grenade; b. 1952; in office: May 7, 2013. **Head of govt.:** Prime Min. Keith Mitchell; b. 1946; in office: Feb. 20, 2013. **Local divisions:** 6 parishes, 1 dependency. **Defense budget/active troops:** NA.

Economy: Industries: food and beverages, textiles, light assembly operations, tourism, constr., education, call-center operations. **Chief agric.:** bananas, cocoa, nutmeg, mace, soursop, citrus, avocados, root crops, corn, vegetables; fish. **Natural resources:** timber, tropical fruit. **Water:** 1,855 cu m per capita. **Electricity prod.:** 214 mil kwH. **Labor force:** agric. 6.8%, industry 15.5%, services 77.7%. **Unemployment:** NA.

Finance: Monetary unit: East Caribbean dollar (XCD) (2.70 = $1 U.S.). **GDP:** $2.0 bil; **per capita GDP:** $17,956; **GDP growth:** 3.1%. **Imports:** $316 mil; U.S. 31.7%, Trinidad and Tobago 24.9%, China 6.7%. **Exports:** $39.9 mil; U.S. 25.3%, Japan 10.1%, Guyana 8.7%, Dominica 6.6%, St. Lucia 6.4%. **Tourism:** $170 mil. **Budget:** $252.3 mil. **Inflation** (2017-18): 0.8%.

Transport: Airports: 3.

Communications: Telephone (2017): 29.3 per 100 pop. **Mobile** (2017): 102.1 per 100 pop. **Broadband:** 89.2 per 100 pop. **Internet:** 59.1%.

Health: Expend.: 4.8%. **Life expect.:** 72.6 male; 78.1 female.

Births: 14.6 per 1,000 pop. **Deaths:** 8.3 per 1,000 pop. **Infant mortality:** 8.9 per 1,000 live births. **Undernourished:** NA. **HIV** (2018): 0.5%.

Education: Compulsory: ages 5-16. **Literacy:** NA.

Embassy: 1701 New Hampshire Ave. NW 20009; 265-2561.

Website: www.gov.gd

Christopher Columbus sighted Grenada in 1498. The first European settlers were French, 1650. The island was held alternately by France and England until final British occupation, 1784. Grenada became fully independent Feb. 7, 1974, during a general strike.

On Oct. 14, 1983, a military coup ousted Prime Min. Maurice Bishop, who was put under house arrest, later freed by supporters, rearrested, and executed Oct. 19. U.S. forces, with a token force from six area nations, invaded Grenada, Oct. 25. Resistance from the Grenadian army and Cuban advisors was quickly overcome, and U.S. troops left Grenada in June 1985.

Hurricane Ivan slammed into Grenada, Sept. 7, 2004, killing 39 people and damaging an estimated 90% of the buildings on the island. The New National Party (NNP) won all 15 seats in 2013 and 2018 legislative elections; the NNP's Keith Mitchell became prime min., Feb. 20, 2013.

Guatemala
Republic of Guatemala

People: Population: 17,153,288 (68). **Age distrib.:** <15: 33.7%; 65+: 4.7%. **Growth:** 1.7%. **Migrants:** 0.5%. **Pop. density:** 414.6 per sq mi, 160.1 per sq km. **Urban:** 51.8%. **Ethnic groups:** mestizo or Ladino (mixed Amerindian/Spanish) 56%, Maya 41.7%, Xinca (Indigenous, non-Maya) 1.8%. **Languages:** Spanish (official), Maya langs. (incl. K'iche, Q'eqchi, Mam, Kaqchikel). **Religions:** Christian 97.2% (Catholic [official] 66.5%, Protestant 18.8%, independent 10.8%).

Geography: Total area: 42,042 sq mi, 108,889 sq km (105); **Land area:** 41,374 sq mi, 107,159 sq km. **Location:** Central America. Mexico on N and W, El Salvador on S, Honduras and Belize on E. **Topography:** Central highland and mountain areas bordered by a narrow Pacific coast and lowlands and fertile river valleys on the Caribbean. Numerous volcanoes in S, more than half a dozen over 11,000 ft. **Arable land:** 8.0%. **Capital:** Guatemala City, 2,934,841.

Government: Type: Presidential republic. **Head of state and govt.:** Pres. Alejandro Giammattei; b. 1956; in office: Jan. 14, 2020. **Local divisions:** 22 departments. **Defense budget:** $307 mil. **Active troops:** 18,050.

Economy: Industries: sugar, textiles/clothing, furniture, chemicals, petroleum, metals, rubber, tourism. **Chief agric.:** sugarcane, corn, bananas, coffee, beans, cardamom; cattle, sheep. **Natural resources:** petroleum, nickel, rare woods, fish, chicle, hydropower. **Water:** 7,562 cu m per capita. **Crude oil reserves:** 89.4 mil bbls. **Electricity prod.:** 12.5 bil kwH. **Labor force:** agric. 31.3%, industry 18.4%, services 50.3%. **Unemployment:** 2.5%.

Finance: Monetary unit: Quetzal (GTQ) (7.71 = $1 U.S.). **GDP:** $149.4 bil; **per capita GDP:** $8,996; **GDP growth:** 3.8%. **Imports:** $17.1 bil; U.S. 39.8%, China 10.7%, Mexico 10.7%, El Salvador 5.3%. **Exports:** $11.1 bil; U.S. 33.8%, El Salvador 11.1%, Honduras 8.8%, Nicaragua 5.1%. **Tourism:** $1.2 bil. **Budget:** $9.2 bil. **Inflation:** 3.7%.

Transport: Railways: 497 mi. **Motor vehicles:** 129.3 per 1,000 pop. **Airports:** 16.

Communications: Telephone: 14.1 per 100 pop. **Mobile:** 118.7 per 100 pop. **Broadband:** 16.5 per 100 pop. **Internet:** 65%.

Health: Expend.: 5.8%. **Life expect.:** 70.3 male; 74.5 female.

Births: 23.3 per 1,000 pop. **Deaths:** 4.9 per 1,000 pop. **Infant mortality:** 21.8 per 1,000 live births. **Undernourished:** 16.1%. **HIV:** 0.3%.

Education: Compulsory: ages 6-15. **Literacy:** 81.5%.

Embassy: 2220 R St. NW 20008; 745-4953.

Website: www.guatemala.gob.gt or www.presidencia.gob.gt

A Mayan Indian empire flourished in present-day Guatemala for over 1,000 years before Spaniards came. Guatemala was a Spanish colony 1524-1821. A republic was established in 1839.

In 1954, the U.S. Central Intelligence Agency engineered the overthrow of elected Pres. Jacobo Arbenz Guzmán, a left-wing reformer. Since then, the country has experienced a variety of military and civilian governments and periods of insurgency, repression, paramilitary violence, and civil war.

The Guatemalan government and leftist rebels signed a peace accord Dec. 29, 1996. During more than 35 years of armed conflict, some 200,000 people were killed or "disappeared"; most casualties were attributed to the government and its paramilitary allies. Gen. Efraín Ríos Montt, dictator in 1982-83, was found guilty of genocide May 10, 2013, but the Constitutional Court overturned his conviction May 20; Ríos Montt died, Apr. 1, 2018, during a retrial. Four former high-level military officers were convicted, May 23, 2018, of crimes against humanity and other charges.

Former Pres. Alfonso Portillo was extradited to the U.S. May 24, 2013, and pleaded guilty to money laundering, Mar. 18, 2014. Drug trafficking, arms smuggling, police corruption, and gang violence posed threats to national stability. Hundreds of thousands of Guatemalans were among the Central American asylum seekers and other migrants detained trying to enter the U.S. from Mexico 2013-19. Facing U.S. sanctions, Guatemala signed, July 26, 2019, an agreement to accept Honduran and Salvadoran migrants who had sought asylum in the U.S.

Vice Pres. Roxana Baldetti resigned, May 2015, and was sentenced, Oct. 9, 2018, to 15.5 years in prison following a corruption conviction. Following large-scale protests, Pres. Otto Pérez Molina resigned Sept. 2, 2015; he was ordered, Sept. 8, to stand trial on corruption charges. Former comedian Jimmy Ernesto Morales Cabrera won a runoff election for president, Oct. 25, 2015. Under investigation by a UN-sponsored anti-corruption panel, Morales, 2018-19, took steps to block the panel's work. Conservative Alejandro Giammattei won an Aug. 11, 2019, presidential runoff election.

The 2020 COVID-19 pandemic caused about 91,000 cases in Guatemala and over 3,200 deaths as of Sept. 30.

Guinea
Republic of Guinea

People: Population: 12,527,440 (76). **Age distrib.:** <15: 41.2%; 65+: 3.9%. **Growth:** 2.8%. **Migrants:** 0.9%. **Pop. density:** 132.0 per sq mi, 51.0 per sq km. **Urban:** 36.9%. **Ethnic groups:** Fulani (Peuhl) 33.4%, Malinke 29.4%, Susu 21.2%, Guerze 7.8%, Kissi 6.2%, Toma 1.6%. **Languages:** French (official), ethnic group-specific langs. **Religions:** Muslim 88.5% (Sunni), ethnic religionist 7.9%, Christian 3.4%.

Geography: Total area: 94,926 sq mi, 245,857 sq km (77); **Land area:** 94,872 sq mi, 245,717 sq km. **Location:** Atlantic coast of W Africa. Guinea-Bissau, Senegal, Mali on N; Côte d'Ivoire on E; Liberia, Sierra Leone on S. **Topography:** Narrow coastal belt leads to mountainous middle region, source of the Gambia, Senegal, and Niger Rivers. Upper Guinea, farther inland, is cooler upland. The SE is forested. **Arable land:** 12.6%. **Capital:** Conakry, 1,938,272.

Government: Type: Presidential republic. **Head of state:** Pres. Alpha Condé; b. 1938; in office: Dec. 21, 2010. **Head of govt.:** Prime Min. Ibrahima Kassory Fofana; in office: May 22, 2018. **Local divisions:** 7 regions, 1 governorate. **Defense budget:** $191 mil. **Active troops:** 9,700.

Economy: Industries: bauxite, gold, diamonds, iron ore; light mfg.; agric. proc. **Chief agric.:** rice, coffee, pineapples, mangoes, palm kernels, cocoa, cassava, bananas, potatoes; cattle, sheep, goats. **Natural resources:** bauxite, iron ore, diamonds, gold, uranium, hydropower, fish, salt. **Water:** 17,771 cu m per capita. **Electricity prod.:** 1.6 bil kwH. **Labor force:** agric. 61.3%, industry 6.2%, services 32.5%. **Unemployment:** 4.3%.

Finance: Monetary unit: Franc (GNF) (9,654.71 = $1 U.S.). **GDP:** $34.1 bil; **per capita GDP:** $2,670; **GDP growth:** 5.6%. **Imports:** $4.8 bil; Netherlands 17.2%, China 13.2%, India 11.8%, Belgium 10%, France 6.9%. **Exports:** $3.5 bil; China 35.8%, Ghana 20.1%, UAE 11.6%. **Tourism:** $6 mil. **Budget:** $1.7 bil. **Inflation:** 9.5%.

Transport: Railways: 675 mi. **Airports:** 4.

Communications: Telephone (2011): 0.2 per 100 pop. **Mobile:** 96.1 per 100 pop. **Broadband:** 15.7 per 100 pop. **Internet:** 18%.

Health: Expend.: 4.1%. **Life expect.:** 61.3 male; 65.0 female.

Births: 36.1 per 1,000 pop. **Deaths:** 8.4 per 1,000 pop. **Infant mortality:** 52.4 per 1,000 live births. **Undernourished:** NA. **HIV:** 1.4%.

Education: Compulsory: ages 7-12. **Literacy:** 30.4%.

Embassy: 2112 Leroy Pl. NW 20008; 986-4300.

Website: www.presidence.gov.gn

Guinea, a French colony, attained independence Oct. 2, 1958. Sékou Touré, Guinea's first president (1958-84), turned to Communist nations for support and set up a one-party state. Thousands of opponents were jailed and tortured, and many were killed in the 1970s after an unsuccessful Portuguese invasion.

The military took control in a bloodless coup after the Mar. 1984 death of Touré. A new constitution was approved in 1991, but movement toward democracy was slow. Gen. Lansana Conté, the incumbent, won a long-awaited presidential election in Dec. 1993, which outside monitors called flawed. Conté suppressed an army mutiny in Conakry, Feb. 2-3, 1996, and won reelection in 1998.

Major opposition parties boycotted the 2003 presidential election, in which the ailing Conté won 95.6% of the vote. More than 120 died in Jan.-Feb. 2007 strikes and protests that pressured Conté to name a new prime min. from a union-leader approved list; protests followed Prime Min. Lansana Kouyate's ouster by Conté in May 2008. After Conté's death Dec. 22, a military junta took power. More than 150 people were reportedly killed Sept. 28, 2009, when Guinean troops fired into a crowd of about 50,000 anti-government protesters in Conakry. After an assassination attempt Dec. 3, 2009, by a former aide left Pres. Moussa Dadis Camara seriously wounded, Vice Pres. Sékouba Konaté became interim head of state.

Presidential elections June-Nov. 2010 brought a civilian government headed by Alpha Condé to power Dec. 21. Condé won reelection, Oct. 11, 2015. A new constitution, approved in a Mar. 22, 2020, referendum that was boycotted by the opposition, permitted Condé to seek another term in scheduled Oct. 2020 elections; demonstrations against constitutional changes left dozens dead.

The largest known outbreak of Ebola virus disease (EVD) began in Guinea in Dec. 2013 and spread rapidly to Liberia and Sierra Leone. The WHO lifted its public health emergency in West Africa, Mar. 29, 2016. By June 10, 2016, the WHO had recorded 28,616 EVD cases in the 3 countries (including 3,814 in Guinea) and 11,310 deaths (2,544 in Guinea). Guinea declared an end to the epidemic there, June 1. The 2020 COVID-19 pandemic caused about 10,600 cases in Guinea and 66 deaths as of Sept. 30.

Guinea-Bissau
Republic of Guinea-Bissau

People: Population: 1,927,104 (148). **Age distrib.:** <15: 43.2%; 65+: 3.1%. **Growth:** 2.5%. **Migrants:** 1.4%. **Pop. density:** 177.5 per sq mi, 68.5 per sq km. **Urban:** 44.2%. **Ethnic groups:** Fulani 28.5%, Balanta 22.5%, Mandinga 14.7%, Papel 9.1%, Manjaco 8.3%, Beafada 3.5%, Mancanha 3.1%, Bijago 2.1%. **Languages:** Crioulo (lingua franca), Portuguese (official), Pular, Mandingo. **Religions:** Muslim 46.4% (Sunni), ethnic religionist 39.8%, Christian 12.8%.

Geography: Total area: 13,948 sq mi, 36,125 sq km (134); **Land area:** 10,857 sq mi, 28,120 sq km. **Location:** Atlantic coast of W Africa. Senegal on N, Guinea on E and S. **Topography:** A swampy coastal plain covers most of country. Low savanna region to E. **Arable land:** 10.7%. **Capital:** Bissau, 599,714.

Government: Type: Semi-presidential republic. **Head of state:** Pres. Umaro Cissoko Embaló; b. 1972; in office: Feb. 27, 2020. **Head of govt.:** Prime Min. Nuno Nabiam; b. 1966; in office: Feb. 27, 2020. **Local divisions:** 9 regions. **Defense budget:** NA. **Active troops:** 4,450.

Economy: Industries: agric. prods. proc., beer, soft drinks. **Chief agric.:** rice, corn, beans, cassava, cashew nuts, peanuts, palm kernels, cotton; fish. **Natural resources:** fish, timber, phosphates, bauxite, clay, granite, limestone, unexploited petroleum deposits. **Water:** 16,873 cu m per capita. **Electricity prod.:** 36 mil kWh. **Labor force:** agric. 67.8%, industry 7.0%, services 25.2%. **Unemployment:** 2.5%.

Finance: Monetary unit: CFA Franc (XOF) (553.52 = $1 U.S.). **GDP:** $4.0 bil; **per capita GDP:** $2,072; **GDP growth:** 4.6%. **Imports:** $283.5 mil; Portugal 47.8%, Senegal 12.1%, China 10.4%, Netherlands 8.1%, Pakistan 5.4%. **Exports:** $328.1 mil; India 67.1%, Vietnam 21.1%. **Tourism:** $20 mil. **Budget:** $263.5 mil. **Inflation** (2016-17): 1.4%.

Transport: Airports: 2.

Communications: Telephone (2009): 0.3 per 100 pop. **Mobile:** 79 per 100 pop. **Broadband:** 7.3 per 100 pop. **Internet:** 3.9%.

Health: Expend.: 7.2%. **Life expect.:** 60.6 male; 65.1 female. **Births:** 36.9 per 1,000 pop. **Deaths:** 7.9 per 1,000 pop. **Infant mortality:** 51.9 per 1,000 live births. **Undernourished:** NA. **HIV:** 3.4%.

Education: Compulsory: ages 6-14. **Literacy:** 59.9%.

Permanent UN mission: 336 E. 45th St., 13th Fl., New York, NY 10017; (212) 896-8311.

Website: www.state.gov/countries-areas/guinea-bissau/

Portuguese mariners explored the area in the mid-15th cent.; the slave trade flourished in the 17th and 18th cents., and colonization began in the 19th. Independence came Sept. 10, 1974, ending 13 years of guerrilla warfare against the Portuguese regime.

A Nov. 1980 coup gave army chief João Bernardo Vieira absolute power. Vieira eventually initiated political liberalization; multiparty elections were held in 1994. A 1998 army uprising triggered a civil war; rebel troops ousted Vieira on May 7, 1999.

Civilian rule returned with 1999-2000 elections, but top military officers staged a coup Sept. 14, 2003. Vieira won a presidential runoff election, July 24, 2005. A group of soldiers murdered Vieira, Mar. 2, 2009. Political violence continued as the 2009 presidential election approached; the ruling party (PAIGC) candidate, Malam Bacai Sanhá, won a runoff vote July 26. He died Jan. 9, 2012. After a coup, Apr. 12, the military appointed Manuel Serifo Nhamadjo to lead a transitional government. Drug trafficking increased substantially, with the support of the military. José Mário Vaz of the PAIGC won a May 18, 2014, presidential runoff. In a Dec. 29, 2019, presidential runoff, Umaro Sissoco Embaló defeated the candidate of the PAIGC, which disputed the result.

The 2020 COVID-19 pandemic caused more than 2,300 cases and 39 deaths in Guinea-Bissau as of Sept. 30.

Guyana
Cooperative Republic of Guyana

People: Population: 750,204 (162). **Age distrib.:** <15: 23.9%; 65+: 7.0%. **Growth:** 0.8%. **Migrants:** 0.2%. **Pop. density:** 9.9 per sq mi, 3.8 per sq km. **Urban:** 26.8%. **Ethnic groups:** East Indian 39.8%, African descent 29.3%, mixed 19.9%, Amerindian 10.5%. **Languages:** English (official), Guyanese Creole, Amerindian langs., Indian langs., Chinese. **Religions:** Christian 54.5% (Protestant 34.3%, independent 11.3%), Hindu 30.2%, Muslim 7.9% (Sunni 7%, Shia 1%).

Geography: Total area: 83,000 sq mi, 214,969 sq km (83); **Land area:** 76,004 sq mi, 196,849 sq km. **Location:** N coast of S America. Venezuela on W, Brazil on S, Suriname on E. **Topography:** Dense tropical forests cover much of land. A grassy savanna divides it from flat coastal area, where 90% of the pop. lives, with its rich alluvial soil. **Arable land:** 2.1%. **Capital:** Georgetown, 109,934.

Government: Type: Parliamentary republic. **Head of state and govt.:** Pres. Mohammed Irfaan Ali; b. 1980; in office: Aug. 2, 2020. **Local divisions:** 10 regions. **Defense budget:** $68 mil. **Active troops:** 3,400.

Economy: Industries: bauxite, sugar, rice milling, timber, textiles, gold mining. **Chief agric.:** sugarcane, rice, edible oils; beef, pork, poultry; shrimp, fish. **Natural resources:** bauxite, gold, diamonds, timber, shrimp, fish. **Water:** 348,374 cu m per capita. **Electricity prod.:** 1.0 bil kwH. **Labor force:** agric. 16.8%, industry 22.9%, services 60.3%. **Unemployment:** 11.8%.

Finance: Monetary unit: Dollar (GYD) (208.80 = $1 U.S.). **GDP:** $7.9 bil; **per capita GDP:** $10,105; **GDP growth:** 4.7%. **Imports:** $1.6 bil; Trinidad and Tobago 27.5%, U.S. 26.5%, China 8.9%, Suriname 6.1%. **Exports:** $1.4 bil; Canada 24.9%, U.S. 16.5%, Panama 9.6%, UK 7.7%, Jamaica 5.1%, Trinidad and Tobago 5%. **Tourism:** $28 mil. **Budget:** $1.2 bil. **Inflation:** 2.1%.

Transport: Motor vehicles: 132.2 per 1,000 pop. **Airports:** 11.

Communications: Telephone: 17.5 per 100 pop. **Mobile** (2017): 83 per 100 pop. **Broadband:** 26.3 per 100 pop. **Internet:** 37.3%.

Health: Expend.: 4.9%. **Life expect.:** 66.5 male; 72.6 female. **Births:** 15.5 per 1,000 pop. **Deaths:** 7.5 per 1,000 pop. **Infant mortality:** 27.6 per 1,000 live births. **Undernourished:** 5.7%. **HIV:** 1.4%.

Education: Compulsory: ages 6-11. **Literacy:** 88.5%.

Embassy: 2490 Tracy Pl. NW 20008; 265-6900.

Website: parliament.gov.gy

Guyana became a Dutch possession in the 17th cent., but sovereignty passed to Britain in 1815. Indentured servants from India soon outnumbered African slaves. Guyana became independent May 26, 1966.

The Port Kaituma ambush of U.S. Rep. Leo J. Ryan and others investigating mistreatment of American followers of the Rev. Jim Jones's Peoples Temple cult triggered a mass suicide-execution of more than 900 at their commune in Jonestown, Nov. 18, 1978.

An Oct. 1992 election victory began more than two decades of People's Progressive Party/Civic (PPP/C) governance. An opposition coalition won May 11, 2015, elections, and coalition leader David Granger became president, May 16. Major offshore oil discoveries were announced in 2015-19. A Mar. 2, 2020, election returned the PPP/C to power.

The 2020 COVID-19 pandemic caused almost 2,800 cases in Guyana as of Sept. 30 and 78 deaths.

Haiti
Republic of Haiti

People: Population: 11,067,777 (82). **Age distrib.:** <15: 31.2%; 65+: 4.3%. **Growth:** 1.3%. **Migrants:** 0.2%. **Pop. density:** 1,040.1 per sq mi, 401.6 per sq km. **Urban:** 57.1%. **Ethnic groups:** Black 95%, mixed and white 5%. **Languages:** French, Creole (both official). **Religions:** Christian 94% (Catholic [official] 67.4%, Protestant 19.5%), agnostic 2.9%, Spiritist 2.7%.

Geography: Total area: 10,714 sq mi, 27,750 sq km (144); **Land area:** 10,641 sq mi, 27,560 sq km. **Location:** In Caribbean; occupies western third of isl. of Hispaniola. Dominican Republic on E, Cuba to W. **Topography:** About two-thirds is mountainous. Much of rest is semiarid. Coastal areas are warm and moist. **Arable land:** 38.8%. **Capital:** Port-au-Prince, 2,773,553.

Government: Type: Semi-presidential republic. **Head of state:** Pres. Jovenel Moise; b. 1968; in office: Feb. 7, 2017. **Head of govt.:** Prime Min. Joseph Jouthe; b. 1961; in office: Mar. 4, 2020. **Local divisions:** 10 departments. **Defense budget:** $13 mil. **Active troops:** 400. UN mission MINUJUSTH, est. Oct. 2017, is assisting Haiti in developing a national police.

Economy: Industries: textiles, sugar refining, flour milling, cement, light assembly using imported parts. **Chief agric.:** coffee, mangoes, cocoa, sugarcane, rice, corn, sorghum. **Natural resources:** bauxite, copper, calcium carbonate, gold, marble, hydropower. **Water:** 1,278 cu m per capita. **Electricity prod.:** 1.0 bil kwH. **Labor force:** agric. 28.3%, industry 6.6%, services 65.0%. **Unemployment:** 13.9%.

Finance: Monetary unit: Gourde (HTG) (112.05 = $1 U.S.). **GDP:** $20.3 bil; **per capita GDP:** $1,801; **GDP growth:** –0.9%. **Imports:** $3.6 bil; U.S. 20.7%, China 18.8%, Netherlands Antilles 15.7%, Indonesia 8.5%. **Exports:** $980.2 mil; U.S. 80.6%. **Tourism:** $620 mil. **Budget:** $1.7 bil. **Inflation:** 18.7%.

Transport: Motor vehicles: 9 per 1,000 pop. **Airports:** 4.
Communications: Telephone: 0.05 per 100 pop. **Mobile:** 57.5 per 100 pop. **Broadband:** 27.1 per 100 pop. **Internet** (2018): 32.5%.
Health: Expend.: 8.0%. **Life expect.:** 62.6 male; 68.0 female.
Births: 21.7 per 1,000 pop. **Deaths:** 7.4 per 1,000 pop. **Infant mortality:** 42.6 per 1,000 live births. **Undernourished:** 48.2%. **HIV:** 1.9%.
Education: Compulsory: ages 6-11. **Literacy:** 83.0%.
Embassy: 2311 Massachusetts Ave. NW 20008; 332-4090.
Website: primature.gouv.ht or www.haiti.org

Haiti, visited by Christopher Columbus in 1492 and a French colony from 1697, attained its independence, 1804, following a rebellion led by former slave Toussaint L'Ouverture. After a period of political violence, the U.S. occupied the country 1915-34.

François Duvalier, known as Papa Doc, was elected president in 1957; in 1964 he was named president for life. Upon his death in 1971, he was succeeded by his son, Jean Claude Duvalier, known as Baby Doc. Following weeks of unrest, Jean Claude fled Haiti aboard a U.S. Air Force jet Feb. 7, 1986. His departure ended the Duvalier family's brutal 28-year dictatorship, but political violence, corruption, poverty, AIDS, and other health problems have continued to plague Haiti.

Jean-Bertrand Aristide was elected president in 1990, but the military arrested and expelled him from the country in Sept. 1991. The U.S. Coast Guard intercepted some 35,000 Haitian refugees as they tried to enter the U.S., 1991-92. Most were returned to Haiti. There was a new upsurge of refugees starting in late 1993.

The UN authorized in 1994 an invasion of Haiti by a U.S.-led multinational force. A full-scale invasion was averted, Sept. 18, when military leaders agreed to step down. Aristide was restored to office Oct. 15. A UN peacekeeping force exercised responsibility in Haiti from 1995 to 1997. Aristide transferred power to his elected successor, René Préval, in 1996.

Aristide won the 2000 presidency in an election boycotted by opposition groups. An armed uprising in early 2004 and pressure from France and the U.S. toppled Aristide, who went into exile Feb. 29. A U.S.-led contingent, sent in after the upheaval, yielded authority June 1, 2004, to a UN stabilization force (MINUSTAH). MINUSTAH's mission ended Oct. 15, 2017; the force was replaced by MINUJUSTH, intended to strengthen the rule of law, which completed its mandate Oct. 15, 2019.

Préval was again elected president in 2006. Skyrocketing prices for food imports sparked riots and mass protests in Apr. 2008. A succession of hurricanes and tropical storms, Aug.-Sept. 2008, left more than 550 Haitians dead and up to 1 mil homeless.

An earthquake Jan. 12, 2010, near Port-au-Prince caused cataclysmic damage. More than 220,000 people were killed, at least 300,000 were injured, and more than 1.5 mil were left homeless. In the following years, rebuilding proceeded slowly. In Nov. 2017, the Trump administration announced it would end temporary residency status for almost 59,000 Haitians permitted to live in the U.S. after the 2010 earthquake; U.S. court challenges delayed implementation.

A severe cholera epidemic began soon after the 2010 earthquake. By 2018 the number of new cases had dropped sharply, but through 2018, about 820,000 total cases had been reported and almost 9,800 people had died. The UN publicly acknowledged responsibility for the epidemic Dec. 1, 2016.

Michel Martelly, an entertainer, won a Mar. 20, 2011, presidential runoff election. After allegations of widespread fraud in the Oct. 25, 2015, first-round election for a new president, an electoral commission ruled that the balloting should be held again Oct. 9, 2016. Postponed, Oct. 5, 2016, after Hurricane Matthew caused widespread damage and about 1,000 deaths, the Nov. 20, 2016, re-vote was won by businessman Jovenel Moïse. Government-announced fuel price increases led to violent protests, July 2018, leaving several dead; the increases were suspended. Renewed protests, against corruption and economic hardship (and calling for Moïse's resignation), occurred in 2019; Oct. legislative elections were postponed. A Feb. 2020 police protest in Port-au-Prince over working conditions resulted in a gun battle with soldiers.

Impacted in 2020 by the COVID-19 pandemic, Haiti had more than 8,700 cases and over 200 deaths by Sept. 30.

Honduras
Republic of Honduras

People: Population: 9,235,340 (95). **Age distrib.:** <15: 30.2%; 65+: 5.4%. **Growth:** 1.3%. **Migrants:** 0.4%. **Pop. density:** 213.8 per sq mi, 82.5 per sq km. **Urban:** 58.4%. **Ethnic groups:** mestizo (mixed Amerindian/European) 90%, Amerindian 7%, Black 2%. **Languages:** Spanish (official), Amerindian dialects. **Religions:** Christian 95.7% (Catholic [official] 71.4%, Protestant 16.5%).
Geography: Total area: 43,278 sq mi, 112,090 sq km (101); **Land area:** 43,201 sq mi, 111,890 sq km. **Location:** Central America. Guatemala on W; El Salvador, Nicaragua on S. **Topography:** Caribbean coast is 500 mi long. Pacific coast, on Gulf of Fonseca, is 40 mi long. Mountainous, with wide fertile valleys and rich forests. **Arable land:** 9.1%. **Capital:** Tegucigalpa, 1,444,085.
Government: Type: Presidential republic. **Head of state and govt.:** Pres. Juan Orlando Hernandez Alvarado; b. 1968; in office:

Jan. 27, 2014. **Local divisions:** 18 departments. **Defense budget:** $341 mil. **Active troops:** 14,950.
Economy: Industries: sugar proc., coffee, woven and knit apparel, wood prods., cigars. **Chief agric.:** bananas, coffee, citrus, corn, African palm; beef; shrimp, tilapia, lobster. **Natural resources:** timber, gold, silver, copper, lead, zinc, iron ore, antimony, coal, fish, hydropower. **Water:** 9,947 cu m per capita. **Electricity prod.:** 9.0 bil kWh. **Labor force:** agric. 30.1%, industry 19.7%, services 50.2%. **Unemployment:** 5.2%.
Finance: Monetary unit: Lempira (HNL) (24.64 = $1 U.S.). **GDP:** $58.1 bil; **per capita GDP:** $5,965; **GDP growth:** 2.7%. **Imports:** $11.3 bil; U.S. 40.3%, Guatemala 10.5%, China 8.5%, Mexico 6.2%, El Salvador 5.7%. **Exports:** $8.7 bil; U.S. 34.5%, Germany 8.9%, Belgium 7.7%, El Salvador 7.3%, Netherlands 7.2%, Guatemala 5.2%. **Tourism:** $547 mil. **Budget:** $5.3 bil. **Inflation:** 4.4%.
Transport: Railways: 434 mi. **Motor vehicles:** 20.6 per 1,000 pop. **Airports:** 13.
Communications: Telephone: 5.5 per 100 pop. **Mobile:** 79.2 per 100 pop. **Broadband:** 24.5 per 100 pop. **Internet:** 31.7%.
Health: Expend.: 7.9%. **Life expect.:** 71.1 male; 78.3 female.
Births: 18.5 per 1,000 pop. **Deaths:** 4.7 per 1,000 pop. **Infant mortality:** 14.6 per 1,000 live births. **Undernourished:** 13.6%. **HIV:** 0.3%.
Education: Compulsory: ages 5-16. **Literacy:** 96.5%.
Embassy: 3007 Tilden St. NW, Ste. 4-M, 20008; 966-7702.
Website: www.presidencia.gob.hn

Mayan civilization flourished in Honduras in the 1st millennium CE. Columbus arrived in 1502. Honduras became independent after freeing itself from Spain, 1821, and from the Fed. of Central America, 1838.

In 1975, the army ousted Gen. Oswaldo Lopez Arellano, president for most of the time since 1963, over charges of pervasive bribery by United Brands Co. of the U.S. An elected civilian government took power in 1982.

Hurricane Mitch, Oct. 1998, killed at least 5,600. On May 4, 2018, the Trump administration announced it would terminate temporary residency status for about 86,000 Hondurans permitted to live in the U.S. after Mitch; court challenges delayed implementation.

Juan Orlando Hernández of the conservative National Party won the Nov. 2013 presidential election. After the Supreme Court, 2015, struck down presidential term limits, Hernández won reelection, Nov. 26, 2017.

Honduras has become a transshipment point for illegal drugs being smuggled to the U.S. Hernández was an unindicted co-conspirator in the 2019 U.S. drug-crimes trial of his brother (convicted Oct. 18). Drug-gang violence and other crime apparently contributed to an increase in Honduran migrants and asylum seekers trying to enter the U.S. along the Mexican border, 2013-19. Under a 2019 agreement with the U.S., Honduras would accept asylum seekers from other countries trying to reach the U.S.

Environmental activist Berta Cáceres was shot to death, Mar. 3, 2016. The NGO Global Witness estimated in mid-2017 that more than 120 environmental activists or opponents of land seizures for development had been killed since 2009. On Nov. 29, 2018, seven men were convicted of the Cáceres murder, apparently ordered by a company facing delays on a dam project.

The 2020 COVID-19 pandemic caused more than 75,500 Honduran cases (including Pres. Hernández) and over 2,300 deaths by Sept. 30.

Hungary

People: Population: 9,771,827 (93). **Age distrib.:** <15: 14.5%; 65+: 20.7%. **Growth:** −0.3%. **Migrants:** 5.3%. **Pop. density:** 282.4 per sq mi, 109.1 per sq km. **Urban:** 71.9%. **Ethnic groups:** Hungarian 85.6%, Romani 3.2%. **Languages:** Hungarian (official), English, German. **Religions:** Christian 87.3% (Catholic 58.3%, Protestant 25.6%), agnostic 7.6%, atheist 4.1%.
Geography: Total area: 35,918 sq mi, 93,028 sq km (108); **Land area:** 34,598 sq mi, 89,608 sq km. **Location:** Central Europe. Ukraine, Slovakia on N; Austria on W; Slovenia, Croatia, Serbia on S; Romania on E. **Topography:** Danube R. forms Slovak border in NW, then swings S to bisect country. Eastern half of Hungary is mainly a great fertile plain, the Alfold. Hilly in W and N. **Arable land:** 47.4%. **Capital:** Budapest, 1,768,073.
Government: Type: Parliamentary republic. **Head of state:** Pres. János Áder; b. 1959; in office: May 10, 2012. **Head of govt.:** Prime Min. Viktor Orbán; b. 1963; in office: May 29, 2010. **Local divisions:** 19 counties, 23 cities with county rights, 1 capital city. **Defense budget:** $2 bil. **Active troops:** 27,800.
Economy: Industries: mining, metallurgy, constr. materials, processed foods, textiles, chemicals (espec. pharmaceuticals), motor vehicles. **Chief agric.:** wheat, corn, sunflower seeds, potatoes, sugar beets; pigs, cattle. **Natural resources:** bauxite, coal, nat. gas. **Water:** 10,697 cu m per capita. **Crude oil reserves:** 18 mil bbls. **Electricity prod.** (2018): 30.3 bil kWh. **Labor force:** agric. 4.6%, industry 32.8%, services 62.6%. **Unemployment:** 3.5%.
Finance: Monetary unit: Forint (HUF) (303.88 = $1 U.S.). **GDP:** $332.0 bil; **per capita GDP:** $33,979; **GDP growth:** 4.9%. **Imports:** $96.3 bil; Germany 26.2%, Austria 6.3%, China 5.9%, Poland 5.5%, Slovakia 5.3%, Netherlands 5%. **Exports:** $98.7 bil; Germany 27.7%, Romania 5.4%, Italy 5.1%, Austria 5%. **Tourism:** $7.3 bil. **Budget:** $64.7 bil. **Inflation:** 3.3%.

Transport: Railways: 5,001 mi. **Motor vehicles:** 421.9 per 1,000 pop. **Airports:** 20.

Communications: Telephone: 31.1 per 100 pop. **Mobile:** 103.4 per 100 pop. **Broadband:** 49.1 per 100 pop. **Internet** (2018): 76.1%.

Health: Expend.: 6.9%. **Life expect.:** 73.0 male; 80.6 female. **Births:** 8.8 per 1,000 pop. **Deaths:** 12.9 per 1,000 pop. **Infant mortality:** 4.7 per 1,000 live births. **Undernourished:** <2.5%. **HIV** (2018): <0.1%.

Education: Compulsory: ages 4-16. **Literacy:** 99.4%.

Embassy: 3910 Shoemaker St. NW 20008; 362-6730.

Website: www.kormany.hu

Earliest settlers, chiefly Slav and Germanic, were overrun by Magyars from the east. Stephen I (997-1038) was made king by Pope Sylvester II in 1000 CE. The country suffered repeated Turkish invasions in the 15th-17th cents. After the Turks were defeated, 1686-97, Austria dominated, but Hungary obtained concessions, and regained internal independence in 1867 under a dual monarchy with the emperor of Austria. Defeated with the Central Powers at the end of WWI in 1918, Hungary lost Transylvania to Romania, Croatia and Bacska to Yugoslavia, and Slovakia and Carpatho-Ruthenia to Czechoslovakia. All had large Hungarian minorities. A republic under Michael Karolyi and a Bolshevist revolt under Bela Kun were followed by a vote for a monarchy in 1920 with Adm. Nicholas Horthy as regent.

Hungary allied with Germany before WWII and was allowed to annex, 1938-41, most of its lost territories. Russian troops captured the country, 1944-45. Hungary returned to its borders of 1937.

A republic was declared Feb. 1, 1946. In 1947 a hard-line Communist, pro-Soviet government was installed. Demonstrations against Communist rule developed into open revolt in 1956. Soviet forces launched a massive attack Nov. 4 against Budapest. About 200,000 persons fled the country. Thousands were arrested and executed.

Major economic reforms were launched early in 1968, switching from a central planning system to one based on market forces and profit. In 1989 Parliament legalized freedom of assembly and association as Hungary shifted away from Communism. In Oct. the Communist Party was formally dissolved. The last Soviet troops left June 19, 1991. Hungary became a full member of NATO in 1999 and of the EU in 2004.

The IMF, EU, and World Bank agreed Oct. 2008 to extend $25.1 bil to rescue Hungary's economy, battered by a global financial crisis. The center-right Fidesz party ousted the Socialists in 2010 parliamentary elections, and Viktor Orbán became prime min. A fiscally and socially conservative constitution went into force Jan. 1, 2012. Fidesz won Apr. 6, 2014, elections and, after an anti-immigration campaign, increased its majority in Apr. 8, 2018, voting. The EU in 2018 began consideration of disciplinary measures against Hungary, in part over limits on press and other freedoms. Dec. 2018 Hungarian legislation limited judicial independence. May 2020 legislation repealed legal rights of transgender people.

Hungary was a major transit route in 2015 for migrants from the Balkans, SW Asia, the Middle East, and Africa trying to reach N Europe. More than 411,000 migrants entered or tried to enter Hungary in 2015, almost all before the end of Oct., by which time Hungary had built more than 300 mi of security fencing along its southern borders with Serbia and Croatia. The government refused to participate in a 2015 EU refugee resettlement program.

In 2020, the COVID-19 pandemic caused more than 26,000 cases and 765 deaths in Hungary by Sept. 30. Ostensibly pandemic-related legislation, Mar. 30, gave Orbán sweeping emergency powers; June laws to end emergency rule gave Orbán authority to reinstate it at any time.

Iceland
Republic of Iceland

People: Population: 350,734 (172). **Age distrib.:** <15: 20.3%; 65+: 15.5%. **Growth:** 1.0%. **Migrants:** 15.5%. **Pop. density:** 9.1 per sq mi, 3.5 per sq km. **Urban:** **Ethnic groups:** homogeneous mix of Norse-Celt descend or born in a background (immigrant or one parent born abroad): **Languages:** Icelandic, English, Nordic langs., German. **Religion:** Christian 92% (Protestant 80.8%), agnostic 5.4%.

Geography: Total area: 39,769 sq mi, 103,000 sq km (106). **Land area:** 38,707 sq mi, 100,250 sq km. **Location:** Isl. at N end of Atlantic O. Nearest neighbor is Greenland (Den.) to W. **Topography:** Recent volcanic origin. Three-quarters of surface is wasteland: glaciers, lakes, lava desert, geysers, and hot springs. The climate is moderated by the Gulf Stream. **Arable land:** 1.2%. **Capital:** Reykjavik, 216,364.

Government: Type: Unitary parliamentary republic. **Head of state:** Pres. Gudni Thorlacius Johannesson; b. 1968; in office: Aug. 1, 2016. **Head of govt.:** Prime Min. Katrin Jakobsdottir; b. 1976; in office: Nov. 30, 2017. **Local divisions:** 74 municipalities. **Defense budget:** $55 mil (Coast Guard budget). **Active troops:** No armed forces; 250 Coast Guard. Relies on NATO allies for air policing and defense.

Economy: Industries: tourism, fish proc., aluminum smelting, geothermal power, hydropower, medical/pharmaceutical prods. **Chief agric.:** potatoes, carrots, green vegetables; mutton, chicken; fish. **Natural resources:** fish, hydropower, geothermal power, diatomite. **Water:** 507,463 cu m per capita. **Electricity prod.** (2018):

19.6 bil kWh. **Labor force:** agric. 3.8%, industry 16.1%, services 80.1%. **Unemployment:** 3.2%.

Finance: Monetary unit: Krona (ISK) (138.99 = $1 U.S.). **GDP:** $21.7 bil; **per capita GDP:** $60,061; **GDP growth:** 1.9%. **Imports:** $6.5 bil; Germany 10.7%, Norway 9.2%, China 7%, Netherlands 6.7%, U.S. 6.4%, Denmark 6.2%, UK 5.7%. **Exports:** $5.0 bil; Netherlands 25.5%, Spain 13.6%, UK 9.4%, Germany 7.6%, U.S. 7%, France 6.3%. **Tourism:** $2.7 bil. **Budget:** $10.0 bil. **Inflation:** 3.0%.

Transport: Motor vehicles: 873.9 per 1,000 pop. **Airports:** 7.

Communications: Telephone: 40.6 per 100 pop. **Mobile:** 126.1 per 100 pop. **Broadband:** 113.3 per 100 pop. **Internet** (2018): 99%.

Health: Expend.: 8.3%. **Life expect.:** 81.0 male; 85.6 female. **Births:** 13.3 per 1,000 pop. **Deaths:** 6.6 per 1,000 pop. **Infant mortality:** 2.1 per 1,000 live births. **Undernourished:** <2.5%. **HIV** (2018): 0.1%.

Education: Compulsory: ages 6-15. **Literacy:** 99%.

Embassy: 2900 K St. NW, Ste. 509, 20007; 265-6653.

Website: www.iceland.is

Iceland was an independent republic from 930 to 1262, when it joined with Norway. Its language has maintained its purity for 1,000 years. The Althing, or assembly, established in 930, is the world's oldest surviving parliament. Danish rule lasted 1380-1918; the last ties with the Danish crown were severed in 1944.

Iceland's banking system and currency collapsed amid the global financial crisis in Oct. 2008. More than $10 bil in loans from the IMF and European governments restored financial stability; austerity measures were imposed, and the nation entered a deep recession. Soaring inflation and unemployment led to the Feb. 2009 installation of a center-left government. An Apr. 2010 eruption of the Eyjafjallajökull volcano disrupted European air traffic. After Apr. 28, 2013, parliamentary elections, center-right parties came to power. Following Oct. 28, 2017, elections, Katrin Jakobsdottir of the Left-Green Movement became prime min., forming a coalition with center-right parties.

Affected by the 2020 COVID-19 pandemic, Iceland instituted a testing, tracing, and isolation program to slow transmission. As of Sept. 30, the country had about 2,700 total cases and 10 deaths.

Iceland's glaciers have been shrinking, an apparent effect of climate change.

India
Republic of India

People: Population: 1,326,093,247 (2). **Age distrib.:** <15: 26.3%; 65+: 6.7%. **Growth:** 1.1%. **Migrants:** 0.4%. **Pop. density:** 1,155.2 per sq mi, 446.0 per sq km. **Urban:** 34.9%. **Ethnic groups:** Indo-Aryan 72%, Dravidian 25%, Mongoloid and other 3%. **Languages:** Hindi (most widely spoken); 22 other official langs. (incl. Bengali, Telugu, Marathi, Tamil, Urdu, Gujarati); English (subsidiary official lang.; crucial for natl., political, commercial communication); Hindustani (variant of Hindi/Urdu widely spoken throughout N). **Religions:** Hindu 72.5% (Vaishnavite 28%, Shaivite 26%, Saktist 19%), Muslim 14.5% (Sunni 13%, Shia 1%), Christian 4.9%, ethnic religionist 3.5%, Sikh 1.9%, agnostic 1.2%.

Geography: Total area: 1,269,219 sq mi, 3,287,263 sq km (7); **Land area:** 1,147,956 sq mi, 2,973,193 sq km. **Location:** Occupies most of Indian subcontinent in S Asia. Pakistan on W; China, Nepal, Bhutan on N; Myanmar, Bangladesh on E. **Topography:** The Himalayan Mts., highest in world, stretch across northern borders. The Ganges Plain below is among the world's most densely populated regions. The climate varies from tropical heat in S to near-Arctic cold in N. Rajasthan Desert in NW. NE Assam Hills get 400 in. of rain a year. **Arable land:** 52.6%. **Capital:** Delhi, 30,290,936. **Cities:** Mumbai (Bombay), 20,411,274; Kolkata (Calcutta), 14,850,066; Bangalore, 12,326,532; Chennai (Madras), 10,971,108; Hyderabad, 10,004,144; Ahmadabad, 8,059,441; Surat, 7,184,590; Pune (Poona), 6,629,347; Srinagar, 1,585,774; Jammu, 702,085.

Government: Type: Federal parliamentary republic. **Head of state:** Pres. Ram Nath Kovind; b. 1945; in office: July 25, 2017. **Head of govt.:** Prime Min. Narendra Modi; b. 1950; in office: May 26, 2014. **Local divisions:** 28 states, 8 union territories. **Defense budget:** $60.5 bil. **Active troops:** 1,455,550.

Economy: Industries: textiles, chemicals, food proc., steel, transp. equip., cement, mining, petroleum, machinery, software, pharmaceuticals. **Chief agric.:** rice, wheat, oilseed, cotton, jute, tea, sugarcane, lentils, onions, potatoes; dairy prods., sheep, goats; fish. **Natural resources:** coal, iron ore, manganese, mica, bauxite, rare earth elements, titanium ore, chromite, nat. gas, diamonds, petroleum, limestone. **Water:** 1,427 cu m per capita. **Crude oil reserves:** 4.4 bil bbls. **Electricity prod.** (2018): 1.5 tril kWh. **Labor force:** agric. 41.5%, industry 26.2%, services 32.3%. **Unemployment:** 5.4%.

Finance: Monetary unit: Rupee (INR) (73.26 = $1 U.S.). **GDP:** $9.6 tril; **per capita GDP:** $7,034; **GDP growth:** 5.0%. **Imports:** $452.2 bil; China 16.3%, U.S. 5.5%, UAE 5.2%. **Exports:** $304.1 bil; U.S. 15.6%, UAE 10.2%. **Tourism:** $30 bil. **Budget:** $329.0 bil. **Inflation:** 7.7%.

Transport: Railways: 42,579 mi. **Motor vehicles:** 43.5 per 1,000 pop. **Airports:** 253.

Communications: Telephone: 1.6 per 100 pop. **Mobile:** 86.9 per 100 pop. **Broadband:** 25.8 per 100 pop. **Internet:** 34.5%.
Health: Expend.: 3.5%. **Life expect.:** 68.4 male; 71.2 female.
Births: 18.2 per 1,000 pop. **Deaths:** 7.3 per 1,000 pop. **Infant mortality:** 35.4 per 1,000 live births. **Undernourished:** 14.0%. **HIV:** NA.
Education: Compulsory: ages 6-13. **Literacy:** 91.7%.
Embassy: 2107 Massachusetts Ave. NW 20008; 939-7000.
Website: www.india.gov.in

India has one of the oldest civilizations in the world. Excavations trace the Indus Valley civilization back for at least 5,000 years. Paintings in the mountain caves of Ajanta, richly carved temples, the Taj Mahal in Agra, and the Kutab Minar in Delhi are among treasured relics of the past.

Aryan tribes, speaking Sanskrit, invaded from the NW around 1500 BCE. Asoka ruled most of the Indian subcontinent in the 3rd cent. BCE and established Buddhism. But Hinduism revived and eventually predominated. Under the Guptas, 4th-6th cent. CE, science, literature, and the arts enjoyed a golden age. Arab invaders established a Muslim foothold in the west in the 8th cent., and Turkish Muslims gained control of North India by 1200. The Mughal emperors ruled 1526-1857.

Vasco da Gama established Portuguese trading posts 1498-1503. The Dutch followed. The British East India Co. sent Capt. William Hawkins, 1609, to get concessions from the Mughal emperor for spices and textiles. Operating as the East India Co., the British gained control of most of India. The British parliament assumed political direction; under Lord Bentinck, 1828-35, rule by rajahs (princes) was curbed. After the Sepoy troops mutinied, 1857-58, the British supported the native rulers.

Nationalism grew after WWI. The Indian National Congress and the Muslim League demanded constitutional reform. A leader emerged in Mohandas K. Gandhi (called Mahatma, or Great Soul) (b. Oct. 2, 1869), who advocated self-rule, nonviolence, and an end to caste discrimination against "untouchables." In 1930 he launched a program of civil disobedience, boycotting British goods and rejecting taxes without representation. He was assassinated Jan. 30, 1948.

In 1935, Britain gave India a constitution providing a bicameral federal congress. Muhammad Ali Jinnah, head of the Muslim League, sought creation of a Muslim nation, Pakistan.

The British government partitioned British India into the dominions of India and Pakistan. India became a member of the UN in 1945, a self-governing member of the Commonwealth in 1947, and a democratic republic, Jan. 26, 1950. More than 12 mil Hindu and Muslim refugees crossed the India-Pakistan borders in 1947; about 200,000 were killed in communal fighting.

After Pakistan troops began attacks on Bengali separatists in East Pakistan, Mar. 25, 1971, some 10 mil refugees fled to India. India and Pakistan went to war Dec. 3, 1971, on both the east and west fronts. Pakistan troops, Dec. 16, surrendered in the east, which became Bangladesh; Pakistan agreed to a cease-fire in the west Dec. 17.

Indira Gandhi, India's prime minister since Jan. 1966, invoked emergency powers in June 1975. Thousands of opponents were arrested and press censorship imposed. These and other actions, including population control through forced vasectomies, were widely resented. Opposition parties, united in the Janata coalition, won the 1977 elections.

Gandhi became prime minister for the second time in 1980. She was assassinated by two of her Sikh bodyguards Oct. 31, 1984, in response to the government suppression in June 1984 of a Sikh uprising in Punjab, which included an assault on the Golden Temple at Amritsar, the holiest Sikh shrine. Widespread rioting followed the assassination; thousands of Sikhs were killed and some 50,000 left homeless. Rajiv, Indira Gandhi's son, replaced her as prime min. A gas leak at a Union Carbide chemical plant in Bhopal, Dec. 1984, eventually killed some 14,000 people.

Many died in religious, ethnic, and political conflicts during the late 1980s and early '90s. To suppress the Sikh insurgency in Punjab, Indian government troops attacked the Golden Temple again in 1988. Rajiv Gandhi, swept from office in 1989, was assassinated May 21, 1991. Nationwide riots followed the destruction of a 16th-cent. mosque in Ayodhya by Hindu militants in Dec. 1992. Ethnic clashes in Assam, in NE India, killed thousands in Feb. 1993. Bombs jolted Mumbai and Kolkata, Mar. 12-19, killing over 300.

India conducted a series of nuclear tests in mid-May 1998, raising tensions with Pakistan. India blamed Pakistani-sponsored terrorist groups for an Oct. 1, 2001, suicide attack on the state legislature in Jammu and Kashmir (see below), in which at least 40 people died, and a Dec. 13 assault on the Indian parliament in New Delhi that left 13 people dead. Hindu-Muslim clashes in Gujarat Feb.-Mar. 2002 claimed more than 700 lives.

The Congress Party won the most seats in 2004 parliamentary elections.

The Indian Ocean tsunami of Dec. 26, 2004, left more than 16,000 people dead and over 647,000 displaced in India. Islamic extremists set off 7 bombs on commuter trains in Mumbai, July 11, 2006, killing some 200 people. The unmanned *Chandrayaan-1*, India's first lunar survey mission, was launched into space Oct. 22, 2008.

Ten Pakistanis linked to a Kashmir militant group stormed several sites in Mumbai, Nov. 2008, killing 163 people.

In 2009 parliamentary elections, the United Progressive Alliance, headed by the Congress Party, gained a resounding victory. A triple bombing in Mumbai July 13, 2011, killed 26 people and injured about 140. Electricity blackouts July 30-31, 2012, left 670 mil people without power.

Several rapes in New Delhi in Nov.-Dec. 2012 prompted protests for their mishandling by police and government inaction. Tougher laws against sexual violence were passed Feb. 4, 2013. The Hindu nationalist Bharatiya Janata party (BJP) won a large majority in Apr.-May 2014 parliamentary elections; Narendra Modi became prime min.

Development of high-tech industries has propelled rapid economic growth in most years since the 1990s; hundreds of millions have emerged from extreme poverty, although distribution of wealth remains highly uneven. Since 2011, India has had the world's third-largest GDP. To combat climate change, the government released a plan, Oct. 1, 2015, for reducing the rate of growth in India's carbon emissions. WHO data released in 2018 showed that 11 of the 12 world cities with the worst air pollution were in India.

The Supreme Court, Sept. 6, 2018, struck down a 19th-cent. law that made consensual gay sex a criminal offense. The BJP increased its majority in Apr.-May 2019 elections. Objecting to what were characterized as protectionist Indian trade practices, the U.S. took steps in 2019 to increase tariffs on various Indian exports. A check of citizenship status in Assam produced a list, released Aug. 31, 2019, of 1.9 mil people, mostly Muslim ethnic Bengalis, judged to be noncitizens and subject to deportation. Dec. 2019 legislation facilitated citizenship for some migrants from Bangladesh, Pakistan, or Afghanistan—not including Muslims. On Aug. 5, 2020, Modi participated in a groundbreaking ceremony for a Hindu temple to be built on the site of the destroyed Ayodhya mosque.

As the COVID-19 pandemic spread to India, the government ordered a strict nationwide lockdown as of Mar. 25, 2020, to slow disease transmission. The severe economic impact (GDP fell almost 24% in Q2) led to easing of the lockdown beginning in May, although new cases were rising. They increased more sharply in subsequent months. By Sept. 30, India had more than 6.2 mil cases (2nd-highest in the world), and about 97,500 people had died (3rd-highest).

Sikkim, bordered by Tibet, Bhutan, and Nepal, formerly British protected, became a protectorate of India in 1950. Area 2,740 sq mi; pop. (2011 census) 610,577; capital is Gangtok. In Sept. 1974, India's parliament voted to make Sikkim an associate Indian state, absorbing it into India.

Kashmir is a predominantly Muslim region in the NW that borders India, Pakistan, Afghanistan, and China. Muslim rule of the previously Hindu kingdom began in 1341; after almost 200 years under the Mughals, the area was incorporated into British India in 1846. Fighting broke out in the region between India and Pakistan in 1947 following independence from Britain. A cease-fire was negotiated by the UN Jan. 1, 1949; it gave Pakistan control of one-third of the area as Azad Kashmir, in the W and NW, and India the remaining two-thirds, as the Indian state of Jammu and Kashmir. Area 39,146 sq mi; pop. (2011 census) 12,541,302. Capitals: Srinagar (summer), pop. (2019 est.) 1,549,803; Jammu (winter), pop. (2019 est.) 696,856. Fighting in the area resumed during 1965 and 1971. China occupied about 14,000 sq mi in the Ladakh district after a war with India in 1962. India separated Ladakh from Jammu and Kashmir in 2019. On June 15, 2020, at least 20 Indian soldiers were killed in fighting with Chinese troops in a disputed border area of Ladakh, and tensions remained high in subsequent months.

Since 1989, Indian security forces in Jammu and Kashmir have battled Islamic separatist fighters. India has charged Pakistan with aiding the separatists. A cease-fire between Indian and Pakistani troops along the line of control took effect Nov. 2003. Some breaches occurred, and fighting between Indian forces and Islamic militants continued. After a period of intense cross-border shelling, India and Pakistan agreed on a new cease-fire, May 29, 2018. More than 40 Indian paramilitary troops in Kashmir were killed in a terrorist bombing, Feb. 14, 2019. Fighting between Indian forces and separatists continued in 2020. Estimates of conflict-related deaths since 1989 range from 40,000 to over 80,000.

The Indian government revoked statehood for Jammu and Kashmir, effective Oct. 31, 2019, to create two federally administered territories; India increased security forces and reportedly detained thousands.

France, 1952-54, peacefully yielded to India its five colonies, former French India: Pondicherry, Karikal, Mahe, and Yanaon were merged to become Pondicherry, now Puducherry, area 185 sq mi; pop. (2011 census) 1,247,953. The colony of Chandernagor was incorporated into the state of West Bengal.

SCIENCE & TECHNOLOGY

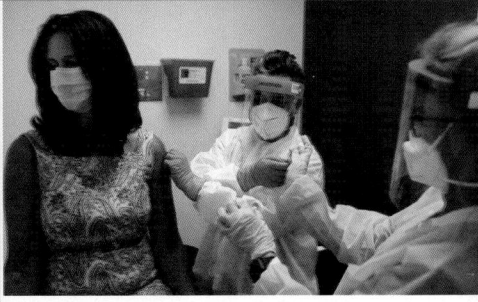

HIDING IN PLAIN SIGHT Researchers May 6, 2020, announced their discovery of the closest-known black hole to Earth, just 1,000 light-years away.

MOON SHOT Pharmaceutical companies and public health authorities raced to develop a potential vaccine to prevent the spread of COVID-19, with several vaccines reaching the clinical trial phase by summer 2020.

PLAGUE AND PESTILENCE
Locust swarms destroyed farmland and threatened already precarious food security in 2020, particularly in hard-hit East African countries, including Kenya, Somalia, and Ethiopia.

SPACE MILESTONE
SpaceX became the first private company to launch humans into orbit May 30, 2020, when it ferried two NASA astronauts to the International Space Station.

SPORTS

CHANGING TIMES Some fans resisted NASCAR's June 10, 2020, move to ban the Confederate flag at all of its facilities and events.

PUBLIC GRIEF
NBA fans mourned the sudden death of 41-year-old former L.A. Lakers star Kobe Bryant, who died along with eight others in a helicopter crash, Jan. 26, 2020.

RECORD-SETTER
Heisman winner Joe Burrow notched a handful of records as he led LSU to a College Football Playoff Championship win, 42-25, over Clemson Jan. 13, 2020.

COMEBACK KID Kansas City quarterback Patrick Mahomes led a 2nd-half charge to defeat the San Francisco 49ers in Super Bowl LIV, 31-20, Feb. 2, 2020.

EARLY SUCCESS American 23-year-old Collin Morikawa claimed the PGA Championship title Aug. 9, 2020.

HEAD START The NWSL was the first professional league to restart and complete their pandemic-shortened 2020 season, with Rachel Daly and the Houston Dash taking the championship over Chicago July 26, 2020.

SHUT OUT As professional sports emerged from COVID-19-related season delays in July 2020, stadiums and arenas remained largely unoccupied out of safety concerns.

MATCH POINT Naomi Osaka won an emotional U.S. Open singles title over Victoria Azarenka Sept. 12, 2020, and made a statement throughout the tournament wearing face masks bearing the names of Black people who were victims of violence.

ANOTHER CROWN
LeBron James led the L.A. Lakers to the NBA title, Oct. 11, 2020, over the Miami Heat, earning his fourth NBA Finals MVP Award.

ARTS

A STAR IS BORN 18-year-old pop talent Billie Eilish won all four major award categories at the Grammy Awards Jan. 26, 2020, while her brother, producer Finneas O'Connell, won five.

SHOW STOPPERS Ariana Grande and Lady Gaga each claimed multiple awards and performed together at the MTV Video Music Awards Aug. 30, 2020.

WINNING THE DAY South Korea's Bong Joon-ho and *Parasite* made Academy Awards history Feb. 9, 2020, with the first non-English-language film ever to win Best Picture.

"SIMPLY THE BEST" Canadian sitcom *Schitt's Creek* swept the comedy categories at the 72nd Emmy Awards, held largely remotely Sept. 20, 2020, taking best comedy series and all four acting prizes, which went to stars Eugene Levy, Annie Murphy, Daniel Levy, and Catherine O'Hara.

PEOPLE

JUDGMENT DAY
Movie producer Harvey Weinstein was convicted of rape in New York and sentenced to 23 years in prison Mar. 11, 2020; other sexual assault charges were pending in Los Angeles.

STEPPING BACK
Prince Harry and Meghan Markle Jan. 8, 2020, announced they were retreating from their royal duties, raising eyebrows among UK royal watchers.

CALL THE DOCTOR
Anthony Fauci, the director of the National Institute of Allergy and Infectious Diseases, became a familiar face in the U.S. government's pandemic response briefings in spring 2020.

U.S. v. Ghislaine Maxwell

- Maxwell has been charged with facilitating the sexual abuse of underaged girls by Jeffrey Epstein.
- The charged conduct occurred in New York City, Palm Beach, Florida, Santa Fe, New Mexico, and London, England.
- If you recognize either of these persons and feel you may be a victim, please call the following number:

1-800-CALL FBI

IN FEDERAL CUSTODY
Ghislaine Maxwell, the alleged accomplice of deceased accused sex-trafficker Jeffrey Epstein, was arrested July 2, 2020.

FAREWELL

CHADWICK BOSEMAN
Nov. 29, 1976-Aug. 28, 2020

KOBE BRYANT
Aug. 23, 1978-Jan. 26, 2020

HERMAN CAIN
Dec. 13, 1945-July 30, 2020

CHRISTO
June 13, 1935-May 31, 2020

MARY HIGGINS CLARK
Dec. 24, 1927-Jan. 31, 2020

CHARLIE DANIELS
Oct. 28, 1936-July 6, 2020

OLIVIA DE HAVILLAND
July 1, 1916-July 26, 2020

BRIAN DENNEHY
July 9, 1938-Apr. 15, 2020

KIRK DOUGLAS
Dec. 9, 1916-Feb. 5, 2020

HUGH DOWNS
Feb. 14, 1921-July 1, 2020

WHITEY FORD
Oct. 21, 1928-Oct. 8, 2020

BOB GIBSON
Nov. 9, 1935-Oct. 2, 2020

RUTH BADER GINSBURG
Mar. 15, 1933-Sept. 18, 2020

KATHERINE JOHNSON
Aug. 26, 1918-Feb. 24, 2020

TERRY JONES
Feb. 1, 1942-Jan. 21, 2020

IRRFAN KHAN
Jan. 7, 1967-Apr. 29, 2020

LARRY KRAMER
June 25, 1935-May 27, 2020

JIM LEHRER
May 19, 1934-Jan. 23, 2020

JOHN LEWIS
Feb. 21, 1940-July 17, 2020

LITTLE RICHARD
Dec. 5, 1932-May 9, 2020

TERRENCE MCNALLY
Nov. 3, 1938-Mar. 24, 2020

REGIS PHILBIN
Aug. 25, 1931-July 24, 2020

JOHN PRINE
Oct. 10, 1946-Apr. 7, 2020

CARL REINER
Mar. 20, 1922-June 29, 2020

FAREWELL

DIANA RIGG
July 20, 1938-Sept. 10, 2020

NAYA RIVERA
Jan. 12, 1987-July 8, 2020

KENNY ROGERS
Aug. 21, 1938-Mar. 20, 2020

GALE SAYERS
May 30, 1943-Sept. 23, 2020

TOM SEAVER
Nov. 17, 1944-Aug. 31, 2020

JERRY STILLER
June 8, 1927-May 11, 2020

LINDA TRIPP
Nov. 24, 1949-Apr. 8, 2020

EDDIE VAN HALEN
Jan. 26, 1955-Oct. 6, 2020

MAX VON SYDOW
Apr. 10, 1929-Mar. 8, 2020

FRED WILLARD
Sept. 18, 1933-May 15, 2020

BILL WITHERS
July 4, 1938-Mar. 30, 2020

MICKEY WRIGHT
Feb. 14, 1935-Feb. 17, 2020

Indonesia
Republic of Indonesia

People: Population: 267,026,366 (4). **Age distrib.:** <15: 23.9%; 65+: 7.8%. **Growth:** 0.8%. **Migrants:** 0.1%. **Pop. density:** 381.8 per sq mi, 147.4 per sq km. **Urban:** 56.6%. **Ethnic groups:** Javanese 40.1%, Sundanese 15.5%, Malay 3.7%, Batak 3.6%, Madurese 3%, Betawi 2.9%, Minangkabau 2.7%, Buginese 2.7%, Bantenese 2%. **Languages:** Bahasa Indonesia (official; modified form of Malay), English, Dutch, local dialects (Javanese most widely spoken). **Religions:** Muslim 79.6% (Sunni), Christian 12.2%.

Geography: Total area: 735,358 sq mi, 1,904,569 sq km (14); **Land area:** 699,451 sq mi, 1,811,569 sq km. **Location:** Archipelago SE of Asian mainland along the equator. Malaysia on N, Papua New Guinea on E, Timor-Leste on S. **Topography:** Comprises 17,508 islands (about 6,000 inhabited), including Java, Sumatra, Kalimantan (most of Borneo), Sulawesi (Celebes), and West Irian (Irian Jaya, the W half of New Guinea). Also Bangka, billiton, Madura, Bali, Timor. Cooler climate in mountains and plateaus on the major isls.; tropical lowlands. **Arable land:** 14.0%. **Capital:** Jakarta, 10,770,487. **Cities:** Bekasi, 3,394,273; Surabaya, 2,944,403; Depok, 2,727,209; Bandung, 2,580,191.

Government: Type: Presidential republic. **Head of state and govt.:** Pres. Joko Widodo; b. 1961; in office: Oct. 20, 2014. **Local divisions:** 31 provinces, 1 autonomous province, 1 special region, 1 national capital district. **Defense budget:** $7.4 bil. **Active troops:** 395,500.

Economy: Industries: petroleum and nat. gas, textiles, automotive, elec. appliances, apparel, footwear, mining, cement, medical instruments and appliances. **Chief agric.:** rubber, palm oil, poultry, beef, shrimp, cocoa, coffee, medicinal herbs. **Natural resources:** petroleum, tin, nat. gas, nickel, timber, bauxite, copper, coal, gold, silver. **Water:** 7,648 cu m per capita. **Crude oil reserves:** 3.2 bil bbls. **Electricity prod.:** 241.3 bil kwH. **Labor force:** agric. 27.7%, industry 22.7%, services 49.6%. **Unemployment:** 4.8%.

Finance: Monetary unit: Rupiah (IDR) (14,744.40 = $1 U.S.). **GDP:** $3.3 tril; **per capita GDP:** $12,302; **GDP growth:** 5.0%. **Imports:** $150.1 bil; China 23.2%, Singapore 10.9%, Japan 10%, Thailand 6%, Malaysia 5.6%, South Korea 5.3%, U.S. 5.2%. **Exports:** $168.9 bil; China 13.6%, U.S. 10.6%, Japan 10.5%, India 8.4%, Singapore 7.6%, Malaysia 5.1%. **Tourism:** $16.9 bil. **Budget:** $159.6 bil. **Inflation:** 3.0%.

Transport: Railways: 5,070 mi (only partly operational). **Motor vehicles:** 102.2 per 1,000 pop. **Airports:** 186.

Communications: Telephone: 4.2 per 100 pop. **Mobile:** 119.8 per 100 pop. **Broadband:** 95.7 per 100 pop. **Internet** (2018): 39.8%.

Health: Expend.: 3.0%. **Life expect.:** 71.1 male; 76.5 female. **Births:** 15.4 per 1,000 pop. **Deaths:** 6.6 per 1,000 pop. **Infant mortality:** 20.4 per 1,000 live births. **Undernourished:** 9.0%. **HIV** (2018): 0.4%.

Education: Compulsory: ages 7-15. **Literacy:** 99.7%.
Embassy: 2020 Massachusetts Ave. NW 20036; 775-5200.
Website: www.indonesia.go.id

Hindu and Buddhist civilization from India reached Indonesia nearly 2,000 years ago, taking root especially in Java. Islam spread along the maritime trade routes in the 15th cent. and became predominant by the 16th cent. The Dutch replaced the Portuguese as the area's most important European trade power in the 17th cent., securing territorial control over Java by 1750. The other islands were subdued in the early 20th cent.

Following Japanese occupation, 1942-45, nationalists led by Sukarno and Hatta declared independence. The Netherlands ceded sovereignty in 1949. A republic was declared, Aug. 17, 1950, with Sukarno as president.

Irian Jaya, on New Guinea, remained under Dutch control but was transferred by the UN to Indonesia in 1963; it became the provinces of Papua and West Papua in the early 2000s. Pro-independence protests and an armed separatist movement have been met by a harsh government crackdown in recent years. Protests, sometimes violent, in Aug.-Sept. 2019 resulted in dozens of deaths, including at the hands of security or paramilitary forces.

Sukarno suspended parliament in 1960 and was named president for life in 1963. He made close alliances with Communist governments. In Sept. 1965 an attempted coup was successfully put down, but Sukarno was forced to cede power to the army, led by Gen. Suharto. The regime blamed the coup on the Communist Party; more than 300,000 alleged Communists were killed in army-initiated massacres.

Parliament reelected Suharto to a seventh consecutive presidential term in 1998, as a severe economic downturn focused public anger on nepotism, cronyism, and corruption in the Suharto regime. Suharto resigned May 21, 1998. Abdurrahman Wahid, leader of Indonesia's largest Muslim organization, was elected president in 1999. In Aug. 2000, under pressure from the legislature, he agreed to share power with Vice Pres. Megawati Sukarnoputri, the daughter of the late Pres. Sukarno. Charging Wahid with incompetence and corruption, the legislature ousted him July 23, 2001, and Megawati became Indonesia's first woman president.

Clashes between Muslims and Christians in the Maluku (Molucca) Isls., 1999-2002, claimed about 5,000 lives. East Timor,

a former Portuguese colony that Indonesia invaded in Dec. 1975 and controlled until Oct. 1999, became a fully independent country May 20, 2002, as Timor-Leste.

Separatists in Aceh, NW Sumatra, fought government troops, 1980s-2000s. A peace agreement granting Aceh greater autonomy was signed Aug. 15, 2005. Aceh adopted a strict penal code based on sharia law and sometimes enforced by vigilantes.

Investigators blamed Islamic terrorists for bombings that killed 202 people, mostly foreign tourists, at nightclubs in Bali, Oct. 12, 2002, and 12 people at a Marriott hotel in Jakarta, Aug. 5, 2003. A car bomb outside the Australian embassy, Sept. 9, 2004, killed 9. Susilo Bambang Yudhoyono, a retired general, defeated Megawati in a 2004 direct presidential runoff vote.

A massive earthquake off NW Sumatra, Dec. 26, 2004, triggered tsunamis that wreaked havoc in the Indian Ocean region. The death toll in Indonesia alone exceeded 165,000.

Pres. Yudhoyono won a second 5-year term July 8, 2009. Suicide bombings at two Jakarta hotels July 17 left nine people dead.

The General Elections Commission, July 22, 2014, declared populist Jakarta governor Joko Widodo the presidential election winner. All 162 people aboard an AirAsia Indonesia flight were killed, Dec. 28, 2014, when the plane crashed into the Java Sea near Borneo.

Assaults by terrorist gunmen and bombers in Jakarta, Jan. 14, 2016, left 8 dead, including 4 attackers; ISIS claimed responsibility. A series of ISIS-inspired suicide bombings at churches and attacks on police, May 2018, left 13 victims dead.

Rainforest destruction and air pollution from fires to clear areas for agriculture have been major environmental problems in recent years. A Sept. 2016 study estimated that especially severe pollution from 2015 fires may have caused more than 100,000 premature deaths.

All 189 on board an Indonesian Lion Air flight were killed, Oct. 29, 2018, when the Boeing 737 Max 8 plane crashed shortly after takeoff from Jakarta; a faulty anti-stall system on the aircraft was suspected.

Pres. Widodo won reelection in Apr. 17, 2019, voting. Severely affected by the 2020 COVID-19 pandemic, Indonesia had almost 283,000 cases and over 10,600 deaths by Sept. 30.

Iran
Islamic Republic of Iran

People: Population: 84,923,314 (17). **Age distrib.:** <15: 24.1%; 65+: 5.9%. **Growth:** 1.1%. **Migrants:** 3.2%. **Pop. density:** 143.6 per sq mi, 55.4 per sq km. **Urban:** 75.9%. **Ethnic groups:** Persian, Azeri, Kurd, Lur, Baloch, Arab, Turkmen and Turkic tribes. **Languages:** Persian Farsi (official), Azeri Turkic and Turkic dialects, Kurdish, Gilaki and Mazandarani, Luri, Balochi, Arabic. **Religions:** Muslim 98.6% (Shia [official] 81%, Sunni 17%).

Geography: Total area: 636,372 sq mi, 1,648,195 sq km (17); **Land area:** 591,352 sq mi, 1,531,595 sq km. **Location:** Between the Middle East and S Asia. Iraq, Turkey on W; Armenia, Azerbaijan, Turkmenistan on N; Afghanistan, Pakistan on E. **Topography:** Interior highlands and plains surrounded by high mountains, up to 18,000 ft. Large salt deserts cover much of area, though there are oases and forests. Most of pop. inhabits N and NW. **Arable land:** 9.0%. **Capital:** Tehran, 9,134,708. **Cities:** Mashhad, 3,208,336; Esfahan, 2,132,037.

Government: Type: Theocratic republic. **Religious head:** Ayatollah Sayyed Ali Khamenei; b. 1939; in office: June 4, 1989. **Head of state and govt.:** Pres. Hassan Rouhani; b. 1948; in office: Aug. 4, 2013. **Local divisions:** 31 provinces. **Defense budget:** $17.4 bil. **Active troops:** 610,000.

Economy: Industries: petroleum, petrochemicals, gas, fertilizer, caustic soda, textiles, cement and other constr. materials. **Chief agric.:** wheat, rice, other grains, sugar beets, sugarcane, fruits, nuts, cotton; dairy prods., wool; caviar. **Natural resources:** petroleum, nat. gas, coal, chromium, copper, iron ore, lead, manganese, zinc, sulfur. **Water:** 1,688 cu m per capita. **Crude oil reserves:** 155.6 bil bbls. **Electricity prod.:** 289.6 bil kWH. **Labor force:** agric. 17.8%, industry 30.3%, services 51.9%. **Unemployment:** 11.2%.

Finance: Monetary unit: Rial (IRR) (42,059.99 = $1 U.S.). **GDP** (2017): $1.2 tril; **per capita GDP** (2017): $14,536; **GDP growth** (2017): 3.8%. **Imports:** $76.4 bil; UAE 29.8%, China 12.7%. **Exports:** $101.4 bil; China 27.5%, India 15.1%, South Korea 11.4%, Turkey 11.1%, Italy 5.7%, Japan 5.3%. **Tourism** (2017): $4.4 bil. **Budget:** $84.5 bil. **Inflation:** 39.9%.

Transport: Railways: 5,272 mi. **Motor vehicles:** 69.3 per 1,000 pop. **Airports:** 140.

Communications: Telephone: 37.3 per 100 pop. **Mobile:** 108.5 per 100 pop. **Broadband:** 68.2 per 100 pop. **Internet** (2018): 70%.

Health: Expend.: 8.7%. **Life expect.:** 73.1 male; 76.0 female. **Births:** 16.3 per 1,000 pop. **Deaths:** 5.3 per 1,000 pop. **Infant mortality:** 14.9 per 1,000 live births. **Undernourished:** 4.7%. **HIV:** <0.1%.

Education: Compulsory: ages 6-14. **Literacy:** 98.1%.
Permanent UN mission: 622 Third Ave., 34th Fl., New York, NY 10017; (212) 687-2020.
Website: www.president.ir

Ancestors of inhabitants of Iran, formerly known as Persia, came from the east during the second millennium BCE; they were an

Indo-European group related to the Aryans of India. In 549 BCE, Cyrus the Great united the Medes and Persians in the Persian Empire; he conquered Babylonia in 538 BCE, and restored Jerusalem to the Jews. Alexander the Great conquered Persia in 333 BCE, but Persians regained independence in the next century under the Parthians, themselves succeeded by Sassanian Persians in 226 CE. Arabs brought Islam to Persia in the 7th cent., replacing the Indigenous Zoroastrian faith. After Persian political and cultural autonomy was reasserted in the 9th cent., arts and sciences flourished.

Turks and Mongols ruled Persia in turn from the 11th cent. to 1502, when Ismael I established the Iranian Safavid dynasty and made Shiite Islam the official religion. The dynasty lasted until 1722. The British and Russian empires vied for influence in the 19th cent.; Britain severed Afghanistan from Iran in 1857.

Reza Khan, a military officer, became prime min., 1923, and shah in 1925. He began modernization, curbed foreign influence, and officially changed the country's name from Persia to Iran in 1935. Fearing the shah's Axis sympathies, British and Soviet troops forced him to abdicate, 1941; he was succeeded by his son, Mohammad Reza Pahlavi. The U.S. Central Intelligence Agency had a major role in the ouster, 1953, of Prime Min. Muhammad Mossadegh, who had nationalized the oil industry.

With U.S. backing, the shah brought economic and social change to Iran (White Revolution), but repression of opposition groups grew severe. Violent protests in 1978 eventually forced the shah to depart, Jan. 16, 1979. Shiite leader Ayatollah Ruhollah Khomeini, exiled by the shah in 1963, returned to Tehran, Feb. 1. Pro-Khomeini forces defeated government troops, Feb 11. Khomeini established an Islamic theocracy.

Iranian militants seized the U.S. embassy in Tehran Nov. 4, 1979, and took hostages, including 62 Americans. Despite international condemnations and U.S. efforts, including an abortive Apr. 1980 rescue attempt, the crisis continued. The U.S. broke diplomatic relations with Iran, Apr. 7. The shah died in Egypt, July 27. The hostage drama ended Jan. 20, 1981, when an accord, involving the release of frozen Iranian assets, was reached.

War between Iran and Iraq, 1980-88, killed hundreds of thousands. In Nov. 1986 it became known that the U.S., which had generally sided with Iraq during the war, had secretly shipped arms to Iran to gain help in obtaining the release of U.S. hostages held in Lebanon.

A U.S. Navy warship shot down an Iranian airliner, July 3, 1988, after mistaking it for an F-14 fighter jet; all 290 aboard died.

An earthquake struck northern Iran June 21, 1990, killing more than 45,000 and leaving 400,000 homeless. Some 1 mil Kurdish refugees fled from Iraq to Iran following the Persian Gulf War of 1991. To curb Iran's alleged support for international terrorism, the U.S. in 1996 authorized sanctions on foreign companies that invested there.

Mohammad Khatami, a moderate Shiite Muslim cleric, was elected president in 1997. He was reelected in 2001 but faced ongoing resistance from religious conservatives.

An earthquake Dec. 26, 2003, in Bam, SE Iran, killed about 26,000 people. After the Guardian Council, dominated by religious conservatives, disqualified some 2,400 reformist candidates, hardliners won legislative elections Feb. 20, 2004.

The religiously conservative mayor of Tehran, Mahmoud Ahmadinejad, defeated former Pres. Hashemi Rafsanjani in a 2005 runoff election. U.S. Pres. George W. Bush's administration accused Iran of seeking to build nuclear weapons, aiding Shiite militias opposing government forces in the U.S.-led war in Iraq (2003-11), and supplying rockets to Hezbollah fighters in Lebanon for use against Israel.

Seeking to halt Iran's uranium-enrichment program, the UN Security Council imposed sanctions, 2006-07.

Ahmadinejad won the 2009 presidential election. His main opponent claimed the vote count was fraudulent. Huge post-election protests in Tehran and other major cities were crushed. Tensions with the U.S. and European governments were heightened in 2009 by disclosures that Iran had been secretly enriching uranium at an underground site near Qom, and by Iranian tests of medium-range missiles.

The UN and U.S. toughened sanctions, June-July 2010. Iran accused Israel, the U.S., and other Western powers of carrying out cyberattacks against the country's nuclear facilities and of assassinating Iranian scientists. Iran announced, Jan. 2012, it was enriching uranium at its underground Fordo nuclear facility.

The moderate cleric Hassan Rouhani was elected president June 14, 2013. An agreement—signed July 14, 2015, by the U.S., UK, France, Germany, Russia, China, Iran, and the EU—required Iran to limit and partly dismantle its nuclear program and submit to international inspections in return for the lifting of most sanctions. Rouhani won reelection as president, May 19, 2017. Large-scale protests, mainly against poor economic conditions, occurred in dozens of cities around Iran, Dec. 2017-Jan. 2018, until suppressed by forces of the Islamic Revolutionary Guard Corps (IRGC). Pres. Donald Trump announced, May 8, 2018, that the U.S. would withdraw from the 2015 nuclear agreement and reimpose U.S. sanctions. Beginning in July 2019, Iran took nuclear program actions in violation of the 2015 accord.

The U.S. blamed Iran for May and June 2019 attacks on oil tankers in the Persian Gulf region.

Playing a role in regional conflicts, Iran supported the Syrian government in its civil war, beginning 2012; Shiite militia forces in Iraq, beginning 2014; and Houthi rebels in Yemen's civil war, beginning 2014. ISIS claimed responsibility for two terrorist attacks in Tehran, June 7, 2017, that left at least 17 people dead. A Sept. 22, 2018, terrorist attack on a military parade in Ahvaz killed at least 25. The U.S. and Saudi Arabia blamed Iran for Sept. 14, 2019, drone and cruise missile strikes on two Saudi oil facilities; Houthi rebels had claimed responsibility. New U.S. sanctions were announced in Sept. 2019. Widespread demonstrations protesting economic conditions were suppressed, Nov. 2019; up to 1,500 protesters may have been killed.

A U.S. drone strike in Iraq, Jan. 3, 2020, killed IRGC general Qassem Soleimani, in charge of the corps' foreign operations. Iran, Jan. 7, fired missiles at two Iraqi military bases housing U.S. troops. On Jan. 8, Iran mistakenly shot down a Ukrainian airliner shortly after its takeoff from Tehran, killing all 176 onboard.

An explosion and fire caused extensive damage, July 2, 2020, at a key Iranian nuclear facility; Israeli sabotage was suspected. Several similar disasters occurred, June-July, at Iranian industrial or infrastructure sites. The U.S. further strengthened sanctions (opposed by the UK, France, and Germany), Sept. 2020.

Hard-hit by the 2020 COVID-19 pandemic, Iran had more than 453,000 cases and about 26,000 deaths as of Sept. 30.

Iraq
Republic of Iraq

People: Population: 38,872,655 (36). **Age distrib.:** <15: 37.0%; 65+: 3.3%. **Growth:** 2.1%. **Migrants:** 0.9%. **Pop. density:** 230.2 per sq mi, 88.9 per sq km. **Urban:** 70.9%. **Ethnic groups:** Arab 75%-80%, Kurdish 15%-20%, other (incl. Turkmen, Yezidi, Shabak, Kaka'i) 5%. **Languages:** Arabic, Kurdish (both official); Turkmen, Syriac, Armenian (official in areas). **Religions:** Muslim (official) 97.7% (Shia 61%, Sunni 36%).

Geography: Total area: 169,235 sq mi, 438,317 sq km (58). **Land area:** 168,868 sq mi, 437,367 sq km. **Location:** Middle East, occupying most of historic Mesopotamia. Jordan, Syria on W; Turkey on N; Iran on E; Kuwait, Saudi Arabia on S. **Topography:** Mostly an alluvial plain, including the Tigris and Euphrates Rivers, descending from mountains in N to desert in SW. Persian Gulf region is marshland. **Arable land:** 11.5%. **Capital:** Baghdad, 7,144,260. **Cities:** Mosul, 1,629,932; Basra, 1,352,210; Kirkuk, 1,012,614; Najaf, 873,744; Erbil, 846,374.

Government: Type: Federal parliamentary republic. **Head of state:** Pres. Barham Salih; b. 1960; in office Oct. 2, 2018. **Head of govt.:** Prime Min. Mustafa al-Kadhimi; b. 1967; in office: May 7, 2020. **Local divisions:** 18 governorates, 1 region (Kurdistan Regional Govt.). **Defense budget:** $20.5 bil. **Active troops:** 193,000.

Economy: Industries: petroleum, chemicals, textiles, leather, constr. materials, food proc., fertilizer, metal fabrication/proc. **Chief agric.:** wheat, barley, rice, vegetables, dates, cotton; cattle, sheep, poultry. **Natural resources:** petroleum, nat. gas, phosphates, sulfur. **Water:** 2,348 cu m per capita. **Crude oil reserves:** 145 bil bbls. **Electricity prod.:** 82.3 bil kWh. **Labor force:** agric. 17.8%, industry 22.4%, services 59.9%. **Unemployment:** 12.8%.

Finance: Monetary unit: Dinar (IQD) (1,189.59 = $1 U.S.). **GDP:** $445.5 bil; **per capita GDP:** $11,332; **GDP growth:** 4.4%. **Imports:** $39.5 bil; Turkey 27.8%, China 25.7%. **Exports:** $61.4 bil; India 21.2%, China 20.2%, U.S. 15.8%, South Korea 9.4%, Greece 5.3%. **Tourism:** $3.6 bil. **Budget:** $76.8 bil. **Inflation** (2017-18): 0.4%.

Transport: Railways: 1,412 mi. **Motor vehicles:** 58.5 per 1,000 pop. **Airports:** 72.

Communications: Telephone: 7 per 100 pop. **Mobile:** 94.9 per 100 pop. **Broadband:** 25.1 per 100 pop. **Internet:** 49.4%.

Health: Expend.: 4.2%. **Life expect.:** 70.7 male; 74.6 female. **Births:** 25.7 per 1,000 pop. **Deaths:** 3.9 per 1,000 pop. **Infant mortality:** 19.5 per 1,000 live births. **Undernourished:** 23.7%. **HIV:** NA.

Education: Compulsory: ages 6-11. **Literacy:** 93.5%.

Embassy: 3421 Massachusetts Ave. NW 20007; 742-1600.

Website: www.pmo.iq

The Tigris-Euphrates valley, formerly called Mesopotamia, was the site of one of the earliest civilizations in the world. Mesopotamia ceased to be a separate entity after Persian, Greek, and Arab conquests. The Arabs founded Baghdad, from where the caliph ruled a vast Islamic empire in the 8th and 9th cents. Mongol and Turkish conquests led to a decline in the region's population, economy, cultural life, and irrigation system.

Britain secured a League of Nations mandate over Iraq after WWI. Independence under a king came in 1932. Rebellious army officers killed King Faisal II, July 1958, and established a leftist, pan-Arab republic. The Baath Arab Socialist Party increasingly dominated successive regimes. A Baath leader, Saddam Hussein, became president in 1979. He ruled as a dictator for more than two decades, repressing Iraq's Kurds and Shiites. Israeli planes destroyed a nuclear reactor near Baghdad in 1981, claiming it could be used to produce nuclear weapons.

After skirmishing intermittently for 10 months, Iraq and Iran entered into open warfare on Sept. 22, 1980. Iran repulsed early Iraqi advances, producing a long and costly stalemate; hundreds of thousands of Iraqis lost their lives during the 8-year conflict. Saddam used poison gas against Iraqi Kurds in 1988, killing more than 5,000 people in Halabja, the first mass use of poison gas against civilians since the Holocaust.

Iraq invaded Kuwait in 1990. Backed by the UN, a U.S.-led coalition launched air and missile attacks on Iraq, Jan. 16, 1991, and began a ground attack to retake Kuwait Feb. 23. Iraqi forces were defeated in four days. Some 175,000 Iraqis were taken prisoner, and Iraqi casualties were estimated at over 85,000. As part of the cease-fire agreement, Iraq agreed to scrap all poison gas and germ weapons and allow UN observers to inspect the sites.

Iraqi cooperation with UN weapons inspection teams was intermittent throughout the 1990s. Standoffs over inspections culminated in intensive U.S. and British aerial bombardment of Iraqi military targets, Dec. 16-19, 1998. After two years of sporadic activity, U.S. and British warplanes struck sites near Baghdad mid-Feb. 2001.

Despite opposition from some countries, including France, Germany, and Russia, a U.S.-led coalition invaded Iraq Mar. 19, 2003. By Apr. 6 the British controlled Basra and other areas in the south, and the U.S. entered Baghdad Apr. 7. Saddam disappeared, the Iraqi government collapsed, and most of Iraq's armed forces dissolved into the civilian population. On May 1, U.S. Pres. George W. Bush declared the end of major combat. Searches failed to find chemical, biological, or nuclear weapons that the U.S. and other countries claimed Iraq had stockpiled.

The U.S.-led Coalition Provisional Authority was unable to maintain order following Saddam's fall. Reconstruction efforts were hampered by guerrilla attacks from Baath remnants, Islamic extremists, and others. U.S. troops killed two of Saddam's sons, Uday and Qusay, July 22, 2003, in Mosul. Saddam Hussein was captured in an underground hideout mid-Dec. 2003; tried and convicted for committing crimes against humanity in the 1980s, he was executed Dec. 30, 2006.

Photographs released in Apr. 2004 showed instances of physical abuse and sexual humiliation of Iraqi inmates by U.S. military personnel at Baghdad's Abu Ghraib prison in 2003.

On June 28, 2004, U.S. authorities transferred sovereignty to a transitional Iraqi government. Despite insurgent threats, an estimated 8 mil people in Iraq, mostly Shiites and Kurds, cast ballots Jan. 30, 2005, for a transitional national assembly. Insurgents launched new waves of attacks. Rumors of a suicide bomber set off a stampede of Shiite pilgrims in northern Baghdad Aug. 31, killing close to 1,000 people. The U.S. blamed Jordanian militant Abu Musab al-Zarqawi, leader of al-Qaeda in Iraq, for directing a series of kidnappings, beheadings, and suicide bombings. He was killed by a U.S. airstrike, June 2006.

A new government elected in legislative elections Dec. 15, 2005, was installed May 20, 2006, headed by Shiite leader Nouri Kamel al-Maliki. The Iraqi civilian death toll averaged more than 2,800 per month in 2006.

A 2007 "surge" elevated U.S. troop strength from 132,000 in Jan. to 171,000 in Oct. Military and civilian casualties began dropping after mid-2007. A cease-fire by Shiite militias and a shift by Sunni clan leaders against al-Qaeda in Iraq contributed to the reduction in violence.

A Nov. 2008 agreement called for all U.S. forces to leave Iraq by Dec. 31, 2011. Inconclusive legislative elections were held Mar. 7, 2010. On Aug. 31, Pres. Barack Obama formally declared an end to the U.S. combat role, and Operation Iraqi Freedom was succeeded by Operation New Dawn. More than 9 months of political deadlock ended when Prime Min. Maliki was sworn in for a second term Dec. 21.

U.S. troops completed their withdrawal from Iraq Dec. 15, 2011. From Mar. 2003 through Dec. 2011, more than 4,500 U.S. service members died in operations in Iraq; another 32,000 were wounded. British troop losses totaled 179; other allies, 139. More than 115,000 Iraqi civilians and over 10,000 police and security forces were killed. U.S. budgeted costs of the Iraq war exceeded $820 bil for the 2003-12 period.

Tensions manifested between Sunnis and Shiites after the U.S. departure. The Sunni insurgent group al-Qaeda in Iraq was blamed for ongoing violence; in periodic assaults throughout 2012, 4,573 civilians were killed. Violence accelerated. In 2013-14, more than 20,000 civilians were killed.

In parliamentary elections Apr. 30, 2014, Maliki's coalition won the largest bloc of seats. Shiite Haider al-Abadi, of Maliki's Dawa Party, became prime min. Sept. 8.

In Dec. 2013, the Sunni extremist Islamic State in Iraq and Syria (ISIS) began crossing from Syria into Iraq and seizing territory. The ISIS offensive intensified beginning in June 2014. The group took control of large areas of northern and central Iraq, including the cities of Mosul (Iraq's second-largest) and Tikrit, where ISIS killed 1,700 captured Shiite soldiers. ISIS imposed Islamic law, with harsh punishments, in areas it controlled while suppressing, killing, and sexually assaulting civilians who were non-Sunni Muslims or members of the Yazidi sect and other religious minorities. (Nadia Murad, a Yazidi sexual assault survivor, shared the 2018 Nobel Peace Prize for her activism against sexual violence in war.) The U.S., later joined by other nations, began, Aug. 8, airstrikes against ISIS targets; the U.S. provided military aid to Iraqi government forces and Kurdish fighters opposing ISIS, including ground troops to serve as advisers and trainers beginning in mid-2014.

Forces fighting ISIS in 2015-17 included government troops, Shiite militias (often backed by Iran), Sunni tribal militias, and Kurdish troops. Kurdish fighters made gains in northern Iraq, and government and Shiite forces completed recapturing Tikrit, Apr. 1, 2015. After a

bloody 9-month campaign, Abadi proclaimed the recapture of Mosul, July 9, 2017. Abadi announced, Dec. 9, 2017, that all ISIS territory in Iraq had been retaken. However, thousands of ISIS fighters remained in the country, attacking civilians and security forces.

In a Sept. 25, 2017, referendum, called by the Kurdistan Regional Government—but deemed illegal by the Iraqi government—92.7% of participants voted for Kurdistan's independence from Iraq. Iraqi-government and Shiite-militia forces responded by driving Kurdish troops from territory outside the Kurdistan autonomous region that the Kurds had occupied during the fight against ISIS.

The U.S. deactivated, Apr. 30, 2018, its land forces command in Baghdad, but more than 5,000 U.S. troops remained in Iraq. The U.S. announced, Sept. 9, 2020, a force reduction to about 3,000.

Following May 12, 2018, parliamentary elections, on Oct. 2, 2018, parliament elected Kurdish politician Barham Salih as president, and Shiite consensus candidate Adel Abdul Mahdi was designated prime min. After two months of protests against economic conditions, corruption, and Iranian influence—in which hundreds were killed by security forces—the prime min. resigned, Nov. 29, 2019. Protests continued into 2020. Iran-backed militia forces attacked the U.S. embassy in Baghdad, Dec. 31, 2019; rocket attacks on the embassy and other U.S. facilities continued in 2020. Compromise candidate Mustafa al-Kadhimi was chosen as the new prime min., May 7, 2020.

The 2020 COVID-19 pandemic caused about 358,000 Iraqi cases and over 9,000 deaths as of Sept. 30. The global recession accompanying the pandemic sharply reduced oil revenue.

Ireland

People: Population: 5,176,569 (121). **Age distrib.:** <15: 21.2%; 65+: 13.8%. **Growth:** 1.0%. **Migrants:** 17.1%. **Pop. density:** 194.6 per sq mi, 75.2 per sq km. **Urban:** 63.7%. **Ethnic groups:** Irish 82.2%, other white 9.5%, Asian 2.1%. **Languages:** English (official; generally used), Irish (Gaelic or Gaeilge) (official; spoken mainly on western coast). **Religions:** Christian 90.4% (Catholic 84.8%), agnostic 7.2%.

Geography: Total area: 27,133 sq mi, 70,273 sq km (118); **Land area:** 26,596 sq mi, 68,883 sq km. **Location:** Atlantic O. just W of Great Britain. Northern Ireland (UK) on E. **Topography:** Central plateau surrounded by isolated groups of hills and mountains. Heavily indented Atlantic coastline. **Arable land:** 6.4%. **Capital:** Dublin, 1,228,179.

Government: Type: Parliamentary republic. **Head of state:** Pres. Michael D. Higgins; b. 1941; in office: Nov. 11, 2011. **Head of govt.:** Prime Min. Micheál Martin; b. 1960; in office: June 27, 2020. **Local divisions:** 28 counties, 3 cities. **Defense budget:** $1.1 bil. **Active troops:** 8,650.

Economy: Industries: pharmaceuticals, chemicals, computer hardware and software, food prods., beverages and brewing, medical devices. **Chief agric.:** barley, potatoes, wheat; beef, dairy prods. **Natural resources:** nat. gas, peat, copper, lead, zinc, silver, barite, gypsum, limestone, dolomite. **Water:** 10,920 cu m per capita. **Electricity prod.** (2018): 29.3 bil kwH. **Labor force:** agric. 4.5%, industry 18.5%, services 77.0%. **Unemployment:** 5.2%.

Finance: Monetary unit: Euro (EUR) (0.84 = $1 U.S.). **GDP:** $436.0 bil; **per capita GDP:** $88,241; **GDP growth:** 5.5%. **Imports:** $98.1 bil; UK 29%, U.S. 18.9%, France 12.1%, Germany 9.6%. **Exports:** $219.7 bil; U.S. 27.1%, UK 13.4%, Belgium 11%, Germany 8.1%, Switzerland 5.1%. **Tourism:** $5.8 bil. **Budget:** $87.2 bil. **Inflation:** 0.9%.

Transport: Railways: 2,673 mi. **Motor vehicles:** 508.6 per 1,000 cap. **Airports:** 16.

Communications: Telephone: 38 per 100 pop. **Mobile:** 103.2 per 100 pop. **Broadband:** 102 per 100 pop. **Internet** (2018): 84.5%.

Health: Expend.: 7.2%. **Life expect.:** 78.9 male; 83.7 female. **Births:** 13 per 1,000 pop. **Deaths:** 6.8 per 1,000 pop. **Infant mortality:** 3.6 per 1,000 live births. **Undernourished:** <2.5%. **HIV:** 0.2%.

Education: Compulsory: ages 6-15. **Literacy:** 99%.

Embassy: 2234 Massachusetts Ave. NW 20008; 462-3939.

Website: www.gov.ie

Celtic tribes invaded the islands about the 4th cent. BCE; their Gaelic culture and literature flourished in the 5th cent. CE, the same century in which St. Patrick converted the Irish to Christianity. Norse invasions began in the 8th cent., ending with defeat of the Danes by the Irish King Brian Boru in 1014. English invasions started in the 12th cent. For over 700 years the Anglo-Irish struggle continued with bitter rebellions and savage repressions. In the Irish Potato Famine, failure of the staple potato crop, 1845-49, caused 1 mil deaths from starvation and related diseases; up to 2 mil people emigrated, many to the U.S.

The Easter Monday Rebellion in 1916 failed but was followed by guerrilla warfare and harsh reprisals by British troops called the Black and Tans. The Dail Eireann (Irish parliament) reaffirmed independence in Jan. 1919. The British offered dominion status to Ulster (6 counties) and southern Ireland (26 counties) Dec. 1921. The constitution of the Irish Free State, a British dominion, was adopted Dec. 11, 1922. Northern Ireland remained part of the UK (see United Kingdom—Northern Ireland).

A new constitution adopted by plebiscite came into operation Dec. 29, 1937. It declared the name of the state Eire in the Irish language (Ireland in the English) and declared it a sovereign democratic state. On Dec. 21, 1948, the country was declared a republic rather than a dominion and withdrew from the Commonwealth. The British Parliament recognized both actions, 1949, but the six north-eastern counties remained in the UK.

Irish governments have favored peaceful unification of all Ireland and cooperated with Britain against terrorist groups. After negotiators in Northern Ireland approved a peace settlement on Good Friday, Apr. 10, 1998, voters in the Irish Republic endorsed the accord, on May 22, and the Irish gave up their constitution's territorial claims on the north.

Expansion of educational opportunities and foreign investment in high-tech industries in the 1990s boosted Ireland's prosperity. In 1990, Mary Robinson became Ireland's first woman president.

Responding to allegations of child sex abuse by Catholic clergy in Ireland, Pope Benedict XVI issued a public apology to victims and their families Mar. 2010.

After a 2008-10 financial crisis, the EU approved an 85-bil euro emergency loan package that obligated Ireland to impose unpopular austerity measures. Fianna Fáil, the party that had dominated Irish politics since the 1930s, was defeated in Feb. 2011 elections, and Enda Kenny of the center-right Fine Gael became prime minister. Leo Varadkar of Fine Gael succeeded Kenny, June 14, 2017. Inconclusive Feb. 8, 2020, elections saw the nationalist Sinn Féin party make gains. On June 27, a coalition government of Fianna Fáil, Fine Gael, and the Green Party took office, initially headed by Fianna Fáil's Micheál Martin; he was to be succeeded by Fine Gael's leader in 2022.

In a national referendum, May 22, 2015, voters legalized same-sex marriage. In a May 25, 2018, referendum, voters essentially legalized almost all abortions.

Affected by the 2020 COVID-19 pandemic, Ireland had almost 36,000 cases by Sept. 30, and over 1,800 people had died.

Israel
State of Israel

People: Population: 8,675,475 (98). **Age distrib.:** <15: 26.8%; 65+: 12.0%. **Growth:** 1.5%. **Migrants:** 23.0%. **Pop. density:** 1,045.2 per sq mi, 403.6 per sq km. **Urban:** 92.6%. **Ethnic groups:** Jewish 74.4% (Israel-born 76.9%, Europe/America/Oceania-born 15.9%, Africa-born 4.6%, Asia-born 2.6%), Arab 20.9%. **Languages:** Hebrew (official), Arabic, English. **Religions:** Jewish (official) 70.5%, Muslim 20% (Sunni), agnostic 5.3%.

Geography: Total area: 8,470 sq mi, 21,937 sq km (149); **Land area:** 8,300 sq mi, 21,497 sq km. **Location:** Middle East, on E end of Mediterranean Sea. Lebanon on N; Syria, West Bank, Jordan on E; Gaza Strip, Egypt on W. **Topography:** The Mediterranean coastal plain is fertile and well-watered. Judean Plateau in center. Semi-desert Negev region extends to apex at head of Gulf of Aqaba. The E border drops sharply into the Jordan Rift Valley, which incl. Lake Tiberias (Sea of Galilee) and the Dead Sea (1,339 ft below sea level), lowest point in Asia. **Arable land:** 17.9%. **Capital:** Jerusalem, 931,756. **Cities:** Tel Aviv-Jaffa, 4,181,480; Haifa, 1,147,431.

Government: Type: Parliamentary democracy. **Head of state:** Pres. Reuven Rivlin; b. 1939; in office: July 27, 2014. **Head of govt.:** Prime Min. Benjamin Netanyahu; b. 1949; in office: Mar. 31, 2009. **Local divisions:** 6 districts. **Defense budget:** $19.3 bil. **Active troops:** 169,500.

Economy: Industries: high-tech prods. (incl. aviation, communications, computer-aided design and manufactures, medical electronics, fiber optics), wood and paper prods. **Chief agric.:** citrus, vegetables, cotton; beef, poultry. **Natural resources:** timber, potash, copper ore, nat. gas, phosphate rock, magnesium bromide, clays, sand. **Water:** 214 cu m per capita. **Crude oil reserves:** 12.7 mil bbls. **Electricity prod.:** 63.5 bil kWH. **Labor force:** agric. 0.9%, industry 16.8%, services 82.3%. **Unemployment:** 3.8%.

Finance: Monetary unit: Shekel (ILS) (3.37 = $1 U.S.). **GDP:** $382.0 bil; **per capita GDP:** $42,194; **GDP growth:** 3.5%. **Imports:** $68.6 bil; U.S. 11.7%, China 9.5%, Switzerland 8%, Germany 6.8%, UK 6.2%, Belgium 5.9%. **Exports:** $58.7 bil; U.S. 28.8%, UK 8.2%, Hong Kong 5%, China 5.4%. **Tourism:** $7.6 bil. **Budget:** $100.2 bil. **Inflation:** 0.8%.

Transport: Railways: 860 mi. **Motor vehicles:** 397.7 per 1,000 pop. **Airports:** 33.

Communications: Telephone: 38.2 per 100 pop. **Mobile:** 127.7 per 100 pop. **Broadband:** 105.1 per 100 pop. **Internet:** 81.6%.

Health: Expend.: 7.4%. **Life expect.:** 81.1 male; 85.0 female. **Births:** 17.6 per 1,000 pop. **Deaths:** 5.3 per 1,000 pop. **Infant mortality:** 3.3 per 1,000 live births. **Undernourished:** <2.5%. **HIV (2018):** 0.2%.

Education: Compulsory: ages 3-17. **Literacy:** 97.8%.
Embassy: 3514 International Dr. NW 20008; 364-5500.
Website: www.gov.il

Occupying the southwest corner of the ancient Fertile Crescent, Israel contains some of the oldest known evidence of agriculture and of primitive town life. The Hebrews probably arrived early in the 2nd millennium BCE. Under King David and his successors (c. 1000 BCE-597 BCE), Judaism was developed and secured. After conquest by Babylonians, Persians, and Greeks, an independent Jewish kingdom was revived, 168 BCE, but Rome took over in the next century,

suppressed Jewish revolts in 70 CE and 135 CE, and renamed Judea Palestine, after the earlier coastal inhabitants, the Philistines.

Arab invaders conquered Palestine in 636. The Arabic language and Islam prevailed within a few centuries, but a Jewish minority remained. The land was ruled from the 11th cent. as a part of non-Arab empires by Seljuks, Mamluks, and Ottomans (with a Crusader interval, 1098-1291).

After four centuries of Ottoman rule, the land was taken in 1917 by Britain, which pledged in the Balfour Declaration to support a Jewish homeland. In 1920 a British Palestine Mandate was recognized; in 1922 the land east of the Jordan R. was detached.

Jewish immigration, begun in the late 19th cent., swelled in the 1930s and 1940s with refugees from Nazi Germany and survivors of the Holocaust; heavy Arab immigration from Syria and Lebanon also occurred. Arab opposition to Jewish immigration turned violent in 1920, 1921, 1929, and 1936. The UN General Assembly voted in 1947 to partition Palestine into an Arab and a Jewish state. Britain withdrew in May 1948.

Israel was declared independent May 14, 1948; Arabs rejected partition. Egypt, Jordan, Syria, Lebanon, Iraq, and Saudi Arabia invaded but failed to destroy the Jewish state, which gained territory. Separate armistices with the Arab nations were signed in 1949; Jordan occupied the West Bank, Egypt occupied Gaza. Neither granted Palestinian autonomy.

After persistent terrorist raids, Israel invaded Egypt's Sinai, Oct. 29, 1956, aided briefly by British and French forces. A UN cease-fire was arranged Nov. 6.

An uneasy truce between Israel and the Arab countries lasted until 1967, when Egypt reoccupied the Gaza Strip and closed the Gulf of Aqaba to Israeli shipping. In the Six-Day War, starting June 5, the Israelis took the Gaza Strip, occupied the Sinai Peninsula to the Suez Canal, and captured East Jerusalem, Syria's Golan Heights, and Jordan's West Bank.

Egypt and Syria attacked Israel, Oct. 6, 1973 (Yom Kippur, the most solemn day in the Jewish calendar). Israel counterattacked, driving the Syrians back, and crossed the Suez Canal. A cease-fire took effect Oct. 24 and a UN peacekeeping force arrived. Under a 1974 disengagement agreement, Israel withdrew from the canal's west bank. Israeli forces raided Entebbe, Uganda, in 1976 and rescued 103 hostages who had been seized by Arab and German terrorists.

Israel's prime ministers, including David Ben-Gurion, Golda Meir, and Yitzhak Rabin, pursued a moderate socialist program, 1948-77. In 1977, the conservative opposition, led by Menachem Begin, was voted into office for the first time. Egypt's Pres. Anwar al-Sadat visited Jerusalem in 1977, and on Mar. 26, 1979, Egypt and Israel signed a formal peace treaty, ending 30 years of war. Israel returned the Sinai to Egypt in 1982.

Israeli forces invaded Lebanon, June 6, 1982, to destroy Palestine Liberation Organization (PLO) strongholds. After massive Israeli bombing of West Beirut, the PLO agreed to evacuate the city. Israeli troops entered West Beirut Sept. 14. Israel drew widespread condemnation when Lebanese Christian forces, Sept. 16, entered two West Beirut refugee camps and slaughtered hundreds of Palestinians.

In 1989, violence escalated over the Israeli military occupation of the West Bank and Gaza Strip. In a series of uprisings known as the first intifada, Palestinian protesters defied Israeli troops, who forcibly retaliated. During the Persian Gulf War, 1991, Iraq fired Scud missiles at Israel.

Ongoing peace talks led to historic agreements between Israel and the PLO, Sept. 1993. The PLO recognized Israel's right to exist; Israel recognized the PLO as the Palestinians' representative. The two sides then signed, Sept. 13, an agreement (known as the Oslo Accord) for limited Palestinian self-rule in the West Bank and Gaza. A follow-up Sept. 1995 agreement (Oslo II) essentially divided the West Bank into areas under Israeli or Palestinian control. Israel and Jordan signed, July 25, 1994, in Washington, DC, a declaration ending their 46-year state of war.

On Nov. 4, 1995, an Orthodox Jewish Israeli assassinated Labor Party Prime Min. Yitzhak Rabin in Tel Aviv. Support for Rabin's successor, Shimon Peres, was shaken by a series of suicide bombings and rocket attacks by Islamic militants. Emphasizing security issues, the candidate of the conservative Likud bloc, Benjamin Netanyahu, was elected prime minister on May 29, 1996.

Under an interim accord signed by Netanyahu and PLO leader Yasir Arafat, Oct. 23, 1998, Israel agreed to yield more West Bank territory to the Palestinians, in exchange for new security guarantees. After May 1999 elections, the Labor Party's Ehud Barak replaced Netanyahu as prime minister.

Israel pulled virtually all its troops out of southern Lebanon in May 2000. Marathon summit talks in the U.S. between Barak and Arafat, July 11-25, failed. A second intifada began in late Sept. in Israel and the Palestinian territories. Barak called new elections for prime minister but lost Feb. 2001 to Ariel Sharon, a hardliner. The bloodshed intensified during the summer, as Palestinian suicide bombers attacked Israeli civilians, and Israel struck at Palestinian-controlled territory attempting to assassinate suspected terrorists.

Israel launched a major West Bank offensive Mar. 29, 2002, two days after a suicide bomber killed 26 Israeli Jews at a Passover celebration in Netanya.

Sharon's decision to pull all Israeli settlers and troops out of Gaza was approved by the cabinet Feb. 2005. Sharon and Deputy Prime Min. Ehud Olmert then formed the centrist Kadima Party. Sharon suffered a massive stroke Jan. 4, 2006. Olmert became prime minister, led Kadima to victory in Mar. elections, and formed a broad coalition government.

Clashes in mid-2006 along the Gaza and Lebanon borders rapidly escalated into full-scale war. By Aug. 14, a UN-sponsored cease-fire had taken hold. Olmert, targeted in multiple corruption inquiries, announced his resignation July 30, 2008. (He was convicted on bribery charges, 2014 and 2015.) After a campaign overshadowed by a three-week war between Israel and Hamas in Gaza, both Kadima and Likud fell far short of a majority in Feb. 2009 elections. On Mar. 31, Netanyahu became prime min. for a second time.

Israel's relations with allies were strained when the Israeli government announced in Mar. 2010 that it would build 1,600 homes in Ramat Shlomo (a Jewish settlement in mostly Arab East Jerusalem) and when Israeli commandos killed 9 Turkish pro-Palestinian activists in clashes May 31 on board the *Mavi Marmara*, part of a flotilla seeking to break Israel's blockade of Gaza.

Israel clashed with Palestinians in Gaza Oct.-Nov. 2012.

Netanyahu's right-wing Likud-Yisrael Beitenu political bloc narrowly won Jan. 22, 2013, parliamentary elections. After Mar. 17, 2015, elections, Netanyahu assembled a new coalition government.

Conflict between Israel and Hamas escalated in 2014. Rocket attacks from Gaza into Israel increased beginning in June. Israel launched air and artillery attacks on targets in Gaza, and Israeli ground forces entered Gaza July 17, in part to destroy tunnels used to infiltrate fighters into Israel. Israeli ground and air attacks caused high civilian casualties. Israel pulled out ground troops Aug. 5. A cease-fire was agreed Aug. 26.

Tensions between Iran and Israel have grown over Iran's nuclear and missile programs, which Israel sees as existential threats, as well as over Iranian support for regional anti-Israel militias and governments. Israeli airstrikes have targeted Iranian military assets or Iranian-backed forces in Syria, Iraq, and Lebanon.

On May 14, 2018, the U.S. officially moved its embassy from Tel Aviv, where most embassies are located, to Jerusalem. The U.S., Aug.-Sept. 2018, announced the cutoff of hundreds of millions of dollars in direct and UN-administered Palestinian aid. A proclamation signed Mar. 25, 2019, by U.S. Pres. Donald Trump recognized Israeli sovereignty over the Golan Heights. The U.S. announced, Nov. 18, that it did not consider Israeli West Bank settlements to be in violation of international law.

Controversial July 2018 legislation declared that "the Jewish people … have an exclusive right to national self-determination" in Israel. With Netanyahu plagued by corruption scandals, Likud finished in a virtual tie with the centrist opposition Blue and White alliance, led by Benny Gantz, in Apr. 9 and Sept. 17, 2019, elections. After a third election, Mar. 2, 2020, produced a similar stalemate, Netanyahu and Gantz reached a power-sharing agreement. Netanyahu was sworn in May 17 for a new term as prime minister, to be succeeded by Gantz 18 months later. Netanyahu had been formally indicted, Jan. 28, on bribery, fraud, and breach of trust charges.

The U.S., Israel, and the United Arab Emirates announced, Aug. 13, 2020, that Israel and the UAE would normalize relations; Israel agreed to suspend plans to annex portions of the West Bank. Israel, Bahrain, and the U.S. announced, Sept. 11, that Israel and Bahrain would establish diplomatic ties. Netanyahu signed agreements with the UAE and with Bahrain Sept. 15 in Washington, D.C.

Israel instituted lockdown measures in Mar. 2020 to combat the COVID-19 pandemic. New cases spiked after measures were eased in May, and a second lockdown began Sept. 18. By Sept. 30, Israel had more than 233,000 COVID-19 cases and over 1,500 deaths.

Palestinian Territories

The Palestinian territories comprise the Gaza Strip, often called Gaza, and the West Bank, both occupied by Israel in 1967. Since 1996 the Palestinian Authority has been responsible for civil government in the territories. Elected president Jan. 20, 1996, PLO leader Yasir Arafat headed the Palestinian Authority until his death Nov. 11, 2004. Mahmoud Abbas, of the PLO's Fatah faction, was elected president Jan. 2005. A victory by Hamas militants in Jan. 2006 legislative elections led to a power struggle with Abbas. In bitter fighting, Hamas ousted Fatah from Gaza, June 2007, but Abbas retained power in the West Bank. As of Sept. 2020, Gaza remained largely in Hamas control.

The UN General Assembly voted, Nov. 29, 2012, to make Palestine a non-member observer state. Speaking at the UN Sept. 30, 2015, Abbas said the Palestinian Authority would no longer be bound by the Oslo Accords, which he alleged Israel had violated.

The **Gaza Strip** extends NE from the Sinai Peninsula for 25 mi, with the Mediterranean Sea to the W and Israel to the E. Nearly all the inhabitants are Palestinian Arabs. Area 139 sq mi; pop. (2020 est.) 1,918,221. Hamas's security force, the Izz al-Din al-Qassam Brigades, numbers 15,000-20,000.

Israel captured Gaza from Egypt in the 1967 war. It remained under Israeli occupation until May 1994, when the Israeli Defense Forces largely withdrew. Agreements between Israel and the PLO in 1993 and 1994 provided for interim self-rule in Gaza, but Israel

retained control over security. Israel forcibly evacuated all 9,000 Jewish settlers from Gaza by Aug. 22, 2005, and the last remaining Israeli soldiers pulled out Sept. 12. Israel established a fortified barrier on its Gaza border to block Palestinian infiltrators.

After the Hamas takeover, Israel declared Gaza a "hostile entity," Sept. 19, 2007, and intensified military and economic pressures. Hamas thwarted an Israeli blockade, Jan. 2008, blowing up part of the border wall between Gaza and Egypt. Retaliating for Hamas rocket and mortar attacks, Israel launched an aerial assault and ground offensive in Gaza, Dec. 2008-Jan. 2009. After the *Mavi Marmara* incident, Israel June 2010 eased some restrictions on the flow of goods to Gaza. Egypt's new Islamist govt. lifted the blockade along its Gaza border May 28, 2011. However, Egypt's subsequent military government re-closed the border in 2013 and sought to destroy tunnels dug by Hamas to bring military and other equipment into Gaza. Egypt opened the Gaza border intermittently beginning in 2015.

Members of the Israeli Air Force, Oct. 31, 2012, assassinated Hamas's military chief, Ahmed al-Jabari, in the Gaza Strip. In 2017, Israel began building a below-ground barrier on the Gaza border in an effort to block Hamas tunneling. Large-scale, sometimes violent protests occurred, Mar.-May 2018, on the Gaza side of the Israeli border wall, accompanied by attempts to storm the wall and firing across the border into Israel; more than 100 protesters were killed by Israeli security forces. Cross-border violence flared again later in 2018 and continued in 2019-20.

The **West Bank** is located W of the Jordan R. and Dead Sea, bounded by Jordan on the E and by Israel on the N, W, and S. The Palestinian Authority administers several major cities, but Israel retains control over much land, including Jewish settlements. Total area 2,263 sq mi, land area 2,178 sq mi; pop. (2020 est.) 2,900,034 (Palestinian only). The Palestinian Authority's National Security Force is a paramilitary organization of about 10,000 that maintains internal security in the West Bank.

In June 2002 the Israeli government began building a controversial security barrier in the West Bank to restrict Palestinian access to Israel and reduce infiltration by suicide bombers. In a nonbinding ruling, July 9, 2004, the World Court said the barrier violated international law. Israel has continued to allow the expansion of Jewish settlements; by 2020, more than 460,000 Jewish settlers were living in the West Bank (not including more than 200,000 in East Jerusalem, which Israel annexed in 1967).

The Palestinian Authority ordered lockdown measures against COVID-19 in the West Bank. By Sept. 30, 2020, more than 50,000 cases and 360 deaths had been reported in the Palestinian territories.

Italy
Italian Republic

People: Population: 62,402,659 (23). **Age distrib.:** <15: 13.4%; 65+: 22.1%. **Growth:** 0.1%. **Migrants:** 10.4%. **Pop. density:** 549.5 per sq mi, 212.2 per sq km. **Urban:** 71.0%. **Ethnic groups:** Italian (incl. small clusters of German-, French-, and Slovene-Italians in N; Albanian- and Greek-Italians in S). **Languages:** Italian (official), German, French, Slovene. **Religions:** Christian 75.5% (Catholic [official] 71.1%), agnostic 13.2%, Muslim 6.2% (Sunni), atheist 4%.

Geography: Total area: 116,348 sq mi, 301,340 sq km (71); **Land area:** 113,568 sq mi, 294,140 sq km. **Location:** Southern Europe, jutting into Mediterranean Sea. France on W; Switzerland, Austria on N; Slovenia on E. **Topography:** Long boot-shaped peninsula, with Apennine Mts. running its length, extending SE from the Alps into Mediterranean, with islands of Sicily and Sardinia offshore. The alluvial Po Valley drains most of N. Rest of the country is rugged and mountainous, except for intermittent coastal plains like the Campania S of Rome. **Arable land:** 22.9%. **Capital:** Rome, 4,257,056. **Cities:** Milan, 3,140,181; Naples, 2,186,853; Turin, 1,792,163.

Government: Type: Parliamentary republic. **Head of state:** Pres. Sergio Mattarella; b. 1941; in office: Feb. 3, 2015. **Head of govt.:** Prime Min. Giuseppe Conte; b. 1964; in office: June 1, 2018. **Local divisions:** 20 regions (5 autonomous). **Defense budget:** $27.1 bil. **Active troops:** 165,500.

Economy: Industries: tourism, machinery, iron and steel, chemicals, food proc., textiles, motor vehicles, clothing, footwear. **Chief agric.:** fruits, vegetables, grapes, potatoes, sugar beets, soybeans, grain, olives; beef, dairy prods.; fish. **Natural resources:** coal, antimony, mercury, zinc, potash, marble, barite, asbestos, pumice, fluorspar, feldspar, pyrite (sulfur), nat. gas/crude oil reserves, fish. **Water:** 3,223 cu m per capita. **Crude oil reserves:** 517.9 mil bbls. **Electricity prod.** (2018): 276.4 bil kWh. **Labor force:** agric. 3.6%, industry 25.6%, services 70.8%. **Unemployment:** 9.8%.

Finance: Monetary unit: Euro (EUR) (0.84 = $1 U.S.). **GDP:** $2.7 tril; **per capita GDP:** $44,197; **GDP growth:** 0.3%. **Imports:** $432.9 bil; Germany 16.3%, France 8.8%, China 7.1%, Netherlands 5.6%, Spain 5.3%. **Exports:** $496.3 bil; Germany 12.5%, France 10.3%, U.S. 9%, Spain 5.2%, UK 5.2%. **Tourism:** $49.6 bil. **Budget:** $948.1 bil. **Inflation:** 0.6%.

Transport: Railways: 12,541 mi. **Motor vehicles:** 709.6 per 1,000 pop. **Airports:** 98.

Communications: Telephone: 33.6 per 100 pop. **Mobile:** 137.5 per 100 pop. **Broadband:** 87.9 per 100 pop. **Internet** (2018): 74.4%.

Health: Expend.: 8.8%. **Life expect.:** 79.8 male; 85.3 female. **Births:** 8.4 per 1,000 pop. **Deaths:** 10.7 per 1,000 pop. **Infant mortality:** 3.2 per 1,000 live births. **Undernourished:** <2.5%. **HIV:** 0.2%. **Education:** Compulsory: ages 6-17. **Literacy:** 99.9%.
Embassy: 3000 Whitehaven St. NW 20008; 612-4400.
Website: www.governo.it

Rome emerged as the major power in Italy after 500 BCE, dominating the Etruscans to the north and Greeks to the south. Under the Empire, which lasted until the 5th cent. CE, Rome ruled most of Western Europe, the Balkans, the Middle East, and North Africa. After Rome fell, Italy became a patchwork of kingdoms, principalities, and city-states until reunified, 1870.

The Fascist leader Benito Mussolini came to power, 1922, and aligned Italy with Nazi Germany in WWII. After Fascism was overthrown in 1943, Italy declared war on Germany and Japan and contributed to the Allied victory. It surrendered conquered lands and lost its colonies. Mussolini was killed by partisans Apr. 28, 1945. Victor Emmanuel III abdicated May 9, 1946; his son Humbert II was king until June 10, when Italy became a republic after a referendum, June 2-3. In the postwar decades, Italy had a succession of short-lived governments.

Christian Democratic leader and former Prime Min. Aldo Moro was abducted and murdered in 1978 by Red Brigade terrorists. A wave of left-wing political violence continued into the 1980s.

In Mar. 1994 voting, right-wing parties won a majority, dislodging Italy's long-powerful Christian Democratic Party. Italy led a 7,000-member peacekeeping force in Albania, Apr.-Aug. 1997, and contributed troops to the NATO-led security force (KFOR) that entered Kosovo in June 1999.

Supporters of Silvio Berlusconi, a multibillionaire media magnate, won the 2001 parliamentary elections. Berlusconi backed American-led military operations in Afghanistan (2001) and Iraq (2003). As of mid-2020, about 900 Italian troops were serving with the NATO mission in Afghanistan.

Berlusconi lost 2006 parliamentary elections but returned at the head of a center-right coalition after Apr. 2008 elections. Sluggish economic growth and rising public debt raised investors' concerns about Italy's financial stability. Berlusconi resigned Nov. 12, 2011, but Italy's economic problems worsened. After Feb. 25, 2013, elections, a coalition government was announced Apr. 27, 2013, led by the center-left Democratic Party (PD), which promised political and economic reforms. Berlusconi was convicted in 2012 of tax fraud and in 2015 of bribing a senator. Legalization of civil unions between same-sex couples won final parliamentary approval, May 11, 2016. Proposed government reforms were defeated in a Dec. 4, 2016, referendum.

About 625,000 African, Middle Eastern, and SW Asian migrants fleeing violence and economic hardship crossed the Mediterranean from North Africa (mainly Libya) to Italy, 2014-17. More than 13,000 died trying to make the crossing. Beginning in 2017, Italy worked with various Libyan authorities to reduce migrant crossings. Migrant arrivals, 2018 to mid-Sept. 2020, totaled about 57,000.

In Mar. 4, 2018, elections, the populist Five Star Movement (M5S) and the anti-immigration League made strong showings. A League-M5S coalition government took office June 1, 2018, with Giuseppe Conte as prime minister. With League-M5S disputes increasing, the economy stagnant, and debt rising, Conte resigned, Aug. 20, 2019. M5S and the PD agreed, Aug. 28, to form a new coalition government; Conte returned as prime minister.

Italy was one of the first European countries severely impacted by the 2020 COVID-19 pandemic. With cases and deaths, especially in the N, rising rapidly, strict nationwide lockdown measures were instituted in Mar. Many measures were eased in May as new cases declined. With new cases rising again in Aug.-Sept., by Sept. 30, Italy had a total of about 313,000 cases; almost 36,000 people had died. The pandemic devastated the tourism industry and the economy overall—GDP in Q2 2020 was down more than 17% from a year earlier.

Sicily, 9,927 sq mi, pop. (2014 est.) 5,094,937, is an island 180 by 120 mi, seat of an autonomous region that embraces the island of Pantelleria, 32 sq mi, and the Lipari group, 44 sq mi, including two active volcanoes: Vulcano (1,637 ft) and Stromboli (3,031 ft). From prehistoric times Sicily has been settled by various peoples; a Greek state had its capital at Syracuse. Rome took Sicily from Carthage 215 BCE. Mt. Etna, a 10,925-ft active volcano, is its tallest peak.

Sardinia, 9,301 sq mi, pop. (2014 est.) 1,663,859, lies in the Mediterranean, 115 mi W of Italy and 7½ mi S of Corsica. It is 160 mi long, 68 mi wide, and mountainous. Mining, historically important, has declined in recent decades, and tourism has increased. In 1720, Sardinia was added to the possessions of the Dukes of Savoy in Piedmont and Savoy to form the Kingdom of Sardinia. Elba, 86 sq mi, lies 6 mi W of Tuscany. Napoleon I lived in exile on Elba 1814-15.

Jamaica

People: Population: 2,808,570 (137). **Age distrib.:** <15: 25.2%; 65+: 9.2%. **Growth:** –0.1%. **Migrants:** 0.8%. **Pop. density:** 671.6 per sq mi, 259.3 per sq km. **Urban:** 56.3%. **Ethnic groups:** Black 92.1%, mixed 6.1%. **Languages:** English, English patois. **Religions:** Christian 84.9% (Protestant 61.4%, independent 18.4%), Spiritist 9.8%, agnostic 4.2%.
Geography: Total area: 4,244 sq mi, 10,991 sq km (161); **Land area:** 4,182 sq mi, 10,831 sq km. **Location:** W Indies. Cuba to N,

Haiti to E. **Topography:** Four-fifths of country is covered by mountains. **Arable land:** 11.1%. **Capital:** Kingston, 590,940.
Government: Type: Parliamentary democracy under constitutional monarchy. **Head of state:** Queen Elizabeth II, rep. by Gov.-Gen. Patrick Allen; b. 1951; in office: Feb. 26, 2009. **Head of govt.:** Prime Min. Andrew Holness; b. 1972; in office: Mar. 3, 2016. **Local divisions:** 14 parishes. **Defense budget:** $262 mil. **Active troops:** 5,950.
Economy: Industries: agriculture, mining, manufacture, constr., financial and insurance services, tourism, telecom. **Chief agric.:** sugarcane, bananas, coffee, citrus, yams, ackees, vegetables; poultry, goats, milk; shellfish. **Natural resources:** bauxite, gypsum, limestone. **Water:** 3,744 cu m per capita. **Electricity prod.:** 4.2 bil kWh. **Labor force:** agric. 15.7%, industry 16.2%, services 68.1%. **Unemployment:** 8.0%.
Finance: Monetary unit: Dollar (JMD) (149.41 = $1 U.S.). **GDP:** $30.0 bil; **per capita GDP:** $10,166; **GDP growth:** 0.7%. **Imports:** $5.2 bil; U.S. 40.6%, Colombia 6.8%, Japan 5.8%, China 5.8%. **Exports:** $1.3 bil; U.S. 39.1%, Netherlands 12.3%, Canada 8.4%. **Tourism:** $3.1 bil. **Budget:** $4.3 bil. **Inflation:** 3.9%.
Transport: Motor vehicles: 71.4 per 1,000 pop. **Airports:** 11.
Communications: Telephone: 12.4 per 100 pop. **Mobile:** 101 per 100 pop. **Broadband:** 48.9 per 100 pop. **Internet:** 55.1%.
Health: Expend.: 6.0%. **Life expect.:** 73.4 male; 77.1 female. **Births:** 16.1 per 1,000 pop. **Deaths:** 7.5 per 1,000 pop. **Infant mortality:** 11.6 per 1,000 live births. **Undernourished:** 8.7%. **HIV:** 1.4%. **Education:** Compulsory: ages 6-11. **Literacy:** 96.3%.
Embassy: 1520 New Hampshire Ave. NW 20036; 452-0660.
Website: jis.gov.jm

Jamaica was visited by Christopher Columbus, 1494, and ruled by Spain (under whom Arawak Indians died out) until seized by Britain, 1655. Jamaica won independence Aug. 6, 1962. The island's rich musical innovations include ska and reggae. Rastafarianism is an influential religious movement.

In 1974 Jamaica sought an increase in taxes paid by U.S. and Canadian bauxite mines. The socialist government acquired 50% ownership of the companies' Jamaican interests in 1976. Rudimentary welfare state measures were passed. Relations with the U.S. improved in the 1980s when Jamaican politics entered a more conservative phase.

Portia Simpson-Miller of the People's National Party (PNP) became Jamaica's first female prime min., Mar. 30, 2006. The Jamaica Labour Party (JLP) won Sept. 3, 2007, elections. While trying to arrest alleged gang leader Christopher (Dudus) Coke, police and soldiers clashed with residents in a section of Kingston in May 2010, leaving 76 people dead. Coke pleaded guilty in the U.S. to racketeering charges in 2011. The PNP won Dec. 2011 elections; Simpson-Miller again became prime min. After she implemented unpopular austerity measures to obtain IMF aid, the JLP won Feb. 25, 2016, elections; Andrew Holness became prime min. The JLP won Sept. 3, 2020, elections.

The 2020 COVID-19 pandemic caused about 6,400 cases, with over 100 deaths, by Sept. 30.

Japan

People: Population: 125,507,472 (11). **Age distrib.:** <15: 12.5%; 65+: 29.2%. **Growth:** –0.3%. **Migrants:** 2.0%. **Pop. density:** 891.8 per sq mi, 344.3 per sq km. **Urban:** 91.8%. **Ethnic groups:** Japanese 98.1%. **Languages:** Japanese. **Religions:** Buddhist 56.3%, new religionist 25.9%, agnostic 10.2%, atheist 2.9%.
Geography: Total area: 145,914 sq mi, 377,915 sq km (61); **Land area:** 140,728 sq mi, 364,485 sq km. Consists of 4 main islands: Honshu ("mainland"), 87,805 sq mi; Hokkaido, 30,144 sq mi; Kyushu, 14,114 sq mi; Shikoku, 7,049 sq mi. **Location:** Archipelago off E coast of Asia. Russia to N, N. Korea and S. Korea to W. **Topography:** Deeply indented coast. The northern islands are continuation of the Sakhalin Mts. China's Kunlun range continues into southern islands. The ranges meet in Japanese Alps. Group of mostly extinct or inactive volcanoes, incl. Mt. Fuji (Fujiyama) (12,388 ft), cross Honshu E W in a vast transverse fissure. **Arable land:** 11.4%. **Capital:** Tokyo, 37,393,129 (Major Metro Area [MMA]). **Cities:** Kinki MMA (Osaka), 19,165,340; Chukyo MMA (Nagoya), 9,552,132; Kitakyushu-Fukuoka MMA, 5,528,632; Shizuoka-Hamamatsu MMA, 2,922,320; Sapporo, 2,669,680; Sendai, 2,327,417; Hiroshima, 2,083,223.
Government: Type: Parliamentary constitutional monarchy. **Head of state:** Emperor Naruhito; b. 1960; in office: May 1, 2019. **Head of govt.:** Prime Min. Yoshihide Suga; b. 1948; in office Sept. 16, 2020. **Local divisions:** 47 prefectures. **Defense budget:** $48.6 bil. **Active troops:** 247,150.
Economy: Industries: motor vehicles, electronic equip., machine tools, steel and nonferrous metals, ships, chemicals. **Chief agric.:** vegetables, rice, fish, poultry, fruit, dairy prods., pork, beef, flowers, potatoes/taros/yams, sugarcane, tea, legumes. **Natural resources:** negligible mineral resources, fish. **Water:** 3,373 cu m per capita. **Crude oil reserves:** 44.1 mil bbls. **Electricity prod.** (2018): 952.1 bil kwH. **Labor force:** agric. 3.4%, industry 24.1%, services 72.6%. **Unemployment:** 2.3%.
Finance: Monetary unit: Yen (JPY) (106.22 = $1 U.S.). **GDP:** $5.5 tril; **per capita GDP:** $43,236; **GDP growth:** 0.7%. **Imports:** $644.7 bil; China 24.5%, U.S. 11%, Australia 5.8%. **Exports:** $688.9 bil; U.S. 19.4%, China 19%, South Korea 7.6%, Hong Kong 5.1%. **Tourism:** $46.1 bil. **Budget:** $1.9 tril. **Inflation:** 0.5%.

Transport: Railways: 16,970 mi. **Motor vehicles:** 606.8 per 1,000 pop. **Airports:** 142.

Communications: Telephone: 49.9 per 100 pop. **Mobile:** 139.2 per 100 pop. **Broadband:** 133.2 per 100 pop. **Internet:** 84.6%.

Health: Expend.: 10.9%. **Life expect.:** 82.7 male; 89.5 female. **Births:** 7.3 per 1,000 pop. **Deaths:** 10.2 per 1,000 pop. **Infant mortality:** 1.9 per 1,000 live births. **Undernourished:** <2.5%. **HIV** (2018): <0.1%.

Education: Compulsory: ages 6-14. **Literacy:** 99%.

Embassy: 2520 Massachusetts Ave. NW 20008; 238-6700.

Website: www.japan.go.jp

According to Japanese legend, the empire was founded by Emperor Jimmu, 660 BCE, but earliest records of a unified Japan date from 1,000 years later. Chinese influence was strong in the formation of Japanese civilization. Buddhism was introduced before the 6th cent. CE.

A feudal system, with locally powerful noble families and their samurai warrior retainers, dominated from 1192. Central power was held by successive families of shoguns (military dictators), 1192-1867, until recovered by Emperor Meiji, 1868. The Portuguese and Dutch had minor trade with Japan in the 16th and 17th cents.; U.S. Commodore Matthew C. Perry opened the country to U.S. trade in a treaty ratified 1854. Industrialization began in the late 19th cent. Military conflicts won Taiwan from China, 1894-95, and the southern half of Sakhalin from Russia, 1904-05. Japan annexed Korea, 1910.

In WWI Japan ousted Germany from Shandong in China and took over German Pacific islands. Japan took Manchuria in 1931 and launched full-scale war in China in 1937. In WWII, Japan attacked Pearl Harbor, Dec. 7, 1941, launching war with the U.S. The U.S. dropped atomic bombs on Hiroshima, Aug. 6, and Nagasaki, Aug. 9, 1945. Japan surrendered Aug. 14.

In a new constitution adopted May 3, 1947, Japan renounced the right to wage war; the emperor renounced claims to divinity; and the Diet became the sole lawmaking authority. The U.S. and 48 other non-Communist nations signed a peace treaty with Japan on Sept. 8, 1951; on the same day, the U.S. signed a bilateral defense agreement with Japan. The peace treaty restored Japan's sovereignty effective Apr. 28, 1952.

Rebuilding after WWII, Japan emerged as one of the most powerful economies in the world. Japan's restrictive import policies allowed it to accumulate huge trade surpluses.

In 1968, the U.S. returned control of the Bonin Isls., Volcano Isls. (including Iwo Jima), and Marcus Isls to Japan. In 1972, the U.S. returned Okinawa, the other Ryukyu Isls., and the Daito Isls., but the U.S. continued to maintain military bases on Okinawa.

The Liberal Democratic Party (LDP) governed Japan from the mid-1950s through early 1990s. In 1994, Tomiichi Murayama became Japan's first Socialist premier since 1947-48. With the country mired in a lengthy recession, the LDP regained power in 1996.

For the first time since WWII, Japan sent troops to an overseas war zone, when about 600 noncombat troops served in Iraq Feb. 2004-July 2006. Legislation formalizing a new constitutional interpretation allowing the military to take offensive action to aid an ally, such as the U.S., won final passage Sept. 19, 2015.

The 2008-09 global recession hit Japan hard, prompting a series of economic stimulus plans. The LDP suffered a crushing defeat in 2009 parliamentary elections, won by the opposition Democratic Party of Japan (DPJ).

A 9.0 magnitude earthquake and tsunami off Japan's east coast Mar. 11, 2011, left almost 21,000 people dead. The Fukushima Daiichi nuclear power plant experienced meltdowns, spewing radiation over a large area. Japan temporarily shut down its nuclear reactors and revised safety guidelines.

Elections swept LDP candidates into office in Dec. 2012, and former Prime Min. Shinzo Abe became prime minister. Abe's LDP won Dec. 14, 2014, and Oct. 22, 2017, elections.

After the U.S. withdrew, Jan. 23, 2017, from the 12-nation Trans-Pacific Partnership trade agreement, Japan signed, Mar. 8, 2018, a revised 11-nation pact. Japan and the EU signed, July 17, 2018, a trade liberalization agreement. New U.S. tariffs on Japanese steel imports went into effect, Mar. 23, 2018. A limited Japan-U.S. trade agreement was signed Sept. 25, 2019.

Emperor Akihito, 85, abdicated, Apr. 30, 2019; he was succeeded, May 1, by son Naruhito.

Abe, Apr. 2020, declared a state of emergency, involving business closures and other measures to combat the COVID-19 pandemic. With new cases declining, many restrictions were eased in May, but spikes in cases continued. As of Sept. 30, Japan had a total of about 83,000 cases; 1,564 people had died. The pandemic caused a steep economic decline—GDP fell almost 8% in Q2 2020. The 2020 Summer Olympics in Tokyo were rescheduled for 2021.

Abe announced, Aug. 28, 2020, that he would resign because of ill health. The LDP's Yoshihide Suga became prime minister Sept. 16.

Jordan
Hashemite Kingdom of Jordan

People: Population: 10,820,644 (84). **Age distrib.:** <15: 33.1%; 65+: 3.7%. **Growth:** 0.8%. **Migrants:** 33.1%. **Pop. density:** 315.6 per sq mi, 121.9 per sq km. **Urban:** 91.4%. **Ethnic groups:** Jordanian 69.3%, Syrian 13.3%, Palestinian 6.7%, Egyptian 6.7%.

Languages: Arabic (official), English (widely understood among upper and middle classes). **Religions:** Muslim 95.6% (Sunni [official] 93%, Shia 2%).

Geography: Total area: 34,495 sq mi, 89,342 sq km (110); **Land area:** 34,287 sq mi, 88,802 sq km. **Location:** Middle East. Israel, West Bank on W; Saudi Arabia on S; Iraq on E; Syria on N. **Topography:** About 88% is arid. Fertile areas in W. Only port is on short Aqaba Gulf coast. Country shares Dead Sea (1,339 ft below sea level) with Israel. **Arable land:** 2.1%. **Capital:** Amman, 2,148,293.

Government: Type: Parliamentary constitutional monarchy. **Head of state:** King Abdullah II; b. 1962; in office: Feb. 7, 1999. **Head of govt.:** Prime Min. Omar al-Razzaz; b. 1960; in office: June 4, 2018. **Local divisions:** 12 governorates. **Defense budget:** $1.7 bil. **Active troops:** 100,500.

Economy: Industries: tourism, information tech., clothing, fertilizer, potash, phosphate mining, pharmaceuticals. **Chief agric.:** citrus, tomatoes, cucumbers, olives, strawberries, stone fruits; sheep, poultry, dairy. **Natural resources:** phosphates, potash, shale oil. **Water:** 97 cu m per capita. **Crude oil reserves:** 1 mil bbls. **Electricity prod.:** 19.6 bil kWh. **Labor force:** agric. 3.0%, industry 24.4%, services 72.6%. **Unemployment:** 14.6%.

Finance: Monetary unit: Dinar (JOD) (0.71 = $1 U.S.). **GDP:** $104.2 bil; **per capita GDP:** $10,317; **GDP growth:** 2.0%. **Imports:** $18.2 bil; China 13.6%, Saudi Arabia 13.6%, U.S. 9.9%. **Exports:** $7.5 bil; U.S. 24.9%, Saudi Arabia 12.8%, India 8.2%, Iraq 8.2%, Kuwait 5.4%. **Tourism:** $5.8 bil. **Budget:** $11.5 bil. **Inflation:** 0.8%.

Transport: Railways: 316 mi. **Motor vehicles:** 108.5 per 1,000 pop. **Airports:** 16.

Communications: Telephone: 3.2 per 100 pop. **Mobile:** 87.6 per 100 pop. **Broadband:** 100 per 100 pop. **Internet:** 66.8%.

Health: Expend.: 8.1%. **Life expect.:** 74.0 male; 77.1 female. **Births:** 23 per 1,000 pop. **Deaths:** 3.4 per 1,000 pop. **Infant mortality:** 12.8 per 1,000 live births. **Undernourished:** 8.5%. **HIV** (2018): <0.1%.

Education: Compulsory: ages 6-15. **Literacy:** 99.3%.

Embassy: 3504 International Dr. NW 20008; 966-2664.

Website: jordan.gov.jo

From ancient times to 1922 the lands to the east of the Jordan R. were culturally and politically united with the lands to the W. Arabs conquered the area in the 7th cent.; the Ottomans took control in the 16th. Britain's 1920 Palestine Mandate covered both sides of the Jordan. In 1921, Abdullah, son of the ruler of Hejaz in Arabia, was installed by Britain as emir of an autonomous Transjordan, covering two-thirds of Palestine. An independent kingdom was proclaimed, 1946.

During the 1948 Arab-Israeli war, the West Bank and East Jerusalem were added to the kingdom, which changed its name to Jordan. These territories were lost to Israel in 1967, which swelled the number of Arab refugees on the East Bank.

Jordan and Israel signed a peace treaty, Oct. 26, 1994. King Hussein died Feb. 7, 1999, ending a nearly 47-year reign; his eldest son assumed the throne as Abdullah II. The king responded to Arab Spring protests, 2011-12, by somewhat liberalizing parliamentary election laws.

In 2014, Jordan joined the U.S.-led campaign of airstrikes and other military action against ISIS in Syria and Iraq. About 660,000 Syrians fleeing civil war were living in Jordan as of Sept. 2020; 67,000 Iraqi refugees were in Jordan as of Aug. 31, 2020.

Travel restrictions and other measures to combat COVID-19 hurt the tourism industry in 2020. As of Sept. 30, Jordan had over 10,000 cases and 57 deaths.

Kazakhstan
Republic of Kazakhstan

People: Population: 19,091,949 (64). **Age distrib.:** <15: 26.1%; 65+: 8.4%. **Growth:** 0.9%. **Migrants:** 20.0%. **Pop. density:** 18.3 per sq mi, 7.1 per sq km. **Urban:** 57.7%. **Ethnic groups:** Kazakh (Qazaq) 68%, Russian 19.3%, Uzbek 3.2%. **Languages:** Kazakh or Qazaq, Russian (both official). **Religions:** Muslim 71% (Sunni), Christian 25.8% (Orthodox 24.1%), agnostic 2.5%.

Geography: Total area: 1,052,090 sq mi, 2,724,900 sq km (9); **Land area:** 1,042,360 sq mi, 2,699,700 sq km. **Location:** Central Asia. Russia on N; China on E; Kyrgyzstan, Uzbekistan, Turkmenistan on S. **Topography:** Extends from lower reaches of Volga in Europe to Altay Mts. on Chinese border. **Arable land:** 10.9%. **Capital:** Nur-Sultan (fmr. Astana), 1,165,983. **Cities:** Almaty, 1,895,742.

Government: Type: Presidential republic. **Head of state:** Pres. Kassym-Jomart Tokayev; b. 1953; in office: Mar. 20, 2019. **Head of govt.:** Prime Min. Askar Mamin; b. 1965; in office: Feb. 21, 2019. **Local divisions:** 14 provinces, 4 cities. **Defense budget:** $1.6 bil. **Active troops:** 39,000.

Economy: Industries: oil, coal, iron ore, manganese, chromite, lead, zinc, copper, titanium, bauxite, gold, silver, phosphates, sulfur, uranium. **Chief agric.:** grain (mostly spring wheat, barley), potatoes, vegetables, melons; livestock. **Natural resources:** petroleum, nat. gas, coal, iron ore, manganese, chrome ore, nickel, cobalt, copper, molybdenum, lead, zinc, bauxite, gold, uranium. **Water:** 5,955 cu m per capita. **Crude oil reserves:** 30 bil bbls. **Electricity prod.** (2018): 101.2 bil kWh. **Labor force:** agric. 15.5%, industry 20.5%, services 64.1%. **Unemployment:** 4.8%.

Finance: Monetary unit: Tenge (KZT) (420.74 = $1 U.S.). **GDP:** $508.1 bil; **per capita GDP:** $27,444; **GDP growth:** 4.5%. **Imports:** $31.9 bil; Russia 38.9%, China 16.1%, Germany 5.1%.

Exports: $49.3 bil; Italy 17.9%, China 11.9%, Netherlands 9.8%, Russia 9.3%, Switzerland 6.4%, France 5.9%. **Tourism:** $2.5 bil.
Budget: $38.3 bil. **Inflation** (2016-17): 7.4%.
Transport: Railways: 10,323 mi. **Airports:** 63.
Communications: Telephone: 18.3 per 100 pop. **Mobile:** 142 per 100 pop. **Broadband:** 75.1 per 100 pop. **Internet** (2018): 78.9%.
Health: Expend.: 3.1%. **Life expect.:** 66.8 male; 76.8 female.
Births: 16.4 per 1,000 pop. **Deaths:** 8.2 per 1,000 pop. **Infant mortality:** 17.9 per 1,000 live births. **Undernourished:** <2.5%. **HIV:** 0.3%.
Education: Compulsory: ages 7-15. **Literacy:** 99.9%.
Embassy: 1401 16th St. NW 20036; 232-5488.
Website: www.government.kz
The region came under the Mongols' rule in the 13th cent. and gradually came under Russian rule, 1730-1853. It was admitted to the USSR as a constituent republic in 1936.

Kazakhstan became independent when the Soviet Union dissolved Dec. 26, 1991. The Communist Party chief, Nursultan Nazarbayev, was elected president unopposed. Dissent was suppressed. Nazarbayev encouraged Western investment in the oil industry, helping the economy. Regular production began, Oct. 2016, at the large Kashagan oil field in the Caspian Sea.

Kazakhstan agreed, Feb. 1994, to dismantle nuclear missiles. Private land ownership was legalized Dec. 1995. Astana (formerly Akmola) became the nation's new capital, June 9, 1998; it was renamed Nur-Sultan, Mar. 23, 2019.

Pres. Nazarbayev was reelected in 1999, 2005, 2011, and 2015 (the last time with almost 98% of the vote). His Nur Otan party won 2016 parliamentary elections. Nazarbayev resigned, Mar. 20, 2019, retaining influence as "first president." Upper-house speaker Kassym-Jomart Tokayev of Nur Otan became acting president and won a June 9, 2019, presidential election.

An agreement to create a limited economic union of Kazakhstan, Russia, and Belarus was signed May 29, 2014 (Armenia and Kyrgyzstan joined in 2015).

Hard-hit by the 2020 COVID-19 pandemic, Kazakhstan imposed strict lockdown measures. As of Sept. 30, Kazakhstan had almost 141,000 cases and over 2,000 deaths.

Kenya
Republic of Kenya

People: Population: 53,527,936 (27). **Age distrib.:** <15: 38.7%; 65+: 3.1%. **Growth:** 2.2%. **Migrants:** 2.0%. **Pop. density:** 243.6 per sq mi, 94.1 per sq km. **Urban:** 28.0%. **Ethnic groups:** Kikuyu 17.1%, Luhya 14.3%, Kalenjin 13.4%, Luo 10.7%, Kamba 9.8%, Somali 5.8%, Kisii 5.7%, Mijikenda 5.2%, Meru 4.2%, Maasai 2.5%, Turkana 2.1%. **Languages:** English, Kiswahili (both official); numerous Indigenous langs.
Religions: Christian 82.5% (Protestant 45.2%, Catholic 21.1%, independent 15.5%), ethnic religionist 7.9%, Muslim 7.8% (Sunni).
Geography: Total area: 224,081 sq mi, 580,367 sq km (48); **Land area:** 219,746 sq mi, 569,140 sq km. **Location:** E Africa, on coast of Indian O. Uganda on W, Tanzania on S, Somalia on E, Ethiopia on N, South Sudan on NW. **Topography:** Northern three-fifths of country is arid. A low coastal area and a plateau 3,000-10,000-ft high is in S. The Great Rift Valley enters the country N-S, flanked by high mountains. **Arable land:** 10.2%. **Capital:** Nairobi, 4,734,881. **Cities:** Mombasa, 1,295,975.
Government: Type: Presidential republic. **Head of state and govt.:** Pres. Uhuru Kenyatta; b. 1961; in office: Apr. 9, 2013. **Local divisions:** 47 counties. **Defense budget:** $1.2 bil. **Active troops:** 24,100.
Economy: Industries: small-scale consumer goods (plastic, furniture, batteries, textiles, clothing, soap, cigarettes, flour), agric. prods., horticulture, oil refining, aluminum, steel, lead, cement. **Chief agric.:** tea, coffee, corn, wheat, sugarcane, fruit, vegetables; dairy prods., beef, fish, pork. **Natural resources:** limestone, soda ash, salt, gems, fluorspar, zinc, diatomite, gypsum, wildlife, hydropower. **Water:** 618 cu m per capita. **Electricity prod.:** 10.1 bil kwH. **Labor force:** agric. 53.8%, industry 7.4%, services 38.7%. **Unemployment:** 2.7%.
Finance: Monetary unit: Shilling (KES) (108.39 = $1 U.S.).
GDP: $237.1 bil; **per capita GDP:** $4,509; **GDP growth:** 5.4%.
Imports: $16 bil; China 22.5%, India 9.9%, UAE 8.7%, Saudi Arabia 5.1%. **Exports:** $5.8 bil; Uganda 10.8%, Pakistan 10.6%, U.S. 8.1%, Netherlands 7.3%, UK 6.4%. **Tourism** (2018): $1.1 bil. **Budget:** $19.2 bil. **Inflation** (2017-18): 4.7%.
Transport: Railways: 2,373 mi. **Motor vehicles:** 35 per 1,000 pop. **Airports:** 16.
Communications: Telephone: 0.1 per 100 pop. **Mobile:** 96.3 per 100 pop. **Broadband:** 35.7 per 100 pop. **Internet:** 17.8%.
Health: Expend.: 4.8%. **Life expect.:** 67.3 male; 70.6 female.
Births: 27.2 per 1,000 pop. **Deaths:** 5.2 per 1,000 pop. **Infant mortality:** 29.8 per 1,000 live births. **Undernourished:** 23.0%. **HIV:** 4.5%.
Education: Compulsory: ages 6-17. **Literacy:** 87.8%.
Embassy: 2249 R St. NW 20008; 387-6101.
Website: www.president.go.ke
Arab colonies exported spices and slaves from the Kenya coast as early as the 8th cent. Britain obtained control in the 19th century. Kenya won independence Dec. 12, 1963, four years after the end of the violent Mau Mau uprising. Jomo Kenyatta, the country's leader since independence, died Aug. 22, 1978. He was succeeded by his vice president, Daniel arap Moi.

During the first half of the 1990s, Kenya suffered widespread unemployment and high inflation. Tribal clashes in the western provinces claimed thousands of lives. Pres. Moi won a fourth term in Dec. 1997, in an election plagued by irregularities. A truck bomb explosion at the U.S. embassy in Nairobi, Aug. 7, 1998, killed more than 200 people and injured about 5,000. The U.S. blamed the attack on al-Qaeda.

Pres. Moi was succeeded, Dec. 2002, by Mwai Kibaki of the opposition Democratic Party. After a disputed election Dec. 2007, Kenya's electoral commission declared Kibaki the winner over challenger Raila Odinga. Weeks of factional violence followed, leaving some 1,500 people dead and 600,000 displaced. Uhuru Kenyatta (Jomo Kenyatta's son) was declared, Mar. 10, 2013, the winner over Odinga in the Mar. 4 presidential election, amid accusations of vote-rigging. On Aug. 11, 2017, Kenyatta was again declared the victor over Odinga in Aug. 8 presidential voting; Odinga charged electoral fraud. After the Supreme Court, Sept. 1, nullified the result, Kenyatta won an Oct. 26 re-vote boycotted by Odinga.

Kenya sent troops into Somalia in 2011 (they joined with the African Union's AMISOM force in 2012) to combat the Somali Islamist extremist group al-Shabab. Al-Shabab carried out a series of deadly terrorist attacks in Kenya. An Apr. 2, 2015, attack on Garissa Univ. College killed 148 people. Scores of Kenyan troops have been killed by al-Shabab fighters in Somalia. The UNHCR estimated that about 266,000 Somali refugees were living in Kenya as of mid-2020, a decline of almost 75,000 from four years earlier—when tens of thousands of people were repatriated to Somalia, amid allegations of forced returns.

Kenya's High Court, May 24, 2019, upheld the constitutionality of a 19th-cent. law criminalizing gay sex.

Impacted by the 2020 COVID-19 pandemic, Kenya had about 38,000 cases and over 700 deaths by Sept. 30.

Kiribati
Republic of Kiribati

People: Population: 111,796 (180). **Age distrib.:** <15: 28.5%; 65+: 4.6%. **Growth:** 1.1%. **Migrants:** 2.6%. **Pop. density:** 357.0 per sq mi, 137.8 per sq km. **Urban:** 55.6%. **Ethnic groups:** I-Kiribati 96.2%. **Languages:** I-Kiribati, English (both official). **Religions:** Christian 96.9% (Catholic 44%, Protestant 37.3%, independent 15.5%), Baha'i 2.3%.
Geography: Total area: 313 sq mi, 811 sq km (173); **Land area:** 313 sq mi, 811 sq km. **Location:** 33 atolls (Gilbert, Line, and Phoenix Isls.) in mid-Pacific scattered over an area of about 1.35 mil sq mi around the point where the International Date Line formerly crossed the Equator. The Date Line was moved in 1997 to follow Kiribati's E border. Nearest neighbors are Nauru to SW, Tuvalu and Tokelau Isls. (N.Z.) to S. **Topography:** Except Banaba (Ocean) Isl., all are low-lying, with soil of coral sand and rock fragments, subject to erratic rainfall. **Arable land:** 2.5%. **Capital:** Tarawa, 64,011 (figure is for Tarawa Isl.).
Government: Type: Presidential republic. **Head of state and govt.:** Pres. Taneti Maamau; b. 1960; in office: Mar. 11, 2016. **Local divisions:** 3 geographical units (no first-order admin. divisions). **Defense budget/active troops:** NA.
Economy: Industries: fishing, handicrafts. **Chief agric.:** copra, breadfruit, fish. **Natural resources:** phosphate (production discontinued in 1979), coconuts, fish. **Water:** NA. **Electricity prod.:** 30 mil kwH. **Labor force:** agric. 24.3%, industry 18.2%, services 57.5%. **Unemployment:** NA.
Finance: Monetary unit: Australian Dollar (AUD) (1.37 = $1 U.S.). **GDP:** $278.7 mil; **per capita GDP:** $2,369; **GDP growth:** 2.2%. **Imports** (2016): $107.1 mil; Australia 29.3%, Fiji 17.3%, New Zealand 10.1%, China 5.8%, U.S. 5.8%, Singapore 5.1%. **Exports** (2013): $84.8 mil; Philippines 50.8%, Malaysia 17.2%, U.S. 11.4%, Bangladesh 5.8%, Fiji 5.4%. **Tourism:** $3 mil. **Budget:** $277.5 mil. **Inflation** (2014-15): 0.6%.
Transport: Airports: 4.
Communications: Telephone (2017): 0.7 per 100 pop. **Mobile:** 46.6 per 100 pop. **Broadband:** 42 per 100 pop. **Internet:** 14.6%.
Health: Expend.: 10.8%. **Life expect.:** 65.0 male; 70.2 female.
Births: 20.5 per 1,000 pop. **Deaths:** 6.9 per 1,000 pop. **Infant mortality:** 29.2 per 1,000 live births. **Undernourished:** 3.0%. **HIV:** NA.
Education: Compulsory: ages 6-14. **Literacy:** 97.7%.
Permanent UN mission: 800 Second Ave., Ste. 400A, New York, NY 10017; (212) 867-3310.
Website: www.president.gov.ki
A British protectorate since 1892, the Gilbert and Ellice Islands colony was completed with the inclusion of the Phoenix Islands, 1937. Tarawa Atoll was the scene of some of the bloodiest fighting in the Pacific during WWII.

Self-rule was granted 1971; the Ellice Islands separated from the colony in 1975 and became independent Tuvalu, 1978. Kiribati (pronounced *Kiribass*) independence was attained July 12, 1979. Kiribati's land area is shrinking as a result of rising sea levels; in 2014, the government began buying land in Fiji for agriculture and possible future resettlement.

Opposition candidate Taneti Maamau won the Mar. 9, 2016, presidential election. With Chinese investment increasing, Kiribati broke relations with Taiwan, Sept. 20, 2019. Maamau won a second term as president, June 22, 2020.

Korea, North
Democratic People's Republic of Korea

People: Population: 25,643,466 (54). **Age distrib.:** <15: 20.5%; 65+: 9.7%. **Growth:** 0.5%. **Migrants:** 0.2%. **Pop. density:** 551.6 per sq mi, 213.0 per sq km. **Urban:** 62.4%. **Ethnic groups:** racially homogeneous; small Chinese community, a few ethnic Japanese. **Languages:** Korean. **Religions:** agnostic 58.3%, atheist 15.2%, new religionist 12.5%, ethnic religionist 11.9%.

Geography: Total area: 46,540 sq mi, 120,538 sq km (97); **Land area:** 46,490 sq mi, 120,408 sq km. **Location:** Northern E Asia. China and Russia on N, S. Korea on S. **Topography:** Mountains and hills cover nearly entire country, with narrow valleys and small plains in between. N and E coasts are most rugged areas. **Arable land:** 19.5%. **Capital:** P'yongyang, 3,084,244.

Government: Type: Dictatorship, single-party state. **Head of govt.:** Kim Jong Un; b. 1983; officially assumed post Dec. 17, 2011. **Chief of state:** Supreme People's Assembly Pres. Choe Ryong Hae; in office: Apr. 11, 2019. **Local divisions:** 9 provinces, 3 cities. **Defense budget:** NA. **Active troops:** 1,280,000.

Economy: Industries: military prods.; machine building, elec. power, chemicals; mining, metallurgy; textiles, food proc.; tourism. **Chief agric.:** rice, corn, potatoes, wheat, soybeans, pulses, beef, pork. **Natural resources:** coal, iron ore, limestone, magnesite, graphite, copper, zinc, lead, prec. metals, hydropower. **Water:** 3,027 cu m per capita. **Electricity prod.:** 16.1 bil kWh. **Labor force:** agric. 51.1%, industry 13.2%, services 35.7%. **Unemployment:** 2.8%.

Finance: Monetary unit: Won (KPW) (900.04 = $1 U.S.). **GDP:** NA; **per capita GDP:** NA; **GDP growth:** NA. **Imports** (2018): $2.3 bil; China 91.9%. **Exports** (2018): $222 mil; China 86.3%. **Budget** (2007): $3.3 bil. **Inflation:** NA.

Transport: Railways: 4,620 mi. **Airports:** 39.

Communications: Telephone (2017): 4.6 per 100 pop. **Mobile** (2017): 15 per 100 pop. **Broadband:** NA. **Internet:** NA.

Health: Expend.: NA. **Life expect.:** 67.7 male; 75.6 female. **Births:** 14.5 per 1,000 pop. **Deaths:** 9.4 per 1,000 pop. **Infant mortality:** 20.0 per 1,000 live births. **Undernourished:** 47.6%. **HIV:** NA.

Education: Compulsory: ages 6-16. **Literacy:** 100%.

Permanent UN mission: 820 Second Ave., 13th Fl., New York, NY 10017; (212) 972-3105.

Website: www.korea-dpr.com

The Democratic People's Republic of Korea was founded May 1, 1948, in the zone occupied by Russia after WWII. Its armies tried to conquer the south, 1950. After three years of fighting, with Chinese and U.S. intervention, a cease-fire was proclaimed. A demilitarized zone (DMZ) was established, straddling the cease-fire line.

For the next four decades, a hard-line Communist regime headed by Kim Il Sung kept tight control over the nation's political, economic, and cultural life. The nation used its mineral and hydroelectric resources to develop its military strength. By the early 1990s, North Korea was widely believed to be developing nuclear weapons. The U.S. and North Korea signed an agreement, Oct. 21, 1994, providing for phased dismantling of North Korea's nuclear development program in return for U.S. energy aid and improved ties with the U.S.

Kim Il Sung died July 8, 1994. He was succeeded by his son, Kim Jong Il. Defections by high officials, a deteriorating economy, and severe food shortages plagued North Korea, beginning in the late 1990s. North Korea and Japan agreed to normalize relations in a Sept. 2002 summit.

In Oct. 2002, North Korea admitted to pursuing a secret nuclear weapons program in violation of past agreements. During 2003-09, as six-nation talks sponsored by China sought to resolve the nuclear issue, North Korea alternately stopped and resumed its nuclear program. North Korea conducted its first nuclear explosion Oct. 9, 2006.

In Apr.-May 2009, North Korea suspended participation in the six-nation talks, expelled IAEA inspectors, tested multiple missiles, and exploded a nuclear device underground. The UN Security Council June 12 toughened sanctions on North Korea.

Kim Jong Il died Dec. 17, 2011. He was succeeded by his son Kim Jong Un. In Dec. 2013, Kim Jong Un ordered the execution of his politically powerful uncle, Jang Song Thaek.

North Korea conducted a nuclear test Feb. 10, 2013, and it negated, Mar. 11, 2013, the cease-fire agreement with the South that ended the Korean War. It conducted numerous short- and medium-range missile tests 2013-15. North Korea was apparently responsible for cyberattacks on Sony Pictures Entertainment, Nov. 2014, related to a comedy film about Kim Jong Un. North Korea conducted its fourth nuclear weapons test on Jan. 6, 2016, and its fifth on Sept. 9. North Korea continued missile tests, 2016-17, including its first ICBM launch, July 4, 2017. U.S. and UN sanctions were strengthened in 2016 and again in 2017. North Korea conducted its sixth nuclear test, Sept. 3, 2017.

On Apr. 27, 2018, Kim Jong Un met in the DMZ with South Korean Pres. Moon Jae-in. They agreed to work toward a peace treaty and denuclearization of the Korean Peninsula. North Korea said it destroyed, May 24, its nuclear test site. At a June 12 summit meeting in Singapore with U.S. Pres. Donald Trump, Kim again made a general denuclearization pledge. As post-summit U.S.-North Korea talks continued, North Korea began dismantling a missile test site in July. However, U.S. officials, and an Aug. 2018 UN report, concluded that North Korea was continuing its nuclear and missile programs. A second Trump-Kim summit, Feb. 2019 in Hanoi, Vietnam, ended without resolution. Beginning May 2019, North Korea fired a number of short-range missiles, its first missile tests since 2017. A Trump-Kim meeting at the DMZ on June 30, 2019, produced no immediate results. North Korean missile tests continued in 2020.

North Korea claimed to have virtually no COVID-19 cases as of Sept. 2020. Measures to combat disease spread, such as closing the border with key trading partner China, as well as severe flooding, hurt an already weak economy.

Korea, South
Republic of Korea

People: Population: 51,835,110 (28). **Age distrib.:** <15: 12.8%; 65+: 15.9%. **Growth:** 0.4%. **Migrants:** 2.3%. **Pop. density:** 1,385.2 per sq mi, 534.8 per sq km. **Urban:** 81.4%. **Ethnic groups:** homogeneous. **Languages:** Korean, English (widely taught). **Religions:** Christian 33.6% (independent 13.9%, Protestant 12.9%), Buddhist 24.5%, ethnic religionist 15.1%, new religionist 14.2%, Confucianist 10.6%.

Geography: Total area: 38,502 sq mi, 99,720 sq km (107); **Land area:** 37,421 sq mi, 96,920 sq km. **Location:** Northern E Asia. N. Korea on N. **Topography:** Mountainous, with a rugged E coast. W and S coasts are deeply indented, with many islands and harbors. **Arable land:** 14.3%. **Capital:** Seoul, 9,963,452. **Cities:** Busan, 3,465,190; Incheon, 2,801,039; Daegu, 2,198,962.

Government: Type: Presidential republic. **Head of state:** Pres. Moon Jae-in; b. 1953; in office: May 10, 2017. **Head of govt.:** Prime Min. Chung Sye-kyun; b. 1950; in office: Jan. 14, 2020. **Local divisions:** 9 provinces, 6 metropolitan cities, 1 special city, 1 special self-governing city. **Defense budget:** $39.8 bil. **Active troops:** 599,000.

Economy: Industries: electronics, telecom, auto prod., chemicals, shipbuilding, steel. **Chief agric.:** rice, root crops, barley, vegetables, fruit, cattle, pigs, chickens, milk, eggs, fish. **Natural resources:** coal, tungsten, graphite, molybdenum, lead. **Water:** 1,367 cu m per capita. **Electricity prod.** (2018): 542.8 bil kWh. **Labor force:** agric. 4.8%, industry 25.0%, services 70.2%. **Unemployment:** 4.6%.

Finance: Monetary unit: Won (KRW) (1,188.37 = $1 U.S.). **GDP:** $2.2 tril; **per capita GDP:** $43,029; **GDP growth:** 2.0%. **Imports:** $457.5 bil; China 20.5%, Japan 11.5%, U.S. 10.5%. **Exports:** $577.4 bil; China 25.1%, U.S. 12.2%, Vietnam 8.2%, Hong Kong 6.9%. **Tourism:** $21.6 bil. **Budget:** $335.8 bil. **Inflation:** 0.4%.

Transport: Railways: 2,472 mi. **Motor vehicles:** 451.3 per 1,000 pop. **Airports:** 71.

Communications: Telephone: 50.6 per 100 pop. **Mobile:** 129.7 per 100 pop. **Broadband:** 112.8 per 100 pop. **Internet** (2018): 95.9%.

Health: Expend.: 7.6%. **Life expect.:** 79.4 male; 85.9 female. **Births:** 8.2 per 1,000 pop. **Deaths:** 6.8 per 1,000 pop. **Infant mortality:** 3.0 per 1,000 live births. **Undernourished:** <2.5%. **HIV:** NA.

Education: Compulsory: ages 6-14. **Literacy:** NA.

Embassy: 2450 Massachusetts Ave. NW 20008; 939-5600.

Website: www.korea.net

The recorded history of Korea, once called the Hermit Kingdom, dates back to the 1st cent. BCE. It was united in a kingdom under the Silla Dynasty, 668 CE. It was at times associated with the Chinese empire; the treaty that concluded the Sino-Japanese war of 1894-95 recognized Korea's complete independence. In 1910 Japan forcibly annexed Korea as Chosun.

At the Potsdam conference, July 1945, near the end of WWII, the 38th parallel was designated as the line dividing Soviet (north) and U.S. (south) occupation zones. Soviet troops entered Korea Aug. 10, 1945; U.S. troops entered Sept. 8.

The South Koreans formed the Republic of Korea in May 1948 with Seoul as the capital. Dr. Syngman Rhee was chosen president. A separate, Communist regime was formed in the North; its army attacked the south in June 1950, initiating the Korean War. UN troops, under U.S. command, supported South Korea in the war, which ended in an armistice (July 1953) leaving Korea divided by a demilitarized zone (DMZ) along the 38th parallel. The U.S. kept troops in South Korea (about 28,500 in 2020).

Rhee's authoritarian rule became increasingly unpopular, forcing his resignation Apr. 26, 1960. In an army coup May 16, 1961, Gen. Park Chung-hee became chairman of a ruling junta. First elected president, 1963, Park was assassinated by the chief of the Korean intelligence agency, Oct. 26, 1979.

In May 1980, Gen. Chun Doo-hwan, head of military intelligence, ordered the brutal suppression of pro-democracy demonstrations in Kwangju. Chun became president, Aug. 27, 1980. On July 1, 1987, following anti-government protests, Chun agreed to democratic reforms. In Dec., Roh Tae-woo, a longtime ally of Chun's, was elected president.

Pres. Kim Young-sam took office in 1993. Convicted of mutiny, treason, and corruption, Chun was sentenced to death by a Seoul court, Aug. 26, 1996, for his role in the 1979 coup and 1980 Kwangju massacre; Roh received a 225-year prison sentence. Kim Dae-jung, a longtime dissident, won the presidential election Dec. 18, 1997. Chun and Roh were released and pardoned Dec. 22.

At a summit meeting in Pyongyang, June 13-15, 2000, Pres. Kim Dae-jung and North Korean leader Kim Jong Il agreed to work for reconciliation and eventual reunification of their two countries. On Oct. 13, 2000, Kim Dae-jung was named the winner of the Nobel Peace Prize. Roh Moo-hyun won the 2002 presidential election.

The IAEA, Sept. 2, 2004, said South Korea had acknowledged having secretly processed a small amount of uranium to near weapons-grade level in 2000, violating the Nuclear Non-Proliferation Treaty and a bilateral accord with North Korea (North Korea, 2006-17, conducted 6 nuclear weapons tests).

Conservative Park Geun-hye became South Korea's first female president in Dec. 19, 2012, elections. Pres. Park was impeached for corruption by the National Assembly, Dec. 9, 2016, and removed from office, Mar. 10, 2017; a criminal trial ended, Apr. 6, 2018, in a conviction and prison sentence.

Following a series of North Korean missile tests, a U.S.-South Korean agreement to deploy an advanced U.S. missile defense system known as THAAD in South Korea was announced July 8, 2016.

Moon Jae-in of the Democratic Party, who campaigned on a policy of diplomatic engagement with North Korea, won the May 9, 2017, presidential election. Moon met with North Korean leader Kim Jong Un in the DMZ, Apr. 27, 2018; they agreed to work toward a peace treaty and denuclearization. With North-South tensions increasing in 2020, North Korea blew up a liaison-office building near the border, June 16.

A U.S.-South Korea trade liberalization agreement went into effect Mar. 15, 2012. Revisions signed Sept. 24, 2018, were aimed in part at increasing U.S. auto exports.

The Constitutional Court struck down, Apr. 11, 2019, a 1953 law banning almost all abortions; the decision gave the legislature until the end of 2020 to change the law.

Affected by late Jan. 2020 by the COVID-19 pandemic, South Korea instituted an intensive program of testing and contact tracing to combat the disease's spread. New cases dropped from a late Feb.-early Mar. peak, but clusters of new cases continued. As of Sept. 30, South Korea had totals of almost 24,000 cases and 413 deaths.

Kosovo
Republic of Kosovo

People: Population: 1,932,774 (147). **Age distrib.:** <15: 24.1%; 65+: 7.8%. **Growth:** 0.7%. **Pop. density:** 459.8 per sq mi, 177.5 per sq km. **Ethnic groups:** Albanian 92.9%, Bosniak 1.6%, Serb 1.5%, Turk 1.1%. **Languages:** Albanian, Serbian (both official); Bosnian. **Religions:** Muslim 92.5% (Sunni), Christian 6.3%.

Geography: Total area: 4,203 sq mi, 10,887 sq km (162); **Land area:** 4,203 sq mi, 10,887 sq km. **Location:** SE Europe. Serbia on N, Montenegro on NW, Albania on SW, North Macedonia on SE. **Topography:** Low flood basins surrounded by several high mountain ranges. **Arable land:** 44.9%. **Capital:** Pristina.

Government: Type: Parliamentary republic. **Head of state:** Pres. Hashim Thaci; b. 1968; in office: Apr. 7, 2016. **Head of govt.:** Prime Min. Avdullah Hoti; b. 1976; in office: June 3, 2020. **Local divisions:** 38 municipalities. **Defense budget:** NA. **Active troops:** Kosovo Security Force (non-military) only.

Economy: Industries: mineral mining, constr. materials, base metals, leather, machinery, appliances, foodstuffs and beverages. **Chief agric.:** wheat, corn, berries, potatoes, peppers, fruit; dairy; fish. **Natural resources:** nickel, lead, zinc, magnesium, lignite, kaolin, chrome, bauxite. **Water:** NA. **Electricity prod.** (2018): 5.1 bil kWh. **Labor force:** agric. 3.5%, industry 26.2%, services 70.3%. **Unemployment:** NA.

Finance: Monetary unit: Euro (EUR) (0.84 = $1 U.S.). **GDP:** $21.2 bil; **per capita GDP:** $11,839; **GDP growth:** 4.2%. **Imports:** $3.2 bil; Germany 12.4%, Serbia 12.3%, Turkey 9.6%, China 9.1%, Italy 6.4%, North Macedonia 5.1%, Albania 5%. **Exports:** $428 mil; Albania 16%, India 14%, North Macedonia 12.1%, Serbia 10.6%, Switzerland 5.6%, Germany 5.4%. **Budget:** $2.2 bil. **Inflation:** 2.7%.

Transport: Railways: 207 mi. **Airports:** 3.

Communications: NA.

Health: Expend.: NA. **Life expect.:** 70.5 male; 75.1 female. **Births:** 15.4 per 1,000 pop. **Deaths:** 7 per 1,000 pop. **Infant mortality:** 30.2 per 1,000 live births. **Undernourished:** NA. **HIV:** NA.

Education: Compulsory: ages 6-15. **Literacy:** 91.9%.

Embassy: 2175 K St. NW, Ste. 300, 20037; 380-3581.

Website: www.rks-gov.net

Kosovo was part of the Roman and Byzantine empires before Serbs, a Slavic people, took control in the Middle Ages. After Ottoman Turks defeated Serb forces, 1389, Kosovo's population became predominantly Muslim and Kosovar (ethnic Albanian). Serbia regained control in the First Balkan War (1912-13). Kosovo entered the Kingdom of Serbs, Croats, and Slovenes as part of Serbia after World War I and became an autonomous province of Serbia, a constituent republic of Yugoslavia, after World War II.

Revoking provincial autonomy, Serbia began ruling Kosovo by force in 1989. Albanian secessionists proclaimed an independent Republic of Kosovo in July 1990. As Yugoslavia collapsed, the

republics of Serbia (incl. Kosovo) and Montenegro proclaimed a new Federal Republic of Yugoslavia, 1992. Guerrilla attacks by the Kosovo Liberation Army (KLA) in 1997 brought a ferocious counteroffensive by Serbian authorities.

Fearful that the Serbs were employing "ethnic cleansing" tactics, NATO launched an air war against Yugoslavia, Mar.-June 1999; the Serbs retaliated by terrorizing the Kosovars. Hundreds of thousands fled, mostly to Albania and Macedonia (now North Macedonia). A 50,000-member multinational force (KFOR) entered Kosovo in June, and most refugees returned by Sept. 1, 1999. (About 3,400 KFOR troops remained in Kosovo as of mid-2020.)

From June 1999, Kosovo was administered by a UN mission (UNMIK). Kosovo declared independence, Feb. 17, 2008. More than 100 nations, including the U.S. and most EU members, have recognized Kosovo; Serbia and Russia have not. Kosovo and Serbia, Apr. 19, 2013, completed a power-sharing agreement between N Kosovo regions with a Serb majority and the Kosovo central government; implementation was suspended by Kosovo's constitutional court, Nov. 10, 2015.

An EU special prosecutor reported, July 29, 2014, evidence of ethnic cleansing against Serbs by the KLA in the late 1990s. Prime Min. Hashim Thaçi, who headed the KLA at that time, had denied any wrongdoing. Isa Mustafa replaced Thaçi as prime min., Dec. 9, 2014. Parliament elected Thaçi president of Kosovo, Feb. 26, 2016. Former KLA commander Ramush Haradinaj became prime min., Sept. 9, 2017. Facing questioning by a war crimes tribunal, Haradinaj resigned, July 19, 2019. Avdullah Hoti, backed by Thaçi, became prime min., June 3, 2020. An indictment against Thaçi for war crimes was announced June 24.

Kosovo and Serbia signed an agreement, Sept. 4, 2020, to move toward normalizing economic relations.

The 2020 COVID-19 pandemic caused more than 15,500 cases and over 600 deaths in Kosovo as of Sept. 30.

Kuwait
State of Kuwait

People: Population: 2,993,706 (136). **Age distrib.:** <15: 24.3%; 65+: 2.9%. **Growth:** 1.2%. **Migrants:** 72.1%. **Pop. density:** 435.2 per sq mi, 168.0 per sq km. **Urban:** 100.0%. **Ethnic groups:** Asian 40.3%, Kuwaiti 30.4%, other Arab 27.4%, African 1%. **Languages:** Arabic (official), English (widely spoken). **Religions:** Muslim (official) 82.9% (Sunni 66%, Shia 17%), Christian 11.9%, Hindu 3.7%.

Geography: Total area: 6,880 sq mi, 17,818 sq km (153); **Land area:** 6,880 sq mi, 17,818 sq km. **Location:** Middle East, at N end of Persian Gulf. Iraq on N, Saudi Arabia on S. **Topography:** Flat, very dry, and extremely hot. **Arable land:** 0.5%. **Capital:** Kuwait City, 3,114,553.

Government: Type: Constitutional monarchy (emirate). **Head of state:** Emir Sheikh Sabah al-Ahmad al-Jabir al-Sabah; b. 1929; in office: Jan. 29, 2006. **Head of govt.:** Prime Min. Sheikh Jaber al-Mubarak al-Hamad al-Sabah; b. 1942; in office: Nov. 30, 2011. **Local divisions:** 6 governorates. **Defense budget:** $6.4 bil. **Active troops:** 17,500.

Economy: Industries: petroleum, petrochemicals, cement, shipbuilding and repair, water desalination, food proc., constr. materials. **Chief agric.:** fish. **Natural resources:** petroleum, fish, shrimp, nat. gas. **Water:** 5 cu m per capita. **Crude oil reserves:** 101.5 bil bbls (incl. half of Neutral Zone reserves). **Electricity prod.:** 68.4 bil kWh. **Labor force:** agric. 2.0%, industry 24.4%, services 73.7%. **Unemployment:** 2.3%.

Finance: Monetary unit: Dinar (KWD) (0.31 = $1 U.S.). **GDP:** $218.4 bil; **per capita GDP:** $51,912; **GDP growth:** 0.4%. **Imports:** $29.5 bil; China 13.5%, U.S. 13.3%, UAE 9.5%, Saudi Arabia 5.8%, Germany 5.4%, Japan 5%. **Exports:** $55.2 bil; South Korea 18.3%, China 17.4%, Japan 11.5%, India 11.2%, Singapore 6.3%, U.S. 5.7%. **Tourism:** $700 mil. **Budget:** $62.6 bil. **Inflation:** 1.1%.

Transport: Motor vehicles: 809.6 per 1,000 pop. **Airports:** 4.

Communications: Telephone: 12.5 per 100 pop. **Mobile:** 178.6 per 100 pop. **Broadband:** 127.3 per 100 pop. **Internet** (2018): 99.6%.

Health: Expend.: 5.3%. **Life expect.:** 77.2 male; 80.2 female. **Births:** 18 per 1,000 pop. **Deaths:** 2.3 per 1,000 pop. **Infant mortality:** 6.5 per 1,000 live births. **Undernourished:** <2.5%. **HIV** (2018): <0.1%.

Education: Compulsory: ages 6-14. **Literacy:** 99.1%.

Embassy: 2940 Tilden St. NW 20008; 966-0702.

Website: www.pm.gov.kw

Kuwait is ruled by the Sabah dynasty, founded 1759. Britain ran foreign relations and defense from 1899 until independence in 1961. More than two-thirds of the population is non-Kuwaiti, including many Palestinians and non-Arab Asians, and cannot vote.

Oil exports provide most of Kuwait's income. Oil pays for free medical care and education for citizens. There is no income tax. Low global oil prices beginning in 2014 hurt the economy; government efforts to diversify the economy proceeded slowly.

Kuwait was attacked and overrun by Iraqi forces Aug. 1990. In Operation Desert Storm a U.S.-led coalition, with authorization from the UN Security Council, began bombing Iraq and Iraqi forces in Kuwait, Jan. 1991, then launched a ground assault Feb. 23. By Feb. 27, Iraqi forces were routed and Kuwait liberated.

Political rights were extended to women, May 16, 2005; the first female cabinet member was appointed June 12. Kuwait enacted a

$5.2-bil program Mar. 2009 to bail out banks and investment companies battered by the global financial crisis. In Nov. 26, 2016, elections, opposition candidates won 24 of 65 seats in the National Assembly; one woman was elected. A suicide bomber killed 27 people and wounded more than 200 at a Shiite mosque, June 26, 2015; an ISIS-affiliated Sunni extremist group claimed responsibility. The 2020 COVID-19 pandemic caused more than 104,000 Kuwaiti cases as of Sept. 30; over 600 people had died.

Kyrgyzstan
Kyrgyz Republic

People: Population: 5,964,897 (113). **Age distrib.:** <15: 30.4%; 65+: 5.8%. **Growth:** 0.9%. **Migrants:** 3.1%. **Pop. density:** 80.5 per sq mi, 31.1 per sq km. **Urban:** 36.9%. **Ethnic groups:** Kyrgyz 73.5%, Uzbek 14.7%, Russian 5.5%, other (incl. Uyghur, Tajik, Turk, Kazakh, Tatar, Ukrainian, Korean, German) 5.2%. **Languages:** Kyrgyz, Russian (both official); Uzbek. **Religions:** Muslim 87.6% (Sunni), agnostic 6.3%, Christian 4.2%.

Geography: Total area: 77,202 sq mi, 199,951 sq km (85); **Land area:** 74,055 sq mi, 191,801 sq km. **Location:** Central Asia. Kazakhstan on N, China on E, Uzbekistan on W, Tajikistan on S. **Topography:** Landlocked country nearly covered by Tien Shan and Pamir Mts.; avg. elevation 9,020 ft. Issyk-Kul, a large salt lake in NE, is 1 mi above sea level. **Arable land:** 6.7%. **Capital:** Bishkek, 1,038,429.

Government: Type: Parliamentary republic. **Head of state:** Pres. Sooronbay Jeenbekov; b. 1958; in office: Nov. 24, 2017. **Head of govt.:** Prime Min. Kubatbek Boronov; b. 1964; in office: June 17, 2020. **Local divisions:** 7 provinces, 2 cities. **Defense budget:** NA. **Active troops:** 10,900.

Economy: Industries: small machinery, textiles, food proc., cement, shoes, lumber, refrigerators, furniture, elec. motors. **Chief agric.:** cotton, potatoes, vegetables, grapes, fruits and berries; sheep, goats, cattle, wool. **Natural resources:** hydropower, gold, rare earth metals, coal, oil, nat. gas, nepheline, mercury, bismuth, lead, zinc. **Water:** 3,907 cu m per capita. **Crude oil reserves:** 40 mil bbls. **Electricity prod.:** 15.3 bil kWh. **Labor force:** agric. 20.4%, industry 24.7%, services 54.9%. **Unemployment:** 6.6%.

Finance: Monetary unit: Som (KGS) (78.69 = $1 U.S.). **GDP:** $35.3 bil; **per capita GDP:** $5,471; **GDP growth:** 4.5%. **Imports:** $4.2 bil; China 32.6%, Russia 24.8%, Kazakhstan 16.4%. **Exports:** $1.8 bil; Switzerland 59.1%, Uzbekistan 9.4%, Kazakhstan 5.1%. **Tourism:** $644 mil. **Budget:** $2.4 bil. **Inflation:** 1.1%.

Transport: Railways: 263 mi. **Airports:** 18.

Communications: Telephone: 5.3 per 100 pop. **Mobile:** 122.6 per 100 pop. **Broadband:** 73.7 per 100 pop. **Internet:** 38%.

Health: Expend.: 6.2%. **Life expect.:** 67.7 male; 76.2 female. **Births:** 20.6 per 1,000 pop. **Deaths:** 6.3 per 1,000 pop. **Infant mortality:** 23.3 per 1,000 live births. **Undernourished:** 6.4%. **HIV:** 0.2%.

Education: Compulsory: ages 6-15. **Literacy:** 99.8%.

Embassy: 2360 Massachusetts Ave. NW 20008; 449-9822.

Website: www.gov.kg

The region was inhabited around the 13th cent. by the Kyrgyz. It was annexed to Russia, 1864, and became a constituent republic of the USSR in 1936. Kyrgyzstan declared independence Aug. 31, 1991, ahead of the USSR disbanding Dec. 26, 1991.

In power since 1990, Pres. Askar Akayev won a third 5-year term in the 2000 election. Fraud by Akayev loyalists in parliamentary elections Feb.-Mar. 2005 sparked protests. Akayev fled the country, Mar. 24, and formally resigned, Apr. 4. His interim successor, former Prime Min. Kurmanbek Bakiyev, a leader of the "tulip revolution," won the 2005 presidential vote and was reelected 2009, when monitors reported numerous irregularities. He was ousted by opposition parties Apr. 7, 2010, after clashes between protesters and government security forces left at least 77 people dead.

Fighting in mid-June 2010 between majority Kyrgyz and minority Uzbeks in the southern cities of Osh and Jalalabad claimed up to 2,000 lives. Almazbek Atambayev won the 2011 presidential election. Constitutional changes approved in a Dec. 2016 referendum strengthened the powers of the executive branch. Former Prime Min. Sooronbay Jeenbekov won the Oct. 15, 2017, presidential election. Jeenbekov ally Mukhammedkaly Abylgaziyev became prime min., Apr. 20, 2018. Two days after Abylgaziyev resigned in a corruption scandal, Kubatbek Boronov became prime minister, June 17, 2020. By Aug. 31, 2020, the COVID-19 pandemic had caused more than 46,000 cases in Kyrgyzstan; over 1,000 people had died.

Laos
Lao People's Democratic Republic

People: Population: 7,447,396 (101). **Age distrib.:** <15: 31.2%; 65+: 4.1%. **Growth:** 1.4%. **Migrants:** 0.7%. **Pop. density:** 83.6 per sq mi, 32.3 per sq km. **Urban:** 36.3%. **Ethnic groups:** Lao 53.2%, Khmou 11%, Hmong 9.2%, Phouthay 3.4%, Tai 3.1%, Makong 2.5%, Katong 2.2%, Lue 2%. **Languages:** Lao (official), French, English, ethnic langs. **Religions:** Buddhist 53.4%, ethnic religionist 41.7%, Christian 2.8%.

Geography: Total area: 91,429 sq mi, 236,800 sq km (82); **Land area:** 89,112 sq mi, 230,800 sq km. **Location:** Indochina Peninsula in SE Asia. Myanmar, China on N; Vietnam on E; Cambodia on S; Thailand

on W. **Topography:** Landlocked, dominated by jungle. Mountains along E border are source of E-W rivers. Mekong R. defines most of W border. **Arable land:** 6.7%. **Capital:** Vientiane, 682,542.

Government: Type: Communist state. **Head of state:** Pres. Bounnhang Vorachit; b. 1937; in office: Apr. 20, 2016. **Head of govt.:** Prime Min. Thongloun Sisoulith; b. 1945; in office: Apr. 20, 2016. **Local divisions:** 17 provinces, 1 prefecture. **Defense budget:** NA. **Active troops:** 29,100.

Economy: Industries: mining, timber, elec. power, agric. proc., rubber, constr., garments. **Chief agric.:** sweet potatoes, vegetables, corn, coffee, sugarcane, tobacco, cotton, tea, peanuts, rice, cassava; water buffalo, pigs. **Natural resources:** timber, hydropower, gypsum, tin, gold, gems. **Water:** 48,629 cu m per capita. **Electricity prod.:** 27.9 bil kWh. **Labor force:** agric. 61.7%, industry 12.2%, services 26.4%. **Unemployment:** 0.6%.

Finance: Monetary unit: Kip (LAK) (9,093.59 = $1 U.S.). **GDP:** $58.4 bil; **per capita GDP:** $8,151; **GDP growth:** 4.7%. **Imports:** $5 bil; Thailand 59.1%, China 21.5%, Vietnam 9.8%. **Exports:** $3.7 bil; Thailand 42.6%, China 28.7%, Vietnam 10.4%. **Tourism:** $734 mil. **Budget:** $4.0 bil. **Inflation:** 3.3%.

Transport: Airports: 8.

Communications: Telephone: 21 per 100 pop. **Mobile:** 51.9 per 100 pop. **Broadband:** 40 per 100 pop. **Internet:** 25.5%.

Health: Expend.: 2.5%. **Life expect.:** 63.6 male; 67.9 female. **Births:** 22.4 per 1,000 pop. **Deaths:** 7.2 per 1,000 pop. **Infant mortality:** 45.6 per 1,000 live births. **Undernourished:** NA. **HIV:** 0.3%.

Education: Compulsory: ages 6-14. **Literacy:** 92.5%.

Embassy: 2222 S St. NW 20008; 332-6416.

Website: www.na.gov.la

Laos became a French protectorate in 1893, but regained independence as a constitutional monarchy July 19, 1949. Conflicts among neutralist, Communist, and conservative factions created a chaotic political situation. Armed conflict increased after 1960.

The three factions formed a coalition government in June 1962 with neutralist Prince Souvanna Phouma as premier. A 14-nation conference in Geneva signed agreements, 1962, guaranteeing independence. By 1964 the leftist Pathet Lao had withdrawn from the coalition, and, with aid from North Vietnamese troops, renewed attacks. During the Vietnam War, U.S. planes (1964-73) dropped more than 2 mil tons of bombs on targets in Laos, principally the Ho Chi Minh trail, a supply line from North Vietnam to Communist forces in Laos, South Vietnam, and Cambodia. (Beginning in the 1990s, the U.S., other nations, and the UN provided aid to dismantle unexploded bombs.)

After Pathet Lao military gains in Laos, Souvanna Phouma, May 1975, ordered government troops to cease fighting; the Pathet Lao took control. The Lao People's Democratic Republic was proclaimed Dec. 3, 1975.

From the mid-1970s through the 1980s, Laos relied on Vietnam for military and financial aid. After easing its finance laws in 1988, Laos attracted investment from Thailand, China, South Korea, the U.S., and other nations. Laos was admitted to the Assn. of SE Asian Nations in 1997. The U.S. Congress approved normalization of trade with Laos in 2004. Laos opened its first stock exchange Jan. 11, 2011.

Despite environmental and safety concerns, since the 1990s, dozens of dams have been built or planned on Mekong R. tributaries, providing hydroelectricity for domestic use and export. A dam collapse in southern Laos, July 23, 2018, killed at least 35 and displaced thousands.

Latvia
Republic of Latvia

People: Population: 1,881,232 (149). **Age distrib.:** <15: 15.3%; 65+: 20.5%. **Growth:** –1.1%. **Migrants:** 12.4%. **Pop. density:** 78.3 per sq mi, 30.2 per sq km. **Urban:** 68.3%. **Ethnic groups:** Latvian 62.2%, Russian 25.2%, Belarusian 3.2%, Ukrainian 2.2%, Polish 2.1%. **Languages:** Latvian (official), Russian. **Religions:** Christian 82.9% (Protestant 36.6%, Catholic 23.2%, Orthodox 22.6%), agnostic 13.3%, atheist 3%.

Geography: Total area: 24,938 sq mi, 64,589 sq km (122); **Land area:** 24,034 sq mi, 62,249 sq km. **Location:** E Europe, on Baltic Sea. Estonia on N; Russia on E; Belarus, Lithuania on S. **Topography:** Lowland with numerous lakes, marshes, and peat bogs. Principal river is W. Dvina (Daugava). Glacial hills in E. **Arable land:** 20.8%. **Capital:** Riga, 630,692.

Government: Type: Parliamentary republic. **Head of state:** Pres. Egils Levits; b. 1955; in office: July 8, 2019. **Head of govt.:** Prime Min. Arturs Krisjanis Karins; b. 1964; in office: Jan. 23, 2019. **Local divisions:** 110 municipalities, 9 cities. **Defense budget:** $712 mil. **Active troops:** 6,900.

Economy: Industries: processed foods, processed wood prods., textiles, processed metals, pharmaceuticals, railroad cars, synthetic fibers. **Chief agric.:** grain, rapeseed, potatoes, vegetables; pork, poultry; fish. **Natural resources:** peat, limestone, dolomite, amber, hydropower, timber. **Water:** 17,918 cu m per capita. **Electricity prod.** (2018): 6.5 bil kWh. **Labor force:** agric. 6.5%, industry 23.7%, services 69.8%. **Unemployment:** 6.5%.

Finance: Monetary unit: Euro (EUR) (0.84 = $1 U.S.). **GDP:** $61.6 bil; **per capita GDP:** $32,204; **GDP growth:** 2.2%. **Imports:** $15.8 bil; Lithuania 17.6%, Germany 11.7%, Poland 8.7%, Estonia

7.6%, Russia 7.1%. **Exports:** $12.8 bil; Lithuania 15.8%, Russia 14%, Estonia 10.9%, Germany 6.9%, Sweden 5.7%. **Tourism:** $1 bil. **Budget:** $11.5 bil. **Inflation:** 2.8%.

Transport: Railways: 1,156 mi. **Motor vehicles:** 416.8 per 1,000 pop. **Airports:** 18.

Communications: Telephone: 13.8 per 100 pop. **Mobile:** 107.3 per 100 pop. **Broadband:** 117.9 per 100 pop. **Internet** (2018): 83.6%.

Health: Expend.: 6.0%. **Life expect.:** 70.9 male; 80.1 female. **Births:** 9.2 per 1,000 pop. **Deaths:** 14.6 per 1,000 pop. **Infant mortality:** 5.0 per 1,000 live births. **Undernourished:** <2.5%. **HIV:** 0.5%.

Education: Compulsory: ages 5-15. **Literacy:** 99.8%.

Embassy: 2306 Massachusetts Ave. NW 20008; 328-2840.

Website: www.mk.gov.lv or latvia.lv

Prior to 1918, Latvia was occupied by the Russians and Germans. It was an independent republic, 1918-39. The Aug. 1939 Soviet-German agreement assigned Latvia to the Soviet sphere of influence. It was officially absorbed by the USSR in 1940. It was overrun by the German army in 1941, but retaken in 1945.

Latvia declared independence, Aug. 21, 1991. The last Russian troops in Latvia withdrew by Aug. 31, 1994. Responding to international pressure, Latvian voters, 1998, eased citizenship laws that had discriminated against some 500,000 ethnic Russians. Latvia joined the EU and NATO in 2004. It began using the euro as its currency Jan. 1, 2014.

Hit hard by recession, Latvia reached agreement Dec. 2008 on a $10.4-bil emergency loan from the EU, IMF, World Bank, and Nordic countries. Angered by the economic downturn and influence of wealthy oligarchs, voters approved a July 2011 referendum dissolving parliament. Prime Min. Valdis Dombrovskis's center-right Unity Party came in third in Sept. 2011 elections, but he remained prime min. After more than 50 people died, Nov. 21, 2013, in a Riga supermarket roof collapse, Dombrovskis resigned. Laimdota Straujuma became Latvia's first woman prime min., Jan. 22, 2014. She resigned, Dec. 7, 2015, after agreeing to an unpopular EU refugee resettlement program. NATO announced, Feb. 5, 2016, it would station troops in Latvia to deter Russian aggression. After money-laundering scandals, populist parties did well in inconclusive Oct. 6, 2018, elections. Krisjanis Karins of New Unity formed a coalition and became prime min., Jan. 23, 2019.

The 2020 COVID-19 pandemic caused about 1,700 cases in Latvia as of Sept. 30; 37 people had died.

Lebanon
Lebanese Republic

People: Population: 5,469,612 (117). **Age distrib.:** <15: 20.8%; 65+: 8.0%. **Growth:** −8.1%. **Migrants:** 27.2%. **Pop. density:** 1,384.8 per sq mi, 534.7 per sq km. **Urban:** 88.9%. **Ethnic groups:** Arab 95%, Armenian 4%. (Many Christian Lebanese identify not as Arab but as Phoenician, descendants of ancient Canaanites.) **Languages:** Arabic (official), French, English, Armenian. **Religions:** Muslim 58.6% (Shia 28%, Sunni 26%, Islamic schismatic 5%), Christian 35.2% (Catholic 28.4%), agnostic 3%, Buddhist 2.1%.

Geography: Total area: 4,015 sq mi, 10,400 sq km (163). **Land area:** 3,950 sq mi, 10,230 sq km. **Location:** Middle East, on E end of Mediterranean Sea. Syria on E, Israel on S. **Topography:** Narrow coastal strip. Two N-S mountain ranges enclose the fertile Beqaa Valley. The Litani R. runs S through the valley. **Arable land:** 12.9%. **Capital:** Beirut, 2,424,425.

Government: Type: Parliamentary republic. **Head of state:** Pres. Michel Aoun; b. 1933; in office: Oct. 31, 2016. **Head of govt.:** Vacant as of Oct. 1, 2020. **Local divisions:** 8 governorates. **Defense budget:** $1.9 bil. **Active troops:** 60,000.

Economy: Industries: banking, tourism, real estate and constr., food proc., wine, jewelry, cement, textiles, mineral and chem. prods., wood and furniture prods. **Chief agric.:** citrus, grapes, tomatoes, apples, vegetables, potatoes, olives, tobacco; sheep, goats. **Natural resources:** limestone, iron ore, salt, water (surplus in a water-deficit region). **Water:** 740 cu m per capita. **Electricity prod.:** 19.0 bil kWh. **Labor force:** agric. 13.4%, industry 22.3%, services 64.3%. **Unemployment:** 6.3%.

Finance: Monetary unit: Pound (LBP) (1,507.50 = $1 U.S.). **GDP:** $105.1 bil; **per capita GDP:** $15,327; **GDP growth:** −5.6%. **Imports:** $18.3 bil; China 10.2%, Italy 8.9%, Greece 7%, Germany 6.6%, U.S. 6.3%. **Exports:** $3.5 bil; China 13%, UAE 9.9%, South Africa 7.5%, Saudi Arabia 6.5%, Syria 6.5%, Iraq 5.8%. **Tourism:** $8.6 bil. **Budget:** $15.4 bil. **Inflation:** 3.0%.

Transport: Railways: 249 mi (unusable due to damage from fighting). **Motor vehicles:** 135.2 per 1,000 pop. **Airports:** 5.

Communications: Telephone: 13 per 100 pop. **Mobile:** 64.5 per 100 pop. **Broadband:** 60.9 per 100 pop. **Internet:** 78.2%.

Health: Expend.: 8.2%. **Life expect.:** 76.9 male; 79.8 female. **Births:** 13.6 per 1,000 pop. **Deaths:** 5.4 per 1,000 pop. **Infant mortality:** 6.8 per 1,000 live births. **Undernourished:** 5.7%. **HIV:** <0.1%.

Education: Compulsory: ages 5-15. **Literacy:** 99.8%.

Embassy: 2560 28th St. NW 20008; 939-6300.

Website: www.pcm.gov.lb or www.presidency.gov.lb

Formed from five former Turkish Empire districts, Lebanon became independent Sept. 1, 1920, and was administered under French mandate 1920-41. French troops withdrew in 1946.

Under the 1943 National Covenant, all public positions were divided among the various religious communities, with Christians in the majority. By the 1970s, Muslims became the majority and demanded a larger political and economic role.

U.S. Marines intervened, May-Oct. 1958, during a Syrian-aided revolt. Continued raids against Israeli civilians, 1970-75, brought Israeli retaliation in southern Lebanon.

An estimated 60,000 were killed in a 1975-76 civil war. Palestinian units and leftist Muslims fought against Maronite militia (the Phalange) and other Christians. Several Arab countries provided support to various factions, while Israel aided Christian forces. Syria, which intervened in 1976 to fight Palestinian groups, largely policed a cease-fire.

Israeli forces invaded Lebanon June 6, 1982, attacking strongholds of the Palestine Liberation Organization (PLO). Israeli and Syrian forces engaged in the Bekaa Valley. On Aug. 21, the PLO evacuated W Beirut after massive Israeli bombings. Israeli troops entered W Beirut following the Sept. 14 assassination of newly elected Lebanese Pres. Bashir Gemayel. On Sept. 16, 1982, Lebanese Christian troops entered the Sabra and Shatila refugee camps and massacred hundreds of Palestinian civilians. An agreement May 17, 1983, between Lebanon, Israel, and the U.S. (but not Syria) provided for the withdrawal of Israeli troops; at least 30,000 Syrian troops remained in Lebanon, and Israel held onto a "security zone" in the south.

In 1983, some 50 people were killed in an explosion at the U.S. embassy, Apr. 18; 241 U.S. service members and 58 French soldiers died in separate Islamist suicide attacks, Oct. 23. The 1980s witnessed kidnappings of U.S., British, French, and Soviet citizens by Islamic militants.

A treaty signed May 22, 1991, between Lebanon and Syria recognized Lebanon as a separate state for the first time since 1943.

Israeli forces conducted air raids and artillery strikes against guerrilla bases and villages in southern Lebanon, causing over 200,000 to flee their homes July 25-29, 1993. Some 500,000 civilians fled in Apr. 1996 when Israel struck suspected guerrilla bases in the south. The economy revived in the 1990s, but Syria continued to dominate Lebanon's political affairs. Israel withdrew virtually all its troops from southern Lebanon by May 2000, leaving Hezbollah, an Iranian-backed Shiite Muslim guerrilla group, in control of much of the region.

Rafik al-Hariri, a former prime min. (1992-98, 2000-04), was killed by a truck bomb, Feb. 14, 2005. Many Lebanese blamed Syria or Hezbollah. As anti-Syrian protests mounted, Syrian troops left Lebanon. A Hezbollah official was convicted in absentia by a UN tribunal, Aug. 18, 2020, of conspiracy in connection with the bombing.

Beginning July 2006, Hezbollah bombarded northern Israel with thousands of rockets, and Israeli air and ground forces assaulted suspected Hezbollah strongholds in southern Lebanon and southern Beirut. By Aug. 14, 2006, when a UN-sponsored cease-fire took hold, the war dead included nearly 1,150 Lebanese. To enforce the truce, thousands of Lebanese troops moved into southern Lebanon, and the small UN force already in Lebanon (UNIFIL) was expanded. In mid-2020, UNIFIL had more than 10,000 uniformed personnel in Lebanon.

After more than 3 months of fighting in which over 400 people died, Lebanese forces Sept. 2, 2007, defeated Islamic militants at the Nahr al-Bared Palestinian refugee camp north of Tripoli. A 2008 power-sharing accord between the government and Hezbollah eased factional violence and paved the way for Gen. Michel Suleiman to become president, ending an 18-month stalemate. Factional disputes in parliament led to a lengthy delay in electing a successor when Suleiman's term expired in May 2014. Maronite Christian Michel Aoun, after gaining the support of Hezbollah, was elected president Oct. 31, 2016. Saad al-Hariri, a Sunni Muslim, became prime min., Dec. 18, 2016. Hezbollah and allied Shiite parties made gains in May 6, 2018, parliamentary elections.

The Syrian civil war, in which Hezbollah fighters supported Syria's government (dominated by followers of the Alawite sect of Shiite Islam) and many opposition fighters were Sunni Muslims, spilled over into Lebanon beginning in 2012—involving factional fighting and terrorist attacks within the country and border fighting with various Syrian forces. Hezbollah announced, May 14, 2016, that its top military commander had been killed by shellfire in Syria. About 880,000 Syrian refugees were in Lebanon as of Aug. 31, 2020.

Months of protests against deteriorating economic conditions began in Oct. 2019. Prime Min. Hariri resigned, Oct. 29. Hassan Diab replaced him, Jan. 21, 2020. The economic crisis deepened in the following months, aggravated by the COVID-19 pandemic. As of Sept. 30, Lebanon had more than 38,000 cases and 361 deaths.

A massive explosion in Beirut, Aug. 4, 2020, at a warehouse storing dangerous chemicals caused at least 190 deaths and 6,500 injuries and displaced about 300,000 people. Protests against government corruption and inefficiency followed. Diab resigned Aug. 10. Pres. Aoun designated diplomat Mustapha Adib to replace Diab, but Adib failed in Sept. to form a new government.

Lesotho
Kingdom of Lesotho

People: Population: 1,969,334 (146). **Age distrib.:** <15: 31.3%; 65+: 5.6%. **Growth:** 0.2%. **Migrants:** 0.3%. **Pop. density:**

168.0 per sq mi, 64.9 per sq km. **Urban:** 29.0%. **Ethnic groups:** Sotho 99.7%. **Languages:** Sesotho, English (both official); Zulu; Xhosa. **Religions:** Christian 93.2% (Catholic 50.8%, Protestant 32.5%), ethnic religionist 5.4%.

Geography: Total area: 11,720 sq mi, 30,355 sq km (138); **Land area:** 11,720 sq mi, 30,355 sq km. **Location:** Southern Africa. Completely surrounded by South Africa. **Topography:** Landlocked and mountainous, 5,000 to 11,000 ft in elevation. **Arable land:** 13.6%. **Capital:** Maseru, 201,851.

Government: Type: Parliamentary constitutional monarchy. **Head of state:** King Letsie III; b. 1963; in office: Feb. 7, 1996. **Head of govt.:** Prime Min. Moeketsi Majoro; b. 1961; in office: May 20, 2020. **Local divisions:** 10 districts. **Defense budget:** $43 mil. **Active troops:** 2,000.

Economy: Industries: food, beverages, textiles, apparel assembly, handicrafts, constr., tourism. **Chief agric.:** corn, wheat, pulses, sorghum, barley; livestock. **Natural resources:** water, diamonds, sand, clay, building stone. **Water:** 1,353 cu m per capita. **Electricity prod.:** 501 mil kWh. **Labor force:** agric. 8.4%, industry 41.9%, services 49.6%. **Unemployment:** 22.8%.

Finance: Monetary unit: Loti (LSL) (16.57 = $1 U.S.). **GDP:** $6.1 bil; **per capita GDP:** $2,882; **GDP growth:** 1.5%. **Imports:** $1.8 bil; South Africa 87.2%. **Exports:** $1.0 bil; South Africa 57%, U.S. 33.5%. **Tourism:** $22 mil. **Budget:** $1.3 bil. **Inflation:** 5.2%.

Transport: Airports: 3.

Communications: Telephone: 0.4 per 100 pop. **Mobile** (2017): 113.8 per 100 pop. **Broadband:** 49 per 100 pop. **Internet:** 29%.

Health: Expend.: 8.8%. **Life expect.:** 53.1 male; 53.0 female. **Births:** 23.2 per 1,000 pop. **Deaths:** 15.4 per 1,000 pop. **Infant mortality:** 41.5 per 1,000 live births. **Undernourished:** 32.6%. **HIV:** 22.8%.

Education: Compulsory: ages 6-12. **Literacy:** 79.4%.

Embassy: 2511 Massachusetts Ave. NW 20008; 797-5533.

Website: www.gov.ls or www.lesothoemb-usa.gov.ls

Lesotho (once called Basutoland) became a British protectorate in 1868. Independence came Oct. 4, 1966. Livestock raising is a major industry; textiles, clothing, and diamonds are leading exports. Cultivation of marijuana is a significant source of income.

Letsie III became king Nov. 12, 1990. In Mar. 1993, Ntsu Mokhehle, a civilian, was elected prime minister, ending 23 years of military rule. After a series of violent disturbances, the king dismissed the Mokhehle government Aug. 17, 1994; constitutional rule was restored Sept. 14.

Letsie abdicated, Jan. 25, 1995. King Moshoeshoe died, Jan. 15, 1996, and Letsie returned to power Feb. 7. After parliamentary elections May 26, 2012, the left-leaning Thomas Motsoahae Thabane became prime min. He fled to South Africa, Aug.-Sept. 2014, when units of the military, which backed a political rival, attacked police forces loyal to Thabane. June 3, 2017, elections returned Thabane to office. He resigned May 19, 2020, after allegations he was involved in the 2017 murder of his wife (his current wife had been charged with murder Feb. 4). Finance Min. Moeketsi Majoro became prime min. May 20.

The COVID-19 pandemic caused 1,565 cases and 35 deaths in Lesotho by Aug. 31, 2020.

Liberia
Republic of Liberia

People: Population: 5,073,296 (123). **Age distrib.:** <15: 43.4%; 65+: 2.8%. **Growth:** 2.8%. **Migrants:** 1.9%. **Pop. density:** 136.4 per sq mi, 52.7 per sq km. **Urban:** 52.1%. **Ethnic groups:** Kpelle 20.3%, Bassa 13.4%, Grebo 10%, Gio 8%, Mano 7.9%, Kru 6%, Lorma 5.1%, Kissi 4.8%, Gola 4.4%, Krahn 4%, Vai 4%, Mandingo 3.2%, Gbandi 3%. **Languages:** English (official), about 20 ethnic-group langs. **Religions:** Christian 42.8% (Protestant 19.8%, independent 13.7%), ethnic religionist 39%, Muslim 16.1% (Sunni).

Geography: Total area: 43,000 sq mi, 111,369 sq km (102); **Land area:** 37,189 sq mi, 96,320 sq km. **Location:** SW coast of W Africa. Sierra Leone on W, Guinea on N, Côte d'Ivoire on E. **Topography:** Marshy Atlantic coastline rises to low mountains and plateaus in forested interior. Six major rivers flow in parallel courses to the ocean. **Arable land:** 5.2%. **Capital:** Monrovia, 1,517,235.

Government: Type: Presidential republic. **Head of state and govt.:** Pres. George Weah; b. 1966; in office: Jan. 22, 2018. **Local divisions:** 15 counties. **Defense budget:** $14 mil. **Active troops:** 2,010.

Economy: Industries: mining, rubber and palm oil proc., diamonds. **Chief agric.:** rubber, coffee, cocoa, rice, cassava, palm oil, sugarcane, bananas; sheep, goats. **Natural resources:** iron ore, timber, diamonds, gold, hydropower. **Water:** 49,028 cu m per capita. **Electricity prod.:** 403 mil kWh. **Labor force:** agric. 43.0%, industry 10.1%, services 46.9%. **Unemployment:** 2.7%.

Finance: Monetary unit: Dollar (LRD) (199.31 = $1 U.S.). **GDP:** $7.3 bil; **per capita GDP:** $1,487; **GDP growth:** -2.3%. **Imports:** $1.2 bil; Singapore 29.8%, China 24.4%, South Korea 17.5%, Japan 9.4%. **Exports:** $260.6 mil; Germany 36.2%, Switzerland 14.2%, UAE 8.8%, U.S. 6.8%. **Tourism** (2015): $46 mil. **Budget:** $693.8 mil. **Inflation** (2017-18): 23.6%.

Transport: Railways: 267 mi (mostly inoperable due to damage from fighting). **Motor vehicles:** 15.2 per 1,000 pop. **Airports:** 2.

Communications: Telephone (2016): 0.2 per 100 pop. **Mobile** (2017): 56.6 per 100 pop. **Broadband:** 11.6 per 100 pop. **Internet:** 8%.

Health: Expend.: 8.2%. **Life expect.:** 62.5 male; 67.0 female. **Births:** 37.3 per 1,000 pop. **Deaths:** 7 per 1,000 pop. **Infant mortality:** 47.4 per 1,000 live births. **Undernourished:** 37.5%. **HIV:** 1.5%.

Education: Compulsory ages: 6-11. **Literacy:** 55.4%.

Embassy: 5201 16th St. NW 20011; 723-0437.

Website: www.emansion.gov.lr

Liberia was founded in 1822 by freed Black slaves from the U.S. who settled at Monrovia with the aid of colonization societies. It became a republic July 26, 1847, with a constitution modeled on that of the U.S. Descendants of freed slaves dominated politics for much of the 19th and 20th cents.

Under Pres. William V. S. Tubman, Liberia was a founding member of the UN in 1945. Tubman died in 1971 and was succeeded by his vice president, William R. Tolbert Jr. Charging rampant corruption, an Army Redemption Council of enlisted men staged a bloody predawn coup, Apr. 12, 1980, killing Pres. Tolbert and installing Sgt. Samuel Doe, an Indigenous African, as head of state. In 1985, Doe was chosen president in a disputed election.

A civil war began Dec. 1989. In Sept. 1990, Pres. Doe was executed. Despite the introduction of a multinational peacekeeping force, the conflict intensified. Factional fighting devastated Monrovia in Apr. 1996. Ruth Perry became modern Africa's first female head of state Sept. 3, 1996, leading a transitional government. By then, the civil war had claimed more than 150,000 lives.

Former rebel leader Charles Taylor was elected president July 1997. The UN imposed sanctions in 2001, to punish Liberia for aiding an insurgency in Sierra Leone.

A UN-sponsored war crimes tribunal indicted Taylor, June 2003, for his role in the Sierra Leone conflict. With Liberian rebels threatening Monrovia, Taylor resigned Aug. 11 and went into exile. The UN authorized a 15,000-member peacekeeping force (UNMIL) Sept. 19. (UNMIL officially ended Mar. 30, 2018.) A businessman, Charles Gyude Bryant, was sworn in Oct. 14, 2003, to head a power-sharing interim government. Ellen Johnson-Sirleaf won presidential elections in 2005 and 2011, and shared the 2011 Nobel Peace Prize. Charles Taylor was convicted at The Hague in 2012 of aiding and abetting war crimes and crimes against humanity, and sentenced to 50 years in prison. Former soccer star George Weah succeeded Johnson-Sirleaf after winning a Dec. 26, 2017, presidential runoff election. The U.S., Mar. 27, 2018, said it would end temporary residency status for thousands of Liberians permitted to live in the U.S. since the 1990s civil war, requiring them to leave the country by Mar. 31, 2019—later extended to Jan. 10, 2021.

Liberia was seriously affected, 2014-16, by an Ebola virus epidemic; the WHO reported a total of 10,675 Liberian cases, which caused 4,809 deaths. The 2020 COVID-19 pandemic caused more than 1,300 Liberian cases by Sept. 30; over 80 people had died.

Libya
State of Libya

People: Population: 6,890,535 (106). **Age distrib.:** <15: 33.7%; 65+: 4.0%. **Growth:** 1.9%. **Migrants:** 12.1%. **Pop. density:** 10.1 per sq mi, 3.9 per sq km. **Urban:** 80.7%. **Ethnic groups:** Berber and Arab 97%, other (incl. Greek, Maltese, Italian, Egyptian, Pakistani, Turkish, Indian, Tunisian) 3%. **Languages:** Arabic (official), Italian, English, Berber. **Religions:** Muslim 99% (Sunni [official] 94%, Islamic schismatic 5%).

Geography: Total area: 679,362 sq mi, 1,759,540 sq km (16); **Land area:** 679,362 sq mi, 1,759,540 sq km. **Location:** Mediterranean coast of N Africa. Tunisia, Algeria on W; Niger, Chad on S; Sudan, Egypt on E. **Topography:** Desert and semidesert regions cover 92% of land with low mountains in N, higher mountains in S, and a narrow coastal zone. **Arable land:** 1.0%. **Capital:** Tripoli, 1,165,085.

Government: Type: In transition. **Head of state and govt.:** Prime Min. Faiez Mustafa Serraj is head of the internationally backed Government of National Accord; in office: Jan. 25, 2016. Competing leaders include Gen. Khalifa Haftar in eastern Libya. **Local divisions:** 22 governorates. **Defense budget/active troops:** NA.

Economy: Industries: petroleum, petrochemicals, aluminum, iron and steel, food proc., textiles, handicrafts, cement. **Chief agric.:** wheat, barley, olives, dates, citrus, vegetables, peanuts, soybeans; cattle. **Natural resources:** petroleum, nat. gas, gypsum. **Water:** 110 cu m per capita. **Crude oil reserves:** 48.4 bil bbls. **Electricity prod.:** 34.6 bil kWh. **Labor force:** agric. 18.8%, industry 21.7%, services 59.5%. **Unemployment:** 18.6%.

Finance: Monetary unit: Dinar (LYD) (1.36 = $1 U.S.). **GDP:** $107.1 bil; **per capita GDP:** $15,803; **GDP growth:** 2.5%. **Imports:** $11.4 bil; China 13.5%, Turkey 11.3%, Italy 6.9%, South Korea 5.9%. **Exports:** $18.4 bil; Italy 19%, Spain 12.5%, France 11%, Egypt 8.6%, Germany 8.6%, China 8.3%. **Tourism** (2010): $60 mil. **Budget:** $23.5 bil. **Inflation** (2016-17): 28.5%.

Transport: Motor vehicles: 470.2 per 1,000 pop. **Airports:** 68.

Communications: Telephone (2017): 23.9 per 100 pop. **Mobile** (2017): 91.5 per 100 pop. **Broadband:** 36.9 per 100 pop. **Internet:** 21.8%.

Health: Expend. NA. **Life expect.:** 74.4 male; 79.1 female. **Births:** 23 per 1,000 pop. **Deaths:** 3.5 per 1,000 pop. **Infant mortality:** 11.5 per 1,000 live births. **Undernourished:** NA. **HIV:** 0.2%.
Education: Compulsory: ages 6-14. **Literacy:** 91%.
Embassy: 1460 Dahlia St. NW, 20012; 944-9601.
Website: www.pm.gov.ly or www.embassyoflibyadc.org

First settled by Berbers, Libya was ruled in succession by Carthage, Rome, the Vandals, and the Ottomans. Italy ruled from 1912, and Britain and France after WWII. Libya became an independent constitutional monarchy Jan. 2, 1952. In 1969 a junta led by Col. Muammar al-Qaddafi seized power.

Under Qaddafi's dictatorship, dissent was suppressed and wars were waged with Egypt and Chad. During the 1980s, Libya was accused of promoting terrorism, such as the Apr. 5, 1986, bombing of a West Berlin nightclub, which killed 3, including a U.S. serviceman. The U.S. attacked what it called "terrorist-related targets" in Libya, Apr. 14, including Qaddafi's barracks.

Libya agents were accused of planting bombs that blew up Pan Am Flight 103 over Lockerbie, Scotland, killing 270 people Dec. 21, 1988, and French UTA Flight 772 over Niger, killing 170 people Sept. 19, 1989. The UN imposed sanctions in 1992 for Libya's failure to cooperate in the Lockerbie and UTA cases.

Libya agreed in 2003 to renounce terrorism and settle compensation cases for the families of the Lockerbie and UTA bombing victims. The UN lifted sanctions in Sept., and in Dec., Libya renounced nuclear, chemical, and biological weapons and long-range missiles.

Arab Spring rebels fought Qaddafi's forces throughout the spring of 2011. With diplomatic backing from the Arab League and the UN, NATO forces imposed an arms embargo and no-fly zone against Qaddafi. Aided by NATO, rebels took control of Tripoli Aug. 23, 2011. Rebels killed Qaddafi Oct. 20, 2011. Ansar al-Shariah terrorists attacked the U.S. consulate and a CIA base in Benghazi Sept. 11, 2012, killing Ambassador J. Christopher Stephens and three other Americans. The U.S. captured, June 15, 2014, the alleged leader of the attack, Ahmed Abu Khattala; he was convicted, Nov. 28, 2017, on terrorism-related charges.

Violence between Islamists, rival militia groups, and pro-government forces continued, 2013-20. Parliamentary elections marred by violence were held June 25, 2014. The new parliament met in Tobruk because of Islamist militia control of Tripoli. A UN-backed Government of National Accord (GNA) was formed in Jan. 2016. The GNA had largely taken control in Tripoli by Apr. 2016 but was not recognized by the Tobruk government. ISIS seized territory in Libya by early 2016. An offensive by pro-GNA and other militia forces, aided by U.S. airstrikes and special operations troops, had retaken most ISIS territory by Dec. 2016, although some ISIS fighters remained active. By mid-2017, forces led by former Libyan army Gen. Khalifa Haftar (loosely allied with the Tobruk government) gained control of eastern Libya.

Haftar's forces began, Apr. 2019, an offensive toward Tripoli; they were supported by Russian military aid but ended their unsuccessful offensive June 2020. The GNA forces, plus various militias and other armed groups that opposed Haftar, received Turkish military support.

Beginning in 2014, Libya was a major transit route for African and other migrants trying to reach Europe. By mid-2017, efforts by Italy and other EU nations reduced migrant crossings of the Mediterranean. In 2020, about 650,000 migrants were in Libya, some living in harsh conditions in detention camps.

The 2020 COVID-19 pandemic caused about 34,000 Libyan cases and 540 deaths as of Sept. 30.

Liechtenstein
Principality of Liechtenstein

People: Population: 39,137 (190). **Age distrib.:** <15: 15.2%; 65+: 18.9%. **Growth:** 0.7%. **Migrants:** 67.0%. **Pop. density:** 633.5 per sq mi, 244.6 per sq km. **Urban:** 14.4%. **Ethnic groups:** Liechtensteiner 66%, Swiss 9.6%, Austrian 5.8%, German 4.3%, Italian 3.1%. **Languages:** German (official). **Religions:** Christian 87.6% (Catholic [official] 75.2%, Protestant 10.6%), Muslim 6.8% (Sunni), agnostic 5.3%.

Geography: Total area: 62 sq mi, 160 sq km (191); **Land area:** 62 sq mi, 160 sq km. **Location:** Central Europe, in Alps. Switzerland on W, Austria on E. **Topography:** Rhine Valley occupies one-third of country, Alps in the rest. **Arable land:** 13.5%. **Capital:** Vaduz, 5,470.

Government: Type: Constitutional monarchy. **Head of state:** Prince Hans-Adam II; b. 1945; in office: Nov. 13, 1989. **Head of govt.:** Prime Min. Adrian Hasler; b. 1964; in office: Mar. 27, 2013. **Local divisions:** 11 communes. **Defense budget/active troops:** NA.

Economy: Industries: electronics, metal mfg., dental prods., ceramics, pharmaceuticals, food prods., precision instruments, tourism, optical instruments. **Chief agric.:** wheat, barley, corn, potatoes; livestock. **Natural resources:** hydroelectric potential. **Water:** NA. **Labor force:** services 70.5%, industry 28.5%, agric. 1%. **Unemployment:** NA.

Finance: Monetary unit: Swiss Franc (CHF) (0.91 = $1 U.S.). **GDP:** NA; **per capita GDP:** NA; **GDP growth:** NA. **Imports** (2014): $2.2 bil. **Exports** (2015): $3.2 bil. Data excl. trade with Switzerland. **Budget** (2011): $890.4 mil. **Inflation** (2015-16): −0.4%.

Transport: Railways: 6 mi (owned by Austrian Railway System). **Communications: Telephone:** 40.2 per 100 pop. **Mobile:** 124.6 per 100 pop. **Broadband:** 122.6 per 100 pop. **Internet:** 98.1%.
Health: Expend.: NA. **Life expect.:** 79.9 male; 85.0 female. **Births:** 10.4 per 1,000 pop. **Deaths:** 7.8 per 1,000 pop. **Infant mortality:** 4.2 per 1,000 live births. **Undernourished:** NA. **HIV:** NA.
Education: Compulsory: ages 6-14. **Literacy:** 100%.
Embassy: 2900 K St. NW, Ste. 602B, 20007; 331-0590.
Website: www.liechtenstein.li

Liechtenstein became sovereign in 1806. It is united with Switzerland by a customs and monetary union. Many workers commute daily from Austria, Switzerland, and Germany.

On Aug. 15, 2004, Prince Hans-Adam II assigned day-to-day responsibilities for running the country to his son, Crown Prince Alois. Long regarded as a tax haven, Liechtenstein took steps, 2008-13, to ease banking secrecy laws.

Lithuania
Republic of Lithuania

People: Population: 2,731,464 (138). **Age distrib.:** <15: 15.3%; 65+: 20.4%. **Growth:** −1.1%. **Migrants:** 4.2%. **Pop. density:** 112.9 per sq mi, 43.6 per sq km. **Urban:** 68.0%. **Ethnic groups:** Lithuanian 84.1%, Polish 6.6%, Russian 5.8%. **Languages:** Lithuanian (official), Russian, Polish. **Religions:** Christian 89.3% (Catholic 81.4%), agnostic 9.7%.

Geography: Total area: 25,212 sq mi, 65,300 sq km (121); **Land area:** 24,201 sq mi, 62,680 sq km. **Location:** Eastern Europe, on SE coast of Baltic. Latvia on N; Belarus on E, S; Poland, Russia on W. **Topography:** Lowland with hills in W and S. Many small lakes and rivers with marshes espec. in N and W. **Arable land:** 33.6%. **Capital:** Vilnius, 538,894.

Government: Type: Semi-presidential republic. **Head of state:** Gitanas Nauseda; b. 1964; in office: July 12, 2019. **Head of govt.:** Prime Min. Saulius Skvernelis; b. 1970; in office: Dec. 13, 2016. **Local divisions:** 60 municipalities. **Defense budget:** $1.1 bil. **Active troops:** 20,650.

Economy: Industries: metal-cutting machine tools, elec. motors, TVs, refrigerators and freezers, petroleum refining, shipbuilding, furniture. **Chief agric.:** grain, potatoes, sugar beets, flax, vegetables; beef, milk, eggs; fish. **Natural resources:** peat, amber. **Water:** 8,478 cu m per capita. **Crude oil reserves:** 12 mil bbls. **Electricity prod.** (2018): 2.4 bil kWh. **Labor force:** agric. 6.6%, industry 25.9%, services 67.4%. **Unemployment:** 6.3%.

Finance: Monetary unit: Euro (EUR) (0.84 = $1 U.S.). **GDP:** $106.5 bil; **per capita GDP:** $38,214; **GDP growth:** 3.9%. **Imports:** $31.6 bil; Russia 13%, Germany 12.3%, Poland 10.6%, Latvia 7.1%, Italy 5.2%, Netherlands 5.1%. **Exports:** $29.1 bil; Russia 15%, Latvia 9.9%, Poland 8.1%, Germany 7.3%, U.S. 5.2%, Estonia 5%. **Tourism:** $1.5 bil. **Budget:** $15.7 bil. **Inflation:** 2.3%.
Transport: Railways: 1,099 mi. **Motor vehicles:** 559.8 per 1,000 pop. **Airports:** 22.
Communications: Telephone: 15.2 per 100 pop. **Mobile:** 164.3 per 100 pop. **Broadband:** 79.8 per 100 pop. **Internet** (2018): 79.7%.
Health: Expend.: 6.5%. **Life expect.:** 70.3 male; 81.1 female. **Births:** 9.5 per 1,000 pop. **Deaths:** 15 per 1,000 pop. **Infant mortality:** 3.8 per 1,000 live births. **Undernourished:** <2.5%. **HIV:** 0.2%.
Education: Compulsory: ages 7-16. **Literacy:** 99.8%.
Embassy: 2622 16th St. NW 20009; 234-5860.
Website: lrvk.lrv.lt

Lithuania, briefly occupied by the German army, 1914-18, was annexed by the Soviet Union until 1919. In 1939 it rejoined the Soviet sphere of influence and was annexed by the USSR Aug. 3, 1940.

Lithuania declared its independence Mar. 11, 1990; independence was ratified by the Soviet Union Sept. 1991. The country became a full member of NATO and the EU in 2004; it began using the euro as its currency, Jan. 1, 2015. The center-left Social Democrats won Oct. 2012 parliamentary elections. After the Peasants and Greens party won Oct. 2016 parliamentary elections, Saulius Skvernelis became prime min. Independent Gitanas Nauseda won a presidential runoff election, May 26, 2019.

By Sept. 30, 2020, the COVID-19 pandemic had caused almost 4,600 Lithuanian cases and 92 deaths.

Luxembourg
Grand Duchy of Luxembourg

People: Population: 628,381 (164). **Age distrib.:** <15: 16.7%; 65+: 15.4%. **Growth:** 1.8%. **Migrants:** 47.4%. **Pop. density:** 629.4 per sq mi, 243.0 per sq km. **Urban:** 91.5%. **Ethnic groups:** Luxembourger 51.1%, Portuguese 15.7%, French 7.5%, Italian 3.6%, Belgian 3.3%, German 2.1%. **Languages:** Luxembourgish (national lang.), French, German (all official admin. and judicial langs.); Portuguese; Italian; English. **Religions:** Christian 76.1% (Catholic 73.4%), agnostic 18.4%, Muslim 3.5% (Sunni).

Geography: Total area: 998 sq mi, 2,586 sq km (169); **Land area:** 998 sq mi, 2,586 sq km. **Location:** Western Europe. Belgium on W, France on S, Germany on E. **Topography:** Heavy forests (Ardennes) cover N. Low, open plateau in S. **Arable land:** 25.5%. **Capital:** Luxembourg, 119,752.

Government: Type: Constitutional monarchy. **Head of state:** Grand Duke Henri; b. 1955; in office: Oct. 7, 2000. **Head of govt.:** Prime Min. Xavier Bettel; b. 1973; in office: Dec. 4, 2013. **Local divisions:** 12 cantons. **Defense budget:** $344 mil. **Active troops:** 900.

Economy: Industries: banking and financial services; constr.; real estate services; iron, metals, steel; information tech.; telecom; cargo transp. and logistics. **Chief agric.:** grapes, barley, oats, potatoes, wheat, fruits; dairy and livestock prods. **Natural resources:** iron ore (no longer exploited). **Water:** 5,998 cu m per capita. **Electricity prod.** (2018): 335 mil kWh. **Labor force:** agric. 1.0%, industry 11.5%, services 87.5%. **Unemployment:** 5.2%.

Finance: Monetary unit: Euro (EUR) (0.84 = $1 U.S.). **GDP:** $75.2 bil; **per capita GDP:** $121,293; **GDP growth:** 2.3%. **Imports:** $20.7 bil; Belgium 32%, Germany 24.9%, France 11.1%, U.S. 5.7%. **Exports:** $16 bil; Germany 25.6%, Belgium 17.6%, France 14%, Netherlands 5.1%. **Tourism:** $4.9 bil. **Budget:** $26.8 bil. **Inflation:** 1.7%.

Transport: Railways: 171 mi. **Motor vehicles:** 768.8 per 1,000 pop. **Airports:** 1.

Communications: Telephone: 45.3 per 100 pop. **Mobile:** 132.2 per 100 pop. **Broadband:** 88.1 per 100 pop. **Internet** (2018): 97.1%.

Health: Expend.: 5.5%. **Life expect.:** 80.1 male; 85.2 female. **Births:** 11.6 per 1,000 pop. **Deaths:** 7.3 per 1,000 pop. **Infant mortality:** 3.3 per 1,000 live births. **Undernourished:** <2.5%. **HIV** (2018): 0.3%.

Education: Compulsory: ages 4-15. **Literacy:** 100%.

Embassy: 2200 Massachusetts Ave. NW 20008; 265-4171.

Website: www.gouvernement.lu

Luxembourg, founded about 963, was ruled by Burgundy, Spain, Austria, and France from 1448 to 1815. It left the Germanic Confederation in 1866. Overrun by Germany in two world wars, Luxembourg ended its neutrality in 1948, when a customs union with Belgium and the Netherlands was adopted. Luxembourg was one of the six founding members (1951) of what became the European Union.

After Oct. 20, 2013, elections, the Democratic Party's Xavier Bettel formed a center-left coalition and became prime min. Same-sex marriage was legalized in 2014. Bettel, May 15, 2015, became the first EU government head to marry a same-sex partner. Bettel's coalition retained power in Oct. 14, 2018, elections.

To reduce traffic, the government made public transportation free as of Mar. 1, 2020. Affected by the 2020 COVID-19 pandemic, Luxembourg had more than 8,400 cases and 124 deaths as of Sept. 30.

Madagascar
Republic of Madagascar

People: Population: 26,955,737 (53). **Age distrib.:** <15: 38.9%; 65+: 3.5%. **Growth:** 2.4%. **Migrants:** 0.1%. **Pop. density:** 120.1 per sq mi, 46.4 per sq km. **Urban:** 38.5%. **Ethnic groups:** Malayo-Indonesian (Merina and related Betsileo), Cotiers (mixed African/Malayo-Indonesian/Arab ancestry), French, Indian, Creole, Comoran. **Languages:** French, Malagasy (both official); English.

Religions: Christian 58.6% (Protestant 29.9%, Catholic 24.3%), ethnic religionist 38.7%.

Geography: Total area: 226,658 sq mi, 587,041 sq km (46); **Land area:** 224,534 sq mi, 581,540 sq km. **Location:** In Indian O., off SE coast of Africa. Comoro Isls. to NW, Mozambique to W. **Topography:** Humid coastal strip in E, fertile valleys in mountainous center plateau region, and a wider coastal strip on W. **Arable land:** 5.2%. **Capital:** Antananarivo, 3,368,585.

Government: Type: Semi-presidential republic. **Head of state:** Pres. Andry Rajoelina; b. 1974; in office: Jan. 19, 2019. **Head of govt.:** Prime Min. Christian Ntsay; b. 1961; in office: June 6, 2018. **Local divisions:** 6 provinces. **Defense budget:** $77 mil. **Active troops:** 13,500.

Economy: Industries: meat proc., seafood, soap, beer, leather, sugar, textiles, glassware, cement, auto assembly. **Chief agric.:** coffee, vanilla, sugarcane, cloves, cocoa, rice, cassava, beans, bananas, peanuts. **Natural resources:** graphite, chromite, coal, bauxite, rare earth elements, salt, quartz, tar sands, semiprec. stones, mica, fish, hydropower. **Water:** 13,179 cu m per capita. **Electricity prod.:** 1.7 bil kWh. **Labor force:** agric. 63.8%, industry 9.1%, services 27.1%. **Unemployment:** 1.8%.

Finance: Monetary unit: Ariary (MGA) (3,844.59 = $1 U.S.). **GDP:** $46.2 bil; **per capita GDP:** $1,714; **GDP growth:** 4.8%. **Imports:** $2.7 bil; China 18.7%, India 9.3%, France 6.4%, South Africa 5.6%, UAE 5.3%. **Exports:** $2.3 bil; France 24.8%, U.S. 16.5%, China 6.7%, Germany 6.5%, Japan 6%. **Tourism:** $193 mil. **Budget:** $2.1 bil. **Inflation:** 5.6%.

Transport: Railways: 519 mi. **Motor vehicles:** 13.6 per 1,000 pop. **Airports:** 26.

Communications: Telephone: 0.3 per 100 pop. **Mobile:** 40.6 per 100 pop. **Broadband:** 13 per 100 pop. **Internet:** 9.8%.

Health: Expend.: 5.5%. **Life expect.:** 65.7 male; 68.9 female. **Births:** 29.9 per 1,000 pop. **Deaths:** 6.2 per 1,000 pop. **Infant mortality:** 37.8 per 1,000 live births. **Undernourished:** 41.7%. **HIV:** 0.3%.

Education: Compulsory: ages 6-10. **Literacy:** 81.2%.

Embassy: 2374 Massachusetts Ave. NW 20008; 265-5525.

Website: www.primature.gov.mg

Madagascar was settled 2,000 years ago by Malayan-Indonesian people, whose descendants still predominate. A unified kingdom

ruled in the 18th and 19th cent. The island became a French protectorate, 1885, and a colony, 1896. Independence came June 26, 1960.

Discontent with inflation and French domination led to a coup in 1972. The new regime nationalized French-owned financial interests, closed French bases and a U.S. space-tracking station, and obtained Chinese aid. The government conducted a program of arrests, expulsion of foreigners, and repression of strikes in 1979.

In 1990, Madagascar ended a on multiparty politics that had existed since 1975. Albert Zafy won the 1993 presidential election, ending the 17-year rule of Adm. Didier Ratsiraka, but was impeached and removed from office in 1996.

Marc Ravalomanana won a contentious presidential election over Ratsiraka Dec. 2001 and was reelected in 2006. A power struggle between Ravalomanana and the military-backed Andry Rajoelina led to Rajoelina's installation as head of a transitional regime, Mar. 17, 2009. Postponed presidential elections, held in late 2013, were won by Hery Rajaonarimampianina. Rajoelina defeated Ravalomanana in a disputed Dec. 19, 2018, presidential runoff election. A coalition allied with Rajoelina won May 27, 2019, parliamentary elections. The 2020 COVID-19 pandemic caused more than 16,000 cases and over 200 deaths in Madagascar as of Sept. 30.

Malawi
Republic of Malawi

People: Population: 21,196,629 (60). **Age distrib.:** <15: 45.9%; 65+: 2.7%. **Growth:** 3.3%. **Migrants:** 1.3%. **Pop. density:** 583.5 per sq mi, 225.3 per sq km. **Urban:** 17.4%. **Ethnic groups:** Chewa 34.3%, Lomwe 18.8%, Yao 13.2%, Ngoni 10.4%, Tumbuka 9.2%, Sena 3.8%, Mang'anja 3.2%. **Languages:** English (official), Chichewa (common), Chinyanja, Chiyao, Chitumbuka, Chilomwe, Chinkhonde. **Religions:** Christian 81.1% (Protestant 37.2%, Catholic 33%, independent 10.9%), Muslim 13.4% (Sunni), ethnic religionist 4.7%.

Geography: Total area: 45,747 sq mi, 118,484 sq km (98); **Land area:** 36,324 sq mi, 94,080 sq km. **Location:** SE Africa. Zambia on W, Mozambique on S and E, Tanzania on N. **Topography:** 560 mi N-S along Lake Nyasa (Lake Malawi), most of which belongs to Malawi. High plateaus and mountains line the Rift Valley along length of nation. **Arable land:** 38.2%. **Capital:** Lilongwe, 1,121,720.

Government: Type: Presidential republic. **Head of state and govt.:** Pres. Lazarus Chakwera; b. 1955; in office: June 28, 2020. **Local divisions:** 28 districts. **Defense budget:** $67 mil. **Active troops:** 10,700.

Economy: Industries: tobacco, tea, sugar, sawmill prods., cement, consumer goods. **Chief agric.:** tobacco, sugarcane, tea, corn, potatoes, cassava, sorghum, pulses, cotton, groundnuts, macadamia nuts, coffee; cattle, goats. **Natural resources:** limestone; hydropower; unexploited deposits of uranium, coal, bauxite. **Water:** 928 cu m per capita. **Electricity prod.:** 2.1 bil kWh. **Labor force:** agric. 43.2%, industry 13.8%, services 43.0%. **Unemployment:** 5.7%.

Finance: Monetary unit: Kwacha (MWK) (747.08 = $1 U.S.). **GDP:** $20.6 bil; **per capita GDP:** $1,104; **GDP growth:** 4.4%. **Imports:** $2.3 bil; South Africa 20.7%, China 14.2%, India 11.6%, UAE 7%. **Exports:** $1.4 bil; Zimbabwe 13.1%, Mozambique 11.8%, Belgium 10.7%, South Africa 6.3%, Netherlands 5%. **Tourism:** $42 mil. **Budget:** $1.6 bil. **Inflation:** 9.4%.

Transport: Railways: 477 mi. **Motor vehicles:** 2.1 per 1,000 pop. **Airports:** 7.

Communications: Telephone: 0.1 per 100 pop. **Mobile:** 39 per 100 pop. **Broadband:** 25.5 per 100 pop. **Internet:** 13.8%.

Health: Expend.: 9.6%. **Life expect.:** 61.2 male; 65.3 female. **Births:** 40.1 per 1,000 pop. **Deaths:** 7.2 per 1,000 pop. **Infant mortality:** 39.5 per 1,000 live births. **Undernourished:** 18.8%. **HIV:** 8.9%.

Education: Compulsory: ages 6-13. **Literacy:** 72.9%.

Embassy: 2408 Massachusetts Ave. NW 20008; 721-0270.

Website: www.malawi.gov.mw

Bantus came to the land in the 16th cent., Arab slavers in the 19th. The area became the British protectorate Nyasaland in 1891. It became independent July 6, 1964, and a republic in 1966. After three decades as a one-party state under Pres. Hastings Kamuzu Banda, Malawi adopted a new constitution and, in multiparty elections held May 17, 1994, chose a new leader, Bakili Muluzi.

Ruling-party candidate Bingu wa Mutharika won a disputed 2004 presidential election. He won reelection May 2009. Joyce Banda became Malawi's first female pres. after the death of Mutharika Apr. 5, 2012. In May 20-22, 2014, presidential elections, Peter Mutharika (the former president's brother) was declared the winner. Drought affected up to 8 mil in 2016. After Peter Mutharika appeared to narrowly win reelection, May 21, 2019, opposition candidate Lazarus Chakwera claimed voting irregularities, and the Constitutional Court, Feb. 3, 2020, annulled the result. Chakwera won a June 23 re-vote.

By Sept. 30, 2020, the COVID-19 pandemic had caused almost 5,800 cases and 179 deaths in Malawi.

Malaysia

People: Population: 32,652,083 (42). **Age distrib.:** <15: 26.8%; 65+: 6.9%. **Growth:** 1.3%. **Migrants:** 10.7%. **Pop. density:** 257.3 per sq mi, 99.4 per sq km. **Urban:** 77.2%. **Ethnic groups:** Bumiputera 62% (Malays and Indigenous, incl. Orang Asli, Dayak,

Anak Negeri), Chinese 20.6%, Indian 5.7%, non-citizen 10.3%. **Languages:** Bahasa Malaysia (official), English, Chinese, Tamil, Telugu, Malayalam, Panjabi, Thai. **Religions:** Muslim 57.7% (Sunni [official]), Chinese folk-religionist 19%, Christian 6.7%, Hindu 6.5%, Buddhist 5.5%, ethnic religionist 3.4%.

Geography: Total area: 127,355 sq mi, 329,847 sq km (66); **Land area:** 126,895 sq mi, 328,657 sq km. **Location:** SE tip of Asia, plus N coast of the island of Borneo. Thailand, Brunei on N; Indonesia on S. **Topography:** Most of W is covered by tropical jungle, including a central mountain range that runs N-S through the peninsula. Marshy W coast, sandy E coast. Wide swampy coastal plain with interior jungles and mountains in E. **Arable land:** 2.6%. **Capital:** Kuala Lumpur, 7,996,830. **Cities:** Johor Bahru, 1,023,900.

Government: Type: Federal parliamentary constitutional monarchy. **Head of state:** King Sultan Abdullah Sultan Ahmad Shah; b. 1959; in office: Jan. 24, 2019. **Head of govt.:** Prime Min. Tan Sri Muhyiddin Yassin; b. 1947; in office: Mar. 1, 2020. **Local divisions:** 13 states, 1 federal territory. **Defense budget:** $3.3 bil. **Active troops:** 113,000.

Economy: Industries: rubber and palm oil proc. and mfg., petroleum and nat. gas, light mfg., pharmaceuticals, medical tech., logging. **Chief agric.:** palm oil, rubber, cocoa, rice, pepper. **Natural resources:** tin, petroleum, timber, copper, iron ore, nat. gas, bauxite. **Water:** 18,341 cu m per capita. **Crude oil reserves:** 3.6 bil bbls. **Electricity prod.:** 156.0 bil kWh. **Labor force:** agric. 10.1%, industry 26.8%, services 63.1%. **Unemployment:** 4.3%.

Finance: Monetary unit: Ringgit (MYR) (4.15 = $1 U.S.). **GDP:** $943.3 bil; **per capita GDP:** $29,526; **GDP growth:** 4.3%. **Imports:** $160.7 bil; China 19.9%, Singapore 10.8%, U.S. 8.4%, Japan 7.6%, Thailand 5.8%. **Exports:** $187.9 bil; Singapore 15.1%, China 12.6%, U.S. 9.4%, Japan 8.2%, Thailand 5.7%. **Tourism:** $19.8 bil. **Budget:** $60.6 bil. **Inflation:** 0.7%.

Transport: Railways: 1,150 mi. **Motor vehicles:** 483.1 per 1,000 pop. **Airports:** 39.

Communications: Telephone: 20.4 per 100 pop. **Mobile:** 134.5 per 100 pop. **Broadband:** 111.5 per 100 pop. **Internet** (2018): 81.2%.

Health: Expend.: 3.8%. **Life expect.:** 73.0 male; 78.9 female. **Births:** 18.3 per 1,000 pop. **Deaths:** 5.3 per 1,000 pop. **Infant mortality:** 11.4 per 1,000 live births. **Undernourished:** 3.0%. **HIV:** 0.4%.

Education: Compulsory: ages 6-11. **Literacy:** 96.9%.

Embassy: 3516 International Ct. NW 20008; 572-9700.

Website: www.malaysia.gov.my

European traders visited in the 16th cent.; Britain established control in 1867. Malaysia was created Sep. 16, 1963. It included Malaya (which gained independence in 1957 after the suppression of Communist rebels), plus the formerly British Singapore, Sabah (N Borneo), and Sarawak (NW Borneo). Singapore was separated in 1965.

Malaysia has abundant natural resources, though rainforest destruction has become a major environmental problem. Work on a federal administrative center at Putrajaya, south of Kuala Lumpur, was completed in 1999; it is linked by rail with Kuala Lumpur's city center and Cyberjaya, a hub for high-tech manufacturing and research.

National Front leader Najib Razak took over the premiership in 2009. In a close election (deemed fraudulent by the opposition), May 5, 2013, the governing coalition was returned to power.

A Malaysia Airlines flight to Beijing, carrying 239 passengers and crew, lost contact with air traffic control Mar. 8, 2014, shortly after takeoff from Kuala Lumpur and was presumed lost in the Indian Ocean. On July 17, 2014, a Malaysia Airlines flight from Amsterdam to Kuala Lumpur was shot down by a missile over eastern Ukraine, killing all 298 people onboard. An international team of investigators concluded, Sept. 2016, that the missile was Russian made and had been fired from an area controlled by pro-Russian separatists.

A security law enacted Dec. 3, 2015, gave the Malaysian government sweeping powers to conduct surveillance and searches and to suppress protests.

Beginning in 2015, Malaysian authorities (as well as officials in other countries) investigated possible misappropriation of more than $4.5 bil from a government development fund (known as 1MDB), including up to $1 bil in transfers to bank accounts controlled by Prime Min. Najib, who denied wrongdoing. After the National Front lost May 9, 2018, elections and new Prime Min. Mahathir Mohamad took office, Najib was charged, in 2018, with dozens of corruption-related offenses. He was convicted, July 28, 2020, on 7 corruption counts. With his coalition fracturing, Mahathir resigned, Feb. 24, 2020. Muhyiddin Yassin, backed by Najib's party, became prime minister Mar. 1.

Affected by the 2020 COVID-19 pandemic, Malaysia had more than 11,000 cases and 134 deaths as of Sept. 30.

Maldives
Republic of Maldives

People: Population: 391,904 (171). **Age distrib.:** <15: 22.1%; 65+: 4.8%. **Growth:** –0.1%. **Migrants:** 13.0%. **Pop. density:** 3,406.1 per sq mi, 1,315.1 per sq km. **Urban:** 40.7%. **Ethnic groups:** homogeneous mixture of Sinhalese, Dravidian, Arab, Australasian, and African. **Languages:** Dhivehi (official), English (spoken by most govt. officials). **Religions:** Muslim 98.7% (Sunni [official]).

Geography: Total area: 115 sq mi, 298 sq km (188); **Land area:** 115 sq mi, 298 sq km. **Location:** In Indian O. Nearest neighbor is India to NE. **Topography:** 19 atolls with 1,190 islands, 200 inhabited. None of the islands are over 5 sq mi in area; all are nearly flat. **Arable land:** 13.0%. **Capital:** Male, 176,851.

Government: Type: Presidential republic. **Head of state and govt.:** Pres. Ibrahim Mohamed Solih; b. 1962; in office: Nov. 17, 2018. **Local divisions:** 21 admin. atolls. **Defense budget/active troops:** NA.

Economy: Industries: tourism, fish proc., shipping, boat building, coconut proc., woven mats, rope. **Chief agric.:** coconuts, corn, sweet potatoes; fish. **Natural resources:** fish. **Water:** 69 cu m per capita. **Electricity prod.:** 424 mil kWh. **Labor force:** agric. 8.2%, industry 18.3%, services 73.4%. **Unemployment:** 6.4%.

Finance: Monetary unit: Rufiyaa (MVR) (15.40 = $1 U.S.). **GDP:** $10.5 bil; **per capita GDP:** $19,698; **GDP growth:** 5.2%. **Imports** (2016): $2.1 bil; UAE 17.1%, India 13.5%, Singapore 13.3%, China 10.8%, Sri Lanka 6.7%, Malaysia 6%. **Exports** (2016): $256.2 mil; Thailand 42.8%, Sri Lanka 8.7%, Bangladesh 6.4%, France 6.2%, U.S. 6.1%, Germany 5%. **Tourism:** $3.2 bil. **Budget** (2016): $1.6 bil. **Inflation** (2016-17): 2.3%.

Transport: Airports: 7.

Communications: Telephone: 3.6 per 100 pop. **Mobile:** 166.4 per 100 pop. **Broadband:** 63.5 per 100 pop. **Internet:** 63.2%.

Health: Expend.: 9.0%. **Life expect.:** 74.0 male; 78.9 female. **Births:** 16 per 1,000 pop. **Deaths:** 4.1 per 1,000 pop. **Infant mortality:** 19.8 per 1,000 live births. **Undernourished:** NA. **HIV:** NA.

Education: Compulsory: NA. **Literacy:** 98.8%.

Embassy: 800 Second Ave., Ste. 400E, New York, NY 10017; (212) 599-6195.

Website: presidency.gov.mv

A British protectorate since 1887, the nation achieved independence July 26, 1965; long a sultanate, the Maldives became a republic in 1968. Rising sea levels threaten the island nation. The Indian Ocean tsunami of Dec. 26, 2004, killed at least 82 people in the Maldives.

Pres. Maumoon Abdul Gayoom, in office 1978-2008, lost a 2008 runoff election to pro-democracy leader and former political prisoner Mohamed (Anni) Nasheed. Following protests over the arrest of a judge, Nasheed resigned Feb. 2012. He ran for president in 2013 but lost the Nov. 16 runoff to Abdulla Yameen Abdul Gayoom (the former president's half-brother). Nasheed, Mar. 2015, was convicted on terrorism charges and sentenced to 13 years in prison; while the case was appealed, Nasheed received political asylum in the UK in May 2016. In 2017, the government detained political opponents. Troops intervened in July and Aug. 2017 to prevent opposition lawmakers from impeaching the parliament's speaker, an ally of Pres. Yameen. Opposition candidate Ibrahim Mohamed Solih defeated Yameen in the Sept. 23, 2018, presidential election. Nasheed returned to the Maldives, Nov. 1, 2018. Solih's party won a landslide victory in Apr. 6, 2019, parliamentary elections.

The 2020 COVID-19 pandemic caused more than 10,000 cases and 34 deaths in the Maldives as of Sept. 30.

Mali
Republic of Mali

People: Population: 19,553,397 (62). **Age distrib.:** <15: 47.7%; 65+: 3.0%. **Growth:** 2.9%. **Migrants:** 2.4%. **Pop. density:** 41.5 per sq mi, 16.0 per sq km. **Urban:** 49.5%. **Ethnic groups:** Bambara 33.3%, Fulani (Peuhl) 13.3%, Sarakole/Soninke/Marka 9.8%, Senufo/Manianka 9.6%, Malinke 8.8%, Dogon 8.7%, Sonrai 5.9%, Bobo 2.1%, Tuareg/Bella 1.7%. **Languages:** French (official), Bambara, Peuhl/Foulfoulbe, Dogon, Maraka/Soninke, Malinke, Sonrhai/Djerma, Minianka, Tamacheq. **Religions:** Muslim 88.9% (Sunni), ethnic religionist 8.8%.

Geography: Total area: 478,841 sq mi, 1,240,192 sq km (23); **Land area:** 471,118 sq mi, 1,220,190 sq km. **Location:** W Africa. Mauritania, Senegal on W; Guinea, Côte d'Ivoire, Burkina Faso on S; Niger on E; Algeria on N. **Topography:** Landlocked grassy plain in upper basins of the Senegal and Niger R., extending N into the Sahara. **Arable land:** 5.3%. **Capital:** Bamako, 2,617,686.

Government: Type: Semi-presidential republic. **Head of state:** Transitional govt. Pres. Bah Ndaw; b. 1950; in office: Sept. 25, 2020. **Head of govt.:** Prime Min. Moctar Ouane; b. 1955; in office: Sept. 27, 2020. **Local divisions:** 10 regions, 1 district. **Defense budget:** $727 mil. **Active troops:** 13,000.

Economy: Industries: food proc., constr., phosphate and gold mining. **Chief agric.:** cotton, millet, rice, corn, vegetables, peanuts; cattle, sheep, goats. **Natural resources:** gold, phosphates, kaolin, salt, limestone, uranium, gypsum, granite, hydropower. **Water:** 6,472 cu m per capita. **Electricity prod.:** 2.6 bil kWh. **Labor force:** agric. 62.3%, industry 7.6%, services 30.2%. **Unemployment:** 7.3%.

Finance: Monetary unit: CFA Franc (XOF) (553.52 = $1 U.S.). **GDP:** $47.6 bil; **per capita GDP:** $2,424; **GDP growth:** 5.0%. **Imports:** $3.6 bil; Senegal 24.4%, China 13.2%, Côte d'Ivoire 9%, France 7.3%. **Exports:** $3.1 bil; Switzerland 31.8%, UAE 15.4%, Burkina Faso 7.8%, Côte d'Ivoire 7.3%, South Africa 5%. **Tourism:** $227 mil. **Budget:** $3.5 bil. **Inflation:** –1.7%.

Transport: Railways: 368 mi. **Motor vehicles:** 1.8 per 1,000 pop. **Airports:** 8.

Communications: Telephone: 1.2 per 100 pop. **Mobile:** 115.1 per 100 pop. **Broadband:** 26.6 per 100 pop. **Internet:** 13%.
Health: Expend.: 3.8%. **Life expect.:** 59.4 male; 63.9 female.
Births: 42.2 per 1,000 pop. **Deaths:** 9 per 1,000 pop. **Infant mortality:** 64.0 per 1,000 live births. **Undernourished:** 5.1%. **HIV:** 1.2%.
Education: Compulsory: ages 7-15. **Literacy:** 50.1%.
Embassy: 2130 R St. NW 20008; 332-2249.
Website: primature.gov.ml

Until the 15th cent. the area was part of the great Mali Empire. Timbuktu (Tombouctou) was a center of Islamic study. French rule was secured, 1898. The Sudanese Rep. and Senegal became independent as the Mali Federation in 1960, but Senegal withdrew, and the Sudanese Rep. was renamed Mali.

A coup toppled a socialist regime led, 1960-68, by Pres. Modibo Keita. Famine struck in 1973-74, killing as many as 100,000 people.

The military, Mar. 1991, overthrew Pres. Moussa Traoré, who had ruled since 1968. The government and a Tuareg rebel group signed a peace accord in 1994, but Taureg separatists remained active in the north.

Amadou Toumani Touré, who led the 1991 coup, was elected president in 2002 and reelected 2007. After a Mar. 2012 coup, Islamist rebels, allied with Taureg groups, seized control of the country's north. In Jan. 2013, France and West African regional forces entered the fight against the Islamists, who were pushed out of most areas they had seized. The UN Stabilization Mission in Mali (MINUSMA) was approved Apr. 25, 2013. Ibrahim Boubacar Keita was elected president Aug. 11, 2013. Attacks by Taureg rebels, as well as fighting against Islamists, continued in 2014 and early 2015. A new peace agreement with Taureg fighters was signed in mid-2015, but violence, including Islamist extremist attacks, continued. A suicide bombing, Jan. 18, 2017, at a N Mali military camp left at least 75 dead. Ethnic violence and other fighting in central Mali left hundreds dead in 2019. About 14,000 MINUSMA uniformed personnel, as well as French and "G5" West African troops, were in Mali as of mid-2020. French forces, June 3, 2020, killed the leader of the terrorist group al-Qaeda in the Islamic Maghreb.

Keita won a second a second term in 2018. Beginning in June 2020, large-scale demonstrations protested corruption, economic conditions, and disputed Mar.-Apr. parliamentary elections. Keita and his prime minister, Boubou Cissé, were ousted, Aug. 18, in a military coup led by Col. Assimi Goïta. Goïta announced, Sept. 21, that retired Col. Bah N'Daou would serve as interim president until promised 2022 elections.

The 2020 COVID-19 pandemic caused about 3,100 cases in Mali and 131 deaths as of Sept. 30.

Malta
Republic of Malta

People: Population: 457,267 (169). **Age distrib.:** <15: 14.4%; 65+: 21.3%. **Growth:** 0.8%. **Migrants:** 19.3%. **Pop. density:** 3,747.8 per sq mi, 1,447.0 per sq km. **Urban:** 94.7%. **Ethnic groups:** Maltese (descendants of ancient Carthaginians and Phoenicians with Italian, other Mediterranean stock). **Languages:** Maltese, English (both official). **Religions:** Christian 95.6% (Catholic [official] 93.6%).
Geography: Total area: 122 sq mi, 316 sq km (187); **Land area:** 122 sq mi, 316 sq km. Island of Malta is 95 sq mi. Gozo, 26 sq mi, and Comino, 1 sq mi, are other islands in group. **Location:** Center of Mediterranean Sea. Nearest neighbor is Italy to N. **Topography:** Heavily indented coastline. Low hills cover interior. **Arable land:** 28.3%. **Capital:** Valletta, 212,768.
Government: Type: Parliamentary republic. **Head of state:** Pres. George Vella; b. 1942; in office: Apr. 4, 2019. **Head of govt.:** Prime Min. Robert Abela; b. 1977; in office: Jan. 13, 2020. **Local divisions:** 68 localities. **Defense budget:** $84 mil. **Active troops:** 1,750.
Economy: Industries: tourism, electronics, shipbuilding and repair, constr., food and beverages, pharmaceuticals, footwear. **Chief agric.:** potatoes, cauliflower, grapes, wheat, barley, tomatoes, citrus, cut flowers, green peppers; pork, milk. **Natural resources:** limestone, salt. **Water:** 117 cu m per capita. **Electricity prod.:** 1.6 bil kwH. **Labor force:** agric. 0.9%, industry 18.0%, services 81.0%. **Unemployment:** 3.4%.
Finance: Monetary unit: Euro (EUR) (0.84 = $1 U.S.). **GDP:** $22.9 bil; **per capita GDP:** $45,652; **GDP growth:** 4.4%. **Imports:** $5 bil; Italy 23%, Germany 7.9%, UK 7.7%, Spain 5%. **Exports:** $3.3 bil; Germany 17.3%, France 10.2%, Italy 9.4%, Singapore 5.9%, Hong Kong 5.8%, U.S. 5.7%. **Tourism:** $1.9 bil. **Budget:** $4.6 bil. **Inflation:** 1.6%.
Transport: Motor vehicles: 789.8 per 1,000 pop. **Airports:** 1.
Communications: Telephone: 58.2 per 100 pop. **Mobile:** 140.2 per 100 pop. **Broadband:** 102.5 per 100 pop. **Internet** (2018): 81.4%.
Health: Expend.: 9.3%. **Life expect.:** 80.7 male; 85.0 female.
Births: 9.9 per 1,000 pop. **Deaths:** 8.3 per 1,000 pop. **Infant mortality:** 4.6 per 1,000 live births. **Undernourished:** <2.5%. **HIV:** NA.
Education: Compulsory: ages 5-15. **Literacy:** 99.3%.
Embassy: 2017 Connecticut Ave. NW 20008; 462-3611.
Website: www.gov.mt

Malta was ruled by Phoenicians, Romans, Arabs, Normans, the Knights of Malta, France, and Britain (since 1814). It became independent Sept. 21, 1964, and a republic in 1974.

Malta became a full member of the EU May 1, 2004. Same-sex marriage was legalized in 2017.

The Labour Party won June 3, 2017, elections, called early by Prime Min. Joseph Muscat in the face of corruption allegations. Daphne Caruana Galizia, a journalist reporting on corruption, was killed by a car bomb, Oct. 16, 2017. Labour's Robert Abela replaced Muscat in Jan. 2020.

By Sept. 30, 2020, Malta had more than 3,000 COVID-19 cases and 34 deaths.

Marshall Islands
Republic of the Marshall Islands

People: Population: 77,917 (187). **Age distrib.:** <15: 32.9%; 65+: 4.7%. **Growth:** 1.4%. **Migrants:** 5.6%. **Pop. density:** 1,114.9 per sq mi, 430.5 per sq km. **Urban:** 77.8%. **Ethnic groups:** Marshallese 92.1%, mixed Marshallese 5.9%. **Languages:** Marshallese, English (both official). **Religions:** Christian 94.3% (Protestant 71.5%, independent 14.7%), Baha'i 3.2%.
Geography: Total area: 70 sq mi, 181 sq km (190); **Land area:** 70 sq mi, 181 sq km. **Location:** In N Pacific O.; made up of two 800-mi-long island chains, including atolls of Bikini, Enewetak, Kwajalein, Majuro, Rongelap, and Utirik. Nearest neighbors are Micronesia to W, Nauru and Kiribati to S. **Topography:** Low coral limestone and sand islands. **Arable land:** 11.1%. **Capital:** Majuro, 30,661.
Government: Type: Mixed presidential-parliamentary system in free association with U.S. **Head of state and govt.:** Pres. David Kabua; b. 1951; in office: Jan. 13, 2020. **Local divisions:** 24 municipalities. **Defense budget/active troops:** NA.
Economy: Industries: copra, tuna proc., tourism, craft items. **Chief agric.:** coconuts, tomatoes, melons, taro, breadfruit, fruits; pigs, chickens. **Natural resources:** coconut prods., marine prods., deep-seabed minerals. **Water:** NA. **Labor force:** agric. 11%, industry 16.3%, services 72.7%. **Unemployment:** NA.
Finance: Monetary unit: U.S. Dollar (USD) (1.00 = $1 U.S.). **GDP** (2018): $232.8 mil; **per capita GDP** (2018): $3,986; **GDP growth** (2018): 3.6%. **Imports** (2016): $103.8 mil. **Exports:** NA. **Tourism:** $9 mil. **Budget** (2013): $113.9 mil. **Inflation** (2016-17): 0%.
Transport: Airports: 4.
Communications: Telephone (2014): 4.1 per 100 pop. **Mobile** (2017): 27.6 per 100 pop. **Broadband:** NA. **Internet:** 38.7%.
Health: Expend.: 16.4%. **Life expect.:** 71.8 male; 76.5 female.
Births: 22.8 per 1,000 pop. **Deaths:** 4.3 per 1,000 pop. **Infant mortality:** 17.4 per 1,000 live births. **Undernourished:** NA. **HIV:** NA.
Education: Compulsory: ages 5-17. **Literacy:** 98.3%.
Embassy: 2433 Massachusetts Ave. NW, 1st Fl., 20008; 234-5414.
Website: www.rmiparliament.org

The Marshall Islands were a German possession until WWI and were administered by Japan between the World Wars. After WWII, they were administered by the U.S. as part of the UN Trust Territory of the Pacific Islands. During 1946-58, Bikini and Enewetak Atolls were used as test sites for U.S. nuclear weapons.

The Compact of Free Association, ratified by the U.S. in 1986, gave the islands their independence. In the compact, the U.S. agreed to provide financial aid to the islands, maintain their defense, and compensate victims of nuclear testing; it was renewed Dec. 2003. Elected by parliament, Jan. 27, 2016, Hilda Heine became the country's first female president. David Kabua replaced her in Jan. 2020. The Marshall Islands is considered highly vulnerable to rising sea levels resulting from climate change.

Mauritania
Islamic Republic of Mauritania

People: Population: 4,005,475 (127). **Age distrib.:** <15: 37.6%; 65+: 3.9%. **Growth:** 2.1%. **Migrants:** 3.8%. **Pop. density:** 10.1 per sq mi, 3.9 per sq km. **Urban:** 55.3%. **Ethnic groups:** Black Moor (Arab-speaking slaves, former slaves, and their descendants of African origin, enslaved by white Moors) 40%, white Moor or Beydane (Arab-Berber descent) 30%, Sub-Saharan Mauritanian (non-Arabic speaking) 30%. **Languages:** Arabic (official and national); Pular, Soninke, Wolof (all national langs.); French. **Religions:** Muslim 99.3% (Sunni [official]).
Geography: Total area: 397,955 sq mi, 1,030,700 sq km (28); **Land area:** 397,955 sq mi, 1,030,700 sq km. **Location:** NW Africa. Western Sahara on N; Algeria, Mali on E; Senegal on S. **Topography:** Fertile Senegal R. valley in S gives way to wide central region of sandy plains and scrub trees. N is arid and extends into the Sahara. **Arable land:** 0.4%. **Capital:** Nouakchott, 1,314,636.
Government: Type: Presidential republic. **Head of state:** Pres. Mohamed Cheikh El Ghazouani; b. 1956; in office: Aug. 1, 2019. **Head of govt.:** Prime Min. Mohamed Ould Bilal; b. 1963; in office: Aug. 6, 2020. **Local divisions:** 15 regions. **Defense budget:** $160 mil. **Active troops:** 15,850.
Economy: Industries: fish proc., oil prod., mining. **Chief agric.:** dates, millet, sorghum, rice, corn; cattle. **Natural resources:** iron ore, gypsum, copper, phosphate, diamonds, gold, oil, fish. **Water:** 2,579 cu m per capita. **Crude oil reserves:** 20 mil bbls. **Electricity prod.:** 1.1 bil kwH. **Labor force:** agric. 50.6%, industry 13.1%, services 36.3%. **Unemployment:** 9.6%.

Finance: Monetary unit: Ouguiya (MRU) (36.97 = $1 U.S.). **GDP:** $24.5 bil; **per capita GDP:** $5,412; **GDP growth:** 5.9%. **Imports:** $2.1 bil; Belgium 11.5%, UAE 11.3%, U.S. 9.2%, China 7.5%, France 7.4%, Netherlands 6.1%, Morocco 6%. **Exports:** $1.7 bil; China 31.2%, Switzerland 14.4%, Spain 10.1%, Germany 8.2%, Japan 8.1%. **Tourism:** $4 mil. **Budget:** $1.4 bil. **Inflation:** 2.3%.

Transport: Railways: 452 mil. **Motor vehicles:** 8.2 per 1,000 pop. **Airports:** 9.

Communications: Telephone: 1.4 per 100 pop. **Mobile:** 103.7 per 100 pop. **Broadband:** 30.3 per 100 pop. **Internet:** 20.8%.

Health: Expend.: 4.4%. **Life expect.:** 62.1 male; 67.0 female. **Births:** 29 per 1,000 pop. **Deaths:** 7.5 per 1,000 pop. **Infant mortality:** 47.9 per 1,000 live births. **Undernourished:** 11.9%. **HIV:** 0.2%.

Education: Compulsory: ages 6-14. **Literacy:** 63.9%.

Embassy: 2129 Leroy Pl. NW 20008; 232-5700.

Website: primature.gov.mr

A French protectorate from 1903, Mauritania became independent Nov. 28, 1960. It annexed the south of former Spanish Sahara (now Morocco-claimed Western Sahara) in 1976 but renounced its claim to the region after signing a peace treaty with the Saharan guerrillas of the Polisario Front, 1979.

Up to 10,000 people tried to emigrate in handmade boats to Spain's Canary Islands Jan.-June 2006; more than 1,700 died. After decades of military rule, civilian rule was restored, 2006-07, but a 2008 military coup toppled the elected government. The coup leader, Gen. Mohamed Ould Abdel Aziz, won disputed presidential elections in 2009 and 2014. Mohamed Ould Ghazouani, backed by Aziz, won a disputed June 22, 2019, presidential election. Amid corruption allegations, Ghazouani named a new prime minister, Aug. 6, 2020.

In 2013, U.S. troops began training and equipping Mauritanian counterterrorism forces combatting Islamic extremists. In 2017, Mauritania and four other nations created the anti-terrorism G5 Sahel Cross-Border Joint Force.

Major oil finds have recently been developed. Slavery, repeatedly abolished, continues to exist in Mauritania. An estimated 90,000 people lived under conditions of servitude in 2019.

The 2020 COVID-19 pandemic caused about 7,500 cases and more than 160 deaths in Mauritania as of Sept. 30.

Mauritius
Republic of Mauritius

People: Population: 1,379,365 (152). **Age distrib.:** <15: 19.4%; 65+: 11.1%. **Growth:** 0.5%. **Migrants:** 2.3%. **Pop. density:** 1,759.9 per sq mi, 679.5 per sq km. **Urban:** 40.8%. **Ethnic groups:** Indo-Mauritian (approx. two-thirds of pop.), Creole, Sino-Mauritian, Franco-Mauritian. **Languages:** Creole, Bhojpuri, French, English. **Religions:** Hindu 58.5% (Shaivites 20%, Vaishnavites 19%, Saktists 19%), Muslim 21.2% (Sunni 17%, Islamic schismatic 4%), Christian 12.2% (Catholic 7.9%, Protestant 4%).

Geography: Total area: 788 sq mi, 2,040 sq km (171); **Land area:** 784 sq mi, 2,030 sq km. **Location:** In Indian O., 500 mi E of Madagascar, its nearest neighbor. **Topography:** A volcanic island nearly surrounded by coral reefs. A central plateau is encircled by peaks. **Arable land:** 36.9%. **Capital:** Port Louis, 149,365.

Government: Type: Parliamentary republic. **Head of state:** Pres. Prithvirajsing Roopun; b. 1959; in office: Dec. 2, 2019. **Head of govt.:** Prime Min. Pravind Jugnauth; b. 1961; in office: Jan. 23, 2017. **Local divisions:** 9 districts, 3 dependencies. **Defense budget:** $220 mil. **Active troops:** No standing armed forces; 2,550 paramilitary. Special Mobile Force (part of police) and coast guard provide security.

Economy: Industries: food proc. (largely sugar milling), textiles, clothing, mining, chemicals, metal prods. **Chief agric.:** sugarcane, tea, corn, potatoes, bananas, pulses; cattle, goats; fish. **Natural resources:** fish. **Water:** 2,175 cu m per capita. **Electricity prod.:** 3.0 bil kWh. **Labor force:** agric. 5.9%, industry 25.1%, services 69.0%. **Unemployment:** 6.7%.

Finance: Monetary unit: Rupee (MUR) (39.77 = $1 U.S.). **GDP:** $30.3 bil; **per capita GDP:** $23,942; **GDP growth:** 3.6%. **Imports:** $5 bil; India 17.9%, China 15.7%, France 11.1%, South Africa 9.7%. **Exports:** $2.4 bil; France 16.7%, U.S. 12.5%, UK 12%, South Africa 9%, Madagascar 6.7%, Italy 6.6%, Spain 5.2%. **Tourism:** $1.8 bil. **Budget:** $3.0 bil. **Inflation:** 0.4%.

Transport: Motor vehicles: 246.8 per 1,000 pop. **Airports:** 2.

Communications: Telephone: 34.3 per 100 pop. **Mobile:** 151.4 per 100 pop. **Broadband:** 59 per 100 pop. **Internet** (2018): 58.6%.

Health: Expend.: 5.7%. **Life expect.:** 73.0 male; 80.1 female. **Births:** 12.6 per 1,000 pop. **Deaths:** 7.3 per 1,000 pop. **Infant mortality:** 9.0 per 1,000 live births. **Undernourished:** 5.3%. **HIV:** 1.2%.

Education: Compulsory: ages 5-15. **Literacy:** 99.0%.

Embassy: 1709 N St. NW 20036; 244-1491.

Website: www.govmu.org

Mauritius was uninhabited when settled in 1638 by the Dutch, who introduced sugarcane. France took over in 1721, bringing African slaves. Britain ruled from 1810, bringing Indian workers. Mauritius became independent, Mar. 12, 1968, and a republic, Mar. 12, 1992.

Prime Min. Pravind Jugnauth's party won Nov. 7, 2019, elections. The National Assembly, Dec. 2, chose Prithvirajsing Roopun as the country's president. An oil tanker ran aground off the SE coast, July 25, 2020, spilling 1,000 tons of fuel.

Mexico
United Mexican States

People: Population: 128,649,565 (10). **Age distrib.:** <15: 26.0%; 65+: 7.7%. **Growth:** 1.0%. **Migrants:** 0.8%. **Pop. density:** 171.4 per sq mi, 66.2 per sq km. **Urban:** 80.7%. **Ethnic groups:** mestizo (Amerindian-Spanish) 62%, predom. Amerindian 21%, Amerindian 7%. **Languages:** Spanish, Indigenous langs. (incl. Mayan, Nahuatl). **Religions:** Christian 95.8% (Catholic 85.4%), agnostic 2.9%.

Geography: Total area: 758,449 sq mi, 1,964,375 sq km (13); **Land area:** 750,561 sq mi, 1,943,945 sq km. **Location:** Southern N America. U.S. on N, Guatemala and Belize on S. **Topography:** The Sierra Madre Occidental Mts. run NW-SE near the W coast; the Sierra Madre Oriental Mts. are near Gulf of Mexico. They join S of Mexico City. In between lies a dry central plateau (5,000-8,000 ft) with temperate vegetation. Coastal lowlands are tropical. About 45% of land is arid. **Arable land:** 12.3%. **Capital:** Mexico City, 21,782,378. **Cities:** Guadalajara, 5,179,479; Monterrey, 4,874,095; Puebla, 3,194,848; Toluca de Lerdo, 2,467,241; Tijuana, 2,140,398.

Government: Type: Federal presidential republic. **Head of state and govt.:** Pres. Andrés Manuel López Obrador; b. 1953; in office: Dec. 1, 2018. **Local divisions:** 32 states. **Defense budget:** $5.1 bil. **Active troops:** 236,450.

Economy: Industries: food/beverages, tobacco, chemicals, iron and steel, petroleum, mining, textiles, clothing, motor vehicles. **Chief agric.:** corn, wheat, soybeans, rice, beans, cotton, coffee, fruit, tomatoes; beef, poultry, dairy prods. **Natural resources:** petroleum, silver, antimony, copper, gold, lead, zinc, nat. gas, timber. **Water:** 3,576 cu m per capita. **Crude oil reserves:** 5.8 bil bbls. **Electricity prod.** (2018): 323.2 bil kWh. **Labor force:** agric. 12.4%, industry 26.2%, services 61.4%. **Unemployment:** 3.7%.

Finance: Monetary unit: Peso (MXN) (21.52 = $1 U.S.). **GDP:** $2.6 tril; **per capita GDP:** $20,411; **GDP growth:** −0.1%. **Imports:** $420.8 bil; U.S. 46.4%, China 17.7%. **Exports:** $409.8 bil; U.S. 79.9%. **Tourism:** $24.6 bil. **Budget:** $273.8 bil. **Inflation:** 3.6%.

Transport: Railways: 12,940 mi. **Motor vehicles:** 343 per 1,000 pop. **Airports:** 243.

Communications: Telephone: 16.9 per 100 pop. **Mobile:** 93 per 100 pop. **Broadband:** 63.6 per 100 pop. **Internet** (2018): 65.8%.

Health: Expend.: 5.5%. **Life expect.:** 73.9 male; 79.6 female. **Births:** 17.6 per 1,000 pop. **Deaths:** 5.4 per 1,000 pop. **Infant mortality:** 10.7 per 1,000 live births. **Undernourished:** 7.1%. **HIV** (2018): 0.2%.

Education: Compulsory: ages 4-17. **Literacy:** 99.3%.

Embassy: 1911 Pennsylvania Ave. NW 20006; 728-1600.

Website: www.gob.mx

Mexico was the site of advanced civilizations. The Mayans, an agricultural people, moved up from Yucatan, built huge stone pyramids, and invented a calendar. The Toltecs were overcome by the Aztecs, who founded Tenochtitlan 1325 CE, now Mexico City. Hernán Cortés, Spanish conquistador, destroyed the Aztec empire, 1519-21. After three centuries of Spanish rule the people revolted, beginning in 1810. Spain recognized Mexican independence, 1821. A republic was declared in 1823.

Mexican territory extended into the present-day United States. Texas established a republic in 1836, and Mexico lost California and most of the SW in the U.S.-Mexican War, 1846-48.

The French supported an Austrian archduke on the Mexican throne as Maximilian I, 1864-67. He was deposed in an uprising led by Benito Juárez. Dictatorial rule by Porfirio Díaz, president 1877-80, 1884-1911, led to a period of rebellion and factional fighting. A new constitution in 1917 brought reform.

The Institutional Revolutionary Party (PRI) dominated politics from 1929 until the late 1990s. Gains in agriculture, industry, and social services were achieved, but poverty remained widespread. Vast oil reserves were discovered, 1970s-80s. About 10,000 people died when a magnitude 8.0 earthquake struck near Mexico City, Sept. 19, 1985.

The National Action Party won the 2000 and 2006 presidential elections. Despite a government crackdown on drug cartels, drug-related violence intensified (47,500 killed, Dec. 2006-Sept. 2012). Enrique Peña Nieto (PRI) won the 2012 presidential election. Notorious drug cartel leader Joaquín Guzmán Loera, known as El Chapo, was captured, Feb. 22, 2014. After an escape, recapture, and extradition to the U.S., he was convicted, Feb. 12, 2019, of drug trafficking and sentenced, July 17, to life in prison.

Vowing to reduce violence and corruption and to combat poverty, leftist Andrés Manuel López Obrador of the Moreno Party easily won the July 1, 2018, presidential election. However, drug cartel and other violence continued.

A Supreme Court decision, June 3, 2015, in effect legalized same-sex marriage nationwide.

The North American Free Trade Agreement (NAFTA) with the U.S. and Canada took effect Jan. 1, 1994. At U.S. insistence, negotiations on revising NAFTA began Aug. 16, 2017. A revised pact, renamed the U.S.-Mexico-Canada Agreement (USMCA) leaving much of the original NAFTA in place, was signed Nov. 30, 2018—then further revised to gain U.S. congressional approval (including strengthening labor and environmental provisions). The USMCA came into force July 1, 2020.

With hundreds of thousands of Central American asylum-seekers and other migrants crossing from Mexico into the U.S. in 2019, Mexico agreed, June 7, to increase troops at its southern border with Guatemala. By 2020, under a 2019 U.S. policy, tens of thousands of asylum seekers were forced to wait in Mexico, often in harsh conditions, while their cases were pending.

Hard-hit by the 2020 COVID-19 pandemic, Mexico had almost 734,000 cases and over 76,600 deaths by Sept. 30. The pandemic worsened an already struggling economy.

Micronesia
Federated States of Micronesia

People: Population: 102,436 (182). **Age distrib.:** <15: 28.9%; 65+: 4.6%. **Growth:** –0.6%. **Migrants:** 2.5%. **Pop. density:** 377.9 per sq mi, 145.9 per sq km. **Urban:** 22.9%. **Ethnic groups:** Chuukese/Mortlockese 49.3%, Pohnpeian 29.8%, Kosraean 6.3%, Yapese 5.7%, Yap outer islander 5.1%. **Languages:** English (official), Chuukese, Kosrean, Pohnpeian, Yapese, Ulithian, Woleaian, Nukuoro, Kapingamarangi. **Religions:** Christian 94.5% (Catholic 49.8%, Protestant 37.7%), ethnic religionist 2.9%.

Geography: Total area: 271 sq mi, 702 sq km (178); **Land area:** 271 sq mi, 702 sq km. **Location:** Consists of 607 islands in four major island groups in W Pacific O. **Topography:** Mountainous islands and coral atolls; volcanic outcroppings on Pohnpei, Kosrae, and Truk. Tropical climate. **Arable land:** 2.9%. **Capital:** Palikir, 6,996.

Government: Type: Federal republic in free association with U.S. **Head of state and govt.:** Pres. David W. Panuelo; b. 1964; in office: May 11, 2019. **Local divisions:** 4 states. **Defense budget/ active troops:** NA.

Economy: Industries: tourism, constr., specialized aquaculture, craft items. **Chief agric.:** taro, yams, coconuts, bananas, cassava, kava, Kosraen citrus, betel nuts, black pepper, fish, pigs, chickens. **Natural resources:** timber, marine prods., deep-seabed minerals, phosphate. **Water:** NA. **Labor force:** agric. 34.6%, industry 6.2%, services 44.2%. **Unemployment:** NA.

Finance: Monetary unit: U.S. Dollar (USD) (1.00 = $1 U.S.). **GDP** (2018): $399.9 mil; **per capita GDP** (2018): $3,550; **GDP growth** (2018): 0.2%. **Imports** (2015): $167.8 mil. **Exports** (2013): $88.3 mil. **Tourism** (2015): $25 mil. **Budget** (FY2012/13): $192.1 mil. **Inflation** (2016-17): 0.5%.

Transport: Airports: 6.

Communications: Telephone (2017): 6.2 per 100 pop. **Mobile** (2017): 20.7 per 100 pop. **Broadband:** NA. **Internet:** 35.3%.

Health: Expend.: 12.4%. **Life expect.:** 71.8 male; 76.1 female. **Births:** 18.9 per 1,000 pop. **Deaths:** 4.3 per 1,000 pop. **Infant mortality:** 17.8 per 1,000 live births. **Undernourished:** NA. **HIV:** NA. **Education:** Compulsory: NA. **Literacy:** 90.4%. **Embassy:** 1725 N St. NW 20036; 223-4383. **Website:** micronesia.fm

Micronesia, formerly known as the Caroline Islands, was ruled successively by Spain, Germany, Japan, and the U.S. The nation gained independence under a compact of free association with the U.S., Nov. 1986, and was admitted to the UN in 1991. Micronesian officials have repeatedly warned of the dangers to their country of rising sea levels linked to climate change.

Moldova
Republic of Moldova

People: Population: 3,364,496 (132). **Age distrib.:** <15: 18.3%; 65+: 14.0%. **Growth:** –1.1%. **Migrants:** 2.6%. **Pop. density:** 264.9 per sq mi, 102.3 per sq km. **Urban:** 42.8%. **Ethnic groups:** Moldovan 75.1%, Romanian 7%, Ukrainian 6.6%, Gagauz 4.6%, Russian 4.1%. **Languages:** Moldovan/Romanian (official), Russian, Gagauz, Ukrainian. **Religions:** Christian 97.5% (Orthodox [official] 94.5%).

Geography: Total area: 13,070 sq mi, 33,851 sq km (136); **Land area:** 12,699 sq mi, 32,891 sq km. **Location:** Eastern Europe. Romania on W; Ukraine on N, E, and S. **Topography:** Landlocked; mainly hilly plains with steppelands in S near Black Sea. **Arable land:** 52.8%. **Capital:** Chisinau, 504,342.

Government: Type: Parliamentary republic. **Head of state:** Pres. Igor Dodon; b. 1975; in office: Dec. 23, 2016. **Head of govt.:** Prime Min. Ion Chicu; b. 1972; in office: Nov. 14, 2019. **Local divisions:** 32 raions, 3 municipalities, 2 territorial units (1 autonomous). **Defense budget:** $42 mil. **Active troops:** 5,150.

Economy: Industries: sugar proc., vegetable oil, food proc., agric. machinery, foundry equip., refrigerators and freezers. **Chief agric.:** vegetables, fruits, grapes, grain, sugar beets, sunflower seeds, tobacco; beef, milk; wine. **Natural resources:** lignite, phosphorites, gypsum, limestone. **Water:** 3,029 cu m per capita. **Electricity prod.:** 4.7 bil kWh. **Labor force:** agric. 35.4%, industry 17.1%, services 47.5%. **Unemployment:** 5.4%.

Finance: Monetary unit: Leu (MDL) (16.61 = $1 U.S.). **GDP:** $36.1 bil; **per capita GDP:** $13,574; **GDP growth:** 3.5%. **Imports:** $4.4 bil; Romania 15.5%, Ukraine 11.4%, Russia 10.6%, China 10.4%, Germany 8.9%, Italy 6.9%, Turkey 6.1%. **Exports:** $1.9 bil;

Romania 24.6%, Russia 13.7%, Italy 9.1%, Germany 6.2%, Ukraine 5.3%. **Tourism:** $396 mil. **Budget:** $2.9 bil (natl. public). **Inflation:** 4.8%.

Transport: Railways: 728 mi. **Airports:** 5.

Communications: Telephone: 27.3 per 100 pop. **Mobile:** 88 per 100 pop. **Broadband:** 60 per 100 pop. **Internet:** 76.1%.

Health: Expend.: 7.0%. **Life expect.:** 68.0 male; 76.0 female. **Births:** 10.7 per 1,000 pop. **Deaths:** 12.6 per 1,000 pop. **Infant mortality:** 11.1 per 1,000 live births. **Undernourished:** NA. **HIV:** 0.7%.

Education: Compulsory: ages 7-17. **Literacy:** 99.4%. **Embassy:** 2101 S St. NW 20008; 667-1130. **Website:** www.moldova.md

In 1918, Romania annexed Bessarabia, west of the Dniester R. In 1924, the Soviet Union established the Moldavian Autonomous Soviet Socialist Republic on the eastern bank of the Dniester R (Trans-Dniester region, or Transnistria). It was merged with the Romanian-speaking districts of Bessarabia in 1940 to form the Moldavian SSR. During WWII, Romania, allied with Germany, occupied the area. It was recaptured by the USSR in 1944. Moldova declared independence Aug. 27, 1991, prior to the dissolution of the USSR Dec. 26, 1991.

Fighting erupted Mar. 1992 in Transnistria between Moldovan security forces and Slavic separatists—ethnic Russians and ethnic Ukrainians—who feared Moldova's merging with neighboring Romania. In a 1994 plebiscite, voters in Moldova supported independence. Defying the Moldovan government, voters in the breakaway Transnistria held legislative elections and approved a separatist constitution in 1995. A peace accord with Transnistria separatists was signed in Moscow in 1997. In a 2006 referendum, Transnistria voters overwhelmingly supported independence from Moldova and eventual union with Russia, which has troops in the region.

Pro-Western parties won Moldova's parliamentary elections in 2009, 2010, and 2014. Moldova and the EU signed an Association Agreement, June 27, 2014. A banking scandal involving about $1 bil in bad loans, 2010-14, caused political turmoil. Pavel Filip became prime min., Jan. 20, 2016, pledging to fight corruption. In Moldova's first direct presidential election, pro-Russian Socialist Party (PSRM) candidate Igor Dodon won a Nov. 13, 2016, runoff. Following Feb. 24, 2019, parliamentary elections, pro-EU Maia Sandu became prime min. in June. After she lost a no-confidence vote, Dodon supporter Ion Chicu replaced her, Nov. 14.

The 2020 COVID-19 pandemic caused about 52,000 cases and over 1,300 deaths in Moldova by Sept. 30.

Monaco
Principality of Monaco

People: Population: 30,940 (192). (Immigrants made up almost 68% of pop. in 2019.) **Age distrib.:** <15: 9.4%; 65+: 35.1%. **Growth:** 0.4%. **Migrants:** 68.0%. **Pop. density:** 40,067.1 per sq mi, 15,470.0 per sq km. **Urban:** 100.0%. **Ethnic groups (by birth country):** Monegasque 32.1%, French 19.9%, Italian 15.3%, British 5%, Belgian 2.3%, Swiss 2%. **Languages:** French (official), English, Italian, Monegasque. **Religions:** Christian 85% (Catholic [official] 82.3%), agnostic 10.8%, atheist 2.1%, Jewish 1.5%.

Geography: Total area: 0.77 sq mi, 2 sq km (195); **Land area:** 0.77 sq mi, 2 sq km. **Location:** NW Mediterranean coast. France to W, N, and E. **Topography:** Principality rises from port up to Monaco-Ville on a high promontory. **Arable land:** 0%. **Capital:** Monaco.

Government: Type: Constitutional monarchy. **Head of state:** Prince Albert II; b. 1958; in office: Apr. 6, 2005. **Head of govt.:** Min. of State Serge Telle; b. 1955; in office: Feb. 1, 2016. **Local divisions:** no first-order admin. divisions. **Defense budget/active troops:** NA.

Economy: Industries: banking, insurance, tourism, constr. **Chief agric.:** none. **Natural resources:** none. **Water:** NA. **Labor force:** industry 16.1%, services 83.9%. **Unemployment:** NA.

Finance: Monetary unit: Euro (EUR) (0.84 = $1 U.S.). **GDP:** NA; **per capita GDP:** NA; **GDP growth** (2018): 6.1%. **Imports:** $1.4 bil. **Exports:** $964.6 mil. Full customs integration with France. **Budget** (2011): $953.6 mil. **Inflation** (2009-10): 1.5%.

Transport: NA.

Communications: Telephone: 112.1 per 100 pop. **Mobile:** 84.5 per 100 pop. **Broadband:** 80.1 per 100 pop. **Internet:** 97.1%.

Health: Expend.: 1.8%. **Life expect.:** 85.4 male; 93.3 female. **Births:** 6.4 per 1,000 pop. **Deaths:** 10.8 per 1,000 pop. **Infant mortality:** 1.9 per 1,000 live births. **Undernourished:** NA. **HIV:** NA. **Education:** Compulsory: ages 6-16. **Literacy:** 99%. **Embassy:** 3400 International Dr. NW, Ste. 2K-100, 20008; 234-1530. **Website:** www.gouv.mc

Monaco has belonged to the House of Grimaldi almost continuously since 1297. It was annexed by France in 1793 and was placed under the protectorate of Sardinia in 1815. An 1861 treaty restored independence. The Prince of Monaco was an absolute ruler until the 1911 constitution. Monaco is noted for its climate, scenery, casinos, and Formula One Grand Prix auto race (canceled in 2020 because of the COVID-19 pandemic). Monaco is a tourist destination and tax haven for the wealthy. Prince Rainier III, ruler from 1949, died in 2005 and was succeeded by his son, Albert II.

Mongolia

People: Population: 3,168,026 (133). **Age distrib.:** <15: 27.0%; 65+: 4.8%. **Growth:** 1.0%. **Migrants:** 0.7%. **Pop. density:** 5.3 per sq mi, 2.0 per sq km. **Urban:** 68.7%. **Ethnic groups:** Khalkh 84.5%, Kazak 3.9%, Dorvod 2.4%. **Languages:** Mongolian (official) (Khalkha dialect predom.), Turkic, Russian. **Religions:** Buddhist 58.6%, ethnic religionist 18%, agnostic 14%, Muslim 5% (Sunni).

Geography: Total area: 603,909 sq mi, 1,564,116 sq km (18); **Land area:** 599,831 sq mi, 1,553,556 sq km. **Location:** E Central Asia. Russia on N, China on E, W, and S. **Topography:** Mostly high plateau with mountains, salt lakes, and vast grasslands. Gobi Desert in S. **Arable land:** 0.4%. **Capital:** Ulaanbaatar, 1,584,358.

Government: Type: Semi-presidential republic. **Head of state:** Pres. Khaltmaa Battulga; b. 1963; in office: July 10, 2017. **Head of govt.:** Prime. Min. Ukhnaa Khurelsukh; b. 1968; in office: Oct. 4, 2017. **Local divisions:** 21 provinces, 1 municipality. **Defense budget:** $96 mil. **Active troops:** 9,700.

Economy: Industries: constr. and constr. materials, mining, oil, food and beverages, animal prods. proc., cashmere and natural fiber mfg. **Chief agric.:** wheat, barley, vegetables, forage crops; sheep, goats, cattle, camels, horses. **Natural resources:** oil, coal, copper, molybdenum, tungsten, phosphates, tin, nickel, zinc, fluorspar, gold, silver, iron. **Water:** 11,313 cu m per capita. **Electricity prod.:** 5.7 bil kWh. **Labor force:** agric. 26.9%, industry 19.5%, services 53.6%. **Unemployment:** 6.0%.

Finance: Monetary unit: Tughrik (MNT) (2,863.66 = $1 U.S.). **GDP:** $41.3 bil; **per capita GDP:** $12,820; **GDP growth:** 5.1%. **Imports** (2018): $5.9 bil; China 32.6%, Russia 28.1%, Japan 8.4%. **Exports** (2018): $7.0 bil; China 93.3%. **Tourism:** $513 mil. **Budget:** $3.7 bil. **Inflation:** 7.3%.

Transport: Railways: 1,128 mi. **Airports:** 15.

Communications: Telephone: 11.7 per 100 pop. **Mobile:** 133.2 per 100 pop. **Broadband:** 80.8 per 100 pop. **Internet:** 23.7%.

Health: Expend.: 4.0%. **Life expect.:** 66.6 male; 75.2 female. **Births:** 16.6 per 1,000 pop. **Deaths:** 6.3 per 1,000 pop. **Infant mortality:** 19.2 per 1,000 live births. **Undernourished:** 21.3%. **HIV:** <0.1%.

Education: Compulsory: ages 6-17. **Literacy:** 98.6%.

Embassy: 2833 M St. NW 20007; 333-7117.

Website: zasag.mn

Mongolia reached the zenith of its power in the 13th cent. when Genghis Khan and his successors conquered all of China and extended their influence as far west as Hungary and Poland. In later centuries, the empire dissolved, and Mongolia became a province of China.

With the advent of the 1911 Chinese revolution, Mongolia, with Russian backing, declared its independence, 1921. A Communist regime was established, 1921. The Mongolian People's Revolutionary Party (MPRP) yielded its monopoly on power, 1990. A new constitution took effect, 1992.

Riots followed 2008 parliamentary elections, won by the ruling MPRP (renamed the Mongolian People's Party, or MPP, in 2010). The Democratic Party (DP) won the 2009 presidential election and 2012 legislative elections. Low commodity prices and reduced exports to China caused the economy to slump, and the MPP won June 29, 2016, parliamentary elections. The IMF approved a $5.5-bil bailout package, May 24, 2017. The DP's Khaltmaa Battulga won a July 7 presidential runoff vote. Parliament voted, Sept. 7, to oust Prime Min. Jargaltulga Erdenebat, whose government was accused of corruption. The MPP's Ukhnaa Khurelsukh replaced Erdenebat—and stayed in office when his party won June 24, 2020, legislative elections.

Montenegro

People: Population: 609,859 (165). **Age distrib.:** <15: 18.1%; 65+: 16.0%. **Growth:** −0.4%. **Migrants:** 11.3%. **Pop. density:** 117.4 per sq mi, 45.3 per sq km **Urban:** 67.5%. **Ethnic groups:** Montenegrin 45%, Serbian 28.7%, Bosniak 8.7%, Albanian 4.9%, Muslim 3.3%. **Languages:** Serbian, Montenegrin (official), Bosnian, Albanian, Serbo-Croat. **Religions:** Christian 79.2% (Orthodox 71.2%), Muslim 17.5% (Sunni), agnostic 2.8%.

Geography: Total area: 5,333 sq mi, 13,812 sq km (157); **Land area:** 5,194 sq mi, 13,452 sq km. **Location:** Balkan Peninsula in SE Europe. Bosnia and Herzegovina on N and W, Serbia on E, Albania on SE, Croatia on W. **Topography:** Mostly rugged and mountainous, with few arable regions, mostly along the Zeta R. Highly indented narrow coastline. **Arable land:** 0.7%. **Capital:** Podgorica, 177,177. Cetinje holds status of "Old Royal Capital."

Government: Type: Parliamentary republic. **Head of state:** Pres. Milo Djukanovic; b. 1958; in office: May 20, 2018. **Head of govt.:** Prime. Min. Dusko Markovic; b. 1958; in office: Nov. 28, 2016. **Local divisions:** 24 municipalities. **Defense budget:** $74 mil. **Active troops:** 2,350.

Economy: Industries: steelmaking, aluminum, agric. proc., consumer goods, tourism. **Chief agric.:** tobacco, potatoes, citrus fruits, olives, grapes; sheep; wine. **Natural resources:** bauxite, hydroelectricity. **Water:** NA. **Electricity prod.** (2018): 3.7 bil kWh. **Labor force:** agric. 7.8%, industry 19.2%, services 73.0%. **Unemployment:** 14.8%.

Finance: Monetary unit: Euro (EUR) (0.84 = $1 U.S.). **GDP:** $14.3 bil; **per capita GDP:** $22,989; **GDP growth:** 3.6%. **Imports:** $2.6 bil. **Exports:** $422.2 mil. **Tourism:** $1.2 bil. **Budget:** $2.1 bil. **Inflation** (2017-18): 2.6%.

Transport: Railways: 155 mi. **Airports:** 5.

Communications: Telephone: 27.5 per 100 pop. **Mobile:** 180.7 per 100 pop. **Broadband:** 66.5 per 100 pop. **Internet** (2018): 71.5%.

Health: Expend.: NA. **Life expect.:** 74.8 male; 79.8 female. **Births:** 11.5 per 1,000 pop. **Deaths:** 10.4 per 1,000 pop. **Infant mortality:** 3.4 per 1,000 live births. **Undernourished:** <2.5%. **HIV:** <0.1%.

Education: Compulsory: ages 6-14. **Literacy:** 99.1%.

Embassy: 1610 New Hampshire Ave. NW 20009; 234-6108.

Website: www.gov.me

Part of the medieval Serbian Kingdom, Montenegro preserved its autonomy for centuries because of its mountainous terrain. After WWI, it was part of the Kingdom of Serbs, Croats, and Slovenes, later renamed Yugoslavia. Italian forces occupied parts of Montenegro during WWII. In 1945, with the establishment of a federal Yugoslavia under Communist rule, Montenegro became one of six constituent republics.

In Apr. 1992, after four other republics had declared independence, Montenegro and Serbia reconstituted themselves as the Federal Republic of Yugoslavia. On June 3, 2006, Montenegro declared independence. It applied, Dec. 15, 2008, to join the EU. The governing, pro-Western Democratic Party of Socialists (DPS) won the most seats in Oct. 16, 2016, parliamentary elections; 20 Serbian nationals were arrested on election day, accused of plotting a coup, allegedly with Russian backing. Montenegro became a member of NATO, June 5, 2017. The DPS's Milo Djukanovic won the Apr. 15, 2018, presidential election. Parliament legalized same-sex partnerships, July 1, 2020. In Aug. 30 parliamentary elections, a coalition of opposition parties won a majority of seats; they agreed, Sept. 9, to form a new government.

The 2020 COVID-19 pandemic caused about 10,600 cases and 164 deaths in Montenegro as of Sept. 30.

Morocco
Kingdom of Morocco

People: Population: 35,561,654 (40). **Age distrib.:** <15: 27.0%; 65+: 7.1%. **Growth:** 1.0%. **Migrants:** 0.3%. **Pop. density:** 206.4 per sq mi, 79.7 per sq km. **Urban:** 63.5%. **Ethnic groups:** Arab-Berber 99%. **Languages:** Arabic (official), Berber langs. (incl. Tamazight [official]), French (lang. of business, govt., diplomacy). **Religions:** Muslim 99.7% (Sunni [official]).

Geography: Total area: 172,414 sq mi, 446,550 sq km (57); **Land area:** 172,317 sq mi, 446,300 sq km. **Location:** NW coast of Africa. Western Sahara on S, Algeria on E, Spain to N. **Topography:** Consists of 5 natural regions: mountain ranges (Riff in N, Middle Atlas, Upper Atlas, and Anti-Atlas); rich plains in W; alluvial plains in SW; well-cultivated plateaus in center; pre-Sahara arid zone extending from SE. **Arable land:** 17.5%. **Capital:** Rabat, 1,884,802. **Cities:** Dar-el-Beida (Casablanca), 3,752,357.

Government: Type: Parliamentary constitutional monarchy. **Head of state:** King Mohammed VI; b. 1963; in office: July 30, 1999. **Head of govt.:** Prime Min. Saad-Eddine al-Othmani; b. 1956; in office: Mar. 17, 2017. **Local divisions:** 11 regions (recognized; not incl. claimed region in territory of disputed Western Sahara). **Defense budget:** $3.6 bil. **Active troops:** 195,800.

Economy: Industries: automotive parts, phosphate mining and proc., aerospace, food proc., leather goods. **Chief agric.:** barley, wheat, citrus fruits, grapes, vegetables, olives. **Natural resources:** phosphates, iron ore, manganese, lead, zinc, fish, salt. **Water:** 811 cu m per capita. **Crude oil reserves:** 684,000 bbls. **Electricity prod.:** 29.8 bil kWh. **Labor force:** agric. 34.1%, industry 21.8%, services 44.0%. **Unemployment:** 9.0%.

Finance: Monetary unit: Dirham (MAD) (9.19 = $1 U.S.). **GDP:** $290.0 bil; **per capita GDP:** $7,826; **GDP growth:** 2.3%. **Imports:** $39.6 bil; Spain 16.7%, France 12.2%, China 9.2%, U.S. 6.9%, Germany 6%, Italy 5.9%. **Exports:** $21.5 bil; Spain 23.2%, France 22.6%. **Tourism:** $8.2 bil. **Budget:** $26.8 bil. **Inflation:** 0.2%.

Transport: Railways: 1,284 mi. **Motor vehicles:** 119.7 per 1,000 pop. **Airports:** 31.

Communications: Telephone: 6.1 per 100 pop. **Mobile:** 124.2 per 100 pop. **Broadband:** 58.3 per 100 pop. **Internet** (2018): 64.8%.

Health: Expend.: 5.2%. **Life expect.:** 71.6 male; 75.1 female. **Births:** 17.9 per 1,000 pop. **Deaths:** 6.6 per 1,000 pop. **Infant mortality:** 18.2 per 1,000 live births. **Undernourished:** 4.3%. **HIV:** <0.1%.

Education: Compulsory: ages 6-14. **Literacy:** 97.7%.

Embassy: 1601 21st St. NW 20009; 462-7980.

Website: www.egov.ma

Berbers were the region's original inhabitants, followed by Carthaginians and Romans. Arabs conquered it in 683. In the 11th and 12th cents., a Berber empire ruled all NW Africa and most of Spain from Morocco.

Part of Morocco came under Spanish rule in the 19th cent.; France controlled the rest in the early 20th. Tribal uprisings lasted from 1911 to 1933. Independence was achieved Mar. 2, 1956. Tangier, an internationalized seaport, was incorporated into Morocco, 1956. Ifni, a Spanish enclave, was ceded in 1969.

King Hassan II assumed the throne in 1961, reigning until his death in 1999; he was succeeded by his eldest son. A bicameral legislature was established in 1997.

Five terrorist attacks, linked to al-Qaeda, in Casablanca May 16, 2003, left 45 people dead, including 12 suicide bombers. Following a series of suicide bombings in 2007, the government stepped up its campaign against militant Islamists. After Arab Spring street demonstrations Feb.-Mar. 2011, the monarchy implemented modest constitutional reforms. Throughout 2011, Moroccans staged protests over persistent unemployment, alleged unjust detentions, and lack of free speech. The moderate Islamist Justice and Development Party (PJD) won a plurality in Oct. 7, 2016, parliamentary elections; the PJD's Saad-Eddine al-Othmani became prime min., Mar. 17, 2017. Large protests in the impoverished Rif region, 2017-18, prompted a harsh response by security forces. Morocco completed, Dec. 2018, one of the world's largest concentrated solar power complexes.

The 2020 COVID-19 pandemic caused more than 121,000 cases and over 2,100 deaths in Morocco as of Sept. 30.

Western Sahara

Western Sahara, formerly the protectorate of Spanish Sahara, is bounded on the N by Morocco, the NE by Algeria, the E and S by Mauritania, and the W by the Atlantic O. Phosphates are the major resource. Area 102,703 sq mi; pop. (2020 est.) 652,271. Capital is Laayoune; pop. (2018 est.) 232,388.

Spain withdrew in Feb. 1976. On Apr. 14, 1976, Morocco annexed over 70,000 sq mi, with the remainder annexed by Mauritania. The Polisario Front guerrilla movement, which proclaimed the region independent Feb. 27, launched attacks with Algerian support. After Mauritania signed a treaty with Polisario Aug. 5, 1979, Morocco occupied Mauritania's portion of Western Sahara.

After years of bitter fighting, Morocco controlled the main urban areas, and Polisario vast, sparsely populated desert areas. The two sides implemented a cease-fire in 1991, when a UN peacekeeping force (MINURSO) was established with a mandate to prepare for a referendum on self-determination as early as 1992. In mid-2020, MINURSO had almost 200 personnel in Western Sahara. A referendum had still not been held. Morocco, which left the predecessor of the African Union (AU) in 1984 over recognition of Western Sahara, was readmitted to the AU, Jan. 31, 2017.

Mozambique
Republic of Mozambique

People: Population: 30,098,197 (47). **Age distrib.:** <15: 45.6%; 65+: 2.9%. **Growth:** 2.6%. **Migrants:** 1.1%. **Pop. density:** 99.1 per sq mi, 38.3 per sq km. **Urban:** 37.1%. **Ethnic groups:** African (incl. Makhuwa, Tsonga, Lomwe, Sena) 99%. **Languages:** Emakhuwa, Portuguese (official), Xichangana, Cinyanja, Cisena, Elomwe, Echuwabo, other Mozambican langs. **Religions:** Christian 54.2% (Catholic 24%, Protestant 15.2%, independent 15%), ethnic religionist 27.8%, Muslim 17.4% (Sunni).

Geography: Total area: 308,642 sq mi, 799,380 sq km (34); **Land area:** 303,623 sq mi, 786,380 sq km. **Location:** SE coast of Africa. Tanzania on N; Malawi, Zambia, Zimbabwe on W; South Africa, Swaziland on S. **Topography:** Coastal lowlands comprise nearly half the country with plateaus rising in steps to mountains along western border. **Arable land:** 7.2%. **Capital:** Maputo, 1,110,477. **Cities:** Matola, 1,705,886.

Government: Type: Presidential republic. **Head of state and govt.:** Pres. Filipe Jacinto Nyusi; b. 1959; in office: Jan. 15, 2015. **Local divisions:** 10 provinces, 1 city. **Defense budget:** $127 mil. **Active troops:** 11,200.

Economy: Industries: aluminum, petroleum prods., chemicals, textiles, cement, glass, asbestos, tobacco, food, beverages. **Chief agric.:** cotton, cashew nuts, sugarcane, tea, cassava, corn, coconuts, sisal, citrus and tropical fruits, potatoes, sunflowers; beef, poultry. **Natural resources:** coal, titanium, nat. gas, hydropower, tantalum, graphite. **Water:** 7,317 cu m per capita. **Electricity prod.:** 16.7 bil kWh. **Labor force:** agric. 69.9%, industry 8.6%, services 21.5%. **Unemployment:** 3.2%.

Finance: Monetary unit: Metical (MZN) (71.53 = $1 U.S.). **GDP:** $40.5 bil; **per capita GDP:** $1,334; **GDP growth:** 2.2%. **Imports:** $5.2 bil; South Africa 36.8%, China 7%, UAE 6.8%, India 6.2%. **Exports:** $4.7 bil; India 28.1%, Netherlands 24.4%, South Africa 16.7%. **Tourism:** $252 mil. **Budget:** $4.1 bil. **Inflation:** 2.8%.

Transport: Railways: 2,975 mi. **Motor vehicles:** 3.6 per 1,000 pop. **Airports:** 21.

Communications: Telephone: 0.2 per 100 pop. **Mobile:** 47.7 per 100 pop. **Broadband:** 25.7 per 100 pop. **Internet:** 10%.

Health: Expend.: 4.9%. **Life expect.:** 54.4 male; 57.4 female. **Births:** 38.6 per 1,000 pop. **Deaths:** 11 per 1,000 pop. **Infant mortality:** 64.7 per 1,000 live births. **Undernourished:** 32.6%. **HIV:** 12.4%.

Education: Compulsory: ages 6-12. **Literacy:** 70.9%.

Embassy: 1525 New Hampshire Ave. NW 20036; 293-7146.

Website: www.portaldogoverno.gov.mz

The first Portuguese post on the Mozambique coast was established in 1505 on the trade route to Asia. Mozambique

became independent June 25, 1975, after a 10-year war against Portuguese rule led by Frelimo (Front for the Liberation of Mozambique).

The Frelimo government, headed by Pres. Samora Machel, transitioned to a Communist system. Most of the country's whites emigrated. In the 1980s, severe drought and civil war caused famine and heavy loss of life. Pres. Machel was killed in a plane crash, Oct. 19, 1986. Frelimo formally abandoned Marxist-Leninism in 1989, and a new constitution, effective Nov. 30, 1990, established multiparty elections and a free-market economy.

A 1992 peace agreement ended 15 years of hostilities (up to 1 mil killed) between the government and the Mozambique National Resistance (Renamo), which became the main opposition party. Repatriation of 1.7 mil Mozambican refugees ended June 1995.

Devastating floods occurred Feb.-Mar. 2000 and Jan.-Mar. 2008.

Frelimo retained power under Pres. Joaquim Chissano (1986-2005) and Pres. Armando Guebuza (2005-15). Filipe Jacinto Nyusi of Frelimo won the Oct. 15, 2014, presidential election. Clashes began in 2013 between government forces and Renamo, which challenged 2014 election results. A truce beginning Dec. 2016 paved the way for May 2018 constitutional amendments decentralizing political power. Nyusi was reelected Oct. 15, 2019.

Natural gas reserves are estimated at more than 100 tril cu ft (third-largest in Africa). Beginning Oct. 2017, Islamist militants staged a series of attacks in the gas-rich Cabo Delgado region. Violence escalated in 2020. The UNHCR estimated that, by mid-2020, about 250,000 people in Cabo Delgado had been internally displaced since 2017.

Cyclone Idai, Mar. 2019, killed more than 600 and displaced hundreds of thousands.

In 2020, the COVID-19 pandemic caused more than 8,500 Mozambican cases and 59 deaths by Sept. 30.

Myanmar
(Burma)
Union of Myanmar

People: Population: 56,590,071 (25). **Age distrib.:** <15: 26.0%; 65+: 6.0%. **Growth:** 0.8%. **Migrants:** 0.1%. **Pop. density:** 224.3 per sq mi, 86.6 per sq km. **Urban:** 31.1%. **Ethnic groups:** Burman (Bamar) 68%, Shan 9%, Karen 7%, Rakhine 4%, Chinese 3%, Indian 2%, Mon 2%. **Languages:** Burmese (official). **Religions:** Buddhist (official) 76.6%, Christian 8%, ethnic religionist 7.9%, Muslim 3.6% (Sunni).

Geography: Total area: 261,228 sq mi, 676,578 sq km (39); **Land area:** 252,321 sq mi, 653,508 sq km. **Location:** Between S and SE Asia, on Bay of Bengal. Bangladesh, India on W; China, Laos, Thailand on E. **Topography:** Surrounding mountains on W, N, and E. Dense forests cover much of nation. N-S rivers provide habitable valleys, especially the Irrawaddy, navigable for 900 mi. Tropical monsoon climate. **Arable land:** 16.9%. **Capital:** Yangon (Rangoon), 5,331,800; Nay Pyi Taw (admin.), 593,596. **Cities:** Mandalay, 1,437,554.

Government: Type: Parliamentary republic. **Head of state and govt.:** Pres. Win Myint; b. 1951; in office: Mar. 30, 2018. **Local divisions:** 7 regions, 7 states, 1 union territory. **Defense budget:** $2.1 bil. **Active troops:** 406,000.

Economy: Industries: agric. proc.; wood/wood prods.; copper, tin, tungsten, iron; cement, constr. materials; pharmaceuticals; fertilizer. **Chief agric.:** rice, pulses, beans, sesame, groundnuts, sugarcane; fish. **Natural resources:** petroleum, timber, tin, antimony, zinc, copper, tungsten, lead, coal, marble, limestone, prec. stones, nat. gas, hydropower. **Water:** 21,885 cu m per capita. **Crude oil reserves:** 139 mil bbls. **Electricity prod.:** 21.8 bil kWh. **Labor force:** agric. 48.1%, industry 16.3%, services 35.6%. **Unemployment:** 1.7%.

Finance: Monetary unit: Kyat (MMK) (1,329.89 = $1 U.S.). **GDP:** $289.4 bil; **per capita GDP:** $5,355; **GDP growth:** 2.9%. **Imports:** $15.8 bil; China 31.4%, Singapore 15%, Thailand 11.1%, Saudi Arabia 7.5%, Malaysia 6.2%, Japan 6%, India 5.5%. **Exports:** $9.8 bil; China 36.5%, Thailand 21.8%, Japan 6.6%, Singapore 6.4%, India 5.9%. Trade figures are underestimates due to value of goods smuggled in from Thailand, China, Malaysia, India and smuggled out to Thailand, China, Bangladesh. **Tourism:** $2.5 bil. **Budget:** $11.2 bil. **Inflation:** 8.8%.

Transport: Railways: 3,126 mi. **Motor vehicles:** 0.8 per 1,000 pop. **Airports:** 36.

Communications: Telephone: 1 per 100 pop. **Mobile:** 113.8 per 100 pop. **Broadband:** 75.1 per 100 pop. **Internet:** 30.7%.

Health: Expend.: 4.6%. **Life expect.:** 67.7 male; 71.1 female. **Births:** 17 per 1,000 pop. **Deaths:** 7.2 per 1,000 pop. **Infant mortality:** 31.7 per 1,000 live births. **Undernourished:** 14.1%. **HIV:** 0.7%.

Education: Compulsory: ages 5-9. **Literacy:** 84.8%.

Embassy: 2300 S St. NW 20008; 332-3344.

Website: www.president-office.gov.mm

The Burmese arrived from Tibet before the 9th cent., displacing earlier cultures, and a Buddhist monarchy was established by the 11th cent. Burma was conquered by China's Mongol dynasty in

1272, then ruled by the Shan people as a Chinese tributary until the 16th cent. Britain subjugated Burma in three wars, 1824-84, and ruled the country as part of India until 1937, when Burma became self-governing. Full independence was achieved Jan. 4, 1948.

Gen. Ne Win dominated politics from 1962 to 1988, first as military ruler, then as constitutional president, advancing policies that increased economic socialization and international isolation. Ne Win resigned July 1988, following antigovernment riots. In Sept., the military seized power, under Gen. Saw Maung. In 1989 the country's name was changed to Myanmar.

Although the main opposition party won a decisive victory in 1990 multiparty elections, the military refused to surrender power. A key opposition leader, Aung San Suu Kyi, was held under house arrest, 1989-95, 2000-02, and 2003-10.

In late Sept. 2007, thousands of Buddhist monks led mass protests in Yangon; security forces cracked down by raiding monasteries, arresting monks, and firing on demonstrators. Cyclone Nargis, May 2-3, 2008, killed more than 138,000.

After the military dominated Nov. 2010 parliamentary elections, the ruling council was dissolved and an initially nominal civilian government returned, Mar. 30, 2011. Suu Kyi's National League for Democracy (NLD) won 43 of 45 parliamentary seats in an Apr. 1, 2012, election, and Suu Kyi traveled to Oslo, Norway, to accept the Nobel Peace Prize (awarded in 1991). The NLD won Nov. 8, 2015, parliamentary elections. NLD candidates were elected president by the parliament, 2016 and 2018. Suu Kyi, constitutionally barred from the presidency, assumed the newly created post of state counsellor, Apr. 6, 2016, becoming the country's de facto leader.

Following the 2011 breakdown of a cease-fire, fighting resumed between government forces and rebels in northern Kachin state.

Violence against Rohingya Muslims, in Rakhine state in the W, intensified beginning in 2012. Almost all of Myanmar's Rohingya are not recognized as citizens by the government. Almost 100,000 Rohingya fled by boat, 2014-15, seeking asylum. Attacks by the military beginning in Oct. 2016 left hundreds of civilians dead and caused about 75,000 Rohingya to flee to Bangladesh by early 2017. New military and vigilante attacks on Rohingya in which at least 10,000 were killed led almost three-quarters of a million Rohingya to flee to Bangladesh beginning in Aug. 2017. A UN panel recommended, Aug. 27, 2018, that Myanmar military leaders face trial for genocide. A UN official reported, July 2019, that about 128,000 Rohingya in Myanmar were confined to "concentration camps." As of Aug. 31, 2020, Bangladesh hosted more than 860,000 Rohingya refugees. A UN official, Apr. 2020, accused the military of atrocities against Buddhist civilians in Rakhine as it intensified its fight against Arakan Army rebels.

The 2020 COVID-19 pandemic caused 12,425 cases and 284 deaths in Myanmar by Sept. 30.

Namibia
Republic of Namibia

People: Population: 2,630,073 (139). **Age distrib.:** <15: 35.7%; 65+: 3.9%. **Growth:** 1.8%. **Migrants:** 4.3%. **Pop. density:** 8.3 per sq mi, 3.2 per sq km. **Urban:** 52.0%. **Ethnic groups:** Ovambo 50%, Kavangos 9%, Herero 7%, Damara 7%, European and African ancestry 6.5%, European 6%, Nama 5%, Caprivian 4%, San 3%. **Languages:** Oshiwambo langs., Nama/Damara, Kavango langs., Afrikaans (common), Herero langs., Zambezi langs., English (official). **Religions:** Christian 91.4% (Protestant 64.1%, Catholic 17.6%), ethnic religionist 5.2%.

Geography: Total area: 318,261 sq mi, 824,292 sq km (33). **Land area:** 317,874 sq mi, 823,290 sq km. **Location:** Southern Africa on Atlantic coast. Angola on N; Botswana, Zambia on E; South Africa on S. **Topography:** Three distinct regions incl. Namib Desert along the Atlantic, a mountainous central plateau with woodland savanna, and Kalahari Desert in E. True forests found in NE. Four rivers but little other surface water. **Arable land:** 1.0%. **Capital:** Windhoek, 431,171.

Government: Type: Presidential republic. **Head of state and govt.:** Pres. Hage Geingob; b. 1941; in office: Mar. 21, 2015. **Local divisions:** 14 regions. **Defense budget:** $422 mil. **Active troops:** 9,900.

Economy: Industries: meatpacking, fish proc., dairy prods., pasta, beverages, mining. **Chief agric.:** millet, sorghum, peanuts, grapes; livestock; fish. **Natural resources:** diamonds, copper, uranium, gold, silver, lead, tin, lithium, cadmium, tungsten, zinc, salt, hydropower, fish. **Water:** 15,750 cu m per capita. **Electricity prod.:** 1.8 bil kWh. **Labor force:** agric. 21.8%, industry 16.4%, services 61.8%. **Unemployment:** 20.6%.

Finance: Monetary unit: Dollar (NAD) (16.57 = $1 U.S.). **GDP:** $25.0 bil; **per capita GDP:** $10,037; **GDP growth:** –1.1%. **Imports:** $5.4 bil; South Africa 61.4%. **Exports:** $4 bil; South Africa 27.1%, Botswana 14.9%, Switzerland 12%, Zambia 5.7%. **Tourism:** $350 mil. **Budget:** $5.0 bil. **Inflation:** 3.7%.

Transport: Railways: 1,633 mi. **Motor vehicles:** 120.8 per 1,000 pop. **Airports:** 19.

Communications: Telephone: 6.9 per 100 pop. **Mobile:** 112.7 per 100 pop. **Broadband:** 59.3 per 100 pop. **Internet:** 51%.

Health: Expend.: 8.6%. **Life expect.:** 63.3 male; 67.3 female. **Births:** 25.7 per 1,000 pop. **Deaths:** 7.3 per 1,000 pop. **Infant mortality:** 31.4 per 1,000 live births. **Undernourished:** 14.7%. **HIV:** 11.5%.

Education: Compulsory: ages 7-13. **Literacy:** 95.2%.
Embassy: 1605 New Hampshire Ave. NW 20009; 986-0540.
Website: www.gov.na

Namibia was declared a German protectorate in 1890 and officially called South-West Africa. German troops putting down a rebellion killed tens of thousands of Herero and Nama people, 1904-08. South Africa seized the territory in 1915 during WWI. In 1966, the Marxist South-West Africa People's Organization (SWAPO) launched a guerrilla war for independence, aided by Angola and Cuba. The UN General Assembly named the area Namibia in 1968.

South Africa, Angola, and Cuba signed a U.S.-mediated agreement Dec. 22, 1988, to end South African administration of Namibia. A constitution providing for multiparty government was adopted Feb. 9, 1990, and Namibia gained independence Mar. 21.

Walvis Bay, the principal deepwater port, was returned to Namibia by South Africa in 1994.

SWAPO, the leading political group since independence, won Nov. 2019 presidential and parliamentary elections but saw its vote decline amid a corruption scandal and a slumping economy.

In 2020, the COVID-19 pandemic caused 11,140 cases and 121 deaths in Namibia as of Sept. 30.

Nauru
Republic of Nauru

People: Population: 9,785 (195). **Age distrib.:** <15: 30.9%; 65+: 3.5%. **Growth:** 0.5%. **Migrants:** 19.7%. **Pop. density:** 1,206.8 per sq mi, 466.0 per sq km. **Urban:** 100.0%. **Ethnic groups:** Nauruan 88.9%, part Nauruan 6.6%, I-Kiribati 2%. **Languages:** Nauruan (official), English (used in govt. and commerce). **Religions:** Christian 74% (Protestant 43.3%, Catholic 24.5%), Chinese folk-religionist 10.7%, Baha'i 9.4%, agnostic 4.4%.

Geography: Total area: 8.1 sq mi, 21 sq km (194); **Land area:** 8.1 sq mi, 21 sq km. **Location:** In W Pacific O. just S of equator. Nearest neighbor is Kiribati to E. **Topography:** Mostly a plateau bearing high-grade phosphate deposits, surrounded by a sandy shore and coral reef in concentric rings. **Arable land:** 0%. **Capital:** None official; govt. offices in Yaren district.

Government: Type: Parliamentary republic. **Head of state and govt.:** Pres. Lionel Aingimea; in office: Aug. 27, 2019. **Local divisions:** 14 districts. **Defense budget/active troops:** NA.

Economy: Industries: phosphate mining, offshore banking, coconut prods. **Chief agric.:** coconuts. **Natural resources:** phosphates, fish. **Water:** NA. **Electricity prod.:** 25 mil kWH. **Labor force:** agric. 2.7%, industry 24.9%, services 68.6%. **Unemployment:** NA.

Finance: Monetary unit: Australian Dollar (AUD) (1.37 = $1 U.S.). **GDP:** $152.0 mil; **per capita GDP:** $12,080; **GDP growth:** 0.0%. **Imports** (2016): $64.9 mil; Australia 67.5%, Fiji 9.2%, India 8.1%, Singapore 5.4%. **Exports** (2013): $125 mil; Nigeria 38.6%, Japan 16.6%, Australia 15.9%, South Korea 13.7%, New Zealand 5.7%. **Budget:** $113.4 mil. **Inflation** (2016-17): 5.1%.

Transport: Airports: 1.

Communications: Telephone (2009): 19.1 per 100 pop. **Mobile** (2017): 94.6 per 100 pop. **Broadband:** 35.2 per 100 pop. **Internet:** 57%.

Health: Expend.: 11.0%. **Life expect.:** 64.3 male; 71.9 female. **Births:** 21.9 per 1,000 pop. **Deaths:** 6 per 1,000 pop. **Infant mortality:** 7.4 per 1,000 live births. **Undernourished:** NA. **HIV:** NA.

Education: Compulsory: ages 4-17. **Literacy:** NA.
Permanent UN mission: 801 2nd Ave., 3rd Fl., New York, NY 10017; (212) 937-0074.
Website: www.naurugov.nr

The British reached the island in 1798, but it was annexed by the German Empire in 1886. After WWI, Australia administered Nauru under a League of Nations mandate. Japan occupied the island during WWII. In 1947 Nauru was made a UN trust territory, administered by Australia. It became an independent republic Jan. 31, 1968.

Phosphate exports provided Nauru with high per capita revenues. Phosphate reserves, however, are nearly depleted, and environmental damage from strip mining has been severe. Rising sea levels linked to global climate change have eroded Nauru's coastline.

A Nov. 20, 2012, Amnesty Intl. report found inhumane living conditions at Australia's detention center on Nauru for refugees and undocumented immigrants intercepted trying to enter Australia by boat. An Australian government report, released Mar. 20, 2015, confirmed abuse of detainees by staff. Under a 2016 Australia-U.S. resettlement agreement, several hundred refugees left Nauru for the U.S.; hundreds of others were returned to their country of origin. A Feb. 2019 Australian law allowing detainees to receive medical treatment in Australia was repealed in Dec. By 2020, more than 200 refugees remained in Nauru.

Nepal
Federal Democratic Republic of Nepal

People: Population: 30,327,877 (46). **Age distrib.:** <15: 28.4%; 65+: 5.7%. **Growth:** 0.9%. **Migrants:** 1.7%. **Pop. density:** 547.9 per sq mi, 211.6 per sq km. **Urban:** 20.6%. **Ethnic groups:** Chhetri 16.6%, Brahman-Hill 12.2%, Magar 7.1%, Tharu 6.6%,

Tamang 5.8%, Newar 5%, Kami 4.8%, Muslim 4.4%, Yadav 4%, Rai 2.3%, Gurung 2%. **Languages:** Nepali (official), Maithali, Bhojpuri, Tharu, Tamang, Newar, Bajjika, Magar, Doteli, Urdu. **Religions:** Hindu 65.8.% (Shaivites 30%, Vaishnavites 29%, Saktists 6%), ethnic religionist 12.8%, Buddhist 12.2%, Christian 4.3%, Muslim 4.3% (Sunni).

Geography: Total area: 56,827 sq mi, 147,181 sq km (93); **Land area:** 55,348 sq mi, 143,351 sq km. **Location:** Astride Himalaya Mts. China on N, India on S. **Topography:** The Himalayas across the N, hill country with fertile valleys across the center. S border region is part of flat, subtropical Ganges Plain. **Arable land:** 14.7%. **Capital:** Kathmandu, 1,423,515.

Government: Type: Federal parliamentary republic. **Head of state:** Pres. Bidhya Devi Bhandari; b. 1961; in office: Oct. 29, 2015. **Head of govt.:** Prime Min. KP Sharma Oli; b. 1952; in office: Feb. 15, 2018. **Local divisions:** 7 provinces. **Defense budget:** $387 mil. **Active troops:** 96,600.

Economy: Industries: tourism, carpets, textiles; small rice, jute, sugar, oilseed mills; cigarettes, cement, brick prod. **Chief agric.:** pulses, rice, corn, wheat, sugarcane, jute, root crops; milk, water buffalo meat. **Natural resources:** quartz, water, timber, hydropower, lignite, copper, cobalt, iron ore. **Water:** 7,173 cu m per capita. **Electricity prod.:** 4.7 bil kWh. **Labor force:** agric. 64.5%, industry 15.3%, services 20.2%. **Unemployment:** 1.5%.

Finance: Monetary unit: Rupee (NPR) (117.76 = $1 U.S.). **GDP:** $101.8 bil; **per capita GDP:** $3,558; **GDP growth:** 7.0%. **Imports:** $10 bil; India 70.2%, China 7.5%. **Exports:** $818.7 mil; India 53.1%, U.S. 11.8%, Turkey 7.2%. **Tourism:** $701 mil. **Budget:** $5.9 bil. **Inflation:** 5.6%.

Transport: Railways: 37 mi. **Airports:** 11.

Communications: Telephone: 2.8 per 100 pop. **Mobile:** 139.4 per 100 pop. **Broadband:** 52.4 per 100 pop. **Internet:** 34%.

Health: Expend.: 5.6%. **Life expect.:** 71.1 male; 72.6 female. **Births:** 18.1 per 1,000 pop. **Deaths:** 5.7 per 1,000 pop. **Infant mortality:** 25.1 per 1,000 live births. **Undernourished:** 6.1%. **HIV:** 0.1%.

Education: Compulsory: 4-12. **Literacy:** 92.4%.
Embassy: 2131 Leroy Pl. NW 20008; 667-4550.
Website: nepal.gov.np

Nepal was originally a group of principalities, with the Gurkha principality becoming dominant about 1769. In 1951 King Tribhubana Bir Bikram, member of the Shah family, ended the system of rule by hereditary premiers of the Ranas family, who had kept the kings virtual prisoners, and established a cabinet system of government. Polygamy, child marriage, and the caste system were officially abolished in 1963. Political parties were legalized in 1990.

Nine members of Nepal's royal family, including King Birendra, died in a June 1, 2001, massacre. The killings were blamed on a 10th family member, Crown Prince Dipendra, who reportedly killed himself, allowing Birendra's brother Gyanendra Bir Bikram Shah Dev to take the throne.

Citing the government's failure to stop a Maoist insurgency, King Gyanendra assumed absolute authority, Feb. 1, 2005, but after protests, he agreed, Apr. 24, 2006, to reinstate parliament. A new government signed a peace accord with Maoist rebels Nov. 21 ending a decade-long civil war that claimed 13,000 lives. Maoists joined an interim parliament and cabinet in 2007. A constituent assembly voted May 2008 to abolish the monarchy and make Nepal a republic. Maoist Baburam Bhattarai became prime min. Aug. 29, 2011, but Maoists suffered a defeat in Nov. 19, 2013, elections.

A new constitution, establishing a federal system with seven states, was adopted Sept. 20, 2015. Khadga Prasad Sharma Oli, leader of a non-Maoist Communist party, was elected prime min. by parliament, Oct. 11, 2015. Bidhya Devi Bhandari (of Oli's party) was elected by parliament, Oct. 28, 2015, as Nepal's first female president. Oli, facing a no-confidence vote, announced his resignation, July 23, 2016. After a coalition of Communist parties won late 2017 legislative elections, Oli returned as prime min., Feb. 15, 2018.

A magnitude 7.8 earthquake near Kathmandu, Apr. 25, 2015, killed more than 8,000 people and displaced 2.8 mil. Historic tem-ples and other sites were heavily damaged. A second quake, May 12, brought the combined death toll to over 8,600. Overcrowding contributed to at least 11 deaths (9 in Nepal) on Mt. Everest during the 2019 climbing season, one of the highest annual death tolls. The government canceled the 2020 climbing season in response to the COVID-19 pandemic, which devastated Nepal's important tourism industry. By Aug. 31, Nepal had more than 76,000 COVID-19 cases and almost 500 deaths.

Netherlands
Kingdom of the Netherlands

People: Population: 17,280,397 (67). **Age distrib.:** <15: 16.1%; 65+: 19.8%. **Growth:** 0.4%. **Migrants:** 13.4%. **Pop. density:** 1,320.5 per sq mi, 509.9 per sq km. **Urban:** 92.2%. **Ethnic groups:** Dutch 76.9%, EU 6.4%, Turkish 2.4%, Moroccan 2.3%, Indonesian 2.1%, German 2.1%, Surinamese 2%. **Languages:** Dutch (official). **Religions:** Christian 54.8% (Catholic 31.6%, Protestant 20.1%), agnostic 32.5%, Muslim 7.4% (Sunni), atheist 2.8%.

Geography: Total area: 16,040 sq mi, 41,543 sq km (131); **Land area:** 13,086 sq mi, 33,893 sq km. **Location:** NW Europe on North Sea. Germany on E, Belgium on S. **Topography:** Land is flat with avg. elevation of 37 ft above sea level; much of land reclaimed and protected by some 1,500 mi of dikes. **Arable land:** 30.8%. **Capital:** Amsterdam, 1,148,972; s-Gravenhage (The Hague) (seat), 697,564. **Cities:** Rotterdam, 1,010,026.

Government: Type: Parliamentary constitutional monarchy. **Head of state:** King Willem-Alexander; b. 1967; in office: Apr. 30, 2013. **Head of govt.:** Prime Min. Mark Rutte; b. 1967; in office: Oct. 14, 2010. **Local divisions:** 12 provinces. **Defense budget:** $12.1 bil. **Active troops:** 35,400.

Economy: Industries: agroindustries, metal/engineering prods., elec. machinery/equip., chemicals. **Chief agric.:** vegetables, ornamentals, dairy, poultry and livestock prods. **Natural resources:** nat. gas, petroleum, peat, limestone, salt, sand and gravel. **Water:** 5,342 cu m per capita. **Crude oil reserves:** 114.5 mil bbls. **Electricity prod.** (2018): 108 bil kWh. **Labor force:** agric. 2.0%, industry 15.8%, services 82.2%. **Unemployment:** 3.0%.

Finance: Monetary unit: Euro (EUR) (0.84 = $1 U.S.). **GDP:** $1.0 tril; **per capita GDP:** $59,687; **GDP growth:** 1.8%. **Imports:** $453.8 bil; China 16.4%, Germany 15.3%, Belgium 8.5%, U.S. 6.9%, UK 5.1%. **Exports:** $555.6 bil; Germany 24.2%, Belgium 10.7%, UK 8.8%, France 8.8%. **Tourism:** $18.5 bil. **Budget:** $352.4 bil. **Inflation:** 2.6%.

Transport: Railways: 1,900 mi. **Motor vehicles:** 580.2 per 1,000 pop. **Airports:** 23.

Communications: Telephone: 34.6 per 100 pop. **Mobile** (2017): 120.6 per 100 pop. **Broadband:** 90.8 per 100 pop. **Internet** (2018): 94.7%.

Health: Expend.: 10.1%. **Life expect.:** 79.5 male; 84.1 female. **Births:** 11 per 1,000 pop. **Deaths:** 9.2 per 1,000 pop. **Infant mortality:** 3.5 per 1,000 live births. **Undernourished:** <2.5%. **HIV:** 0.2%.

Education: Compulsory: ages 5-17. **Literacy:** 99%.
Embassy: 4200 Linnean Ave. NW 20008; 244-5300.
Website: www.government.nl

Julius Caesar conquered the region in 55 BCE, when it was inhabited by Celtic and Germanic tribes. After the empire of Charlemagne fell apart, the Netherlands (Holland, Belgium, Flanders) split among counts, dukes, and bishops, passed to Burgundy and thence to Spain. William the Silent, prince of Orange, led a confederation of the northern provinces, called Estates, in the Union of Utrecht, 1579; in 1581 they repudiated allegiance to Spain. The rise of the Dutch republic to naval, economic, and artistic eminence came in the 17th cent.

After a period of French hegemony, 1795-1813, the Congress of Vienna in 1815 formed a kingdom of the Netherlands, including Belgium, under William I. In 1830, Belgium seceded.

The Netherlands maintained its neutrality in WWI but was invaded during WWII and occupied by Germany, 1940-45. In 1949, after several years of fighting, the Netherlands granted independence to Indonesia.

The murder May 6, 2002, of right-wing populist leader Pim Fortuyn marked the first political assassination in modern Dutch history. On Apr. 30, 2009, an attempt to assassinate Queen Beatrix failed (but left 8 dead). Beatrix, 75, abdicated the throne to her son, Willem-Alexander, Apr. 30, 2013. A Malaysia Airlines flight from Amsterdam to Kuala Lumpur was shot down over eastern Ukraine, July 17, 2014; nearly 200 Dutch passport holders were among 298 killed. Prime Min. Mark Rutte's center-right People's Party won Mar. 15, 2017, parliamentary elections, holding off a challenge from the anti-Islamic, right-wing Freedom Party. Legislation in 2018 prohibited wearing face-covering garments such as the burqa in public facilities.

To combat the COVID-19 pandemic, the Netherlands instituted limited lockdown measures in Mar. 2020 (eased beginning in May). New cases rose again, July-Sept. As of Sept. 30, the country had more than 117,000 cases and almost 6,400 deaths. The important tourism industry was hard hit, both in the Netherlands itself and in its Caribbean dependencies.

Dutch Dependencies

Constitutional changes effective Oct. 10, 2010, dissolved the political entity known as the Netherlands Antilles. Curaçao (area 171 sq mi), an island near the coast of Venezuela, and Sint Maarten (13 sq mi), occupying the southern one-third of the island of St. Martin, SE of Puerto Rico, were elevated to the status of autonomous countries. Bonaire, Saba, and Sint Eustatius became special municipalities. Sint Maarten suffered extensive damage from Hurricane Luis, Sept. 1995, and Hurricane Irma, Sept. 2017. Pop. of Curaçao, 151,345 (2020 est.); that of its capital, Willemstad, 144,037 (2018 est.). Sint Maarten, pop. 43,847 (2020 est.); capital is Philipsburg. Principal industries: Curaçao, tourism, petroleum refining and transshipment, light mfg.; Sint Maarten, tourism, light industry. International tourism receipts were $593 mil (2018) for Curaçao, $682 mil (2019) for Sint Maarten. Per capita GDP of Sint Maarten was $32,256 (2017), Curaçao, $25,572 (2018). **Websites:** www.gobiernu.cw (Curaçao); www.sintmaartengov.org (Sint Maarten)

Aruba, about 26 mi west of Curaçao, was separated from the Netherlands Antilles on Jan. 1, 1986; it is an autonomous component of the Netherlands, with a status similar to Curaçao and Sint Maarten. Area: 69 sq mi; pop. (2019 est.) 118,013. Capital: Oranjestad; pop. (2018 est.) 29,877. Chief industries are tourism, petroleum transshipment facilities, banking. **Website:** www.kabga.aw

New Zealand

People: Population: 4,925,477 (125). **Age distrib.:** <15: 19.6%; 65+: 15.5%. **Growth:** 1.4%. **Migrants:** 22.3%. **Pop. density:** 48.2 per sq mi, 18.6 per sq km. **Urban:** 86.7%. **Ethnic groups:** European 64.1%, Maori 16.5%, Chinese 4.9%, Indian 4.7%, Samoan 3.9%, Tongan 1.8%, Cook Islands Maori 1.7%, English 1.5%, Filipino 1.5%, New Zealander 1%. Respondents could identify more than one ethnic group. **Languages:** English (de facto official), Maori (de jure official), Samoan. **Religions:** Christian 53.8% (Protestant 31.9%, Catholic 13.4%), agnostic 35.2%, Buddhist 3.5%.

Geography: Total area: 103,799 sq mi, 268,838 sq km (75); **Land area:** 102,138 sq mi, 264,537 sq km. **Location:** SW Pacific O. Nearest neighbors are Australia to W, Fiji and Tonga to N. **Topography:** Two main islands (North and South Isls.) are hilly and mountainous. The E coasts consist of fertile plains, incl. Canterbury Plains on South Isl. Volcanic plateau in center of North Isl. Glaciers and 15 peaks over 10,000 ft on South Isl. **Arable land:** 2.2%. **Capital:** Wellington, 414,818. **Cities:** Auckland, 1,606,564.

Government: Type: Parliamentary democracy under constitutional monarchy. **Head of state:** Queen Elizabeth II, rep. by Gov.-Gen. Patricia Lee Reddy; b. 1954; in office: Sept. 28, 2016. **Head of govt.:** Prime Min. Jacinda Ardern; b. 1980; in office: Oct. 26, 2017. **Local divisions:** 16 regions, 1 territory. **Defense budget:** $2.7 bil. **Active troops:** 9,400.

Economy: Industries: agric., forestry, fishing, logs and wood articles, mfg., mining, constr., financial services, real estate services, tourism. **Chief agric.:** dairy prods., sheep, beef, poultry, fruit, vegetables, wine, seafood, wheat, barley. **Natural resources:** nat. gas, iron ore, sand, coal, timber, hydropower, gold, limestone. **Water:** 69,486 cu m per capita. **Crude oil reserves:** 43.3 mil bbls. **Electricity prod.** (2018): 43.3 bil kWh. **Labor force:** agric. 5.6%, industry 19.4%, services 75.1%. **Unemployment:** 4.0%.

Finance: Monetary unit: Dollar (NZD) (1.49 = $1 U.S.). **GDP:** $216.1 bil; **per capita GDP:** $43,953; **GDP growth:** 2.2%. **Imports:** $39.7 bil; China 19%, Australia 12.1%, U.S. 10.5%, Japan 7.3%, Germany 5.3%. **Exports:** $37.4 bil; China 22.4%, Australia 16.4%, U.S. 9.9%, Japan 6.1%. **Tourism** (2018): $10.9 bil. **Budget:** $71.0 bil. **Inflation:** 1.6%.

Transport: Railways: 2,565 mi. **Motor vehicles:** 914.8 per 1,000 pop. **Airports:** 39.

Communications: Telephone: 37.1 per 100 pop. **Mobile:** 134.9 per 100 pop. **Broadband:** 101.6 per 100 pop. **Internet:** 90.8%.

Health: Expend.: 9.2%. **Life expect.:** 80.4 male; 84.0 female. **Births:** 12.8 per 1,000 pop. **Deaths:** 6.9 per 1,000 pop. **Infant mortality:** 3.5 per 1,000 live births. **Undernourished:** <2.5%. **HIV:** <0.1%.

Education: Compulsory: ages 6-15. **Literacy:** 99%.

Embassy: 37 Observatory Cir. NW 20008; 328-4800.

Website: www.govt.nz

New Zealand comprises North Island, 43,911 sq mi; South Island, 58,084 sq mi; Stewart Island, 649 sq mi; Chatham Isls., 373 sq mi; and several groups of smaller islands. The Maori, a Polynesian group from the eastern Pacific, reached New Zealand before and during the 14th cent. The first European to sight New Zealand was Dutch navigator Abel Janszoon Tasman. The Maori refused to allow him to land. British Capt. James Cook explored the coasts, 1769-70.

British sovereignty was proclaimed and Maori land rights were recognized in the Treaty of Waitangi, 1840, with organized settlement beginning the same year. Representative institutions were granted in 1853. The Maori Wars, or New Zealand Wars, ended in 1870 with British victory. The colony became a dominion in 1907 and gained full independence in 1947.

A progressive tradition in politics began in the 19th cent. Much of the nation's economy has been deregulated since the 1980s. Jenny Shipley of the National Party became the nation's first female prime min., Dec. 8, 1997. The Labour Party won Nov. 27, 1999, elections.

A measure establishing a supreme court and ending appeals to the UK Privy Council passed Oct. 14, 2003. A major settlement of Maori land claims was signed June 25, 2008.

A Christchurch earthquake, Feb. 22, 2011, killed 181 people and caused extensive damage. Parliament legalized same-sex marriage Apr. 17, 2013.

After the National Party (in office since 2008) fell short of a majority in Sept. 23, 2017, elections, Labour Party head Jacinda Ardern formed a coalition government.

A gunman killed 51 in attacks at two Christchurch-area mosques, Mar. 15, 2019. Parliament, Apr. 10, outlawed many types of semi-automatic weapons. 2020 legislation legalized most abortions.

Affected by the 2020 COVID-19 pandemic, New Zealand instituted strict lockdown measures, Mar. 25. With new cases near zero, the government began easing restrictions Apr. 28. There was a spike in new cases in Aug. By Sept. 30, the country had 1,480 cases; 25 people had died. Scheduled Sept. elections were delayed until Oct. 17.

In 1965, the **Cook Islands** (area: 91 sq mi; 2019 est. pop.: 8,799), halfway between New Zealand and Hawaii, became self-governing. New Zealand retains responsibility for defense and foreign affairs. **Niue** (area: 100 sq mi; 2017 est. pop.: 1,618) attained the same status in 1974; it lies about 675 mi W of Cook Isls. **Tokelau** (area: 4.6 sq mi; 2016 est. pop.: 1,499) comprises three atolls 300 mi N of Samoa. Referendums in 2006 and 2007 on Tokelau self-government failed to gain the required two-third majority. **Ross Dependency**, administered by New Zealand since 1923, comprises 160,000 sq mi of Antarctic territory. **Websites:** www.cookislands.gov.ck; www.gov.nu; www.tokelau.org.nz

Nicaragua
Republic of Nicaragua

People: Population: 6,203,441 (110). **Age distrib.:** <15: 25.6%; 65+: 5.8%. **Growth:** 1.0%. **Migrants:** 0.6%. **Pop. density:** 133.9 per sq mi, 51.7 per sq km. **Urban:** 59.0%. **Ethnic groups:** mestizo (mixed Amerindian/white) 69%, white 17%, Black 9%, Amerindian 5%. **Languages:** Spanish (official), Miskito, Mestizo on Carib. coast. **Religions:** Christian 94.7% (Catholic 69.3%, Protestant 19.1%).

Geography: Total area: 50,336 sq mi, 130,370 sq km (96); **Land area:** 46,328 sq mi, 119,990 sq km. **Location:** Central America. Honduras on N, Costa Rica on S. **Topography:** Both Caribbean and Pacific coasts are over 200 mi long. Cordillera Mts., with many volcanic peaks, run NW-SE through middle of country. **Arable land:** 12.5%. **Capital:** Managua, 1,063,698.

Government: Type: Presidential republic. **Head of state and govt.:** Pres. Daniel Ortega Saavedra; b. 1945; in office: Jan. 10, 2007. **Local divisions:** 15 departments, 2 autonomous regions. **Defense budget:** $78 mil. **Active troops:** 12,000.

Economy: Industries: food proc., chemicals, machinery and metal prods., knit and woven apparel, petroleum refining and distrib. **Chief agric.:** coffee, bananas, sugarcane, rice, corn, tobacco, cotton, sesame, soya, beans, beef, veal, pork, poultry, dairy prods., shrimp, lobsters, peanuts. **Natural resources:** gold, silver, copper, tungsten, lead, zinc, timber, fish. **Water:** 26,455 cu m per capita. **Electricity prod.:** 4.4 bil kWh. **Labor force:** agric. 30.6%, industry 15.6%, services 53.8%. **Unemployment:** 7.4%.

Finance: Monetary unit: Cordoba (NIO) (34.76 = $1 U.S.). **GDP:** $36.9 bil; **per capita GDP:** $5,631; **GDP growth:** −3.9%. **Imports:** $6.6 bil; U.S. 20.8%, China 14.3%, Mexico 11.1%, Costa Rica 7.9%, Guatemala 7%, El Salvador 5.6%. **Exports:** $3.8 bil; U.S. 44.2%, El Salvador 6.4%, Venezuela 5.5%, Costa Rica 5.5%. **Tourism:** $544 mil. **Budget:** $4.2 bil. **Inflation:** 5.4%.

Transport: Motor vehicles: 56.3 per 1,000 pop. **Airports:** 12.

Communications: Telephone: 5 per 100 pop. **Mobile:** 115.1 per 100 pop. **Broadband:** 30.4 per 100 pop. **Internet:** 27.9%.

Health: Expend.: 8.6%. **Life expect.:** 72.0 male; 76.6 female. **Births:** 17.1 per 1,000 pop. **Deaths:** 5.2 per 1,000 pop. **Infant mortality:** 16.5 per 1,000 live births. **Undernourished:** 17.2%. **HIV:** 0.2%.

Education: Compulsory: ages 5-11. **Literacy:** 91.6%.

Embassy: 1627 New Hampshire Ave. NW 20009; 939-6570.

Website: www.asamblea.gob.ni

Nicaragua, inhabited by various Indian tribes, was conquered by Spain in 1552. After gaining independence from Spain, 1821, Nicaragua was united for a short period with Mexico, then with the United Provinces of Central America, before becoming an independent republic, 1838. U.S. Marines occupied the country at times in the early 20th cent., the last time from 1926 to 1933.

Gen. Anastasio Somoza Debayle held the presidency 1967-72, 1974-79. Martial law was imposed in Dec. 1974, after officials were kidnapped by Marxist Sandinista guerrillas. Nationwide strikes touched off a civil war, 1978, which ended when Somoza fled Nicaragua and the Sandinistas took control of Managua, July 1979. Somoza was assassinated in Paraguay, Sept. 17, 1980.

Relations with the U.S. were strained as a result of Nicaragua's aid to leftist guerrillas in El Salvador and U.S. backing of anti-Sandinista contra guerrilla groups, which fought the Sandinista government throughout the 1980s. In 1985 the U.S. House rejected Pres. Ronald Reagan's request for military aid to the contras. The U.S. later secretly diverted funds to the contras.

In a stunning upset, Violeta Barrios de Chamorro defeated Sandinista leader Daniel Ortega Saavedra in national elections, Feb. 25, 1990. Conservative candidates won the 1996 and 2001 presidential elections. Drought and a drop in coffee prices precipitated an economic crisis in 2001.

Ortega won the Nov. 2006 presidential election and was reelected Nov. 6, 2011. After presidential term limits were removed (2014), Ortega won the Nov. 6, 2016, presidential election; Rosario Murillo Zambrana, Ortega's wife, was elected vice president.

Months of protests, beginning Apr. 2018, against the Ortega government's policies and authoritarian rule resulted in hundreds of deaths, most at the hands of security forces or allied paramilitary groups. Hundreds were arrested, some reportedly tortured in detention. By early 2020, more than 100,000 Nicaraguans had fled the country. June 8, 2019, legislation amnestied police and other forces for their acts against demonstrators.

The 2020 COVID-19 pandemic caused more than 4,100 cases and over 150 deaths as of Sept. 30. The government did not adopt lockdown measures, and critics claimed the true numbers were significantly higher.

Niger
Republic of Niger

People: Population: 22,772,361 (58). **Age distrib.:** <15: 50.6%; 65+: 2.7%. **Growth:** 3.7%. **Migrants:** 1.3%. **Pop. density:** 46.6 per sq mi, 18.0 per sq km. **Urban:** 16.6%. **Ethnic groups:** Hausa 53.1%, Zarma/Songhai 21.2%, Tuareg 11%, Fulani (Peuhl) 6.5%, Kanuri 5.9%. **Languages:** French (official), Hausa, Djerma. **Religions:** Muslim 96.6% (Sunni), ethnic religionist 3%.

Geography: Total area: 489,191 sq mi, 1,267,000 sq km (21); **Land area:** 489,076 sq mi, 1,266,700 sq km. **Location:** Interior of N Africa. Libya, Algeria on N; Mali, Burkina Faso on W; Benin, Nigeria on S; Chad on E. **Topography:** Mostly arid desert and mountains. Narrow savanna in S and Niger R. basin in the SW. **Arable land:** 14.0%. **Capital:** Niamey, 1,291,848.

Government: Type: Semi-presidential republic. **Head of state:** Pres. Mahamadou Issoufou; b. 1952; in office: Apr. 7, 2011. **Head of govt.:** Prime Min. Brigi Rafini; b. 1953; in office: Apr. 7, 2011. **Local divisions:** 7 regions, 1 capital district. **Defense budget:** $176 mil. **Active troops:** 5,300.

Economy: Industries: uranium mining, petroleum, cement, brick, soap, textiles, food proc., chemicals, slaughterhouses. **Chief agric.:** cowpeas, cotton, peanuts, millet, sorghum, cassava, rice; cattle, sheep, goats, camels, donkeys. **Natural resources:** uranium, coal, iron ore, tin, phosphates, gold, molybdenum, gypsum, salt, petroleum. **Water:** 1,585 cu m per capita. **Crude oil reserves:** 150 mil bbls. **Electricity prod.:** 529 mil kWh. **Labor force:** agric. 74.9%, industry 7.2%, services 18.0%. **Unemployment:** 0.5%.

Finance: Monetary unit: CFA Franc (XOF) (553.52 = $1 U.S.). **GDP:** $29.6 bil; **per capita GDP:** $1,270; **GDP growth:** 5.8%. **Imports:** $1.8 bil; France 28.8%, China 14.4%, Malaysia 5.7%, Nigeria 5.4%, Thailand 5.3%, U.S. 5.1%. **Exports:** $4.1 bil; France 30.2%, Thailand 18.3%, Malaysia 9.9%, Nigeria 8.3%, Mali 5%. **Tourism:** $98 mil. **Budget:** $2.2 bil. **Inflation:** −2.5%.

Transport: Motor vehicles: 13.6 per 1,000 pop. **Airports:** 10. **Communications: Telephone** (2017): 0.5 per 100 pop. **Mobile** (2017): 40.6 per 100 pop. **Broadband:** 4 per 100 pop. **Internet** (2018): 5.3%.

Health: Expend.: 7.7%. **Life expect.:** 57.8 male; 60.8 female. **Births:** 47.5 per 1,000 pop. **Deaths:** 10.2 per 1,000 pop. **Infant mortality:** 67.7 per 1,000 live births. **Undernourished:** NA. **HIV:** 0.2%.

Education: Compulsory: NA. **Literacy:** 19.1%.
Embassy: 2204 R St. NW 20008; 483-4224.
Website: www.gouv.ne

Niger was part of ancient and medieval African empires. European explorers reached the area in the late 18th cent. The French colony of Niger was established 1900-22 after the defeat of Tuareg fighters, who had invaded the area from the north a century before. The country became independent Aug. 3, 1960.

In 1993, Niger held its first free and open elections since independence. A peace accord Apr. 24, 1995, ended a Tuareg rebellion that began in 1990. After a coup, Jan. 27, 1996, the military retained control. On Apr. 9, 1999, Gen. Ibrahim Bare Mainassara, president since 1996, was assassinated. Oct.-Nov. elections, under a new constitution, restored civilian rule.

Popularly elected in 1999 and 2004, Pres. Mamadou Tandja invoked emergency powers in 2009 to remain in office. He was overthrown by a military junta Feb. 18, 2010. Civilian rule returned following 2011 elections. Pres. Mahamadou Issoufou won reelection in 2016.

Beginning in Feb. 2015, the Nigeria-based Islamist extremist group Boko Haram staged attacks in southern Niger. Niger's parliament approved, Feb. 9, sending troops into Nigeria to fight Boko Haram. Niger joined 4 other regional nations in establishing, July 2, 2017, the G5 Sahel Cross-Border Joint Force to combat Islamist terrorism and other crime. An attack in W Niger by ISIS-affiliated militants, Oct. 4, 2017, killed 4 Niger soldiers, an interpreter, and 4 U.S. special operations troops. More than 170 Niger troops died in Islamist attacks, Dec. 2019-Jan. 2020. Niger said 120 extremist fighters were killed in a Feb. operation. As of Aug. 31, 2020, Niger had more than 265,000 internally displaced persons and hosted more than 167,000 refugees from Nigeria, as well as over 59,000 from Mali.

The 2020 COVID-19 pandemic caused almost 1,200 Nigerien cases and 69 deaths by Sept. 30.

Nigeria
Federal Republic of Nigeria

People: Population: 214,028,302 (6). **Age distrib.:** <15: 41.7%; 65+: 3.3%. **Growth:** 2.5%. **Migrants:** 0.6%. **Pop. density:** 608.6 per sq mi, 235.0 per sq km. **Urban:** 52.0%. **Ethnic groups:** Hausa 30%, Yoruba 15.5%, Igbo (Ibo) 15.2%, Fulani 6%, Tiv 2.4%, Kanuri/Beriberi 2.4%, Ibibio 1.8%, Ijaw/Izon 1.8%. **Languages:** English (official), Hausa, Yoruba, Igbo (Ibo), Fulani, 500+ Indig-

enous langs. **Religions:** Muslim 46.3% (Sunni), Christian 46.2% (Protestant 24.8%, independent 11.2%, Catholic 10.2%), ethnic religionist 7.1%.

Geography: Total area: 356,669 sq mi, 923,768 sq km (31); **Land area:** 351,649 sq mi, 910,768 sq km. **Location:** S coast of W Africa. Benin on W, Niger on N, Chad and Cameroon on E. **Topography:** 4 E-W regions: a coastal mangrove swamp, a tropical rain forest, a plateau of savanna and open woodland, and semi-desert in N. **Arable land:** 37.3%. **Capital:** Abuja, 3,277,740. **Cities:** Lagos, 14,368,332; Kano, 3,999,050; Ibadan, 3,551,961; Port Harcourt, 3,020,232.

Government: Type: Federal presidential republic. **Head of state and govt.:** Pres. Muhammadu Buhari; b. 1942; in office: May 29, 2015. **Local divisions:** 36 states, 1 territory. **Defense budget:** $1.8 bil. **Active troops:** 143,000.

Economy: Industries: crude oil, coal, tin, columbite; rubber prods., wood; hides/skins, textiles, cement and other constr. materials. **Chief agric.:** cocoa, peanuts, cotton, palm oil, corn, rice, sorghum, millet, cassava, yams, rubber; cattle, sheep; fish. **Natural resources:** nat. gas, petroleum, tin, iron ore, coal, limestone, niobium, lead, zinc. **Water:** 1,499 cu m per capita. **Crude oil reserves:** 37.0 bil bbls. **Electricity prod.:** 30.6 bil kWh. **Labor force:** agric. 34.7%, industry 12.2%, services 53.1%. **Unemployment:** 8.0%.

Finance: Monetary unit: Naira (NGN) (380.92 = $1 U.S.). **GDP:** $1.1 tril; **per capita GDP:** $5,348; **GDP growth:** 2.2%. **Imports:** $32.7 bil; China 21.1%, Belgium 8.7%, U.S. 8.4%, South Korea 7.5%. **Exports:** $1.1 bil; India 30.6%, U.S. 12.1%, Spain 6.6%, China 5.6%, France 5.5%. **Tourism:** $1.4 bil. **Budget:** $19.5 bil. **Inflation:** 11.4%.

Transport: Railways: 2,360 mi. **Motor vehicles:** 8.4 per 1,000 pop. **Airports:** 40.
Communications: Telephone: 0.1 per 100 pop. **Mobile:** 88.2 per 100 pop. **Broadband:** 19.9 per 100 pop. **Internet:** 42%.

Health: Expend.: 3.8%. **Life expect.:** 58.6 male; 62.3 female. **Births:** 34.6 per 1,000 pop. **Deaths:** 9.1 per 1,000 pop. **Infant mortality:** 59.8 per 1,000 live births. **Undernourished:** 12.6%. **HIV:** 1.3%.

Education: Compulsory: ages 6-14. **Literacy:** 75.0%.
Embassy: 3519 International Ct. NW 20008; 986-8400.
Website: www.nigeria.gov.ng

Early cultures in Nigeria date back to at least 700 BCE. From the 12th to the 14th cent., more advanced cultures developed in the Yoruba area, at Ife, and in the north, where Muslim influence prevailed. Portuguese and British slavers appeared in the 15th-16th cent. Britain seized Lagos, 1861, and gradually extended control inland until 1900. Nigeria became independent Oct. 1, 1960, and a republic Oct. 1, 1963.

On May 30, 1967, the Eastern Region seceded, proclaiming itself the Republic of Biafra, plunging the country into civil war. Casualties were estimated at over 1 mil, including many Biafrans (mostly Igbos) who died of starvation despite international relief efforts. The secessionists capitulated Jan. 12, 1970.

Nigeria emerged as one of the world's leading oil exporters in the 1970s, but much of the revenue has been squandered through corruption and mismanagement. Oil spills have polluted much of the Niger Delta region.

After 13 years of military rule, the nation made a peaceful return to civilian government Oct. 1979. Military rule resumed Dec. 31, 1983. An interim civilian government (in office Aug. 26, 1993) was ousted Nov. 17, 1993, in a coup led by Gen. Sani Abacha. His brutal rule ended June 8, 1998, when he died of an apparent heart attack. Olusegun Obasanjo won a presidential election Feb. 27, 1999, to lead Nigeria's first civilian government in 15 years.

The imposition of strict Islamic law in northern states led to clashes, Jan.-Mar. 2000, in which at least 800 people died. Fighting between Muslims and Christians Sept. 7-12 and Oct. 13-14, 2001, claimed an est. 600 lives. Christian militia members massacred about 630 Muslims at Yelwa, central Nigeria, May 2, 2004. Vice Pres. Goodluck Jonathan, a southern Christian, became president in 2010 when his predecessor died. Jonathan won reelection Apr. 16, 2011, over Muhammadu Buhari, a northern-based Muslim.

Boko Haram, a radical Islamist group based in NE Nigeria that seeks to establish an Islamist state, began terrorist attacks in 2009 against government forces and civilian targets. The group gained control of a large area in the NE and terrorist attacks escalated, 2013-15. In a message released Mar. 7, 2015, the group claimed allegiance to ISIS (Boko Haram split, in 2016, into ISIS-affiliated and non-affiliated factions). Boko Haram also staged attacks in neighboring Chad, Cameroon, and Niger; troops from those countries fought Boko Haram in Nigeria beginning in 2015. Vowing tougher action against Boko Haram, Buhari defeated Jonathan in the Mar. 28-29, 2015, presidential election. Subsequent government offensives retook a significant portion of the territory Boko Haram had seized, but in 2016-20, Boko Haram forces, including the ISIS-affiliated militants, continued to control some areas of NE Nigeria and stage deadly attacks against civilians and security forces. Boko Haram kidnapped thousands of Nigerians and foreigners, including 276 girls from a boarding school in Chibok, Apr. 14, 2014; after a series of escapes, rescues, and releases, 112 girls remained in custody or unaccounted for six years later.

Amid ongoing Islamist, as well as other religious and ethnic, violence, Buhari won reelection, Feb. 23, 2019. The Council on Foreign Relations estimated that, by Aug. 1, 2020, more than 39,000 people had been killed as a result of Boko Haram attacks, clashes with security forces, and related actions. The UNHCR estimated that, as of Aug. 31, 2020, more than 299,000 Nigerian refugees were in Niger, Cameroon, or Chad; over 2.8 mil Nigerians were internally displaced.

As the 2020 COVID-19 pandemic spread through Africa, Nigeria recorded more than 58,600 cases and over 1,100 deaths as of Sept. 30.

North Macedonia
Republic of North Macedonia

(Under the terms of the Prespa Agreement, in force as of Feb. 12, 2019, Macedonia and Greece agreed to recognize the former under the name North Macedonia, ending a longstanding regional dispute.)

People: Population: 2,125,971 (144). **Age distrib.:** <15: 16.2%; 65+: 14.2%. **Growth:** 0.1%. **Migrants:** 6.3%. **Pop. density:** 216.5 per sq mi, 83.6 per sq km. **Urban:** 58.5%. **Ethnic groups:** Macedonian 64.2%, Albanian 25.2%, Turkish 3.9%, Romani 2.7%. **Languages:** Macedonian (official), Albanian, Turkish. **Religions:** Christian 64% (Orthodox [official] 62.2%), Muslim 32.7% (Sunni), agnostic 2.9%.

Geography: Total area: 9,928 sq mi, 25,713 sq km (146); **Land area:** 9,820 sq mi, 25,433 sq km. **Location:** SE Europe. Bulgaria on E, Greece on S, Albania on W, Serbia on N. **Topography:** Landlocked, mostly mountainous with deep river valleys, 3 large lakes. Country is bisected by Vardar R. **Arable land:** 16.5%. **Capital:** Skopje, 595,275.

Government: Type: Parliamentary republic. **Head of state:** Pres. Stevo Pendarovski; b. 1963; in office: May 12, 2019. **Head of govt.:** Prime Min. Zoran Zaev; b. 1974; in office: Aug. 30, 2020. **Local divisions:** 70 municipalities, 1 city. **Defense budget:** $152 mil. **Active troops:** 8,000.

Economy: Industries: food proc., beverages, textiles, chemicals, iron, steel, cement, energy, pharmaceuticals. **Chief agric.:** grapes, tobacco, vegetables, fruits; milk, eggs. **Natural resources:** iron ore, copper, lead, zinc, chromite, manganese, nickel, tungsten, gold, silver, asbestos, gypsum, timber. **Water:** 3,072 cu m per capita. **Electricity prod.:** 5.3 bil kWh. **Labor force:** agric. 15.1%, industry 31.4%, services 53.5%. **Unemployment:** 16.4%.

Finance: Monetary unit: Denar (MKD) (52.07 = $1 U.S.). **GDP:** $37.1 bil; **per capita GDP:** $17,815; **GDP growth:** 3.6%. **Imports:** $6.6 bil; Germany 11.9%, UK 10%, Greece 8%, Serbia 7.1%, China 5.9%, Italy 5.5%. **Exports:** $4.6 bil; Germany 46.7%, Bulgaria 6.1%. **Tourism:** $396 mil. **Budget:** $3.6 bil. **Inflation:** 0.8%.

Transport: Railways: 575 mi. **Airports:** 8.

Communications: Telephone: 18 per 100 pop. **Mobile:** 98.5 per 100 pop. **Broadband:** 63.9 per 100 pop. **Internet** (2018): 79.2%.

Health: Expend.: 6.1%. **Life expect.:** 74.2 male; 78.6 female. **Births:** 10.7 per 1,000 pop. **Deaths:** 9.6 per 1,000 pop. **Infant mortality:** 7.4 per 1,000 live births. **Undernourished:** 3.1%. **HIV** (2018): <0.1%.

Education: Compulsory: ages 6-18. **Literacy:** 97%.
Embassy: 2129 Wyoming Ave. NW 20008; 667-0501.
Website: www.vlada.mk

Muslim Turks ruled present-day North Macedonia from 1389 to 1912. In 1913, the area was incorporated into Serbia, which in 1918 became part of the Kingdom of Serbs, Croats, and Slovenes (later Yugoslavia). In 1946, the area, then called Macedonia, became a constituent republic of Yugoslavia.

Macedonia declared its independence Sept. 8, 1991, and was admitted to the UN in 1993. For decades, Greece, objecting to Macedonia's use of what it considered a Hellenic name, blocked Macedonia's bids to join NATO and the EU.

Ethnic Albanian guerrillas launched an offensive Mar. 2001 in NW Macedonia. An accord signed Aug. 13 paved the way for a NATO peacekeeping force. A law broadening the rights of ethnic Albanians was enacted Jan. 2002.

In 2015 and early 2016, tens of thousands of migrants from the Middle East and SW Asia who landed in Greece tried to cross Macedonia on their way to N Europe. After building border fencing and taking other steps to restrict access, Macedonia announced, Mar. 9, 2016, that its border with Greece was closed to migrants.

After a government wiretapping and corruption scandal, conservative Prime Min. Nikola Gruevski resigned Jan. 15, 2016. Following parliamentary elections in Dec. 2016, Social Democrat Zoran Zaev formed a coalition and became prime min. May 31, 2017. On June 17, 2018, Macedonia and Greece signed an agreement for the former to change its name to North Macedonia. The agreement took effect Feb. 12, 2019. Pro-EU, pro-NATO candidate Stevo Pendarovski won a May 5 presidential runoff election. North Macedonia joined NATO Mar. 27, 2020. With EU talks stalled, Prime Min. Zaev

resigned, Jan. 3, 2020. After July 15 elections, Zaev formed a new coalition government.

The 2020 COVID-19 pandemic caused almost 17,800 cases and over 700 deaths in North Macedonia as of Sept. 30.

Norway
Kingdom of Norway

People: Population: 5,467,439 (118). **Age distrib.:** <15: 18.0%; 65+: 17.4%. **Growth:** 0.8%. **Migrants:** 16.1%. **Pop. density:** 46.5 per sq mi, 18.0 per sq km. **Urban:** 83.0%. **Ethnic groups:** Norwegian (incl. Sami) 83.2%, other European 8.3%. **Languages:** Bokmal Norwegian, Nynorsk Norwegian (both official); Sami (official in 9 municipalities). **Religions:** Christian 84.2% (Protestant 78.5%), agnostic 7.5%, Muslim 6.4% (Sunni).

Geography: Total area: 125,021 sq mi, 323,802 sq km (67); **Land area:** 117,484 sq mi, 304,282 sq km. **Location:** W part of Scandinavian peninsula in NW Europe (extends farther N than any European land). Sweden, Finland, Russia on E. **Topography:** Highly indented coast lined with tens of thousands of islands. Mountains and plateaus cover most of country, which is only 33% forested. **Arable land:** 2.2%. **Capital:** Oslo, 1,041,378.

Government: Type: Parliamentary constitutional monarchy. **Head of state:** King Harald V; b. 1937; in office: Jan. 17, 1991. **Head of govt.:** Prime Min. Erna Solberg; b. 1961; in office: Oct. 16, 2013. **Local divisions:** 18 counties. **Defense budget:** $6.7 bil. **Active troops:** 23,250.

Economy: Industries: petroleum and gas, shipping, fishing, aquaculture, food proc., shipbuilding, pulp/paper prods. **Chief agric.:** barley, wheat, potatoes; pork, beef, veal, milk; fish. **Natural resources:** petroleum, nat. gas, iron ore, copper, lead, zinc, titanium, pyrites, nickel, fish, timber, hydropower. **Water:** 74,081 cu m per capita. **Crude oil reserves:** 8.2 bil bbls. **Electricity prod.** (2018): 144 bil kWh. **Labor force:** agric. 2.0%, industry 19.1%, services 78.9%. **Unemployment:** 3.3%.

Finance: Monetary unit: Krone (NOK) (8.90 = $1 U.S.). **GDP:** $357.4 bil; **per capita GDP:** $66,832; **GDP growth:** 1.2%. **Imports:** $95.1 bil; Sweden 11.4%, Germany 11%, China 9.8%, U.S. 6.8%, South Korea 6.7%, Denmark 5.4%. **Exports:** $102.8 bil; UK 21.1%, Germany 15.5%, Netherlands 9.9%, Sweden 6.6%, France 6.4%. **Tourism:** $5 bil. **Budget:** $199.5 bil. **Inflation:** 2.2%.

Transport: Railways: 2,610 mi. **Motor vehicles:** 621.8 per 1,000 pop. **Airports:** 67.

Communications: Telephone: 10.6 per 100 pop. **Mobile:** 107.2 per 100 pop. **Broadband:** 95.1 per 100 pop. **Internet** (2018): 96.5%.

Health: Expend.: 10.4%. **Life expect.:** 80.0 male; 84.4 female. **Births:** 12.2 per 1,000 pop. **Deaths:** 8.1 per 1,000 pop. **Infant mortality:** 2.5 per 1,000 live births. **Undernourished:** <2.5%. **HIV** (2018): 0.1%.

Education: Compulsory: ages 6-15. **Literacy:** 100%.
Embassy: 2720 34th St. NW 20008; 333-6000.
Website: www.regjeringen.no

The first ruler of Norway was Harald the Fairhaired, who came to power in 872 ce. Between 800 and 1000, Norway's Vikings raided and occupied widely dispersed parts of Europe. The country was united with Denmark, 1381-1814, and with Sweden, 1814-1905. In 1905, the country became independent with Prince Charles of Denmark as king.

Norway remained neutral during WWI. In WWII, Germany attacked Norway Apr. 9, 1940, and held it until liberation May 8, 1945. The country abandoned its neutrality after the war and joined NATO. In a referendum Nov. 28, 1994, Norwegian voters rejected European Union membership.

Norway has one of the highest living standards in the world. Hydropower accounts for more than 90% of electricity production. The country is a leading producer and exporter of crude oil, with extensive reserves in the North Sea, and natural gas production has increased in recent years. Norway has used oil revenue to build up the world's largest sovereign wealth fund (about $1 tril in 2020).

A right-wing extremist, Anders Behring Breivik, confessed to killing 8 people with a car bomb in central Oslo and murdering another 69 at an island camp sponsored by the Labor Party's youth wing July 22, 2011. He was sentenced Aug. 24, 2012, to 21 years in prison. Parliament voted June 18, 2013, to make military service compulsory for women as well as men. Rightist and anti-immigration parties won the most seats in Sept. 9, 2013, elections; Conservative Party leader Erna Solberg became prime min. In 2015, about 31,000 migrants from the Middle East, SW Asia, and Africa applied for asylum in Norway. Solberg's coalition won Sept. 11, 2017, elections.

The 2020 COVID-19 pandemic caused almost 14,000 cases and 274 deaths in Norway as of Sept. 30. A pandemic-related global recession caused a sharp drop in Norway's oil revenue.

Svalbard is a group of mountainous islands in the Arctic O., area 23,956 sq mi, pop. (2017 est.) 2,583. The largest, Spitsbergen (formerly called West Spitsbergen), 14,546 sq mi, seat of the governor, is about 370 mi N of Norway. By the 1920 Svalbard Treaty (in force

1925), major European powers recognized Norway's sovereignty over the archipelago.

Jan Mayen, area 146 sq mi, is a volcanic island located about 565 mi W-NW of Norway; it was annexed in 1929. The only people on Jan Mayen are military personnel and researchers. Norway operates a research station on volcanic Bouvet Isl. (annexed 1930), area 19 sq mi, in the South Atlantic O., about midway between South Africa and Antarctica.

Oman
Sultanate of Oman

People: Population: 3,634,689 (130). **Age distrib.:** <15: 30.1%; 65+: 3.7%. **Growth:** 1.9%. **Migrants:** 46.0%. **Pop. density:** 30.4 per sq mi, 11.7 per sq km. **Urban:** 86.3%. **Ethnic groups:** Arab, Baluchi, South Asian (Indian, Pakistani, Sri Lankan, Bangladeshi), African. **Languages:** Arabic (official), English, Baluchi, Swahili, Urdu, Indian dialects. **Religions:** Muslim (official) 90.6% (Sunni 48%, Islamic schismatic 36%, Shia 7%), Hindu 4.6%, Christian 3.6%.

Geography: Total area: 119,499 sq mi, 309,500 sq km (70); **Land area:** 119,499 sq mi, 309,500 sq km. **Location:** SE coast of Arabian peninsula. United Arab Emirates, Saudi Arabia, Yemen on W. **Topography:** A narrow coastal plain, a range of barren mountains reaching 9,900 ft, and a wide, stony, mostly waterless plateau, avg. elevation 1,000 ft. An exclave at the tip of the Musandam peninsula controls access to the Persian Gulf. **Arable land:** 0.2%. **Capital:** Muscat, 1,549,729.

Government: Type: Absolute monarchy. **Head of state and govt.:** Sultan and Prime Min. Haitham bin Tariq bin Taimur al-Said b. 1954; in office: Jan. 11, 2020. **Local divisions:** 11 governorates. **Defense budget:** $9 bil. **Active troops:** 42,600.

Economy: Industries: crude oil prod. and refining, nat. and liquefied nat. gas prod., constr., cement, copper, steel, chemicals, optic fiber. **Chief agric.:** dates, limes, bananas, alfalfa, vegetables; camels, cattle; fish. **Natural resources:** petroleum, copper, asbestos, marble, limestone, chromium, gypsum, nat. gas. **Water:** 302 cu m per capita. **Crude oil reserves:** 5.4 bil bbls. **Electricity prod.:** 34.0 bil kWh. **Labor force:** agric. 4.5%, industry 32.8%, services 62.7%. **Unemployment:** 2.6%.

Finance: Monetary unit: Rial (OMR) (0.38 = $1 U.S.). **GDP:** $144.5 bil; **per capita GDP:** $29,052; **GDP growth:** 0.5%. **Imports:** $24.1 bil; UAE 35.5%, U.S. 27.8%. **Exports:** $103.3 bil; China 43.7%, UAE 11%, South Korea 7.9%. **Tourism:** $1.8 bil. **Budget:** $31.9 bil. **Inflation:** 0.1%.

Transport: Motor vehicles: 222.6 per 1,000 pop. **Airports:** 13. **Communications: Telephone:** 11.6 per 100 pop. **Mobile:** 133.4 per 100 pop. **Broadband:** 93.9 per 100 pop. **Internet:** 80.2%.

Health: Expend.: 3.8%. **Life expect.:** 74.4 male; 78.4 female. **Births:** 23.1 per 1,000 pop. **Deaths:** 3.3 per 1,000 pop. **Infant mortality:** 11.7 per 1,000 live births. **Undernourished:** 7.8%. **HIV:** <0.1%.

Education: Compulsory: ages 6-15. **Literacy:** 98.6%.
Embassy: 2535 Belmont Rd. NW 20008; 387-1980.
Website: www.oman.om
Oman was originally called Muscat and Oman. A long history of rule by other lands, including Portugal in the 16th cent., ended with the ouster of the Persians in 1744. By the early 19th cent., Muscat and Oman controlled much of the Persian and Pakistani coasts.

British influence was confirmed in a 1951 treaty, and Britain helped suppress an uprising by interior tribes in the 1950s.

On July 23, 1970, Sultan Qaboos bin Said al-Said became ruler. He changed the nation's name to Sultanate of Oman. Petroleum and natural gas are major sources of income. Oman has strong ties to the U.S. but also favorable relations with Iran. After Arab Spring protests Feb. 2011, Sultan Qaboos expanded the powers of the lower house of parliament, Oct. 20, 2011. Sultan Qaboos died, Jan. 10, 2020; he was succeeded the next day by his cousin Haitham bin Tariq al-Said.

The 2020 COVID-19 pandemic caused more than 98,000 cases and 935 deaths in Oman by Sept. 30.

Pakistan
Islamic Republic of Pakistan

People: Population: 233,500,636 (5). **Age distrib.:** <15: 36.0%; 65+: 4.4%. **Growth:** 2.0%. **Migrants:** 1.5%. **Pop. density:** 784.5 per sq mi, 302.9 per sq km. **Urban:** 37.2%. **Ethnic groups:** Punjabi 44.7%, Pashtun (Pathan) 15.4%, Sindhi 14.1%, Saraiki 8.4%, Muhajir 7.6%, Balochi 3.6%. **Languages:** Punjabi, Sindhi, Saraiki, Pashto or Pashtu, Urdu (official), Balochi, Hindko, English (official; lingua franca of elite and most govt. ministries). **Religions:** Muslim (official) 96.4% (Sunni 84%, Shia 10%, Islamic schismatic 3%), Christian 1.9%, Hindu 1.3%.

Geography: Total area: 307,374 sq mi, 796,095 sq km (35); **Land area:** 297,637 sq mi, 770,875 sq km. **Location:** W part of S Asia. Iran on W, Afghanistan and China on N, India on E. **Topography:** The Indus R. rises in the Hindu Kush and Himalaya Mts. in the N, then flows 1,000 mi into Arabian Sea. Thar Desert, Eastern Plains flank Indus Valley. **Arable land:** 40.5%. **Capital:** Islamabad, 1,129,198. **Cities:** Karachi, 16,093,786; Lahore, 12,642,423; Faisalabad, 3,462,295; Rawalpindi, 2,236,905; Gujranwala, 2,229,220; Peshawar, 2,202,946.

Government: Type: Federal parliamentary republic. **Head of state:** Pres. Arif Alvi; b. 1949; in office: Sept. 9, 2018. **Head of govt.:** Prime Min. Imran Khan; b. 1952; in office: Aug. 18, 2018. **Local divisions:** 4 provinces, 1 capital territory, 2 admin. entities in Pakistan-administered part of disputed Jammu and Kashmir region. **Defense budget:** $10.3 bil. **Active troops:** 653,800.

Economy: Industries: textiles and apparel, food proc., pharmaceuticals, surgical instruments, constr. materials, paper prods., fertilizer, shrimp. **Chief agric.:** cotton, wheat, rice, sugarcane, fruits, vegetables; milk, beef, mutton, eggs. **Natural resources:** nat. gas, limited petroleum, poor quality coal, iron ore, copper, salt, limestone. **Water:** 1,253 cu m per capita. **Crude oil reserves:** 342.8 mil bbls. **Electricity prod.:** 126.5 bil kWh. **Labor force:** agric. 35.9%, industry 25.8%, services 38.3%. **Unemployment:** 4.5%.

Finance: Monetary unit: Rupee (PKR) (165.88 = $1 U.S.). **GDP:** $1.1 tril; **per capita GDP:** $4,885; **GDP growth:** 1.0%. **Imports:** $53.1 bil; China 27.4%, UAE 13.7%. **Exports:** $32.9 bil; U.S. 17.7%, UK 7.7%, China 6%, Germany 5.8%, Afghanistan 5.2%. **Tourism:** $494 mil. **Budget:** $64.5 bil. **Inflation:** 10.6%.

Transport: Railways: 7,383 mi. **Motor vehicles:** 18.7 per 1,000 pop. **Airports:** 108.

Communications: Telephone: 1.3 per 100 pop. **Mobile:** 72.6 per 100 pop. **Broadband:** 24.7 per 100 pop. **Internet:** 15.5%.

Health: Expend.: 2.9%. **Life expect.:** 67.2 male; 71.3 female. **Births:** 27.4 per 1,000 pop. **Deaths:** 6.2 per 1,000 pop. **Infant mortality:** 52.3 per 1,000 live births. **Undernourished:** 12.3%. **HIV:** 0.1%.

Education: Compulsory: ages 5-16. **Literacy:** 74.5%.
Embassy: 3517 International Ct. NW 20008; 243-6500.
Website: www.pakistan.gov.pk
Pakistan shares the 5,000-year history of the India-Pakistan subcontinent. At present-day Harappa and Mohenjo Daro, the Indus Valley civilization, with large cities and elaborate irrigation systems, flourished c. 4,000-2,500 BCE. Aryan invaders from the northwest conquered the region around 1,500 BCE, forging the Vedic civilization that dominated the region for over a thousand years. The first Arab invasion, 712 CE, introduced Islam. Present-day Pakistan and India were part of the Mughal Empire from 1526 to 1857. Muslim power faded by the end of the 19th cent. as the British gained control.

Muhammad Ali Jinnah (1876-1948) was the principal architect of Pakistan. When the British withdrew, Aug. 14, 1947, two largely Islamic regions of British India acquired self-government as Pakistan, with dominion status in the Commonwealth. Pakistan was divided into West Pakistan and East Pakistan, nearly 1,000 mi apart on opposite sides of India. Kashmir, a predominantly Muslim region divided between Pakistan and India, has remained a source of conflict between the two countries.

Rioting and strikes broke out in the East after Pakistan's government, Mar. 1, 1971, postponed the constituent assembly, dominated by supporters of regional autonomy for East Pakistan. Armed conflict between East and West lasted from Mar. to Dec. 1971, with India siding with Easterners, who proclaimed the independent nation of Bangladesh. Thousands were killed, and some 10 mil Easterners fled to India. Full-scale war erupted between India and Pakistan, but Pakistan troops in the East surrendered Dec. 16; Pakistan agreed to a cease-fire in the West Dec. 17. On July 3, 1972, Pakistan and India signed a pact providing for troop withdrawals.

Zulfikar Ali Bhutto, who became president in 1971 and prime min. in 1973, was overthrown in a military coup July 1977. Convicted of complicity in a 1974 political murder, he was executed Apr. 4, 1979. Millions of Afghan refugees entered Pakistan after the USSR invaded Afghanistan Dec. 1979 and after U.S.-led forces began fighting the Taliban in Afghanistan in 2001. Although millions of refugees have been repatriated, including those reportedly forced by Pakistan to return, about 1.4 mil Afghan refugees were living in Pakistan in 2020.

Pres. Mohammad Zia ul-Haq was killed when his plane exploded in Aug. 1988. Following Nov. elections, Benazir Bhutto, daughter of Zulfikar Ali Bhutto, became prime min. and the first elected woman leader of a Muslim nation. She was accused of corruption and dismissed by the president, Aug. 1990. Bhutto returned to power Oct. 1993 but was dismissed Nov. 1996 amid further corruption charges. Responding to India's nuclear weapons tests, Pakistan conducted its own tests in 1998.

Prime Min. Nawaz Sharif fired, Oct. 1999, army chief Gen. Pervez Musharraf, whose supporters staged a bloodless coup. Musharraf assumed the presidency June 20, 2001. Following the Sept. 11, 2001, terrorist attacks on the U.S., Pres. Musharraf pledged cooperation with the U.S. in fighting Taliban and al-Qaeda militants within Pakistan and in neighboring Afghanistan. In return, the U.S. waived 1998 sanctions and offered Pakistan financial aid and debt relief. An earthquake that rocked Pakistan and the Pakistani-held region of Kashmir Oct. 8, 2005, killed about 80,000 people.

More than 140 people died Oct. 18, 2007, when suicide bombers struck Benazir Bhutto's convoy upon her return from more than eight years in exile. Musharraf, who had won the Oct. 6 presidential election, gave up his post Nov. 25 and was sworn in as civilian president the next day. Bhutto was assassinated Dec. 27, 2007, after a rally in Rawalpindi.

Headed by Bhutto's widower, Asif Ali Zardari, the Pakistan Peoples Party led in parliamentary elections Feb. 18, 2008. Musharraf resigned Aug. 18 under threat of impeachment, and Zardari became president Sept. 9. Amid deteriorating security, U.S. and Pakistani forces clashed with the Taliban near the Afghan border, and Islamists carried out new suicide attacks. The government announced Feb. 16, 2009, a truce conceding de facto control of the strategic Swat Valley to the Taliban, but in May, government forces launched an offensive that reclaimed most of the region; the fighting displaced nearly 2 mil civilians. Catastrophic floods and monsoon rains, July-Aug. 2010, inundated one-fifth of Pakistan, leaving more than 1,750 people dead and displacing up to 20 mil.

On May 2, 2011, U.S. commandos killed al-Qaeda leader Osama bin Laden in Abbottabad. The raid, carried out by helicopter from Afghanistan, was launched without prior warning to Pakistani authorities. The U.S. has suspected some Pakistani military and other officials of covert links and assistance to Islamist extremist groups such as the Taliban and al-Qaeda.

On Oct. 9, 2012, 15-year-old Malala Yousafzai, who advocated for education rights for girls in Pakistan, was shot by the Taliban, sparking worldwide outrage. After treatment at a British hospital, she resumed her advocacy, for which she shared the 2014 Nobel Peace Prize. Two arrested Sept. 12, 2014, were convicted in Apr. 2015.

Musharraf returned to Pakistan Mar. 24, 2013, to attempt a political comeback. Charged with treason in 2014, he was convicted in absentia, Dec. 2019. He had been allowed to leave the country, Mar. 18, 2016, for medical treatment in Dubai. Former Prime Min. Nawaz Sharif was returned to office in May 11, 2013, elections. With Sharif accused of corruption, a Supreme Court ruling, July 28, 2017, forced him to step down as prime min. Sharif was convicted on corruption charges, July and Dec. 2018; he was allowed to leave the country for medical treatment in the UK, Nov. 2019.

The party of former cricket star Imran Khan, the Pakistan Movement for Justice, with apparent backing from the military, won the most seats in July 25, 2018, parliamentary elections; Khan became prime min. Aug. 18. Arif Alvi, from Khan's party, was elected president Sept. 4, 2018.

A terrorist attack on a Peshawar school, Dec. 16, 2014, left about 150 dead. In 2007-14, an estimated 7,500 people died in terrorist attacks. Fighting between Pakistani forces and Islamic extremists resulted in more than 17,000 fatalities, 2007-14. Terrorist attacks and conflict between Islamic extremists and Pakistani forces, sometimes supported by U.S. drone strikes, continued. A suicide bomber killed about 70 people in a Lahore park, Mar. 27, 2016; a Taliban offshoot group claimed responsibility. An Aug. 8 Islamist suicide bombing at a hospital in Quetta killed more than 70. At least 90 people were killed, Feb. 16, 2017, in a suicide bombing in Sehwan for which ISIS claimed responsibility. A July 13, 2018, Islamist extremist suicide bombing in Mastung left at least 149 dead.

Fearing the impact on Pakistan's economy, the government resisted strict nationwide lockdown measures to combat the 2020 COVID-19 pandemic. As of Sept. 30, Pakistan had more than 312,000 cases and almost 6,500 had died.

Palau
Republic of Palau

People: **Population:** 21,085 (193). **Age distrib.:** <15: 18.7%; 65+: 9.4%. **Growth:** 0.4%. **Migrants:** 28.1%. **Pop. density:** 122.4 per sq mi, 47.2 per sq km. **Urban:** 81.0%. **Ethnic groups:** Palauan (Micronesian with Malayan/Melanesian admixtures) 73%, Asian 21.7%, Carolinian 2%. **Languages:** Palauan (official on most islands), English (official), Filipino. **Religions:** Christian 91.3% (Protestant 43%, Catholic 37.4%, independent 10.9%), agnostic 3.2%, Muslim 2.8% (Sunni).

Geography: **Total area:** 177 sq mi, 459 sq km (181); **Land area:** 177 sq mi, 459 sq km. **Location:** Archipelago (26 islands, more than 300 islets) in W Pacific O., about 530 mi SE of the Philippines. Micronesia to E, Indonesia to S. **Topography:** A mountainous main island and low coral atolls, usually fringed with large barrier reefs. **Arable land:** 2.2%. **Capital:** Ngerulmud.

Government: **Type:** Presidential republic in free association with U.S. **Head of state and govt.:** Pres. Tommy Remengesau; b. 1956; in office: Jan. 17, 2013. **Local divisions:** 16 states. **Defense budget/active troops:** NA.

Economy: **Industries:** tourism, fishing, subsistence agriculture. **Chief agric.:** coconuts, cassava, sweet potatoes; fish, pigs, chickens, eggs. **Natural resources:** forests, minerals (espec. gold), marine prods., deep-seabed minerals. **Water:** NA. **Labor**

force: agric. 1.2%, industry 12.4%, services 86.4%. **Unemployment:** 0.0%.

Finance: **Monetary unit:** U.S. Dollar (USD) (1.00 = $1 U.S.). **GDP** (2018): $331.2 mil; **per capita GDP** (2018): $18,496; **GDP growth** (2018): 1.7%. **Imports** (2018): $4.7 bil; U.S. 33.4%, Guam 15.8%, Japan 15.7%, China 13.5%, South Korea 5.3%. **Exports:** $23.2 bil; Japan 51.3%, U.S. 15.8%, India 13.8%, Guam 8%. **Tourism** (2017): $116 mil. **Budget** (2012): $167.3 mil. **Inflation** (2016-17): 1.3%.

Transport: **Airports:** 1.

Communications: **Telephone** (2015): 40.8 per 100 pop. **Mobile** (2015): 134.4 per 100 pop. **Broadband:** NA. **Internet:** NA.

Health: **Expend.:** 12.0%. **Life expect.:** 70.9 male; 77.5 female. **Births:** 11.3 per 1,000 pop. **Deaths:** 8.3 per 1,000 pop. **Infant mortality:** 9.8 per 1,000 live births. **Undernourished:** NA. **HIV:** NA.

Education: Compulsory: ages 6-17. **Literacy:** 96.6%.

Embassy: 1701 Pennsylvania Ave. NW, Ste. 300, 20036; 349-8598.

Website: palaugov.pw

Spain acquired the Palau Islands, 1886, and sold them to Germany, 1899. Japan seized them in 1914. U.S. forces occupied the islands in 1944; in 1947, they became part of the U.S.-administered UN Trust Territory of the Pacific Islands. In 1981, Palau became an autonomous republic. It ratified a compact of free association with the U.S. in 1993 and became an independent nation, Oct. 1, 1994. Oct. 2015 legislation provided for the creation of a 193,000 sq mi marine sanctuary, in which fishing and mineral development would be prohibited.

Panama
Republic of Panama

People: **Population:** 3,894,082 (128). **Age distrib.:** <15: 25.6%; 65+: 9.0%. **Growth:** 1.2%. **Migrants:** 4.4%. **Pop. density:** 135.7 per sq mi, 52.4 per sq km. **Urban:** 68.4%. **Ethnic groups:** mestizo (mixed Amerindian/white) 65%, Native American (incl. Ngabe 7.6%, Kuna 2.4%) 12.3%, Black or African descent 9.2%, mulatto 6.8%, white 6.7%. **Languages:** Spanish (official), Indigenous langs. **Religions:** Christian 90.1% (Catholic [official] 73.5%, Protestant 10.4%), agnostic 4%.

Geography: **Total area:** 29,120 sq mi, 75,420 sq km (116); **Land area:** 28,703 sq mi, 74,340 sq km. **Location:** Central America. Costa Rica on W, Colombia on E. **Topography:** Two mountain ranges run length of isthmus. Tropical rain forests cover the Caribbean coast and E. **Arable land:** 7.6%. **Capital:** Panama City, 1,860,291.

Government: **Type:** Presidential republic. **Head of state and govt.:** Pres. Laurentino "Nito" Cortizo; b. 1953; in office: July 1, 2019. **Local divisions:** 10 provinces, 3 Indigenous regions. **Defense budget:** $805 mil. **Active troops:** No armed forces. 26,000 paramilitary only.

Economy: **Industries:** constr., brewing, cement/other constr. materials, sugar milling. **Chief agric.:** bananas, rice, corn, coffee, sugarcane, vegetables; livestock; shrimp. **Natural resources:** copper, mahogany forests, shrimp, hydropower. **Water:** 33,984 cu m per capita. **Electricity prod.:** 10.8 bil kWh. **Labor force:** agric. 13.7%, industry 18.8%, services 67.5%. **Unemployment:** 3.8%.

Finance: **Monetary unit:** Balboa (PAB) (1.00 = $1 U.S.). **GDP:** $139.1 bil; **per capita GDP:** $32,762; **GDP growth:** 3.0%. **Imports:** $21.9 bil; U.S. 24.4%, China 9.8%. **Exports:** $15.5 bil. Trade data incl. Colón Free Zone. U.S. 18.9%, Netherlands 16.5%, China 6.5%, Costa Rica 5.4%, India 5.1%, Vietnam 5%. **Tourism:** $4.5 bil. **Budget:** $13.4 bil. **Inflation:** −0.4%.

Transport: **Railways:** 48 mi. **Motor vehicles:** 225.7 per 1,000 pop. **Airports:** 57.

Communications: **Telephone:** 16.1 per 100 pop. **Mobile:** 130.1 per 100 pop. **Broadband:** 60.7 per 100 pop. **Internet:** 57.9%.

Health: **Expend.:** 7.3%. **Life expect.:** 76.4 male; 82.2 female. **Births:** 17.1 per 1,000 pop. **Deaths:** 5.1 per 1,000 pop. **Infant mortality:** 9.1 per 1,000 live births. **Undernourished:** 6.9%. **HIV** (2018): 0.9%.

Education: Compulsory: ages 4-14. **Literacy:** 99.1%.

Embassy: 2862 McGill Ter. NW 20008; 483-1407.

Website: www.presidencia.gob.pa

The coast of Panama was sighted by Rodrigo de Bastidas, sailing with Columbus for Spain in 1501, and was visited by Columbus in 1502. Vasco Núñez de Balboa crossed the isthmus and "discovered" the Pacific Ocean, Sept. 13, 1513. Spanish colonies were ravaged by Francis Drake, 1572-95, and Henry Morgan, 1668-71. Morgan destroyed the old city of Panama, which was founded in 1519. Freed from Spain, Panama joined Colombia in 1821.

Panama declared independence from Colombia Nov. 3, 1903, and granted control of the Canal Zone to the U.S. Feb. 26, 1904. The U.S.-built Panama Canal opened Aug. 15, 1914. A 1978 treaty provided for its gradual return to Panama—completed Dec. 31, 1999. A $5.3-bil expansion was approved by referendum Oct. 22, 2006. The first ship crossed the new wider channel June 26, 2016.

Pres. Eric Arturo Delvalle was ousted by the National Assembly, Feb. 26, 1988, after he tried to fire Gen. Manuel Antonio Noriega, who was under a U.S. indictment on drug charges. U.S. troops invaded Panama Dec. 20, 1989, and Noriega surrendered Jan. 3, 1990. After two decades in a U.S. prison, Noriega was extradited to France, 2010, and then to Panama, 2011. While serving a 20-year sentence in Panama, Noriega died May 29, 2017.

Information published beginning Apr. 3, 2016, from "Panama Papers" documents—leaked from a Panama City law firm—linked public officials and others in various countries to offshore bank accounts and companies created to conceal wealth or avoid taxes. Vowing to fight corruption, Laurentino Cortizo of the Democratic Revolutionary Party narrowly won the May 5, 2019, presidential election.

Hard-hit by the 2020 COVID-19 pandemic, Panama had one of the highest per-capita infection rates in Latin America. As of Sept. 30, the country had more than 111,000 cases; more than 2,300 people had died.

Papua New Guinea
Independent State of Papua New Guinea

People: Population: 7,259,456 (102). **Age distrib.:** <15: 32.0%; 65+: 4.6%. **Growth:** 1.6%. **Migrants:** 0.4%. **Pop. density:** 41.5 per sq mi, 16.0 per sq km. **Urban:** 13.3%. **Ethnic groups:** Melanesian, Papuan, Negrito, Micronesian, Polynesian. **Languages:** Tok Pisin, English, Hiri Motu (all official); some 839 Indigenous langs. (many spoken by fewer than 1,000). **Religions:** Christian (official) 95.3% (Protestant 58.4%, Catholic 31%), ethnic religionist 2.9%.

Geography: Total area: 178,704 sq mi, 462,840 sq km (54); **Land area:** 174,850 sq mi, 452,860 sq km. **Location:** SE Asia; E half of island of New Guinea and about 600 nearby islands. Indonesia on W, Australia on S. **Topography:** Thickly forested mountains cover much of center, with lowlands along the coasts. Incl. some islands of Bismarck and Solomon groups, such as Admiralty Isls., New Ireland, New Britain, and Bougainville. **Arable land:** 0.7%. **Capital:** Port Moresby, 382,516.

Government: Type: Parliamentary democracy under constitutional monarchy. **Head of state:** Queen Elizabeth II, rep. by Gov.-Gen. Bob Dadae; in office: Feb. 28, 2017. **Head of govt.:** Prime Min. James Marape; in office: May 30, 2019. **Local divisions:** 20 provinces, 1 autonomous region, 1 district. **Defense budget:** $79 mil. **Active troops:** 3,600.

Economy: Industries: copra crushing, palm oil proc., plywood prod., wood chip prod., mining, crude oil/petroleum prods. **Chief agric.:** coffee, cocoa, copra, palm kernels, tea, sugar, rubber, sweet potatoes; poultry, pork; shellfish. **Natural resources:** gold, copper, silver, nat. gas, timber, oil, fisheries. **Water:** 97,079 cu m per capita. **Crude oil reserves:** 158.2 mil bbls. **Electricity prod.:** 3.9 bil kWh. **Labor force:** agric. 57.8%, industry 6.7%, services 35.5%. **Unemployment:** 2.5%.

Finance: Monetary unit: Kina (PGK) (3.48 = $1 U.S.). **GDP:** $40.1 bil; **per capita GDP:** $4,569; **GDP growth:** 5.6%. **Imports:** $1.9 bil; Australia 30.1%, China 17.3%, Singapore 10.2%, Malaysia 8.2%. **Exports:** $8.5 bil; Australia 18.9%, Singapore 17.5%, Japan 13.8%, China 12.7%. **Tourism:** $3 mil. **Budget:** $4.6 bil. **Inflation:** 3.6%.

Transport: Motor vehicles: 21.9 per 1,000 pop. **Airports:** 21. **Communications: Telephone** (2017): 1.9 per 100 pop. **Mobile** (2017): 47.6 per 100 pop. **Broadband:** 11.1 per 100 pop. **Internet:** 11.2%.

Health: Expend.: 2.5%. **Life expect.:** 65.6 male; 70.0 female. **Births:** 22.5 per 1,000 pop. **Deaths:** 6.7 per 1,000 pop. **Infant mortality:** 33.2 per 1,000 live births. **Undernourished:** NA. **HIV:** 0.9%.

Education: Compulsory: NA. **Literacy:** 64.2%.
Embassy: 1779 Massachusetts Ave. NW, Ste. 805, 20036; 745-3680.

Website: www.pm.gov.pg

Human remains dating back at least 10,000 years have been found in the interior of New Guinea. European colonization began in the 19th cent., when the Dutch took control of the island's western half (now part of Indonesia). The southern half of eastern New Guinea was claimed by Britain in 1884 and transferred to Australia in 1905. Germany claimed the northern half in 1884, but Australia captured it in WWI. Self-government was achieved Dec. 1, 1973, and independence Sept. 16, 1975.

Secessionist rebels clashed with government forces on Bougainville 1988-97, claiming some 20,000 lives. A Bougainville autonomy agreement was signed Aug. 30, 2001. In a late-2019 nonbinding referendum, 98% of Bougainville voters favored independence. Independence advocate and former rebel leader Ishmael Toroama was elected president of Bougainville in Sept. 2020.

Sir Michael Somare, the nation's first prime min. (1975-80, 1982-85), regained the office in 2002 and was reelected by parliament Aug. 13, 2007. Somare took indefinite medical leave Apr. 2011. After June-July 2012 parliamentary elections, Peter O'Neill served as prime min. beginning Aug. 3, 2012. Losing support over

economic conditions and corruption, O'Neill resigned, May 26, 2019. James Marape was elected prime minister by parliament, May 30, 2019.

The Supreme Court, Apr. 26, 2016, ruled illegal Australia's detention center on Manus Island for migrants intercepted trying to reach Australia by boat. The center, where detainees endured harsh living conditions, was closed Oct. 31, 2017. Approximately 600 detainees, all male, were initially relocated to other Australian-run camps. By 2020, several hundred detainees had gone to the U.S. under a 2016 Australia-U.S. resettlement agreement; other migrants had been relocated to Port Moresby.

The country has extensive energy resources. Shipments of liquefied natural gas through a new processing and shipping facility near Port Moresby began in May 2014.

Paraguay
Republic of Paraguay

People: Population: 7,191,685 (103). **Age distrib.:** <15: 23.4%; 65+: 7.9%. **Growth:** 1.2%. **Migrants:** 2.3%. **Pop. density:** 46.9 per sq mi, 18.1 per sq km. **Urban:** 62.2%. **Ethnic groups:** mestizo (mixed Spanish/Amerindian) 95%. **Languages:** Spanish, Guaraní (both official). **Religions:** Christian 95.1% (Catholic [official] 84.8%).

Geography: Total area: 157,048 sq mi, 406,752 sq km (59); **Land area:** 153,399 sq mi, 397,302 sq km. **Location:** Landlocked country in central S America. Bolivia on N, Argentina on S, Brazil on E. **Topography:** Paraguay R. bisects country. Fertile plains, wooded slopes, grasslands to E. Gran Chaco plain, with marshes and scrub trees, to W. Extreme W is arid. **Arable land:** 12.2%. **Capital:** Asunción, 3,336,562.

Government: Type: Presidential republic. **Head of state and govt.:** Pres. Mario Abdo Benítez; b. 1971; in office: Aug. 15, 2018. **Local divisions:** 17 departments, 1 capital city. **Defense budget:** $288 mil. **Active troops:** 13,950.

Economy: Industries: sugar proc., cement, textiles, beverages, wood prods., steel. **Chief agric.:** cotton, sugarcane, soybeans, corn, wheat, tobacco, cassava, fruits, vegetables; beef, pork, eggs, milk. **Natural resources:** hydropower, timber, iron ore, manganese, limestone. **Water:** 56,937 cu m per capita. **Electricity prod.:** 59.2 bil kWh. **Labor force:** agric. 19.9%, industry 17.9%, services 62.1%. **Unemployment:** 4.8%.

Finance: Monetary unit: Guarani (PYG) (6,968.55 = $1 U.S.). **GDP:** $93.1 bil; **per capita GDP:** $13,210; **GDP growth:** 0.0%. **Imports:** $11.4 bil; China 31.3%, Brazil 23.4%, Argentina 12.9%, U.S. 7.4%. **Exports:** $11.7 bil; Brazil 31.9%, Argentina 15.9%, Chile 6.9%, Russia 5.9%. **Tourism:** $379 mil. **Budget:** $6.0 bil. **Inflation:** 2.8%.

Transport: Railways: 19 mi. **Motor vehicles:** 96.8 per 1,000 pop. **Airports:** 15.

Communications: Telephone: 4.4 per 100 pop. **Mobile:** 107 per 100 pop. **Broadband:** 47.9 per 100 pop. **Internet** (2018): 65%.

Health: Expend.: 6.7%. **Life expect.:** 75.2 male; 80.7 female. **Births:** 16.6 per 1,000 pop. **Deaths:** 4.9 per 1,000 pop. **Infant mortality:** 16.9 per 1,000 live births. **Undernourished:** 8.8%. **HIV:** 0.5%.

Education: Compulsory: ages 5-17. **Literacy:** 98.3%.
Embassy: 2209 Massachusetts Ave. NW 20008; 483-6960.
Website: www.presidencia.gov.py

Guaraní Indians preceded Europeans in Paraguay, which was visited by Sebastian Cabot in 1527 and became a Spanish possession in 1535. Paraguay gained independence from Spain in 1811. It lost half its population and much of its territory to Brazil, Uruguay, and Argentina in the War of the Triple Alliance, 1865-70. Large areas were won from Bolivia in the Chaco War, 1932-35. Gen. Alfredo Stroessner held the presidency 1954-89, until his ouster in a military coup.

Power struggles ensued between civilian and military leaders, 1993-97. The assassination of Vice Pres. Luis María Argaña, Mar. 23, 1999, was widely attributed to Pres. Raúl Cubas Grau and triggered protests and an impeachment vote; Cubas resigned Mar. 28. An attempted military coup was suppressed May 18, 2000.

Mass protests over the depressed economy led to the proclamation of a state of emergency July 15, 2002. Nicanor Duarte Frutos of the conservative Colorado Party won the presidency, Apr. 27, 2003.

Paraguayan authorities blamed a leftist group for the Sept. 2004 kidnapping and subsequent murder of Cecilia Cubas, daughter of former Pres. Cubas. Fernando Lugo, a former Catholic cleric known as the "bishop of the poor," won a presidential election Apr. 20, 2008, ending over six decades of Colorado rule. On June 22, 2012, Lugo was removed from office after his handling of a dispute between landless peasants and police left 17 dead June 15. Colorado candidate Horacio Cartes, a former tobacco magnate, was elected president Apr. 21, 2013. Mario Abdo Benítez of the Colorado Party narrowly won the Apr. 22, 2018, presidential election.

The 2020 COVID-19 pandemic caused more than 39,000 cases and over 800 deaths in Paraguay as of Sept. 30.

Peru
Republic of Peru

People: Population: 31,914,989 (44). **Age distrib.:** <15: 25.4%; 65+: 8.0%. **Growth:** 0.9%. **Migrants:** 2.4%. **Pop. density:** 64.6 per sq mi, 24.9 per sq km. **Urban:** 78.3%. **Ethnic groups:** mestizo (mixed Amerindian/white) 60.2%, Amerindian 25.8%, white 5.9%, African descent 3.6%. **Languages:** Spanish, Quechua, Aymara (all official). **Religions:** Christian 96.4% (Catholic [official] 84.1%).

Geography: Total area: 496,225 sq mi, 1,285,216 sq km (19); **Land area:** 494,209 sq mi, 1,279,996 sq km. **Location:** Pacific coast of S America. Ecuador, Colombia on N; Brazil, Bolivia on E; Chile on S. **Topography:** An arid coastal strip, 10-100 mi wide. The Andes cover one-quarter of land area. The uplands are well-watered, as are the eastern slopes reaching the Amazon Basin, which covers half of country. **Arable land:** 2.7%. **Capital:** Lima, 10,719,188. **Cities:** Arequipa, 922,999.

Government: Type: Presidential republic. **Head of state and govt.** Pres. Martín Vizcarra; b. 1963; in office: Mar. 23, 2018. **Local divisions:** 25 regions, 1 province. **Defense budget:** $2.2 bil. **Active troops:** 81,000.

Economy: Industries: mining, refining of minerals; steel, metal fabrication; petroleum extraction/refining. nat. gas and nat. gas liquefaction; fishing/fish proc., cement, glass, textiles. **Chief agric.:** artichokes, asparagus, avocados, blueberries, coffee, cocoa, cotton, sugarcane, rice, potatoes, corn, plantains, grapes and other fruits; poultry, beef, pork, dairy prods.; guinea pigs; fish. **Natural resources:** copper, silver, gold, petroleum, timber, fish, iron ore, coal, phosphate, potash, hydropower, nat. gas. **Water:** 58,449 cu m per capita. **Crude oil reserves:** 985.1 mil bbls. **Electricity prod.:** 51.3 bil kWh. **Labor force:** agric. 27.2%, industry 15.3%, services 57.5%. **Unemployment:** 3.2%.

Finance: Monetary unit: Sol (PEN) (3.53 = $1 U.S.). **GDP:** $435.0 bil; **per capita GDP:** $13,380; **GDP growth:** 2.2%. **Imports:** $38.7 bil; China 22.3%, U.S. 20.1%, Brazil 6% **Exports:** $44.9 bil; China 26.5%, U.S. 15.2%, Switzerland 5.2%. **Tourism:** $3.8 bil. **Budget:** $64.8 bil. **Inflation:** 2.1%.

Transport: Railways: 1,152 mi. **Motor vehicles:** 87.9 per 1,000 pop. **Airports:** 59.

Communications: Telephone (2017): 9.8 per 100 pop. **Mobile** (2017): 123.8 per 100 pop. **Broadband:** 64.2 per 100 pop. **Internet** (2018): 52.5%.

Health: Expend.: 5.0%. **Life expect.:** 72.6 male; 76.9 female. **Births:** 17 per 1,000 pop. **Deaths:** 6.2 per 1,000 pop. **Infant mortality:** 16.7 per 1,000 live births. **Undernourished:** 6.7%. **HIV:** 0.3%.

Education: Compulsory: ages 3-16. **Literacy:** 99.0%.

Embassy: 1700 Massachusetts Ave. NW 20036; 833-9860.

Website: www.peru.gob.pe

The powerful Inca Empire had its seat at Cuzco in the Andes and covered much of western S America. A civil war had weakened the empire when Spaniard Francisco Pizarro began raiding Peru for its wealth, 1532. In 1533 he executed the Inca ruler, Atahualpa, and enslaved the people.

José de San Martin captured Lima from the Spanish in 1821; Simón Bolívar routed Spanish forces in 1824, and for much of the 19th cent., the country was governed by military leaders. Chile defeated Peru in the War of the Pacific, 1879-83. Right-wing groups allied with the military and the leftist APRA party vied for power in the first half of the 20th cent.

Peru returned to democratic leadership in 1980 but was plagued by economic problems and by leftist Shining Path (Sendero Luminoso) guerrillas. Conflict between guerrillas and government troops, 1980-2000, killed more than 69,000.

Elected president in June 1990, Alberto Fujimori dissolved Congress, suspended parts of the constitution, and initiated press censorship, Apr. 1992. The leader of Shining Path was captured Sept. 12. Fujimori won reelection in 1995 and 2000, but his repressive antiterrorism tactics drew international criticism.

Scandals involving a top aide led Fujimori to leave office, Nov. 2000. He was convicted, 2007-15, on charges that included complicity in a paramilitary death squad's killings and misusing public funds.

In a presidential runoff election June 5, 2011, leftist Ollanta Humala Tasso defeated Keiko Fujimori, daughter of the former president. Pedro Pablo Kuczynski defeated Keiko Fujimori, June 5, 2016. Facing impeachment over a corruption scandal, Kuczynski resigned and was replaced, Mar. 2018, by Vice Pres. Martín Vizcarra. In a Dec. 9, 2018, referendum, voters approved anti-corruption reforms. To break a deadlock with the legislature, Vizcarra said, Sept. 30, 2019, he was dissolving Congress; centrist parties made gains in Jan. 26, 2020, congressional elections. Vizcarra, Sept. 18, 2020, survived a congressional impeachment vote over obstruction of justice allegations.

About 477,000 Venezuelans, escaping economic hardship and repression, were in Peru as of Aug. 2020 and had applied for asylum or obtained temporary residence status.

Peru was one of the worst affected countries in Latin America by the 2020 COVID-19 pandemic, severely straining the health care system. By Sept. 30, the country had almost 809,000 cases and over 32,000 people had died.

Philippines
Republic of the Philippines

People: Population: 109,180,815 (12). **Age distrib.:** <15: 32.4%; 65+: 4.9%. **Growth:** 1.5%. **Migrants:** 0.2%. **Pop. density:** 948.4 per sq mi, 366.2 per sq km. **Urban:** 47.4%. **Ethnic groups:** Tagalog 24.4%, Bisaya/Binisaya 11.4%, Cebuano 9.9%, Ilocano 8.8%, Hiligaynon/Ilonggo 8.4%, Bikol/Bicol 6.8%, Waray 4%. **Languages:** Filipino (based on Tagalog), English (both official); 8 major dialects (incl. Tagalog). **Religions:** Christian 90.8% (Catholic 69.4%, independent 16%), Muslim 5.4% (Sunni).

Geography: Total area: 115,831 sq mi, 300,000 sq km (72); **Land area:** 115,124 sq mi, 298,170 sq km. **Location:** Archipelago in SE Asia. Malaysia, Indonesia on S; Taiwan on N. **Topography:** Comprises some 7,107 islands stretching 1,100 mi N-S. About 95% of area and pop. are on 11 largest islands, which are mountainous, except for the heavily indented coastlines and central plain on Luzon. **Arable land:** 18.7%. **Capital:** Manila, 13,923,452. **Cities:** Davao City, 1,825,450; Cebu City, 980,070.

Government: Type: Presidential republic. **Head of state and govt.:** Pres. Rodrigo Roa Duterte; b. 1945; in office: June 30, 2016. **Local divisions:** 81 provinces, 38 chartered cities. **Defense budget:** $3.5 bil. **Active troops:** 142,350.

Economy: Industries: semiconductors and electronics assembly, business process outsourcing, food/beverage mfg., constr. **Chief agric.:** rice, fish, livestock, poultry, bananas, coconuts/copra, corn, sugarcane. **Natural resources:** timber, petroleum, nickel, cobalt, silver, gold, salt, copper. **Water:** 4,565 cu m per capita. **Crude oil reserves:** 138.5 mil bbls. **Electricity prod.:** 90.0 bil kWh. **Labor force:** agric. 22.5%, industry 19.8%, services 57.6%. **Unemployment:** 2.2%.

Finance: Monetary unit: Peso (PHP) (48.58 = $1 U.S.). **GDP:** $1.0 tril; **per capita GDP:** $9,277; **GDP growth:** 6.0%. **Imports:** $89.4 bil; China 18.1%, Japan 11.4%, South Korea 8.8%, U.S. 7.4%, Thailand 7.1%, Indonesia 6.7%, Singapore 5.9%. **Exports:** $48.2 bil; Japan 16.4%, U.S. 14.6%, Hong Kong 13.7%, China 11%, Singapore 6.1%. **Tourism:** $9.8 bil. **Budget:** $56.0 bil. **Inflation:** 2.5%.

Transport: Railways: 48 mi. **Motor vehicles:** 41.5 per 1,000 pop. **Airports:** 89.

Communications: Telephone (2017): 4 per 100 pop. **Mobile** (2017): 110.1 per 100 pop. **Broadband:** 68.6 per 100 pop. **Internet:** 60.1%.

Health: Expend.: 4.4%. **Life expect.:** 66.5 male; 73.8 female. **Births:** 22.9 per 1,000 pop. **Deaths:** 6 per 1,000 pop. **Infant mortality:** 20.0 per 1,000 live births. **Undernourished:** 14.5%. **HIV:** 0.2%.

Education: Compulsory: ages 5-15. **Literacy:** 99.1%.

Embassy: 1600 Massachusetts Ave. NW 20036; 467-9300.

Website: www.gov.ph

Originally inhabited by Malay peoples, the archipelago was visited by Magellan, 1521. The Spanish founded Manila, 1571. Spain ceded the islands, named for King Philip II of Spain, to the U.S. for $20 mil, 1898, following the Spanish-American War. U.S. troops suppressed a guerrilla uprising in a brutal war, 1899-1905. Japan attacked the Philippines Dec. 8, 1941, and occupied the islands during WWII. Independence was proclaimed, July 4, 1946. A republic was established.

The repressive and corrupt regime of Pres. Ferdinand Marcos and his wife, Imelda, was in place 1965-86. The assassination of prominent opposition leader Benigno S. Aquino Jr., Aug. 21, 1983, sparked calls for Marcos's resignation. Marcos defeated Corazon Aquino, widow of the slain opposition leader, Feb. 16, 1986, in an allegedly fraudulent election. Mass protests and international pressure forced Marcos to flee the country Feb. 25, and Aquino became president.

Her government was plagued by a weak economy, widespread poverty, and Communist and Muslim insurgencies. Fidel Ramos won the May 1992 presidential election. A treaty with Muslim separatist guerrillas providing for expansion and development of an autonomous Muslim region on Mindanao, in the southern Philippines, was signed Sept. 2, 1996; the rebellion had claimed more than 120,000 lives since 1972.

Joseph (Erap) Estrada, a former movie actor, won the presidential election, May 11, 1998, but was impeached on bribery and corruption charges Nov. 13, 2000. Vice Pres. Gloria Macapagal Arroyo became president Jan. 20, 2001, and won reelection May 10, 2004. After Estrada was convicted in 2007 of taking more than $85 mil in bribes and kickbacks while in office, then pardoned, Benigno "NoyNoy" Aquino III, the son of former Pres. Aquino, defeated Estrada in the May 10, 2010, presidential election.

The government, 2012 and 2014, signed new peace and autonomy deals with Muslim rebels on Mindanao; violence had persisted after the 1996 accord. However, the Abu Sayyaf Islamist guerrilla group and the rebel group Maute, both of which claimed allegiance to ISIS, continued to stage attacks.

Typhoon Haiyan, Nov. 8, 2013, killed more than 6,200 people and displaced over 4 mil.

Vowing a tough crackdown on drug crime, Rodrigo Duterte was elected president, May 9, 2016. By the end of 2017, an estimated 12,000 drug suspects had been killed by police or vigilantes since Duterte took office, including about 4,000 acknowledged police killings; 1.3 mil drug suspects had surrendered as of mid-2017, according to government figures. The death toll in the war on drugs was estimated as high as 25,000 by mid-2020.

Duterte's government completed a new cease-fire agreement with Communist rebels, Aug. 26, 2016. Muslim rebels held part of the city of Marawi, May–Oct. 2017. Legislation to implement the 2014 autonomy agreement was signed in July 2018. Jan. 21 and Feb. 6, 2019, referenda in the south endorsed a new Bangsamoro autonomous region, although extremist attacks continued. Duterte signed, July 3, 2020, an antiterrorism bill giving security forces sweeping powers that critics feared could also be used in the government's ongoing suppression of dissidents and journalists.

Severely affected by the 2020 COVID-19 pandemic, the Philippines had more than 309,000 cases and over 5,400 deaths by Sept. 30.

Poland
Republic of Poland

People: Population: 38,282,325 (37). **Age distrib.:** <15: 14.8%; 65+: 18.7%. **Growth:** –0.2%. **Migrants:** 1.7%. **Pop. density:** 325.9 per sq mi, 125.8 per sq km. **Urban:** 60.0%. **Ethnic groups:** Polish 96.9%. **Languages:** Polish (official). **Religions:** Christian 95.9% (Catholic 93.2%), agnostic 3.6%.

Geography: Total area: 120,728 sq mi, 312,685 sq km (69); **Land area:** 117,474 sq mi, 304,255 sq km. **Location:** On Baltic Sea in E central Europe. Germany on W; Czech Rep., Slovakia on S; Lithuania, Belarus, Ukraine on E; Russia on N. **Topography:** Mostly lowlands forming part of the Northern European Plain. The Carpathian Mts. along S border rise to 8,200 ft. **Arable land:** 35.6%. **Capital:** Warsaw, 1,783,251. **Cities:** Kraków, 768,731.

Government: Type: Parliamentary republic. **Head of state:** Pres. Andrzej Duda; b. 1972; in office: Aug. 6, 2015. **Head of govt.:** Prime Min. Mateusz Morawiecki; b. 1968; in office: Dec. 11, 2017. **Local divisions:** 16 provinces. **Defense budget:** $11.4 bil. **Active troops:** 123,700.

Economy: Industries: machine building, iron and steel, coal mining, chemicals, shipbuilding, food proc., glass, beverages, textiles. **Chief agric.:** potatoes, fruits, vegetables, wheat; poultry, eggs, pork, dairy. **Natural resources:** coal, sulfur, copper, nat. gas, silver, lead, salt, amber. **Water:** 1,585 cu m per capita. **Crude oil reserves:** 119 mil bbls. **Electricity prod.** (2018): 159.9 bil kWh. **Labor force:** agric. 8.9%, industry 32.0%, services 59.1%. **Unemployment:** 3.0%.

Finance: Monetary unit: Zloty (PLN) (3.76 = $1 U.S.). **GDP:** $1.3 tril; **per capita GDP:** $34,218; **GDP growth:** 4.1%. **Imports:** $223.8 bil; Germany 27.9%, China 8%, Russia 6.4%, Netherlands 6%, Italy 5.3%. **Exports:** $224.6 bil; Germany 27.4%, Czechia 6.4%, UK 6.4%, France 5.6%. **Tourism:** $13.9 bil. **Budget:** $216.2 bil. **Inflation:** 2.2%.

Transport: Railways: 11,950 mi. **Motor vehicles:** 718.3 per 1,000 pop. **Airports:** 87.

Communications: Telephone (2017): 19.5 per 100 pop. **Mobile:** 134.7 per 100 pop. **Broadband:** 154.1 per 100 pop. **Internet** (2018): 77.5%.

Health: Expend.: 6.5%. **Life expect.:** 74.5 male; 82.3 female. **Births:** 8.9 per 1,000 pop. **Deaths:** 10.6 per 1,000 pop. **Infant mortality:** 4.3 per 1,000 live births. **Undernourished:** <2.5%. **HIV:** NA.

Education: Compulsory: ages 6-15. **Literacy:** 99.8%.

Embassy: 2640 16th St. NW 20009; 499-1700.

Website: www.poland.gov.pl

Slavic tribes in the area were converted to Latin Christianity in the 10th cent. Poland was a great power from the 14th to the 17th cent. In three partitions (1772, 1793, 1795) it was apportioned among Prussia, Russia, and Austria. Overrun by the Austro-German armies in WWI, it declared its independence on Nov. 11, 1918, and was recognized as independent by the Treaty of Versailles, June 28, 1919. Large territories to the east were taken in a war with Russia, 1921.

Germany and the USSR invaded Poland Sept. 1939 and divided the country. During the war, Nazis killed some 6 mil Polish citizens, half of them Jews. (Controversial 2018 legislation outlawed attributing to Poland any role in Nazi atrocities.) In compensation for territory ceded to the USSR when WWII ended, Poland received German territory comprising Silesia, Pomerania, West Prussia, and part of East Prussia. Communists, who aligned themselves with the USSR, dominated the 1947 election.

In 12 years of rule by Stalinists, large estates were abolished, industries nationalized, schools secularized, and Roman Catholic prelates jailed. Farm production fell off. Harsh working conditions caused a riot in Poznan, June 28-29, 1956. A new Politburo, committed to a more independent Polish Communism, was named Oct. 1956, with Wladyslaw Gomulka as first secretary of the party.

Collectivization of farms was ended. Gomulka agreed to increase religious liberty.

After worker riots over price rises and new wage rules, Gomulka resigned, Dec. 20, 1970; he was succeeded by Edward Gierek. The rules were dropped and price rises revoked.

Independent trade union Solidarity gained strength in the 1980s, organizing strikes and making bold demands. Led by Lech Walesa, Solidarity helped to win political and economic reforms, including free elections, in an Apr. 5, 1989, accord. Candidates endorsed by Solidarity swept the parliamentary elections, June 4. Walesa became president Dec. 22, 1990.

Policies to transform the economy into a free-market system led to inflation, unemployment, and a return to the political left in 1993 parliamentary elections. A former Communist, Aleksander Kwasniewski, defeated Walesa in the 1995 presidential election and was reelected 5 years later. Poland became a full member of NATO, Mar. 12, 1999, and entered the European Union May 1, 2004.

Lech Kaczynski of the conservative Law and Justice (PiS) party won a presidential runoff election Oct. 23, 2005. After Pres. Kaczynski was killed in a plane crash, Apr. 10, 2010, Parliament Speaker Bronislaw Komorowski of the center-right Civic Platform party became president. He was defeated by Andrzej Duda of PiS in a May 24, 2015, presidential runoff. PiS won Oct. 25, 2015, parliamentary elections. July 2017 legislation allowing the justice minister to appoint lower court judges drew criticism from EU leaders as a threat to judicial independence. Legislation effective July 2018 forcing the retirement of about two dozen Supreme Court judges prompted widespread protests. PiS won a slim majority in Oct. 13, 2019, parliamentary elections. Duda narrowly won reelection in a July 12, 2020, presidential runoff.

As of Sept. 30, the 2020 COVID-19 pandemic had caused about 90,000 cases and almost 2,500 deaths in Poland.

Portugal
Portuguese Republic

People: Population: 10,302,674 (89). **Age distrib.:** <15: 13.6%; 65+: 20.9%. **Growth:** –0.2%. **Migrants:** 8.7%. **Pop. density:** 291.7 per sq mi, 112.6 per sq km. **Urban:** 66.3%. **Ethnic groups:** homogeneous Mediterranean pop. **Languages:** Portuguese, Mirandese (both official). **Religions:** Christian 89.1% (Catholic [official] 83.6%), agnostic 7.6%.

Geography: Total area: 35,556 sq mi, 92,090 sq km (109); **Land area:** 35,317 sq mi, 91,470 sq km. **Location:** SW extreme of Europe. Spain on N, E. **Topography:** Tajus R. bisects country NE-SW. N is cool and rainy, mountainous. S is drier, with warm climate and rolling plains. **Arable land:** 10.3%. **Capital:** Lisbon, 2,956,879. **Cities:** Porto, 1,312,947.

Government: Type: Semi-presidential republic. **Head of state:** Pres. Marcelo Rebelo de Sousa; b. 1948; in office: Mar. 9, 2016. **Head of govt.:** Prime Min. António Costa; b. 1961; in office: Nov. 24, 2015. **Local divisions:** 18 districts, 2 autonomous regions. **Defense budget:** $2.7 bil. **Active troops:** 27,250.

Economy: Industries: textiles, clothing, footwear, wood and cork, paper and pulp, chemicals, fuels and lubricants, automobiles/auto parts, base metals. **Chief agric.:** grain, potatoes, tomatoes, olives, grapes; sheep, cattle, goats. **Natural resources:** fish, forests (cork), iron ore, copper, zinc, tin, tungsten, silver, gold, uranium, marble, clay, gypsum, salt, hydropower. **Water:** 7,493 cu m per capita. **Electricity prod.** (2018): 55.3 bil kWh. **Labor force:** agric. 5.7%, industry 24.6%, services 69.8%. **Unemployment:** 5.9%.

Finance: Monetary unit: Euro (EUR) (0.84 = $1 U.S.). **GDP:** $374.5 bil; **per capita GDP:** $36,471; **GDP growth:** 2.2%. **Imports:** $74.7 bil; Spain 32%, Germany 13.7%, France 7.4%, Italy 5.5%, Netherlands 5.4%. **Exports:** $61 bil; Spain 25.2%, France 12.5%, Germany 11.3%, UK 6.6%, U.S. 5.2%. **Tourism:** $20.6 bil. **Budget:** $100.0 bil. **Inflation:** 0.3%.

Transport: Railways: 1,911 mi. **Motor vehicles:** 570.6 per 1,000 pop. **Airports:** 43.

Communications: Telephone: 49.5 per 100 pop. **Mobile:** 115.6 per 100 pop. **Broadband:** 68.9 per 100 pop. **Internet** (2018): 74.7%.

Health: Expend.: 9.0%. **Life expect.:** 77.9 male; 84.4 female. **Births:** 8.1 per 1,000 pop. **Deaths:** 10.8 per 1,000 pop. **Infant mortality:** 2.6 per 1,000 live births. **Undernourished:** <2.5%. **HIV** (2018): 0.5%.

Education: Compulsory: ages 6-17. **Literacy:** 99.7%.

Embassy: 2012 Massachusetts Ave. NW 20036; 350-5400.

Website: www.portugal.gov.pt

Portugal, an independent state since the 12th cent., was a kingdom until a 1910 revolution drove out King Manoel II and a republic was proclaimed. Beginning in 1932, Prime Min. Antonio de Oliveira Salazar headed a repressive government. Illness forced his retirement in Sept. 1968.

On Apr. 25, 1974, a military junta led by Gen. Antonio de Spinola seized the government; Spinola became president. The new government granted independence to Guinea-Bissau, Mozambique, Cabo Verde, Angola, and São Tomé and Príncipe.

With the economy lagging, the Socialists won 2005 and 2009 parliamentary elections. After Portugal was given a 78-bil-euro bailout package from international lenders to avert default, the center-right Social Democratic Party won parliamentary elections June 2011. Austerity cuts caused widespread protests in Nov. 2012. Portugal exited the bailout program in May 2014. After parliamentary elections Oct. 4, 2015, Socialist António Costa became prime min., Nov. 24, leading an anti-austerity leftist coalition. Former Prime Min. António Guterres became UN secretary general, Jan. 1, 2017. Costa retained office after the Socialists increased their number of seats in Oct. 6, 2019, elections.

Affected by the 2020 COVID-19 pandemic, Portugal recorded almost 75,000 cases and nearly 2,000 deaths by Sept. 30.

Azores Isls., in the Atlantic, 740 mi W of Portugal, have an area of 868 sq mi and a pop. (2014 est.) of 246,353. A 1951 agreement gave the U.S. rights to use defense facilities in the Azores. The **Madeira Isls.**, 350 mi off the NW coast of Africa, have an area of 306 sq mi and a pop. (2014 est.) of 258,686. Both groups were offered partial autonomy in 1976.

Qatar
State of Qatar

People: Population: 2,444,174 (140). **Age distrib.:** <15: 12.8%; 65+: 1.2%. **Growth:** 1.4%. **Migrants:** 78.7%. **Pop. density:** 546.4 per sq mi, 211.0 per sq km. **Urban:** 99.2%. **Ethnic groups:** non-Qatari 88.4%, Qatari 11.6%. **Languages:** Arabic (official), English. **Religions:** Muslim 80% (Sunni [official] 67%, Shia 13%), Christian 12.9% (Catholic 11.6%), Hindu 3%.

Geography: Total area: 4,473 sq mi, 11,586 sq km (159); **Land area:** 4,473 sq mi, 11,586 sq km. **Location:** Middle East, occupying peninsula on W coast of Persian Gulf. Saudi Arabia on S. **Topography:** Mostly flat desert with some limestone ridges; scarce vegetation. **Arable land:** 1.2%. **Capital:** Doha (Ad-Dawhah) 641,380.

Government: Type: Absolute monarchy. **Head of state:** Sheikh Tamim bin Hamad al-Thani; b. 1980; in office: June 25, 2013. **Head of govt.:** Prime Min. Khalid bin Khalifa bin Abdul Aziz Al Thani; b. 1968; in office: Jan. 28, 2020. **Local divisions:** 8 municipalities. **Defense budget:** NA. **Active troops:** 16,500.

Economy: Industries: liquefied nat. gas, crude oil prod./refining, ammonia, fertilizer, petrochemicals, steel reinforcing bars. **Chief agric.:** fruits, vegetables; poultry, dairy prods., beef; fish. **Natural resources:** petroleum, fish, nat. gas. **Water:** 22 cu m per capita. **Crude oil reserves:** 25.2 bil bbls. **Electricity prod.:** 42.9 bil kwH. **Labor force:** agric. 1.2%, industry 54.4%, services 44.5%. **Unemployment:** 0.1%.

Finance: Monetary unit: Riyal (QAR) (3.64 = $1 U.S.). **GDP:** $273.3 bil; **per capita GDP:** $96,491; **GDP growth:** −0.2%. **Imports:** $30.8 bil; China 10.9%, U.S. 8.9%, UAE 8.5%, Germany 8.1%, UK 5.5%, India 5.4%, Japan 5.3%. **Exports:** $67.5 bil; Japan 17.3%, South Korea 16%, India 12.6%, China 11.2%, Singapore 8.2%, UAE 6.4%. **Tourism:** $5.4 bil. **Budget:** $53.8 bil. **Inflation:** −0.7%.

Transport: Motor vehicles: 189.8 per 1,000 pop. **Airports:** 4. **Communications: Telephone:** 16.3 per 100 pop. **Mobile:** 141.9 per 100 pop. **Broadband:** 117.4 per 100 pop. **Internet** (2018): 99.7%.

Health: Expend.: 2.6%. **Life expect.:** 77.2 male; 81.6 female. **Births:** 9.3 per 1,000 pop. **Deaths:** 1.6 per 1,000 pop. **Infant mortality:** 5.7 per 1,000 live births. **Undernourished:** NA. **HIV:** NA. **Education:** Compulsory: ages 6-14. **Literacy:** 94.6%. **Embassy:** 2555 M St. NW 20037; 274-1600. **Website:** portal.www.gov.qa

Qatar was under Bahrain's control until the Ottoman Turks took power, 1872 to 1915. In a treaty signed 1916, Qatar gave Great Britain responsibility for its defense and foreign relations. Qatar declared itself independent, Sept. 1, 1971. In municipal elections held Mar. 8, 1999, women participated for the first time as candidates and voters. Qatar's emir, Sheikh Hamad bin Kha-lifa al-Thani, abdicated in favor of his son, Sheikh Tamim bin Hamad al-Thani, June 25, 2013. A major producer and exporter of oil and natural gas, Qatar is one of the world's wealthiest nations per capita.

Since the early 2000s, Qatar has hosted U.S. military facilities and forces. Qatar joined Saudi-led airstrikes, beginning Mar. 2015, against Shiite Houthi rebels in Yemen but was expelled from that effort June 5, 2017. Beginning June 5, a Saudi-led group of Arab nations, alleging Qatari support for terrorist and sectarian groups, broke diplomatic relations with Qatar and imposed a travel and trade ban. On Aug. 24, Qatar restored full diplomatic relations with Iran (severed in 2016). A member of OPEC since 1961, Qatar left the organization Jan. 1, 2019. Global recession triggered by the 2020 COVID-19 pandemic hurt oil and gas revenue. Hard hit by the pandemic, Qatar had more than 125,000 COVID-19 cases and over 200 deaths by Sept. 30.

Romania

People: Population: 21,302,893 (59). **Age distrib.:** <15: 14.1%; 65+: 17.6%. **Growth:** −0.4%. **Migrants:** 2.4%. **Pop. density:** 240.0 per sq mi, 92.7 per sq km. **Urban:** 54.2%. **Ethnic**

groups: Romanian 83.4%, Hungarian 6.1%, Romani 3.1%. **Languages:** Romanian (official), Hungarian. **Religions:** Christian 98.6% (Orthodox 81.3%).

Geography: Total area: 92,043 sq mi, 238,391 sq km (81); **Land area:** 88,761 sq mi, 229,891 sq km. **Location:** SE Europe, on the Black Sea. Moldova on E, Ukraine on N, Hungary and Serbia on W, Bulgaria on S. **Topography:** The Carpathian Mts. surround the N central Transylvanian plateau. The lower reaches of the Danube river system flow through plains S and E of the mountains. **Arable land:** 37.1%. **Capital:** Bucharest, 1,803,247.

Government: Type: Semi-presidential republic. **Head of state:** Pres. Klaus Iohannis; b. 1959; in office: Dec. 21, 2014. **Head of govt.:** Prime Min. Ludovic Orban; b. 1963; in office: Nov. 4, 2019. **Local divisions:** 41 counties, 1 municipality. **Defense budget:** $5 bil. **Active troops:** 69,600.

Economy: Industries: elec. machinery/equip., auto assembly, textiles/footwear, light machinery, metallurgy, chemicals, food proc. **Chief agric.:** wheat, corn, barley, sugar beets, sunflower seeds, potatoes, grapes; eggs, sheep. **Natural resources:** petroleum, timber, nat. gas, coal, iron ore, salt, hydropower. **Water:** 10,773 cu m per capita. **Crude oil reserves:** 600 mil bbls. **Electricity prod.** (2018): 61.2 bil kWH. **Labor force:** agric. 21.3%, industry 30.1%, services 48.6%. **Unemployment:** 3.9%.

Finance: Monetary unit: Leu (RON) (4.10 = $1 U.S.). **GDP:** $625.2 bil; **per capita GDP:** $32,297; **GDP growth:** 4.1%. **Imports:** $78.1 bil; Germany 20%, Italy 10%, Hungary 7.5%, Poland 5.5%, France 5.3%, China 5%. **Exports:** $64.6 bil; Germany 23%, Italy 11.2%, France 6.8%. **Tourism:** $3.6 bil. **Budget:** $68.1 bil. **Inflation:** 3.8%.

Transport: Railways: 7,002 mi. **Motor vehicles:** 350.5 per 1,000 pop. **Airports:** 26.

Communications: Telephone: 18.8 per 100 pop. **Mobile:** 116.2 per 100 pop. **Broadband:** 82.9 per 100 pop. **Internet** (2018): 70.7%.

Health: Expend.: 5.2%. **Life expect.:** 72.6 male; 79.7 female. **Births:** 8.5 per 1,000 pop. **Deaths:** 12 per 1,000 pop. **Infant mortality:** 8.7 per 1,000 live births. **Undernourished:** <2.5%. **HIV:** 0.1%. **Education:** Compulsory: ages 7-16. **Literacy:** 99.4%. **Embassy:** 1607 23rd St. NW 20008; 332-4846. **Website:** gov.ro

Romania's earliest known people merged with invading Proto-Thracians, preceding by centuries the Dacians. Rome occupied the Dacian kingdom, 106-271 CE; people and language were Romanized. The Turkey-dominated principalities of Wallachia and Moldavia were united in 1859, became Romania in 1861, and gained recognition as an independent kingdom, 1881.

After WWI, Romania acquired Bessarabia, Bukovina, Transylvania, and Banat. In 1940 it ceded Bessarabia and Northern Bukovina to the USSR, part of southern Dobrudja to Bulgaria, and northern Transylvania to Hungary. In 1941, Prem. Marshal Ion Antonescu led Romania in support of Germany against the USSR. He was overthrown in 1944, and Romania joined the Allies. After occupation by Soviet troops, a People's Republic was proclaimed, Dec. 30, 1947.

The domestic policies of Nicolae Ceausescu (in power 1965) were repressive. All industry was state-owned, and state farms and cooperatives owned almost all arable land. Ceausescu's security forces fired on anti-government demonstrators, Dec. 1989, killing hundreds, but when the army sided with the protesters, his regime fell. Ceausescu and his wife were executed Dec. 25, 1989.

A new constitution providing for a multiparty system took effect Dec. 8, 1991. Many state-owned companies were privatized in 1996. Romania became a full NATO member in 2004. It entered the European Union Jan. 1, 2007.

The Social Democratic Party's (PSD) Victor-Viorel Ponta became prime min. May 7, 2012. He ran for president in 2014 but lost the runoff to centrist Klaus Iohannis. Large protests, blaming government incompetence for the deaths of more than 60 in a Bucharest nightclub fire, Oct. 30, 2015, led to the resignation, Nov. 4, 2015, of Ponta, already weakened by corruption allegations. The PSD won Dec. 11, 2016, parliamentary elections. The PSD's Viorica Dancila, a close ally of party leader Liviu Dragnea, became Romania's first female prime min. Jan. 29, 2018. Dragnea was convicted, June 2018, on corruption-related charges. After Dancila, Oct. 10, 2019, lost a no-confidence vote, Ludovic Orban of the center-right National Liberal Party became prime min., Nov. 4. Iohannis won reelection in a Nov. 24 presidential runoff (defeating Dancila).

After new cases rose sharply July-Sept., the 2020 COVID-19 pandemic had caused more than 125,000 total cases and about 4,800 deaths in Romania by Sept. 30.

Russia
Russian Federation

People: Population: 141,722,205 (9). **Age distrib.:** <15: 17.2%; 65+: 15.5%. **Growth:** −0.2%. **Migrants:** 8.0%. **Pop. density:** 22.4 per sq mi, 8.7 per sq km. **Urban:** 74.8%. **Ethnic groups:** Russian 77.7%, Tatar 3.7%. **Languages:** Russian (official), Tatar. **Religions:** Christian 81.9% (Orthodox 79%), Muslim 12.7% (Sunni), agnostic 3.8%.

Geography: Total area: 6,601,668 sq mi, 17,098,242 sq km (1); **Land area:** 6,323,482 sq mi, 16,377,742 sq km, more than 76%

of total area of the former USSR and the largest country in the world. **Location:** Stretches from Eastern Europe across N Asia to the Pacific O. Finland, Norway, Estonia, Latvia, Belarus, Ukraine on W; Georgia, Azerbaijan, Kazakhstan, China, Mongolia, N. Korea on S; Kaliningrad exclave bordered by Poland on the S, Lithuania on the N and E. **Topography:** Every type of climate except distinctly tropical. European portion is low plain, grassy in S, wooded in N, with Ural Mts. on E, and Caucasus Mts. on S. Urals stretch N-S for 2,500 mi. Asiatic portion is vast plain, with mountains on S and in E; tundra covers extreme N with forest belt below; plains, marshes in W, desert in SW. **Arable land:** 7.4%. **Capital:** Moscow, 12,537,954. **Cities:** Saint Petersburg, 5,467,808; Novosibirsk, 1,663,748; Yekaterinburg, 1,503,812; Kazan, 1,272,063; Nizhniy Novgorod, 1,257,754; Chelyabinsk, 1,227,795.

Government: Type: Semi-presidential federation. **Head of state:** Pres. Vladimir Putin; b. 1952; in office: May 7, 2012. **Head of govt.:** Prime Min. Mikhail Mishustin; b. 1966; in office: Jan. 16, 2020. **Local divisions:** 46 provinces (oblasts), 21 republics, 4 autonomous okrugs, 9 krays, 2 federal cities, 1 autonomous oblast. **Defense budget:** $48.2 bil. **Active troops:** 900,000.

Economy: Industries: coal, oil, gas, chemicals, metals; machine building; defense (incl. radar, missile prod.); shipbuilding; road, rail transp. equip.; communications equip.; agric. machinery, tractors, constr. equip. **Chief agric.:** grain, sugar beets, sunflower seeds, vegetables, fruits; beef, milk. **Natural resources:** oil, nat. gas, coal, minerals, bauxite, rare earth elements, timber. Climate, terrain, and distance are obstacles to resource exploitation. **Water:** 31,426 cu m per capita. **Crude oil reserves:** 80 bil bbls. **Electricity prod.** (2018): 1 tril kWh. **Labor force:** agric. 5.6%, industry 26.6%, services 67.8%. **Unemployment:** 4.4%.

Finance: Monetary unit: Ruble (RUB) (75.25 = $1 U.S.). **GDP:** $4.3 tril; **per capita GDP:** $29,181; **GDP growth:** 1.3%. **Imports:** $238 bil; China 21.2%, Germany 10.7%, U.S. 5.6%, Belarus 5%. **Exports:** $353 bil; China 10.9%, Netherlands 10%, Germany 7.1%, Belarus 5.1%. **Tourism:** $11 bil. **Budget:** $281.4 bil. **Inflation:** 4.5%.

Transport: Railways: 54,157 mi. **Motor vehicles:** 411.1 per 1,000 pop. **Airports:** 594.

Communications: Telephone (2017): 22 per 100 pop. **Mobile:** 157.4 per 100 pop. **Broadband:** 80.8 per 100 pop. **Internet** (2018): 80.9%.

Health: Expend.: 5.3%. **Life expect.:** 66.3 male; 77.8 female. **Births:** 10 per 1,000 pop. **Deaths:** 13.4 per 1,000 pop. **Infant mortality:** 6.5 per 1,000 live births. **Undernourished:** <2.5%. **HIV:** NA.

Education: Compulsory: ages 7-17. Literacy: 99.7%.

Embassy: 2650 Wisconsin Ave. NW 20007; 298-5700.

Website: government.ru

Slavic tribes began migrating into Russia from the W in the 5th cent. The first Russian state, centered in Novgorod and Kyiv, was founded by Scandinavian chieftains in the 9th cent. In the 13th cent., Mongols overran the country. It recovered under the grand dukes and princes of Muscovy, or Moscow, and by 1480 freed itself from the Mongols. Ivan the Terrible was proclaimed Tsar, 1547. Peter the Great (1682-1725) extended the domain and, in 1721, founded the Russian empire. Western ideas and the beginnings of modernization spread through the empire in the 19th and early 20th cent.

Military reverses in the 1905 war with Japan and in WWI led to the breakdown of the Tsarist regime. The 1917 Revolution began in Mar. with a series of sporadic strikes for higher wages by factory workers. A provisional democratic government under Prince Georgi Lvov was established but a second provisional government, under Alexander Kerensky, followed in May. Vladimir Ilyich Lenin, Nov. 7, overthrew the Kerensky government and the freely elected Constituent Assembly in a Communist coup.

Soviet Union. Lenin's death Jan. 21, 1924, led to an internal power struggle won by Joseph Stalin. His brutal tactics, including purge trials, mass executions, and exile to work camps, resulted in millions of deaths.

Despite a Germany-USSR non-aggression pact signed in Aug. 1939, Germany invaded the Soviet Union, June 1941. Russian winter counterthrusts, 1941-42 and 1942-43; victory at Stalingrad (now Volgograd), Feb. 2, 1943 (2 mil total casualties); and resistance to the siege of Leningrad (now St. Petersburg) stopped the German advance. Russian armies drove the Germans from Eastern Europe and the Balkans in the next two years.

After WWII, Communists took over in countries throughout the region, extending the Soviet sphere of influence. The USSR and the U.S., the world's leading nuclear superpowers, became Cold War rivals. After Stalin died, Mar. 5, 1953, Nikita Khrushchev gained power and denounced Stalin, 1956, beginning "de-Stalinization."

Under Khrushchev the open antagonism of Poles and Hungarians toward Moscow's domination was suppressed in 1956. He aided the Cuban revolution under Fidel Castro but withdrew Soviet missiles from Cuba during a confrontation with U.S. Pres. John Kennedy, Sept.-Oct. 1962. Khrushchev was deposed, Oct. 1964, and replaced by Leonid I. Brezhnev. In Aug. 1968, Soviet forces invaded Czechoslovakia, crushing liberalization there.

Massive Soviet military aid to North Vietnam in the late 1960s and early 1970s helped ensure Communist victories throughout Indochina. In Dec. 1979, Soviet forces entered Afghanistan to support a pro-Soviet regime against U.S.-supported Muslim resistance fighters. In Apr. 1988, the Soviets agreed to withdraw their troops, ending a futile 8-year war.

Mikhail Gorbachev was chosen Communist Party gen. sec., Mar. 1985. In 1987 he initiated a program of political and economic reforms through openness (*glasnost*) and restructuring (*perestroika*). Gorbachev faced economic problems as well as ethnic and nationalist unrest in the republics. A coup by Communist hardliners Aug. 1991 was foiled with help from Russian Republic Pres. Boris Yeltsin. On Aug. 24, Gorbachev resigned as leader of the Communist Party. Several republics declared their independence. On Aug. 29, the Soviet Parliament voted to suspend all activities of the Communist Party. The Soviet Union officially broke up Dec. 26, 1991.

Russian Federation. Under Pres. Yeltsin, Russia took steps toward privatization, which caused inflation and a severe economic downturn. In June 1992, Yeltsin and U.S. Pres. George H. W. Bush agreed to massive arms reductions. In a referendum Dec. 12, 1993, a new constitution was approved. Russian troops fought rebels in the breakaway republic of Chechnya Dec. 1994-Aug. 1996, when a peace accord temporarily ended the conflict. Yeltsin was reelected in 1996.

An Aug. 1999 operation to suppress Islamic rebels in the republic of Dagestan reignited the war in neighboring Chechnya, where Russia launched a full-scale assault. Yeltsin unexpectedly resigned Dec. 31, 1999, naming Prime Min. Vladimir Putin as his interim successor. Putin won presidential elections Mar. 2000 and Mar. 2004. Putin's allies won legislative elections, Dec. 2003.

A bomb in Grozny, May 9, 2004, killed Chechnya's pro-Moscow president, Akhmad Kadyrov. In another terrorist act linked to the Chechnya conflict, two passenger planes exploded in midair after taking off from Moscow Aug. 24, killing 90 people. After Chechen rebels, Sept. 1, 2004, seized control of a school in Beslan, North Ossetia, Russian troops stormed the school Sept. 3; more than 330 people, including 186 children, died. Putin cited the terrorist threat Sept. 13 in proposing a government overhaul that tightened his control over parliament and regional officeholders. Russian forces killed Chechen rebel leader Aslan Maskha-dov, Mar. 8, 2005, and Chechen guerrilla leader Shamil Basayev, organizer of the Beslan attack, July 10, 2006.

Constitutionally barred from seeking another term, Pres. Putin backed his protégé Prime Min. Dmitri Medvedev, who won the presidential election Mar. 2, 2008. Medvedev named Putin as prime min. A long-simmering conflict with Georgia erupted into open warfare Aug. 7-16. Russian troops supported secessionists in the enclaves of South Ossetia and Abkhazia, which Russia recognized as independent, Aug. 26, 2008.

Russia declared, Apr. 16, 2009, that it had ended counterterrorism operations in Chechnya; from June through Aug., there was an upsurge of insurgent violence in Chechnya and neighboring Dagestan and Ingushetia. Suicide bombers from Dagestan struck two Moscow subway stations Mar. 29, 2010, killing 40 people.

Medvedev and U.S. Pres. Barack Obama, Apr. 8, 2010, signed a nuclear arms reduction treaty known as New START. Putin won the Mar. 4, 2012, presidential election, though there were claims of fraud. Three members of the anti-Putin punk-protest band Pussy Riot were convicted of hooliganism Aug. 17, 2012. Putin signed a law, June 30, 2013, effectively making it illegal to advocate publicly for gay rights. Persecution of LBGTQ people increased in subsequent years. A 2020 constitutional amendment defined marriage as only between a man and a woman.

After Ukraine's pro-Russian president was removed from office Feb. 22, 2014, Russia sent troops into Ukraine's Crimean Peninsula and annexed Crimea Mar. 18. Russia also apparently provided military equipment and troops to pro-Russian separatists in eastern Ukraine fighting Ukrainian government forces beginning in Apr. 2014. The U.S. and EU imposed economic sanctions to protest Russia's Ukraine policies.

Russia supported Pres. Bashar al-Assad in Syria's civil war (2011-). In Sept. 2015, Russia sent combat aircraft and troops to Syria. Russian airstrikes against various rebel forces, including ISIS and an al-Qaeda affiliate, and against rebel-held areas caused high civilian casualties. An ISIS-affiliated group claimed responsibility for planting a bomb on a Russian airliner that crashed in Egypt, Oct. 31, 2015, killing all 224 onboard.

More than 100 Russian athletes were barred from the 2016 Summer Olympics after the World Anti-Doping Agency presented evidence of a widespread state-sponsored program to provide athletes with banned drugs. Russia was officially barred from the 2018 Winter Olympics, although 169 individual Russian athletes were allowed to compete.

Putin's United Russia party won Sept. 18, 2016, parliamentary elections. With the media tightly controlled and amid allegations of fraud, Putin won a new 6-year term as president, Mar. 18, 2018. Leading dissident Aleksei Navalny was barred from running against Putin.

U.S. government security agencies concluded in Dec. 2016 that Russia attempted to interfere in the 2016 U.S. presidential election, apparently to assist the candidacy of Donald Trump, using tactics including cyberattacks and manipulation of social media. The U.S. indicted, Feb. and July 2018, 16 Russian individuals or companies and 12 Russian intelligence officials on charges related to 2016 election interference.

At a July 16, 2018, meeting with Pres. Trump, Putin denied Russia had interfered in U.S. elections; speaking after the meeting, Trump appeared to accept the denial. At an Aug. 2 briefing, top Trump-administration intelligence officials stated that Russia was working to affect the 2018 elections. U.S. officials concluded in 2019 and 2020 that Russian election interference was ongoing.

Russian agents were apparently responsible for the poisoning, in the UK in Mar. 2018, of a former Russian intelligence officer. Navalny, while traveling in Siberia Aug. 20, 2020, was apparently poisoned, according to officials in Germany, where he was transferred for treatment.

Beginning in 2014, the U.S. accused Russia of violating the 1987 Intermediate-Range Nuclear Forces (INF) Treaty. The U.S. withdrew from the INF treaty Aug. 2, 2019.

Constitutional changes approved in 2020 allowed Putin serve two more 6-year terms as president after his current term expires in 2024.

Russia was one of the world's most severely affected countries by the 2020 COVID-19 pandemic, with more than 1,176,000 cases by Sept. 30 and almost 21,000 deaths (under-reporting was suspected). Lockdown measures to impede disease transmission, as well as pandemic-related declines in oil and natural gas revenue, hurt the economy. Putin announced, Aug. 11, that a Russian-developed vaccine had been approved for use—although it had not yet gone through large-scale clinical trials.

Rwanda
Republic of Rwanda

People: Population: 12,712,431 (75). **Age distrib.:** <15: 40.0%; 65+: 2.6%. **Growth:** 1.9%. **Migrants:** 4.3%. **Pop. density:** 1,334.7 per sq mi, 515.3 per sq km. **Urban:** 17.4%. **Ethnic groups:** Hutu, Tutsi, Twa (Pygmy). **Languages:** Kinyarwanda (universal Bantu vernacular), French, English (all official). **Religions:** Christian 91.2% (Catholic 44.3%, Protestant 34.9%, independent 12%), Muslim 5.6% (Sunni).

Geography: Total area: 10,169 sq mi, 26,338 sq km (145); **Land area:** 9,524 sq mi, 24,668 sq km. **Location:** E central Africa. Uganda on N, Dem. Rep. of the Congo on W, Burundi on S, Tanzania on E. **Topography:** Grassy uplands and hills cover most of country, with chain of volcanoes in NW. Nile R. source is in headwaters of the Kagera (Akagera) R. **Arable land:** 46.7%. **Capital:** Kigali, 1,132,101.

Government: Type: Presidential republic. **Head of state:** Pres. Paul Kagame; b. 1957; in office: Apr. 22, 2000 (de facto from Mar. 24). **Head of govt.:** Prime Min. Edouard Ngirente; b. 1973; in office: Aug. 30, 2017. **Local divisions:** 4 provinces, 1 city. **Defense budget:** $112 mil. **Active troops:** 33,000.

Economy: Industries: cement, agric. prods., small-scale beverages, soap, furniture, shoes, plastic goods, textiles, cigarettes. **Chief agric.:** coffee, tea, pyrethrum (insecticide made from chrysanthemums), bananas, beans, sorghum, potatoes; livestock. **Natural resources:** gold, tin ore, tungsten ore, methane, hydropower. **Water:** 1,089 cu m per capita. **Electricity prod.:** 771 mil kwH. **Labor force:** agric. 61.7%, industry 9.1%, services 29.2%. **Unemployment:** 1.0%.

Finance: Monetary unit: Franc (RWF) (965.41 = $1 U.S.). **GDP:** $29.3 bil; **per capita GDP:** $2,318; **GDP growth:** 9.4%. **Imports:** $1.9 bil; China 20.4%, Uganda 11%, India 7.2%, Kenya 7.1%, Tanzania 5.3%, UAE 5.1%. **Exports:** $1.1 bil; UAE 38.3%, Kenya 15.1%, Switzerland 9.9%, Dem. Rep. of the Congo 9.5%. **Tourism:** $374 mil. **Budget:** $2.3 bil. **Inflation:** 3.4%.

Transport: Airports: 4.

Communications: Telephone: 0.1 per 100 pop. **Mobile:** 78.9 per 100 pop. **Broadband:** 35 per 100 pop. **Internet:** 21.8%.

Health: Expend.: 6.6%. **Life expect.:** 63.2 male; 67.1 female. **Births:** 27.9 per 1,000 pop. **Deaths:** 6.1 per 1,000 pop. **Infant mortality:** 28.0 per 1,000 live births. **Undernourished:** 35.6%. **HIV:** 2.6%.

Education: Compulsory: ages 7-12. **Literacy:** 86.5%.

Embassy: 1875 Connecticut Ave. NW, Ste. 540, 20009; 232-2882. **Website:** www.gov.rw

For centuries, the Tutsi dominated the Hutu majority. A civil war broke out in 1959 and Tutsi power was ended. Many Tutsi went into exile. Rwanda, which had been part of the Belgian UN trusteeship of Rwanda-Urundi, became independent July 1, 1962.

A large-scale massacre of Tutsi occurred in 1963. Hutu rivalries led to a bloodless coup July 1973 in which Hutu army officer Juvénal Habyarimana took power. After an invasion and coup attempt by Tutsi exiles in 1990, a multiparty democracy was established.

Renewed ethnic strife led to an Aug. 1993 peace accord between the government and rebels of the Tutsiled Rwandan Patriotic Front (RPF). But after Habyarimana and Burundi Pres. Cyprien Ntaryamira were killed Apr. 6, 1994, in a suspicious plane crash, violence broke out. More than 1 mil may have died in massacres, mostly of Tutsi by Hutu militias, and in civil warfare as the RPF

sought power. About 2 mil Tutsi and Hutu fled to camps in Zaire (now Dem. Rep. of the Congo, or DRC) and other countries; many died of disease. French troops under a UN mandate moved into SW Rwanda June 23 to establish a safe zone. The RPF claimed victory, installing a government led by a moderate Hutu premier in July. French troops pulled out Aug. 22. A UN peacekeeping mission ended Mar. 8, 1996. More than 1 mil refugees, mostly Hutu, returned to Rwanda in Nov.-Dec. 1996.

Former Prime Min. Jean Kambanda pleaded guilty to genocide, May 1, 1998, before the UN-backed Intl. Criminal Tribunal for Rwanda (ICTR); he received a life sentence Sept. 4, 1998. RPF leader Maj. Gen. Paul Kagame became Rwanda's first Tutsi president Apr. 22, 2000.

Rwandans approved a new constitution, May 26, 2003, and reelected Pres. Kagame, Aug. 25. Rwanda cut diplomatic ties with France Nov. 24, 2006, after a French judge linked Kagame to the 1994 deaths of Habyarimana and Ntaryamira. The country restored relations with France, Nov. 2009, the same month Rwanda joined the Commonwealth. Accused of being one of the architects of the 1994 genocide, Col. Theoneste Bagosora was convicted and sentenced to prison by the ICTR, Dec. 18, 2008. A Rwandan court Jan. 20, 2009, sentenced former Justice Min. Agnes Ntamabyariro to life in prison for her role in inciting the massacres. Up to 4,000 Rwandan troops fought that month alongside Congolese forces against Hutu militias in eastern DRC. After a campaign criticized as repressive by human rights groups, Pres. Kagame won reelection Aug. 9, 2010.

An Oct. 17, 2012, UN report found that the Rwanda military was backing a rebellion (2012-13) by the mostly-Tutsi M23 group in the DRC. Shortly before the ICTR ceased operations, Dec. 31, 2015, one of its most-wanted fugitives, Ladislas Ntaganzwa, was arrested by Interpol in the DRC. His genocide trial in Rwanda ended in a conviction and life sentence, May 28, 2020. Suppressing political opposition, Kagame won—with almost 99% of the vote—a new term as president in an Aug. 4, 2017, election. Dissident Paul Rusesabagina, whose protection of over 1,200 Tutsi from the 1994 genocide was dramatized in the film *Hotel Rwanda*, was arrested, Aug. 2020, on terrorism charges.

The 2020 COVID-19 pandemic caused about 4,800 cases and 29 deaths in Rwanda by Sept. 30.

Saint Kitts and Nevis
Federation of Saint Kitts and Nevis

People: Population: 53,821 (189). **Age distrib.:** <15: 19.9%; 65+: 10.0%. **Growth:** 0.7%. **Migrants:** 14.4%. **Pop. density:** 534.1 per sq mi, 206.2 per sq km. **Urban:** 30.8%. **Ethnic groups:** African descent 92.5%, mixed 3%, white 2.1%. **Languages:** English (official). **Religions:** Christian 94.1% (Protestant 77.2%).

Geography: Total area: 101 sq mi, 261 sq km (189); **Land area:** 101 sq mi, 261 sq km. **Location:** In N part of the Leeward group of Lesser Antilles in E Caribbean Sea. Antigua and Barbuda to E. **Topography:** Forested volcanic slopes on St. Kitts; beaches rising to central peak on Nevis. Tropical climate moderated by sea breezes. **Arable land:** 19.2%. **Capital:** Basseterre, 14,434.

Government: Type: Federal parliamentary democracy under constitutional monarchy. **Head of state:** Queen Elizabeth II, rep. by Gov.-Gen. Samuel W. T. Seaton; b. 1950; in office: Sept. 1, 2015. **Head of govt.:** Prime Min. Timothy Harris; b. 1964; in office: Feb. 18, 2015. **Local divisions:** 14 parishes. **Defense budget/active troops:** NA.

Economy: Industries: tourism, cotton, salt, copra, clothing, footwear, beverages. **Chief agric.:** sugarcane, rice, yams, vegetables, bananas; fish. **Water:** 434 cu m per capita. **Electricity prod.:** 198 mil kwH. **Labor force:** NA. **Unemployment:** NA.

Finance: Monetary unit: East Caribbean Dollar (XCD) (2.70 = $1 U.S.). **GDP:** $1.4 bil; **per capita GDP:** $27,449; **GDP growth:** 2.5%. **Imports:** $335.3 mil; (2016) U.S. 56.8%, Trinidad and Tobago 6.8%, Cyprus 6.2%. **Exports:** $57.4 mil; (2016) U.S. 49.6%, Poland, 15.2%, Turkey 11.6%. **Tourism:** $202 mil. **Budget:** $291.1 mil. **Inflation** (2017-18): −1.0%.

Transport: Railways: 31 mi. **Airports:** 2.

Communications: Telephone (2017): 33.2 per 100 pop. **Mobile** (2017): 147.7 per 100 pop. **Broadband:** 84.9 per 100 pop. **Internet:** 80.7%.

Health: Expend.: 5.0%. **Life expect.:** 74.1 male; 79.1 female. **Births:** 12.6 per 1,000 pop. **Deaths:** 7.3 per 1,000 pop. **Infant mortality:** 7.8 per 1,000 live births. **Undernourished:** NA. **HIV** (2018): 0.5%.

Education: Compulsory: ages 5-16. **Literacy:** 98%.

Embassy: 3216 New Mexico Ave. NW, 20016; 686-2636. **Website:** www.gov.kn

St. Kitts (formerly St. Christopher; known by Indigenous peoples as Liamuiga) and Nevis were reached by Columbus in 1493. They were settled by Britain in 1623 (ownership was disputed with France until 1713). The colony achieved self-government in 1967, becoming independent, Sept. 19, 1983. A secession referendum on Nevis, Aug. 10, 1998, fell short of the two-thirds majority required. Twenty years of Labour Party governments ended when an opposition coalition won Feb. 16, 2015, legislative elections. The coalition won June 5, 2020, elections.

Saint Lucia

People: Population: 166,487 (178). **Age distrib.:** <15: 19.2%; 65+: 13.1%. **Growth:** 0.3%. **Migrants:** 4.6%. **Pop. density:** 711.6 per sq mi, 274.7 per sq km. **Urban:** 18.8%. **Ethnic groups:** Black/African descent 85.3%, mixed 10.9%, East Indian 2.2%. **Languages:** English (official), French patois. **Religions:** Christian 95.6% (Catholic 69.7%, Protestant 22.8%).

Geography: Total area: 238 sq mi, 616 sq km (179); **Land area:** 234 sq mi, 606 sq km. **Location:** E Caribbean, second largest of Windward Isls. Martinique (Fr.) to N, St. Vincent to S. **Topography:** Mountainous, volcanic in origin; Soufrière Volcanic Centre in S. Wooded mountains run N-S. **Arable land:** 4.9%. **Capital:** Castries, 22,258.

Government: Type: Parliamentary democracy under constitutional monarchy. **Head of state:** Queen Elizabeth II, rep. by Gov.-Gen. Neville Cenac, b. 1939; in office: Jan. 12, 2018. **Head of govt.:** Prime Min. Allen Chastanet; in office: June 7, 2016. **Local divisions:** 10 districts. **Defense budget/active troops:** NA.

Economy: Industries: tourism, clothing, electronic components assembly, beverages, corrugated cardboard boxes, lime proc. **Chief agric.:** bananas, coconuts, vegetables, citrus, root crops, cocoa. **Natural resources:** forests, sandy beaches, pumice, mineral springs. **Water:** 1,678 cu m per capita. **Electricity prod.:** 377 mil kWh. **Labor force:** agric. 17.0%, industry 18.3%, services 64.7%. **Unemployment:** 20.2%.

Finance: Monetary unit: East Caribbean Dollar (XCD) (2.70 = $1 U.S.). **GDP:** $2.9 bil; **per capita GDP:** $16,089; **GDP growth:** 1.7%. **Imports:** $600 mil; U.S. 53.3%, Trinidad and Tobago 10.8%. **Exports:** $185.1 mil; U.S. 67.6%, UK 5.9%, Trinidad and Tobago 5.5%. **Tourism:** $999 mil. **Budget:** $392.8 mil. **Inflation** (2017-18): 1.9%.

Transport: Airports: 2.

Communications: Telephone: 20.1 per 100 pop. **Mobile:** 101.7 per 100 pop. **Broadband:** 40.8 per 100 pop. **Internet:** 50.8%.

Health: Expend.: 4.5%. **Life expect.:** 75.7 male; 81.4 female. **Births:** 12.5 per 1,000 pop. **Deaths:** 8.1 per 1,000 pop. **Infant mortality:** 10.1 per 1,000 live births. **Undernourished:** NA. **HIV** (2018): 0.6%.

Education: Compulsory: ages 5-14. **Literacy:** NA.
Embassy: 1629 K St. NW, Ste. 1250, 20006; 364-6792.
Website: www.govt.lc

St. Lucia, ceded to Britain by France with the Treaty of Paris, 1814, gained independence Feb. 22, 1979. Investigation results announced Mar. 8, 2015, by Prime Min. Kenny Anthony found that 12 suspected criminals were put on a "death list" and killed by police in 2010-11. Pledging a tax cut and resolution of the police scandal, the conservative United Workers Party (UWP) defeated Anthony's Labor Party in June 6, 2016, elections; UWP leader Allen Chastanet became prime min.

Saint Vincent and the Grenadines

People: Population: 101,390 (183). **Age distrib.:** <15: 20.1%; 65+: 10.7%. **Growth:** −0.2%. **Migrants:** 4.2%. **Pop. density:** 675.1 per sq mi, 260.6 per sq km. **Urban:** 53.0%. **Ethnic groups:** African descent 71.2%, mixed 23%, Indigenous 3%. **Languages:** English, Vincentian Creole English, French patois. **Religions:** Christian 88.6% (Protestant 60%, independent 22.7%), Hindu 3.4%, agnostic 2.5%.

Geography: Total area: 150 sq mi, 389 sq km (185); **Land area:** 150 sq mi, 389 sq km. **Location:** E Caribbean; St. Vincent (133 sq mi) and the northern islets of the Grenadines form a part of Windward chain. St. Lucia to N, Barbados to E, Grenada to S. **Topography:** St. Vincent is volcanic, with a ridge of thickly wooded mountains running its length. **Arable land:** 12.8%. **Capital:** Kingstown, 26,636.

Government: Type: Parliamentary democracy under constitutional monarchy. **Head of state:** Queen Elizabeth II, rep. by Gov.-Gen. Susan Dougan; in office: Aug. 1, 2019. **Head of govt.:** Prime Min. Ralph Gonsalves; b. 1946; in office: Mar. 29, 2001. **Local divisions:** 6 parishes. **Defense budget/active troops:** NA.

Economy: Industries: tourism, food proc., cement, furniture, clothing, starch. **Chief agric.:** bananas, coconuts, sweet potatoes, spices. **Natural resources:** hydropower. **Water:** 910 cu m per capita. **Electricity prod.:** 118 mil kWh. **Labor force:** agric. 10.5%, industry 19.9%, services 69.5%. **Unemployment:** 18.9%.

Finance: Monetary unit: East Caribbean Dollar (XCD) (2.70 = $1 U.S.). **GDP:** $1.4 bil; **per capita GDP:** $12,983; **GDP growth:** 0.3%. **Imports:** $295.9 mil; U.S. 36.8%, Trinidad and Tobago 19.1%, UK 7%, China 5.8%. **Exports:** $48.6 mil; Jordan 40.7%, France 12.5%, Barbados 7%, St. Lucia 6.8%, Antigua and Barbuda 5.7%, U.S. 5.5%. **Tourism:** $118 mil. **Budget:** $230.0 mil. **Inflation** (2017-18): 2.3%.

Transport: Airports: 5.

Communications: Telephone: 17.4 per 100 pop. **Mobile:** 96.1 per 100 pop. **Broadband:** 49.6 per 100 pop. **Internet** (2018): 22.4%.

Health: Expend.: 4.5%. **Life expect.:** 74.1 male; 78.3 female. **Births:** 12.6 per 1,000 pop. **Deaths:** 7.6 per 1,000 pop. **Infant mortality:** 11.0 per 1,000 live births. **Undernourished:** 5.7%. **HIV** (2018): 1.5%.

Education: Compulsory: ages 5-16. **Literacy:** 88%.
Embassy: 1627 K St. NW, Ste. 1202, 20006; 364-6730.
Website: www.gov.vc

St. Vincent received its name because of the belief (not supported by evidence) that Christopher Columbus landed there on Jan. 22, 1498 (St. Vincent's Day). Britain and France both laid claim to the island in the 17th and 18th cent.; the Treaty of Versailles, 1783, ceded it to Britain. Independence was attained Oct. 27, 1979.

Samoa
Independent State of Samoa

People: Population: 203,774 (177). **Age distrib.:** <15: 29.3%; 65+: 6.2%. **Growth:** 0.6%. **Migrants:** 2.0%. **Pop. density:** 187.1 per sq mi, 72.2 per sq km. **Urban:** 17.9%. **Ethnic groups:** Samoan 96%, Samoan/New Zealander 2%. **Languages:** Samoan (Polynesian), English (both official). **Religions:** Christian (official) 98.8% (Protestant 50.1%, independent 33.4%, Catholic 15.3%).

Geography: Total area: 1,093 sq mi, 2,831 sq km (168); **Land area:** 1,089 sq mi, 2,821 sq km. **Location:** S Pacific O. Nearest neighbors are Fiji to SW, Tonga to S. **Topography:** Main islands, Savaii (659 sq mi) and Upolu (432 sq mi), both ruggedly mountainous. Small islands of Manono and Apolima. **Arable land:** 2.8%. **Capital:** Apia, 36,066.

Government: Type: Parliamentary republic. **Head of state:** Tuimaleali'ifano Va'aletoa Sualauvi II; b. 1947; in office: July 21, 2017. **Head of govt.:** Prime Min. Tuila'epa Sailele Malielegaoi; b. 1945; in office: Nov. 23, 1998. **Local divisions:** 11 districts. **Defense budget/active troops:** NA.

Economy: Industries: food proc., building materials, auto parts. **Chief agric.:** coconuts, nonu, bananas, taro, yams, coffee, cocoa. **Natural resources:** hardwood forests, fish, hydropower. **Water:** NA. **Electricity prod.:** 132 mil kWh. **Labor force:** agric. 29.9%, industry 23.3%, services 46.9%. **Unemployment:** 8.4%.

Finance: Monetary unit: Tala (WST) (2.60 = $1 U.S.). **GDP:** $1.3 bil; **per capita GDP:** $6,787; **GDP growth:** 3.5%. **Imports** (2018): $89.3 bil; New Zealand 22%, Singapore 20.7%, U.S. 12.5%, China 10.1%, Australia 8.6%, Fiji 5.2%. **Exports** (2014): $27.5 mil; Australia 22.9%, New Zealand 22.8%, American Samoa 22.1%, Afghanistan 14.9%, U.S. 5.9%. **Tourism:** $199 mil. **Budget:** $276.8 mil. **Inflation:** 1.0%.

Transport: Airports: 1.

Communications: Telephone (2017): 4.3 per 100 pop. **Mobile** (2017): 63.6 per 100 pop. **Broadband:** 29.8 per 100 pop. **Internet:** 33.6%.

Health: Expend.: 5.5%. **Life expect.:** 71.7 male; 77.7 female. **Births:** 19.6 per 1,000 pop. **Deaths:** 5.4 per 1,000 pop. **Infant mortality:** 17.0 per 1,000 live births. **Undernourished:** <2.5%. **HIV:** NA.

Education: Compulsory: ages 5-12. **Literacy:** 99.1%.
Embassy: 800 Second Ave., 4th Fl., New York, NY 10017; (212) 599-6196.
Website: www.samoagovt.ws

Samoa (formerly Western Samoa) was a German colony, 1899 to 1914, when New Zealand landed troops and took over. It became a New Zealand mandate under the League of Nations and, in 1945, a New Zealand UN Trusteeship. An elected local government took office in Oct. 1959, and the country became fully independent Jan. 1, 1962. In 2011, Samoa moved west of the Intl. Date Line to reduce time differences with Australia and New Zealand. "Panama Papers" documents showed, in 2016, that the law firm from which the files leaked had set up thousands of shell companies in Samoa. The Legislative Assembly, July 4, 2017, elected Tuimaleali'ifano Va'aletoa Sualauvi II to a 5-year term as head of state.

San Marino
Republic of San Marino

People: Population: 34,232 (191). **Age distrib.:** <15: 14.7%; 65+: 20.2%. **Growth:** 0.6%. **Migrants:** 16.3%. **Pop. density:** 1,453.5 per sq mi, 561.2 per sq km. **Urban:** 97.5%. **Ethnic groups:** Sammarinese, Italian. **Languages:** Italian. **Religions:** Christian 91.5% (Catholic 90.7%), agnostic 5.6%.

Geography: Total area: 24 sq mi, 61 sq km (192); **Land area:** 24 sq mi, 61 sq km. **Location:** Completely surrounded by Italy, in N center of that country, near Adriatic coast. **Topography:** On slopes of Mt. Titano. **Arable land:** 16.7%. **Capital:** San Marino, 4,465.

Government: Type: Parliamentary republic. **Heads of state:** Two captains regent, elected by parliament from among its members, to 6-month term each. **Head of govt.:** Sec. of State for Foreign and Political Affairs Luca Beccari; b. 1974; in office: Jan. 8, 2020. **Local divisions:** 9 municipalities. **Defense budget/active troops:** NA.

Economy: Industries: tourism, banking, textiles, electronics, ceramics, cement, wine. **Chief agric.:** wheat, grapes, corn, olives;

cattle, pigs, horses, beef, cheese, hides. **Natural resources:** building stone. **Water:** NA. **Labor force:** agric. 0.3%, industry 42.4%, services 57.3%. **Unemployment:** NA.

Finance: Monetary unit: Euro (EUR) (0.84 = $1 U.S.). **GDP** (2018): $2.1 bil; **per capita GDP** (2018): $60,750; **GDP growth** (2018): 1.2%. **Imports** (2011): $2.5 bil. **Exports** (2011): $3.8 bil. **Budget** (2011): $715.3 mil. **Inflation** (2016-17): 1.0%.

Transport: NA.

Communications: Telephone (2017): 53.5 per 100 pop. **Mobile** (2017): 112.9 per 100 pop. **Broadband:** NA. **Internet:** 60.2%.

Health: Expend.: 7.4%. **Life expect.:** 80.9 male; 86.3 female. **Births:** 8.8 per 1,000 pop. **Deaths:** 9 per 1,000 pop. **Infant mortality:** 4.2 per 1,000 live births. **Undernourished:** NA. **HIV:** NA.

Education: Compulsory: ages 6-15. **Literacy:** 100.0%.

Embassy: 1711 N St. NW, 2nd Fl., 20036; 223-2418.

Website: www.sanmarino.sm

San Marino, founded in the 4th cent., claims to be the world's oldest republic. It has had a treaty of friendship with Italy since 1862. The Sammarinese Christian Democratic Party (PDCS) won the most seats in Dec. 8, 2019, parliamentary elections. Luca Beccari of the PDCS became head of a coalition government Jan. 8, 2020.

São Tomé and Príncipe
Democratic Republic of São Tomé and Príncipe

People: Population: 211,122 (176). **Age distrib.:** <15: 39.8%; 65+: 2.9%. **Growth:** 1.6%. **Migrants:** 1.0%. **Pop. density:** 567.2 per sq mi, 219.0 per sq km. **Urban:** 74.4%. **Ethnic groups:** mestico, angolares (descendants of Angolan slaves), forros (descendants of freed slaves), servicais (contract laborers fr. Angola, Mozambique, Cabo Verde), tongas (children of servicais born on islands), Europeans (primarily Portuguese), Asians (mostly Chinese). **Languages:** Portuguese (official), Forro, Cabo Verdian, French, Angolar, English. **Religions:** Christian 96.1% (Catholic 71.6%, independent 16.6%), Baha'i 2.2%.

Geography: Total area: 372 sq mi, 964 sq km (172); **Land area:** 372 sq mi, 964 sq km. **Location:** Gulf of Guinea about 125 mi off W central Africa. Gabon, Equatorial Guinea to E. **Topography:** Part of an extinct volcano chain; lush forests and croplands. **Arable land:** 4.2%. **Capital:** São Tomé, 80,099.

Government: Type: Semi-presidential republic. **Head of state:** Pres. Evaristo Carvalho; b. 1941; in office: Sept. 3, 2016. **Head of govt.:** Prime Min. Jorge Bom Jesus; in office: Dec. 3, 2018. **Local divisions:** 6 districts, 1 autonomous region. **Defense budget/ active troops:** NA.

Economy: Industries: light constr., textiles, soap, beer, fish proc., timber. **Chief agric.:** cocoa, coconuts, palm kernels, copra, cinnamon, pepper, coffee, bananas, papayas, beans; poultry; fish. **Natural resources:** fish, hydropower. **Water:** 10,671 cu m per capita. **Electricity prod.:** 87 mil kWh. **Labor force:** agric. 18.7%, industry 18.4%, services 62.9%. **Unemployment:** 13.7%.

Finance: Monetary unit: Dobra (STN) (20.73 = $1 U.S.). **GDP** $887.8 mil; **per capita GDP:** $4,128; **GDP growth:** 2.4%. **Imports:** $127.7 mil; Portugal 54.7%, Angola 16.5%, China 5.6%. **Exports:** $15.6 mil; Guyana 43.7%, Germany 23.6%, Portugal 6%, Netherlands 5.5%. **Tourism:** $44 mil. **Budget:** $112.4 mil. **Inflation** (2017-18): 7.9%.

Transport: Airports: 2.

Communications: Telephone: 2.5 per 100 pop. **Mobile:** 77.1 per 100 pop. **Broadband:** 33.9 per 100 pop. **Internet:** 29.9%.

Health: Expend.: 6.2%. **Life expect.:** 64.9 male; 67.8 female. **Births:** 29.7 per 1,000 pop. **Deaths:** 6.3 per 1,000 pop. **Infant mortality:** 41.7 per 1,000 live births. **Undernourished:** 12.0%. **HIV** (2018): 0.7%.

Education: Compulsory: ages 6-11. **Literacy:** 97.8%.

Permanent UN mission: 675 Third Ave., Ste. 1807, New York, NY 10017; (212) 651-8116.

Website: www.parlamento.st

The Portuguese reached the islands in 1471 and brought the first inhabitants—convicts and exiled Jews. Sugarcane planting was replaced by the slave trade as the chief economic activity until coffee and cocoa were introduced in the 19th century.

Portugal agreed, 1974, to turn the colony over to the Gabon-based Movement for the Liberation of São Tomé and Príncipe; its East German-trained leader, Manuel Pinto da Costa, became the country's first president. Independence came July 12, 1975. Democratic reforms were instituted in 1987. In 1991, Miguel Trovoada won the first free presidential election.

The Independent Democratic Action (ADI) party won Oct. 12, 2014, legislative elections and an Aug. 7, 2016, presidential runoff. The country, one of the world's poorest, has sought to develop oil deposits in the Gulf of Guinea and tourism. Seeking aid and investment, São Tomé broke diplomatic ties with Taiwan and established relations with China, Dec. 2016. In Oct. 7, 2018, elections, the ADI lost its parliamentary majority, and an opposition coalition formed a government.

Saudi Arabia
Kingdom of Saudi Arabia

People: Population: 34,173,498 (41). **Age distrib.:** <15: 24.8%; 65+: 3.6%. **Growth:** 1.6%. **Migrants:** 38.3%. **Pop. density:** 41.2 per sq mi, 15.9 per sq km. **Urban:** 84.3%. **Ethnic groups:** Arab 90%, Afro-Asian 10%. **Languages:** Arabic (official). **Religions:** Muslim 90.6% (Sunni [official] 81%, Shia 9%), Christian 5.8%.

Geography: Total area: 830,000 sq mi, 2,149,690 sq km (12); **Land area:** 830,000 sq mi, 2,149,690 sq km. **Location:** Occupies most of Arabian Peninsula in Middle East. Kuwait, Iraq, Jordan on N; Yemen, Oman on S; UAE, Qatar on E. **Topography:** Bordered by Red Sea on W. Highlands in W slope as barren desert to the Persian Gulf on E. **Arable land:** 1.6%. **Capital:** Riyadh, 7,231,447. **Cities:** Jeddah, 4,610,176; Mecca, 2,042,106; Medina, 1,488,782; Ad-Dammam, 1,252,523.

Government: Type: Absolute monarchy. **Head of state and govt.:** King Salman bin Abdul Aziz; b. 1924; in office: Jan. 23, 2015. **Local divisions:** 13 regions. **Defense budget:** $78.4 bil. **Active troops:** 227,000.

Economy: Industries: crude oil prod., petroleum refining, basic petrochemicals, ammonia, industrial gases, caustic soda, cement, fertilizer. **Chief agric.:** wheat, barley, tomatoes, melons, dates, citrus; mutton, chickens, eggs, milk. **Natural resources:** petroleum, nat. gas, iron ore, gold, copper. **Water:** 73 cu m per capita. **Crude oil reserves:** 267 bil bbls (incl. half of Neutral Zone reserves). **Electricity prod.:** 327.0 bil kWh. **Labor force:** agric. 2.3%, industry 24.8%, services 72.9%. **Unemployment:** 5.9%.

Finance: Monetary unit: Riyal (SAR) (3.75 = $1 U.S.). **GDP:** $1.7 tril; **per capita GDP:** $48,908; **GDP growth:** 0.3%. **Imports:** $119.3 bil; China 15.4%, U.S. 13.6%, UAE 6.5%, Germany 5.8%. **Exports:** $221.1 bil; Japan 12.2%, China 11.7%, South Korea 9%, India 8.9%, U.S. 8.3%, UAE 6.7%. **Tourism:** $16.4 bil. **Budget:** $241.8 bil. **Inflation:** −2.1%.

Transport: Railways: 3,362 mi. **Motor vehicles:** 239.4 per 1,000 pop. **Airports:** 82.

Communications: Telephone: 16 per 100 pop. **Mobile:** 122.6 per 100 pop. **Broadband:** 90 per 100 pop. **Internet** (2018): 93.3%.

Health: Expend. (2016): 5.8%. **Life expect.:** 74.6 male; 77.8 female. **Births:** 14.7 per 1,000 pop. **Deaths:** 3.4 per 1,000 pop. **Infant mortality:** 11.3 per 1,000 live births. **Undernourished:** 4.8%. **HIV:** NA.

Education: Compulsory: ages 6-14. **Literacy:** 99.3%.

Embassy: 601 New Hampshire Ave. NW 20037; 342-3800.

Website: www.saudi.gov.sa

Arabia was divided among numerous warring groups and small kingdoms before Muhammad united it in the early 7th cent. His successors conquered the entire Middle East and North Africa, bringing Islam and the Arabic language. But Arabia soon returned to its former status.

Nejd, in central Arabia, long an independent state and center of the Wahhabi sect, fell under Turkish rule in the 18th cent. Ibn Saud, founder of the Saudi dynasty, overthrew the Turks, 1913. He captured Hasa, a Turkish province in eastern Arabia, also 1913; the Hejaz region in western Arabia, 1925; and most of Asir, in SW Arabia, by 1926. The discovery of oil in the 1930s trans-formed the nation. The Hejaz contains the holy cities of Islam—Medina and Mecca.

Ibn Saud reigned until his death, Nov. 1953. Subsequent kings as of 2020 have been his sons. King Salman, June 21, 2017, named as crown prince (heir to the throne) his son Mohammed bin Salman. Known as MBS, the crown prince took on increasing responsibilities. The Islamic religious code is the law of the land. Alcohol and public entertainments are restricted, although the government announced, Dec. 11, 2017, it would end a 35-year ban on movie theaters.

Saudi Arabia has often allied itself with and purchased arms from the U.S. and other Western nations. Saudi units, nevertheless, fought against Western ally Israel in the 1948 and 1973 Arab-Israeli wars. Saudi Arabia played a leading role in the 1973-74 Arab oil embargo against the U.S. and other nations.

After Iraq invaded Kuwait, Aug. 2, 1990, Saudi Arabia accepted the Kuwait royal family and more than 400,000 Kuwaiti refugees. Western and Arab troops also deployed on Saudi soil before and during the 1991 Persian Gulf War.

When 15 of the 19 al-Qaeda hijackers who carried out the Sept. 11, 2001, attacks on the U.S. were found to be Saudi, some in the U.S. blamed the Saudi government for allowing Muslim extremism to flourish in Saudi Arabia.

In 2012, Saudi women competed in the Olympics for the first time. A royal decree, Jan. 11, 2013, permitted women to hold 30 of the 150 seats on the government's advisory Shura council. Women were allowed to vote and run for office in municipal elections for the first time in 2015. The male guardianship system that subordinated women was loosened in the late 2010s. A royal decree, effective June 24, 2018, made it legal for women to drive. Decrees issued Aug. 2, 2019, gave women the rights to obtain passports and travel freely, as well as increasing rights in employment and family matters.

Middle East Respiratory Syndrome (MERS), a disease caused by a coronavirus, was first recognized in Saudi Arabia in 2012 and had spread to 26 other countries as of 2020, causing more than 2,500 cases and over 850 deaths.

Saudi Arabia supplied weapons to rebels in Syria's civil war (2011–). Beginning in 2014, Saudi warplanes participated in U.S.-led airstrikes against ISIS in Syria. ISIS staged terrorist attacks inside Saudi Arabia in 2014 and subsequent years.

Saudi Arabia led a coalition of Sunni nations that began airstrikes, Mar. 25, 2015, and took other military action against Iran-backed Shiite Houthi rebels in Yemen, causing high civilian casualties. Rebels launched drone and missile strikes on targets in Saudi Arabia and claimed credit for attacks, Sept. 14, 2019, on two major oil installations. Saudi Arabia blamed Iran for the Sept. 14 attacks.

In June 2017, Saudi Arabia, concerned in part with Qatar's support for closer ties with Iran, led a group of Arab nations that broke diplomatic relations with Qatar and imposed a travel and trade boycott.

Low oil prices reduced government revenue beginning in 2015. King Salman announced, Apr. 25, 2016, a plan for economic diversification and privatization by the year 2030. In what was said to be a government anti-corruption campaign, hundreds of business leaders and royal family members were detained, Nov. 2017-Jan. 2018, and more than $100 bil in assets were taken.

Saudi dissident and journalist Jamal Khashoggi was killed, Oct. 2, 2018, inside the Saudi consulate in Istanbul, Turkey. A CIA assessment concluded with "high confidence" in Nov. 2018 that MBS ordered the killing; the Saudi government denied MBS involvement. After a trial in Riyadh, 8 people (not including any high-level officials) were given final sentences, Sept. 7, 2020, of lengthy prison terms for Khashoggi's killing, which the prosecutor claimed was not planned in advance.

In 2020, Saudi Arabia was severely affected by the COVID-19 pandemic; by Sept. 30, there were more than 334,000 Saudi cases and over 4,700 deaths. To combat COVID-19 spread, Saudi Arabia barred foreigners (usually over 2 mil) from making the hajj, or pilgrimage, to Mecca in 2020 and strictly limited the number of Saudi pilgrims.

Senegal
Republic of Senegal

People: Population: 15,736,368 (72). **Age distrib.:** <15: 40.4%; 65+: 3.1%. **Growth:** 2.3%. **Migrants:** 1.7%. **Pop. density:** 211.7 per sq mi, 81.7 per sq km. **Urban:** 48.1%. **Ethnic groups:** Wolof 37.1%, Pular 26.2%, Serer 17%, Mandinka 5.6%, Jola 4.5%, other (incl. Europeans, persons of Lebanese descent) 8.3%. **Languages:** French (official), Wolof, Pular, Jola, Mandinka. **Religions:** Muslim 91.5% (Sunni), Christian 4.9%, ethnic religionist 3.2%.

Geography: Total area: 75,955 sq mi, 196,722 sq km (86). **Land area:** 74,336 sq mi, 192,530 sq km. **Location:** W extreme of Africa. Mauritania on N, Mali on E, Guinea and Guinea-Bissau on S; surrounds The Gambia on three sides. **Topography:** Mostly low rolling plains, rising somewhat in SE. Swamp and jungles in SW. **Arable land:** 16.6%. **Capital:** Dakar, 3,140,442.

Government: Type: Presidential republic. **Head of state and govt.:** Pres. Macky Sall; b. 1961; in office: Apr. 2, 2012. (Parliament approved the abolishment of the post of prime minister, May 2019.) **Local divisions:** 14 regions. **Defense budget:** $343 mil. **Active troops:** 13,600.

Economy: Industries: agric. and fish proc., phosphate mining, fertilizer prod., petroleum refining, zircon and gold mining, constr. materials, ship constr. and repair. **Chief agric.:** peanuts, millet, corn, sorghum, rice, cotton, tomatoes, green vegetables; cattle, poultry, pigs; fish. **Natural resources:** fish, phosphates, iron ore. **Water:** 2,459 cu m per capita. **Electricity prod.:** 4.5 bil kWh. **Labor force:** agric. 29.4%, industry 13.6%, services 56.9%. **Unemployment:** 6.7%.

Finance: Monetary unit: CFA Franc (XOF) (553.52 = $1 U.S.). **GDP:** $57.6 bil; **per capita GDP:** $3,536; **GDP growth:** 5.3%. **Imports:** $5.2 bil; France 16.3%, China 10.4%, Nigeria 8%, India 7.2%. **Exports:** $2.4 bil; Mali 14.8%, Switzerland 11.4%, India 6%, Côte d'Ivoire 5.3%, UAE 5.1%. **Tourism:** $496 mil. **Budget:** $4.9 bil. **Inflation:** 1.8%.

Transport: Railways: 563 mi (only partly operational). **Airports:** 9. **Communications: Telephone:** 1.9 per 100 pop. **Mobile:** 104.5 per 100 pop. **Broadband:** 26.9 per 100 pop. **Internet:** 46%.

Health: Expend.: 4.1%. **Life expect.:** 61.1 male; 65.4 female. **Births:** 31.8 per 1,000 pop. **Deaths:** 7.6 per 1,000 pop. **Infant mortality:** 45.7 per 1,000 live births. **Undernourished:** 9.4%. **HIV:** 0.4%.

Education: Compulsory: ages 6-16. **Literacy:** 69.5%.
Embassy: 2215 M St. NW 20037; 234-0540.
Website: www.sec.gouv.sn

Portuguese settlers arrived in the 15th cent., but French control grew from the 17th cent. The last independent Muslim state was subdued in 1893. Senegal became an independent republic Aug. 20, 1960, but French political and economic influence remained strong. Senegambia, a loose confederation of Senegal and The Gambia, was established in 1982 but dissolved seven years later.

Forty years of Socialist Party rule ended when Abdoulaye Wade of the Senegalese Democratic Party won a presidential runoff election, Mar. 19, 2000. A Senegalese ferry capsized Sept. 26, 2002, killing at least 1,863 people. Pres. Wade, reelected Feb. 25, 2007, lost his bid for a third term Mar. 26, 2012, to Macky Sall. After a campaign marred by violence, Sall's coalition won July 30, 2017, legislative elections. Sall won the Feb. 24, 2019, presidential election; leading opposition candidates were barred.

The 2020 COVID-19 pandemic caused about 15,000 cases and over 300 deaths in Senegal by Sept. 30.

Serbia
Republic of Serbia

People: Population: 7,012,165 (104). **Age distrib.:** <15: 14.1%; 65+: 20.0%. **Growth:** –0.5%. **Migrants:** 9.4%. **Pop. density:** 234.4 per sq mi, 90.5 per sq km. **Urban:** 56.4%. **Ethnic groups:** Serb 83.3%, Hungarian 3.5%, Romani 2.1%, Bosniak 2%. **Languages:** Serbian (official), Hungarian. **Religions:** Christian 89.5% (Orthodox 81.8%), Muslim 7.4% (Sunni), agnostic 2.5%.

Geography: Total area: 29,913 sq mi, 77,474 sq km (115); **Land area:** 29,913 sq mi, 77,474 sq km. **Location:** Balkan Peninsula in SE Europe. Croatia, Bosnia and Herzegovina on W; Hungary on N; Romania, Bulgaria on E; Montenegro, Albania, Macedonia on S. **Topography:** Terrain varies widely—fertile plains drained by Danube, other rivers in N; limestone basins in E; mountains, hills in SE. **Arable land:** 29.7%. **Capital:** Belgrade, 1,397,939.

Government: Type: Parliamentary republic. **Head of state:** Pres. Aleksandar Vucic; b. 1970; in office: May 31, 2017. **Head of govt.:** Prime Min. Ana Brnabic; b. 1975; in office: June 29, 2017. **Local divisions:** 119 municipalities, 26 cities (of which 37 municipalities, 8 cities comprise the autonomous province of Vojvodina). **Defense budget:** $906 mil. **Active troops:** 28,150.

Economy: Industries: automobiles, base metals, furniture, food proc., machinery, chemicals, sugar, tires. **Chief agric.:** wheat, maize, sunflowers, sugar beets, grapes/wine, fruits (raspberries, apples, sour cherries); vegetables; beef, pork. **Natural resources:** oil, gas, coal, iron ore, copper, zinc, antimony, chromite, gold, silver, magnesium, pyrite, limestone, marble, salt. **Water:** 18,451 cu m per capita. **Crude oil reserves:** 77.5 mil bbls. **Electricity prod.** (2018): 35.5 bil kWh. **Labor force:** agric. 15.1%, industry 27.4%, services 57.6%. **Unemployment:** 12.7%.

Finance: Monetary unit: Dinar (RSD) (99.20 = $1 U.S.). **GDP:** $131.9 bil; **per capita GDP:** $18,989; **GDP growth:** 4.2%. **Imports:** $20.4 bil; Germany 12.7%, Italy 10%, China 8.2%, Russia 7.3%. **Exports:** $15.9 bil; Italy 13.5%, Germany 12.8%, Bosnia and Herzegovina 8.2%, Russia 6%. **Tourism:** $1.6 bil. **Budget:** $17.6 bil (incl. central and local govt.). **Inflation:** 1.8%.

Transport: Railways: 2,367 mi. **Motor vehicles:** 329.5 per 1,000 pop. **Airports:** 10.

Communications: Telephone: 27.6 per 100 pop. **Mobile** (2017): 97.6 per 100 pop. **Broadband:** 77.1 per 100 pop. **Internet** (2018): 73.4%.

Health: Expend.: 8.4%. **Life expect.:** 73.4 male; 79.4 female. **Births:** 8.8 per 1,000 pop. **Deaths:** 13.5 per 1,000 pop. **Infant mortality:** 5.6 per 1,000 live births. **Undernourished:** 4.6%. **HIV:** <0.1%.

Education: Compulsory: ages 7-14. **Literacy:** 99.7%.
Embassy: 2233 Wisconsin Ave. NW, Ste. 410, 20007; 332-0333.
Website: www.srbija.gov.rs

Serbia was a vassal principality of Turkey from 1389 to 1878, when the Treaty of Berlin established it as an independent kingdom. After the Balkan wars, Serbia annexed Old Serbia and Macedonia, 1913.

When the Austro-Hungarian empire collapsed after WWI, the Kingdom of Serbs, Croats, and Slovenes—Yugoslavia after 1929—was formed from the provinces of Croatia, Dalmatia, Bosnia, Herzegovina, Slovenia, Vojvodina, and the independent state of Montenegro.

After Nazi Germany's occupation 1941-45, Yugoslavia became a federal republic, headed by Josip Broz, a Communist, known as Marshal Tito. He rejected Stalin's dictatorship and accepted economic and military aid from the West. After Tito died in 1980, Yugoslavia held together for a decade before breaking apart. During 1991-95, Serbia, under Pres. Slobodan Milosevic, supported ethnic Serb fighters in Croatia and in Bosnia and Herzegovina, which had declared independence. The republics of Serbia and Montenegro proclaimed a new Federal Republic of Yugoslavia, Apr. 17, 1992. The UN imposed sanctions on the newly reconstituted Yugoslavia to end the bloodshed in Bosnia.

A peace agreement was reached in 1995. A UN-backed war crimes tribunal began in May 1996 to try suspects from the former Yugoslavia. Barred from running for a third term as Serbian president, Milosevic had himself inaugurated as president of Yugoslavia, July 23, 1997.

Serbian efforts to suppress a secessionist movement in Kosovo led in Mar.-June 1999 to a war with the U.S. and its NATO allies; they accused Milosevic of pursuing a policy of ethnic cleansing against the predominantly Muslim Kosovars (ethnic Albanians).

NATO stationed a multinational force in Kosovo, which was placed under UN administration.

Milosevic initially refused to accept defeat by opposition leader Vojislav Kostunica in a 2000 presidential election but resigned Oct. 6 after mass demonstrations. After surrendering to Serbian authorities Apr. 1, 2001, Milosevic was extradited June 28 to The Hague, Netherlands, where a UN tribunal had indicted him for war crimes. He was found dead in prison Mar. 11, 2006, before his trial was completed.

A pact to reconstitute Yugoslavia as a new union of Serbia and Montenegro took effect Feb. 4, 2003. Zoran Djindjic, premier of the Republic of Serbia, was assassinated Mar. 12 in Belgrade, triggering a roundup of more than 4,500 people associated with organized crime and the Milosevic regime. Montenegrins voted for separation in a referendum May 21, 2006, and Montenegro became an independent republic June 3.

Kosovo declared independence from Serbia Feb. 17, 2008, but Serbia refused to recognize the new country. Following parliamentary elections in Serbia May 11, a pro-Western government took office. To meet a requirement for EU membership, Serbia arrested, in 2008, former Bosnian Serb leader Radovan Karadzic; he was convicted at The Hague of genocide and crimes against humanity, Mar. 24, 2016. Serbia's parliament passed a resolution Mar. 31, 2010, apologizing for the 1995 massacre of 8,000 Bosniaks (primarily Muslim ethnic group) by Bosnian Serbs at Srebrenica. Ratko Mladic, the former Bosnian Serb military commander accused of directing the Srebrenica massacre, was arrested in Serbia, May 2011, and sent to The Hague; he was convicted, Nov. 22, 2017, of genocide, war crimes, and crimes against humanity. Serbia began accession negotiations for EU membership Jan. 21, 2014. Aleksandar Vucic, an advocate of EU membership and also close ties to Russia, became prime min. following Mar. 16, 2014, elections.

An estimated 900,000 refugees and other migrants, largely from the Middle East and SW Asia, passed through Serbia in 2015 and early 2016, most en route to N Europe. The government essentially closed Serbia's borders Mar. 9, 2016.

Vucic was elected president, Apr. 2, 2017. Ana Brnabic took office, June 29, as Serbia's first female prime min. Months of anti-Vucic demonstrations began in late 2018, protesting authoritarian policies and control of the media. In June 21, 2020, parliamentary elections boycotted by leading opposition parties, Vucic's coalition won a landslide victory. Serbia signed an agreement with Kosovo, Sept. 4, 2020, on normalizing economic relations.

By Sept. 30, 2020, the COVID-19 pandemic had caused about 33,500 cases and almost 750 deaths in Serbia.

Vojvodina (8,304 sq mi) is a nominally autonomous province in northern Serbia with a pop. (2011 census) of 1,931,809, mostly Serbian. The capital is Novi Sad. **Website:** www.vojvodina.gov.rs

Seychelles
Republic of Seychelles

People: Population: 95,981 (185). **Age distrib.:** <15: 18.9%; 65+: 8.3%. **Growth:** 0.7%. **Migrants:** 13.2%. **Pop. density:** 546.4 per sq mi, 210.9 per sq km. **Urban:** 57.5%. **Ethnic groups:** predominantly creole (mainly of East African and Malagasy heritage); also French, Indian, Chinese, and Arab pops. **Languages:** Seychellois Creole, English, French (all official). **Religions:** Christian 94.5% (Catholic 83.3%, Protestant 10.2%), agnostic 2.3%.

Geography: Total area: 176 sq mi, 455 sq km (182). **Land area:** 176 sq mi, 455 sq km. **Location:** In Indian O. 700 mi NE of Madagascar. Nearest neighbors are Madagascar and Somalia on NW. **Topography:** Archipelago of over 116 islands. One group is composed of coral; the Mahe group of isls., predominantly mountainous, is granite. **Arable land:** 0.3%. **Capital:** Victoria, 28,091.

Government: Type: Presidential republic. **Head of state and govt.:** Pres. Danny Faure; b. 1962; in office: Oct. 16, 2016. **Local divisions:** 27 admin. districts. **Defense budget:** NA. **Active troops:** 420.

Economy: Industries: fishing, tourism, beverages. **Chief agric.:** coconuts, cinnamon, vanilla, sweet potatoes, cassava, copra, bananas; tuna. **Natural resources:** fish, coconuts, cinnamon trees. **Water:** NA. **Electricity prod.:** 403 mil kWh. **Labor force:** agric. 2.5%, industry 13.8%, services 83.7%. **Unemployment:** NA.

Finance: Monetary unit: Rupee (SCR) (17.95 = $1 U.S.). **GDP:** $3.0 bil; **per capita GDP:** $30,260; **GDP growth:** 4.7%. **Imports:** $1.2 bil; UAE 13.4%, France 9.4%, Spain 5.7%, South Africa 5%. **Exports:** $564.8 mil; UAE 28.5%, France 24%, UK 13.8%, Italy 8.9%. **Tourism:** $590 mil. **Budget:** $600.7 mil. **Inflation:** 1.8%.

Transport: Airports: 7.

Communications: Telephone: 20.9 per 100 pop. **Mobile:** 184.3 per 100 pop. **Broadband:** 76 per 100 pop. **Internet:** 58.8%.

Health: Expend.: 5.0%. **Life expect.:** 71.1 male; 80.2 female. **Births:** 12.8 per 1,000 pop. **Deaths:** 7.1 per 1,000 pop. **Infant mortality:** 9.3 per 1,000 live births. **Undernourished:** NA. **HIV:** NA.

Education: Compulsory: ages 6-15. **Literacy:** 99.1%.

Permanent UN mission: 800 Second Ave., Ste. 400C, New York, NY 10017; (212) 972-1785.

Website: www.egov.sc

The islands were occupied by France in 1768 and seized by Britain in 1794. Ruled as part of Mauritius from 1814, Seychelles became a separate colony in 1903 and declared independence June 29, 1976. Tourism, a major driver of economic growth, was hurt in 2020 by the COVID-19 pandemic.

The country's first president was ousted in a 1977 coup by socialist leader France Albert René. A new constitution, approved June 1993, provided for a multiparty state. René resigned Apr. 14, 2004. Vice Pres. James Michel succeeded him and won 2006, 2011, and 2015 elections. After his party lost Sept. 2016 legislative elections, Michel resigned effective Oct. 16, and Vice Pres. Danny Faure became president.

Sierra Leone
Republic of Sierra Leone

People: Population: 6,624,933 (107). **Age distrib.:** <15: 41.4%; 65+: 3.7%. **Growth:** 2.4%. **Migrants:** 0.7%. **Pop. density:** 239.6 per sq mi, 92.5 per sq km. **Urban:** 42.9%. **Ethnic groups:** Temne 35.5%, Mende 33.2%, Limba 6.4%, Kono 4.4%, Fullah 3.4%, Loko 2.9%, Koranko 2.8%, Sherbro 2.6%, Mandingo 2.4%. **Languages:** English (official), Mende (principal vernacular in S), Temne (principal vernacular in N), Krio (English-based Creole, a lingua franca). **Religions:** Muslim 66.9% (Sunni), ethnic religionist 20.4%, Christian 11.1%.

Geography: Total area: 27,699 sq mi, 71,740 sq km (117); **Land area:** 27,653 sq mi, 71,620 sq km. **Location:** W coast of W Africa. Guinea on N and E, Liberia on S. **Topography:** Mangrove swamps in heavily indented, 210-mi coastline. Wooded hills rise to a plateau and mountains in E. **Arable land:** 21.9%. **Capital:** Freetown, 1,201,900.

Government: Type: Presidential republic. **Head of state and govt.:** Pres. Julius Maada Bio; b. 1964; in office: Apr. 4, 2018. **Local divisions:** 4 provinces, 1 area. **Defense budget:** $11 mil. **Active troops:** 8,500.

Economy: Industries: diamond mining, iron ore, rutile and bauxite mining, small-scale mfg. (beverages, textiles, footwear). **Chief agric.:** rice, coffee, cocoa, palm kernels, palm oil, peanuts, cashews; poultry, cattle, sheep, pigs; fish. **Natural resources:** diamonds, titanium ore, bauxite, iron ore, gold, chromite. **Water:** 21,172 cu m per capita. **Electricity prod.:** 215 mil kWh. **Labor force:** agric. 54.4%, industry 6.5%, services 39.1%. **Unemployment:** 4.4%.

Finance: Monetary unit: Leone (SLL) (10,000.31 = $1 U.S.). **GDP:** $14.0 bil; **per capita GDP:** $1,790; **GDP growth:** 5.5%. **Imports:** $1.1 bil; China 11.5%, U.S. 9.2%, Belgium 8.8%, UAE 7.7%, India 7.4%, Turkey 5.2%, Senegal 5.1%. **Exports:** $808.4 mil; Côte d'Ivoire 37.7%, Belgium 20.5%, U.S. 15.7%, China 10.2%, Netherlands 6.1%. **Tourism:** $39 mil. **Budget:** $846.4 mil. **Inflation:** 14.8%.

Transport: Motor vehicles: 5.2 per 1,000 pop. **Airports:** 1. **Communications: Telephone** (2017): 0.2 per 100 pop. **Mobile** (2017): 88.5 per 100 pop. **Broadband:** 25.6 per 100 pop. **Internet:** 9%.

Health: Expend.: 13.4%. **Life expect.:** 57.1 male; 62.6 female. **Births:** 35.4 per 1,000 pop. **Deaths:** 9.8 per 1,000 pop. **Infant mortality:** 63.6 per 1,000 live births. **Undernourished:** 26.0%. **HIV:** 1.6%.

Education: Compulsory: ages 6-14. **Literacy:** 66.6%.

Embassy: 1701 19th St. NW 20009; 939-9261.

Website: statehouse.gov.sl

The British founded Freetown, 1787, as a haven for freed slaves. Full independence arrived Apr. 27, 1961. A one-party state was established by referendum in 1978.

Mutinous soldiers ousted Pres. Joseph Momoh, Apr. 30, 1992. A coup, Jan. 16, 1996, paved the way for multiparty elections and a return to civilian rule. A peace accord, signed Nov. 30 with the Revolutionary United Front (RUF), brought a temporary halt to a civil war that had claimed over 10,000 lives in five years.

After a May 25, 1997, coup, Nigeria's military restored Pres. Ahmad Tejan Kabbah to power on Mar. 10, 1998, but RUF rebels mounted a guerrilla counteroffensive, killing thousands of civilians and mutilating thousands more. A power-sharing agreement between the Kabbah government and the RUF, July 1999, collapsed in early May 2000, but rebel leader Foday Sankoh was captured in Freetown, May 17 (he died in UN custody, July 29, 2003). A UN-sponsored disarmament program in 2001 reduced the level of violence. Government and rebel leaders declared an official end to the war Jan. 18, 2002; more than 50,000 people had died in the conflict. Kabbah won the May 14, 2002, presidential election.

Opposition leader Ernest Bai Koroma won a presidential runoff vote, Sept. 8, 2007. Three former RUF leaders were convicted of war crimes, Feb. 25, 2009. A 2012 cholera epidemic caused about 23,000 cases and 300 deaths. Koroma won reelection Nov. 17, 2012. An Ebola virus epidemic that began in Guinea in Dec. 2013 caused 14,124 cases and 3,956 deaths in Sierra Leone by the time the WHO declared its public health emergency over, Mar. 29, 2016. After a campaign marred by violence, Julius Maada Bio, a leader of the 1992 mutiny and 1996 coup, was declared the winner, Apr. 4, 2018, of a presidential runoff election. On Feb. 7, 2019,

Bio declared a national emergency in response to the high incidence of rape and other sexual violence against women. The 2020 COVID-19 pandemic caused about 2,200 cases and 72 deaths by Sept. 30.

Singapore
Republic of Singapore

People: Population: 6,209,660 (109). **Age distrib.:** <15: 12.8%; 65+: 10.9%. **Growth:** 1.7%. **Migrants:** 37.1%. **Pop. density:** 22,677.6 per sq mi, 8,755.9 per sq km. **Urban:** 100.0%. **Ethnic groups:** Chinese 74.3%, Malay 13.4%, Indian 9%, other (incl. Eurasian, Caucasian, Japanese, Filipino, Vietnamese) 3.2%. **Languages:** English, Mandarin, Malay, Tamil (all official); other Chinese dialects (incl. Hokkien, Cantonese, Teochew). **Religions:** Chinese folk-religionist 37.1%, Christian 20.5%, Muslim 15.4% (Sunni), Buddhist 15.2%, Hindu 5%, agnostic 4.8%.

Geography: Total area: 278 sq mi, 719 sq km (177); **Land area:** 274 sq mi, 709 sq km. **Location:** Off tip of Malayan Peninsula in SE Asia. Nearest neighbors are Malaysia on N, Indonesia on S. **Topography:** Flat, formerly swampy island with 40 nearby islets. **Arable land:** 0.8%. **Capital:** Singapore, 5,935,053.

Government: Type: Parliamentary republic. **Head of state:** Pres. Halimah Yacob; b. 1954; in office: Sept. 14, 2017. **Head of govt.:** Prime Min. Lee Hsien Loong; b. 1952; in office: Aug. 12, 2004. **Local divisions:** none. **Defense budget:** $11.3 bil. **Active troops:** 51,000.

Economy: Industries: electronics, chemicals, financial services, oil drilling equip., petroleum refining, biomedical prods., scientific instruments. **Chief agric.:** vegetables; poultry, eggs; fish, ornamental fish, orchids. **Natural resources:** fish, deepwater ports. **Water:** 105 cu m per capita. **Electricity prod.** (2018): 49.8 bil kWh. **Labor force:** agric. 0.7%, industry 15.2%, services 84.1%. **Unemployment:** 4.4%.

Finance: Monetary unit: Dollar (SGD) (1.36 = $1 U.S.). **GDP:** $578.2 bil; **per capita GDP:** $101,376; **GDP growth:** 0.7%. **Imports:** $312.1 bil; China 13.9%, Malaysia 12%, U.S. 10.7%, Japan 6.3%, South Korea 5%. **Exports:** $396.8 bil; China 14.7%, Hong Kong 12.6%, Malaysia 10.8%, U.S. 6.6%, Indonesia 5.8%. **Tourism:** $20.1 bil. **Budget:** $51.9 bil (incl. operational and development expenditures). **Inflation:** 0.6%.

Transport: Motor vehicles: 136.8 per 1,000 pop. **Airports:** 9.

Communications: Telephone: 34.2 per 100 pop. **Mobile:** 145.7 per 100 pop. **Broadband:** 148.2 per 100 pop. **Internet** (2018): 88.2%.

Health: Expend.: 4.4%. **Life expect.:** 83.3 male; 88.9 female. **Births:** 8.9 per 1,000 pop. **Deaths:** 3.6 per 1,000 pop. **Infant mortality:** 2.3 per 1,000 live births. **Undernourished:** NA. **HIV:** 0.2%.

Education: Compulsory: ages 6-11. **Literacy:** 99.9%.

Embassy: 3501 International Pl. NW 20008; 537-3100.

Website: www.gov.sg

Founded in 1819 by Sir Thomas Stamford Raffles, Singapore was a British colony until 1959, when it became autonomous within the Commonwealth. On Sept. 16, 1963, it joined with Malaya, Sarawak, and Sabah to form the Federation of Malaysia. Tensions between Malays, dominant in the federation, and ethnic Chinese, dominant in Singapore, led to an accord under which Singapore became a separate nation, Aug. 9, 1965.

Singapore is a major port and manufacturing, banking, and commerce center. Asian immigrant workers hold many low-paying jobs. The government, dominated by the People's Action Party (PAP), has taken strong actions to keep order and suppress dissent.

Singapore's first prime min., Lee Kuan Yew (in office 1959-90), credited with building the country's strong economy, died Mar. 23, 2015. His son, Lee Hsien Loong, took office as prime min., Aug. 12, 2004. Halimah Yacob became Singapore's first fe-male president, Sept. 14, 2017.

In 2020, the COVID-19 pandemic caused more than 57,700 cases in Singapore by Sept. 30, and 27 people had died. GDP fell sharply.

Slovakia
Slovak Republic

People: Population: 5,440,602 (119). **Age distrib.:** <15: 15.1%; 65+: 17.0%. **Growth:** −0.1%. **Migrants:** 3.4%. **Pop. density:** 292.9 per sq mi, 113.1 per sq km. **Urban:** 53.8%. **Ethnic groups:** Slovak 80.7%, Hungarian 8.5%, Romani 2%. **Languages:** Slovak (official), Hungarian, Roma. **Religions:** Christian 84.5% (Catholic 75.1%), agnostic 12.2%, atheist 3.2%.

Geography: Total area: 18,933 sq mi, 49,035 sq km (127); **Land area:** 18,573 sq mi, 48,105 sq km. **Location:** E central Europe. Poland on N, Hungary on S, Austria and Czech Rep. on W, Ukraine on E. **Topography:** Carpathian Mts. in N, fertile Danube plain in S. **Arable land:** 27.9%. **Capital:** Bratislava, 434,926.

Government: Type: Parliamentary republic. **Head of state:** Pres. Zuzana Caputová; b. 1973; in office: June 15, 2019. **Head of govt.:** Prime Min. Igor Matovič; b. 1973; in office: Mar. 21, 2020.

Local divisions: 8 regions. **Defense budget:** $1.9 bil. **Active troops:** 15,850.

Economy: Industries: automobiles; metal and metal prods.; electricity, gas, coke, oil, nuclear fuel; chemicals, synthetic fibers, wood and paper prods.; machinery. **Chief agric.:** grains, potatoes, sugar beets, hops, fruit; pigs, cattle, poultry. **Natural resources:** lignite, iron ore, copper and manganese ore, salt. **Water:** 9,196 cu m per capita. **Crude oil reserves:** 9 mil bbls. **Electricity prod** (2018): 23.6 bil kWh. **Labor force:** agric. 2.1%, industry 36.1%, services 61.8%. **Unemployment:** 5.1%.

Finance: Monetary unit: Euro (EUR) (0.84 = $1 U.S.). **GDP:** $186.4 bil; **per capita GDP:** $34,178; **GDP growth:** 2.4%. **Imports:** $80.1 bil; Germany 19.1%, Czechia 16.3%, Austria 10.3%, Poland 6.5%, Hungary 6.4%. **Exports:** $80.8 bil; Germany 20.7%, Czechia 11.6%, Poland 7.7%, France 6.3%, Italy 6.1%, UK 6%, Hungary 6%, Austria 6%. **Tourism:** $3.2 bil. **Budget:** $38.8 bil. **Inflation:** 2.7%.

Transport: Railways: 2,225 mi. **Motor vehicles:** 490.6 per 1,000 pop. **Airports:** 19.

Communications: Telephone: 13.3 per 100 pop. **Mobile:** 132.8 per 100 pop. **Broadband:** 82.6 per 100 pop. **Internet** (2018): 80.7%.

Health: Expend.: 6.7%. **Life expect.:** 74.3 male; 81.6 female. **Births:** 9.3 per 1,000 pop. **Deaths:** 10.1 per 1,000 pop. **Infant mortality:** 4.9 per 1,000 live births. **Undernourished:** 6.1%. **HIV** (2018): <0.1%.

Education: Compulsory: ages 6-15. **Literacy:** NA.

Embassy: 3523 International Ct. NW 20008; 237-1054.

Website: www.government.gov.sk

Settled by Illyrian, Celtic, and Germanic peoples, Slovakia was incorporated into Great Moravia in the 9th cent. It became part of Hungary in the 11th cent. Overrun by Czech Hussites in the 15th cent., it was restored to Hungarian rule in 1526. After WWI, the Slovaks joined the Czechs of Bohemia to form the Republic of Czechoslovakia, Oct. 28, 1918.

Germany invaded Czechoslovakia, 1939, and declared Slovakia independent. Slovakia rejoined Czechoslovakia in 1945. Czechoslovakia split into two separate states—the Czech Republic and Slovakia—on Jan. 1, 1993.

Slovakia joined the EU and NATO in 2004. Following Mar. 10, 2012, legislative elections, Robert Fico of the social-democratic Smer party became prime min. After a political scandal involving alleged links to organized crime, Peter Pellegrini of Smer replaced Fico, Mar. 22, 2018. Anti-corruption activist Zuzana Caputová won a Mar. 30, 2019, runoff election to become Slovakia's first female president. A center-right party headed by Igor Matovič, who ran an anti-corruption campaign, outpolled Smer in Feb. 29, 2020, legislative elections; Matovič became prime min. Mar. 21. The 2020 COVID-19 pandemic caused almost 9,600 cases and 45 deaths in Slovakia as of Sept. 30.

Slovenia
Republic of Slovenia

People: Population: 2,102,678 (145). **Age distrib.:** <15: 14.8%; 65+: 21.2%. **Growth:** 0.0%. **Migrants:** 12.2%. **Pop. density:** 270.3 per sq mi, 104.3 per sq km. **Urban:** 55.1%. **Ethnic groups:** Slovene 83.1%, Serb 2%, Croat 1.8%. **Languages:** Slovenian (official), Serbo-Croatian. **Religions:** Christian 82.1% (Catholic 76.7%), agnostic 11.2%, Muslim 4% (Sunni).

Geography: Total area: 7,827 sq mi, 20,273 sq km (151); **Land area:** 7,780 sq mi, 20,151 sq km. **Location:** SE Europe. Italy on W, Austria on N, Hungary on NE, Croatia on SE, S. **Topography:** Mostly hilly; more than half forested. **Arable land:** 9.1%. **Capital:** Ljubljana, 286,491.

Government: Type: Parliamentary republic. **Head of state:** Pres. Borut Pahor; b. 1963; in office: Dec. 22, 2012. **Head of govt.:** Prime Min. Janez Janša; b. 1958; in office: Mar. 13, 2020. **Local divisions:** 201 municipalities, 11 urban municipalities. **Defense budget:** $630 mil. **Active troops:** 7,250.

Economy: Industries: ferrous metallurgy and aluminum prods., lead and zinc smelting, electronics (incl. military), trucks, automobiles, elec. power equip., wood prods. **Chief agric.:** hops, wheat, coffee, corn, apples, pears; cattle, sheep, poultry. **Natural resources:** lignite, lead, zinc, building stone, hydropower, forests. **Water:** 15,322 cu m per capita. **Electricity prod** (2018): 15.3 bil kWh. **Labor force:** agric. 5.1%, industry 33.5%, services 61.5%. **Unemployment:** 3.8%.

Finance: Monetary unit: Euro (EUR) (0.84 = $1 U.S.). **GDP:** $84.9 bil; **per capita GDP:** $40,657; **GDP growth:** 2.4%. **Imports:** $30.4 bil; Germany 16.5%, Italy 13.5%, Austria 9.3%, Turkey 5.8%. **Exports:** $32.1 bil; Germany 18.9%, Italy 10.7%, Austria 7.4%, Croatia 7.1%. **Tourism:** $3.1 bil. **Budget:** $21.1 bil. **Inflation:** 1.6%.

Transport: Railways: 764 mi. **Motor vehicles:** 606.3 per 1,000 pop. **Airports:** 9.

Communications: Telephone: 33.4 per 100 pop. **Mobile:** 118.7 per 100 pop. **Broadband:** 70 per 100 pop. **Internet** (2018): 79.7%.

Health: Expend.: 8.2%. **Life expect.:** 78.5 male; 84.4 female. **Births:** 8.7 per 1,000 pop. **Deaths:** 10.3 per 1,000 pop. **Infant mortality:** 1.7 per 1,000 live births. **Undernourished:** <2.5%. **HIV** (2018): <0.1%.

Education: Compulsory: ages 6-14. **Literacy:** 99.8%.

Embassy: 2410 California St. NW 20008; 386-6601. **Website:** www.vlada.si or e-uprava.gov.si

The Slovenes settled in their current territory during the 6th to 8th cent. They fell under German domination in the 9th cent. After 1848, the Slovenes, divided among several Austrian provinces, began their struggle for unification. In 1918 a majority of Slovenes became part of the Kingdom of Serbs, Croats, and Slovenes, later renamed Yugoslavia.

Slovenia declared independence June 25, 1991; attained full membership in the EU and NATO in 2004; and adopted the euro Jan. 1, 2007. After about 474,000 migrants (many from the Middle East and SW Asia) trying to reach N Europe entered Slovenia Oct. 1, 2015-Mar. 8, 2016, Slovenia announced, Mar. 8, it was essentially closing its border to migrants. The rightist, anti-immigration Slovenian Democratic Party (SDS) won the most seats in June 3, 2018, National Assembly elections, but 5 center-left parties agreed, Aug. 29, to form a coalition minority government. Unable to pass legislation, Prime Min. Marjan Šarec resigned, Jan. 27, 2020. Janez Jansa of SDS became prime minister, Mar. 13. As of Sept. 30, the COVID-19 pandemic had caused about 5,500 Slovenian cases and 138 deaths.

Solomon Islands

People: Population: 685,097 (163). **Age distrib.:** <15: 33.0%; 65+: 4.5%. **Growth:** 1.8%. **Migrants:** 0.4%. **Pop. density:** 63.4 per sq mi, 24.5 per sq km. **Urban:** 24.7%. **Ethnic groups:** Melanesian 95.3%, Polynesian 3.1%. **Languages:** Melanesian pidgin (lingua franca in much of country), English (official), 120 Indigenous langs. **Religions:** Christian 95% (Protestant 67.4%, Catholic 20.5%), ethnic religionist 3.3%.

Geography: Total area: 11,157 sq mi, 28,896 sq km (140); **Land area:** 10,805 sq mi, 27,986 sq km. **Location:** Melanesian Archipelago in W Pacific O. Nearest neighbor is Papua New Guinea to W. **Topography:** 10 large volcanic, rugged islands; 4 groups of smaller islands. **Arable land:** 0.7%. **Capital:** Honiara, 81,801.

Government: Type: Parliamentary democracy under constitutional monarchy. **Head of state:** Queen Elizabeth II, rep. by Gov.-Gen. David Vunagi; in office: July 7, 2019. **Head of govt.:** Prime Min. Manasseh Sogavare; b. 1955; in office: Apr. 24, 2019. **Local divisions:** 9 provinces, 1 city. **Defense budget/active troops:** NA.

Economy: Industries: fish (tuna), mining, timber. **Chief agric.:** cocoa, coconuts, palm kernels, rice, fruit; cattle, pigs; fish. **Natural resources:** fish, forests, gold, bauxite, phosphates, lead, zinc, nickel. **Water:** 73,123 cu m per capita. **Electricity prod.:** 107 mil kWh. **Labor force:** agric. 37.1%, industry 9.6%, services 53.4%. **Unemployment:** 0.5%.

Finance: Monetary unit: Dollar (SBD) (8.13 = $1 U.S.). **GDP:** $1.7 bil; **per capita GDP:** $2,466; **GDP growth:** 2.7%. **Imports:** $462.1 mil; China 21.9%, Australia 19.6%, Singapore 10.7%, Vietnam 7.5%, New Zealand 6.2%, Papua New Guinea 5%. **Exports:** $468.6 mil; China 64.5%, Italy 6.2%. **Tourism:** $70 mil. **Budget:** $570.5 mil. **Inflation:** 1.6%.

Transport: Airports: 1.

Communications: Telephone: 1.1 per 100 pop. **Mobile:** 73.8 per 100 pop. **Broadband:** 18.7 per 100 pop. **Internet:** 11.9%.

Health: Expend.: 4.7%. **Life expect.:** 73.5 male; 79.0 female. **Births:** 23.6 per 1,000 pop. **Deaths:** 3.8 per 1,000 pop. **Infant mortality:** 13.4 per 1,000 live births. **Undernourished:** 13.2%. **HIV:** NA.

Education: Compulsory: NA. **Literacy:** 84.1%.

Permanent UN Mission: 800 Second Ave., Ste. 400L, New York, NY 10017; (212) 599-6192.

Website: www.parliament.gov.sb

The Solomon Isls., inhabited by Melanesians, were sighted 1568 by an expedition from Peru. Britain established a protectorate in the 1890s over most of the group. The islands, including Guadalcanal, saw major WWII battles. They achieved self-government, Jan. 2, 1976, and formal independence, July 7, 1978.

To restore order after years of factional violence, an Australian-led regional security force (RAMSI) arrived in July 2003.

Following Apr. 2006 elections, the first since RAMSI began, parliament's choice of Snyder Rini as prime min. led to two days of rioting in Honiara over alleged influence-buying by the ethnic Chinese business community Rini resigned, Apr. 26, 2006. Former prime min. Manasseh Sogavare (2000-01, 2006-07) again became head of government following Nov. 19, 2014, parliamentary elections. RAMSI formally ended June 2017. Sogavare, Nov. 6, 2017, lost a no-confidence vote, but he returned as prime minister after Apr. 3, 2019, elections. Seeking Chinese development assistance, the government decided, Sept. 2019, to switch diplomatic relations from Taiwan to China.

Somalia
Federal Republic of Somalia

People: Population: 11,757,124 (78). **Age distrib.:** <15: 42.4%; 65+: 2.3%. **Growth:** 2.3%. **Migrants:** 0.3%. **Pop. density:** 48.5 per sq mi, 18.7 per sq km. **Urban:** 46.1%. **Ethnic groups:** Somali 85%, Bantu and other non-Somali 15%. **Languages:** Somali, Arabic (both official); Italian; English. **Religions:** Muslim 99.9% (Sunni [official] 98%, Shia 1%).

Geography: Total area: 246,201 sq mi, 637,657 sq km (43); **Land area:** 242,216 sq mi, 627,337 sq km. **Location:** Eastern horn of Africa. Djibouti, Ethiopia, Kenya on W. **Topography:** Coastline extends for 1,700 mi. Hills cover the N; center and S are flat. **Arable land:** 1.8%. **Capital:** Mogadishu, 2,282,009.

Government: Type: Federal parliamentary republic. **Head of state:** Pres. Mohamed Abdullahi Mohamed "Farmaajo"; b. 1962; in office: Feb. 8, 2017. **Head of govt.:** Prime Min. Mohamed Hussein Roble; b. 1963; in office: Sept. 23, 2020. **Local divisions:** 18 regions. **Defense budget:** NA. **Active troops:** 19,800.

Economy: Industries: light industries incl. sugar refining, textiles, wireless communication. **Chief agric.:** bananas, sorghum, corn, coconuts, rice, sugarcane, mangoes, sesame seeds, beans; cattle, sheep, goats; fish. **Natural resources:** uranium, largely unexploited reserves of iron ore, tin, gypsum, bauxite, copper, salt, nat. gas. **Water:** 997 cu m per capita. **Electricity prod.:** 347 mil kWh. **Labor force:** agric. 83.0%, industry 3.5%, services 13.4%. **Unemployment:** 11.4%.

Finance: Monetary unit: Shilling (SOS) (576.44 = $1 U.S.). **GDP:** NA; **per capita GDP:** NA; **GDP growth:** NA. **Imports** (2018): $94.4 bil; China 17.6%, India 17.2%, Ethiopia 10.5%, Oman 10.3%, Kenya 6.9%, Turkey 5.3%. **Exports** (2014): $819 mil; Oman 31.7%, Saudi Arabia 18.7%, UAE 16.3%, Nigeria 5.1%. **Budget** (2014): $151.1 mil. **Inflation** (2016-17): 1.5%.

Transport: Airports: 8.

Communications: Telephone (2017): <0.01 per 100 pop. **Mobile** (2017): 48.8 per 100 pop. **Broadband:** 2.4 per 100 pop. **Internet:** 2%.

Health: Expend.: NA. **Life expect.:** 51.8 male; 56.2 female. **Births:** 38.7 per 1,000 pop. **Deaths:** 12.4 per 1,000 pop. **Infant mortality:** 89.5 per 1,000 live births. **Undernourished:** NA. **HIV:** 0.1%.

Education: Compulsory: NA. **Literacy:** NA.

Embassy: 1705 Desales St., Ste. 300, 20036; 296-0570.

Website: www.villasomalia.gov.so or www.state.gov/p/af/ci/so/

British Somaliland (present-day N Somalia) was formed in the 19th cent., as was Italian Somaliland (now central and S Somalia). Italy lost its African colonies in WWII. British Somaliland gained independence, June 26, 1960, and by prearrangement, merged, July 1, with the UN Trust Territory of Somalia to create the independent Somali Republic.

On Oct. 15, 1969, Somalia's first civilian president, Abdirashid Ali Sharmarke, was assassinated. Six days later, Maj. Gen. Muhammad Siad Barre led a military coup. In 1970, he declared the country a socialist state.

Somalia has laid claim to Ogaden, the huge eastern region of Ethiopia, peopled mostly by Somalis. Some 11,000 Cuban troops with Soviet arms defeated Somali army troops and ethnic Somali rebels in Ethiopia, 1978. As many as 1.5 mil refugees entered Somalia. Guerrilla fighting in Ogaden continued until 1988, when a peace agreement was reached with Ethiopia.

Fighting in Mogadishu led Siad Barre to flee the capital, Jan. 1991. Fighting between rival factions caused 40,000 casualties, 1991-92, and by mid-1992, the civil war, drought, and banditry combined to produce a famine that threatened some 1.5 mil people.

U.S. troops and the UN worked to safeguard food delivery, 1991-93, resulting in significant U.S. and other casualties; a failed mission Oct. 3-4, 1993, left 18 U.S. troops and more than 500 Somalis dead. The U.S. withdrew its peacekeeping forces Mar. 25, 1994.

When the last UN troops pulled out, Mar. 3, 1995, armed factions controlled different regions. A peace deal Jan. 29, 2004, led to the Aug. 22 inauguration of a transitional parliament, Somalia's first legislature in 13 years. Meeting in Nairobi, Kenya, the parliament chose Abdullahi Yusuf Ahmed as president; Mogadishu was held by his rivals. On June 5, 2005, an Islamist militia took over Mogadishu, defeating U.S.-backed secular warlords. Islamists held much of the central and southern regions.

With aid from Ethiopian troops, transitional govt. forces recaptured Mogadishu in Dec. 2006. The UN Security Council authorized, Feb. 20, 2007, an African Union peacekeeping mission to Somalia (AMISOM). An upsurge of fighting in Mogadishu, Feb.-Apr., killed hundreds of people and caused 350,000 to flee. Bombings and kidnappings escalated in 2007-08; many of the attacks on transitional authorities and their allies were blamed on al-Shabab, an al-Qaeda ally.

After Pres. Yusuf resigned Dec. 29, 2008, the transitional parliament, meeting in Djibouti Jan. 31, 2009, elected a moderate Islamist, Sheikh Sharif Sheikh Ahmed. Meanwhile, pirates carried out more than 200 attacks off the Horn of Africa in 2009. Pirates and Islamist insurgents continued to disrupt famine relief efforts in 2010-11. Pressured by AMISOM forces, al-Shabab pulled out of Mogadishu, Aug. 6, 2011, but continued to control much of southern Somalia. Somali leaders, meeting in Feb. 2012 in Garowe, Somalia, established the conditions to install the caretaker government sworn in Aug. 20. The new parliament elected Hassan Sheik Mohamud president Sept. 10, 2012. Bombings and other attacks by al-Shabab, in Mogadishu and elsewhere, continued. Al-Shabab leader Ahmed Abdi Godane was killed by a U.S. airstrike Sept. 1, 2014, and U.S. drone strikes killed other high-ranking members of the group, 2014-15. AMISOM and Somali forces had pushed al-Shabab out of major towns by mid-2015. However, the group's terrorist attacks continued, and it retook some towns by 2016.

Delayed by violence, late 2016 indirect elections resulted in the seating of a new bicameral parliament Dec. 27. Parliament, Feb. 8, 2017, elected former Prime Min. Mohamed Abdullahi Mohamed (2010-11) as Somalia's president. He pledged stronger action against Islamist militants, but further deadly al-Shabab attacks occurred. A truck bombing in Mogadishu, Oct. 14, 2017, killed more than 500. Drought and warfare caused famine affecting more than 6 mil Somalis by 2017. Combat and terrorist attacks continued, 2018-20. U.S. troops (about 650-700 in mid-2020) assisted AMISOM forces (over 20,000 in 2020) and Somali government forces. Ongoing warfare, as well as a 2020 locust invasion, continued to threaten food supplies. The 2020 COVID-19 pandemic also affected Somalia, which had about 3,600 cases and 99 deaths by Sept. 30.

South Africa
Republic of South Africa

People: Population: 56,463,617 (26). **Age distrib.:** <15: 27.9%; 65+: 6.1%. **Growth:** 1.0%. **Migrants:** 7.2%. **Pop. density:** 120.4 per sq mi, 46.5 per sq km. **Urban:** 67.4%. **Ethnic groups:** Black African 80.9%, colored (South African term for persons of mixed-race ancestry) 8.8%, white 7.8%, Indian/Asian 2.5%. **Languages:** isiZulu, isiXhosa, Afrikaans, Sepedi, Setswana, English, Sesotho, Xitsonga, siSwati, Tshivenda, isiNdebele (all official). **Religions:** Christian 82.1% (independent 48.1%, Protestant 26.3%), ethnic religionist 6.8%, agnostic 5.5%.

Geography: Total area: 470,693 sq mi, 1,219,090 sq km (24); **Land area:** 468,909 sq mi, 1,214,470 sq km. **Location:** Southern extreme of Africa. Namibia, Botswana, Zimbabwe on N; Mozambique, Swaziland on E; surrounds Lesotho. **Topography:** Large interior plateau reaches close to the country's 1,739-mi coastline. Few major rivers or lakes. Rainfall is sparse in W, more plentiful in E. **Arable land:** 9.9%. **Capital:** Pretoria (admin.), 2,565,660; Cape Town (legis.), 4,617,560; Bloemfontein (judicial), 567,029. **Cities:** Johannesburg, 5,782,747; Ekurhuleni, 3,894,262; Durban, 3,158,313; Port Elizabeth, 1,253,742.

Government: Type: Parliamentary republic. **Head of state and govt.:** Pres. Cyril Ramaphosa; b. 1952; in office: Feb. 15, 2018. **Local divisions:** 9 provinces. **Defense budget:** $3.5 bil. **Active troops:** 74,850.

Economy: Industries: mining (platinum, gold, chromium), auto assembly, metalworking, machinery, textiles, iron and steel, chemicals, fertilizer, foodstuffs. **Chief agric.:** corn, wheat, sugarcane, fruits, vegetables; beef, poultry, mutton, wool, dairy prods. **Natural resources:** gold, chromium, antimony, coal, iron ore, manganese, nickel, phosphates, tin, rare earth elements, uranium, gem diamonds, platinum, copper, vanadium, salt, nat. gas. **Water:** 905 cu m per capita. **Crude oil reserves:** 15 mil bbls. **Electricity prod.:** 237.5 bil kWh. **Labor force:** agric. 5.0%, industry 22.7%, services 72.3%. **Unemployment:** 28.5%.

Finance: Monetary unit: Rand (ZAR) (16.57 = $1 U.S.). **GDP:** $761.2 bil; **per capita GDP:** $12,999; **GDP growth:** 0.2%. **Imports:** $89.4 bil; China 18.3%, Germany 11.9%, U.S. 6.6%. **Exports:** $94.9 bil; China 9.5%, U.S. 7.7%, Germany 7.1%. **Tourism:** $8.4 bil. **Budget:** $108.3 bil. **Inflation:** 4.1%.

Transport: Railways: 13,040 mi. **Motor vehicles:** 234.8 per 1,000 pop. **Airports:** 130.

Communications: Telephone: 5.4 per 100 pop. **Mobile:** 153.2 per 100 pop. **Broadband:** 70 per 100 pop. **Internet:** 56.2%.

Health: Expend.: 8.1%. **Life expect.:** 63.4 male; 66.2 female. **Births:** 19.2 per 1,000 pop. **Deaths:** 9.3 per 1,000 pop. **Infant mortality:** 27.8 per 1,000 live births. **Undernourished:** 5.7%. **HIV:** 19.0%.

Education: Compulsory: ages 7-15. **Literacy:** 95.3%.
Embassy: 3051 Massachusetts Ave. NW 20008; 232-4400.
Website: www.gov.za

San and KhoiKhoi people were the original inhabitants. Bantus, including Zulu, Xhosa, Swazi, and Sotho, occupied the area from northeastern to southern South Africa before the 17th cent.

The Dutch settled the Cape of Good Hope area, beginning in the 17th cent. Britain seized the Cape, 1806. Many Dutch trekked north and founded two republics, Transvaal and Orange Free State. Diamonds were discovered, 1867, and gold, 1886. The Dutch (Boers) resented encroachments by the British and others; the Anglo-Boer War followed, 1899-1902. Britain won and created, May 31, 1910, the Union of South Africa, incorporating two British colonies (Cape and Natal) with Transvaal and Orange Free State. After a referendum, the Union became the Republic of South Africa, May 31, 1961, and withdrew from the Commonwealth (it rejoined in 1994).

Daniel Malan's National Party, elected in 1948, made the policy of separate development of the races, or apartheid, official. Under apartheid, the majority-Black population was restricted to living and working in designated areas, attended separate schools, could hold only certain jobs, and were paid less than whites for similar

work. Only whites could vote or run for public office. Persons of Asian Indian ancestry and those of mixed race ("coloureds") had limited political rights.

Protests against apartheid were suppressed. At Sharpeville on Mar. 21, 1960, government troops killed 69 Black protesters. At least 600 persons, mostly Bantus, were killed in 1976 anti-apartheid riots. In 1986, Nobel Peace Prize winner Bishop Desmond Tutu called for Western nations to apply sanctions against South Africa to force an end to apartheid. On May 19, South Africa attacked three neighboring countries—Zimbabwe, Botswana, Zambia—striking at guerrilla strongholds of the anti-apartheid African National Congress (ANC).

Some 2 mil South African Black workers staged a strike, June 6-8, 1988. Pres. P. W. Botha, head of the government since 1978, resigned Aug. 14, 1989, and was replaced by F. W. de Klerk. In 1990 the government lifted its ban on the ANC. Anti-apartheid leader Nelson Mandela was freed Feb. 11 after more than 27 years in prison. In Feb. 1991, Pres. de Klerk pledged to end apartheid laws.

In 1993 negotiators agreed on basic principles for a new democratic constitution, and Mandela and de Klerk shared the Nobel Peace Prize. South Africa's partially self-governing Black territories, or "homelands," were incorporated into a national system of nine provinces. The ANC won elections Apr. 26-29, 1994, making Mandela president. The predominantly-Zulu Inkatha Freedom Party won control of the legislature in a mainly Zulu province. By then, fighting between the ANC and Inkatha (aided, during the apartheid era, by South African defense forces) had killed more than 14,000 people in the Zulu region.

A post-apartheid constitution became law Dec. 10, 1996. The ANC won elections, June 2, 1999, and ANC leader Thabo Mbeki became president. South Africa, Nov. 30, 2006, became the first African country to legalize same-sex marriage.

Mbeki's former deputy president, Jacob Zuma, became president after Apr. 22, 2009, elections. Despite corruption charges, Zuma was reelected president by the National Assembly, May 21, 2014. With the economy weak and claims of corruption continuing, Zuma bowed to pressure from ANC leaders and resigned Feb. 14, 2018. Cyril Ramaphosa, head of the ANC since Dec. 2017, was elected president by the National Assembly, Feb. 15, 2018. The ANC retained a parliamentary majority in May 8, 2019, elections, and the National Assembly reelected Ramaphosa president, May 22, 2019.

South Africa was the hardest-hit country in Africa by the 2020 COVID-19 pandemic. Despite lockdown measures, the country had more than 672,000 cases and almost 16,700 deaths by Sept. 30.

South Sudan
Republic of South Sudan

People: Population: 10,561,244 (87). **Age distrib.:** <15: 41.6%; 65+: 2.5%. **Growth:** 2.8%. **Migrants:** 7.8%. **Pop. density:** 42.5 per sq mi, 16.4 per sq km. **Urban:** 20.2%. **Ethnic groups:** Dinka (Jieng) 35.8%, Nuer (Naath) 15.6%, Shilluk (Chollo), Azande, Bari, Kakwa, Kuku, Murle, Mandari, Didinga. **Languages:** English (official), Arabic (incl. Juba, Sudanese variants). **Religions:** Christian 62% (Catholic 41.5%, Protestant 19.4%), ethnic religionist 31.4%, Muslim 6.2% (Sunni).

Geography: Total area: 248,777 sq mi, 644,329 sq km (41). **Location:** NE Africa. Sudan on N, Uganda and Kenya on S, Ethiopia on E, Central African Rep. and Dem. Rep. of the Congo on W. **Topography:** The White Nile R. flows N through center of country and feeds the Sudd, a swampy area occupying more than 15% of the country's center; it is one of the world's largest wetlands. **Arable land:** 0%. **Capital:** Juba, 403,215.

Government: Type: Presidential republic. **Head of state and govt.:** Pres. Salva Kiir Mayardit; b. 1951; in office: July 9, 2011. **Local divisions:** 10 states. **Defense budget:** $70 mil. **Active troops:** 185,000.

Economy: Chief agric.: sorghum, maize, rice, millet, wheat, gum arabic, sugarcane, mangoes, papayas, bananas, sweet potatoes, sunflower seeds, cotton, sesame seeds; cattle, sheep. **Natural resources:** hydropower, gold, diamonds, petroleum, hardwoods, limestone, iron ore, copper, chromium ore, zinc, tungsten, mica, silver. **Water:** 3,936 cu m per capita. **Crude oil reserves** (2017): 3.5 bil bbls. **Electricity prod.:** 510 mil kWh. **Labor force:** agric. 56.1%, industry 14.1%, services 29.7%. **Unemployment:** 12.3%.

Finance: Monetary unit: Pound (SSP) (164.20 = 1 U.S.). **Imports** (2016): $3.8 bil. **Exports** (2016): $1.1 bil. **Budget:** $298.6 mil. **Inflation** (2016-17): 187.9%.

Transport: Railways: 154 mi. **Airports:** 4.

Communications: Telephone (2012): <0.01 per 100 pop. **Mobile:** 33.5 per 100 pop. **Broadband:** 1.1 per 100 pop. **Internet:** 8%.

Health: Expend.: 9.8%. **Life expect.:** 54.6 male; 56.5 female. **Births:** 38.8 per 1,000 pop. **Deaths:** 11.4 per 1,000 pop. **Infant mortality:** 69.9 per 1,000 live births. **Undernourished:** NA. **HIV:** 2.5%.

Education: Compulsory: ages 6-13. **Literacy:** 47.9%.
Embassy: 1015 31st St. NW, Ste. 300, 20007; 293-7940.
Website: www.state.gov/countries-areas/south-sudan/

South Sudan was a region of the Republic of the Sudan when that country became independent in 1956. Northerners (mostly Arab Muslims) dominated, while southerners (mostly Black Africans who practiced Christianity or traditional religions) were marginalized. Southern rebels waged war against the north, 1955-72, until an agreement was reached offering regional self-government for the south. Oil was discovered in the south in 1978.

Civil war broke out again in 1983. Fighting and related famine cost an estimated 2 mil lives and displaced millions of southerners. A peace accord was signed in 2005. A power-sharing agreement allowed for an independence referendum.

Almost 99% of southern Sudanese who voted in the referendum, Jan. 9-15, 2011, supported secession. The UN Security Council, July 8, authorized a peacekeeping force (UNMISS) for the area. South Sudan attained full independence July 9, 2011.

Pres. Salva Kiir fired Vice Pres. Riek Machar, July 23, 2013. Heavy fighting broke out in Juba in Dec. 2013 between government troops and rebels led by Machar (who belong to different ethnic groups) battled throughout the country in 2014-15. Kiir and Machar signed a peace accord Aug. 2015. Renewed heavy fighting began July 7, 2016. A new peace agreement was signed Sept. 12, 2018. A U.S.-funded study reported, Sept. 26, 2018, that South Sudan's civil war had caused about 383,000 "excess deaths" since late 2013. Some violence continued in 2019. After Kiir and Machar agreed in Feb. 2020 on a new transitional government, leading to elections in three years, Machar was sworn in as first vice president Feb. 22. At that time, more than 1.6 mil people were internally displaced. As of Aug. 31, over 2.2 mil South Sudanese were refugees in neighboring countries. UNMISS had more than 16,000 uniformed personnel in South Sudan as of Aug. 31.

The 2020 COVID-19 pandemic caused about 2,700 cases and almost 50 deaths in South Sudan by Sept. 30.

Spain
Kingdom of Spain

People: Population: 50,015,792 (29). **Age distrib.:** <15: 15.0%; 65+: 18.5%. **Growth:** 0.7%. **Migrants:** 13.1%. **Pop. density:** 259.6 per sq mi, 100.2 per sq km. **Urban:** 80.8%. **Ethnic groups** (by birth country): Spanish 86.4%, other 10.5%. **Languages:** Castilian Spanish (official); Catalan, Galician, Basque (all official in areas). **Religions:** Christian 85.6% (Catholic [official] 82.4%), agnostic 9.2%, Muslim 3.2% (Sunni).

Geography: Total area: 195,124 sq mi, 505,370 sq km (51); **Land area:** 192,657 sq mi, 498,980 sq km. **Location:** SW Europe. Portugal on W; France, Andorra on N; Morocco to S. **Topography:** High, arid plateau broken by mountain ranges and river valleys in interior. The NW is heavily watered, the S has lowlands and a Medit. climate. **Arable land:** 24.5%. **Capital:** Madrid, 6,617,513. **Cities:** Barcelona, 5,585,556.

Government: Type: Parliamentary constitutional monarchy. **Head of state:** King Felipe VI; b. 1968; in office: June 19, 2014. **Head of govt.:** Pres. Pedro Sánchez Pérez-Castejón; b. 1972; in office: June 2, 2018. **Local divisions:** 17 autonomous communities, 2 autonomous cities. **Defense budget:** $12.9 bil. **Active troops:** 120,350.

Economy: Industries: textiles/apparel (incl. footwear), food/beverages, metals/metal manufactures, chemicals, shipbuilding, automobiles, machine tools, tourism. **Chief agric.:** grain, vegetables, olives, wine grapes, sugar beets, citrus; beef, pork, poultry, dairy prods.; fish. **Natural resources:** coal, lignite, iron ore, copper, lead, zinc, uranium, tungsten, mercury, pyrites, magnesite, fluorspar, gypsum, sepiolite, kaolin, potash, hydropower. **Water:** 2,405 cu m per capita. **Crude oil reserves:** 150 mil bbls. **Electricity prod** (2018): 259.1 bil kWh. **Labor force:** agric. 4.0%, industry 20.2%, services 75.8%. **Unemployment:** 13.0%.

Finance: Monetary unit· Euro (EUR) (0.84 = $1 U.S.). **GDP:** $2.0 tril; **per capita GDP:** $42,214; **GDP growth:** 2.0%. **Imports:** $338.6 bil; Germany 14.2%, France 11.9%, China 6.9%, Italy 6.8%, Netherlands 5.1%. **Exports:** $313.7 bil; France 15.1%, Germany 11.3%, Italy 7.8%, Portugal 7.1%, UK 6.9%. **Tourism:** $79.7 bil. **Budget:** $539.0 bil. **Inflation:** 0.7%.

Transport: Railways: 9,527 mi. **Motor vehicles:** 504.9 per 1,000 pop. **Airports:** 102.

Communications: Telephone: 42.1 per 100 pop. **Mobile:** 115.9 per 100 pop. **Broadband:** 95.5 per 100 pop. **Internet** (2018): 86.1%.

Health: Expend.: 8.9%. **Life expect.:** 79.0 male; 85.2 female. **Births:** 8.7 per 1,000 pop. **Deaths:** 9.3 per 1,000 pop. **Infant mortality:** 3.2 per 1,000 live births. **Undernourished:** <2.5%. **HIV:** 0.4%.

Education: Compulsory: ages 6-15. **Literacy:** 99.7%. **Embassy:** 2375 Pennsylvania Ave. NW 20037; 452-0100. **Website:** www.lamoncloa.gob.es

Settled by Iberians, Basques, and Celts, Spain was successively ruled (wholly or in part) by Carthage, Rome, and the Visigoths. Muslims invaded Iberia from N Africa in 711. Reconquest of the peninsula by Christians from the N laid the foundations of modern Spain. In 1469 the kingdoms of Aragon and Castile were united by the marriage of Ferdinand II and Isabella I. Moorish rule ended with the fall of Granada, 1492, the year Spain's large Jewish community was expelled.

Spain established a colonial empire after Columbus's 1492 "discovery" of America. Cortés conquered Mexico, and Pizarro conquered Peru. Spain lost most of its American colonies in the early 19th cent. and Cuba, the Philippines, and Puerto Rico in the Spanish-American War, 1898.

Primo de Rivera became dictator, 1923. King Alfonso XIII revoked the dictatorship, 1930, but was forced into exile in 1931. A republic was proclaimed, which disestablished the church, curtailed its privileges, and secularized education. A Popular Front of socialists, Communists, republicans, and anarchists governed 1936-39.

Army officers under Francisco Franco revolted, 1936. Some 500,000 to 1 mil died in the Spanish Civil War before Franco's Nationalist forces won a complete victory Apr. 1, 1939. Franco ruled as a dictator. Spain was officially neutral in WWII but had cordial relations with Nazi Germany for most of the war.

After Franco's death, Nov. 20, 1975, Prince Juan Carlos became king. In free elections, June 1977, moderates and democratic socialists won the most votes. The king thwarted a 1981 coup attempt by right-wing military officers. The Socialist Workers' Party (PSOE), under Felipe González Márquez, won four consecutive general elections, 1982-93, but lost to a coalition of conservative and regional parties, 1996.

Islamic extremists bombed four commuter trains in central Madrid, Mar. 11, 2004, killing 191 people. The PSOE won elections three days later. Spain legalized same-sex marriage in 2005.

Spain's economy suffered during the worldwide financial crisis that began in 2008; in May 2010, as the budget deficit mounted, the government introduced austerity measures to reassure international lenders. Mariano Rajoy's conservative Popular Party (PP) won Nov. 2011 elections. Spain received a 100-bil-euro EU bailout for its ailing banks in 2012. Spain's unemployment rate surpassed 26% in 2013. GDP began growing in 2014, after five years of decline, but unemployment remained high.

Juan Carlos abdicated in favor of his son, who became King Felipe VI, June 19, 2014. Hurt by corruption scandals, the PP lost support in Dec. 20, 2015, and June 26, 2016, legislative elections, but Rajoy was sworn in as head of a minority govt., Oct. 31, 2016. Rajoy lost a no-confidence vote, June 1, 2018; the PSOE's Pedro Sánchez became prime min. The PSOE won the most seats but not a majority in Apr. 28 and Nov. 10, 2019, elections. Sánchez formed a new coalition minority government, Jan. 7, 2020.

In one of a series of events linked by police to an Islamist extremist cell in Catalonia, 14 people were killed and more than 100 injured in Barcelona, Aug. 17, 2017, when a terrorist drove a van through a crowded pedestrian area; he then apparently killed the driver of a car he stole.

Spain was the European entry point for more than 65,000 African and Middle Eastern migrants (most arriving by boat) in 2018. About 50,000 arrived, 2019 through mid-Sept. 2020.

Hard-hit by Mar. 2020 by the COVID-19 pandemic, Spain instituted a nationwide lockdown to slow disease spread. With new cases declining, the nationwide state of emergency was ended June 21, but cases rose sharply again in Aug.-Sept. By Sept. 30, Spain had more than 716,000 total cases and over 31,000 deaths. The pandemic had a severe impact on the tourism industry and the rest of the economy; GDP in Q2 2020 declined 22% from the same period in 2019.

Catalonia and the **Basque Country** were granted autonomy, Jan. 1980, following approval in referendums. But Basque extremists pushed for independence. The Basque separatist group ETA carried out bombings that killed about 830 since 1968. ETA declared a unilateral cease-fire in 2011 and said in 2018 that it was disbanding. In Catalonia, voters approved expanded home-rule, June 18, 2006. Separatist parties won Catalonia's regional parliamentary elections Sept. 27, 2015. Catalonia scheduled a separation referendum for Oct. 1, 2017, but Spanish authorities took steps to interfere with balloting. After the regional parliament, Oct. 27, voted to declare independence, the national government dissolved the parliament and removed pro-independence regional president Carles Puigdemont from office. In new regional parliamentary elections, Dec. 21, separatists again won a majority; the parliament elected separatist Quim Torra as regional president, May 14, 2018. On Oct. 14, 2019, 9 separatist leaders were convicted and given prison terms for their roles in the 2017 secession attempt. Spain's Supreme Court ruled, Sept. 28, 2020, that Torra could not hold office. **Website:** web.gencat.cat

The **Balearic Isls.** in the W Mediterranean, 1,927 sq mi, is an autonomous community of Spain; the islands include Majorca (Mallorca; capital Palma de Mallorca), Minorca, Cabrera, Ibiza, and Formentera. The **Canary Isls.**, 2,807 sq mi, an autonomous community in the Atlantic W of Morocco, includes the islands of Tenerife, Palma, Gomera, Hierro, Grand Canary, Fuerteventura, and Lanzarote; Las Palmas and Santa Cruz are thriving ports.

Ceuta and **Melilla**, small Spanish enclaves on Morocco's Mediterranean coast, gained limited autonomy in Sept. 1994. In 2014-20, thousands of African and Middle Eastern migrants crossed the borders between Morocco and the enclaves.

Spain has sought the return of **Gibraltar**, in British hands since 1704.

Sri Lanka
Democratic Socialist Republic of Sri Lanka

People: Population: 22,889,201 (57). **Age distrib.:** <15: 23.1%; 65+: 10.6%. **Growth:** 0.7%. **Migrants:** 0.2%. **Pop. density:** 917.3 per sq mi, 354.2 per sq km. **Urban:** 18.7%. **Ethnic groups:** Sinhalese 74.9%, Sri Lankan Tamil 11.2%, Sri Lankan Moor 9.2%, Indian Tamil 4.2%. **Languages:** Sinhala, Tamil (both official and national); English (commonly used in govt.). **Religions:** Buddhist (official) 67.8%, Hindu 13%, Muslim 9.3% (Sunni), Christian 9.1%.

Geography: Total area: 25,332 sq mi, 65,610 sq km (120); **Land area:** 24,954 sq mi, 64,630 sq km. **Location:** Indian O. off SE coast of India. **Topography:** Coastal area and N half are flat; S central area is hilly and mountainous. **Arable land:** 20.7%. **Capital:** Colombo, 612,535; Sri Jayewardenepura Kotte (legis.), 103,248.

Government: Type: Presidential republic. **Head of state and govt.:** Pres. Gotabaya Rajapaksa; b. 1949; in office: Nov. 18, 2019. **Local divisions:** 9 provinces. **Defense budget:** $1.7 bil. **Active troops:** 255,000.

Economy: Industries: rubber, tea, coconuts, tobacco and other agric. commodities; telecom, insurance, banking; tourism, shipping; clothing, textiles; cement, petroleum refining. **Chief agric.:** rice, sugarcane, grains, pulses, oilseed, spices, vegetables, fruit, tea, rubber, coconuts; milk, eggs, hides, beef; fish. **Natural resources:** limestone, graphite, mineral sands, gems, phosphates, clay, hydropower. **Water:** 2,529 cu m per capita. **Electricity prod.:** 15.1 bil kWh. **Labor force:** agric. 23.7%, industry 30.4%, services 45.9%. **Unemployment:** 4.2%.

Finance: Monetary unit: Rupee (LKR) (185.04 = $1 U.S.). **GDP:** $297.0 bil; **per capita GDP:** $13,620; **GDP growth:** 2.3%. **Imports:** $21 bil; India 22%, China 19.9%, Singapore 6.9%, UAE 5.7%. **Exports:** $11.4 bil; U.S. 24.6%, UK 9%, India 5.8%. **Tourism:** $3.6 bil. **Budget:** $16.9 bil. **Inflation:** 3.5%.

Transport: Railways: 971 mi. **Motor vehicles:** 49.2 per 1,000 pop. **Airports:** 11.

Communications: Telephone: 11.6 per 100 pop. **Mobile:** 115.1 per 100 pop. **Broadband:** 22.4 per 100 pop. **Internet:** 34.1%.

Health: Expend.: 3.8%. **Life expect.:** 74.0 male; 81.1 female. **Births:** 14.2 per 1,000 pop. **Deaths:** 6.5 per 1,000 pop. **Infant mortality:** 7.8 per 1,000 live births. **Undernourished:** 7.6%. **HIV:** <0.1%.

Education: Compulsory: ages 5-15. **Literacy:** 98.8%.

Embassy: 3025 Whitehaven St. NW 20008; 483-4025.

Website: www.gov.lk

The island was known to the ancient world as Taprobane (Greek for copper-colored) and later as Serendip (from Arabic). Colonists from N India subdued the Indigenous Veddahs about 543 BCE; their descendants, the Buddhist Sinhalese, still form most of the population. Hindu descendants of Tamil immigrants from S India are the largest minority ethnic group.

Parts were occupied by the Portuguese in 1505 and the Dutch in 1658. The British seized the island in 1796. It became an independent member of the Commonwealth as Ceylon in 1948 before changing its name to Sri Lanka May 22, 1972.

Prime Min. Solomon W. R. D. Bandaranaike was assassinated Sept. 25, 1959. His widow, Sirimavo Bandaranaike, served as prime min. 1960-65, 1970-77, 1994-2000. In the 1970s, thousands of ultra-leftists were executed, while massive land reform and nationalization of foreign-owned plantations took place.

Tensions between Sinhalese and Tamil separatists erupted in the early 1980s and turned into a 20-year civil war that killed more than 60,000; another 20,000, mostly young Tamils, "disappeared" while in government custody. Pres. Ranasinghe Premadasa was assassinated May 1, 1993, by a Tamil rebel. A truce intended to bring an end to the civil war was signed Feb. 22, 2002.

More than 31,000 died in the Dec. 26, 2004, Indian Ocean tsunami. Prime Min. Mahinda Rajapaksa won the 2005 presidential election and was reelected in 2010. Thousands died during more than three years of fighting among government forces, paramilitary groups, and Tamil rebels beginning in Dec. 2005. Tamil leader Vellupillai Prabhakaran was killed May 18-19, 2009, and Pres. Rajapaksa formally declared victory. Maithripala Sirisena defeated Rajapaksa in the Jan. 8, 2015, presidential election. A Sept. 16, 2015, UN report documented widespread torture of detainees by government security forces during Sri Lanka's civil war; 2017 and 2018 UN reports concluded that torture of national-security detainees continued. The WHO announced, Sept. 5, 2016, that Sri Lanka had eradicated malaria.

Loans and investments from China have financed large infrastructure projects in recent years. More than 250 died Easter Sunday, Apr. 21, 2019, in suicide bombings at churches and other sites carried out by Islamist extremists. Gotabaya Rajapaksa, brother of the former president, won the Nov. 16, 2019, presidential election. He named Mahinda Rajapaksa prime min. The ruling party won Aug. 5, 2020, parliamentary elections.

The 2020 COVID-19 pandemic caused almost 3,400 cases and 13 deaths as of Sept. 30.

Sudan
Republic of the Sudan

(Pre-2012 data include South Sudan, which became independent July 9, 2011.)

People: Population: 45,561,556 (31). **Age distrib.:** <15: 42.0%; 65+: 3.0%. **Growth:** 2.7%. **Migrants:** 2.9%. **Pop. density:** 63.4 per sq mi, 24.5 per sq km. **Urban:** 35.3%. **Ethnic groups:** Sudanese Arab (approx. 70%), Fur, Beja, Nuba, Fallata. **Languages:** Arabic, English (both official); Nubian; Ta Bedawie; Fur. **Religions:** Muslim (official) 91.8% (Sunni), Christian 4.4%, ethnic religionist 2.6%.

Geography: Total area: 718,723 sq mi, 1,861,484 sq km (15). **Location:** E end of Sahara desert zone. Egypt on N; Libya, Chad, Central African Republic on W; South Sudan on S; Ethiopia, Eritrea on E. **Topography:** The N consists of Libyan Desert in W and the mountainous Nubia Desert in E, with narrow Nile Valley between. Large rainy areas with fields, pastures, and forests in center. The S has rich soil, heavy rain. **Arable land** (2011): 15.7%. **Capital:** Khartoum, 5,828,858.

Government: Type: Presidential republic. **Head of state:** Sovereign Council Chief Lt. Gen. Abdel Fattah Abdelrahman Burhan; b. 1960; in office: Aug. 21, 2019. **Head of govt.:** Prime Min. Abdalla Hamdok; b. 1956; in office: Aug. 21, 2019. (Under an Aug. 2019 power-sharing agreement between the military and civilian protesters, a 39-month transitional government will be followed by elections.) **Local divisions:** 18 states. **Defense budget:** NA. **Active troops:** 104,300.

Economy: Industries: oil, cotton ginning, textiles, cement, edible oils, sugar, soap distilling, shoes, petroleum refining, pharmaceuticals, armaments. **Chief agric.:** cotton, groundnuts, sorghum, millet, wheat, gum arabic, sugarcane, cassava, mangoes, papayas, bananas, sweet potatoes, sesame seeds; animal feed, sheep. **Natural resources:** petroleum; small reserves of iron ore, copper, chromium ore, zinc, tungsten, mica, silver, gold; hydropower. **Water:** 933 cu m per capita. **Crude oil reserves:** 5 bil bbls. **Electricity prod.:** 15.2 bil kWh. **Labor force:** agric. 39.7%, industry 15.9%, services 44.4%. **Unemployment:** 16.6%.

Finance: Monetary unit: Pound (SDG) (55.25 = $1 U.S.). **GDP:** $176.5 bil; **per capita GDP:** $4,123; **GDP growth:** -2.6%. **Imports:** $8.2 bil; UAE 12.7%, Egypt 10.6%, India 10.5%, Turkey 10.2%, Japan 7.6%, Saudi Arabia 6%. **Exports:** $4.1 bil; UAE 55.5%, Egypt 14.7%, Saudi Arabia 8.8%. **Tourism:** $821 mil. **Budget:** $13.4 bil. **Inflation:** 51.0%.

Transport: Railways: 4,506 mi. **Motor vehicles:** 2.9 per 1,000 pop. **Airports:** 17.

Communications: Telephone: 0.3 per 100 pop. **Mobile:** 72 per 100 pop. **Broadband:** 30.5 per 100 pop. **Internet:** 30.9%.

Health: Expend.: 6.3%. **Life expect.:** 64.3 male; 68.8 female. **Births:** 33.8 per 1,000 pop. **Deaths:** 6.5 per 1,000 pop. **Infant mortality:** 41.8 per 1,000 live births. **Undernourished:** 12.4%. **HIV:** 0.2%.

Education: Compulsory: ages 6-13. **Literacy:** 73.0%.

Embassy: 2210 Massachusetts Ave. NW 20008; 338-8565.

Website: www.presidency.gov.sd

Northern Sudan, ancient Nubia, was settled by Egyptians in antiquity. The population was converted to Coptic Christianity in the 6th cent. Arab conquests brought Islam to the area in the 15th cent. In the 1820s, Egypt took over Sudan, defeating the last of the earlier empires, including the Fung. In the 1880s, Muhammad Ahmad, who called himself the Mahdi (leader of the faithful), and his followers, the dervishes, led a revolution. An Anglo-Egyptian force crushed the Mahdi's successors, 1898.

Sudan gained independence Jan. 1, 1956. In 1969, a Revolutionary Council took power, led by authoritarian Pres. Gaafar al-Nimeiry. He was overthrown, Apr. 6, 1985. Sudan held democratic elections in 1986. Brig. Omar Hassan Ahmad al-Bashir staged a coup, June 30, 1989. He became president in 1993.

During 1955-72 and 1983-2005, rebels in the south (primarily Christians and followers of traditional religions) fought against government domination by mostly Arab-Muslim northern Sudan. War and famine cost an estimated 2 mil lives. An accord largely ended the rebellion Jan. 9, 2005, but violence increased beginning in 2011.

A rebellion in the Darfur region of western Sudan caused a new crisis, 2003-11. Marauding Arab militias, the *janjaweed*, reportedly acting in collusion with Sudanese government troops, looted and burned homes in Darfur. More than 7,000 African Union (AU) peacekeepers were ineffectual. By Sept. 2009, the Darfur war had killed about 300,000 people and displaced another 2.7 mil. A joint UN-AU force of up to 26,000 peacekeepers (UNMIS) was deployed Aug. 2007-July 2011.

After northern Sudanese voted overwhelmingly for secession, Jan. 9-15, 2011, South Sudan attained full independence July 9. Conflict in Darfur flared up again in 2014-16. A UN-AU peacekeeping mission in Darfur (UNAMID) included almost 16,000 uniformed personnel as of Aug. 31, 2017. Although some violence continued, the UN reduced UNAMID personnel to about 6,000 by Aug. 31,

2020. The government reached a peace agreement, Aug. 31, with some Darfur and southern rebel groups.

After months of deadly protests triggered by economic hardship, Bashir was ousted in a military coup, Apr. 11, 2019. Protests continued, demanding civilian rule. An agreement signed Aug. 17, 2019, by military and protest leaders provided for a 39-month power-sharing transition government, followed by a democratically elected government. Bashir was convicted on corruption charges, Dec. 14, 2019, and went on trial, July 21, 2020, on charges related to the 1989 coup. He also faced war crimes charges at the Intl. Criminal Court in The Hague.

The 2020 COVID-19 pandemic caused more than 13,600 cases and over 800 deaths in Sudan as of Sept. 30.

Suriname
Republic of Suriname

People: Population: 609,569 (166). **Age distrib.:** <15: 23.4%; 65+: 6.5%. **Growth:** 0.9%. **Migrants:** 7.9%. **Pop. density:** 10.1 per sq mi, 3.9 per sq km. **Urban:** 66.1%. **Ethnic groups:** Hindustani or East Indian (descended fr. 19th-cent. emigrants fr. northern India) 27.4%, Maroon (descendants of escaped African slaves) 21.7%, Creole (mixed white/Black) 15.7%, Javanese 13.7%, mixed 13.4%. **Languages:** Dutch (official), English (widely spoken), Sranang Tongo (Surinamese), Caribbean Hindustani, Javanese. **Religions:** Christian 51.6% (Catholic 30.8%, Protestant 15.6%), Hindu 20.4%, Muslim 15.8% (Sunni), agnostic 4.9%.

Geography: Total area: 63,251 sq mi, 163,820 sq km (90); **Land area:** 60,232 sq mi, 156,000 sq km. **Location:** N shore of S America. Guyana on W, Brazil on S, French Guiana on E. **Topography:** Flat Atlantic coast, where dikes permit agriculture. Inland is forest belt. To S, hills cover three-fourths of country. **Arable land:** 0.4%. **Capital:** Paramaribo, 239,457.

Government: Type: Presidential republic. **Head of state and govt.:** Pres. Chandrikapersad Santokhi; b. 1959; in office: July 16, 2020. **Local divisions:** 10 districts. **Defense budget:** NA. **Active troops:** 1,840.

Economy: Industries: gold mining, oil, lumber, food proc., fishing. **Chief agric.:** rice, bananas, seabob shrimp, yellow-fin tuna, vegetables. **Natural resources:** timber, hydropower, fish, kaolin, shrimp, bauxite, gold; small amounts of nickel, copper, platinum, iron ore. **Water:** 175,719 cu m per capita. **Crude oil reserves:** 74.4 mil bbls. **Electricity prod.:** 1.8 bil kWh. **Labor force:** agric. 7.5%, industry 23.5%, services 69.1%. **Unemployment:** 7.5%.

Finance: Monetary unit: Dollar (SRD) (7.46 = $1 U.S.). **GDP:** $9.9 bil; **per capita GDP:** $17,005; **GDP growth:** −0.8%. **Imports:** $1.3 bil; U.S. 30.6%, Netherlands 14.8%, Trinidad and Tobago 11.4%, China 7.6%. **Exports:** $2.0 bil; Switzerland 38%, Hong Kong 21.9%, Belgium 10.1%, UAE 7.2%, Guyana 6.1%. **Tourism:** $53 mil. **Budget:** $827.8 mil. **Inflation** (2016-17): 22.0%.

Transport: Motor vehicles: 277.3 per 1,000 pop. **Airports:** 6. **Communications: Telephone:** 15.3 per 100 pop. **Mobile** (2017): 139.5 per 100 pop. **Broadband:** 46.9 per 100 pop. **Internet:** 48.9%.

Health: Expend.: 6.2%. **Life expect.:** 70.8 male; 75.9 female. **Births:** 14.9 per 1,000 pop. **Deaths:** 6.2 per 1,000 pop. **Infant mortality:** 22.1 per 1,000 live births. **Undernourished:** 8.1%. **HIV:** 1.3%.

Education: Compulsory: ages 7-12. **Literacy:** 98.6%.

Embassy: 4201 Connecticut Ave. NW, Ste. 400, 20008; 629-4302.

Website: www.gov.sr or www.surinameembassy.org

The Netherlands acquired Suriname in 1667 from Britain. The 1954 Dutch constitution raised the colony to a level of equality with the Netherlands. Independence was granted Nov. 25, 1975; some 40% of the population (mostly E Indians, who opposed independence) immigrated to the Netherlands.

Désiré "Dési" Bouterse, who masterminded coups in 1982 and 1990, was elected president by the National Assembly, July 19, 2010. Bouterse had been convicted in absentia in the Netherlands, 1999, for drug trafficking. Named by the U.S. as a transshipment point for cocaine, Suriname agreed in 2012 to improve shipping inspections. Bouterse's son Dino pleaded guilty in the U.S., Aug. 29, 2014, to drug trafficking and terrorism charges. Bouterse was reelected by the National Assembly, July 14, 2015. He was convicted, in Surname Nov. 29, 2019, of murder in connection with the 1982 coup; he appealed. Following an opposition victory in May 25, 2020, elections, the new National Assembly elected Chandrikapersad Santokhi president, July 13.

Suriname was affected, 2015-17, by a Zika virus outbreak (about 3,500 cases). The 2020 COVID-19 pandemic caused over 4,800 cases and 102 deaths in Suriname as of Sept. 30.

Sweden
Kingdom of Sweden

People: Population: 10,202,491 (91). **Age distrib.:** <15: 17.7%; 65+: 20.6%. **Growth:** 0.8%. **Migrants:** 20.0%. **Pop. density:** 64.4 per sq mi, 24.9 per sq km. **Urban:** 88.0%. **Ethnic groups** (by birth country): Swedish 80.9%, Syrian 1.8%, Finnish 1.4%, Iraqi 1.4%; Indigenous Sami. **Languages:** Swedish (official). **Religions:** Christian 57.4% (Protestant 54.3%), agnostic 20.4%, atheist 11.9%, Muslim 9.1% (Sunni 7%, Shia 2%).

Geography: Total area: 173,860 sq mi, 450,295 sq km (55); **Land area:** 158,431 sq mi, 410,335 sq km. **Location:** Scandinavian Peninsula in N Europe. Norway on W, Denmark on S (across Kattegat strait), Finland on E. **Topography:** Mountains along NW border cover 25% of Sweden. Flat or rolling terrain with several large lakes across central and southern areas. **Arable land:** 6.3%. **Capital:** Stockholm, 1,632,798.

Government: Type: Parliamentary constitutional monarchy. **Head of state:** King Carl XVI Gustaf; b. 1946; in office: Sept. 15, 1973. **Head of govt.:** Prime Min. Stefan Löfven; b. 1957; in office: Oct. 3, 2014. **Local divisions:** 21 counties. **Defense budget:** $6.4 bil. **Active troops:** 15,150.

Economy: Industries: iron and steel, precision equip. (bearings, radio and phone parts, armaments), wood pulp and paper prods., processed foods, motor vehicles. **Chief agric.:** barley, wheat, sugar beets; meat, milk. **Natural resources:** iron ore, copper, lead, zinc, gold, silver, tungsten, uranium, arsenic, feldspar, timber, hydropower. **Water:** 17,556 cu m per capita. **Electricity prod.** (2018): 156.5 bil kWh. **Labor force:** agric. 1.6%, industry 17.7%, services 80.7%. **Unemployment:** 6.7%.

Finance: Monetary unit: Krona (SEK) (8.73 = $1 U.S.). **GDP:** $574.1 bil; **per capita GDP:** $55,815; **GDP growth:** 1.2%. **Imports:** $153.2 bil; Germany 18.7%, Netherlands 8.9%, Norway 7.7%, Denmark 7.2%, China 5.5%, UK 5.1%. **Exports:** $165.6 bil; Germany 11%, Norway 10.2%, Finland 6.9%, U.S. 6.9%, Denmark 6.9%, UK 6.2%, Netherlands 5.5%. **Tourism:** $15.2 bil. **Budget:** $264.4 bil. **Inflation:** 1.8%.

Transport: Railways: 8,778 mi. **Motor vehicles:** 553.3 per 1,000 pop. **Airports:** 149.

Communications: Telephone: 24 per 100 pop. **Mobile:** 125.1 per 100 pop. **Broadband:** 122.6 per 100 pop. **Internet** (2018): 92.1%.

Health: Expend.: 11.0%. **Life expect.:** 80.4 male; 84.5 female. **Births:** 12.1 per 1,000 pop. **Deaths:** 9.4 per 1,000 pop. **Infant mortality:** 2.6 per 1,000 live births. **Undernourished:** <2.5%. **HIV:** NA.

Education: Compulsory: ages 6-15. **Literacy:** 99%.

Embassy: 2900 K St. NW 20007; 467-2600.

Website: sweden.se

The Swedes have lived in present-day Sweden for at least 5,000 years. Gothic tribes from Sweden played a major role in the disintegration of the Roman Empire. Other Swedes helped create the first Russian state in the 9th cent. The Swedes were Christianized from the 11th cent., and a strong centralized monarchy developed. The Riksdag, the first European parliament to represent all classes of society, was first called in 1435.

A revolt led by Gustavus I in 1521-23 freed Sweden from Danish rule (dating from 1397); he built up the government and military and established the Lutheran Church. In the 17th cent. Sweden was a major European power, gaining most of the Baltic seacoast. The Napoleonic wars, 1799-1815, in which Sweden acquired Norway (it became independent 1905), were the last in which Sweden participated.

The Social Democratic Party (SAP) has governed Sweden for most of the period since World War II. Prime Min. Olof Palme was shot to death in Stockholm, Feb. 28, 1986. Sweden entered the EU, Jan. 1, 1995. A center-right alliance defeated the SAP in 2006 and 2010 parliamentary elections. Parliament voted Apr. 1, 2009, to legalize same-sex marriage. The SAP won the largest bloc of seats in Sept. 14, 2014, elections, in which the anti-immigration Sweden Democrats (SD) won 49 seats. The SAP's Stefan Löfven became prime min., Oct. 3. Parliament approved, 2016, defense cooperation agreements with NATO and the U.S. In 2017, Sweden adopted (for men and women) a military draft.

About 238,000 migrants, mostly from the Middle East, SW Asia, and Africa, applied for asylum in Sweden in 2015-18. Legislation tightening asylum rules was enacted June 21, 2016. Of applications decided, 2015-18, the government granted asylum in about 50% of cases.

In Sept. 9, 2018, elections, an SAP-led center-left coalition fell short of a majority; the SD won 62 seats. Löfven formed a minority government, Jan. 21, 2019.

The government resisted strict lockdown measures to combat the 2020 COVID-19 pandemic. As of Sept. 30, Sweden had over 92,000 cases and about 5,900 deaths (both figures the highest per capita for any Nordic country).

Switzerland
Swiss Confederation

People: Population: 8,403,994 (100). **Age distrib.:** <15: 15.3%; 65+: 18.7%. **Growth:** 0.7%. **Migrants:** 29.9%. **Pop. density:** 544.2 per sq mi, 210.1 per sq km. **Urban:** 73.9%. **Ethnic groups** (by birth country): Swiss 69.5%, German 4.2%, Italian 3.2%, Portuguese 2.6%, French 2%. **Languages:** German, French, Italian, Romansch (all official); English; Portuguese; Albanian; Serbo-Croatian; Spanish. **Religions:** Christian 73.7% (Catholic 39.7%, Protestant 29.7%), agnostic 17%, Muslim 6.5% (Sunni).

Geography: Total area: 15,937 sq mi, 41,277 sq km (132); **Land area:** 15,443 sq mi, 39,997 sq km. **Location:** In Alps Mts. in central Europe. France on W; Italy on S; Liechtenstein, Austria on E; Germany on N. **Topography:** The Alps cover 60% of land area; the Jura, near France, 10%. The midlands run NE-SW in-between. **Arable land:** 10.1%. **Capital:** Bern, 429,734. **Cities:** Zürich, 1,395,356; Genève, 613,373.

Government: Type: Federal republic (formally a confederation). **Head of state and govt.:** President chosen on rotating basis from among 7-member Federal Council for 1-year term. **Local divisions:** 26 cantons. **Defense budget:** $5.4 bil. **Active troops:** 21,450.

Economy: Industries: machinery, chemicals, watches, textiles, precision instruments, tourism, banking, insurance. **Chief agric.:** grains, fruits, vegetables; meat, eggs, dairy prods. **Natural resources:** timber, salt. **Water:** 6,312 cu m per capita. **Electricity prod.** (2018): 63.6 bil kWh. **Labor force:** agric. 2.9%, industry 20.0%, services 77.2%. **Unemployment:** 4.9%.

Finance: Monetary unit: Franc (CHF) (0.91 = $1 U.S.). **GDP:** $608.7 bil; **per capita GDP:** $70,989; **GDP growth:** 0.9%. **Imports:** $264.5 bil; Germany 20.9%, U.S. 7.9%, Italy 7.6%, UK 7.3%, France 6.8%, China 5%. **Exports:** $313.5 bil; Germany 15.2%, U.S. 12.3%, China 8.2%, India 6.7%, France 5.7%, UK 5.7%, Hong Kong 5.4%, Italy 5.3%. **Tourism:** $17.1 bil. **Budget:** $234.4 bil (federal, cantonal, and municipal). **Inflation:** 0.4%.

Transport: Railways: 3,536 mi. **Motor vehicles:** 624.8 per 1,000 pop. **Airports:** 40.

Communications: Telephone: 39.2 per 100 pop. **Mobile:** 129.6 per 100 pop. **Broadband:** 99.7 per 100 pop. **Internet:** 89.7%.

Health: Expend.: 12.3%. **Life expect.:** 80.5 male; 85.3 female. **Births:** 10.5 per 1,000 pop. **Deaths:** 8.5 per 1,000 pop. **Infant mortality:** 3.5 per 1,000 live births. **Undernourished:** <2.5%. **HIV:** 0.2%.

Education: Compulsory: ages 5-15. **Literacy:** 99%.

Embassy: 2201 Wisconsin Ave. NW, #300, 20007; 745-7900.

Website: www.ch.ch

Switzerland, the former Roman province of Helvetia, traces its modern history to 1291, when three cantons created a defensive league. Other cantons were subsequently admitted to the Swiss Confederation, which obtained its independence from the Holy Roman Empire through the Peace of Westphalia (1648). The cantons were joined under a federal constitution in 1848.

Switzerland has maintained an armed neutrality since 1815 and has not been involved in a foreign war since 1515. It is the seat of many UN and other international agencies but only became a full UN member on Sept. 10, 2002.

Switzerland is a world banking center. The government announced, Mar. 1997, a $4.7-bil fund to compensate victims of the Nazi Holocaust and other catastrophes. Swiss banks agreed Aug. 12, 1998, to pay $1.25 bil in reparations. A June 2002 referendum decriminalized abortion. Referenda in 2005 harmonized many policies with the EU; more rights for same-sex couples were also endorsed June 5, 2005.

The Swiss government bailed out the troubled banking giant UBS during the international financial crisis in Oct. 2008. In a Nov. 2009 referendum reflecting anti-Muslim sentiment, voters approved a constitutional ban on construction of new minarets on mosques. In a Feb. 9, 2014, referendum, voters called on the government to set immigration quotas; however, Dec. 2016 immigration legislation rejected quotas, which could have jeopardized Switzerland's access to the EU single market. In a May 19, 2019, referendum, voters approved stricter gun controls.

Switzerland officially opened the 35-mi Gotthard Base Tunnel, the world's longest railway tunnel, June 1, 2016.

The 2020 COVID-19 pandemic caused about 53,000 cases and almost 1,800 deaths in Switzerland as of Sept. 30.

Syria
Syrian Arab Republic

People: Population: 19,398,448 (63). **Age distrib.: <15:** 33.5%; **65+:** 4.5%. **Growth:** 4.6%. **Migrants:** 5.1%. **Pop. density:** 270.3 per sq mi, 104.4 per sq km. **Urban:** 55.5%. **Ethnic groups:** Arab 50%, Alawite 15%, Kurd 10%, Levantine 10%, other 15% (incl. Druze, Ismaili, Imami, Nusairi, Assyrian, Turkoman, Armenian). **Languages:** Arabic (official), Kurdish, Armenian, Aramaic, Circassian, French, English. **Religions:** Muslim (official) 94.7% (Sunni 79%, Shia 15%), Christian 3.2%.

Geography: Total area: 72,370 sq mi, 187,437 sq km (87); **Land area:** 70,900 sq mi, 183,630 sq km. (500 sq mi of area is occupied by Israel.) **Location:** Middle East, at E end of Medit. Sea. Lebanon, Israel on W; Jordan on S; Iraq on E; Turkey on N. **Topography:** A short Medit. coastline stretches E and S with fertile lowlands and plains, alternating with mountains and large desert areas. **Arable land:** 24.4%. **Capital:** Damascus, 2,392,045. **Cities:** Aleppo (Halab), 1,916,781; Homs (Hims), 1,335,804. (Pop. ests. are not based on solid evidence because of wartime instability.)

Government: Type: Presidential republic; highly authoritarian regime. **Head of state:** Pres. Bashar al-Assad; b. 1965; in office:

July 17, 2000. **Head of govt.:** Prime Min. Hussein Arnous; b. 1953; in office: Aug. 31, 2020. **Local divisions:** 14 provinces. **Defense budget:** NA. **Active troops:** 169,000.

Economy: Industries: petroleum, textiles, food proc., beverages, tobacco, phosphate rock mining, cement. **Chief agric.:** wheat, barley, cotton, lentils, chickpeas, olives, sugar beets; beef, mutton. **Natural resources:** petroleum, phosphates, chrome and manganese ores, asphalt, iron ore, rock salt, marble, gypsum, hydropower. **Water:** 920 cu m per capita. **Crude oil reserves:** 2.5 bil bbls. **Electricity prod.:** 17.2 bil kwH. **Labor force:** agric. 10.5%, industry 26.5%, services 63.0%. **Unemployment:** 8.5%.

Finance: Monetary unit: Pound (SYP) (511.29 = $1 U.S.). **GDP:** NA; **per capita GDP:** NA; **GDP growth:** NA. **Imports:** $6.3 bil; Russia 32.4%, Turkey 16.7%, China 9.5%. **Exports:** $1.9 bil; Lebanon 31.5%, Iraq 10.3%, Jordan 8.8%, China 7.8%, Turkey 7.5%, Spain 7.3%. **Tourism** (2010): $6.2 bil. **Budget:** $3.2 bil (govt. projections for FY2016). **Inflation** (2016-17): 28.1%.

Transport: Railways: 1,275 mi. **Motor vehicles:** 135.8 per 1,000 pop. **Airports:** 29.

Communications: Telephone: 16.2 per 100 pop. **Mobile:** 98.4 per 100 pop. **Broadband:** 12.7 per 100 pop. **Internet:** 34.3%.

Health: Expend. (2012): 3.6%. **Life expect.:** 72.3 male; 75.3 female. **Births:** 23.8 per 1,000 pop. **Deaths:** 4.5 per 1,000 pop. **Infant mortality:** 16.5 per 1,000 live births. **Undernourished:** NA. **HIV:** <0.1%.

Education: Compulsory: ages 6-14. **Literacy:** 86.4%.

Embassy: 2215 Wyoming Ave. NW 20008; 232-6313.

Website: www.egov.sy

Syria was the center of the Seleucid Empire but later was absorbed into the Roman and Arab empires. Ottoman rule prevailed for four cents., until the end of WWI.

The state of Syria was formed from former Turkish districts, separated by the Treaty of Sevres, 1920, and divided into the states of Syria and Greater Lebanon. Both were administered under a French League of Nations mandate, 1920-41. The occupying French proclaimed Syria a republic Sept. 16, 1941; independence came Apr. 17, 1946. Syria joined the Arab invasion of Israel in 1948.

Syria belonged to the United Arab Republic from Feb. 1958 to Sept. 1961. The Socialist Baath party seized power Mar. 1963 and became the only legal party. The Alawite minority has dominated the government (Alawism is a sect of Shiite Islam).

In the June 1967 Arab-Israeli war, Israel seized and occupied the Golan Heights, from which Syria had shelled Israeli settlements. On Oct. 6, 1973, Syria and Egypt attacked Israel but failed to recapture the Golan Heights. Syrian troops entered Lebanon in 1976, during the Lebanese civil war, and remained a strong presence in the country. Syria sided with Iran during the Iran-Iraq War, 1980-88.

Thousands died in the city of Hama Feb. 1982 when government forces crushed a Muslim Brotherhood uprising. Following Israel's invasion of Lebanon, June 6, 1982, Israeli planes destroyed Syrian planes and antiaircraft missile batteries in the Bekaa Valley, June 9.

Hafez al-Assad, president of Syria since 1971, died June 10, 2000, and was succeeded by his son Bashar al-Assad. Syria aided fighters of the Lebanon-based Shiite group Hezbollah in their conflict with Israel and gave about 180,000 Lebanese temporary refuge when Israeli forces targeted Hezbollah, July-Aug. 2006. On Sept. 6, 2007, Israel bombed a secret site in N Syria where the Israelis believed Syria and North Korea were developing a nuclear facility; both countries denied the claim.

The Assad regime used troops and tanks during Arab Spring demonstrations in Mar. 2011, but the confrontations escalated into outright rebellion. A number of armed opposition groups fought Assad's forces and each other for control of territory. Hezbollah forces fought on the side of the Assad government, which was also backed by Iran. The U.S., Aug. 18, 2011, called on Assad to step down and imposed economic sanctions.

International intelligence communities announced, May 2013, increasing evidence that Assad's forces had used chemical and biological weapons. The EU and U.S., 2013, began to supply military support to rebel groups. A chemical attack on an opposition-controlled Damascus suburb Aug. 21, 2013, killed more than 1,400. Russian and U.S. negotiators reached an agreement with Syria requiring the Assad government to relinquish chemical weapons. The last known covered chemical weapons were believed to have been removed June 23, 2014. A UN report, Aug. 24, 2016, confirmed allegations that Assad's forces were using chlorine gas (not covered by the 2013 agreement). Syrian aircraft dropped chemical weapons prohibited by the 2013 agreement on a rebel-held town, Apr. 4, 2017; the U.S., Apr. 6, launched a cruise missile attack on the air base used by the planes. Israeli war-planes reportedly attacked, Sept. 7, 2017, Syrian military sites producing chemical weapons and missiles. An apparent chemical attack, Apr. 7, 2018, that killed dozens in a then-rebel-held area east of Damascus prompted U.S., UK, and French retaliatory airstrikes, Apr. 13. The U.S. announced, Sept. 26, 2019, that Assad's forces had used chlorine gas in a May 2019 attack on rebels.

By summer 2014, the Sunni extremist group ISIS (Islamic State in Iraq and Syria) controlled large areas in eastern and northern Syria. The night of Sept. 22-23, 2014, the U.S. began a campaign of airstrikes against ISIS and other Islamist extremist groups in Syria, supported by several Middle East countries and European and other allies. Russia, which backed Assad, sent warplanes and troops to Syria in Sept. 2015 and began its own air campaign, Sept. 30, against anti-government forces. Heavy Russian airstrikes helped the Assad regime regain control of large areas, 2016-18, often with high civilian casualties. Syrian Kurdish and other rebel groups making up the Syrian Democratic Forces (SDF), with support from U.S. airstrikes and special operations troops, retook territory in northern and eastern Syria from ISIS, 2015-17, including Raqqa (ISIS's self-proclaimed capital), Oct. 2017. The SDF said it captured the last ISIS-controlled area in Mar. 2019, although ISIS members remained active. ISIS leader Abu Bakr al-Baghdadi died (an apparent suicide) in a U.S. raid on his N Syria compound, Oct. 26, 2019.

The U.S., in early 2019, announced plans to reduce its ground troops in Syria.

In 2016-19, Turkish troops and groups aligned with them attacked Syrian Kurdish forces and tried to limit Kurdish-controlled areas in northern Syria. When the U.S., Oct. 2019, pulled back troops in northern Syria, Turkish and allied forces launched a new attack on the SDF, displacing tens of thousands of people and shrinking Kurdish-controlled territory.

By 2019, non-Kurdish rebels had largely retreated to Idlib Province in NW Syria; a Syrian government offensive, supported by Russian airstrikes, began Apr. 2019 and continued in 2020; Turkish troops supported some Idlib rebel groups. A Mar. 2020 cease-fire reduced violence.

Estimates of the total death toll in Syria's civil war since Mar. 2011 varied widely; the Syrian Observatory for Human Rights released an estimate of almost 585,000 in early 2020. The UNHCR reported the number of Syrian refugees in Turkey, the Middle East, and North Africa at more than 5.5 mil as of mid-Sept. 2020. About 1 mil Syrians had applied for asylum in Europe. About 6.1 mil people were displaced within Syria as of mid-2020. The impact of the 2020 COVID-19 pandemic on war-torn Syria was difficult to assess; the WHO reported 4,148 cases and 197 deaths as of Sept. 30.

Taiwan

People: Population: 23,603,049 (56). **Age distrib.:** <15: 12.4%; 65+: 15.7%. **Growth:** 0.1%. **Pop. density:** 1,895.0 per sq mi, 731.7 per sq km. **Urban:** 78.9%. **Ethnic groups:** Han Chinese 95%+ (incl. Hoklo [approx. 70% of pop.], Hakka, other groups originating in mainland China), Indigenous Malayo-Polynesian peoples 2.3%. **Languages:** Mandarin Chinese (official), Taiwanese (Min Nan), Hakka dialects. **Religions:** Chinese folk-religionist 42.3%, Buddhist 26.7%, Daoist 12.8%, new religionist 6.8%, Christian 6.2%, agnostic 4.3%.

Geography: Total area: 13,892 sq mi, 35,980 sq km (135); **Land area:** 12,456 sq mi, 32,260 sq km. **Location:** Off SE coast of China, between E and S China Seas. **Topography:** A mountain range forms backbone of island. The eastern half is very steep and craggy; western slope is flat, fertile, and well cultivated. **Arable land:** 16.6%. **Capital:** Taipei, 2,721,485. **Cities:** Xinbei, 4,398,383; Taoyuan, 2,245,162.

Government: Type: Semi-presidential republic. **Head of state:** Pres. Tsai Ing-wen; b. 1956; in office: May 20, 2016. **Head of govt.:** Prem. Su Tseng-chang; b. 1947; in office: Jan. 11, 2019. **Local divisions:** 13 counties, 3 cities, 6 special municipalities. **Defense budget:** $10.9 bil. **Active troops:** 163,000.

Economy: Industries: electronics, communications and information tech. prods., petroleum refining, chemicals, textiles, iron and steel, machinery, cement, food proc. **Chief agric.:** rice, vegetables, fruit, tea, flowers; pigs, poultry; fish. **Natural resources:** coal, nat. gas, limestone, marble, asbestos. **Water:** NA. **Crude oil reserves:** 2.4 mil bbls. **Electricity prod.:** 249.5 bil kWh. **Labor force:** agric. 4.9%, industry 36.7%, services 58.5%. **Unemployment:** 3.8%.

Finance: Monetary unit: New Dollar (TWD) (29.34 = $1 U.S.). **GDP:** NA; **per capita GDP:** NA; **GDP growth:** NA. **Imports:** $259 bil; China 19.3%, Japan 16.2%, ASEAN 12%, U.S. 11.7%, EU 10%, South Korea 6.5%. **Exports:** $349.8 bil; (2018): China 28.8%, Hong Kong 12.4%, U.S. 11.8%, Japan 6.9%, Singapore 5.7%. **Tourism:** $14.4 bil. **Budget:** $92.0 bil. **Inflation** (2016-17): 1.1%.

Transport: Railways: 1,002 mi. **Motor vehicles:** 338.5 per 1,000 pop. **Airports:** 35.

Communications: Telephone: 55.5 per 100 pop. **Mobile:** 123.7 per 100 pop. **Broadband:** NA. **Internet:** 92.8%.

Health: Expend.: NA. **Life expect.:** 77.5 male; 83.9 female. **Births:** 8 per 1,000 pop. **Deaths:** 7.9 per 1,000 pop. **Infant mortality:** 4.2 per 1,000 live births. **Undernourished:** 3.5%. **HIV:** NA.

Education: Compulsory: ages 6-15. **Literacy:** 98.5%.

Taipei Economic and Cultural Representative Office: 4201 Wisconsin Ave. NW 20016; 895-1800.

Website: www.taiwan.gov.tw

Large-scale immigration from China began in the 17th cent. The island came under mainland control after an interval of Dutch rule, 1620-62. Japan ruled Taiwan (also called Formosa), 1895-1945. The Kuomintang (Chinese Nationalist Party) government fled to Taiwan in 1949 and established the Republic of China under Chiang Kaishek, who ruled until his death in 1975. The U.S. provided military aid to deter a Communist invasion.

In 1971, the UN expelled Taiwan and recognized the mainland government. The U.S. acknowledged the People's Republic of China, Dec. 15, 1978, and severed diplomatic relations with Taiwan. The U.S. and Taiwan have maintained strong economic, defense, and unofficial ties. After opportunities for Chinese aid and investment led a number of countries to break relations in the 2010s, Taiwan maintained diplomatic ties with 15 countries as of Sept. 30, 2020.

Land reform, government planning, U.S. aid and investment, and free universal education brought advances in industry, agriculture, and living standards. In 1987 martial law was lifted after 38 years, and in 1991 more than four decades of emergency rule ended. Taiwan held its first direct presidential election Mar. 23, 1996.

Five decades of Kuomintang rule ended when Chen Shui-bian, leader of the pro-independence Democratic Progressive Party (DPP), won the Mar. 2000 presidential election. Chen was wounded in an apparent assassination attempt Mar. 19, 2004, one day before he won a second term as president. Promising increased cooperation with China, Kuomintang candidate Ma Ying-jeou won the 2008 and 2012 presidential elections.

The People's Republic considers Taiwan a rebel province of the mainland; in 1991, the Kuomintang dropped its claim to be the sole government of both. The first formal talks between Taiwan and China were held Feb. 11, 2014. Concern over recent Kuomintang pro-China policies helped the DPP win Jan. 16, 2016, presidential and legislative elections. The DPP's Tsai Ingwen became Taiwan's first female president. She was reelected and the DPP won legislative elections, Jan. 11, 2020.

In accordance with a Constitutional Court ruling, legislation legalizing same-sex marriage went into effect May 24, 2019.

In early 2020, the government instituted border controls and other measures to combat the COVID-19 pandemic. By Sept. 30, Taiwan had 513 cases and 7 deaths (Johns Hopkins Univ. data).

The **Penghu Isls.** (Pescadores), 49 sq mi, pop. (2011 est.) 96,597, lie between Taiwan and the mainland. Kinmen, fmr. Quemoy, pop. (2011 est.) 99,691, and Matsu, pop. (2011 est.) 10,106, lie just off the mainland.

Tajikistan
Republic of Tajikistan

People: Population: 8,873,669 (96). **Age distrib.:** <15: 31.4%; 65+: 3.6%. **Growth:** 1.5%. **Migrants:** 2.9%. **Pop. density:** 162.4 per sq mi, 62.7 per sq km. **Urban:** 27.5%. **Ethnic groups:** Tajik 84.3% (incl. Pamiri, Yagnobi), Uzbek 13.8%, other 2% (incl. Kyrgyz, Russian, Turkmen, Tatar, Arab). **Languages:** Tajik (official), Uzbek, Russian (used in govt. and business). **Religions:** Muslim 98% (Sunni [official] 88%, Shia 10%).

Geography: Total area: 55,637 sq mi, 144,100 sq km (94). **Land area:** 54,637 sq mi, 141,510 sq km. **Location:** Central Asia. Uzbekistan on N and W, Kyrgyzstan on N, China on E, Afghanistan on S. **Topography:** Mountainous; contains the Pamirs, Trans-Alai mountain system. **Arable land:** 5.2%. **Capital:** Dushanbe, 915,712.

Government: Type: Presidential republic. **Head of state:** Pres. Emomali Rahmon; b. 1952; in office: Nov. 6, 1994. **Head of govt.:** Prime Min. Qohir Rasulzoda; b. 1961; in office: Nov. 23, 2013. **Local divisions:** 2 provinces, 1 autonomous province, 1 capital region, 1 district under republic admin. **Defense budget:** $187 mil. **Active troops:** 8,800.

Economy: Industries: aluminum, cement, coal, gold, silver. **Chief agric.:** cotton, grain, fruits, grapes, vegetables; cattle, sheep, goats. **Natural resources:** hydropower, petroleum, uranium, mercury, brown coal, lead, zinc, antimony, tungsten, silver, gold. **Water:** 2,456 cu m per capita. **Crude oil reserves:** 12 mil bbls. **Electricity prod.:** 17.9 bil kWh. **Labor force:** agric. 44.2%, industry 16.0%, services 39.9%. **Unemployment:** 11.0%.

Finance: Monetary unit: Somoni (TJS) (10.28 = $1 U.S.). **GDP:** $32.8 bil; **per capita GDP:** $3,520; **GDP growth:** 7.0%. **Imports:** $2.4 bil; Russia 38%, Kazakhstan 19%, China 8.7%. **Exports:** $873.1 mil; Turkey 27.5%, China 17.7%, Russia 13.4%, Switzerland 12.5%, Algeria 8.2%, Iran 7.1%. **Tourism:** $14 mil. **Budget:** $2.4 bil. **Inflation** (2015-16): 6.0%.

Transport: Railways: 423 mi. **Airports:** 17.

Communications: Telephone (2017): 5.4 per 100 pop. **Mobile** (2017): 111.5 per 100 pop. **Broadband:** 22.7 per 100 pop. **Internet:** 22%.

Health: Expend.: 7.2%. **Life expect.:** 65.9 male; 72.3 female. **Births:** 21.8 per 1,000 pop. **Deaths:** 5.8 per 1,000 pop. **Infant mortality:** 28.8 per 1,000 live births. **Undernourished:** NA. **HIV:** 0.2%.

Education: Compulsory: ages 7-15. **Literacy:** 99.8%.

Embassy: 1005 New Hampshire Ave. NW 20037; 223-6090.

Website: www.president.tj

Societies were settled in the region from about 3000 BCE. Invaders have included Iranians, Arabs (who converted the population to Islam), Mongols, Uzbeks, Afghans, and Russians. The USSR gained control 1918-25, making the region a part of the Uzbek SSR until the Tajik SSR was proclaimed, 1929.

Tajikistan declared independence Sept. 9, 1991. Factional fighting led to the installation of a pro-Communist regime, Jan. 1993. A new constitution establishing a presidential system was approved by referendum in 1994.

About 55,000 died in clashes between Muslim rebels and loyalist troops (supported by Russia) by mid-1997. Pres. Emomali Rakhmonov, first elected in 1994, won a Nov. 1999 election called a farce by human-rights observers. Leading opposition groups boycotted the Nov. 2006 election, again won by Rakhmonov (who changed his name to Rahmon in 2007). He won the Nov. 2013 election with 84% of the vote. The 2020 election was scheduled for Oct.11.

Poverty and corruption are widespread. Much of the nation's income is supplied by international donors and by remittances from Tajiks working in Russia. After rebels murdered a Tajik general, July 21, 2012, the army killed about 30 militants, July 24. A former warlord surrendered, Aug. 13, in exchange for a troop withdrawal. In the 2010s, an estimated 1,300 Tajiks joined ISIS forces in Syria and Iraq. In an assault claimed by ISIS, four tourists (two U.S., two European) were fatally attacked while cycling in Tajikistan, July 29, 2018. Islamist militant prison riots, Nov. 2018 and May 2019, left at least 55 inmates and guards dead.

The 2020 COVID-19 pandemic caused about 9,700 cases and 75 deaths by Sept. 30.

Tanzania
United Republic of Tanzania

People: Population: 58,552,845 (24). **Age distrib.:** <15: 42.7%; 65+: 3.1%. **Growth:** 2.7%. **Migrants:** 0.9%. **Pop. density:** 171.2 per sq mi, 66.1 per sq km. **Urban:** 35.2%. **Ethnic groups:** African 99% (of which 95% are Bantu consisting of 130+ tribes). **Languages:** Kiswahili or Swahili, English (primary lang. of commerce, admin., higher ed.) (both official); Arabic (widely spoken in Zanzibar). **Religions:** Christian 56.8% (Protestant 28%, Catholic 26.7%), Muslim 31% (Sunni), ethnic religionist 10.5%.

Geography: Total area: 365,755 sq mi, 947,300 sq km (30); **Land area:** 342,009 sq mi, 885,800 sq km. **Location:** Coast of E Africa. Kenya, Uganda on N; Rwanda, Burundi, Dem. Rep. of the Congo on W; Zambia, Malawi, Mozambique on S. **Topography:** Hot, arid central plateau surrounded by lake region in W. Temperate highlands in N and S; coastal plains. Mt. Kilimanjaro (19,341 ft) is highest in Africa. **Arable land:** 15.2%. **Capital:** Dodoma (official; legis.), 261,645; Dar es Salaam (de facto; exec. branch offices), 6,701,650. **Cities:** Mwanza, 1,120,430.

Government: Type: Presidential republic. **Head of state and govt.:** Pres. John Magufuli; b. 1959; in office: Nov. 5, 2015. **Local divisions:** 31 regions. **Defense budget:** $827 mil. **Active troops:** 27,000.

Economy: Industries: agric. proc.; mining; salt, soda ash; cement, oil refining, shoes, apparel, wood prods., fertilizer. **Chief agric.:** coffee, sisal, tea, cotton, pyrethrum (insecticide made from chrysanthemums), cashews, tobacco, cloves, corn, wheat, cassava; cattle, sheep, goats. **Natural resources:** hydropower, tin, phosphates, iron ore, coal, diamonds, gems, gold, nat. gas, nickel. **Water:** 1,680 cu m per capita. **Electricity prod.:** 7.6 bil kWh. **Labor force:** agric. 64.9%, industry 6.8%, services 28.3%. **Unemployment:** 2.0%.

Finance: Monetary unit: Shilling (TZS) (2,319.65 = $1 U.S.). **GDP:** $156.0 bil; **per capita GDP:** $2,771; **GDP growth:** 5.8%. **Imports:** $7.9 bil; India 16.5%, China 15.8%, UAE 9.2%, Saudi Arabia 7.9%, South Africa 5.1%. **Exports:** $5 bil; India 21.8%, South Africa 17.9%, Kenya 8.8%, Switzerland 6.7%, Belgium 5.9%, Dem. Rep. of the Congo 5.8%. **Tourism:** $2.6 bil. **Budget:** $8.8 bil. **Inflation:** 3.5%.

Transport: Railways: 2,838 mi. **Motor vehicles:** 1.9 per 1,000 pop. **Airports:** 10.

Communications: Telephone: 0.2 per 100 pop. **Mobile:** 77.2 per 100 pop. **Broadband:** 8.7 per 100 pop. **Internet:** 25%.

Health: Expend.: 3.6%. **Life expect.:** 62.3 male; 65.5 female. **Births:** 34.6 per 1,000 pop. **Deaths:** 7.1 per 1,000 pop. **Infant mortality:** 36.4 per 1,000 live births. **Undernourished:** 25.0%. **HIV:** 4.8%.

Education: Compulsory: ages 7-13. **Literacy:** 85.8%.
Embassy: 1232 22nd St. NW 20037; 939-6125.
Website: www.tanzania.go.tz

Arab colonization and slaving in Tanganyika began in the 8th cent.; Portuguese sailors explored the coast around 1500. Other Europeans followed.

In 1885 Germany established German East Africa, of which Tanganyika formed the bulk. Under Britain, it became a League of Nations mandate and after 1946, a UN trust territory. It became independent, Dec. 9, 1961, and a republic within the Commonwealth a year later.

Zanzibar, the Isle of Cloves, has an area of 640 sq mi and lies 23 mi off mainland Tanzania. The island of Pemba, area 380 sq mi, is 25 mi to the NE. Ethnic groups in Zanzibar include Arabs and Africans. Zanzibar and Pemba are major producers of cloves and clove oil.

Zanzibar was for centuries the center for Arab slave traders. Portugal ruled the region for two centuries until ousted by Arabs around 1700. Zanzibar became a British Protectorate in 1890; independence came Dec. 10, 1963. Revolutionary forces overthrew the Sultan, Jan. 12, 1964. The new government ousted Western diplomats and journalists, slaughtered thousands of Arabs, and nationalized farms.

The Republic of Tanganyika and the Republic of Zanzibar joined to form the United Republic of Tanzania, Apr. 26, 1964. Zanzibar retains internal self-government.

Until resigning as president in 1985, Julius K. Nyerere, a former Tanganyikan independence leader, dominated Tanzania's single-party government, which emphasized government planning and economic control. A multiparty system was established in 1992, and the economy was privatized in the 1990s.

A bomb at the U.S. embassy in Dar es Salaam, Aug. 7, 1998, killed 11 and injured at least 70. The U.S. blamed the attack on Islamic terrorists associated with Osama bin Laden.

John Magufuli of the ruling Chama Cha Mapinduzi (CCM) won the Oct. 25, 2015, presidential election. Zanzibar regional elections the same day were annulled because of voting irregularities and rerun Mar. 20, 2016; the CCM incumbent won Zanzibar's presidency in voting boycotted by the opposition. Magufuli suppressed press freedom and political opposition. He denied the 2020 COVID-19 pandemic was a problem in Tanzania (opponents disagreed) and limited cooperation with the WHO.

Large natural gas deposits (57 tril cu ft) have been discovered in recent years.

Thailand
Kingdom of Thailand

People: Population: 68,977,400 (20). **Age distrib.:** <15: 16.4%; 65+: 11.8%. **Growth:** 0.2%. **Migrants:** 5.2%. **Pop. density:** 349.7 per sq mi, 135.0 per sq km. **Urban:** 51.4%. **Ethnic groups:** Thai 97.5%. **Languages:** Thai (official), English (secondary lang. of elite). **Religions:** Buddhist (official) 86.5%, Muslim 6.1% (Sunni).

Geography: Total area: 198,117 sq mi, 513,120 sq km (50); **Land area:** 197,256 sq mi, 510,890 sq km. **Location:** On Indochinese and Malayan peninsulas in SE Asia. Myanmar on W and N, Laos on N, Cambodia on E, Malaysia on S. **Topography:** A plateau dominates NE third of Thailand, dropping to fertile alluvial valley of Chao Phraya R. in center. Forested mountains with narrow fertile valleys are in N. Rain forests cover S peninsula region. **Arable land:** 32.9%. **Capital:** Bangkok (Krung Thep), 10,539,415. **Cities:** Chon Buri, 1,398,645.

Government: Type: Constitutional monarchy. **Head of state:** King Vajiralongkorn; b. 1952; in office: Dec. 1, 2016. **Head of govt.:** Prime Min. Prayuth Chan-ocha; b. 1954; in office: Aug. 25, 2014. **Local divisions:** 76 provinces, 1 municipality. **Defense budget:** $7.1 bil. **Active troops:** 360,850.

Economy: Industries: tourism, textiles and garments, agric. proc., beverages, tobacco, cement, light mfg. (jewelry, elec. appliances, computers and parts, integrated circuits, furniture). **Chief agric.:** rice, cassava, rubber, corn, sugarcane, coconuts, palm oil, pineapples, livestock, fish prods. **Natural resources:** tin, rubber, nat. gas, tungsten, tantalum, timber, lead, fish, gypsum, lignite, fluorite. **Water:** 6,353 cu m per capita. **Crude oil reserves:** 292.6 mil bbls. **Electricity prod.:** 171.8 bil kWh. **Labor force:** agric. 31.2%, industry 22.5%, services 46.3%. **Unemployment:** 0.8%.

Finance: Monetary unit: Baht (THB) (31.37 = $1 U.S.). **GDP:** $1.3 tril; **per capita GDP:** $19,228; **GDP growth:** 2.4%. **Imports:** $203.2 bil; China 20%, Japan 14.5%, U.S. 6.8%, Malaysia 5.4%. **Exports:** $235.1 bil; China 12.4%, U.S. 11.2%, Japan 9.5%, Hong Kong 5.2%. **Tourism:** $60.5 bil. **Budget:** $85.1 bil. **Inflation:** 0.7%.

Transport: Railways: 2,564 mi. **Motor vehicles:** 259.2 per 1,000 pop. **Airports:** 63.

Communications: Telephone: 4.2 per 100 pop. **Mobile:** 180.2 per 100 pop. **Broadband:** 99 per 100 pop. **Internet** (2018): 56.8%.

Health: Expend.: 3.7%. **Life expect.:** 72.4 male; 78.9 female. **Births:** 10.7 per 1,000 pop. **Deaths:** 8.3 per 1,000 pop. **Infant mortality:** 8.6 per 1,000 live births. **Undernourished:** 9.3%. **HIV:** 1.0%.

Education: Compulsory: ages 6-14. **Literacy:** 98.1%.
Embassy: 1024 Wisconsin Ave. NW 20007; 944-3600.
Website: www.thaigov.go.th

Thais began migrating from southern China during the 11th cent. and established a unified Thai kingdom, 1350. Known as Siam until 1939, Thailand is the only country in SE Asia never colonized by Europeans. King Mongkut and his son King Chulalongkorn, ruling successively from 1851 to 1910, modernized the country and signed trade treaties with Britain and France. A bloodless revolution in 1932 limited the monarchy. Thailand was an ally of Japan during WWII and of the U.S. during the postwar period. For decades, the military had a dominant role in governing the country.

By the end of the 1990s, according to UN estimates, more than 750,000 people in Thailand had HIV/AIDS, with 143,000 new infections in 1991 alone. A nationwide prevention campaign reduced the number of new HIV infections.

Beginning in 2004, security forces tried to suppress a Muslim insurgency in southern Thailand. By 2020, about 7,000 people, mostly civilians, had been killed in insurgent attacks and bombings and in actions by security forces.

Following elections in Jan. 2001, Thaksin Shinawatra became prime min. A military junta took power in a bloodless coup Sept. 19, 2006. Thaksin supporters won Dec. 2007 elections, and Samak Sundaravej became prime min. after civilian rule was restored Jan. 22, 2008. Thailand's Constitutional Court ousted Samak in Sept., and Thaksin's brother-in-law Somchai Wongsawat became prime min. Sept. 18. But a Constitutional Court ruling, Dec. 2, barred him from politics.

On Feb. 26, 2010, Thailand's Supreme Court ordered the seizure of about $1.4 bil of Thaksin's family assets. After Thaksin supporters, known as Red Shirts, staged mass rallies and began to build a fortified compound in Bangkok, a crackdown by Thai security forces May 14-19, 2010, left more than 90 people dead. Thaksin's sister, Yingluck Shinawatra, became Thailand's first female prime min. after parliamentary elections July 3, 2011. On May 7, 2014, she was removed from office by the Constitutional Court, and the military seized power in a May 22 coup. An interim legislature, with a majority of military members, was appointed July 31; it named coup leader Gen. Prayuth Chan-ocha as prime min. Aug. 21, 2014. Tried for criminal negligence, Yingluck fled the country before a guilty verdict was announced Sept. 27, 2017.

A 2015 investigation resulted in charges against more than 100, including government and military officials, for involvement in human trafficking of migrants from Myanmar and Bangladesh. More than 60 traffickers were convicted, July 19, 2017. A bombing at the Erawan shrine in Bangkok, Aug. 17, 2015, killed 20. Thai police arrested two suspects, Aug. 29 and Sept. 1, said to be Uighur militants; in July, Thailand had deported more than 100 Uighur migrants to China. In an Aug. 7, 2016, referendum (opposition campaigning had been barred), voters approved a military-drafted new constitution and a companion measure giving the military a strong role in selecting prime ministers after a return to civilian rule.

King Bhumibol, monarch since June 1946, died Oct. 13, 2016; crown prince Maha Vajiralongkorn succeeded him Dec. 1.

Following disputed Mar. 24, 2019, legislative elections, the National Assembly, June 5, elected Prayuth to remain prime min. A Feb. 2020 court ruling barred a popular opposition party. Months of large student-led protests, beginning in July 2020, demanded political reforms.

The 2020 COVID-19 pandemic caused more than 3,500 cases and 59 deaths in Thailand by Sept. 30. The economically important tourism industry was severely hurt.

Timor-Leste
Democratic Republic of Timor-Leste

People: Population: 1,383,723 (151). **Age distrib.:** <15: 40.0%; 65+: 4.1%. **Growth:** 2.3%. **Migrants:** 0.7%. **Pop. density:** 240.9 per sq mi, 93.0 per sq km. **Urban:** 31.3%. **Ethnic groups:** Austronesian (Malayo-Polynesian), Melanesian-Papuan, small Chinese minority. **Languages:** Tetun Prasa, Portuguese (both official); Indonesian, English (working langs.); about 32 Indigenous langs. **Religions:** Christian 88.7% (Catholic 84.3%), ethnic religionist 6.3%, Muslim 3.9% (Sunni).

Geography: Total area: 5,743 sq mi, 14,874 sq km (155); **Land area:** 5,743 sq mi, 14,874 sq km. **Location:** E half of Timor Isl. in SW Pacific O. Indonesia on W half of island. **Topography:** Rugged terrain, rising to 9,721 ft at Mt. Ramelau. **Arable land:** 10.4%. **Capital:** Dili, 281,135.

Government: Type: Semi-presidential republic. **Head of state:** Pres. Francisco Guterres; b. 1954; in office: May 20, 2017. **Head of govt.:** Prime Min. Taur Matan Ruak; b. 1956; in office: June 22, 2018. **Local divisions:** 12 municipalities, 1 special admin. region. **Defense budget:** $31 mil. **Active troops:** 2,280.

Economy: Industries: printing, soap mfg., handicrafts, woven cloth. **Chief agric.:** coffee, rice, corn, cassava, sweet potatoes, soybeans, cabbages, mangoes, bananas, vanilla. **Natural resources:** gold, petroleum, nat. gas, manganese, marble. **Water:** 6,339 cu m per capita. **Labor force:** agric. 43.7%, industry 9.8%, services 46.4%. **Unemployment:** 4.6%.

Finance: Monetary unit: U.S. Dollar (USD) (1.00 = $1 U.S.). **GDP:** $4.2 bil; **per capita GDP:** $3,253; **GDP growth:** 3.4%. **Imports:** $681.2 mil. **Exports:** $16.7 mil. **Tourism:** $70 mil. **Budget:** $2.4 bil. **Inflation** (2017-18): 2.6%.

Transport: Airports: 2.

Communications: Telephone: 0.2 per 100 pop. **Mobile:** 103.2 per 100 pop. **Broadband:** 33.6 per 100 pop. **Internet:** 27.5%.

Health: Expend.: 3.9%. **Life expect.:** 67.6 male; 71.1 female. **Births:** 32 per 1,000 pop. **Deaths:** 5.7 per 1,000 pop. **Infant mortality:** 31.7 per 1,000 live births. **Undernourished:** 30.9%. **HIV:** 0.2%.

Education: Compulsory: ages 6-14. **Literacy:** 83.5%.

Embassy: 4201 Connecticut Ave. NW, Ste. 504, 20008; 966-3202.

Website: timor-leste.gov.tl

The collapse of Portuguese rule in East Timor led to factional fighting, Aug. 1975, and an invasion by Indonesia in Dec. Indonesia annexed East Timor in 1976. In over two decades, some 200,000 Timorese died due to civil war, famine, and persecution by Indonesian authorities. In a referendum held Aug. 1999 under UN auspices,

Timorese voted overwhelmingly for independence but were then terrorized by pro-Indonesian militias. An international peacekeeping force entered in Sept.; a UN interim administration formally took command Oct. 26, 1999. Pro-independence forces won elections for a constituent assembly Aug. 2001. Xanana Gusmão, a former guerrilla leader, won the presidential election Apr. 2002. As Timor-Leste, the territory became independent May 20.

José Ramos-Horta, a Nobel Peace Prize laureate, won a presidential runoff vote May 2007. After inconclusive parliamentary elections June 30, Ramos-Horta chose Gusmão as prime min. Gusmão-supported independent Taur Matan Ruak became president in a May 2012 runoff election. Gusmão's CNRT party won July parliamentary elections. The UN peacekeeping mission ended Dec. 31, 2012. Beginning in 2005, much of East Timor's budget consisted of revenue from offshore oil and natural gas deposits. Lower oil prices beginning in 2014, as well as depletion of oil fields and costly infrastructure projects, hurt the economy. Gusmão resigned Feb. 6, 2015, and was replaced as prime min. by Rui Maria de Araújo of the FRETILIN party. FRETILIN's Francisco Guterres won the Mar. 20, 2017, presidential election. After inconclusive July 22 parliamentary elections, FRETILIN's Mari Alkatiri became prime min. A coalition including the CNRT won new elections, May 12, 2018; Taur Matan Ruak became prime min. Ending a long dispute, Timor-Leste and Australia signed a treaty, Mar. 6, 2018, establishing the boundary between in an oil- and gas-rich area of the Timor Sea.

Togo
Togolese Republic

People: Population: 8,608,444 (99). **Age distrib.:** <15: 39.7%; 65+: 3.6%. **Growth:** 2.6%. **Migrants:** 3.5%. **Pop. density:** 410.0 per sq mi, 158.3 per sq km. **Urban:** 42.8%. **Ethnic groups:** Adja-Ewe/Mina 42.4%, Kabye/Tem 25.9%, Para-Gourma/Akan 17.1%, Akposso/Akebu 4.1%, Ana-Ife 3.2%. **Languages:** French (official, lang. of commerce), Ewe and Mina (in S), Kabye and Dagomba (in N). **Religions:** Christian 48.1% (Catholic 30.2%, Protestant 14.5%), ethnic religionist 32.6%, Muslim 18.5% (Sunni).

Geography: Total area: 21,925 sq mi, 56,785 sq km (123); **Land area:** 20,998 sq mi, 54,385 sq km. **Location:** S coast of W Africa. Ghana on W, Burkina Faso on N, Benin on E. **Topography:** Hills running SW-NE split Togo into two savanna plains regions. **Arable land:** 48.7%. **Capital:** Lomé 1,827,878.

Government: Type: Presidential republic. **Head of state:** Pres. Faure Gnassingbé; b. 1966; in office: May 4, 2005. **Head of govt.:** Prime Min. Komi Klassou; b. 1960; in office: June 5, 2015. **Local divisions:** 5 regions. **Defense budget:** $107 mil. **Active troops:** 8,550.

Economy: Industries: phosphate mining, agric. proc., cement, handicrafts, textiles, beverages. **Chief agric.:** coffee, cocoa, cotton, yams, cassava, corn, beans, rice, millet, sorghum; livestock; fish. **Natural resources:** phosphates, limestone, marble. **Water:** 1,885 cu m per capita. **Electricity prod.:** 233 mil kWh. **Labor force:** agric. 37.2%, industry 12.9%, services 49.9%. **Unemployment:** 2.0%.

Finance: Monetary unit: CFA Franc (XOF) (553.52 = $1 U.S.). **GDP:** $13.4 bil; **per capita GDP:** $1,662; **GDP growth:** 5.3%. **Imports:** $2 bil; China 27.5%, France 9.1%. **Exports:** $1 bil; Benin 16.7%, Burkina Faso 15.2%, Niger 8.9%, India 7.3%, Mali 6.7%, Ghana 5.5%, Côte d'Ivoire 5.4%. **Tourism:** $153 mil. **Budget:** $1.2 bil. **Inflation:** 0.7%.

Transport: Railways: 353 mi. **Motor vehicles:** 27 per 1,000 pop. **Airports:** 2.

Communications: Telephone: 0.5 per 100 pop. **Mobile:** 77.9 per 100 pop. **Broadband:** 20.7 per 100 pop. **Internet:** 12.4%.

Health: Expend.: 6.2%. **Life expect.:** 63.9 male; 69.3 female. **Births:** 32 per 1,000 pop. **Deaths:** 6.5 per 1,000 pop. **Infant mortality:** 38.5 per 1,000 live births. **Undernourished:** 20.7%. **HIV:** 2.2%.

Education: Compulsory: ages 6-15. **Literacy:** 84.3%.

Embassy: 2208 Massachusetts Ave. NW 20008; 234-4212.

Website: www.primature.gouv.tg or www.state.gov/p/af/ci/to/

Togoland was administered by Germany and then by France and Britain. The French sector became the republic of Togo Apr. 27, 1960. In office since 1967, Pres. Gnassingbé Eyadéma was Africa's longest-serving head of state until his death Feb. 5, 2005. His son, Faure Gnassingbé, was installed as president and won an Apr. 24 election. Opposition parties disputed the result, and protests led to violent clashes in Lomé.

After a shootout at his home Apr. 12, 2009, former Defense Min. Kpatcha Gnassingbé, the president's brother, was arrested and accused of plotting a coup. Pres. Gnassingbé won reelection Mar. 4, 2010, to a second 5-year term. Weeks of anti-government protests led Prime Min. Gilbert Fossoun Houngbo to resign, July 13, 2012. Pres. Gnassingbé won a third term in Apr. 25, 2015, elections; the opposition disputed the result. More than a dozen people died and dozens were injured in large-scale anti-government protests, beginning Aug. 2017. Gnassingbé's party won Dec. 20, 2018, legislative elections, and Gnassingbé won a new term as president, Feb. 22, 2020.

The 2020 COVID-19 pandemic caused more than 1,700 cases and 48 deaths by Sept. 30.

Tonga
Kingdom of Tonga

People: Population: 106,095 (181). **Age distrib.:** <15: 32.0%; 65+: 6.8%. **Growth:** –0.2%. **Migrants:** 3.6%. **Pop. density:** 383.2 per sq mi, 148.0 per sq km. **Urban:** 23.1%. **Ethnic groups:** Tongan 97%. **Languages:** Tongan, English (both official). **Religions:** Christian 95.7% (independent 55.6%, Protestant 30.4%, Catholic 9.6%), Baha'i 3.6%.

Geography: Total area: 288 sq mi, 747 sq km (176); **Land area:** 277 sq mi, 717 sq km. **Location:** Western S Pacific O. Nearest neighbors are Fiji to NW, Samoa to NE. **Topography:** Comprises 170 volcanic and coral islands, 36 inhabited. **Arable land:** 25.0%.

Capital: Nuku'alofa, 22,904.

Government: Type: Constitutional monarchy. **Head of state:** King Tupou VI; b. 1959; in office: Mar. 18, 2012. **Head of govt.:** Prime Min. Pohiva Tu'i'onetoa; b. 1961; in office: Sept. 27, 2019. **Local divisions:** 5 island divisions. **Defense budget/active troops:** NA.

Economy: Industries: tourism, constr., fishing. **Chief agric.:** squash, coconuts, copra, bananas, vanilla beans, cocoa, coffee, sweet potatoes, cassava, taro, kava. **Natural resources:** fish. **Water:** NA. **Electricity prod.:** 52 mil kWh. **Labor force:** agric. 23.7%, industry 29.2%, services 47.1%. **Unemployment:** 1.2%.

Finance: Monetary unit: Pa'anga (TOP) (2.26 = $1 U.S.). **GDP** (2018): $662.0 mil; **per capita GDP** (2018): $6,415; **GDP growth** (2018): 0.3%. **Imports:** $250.2 mil; New Zealand 33.3%, Fiji 11.7%, U.S. 9.8%, Singapore 9%, Australia 8.9%, China 7.9%, Japan 5.9%. **Exports:** $18.4 mil; Hong Kong 25.1%, New Zealand 22.6%, U.S. 14.3%, Japan 12.8%, Australia 10.5%. **Tourism:** $57 mil. **Budget:** $181.2 mil. **Inflation** (2016-17): 7.4%.

Transport: Airports: 1.

Communications: Telephone (2017): 14.4 per 100 pop. **Mobile** (2017): 105.8 per 100 pop. **Broadband:** 59.2 per 100 pop. **Internet:** 41.2%.

Health: Expend.: 5.3%. **Life expect.:** 75.4 male; 78.8 female. **Births:** 21 per 1,000 pop. **Deaths:** 4.9 per 1,000 pop. **Infant mortality:** 10.3 per 1,000 live births. **Undernourished:** NA. **HIV:** NA.

Education: Compulsory: ages 4-18. **Literacy:** 99.4%.

Permanent UN mission: 250 E. 51st St., New York, NY 10022; (917) 369-1025.

Website: www.gov.to

First inhabited by ancestors of Polynesians c. 2000 BCE, Tonga was visited by the Dutch in the early 17th cent. and by British explorer James Cook in the 1770s. A series of civil wars ended, 1845, with establishment of the Tupou dynasty. In 1900, Tonga became a British protectorate. Tonga gained independence June 1970 and joined the Commonwealth. It joined the UN in 1999. George Tupou VI became king Mar. 18, 2012. Elections in Nov. 2010 gave the country its first democratically elected parliament. Prime Min. 'Akilisi Pohiva of the Democratic Party died, Sept. 12, 2019, while receiving medical treatment in New Zealand. Pohiva Tu'i'onetoa of the newly formed People's Party was elected prime minister by parliament, Sept. 27.

Trinidad and Tobago
Republic of Trinidad and Tobago

People: Population: 1,208,789 (155). **Age distrib.:** <15: 19.0%; 65+: 12.1%. **Growth:** –0.3%. **Migrants:** 4.2%. **Pop. density:** 610.5 per sq mi, 235.7 per sq km. **Urban:** 53.2%. **Ethnic groups:** East Indian 35.4%, African 34.2%, mixed-other 15.3%, mixed African/East Indian 7.7%. **Languages:** English (official), Trinidadian Creole English, Tobagonian Creole English, Caribbean Hindustani, Trinidadian Creole French, Spanish, Chinese. **Religions:** Christian 63.8% (Catholic 26.8%, Protestant 25%, independent 11.2%), Hindu 23.9%, Muslim 6.5% (Sunni 6%).

Geography: Total area: 1,980 sq mi, 5,128 sq km (166); **Land area:** 1,980 sq mi, 5,128 sq km. **Location:** In Caribbean, off E coast of Venezuela. **Topography:** Three low mountain ranges cross Trinidad E-W, with a well-watered plain between N and central ranges. Parts of E and W coasts are swamps. Tobago, 116 sq mi, lies 20 mi NE. **Arable land:** 4.9%. **Capital:** Port of Spain, 544,207.

Government: Type: Parliamentary republic. **Head of state:** Pres. Paula-Mae Weekes; b. 1958; in office: Mar. 19, 2018. **Head of govt.:** Prime Min. Keith Rowley; b. 1949; in office: Sept. 9, 2015. **Local divisions:** 9 regions, 3 boroughs, 2 cities, 1 ward. **Defense budget:** $904 mil. **Active troops:** 4,050.

Economy: Industries: petroleum and petroleum prods., liquefied nat. gas, methanol, ammonia, urea, steel prods., beverages. **Chief agric.:** cocoa, dasheen, pumpkin, cassava, tomatoes, cucumbers, eggplant, hot pepper, pommecythere, coconut water, poultry. **Natural resources:** petroleum, nat. gas, asphalt. **Water:** 2,805 cu m per capita. **Crude oil reserves:** 243 mil bbls. **Electricity prod.:** 10.4 bil kWh. **Labor force:** agric. 2.9%, industry 26.6%, services 70.5%. **Unemployment:** 2.8%.

Finance: Monetary unit: Dollar (TTD) (6.77 = $1 U.S.). **GDP:** $38.0 bil; **per capita GDP:** $27,261; **GDP growth:** 0.0%. **Imports:** $6.1 bil; U.S. 23.8%, Russia 15.3%, Colombia 11.1%, Gabon 10.5%, China 7.3%. **Exports:** $9.9 bil; U.S. 34.8%, Argentina 9%. **Tourism:** $439 mil. **Budget:** $7.4 bil. **Inflation** (2017-18): 1.0%.

Transport: Motor vehicles: 345.5 per 1,000 pop. **Airports:** 2.

Communications: Telephone: 23.1 per 100 pop. **Mobile:** 140.1 per 100 pop. **Broadband:** 46.1 per 100 pop. **Internet:** 77.3%.

Health: Expend.: 7.0%. **Life expect.:** 70.9 male; 76.9 female. **Births:** 11.4 per 1,000 pop. **Deaths:** 9.1 per 1,000 pop. **Infant mortality:** 20.1 per 1,000 live births. **Undernourished:** 5.5%. **HIV:** 0.7%.

Education: Compulsory: ages 6-11. **Literacy:** 99%.

Embassy: 1708 Massachusetts Ave. NW 20036; 467-6490.

Website: www.ttconnect.gov.tt

Christopher Columbus sighted Trinidad in 1498. It became a British possession in 1802; in the 1800s tens of thousands of indentured servants and their families were brought from India to work in agriculture. Trinidad and Tobago won independence Aug. 31, 1962. It became a republic in 1976. The nation, among the most prosperous in the Caribbean, produces oil and natural gas.

In July 1990, Muslim extremists captured the Parliament building and TV station and held about 50 hostages, including Prime Min. Arthur N. R. Robinson, for 6 days.

Basdeo Panday was the nation's first prime min. of Indian ancestry (1995-2001). The country's first female prime min., Kamla Persad-Bissessar, took office May 26, 2010. After Sept. 7, 2015, elections, Keith Rowley became prime min. On Mar. 19, 2018, Paula-Mae Weekes became Trinidad's first female president. The PNM narrowly won Aug. 10, 2020, elections.

The 2020 COVID-19 pandemic caused more than 4,400 cases and 74 deaths by Sept. 30.

Tunisia
Republic of Tunisia

People: Population: 11,721,177 (79). **Age distrib.:** <15: 25.3%; 65+: 8.9%. **Growth:** 0.8%. **Migrants:** 0.5%. **Pop. density:** 195.4 per sq mi, 75.4 per sq km. **Urban:** 69.6%. **Ethnic groups:** Arab 98%. **Languages:** Arabic (official), French (used in commerce); Berber (Tamazight). **Religions:** Muslim (official) 99.5% (Sunni 98%, Islamic schismatic 2%).

Geography: Total area: 63,170 sq mi, 163,610 sq km (91); **Land area:** 59,985 sq mi, 155,360 sq km. **Location:** N coast of Africa. Algeria on W, Libya on E. **Topography:** The N is wooded and fertile. Grazing lands and orchards are in central coastal plains. The S is arid, approaching Sahara Desert. **Arable land:** 18.6%. **Capital:** Tunis, 2,365,201.

Government: Type: Parliamentary republic. **Head of state:** Pres. Kais Saied; b. 1958; in office: Oct. 23, 2019. **Head of govt.:** Prime Min. Hichem Mechichi; b. 1974; in office: Sept. 2, 2020. **Local divisions:** 24 governorates. **Defense budget:** $993 mil. **Active troops:** 35,800.

Economy: Industries: petroleum, mining, tourism, textiles, footwear, agribusiness, beverages. **Chief agric.:** olives, olive oil, grain, tomatoes, citrus fruit, sugar beets, dates, almonds; beef, dairy prods. **Natural resources:** petroleum, phosphates, iron ore, lead, zinc, salt. **Water:** 400 cu m per capita. **Crude oil reserves:** 425 mil bbls. **Electricity prod.:** 19.2 bil kWh. **Labor force:** agric. 12.7%, industry 32.5%, services 54.8%. **Unemployment:** 16.2%.

Finance: Monetary unit: Dinar (TND) (2.72 = $1 U.S.). **GDP:** $131.0 bil; **per capita GDP:** $11,201; **GDP growth:** 1.0%. **Imports:** $19.1 bil; Italy 15.8%, France 15.1%, China 9.2%, Germany 8.1%. **Exports:** $13.8 bil; France 32.1%, Italy 17.3%, Germany 12.4%. **Tourism:** $1.7 bil. **Budget:** $12.2 bil. **Inflation:** 6.7%.

Transport: Railways: 1,350 mi (only partly operational). **Motor vehicles:** 150 per 1,000 pop. **Airports:** 15.

Communications: Telephone: 11.3 per 100 pop. **Mobile:** 127.7 per 100 pop. **Broadband:** 65 per 100 pop. **Internet** (2018): 64.2%.

Health: Expend.: 7.2%. **Life expect.:** 74.6 male; 78.1 female. **Births:** 15.9 per 1,000 pop. **Deaths:** 6.4 per 1,000 pop. **Infant mortality:** 11.0 per 1,000 live births. **Undernourished:** <2.5%. **HIV:** <0.1%.

Education: Compulsory: ages 6-14. **Literacy:** 81.8%.

Embassy: 1515 Massachusetts Ave. NW 20005; 862-1850.

Website: www.tunisie.gov.tn or www.pm.gov.tn

Site of ancient Carthage and a former Barbary state under the suzerainty of Turkey, Tunisia became a protectorate of France, May 12, 1881. The nation became independent Mar. 20, 1956, and ended the monarchy the following year. Habib Bourguiba, an independence leader, served as president until 1987, when he was deposed by his prime min., Zine al-Abidine Ben Ali, who then won five presidential elections, 1989-2009, all tightly controlled.

Arab Spring protests, which began Dec. 2010, ousted Ben Ali, Jan. 14, 2011. Prime Min. Hamadi Jebali of the moderate Islamist Ennahda party, took office after his party won Oct. 2011 elections. Jebali resigned Feb. 19, 2013, after failing to institute promised reforms. After a new constitution was approved, Jan. 26, 2014, the secular Nida Tunis party won Oct. 26 legislative elections; Nida Tunis leader Beji Caid Essebsi was elected pres., Dec. 21, 2014.

Three Islamist extremist gunmen attacked a museum in Tunis, Mar. 18, 2015, killing 22. A gunman killed 38 foreign tourists at a resort hotel in Sousse, June 26; ISIS claimed responsibility. An ISIS suicide bombing in Tunis, Nov. 24, left 12 victims dead.

July 2017 legislation gave women greater protection from abuse and sexual harassment. In Sept. 2017, the government lifted a ban on women marrying non-Muslims.

Pres. Essebsi died, July 25, 2019. In an Oct. 13 presidential run-off, law professor Kais Saied, an independent, won election. After inconclusive Oct. 6 legislative elections, Elyes Fakhfakh became prime minister, Feb. 27, 2020—but resigned July 15 amid conflict of interest allegations. Pres. Saied, July 25, named Interior Min. Hichem Mechichi to succeed Fakhfakh.

The 2020 COVID-19 pandemic further hurt an already weak economy. By Sept. 30, Tunisia had about 17,400 cases and 246 deaths.

Turkey
Republic of Turkey

People: Population: 82,017,514 (18). **Age distrib.:** <15: 23.4%; 65+: 8.4%. **Growth:** 0.4%. **Migrants:** 7.0%. **Pop. density:** 276.0 per sq mi, 106.6 per sq km. **Urban:** 76.1%. **Ethnic groups:** Turkish 70%-75%, Kurdish 19%. **Languages:** Turkish (official), Kurdish. **Religions:** Muslim 98.3% (Sunni 83%, Shia 15%).

Geography: Total area: 302,535 sq mi, 783,562 sq km (36). **Land area:** 297,157 sq mi, 769,632 sq km. **Location:** Asia Minor, stretching into continental Europe; borders on Medit. and Black Seas. Bulgaria, Greece on W; Georgia, Armenia on N; Iran on E; Iraq, Syria on S. **Topography:** Center has wide plateaus with hot, dry summers and cold winters. High mountains ring the interior on all but W, with more than 20 peaks over 10,000 ft. Rolling plains in W; mild, fertile coastal plains in S and W. **Arable land:** 26.0%. **Capital:** Ankara, 5,117,603. **Cities:** Istanbul, 15,190,336; Izmir, 2,992,953; Bursa, 1,986,268; Adana, 1,770,850; Gaziantep, 1,704,118.

Government: Type: Presidential republic. **Head of state and govt.:** Pres. Recep Tayyip Erdogan; b. 1954; in office: Aug. 28, 2014. (The position of prime minister was eliminated in June 2018.) **Local divisions:** 81 provinces. **Defense budget:** $8.1 bil. **Active troops:** 355,200.

Economy: Industries: textiles, food proc., automobiles, electronics, mining, steel, petroleum, constr., lumber, paper. **Chief agric.:** tobacco, cotton, grain, olives, sugar beets, hazelnuts, pulses, citrus; livestock. **Natural resources:** coal, iron ore, copper, chromium, antimony, mercury, gold, barite, borate, strontium, emery, feldspar, limestone, magnesite, marble, perlite, pumice, pyrites (sulfur), clay, hydropower. **Water:** 2,621 cu m per capita. **Crude oil reserves:** 366 mil bbls. **Electricity prod.** (2018): 289.2 bil kwH. **Labor force:** agric. 18.0%, industry 26.1%, services 55.9%. **Unemployment:** 12.9%.

Finance: Monetary unit: Lira (TRY) (7.44 = $1 U.S.). **GDP:** $2.3 tril; **per capita GDP:** $27,875; **GDP growth:** 0.9%. **Imports:** $225.1 bil; China 10%, Germany 9.1%, Russia 8.4%, U.S. 5.1%. **Exports:** $166.2 bil; Germany 9.6%, UK 6.1%, UAE 5.9%, Iraq 5.8%, U.S. 5.5%, Italy 5.4%. **Tourism:** $29.8 bil. **Budget:** $185.8 bil. **Inflation:** 15.2%.

Transport: Railways: 7,898 mi. **Motor vehicles:** 218.7 per 1,000 pop. **Airports:** 91.

Communications: Telephone: 14.1 per 100 pop. **Mobile:** 97.3 per 100 pop. **Broadband:** 70.5 per 100 pop. **Internet** (2018): 71%.

Health: Expend.: 4.2%. **Life expect.:** 73.3 male; 78.2 female. **Births:** 14.8 per 1,000 pop. **Deaths:** 6.1 per 1,000 pop. **Infant mortality:** 15.8 per 1,000 live births. **Undernourished:** <2.5%. **HIV:** NA.

Education: Compulsory: ages 6-17. **Literacy:** 99.8%.

Embassy: 2525 Massachusetts Ave. NW 20008; 612-6700.

Website: www.tccb.gov.tr

Ancient inhabitants of Turkey were among the world's first agriculturalists. Such civilizations as the Hittite, Phrygian, and Lydian flourished in Asiatic Turkey (Asia Minor), as did much of Greek civilization. After the fall of Rome in the 5th cent., Constantinople (now Istanbul) was the capital of the Byzantine Empire for 1,000 years. It fell in 1453 to Ottoman Turks, who ruled a vast empire for over 400 years.

Just before WWI, Turkey, or the Ottoman Empire, ruled what is now Syria, Lebanon, Iraq, Jordan, Israel, Saudi Arabia, Yemen, and islands in the Aegean Sea. Turkey joined Germany and Austria in WWI, and its defeat resulted in the loss of territory and the fall of the sultanate. A secular republic was established Oct. 29, 1923. The first pres., Mustafa Kemal (later Kemal Ataturk), led Turkey until his death in 1938.

Turkey kept neutral during most of WWII. The country became a full member of NATO in 1952. Military coups overthrew civilian governments in 1960 and 1980. Turkey invaded nearby Cyprus July 20, 1974, to prevent that country from uniting with Greece, and Cyprus was divided into Greek and Turkish zones.

Turkey joined the U.S.-led force that ousted Iraq from Kuwait, 1991. Millions of Iraqi Kurdish refugees fled to Turkey's SE border region after the war. Turkish offensives in Kurdish areas of Turkey

caused heavy casualties among separatist guerrillas and civilians. Kurdish militants raided Turkish diplomatic missions in some 25 Western European cities, June 24, 1993.

Tansu Ciller became Turkey's first woman prime min. July 5, 1993. The Islamic Welfare Party gained strength in the 1990s, and in June 1996, a coalition with Ciller's True Path Party was formed. The pro-Islamic government resigned June 18, 1997, under pressure from the military, which stepped up its campaign against Islamic fundamentalism in 1998.

Kurdish rebel leader Abdullah Öcalan was captured Feb. 15, 1999, and convicted of terrorism June 29. His organization, the Kurdistan Workers' Party (PKK), announced in 1999 that it would abandon its 14-year-old insurgency. Violence continued at a lower level, however.

Earthquakes in Apr. and Nov. 1999 killed over 17,000 people. The Islamic Justice and Development Party (AKP) led by Recep Tayyip Erdogan won Nov. 3, 2002, parliamentary elections. Erdogan became prime min., May 14, 2003. His party scored a landslide win in 2007 parliamentary elections.

Erdogan won an Aug. 10, 2014, election to become Turkey's first popularly elected president. In an Apr. 16, 2017, referendum, accompanied by allegations of irregularities, voters narrowly approved constitutional amendments strengthening the president's powers and abolishing the post of prime minister after the next elections. Erdogan won the June 24, 2018, presidential election; the AKP won parliamentary elections the same day.

During Syria's civil war (2011-), Turkey became a haven for Syrian refugees (more than 3.6 mil as of mid-Sept. 2020). Turkey was also a major transit route for hundreds of thousands of Syrian and other migrants trying to reach Europe. Under a Turkey-EU agreement, effective Mar. 20, 2016, Turkey pledged to crack down on smugglers ferrying migrants to Greece. The EU pledged to provide aid to help Turkey care for refugees and to resettle some Syrians from Turkish refugee camps. Migrant crossings dropped following the agreement.

Turkish government forces launched a new offensive against the PKK in SE Turkey, beginning in mid-2015, and Kurdish extremists staged terrorist attacks in Turkish cities, as well as attacks on government troops. Turkey began airstrikes, July 24, 2015, against PKK strongholds in N Iraq and later launched attacks on Syrian Kurdish fighters said to be affiliated with the PKK. Turkish ground troops fought in Syria beginning in 2016, mainly to limit areas controlled by Syrian Kurds (allied with the U.S. in fighting ISIS in Syria). After the U.S., Oct. 2019, pulled back troops from N Syria, a new offensive by Turkish and allied Syrian militia forces drove Syrian Kurdish fighters out of areas near the Turkish border.

Terrorist attacks within Turkey attributed to ISIS included suicide bombings at Istanbul's main airport, June 28, 2016, that killed at least 45. On Aug. 20, a suicide bomber killed at least 54 at a wedding in SE Turkey. A gunman killed 39 at an Istanbul nightclub, Jan. 1, 2017.

A coup attempt against Erdogan by elements of the military, July 15-16, 2016, was put down by loyal military units. The government blamed the coup on Muslim cleric Fethullah Gülen, living in the U.S. The abortive coup left at least 240 dead, and some 50,000 soldiers, government officials, and civilians (including journalists) were detained. Intensifying an ongoing crackdown on dissent, the government closed more than 100 media outlets and fired or suspended tens of thousands of judges, government officials, and teachers. July 2020 legislation increased government control of social media platforms in Turkey.

Tensions in U.S.-Turkish relations, along with economic problems, contributed to a sharp drop in the lira's value, 2018-19. U.S. tariffs on Turkish steel and aluminum were imposed, Mar. 23, 2018. The U.S., May 16, 2019, removed Turkey from a trade-preference program. After Turkey began receiving, July 2019, sophisticated missiles purchased from Russia, the U.S. canceled a sale to Turkey of advanced fighter planes. A weak economy, causing a further drop in the lira's value, was aggravated in 2020 by the COVID-19 pandemic. Severely affected by the pandemic, Turkey had more than 317,000 cases by Sept. 30; over 8,100 people had died.

Under a July 2020 decree issued by Erdogan, Istanbul's Hagia Sophia—built as a Christian church in the 6th cent., used as a mosque 1453-1934, and a museum since 1934—once again was converted to a mosque.

Turkmenistan

People: Population: 5,528,627 (116). **Age distrib.:** <15: 25.4%; 65+: 5.4%. **Growth:** 1.1%. **Migrants:** 3.3%. **Pop. density:** 30.5 per sq mi, 11.8 per sq km. **Urban:** 52.5%. **Ethnic groups:** Turkmen 85%, Uzbek 5%, Russian 4%. **Languages:** Turkmen (official), Russian, Uzbek. **Religions:** Muslim (official) 96.9% (Sunni).

Geography: Total area: 188,456 sq mi, 488,100 sq km (52). **Land area:** 181,441 sq mi, 469,930 sq km. **Location:** Central Asia. Kazakhstan on N; Uzbekistan on N and E; Afghanistan, Iran on S. **Topography:** Kara Kum Desert occupies 80% of country. Bordered on W by Caspian Sea. **Arable land:** 4.1%. **Capital:** Ashgabat, 846,255.

Government: Type: Presidential republic; authoritarian. **Head of state and govt.:** Pres. Gurbanguly Berdymukhammedov; b.

1957; in office: Feb. 14, 2007 (acting from Dec. 21, 2006). **Local divisions:** 5 provinces, 1 independent city. **Defense budget:** NA. **Active troops:** 36,500.

Economy: Industries: nat. gas, oil, petroleum prods., textiles, food proc. **Chief agric.:** cotton, grain, melons; livestock. **Natural resources:** petroleum, nat. gas, sulfur, salt. **Water:** 4,302 cu m per capita. **Crude oil reserves:** 600 mil bbls. **Electricity prod.:** 21.2 bil kWh. **Labor force:** agric. 19.5%, industry 42.6%, services 37.9%. **Unemployment:** 4.1%.

Finance: Monetary unit: Manat (TMT) (3.50 = $1 U.S.). **GDP** (2018): $88.9 bil; **per capita GDP** (2018): $15,196; **GDP growth** (2018): 6.2%. **Imports:** $4.6 bil; Turkey 24.2%, Algeria 14.4%, Germany 9.8%, China 8.9%, Russia 8%, U.S. 6.6%. **Exports:** $7.5 bil; China 83.7%, Turkey 5.1%. **Budget:** $6.7 bil. **Inflation** (2016-17): 8%.

Transport: Railways: 3,177 mi. **Airports:** 21.

Communications: Telephone (2017): 11.8 per 100 pop. **Mobile** (2017): 162.9 per 100 pop. **Broadband:** 15.3 per 100 pop. **Internet:** 21.3%.

Health: Expend.: 6.9%. **Life expect.:** 68.2 male; 74.5 female. **Births:** 18.3 per 1,000 pop. **Deaths:** 6.1 per 1,000 pop. **Infant mortality:** 30.8 per 1,000 live births. **Undernourished:** 4.0%. **HIV:** NA.

Education: Compulsory: ages 6-17. **Literacy:** 99.7%.

Embassy: 2207 Massachusetts Ave. NW 20008; 588-1500.

Website: www.turkmenistan.gov.tm

The region has been inhabited by Turkic peoples since the 10th cent. It became part of Russian Turkestan in 1881, and a constituent republic of the USSR in 1925. Turkmenistan declared independence Oct. 27, 1991, and became an independent state when the USSR disbanded Dec. 26, 1991.

Turkmenistan has extensive natural gas reserves and also oil reserves. Political power centers on the former Communist Party apparatus and authoritarian leadership. Gurbanguly Berdymukhammedov won the Feb. 2007 presidential election, considered fraudulent by international observers. He was reelected with 97% of the vote, Feb. 12, 2012, and with 98%, Feb. 12, 2017. Despite international skepticism, the government claimed Turkmenistan was not affected by the 2020 COVID-19 pandemic.

Tuvalu

People: Population: 11,342 (194). **Age distrib.:** <15: 29.4%; 65+: 6.7%. **Growth:** 0.9%. **Migrants:** 2.0%. **Pop. density:** 1,129.8 per sq mi, 436.2 per sq km. **Urban:** 64.0%. **Ethnic groups:** Tuvaluan 86.8%, Tuvaluan/I-Kiribati 5.6%, Tuvaluan/other 6.7%. **Languages:** Tuvaluan, English (both official); Samoan. **Religions:** Christian 94.8% (Protestant [official] 85.5%), agnostic 2.9%.

Geography: Total area: 10 sq mi, 26 sq km (193); **Land area:** 10 sq mi, 26 sq km. **Location:** 9 islands forming NW-SE chain 360 mi long in SW Pacific O. Nearest neighbors are Kiribati to NE, Fiji to S. **Topography:** All low-lying atolls, no more than 15 ft above sea level, composed of coral reefs. **Arable land:** 0%. **Capital:** Funafuti, 7,042.

Government: Type: Parliamentary democracy under constitutional monarchy. **Head of state:** Queen Elizabeth II, rep. by Gov.-Gen. Iakoba Taeia Italeli; in office: Apr. 16, 2010. **Head of govt.:** Prime Min. Kausea Natano; b. 1957; in office: Sept. 19, 2019. **Local divisions:** 7 island councils, 1 town council. **Defense budget/ active troops:** NA.

Economy: Industries: fishing. **Chief agric.:** coconuts; fish. **Natural resources:** fish, coconuts. **Water:** NA. **Labor force:** agric. 27%, industry 9.5%, services 56.7%. **Unemployment:** NA.

Finance: Monetary unit: Australian Dollar (AUD) (1.37 = $1 U.S.). **GDP:** $52.0 mil; **per capita GDP:** $4,465; **GDP growth:** 9.8%. **Imports** (2018): $20.7 bil; Singapore 33.4%, South Korea 11.5%, Australia 10.8%, New Zealand 8%, Fiji 7.5%, Chile 6.1%, South Africa 5%, Japan 5%. **Exports** (2010): $600,000; U.S. 18.2%, Bosnia and Herzegovina 17%, Fiji 14.8%, Nigeria 14.2%, Germany 8.2%, South Africa 5.9%, Colombia 5.1%. **Tourism** (2010): $2 mil. **Budget:** $32.5 mil. **Inflation** (2016-17): 4.1%.

Transport: NA.

Communications: Telephone (2017): 17.6 per 100 pop. **Mobile** (2017): 70.4 per 100 pop. **Broadband:** NA. **Internet:** 49.3%.

Health: Expend.: 17.1%. **Life expect.:** 65.6 male; 70.2 female. **Births:** 23.4 per 1,000 pop. **Deaths:** 8.2 per 1,000 pop. **Infant mortality:** 26.6 per 1,000 live births. **Undernourished:** NA. **HIV:** NA.

Education: Compulsory: ages 7-14. **Literacy:** NA.

Permanent UN Mission: 800 Second Ave., Ste. 400D, New York, NY 10017; (212) 490-0534.

Website: www.timelesstuvalu.com or www.state.gov/countriesareas/tuvalu/

The Ellice Islands separated from the British Gilbert and Ellice Islands Colony in 1975 and became Tuvalu; independence came Oct. 1, 1978. In 2000, Tuvalu joined the United Nations. A major drought that began in Nov. 2010 obliged the government to declare a state of emergency Sept. 28, 2011. Following Sept. 9, 2019, elections, the legislature elected Kausea Natano prime minister, Sept. 19. Rising sea levels due to climate change are threatening to submerge the tiny island nation.

Uganda
Republic of Uganda

People: Population: 43,252,966 (34). **Age distrib.:** <15: 48.2%; 65+: 2.4%. **Growth:** 3.4%. **Migrants:** 3.9%. **Pop. density:** 568.4 per sq mi, 219.4 per sq km. **Urban:** 25.0%. **Ethnic groups:** Baganda 16.5%, Banyankole 9.6%, Basoga 8.8%, Bakiga 7.1%, Iteso 7%, Langi 6.3%, Bagisu 4.9%, Acholi 4.4%, Lugbara 3.3%. **Languages:** English, Swahili (both official); Ganda or Luganda (most widely used Niger-Congo lang.). **Religions:** Christian 84.9% (Catholic 41.4%, Protestant 41.1%), Muslim 11.7% (Sunni).

Geography: Total area: 93,065 sq mi, 241,038 sq km (79); **Land area:** 76,101 sq mi, 197,100 sq km. **Location:** E Central Africa. South Sudan on N, Dem. Rep. of the Congo on W, Rwanda and Tanzania on S, Kenya on E. **Topography:** Mostly high plateau 3,000-6,000 ft high, with Ruwenzori Range in W (Mt. Margherita, 16,765 ft), volcanoes in SW. NE is arid, SW and SW rainy. Lakes Victoria, Edward, Albert form much of borders. **Arable land:** 34.4%. **Capital:** Kampala, 3,298,364.

Government: Type: Presidential republic. **Head of state and govt.:** Pres. Yoweri Kaguta Museveni; b. 1944; in office: Jan. 29, 1986. **Local divisions:** 134 districts, 1 capital city. **Defense budget:** $547 mil. **Active troops:** 45,000.

Economy: Industries: sugar proc., brewing, tobacco, cotton textiles, cement, steel prod. **Chief agric.:** coffee, tea, cotton, tobacco, cassava, potatoes, corn, millet, pulses, cut flowers; beef, goat meat, milk, poultry, fish. **Natural resources:** copper, cobalt, hydropower, limestone, salt, gold. **Water:** 1,402 cu m per capita. **Crude oil reserves:** 2.5 bil bbls. **Electricity prod.:** 3.9 bil kwH. **Labor force:** agric. 72.4%, industry 6.9%, services 20.9%. **Unemployment:** 1.9%.

Finance: Monetary unit: Shilling (UGX) (3,687.34 = $1 U.S.). **GDP:** $100.6 bil; **per capita GDP:** $2,272; **GDP growth:** 6.5%. **Imports:** $5.0 bil; China 17.4%, India 13.4%, UAE 12.2%, Kenya 7.9%, Japan 6.4%, Saudi Arabia 6.3%. **Exports:** $3.3 bil; Kenya 17.7%, UAE 16.7%, Dem. Rep. of the Congo 6.6%, Rwanda 6.1%. **Tourism:** $1.2 bil. **Budget:** $4.9 bil. **Inflation:** 2.9%.

Transport: Railways: 773 mi. **Motor vehicles:** 12 per 1,000 pop. **Airports:** 5.

Communications: Telephone: 0.4 per 100 pop. **Mobile:** 57.3 per 100 pop. **Broadband:** 23.4 per 100 pop. **Internet:** 23.7%.

Health: Expend.: 6.3%. **Life expect.:** 66.0 male; 70.5 female. **Births:** 42.3 per 1,000 pop. **Deaths:** 5.3 per 1,000 pop. **Infant mortality:** 32.6 per 1,000 live births. **Undernourished:** NA. **HIV:** 5.8%.

Education: Compulsory: ages 6-12. **Literacy:** 89.4%.

Embassy: 5911 16th St. NW 20011; 726-0416.

Website: www.statehouse.go.ug

Britain obtained a protectorate over Uganda in 1894. The country became independent Oct. 9, 1962, and a republic within the Commonwealth a year later. In 1967, the traditional kingdoms, including the powerful Buganda state, were abolished.

Gen. Idi Amin seized power from Prime Min. Milton Obote in 1971. During his 8-year dictatorship, he was responsible for the deaths of up to 300,000 of his opponents. In 1972 he expelled nearly all of Uganda's 45,000 Asians. Tanzanian troops and Ugandan exiles and rebels ousted Amin, Apr. 11, 1979.

Obote, president from Dec. 1980, was ousted in a military coup July 1985. Guerrilla war and rampant human rights abuses had plagued Uganda under Obote's regime.

Conditions improved after Yoweri Museveni took power in Jan. 1986. In 1993 the Buganda and other traditional monarchies were restored for ceremonial purposes. Uganda helped Laurent Kabila seize power in the Dem. Rep. of the Congo (DRC; formerly Zaire) in 1997 but sent troops in 1998 to aid insurgents seeking his ouster. A withdrawal accord was signed Sept. 2002.

Pres. Museveni won reelection in 2001, 2006, 2011, and 2016; his political opponents, the U.S., and the EU considered the elections flawed. Several opposition politicians were arrested, Aug. 2018; anti-government protests were violently suppressed.

The rebel Lord's Resistance Army (LRA), led by Joseph Kony, began an insurgency against the Museveni government in 1986 and abducted tens of thousands of children to serve as soldiers and sex slaves. According to UN estimates, the LRA, 1987-2012, killed more than 100,000 people and displaced some 2.5 mil in Uganda and neighboring countries. Peace talks brokered by Sudan began July 2006, and LRA violence in Uganda diminished. A cease-fire accord was signed Feb. 23, 2008, by which time the LRA had largely moved its activities to the DRC and Central African Rep. Kony had been charged with war crimes by the Intl. Criminal Court in 2005. As of Sept. 2020, he remained at large.

In 2007, Uganda began supplying troops to the African Union's peacekeeping force in Somalia. Suicide bombings July 11, 2010, killed 76 people watching a World Cup soccer match on outdoor video screens in Kampala; al-Shabab, a Somali al-Qaeda-linked Islamist group, claimed responsibility.

The UNHCR estimated that, as of Aug. 31, 2020, 882,000 refugees from South Sudan were living in Uganda, which also hosted more than 418,000 refugees from the DRC.

Uganda instituted curfews, border controls, and other measures to combat the 2020 COVID-19 pandemic. As of Sept. 30, the country had about 8,000 cases; 75 people had died.

Ukraine

People: Population: 43,922,939 (33). **Age distrib.:** <15: 16.2%; 65+: 17.0%. **Growth:** −0.2%. **Migrants:** 11.3%. **Pop. density:** 196.4 per sq mi, 75.8 per sq km. **Urban:** 69.6%. **Ethnic groups:** Ukrainian 77.8%, Russian 17.3%. **Languages:** Ukrainian (official), Russian. **Religions:** Christian 86.8% (Orthodox 71.9%, Catholic 11.1%), agnostic 9.6%.

Geography: Total area: 233,032 sq mi, 603,550 sq km (About 7.1% is occupied by Russia.) (45); **Land area:** 223,681 sq mi, 579,330 sq km. **Location:** Eastern Europe. Belarus on N; Russia on NE and E; Moldova, Romania on SW; Hungary, Slovakia, Poland on W. **Topography:** Part of E European plain with arable black soil. Carpathians in the SW, Crimean chain in the S. **Arable land:** 56.6%. **Capital:** Kiev, 2,988,176. **Cities:** Kharkiv, 1,429,004; Odesa, 1,009,289.

Government: Type: Semi-presidential republic. **Head of state:** Pres. Volodymyr Zelensky; b. 1978; in office: May 20, 2019. **Head of govt.:** Prime Min. Denys Shmyhal b. 1975; in office: Mar. 4, 2020. **Local divisions:** 24 provinces, 1 autonomous republic, 2 municipalities. **Defense budget:** $3.8 bil. **Active troops:** 209,000.

Economy: Industries: coal, elec. power, metals, machinery and transp. equip., chemicals, food proc. **Chief agric.:** grain, sugar beets, sunflower seeds, vegetables; beef, milk. **Natural resources:** iron ore, coal, manganese, nat. gas, oil, salt, sulfur, graphite, titanium, magnesium, kaolin, nickel, mercury, timber. **Water:** 3,964 cu m per capita. **Crude oil reserves:** 395 mil bbls. **Electricity prod.:** 145.7 bil kWH. **Labor force:** agric. 14.1%, industry 24.8%, services 61.1%. **Unemployment:** 8.9%.

Finance: Monetary unit: Hryvnia (UAH) (27.75 = $1 U.S.). **GDP:** $560.7 bil; **per capita GDP:** $13,341; **GDP growth:** 3.2%. **Imports:** $49.1 bil; Russia 14.5%, China 11.3%, Germany 11.2%, Poland 7%, Belarus 6.7%, U.S. 5.1%. **Exports:** $39.7 bil; Russia 9.2%, Poland 6.5%, Turkey 5.6%, India 5.5%, Italy 5.2%. **Tourism:** $1.6 bil. **Budget:** $31.6 bil (planned and consolidated). **Inflation:** 7.9%.

Transport: Railways: 13,504 mi. **Motor vehicles:** 234.6 per 1,000 pop. **Airports:** 108.

Communications: Telephone: 13.8 per 100 pop. **Mobile:** 122.6 per 100 pop. **Broadband:** 41.7 per 100 pop. **Internet:** 58.9%.

Health: Expend.: 7.0%. **Life expect.:** 68.2 male; 77.9 female. **Births:** 9.6 per 1,000 pop. **Deaths:** 14 per 1,000 pop. **Infant mortality:** 7.4 per 1,000 live births. **Undernourished:** 3.5%. **HIV:** 1.0%.

Education: Compulsory: ages 6-16. **Literacy:** 99.8%.

Embassy: 3350 M St. NW 20007; 349-2920.

Website: www.kmu.gov.ua

Ukrainians' Slavic ancestors inhabited the region well before the 1st cent. CE. In the 9th cent., the princes of Kyiv established a strong state called Kyivan Rus, which included much of present-day Ukraine. Internal conflicts led to the disintegration of the Ukrainian state by the 13th cent. Mongol rule was supplanted by Poland and Lithuania in the 14th and 15th cent. The N Black Sea coast and Crimea came under Turkish control in 1478. Ukrainian Cossacks, starting in the late 16th cent., rebelled against the occupiers of Ukraine: Russia, Poland, and Turkey.

An independent Ukrainian National Republic was proclaimed on Jan. 22, 1918. But in 1921, Ukraine's neighbors occupied and divided Ukrainian territory. In 1922, Ukraine became a constituent republic of the USSR. In 1932-33, the Soviet government engineered a famine in eastern Ukraine, and 6-7 mil Ukrainians died. During WWII the Ukrainian nationalist underground fought Nazi and Soviet forces. Over 5 mil Ukrainians died in the war. The reoccupation of Ukraine by Soviet troops in 1944 brought a renewed wave of repression.

The world's worst nuclear power plant disaster occurred in Chernobyl, Ukraine, in Apr. 1986; many thousands were killed or disabled as a result of the radiation leak.

Ukrainian independence was restored, Dec. 1991, with the Soviet Union's dissolution. Following a 1994 accord with Russia and the U.S., Ukraine's large nuclear arsenal was transferred to Russia for destruction.

President since 1994, Leonid Kuchma attempted to engineer the 2004 election of his handpicked successor, the Russian-backed Prime Min. Viktor Yanukovych. After Yanukovych was declared the winner in Nov., massive protests (the Orange Revolution) forced an election rerun, Dec. 26, won by Viktor Yushchenko. Yanukovych was the winner in the Feb. 2010 presidential election.

Large anti-Yanukovych protests began in Nov. 2013, following his decision not to sign a free trade pact with the EU. After dozens were killed in violent protests in Kyiv, Feb. 18-20, 2014, parliament removed Yanukovych from office, Feb. 22. Pro-EU candidate Petro Poroshenko won a May 25, 2014, presidential election. The EU agreement was completed Sept. 16.

Hurt by corruption and a weak economy, Poroshenko lost an Apr. 21, 2019, presidential runoff election to entertainer and businessman Volodymyr Zelensky. Zelensky's Servant of the People party won July 21, 2019, parliamentary elections.

In a July 25, 2019, phone call, U.S. Pres. Donald Trump urged Zelensky to investigate actions of former U.S. Vice Pres. Joe Biden, a Trump political rival, and Biden's son Hunter. (Trump was acquitted, Feb. 5, 2020, on impeachment charges related to the call.)

Aiding pro-Russian separatists, Russian forces entered Crimea in Mar. 2014, and Russia annexed the region Mar. 18. Fighting began in Apr. 2014 in eastern Ukraine between Ukrainian forces and pro-Russian separatists, widely reported to be aided by Russian military equipment and troops. A Russian missile fired by separatists or Russians apparently shot down a Malaysian airliner over eastern Ukraine, July 17, 2014, killing all 298 on board. A Feb. 12, 2015, cease-fire (known as the Minsk II Agreement) reduced violence, but fighting continued along the cease-fire line. By 2020, the death toll in Ukraine's civil war was at least 13,000. In mid-2020, the UNHCR estimated that 2.4 mil people were internally displaced or "conflict affected."

Shortly after takeoff from Tehran, a Ukrainian airliner was mistakenly shot down by the Iranian military, Jan. 8, 2020; all 176 on board were killed.

The 2020 COVID-19 pandemic caused about 209,000 Ukrainian cases and over 4,100 deaths by Sept. 30.

United Arab Emirates

People: Population: 9,992,083 (92). **Age distrib.:** <15: 14.4%; 65+: 1.9%. **Growth:** 1.5%. **Migrants:** 87.9%. **Pop. density:** 309.6 per sq mi, 119.5 per sq km. **Urban:** 87.0%. **Ethnic groups:** South Asian 59.4% (incl. Indian 38.2%, Bangladeshi 9.5%, Pakistani 9.4%), Emirati 11.6%, Egyptian 10.2%, Filipino 6.1%. About 85% of pop. are noncitizens. **Languages:** Arabic (official), English, Hindi, Malayam, Urdu. **Religions:** Muslim 78.6% (Sunni [official] 67%, Shia 7%, Islamic schismatic 5%), Christian 10.9% (Catholic 9.6%), Hindu 6.2%.

Geography: Total area: 32,278 sq mi, 83,600 sq km (113). **Land area:** 32,278 sq mi, 83,600 sq km. **Location:** Middle East, on S shore of the Persian Gulf. Saudi Arabia on W and S, Oman on E. **Topography:** A barren, flat coastal plain gives way to uninhabited sand dunes on S. Hajar Mts. in E. **Arable land:** 0.6%. **Capital:** Abu Dhabi, 1,482,816. **Cities:** Dubai, 2,878,344; Sharjah, 1,684,649.

Government: Type: Federation of monarchies. **Head of state:** Pres. Sheikh Khalifa bin Zayed al Nahyan; b. 1948; in office: Nov. 3, 2004. **Head of govt.:** Prime Min. Sheikh Muhammad bin Rashid al-Maktum; b. 1949; in office: Jan. 5, 2006. **Local divisions:** 7 emirates: Abu Dhabi, Ajman, Dubai, Fujaira, Ras al-Khaimah, Sharjah, Umm al-Qaiwain. **Defense budget:** NA. **Active troops:** 63,000.

Economy: Industries: petroleum and petrochemicals, fishing, aluminum, cement, fertilizer, commercial ship repair, constr. materials. **Chief agric.:** dates, vegetables, watermelons; poultry, eggs; fish. **Natural resources:** petroleum, nat. gas. **Water:** 16 cu m per capita. **Crude oil reserves:** 97.8 bil bbls. **Electricity prod.:** 126.5 bil kWH. **Labor force:** agric. 1.4%, industry 34.2%, services 64.4%. **Unemployment:** 2.5%.

Finance: Monetary unit: Dirham (AED) (3.67 = $1 U.S.). **GDP:** $683.0 bil; **per capita GDP:** $69,901; **GDP growth:** 1.7%. **Imports:** $229.2 bil; China 8.5%, U.S. 6.8%, India 6.6%. **Exports:** $308.5 bil; India 10.1%, Iran 9.9%, Japan 9.3%, China 5.4%, Oman 5%. **Tourism:** $21.4 bil (Dubai only). **Budget:** $111.1 bil (not incl. emirate-level spending in Abu Dhabi and Dubai). **Inflation:** −1.9%.

Transport: Motor vehicles: 322.1 per 1,000 pop. **Airports:** 25.

Communications: Telephone: 24.3 per 100 pop. **Mobile:** 208.5 per 100 pop. **Broadband:** 243.4 per 100 pop. **Internet** (2018): 98.5%.

Health: Expend.: 3.3%. **Life expect.:** 77.6 male; 80.5 female. **Births:** 9.5 per 1,000 pop. **Deaths:** 2 per 1,000 pop. **Infant mortality:** 5.3 per 1,000 live births. **Undernourished:** 3.1%. **HIV:** NA.

Education: Compulsory: ages 6-11. **Literacy:** 99.4%.

Embassy: 3522 International Ct. NW 20008; 243-2400.

Website: www.government.ae

The 7 "Trucial Sheikdoms" gave Britain control of defense and foreign relations in the 19th cent. They merged to become an independent state Dec. 2, 1971. Oil revenues have made the UAE one of the world's wealthiest countries. Banking, construction, and tourism have boomed in recent years. The economy was hurt in 2020 by the COVID-19 pandemic, which caused about 93,000 cases and over 400 deaths in the UAE by Sept. 30.

In Mar. 2015, the UAE joined a Saudi-led coalition conducting airstrikes against Shiite Houthi rebels in Yemen's civil war. UAE troops trained anti-Houthi forces and assisted in combat operations. By 2020, the UAE backed southern separatists in Yemen. The UAE and Israel signed an agreement, Sept. 15, 2020, to normalize relations.

United Kingdom
United Kingdom of Great Britain and Northern Ireland

People: Population: 65,761,117 (22). **Age distrib.:** <15: 17.6%; 65+: 18.5%. **Growth:** 0.5%. **Migrants:** 14.1%. **Pop. density:** 704.0 per sq mi, 271.8 per sq km. **Urban:** 83.9%. **Ethnic groups:** white 87.2%, Black/African/Caribbean/Black British 3%, Asian/Asian British: Indian 2.3%. **Languages:** English; Scots, Scottish Gaelic, Welsh, Irish (all recognized regional langs.). **Reli-

gions: Christian 66.7% (Protestant 48.8%, Catholic 11.7%), agnostic 21.8%, Muslim 7% (Sunni), atheist 1.4%, Hindu 1.1%.

Geography: Total area: 94,058 sq mi, 243,610 sq km (78); **Land area:** 93,410 sq mi, 241,930 sq km. **Location:** Off NW coast of Europe, across English Channel, Strait of Dover, North Sea. Ireland to W, France to SE. **Topography:** England is mostly rolling land, rising to Uplands of southern Scotland. Lowlands in center of Scotland, granite highlands in N. British Isles have milder climate than N Europe due to Gulf Stream and ample rainfall. Severn, 220 mi, and Thames, 215 mi, are longest rivers. **Arable land:** 25.1%.

Capital: London, 9,304,016. **Cities:** Manchester, 2,730,076; Birmingham (West Midlands), 2,607,437; West Yorkshire, 1,889,095; Glasgow, 1,673,332; Belfast, 630,632; Edinburgh, 536,775; Cardiff, 477,627.

Government: Type: Parliamentary constitutional monarchy. **Head of state:** Queen Elizabeth II; b. 1926; in office: Feb. 6, 1952. **Head of govt.:** Prime Min. Boris Johnson; b. 1964; in office: July 24, 2019. **Local divisions:** 228 local authorities (England: 151; Wales: 22; Scotland: 32; Northern Ireland: 11; 12 other dependent areas). **Defense budget:** $54.8 bil. **Active troops:** 148,450.

Economy: Industries: machine tools, elec. power equip., automation equip., railroad equip., shipbuilding, aircraft, motor vehicles and parts, electronics and communications equip. **Chief agric.:** cereals, oilseed, potatoes, vegetables; cattle, sheep, poultry; fish. **Natural resources:** coal, petroleum, nat. gas, iron ore, lead, zinc, gold, tin, limestone, salt, clay, chalk, gypsum, potash, silica sand, slate. **Water:** 2,221 cu m per capita. **Crude oil reserves:** 2.7 bil bbls. **Electricity prod** (2018): 315.4 bil kwH. **Labor force:** agric. 1.0%, industry 17.7%, services 81.3%. **Unemployment:** 4.1%.

Finance: Monetary unit: Pound (GBP) (0.75 = $1 U.S.). **GDP:** $3.3 tril; **per capita GDP:** $48,710; **GDP growth:** 1.4%. **Imports:** $615.9 bil; Germany 13.7%, U.S. 9.5%, China 9.3%, Netherlands 8%, France 5.4%, Belgium 5%. **Exports:** $441.2 bil; U.S. 13.2%, Germany 10.5%, France 7.4%, Netherlands 6.2%, Ireland 5.6%. **Tourism:** $50.4 bil. **Budget:** $1.1 tril. **Inflation:** 1.7%.

Transport: Railways: 10,462 mi. **Motor vehicles:** 620.7 per 1,000 pop. **Airports:** 271.

Communications: Telephone: 47.6 per 100 pop. **Mobile:** 117.5 per 100 pop. **Broadband:** 88.1 per 100 pop. **Internet** (2018): 94.9%.

Health: Expend.: 9.6%. **Life expect.:** 78.8 male; 83.5 female. **Births:** 11.9 per 1,000 pop. **Deaths:** 9.5 per 1,000 pop. **Infant mortality:** 4.1 per 1,000 live births. **Undernourished:** <2.5%. **HIV** (2017): 0.2%.

Education: Compulsory: ages 5-15. **Literacy:** 99%.

Embassy: 3100 Massachusetts Ave. NW 20008; 588-6500.

Website: www.gov.uk

The United Kingdom of Great Britain and Northern Ireland comprises England, Wales, Scotland, and Northern Ireland.

Queen and Royal Family. The ruling sovereign is Elizabeth II of the House of Windsor, elder daughter of King George VI. She succeeded to the throne Feb. 6, 1952, and was crowned June 2, 1953. She was married Nov. 20, 1947, to Lt. Philip Mountbatten (b. June 10, 1921), former Prince of Greece. He was created Duke of Edinburgh, and given the title H.R.H., Nov. 19, 1947; he was named Prince of the United Kingdom and Northern Ireland Feb. 22, 1957. Prince Charles Philip Arthur George (b. Nov. 14, 1948) is the Prince of Wales and heir apparent. His first son, William Philip Arthur Louis (b. June 21, 1982), is second in line to the throne. William married Catherine (Kate) Middleton, Apr. 29, 2011. Their son George Alexander Louis (b. July 22, 2013) is third in line; Charlotte Elizabeth Diana (b. May 2, 2015) is fourth; Louis Arthur Charles (b. Apr. 23, 2018) is fifth. On May 19, 2018, Prince Charles's younger son, Henry Charles Albert David (Harry; sixth in line) married American actor Meghan Markle. Their first child, Archie Harrison (seventh in line), was born May 6, 2019. Harry and Meghan stepped back from official duties as of Mar. 31, 2020. Prince Andrew, younger brother of Prince Charles, stepped back from official duties Nov. 20, 2019, following allegations related to his friendship with convicted sex offender Jeffrey Epstein.

Parliament is the UK's legislative body, with certain powers over dependent units. It consists of two houses. The House of Commons has 650 members, elected by direct ballot and divided as follows: England, 533; Wales, 40; Scotland, 59; Northern Ireland, 18. The House of Lords (June 2020) comprised 778 members: 87 hereditary peers, 666 life peers, and 25 archbishops and bishops of the Church of England.

Resources and industries. Great Britain is a global trade and financial services center. As of 2017, service industries accounted for more than 79% of GDP; industry, about 20%; agriculture, less than 1%. Manufacturing, historically important since the Industrial Revolution, has declined in economic significance, while finance, centered in London, has grown in importance. Coal production, also historically important, has declined by more than 90% since 1970. Large oil and gas fields in the North Sea began commercial oil production in 1975, but proved reserves were declining in the 21st cent. Hornsea One in the North Sea (fully operational Dec. 2019) is the world's largest offshore wind farm.

Religion and Education. The Church of England is Protestant Episcopal. The queen is its temporal head, with rights of appointments to archbishoprics, bishoprics, and other offices. There are two provinces, Canterbury and York, each headed by an archbishop. Westminster Abbey (1050-1760) is the site of coronations and the tombs of Elizabeth I, Mary, Queen of Scots, kings, poets, and the Unknown Warrior. Celebrated British universities Oxford and Cambridge each date to the 13th cent.

History. Britain was separated from the European continent at least 200,000 years ago by catastrophic flooding that created the English Channel. Migrants across the Channel included the Celts, who arrived 2,500 to 3,000 years ago. Their language survives in Welsh and Gaelic enclaves.

England was part of the Roman Empire 43-410 CE, after which waves of Jutes, Angles, and Saxons arrived from German lands, followed by Danish raiders from the 8th through 11th cent. French-speaking Normans invaded in 1066, uniting the country with their dominions in France.

Opposition by nobles to royal authority forced King John to agree to the Magna Carta in 1215, a guarantee of rights and the rule of law. In the ensuing decades, the foundations of the parliamentary system were laid.

English dynastic claims to large parts of France led to the Hundred Years War, 1338-1453, an unsuccessful campaign. A long civil war, the War of the Roses, 1455-85, ended with the establishment of the Tudor monarchy. The economy prospered over long periods of domestic peace unmatched in continental Europe. The Church of England separated from the authority of the pope, 1534.

During the reign of Queen Elizabeth I, 1558-1603, England became a major naval power, leading to the founding of colonies in the New World and the expansion of trade with Europe and Asia. Scotland and England shared a single monarch after James VI of Scotland was crowned James I of England in 1603.

A struggle between Parliament and the Stuart kings led to a civil war, 1642-49, and the establishment of a republic under the Puritan Oliver Cromwell. The monarchy was restored in 1660, but the Glorious Revolution of 1688 confirmed the sovereignty of Parliament: a Bill of Rights was granted 1689. Scotland was united with England after the ratification of the Articles of Union of Scotland and England, May 1707.

Technological and entrepreneurial innovations led to the Industrial Revolution in the 18th cent. The 13 N American colonies were lost but replaced by growing empires in Canada, India, Australia, and elsewhere. Britain's role in the defeat of Napoleon, 1815, strengthened its position as the leading world power.

The limited extension of voting rights in 1832, 1867, and 1884; the formation of trade unions; and the development of universal public education were among the social changes that accompanied the spread of industrialization and urbanization in the 19th cent. (Men gained full voting rights in 1918 and women in 1928.) Large parts of Africa and Asia were added to the empire during the reign of Queen Victoria, 1837-1901.

Though victorious in WWI, Britain suffered huge casualties and economic dislocation. Ireland became independent in 1921, and independence movements became active in India and other colonies. The country suffered major bombing damage in WWII but rallied behind Prime Min. Winston Churchill and held off Germany until Allied victory was achieved, 1945.

In the postwar period, Britain lost its world leadership position to other powers. Labour governments nationalized some basic industries and expanded social welfare programs. In 1973, the UK joined the European Economic Community, which became the European Union (EU). Prime Min. Margaret Thatcher's Conservative governments, 1979-90, fostered private enterprise and began denationalization of key industries. The Channel Tunnel linking Britain to the Continent was opened May 6, 1994.

Diana, Princess of Wales, died in a car crash in Paris, Aug. 31, 1997.

After the Sept. 11 attacks on the U.S., the UK participated, beginning in 2001, in the Afghanistan war, maintaining as many as 9,500 troops in the country. About 950 were in Afghanistan in mid-2020. Labour Prime Min. Tony Blair committed British troops to the 2003 U.S.-led invasion of Iraq. UK forces, which numbered 46,000 at the height of combat operations, almost entirely pulled out by mid-2009. The UK joined (2014-19) U.S.-led airstrikes against ISIS forces in Iraq and Syria.

Suicide bombings on 3 London underground trains and a bus, July 7, 2005, left 56 people dead.

Legislation in 2005 established a Supreme Court, to replace the House of Lords as the UK's highest court. Blair, who had won three elections, was succeeded by Labour's Gordon Brown, June 2007. Responding Oct. 13, 2008, to the worldwide financial crisis, Prime Min. Brown initiated a plan to provide three of Britain's largest banks with a capital infusion of up to $63 bil.

In the wake of Britain's deepest recession since WWII, voters rejected the Labour Party in May 2010 elections. Conservative Prime Min. David Cameron responded to the fiscal crisis with austerity measures. Parliament voted in favor of same-sex marriage July 16, 2013. The Conservatives won May 7, 2015, elections. Tens of thousands of migrants to Europe from Africa, the Middle East, and SW Asia in 2015 tried to enter Britain. Anti-immigrant sentiment, including concerns about immigration from elsewhere in the EU, contributed to a 51.9%-48.1% referendum vote, June 23, 2016, favoring Britain's exit from the EU ("Brexit"). Conservative Theresa May replaced Cameron, July 13. After June 8, 2017, elections, May remained prime min.

A suicide bomber apparently with ISIS connections killed 22 victims and injured more than 100 at a concert in Manchester, May 22, 2017. In London, June 3, three attackers fatally ran down with a van or stabbed 8 victims; ISIS claimed responsibility.

Russia was the "highly likely" perpetrator, Prime Min. May said Mar. 12, 2018, of the Mar. 4 poisoning in Salisbury of a former Russian intelligence officer who became a British spy and his daughter; both survived.

Prime Min. May and EU leaders completed, Nov. 2018, a separation agreement, but Parliament, Jan.-Mar. 2019, rejected it three times. Conservative Boris Johnson, a Brexit hardliner, replaced May as prime min., July 24, 2019, and negotiated a revised EU agreement that kept Northern Ireland largely aligned with EU policies, to prevent a "hard" border between Northern Ireland and the Irish Republic (an EU member). Campaigning to "get Brexit done," Johnson and the Conservatives won a sweeping victory in Dec. 12 elections. After the new Parliament and the EU approved the revised separation agreement, Britain formally exited the EU Jan. 31, 2020. With the UK then in a transition period, Johnson faced a Dec. 31, 2020, deadline to negotiate a new EU trade pact. A bill introduced by Johnson's government Sept. 9, 2020, and passed by the House of Commons Sept. 29 contradicted separation agreement provisions regarding Northern Ireland, complicating ongoing UK-EU negotiations.

Initially slow, then somewhat inconsistent in implementing lockdown measures, Britain was one of the hardest-hit Western European countries by the 2020 COVID-19 pandemic, with more than 446,000 cases (including Prime Min. Johnson in Apr.) and over 42,000 deaths by Sept. 30. Government stimulus programs aimed to alleviate economic damage—GDP dropped 20% in Q2.

When Cyprus gained independence, the UK retained the sovereign base areas of Akrotiri (47 sq mi) and Dhekelia (51 sq mi) on the island.

Wales

The Principality of Wales in western Britain has an area of 8,019 sq mi and a population (2019 est.) of 3,152,879. Cardiff is the capital, pop. (2020 est.) 477,627.

The creation of a 60-seat elected Welsh assembly with limited powers passed by a thin margin in a Sept. 18, 1997, referendum.

Early Anglo-Saxon invaders drove Celtic peoples into the mountains of Wales, where they developed a distinct nationality. Members of the ruling house of Gwynedd in the 13th cent. fought England but were crushed, 1283. Edward of Caernarvon, son of Edward I of England, was created Prince of Wales, 1301. **Website:** gov.wales

Scotland

Scotland occupies the northern 37% of the main British island, and the Hebrides, Orkney, Shetland, and smaller islands. Length 275 mi, breadth approx. 150 mi, area 30,414 sq mi, pop. (2019 est.) 5,463,300.

The Lowlands, a belt of land approx. 60 mi wide from the Firth of Clyde to the Firth of Forth, divide the farming region of the Southern Uplands from the granite Highlands of the N; they contain 75% of the population and most of the industry. The Highlands, famous for hunting and fishing, have been opened to industry by many hydroelectric power stations.

Edinburgh, pop. (2019 est.) 536,775, is the capital. Glasgow, pop. (2020 est.) 1,673,332, is Scotland's major port and shipbuilding center and has developed a services-based economy in the 21st cent., including financial services, healthcare, and engineering. Aberdeen, pop. (2019 est.) 228,670, is a major port and center of granite, fish-processing, and North Sea oil industries. Dundee, pop. (2019 est.) 149,320, NE of Edinburgh, is an industrial and fish-processing center.

History. Scotland was called Caledonia by the Romans who battled early Celtic tribes and occupied southern areas from the 1st to the 4th cent. Missionaries from England introduced Christianity in the 4th cent.; St. Columba, an Irish monk, converted most of Scotland in the 6th cent.

The Kingdom of Scotland was founded in 1018. William Wallace and Robert Bruce both defeated English armies 1297 and 1314, respectively. In 1603, James VI of Scotland, son of Mary, Queen of Scots, succeeded to the English throne as James I, and effected the Union of the Crowns. In 1707 Scotland received representation in the British Parliament. A 1997 proposal to create a regional legislature passed by a landslide; the Scottish Parliament has limited taxing authority and autonomy in areas such as education and social welfare. In 2011 elections for the 129-seat parliament, the pro-independence Scottish National Party (SNP) won a majority. In a referendum on independence Sept. 18, 2014, 55% of Scottish voters opposed separating from the UK. The SNP remained in power but lost its majority in May 5, 2016, parliamentary elections.

Memorials of Robert Burns, Sir Walter Scott, John Knox, and Mary, Queen of Scots, draw many tourists, as do the beauties of the Trossachs, Loch Katrine, Loch Lomond, and abbey ruins.

Industries. Engineering products are a key industry, with growing emphasis on office machinery, autos, electronics, and other consumer goods. Oil discoveries offshore in the North Sea stimulated onshore support industries.

Scotland produces fine woolens, worsteds, tweeds, silks, fine linens, and jute. It is known for its special breeds of cattle and sheep. Commercial fishing is an important industry. Whisky is a major export.

The Hebrides are a group of about 500 islands, 100 inhabited, off the W coast. The **Inner Hebrides** include Skye, Mull, and Iona, the last famous for the arrival of St. Columba, 563 CE. The **Outer Hebrides** include Lewis and Harris. Industries include sheep raising and weaving. The approx. 70 **Orkney Isls.** are to the NE. The capital is Kirkwall, on Pomona Isl. Fish curing, sheep raising, and weaving are occupations. NE of Orkney are the 200 **Shetland Isls.**, 24 inhabited, home of Shetland ponies. Orkney and Shetland are centers for the North Sea oil industry. **Website:** www.gov.scot

Northern Ireland

Northern Ireland was constituted in 1920 from 6 of the 9 counties of Ulster, the NE corner of Ireland. Area 5,452 sq mi, pop. (2019 est.) 1,893,667. Capital and chief industrial center, Belfast, pop. (2020 est.) 630,632.

Industries. Shipbuilding, including large tankers, has long been an important industry, centered in Belfast, the largest port. Linen is manufactured, along with apparel, rope, and twine. Growing diversification has added engineering products, synthetic fibers, and electronics. Major farm products include livestock, poultry, potatoes, and dairy foods.

Government and History. An act of the British Parliament, 1920, divided Northern from Southern Ireland, each with a parliament and government. When Ireland became a dominion, 1921, and later a republic, Northern Ireland chose to remain a part of the UK.

During 1968-69, the Roman Catholic minority claimed discrimination in voting rights, housing, and employment. Violence and terrorism intensified, involving branches of the Irish Republican Army (IRA; outlawed in the Irish Republic), Protestant groups, police, and British troops. Between 1969 and 2001, more than 3,500 were killed in sectarian violence in Northern Ireland, Ireland, England, and elsewhere. For most of this period, Britain imposed direct rule.

A settlement reached on Good Friday, Apr. 10, 1998, and approved May 22 by voters in Northern Ireland and the Irish Republic, restored home rule and election of a 108-member assembly with safeguards for minority rights. Both Ireland and Great Britain agreed to relinquish constitutional claims on Northern Ireland. IRA dissidents detonated a bomb at Omagh Aug. 15 that killed 29 people and injured over 330.

London transferred authority to a Northern Ireland power-sharing government in 1999. The IRA July 2005 renounced violence and ordered all units to disarm; Britain reduced its military presence. A dispute between the pro-UK Democratic Unionist Party and the Irish nationalist party Sinn Fein caused the government to collapse in Jan. 2017. After inconclusive Mar. 2017 elections for the Northern Ireland assembly, a new power-sharing government was not formed until Jan. 2020. Under 2019 UK Parliament legislation, same-sex marriage and most abortions became legal in Northern Ireland in 2020.

Religion and Education. According to the 2011 census, the population of Northern Ireland was about 42% Protestant and other Christian, almost 41% Catholic, and more than 17% other religions, no religion, or not stated. Education is compulsory between the ages of 4 and 16 years. **Website:** www.northernireland.gov.uk

Channel Islands

The Channel Islands, area 75 sq mi, off the NW coast of France, the only parts of the former Dukedom of Normandy belonging to England, are Jersey, Guernsey, and the dependencies of Guernsey—Alderney, Brecqhou, Herm, Jethou, Lihou, and Sark. The Bailiwicks of **Jersey**, area 45 sq mi, pop. (2020 est.) 101,073, capital St. Helier, and **Guernsey**, area 30 sq mi, pop. (2020 est.) 67,052, capital St. Peter Port, have separate legal existences and lieutenant governors named by the Crown. The islands were the only British soil occupied by German troops in WWII. **Websites:** www.gov.je; www.gov.gg

Isle of Man

The Isle of Man, area 221 sq mi, pop. (2020 est.) 90,499, is in the Irish Sea, 20 mi from Scotland, 30 mi from Cumberland. It is rich in lead and iron. The island has its own laws and a lieutenant governor appointed by the Crown. The Tynwald (legislature) consists of the Legislative Council, partly elected, and House of Keys, elected. Capital: Douglas; pop. (2018 est.) 27,000. Leading employment sectors in 2016 were professional, education, medical, and scientific services 22.6%; insurance, banking, finance, and business services 20.9%; and misc. services 9.3%. Man is famous for the Manx tailless cat. **Website:** www.gov.im

Gibraltar

A dependency on the S coast of Spain, Gibraltar guards the entrance to the Mediterranean. Known as the Rock, Gibraltar has been in British possession since 1704. It is 3 mi long and 0.75 mi wide (total area, 2.25 sq mi) and reaches a max. elevation of 1,396 ft. A narrow isthmus connects it with the rest of the Iberian Peninsula. Pop. (2020 est.) 29,581.

Gibraltar has historically been—and remains—an object of contention between Britain and Spain. In 1967, residents voted almost unanimously to remain under British rule. A 1969 constitution increased Gibraltarian control of domestic affairs. Voters rejected a plan for the UK and Spain to share sovereignty, Nov. 7, 2002. Residents approved a new constitution Nov. 30, 2006. **Website:** www.gibraltar.gov.gi

British West Indies

A number of the Leeward Isls. are self-governing British possessions. Universal suffrage was instituted 1951-54; ministerial systems were set up 1956-60.

The Leeward Isls. associated with the UK are **Montserrat**, area 39 sq mi, pop. (2020 est.) 5,373. Brades Estate (2018 est. pop., 472) is de facto capital after Plymouth was abandoned in 1997 due to volcanic activity. The **British Virgin Isls.**, 58 sq mi, pop. (2020 est.) 37,381, capital Road Town (2018 est. pop., 15,137); and **Anguilla**, 35 sq mi, pop. (2020 est.) 18,090, capital The Valley (2018 est. pop., 1,402). Montserrat was devastated by the Soufrière Hills volcano, which began erupting July 18, 1995.

The three **Cayman Isls.**, a dependency, lie S of Cuba, NW of Jamaica. Pop. (2020 est.) 61,944, most of it on Grand Cayman. It is a free port; in the 1970s Grand Cayman became a tax-free refuge for foreign funds and branches of many Western banks were opened there. International tourism receipts in 2018 were $880 mil. Total area 102 sq mi. Capital: George Town; pop. (2018 est.) 34,875.

The **Turks and Caicos Isls.** are a dependency at the SE end of the Bahama Islands. Of about 40 islands, only 8 are inhabited; area 366 sq mi, pop. (2020 est.) 55,926; capital Cockburn Town (Grand Turk). Salt, shellfish, and conch shells are the main exports.

In Sept. 2017, Anguilla, the British Virgin Isls., and the Turks and Caicos Isls. suffered severe damage from Hurricane Irma. Hurricane Maria further damaged the Turks and Caicos Isls.

Bermuda

Bermuda is a British dependency governed by a royal governor and an assembly, dating from 1620, the oldest legislative body among British dependencies. It is a group of about 150 small islands of coral formation, 20 inhabited, comprising 21 sq mi in the western Atlantic, 580 mi E of N. Carolina. Pop. (2020 est.) 71,750 (about 54% of African descent). Pop. density is high. Capital: Hamilton; pop. (2018 est.) 10,073.

Tourism is the major industry; tourism receipts in 2019 were $590 mil. Bermuda is also a haven for the offshore insurance industry. Exports include petroleum products, medicine. GDP per capita in 2016 was $99,400. In a referendum Aug. 15, 1995, voters rejected independence by nearly a 3-to-1 majority. **Website:** www.gov.bm

South Atlantic Territories

The **Falkland Isls.**, a dependency, lie 300 mi E of the Strait of Magellan at the southern end of S America.

The Falklands include 2 large islands and about 200 smaller ones, area 4,700 sq mi, pop. (2016 est.) 3,198. Capital Stanley, pop. (2018 est.) 2,269. The licensing of foreign fishing vessels is a major source of revenue. Fishing, tourism, and sheep farming are main industries; wool is the leading export. There are indications of large oil and gas deposits. Argentina claims the islands as Islas Malvinas; 97% of inhabitants are of British origin. Argentina invaded the islands Apr. 2, 1982. A British military task force sent to the area forced an Argentine surrender at Port Stanley, June 14, 1982. **Website:** www.falklands.gov.fk

British Antarctic Territory, S of 60° S lat., formerly a dependency of the Falkland Isls., was made a separate colony in 1962 and includes the South Shetland Isls., the South Orkney Isls., and the Antarctic Peninsula. A chain of meteorological stations is maintained.

South Georgia and the **South Sandwich Isls.**, formerly administered by the Falklands Isls., became a separate dependency in 1985. Total area of 1,507 sq mi. South Georgia, with no permanent population, is about 800 mi SE of the Falklands; the South Sandwich Isls. are uninhabited, about 470 mi SE of South Georgia. **Website:** www.gov.gs

St. Helena, an island 1,200 mi off the W coast of Africa and 1,800 mi E of S America, 47 sq mi. Total area of St. Helena, Ascension, and Tristan da Cunha is 152 sq mi; total pop. (2020 est.) 7,862. Construction, crafts, fishing are chief industries. After Napoleon Bonaparte was defeated at Waterloo the Allies exiled him to St. Helena, where he lived from Oct. 16, 1815, to his death, May 5,

1821. Capital: Jamestown; pop. (2018 est.) 603. **Website:** www.sainthelena.gov.sh

Tristan da Cunha is the principal island, area 38 sq mi, in a group of islands of volcanic origin, total area 71 sq mi, halfway between the Cape of Good Hope and S America. The islands are part of the British overseas territory of St. Helena, Ascension, and Tristan da Cunha.

Ascension is an island of volcanic origin, 34 sq mi in area, 700 mi NW of St. Helena. It is part of the British overseas territory of St. Helena, Ascension, and Tristan da Cunha. It is a communications relay center for Britain and has a U.S. satellite tracking center. The island is noted for sea turtles. **Website:** www.ascension-island.gov.ac

British Indian Ocean Territory (BIOT)

Formed Nov. 1965, with islands formerly dependencies of Mauritius (the Chagos Archipelago, including Diego Garcia) or Seychelles (Aldabra, Farquhar, and Des Roches—transferred back to Seychelles, which became independent in 1976). Total area 21,004 sq mi, land area 23 sq mi. The Chagos civilian population was removed by the UK in the 1970s to make way for expansion of the U.S. military base on Diego Garcia. The UK has opposed islanders' efforts to return home. In 2019, a UN court advisory opinion and General Assembly resolution termed UK control of the Chagos illegal.

Pacific Ocean Territories

Pitcairn Isl. is in the Pacific, halfway between S America and Australia. The island was discovered in 1767 by Philip Carteret but was not inhabited until 23 years later when the mutineers of the *Bounty* landed there. Pop. (2020 est.) 50; descendants of mutineers and their Tahitian wives. It is administered by a British High Commissioner in New Zealand and a local Council. The uninhabited islands of Henderson, Ducie, and Oeno are in the Pitcairn group, area 18 sq mi. **Website:** www.government.pn

United States
United States of America

(Figures for U.S. may differ elsewhere in The World Almanac.*)*

People: Population: 332,639,102 (3). **Age distrib.:** <15: 18.5%; 65+: 16.9%. **Growth:** 0.7%. **Migrants:** 15.4%. **Pop. density:** 94.2 per sq mi, 36.4 per sq km. **Urban:** 82.7%. **Ethnic groups:** white 72.4%, Black 12.6%, Asian 4.8%. About 16.3% of pop. is Hispanic (any race). **Languages:** English, Spanish, Chinese; Hawaiian official in Hawaii, Indigenous langs. official in Alaska. No official natl. lang. **Religions:** Christian 73.5% (Catholic 27.3%, independent 23.6%, Protestant 19.9%), agnostic 16.9%, atheist 3.3%, Jewish 1.7%, Muslim 1.5%, Buddhist 1.3%.

Geography: Total area: 3,796,742 sq mi, 9,833,517 sq km (3). **Land area:** 3,532,315 sq mi, 9,148,655 sq km. (Area is for 50 states and DC only.) **Location:** Primarily N America. Canada on N, Mexico on S; Pacific on W, Atlantic on E. **Topography:** Vast central plain, mountains in W, hills and low mountains in E. **Arable land:** 17.3%. **Capital:** Washington, DC, 5,321,730.

Government: Type: Constitutional federal republic. **Head of state and govt.:** Pres. Donald J. Trump; b. 1946; in office: Jan. 20, 2017. **Local divisions:** 50 states, 1 district. **Defense budget:** $684.6 bil. **Active troops:** 1,379,800.

Economy: Industries: petroleum, steel, motor vehicles, aerospace, telecom, chemicals, electronics, food proc., consumer goods, lumber, mining. **Chief agric.:** wheat, corn, other grains, fruits, vegetables, cotton; beef, pork, poultry, dairy prods.; fish; forest prods. **Natural resources:** coal, copper, lead, molybdenum, phosphates, rare earth elements, uranium, bauxite, gold, iron, mercury, nickel, potash, silver, tungsten, zinc, petroleum, nat. gas, timber. **Water:** 9,459 cu m per capita. **Crude oil reserves** (2019): 47.1 bil bbls. **Electricity prod.** (2019): 4.1 tril kWh. **Labor force:** agric. 1.3%, industry 19.7%, services 79.0%. **Unemployment:** 3.9%.

Finance: Monetary unit: Dollar (USD) (1.00 = $1 U.S.). **GDP:** $21.4 tril; **per capita GDP:** $65,281; **GDP growth:** 2.3%. **Imports:** $2.4 tril; China 21.6%, Mexico 13.4%, Canada 12.8%, Japan 5.8%, Germany 5%. **Exports:** $1.6 tril; Canada 18.3%, Mexico 15.7%, China 8.4%. **Tourism:** $214.1 bil. **Budget:** $4 tril (excl. approx. $2.3 tril of social benefits). **Inflation:** 1.8%.

Transport: Railways: 182,412 mi. **Motor vehicles:** 855 per 1,000 pop. **Airports:** 5,054.

Communications: Telephone: 35.7 per 100 pop. **Mobile:** 123.7 per 100 pop. **Broadband:** 132.9 per 100 pop. **Internet:** 87.3%.

Health: Expend.: 17.1%. **Life expect.:** 78.0 male; 82.5 female. **Births:** 12.4 per 1,000 pop. **Deaths:** 8.3 per 1,000 pop. **Infant mortality:** 5.3 per 1,000 live births. **Undernourished:** <2.5%. **HIV** (2018): 0.4%.

Education: Compulsory: ages 6-17. **Literacy:** 99%.

Website: www.usa.gov

See also U.S. History chapter; Chronology of the Year's Events.

Uruguay
Oriental Republic of Uruguay

People: Population: 3,387,605 (131). **Age distrib.:** <15: 19.5%; 65+: 14.7%. **Growth:** 0.3%. **Migrants:** 2.4%. **Pop. density:** 50.1 per sq mi, 19.4 per sq km. **Urban:** 95.5%. **Ethnic groups:** white 87.7%, Black 4.6%, Indigenous 2.4%. **Languages:** Spanish (official). **Religions:** Christian 61.9% (Catholic 51.4%), agnostic 30.1%, atheist 6.9%.

Geography: Total area: 68,037 sq mi, 176,215 sq km (89); **Land area:** 67,574 sq mi, 175,015 sq km. **Location:** Southern S America, on Atlantic O. Argentina on W, Brazil on N. **Topography:** Rolling, grassy plains and hills, well-watered by rivers flowing W to Uruguay R. **Arable land:** 13.9%. **Capital:** Montevideo, 1,752,388.

Government: Type: Presidential republic. **Head of state and govt.:** Pres. Luis Alberto Lacalle Pou; b. 1973; in office: Mar. 1, 2020. **Local divisions:** 19 departments. **Defense budget:** $442 mil. **Active troops:** 21,100.

Economy: Industries: food proc., elec. machinery, transp. equip., petroleum prods., textiles, chemicals, beverages. **Chief agric.:** cellulose, beef, soybeans, rice, wheat; dairy prods.; fish. **Natural resources:** hydropower, minor minerals, fish. **Water:** 49,812 cu m per capita. **Electricity prod.:** 13.5 bil kWh. **Labor force:** agric. 7.9%, industry 18.7%, services 73.4%. **Unemployment:** 8.8%.

Finance: Monetary unit: Peso (UYU) (42.45 = $1 U.S.). **GDP:** $77.7 bil; **per capita GDP:** $22,455; **GDP growth:** 0.2%. **Imports:** $8.6 bil; China 20%, Brazil 19.5%, Argentina 12.6%, U.S. 10.9%. **Exports:** $11.4 bil; China 19%, Brazil 16.1%, U.S. 5.7%, Argentina 5.4%. **Tourism:** $2 bil. **Budget:** $19.7 bil. **Inflation:** 7.9%.

Transport: Railways: 1,040 mi (operational). **Motor vehicles:** 340.8 per 1,000 pop. **Airports:** 3.

Communications: Telephone: 33.4 per 100 pop. **Mobile:** 149.9 per 100 pop. **Broadband:** 112.1 per 100 pop. **Internet:** 68.3%.

Health: Expend.: 9.3%. **Life expect.:** 74.8 male; 81.2 female. **Births:** 12.9 per 1,000 pop. **Deaths:** 9.3 per 1,000 pop. **Infant mortality:** 7.8 per 1,000 live births. **Undernourished:** <2.5%. **HIV (2018):** 0.6%.

Education: Compulsory: ages 4-17. **Literacy:** 98.9%.

Embassy: 1913 I St. NW 20006; 331-1313.

Website: www.gub.uy

Spanish settlers began to supplant the Indigenous Charrua Indians in 1624. Uruguay was attached to the Spanish Viceroyalty of Rio de la Plata in the 18th cent. Rebels fought against Spain beginning in 1810, with independence declared Aug. 25, 1825. To suppress Tupamaro guerrilla activities, a repressive military regime took power in 1973. Constitutional government was restored in 1985.

Same-sex marriage and marijuana use were legalized in 2013.

José (Pepe) Mujica, a former guerrilla, transformed his Marxist Tupamaro movement into a mainstream political party. Tabaré Vázquez, the candidate of Mujica's Broad Front coalition, won a presidential runoff election, Nov. 30, 2014. Conservative Luis Lacalle Pou narrowly defeated the Broad Front candidate in a Nov. 24, 2019, runoff.

The 2020 COVID-19 pandemic caused about 2,000 cases and 47 deaths in Uruguay as of Sept. 30.

Uzbekistan
Republic of Uzbekistan

People: Population: 30,565,411 (45). **Age distrib.:** <15: 23.2%; 65+: 5.9%. **Growth:** 0.9%. **Migrants:** 3.5%. **Pop. density:** 186.1 per sq mi, 71.9 per sq km. **Urban:** 50.4%. **Ethnic groups:** Uzbek 83.8%, Tajik 4.8%, Kazakh 2.5%, Russian 2.3%, Karakalpak 2.2%. **Languages:** Uzbek (official), Russian, Tajik. **Religions:** Muslim (official) 96.3% (Sunni).

Geography: Total area: 172,742 sq mi, 447,400 sq km (56); **Land area:** 164,248 sq mi, 425,400 sq km. **Location:** Central Asia. Kazakhstan on N and W; Kyrgyzstan, Tajikistan on E; Afghanistan, Turkmenistan on S. **Topography:** Mostly plains and desert. **Arable land:** 9.5%. **Capital:** Tashkent, 2,517,381.

Government: Type: Presidential republic; highly authoritarian. **Head of state:** Pres. Shavkat Mirziyoyev; b. 1957; in office: Sept. 8, 2016. **Head of govt.:** Prime Min. Abdulla Aripov; b. 1961; in office: Dec. 14, 2016. **Local divisions:** 12 provinces, 1 autonomous republic, 1 city. **Defense budget:** NA. **Active troops:** 48,000.

Economy: Industries: textiles, food proc., machine building, metallurgy, mining, hydrocarbon extraction, chemicals. **Chief agric.:** cotton, vegetables, fruits, grain; livestock. **Natural resources:** nat. gas, petroleum, coal, gold, uranium, silver, copper, lead, zinc, tungsten, molybdenum. **Water:** 1,531 cu m per capita. **Crude oil reserves:** 594 mil bbls. **Electricity prod.:** 58.5 bil kWh. **Labor force:** agric. 23.3%, industry 29.9%, services 46.8%. **Unemployment:** 6.1%.

Finance: Monetary unit: Som (UZS) (10,269.37 = $1 U.S.). **GDP:** $244.8 bil; **per capita GDP:** $7,289; **GDP growth:** 5.6%. **Imports:** $11.4 bil; China 23.7%, Russia 22.5%, Kazakhstan 10.7%, South Korea 9.8%, Turkey 5.8%, Germany 5.6%. **Exports:** $11.5 bil; Switzerland 38.7%, China 15.5%, Russia 10.7%, Turkey

8.6%, Kazakhstan 7.7%. **Tourism:** $1.5 bil. **Budget:** $15.1 bil. **Inflation** (2016-17): 12.5%.

Transport: Railways: 2,884 mi. **Motor vehicles:** 82.6 per 1,000 pop. **Airports:** 33.

Communications: Telephone (2017): 10.8 per 100 pop. **Mobile** (2017): 75.9 per 100 pop. **Broadband:** 59.4 per 100 pop. **Internet:** 52.3%.

Health: Expend.: 6.4%. **Life expect.:** 71.7 male; 78.0 female. **Births:** 16.1 per 1,000 pop. **Deaths:** 5.4 per 1,000 pop. **Infant mortality:** 16.3 per 1,000 live births. **Undernourished:** 2.6%. **HIV:** 0.2%.

Education: Compulsory: ages 7-18. **Literacy:** 100.0%.

Embassy: 1746 Massachusetts Ave. NW 20036; 293-6803.

Website: www.gov.uz

The region was overrun by the Mongols under Genghis Khan in 1220. In the 14th cent., Uzbekistan became the center of a native Timurid empire. In later centuries Muslim feudal states emerged. Russian military conquest began in the 19th cent. The Uzbek SSR became a Soviet republic in 1925.

Uzbekistan gained independence when the Soviet Union disbanded Dec. 26, 1991, and was led by the authoritarian government of a former Communist, Islam A. Karimov.

Attacks by Islamic militants, Mar.-July 2004, killed more than 50 people. In June 2004, Russia's OAO Lukoil signed a $1-bil deal to develop Uzbekistan's natural gas fields.

After armed dissidents at Andizhan attacked government buildings and freed hundreds of prisoners, May 2005, security forces killed many rebels and unarmed demonstrators. Karimov then launched a general crackdown on human rights activists. Karimov signed a military cooperation agreement with Russia, Nov. 2005.

Karimov remained in office following the expiration of his presidential term Jan. 22, 2007, despite a two-term constitutional limit. He won a third term Dec. 23 (88.1% of the vote) and a fourth term, Mar. 29, 2015 (90.4%). The government announced, Sept. 2, 2016, that Karimov had died. Prime Min. Shavkat Mirziyoyev became interim president and won (88.6%) a flawed Dec. 4 presidential election. Mirziyoyev took steps to reduce repression, including freeing some jailed dissidents, arresting some security officers accused of torture, and reducing forced labor in the cotton harvests.

The 2020 COVID-19 pandemic caused more than 56,000 cases and almost 500 deaths in Uzbekistan as of Sept. 30.

Vanuatu
Republic of Vanuatu

People: Population: 298,333 (174). **Age distrib.:** <15: 33.6%; 65+: 4.4%. **Growth:** 1.7%. **Migrants:** 1.1%. **Pop. density:** 63.4 per sq mi, 24.5 per sq km. **Urban:** 25.5%. **Ethnic groups:** Melanesian 99.2%. **Languages:** 100+ local langs.; Bislama (creole), English, French (all official). **Religions:** Christian (official) 93.5% (Protestant 73.1%, Catholic 10.6%), ethnic religionist 4.4%.

Geography: Total area: 4,706 sq mi, 12,189 sq km (158); **Land area:** 4,706 sq mi, 12,189 sq km. **Location:** More than 80 islands (about 65 inhabited) in SW Pacific, 1,200 mi NE of Brisbane, Australia. Fiji to E, Solomon Isls. to NW. **Topography:** Dense forest with narrow coastal strips of cultivated land. **Arable land:** 1.6%. **Capital:** Port Vila, 52,690.

Government: Type: Parliamentary republic. **Head of state:** Pres. Tallis Obed Moses; in office: July 6, 2017. **Head of govt.:** Prime Min. Bob Loughman b. 1961; in office: Apr. 20, 2020. **Local divisions:** 6 provinces. **Defense budget/active troops:** NA.

Economy: Industries: food and fish freezing, wood proc., meat canning. **Chief agric.:** copra, coconuts, cocoa, coffee, taro, yams, fruits, vegetables; beef; fish. **Natural resources:** manganese, hardwood forests, fish. **Water:** 36,206 cu m per capita. **Electricity prod.:** 59 mil kWh. **Labor force:** agric. 55.3%, industry 6.3%, services 38.4%. **Unemployment:** 4.4%.

Finance: Monetary unit: Vatu (VUV) (112.71 = $1 U.S.). **GDP:** $981.8 mil; **per capita GDP:** $3,274; **GDP growth:** 2.9%. **Imports:** $273.7 mil; Russia 35.2%, Australia 19.8%, New Zealand 9.8%, China 6.3%, Fiji 5.5%. **Exports:** $44.7 mil; Philippines 23.9%, Australia 16.5%, U.S. 10.4%, Japan 8.8%, Venezuela 8%. **Tourism:** $295 mil. **Budget:** $244.1 mil. **Inflation:** 2.8%.

Transport: Motor vehicles: 58 per 1,000 pop. **Airports:** 3.

Communications: Telephone (2017): 1.6 per 100 pop. **Mobile** (2017): 79.9 per 100 pop. **Broadband:** 45.4 per 100 pop. **Internet:** 25.7%.

Health: Expend.: 3.3%. **Life expect.:** 72.9 male; 76.4 female. **Births:** 22.4 per 1,000 pop. **Deaths:** 4 per 1,000 pop. **Infant mortality:** 12.7 per 1,000 live births. **Undernourished:** 9.8%. **HIV:** NA.

Education: Compulsory: NA. **Literacy:** 96.3%.

Permanent UN mission: 800 Second Ave., Ste. 400B, New York, NY 10017; (212) 661-4303.

Website: parliament.gov.vu

The Anglo-French condominium of the New Hebrides, administered jointly since 1906, became the independent Republic of Vanuatu on July 30, 1980. Cyclone Pam, Mar. 13-14, 2015, destroyed 96% of the country's crops and left 166,000 people in need of emergency assistance; the official death toll was 11. Following Mar. 19-20, 2020, legislative elections, Bob Loughman was elected prime min. by parliament, Apr. 20. The COVID-19 pandemic caused tourism revenue to plunge in 2020. Selling citizenship to affluent foreigners has become a significant source of revenue in recent years.

Vatican City
The Holy See (Vatican City State)

People: Population (2019): 1,000 (196). **Migrants:** 100.0%. **Pop. density** (2017): 5,886.3 per sq mi, 2,272.7 per sq km. **Urban:** 100.0%. **Ethnic groups:** Italian, Swiss, Argentinian, other nationalities. **Languages:** Italian, Latin, French. **Religions:** Roman Catholic (official).

Geography: Total area: 0.17 sq mi, 0.44 sq km (196); **Land area:** 0.17 sq mi, 0.44 sq km. **Location:** Within the city of Rome, completely surrounded by Italy.

Economy: Industries: printing; coin, medal, postage stamp prod.; mosaics, staff uniforms; worldwide banking, financial activities. **Water:** NA. **Labor force:** Essentially services with small amount of industry; nearly all dignitaries, priests, nuns, guards, and approx. 3,000 lay workers live outside the Vatican.

Finance: Monetary unit: Euro (EUR) (0.84 = $1 U.S.). **GDP: NA; per capita GDP:** NA; **GDP growth:** NA. **Budget** (2013): $348 mil.

Apostolic Nunciature: 3339 Massachusetts Ave. NW 20008; 333-7171.

Website: www.vatican.va or www.vaticanstate.va

The popes for many centuries, held temporal sovereignty over mid-Italy (the so-called Papal States), comprising an area of some 16,000 sq mi, with a population in the 19th cent. of more than 3 mil. This territory was incorporated in the new Kingdom of Italy (1861), the sovereignty of the pope being confined to the palaces of the Vatican and the Lateran in Rome and the villa of Castel Gandolfo, by an Italian law, May 13, 1871.

A Treaty of Conciliation, a concordat, and a financial convention with Italy were signed Feb. 11, 1929. They established the independent state of Vatican City and gave the Roman Catholic Church special status in Italy. The treaty (Lateran Agreement) was incorporated into Italy's Constitution (Article 7) in 1947. Italy and the Vatican signed an agreement in 1984 eliminating Roman Catholicism as the state religion and ending required religious education in Italian schools.

Vatican City includes the Basilica of Saint Peter, the Vatican Palace and Museum, the Vatican gardens, and neighboring buildings; 13 buildings in Rome, outside the boundaries, enjoy extraterritorial rights. The legal system is based on the code of canon law, the apostolic constitutions, and laws especially promulgated for Vatican City by the pope.

Pope Benedict XVI, elected Apr. 19, 2005, announced he would resign Feb. 11, 2013, the first pontiff to do so since 1415. He became Pope Emeritus Feb. 28. Cardinal Jorge Mario Bergoglio, from Argentina, was elected Mar. 13, taking the name Francis. He became the first Latin American and first Jesuit pope.

Cardinal George Pell, prefect of the Vatican's Secretariat for the Economy, was charged in Australia in 2017 with child sex abuse; his 2018 conviction was overturned on appeal, Apr. 7, 2020. Former cardinal and archbishop of Washington, DC, Theodore McCarrick was defrocked by the Vatican, Feb. 2019, for sexual abuse of minors. A May 9, 2019, papal edict required priests and nuns to report to church authorities sexual abuse or attempted cover-ups.

Venezuela
Bolivarian Republic of Venezuela

People: Population: 28,644,603 (50). **Age distrib.:** <15: 25.7%; 65+: 8.2%. **Growth:** 0.7%. **Migrants:** 4.8%. **Pop. density:** 84.1 per sq mi, 32.5 per sq km. **Urban:** 88.3%. **Ethnic groups:** Spanish, Italian, Portuguese, Arab, German, African, Indigenous. **Languages:** Spanish (official), Indigenous dialects. **Religions:** Christian 91.9% (Catholic [official] 80.2%), agnostic 4.9%.

Geography: Total area: 352,144 sq mi, 912,050 sq km (32); **Land area:** 340,561 sq mi, 882,050 sq km. **Location:** Carib. coast of S America. Colombia on W, Brazil on S, Guyana on E. **Topography:** Plains, called llanos, extend between Andes Mts. and Orinoco Delta. Orinoco stretches 1,600 mi and drains 80% of country. **Arable land:** 2.9%. **Capital:** Caracas, 2,938,992. **Cities:** Maracaibo, 2,257,999; Valencia, 1,910,188.

Government: Type: Federal presidential republic. **Head of state and govt.:** Pres. Nicolás Maduro Moros; b. 1962; in office: Apr. 19, 2013. (More than 50 countries, inc. the U.S., recognize National Assembly leader Juan Guaidó [b. 1983] as interim pres.) **Local divisions:** 23 states, 1 capital district, 1 federal dependency consisting of 11 fed. controlled island groups. **Defense budget** (2017): $741 mil. **Active troops:** 123,000.

Economy: Industries: agric. prods., livestock, raw materials, machinery and equip., transp. equip., constr. materials, medical equip., pharmaceuticals. **Chief agric.:** corn, sorghum, sugarcane, rice, bananas, vegetables, coffee; beef, pork, milk, eggs; fish. **Natural resources:** petroleum, nat. gas, iron ore, gold, bauxite, hydropower, diamonds. **Water:** 41,436 cu m per capita. **Crude oil**

reserves: 302.8 bil bbls. **Electricity prod:** 103.9 bil kWh. **Labor force:** agric. 8.4%, industry 16.1%, services 75.5%. **Unemployment:** 9.4%.

Finance: Monetary unit: Bolivar (VEF) (9.99 = $1 U.S.). The govt., Aug. 20, 2018, introduced the sovereign bolivar (VES), which is equal to 100,000 of the former currency. **GDP** (2014): $543.9 bil; **per capita GDP** (2014): $18,102; **GDP growth** (2014): –3.9%. **Imports:** $11 bil; U.S. 24.8%, China 14.2%, Mexico 9.5%. **Exports:** $32.1 bil; U.S. 34.8%, India 17.2%, China 16%, Netherlands Antilles 8.2%, Singapore 6.3%. **Tourism** (2016): $473 mil. **Budget:** $189.7 bil. **Inflation** (2015-16): 254.9%.

Transport: Railways: 278 mi. **Motor vehicles:** 115.5 per 1,000 pop. **Airports:** 127.

Communications: Telephone: 19.2 per 100 pop. **Mobile:** 71.8 per 100 pop. **Broadband:** 50.1 per 100 pop. **Internet:** 72%.

Health: Expend.: 1.2%. **Life expect.:** 67.5 male; 74.7 female. **Births:** 17.9 per 1,000 pop. **Deaths:** 7.5 per 1,000 pop. **Infant mortality:** 27.9 per 1,000 live births. **Undernourished:** 31.4%. **HIV:** 0.6%.

Education: Compulsory: ages 3-19. **Literacy:** 98.8%.

Embassy: 1099 30th St. NW 20007; 342-2214.

Website: www.presidencia.gob.ve

Columbus first set foot on the South American continent on the peninsula of Paria, Aug. 1498. Alonso de Ojeda, 1499, called the land Venezuela, or Little Venice, because the native people had houses on stilts. Spanish colonialists dominated Venezuela until Simón Bolívar's victory near Carabobo in June 1821. The republic was formed after secession from the Colombian Federation in 1830. Military strongmen ruled Venezuela for much of its history. Beginning in 1959, the country had democratically elected governments.

Venezuela has the world's largest crude oil reserves, and the economy in recent decades has been heavily dependent on oil revenues. The government, Jan. 1, 1976, nationalized the oil industry. The country also has large reserves of natural gas.

Two attempted coups were thwarted by loyalist troops in Feb. and Nov. 1992. Coup leader Hugo Chávez, who ran as a populist, was elected president Dec. 1998. That month, voters approved a new constitution greatly increasing his powers.

Popular among the poor, Chávez alienated middle- and upper-class Venezuelans with economic and political reforms, and his foreign policy antagonized the U.S. With the economy surging, he won the Dec. 2006 presidential election. Suffering from cancer, Chávez won reelection, Oct. 7, 2012. He died Mar. 5, 2013, before he could be sworn in. Vice Pres. Nicolás Maduro Moros won a narrow victory in Apr. 14, 2013, elections.

With the economy hurt by low oil prices, declining oil production, and tight currency and price controls, GDP declined sharply beginning in 2014 and inflation soared. Shortages of food, medicine, and other goods were widespread. A political crisis intensified economic problems. Beginning in 2015, millions of Venezuelans emigrated, largely to other South American nations. The UNHCR estimated, Sept. 2020, that about 5.1 mil Venezuelans were migrants, refugees, or asylum seekers.

Large anti-Maduro protests, Feb.-June 2014, were met with a harsh crackdown; more than 40 people died. An opposition coalition won Dec. 6, 2015, National Assembly elections, but the Supreme Court often overturned legislation. Looting and sometimes violent demonstrations were widespread in 2016-17. Members of a constituent assembly, mainly Maduro supporters, were chosen July 30, 2017, in an election widely criticized as fraudulent. The constituent assembly, in a decree, Aug. 18, largely took over the interim power to legislate. In a flawed election, May 20, 2018, Maduro won a new term as president. The National Assembly, Jan. 15, 2019, declared Maduro's presidency illegitimate. National Assembly head Juan Guaidó, Jan. 23, 2019, declared himself interim president. Dozens of countries, including the U.S., recognized Guaidó, but Maduro clung to power. The military cracked down on protesters. UN reports in 2019 and 2020 concluded that detainees were being tortured and that security forces and death squads had committed thousands of extrajudicial killings. A May 2020 raid, organized by U.S. mercenaries and apparently intended to overthrow Maduro, failed. The 2020 COVID-19 pandemic added to the country's suffering. Venezuela had about 73,500 cases and over 600 deaths as of Sept. 30; critics accused the government of concealing the true scope of the health crisis.

Vietnam
Socialist Republic of Vietnam

People: Population: 98,721,275 (16). **Age distrib.:** <15: 22.6%; 65+: 6.9%. **Growth:** 0.8%. **Migrants:** 0.1%. **Pop. density:** 824.6 per sq mi, 318.4 per sq km. **Urban:** 37.3%. **Ethnic groups:** Kinh (Viet) 85.7%. **Languages:** Vietnamese (official), English, French, Chinese, Khmer. **Religions:** Buddhist 50.4%, agnostic 11.9%, new religionist 10.8%, ethnic religionist 10%, Christian 9.2% (Catholic 7.1%), atheist 6%.

Geography: Total area: 127,881 sq mi, 331,210 sq km (65); **Land area:** 119,719 sq mi, 310,070 sq km. **Location:** SE Asia, on E coast of Indochinese Peninsula. China on N; Laos, Cambodia on

W. **Topography:** Long and narrow, with 1,400-mi coast. Densely settled Red R. Valley in N; narrow coastal plains in center; wide, often marshy Mekong R. Delta in S. Semi-arid plateaus and barren mountains, with some stretches of tropical rain forest, in rest of country. **Arable land:** 22.5%. **Capital:** Hanoi, 4,678,198. **Cities:** Ho Chi Minh City, 8,602,317; Can Tho, 1,617,602; Hai Phòng, 1,300,088; Da Nang, 1,125,316.

Government: Type: Communist state. **Head of state:** Pres. Nguyen Phu Trong; b. 1944; in office: Oct. 23, 2018. **Head of govt.:** Prime Min. Nguyen Xuan Phuc; b. 1954; in office: Apr. 7, 2016. **Local divisions:** 58 provinces, 5 municipalities. **Defense budget:** $5.2 bil. **Active troops:** 482,000.

Economy: Industries: food proc., garments, shoes, machine-building, mining, coal, steel, cement, chemical fertilizer. **Chief agric.:** rice, coffee, rubber, tea, pepper, soybeans, cashews, sugarcane, peanuts, bananas; pork, poultry; seafood. **Natural resources:** antimony, phosphates, coal, manganese, rare earth elements, bauxite, chromate, offshore oil and gas deposits, timber, hydropower. **Water:** 9,254 cu m per capita. **Crude oil reserves:** 4.4 bil bbls. **Electricity prod.:** 173.3 bil kWh. **Labor force:** agric. 36.2%, industry 28.4%, services 35.4%. **Unemployment:** 2.0%.

Finance: Monetary unit: Dong (VND) (23,292.40 = $1 U.S.). **GDP:** $807.8 bil; **per capita GDP:** $8,374; **GDP growth:** 7.0%. **Imports:** $202.6 bil; China 25.8%, South Korea 20.5%, Japan 7.8%. **Exports:** $214.1 bil; U.S. 20.1%, China 14.5%, Japan 8%, South Korea 6.8%. **Tourism:** $11.8 bil. **Budget:** $69.4 bil. **Inflation:** 2.8%.

Transport: Railways: 1,616 mi. **Motor vehicles:** 5.5 per 1,000 pop. **Airports:** 38.

Communications: Telephone: 15 per 100 pop. **Mobile:** 147.2 per 100 pop. **Broadband:** 46.9 per 100 pop. **Internet** (2018): 70.3%.

Health: Expend.: 5.5%. **Life expect.:** 71.9 male; 77.1 female. **Births:** 14.5 per 1,000 pop. **Deaths:** 6 per 1,000 pop. **Infant mortality:** 15.7 per 1,000 live births. **Undernourished:** 6.4%. **HIV:** 0.3%.

Education: Compulsory: ages 5-14. **Literacy:** 98.4%.
Embassy: 1233 20th St. NW, Ste. 400, 20036; 861-0737.
Website: vietnam.gov.vn

Settled by Viets from central China, Vietnam was held by China, 111 BCE-939 CE, and was a vassal state during subsequent periods. Conquest by France began in 1858 and ended in 1884 with the protectorates of Tonkin and Annam in the N and the colony of Cochin-China in the S.

Japan occupied Vietnam in 1940. Several groups formed the Vietminh (Independence) League, headed by Communist guerrilla leader Ho Chi Minh. In Aug. 1945, the Vietminh forced out Bao Dai, former emperor of Annam and head of a Japan-sponsored regime. France, seeking to reestablish colonial control, unsuccessfully battled Communist and nationalist forces, 1946-54.

Separate states formed in N. and S. Vietnam, with Communists under Ho Chi Minh (backed by Russia and China) controlling N. Vietnam and a non-Communist government (backed by the U.S.) controlling S. Vietnam. N. Vietnam aided Vietcong guerrillas who sought to take over S. Vietnam. U.S. troops and the S. Vietnamese army fought N. Vietnamese and Vietcong forces, including in border areas of Laos and Cambodia. Combat deaths included: U.S. 47,434 (Aug. 4, 1964-Jan. 27, 1973); S. Vietnam more than 200,000; other allied forces 5,225. Total U.S. fatalities exceeded 58,000. Vietnamese civilian casualties were more than 1 mil. The war displaced more than 6.5 mil in S. Vietnam.

A never-implemented cease-fire agreement was signed in Paris Jan. 27, 1973, by the U.S., N. and S. Vietnam, and the Vietcong. The last U.S. troops left Vietnam Mar. 27, 1973. S. Vietnam surrendered Apr. 30, 1975. N. Vietnam assumed control. The country was officially reunited July 2, 1976.

Heavy fighting with Cambodia took place, 1977-80. China cut off economic aid, 1978, when 140,000 ethnic Chinese fled discrimination in Vietnam. Reacting to Vietnam's 1979 invasion of Cambodia, China attacked four Vietnamese border provinces, Feb. 1979.

Vietnam announced in 1987 reforms aimed at reducing central control of the economy. The U.S. ended, Feb. 1994, a 19-year embargo on trade with Vietnam, and it extended full diplomatic recognition to Vietnam July 11, 1995. The U.S. lifted in 2016 its embargo on lethal arms sales to Vietnam.

Vietnam used a lockdown and extensive testing, Apr. 2020, to combat the COVID-19 pandemic and sharply reduce cases. New cases spiked in some areas in July-Aug. By Sept. 30, Vietnam had totals of 1,094 cases and 35 deaths.

Yemen
Republic of Yemen

People: Population: 29,884,405 (48). **Age distrib.:** <15: 37.7%; 65+: 2.9%. **Growth:** 2.0%. **Migrants:** 1.3%. **Pop. density:** 146.6 per sq mi, 56.6 per sq km. **Urban:** 37.9%. **Ethnic groups:** predom. Arab; also Afro-Arab, South Asian, European. **Languages:** Arabic (official). **Religions:** Muslim (official) 99.2% (Shia 55%, Sunni 44%).

Geography: Total area: 203,850 sq mi, 527,968 sq km (49); **Land area:** 203,850 sq mi, 527,968 sq km. **Location:** Middle East, on S coast of the Arabian Peninsula. Saudi Arabia on N, Oman on E. **Topography:** Sandy coastal strip; well-watered fertile mountains in interior. **Arable land:** 2.1%. **Capital:** Sanaa, 2,972,988.

Government: Type: In transition. **Head of state:** Pres. Abd Rabbuh Mansur Hadi; b. 1950; in office: Feb. 25, 2012. **Head of govt.:** Prime Min. Maeen Abdulmalik Saeed; in office: Oct. 15, 2018. **Local divisions:** 22 governorates. **Defense budget:** NA. **Active troops:** 40,000. (20,000 insurgent forces in territory where govt. does not exercise effective control.)

Economy: Industries: crude oil prod. and petroleum refining, small-scale prod. of cotton textiles and leather goods, food proc., handicrafts, aluminum prods. **Chief agric.:** grains, fruits, vegetables, pulses, khat, coffee, cotton; dairy prods., livestock, poultry; fish. **Natural resources:** petroleum; fish; rock salt; marble; small deposits of coal, gold, lead, nickel, copper. **Water:** 74 cu m per capita. **Crude oil reserves:** 3 bil bbls. **Electricity prod.:** 4.5 bil kWh. **Labor force:** agric. 28.6%, industry 10.0%, services 61.4%. **Unemployment:** 12.8%.

Finance: Monetary unit: Rial (YER) (250.35 = $1 U.S.). **GDP:** NA; **per capita GDP:** NA; **GDP growth** (2018): 0.8%. **Imports:** $4.1 bil; UAE 12.2%, China 12.1%, Turkey 8.7%, Brazil 7.3%, Saudi Arabia 6.5%, Argentina 5.5%. **Exports:** $384.5 mil; Egypt 29.4%, Thailand 16.7%, Belarus 13.5%, Oman 10.5%, UAE 6.5%, Saudi Arabia 5%. **Tourism** (2015): $100 mil. **Budget:** $4.5 bil. **Inflation** (2016-17): 24.7%.

Transport: Motor vehicles: 31.3 per 1,000 pop. **Airports:** 17.

Communications: Telephone (2017): 4.3 per 100 pop. **Mobile** (2017): 55.2 per 100 pop. **Broadband:** 5.9 per 100 pop. **Internet:** 26.7%.

Health: Expend. (2015): 4.2%. **Life expect.:** 64.7 male; 69.3 female. **Births:** 25.8 per 1,000 pop. **Deaths:** 5.6 per 1,000 pop. **Infant mortality:** 41.9 per 1,000 live births. **Undernourished:** NA. **HIV:** <0.1%.

Education: Compulsory: ages 6-14. **Literacy:** 70.1%.
Embassy: 2319 Wyoming Ave. NW 20008; 965-4760.
Website: www.yemen.gov.ye or www.yemenembassy.org

Yemen's territory once was part of the ancient biblical Kingdom of Sheba, or Saba. Yemen became independent in 1918, after centuries of Ottoman Turkish rule.

Imam Yahya ibn Muhammad ruled, 1904-48, and after his assassination was succeeded by his son, Imam Ahmed, 1948-62. Army officers headed by Brig. Gen. Abdullah al-Salal declared the country the Yemen Arab Republic, Sept. 1962. Ahmed's heir, the Imam Mohamad al-Badr, fled to the mountains where tribesmen joined royalist forces, aided by the Saudi monarchy. Fighting between royalists and republicans killed about 150,000 people until hostilities ended in 1970.

South Yemen, formed from the British colony of Aden and the British protectorate of South Arabia, became independent Nov. 1967. A Marxist state and a Soviet ally, it took the name People's Democratic Republic of Yemen in 1970. More than 300,000 Yemenis fled from the S to the N after independence, contributing to two decades of hostility between the two states.

The two countries were formally united May 21, 1990, but regional clan-based rivalries led to full-scale civil war in 1994. Northern troops captured the former southern capital of Aden in July.

While on a refueling stop in Aden, Oct. 12, 2000, the destroyer USS Cole was bombed, killing 17 Americans; the U.S. blamed the attack on al-Qaeda terrorists.

Clashes beginning in June 2004 between Yemeni government forces and Shiite rebels led by an anti-U.S. cleric, Hussein al-Houthi, left more than 200 people dead. The government announced Sept. 10 that Yemeni troops had killed al-Houthi.

During 2007-10, Shiite rebels in the northwest, secessionists in the south, Sunni militants in the east affiliated with al-Qaeda in the Arabian Peninsula (AQAP), and pirates in coastal waters challenged Yemeni government authority. Pres. Ali Abdullah Saleh was severely wounded June 3, 2011, in a rocket attack. Vice Pres. Abd Rabbuh Mansur Hadi became acting president and won an uncontested Feb. 2012 election. Anwar al-Awlaki, a U.S. citizen and radical Muslim cleric linked to several plots against the U.S., was killed Sept. 30, 2011, by a U.S. missile in northern Yemen.

Shiite rebels known as Houthis took over Sanaa in Sept. 2014 and gained control of much of western Yemen. A coalition of Sunni nations led by Saudi Arabia, which backed Hadi, began, Mar. 25, 2015, airstrikes against Houthi fighters and Houthi-controlled areas. The U.S. provided weaponry and logistical support. UAE ground troops aided forces combating Houthi rebels. Airstrikes (including bombings of hospitals, markets, and schoolchildren) and other fighting caused high civilian casualties. Houthi rebels were aided by Iran. Houthi forces reportedly killed Saleh, Dec. 4, 2017. AQAP seized control of parts of southern Yemen. U.S. airstrikes and special operations troops aided the fight against AQAP; the U.S. said the head of AQAP was killed in a Jan. 2020 drone strike. The Sunni extremist group ISIS staged attacks, 2015-20. Houthi forces launched missile and drone attacks on targets in Saudi Arabia. Southern separatists fought government troops in 2019-20; Saudi Arabia and the UAE sought to implement a power-sharing agreement.

By 2020, the death toll in Yemen's civil war since 2015 was estimated to be at least 100,000. By mid-2020, more than 3.6 mil people had been internally displaced since 2015. More than 24 mil people needed humanitarian assistance. A cholera epidemic that began in late 2016 had caused more than 2.4 mil cases and about 4,000 deaths by mid-2020. Although the impact of the 2020 COVID-19 pandemic on Yemen, with a decimated health care system, was difficult to assess, the WHO reported more than 2,000 cases and almost 600 deaths by Sept. 30.

Zambia
Republic of Zambia

People: Population: 17,426,623 (66). **Age distrib.:** <15: 45.7%; 65+: 2.3%. **Growth:** 2.9%. **Migrants:** 1.0%. **Pop. density:** 60.7 per sq mi, 23.4 per sq km. **Urban:** 44.6%. **Ethnic groups:** Bemba 21%, Tonga 13.6%, Chewa 7.4%, Lozi 5.7%, Nsenga 5.3%, Tumbuka 4.4%, Ngoni 4%, Lala 3.1%, Kaonde 2.9%, Namwanga 2.8%, Lunda (northwestern) 2.6%, Mambwe 2.5%, Luvale 2.2%, Lamba 2.1%. **Languages:** Bantu langs. (incl. Bemba, Nyanja, Tonga, Lozi, Chewa, Nsenga, Tumbuka); English (official). **Religions:** Christian (official) 85.7% (Protestant 35.6%, Catholic 33.5%, independent 16.6%), ethnic religionist 11.1%.

Geography: Total area: 290,587 sq mi, 752,618 sq km (38). **Land area:** 287,028 sq mi, 743,398 sq km. **Location:** S central Africa. Dem. Rep. of the Congo on N; Tanzania, Malawi, Mozambique on E; Zimbabwe, Namibia on S; Angola on W. **Topography:** Mostly high plateau with thick forests, drained by several important rivers, including the Zambezi. **Arable land:** 5.1%. **Capital:** Lusaka, 2,774,133.

Government: Type: Presidential republic. **Head of state and govt.:** Pres. Edgar Lungu; b. 1956; in office: Jan. 25, 2015. **Local divisions:** 10 provinces. **Defense budget:** $387 mil. **Active troops:** 15,100.

Economy: Industries: copper mining and proc., emerald mining, constr., foodstuffs, beverages, chemicals, textiles, fertilizer, horticulture. **Chief agric.:** corn, sorghum, rice, peanuts, sunflower seeds, vegetables, flowers, tobacco, cotton, sugarcane, cassava, coffee; cattle, goats, pigs, poultry, milk, eggs, hides. **Natural resources:** copper, cobalt, zinc, lead, coal, emeralds, gold, silver, uranium, hydropower. **Water:** 6,131 cu m per capita. **Electricity prod.:** 14.0 bil kWh. **Labor force:** agric. 48.5%, industry 10.8%, services 40.7%. **Unemployment:** 11.4%.

Finance: Monetary unit: Kwacha (ZMW) (19.61 = $1 U.S.). **GDP:** $64.7 bil; **per capita GDP:** $3,624; **GDP growth:** 1.7%. **Imports:** $7.9 bil; South Africa 28.2%, Dem. Rep. of the Congo 20.8%, China 12.9%, Kuwait 5.4%. **Exports:** $8.2 bil; Switzerland 44.8%, China 16.1%, Dem. Rep. of the Congo 6.2%, Singapore 6%, South Africa 5.9%. **Tourism:** $819 mil. **Budget:** $6.4 bil. **Inflation:** 9.2%.

Transport: Railways: 1,942 mi (incl. 1,156 mi of Tanzania-Zambia Railway Authority). **Motor vehicles:** 23.2 per 1,000 pop. **Airports:** 8.

Communications: Telephone: 0.6 per 100 pop. **Mobile:** 89.2 per 100 pop. **Broadband:** 45.2 per 100 pop. **Internet** (2018): 14.3%.

Health: Expend.: 4.5%. **Life expect.:** 51.9 male; 55.3 female. **Births:** 40.4 per 1,000 pop. **Deaths:** 11.6 per 1,000 pop. **Infant mortality:** 56.0 per 1,000 live births. **Undernourished:** NA. **HIV:** 11.5%.

Education: Compulsory: ages 7-13. **Literacy:** 92.1%.
Embassy: 2200 R St. NW 20008; 234-4009.
Website: www.parliament.gov.zm

Ruled by the British as Northern Rhodesia, the country became the independent republic of Zambia within the Commonwealth Oct. 24, 1964. Independence leader Kenneth Kaunda governed as president, 1964-91. A Zambian government corporation in 1970 took over 51% of two foreign-owned copper-mining companies. Privately held land and other enterprises were nationalized in 1975. In the 1980s and 1990s, lowered copper prices hurt the economy and severe drought caused famine.

Oct. 1991 elections brought an end to Kaunda's one-party rule. The new government sought to sell state enterprises, including the copper industry. Pres. Frederick Chiluba won reelection Nov. 1996. In 2001, Chiluba endorsed Levy Patrick Mwanawasa, who won a disputed Dec. election. Food shortages threatened more than 2 mil Zambians in 2002. Mwanawasa won a second term in 2006.

Pres. Mwanawasa died Aug. 19, 2008. Vice Pres. Rupiah Banda became acting pres. He narrowly won the presidency in the Oct. 2008 election but lost to opposition leader Michael Sata Sept. 2011. Sata died in office, Oct. 28, 2014. Edgar Lungu of Sata's Patriotic Front party narrowly won a Jan. 2015 special election. Lungu narrowly won a new term in Aug. 11, 2016, elections that his main opponent claimed were marred by fraud. Lungu invoked emergency powers for 3 months, beginning in July 2017,

after blaming opposition parties for a series of arson fires. Several European countries suspended aid payments, Sept. 2018, after allegations of government corruption and embezzlement of aid money.

The country has made progress in treating HIV/AIDS, but the disease afflicted 1.2 mil Zambians as of 2018. The 2020 COVID-19 pandemic caused almost 15,000 cases and 332 deaths in Zambia as of Sept. 30.

Zimbabwe
Republic of Zimbabwe

People: Population: 14,546,314 (73). **Age distrib.:** <15: 38.3%; 65+: 4.5%. **Growth:** 1.9%. **Migrants:** 2.8%. **Pop. density:** 97.4 per sq mi, 37.6 per sq km. **Urban:** 32.2%. **Ethnic groups:** African (predom. Shona; Ndebele is second-largest ethnic group) 99.4%. **Languages:** Shona, Ndebele (both official and most widely spoken); English (official, used in business), 13 official minority langs. **Religions:** Christian 83.1% (independent 37.8%, Protestant 34.7%, Catholic 10.6%), ethnic religionist 14.5%.

Geography: Total area: 150,872 sq mi, 390,757 sq km (60). **Land area:** 149,362 sq mi, 386,847 sq km. **Location:** Southern Africa. Zambia on N, Botswana on W, South Africa on S, Mozambique on E. **Topography:** High plateau rising to mountains on E border, sloping down on other borders. **Arable land:** 10.3%. **Capital:** Harare, 1,529,920.

Government: Type: Presidential republic. **Head of state and govt.:** Pres. Emmerson Mnangagwa; b. 1942; in office: Nov. 24, 2017. **Local divisions:** 8 provinces, 2 cities with provincial status. **Defense budget:** $72 mil. **Active troops:** 29,000.

Economy: Industries: mining, steel, wood prods., cement, chemicals, fertilizer, clothing and footwear, foodstuffs, beverages. **Chief agric.:** tobacco, corn, cotton, wheat, coffee, sugarcane, peanuts; sheep, goats, pigs. **Natural resources:** coal, chromium ore, asbestos, gold, nickel, copper, iron ore, vanadium, lithium, tin, platinum group metals. **Water:** 1,310 cu m per capita. **Electricity prod.:** 7.3 bil kWh. **Labor force:** agric. 66.3%, industry 6.5%, services 27.2%. **Unemployment:** 5.0%.

Finance: Monetary unit: Dollar (ZWD) (361.90 = $1 U.S.). **GDP:** $43.3 bil; **per capita GDP:** $2,953; **GDP growth:** −8.1%. **Imports:** $5.5 bil; South Africa 47.8%, Zambia 20.5%. **Exports:** $4.4 bil; South Africa 50.3%, Mozambique 22.5%, UAE 9.8%. **Tourism** (2017): $149 mil. **Budget:** $5.5 bil. **Inflation** (2016-17): 0.9%.

Transport: Railways: 2,129 mi. **Motor vehicles:** 47.7 per 1,000 pop. **Airports:** 17.

Communications: Telephone: 1.9 per 100 pop. **Mobile:** 89.4 per 100 pop. **Broadband:** 41.3 per 100 pop. **Internet:** 27.1%.

Health: Expend.: 6.6%. **Life expect.:** 60.2 male; 64.5 female. **Births:** 33.6 per 1,000 pop. **Deaths:** 9.3 per 1,000 pop. **Infant mortality:** 30.3 per 1,000 live births. **Undernourished:** NA. **HIV:** 12.8%.

Education: Compulsory: ages 6-12. **Literacy:** 86.5%.
Embassy: 1608 New Hampshire Ave. NW 20009; 332-7100.
Website: www.zim.gov.zw

Britain took over the area as Southern Rhodesia in 1923 from the British South Africa Co. (which, under Cecil Rhodes, had conquered it by 1897) and granted internal self-government. A 1961 constitution restricted voting to keep whites in power.

On Nov. 11, 1965, Prime Min. Ian D. Smith unilaterally declared independence. Britain termed the act illegal and demanded that the country (known as Rhodesia until 1980) enfranchise the Black African majority. The UN imposed sanctions, and Black nationalists launched guerrilla attacks.

After the country held its first universal-franchise election, Apr. 21, 1979, all parties accepted a cease-fire, Dec. 5. The country changed its name to Zimbabwe upon independence, Apr. 18, 1980. Robert Mugabe, the nation's first prime min., became executive president in 1987. From the late 1990s, Mugabe's rule became increasingly repressive. A land redistribution campaign triggered violent attacks in Apr. 2000 against some white farmers. Whites made up less than 1% of the population but had held 70% of the land. Production of corn, the nation's food staple, subsequently declined sharply. Mugabe, relying on fraud and intimidation, won the Mar. 9-11, 2002, presidential election. During 2006-08, inflation soared to a yearly rate of more than 100,000%.

Mugabe clung to power after a widely discredited 2008 presidential election and intensified a crackdown on dissidents. Mugabe won the July 31, 2013, presidential election.

Drought caused food shortages in 2016. Police suppressed strikes and demonstrations protesting economic conditions. Mugabe lost the support of the military and his ZANU-PF party, and he resigned, Nov. 21, 2017. Vice Pres. Emmerson Mnangagwa became president, Nov. 24, and narrowly won a disputed July 30, 2018, presidential election. Security forces cracked down violently after Jan. 2019 protests and looting, triggered by food and fuel shortages. Hyperinflation and repression of dissent continued, 2019-20. As the 2020 COVID-19 pandemic spread to Zimbabwe, the health minister, charged with corruption, was dismissed July 7. By Sept. 30, the country had more than 7,800 cases and over 200 deaths.

WORLD ALMANAC EDITORS' PICKS:
MEMORABLE MOMENTS OF THE SUMMER OLYMPIC GAMES

It's possible that the most memorable thing about the 2020 Olympics will be that they were pushed back to summer 2021 (assuming the COVID-19 pandemic has ebbed to make it safe by then). Until then, relive some memorable moments from the previous 28 Summer Games.

1936, Berlin: Jesse Owens Repudiates White Supremacy

Adolf Hitler hoped the 1936 Games would confirm his doctrine of Aryan racial superiority. But Jesse Owens, a Black track-and-field phenom, laid waste to that belief, becoming the first American to win four gold medals in track and field in a single Olympics. Owens broke the Olympic records in the 100-m and 200-m dashes, and with his 4x100-m relay team. He won his fourth gold, setting another Olympic record, in the long jump, by besting Germany's own Luz Long, who publicly congratulated Owens. "It took a lot of courage for him to befriend me … Hitler must have gone crazy watching us embrace," Owens said. While he received a ticker-tape parade in the U.S., there was no customary invitation to meet Pres. Franklin Roosevelt. "Hitler didn't snub me; it was our president who snubbed me," Owens said.

1964, Tokyo: The Greatest Gymnast Ever?

By the time she appeared at her third straight Olympics in Tokyo, Soviet gymnast Larisa Latynina had amassed 12 medals in Olympic competition: four gold, a silver, and a bronze in Melbourne in 1956 and three gold, two silver, and a bronze in Rome (1960). At age 29, the Ukraine-born Latynina dominated once again in Tokyo, winning two gold, two silver, and two bronze. Her career nine gold medals are the most ever for a gymnast, and her total medal haul of 18 stood as a record for 48 years.

1968, Mexico City: Black Power

U.S. sprinter Tommie Smith broke the world record and won gold in the 200-m event, but his medal ceremony made an even bigger impression. Smith and fellow American John Carlos, who won bronze, ascended the podium shoeless in black socks as a protest against Black poverty. Each man also raised a black-gloved hand, a salute to the "Black power" faction of the civil rights movement. Smith and Carlos were immediately ushered out of the stadium amid jeers and racial epithets, suspended from the U.S. Olympic team, and ordered to return home.

1972, Munich: The Munich Massacre

U.S. swimmer Mark Spitz won a then-record seven gold medals in one Olympiad. Olga Korbut, a 17-year-old Soviet gymnast, ushered in the era of teens dominating the sport. But once again, events outside the athletic arena imprinted the most indelible memory of the Games. Eight militants from the Palestinian group Black September stormed Munich's Olympic Village Sept. 5, killed two members of the Israeli team, and held nine others hostage. Helicopters took the terrorists and hostages to a military base, where a shootout killed all nine hostages and five terrorists. After a 34-hour interval, the Intl. Olympic Committee ordered competition to resume.

1976, Montréal: Perfect Tens

No gymnast had ever received a perfect 10.0 score in any event until 1976, when 14-year-old Nadia Comaneci of Romania did it on the uneven bars. The scoreboard held only three digits, so her score actually appeared as 1.00. She logged a total of seven perfect tens, winning three gold medals, a silver, and a bronze. She remains the youngest all-around gymnastics champion.

1980, Moscow: The Cold War Infiltrates Sports

Despite the protestations of the IOC, the Games have always been political. In 1920, five countries defeated in World War I were not invited to the Antwerp Games. In 1976, 28 African countries boycotted because the IOC refused to ban New Zealand, whose rugby team had toured South Africa despite an informal international embargo because of that country's apartheid policy. The U.S. upped the political ante in 1980 when it refused to participate in the Moscow Games following the 1979 Soviet invasion of Afghanistan. A total of 65 countries joined in the boycott, including Canada and West Germany. Four years later, 14 Eastern bloc nations retaliated by refusing to send teams to the Los Angeles Games.

1984, Los Angeles: A Hollywood Story

When the 1976 Games proved a financial fiasco for Montréal, only Los Angeles bid to host the 1984 Olympics. To avoid the same fate, the L.A. Olympic Organizing Committee and chairman Peter Ueberroth repurposed existing athletic facilities and enlisted dozens of corporate sponsors, creating now-typical claims to be the official car, hamburger, or beverage of the Games. These Games turned a $223-mil profit and remain the only profitable Olympics in history. Gymnast Mary Lou Retton became America's sweetheart after winning five medals, including gold in the all-around. She later became the first woman to grace the front of a Wheaties box.

1992, Barcelona: The Dream Team

Basketball's governing body first allowed U.S. professional athletes to compete in the Olympics in 1992. The "Dream Team" roster included co-captains Magic Johnson and Larry Bird, along with Michael Jordan, Scottie Pippen, John Stockton, Karl Malone, Patrick Ewing, Chris Mullin, David Robinson, Charles Barkley, Clyde Drexler, and Duke's Christian Laettner, the lone collegian. The Dream Team cruised through their games, beating their opponents by an average of nearly 44 points en route to a 117-85 drubbing of Croatia in the gold-medal game.

1996, Atlanta: Violence Mars the Games Again

The Atlanta Games will always be remembered for the terrorist bombing of Centennial Olympic Park that killed two people and injured 110 others. Another lasting image from these Games, however, is coach Bela Karolyi carrying 4'9" gymnast Kerri Strug in his arms to the podium to receive her medal. Despite a severely sprained ankle, Strug propelled the U.S. team to its first team gold medal by nailing her landing in the vault event before collapsing to the floor.

2004, 2008, 2012, 2016: Phenomenal Phelps

"It was about becoming the first Michael Phelps, not the second Mark Spitz," Phelps said after winning eight medals (six gold) at the 2004 Olympics in Athens. Fellow Olympic swimming champion Spitz was soon in Phelps's rearview mirror, as Phelps became the most decorated Olympian in history with 28 medals, including 8 more gold in Beijing (2008), 4 in London (2012), and 5 in Rio de Janeiro (2016). As of 2020, Phelps was still the Olympic record-holder in the 200-m freestyle, 200-m butterfly, 200-m individual medley, and 400-m individual medley, and teams he anchored hold the Olympic records in all three relays.

2008, 2012, 2016: Fastest Man Alive

The winner of the men's 100-m dash is often deemed the fastest man alive. For a century, the only man to successfully defend that title was Carl Lewis (1984, 1988). But in 2008 in Beijing, Jamaican sprinter Usain Bolt cruised to gold (and a new world record) in that event. He also set a new world record in the 200-m sprint. Bolt bested both of his records a year later at the IAAF World Championships, and repeated his Olympic dominance in London in 2012, winning both sprint events and anchoring the 4x100-m relay. In Rio in 2016, Bolt's times were slower but still good enough for gold in all three events once again.

OLYMPIC GAMES

General Olympic Information

The modern Olympic Games, first held in Athens, Greece, in 1896, were the result of efforts by Baron Pierre de Coubertin, a French educator, to promote interest in education and culture and to foster better international understanding through love of athletics. His inspiration was the ancient Greek Olympic Games, most notable of the four Panhellenic celebrations. The games were combined patriotic, religious, and athletic festivals held every four years. The first such recorded festival was held in 776 BCE, when the Greeks began to keep their calendar by "Olympiads," or four-year spans between the games.

Coubertin enlisted 14 nations to send athletes to the first modern Olympics. Now athletes from more than 200 nations and territories compete in the Summer Olympics. The Winter Olympic Games, started in 1924, draw competitors from about 90 countries and territories.

Symbol: Five rings or circles, linked to represent the sporting friendship of all peoples. They also symbolize five geographic areas—Africa, America, Asia, Australia, and Europe. Each ring is a different color—blue, yellow, black, green, and red—which, with the color white, represent the colors of the world's flags.

Flag: The five-ring symbol on a plain white background.

Creed: "The most important thing in the Olympic Games is not to win but to take part, just as the most important thing in life is not the triumph but the struggle. The essential thing is not to have conquered but to have fought well."

Motto: Citius, Altius, Fortius. ("Faster, higher, stronger" in Latin.)

Oath: "In the name of all the competitors I promise that we shall take part in these Olympic Games, respecting and abiding by the rules which govern them, committing ourselves to a sport without doping and without drugs, in the true spirit of sportsmanship, for the glory of sport and the honor of our teams."

Flame: The modern version of the flame was adopted in 1936. The torch used to kindle it is first lit by the sun's rays in Olympia, Greece, then carried to the site of the Games by relays of runners. Ships and planes are used when necessary.

Winter Olympic Games Sites, 1924-2026

1924	Chamonix, France	1956	Cortina d'Ampezzo, Italy	1980	Lake Placid, NY, U.S.	2006	Turin, Italy
1928	St. Moritz, Switzerland			1984	Sarajevo, Yugoslavia	2010	Vancouver, BC, Can.
1932	Lake Placid, NY, U.S.	1960	Squaw Valley, CA, U.S.	1988	Calgary, AB, Canada	2014	Sochi, Russia
1936	Garmisch-Partenkirchen, Germany	1964	Innsbruck, Austria	1992	Albertville, France	2018	Pyeongchang, South Korea
		1968	Grenoble, France	1994	Lillehammer, Norway		
1948	St. Moritz, Switzerland	1972	Sapporo, Japan	1998	Nagano, Japan	2022	Beijing, China
1952	Oslo, Norway	1976	Innsbruck, Austria	2002	Salt Lake City, UT, U.S.	2026	Milan-Cortina, Italy

Summer Olympic Games Sites, 1896-2028

1896	Athens, Greece	1928	Amsterdam, Netherlands	1968	Mexico City, Mexico	2000	Sydney, Australia
1900	Paris, France	1932	Los Angeles, CA, U.S.	1972	Munich, W. Germany	2004	Athens, Greece
1904	St. Louis, MO, U.S.	1936	Berlin, Germany	1976	Montréal, QC, Canada	2008	Beijing, China
1906	Athens, Greece*	1948	London, England, UK	1980	Moscow, USSR	2012	London, England, UK
1908	London, England, UK	1952	Helsinki, Finland	1984	Los Angeles, CA, U.S.	2016	Rio de Janeiro, Brazil
1912	Stockholm, Sweden	1956	Melbourne, Australia	1988	Seoul, South Korea	2020	Tokyo, Japan
1920	Antwerp, Belgium	1960	Rome, Italy	1992	Barcelona, Spain	2024	Paris, France
1924	Paris, France	1964	Tokyo, Japan	1996	Atlanta, GA, U.S.	2028	Los Angeles, CA, U.S.

* = Games not recognized by International Olympic Committee. **Note:** Games VI (1916), XII (1940), and XIII (1944) were not celebrated.

2020 Summer Olympic Games: Preview
Tokyo, Japan, July 23-Aug. 8, 2021

The XXXII Summer Olympics was scheduled to bring the games to Tokyo, Japan, for the first time in over a half-century, with some competitions set to take place on the same sites as the 1964 Games. Five sports (baseball/softball, karate, skateboarding, sport climbing, and surfing) were added to this edition of the Games for a total of 339 medal events across 33 sports. There were also events added in existing sports, including more mixed-gender competitions. More than 11,000 athletes representing 206 nations were expected to compete.

Originally scheduled to be held July 24-Aug. 9, 2020, the Games were postponed by one year in Mar. 2020 because of the coronavirus pandemic. The Games were still formally to be known as the 2020 Summer Olympic Games. The 2020 Summer Paralympic Games were likewise delayed until Aug.-Sept. 2021.

2016 Summer Olympic Games
Rio de Janeiro, Brazil, Aug. 5-21, 2016

The first-ever Olympic Games in South America set records for number of athletes (11,303) and nations participating (206, plus teams composed of refugees and of independent athletes). Thirty-two venues hosted 306 events in 28 different sports.

U.S. swimmer Michael Phelps won five gold medals and one silver, bringing the 31-year-old's career haul to 28 (including 23 gold medals) over four Olympiads. Fellow U.S. swimmer Katie Ledecky was the most decorated female athlete in Rio, with four golds and one silver, along with two new Olympic records. The U.S. cruised to the team gold medal in women's gymnastics behind the performances of 19-year-old Simone Biles and 22-year-old Aly Raisman. Biles and Raisman finished 1-2 in both the floor exercise and the individual all-around competitions; Biles also captured gold in the vault and bronze on the balance beam.

Jamaica's Usain Bolt became the first man in history to win the 100-m run, the 200-m run, and the 4x100-m relay in three consecutive Olympics.

Brazil's national team won its first-ever gold medal in soccer, a balm for months of speculation about whether Brazil could pull off staging the Games. Even in the last days before competition began, concerns lingered about public safety, incomplete facilities, water quality for the sailing and canoeing events, and the threat of Zika virus.

Less than a month before the Games began, the World Anti-Doping Agency released evidence of a comprehensive state-run doping program in Russia, and recommended banning all Russian athletes from the Games. The International Olympic Committee took a less punitive stance, and ultimately cleared more than two-thirds of Russia's contingent to compete at Rio.

2016 Summer Olympic Games: Final Medal Standings

(G = Gold, S = Silver, B = Bronze, T = Total medals)

Country	G	S	B	T	Country	G	S	B	T	Country	G	S	B	T
United States ..	46	37	38	121	Colombia	3	2	3	8	Independent				
China	26	18	26	70	Iran	3	1	4	8	Olympic				
Great Britain ...	27	23	17	67	Serbia........	2	4	2	8	Athletes.....	1	0	1	2
Russia........	19	18	19	56	Turkey........	1	3	4	8	Algeria	0	2	0	2
Germany.......	17	10	15	42	Ethiopia.......	1	2	5	8	Ireland........	0	2	0	2
France.......	10	18	14	42	Switzerland ...	3	2	2	7	India	0	1	1	2
Japan	12	8	21	41	North Korea ...	2	3	2	7	Mongolia	0	1	1	2
Australia	8	11	10	29	Georgia	2	1	4	7	Israel........	0	0	2	2
Italy..........	8	12	8	28	Greece	3	1	2	6	Fiji............	1	0	0	1
Canada.......	4	3	15	22	Belgium.......	2	2	2	6	Jordan........	1	0	0	1
South Korea ...	9	3	9	21	Thailand	2	2	2	6	Kosovo	1	0	0	1
Netherlands ...	8	7	4	19	Romania	1	1	3	5	Puerto Rico...	1	0	0	1
Brazil.........	7	6	6	19	Malaysia	0	4	1	5	Singapore	1	0	0	1
New Zealand ..	4	9	5	18	Mexico	0	3	2	5	Tajikistan......	1	0	0	1
Azerbaijan.....	1	7	10	18	Argentina	3	1	0	4	Burundi	0	1	0	1
Spain	7	4	6	17	Slovakia	2	2	0	4	Grenada	0	1	0	1
Kazakhstan....	3	5	9	17	Armenia	1	3	0	4	Niger.........	0	1	0	1
Hungary	8	3	4	15	Slovenia	1	2	1	4	Philippines ...	0	1	0	1
Denmark.......	2	6	7	15	Lithuania	0	1	3	4	Qatar	0	1	0	1
Kenya	6	6	1	13	Norway	0	0	4	4	Austria	0	0	1	1
Uzbekistan	4	2	7	13	Indonesia	1	2	0	3	Dominican Rep.	0	0	1	1
Jamaica	6	3	2	11	Taiwan	1	0	2	3	Estonia	0	0	1	1
Cuba.........	5	2	4	11	Bulgaria	0	1	2	3	Finland	0	0	1	1
Sweden.......	2	6	3	11	Venezuela.....	0	1	2	3	Moldova	0	0	1	1
Ukraine.......	2	5	4	11	Egypt	0	0	3	3	Morocco	0	0	1	1
Poland	2	3	6	11	Tunisia	0	0	3	3	Nigeria	0	0	1	1
Croatia	5	3	2	10	Bahrain	1	1	0	2	Portugal	0	0	1	1
South Africa ...	2	6	2	10	Vietnam	1	1	0	2	Trinidad and				
Czech Republic	1	2	7	10	The Bahamas..	1	0	1	2	Tobago	0	0	1	1
Belarus.......	1	4	4	9	Côte d'Ivoire...	1	0	1	2	UAE	0	0	1	1

Summer Olympic Games Champions, 1896-2016

* = Olympic record; (w) wind-aided; times are shown in hour:minute:sec.

The 1980 games were boycotted by 62 nations, including the U.S. The 1984 games were boycotted by the USSR and most Eastern bloc nations. East and West Germany competed separately, 1968-88. The 1992 Unified Team consisted of 12 former Soviet republics. The 1992 Independent Olympic Participants (IOP) were from Serbia, Montenegro, and Macedonia.

Not all sports are listed here, and many events are omitted, even within listed sports, particularly if the event has not been held in more recent Games. Point systems for scoring events have changed many times. Points shown are those under the point system in use at the time.

Basketball

Men

1936	United States, Canada, Mexico
1948	United States, France, Brazil
1952	United States, USSR, Uruguay
1956	United States, USSR, Uruguay
1960	United States, USSR, Brazil
1964	United States, USSR, Brazil
1968	United States, Yugoslavia, USSR
1972	USSR, United States, Cuba
1976	United States, Yugoslavia, USSR
1980	Yugoslavia, Italy, USSR
1984	United States, Spain, Yugoslavia

Men

1988	USSR, Yugoslavia, United States
1992	United States, Croatia, Lithuania
1996	United States, Yugoslavia, Lithuania
2000	United States, France, Lithuania
2004	Argentina, Italy, United States
2008	United States, Spain, Argentina
2012	United States, Spain, Russia
2016	United States, Serbia, Spain

Women

1976	USSR, United States, Bulgaria
1980	USSR, Bulgaria, Yugoslavia

Women

1984	United States, South Korea, China
1988	United States, Yugoslavia, USSR
1992	Unified Team, China, United States
1996	United States, Brazil, Australia
2000	United States, Australia, Brazil
2004	United States, Australia, Russia
2008	United States, Australia, Russia
2012	United States, France, Australia
2016	United States, Spain, Serbia

Boxing—Men

Weight class limits have changed many times since the first Olympic boxing events were held in 1904. The limits shown were used in the 2016 Olympic Games. The Super Heavyweight class was known as Heavyweight 1904-80.

Lt. Flyweight (49 kg/108 lbs)

1968	Francisco Rodriguez, Venezuela
1972	Gyorgy Gedo, Hungary
1976	Jorge Hernandez, Cuba
1980	Shamil Sabyrov, USSR
1984	Paul Gonzalez, United States
1988	Ivailo Hristov, Bulgaria
1992	Rogelio Marcelo, Cuba
1996	Daniel Petrov, Bulgaria
2000	Brahim Asloum, France
2004	Yan Bhartelemy Varela, Cuba
2008	Zou Shiming, China
2012	Zou Shiming, China
2016	Hasanboy Dusmatov, Uzbekistan

Flyweight (52 kg/115 lbs)

1904	George Finnegan, United States
1920	Frank Di Gennara, United States
1924	Fidel LaBarba, United States
1928	Antal Kocsis, Hungary
1932	Istvan Enekes, Hungary
1936	Willi Kaiser, Germany
1948	Pascual Perez, Argentina

Flyweight (52 kg/115 lbs)

1952	Nathan Brooks, United States
1956	Terence Spinks, Great Britain
1960	Gyula Török, Hungary
1964	Fernando Atzori, Italy
1968	Ricardo Delgado, Mexico
1972	Georgi Kostadinov, Bulgaria
1976	Leo Randolph, United States
1980	Peter Lesov, Bulgaria
1984	Steve McCrory, United States
1988	Kim Kwang-sun, S. Korea
1992	Choi Chol Su, N. Korea
1996	Maikro Romero, Cuba
2000	Wijan Ponlid, Thailand
2004	Yuriorkis Gamboa Toledano, Cuba
2008	Somjit Jongjohor, Thailand
2012	Robeisy Ramírez, Cuba
2016	Shakhobidin Zoirov, Uzbekistan

Bantamweight (56 kg/123 lbs)

1904	Oliver Kirk, United States
1908	A. Henry Thomas, Great Britain
1920	Clarence Walker, South Africa

Bantamweight (56 kg/123 lbs)

1924	William Smith, South Africa
1928	Vittorio Tamagnini, Italy
1932	Horace Gwynne, Canada
1936	Ulderico Sergo, Italy
1948	Tibor Csik, Hungary
1952	Pentti Hamalainen, Finland
1956	Wolfgang Behrendt, E. Germany
1960	Oleg Grigoryev, USSR
1964	Takao Sakurai, Japan
1968	Valery Sokolov, USSR
1972	Orlando Martinez, Cuba
1976	Gu Yong Ju, N. Korea
1980	Juan Hernandez, Cuba
1984	Maurizio Stecca, Italy
1988	Kennedy McKinney, United States
1992	Joel Casamayor, Cuba
1996	Istvan Kovacs, Hungary
2000	Guillermo Rigondeaux, Cuba
2004	Guillermo Rigondeaux, Cuba
2008	Badar-Uugan Enkhbat, Mongolia

Bantamweight (56 kg/123 lbs)
2012 Luke Campbell, Great Britain
2016 Robeisy Ramírez, Cuba

Featherweight (57 kg/125 lbs)
1904 Oliver Kirk, United States
1908 Richard Gunn, Great Britain
1920 Paul Fritsch, France
1924 John Fields, United States
1928 Lambertus van Klaveren, Netherlands
1932 Carmelo Robledo, Argentina
1936 Oscar Casanovas, Argentina
1948 Ernesto Formenti, Italy
1952 Jan Zachara, Czechoslovakia
1956 Vladimir Safronov, USSR
1960 Francesco Musso, Italy
1964 Stanislav Stephashkin, USSR
1968 Antonio Roldan, Mexico
1972 Boris Kousnetsov, USSR
1976 Angel Herrera, Cuba
1980 Rudi Fink, E. Germany
1984 Meldrick Taylor, United States
1988 Giovanni Parisi, Italy
1992 Andreas Tews, Germany
1996 Somluck Kamsing, Thailand
2000 Bekzat Sattarkhanov, Kazakhstan
2004 Alexey Tishchenko, Russia
2008 Vasyl Lomachenko, Ukraine

Lightweight (60 kg/132 lbs)
1904 Harry Spanger, United States
1908 Frederick Grace, Great Britain
1920 Samuel Mosberg, United States
1924 Hans Nielsen, Denmark
1928 Carlo Orlandi, Italy
1932 Lawrence Stevens, South Africa
1936 Imre Harangi, Hungary
1948 Gerald Dreyer, South Africa
1952 Aureliano Bolognesi, Italy
1956 Richard McTaggart, Great Britain
1960 Kazimierz Pazdzior, Poland
1964 Jozef Grudzien, Poland
1968 Ronald Harris, United States
1972 Jan Szczepanski, Poland
1976 Howard Davis, United States
1980 Angel Herrera, Cuba
1984 Pernell Whitaker, United States
1988 Andreas Zülow, E. Germany
1992 Oscar De La Hoya, United States
1996 Hocine Soltani, Algeria
2000 Mario Kindelan, Cuba
2004 Mario Kindelan, Cuba
2008 Alexey Tishchenko, Russia
2012 Vasyl Lomachenko, Ukraine
2016 Robson Conceição, Brazil

Lt. Welterweight (64 kg/141 lbs)
1952 Charles Adkins, United States
1956 Vladimir Yengibaryan, USSR
1960 Bohumil Nemecek, Czechoslovakia
1964 Jerzy Kulej, Poland
1968 Jerzy Kulej, Poland
1972 Ray Seales, United States
1976 Ray Leonard, United States
1980 Patrizio Oliva, Italy
1984 Jerry Page, United States
1988 Viatcheslav Janovski, USSR
1992 Hector Vinent, Cuba
1996 Hector Vinent, Cuba

Lt. Welterweight (64 kg/141 lbs)
2000 Mahamadkadyz Abdullaev, Uzbekistan
2004 Manus Boonjumnong, Thailand
2008 Felix Diaz, Dominican Republic
2012 Roniel Iglesias, Cuba
2016 Fazliddin Gaibnazarov, Uzbekistan

Welterweight (69 kg/152 lbs)
1904 Albert Young, United States
1920 Albert Schneider, Canada
1924 Jean Delarge, Belgium
1928 Edward Morgan, New Zealand
1932 Edward Flynn, United States
1936 Sten Suvio, Finland
1948 Julius Torma, Czechoslovakia
1952 Zygmunt Chychia, Poland
1956 Nicolae Linca, Romania
1960 Giovanni Benvenuti, Italy
1964 Marian Kasprzyk, Poland
1968 Manfred Wolke, E. Germany
1972 Emilio Correa, Cuba
1976 Jochen Bachfeld, E. Germany
1980 Andres Aldama, Cuba
1984 Mark Breland, United States
1988 Robert Wangila, Kenya
1992 Michael Carruth, Ireland
1996 Oleg Saitov, Russia
2000 Oleg Saitov, Russia
2004 Bakhtiyar Artayev, Kazakhstan
2008 Bakhyt Sarsekbayev, Kazakhstan
2012 Serik Sapiyev, Kazakhstan
2016 Daniyar Yeleussinov, Kazakhstan

Lt. Middleweight (71 kg/156 lbs)
1952 Laszlo Papp, Hungary
1956 Laszlo Papp, Hungary
1960 Wilbert McClure, United States
1964 Boris Lagutin, USSR
1968 Boris Lagutin, USSR
1972 Dieter Kottysch, W. Germany
1976 Jerzy Rybicki, Poland
1980 Armando Martinez, Cuba
1984 Frank Tate, United States
1988 Park Si-hun, S. Korea
1992 Juan Lemus, Cuba
1996 David Reid, United States
2000 Yermakhan Ibraimov, Kazakhstan

Middleweight (75 kg/165 lbs)
1904 Charles Mayer, United States
1908 John Douglas, Great Britain
1920 Harry Mallin, Great Britain
1924 Harry Mallin, Great Britain
1928 Piero Toscani, Italy
1932 Carmen Barth, United States
1936 Jean Despeaux, France
1948 Laszlo Papp, Hungary
1952 Floyd Patterson, United States
1956 Gennady Schatkov, USSR
1960 Edward Crook, United States
1964 Valery Popenchenko, USSR
1968 Christopher Finnegan, Great Britain
1972 Vyacheslav Lemechev, USSR
1976 Michael Spinks, United States
1980 Jose Gomez, Cuba
1984 Shin Joon-sup, S. Korea
1988 Henry Maske, E. Germany
1992 Ariel Hernandez, Cuba
1996 Ariel Hernandez, Cuba
2000 Jorge Gutierrez, Cuba
2004 Gaydarbek Gaydarbekov, Russia
2008 James Degale, Great Britain

Middleweight (75 kg/165 lbs)
2012 Ryota Murata, Japan
2016 Arlen López, Cuba

Lt. Heavyweight (81 kg/179 lbs)
1920 Edward Eagan, United States
1924 Harry Mitchell, Great Britain
1928 Victor Avendaño, Argentina
1932 David Carstens, South Africa
1936 Roger Michelot, France
1948 George Hunter, South Africa
1952 Norvel Lee, United States
1956 James Boyd, United States
1960 Cassius Clay, United States
1964 Cosimo Pinto, Italy
1968 Dan Poznyak, USSR
1972 Mate Parlov, Yugoslavia
1976 Leon Spinks, United States
1980 Slobodan Kacar, Yugoslavia
1984 Anton Josipovic, Yugoslavia
1988 Andrew Maynard, United States
1992 Torsten May, Germany
1996 Vassili Jirov, Kazakhstan
2000 Alexander Lebziak, Russia
2004 Andre Ward, United States
2008 Zhang Xiaoping, China
2012 Yegor Mekhontsev, Russia
2016 Julio César la Cruz, Cuba

Heavyweight (91 kg/201 lbs)
1984 Henry Tillman, United States
1988 Ray Mercer, United States
1992 Felix Savon, Cuba
1996 Felix Savon, Cuba
2000 Felix Savon, Cuba
2004 Odlanier Solis Fonte, Cuba
2008 Rakhim Chakhkiev, Russia
2012 Oleksandr Usik, Ukraine
2016 Evgeny Tishchenko, Russia

Super Heavyweight (91+ kg/201+ lbs)
1904 Samuel Berger, United States
1908 Albert Oldham, Great Britain
1920 Ronald Rawson, Great Britain
1924 Otto von Porat, Norway
1928 Arturo Rodriguez Jurado, Argentina
1932 Santiago Lovell, Argentina
1936 Herbert Runge, Germany
1948 Rafael Iglesias, Argentina
1952 H. Edward Sanders, United States
1956 T. Peter Rademacher, United States
1960 Franco De Piccoli, Italy
1964 Joe Frazier, United States
1968 George Foreman, United States
1972 Teofilo Stevenson, Cuba
1976 Teofilo Stevenson, Cuba
1980 Teofilo Stevenson, Cuba
1984 Tyrell Biggs, United States
1988 Lennox Lewis, Canada
1992 Roberto Balado, Cuba
1996 Vladimir Klitchko, Ukraine
2000 Audley Harrison, Great Britain
2004 Alexander Povetkin, Russia
2008 Roberto Cammarelle, Italy
2012 Anthony Joshua, Great Britain
2016 Tony Yoka, France

Boxing—Women

Flyweight (51 kg/112 lbs)
2012 Nicola Adams, Great Britain
2016 Nicola Adams, Great Britain

Lightweight (60 kg/132 lbs)
2012 Katie Taylor, Ireland
2016 Estelle Mossely, France

Middleweight (75 kg/165 lbs)
2012 Claressa Shields, United States
2016 Claressa Shields, United States

Gymnastics—Men

Floor Exercise
1932 István Pelle, Hungary
1936 Georges Miez, Switzerland
1948 Ferenc Pataki, Hungary
1952 William Thoresson, Sweden
1956 Valentin Muratov, USSR
1960 Nobuyuki Aihara, Japan
1964 Franco Menichelli, Italy
1968 Sawao Kato, Japan

Floor Exercise
1972 Nikolay Andrianov, USSR
1976 Nikolay Andrianov, USSR
1980 Roland Brückner, E. Germany
1984 Li Ning, China
1988 Sergei Kharkov, USSR
1992 Li Xiaoshuang, China
1996 Ioannis Melissanidis, Greece
2000 Igors Vihrovs, Latvia

Floor Exercise
2004 Kyle Shewfelt, Canada
2008 Zou Kai, China
2012 Zou Kai, China
2016 Max Whitlock, Great Britain

Horizontal Bar
1896 Hermann Weingärtner, Germany
1904 Anton Heida, United States;
Edward Hennig, United States (tie)

Gymnastics—Men

Horizontal Bar

1924	Leon Stukelj, Yugoslavia
1928	Georges Miez, Switzerland
1932	Dallas Denver Bixler, United States
1936	Aleksanteri Saarvala, Finland
1948	Josef Stalder, Switzerland
1952	Jakob "Jack" Günthard, Switzerland
1956	Takashi Ono, Japan
1960	Takashi Ono, Japan
1964	Boris Shakhlin, USSR
1968	Akinori Nakayama, Japan; Mikhail Voronin, USSR (tie)
1972	Mitsuo Tsukahara, Japan
1976	Mitsuo Tsukahara, Japan
1980	Stoyan Deltchev, Bulgaria
1984	Shinji Morisue, Japan
1988	Vladimir Artemov, USSR; Valeri Liukin, USSR (tie)
1992	Trent Dimas, United States
1996	Andreas Wecker, Germany
2000	Alexei Nemov, Russia
2004	Igor Cassina, Italy
2008	Zou Kai, China
2012	Epke Zonderland, Netherlands
2016	Fabian Hambüchen, Germany

Individual All-Around

1900	Gustave Sandras, France
1904	Julius Lenhart, United States
1908	G. Alberto Braglia, Italy
1912	G. Alberto Braglia, Italy
1920	Giorgio Zampori, Italy
1924	Leon Stukelj, Yugoslavia
1928	Georges Miez, Switzerland
1932	Romeo Neri, Italy
1936	Karl-Alfred Schwarzmann, Germany
1948	Veikko Huhtanen, Finland
1952	Viktor Ivanovich Chukarin, USSR
1956	Viktor Ivanovich Chukarin, USSR
1960	Boris Shakhlin, USSR
1964	Yukio Endo, Japan
1968	Sawao Kato, Japan
1972	Sawao Kato, Japan
1976	Nikolay Andrianov, USSR
1980	Aleksandr Dityatin, USSR
1984	Koji Gushiken, Japan
1988	Vladimir Artemov, USSR
1992	Vitaly Scherbo, Unified Team (Belarus)
1996	Li Xiaoshuang, China
2000	Alexei Nemov, Russia
2004	Paul Hamm, United States
2008	Yang Wei, China
2012	Kohei Uchimura, Japan
2016	Kohei Uchimura, Japan

Parallel Bars

1896	Alfred Flatow, Germany
1904	George Eyser, United States
1924	August Güttinger, Switzerland
1928	Ladislav Vacha, Czechoslovakia
1932	Romeo Neri, Italy
1936	Konrad Frey, Germany
1948	Michael Reusch, Switzerland
1952	Hans Eugster, Switzerland
1956	Viktor Ivanovich Chukarin, USSR
1960	Boris Shakhlin, USSR
1964	Yukio Endo, Japan
1968	Akinori Nakayama, Japan
1972	Sawao Kato, Japan
1976	Sawao Kato, Japan
1980	Aleksandr Tkachev, USSR
1984	Bart Conner, United States
1988	Vladimir Artemov, USSR
1992	Vitaly Scherbo, Unified Team (Belarus)
1996	Roustam Sharipov, Ukraine
2000	Li Xiaopeng, China
2004	Valeri Goncharov, Ukraine
2008	Li Xiaopeng, China
2012	Feng Zhe, China
2016	Oleg Verniaiev, Ukraine

Pommel Horse

1896	Louis Zutter, Switzerland
1904	Anton Heida, United States
1924	Josef Wilhelm, Switzerland
1928	Hermann Hänggi, Switzerland
1932	István Pelle, Hungary
1936	Konrad Frey, Germany
1948	Paavo Johannes Aaltonen, Finland; Veikko Huhtanen, Finland; Heikki Savolainen, Finland (tie)
1952	Viktor Ivanovich Chukarin, USSR
1956	Boris Shakhlin, USSR
1960	Eugen Georg Oskar Ekman, Finland; Boris Shakhlin, USSR (tie)
1964	Miroslav Cerar, Yugoslavia
1968	Miroslav Cerar, Yugoslavia
1972	Viktor Klimenko, USSR
1976	Zoltan Magyar, Hungary
1980	Zoltan Magyar, Hungary
1984	Li Ning, China; Peter Glen Vidmar, United States (tie)
1988	Dmitri Bilozerchev, USSR; Zsolt Borkai, Hungary; Lubomir Geraskov, Bulgaria (tie)
1992	Pae Gil Su, N. Korea; Vitaly Scherbo, Unified Team (Belarus) (tie)
1996	Li Donghua, Switzerland
2000	Marius Daniel Urzica, Romania
2004	Teng Haibin, China
2008	Xiao Qin, China
2012	Krisztián Berki, Hungary
2016	Max Whitlock, Great Britain

Rings

1896	Ioannis Mitropoulos, Greece
1904	Hermann Glass, United States
1924	Francesco Martino, Italy
1928	Leon Stukelj, Yugoslavia
1932	George Gulack, United States
1936	Alois Hudec, Czechoslovakia
1948	Karl Frei, Switzerland
1952	Grant Shaginyan, USSR
1956	Albert Azaryan, USSR
1960	Albert Azaryan, USSR
1964	Takuji Hayata, Japan
1968	Akinori Nakayama, Japan
1972	Akinori Nakayama, Japan
1976	Nikolay Andrianov, USSR
1980	Aleksandr Dityatin, USSR
1984	Koji Gushiken, Japan; Li Ning, China (tie)
1988	Holger Behrendt, E. Germany; Dmitri Bilozerchev, USSR (tie)
1992	Vitaly Scherbo, Unified Team (Belarus)
1996	Juri Chechi, Italy
2000	Szilveszter Csollany, Hungary
2004	Dimosthenis Tampakos, Greece
2008	Chen Yibing, China
2012	Arthur Zanetti, Brazil
2016	Eleftherios Petrounias, Greece

Team Competition

1904	United States, United States, United States
1908	Sweden, Norway, Finland
1912	Italy, Hungary, Great Britain
1920	Italy, Belgium, France
1924	Italy, France, Switzerland
1928	Switzerland, Czechoslovakia, Yugoslavia
1932	Italy, United States, Finland
1936	Germany, Switzerland, Finland
1948	Finland, Switzerland, Hungary
1952	USSR, Switzerland, Finland
1956	USSR, Japan, Finland
1960	Japan, USSR, Italy
1964	Japan, USSR, Unified Team of Germany
1968	Japan, USSR, E. Germany
1972	Japan, USSR, E. Germany
1976	Japan, USSR, E. Germany
1980	USSR, E. Germany, Hungary
1984	United States, China, Japan
1988	USSR, E. Germany, Japan
1992	Unified Team, China, Japan
1996	Russia, China, Ukraine
2000	China, Ukraine, Russia
2004	Japan, United States, Romania
2008	China, Japan, United States
2012	China, Japan, Great Britain
2016	Japan, Russia, China

Vault

1896	Carl Schuhmann, Germany
1904	George Eyser, United States; Anton Heida, United States (tie)
1924	Frank Kriz, United States
1928	Eugen Mack, Switzerland
1932	Savino Guglielmetti, Italy
1936	Karl-Alfred Schwarzmann, Germany
1948	Paavo Johannes Aaltonen, Finland
1952	Viktor Ivanovich Chukarin, USSR
1956	Helmut Bantz, Unified Team of Germany; Valentin Muratov, USSR (tie)
1960	Takashi Ono, Japan; Boris Shakhlin, USSR (tie)
1964	Haruhiro Yamashita, Japan
1968	Mikhail Voronin, USSR
1972	Klaus Köste, E. Germany
1976	Nikolay Andrianov, USSR
1980	Nikolay Andrianov, USSR
1984	Lou Yun, China
1988	Lou Yun, China
1992	Vitaly Scherbo, Unified Team (Belarus)
1996	Alexei Nemov, Russia
2000	Gervasio Deferr, Spain
2004	Gervasio Deferr, Spain
2008	Leszek Blanik, Poland
2012	Yang Hak-seon, South Korea
2016	Ri Se Gwang, North Korea

Gymnastics—Women

Balance Beam

1952	Nina Bocharova, USSR
1956	Agnes Keleti, Hungary
1960	Eva Vechtova-Bosakova, Czechoslovakia
1964	Vera Caslavska, Czechoslovakia
1968	Natalya Kuchinskaya, USSR
1972	Olga Korbut, USSR
1976	Nadia Comaneci, Romania
1980	Nadia Comaneci, Romania
1984	Ecaterina Szabo, Romania; Simona Pauca, Romania (tie)
1988	Daniela Silivas, Romania
1992	Tatiana Lyssenko, Unified Team (Ukraine)
1996	Shannon Miller, United States
2000	Liu Xuan, China
2004	Catalina Ponor, Romania
2008	Shawn Johnson, United States
2012	Deng Linlin, China
2016	Sanne Wevers, Netherlands

Floor Exercise

1952	Agnes Keleti, Hungary
1956	Agnes Keleti, Hungary; Larisa Latynina, USSR (tie)
1960	Larisa Latynina, USSR
1964	Larisa Latynina, USSR

Floor Exercise
1968	Vera Caslavska, Czechoslovakia; Larisa Petrik, USSR (tie)
1972	Olga Korbut, USSR
1976	Nelli Kim, USSR
1980	Nelli Kim, USSR; Nadia Comaneci, Romania (tie)
1984	Ecaterina Szabo, Romania
1988	Daniela Silivas, Romania
1992	Lavinia Milosovici, Romania
1996	Lilia Podkopayeva, Ukraine
2000	Elena Zamolodchikova, Russia
2004	Catalina Ponor, Romania
2008	Sandra Izbasa, Romania
2012	Aly Raisman, United States
2016	Simone Biles, United States

Individual All-Around
1952	Mariya Gorokhovskaya, USSR
1956	Larisa Latynina, USSR
1960	Larisa Latynina, USSR
1964	Vera Caslavska, Czechoslovakia
1968	Vera Caslavska, Czechoslovakia
1972	Lyudmila Turischeva, USSR
1976	Nadia Comaneci, Romania
1980	Elena Davydova, USSR
1984	Mary-Lou Retton, United States
1988	Elena Shushunova, USSR
1992	Tatiana Gutsu, Unified Team (Ukraine)
1996	Lilia Podkopayeva, Ukraine
2000	Simona Amanar, Romania
2004	Carly Patterson, United States
2008	Nastia Liukin, United States
2012	Gabby Douglas, United States
2016	Simone Biles, United States

Team Competition
1928	Netherlands, Italy, Great Britain
1936	Germany, Czechoslovakia, Hungary
1948	Czechoslovakia, Hungary, United States
1952	USSR, Hungary, Czechoslovakia
1956	USSR, Hungary, Romania
1960	USSR, Czechoslovakia, Romania
1964	USSR, Czechoslovakia, Japan
1968	USSR, Czechoslovakia, E. Germany
1972	USSR, E. Germany, Hungary
1976	USSR, Romania, E. Germany
1980	USSR, Romania, E. Germany
1984	Romania, United States, China
1988	USSR, Romania, E. Germany
1992	Unified Team, Romania, United States
1996	United States, Russia, Romania
2000	Romania, Russia, United States
2004	Romania, United States, Russia
2008	China, United States, Romania
2012	United States, Russia, Romania
2016	United States, Russia, China

Uneven Bars
1952	Margit Korondi, Hungary
1956	Agnes Keleti, Hungary
1960	Polina Astakhova, USSR
1964	Polina Astakhova, USSR
1968	Vera Caslavska, Czechoslovakia
1972	Karin Janz, E. Germany

Uneven Bars
1976	Nadia Comaneci, Romania
1980	Maxi Gnauck, E. Germany
1984	Julianne McNamara, United States; Yan-Hong Ma, China (tie)
1988	Daniela Silivas, Romania
1992	Lu Li, China
1996	Svetlana Khorkina, Russia
2000	Svetlana Khorkina, Russia
2004	Emilie LePennec, France
2008	He Kexin, China
2012	Aliya Mustafina, Russia
2016	Aliya Mustafina, Russia

Vault
1952	Ekaterina Kalinchuk, USSR
1956	Larisa Latynina, USSR
1960	Margarita Nikolaeva, USSR
1964	Vera Caslavska, Czechoslovakia
1968	Vera Caslavska, Czechoslovakia
1972	Karin Janz, E. Germany
1976	Nelli Kim, USSR
1980	Natalia Shaposhnikova, USSR
1984	Ecaterina Szabo, Romania
1988	Svetlana Boginskaya, USSR
1992	Henrietta Onodi, Hungary; Lavinia Milosovici, Romania (tie)
1996	Simona Amanar, Romania
2000	Elena Zamolodchikova, Russia
2004	Monica Rosu, Romania
2008	Hong Un Jong, N. Korea
2012	Sandra Izbasa, Romania
2016	Simone Biles, United States

Soccer

Men
1900	Great Britain, France, Belgium
1904	Canada, United States, United States
1908	Great Britain, Denmark, Netherlands
1912	Great Britain, Denmark, Netherlands
1920	Belgium, Spain, Netherlands
1924	Uruguay, Switzerland, Sweden
1928	Uruguay, Argentina, Italy
1936	Italy, Austria, Norway
1948	Sweden, Yugoslavia, Denmark
1952	Hungary, Yugoslavia, Sweden
1956	USSR, Yugoslavia, Bulgaria
1960	Yugoslavia, Denmark, Hungary
1964	Hungary, Czechoslovakia, Unified Team of Germany
1968	Hungary, Bulgaria, Japan
1972	Poland; Hungary; USSR, E. Germany (tie for bronze)
1976	E. Germany, Poland, USSR

Men
1980	Czechoslovakia, E. Germany, USSR
1984	France, Brazil, Yugoslavia
1988	USSR, Brazil, W. Germany
1992	Spain, Poland, Ghana
1996	Nigeria, Argentina, Brazil
2000	Cameroon, Spain, Chile
2004	Argentina, Paraguay, Italy
2008	Argentina, Nigeria, Brazil
2012	Mexico, Brazil, South Korea
2016	Brazil, Germany, Nigeria

Women
1996	United States, China, Norway
2000	Norway, United States, Germany
2004	United States, Brazil, Germany
2008	United States, Brazil, Germany
2012	United States, Japan, Canada
2016	Germany, Sweden, Canada

Swimming and Diving—Men

50-Meter Freestyle
		Time
1988	Matt Biondi, United States	0:22.14
1992	Aleksandr Popov, Unified Team (Rus.)	0:21.91
1996	Aleksandr Popov, Russia	0:22.13
2000	Anthony Ervin, United States	0:21.98
	Gary Hall Jr., United States (tie)	0:21.98
2004	Gary Hall Jr., United States	0:21.93
2008	Cesar Cielo Filho, Brazil	0:21.30*
2012	Florent Manaudou, France	0:21.34
2016	Anthony Ervin, United States	0:21.40

100-Meter Freestyle
		Time
1896	Alfred Hajos, Hungary	1:22.2
1904	Zoltan de Halmay, Hungary (100 yds)	1:02.8
1908	Charles Daniels, United States	1:05.6
1912	Duke P. Kahanamoku, United States	1:03.4
1920	Duke P. Kahanamoku, United States	1:01.4
1924	Johnny Weissmuller, United States	0:59.0
1928	Johnny Weissmuller, United States	0:58.6
1932	Yasuji Miyazaki, Japan	0:58.2
1936	Ferenc Csik, Hungary	0:57.6
1948	Wally Ris, United States	0:57.3
1952	Clarke Scholes, United States	0:57.4
1956	Jon Henricks, Australia	0:55.4
1960	John Devitt, Australia	0:55.2
1964	Don Schollander, United States	0:53.4
1968	Mike Wenden, United States	0:52.2
1972	Mark Spitz, United States	0:51.22
1976	Jim Montgomery, United States	0:49.99
1980	Jorg Woithe, E. Germany	0:50.40
1984	Ambrose "Rowdy" Gaines, United States	0:49.80

100-Meter Freestyle
		Time
1988	Matt Biondi, United States	0:48.63
1992	Aleksandr Popov, Unified Team (Rus.)	0:49.02
1996	Aleksandr Popov, Russia	0:48.74
2000	Pieter van den Hoogenband, Netherlands	0:48.30
2004	Pieter van den Hoogenband, Netherlands	0:48.17
2008	Alain Bernard, France	0:47.21
2012	Nathan Adrian, United States	0:47.52
2016	Kyle Chalmers, Australia	0:47.58

200-Meter Freestyle
		Time
1968	Mike Wenden, Australia	1:55.2
1972	Mark Spitz, United States	1:52.78
1976	Bruce Furniss, United States	1:50.29
1980	Sergei Kopliakov, USSR	1:49.81
1984	Michael Gross, W. Germany	1:47.44
1988	Duncan Armstrong, Australia	1:47.25
1992	Yevgeny Sadovyi, Unified Team (Rus.)	1:46.70
1996	Danyon Loader, New Zealand	1:47.63
2000	Pieter van den Hoogenband, Netherlands	1:45.35
2004	Ian Thorpe, Australia	1:44.71
2008	Michael Phelps, United States	1:42.96*
2012	Yannick Agnel, France	1:43.14
2016	Sun Yang, China	1:44.65

400-Meter Freestyle
		Time
1904	C. M. Daniels, United States (440 yds)	6:16.2
1908	Henry Taylor, Great Britain	5:36.8
1912	George Hodgson, Canada	5:24.4
1920	Norman Ross, United States	5:26.8

400-Meter Freestyle	Time
1924 Johnny Weissmuller, United States	5:04.2
1928 Albert Zorilla, Argentina	5:01.6
1932 Clarence Crabbe, United States	4:48.4
1936 Jack Medica, United States	4:44.5
1948 William Smith, United States	4:41.0
1952 Jean Boiteux, France	4:30.7
1956 Murray Rose, Australia	4:27.3
1960 Murray Rose, Australia	4:18.3
1964 Don Schollander, United States	4:12.2
1968 Mike Burton, United States	4:09.0
1972 Brad Cooper, Australia	4:00.27
1976 Brian Goodell, United States	3:51.93
1980 Vladimir Salnikov, USSR	3:51.31
1984 George DiCarlo, United States	3:51.23
1988 Uwe Dassler, E. Germany	3:46.95
1992 Yevgeny Sadovyi, Unified Team (Rus.)	3:45.00
1996 Danyon Loader, New Zealand	3:47.97
2000 Ian Thorpe, Australia	3:40.59
2004 Ian Thorpe, Australia	3:43.10
2008 Park Tae-hwan, S. Korea	3:41.86
2012 Sun Yang, China	3:40.14*
2016 Mack Horton, Australia	3:41.55

1500-Meter Freestyle	Time
1908 Henry Taylor, Great Britain	22:48.4
1912 George Hodgson, Canada	22:00.0
1920 Norman Ross, United States	22:23.2
1924 Andrew Charlton, Australia	20:06.6
1928 Arne Borg, Sweden	19:51.8
1932 Kusuo Kitamura, Japan	19:12.4
1936 Noboru Terada, Japan	19:13.7
1948 James McLane, United States	19:18.5
1952 Ford Konno, United States	18:30.3
1956 Murray Rose, Australia	17:58.9
1960 John Konrads, Australia	17:19.6
1964 Robert Windle, Australia	17:01.7
1968 Mike Burton, United States	16:38.9
1972 Mike Burton, United States	15:52.58
1976 Brian Goodell, United States	15:02.40
1980 Vladimir Salnikov, USSR	14:58.27
1984 Michael O'Brien, United States	15:05.20
1988 Vladimir Salnikov, USSR	15:00.40
1992 Kieren Perkins, Australia	14:43.48
1996 Kieren Perkins, Australia	14:56.40
2000 Grant Hackett, Australia	14:48.33
2004 Grant Hackett, Australia	14:43.40
2008 Oussama Mellouli, Tunisia	14:40.84
2012 Sun Yang, China	14:31.02*
2016 Gregorio Paltrinieri, Italy	14:34.57

100-Meter Backstroke	Time
1904 Walter Brack, Germany (100 yds)	1:16.8
1908 Arno Bieberstein, Germany	1:24.6
1912 Harry Hebner, United States	1:21.2
1920 Warren Kealoha, United States	1:15.2
1924 Warren Kealoha, United States	1:13.2
1928 George Kojac, United States	1:08.2
1932 Masaji Kiyokawa, Japan	1:08.6
1936 Adolph Kiefer, United States	1:05.9
1948 Allen Stack, United States	1:06.4
1952 Yoshi Oyakawa, United States	1:05.4
1956 David Theile, Australia	1:02.2
1960 David Theile, Australia	1:01.9
1968 Roland Matthes, E. Germany	0:58.7
1972 Roland Matthes, E. Germany	0:56.58
1976 John Naber, United States	0:55.49
1980 Bengt Baron, Sweden	0:56.33
1984 Rick Carey, United States	0:55.79
1988 Daichi Suzuki, Japan	0:55.05
1992 Mark Tewksbury, Canada	0:53.98
1996 Jeff Rouse, United States	0:54.10
2000 Lenny Krayzelburg, United States	0:53.72
2004 Aaron Peirsol, United States	0:54.06
2008 Aaron Peirsol, United States	0:52.54
2012 Matt Grevers, United States	0:52.16
2016 Ryan Murphy, United States	0:51.97*

200-Meter Backstroke	Time
1964 Jed Graef, United States	2:10.3
1968 Roland Matthes, E. Germany	2:09.6
1972 Roland Matthes, E. Germany	2:02.82
1976 John Naber, United States	1:59.19
1980 Sandor Wladar, Hungary	2:01.93
1984 Rick Carey, United States	2:00.23
1988 Igor Polyanski, USSR	1:59.37
1992 Martin Lopez-Zubero, Spain	1:58.47
1996 Brad Bridgewater, United States	1:58.54
2000 Lenny Krayzelburg, United States	1:56.76
2004 Aaron Peirsol, United States	1:54.95

200-Meter Backstroke	Time
2008 Ryan Lochte, United States	1:53.94
2012 Tyler Clary, United States	1:53.41*
2016 Ryan Murphy, United States	1:53.62

100-Meter Breaststroke	Time
1968 Don McKenzie, United States	1:07.79
1972 Nobutaka Taguchi, Japan	1:04.94
1976 John Hencken, United States	1:03.11
1980 Duncan Goodhew, Great Britain	1:03.44
1984 Steve Lundquist, United States	1:01.65
1988 Adrian Moorhouse, Great Britain	1:02.04
1992 Nelson Diebel, United States	1:01.50
1996 Fred Deburghgraeve, Belgium	1:00.60
2000 Domenico Fioravanti, Italy	1:00.46
2004 Kosuke Kitajima, Japan	1:00.08
2008 Kosuke Kitajima, Japan	0:58.91
2012 Cameron van der Burgh, South Africa	0:58.46
2016 Adam Peaty, Great Britain	0:57.13*

200-Meter Breaststroke	Time
1908 Frederick Holman, Great Britain	3:09.2
1912 Walter Bathe, Germany	3:01.8
1920 Hakan Malmrot, Sweden	3:04.4
1924 Robert Skelton, United States	2:56.6
1928 Yoshiyuki Tsuruta, Japan	2:48.8
1932 Yoshiyuki Tsuruta, Japan	2:45.4
1936 Tetsuo Hamuro, Japan	2:41.5
1948 Joseph Verdeur, United States	2:39.3
1952 John Davies, Australia	2:34.4
1956 Masura Furukawa, Japan	2:34.7
1960 William Mulliken, United States	2:37.4
1964 Ian O'Brien, Australia	2:27.8
1968 Felipe Muñoz, Mexico	2:28.7
1972 John Hencken, United States	2:21.55
1976 David Wilkie, Great Britain	2:15.11
1980 Robertas Zhulpa, USSR	2:15.85
1984 Victor Davis, Canada	2:13.34
1988 Jozsef Szabo, Hungary	2:13.52
1992 Mike Barrowman, United States	2:10.16
1996 Norbert Rozsa, Hungary	2:12.57
2000 Domenico Fioravanti, Italy	2:10.87
2004 Kosuke Kitajima, Japan	2:09.44
2008 Kosuke Kitajima, Japan	2:07.64
2012 Dániel Gyurta, Hungary	2:07.28
2016 Dmitriy Balandin, Kazakhstan	2:07.46

100-Meter Butterfly	Time
1968 Doug Russell, United States	0:55.9
1972 Mark Spitz, United States	0:54.27
1976 Matt Vogel, United States	0:54.35
1980 Par Arvidsson, Sweden	0:54.92
1984 Michael Gross, W. Germany	0:53.08
1988 Anthony Nesty, Suriname	0:53.00
1992 Pablo Morales, United States	0:53.32
1996 Denis Pankratov, Russia	0:52.27
2000 Lars Froelander, Sweden	0:52.00
2004 Michael Phelps, United States	0:51.25
2008 Michael Phelps, United States	0:50.58
2012 Michael Phelps, United States	0:51.21
2016 Joseph Schooling, Singapore	0:50.39*

200-Meter Butterfly	Time
1956 William Yorzyk, United States	2:19.3
1960 Michael Troy, United States	2:12.8
1964 Kevin J. Berry, Australia	2:06.6
1968 Carl Robie, United States	2:08.7
1972 Mark Spitz, United States	2:00.70
1976 Mike Bruner, United States	1:59.23
1980 Sergei Fesenko, USSR	1:59.76
1984 Jon Sieben, Australia	1:57.04
1988 Michael Gross, W. Germany	1:56.94
1992 Mel Stewart, United States	1:56.26
1996 Denis Pankratov, Russia	1:56.51
2000 Tom Malchow, United States	1:55.35
2004 Michael Phelps, United States	1:54.04
2008 Michael Phelps, United States	1:52.03*
2012 Chad le Clos, South Africa	1:52.96
2016 Michael Phelps, United States	1:53.36

200-Meter Individual Medley	Time
1968 Charles Hickcox, United States	2:12.0
1972 Gunnar Larsson, Sweden	2:07.17
1984 Alex Baumann, Canada	2:01.42
1988 Tamas Darnyi, Hungary	2:00.17
1992 Tamas Darnyi, Hungary	2:00.76
1996 Attila Czene, Hungary	1:59.91
2000 Massimiliano Rosolino, Italy	1:58.98
2004 Michael Phelps, United States	1:57.14
2008 Michael Phelps, United States	1:54.23*
2012 Michael Phelps, United States	1:54.27
2016 Michael Phelps, United States	1:54.66

400-Meter Individual Medley	Time
1964 Dick Roth, United States	4:45.4
1968 Charles Hickcox, United States	4:48.4
1972 Gunnar Larsson, Sweden	4:31.98
1976 Rod Strachan, United States	4:23.68
1980 Aleksandr Sidorenko, USSR	4:22.89
1984 Alex Baumann, Canada	4:17.41
1988 Tamas Darnyi, Hungary	4:14.75
1992 Tamas Darnyi, Hungary	4:14.23
1996 Tom Dolan, United States	4:14.90
2000 Tom Dolan, United States	4:11.76
2004 Michael Phelps, United States	4:08.26
2008 Michael Phelps, United States	4:03.84*
2012 Ryan Lochte, United States	4:05.18
2016 Kosuke Hagino, Japan	4:06.05

4x100-Meter Freestyle Relay	Time
1964 United States	3:31.2
1968 United States	3:31.7
1972 United States	3:26.42
1984 United States	3:19.03
1988 United States	3:16.53
1992 United States	3:16.74
1996 United States	3:15.41
2000 Australia	3:13.67
2004 South Africa	3:13.17
2008 United States	3:08.24*
2012 France	3:09.93
2016 United States	3:09.92

4x200-Meter Freestyle Relay	Time
1908 Great Britain	10:55.6
1912 Australasia (Australia and New Zealand)	10:11.6
1920 United States	10:04.4
1924 United States	9:53.4
1928 United States	9:36.2
1932 Japan	8:58.4
1936 Japan	8:51.5
1948 United States	8:46.0
1952 United States	8:31.1
1956 Australia	8:23.6
1960 United States	8:10.2
1964 United States	7:52.1
1968 United States	7:52.33
1972 United States	7:35.78
1976 United States	7:23.22
1980 USSR	7:23.50
1984 United States	7:15.69
1988 United States	7:12.51
1992 Unified Team	7:11.95
1996 United States	7:14.84
2000 Australia	7:07.05
2004 United States	7:07.33
2008 United States	6:58.56*
2012 United States	6:59.70
2016 United States	7:00.66

4x100-Meter Medley Relay	Time
1960 United States	4:05.4
1964 United States	3:58.4
1968 United States	3:54.9
1972 United States	3:48.16
1976 United States	3:42.22
1980 Australia	3:45.70
1984 United States	3:39.30
1988 United States	3:36.93
1992 United States	3:36.93
1996 United States	3:34.84
2000 United States	3:33.73
2004 United States	3:30.68
2008 United States	3:29.34
2012 United States	3:29.35
2016 United States	3:27.95*

10-Kilometer Marathon	Time
2008 Maarten van der Weijden, Netherlands	1:51:51.6
2012 Oussama Mellouli, Tunisia	1:49:55.1
2016 Ferry Weertman, Netherlands	1:52:59.8

Platform Diving	Points
1904 Dr. G. E. Sheldon, United States	112.75
1908 Hjalmar Johansson, Sweden	183.75
1912 Erik Adlerz, Sweden	73.94
1920 Clarence Pinkston, United States	100.67
1924 Albert White, United States	97.46
1928 Pete Desjardins, United States	98.74
1932 Harold Smith, United States	124.80
1936 Marshall Wayne, United States	113.58
1948 Sammy Lee, United States	130.05
1952 Sammy Lee, United States	156.28
1956 Joaquin Capilla, Mexico	152.44
1960 Robert Webster, United States	165.56
1964 Robert Webster, United States	148.58
1968 Klaus Dibiasi, Italy	164.18
1972 Klaus Dibiasi, Italy	504.12
1976 Klaus Dibiasi, Italy	600.51
1980 Falk Hoffmann, E. Germany	835.65
1984 Greg Louganis, United States	710.91
1988 Greg Louganis, United States	638.61
1992 Sun Shuwei, China	677.31
1996 Dmitri Sautin, Russia	692.34
2000 Tian Liang, China	724.53
2004 Hu Jia, China	748.08
2008 Matthew Mitcham, Australia	537.95
2012 David Boudia, United States	568.65
2016 Chen Aisen, China	545.35

Springboard Diving	Points
1908 Albert Zurner, Germany	85.50
1912 Paul Guenther, Germany	79.23
1920 Louis Kuehn, United States	675.40
1924 Albert White, United States	97.46
1928 Pete Desjardins, United States	185.04
1932 Michael Galitzen, United States	161.38
1936 Richard Degener, United States	163.57
1948 Bruce Harlan, United States	163.64
1952 David Browning, United States	205.29
1956 Robert Clotworthy, United States	159.56
1960 Gary Tobian, United States	170.00
1964 Kenneth Sitzberger, United States	159.90
1968 Bernie Wrightson, United States	170.15
1972 Vladimir Vasin, USSR	594.09
1976 Phil Boggs, United States	619.52
1980 Aleksandr Portnov, USSR	905.02
1984 Greg Louganis, United States	754.41
1988 Greg Louganis, United States	730.80
1992 Mark Lenzi, United States	676.53
1996 Xiong Ni, China	701.46
2000 Xiong Ni, China	708.72
2004 Peng Bo, China	787.30
2008 He Chong, China	572.90
2012 Ilya Zakharov, Russia	555.90
2016 Cao Yuan, China	547.60

Synchronized Platform Diving	Points
2004 Tian Liang & Yang Jinghui, China	383.88
2008 Lin Yue & Huo Liang, China	468.18
2012 Cao Yuan & Zhang Yanquan, China	486.78
2016 Chen Aisen & Lin Yue, China	496.98

Synchronized Springboard Diving	Points
2004 Nikolaos Siranidis & Thomas Bimis, Greece	353.34
2008 Wang Feng & Qin Kai, China	469.08
2012 Luo Yutong & Qin Kai, China	477.00
2016 Jack Laugher & Chris Mears, Great Britain	454.32

Swimming and Diving—Women

50-Meter Freestyle	Time
1988 Kristin Otto, E. Germany	0:25.49
1992 Yang Wenyi, China	0:24.76
1996 Amy Van Dyken, United States	0:24.87
2000 Inge de Bruijn, Netherlands	0:24.32
2004 Inge de Bruijn, Netherlands	0:24.58
2008 Britta Steffen, Germany	0:24.06
2012 Ranomi Kromowidjojo, Netherlands	0:24.05*
2016 Pernille Blume, Denmark	0:24.07

100-Meter Freestyle	Time
1912 Fanny Durack, Australia	1:22.2
1920 Ethelda Bleibtrey, United States	1:13.6
1924 Ethel Lackie, United States	1:12.4
1928 Albina Osipowich, United States	1:11.0
1932 Helene Madison, United States	1:06.8
1936 Hendrika Mastenbroek, Netherlands	1:05.9

100-Meter Freestyle	Time
1948 Greta Andersen, Denmark	1:06.3
1952 Katalin Szoke, Hungary	1:06.8
1956 Dawn Fraser, Australia	1:02.0
1960 Dawn Fraser, Australia	1:01.2
1964 Dawn Fraser, Australia	0:59.5
1968 Jan Henne, United States	1:00.0
1972 Sandra Neilson, United States	0:58.59
1976 Kornelia Ender, E. Germany	0:55.65
1980 Barbara Krause, E. Germany	0:54.79
1984 Carrie Steinseifer, United States	0:55.92
Nancy Hogshead, United States (tie)	0:55.92
1988 Kristin Otto, E. Germany	0:54.93
1992 Zhuang Yong, China	0:54.64
1996 Li Jingyi, China	0:54.50
2000 Inge de Bruijn, Netherlands	0:53.83

100-Meter Freestyle	Time
2004 Jodie Henry, Australia	0:53.84
2008 Britta Steffen, Germany	0:53.12
2012 Ranomi Kromowidjojo, Netherlands	0:53.00
2016 Simone Manuel, United States	0:52.70*
Penny Oleksiak, Canada (tie)	0:52.70*

200-Meter Freestyle	Time
1968 Debbie Meyer, United States	2:10.5
1972 Shane Gould, Australia	2:03.56
1976 Kornelia Ender, E. Germany	1:59.26
1980 Barbara Krause, E. Germany	1:58.33
1984 Mary Wayte, United States	1:59.23
1988 Heike Friedrich, E. Germany	1:57.65
1992 Nicole Haislett, United States	1:57.90
1996 Claudia Poll, Costa Rica	1:58.16
2000 Susan O'Neill, Australia	1:58.24
2004 Camelia Potec, Romania	1:58.03
2008 Federica Pellegrini, Italy	1:54.82
2012 Allison Schmitt, United States	1:53.61*
2016 Katie Ledecky, United States	1:53.73

400-Meter Freestyle	Time
1924 Martha Norelius, United States	6:02.2
1928 Martha Norelius, United States	5:42.8
1932 Helene Madison, United States	5:28.5
1936 Hendrika Mastenbroek, Netherlands	5:26.4
1948 Ann Curtis, United States	5:17.8
1952 Valerie Gyenge, Hungary	5:12.1
1956 Lorraine Crapp, Australia	4:54.6
1960 Chris von Saltza, United States	4:50.6
1964 Virginia Duenkel, United States	4:43.3
1968 Debbie Meyer, United States	4:31.8
1972 Shane Gould, Australia	4:19.44
1976 Petra Thuemer, E. Germany	4:09.89
1980 Ines Diers, E. Germany	4:08.76
1984 Tiffany Cohen, United States	4:07.10
1988 Janet Evans, United States	4:03.85
1992 Dagmar Hase, Germany	4:07.18
1996 Michelle Smith, Ireland	4:07.25
2000 Brooke Bennett, United States	4:05.80
2004 Laure Manaudou, France	4:05.34
2008 Rebecca Adlington, Great Britain	4:03.22
2012 Camille Muffat, France	4:01.45
2016 Katie Ledecky, United States	3:56.46*

800-Meter Freestyle	Time
1968 Debbie Meyer, United States	9:24.0
1972 Keena Rothhammer, United States	8:53.68
1976 Petra Thuemer, E. Germany	8:37.14
1980 Michelle Ford, Australia	8:28.90
1984 Tiffany Cohen, United States	8:24.95
1988 Janet Evans, United States	8:20.20
1992 Janet Evans, United States	8:25.52
1996 Brooke Bennett, United States	8:27.89
2000 Brooke Bennett, United States	8:19.67
2004 Ai Shibata, Japan	8:24.54
2008 Rebecca Adlington, Great Britain	8:14.10
2012 Katie Ledecky, United States	8:14.63
2016 Katie Ledecky, United States	8:04.79*

100-Meter Backstroke	Time
1924 Sybil Bauer, United States	1:23.2
1928 Marie Braun, Netherlands	1:22.0
1932 Eleanor Holm, United States	1:19.4
1936 Dina Senff, Netherlands	1:18.9
1948 Karen Harup, Denmark	1:14.4
1952 Joan Harrison, South Africa	1:14.3
1956 Judy Grinham, Great Britain	1:12.9
1960 Lynn Burke, United States	1:09.3
1964 Cathy Ferguson, United States	1:07.7
1968 Kaye Hall, United States	1:06.2
1972 Melissa Belote, United States	1:05.78
1976 Ulrike Richter, E. Germany	1:01.83
1980 Rica Reinisch, E. Germany	1:00.86
1984 Theresa Andrews, United States	1:02.55
1988 Kristin Otto, E. Germany	1:00.89
1992 Krisztina Egerszegi, Hungary	1:00.68
1996 Beth Botsford, United States	1:01.19
2000 Diana Mocanu, Romania	1:00.21
2004 Natalie Coughlin, United States	1:00.37
2008 Natalie Coughlin, United States	0:58.96
2012 Missy Franklin, United States	0:58.33
2016 Katinka Hosszú, Hungary	0:58.45

200-Meter Backstroke	Time
1968 Lillian "Pokey" Watson, United States	2:24.8
1972 Melissa Belote, United States	2:19.19
1976 Ulrike Richter, E. Germany	2:13.43
1980 Rica Reinisch, E. Germany	2:11.77
1984 Jolanda de Rover, Netherlands	2:12.38

200-Meter Backstroke	Time
1988 Krisztina Egerszegi, Hungary	2:09.29
1992 Krisztina Egerszegi, Hungary	2:07.06
1996 Krisztina Egerszegi, Hungary	2:07.83
2000 Diana Mocanu, Romania	2:08.16
2004 Kirsty Coventry, Zimbabwe	2:09.19
2008 Kirsty Coventry, Zimbabwe	2:05.24
2012 Missy Franklin, United States	2:04.06*
2016 Maya DiRado, United States	2:05.99

100-Meter Breaststroke	Time
1968 Djurdjica Bjedov, Yugoslavia	1:15.8
1972 Cathy Carr, United States	1:13.58
1976 Hannelore Anke, E. Germany	1:11.16
1980 Ute Geweniger, E. Germany	1:10.22
1984 Petra Van Staveren, Netherlands	1:09.88
1988 Tania Dangalakova, Bulgaria	1:07.95
1992 Yelena Rudkovskaya, Unified Team (Belarus)	1:08.00
1996 Penny Heyns, South Africa	1:07.73
2000 Megan Quann, United States	1:07.05
2004 Luo Xuejuan, China	1:06.64
2008 Leisel Jones, Australia	1:05.17
2012 Ruta Meilutyte, Lithuania	1:05.47
2016 Lilly King, United States	1:04.93*

200-Meter Breaststroke	Time
1924 Lucy Morton, Great Britain	3:33.2
1928 Hilde Schrader, Germany	3:12.6
1932 Clare Dennis, Australia	3:06.3
1936 Hideko Maehata, Japan	3:03.6
1948 Nelly Van Vliet, Netherlands	2:57.2
1952 Eva Szekely, Hungary	2:51.7
1956 Ursula Happe, Germany	2:53.1
1960 Anita Lonsbrough, Great Britain	2:49.5
1964 Galina Prozumenshchikova, USSR	2:46.4
1968 Sharon Wichman, United States	2:44.4
1972 Beverly Whitfield, Australia	2:41.71
1976 Marina Koshevaia, USSR	2:33.35
1980 Lina Kachushite, USSR	2:29.54
1984 Anne Ottenbrite, Canada	2:30.38
1988 Silke Hoerner, E. Germany	2:26.71
1992 Kyoko Iwasaki, Japan	2:26.65
1996 Penny Heyns, South Africa	2:25.41
2000 Agnes Kovacs, Hungary	2:24.35
2004 Amanda Beard, United States	2:23.37
2008 Rebecca Soni, United States	2:20.22
2012 Rebecca Soni, United States	2:19.59*
2016 Rie Kaneto, Japan	2:20.30

100-Meter Butterfly	Time
1956 Shelley Mann, United States	1:11.0
1960 Carolyn Schuler, United States	1:09.5
1964 Sharon Stouder, United States	1:04.7
1968 Lynn McClements, Australia	1:05.5
1972 Mayumi Aoki, Japan	1:03.34
1976 Kornelia Ender, E. Germany	1:00.13
1980 Caren Metschuck, E. Germany	1:00.42
1984 Mary T. Meagher, United States	0:59.26
1988 Kristin Otto, E. Germany	0:59.00
1992 Qian Hong, China	0:58.62
1996 Amy Van Dyken, United States	0:59.13
2000 Inge de Bruijn, Netherlands	0:56.61
2004 Petria Thomas, Australia	0:57.72
2008 Lisbeth Trickett, Australia	0:56.73
2012 Dana Vollmer, United States	0:55.98
2016 Sarah Sjöström, Sweden	0:55.48*

200-Meter Butterfly	Time
1968 Ada Kok, Netherlands	2:24.7
1972 Karen Moe, United States	2:15.57
1976 Andrea Pollack, E. Germany	2:11.41
1980 Ines Geissler, E. Germany	2:10.44
1984 Mary T. Meagher, United States	2:06.90
1988 Kathleen Nord, E. Germany	2:09.51
1992 Summer Sanders, United States	2:08.67
1996 Susan O'Neill, Australia	2:07.76
2000 Misty Hyman, United States	2:05.88
2004 Otylia Jedrzejczak, Poland	2:06.05
2008 Liu Zige, China	2:04.18
2012 Jiao Liuyang, China	2:04.06*
2016 Mireia Belmonte, Spain	2:04.85

200-Meter Individual Medley	Time
1968 Claudia Kolb, United States	2:24.7
1972 Shane Gould, Australia	2:23.07
1984 Tracy Caulkins, United States	2:12.64
1988 Daniela Hunger, E. Germany	2:12.59
1992 Lin Li, China	2:11.65
1996 Michelle Smith, Ireland	2:13.93
2000 Yana Klochkova, Ukraine	2:10.68

200-Meter Individual Medley

		Time
2004	Yana Klochkova, Ukraine	2:11.14
2008	Stephanie Rice, Australia	2:08.45
2012	Ye Shiwen, China	2:07.57
2016	Katinka Hosszú, Hungary	2:06.58*

400-Meter Individual Medley

		Time
1964	Donna de Varona, United States	5:18.7
1968	Claudia Kolb, United States	5:08.5
1972	Gail Neall, Australia	5:02.97
1976	Ulrike Tauber, E. Germany	4:42.77
1980	Petra Schneider, E. Germany	4:36.29
1984	Tracy Caulkins, United States	4:39.24
1988	Janet Evans, United States	4:37.76
1992	Krisztina Egerszegi, Hungary	4:36.54
1996	Michelle Smith, Ireland	4:39.18
2000	Yana Klochkova, Ukraine	4:33.59
2004	Yana Klochkova, Ukraine	4:34.83
2008	Stephanie Rice, Australia	4:29.45
2012	Ye Shiwen, China	4:28.43
2016	Katinka Hosszú, Hungary	4:26.36*

4x100-Meter Freestyle Relay

		Time
1912	Great Britain	5:52.8
1920	United States	5:11.6
1924	United States	4:58.8
1928	United States	4:47.6
1932	United States	4:38.0
1936	Netherlands	4:36.0
1948	United States	4:29.2
1952	Hungary	4:24.4
1956	Australia	4:17.1
1960	United States	4:08.9
1964	United States	4:03.8
1968	United States	4:02.5
1972	United States	3:55.19
1976	United States	3:44.82
1980	East Germany	3:42.71
1984	United States	3:43.43
1988	East Germany	3:40.63
1992	United States	3:39.46
1996	United States	3:39.29
2000	United States	3:36.61
2004	Australia	3:35.94
2008	Netherlands	3:33.76
2012	Australia	3:33.15
2016	Australia	3:30.65*

4x200-Meter Freestyle Relay

		Time
1996	United States	7:59.87
2000	United States	7:57.80
2004	United States	7:53.42
2008	Australia	7:44.31
2012	United States	7:42.92*
2016	United States	7:43.03

4x100-Meter Medley Relay

		Time
1960	United States	4:41.1
1964	United States	4:33.9
1968	United States	4:28.3
1972	United States	4:20.75
1976	East Germany	4:07.95
1980	East Germany	4:06.67
1984	United States	4:08.34
1988	East Germany	4:03.74
1992	United States	4:02.54
1996	United States	4:02.88
2000	United States	3:58.30
2004	Australia	3:57.32
2008	Australia	3:52.69

4x100-Meter Medley Relay

		Time
2012	United States	3:52.05*
2016	United States	3:53.13

10-Kilometer Marathon

		Time
2008	Larisa Ilchenko, Russia	1:59:27.7
2012	Éva Risztov, Hungary	1:57:38.2
2016	Sharon van Rouwendaal, Netherlands	1:56:32.1

Platform Diving

		Points
1912	Greta Johansson, Sweden	39.90
1920	Stefani Fryland-Clausen, Denmark	34.60
1924	Caroline Smith, United States	33.20
1928	Elizabeth B. Pinkston, United States	31.60
1932	Dorothy Poynton, United States	40.26
1936	Dorothy Poynton Hill, United States	33.93
1948	Victoria M. Draves, United States	68.87
1952	Patricia McCormick, United States	79.37
1956	Patricia McCormick, United States	84.85
1960	Ingrid Kramer, Germany	91.28
1964	Lesley Bush, United States	99.80
1968	Milena Duchkova, Czechoslovakia	109.59
1972	Ulrika Knape, Sweden	390.00
1976	Elena Vaytsekhouskaya, USSR	406.59
1980	Martina Jaschke, E. Germany	596.25
1984	Zhou Jihong, China	435.51
1988	Xu Yanmei, China	445.20
1992	Fu Mingxia, China	461.43
1996	Fu Mingxia, China	521.58
2000	Laura Wilkinson, United States	543.75
2004	Chantelle Newbery, Australia	590.31
2008	Chen Ruolin, China	447.70
2012	Chen Ruolin, China	422.30
2016	Ren Qian, China	439.25

Springboard Diving

		Points
1920	Aileen Riggin, United States	539.90
1924	Elizabeth Becker, United States	474.50
1928	Helen Meany, United States	78.62
1932	Georgia Coleman, United States	87.52
1936	Marjorie Gestring, United States	89.27
1948	Victoria M. Draves, United States	108.74
1952	Patricia McCormick, United States	147.30
1956	Patricia McCormick, United States	142.36
1960	Ingrid Kramer, Germany	155.81
1964	Ingrid Engel-Kramer, Germany	145.00
1968	Sue Gossick, United States	150.77
1972	Micki King, United States	450.03
1976	Jenni Chandler, United States	506.19
1980	Irina Kalinina, USSR	725.91
1984	Sylvie Bernier, Canada	530.70
1988	Gao Min, China	580.23
1992	Gao Min, China	572.40
1996	Fu Mingxia, China	547.68
2000	Fu Mingxia, China	609.42
2004	Guo Jingjing, China	633.15
2008	Guo Jingjing, China	415.35
2012	Wu Minxia, China	414.00
2016	Shi Tingmao, China	406.05

Synchronized Platform Diving

		Points
2004	Lao Lishi & Li Ting, China	352.14
2008	Wang Xin & Chen Ruolin, China	363.54
2012	Chen Ruolin & Wang Hao, China	368.40
2016	Chen Ruolin & Liu Huixia, China	354.00

Synchronized Springboard Diving

		Points
2004	Wu Minxia & Guo Jingjing, China	336.90
2008	Guo Jingjing & Wu Minxia, China	343.50
2012	He Zi & Wu Minxia, China	346.20
2016	Wu Minxia & Shi Tingmao, China	345.60

Tennis

Men's Singles

1896	John Boland, Great Britain
1900	Hugh Lawrence Doherty, Great Britain
1904	Beals Wright, United States
1908	Josiah George Ritchie, Great Britain
1912	Charles Lyndhurst Winslow, South Africa
1920	Louis Raymond, South Africa
1924	Vincent Richards, United States
1988	Miloslav Mecir, Czechoslovakia
1992	Marc Rosset, Switzerland
1996	Andre Agassi, United States
2000	Yevgeny Kafelnikov, Russia
2004	Nicolas Massu, Chile
2008	Rafael Nadal, Spain
2012	Andy Murray, Great Britain
2016	Andy Murray, Great Britain

Men's Doubles

1896	John Boland, Great Britain & Friedrick Traun, Germany
1900	Hugh Lawrence Doherty & Reginald Frank Doherty, Great Britain
1904	Edgar Leonard & Beals Wright, U.S.
1908	George Whiteside Hillyard & Reginald Frank Doherty, Great Britain
1912	Harry Austin Kitson & Charles Lyndhurst Winslow, South Africa
1920	Noel Turnbull & Maxwell Woosnam, Great Britain
1924	Vincent Richards & Francis Townsend Hunter, U.S.
1988	Kenneth Flach & Robert A. Seguso, United States
1992	Boris Becker & Michael Stich, Germany
1996	Mark Woodforde & Todd Woodbridge, Australia
2000	Sebastien Lareau & Daniel Nestor, Canada
2004	Fernando Gonzales & Nicolas Massu, Chile

Men's Doubles

2008	Roger Federer & Stanislas Wawrinka, Switzerland
2012	Mike Bryan & Bob Bryan, United States
2016	Marc López & Rafael Nadal, Spain

Women's Singles

1900	Charlotte Cooper, Great Britain
1908	Dorothy Katherine Chambers, Great Britain
1912	Marguerite Broquedis, France
1920	Suzanne Lenglen, France
1924	Helen Wills, United States
1988	Steffi Graf, W. Germany
1992	Jennifer Capriati, United States
1996	Lindsay Davenport, United States
2000	Venus Williams, United States
2004	Justine Henin-Hardenne, Belgium
2008	Elena Dementieva, Russia
2012	Serena Williams, United States
2016	Monica Puig, Puerto Rico

Women's Doubles

1920	Winifred Margaret McNair & Kathleen McKane, Great Britain
1924	Hazel Virginia Wightman & Helen Wills, United States
1988	Pam Shriver & Zina Garrison, United States
1992	Gigi Fernandez & Mary Joe Fernandez, United States
1996	Gigi Fernandez & Mary Joe Fernandez, United States
2000	Venus Williams & Serena Williams, United States
2004	Ting Li & Tian Tian Sun, China
2008	Serena Williams & Venus Williams, United States
2012	Serena Williams & Venus Williams, United States
2016	Ekaterina Makarova & Elena Vesnina, Russia

Mixed Doubles

2012	Victoria Azarenka & Max Mirnyi, Belarus
2016	Bethanie Mattek-Sands & Jack Sock, United States

Track and Field—Men

	100-Meter Run	Time
1896	Thomas Burke, United States	0:12.0
1900	Francis Jarvis, United States	0:11.0
1904	Archie Hahn, United States	0:11.0
1908	Reginald Walker, South Africa	0:10.8
1912	Ralph Craig, United States	0:10.8
1920	Charles Paddock, United States	0:10.8
1924	Harold Abrahams, Great Britain	0:10.6
1928	Percy Williams, Canada	0:10.8
1932	Eddie Tolan, United States	0:10.3
1936	Jesse Owens, United States	0:10.3
1948	Harrison Dillard, United States	0:10.3
1952	Lindy Remigino, United States	0:10.4
1956	Bobby Morrow, United States	0:10.5
1960	Armin Hary, Germany	0:10.2
1964	Bob Hayes, United States	0:10.0
1968	Jim Hines, United States	0:09.95
1972	Valery Borzov, USSR	0:10.14
1976	Hasely Crawford, Trinidad and Tobago	0:10.06
1980	Allan Wells, Great Britain	0:10.25
1984	Carl Lewis, United States	0:09.99
1988	Carl Lewis, United States	0:09.92
1992	Linford Christie, Great Britain	0:09.96
1996	Donovan Bailey, Canada	0:09.84
2000	Maurice Greene, United States	0:09.87
2004	Justin Gatlin, United States	0:09.85
2008	Usain Bolt, Jamaica	0:09.69
2012	Usain Bolt, Jamaica	0:09.63*
2016	Usain Bolt, Jamaica	0:09.81

	200-Meter Run	Time
1900	Walter Tewksbury, United States	0:22.2
1904	Archie Hahn, United States	0:21.6
1908	Robert Kerr, Canada	0:22.6
1912	Ralph Craig, United States	0:21.7
1920	Allan Woodring, United States	0:22.0
1924	Jackson Scholz, United States	0:21.6
1928	Percy Williams, Canada	0:21.8
1932	Eddie Tolan, United States	0:21.2
1936	Jesse Owens, United States	0:20.7
1948	Mel Patton, United States	0:21.1
1952	Andrew Stanfield, United States	0:20.7
1956	Bobby Morrow, United States	0:20.6
1960	Livio Berruti, Italy	0:20.5
1964	Henry Carr, United States	0:20.3
1968	Tommie Smith, United States	0:19.83
1972	Valery Borzov, USSR	0:20.00
1976	Donald Quarrie, Jamaica	0:20.23
1980	Pietro Mennea, Italy	0:20.19
1984	Carl Lewis, United States	0:19.80
1988	Joe DeLoach, United States	0:19.75
1992	Mike Marsh, United States	0:20.01
1996	Michael Johnson, United States	0:19.32
2000	Konstantinos Kenteris, Greece	0:20.09
2004	Shawn Crawford, United States	0:19.79
2008	Usain Bolt, Jamaica	0:19.30*
2012	Usain Bolt, Jamaica	0:19.32
2016	Usain Bolt, Jamaica	0:19.78

	400-Meter Run	Time
1896	Thomas Burke, United States	0:54.2
1900	Maxwell Long, United States	0:49.4
1904	Harry Hillman, United States	0:49.2
1908	Wyndham Halswelle, Gr. Brit. (walkover)	0:50.0
1912	Charles Reidpath, United States	0:48.2

	400-Meter Run	Time
1920	Bevil Rudd, South Africa	0:49.6
1924	Eric Liddell, Great Britain	0:47.6
1928	Ray Barbuti, United States	0:47.8
1932	William Carr, United States	0:46.2
1936	Archie Williams, United States	0:46.5
1948	Arthur Wint, Jamaica	0:46.2
1952	George Rhoden, Jamaica	0:45.9
1956	Charles Jenkins, United States	0:46.7
1960	Otis Davis, United States	0:44.9
1964	Michael Larrabee, United States	0:45.1
1968	Lee Evans, United States	0:43.86
1972	Vincent Matthews, United States	0:44.66
1976	Alberto Juantorena, Cuba	0:44.26
1980	Viktor Markin, USSR	0:44.60
1984	Alonzo Babers, United States	0:44.27
1988	Steve Lewis, United States	0:43.87
1992	Quincy Watts, United States	0:43.50
1996	Michael Johnson, United States	0:43.49
2000	Michael Johnson, United States	0:43.84
2004	Jeremy Wariner, United States	0:44.00
2008	LaShawn Merritt, United States	0:43.75
2012	Kirani James, Grenada	0:43.94
2016	Wayde van Niekerk, South Africa	0:43.03*

	800-Meter Run	Time
1896	Edwin Flack, Australia	2:11.0
1900	Alfred Tysoe, Great Britain	2:01.2
1904	James Lightbody, United States	1:56.0
1908	Mel Sheppard, United States	1:52.8
1912	James "Ted" Meredith, United States	1:51.9
1920	Albert Hill, Great Britain	1:53.4
1924	Douglas Lowe, Great Britain	1:52.4
1928	Douglas Lowe, Great Britain	1:51.8
1932	Thomas Hampson, Great Britain	1:49.8
1936	John Woodruff, United States	1:52.9
1948	Mal Whitfield, United States	1:49.2
1952	Mal Whitfield, United States	1:49.2
1956	Tom Courtney, United States	1:47.7
1960	Peter Snell, New Zealand	1:46.3
1964	Peter Snell, New Zealand	1:45.1
1968	Ralph Doubell, Australia	1:44.3
1972	Dave Wottle, United States	1:45.9
1976	Alberto Juantorena, Cuba	1:43.50
1980	Steve Ovett, Great Britain	1:45.40
1984	Joaquim Cruz, Brazil	1:43.00
1988	Paul Ereng, Kenya	1:43.45
1992	William Tanui, Kenya	1:43.66
1996	Vebjørn Rodal, Norway	1:42.58
2000	Nils Schumann, Germany	1:45.08
2004	Yuriy Borzakovskiy, Russia	1:44.45
2008	Wilfred Bungei, Kenya	1:44.65
2012	David Lekuta Rudisha, Kenya	1:40.91*
2016	David Lekuta Rudisha, Kenya	1:42.15

	1500-Meter Run	Time
1896	Edwin Flack, Australia	4:33.2
1900	Charles Bennett, Great Britain	4:06.2
1904	James Lightbody, United States	4:05.4
1908	Mel Sheppard, United States	4:03.4
1912	Arnold Jackson, Great Britain	3:56.8
1920	Albert Hill, Great Britain	4:01.8
1924	Paavo Nurmi, Finland	3:53.6
1928	Harry Larva, Finland	3:53.2

1500-Meter Run	Time
1932 Luigi Beccali, Italy.	3:51.2
1936 Jack Lovelock, New Zealand	3:47.8
1948 Henry Eriksson, Sweden	3:49.8
1952 Joseph Barthel, Luxembourg	3:45.2
1956 Ron Delany, Ireland	3:41.2
1960 Herb Elliott, Australia	3:35.6
1964 Peter Snell, New Zealand.	3:38.1
1968 Kipchoge Keino, Kenya	3:34.91
1972 Pekka Vasala, Finland	3:36.33
1976 John Walker, New Zealand	3:39.17
1980 Sebastian Coe, Great Britain	3:38.4
1984 Sebastian Coe, Great Britain	3:32.53
1988 Peter Rono, Kenya.	3:35.96
1992 Fermin Cacho Ruiz, Spain	3:40.12
1996 Noureddine Morceli, Algeria	3:35.78
2000 Noah Ngeny, Kenya.	3:32.07*
2004 Hicham El Guerrouj, Morocco	3:34.18
2008 Asbel Kiprop, Kenya[1]	3:33.11
2012 Taoufik Makhloufi, Algeria	3:34.08
2016 Matthew Centrowitz, United States	3:50.00

(1) Originally won by Rashid Ramzi, Bahrain, who was stripped of the gold in 2009 due to doping.

3000-Meter Steeplechase	Time
1920 Percy Hodge, Great Britain	10:00.4
1924 Ville Ritola, Finland.	9:33.6
1928 Toivo Loukola, Finland	9:21.8
1932 Volmari Iso-Hollo, Finland	
(about 3,450 m; extra lap by error)	10:33.4
1936 Volmari Iso-Hollo, Finland.	9:03.8
1948 Tore Sjöstrand, Sweden	9:04.6
1952 Horace Ashenfelter, United States	8:45.4
1956 Chris Brasher, Great Britain	8:41.2
1960 Zdzislaw Krzyszkowiak, Poland	8:34.2
1964 Gaston Roelants, Belgium	8:30.8
1968 Amos Biwott, Kenya	8:51.0
1972 Kipchoge Keino, Kenya.	8:23.64
1976 Anders Garderud, Sweden	8:08.02
1980 Bronislaw Malinowski, Poland.	8:09.7
1984 Julius Korir, Kenya	8:11.80
1988 Julius Kariuki, Kenya.	8:05.51
1992 Matthew Birir, Kenya.	8:08.84
1996 Joseph Keter, Kenya.	8:07.12
2000 Reuben Kosgei, Kenya.	8:21.43
2004 Ezekiel Kemboi, Kenya.	8:05.81
2008 Brimin Kiprop Kirpruto, Kenya.	8:10.34
2012 Ezekiel Kemboi, Kenya.	8:18.56
2016 Conseslus Kipruto, Kenya.	8:03.28*

5000-Meter Run	Time
1912 Hannes Kolehmainen, Finland	14:36.6
1920 Joseph Guillemot, France.	14:55.6
1924 Paavo Nurmi, Finland.	14:31.2
1928 Ville Ritola, Finland.	14:38.0
1932 Lauri Lehtinen, Finland.	14:30.0
1936 Gunnar Höckert, Finland	14:22.2
1948 Gaston Reiff, Belgium.	14:17.6
1952 Emil Zatopek, Czechoslovakia	14:06.6
1956 Vladimir Kuts, USSR	13:39.6
1960 Murray Halberg, New Zealand	13:43.4
1964 Bob Schul, United States	13:48.8
1968 Mohamed Gammoudi, Tunisia	14:05.0
1972 Lasse Viren, Finland.	13:26.4
1976 Lasse Viren, Finland.	13:24.76
1980 Miruts Yifter, Ethiopia	13:20.91
1984 Said Aouita, Morocco	13:05.59
1988 John Ngugi, Kenya.	13:11.70
1992 Dieter Baumann, Germany.	13:12.52
1996 Venuste Niyongabo, Burundi	13:07.96
2000 Million Wolde, Ethiopia	13:35.49
2004 Hicham El Guerrouj, Morocco	13:14.39
2008 Kenenisa Bekele, Ethiopia	12:57.82*
2012 Mo Farah, Great Britain	13:41.66
2016 Mo Farah, Great Britain	13:03.30

10,000-Meter Run	Time
1912 Hannes Kolehmainen, Finland	31:20.8
1920 Paavo Nurmi, Finland.	31:45.8
1924 Ville Ritola, Finland.	30:23.2
1928 Paavo Nurmi, Finland.	30:18.8
1932 Janusz Kusocinski, Poland.	30:11.4
1936 Ilmari Salminen, Finland.	30:15.4
1948 Emil Zatopek, Czechoslovakia	29:59.6
1952 Emil Zatopek, Czechoslovakia	29:17.0

10,000-Meter Run	Time
1956 Vladimir Kuts, USSR	28:45.6
1960 Pyotr Bolotnikov, USSR	28:32.2
1964 Billy Mills, United States	28:24.4
1968 Naftali Temu, Kenya	29:27.4
1972 Lasse Viren, Finland.	27:38.4
1976 Lasse Viren, Finland.	27:40.38
1980 Miruts Yifter, Ethiopia	27:42.7
1984 Alberto Cova, Italy	27:47.54
1988 Brahim Boutayeb, Morocco	27:21.46
1992 Khalid Skah, Morocco.	27:46.70
1996 Haile Gebrselassie, Ethiopia	27:07.34
2000 Haile Gebrselassie, Ethiopia	27:18.20
2004 Kenenisa Bekele, Ethiopia	27:05.10
2008 Kenenisa Bekele, Ethiopia	27:01.17*
2012 Mo Farah, Great Britain	27:30.42
2016 Mo Farah, Great Britain	27:05.17

Marathon	Time
1896 Spyridon Louis, Greece	2:58:50
1900 Michel Theato, France	2:59:45.0
1904 Thomas Hicks, United States	3:28:53.0
1908 John Hayes, United States	2:55:18.4
1912 Kenneth McArthur, South Africa	2:36:54.8
1920 Hannes Kolehmainen, Finland	2:32:35.8
1924 Albin Stenroos, Finland	2:41:22.6
1928 Boughera El Ouafi, France	2:32:57
1932 Juan Zabala, Argentina	2:31:36
1936 Kee-chung Sohn, Japan[1]	2:29:19.2
1948 Delfo Cabrera, Argentina	2:34:51.6
1952 Emil Zatopek, Czechoslovakia	2:23:03.2
1956 Alain Mimoun, France.	2:25:00.0
1960 Abebe Bikila, Ethiopia.	2:15:16.2
1964 Abebe Bikila, Ethiopia.	2:12:11.2
1968 Mamo Wolde, Ethiopia	2:20:26.4
1972 Frank Shorter, United States	2:12:19.8
1976 Waldemar Cierpinski, E. Germany	2:09:55.0
1980 Waldemar Cierpinski, E. Germany	2:11:03.0
1984 Carlos Lopes, Portugal.	2:09:21
1988 Gelindo Bordin, Italy.	2:10:32
1992 Hwang Young-cho, S. Korea	2:13:23
1996 Josia Thugwane, South Africa	2:12:36
2000 Gezahegne Abera, Ethiopia	2:10:11
2004 Stefano Baldini, Italy.	2:10:55
2008 Samuel Kamau Wanjiru, Kenya	2:06:32*
2012 Stephen Kiprotich, Uganda.	2:08:01
2016 Eliud Kipchoge, Kenya	2:08:44

(1) Korean runner who competed under Japanese name Kitei Son.

4x100-Meter Relay	Time
1912 Great Britain	0:42.4
1920 United States	0:42.2
1924 United States	0:41.0
1928 United States	0:41.0
1932 United States	0:40.0
1936 United States	0:39.8
1948 United States	0:40.6
1952 United States	0:40.1
1956 United States	0:39.5
1960 Germany (U.S. disqualified)	0:39.5
1964 United States	0:39.0
1968 United States	0:38.24
1972 United States	0:38.19
1976 United States	0:38.33
1980 USSR	0:38.26
1984 United States	0:37.83
1988 USSR (U.S. disqualified)	0:38.19
1992 United States	0:37.40
1996 Canada	0:37.69
2000 United States	0:37.61
2004 Great Britain	0:38.07
2008 Trinidad and Tobago[1]	0:38.06
2012 Jamaica	0:36.84*
2016 Jamaica	0:37.27

(1) Due to team member Nesta Carter's doping, Jamaica was stripped of the victory in 2017.

4x400-Meter Relay	Time
1908 United States	3:29.4
1912 United States	3:16.6
1920 Great Britain	3:22.2
1924 United States	3:16.0
1928 United States	3:14.2
1932 United States	3:08.2
1936 Great Britain	3:09.0
1948 United States	3:10.4
1952 Jamaica	3:03.9

4x400-Meter Relay	Time
1956 United States	3:04.8
1960 United States	3:02.2
1964 United States	3:00.7
1968 United States	2:56.16
1972 Kenya	2:59.8
1976 United States	2:58.65
1980 USSR	3:01.1
1984 United States	2:57.91
1988 United States	2:56.16
1992 United States	2:55.74
1996 United States	2:55.99
2000 Nigeria[1]	2:58.68
2004 United States	2:55.91
2008 United States	2:55.39*
2012 The Bahamas	2:56.72
2016 United States	2:57.30

(1) The U.S. was stripped of the medal in 2012 after team member Antonio Pettigrew admitted to doping.

20-Kilometer Walk	Time
1956 Leonid Spirin, USSR.	1:31:27.4
1960 Vladimir Golubnichy, USSR	1:34:07.2
1964 Kenneth Matthews, Great Britain	1:29:34.0
1968 Vladimir Golubnichy, USSR	1:33:58.4
1972 Peter Frenkel, E. Germany	1:26:42.4
1976 Daniel Bautista, Mexico	1:24:40.6
1980 Maurizio Damilano, Italy	1:23:35.5
1984 Ernesto Canto, Mexico	1:23:13
1988 Jozef Pribilinec, Czechoslovakia	1:19.57
1992 Daniel Plaza Montero, Spain	1:21:45
1996 Jefferson Perez, Ecuador.	1:20:07
2000 Robert Korzeniowski, Poland	1:18:59
2004 Ivano Brugnetti, Italy.	1:19:40
2008 Valeriy Borchin, Russia	1:19:01
2012 Chen Ding, China	1:18.46*
2016 Wang Zhen, China	1:19.44

50-Kilometer Walk	Time
1932 Thomas "Tommy" Green, Great Britain	4:50.10
1936 Harold Whitlock, Great Britain	4:30:41.4
1948 John Ljunggren, Sweden	4:41.52
1952 Giuseppe Dordoni, Italy	4:28:07.8
1956 Norman Read, New Zealand	4:30:42.8
1960 Donald Thompson, Great Britain	4:25:30
1964 Abdon Pamich, Italy	4:11:12.4
1968 Christoph Höhne, E. Germany	4:20:13.6
1972 Bernd Kannenberg, W. Germany	3:56:11.6
1980 Hartwig Gauder, E. Germany	3:49:24.0
1984 Raúl González, Mexico.	3:47:26
1988 Vyacheslav Ivanenko, USSR	3:38.29
1992 Andrey Perlov, Unified Team (Rus.)	3:50:13
1996 Robert Korzeniowski, Poland	3:43:30
2000 Robert Korzeniowski, Poland	3:42:22
2004 Robert Korzeniowski, Poland	3:38:46
2008 Alex Schwazer, Italy	3:37:09
2012 Jared Tallent, Australia[1]	3:36:53*
2016 Matej Tóth, Slovakia	3:40:58

(1) Russia's Sergey Kirdyapkin was stripped of the gold medal in 2016 for doping.

110-Meter Hurdles	Time
1896 Thomas Curtis, United States.	0:17.6
1900 Alvin Kraenzlein, United States	0:15.4
1904 Frederick Schule, United States	0:16.0
1908 Forrest Smithson, United States.	0:15.0
1912 Frederick Kelly, United States	0:15.1
1920 Earl Thomson, Canada.	0:14.8
1924 Daniel Kinsey, United States	0:15.0
1928 Sydney Atkinson, South Africa	0:14.8
1932 George Saling, United States.	0:14.6
1936 Forrest Towns, United States.	0:14.2
1948 William Porter, United States.	0:13.9
1952 Harrison Dillard, United States	0:13.7
1956 Lee Calhoun, United States.	0:13.5
1960 Lee Calhoun, United States.	0:13.8
1964 Hayes Jones, United States	0:13.6
1968 Willie Davenport, United States	0:13.33
1972 Rod Milburn, United States.	0:13.24
1976 Guy Drut, France	0:13.30
1980 Thomas Munkelt, E. Germany	0:13.39
1984 Roger Kingdom, United States	0:13.20
1988 Roger Kingdom, United States	0:12.98
1992 Mark McKoy, Canada.	0:13.12
1996 Allen Johnson, United States.	0:12.95
2000 Anier Garcia, Cuba.	0:13.00
2004 Liu Xiang, China.	0:12.91*

110-Meter Hurdles	Time
2008 Dayron Robles, Cuba.	0:12.93
2012 Aries Merritt, United States.	0:12.92
2016 Omar McLeod, Jamaica	0:13.05

400-Meter Hurdles	Time
1900 Walter Tewksbury, United States.	0:57.6
1904 Harry Hillman, United States	0:53.0
1908 Charles Bacon, United States	0:55.0
1920 Frank Loomis, United States.	0:54.0
1924 F. Morgan Taylor, United States	0:52.6
1928 David, Lord Burghley, Great Britain.	0:53.4
1932 Bob Tisdall, Ireland.	0:51.7
1936 Glenn Hardin, United States.	0:52.4
1948 Roy Cochran, United States	0:51.1
1952 Charles Moore, United States.	0:50.8
1956 Glenn Davis, United States.	0:50.1
1960 Glenn Davis, United States.	0:49.3
1964 Rex Cawley, United States	0:49.6
1968 David Hemery, Great Britain	0:48.12
1972 John Akii-Bua, Uganda.	0:47.82
1976 Edwin Moses, United States	0:47.64
1980 Volker Beck, E. Germany	0:48.70
1984 Edwin Moses, United States	0:47.75
1988 Andre Phillips, United States	0:47.19
1992 Kevin Young, United States	0:46.78
1996 Derrick Adkins, United States.	0:47.54
2000 Angelo Taylor, United States.	0:47.50
2004 Félix Sánchez, Dominican Republic	0:47.63
2008 Angelo Taylor, United States.	0:47.25
2012 Félix Sánchez, Dominican Republic	0:47.63
2016 Kerron Clement, United States	0:47.73

Note: Event not held in 1912.

Discus Throw	Dist.	
1896 Robert Garrett, United States	29.15m	(95' 7")
1900 Rudolf Bauer, Hungary	36.04m	(118' 3")
1904 Martin Sheridan, United States	39.28m	(128' 10")
1908 Martin Sheridan, United States	40.89m	(134' 1")
1912 Armas Taipale, Finland.	45.21m	(148' 3")
1920 Elmer Niklander, Finland.	44.68m	(146' 7")
1924 Clarence "Bud" Houser, U.S.	46.15m	(151' 4")
1928 Clarence "Bud" Houser, U.S.	47.32m	(155' 3")
1932 John Anderson, United States	49.49m	(162' 4")
1936 Ken Carpenter, United States.	50.48m	(165' 7")
1948 Adolfo Consolini, Italy.	52.78m	(173' 2")
1952 Sim Iness, United States.	55.03m	(180' 6")
1956 Al Oerter, United States.	56.36m	(184' 11")
1960 Al Oerter, United States.	59.18m	(194' 2")
1964 Al Oerter, United States.	61.00m	(200' 1")
1968 Al Oerter, United States.	64.78m	(212' 6")
1972 Ludvik Danek, Czechoslovakia.	64.40m	(211' 3")
1976 Mac Wilkins, United States.	67.50m	(221' 5")
1980 Viktor Rashchupkin, USSR.	66.64m	(218' 8")
1984 Rolf Danneberg, W. Germany.	66.60m	(218' 6")
1988 Jürgen Schult, E. Germany.	68.82m	(225' 9")
1992 Romas Ubartas, Lithuania	65.12m	(213' 8")
1996 Lars Riedel, Germany	69.40m	(227' 8")
2000 Virgilijus Alekna, Lithuania	69.30m	(227' 4")
2004 Virgilijus Alekna, Lithuania	69.89m	(228' 9¾")*
2008 Gerd Kanter, Estonia	68.82m	(225' 9½")
2012 Robert Harting, Germany	68.27m	(224')
2016 Christoph Harting, Germany	68.37m	(224' 3¾")

Hammer Throw	Dist.	
1900 John Flanagan, United States	49.73m	(163' 1")
1904 John Flanagan, United States	51.23m	(168' 1")
1908 John Flanagan, United States	51.92m	(170' 4")
1912 Matt McGrath, United States	54.74m	(179' 7")
1920 Pat Ryan, United States	52.875m	(173' 5¾")
1924 Fred Tootell, United States	53.295m	(174' 10")
1928 Patrick O'Callaghan, Ireland.	51.39m	(168' 7")
1932 Patrick O'Callaghan, Ireland.	53.92m	(176' 11")
1936 Karl Hein, Germany	56.49m	(185' 4")
1948 Imre Németh, Hungary	56.07m	(183' 11½")
1952 József Csérmák, Hungary.	60.34m	(197' 11")
1956 Harold Connolly, United States.	63.19m	(207' 3")
1960 Vasily Rudenkov, USSR.	67.10m	(202' 0")
1964 Romuald Klim, USSR.	69.74m	(228' 10")
1968 Gyula Zsivótzky, Hungary.	73.36m	(240' 8")
1972 Anatoly Bondarchuk, USSR	75.50m	(247' 8")
1976 Yuri Sedykh, USSR	77.52m	(254' 4")
1980 Yuri Sedykh, USSR	81.80m	(268' 4")
1984 Juha Tiainen, Finland.	78.08m	(256' 2")
1988 Sergei Litvinov, USSR	84.80m	(278' 2")*
1992 Andrey Abduvaliyev, Unified Team.	82.54m	(270' 9")
1996 Balázs Kiss, Hungary	81.24m	(266' 6")

	Hammer Throw	Dist.	
2000	Szymon Ziolkowski, Poland	80.02m	(262' 6")
2004	Koji Murofushi, Japan	82.91m	(272')
2008	Primoz Kozmus, Slovenia	82.02m	(269' 1")
2012	Krisztián Pars, Hungary	80.59m	(264' 5")
2016	Dilshod Nazarov, Tajikistan	78.68m	(258' 1¾")

	High Jump	Height	
1896	Ellery Clark, United States	1.81m	(5' 11¼")
1900	Irving Baxter, United States	1.90m	(6' 2¾")
1904	Samuel Jones, United States	1.80m	(5' 11")
1908	Harry Porter, United States	1.90m	(6' 2¾")
1912	Alma Richards, United States	1.93m	(6' 4")
1920	Richmond Landon, United States	1.94m	(6' 4¼")
1924	Harold Osborn, United States	1.98m	(6' 6")
1928	Robert "Bob" King, United States	1.94m	(6' 4¼")
1932	Duncan McNaughton, Canada	1.97m	(6' 5½")
1936	Cornelius Johnson, United States	2.03m	(6' 8")
1948	John Winter, Australia	1.98m	(6' 6")
1952	Walter Davis, United States	2.04m	(6' 8¼")
1956	Charles Dumas, United States	2.12m	(6' 11½")
1960	Robert Shavlakadze, USSR	2.16m	(7' 1")
1964	Valery Brumel, USSR	2.18m	(7' 1¾")
1968	Dick Fosbury, United States	2.24m	(7' 4¼")
1972	Jüri Tarmak, USSR	2.23m	(7' 3¾")
1976	Jacek Wszola, Poland	2.25m	(7' 4½")
1980	Gerd Wessig, E. Germany	2.36m	(7' 8¾")
1984	Dietmar Mögenburg, W. Germany	2.35m	(7' 8½")
1988	Gennadi Avdeyenko, USSR	2.38m	(7' 9¾")
1992	Javier Sotomayor, Cuba	2.34m	(7' 8")
1996	Charles Austin, United States	2.39m	(7' 10")*
2000	Sergey Klyugin, Russia	2.35m	(7' 8½")
2004	Stefan Holm, Sweden	2.36m	(7' 8¾")
2008	Andrey Silnov, Russia	2.36m	(7' 8¾")
2012	Erik Kynard, United States[1]	2.33m	(7' 7¾")
2016	Derek Drouin, Canada	2.38m	(7' 9¾")

(1) Ivan Ukhov, Russia, was stripped of the gold medal in 2019 due to doping; appeal was pending.

	Javelin Throw	Dist.	
1908	Eric Lemming, Sweden	54.82m	(179' 10")
1912	Eric Lemming, Sweden	60.64m	(198' 11")
1920	Jonni Myyrä, Finland	65.78m	(215' 9¾")
1924	Jonni Myyrä, Finland	62.96m	(206' 7")
1928	Erik Lundkvist, Sweden	66.60m	(218' 6")
1932	Matti Järvinen, Finland	72.71m	(238' 6½")
1936	Gerhard Stöck, Germany	71.84m	(235' 8")
1948	Kaj Tapio Rautavaara, Finland	69.77m	(228' 11")
1952	Cy Young, United States	73.78m	(242' 1")
1956	Egil Danielsen, Norway	85.71m	(281' 2½")
1960	Viktor Tsybulenko, USSR	84.64m	(277' 8")
1964	Pauli Nevala, Finland	82.66m	(271' 2")
1968	Janis Lusis, USSR	90.10m	(295' 7")
1972	Klaus Wolfermann, W. Germany	90.48m	(296' 10")
1976	Miklós Németh, Hungary	94.58m	(310' 4")
1980	Dainis Kula, USSR	91.20m	(299' 2")
1984	Arto Härkönen, Finland	86.76m	(284' 8")
1988	Tapio Korjus, Finland	84.28m	(276' 6")
1992	Jan Zelezny, Czechoslovakia	89.66m	(294' 2")
1996	Jan Zelezny, Czech Republic	88.16m	(289' 3")
2000	Jan Zelezny, Czech Republic	90.17m	(295' 9½")
2004	Andreas Thorkildsen, Norway	86.50m	(283' 10")
2008	Andreas Thorkildsen, Norway	90.57m	(297' 1¾")
2012	Keshorn Walcott, Trinidad & Tobago	84.58m	(277' 6")
2016	Thomas Röhler, Germany	90.30m	(296' 3")

	Long Jump	Dist.	
1896	Ellery Clark, United States	6.35m	(20' 10")
1900	Alvin Kraenzlein, United States	7.18m	(23' 6¾")
1904	Meyer Prinstein, United States	7.34m	(24' 1")
1908	Frank Irons, United States	7.48m	(24' 6½")
1912	Albert Gutterson, United States	7.60m	(24' 11¼")
1920	William Petersson, Sweden	7.15m	(23' 5½")
1924	William DeHart Hubbard, U.S.	7.45m	(24' 5¼")
1928	Ed Hamm, United States	7.73m	(25' 4½")
1932	Edward Gordon, United States	7.64m	(25' ¾")
1936	Jesse Owens, United States	8.06m	(26' 5½")
1948	Willie Steele, United States	7.82m	(25' 8")
1952	Jerome Biffle, United States	7.57m	(24' 10")
1956	Gregory Bell, United States	7.83m	(25' 8¼")
1960	Ralph Boston, United States	8.12m	(26' 7¾")
1964	Lynn Davies, Great Britain	8.07m	(26' 5¾")
1968	Bob Beamon, United States	8.90m	(29' 2½")*
1972	Randy Williams, United States	8.24m	(27' ½")
1976	Arnie Robinson, United States	8.35m	(27' 4¾")
1980	Lutz Dombrowski, E. Germany	8.54m	(28' ¼")

	Long Jump	Dist.	
1984	Carl Lewis, United States	8.54m	(28' ¼")
1988	Carl Lewis, United States	8.72m	(28' 7½")
1992	Carl Lewis, United States	8.67m	(28' 5½")
1996	Carl Lewis, United States	8.50m	(27' 10¾")
2000	Ivan Pedroso, Cuba	8.55m	(28' ¾")
2004	Dwight Phillips, United States	8.59m	(28' 2¼")
2008	Irving Saladino, Panama	8.34m	(27' 4¼")
2012	Greg Rutherford, Great Britain	8.31m	(27' 3¼")
2016	Jeff Henderson, United States	8.38m	(27' 6")

	Pole Vault	Height	
1896	William Welles Hoyt, United States	3.30m	(10' 10")
1900	Irving Baxter, United States	3.30m	(10' 10")
1904	Charles Dvorak, United States	3.50m	(11' 6")
1908	Edward Cooke, United States	3.71m	(12' 2")
	Alfred Gilbert, United States (tie)	3.71m	(12' 2")
1912	Harry Stoddard Babcock, U.S.	3.95m	(12' 11½")
1920	Frank Foss, United States	4.09m	(13' 5")
1924	Lee Barnes, United States	3.95m	(12' 11½")
1928	Sabin Carr, United States	4.20m	(13' 9¼")
1932	Bill Miller, United States	4.31m	(14' 1¾")
1936	Earle Meadows, United States	4.35m	(14' 3¼")
1948	Guinn Smith, United States	4.30m	(14' 1¼")
1952	Robert Richards, United States	4.55m	(14' 11¼")
1956	Robert Richards, United States	4.56m	(14' 11½")
1960	Don Bragg, United States	4.70m	(15' 5")
1964	Fred Hansen, United States	5.10m	(16' 8¾")
1968	Bob Seagren, United States	5.40m	(17' 8½")
1972	Wolfgang Nordwig, E. Germany	5.50m	(18' ½")
1976	Tadeusz Slusarski, Poland	5.50m	(18' ½")
1980	Wladyslaw Kozakiewicz, Poland	5.78m	(18' 11½")
1984	Pierre Quinon, France	5.75m	(18' 10¼")
1988	Sergei Bubka, USSR	5.90m	(19' 4¼")
1992	Maksim Tarasov, Unified Team (Rus.)	5.80m	(19' ¼")
1996	Jean Galfione, France	5.92m	(19' 5")
2000	Nick Hysong, United States	5.90m	(19' 4¼")
2004	Timothy Mack, United States	5.95m	(19' 6¼")
2008	Steve Hooker, Australia	5.96m	(19' 6¾")
2012	Renaud Lavillenie, France	5.97m	(19' 7")
2016	Thiago Braz da Silva, Brazil	6.03m	(19' 9½")*

	Shot Put	Dist.	
1896	Robert Garrett, United States	11.22m	(36' 9¾")
1900	Richard Sheldon, United States	14.10m	(46' 3¼")
1904	Ralph Rose, United States	14.81m	(48' 7")
1908	Ralph Rose, United States	14.21m	(46' 7½")
1912	Pat McDonald, United States	15.34m	(50' 4")
1920	Ville Pörhölä, Finland	14.81m	(48' 7¼")
1924	Clarence "Bud" Houser, United States	14.99m	(49' 2¼")
1928	John Kuck, United States	15.87m	(52' ¾")
1932	Leo Sexton, United States	16.00m	(52' 6")
1936	Hans Woellke, Germany	16.20m	(53' 1¾")
1948	Wilbur Thompson, United States	17.12m	(56' 2")
1952	W. Parry O'Brien, United States	17.41m	(57' 1½")
1956	W. Parry O'Brien, United States	18.57m	(60' 11¼")
1960	Bill Nieder, United States	19.68m	(64' 6¾")
1964	Dallas Long, United States	20.33m	(66' 8½")
1968	Randy Matson, United States	20.54m	(67' 4¾")
1972	Wladyslaw Komar, Poland	21.18m	(69' 6")
1976	Udo Beyer, E. Germany	21.05m	(69' ¾")
1980	Vladimir Kiselyov, USSR	21.35m	(70' ½")
1984	Alessandro Andrei, Italy	21.26m	(69' 9")
1988	Ulf Timmermann, E. Germany	22.47m	(73' 8¾")
1992	Michael Stulce, United States	21.70m	(71' 2½")
1996	Randy Barnes, United States	21.62m	(70' 11¼")
2000	Arsi Harju, Finland	21.29m	(69' 10¼")
2004	Adam Nelson, United States[1]	21.16m	(69' 5¼")
2008	Tomasz Majewski, Poland	21.51m	(70' 6¾")
2012	Tomasz Majewski, Poland	21.89m	(71' 9¾")
2016	Ryan Crouser, United States	22.52m	(73' 10½")*

(1) Yuriy Bilonog, Ukraine, was stripped of the gold medal in 2012 due to doping.

	Triple Jump	Dist.	
1896	James Connolly, United States	13.71m	(44' 11¾")
1900	Meyer Prinstein, United States	14.47m	(47' 5¾")
1904	Meyer Prinstein, United States	14.35m	(47' 1")
1908	Tim Ahearne, Gr. Brit.-Ireland	14.92m	(48' 11½")
1912	Gustaf Lindblom, Sweden	14.76m	(48' 5")
1920	Vilho Tuulos, Finland	14.505m	(47' 7")
1924	Anthony Winter, Australia	15.525m	(50' 11¼")
1928	Mikio Oda, Japan	15.21m	(49' 11")
1932	Chuhei Nambu, Japan	15.72m	(51' 7")
1936	Naoto Tajima, Japan	16.00m	(52' 6")
1948	Arne Ahman, Sweden	15.40m	(50' 6¼")

Triple Jump	Dist.
1952 Adhemar Ferreira da Silva, Brazil.... 16.22m	(53' 2¾")
1956 Adhemar Ferreira da Silva, Brazil.... 16.35m	(53' 7¾")
1960 Jozef Schmidt, Poland 16.81m	(55' 1½")
1964 Jozef Schmidt, Poland 16.85m	(55' 3½")
1968 Viktor Saneyev, USSR 17.39m	(57' ¾")
1972 Viktor Saneyev, USSR 17.35m	(56' 11¼")
1976 Viktor Saneyev, USSR 17.29m	(56' 8¾")
1980 Jaak Uudmäe, USSR 17.35m	(56' 11")
1984 Al Joyner, United States........... 17.26m	(56' 7½")
1988 Khristo Markov, Bulgaria 17.61m	(57' 9½")
1992 Mike Conley, United States 18.17m	(59' 7½")(w)
1996 Kenny Harrison, United States...... 18.09m	(59' 4¼")*
2000 Jonathan Edwards, Great Britain 17.71m	(58' 1¼")
2004 Christian Olsson, Sweden 17.79m	(58' 4½")
2008 Nelson Evora, Portugal............ 17.67m	(57' 11¾")
2012 Christian Taylor, United States...... 17.81m	(58' 5¼")
2016 Christian Taylor, United States...... 17.86m	(58' 7¼")

Decathlon	Points
1904 Thomas F. Kiely, Ireland.................... 6,036
1912 Jim Thorpe, United States[1].................8,412.995
1920 Helge Lovland, Norway 6,804.355
1924 Harold Osborn, United States..............7,710.775
1928 Paavo Yrjölä, Finland 8,053.29

Decathlon	Points
1932 James Bausch, United States 8,462.23
1936 Glenn Morris, United States................ 7,900
1948 Robert Mathias, United States 7,139
1952 Robert Mathias, United States.............. 7,887
1956 Milton Campbell, United States 7,937
1960 Rafer Johnson, United States............... 8,392
1964 Willi Holdorf, Germany.................... 7,887
1968 Bill Toomey, United States................. 8,193
1972 Nikolai Avilov, USSR 8,454
1976 Bruce Jenner, United States................ 8,618
1980 Daley Thompson, Great Britain 8,495
1984 Daley Thompson, Great Britain 8,797
1988 Christian Schenk, E. Germany............... 8,488
1992 Robert Zmelik, Czechoslovakia 8,611
1996 Dan O'Brien, United States 8,824
2000 Erki Nool, Estonia........................ 8,641
2004 Roman Sebrle, Czech Republic 8,893*
2008 Bryan Clay, United States 8,791
2012 Ashton Eaton, United States 8,869
2016 Ashton Eaton, United States 8,893*

Note: Event not held in 1908. (1) Thorpe had been stripped of his medal for playing pro baseball) prior to the Olympics. The Intl. Olympic Committee in 1982 posthumously restored his decathlon and pentathlon gold medals.

Track and Field—Women

100-Meter Run	Time
1928 Elizabeth Robinson, United States 0:12.2
1932 Stella Walsh, Poland 0:11.9
1936 Helen Stephens, United States 0:11.5
1948 Fanny Blankers-Koen, Netherlands 0:11.9
1952 Marjorie Jackson, Australia 0:11.5
1956 Betty Cuthbert, Australia................ 0:11.5
1960 Wilma Rudolph, United States 0:11.0
1964 Wyomia Tyus, United States 0:11.4
1968 Wyomia Tyus, United States 0:11.08
1972 Renate Stecher, E. Germany........... 0:11.07
1976 Annegret Richter, W. Germany 0:11.08
1980 Lyudmila Kondratyeva, USSR 0:11.06
1984 Evelyn Ashford, United States 0:10.97
1988 Florence Griffith-Joyner, United States .. 0:10.54*
1992 Gail Devers, United States............. 0:10.82
1996 Gail Devers, United States............. 0:10.94
2000 No winner[1] .... NA
2004 Yuliya Nestsiarenka, Belarus 0:10.93
2008 Shelly-Ann Fraser, Jamaica 0:10.78
2012 Shelly-Ann Fraser-Pryce, Jamaica...... 0:10.75
2016 Elaine Thompson, Jamaica 0:10.71

(1) Marion Jones, U.S., was stripped of her gold medal in 2007 due to doping; the Intl. Olympic Committee declined to award the medal to the runner-up, who was also suspected of doping.

200-Meter Run	Time
1948 Fanny Blankers-Koen, Netherlands 0:24.4
1952 Marjorie Jackson, Australia 0:23.7
1956 Betty Cuthbert, Australia................ 0:23.4
1960 Wilma Rudolph, United States 0:24.0
1964 Edith McGuire, United States........... 0:23.0
1968 Irena Szewinska, Poland 0:22.5
1972 Renate Stecher, E. Germany........... 0:22.40
1976 Bärbel Eckert, E. Germany 0:22.37
1980 Bärbel Wöckel, E. Germany 0:22.03
1984 Valerie Brisco-Hooks, United States 0:21.81
1988 Florence Griffith-Joyner, United States .. 0:21.34*
1992 Gwen Torrence, United States 0:21.81
1996 Marie-Jose Perec, France 0:22.12
2000 Pauline Davis-Thompson, The Bahamas[1] 0:22.27
2004 Veronica Campbell, Jamaica 0:22.05
2008 Veronica Campbell-Brown, Jamaica 0:21.74
2012 Allyson Felix, United States 0:21.88
2016 Elaine Thompson, Jamaica............. 0:21.78

(1) Originally won by Marion Jones, U.S., who was stripped of the gold in 2007 due to doping.

400-Meter Run	Time
1964 Betty Cuthbert, Australia............... 0:52.0
1968 Colette Besson, France 0:52.0
1972 Monika Zehrt, E. Germany 0:51.08
1976 Irena Szewinska, Poland 0:49.29
1980 Marita Koch, E. Germany 0:48.88
1984 Valerie Brisco-Hooks, United States 0:48.83
1988 Olga Bryzgina, USSR................. 0:48.65

400-Meter Run	Time
1992 Marie-Jose Perec, France 0:48.83
1996 Marie-Jose Perec, France 0:48.25*
2000 Cathy Freeman, Australia.............. 0:49.11
2004 Tonique Williams-Darling, The Bahamas ... 0:49.41
2008 Christine Ohuruogu, Great Britain 0:49.62
2012 Sanya Richards-Ross, United States 0:49.55
2016 Shaunae Miller, The Bahamas 0:49.44

800-Meter Run	Time
1928 Lina Radke, Germany.................. 2:16.8
1960 Lyudmila Shevtsova, USSR 2:04.3
1964 Ann Packer, Great Britain.............. 2:01.1
1968 Madeline Manning, United States....... 2:00.9
1972 Hildegard Falck, W. Germany........... 1:58.55
1976 Tatyana Kazankina, USSR 1:54.94
1980 Nadezhda Olizarenko, USSR 1:53.43*
1984 Doina Melinte, Romania 1:57.60
1988 Sigrun Wodars, E. Germany........... 1:56.10
1992 Ellen Van Langen, Netherlands 1:55.54
1996 Svetlana Masterkova, Russia........... 1:57.73
2000 Maria Mutola, Mozambique 1:56.15
2004 Kelly Holmes, Great Britain 1:56.38
2008 Pamela Jelimo, Kenya 1:54.87
2012 Caster Semenya, South Africa[1] 1:57.23
2016 Caster Semenya, South Africa 1:55.28

(1) Russia's Mariya Savinova was stripped of the gold medal for doping.

1500-Meter Run	Time
1972 Lyudmila Bragina, USSR 4:01.04
1976 Tatyana Kazankina, USSR 4:05.48
1980 Tatyana Kazankina, USSR 3:56.06
1984 Gabriella Dorio, Italy 4:03.25
1988 Paula Ivan, Romania 3:53.96*
1992 Hassiba Boulmerka, Algeria 3:55.30
1996 Svetlana Masterkova, Russia........... 4:00.83
2000 Nouria Merah-Benida, Algeria 4:05.10
2004 Kelly Holmes, Great Britain 3:57.90
2008 Nancy Jebet Langat, Kenya 4:00.23
2012 Gamze Bulut, Turkey[1] 4:10.40
2016 Faith Chepngetich Kipyegon, Kenya 4:08.92

(1) Turkey's Asli Cakir Alpetkin was stripped of the gold medal for doping.

3000-Meter Run	Time
1984 Maricica Puica, Romania 8:35.96
1988 Tatyana Samolenko, USSR............. 8:26.53*
1992 Elena Romanova, Unified Team (Rus.) 8:46.04

3000-Meter Steeplechase	Time
2008 Gulnara Galkina-Samitova, Russia....... 8:58.81*
2012 Habiba Ghribi, Tunisia[1] 9:08.37
2016 Ruth Jebet, Bahrain 8:59.75

(1) Russia's Yuliya Zaripova was stripped of the gold medal in 2016 for doping.

5000-Meter Run

		Time
1996	Wang Junxia, China	14:59.88
2000	Gabriela Szabo, Romania	14:40.79
2004	Meseret Defar, Ethiopia	14:45.65
2008	Tirunesh Dibaba, Ethiopia	15:41.40
2012	Meseret Defar, Ethiopia	15:04.25
2016	Vivian Cheruiyot, Kenya	14:26.17*

10,000-Meter Run

		Time
1988	Olga Bondarenko, USSR	31:05.21
1992	Derartu Tulu, Ethiopia	31:06.02
1996	Fernanda Ribeiro, Portugal	31:01.63
2000	Derartu Tulu, Ethiopia	30:17.49
2004	Xing Huina, China	30:24.36
2008	Tirunesh Dibaba, Ethiopia	29:54.66
2012	Tirunesh Dibaba, Ethiopia	30:20.75
2016	Almaz Ayana, Ethiopia	29:17.45*

Marathon

		Time
1984	Joan Benoit, United States	2:24:52
1988	Rosa Mota, Portugal	2:25:40
1992	Valentina Yegorova, Unified Team (Rus.)	2:32:41
1996	Fatuma Roba, Ethiopia	2:26:05
2000	Naoko Takahashi, Japan	2:23:14
2004	Mizuki Noguchi, Japan	2:26:20
2008	Constantina Tomescu, Romania	2:26:44
2012	Tiki Gelana, Ethiopia	2:23:07*
2016	Jemima Jelagat Sumgong, Kenya	2:24:04

4x100-Meter Relay

		Time
1928	Canada	0:48.4
1932	United States	0:46.9
1936	United States	0:46.9
1948	Netherlands	0:47.5
1952	United States	0:45.9
1956	Australia	0:44.5
1960	United States	0:44.5
1964	Poland	0:43.6
1968	United States	0:42.8
1972	West Germany	0:42.81
1976	East Germany	0:42.55
1980	East Germany	0:41.60
1984	United States	0:41.65
1988	United States	0:41.98
1992	United States	0:42.11
1996	United States	0:41.95
2000	The Bahamas	0:41.95
2004	Jamaica	0:41.73
2008	Russia	0:42.31
2012	United States	0:40.82*
2016	United States	0:41.01

4x400-Meter Relay

		Time
1972	East Germany	3:23.0
1976	East Germany	3:19.23
1980	USSR	3:20.2
1984	United States	3:18.29
1988	USSR	3:15.18*
1992	Unified Team	3:20.20
1996	United States	3:20.91
2000	United States[1]	3:22.62
2004	United States[2]	3:19.01
2008	United States	3:18.54
2012	United States	3:16.87
2016	United States	3:19.06

(1) Due to team member Marion Jones's doping, the U.S. was stripped of the victory in 2008. Jones's teammates won an appeal in 2010 to have their medals restored. (2) Team member Crystal Cox was stripped of her gold medal in 2012 due to doping.

20-Kilometer Walk

		Time
2000	Wang Liping, China	1:29:05
2004	Athanasia Tsoumeleka, Greece	1:29:12
2008	Olga Kaniskina, Russia	1:26:31
2012	Elena Lashmanova, Russia	1:25:02*
2016	Liu Hong, China	1:28:35

100-Meter Hurdles

		Time
1972	Annelie Ehrhardt, E. Germany	0:12.59
1976	Johanna Schaller, E. Germany	0:12.77
1980	Vera Komisova, USSR	0:12.56
1984	Benita Fitzgerald-Brown, United States	0:12.84
1988	Yordanka Donkova, Bulgaria	0:12.38
1992	Paraskevi Patoulidou, Greece	0:12.64
1996	Ludmila Engquist, Sweden	0:12.58
2000	Olga Shishigina, Kazakhstan	0:12.65
2004	Joanna Hayes, United States	0:12.37

100-Meter Hurdles

		Time
2008	Dawn Harper, United States	0:12.54
2012	Sally Pearson, Australia	0:12.35*
2016	Brianna Rollins, United States	0:12.48

400-Meter Hurdles

		Time
1984	Nawal El Moutawakel, Morocco	0:54.61
1988	Debra Flintoff-King, Australia	0:53.17
1992	Sally Gunnell, Great Britain	0:53.23
1996	Deon Hemmings, Jamaica	0:52.82
2000	Irina Privalova, Russia	0:53.02
2004	Faní Halkia, Greece	0:52.82
2008	Melaine Walker, Jamaica	0:52.64*
2012	Natalya Antyukh, Russia	0:52.70
2016	Dalilah Muhammad, United States	0:53.13

Discus Throw

		Dist.	
1928	Halina Konopacka, Poland	39.62m	(130' 0")
1932	Lillian Copeland, United States	40.58m	(133' 2")
1936	Gisela Mauermayer, Germany	47.63m	(156' 3")
1948	Micheline Ostermeyer, France	41.92m	(137' 6")
1952	Nina Ponomareva, USSR	51.42m	(168' 8")
1956	Olga Fikotová, Czechoslovakia	53.69m	(176' 1¾")
1960	Nina Ponomareva, USSR	55.10m	(180' 9")
1964	Tamara Press, USSR	57.27m	(187' 10¾")
1968	Lia Manoliu, Romania	58.28m	(191' 2")
1972	Faina Melnik, USSR	66.62m	(218' 7")
1976	Evelin Jahl, E. Germany	69.00m	(226' 4")
1980	Evelin Jahl, E. Germany	69.96m	(229' 6")
1984	Ria Stalman, Netherlands	65.36m	(214' 5")
1988	Martina Hellmann, E. Germany	72.30m	(237' 2")*
1992	Maritza Martén, Cuba	70.06m	(229' 10")
1996	Ilke Wyludda, Germany	69.66m	(228' 6")
2000	Ellina Zvereva, Belarus	68.40m	(224' 5")
2004	Natalya Sadova, Russia	67.02m	(219' 8¾")
2008	Stephanie Brown Trafton, U.S.	64.74m	(212' 4¾")
2012	Sandra Perkovic, Croatia	69.11m	(226' 9")
2016	Sandra Perkovic, Croatia	69.21m	(227' ¾")

Hammer Throw

		Dist.	
2000	Kamila Skolimowska, Poland	71.16m	(233' 5¾")
2004	Olga Kuzenkova, Russia	75.02m	(246' 1")
2008	Yipsi Moreno, Cuba[1]	75.20m	(246' 8¾")
2012	Anita Wlodarczyk, Poland[2]	77.60m	(254' 7")
2016	Anita Wlodarczyk, Poland	82.29m	(269' 11¾")*

(1) Belarus's Aksana Miankova was stripped of the gold medal for doping in 2012. (2) Russia's Tatyana Lysenko was stripped of the gold medal for doping in 2016.

High Jump

		Height	
1928	Ethel Catherwood, Canada	1.59m	(5' 2½")
1932	Jean Shiley, United States	1.67m	(5' 5½")
1936	Ibolya Csák, Hungary	1.60m	(5' 3")
1948	Alice Coachman, United States	1.68m	(5' 6")
1952	Esther Brand, South Africa	1.67m	(5' 5¾")
1956	Mildred McDaniel, United States	1.76m	(5' 9¼")
1960	Iolanda Balas, Romania	1.85m	(6' ¾")
1964	Iolanda Balas, Romania	1.90m	(6' 2¾")
1968	Miloslava Rezková, Czech.	1.82m	(5' 11½")
1972	Ulrike Meyfarth, W. Germany	1.92m	(6' 3½")
1976	Rosemarie Ackermann, E. Germany	1.93m	(6' 4")
1980	Sara Simeoni, Italy	1.97m	(6' 5½")
1984	Ulrike Meyfarth, W. Germany	2.02m	(6' 7½")
1988	Louise Ritter, United States	2.03m	(6' 8")
1992	Heike Henkel, Germany	2.02m	(6' 7½")
1996	Stefka Kostadinova, Bulgaria	2.05m	(6' 8¾")
2000	Yelena Yelesina, Russia	2.01m	(6' 7")
2004	Yelena Slesarenko, Russia	2.06m	(6' 9")*
2008	Tia Hellebaut, Belgium	2.05m	(6' 8¾")
2012	Anna Chicherova, Russia	2.05m	(6' 8¾")
2016	Ruth Beitia, Spain	1.97m	(6' 5½")

Javelin Throw

		Dist.	
1932	"Babe" Didrikson, United States	43.68m	(143' 4")
1936	Tilly Fleischer, Germany	45.18m	(148' 3")
1948	Herma Bauma, Austria	45.57m	(149' 6")
1952	Dana Zátopková, Czechoslovakia	50.47m	(165' 7")
1956	Inese Jaunzeme, USSR	53.86m	(176' 8")
1960	Elvira Ozolina, USSR	55.98m	(183' 8")
1964	Mihaela Penes, Romania	60.54m	(198' 7")
1968	Angéla Németh, Hungary	60.36m	(198' 0")
1972	Ruth Fuchs, E. Germany	63.88m	(209' 7")
1976	Ruth Fuchs, E. Germany	65.94m	(216' 4")
1980	Maria Colón, Cuba	68.40m	(224' 5")

Javelin Throw	Dist.	
1984 Tessa Sanderson, Great Britain.....	69.56m	(228' 2")
1988 Petra Felke, E. Germany.........	74.68m	(245' 0")
1992 Silke Renk, Germany	68.34m	(224' 2")
1996 Heli Rantanen, Finland	67.94m	(222' 11")
2000 Trine Hattestad, Norway	68.91m	(226' 1")
2004 Osleidys Menéndez, Cuba	71.53m	(234' 8")*
2008 Barbora Spotáková, Czech Republic	71.42m	(234' ¾")
2012 Barbora Spotáková, Czech Republic	69.55m	(228' 2¼")
2016 Sara Kolak, Croatia.............	66.18m	(217' 1½")
Note: New records were kept after javelin was modified in 1999.		

Long Jump	Dist.	
1948 Olga Gyarmati, Hungary.........	5.69m	(18' 8")
1952 Yvette Williams, New Zealand	6.24m	(20' 5¼")
1956 Elzbieta Krzesinska, Poland	6.35m	(20' 10")
1960 Vera Krepkina, USSR...........	6.37m	(20' 10¾")
1964 Mary Rand, Great Britain	6.76m	(22' 2¼")
1968 Viorica Viscopoleanu, Romania	6.82m	(22' 4½")
1972 Heidemarie Rosendahl, W. Germany	6.78m	(22' 3")
1976 Angela Voigt, E. Germany........	6.72m	(22' ¾")
1980 Tatyana Kolpakova, USSR	7.06m	(23' 2")
1984 Anisoara Cusmir-Stanciu, Romania..	6.96m	(22' 10")
1988 Jackie Joyner-Kersee, United States	7.40m	(24' 3½")*
1992 Heike Drechsler, Germany	7.14m	(23' 5¼")
1996 Chioma Ajunwa, Nigeria	7.12m	(23' 4¼")
2000 Heike Drechsler, Germany	6.99m	(22' 11¼")
2004 Tatyana Lebedeva, Russia	7.07m	(23' 2½")
2008 Maurren Higa Maggi, Brazil.......	7.04m	(23' 1¼")
2012 Brittney Reese, United States.....	7.12m	(23' 4¼")
2016 Tianna Bartoletta, United States	7.17m	(23' 6¼")

Pole Vault	Height	
2000 Stacy Dragila, United States.......	4.60m	(15' 1")
2004 Elena Isinbayeva, Russia	4.91m	(16' 1¼')
2008 Elena Isinbayeva, Russia	5.05m	(16' 6¾")
2012 Jennifer Suhr, United States.......	4.75m	(15' 7")
2016 Ekateríni Stefanídi, Greece........	4.85m	(15' 11")

Shot Put	Dist.	
1948 Micheline Ostermeyer, France	13.75m	(45' 1½")
1952 Galina Zybina, USSR	15.28m	(50' 1½")
1956 Tamara Tyshkevich, USSR.......	16.59m	(54' 5¼")
1960 Tamara Press, USSR	17.32m	(56' 10")
1964 Tamara Press, USSR	18.14m	(59' 6¼")
1968 Margitta Gummel, E. Germany	19.61m	(64' 4")
1972 Nadezhda Chizhova, USSR	21.03m	(69' 0")
1976 Ivanka Khristova, Bulgaria	21.16m	(69' 5¼")
1980 Ilona Slupianek, E. Germany	22.41m	(73' 6¼")*
1984 Claudia Losch, W. Germany.......	20.48m	(67' 2")
1988 Natalya Lisovskaya, USSR........	22.24m	(72' 11¾")
1992 Svetlana Krivelyova, Unified Team..	21.06m	(69' 1¼")
1996 Astrid Kumbernuss, Germany......	20.56m	(67' 5½")
2000 Yanina Karolchik, Belarus........	20.56m	(67' 5½")
2004 Yumileidi Cumbá, Cuba...........	19.59m	(64' 3¼")
2008 Valerie Vili, New Zealand	20.56m	(67' 5½")
2012 Valerie Adams, New Zealand	20.70m	(67' 11")
2016 Michelle Carter, United States......	20.63m	(67' 8¼")

Triple Jump	Dist.	
1996 Inessa Kravets, Ukraine	15.33m	(50' 3½")
2000 Tereza Marinova, Bulgaria	15.20m	(49' 10½")
2004 Francoise Mbango Etone, Cameroon	15.30m	(50' 2¼")
2008 Francoise Mbango Etone, Cameroon	15.39m	(50' 6")*
2012 Olga Rypakova, Kazakhstan.......	14.98m	(49' 1¾")
2016 Caterine Ibargüen, Colombia.......	15.17m	(49' 9¼")

Heptathlon	Points
1984 Glynis Nunn, Australia	6,390
1988 Jackie Joyner-Kersee, United States.	7,291*
1992 Jackie Joyner-Kersee, United States...	7,044
1996 Ghada Shouaa, Syria	6,780
2000 Denise Lewis, Great Britain........	6,584
2004 Carolina Kluft, Sweden................	6,952
2008 Natallia Dobrynska, Ukraine	6,733
2012 Jessica Ennis, Great Britain	6,955
2016 Nafissatou Thiam, Belgium	6,810

2018 Winter Olympic Games
Pyeongchang, South Korea, Feb. 9-25, 2018

Nearly 3,000 (2,833) athletes representing 92 nations met in Pyeongchang, South Korea, to compete in a record 102 events in 15 sports during the XXIII Olympic Winter Games Feb. 9-25, 2018. South Korea was hosting the Games for the first time since 1988, when the Summer Olympics were held in Seoul. Norway won 39 medals, including 14 gold, to top the final medal count, followed by Germany (31), Canada (29), and the U.S. (23).

Host country South Korea and estranged neighbor North Korea agreed in Jan. 2018 to march together under a unified flag in the opening ceremony and to field a unified women's hockey team. The Intl. Olympic Committee barred Russia from competition due to a state-sponsored doping scandal; Russian athletes granted exemptions by the IOC were allowed to compete under the designation Olympic Athlete(s) from Russia (OAR).

Japanese superstar Yuzuru Hanyu became the first man to win back-to-back singles figure skating gold medals since 1952. OAR teammates Alina Zagitova and Evgenia Medvedeva claimed gold and silver, respectively, in the women's figure skating competition. Czech star Ester Ledecká became the first woman ever to win a gold medal in two different sports at a single Winter Games, claiming the top prize in both the Alpine super-G and snowboarding's parallel giant slalom.

Veteran U.S. snowboarder Shaun White won gold in the men's halfpipe for the third time in his four Olympic appearances, while 17-year-old American rookie Chloe Kim claimed gold in the women's halfpipe event. The U.S. women's hockey team beat Canada in dramatic fashion to claim their first gold medal in the sport since the event began in 1998. U.S. Alpine skiing legend Lindsey Vonn, seeking a comeback after missing the Sochi games due to injury, settled for a bronze medal in downhill; teammate Mikaela Shiffrin claimed gold and silver in the giant slalom and Alpine combined events, respectively. The U.S. men's curling team won gold for the first time since competition officially began in that sport in 1998.

The following six new medal events were introduced in 2018: Alpine skiing team, curling mixed doubles, snowboarding men's/women's big air, and speed skating men's/women's mass start. Two events from the 2014 Games in Sochi, snowboarding men's/women's parallel slalom, were eliminated.

2018 Winter Olympic Games: Final Medal Standings
(G = Gold, S = Silver, B = Bronze, T = Total medals)

Country	G	S	B	T	Country	G	S	B	T	Country	G	S	B	T
Norway	14	14	11	39	Austria	5	3	6	14	Poland	1	0	1	2
Germany	14	10	7	31	Japan	4	5	4	13	Slovenia	0	1	1	2
Canada	11	8	10	29	Italy	3	2	5	10	New Zealand ..	0	0	2	2
United States ..	9	8	6	23	China	1	6	2	9	Spain	0	0	2	2
Netherlands ...	8	6	6	20	Czech Republic	2	2	3	7	Hungary	1	0	0	1
South Korea ..	5	8	4	17	Finland	1	1	4	6	Ukraine	1	0	0	1
OAR	2	6	9	17	Great Britain ..	1	0	4	5	Belgium	0	1	0	1
Switzerland ...	5	6	4	15	Belarus	2	1	0	3	Kazakhstan ...	0	0	1	1
France	5	4	6	15	Slovakia	1	2	0	3	Latvia	0	0	1	1
Sweden	7	6	1	14	Australia	0	2	1	3	Liechtenstein ..	0	0	1	1

OAR = Olympic Athletes from Russia.

Winter Olympic Games Champions, 1924-2018

East and West Germany competed separately, 1968-88. In 1992, the Unified Team represented the former Soviet republics of Russia, Ukraine, Belarus, Kazakhstan, and Uzbekistan. In 2018, Russian athletes competed under the designation Olympic Athlete(s) from Russia (OAR); Russia was banned from competition due to a state-sponsored doping scandal. Not all sports are listed here, and many events are omitted. Point systems used for scoring have changed many times; those shown are of the point system in use at those Games. Times are shown in hour:minute:sec.

Alpine Skiing

Team

2018	Switzerland, Austria, Norway

Men's Downhill

		Time
1948	Henri Oreiller, France	2:55.0
1952	Zeno Colo, Italy	2:30.8
1956	Toni Sailer, Austria	2:52.2
1960	Jean Vuarnet, France	2:06.0
1964	Egon Zimmermann, Austria	2:18.16
1968	Jean-Claude Killy, France	1:59.85
1972	Bernhard Russi, Switzerland	1:51.43
1976	Franz Klammer, Austria	1:45.73
1980	Leonhard Stock, Austria	1:45.50
1984	Bill Johnson, United States	1:45.59
1988	Pirmin Zurbriggen, Switzerland	1:59.63
1992	Patrick Ortlieb, Austria	1:50.37
1994	Tommy Moe, United States	1:45.75
1998	Jean-Luc Cretier, France	1:50.11
2002	Fritz Strobl, Austria	1:39.13
2006	Antoine Deneriaz, France	1:48.80
2010	Didier Defago, Switzerland	1:54.31
2014	Matthias Mayer, Austria	2:06.23
2018	Aksel Lund Svindal, Norway	1:40.25

Men's Giant Slalom

		Time
1952	Stein Eriksen, Norway	2:25.0
1956	Toni Sailer, Austria	3:00.1
1960	Roger Staub, Switzerland	1:48.3
1964	François Bonlieu, France	1:46.71
1968	Jean-Claude Killy, France	3:29.28
1972	Gustavo Thoeni, Italy	3:09.62
1976	Heini Hemmi, Switzerland	3:26.97
1980	Ingemar Stenmark, Sweden	2:40.74
1984	Max Julen, Switzerland	2:41.18
1988	Alberto Tomba, Italy	2:06.37
1992	Alberto Tomba, Italy	2:06.98
1994	Markus Wasmeier, Germany	2:52.46
1998	Hermann Maier, Austria	2:38.51
2002	Stephan Eberharter, Austria	2:23.28
2006	Benjamin Raich, Austria	2:35.00
2010	Carlo Janka, Switzerland	2:37.83
2014	Ted Ligety, United States	2:45.29
2018	Marcel Hirscher, Austria	2:18.04

Men's Slalom

		Time
1948	Edi Reinalter, Switzerland	2:10.3
1952	Othmar Schneider, Austria	2:00.0
1956	Toni Sailer, Austria	3:14.7
1960	Ernst Hinterseer, Austria	2:08.9
1964	Josef Stiegler, Austria	2:11.13
1968	Jean-Claude Killy, France	1:39.73
1972	Francisco Fernandez-Ochoa, Spain	1:49.27
1976	Piero Gros, Italy	2:03.29
1980	Ingemar Stenmark, Sweden	1:44.26
1984	Phil Mahre, United States	1:39.41
1988	Alberto Tomba, Italy	1:39.47
1992	Finn Christian Jagge, Norway	1:44.39
1994	Thomas Stangassinger, Austria	2:02.02
1998	Hans-Petter Buraas, Norway	1:49.31
2002	Jean-Pierre Vidal, France	1:41.06
2006	Benjamin Raich, Austria	1:43.14
2010	Giuliano Razzoli, Italy	1:39.32
2014	Mario Matt, Austria	1:41.84
2018	Andre Myhrer, Sweden	1:38.99

Men's Combined

		Time
1936	Franz Pfnür, Germany	99.25 (pts.)
1948	Henri Oreiller, France	3.27 (pts.)
1988	Hubert Strolz, Austria	36.55 (pts.)
1992	Josef Polig, Italy	14.58 (pts.)
1994	Lasse Kjus, Norway	3:17.53
1998	Mario Reiter, Austria	3:08.06
2002	Kjetil André Aamodt, Norway	3:17.56
2006	Ted Ligety, United States	3:09.35
2010	Bode Miller, United States	2:44.92
2014	Sandro Viletta, Switzerland	2:45.20
2018	Marcel Hirscher, Austria	2:06.52

Men's Super Giant Slalom

		Time
1988	Franck Piccard, France	1:39.66
1992	Kjetil André Aamodt, Norway	1:13.04

Men's Super Giant Slalom

		Time
1994	Markus Wasmeier, Germany	1:32.53
1998	Hermann Maier, Austria	1:34.82
2002	Kjetil André Aamodt, Norway	1:21.58
2006	Kjetil André Aamodt, Norway	1:30.65
2010	Aksel Lund Svindal, Norway	1:30.34
2014	Kjetil Jansrud, Norway	1:18.14
2018	Matthias Mayer, Austria	1:24.44

Women's Downhill

		Time
1948	Hedi Schlunegger, Switzerland	2:28.3
1952	Trude Beiser-Jochum, Austria	1:47.1
1956	Madeleine Berthod, Switzerland	1:40.7
1960	Heidi Biebl, Germany	1:37.6
1964	Christl Haas, Austria	1:55.39
1968	Olga Pall, Austria	1:40.87
1972	Marie-Theres Nadig, Switzerland	1:36.68
1976	Rosi Mittermaier, W. Germany	1:46.16
1980	Annemarie Moser-Proell, Austria	1:37.52
1984	Michela Figini, Switzerland	1:13.36
1988	Marina Kiehl, W. Germany	1:25.86
1992	Kerrin Lee-Gartner, Canada	1:52.55
1994	Katja Seizinger, Germany	1:35.93
1998	Katja Seizinger, Germany	1:28.89
2002	Carole Montillet, France	1:39.56
2006	Michaela Dorfmeister, Austria	1:56.49
2010	Lindsey Vonn, United States	1:44.19
2014	Tina Maze, Slovenia	1:41.57
	Dominique Gisin, Switzerland (tie)	1:41.57
2018	Sofia Goggia, Italy	1:39.22

Women's Giant Slalom

		Time
1952	Andrea Mead Lawrence, United States	2:06.8
1956	Ossi Reichert, Germany	1:56.5
1960	Yvonne Ruegg, Switzerland	1:39.9
1964	Marielle Goitschel, France	1:52.24
1968	Nancy Greene, Canada	1:51.97
1972	Marie-Theres Nadig, Switzerland	1:29.90
1976	Kathy Kreiner, Canada	1:29.13
1980	Hanni Wenzel, Liechtenstein	2:41.66
1984	Debbie Armstrong, United States	2:20.98
1988	Vreni Schneider, Switzerland	2:06.49
1992	Pernilla Wiberg, Sweden	2:12.74
1994	Deborah Compagnoni, Italy	2:30.97
1998	Deborah Compagnoni, Italy	2:50.59
2002	Janica Kostelic, Croatia	2:30.01
2006	Julia Mancuso, United States	2:09.19
2010	Viktoria Rebensburg, Germany	2:27.11
2014	Tina Maze, Slovenia	2:36.87
2018	Mikaela Shiffrin, United States	2:20.02

Note: Beginning in 1980, the event time combined two runs.

Women's Slalom

		Time
1948	Gretchen Fraser, United States	1:57.2
1952	Andrea Mead Lawrence, United States	2:10.6
1956	Renee Colliard, Switzerland	1:52.3
1960	Anne Heggtveit, Canada	1:49.6
1964	Christine Goitschel, France	1:29.86
1968	Marielle Goitschel, France	1:25.86
1972	Barbara Ann Cochran, United States	1:31.24
1976	Rosi Mittermaier, W. Germany	1:30.54
1980	Hanni Wenzel, Liechtenstein	1:25.09
1984	Paoletta Magoni, Italy	1:36.47
1988	Vreni Schneider, Switzerland	1:36.69
1992	Petra Kronberger, Austria	1:32.68
1994	Vreni Schneider, Switzerland	1:56.01
1998	Hilde Gerg, Germany	1:32.40
2002	Janica Kostelic, Croatia	1:46.10
2006	Anja Paerson, Sweden	1:29.04
2010	Maria Riesch, Germany	1:42.89
2014	Mikaela Shiffrin, United States	1:44.54
2018	Frida Hansdotter, Sweden	1:38.63

Women's Combined

		Time
1936	Christl Cranz, Germany	97.06 (pts.)
1948	Trude Beiser-Jochum, Austria	6.58 (pts.)
1988	Anita Wachter, Austria	29.25 (pts.)
1992	Petra Kronberger, Austria	2.55 (pts.)
1994	Pernilla Wiberg, Sweden	3:05.16
1998	Katja Seizinger, Germany	2:40.74
2002	Janica Kostelic, Croatia	2:43.28

Women's Combined	Time
2006 Janica Kostelic, Croatia	2:51.08
2010 Maria Riesch, Germany	2:09.14
2014 Maria Hoefl-Riesch, Germany	2:34.62
2018 Michelle Gisin, Switzerland	2:20.90

Note: In 2010, a one-day super combined event replaced the traditional two-day combined event.

Women's Super Giant Slalom	Time
1988 Sigrid Wolf, Austria	1:19.03
1992 Deborah Compagnoni, Italy	1:21.22
1994 Diann Roffe (Steinrotter), United States	1:22.15
1998 Picabo Street, United States	1:18.02
2002 Daniela Ceccarelli, Italy	1:13.59
2006 Michaela Dorfmeister, Austria	1:32.47
2010 Andrea Fischbacher, Austria	1:20.14
2014 Anna Fenninger, Austria	1:25.52
2018 Ester Ledecká, Czech Republic	1:21.11

Bobsled
(Driver/pilot in parentheses.)

Two-Man Bobsled	Time
1932 United States (Hubert Stevens)	8:14.74
1936 United States (Ivan Brown)	5:29.29
1948 Switzerland (Felix Endrich)	5:29.20
1952 Germany (Andreas Ostler)	5:24.54
1956 Italy (Dalla Costa)	5:30.14
1964 Great Britain (Anthony Nash)	4:21.90
1968 Italy (Eugenio Monti)	4:41.54
1972 W. Germany (Wolfgang Zimmerer)	4:57.07
1976 E. Germany (Meinhard Nehmer)	3:44.42
1980 Switzerland (Erich Schaerer)	4:09.36
1984 E. Germany (Wolfgang Hoppe)	3:25.56
1988 USSR (Janis Kipours)	3:54.19
1992 Switzerland (Gustav Weber)	4:03.26
1994 Switzerland (Gustav Weber)	3:30.81
1998 Canada (Pierre Lueders)	3:37.24
Italy (Guenther Huber) (tie)	3:37.24
2002 Germany II (Christoph Langen)	3:10.11
2006 Germany (Andre Lange)	3:43.38
2010 Germany (Andre Lange)	3:26.65
2014 Germany (Beat Hefti)[1]	3:46.05
2018 Canada (Justin Kripps)	3:16.86
Germany (Francesco Friedrich) (tie)	3:16.86

Four-Man Bobsled	Time
1924 Switzerland (Eduard Scherrer)	5:45.54
1928 United States (William Fiske) (5-man)	3:20.50
1932 United States (William Fiske)	7:53.68
1936 Switzerland (Pierre Musy)	5:19.85
1948 United States (Francis Tyler)	5:20.10
1952 Germany (Andreas Ostler)	5:07.84
1956 Switzerland (Franz Kapus)	5:10.44
1964 Canada (Victor Emery)	4:14.46
1968 Italy (Eugenio Monti) (2 heats)	2:17.39
1972 Switzerland (Jean Wicki)	4:43.07
1976 E. Germany (Meinhard Nehmer)	3:40.43
1980 E. Germany (Meinhard Nehmer)	3:59.92
1984 E. Germany (Wolfgang Hoppe)	3:20.22
1988 Switzerland (Ekkehard Fasser)	3:47.51
1992 Austria (Ingo Appelt)	3:53.90
1994 Germany (Wolfgang Hoppe)	3:27.28
1998 Germany II (Christoph Langen)	2:39.41
2002 Germany II (Andre Lange)	3:07.51
2006 Germany (Andre Lange)	3:40.42
2010 United States (Steven Holcomb)	3:24.46
2014 Latvia (Oskars Melbardis)[1]	3:40.69
2018 Germany (Francesco Friedrich)	3:15.85

Two-Woman Bobsled	Time
2002 United States II (Jill Bakken)	1:37.76
2006 Germany (Sandra Kiriasis)	3:49.98
2010 Canada (Kaillie Humphries)	3:32.28
2014 Canada (Kaillie Humphries)	3:50.61
2018 Germany (Mariama Jamanka)	3:22.45

(1) Awarded gold after Russia's Alexander Zubkov was stripped of medals in both events due to doping.

Cross-Country Skiing

Men's Individual Sprint	Time
2002 Tor Arne Hetland, Norway (1.5 km)	2:56.9
2006 Bjoern Lind, Sweden (1.3 km)	2:26.5
2010 Nikita Kriukov, Russia	3:36.3
2014 Ola Vigen Hattestad, Norway	3:38.39
2018 Johannes Hoesflot Klaebo, Norway	3:05.75

Men's 10 Kilometers	Time
1992 Vegard Ulvang, Norway	27:36.0
1994 Bjoern Daehlie, Norway	24:20.1
1998 Bjoern Daehlie, Norway	27:24.5
2002 Thomas Alsgaard, Norway	49:48.9
Frode Estil, Norway (tie)[1]	49:48.9

(1) Both awarded gold after Johann Muehlegg of Spain was stripped of gold for a drug offense.

Men's 15 Kilometers	Time
1924 Thorleif Haug, Norway	1:14:31
1928 Johan Grottumsbraaten, Norway	1:37:01
1932 Sven Utterstrom, Sweden	1:23:07
1936 Erik-August Larsson, Sweden	1:14:38
1948 Martin Lundstrom, Sweden	1:13:50
1952 Hallgeir Brenden, Norway	1:01:34
1956 Hallgeir Brenden, Norway	0:49:39.0
1960 Haakon Brusveen, Norway	0:51:55.5
1964 Eero Maentyranta, Finland	0:50:54.1
1968 Harald Groenningen, Norway	0:47:54.2
1972 Sven-Ake Lundback, Sweden	0:45:28.24
1976 Nikolai Balukov, USSR	0:43:58.47
1980 Thomas Wassberg, Sweden	0:41:57.63
1984 Gunde Svan, Sweden	0:41:25.6
1988 Mikhail Deviatiarov, USSR	0:41:18.9
1992 Bjoern Daehlie, Norway	0:38:01.9
1994 Bjoern Daehlie, Norway	0:35:48.8
1998 Thomas Alsgaard, Norway	1:07:01.7
2002 Andrus Veerpalu, Estonia	0:37:07.4
2006 Andrus Veerpalu, Estonia	0:38:01.3
2010 Dario Cologna, Switzerland	0:33:36.3
2014 Dario Cologna, Switzerland	0:38:29.7
2018 Dario Cologna, Switzerland	0:33:43.9

Note: Approx. 18-km course 1924-52.

Men's 30-Kilometer Pursuit	Time
1956 Veikko Hakulinen, Finland	1:44:06.0
1964 Eero Maentyranta, Finland	1:30:50.7
1968 Franco Nones, Italy	1:35:39.2
1972 Vyacheslav Vedenine, USSR	1:36:31.15
1976 Sergei Saveliev, USSR	1:30:29.38
1980 Nikolai Zimyatov, USSR	1:27:02.80
1984 Nikolai Zimyatov, USSR	1:28:56.3
1988 Aleksei Prokourorov, USSR	1:24:26.3
1992 Vegard Ulvang, Norway	1:22:27.8
1994 Thomas Alsgaard, Norway	1:12:26.4
1998 Mika Myllylae, Finland	1:33:55.8
2002 Christian Hoffmann, Austria[1]	1:11:31.0
2006 Eugeni Dementiev, Russia	1:17:00.8
2010 Marcus Hellner, Sweden	1:15:11.4

(1) Awarded gold after Johann Muehlegg of Spain was stripped of gold for a drug offense.

Men's Skiathlon	Time
2014 Dario Cologna, Switzerland	1:08:15.4
2018 Simen Hegstad Krüger, Norway	1:16:20.0

Men's 50-Kilometer Mass Start	Time
1924 Thorleif Haug, Norway	3:44:32.0
1928 Per Erik Hedlund, Sweden	4:52:03.0
1932 Veli Saarinen, Finland	4:28:00.0
1936 Elis Wiklund, Sweden	3:30:11.0
1948 Nils Karlsson, Sweden	3:47:48.0
1952 Veikko Hakulinen, Finland	3:33:33.0
1956 Sixten Jernberg, Sweden	2:50:27.0
1960 Kalevi Hamalainen, Finland	2:59:06.3
1964 Sixten Jernberg, Sweden	2:43:52.6
1968 Ole Ellefsaeter, Norway	2:28:45.8
1972 Paal Tyldum, Norway	2:43:14.75
1976 Ivar Formo, Norway	2:37:30.05
1980 Nikolai Zimyatov, USSR	2:27:24.60
1984 Thomas Wassberg, Sweden	2:15:55.8
1988 Gunde Svan, Sweden	2:04:30.9
1992 Bjoern Daehlie, Norway	2:03:41.5
1994 Vladimir Smirnov, Kazakhstan	2:07:20.3
1998 Bjoern Daehlie, Norway	2:05:08.2
2002 Mikhail Ivanov, Russia	2:06:20.8
2006 Giorgio di Centa, Italy	2:06:11.8
2010 Petter Northug, Norway	2:05:35.5
2014 Alexander Legkov, Russia	1:46:55.2
2018 Iivo Niskanen, Finland	2:08:22.1

Men's 4x10-Kilometer Relay

Year		Time
1936	Finland, Norway, Sweden...............	2:41:33.0
1948	Sweden, Finland, Norway..............	2:32:08.0
1952	Finland, Norway, Sweden..............	2:20:16.0
1956	USSR, Finland, Sweden...............	2:15:30.0
1960	Finland, Norway, USSR...............	2:18:45.6
1964	Sweden, Finland, USSR...............	2:18:34.6
1968	Norway, Sweden, Finland.............	2:08:33.5
1972	USSR, Norway, Switzerland............	2:04:47.94
1976	Finland, Norway, USSR...............	2:07:59.72
1980	USSR, Norway, Finland..............	1:57:03.46
1984	Sweden, USSR, Finland..............	1:55:06.30
1988	Sweden, USSR, Czechoslovakia........	1:43:58.60
1992	Norway, Italy, Finland...............	1:39:26.00
1994	Italy, Norway, Finland...............	1:41:15.00
1998	Norway, Italy, Finland...............	1:40:55.70
2002	Norway, Italy, Germany..............	1:32:45.5
2006	Italy, Germany, Sweden..............	1:43:45.7
2010	Sweden, Norway, Czech Republic......	1:45:05.4
2014	Sweden, Russia, France..............	1:28:42.0
2018	Norway, OAR, France................	1:33:04.9

Men's Team Sprint

Year		Time
2006	Bjoern Lind & Thobias Fredriksson, Sweden ..	17:02.9
2010	Oeystein Pettersen & Petter Northug, Norway. .	19:01.0
2014	Sami Jauhojaervi & Iivo Niskanen, Finland	23:14.89
2018	Martin Johnsrud Sundby & Johannes Hoesflot Klaebo, Norway.................	15:56.26

Women's Individual Sprint

Year		Time
2002	Julia Tchepalova, Russia (1.5 km)..........	3:10.6
2006	Chandra Crawford, Canada (1.1 km).......	2:12.3
2010	Marit Bjoergen, Norway................	3:39.2
2014	Maiken Caspersen Falla, Norway.........	2:35.49
2018	Stina Nilsson, Sweden.................	3:03.84

Women's 5 Kilometers

Year		Time
1964	Claudia Boyarskikh, USSR..............	17:50.5
1968	Toini Gustafsson, Sweden..............	16:45.2
1972	Galina Koulacova, USSR...............	17:00.50
1976	Helena Takalo, Finland................	15:48.69
1980	Raisa Smetanina, USSR...............	15:06.92
1984	Marja-Liisa Hamalainen, Finland........	17:04.0
1988	Marjo Matikainen, Finland.............	15:04.0
1992	Marjut Lukkarinen, Finland.............	14:13.8
1994	Lyubov Yegorova, Russia	14:08.8
1998	Larissa Lazutina, Russia...............	17:37.9
2002	Beckie Scott, Canada[1]...............	25:09.9

(1) Awarded gold after Olga Danilova of Russia was stripped of gold and Larissa Lazutina of Russia was stripped of silver for drug offenses.

Women's 10 Kilometers

Year		Time
1952	Lydia Wideman, Finland................	41:40.0
1956	Lyubov Kosyreva, USSR..............	38:11.0
1960	Maria Gusakova, USSR...............	39:46.6
1964	Claudia Boyarskikh, USSR.............	40:24.3
1968	Toini Gustafsson, Sweden.............	36:46.5
1972	Galina Koulacova, USSR..............	34:17.82
1976	Raisa Smetanina, USSR..............	30:13.41
1980	Barbara Petzold, E. Germany..........	30:31.54
1984	Marja-Liisa Hamalainen, Finland	31:44.2
1988	Vida Ventsene, USSR	30:08.3
1992	Lyubov Yegorova, Unified Team (Rus.) ...	25:53.7
1994	Lyubov Yegorova, Russia..............	27:30.1
1998	Larissa Lazutina, Russia..............	46:06.9
2002	Bente Skari, Norway.................	28:05.6
2006	Kristina Smigun, Estonia..............	27:51.4
2010	Charlotte Kalla, Sweden...............	24:58.4
2014	Justyna Kowalczyk, Poland	28:17.8
2018	Ragnhild Haga, Norway	25:00.5

Women's 15-Kilometer Pursuit

Year		Time
1992	Lyubov Yegorova, Unified Team (Rus.) .	42:20.8
1994	Manuela Di Centa, Italy..............	39:44.5
1998	Olga Danilova, Russia	46:55.4
2002	Stefania Belmondo, Italy.............	39:54.4
2006	Kristina Smigun, Estonia.............	42:48.7
2010	Marit Bjoergen, Norway	39:58.1

Women's Skiathlon

Year		Time
2014	Marit Bjoergen, Norway...............	38:33.6
2018	Charlotte Kalla, Sweden	40:44.9

Women's 30-Kilometer Mass Start

Year		Time
1992	Stefania Belmondo, Italy..............	1:22:30.1
1994	Manuela Di Centa, Italy	1:25:41.6

Women's 30-Kilometer Mass Start

Year		Time
1998	Julija Tchepalova, Russia................	1:22:01.5
2002	Gabriella Paruzzi, Italy	1:30:57.1
2006	Katerina Neumannova, Czech Republic......	1:22:25.4
2010	Justyna Kowalczyk, Poland	1:30:33.7
2014	Marit Bjoergen, Norway	1:11:05.2
2018	Marit Bjoergen, Norway	1:22:17.6

Women's 4x5-Kilometer Relay

Year		Time
1956	Finland, USSR, Sweden (15 km)	1:09:01.0
1960	Sweden, USSR, Finland (15 km)	1:04:21.4
1964	USSR, Sweden, Finland (15 km)	0:59:20.2
1968	Norway, Sweden, USSR (15 km)	0:57:30.0
1972	USSR, Finland, Norway (15 km)	0:48:46.15
1976	USSR, Finland, E. Germany	1:07:49.75
1980	E. Germany, USSR, Norway	1:02:11.1
1984	Norway, Czechoslovakia, Finland	1:06:49.7
1988	USSR, Norway, Finland	0:59:51.1
1992	Unified Team, Norway, Italy	0:59:34.8
1994	Russia, Norway, Italy	0:57:12.5
1998	Russia, Norway, Italy	0:55:13.5
2002	Germany, Norway, Switzerland	0:49:30.6
2006	Russia, Germany, Italy	0:54:47.7
2010	Norway, Germany, Finland..............	0:55:19.5
2014	Sweden, Finland, Germany	0:53:02.7
2018	Norway, Sweden, OAR	0:51:24.3

Women's Team Sprint

Year		Time
2006	Lina Andersson & Anna Dahlberg, Sweden ...	16:36.9
2010	Evi Sachenbacher-Stehle & Claudia Nystad, Germany........................	18:03.7
2014	Marit Bjoergen & Ingvild Flugstad Oestberg, Norway.......................	16:04.05
2018	Kikkan Randall & Jessie Diggins, United States	15:56.47

Curling

Men

1998	Switzerland, Canada, Norway
2002	Norway, Canada, Switzerland
2006	Canada, Finland, United States
2010	Canada, Norway, Switzerland
2014	Canada, Great Britain, Sweden
2018	United States, Sweden, Switzerland

Women

1998	Canada, Denmark, Sweden
2002	Britain, Switzerland, Canada
2006	Sweden, Switzerland, Canada
2010	Sweden, Canada, China
2014	Canada, Sweden, Great Britain
2018	Sweden, S. Korea, Japan

Mixed

2018	Canada, Switzerland, Norway

Figure Skating

Men's Singles

1908[1]	Ulrich Salchow, Sweden
1920[1]	Gillis Grafstrom, Sweden
1924	Gillis Grafstrom, Sweden
1928	Gillis Grafstrom, Sweden
1932	Karl Schaefer, Austria
1936	Karl Schaefer, Austria
1948	Richard Button, United States
1952	Richard Button, United States
1956	Hayes Alan Jenkins, United States
1960	David W. Jenkins, United States
1964	Manfred Schnelldorfer, Germany
1968	Wolfgang Schwartz, Austria
1972	Ondrej Nepela, Czechoslovakia
1976	John Curry, Great Britain
1980	Robin Cousins, Great Britain
1984	Scott Hamilton, United States
1988	Brian Boitano, United States
1992	Viktor Petrenko, Unified Team (Ukr.)
1994	Aleksei Urmanov, Russia
1998	Ilya Kulik, Russia
2002	Alexei Yagudin, Russia
2006	Yevgeny Plushenko, Russia
2010	Evan Lysacek, United States
2014	Yuzuru Hanyu, Japan
2018	Yuzuru Hanyu, Japan

(1) Event held during Summer Olympic Games.

Women's Singles

1908[1]	Madge Syers, Great Britain
1920[1]	Magda Julin-Mauroy, Sweden
1924	Herma von Szabo-Planck, Austria
1928	Sonja Henie, Norway

Women's Singles

1932	Sonja Henie, Norway
1936	Sonja Henie, Norway
1948	Barbara Ann Scott, Canada
1952	Jeanette Altwegg, Great Britain
1956	Tenley Albright, United States
1960	Carol Heiss, United States
1964	Sjoukje Dijkstra, Netherlands
1968	Peggy Fleming, United States
1972	Beatrix Schuba, Austria
1976	Dorothy Hamill, United States
1980	Anett Poetzsch, E. Germany
1984	Katarina Witt, E. Germany
1988	Katarina Witt, E. Germany
1992	Kristi Yamaguchi, United States
1994	Oksana Baiul, Ukraine
1998	Tara Lipinski, United States
2002	Sarah Hughes, United States
2006	Shizuka Arakawa, Japan
2010	Kim Yu-na, South Korea
2014	Adelina Sotnikova, Russia
2018	Alina Zagitova, OAR

(1) Event held during Summer Olympic Games.

Pairs

1908[1]	Anna Hubler & Heinrich Burger, Germany
1920[1]	Ludovika Jakobsson & Walter Jakobsson, Finland
1924	Helene Engelman & Alfred Berger, Austria
1928	Andree Joly & Pierre Brunet, France
1932	Andree Joly & Pierre Brunet, France
1936	Maxi Herber & Ernst Baier, Germany
1948	Micheline Lannoy & Pierre Baugniet, Belgium
1952	Ria Falk & Paul Falk, Germany
1956	Elisabeth Schwartz & Kurt Oppelt, Austria
1964	Ludmila Beloussova & Oleg Protopopov, USSR
1968	Ludmila Beloussova & Oleg Protopopov, USSR
1972	Irina Rodnina & Alexei Ulanov, USSR
1976	Irina Rodnina & Aleksandr Zaitsev, USSR
1980	Irina Rodnina & Aleksandr Zaitsev, USSR
1984	Elena Valova & Oleg Vassiliev, USSR
1988	Ekaterina Gordeeva & Sergei Grinkov, USSR
1992	Natalia Mishkutienok & Artur Dimitriev, Unified Team
1994	Ekaterina Gordeeva & Sergei Grinkov, Russia
1998	Oksana Kazakova & Artur Dmitriev, Russia
2002	Elena Berezhnaya & Anton Sikharulidze, Russia; Jamie Salé & David Pelletier, Canada (tie)
2006	Tatyana Totmianina & Maxim Marinin, Russia
2010	Shen Xue & Zhao Hongbo, China
2014	Tatiana Volosozhar & Maxim Trankov, Russia
2018	Aljona Savchenko & Bruno Massot, Germany

(1) Event held during Summer Olympic Games.

Ice Dancing

1976	Ludmila Pakhomova & Aleksandr Gorschkov, USSR
1980	Natalya Linichuk & Gennadi Karponosov, USSR
1984	Jayne Torvill & Christopher Dean, Great Britain
1988	Natalia Bestemianova & Andrei Bukin, USSR
1992	Marina Klimova & Sergei Ponomarenko, Unified Team
1994	Pasha Grishuk & Evgeny Platov, Russia
1998	Pasha Grishuk & Evgeny Platov, Russia
2002	Marina Anissina & Gwendal Peizerat, France
2006	Tatyana Navka & Roman Kostomarov, Russia
2010	Tessa Virtue & Scott Moir, Canada
2014	Meryl Davis & Charlie White, United States
2018	Tessa Virtue & Scott Moir, Canada

Mixed Team

2014	Russia, Canada, United States
2018	Canada, OAR, United States

Freestyle Skiing

Men's Aerials

		Points
1994	Andreas Schoenbaechler, Switzerland	234.67
1998	Eric Bergoust, United States	255.64
2002	Ales Valenta, Czech Republic	257.02
2006	Xiaopeng Han, China	250.77
2010	Alexei Grishin, Belarus	248.41
2014	Anton Kushnir, Belarus	134.50
2018	Oleksandr Abramenko, Ukraine	128.51

Men's Moguls

		Points
1992	Edgar Grospiron, France	25.81
1994	Jean-Luc Brassard, Canada	27.24
1998	Jonny Moseley, United States	26.93
2002	Janne Lahtela, Finland	27.97
2006	Dale Begg-Smith, Australia	26.77
2010	Alex Bilodeau, Canada	26.75
2014	Alex Bilodeau, Canada	26.31
2018	Mikaël Kingsbury, Canada	86.63

Men's Ski Cross

2010	Michael Schmid, Switzerland
2014	Jean Frederic Chapuis, France
2018	Brady Leman, Canada

Men's Ski Halfpipe

		Points
2014	David Wise, United States	92.00
2018	David Wise, United States	97.20

Men's Ski Slopestyle

		Points
2014	Joss Christensen, United States	95.80
2018	Oystein Braaten, Norway	95.00

Women's Aerials

		Points
1994	Lina Tcherjazova, Uzbekistan	166.84
1998	Nikki Stone, United States	193.00
2002	Alisa Camplin, Australia	193.47
2006	Evelyne Leu, Switzerland	202.55
2010	Lydia Lassila, Australia	214.74
2014	Alla Tsuper, Belarus	98.01
2018	Hanna Huskova, Belarus	96.14

Women's Moguls

		Points
1992	Donna Weinbrecht, United States	23.69
1994	Stine Lise Hattestad, Norway	25.97
1998	Tae Satoya, Japan	25.06
2002	Kari Traa, Norway	25.94
2006	Jennifer Heil, Canada	26.50
2010	Hannah Kearney, United States	26.63
2014	Justine Dufour-Lapointe, Canada	22.44
2018	Perrine Laffont, France	78.65

Women's Ski Cross

2010	Ashleigh McIvor, Canada
2014	Marielle Thompson, Canada
2018	Kelsey Serwa, Canada

Women's Ski Halfpipe

		Points
2014	Maddie Bowman, United States	89.00
2018	Cassie Sharpe, Canada	95.80

Women's Ski Slopestyle

		Points
2014	Dara Howell, Canada	94.20
2018	Sarah Höfflin, Switzerland	91.20

Ice Hockey

Men

1920[1]	Canada, United States, Czechoslovakia
1924	Canada, United States, Great Britain
1928	Canada, Sweden, Switzerland
1932	Canada, United States, Germany
1936	Great Britain, Canada, United States
1948	Canada, Czechoslovakia, Switzerland
1952	Canada, United States, Sweden
1956	USSR, United States, Canada
1960	United States, Canada, USSR
1964	USSR, Sweden, Czechoslovakia
1968	USSR, Czechoslovakia, Canada
1972	USSR, United States, Czechoslovakia
1976	USSR, Czechoslovakia, W. Germany
1980	United States, USSR, Sweden
1984	USSR, Czechoslovakia, Sweden
1988	USSR, Finland, Sweden
1992	Unified Team, Canada, Czechoslovakia
1994	Sweden, Canada, Finland
1998	Czech Republic, Russia, Finland
2002	Canada, United States, Russia
2006	Sweden, Finland, Czech Republic
2010	Canada, United States, Finland
2014	Canada, Sweden, Finland
2018	OAR, Germany, Canada

(1) Event held during Summer Olympic Games.

Women

1998	United States, Canada, Finland
2002	Canada, United States, Sweden
2006	Canada, Sweden, United States
2010	Canada, United States, Finland
2014	Canada, United States, Switzerland
2018	United States, Canada, Finland

Luge

Men's Singles

		Time
1964	Thomas Keohler, E. Germany	3:27.77
1968	Manfred Schmid, Austria	2:52.48
1972	Wolfgang Scheidel, E. Germany	3:27.58
1976	Detlef Guenther, E. Germany	3:27.688
1980	Bernhard Glass, E. Germany	2:54.796
1984	Paul Hildgartner, Italy	3:04.258
1988	Jens Mueller, E. Germany	3:05.548
1992	Georg Hackl, Germany	3:02.363
1994	Georg Hackl, Germany	3:21.571
1998	Georg Hackl, Germany	3:18.436

Men's Singles

		Time
2002	Armin Zoeggeler, Italy	2:57.941
2006	Armin Zoeggeler, Italy	3:26.088
2010	Felix Loch, Germany	3:13.085
2014	Felix Loch, Germany	3:27.526
2018	David Gleirscher, Austria	3:10.702

Men's Doubles

		Time
1964	Austria	1:41.62
1968	E. Germany	1:35.85
1972	Italy, E. Germany (tie)	1:28.35
1976	E. Germany	1:25.604
1980	E. Germany	1:19.331
1984	W. Germany	1:23.620
1988	E. Germany	1:31.940
1992	Germany	1:32.053
1994	Italy	1:36.720
1998	Germany	1:41.105
2002	Germany	1:26.082
2006	Austria	1:34.497
2010	Austria	1:22.705
2014	Germany	1:38.933
2018	Germany	1:31.697

Women's Singles

		Time
1964	Ortun Enderlein, Germany	3:24.67
1968	Erica Lechner, Italy	2:28.66
1972	Anna M. Muller, E. Germany	2:59.18
1976	Margit Schumann, E. Germany	2:50.621
1980	Vera Zozulya, USSR	2:36.537
1984	Steffi Martin, E. Germany	2:46.570
1988	Steffi (Martin) Walter, E. Germany	3:03.973
1992	Doris Neuner, Austria	3:06.696
1994	Gerda Weissensteiner, Italy	3:15.517
1998	Silke Kraushaar, Germany	3:23.779
2002	Sylke Otto, Germany	2:52.464
2006	Sylke Otto, Germany	3:07.979
2010	Tatjana Huefner, Germany	2:46.524
2014	Natalie Geisenberger, Germany	3:19.768
2018	Natalie Geisenberger, Germany	3:05.232

Mixed Team Relay

		Time
2014	Germany, Russia, Latvia	2:45.649
2018	Germany, Canada, Austria	2:24.517

Nordic Combined

Men's Individual

1924	Thorleif Haug, Norway
1928	Johan Grottumsbraaten, Norway
1932	Johan Grottumsbraaten, Norway
1936	Oddbjorn Hagen, Norway
1948	Heikki Hasu, Finland
1952	Simon Slattvik, Norway
1956	Sverre Stenersen, Norway
1960	Georg Thoma, W. Germany
1964	Tormod Knutsen, Norway
1968	Franz Keller, W. Germany
1972	Ulrich Wehling, E. Germany
1976	Ulrich Wehling, E. Germany
1980	Ulrich Wehling, E. Germany
1984	Tom Sandberg, Norway
1988	Hippolyt Kempf, Switzerland
1992	Fabrice Guy, France
1994	Fred Barre Lundberg, Norway
1998	Bjarte Engen Vik, Norway
2002	Samppa Lajunen, Finland
2006	Georg Hettich, Germany

Men's 10-Kilometer Large Hill

2010	Bill Demong, United States
2014	Joergen Graabak, Norway
2018	Johannes Rydzek, Germany

Men's 10-Kilometer Normal Hill

2010	Jason Lamy Chappuis, France
2014	Eric Frenzel, Germany
2018	Eric Frenzel, Germany

Men's Team 4x5-Kilometer Relay

1988	W. Germany, Switzerland, Austria
1992	Japan, Norway, Austria
1994	Japan, Norway, Switzerland
1998	Norway, Finland, France
2002	Finland, Germany, France
2006	Austria, Germany, Finland
2010	Austria, United States, Germany
2014	Norway, Germany, Austria
2018	Germany, Norway, Austria

Ski Jumping

Men's Normal Hill

		Points
1964	Veikko Kankkonen, Finland	229.9
1968	Jiri Raska, Czechoslovakia	216.5
1972	Yukio Kasaya, Japan	244.2
1976	Hans-Georg Aschenbach, E. Germany	252.0
1980	Toni Innauer, Austria	266.3
1984	Jens Weissflog, E. Germany	215.2
1988	Matti Nykaenen, Finland	230.5
1992	Ernst Vettori, Austria	222.8
1994	Espen Bredesen, Norway	282.0
1998	Jani Soininen, Finland	234.5
2002	Simon Ammann, Switzerland	269.0
2006	Lars Bystoel, Norway	266.5
2010	Simon Ammann, Switzerland	276.5
2014	Kamil Stoch, Poland	278.0
2018	Andreas Wellinger, Germany	259.3

Men's Large Hill

		Points
1924	Jacob Tullin Thams, Norway	18.960
1928	Alfred Andersen, Norway	19.208
1932	Birger Ruud, Norway	228.1
1936	Birger Ruud, Norway	232.0
1948	Petter Hugsted, Norway	228.1
1952	Arnfinn Bergmann, Norway	226.0
1956	Antti Hyvarinen, Finland	227.0
1960	Helmut Recknagel, E. Germany	227.2
1964	Toralf Engan, Norway	230.7
1968	Vladimir Beloussov, USSR	231.3
1972	Wojciech Fortuna, Poland	219.9
1976	Karl Schnabl, Austria	234.8
1980	Jouko Tormanen, Finland	271.0
1984	Matti Nykaenen, Finland	231.2
1988	Matti Nykaenen, Finland	224.0
1992	Toni Nieminen, Finland	239.5
1994	Jens Weissflog, Germany	274.5
1998	Kazuyoshi Funaki, Japan	272.3
2002	Simon Ammann, Switzerland	281.4
2006	Thomas Morgenstern, Austria	276.9
2010	Simon Ammann, Switzerland	283.6
2014	Kamil Stoch, Poland	278.7
2018	Kamil Stoch, Poland	285.7

Men's Team

		Points
1988	Finland, Yugoslavia, Norway	634.4
1992	Finland, Austria, Czechoslovakia	644.4
1994	Germany, Japan, Austria	970.1
1998	Japan, Germany, Austria	933.0
2002	Germany, Finland, Slovenia	974.1
2006	Austria, Finland, Norway	984.0
2010	Austria, Germany, Norway	1,107.9
2014	Germany, Austria, Japan	1,041.1
2018	Norway, Germany, Poland	1,098.5

Women's Normal Hill

		Points
2014	Carina Vogt, Germany	247.4
2018	Maren Lundby, Norway	264.6

Snowboarding

Men's Big Air

		Points
2018	Sebastien Toutant, Canada	174.25

Men's Halfpipe

		Points
1998	Gian Simmen, Switzerland	85.2
2002	Ross Powers, United States	46.1
2006	Shaun White, United States	46.8
2010	Shaun White, United States	48.4
2014	Iouri Podladtchikov, Switzerland	94.75
2018	Shaun White, United States	97.75

Men's Parallel Giant Slalom

1998	Ross Rebagliati, Canada
2002	Philipp Schoch, Switzerland
2006	Philipp Schoch, Switzerland
2010	Jasey Jay Anderson, Canada
2014	Vic Wild, Russia
2018	Nevin Galmarini, Switzerland

Note: In 2002, the Giant Slalom became the Parallel Giant Slalom.

Men's Parallel Slalom

2014	Vic Wild, Russia

Men's Slopestyle

		Points
2014	Sage Kotsenburg, United States	93.50
2018	Red Gerard, United States	87.16

Men's Snowboard Cross

2006	Seth Wescott, United States
2010	Seth Wescott, United States
2014	Pierre Vaultier, France
2018	Pierre Vaultier, France

Women's Big Air	Points
2018 Anna Gasser, Austria	185.00

Women's Halfpipe	Points
1998 Nicola Thost, Germany	74.6
2002 Kelly Clark, United States	47.9
2006 Hannah Teter, United States	46.4
2010 Torah Bright, Australia	45.0
2014 Kaitlyn Farrington, United States	91.75
2018 Chloe Kim, United States	98.25

Women's Parallel Giant Slalom
1998 Karine Ruby, France
2002 Isabelle Blanc, France
2006 Daniela Meuli, Switzerland
2010 Nicolien Sauerbreij, Netherlands
2014 Patrizia Kummer, Switzerland
2018 Ester Ledecká, Czech Republic
Note: In 2002, the Giant Slalom became the Parallel Giant Slalom.

Women's Parallel Slalom
2014 Julia Dujmovits, Austria

Women's Slopestyle	Points
2014 Jamie Anderson, United States	95.25
2018 Jamie Anderson, United States	83.00

Women's Snowboard Cross
2006 Tanja Frieden, Switzerland
2010 Maelle Ricker, Canada
2014 Eva Samková, Czech Republic
2018 Michela Moioli, Italy

Speed Skating
= Olympic record

Men's 500 Meters	Time
1924 Charles Jewtraw, United States	0:44.0
1928 C. Thunberg, Finland; B. Evensen, Norway (tie)	0:43.4
1932 John A. Shea, United States	0:43.4
1936 Ivar Ballangrud, Norway	0:43.4
1948 Finn Helgesen, Norway	0:43.1
1952 Kenneth Henry, United States	0:43.2
1956 Evgeniy Grishin, USSR	0:40.2
1960 Evgeniy Grishin, USSR	0:40.2
1964 Terry McDermott, United States	0:40.1
1968 Erhard Keller, W. Germany	0:40.3
1972 Erhard Keller, W. Germany	0:39.44
1976 Evgeny Kulikov, USSR	0:39.17
1980 Eric Heiden, United States	0:38.03
1984 Sergei Fokichev, USSR	0:38.19
1988 Uwe-Jens Mey, E. Germany	0:36.45
1992 Uwe-Jens Mey, E. Germany	0:37.14
1994 Aleksandr Golubev, Russia	0:36.33
1998 Hiroyasu Shimizu, Japan	0:35.59
2002 Casey FitzRandolph, United States	0:34.42
2006 Joey Cheek, United States	0:34.82
2010 Mo Tae-bum, S. Korea	0:69.82
2014 Michel Mulder, Netherlands	0:69.312
2018 Havard Lorentzen, Norway	0:34.41*

Note: In 2010 and 2014, results include the total of two 500-km race times.

Men's 1000 Meters	Time
1976 Peter Mueller, United States	1:19.32
1980 Eric Heiden, United States	1:15.18
1984 Gaetan Boucher, Canada	1:15.80
1988 Nikolai Guiliaev, USSR	1:13.03
1992 Olaf Zinke, Germany	1:14.85
1994 Dan Jansen, United States	1:12.43
1998 Ids Postma, Netherlands	1:10.64
2002 Gerard van Velde, Netherlands	1:07.18*
2006 Shani Davis, United States	1:08.89
2010 Shani Davis, United States	1:08.94
2014 Stefan Groothuis, Netherlands	1:08.39
2018 Kjeld Nuis, Netherlands	1:07.95

Men's 1500 Meters	Time
1924 Clas Thunberg, Finland	2:20.8
1928 Clas Thunberg, Finland	2:21.1
1932 John A. Shea, United States	2:57.5
1936 Charles Mathiesen, Norway	2:19.2
1948 Sverre Farstad, Norway	2:17.6
1952 Hjalmar Andersen, Norway	2:20.4
1956 Y. Grishin, USSR; Y. Mikhailov, USSR (tie)	2:08.6
1960 R. Aas, Norway; Y. Grishin, USSR (tie)	2:10.4
1964 Ants Anston, USSR	2:10.3
1968 Cornelis Verkerk, Netherlands	2:03.4
1972 Ard Schenk, Netherlands	2:02.96
1976 Jan Egil Storholt, Norway	1:59.38

Men's 1500 Meters	Time
1980 Eric Heiden, United States	1:55.44
1984 Gaetan Boucher, Canada	1:58.36
1988 Andre Hoffmann, E. Germany	1:52.06
1992 Johann Koss, Norway	1:54.81
1994 Johann Koss, Norway	1:51.29
1998 Aadne Sondral, Norway	1:47.87
2002 Derek Parra, United States	1:43.95*
2006 Enrico Fabris, Italy	1:45.97
2010 Mark Tuitert, Netherlands	1:45.57
2014 Zbigniew Brodka, Poland	1:45.006
2018 Kjeld Nuis, Netherlands	1:44.01

Men's 5000 Meters	Time
1924 Clas Thunberg, Finland	8:39.0
1928 Ivar Ballangrud, Norway	8:50.5
1932 Irving Jaffee, United States	9:40.8
1936 Ivar Ballangrud, Norway	8:19.6
1948 Reidar Liaklev, Norway	8:29.4
1952 Hjalmar Andersen, Norway	8:10.6
1956 Boris Shilkov, USSR	7:48.7
1960 Viktor Kosichkin, USSR	7:51.3
1964 Knut Johannesen, Norway	7:38.4
1968 F. Anton Maier, Norway	7:22.4
1972 Ard Schenk, Netherlands	7:23.61
1976 Sten Stensen, Norway	7:24.48
1980 Eric Heiden, United States	7:02.29
1984 Tomas Gustafson, Sweden	7:12.28
1988 Tomas Gustafson, Sweden	6:44.63
1992 Geir Karlstad, Norway	6:59.97
1994 Johann Koss, Norway	6:34.96
1998 Gianni Romme, Netherlands	6:22.20
2002 Jochem Uytdehaage, Netherlands	6:14.66
2006 Chad Hedrick, United States	6:14.68
2010 Sven Kramer, Netherlands	6:14.60
2014 Sven Kramer, Netherlands	6:10.76
2018 Sven Kramer, Netherlands	6:09.76*

Men's 10,000 Meters	Time
1924 Julius Skutnabb, Finland	18:04.8
1928 Event not held because of thawing of ice	
1932 Irving Jaffee, United States	19:13.6
1936 Ivar Ballangrud, Norway	17:24.3
1948 Ake Seyffarth, Sweden	17:26.3
1952 Hjalmar Andersen, Norway	16:45.8
1956 Sigvard Ericsson, Sweden	16:35.9
1960 Knut Johannesen, Norway	15:46.6
1964 Jonny Nilsson, Sweden	15:50.1
1968 Jonny Hoeglin, Sweden	15:23.6
1972 Ard Schenk, Netherlands	15:01.35
1976 Piet Kleine, Netherlands	14:50.59
1980 Eric Heiden, United States	14:28.13
1984 Igor Malkov, USSR	14:39.90
1988 Tomas Gustafson, Sweden	13:48.20
1992 Bart Veldkamp, Netherlands	14:12.12
1994 Johann Koss, Norway	13:30.55
1998 Gianni Romme, Netherlands	13:15.33
2002 Jochem Uytdehaage, Netherlands	12:58.92
2006 Bob de Jong, Netherlands	13:01.57
2010 Lee Seung-hoon, S. Korea	12:58.55
2014 Jorrit Bergsma, Netherlands	12:44.45
2018 Ted-Jan Bloemen, Canada	12:39.77*

Men's Mass Start
2018 Lee Seung-hoon, S. Korea

Men's Team Pursuit	Time
2006 Italy, Canada, Netherlands	3:44.46
2010 Canada, United States, Netherlands	3:41.37
2014 Netherlands, S. Korea, Poland	3:37.71
2018 Norway, S. Korea, Netherlands	3:37.32

Women's 500 Meters	Time
1960 Helga Haase, Germany	0:45.9
1964 Lydia Skoblikova, USSR	0:45.0
1968 Ludmila Titova, USSR	0:46.1
1972 Anne Henning, United States	0:43.33
1976 Sheila Young, United States	0:42.76
1980 Karin Enke, E. Germany	0:41.78
1984 Christa Rothenburger, E. Germany	0:41.02
1988 Bonnie Blair, United States	0:39.10
1992 Bonnie Blair, United States	0:40.33
1994 Bonnie Blair, United States	0:39.25
1998 Catriona Le May Doan, Canada	0:38.21
2002 Catriona Le May Doan, Canada	0:37.30
2006 Svetlana Zhurova, Russia	0:38.23
2010 Lee Sang-hwa, S. Korea	0:76.09
2014 Lee Sang-hwa, S. Korea	0:74.70
2018 Nao Kodaira, Japan	0:36.94*

Note: In 2010 and 2014, results include the total of two 500-km race times.

Women's 1000 Meters

		Time
1960	Klara Guseva, USSR	1:34.1
1964	Lydia Skoblikova, USSR	1:33.2
1968	Carolina Geijssen, Netherlands	1:32.6
1972	Monika Pflug, W. Germany	1:31.40
1976	Tatiana Averina, USSR	1:28.43
1980	Natalya Petruseva, USSR	1:24.10
1984	Karin Enke, E. Germany	1:21.61
1988	Christa Rothenburger, E. Germany	1:17.65
1992	Bonnie Blair, United States	1:21.90
1994	Bonnie Blair, United States	1:18.74
1998	Marianne Timmer, Netherlands	1:16.51
2002	Chris Witty, United States	1:13.83
2006	Marianne Timmer, Netherlands	1:16.05
2010	Christine Nesbitt, Canada	1:16.56
2014	Zhang Hong, China	1:14.02
2018	Jorien ter Mors, Netherlands	1:13.56*

Women's 1500 Meters

		Time
1960	Lydia Skoblikova, USSR	2:52.2
1964	Lydia Skoblikova, USSR	2:22.6
1968	Kaija Mustonen, Finland	2:22.4
1972	Dianne Holum, United States	2:20.85
1976	Galina Stepanskaya, USSR	2:16.58
1980	Anne Borckink, Netherlands	2:10.95
1984	Karin Enke, E. Germany	2:03.42
1988	Yvonne van Gennip, Netherlands	2:00.68
1992	Jacqueline Boerner, Germany	2:05.87
1994	Emese Hunyady, Austria	2:02.19
1998	Marianne Timmer, Netherlands	1:57.58
2002	Anni Friesinger, Germany	1:54.02
2006	Cindy Klassen, Canada	1:55.27
2010	Ireen Wüst, Netherlands	1:56.89
2014	Jorien ter Mors, Netherlands	1:53.51*
2018	Ireen Wüst, Netherlands	1:54.35

Women's 3000 Meters

		Time
1960	Lydia Skoblikova, USSR	5:14.3
1964	Lydia Skoblikova, USSR	5:14.9
1968	Johanna Schut, Netherlands	4:56.2
1972	Christina Baas-Kaiser, Netherlands	4:52.14
1976	Tatiana Averina, USSR	4:45.19
1980	Bjoerg Eva Jensen, Norway	4:32.13
1984	Andrea Schoene, E. Germany	4:24.79
1988	Yvonne van Gennip, Netherlands	4:11.94
1992	Gunda Niemann, Germany	4:19.90
1994	Svetlana Bazhanova, Russia	4:17.43
1998	Gunda Niemann-Stirnemann, Germany	4:07.29
2002	Claudia Pechstein, Germany	3:57.70*
2006	Ireen Wüst, Netherlands	4:02.43
2010	Martina Sablikova, Czech Republic	4:02.53
2014	Ireen Wüst, Netherlands	4:00.34
2018	Carlijn Achtereekte, Netherlands	3:59.21

Women's 5000 Meters

		Time
1988	Yvonne van Gennip, Netherlands	7:14.13
1992	Gunda Niemann, Germany	7:31.57
1994	Claudia Pechstein, Germany	7:14.37
1998	Claudia Pechstein, Germany	6:59.61
2002	Claudia Pechstein, Germany	6:46.91*
2006	Clara Hughes, Canada	6:59.07
2010	Martina Sablikova, Czech Republic	6:50.91
2014	Martina Sablikova, Czech Republic	6:51.54
2018	Esmee Visser, Netherlands	6:50.23

Women's Mass Start

2018	Nana Takagi, Japan	

Women's Team Pursuit

		Time
2006	Germany, Canada, Russia	3:01.25
2010	Germany, Japan, Poland	3:02.82
2014	Netherlands, Poland, Russia	2:58.05
2018	Japan, Netherlands, United States	2:53.89*

Speed Skating (Short Track)

* = Olympic record

Men's 500 Meters

		Time
1998	Takafumi Nishitani, Japan	0:42.862
2002	Marc Gagnon, Canada	0:41.802
2006	Apolo Anton Ohno, United States	0:41.935
2010	Charles Hamelin, Canada	0:40.981
2014	Victor An, Russia	0:41.312
2018	Wu Dajing, China	0:39.584*

Men's 1000 Meters

		Time
1992	Kim Ki-hoon, S. Korea	1:30.76
1994	Kim Ki-hoon, S. Korea	1:34.57
1998	Kim Dong-sung, S. Korea	1:32.375
2002	Steven Bradbury, Australia	1:29.109
2006	Ahn Hyun-soo, S. Korea	1:26.739
2010	Lee Jung-su, S. Korea	1:23.747
2014	Victor An, Russia	1:25.325
2018	Samuel Girard, Canada	1:24.650

Men's 1500 Meters

		Time
2002	Apolo Anton Ohno, United States	2:18.541
2006	Ahn Hyun-soo, S. Korea	2:25.341
2010	Lee Jung-su, S. Korea	2:17.611
2014	Charles Hamelin, Canada	2:14.985
2018	Lim Hyo-jun, S. Korea	2:10.485*

Men's 5000-Meter Relay

		Time
1992	S. Korea, Canada, Japan	7:14.02
1994	Italy, United States, Australia	7:11.74
1998	Canada, S. Korea, China	7:06.075
2002	Canada, Italy, China	6:51.579
2006	S. Korea, Canada, United States	6:43.376
2010	Canada, S. Korea, United States	6:44.224
2014	Russia, United States, China	6:42.100
2018	Hungary, China, Canada	6:31.971*

Women's 500 Meters

		Time
1992	Cathy Turner, United States	0:47.04
1994	Cathy Turner, United States	0:45.98
1998	Annie Perreault, Canada	0:46.568
2002	Yang Yang (A), China	0:44.187
2006	Wang Meng, China	0:44.345
2010	Wang Meng, China	0:43.048
2014	Li Jianrou, China	0:45.263
2018	Arianna Fontana, Italy	0:42.569

Women's 1000 Meters

		Time
1998	Chun Lee-kyung, S. Korea	1:42.776
2002	Yang Yang (A), China	1:36.391
2006	Jin Sun-yu, S. Korea	1:32.859
2010	Wang Meng, China	1:29.213
2014	Park Seung-hi, S. Korea	1:30.761
2018	Suzanne Schulting, Netherlands	1:29.778

Women's 1500 Meters

		Time
2002	Ko Gi-hyun, S. Korea	2:31.581
2006	Jin Sun-yu, S. Korea	2:23.494
2010	Zhou Yang, China	2:16.993*
2014	Zhou Yang, China	2:19.140
2018	Choi Min-jeong, S. Korea	2:24.948

Women's 3000-Meter Relay

		Time
1992	Canada, United States, Unified Team	4:36.62
1994	S. Korea, Canada, United States	4:26.64
1998	S. Korea, China, Canada	4:16.26
2002	S. Korea, China, Canada	4:12.793
2006	S. Korea, Canada, Italy	4:17.040
2010	China, Canada, United States	4:06.610*
2014	S. Korea, Canada, Italy	4:09.498
2018	S. Korea, Italy, Netherlands	4:07.361

Paralympic Games

Aug. 24-Sept. 5, 2021

The XVI Paralympic Summer Games, originally scheduled for 2020, were postponed to 2021 due to the coronavirus pandemic. More than 4,300 athletes from 159 countries met at the XV Paralympic Summer Games, held Sept. 7-18, 2016, in Rio de Janeiro, Brazil. A total of 529 gold medals were awarded in 23 sports. China claimed 239 total medals, outpacing Great Britain (147), Ukraine (117), and the United States (115). The XII Paralympic Winter Games were held Mar. 9-18, 2018, in the same Olympic venues that hosted the 2018 Winter Games in Pyeongchang, South Korea. A record 567 athletes from 49 delegations competed in 80 medal events across six sports. The United States led the medal tally with 36 total (13 gold), followed by the Neutral Paralympic Athletes (NPA) delegation (Russian athletes) with 24 (8 gold), Canada with 28 (8 gold), and France with 20 (7 gold). The 2022 Winter Paralympics were expected to be held in Mar. in Beijing, China.

The first Olympic Games for athletes with an impairment were held in Rome after the 1960 Summer Olympics; use of the name "paralympic" began with the 1964 games in Tokyo. The Paralympics are held by the Olympic host country in the same year and usually the same city and venue or venues. In 1976, the first Winter Paralympics were held in Ornskoldsvik, Sweden.

COLLEGE SPORTS
COLLEGE FOOTBALL
2019 CFP Championship: LSU Topples Clemson

The No. 1 Louisiana State Univ. Tigers defeated the No. 3 Clemson Tigers, 42-25, Jan. 13, 2020, at the Mercedes-Benz Superdome in New Orleans, LA, in the College Football Playoff Championship. LSU's Heisman Trophy-winning quarterback Joe Burrow threw for 463 yards and five touchdowns—setting a new single-season passing record with 60—and ran for one more TD to take down the defending champion Clemson. The LSU victory, which marked the school's first title of the CFP era and fourth title overall, halted Clemson's 29-game winning streak and gave QB Trevor Lawrence his first college-level loss.

2019 College Football Final Rankings

College Football Playoff Rankings		Associated Press Poll		USA Today Coaches Poll	
Rank, team / **Rank, team**		**Rank, team** / **Rank, team**		**Rank, team** / **Rank, team**	
1. LSU	14. Michigan	1. LSU	14. Auburn	1. LSU	14. Auburn
2. Ohio St.	15. Notre Dame	2. Clemson	15. Iowa	2. Clemson	15. Iowa
3. Clemson	16. Iowa	3. Ohio St.	16. Utah	3. Ohio St.	16. Utah
4. Oklahoma	17. Memphis	4. Georgia	17. Memphis	4. Georgia	17. Memphis
5. Georgia	18. Minnesota	5. Oregon	18. Michigan	5. Oregon	18. Appalachian St.
6. Oregon	19. Boise St.	6. Florida	19. Appalachian St.	6. Oklahoma	19. Michigan
7. Baylor	20. Appalachian St.	7. Oklahoma	20. Navy	7. Florida	20. Navy
8. Wisconsin	21. Cincinnati	8. Alabama	21. Cincinnati	8. Alabama	21. Cincinnati
9. Florida	22. USC	9. Penn St.	22. Air Force	9. Penn St.	22. Boise St.
10. Penn St.	23. Navy	10. Minnesota	23. Boise St.	10. Minnesota	23. Air Force
11. Utah	24. Virginia	11. Wisconsin	24. UCF	11. Notre Dame	24. UCF
12. Auburn	25. Oklahoma St.	12. Notre Dame	25. Texas	12. Baylor	25. Virginia
13. Alabama		13. Baylor		13. Wisconsin	

Note: College Football Playoff ranking is as of Dec. 8, 2019, prior to bowl games and playoffs. Final AP and USA Today polls are as of Jan. 13, 2020 (after all bowls and championship game).

National College Football Championship Game Results, 1998-2019

The Bowl Championship Series (BCS) National Championship game (BCS ranked No. 1 vs. BCS No. 2) determined the NCAA's Football Bowl Subdivision (Div. I-A) champion in 1998-2013. The College Football Playoff (CFP) replaced the BCS at the end of the 2014 regular season. The four-team CFP consists of a semifinal round (rotating among the following six bowl games: Sugar, Rose, Orange, Cotton, Peach, and Fiesta) and a championship game played on a Monday night. A committee ranks 25 teams for the playoffs and selected other bowl games, using guidelines that include strength of schedule, head-to-head results, and won-loss records; preference is given to conference champions. Years shown here are for regular season, not year in which championship was played.

Year	Result	Year	Result	Year	Result
1998	Tennessee 23, Florida St. 16	2006	Florida 41, Ohio St. 14	2013	Florida St. 34, Auburn 31
1999	Florida St. 46, Virginia Tech 29	2007	LSU 38, Ohio St. 24	2014	Ohio St. 42, Oregon 20
2000	Oklahoma 13, Florida St. 2	2008	Florida 24, Oklahoma 14	2015	Alabama 45, Clemson 40
2001	Miami (FL) 37, Nebraska 14	2009	Alabama 37, Texas 21	2016	Clemson 35, Alabama 31
2002	Ohio St. 31, Miami (FL) 24	2010	Auburn 22, Oregon 19	2017	Alabama 26, Georgia 23 (OT)
2003[1]	LSU 21, Oklahoma 14	2011	Alabama 21, LSU 0	2018	Clemson 44, Alabama 16
2004[2]	USC 55, Oklahoma 19	2012	Alabama 42, Notre Dame 14	2019	LSU 42, Clemson 25
2005	Texas 41, USC 38				

(1) AP named USC No. 1 in its final poll despite its not appearing in the BCS No. 1 vs. No. 2 matchup. (2) The BCS's Presidential Oversight Committee vacated USC's 2004 championship due to rules violations.

National College Football Champions, 1936-1997

Unofficial champion(s), as selected by the AP poll of writers and a separate poll of coaches. Where the polls disagreed, both teams are listed with the AP winner first. The AP poll started in 1936, the coaches poll in 1950.

Year	Champion(s)	Year	Champion(s)	Year	Champion(s)	Year	Champion(s)	Year	Champion(s)
1936	Minnesota	1949	Notre Dame	1962	USC	1974	Oklahoma/USC	1986	Penn St.
1937	Pittsburgh	1950	Oklahoma	1963	Texas	1975	Oklahoma	1987	Miami (FL)
1938	Texas Christian	1951	Tennessee	1964	Alabama	1976	Pittsburgh	1988	Notre Dame
1939	Texas A&M	1952	Michigan St.	1965	Alabama/Mich. St.	1977	Notre Dame	1989	Miami (FL)
1940	Minnesota	1953	Maryland	1966	Notre Dame	1978	Alabama/USC	1990	Colorado/GA Tech
1941	Minnesota	1954	Ohio St./UCLA	1967	USC	1979	Alabama	1991	Miami (FL)/Wash.
1942	Ohio St.	1955	Oklahoma	1968	Ohio St.	1980	Georgia	1992	Alabama
1943	Notre Dame	1956	Oklahoma	1969	Texas	1981	Clemson	1993	Florida St.
1944	Army	1957	Auburn/Ohio St.	1970	Nebraska/Texas	1982	Penn St.	1994	Nebraska
1945	Army	1958	LSU	1971	Nebraska	1983	Miami (FL)	1995	Nebraska
1946	Notre Dame	1959	Syracuse	1972	USC	1984	Brigham Young	1996	Florida
1947	Notre Dame	1060	Minnesota	1973	Notre Dame/	1985	Oklahoma	1997	Mich./Nebraska
1948	Michigan	1961	Alabama		Alabama				

Results of Major Bowl Games

Date indicates year the game was played; bowl games are generally played in late Dec. or early Jan. CFP = College Football Playoff semifinal game.

Rose Bowl Results, 1902-2020

Year	Result	Year	Result	Year	Result
1902	(Jan.) Michigan 49, Stanford 0	1928	Stanford 7, Pittsburgh 6	1941	Stanford 21, Nebraska 13
1916	Washington St. 14, Brown 0	1929	Georgia Tech 8, California 7	1942	Oregon St. 20, Duke 16
1917	Oregon 14, Pennsylvania 0	1930	USC 47, Pittsburgh 14	1943	Georgia 9, UCLA 0
1918-19	Service teams	1931	Alabama 24, Washington St. 0	1944	USC 29, Washington 0
1920	Harvard 7, Oregon 6	1932	USC 21, Tulane 12	1945	USC 25, Tennessee 0
1921	California 28, Ohio St. 0	1933	USC 35, Pittsburgh 0	1946	Alabama 34, USC 14
1922	Washington & Jefferson 0,	1934	Columbia 7, Stanford 0	1947	Illinois 45, UCLA 14
	California 0	1935	Alabama 29, Stanford 13	1948	Michigan 49, USC 0
1923	USC 14, Penn St. 3	1936	Stanford 7, SMU 0	1949	Northwestern 20, California 14
1924	Navy 14, Washington 14	1937	Pittsburgh 21, Washington 0	1950	Ohio St. 17, California 14
1925	Notre Dame 27, Stanford 10	1938	California 13, Alabama 0	1951	Michigan 14, California 6
1926	Alabama 20, Washington 19	1939	USC 7, Duke 3	1952	Illinois 40, Stanford 7
1927	Alabama 7, Stanford 7	1940	USC 14, Tennessee 0	1953	USC 7, Wisconsin 0

1954 Michigan St. 28, UCLA 20	1977 USC 14, Michigan 6	2000 Wisconsin 17, Stanford 9
1955 Ohio St. 20, USC 7	1978 Washington 27, Michigan 20	2001 Washington 34, Purdue 24
1956 Michigan St. 17, UCLA 14	1979 USC 17, Michigan 10	2002 Miami (FL) 37, Nebraska 14
1957 Iowa 35, Oregon St. 19	1980 USC 17, Ohio St. 16	2003 Oklahoma 34, Washington St. 14
1958 Ohio St. 10, Oregon 7	1981 Michigan 23, Washington 6	2004 USC 28, Michigan 14
1959 Iowa 38, California 12	1982 Washington 28, Iowa 0	2005 Texas 38, Michigan 37
1960 Washington 44, Wisconsin 8	1983 UCLA 24, Michigan 14	2006 Texas 41, USC 38
1961 Washington 17, Minnesota 7	1984 UCLA 45, Illinois 9	2007 USC 32, Michigan 18
1962 Minnesota 21, UCLA 3	1985 USC 20, Ohio St. 17	2008 USC 49, Illinois 17
1963 USC 42, Wisconsin 37	1986 UCLA 45, Iowa 28	2009 USC 38, Penn St. 24
1964 Illinois 17, Washington 7	1987 Arizona St. 22, Michigan 15	2010 Ohio St. 26, Oregon 17
1965 Michigan 34, Oregon St. 7	1988 Michigan St. 20, USC 17	2011 TCU 21, Wisconsin 19
1966 UCLA 14, Michigan St. 12	1989 Michigan 22, USC 14	2012 Oregon 45, Wisconsin 38
1967 Purdue 14, USC 13	1990 USC 17, Michigan 10	2013 Stanford 20, Wisconsin 14
1968 USC 14, Indiana 3	1991 Washington 46, Iowa 34	2014 Michigan St. 24, Stanford 20
1969 Ohio St. 27, USC 16	1992 Washington 34, Michigan 14	2015 Oregon 59, Florida St. 20 (CFP)
1970 USC 10, Michigan 3	1993 Michigan 38, Washington 31	2016 Stanford 45, Iowa 16
1971 Stanford 27, Ohio St. 17	1994 Wisconsin 21, UCLA 16	2017 USC 52, Penn St. 49
1972 Stanford 13, Michigan 12	1995 Penn St. 38, Oregon 20	2018 Georgia 54, Oklahoma 48 (2 OT)
1973 USC 42, Ohio St. 17	1996 USC 41, Northwestern 32	(CFP)
1974 Ohio St. 42, USC 21	1997 Ohio St. 20, Arizona St. 17	
1975 USC 18, Ohio St. 17	1998 Michigan 21, Washington St. 16	2019 Ohio St. 28, Washington 23
1976 UCLA 23, Ohio St. 10	1999 Wisconsin 38, UCLA 31	2020 Oregon 28, Wisconsin 27

Orange Bowl Results, 1935-2019

1935 (Jan.) Bucknell 26, Miami (FL) 0	1964 Nebraska 13, Auburn 7	1994 Florida St. 18, Nebraska 16
1936 Catholic U. 20, Mississippi 19	1965 Texas 21, Alabama 17	1995 Nebraska 24, Miami (FL) 17
1937 Duquesne 13, Mississippi St. 12	1966 Alabama 39, Nebraska 28	1996 Florida St. 31, Notre Dame 26
1938 Auburn 6, Michigan St. 0	1967 Florida 27, Georgia Tech 12	1996 (Dec.) Nebraska 41,
1939 Tennessee 17, Oklahoma 0	1968 Oklahoma 26, Tennessee 24	Virginia Tech 21
1940 Georgia Tech 21, Missouri 7	1969 Penn St. 15, Kansas 14	1998 (Jan.) Nebraska 42,
1941 Mississippi St. 14,	1970 Penn St. 10, Missouri 3	Tennessee 17
Georgetown 7	1971 Nebraska 17, LSU 12	1999 Florida 31, Syracuse 10
1942 Georgia 40, TCU 26	1972 Nebraska 38, Alabama 6	2000 Michigan 35, Alabama 34 (OT)
1943 Alabama 37, Boston College 21	1973 Nebraska 40, Notre Dame 6	2001 Oklahoma 13, Florida St. 2
1944 LSU 19, Texas A&M 14	1974 Penn St. 16, LSU 9	2002 Florida 56, Maryland 23
1945 Tulsa 26, Georgia Tech 12	1975 Notre Dame 13, Alabama 11	2003 USC 38, Iowa 17
1946 Miami (FL) 13, Holy Cross 6	1976 Oklahoma 14, Michigan 6	2004 Miami (FL) 16, Florida St. 14
1947 Rice 8, Tennessee 0	1977 Ohio St. 27, Colorado 10	2005 USC 55, Oklahoma 19
1948 Georgia Tech 20, Kansas 14	1978 Arkansas 31, Oklahoma 6	2006 Penn St. 26, Florida St. 23 (3 OT)
1949 Texas 41, Georgia 28	1979 Oklahoma 31, Nebraska 24	2007 Louisville 24, Wake Forest 13
1950 Santa Clara 21, Kentucky 13	1980 Oklahoma 24, Florida St. 7	2008 Kansas 24, Virginia Tech 21
1951 Clemson 15, Miami (FL) 14	1981 Oklahoma 18, Florida St. 17	2009 Virginia Tech 20, Cincinnati 7
1952 Georgia Tech 17, Baylor 14	1982 Clemson 22, Nebraska 15	2010 Iowa 24, Georgia Tech 14
1953 Alabama 61, Syracuse 6	1983 Nebraska 21, LSU 20	2011 Stanford 40, Virginia Tech 12
1954 Oklahoma 7, Maryland 0	1984 Miami (FL) 31, Nebraska 30	2012 West Virginia 70, Clemson 33
1955 Duke 34, Nebraska 7	1985 Washington 28, Oklahoma 17	2013 Florida St. 31, Northern Illinois 10
1956 Oklahoma 20, Maryland 6	1986 Oklahoma 25, Penn St. 10	2014 Clemson 40, Ohio St. 35
1957 Colorado 27, Clemson 21	1987 Oklahoma 42, Arkansas 8	2014 (Dec.) Georgia Tech 49,
1958 Oklahoma 48, Duke 21	1988 Miami (FL) 20, Oklahoma 14	Mississippi St. 34
1959 Oklahoma 21, Syracuse 6	1989 Miami (FL) 23, Nebraska 3	2015 Clemson 37, Oklahoma 17 (CFP)
1960 Georgia 14, Missouri 0	1990 Notre Dame 21, Colorado 6	2016 Florida St. 33, Michigan 32
1961 Missouri 21, Navy 14	1991 Colorado 10, Notre Dame 9	2017 Wisconsin 34, Miami (FL) 24
1962 LSU 25, Colorado 7	1992 Miami (FL) 22, Nebraska 0	2018 Alabama 45, Oklahoma 34 (CFP)
1963 Alabama 17, Oklahoma 0	1993 Florida St. 27, Nebraska 14	2019 Florida 36, Virginia 28

Sugar Bowl Results, 1935-2020

1935 (Jan.) Tulane 20, Temple 14	1963 Mississippi 17, Arkansas 13	1992 Notre Dame 39, Florida 28
1936 TCU 3, LSU 2	1964 Alabama 12, Mississippi 7	1993 Alabama 34, Miami (FL) 13
1937 Santa Clara 21, LSU 14	1965 LSU 13, Syracuse 10	1994 Florida 41, West Virginia 7
1938 Santa Clara 6, LSU 0	1966 Missouri 20, Florida 18	1995 Florida St. 23, Florida 17
1939 TCU 15, Carnegie Tech 7	1967 Alabama 34, Nebraska 7	1995 (Dec.) Virginia Tech 28, Texas 10
1940 Texas A&M 14, Tulane 13	1968 LSU 20, Wyoming 13	1997 (Jan.) Florida 52, Florida St. 20
1941 Boston College 19, Tennessee 13	1969 Arkansas 16, Georgia 2	1998 Florida St. 31, Ohio St. 14
1942 Fordham 2, Missouri 0	1970 Mississippi 27, Arkansas 22	1999 Ohio St. 24, Texas A&M 14
1943 Tennessee 14, Tulsa 7	1971 Tennessee 34, Air Force 13	2000 Florida St. 46, Virginia Tech 29
1944 Georgia Tech 20, Tulsa 18	1972 Oklahoma 40, Auburn 22	2001 Miami (FL) 37, Florida 20
1945 Duke 29, Alabama 26	1972 (Dec.) Oklahoma 14, Penn St. 0	2002 LSU 47, Illinois 34
1946 Oklahoma A&M 33,	1973 Notre Dame 24, Alabama 23	2003 Georgia 26, Florida St. 13
St. Mary's (CA) 13	1974 Nebraska 13, Florida 10	2004 LSU 21, Oklahoma 14
1947 Georgia 20, N. Carolina 10	1975 Alabama 13, Penn St. 6	2005 Auburn 16, Virginia Tech 13
1948 Texas 27, Alabama 7	1977 (Jan.) Pittsburgh 27, Georgia 3	2006 West Virginia 38, Georgia 35
1949 Oklahoma 14, N. Carolina 6	1978 Alabama 35, Ohio St. 6	2007 LSU 41, Notre Dame 14
1950 Oklahoma 35, LSU 0	1979 Alabama 14, Penn St. 7	2008 Georgia 41, Hawaii 10
1951 Kentucky 13, Oklahoma 7	1980 Alabama 24, Arkansas 9	2009 Utah 31, Alabama 17
1952 Maryland 28, Tennessee 13	1981 Georgia 17, Notre Dame 10	2010 Florida 51, Cincinnati 24
1953 Georgia Tech 24, Mississippi 7	1982 Pittsburgh 24, Georgia 20	2011 Ohio St. 31, Arkansas 26
1954 Georgia Tech 42, West Virginia 19	1983 Penn St. 27, Georgia 23	2012 Michigan 23, Virginia Tech 20
1955 Navy 21, Mississippi	1984 Auburn 9, Michigan 7	2013 Louisville 33, Florida 23
1956 Georgia Tech 7, Pittsburgh 0	1985 Nebraska 28, LSU 10	2014 Oklahoma 45, Alabama 31
1957 Baylor 13, Tennessee 7	1986 Tennessee 35, Miami (FL) 7	2015 Ohio St. 42, Alabama 35 (CFP)
1958 Mississippi 39, Texas 7	1987 Nebraska 30, LSU 15	2016 Mississippi 48, Oklahoma St. 20
1959 LSU 7, Clemson 0	1988 Syracuse 16, Auburn 16	2017 Oklahoma 35, Auburn 19
1960 Mississippi 21, LSU 0	1989 Florida St. 13, Auburn 7	2018 Alabama 24, Clemson 6 (CFP)
1961 Mississippi 14, Rice 6	1990 Miami (FL) 33, Alabama 25	2019 Texas 28, Georgia 21
1962 Alabama 10, Arkansas 3	1991 Tennessee 23, Virginia 22	2020 Georgia 26, Baylor 14

Cotton Bowl Results, 1937-2019

1937	(Jan.) TCU 16, Marquette 6	1966	LSU 14, Arkansas 7	1995	USC 55, Texas Tech 14
1938	Rice 28, Colorado 14	1966	(Dec.) Georgia 24, SMU 9	1996	Colorado 38, Oregon 6
1939	St. Mary's 20, Texas Tech 13	1968	(Jan.) Texas A&M 20, Alabama 16	1997	Brigham Young 19, Kansas St. 15
1940	Clemson 6, Boston College 3	1969	Texas 36, Tennessee 13	1998	UCLA 29, Texas A&M 23
1941	Texas A&M 13, Fordham 12	1970	Texas 21, Notre Dame 17	1999	Texas 38, Mississippi St. 11
1942	Alabama 29, Texas A&M 21	1971	Notre Dame 24, Texas 11	2000	Arkansas 27, Texas 6
1943	Texas 14, Georgia Tech 7	1972	Penn St. 30, Texas 6	2001	Kansas St. 35, Tennessee 21
1944	Randolph Field 7, Texas 7	1973	Texas 17, Alabama 13	2002	Oklahoma 10, Arkansas 3
1945	Oklahoma A&M 34, TCU 0	1974	Nebraska 19, Texas 3	2003	Texas 35, LSU 20
1946	Texas 40, Missouri 27	1975	Penn St. 41, Baylor 20	2004	Mississippi 31, Oklahoma St. 28
1947	Arkansas 0, LSU 0	1976	Arkansas 31, Georgia 10	2005	Tennessee 38, Texas A&M 7
1948	SMU 13, Penn St. 13	1977	Houston 30, Maryland 21	2006	Alabama 13, Texas Tech 10
1949	SMU 21, Oregon 13	1978	Notre Dame 38, Texas 10	2007	Auburn 17, Nebraska 14
1950	Rice 27, N. Carolina 13	1979	Notre Dame 35, Houston 34	2008	Missouri 38, Arkansas 7
1951	Tennessee 20, Texas 14	1980	Houston 17, Nebraska 14	2009	Mississippi 47, Texas Tech 34
1952	Kentucky 20, TCU 7	1981	Alabama 30, Baylor 2	2010	Mississippi 21, Oklahoma St. 7
1953	Texas 16, Tennessee 0	1982	Texas 14, Alabama 12	2011	LSU 41, Texas A&M 24
1954	Rice 28, Alabama 6	1983	SMU 7, Pittsburgh 3	2012	Arkansas 29, Kansas St. 16
1955	Georgia Tech 14, Arkansas 6	1984	Georgia 10, Texas 9	2013	Texas A&M 41, Oklahoma 13
1956	Mississippi 14, TCU 13	1985	Boston College 45, Houston 28	2014	Missouri 41, Oklahoma St. 31
1957	TCU 28, Syracuse 27	1986	Texas A&M 36, Auburn 16	2015	Michigan St. 42, Baylor 41
1958	Navy 20, Rice 7	1987	Ohio St. 28, Texas A&M 12	2015	(Dec.) Alabama 38, Michigan St.
1959	TCU 0, Air Force 0	1988	Texas A&M 35, Notre Dame 10		0 (CFP)
1960	Syracuse 23, Texas 14	1989	UCLA 17, Arkansas 3	2017	(Jan.) Wisconsin 24, W. Michigan
1961	Duke 7, Arkansas 6	1990	Tennessee 31, Arkansas 27		16
1962	Texas 12, Mississippi 7	1991	Miami (FL) 46, Texas 3	2017	(Dec.) Ohio St. 24, USC 7
1963	LSU 13, Texas 0	1992	Florida St. 10, Texas A&M 2	2018	Clemson 30, Notre Dame 3 (CFP)
1964	Texas 28, Navy 6	1993	Notre Dame 28, Texas A&M 3	2019	Penn St. 53, Memphis 39
1965	Arkansas 10, Nebraska 7	1994	Notre Dame 24, Texas A&M 21		

Peach Bowl Results, 1968-2019

1968	(Dec.) LSU 31, Florida St. 27	1985	Army 31, Illinois 29	2002	Maryland 30, Tennessee 3
1969	West Virginia 14, S. Carolina 3	1986	Virginia Tech 25,	2004	(Jan.) Clemson 27, Tennessee 14
1970	Arizona St. 48, N. Carolina 26		N. Carolina St. 24	2004	(Dec.) Miami (FL) 27, Florida 10
1971	Mississippi 41, Georgia Tech 18	1988	(Jan.) Tennessee 27, Indiana 22	2005	LSU 40, Miami (FL) 3
1972	N. Carolina 49,	1988	(Dec.) N. Carolina St. 28, Iowa 23	2006	Georgia 31, Virginia Tech 24
	West Virginia 13	1989	Syracuse 19, Georgia 18	2007	Auburn 23, Clemson 20 (OT)
1973	Georgia 17, Maryland 16	1990	Auburn 27, Indiana 23	2008	LSU 38, Georgia Tech 3
1974	Vanderbilt 6, Texas Tech 6	1992	(Jan.) E. Carolina 37, N. Carolina	2009	Virginia Tech 37, Tennessee 14
1975	West Virginia 13,		St. 34	2010	Florida St. 26, S. Carolina 17
	N. Carolina St. 10	1993	N. Carolina 21, Mississippi St. 17	2011	Auburn 43, Virginia 24
1976	Kentucky 21, N. Carolina 0	1993	(Dec.) Clemson 14, Kentucky 13	2012	Clemson 25, LSU 24
1977	N. Carolina St. 24, Iowa St. 14	1995	(Jan.) N. Carolina St. 28,	2013	Texas A&M 52, Duke 48
1978	Purdue 41, Georgia Tech 21		Mississippi St. 24	2014	TCU 42, Mississippi 3
1979	Baylor 24, Clemson 18	1995	(Dec.) Virginia 34, Georgia 27	2015	Houston 38, Florida St. 24
1981	(Jan.) Miami (FL) 20, Virginia	1996	LSU 10, Clemson 7	2016	Alabama 24, Washington 7 (CFP)
	Tech 10	1998	(Jan.) Auburn 21, Clemson 17	2018	(Jan.) Central Florida 34,
1981	(Dec.) West Virginia 26, Florida 6	1998	(Dec.) Georgia 35, Virginia 33		Auburn 27
1982	Iowa 28, Tennessee 22	1999	Mississippi St. 27, Clemson 7	2018	(Dec.) Florida 41, Michigan 15
1983	Florida St. 28, N. Carolina 3	2000	LSU 28, Georgia Tech 14	2019	LSU 63, Oklahoma 28 (CFP)
1984	Virginia 27, Purdue 22	2001	N. Carolina 16, Auburn 10		

Fiesta Bowl Results, 1971-2019

1971	(Dec.) Arizona St. 45,	1989	Notre Dame 34, West Virginia 21	2006	Ohio St. 34, Notre Dame 20
	Florida St. 38	1990	Florida St. 41, Nebraska 17	2007	Boise St. 43, Oklahoma 42 (OT)
1972	Arizona St. 49, Missouri 35	1991	Louisville 34, Alabama 7	2008	West Virginia 48, Oklahoma 28
1973	Arizona St. 28, Pittsburgh 7	1992	Penn St. 42, Tennessee 17	2009	Texas 24, Ohio St. 21
1974	Oklahoma St. 16,	1993	Syracuse 26, Colorado 22	2010	Boise St. 17, TCU 10
	Brigham Young 6	1994	Arizona 29, Miami (FL) 0	2011	Oklahoma 48, Connecticut 20
1975	Arizona St. 17, Nebraska 14	1995	Colorado 41, Notre Dame 24	2012	Oklahoma St. 41,
1976	Oklahoma 41, Wyoming 7	1996	Nebraska 62, Florida 24		Stanford 38 (OT)
1977	Penn St. 42, Arizona St. 30	1997	Penn St. 38, Texas 15	2013	Oregon 35, Kansas St. 17
1978	UCLA 10, Arkansas 10	1997	(Dec.) Kansas St. 35,	2014	UCF 52, Baylor 42
1979	Pittsburgh 16, Arizona 10		Syracuse 18	2014	(Dec.) Boise St. 38, Arizona 30
1980	Penn St. 31, Ohio St. 19	1999	(Jan.) Tennessee 23,	2016	(Jan.) Ohio St. 44,
1982	(Jan.) Penn St. 26, USC 10		Florida St. 16		Notre Dame 28
1983	Arizona St. 32, Oklahoma 21	2000	Nebraska 31, Tennessee 21	2016	(Dec.) Clemson 31, Ohio St. 0
1984	Ohio St. 28, Pittsburgh 23	2001	Oregon St. 41, Notre Dame 9		(CFP)
1985	UCLA 39, Miami (FL) 37	2002	Oregon 38, Colorado 16	2017	Penn St. 35, Washington 28
1986	Michigan 27, Nebraska 23	2003	Ohio St. 31, Miami (FL) 24 (2 OT)	2019	(Jan.) LSU 40, UCF 32
1987	Penn St. 14, Miami (FL) 10	2004	Ohio St. 35, Kansas St. 28	2019	(Dec.) Clemson 29, Ohio St. 23
1988	Florida St. 31, Nebraska 28	2005	Utah 35, Pittsburgh 7		(CFP)

Other Select Bowl Results, Dec. 2019-Jan. 2020

Alamo Bowl, San Antonio, TX: Texas 38, Utah 10
Arizona Bowl, Tucson, AZ: Wyoming 38, Georgia St. 17
Armed Forces Bowl, Ft. Worth, TX: Tulane 30, Southern Mississippi 13
Birmingham Bowl, Birmingham, AL: Cincinnati 38, Boston College 6
Camellia Bowl, Montgomery, AL: Arkansas St. 34, Florida Intl. 26
Citrus Bowl, Orlando, FL: Alabama 35, Michigan 16
TaxSlayer Gator Bowl, Jacksonville, FL: Tennessee 23, Indiana 22
Hawai'i Bowl, Honolulu, HI: Hawai'i 38, BYU 34
Independence Bowl, Shreveport, LA: Louisiana Tech 14, Miami (FL) 0

Las Vegas Bowl, Las Vegas, NV: Washington 38, Boise St. 7
Liberty Bowl, Memphis, TN: Navy 20, Kansas 17
Military Bowl, Annapolis, MD: North Carolina 55, Temple 13
Music City Bowl, Nashville, TN: Louisville 38, Mississippi St. 28
New Mexico Bowl, Albuquerque, NM: San Diego St. 48, Central Michigan 11
New Orleans Bowl, New Orleans, LA: Appalachian St. 31, UAB 17
Outback Bowl, Tampa, FL: Minnesota 31, Auburn 24
Pinstripe Bowl, Bronx, NY: Michigan St. 27, Wake Forest 21
Sun Bowl, El Paso, TX: Arizona St. 20, Florida 14
Texas Bowl, Houston, TX: Texas A&M 24, Oklahoma St. 21

All-Time NCAA Bowl Subdivision (FBS) Statistical Leaders

Career Rushing Yards

Player, team	Yrs	Carries	Yds	Avg
Donnel Pumphrey, San Diego St.	2013-16	1,059	6,405	6.05
Ron Dayne, Wisconsin	1996-99	1,115	6,397	5.74
Ricky Williams, Texas	1995-98	1,011	6,279	6.21
Jonathan Taylor, Wisconsin	2017-19	926	6,174	6.67
Tony Dorsett, Pittsburgh	1973-76	1,074	6,082	5.66
DeAngelo Williams, Memphis	2002-05	969	6,026	6.22
Royce Freeman, Oregon	2014-17	947	5,621	5.94
Charles White, USC	1976-79	1,023	5,598	5.47
Travis Prentice, Miami (OH)	1996-99	1,138	5,596	4.92
Cedric Benson, Texas	2001-04	1,112	5,540	4.98

Career Rushing Yards/Game (min. 2,500 yds)

Player, team	Yrs	Carries	Yds	Avg/game
Ed Marinaro, Cornell	1969-71	918	4,715	174.6
O.J. Simpson, USC	1967-68	621	3,124	164.4
Herschel Walker, Georgia	1980-82	994	5,259	159.4
Garrett Wolfe, N. Illinois	2004-06	807	5,164	156.5
LeShon Johnson, N. Illinois	1992-93	592	3,314	150.6
Jonathan Taylor, Wisconsin	2017-19	926	6,174	150.6
Ron Dayne, Wisconsin	1996-99	1,115	6,397	148.8
Marshall Faulk, San Diego St.	1991-93	766	4,589	148.0
George Jones, San Diego St.	1995-96	486	2,810	147.9
Tony Dorsett, Pittsburgh	1973-76	1,074	6,082	141.4
Troy Davis, Iowa St.	1994-96	782	4,382	141.4

Career Passing Yards

Player, team	Yrs	Comp/att	Yds
Case Keenum, Houston	2007-11	1,546/2,229	19,217
Timmy Chang, Hawaii	2000-04	1,388/2,436	17,072
Landry Jones, Oklahoma	2009-12	1,388/2,183	16,646
Graham Harrell, Texas Tech	2005-08	1,403/2,010	15,793
Ty Detmer, BYU	1988-91	958/1,530	15,031
Kellen Moore, Boise St.	2008-11	1,157/1,658	14,667
Baker Mayfield, Texas Tech/Oklahoma	2013, '15-'17	1,026/1,497	14,607
Luke Falk, Washington St.	2013-17	1,404/2,055	14,486
Colt Brennan, Hawaii	2005-07	1,115/1,584	14,193
Rakeem Cato, Marshall	2011-14	1,153/1,838	14,079

Career Receiving Yards

Player, team	Yrs	Rec	Yds	Avg
Corey Davis, W. Michigan	2013-16	332	5,285	15.9
Trevor Insley, Nevada	1996-99	298	5,005	16.8
Ryan Broyles, Oklahoma	2008-11	349	4,586	13.1
Justin Hardy, E. Carolina	2011-14	387	4,541	11.7
Marcus Harris, Wyoming	1993-96	259	4,518	17.4
James Washington, Oklahoma St.	2014-17	225	4,467	19.8
Rashaun Woods, Oklahoma St.	2000-03	293	4,414	15.1
Ryan Yarborough, Wyoming	1990-93	229	4,357	19.03
Troy Edwards, Louisiana Tech	1996-98	280	4,352	15.54
Aaron Turner, Pacific	1989-92	266	4,345	16.33

Note: As of end of 2019 season. Prior to 2002, postseason games were not included in NCAA final football statistics or records. All postseason games were included for the 2002 season and thereafter. Career rushing yards per game rankings do not include active players.

All-Time NCAA Bowl Subdivision (FBS) Team Won-Lost Records

Team	Years	W	L	T	Total games	Pct.	Team	Years	W	L	T	Total games	Pct.
Ohio St.*	130	924	326	53	1,303	0.729	Florida	114	735	420	40	1,195	0.632
Boise St. (1996)	52	460	170	2	632	0.729	Miami (FL)	94	636	367	19	1,022	0.632
Michigan	141	962	346	36	1,344	0.729	Auburn	128	776	445	47	1,268	0.631
Notre Dame*	133	908	326	42	1,276	0.728	Clemson	124	758	460	45	1,263	0.618
Alabama*	128	916	331	43	1,290	0.727	Washington	131	743	454	50	1,247	0.616
Oklahoma	125	908	327	53	1,288	0.726	Virginia Tech	128	751	478	46	1,275	0.607
Texas	127	916	375	33	1,324	0.704	Arizona St.	123	622	399	24	1,045	0.607
USC*	132	847	351	54	1,252	0.698	Texas A&M	126	749	486	48	1,283	0.602
Nebraska	130	902	395	40	1,337	0.690	Michigan St.	124	708	465	44	1,217	0.600
Penn St.	133	898	393	41	1,332	0.690	West Virginia	129	755	504	45	1,304	0.596
Tennessee	129	846	395	53	1,294	0.690	Miami (OH)	132	698	467	44	1,209	0.596
Florida St.*	73	550	264	17	831	0.672	Utah	128	688	467	31	1,186	0.593
LSU	127	812	415	47	1,274	0.656	Central Michigan	123	626	428	36	1,090	0.591
Georgia	128	831	425	54	1,310	0.655	Western Kentucky	107	584	404	30	1,018	0.588
Appalachian St.	56	630	336	29	995	0.648	Georgia Tech*	128	738	511	43	1,292	0.588
Georgia Southern*	57	395	225	10	630	0.635							

* = Record adjusted by action of the NCAA Committee on Infractions. **Note:** As of end of 2019 season. Includes records as senior college only. Bowl and playoff games are included, and each tie game is computed as half won and half lost. Teams must have been in Div. I for at least 25 years to qualify. Tiebreaker rule began with 1996 season.

Heisman Trophy Winners, 1935-2019

The Heisman Memorial Trophy is awarded annually to the nation's outstanding college football player by the Downtown Athletic Club.

Year	Winner, school, position	Year	Winner, school, position	Year	Winner, school, position
1935	Jay Berwanger, Chicago, HB	1964	John Huarte, Notre Dame, QB	1992	Gino Torretta, Miami (FL), QB
1936	Larry Kelley, Yale, E	1965	Mike Garrett, USC, HB	1993	Charlie Ward, Florida St., QB
1937	Clinton Frank, Yale, HB	1966	Steve Spurrier, Florida, QB	1994	Rashaan Salaam, Colorado, RB
1938	David O'Brien, Texas Christian, QB	1967	Gary Beban, UCLA, QB	1995	Eddie George, Ohio St., RB
1939	Nile Kinnick, Iowa, HB	1968	O.J. Simpson, USC, RB	1996	Danny Wuerffel, Florida, QB
1940	Tom Harmon, Michigan, HB	1969	Steve Owens, Oklahoma, RB	1997	Charles Woodson, Michigan, CB
1941	Bruce Smith, Minnesota, HB	1970	Jim Plunkett, Stanford, QB	1998	Ricky Williams, Texas, RB
1942	Frank Sinkwich, Georgia, HB	1971	Pat Sullivan, Auburn, QB	1999	Ron Dayne, Wisconsin, RB
1943	Angelo Bertelli, Notre Dame, QB	1972	Johnny Rodgers, Nebraska, RB-WR	2000	Chris Weinke, Florida St., QB
1944	Leslie Horvath, Ohio St., QB	1973	John Cappelletti, Penn St., RB	2001	Eric Crouch, Nebraska, QB
1945	Felix Blanchard, Army, FB	1974	Archie Griffin, Ohio St., RB	2002	Carson Palmer, USC, QB
1946	Glenn Davis, Army, HB	1975	Archie Griffin, Ohio St., RB	2003	Jason White, Oklahoma, QB
1947	John Lujack, Notre Dame, QB	1976	Tony Dorsett, Pittsburgh, RB	2004	Matt Leinart, USC, QB
1948	Doak Walker, SMU, HB	1977	Earl Campbell, Texas, RB	2005	Reggie Bush, USC, RB[1]
1949	Leon Hart, Notre Dame, E	1978	Billy Sims, Oklahoma, RB	2006	Troy Smith, Ohio St., QB
1950	Vic Janowicz, Ohio St., HB	1979	Charles White, USC, RB	2007	Tim Tebow, Florida, QB
1951	Richard Kazmaier, Princeton, HB	1980	George Rogers, S. Carolina, RB	2008	Sam Bradford, Oklahoma, QB
1952	Billy Vessels, Oklahoma, HB	1981	Marcus Allen, USC, RB	2009	Mark Ingram, Alabama, RB
1953	John Lattner, Notre Dame, HB	1982	Herschel Walker, Georgia, RB	2010	Cam Newton, Auburn, QB
1954	Alan Ameche, Wisconsin, FB	1983	Mike Rozier, Nebraska, RB	2011	Robert Griffin III, Baylor, QB
1955	Howard Cassady, Ohio St., HB	1984	Doug Flutie, Boston College, QB	2012	Johnny Manziel, Texas A&M, QB
1956	Paul Hornung, Notre Dame, QB	1985	Bo Jackson, Auburn, RB	2013	Jameis Winston, Florida St., QB
1957	John Crow, Texas A&M, HB	1986	Vinny Testaverde, Miami (FL), QB	2014	Marcus Mariota, Oregon, QB
1958	Pete Dawkins, Army, HB	1987	Tim Brown, Notre Dame, WR	2015	Derrick Henry, Alabama, RB
1959	Billy Cannon, LSU, HB	1988	Barry Sanders, Oklahoma St., RB	2016	Lamar Jackson, Louisville, QB
1960	Joe Bellino, Navy, HB	1989	Andre Ware, Houston, QB	2017	Baker Mayfield, Oklahoma, QB
1961	Ernest Davis, Syracuse, HB	1990	Ty Detmer, BYU, QB	2018	Kyler Murray, Oklahoma, QB
1962	Terry Baker, Oregon St., QB	1991	Desmond Howard, Michigan, WR	2019	Joe Burrow, LSU, QB
1963	Roger Staubach, Navy, QB				

(1) Bush forfeited the trophy voluntarily Sept. 14, 2010, following revelations of NCAA rules violations while Bush was at USC.

College Football Coach of the Year, 1935-2019

The Coach of the Year has been selected by the American Football Coaches Assn. (AFCA) since 1935 as well as the Football Writers Assn. of America (FWAA) since 1957. When polls disagree, both winners are indicated.

1935 Lynn Waldorf, Northwestern	1968 Joe Paterno, Penn St. (AFCA);	1994 Tom Osborne, Nebraska (AFCA);
1936 Dick Harlow, Harvard	Woody Hayes, Ohio St. (FWAA)	Rich Brooks, Oregon (FWAA)
1937 Edward Mylin, Lafayette	1969 Bo Schembechler, Michigan	1995 Gary Barnett, Northwestern
1938 Bill Kern, Carnegie Tech	1970 Charles McClendon, LSU &	1996 Bruce Snyder, Arizona St.
1939 Eddie Anderson, Iowa	Darrell Royal, Texas (AFCA);	1997 Mike Price, Washington St.
1940 Clark Shaughnessy, Stanford	Alex Agase, Northwestern (FWAA)	1998 Phillip Fulmer, Tennessee
1941 Frank Leahy, Notre Dame	1971 Paul "Bear" Bryant, Alabama (AFCA);	1999 Frank Beamer, Virginia Tech
1942 Bill Alexander, Georgia Tech	Bob Devaney, Nebraska (FWAA)	2000 Bob Stoops, Oklahoma
1943 Amos Alonzo Stagg, Pacific (CA)	1972 John McKay, USC	2001 Larry Coker, Miami (FL) &
1944 Carroll Widdoes, Ohio St.	1973 Paul "Bear" Bryant, Alabama (AFCA);	Ralph Friedgen, Maryland (AFCA);
1945 Bo McMillin, Indiana	Johnny Majors, Pittsburgh (FWAA)	Ralph Friedgen, Maryland (FWAA)
1946 Earl "Red" Blaik, Army	1974 Grant Teaff, Baylor	2002 Jim Tressel, Ohio St.
1947 Fritz Crisler, Michigan	1975 Frank Kush, Arizona St. (AFCA);	2003 Pete Carroll, USC (AFCA);
1948 Bennie Oosterbaan, Michigan	Woody Hayes, Ohio St. (FWAA)	Nick Saban, LSU (FWAA)
1949 Bud Wilkinson, Oklahoma	1976 Johnny Majors, Pittsburgh	2004 Tommy Tuberville, Auburn (AFCA);
1950 Charlie Caldwell, Princeton	1977 Don James, Washington (AFCA);	Urban Meyer, Utah (FWAA)
1951 Chuck Taylor, Stanford	Lou Holtz, Arkansas (FWAA)	2005 Joe Paterno, Penn St. (AFCA);
1952 Biggie Munn, Michigan St.	1978 Joe Paterno, Penn St.	Charlie Weis, Notre Dame (FWAA)
1953 Jim Tatum, Maryland	1979 Earle Bruce, Ohio St.	2006 Jim Grobe, Wake Forest (AFCA);
1954 Henry "Red" Sanders, UCLA	1980 Vince Dooley, Georgia	Greg Schiano, Rutgers (FWAA)
1955 Duffy Daugherty, Michigan St.	1981 Danny Ford, Clemson	2007 Mark Mangino, Kansas
1956 Bowden Wyatt, Tennessee	1982 Joe Paterno, Penn St.	2008 Kyle Whittingham, Utah (AFCA);
1957 Woody Hayes, Ohio St.	1983 Ken Hatfield, Air Force (AFCA);	Nick Saban, Alabama (FWAA)
1958 Paul Dietzel, LSU	Howard Schnellenberger,	2009 Gary Patterson, TCU
1959 Ben Schwartzwalder, Syracuse	Miami (FL) (FWAA)	2010 Chip Kelly, Oregon
1960 Murray Warmath, Minnesota	1984 LaVell Edwards, Brigham Young	2011 Les Miles, LSU (AFCA);
1961 Paul "Bear" Bryant, Alabama (AFCA);	1985 Fisher De Berry, Air Force	Mike Gundy, Oklahoma St. (FWAA)
Darrell Royal, Texas (FWAA)	1986 Joe Paterno, Penn St.	2012 Brian Kelly, Notre Dame
1962 John McKay, USC	1987 Dick MacPherson, Syracuse	2013 David Cutcliffe, Duke (AFCA);
1963 Darrell Royal, Texas	1988 Don Nehlen, W. Virginia (AFCA);	Gus Malzahn, Auburn (FWAA)
1964 Ara Parseghian, Notre Dame &	Lou Holtz, Notre Dame (FWAA)	2014 Gary Patterson, TCU
Frank Broyles, Arkansas (AFCA);	1989 Bill McCartney, Colorado	2015 Dabo Swinney, Clemson (AFCA);
Ara Parseghian, Notre Dame (FWAA)	1990 Bobby Ross, Georgia Tech	Kirk Ferentz, Iowa (FWAA)
1965 Tommy Prothro, UCLA (AFCA);	1991 Don James, Washington	2016 Mike MacIntyre, Colorado
Duffy Daugherty, Mich. St. (FWAA)	1992 Gene Stallings, Alabama	2017 Scott Frost, UCF
1966 Tom Cahill, Army	1993 Barry Alvarez, Wisconsin (AFCA);	2018 Mike Leach, Washington St. (AFCA);
1967 John Pont, Indiana	Terry Bowden, Auburn (FWAA)	Bill Clark, UAB (FWAA)
		2019 Ed Orgeron, LSU

COLLEGE BASKETBALL

2020 NCAA Basketball: No Tournaments, No Champions

In response to the spread of the novel coronavirus in Jan.-Mar. 2020, the NCAA announced Mar. 12, 2020, that the men's and women's basketball tournaments would not be played. At the time of the announcement, 19 men's conference tournaments and 132 games had not been played, with 18 tournaments and 81 games unplayed on the women's side. The cancellation also applied to all other winter and spring NCAA sports seasons, including baseball, gymnastics, softball, and track.

NCAA Men's Basketball Division I Champions, 1939-2019

Year	Champion	Final opponent	Score	Most outstanding player	Winning coach	Site
1939	Oregon	Ohio St.	46-33	Jimmy Hull, Ohio St.	Howard Hobson	Evanston, IL
1940	Indiana	Kansas	60-42	Marv Huffman, Indiana	Branch McCracken	Kansas City, MO
1941	Wisconsin	Washington St.	39-34	John Kotz, Wisconsin	Bud Foster	Kansas City, MO
1942	Stanford	Dartmouth	53-38	Howie Dallmar, Stanford	Everett Dean	Kansas City, MO
1943	Wyoming	Georgetown	46-34	Ken Sailors, Wyoming	Everett Shelton	New York, NY
1944	Utah	Dartmouth	42-40[1]	Arnold Ferrin, Utah	Vadal Peterson	New York, NY
1945	Oklahoma St.[2]	NYU	49-45	Bob Kurland, Oklahoma St.	Henry Iba	New York, NY
1946	Oklahoma St.[2]	North Carolina	43-40	Bob Kurland, Oklahoma St.	Henry Iba	New York, NY
1947	Holy Cross	Oklahoma	58-47	George Kaftan, Holy Cross	Alvin Julian	New York, NY
1948	Kentucky	Baylor	58-42	Alex Groza, Kentucky	Adolph Rupp	New York, NY
1949	Kentucky	Oklahoma St.	46-36	Alex Groza, Kentucky	Adolph Rupp	Seattle, WA
1950	CCNY	Bradley	71-68	Irwin Dambrot, CCNY	Nat Holman	New York, NY
1951	Kentucky	Kansas St.	68-58	Bill Spivey, Kentucky	Adolph Rupp	Minneapolis, MN
1952	Kansas	St. John's (NY)	80-63	Clyde Lovellette, Kansas	Forrest Allen	Seattle, WA
1953	Indiana	Kansas	69-68	B. H. Born, Kansas	Branch McCracken	Kansas City, MO
1954	La Salle	Bradley	92-76	Tom Gola, La Salle	Kenneth Loeffler	Kansas City, MO
1955	San Francisco	La Salle	77-63	Bill Russell, San Francisco	Phil Woolpert	Kansas City, MO
1956	San Francisco	Iowa	83-71	Hal Lear, Temple	Phil Woolpert	Evanston, IL
1957	North Carolina	Kansas	54-53[1]	Wilt Chamberlain, Kansas	Frank McGuire	Kansas City, MO
1958	Kentucky	Seattle	84-72	Elgin Baylor, Seattle	Adolph Rupp	Louisville, KY
1959	California	West Virginia	71-70	Jerry West, West Virginia	Pete Newell	Louisville, KY
1960	Ohio St.	California	75-55	Jerry Lucas, Ohio St.	Fred Taylor	San Francisco, CA
1961	Cincinnati	Ohio St.	70-65[1]	Jerry Lucas, Ohio St.	Edwin Jucker	Kansas City, MO
1962	Cincinnati	Ohio St.	71-59	Paul Hogue, Cincinnati	Edwin Jucker	Louisville, KY
1963	Loyola (IL)	Cincinnati	60-58[1]	Art Heyman, Duke	George Ireland	Louisville, KY
1964	UCLA	Duke	98-83	Walt Hazzard, UCLA	John Wooden	Kansas City, MO
1965	UCLA	Michigan	91-80	Bill Bradley, Princeton	John Wooden	Portland, OR
1966	UTEP[3]	Kentucky	72-65	Jerry Chambers, Utah	Don Haskins	College Park, MD
1967	UCLA	Dayton	79-64	Lew Alcindor[4], UCLA	John Wooden	Louisville, KY
1968	UCLA	North Carolina	78-55	Lew Alcindor[4], UCLA	John Wooden	Los Angeles, CA
1969	UCLA	Purdue	92-72	Lew Alcindor[4], UCLA	John Wooden	Louisville, KY
1970	UCLA	Jacksonville	80-69	Sidney Wicks, UCLA	John Wooden	College Park, MD
1971	UCLA	Villanova*	68-62	Howard Porter, Villanova*	John Wooden	Houston, TX
1972	UCLA	Florida St.	81-76	Bill Walton, UCLA	John Wooden	Los Angeles, CA
1973	UCLA	Memphis[5]	87-66	Bill Walton, UCLA	John Wooden	St. Louis, MO
1974	North Carolina St.	Marquette	76-64	David Thompson, NC State	Norm Sloan	Greensboro, NC

Year	Champion	Final opponent	Score	Most outstanding player	Winning coach	Site
1975	UCLA	Kentucky	92-85	Richard Washington, UCLA	John Wooden	San Diego, CA
1976	Indiana	Michigan	86-68	Kent Benson, Indiana	Bob Knight	Philadelphia, PA
1977	Marquette	North Carolina	67-59	Butch Lee, Marquette	Al McGuire	Atlanta, GA
1978	Kentucky	Duke	94-88	Jack Givens, Kentucky	Joe Hall	St. Louis, MO
1979	Michigan St.	Indiana St.	75-64	Magic Johnson, Michigan St.	Jud Heathcote	Salt Lake City, UT
1980	Louisville	UCLA*	59-54	Darrell Griffith, Louisville	Denny Crum	Indianapolis, IN
1981	Indiana	North Carolina	63-50	Isiah Thomas, Indiana	Bob Knight	Philadelphia, PA
1982	North Carolina	Georgetown	63-62	James Worthy, N. Carolina	Dean Smith	New Orleans, LA
1983	North Carolina St.	Houston	54-52	Hakeem Olajuwon, Houston	Jim Valvano	Albuquerque, NM
1984	Georgetown	Houston	84-75	Patrick Ewing, Georgetown	John Thompson	Seattle, WA
1985	Villanova	Georgetown	66-64	Ed Pinckney, Villanova	Rollie Massimino	Lexington, KY
1986	Louisville	Duke	72-69	Pervis Ellison, Louisville	Denny Crum	Dallas, TX
1987	Indiana	Syracuse	74-73	Keith Smart, Indiana	Bob Knight	New Orleans, LA
1988	Kansas	Oklahoma	83-79	Danny Manning, Kansas	Larry Brown	Kansas City, MO
1989	Michigan	Seton Hall	80-79[1]	Glen Rice, Michigan	Steve Fisher	Seattle, WA
1990	UNLV	Duke	103-73	Anderson Hunt, UNLV	Jerry Tarkanian	Denver, CO
1991	Duke	Kansas	72-65	Christian Laettner, Duke	Mike Krzyzewski	Indianapolis, IN
1992	Duke	Michigan	71-51	Bobby Hurley, Duke	Mike Krzyzewski	Minneapolis, MN
1993	North Carolina	Michigan	77-71	Donald Williams, N. Carolina	Dean Smith	New Orleans, LA
1994	Arkansas	Duke	76-72	Corliss Williamson, Arkansas	Nolan Richardson	Charlotte, NC
1995	UCLA	Arkansas	89-78	Ed O'Bannon, UCLA	Jim Harrick	Seattle, WA
1996	Kentucky	Syracuse	76-67	Tony Delk, Kentucky	Rick Pitino	E. Rutherford, NJ
1997	Arizona	Kentucky	84-79[1]	Miles Simon, Arizona	Lute Olson	Indianapolis, IN
1998	Kentucky	Utah	78-69	Jeff Sheppard, Kentucky	Tubby Smith	San Antonio, TX
1999	Connecticut	Duke	77-74	Richard Hamilton, Connecticut	Jim Calhoun	St. Petersburg, FL
2000	Michigan St.	Florida	89-76	Mateen Cleaves, Michigan St.	Tom Izzo	Indianapolis, IN
2001	Duke	Arizona	82-72	Shane Battier, Duke	Mike Krzyzewski	Minneapolis, MN
2002	Maryland	Indiana	64-52	Juan Dixon, Maryland	Gary Williams	Atlanta, GA
2003	Syracuse	Kansas	81-78	Carmelo Anthony, Syracuse	Jim Boeheim	New Orleans, LA
2004	Connecticut	Georgia Tech	82-73	Emeka Okafor, Connecticut	Jim Calhoun	San Antonio, TX
2005	North Carolina	Illinois	75-70	Sean May, N. Carolina	Roy Williams	St. Louis, MO
2006	Florida	UCLA	73-57	Joakim Noah, Florida	Billy Donovan	Indianapolis, IN
2007	Florida	Ohio St.	84-75	Corey Brewer, Florida	Billy Donovan	Atlanta, GA
2008	Kansas	Memphis	75-68[1]	Mario Chalmers, Kansas	Bill Self	San Antonio, TX
2009	North Carolina	Michigan St.	89-72	Wayne Ellington, N. Carolina	Roy Williams	Detroit, MI
2010	Duke	Butler	61-59	Kyle Singler, Duke	Mike Krzyzewski	Indianapolis, IN
2011	Connecticut	Butler	53-41	Kemba Walker, Connecticut	Jim Calhoun	Houston, TX
2012	Kentucky	Kansas	67-59	Anthony Davis, Kentucky	John Calipari	New Orleans, LA
2013[6]	Louisville	Michigan	82-76	Luke Hancock, Louisville	Rick Pitino	Atlanta, GA
2014	Connecticut	Kentucky	60-54	Shabazz Napier, Connecticut	Kevin Ollie	Arlington, TX
2015	Duke	Wisconsin	68-63	Tyus Jones, Duke	Mike Krzyzewski	Indianapolis, IN
2016	Villanova	North Carolina	77-74	Ryan Arcidiacono, Villanova	Jay Wright	Houston, TX
2017	North Carolina	Gonzaga	71-65	Joel Berry II, N. Carolina	Roy Williams	Glendale, AZ
2018	Villanova	Michigan	79-62	Donte DiVincenzo, Villanova	Jay Wright	San Antonio, TX
2019	Virginia	Texas Tech	85-77[1]	Kyle Guy, Virginia	Tony Bennett	Minneapolis, MN

* = Declared ineligible after the tournament. (1) Overtime. (2) Then known as Oklahoma A&M. (3) Then known as Texas Western. (4) Changed name to Kareem Abdul-Jabbar in 1971. (5) Then known as Memphis State. (6) Title vacated by the NCAA Committee on Infractions in 2018.

All-Time Winningest Men's NCAA Division I Basketball Teams

Team	Yrs	Won	Lost	Pct.	Team	Yrs	Won	Lost	Pct.	Team	Yrs	Won	Lost	Pct.
Kentucky	118	2,318	712	0.765	VCU	52	982	530	0.649	Indiana	120	1,856	1,062	0.636
N. Carolina	110	2,275	818	0.736	Murray St.	95	1,663	903	0.648	Purdue	122	1,819	1,051	0.634
Kansas	122	2,302	862	0.728	Notre Dame	123	1,900	1,040	0.646	Memphis	100	1,585	927	0.631
Duke	115	2,201	893	0.711	Utah	112	1,835	1,019	0.643	Weber St.	58	1,074	632	0.630
UNLV	62	1,279	572	0.691	St. John's (NY)	113	1,871	1,044	0.642	Missouri St.	108	1,686	1,008	0.626
UCLA	101	1,906	864	0.688	Cincinnati	119	1,836	1,025	0.642	Texas	115	1,809	1,097	0.623
Syracuse*	120	1,922	922	0.676	Norfolk St.	67	1,239	692	0.642	BYU	118	1,806	1,101	0.621
W. Kentucky	106	1,815	936	0.660	Connecticut	120	1,701	952	0.641	UAB	42	835	511	0.620
Arizona	116	1,834	957	0.657	Illinois	115	1,811	1,022	0.639	NC St.	108	1,757	1,078	0.620
Villanova	100	1,799	941	0.657	Temple	126	1,940	1,096	0.639	Marquette	104	1,652	1,018	0.619
Louisville*	109	1,746	933	0.652	Arkansas	97	1,708	967	0.639	Penn	124	1,806	1,123	0.617

* = Record adjusted by action of the NCAA Committee on Infractions. **Note:** Through shortened 2019-20 season; winningest teams by percentage. Minimum 25 years as Div. I program.

National Invitation Tournament Champions, 1938-2019

The National Invitation Tournament (NIT), first played in 1938, is the oldest U.S. basketball tournament. The first National Collegiate Athletic Association (NCAA) national championship tournament was played one year later. In 2005, the NCAA purchased the NIT from the five New York City-area colleges that had run it. No tournament was held in 2020 in response to the COVID-19 outbreak.

Year	Champion	Year	Champion	Year	Champion	Year	Champion	Year	Champion
1938	Temple	1955	Duquesne	1972	Maryland	1989	St. John's (NY)	2005	South Carolina
1939	Long Island Univ.	1956	Louisville	1973	Virginia Tech	1990	Vanderbilt	2006	South Carolina
1940	Colorado	1957	Bradley	1974	Purdue	1991	Stanford	2007	West Virginia
1941	Long Island Univ.	1958	Xavier (OH)	1975	Princeton	1992	Virginia	2008	Ohio State
1942	West Virginia	1959	St. John's (NY)	1976	Kentucky	1993	Minnesota	2009	Penn State
1943	St. John's (NY)	1960	Bradley	1977	St. Bonaventure	1994	Villanova	2010	Dayton
1944	St. John's (NY)	1961	Providence	1978	Texas	1995	Virginia Tech	2011	Wichita State
1945	DePaul	1962	Dayton	1979	Indiana	1996	Nebraska	2012	Stanford
1946	Kentucky	1963	Providence	1980	Virginia	1997	Michigan	2013	Baylor
1947	Utah	1964	Bradley	1981	Tulsa	1998	Minnesota	2014	Minnesota
1948	St. Louis	1965	St. John's (NY)	1982	Bradley	1999	California	2015	Stanford
1949	San Francisco	1966	Brigham Young	1983	Fresno State	2000	Wake Forest	2016	George Washington
1950	CCNY	1967	Southern Illinois	1984	Michigan	2001	Tulsa		
1951	Brigham Young	1968	Dayton	1985	UCLA	2002	Memphis	2017	TCU
1952	La Salle	1969	Temple	1986	Ohio State	2003	St. John's (NY)	2018	Penn State
1953	Seton Hall	1970	Marquette	1987	Southern Miss	2004	Michigan	2019	Texas
1954	Holy Cross	1971	North Carolina	1988	Connecticut				

NCAA Men's Basketball Division I All-Time Leaders

Season points

Player, school (season)	G	FG	3-FG	FT	PTS
Pete Maravich, LSU (1970)	31	522	NA	337	1,381
Elvin Hayes, Houston (1968)	33	519	NA	176	1,214
Frank Selvy, Furman (1954)	29	427	NA	355	1,209
Pete Maravich, LSU (1969)	26	433	NA	282	1,148
Pete Maravich, LSU (1968)	26	432	NA	274	1,138
Bo Kimble, Loyola Marymount (1990)	32	404	92	231	1,131
Hersey Hawkins, Bradley (1988)	31	377	87	284	1,125
Austin Carr, Notre Dame (1970)	29	444	NA	218	1,106
Austin Carr, Notre Dame (1971)	29	430	NA	241	1,101
Otis Birdsong, Houston (1977)	36	452	NA	186	1,090

Career points

Player, school (seasons)	G	FG	3-FG	FT	PTS
Pete Maravich, LSU (1968-70)	83	1,387	NA	893	3,667
Freeman Williams, Portland St. (1975-78)	106	1,369	NA	511	3,249
Chris Clemons, Campbell (2016-19)	130	1,024	444	733	3,225
Lionel Simmons, La Salle (1987-90)	131	1,244	56	673	3,217
Alphonso Ford, Mississippi Valley St. (1990-93)	109	1,121	333	590	3,165
Doug McDermott, Creighton (2011-14)	145	1,141	274	594	3,150
Mike Daum, South Dakota St. (2016-19)	137	1,005	271	786	3,067
Harry Kelly, Texas Southern (1980-83)	110	1,234	NA	598	3,066
Keydren Clark, St. Peter's (2003-06)	118	967	435	689	3,058
Hersey Hawkins, Bradley (1985-88)	125	1,100	118	690	3,008

NA = Not available.

Season points per game

Player, school (season)	G	FG	FT	PTS	PPG
Pete Maravich, LSU (1970)	31	522	337	1,381	44.5
Pete Maravich, LSU (1969)	26	433	282	1,148	44.2
Pete Maravich, LSU (1968)	26	432	274	1,138	43.8
Frank Selvy, Furman (1954)	29	427	355	1,209	41.7
Johnny Neumann, Mississippi (1971)	23	366	191	923	40.1
Freeman Williams, Portland St. (1977)	26	417	176	1,010	38.8
Billy McGill, Utah (1962)	26	394	221	1,009	38.8
Calvin Murphy, Niagara (1968)	24	337	242	916	38.2
Austin Carr, Notre Dame (1970)	29	444	218	1,106	38.1
Austin Carr, Notre Dame (1971)	29	430	241	1,101	38.0

Career points per game

Player, school (seasons)	G	FG	FT	PTS	PPG
Pete Maravich, LSU (1968-70)	83	1,387	893	3,667	44.2
Austin Carr, Notre Dame (1969-71)	74	1,017	526	2,560	34.6
Oscar Robertson, Cincinnati (1958-60)	88	1,052	869	2,973	33.8
Calvin Murphy, Niagara (1968-70)	77	947	654	2,548	33.1
Bo Lamar, La.-Lafayette (1972-73)	57	768	326	1,862	32.7
Frank Selvy, Furman (1952-54)	78	922	694	2,538	32.5
Rick Mount, Purdue (1968-70)	72	910	503	2,323	32.3
Darrell Floyd, Furman (1954-56)	71	868	545	2,281	32.1
Nick Werkman, Seton Hall (1962-64)	71	812	649	2,273	32.0
Willie Humes, Idaho St. (1970-71)	48	565	380	1,510	31.5

John R. Wooden Award Winners, 1977-2020

Awarded to the nation's outstanding men's college basketball player by the Los Angeles Athletic Club since 1977; awarded under the same name to women since 2004.

Year	Player, school
1977	Marques Johnson, UCLA
1978	Phil Ford, North Carolina
1979	Larry Bird, Indiana State
1980	Darrell Griffith, Louisville
1981	Danny Ainge, Brigham Young
1982	Ralph Sampson, Virginia
1983	Ralph Sampson, Virginia
1984	Michael Jordan, North Carolina
1985	Chris Mullin, St. John's (NY)
1986	Walter Berry, St. John's (NY)
1987	David Robinson, Navy
1988	Danny Manning, Kansas
1989	Sean Elliott, Arizona
1990	Lionel Simmons, La Salle
1991	Larry Johnson, UNLV
1992	Christian Laettner, Duke
1993	Calbert Cheaney, Indiana
1994	Glenn Robinson, Purdue
1995	Ed O'Bannon, UCLA
1996	Marcus Camby, Massachusetts
1997	Tim Duncan, Wake Forest

Year	Player, school
1998	Antawn Jamison, North Carolina
1999	Elton Brand, Duke
2000	Kenyon Martin, Cincinnati
2001	Shane Battier, Duke
2002	Jay Williams, Duke
2003	T. J. Ford, Texas
2004	(M) Jameer Nelson, St. Joseph's
	(W) Alana Beard, Duke
2005	(M) Andrew Bogut, Utah
	(W) Seimone Augustus, LSU
2006	(M) J. J. Redick, Duke
	(W) Seimone Augustus, LSU
2007	(M) Kevin Durant, Texas
	(W) Candace Parker, Tennessee
2008	(M) Tyler Hansbrough, N. Carolina
	(W) Candace Parker, Tennessee
2009	(M) Blake Griffin, Oklahoma
	(W) Maya Moore, Connecticut
2010	(M) Evan Turner, Ohio State
	(W) Tina Charles, Connecticut

Year	Player, school
2011	(M) Jimmer Fredette, Brigham Young
	(W) Maya Moore, Connecticut
2012	(M) Anthony Davis, Kentucky
	(W) Brittney Griner, Baylor
2013	(M) Trey Burke, Michigan
	(W) Brittney Griner, Baylor
2014	(M) Doug McDermott, Creighton
	(W) Chiney Ogwumike, Stanford
2015	(M) Frank Kaminsky, Wisconsin
	(W) Breanna Stewart, Connecticut
2016	(M) Buddy Hield, Oklahoma
	(W) Breanna Stewart, Connecticut
2017	(M) Frank Mason III, Kansas
	(W) Kelsey Plum, Washington
2018	(M) Jalen Brunson, Villanova
	(W) A'ja Wilson, South Carolina
2019	(M) Zion Williamson, Duke
	(W) Sabrina Ionescu, Oregon
2020	(M) Obi Toppin, Dayton
	(W) Sabrina Ionescu, Oregon

Naismith Coach of the Year, 1987-2020

Year	Men's coach, school	Women's coach, school
1987	Bob Knight, Indiana	Pat Summitt, Tennessee
1988	Larry Brown, Kansas	Leon Barmore, Louisiana Tech
1989	Mike Krzyzewski, Duke	Pat Summitt, Tennessee
1990	Bobby Cremins, Georgia Tech	Tara VanDerveer, Stanford
1991	Randy Ayers, Ohio St.	Debbie Ryan, Virginia
1992	Mike Krzyzewski, Duke	Chris Weller, Maryland
1993	Dean Smith, North Carolina	Vivian Stringer, Iowa
1994	Nolan Richardson, Arkansas	Pat Summitt, Tennessee
1995	Jim Harrick, UCLA	Geno Auriemma, UConn
1996	John Calipari, UMass	Andy Landers, Georgia
1997	Roy Williams, Kansas	Geno Auriemma, UConn
1998	Bill Guthridge, North Carolina	Pat Summitt, Tennessee
1999	Mike Krzyzewski, Duke	Carolyn Peck, Purdue
2000	Mike Montgomery, Stanford	Geno Auriemma, UConn
2001	Rod Barnes, Mississippi	Muffet McGraw, Notre Dame
2002	Ben Howland, Pittsburgh	Geno Auriemma, UConn
2003	Tubby Smith, Kentucky	Gail Goestenkors, Duke
2004	Phil Martelli, St. Joseph's	Pat Summitt, Tennessee

Year	Men's coach, school	Women's coach, school
2005	Bruce Weber, Illinois	Pokey Chatman, LSU
2006	Jay Wright, Villanova	Sylvia Hatchell, North Carolina
2007	Tony Bennett, Washington St.	Gail Goestenkors, Duke
2008	John Calipari, Memphis	Geno Auriemma, UConn
2009	Jamie Dixon, Pittsburgh	Geno Auriemma, UConn
2010	Jim Boeheim, Syracuse	Connie Yori, Nebraska
2011	Steve Fisher, San Diego St.	Tara VanDerveer, Stanford
2012	Bill Self, Kansas	Kim Mulkey, Baylor
2013	Jim Larrañaga, Miami (FL)	Muffet McGraw, Notre Dame
2014	Gregg Marshall, Wichita St.	Muffet McGraw, Notre Dame
2015	John Calipari, Kentucky	Courtney Banghart, Princeton
2016	Jay Wright, Villanova	Geno Auriemma, UConn
2017	Mark Few, Gonzaga	Geno Auriemma, UConn
2018	Tony Bennett, Virginia	Vic Schaefer, Mississippi St.
2019	Rick Barnes, Tennessee	Lisa Bluder, Iowa
2020	Anthony Grant, Dayton	Dawn Staley, South Carolina

Most Coaching Victories in Men's NCAA Division I Basketball Tournament

Coach, school(s), first/latest appearance	Wins	Tournaments	Championships
Mike Krzyzewski, Duke, 1984/2019	97	35	5
Roy Williams; Kansas, North Carolina; 1990/2019	79	29	3
Dean Smith, North Carolina, 1967/1997	65	27	2
Jim Boeheim, Syracuse, 1977/2019	55	34	1
Tom Izzo, Michigan St., 1998/2019	52	22	1
Jim Calhoun; Northeastern, Connecticut; 1981/2012	49	22	3
John Wooden, UCLA, 1950/1975	47	16	10
Lute Olson; Iowa, Arizona; 1979/2007	46	27	1
Bob Knight; Indiana, Texas Tech; 1973/2007	45	28	3
Denny Crum, Louisville, 1972/2000	42	23	2

Note: Through 2019 tournament; 2020 tournament was not held. Coaches active in 2019-20 season in bold. Some records adjusted to reflect vacated victories.

NCAA Women's Basketball Division I Champions, 1982-2019

NCAA canceled the 2020 tournament due to the COVID-19 outbreak.

Year	Champion	Final opponent	Score	Most outstanding player	Winning coach	Site
1982	Louisiana Tech	Cheyney	76-62	Janice Lawrence, LA Tech	Sonja Hogg	Norfolk, VA
1983	USC	Louisiana Tech	69-67	Cheryl Miller, USC	Linda Sharp	Norfolk, VA
1984	USC	Tennessee	72-61	Cheryl Miller, USC	Linda Sharp	Los Angeles, CA
1985	Old Dominion	Georgia	70-65	Tracy Claxton, Old Dominion	Marianne Stanley	Austin, TX
1986	Texas	USC	97-81	Clarissa Davis, Texas	Jody Conradt	Lexington, KY
1987	Tennessee	Louisiana Tech	67-44	Tonya Edwards, Tennessee	Pat Summitt	Austin, TX
1988	Louisiana Tech	Auburn	56-54	Erica Westbrooks, LA Tech	Leon Barmore	Tacoma, WA
1989	Tennessee	Auburn	76-60	Bridgette Gordon, Tennessee	Pat Summitt	Tacoma, WA
1990	Stanford	Auburn	88-81	Jennifer Azzi, Stanford	Tara VanDerveer	Knoxville, TN
1991	Tennessee	Virginia	70-67 (OT)	Dawn Staley, Virginia	Pat Summitt	New Orleans, LA
1992	Stanford	W. Kentucky	78-62	Molly Goodenbour, Stanford	Tara VanDerveer	Los Angeles, CA
1993	Texas Tech	Ohio St.	84-82	Sheryl Swoopes, Texas Tech	Marsha Sharp	Atlanta, GA
1994	North Carolina	Louisiana Tech	60-59	Charlotte Smith, North Carolina	Sylvia Hatchell	Richmond, VA
1995	Connecticut	Tennessee	70-64	Rebecca Lobo, Connecticut	Geno Auriemma	Minneapolis, MN
1996	Tennessee	Georgia	83-65	Michelle Marciniak, Tennessee	Pat Summitt	Charlotte, NC
1997	Tennessee	Old Dominion	68-59	Chamique Holdsclaw, Tennessee	Pat Summitt	Cincinnati, OH
1998	Tennessee	Louisiana Tech	93-75	Chamique Holdsclaw, Tennessee	Pat Summitt	Kansas City, MO
1999	Purdue	Duke	62-45	Ukari Figgs, Purdue	Carolyn Peck	San Jose, CA
2000	Connecticut	Tennessee	71-52	Shea Ralph, Connecticut	Geno Auriemma	Philadelphia, PA
2001	Notre Dame	Purdue	68-66	Ruth Riley, Notre Dame	Muffet McGraw	St. Louis, MO
2002	Connecticut	Oklahoma	82-70	Swin Cash, Connecticut	Geno Auriemma	San Antonio, TX
2003	Connecticut	Tennessee	73-68	Diana Taurasi, Connecticut	Geno Auriemma	Atlanta, GA
2004	Connecticut	Tennessee	70-61	Diana Taurasi, Connecticut	Geno Auriemma	New Orleans, LA
2005	Baylor	Michigan St.	84-62	Sophia Young, Baylor	Kim Mulkey-Robertson	Indianapolis, IN
2006	Maryland	Duke	78-75 (OT)	Laura Harper, Maryland	Brenda Frese	Boston, MA
2007	Tennessee	Rutgers	59-46	Candace Parker, Tennessee	Pat Summitt	Cleveland, OH
2008	Tennessee	Stanford	64-48	Candace Parker, Tennessee	Pat Summitt	Tampa Bay, FL
2009	Connecticut	Louisville	76-54	Tina Charles, Connecticut	Geno Auriemma	St. Louis, MO
2010	Connecticut	Stanford	53-47	Maya Moore, Connecticut	Geno Auriemma	San Antonio, TX
2011	Texas A&M	Notre Dame	76-70	Danielle Adams, Texas A&M	Gary Blair	Indianapolis, IN
2012	Baylor	Notre Dame	80-61	Brittney Griner, Baylor	Kim Mulkey	Denver, CO
2013	Connecticut	Louisville	93-60	Breanna Stewart, Connecticut	Geno Auriemma	New Orleans, LA
2014	Connecticut	Notre Dame	79-58	Breanna Stewart, Connecticut	Geno Auriemma	Nashville, TN
2015	Connecticut	Notre Dame	63-53	Breanna Stewart, Connecticut	Geno Auriemma	Tampa, FL
2016	Connecticut	Syracuse	82-51	Breanna Stewart, Connecticut	Geno Auriemma	Indianapolis, IN
2017	South Carolina	Mississippi St.	67-55	A'ja Wilson, South Carolina	Dawn Staley	Dallas, TX
2018	Notre Dame	Mississippi St.	61-58	Arike Ogunbowale, Notre Dame	Muffet McGraw	Columbus, OH
2019	Baylor	Notre Dame	82-81	Chloe Jackson, Baylor	Kim Mulkey	Tampa, FL

NCAA Women's Basketball Division I All-Time Leaders

	Season points						Season points per game					
Player, school (season)	G	FG	3-FG	FT	PTS	Player, school (season)	G	FG	3-FG	FT	PTS	PPG
Kelsey Plum, Washington (2017)	35	379	115	236	1,109	Patricia Hoskins, Mississippi Valley St. (1989)	27	345	13	205	908	33.6
Jackie Stiles, Missouri St. (2001)	35	365	65	267	1,062	Andrea Congreaves, Mercer (1992)	28	353	77	142	925	33.0
Odyssey Sims, Baylor (2014)	37	362	98	232	1,054	Kelsey Plum, Washington (2017)	35	379	115	236	1,109	31.7
Megan Gustafson, Iowa (2019)	36	412	1	176	1,001	Deborah Temple, Delta St. (1984)	28	373	NA	127	873	31.2
Cindy Brown, Long Beach St. (1987)	35	362	NA	250	974	Andrea Congreaves, Mercer (1993)	26	302	51	150	805	31.0
Jerica Coley, FIU (2014)	33	345	51	231	972	Wanda Ford, Drake (1986)	30	390	NA	139	919	30.6
Genia Miller, Cal St. Fullerton (1991)	33	376	0	217	969	Anucha Browne, Northwestern (1985)	28	341	NA	173	855	30.5
Chiney Ogwumike, Stanford (2014)	37	402	4	159	967	LeChandra LeDay, Grambling (1988)	28	334	36	146	850	30.4
Kelsey Plum, Washington (2016)	37	308	78	266	960	Jackie Stiles, Missouri St. (2001)	35	365	65	267	1,062	30.4
Sheryl Swoopes, Texas Tech (1993)	34	356	32	211	955	Kim Perrot, La.-Lafayette (1990)	28	309	95	128	841	30.0

Career points					
Player, school (seasons)	G	FG	3-FG	FT	PTS
Kelsey Plum, Washington (2014-17)	139	1,136	343	912	3,527
Kelsey Mitchell, Ohio St. (2015-18)	139	1,120	497	665	3,402
Jackie Stiles, Missouri St. (1998-2001)	129	1,160	221	852	3,393
Brittney Griner, Baylor (2010-13)	148	1,247	2	787	3,283
Patricia Hoskins, Mississippi Valley St. (1986-89)	110	1,196	24	706	3,122
Lorri Bauman, Drake (1981-84)	120	1,104	NA	907	3,115
Jerica Coley, FIU (2011-14)	131	1,099	160	749	3,107
Rachel Banham, Minnesota (2012-16)	144	1,081	354	577	3,093
Elena Delle Donne, Delaware (2010-13)	114	1,030	206	773	3,039
Maya Moore, Connecticut (2008-11)	154	1,171	311	383	3,036
Chamique Holdsclaw, Tennessee (1996-99)	148	1,233	36	523	3,025

Career points per game						
Player, school (seasons)	G	FG	3-FG	FT	PTS	PPG
Patricia Hoskins, Mississippi Valley St. (1986-89)	110	1,196	24	706	3,122	28.4
Sandra Hodge, New Orleans (1981-84)	107	1,194	NA	472	2,860	26.7
Elena Delle Donne, Delaware (2010-13)	114	1,030	206	773	3,039	26.7
Jackie Stiles, Missouri St. (1998-2001)	129	1,160	221	852	3,393	26.3
Lorri Bauman, Drake (1981-84)	120	1,104	NA	907	3,115	26.0
Andrea Congreaves, Mercer (1990-93)	108	1,107	153	429	2,796	25.9
Cindy Blodgett, Maine (1995-98)	118	1,055	219	676	3,005	25.5
Valorie Whiteside, Appalachian St. (1985-88)	116	1,153	0	638	2,944	25.4
Kelsey Plum, Washington (2014-17)	139	1,136	343	912	3,527	25.4
Joyce Walker, LSU (1981-84)	117	1,259	NA	388	2,906	24.8
Kelsey Mitchell, Ohio St. (2015-18)	139	1,120	497	665	3,402	24.5

NA = Not available. **Note:** Career leaders played at least three seasons (in a four-year career) or two (in a three-season career) since official NCAA record-keeping began (1981-82).

Wade Trophy Winners, 1978-2020

Awarded by the National Assn. for Girls and Women in Sport and the Women's Basketball Coaches Assn. (WBCA) to the best college women's basketball player in terms of character, leadership, and player performance.

Year	Player, school	Year	Player, school	Year	Player, school
1978	Carol Blazejowski, Montclair St.	1993	Karen Jennings, Nebraska	2007	Candace Parker, Tennessee
1979	Nancy Lieberman, Old Dominion	1994	Carol Ann Shudlick, Minnesota	2008	Candice Wiggins, Stanford
1980	Nancy Lieberman, Old Dominion	1995	Rebecca Lobo, Connecticut	2009	Maya Moore, Connecticut
1981	Lynette Woodard, Kansas	1996	Jennifer Rizzotti, Connecticut	2010	Maya Moore, Connecticut
1982	Pam Kelly, Louisiana Tech	1997	DeLisha Milton, Florida	2011	Maya Moore, Connecticut
1983	LaTaunya Pollard, Long Beach St.	1998	Ticha Penicheiro, Old Dominion	2012	Brittney Griner, Baylor
1984	Janice Lawrence, Louisiana Tech	1999	Stephanie White-McCarty, Purdue	2013	Brittney Griner, Baylor
1985	Cheryl Miller, USC	2000	Edwina Brown, Texas	2014	Odyssey Sims, Baylor
1986	Kamie Ethridge, Texas	2001	Jackie Stiles, Missouri St.	2015	Breanna Stewart, Connecticut
1987	Shelly Pennefeather, Villanova	2002	Sue Bird, Connecticut	2016	Breanna Stewart, Connecticut
1988	Teresa Weatherspoon, Louisiana Tech	2003	Diana Taurasi, Connecticut	2017	Kelsey Plum, Washington
1989	Clarissa Davis, Texas	2004	Alana Beard, Duke	2018	A'ja Wilson, South Carolina
1990	Jennifer Azzi, Stanford	2005	Seimone Augustus, LSU	2019	Sabrina Ionescu, Oregon
1991	Daedra Charles, Tennessee	2006	Seimone Augustus, LSU	2020	Sabrina Ionescu, Oregon
1992	Susan Robinson, Penn St.				

NCAA Men's Baseball Division I Champions, 1947-2019

NCAA canceled the 2020 College World Series due to the COVID-19 outbreak.

Year	Champion	Year	Champion	Year	Champion	Year	Champion	Year	Champion
1947	California	1962	Michigan	1977	Arizona St.	1992	Pepperdine	2006	Oregon St.
1948	USC	1963	USC	1978	USC	1993	LSU	2007	Oregon St.
1949	Texas	1964	Minnesota	1979	Cal St. Fullerton	1994	Oklahoma	2008	Fresno St.
1950	Texas	1965	Arizona St.	1980	Arizona	1995	Cal St. Fullerton	2009	LSU
1951	Oklahoma	1966	Ohio St.	1981	Arizona St.	1996	LSU	2010	South Carolina
1952	Holy Cross	1967	Arizona St.	1982	Miami (FL)	1997	LSU	2011	South Carolina
1953	Michigan	1968	USC	1983	Texas	1998	USC	2012	Arizona
1954	Missouri	1969	Arizona St.	1984	Cal St. Fullerton	1999	Miami (FL)	2013	UCLA
1955	Wake Forest	1970	USC	1985	Miami (FL)	2000	LSU	2014	Vanderbilt
1956	Minnesota	1971	USC	1986	Arizona	2001	Miami (FL)	2015	Virginia
1957	California	1972	USC	1987	Stanford	2002	Texas	2016	Coastal Carolina
1958	USC	1973	USC	1988	Stanford	2003	Rice	2017	Oregon St.
1959	Oklahoma St.	1974	USC	1989	Wichita St.	2004	Cal St. Fullerton	2018	Oregon St.
1960	Minnesota	1975	Texas	1990	Georgia	2005	Texas	2019	Vanderbilt
1961	USC	1976	Arizona	1991	LSU				

NCAA Women's Softball Division I Champions, 1982-2019

NCAA canceled the 2020 Women's College World Series due to the COVID-19 outbreak.

Year	Champion	Year	Champion	Year	Champion	Year	Champion	Year	Champion
1982	UCLA	1990	UCLA	1998	Fresno St.	2006	Arizona	2013	Oklahoma
1983	Texas A&M	1991	Arizona	1999	UCLA	2007	Arizona	2014	Florida
1984	UCLA	1992	UCLA	2000	Oklahoma	2008	Arizona St.	2015	Florida
1985	UCLA	1993	Arizona	2001	Arizona	2009	Washington	2016	Oklahoma
1986	Cal St. Fullerton	1994	Arizona	2002	California	2010	UCLA	2017	Oklahoma
1987	Texas A&M	1995	UCLA	2003	UCLA	2011	Arizona St.	2018	Florida St.
1988	UCLA	1996	Arizona	2004	UCLA	2012	Alabama	2019	UCLA
1989	UCLA	1997	Arizona	2005	Michigan				

NCAA Men's Hockey Division I Champions, 1948-2020

Year	Champion	Year	Champion	Year	Champion	Year	Champion	Year	Champion
1948	Michigan	1963	North Dakota	1978	Boston Univ.	1993	Maine	2007	Michigan St.
1949	Boston College	1964	Michigan	1979	Minnesota	1994	Lake Superior St.	2008	Boston College
1950	Colorado College	1965	Michigan Tech	1980	North Dakota	1995	Boston Univ.	2009	Boston Univ.
1951	Michigan	1966	Michigan St.	1981	Wisconsin	1996	Michigan	2010	Boston College
1952	Michigan	1967	Cornell	1982	North Dakota	1997	North Dakota	2011	Minnesota Duluth
1953	Michigan	1968	Denver	1983	Wisconsin	1998	Michigan	2012	Boston College
1954	Rensselaer	1969	Denver	1984	Bowling Green	1999	Maine	2013	Yale
1955	Michigan	1970	Cornell	1985	Rensselaer	2000	North Dakota	2014	Union College
1956	Michigan	1971	Boston Univ.	1986	Michigan St.	2001	Boston College	2015	Providence
1957	Colorado College	1972	Boston Univ.	1987	North Dakota	2002	Minnesota	2016	North Dakota
1958	Denver	1973	Wisconsin	1988	Lake Superior St.	2003	Minnesota	2017	Denver
1959	North Dakota	1974	Minnesota	1989	Harvard	2004	Denver	2018	Minnesota Duluth
1960	Denver	1975	Michigan Tech	1990	Wisconsin	2005	Denver	2019	Minnesota Duluth
1961	Denver	1976	Minnesota	1991	North Michigan	2006	Wisconsin	2020	No champion
1962	Michigan Tech	1977	Wisconsin	1992	Lake Superior St.				

NCAA Women's Hockey Champions, 2001-20

Year	Champion	Year	Champion	Year	Champion	Year	Champion	Year	Champion
2001	Minnesota Duluth	2005	Minnesota	2009	Wisconsin	2013	Minnesota	2017	Clarkson
2002	Minnesota Duluth	2006	Wisconsin	2010	Minnesota Duluth	2014	Clarkson	2018	Clarkson
2003	Minnesota Duluth	2007	Wisconsin	2011	Wisconsin	2015	Minnesota	2019	Wisconsin
2004	Minnesota	2008	Minnesota Duluth	2012	Minnesota	2016	Minnesota	2020	No champion

NCAA Division I Lacrosse Champions, 1982-2020

Year	Men	Women	Year	Men	Women	Year	Men	Women
1982	North Carolina	Massachusetts	1995	Syracuse	Maryland	2008	Syracuse	Northwestern
1983	Syracuse	Delaware	1996	Princeton	Maryland	2009	Syracuse	Northwestern
1984	Johns Hopkins	Temple	1997	Princeton	Maryland	2010	Duke	Maryland
1985	Johns Hopkins	New Hampshire	1998	Princeton	Maryland	2011	Virginia	Northwestern
1986	North Carolina	Maryland	1999	Virginia	Maryland	2012	Loyola (MD)	Northwestern
1987	Johns Hopkins	Penn St.	2000	Syracuse	Maryland	2013	Duke	North Carolina
1988	Syracuse	Temple	2001	Princeton	Maryland	2014	Duke	Maryland
1989	Syracuse	Penn St.	2002	Syracuse	Princeton	2015	Denver	Maryland
1990	Syracuse[1]	Harvard	2003	Virginia	Princeton	2016	North Carolina	North Carolina
1991	North Carolina	Virginia	2004	Syracuse	Virginia	2017	Maryland	Maryland
1992	Princeton	Maryland	2005	Johns Hopkins	Northwestern	2018	Yale	James Madison
1993	Syracuse	Virginia	2006	Virginia	Northwestern	2019	Virginia	Maryland
1994	Princeton	Princeton	2007	Johns Hopkins	Northwestern	2020	No champion	No champion

Note: NCAA Championships began in 1971 for men, in 1982 for women. (1) Vacated due to an NCAA rules violation.

NCAA Division I Soccer Champions, 1982-2019

Year	Men	Women	Year	Men	Women	Year	Men	Women
1982	Indiana	North Carolina	1995	Wisconsin	Notre Dame	2007	Wake Forest	USC
1983	Indiana	North Carolina	1996	St. John's (NY)	North Carolina	2008	Maryland	North Carolina
1984	Clemson	North Carolina	1997	UCLA	North Carolina	2009	Virginia	North Carolina
1985	UCLA	George Mason	1998	Indiana	Florida	2010	Akron	Notre Dame
1986	Duke	North Carolina	1999	Indiana	North Carolina	2011	North Carolina	Stanford
1987	Clemson	North Carolina	2000	Connecticut	North Carolina	2012	Indiana	North Carolina
1988	Indiana	North Carolina	2001	North Carolina	Santa Clara	2013	Notre Dame	UCLA
1989	Santa Clara;	North Carolina	2002	UCLA	Portland	2014	Virginia	Florida St.
	Virginia (tie)		2003	Indiana	North Carolina	2015	Stanford	Penn St.
1990	UCLA	North Carolina	2004	Indiana	Notre Dame	2016	Stanford	USC
1991	Virginia	North Carolina	2005	Maryland	Portland	2017	Stanford	Stanford
1992	Virginia	North Carolina	2006	UC Santa	North Carolina	2018	Maryland	Florida St.
1993	Virginia	North Carolina		Barbara		2019	Georgetown	Stanford
1994	Virginia	North Carolina						

Note: NCAA Championships began in 1959 for men, in 1982 for women.

NCAA Division I Wrestling Champions, 1964-2020

Year	Champion	Year	Champion	Year	Champion	Year	Champion	Year	Champion
1964	Oklahoma St.	1976	Iowa	1988	Arizona St.	1999	Iowa	2010	Iowa
1965	Iowa St.	1977	Iowa St.	1989	Oklahoma St.	2000	Iowa	2011	Penn St.
1966	Oklahoma St.	1978	Iowa	1990	Oklahoma St.	2001	Minnesota	2012	Penn St.
1967	Michigan St.	1979	Iowa	1991	Iowa	2002	Minnesota	2013	Penn St.
1968	Oklahoma St.	1980	Iowa	1992	Iowa	2003	Oklahoma St.	2014	Penn St.
1969	Iowa St.	1981	Iowa	1993	Iowa	2004	Oklahoma St.	2015	Ohio St.
1970	Iowa St.	1982	Iowa	1994	Oklahoma St.	2005	Oklahoma St.	2016	Penn St.
1971	Oklahoma St.	1983	Iowa	1995	Iowa	2006	Oklahoma St.	2017	Penn St.
1972	Iowa St.	1984	Iowa	1996	Iowa	2007	Minnesota	2018	Penn St.
1973	Iowa St.	1985	Iowa	1997	Iowa	2008	Iowa	2019	Penn St.
1974	Oklahoma	1986	Iowa	1998	Iowa	2009	Iowa	2020	No champion
1975	Iowa	1987	Iowa St.						

Selected NCAA Division I Teams

(Conferences and coaches listed are as of July 2020.)

Team	Nickname	Team colors	Conference	Basketball coach	Football coach
Air Force	Falcons	Blue & silver	Mountain West	Joe Scott	Troy Calhoun
Akron	Zips	Blue & gold	Mid-American	John Groce	Tom Arth
Alabama	Crimson Tide	Crimson & white	Southeastern	Nate Oats	Nick Saban
Appalachian State	Mountaineers	Black & gold	Sun Belt	Dustin Kerns	Shawn Clark
Arizona	Wildcats	Cardinal & navy	Pac-12	Sean Miller	Kevin Sumlin
Arizona State	Sun Devils	Maroon & gold	Pac-12	Bobby Hurley	Herm Edwards
Arkansas	Razorbacks	Cardinal & white	Southeastern	Eric Musselman	Sam Pittman
Arkansas State	Red Wolves	Scarlet & black	Sun Belt	Mike Balado	Blake Anderson
Army	Black Knights	Black, gold, & gray	Independent[1]	Jimmy Allen	Jeff Monken
Auburn	Tigers	Burnt orange & navy blue	Southeastern	Bruce Pearl	Gus Malzahn
Ball State	Cardinals	Cardinal & white	Mid-American	James Whitford	Mike Neu
Baylor	Bears	Green & gold	Big 12	Scott Drew	Dave Aranda
Boise State	Broncos	Blue & orange	Mountain West	Leon Rice	Bryan Harsin
Boston College	Eagles	Maroon & gold	Atlantic Coast	Jim Christian	Jeff Hafley
Bowling Green	Falcons	Orange & brown	Mid-American	Michael Huger	Scot Loeffler
Brigham Young (BYU)	Cougars	Blue & white	Independent[1]	Mark Pope	Kalani Sitake
Brown*	Bears	Brown, red, & white	Ivy League	Mike Martin	James Perry
Butler	Bulldogs	Blue & white	Pioneer League[1]	LaVall Jordan	Jeff Voris
California	Golden Bears	Blue & gold	Pac-12	Mark Fox	Justin Wilcox
Central Michigan	Chippewas	Maroon & gold	Mid-American	Keno Davis	Jim McElwain
Cincinnati	Bearcats	Red & black	American Athletic	John Brannen	Luke Fickell
Citadel*	Bulldogs	Citadel blue & white	Southern	Duggar Baucom	Brent Thompson
Clemson	Tigers	Tiger orange & regalia	Atlantic Coast	Brad Brownell	Dabo Swinney
Colgate*	Raiders	Maroon, gray, & white	Patriot League	Matt Langel	Dan Hunt
Colorado	Buffaloes	Silver, black, & gold	Pac-12	Tad Boyle	Karl Dorrell
Colorado State	Rams	Green & gold	Mountain West	Niko Medved	Steve Addazio
Columbia*	Lions	Columbia blue & white	Ivy League	Jim Engles	Al Bagnoli
Connecticut	Huskies	National flag blue & white	Big East[2]	Dan Hurley	Randy Edsall
Cornell*	Big Red	Carnelian red & white	Ivy League	Brian Earl	David Archer
Dartmouth*	Big Green	Dartmouth green & white	Ivy League	David McLaughlin	Buddy Teevens
Delaware*	Blue Hens	Blue & gold	Colonial Athletic	Martin Ingelsby	Danny Rocco
Duke	Blue Devils	Duke blue & white	Atlantic Coast	Mike Krzyzewski	David Cutcliffe
East Carolina	Pirates	Purple & gold	American Athletic	Joe Dooley	Mike Houston
Eastern Illinois*	Panthers	Blue & gray	Ohio Valley	Jay Spoonhour	Adam Cushing
Eastern Kentucky*	Colonels	Maroon & white	Ohio Valley	A. W. Hamilton	Walt Wells
Eastern Michigan	Eagles	Green & white	Mid-American	Rob Murphy	Chris Creighton
Eastern Washington*	Eagles	Red & white	Big Sky	Shantay Legans	Aaron Best
Florida	Gators	Orange & blue	Southeastern	Mike White	Dan Mullen
Florida A&M*	Rattlers	Orange & green	Mid-Eastern Athletic	Robert McCullum	Willie Simmons
Florida State	Seminoles	Garnet & gold	Atlantic Coast	Leonard Hamilton	Mike Norvell
Fresno State	Bulldogs	Red & blue	Mountain West	Justin Hutson	Kalen DeBoer
Furman*	Paladins	Purple & white	Southern	Bob Richey	Clay Hendrix
Georgia	Bulldogs	Red & black	Southeastern	Tom Crean	Kirby Smart
Georgia Southern	Eagles	Blue & white	Sun Belt	Brian Burg	Chad Lunsford
Georgia Tech	Yellow Jackets	Old gold & white	Atlantic Coast	Josh Pastner	Geoff Collins
Gonzaga	Bulldogs, Zags	Navy blue, white, & red	West Coast	Mark Few	Does not compete
Harvard*	Crimson	Crimson, black, & white	Ivy League	Tommy Amaker	Tim Murphy
Hawaii	Rainbow Warriors	Green, black, white, silver	Mountain West[1]	Eran Ganot	Todd Graham
Holy Cross*	Crusaders	Royal purple	Patriot League	Brett Nelson	Bob Chesney
Houston	Cougars	Scarlet & white	American Athletic	Kelvin Sampson	Dana Holgorsen
Howard*	Bison	Blue & white	Mid-Eastern Athletic	Kenny Blakeney	Larry Scott
Idaho*	Vandals	Silver & vandal gold	Big Sky	Zac Claus	Paul Petrino
Illinois	Fighting Illini	Orange & blue	Big Ten	Brad Underwood	Lovie Smith
Illinois State*	Redbirds	Red & white	Missouri Valley	Dan Muller	Brock Spack
Indiana	Hoosiers	Cream & crimson	Big Ten	Archie Miller	Tom Allen
Indiana State*	Sycamores	Royal blue & white	Missouri Valley	Greg Lansing	Curt Mallory
Iowa	Hawkeyes	Black & gold	Big Ten	Fran McCaffery	Kirk Ferentz
Iowa State	Cyclones	Cardinal & gold	Big 12	Steve Prohm	Matt Campbell
Jackson State*	Tigers	Blue & white	Southwestern Athletic	Wayne Brent	John Hendrick
James Madison*	Dukes	Purple & gold	Colonial Athletic	Mark Byington	Curt Cignetti
Kansas	Jayhawks	Crimson & blue	Big 12	Bill Self	Les Miles
Kansas State	Wildcats	Purple & white	Big 12	Bruce Weber	Chris Klieman
Kent State	Golden Flashes	Navy blue & gold	Mid-American	Rob Senderoff	Sean Lewis
Kentucky	Wildcats	Blue & white	Southeastern	John Calipari	Mark Stoops
Lafayette*	Leopards	Maroon & white	Patriot League	Fran O'Hanlon	John Garrett
Lehigh*	Mountain Hawks	Brown & white	Patriot League	Brett Reed	Tom Gilmore
Liberty	Flames	Red, white, & blue	Independent[1]	Ritchie McKay	Hugh Freeze
Louisiana State (LSU)	Fighting Tigers	Purple & gold	Southeastern	Will Wade	Ed Orgeron
Louisiana Tech	Bulldogs	Red & blue	Conference USA	Eric Konkol	Skip Holtz
Louisiana-Lafayette	Ragin' Cajuns	Vermilion & white	Sun Belt	Bob Marlin	Billy Napier
Louisiana-Monroe	Warhawks	Maroon & gold	Sun Belt	Keith Richard	Matt Viator
Louisville	Cardinals	Red & black	Atlantic Coast	Chris Mack	Scott Satterfield
Maine*	Black Bears	Blue & white	Colonial Athletic[1]	Richard Barron	Nick Charlton
Marshall	Thundering Herd	Kelly green & white	Conference USA	Dan D'Antoni	Doc Holliday
Maryland	Terrapins	Red, white, black, & gold	Big Ten	Mark Turgeon	Michael Locksley
Massachusetts	Minutemen	Maroon & white	Independent[1]	Matt McCall	Walt Bell
Memphis	Tigers	Blue & gray	American Athletic	Anfernee "Penny" Hardaway	Ryan Silverfield
Miami (Florida)	Hurricanes	Orange & green	Atlantic Coast	Jim Larrañaga	Manny Diaz
Miami (Ohio)	RedHawks	Red & white	Mid-American	Jack Owens	Chuck Martin
Michigan	Wolverines	Maize & blue	Big Ten	Juwan Howard	Jim Harbaugh
Michigan State	Spartans	Green & white	Big Ten	Tom Izzo	Mel Tucker
Mid. Tennessee State	Blue Raiders	Royal blue & white	Conference USA	Nick McDevitt	Rick Stockstill
Minnesota	Golden Gophers	Maroon & gold	Big Ten	Richard Pitino	P. J. Fleck
Mississippi (Ole Miss)	Rebels	Cardinal red & navy blue	Southeastern	Kermit Davis	Lane Kiffin

Team	Nickname	Team colors	Conference	Basketball coach	Football coach
Mississippi State	Bulldogs	Maroon & white	Southeastern	Ben Howland	Mike Leach
Missouri	Tigers	Old gold & black	Southeastern	Cuonzo Martin	Eliah Drinkwitz
Montana*	Grizzlies	Maroon & silver	Big Sky	Travis DeCuire	Bobby Hauck
Montana State*	Bobcats	Blue & gold	Big Sky	Danny Sprinkle	Jeff Choate
Morgan State*	Bears	Blue & orange	Mid-Eastern Athletic	Kevin Broadus	Tyrone Wheatley
Murray State*	Racers	Navy & gold	Ohio Valley	Matt McMahon	Dean Hood
Navy	Midshipmen	Navy blue & gold	American Athletic[1]	Ed DeChellis	Ken Niumatalolo
Nebraska	Cornhuskers	Scarlet & cream	Big Ten	Fred Hoiberg	Scott Frost
Nevada	Wolf Pack	Silver & blue	Mountain West	Steve Alford	Jay Norvell
Nevada-Las Vegas (UNLV)	Rebels	Scarlet & gray	Mountain West	T. J. Otzelberger	Marcus Arroyo
New Hampshire*	Wildcats	Blue & white	Colonial Athletic[1]	Bill Herrion	Sean McDonnell
New Mexico	Lobos	Cherry & silver	Mountain West	Paul Weir	Danny Gonzales
New Mexico State	Aggies	Crimson & white	Independent[1]	Chris Jans	Doug Martin
Nicholls State*	Colonels	Red & gray	Southland	Austin Claunch	Tim Rebowe
North Carolina	Tar Heels	Carolina blue & white	Atlantic Coast	Roy Williams	Mack Brown
North Carolina State	Wolfpack	Red & white	Atlantic Coast	Kevin Keatts	Dave Doeren
North Texas	Mean Green	Green & white	Conference USA	Grant McCasland	Seth Littrell
Northern Illinois	Huskies	Cardinal & black	Mid-American	Mark Montgomery	Thomas Hammock
Northern Iowa*	Panthers	Purple & old gold	Missouri Valley	Ben Jacobson	Mark Farley
Northwestern	Wildcats	Purple	Big Ten	Chris Collins	Pat Fitzgerald
Northwestern State*	Demons	Purple, white, & orange	Southland	Mike McConathy	Brad Laird
Notre Dame	Fighting Irish	Blue & gold	Independent[1]	Mike Brey	Brian Kelly
Ohio	Bobcats	Hunter green & white	Mid-American	Jeff Boals	Frank Solich
Ohio State	Buckeyes	Scarlet & gray	Big Ten	Chris Holtmann	Ryan Day
Oklahoma	Sooners	Crimson & cream	Big 12	Lon Kruger	Lincoln Riley
Oklahoma State	Cowboys	Orange & black	Big 12	Mike Boynton Jr.	Mike Gundy
Oregon	Ducks	Green & yellow	Pac-12	Dana Altman	Mario Cristobal
Oregon State	Beavers	Orange & black	Pac-12	Wayne Tinkle	Jonathan Smith
Penn State	Nittany Lions	Blue & white	Big Ten	Patrick Chambers	James Franklin
Pennsylvania*	Quakers	Red & blue	Ivy League	Steve Donahue	Ray Priore
Pittsburgh	Panthers	Gold & blue	Atlantic Coast	Jeff Capel	Pat Narduzzi
Princeton*	Tigers	Orange & black	Ivy League	Mitch Henderson	Bob Surace
Purdue	Boilermakers	Old gold & black	Big Ten	Matt Painter	Jeff Brohm
Rice	Owls	Blue & gray	Conference USA	Scott Pera	Mike Bloomgren
Richmond*	Spiders	Red & blue	Colonial Athletic[1]	Chris Mooney	Russ Huesman
Rutgers	Scarlet Knights	Scarlet	Big Ten	Steve Pikiell	Greg Schiano
Sam Houston State*	Bearkats	Orange & white	Southland	Jason Hooten	K. C. Keeler
San Diego State	Aztecs	Scarlet & black	Mountain West	Brian Dutcher	Brady Hoke
San Jose State	Spartans	Gold, white, & blue	Mountain West	Jean Prioleau	Brent Brennan
South Carolina	Gamecocks	Garnet & black	Southeastern	Frank Martin	Will Muschamp
South Carolina State*	Bulldogs	Garnet & blue	Mid-Eastern Athletic	Murray Garvin	Oliver Pough
South Florida	Bulls	Green & gold	American Athletic	Brian Gregory	Jeff Scott
Southeast Missouri State*	Redhawks	Red, black, & white	Ohio Valley	Brad Korn	Tom Matukewicz
Southern California (USC)	Trojans	Cardinal & gold	Pac-12	Andy Enfield	Clay Helton
Southern Illinois*	Salukis	Maroon & white	Missouri Valley	Bryan Mullins	Nick Hill
Southern Methodist (SMU)	Mustangs	Red & blue	American Athletic	Tim Jankovich	Sonny Dykes
Southern Mississippi	Golden Eagles	Black & gold	Conference USA	Jay Ladner	Jay Hopson
Stanford	Cardinal	Cardinal & white	Pac-12	Jerod Haase	David Shaw
Stephen F. Austin*	Lumberjacks	Purple & white	Southland	Kyle Keller	Colby Carthel
Syracuse	Orange	Orange	Atlantic Coast	Jim Boeheim	Dino Babers
Temple	Owls	Cherry & white	American Athletic	Aaron McKie	Rod Carey
Tennessee	Volunteers	Orange & white	Southeastern	Rick Barnes	Jeremy Pruitt
Tennessee State*	Tigers	Reflex blue & white	Ohio Valley	Brian Collins	Rod Reed
Tennessee Tech*	Golden Eagles	Purple & gold	Ohio Valley	John Pelphrey	Dewayne Alexander
Texas	Longhorns	Burnt orange & white	Big 12	Shaka Smart	Tom Herman
Texas A&M	Aggies	Maroon & white	Southeastern	Buzz Williams	Jimbo Fisher
Texas Christian (TCU)	Horned Frogs	Purple & white	Big 12	Jamie Dixon	Gary Patterson
Texas Southern*	Tigers	Maroon & gray	Southwestern Athletic	Johnny Jones	Clarence McKinney
Texas State	Bobcats	Maroon & gold	Sun Belt	Danny Kaspar	Jake Spavital
Texas Tech	Red Raiders	Scarlet & black	Big 12	Chris Beard	Matt Wells
Toledo	Rockets	Midnight blue & gold	Mid-American	Tod Kowalczyk	Jason Candle
Troy	Trojans	Cardinal, silver, & black	Sun Belt	Scott Cross	Chip Lindsey
Tulane	Green Wave	Olive green & blue	American Athletic	Ron Hunter	Willie Fritz
Tulsa	Golden Hurricane	Old gold, royal blue, & crimson	American Athletic	Frank Haith	Philip Montgomery
UCLA	Bruins	Blue & gold	Pac-12	Mick Cronin	Chip Kelly
Utah	Utes	Red & white	Pac-12	Larry Krystkowiak	Kyle Whittingham
Utah State	Aggies	Navy blue, pewter, & white	Mountain West	Craig Smith	Gary Andersen
UTEP (Texas-El Paso)	Miners	Dark blue, orange, & silver	Conference USA	Rodney Terry	Dana Dimel
Vanderbilt	Commodores	Black & gold	Southeastern	Jerry Stackhouse	Derek Mason
Villanova*	Wildcats	Blue & white	Colonial Athletic[1]	Jay Wright	Mark Ferrante
Virginia	Cavaliers	Orange & blue	Atlantic Coast	Tony Bennett	Bronco Mendenhall
Virginia Tech	Hokies	Chicago maroon & burnt orange	Atlantic Coast	Mike Young	Justin Fuente
Wake Forest	Demon Deacons	Old gold & black	Atlantic Coast	Steve Forbes	Dave Clawson
Washington	Huskies	Purple & gold	Pac-12	Mike Hopkins	Jimmy Lake
Washington State	Cougars	Crimson & gray	Pac-12	Kyle Smith	Nick Rolovich
Weber State*	Wildcats	Purple & white	Big Sky	Randy Rahe	Jay Hill
West Virginia	Mountaineers	Old gold & blue	Big 12	Bob Huggins	Neal Brown
Western Illinois*	Leathernecks	Purple & gold	Missouri Valley[1]	Rob Jeter	Jared Elliott
Western Kentucky	Hilltoppers	Red & white	Conference USA	Rick Stansbury	Tyson Helton
Western Michigan	Broncos	Brown & gold	Mid-American	Clayton Bates	Tim Lester
Wisconsin	Badgers	Cardinal & white	Big Ten	Greg Gard	Paul Chryst
Wyoming	Cowboys	Brown & gold	Mountain West	Jeff Linder	Craig Bohl
Yale*	Elis, Bulldogs	Yale blue & white	Ivy League	James Jones	Tony Reno
Youngstown State*	Penguins	Red & white	Missouri Valley[1]	Jerrod Calhoun	Doug Phillips

* = Football Championship Subdivision (FCS) team (formerly known as I-AA). (1) Team competes in conference listed in football but not in basketball. (2) Team competes in conference listed in basketball but not in football.

FOOTBALL

NFL 2019: Kansas City Wins Title in League's 100th Season

The Kansas City Chiefs ended the NFL's centennial season with their fourth straight AFC West crown and first Super Bowl title in 50 years. The Chiefs advanced to the Super Bowl on three comeback playoff wins, defeating the Houston Texans, 51-31, in the AFC Divisional Playoff game Jan. 12, 2020, at Arrowhead Stadium in Kansas City, MO. Quarterback Patrick Mahomes threw five touchdown passes, three to tight end Travis Kelce, and Damien Williams added a pair of rushing TDs. In the AFC Championship game Jan. 19, 2020, Kansas City defeated Tennessee, 35-24, in Kansas City. Mahomes ran for a 27-yard touchdown and passed for 294 yards.

The defending-champion New England Patriots led the NFL in total defense, allowing only 275.9 yards per game, on the way to their record 11th straight AFC East title. But the Pats season ended in an AFC Wild Card game, losing 20-13, to the Tennessee Titans on Jan. 4, 2020, at Gillette Stadium in Foxborough, MA. After 20 seasons and six Super Bowl championships with New England, 42-year-old Patriots QB Tom Brady signed a two-year contract with Tampa Bay in Mar. 2020.

Titans running back Derrick Henry, who topped the NFL with 1,540 rushing yards in 2019, ran for 182 yards and a touchdown in the upset win over the Patriots. In the AFC Divisional Playoffs, Henry rushed for 195 yards and added a three-yard TD pass in Tennessee's 28-12 win over the top-seeded Baltimore Ravens, Jan. 11, 2020, at M&T Bank Stadium in Baltimore, MD. The Ravens won a franchise-record 14 games with an offense that scored a league-high 531 points and set a single-season NFL record with 3,296 rushing yards. QB Lamar Jackson passed for 3,127 yards and 36 touchdowns, ran for an NFL QB-record 1,206 yards, and was named 2019 NFL Most Valuable Player.

After winning only four games in 2018, the San Francisco 49ers (13-3) went 8-0 to start the season on their way to the NFC West title. The Niners advanced to Super Bowl LIV with a 37-20 win over the Green Bay Packers in the NFC Championship game, Jan. 19, 2020, at Levi's Stadium in Santa Clara, CA. Raheem Mostert rushed for 220 yards and scored four touchdowns in the victory.

The Niners reached the conference title game with a 27-10 win in the NFC Divisional Playoff over Minnesota, Jan. 11, 2020, at Levi's Stadium. The Vikings had beaten NFC South champion New Orleans, 26-20, in an NFC Wild Card playoff Jan. 5, 2020 at the Mercedes-Benz Superdome in New Orleans, LA.

Veteran Saints QB Drew Brees, who missed five games due to a right thumb injury, passed for 208 yards and one TD in the playoff loss. Brees added to his tallies as the NFL all-time leader in passing yards (77,416) and passing TDs (547). Saints wide receiver Michael Thomas caught an NFL-record 149 passes in 2019.

Green Bay (13-3) won the NFC North and advanced to the NFC title game following a 28-23 win over the Seattle Seahawks in a Divisional Playoff, Jan. 12, 2020, at Lambeau Field in Green Bay, WI. Packers QB Aaron Rodgers threw for 243 yards and a pair of touchdowns to Davante Adams, who caught eight passes for 160 yards. Seattle earned an NFC Wild Card berth and QB Russell Wilson passed for 325 yards in the Seahawks' 17-9 Wild Card win over the Philadelphia Eagles, Jan. 5, 2020, at Lincoln Financial Field in Philadelphia, PA.

NFL Playoff Results, 2019

AFC Wild Card Games: Houston 22, Buffalo 19 (OT); Tennessee 20, New England 13.

NFC Wild Card Games: Minnesota 26, New Orleans 20 (OT); Seattle 17, Philadelphia 9.

AFC Divisional Playoff Games: Tennessee 28, Baltimore 12; Kansas City 51, Houston 31.

NFC Divisional Playoff Games: San Francisco 27, Minnesota 10; Green Bay 28, Seattle 23.

AFC Championship Game: Kansas City 35, Tennessee 24.

NFC Championship Game: San Francisco 37, Green Bay 20.

Super Bowl LIV: Kansas City 31, San Francisco 20.

Super Bowl LIV: Kansas City 31, San Francisco 20

The Kansas City Chiefs scored three touchdowns in the fourth quarter to beat the San Francisco 49ers, 31-20, in Super Bowl LIV, Feb. 2, 2020, at Hard Rock Stadium in Miami Gardens, FL. Chiefs QB Patrick Mahomes passed for 286 yards and two TDs to lead Kansas City to its first Super Bowl win in 50 years. Kansas City cut San Francisco's fourth quarter lead to 20-17 with a one-yard TD pass from Mahomes to tight end Travis Kelce, then went ahead 24-20 with under three minutes left when Damien Williams caught a 5-yard touchdown pass from Mahomes, who was voted the Super Bowl's Most Valuable Player. Williams rushed for 104 yards and added a 38-yard TD run for KC's final score.

The teams were tied, 10-10, at halftime, as the NFC's top-rated defense held the 24-year-old Mahomes to 104 passing yards. San Francisco went ahead 13-10 in the third on Robbie Gould's 42-yard field goal, then QB Jimmy Garoppolo led the team on a 55-yard scoring drive capped by Raheem Mostert's 1-yard TD. Garoppolo passed for 219 yards and a touchdown, but each QB threw 2 interceptions.

Kansas City's Andy Reid won his first Super Bowl as a head coach. Reid guided the Philadelphia Eagles to the Super Bowl in 2005, but the team lost to New England, 24-21. The 49ers were appearing in the seventh Super Bowl in franchise history and first since they lost to Baltimore in 2013.

Team	Quarters				
	1	2	3	4	Final
San Francisco	3	7	10	0	20
Kansas City	7	3	0	21	31

Total attendance: 62,417
Game length: 3:29

Team Statistics

	49ers	Chiefs
First downs	21	26
Total net yards	351	397
Rushes-yards	22-141	29-129
Passing yards, net	210	268
Punt returns-yards	1-0	0-0
Kickoff returns-yards	4-61	3-58
Interception returns-yards	2-10	2-1
Field goals made-attempts	2-2	1-1
Pass attempts-completions-interceptions	31-20-2	42-26-2
Sacked-yards lost	1-9	4-18
Punts-average	2-43.0	2-50.0
Fumbles-lost	1-0	3-0
Penalties-yards	5-45	4-24
Time of possession	26:47	33:13

Scoring

San Francisco: Robbie Gould, 38-yard field goal
Kansas City: Patrick Mahomes, 1-yard run (Harrison Butker PAT)
Kansas City: Butker, 31-yard field goal
San Francisco: Kyle Juszczyk 15-yard pass from Jimmy Garoppolo (Gould PAT)
San Francisco: Gould, 42-yard field goal
San Francisco: Raheem Mostert, 1-yard run (Gould PAT)
Kansas City: Travis Kelce, 1-yard pass from Mahomes (Butker PAT)
Kansas City: Damien Williams, 5-yard pass from Mahomes (Butker PAT)
Kansas City: Damien Williams, 38-yard run (Butker PAT)

Individual Statistics

Rushing
San Francisco: Mostert, 12-58; Deebo Samuel, 3-53; Tevin Coleman 5-28; Garoppolo, 2-2.
Kansas City: Damien Williams, 17-104; Mahomes, 9-29; Kelce, 1-2; Darwin Thompson, 1-0; Mecole Hardman, 1-minus-6.

Passing
San Francisco: Garoppolo, 20-31, 219 yards, 1 TD, 2 int.
Kansas City: Mahomes: 26-42, 286 yards, 2 TD, 2 int.

Receiving
San Francisco: Samuel, 5-39; George Kittle, 4-36; Juszczyk, 3-39; Emmanuel Sanders, 3-38; Kendrick Bourne, 2-42; Jeff Wilson, 1-20; Coleman, 1-3; Mostert, 1-2.
Kansas City: Tyreek Hill, 9-105; Kelce, 6-43; Sammy Watkins, 5-98; Damien Williams, 4-29; Blake Bell, 1-9; Hardman, 1-2.

NFL Final Standings, 2019
(playoff seeding in parentheses; * = wild card qualifier for playoffs)

AMERICAN FOOTBALL CONFERENCE

	W	L	T	Pct	PF	PA	Div
East Division							
New England (3)....	12	4	0	.750	420	225	5-1
*Buffalo (5)	10	6	0	.625	314	259	3-3
NY Jets...........	7	9	0	.438	276	359	2-4
Miami	5	11	0	.313	306	494	2-4
North Division							
Baltimore (1)......	14	2	0	.875	531	282	5-1
Pittsburgh	8	8	0	.500	289	303	3-3
Cleveland	6	10	0	.375	335	393	3-3
Cincinnati	2	14	0	.125	279	420	1-5
South Division							
Houston (4)........	10	6	0	.625	378	385	4-2
*Tennessee (6)....	9	7	0	.563	402	331	3-3
Indianapolis	7	9	0	.438	361	373	3-3
Jacksonville	6	10	0	.375	300	397	2-4
West Division							
Kansas City (2)....	12	4	0	.750	451	308	6-0
Denver	7	9	0	.438	282	316	3-3
Oakland	7	9	0	.438	313	419	3-3
L.A. Chargers	5	11	0	.313	337	345	0-6

NATIONAL FOOTBALL CONFERENCE

	W	L	T	Pct	PF	PA	Div
East Division							
Philadelphia (4).....	9	7	0	.563	385	354	5-1
Dallas	8	8	0	.500	434	321	5-1
NY Giants.........	4	12	0	.250	341	451	2-4
Washington........	3	13	0	.188	266	435	0-6
North Division							
Green Bay (2).....	13	3	0	.813	376	313	6-0
*Minnesota (6)	10	6	0	.625	407	303	2-4
Chicago	8	8	0	.500	280	298	4-2
Detroit...........	3	12	1	.219	341	423	0-6
South Division							
New Orleans (3)....	13	3	0	.813	458	341	5-1
Atlanta	7	9	0	.438	381	399	4-2
Tampa Bay	7	9	0	.438	458	449	2-4
Carolina	5	11	0	.313	340	470	1-5
West Division							
San Francisco (1)...	13	3	0	.813	479	310	5-1
*Seattle (5)	11	5	0	.688	405	398	3-3
L.A. Rams	9	7	0	.563	394	364	3-3
Arizona...........	5	10	1	.344	361	442	1-5

NFL Individual Leaders: American Football Conference, 2019

(* = rookie)

PASSING

Player, team	Att	Comp	Pct comp	Yds	Yds/Att	Long	TD	Pct TD	Int	Rating
Ryan Tannehill, Tennessee	286	201	70.3	2,742	9.6	91T	22	7.7	6	117.5
Lamar Jackson, Baltimore	401	265	66.1	3,127	7.8	83T	36	9.0	6	113.3
Patrick Mahomes, Kansas City	484	319	65.9	4,031	8.3	83T	26	5.4	5	105.3
Derek Carr, Oakland	513	361	70.4	4,054	7.9	75	21	4.1	8	100.8
Deshaun Watson, Houston	495	333	67.3	3,852	7.8	54	26	5.3	12	98.0
*Gardner Minshew, Jacksonville	470	285	60.6	3,271	7.0	70T	21	4.5	6	91.2
Philip Rivers, L.A. Chargers	591	390	66.0	4,615	7.8	84T	23	3.9	20	88.5
Jacoby Brissett, Indianapolis	447	272	60.9	2,942	6.6	50	18	4.0	6	88.0
Tom Brady, New England	613	373	60.8	4,057	6.6	59	24	3.9	8	88.0
Ryan Fitzpatrick, Miami	502	311	62.0	3,529	7.0	51	20	4.0	13	85.5
Josh Allen, Buffalo	461	271	58.8	3,089	6.7	53T	20	4.3	9	85.3
Joe Flacco, Denver	262	171	65.3	1,822	7.0	70T	6	2.3	5	85.1
Sam Darnold, NY Jets	441	273	61.9	3,024	6.9	92T	19	4.3	13	84.3
Mason Rudolph, Pittsburgh	283	176	62.2	1,765	6.2	76T	13	4.6	9	82.0
Baker Mayfield, Cleveland	534	317	59.4	3,827	7.2	89T	22	4.1	21	78.8
Andy Dalton, Cincinnati	528	314	59.5	3,494	6.6	66T	16	3.0	14	78.3

RUSHING YARDS

Player, team	Yds	Att	Avg	Long	TD
Derrick Henry, Tennessee	1,540	303	5.1	74T	16
Nick Chubb, Cleveland	1,494	298	5.0	88T	8
Lamar Jackson, Baltimore	1,206	176	6.9	47T	7
Leonard Fournette, Jacksonville	1,152	265	4.3	81	3
*Josh Jacobs, Oakland	1,150	242	4.8	51	7
Joe Mixon, Cincinnati	1,137	278	4.1	41	5
Marlon Mack, Indianapolis	1,091	247	4.4	63T	8
Carlos Hyde, Houston	1,070	245	4.4	58	6
Mark Ingram, Baltimore	1,018	202	5.0	53	10
Phillip Lindsay, Denver	1,011	224	4.5	40	7

RECEPTIONS

Player, team	Rec	Yds	Avg	Long	TD
Keenan Allen, L.A. Chargers	104	1,199	11.5	45	6
DeAndre Hopkins, Houston	104	1,165	11.2	43T	7
Julian Edelman, New England	100	1,117	11.2	44	6
Travis Kelce, Kansas City	97	1,229	12.7	47	5
Austin Ekeler, L.A. Chargers	92	993	10.8	84T	8
Darren Waller, Oakland	90	1,145	12.7	75	3
Tyler Boyd, Cincinnati	90	1,046	11.6	47	5
Jarvis Landry, Cleveland	83	1,174	14.1	65	6
Jamison Crowder, NY Jets	78	833	10.7	41	6
Leonard Fournette, Jacksonville	76	522	6.9	27	0

SCORING—KICKERS

Player, team	PAT	FG	Long	Pts
Harrison Butker, Kansas City	45/48	34/38	56	147
Justin Tucker, Baltimore	57/59	28/29	51	141
Josh Lambo, Jacksonville	19/20	33/34	56	118
Chris Boswell, Pittsburgh	28/28	29/31	51	115
Brandon McManus, Denver	25/26	29/34	53	112
Randy Bullock, Cincinnati	24/25	27/31	57	105
*Austin Seibert, Cleveland	30/35	25/29	53	105

SCORING—NON-KICKERS

Player, team (position)	TD	Rush	Rec	2-Pt	Pts
Derrick Henry, Tennessee (RB)	18	16	2	0	108
Mark Ingram, Baltimore (RB)	15	10	5	2	94
Austin Ekeler, L.A. Chargers (RB)	11	3	8	0	66
Mark Andrews, Baltimore (TE)	10	0	10	0	60
Josh Allen, Buffalo (QB)	9	9	0	1	56
*A.J. Brown, Tennessee (WR)	9	1	8	0	54
Melvin Gordon, L.A. Chargers (RB)	9	8	1	0	54
DeVante Parker, Miami (WR)	9	0	9	0	54
D.J. Chark, Jacksonville (WR)	8	0	8	1	50
Marlon Mack, Indianapolis (RB)	8	8	0	0	50

INTERCEPTIONS

Player, team	No.	Yds	Avg	Long	TD
Stephon Gilmore, New England	6	126	21.0	64T	2
Tre'Davious White, Buffalo	6	57	9.5	49	0
Marcus Peters, L.A. Rams-Baltimore	5	210	42.0	89T	3
Minkah Fitzpatrick, Miami-Pittsburgh	5	130	26.0	96T	1
Darius Leonard, Indianapolis ..	5	92	18.4	80T	1
Kevin Byard, Tennessee	5	79	15.8	28	0
Devin McCourty, New England	5	49	9.8	24	0
J.C. Jackson, New England	5	39	7.8	19	0
Joe Haden, Pittsburgh	5	20	4.0	16	0

KICKOFF RETURNS

Player, team	No.	Yds	Avg	Long	TD
Brandon Wilson, Cincinnati....	20	625	31.3	92T	1
Andre Roberts, Buffalo	25	664	26.6	66	0
*Mecole Hardman, Kansas City	27	704	26.1	104T	1
Jakeem Grant, Miami	23	578	25.1	101T	1
Brandon Bolden, New England	23	515	22.4	38	0
Trevor Davis, Green Bay-Oakland-Miami	23	506	22.0	52	0

PUNTING

Player, team	No.	Yds	Long	Avg
Brett Kern, Tennessee	78	3,672	70	47.1
Ty Long, L.A. Chargers	48	2,256	60	47.0
Logan Cooke, Jacksonville	75	3,507	66	46.8
Bryan Anger, Houston	45	2,094	71	46.5

Player, team	No.	Yds	Long	Avg
Sam Koch, Baltimore	40	1,855	62	46.4
*Jamie Gillan, Cleveland......	63	2,913	71	46.2
*A.J. Cole, Oakland..........	67	3,081	74	46.0

PUNT RETURNS

Player, team	No.	Yds	Avg	Long	TD
Diontae Johnson, Pittsburgh...	20	248	12.4	85T	1
Braxton Berrios, NY Jets	21	240	11.4	26	0
DeAndre Carter, Houston	22	214	9.7	23	0
Gunner Olszewski, New England.............	20	179	9.0	22	0
Andre Roberts, Buffalo	28	223	8.0	22	0
Diontae Spencer, Denver	26	208	8.0	42	0

SACKS

Player, team	No.
T.J. Watt, Pittsburgh	14.5
Joey Bosa, L.A. Chargers....................	11.5
Bud Dupree, Pittsburgh......................	11.5
Justin Houston, Indianapolis..................	11.0
*Josh Allen, Jacksonville....................	10.5
*Maxx Crosby, Oakland	10.0
Myles Garrett, Cleveland.....................	10.0
Matt Judon, Baltimore.......................	9.5
Jordan Phillips, Buffalo......................	9.5
Carlos Dunlap, Cincinnati....................	9.0
Cameron Heyward, Pittsburgh	9.0
Chris Jones, Kansas City	9.0
Harold Landry III, Tennessee.................	9.0

NFL Individual Leaders: National Football Conference, 2019

(* = rookie)

PASSING

Player, team	Att	Comp	Pct comp	Yds	Yds/Att	Long	TD	Pct TD	Int	Rating
Drew Brees, New Orleans	378	281	74.3	2,979	7.9	61T	27	7.1	4	116.3
Kirk Cousins, Minnesota.................	444	307	69.1	3,603	8.1	66	26	5.9	6	107.4
Russell Wilson, Seattle.................	516	341	66.1	4,110	8.0	60T	31	6.0	5	106.3
Matthew Stafford, Detroit	291	187	64.3	2,499	8.6	66	19	6.5	5	106.0
Jimmy Garoppolo, San Francisco........	476	329	69.1	3,978	8.4	75T	27	5.7	13	102.0
Dak Prescott, Dallas	596	388	65.1	4,902	8.2	62	30	5.0	11	99.7
Aaron Rodgers, Green Bay..............	569	353	62.0	4,002	7.0	74T	26	4.6	4	95.4
Carson Wentz, Philadelphia.............	607	388	63.9	4,039	6.7	53T	27	4.4	7	93.1
Matt Ryan, Atlanta	616	408	66.2	4,466	7.3	93T	26	4.2	14	92.1
Case Keenum, Washington	247	160	64.8	1,707	6.9	69T	11	4.5	5	91.3
*Daniel Jones, NY Giants..............	459	284	61.9	3,027	6.6	75T	24	5.2	12	87.7
*Kyler Murray, Arizona	542	349	64.4	3,722	6.9	88T	20	3.7	12	87.4
Jared Goff, L.A. Rams.................	626	394	62.9	4,638	7.4	66	22	3.5	16	86.5
Jameis Winston, Tampa Bay............	626	380	60.7	5,109	8.2	71T	33	5.3	30	84.3
Mitchell Trubisky, Chicago	516	326	63.2	3,138	6.1	53	17	3.3	10	83.0
Kyle Allen, Carolina...................	489	303	62.0	3,322	6.8	52T	17	3.5	16	80.0

RUSHING YARDS

Player, team	Yds	Att	Avg	Long	TD
Christian McCaffrey, Carolina...	1,387	287	4.8	84T	15
Ezekiel Elliott, Dallas	1,357	301	4.5	33T	12
Chris Carson, Seattle	1,230	278	4.4	59	7
Dalvin Cook, Minnesota	1,135	250	4.5	75T	13
Aaron Jones, Green Bay	1,084	236	4.6	56T	16
Saquon Barkley, NY Giants ...	1,003	217	4.6	68T	6
Adrian Peterson, Washington ..	898	211	4.3	32	5
*David Montgomery, Chicago..	889	242	3.7	55	6
Todd Gurley, L.A. Rams	857	223	3.8	25	12
*Miles Sanders, Philadelphia ...	818	179	4.6	65T	3

RECEPTIONS

Player, team	Rec	Yds	Avg	Long	TD
Michael Thomas, New Orleans..	149	1,725	11.6	49	9
Christian McCaffrey, Carolina...	116	1,005	8.7	28	4
Julio Jones, Atlanta...........	99	1,394	14.1	54T	6
Allen Robinson, Chicago	98	1,147	11.7	49	7
Cooper Kupp, L.A. Rams	94	1,161	12.4	66	10
Robert Woods, L.A. Rams	90	1,134	12.6	48	2
Zach Ertz, Philadelphia	88	916	10.4	30	6
D.J. Moore, Carolina	87	1,175	13.5	52T	4
Chris Godwin, Tampa Bay	86	1,333	15.5	71T	9
George Kittle, San Francisco ...	85	1,053	12.4	61T	5

SCORING—KICKERS

Player, team	PAT	FG	Long	Pts
Wil Lutz, New Orleans	48/49	32/36	58	144
Zane Gonzalez, Arizona	34/35	31/35	54	127
*Matt Gay, Tampa Bay	43/48	27/35	58	124
Dan Bailey, Minnesota	40/44	27/29	50	121
Greg Zuerlein, L.A. Rams.......	42/42	24/33	58	114
Matt Prater, Detroit	35/36	26/31	56	113

SCORING—NON-KICKERS

Player, team (position)	TD	Rush	Rec	2-Pt	Pts
Christian McCaffrey, Carolina (RB)	19	15	4	1	116
Aaron Jones, Green Bay (RB) ...	19	16	3	0	114
Todd Gurley, L.A. Rams (RB)	14	12	2	1	86
Ezekiel Elliott, Dallas (RB)	14	12	2	0	84
Dalvin Cook, Minnesota (RB)....	13	13	0	0	78
Kenny Golladay, Detroit (WR)...	11	0	11	0	66
Cooper Kupp, L.A. Rams (WR)....	10	0	10	0	60
Raheem Mostert, San Francisco (RB)...	10	8	2	0	60
Chris Godwin, Tampa Bay (WR)...	9	0	9	1	56
Chris Carson, Seattle (RB)...	9	7	2	0	54
Jared Cook, New Orleans (TE)....	9	0	9	0	54
Marvin Jones, Detroit (WR)	9	0	9	0	54
Michael Thomas, New Orleans (WR)	9	0	9	0	54

INTERCEPTIONS

Player, team	No.	Yds	Avg	Long	TD
Anthony Harris, Minnesota	6	42	7.0	20T	1
Janoris Jenkins, NY Giants- New Orleans.................	5	84	16.8	62	0
Kevin King, Green Bay	5	54	10.8	39	0
Marcus Williams, New Orleans..	4	56	14.0	55T	1
Desmond Trufant, Atlanta.......	4	26	6.5	16	0
Quinton Dunbar, Washington ...	4	6	1.5	6	0

KICKOFF RETURNS

Player, team	No.	Yds	Avg	Long	TD
Cordarrelle Patterson, Chicago...	28	825	29.5	102T	1
*Deonte Harris, New Orleans	24	644	26.8	51	0
*Steven Sims, Washington	32	819	25.6	91T	1
Cody Latimer, NY Giants	24	570	23.8	50	0
Pharoh Cooper, Cincinnati-Arizona	25	561	22.4	39	0
Richie James, San Francisco ...	20	428	21.4	81	0

PUNTING

Player, team	No.	Yds	Long	Avg
Tress Way, Washington..........	79	3,919	79	49.6
Andy Lee, Arizona	61	2,913	64	47.8
Johnny Hekker, L.A. Rams	66	3,128	71	47.4
Cameron Johnston, Philadelphia...	71	3,292	61	46.4
Thomas Morstead, New Orleans..	60	2,770	64	46.2
Riley Dixon, NY Giants	69	3,178	62	46.1
Michael Palardy, Carolina.......	75	3,452	62	46.0
Sam Martin, Detroit.............	76	3,445	62	45.3
Britton Colquitt, Minnesota	62	2,002	59	45.2
Michael Dickson, Seattle	74	3,341	63	45.1

PUNT RETURNS

Player, team	No.	Yds	Avg	Long	TD
*Deonte Harris, New Orleans	36	338	9.4	53T	1
Tarik Cohen, Chicago...........	33	302	9.2	71	0
Richie James, San Francisco ...	33	264	8.0	32	0
Kenjon Barner, Atlanta	35	267	7.6	78T	1

SACKS

Player, team	No.
Shaquil Barrett, Tampa Bay	19.5
Chandler Jones, Arizona	19.0
Cameron Jordan, New Orleans	15.5
Danielle Hunter, Minnesota..................	14.5
Za'Darius Smith, Green Bay	13.5
Aaron Donald, L.A. Rams	12.5
Preston Smith, Green Bay	12.0
Dante Fowler Jr., L.A. Rams.................	11.5
Robert Quinn, Dallas	11.5
Arik Armstead, San Francisco	10.0
Markus Golden, NY Giants..................	10.0

Super Bowl, 1967-2020

The Super Bowl was created as a condition of the merger between the American Football League (AFL, formed in 1959) and National Football League (NFL, formed in 1920). Announced June 8, 1966, the merger agreement stipulated that the leagues would play separate regular season schedules through the 1969 season but meet after each in an AFL-NFL Championship Game, unofficially dubbed the Super Bowl. The first Super Bowl, played at the Memorial Coliseum in Los Angeles on Jan. 15, 1967, did not sell out, unlike every Super Bowl game since. Each player on the victorious Green Bay Packers earned $15,000 for the win; the defeated Kansas City Chiefs each collected $7,500.

No.	Year	Winner	Opponent	Winning coach	Site
I	1967	*Green Bay Packers, 35	Kansas City Chiefs, 10	Vince Lombardi	Memorial Coliseum, Los Angeles, CA
II	1968	Green Bay Packers, 33	*Oakland Raiders, 14	Vince Lombardi	Orange Bowl, Miami, FL
III	1969	*NY Jets, 16	Baltimore Colts, 7	Weeb Ewbank	Orange Bowl, Miami, FL
IV	1970	Kansas City Chiefs, 23	*Minnesota Vikings, 7	Hank Stram	Tulane Stadium, New Orleans, LA
V	1971	Baltimore Colts, 16	*Dallas Cowboys, 13	Don McCafferty	Orange Bowl, Miami, FL
VI	1972	Dallas Cowboys, 24	*Miami Dolphins, 3	Tom Landry	Tulane Stadium, New Orleans, LA
VII	1973	*Miami Dolphins, 14	Washington Redskins, 7	Don Shula	Memorial Coliseum, Los Angeles, CA
VIII	1974	*Miami Dolphins, 24	Minnesota Vikings, 7	Don Shula	Rice Stadium, Houston, TX
IX	1975	*Pittsburgh Steelers, 16	Minnesota Vikings, 6	Chuck Noll	Tulane Stadium, New Orleans, LA
X	1976	Pittsburgh Steelers, 21	*Dallas Cowboys, 17	Chuck Noll	Orange Bowl, Miami, FL
XI	1977	*Oakland Raiders, 32	Minnesota Vikings, 14	John Madden	Rose Bowl, Pasadena, CA
XII	1978	*Dallas Cowboys, 27	Denver Broncos, 10	Tom Landry	Superdome, New Orleans, LA
XIII	1979	Pittsburgh Steelers, 35	*Dallas Cowboys, 31	Chuck Noll	Orange Bowl, Miami, FL
XIV	1980	Pittsburgh Steelers, 31	*L.A. Rams, 19	Chuck Noll	Rose Bowl, Pasadena, CA
XV	1981	Oakland Raiders, 27	*Philadelphia Eagles, 10	Tom Flores	Superdome, New Orleans, LA
XVI	1982	*San Francisco 49ers, 26	Cincinnati Bengals, 21	Bill Walsh	Silverdome, Pontiac, MI
XVII	1983	Washington Redskins, 27	*Miami Dolphins, 17	Joe Gibbs	Rose Bowl, Pasadena, CA
XVIII	1984	*L.A. Raiders, 38	Washington Redskins, 9	Tom Flores	Tampa Stadium, Tampa, FL
XIX	1985	*San Francisco 49ers, 38	Miami Dolphins, 16	Bill Walsh	Stanford Stadium, Stanford, CA
XX	1986	*Chicago Bears, 46	New England Patriots, 10	Mike Ditka	Superdome, New Orleans, LA
XXI	1987	NY Giants, 39	*Denver Broncos, 20	Bill Parcells	Rose Bowl, Pasadena, CA
XXII	1988	*Washington Redskins, 42	Denver Broncos, 10	Joe Gibbs	Jack Murphy Stadium, San Diego, CA
XXIII	1989	*San Francisco 49ers, 20	Cincinnati Bengals, 16	Bill Walsh	Joe Robbie Stadium, Miami, FL
XXIV	1990	San Francisco 49ers, 55	*Denver Broncos, 10	George Seifert	Superdome, New Orleans, LA
XXV	1991	NY Giants, 20	*Buffalo Bills, 19	Bill Parcells	Tampa Stadium, Tampa, FL
XXVI	1992	*Washington Redskins, 37	Buffalo Bills, 24	Joe Gibbs	Metrodome, Minneapolis, MN
XXVII	1993	Dallas Cowboys, 52	*Buffalo Bills, 17	Jimmy Johnson	Rose Bowl, Pasadena, CA
XXVIII	1994	*Dallas Cowboys, 30	Buffalo Bills, 13	Jimmy Johnson	Georgia Dome, Atlanta, GA
XXIX	1995	*San Francisco 49ers, 49	San Diego Chargers, 26	George Seifert	Joe Robbie Stadium, Miami, FL
XXX	1996	*Dallas Cowboys, 27	Pittsburgh Steelers, 17	Barry Switzer	Sun Devil Stadium, Tempe, AZ
XXXI	1997	Green Bay Packers, 35	*New England Patriots, 21	Mike Holmgren	Superdome, New Orleans, LA
XXXII	1998	Denver Broncos, 31	*Green Bay Packers, 24	Mike Shanahan	Qualcomm Stadium, San Diego, CA
XXXIII	1999	Denver Broncos, 34	*Atlanta Falcons, 19	Mike Shanahan	Pro Player Stadium, Miami, FL
XXXIV	2000	*St. Louis Rams, 23	Tennessee Titans, 16	Dick Vermeil	Georgia Dome, Atlanta, GA
XXXV	2001	Baltimore Ravens, 34	*NY Giants, 7	Brian Billick	Raymond James Stadium, Tampa, FL
XXXVI	2002	New England Patriots, 20	*St. Louis Rams, 17	Bill Belichick	Superdome, New Orleans, LA
XXXVII	2003	*Tampa Bay Buccaneers, 48	Oakland Raiders, 21	Jon Gruden	Qualcomm Stadium, San Diego, CA
XXXVIII	2004	New England Patriots, 32	*Carolina Panthers, 29	Bill Belichick	Reliant Stadium, Houston, TX
XXXIX	2005	New England Patriots, 24	*Philadelphia Eagles, 21	Bill Belichick	Alltel Stadium, Jacksonville, FL
XL	2006	Pittsburgh Steelers, 21	*Seattle Seahawks, 10	Bill Cowher	Ford Field, Detroit, MI
XLI	2007	Indianapolis Colts, 29	*Chicago Bears, 17	Tony Dungy	Dolphin Stadium, Miami Gardens, FL
XLII	2008	*NY Giants, 17	New England Patriots, 14	Tom Coughlin	Univ. of Phoenix Stadium, Glendale, AZ
XLIII	2009	Pittsburgh Steelers, 27	**Arizona Cardinals, 23	Mike Tomlin	Raymond James Stadium, Tampa, FL
XLIV	2010	*New Orleans Saints, 31	Indianapolis Colts, 17	Sean Payton	Sun Life Stadium, Miami Gardens, FL
XLV	2011	**Green Bay Packers, 31	Pittsburgh Steelers, 25	Mike McCarthy	Cowboys Stadium, Arlington, TX
XLVI	2012	NY Giants, 21	**New England Patriots, 17	Tom Coughlin	Lucas Oil Stadium, Indianapolis, IN
XLVII	2013	**Baltimore Ravens, 34	San Francisco 49ers, 31	John Harbaugh	Mercedes-Benz Superdome, New Orleans, LA
XLVIII	2014	**Seattle Seahawks, 43	Denver Broncos, 8	Pete Carroll	MetLife Stadium, East Rutherford, NJ
XLIX	2015	New England Patriots, 28	**Seattle Seahawks, 24	Bill Belichick	Univ. of Phoenix Stadium, Glendale, AZ
50 (L)	2016	Denver Broncos, 24	**Carolina Panthers, 10	Gary Kubiak	Levi's Stadium, Santa Clara, CA
LI	2017	New England Patriots, 34 (OT)	**Atlanta Falcons, 28	Bill Belichick	NRG Stadium, Houston, TX
LII	2018	Philadelphia Eagles, 41	**New England Patriots, 33	Doug Pederson	U.S. Bank Stadium, Minneapolis, MN
LIII	2019	New England Patriots, 13	**L.A. Rams, 3	Bill Belichick	Mercedes-Benz Stadium, Atlanta, GA
LIV	2020	Kansas City Chiefs, 31	**San Francisco 49ers, 20	Andy Reid	Hard Rock Stadium, Miami Gardens, FL

* = Team won the coin toss and elected to receive. ** = Team won the coin toss and elected to receive in the second half. OT = Overtime.

Super Bowl Sites, 2021-24

No.	Site	Date	No.	Site	Date
LV	Raymond James Stadium, Tampa, FL ...	Feb. 7, 2021	LVIII	Mercedes-Benz Superdome, New Orleans, LA	Feb. 4, 2024
LVI	SoFi Stadium, Inglewood, CA	Feb. 6, 2022			
LVII	State Farm Stadium, Glendale, AZ	Feb. 5, 2023			

Super Bowl MVPs, 1967-2020

Year	Most valuable player, team	Year	Most valuable player, team	Year	Most valuable player, team
1967	Bart Starr, Green Bay	1985	Joe Montana, San Francisco	2003	Dexter Jackson, Tampa Bay
1968	Bart Starr, Green Bay	1986	Richard Dent, Chicago	2004	Tom Brady, New England
1969	Joe Namath, NY Jets	1987	Phil Simms, NY Giants	2005	Deion Branch, New England
1970	Len Dawson, Kansas City	1988	Doug Williams, Washington	2006	Hines Ward, Pittsburgh
1971	Chuck Howley, Dallas	1989	Jerry Rice, San Francisco	2007	Peyton Manning, Indianapolis
1972	Roger Staubach, Dallas	1990	Joe Montana, San Francisco	2008	Eli Manning, NY Giants
1973	Jake Scott, Miami	1991	Ottis Anderson, NY Giants	2009	Santonio Holmes, Pittsburgh
1974	Larry Csonka, Miami	1992	Mark Rypien, Washington	2010	Drew Brees, New Orleans
1975	Franco Harris, Pittsburgh	1993	Troy Aikman, Dallas	2011	Aaron Rodgers, Green Bay
1976	Lynn Swann, Pittsburgh	1994	Emmitt Smith, Dallas	2012	Eli Manning, NY Giants
1977	Fred Biletnikoff, Oakland	1995	Steve Young, San Francisco	2013	Joe Flacco, Baltimore
1978	Randy White, Harvey Martin; Dallas	1996	Larry Brown, Dallas	2014	Malcolm Smith, Seattle
1979	Terry Bradshaw, Pittsburgh	1997	Desmond Howard, Green Bay	2015	Tom Brady, New England
1980	Terry Bradshaw, Pittsburgh	1998	Terrell Davis, Denver	2016	Von Miller, Denver
1981	Jim Plunkett, Oakland	1999	John Elway, Denver	2017	Tom Brady, New England
1982	Joe Montana, San Francisco	2000	Kurt Warner, St. Louis	2018	Nick Foles, Philadelphia
1983	John Riggins, Washington	2001	Ray Lewis, Baltimore	2019	Julian Edelman, New England
1984	Marcus Allen, L.A. Raiders	2002	Tom Brady, New England	2020	Patrick Mahomes, Kansas City

Super Bowl Single-Game Statistical Leaders

PASSING YARDS

Player, team	Year	Att/comp	Yds	TD
Tom Brady, New England	2018	48/28	505	3
Tom Brady, New England	2017	62/43	466	2
Kurt Warner, St. Louis	2000	45/24	414	2
Kurt Warner, Arizona	2009	43/31	377	3
Nick Foles, Philadelphia	2018	43/28	373	3
Kurt Warner, St. Louis	2002	44/28	365	1
Donovon McNabb, Philadelphia	2005	51/30	357	3
Joe Montana, San Francisco	1989	36/23	357	2

RECEIVING YARDS

Player, team	Year	Rec	Yds	TD
Jerry Rice, San Francisco	1989	11	215	1
Ricky Sanders, Washington	1988	9	193	2
Isaac Bruce, St. Louis	2000	6	162	1

RUSHING YARDS

Player, team	Year	Att	Yds	TD
Timmy Smith, Washington	1988	22	204	2
Marcus Allen, L.A. Raiders	1984	20	191	2
John Riggins, Washington	1983	38	166	1

PASSING TOUCHDOWNS

Player, team	Year	Att/comp	Yds	TD
Steve Young, San Francisco	1995	36/24	325	6
Joe Montana, San Francisco	1990	29/22	297	5
Tom Brady, New England	2015	50/37	328	4
Troy Aikman, Dallas	1993	30/22	273	4
Doug Williams, Washington	1988	29/18	340	4
Terry Bradshaw, Pittsburgh	1979	30/17	318	4

SCORING

Player, team	Year	Pts	
James White, New England	2017	20	(3 TDs, 1 2-pt)
Terrell Davis, Denver	1998	18	(3 TDs)
Jerry Rice, San Francisco	1995	18	(3 TDs)
Ricky Watters, San Francisco	1995	18	(3 TDs)
Jerry Rice, San Francisco	1990	18	(3 TDs)
Roger Craig, San Francisco	1985	18	(3 TDs)
Don Chandler, Green Bay	1968	15	(4 FGs, 3 PATs)
Kevin Butler, Chicago Bears	1986	14	(3 FGs, 5 PATs)
Ray Wersching, San Francisco	1982	14	(4 FGs, 2 PATs)

First-Round Selections in the 2020 NFL Draft

Held Apr. 23-25, 2020.

Team	Player	Pos.	College
1. Cincinnati Bengals	Joe Burrow	QB	LSU
2. Washington	Chase Young	DE	Ohio St.
3. Detroit Lions	Jeff Okudah	CB	Ohio St.
4. NY Giants	Andrew Thomas	OT	Georgia
5. Miami Dolphins	Tua Tagovailoa	QB	Alabama
6. L.A. Chargers	Justin Herbert	QB	Oregon
7. Carolina Panthers	Derrick Brown	DT	Auburn
8. Arizona Cardinals	Isaiah Simmons	LB	Clemson
9. Jacksonville Jaguars	C.J. Henderson	CB	Florida
10. Cleveland Browns	Jedrick Wills	OT	Alabama
11. NY Jets	Mekhi Becton	OT	Louisville
12. Las Vegas Raiders	Henry Ruggs III	WR	Alabama
13. Tampa Bay Buccaneers[1]	Tristan Wirfs	OT	Iowa
14. San Francisco 49ers[2]	Javon Kinlaw	DT	South Carolina
15. Denver Broncos	Jerry Jeudy	WR	Alabama
16. Atlanta Falcons	A.J. Terrell	CB	Clemson
17. Dallas Cowboys	CeeDee Lamb	WR	Oklahoma
18. Miami Dolphins[3]	Austin Jackson	OT	USC
19. Las Vegas Raiders[4]	Damon Arnette	CB	Ohio St.
20. Jacksonville Jaguars[5]	K'Lavon Chaisson	LB	LSU
21. Philadelphia Eagles	Jalen Reagor	WR	TCU
22. Minnesota Vikings[6]	Justin Jefferson	WR	LSU
23. L.A. Chargers[7]	Kenneth Murray	LB	Oklahoma
24. New Orleans Saints	Cesar Ruiz	C	Michigan
25. San Francisco 49ers[8]	Brandon Aiyuk	WR	Arizona St.
26. Green Bay Packers[9]	Jordan Love	QB	Utah St.
27. Seattle Seahawks	Jordyn Brooks	LB	Texas Tech
28. Baltimore Ravens	Patrick Queen	LB	LSU
29. Tennessee Titans	Isaiah Wilson	OT	Georgia
30. Miami Dolphins[10]	Noah Igbinoghene	CB	Auburn
31. Minnesota Vikings[11]	Jeff Gladney	CB	TCU
32. Kansas City Chiefs	Clyde Edwards-Helaire	RB	LSU

(1) From Indianapolis through San Francisco. (2) From Tampa Bay. (3) From Pittsburgh. (4) From Chicago. (5) From L.A. Rams. (6) From Buffalo. (7) From New England. (8) From Minnesota. (9) From Houston through Miami. (10) From Green Bay. (11) From San Francisco.

Number One NFL Draft Choices, 1960-2020

Year	Team	Player, pos., college	Year	Team	Player, pos., college
1960	L.A. Rams	Billy Cannon, HB, LSU	1991	Dallas	Russell Maryland, DL, Miami (FL)
1961	Minnesota	Tommy Mason, HB, Tulane	1992	Indianapolis	Steve Emtman, DL, Washington
1962	Washington	Ernie Davis, HB, Syracuse	1993	New England	Drew Bledsoe, QB, Washington St.
1963	L.A. Rams	Terry Baker, QB, Oregon St.	1994	Cincinnati	Dan Wilkinson, DT, Ohio St.
1964	San Francisco	Dave Parks, E, Texas Tech	1995	Cincinnati	Ki-Jana Carter, RB, Penn St.
1965	NY Giants	Tucker Frederickson, RB, Auburn	1996	NY Jets	Keyshawn Johnson, WR, USC
1966	Atlanta	Tommy Nobis, LB, Texas	1997	St. Louis	Orlando Pace, OT, Ohio St.
1967	Baltimore Colts	Bubba Smith, DE, Michigan St.	1998	Indianapolis	Peyton Manning, QB, Tennessee
1968	Minnesota	Ron Yary, OT, USC	1999	Cleveland	Tim Couch, QB, Kentucky
1969	Buffalo	O.J. Simpson, RB, USC	2000	Cleveland	Courtney Brown, DE, Penn St.
1970	Pittsburgh	Terry Bradshaw, QB, LA Tech	2001	Atlanta	Michael Vick, QB, Virginia Tech
1971	New England	Jim Plunkett, QB, Stanford	2002	Houston	David Carr, QB, Fresno St.
1972	Buffalo	Walt Patulski, DE, Notre Dame	2003	Cincinnati	Carson Palmer, QB, USC
1973	Houston	John Matuszak, DE, Tampa	2004	San Diego	Eli Manning, QB, Mississippi
1974	Dallas	Ed "Too Tall" Jones, DE, Tenn. St.	2005	San Francisco	Alex D. Smith, QB, Utah
1975	Atlanta	Steve Bartkowski, QB, California	2006	Houston	Mario Williams, DE, NC State
1976	Tampa Bay	Lee Roy Selmon, DE, Oklahoma	2007	Oakland	JaMarcus Russell, QB, LSU
1977	Tampa Bay	Ricky Bell, RB, USC	2008	Miami	Jake Long, OT, Michigan
1978	Houston	Earl Campbell, RB, Texas	2009	Detroit	Matthew Stafford, QB, Georgia
1979	Buffalo	Tom Cousineau, LB, Ohio St.	2010	St. Louis	Sam Bradford, QB, Oklahoma
1980	Detroit	Billy Sims, RB, Oklahoma	2011	Carolina	Cam Newton, QB, Auburn
1981	New Orleans	George Rogers, RB, S. Carolina	2012	Indianapolis	Andrew Luck, QB, Stanford
1982	New England	Kenneth Sims, DT, Texas	2013	Kansas City	Eric Fisher, OT, Central Michigan
1983	Baltimore Colts	John Elway, QB, Stanford	2014	Houston	Jadeveon Clowney, DE, S. Carolina
1984	New England	Irving Fryar, WR, Nebraska	2015	Tampa Bay	Jameis Winston, QB, Florida St.
1985	Buffalo	Bruce Smith, DE, Virginia Tech	2016	L.A. Rams	Jared Goff, QB, California
1986	Tampa Bay	Bo Jackson, RB, Auburn	2017	Cleveland	Myles Garrett, DE, Texas A&M
1987	Tampa Bay	Vinny Testaverde, QB, Miami (FL)	2018	Cleveland	Baker Mayfield, QB, Oklahoma
1988	Atlanta	Aundray Bruce, LB, Auburn	2019	Arizona	Kyler Murray, QB, Oklahoma
1989	Dallas	Troy Aikman, QB, UCLA	2020	Cincinnati	Joe Burrow, QB, LSU
1990	Indianapolis	Jeff George, QB, Illinois			

American Football League Champions, 1960-69

Year	Eastern (W-L-T)	Western (W-L-T)	Championship
1960	Houston Oilers (10-4-0)	L.A. Chargers (10-4-0)	Houston 24, L.A. 16
1961	Houston Oilers (10-3-1)	San Diego Chargers (12-2-0)	Houston 10, San Diego 3
1962	Houston Oilers (11-3-0)	Dallas Texans (11-3-0)	Dallas 20, Houston 17 (2 OT)
1963	Boston Patriots (7-6-1)[1]	San Diego Chargers (11-3-0)	San Diego 51, Boston 10
1964	Buffalo Bills (12-2-0)	San Diego Chargers (8-5-1)	Buffalo 20, San Diego 7
1965	Buffalo Bills (10-3-1)	San Diego Chargers (9-2-3)	Buffalo 23, San Diego 0
1966	Buffalo Bills (9-4-1)	Kansas City Chiefs (11-2-1)	Kansas City 31, Buffalo 7
1967	Houston Oilers (9-4-1)	Oakland Raiders (13-1-0)	Oakland 40, Houston 7
1968	NY Jets (11-3-0)	Oakland Raiders (12-2-0)[2]	NY Jets 27, Oakland 23
1969	NY Jets (10-4-0)	Oakland Raiders (12-1-1)	Kansas City 17, Oakland 7[3]

(1) Defeated conference champion Buffalo Bills in divisional playoff. (2) Defeated conference champion Kansas City Chiefs in divisional playoff. (3) Kansas City Chiefs defeated NY Jets, and Oakland Raiders defeated Houston Oilers in divisional playoffs.

National Football League Champions, 1933-69

Year	Eastern (W-L-T)	Western (W-L-T)	Championship
1933	NY Giants (11-3-0)	Chicago Bears (10-2-1)	Chicago Bears 23, NY Giants 21
1934	NY Giants (8-5-0)	Chicago Bears (13-0-0)	NY Giants 30, Chicago Bears 13
1935	NY Giants (9-3-0)	Detroit Lions (7-3-2)	Detroit 26, NY Giants 7
1936	Boston Redskins (7-5-0)	Green Bay Packers (10-1-1)	Green Bay 21, Boston 6
1937	Washington Redskins (8-3-0)	Chicago Bears (9-1-1)	Washington 28, Chicago Bears 21
1938	NY Giants (8-2-1)	Green Bay Packers (8-3-0)	NY Giants 23, Green Bay 17
1939	NY Giants (9-1-1)	Green Bay Packers (9-2-0)	Green Bay 27, NY Giants 0
1940	Washington Redskins (9-2-0)	Chicago Bears (8-3-0)	Chicago Bears 73, Washington 0
1941	NY Giants (8-3-0)	Chicago Bears (10-1-0)[1]	Chicago Bears 37, NY Giants 9
1942	Washington Redskins (10-1-0)	Chicago Bears (11-0-0)	Washington 14, Chicago Bears 6
1943	Washington Redskins (6-3-1)[1]	Chicago Bears (8-1-1)	Chicago Bears, 41, Washington 21
1944	NY Giants (8-1-1)	Green Bay Packers (8-2-0)	Green Bay 14, NY Giants 7
1945	Washington Redskins (8-2-0)	Cleveland Rams (9-1-0)	Cleveland Rams 15, Washington 14
1946	NY Giants (7-3-1)	Chicago Bears (8-2-1)	Chicago Bears 24, NY Giants 14
1947	Philadelphia Eagles (8-4-0)[1]	Chicago Cardinals (9-3-0)	Chicago Cardinals 28, Philadelphia 21
1948	Philadelphia Eagles (9-2-1)	Chicago Cardinals (11-1-0)	Philadelphia 7, Chicago Cardinals 0
1949	Philadelphia Eagles (11-1-0)	L.A. Rams (8-2-2)	Philadelphia 14, L.A. Rams 0
1950	Cleveland Browns (10-2-0)[1]	L.A. Rams (9-3-0)[1]	Cleveland Browns 30, L.A. Rams 28
1951	Cleveland Browns (11-1-0)	L.A. Rams (8-4-0)	L.A. Rams 24, Cleveland Browns 17
1952	Cleveland Browns (8-4-0)	Detroit Lions (9-3-0)[1]	Detroit 17, Cleveland Browns 7
1953	Cleveland Browns (11-1-0)	Detroit Lions (10-2-0)	Detroit 17, Cleveland Browns 16
1954	Cleveland Browns (9-3-0)	Detroit Lions (9-2-1)	Cleveland Browns 56, Detroit 10
1955	Cleveland Browns (9-2-1)	L.A. Rams (8-3-1)	Cleveland Browns 38, L.A. Rams 14
1956	NY Giants (8-3-1)	Chicago Bears (9-2-1)	NY Giants 47, Chicago Bears 7
1957	Cleveland Browns (9-2-1)	Detroit Lions (8-4-0)[1]	Detroit 59, Cleveland Browns 14
1958	NY Giants (9-3-0)[1]	Baltimore Colts (9-3-0)	Baltimore 23, NY Giants 17[2]
1959	NY Giants (10-2-0)	Baltimore Colts (9-3-0)	Baltimore 31, NY Giants 16

Year	Eastern (W-L-T)	Western (W-L-T)	Championship
1960	Philadelphia Eagles (10-2-0)	Green Bay Packers (8-4-0)	Philadelphia 17, Green Bay 13
1961	NY Giants (10-3-1)	Green Bay Packers (11-3-0)	Green Bay 37, NY Giants 0
1962	NY Giants (12-2-0)	Green Bay Packers (13-1-0)	Green Bay 16, NY Giants 7
1963	NY Giants (11-3-0)	Chicago Bears (11-1-2)	Chicago 14, NY Giants 10
1964	Cleveland Browns (10-3-1)	Baltimore Colts (12-2-0)	Cleveland Browns 27, Baltimore 0
1965	Cleveland Browns (11-3-0)	Green Bay Packers (10-3-1)[1]	Green Bay 23, Cleveland Browns 12
1966	Dallas Cowboys (10-3-1)	Green Bay Packers (12-2-0)	Green Bay 34, Dallas 27
1967	Dallas Cowboys (9-5-0)	Green Bay Packers (9-4-1)	Green Bay 21, Dallas 17
1968	Cleveland Browns (10-4-0)	Baltimore Colts (13-1-0)	Baltimore 34, Cleveland Browns 0
1969	Cleveland Browns (10-3-1)	Minnesota Vikings (12-2-0)	Minnesota 27, Cleveland Browns 7

Note: Conference title games preceded NFL Championship from 1967-69. (1) Won divisional or conference playoff. (2) Won at 8:15 of sudden death overtime period.

NFL Divisional Champions and Wild Cards, 1970-95

The American Football League and National Football League officially merged in 1966. At the beginning of the 1970 season, the two leagues became the AFC and NFC conferences in the new NFL. Regular-season (W-L-T) records are in parentheses.

AMERICAN FOOTBALL CONFERENCE

Year	Eastern	Central	Western	Wild card
1970	Baltimore Colts (11-2-1)	Cincinnati Bengals (8-6-0)	Oakland Raiders (8-4-2)	Miami Dolphins (10-4-0)
1971	Miami Dolphins (10-3-1)	Cleveland Browns (9-5-0)	Kansas City Chiefs (11-3-0)	Baltimore Colts (10-4-0)
1972	Miami Dolphins (14-0-0)	Pittsburgh Steelers (11-3-0)	Oakland Raiders (10-3-1)	Cleveland Browns (10-4-0)
1973	Miami Dolphins (12-2-0)	Cincinnati Bengals (10-4-0)	Oakland Raiders (9-4-1)	Pittsburgh Steelers (10-4-0)
1974	Miami Dolphins (11-3-0)	Pittsburgh Steelers (10-3-1)	Oakland Raiders (12-2-0)	Buffalo Bills (9-5-0)
1975	Baltimore Colts (10-4-0)	Pittsburgh Steelers (12-2-0)	Oakland Raiders (11-3-0)	Cincinnati Bengals (11-3-0)
1976	Baltimore Colts (11-3-0)	Pittsburgh Steelers (10-4-0)	Oakland Raiders (13-1-0)	New England Patriots (11-3-0)
1977	Baltimore Colts (10-4-0)	Pittsburgh Steelers (9-5-0)	Denver Broncos (12-2-0)	Oakland Raiders (11-3-0)
1978	New England Patriots (11-5-0)	Pittsburgh Steelers (14-2-0)	Denver Broncos (10-6-0)	Houston Oilers (10-6-0) Miami Dolphins (11-5-0)
1979	Miami Dolphins (10-6-0)	Pittsburgh Steelers (12-4-0)	San Diego Chargers (12-4-0)	Houston Oilers (11-5-0) Denver Broncos (10-6-0)
1980	Buffalo Bills (11-5-0)	Cleveland Browns (11-5-0)	San Diego Chargers (11-5-0)	Houston Oilers (11-5-0) Oakland Raiders (11-5-0)
1981	Miami Dolphins (11-4-1)	Cincinnati Bengals (12-4-0)	San Diego Chargers (10-6-0)	Buffalo Bills (10-6-0) NY Jets (10-5-1)
1982	Strike abbreviated season. See note.			
1983	Miami Dolphins (12-4-0)	Pittsburgh Steelers (10-6-0)	L.A. Raiders (12-4-0)	Denver Broncos (9-7-0) Seattle Seahawks (9-7-0)
1984	Miami Dolphins (14-2-0)	Pittsburgh Steelers (9-7-0)	Denver Broncos (13-3-0)	L.A. Raiders (11-5-0) Seattle Seahawks (12-4-0)
1985	Miami Dolphins (12-4-0)	Cleveland Browns (8-8-0)	L.A. Raiders (12-4-0)	New England Patriots (11-5-0) NY Jets (11-5-0)
1986	New England Patriots (11-5-0)	Cleveland Browns (12-4-0)	Denver Broncos (11-5-0)	Kansas City Chiefs (10-6-0) NY Jets (10-6-0)
1987	Indianapolis Colts (9-6-0)	Cleveland Browns (10-5-0)	Denver Broncos (10-4-1)	Houston Oilers (9-6-0) Seattle Seahawks (9-6-0)
1988	Buffalo Bills (12-4-0)	Cincinnati Bengals (12-4-0)	Seattle Seahawks (9-7-0)	Cleveland Browns (10-6-0) Houston Oilers (10-6-0)
1989	Buffalo Bills (9-7-0)	Cleveland Browns (9-6-1)	Denver Broncos (11-5-0)	Houston Oilers (9-7-0) Pittsburgh Steelers (9-7-0)
1990	Buffalo Bills (13-3-0)	Cincinnati Bengals (9-7-0)	L.A. Raiders (12-4-0)	Houston Oilers (9-7-0) Kansas City Chiefs (11-5-0) Miami Dolphins (12-4-0)
1991	Buffalo Bills (13-3-0)	Houston Oilers (11-5-0)	Denver Broncos (12-4-0)	Kansas City Chiefs (10-6-0) L.A. Raiders (9-7-0) NY Jets (8-8-0)
1992	Miami Dolphins (11-5-0)	Pittsburgh Steelers (11-5-0)	San Diego Chargers (11-5-0)	Buffalo Bills (11-5-0) Houston Oilers (10-6-0) Kansas City Chiefs (10-6-0)
1993	Buffalo Bills (12-4-0)	Houston Oilers (12-4-0)	Kansas City Chiefs (11-5-0)	Denver Broncos (9-7-0) L.A. Raiders (10-6-0) Pittsburgh Steelers (9-7-0)
1994	Miami Dolphins (10-6-0)	Pittsburgh Steelers (12-4-0)	San Diego Chargers (11-5-0)	Cleveland Browns (11-5-0) Kansas City Chiefs (9-7-0) New England Patriots (10-6-0)
1995	Buffalo Bills (10-6-0)	Pittsburgh Steelers (11-5-0)	Kansas City Chiefs (13-3-0)	Miami Dolphins (9-7-0) Indianapolis Colts (9-7-0) San Diego Chargers (9-7-0)

NATIONAL FOOTBALL CONFERENCE

Year	Eastern	Central	Western	Wild card
1970	Dallas Cowboys (10-4-0)	Minnesota Vikings (12-2-0)	San Francisco 49ers (10-3-1)	Detroit Lions (10-4-0)
1971	Dallas Cowboys (11-3-0)	Minnesota Vikings (11-3-0)	San Francisco 49ers (9-5-0)	Washington Redskins (9-4-1)
1972	Washington Redskins (11-3-0)	Green Bay Packers (10-4-0)	San Francisco 49ers (8-5-1)	Dallas Cowboys (10-4-0)
1973	Dallas Cowboys (10-4-0)	Minnesota Vikings (12-2-0)	L.A. Rams (12-2-0)	Washington Redskins (10-4-0)
1974	St. Louis Cardinals (10-4-0)	Minnesota Vikings (10-4-0)	L.A. Rams (10-4-0)	Washington Redskins (10-4-0)
1975	St. Louis Cardinals (11-3-0)	Minnesota Vikings (12-2-0)	L.A. Rams (12-2-0)	Dallas Cowboys (10-4-0)

Year	Eastern	Central	Western	Wild card
1976	Dallas Cowboys (11-3-0)	Minnesota Vikings (11-2-1)	L.A. Rams (10-3-1)	Washington Redskins (10-4-0)
1977	Dallas Cowboys (12-2-0)	Minnesota Vikings (9-5-0)	L.A. Rams (10-4-0)	Chicago Bears (9-5-0)
1978	Dallas Cowboys (12-4-0)	Minnesota Vikings (8-7-1)	L.A. Rams (12-4-0)	Atlanta Falcons (9-7-0) Philadelphia Eagles (9-7-0)
1979	Dallas Cowboys (11-5-0)	Tampa Bay Buccaneers (10-6-0)	L.A. Rams (9-7-0)	Chicago Bears (10-6-0) Philadelphia Eagles (11-5-0)
1980	Philadelphia Eagles (12-4-0)	Minnesota Vikings (9-7-0)	Atlanta Falcons (12-4-0)	Dallas Cowboys (12-4-0) L.A. Rams (11-5-0)
1981	Dallas Cowboys (12-4-0)	Tampa Bay Buccaneers (9-7-0)	San Francisco 49ers (13-3-0)	NY Giants (9-7-0) Philadelphia Eagles (10-6-0)
1982	Strike abbreviated season. See note.			
1983	Washington Redskins (14-2-0)	Detroit Lions (9-7-0)	San Francisco 49ers (10-6-0)	Dallas Cowboys (12-4-0) L.A. Rams (9-7-0)
1984	Washington Redskins (11-5-0)	Chicago Bears (10-6-0)	San Francisco 49ers (15-1-0)	L.A. Rams (10-6-0) NY Giants (9-7-0)
1985	Dallas Cowboys (10-6-0)	Chicago Bears (15-1-0)	L.A. Rams (11-5-0)	NY Giants (10-6-0) San Francisco 49ers (10-6-0)
1986	NY Giants (14-2-0)	Chicago Bears (14-2-0)	San Francisco 49ers (10-5-1)	L.A. Rams (10-6-0) Washington Redskins (12-4-0)
1987	Washington Redskins (11-4-0)	Chicago Bears (11-4-0)	San Francisco 49ers (13-2-0)	Minnesota Vikings (8-7-0) New Orleans Saints (12-3-0)
1988	Philadelphia Eagles (10-6-0)	Chicago Bears (12-4-0)	San Francisco 49ers (10-6-0)	L.A. Rams (10-6-0) Minnesota Vikings (11-5-0)
1989	NY Giants (12-4-0)	Minnesota Vikings (10-6-0)	San Francisco 49ers (14-2-0)	L.A. Rams (11-5-0) Philadelphia Eagles (11-5-0)
1990	NY Giants (13-3-0)	Chicago Bears (11-5-0)	San Francisco 49ers (14-2-0)	New Orleans Saints (8-8-0) Philadelphia Eagles (10-6-0) Washington Redskins (10-6-0)
1991	Washington Redskins (14-2-0)	Detroit Lions (12-4-0)	New Orleans Saints (11-5-0)	Atlanta Falcons (10-6-0) Chicago Bears (11-5-0) Dallas Cowboys (11-5-0)
1992	Dallas Cowboys (13-3-0)	Minnesota Vikings (11-5-0)	San Francisco 49ers (14-2-0)	New Orleans Saints (12-4-0) Philadelphia Eagles (11-5-0) Washington Redskins (9-7-0)
1993	Dallas Cowboys (12-4-0)	Detroit Lions (10-6-0)	San Francisco 49ers (10-6-0)	Green Bay Packers (9-7-0) Minnesota Vikings (9-7-0) NY Giants (11-5-0)
1994	Dallas Cowboys (12-4-0)	Minnesota Vikings (10-6-0)	San Francisco 49ers (13-3-0)	Chicago Bears (9-7-0) Detroit Lions (9-7-0) Green Bay Packers (9-7-0)
1995	Dallas Cowboys (12-4-0)	Green Bay Packers (11-5-0)	San Francisco 49ers (11-5-0)	Philadelphia Eagles (10-6-0) Detroit Lions (10-6-0) Atlanta Falcons (9-7-0)

Note: A strike shortened the 1982 season from 16 to 9 games. The top eight teams in each conference played in a tournament to determine the conference champion.

NFL Playoff Results, 1996-2019

Year	Conference	Division	Winner (W-L-T)	Playoffs[1]	Year
1996	American	Eastern	New England Patriots (11-5-0)	Jacksonville* 30, Denver 27	1996
		Central	Pittsburgh Steelers (10-6-0)	New England 28, Pittsburgh 3	
		Western	Denver Broncos (13-3-0)	New England 20, Jacksonville* 6	
	National	Eastern	Dallas Cowboys (10-6-0)	Green Bay 35, San Francisco* 14	
		Central	Green Bay Packers (13-3-0)	Carolina 26, Dallas 17	
		Western	Carolina Panthers (12-4-0)	Green Bay 30, Carolina 13	
1997	American	Eastern	New England Patriots (10-6-0)	Pittsburgh 7, New England 6	1997
		Central	Pittsburgh Steelers (11-5-0)	Denver* 14, Kansas City 10	
		Western	Kansas City Chiefs (13-3-0)	Denver* 24, Pittsburgh 21	
	National	Eastern	NY Giants (10-5-1)	San Francisco 38, Minnesota* 22	
		Central	Green Bay Packers (13-3-0)	Green Bay 21, Tampa Bay* 7	
		Western	San Francisco 49ers (13-3-0)	Green Bay 23, San Francisco 10	
1998	American	Eastern	NY Jets (12-4-0)	Denver 38, Miami* 3	1998
		Central	Jacksonville Jaguars (11-5-0)	NY Jets 34, Jacksonville 24	
		Western	Denver Broncos (14-2-0)	Denver 23, NY Jets 10	
	National	Eastern	Dallas Cowboys (10-6-0)	Atlanta 20, San Francisco* 18	
		Central	Minnesota Vikings (15-1-0)	Minnesota 41, Arizona* 21	
		Western	Atlanta Falcons (14-2-0)	Atlanta 30, Minnesota 27 (OT)	
1999	American	Eastern	Indianapolis Colts (13-3-0)	Jacksonville 62, Miami* 7	1999
		Central	Jacksonville Jaguars (14-2-0)	Tennessee* 19, Indianapolis 16	
		Western	Seattle Seahawks (9-7-0)	Tennessee* 33, Jacksonville 14	
	National	Eastern	Washington Redskins (10-6-0)	Tampa Bay 14, Washington 13	
		Central	Tampa Bay Buccaneers (11-5-0)	St. Louis 49, Minnesota* 37	
		Western	St. Louis Rams (13-3-0)	St. Louis 11, Tampa Bay 6	

Year	Conference	Division	Winner (W-L-T)	Playoffs[1]	Year
2000	American	Eastern	Miami Dolphins (11-5-0)	Oakland 27, Miami 0	2000
		Central	Tennessee Titans (13-3-0)	Baltimore* 24, Tennessee 10	
		Western	Oakland Raiders (12-4-0)	Baltimore* 16, Oakland 3	
	National	Eastern	NY Giants (12-4-0)	Minnesota 34, New Orleans 16	
		Central	Minnesota Vikings (11-5-0)	NY Giants 20, Philadelphia* 10	
		Western	New Orleans Saints (10-6-0)	NY Giants 41, Minnesota 0	
2001	American	Eastern	New England Patriots (11-5-0)	New England 16, Oakland 13 (OT)	2001
		Central	Pittsburgh Steelers (13-3-0)	Pittsburgh 27, Baltimore* 10	
		Western	Oakland Raiders (10-6-0)	New England 24, Pittsburgh 17	
	National	Eastern	Philadelphia Eagles (11-5-0)	Philadelphia 33, Chicago 19	
		Central	Chicago Bears (13-3-0)	St. Louis 45, Green Bay* 17	
		Western	St. Louis Rams (14-2-0)	St. Louis 29, Philadelphia 24	
2002	American	East	NY Jets (9-7-0)		2002
		North	Pittsburgh Steelers (10-5-1)	Oakland 30, NY Jets 10	
		South	Tennessee Titans (11-5-0)	Tennessee 34, Pittsburgh 31 (OT)	
		West	Oakland Raiders (11-5-0)	Oakland 41, Tennessee 24	
	National	East	Philadelphia Eagles (12-4-0)		
		North	Green Bay Packers (12-4-0)	Philadelphia 20, Atlanta* 6	
		South	Tampa Bay Buccaneers (12-4-0)	Tampa Bay 31, San Francisco 6	
		West	San Francisco 49ers (10-6-0)	Tampa Bay 27, Philadelphia 10	
2003	American	East	New England Patriots (14-2-0)		2003
		North	Baltimore Ravens (10-6-0)	Indianapolis 38, Kansas City 31	
		South	Indianapolis Colts (12-4-0)	New England 17, Tennessee* 14	
		West	Kansas City Chiefs (13-3-0)	New England 24, Indianapolis 14	
	National	East	Philadelphia Eagles (12-4-0)		
		North	Green Bay Packers (10-6-0)	Carolina 29, St. Louis 23 (2 OT)	
		South	Carolina Panthers (11-5-0)	Philadelphia 20, Green Bay 17 (OT)	
		West	St. Louis Rams (12-4-0)	Carolina 14, Philadelphia 3	
2004	American	East	New England Patriots (14-2-0)		2004
		North	Pittsburgh Steelers (15-1-0)	Pittsburgh 20, NY Jets* 17 (OT)	
		South	Indianapolis Colts (12-4-0)	New England 20, Indianapolis 3	
		West	San Diego Chargers (12-4-0)	New England 41, Pittsburgh 27	
	National	East	Philadelphia Eagles (13-3-0)		
		North	Green Bay Packers (10-6-0)	Atlanta 47, St. Louis* 17	
		South	Atlanta Falcons (11-5-0)	Philadelphia 27, Minnesota* 14	
		West	Seattle Seahawks (9-7-0)	Philadelphia 27, Atlanta 10	
2005	American	East	New England Patriots (10-6-0)		2005
		North	Cincinnati Bengals (11-5-0)	Denver 27, New England 13	
		South	Indianapolis Colts (14-2-0)	Pittsburgh* 21, Indianapolis 18	
		West	Denver Broncos (13-3-0)	Pittsburgh* 34, Denver 17	
	National	East	NY Giants (11-5-0)		
		North	Chicago Bears (11-5-0)	Seattle 20, Washington* 10	
		South	Tampa Bay Buccaneers (11-5-0)	Carolina* 29, Chicago 21	
		West	Seattle Seahawks (13-3-0)	Seattle 34, Carolina* 14	
2006	American	East	New England Patriots (12-4-0)		2006
		North	Baltimore Ravens (13-3-0)	Indianapolis 15, Baltimore 6	
		South	Indianapolis Colts (12-4-0)	New England 24, San Diego 21	
		West	San Diego Chargers (14-2-0)	Indianapolis 38, New England 34	
	National	East	Philadelphia Eagles (10-6-0)		
		North	Chicago Bears (13-3-0)	New Orleans 27, Philadelphia 24	
		South	New Orleans Saints (10-6-0)	Chicago 27, Seattle 24 (OT)	
		West	Seattle Seahawks (9-7-0)	Chicago 39, New Orleans 14	
2007	American	East	New England Patriots (16-0-0)		2007
		North	Pittsburgh Steelers (10-6-0)	New England 31, Jacksonville* 20	
		South	Indianapolis Colts (13-3-0)	San Diego 28, Indianapolis 24	
		West	San Diego Chargers (11-5-0)	New England 21, San Diego 12	
	National	East	Dallas Cowboys (13-3-0)		
		North	Green Bay Packers (13-3-0)	Green Bay 42, Seattle 20	
		South	Tampa Bay Buccaneers (9-7-0)	NY Giants* 21, Dallas 17	
		West	Seattle Seahawks (10-6-0)	NY Giants* 23, Green Bay 20 (OT)	
2008	American	East	Miami Dolphins (11-5-0)		2008
		North	Pittsburgh Steelers (12-4-0)	Baltimore* 13, Tennessee 10	
		South	Tennessee Titans (13-3-0)	Pittsburgh 35, San Diego 24	
		West	San Diego Chargers (8-8-0)	Pittsburgh 23, Baltimore* 14	
	National	East	NY Giants (12-4-0)		
		North	Minnesota Vikings (10-6-0)	Arizona 33, Carolina 13	
		South	Carolina Panthers (12-4-0)	Philadelphia* 23, NY Giants 11	
		West	Arizona Cardinals (9-7-0)	Arizona 32, Philadelphia* 25	
2009	American	East	New England Patriots (10-6-0)		2009
		North	Cincinnati Bengals (10-6-0)	Indianapolis 20, Baltimore* 3	
		South	Indianapolis Colts (14-2-0)	NY Jets* 17, San Diego 14	
		West	San Diego Chargers (13-3-0)	Indianapolis 30, NY Jets* 17	
	National	East	Dallas Cowboys (11-5-0)		
		North	Minnesota Vikings (12-4-0)	New Orleans 45, Arizona 14	
		South	New Orleans Saints (13-3-0)	Minnesota 34, Dallas 3	
		West	Arizona Cardinals (10-6-0)	New Orleans 31, Minnesota 28 (OT)	

Year	Conference	Division	Winner (W-L-T)	Playoffs[1]	Year
2010	American	East	New England Patriots (14-2-0)		2010
		North	Pittsburgh Steelers (12-4-0)	Pittsburgh 31, Baltimore* 24	
		South	Indianapolis Colts (10-6-0)	NY Jets* 28, New England 21	
		West	Kansas City Chiefs (10-6-0)	Pittsburgh 24, NY Jets* 19	
	National	East	Philadelphia Eagles (10-6-0)		
		North	Chicago Bears (11-5-0)	Green Bay* 48, Atlanta 21	
		South	Atlanta Falcons (13-3-0)	Chicago 35, Seattle 24	
		West	Seattle Seahawks (7-9-0)	Green Bay* 21, Chicago 14	
2011	American	East	New England Patriots (13-3-0)		2011
		North	Baltimore Ravens (12-4-0)	New England 45, Denver 10	
		South	Houston Texans (10-6-0)	Baltimore 20, Houston 13	
		West	Denver Broncos (8-8-0)	New England 23, Baltimore 20	
	National	East	NY Giants (9-7-0)		
		North	Green Bay Packers (15-1-0)	San Francisco 36, New Orleans 32	
		South	New Orleans Saints (13-3-0)	NY Giants 37, Green Bay 20	
		West	San Francisco 49ers (13-3-0)	NY Giants 20, San Francisco 17 (OT)	
2012	American	East	New England Patriots (12-4-0)		2012
		North	Baltimore Ravens (10-6-0)	Baltimore 38, Denver 35 (2 OT)	
		South	Houston Texans (12-4-0)	New England 41, Houston 28	
		West	Denver Broncos (13-3-0)	Baltimore 28, New England 13	
	National	East	Washington Redskins (10-6-0)		
		North	Green Bay Packers (11-5-0)	San Francisco 45, Green Bay 31	
		South	Atlanta Falcons (13-3-0)	Atlanta 30, Seattle* 28	
		West	San Francisco 49ers (11-4-1)	San Francisco 28, Atlanta 24	
2013	American	East	New England Patriots (12-4-0)		2013
		North	Cincinnati Bengals (11-5-0)	New England 43, Indianapolis 22	
		South	Indianapolis Colts (11-5-0)	Denver 24, San Diego* 17	
		West	Denver Broncos (13-3-0)	Denver 26, New England 16	
	National	East	Philadelphia Eagles (10-6-0)		
		North	Green Bay Packers (8-7-1)	Seattle 23, New Orleans* 15	
		South	Carolina Panthers (12-4-0)	San Francisco* 23, Carolina 10	
		West	Seattle Seahawks (13-3-0)	Seattle 23, San Francisco* 17	
2014	American	East	New England Patriots (12-4-0)		2014
		North	Pittsburgh Steelers (11-5-0)	New England 35, Baltimore* 31	
		South	Indianapolis Colts (11-5-0)	Indianapolis 24, Denver 13	
		West	Denver Broncos (12-4-0)	New England 45, Indianapolis 7	
	National	East	Dallas Cowboys (12-4-0)		
		North	Green Bay Packers (12-4-0)	Seattle 31, Carolina 17	
		South	Carolina Panthers (7-8-1)	Green Bay 26, Dallas 21	
		West	Seattle Seahawks (12-4-0)	Seattle 28, Green Bay 22 (OT)	
2015	American	East	New England Patriots (12-4-0)		2015
		North	Cincinnati Bengals (12-4-0)	New England 27, Kansas City* 20	
		South	Houston Texans (9-7-0)	Denver 23, Pittsburgh* 16	
		West	Denver Broncos (12-4-0)	Denver 20, New England 18	
	National	East	Washington Redskins (9-7-0)		
		North	Minnesota Vikings (11-5-0)	Arizona 26, Green Bay* 20 (OT)	
		South	Carolina Panthers (15-1-0)	Carolina 31, Seattle* 24	
		West	Arizona Cardinals (13-3-0)	Carolina 49, Arizona 15	
2016	American	East	New England Patriots (14-2-0)		2016
		North	Pittsburgh Steelers (11-5-0)	New England 34, Houston 16	
		South	Houston Texans (9-7-0)	Pittsburgh 18, Kansas City 16	
		West	Kansas City Chiefs (12-4-0)	New England 36, Pittsburgh 17	
	National	East	Dallas Cowboys (13-3-0)		
		North	Green Bay Packers (10-6-0)	Atlanta 36, Seattle 20	
		South	Atlanta Falcons (11-5-0)	Green Bay 34, Dallas 31	
		West	Seattle Seahawks (10-5-1)	Atlanta 44, Green Bay 21	
2017	American	East	New England Patriots (13-3-0)		2017
		North	Pittsburgh Steelers (13-3-0)	New England 35, Tennessee* 14	
		South	Jacksonville Jaguars (10-6-0)	Jacksonville 45, Pittsburg 42	
		West	Kansas City Chiefs (10-6-0)	New England 24, Jacksonville 20	
	National	East	Philadelphia Eagles (13-3-0)		
		North	Minnesota Vikings (13-3-0)	Philadelphia 15, Atlanta* 10	
		South	New Orleans Saints (11-5-0)	Minnesota 29, New Orleans 24	
		West	Los Angeles Rams (11-5-0)	Philadelphia 38, Minnesota 7	
2018	American	East	New England Patriots (11-5-0)		2018
		North	Baltimore Ravens (10-6-0)	Kansas City 31, Indianapolis 13	
		South	Houston Texans (11-5-0)	New England 41, L.A. Chargers* 28	
		West	Kansas City Chiefs (12-4-0)	New England 37, Kansas City 31 (OT)	
	National	East	Dallas Cowboys (10-6-0)		
		North	Chicago Bears (12-4-0)	L.A. Rams 30, Dallas 22	
		South	New Orleans Saints (13-3-0)	New Orleans 20, Philadelphia* 14	
		West	L.A. Rams (13-3-0)	L.A. Rams 26, New Orleans 23 (OT)	
2019	American	East	New England Patriots (12-4-0)		2019
		North	Baltimore Ravens (14-2-0)	Tennessee* 28, Baltimore 12	
		South	Houston Texans (10-6-0)	Kansas City 51, Houston 31	
		West	Kansas City Chiefs (12-4-0)	Kansas City 35, Tennessee* 24	
	National	East	Philadelphia Eagles (9-7-0)		
		North	Green Bay Packers (13-3-0)	San Francisco 27, Minnesota* 10	
		South	New Orleans Saints (13-3-0)	Green Bay 28, Seattle* 23	
		West	San Francisco 49ers (13-3-0)	San Francisco 37, Green Bay 20	

* = Wild card team. (1) Only the final two conference playoff rounds are shown.

American Football Conference Leaders, 1960-2019
(American Football League, 1960-69)

PASSING (BASED ON QB RATING POINTS) — RECEPTIONS

Player, team	Rating	Att	Comp	Yds	TD	Year	Player, team	Rec	Yds	TD
Jack Kemp, L.A. Chargers	NA	406	211	3,018	20	1960	Lionel Taylor, Denver	92	1,235	12
George Blanda, Houston	NA	362	187	3,330	36	1961	Lionel Taylor, Denver	100	1,176	4
Len Dawson, Dallas Texans	NA	310	189	2,759	29	1962	Lionel Taylor, Denver	77	908	4
Tobin Rote, San Diego	NA	286	170	2,510	20	1963	Lionel Taylor, Denver	78	1,101	10
Len Dawson, Kansas City	NA	354	199	2,879	30	1964	Charley Hennigan, Houston	101	1,546	8
John Hadl, San Diego	NA	348	174	2,798	20	1965	Lionel Taylor, Denver	85	1,131	6
Len Dawson, Kansas City	NA	284	159	2,527	26	1966	Lance Alworth, San Diego	73	1,383	13
Daryle Lamonica, Oakland	NA	425	220	3,228	30	1967	George Sauer, NY Jets	75	1,189	6
Len Dawson, Kansas City	NA	224	131	2,109	17	1968	Lance Alworth, San Diego	68	1,312	10
Greg Cook, Cincinnati	NA	197	106	1,854	15	1969	Lance Alworth, San Diego	64	1,003	4
Daryle Lamonica, Oakland	NA	356	179	2,516	22	1970	Marlin Briscoe, Buffalo	57	1,036	8
Bob Griese, Miami	NA	263	145	2,089	19	1971	Fred Biletnikoff, Oakland	61	929	9
Earl Morrall, Miami	NA	150	83	1,360	11	1972	Fred Biletnikoff, Oakland	58	802	7
Ken Stabler, Oakland	88.3	260	163	1,997	14	1973	Fred Willis, Houston	57	371	1
Ken Anderson, Cincinnati	95.7	328	213	2,667	18	1974	Lydell Mitchell, Baltimore Colts	72	544	2
Ken Anderson, Cincinnati	93.9	377	228	3,169	21	1975	Reggie Rucker, Cleveland	60	770	3
							Lydell Mitchell, Baltimore Colts	60	544	4
Ken Stabler, Oakland	103.4	291	194	2,737	27	1976	MacArthur Lane, Kansas City	66	686	1
Bob Griese, Miami	87.8	307	180	2,252	22	1977	Lydell Mitchell, Baltimore Colts	71	620	4
Terry Bradshaw, Pittsburgh	84.7	368	207	2,915	28	1978	Steve Largent, Seattle	71	1,168	8
Dan Fouts, San Diego	82.6	530	332	4,082	24	1979	Joe Washington, Baltimore Colts	82	750	3
Brian Sipe, Cleveland	91.4	554	337	4,132	30	1980	Kellen Winslow, San Diego	89	1,290	9
Ken Anderson, Cincinnati	98.4	479	300	3,754	29	1981	Kellen Winslow, San Diego	88	1,075	10
Ken Anderson, Cincinnati	95.3	309	218	2,495	12	1982	Kellen Winslow, San Diego	54	721	6
Dan Marino, Miami	96.0	296	173	2,210	20	1983	Todd Christensen, L.A. Raiders	92	1,247	12
Dan Marino, Miami	108.9	564	362	5,084	48	1984	Ozzie Newsome, Cleveland	89	1,001	5
Ken O'Brien, NY Jets	96.2	488	297	3,888	25	1985	Lionel James, San Diego	86	1,027	6
Dan Marino, Miami	92.5	623	378	4,746	44	1986	Todd Christensen, L.A. Raiders	95	1,153	8
Bernie Kosar, Cleveland	95.4	389	241	3,033	22	1987	Al Toon, NY Jets	68	976	5
Boomer Esiason, Cincinnati	97.4	388	223	3,572	28	1988	Al Toon, NY Jets	93	1,067	5
Boomer Esiason, Cincinnati	92.1	455	258	3,525	28	1989	Andre Reed, Buffalo	88	1,312	9
Jim Kelly, Buffalo	101.2	346	219	2,829	24	1990	Haywood Jeffires, Houston	74	1,048	8
							Drew Hill, Houston	74	1,019	5
Jim Kelly, Buffalo	97.6	474	304	3,844	33	1991	Haywood Jeffires, Houston	100	1,181	7
Warren Moon, Houston	89.3	346	224	2,521	18	1992	Haywood Jeffires, Houston	90	913	9
John Elway, Denver	92.8	551	348	4,030	25	1993	Reggie Langhorne, Indianapolis	85	1,038	3
Dan Marino, Miami	89.2	615	385	4,453	30	1994	Ben Coates, New England	96	1,174	7
Jim Harbaugh, Indianapolis	100.7	314	200	2,575	17	1995	Carl Pickens, Cincinnati	99	1,234	17
John Elway, Denver	89.2	466	287	3,328	26	1996	Carl Pickens, Cincinnati	100	1,180	12
Mark Brunell, Jacksonville	91.2	435	264	3,281	18	1997	Tim Brown, Oakland	104	1,408	5
Vinny Testaverde, NY Jets	101.6	421	259	3,256	29	1998	O.J. McDuffie, Miami	90	1,050	7
Peyton Manning, Indianapolis	90.7	533	331	4,135	26	1999	Jimmy Smith, Jacksonville	116	1,636	6
Brian Griese, Denver	102.9	336	216	2,688	19	2000	Marvin Harrison, Indianapolis	102	1,413	14
Rich Gannon, Oakland	95.5	549	361	3,828	27	2001	Rod Smith, Denver	113	1,343	11
Chad Pennington, NY Jets	104.2	399	275	3,120	22	2002	Marvin Harrison, Indianapolis	143	1,722	11
Steve McNair, Tennessee	100.4	400	250	3,215	24	2003	LaDainian Tomlinson, San Diego	100	725	4
Peyton Manning, Indianapolis	121.1	497	336	4,557	49	2004	Tony Gonzalez, Kansas City	102	1,258	7
Peyton Manning, Indianapolis	104.1	453	305	3,747	28	2005	Chad Johnson, Cincinnati	97	1,432	9
Peyton Manning, Indianapolis	101.0	557	362	4,397	31	2006	Andre Johnson, Houston	103	1,147	5
Tom Brady, New England	117.2	578	398	4,806	50	2007	Wes Welker, New England	112	1,175	8
							T.J. Houshmandzadeh, Cincinnati	112	1,143	12
Philip Rivers, San Diego	105.5	478	312	4,009	34	2008	Andre Johnson, Houston	115	1,575	8
Philip Rivers, San Diego	104.4	486	317	4,254	28	2009	Wes Welker, New England	123	1,348	4
Tom Brady, New England	111.0	492	324	3,900	36	2010	Reggie Wayne, Indianapolis	111	1,355	6
Tom Brady, New England	105.6	611	401	5,235	39	2011	Wes Welker, New England	122	1,569	9
Peyton Manning, Denver	105.8	583	400	4,659	37	2012	Wes Welker, New England	118	1,354	6
Peyton Manning, Denver	115.1	659	450	5,477	55	2013	Antonio Brown, Pittsburgh	110	1,499	8
Ben Roethlisberger, Pittsburgh	103.3	608	408	4,952	32	2014	Antonio Brown, Pittsburgh	129	1,698	13
Andy Dalton, Cincinnati	106.2	386	255	3,250	25	2015	Antonio Brown, Pittsburgh	136	1,834	10
Tom Brady, New England	112.2	432	291	3,554	28	2016	Antonio Brown, Pittsburgh	106	1,284	12
Alex Smith, Kansas City	104.7	505	341	4,042	26	2017	Jarvis Landry, Miami	112	987	9
Patrick Mahomes, Kansas City	113.8	580	383	5,097	50	2018	DeAndre Hopkins, Houston	115	1,572	11
Ryan Tannehill, Tennessee	117.5	286	201	2,742	22	2019	Keenan Allen, L.A. Chargers	104	1,199	6
							DeAndre Hopkins, Houston	104	1,165	7

SCORING — RUSHING YARDS

Player, team	TD	XPM	FGM	Pts	Year	Player, team	Yds	Att	TD
Gene Mingo, Denver	6	33	18	123	1960	Abner Haynes, Dallas Texans	875	156	9
Gino Cappelletti, Boston	8	48	17	147	1961	Billy Cannon, Houston	948	200	6
Gene Mingo, Denver	4	32	27	137	1962	Cookie Gilchrist, Buffalo	1,096	214	13
Gino Cappelletti, Boston	2	35	22	113	1963	Clem Daniels, Oakland	1,099	215	3
Gino Cappelletti, Boston	7	36	25	155	1964	Cookie Gilchrist, Buffalo	981	230	6
Gino Cappelletti, Boston	9	27	17	132	1965	Paul Lowe, San Diego	1,121	222	7
Gino Cappelletti, Boston	6	35	16	119	1966	Jim Nance, Boston	1,458	299	11
George Blanda, Oakland	0	56	20	116	1967	Jim Nance, Boston	1,216	269	7
Jim Turner, NY Jets	0	43	34	145	1968	Paul Robinson, Cincinnati	1,023	238	8

SCORING Player, team	TD	XPM	FGM	Pts	Year	RUSHING YARDS Player, team	Yds	Att	TD
Jim Turner, NY Jets	0	33	32	129	1969	Dickie Post, San Diego	873	182	6
Jan Stenerud, Kansas City	0	26	30	116	1970	Floyd Little, Denver	901	209	3
Garo Yepremian, Miami	0	33	28	117	1971	Floyd Little, Denver	1,133	284	6
Bobby Howfield, NY Jets	0	40	27	121	1972	O.J. Simpson, Buffalo	1,251	292	6
Roy Gerela, Pittsburgh	0	36	29	123	1973	O.J. Simpson, Buffalo	2,003	332	12
Roy Gerela, Pittsburgh	0	33	20	93	1974	Otis Armstrong, Denver	1,407	263	9
O.J. Simpson, Buffalo	23	0	0	138	1975	O.J. Simpson, Buffalo	1,817	329	16
Toni Linhart, Baltimore Colts	0	49	20	109	1976	O.J. Simpson, Buffalo	1,503	290	8
Errol Mann, Oakland	0	39	20	99	1977	Mark van Eeghen, Oakland	1,273	324	7
Pat Leahy, NY Jets	0	41	22	107	1978	Earl Campbell, Houston	1,450	302	13
John Smith, New England	0	46	23	115	1979	Earl Campbell, Houston	1,697	368	19
John Smith, New England	0	51	26	129	1980	Earl Campbell, Houston	1,934	373	13
Jim Breech, Cincinnati	0	49	22	115	1981	Earl Campbell, Houston	1,376	361	10
Nick Lowery, Kansas City	0	37	26	115	1982	Freeman McNeil, NY Jets	786	151	6
Marcus Allen, L.A. Raiders	14	0	0	84	1983	Curt Warner, Seattle	1,449	335	13
Gary Anderson, Pittsburgh	0	38	27	119	1984	Earnest Jackson, San Diego	1,179	296	8
Gary Anderson, Pittsburgh	0	45	24	117	1985	Marcus Allen, L.A. Raiders	1,759	380	11
Gary Anderson, Pittsburgh	0	40	33	139	1986	Curt Warner, Seattle	1,481	319	13
Tony Franklin, New England	0	44	32	140	1987	Eric Dickerson, L.A. Rams-Ind.	1,288*	283	6
Jim Breech, Cincinnati	0	25	24	97	1988	Eric Dickerson, Indianapolis	1,659	388	14
Scott Norwood, Buffalo	0	33	32	129	1989	Christian Okoye, Kansas City	1,480	370	12
David Treadwell, Denver	0	39	27	120	1990	Thurman Thomas, Buffalo	1,297	271	11
Nick Lowery, Kansas City	0	37	34	139	1991	Thurman Thomas, Buffalo	1,407	288	7
Pete Stoyanovich, Miami	0	28	31	121	1992	Barry Foster, Pittsburgh	1,690	390	11
Pete Stoyanovich, Miami	0	34	30	124	1993	Thurman Thomas, Buffalo	1,315	355	6
Jeff Jaeger, L.A. Raiders	0	27	35	132	1994	Chris Warren, Seattle	1,545	333	9
John Carney, San Diego	0	33	34	135	1995	Curtis Martin, New England	1,487	368	14
Norm Johnson, Pittsburgh	0	39	34	141	1996	Terrell Davis, Denver	1,538	345	13
Cary Blanchard, Indianapolis	0	27	36	135	1997	Terrell Davis, Denver	1,750	369	15
Mike Hollis, Jacksonville	0	41	31	134	1998	Terrell Davis, Denver	2,008	392	21
Steve Christie, Buffalo	0	41	33	140	1999	Edgerrin James, Indianapolis	1,553	369	13
Mike Vanderjagt, Indianapolis	0	43	34	145	2000	Edgerrin James, Indianapolis	1,709	387	13
Matt Stover, Baltimore	0	30	35	135	2001	Priest Holmes, Kansas City	1,555	327	8
Mike Vanderjagt, Indianapolis	0	41	28	125	2002	Ricky Williams, Miami	1,853	383	16
Priest Holmes, Kansas City	24	0	0	144	2003	Jamal Lewis, Baltimore	2,066	387	14
Priest Holmes, Kansas City	27	0	0	162	2004	Curtis Martin, NY Jets	1,697	371	12
Adam Vinatieri, New England	0	48	31	141	2005	Larry Johnson, Kansas City	1,750	336	20
Shayne Graham, Cincinnati	0	47	28	131	2006	LaDainian Tomlinson, San Diego	1,815	348	28
LaDainian Tomlinson, San Diego	31	0	0	186	2007	LaDainian Tomlinson, San Diego	1,474	315	15
Randy Moss, New England	23	0	0	138	2008	Thomas Jones, NY Jets	1,312	290	13
Stephen Gostkowski, New England	0	40	36	148	2009	Chris Johnson, Tennessee	2,006	358	14
Nate Kaeding, San Diego	0	50	32	146	2010	Arian Foster, Houston	1,616	327	16
Sebastian Janikowski, Oakland	0	43	33	142	2011	Maurice Jones-Drew, Jacksonville	1,606	343	8
Stephen Gostkowski, New England	0	59	28	143	2012	Jamaal Charles, Kansas City	1,509	285	5
Stephen Gostkowski, New England	0	66	29	153	2013	Jamaal Charles, Kansas City	1,287	259	12
Stephen Gostkowski, New England	0	44	38	158	2014	Le'Veon Bell, Pittsburgh	1,361	290	8
Stephen Gostkowski, New England	0	51	35	156	2015	Chris Ivory, NY Jets	1,070	247	7
Justin Tucker, Baltimore	0	52	33	151	2016	DeMarco Murray, Tennessee	1,287	293	9
Stephen Gostkowski, New England	0	27	38	141	2017	Kareem Hunt, Kansas City	1,327	272	8
Ka'imi Fairbairn, Houston	0	45	37	156	2018	Joe Mixon, Cincinnati	1,168	237	8
Harrison Butker, Kansas City	0	45	34	147	2019	Derrick Henry, Tennessee	1,540	303	16

* = Includes 277 yards after being traded to NFC; 1,011 yards led AFC. NA = Not applicable/available. **Note:** Passer ratings for years prior to 1973 were determined by different measures and are not directly comparable to current passer ratings.

National Football Conference Leaders, 1960-2019

(National Football League, 1960-69)

PASSING (BASED ON QB RATING POINTS) Player, team	Rating	Att	Comp	Yds	TD	Year	RECEPTIONS Player, team	Rec	Yds	TD
Milt Plum, Cleveland	NA	250	151	2,297	21	1960	Raymond Berry, Baltimore Colts	74	1,298	10
Milt Plum, Cleveland	NA	302	177	2,416	18	1961	Jim Phillips, L.A. Rams	78	1,092	5
Bart Starr, Green Bay	NA	285	178	2,438	12	1962	Bobby Mitchell, Washington	72	1,384	11
Y.A. Tittle, NY Giants	NA	367	221	3,145	36	1963	Bobby Joe Conrad, St. Louis Cardinals	73	967	10
Bart Starr, Green Bay	NA	272	163	2,144	15	1964	Johnny Morris, Chicago	93	1,200	10
Rudy Bukich, Chicago	NA	312	176	2,641	20	1965	Dave Parks, San Francisco	80	1,344	12
Bart Starr, Green Bay	NA	251	156	2,257	14	1966	Charley Taylor, Washington	72	1,119	12
Sonny Jurgensen, Washington	NA	508	288	3,747	31	1967	Charley Taylor, Washington	70	990	9
Earl Morrall, Baltimore Colts	NA	317	182	2,909	26	1968	Clifton McNeil, San Francisco	71	994	7
Sonny Jurgensen, Washington	NA	442	274	3,102	22	1969	Dan Abramowicz, New Orleans	73	1,015	7
John Brodie, San Francisco	NA	378	223	2,941	24	1970	Dick Gordon, Chicago	71	1,026	13
Roger Staubach, Dallas	NA	211	126	1,882	15	1971	Bob Tucker, NY Giants	59	791	4
Norm Snead, NY Giants	NA	325	196	2,307	17	1972	Harold Jackson, Philadelphia	62	1,048	4
Roger Staubach, Dallas	94.6	286	179	2,428	23	1973	Harold Carmichael, Philadelphia	67	1,116	9
Sonny Jurgensen, Washington	94.5	167	107	1,185	11	1974	Charles Young, Philadelphia	63	696	3

PASSING (BASED ON QB RATING POINTS)

Year	Player, team	Rating	Att	Comp	Yds	TD
1975	Fran Tarkenton, Minnesota	91.8	425	273	2,994	25
1976	James Harris, L.A. Rams	89.6	158	91	1,460	8
1977	Roger Staubach, Dallas	87.0	361	210	2,620	18
1978	Roger Staubach, Dallas	84.9	413	231	3,190	25
1979	Roger Staubach, Dallas	92.3	461	267	3,586	27
1980	Ron Jaworski, Philadelphia	91.0	451	257	3,529	27
1981	Joe Montana, San Francisco	88.4	488	311	3,565	19
1982	Joe Theismann, Washington	91.3	252	161	2,033	13
1983	Steve Bartkowski, Atlanta	97.6	432	274	3,167	22
1984	Joe Montana, San Francisco	102.9	432	279	3,630	28
1985	Joe Montana, San Francisco	91.3	494	303	3,653	27
1986	Tommy Kramer, Minnesota	92.6	372	208	3,000	24
1987	Joe Montana, San Francisco	102.1	398	266	3,054	31
1988	Wade Wilson, Minnesota	91.5	332	204	2,746	15
1989	Joe Montana, San Francisco	112.4	386	271	3,521	26
1990	Phil Simms, NY Giants	92.7	311	184	2,284	15
1991	Steve Young, San Francisco	101.8	279	180	2,517	17
1992	Steve Young, San Francisco	107.0	402	268	3,465	25
1993	Steve Young, San Francisco	101.5	462	314	4,023	29
1994	Steve Young, San Francisco	112.8	461	324	3,969	35
1995	Brett Favre, Green Bay	99.5	570	359	4,413	38
1996	Steve Young, San Francisco	97.2	316	214	2,410	14
1997	Steve Young, San Francisco	104.7	356	241	3,029	19
1998	Randall Cunningham, Minnesota	106.0	425	259	3,704	34
1999	Kurt Warner, St. Louis	109.2	499	325	4,353	41
2000	Trent Green, St. Louis	101.8	240	145	2,063	16
2001	Kurt Warner, St. Louis	101.4	546	375	4,830	36
2002	Brad Johnson, Tampa Bay	92.9	451	281	3,049	22
2003	Daunte Culpepper, Minnesota	96.4	454	295	3,479	25
2004	Daunte Culpepper, Minnesota	110.9	548	379	4,717	39
2005	Matt Hasselbeck, Seattle	98.2	449	294	3,459	24
2006	Drew Brees, New Orleans	96.2	554	356	4,418	26
2007	Tony Romo, Dallas	97.4	520	335	4,211	36
2008	Kurt Warner, Arizona	96.9	598	401	4,583	30
2009	Drew Brees, New Orleans	109.6	514	363	4,388	34
2010	Aaron Rodgers, Green Bay	101.2	475	312	3,922	28
2011	Aaron Rodgers, Green Bay	122.5	502	343	4,643	45
2012	Aaron Rodgers, Green Bay	108.0	552	371	4,295	39
2013	Nick Foles, Philadelphia	119.2	317	203	2,891	27
2014	Tony Romo, Dallas	113.2	435	304	3,705	34
2015	Russell Wilson, Seattle	110.1	483	329	4,024	34
2016	Matt Ryan, Atlanta	117.1	534	373	4,944	38
2017	Drew Brees, New Orleans	103.9	536	386	4,334	23
2018	Drew Brees, New Orleans	115.7	489	364	3,992	32
2019	Drew Brees, New Orleans	116.3	378	281	2,979	27

RECEPTIONS

Year	Player, team	Rec	Yds	TD
1975	Chuck Foreman, Minnesota	73	691	9
1976	Drew Pearson, Dallas	58	806	6
1977	Ahmad Rashad, Minnesota	51	681	2
1978	Rickey Young, Minnesota	88	704	5
1979	Ahmad Rashad, Minnesota	80	1,156	9
1980	Earl Cooper, San Francisco	83	567	4
1981	Dwight Clark, San Francisco	85	1,105	4
1982	Dwight Clark, San Francisco	60	913	5
1983	Roy Green, St. Louis Cardinals	78	1,227	14
	Charlie Brown, Washington	78	1,225	8
	Earnest Gray, NY Giants	78	1,139	5
1984	Art Monk, Washington	106	1,372	7
1985	Roger Craig, San Francisco	92	1,016	6
1986	Jerry Rice, San Francisco	86	1,570	15
1987	J. T. Smith, St. Louis Cardinals	91	1,117	8
1988	Henry Ellard, L.A. Rams	86	1,414	10
1989	Sterling Sharpe, Green Bay	90	1,423	12
1990	Jerry Rice, San Francisco	100	1,502	13
1991	Michael Irvin, Dallas	93	1,523	8
1992	Sterling Sharpe, Green Bay	108	1,461	13
1993	Sterling Sharpe, Green Bay	112	1,274	11
1994	Cris Carter, Minnesota	122	1,256	7
1995	Herman Moore, Detroit	123	1,686	14
1996	Jerry Rice, San Francisco	108	1,254	8
1997	Herman Moore, Detroit	104	1,293	8
1998	Frank Sanders, Arizona	89	1,145	3
1999	Muhsin Muhammad, Carolina	96	1,253	8
2000	Muhsin Muhammad, Carolina	102	1,183	6
2001	Keyshawn Johnson, Tampa Bay	106	1,266	1
2002	Randy Moss, Minnesota	106	1,347	7
2003	Torry Holt, St. Louis	117	1,696	12
2004	Joe Horn, New Orleans	94	1,399	11
	Torry Holt, St. Louis	94	1,372	10
2005	Steve Smith, Carolina	103	1,563	12
	Larry Fitzgerald, Arizona	103	1,409	10
2006	Mike Furrey, Detroit	98	1,086	6
2007	Larry Fitzgerald, Arizona	100	1,409	10
2008	Larry Fitzgerald, Arizona	96	1,431	12
2009	Steve Smith, NY Giants	107	1,220	7
2010	Roddy White, Atlanta	115	1,389	10
2011	Roddy White, Atlanta	100	1,296	8
2012	Calvin Johnson, Detroit	122	1,964	5
2013	Pierre Garcon, Washington	113	1,346	5
2014	Julio Jones, Atlanta	104	1,593	6
2015	Julio Jones, Atlanta	136	1,871	8
2016	Larry Fitzgerald, Arizona	107	1,023	6
2017	Larry Fitzgerald, Arizona	109	1,156	6
2018	Michael Thomas, New Orleans	125	1,405	9
2019	Michael Thomas, New Orleans	149	1,725	9

SCORING

Year	Player, team	TD	XPM	FGM	Pts
1960	Paul Hornung, Green Bay	15	41	15	176
1961	Paul Hornung, Green Bay	10	41	15	146
1962	Jim Taylor, Green Bay	19	0	0	114
1963	Don Chandler, NY Giants	0	52	18	106
1964	Lenny Moore, Baltimore Colts	20	0	0	120
1965	Gale Sayers, Chicago	22	0	0	132
1966	Bruce Gossett, L.A. Rams	0	29	28	113
1967	Jim Bakken, St. Louis Cardinals	0	36	27	117
1968	Leroy Kelly, Cleveland	20	0	0	120
1969	Fred Cox, Minnesota	0	43	26	121
1970	Fred Cox, Minnesota	0	35	30	125
1971	Curt Knight, Washington	0	27	29	114
1972	Chester Marcol, Green Bay	0	29	33	128
1973	David Ray, L.A. Rams	0	40	30	130
1974	Chester Marcol, Green Bay	0	19	25	94
1975	Chuck Foreman, Minnesota	22	0	0	132
1976	Mark Moseley, Washington	0	31	22	97
1977	Walter Payton, Chicago	16	0	0	96
1978	Frank Corral, L.A. Rams	0	31	29	118
1979	Mark Moseley, Washington	0	39	25	114
1980	Ed Murray, Detroit	0	35	27	116
1981	Ed Murray, Detroit	0	46	25	121
	Rafael Septien, Dallas	0	40	27	121
1982	Wendell Tyler, L.A. Rams	13	0	0	78
1983	Mark Moseley, Washington	0	62	33	161

RUSHING YARDS

Year	Player, team	Yds	Att	TD
1960	Jim Brown, Cleveland	1,257	215	9
1961	Jim Brown, Cleveland	1,408	305	8
1962	Jim Taylor, Green Bay	1,474	272	19
1963	Jim Brown, Cleveland	1,863	291	12
1964	Jim Brown, Cleveland	1,446	280	7
1965	Jim Brown, Cleveland	1,544	289	17
1966	Gale Sayers, Chicago	1,231	229	8
1967	Leroy Kelly, Cleveland	1,205	235	11
1968	Leroy Kelly, Cleveland	1,239	248	16
1969	Gale Sayers, Chicago	1,032	236	8
1970	Larry Brown, Washington	1,125	237	5
1971	John Brockington, Green Bay	1,105	216	4
1972	Larry Brown, Washington	1,216	285	8
1973	John Brockington, Green Bay	1,144	265	3
1974	Lawrence McCutcheon, L.A. Rams	1,109	236	3
1975	Jim Otis, St. Louis Cardinals	1,076	269	5
1976	Walter Payton, Chicago	1,390	311	13
1977	Walter Payton, Chicago	1,852	339	14
1978	Walter Payton, Chicago	1,395	333	11
1979	Walter Payton, Chicago	1,610	369	14
1980	Walter Payton, Chicago	1,460	317	6
1981	George Rogers, New Orleans	1,674	378	13
1982	Tony Dorsett, Dallas	745	177	5
1983	Eric Dickerson, L.A. Rams	1,808	390	18

SCORING

Player, team	TD	XPM	FGM	Pts
Ray Wersching, San Francisco	0	56	25	131
Kevin Butler, Chicago	0	51	31	144
Kevin Butler, Chicago	0	36	28	120
Jerry Rice, San Francisco	23	0	0	138
Mike Cofer, San Francisco	0	40	27	121
Mike Cofer, San Francisco	0	49	29	136
Chip Lohmiller, Washington	0	41	30	131
Chip Lohmiller, Washington	0	56	31	149
Morten Andersen, New Orleans	0	33	29	120
Chip Lohmiller, Washington	0	30	30	120
Jason Hanson, Detroit	0	28	34	130
Fuad Reveiz, Minnesota	0	30	34	132
Emmitt Smith, Dallas	22	0	0	132
Emmitt Smith, Dallas	25	0	0	150
John Kasay, Carolina	0	34	37	145
Richie Cunningham, Dallas	0	24	34	126
Gary Anderson, Minnesota	0	59	35	164
Jeff Wilkins, St. Louis	0	64	20	124
Marshall Faulk, St. Louis	26	0	0	160
Marshall Faulk, St. Louis	21	0	0	128
Jay Feely, Atlanta	0	42	32	138
Jeff Wilkins, St. Louis	0	46	39	163
David Akers, Philadelphia	0	41	27	122
Shaun Alexander, Seattle	28	0	0	168
Robbie Gould, Chicago	0	47	32	143
Mason Crosby, Green Bay	0	48	31	141
David Akers, Philadelphia	0	45	33	144
David Akers, Philadelphia	0	43	32	139
David Akers, Philadelphia	0	47	32	143
David Akers, San Francisco	0	34	44	166
Lawrence Tynes, NY Giants	0	46	33	145
Steven Hauschka, Seattle	0	44	33	143
Cody Parkey, Philadelphia	0	54	32	150
Graham Gano, Carolina	0	56	30	146
Matt Bryant, Atlanta	0	56	34	158
Greg Zuerlein, L.A. Rams	0	44	38	158
Wil Lutz, New Orleans	0	52	28	136
Wil Lutz, New Orleans	0	48	32	144

RUSHING YARDS

Year	Player, team	Yds	Att	TD
1984	Eric Dickerson, L.A. Rams	2,105	379	14
1985	Gerald Riggs, Atlanta	1,719	397	10
1986	Eric Dickerson, L.A. Rams	1,821	404	11
1987	Charles White, L.A. Rams	1,374	324	11
1988	Herschel Walker, Dallas	1,514	361	5
1989	Barry Sanders, Detroit	1,470	280	14
1990	Barry Sanders, Detroit	1,304	255	13
1991	Emmitt Smith, Dallas	1,563	365	12
1992	Emmitt Smith, Dallas	1,713	373	18
1993	Emmitt Smith, Dallas	1,486	283	9
1994	Barry Sanders, Detroit	1,883	331	7
1995	Emmitt Smith, Dallas	1,773	377	25
1996	Barry Sanders, Detroit	1,553	307	11
1997	Barry Sanders, Detroit	2,053	335	11
1998	Jamal Anderson, Atlanta	1,846	410	14
1999	Stephen Davis, Washington	1,405	290	17
2000	Robert Smith, Minnesota	1,521	295	7
2001	Stephen Davis, Washington	1,432	356	5
2002	Deuce McAllister, New Orleans	1,388	325	13
2003	Ahman Green, Green Bay	1,883	355	15
2004	Shaun Alexander, Seattle	1,696	353	16
2005	Shaun Alexander, Seattle	1,880	370	27
2006	Frank Gore, San Francisco	1,695	312	8
2007	Adrian Peterson, Minnesota	1,341	238	12
2008	Adrian Peterson, Minnesota	1,760	363	10
2009	Steven Jackson, St. Louis	1,416	324	4
2010	Michael Turner, Atlanta	1,371	334	12
2011	Michael Turner, Atlanta	1,340	301	11
2012	Adrian Peterson, Minnesota	2,097	348	12
2013	LeSean McCoy, Philadelphia	1,607	314	9
2014	DeMarco Murray, Dallas	1,845	392	13
2015	Adrian Peterson, Minnesota	1,485	327	11
2016	Ezekiel Elliott, Dallas	1,631	322	15
2017	Todd Gurley, L.A. Rams	1,305	279	13
2018	Ezekiel Elliott, Dallas	1,434	304	6
2019	Christian McCaffrey, Carolina	1,387	287	15

NA = Not applicable/available. **Note:** Passer ratings for years prior to 1973 were determined by different measures and are not directly comparable to current passer ratings.

NFL Most Valuable Player, 1957-2019

The Most Valuable Player is one of many awards given out annually by the Associated Press. Many other organizations give out annual awards honoring the NFL's best players, and those winners may differ from this list.

Year	Player, team	Year	Player, team	Year	Player, team
1957	Jim Brown, Cleveland	1979	Earl Campbell, Houston	2000	Marshall Faulk, St. Louis
1958	Jim Brown, Cleveland	1980	Brian Sipe, Cleveland	2001	Kurt Warner, St. Louis
1959	Charlie Conerly, NY Giants	1981	Ken Anderson, Cincinnati	2002	Rich Gannon, Oakland
1960	Norm Van Brocklin, Philadelphia	1982	Mark Moseley, Washington	2003	Peyton Manning, Indianapolis;
1961	Paul Hornung, Green Bay	1983	Joe Theismann, Washington		Steve McNair, Tennessee
1962	Jim Taylor, Green Bay	1984	Dan Marino, Miami	2004	Peyton Manning, Indianapolis
1963	Y. A. Tittle, NY Giants	1985	Marcus Allen, Los Angeles	2005	Shaun Alexander, Seattle
1964	Johnny Unitas, Baltimore	1986	Lawrence Taylor, NY Giants	2006	LaDainian Tomlinson, San Diego
1965	Jim Brown, Cleveland	1987	John Elway, Denver	2007	Tom Brady, New England
1966	Bart Starr, Green Bay	1988	Boomer Esiason, Cincinnati	2008	Peyton Manning, Indianapolis
1967	Johnny Unitas, Baltimore	1989	Joe Montana, San Francisco	2009	Peyton Manning, Indianapolis
1968	Earl Morrall, Baltimore	1990	Joe Montana, San Francisco	2010	Tom Brady, New England
1969	Roman Gabriel, Los Angeles	1991	Thurman Thomas, Buffalo	2011	Aaron Rodgers, Green Bay
1970	John Brodie, San Francisco	1992	Steve Young, San Francisco	2012	Adrian Peterson, Minnesota
1971	Alan Page, Minnesota	1993	Emmitt Smith, Dallas	2013	Peyton Manning, Denver
1972	Larry Brown, Washington	1994	Steve Young, San Francisco	2014	Aaron Rodgers, Green Bay
1973	O.J. Simpson, Buffalo	1995	Brett Favre, Green Bay	2015	Cam Newton, Carolina
1974	Ken Stabler, Oakland	1996	Brett Favre, Green Bay	2016	Matt Ryan, Atlanta
1975	Fran Tarkenton, Minnesota	1997	Brett Favre, Green Bay;	2017	Tom Brady, New England
1976	Bert Jones, Baltimore		Barry Sanders, Detroit	2018	Patrick Mahomes, Kansas City
1977	Walter Payton, Chicago	1998	Terrell Davis, Denver	2019	Lamar Jackson, Baltimore
1978	Terry Bradshaw, Pittsburgh	1999	Kurt Warner, St. Louis		

All-Time Professional (NFL and AFL) Football Records

(at end of 2019 season; * = active in 2019; (a) includes AFL statistics; ** = 2-pt conversions scored)

All-Time Defensive Leaders

Interceptions, career: 81, Paul Krause, Washington-Minnesota, 1964-79.
Interceptions, season: 14, Dick "Night Train" Lane, L.A. Rams, 1952.
Interception touchdowns, career: 12, Rod Woodson, Pittsburgh-San Francisco-Baltimore Ravens-Oakland, 1987-2003.

Interception touchdowns, season: 4; Ken Houston, Houston, 1971; Jim Kearney, Kansas City, 1972; Eric Allen, Philadelphia, 1993.
Sacks, career (since 1982): 200.0, Bruce Smith, Buffalo-Washington, 1985-2003.
Sacks, season (since 1982): 22.5, Michael Strahan, NY Giants, 2001.

All-Time Scoring Leaders by Points

Player	Yrs	TD	PAT	FG	Total
Adam Vinatieri*	24	0	874**	599	2,673
Morten Andersen	25	0	849	565	2,544
Gary Anderson	23	0	820	538	2,434
Jason Hanson	21	0	665	495	2,150
John Carney	23	0	628	478	2,062
Matt Stover	19	0	591	471	2,004
George Blanda (a)	26	9	943	335	2,002
Jason Elam	17	0	675	436	1,983
John Kasay	20	0	587	461	1,970
Sebastian Janikowski	18	0	605	436	1,913
Phil Dawson	20	1	518	441	1,847
Stephen Gostkowski*	14	0	653	374	1,775
Matt Bryant*	18	0	567	397	1,758
Norm Johnson	18	0	638	366	1,736
David Akers	16	0	563	386	1,721

Points, season: 186, LaDainian Tomlinson, San Diego, 2006 (31 TDs).
Points, game: 40, Ernie Nevers, Chicago Cardinals vs. Chicago Bears, Nov. 28, 1929 (6 TDs, 4 PATs).
Touchdowns, season: 31, LaDainian Tomlinson, San Diego, 2006.
Touchdowns, game: 6; Ernie Nevers, Chicago Cardinals vs. Chicago Bears, Nov. 28, 1929 (6 rushing); Dub Jones, Cleveland Browns vs. Chicago Bears, Nov. 25, 1951 (4 rushing, 2 pass receptions); Gale Sayers, Chicago Bears vs. San Francisco, Dec. 12, 1965 (4 rushing, 1 pass reception, 1 punt return).

All-Time Scoring Leaders by Touchdowns

Player	Yrs	Rush	Rec	Ret	TD
Jerry Rice	20	10	197	1	208
Emmitt Smith	15	164	11	0	175
LaDainian Tomlinson	11	145	17	0	162
Randy Moss	14	0	156	1	157
Terrell Owens	15	3	153	0	156
Marcus Allen	16	123	21	1	145
Marshall Faulk	12	100	36	0	136
Cris Carter	16	0	130	1	131
Marvin Harrison	13	0	128	0	128
Jim Brown	9	106	20	0	126
Walter Payton	13	110	15	0	125
Larry Fitzgerald*	16	0	120	0	120
Adrian Peterson*	13	111	6	0	117
Antonio Gates	16	0	116	0	116
John Riggins	14	104	12	0	116

Points after TD, season: 75, Matt Prater, Denver, 2013.
Consecutive points after TD: 523, Stephen Gostkowski, New England, 2006-16.
Field goals, career: 599, Adam Vinatieri, New England-Indianapolis, 1996-2019.
Field goals, season: 44, David Akers, San Francisco, 2011.
Field goals, game: 8, Rob Bironas, Tennessee vs. Houston, Oct. 21, 2007.
Longest field goal: 64 yards, Matt Prater, Denver vs. Tennessee, Dec. 8, 2013.

All-Time Rushing Leaders
(ranked by rushing yards)

Player	Yrs	Att	Yds	Avg	Long	TD
Emmitt Smith	15	4,409	18,355	4.2	75T	164
Walter Payton	13	3,838	16,726	4.4	76	110
Frank Gore*	15	3,548	15,347	4.3	80T	79
Barry Sanders	10	3,062	15,269	5.0	85	99
Adrian Peterson*	13	3,036	14,216	4.7	90T	111
Curtis Martin	11	3,518	14,101	4.0	70T	90
LaDainian Tomlinson	11	3,174	13,684	4.3	85T	145
Jerome Bettis	13	3,479	13,662	3.9	71T	91
Eric Dickerson	11	2,996	13,259	4.4	85T	90
Tony Dorsett	12	2,936	12,739	4.3	99T	77
Jim Brown	9	2,359	12,312	5.2	80T	106
Marshall Faulk	12	2,836	12,279	4.3	71T	100
Edgerrin James	11	3,028	12,246	4.0	72	80
Marcus Allen	16	3,022	12,243	4.1	61T	123
Franco Harris	13	2,949	12,120	4.1	75T	91
Thurman Thomas	13	2,877	12,074	4.2	80T	65
Fred Taylor	13	2,534	11,695	4.6	80T	66
Steven Jackson	12	2,764	11,438	4.1	59T	69
John Riggins	14	2,916	11,352	3.9	66T	104
Corey Dillon	13	2,618	11,241	4.3	96T	82

Yards gained, season: 2,105, Eric Dickerson, L.A. Rams, 1984.
Yards gained, game: 296, Adrian Peterson, Minnesota vs. San Diego, Nov. 4, 2007.
Rushing TDs, career: 164, Emmitt Smith, Dallas-Arizona, 1990-2004.
Rushing TDs, season: 28, LaDainian Tomlinson, San Diego, 2006.
Rushing TDs, game: 6, Ernie Nevers, Chicago Cardinals vs. Chicago Bears, Nov. 28, 1929.
Rushing attempts, game: 45, Jamie Morris, Washington vs. Cincinnati, Dec. 17, 1988 (OT).
Longest run from scrimmage: 99 yards (TD), Tony Dorsett, Dallas vs. Minnesota, Jan. 3, 1983; Derrick Henry, Tennessee vs. Jacksonville, Dec. 6, 2018.

All-Time Receiving Leaders
(ranked by number of receptions)

Player	Yrs	No.	Yds	Avg	Long	TD
Jerry Rice	20	1,549	22,895	14.8	96T	197
Larry Fitzgerald*	16	1,378	17,083	12.4	80T	120
Tony Gonzalez	17	1,325	15,127	11.4	73T	111
Jason Witten*	16	1,215	12,977	10.7	69	72
Marvin Harrison	13	1,102	14,580	13.2	80T	128
Cris Carter	16	1,101	13,899	12.6	80T	130
Tim Brown	17	1,094	14,934	13.7	80T	100
Terrell Owens	15	1,078	15,934	14.8	98T	153
Anquan Boldin	14	1,076	13,779	12.8	79T	82
Reggie Wayne	14	1,070	14,345	13.4	80	82
Andre Johnson	14	1,062	14,185	13.4	77T	70
Steve Smith Sr.	16	1,031	14,731	14.3	80T	81
Isaac Bruce	16	1,024	15,208	14.9	80T	91
Hines Ward	14	1,000	12,083	12.1	85T	85
Randy Moss	14	982	15,292	15.6	82T	156
Brandon Marshall	13	970	12,351	12.7	75T	83
Antonio Gates	16	955	11,841	12.4	72T	116
Andre Reed	16	951	13,198	13.9	83T	87
Derrick Mason	15	943	12,061	12.8	79T	66
Art Monk	16	940	12,721	13.5	79T	68

Yards gained, career: 22,895, Jerry Rice, San Francisco-Oakland-Seattle, 1985-2004.
Yards gained, season: 1,964, Calvin Johnson, Detroit, 2012.
Yards gained, game: 336, Willie "Flipper" Anderson, L.A. Rams vs. New Orleans, Nov. 26, 1989 (OT).
Pass receptions, season: 149, Michael Thomas, New Orleans, 2019.
Pass receptions, game: 21, Brandon Marshall, Denver vs. Indianapolis, Dec. 13, 2009.

Touchdown receptions, career: 197, Jerry Rice, San Francisco-Oakland-Seattle, 1985-2004.
Touchdown receptions, season: 23, Randy Moss, New England, 2007.
Touchdown receptions, game: 5; Bob Shaw, Chicago Cardinals vs. Baltimore Colts, Oct. 2, 1950; Kellen Winslow, San Diego vs. Oakland, Nov. 22, 1981; Jerry Rice, San Francisco vs. Atlanta, Oct. 14, 1990.

All-Time Passing Leaders
(minimum 1,500 attempts; ranked by quarterback rating points)

Player	Yrs	Att	Comp	Yds	TD	Int	Rate[1]
Aaron Rodgers*	15	6,061	3,913	46,946	364	84	102.4
Russell Wilson*	8	3,777	2,436	29,734	227	68	101.2
Drew Brees	19	10,161	6,867	77,416	547	237	98.4
Tony Romo	13	4,335	2,829	34,183	248	117	97.1
Dak Prescott*	4	2,071	1,363	15,778	97	36	97.0
Tom Brady*	20	9,988	6,377	74,571	541	179	97.0
Steve Young	15	4,149	2,667	33,124	232	107	96.8
Kirk Cousins*	8	3,146	2,104	24,107	155	71	96.8
Peyton Manning	17	9,380	6,125	71,940	539	251	96.5
Philip Rivers*	16	7,591	4,908	59,271	397	198	95.1
Matt Ryan*	12	6,817	4,460	51,186	321	147	94.6
Ben Roethlisberger*	16	7,230	4,651	56,545	363	191	94.0
Kurt Warner	12	4,070	2,666	32,344	208	128	93.7
Carson Wentz*	4	2,055	1,311	14,191	97	35	92.7
Joe Montana	15	5,391	3,409	40,551	273	139	92.3
Jared Goff*	4	1,869	1,166	14,219	87	42	91.9
Derek Carr*	6	3,313	2,120	22,793	143	62	91.0
Chad Pennington	11	2,471	1,632	17,823	102	64	90.1
Ryan Tannehill*	7	3,197	2,030	23,176	145	81	89.8
Marcus Mariota*	5	1,765	1,110	13,207	76	44	89.6

(1) Rating points based on performances in the following categories: percentage of completions, percentage of touchdown passes, percentage of interceptions, and average gain per pass attempt.

Yards gained, career: 77,416, Drew Brees, San Diego-New Orleans, 2001-19.
Yards gained, season: 5,477, Peyton Manning, Denver, 2013.
Yards gained, game: 554, Norm Van Brocklin, L.A. Rams vs. NY Yanks, Sept. 28, 1951 (27 completions in 41 attempts).
Touchdowns passing, career: 547, Drew Brees, San Diego-New Orleans, 2001-19.
Touchdowns passing, season: 55, Peyton Manning, Denver, 2013.
Touchdowns passing, game: 7; Sid Luckman, Chicago Bears vs. NY Giants, Nov. 14, 1943; Adrian Burk, Philadelphia vs. Washington, Oct. 17, 1954; George Blanda, Houston vs. NY

Titans, Nov. 19, 1961; Y. A. Tittle, NY Giants vs. Washington, Oct. 28, 1962; Joe Kapp, Minnesota vs. Baltimore Colts, Sept. 28, 1969; Peyton Manning, Denver vs. Baltimore, Sept. 5, 2013; Nick Foles, Philadelphia vs. Oakland, Nov. 3, 2013; Drew Brees, New Orleans vs. NY Giants, Nov. 1, 2015.
Passes completed, career: 6,867, Drew Brees, San Diego-New Orleans, 2001-19.
Passes completed, season: 471, Drew Brees, New Orleans, 2016.
Passes completed, game: 45, Drew Bledsoe, New England vs. Minnesota, Nov. 13, 1994 (OT); Jared Goff, L.A. Rams vs. Tampa Bay, Sept. 29, 2019.

National Football League Franchise Origins

(Team: founding year, league. Home stadium location; subsequent history.)

Arizona Cardinals: 1920, American Professional Football Association (APFA)[1]. Chicago, 1920-59; St. Louis, 1960-87; Tempe, AZ, 1988-2005; Glendale, AZ, 2006-present.
Atlanta Falcons: 1966, NFL. Atlanta, GA, 1966-present.
Baltimore Ravens: 1996, NFL. Baltimore, 1996-present.
Buffalo Bills: 1960, American Football League (AFL)[2]. Buffalo, 1960-72; Orchard Park, NY, 1973-present.
Carolina Panthers: 1995, NFL. Clemson, SC, 1995; Charlotte, NC, 1996-present.
Chicago Bears: 1920, APFA. Decatur, IL, 1920; Chicago, 1921-present.
Cincinnati Bengals: 1968, AFL. Cincinnati, 1968-present.
Cleveland Browns: 1946, All-America Football Conference (AAFC)[3]. Cleveland, 1946-95; 1999-present.
Dallas Cowboys: 1960, NFL. Dallas, 1960-70; Irving, TX, 1971-2008; Arlington, TX, 2009-present.
Denver Broncos: 1960, AFL. Denver, 1960-present.
Detroit Lions: 1930, NFL. Portsmouth, OH, 1930-33; Detroit, 1934-74; Pontiac, MI, 1975-2001; Detroit, 2002-present.
Green Bay Packers: 1921, APFA. Green Bay, WI, 1921-present.
Houston Texans: 2002, NFL. Houston, 2002-present.
Indianapolis Colts: 1953, NFL[3]. Baltimore, 1953-83; Indianapolis, 1984-present.
Jacksonville Jaguars: 1995, NFL. Jacksonville, FL, 1995-present.
Kansas City Chiefs: 1960, AFL. Dallas, 1960-62; Kansas City, MO, 1963-present.
L.A. Chargers: 1960, AFL. Los Angeles, 1960; San Diego, 1961-2016. Los Angeles, 2017-present.

L.A. Rams: 1937, NFL. Cleveland, 1937-45; Los Angeles, 1946-79; Anaheim, CA, 1980-94; St. Louis, 1995-2015; L.A., 2016-present.
Miami Dolphins: 1966, AFL. Miami, 1966-1986; Miami Gardens, FL, 1987-present.
Minnesota Vikings: 1961, NFL. Bloomington, MN, 1961-81; Minneapolis, 1982-present.
New England Patriots: 1960, AFL. Boston, 1960-70; Foxborough, MA, 1971-present.
New Orleans Saints: 1967, NFL. New Orleans, 1967-2004; Baton Rouge and San Antonio, 2005; New Orleans, 2006-present.
NY Giants: 1925, NFL. New York, NY, 1925-73; 1975; New Haven, CT, 1973-74; E. Rutherford, NJ, 1976-present.
NY Jets: 1960, AFL. New York, NY, 1960-83; E. Rutherford, NJ, 1984-present.
Oakland Raiders: 1960, AFL. San Francisco, 1960-61; Oakland, CA, 1962-81; Los Angeles, 1982-94; Oakland, CA, 1995-present. The Raiders gained league approval, Mar. 2017, to move the franchise to Las Vegas, NV, for the start of the 2020 season.
Philadelphia Eagles: 1933, NFL. Philadelphia, 1933-present.
Pittsburgh Steelers: 1933, NFL. Pittsburgh, 1933-present.
San Francisco 49ers: 1946, AAFC. San Francisco, 1946-2013; Santa Clara, CA, 2014-present.
Seattle Seahawks: 1976, NFL. Seattle, 1976-present.
Tampa Bay Buccaneers: 1976, NFL. Tampa, FL, 1976-present.
Tennessee Titans: 1960, AFL. Houston, 1960-96; Memphis, 1997; Nashville, 1998-present.
Washington: 1932, NFL, as Redskins. Boston, 1932-36; Washington, DC, 1937-96; Landover, MD, 1997-present.

(1) The American Professional Football Association (APFA) was formed in 1920 to standardize the rules of professional football. In 1922, the name was changed to the National Football League (NFL). (2) The most successful of four leagues called the American Football League, or AFL (1926; 1936-37; 1940-41; 1960-69). Congress approved an NFL/AFL merger in 1966. Baltimore, Cleveland, and Pittsburgh agreed to join the 10 incoming AFL teams to form the American Football Conference. The unified NFL began play in 1970 with 26 teams. (3) The All-America Football Conference (AAFC), 1946-49. In 1950, three of its teams joined the NFL (Baltimore, Cleveland, and San Francisco). The Baltimore franchise failed, but the NFL awarded the city a second one, also called the Colts, in 1953.

NFL Stadiums

(**A** = A-Turf Titan, **F** = FieldTurf, **G** = Grass, **M** = Matrix SoftTop Convertible Turf,
N = Natural grass, **S** = Synthetic, **SI** = SISGrass, **TNS** = Turf-Nation-S5, **U** = UBU Speed Series S5-M)

Team: stadium, location, surface (year built)	Capacity[1]	Team: stadium, location, surface (year built)	Capacity[1]
Bears: Soldier Field[2], Chicago, IL, N (1924)	61,500	**Giants:** MetLife Stadium[10], East Rutherford, NJ, U (2010)	82,500
Bengals: Paul Brown Stadium, Cincinnati, OH, S (2000)	65,515	**Jaguars:** TIAA Bank Field[11], Jacksonville, FL, G (1995)	67,862
Bills: New Era Field[3], Orchard Park, NY, A (1973).	71,870	**Jets:** MetLife Stadium[10], East Rutherford, NJ, U (2010)	82,500
Broncos: Empower Field at Mile High[4], Denver, CO, N (2001)	76,125	**Lions:** Ford Field, Detroit, MI, F (2002)	64,500
Browns: FirstEnergy Stadium[5], Cleveland, OH, G (1999)	67,431	**Packers:** Lambeau Field[12], Green Bay, WI (1957)	81,441
Buccaneers: Raymond James Stadium, Tampa, FL, G (1998)	65,618	**Panthers:** Bank of America Stadium[13], Charlotte, NC, G (1996)	73,778
Cardinals: State Farm Stadium[6], Glendale, AZ, G (2006)	65,000	**Patriots:** Gillette Stadium, Foxborough, MA, F (2002)	65,878
Chargers: Dignity Health Sports Park[7], Carson, CA, G (2003)	27,000	**Raiders:** Oakland-Alameda County Coliseum[14], Oakland, CA, G (1966)	55,997
Chiefs: Arrowhead Stadium, Kansas City, MO, G (1972; fully renovated 2010)	76,416	**Rams:** Los Angeles Memorial Coliseum[15], Los Angeles, CA, N (1923)	76,750
Colts: Lucas Oil Stadium, Indianapolis, IN, F (2008)	63,000	**Ravens:** M&T Bank Stadium[16], Baltimore, MD, G (1998)	71,008
Cowboys: AT&T Stadium[8], Arlington, TX, M (2009)	80,000	**Saints:** Mercedes-Benz Superdome[17], New Orleans, LA, TNS (1975)	73,000
Dolphins: Hard Rock Stadium[9], Miami Gardens, FL, G (1987)	64,767	**Seahawks:** CenturyLink Field[18], Seattle, WA, F (2002)	68,740
Eagles: Lincoln Financial Field, Philadelphia, PA, N (2003)	69,696	**Steelers:** Heinz Field, Pittsburgh, PA, N (2001)	68,400
Falcons: Mercedes-Benz Stadium, Atlanta, GA, F (2017)	71,000	**Texans:** NRG Stadium[19], Houston, TX, S (2002)	71,995
49ers: Levi's Stadium, Santa Clara, CA, N (2014)	68,500	**Titans:** Nissan Stadium[20], Nashville, TN, N (1999)	69,143
		Vikings: U.S. Bank Stadium, Minneapolis, MN, U (2016)	66,655
		Washington: FedExField[21], Landover, MD, N (1997)	82,000

(1) As of the start of the 2019 season. (2) Renovation in 2002 replaced interior of stadium. (3) Formerly Rich Stadium (1973-98); Ralph Wilson Stadium (1998-2015). (4) Formerly INVESCO Field at Mile High (2001-11); Sports Authority Field at Mile High (2011-18); Broncos Stadium at Mile High (2018). (5) Formerly Cleveland Browns Stadium (1999-2012). (6) Formerly University of Phoenix Stadium (2006-18). (7) The Chargers relocated to Los Angeles prior to the 2017 season and played at StubHub Center, which was renamed Dignity Health Sports Park in 2019. (8) Formerly Cowboys Stadium (2009-12). (9) Formerly Joe Robbie Stadium (1987-96); Pro Player Park/Stadium (1996-2005); Dolphin's Stadium (2005-09; 2010); Land Shark Stadium (2009); Sun Life Stadium (2010-16); New Miami Stadium (2016). (10) Formerly New Meadowlands Stadium (2010-11). (11) Formerly Alltel Stadium (1997-2007); Jacksonville Municipal Stadium (1994-97, 2007-09); EverBank Field (2010-17). (12) Formerly City Stadium (1957-65). Renovation completed in 2003 added 11,625 seats. (13) Formerly Ericsson Stadium (1996-2003). (14) Formerly Oakland-Alameda County Coliseum (1966-98); Network Associates Coliseum (1998-2004); McAfee Stadium (2004-08); Oakland Coliseum (2008-11); O.co Coliseum (2011-15). (15) The Rams relocated to Los Angeles prior to the 2016 season. (16) Formerly PSINet Stadium (1998-2002); Ravens Stadium (2002-03). (17) Formerly Louisiana Superdome (1975-2011). (18) Formerly Seahawks Stadium (2002-04); Qwest Field (2004-11). (19) Formerly Reliant Stadium (2002-13). (20) Formerly Adelphia Coliseum (1999-2002); The Coliseum (2002-06); LP Field (2006-15). (21) Formerly Jack Kent Cooke Stadium (1997-99).

Pro Football Hall of Fame

Located in Canton, OH. * = Member elected in Feb. 2020 and scheduled to be inducted Aug. 7, 2021. www.profootballhof.com

Herb Adderley
Troy Aikman
George Allen
Larry Allen
Marcus Allen
Lance Alworth
Morten Andersen
Doug Atkins
*Steve Atwater
Morris "Red" Badgro
Champ Bailey
Lem Barney
Cliff Battles
Sammy Baugh
Bobby Beathard
Chuck Bednarik
Bert Bell
Bobby Bell
Raymond Berry
Elvin Bethea
Jerome Bettis
Charles Bidwill
Fred Biletnikoff
George Blanda
Mel Blount
Pat Bowlen
Terry Bradshaw
Gil Brandt
Robert Brazile
Derrick Brooks
Bob Brown
Jim Brown
Paul Brown
Roosevelt Brown
Tim Brown
Willie Brown
*Isaac Bruce
Junious "Buck"
  Buchanan
Nick Buoniconti
Dick Butkus
Jack Butler
Earl Campbell
Tony Canadeo
*Harold Carmichael
Joe Carr
Harry Carson
Cris Carter
Dave Casper
Guy Chamberlin
Jack Christiansen
Earl "Dutch" Clark
George Connor
Jim Conzelman
*Jimbo Covert
*Bill Cowher
Lou Creekmur
Larry Csonka
Curley Culp
Al Davis
Terrell Davis
Willie Davis
Dermontti Dawson
Len Dawson
Fred Dean
Edward DeBartolo Jr.
Joe DeLamielleure
Richard Dent
Eric Dickerson
Dan Dierdorf

*Bobby Dillon
Mike Ditka
Chris Doleman
Art Donovan
Tony Dorsett
John "Paddy" Driscoll
Bill Dudley
Tony Dungy
Kenny Easley
Glen "Turk" Edwards
Carl Eller
John Elway
Weeb Ewbank
Marshall Faulk
Brett Favre
Tom Fears
Jim Finks
Ray Flaherty
Len Ford
Dr. Daniel Fortmann
Dan Fouts
Benny Friedman
Frank Gatski
Bill George
Joe Gibbs
Frank Gifford
Sid Gillman
Tony Gonzalez
Otto Graham
Harold "Red" Grange
Bud Grant
Darrell Green
Joe Greene
Kevin Greene
Forrest Gregg
Bob Griese
Russ Grimm
Lou Groza
Ray Guy
Joe Guyon
George Halas
Charles Haley
Jack Ham
Dan Hampton
Chris Hanburger
John Hannah
*Cliff Harris
Franco Harris
Marvin Harrison
Bob Hayes
Mike Haynes
Ed Healey
Mel Hein
Ted Hendricks
Wilbur "Pete" Henry
Arnold Herber
Bill Hewitt
Gene Hickerson
*Winston Hill
Clarke Hinkle
Elroy "Crazylegs" Hirsch
Paul Hornung
Ken Houston
Robert "Cal" Hubbard
Sam Huff
Claude Humphrey
Lamar Hunt
*Steve Hutchinson
Don Hutson
Michael Irvin

Rickey Jackson
*Edgerrin James
Jimmy Johnson
*Jimmy Johnson
  (coach)
John Henry Johnson
Charlie Joiner
David "Deacon" Jones
Jerry Jones
Stan Jones
Walter Jones
Henry Jordan
Sonny Jurgensen
*Alex Karras
Jim Kelly
Leroy Kelly
Cortez Kennedy
Walt Kiesling
Frank "Bruiser" Kinard
Jerry Kramer
Paul Krause
Earl "Curly" Lambeau
Jack Lambert
Tom Landry
Dick "Night Train" Lane
Jim Langer
Willie Lanier
Steve Largent
Yale Lary
Dante Lavelli
Ty Law
Bobby Layne
Dick LeBeau
Alphonse "Tuffy"
  Leemans
Marv Levy
Ray Lewis
Bob Lilly
Floyd Little
Larry Little
James Lofton
Vince Lombardi
Howie Long
Ronnie Lott
Sid Luckman
Roy "Link" Lyman
Tom Mack
John Mackey
John Madden
Tim Mara
Wellington Mara
Gino Marchetti
Dan Marino
George Preston Marshall
Curtis Martin
Ollie Matson
Bruce Matthews
Kevin Mawae
Don Maynard
George McAfee
Mike McCormack
Randall McDaniel
Tommy McDonald
Hugh McElhenny
Johnny "Blood" McNally
Mike Michalske
Wayne Millner
Bobby Mitchell
Ron Mix
Art Monk

Joe Montana
Warren Moon
Lenny Moore
Randy Moss
Marion Motley
Mike Munchak
Anthony Muñoz
George Musso
Bronko Nagurski
Joe Namath
Earle "Greasy" Neale
Ernie Nevers
Ozzie Newsome
Ray Nitschke
Chuck Noll
Leo Nomellini
Jonathan Ogden
Merlin Olsen
Jim Otto
Steve Owen
Terrell Owens
Orlando Pace
Alan Page
Bill Parcells
Clarence "Ace" Parker
Jim Parker
Walter Payton
Joe Perry
Pete Pihos
*Troy Polamalu
Bill Polian
Fritz Pollard
John Randle
Hugh "Shorty" Ray
Andre Reed
Ed Reed
Dan Reeves
Mel Renfro
Jerry Rice
Les Richter
John Riggins
Jim Ringo
Willie Roaf
Dave Robinson
Johnny Robinson
Andy Robustelli
Art Rooney
Dan Rooney
Pete Rozelle
Ed Sabol
*Steve Sabol
Bob St. Clair
Barry Sanders
Charlie Sanders
Deion Sanders
Warren Sapp
Gale Sayers
Joe Schmidt
Tex Schramm
Junior Seau
Lee Roy Selmon
Shannon Sharpe
Billy Shaw
Art Shell
*Donnie Shell
Will Shields
Don Shula
O.J. Simpson
Mike Singletary

*Duke Slater
Jackie Slater
Bruce Smith
Emmitt Smith
Jackie Smith
*Mac Speedie
*Ed Sprinkle
Ken Stabler
John Stallworth
Dick Stanfel
Bart Starr
Roger Staubach
Ernie Stautner
Jan Stenerud
Dwight Stephenson
Michael Strahan
Hank Stram
Ken Strong
Joe Stydahar
Lynn Swann
*Paul Tagliabue
Fran Tarkenton
Charley Taylor
Jason Taylor
Jim Taylor
Lawrence "LT" Taylor
Derrick Thomas
Emmitt Thomas
Thurman Thomas
Jim Thorpe
Mick Tingelhoff
Andre Tippett
Y. A. Tittle
LaDainian Tomlinson
George Trafton
Charley Trippi
Emlen Tunnell
Clyde "Bulldog" Turner
Johnny Unitas
Gene Upshaw
Brian Urlacher
Norm Van Brocklin
Steve Van Buren
Doak Walker
Bill Walsh
Paul Warfield
Kurt Warner
Bob Waterfield
Mike Webster
Roger Wehrli
Arnie Weinmeister
Randy White
Reggie White
Dave Wilcox
Aeneas Williams
Bill Willis
Larry Wilson
Ralph Wilson Jr.
Kellen Winslow
Alex Wojciechowicz
Ron Wolf
Willie Wood
Rod Woodson
Rayfield Wright
Ron Yary
*George Young
Steve Young
Jack Youngblood
Gary Zimmerman

All-Time NFL Coaching Victories

(at end of 2019 season; ranked by overall career wins; * = active in 2019)

Coach	Team	Yrs	Regular Season				Overall			
			W	L	T	Pct	W	L	T	Pct
Don Shula	Colts, Dolphins	33	328	156	6	.677	347	173	6	.666
George Halas	Bears	40	318	148	31	.682	324	151	31	.682
Bill Belichick*	Browns, Patriots	25	273	127	0	.683	304	139	0	.686
Tom Landry	Cowboys	29	250	162	6	.607	270	178	6	.603
Earl (Curly) Lambeau	Packers, Cardinals, Redskins	33	226	132	22	.631	229	134	22	.631
Andy Reid*	Eagles, Chiefs	21	207	128	1	.618	222	142	1	.610
Chuck Noll	Steelers	23	193	148	1	.566	209	156	1	.572
Marty Schottenheimer	Browns, Chiefs, Redskins, Chargers	21	200	126	1	.613	205	139	1	.596
Dan Reeves	Broncos, Giants, Falcons	23	190	165	2	.535	201	174	2	.536
Chuck Knox	L.A. Rams, Bills, Seahawks	22	186	147	1	.558	193	158	1	.550
Bill Parcells	Giants, Patriots, Jets, Cowboys	19	172	130	1	.569	183	138	1	.570
Tom Coughlin	Jaguars, Giants	20	170	150	0	.531	182	157	0	.537
Mike Shanahan	L.A. Raiders, Broncos, Redskins	20	170	138	0	.552	178	144	0	.553
Jeff Fisher	Houston/Tennessee Oilers, Titans, St. Louis/ L.A. Rams	22	173	165	1	.512	178	171	1	.510
Mike Holmgren	Packers, Seahawks	17	161	111	0	.592	174	122	0	.588

Note: Official NFL records do not include All-America Football Conference statistics.

BASEBALL

Playoff Results, 2020

American League

American League Wild Card Series (best-of-three): Tampa Bay 2, Toronto 0; Oakland 2, Chicago White Sox 1; Houston 2, Minnesota 0; NY Yankees 2, Cleveland 0.

American League Division Series (ALDS): Tampa Bay 3, NY Yankees 2; Houston 3, Oakland 1.

American League Championship Series (ALCS): Tampa Bay 4, Houston 3.

National League

National League Wild Card Series (best-of-three): L.A. Dodgers 2, Milwaukee 0; Atlanta 2, Cincinnati 0; Miami 2, Chicago Cubs 0; San Diego 2, St. Louis 1.

National League Division Series (NLDS): L.A. Dodgers 3, San Diego 0; Atlanta 3, Miami 0.

National League Championship Series (NLCS): L.A. Dodgers 4, Atlanta 3.

World Series, 2020: L.A. Dodgers Win World Series Amid COVID-19 Pandemic

The Los Angeles Dodgers won their first World Series since 1988, defeating the Tampa Bay Rays in six games and ending a shortened 2020 season that was unique and challenging due to the coronavirus pandemic. Dodgers outfielder Mookie Betts scored the go-ahead run in the bottom of the sixth inning and added a solo home run in the eighth in a 3-1, Game 6 victory, Oct. 27, 2020, at Globe Life Field in Arlington, TX. Julio Urías retired all seven batters he faced for the save.

Corey Seager batted .400 for the Dodgers in the series with a pair of homers and was named World Series MVP. Seager and Justin Turner each had four hits for L.A. in Game 4 on Oct. 24, but the Rays pulled out a dramatic 8-7 win that tied the series. With two outs and two base runners in the bottom of the ninth, Brett Phillips singled off Kenley Jansen, scoring Kevin Kiermaier from 2nd with the game-tying run. Chris Taylor mishandled the ball in right-center and Randy Arozarena scored the game-winner when catcher Will Smith missed the relay throw from Max Muncy. Arozarena, who batted .364 with three home runs in the World Series, set MLB records for a single postseason with 10 homers and 29 hits in 2020.

Veteran left-hander Clayton Kershaw earned two wins, striking out eight in an 8-3 Dodgers' Game 1 victory, Oct. 20, and aided by home runs from Joc Pederson and Max Muncy in a 4-2 Game 5 victory Oct. 25.

Justin Turner was taken out of Game 6 after seven innings because he had tested positive for COVID-19. The veteran third baseman was criticized for appearing without a mask on the field during the Dodgers' victory celebration.

Game 1
Oct. 20 at Globe Life Field, Arlington, TX. Attendance: 11,388. Game time: 3:24.

	1	2	3	4	5	6	7	8	9		R	H	E
Tampa Bay Rays	0	0	0	0	1	0	2	0	0		3	6	0
L.A. Dodgers	0	0	0	2	4	2	0	0	X		8	10	0

Winning pitcher: Clayton Kershaw
Losing pitcher: Tyler Glasnow

Game 2
Oct. 21 at Globe Life Field, Arlington, TX. Attendance: 11,472. Game time: 3:40.

	1	2	3	4	5	6	7	8	9		R	H	E
Tampa Bay Rays	1	0	0	2	2	1	0	0	0		6	10	0
L.A. Dodgers	0	0	0	2	0	1	0	1	0		4	5	1

Winning pitcher: Nick Anderson
Losing pitcher: Tony Gonsolin
Save: Diego Castillo

Game 3
Oct. 23 at Globe Life Field, Arlington, TX. Attendance: 11,447. Game time: 3:14.

	1	2	3	4	5	6	7	8	9		R	H	E
L.A. Dodgers	1	0	2	2	0	1	0	0	0		6	10	0
Tampa Bay Rays	0	0	0	0	1	0	0	0	1		2	4	0

Winning pitcher: Walker Buehler
Losing pitcher: Charlie Morton

Game 4
Oct. 24 at Globe Life Field, Arlington, TX. Attendance: 11,441. Game time: 4:10.

	1	2	3	4	5	6	7	8	9		R	H	E
L.A. Dodgers	1	0	1	0	1	1	2	1	0		7	15	2
Tampa Bay Rays	0	0	0	1	1	3	1	0	2		8	10	0

Winning pitcher: John Curtiss
Losing pitcher: Kenley Jansen

Game 5
Oct. 25 at Globe Life Field, Arlington, TX. Attendance: 11,437. Game time: 3:30.

	1	2	3	4	5	6	7	8	9		R	H	E
L.A. Dodgers	2	1	0	0	1	0	0	0	0		4	6	1
Tampa Bay Rays	0	0	2	0	0	0	0	0	0		2	7	0

Winning pitcher: Clayton Kershaw
Losing pitcher: Tyler Glasnow
Save: Blake Treinen

Game 6
Oct. 27 at Globe Life Field, Arlington, TX. Attendance: 11,437. Game time: 3:28.

	1	2	3	4	5	6	7	8	9		R	H	E
Tampa Bay Rays	1	0	0	0	0	0	0	0	0		1	5	0
L.A. Dodgers	0	0	0	0	0	2	0	1	X		3	5	0

Winning pitcher: Victor González
Losing pitcher: Nick Anderson
Save: Julio Urías

MLB 2020: Los Angeles Dodgers Win World Series

The coronavirus pandemic forced a months-long delay to the 2020 Major League Baseball regular season, which began on July 23, 2020. Spring training had been suspended on Mar. 12, and the planned Mar. 26 start date was initially delayed two weeks. But the Centers for Disease Control and Prevention Mar. 15 recommended canceling or postponing events with more than 50 people for eight weeks. After lengthy negotiations with the players association, MLB announced plans for a regular season reduced from its standard 162 games to 60 and with an expanded 16-team postseason with a best-of-three Wild Card round. All playoff games after the wild card round were played at neutral sites. The 2020 regular season also featured the use of designated hitters in both leagues, seven-inning doubleheaders, and adjusted extra-inning rules. Regular season games were played at each team's home stadium without fans in attendance, and MLB implemented extensive health and safety protocols to try to prevent the spread of COVID-19. Several series were postponed due to multiple positive coronavirus tests, yet all but two teams (St. Louis and Detroit) completed the entire 60-game slate.

The L.A. Dodgers (43-17) topped the majors with 118 homers and had MLB's best team ERA (3.02) on the way to their eighth consecutive National League West title. The Dodgers topped Atlanta in the National League Championship Series after dropping three of the first four games. Cody Bellinger hit a tiebreaking solo homer off the Braves' Chris Martin in the seventh inning of Game 7, and L.A. won, 4-3, Oct. 18, at Globe Life Field in Arlington, TX. Dodgers shortstop Corey Seager set NLCS records with five homers and 11 RBI and was voted NLCS Most Valuable Player.

The Dodgers-Braves series marked the first games in 2020 that MLB allowed fans to attend. The NLCS averaged just under 11,000 fans per game at 40,300-capacity Globe Life Field, the Texas Rangers' stadium, which opened in 2020. The Dodgers reached their fourth NLCS in the last five seasons with an NL Division Series sweep over the San Diego Padres. The NL East champion Braves reached the NLCS with an NL Division Series sweep over the Marlins, who reached the postseason after losing 105 games in 2019.

The Tampa Bay Rays won the AL East Division and defeated the NY Yankees in five games in their AL Division Series. The Rays then beat the Houston Astros in seven games in the American League Championship Series at Petco Park in San Diego. Tampa Bay won the first three games of the series before Houston took the next three. In the series finale Oct. 17, Charlie Morton won his second game of the series in a 4-2 victory. Rays outfielder Randy Arozarena, who had tested positive for the coronavirus during the season, batted .321 with four homers against Houston to win the ALCS MVP.

Yankees infielder DJ LeMahieu led the majors with a .364 batting average, becoming the first player in the modern era to win undisputed batting titles in both leagues. Yankees first baseman Luke Voit topped the majors with 22 home runs in the abbreviated season, and Washington's Juan Soto became the NL's youngest-ever batting champ with a .351 batting average. The 21-year-old Nationals outfielder also led MLB in slugging (.695) and on-base percentage (.490).

Cleveland's Shane Bieber led the majors with a 1.63 ERA and 122 strikeouts. The shortened season produced two no-hitters. Chicago White Sox right-hander Lucas Giolito struck out 13 in a 4-0 win over the Pittsburgh Pirates, Aug. 25, at Guaranteed Rate Field in Chicago. The Cubs' Alec Mills tossed a 12-0 no-hitter against the Brewers at Miller Park in Milwaukee, Sept. 13.

National League Final Standings, 2020

(* = wild card)

Eastern Division

Team	W	L	PCT	GB	Home	Road	vs. East	vs. Central	vs. West	vs. AL
Atlanta	35	25	.583	–	19-11	16-14	24-16	0-0	0-0	11-9
Miami	31	29	.517	4	11-15	20-14	21-19	0-0	0-0	10-10
Philadelphia	28	32	.467	7	19-13	9-19	21-19	0-0	0-0	7-13
NY Mets	26	34	.433	9	12-17	14-17	17-23	0-0	0-0	9-11
Washington	26	34	.433	9	15-18	11-16	17-23	0-0	0-0	9-11

Central Division

Team	W	L	PCT	GB	Home	Road	vs. East	vs. Central	vs. West	vs. AL
Chicago Cubs	34	26	.567	–	19-14	15-12	0-0	22-18	0-0	12-8
St. Louis	30	28	.517	3	14-13	16-15	0-0	22-18	0-0	8-10
Cincinnati*	31	29	.517	3	16-13	15-16	0-0	21-19	0-0	10-10
Milwaukee*	29	31	.483	5	15-14	14-17	0-0	19-21	0-0	10-10
Pittsburgh	19	41	.317	15	13-19	6-22	0-0	16-24	0-0	3-17

Western Division

Team	W	L	PCT	GB	Home	Road	vs. East	vs. Central	vs. West	vs. AL
L.A. Dodgers	43	17	.717	–	21-9	22-8	0-0	0-0	27-13	16-4
San Diego	37	23	.617	6	21-11	16-12	0-0	0-0	24-16	13-7
San Francisco	29	31	.483	14	19-14	10-17	0-0	0-0	18-22	11-9
Colorado	26	34	.433	17	12-18	14-16	0-0	0-0	17-23	9-11
Arizona	25	35	.417	18	16-14	9-21	0-0	0-0	14-26	11-9

American League Final Standings, 2020

(* = wild card)

Eastern Division

Team	W	L	PCT	GB	Home	Road	vs. East	vs. Central	vs. West	vs. NL
Tampa Bay	40	20	.667	–	20-9	20-11	27-13	0-0	0 0	13-7
NY Yankees	33	27	.550	7	22-9	11-18	23-17	0-0	0-0	10-10
Toronto*	32	28	.533	8	17-9	15-19	22-18	0-0	0-0	10-10
Baltimore	25	35	.417	15	13-20	12-15	14-26	0-0	0-0	11-9
Boston	24	36	.400	16	11-20	13-16	14-26	0-0	0-0	10-10

Central Division

Team	W	L	PCT	GB	Home	Road	vs. East	vs. Central	vs. West	vs. NL
Minnesota	36	24	.600	–	24-7	12-17	0-0	23-17	0-0	13-7
Cleveland	35	25	.583	1	18-12	17-13	0-0	23-17	0-0	12-8
Chicago White Sox*	35	25	.583	1	18-12	17-13	0-0	25-15	0-0	10-10
Kansas City	26	34	.433	10	15-15	11-19	0-0	17-23	0-0	9-11
Detroit	23	35	.397	12	15-15	11-20	0-0	12-28	0-0	11-7

Western Division

Team	W	L	PCT	GB	Home	Road	vs. East	vs. Central	vs. West	vs. NL
Oakland	36	24	.600	–	22-10	14-14	0-0	0-0	26-14	10-10
Houston	29	31	.483	7	20-8	9-23	0-0	0-0	19-21	10-10
Seattle	27	33	.450	9	14-10	13-23	0-0	0-0	20-20	7-13
L.A. Angels	26	34	.433	10	16-15	10-19	0-0	0-0	19-21	7-13
Texas	22	38	.367	14	16-14	6-24	0-0	0-0	16-24	6-14

Note: Teams played a 60-game regular season (well below the standard 162 games) due to the coronavirus pandemic. Cleveland finished second in the AL Central over the Chicago White Sox due to a better record in head-to-head games (8-2); Milwaukee earned the second NL wild card slot over San Francisco due to a better intradivision record (19-21).

National League Team Statistics, 2020

Team Batting

Team	AVG	AB	R	H	HR	RBI
NY Mets	.272	2,023	286	551	86	278
Atlanta Braves	.268	2,074	348	556	103	338
Washington Nationals	.264	1,968	293	519	66	279
San Francisco Giants	.263	2,019	299	532	81	290
Colorado Rockies	.257	2,057	275	528	63	264
Philadelphia Phillies	.257	1,948	306	500	82	289
San Diego Padres	.257	1,972	325	506	95	312
L.A. Dodgers	.256	2,042	349	523	118	327
Miami Marlins	.244	1,935	263	472	60	247
Arizona Diamondbacks	.241	1,997	269	482	58	255
St. Louis Cardinals	.234	1,752	240	410	51	231
Milwaukee Brewers	.223	1,920	247	429	75	238
Chicago Cubs	.220	1,918	265	422	74	248
Pittsburgh Pirates	.220	1,932	219	425	59	210
Cincinnati Reds	.212	1,842	243	390	90	237

Team Pitching

Team	ERA	IP	H	BB	K	SV
L.A. Dodgers	3.02	538.2	424	145	517	15
Cincinnati Reds	3.84	504.0	401	213	615	9
San Diego Padres	3.86	520.1	456	170	565	13
St. Louis Cardinals	3.90	473.0	376	204	464	13
Chicago Cubs	3.99	518.1	451	182	523	16
Milwaukee Brewers	4.16	517.1	446	189	614	14
Atlanta Braves	4.41	524.1	494	220	506	13
San Francisco Giants	4.64	517.2	474	210	488	13
Pittsburgh Pirates	4.68	513.0	451	249	536	6
Arizona Diamondbacks	4.84	518.1	506	235	524	13
Miami Marlins	4.86	504.0	506	226	451	18
NY Mets	4.98	513.1	511	219	574	11
Washington Nationals	5.09	503.2	548	216	508	12
Philadelphia Phillies	5.14	497.0	550	185	532	11
Colorado Rockies	5.59	526.1	579	205	393	16

American League Team Statistics, 2020

Team Batting

Team	AVG	AB	R	H	HR	RBI
Boston Red Sox	.265	2,083	292	552	81	278
Chicago White Sox	.261	2,047	306	534	96	294
Baltimore Orioles	.258	2,026	274	523	77	264
Toronto Blue Jays	.255	2,023	302	516	88	288
L.A. Angels	.248	2,020	294	501	85	285
NY Yankees	.247	1,915	315	473	94	301
Detroit Tigers	.245	1,893	249	463	62	242
Kansas City Royals	.244	1,988	248	485	68	237
Minnesota Twins	.242	1,937	269	468	91	258
Houston Astros	.240	1,992	279	478	69	268
Tampa Bay Rays	.238	1,975	289	470	80	274
Cleveland Indians	.228	1,959	248	446	59	234
Seattle Mariners	.226	1,929	254	435	60	244
Oakland Athletics	.225	1,908	274	430	71	264
Texas Rangers	.217	1,936	224	420	62	204

Team Pitching

Team	ERA	IP	H	BB	K	SV
Cleveland Indians	3.29	536.0	440	157	621	20
Tampa Bay Rays	3.56	527.2	475	168	552	23
Minnesota Twins	3.58	513.1	448	170	535	17
Oakland Athletics	3.77	515.1	471	165	506	17
Chicago White Sox	3.81	527.0	448	217	523	13
Kansas City Royals	4.30	517.0	500	211	517	19
Houston Astros	4.31	524.0	472	217	526	16
NY Yankees	4.35	500.2	455	168	528	14
Baltimore Orioles	4.51	518.2	489	192	487	11
Toronto Blue Jays	4.60	524.2	517	250	519	17
Texas Rangers	5.02	516.2	479	236	489	10
Seattle Mariners	5.03	516.2	482	230	469	15
L.A. Angels	5.09	525.1	492	199	523	12
Boston Red Sox	5.58	524.0	587	252	537	14
Detroit Tigers	5.63	492.1	511	192	444	11

Major League Leaders, 2020
National League Leaders, 2020

Batting Average: Juan Soto, Washington, .351; Freddie Freeman, Atlanta, .341; Marcell Ozuna, Atlanta, .338; Trea Turner, Washington, .335; Donovan Solano, San Francisco, .326; Michael Conforto, NY Mets, .322.

On-base percentage: Juan Soto, Washington, .490; Freddie Freeman, Atlanta, .462; Marcell Ozuna, Atlanta, .431; Bryce Harper, Philadelphia, .420; Paul Goldschmidt, St. Louis, .417; Michael Conforto, NY Mets, .412.

Slugging: Juan Soto, Washington, .695; Freddie Freeman, Atlanta, .640; Marcell Ozuna, Atlanta, .636; Dominic Smith, NY Mets, .616; Wil Myers, San Diego, .606; Trea Turner, Washington, .588.

Runs Scored: Freddie Freeman, Atlanta, 51; Fernando Tatís Jr., San Diego, 50; Dansby Swanson, Atlanta, 49; Mookie Betts, L.A. Dodgers, 47; Trea Turner, Washington, 46; Ronald Acuña Jr., Atlanta, 46.

Runs Batted In: Marcell Ozuna, Atlanta, 56; Freddie Freeman, Atlanta, 53; Manny Machado, San Diego, 47; Fernando Tatís Jr., San Diego, 45; Charlie Blackmon, Colorado, 42; Dominic Smith, NY Mets, 42.

Hits: Trea Turner, Washington, 78; Marcell Ozuna, Atlanta, 77; Freddie Freeman, Atlanta, 73; Manny Machado, San Diego, 68; Trevor Story, Colorado, 68; Charlie Blackmon, Colorado, 67.

Doubles: Freddie Freeman, Atlanta, 23; Dominic Smith, NY Mets, 21; Christian Walker, Arizona, 18; Nick Markakis, Atlanta, 15; Donovan Solano, San Francisco, 15; Trea Turner, Washington, 15; Dansby Swanson, Atlanta, 15; Jake Cronenworth, San Diego, 15.

Triples: Trevor Story, Colorado, 4; Mike Yastrzemski, San Francisco, 4; Trea Turner, Washington, 4; Asdrúbal Cabrera, Washington, 3; Eduardo Escobar, Arizona, 3; Brandon Nimmo, NY Mets, 3; Trent Grisham, San Diego, 3; Jake Cronenworth, San Diego, 3; Garrett Hampson, Colorado, 3.

Home Runs: Marcell Ozuna, Atlanta, 18; Fernando Tatís Jr., San Diego, 17; AJ Pollock, L.A. Dodgers, 16; Manny Machado, San Diego, 16; Kole Calhoun, Arizona, 16; Adam Duvall, Atlanta, 16; Mookie Betts, L.A. Dodgers, 16; Pete Alonso, NY Mets, 16.

Stolen Bases: Trevor Story, Colorado, 15; Roman Quinn, Philadelphia, 12; Trea Turner, Washington, 12; Fernando Tatís Jr., San Diego, 11; Starling Marte, Miami-Arizona, 10; Mookie Betts, L.A. Dodgers, 10; Trent Grisham, San Diego, 10.

Pitching Wins: Yu Darvish, Chicago Cubs, 8; Max Fried, Atlanta, 7; Zach Davies, San Diego, 7; Clayton Kershaw, L.A. Dodgers, 6; Kyle Hendricks, Chicago Cubs, 6; Pablo López, Miami, 6; David Peterson, NY Mets, 6.

Earned Run Average: Trevor Bauer, Cincinnati, 1.73; Yu Darvish, Chicago Cubs, 2.01; Dinelson Lamet, San Diego, 2.09; Jacob deGrom, NY Mets, 2.38; Zach Davies, San Diego, 2.73; Zac Gallen, Arizona, 2.75.

Strikeouts: Jacob deGrom, NY Mets, 104; Trevor Bauer, Cincinnati, 100; Aaron Nola, Philadelphia, 96; Yu Darvish, Chicago Cubs, 93; Dinelson Lamet, San Diego, 93; Max Scherzer, Washington, 92.

Saves: Josh Hader, Milwaukee, 13; Brandon Kintzler, Miami, 12; Mark Melancon, Atlanta, 11; Kenley Jansen, L.A. Dodgers, 11; Daniel Hudson, Washington, 10; Jeremy Jeffress, Chicago Cubs, 8; Raisel Iglesias, Cincinnati, 8.

American League Leaders, 2020

Batting Average: DJ LeMahieu, NY Yankees, .364; Tim Anderson, Chicago White Sox, .322; David Fletcher, L.A. Angels, .319; José Abreu, Chicago White Sox, .317; Alex Verdugo, Boston, .308; Lourdes Gurriel Jr., Toronto, .308.

On-Base Percentage: DJ LeMahieu, NY Yankees, .421; Anthony Rendon, L.A. Angels, .418; Nelson Cruz, Minnesota, .397; Mike Trout, L.A. Angels, .390; Mark Canha, Oakland, .387; José Ramírez, Cleveland, .386.

Slugging: José Abreu, Chicago White Sox, .617; Luke Voit, NY Yankees, .610; José Ramírez, Cleveland, .607; Mike Trout, L.A. Angels, .603; Nelson Cruz, Minnesota, .595; DJ LeMahieu, NY Yankees, .590.

Runs Scored: José Ramírez, Cleveland, 45; Tim Anderson, Chicago White Sox, 45; José Abreu, Chicago White Sox, 43; DJ LeMahieu, NY Yankees, 41; Mike Trout, L.A. Angels, 41; Luke Voit, NY Yankees, 41; Cavan Biggio, Toronto, 41.

Runs Batted In: José Abreu, Chicago White Sox, 60; Luke Voit, NY Yankees, 52; Mike Trout, L.A. Angels, 46; José Ramírez, Cleveland, 46; Rafael Devers, Boston, 43; Eddie Rosario, Minnesota, 42; Matt Olson, Oakland, 42; Kyle Tucker, Houston, 42.

Hits: José Abreu, Chicago White Sox, 76; DJ LeMahieu, NY Yankees, 71; Whit Merrifield, Kansas City, 70; Tim Anderson, Chicago White Sox, 67; César Hernández, Cleveland, 66; David Fletcher, L.A. Angels, 66.

Doubles: César Hernández, Cleveland, 20; José Iglesias, Baltimore, 17; J.D. Martinez, Boston, 16; Maikel Franco, Kansas City, 16; José Ramírez, Cleveland, 16; Alex Verdugo, Boston, 16; Rafael Devers, Boston, 16; Cavan Biggio, Toronto, 16.

Triples: Kyle Tucker, Houston, 6; Kevin Kiermaier, Tampa Bay, 3; Jeimer Candelario, Detroit, 3; Adalberto Mondesi, Kansas City, 3; Isiah Kiner-Falefa, Texas, 3; Yoan Moncada, Chicago White Sox, 3; Cedric Mullins, Baltimore, 3.

Home Runs: Luke Voit, NY Yankees, 22; José Abreu, Chicago White Sox, 19; Mike Trout, L.A. Angels, 17; José Ramírez, Cleveland, 17; Nelson Cruz, Minnesota, 16; Teoscar Hernández, Toronto, 16.

Stolen Bases: Adalberto Mondesi, Kansas City, 24; Whit Merrifield, Kansas City, 12; Manuel Margot, Tampa Bay, 12; Dylan Moore, Seattle, 12; José Ramírez, Cleveland, 10; Luis Robert, Chicago White Sox, 9.

Pitching Wins: Shane Bieber, Cleveland, 8; Gerrit Cole, NY Yankees, 7; Marco Gonzales, Seattle, 7; eight pitchers tied with 6.

Earned Run Average: Shane Bieber, Cleveland, 1.63; Dallas Keuchel, Chicago White Sox, 1.99; Chris Bassitt, Oakland, 2.29; Hyun-jin Ryu, Toronto, 2.69; Kenta Maeda, Minnesota, 2.70; Gerrit Cole, NY Yankees, 2.84.

Strikeouts: Shane Bieber, Cleveland, 122; Lucas Giolito, Chicago White Sox, 97; Gerrit Cole, NY Yankees, 94; Tyler Glasnow, Tampa Bay, 91; Lance Lynn, Texas, 89; Carlos Carrasco, Cleveland, 82.

Saves: Brad Hand, Cleveland, 16; Liam Hendriks, Oakland, 14; Alex Colomé, Chicago White Sox, 12; Ryan Pressly, Houston, 12; Matt Barnes, Boston, 9; Taylor Rogers, Minnesota, 9.

All-Time Major League Single-Season Leaders

Source: www.mlb.com; * = Active in 2020 season; records for "modern" era beginning in 1901.

Home Runs

Barry Bonds (2001)	73
Mark McGwire (1998)	70
Sammy Sosa (1998)	66
Mark McGwire (1999)	65
Sammy Sosa (2001)	64
Sammy Sosa (1999)	63
Roger Maris (1961)	61
Babe Ruth (1927)	60

Runs Scored

Babe Ruth (1921)	177
Lou Gehrig (1936)	167
Lou Gehrig (1931)	163
Babe Ruth (1928)	163
Chuck Klein (1930)	158
Babe Ruth (1920, 1927)	158
Rogers Hornsby (1929)	156
Kiki Cuyler (1930)	155

Hits

Ichiro Suzuki (2004)	262
George Sisler (1920)	257
Lefty O'Doul (1929)	254
Bill Terry (1930)	254
Al Simmons (1925)	253
Rogers Hornsby (1922)	250
Chuck Klein (1930)	250
Ty Cobb (1911)	248

Runs Batted In

Hack Wilson (1930)	191
Lou Gehrig (1931)	184
Hank Greenberg (1937)	183
Jimmie Foxx (1938)	175
Lou Gehrig (1927)	175
Lou Gehrig (1930)	174
Babe Ruth (1921)	171
Hank Greenburg (1935)	170
Chuck Klein (1930)	170

Batting Average

Rogers Hornsby (1924)	.424
Nap Lajoie (1901)	.421
George Sisler (1922)	.420
Ty Cobb (1911)	.420
Ty Cobb (1912)	.410
Joe Jackson (1911)	.408
George Sisler (1920)	.407
Ted Williams (1941)	.406

Stolen Bases

Rickey Henderson (1982)	130
Lou Brock (1974)	118
Vince Coleman (1985)	110
Vince Coleman (1987)	109
Rickey Henderson (1983)	108
Vince Coleman (1986)	107
Maury Wills (1962)	104
Rickey Henderson (1980)	100

Walks (Batter)

Barry Bonds (2004)	232
Barry Bonds (2002)	198
Barry Bonds (2001)	177
Babe Ruth (1923)	170
Mark McGwire (1998)	162
Ted Williams (1947, 1949)	162
Ted Williams (1946)	156

Strikeouts (Batter)

Mark Reynolds (2009)	223
Adam Dunn (2012)	222
Chris Davis* (2016)	219
Yoán Moncada* (2018)	217
Chris Carter (2013)	212
Mark Reynolds (2010)	211
Giancarlo Stanton (2018)	211
Chris Davis (2015)	208
Aaron Judge (2017)	208

Earned Run Average

Dutch Leonard (1914)	0.96
Mordecai "Three Finger" Brown (1906)	1.04
Bob Gibson (1968)	1.12
Christy Mathewson (1909)	1.14
Walter Johnson (1913)	1.14
Jack Pfiester (1907)	1.15
Addie Joss (1908)	1.16
Carl Lundgren (1907)	1.17

Wins (Pitcher)

Jack Chesbro (1904)	41
Ed Walsh (1908)	40
Christy Mathewson (1908)	37
Walter Johnson (1913)	36
Joe McGinnity (1904)	35
Grover Alexander (1916)	33
Walter Johnson (1912)	33
Cristy Mathewson (1904)	33
Cy Young (1901)	33

Strikeouts (Pitcher)

Nolan Ryan (1973)	383
Sandy Koufax (1965)	382
Randy Johnson (2001)	372
Nolan Ryan (1974)	367
Randy Johnson (1999)	364
Rube Waddell (1904)	349
Bob Feller (1946)	348
Randy Johnson (2000)	347

Saves

Francisco Rodríguez (2008)	62
Edwin Díaz* (2018)	57
Bobby Thigpen (1990)	57
Eric Gagne (2003)	55
John Smoltz (2002)	55
Trevor Hoffman (1998)	53
Randy Myers (1993)	53
Mariano Rivera (2004)	53

All-Time Major League Leaders

Source: www.mlb.com; * = Active in 2020 season; career records for players in "modern" era beginning in 1901 may include statistics from preceding years.

Games

Pete Rose	3,562
Carl Yastrzemski	3,308
Hank Aaron	3,298
Rickey Henderson	3,081
Ty Cobb	3,035
Eddie Murray	3,026
Stan Musial	3,026
Cal Ripken Jr.	3,001
Willie Mays	2,992
Barry Bonds	2,986

At Bats

Pete Rose	14,053
Hank Aaron	12,364
Carl Yastrzemski	11,988
Cal Ripken Jr.	11,551
Ty Cobb	11,429
Eddie Murray	11,336
Derek Jeter	11,195
Adrián Beltré	11,068
Robin Yount	11,008
Dave Winfield	11,003

Runs Batted In

Hank Aaron	2,297
Babe Ruth	2,213
Albert Pujols*	2,100
Alex Rodriguez	2,086
Barry Bonds	1,996
Lou Gehrig	1,995
Stan Musial	1,951
Ty Cobb	1,938
Jimmie Foxx	1,922
Eddie Murray	1,917

Runs

Rickey Henderson	2,295
Ty Cobb	2,246
Barry Bonds	2,227
Hank Aaron	2,174
Babe Ruth	2,174
Pete Rose	2,165
Willie Mays	2,062
Alex Rodriguez	2,021
Stan Musial	1,949
Derek Jeter	1,923

Stolen Bases

Rickey Henderson	1,406
Lou Brock	938
Billy Hamilton	912
Ty Cobb	892
Tim Raines	808
Vince Coleman	752
Eddie Collins	745
Arlie Latham	739
Max Carey	738
Honus Wagner	722

Triples

Sam Crawford	309
Ty Cobb	297
Honus Wagner	252
Jake Beckley	243
Roger Connor	233
Tris Speaker	222
Fred Clarke	220
Dan Brouthers	205
Joe Kelley	194
Paul Waner	191

Batting Average

Ty Cobb	.367
Rogers Hornsby	.358
Joe Jackson	.356
Ed Delahanty	.346
Tris Speaker	.345
Ted Williams	.344
Billy Hamilton	.344
Dan Brouthers	.342
Babe Ruth	.342
Harry Heilmann	.342

Walks (Batter)

Barry Bonds	2,558
Rickey Henderson	2,190
Babe Ruth	2,062
Ted Williams	2,019
Joe Morgan	1,865
Carl Yastrzemski	1,845
Jim Thome	1,747
Mickey Mantle	1,733
Mel Ott	1,708
Frank Thomas	1,667

Strikeouts (Pitcher)

Nolan Ryan	5,714
Randy Johnson	4,875
Roger Clemens	4,672
Steve Carlton	4,136
Bert Blyleven	3,701
Tom Seaver	3,640
Don Sutton	3,574
Gaylord Perry	3,534
Walter Johnson	3,508
Greg Maddux	3,371

Saves

Mariano Rivera	652
Trevor Hoffman	601
Lee Smith	478
Francisco Rodríguez	437
John Franco	424
Billy Wagner	422
Dennis Eckersley	390
Joe Nathan	377
Jonathan Papelbon	368
Jeff Reardon	367

Shutouts

Walter Johnson	110
Grover Alexander	90
Christy Mathewson	79
Cy Young	76
Eddie Plank	69
Warren Spahn	63
Nolan Ryan	61
Tom Seaver	61
Bert Blyleven	60
Don Sutton	58

Losses

Cy Young	316
Nolan Ryan	292
Walter Johnson	279
Phil Niekro	274
Gaylord Perry	265
Don Sutton	256
Jack Powell	254
Eppa Rixey	251
Bert Blyleven	250
Robin Roberts	245
Warren Spahn	245

All-Time Home Run Leaders

Source: www.mlb.com; * = Active in 2020 season.

Player	HR	Player	HR	Player	HR	Player	HR
Barry Bonds	762	Manny Ramirez	555	Fred McGriff	493	Jason Giambi	440
Hank Aaron	755	Mike Schmidt	548	Miguel Cabrera*	487	Paul Konerko	439
Babe Ruth	714	David Ortiz	541	Adrián Beltré	477	Andre Dawson	438
Alex Rodriguez	696	Mickey Mantle	536	Stan Musial	475	Carlos Beltrán	435
Albert Pujols*	662	Jimmie Foxx	534	Willie Stargell	475	Juan Gonzalez	434
Willie Mays	660	Willie McCovey	521	Carlos Delgado	473	Andruw Jones	434
Ken Griffey Jr.	630	Frank Thomas	521	Chipper Jones	468	Cal Ripken Jr.	431
Jim Thome	612	Ted Williams	521	Dave Winfield	465	Mike Piazza	427
Sammy Sosa	609	Ernie Banks	512	Jose Canseco	462	Billy Williams	426
Frank Robinson	586	Eddie Mathews	512	Adam Dunn	462	Edwin Encarnación*	424
Mark McGwire	583	Mel Ott	511	Carl Yastrzemski	452	Nelson Cruz*	417
Harmon Killebrew	573	Gary Sheffield	509	Jeff Bagwell	449	Darrell Evans	414
Rafael Palmeiro	569	Eddie Murray	504	Vladimir Guerrero	449	Alfonso Soriano	412
Reggie Jackson	563	Lou Gehrig	493	Dave Kingman	442	Mark Teixeira	409

Players With 3,000 Major League Hits

Source: www.mlb.com; * = Active in 2020 season.

Player	Hits	Player	Hits	Player	Hits	Player	Hits
Pete Rose	4,256	Paul Molitor	3,319	George Brett	3,154	Rickey Henderson	3,055
Ty Cobb	4,191	Eddie Collins	3,314	Paul Waner	3,152	Rod Carew	3,053
Hank Aaron	3,771	Willie Mays	3,283	Robin Yount	3,142	Lou Brock	3,023
Stan Musial	3,630	Eddie Murray	3,255	Tony Gwynn	3,141	Rafael Palmeiro	3,020
Tris Speaker	3,515	Nap Lajoie	3,252	Alex Rodriguez	3,115	Cap Anson	3,011
Derek Jeter	3,465	Albert Pujols*	3,236	Dave Winfield	3,110	Wade Boggs	3,010
Honus Wagner	3,430	Cal Ripken Jr.	3,184	Ichiro Suzuki	3,089	Al Kaline	3,007
Carl Yastrzemski	3,419	Adrián Beltré	3,166	Craig Biggio	3,060	Roberto Clemente	3,000

50 Home Run Club

Only Barry Bonds and Mark McGwire hit 70 or more home runs in a season. Five players—including Babe Ruth and Roger Maris—hit 60 or more, a feat Sammy Sosa accomplished for the third time in 2001.

HR	Player, team	Year	HR	Player, team	Year
73	Barry Bonds, San Francisco Giants	2001	54	Alex Rodriguez, NY Yankees	2007
70	Mark McGwire, St. Louis Cardinals	1998	54	Babe Ruth, NY Yankees	1920
66	Sammy Sosa, Chicago Cubs	1998	54	Babe Ruth, NY Yankees	1928
65	Mark McGwire, St. Louis Cardinals	1999	53	Pete Alonso, NY Mets	2019
64	Sammy Sosa, Chicago Cubs	2001	53	Chris Davis, Baltimore Orioles	2013
63	Sammy Sosa, Chicago Cubs	1999	52	George Foster, Cincinnati Reds	1977
61	Roger Maris, NY Yankees	1961	52	Aaron Judge, NY Yankees	2017
60	Babe Ruth, NY Yankees	1927	52	Mickey Mantle, NY Yankees	1956
59	Babe Ruth, NY Yankees	1921	52	Willie Mays, San Francisco Giants	1965
59	Giancarlo Stanton, Miami Marlins	2017	52	Mark McGwire, Oakland A's	1996
58	Jimmie Foxx, Philadelphia Athletics	1932	52	Alex Rodriguez, Texas Rangers	2001
58	Hank Greenberg, Detroit Tigers	1938	52	Jim Thome, Cleveland Indians	2002
58	Ryan Howard, Philadelphia Phillies	2006	51	Cecil Fielder, Detroit Tigers	1990
58	Mark McGwire, Oakland A's/St. Louis Cardinals	1997	51	Andruw Jones, Atlanta Braves	2005
57	Luis Gonzalez, Arizona Diamondbacks	2001	51	Ralph Kiner, Pittsburgh Pirates	1947
57	Alex Rodriguez, Texas Rangers	2002	51	Willie Mays, NY Giants	1955
56	Ken Griffey Jr., Seattle Mariners	1997	51	Johnny Mize, NY Giants	1947
56	Ken Griffey Jr., Seattle Mariners	1998	50	Brady Anderson, Baltimore Orioles	1996
56	Hack Wilson, Chicago Cubs	1930	50	Albert Belle, Cleveland Indians	1995
54	José Bautista, Toronto Blue Jays	2010	50	Prince Fielder, Milwaukee Brewers	2007
54	Ralph Kiner, Pittsburgh Pirates	1949	50	Jimmie Foxx, Boston Red Sox	1938
54	Mickey Mantle, NY Yankees	1961	50	Sammy Sosa, Chicago Cubs	2000
54	David Ortiz, Boston Red Sox	2006	50	Greg Vaughn, San Diego Padres	1998

Pitchers With 300 Major League Wins

Source: www.mlb.com

Pitcher	Wins	Pitcher	Wins	Pitcher	Wins	Pitcher	Wins
Cy Young	511	Charles "Kid" Nichols	361	Eddie Plank	326	Charley Radbourn	309
Walter Johnson	417	Greg Maddux	355	Nolan Ryan	324	Mickey Welch	307
Grover Alexander	373	Roger Clemens	354	Don Sutton	324	Tom Glavine	305
Christy Mathewson	373	Tim Keefe	342	Phil Niekro	318	Randy Johnson	303
Warren Spahn	363	Steve Carlton	329	Gaylord Perry	314	Robert "Lefty" Grove	300
James "Pud" Galvin	361	John Clarkson	328	Tom Seaver	311	Early "Gus" Wynn	300

Official Major League Perfect Games Since 1901

Date	Pitcher	Teams	Date	Pitcher	Teams
5/5/1904	Cy Young	Boston 3 vs. Phil. 0 (AL)	7/28/1994	Kenny Rogers	Texas 4 vs. California 0 (AL)
10/2/1908	Addie Joss	Clev. 1 vs. Chicago 0 (AL)	5/17/1998	David Wells	NY 4 vs. Minn. 0 (AL)
4/30/1922	Charlie Robertson	Chicago 2 vs. Detroit 0 (AL)	7/18/1999	David Cone	NY 6 vs. Montréal 0 (AL)
10/8/1956	Don Larsen	NY 2 (AL) vs. Brooklyn 0* (NL)	5/18/2004	Randy Johnson	Arizona 2 vs. Atlanta 0 (NL)
6/21/1964	Jim Bunning	Phil. 6 vs. NY 0 (NL)	7/23/2009	Mark Buehrle	Chicago 5 vs. Tampa Bay 0 (AL)
9/9/1965	Sandy Koufax	L.A. 1 vs. Chicago 0 (NL)	5/9/2010	Dallas Braden	Oakland 4 vs. Tampa Bay 0 (AL)
5/8/1968	Jim "Catfish" Hunter	Oakland 4 vs. Minn. 0 (AL)	5/29/2010	Roy Halladay	Phil. 1 vs. Florida 0 (NL)
5/15/1981	Len Barker	Clev. 3 vs. Toronto 0 (AL)	4/21/2012	Philip Humber	Chicago 4 vs. Seattle 0 (AL)
9/30/1984	Mike Witt	California 1 vs. Texas 0 (AL)	6/13/2012	Matt Cain	S.F. 10 vs. Houston 0 (NL)
9/16/1988	Tom Browning	Cincinnati 1 vs. L.A. 0 (NL)	8/15/2012	Felix Hernandez	Seattle 1 vs. Tampa Bay 0 (AL)
7/28/1991	Dennis Martinez	Montréal 2 vs. L.A. 0 (NL)			

* = World Series game. **Note:** Two pre-1901 National League pitchers are also credited with perfect games. Within one week in 1880, Lee Richmond (June 12, Worcester 1, Cleveland 0) and John "Monte" Ward (June 17, Providence 5, Buffalo 0) each threw a perfect game.

Most Career Major League No-Hitters

No.	Pitcher	No.	Pitcher
7	Nolan Ryan	2	Jake Arrieta, Homer Bailey, Mark Buehrle, Jim Bunning, Steve Busby, Carl Erskine, Mike Fiers, Bob Forsch, James "Pud" Galvin, Roy Halladay, Ken Holtzman, Randy Johnson, Addie Joss, Dutch Leonard, Tim Lincecum, Jim Maloney, Christy Mathewson, Hideo Nomo, Allie Reynolds, Max Scherzer, Frank Smith, Warren Spahn, Bill Stoneman, Virgil Trucks, Johnny Vander Meer, Don Wilson
4	Sandy Koufax		
3	Larry Corcoran, Bob Feller, Justin Verlander, Cy Young		

Home Run Leaders by Season, 1901-2020

* = All-time single-season record for league since beginning of "modern" era in 1901.

	National League			American League	
Year	Player, team	HR	Year	Player, team	HR
1901	Sam Crawford, Cincinnati	16	1901	Nap Lajoie, Philadelphia	14
1902	Thomas Leach, Pittsburgh	6	1902	Socks Seybold, Philadelphia	16
1903	James Sheckard, Brooklyn	9	1903	Buck Freeman, Boston	13
1904	Harry Lumley, Brooklyn	9	1904	Harry Davis, Philadelphia	10
1905	Fred Odwell, Cincinnati	9	1905	Harry Davis, Philadelphia	8
1906	Timothy Jordan, Brooklyn	12	1906	Harry Davis, Philadelphia	12
1907	David Brain, Boston	10	1907	Harry Davis, Philadelphia	8
1908	Timothy Jordan, Brooklyn	12	1908	Sam Crawford, Detroit	7
1909	Red Murray, New York	7	1909	Ty Cobb, Detroit	9
1910	Fred Beck, Boston; Frank Schulte, Chicago	10	1910	Jake Stahl, Boston	10
1911	Frank Schulte, Chicago	21	1911	J. Franklin Baker, Philadelphia	11
1912	Henry Zimmerman, Chicago	14	1912	J. Franklin Baker, Phil.; Tris Speaker, Boston	10
1913	Gavvy Cravath, Philadelphia	19	1913	J. Franklin Baker, Philadelphia	12
1914	Gavvy Cravath, Philadelphia	19	1914	J. Franklin Baker, Philadelphia	9
1915	Gavvy Cravath, Philadelphia	24	1915	Robert Roth, Chicago-Cleveland	7
1916	Dave Robertson, NY; Fred "Cy" Williams, Chicago	12	1916	Wally Pipp, New York	12
1917	Gavvy Cravath, Phil.; Dave Robertson, NY	12	1917	Wally Pipp, New York	9

National League			American League		
Year	**Player, team**	**HR**	**Year**	**Player, team**	**HR**
1918	Gavvy Cravath, Philadelphia	8	1918	Babe Ruth, Boston; Tilly Walker, Philadelphia	11
1919	Gavvy Cravath, Philadelphia	12	1919	Babe Ruth, Boston	29
1920	Cy Williams, Philadelphia	15	1920	Babe Ruth, New York	54
1921	George Kelly, New York	23	1921	Babe Ruth, New York	59
1922	Rogers Hornsby, St. Louis	42	1922	Ken Williams, St. Louis	39
1923	Cy Williams, Philadelphia	41	1923	Babe Ruth, New York	41
1924	Jacques Fournier, Brooklyn	27	1924	Babe Ruth, New York	46
1925	Rogers Hornsby, St. Louis	39	1925	Bob Meusel, New York	33
1926	Hack Wilson, Chicago	21	1926	Babe Ruth, New York	47
1927	Hack Wilson, Chicago; Cy Williams, Philadelphia	30	1927	Babe Ruth, New York	60
1928	Hack Wilson, Chicago; Jim Bottomley, St. Louis	31	1928	Babe Ruth, New York	54
1929	Chuck Klein, Philadelphia	43	1929	Babe Ruth, New York	46
1930	Hack Wilson, Chicago	56	1930	Babe Ruth, New York	49
1931	Chuck Klein, Philadelphia	31	1931	Lou Gehrig, New York; Babe Ruth, New York	46
1932	Chuck Klein, Philadelphia; Mel Ott, New York	38	1932	Jimmie Foxx, Philadelphia	58
1933	Chuck Klein, Philadelphia	28	1933	Jimmie Foxx, Philadelphia	48
1934	Rip Collins, St. Louis; Mel Ott, New York	35	1934	Lou Gehrig, New York	49
1935	Walter Berger, Boston	34	1935	Jimmie Foxx, Phil.; Hank Greenberg, Detroit	36
1936	Mel Ott, New York	33	1936	Lou Gehrig, New York	49
1937	Joe Medwick, St. Louis; Mel Ott, New York	31	1937	Joe DiMaggio, New York	46
1938	Mel Ott, New York	36	1938	Hank Greenberg, Detroit	58
1939	John Mize, St. Louis	28	1939	Jimmie Foxx, Boston	35
1940	John Mize, St. Louis	43	1940	Hank Greenberg, Detroit	41
1941	Dolph Camilli, Brooklyn	34	1941	Ted Williams, Boston	37
1942	Mel Ott, New York	30	1942	Ted Williams, Boston	36
1943	Bill Nicholson, Chicago	29	1943	Rudy York, Detroit	34
1944	Bill Nicholson, Chicago	33	1944	Nick Etten, New York	22
1945	Tommy Holmes, Boston	28	1945	Vern Stephens, St. Louis	24
1946	Ralph Kiner, Pittsburgh	23	1946	Hank Greenberg, Detroit	44
1947	Ralph Kiner, Pittsburgh; John Mize, New York	51	1947	Ted Williams, Boston	32
1948	Ralph Kiner, Pittsburgh; John Mize, New York	40	1948	Joe DiMaggio, New York	39
1949	Ralph Kiner, Pittsburgh	54	1949	Ted Williams, Boston	43
1950	Ralph Kiner, Pittsburgh	47	1950	Al Rosen, Cleveland	37
1951	Ralph Kiner, Pittsburgh	42	1951	Gus Zernial, Chicago-Philadelphia	33
1952	Ralph Kiner, Pittsburgh; Hank Sauer, Chicago	37	1952	Larry Doby, Cleveland	32
1953	Ed Mathews, Milwaukee	47	1953	Al Rosen, Cleveland	43
1954	Ted Kluszewski, Cincinnati	49	1954	Larry Doby, Cleveland	32
1955	Willie Mays, New York	51	1955	Mickey Mantle, New York	37
1956	Duke Snider, Brooklyn	43	1956	Mickey Mantle, New York	52
1957	Hank Aaron, Milwaukee	44	1957	Roy Sievers, Washington	42
1958	Ernie Banks, Chicago	47	1958	Mickey Mantle, New York	42
1959	Ed Mathews, Milwaukee	46	1959	Rocky Colavito, Clev.; Harmon Killebrew, Wash.	42
1960	Ernie Banks, Chicago	41	1960	Mickey Mantle, New York	40
1961	Orlando Cepeda, San Francisco	46	1961	Roger Maris, New York	61*
1962	Willie Mays, San Francisco	49	1962	Harmon Killebrew, Minnesota	48
1963	Hank Aaron, Milwaukee; Willie McCovey, S.F.	44	1963	Harmon Killebrew, Minnesota	45
1964	Willie Mays, San Francisco	47	1964	Harmon Killebrew, Minnesota	49
1965	Willie Mays, San Francisco	52	1965	Tony Conigliaro, Boston	32
1966	Hank Aaron, Atlanta	44	1966	Frank Robinson, Baltimore	49
1967	Hank Aaron, Atlanta	39	1967	Harmon Killebrew, Minn.; Carl Yastrzemski, Boston	44
1968	Willie McCovey, San Francisco	36	1968	Frank Howard, Washington	44
1969	Willie McCovey, San Francisco	45	1969	Harmon Killebrew, Minnesota	49
1970	Johnny Bench, Cincinnati	45	1970	Frank Howard, Washington	44
1971	Willie Stargell, Pittsburgh	48	1971	Bill Melton, Chicago	33
1972	Johnny Bench, Cincinnati	40	1972	Dick Allen, Chicago	37
1973	Willie Stargell, Pittsburgh	44	1973	Reggie Jackson, Oakland	32
1974	Mike Schmidt, Philadelphia	36	1974	Dick Allen, Chicago	32
1975	Mike Schmidt, Philadelphia	38	1975	Reggie Jackson, Oak.; George Scott, Milw.	36
1976	Mike Schmidt, Philadelphia	38	1976	Graig Nettles, New York	32
1977	George Foster, Cincinnati	52	1977	Jim Rice, Boston	39
1978	George Foster, Cincinnati	40	1978	Jim Rice, Boston	46
1979	Dave Kingman, Chicago	48	1979	Gorman Thomas, Milwaukee	45
1980	Mike Schmidt, Philadelphia	48	1980	Reggie Jackson, New York; Ben Oglivie, Milw.	41
1981	Mike Schmidt, Philadelphia	31	1981	Tony Armas, Oakland; Dwight Evans, Boston; Bobby Grich, Cal.; Eddie Murray, Baltimore	22
1982	Dave Kingman, New York	37	1982	Gorman Thomas, Milw.; Reggie Jackson, Cal.	39
1983	Mike Schmidt, Philadelphia	40	1983	Jim Rice, Boston	39
1984	Dale Murphy, Atlanta; Mike Schmidt, Philadelphia	36	1984	Tony Armas, Boston	43
1985	Dale Murphy, Atlanta	37	1985	Darrell Evans, Detroit	40
1986	Mike Schmidt, Philadelphia	37	1986	Jesse Barfield, Toronto	40
1987	Andre Dawson, Chicago	49	1987	Mark McGwire, Oakland	49
1988	Darryl Strawberry, New York	39	1988	Jose Canseco, Oakland	42
1989	Kevin Mitchell, San Francisco	47	1989	Fred McGriff, Toronto	36
1990	Ryne Sandberg, Chicago	40	1990	Cecil Fielder, Detroit	51
1991	Howard Johnson, New York	38	1991	Jose Canseco, Oakland; Cecil Fielder, Detroit	44
1992	Fred McGriff, San Diego	35	1992	Juan Gonzalez, Texas	43
1993	Barry Bonds, San Francisco	46	1993	Juan Gonzalez, Texas	46
1994	Matt Williams, San Francisco	43	1994	Ken Griffey Jr., Seattle	40
1995	Dante Bichette, Colorado	40	1995	Albert Belle, Cleveland	50
1996	Andres Galarraga, Colorado	47	1996	Mark McGwire, Oakland	52
1997[1]	Larry Walker, Colorado	49	1997[1]	Ken Griffey Jr., Seattle	56
1998	Mark McGwire, St. Louis	70	1998	Ken Griffey Jr., Seattle	56
1999	Mark McGwire, St. Louis	65	1999	Ken Griffey Jr., Seattle	48
2000	Sammy Sosa, Chicago	50	2000	Troy Glaus, Anaheim	47
2001	Barry Bonds, San Francisco	73*	2001	Alex Rodriguez, Texas	52
2002	Sammy Sosa, Chicago	49	2002	Alex Rodriguez, Texas	57
2003	Jim Thome, Philadelphia	47	2003	Alex Rodriguez, Texas	47
2004	Adrián Beltré, Los Angeles	48	2004	Manny Ramirez, Boston	43
2005	Andruw Jones, Atlanta	51	2005	Alex Rodriguez, New York	48

Year	National League — Player, team	HR	Year	American League — Player, team	HR
2006	Ryan Howard, Philadelphia	58	2006	David Ortiz, Boston	54
2007	Prince Fielder, Milwaukee	50	2007	Alex Rodriguez, New York	54
2008	Ryan Howard, Philadelphia	48	2008	Miguel Cabrera, Detroit	37
2009	Albert Pujols, St. Louis	47	2009	Carlos Peña, Tampa Bay; Mark Teixeira, New York	39
2010	Albert Pujols, St. Louis	42	2010	José Bautista, Toronto	54
2011	Matt Kemp, Los Angeles	39	2011	José Bautista, Toronto	43
2012	Ryan Braun, Milwaukee	41	2012	Miguel Cabrera, Detroit	44
2013	Pedro Alvarez, Pitt.; Paul Goldschmidt, Arizona	36	2013	Chris Davis, Baltimore	53
2014	Giancarlo Stanton, Miami	37	2014	Nelson Cruz, Baltimore	40
2015	Nolan Arenado, Colorado; Bryce Harper, Washington	42	2015	Chris Davis, Baltimore	47
2016	Nolan Arenado, Colorado; Chris Carter, Milwaukee	41	2016	Mark Trumbo, Baltimore	47
2017	Giancarlo Stanton, Miami	59	2017	Aaron Judge, New York	52
2018	Nolan Arenado, Colorado	38	2018	Khris Davis, Oakland	48
2019	Pete Alonso, NY Mets	53	2019	Jorge Soler, Kansas City	48
2020	Marcell Ozuna, Atlanta	18	2020	Luke Voit, New York	22

(1) In 1997, Mark McGwire hit 58 home runs, 34 with the Oakland Athletics (AL) and 24 with the St. Louis Cardinals (NL).

Batting Champions by Season, 1901-2020

* = All-time single-season record for league since beginning of "modern" era in 1901.

Year	National League — Player, team	AVG	Year	American League — Player, team	AVG
1901	Jesse C. Burkett, St. Louis	.376	1901[1]	Nap Lajoie, Philadelphia	.426*
1902	Clarence Beaumont, Pittsburgh	.357	1902	Ed Delahanty, Washington	.376
1903	Honus Wagner, Pittsburgh	.355	1903	Nap Lajoie, Cleveland	.357
1904	Honus Wagner, Pittsburgh	.349	1904	Nap Lajoie, Cleveland	.382
1905	James Seymour, Cincinnati	.377	1905	Elmer Flick, Cleveland	.308
1906	Honus Wagner, Pittsburgh	.339	1906	George Stone, St. Louis	.358
1907	Honus Wagner, Pittsburgh	.350	1907	Ty Cobb, Detroit	.350
1908	Honus Wagner, Pittsburgh	.354	1908	Ty Cobb, Detroit	.324
1909	Honus Wagner, Pittsburgh	.339	1909	Ty Cobb, Detroit	.377
1910	Sherwood Magee, Philadelphia	.331	1910[2]	Ty Cobb, Detroit	.385
1911	Honus Wagner, Pittsburgh	.334	1911	Ty Cobb, Detroit	.420
1912	Henry Zimmerman, Chicago	.372	1912	Ty Cobb, Detroit	.410
1913	Jacob Daubert, Brooklyn	.350	1913	Ty Cobb, Detroit	.390
1914	Jacob Daubert, Brooklyn	.329	1914	Ty Cobb, Detroit	.368
1915	Larry Doyle, New York	.320	1915	Ty Cobb, Detroit	.369
1916	Hal Chase, Cincinnati	.339	1916	Tris Speaker, Cleveland	.386
1917	Edd Roush, Cincinnati	.341	1917	Ty Cobb, Detroit	.383
1918	Zack Wheat, Brooklyn	.335	1918	Ty Cobb, Detroit	.382
1919	Edd Roush, Cincinnati	.321	1919	Ty Cobb, Detroit	.384
1920	Rogers Hornsby, St. Louis	.370	1920	George Sisler, St. Louis	.407
1921	Rogers Hornsby, St. Louis	.397	1921	Harry Heilmann, Detroit	.394
1922	Rogers Hornsby, St. Louis	.401	1922	George Sisler, St. Louis	.420
1923	Rogers Hornsby, St. Louis	.384	1923	Harry Heilmann, Detroit	.403
1924	Rogers Hornsby, St. Louis	.424*	1924	Babe Ruth, New York	.378
1925	Rogers Hornsby, St. Louis	.403	1925	Harry Heilmann, Detroit	.393
1926	Eugene Hargrave, Cincinnati	.353	1926	Henry Manush, Detroit	.378
1927	Paul Waner, Pittsburgh	.380	1927	Harry Heilmann, Detroit	.398
1928	Rogers Hornsby, Boston	.387	1928	Goose Goslin, Washington	.379
1929	Lefty O'Doul, Philadelphia	.398	1929	Lew Fonseca, Cleveland	.369
1930	Bill Terry, New York	.401	1930	Al Simmons, Philadelphia	.381
1931	Chick Hafey, St. Louis	.349	1931	Al Simmons, Philadelphia	.390
1932	Lefty O'Doul, Brooklyn	.368	1932	Dale Alexander, Detroit-Boston	.367
1933	Chuck Klein, Philadelphia	.368	1933	Jimmie Foxx, Philadelphia	.356
1934	Paul Waner, Pittsburgh	.362	1934	Lou Gehrig, New York	.363
1935	Arky Vaughan, Pittsburgh	.385	1935	Buddy Myer, Washington	.349
1936	Paul Waner, Pittsburgh	.373	1936	Luke Appling, Chicago	.388
1937	Joe Medwick, St. Louis	.374	1937	Charlie Gehringer, Detroit	.371
1938	Ernie Lombardi, Cincinnati	.342	1938	Jimmie Foxx, Boston	.349
1939	John Mize, St. Louis	.349	1939	Joe DiMaggio, New York	.381
1940	Debs Garms, Pittsburgh	.355	1940	Joe DiMaggio, New York	.352
1941	Pete Reiser, Brooklyn	.343	1941	Ted Williams, Boston	.406
1942	Ernie Lombardi, Boston	.330	1942	Ted Williams, Boston	.356
1943	Stan Musial, St. Louis	.357	1943	Luke Appling, Chicago	.328
1944	Dixie Walker, Brooklyn	.357	1944	Lou Boudreau, Cleveland	.327
1945	Phil Cavarretta, Chicago	.355	1945	George Stirnweiss, New York	.309
1946	Stan Musial, St. Louis	.365	1946	Mickey Vernon, Washington	.353
1947	Harry Walker, St. Louis-Philadelphia	.363	1947	Ted Williams, Boston	.343
1948	Stan Musial, St. Louis	.376	1948	Ted Williams, Boston	.369
1949	Jackie Robinson, Brooklyn	.342	1949	George Kell, Detroit	.343
1950	Stan Musial, St. Louis	.346	1950	Billy Goodman, Boston	.354
1951	Stan Musial, St. Louis	.355	1951	Ferris Fain, Philadelphia	.344
1952	Stan Musial, St. Louis	.336	1952	Ferris Fain, Philadelphia	.327
1953	Carl Furillo, Brooklyn	.344	1953	Mickey Vernon, Washington	.337
1954	Willie Mays, New York	.345	1954	Roberto Avila, Cleveland	.341
1955	Richie Ashburn, Philadelphia	.338	1955	Al Kaline, Detroit	.340
1956	Hank Aaron, Milwaukee	.328	1956	Mickey Mantle, New York	.353
1957	Stan Musial, St. Louis	.351	1957	Ted Williams, Boston	.388
1958	Richie Ashburn, Philadelphia	.350	1958	Ted Williams, Boston	.328
1959	Hank Aaron, Milwaukee	.355	1959	Harvey Kuenn, Detroit	.353
1960	Dick Groat, Pittsburgh	.325	1960	Pete Runnels, Boston	.320
1961	Roberto Clemente, Pittsburgh	.351	1961	Norm Cash, Detroit	.361
1962	Tommy Davis, Los Angeles	.346	1962	Pete Runnels, Boston	.326
1963	Tommy Davis, Los Angeles	.326	1963	Carl Yastrzemski, Boston	.321
1964	Roberto Clemente, Pittsburgh	.339	1964	Tony Oliva, Minnesota	.323
1965	Roberto Clemente, Pittsburgh	.329	1965	Tony Oliva, Minnesota	.321
1966	Matty Alou, Pittsburgh	.342	1966	Frank Robinson, Baltimore	.316
1967	Roberto Clemente, Pittsburgh	.357	1967	Carl Yastrzemski, Boston	.326
1968	Pete Rose, Cincinnati	.335	1968	Carl Yastrzemski, Boston	.301
1969	Pete Rose, Cincinnati	.348	1969	Rod Carew, Minnesota	.332
1970	Rico Carty, Atlanta	.366	1970	Alex Johnson, California	.329
1971	Joe Torre, St. Louis	.363	1971	Tony Oliva, Minnesota	.337
1972	Billy Williams, Chicago	.333	1972	Rod Carew, Minnesota	.318

Year	National League Player, team	AVG	Year	American League Player, team	AVG
1973	Pete Rose, Cincinnati	.338	1973	Rod Carew, Minnesota	.350
1974	Ralph Garr, Atlanta	.353	1974	Rod Carew, Minnesota	.364
1975	Bill Madlock, Chicago	.354	1975	Rod Carew, Minnesota	.359
1976	Bill Madlock, Chicago	.339	1976	George Brett, Kansas City	.333
1977	Dave Parker, Pittsburgh	.338	1977	Rod Carew, Minnesota	.388
1978	Dave Parker, Pittsburgh	.334	1978	Rod Carew, Minnesota	.333
1979	Keith Hernandez, St. Louis	.344	1979	Fred Lynn, Boston	.333
1980	Bill Buckner, Chicago	.324	1980	George Brett, Kansas City	.390
1981	Bill Madlock, Pittsburgh	.341	1981	Carney Lansford, Boston	.336
1982	Al Oliver, Montréal	.331	1982	Willie Wilson, Kansas City	.332
1983	Bill Madlock, Pittsburgh	.323	1983	Wade Boggs, Boston	.361
1984	Tony Gwynn, San Diego	.351	1984	Don Mattingly, New York	.343
1985	Willie McGee, St. Louis	.353	1985	Wade Boggs, Boston	.368
1986	Tim Raines, Montréal	.334	1986	Wade Boggs, Boston	.357
1987	Tony Gwynn, San Diego	.370	1987	Wade Boggs, Boston	.363
1988	Tony Gwynn, San Diego	.313	1988	Wade Boggs, Boston	.366
1989	Tony Gwynn, San Diego	.336	1989	Kirby Puckett, Minnesota	.339
1990	Willie McGee, St. Louis	.335	1990	George Brett, Kansas City	.329
1991	Terry Pendleton, Atlanta	.319	1991	Julio Franco, Texas	.341
1992	Gary Sheffield, San Diego	.330	1992	Edgar Martinez, Seattle	.343
1993	Andres Galarraga, Colorado	.370	1993	John Olerud, Toronto	.363
1994	Tony Gwynn, San Diego	.394	1994	Paul O'Neill, New York	.359
1995	Tony Gwynn, San Diego	.368	1995	Edgar Martinez, Seattle	.356
1996	Tony Gwynn, San Diego	.353	1996	Alex Rodriguez, Seattle	.358
1997	Tony Gwynn, San Diego	.372	1997	Frank Thomas, Chicago	.347
1998	Larry Walker, Colorado	.363	1998	Bernie Williams, New York	.339
1999	Larry Walker, Colorado	.379	1999	Nomar Garciaparra, Boston	.357
2000	Todd Helton, Colorado	.372	2000	Nomar Garciaparra, Boston	.372
2001	Larry Walker, Colorado	.350	2001	Ichiro Suzuki, Seattle	.350
2002	Barry Bonds, San Francisco	.370	2002	Manny Ramirez, Boston	.349
2003	Albert Pujols, St. Louis	.359	2003	Bill Mueller, Boston	.326
2004	Barry Bonds, San Francisco	.362	2004	Ichiro Suzuki, Seattle	.372
2005	Derrek Lee, Chicago	.335	2005	Michael Young, Texas	.331
2006	Freddy Sanchez, Pittsburgh	.344	2006	Joe Mauer, Minnesota	.347
2007	Matt Holliday, Colorado	.340	2007	Magglio Ordoñez, Detroit	.363
2008	Chipper Jones, Atlanta	.364	2008	Joe Mauer, Minnesota	.328
2009	Hanley Ramirez, Florida	.342	2009	Joe Mauer, Minnesota	.365
2010	Carlos Gonzalez, Colorado	.336	2010	Josh Hamilton, Texas	.359
2011	José Reyes, New York	.337	2011	Miguel Cabrera, Detroit	.344
2012	Buster Posey, San Francisco	.336	2012	Miguel Cabrera, Detroit	.330
2013	Michael Cuddyer, Colorado	.331	2013	Miguel Cabrera, Detroit	.348
2014	Justin Morneau, Colorado	.319	2014	José Altuve, Houston	.341
2015	Dee Gordon, Miami	.333	2015	Miguel Cabrera, Detroit	.338
2016	DJ LeMahieu, Colorado	.348	2016	José Altuve, Houston	.338
2017	Charlie Blackmon, Colorado	.331	2017	José Altuve, Houston	.346
2018	Christian Yelich, Milwaukee	.326	2018	Mookie Betts, Boston	.346
2019	Christian Yelich, Milwaukee	.329	2019	Tim Anderson, Chicago	.335
2020	Juan Soto, Washington	.351	2020	DJ LeMahieu, New York	.364

(1) Nap Lajoie's 1901 batting average varies in historical records from .421 to .426. (2) Some baseball researchers have concluded that Ty Cobb actually hit .382 in 1910 while Nap Lajoie, Cleveland, hit .383.

Earned Run Average Leaders by Season, 1977-2020

Year	National League Pitcher, team	G	IP	ERA	Year	American League Pitcher, team	G	IP	ERA
1977	John Candelaria, Pittsburgh	33	230.2	2.34	1977	Frank Tanana, California	31	241.1	2.54
1978	Craig Swan, New York	29	207.1	2.43	1978	Ron Guidry, New York	35	273.2	1.74
1979	J. R. Richard, Houston	38	292.1	2.71	1979	Ron Guidry, New York	33	236.1	2.78
1980	Don Sutton, Los Angeles	32	212.1	2.20	1980	Rudy May, New York	41	175.1	2.46
1981	Nolan Ryan, Houston	21	149.0	1.69	1981	Sammy Stewart, Baltimore	29	112.1	2.32
1982	Steve Rogers, Montréal	35	277.0	2.40	1982	Rick Sutcliffe, Cleveland	34	216.0	2.96
1983	Atlee Hammaker, San Francisco	23	172.1	2.25	1983	Rick Honeycutt, Texas	25	174.2	2.42
1984	Alejandro Peña, Los Angeles	28	199.1	2.48	1984	Mike Boddicker, Baltimore	34	261.1	2.79
1985	Dwight Gooden, New York	35	276.2	1.53	1985	Dave Stieb, Toronto	36	265.0	2.48
1986	Mike Scott, Houston	37	275.1	2.22	1986	Roger Clemens, Boston	33	254.0	2.48
1987	Nolan Ryan, Houston	34	211.2	2.76	1987	Jimmy Key, Toronto	36	261.0	2.76
1988	Joe Magrane, St. Louis	24	165.1	2.18	1988	Allan Anderson, Minnesota	30	202.1	2.45
1989	Scott Garrelts, San Francisco	30	193.1	2.28	1989	Bret Saberhagen, Kansas City	36	262.1	2.16
1990	Danny Darwin, Houston	48	162.2	2.21	1990	Roger Clemens, Boston	31	228.1	1.93
1991	Dennis Martinez, Montréal	31	222.0	2.39	1991	Roger Clemens, Boston	35	271.1	2.62
1992	Bill Swift, San Francisco	30	164.2	2.08	1992	Roger Clemens, Boston	32	246.2	2.41
1993	Greg Maddux, Atlanta	36	267.0	2.36	1993	Kevin Appier, Kansas City	34	238.2	2.56
1994	Greg Maddux, Atlanta	25	202.0	1.56	1994	Steve Ontiveros, Oakland	27	115.1	2.65
1995	Greg Maddux, Atlanta	28	209.2	1.63	1995	Randy Johnson, Seattle	30	214.1	2.48
1996	Kevin Brown, Florida	32	233.0	1.89	1996	Juan Guzmán, Toronto	27	187.2	2.93
1997	Pedro Martinez, Montréal	31	241.1	1.90	1997	Roger Clemens, Toronto	34	264.0	2.05
1998	Greg Maddux, Atlanta	34	251.0	2.22	1998	Roger Clemens, Toronto	33	234.2	2.65
1999	Randy Johnson, Arizona	35	271.2	2.48	1999	Pedro Martinez, Boston	31	213.1	2.07
2000	Kevin Brown, Los Angeles	33	230.0	2.58	2000	Pedro Martinez, Boston	29	217.0	1.74
2001	Randy Johnson, Arizona	35	249.2	2.49	2001	Freddy Garcia, Seattle	34	238.2	3.05
2002	Randy Johnson, Arizona	35	260.0	2.32	2002	Pedro Martinez, Boston	30	199.1	2.26
2003	Jason Schmidt, San Francisco	29	207.2	2.34	2003	Pedro Martinez, Boston	29	186.2	2.22
2004	Jake Peavy, San Diego	27	166.1	2.27	2004	Johan Santana, Minnesota	34	228.0	2.61
2005	Roger Clemens, Houston	32	211.1	1.87	2005	Kevin Millwood, Cleveland	30	192.0	2.86
2006	Roy Oswalt, Houston	33	220.2	2.98	2006	Johan Santana, Minnesota	34	233.2	2.77
2007	Jake Peavy, San Diego	34	223.1	2.54	2007	John Lackey, Los Angeles	33	224.0	3.01
2008	Johan Santana, New York	34	234.1	2.53	2008	Cliff Lee, Cleveland	31	223.1	2.54
2009	Chris Carpenter, St. Louis	28	192.2	2.24	2009	Zack Greinke, Kansas City	33	229.1	2.16
2010	Josh Johnson, Florida	28	183.2	2.30	2010	Felix Hernandez, Seattle	34	249.2	2.27
2011	Clayton Kershaw, Los Angeles	33	233.1	2.28	2011	Justin Verlander, Detroit	34	251.0	2.40
2012	Clayton Kershaw, Los Angeles	33	227.2	2.53	2012	David Price, Tampa Bay	31	211.0	2.56
2013	Clayton Kershaw, Los Angeles	33	236.0	1.83	2013	Anibal Sanchez, Detroit	29	182.0	2.57
2014	Clayton Kershaw, Los Angeles	27	198.1	1.77	2014	Felix Hernandez, Seattle	34	236.0	2.14
2015	Zack Greinke, Los Angeles	32	222.2	1.66	2015	David Price, Detroit-Toronto	32	220.1	2.45
2016	Kyle Hendricks, Chicago	31	190.0	2.13	2016	Aaron Sanchez, Toronto	30	192.0	3.00
2017	Clayton Kershaw, Los Angeles	27	175.0	2.31	2017	Corey Kluber, Cleveland	29	203.2	2.25
2018	Jacob deGrom, NY Mets	32	217.0	1.70	2018	Blake Snell, Tampa Bay	31	180.2	1.89
2019	Hyun-jin Ryu, Los Angeles	29	182.2	2.32	2019	Gerrit Cole, Houston	33	212.1	2.50
2020	Trevor Bauer, Cincinnati	11	73.0	1.73	2020	Shane Bieber, Cleveland	12	77.1	1.63

Strikeout Leaders by Season, 1901-2020

* = All-time single-season record for league since beginning of "modern" era in 1901.

	National League			American League	
Year	Pitcher, team	SO	Year	Pitcher, team	SO
1901	Noodles Hahn, Cincinnati	239	1901	Cy Young, Boston	158
1902	Vic Willis, Boston	225	1902	Rube Waddell, Philadelphia	210
1903	Christy Mathewson, New York	267	1903	Rube Waddell, Philadelphia	302
1904	Christy Mathewson, New York	212	1904	Rube Waddell, Philadelphia	349
1905	Christy Mathewson, New York	206	1905	Rube Waddell, Philadelphia	287
1906	Fred Beebe, Chicago-St. Louis	171	1906	Rube Waddell, Philadelphia	196
1907	Christy Mathewson, New York	178	1907	Rube Waddell, Philadelphia	232
1908	Christy Mathewson, New York	259	1908	Ed Walsh, Chicago	269
1909	Orval Overall, Chicago	205	1909	Frank Smith, Chicago	177
1910	Earl Moore, Philadelphia	185	1910	Walter Johnson, Washington	313
1911	Rube Marquard, New York	237	1911	Ed Walsh, Chicago	255
1912	Grover Alexander, Philadelphia	195	1912	Walter Johnson, Washington	303
1913	Tom Seaton, Philadelphia	168	1913	Walter Johnson, Washington	243
1914	Grover Alexander, Philadelphia	214	1914	Walter Johnson, Washington	225
1915	Grover Alexander, Philadelphia	241	1915	Walter Johnson, Washington	203
1916	Grover Alexander, Philadelphia	167	1916	Walter Johnson, Washington	228
1917	Grover Alexander, Philadelphia	200	1917	Walter Johnson, Washington	188
1918	Hippo Vaughn, Chicago	148	1918	Walter Johnson, Washington	162
1919	Hippo Vaughn, Chicago	141	1919	Walter Johnson, Washington	147
1920	Grover Alexander, Chicago	173	1920	Stan Coveleski, Cleveland	133
1921	Burleigh Grimes, Brooklyn	136	1921	Walter Johnson, Washington	143
1922	Dazzy Vance, Brooklyn	134	1922	Urban Shocker, St. Louis	149
1923	Dazzy Vance, Brooklyn	197	1923	Walter Johnson, Washington	130
1924	Dazzy Vance, Brooklyn	262	1924	Walter Johnson, Washington	158
1925	Dazzy Vance, Brooklyn	221	1925	Lefty Grove, Philadelphia	116
1926	Dazzy Vance, Brooklyn	140	1926	Lefty Grove, Philadelphia	194
1927	Dazzy Vance, Brooklyn	184	1927	Lefty Grove, Philadelphia	174
1928	Dazzy Vance, Brooklyn	200	1928	Lefty Grove, Philadelphia	183
1929	Pat Malone, Chicago	166	1929	Lefty Grove, Philadelphia	170
1930	Bill Hallahan, St. Louis	177	1930	Lefty Grove, Philadelphia	209
1931	Bill Hallahan, St. Louis	159	1931	Lefty Grove, Philadelphia	175
1932	Dizzy Dean, St. Louis	191	1932	Red Ruffing, New York	190
1933	Dizzy Dean, St. Louis	199	1933	Lefty Gomez, New York	163
1934	Dizzy Dean, St. Louis	195	1934	Lefty Gomez, New York	158
1935	Dizzy Dean, St. Louis	190	1935	Tommy Bridges, Detroit	163
1936	Van Lingle Mungo, Brooklyn	238	1936	Tommy Bridges, Detroit	175
1937	Carl Hubbell, New York	159	1937	Lefty Gomez, New York	194
1938	Clay Bryant, Chicago	135	1938	Bob Feller, Cleveland	240
1939	Claude Passeau, Philadelphia-Chicago; Bucky Walters, Cincinnati	137	1939	Bob Feller, Cleveland	246
1940	Kirby Higbe, Philadelphia	137	1940	Bob Feller, Cleveland	261
1941	John Vander Meer, Cincinnati	202	1941	Bob Feller, Cleveland	260
1942	John Vander Meer, Cincinnati	186	1942	Tex Hughson, Boston; Bobo Newsom, Washington	113
1943	John Vander Meer, Cincinnati	174	1943	Allie Reynolds, Cleveland	151
1944	Bill Voiselle, New York	161	1944	Hal Newhouser, Detroit	187
1945	Preacher Roe, Pittsburgh	148	1945	Hal Newhouser, Detroit	212
1946	Johnny Schmitz, Chicago	135	1946	Bob Feller, Cleveland	348
1947	Ewell Blackwell, Cincinnati	193	1947	Bob Feller, Cleveland	196
1948	Harry Brecheen, St. Louis	149	1948	Bob Feller, Cleveland	164
1949	Warren Spahn, Boston	151	1949	Virgil Trucks, Detroit	153
1950	Warren Spahn, Boston	191	1950	Bob Lemon, Cleveland	170
1951	Warren Spahn, Boston; Don Newcombe, Brooklyn	164	1951	Vic Raschi, New York	164
1952	Warren Spahn, Boston	183	1952	Allie Reynolds, New York	160
1953	Robin Roberts, Philadelphia	198	1953	Billy Pierce, Chicago	186
1954	Robin Roberts, Philadelphia	185	1954	Bob Turley, Baltimore	185
1955	Sam Jones, Chicago	198	1955	Herb Score, Cleveland	245
1956	Sam Jones, Chicago	176	1956	Herb Score, Cleveland	263
1957	Jack Sanford, Philadelphia	188	1957	Early Wynn, Cleveland	184
1958	Sam Jones, St. Louis	225	1958	Early Wynn, Chicago	179
1959	Don Drysdale, Los Angeles	242	1959	Jim Bunning, Detroit	201
1960	Don Drysdale, Los Angeles	246	1960	Jim Bunning, Detroit	201
1961	Sandy Koufax, Los Angeles	269	1961	Camilo Pascual, Minnesota	221
1962	Don Drysdale, Los Angeles	232	1962	Camilo Pascual, Minnesota	206
1963	Sandy Koufax, Los Angeles	306	1963	Camilo Pascual, Minnesota	202
1964	Bob Veale, Pittsburgh	250	1964	Al Downing, New York	217
1965	Sandy Koufax, Los Angeles	382*	1965	Sam McDowell, Cleveland	325
1966	Sandy Koufax, Los Angeles	317	1966	Sam McDowell, Cleveland	225
1967	Jim Bunning, Philadelphia	253	1967	Jim Lonborg, Boston	246
1968	Bob Gibson, St. Louis	268	1968	Sam McDowell, Cleveland	283
1969	Ferguson Jenkins, Chicago	273	1969	Sam McDowell, Cleveland	279
1970	Tom Seaver, New York	283	1970	Sam McDowell, Cleveland	304
1971	Tom Seaver, New York	289	1971	Mickey Lolich, Detroit	308
1972	Steve Carlton, Philadelphia	310	1972	Nolan Ryan, California	329
1973	Tom Seaver, New York	251	1973	Nolan Ryan, California	383*
1974	Steve Carlton, Philadelphia	240	1974	Nolan Ryan, California	367
1975	Tom Seaver, New York	243	1975	Frank Tanana, California	269
1976	Tom Seaver, New York	235	1976	Nolan Ryan, California	327
1977	Phil Niekro, Atlanta	262	1977	Nolan Ryan, California	341
1978	J. R. Richard, Houston	303	1978	Nolan Ryan, California	260

National League			American League		
Year	Pitcher, team	SO	Year	Pitcher, team	SO
1979	J. R. Richard, Houston	313	1979	Nolan Ryan, California	223
1980	Steve Carlton, Philadelphia	286	1980	Len Barker, Cleveland	187
1981	Fernando Valenzuela, Los Angeles	180	1981	Len Barker, Cleveland	127
1982	Steve Carlton, Philadelphia	286	1982	Floyd Bannister, Seattle	209
1983	Steve Carlton, Philadelphia	275	1983	Jack Morris, Detroit	232
1984	Dwight Gooden, New York	276	1984	Mark Langston, Seattle	204
1985	Dwight Gooden, New York	268	1985	Bert Blyleven, Cleveland-Minnesota	206
1986	Mike Scott, Houston	306	1986	Mark Langston, Seattle	245
1987	Nolan Ryan, Houston	270	1987	Mark Langston, Seattle	262
1988	Nolan Ryan, Houston	228	1988	Roger Clemens, Boston	291
1989	Jose DeLeon, St. Louis	201	1989	Nolan Ryan, Texas	301
1990	David Cone, New York	233	1990	Nolan Ryan, Texas	232
1991	David Cone, New York	241	1991	Roger Clemens, Boston	241
1992	John Smoltz, Atlanta	215	1992	Randy Johnson, Seattle	241
1993	José Rijo, Cincinnati	227	1993	Randy Johnson, Seattle	308
1994	Andy Benes, San Diego	189	1994	Randy Johnson, Seattle	204
1995	Hideo Nomo, Los Angeles	236	1995	Randy Johnson, Seattle	294
1996	John Smoltz, Atlanta	276	1996	Roger Clemens, Boston	257
1997	Curt Schilling, Philadelphia	319	1997	Roger Clemens, Toronto	292
1998	Curt Schilling, Philadelphia	300	1998	Roger Clemens, Toronto	271
1999	Randy Johnson, Arizona	364	1999	Pedro Martinez, Boston	313
2000	Randy Johnson, Arizona	347	2000	Pedro Martinez, Boston	284
2001	Randy Johnson, Arizona	372	2001	Hideo Nomo, Boston	220
2002	Randy Johnson, Arizona	334	2002	Pedro Martinez, Boston	239
2003	Kerry Wood, Chicago	266	2003	Esteban Loaiza, Chicago	207
2004	Randy Johnson, Arizona	290	2004	Johan Santana, Minnesota	265
2005	Jake Peavy, San Diego	216	2005	Johan Santana, Minnesota	238
2006	Aaron Harang, Cincinnati	216	2006	Johan Santana, Minnesota	245
2007	Jake Peavy, San Diego	240	2007	Scott Kazmir, Tampa Bay	239
2008	Tim Lincecum, San Francisco	265	2008	A. J. Burnett, Toronto	231
2009	Tim Lincecum, San Francisco	261	2009	Justin Verlander, Detroit	269
2010	Tim Lincecum, San Francisco	231	2010	Jered Weaver, Los Angeles	233
2011	Clayton Kershaw, Los Angeles	248	2011	Justin Verlander, Detroit	250
2012	R.A. Dickey, New York	230	2012	Justin Verlander, Detroit	239
2013	Clayton Kershaw, Los Angeles	232	2013	Yu Darvish, Texas	277
2014	Johnny Cueto, Cincinnati; Stephen Strasburg, Washington	242	2014	David Price, Tampa Bay-Detroit	271
2015	Clayton Kershaw, Los Angeles	301	2015	Chris Sale, Chicago	274
2016	Max Scherzer, Washington	284	2016	Justin Verlander, Detroit	254
2017	Max Scherzer, Washington	268	2017	Chris Sale, Boston	308
2018	Max Scherzer, Washington	300	2018	Justin Verlander, Houston	290
2019	Jacob deGrom, New York	255	2019	Gerrit Cole, Houston	326
2020	Jacob deGrom, New York	104	2020	Shane Bieber, Cleveland	122

Cy Young Award Winners, 1956-2019

Year	Pitcher, team	Year	Pitcher, team	Year	Pitcher, team
1956	Don Newcombe, Brooklyn	1980	(NL) Steve Carlton, Philadelphia	1999	(NL) Randy Johnson, Arizona
1957	Warren Spahn, Milwaukee		(AL) Steve Stone, Baltimore		(AL) Pedro Martinez, Boston
1958	Bob Turley, NY Yankees	1981	(NL) Fernando Valenzuela, L.A.	2000	(NL) Randy Johnson, Arizona
1959	Early Wynn, Chicago White Sox		(AL) Rollie Fingers, Milwaukee		(AL) Pedro Martinez, Boston
1960	Vernon Law, Pittsburgh	1982	(NL) Steve Carlton, Philadelphia	2001	(NL) Randy Johnson, Arizona
1961	Whitey Ford, NY Yankees		(AL) Pete Vuckovich, Milwaukee		(AL) Roger Clemens, NY
1962	Don Drysdale, L.A. Dodgers	1983	(NL) John Denny, Philadelphia	2002	(NL) Randy Johnson, Arizona
1963	Sandy Koufax, L.A. Dodgers		(AL) LaMarr Hoyt, Chicago		(AL) Barry Zito, Oakland
1964	Dean Chance, L.A. Angels	1984	(NL) Rick Sutcliffe, Chicago	2003	(NL) Eric Gagne, L.A.
1965	Sandy Koufax, L.A. Dodgers		(AL) Willie Hernandez, Detroit		(AL) Roy Halladay, Toronto
1966	Sandy Koufax, L.A. Dodgers	1985	(NL) Dwight Gooden, NY	2004	(NL) Roger Clemens, Houston
1967	(NL) Mike McCormick, S.F.		(AL) Bret Saberhagen, Kansas City		(AL) Johan Santana, Minnesota
	(AL) Jim Lonborg, Boston	1986	(NL) Mike Scott, Houston	2005	(NL) Chris Carpenter, St. Louis
1968	(NL) Bob Gibson, St. Louis		(AL) Roger Clemens, Boston		(AL) Bartolo Colon, L.A.
	(AL) Denny McLain, Detroit	1987	(NL) Steve Bedrosian, Phil.	2006	(NL) Brandon Webb, Arizona
1969	(NL) Tom Seaver, NY		(AL) Roger Clemens, Boston		(AL) Johan Santana, Minnesota
	(AL) Denny McLain, Detroit; Mike Cuellar, Baltimore	1988	(NL) Orel Hershiser, L.A.	2007	(NL) Jake Peavy, San Diego
			(AL) Frank Viola, Minnesota		(AL) CC Sabathia, Cleveland
1970	(NL) Bob Gibson, St. Louis	1989	(NL) Mark Davis, San Diego	2008	(NL) Tim Lincecum, S.F.
	(AL) Jim Perry, Minnesota		(AL) Bret Saberhagen, Kansas City		(AL) Cliff Lee, Cleveland
1971	(NL) Ferguson Jenkins, Chicago	1990	(NL) Doug Drabek, Pittsburgh	2009	(NL) Tim Lincecum, S.F.
	(AL) Vida Blue, Oakland		(AL) Bob Welch, Oakland		(AL) Zack Greinke, Kansas City
1972	(NL) Steve Carlton, Philadelphia	1991	(NL) Tom Glavine, Atlanta	2010	(NL) Roy Halladay, Philadelphia
	(AL) Gaylord Perry, Cleveland		(AL) Roger Clemens, Boston		(AL) Felix Hernandez, Seattle
1973	(NL) Tom Seaver, NY	1992	(NL) Greg Maddux, Chicago	2011	(NL) Clayton Kershaw, L.A.
	(AL) Jim Palmer, Baltimore		(AL) Dennis Eckersley, Oakland		(AL) Justin Verlander, Detroit
1974	(NL) Mike Marshall, L.A.	1993	(NL) Greg Maddux, Atlanta	2012	(NL) R.A. Dickey, NY
	(AL) Jim "Catfish" Hunter, Oakland		(AL) Jack McDowell, Chicago		(AL) David Price, Tampa Bay
1975	(NL) Tom Seaver, NY	1994	(NL) Greg Maddux, Atlanta	2013	(NL) Clayton Kershaw, L.A.
	(AL) Jim Palmer, Baltimore		(AL) David Cone, Kansas City		(AL) Max Scherzer, Detroit
1976	(NL) Randy Jones, San Diego	1995	(NL) Greg Maddux, Atlanta	2014	(NL) Clayton Kershaw, L.A.
	(AL) Jim Palmer, Baltimore		(AL) Randy Johnson, Seattle		(AL) Corey Kluber, Cleveland
1977	(NL) Steve Carlton, Philadelphia	1996	(NL) John Smoltz, Atlanta	2015	(NL) Jake Arrieta, Chicago
	(AL) Sparky Lyle, NY		(AL) Pat Hentgen, Toronto		(AL) Dallas Keuchel, Houston
1978	(NL) Gaylord Perry, San Diego	1997	(NL) Pedro Martinez, Montréal	2016	(NL) Max Scherzer, Washington
	(AL) Ron Guidry, NY		(AL) Roger Clemens, Toronto		(AL) Rick Porcello, Boston
1979	(NL) Bruce Sutter, Chicago	1998	(NL) Tom Glavine, Atlanta	2017	(NL) Max Scherzer, Washington
	(AL) Mike Flanagan, Baltimore		(AL) Roger Clemens, Toronto		(AL) Corey Kluber, Cleveland
				2018	(NL) Jacob deGrom, NY
					(AL) Blake Snell, Tampa Bay
				2019	(NL) Jacob deGrom, NY
					(AL) Justin Verlander, Houston

Most Valuable Players, 1931-2019

As selected by the Baseball Writers' Assn. of America. Prior to 1931, MVP honors were named by various sources.

National League

Year	Player, team	Year	Player, team	Year	Player, team
1931	Frank Frisch, St. Louis	1961	Frank Robinson, Cincinnati	1990	Barry Bonds, Pittsburgh
1932	Chuck Klein, Philadelphia	1962	Maury Wills, Los Angeles	1991	Terry Pendleton, Atlanta
1933	Carl Hubbell, New York	1963	Sandy Koufax, Los Angeles	1992	Barry Bonds, Pittsburgh
1934	Dizzy Dean, St. Louis	1964	Ken Boyer, St. Louis	1993	Barry Bonds, San Francisco
1935	Gabby Hartnett, Chicago	1965	Willie Mays, San Francisco	1994	Jeff Bagwell, Houston
1936	Carl Hubbell, New York	1966	Roberto Clemente, Pittsburgh	1995	Barry Larkin, Cincinnati
1937	Joe Medwick, St. Louis	1967	Orlando Cepeda, St. Louis	1996	Ken Caminiti, San Diego
1938	Ernie Lombardi, Cincinnati	1968	Bob Gibson, St. Louis	1997	Larry Walker, Colorado
1939	Bucky Walters, Cincinnati	1969	Willie McCovey, San Francisco	1998	Sammy Sosa, Chicago
1940	Frank McCormick, Cincinnati	1970	Johnny Bench, Cincinnati	1999	Chipper Jones, Atlanta
1941	Dolph Camilli, Brooklyn	1971	Joe Torre, St. Louis	2000	Jeff Kent, San Francisco
1942	Mort Cooper, St. Louis	1972	Johnny Bench, Cincinnati	2001	Barry Bonds, San Francisco
1943	Stan Musial, St. Louis	1973	Pete Rose, Cincinnati	2002	Barry Bonds, San Francisco
1944	Martin Marion, St. Louis	1974	Steve Garvey, Los Angeles	2003	Barry Bonds, San Francisco
1945	Phil Cavarretta, Chicago	1975	Joe Morgan, Cincinnati	2004	Barry Bonds, San Francisco
1946	Stan Musial, St. Louis	1976	Joe Morgan, Cincinnati	2005	Albert Pujols, St. Louis
1947	Bob Elliott, Boston	1977	George Foster, Cincinnati	2006	Ryan Howard, Philadelphia
1948	Stan Musial, St. Louis	1978	Dave Parker, Pittsburgh	2007	Jimmy Rollins, Philadelphia
1949	Jackie Robinson, Brooklyn	1979	Keith Hernandez, St. Louis;	2008	Albert Pujols, St. Louis
1950	Jim Konstanty, Philadelphia		Willie Stargell, Pittsburgh	2009	Albert Pujols, St. Louis
1951	Roy Campanella, Brooklyn	1980	Mike Schmidt, Philadelphia	2010	Joey Votto, Cincinnati
1952	Hank Sauer, Chicago	1981	Mike Schmidt, Philadelphia	2011	Ryan Braun, Milwaukee
1953	Roy Campanella, Brooklyn	1982	Dale Murphy, Atlanta	2012	Buster Posey, San Francisco
1954	Willie Mays, New York	1983	Dale Murphy, Atlanta	2013	Andrew McCutchen, Pittsburgh
1955	Roy Campanella, Brooklyn	1984	Ryne Sandberg, Chicago	2014	Clayton Kershaw, Los Angeles
1956	Don Newcombe, Brooklyn	1985	Willie McGee, St. Louis	2015	Bryce Harper, Washington
1957	Hank Aaron, Milwaukee	1986	Mike Schmidt, Philadelphia	2016	Kris Bryant, Chicago
1958	Ernie Banks, Chicago	1987	Andre Dawson, Chicago	2017	Giancarlo Stanton, Miami
1959	Ernie Banks, Chicago	1988	Kirk Gibson, Los Angeles	2018	Christian Yelich, Milwaukee
1960	Dick Groat, Pittsburgh	1989	Kevin Mitchell, San Francisco	2019	Cody Bellinger, Los Angeles

American League

Year	Player, team	Year	Player, team	Year	Player, team
1931	Lefty Grove, Philadelphia	1960	Roger Maris, New York	1990	Rickey Henderson, Oakland
1932	Jimmie Foxx, Philadelphia	1961	Roger Maris, New York	1991	Cal Ripken Jr., Baltimore
1933	Jimmie Foxx, Philadelphia	1962	Mickey Mantle, New York	1992	Dennis Eckersley, Oakland
1934	Mickey Cochrane, Detroit	1963	Elston Howard, New York	1993	Frank Thomas, Chicago
1935	Hank Greenberg, Detroit	1964	Brooks Robinson, Baltimore	1994	Frank Thomas, Chicago
1936	Lou Gehrig, New York	1965	Zoilo Versalles, Minnesota	1995	Mo Vaughn, Boston
1937	Charlie Gehringer, Detroit	1966	Frank Robinson, Baltimore	1996	Juan Gonzalez, Texas
1938	Jimmie Foxx, Boston	1967	Carl Yastrzemski, Boston	1997	Ken Griffey Jr., Seattle
1939	Joe DiMaggio, New York	1968	Denny McLain, Detroit	1998	Juan Gonzalez, Texas
1940	Hank Greenberg, Detroit	1969	Harmon Killebrew, Minnesota	1999	Ivan Rodriguez, Texas
1941	Joe DiMaggio, New York	1970	John "Boog" Powell, Baltimore	2000	Jason Giambi, Oakland
1942	Joe Gordon, New York	1971	Vida Blue, Oakland	2001	Ichiro Suzuki, Seattle
1943	Spurgeon "Spud" Chandler, New York	1972	Dick Allen, Chicago	2002	Miguel Tejada, Oakland
		1973	Reggie Jackson, Oakland	2003	Alex Rodriguez, Texas
1944	Hal Newhouser, Detroit	1974	Jeff Burroughs, Texas	2004	Vladimir Guerrero, Anaheim
1945	Hal Newhouser, Detroit	1975	Fred Lynn, Boston	2005	Alex Rodriguez, New York
1946	Ted Williams, Boston	1976	Thurman Munson, New York	2006	Justin Morneau, Minnesota
1947	Joe DiMaggio, New York	1977	Rod Carew, Minnesota	2007	Alex Rodriguez, New York
1948	Lou Boudreau, Cleveland	1978	Jim Rice, Boston	2008	Dustin Pedroia, Boston
1949	Ted Williams, Boston	1979	Don Baylor, California	2009	Joe Mauer, Minnesota
1950	Phil Rizzuto, New York	1980	George Brett, Kansas City	2010	Josh Hamilton, Texas
1951	Yogi Berra, New York	1981	Rollie Fingers, Milwaukee	2011	Justin Verlander, Detroit
1952	Bobby Shantz, Philadelphia	1982	Robin Yount, Milwaukee	2012	Miguel Cabrera, Detroit
1953	Al Rosen, Cleveland	1983	Cal Ripken Jr., Baltimore	2013	Miguel Cabrera, Detroit
1954	Yogi Berra, New York	1984	Willie Hernandez, Detroit	2014	Mike Trout, Los Angeles
1955	Yogi Berra, New York	1985	Don Mattingly, New York	2015	Josh Donaldson, Toronto
1956	Mickey Mantle, New York	1986	Roger Clemens, Boston	2016	Mike Trout, Los Angeles
1957	Mickey Mantle, New York	1987	George Bell, Toronto	2017	José Altuve, Houston
1958	Jackie Jensen, Boston	1988	Jose Canseco, Oakland	2018	Mookie Betts, Boston
1959	Nellie Fox, Chicago	1989	Robin Yount, Milwaukee	2019	Mike Trout, Los Angeles

Rookie of the Year, 1949-2019

(as selected by the Baseball Writers' Assn. of America)

1947: Jackie Robinson, Brooklyn, 1B (combined selection); 1948: Alvin Dark, Boston (NL), SS (combined selection).

National League

Year	Player, team, position	Year	Player, team, position	Year	Player, team, position
1949	Don Newcombe, Brooklyn, P	1956	Frank Robinson, Cincinnati, OF	1963	Pete Rose, Cincinnati, 2B
1950	Sam Jethroe, Boston, OF	1957	Jack Sanford, Philadelphia, P	1964	Richie Allen, Philadelphia, 3B
1951	Willie Mays, NY, OF	1958	Orlando Cepeda, San Francisco, 1B	1965	Jim Lefebvre, L.A., 2B
1952	Joe Black, Brooklyn, P	1959	Willie McCovey, San Francisco, 1B	1966	Tommy Helms, Cincinnati, 2B
1953	Jim Gilliam, Brooklyn, 2B	1960	Frank Howard, L.A., OF	1967	Tom Seaver, NY, P
1954	Wally Moon, St. Louis, OF	1961	Billy Williams, Chicago, OF	1968	Johnny Bench, Cincinnati, C
1955	Bill Virdon, St. Louis, OF	1962	Ken Hubbs, Chicago, 2B	1969	Ted Sizemore, L.A., 2B

Year	Player, team, position	Year	Player, team, position	Year	Player, team, position
1970	Carl Morton, Montréal, P	1986	Todd Worrell, St. Louis, P	2003	Dontrelle Willis, Florida, P
1971	Earl Williams, Atlanta, C	1987	Benito Santiago, San Diego, C	2004	Jason Bay, Pittsburgh, OF
1972	Jon Matlack, NY, P	1988	Chris Sabo, Cincinnati, 3B	2005	Ryan Howard, Philadelphia, 1B
1973	Gary Matthews, San Francisco, OF	1989	Jerome Walton, Chicago, OF	2006	Hanley Ramirez, Florida, SS
1974	Bake McBride, St. Louis, OF	1990	Dave Justice, Atlanta, 1B	2007	Ryan Braun, Milwaukee, 3B
1975	John Montefusco, San Francisco, P	1991	Jeff Bagwell, Houston, 1B	2008	Geovany Soto, Chicago, C
1976	Butch Metzger, San Diego, P;	1992	Eric Karros, L.A., 1B	2009	Chris Coghlan, Florida, OF
	Pat Zachry, Cincinnati, P	1993	Mike Piazza, L.A., C	2010	Buster Posey, San Francisco, C
1977	Andre Dawson, Montréal, OF	1994	Raul Mondesi, L.A., OF	2011	Craig Kimbrel, Atlanta, P
1978	Bob Horner, Atlanta, 3B	1995	Hideo Nomo, L.A., P	2012	Bryce Harper, Washington, OF
1979	Rick Sutcliffe, L.A., P	1996	Todd Hollandsworth, L.A., OF	2013	José Fernández, Miami, P
1980	Steve Howe, L.A., P	1997	Scott Rolen, Philadelphia, 3B	2014	Jacob deGrom, NY, P
1981	Fernando Valenzuela, L.A., P	1998	Kerry Wood, Chicago, P	2015	Kris Bryant, Chicago, 3B
1982	Steve Sax, L.A., 2B	1999	Scott Williamson, Cincinnati, P	2016	Corey Seager, L.A., SS
1983	Darryl Strawberry, NY, OF	2000	Rafael Furcal, Atlanta, SS	2017	Cody Bellinger, L.A., 1B
1984	Dwight Gooden, NY, P	2001	Albert Pujols, St. Louis, OF	2018	Ronald Acuña Jr., Atlanta, OF
1985	Vince Coleman, St. Louis, OF	2002	Jason Jennings, Colorado, P	2019	Pete Alonso, NY, 1B

American League

Year	Player, team, position	Year	Player, team, position	Year	Player, team, position
1949	Roy Sievers, St. Louis, OF	1973	Al Bumbry, Baltimore, OF	1996	Derek Jeter, NY, SS
1950	Walt Dropo, Boston, 1B	1974	Mike Hargrove, Texas, 1B	1997	Nomar Garciaparra, Boston, SS
1951	Gil McDougald, NY, 3B	1975	Fred Lynn, Boston, OF	1998	Ben Grieve, Oakland, OF
1952	Harry Byrd, Philadelphia, P	1976	Mark Fidrych, Detroit, P	1999	Carlos Beltran, Kansas City, OF
1953	Harvey Kuenn, Detroit, SS	1977	Eddie Murray, Baltimore, DH	2000	Kazuhiro Sasaki, Seattle, P
1954	Bob Grim, NY, P	1978	Lou Whitaker, Detroit, 2B	2001	Ichiro Suzuki, Seattle, OF
1955	Herb Score, Cleveland, P	1979	John Castino, Minnesota, 3B;	2002	Eric Hinske, Toronto, 3B
1956	Luis Aparicio, Chicago, SS		Alfredo Griffin, Toronto, SS	2003	Angel Berroa, Kansas City, SS
1957	Tony Kubek, NY, IF-OF	1980	Joe Charboneau, Cleveland, OF	2004	Bobby Crosby, Oakland, SS
1958	Albie Pearson, Washington, OF	1981	Dave Righetti, NY, P	2005	Huston Street, Oakland, P
1959	Bob Allison, Washington, OF	1982	Cal Ripken Jr., Baltimore, SS	2006	Justin Verlander, Detroit, P
1960	Ron Hansen, Baltimore, SS	1983	Ron Kittle, Chicago, OF	2007	Dustin Pedroia, Boston, 2B
1961	Don Schwall, Boston, P	1984	Alvin Davis, Seattle, 1B	2008	Evan Longoria, Tampa Bay, 3B
1962	Tom Tresh, NY, IF-OF	1985	Ozzie Guillen, Chicago, SS	2009	Andrew Bailey, Oakland, P
1963	Gary Peters, Chicago, P	1986	Jose Canseco, Oakland, OF	2010	Neftali Feliz, Texas, P
1964	Tony Oliva, Minnesota, OF	1987	Mark McGwire, Oakland, 1B	2011	Jeremy Hellickson, Tampa Bay, P
1965	Curt Blefary, Baltimore, OF	1988	Walt Weiss, Oakland, SS	2012	Mike Trout, L.A., OF
1966	Tommie Agee, Chicago, OF	1989	Gregg Olson, Baltimore, P	2013	Wil Myers, Tampa Bay, OF
1967	Rod Carew, Minnesota, 2B	1990	Sandy Alomar Jr., Cleveland, C	2014	José Abreu, Chicago, 1B
1968	Stan Bahnsen, NY, P	1991	Chuck Knoblauch, Minnesota, 2B	2015	Carlos Correa, Houston, SS
1969	Lou Piniella, Kansas City, OF	1992	Pat Listach, Milwaukee, SS	2016	Michael Fulmer, Detroit, P
1970	Thurman Munson, NY, C	1993	Tim Salmon, California, OF	2017	Aaron Judge, NY, OF
1971	Chris Chambliss, Cleveland, 1B	1994	Bob Hamelin, Kansas City, DH	2018	Shohei Ohtani, L.A., DH/P
1972	Carlton Fisk, Boston, C	1995	Marty Cordova, Minnesota, OF	2019	Yordan Álvarez, Houston, OF

Major League Pennant Winners, 1901-75

	National League						American League				
Year	Winner	W	L	PCT	Manager	Year	Winner	W	L	PCT	Manager
1901	Pittsburgh	90	49	.647	Clarke	1901	Chicago	83	53	.610	Griffith
1902	Pittsburgh	103	36	.741	Clarke	1902	Philadelphia	83	53	.610	Mack
1903	Pittsburgh	91	49	.650	Clarke	1903	Boston	91	47	.659	Collins
1904	New York	106	47	.693	McGraw	1904	Boston	95	59	.617	Collins
1905	New York	105	48	.686	McGraw	1905	Philadelphia	92	56	.622	Mack
1906	Chicago	116	36	.763	Chance	1906	Chicago	93	58	.616	Jones
1907	Chicago	107	45	.704	Chance	1907	Detroit	92	58	.613	Jennings
1908	Chicago	99	55	.643	Chance	1908	Detroit	90	63	.588	Jennings
1909	Pittsburgh	110	42	.724	Clarke	1909	Detroit	98	54	.645	Jennings
1910	Chicago	104	50	.675	Chance	1910	Philadelphia	102	48	.680	Mack
1911	New York	99	54	.647	McGraw	1911	Philadelphia	101	50	.669	Mack
1912	New York	103	48	.682	McGraw	1912	Boston	105	47	.691	Stahl
1913	New York	101	51	.664	McGraw	1913	Philadelphia	96	57	.627	Mack
1914	Boston	94	59	.614	Stallings	1914	Philadelphia	99	53	.651	Mack
1915	Philadelphia	90	62	.592	Moran	1915	Boston	101	50	.669	Carrigan
1916	Brooklyn	94	60	.610	Robinson	1916	Boston	91	63	.591	Carrigan
1917	New York	98	56	.636	McGraw	1917	Chicago	100	54	.649	Rowland
1918	Chicago	84	45	.651	Mitchell	1918	Boston	75	51	.595	Barrow
1919	Cincinnati	96	44	.686	Moran	1919	Chicago	88	52	.629	Gleason
1920	Brooklyn	93	61	.604	Robinson	1920	Cleveland	98	56	.636	Speaker
1921	New York	94	59	.614	McGraw	1921	New York	98	55	.641	Huggins
1922	New York	93	61	.604	McGraw	1922	New York	94	60	.610	Huggins
1923	New York	95	58	.621	McGraw	1923	New York	98	54	.645	Huggins
1924	New York	93	60	.608	McGraw	1924	Washington	92	62	.597	Harris
1925	Pittsburgh	95	58	.621	McKechnie	1925	Washington	96	55	.636	Harris
1926	St. Louis	89	65	.578	Hornsby	1926	New York	91	63	.591	Huggins
1927	Pittsburgh	94	60	.610	Bush	1927	New York	110	44	.714	Huggins
1928	St. Louis	95	59	.617	McKechnie	1928	New York	101	53	.656	Huggins
1929	Chicago	98	54	.645	McCarthy	1929	Philadelphia	104	46	.693	Mack
1930	St. Louis	92	62	.597	Street	1930	Philadelphia	102	52	.662	Mack
1931	St. Louis	101	53	.656	Street	1931	Philadelphia	107	45	.704	Mack
1932	Chicago	90	64	.584	Hornsby, Grimm	1932	New York	107	47	.695	McCarthy

		National League						American League			
Year	Winner	W	L	PCT	Manager	Year	Winner	W	L	PCT	Manager
1933	New York	91	61	.599	Terry	1933	Washington	99	53	.651	Cronin
1934	St. Louis	95	58	.621	Frisch	1934	Detroit	101	53	.656	Cochrane
1935	Chicago	100	54	.649	Grimm	1935	Detroit	93	58	.616	Cochrane
1936	New York	92	62	.597	Terry	1936	New York	102	51	.667	McCarthy
1937	New York	95	57	.625	Terry	1937	New York	102	52	.662	McCarthy
1938	Chicago	89	63	.586	Grimm, Hartnett	1938	New York	99	53	.651	McCarthy
1939	Cincinnati	97	57	.630	McKechnie	1939	New York	106	45	.702	McCarthy
1940	Cincinnati	100	53	.654	McKechnie	1940	Detroit	90	64	.584	Baker
1941	Brooklyn	100	54	.649	Durocher	1941	New York	101	53	.656	McCarthy
1942	St. Louis	106	48	.688	Southworth	1942	New York	103	51	.669	McCarthy
1943	St. Louis	105	49	.682	Southworth	1943	New York	98	56	.636	McCarthy
1944	St. Louis	105	49	.682	Southworth	1944	St. Louis	89	65	.578	Sewell
1945	Chicago	98	56	.636	Grimm	1945	Detroit	88	65	.575	O'Neill
1946	St. Louis	98	58	.628	Dyer	1946	Boston	104	50	.675	Cronin
1947	Brooklyn	94	60	.610	Shotton	1947	New York	97	57	.630	Harris
1948	Boston	91	62	.595	Southworth	1948	Cleveland	97	58	.626	Boudreau
1949	Brooklyn	97	57	.630	Shotton	1949	New York	97	57	.630	Stengel
1950	Philadelphia	91	63	.591	Sawyer	1950	New York	98	56	.636	Stengel
1951	New York	98	59	.624	Durocher	1951	New York	98	56	.636	Stengel
1952	Brooklyn	96	57	.627	Dressen	1952	New York	95	59	.617	Stengel
1953	Brooklyn	105	49	.682	Dressen	1953	New York	99	52	.656	Stengel
1954	New York	97	57	.630	Durocher	1954	Cleveland	111	43	.721	Lopez
1955	Brooklyn	98	55	.641	Alston	1955	New York	96	58	.623	Stengel
1956	Brooklyn	93	61	.604	Alston	1956	New York	97	57	.630	Stengel
1957	Milwaukee	95	59	.617	Haney	1957	New York	98	56	.636	Stengel
1958	Milwaukee	92	62	.597	Haney	1958	New York	92	62	.597	Stengel
1959	Los Angeles	88	68	.564	Alston	1959	Chicago	94	60	.610	Lopez
1960	Pittsburgh	95	59	.617	Murtaugh	1960	New York	97	57	.630	Stengel
1961	Cincinnati	93	61	.604	Hutchinson	1961	New York	109	53	.673	Houk
1962	San Francisco	103	62	.624	Dark	1962	New York	96	66	.593	Houk
1963	Los Angeles	99	63	.611	Alston	1963	New York	104	57	.646	Houk
1964	St. Louis	93	69	.574	Keane	1964	New York	99	63	.611	Berra
1965	Los Angeles	97	65	.599	Alston	1965	Minnesota	102	60	.630	Mele
1966	Los Angeles	95	67	.586	Alston	1966	Baltimore	97	63	.606	Bauer
1967	St. Louis	101	60	.627	Schoendienst	1967	Boston	92	70	.568	Williams
1968	St. Louis	97	65	.599	Schoendienst	1968	Detroit	103	59	.636	Smith
1969	New York	100	62	.617	Hodges	1969	Baltimore	109	53	.673	Weaver
1970	Cincinnati	102	60	.630	Anderson	1970	Baltimore	108	54	.667	Weaver
1971	Pittsburgh	97	65	.599	Murtaugh	1971	Baltimore	101	57	.639	Weaver
1972	Cincinnati	95	59	.617	Anderson	1972	Oakland	93	62	.600	Williams
1973	New York	82	79	.509	Berra	1973	Oakland	94	68	.580	Williams
1974	Los Angeles	102	60	.630	Alston	1974	Oakland	90	72	.556	Dark
1975	Cincinnati	108	54	.667	Anderson	1975	Boston	95	65	.594	Johnson

Major League Pennant Winners, 1976-2020

National League

Year	East winner	W	L	PCT	Manager	West winner	W	L	PCT	Manager	Pennant winner
1976	Philadelphia	101	61	.623	Ozark	Cincinnati	102	60	.630	Anderson	Cincinnati
1977	Philadelphia	101	61	.623	Ozark	Los Angeles	98	64	.605	Lasorda	Los Angeles
1978	Philadelphia	90	72	.556	Ozark	Los Angeles	95	67	.586	Lasorda	Los Angeles
1979	Pittsburgh	98	64	.605	Tanner	Cincinnati	90	71	.559	McNamara	Pittsburgh
1980	Philadelphia	91	71	.562	Green	Houston	93	70	.571	Virdon	Philadelphia
1981(a)	Philadelphia	34	21	.618	Green	Los Angeles	36	21	.632	Lasorda	(c)
1981(b)	Montréal	30	23	.566	Williams, Fanning	Houston	33	20	.623	Virdon	Los Angeles
1982	St. Louis	92	70	.568	Herzog	Atlanta	89	73	.549	Torre	St. Louis
1983	Philadelphia	90	72	.558	Corrales, Owens	Los Angeles	91	71	.562	Lasorda	Philadelphia
1984	Chicago	96	65	.596	Frey	San Diego	92	70	.568	Williams	San Diego
1985	St. Louis	101	61	.623	Herzog	Los Angeles	95	67	.586	Lasorda	St. Louis
1986	New York	108	54	.667	Johnson	Houston	96	66	.593	Lanier	New York
1987	St. Louis	95	67	.586	Herzog	San Francisco	90	72	.556	Craig	St. Louis
1988	New York	100	60	.625	Johnson	Los Angeles	94	67	.584	Lasorda	Los Angeles
1989	Chicago	93	69	.574	Zimmer	San Francisco	92	70	.568	Craig	San Francisco
1990	Pittsburgh	95	67	.586	Leyland	Cincinnati	91	71	.562	Piniella	Cincinnati
1991	Pittsburgh	98	64	.605	Leyland	Atlanta	94	68	.580	Cox	Atlanta
1992	Pittsburgh	96	66	.593	Leyland	Atlanta	98	64	.605	Cox	Atlanta
1993	Philadelphia	97	65	.599	Fregosi	Atlanta	104	58	.642	Cox	Philadelphia

Year	Division	Winner	W	L	PCT	Manager	Playoffs	Pennant winner
1994(d)	East	Montréal	74	40	.649	Alou	—	—
	Central	Cincinnati	66	48	.579	Johnson		
	West	Los Angeles	58	56	.509	Lasorda		
1995	East	Atlanta	90	54	.625	Cox	Atlanta 3, Colorado* 1	Atlanta
	Central	Cincinnati	85	59	.590	Johnson	Cincinnati 3, Los Angeles 0	
	West	Los Angeles	78	66	.542	Lasorda	Atlanta 4, Cincinnati 0	
1996	East	Atlanta	96	66	.593	Cox	Atlanta 3, Los Angeles* 0	Atlanta
	Central	St. Louis	88	74	.543	La Russa	St. Louis 3, San Diego 0	
	West	San Diego	91	71	.562	Bochy	Atlanta 4, St. Louis 3	

Year	Division	Winner	W	L	PCT	Manager	Playoffs	Pennant winner
1997	East	Atlanta	101	61	.623	Cox	Atlanta 3, Houston 0	Florida*
	Central	Houston	84	78	.519	Dierker	Florida* 3, San Francisco 0	(Leyland)
	West	San Francisco	90	72	.556	Baker	Florida* 4, Atlanta 2	
1998	East	Atlanta	106	56	.654	Cox	Atlanta 3, Chicago* 0	San Diego
	Central	Houston	102	60	.630	Dierker	San Diego 3, Houston 1	
	West	San Diego	98	64	.605	Bochy	San Diego 4, Atlanta 2	
1999	East	Atlanta	103	59	.636	Cox	Atlanta 3, Houston 1	Atlanta
	Central	Houston	97	65	.599	Dierker, Galante	New York* 3, Arizona 1	
	West	Arizona	100	62	.617	Showalter	Atlanta 4, New York* 2	
2000	East	Atlanta	95	67	.586	Cox	St. Louis 3, Atlanta 0	New York*
	Central	St. Louis	95	67	.586	La Russa	New York* 3, San Francisco 1	(Valentine)
	West	San Francisco	97	65	.599	Baker	New York* 4, St. Louis 1	
2001	East	Atlanta	88	74	.543	Cox	Atlanta 3, Houston 0	Arizona
	Central	Houston	93	69	.574	Dierker	Arizona 3, St. Louis* 2	
	West	Arizona	92	70	.568	Brenly	Arizona 4, Atlanta 1	
2002	East	Atlanta	101	59	.631	Cox	St. Louis 3, Arizona 0	San Francisco*
	Central	St. Louis	97	65	.599	La Russa	San Francisco* 3, Atlanta 2	(Baker)
	West	Arizona	98	64	.605	Brenly	San Francisco* 4, St. Louis 1	
2003	East	Atlanta	101	61	.623	Cox	Chicago 3, Atlanta 2	Florida*
	Central	Chicago	88	74	.543	Baker	Florida* 3, San Francisco 1	(McKeon, Torborg)
	West	San Francisco	100	61	.621	Alou	Florida* 4, Chicago 3	
2004	East	Atlanta	96	66	.593	Cox	Houston* 3, Atlanta 2	St. Louis
	Central	St. Louis	105	57	.648	La Russa	St. Louis 3, Los Angeles 1	
	West	Los Angeles	93	69	.574	Tracy	St. Louis 4, Houston* 3	
2005	East	Atlanta	90	72	.556	Cox	St. Louis 3, San Diego 0	Houston*
	Central	St. Louis	100	62	.617	La Russa	Houston* 3, Atlanta 1	(Garner)
	West	San Diego	82	80	.506	Bochy	Houston* 4, St. Louis 2	
2006	East	New York	97	65	.599	Randolph	New York 3, Los Angeles* 0	St. Louis
	Central	St. Louis	83	78	.516	La Russa	St. Louis 3, San Diego 1	
	West	San Diego	88	74	.543	Bochy	St. Louis 4, New York 3	
2007	East	Philadelphia	89	73	.549	Manuel	Colorado* 3, Philadelphia 0	Colorado*
	Central	Chicago	85	77	.525	Piniella	Arizona 3, Chicago 0	(Hurdle)
	West	Arizona	90	72	.556	Melvin	Colorado* 4, Arizona 0	
2008	East	Philadelphia	92	70	.568	Manuel	Philadelphia 3, Milwaukee* 1	Philadelphia
	Central	Chicago	97	64	.602	Piniella	Los Angeles 3, Chicago 0	
	West	Los Angeles	84	78	.519	Torre	Philadelphia 4, Los Angeles 1	
2009	East	Philadelphia	93	69	.574	Manuel	Philadelphia 3, Colorado* 1	Philadelphia
	Central	St. Louis	91	71	.562	La Russa	Los Angeles 3, St. Louis 0	
	West	Los Angeles	95	67	.586	Torre	Philadelphia 4, Los Angeles 1	
2010	East	Philadelphia	97	65	.599	Manuel	San Francisco 3, Atlanta* 1	San Francisco
	Central	Cincinnati	91	71	.562	Baker	Philadelphia 3, Cincinnati 0	
	West	San Francisco	92	70	.568	Bochy	San Francisco 4, Philadelphia 2	
2011	East	Philadelphia	102	60	.630	Manuel	Milwaukee 3, Arizona 2	St. Louis*
	Central	Milwaukee	96	66	.593	Roenicke	St. Louis* 3, Philadelphia 2	(La Russa)
	West	Arizona	94	68	.580	Gibson	St. Louis* 4, Milwaukee 2	
2012	East	Washington	98	64	.605	Johnson	#St. Louis* 6, Atlanta* 3	San Francisco
	Central	Cincinnati	97	65	.599	Baker	St. Louis* 3, Washington 2	
	West	San Francisco	94	68	.580	Bochy	San Francisco 3, Cincinnati 2	
							San Francisco 4, St. Louis* 3	
2013	East	Atlanta	96	66	.593	González	#Pittsburgh* 6, Cincinnati* 2	St. Louis
	Central	St. Louis	97	65	.599	Matheny	St. Louis 3, Pittsburgh* 2	
	West	Los Angeles	92	70	.568	Mattingly	Los Angeles 3, Atlanta 1	
							St. Louis 4, Los Angeles 2	
2014	East	Washington	96	66	.593	Williams	#San Francisco* 8, Pittsburgh* 0	San Francisco*
	Central	St. Louis	90	72	.556	Matheny	San Francisco* 3, Washington 1	(Bochy)
	West	Los Angeles	94	68	.580	Mattingly	St. Louis 3, Los Angeles 1	
							San Francisco* 4, St. Louis 1	
2015	East	New York	90	72	.556	Collins	#Chicago* 4, Pittsburgh* 0	New York
	Central	St. Louis	100	62	.617	Matheny	Chicago* 3, St. Louis 1	
	West	Los Angeles	92	70	.568	Mattingly	New York 3, Los Angeles 2	
							New York 4, Chicago* 0	
2016	East	Washington	95	67	.586	Baker	#San Francisco* 3, New York* 0	Chicago
	Central	Chicago	103	58	.640	Maddon	Chicago 3, San Francisco* 1	
	West	Los Angeles	91	71	.562	Roberts	Los Angeles 3, Washington 2	
							Chicago 4, Los Angeles 2	
2017	East	Washington	97	65	.599	Baker	#Arizona* 11, Colorado* 8	Los Angeles
	Central	Chicago	92	70	.568	Maddon	Chicago 3, Washington 2	
	West	Los Angeles	104	58	.642	Roberts	Los Angeles 3, Arizona* 0	
							Los Angeles 4, Chicago 1	
2018	East	Atlanta	90	72	.556	Snitker	#Colorado* 2, Chicago* 1	Los Angeles
	Central	Milwaukee	96	67	.589	Counsell	Milwaukee 3, Colorado* 0	
	West	Los Angeles	92	71	.564	Roberts	Los Angeles 3, Atlanta 1	
							Los Angeles 4, Milwaukee 3	
2019	East	Atlanta	97	65	.599	Snitker	#Washington* 4, Milwaukee* 3	Washington*
	Central	St. Louis	91	71	.562	Shildt	St. Louis 3, Atlanta 2	(Martinez)
	West	Los Angeles	106	56	.654	Roberts	Washington* 3, Los Angeles 2	
							Washington* 4, St. Louis 0	
2020	East	Atlanta	35	25	.583	Snitker	Los Angeles 3, San Diego* 0	Los Angeles
	Central	Chicago	34	26	.567	Ross	Atlanta 3, Miami* 0	
	West	Los Angeles	43	17	.717	Roberts	Los Angeles 4, Atlanta 3	

American League

Year	East winner	W	L	PCT	Manager	West winner	W	L	PCT	Manager	Pennant winner
1976	New York	97	62	.610	Martin	Kansas City	90	72	.556	Herzog	New York
1977	New York	100	62	.617	Martin	Kansas City	102	60	.630	Herzog	New York
1978	New York	100	63	.613	Martin, Lemon	Kansas City	92	70	.568	Herzog	New York
1979	Baltimore	102	57	.642	Weaver	California	88	74	.543	Fregosi	Baltimore
1980	New York	103	59	.636	Howser	Kansas City	97	65	.599	Frey	Kansas City
1981(a)	New York	34	22	.607	Michael, Lemon	Oakland	37	23	.617	Martin	(c)
1981(b)	Milwaukee	31	22	.585	Rodgers	Kansas City	30	23	.566	Frey, Howser	New York
1982	Milwaukee	95	67	.586	Rodgers, Kuenn	California	93	69	.574	Mauch	Milwaukee
1983	Baltimore	98	64	.605	Altobelli	Chicago	99	63	.611	La Russa	Baltimore
1984	Detroit	104	58	.642	Anderson	Kansas City	84	78	.519	Howser	Detroit
1985	Toronto	99	62	.615	Cox	Kansas City	91	71	.562	Howser	Kansas City
1986	Boston	95	66	.590	McNamara	California	92	70	.568	Mauch	Boston
1987	Detroit	98	64	.605	Anderson	Minnesota	85	77	.525	Kelly	Minnesota
1988	Boston	89	73	.549	McNamara, Morgan	Oakland	104	58	.642	La Russa	Oakland
1989	Toronto	89	73	.549	Williams, Gaston	Oakland	99	63	.611	La Russa	Oakland
1990	Boston	88	74	.543	Morgan	Oakland	103	59	.636	La Russa	Oakland
1991	Toronto	91	71	.562	Gaston, Tenace	Minnesota	95	67	.586	Kelly	Minnesota
1992	Toronto	96	66	.593	Gaston	Oakland	96	66	.593	La Russa	Toronto
1993	Toronto	95	67	.586	Gaston	Chicago	94	68	.580	Lamont	Toronto

Year	Division	Winner	W	L	PCT	Manager	Playoffs	Pennant winner
1994(d)	East	New York	70	43	.619	Showalter	—	—
	Central	Chicago	67	46	.593	Lamont		
	West	Texas	52	62	.456	Kennedy		
1995	East	Boston	86	58	.597	Kennedy	Cleveland 3, Boston 0	Cleveland
	Central	Cleveland	100	44	.694	Hargrove	Seattle 3, New York* 2	
	West	Seattle	79	66	.545	Piniella	Cleveland 3, Seattle 2	
1996	East	New York	92	70	.568	Torre	Baltimore* 3, Cleveland 1	New York
	Central	Cleveland	99	62	.615	Hargrove	New York 3, Texas 1	
	West	Texas	90	72	.556	Oates	New York 4, Baltimore* 1	
1997	East	Baltimore	98	64	.605	Johnson	Baltimore 3, Seattle 1	Cleveland
	Central	Cleveland	86	75	.534	Hargrove	Cleveland 3, New York* 2	
	West	Seattle	90	72	.556	Piniella	Cleveland 4, Baltimore 2	
1998	East	New York	114	48	.704	Torre	New York 3, Texas 0	New York
	Central	Cleveland	89	73	.549	Hargrove	Cleveland 3, Boston* 1	
	West	Texas	88	74	.543	Oates	New York 4, Cleveland 2	
1999	East	New York	98	64	.605	Torre	New York 3, Texas 0	New York
	Central	Cleveland	97	65	.599	Hargrove	Boston* 3, Cleveland 2	
	West	Texas	95	67	.586	Oates	New York 4, Boston* 1	
2000	East	New York	87	74	.540	Torre	New York 3, Oakland 2	New York
	Central	Chicago	95	67	.586	Manuel	Seattle* 3, Chicago 0	
	West	Oakland	91	70	.565	Howe	New York 4, Seattle* 2	
2001	East	New York	95	65	.594	Torre	Seattle 3, Cleveland 2	New York
	Central	Cleveland	91	71	.562	Manuel	New York 3, Oakland* 2	
	West	Seattle	116	46	.716	Piniella	New York 4, Seattle 1	
2002	East	New York	103	58	.640	Torre	Anaheim* 3, New York 1	Anaheim*
	Central	Minnesota	94	67	.584	Gardenhire	Minnesota 3, Oakland 2	(Scioscia)
	West	Oakland	103	59	.636	Howe	Anaheim* 4, Minnesota 1	
2003	East	New York	101	61	.623	Torre	New York 3, Minnesota 1	New York
	Central	Minnesota	90	72	.556	Gardenhire	Boston* 3, Oakland 2	
	West	Oakland	96	66	.593	Macha	New York 4, Boston* 3	
2004	East	New York	101	61	.623	Torre	New York 3, Minnesota 1	Boston*
	Central	Minnesota	92	70	.568	Gardenhire	Boston* 3, Anaheim 0	(Francona)
	West	Anaheim	92	70	.568	Scioscia	Boston* 4, New York 3	
2005	East	New York	95	67	.586	Torre	Chicago 3, Boston* 0	Chicago
	Central	Chicago	99	63	.611	Guillen	Los Angeles 3, New York 2	
	West	Los Angeles	95	67	.586	Scioscia	Chicago 4, Los Angeles 1	
2006	East	New York	97	65	.599	Torre	Oakland 3, Minnesota 0	Detroit*
	Central	Minnesota	96	66	.593	Gardenhire	Detroit* 3, New York 1	(Leyland)
	West	Oakland	93	69	.574	Macha	Detroit* 4, Oakland 0	
2007	East	Boston	96	66	.593	Francona	Boston 3, Los Angeles 0	Boston
	Central	Cleveland	96	66	.593	Wedge	Cleveland 3, New York* 1	
	West	Los Angeles	94	68	.580	Scioscia	Boston 4, Cleveland 3	
2008	East	Tampa Bay	97	65	.599	Maddon	Tampa Bay 3, Chicago 1	Tampa Bay
	Central	Chicago	89	74	.546	Guillen	Boston* 3, Los Angeles 1	
	West	Los Angeles	100	62	.617	Scioscia	Tampa Bay 4, Boston* 3	
2009	East	New York	103	59	.636	Girardi	New York 3, Minnesota 0	New York
	Central	Minnesota	87	76	.534	Gardenhire	Los Angeles 3, Boston* 0	
	West	Los Angeles	97	65	.599	Scioscia	New York 4, Los Angeles 2	
2010	East	Tampa Bay	96	66	.593	Maddon	New York* 3, Minnesota 0	Texas
	Central	Minnesota	94	68	.580	Gardenhire	Texas 3, Tampa Bay 2	
	West	Texas	90	72	.556	Washington	Texas 4, New York* 2	
2011	East	New York	97	65	.599	Girardi	Detroit 3, New York 2	Texas
	Central	Detroit	95	67	.586	Leyland	Texas 3, Tampa Bay* 1	
	West	Texas	96	66	.593	Washington	Texas 4, Detroit 2	
2012	East	New York	95	67	.586	Girardi	#Baltimore* 5, Texas* 1	Detroit
	Central	Detroit	88	74	.543	Leyland	New York 3, Baltimore* 2	
	West	Oakland	94	68	.580	Melvin	Detroit 3, Oakland 2	
							Detroit 4, New York 0	
2013	East	Boston	97	65	.599	Farrell	#Tampa Bay* 4, Cleveland* 0	Boston
	Central	Detroit	93	69	.574	Leyland	Boston 3, Tampa Bay* 1	
	West	Oakland	96	66	.593	Melvin	Detroit 3, Oakland 2	
							Boston 4, Detroit 2	
2014	East	Baltimore	96	66	.593	Showalter	#Kansas City* 9, Oakland* 8	Kansas City*
	Central	Detroit	90	72	.556	Ausmus	Kansas City* 3, Los Angeles 0	(Yost)
	West	Los Angeles	98	64	.605	Scioscia	Baltimore 3, Detroit 0	
							Kansas City* 4, Baltimore 0	
2015	East	Toronto	93	69	.574	Gibbons	#Houston* 3, New York* 0	Kansas City
	Central	Kansas City	95	67	.586	Yost	Kansas City 3, Houston* 2	
	West	Texas	88	74	.543	Banister	Toronto 3, Texas 2	
							Kansas City 4, Toronto 2	
2016	East	Boston	93	69	.574	Farrell	#Toronto* 5, Baltimore* 2	Cleveland
	Central	Cleveland	94	67	.584	Francona	Toronto* 3, Texas 0	
	West	Texas	95	67	.586	Banister	Cleveland 3, Boston 0	
							Cleveland 4, Toronto* 1	
2017	East	Boston	93	69	.574	Farrell	#New York* 8, Minnesota* 4	Houston
	Central	Cleveland	102	60	.630	Francona	Houston 3, Boston 1	
	West	Houston	101	61	.623	Hinch	New York* 3, Cleveland 2	
							Houston 4, New York* 3	
2018	East	Boston	108	54	.667	Cora	#New York* 7, Oakland* 2	Boston
	Central	Cleveland	91	71	.562	Francona	Boston 3, New York* 1	
	West	Houston	103	59	.636	Hinch	Houston 3, Cleveland 0	
							Boston 4, Houston 1	
2019	East	New York	103	59	.636	Boone	#Tampa Bay* 5, Oakland* 1	Houston
	Central	Minnesota	101	61	.623	Baldelli	New York 3, Minnesota 0	
	West	Houston	107	55	.660	Hinch	Houston 3, Tampa Bay* 2	
							Houston 4, New York 2	
2020	East	Tampa Bay	40	20	.667	Cash	Tampa Bay 3, New York* 2	Tampa Bay
	Central	Minnesota	36	24	.600	Baldelli	Houston* 3, Oakland 1	
	West	Oakland	36	24	.600	Melvin	Tampa Bay 4, Houston* 3	

* = Wild-card team. If pennant winner is wild-card team, manager's name is given in parentheses. # = Single-game wild-card playoff (debuted in 2012). **Note:** In 2020, a best-of-three wild-card round included 8 teams in each league. (a) First half. (b) Second half. (c) Montréal, L.A., NY Yankees, and Oakland won the divisional playoffs. (d) In Aug. 1994, a players' strike began that caused the cancelation of the remainder of the season, the playoffs, and the World Series. Teams listed as division "winners" for 1994 were leading their divisions at the time of the strike.

World Series Results, 1903-2020

1903 Boston AL 5, Pittsburgh NL 3	1942 St. Louis NL 4, New York AL 1	1981 Los Angeles NL 4, New York AL 2
1904 No series	1943 New York AL 4, St. Louis NL 1	1982 St. Louis NL 4, Milwaukee AL 3
1905 New York NL 4, Philadelphia AL 1	1944 St. Louis NL 4, St. Louis AL 2	1983 Baltimore AL 4, Philadelphia NL 1
1906 Chicago AL 4, Chicago NL 2	1945 Detroit AL 4, Chicago NL 3	1984 Detroit AL 4, San Diego NL 1
1907 Chicago NL 4, Detroit AL 0, 1 tie	1946 St. Louis NL 4, Boston AL 3	1985 Kansas City AL 4, St. Louis NL 3
1908 Chicago NL 4, Detroit AL 1	1947 New York AL 4, Brooklyn NL 3	1986 New York NL 4, Boston AL 3
1909 Pittsburgh NL 4, Detroit AL 3	1948 Cleveland AL 4, Boston NL 2	1987 Minnesota AL 4, St. Louis NL 3
1910 Philadelphia AL 4, Chicago NL 1	1949 New York AL 4, Brooklyn NL 1	1988 Los Angeles NL 4, Oakland AL 1
1911 Philadelphia AL 4, New York NL 2	1950 New York AL 4, Philadelphia NL 0	1989 Oakland AL 4, San Francisco NL 0
1912 Boston AL 4, New York NL 3, 1 tie	1951 New York AL 4, New York NL 2	1990 Cincinnati NL 4, Oakland AL 0
1913 Philadelphia AL 4, New York NL 1	1952 New York AL 4, Brooklyn NL 3	1991 Minnesota AL 4, Atlanta NL 3
1914 Boston NL 4, Philadelphia AL 0	1953 New York AL 4, Brooklyn NL 2	1992 Toronto AL 4, Atlanta NL 2
1915 Boston AL 4, Philadelphia NL 1	1954 New York NL 4, Cleveland AL 0	1993 Toronto AL 4, Philadelphia NL 2
1916 Boston AL 4, Brooklyn NL 1	1955 Brooklyn NL 4, New York AL 3	1994 No series due to strike
1917 Chicago AL 4, New York NL 2	1956 New York AL 4, Brooklyn NL 3	1995 Atlanta NL 4, Cleveland AL 2
1918 Boston AL 4, Chicago NL 2	1957 Milwaukee NL 4, New York AL 3	1996 New York AL 4, Atlanta NL 2
1919 Cincinnati NL 5, Chicago AL 3	1958 New York AL 4, Milwaukee NL 3	1997 Florida NL 4, Cleveland AL 3
1920 Cleveland AL 5, Brooklyn NL 2	1959 Los Angeles NL 4, Chicago AL 2	1998 New York AL 4, San Diego NL 0
1921 New York NL 5, New York AL 3	1960 Pittsburgh NL 4, New York AL 3	1999 New York AL 4, Atlanta NL 0
1922 New York NL 4, New York AL 0, 1 tie	1961 New York AL 4, Cincinnati NL 1	2000 New York AL 4, New York NL 1
1923 New York AL 4, New York NL 2	1962 New York AL 4, San Francisco NL 3	2001 Arizona NL 4, New York AL 3
1924 Washington AL 4, New York NL 3	1963 Los Angeles NL 4, New York AL 0	2002 Anaheim AL 4, San Francisco NL 3
1925 Pittsburgh NL 4, Washington AL 3	1964 St. Louis NL 4, New York AL 3	2003 Florida NL 4, New York AL 2
1926 St. Louis NL 4, New York AL 3	1965 Los Angeles NL 4, Minnesota AL 3	2004 Boston AL 4, St. Louis NL 0
1927 New York AL 4, Pittsburgh NL 0	1966 Baltimore AL 4, Los Angeles NL 0	2005 Chicago AL 4, Houston NL 0
1928 New York AL 4, St. Louis NL 0	1967 St. Louis NL 4, Boston AL 3	2006 St. Louis NL 4, Detroit AL 1
1929 Philadelphia AL 4, Chicago NL 1	1968 Detroit AL 4, St. Louis NL 3	2007 Boston AL 4, Colorado NL 0
1930 Philadelphia AL 4, St. Louis NL 2	1969 New York NL 4, Baltimore AL 1	2008 Philadelphia NL 4, Tampa Bay AL 1
1931 St. Louis NL 4, Philadelphia AL 3	1970 Baltimore AL 4, Cincinnati NL 1	2009 New York AL 4, Philadelphia NL 2
1932 New York AL 4, Chicago NL 0	1971 Pittsburgh NL 4, Baltimore AL 3	2010 San Francisco NL 4, Texas AL 1
1933 New York NL 4, Washington AL 1	1972 Oakland AL 4, Cincinnati NL 3	2011 St. Louis NL 4, Texas AL 3
1934 St. Louis NL 4, Detroit AL 3	1973 Oakland AL 4, New York NL 3	2012 San Francisco NL 4, Detroit AL 0
1935 Detroit AL 4, Chicago NL 2	1974 Oakland AL 4, Los Angeles NL 1	2013 Boston AL 4, St. Louis NL 2
1936 New York AL 4, New York NL 2	1975 Cincinnati NL 4, Boston AL 3	2014 San Fran. NL 4, Kansas City AL 3
1937 New York AL 4, New York NL 1	1976 Cincinnati NL 4, New York AL 0	2015 Kansas City AL 4, New York NL 1
1938 New York AL 4, Chicago NL 0	1977 New York AL 4, Los Angeles NL 2	2016 Chicago NL 4, Cleveland AL 3
1939 New York AL 4, Cincinnati NL 0	1978 New York AL 4, Los Angeles NL 2	2017 Houston AL 4, Los Angeles NL 3
1940 Cincinnati NL 4, Detroit AL 3	1979 Pittsburgh NL 4, Baltimore AL 3	2018 Boston AL 4, Los Angeles NL 1
1941 New York AL 4, Brooklyn NL 1	1980 Philadelphia NL 4, Kansas City AL 2	2019 Washington NL 4, Houston AL 3
		2020 Los Angeles NL 4, Tampa Bay AL 2

World Series Most Valuable Player, 1955-2020

Year	Player, position, team	Year	Player, position, team	Year	Player, position, team
1955	Johnny Podres, P, Brooklyn	1978	Bucky Dent, SS, NY (AL)	1999	Mariano Rivera, P, NY (AL)
1956	Don Larsen, P, NY (AL)	1979	Willie Stargell, 1B, Pittsburgh	2000	Derek Jeter, SS, NY (AL)
1957	Lew Burdette, P, Milwaukee (NL)	1980	Mike Schmidt, 3B, Philadelphia	2001	Curt Schilling, P, Arizona;
1958	Bob Turley, P, NY (AL)	1981	Ron Cey, 3B, Los Angeles (NL);		Randy Johnson, P, Arizona
1959	Larry Sherry, P, Los Angeles (NL)		Pedro Guerrero, OF, Los Angeles;	2002	Troy Glaus, 3B, Anaheim
1960[1]	Bobby Richardson, 2B, NY (AL)		Steve Yeager, C, Los Angeles	2003	Josh Beckett, P, Florida
1961	Whitey Ford, P, NY (AL)	1982	Darrell Porter, C, St. Louis	2004	Manny Ramirez, OF, Boston
1962	Ralph Terry, P, NY (AL)	1983	Rick Dempsey, C, Baltimore	2005	Jermaine Dye, OF, Chicago (AL)
1963	Sandy Koufax, P, Los Angeles (NL)	1984	Alan Trammell, SS, Detroit	2006	David Eckstein, SS, St. Louis
1964	Bob Gibson, P, St. Louis	1985	Bret Saberhagen, P, Kansas City	2007	Mike Lowell, 3B, Boston
1965	Sandy Koufax, P, Los Angeles (NL)	1986	Ray Knight, 3B, NY (NL)	2008	Cole Hamels, P, Philadelphia
1966	Frank Robinson, OF, Baltimore	1987	Frank Viola, P, Minnesota	2009	Hideki Matsui, DH, NY (AL)
1967	Bob Gibson, P, St. Louis	1988	Orel Hershiser, P, Los Angeles (NL)	2010	Edgar Renteria, SS, San Francisco
1968	Mickey Lolich, P, Detroit	1989	Dave Stewart, P, Oakland	2011	David Freese, 3B, St. Louis
1969	Donn Clendenon, 1B, NY (NL)	1990	José Rijo, P, Cincinnati	2012	Pablo Sandoval, 3B, San Francisco
1970	Brooks Robinson, 3B, Baltimore	1991	Jack Morris, P, Minnesota	2013	David Ortiz, DH, Boston
1971	Roberto Clemente, P, Pittsburgh	1992	Pat Borders, C, Toronto	2014	Madison Bumgarner, P, San Francisco
1972	Gene Tenace, C, Oakland	1993	Paul Molitor, DH, Toronto	2015	Salvador Pérez, C, Kansas City
1973	Reggie Jackson, OF, Oakland	1994	No series due to strike	2016	Ben Zobrist, OF, Chicago (NL)
1974	Rollie Fingers, P, Oakland	1995	Tom Glavine, P, Atlanta	2017	George Springer, OF, Houston
1975	Pete Rose, 3B, Cincinnati	1996	John Wetteland, P, NY (AL)	2018	Steve Pearce, 1B, Boston
1976	Johnny Bench, C, Cincinnati	1997	Livan Hernandez, P, Florida	2019	Stephen Strasburg, P, Washington
1977	Reggie Jackson, OF, NY (AL)	1998	Scott Brosius, 3B, NY (AL)	2020	Corey Seager, SS, Los Angeles (NL)

Note: World Series canceled in 1994 due to strike. (1) Richardson won the MVP although Pittsburgh beat New York.

World Series Won-Lost Records, by Franchise

Since beginning of "modern" era in 1901. Figures represent overall Series wins, not individual games.

Team	Wins	Losses	Team	Wins	Losses
New York Yankees	27	13	Toronto Blue Jays	2	0
St. Louis Cardinals	11	8	Kansas City Royals	2	2
Boston Red Sox	9	4	New York Mets	2	3
Philadelphia/Kansas City/Oakland A's	9	5	Cleveland Indians	2	4
New York/San Francisco Giants	8	12	Philadelphia Phillies	2	5
Brooklyn/Los Angeles Dodgers	7	14	Houston Astros	1	2
Pittsburgh Pirates	5	2	Arizona Diamondbacks	1	0
Cincinnati Reds	5	4	L.A./California/Anaheim/L.A. Angels	1	0
Detroit Tigers	4	7	Montréal Expos/Washington Nationals	1	0
Chicago White Sox	3	2	Colorado Rockies	0	1
Washington Senators/Minnesota Twins	3	3	Seattle Pilots/Milwaukee Brewers	0	1
St. Louis Browns/Baltimore Orioles	3	4	San Diego Padres	0	2
Boston/Milwaukee/Atlanta Braves	3	6	Tampa Bay Rays	0	2
Chicago Cubs	3	8	Texas Rangers	0	2
Florida/Miami Marlins	2	0	Seattle Mariners	0	0

All-Time World Series Career Leaders
(through 2020)

Batting Leaders

Batter (min. 50 PA)	H	AB	AVG	Batter (min. 50 PA)	H	AB	AVG
1. David Ortiz	20	44	.455	6. Hal McRae	18	45	.400
2. Pablo Sandoval	20	47	.426	7. Lou Brock	34	87	.391
3. Johnny "Pepper" Martin	23	55	.418	8. Marquis Grissom	30	77	.390
4. Paul Molitor	23	55	.418	9. Thurman Munson	25	67	.373
5. Lance Berkman	16	39	.410	10. George Brett	19	51	.373

Games Played
Yogi Berra 75
Mickey Mantle 65
Elston Howard 54
Hank Bauer 53
Gil McDougald 53
Phil Rizzuto 52
Joe DiMaggio 51
Frankie Frisch 50
Pee Wee Reese 44
Roger Maris 41
Babe Ruth 41

Runs Batted In
Mickey Mantle 40
Yogi Berra 39
Lou Gehrig 35
Babe Ruth 33
Joe DiMaggio 30
Bill Skowron 29
Duke Snider 26

Hits
Yogi Berra 71
Mickey Mantle 59
Frankie Frisch 58
Joe DiMaggio 54
Derek Jeter 50
Hank Bauer 46
Pee Wee Reese 46
Gil McDougald 45
Phil Rizzuto 45
Lou Gehrig 43

Home Runs
Mickey Mantle 18
Babe Ruth 15
Yogi Berra 12
Duke Snider 11
Lou Gehrig 10
Reggie Jackson 10
Joe DiMaggio 8
Frank Robinson 8
Bill Skowron 8

Runs
Mickey Mantle 42
Yogi Berra 41
Babe Ruth 37
Derek Jeter 32
Lou Gehrig 30
Joe DiMaggio 27
Roger Maris 26
Elston Howard 25
Gil McDougald 23
Jackie Robinson 22

Stolen Bases
Lou Brock 14
Eddie Collins 14
Frank Chance 10
Dave Lopes 10
Phil Rizzuto 10
Frankie Frisch 9
Kenny Lofton 9
Honus Wagner 9
Johnny Evers 8

Pitching Leaders

Games Pitched
Mariano Rivera 24
Whitey Ford 22
Mike Stanton 20
Rollie Fingers 16
Ryan Madson 16
Jeff Nelson 16
Allie Reynolds 15
Bob Turley 15
Clay Carroll 14
Andy Pettitte 13
Clem Labine 13
Mark Wohlers 13
Jeremy Affeldt 12
Waite Hoyt 12
Catfish Hunter 12
Art Nehf 12

Wins
Whitey Ford 10
Bob Gibson 7
Allie Reynolds 7
Red Ruffing 7
Chief Bender 6
Lefty Gomez 6
Waite Hoyt 6
Three Finger Brown 5
Jack Coombs 5
Catfish Hunter 5
Christy Mathewson 5
Herb Pennock 5
Andy Pettitte 5
Vic Raschi 5

Strikeouts
Whitey Ford 94
Bob Gibson 92
Allie Reynolds 62
Sandy Koufax 61
Red Ruffing 61
Chief Bender 59
George Earnshaw 56
Andy Pettitte 56
John Smoltz 52
Roger Clemens 49
Waite Hoyt 49
Christy Mathewson . . . 48
Bob Turley 46

Saves
Mariano Rivera 11
Rollie Fingers 6
Johnny Murphy 4
Robb Nen 4
Allie Reynolds 4
John Wetteland 4
Roy Face 3
Neftali Feliz 3
Firpo Marberry 3
Will McEnaney 3
Tug McGraw 3
Jonathan Papelbon 3
Herb Pennock 3
Troy Percival 3
Sergio Romo 3
Kent Tekulve 3
Todd Worrell 3

MLB Stadiums, 2020

Team	Stadium (year opened)	Surface	Distances (ft) LF	Center	RF	Seating capacity[1]
Arizona Diamondbacks	Chase Field (1998)	Turf	330	407	335	48,405
Atlanta Braves	Truist Park (2017)	Grass	335	400	325	41,184
Chicago Cubs	Wrigley Field (1914)	Grass	355	400	353	41,298
Cincinnati Reds	Great American Ball Park (2003)	Grass	328	404	325	42,319
Colorado Rockies	Coors Field (1995)	Grass	347	415	350	50,144
Los Angeles Dodgers	Dodger Stadium (1962)	Grass	330	395	330	56,000
Miami Marlins	Marlins Park (2012)	Turf	340	400	335	37,446
Milwaukee Brewers	Miller Park (2001)	Grass	342	400	345	41,700
New York Mets	Citi Field (2009)	Grass	335	408	330	41,922
Philadelphia Phillies	Citizens Bank Park (2004)	Grass	329	401	330	42,792
Pittsburgh Pirates	PNC Park (2001)	Grass	325	399	320	38,747
St. Louis Cardinals	Busch Stadium (2006)	Grass	336	400	335	44,383
San Diego Padres	Petco Park (2004)	Grass	336	396	322	40,019
San Francisco Giants	Oracle Park (2000)	Grass	339	391	309	41,314
Washington Nationals	Nationals Park (2008)	Grass	336	402	335	41,380
Baltimore Orioles	Oriole Park at Camden Yards (1992)	Grass	333	410	318	45,971
Boston Red Sox	Fenway Park (1912)	Grass	310	390	302	37,305[2]
Chicago White Sox	Guaranteed Rate Field (1991)	Grass	330	400	335	40,615
Cleveland Indians	Progressive Field (1994)	Grass	325	405	325	34,830
Detroit Tigers	Comerica Park (2000)	Grass	345	420	330	41,083
Houston Astros	Minute Maid Park (2000)	Grass	315	409	326	41,168
Kansas City Royals	Kauffman Stadium (1973)	Grass	330	410	330	37,903
Los Angeles Angels	Angel Stadium of Anaheim (1966)	Grass	347	396	348	45,517
Minnesota Twins	Target Field (2010)	Grass	339	404	328	38,544
New York Yankees	Yankee Stadium (2009)	Grass	318	408	314	46,537
Oakland Athletics	Oakland Coliseum (1966)	Grass	330	400	330	46,847
Seattle Mariners	T-Mobile Park (1999)	Grass	331	401	326	47,500
Tampa Bay Rays	Tropicana Field (1990)	Turf	315	404	322	25,025
Texas Rangers	Globe Life Field (2020)	Turf	329	407	326	40,300
Toronto Blue Jays	Rogers Centre (1989)	Astroturf	328	400	328	49,286

(1) As of 2020 season. (2) For day games; night game capacity is 37,755.

Major League Franchise Shifts and Additions

1953: Boston Braves (NL) became Milwaukee Braves.
1954: St. Louis Browns (AL) became Baltimore Orioles.
1955: Philadelphia Athletics (AL) became Kansas City Athletics.
1958: New York Giants (NL) became San Francisco Giants.
1958: Brooklyn Dodgers (NL) became L.A. Dodgers.
1961: Washington Senators (AL) became Minnesota Twins.
1961: L.A. Angels enfranchised by the AL.
1961: Washington Senators II enfranchised by the AL, replacing Washington Senators I, whose franchise moved to Minneapolis-St. Paul and became Minnesota Twins.
1962: Houston Colt .45s enfranchised by the NL.
1962: New York Mets enfranchised by the NL.
1966: Milwaukee Braves (NL) became Atlanta Braves.
1968: Kansas City Athletics (AL) became Oakland Athletics.

1969: Kansas City Royals and Seattle Pilots enfranchised by the AL; Montréal Expos and San Diego Padres enfranchised by the NL.
1970: Seattle Pilots (AL) became Milwaukee Brewers.
1972: Washington Senators II (AL) became Texas Rangers (Dallas-Fort Worth area).
1977: Toronto Blue Jays and Seattle Mariners enfranchised by the AL.
1993: Colorado Rockies (Denver) and Florida Marlins (Miami) enfranchised by the NL.
1998: Tampa Bay Devil Rays began play in the AL; Arizona Diamondbacks (Phoenix) began play in the NL (both teams enfranchised in 1995). Milwaukee Brewers moved from the AL to the NL.
2005: Montréal Expos (NL) became Washington Nationals.
2013: Houston Astros moved from the NL to the AL.

National Baseball Hall of Fame and Museum

Located in Cooperstown, NY. # = Player chosen in first year of eligibility (five seasons after retirement) or earlier. * = 2020 inductee.
www.baseballhall.org

#Aaron, Hank
Alexander, Grover
Alomar, Roberto
Alston, Walt
Anderson, George
Anson, Cap
Aparicio, Luis
Appling, Luke
Ashburn, Richie
Averill, Earl
Bagwell, Jeff
Baines, Harold
Baker, Frank "Home Run"
Bancroft, Dave
#Banks, Ernie
Barlick, Al
Barrow, Edward G.
Beckley, Jake
Bell, James "Cool Papa"
#Bench, Johnny
Bender, Charles "Chief"
Berra, Lawrence "Yogi"
Biggio, Craig
Blyleven, Bert
#Boggs, Wade
Bottomley, Jim
Boudreau, Lou
Bresnahan, Roger
#Brett, George
#Brock, Lou
Brouthers, Dan
Brown, Mordecai
Brown, Ray
Brown, Willard
Bulkeley, Morgan C.
Bunning, Jim
Burkett, Jesse C.
Campanella, Roy
#Carew, Rod
Carey, Max
#Carlton, Steve
Carter, Gary
Cartwright, Alexander
Cepeda, Orlando
Chadwick, Henry
Chance, Frank
Chandler, Albert "Happy"
Charleston, Oscar
Chesbro, John
Chylak, Nestor
Clarke, Fred
Clarkson, John
#Clemente, Roberto
Cobb, Ty[1]
Cochrane, Mickey
Collins, Eddie
Collins, James
Combs, Earle
Comiskey, Charles A.
Conlan, John "Jocko"
Connolly, Thomas H.
Connor, Roger
Cooper, Andy
Coveleski, Stan
Cox, Bobby
Crawford, Sam
Cronin, Joe

Cummings, W. A. "Candy"
Cuyler, Hazen "Kiki"
Dandridge, Ray
Davis, George
Dawson, Andre
Day, Leon
Dean, Jay Hanna "Dizzy"
Delahanty, Ed
Dickey, Bill
Dihigo, Martín
#DiMaggio, Joe
#Doby, Larry
Doerr, Bobby
Dreyfuss, Barney
Drysdale, Don
Duffy, Hugh
Durocher, Leo
#Eckersley, Dennis
Evans, Billy
Evers, John
Ewing, Buck
Faber, Urban "Red"
#Feller, Bob
Ferrell, Rick
Fingers, Rollie
Fisk, Carlton
Flick, Elmer H.
Ford, Whitey
Foster, Andrew "Rube"
Foster, Bill
Fox, Nellie
Foxx, Jimmie
Frick, Ford
Frisch, Frank
Galvin, James "Pud"
#Gehrig, Lou
Gehringer, Charles
#Gibson, Bob
Gibson, Josh
Giles, Warren
Gillick, Pat
#Glavine, Tom
Gomez, Lefty
Gordon, Joe
Goslin, Leon "Goose"
Gossage, Rich
Grant, Frank
Greenberg, Hank
#Griffey, Ken, Jr.
Griffith, Clark
Grimes, Burleigh
Grove, Lefty
Guerrero, Vladimir
#Gwynn, Tony
Hafey, Charles "Chick"
Haines, Jesse
#Halladay, Roy
Hamilton, Bill
Hanlon, Ned
Harridge, Will
Harris, Bucky
Hartnett, Gabby
Harvey, Doug
Heilmann, Harry
#Henderson, Rickey
Herman, Billy
Herzog, Whitey

Hill, Pete
Hoffman, Trevor
Hooper, Harry
Hornsby, Rogers
Hoyt, Waite
Hubbard, Cal
Hubbell, Carl
Huggins, Miller
Hulbert, William
Hunter, James "Catfish"
Irvin, Monte
#Jackson, Reggie
Jackson, Travis
Jenkins, Ferguson
Jennings, Hugh
*#Jeter, Derek
Johnson, Byron "Ban"
#Johnson, Randy
Johnson, Walter[1]
Johnson, William "Judy"
#Jones, Chipper
Joss, Addie
#Kaline, Al
Keefe, Timothy
Keeler, William
Kell, George
Kelley, Joe
Kelly, George
Kelly, King
Killebrew, Harmon
Kiner, Ralph
Klein, Chuck
Klem, Bill
#Koufax, Sandy
Kuhn, Bowie
La Russa, Tony
Lajoie, Nap
Landis, Kenesaw M.
Larkin, Barry
Lasorda, Tommy
Lazzeri, Tony
Lemon, Bob
Leonard, Buck
Lindstrom, Fred
Lloyd, Pop
Lombardi, Ernie
Lopez, Al
Lyons, Ted
Mack, Connie
Mackey, James "Biz"
MacPhail, Larry
MacPhail, Lee
#Maddux, Greg
Manley, Effa
#Mantle, Mickey
Manush, Henry
Maranville, Walter
Marichal, Juan
Marquard, Rube
Martinez, Edgar
#Martínez, Pedro
Mathews, Eddie
Mathewson, Christy[1]
#Mays, Willie
Mazeroski, Bill
McCarthy, Joe
McCarthy, Thomas

#McCovey, Willie
McGinnity, Joe
McGowan, Bill
McGraw, John
McKechnie, Bill
McPhee, John "Bid"
Medwick, Joe
Mendez, Jose
*Miller, Marvin
Mize, Johnny
#Molitor, Paul
#Morgan, Joe
Morris, Jack
#Murray, Eddie
#Musial, Stan
Mussina, Mike
Newhouser, Hal
Nichols, Kid
Niekro, Phil
O'Day, Hank
O'Malley, Walter
O'Rourke, Jim
Ott, Mel
Paige, Satchel
#Palmer, Jim
Pennock, Herb
Perez, Tony
Perry, Gaylord
Piazza, Mike
Plank, Ed
Pompez, Alex
Posey, Cum(berland)
#Puckett, Kirby
Radbourn, Charlie
Raines, Tim
Reese, Pee Wee
Rice, Jim
Rice, Sam
Rickey, Branch
#Ripken, Cal, Jr.
#Rivera, Mariano
Rixey, Eppa
Rizzuto, Phil "Scooter"
Roberts, Robin
#Robinson, Brooks
#Robinson, Frank
#Robinson, Jackie
Robinson, Wilbert
#Rodríguez, Iván
Rogan, Joe "Bullet"
Roush, Edd
Ruffing, Red
Ruppert, Jacob
Rusie, Amos
#Ruth, Babe[1]
#Ryan, Nolan
Sandberg, Ryne
Santo, Ron
Santop, Louis
Schalk, Ray
#Schmidt, Mike
Schoendienst, Red
Schuerholz, John
#Seaver, Tom
Selee, Frank
Selig, Bud
Sewell, Joe

Simmons, Al
*Simmons, Ted
Sisler, George
Slaughter, Enos
Smith, Hilton
Smith, Lee
#Smith, Ozzie
#Smoltz, John
Snider, Duke
Southworth, Billy
#Spahn, Warren
Spalding, Albert
Speaker, Tris
#Stargell, Willie
Stearnes, Norman
Stengel, Casey
Sutter, Bruce
Suttles, George "Mule"
Sutton, Don
Taylor, Ben
Terry, Bill
#Thomas, Frank
#Thome, Jim
Thompson, Sam
Tinker, Joe
Torre, Joe
Torriente, Cristobal
Trammell, Alan
Traynor, Harold J. "Pie"
Vance, Arthur "Dazzy"
Vaughan, Joseph "Arky"
Veeck, Bill
Waddell, Rube
Wagner, Honus[1]
*Walker, Larry
Wallace, Roderick
Walsh, Ed
Waner, Lloyd
Waner, Paul
Ward, John
Weaver, Earl
Weiss, George
Welch, Mickey
Wells, Willie
Wheat, Zach
White, Deacon
White, Sol
Wilhelm, Hoyt
Wilkinson, J. L.
Williams, Billy
Williams, Dick
Williams, Joe
#Williams, Ted
Willis, Vic
Wilson, Hack
Wilson, Jud
#Winfield, Dave
Wright, George
Wright, Harry
Wynn, Early
#Yastrzemski, Carl
Yawkey, Tom
Young, Cy
Youngs, Ross
#Yount, Robin

(1) Player inducted in 1936, the year of the first Hall of Fame election.

BASKETBALL

Lakers Win 2020 NBA Championship

The Los Angeles Lakers won the NBA Championship in a 2019-20 season that was marred by tragedy and interrupted by the coronavirus pandemic. The Lakers' first title in ten years came as the franchise endured the death of former star Kobe Bryant, who died in a helicopter crash in California on Jan. 26, 2020, at age 41. Among the nine crash victims was Bryant's 13-year-old daughter Gianna. Bryant retired in 2016 after a 20-year career with the Lakers that produced five NBA championships.

The NBA suspended play on Mar. 11 after Utah Jazz center Rudy Gobert tested positive for COVID-19. Teams were sidelined until July, when the season resumed with spectatorless games at the ESPN Wide World of Sports Complex at Walt Disney World Resort outside Orlando, FL. Of the 30 teams, the 22 participating in the so-called Bubble consisted of the top eight teams in each conference and six teams that were six games or fewer behind the No. 8 seed in their respective conference.

All-Star forward LeBron James scored 28 points in the Lakers' 106-93 win over the Miami Heat in Game 6 of the NBA Finals, Oct. 11, 2020. James, playing in the 10th NBA Finals of his career, averaged 29.8 points to earn his fourth NBA Finals Most Valuable Player award. Teammate Anthony Davis averaged 25 ppg in the Finals as the Lakers earned their 17th title in franchise history. The Miami Heat reached the Finals in 2020 after beating the Boston Celtics in the Eastern Conference Finals and top-seeded Milwaukee in the semifinals. The Bucks had compiled the league's best record (56-17) behind forward Giannis Antetokounmpo, who averaged 29.5 points and 13.6 rebounds to earn his second straight NBA MVP Award.

Occurring in the wake of the police killing of George Floyd in Minneapolis and subsequent major protests, the season restart allowed for an official embrace of racial justice issues, with players allowed to wear advocacy messages on their uniforms. Milwaukee did not take the court for Game 5 of their first-round playoff series against Orlando on Aug. 26 due to the police shooting of Jacob Blake in Kenosha, WI, Aug. 23. The league postponed the day's entire slate of playoff games and resumed the postseason Aug. 29.

Houston's James Harden (34.3 ppg) led the league in scoring for the third straight season. The veteran guard scored 50 or more points in a game five times, including a 60-point effort in a 158-111 win over the Atlanta Hawks, Nov. 30, 2019, at Toyota Center in Houston. But Portland's Damian Lillard scored a single-game season-high 61 points twice. He reached 61 in a 129-124 overtime win over the Golden State Warriors, Jan. 20, 2020, at Moda Center in Portland, OR, and again in a 134-131 victory over Dallas, Aug. 11, 2020, at the HP Field House at the Disney complex.

Former NBA commissioner David Stern died on Jan. 1, 2020, at age 77. Stern became the league's fourth commissioner in 1984 and guided the NBA through 30 years of tremendous growth.

NBA Final Standings, 2019-20

The NBA suspended the regular season Mar. 11, 2020, due to the coronavirus pandemic and resumed in a "Bubble" without fans in attendance near Orlando, FL, on July 30. A total of 22 teams competed in "seeding games": 16 teams that were in playoff positions when the season was suspended and 6 teams that were 6 games or fewer behind the 8th seed in their respective conferences. A traditional, conference-based playoff format followed.

(playoff seeding in parentheses)

Eastern Conference

Atlantic Division	W	L	PCT	GB
Toronto Raptors (2)	53	19	.736	—
Boston Celtics (3)	48	24	.667	5
Philadelphia 76ers (6)	43	30	.589	10.5
Brooklyn Nets (7)	35	37	.486	18
New York Knicks	21	45	.318	29

Central Division	W	L	PCT	GB
Milwaukee Bucks (1)	56	17	.767	—
Indiana Pacers (4)	45	28	.616	11
Chicago Bulls	22	43	.338	30
Detroit Pistons	20	46	.303	32.5
Cleveland Cavaliers	19	46	.292	33

Southeast Division	W	L	PCT	GB
Miami Heat (5)	44	29	.603	—
Orlando Magic (8)	33	40	.452	11
Charlotte Hornets	23	42	.354	17
Washington Wizards	25	47	.347	18.5
Atlanta Hawks	20	47	.299	21

Western Conference

Northwest Division	W	L	PCT	GB
Denver Nuggets (3)	46	27	.630	—
Oklahoma City Thunder (5)	44	28	.611	1.5
Utah Jazz (6)	44	28	.611	1.5
Portland Trail Blazers (8)	35	39	.473	11.5
Minnesota Timberwolves	19	45	.297	22.5

Pacific Division	W	L	PCT	GB
L.A. Lakers (1)	52	19	.732	—
L.A. Clippers (2)	49	23	.681	3.5
Phoenix Suns	34	39	.466	19
Sacramento Kings	31	41	.431	21.5
Golden State Warriors	15	50	.231	34

Southwest Division	W	L	PCT	GB
Houston Rockets (4)	44	28	.611	—
Dallas Mavericks (7)	43	32	.573	2.5
Memphis Grizzlies	34	39	.466	10.5
San Antonio Spurs	32	39	.451	11.5
New Orleans Pelicans	30	42	.417	14

Note: Oklahoma City earned the No. 5 seed due to a better head-to-head record (2-1) over Utah.

NBA Playoff Results, 2020

Eastern Conference
Milwaukee defeated Orlando, 4 games to 1
Toronto defeated Brooklyn, 4 games to 0
Boston defeated Philadelphia, 4 games to 0
Miami defeated Indiana, 4 games to 0
Miami defeated Milwaukee, 4 games to 1
Boston defeated Toronto, 4 games to 3
Miami defeated Boston, 4 games to 2

Western Conference
L.A. Lakers defeated Portland, 4 games to 1
L.A. Clippers defeated Dallas, 4 games to 2
Denver defeated Utah, 4 games to 3
Houston defeated Oklahoma City, 4 games to 3
L.A. Lakers defeated Houston, 4 games to 1
Denver defeated L.A. Clippers, 4 games to 3
L.A. Lakers defeated Denver, 4 games to 1

Championship
L.A. Lakers defeated Miami, 4 games to 2 (116-98, 124-114, 104-115, 102-96, 108-111, 106-93)

NBA Regular Season Individual Highs, 2019-20

Minutes, game: 52, P.J. Tucker, Houston v. San Antonio, Dec. 3
Points, game: 61, Damian Lillard, Portland v. Golden State, Jan. 20 (OT); Portland v. Dallas, Aug. 11
Field goals, game: 20, Anthony Davis, L.A. Lakers v. Minnesota, Dec. 8; James Harden, Houston v. Cleveland, Dec. 11; T.J. Warren, Indiana v. Philadelphia, Aug. 1
Field goal attempts, game: 41, James Harden, Houston v. Minnesota, Nov. 16
3-pointers, game: 13, Zach LaVine, Chicago v. Charlotte, Nov. 23
3-point attempts, game: 22, James Harden, Houston v. Minnesota, Nov. 16; Marcus Smart, Boston v. Phoenix, Jan. 18
Free throws, game: 26, Anthony Davis, L.A. Lakers v. Memphis, Oct. 29

Free throw attempts, game: 27, Anthony Davis, L.A. Lakers v. Memphis, Oct. 29
Rebounds, game: 25, Jonas Valanciunas, Memphis v. Sacramento, Feb. 28
Assists, game: 19, Luka Doncic, Dallas v. Milwaukee, Aug. 8; LeBron James, L.A. Lakers v. Orlando, Jan. 15
Steals, game: 7, achieved eight times by seven players
Blocks, game: 10, Hassan Whiteside, Portland v. Chicago, Nov. 29
Minutes played, season: 2,557, CJ McCollum, Portland
Off. rebounds, season: 258, Hassan Whiteside, Portland
Def. rebounds, season: 716, Giannis Antetokounmpo, Milwaukee
Personal fouls, season: 278, Dillon Brooks, Memphis

NBA Finals MVP, 1969-2020

Year	Player, team	Year	Player, team	Year	Player, team
1969	Jerry West, L.A. Lakers	1986	Larry Bird, Boston	2004	Chauncey Billups, Detroit
1970	Willis Reed, New York	1987	Magic Johnson, L.A. Lakers	2005	Tim Duncan, San Antonio
1971	Lew Alcindor (Kareem Abdul-Jabbar), Milwaukee	1988	James Worthy, L.A. Lakers	2006	Dwyane Wade, Miami
		1989	Joe Dumars, Detroit	2007	Tony Parker, San Antonio
1972	Wilt Chamberlain, L.A. Lakers	1990	Isiah Thomas, Detroit	2008	Paul Pierce, Boston
1973	Willis Reed, New York	1991	Michael Jordan, Chicago	2009	Kobe Bryant, L.A. Lakers
1974	John Havlicek, Boston	1992	Michael Jordan, Chicago	2010	Kobe Bryant, L.A. Lakers
1975	Rick Barry, Golden State	1993	Michael Jordan, Chicago	2011	Dirk Nowitzki, Dallas
1976	Jo Jo White, Boston	1994	Hakeem Olajuwon, Houston	2012	LeBron James, Miami
1977	Bill Walton, Portland	1995	Hakeem Olajuwon, Houston	2013	LeBron James, Miami
1978	Wes Unseld, Washington	1996	Michael Jordan, Chicago	2014	Kawhi Leonard, San Antonio
1979	Dennis Johnson, Seattle	1997	Michael Jordan, Chicago	2015	Andre Iguodala, Golden State
1980	Magic Johnson, L.A. Lakers	1998	Michael Jordan, Chicago	2016	LeBron James, Cleveland
1981	Cedric Maxwell, Boston	1999	Tim Duncan, San Antonio	2017	Kevin Durant, Golden State
1982	Magic Johnson, L.A. Lakers	2000	Shaquille O'Neal, L.A. Lakers	2018	Kevin Durant, Golden State
1983	Moses Malone, Philadelphia	2001	Shaquille O'Neal, L.A. Lakers	2019	Kawhi Leonard, Toronto
1984	Larry Bird, Boston	2002	Shaquille O'Neal, L.A. Lakers	2020	LeBron James, L.A. Lakers
1985	Kareem Abdul-Jabbar, L.A. Lakers	2003	Tim Duncan, San Antonio		

NBA Finals All-Time Statistical Leaders

(* = Active in 2019-20 season; ** = not active in 2019-20 but not retired. Minimum 10 games played.)

Scoring average	GP	FG	FT	PTS	AVG	Scoring average	GP	FG	FT	PTS	AVG
Rick Barry	10	138	87	363	36.3	Bob Pettit	25	241	227	709	28.4
Michael Jordan	35	438	258	1,176	33.6	*LeBron James	55	588	285	1,562	28.4
Jerry West	55	612	455	1,679	30.5	*Kyrie Irving	13	140	50	360	27.7
**Kevin Durant	15	160	92	455	30.3	Hakeem Olajuwon	17	187	91	467	27.5
Shaquille O'Neal	30	340	185	865	28.8	*Stephen Curry	28	234	152	741	26.5

Games Played		Points		Rebounds		Assists	
Bill Russell	70	Jerry West	1,679	Bill Russell	1,718	Magic Johnson	584
Sam Jones	64	*LeBron James	1,562	Wilt Chamberlain	862	*LeBron James	430
Kareem Abdul-Jabbar	56	Kareem Abdul-Jabbar	1,317	Elgin Baylor	593	Bob Cousy	400
Jerry West	55	Michael Jordan	1,176	*LeBron James	561	Bill Russell	315
*LeBron James	55	Elgin Baylor	1,161	Kareem Abdul-Jabbar	507	Jerry West	306

NBA Most Valuable Player, 1956-2020

Year	Player, team	Year	Player, team	Year	Player, team
1956	Bob Pettit, St. Louis	1978	Bill Walton, Portland	2000	Shaquille O'Neal, L.A. Lakers
1957	Bob Cousy, Boston	1979	Moses Malone, Houston	2001	Allen Iverson, Philadelphia
1958	Bill Russell, Boston	1980	Kareem Abdul-Jabbar, L.A. Lakers	2002	Tim Duncan, San Antonio
1959	Bob Pettit, St. Louis	1981	Julius Erving, Philadelphia	2003	Tim Duncan, San Antonio
1960	Wilt Chamberlain, Philadelphia	1982	Moses Malone, Houston	2004	Kevin Garnett, Minnesota
1961	Bill Russell, Boston	1983	Moses Malone, Philadelphia	2005	Steve Nash, Phoenix
1962	Bill Russell, Boston	1984	Larry Bird, Boston	2006	Steve Nash, Phoenix
1963	Bill Russell, Boston	1985	Larry Bird, Boston	2007	Dirk Nowitzki, Dallas
1964	Oscar Robertson, Cincinnati	1986	Larry Bird, Boston	2008	Kobe Bryant, L.A. Lakers
1965	Bill Russell, Boston	1987	Magic Johnson, L.A. Lakers	2009	LeBron James, Cleveland
1966	Wilt Chamberlain, Philadelphia	1988	Michael Jordan, Chicago	2010	LeBron James, Cleveland
1967	Wilt Chamberlain, Philadelphia	1989	Magic Johnson, L.A. Lakers	2011	Derrick Rose, Chicago
1968	Wilt Chamberlain, Philadelphia	1990	Magic Johnson, L.A. Lakers	2012	LeBron James, Miami
1969	Wes Unseld, Baltimore	1991	Michael Jordan, Chicago	2013	LeBron James, Miami
1970	Willis Reed, New York	1992	Michael Jordan, Chicago	2014	Kevin Durant, Oklahoma City
1971	Lew Alcindor (Abdul-Jabbar), Milw.	1993	Charles Barkley, Phoenix	2015	Stephen Curry, Golden State
1972	Kareem Abdul-Jabbar, Milwaukee	1994	Hakeem Olajuwon, Houston	2016	Stephen Curry, Golden State
1973	Dave Cowens, Boston	1995	David Robinson, San Antonio	2017	Russell Westbrook, Oklahoma City
1974	Kareem Abdul-Jabbar, Milwaukee	1996	Michael Jordan, Chicago	2018	James Harden, Houston
1975	Bob McAdoo, Buffalo	1997	Karl Malone, Utah	2019	Giannis Antetokounmpo, Milwaukee
1976	Kareem Abdul-Jabbar, L.A. Lakers	1998	Michael Jordan, Chicago	2020	Giannis Antetokounmpo, Milwaukee
1977	Kareem Abdul-Jabbar, L.A. Lakers	1999	Karl Malone, Utah		

NBA Scoring Leaders, 1947-2020

(Average points per game; minimum games for eligibility varied.)

Year	Player, team	PTS	AVG	Year	Player, team	PTS	AVG
1947	Joe Fulks, Philadelphia	1,389	23.2	1969	Elvin Hayes, San Diego	2,327	28.4
1948	Max Zaslofsky, Chicago	1,007	21.0	1970	Jerry West, L.A. Lakers	2,309	31.2
1949	George Mikan, Minneapolis	1,698	28.3	1971	Lew Alcindor (Kareem Abdul-Jabbar), Milw.	2,596	31.7
1950	George Mikan, Minneapolis	1,865	27.4	1972	Kareem Abdul-Jabbar, Milwaukee	2,822	34.8
1951	George Mikan, Minneapolis	1,932	28.4	1973	Nate Archibald, Kansas City-Omaha	2,719	34.0
1952	Paul Arizin, Philadelphia	1,674	25.4	1974	Bob McAdoo, Buffalo	2,261	30.6
1953	Neil Johnston, Philadelphia	1,564	22.3	1975	Bob McAdoo, Buffalo	2,831	34.5
1954	Neil Johnston, Philadelphia	1,759	24.4	1976	Bob McAdoo, Buffalo	2,427	31.1
1955	Neil Johnston, Philadelphia	1,631	22.7	1977	Pete Maravich, New Orleans	2,273	31.1
1956	Bob Pettit, St. Louis	1,849	25.7	1978	George Gervin, San Antonio	2,232	27.2
1957	Paul Arizin, Philadelphia	1,817	25.6	1979	George Gervin, San Antonio	2,365	29.6
1958	George Yardley, Detroit	2,001	27.8	1980	George Gervin, San Antonio	2,585	33.1
1959	Bob Pettit, St. Louis	2,105	29.2	1981	Adrian Dantley, Utah	2,452	30.7
1960	Wilt Chamberlain, Philadelphia	2,707	37.6	1982	George Gervin, San Antonio	2,551	32.3
1961	Wilt Chamberlain, Philadelphia	3,033	38.4	1983	Alex English, Denver	2,326	28.4
1962	Wilt Chamberlain, Philadelphia	4,029	50.4	1984	Adrian Dantley, Utah	2,418	30.6
1963	Wilt Chamberlain, San Francisco	3,586	44.8	1985	Bernard King, New York	1,809	32.9
1964	Wilt Chamberlain, San Francisco	2,948	36.9	1986	Dominique Wilkins, Atlanta	2,366	30.3
1965	Wilt Chamberlain, San Francisco-Phil.	2,534	34.7	1987	Michael Jordan, Chicago	3,041	37.1
1966	Wilt Chamberlain, Philadelphia	2,649	33.5	1988	Michael Jordan, Chicago	2,868	35.0
1967	Rick Barry, San Francisco	2,775	35.6	1989	Michael Jordan, Chicago	2,633	32.5
1968	Dave Bing, Detroit	2,142	27.1	1990	Michael Jordan, Chicago	2,753	33.6

Year	Player, team	PTS	AVG	Year	Player, team	PTS	AVG
1991	Michael Jordan, Chicago	2,580	31.5	2006	Kobe Bryant, L.A. Lakers	2,832	35.4
1992	Michael Jordan, Chicago	2,404	30.1	2007	Kobe Bryant, L.A. Lakers	2,430	31.6
1993	Michael Jordan, Chicago	2,541	32.6	2008	LeBron James, Cleveland	2,250	30.0
1994	David Robinson, San Antonio	2,383	29.8	2009	Dwyane Wade, Miami	2,386	30.2
1995	Shaquille O'Neal, Orlando	2,315	29.3	2010	Kevin Durant, Oklahoma City	2,472	30.1
1996	Michael Jordan, Chicago	2,491	30.4	2011	Kevin Durant, Oklahoma City	2,161	27.7
1997	Michael Jordan, Chicago	2,431	29.6	2012	Kevin Durant, Oklahoma City	1,850	28.0
1998	Michael Jordan, Chicago	2,357	28.7	2013	Carmelo Anthony, New York	1,920	28.7
1999	Allen Iverson, Philadelphia	1,284	26.8	2014	Kevin Durant, Oklahoma City	2,593	32.0
2000	Shaquille O'Neal, L.A. Lakers	2,344	29.7	2015	Russell Westbrook, Oklahoma City	1,886	28.1
2001	Allen Iverson, Philadelphia	2,207	31.1	2016	Stephen Curry, Golden State	2,375	30.1
2002	Allen Iverson, Philadelphia	1,883	31.4	2017	Russell Westbrook, Oklahoma City	2,558	31.6
2003	Tracy McGrady, Orlando	2,407	32.1	2018	James Harden, Houston	2,191	30.4
2004	Tracy McGrady, Orlando	1,878	28.0	2019	James Harden, Houston	2,818	36.1
2005	Allen Iverson, Philadelphia	2,302	30.7	2020	James Harden, Houston	2,335	34.3

NBA Champions, 1947-2020

Year	Eastern champion	Western champion (Regular season)	Champion	Winning coach (Playoffs)	Opponent
1947	Washington Capitols	Chicago Stags	Philadelphia	Ed Gottlieb	Chicago
1948	Philadelphia Warriors	St. Louis Bombers	Baltimore	Buddy Jeannette	Philadelphia
1949	Washington Capitols	Rochester	Minneapolis	John Kundla	Washington
1950[1]	Syracuse	Indianapolis	Minneapolis	John Kundla	Syracuse
1951	Philadelphia Warriors	Minneapolis	Rochester	Lester Harrison	New York
1952	Syracuse	Rochester	Minneapolis	John Kundla	New York
1953	New York	Minneapolis	Minneapolis	John Kundla	New York
1954	New York	Minneapolis	Minneapolis	John Kundla	Syracuse
1955	Syracuse	Ft. Wayne	Syracuse	Al Cervi	Ft. Wayne
1956	Philadelphia Warriors	Ft. Wayne	Philadelphia	George Senesky	Ft. Wayne
1957	Boston	St. Louis	Boston	Red Auerbach	St. Louis
1958	Boston	St. Louis	St. Louis	Alex Hannum	Boston
1959	Boston	St. Louis	Boston	Red Auerbach	Minneapolis
1960	Boston	St. Louis	Boston	Red Auerbach	St. Louis
1961	Boston	St. Louis	Boston	Red Auerbach	St. Louis
1962	Boston	L.A. Lakers	Boston	Red Auerbach	L.A. Lakers
1963	Boston	L.A. Lakers	Boston	Red Auerbach	L.A. Lakers
1964	Boston	San Francisco	Boston	Red Auerbach	San Francisco
1965	Boston	L.A. Lakers	Boston	Red Auerbach	L.A. Lakers
1966	Philadelphia	L.A. Lakers	Boston	Red Auerbach	L.A. Lakers
1967	Philadelphia	San Francisco	Philadelphia	Alex Hannum	San Francisco
1968	Philadelphia	St. Louis	Boston	Bill Russell	L.A. Lakers
1969	Baltimore	L.A. Lakers	Boston	Bill Russell	L.A. Lakers
1970	New York	Atlanta	New York	Red Holzman	L.A. Lakers

Year	Atlantic	Central	Midwest	Pacific	Champion	Winning coach	Opponent
1971	New York	Baltimore	Milwaukee	L.A. Lakers	Milwaukee	Larry Costello	Baltimore
1972	Boston	Baltimore	Milwaukee	L.A. Lakers	L.A. Lakers	Bill Sharman	New York
1973	Boston	Baltimore	Milwaukee	L.A. Lakers	New York	Red Holzman	L.A. Lakers
1974	Boston	Capital	Milwaukee	L.A. Lakers	Boston	Tom Heinsohn	Milwaukee
1975	Boston	Washington	Chicago	Golden State	Golden State	Al Attles	Washington
1976	Boston	Cleveland	Milwaukee	Golden State	Boston	Tom Heinsohn	Phoenix
1977	Philadelphia	Houston	Denver	L.A. Lakers	Portland	Jack Ramsay	Philadelphia
1978	Philadelphia	San Antonio	Denver	Portland	Washington	Dick Motta	Seattle
1979	Washington	San Antonio	Kansas City	Seattle	Seattle	Len Wilkens	Washington
1980	Boston	Atlanta	Milwaukee	L.A. Lakers	L.A. Lakers	Paul Westhead	Philadelphia
1981	Boston	Milwaukee	San Antonio	Phoenix	Boston	Bill Fitch	Houston
1982	Boston	Milwaukee	San Antonio	L.A. Lakers	L.A. Lakers	Pat Riley	Philadelphia
1983	Philadelphia	Milwaukee	San Antonio	L.A. Lakers	Philadelphia	Billy Cunningham	L.A. Lakers
1984	Boston	Milwaukee	Utah	L.A. Lakers	Boston	K. C. Jones	L.A. Lakers
1985	Boston	Milwaukee	Denver	L.A. Lakers	L.A. Lakers	Pat Riley	Boston
1986	Boston	Milwaukee	Houston	L.A. Lakers	Boston	K. C. Jones	Houston
1987	Boston	Atlanta	Dallas	L.A. Lakers	L.A. Lakers	Pat Riley	Boston
1988	Boston	Detroit	Denver	L.A. Lakers	L.A. Lakers	Pat Riley	Detroit
1989	New York	Detroit	Utah	L.A. Lakers	Detroit	Chuck Daly	L.A. Lakers
1990	Philadelphia	Detroit	San Antonio	L.A. Lakers	Detroit	Chuck Daly	Portland
1991	Boston	Chicago	San Antonio	Portland	Chicago	Phil Jackson	L.A. Lakers
1992	Boston	Chicago	Utah	Portland	Chicago	Phil Jackson	Portland
1993	New York	Chicago	Houston	Phoenix	Chicago	Phil Jackson	Phoenix
1994	New York	Atlanta	Houston	Seattle	Houston	Rudy Tomjanovich	New York
1995	Orlando	Indiana	San Antonio	Phoenix	Houston	Rudy Tomjanovich	Orlando
1996	Orlando	Chicago	San Antonio	Seattle	Chicago	Phil Jackson	Seattle
1997	Miami	Chicago	Utah	Seattle	Chicago	Phil Jackson	Utah
1998	Miami	Chicago	Utah	L.A. Lakers	Chicago	Phil Jackson	Utah
1900	Miami	Indiana	San Antonio	Portland	San Antonio	Gregg Popovich	New York
2000	Miami	Indiana	Utah	L.A. Lakers	L.A. Lakers	Phil Jackson	Indiana
2001	Philadelphia	Milwaukee	San Antonio	L.A. Lakers	L.A. Lakers	Phil Jackson	Philadelphia
2002	New Jersey	Detroit	San Antonio	Sacramento	L.A. Lakers	Phil Jackson	New Jersey
2003	New Jersey	Detroit	San Antonio	Sacramento	San Antonio	Gregg Popovich	New Jersey
2004	New Jersey	Indiana	Minnesota	L.A. Lakers	Detroit	Larry Brown	L.A. Lakers

Year	Atlantic	Central	Southeast	Northwest	Pacific	Southwest	Champion	Winning coach	Opponent
2005	Boston	Detroit	Miami	Seattle	Phoenix	San Antonio	San Antonio	Gregg Popovich	Detroit
2006	New Jersey	Detroit	Miami	Denver	Phoenix	San Antonio	Miami	Pat Riley	Dallas
2007	Toronto	Detroit	Miami	Utah	Phoenix	Dallas	San Antonio	Gregg Popovich	Cleveland
2008	Boston	Detroit	Orlando	Utah	L.A. Lakers	New Orleans	Boston	Glenn "Doc" Rivers	L.A. Lakers
2009	Boston	Cleveland	Orlando	Denver	L.A. Lakers	San Antonio	L.A. Lakers	Phil Jackson	Orlando
2010	Boston	Cleveland	Orlando	Denver	L.A. Lakers	Dallas	L.A. Lakers	Phil Jackson	Boston
2011	Boston	Chicago	Miami	OK City	L.A. Lakers	San Antonio	Dallas	Rick Carlisle	Miami
2012	Boston	Chicago	Miami	OK City	L.A. Lakers	San Antonio	Miami	Erik Spoelstra	OK City
2013	New York	Indiana	Miami	OK City	L.A. Clippers	San Antonio	Miami	Erik Spoelstra	San Antonio
2014	Toronto	Indiana	Miami	OK City	L.A. Clippers	San Antonio	San Antonio	Gregg Popovich	Miami
2015	Toronto	Cleveland	Atlanta	Portland	Golden State	Houston	Golden State	Steve Kerr	Cleveland
2016	Toronto	Cleveland	Miami	OK City	Golden State	San Antonio	Cleveland	Tyronn Lue	Golden State
2017	Boston	Cleveland	Washington	Utah	Golden State	San Antonio	Golden State	Steve Kerr	Cleveland
2018	Toronto	Cleveland	Miami	Portland	Golden State	Houston	Golden State	Steve Kerr	Cleveland
2019	Toronto	Milwaukee	Orlando	Denver	Golden State	Houston	Toronto	Nick Nurse	Golden State
2020	Toronto	Milwaukee	Miami	Denver	L.A. Lakers	Houston	L.A. Lakers	Frank Vogel	Miami

(1) The newly formed NBA combined the 11-team BAA (Basketball Assn. of Amer.) and six NBL (Natl. Basketball League) teams in the 1949-50 season and had three divisions for one year. The Minneapolis Lakers were co-champions of the soon-defunct Central Division.

All-NBA and All-Defensive Teams, 2019-20

	All-NBA Team			All-Defensive Team	
First Team	Second Team	Position	First Team		Second Team
Giannis Antetokounmpo, Milwaukee	Kawhi Leonard, L.A. Clippers	Forward	Giannis Antetokounmpo, Milwaukee		Kawhi Leonard, L.A. Clippers
LeBron James, L.A. Lakers	Pascal Siakam, Toronto	Forward	Anthony Davis, L.A. Lakers		Bam Adebayo, Miami
Anthony Davis, L.A. Lakers	Nikola Jokic, Denver	Center	Rudy Gobert, Utah		Brook Lopez, Milwaukee
Luka Doncic, Dallas	Chris Paul, Oklahoma City	Guard	Marcus Smart, Boston		Patrick Beverley, L.A. Clippers
James Harden, Houston	Damian Lillard, Portland	Guard	Ben Simmons, Philadelphia		Eric Bledsoe, Milwaukee

NBA Statistical Leaders, 2019-20

To qualify for averaged categories, player must be on pace to play 58 games in an 82-game season. Minimums in 2019-20 based on team games played.

Scoring Average

Player, team	GP	FG	FT	PTS	AVG
James Harden, Houston	68	672	692	2,335	34.3
Bradley Beal, Washington	57	593	385	1,741	30.5
Damian Lillard, Portland	66	624	460	1,978	30.0
Trae Young, Atlanta	60	546	481	1,778	29.6
Giannis Antetokounmpo, Milwaukee	63	685	398	1,857	29.5
Luka Doncic, Dallas	61	581	426	1,759	28.8
Russell Westbrook, Houston	57	604	290	1,553	27.2
Kawhi Leonard, L.A. Clippers	57	532	356	1,543	27.1
Devin Booker, Phoenix	70	627	468	1,863	26.6
Anthony Davis, L.A. Lakers	62	551	444	1,618	26.1

Field Goal Percentage
(Minimum in 2019-20 based on team games played)

Player, team	FGM	FGA	PCT
Mitchell Robinson, New York	253	341	.742
Rudy Gobert, Utah	386	557	.693
Jarrett Allen, Brooklyn	302	465	.649
Hassan Whiteside, Portland	436	702	.621
Brandon Clarke, Memphis	296	479	.618
Steven Adams, Oklahoma City	283	478	.592
Jonas Valanciunas, Memphis	432	739	.585
John Collins, Atlanta	353	605	.583
Montrezl Harrell, L.A. Clippers	471	812	.580
Ben Simmons, Philadelphia	375	647	.580

Free Throw Percentage
(Minimum in 2019-20 based on team games played)

Player, team	FTM	FTA	PCT
Brad Wanamaker, Boston	126	136	.926
Devin Booker, Phoenix	468	509	.919
Khris Middleton, Milwaukee	208	227	.916
Chris Paul, Oklahoma City	253	279	.907
Bojan Bogdanovic, Utah	250	277	.903
Danilo Gallinari, Oklahoma City	266	298	.893
Malcolm Brogdon, Indiana	166	186	.892
JJ Redick, New Orleans	165	185	.892
D.J. Augustin, Orlando	161	181	.890
Damian Lillard, Portland	460	518	.888

3-Point Field Goal Percentage
(Minimum in 2019-20 based on team games played)

Player, team	3FGM	3FGA	PCT
George Hill, Milwaukee	81	176	.460
JJ Redick, New Orleans	180	397	.453
Seth Curry, Dallas	145	321	.452
Duncan Robinson, Miami	270	606	.446
Doug McDermott, Indiana	128	294	.435
Davis Bertans, Washington	200	472	.424
Joe Harris, Brooklyn	172	406	.424
Nemanja Bjelica, Sacramento	134	320	.419
Gary Trent Jr., Portland	112	268	.418
Kyle Korver, Milwaukee	99	237	.418

Rebounds per Game

Player, team	GP	OFF	DEF	TOT	AVG
Andre Drummond, Detroit-Cleveland	57	250	614	864	15.2
Giannis Antetokounmpo, Milwaukee	63	140	716	856	13.6
Hassan Whiteside, Portland	67	258	647	905	13.5
Rudy Gobert, Utah	68	230	686	916	13.5
Domantas Sabonis, Indiana	62	189	582	771	12.4
Jonas Valanciunas, Memphis	70	213	575	788	11.3
Nikola Vucevic, Orlando	62	140	533	673	10.9
Bam Adebayo, Miami	72	176	559	735	10.2
Tristan Thompson, Cleveland	57	226	351	577	10.1
DeAndre Jordan, Brooklyn	56	141	420	561	10.0

Assists per Game

Player, team	GP	AST	APG
LeBron James, L.A. Lakers	67	684	10.2
Trae Young, Atlanta	60	560	9.3
Luka Doncic, Dallas	61	538	8.8
Ricky Rubio, Phoenix	65	570	8.8
Damian Lillard, Portland	66	530	8.0
Ben Simmons, Philadelphia	57	455	8.0
James Harden, Houston	68	512	7.5
Devonte' Graham, Charlotte	63	471	7.5
Kyle Lowry, Toronto	58	433	7.5
Ja Morant, Memphis	67	488	7.3

Steals per Game

Player, team	GP	STL	AVG
Ben Simmons, Philadelphia	57	119	2.09
Kris Dunn, Chicago	51	101	1.98
Andre Drummond, Detroit-Cleveland	57	109	1.91
Fred VanVleet, Toronto	54	100	1.85
James Harden, Houston	68	125	1.84
Kawhi Leonard, L.A. Clippers	57	103	1.81
Jimmy Butler, Miami	58	103	1.78
Marcus Smart, Boston	60	101	1.68
Dejounte Murray, San Antonio	66	111	1.68
Robert Covington, Minnesota-Houston	70	115	1.64

Blocked Shots per Game

Player, team	GP	BLK	AVG
Hassan Whiteside, Portland	67	196	2.93
Brook Lopez, Milwaukee	68	163	2.40
Anthony Davis, L.A. Lakers	62	143	2.31
Myles Turner, Indiana	62	132	2.13
Kristaps Porzingis, Dallas	57	115	2.02
Rudy Gobert, Utah	68	135	1.97
Mitchell Robinson, New York	61	119	1.95
LaMarcus Aldridge, San Antonio	53	87	1.64
Andre Drummond, Detroit-Cleveland	57	93	1.63
Jaren Jackson Jr., Memphis	57	92	1.61

NBA Defensive Player of the Year, 1983-2020

Year	Player, team	Year	Player, team	Year	Player, team
1983	Sidney Moncrief, Milwaukee	1997	Dikembe Mutombo, Atlanta	2009	Dwight Howard, Orlando
1984	Sidney Moncrief, Milwaukee	1998	Dikembe Mutombo, Atlanta	2010	Dwight Howard, Orlando
1985	Mark Eaton, Utah	1999	Alonzo Mourning, Miami	2011	Dwight Howard, Orlando
1986	Alvin Robertson, San Antonio	2000	Alonzo Mourning, Miami	2012	Tyson Chandler, New York
1987	Michael Cooper, L.A. Lakers	2001	Dikembe Mutombo, Philadelphia-Atlanta	2013	Marc Gasol, Memphis
1988	Michael Jordan, Chicago			2014	Joakim Noah, Chicago
1989	Mark Eaton, Utah	2002	Ben Wallace, Detroit	2015	Kawhi Leonard, San Antonio
1990	Dennis Rodman, Detroit	2003	Ben Wallace, Detroit	2016	Kawhi Leonard, San Antonio
1991	Dennis Rodman, Detroit	2004	Ron Artest, Indiana	2017	Draymond Green, Golden State
1992	David Robinson, San Antonio	2005	Ben Wallace, Detroit	2018	Rudy Gobert, Utah
1993	Hakeem Olajuwon, Houston	2006	Ben Wallace, Detroit	2019	Rudy Gobert, Utah
1994	Hakeem Olajuwon, Houston	2007	Marcus Camby, Denver	2020	Giannis Antetokounmpo, Milwaukee
1995	Dikembe Mutombo, Denver	2008	Kevin Garnett, Boston		
1996	Gary Payton, Seattle				

NBA Rookie of the Year, 1953-2020

Year	Player, team	Year	Player, team	Year	Player, team
1953	Don Meineke, Ft. Wayne	1975	Jamaal Wilkes, Golden State	1998	Tim Duncan, San Antonio
1954	Ray Felix, Baltimore	1976	Alvan Adams, Phoenix	1999	Vince Carter, Toronto
1955	Bob Pettit, Milwaukee	1977	Adrian Dantley, Buffalo	2000	Elton Brand, Chicago;
1956	Maurice Stokes, Rochester	1978	Walter Davis, Phoenix		Steve Francis, Houston
1957	Tom Heinsohn, Boston	1979	Phil Ford, Kansas City	2001	Mike Miller, Orlando
1958	Woody Sauldsberry, Philadelphia	1980	Larry Bird, Boston	2002	Pau Gasol, Memphis
1959	Elgin Baylor, Minneapolis	1981	Darrell Griffith, Utah	2003	Amar'e Stoudemire, Phoenix
1960	Wilt Chamberlain, Philadelphia	1982	Buck Williams, New Jersey	2004	LeBron James, Cleveland
1961	Oscar Robertson, Cincinnati	1983	Terry Cummings, San Diego	2005	Emeka Okafor, Charlotte
1962	Walt Bellamy, Chicago	1984	Ralph Sampson, Houston	2006	Chris Paul, New Orl./OK City
1963	Terry Dischinger, Chicago	1985	Michael Jordan, Chicago	2007	Brandon Roy, Portland
1964	Jerry Lucas, Cincinnati	1986	Patrick Ewing, New York	2008	Kevin Durant, Seattle
1965	Willis Reed, New York	1987	Chuck Person, Indiana	2009	Derrick Rose, Chicago
1966	Rick Barry, San Francisco	1988	Mark Jackson, New York	2010	Tyreke Evans, Sacramento
1967	Dave Bing, Detroit	1989	Mitch Richmond, Golden State	2011	Blake Griffin, L.A. Clippers
1968	Earl Monroe, Baltimore	1990	David Robinson, San Antonio	2012	Kyrie Irving, Cleveland
1969	Wes Unseld, Baltimore	1991	Derrick Coleman, New Jersey	2013	Damian Lillard, Portland
1970	Lew Alcindor (Kareem	1992	Larry Johnson, Charlotte	2014	Michael Carter-Williams, Philadelphia
	Abdul-Jabbar), Milwaukee	1993	Shaquille O'Neal, Orlando	2015	Andrew Wiggins, Minnesota
1971	Dave Cowens, Boston;	1994	Chris Webber, Golden State	2016	Karl-Anthony Towns, Minnesota
	Geoff Petrie, Portland	1995	Grant Hill, Detroit;	2017	Malcolm Brogdon, Milwaukee
1972	Sidney Wicks, Portland		Jason Kidd, Dallas	2018	Ben Simmons, Philadelphia
1973	Bob McAdoo, Buffalo	1996	Damon Stoudamire, Toronto	2019	Luka Doncic, Dallas
1974	Ernie DiGregorio, Buffalo	1997	Allen Iverson, Philadelphia	2020	Ja Morant, Memphis

NBA Sixth Man Award, 1983-2020

Year	Player, team	Year	Player, team	Year	Player, team
1983	Bobby Jones, Philadelphia	1996	Toni Kukoc, Chicago	2009	Jason Terry, Dallas
1984	Kevin McHale, Boston	1997	John Starks, New York	2010	Jamal Crawford, Atlanta
1985	Kevin McHale, Boston	1998	Danny Manning, Phoenix	2011	Lamar Odom, L.A. Lakers
1986	Bill Walton, Boston	1999	Darrell Armstrong, Orlando	2012	James Harden, Oklahoma City
1987	Ricky Pierce, Milwaukee	2000	Rodney Rogers, Phoenix	2013	J.R. Smith, New York
1988	Roy Tarpley, Dallas	2001	Aaron McKie, Philadelphia	2014	Jamal Crawford, L.A. Clippers
1989	Eddie Johnson, Phoenix	2002	Corliss Williamson, Detroit	2015	Lou Williams, Toronto
1990	Ricky Pierce, Milwaukee	2003	Bobby Jackson, Sacramento	2016	Jamal Crawford, L.A. Clippers
1991	Detlef Schrempf, Indiana	2004	Antawn Jamison, Dallas	2017	Eric Gordon, Houston
1992	Detlef Schrempf, Indiana	2005	Ben Gordon, Chicago	2018	Lou Williams, L.A. Clippers
1993	Clifford Robinson, Portland	2006	Mike Miller, Memphis	2019	Lou Williams, L.A. Clippers
1994	Dell Curry, Charlotte	2007	Leandro Barbosa, Phoenix	2020	Montrezl Harrell, L.A. Clippers
1995	Anthony Mason, New York	2008	Manu Ginobili, San Antonio		

NBA Player Draft First-Round Picks, 2019

(June 20, 2019; 2020 draft was scheduled for Nov. 18, 2020)

Team	Player, position, school/team	Team	Player, position, school/team
1. New Orleans	Zion Williamson, F, Duke	16. Orlando	Chuma Okeke, F, Auburn
2. Memphis	Ja Morant, G, Murray St.	17. Brooklyn[6]	Nickeil Alexander-Walker, G, Virginia Tech
3. NY Knicks	RJ Barrett, F, Duke	18. Indiana	Goga Bitadze, C, KK Mega Leks (Serbia)
4. L.A. Lakers[1]	De'Andre Hunter, F, Virginia	19. San Antonio	Luka Samanic, F, KK Olimpija (Slovenia)
5. Cleveland	Darius Garland, G, Vanderbilt	20. Boston[7]	Matisse Thybulle, F, Washington
6. Phoenix[2]	Jarrett Culver, F, Texas Tech	21. Oklahoma City[8]	Brandon Clarke, F, Gonzaga
7. Chicago	Coby White, G, North Carolina	22. Boston	Grant Williams, F, Tennessee
8. Atlanta[3]	Jaxson Hayes, C, Texas	23. Utah[9]	Darius Bazley, F, Princeton HS (OH)
9. Washington	Rui Hachimura, F, Gonzaga	24. Philadelphia[10]	Ty Jerome, G, Virginia
10. Atlanta	Cam Reddish, F, Duke	25. Portland	Nassir Little, F, North Carolina
11. Minnesota[4]	Cameron Johnson, F, North Carolina	26. Cleveland[11]	Dylan Windler, F, Belmont
12. Charlotte	PJ Washington Jr., F, Kentucky	27. Brooklyn[12]	Mfiondu Kabengele, C, Florida St.
13. Miami	Tyler Herro, G, Kentucky	28. Golden State	Jordan Poole, G, Michigan
14. Boston[5]	Romeo Langford, F, Indiana	29. San Antonio[13]	Keldon Johnson, F, Kentucky
15. Detroit	Sekou Doumbouya, F, Limoges (France)	30. Milwaukee[14]	Kevin Porter Jr., G, USC

(1) Rights traded to New Orleans, who traded the pick to Atlanta. (2) Rights traded to New Orleans. (3) Rights traded to Minnesota. (4) Rights traded to Phoenix. (5) From Sacramento through Philadelphia. (6) Rights traded to Atlanta, who traded the pick to New Orleans. (7) From L.A. Clippers through Memphis, rights traded to Philadelphia. (8) Rights traded to Memphis. (9) Rights traded to Memphis, who traded the pick to Oklahoma City. (10) Rights traded to Boston, who traded the pick to Phoenix. (11) From Houston. (12) From Denver, rights traded to L.A. Clippers. (13) From Toronto. (14) Rights traded to Detroit, who traded the pick to Cleveland.

Number-One First-Round NBA Draft Picks, 1966-2019

Year	Team	Player, school/team	Year	Team	Player, school/team
1966	New York	Cazzie Russell, Michigan	1984	Houston	Hakeem Olajuwon, Houston
1967	Detroit	Jimmy Walker, Providence	1985	New York	Patrick Ewing, Georgetown
1968	San Diego	Elvin Hayes, Houston	1986	Cleveland	Brad Daugherty, North Carolina
1969	Milwaukee	Lew Alcindor (Kareem Abdul-Jabbar), UCLA	1987	San Antonio	David Robinson, Navy
1970	Detroit	Bob Lanier, St. Bonaventure	1988	L.A. Clippers	Danny Manning, Kansas
1971	Cleveland	Austin Carr, Notre Dame	1989	Sacramento	Pervis Ellison, Louisville
1972	Portland	LaRue Martin, Loyola-Chicago	1990	New Jersey	Derrick Coleman, Syracuse
1973	Philadelphia	Doug Collins, Illinois State	1991	Charlotte	Larry Johnson, UNLV
1974	Portland	Bill Walton, UCLA	1992	Orlando	Shaquille O'Neal, LSU
1975	Atlanta	David Thompson[1], NC State	1993	Orlando	Chris Webber[2], Michigan
1976	Houston	John Lucas, Maryland	1994	Milwaukee	Glenn Robinson, Purdue
1977	Milwaukee	Kent Benson, Indiana	1995	Golden State	Joe Smith, Maryland
1978	Portland	Mychal Thompson, Minnesota	1996	Philadelphia	Allen Iverson, Georgetown
1979	L.A. Lakers	Earvin "Magic" Johnson, Michigan State	1997	San Antonio	Tim Duncan, Wake Forest
1980	Golden State	Joe Barry Carroll, Purdue	1998	L.A. Clippers	Michael Olowokandi, Pacific (CA)
1981	Dallas	Mark Aguirre, DePaul	1999	Chicago	Elton Brand, Duke
1982	L.A. Lakers	James Worthy, North Carolina	2000	New Jersey	Kenyon Martin, Cincinnati
1983	Houston	Ralph Sampson, Virginia	2001	Washington	Kwame Brown, Glynn Academy (HS)

Year	Team	Player, school/team	Year	Team	Player, school/team
2002	Houston	Yao Ming, Shanghai Sharks (China)	2011	Cleveland	Kyrie Irving, Duke
2003	Cleveland	LeBron James, St. Vincent-St. Mary (HS)	2012	New Orleans	Anthony Davis, Kentucky
2004	Orlando	Dwight Howard, Southwest Atlanta Christian Academy (HS)	2013	Cleveland	Anthony Bennett, UNLV
			2014	Cleveland	Andrew Wiggins, Kansas
2005	Milwaukee	Andrew Bogut, Utah	2015	Minnesota	Karl-Anthony Towns, Kentucky
2006	Toronto	Andrea Bargnani, Benetton Treviso (Italy)	2016	Philadelphia	Ben Simmons, LSU
2007	Portland	Greg Oden, Ohio State	2017	Philadelphia	Markelle Fultz, Washington
2008	Chicago	Derrick Rose, Memphis	2018	Phoenix	Deandre Ayton, Arizona
2009	L.A. Clippers	Blake Griffin, Oklahoma	2019	New Orleans	Zion Williamson, Duke
2010	Washington	John Wall, Kentucky			

HS = High school. (1) Signed with Denver of the American Basketball Association (ABA). (2) Traded to Golden State for rights to Anfernee Hardaway and three future first-round draft choices.

All-Time NBA Statistical Leaders

(At the end of the 2019-20 season. * = Active in 2019-20 season; ** = not active in 2019-20 but not retired.)

Scoring Average
(Minimum 400 games or 10,000 points)

	GP	PTS	AVG
Michael Jordan	1,072	32,292	30.1
Wilt Chamberlain	1,045	31,419	30.1
Elgin Baylor	846	23,149	27.4
*LeBron James	1,265	34,241	27.1
Jerry West	932	25,192	27.0
**Kevin Durant	849	22,940	27.0
Allen Iverson	914	24,368	26.7
Bob Pettit	792	20,880	26.4
George Gervin	791	20,708	26.2
Oscar Robertson	1,040	26,710	25.7

3-Point Field Goal Percentage
(Minimum 250 3-point field goals made)

	3-FGM	3-FGA	PCT
Steve Kerr	726	1,599	45.4
*Seth Curry	446	1,007	44.3
Hubert Davis	728	1,651	44.1
Drazen Petrovic	255	583	43.7
*Duncan Robinson	280	641	43.7
*Stephen Curry	2,495	5,739	43.5
Jason Kapono	457	1,054	43.4
Tim Legler	260	603	43.1
Steve Novak	575	1,337	43.0
*Kyle Korver	2,450	5,715	42.9

Free Throw Percentage
(Minimum 1,200 free throws made)

	FTM	FTA	PCT
*Stephen Curry	2,560	2,827	90.6
Steve Nash	3,060	3,384	90.4
Mark Price	2,135	2,362	90.4
Rick Barry	3,818	4,243	90.0
Peja Stojakovic	2,237	2,500	89.5
Chauncey Billups	4,496	5,029	89.4
Ray Allen	4,398	4,920	89.4
Calvin Murphy	3,445	3,864	89.2
*JJ Redick	2,011	2,258	89.1
Scott Skiles	1,548	1,741	88.9

Field Goal Percentage
(Minimum 2,000 field goals made)

	FGM	FGA	PCT
*DeAndre Jordan	3,337	4,985	66.9
*Rudy Gobert	2,043	3,193	64.0
Artis Gilmore	5,732	9,570	59.9
*Tyson Chandler	3,558	5,964	59.7
*Steven Adams	2,157	3,664	58.9
*Dwight Howard	6,739	11,494	58.6
Shaquille O'Neal	11,330	19,457	58.2
*Hassan Whiteside	2,346	4,029	58.2
Mark West	2,528	4,356	58.0
*JaVale McGee	2,364	4,113	57.5

Minutes Played

Kareem Abdul-Jabbar	57,446
Karl Malone	54,852
Dirk Nowitzki	51,369
Kevin Garnett	50,418
Jason Kidd	50,110
Elvin Hayes	50,000
Kobe Bryant	48,638
*LeBron James	48,550
Wilt Chamberlain	47,859
John Stockton	47,764

Field Goals Attempted

Kareem Abdul-Jabbar	28,307
Karl Malone	26,210
Kobe Bryant	26,200
*LeBron James	24,781
Michael Jordan	24,537
Elvin Hayes	24,272
John Havlicek	23,930
Dirk Nowitzki	23,734
Wilt Chamberlain	23,497
Dominique Wilkins	21,589

Points

Kareem Abdul-Jabbar	38,387
Karl Malone	36,928
*LeBron James	34,241
Kobe Bryant	33,643
Michael Jordan	32,292
Dirk Nowitzki	31,560
Wilt Chamberlain	31,419
Shaquille O'Neal	28,596
Moses Malone	27,409
Elvin Hayes	27,313

Games Played

Robert Parish	1,611
Kareem Abdul-Jabbar	1,560
*Vince Carter	1,541
Dirk Nowitzki	1,522
John Stockton	1,504
Karl Malone	1,476
Kevin Garnett	1,462
Kevin Willis	1,424
Jason Terry	1,410
Tim Duncan	1,392

Field Goals Made

Kareem Abdul-Jabbar	15,837
Karl Malone	13,528
Wilt Chamberlain	12,681
*LeBron James	12,481
Michael Jordan	12,192
Kobe Bryant	11,719
Shaquille O'Neal	11,330
Dirk Nowitzki	11,169
Elvin Hayes	10,976
Hakeem Olajuwon	10,749

Rebounds

Wilt Chamberlain	23,924
Bill Russell	21,620
Kareem Abdul-Jabbar	17,440
Elvin Hayes	16,279
Moses Malone	16,212
Tim Duncan	15,091
Karl Malone	14,968
Robert Parish	14,715
Kevin Garnett	14,662
Nate Thurmond	14,464

Personal Fouls

Kareem Abdul-Jabbar	4,657
Karl Malone	4,578
Robert Parish	4,443
Charles Oakley	4,421
Hakeem Olajuwon	4,383
Buck Williams	4,267
Elvin Hayes	4,193
Clifford Robinson	4,175
Kevin Willis	4,172
Shaquille O'Neal	4,146
Otis Thorpe	4,146

3-Point Field Goals Attempted

Ray Allen	7,429
Reggie Miller	6,486
*James Harden	6,394
*Jamal Crawford	6,379
*Vince Carter	6,168
Jason Terry	6,010
Paul Pierce	5,816
*Stephen Curry	5,739
*Kyle Korver	5,715
Jason Kidd	5,701

Assists

John Stockton	15,806
Jason Kidd	12,091
Steve Nash	10,335
Mark Jackson	10,334
Magic Johnson	10,141
Oscar Robertson	9,887
*Chris Paul	9,653
*LeBron James	9,346
Isiah Thomas	9,061
Gary Payton	8,966

Blocked Shots

Hakeem Olajuwon	3,830
Dikembe Mutombo	3,289
Kareem Abdul-Jabbar	3,189
Mark Eaton	3,064
Tim Duncan	3,020
David Robinson	2,954
Patrick Ewing	2,894
Shaquille O'Neal	2,732
Tree Rollins	2,542
Robert Parish	2,361

3-Point Field Goals Made

Ray Allen	2,973
Reggie Miller	2,560
*Stephen Curry	2,495
*Kyle Korver	2,450
*James Harden	2,324
*Vince Carter	2,290
Jason Terry	2,282
*Jamal Crawford	2,221
Paul Pierce	2,143
Jason Kidd	1,988

Steals

John Stockton	3,265
Jason Kidd	2,684
Michael Jordan	2,514
Gary Payton	2,445
Maurice Cheeks	2,310
Scottie Pippen	2,307
*Chris Paul	2,233
Clyde Drexler	2,207
Hakeem Olajuwon	2,162
Alvin Robertson	2,112

NBA Coach of the Year, 1963-2020

Year	Coach, team	Year	Coach, team	Year	Coach, team
1963	Harry Gallatin, St. Louis	1983	Don Nelson, Milwaukee	2002	Rick Carlisle, Detroit
1964	Alex Hannum, San Francisco	1984	Frank Layden, Utah	2003	Gregg Popovich, San Antonio
1965	Red Auerbach, Boston	1985	Don Nelson, Milwaukee	2004	Hubie Brown, Memphis
1966	Dolph Schayes, Philadelphia	1986	Mike Fratello, Atlanta	2005	Mike D'Antoni, Phoenix
1967	Johnny Kerr, Chicago	1987	Mike Schuler, Portland	2006	Avery Johnson, Dallas
1968	Richie Guerin, St. Louis	1988	Doug Moe, Denver	2007	Sam Mitchell, Toronto
1969	Gene Shue, Baltimore	1989	Cotton Fitzsimmons, Phoenix	2008	Byron Scott, New Orleans
1970	Red Holzman, New York	1990	Pat Riley, L.A. Lakers	2009	Mike Brown, Cleveland
1971	Dick Motta, Chicago	1991	Don Chaney, Houston	2010	Scott Brooks, Oklahoma City
1972	Bill Sharman, L.A. Lakers	1992	Don Nelson, Golden State	2011	Tom Thibodeau, Chicago
1973	Tom Heinsohn, Boston	1993	Pat Riley, New York	2012	Gregg Popovich, San Antonio
1974	Ray Scott, Detroit	1994	Lenny Wilkens, Atlanta	2013	George Karl, Denver
1975	Phil Johnson, Kansas City-Omaha	1995	Del Harris, L.A. Lakers	2014	Gregg Popovich, San Antonio
1976	Bill Fitch, Cleveland	1996	Phil Jackson, Chicago	2015	Mike Budenholzer, Atlanta
1977	Tom Nissalke, Houston	1997	Pat Riley, Miami	2016	Steve Kerr, Golden State
1978	Hubie Brown, Atlanta	1998	Larry Bird, Indiana	2017	Mike D'Antoni, Houston
1979	Cotton Fitzsimmons, Kansas City	1999	Mike Dunleavy, Portland	2018	Dwane Casey, Toronto
1980	Bill Fitch, Boston	2000	Glenn "Doc" Rivers, Orlando	2019	Mike Budenholzer, Milwaukee
1981	Jack McKinney, Indiana	2001	Larry Brown, Philadelphia	2020	Nick Nurse, Toronto
1982	Gene Shue, Washington				

National Basketball Association Franchise Origins

Team, founding year (in NBA, Basketball Assn. of Amer. [BAA], or Amer. Basketball Assn. [ABA]), location, and subsequent history. Neutral sites and arena sites in the same metropolitan area not listed separately.

Atlanta Hawks: 1949, NBA, as Tri-Cities Blackhawks, 1949-51, Moline, IL. Milwaukee Hawks, 1951-55; St. Louis Hawks, 1955-68; Atlanta Hawks, 1968-present.

Boston Celtics: 1946, BAA, Boston, MA, 1946-present.

Brooklyn Nets: 1967, ABA, as New Jersey Americans, 1967-68; Teaneck, NJ. New York Nets, 1968-77; New Jersey Nets, 1977-2012; Brooklyn Nets, 2012-present.

Charlotte Hornets: 2004, NBA, as Charlotte Bobcats, 2004-14, Charlotte, NC. Charlotte Hornets, 2014-present.

Chicago Bulls: 1966, NBA, Chicago, IL, 1966-present.

Cleveland Cavaliers: 1970, NBA, Cleveland, OH, 1970-present.

Dallas Mavericks: 1980, NBA, Dallas, TX, 1980-present.

Denver Nuggets: 1967, ABA, as Denver Rockets, 1967-74; Denver, CO. Denver Nuggets, 1974-present.

Detroit Pistons: 1948, NBA, as Ft. Wayne Pistons, 1948-57, Ft. Wayne, IN. Detroit Pistons, 1957-present.

Golden State Warriors: 1946, BAA, as Philadelphia Warriors, 1946-62, Philadelphia, PA. San Francisco Warriors, 1962-71; Golden State Warriors, 1971-2019, Oakland, CA; 2019-present, San Francisco, CA.

Houston Rockets: 1967, NBA, as San Diego Rockets, 1967-71, San Diego, CA. Houston Rockets, 1971-present.

Indiana Pacers: 1967, ABA, Indianapolis, IN, 1974-present.

L.A. Clippers: 1970, NBA, as Buffalo Braves, 1970-78, Buffalo, NY. San Diego Clippers, 1978-84; L.A. Clippers, 1984-present.

L.A. Lakers: 1948, BAA, as Minneapolis Lakers, 1948-60, Minneapolis, MN. L.A. Lakers, 1960-present.

Memphis Grizzlies: 1995, NBA, as Vancouver Grizzlies, 1995-2001, Vancouver, BC, Canada. Memphis Grizzlies, 2001-present.

Miami Heat: 1988, NBA, Miami, FL, 1988-present.

Milwaukee Bucks: 1968, NBA, Milwaukee, WI, 1968-present.

Minnesota Timberwolves: 1989, NBA, Minneapolis, MN, 1989-present.

New Orleans Pelicans: 1988, NBA, as Charlotte Hornets, 1988-2002, Charlotte, NC. New Orleans Hornets, 2002-13 (Hornets played most home games in Oklahoma City, 2005-07, as city repaired Hurricane Katrina damage); New Orleans Pelicans, 2013-present.

New York Knicks: 1946, BAA, New York, NY, 1946-present.

Oklahoma City Thunder: 1967, NBA, as Seattle SuperSonics, 1967-2008, Seattle, WA. Oklahoma City Thunder, 2008-present.

Orlando Magic: 1989, NBA, Orlando, FL, 1989-present.

Philadelphia 76ers: 1949, NBA, as Syracuse Nationals, 1949-63, Syracuse, NY. Philadelphia 76ers, 1963-present.

Phoenix Suns: 1968, NBA, Phoenix, AZ, 1968-present.

Portland Trail Blazers: 1970, NBA, Portland, OR, 1970-present.

Sacramento Kings: 1948, BAA, as Rochester Royals, 1948-57, Rochester, NY. Cincinnati Royals, 1957-72; Kansas City-Omaha Kings, 1972-75; Kansas City Kings, 1975-85; Sacramento Kings, 1985-present.

San Antonio Spurs: ABA, as Dallas Chaparrals, 1967-73, Dallas, TX. San Antonio Spurs, 1973-present.

Toronto Raptors: 1995, NBA, Toronto, ON, Canada, 1995-present.

Utah Jazz: 1974, NBA, as New Orleans Jazz, 1974-79, New Orleans, LA. Utah Jazz, 1979-present, Salt Lake City.

Washington Wizards: 1961, NBA, as Chicago Packers, 1961-62, Chicago, IL. Chicago Zephyrs, 1962-63; Baltimore Bullets, 1963-73; Capital Bullets, 1973-74; Landover, MD; Washington Bullets, 1974-97; Washington Wizards, 1997-present.

NBA Home Courts

Team	Name (year built)	Capacity[1]	Team	Name (year built)	Capacity[1]
Atlanta	State Farm Arena[2] (1999)	16,880	Miami	AmericanAirlines Arena (1999)	19,600
Boston	TD Garden[3] (1995)	18,624	Milwaukee	Fiserv Forum (2018)	17,341
Brooklyn	Barclays Center[4] (2012)	17,732	Minnesota	Target Center (1990)	18,978
Charlotte	Spectrum Center[5] (2005)	19,077	New Orleans	Smoothie King Center[8] (1999)	16,867
Chicago	United Center (1994)	20,917	New York	Madison Square Garden (IV) (1968)	19,812
Cleveland	Rocket Mortgage FieldHouse[6] (1994)	19,432	Oklahoma City	Chesapeake Energy Arena[9] (2002)	18,203
Dallas	American Airlines Center (2001)	19,200	Orlando	Amway Center (2010)	18,846
Denver	Pepsi Center (1999)	19,520	Philadelphia	Wells Fargo Center[10] (1996)	20,155
Detroit	Little Caesars Arena (2017)	20,332	Phoenix	Talking Stick Resort Arena[11] (1992)	18,055
Golden State	Chase Center (2019)	18,064	Portland	Moda Center[12] (1995)	19,441
Houston	Toyota Center (2003)	18,055	Sacramento	Golden 1 Center (2016)	17,583
Indiana	Bankers Life Fieldhouse[7] (1999)	17,923	San Antonio	AT&T Center[13] (2002)	18,354
L.A. Clippers	Staples Center (1999)	19,068	Toronto	Scotiabank Arena[14] (1999)	19,800
L.A. Lakers	Staples Center (1999)	18,997	Utah	Vivint Smart Home Arena[15] (1991)	18,306
Memphis	FedExForum (2004)	17,794	Washington	Capital One Arena[16] (1997)	20,362

(1) At the end of the 2019-20 season, unless noted. (2) Philips Arena, 1999-2018. (3) FleetCenter, 1995-2005; TD Banknorth Garden, 2005-09. (4) The New Jersey Nets relocated to Brooklyn prior to the 2012-13 season. (5) Charlotte Bobcats Arena, 2005-08; Time Warner Cable Arena, 2008-16. (6) Gund Arena, 1994-2005; Quicken Loans Arena, 2005-19. (7) Conseco Fieldhouse, 1999-2011. (8) New Orleans Arena, 1999-2014; because of damage to New Orleans Arena due to Hurricane Katrina, the Hornets played 35 games in the Ford Center in Oklahoma City, OK, 3 games in New Orleans Arena, and 3 games at other locations during the 2005-06 season; in 2006-07, the Hornets played 35 games at the Ford Center and 6 games in New Orleans Arena. (9) Ford Center, 2008-11; the Seattle SuperSonics relocated to Oklahoma City prior to the 2008-09 season. (10) CoreStates Center, 1996-98; First Union Center, 1998-2003; Wachovia Center, 2003-10. (11) America West Arena, 1992-2006; US Airways Center, 2006-15. (12) The Rose Garden, 1995-2013. (13) SBC Center, 2002-06. (14) Air Canada Centre, 1999-2018. (15) Delta Center, 1991-2006; EnergySolutions Arena, 2006-15. (16) MCI Center, 1997-2006; Verizon Center, 2006-17.

All-Time NBA Regular Season Coaching Victories

(At the end of the 2019-20 season, ranked by wins. * = Active in 2019-20 season.)

Coach	W	L	PCT	Coach	W	L	PCT	Coach	W	L	PCT
Don Nelson	1,335	1,063	.557	Larry Brown	1,098	904	.548	Cotton Fitzsimmons	832	775	.518
Lenny Wilkens	1,332	1,155	.536	Rick Adelman	1,042	749	.582	*Rick Carlisle	794	659	.546
*Gregg Popovich	1,277	614	.675	Bill Fitch	944	1,106	.460	Gene Shue	784	861	.477
Jerry Sloan	1,221	803	.603	*Doc Rivers	943	681	.581	John MacLeod	707	657	.518
Pat Riley	1,210	694	.636	Red Auerbach	938	479	.662	Red Holzman	696	603	.536
George Karl	1,175	824	.588	Dick Motta	935	1,017	.479	*Mike D'Antoni	672	527	.560
Phil Jackson	1,155	485	.704	Jack Ramsay	864	783	.525				

Naismith Memorial Basketball Hall of Fame

Located in Springfield, MA. * = 2020 inductee. + = Enshrined as both a player and coach. Referee inductees not shown.
www.hoophall.com

Players
Abdul-Jabbar, Kareem
Allen, Ray
Archibald, Nate
Arizin, Paul
Barkley, Charles
Barlow, Thomas
Barry, Rick
Baylor, Elgin
Beaty, Zelmo
Beckman, John
Bellamy, Walt
Belov, Sergei
Bing, Dave
Bird, Larry
Blazejowski, Carol
Borgmann, Bennie
Bradley, Bill
Braun, Carl
Brennan, Joseph
Brown, Roger
*Bryant, Kobe
*Catchings, Tamika
Cervi, Al
Chamberlain, Wilt
Cheeks, Maurice
Clayton, Zack
Cooper, Charles
Cooper, Charles "Chuck"
Cooper, Cynthia
Cosic, Kresimir
Cousy, Bob
Cowens, Dave
Crawford, Joan
Cunningham, Billy
Curry, Denise
Dalipagic, Drazen
Dampier, Louis
Daniels, Mel
Dantley, Adrian
Davies, Bob
DeBernardi, Forrest
DeBusschere, Dave
Dehnert, Henry "Dutch"
Divac, Vlade
Donovan, Anne
Drexler, Clyde
Dumars, Joe
*Duncan, Tim
Edwards, Teresa
Endacott, Paul
English, Alex
Erving, Julius
Ewing, Patrick
Foster, Bud
Frazier, Walt
Friedman, Max
Fulks, Joe
Gale, Lauren
Galis, Nick
Gallatin, Harry
*Garnett, Kevin
Gates, William "Pop"
Gervin, George
Gilmore, Artis
Gola, Tom
Goodrich, Gail
Greer, Hal
Gruenig, Robert "Ace"
Guerin, Richard
Hagan, Cliff
Hanson, Victor
Harris-Stewart, Lusia
Havlicek, John
Hawkins, Cornelius "Connie"
Hayes, Elvin
Haynes, Marques
Haywood, Spencer
*Heinsohn, Tom
Hill, Grant
Holman, Nat
Houbregs, Bob
Howell, Bailey
Hyatt, Chuck
Isaacs, John
Issel, Dan
Iverson, Allen
Jeannette, Harry "Buddy"
Johnson, Dennis
Johnson, Earvin "Magic"
Johnson, Gus
Johnson, William
Johnston, Neil
Jones, Bobby
Jones, K. C.
Jones, Sam
Jordan, Michael
Kidd, Jason
King, Bernard
Krause, Ed "Moose"
Kurland, Bob
Lanier, Bob
Lapchick, Joe
Leslie, Lisa
Lieberman, Nancy
Lovellette, Clyde
Lucas, Jerry
Luisetti, Angelo "Hank"
Macauley, Ed
Malone, Karl
Malone, Moses
Maravich, Pete
Marcari, Hortencia
Marciulionis, Sarunas
Martin, Slater
McAdoo, Bob
McClain, Katrina
McCracken, Emmett "Branch"
McCracken, Jack
McDermott, Bobby
McGinnis, George
McGrady, Tracy
McGuire, Dick
McHale, Kevin
Meneghin, Dino
Meyers, Ann
Mikan, George
Mikkelsen, Vern
Miller, Cheryl
Miller, Reggie
Ming, Yao
Moncrief, Sidney
Monroe, Earl
Mourning, Alonzo
Mullin, Chris
Murphy, Calvin
Murphy, Charles "Stretch"
Mutombo, Dikembe
Nash, Steve
Olajuwon, Hakeem
O'Neal, Shaquille
Page, Harlan "Pat"
Parish, Robert
Payton, Gary
Pereira, Maciel "Ubiratan"
Petrovic, Drazen
Pettit, Bob
Phillip, Andy
Pippen, Scottie
Pollard, Jim
Posey, Cumberland
Radja, Dino
Ramsay, Frank
Reed, Willis
Richmond, Mitch
Risen, Arnie
Robertson, Oscar
Robinson, David
Rodgers, Guy
Rodman, Dennis
Roosma, John
Russell, Bill
Russell, John "Honey"
Sabonis, Arvydas
Sampson, Ralph
Schayes, Adolph
Schmidt, Ernest
Schmidt, Oscar
Schommer, John
Scott, Charlie
Sedran, Barney
Semjonova, Uljana
+Sharman, Bill
Sikma, Jack
Smith, Katie
Staley, Dawn
Steinmetz, Chris
Stockton, John
Stokes, Maurice
Swoopes, Sheryl
Tatum, Reece "Goose"
Thomas, Isiah
Thompson, David
Thompson, John
Thompson, Tina
Thurmond, Nate
Twyman, Jack
Unseld, Wes
Vandivier, Robert "Fuzzy"
Wachter, Ed
Walker, Chet
Walton, Bill
Wanzer, Bobby
Washington, Ora Mae
Weatherspoon, Teresa
West, Jerry
Westphal, Paul
White, Jo Jo
White, Nera
+Wilkens, Lenny
Wilkes, Jamaal
Wilkins, Dominique
Woodard, Lynette
+Wooden, John
Worthy, James
Yardley, George

Coaches
Alexeeva, Lidia
Allen, Forrest C. "Phog"
Anderson, Harold
Auerbach, Arnold "Red"
Auriemma, Geno
Barmore, Leon
Barry, Justin "Sam"
Blood, Ernest
Boeheim, Jim
Brown, Larry
Calhoun, Jim
Calipari, John
Cann, Howard
Carlson, Clifford
Carnesecca, Lou
Carnevale, Ben
Carril, Pete
Case, Everett
Chancellor, Van
Chaney, John
Conradt, Jody
Crum, Denzil "Denny"
Daly, Chuck
Dean, Everett
Diaz-Miguel, Antonio
Diddle, Edgar
Drake, Bruce
Driesell, Charles "Lefty"
Ferrándiz, Pedro
Fitch, Bill
Gaines, Clarence
Gamba, Sandro
Gardner, James "Jack"
Gaze, Lindsay
Gill, Amory "Slats"
Gomelsky, Aleksandr
Gunter, Sue
Hannum, Alex
Harshman, Marv
Haskins, Don
Hatchell, Sylvia
+Heinsohn, Tom
Hickey, Edgar
Hobson, Howard
Holzman, William "Red"
Hughes, Robert
Hurley, Bob, Sr.
Iba, Hank
Izzo, Tom
Jackson, Phil
Julian, Alvin
Keaney, Frank
Keogan, George
Knight, Bob
Krzyzewski, Mike
Kundla, John
Lambert, Ward
Leonard, Bob
Lewis, Guy V.
Litwack, Harry
Loeffler, Kenneth
Lonborg, Arthur "Dutch"
Magee, Herb
McCutchan, Arad
McGraw, Muffet
McGuire, Al
McGuire, Frank
McLendon, John
Meanwell, Dr. Walter
Meyer, Ray
Miller, Ralph
Moore, Billie
*Mulkey, Kim
Nelson, Don
Newell, Pete
Nikolic, Aleksandar
Novosel, Mirko
Olson, Robert "Lute"
Pitino, Rick
Ramsay, John "Jack"
Richardson, Nolan
Riley, Pat
Rubini, Cesare
Rupp, Adolph
Rush, Cathy
Sachs, Leonard
Self, Bill
+Sharman, Bill
Shelton, Everett
Sloan, Jerry
Smith, Dean
*Stevens, Barbara
Stringer, C. Vivian
Summitt, Pat
*Sutton, Eddie
Tarkanian, Jerry
Taylor, Fred
Teague, Bertha
Thompson, John R.
*Tomjanovich, Rudy
VanDerveer, Tara
Wade, Margaret
Watts, Stan
+Wilkens, Lenny
Williams, Gary
Williams, Roy
Winter, Tex
*Wooden, John
Woolpert, Phil
Wootten, Morgan
Yow, Kay

Teams
1948-82 Wayland Baptist (women's teams)
1957-59 Tennessee A&I (men's teams)
1960 USA Men's Olympic Team
1966 Texas Western
1972-73-74 Immaculata Coll.
1992 USA Men's Olympic "Dream Team"
All American Red Heads
Buffalo Germans
First Team
Harlem Globetrotters
New York Renaissance
Original Celtics

Contributors
Abbott, Senda Berenson
McGuire, Al
Barksdale, Don
*Baumann, Patrick
Bee, Clair
Biasone, Danny
Brown, Hubert "Hubie"
Brown, Walter
Bunn, John
Buss, Jerry
Clifton, Nat
Colangelo, Jerry
Davidson, Bill
Douglas, Bob
Duer, Al
Embry, Wayne
Fagan, Cliff
Fisher, Harry
Fleisher, Larry
Gavitt, David
Gottlieb, Edward
Granik, Russ
Gulick, Dr. Luther
Harrison, Lester
Hearn, Francis "Chick"
Henderson, E. B.
Hepp, Dr. Ferenc
Hickox, Edward
Hinkle, Tony
Irish, Edward "Ned"
Jackson, Mannie
Jernstedt, Tom
Jones, R. William
Kennedy, Walter
Knight, Phil
Krause, Jerry
Lemon, Meadowlark
Liston, Emil
Lloyd, Earl
Lobo, Rebecca
McLendon, John
Mokray, Bill
Morgan, Ralph
Morgenweck, Frank
Naismith, Dr. James
Newton, C. M.
O'Brien, John
O'Brien, Larry
Olsen, Harold
Podoloff, Maurice
Porter, Henry V.
Raveling, George
Reid, William
Reinsdorf, Jerry
Ripley, Elmer
St. John, Lynn
Sanders, Tom "Satch"
Saperstein, Abe
Schabinger, Arthur
Stagg, Alonzo
Stankovic, Boris
Steitz, Edward
Stern, David
Taylor, Chuck
Thorn, Rod
Tower, Oswald
Trester, Arthur
Vitale, Dick
Wells, Clifford
Welts, Rick
Wilke, Lou
Zollner, Fred

Attles, Al

Seattle Storm Win 2020 WNBA Championship

The Seattle Storm won their second WNBA title in three years in a 2020 season shortened due to the coronavirus pandemic. The regular season began on July 25 and each team played 22 games, all of which were contested without fans in attendance at the IMG Academy in Bradenton, FL. Breanna Stewart, who missed the 2019 WNBA season due to an Achilles injury, scored 26 points in Seattle's 92-59 win over the Las Vegas Aces, Oct. 6, 2020, to complete a three-game sweep in the WNBA Finals.

WNBA Final Standings, 2020

(playoff seeds in parentheses; top eight teams by PCT advance, regardless of conference; top two seeds receive a bye to the semifinals, and the third and fourth seeds receive a bye to the second round. Delayed start reduced the 2020 regular season to 22 games.)

Eastern Conference	W	L	PCT	GB	Western Conference	W	L	PCT	GB
Chicago Sky (6)	12	10	.545	—	Las Vegas Aces (1)	18	4	.818	—
Connecticut Sun (7)	10	12	.455	2	Seattle Storm (2)	18	4	.818	—
Washington Mystics (8)	9	13	.409	3	Los Angeles Sparks (3)	15	7	.682	3
Atlanta Dream	7	15	.318	5	Minnesota Lynx (4)	14	8	.636	4
Indiana Fever	6	16	.273	6	Phoenix Mercury (5)	13	9	.591	5
New York Liberty	2	20	.091	10	Dallas Wings	8	14	.364	10

Note: Las Vegas earned the No. 1 seed over Seattle due to a better head-to-head record.

WNBA Playoff Results, 2020

First Round (single elimination)
(7) Connecticut 94, (6) Chicago 81
(5) Phoenix 85, (8) Washington 84

Second Round (single elimination)
(4) Minnesota 80, (5) Phoenix 79
(7) Connecticut 73, (3) Los Angeles 59

Semifinals (best-of-five)
(1) Las Vegas defeated (7) Connecticut, 3 games to 2
(2) Seattle defeated (4) Minnesota, 3 games to 0

WNBA Championship
Seattle defeated Las Vegas, 3 games to 0 (93-80, 104-91, 92-59)

WNBA Statistical Leaders, 2020

Minutes played: 752, Napheesa Collier, Minnesota
Total points: 501, Arike Ogunbowale, Dallas
Points per game: 22.8, Arike Ogunbowale, Dallas
Field goal pct.: .605, Brionna Jones, Connecticut
3-point field goal pct.: .522, Alysha Clark, Seattle

Free throw pct.: .951, Tiffany Mitchell, Indiana
Rebounds: 214: Candace Parker, Los Angeles
Assists: 220: Courtney Vandersloot, Chicago
Steals: 42, Alyssa Thomas, Connecticut
Blocks: 44, Aja Wilson, Las Vegas

WNBA Champions, 1997-2020

Year	Eastern champion	Western champion	Champion	Winning coach	Opponent
		Regular Season		Playoffs	
1997	Houston Comets	Phoenix Mercury	Houston	Van Chancellor	New York
1998	Cleveland Rockers	Houston Comets	Houston	Van Chancellor	Phoenix
1999	New York Liberty	Houston Comets	Houston	Van Chancellor	New York
2000	New York Liberty	Los Angeles Sparks	Houston	Van Chancellor	New York
2001	Cleveland Rockers	Los Angeles Sparks	Los Angeles	Michael Cooper	Charlotte
2002	New York Liberty	Los Angeles Sparks	Los Angeles	Michael Cooper	New York
2003	Detroit Shock	Los Angeles Sparks	Detroit	Bill Laimbeer	Los Angeles
2004	Connecticut Sun	Los Angeles Sparks	Seattle	Anne Donovan	Connecticut
2005	Connecticut Sun	Sacramento Monarchs	Sacramento	John Whisenant	Connecticut
2006	Connecticut Sun	Los Angeles Sparks	Detroit	Bill Laimbeer	Sacramento
2007	Detroit Shock	Phoenix Mercury	Phoenix	Paul Westhead	Detroit
2008	Detroit Shock	San Antonio Silver Stars	Detroit	Bill Laimbeer	San Antonio
2009	Indiana Fever	Phoenix Mercury	Phoenix	Corey Gaines	Indiana
2010	Washington Mystics	Seattle Storm	Seattle	Brian Agler	Atlanta
2011	Indiana Fever	Minnesota Lynx	Minnesota	Cheryl Reeve	Atlanta
2012	Connecticut Sun	Minnesota Lynx	Indiana	Lin Dunn	Minnesota
2013	Chicago Sky	Minnesota Lynx	Minnesota	Cheryl Reeve	Atlanta
2014	Atlanta Dream	Phoenix Mercury	Phoenix	Sandy Brondello	Chicago
2015	New York Liberty	Minnesota Lynx	Minnesota	Cheryl Reeve	Indiana
2016	New York Liberty	Minnesota Lynx	Los Angeles	Brian Agler	Minnesota
2017	New York Liberty	Minnesota Lynx	Minnesota	Cheryl Reeve	Los Angeles
2018	Atlanta Dream	Seattle Storm	Seattle	Dan Hughes	Washington
2019	Washington Mystics	Los Angeles Sparks	Washington	Mike Thibault	Connecticut
2020	Chicago Sky	Las Vegas Aces	Seattle	Gary Kloppenburg[1]	Las Vegas

(1) Seattle head coach Dan Hughes was not medically cleared for the 2020 season.

WNBA Finals MVP, 1997-2020

Year	Player, team	Year	Player, team	Year	Player, team
1997	Cynthia Cooper, Houston	2005	Yolanda Griffith, Sacramento	2013	Maya Moore, Minnesota
1998	Cynthia Cooper, Houston	2006	Deanna Nolan, Detroit	2014	Diana Taurasi, Phoenix
1999	Cynthia Cooper, Houston	2007	Cappie Pondexter, Phoenix	2015	Sylvia Fowles, Minnesota
2000	Cynthia Cooper, Houston	2008	Katie Smith, Detroit	2016	Candace Parker, Los Angeles
2001	Lisa Leslie, Los Angeles	2009	Diana Taurasi, Phoenix	2017	Sylvia Fowles, Minnesota
2002	Lisa Leslie, Los Angeles	2010	Lauren Jackson, Seattle	2018	Breanna Stewart, Seattle
2003	Ruth Riley, Detroit	2011	Seimone Augustus, Minnesota	2019	Emma Meesseman, Wash.
2004	Betty Lennox, Seattle	2012	Tamika Catchings, Indiana	2020	Breanna Stewart, Seattle

WNBA Most Valuable Player, 1997-2020

Year	Player, team	Year	Player, team	Year	Player, team
1997	Cynthia Cooper, Houston	2005	Sheryl Swoopes, Houston	2013	Candace Parker, Los Angeles
1998	Cynthia Cooper, Houston	2006	Lisa Leslie, Los Angeles	2014	Maya Moore, Minnesota
1999	Yolanda Griffith, Sacramento	2007	Lauren Jackson, Seattle	2015	Elena Delle Donne, Chicago
2000	Sheryl Swoopes, Houston	2008	Candace Parker, Los Angeles	2016	Nneka Ogwumike, Los Angeles
2001	Lisa Leslie, Los Angeles	2009	Diana Taurasi, Phoenix	2017	Sylvia Fowles, Minnesota
2002	Sheryl Swoopes, Houston	2010	Lauren Jackson, Seattle	2018	Breanna Stewart, Seattle
2003	Lauren Jackson, Seattle	2011	Tamika Catchings, Indiana	2019	Elena Delle Donne, Wash.
2004	Lisa Leslie, Los Angeles	2012	Tina Charles, Connecticut	2020	A'ja Wilson, Las Vegas

WNBA Rookie of the Year, 1997-2020

Year	Player, team	Year	Player, team	Year	Player, team
1997	No award	2005	Temeka Johnson, Washington	2013	Elena Delle Donne, Chicago
1998	Tracy Reid, Charlotte	2006	Seimone Augustus, Minnesota	2014	Chiney Ogwumike, Connecticut
1999	Chamique Holdsclaw, Washington	2007	Armintie Price, Chicago	2015	Jewell Loyd, Seattle
2000	Betty Lennox, Minnesota	2008	Candace Parker, Los Angeles	2016	Breanna Stewart, Seattle
2001	Jackie Stiles, Portland	2009	Angel McCoughtry, Atlanta	2017	Allisha Gray, Dallas
2002	Tamika Catchings, Indiana	2010	Tina Charles, Connecticut	2018	A'ja Wilson, Las Vegas
2003	Cheryl Ford, Detroit	2011	Maya Moore, Minnesota	2019	Napheesa Collier, Minnesota
2004	Diana Taurasi, Phoenix	2012	Nneka Ogwumike, Los Angeles	2020	Crystal Dangerfield, Minnesota

WNBA Scoring Leaders, 1997-2020

(Average points per game; 24 games or 480 point minimum, 2004-19; 16 games in 2020; prior season minimums vary.)

Year	Player, team	PTS	AVG	Year	Player, team	PTS	AVG
1997	Cynthia Cooper, Houston	621	22.2	2009	Diana Taurasi, Phoenix	631	20.4
1998	Cynthia Cooper, Houston	680	22.7	2010	Diana Taurasi, Phoenix	702	22.6
1999	Cynthia Cooper, Houston	686	22.1	2011	Diana Taurasi, Phoenix	692	21.6
2000	Sheryl Swoopes, Houston	643	20.7	2012	Angel McCoughtry, Atlanta	514	21.4
2001	Katie Smith, Minnesota	739	23.1	2013	Angel McCoughtry, Atlanta	711	21.5
2002	Chamique Holdsclaw, Washington	397	19.9	2014	Maya Moore, Minnesota	812	23.9
2003	Lauren Jackson, Seattle	698	21.2	2015	Elena Delle Donne, Chicago	725	23.4
2004	Lauren Jackson, Seattle	634	20.5	2016	Tina Charles, New York	688	21.5
2005	Sheryl Swoopes, Houston	614	18.6	2017	Brittney Griner, Phoenix	569	21.9
2006	Diana Taurasi, Phoenix	860	25.3	2018	Liz Cambage, Dallas	737	23.0
2007	Lauren Jackson, Seattle	739	23.8	2019	Brittney Griner, Phoenix	642	20.7
2008	Diana Taurasi, Phoenix	820	24.1	2020	Arike Ogunbowale, Dallas	501	22.8

WNBA Rebounding Leaders, 1997-2020

(Average rebounds per game; 24 games or 240 rebounds minimum, 2004-19; 16 games in 2020; prior season minimums vary.)

Year	Player, team	REB	RPG	Year	Player, team	REB	RPG
1997	Lisa Leslie, Los Angeles	266	9.5	2009	Candace Parker, Los Angeles	244	9.8
1998	Lisa Leslie, Los Angeles	285	10.2	2010	Tina Charles, Connecticut	398	11.7
1999	Yolanda Griffith, Sacramento	329	11.3	2011	Tina Charles, Connecticut	374	11.0
2000	Natalie Williams, Utah	336	11.6	2012	Tina Charles, Connecticut	345	10.5
2001	Yolanda Griffith, Sacramento	357	11.2	2013	Sylvia Fowles, Chicago	369	11.5
2002	Chamique Holdsclaw, Washington	232	11.6	2014	Courtney Paris, Tulsa	347	10.2
2003	Chamique Holdsclaw, Washington	294	10.9	2015	Courtney Paris, Tulsa	317	9.3
2004	Lisa Leslie, Los Angeles	336	9.9	2016	Tina Charles, New York	317	9.9
2005	Cheryl Ford, Detroit	322	9.8	2017	Jonquel Jones, Connecticut	403	11.9
2006	Cheryl Ford, Detroit	363	11.3	2018	Sylvia Fowles, Minnesota	404	11.9
2007	Lauren Jackson, Seattle	300	9.7	2019	Jonquel Jones, Connecticut	330	9.7
2008	Candace Parker, Los Angeles	313	9.5	2020	Candace Parker, Los Angeles	214	9.7

WNBA Assist Leaders, 1997-2020

(Average assists per game; 24 games or 140 assists minimum, 2004-19; 16 games in 2020; prior season minimums vary.)

Year	Player, team	AST	APG	Year	Player, team	AST	APG
1997	Teresa Weatherspoon, New York	172	6.1	2009	Sue Bird, Seattle	179	5.8
1998	Ticha Penicheiro, Sacramento	224	7.5	2010	Ticha Penicheiro, Los Angeles	220	6.9
1999	Ticha Penicheiro, Sacramento	226	7.1	2011	Lindsay Whalen, Minnesota	199	5.9
2000	Ticha Penicheiro, Sacramento	236	7.9	2012	Lindsay Whalen, Minnesota	178	5.4
2001	Ticha Penicheiro, Sacramento	172	7.5	2013	Danielle Robinson, San Antonio	168	6.7
2002	Ticha Penicheiro, Sacramento	192	8.0	2014	Diana Taurasi, Phoenix	185	5.6
2003	Ticha Penicheiro, Sacramento	229	6.7	2015	Courtney Vandersloot, Chicago	198	5.8
2004	Nikki Teasley, Los Angeles	207	6.1	2016	Sue Bird, Seattle	196	5.8
2005	Sue Bird, Seattle	176	5.9	2017	Courtney Vandersloot, Chicago	218	8.1
2006	Nikki Teasley, Washington	183	5.4	2018	Courtney Vandersloot, Chicago	258	8.6
2007	Becky Hammon, San Antonio	140	5.0	2019	Courtney Vandersloot, Chicago	300	9.1
2008	Lindsay Whalen, Connecticut	166	5.4	2020	Courtney Vandersloot, Chicago	220	10.0

All-Time WNBA Statistical Leaders

(At the end of the 2020 season. * = Active in 2020 season; ** = not active in 2020 but not retired.)

Scoring Average
(Minimum 100 games)

Player	G	PTS	AVG	Player	G	PTS	AVG
Cynthia Cooper	124	2,601	21.0	*Angel McCoughtry	308	5,785	18.8
**Elena Delle Donne	190	3,853	20.3	**Maya Moore	271	4,984	18.4
*Breanna Stewart	121	2,413	19.9	**Tina Charles	330	5,982	18.1
*Diana Taurasi	456	8,931	19.6	*Brittney Griner	224	3,879	17.3
Lauren Jackson	317	6,007	18.9	Lisa Leslie	363	6,263	17.3

Points		Rebounds		Steals	
*Diana Taurasi	8,931	*Sylvia Fowles	3,400	Tamika Catchings	1,074
Tina Thompson	7,488	Rebekkah Brunson	3,356	Ticha Penicheiro	764
Tamika Catchings	7,380	Tamika Catchings	3,316	Alana Beard	710
Cappie Pondexter	6,811	Lisa Leslie	3,307	*Sue Bird	659
*Candace Dupree	6,728	**Tina Charles	3,133	Sheryl Swoopes	657
Katie Smith	6,452	*Candace Dupree	3,071	Jia Perkins	635
Lisa Leslie	6,263	Tina Thompson	3,070	Sancho Lyttle	634
*Sue Bird	6,262	Taj McWilliams-Franklin	3,013	*Angel McCoughtry	626

3-Point Field Goals Made		Assists		Blocked Shots	
*Diana Taurasi	1,164	*Sue Bird	2,888	Margo Dydek	877
Katie Smith	906	Ticha Penicheiro	2,599	Lisa Leslie	822
*Sue Bird	878	Lindsay Whalen	2,348	*Brittney Griner	658
Becky Hammon	829	*Diana Taurasi	1,953	*Sylvia Fowles	629
Tina Thompson	748	*Courtney Vandersloot	1,905	Lauren Jackson	586
Katie Douglas	727	Becky Hammon	1,708	Tangela Smith	557
Tamika Catchings	606	Cappie Pondexter	1,578	Tammy Sutton-Brown	555
**Kristi Toliver	600	Tamika Catchings	1,488	*Candace Parker	545

HOCKEY

Tampa Bay Lightning Win 2020 Stanley Cup

The Tampa Bay Lightning won their second Stanley Cup championship in franchise history, capping a 2019-20 season that was stalled for five months due to the coronavirus pandemic. Tampa Bay's Andrei Vasilevskiy stopped 22 shots, and goals from Brayden Point and Blake Coleman gave the Lightning a 2-0 win over the Dallas Stars in Game 6 of the Stanley Cup Final, Sept. 28, 2020, at Rogers Place in Edmonton, AB, Canada. Lightning defenseman Victor Hedman scored 10 postseason goals and won the Conn Smythe Trophy as Most Valuable Player of the playoffs.

The NHL suspended play Mar. 12, 2020, with 189 regular-season games unplayed. The Boston Bruins (44-14-12) won the Presidents' Trophy in the abbreviated 2019-20 regular season with the league's best record. Play resumed in Aug. with a round-robin series and qualifying-round tournaments to determine the playoff matchups. A total of 24 teams participated in the season's restart. All postseason games were played without fans in attendance in Canadian hub cities of Toronto, ON, and Edmonton, AB.

The Lightning earned the second seed in the East in their round-robin series. Brayden Point led all skaters with 14 playoff goals, including an overtime goal in a 5-OT Game 1 and another in Game 5 for a 5-4, series-clinching first-round victory over Columbus, Aug. 19, at Scotiabank Arena in Toronto. The Lightning defeated the NY Islanders in six games in the Eastern Conference Finals at Rogers Place in Edmonton. Anthony Cirelli scored the winning goal in overtime in Game 6 to lift Tampa Bay to a 2-1 win, Sept. 17.

The Dallas Stars reached the Stanley Cup Final for the first time since 2000. Dallas lost two of three games in its round-robin series and earned the West's No. 3 playoff seed. Denis Gurianov's Game 5, overtime goal lifted the Stars over the Vegas Golden Knights, 3-2, to win the Western Conference Final, Sept. 14, 2020, at Rogers Place in Edmonton.

Final NHL Standings, 2019-20

(* = clinched playoff berth; seeds earned in round-robin play shown in parentheses)

Standings are determined by total points. Teams earn two points for each win and one point for each game lost in overtime or in a shootout. ROW, which stands for Regulation plus Overtime Wins, is used to break ties between teams with the same number of points.

Due to the COVID-19 pandemic, 24 teams—the top 12 in each Conference on the basis of points percentage at the time of the pause—competed in Seeding Round Robins, a Qualifying Round, and Conference-based Stanley Cup Playoffs in two "hub" cities.

Eastern Conference

Atlantic Division	W	L	OT	GF	GA	ROW	PTS	PCT
Boston* (4)	44	14	12	227	174	44	100	.714
Tampa Bay* (2)	43	21	6	245	195	41	92	.657
Toronto	36	25	9	238	227	35	81	.579
Florida	35	26	8	231	228	32	78	.565
Montréal*	31	31	9	212	221	27	71	.500
Buffalo	30	31	8	195	217	28	68	.493
Ottawa	25	34	12	191	243	24	62	.437
Detroit	17	49	5	145	267	14	39	.275

Metropolitan Division	W	L	OT	GF	GA	ROW	PTS	PCT
Washington* (3)	41	20	8	240	215	37	90	.652
Philadelphia* (1)	41	21	7	232	196	36	89	.645
Pittsburgh	40	23	6	224	196	37	86	.623
Carolina*	38	25	5	222	193	33	81	.596
NY Islanders*	35	23	10	192	193	32	80	.588
Columbus*	33	22	15	180	187	33	81	.579
NY Rangers	37	28	5	234	222	36	79	.564
New Jersey	28	29	12	189	230	24	68	.493

Western Conference

Central Division	W	L	OT	GF	GA	ROW	PTS	PCT
St. Louis* (4)	42	19	10	225	193	40	94	.662
Colorado* (2)	42	20	8	237	191	41	92	.657
Dallas* (3)	37	24	8	180	177	35	82	.594
Nashville	35	26	8	215	217	32	78	.565
Winnipeg	37	28	6	216	203	34	80	.563
Minnesota	35	27	7	220	220	33	77	.558
Chicago*	32	30	8	212	218	28	72	.514

Pacific Division	W	L	OT	GF	GA	ROW	PTS	PCT
Vegas* (1)	39	24	8	227	211	36	86	.606
Edmonton	37	25	9	225	217	35	83	.585
Vancouver*	36	27	6	228	217	32	78	.565
Calgary*	36	27	7	210	215	30	79	.564
Arizona*	33	29	8	195	187	28	74	.529
Anaheim	29	33	9	187	226	24	67	.472
Los Angeles	29	35	6	178	212	28	64	.457
San Jose	29	36	5	182	226	27	63	.450

Qualifying Rounds and Stanley Cup Playoff Results, 2020

Qualifying Rounds
Montréal defeated Pittsburgh, 3-1
Carolina defeated NY Rangers, 3-0
NY Islanders defeated Florida, 3-1
Columbus defeated Toronto, 3-2
Chicago defeated Edmonton, 3-1
Arizona defeated Nashville, 3-1
Vancouver defeated Minnesota, 3-1
Calgary defeated Winnipeg, 3-1

Eastern Conference Finals
Philadelphia defeated Montréal, 4-2
Tampa Bay defeated Columbus, 4-1
NY Islanders defeated Washington, 4-1
Boston defeated Carolina, 4-1
NY Islanders defeated Philadelphia, 4-3
Tampa Bay defeated Boston, 4-1
Tampa Bay defeated NY Islanders, 4-2

Western Conference Finals
Vegas defeated Chicago, 4-1
Colorado defeated Arizona, 4-1
Dallas defeated Calgary, 4-2
Vancouver defeated St. Louis, 4-2
Vegas defeated Vancouver, 4-3
Dallas defeated Colorado, 4-3
Dallas defeated Vegas, 4-1

Stanley Cup Final
Tampa Bay defeated Dallas, 4-2 (1-4, 3-2, 5-2, 5-4 [OT], 2-3 [2OT], 2-0)

Stanley Cup Champions, 1927-2020

Year	Champion	Coach	Final opponent	Year	Champion	Coach	Final opponent
1927	Ottawa	Dave Gill	Boston	1946	Montréal	Dick Irvin	Boston
1928	NY Rangers	Lester Patrick	Montréal Maroons	1947	Toronto	Hap Day	Montréal
				1948	Toronto	Hap Day	Detroit
1929	Boston	Art Ross	NY Rangers	1949	Toronto	Hap Day	Detroit
1930	Montréal Canadiens	Cecil Hart	Boston	1950	Detroit	Tommy Ivan	NY Rangers
1931	Montréal Canadiens	Cecil Hart	Chicago	1951	Toronto	Joe Primeau	Montréal
1932	Toronto	Dick Irvin	NY Rangers	1952	Detroit	Tommy Ivan	Montréal
1933	NY Rangers	Lester Patrick	Toronto	1953	Montréal	Dick Irvin	Boston
1934	Chicago	Tommy Gorman	Detroit	1954	Detroit	Tommy Ivan	Montréal
1935	Montréal Maroons	Tommy Gorman	Toronto	1955	Detroit	Jimmy Skinner	Montréal
1936	Detroit	Jack Adams	Toronto	1956	Montréal	Toe Blake	Detroit
1937	Detroit	Jack Adams	NY Rangers	1957	Montréal	Toe Blake	Boston
1938	Chicago	Bill Stewart	Toronto	1958	Montréal	Toe Blake	Boston
1939	Boston	Art Ross	Toronto	1959	Montréal	Toe Blake	Toronto
1940	NY Rangers	Frank Boucher	Toronto	1960	Montréal	Toe Blake	Toronto
1941	Boston	Cooney Weiland	Detroit	1961	Chicago	Rudy Pilous	Detroit
1942	Toronto	Hap Day	Detroit	1962	Toronto	Punch Imlach	Chicago
1943	Detroit	Jack Adams	Boston	1963	Toronto	Punch Imlach	Detroit
1944	Montréal	Dick Irvin	Chicago	1964	Toronto	Punch Imlach	Detroit
1945	Toronto	Hap Day	Detroit	1965	Montréal	Toe Blake	Chicago

Year	Champion	Coach	Final opponent	Year	Champion	Coach	Final opponent
1966	Montréal	Toe Blake	Detroit	1994	NY Rangers	Mike Keenan	Vancouver
1967	Toronto	Punch Imlach	Montréal	1995	New Jersey	Jacques Lemaire	Detroit
1968	Montréal	Toe Blake	St. Louis	1996	Colorado	Marc Crawford	Florida
1969	Montréal	Claude Ruel	St. Louis	1997	Detroit	Scotty Bowman	Philadelphia
1970	Boston	Harry Sinden	St. Louis	1998	Detroit	Scotty Bowman	Washington
1971	Montréal	Al MacNeil	Chicago	1999	Dallas	Ken Hitchcock	Buffalo
1972	Boston	Tom Johnson	NY Rangers	2000	New Jersey	Larry Robinson	Dallas
1973	Montréal	Scotty Bowman	Chicago	2001	Colorado	Bob Hartley	New Jersey
1974	Philadelphia	Fred Shero	Boston	2002	Detroit	Scotty Bowman	Carolina
1975	Philadelphia	Fred Shero	Buffalo	2003	New Jersey	Pat Burns	Anaheim
1976	Montréal	Scotty Bowman	Philadelphia	2004	Tampa Bay	John Tortorella	Calgary
1977	Montréal	Scotty Bowman	Boston	2005	No competition (labor dispute; season canceled)		
1978	Montréal	Scotty Bowman	Boston	2006	Carolina	Peter Laviolette	Edmonton
1979	Montréal	Scotty Bowman	NY Rangers	2007	Anaheim	Randy Carlyle	Ottawa
1980	NY Islanders	Al Arbour	Philadelphia	2008	Detroit	Mike Babcock	Pittsburgh
1981	NY Islanders	Al Arbour	Minnesota	2009	Pittsburgh	Dan Bylsma	Detroit
1982	NY Islanders	Al Arbour	Vancouver	2010	Chicago	Joel Quenneville	Philadelphia
1983	NY Islanders	Al Arbour	Edmonton	2011	Boston	Claude Julien	Vancouver
1984	Edmonton	Glen Sather	NY Islanders	2012	Los Angeles	Darryl Sutter	New Jersey
1985	Edmonton	Glen Sather	Philadelphia	2013	Chicago	Joel Quenneville	Boston
1986	Montréal	Jean Perron	Calgary	2014	Los Angeles	Darryl Sutter	NY Rangers
1987	Edmonton	Glen Sather	Philadelphia	2015	Chicago	Joel Quenneville	Tampa Bay
1988	Edmonton	Glen Sather	Boston	2016	Pittsburgh	Mike Sullivan	San Jose
1989	Calgary	Terry Crisp	Montréal	2017	Pittsburgh	Mike Sullivan	Nashville
1990	Edmonton	John Muckler	Boston	2018	Washington	Barry Trotz	Vegas
1991	Pittsburgh	Bob Johnson	Minnesota	2019	St. Louis	Craig Berube	Boston
1992	Pittsburgh	Scotty Bowman	Chicago	2020	Tampa Bay	Jon Cooper	Dallas
1993	Montréal	Jacques Demers	Los Angeles				

Presidents' Trophy, 1986-2020

Awarded annually to club with best regular season record. Records are Win-Loss-Tie, 1986-99; Win-Loss-Tie-Overtime Loss, 2000-04; Win-Loss-Overtime Loss, 2006-present. (Because of a labor dispute, the 2005 season was canceled.)

Year	Team	Record	Points	Year	Team	Record	Points	Year	Team	Record	Points
1986	Edmonton	56-17-7	119	1998	Dallas	49-22-11	109	2010	Washington	54-15-13	121
1987	Edmonton	50-24-6	106	1999	Dallas	51-19-12	114	2011	Vancouver	54-19-9	117
1988	Calgary	48-23-9	105	2000	St. Louis	51-19-11-1	114	2012	Vancouver	51-22-9	111
1989	Calgary	54-17-9	117	2001	Colorado	52-16-10-4	118	2013	Chicago	36-7-5	77
1990	Boston	46-25-9	101	2002	Detroit	51-17-10-4	116	2014	Boston	54-19-9	117
1991	Chicago	49-23-8	106	2003	Ottawa	52-21-8-1	113	2015	NY Rangers	53-22-7	113
1992	NY Rangers	50-25-5	105	2004	Detroit	48-21-11-2	109	2016	Washington	56-18-8	120
1993	Pittsburgh	56-21-7	119	2006	Detroit	58-16-8	124	2017	Washington	55-19-8	118
1994	NY Rangers	52-24-8	112	2007	Buffalo	53-22-7	113	2018	Nashville	53-18-11	117
1995	Detroit	33-11-4	70	2008	Detroit	54-21-7	115	2019	Tampa Bay	62-16-4	128
1996	Detroit	62-13-7	131	2009	San Jose	53-18-11	117	2020	Boston Bruins	44-14-12	100
1997	Colorado	49-24-9	107								

Most NHL Goals in a Season

Player	Team	Season	Goals	Player	Team	Season	Goals
Wayne Gretzky	Edmonton	1981-82	92	Wayne Gretzky	Edmonton	1982-83	71
Wayne Gretzky	Edmonton	1983-84	87	Jari Kurri	Edmonton	1984-85	71
Brett Hull	St. Louis	1990-91	86	Mario Lemieux	Pittsburgh	1987-88	70
Mario Lemieux	Pittsburgh	1988-89	85	Bernie Nicholls	Los Angeles	1988-89	70
Phil Esposito	Boston	1970-71	76	Brett Hull	St. Louis	1991-92	70
Alexander Mogilny	Buffalo	1992-93	76	Mike Bossy	NY Islanders	1978-79	69
Teemu Selanne	Winnipeg	1992-93	76	Mario Lemieux	Pittsburgh	1992-93	69
Wayne Gretzky	Edmonton	1984-85	73	Mario Lemieux	Pittsburgh	1995-96	69
Brett Hull	St. Louis	1989-90	72				

NHL Regular Season Career Scoring Leaders

(Through end of 2019-20 season. * = Active in 2019-20 season.)

Player	Goals	Assists	Points	Player	Goals	Assists	Points	Player	Goals	Assists	Points
Wayne Gretzky	894	1,963	2,857	Stan Mikita	541	926	1,467	Mats Sundin	564	785	1,349
Jaromir Jagr	766	1,155	1,921	Teemu Selanne	684	773	1,457	Dave Andreychuk	640	698	1,338
Mark Messier	694	1,193	1,887	Bryan Trottier	524	901	1,425	Denis Savard	473	865	1,338
Gordie Howe	801	1,049	1,850	Adam Oates	341	1,079	1,420	Mike Gartner	708	627	1,335
Ron Francis	549	1,249	1,798	Doug Gilmour	450	964	1,414	Pierre Turgeon	515	812	1,327
Marcel Dionne	731	1,040	1,771	Dale Hawerchuk	518	891	1,409	Gilbert Perreault	512	814	1,326
Steve Yzerman	692	1,063	1,755	Jari Kurri	601	797	1,398	Jarome Iginla	625	675	1,300
Mario Lemieux	690	1,033	1,723	Luc Robitaille	668	726	1,394	Alex Delvecchio	456	825	1,281
Joe Sakic	625	1,016	1,641	Brett Hull	741	650	1,391	*Alexander Ovechkin	706	572	1,278
Phil Esposito	717	873	1,590	Mike Modano	561	813	1,374	Al MacInnis	340	934	1,274
Ray Bourque	410	1,169	1,579	Johnny Bucyk	556	813	1,369	Jean Ratelle	491	776	1,267
Mark Recchi	577	956	1,533	Brendan Shanahan	656	698	1,354	*Sidney Crosby	462	801	1,263
Paul Coffey	396	1,135	1,531	Guy Lafleur	560	793	1,353				
*Joe Thornton	420	1,089	1,509								

Leading NHL Career Goaltenders

(Through end of 2019-20 season. * = Active in 2019-20 season.)

Ranked by Shutouts				Ranked by Wins			
Martin Brodeur	125	Lorne Chabot	71	Martin Brodeur	691	Glenn Hall	407
Terry Sawchuk	103	Harry Lumley	71	Patrick Roy	551	Grant Fuhr	403
George Hainsworth	94	Roy Worters	67	Roberto Luongo	489	Chris Osgood	401
Glenn Hall	84	Patrick Roy	66	Ed Belfour	484	Dominik Hasek	389
Jacques Plante	82	*Henrik Lundqvist	64	*Marc-Andre Fleury	466	*Ryan Miller	387
Alec Connell	81	Turk Broda	61	*Henrik Lundqvist	459	Mike Vernon	385
Tiny Thompson	81	*Marc-Andre Fleury	61	Curtis Joseph	454	John Vanbiesbrouck	374
Dominik Hasek	81	Evgeni Nabokov	59	Terry Sawchuk	445	Andy Moog	372
Roberto Luongo	77	John Ross Roach	58	Jacques Plante	437	Tom Barrasso	369
Ed Belfour	76	*Pekka Rinne	58	Tony Esposito	423	*Pekka Rinne	359
Tony Esposito	76						

Hart Memorial Trophy (MVP), 1927-2020

Year	Player, team	Year	Player, team	Year	Player, team
1927	Herb Gardiner, Montréal Canadiens	1958	Gordie Howe, Detroit	1989	Wayne Gretzky, Los Angeles
1928	Howie Morenz, Montréal Canadiens	1959	Andy Bathgate, NY Rangers	1990	Mark Messier, Edmonton
1929	Roy Worters, NY Americans	1960	Gordie Howe, Detroit	1991	Brett Hull, St. Louis
1930	Nels Stewart, Montréal Maroons	1961	Bernie Geoffrion, Montréal	1992	Mark Messier, NY Rangers
1931	Howie Morenz, Montréal Canadiens	1962	Jacques Plante, Montréal	1993	Mario Lemieux, Pittsburgh
1932	Howie Morenz, Montréal Canadiens	1963	Gordie Howe, Detroit	1994	Sergei Fedorov, Detroit
1933	Eddie Shore, Boston	1964	Jean Beliveau, Montréal	1995	Eric Lindros, Philadelphia
1934	Aurel Joliat, Montréal Canadiens	1965	Bobby Hull, Chicago	1996	Mario Lemieux, Pittsburgh
1935	Eddie Shore, Boston	1966	Bobby Hull, Chicago	1997	Dominik Hasek, Buffalo
1936	Eddie Shore, Boston	1967	Stan Mikita, Chicago	1998	Dominik Hasek, Buffalo
1937	Babe Siebert, Montréal Canadiens	1968	Stan Mikita, Chicago	1999	Jaromir Jagr, Pittsburgh
1938	Eddie Shore, Boston	1969	Phil Esposito, Boston	2000	Chris Pronger, St. Louis
1939	Toe Blake, Montréal	1970	Bobby Orr, Boston	2001	Joe Sakic, Colorado
1940	Ebbie Goodfellow, Detroit	1971	Bobby Orr, Boston	2002	Jose Theodore, Montréal
1941	Bill Cowley, Boston	1972	Bobby Orr, Boston	2003	Peter Forsberg, Colorado
1942	Tom Anderson, Brooklyn Americans	1973	Bobby Clarke, Philadelphia	2004	Martin St. Louis, Tampa Bay
1943	Bill Cowley, Boston	1974	Phil Esposito, Boston	2006	Joe Thornton, San Jose
1944	Babe Pratt, Toronto	1975	Bobby Clarke, Philadelphia	2007	Sidney Crosby, Pittsburgh
1945	Elmer Lach, Montréal	1976	Bobby Clarke, Philadelphia	2008	Alexander Ovechkin, Washington
1946	Max Bentley, Chicago	1977	Guy Lafleur, Montréal	2009	Alexander Ovechkin, Washington
1947	Maurice Richard, Montréal	1978	Guy Lafleur, Montréal	2010	Henrik Sedin, Vancouver
1948	Buddy O'Connor, NY Rangers	1979	Bryan Trottier, NY Islanders	2011	Corey Perry, Anaheim
1949	Sid Abel, Detroit	1980	Wayne Gretzky, Edmonton	2012	Evgeni Malkin, Pittsburgh
1950	Chuck Rayner, NY Rangers	1981	Wayne Gretzky, Edmonton	2013	Alexander Ovechkin, Washington
1951	Milt Schmidt, Boston	1982	Wayne Gretzky, Edmonton	2014	Sidney Crosby, Pittsburgh
1952	Gordie Howe, Detroit	1983	Wayne Gretzky, Edmonton	2015	Carey Price, Montréal
1953	Gordie Howe, Detroit	1984	Wayne Gretzky, Edmonton	2016	Patrick Kane, Chicago
1954	Al Rollins, Chicago	1985	Wayne Gretzky, Edmonton	2017	Connor McDavid, Edmonton
1955	Ted Kennedy, Toronto	1986	Wayne Gretzky, Edmonton	2018	Taylor Hall, New Jersey
1956	Jean Beliveau, Montréal	1987	Wayne Gretzky, Edmonton	2019	Nikita Kucherov, Tampa Bay
1957	Gordie Howe, Detroit	1988	Mario Lemieux, Pittsburgh	2020	Leon Draisaitl, Edmonton

Conn Smythe Trophy (MVP in Playoffs), 1965-2020

Year	Player, team	Year	Player, team	Year	Player, team
1965	Jean Beliveau, Montréal	1984	Mark Messier, Edmonton	2002	Nicklas Lidstrom, Detroit
1966	Roger Crozier, Detroit	1985	Wayne Gretzky, Edmonton	2003	Jean-Sebastien Giguere, Anaheim
1967	Dave Keon, Toronto	1986	Patrick Roy, Montréal	2004	Brad Richards, Tampa Bay
1968	Glenn Hall, St. Louis	1987	Ron Hextall, Philadelphia	2006	Cam Ward, Carolina
1969	Serge Savard, Montréal	1988	Wayne Gretzky, Edmonton	2007	Scott Niedermayer, Anaheim
1970	Bobby Orr, Boston	1989	Al MacInnis, Calgary	2008	Henrik Zetterberg, Detroit
1971	Ken Dryden, Montréal	1990	Bill Ranford, Edmonton	2009	Evgeni Malkin, Pittsburgh
1972	Bobby Orr, Boston	1991	Mario Lemieux, Pittsburgh	2010	Jonathan Toews, Chicago
1973	Yvan Cournoyer, Montréal	1992	Mario Lemieux, Pittsburgh	2011	Tim Thomas, Boston
1974	Bernie Parent, Philadelphia	1993	Patrick Roy, Montréal	2012	Jonathan Quick, Los Angeles
1975	Bernie Parent, Philadelphia	1994	Brian Leetch, NY Rangers	2013	Patrick Kane, Chicago
1976	Reggie Leach, Philadelphia	1995	Claude Lemieux, New Jersey	2014	Justin Williams, Los Angeles
1977	Guy Lafleur, Montréal	1996	Joe Sakic, Colorado	2015	Duncan Keith, Chicago
1978	Larry Robinson, Montréal	1997	Mike Vernon, Detroit	2016	Sidney Crosby, Pittsburgh
1979	Bob Gainey, Montréal	1998	Steve Yzerman, Detroit	2017	Sidney Crosby, Pittsburgh
1980	Bryan Trottier, NY Islanders	1999	Joe Nieuwendyk, Dallas	2018	Alex Ovechkin, Washington
1981	Butch Goring, NY Islanders	2000	Scott Stevens, New Jersey	2019	Ryan O'Reilly, St. Louis
1982	Mike Bossy, NY Islanders	2001	Patrick Roy, Colorado	2020	Víctor Hedman, Tampa Bay
1983	Billy Smith, NY Islanders				

Calder Memorial Trophy (Best Rookie), 1933-2020

Year	Player, team	Year	Player, team	Year	Player, team
1933	Carl Voss, Detroit	1962	Bobby Rousseau, Montréal	1991	Ed Belfour, Chicago
1934	Russ Blinco, Montréal Maroons	1963	Kent Douglas, Toronto	1992	Pavel Bure, Vancouver
1935	Dave Schriner, NY Americans	1964	Jacques Laperrière, Montréal	1993	Teemu Selanne, Winnipeg
1936	Mike Karakas, Chicago	1965	Roger Crozier, Detroit	1994	Martin Brodeur, New Jersey
1937	Syl Apps, Toronto	1966	Brit Selby, Toronto	1995	Peter Forsberg, Quebec
1938	Cully Dahlstrom, Chicago	1967	Bobby Orr, Boston	1996	Daniel Alfredsson, Ottawa
1939	Frank Brimsok, Boston	1968	Derek Sanderson, Boston	1997	Bryan Berard, NY Islanders
1940	Kilby MacDonald, NY Rangers	1969	Danny Grant, Minnesota	1998	Sergei Samsonov, Boston
1941	John Quilty, Montréal	1970	Tony Esposito, Chicago	1999	Chris Drury, Colorado
1942	Grant Warwick, NY Rangers	1971	Gilbert Perreault, Buffalo	2000	Scott Gomez, New Jersey
1943	Gaye Stewart, Toronto	1972	Ken Dryden, Montréal	2001	Evgeni Nabokov, San Jose
1944	Gus Bodnar, Toronto	1973	Steve Vickers, NY Rangers	2002	Dany Heatley, Atlanta
1945	Frank McCool, Toronto	1974	Denis Potvin, NY Islanders	2003	Barret Jackman, St. Louis
1946	Edgar Laprade, NY Rangers	1975	Eric Vail, Atlanta	2004	Andrew Raycroft, Boston
1947	Howie Meeker, Toronto	1976	Bryan Trottier, NY Islanders	2006	Alexander Ovechkin, Washington
1948	Jim McFadden, Detroit	1977	Willi Plett, Atlanta	2007	Evgeni Malkin, Pittsburgh
1949	Pentti Lund, NY Rangers	1978	Mike Bossy, NY Islanders	2008	Patrick Kane, Chicago
1950	Jack Gelineau, Boston	1979	Bobby Smith, Minnesota	2009	Steve Mason, Columbus
1951	Terry Sawchuk, Detroit	1980	Ray Bourque, Boston	2010	Tyler Myers, Buffalo
1952	Bernie Geoffrion, Montréal	1981	Peter Stastny, Quebec	2011	Jeff Skinner, Carolina
1953	Gump Worsley, NY Rangers	1982	Dale Hawerchuk, Winnipeg	2012	Gabriel Landeskog, Colorado
1954	Camille Henry, NY Rangers	1983	Steve Larmer, Chicago	2013	Jonathan Huberdeau, Florida
1955	Ed Litzenberger, Chicago	1984	Tom Barrasso, Buffalo	2014	Nathan MacKinnon, Colorado
1956	Glenn Hall, Detroit	1985	Mario Lemieux, Pittsburgh	2015	Aaron Ekblad, Florida
1957	Larry Regan, Boston	1986	Gary Suter, Calgary	2016	Artemi Panarin, Chicago
1958	Frank Mahovlich, Toronto	1987	Luc Robitaille, Los Angeles	2017	Auston Matthews, Toronto
1959	Ralph Backstrom, Montréal	1988	Joe Nieuwendyk, Calgary	2018	Mathew Barzal, NY Islanders
1960	Bill Hay, Chicago	1989	Brian Leetch, NY Rangers	2019	Elias Pettersson, Vancouver
1961	Dave Keon, Toronto	1990	Sergei Makarov, Calgary	2020	Cale Makar, Colorado

Lady Byng Memorial Trophy (Most Gentlemanly Player), 1925-2020

Year	Player, team	Year	Player, team	Year	Player, team
1925	Frank Nighbor, Ottawa	1957	Andy Hebenton, NY Rangers	1989	Joe Mullen, Calgary
1926	Frank Nighbor, Ottawa	1958	Camille Henry, NY Rangers	1990	Brett Hull, St. Louis
1927	Billy Burch, NY Americans	1959	Alex Delvecchio, Detroit	1991	Wayne Gretzky, Los Angeles
1928	Frank Boucher, NY Rangers	1960	Don McKenney, Boston	1992	Wayne Gretzky, Los Angeles
1929	Frank Boucher, NY Rangers	1961	Red Kelly, Toronto	1993	Pierre Turgeon, NY Islanders
1930	Frank Boucher, NY Rangers	1962	Dave Keon, Toronto	1994	Wayne Gretzky, Los Angeles
1931	Frank Boucher, NY Rangers	1963	Dave Keon, Toronto	1995	Ron Francis, Pittsburgh
1932	Joe Primeau, Toronto	1964	Ken Wharram, Chicago	1996	Paul Kariya, Anaheim
1933	Frank Boucher, NY Rangers	1965	Bobby Hull, Chicago	1997	Paul Kariya, Anaheim
1934	Frank Boucher, NY Rangers	1966	Alex Delvecchio, Detroit	1998	Ron Francis, Pittsburgh
1935	Frank Boucher, NY Rangers	1967	Stan Mikita, Chicago	1999	Wayne Gretzky, NY Rangers
1936	Doc Romnes, Chicago	1968	Stan Mikita, Chicago	2000	Pavol Demitra, St. Louis
1937	Marty Barry, Detroit	1969	Alex Delvecchio, Detroit	2001	Joe Sakic, Colorado
1938	Gordie Drillon, Toronto	1970	Phil Goyette, St. Louis	2002	Ron Francis, Carolina
1939	Clint Smith, NY Rangers	1971	John Bucyk, Boston	2003	Alexander Mogilny, Toronto
1940	Bobby Bauer, Boston	1972	Jean Ratelle, NY Rangers	2004	Brad Richards, Tampa Bay
1941	Bobby Bauer, Boston	1973	Gil Perreault, Buffalo	2006	Pavel Datsyuk, Detroit
1942	Syl Apps, Toronto	1974	John Bucyk, Boston	2007	Pavel Datsyuk, Detroit
1943	Max Bentley, Chicago	1975	Marcel Dionne, Detroit	2008	Pavel Datsyuk, Detroit
1944	Clint Smith, Chicago	1976	Jean Ratelle, NYR-Boston	2009	Pavel Datsyuk, Detroit
1945	Bill Mosienko, Chicago	1977	Marcel Dionne, Los Angeles	2010	Martin St. Louis, Tampa Bay
1946	Toe Blake, Montréal	1978	Butch Goring, Los Angeles	2011	Martin St. Louis, Tampa Bay
1947	Bobby Bauer, Boston	1979	Bob MacMillan, Atlanta	2012	Brian Campbell, Florida
1948	Buddy O'Connor, NY Rangers	1980	Wayne Gretzky, Edmonton	2013	Martin St. Louis, Tampa Bay
1949	Bill Quackenbush, Detroit	1981	Rick Kehoe, Pittsburgh	2014	Ryan O'Reilly, Colorado
1950	Edgar Laprade, NY Rangers	1982	Rick Middleton, Boston	2015	Jiri Hudler, Calgary
1951	Red Kelly, Detroit	1983	Mike Bossy, NY Islanders	2016	Anze Kopitar, Los Angeles
1952	Sid Smith, Toronto	1984	Mike Bossy, NY Islanders	2017	Johnny Gaudreau, Calgary
1953	Red Kelly, Detroit	1985	Jari Kurri, Edmonton	2018	William Karlsson, Vegas
1954	Red Kelly, Detroit	1986	Mike Bossy, NY Islanders	2019	Aleksander Barkov, Florida
1955	Sid Smith, Toronto	1987	Joe Mullen, Calgary	2020	Nathan MacKinnon, Colorado
1956	Dutch Reibel, Detroit	1988	Mats Naslund, Montréal		

James Norris Memorial Trophy (Best Defenseman), 1954-2020

Year	Player, team	Year	Player, team	Year	Player, team
1954	Red Kelly, Detroit	1976	Denis Potvin, NY Islanders	1998	Rob Blake, Los Angeles
1955	Doug Harvey, Montréal	1977	Larry Robinson, Montréal	1999	Al MacInnis, St. Louis
1956	Doug Harvey, Montréal	1978	Denis Potvin, NY Islanders	2000	Chris Pronger, St. Louis
1957	Doug Harvey, Montréal	1979	Denis Potvin, NY Islanders	2001	Nicklas Lidstrom, Detroit
1958	Doug Harvey, Montréal	1980	Larry Robinson, Montréal	2002	Nicklas Lidstrom, Detroit
1959	Tom Johnson, Montréal	1981	Randy Carlyle, Pittsburgh	2003	Nicklas Lidstrom, Detroit
1960	Doug Harvey, Montréal	1982	Doug Wilson, Chicago	2004	Scott Niedermayer, New Jersey
1961	Doug Harvey, Montréal	1983	Rod Langway, Washington	2006	Nicklas Lidstrom, Detroit
1962	Doug Harvey, NY Rangers	1984	Rod Langway, Washington	2007	Nicklas Lidstrom, Detroit
1963	Pierre Pilote, Chicago	1985	Paul Coffey, Edmonton	2008	Nicklas Lidstrom, Detroit
1964	Pierre Pilote, Chicago	1986	Paul Coffey, Edmonton	2009	Zdeno Chara, Boston
1965	Pierre Pilote, Chicago	1987	Ray Bourque, Boston	2010	Duncan Keith, Chicago
1966	Jacques Laperrière, Montréal	1988	Ray Bourque, Boston	2011	Nicklas Lidstrom, Detroit
1967	Harry Howell, NY Rangers	1989	Chris Chelios, Montréal	2012	Erik Karlsson, Ottawa
1968	Bobby Orr, Boston	1990	Ray Bourque, Boston	2013	P. K. Subban, Montréal
1969	Bobby Orr, Boston	1991	Ray Bourque, Boston	2014	Duncan Keith, Chicago
1970	Bobby Orr, Boston	1992	Brian Leetch, NY Rangers	2015	Erik Karlsson, Ottawa
1971	Bobby Orr, Boston	1993	Chris Chelios, Chicago	2016	Drew Doughty, Los Angeles
1972	Bobby Orr, Boston	1994	Ray Bourque, Boston	2017	Brent Burns, San Jose
1973	Bobby Orr, Boston	1995	Paul Coffey, Detroit	2018	Victor Hedman, Tampa Bay
1974	Bobby Orr, Boston	1996	Chris Chelios, Chicago	2019	Mark Giordano, Calgary
1975	Bobby Orr, Boston	1997	Brian Leetch, NY Rangers	2020	Roman Josi, Nashville

Art Ross Trophy (Highest Scorer), 1947-2020

Year	Player, team	Year	Player, team	Year	Player, team
1947	Max Bentley, Chicago	1972	Phil Esposito, Boston	1996	Mario Lemieux, Pittsburgh
1948	Elmer Lach, Montréal	1973	Phil Esposito, Boston	1997	Mario Lemieux, Pittsburgh
1949	Roy Conacher, Chicago	1974	Phil Esposito, Boston	1998	Jaromir Jagr, Pittsburgh
1950	Ted Lindsay, Detroit	1975	Bobby Orr, Boston	1999	Jaromir Jagr, Pittsburgh
1951	Gordie Howe, Detroit	1976	Guy Lafleur, Montréal	2000	Jaromir Jagr, Pittsburgh
1952	Gordie Howe, Detroit	1977	Guy Lafleur, Montréal	2001	Jaromir Jagr, Pittsburgh
1953	Gordie Howe, Detroit	1978	Guy Lafleur, Montréal	2002	Jarome Iginla, Calgary
1954	Gordie Howe, Detroit	1979	Bryan Trottier, NY Islanders	2003	Peter Forsberg, Colorado
1955	Bernie Geoffrion, Montréal	1980	Marcel Dionne, Los Angeles	2004	Martin St. Louis, Tampa Bay
1956	Jean Beliveau, Montréal	1981	Wayne Gretzky, Edmonton	2006	Joe Thornton, Boston/San Jose
1957	Gordie Howe, Detroit	1982	Wayne Gretzky, Edmonton	2007	Sidney Crosby, Pittsburgh
1958	Dickie Moore, Montréal	1983	Wayne Gretzky, Edmonton	2008	Alexander Ovechkin, Washington
1959	Dickie Moore, Montréal	1984	Wayne Gretzky, Edmonton	2009	Evgeni Malkin, Pittsburgh
1960	Bobby Hull, Chicago	1985	Wayne Gretzky, Edmonton	2010	Henrik Sedin, Vancouver
1961	Bernie Geoffrion, Montréal	1986	Wayne Gretzky, Edmonton	2011	Daniel Sedin, Vancouver
1962	Bobby Hull, Chicago	1987	Wayne Gretzky, Edmonton	2012	Evgeni Malkin, Pittsburgh
1963	Gordie Howe, Detroit	1988	Mario Lemieux, Pittsburgh	2013	Martin St. Louis, Tampa Bay
1964	Stan Mikita, Chicago	1989	Mario Lemieux, Pittsburgh	2014	Sidney Crosby, Pittsburgh
1965	Stan Mikita, Chicago	1990	Wayne Gretzky, Los Angeles	2015	Jamie Benn, Dallas
1966	Bobby Hull, Chicago	1991	Wayne Gretzky, Los Angeles	2016	Patrick Kane, Chicago
1967	Stan Mikita, Chicago	1992	Mario Lemieux, Pittsburgh	2017	Connor McDavid, Edmonton
1968	Stan Mikita, Chicago	1993	Mario Lemieux, Pittsburgh	2018	Connor McDavid, Edmonton
1969	Phil Esposito, Boston	1994	Wayne Gretzky, Los Angeles	2019	Nikita Kucherov, Tampa Bay
1970	Bobby Orr, Boston	1995	Jaromir Jagr, Pittsburgh	2020	Leon Draisaitl, Edmonton
1971	Phil Esposito, Boston				

Vezina Trophy (Best Goaltender), 1927-2020

Year	Player, team	Year	Player, team	Year	Player, team
1927	George Hainsworth, Montréal Canadiens	1929	George Hainsworth, Montréal Canadiens	1932	Charlie Gardiner, Chicago
		1930	Tiny Thompson, Boston	1933	Tiny Thompson, Boston
1928	George Hainsworth, Montréal Canadiens	1931	Roy Worters, NY Americans	1934	Charlie Gardiner, Chicago
				1935	Lorne Chabot, Chicago

Year	Player, team	Year	Player, team	Year	Player, team
1936	Tiny Thompson, Boston	1965	Sawchuk, Bower; Toronto	1991	Ed Belfour, Chicago
1937	Normie Smith, Detroit	1966	Lorne Worsley, Hodge; Montréal	1992	Patrick Roy, Montréal
1938	Tiny Thompson, Boston	1967	Hall, Denis DeJordy; Chicago	1993	Ed Belfour, Chicago
1939	Frank Brimsek, Boston	1968	Worsley, Rogatien Vachon; Montréal	1994	Dominik Hasek, Buffalo
1940	Dave Kerr, NY Rangers	1969	Hall, Plante; St. Louis	1995	Dominik Hasek, Buffalo
1941	Turk Broda, Toronto	1970	Tony Esposito, Chicago	1996	Jim Carey, Washington
1942	Frank Brimsek, Boston	1971	Ed Giacomin, Gilles Villemure;	1997	Dominik Hasek, Buffalo
1943	Johnny Mowers, Detroit		NY Rangers	1998	Dominik Hasek, Buffalo
1944	Bill Durnan, Montréal	1972	Esposito, Gary Smith; Chicago	1999	Dominik Hasek, Buffalo
1945	Bill Durnan, Montréal	1973	Ken Dryden, Montréal	2000	Olaf Kolzig, Washington
1946	Bill Durnan, Montréal	1974	Bernie Parent, Philadelphia;	2001	Dominik Hasek, Buffalo
1947	Bill Durnan, Montréal		Tony Esposito, Chicago	2002	Jose Theodore, Montréal
1948	Turk Broda, Toronto	1975	Bernie Parent, Philadelphia	2003	Martin Brodeur, New Jersey
1949	Bill Durnan, Montréal	1976	Ken Dryden, Montréal	2004	Martin Brodeur, New Jersey
1950	Bill Durnan, Montréal	1977	Dryden, Michel Larocque; Montréal	2006	Miikka Kiprusoff, Calgary
1951	Al Rollins, Toronto	1978	Dryden, Larocque; Montréal	2007	Martin Brodeur, New Jersey
1952	Terry Sawchuk, Detroit	1979	Dryden, Larocque; Montréal	2008	Martin Brodeur, New Jersey
1953	Terry Sawchuk, Detroit	1980	Bob Sauve, Don Edwards; Buffalo	2009	Tim Thomas, Boston
1954	Harry Lumley, Toronto	1981	Richard Sevigny, Michel Larocque,	2010	Ryan Miller, Buffalo
1955	Terry Sawchuk, Detroit		Denis Herron; Montréal	2011	Tim Thomas, Boston
1956	Jacques Plante, Montréal	1982	Bill Smith, NY Islanders	2012	Henrik Lundqvist, NY Rangers
1957	Jacques Plante, Montréal	1983	Pete Peeters, Boston	2013	Sergei Bobrovsky, Columbus
1958	Jacques Plante, Montréal	1984	Tom Barrasso, Buffalo	2014	Tuukka Rask, Boston
1959	Jacques Plante, Montréal	1985	Pelle Lindbergh, Philadelphia	2015	Carey Price, Montréal
1960	Jacques Plante, Montréal	1986	John Vanbiesbrouck, NY Rangers	2016	Braden Holtby, Washington
1961	Johnny Bower, Toronto	1987	Ron Hextall, Philadelphia	2017	Sergei Bobrovsky, Columbus
1962	Jacques Plante, Montréal	1988	Grant Fuhr, Edmonton	2018	Pekka Rinne, Nashville
1963	Glenn Hall, Chicago	1989	Patrick Roy, Montréal	2019	Andrei Vasilevskiy, Tampa Bay
1964	Charlie Hodge, Montréal	1990	Patrick Roy, Montréal	2020	Connor Hellebuyck, Winnipeg

National Hockey League Franchise Origins

Team: founding year, league (NHL, World Hockey Association [WHA], or National Hockey Association of Canada [NHA]). Original location; subsequent history. Neutral sites and arena sites in the same metropolitan area not shown. * = Joined NHL in 1979 from defunct WHA.

Anaheim Ducks: 1993, NHL, as Mighty Ducks of Anaheim. Anaheim, CA, 1993-present. (Ducks, 2006-present.)
*Arizona Coyotes: 1972, WHA, as Winnipeg Jets. Winnipeg, MB, Canada, 1979-96; Phoenix Coyotes, 1996-2014; Arizona Coyotes, Glendale, AZ, 2014-present.
Boston Bruins: 1924, NHL. Boston, 1924-present.
Buffalo Sabres: 1970, NHL. Buffalo, NY, 1970-present.
Calgary Flames: 1972, NHL, as Atlanta Flames. Atlanta, GA, 1972-80; Calgary, AB, Canada, 1980-present.
*Carolina Hurricanes: 1972, WHA, as Hartford Whalers. Hartford, CT, 1979-97; Carolina Hurricanes, Greensboro, NC, 1997-99; Raleigh, NC, 1999-present.
Chicago Blackhawks: 1926, NHL, as Chicago Black Hawks. Chicago, 1926-present. (Blackhawks, 1986-present.)
*Colorado Avalanche: 1972, WHA, as Quebec Nordiques. Quebec City, QC, Canada, 1979-95; Colorado Avalanche, Denver, 1995-present.
Columbus Blue Jackets: 2000, NHL. Columbus, OH, 2000-present.
Dallas Stars: 1967, NHL, as Minnesota North Stars. Bloomington, MN, 1967-93; Dallas Stars, Dallas, 1993-present.
Detroit Red Wings: 1926, NHL, as Detroit Cougars, 1926-30. Detroit Falcons, 1930-32; Detroit Red Wings, 1932-present.
*Edmonton Oilers: 1972, WHA. Edmonton, AB, Canada, 1979-present.
Florida Panthers: 1993, NHL. Miami, FL, 1993-98; Sunrise, FL, 1998-present.
Los Angeles Kings: 1967, NHL. Los Angeles, 1967-present.
Minnesota Wild: 2000, NHL. St. Paul, MN, 2000-present.

Montréal Canadiens: 1909, NHA; joined NHL, 1917. Montréal, QC, Canada, 1909-present.
Nashville Predators: 1998, NHL. Nashville, TN, 1998-present.
New Jersey Devils: 1974, NHL, as Kansas City Scouts. Kansas City, MO, 1974-76; Colorado Rockies, Denver, CO, 1976-82; New Jersey Devils, East Rutherford, NJ, 1982-2007; Newark, NJ, 2007-present.
New York Islanders: 1972, NHL. Uniondale, NY, 1972-2015; Brooklyn, NY, 2015-present.
New York Rangers: 1926, NHL. New York City, 1926-present.
Ottawa Senators: 1992, NHL. Ottawa, ON, Canada, 1992-present.
Philadelphia Flyers: 1967, NHL. Philadelphia, 1967-present.
Pittsburgh Penguins: 1967, NHL. Pittsburgh, 1967-present.
St. Louis Blues: 1967, NHL. St. Louis, MO, 1967-present.
San Jose Sharks: 1991, NHL. Daly City, CA, 1991-93; San Jose, CA, 1993-present.
Tampa Bay Lightning: 1992, NHL. Tampa, FL, 1992-93; St. Petersburg, FL, 1993-96; Tampa, FL, 1996-present.
Toronto Maple Leafs: 1917, NHL, as Toronto (ON, Canada) Arenas, 1917-19. Toronto St. Patricks, 1919-26; Toronto Maple Leafs, 1926-present.
Vancouver Canucks: 1970, NHL. Vancouver, BC, Canada, 1970-present.
Vegas Golden Knights: 2017, NHL. Las Vegas, NV, 2017-present.
Washington Capitals: 1974, NHL. Landover, MD, 1974-97; Washington, DC, 1997-present.
Winnipeg Jets: 1999, NHL, as Atlanta Thrashers. Atlanta, GA, 1999-2011; Winnipeg, MB, Canada, 2011-present.

NHL Home Ice

Team	Name (year play began)	Capacity[1]	Team	Name (year play began)	Capacity[1]
Anaheim	Honda Center[2] (1993)	17,174	Nashville	Bridgestone Arena[10] (1997)	17,159
Arizona	Gila River Arena[3] (2003)	17,125	New Jersey	Prudential Center (2007)	16,514
Boston	TD Garden[4] (1995)	17,565	NY Islanders	Barclays Center[11] (2015)	15,795
Buffalo	KeyBank Center[5] (1996)	19,070	NY Rangers	Madison Square Garden (IV) (1968)	18,006
Calgary	Scotiabank Saddledome[6] (1983)	19,289	Ottawa	Canadian Tire Centre[12] (1996)	18,652
Carolina	PNC Arena[7] (1999)	18,680	Philadelphia	Wells Fargo Center[13] (1996)	19,306
Chicago	United Center (1994)	19,717	Pittsburgh	PPG Paints Arena[14] (2010)	18,387
Colorado	Pepsi Center (1999)	17,809	St. Louis	Enterprise Center (1994)	18,096
Columbus	Nationwide Arena (2000)	18,144	San Jose	SAP Center at San Jose[16] (1993)	17,562
Dallas	American Airlines Center (2001)	18,532	Tampa Bay	Amalie Arena[17] (1996)	19,092
Detroit	Little Caesars Arena (2017)	19,515	Toronto	Scotiabank Arena[18] (1999)	18,819
Edmonton	Rogers Place (2016)	18,347	Vancouver	Rogers Arena[19] (1995)	18,870
Florida	BB&T Center[8] (1998)	19,638	Vegas	T-Mobile Arena (2017)	17,367
Los Angeles	Staples Center (1999)	18,230	Washington	Capital One Arena[20] (1997)	18,573
Minnesota	Xcel Energy Center (2000)	17,954	Winnipeg	Bell MTS Place[21] (2004)	15,294
Montréal	Le Centre Bell[9] (1996)	21,302			

(1) At the end of the 2019-20 season unless otherwise noted. (2) The Arrowhead Pond of Anaheim, 1993-2006; Jobing.com Arena, 2006-14. (3) Glendale Arena, 2003-06; Jobing.com Arena, 2006-14. (4) FleetCenter, 1995-2005; TD Banknorth Garden, 2005-09. (5) Marine Midland Arena, 1996-99; HSBC Arena, 1999-2011; First Niagara Center, 2011-16. (6) Olympic Saddledome, 1983-96; Canadian Airlines Saddledome, 1996-2000; Pengrowth Saddledome, 2000-10. (7) Raleigh Entertainment and Sports Arena, 1999-2002; RBC Center, 2002-11. (8) National Car Rental Center, 1998-2002; Office Depot Center, 2002-05; BankAtlantic Center, 2005-12. (9) Le Centre Molson, 1996-2002. (10) Nashville Arena, 1997-99; Gaylord Entertainment Center, 1999-2007; Sommet Center, 2007-10. (11) The Islanders played 24 regular season home games in 2019-20 at Nassau Veterans Memorial Coliseum, Uniondale, NY. (12) Corel Centre, 1996-2006; Scotiabank Place, 2006-13. (13) CoreStates Center, 1996-98; First Union Center, 1998-2003; Wachovia Center, 2003-10. (14) CONSOL Energy Center, 2010-16. (15) Kiel Center, 1994-2000; Savvis Center, 2000-06; Scottrade Center, 2006-18. (16) San Jose Arena, 1993-2001; Compaq Center, 2001-02; HP Pavilion at San Jose, 2002-13. (17) Ice Palace, 1996-2002; St. Pete Times Forum, 2002-12; Tampa Bay Times Forum, 2012-14. (18) Air Canada Centre, 1999-2018. (19) General Motors Place, 1995-2010. (20) MCI Center, 1997-2006; Verizon Center, 2006-17. (21) MTS Centre, 2004-17.

SOCCER

Houston Wins First NWSL Title in 2020

The Houston Dash won their first ever National Women's Soccer League's Challenge Cup final with a 2-0 victory over the Chicago Red Stars July 26, 2020, at Rio Tinto Stadium in Sandy, UT. The NWSL became the first major U.S. sports league to return from coronavirus imposed shutdowns, with a shortened season reformatted as a monthlong tournament in which 8 of 9 NWSL teams participated. (Orlando withdrew before play began due to positive coronavirus tests.)

Women's Professional Soccer Champions

Year	Winner	Final opponent	Score	Site	MVP
		Women's United Soccer Association champions			
2001	Bay Area CyberRays	Atlanta Beat	3-3 (4-2)*	Foxborough, MA	Julie Murray
2002	Carolina Courage	Washington Freedom	3-2	Atlanta, GA	Birgit Prinz
2003	Washington Freedom	Atlanta Beat	2-1	San Diego, CA	Abby Wambach
		Women's Professional Soccer champions			
2009	Sky Blue FC	Los Angeles Sol	1-0	Carson, CA	Heather O'Reilly
2010	FC Gold Pride	Philadelphia Independence	4-1	Hayward, CA	Marta
2011	Western New York Flash	Philadelphia Independence	1-1 (5-4)*	Rochester, NY	Christine Sinclair
		National Women's Soccer League champions			
2013	Portland Thorns FC	Western New York Flash	2-0	Rochester, NY	Tobin Heath
2014	FC Kansas City	Seattle Reign FC	2-1	Tukwila, WA	Lauren Holiday
2015	FC Kansas City	Seattle Reign FC	1-0	Portland, OR	Amy Rodriguez
2016	Western New York Flash	Washington Spirit	2-2 (3-2)*	Houston, TX	Sabrina D'Angelo
2017	Portland Thorns FC	North Carolina Courage	1-0	Orlando, FL	Lindsey Horan
2018	North Carolina Courage	Portland Thorns FC	3-0	Portland, OR	Jess McDonald
2019	North Carolina Courage	Chicago Red Stars	4-0	Cary, NC	Debinha
2020	Houston Dash	Chicago Red Stars	2-0	Sandy, UT	Rachel Daly

* = Match decided on penalty kicks (shootout score in parentheses). **Note:** The Women's United Soccer Association (WUSA) folded in 2003. Women's Professional Soccer (WPS) stopped operating in 2012, suspending its fourth season. In Apr. 2013, the National Women's Soccer League (NWSL) began play with eight teams competing: Boston Breakers, Chicago Red Stars, FC Kansas City, Portland Thorns FC, Seattle Reign FC, Sky Blue FC (New York/New Jersey), Washington Spirit (DC), and Western New York Flash. The Houston Dash began play as an NWSL expansion team for the 2014 season; Orlando joined the league in 2016. In Jan. 2017, the Western New York Flash relocated to North Carolina and were renamed the North Carolina Courage. Kansas City and Boston ceased operation in 2017. The Utah Royals joined the league in 2018 with former FC Kansas City assets.

U.S. Wins 2019 Women's World Cup

The U.S. women's national soccer team won the 2019 FIFA World Cup with a 2-0 victory over Netherlands July 7, 2019, at Stade de Lyon in Lyon, France. Held scoreless for the first hour of the final, the U.S. scored in the 61st minute, a penalty-spot goal by 34-year-old standout Megan Rapinoe, followed by midfielder Rose Lavelle's low shot for a second goal less than 10 minutes later. Rapinoe won both the Golden Ball award as the tournament's top player and the Golden Boot award as its top scorer. Alex Morgan, who tied Rapinoe with six goals and three assists in the tournament (Rapinoe led in minutes-per-goal), won the Silver Boot. Dutch goalie Sari van Veenendaal claimed the Golden Glove as the best goalkeeper in the competition.

The U.S. team, led by coach Jill Ellis, scored 26 goals—a tournament record that also included a 13-0 record win over Thailand in their first game of the tournament—and never fell behind in any of their seven 2019 World Cup matches.

The United States became the first team to reach three consecutive Women's World Cup Finals, and was the first squad to repeat as champs since Germany won titles in 2003 and 2007.

Women's World Cup Results, 2019

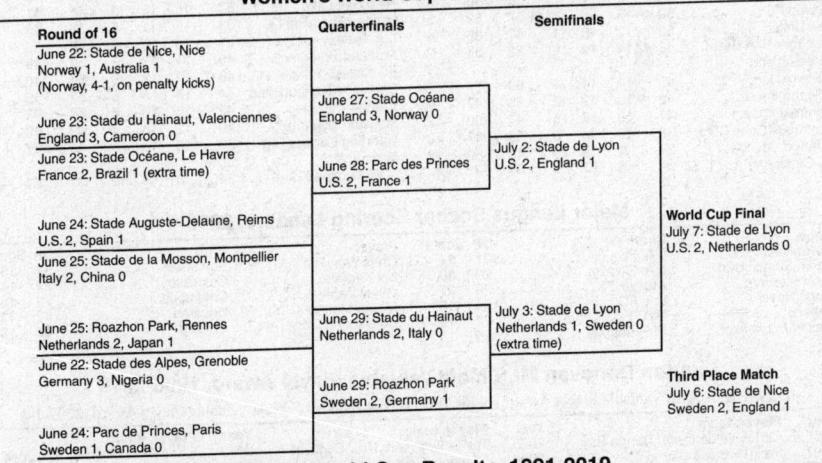

Round of 16

June 22: Stade de Nice, Nice
Norway 1, Australia 1
(Norway, 4-1, on penalty kicks)

June 23: Stade du Hainaut, Valenciennes
England 3, Cameroon 0

June 23: Stade Océane, Le Havre
France 2, Brazil 1 (extra time)

June 24: Stade Auguste-Delaune, Reims
U.S. 2, Spain 1

June 25: Stade de la Mosson, Montpellier
Italy 2, China 0

June 25: Roazhon Park, Rennes
Netherlands 2, Japan 1

June 22: Stade des Alpes, Grenoble
Germany 3, Nigeria 0

June 24: Parc de Princes, Paris
Sweden 1, Canada 0

Quarterfinals

June 27: Stade Océane
England 3, Norway 0

June 28: Parc des Princes
U.S. 2, France 1

June 29: Stade du Hainaut
Netherlands 2, Italy 0

June 29: Roazhon Park
Sweden 2, Germany 1

Semifinals

July 2: Stade de Lyon
U.S. 2, England 1

July 3: Stade de Lyon
Netherlands 1, Sweden 0
(extra time)

World Cup Final
July 7: Stade de Lyon
U.S. 2, Netherlands 0

Third Place Match
July 6: Stade de Nice
Sweden 2, England 1

Women's World Cup Results, 1991-2019

Year	Winner	Final opponent	Score	Site	Year	Winner	Final opponent	Score	Site
1991	U.S.	Norway	2-1	China	2007	Germany	Brazil	2-0	China
1995	Norway	Germany	2-0	Sweden	2011	Japan	U.S.	2-2 (3-1)*	Germany
1999	U.S.	China	0-0 (5-4)*	Pasadena, CA, U.S.	2015	U.S.	Japan	5-2	Canada
2003	Germany	Sweden	2-1#	Carson, CA, U.S.	2019	U.S.	Netherlands	2-0	France

* = Match decided in penalty kicks (shootout score in parentheses). # = Match decided in extra time.

MLS 2019: Sounders Take MLS Cup

Facing off in the MLS Cup for the third time in four years, the Seattle Sounders defeated Toronto FC, 3-1, to take the Major League Soccer title on Nov. 10, 2019. Spanish right winger Víctor Rodríguez, who scored the Sounders' second goal, was named the MLS Cup MVP. Seattle won the Cup at home for the first time, before a record-setting crowd of 69,274 fans at a sold-out CenturyLink Field.

Seattle beat Supporters' Shield-winning L.A. FC in the Western Conference final to reach the MLS Cup. L.A. FC forward Carlos Vela set an MLS single-season goals record (34) in 2019 and was named the 2019 league MVP. The 2018 champion Atlanta United again reached the Eastern Conference finals but was eliminated by Toronto, 2-1, Oct. 30, at at Mercedes-Benz Stadium in Atlanta.

Atlético Madrid defeated the MLS All-Stars, 3-0, at Exploria Stadium in Orlando, FL, in the MLS All-Star Game July 31, 2019.

Major League Soccer (MLS) Cup Results, 1996-2019

Year	Winner	Final opponent	Score	Site	MVP
1996	DC United	Los Angeles Galaxy	3-2 (OT)	Foxborough, MA	Marco Etcheverry
1997	DC United	Colorado Rapids	2-1	Washington, DC	Jaime Moreno
1998	Chicago Fire	DC United	2-0	Pasadena, CA	Peter Nowak
1999	DC United	Los Angeles Galaxy	2-0	Foxborough, MA	Ben Olsen
2000	Kansas City Wizards	Chicago Fire	1-0	Washington, DC	Tony Meola
2001	San Jose Earthquakes	Los Angeles Galaxy	2-1 (OT)	Columbus, OH	Dwayne De Rosario
2002	Los Angeles Galaxy	New England Revolution	1-0 (OT)	Foxborough, MA	Carlos Ruiz
2003	San Jose Earthquakes	Chicago Fire	4-2	Carson, CA	Landon Donovan
2004	DC United	Kansas City Wizards	3-2	Carson, CA	Alecko Eskandarian
2005	Los Angeles Galaxy	New England Revolution	1-0 (OT)	Frisco, TX	Guillermo Ramírez
2006	Houston Dynamo	New England Revolution	1-1 (4-3)*	Frisco, TX	Brian Ching
2007	Houston Dynamo	New England Revolution	2-1	Washington, DC	Dwayne De Rosario
2008	Columbus Crew	New York Red Bulls	3-1	Carson, CA	Guillermo Barros Schelotto
2009	Real Salt Lake	Los Angeles Galaxy	1-1 (5-4)*	Seattle, WA	Nick Rimando
2010	Colorado Rapids	FC Dallas	2-1 (OT)	Toronto, ON, Canada	Conor Casey
2011	Los Angeles Galaxy	Houston Dynamo	1-0	Carson, CA	Landon Donovan
2012	Los Angeles Galaxy	Houston Dynamo	3-1	Carson, CA	Omar Gonzalez
2013	Sporting Kansas City	Real Salt Lake	1-1 (7-6)*	Kansas City, KS	Aurelien Collin
2014	Los Angeles Galaxy	New England Revolution	2-1 (OT)	Carson, CA	Robbie Keane
2015	Portland Timbers	Columbus Crew	2-1	Columbus, OH	Diego Valeri
2016	Seattle Sounders FC	Toronto FC	0-0 (5-4)*	Toronto, ON, Canada	Stefan Frei
2017	Toronto FC	Seattle Sounders FC	2-0	Toronto, ON, Canada	Jozy Altidore
2018	Atlanta United FC	Portland Timbers	2-0	Atlanta, GA	Josef Martínez
2019	Seattle Sounders	Toronto FC	3-1	Seattle, WA	Víctor Rodríguez

* = Match decided in penalty kicks (shootout score in parentheses). OT = Overtime.

Major League Soccer Final Standings, 2019
(Does not include playoff games)

Eastern Conference	PTS	W	L	T	GF	GA	GD	Western Conference	PTS	W	L	T	GF	GA	GD
New York City FC	64	18	6	10	63	42	21	Los Angeles FC	72	21	4	9	85	37	48
Atlanta United FC....	58	18	12	4	58	43	15	Seattle Sounders FC	56	16	10	8	52	49	3
Philadelphia Union ...	55	16	11	7	58	50	8	Real Salt Lake	53	16	13	5	46	41	5
Toronto FC	50	13	10	11	57	52	5	Minnesota United FC..	53	15	11	8	52	43	9
D.C. United	50	13	10	11	42	38	4	L.A. Galaxy	51	16	15	3	58	59	−1
New York Red Bulls ..	48	14	14	6	53	51	2	Portland Timbers	49	14	13	7	52	49	3
New England								FC Dallas	48	13	12	9	54	46	8
Revolution........	45	11	11	12	50	57	−7	San Jose Earthquakes	44	13	16	5	52	55	−3
Chicago Fire FC.....	42	10	12	12	55	47	−8	Colorado Rapids.....	42	12	16	6	58	63	−5
Montreal Impact	41	12	17	5	47	60	−13	Houston Dynamo	40	12	18	4	49	59	−10
Columbus Crew SC ..	38	10	16	8	39	47	−8	Sporting Kansas City	38	10	16	8	49	67	−18
Orlando City SC.....	37	9	15	10	44	52	−8	Vancouver							
FC Cincinnati	24	6	22	6	31	75	−44	Whitecaps FC	34	8	16	10	37	59	−22

Major League Soccer Scoring Leaders, 2019

Player	Club	GP	Goals	Player	Club	GP	Goals
Carlos Vela	L.A. FC	31	34	Chris Wondolowski	San Jose............	32	15
Zlatan Ibrahimovic	L.A. Galaxy	29	30	Kei Kamara...........	Colorado............	29	14
Josef Martinez	Atlanta	29	27	Gyasi Zardes	Columbus	28	13
Diego Rossi	L.A. FC	34	16	Mauro Manotas.......	Houston	32	13
Heber	NYC FC	22	15	CJ Sapong	Chicago	32	13
Kacper Przybylko	Philadelphia	26	15				

Landon Donovan MLS Most Valuable Player Award, 1996-2019
(Honda MLS Most Valuable Player Award, 1996-2007; Volkswagen MLS Most Valuable Player Award, 2007-14)

Year	Player, team	Year	Player, team	Year	Player, team
1996	Carlos Valderrama, Tampa Bay	2005	Taylor Twellman, New England	2012	Chris Wondolowski, San Jose
1997	Preki, Kansas City	2006	Christian Gómez, DC	2013	Mike Magee, Chicago
1998	Marco Etcheverry, DC	2007	Luciano Emilio, DC	2014	Robbie Keane, L.A. Galaxy
1999	Jason Kreis, Dallas	2008	Guillermo Barros Schelotto,	2015	Sebastian Giovinco, Toronto
2000	Tony Meola, Kansas City		Columbus	2016	David Villa, New York City
2001	Alex Pineda Chacón, Miami	2009	Landon Donovan, L.A. Galaxy	2017	Diego Valeri, Portland
2002	Carlos Ruiz, L.A. Galaxy	2010	David Ferreira, Dallas	2018	Josef Martínez, Atlanta
2003	Preki, Kansas City	2011	Dwayne De Rosario, DC	2019	Carlos Vela, L.A. FC
2004	Amado Guevara, NY/NJ				

France Wins 2018 FIFA Men's World Cup

France won its second FIFA World Cup men's soccer title with a 4-2 victory over Croatia, July 15, 2018, at Luzhniki Stadium in Moscow, Russia. Les Bleus scored first on a free kick by Antoine Griezmann, ruled an own goal by Croatia's Mario Mandzukic after he deflected the ball into Croatia's net. The new Video Assistant Referee (VAR) technology was used for the first time at the 2018 Men's World Cup tournament. When a video review confirmed a handball by Croatia's Ivan Perisic, France was awarded a penalty kick, which Griezmann converted to give Les Bleus a 2-1 lead. France added second-half goals by Paul Pogba and 19-year-old Kylian Mbappé—who became the first teenager to score a goal in a World Cup final match since 17-year-old Pelé in 1958—for a final score of 4-2, making it the highest scoring men's World Cup final since 1966.

Les Bleus goaltender and team captain Hugo Lloris recorded a pair of clean sheets en route to the finals, eliminating Uruguay in the quarterfinals, 2-0, July 6. Samuel Umtiti scored the only goal of the match in France's 1-0 semifinal win over Belgium, July 10. The Belgian squad won the third-place match, 2-0, against England, July 14 at St. Petersburg Stadium.

Croatia reached its first-ever World Cup final when Mandzukic scored in the 109th minute to defeat England, 2-1, in extra time in the semifinals, July 11. After playing to a 2-2 tie through extra time, Croatia won on penalty kicks, 4-3, defeating host Russia in the quarterfinals on July 7 at Fisht Stadium in Sochi.

England reached the semifinals for the first time since 1990. The Three Lions shut out Sweden, 2-0, in the quarterfinals July 7 at Samara Arena in Samara before their semifinal loss to Croatia. Defending champion Germany managed just one group match victory, 2-1, over Sweden June 23 at Fisht Stadium and failed to move on.

England's Harry Kane topped all scorers in the tournament with six goals and won the Golden Boot award. Veteran Croatia midfielder Luka Modric was voted the best player of the competition, taking home the Golden Ball award.

Men's World Cup Results, 2018

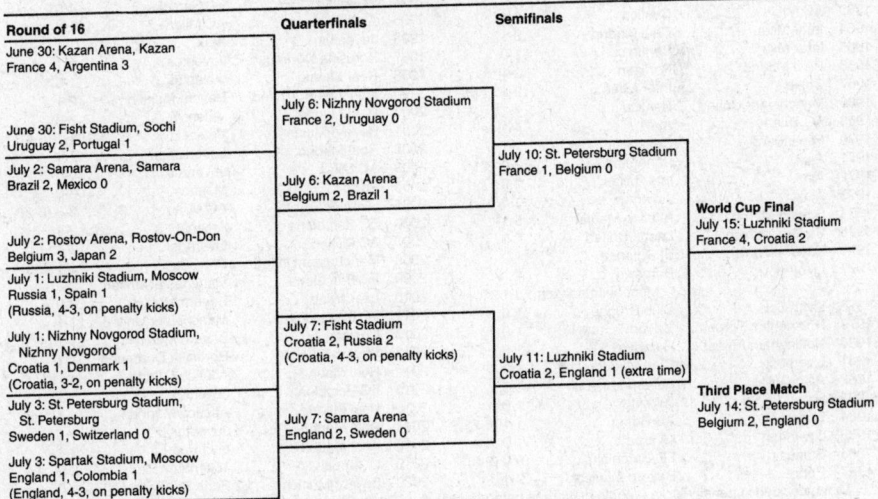

Round of 16

June 30: Kazan Arena, Kazan
France 4, Argentina 3

June 30: Fisht Stadium, Sochi
Uruguay 2, Portugal 1

July 2: Samara Arena, Samara
Brazil 2, Mexico 0

July 2: Rostov Arena, Rostov-On-Don
Belgium 3, Japan 2

July 1: Luzhniki Stadium, Moscow
Russia 1, Spain 1
(Russia, 4-3, on penalty kicks)

July 1: Nizhny Novgorod Stadium,
  Nizhny Novgorod
Croatia 1, Denmark 1
(Croatia, 3-2, on penalty kicks)

July 3: St. Petersburg Stadium,
  St. Petersburg
Sweden 1, Switzerland 0

July 3: Spartak Stadium, Moscow
England 1, Colombia 1
(England, 4-3, on penalty kicks)

Quarterfinals

July 6: Nizhny Novgorod Stadium
France 2, Uruguay 0

July 6: Kazan Arena
Belgium 2, Brazil 1

July 7: Fisht Stadium
Croatia 2, Russia 2
(Croatia, 4-3, on penalty kicks)

July 7: Samara Arena
England 2, Sweden 0

Semifinals

July 10: St. Petersburg Stadium
France 1, Belgium 0

July 11: Luzhniki Stadium
Croatia 2, England 1 (extra time)

World Cup Final
July 15: Luzhniki Stadium
France 4, Croatia 2

Third Place Match
July 14: St. Petersburg Stadium
Belgium 2, England 0

Men's World Cup Group Standings, 2018

(* = advanced to round of 16)

GROUP A	MP	W	D	L	GF	GA	+/−	PTS
Uruguay*	3	3	0	0	5	0	5	9
Russia*	3	2	0	1	8	4	4	6
Saudi Arabia	3	1	0	2	2	7	−5	3
Egypt	3	0	0	3	2	6	−4	0
GROUP B								
Spain*	3	1	2	0	6	5	1	5
Portugal*	3	1	2	0	5	4	1	5
Iran	3	1	1	1	2	2	0	4
Morocco	3	0	1	2	2	4	−2	1
GROUP C								
France*	3	2	1	0	3	1	2	7
Denmark*	3	1	2	0	2	1	1	5
Peru	3	1	0	2	2	2	0	3
Australia	3	0	1	2	2	5	−3	1
GROUP D								
Croatia*	3	3	0	0	7	1	6	9
Argentina*	3	1	1	1	3	5	−2	4
Nigeria	3	1	0	2	3	4	−1	3
Iceland	3	0	1	2	2	5	−3	1

GROUP E	MP	W	D	L	GF	GA	+/−	PTS
Brazil*	3	2	1	0	5	1	4	7
Switzerland*	3	1	2	0	5	4	1	5
Serbia	3	1	0	2	2	4	−2	3
Costa Rica	3	0	1	2	2	5	−3	1
GROUP F								
Sweden*	3	2	0	1	5	2	3	6
Mexico*	3	2	0	1	3	4	−1	6
South Korea	3	1	0	2	3	3	0	3
Germany	3	1	0	2	2	4	−2	3
GROUP G								
Belgium*	3	3	0	0	9	2	7	9
England*	3	2	0	1	8	3	5	6
Tunisia	3	1	0	2	5	8	−3	3
Panama	3	0	0	3	2	11	−9	0
GROUP H								
Colombia*	3	2	0	1	5	2	3	6
Japan*	3	1	1	1	4	4	0	4
Senegal	3	1	1	1	4	4	0	4
Poland	3	1	0	2	2	5	−3	3

Men's World Cup Results, 1930-2018

Year	Winner	Final opponent	Score	Site	Year	Winner	Final opponent	Score	Site
1930	Uruguay	Argentina	4-2	Uruguay	1982	Italy	W. Germany	3-1	Spain
1934	Italy	Czechoslovakia	2-1#	Italy	1986	Argentina	W. Germany	3-2	Mexico
1938	Italy	Hungary	4-2	France	1990	W. Germany	Argentina	1-0	Italy
1950	Uruguay	Brazil	2-1	Brazil	1994	Brazil	Italy	0-0 (3-2)*	U.S.
1954	W. Germany	Hungary	3-2	Switzerland	1998	France	Brazil	3-0	France
1958	Brazil	Sweden	5-2	Sweden	2002	Brazil	Germany	2-0	Japan/S. Korea
1962	Brazil	Czechoslovakia	3-1	Chile	2006	Italy	France	1-1 (5-3)*	Germany
1966	England	W. Germany	4-2#	England	2010	Spain	Netherlands	1-0#	South Africa
1970	Brazil	Italy	4-1	Mexico	2014	Germany	Argentina	1-0#	Brazil
1974	W. Germany	Netherlands	2-1	W. Germany	2018	France	Croatia	4-2	Russia
1978	Argentina	Netherlands	3-1#	Argentina					

* = Match decided in penalty kicks (shootout score in parentheses). # = Match decided in extra time.

UEFA Champions League Results, 1956-2020

Year	Winner	Final opponent	Score	Year	Winner	Final opponent	Score
1956	Real Madrid	Reims	4-3	1988	PSV	Benfica	0-0 (6-5)*
1957	Real Madrid	Fiorentina	2-0	1989	AC Milan	Steaua	4-0
1958	Real Madrid	AC Milan	3-2#	1990	AC Milan	Benfica	1-0
1959	Real Madrid	Reims	2-0	1991	Crvena Zvezda	Marseille	0-0 (5-3)*
1960	Real Madrid	Eintracht Frankfurt	7-3	1992	FC Barcelona	Sampdoria	1-0#
1961	Benfica	FC Barcelona	3-2	1993	Marseille	AC Milan	1-0
1962	Benfica	Real Madrid	5-3	1994	AC Milan	FC Barcelona	4-0
1963	AC Milan	Benfica	2-1	1995	Ajax	AC Milan	1-0
1964	Inter Milan	Real Madrid	3-1	1996	Juventus	Ajax	1-1 (4-2)*
1965	Inter Milan	Benfica	1-0	1997	Borussia Dortmund	Juventus	3-1
1966	Real Madrid	Partizan	2-1	1998	Real Madrid	Juventus	1-0
1967	Celtic	Inter Milan	2-1	1999	Manchester United	Bayern Munich	2-1
1968	Manchester United	Benfica	4-1#	2000	Real Madrid	Valencia	3-0
1969	AC Milan	Ajax	4-1	2001	Bayern Munich	Valencia	1-1 (5-4)*
1970	Feyenoord	Celtic	2-1#	2002	Real Madrid	Leverkusen	2-1
1971	Ajax	Panathinaikos	2-0	2003	AC Milan	Juventus	0-0 (3-2)*
1972	Ajax	Inter Milan	2-0	2004	Porto	Monaco	3-0
1973	Ajax	Juventus	1-0	2005	Liverpool	AC Milan	3-3 (3-2)*
1974	Bayern Munich	Atlético Madrid	5-1[1]	2006	FC Barcelona	Arsenal	2-1
1975	Bayern Munich	Leeds United	2-0	2007	AC Milan	Liverpool	2-1
1976	Bayern Munich	St.-Étienne	1-0	2008	Manchester United	Chelsea	1-1 (6-5)*
1977	Liverpool	Borussia Mönchengladbach	3-1	2009	FC Barcelona	Manchester United	2-0
1978	Liverpool	Club Brugge	1-0	2010	Inter Milan	Bayern Munich	2-0
1979	Nottingham Forest	Malmö	1-0	2011	FC Barcelona	Manchester United	3-1
1980	Nottingham Forest	Hamburg SV	1-0	2012	Chelsea	Bayern Munich	1-1 (4-3)*
1981	Liverpool	Real Madrid	1-0	2013	Bayern Munich	Borussia Dortmund	2-1
1982	Aston Villa	Bayern Munich	1-0	2014	Real Madrid	Atlético Madrid	4-1#
1983	Hamburg SV	Juventus	1-0	2015	FC Barcelona	Juventus	3-1
1984	Liverpool	AS Roma	1-1 (4-2)*	2016	Real Madrid	Atlético Madrid	1-1 (5-3)*
1985	Juventus	Liverpool	1-0	2017	Real Madrid	Juventus	4-1
1986	Steaua	FC Barcelona	0-0 (2-0)*	2018	Real Madrid	Liverpool	3-1
1987	Porto	Bayern Munich	2-1	2019	Liverpool	Tottenham	2-0
				2020	Bayern Munich	Paris St.-Germain	1-0

* = Match decided in penalty kicks (shootout score in parentheses). # = Match decided in extra time. (1) Aggregate score. First game, 1-1; second, 4-0.

UEFA European Football Championships, 1960-2016

The final rounds of the 2016 Union of European Football Associations (UEFA) European Championships were hosted by France and opened June 10, 2016, when the host country defeated Romania, 2-1, at Stade de France in Saint-Denis. France advanced to the Euro 2016 final match against Portugal, but Portugal prevailed, 1-0, in extra time on a goal by Éder in the 109th minute July 10 at Stade de France. Portugal had reached the final with a 2-0 victory over Wales on July 6 at Stade de Lyon in Lyon. France had defeated Germany, 2-0, in the other semifinal match July 7 at Stade Vélodrome in Marseilles. France's Antoine Griezmann was voted player of the tournament, with six goals and two assists.

The 2020 tournament was pushed back to June 11-July 11, 2021, as a result of the COVID-19 pandemic.

Year	Winner	Final opponent	Score	Site	Year	Winner	Final opponent	Score	Site
1960	USSR	Yugoslavia	2-1#	France	1992	Denmark	Germany	2-0	Sweden
1964	Spain	USSR	2-1	Spain	1996	Germany	Czech Rep.	2-1#	England
1968	Italy	Yugoslavia	2-0	Italy	2000	France	Italy	2-1#	Belgium/Neth.
1972	W. Germany	USSR	3-0	Belgium	2004	Greece	Portugal	1-0	Portugal
1976	Czechoslovakia	W. Germany	2-2 (5-3)*	Yugoslavia	2008	Spain	Germany	1-0	Austria/Switz.
1980	W. Germany	Belgium	2-1	Italy	2012	Spain	Italy	4-0	Poland/Ukr.
1984	France	Spain	2-0	France	2016	Portugal	France	1-0#	France
1988	Netherlands	USSR	2-0	W. Germany					

* = Match decided in penalty kicks (shootout score in parentheses). # = Match decided in extra time.

Selected European Soccer League Champions, 1950-2020

Season	England: Premier League[1]	Spain: La Liga	Italy: Serie A	Germany: Bundesliga[2]
1949-50	Portsmouth FC	Atlético Madrid	Juventus	VfB Stuttgart
1950-51	Tottenham Hotspur	Atlético Madrid	AC Milan	Kaiserslautern
1951-52	Manchester United	FC Barcelona	Juventus	VfB Stuttgart
1952-53	Arsenal	FC Barcelona	Inter Milan	Kaiserslautern
1953-54	Wolverhampton Wanderers	Real Madrid	Inter Milan	Hannoverscher SV 96
1954-55	Chelsea	Real Madrid	AC Milan	Rot-Weiss Essen
1955-56	Manchester United	Athletic Bilbao	Fiorentina	Borussia Dortmund
1956-57	Manchester United	Real Madrid	AC Milan	Borussia Dortmund
1957-58	Wolverhampton Wanderers	Real Madrid	Juventus	Schalke 04
1958-59	Wolverhampton Wanderers	FC Barcelona	AC Milan	Eintracht Frankfurt
1959-60	Burnley FC	FC Barcelona	Juventus	Hamburg SV
1960-61	Tottenham Hotspur	Real Madrid	Juventus	FC Nuremberg
1961-62	Ipswich Town	Real Madrid	AC Milan	FC Cologne
1962-63	Everton	Real Madrid	Inter Milan	Borussia Dortmund
1963-64	Liverpool	Real Madrid	Bologna	FC Cologne
1964-65	Manchester United	Real Madrid	Inter Milan	Werder Bremen
1965-66	Liverpool	Atlético Madrid	Inter Milan	TSV 1860 Munich
1966-67	Manchester United	Real Madrid	Juventus	Eintracht Braunschweig
1967-68	Manchester City	Real Madrid	AC Milan	FC Nuremberg
1968-69	Leeds United	Real Madrid	Fiorentina	Bayern Munich
1969-70	Everton	Atlético Madrid	Cagliari	Borussia Mönchengladbach
1970-71	Arsenal	Valencia	Inter Milan	Borussia Mönchengladbach
1971-72	Derby County	Real Madrid	Juventus	Bayern Munich
1972-73	Liverpool	Atlético Madrid	Juventus	Bayern Munich
1973-74	Leeds United	FC Barcelona	Lazio	Borussia Mönchengladbach
1974-75	Derby County	Real Madrid	Juventus	Borussia Mönchengladbach
1975-76	Liverpool	Real Madrid	Torino	Borussia Mönchengladbach
1976-77	Liverpool	Atlético Madrid	Juventus	FC Cologne
1977-78	Nottingham Forest	Real Madrid	Juventus	Hamburg SV
1978-79	Liverpool	Real Madrid	AC Milan	Bayern Munich
1979-80	Liverpool	Real Madrid	Inter Milan	Bayern Munich
1980-81	Aston Villa	Real Sociedad	Juventus	Hamburg SV
1981-82	Liverpool	Real Sociedad	AS Roma	Hamburg SV
1982-83	Liverpool	Athletic Bilbao	Juventus	VfB Stuttgart
1983-84	Liverpool	Athletic Bilbao	Verona	Bayern Munich
1984-85	Everton	FC Barcelona	Juventus	Bayern Munich
1985-86	Liverpool	Real Madrid	Napoli	Werder Bremen
1986-87	Everton	Real Madrid	AC Milan	Bayern Munich
1987-88	Liverpool	Real Madrid	Inter Milan	Bayern Munich
1988-89	Arsenal	Real Madrid	Napoli	FC Kaiserslautern
1989-90	Liverpool	Real Madrid	Sampdoria	VfB Stuttgart
1990-91	Arsenal	FC Barcelona	AC Milan	Werder Bremen
1991-92	Leeds United	FC Barcelona	AC Milan	Bayern Munich
1992-93	Manchester United	FC Barcelona	AC Milan	Borussia Dortmund
1993-94	Manchester United	FC Barcelona	Juventus	Borussia Dortmund
1994-95	Blackburn Rovers	Real Madrid	AC Milan	Bayern Munich
1995-96	Manchester United	Atlético Madrid	Juventus	FC Kaiserslautern
1996-97	Manchester United	Real Madrid	Juventus	Bayern Munich
1997-98	Arsenal	FC Barcelona	AC Milan	Bayern Munich
1998-99	Manchester United	FC Barcelona	Lazio	Bayern Munich
1999-2000	Manchester United	Deportivo Coruña	AS Roma	Bayern Munich
2000-01	Manchester United	Real Madrid	Juventus	Borussia Dortmund
2001-02	Arsenal	Valencia	Juventus	Bayern Munich
2002-03	Manchester United	Real Madrid	AC Milan	Werder Bremen
2003-04	Arsenal	Valencia	None[3]	Bayern Munich
2004-05	Chelsea	FC Barcelona	Inter Milan[3]	Bayern Munich
2005-06	Chelsea	FC Barcelona	Inter Milan	VfB Stuttgart
2006-07	Manchester United	Real Madrid	Inter Milan	Bayern Munich
2007-08	Manchester United	Real Madrid	Inter Milan	VfL Wolfsburg
2008-09	Manchester United	FC Barcelona	Inter Milan	Bayern Munich
2009-10	Chelsea	FC Barcelona	AC Milan	Borussia Dortmund
2010-11	Manchester United	Real Madrid	Juventus	Borussia Dortmund
2011-12	Manchester City	Real Madrid	Juventus	Bayern Munich
2012-13	Manchester United	FC Barcelona	Juventus	Bayern Munich
2013-14	Manchester City	Atlético Madrid	Juventus	Bayern Munich
2014-15	Chelsea	FC Barcelona	Juventus	Bayern Munich
2015-16	Leicester City	FC Barcelona	Juventus	Bayern Munich
2016-17	Chelsea	Real Madrid	Juventus	Bayern Munich
2017-18	Manchester City	FC Barcelona	Juventus	Bayern Munich
2018-19	Manchester City	FC Barcelona	Juventus	Bayern Munich
2019-20	Liverpool	Real Madrid	Juventus	Bayern Munich

(1) Football League champions are listed prior to 1992-93 season, when the Premier League formed. (2) Regional champions are listed prior to 1963-64 season, when National Bundesliga formed. (3) Juventus was stripped of two titles in 2006 because of match-fixing.

FIFA Confederations Cup Results, 1997-2017

The FIFA Confederations Cup was a tournament contested by six continental champions, the World Cup winner, and the host country. FIFA announced in Mar. 2019 that it will hold a new 24-team FIFA Club World Cup in June-July of 2021.

Year	Winner	Final opponent	Score	Third place	Fourth place	Site
1997	Brazil	Australia	6-0	Czech Republic	Uruguay	Saudi Arabia
1999	Mexico	Brazil	4-3	U.S.	Saudi Arabia	Mexico
2001	France	Japan	1-0	Australia	Brazil	S. Korea/Japan
2003	France	Cameroon	1-0#	Turkey	Colombia	France
2005	Brazil	Argentina	4-1	Germany	Mexico	Germany
2009	Brazil	U.S.	3-2	Spain	South Africa	South Africa
2013	Brazil	Spain	3-0	Italy	Uruguay	Brazil
2017	Germany	Chile	1-0	Portugal	Mexico	Russia

= Match decided in extra time.

GOLF

Men's All-Time Leading Major Professional Championship Winners
Through Sept. 2020. * = Active PGA player in 2020; (a) = amateur.

Player	Masters	U.S. Open	British Open	PGA	Total
Jack Nicklaus	1963, '65-'66, '72, '75, '86	1962, '67, '72, '80	1966, '70, '78	1963, '71, '73, '75, '80	18
Tiger Woods*	1997, 2001-02, '05, '19	2000, '02, '08	2000, '05-'06	1999-2000, '06-'07	15
Walter Hagen	—	1914, '19	1922, '24, '28-'29	1921, '24-'27	11
Ben Hogan	1951, '53	1948, '50-'51, '53	1953	1946, '48	9
Gary Player	1961, '74, '78	1965	1959, '68, '74	1962, '72	9
Tom Watson	1977, '81	1982	1975, '77, '80, '82-'83	—	8
Bobby Jones (a)	—	1923, '26, '29-'30	1926-27, '30	—	7
Arnold Palmer	1958, '60, '62, '64	1960	1961-62	—	7
Gene Sarazen	1935	1922, '32	1932	1922-23, '33	7
Sam Snead	1949, '52, '54	—	1946	1942, '49, '51	7
Harry Vardon	—	1900	1896, '98-'99, 1903, '11, '14	—	7
Nick Faldo	1989-90, '96	—	1987, '90, '92	—	6
Lee Trevino	—	1968, '71	1971-72	1974, '84	6

Men's All-Time Leading PGA Tournament Winners
Ranked by career wins in PGA Tour co-sponsored and/or approved tournaments through 2019-20 season. * = Active PGA player in 2019-20 season.

Player	Wins	Majors	Player	Wins	Majors	Player	Wins	Majors
Sam Snead	82	7	*Vijay Singh	34	3	*Dustin Johnson	23	1
*Tiger Woods	82	15	Jimmy Demaret	31	3	Jim Barnes	22	4
Jack Nicklaus	73	18	Horton Smith	30	2	Raymond Floyd	22	4
Ben Hogan	64	9	Lee Trevino	29	6	Johnny Farrell	22	1
Arnold Palmer	62	7	Gene Littler	29	1	Craig Wood	21	2
Byron Nelson	52	5	Harry Cooper	29	0	*Davis Love III	21	1
Billy Casper	51	3	Leo Diegel	28	2	Willie Macfarlane	21	1
Walter Hagen	45	11	Paul Runyan	28	2	Lanny Wadkins	21	1
*Phil Mickelson	44	5	Henry Picard	26	2	Hale Irwin	20	3
Tom Watson	39	8	Tommy Armour	25	3	Greg Norman	20	2
Cary Middlecoff	39	3	Johnny Miller	25	2	Johnny Revolta	20	1
Gene Sarazen	38	7	Gary Player	24	9	Doug Sanders	20	0
Lloyd Mangrum	36	1	Macdonald Smith	24	0			

Professional Golfers' Association Leading Money Winners, 1946-2020

Year	Player	Earnings	Year	Player	Earnings	Year	Player	Earnings
1946	Ben Hogan	$42,556	1971	Jack Nicklaus	$244,490	1996	Tom Lehman	$1,780,159
1947	Jimmy Demaret	27,936	1972	Jack Nicklaus	320,542	1997	Tiger Woods	2,066,833
1948	Ben Hogan	32,112	1973	Jack Nicklaus	308,362	1998	David Duval	2,591,031
1949	Sam Snead	31,593	1974	Johnny Miller	353,021	1999	Tiger Woods	6,616,585
1950	Sam Snead	35,758	1975	Jack Nicklaus	298,149	2000	Tiger Woods	9,188,321
1951	Lloyd Mangrum	26,088	1976	Jack Nicklaus	266,438	2001	Tiger Woods	5,687,777
1952	Julius Boros	37,032	1977	Tom Watson	310,653	2002	Tiger Woods	6,912,625
1953	Lew Worsham	34,002	1978	Tom Watson	362,429	2003	Vijay Singh	7,573,907
1954	Bob Toski	65,819	1979	Tom Watson	462,636	2004	Vijay Singh	10,905,166
1955	Julius Boros	63,121	1980	Tom Watson	530,808	2005	Tiger Woods	10,628,024
1956	Ted Kroll	72,835	1981	Tom Kite	375,699	2006	Tiger Woods	9,941,563
1957	Dick Mayer	65,835	1982	Craig Stadler	446,462	2007	Tiger Woods	10,867,052
1958	Arnold Palmer	42,607	1983	Hal Sutton	426,668	2008	Vijay Singh	6,601,094
1959	Art Wall Jr.	53,167	1984	Tom Watson	476,260	2009	Tiger Woods	10,508,163
1960	Arnold Palmer	75,262	1985	Curtis Strange	542,321	2010	Matt Kuchar	4,910,477
1961	Gary Player	64,540	1986	Greg Norman	653,296	2011	Luke Donald	6,683,214
1962	Arnold Palmer	81,448	1987	Curtis Strange	925,941	2012	Rory McIlroy	8,047,952
1963	Arnold Palmer	128,230	1988	Curtis Strange	1,147,644	2013	Tiger Woods	8,553,439
1964	Jack Nicklaus	113,284	1989	Tom Kite	1,395,278	2014	Rory McIlroy	8,280,096
1965	Jack Nicklaus	140,752	1990	Greg Norman	1,165,477	2015	Jordan Spieth	12,030,465
1966	Billy Casper	121,944	1991	Corey Pavin	979,430	2016	Dustin Johnson	9,365,185
1967	Jack Nicklaus	188,998	1992	Fred Couples	1,344,188	2017	Justin Thomas	9,921,560
1968	Billy Casper	205,168	1993	Nick Price	1,478,557	2018	Justin Thomas	8,694,821
1969	Frank Beard	164,707	1994	Nick Price	1,499,927	2019	Brooks Koepka	9,684,006
1970	Lee Trevino	157,037	1995	Greg Norman	1,654,959	2020	Justin Thomas	7,344,040

Note: The PGA tour introduced a new split season format in Oct. 2013, which concluded with the FedEx Cup in Sept. 2014. From 2014 on, year shown is the one in which season ended.

FedEx Cup Winners, 2007-20
The FedEx Cup, a season-long competition with points awarded by finishing rank in each tournament, divides the PGA Tour into a regular season consisting of 43 events, combined with a 3-event playoff that ends with the Tour Championship. The coronavirus pandemic reduced the 2019-20 season to a total of 36 tournaments. The winner's share of the prize pool increased from $10 mil to $15 mil in 2019.

Year	Winner	Year	Winner	Year	Winner	Year	Winner	Year	Winner
2007	Tiger Woods	2010	Jim Furyk	2013	Henrik Stenson	2016	Rory McIlroy	2019	Rory McIlroy
2008	Vijay Singh	2011	Bill Haas	2014	Billy Horschel	2017	Justin Thomas	2020	Dustin Johnson
2009	Tiger Woods	2012	Brandt Snedeker	2015	Jordan Spieth	2018	Justin Rose		

Masters Golf Tournament Winners, 1940-2019

First contested in 1934 as Augusta National Invitation Tournament (name changed in 1939); not played, 1943-45.

Year	Winner	Year	Winner	Year	Winner	Year	Winner	Year	Winner
1940	Jimmy Demaret	1959	Art Wall Jr.	1975	Jack Nicklaus	1991	Ian Woosnam	2005	Tiger Woods
1941	Craig Wood	1960	Arnold Palmer	1976	Ray Floyd	1992	Fred Couples	2006	Phil Mickelson
1942	Byron Nelson	1961	Gary Player	1977	Tom Watson	1993	Bernhard Langer	2007	Zach Johnson
1946	Herman Keiser	1962	Arnold Palmer	1978	Gary Player	1994	José María	2008	Trevor Immelman
1947	Jimmy Demaret	1963	Jack Nicklaus	1979	Fuzzy Zoeller		Olazábal	2009	Angel Cabrera
1948	Claude Harmon	1964	Arnold Palmer	1980	Seve Ballesteros	1995	Ben Crenshaw	2010	Phil Mickelson
1949	Sam Snead	1965	Jack Nicklaus	1981	Tom Watson	1996	Nick Faldo	2011	Charl Schwartzel
1950	Jimmy Demaret	1966	Jack Nicklaus	1982	Craig Stadler	1997	Tiger Woods	2012	Bubba Watson
1951	Ben Hogan	1967	Gay Brewer Jr.	1983	Seve Ballesteros	1998	Mark O'Meara	2013	Adam Scott
1952	Sam Snead	1968	Bob Goalby	1984	Ben Crenshaw	1999	José María	2014	Bubba Watson
1953	Ben Hogan	1969	George Archer	1985	Bernhard Langer		Olazábal	2015	Jordan Spieth
1954	Sam Snead	1970	Billy Casper	1986	Jack Nicklaus	2000	Vijay Singh	2016	Danny Willett
1955	Cary Middlecoff	1971	Charles Coody	1987	Larry Mize	2001	Tiger Woods	2017	Sergio García
1956	Jack Burke	1972	Jack Nicklaus	1988	Sandy Lyle	2002	Tiger Woods	2018	Patrick Reed
1957	Doug Ford	1973	Tommy Aaron	1989	Nick Faldo	2003	Mike Weir	2019	Tiger Woods
1958	Arnold Palmer	1974	Gary Player	1990	Nick Faldo	2004	Phil Mickelson		

U.S. Open Winners, 1940-2020

First contested in 1895; not played, 1942-45.

Year	Winner	Year	Winner	Year	Winner	Year	Winner	Year	Winner
1940	Lawson Little	1960	Arnold Palmer	1976	Jerry Pate	1992	Tom Kite	2007	Angel Cabrera
1941	Craig Wood	1961	Gene Littler	1977	Hubert Green	1993	Lee Janzen	2008	Tiger Woods
1946	Lloyd Mangrum	1962	Jack Nicklaus	1978	Andy North	1994	Ernie Els	2009	Lucas Glover
1947	Lew Worsham	1963	Julius Boros	1979	Hale Irwin	1995	Corey Pavin	2010	Graeme McDowell
1948	Ben Hogan	1964	Ken Venturi	1980	Jack Nicklaus	1996	Steve Jones	2011	Rory McIlroy
1949	Cary Middlecoff	1965	Gary Player	1981	David Graham	1997	Ernie Els	2012	Webb Simpson
1950	Ben Hogan	1966	Billy Casper	1982	Tom Watson	1998	Lee Janzen	2013	Justin Rose
1951	Ben Hogan	1967	Jack Nicklaus	1983	Larry Nelson	1999	Payne Stewart	2014	Martin Kaymer
1952	Julius Boros	1968	Lee Trevino	1984	Fuzzy Zoeller	2000	Tiger Woods	2015	Jordan Spieth
1953	Ben Hogan	1969	Orville Moody	1985	Andy North	2001	Retief Goosen	2016	Dustin Johnson
1954	Ed Furgol	1970	Tony Jacklin	1986	Ray Floyd	2002	Tiger Woods	2017	Brooks Koepka
1955	Jack Fleck	1971	Lee Trevino	1987	Scott Simpson	2003	Jim Furyk	2018	Brooks Koepka
1956	Cary Middlecoff	1972	Jack Nicklaus	1988	Curtis Strange	2004	Retief Goosen	2019	Gary Woodland
1957	Dick Mayer	1973	Johnny Miller	1989	Curtis Strange	2005	Michael Campbell	2020	Bryson
1958	Tommy Bolt	1974	Hale Irwin	1990	Hale Irwin	2006	Geoff Ogilvy		DeChambeau
1959	Billy Casper	1975	Lou Graham	1991	Payne Stewart				

British Open Winners, 1946-2019

Officially called the Open Championship. First contested in 1860; not played, 1940-45, 2020.

Year	Winner	Year	Winner	Year	Winner	Year	Winner	Year	Winner
1946	Sam Snead	1961	Arnold Palmer	1976	Johnny Miller	1991	Ian Baker-Finch	2006	Tiger Woods
1947	Fred Daly	1962	Arnold Palmer	1977	Tom Watson	1992	Nick Faldo	2007	Padraig Harrington
1948	Henry Cotton	1963	Bob Charles	1978	Jack Nicklaus	1993	Greg Norman	2008	Padraig Harrington
1949	Bobby Locke	1964	Tony Lema	1979	Seve Ballesteros	1994	Nick Price	2009	Stewart Cink
1950	Bobby Locke	1965	Peter Thomson	1980	Tom Watson	1995	John Daly	2010	Louis Oosthuizen
1951	Max Faulkner	1966	Jack Nicklaus	1981	Bill Rogers	1996	Tom Lehman	2011	Darren Clarke
1952	Bobby Locke	1967	Roberto de Vicenzo	1982	Tom Watson	1997	Justin Leonard	2012	Ernie Els
1953	Ben Hogan	1968	Gary Player	1983	Tom Watson	1998	Mark O'Meara	2013	Phil Mickelson
1954	Peter Thomson	1969	Tony Jacklin	1984	Seve Ballesteros	1999	Paul Lawrie	2014	Rory McIlroy
1955	Peter Thomson	1970	Jack Nicklaus	1985	Sandy Lyle	2000	Tiger Woods	2015	Zach Johnson
1956	Peter Thomson	1971	Lee Trevino	1986	Greg Norman	2001	David Duval	2016	Henrik Stenson
1957	Bobby Locke	1972	Lee Trevino	1987	Nick Faldo	2002	Ernie Els	2017	Jordan Spieth
1958	Peter Thomson	1973	Tom Weiskopf	1988	Seve Ballesteros	2003	Ben Curtis	2018	Francesco Molinari
1959	Gary Player	1974	Gary Player	1989	Mark Calcavecchia	2004	Todd Hamilton	2019	Shane Lowry
1960	Kel Nagle	1975	Tom Watson	1990	Nick Faldo	2005	Tiger Woods		

PGA Championship Winners, 1940-2020

First contested in 1916; not played, 1943.

Year	Winner	Year	Winner	Year	Winner	Year	Winner	Year	Winner
1940	Byron Nelson	1957	Lionel Hebert	1973	Jack Nicklaus	1989	Payne Stewart	2005	Phil Mickelson
1941	Victor Ghezzi	1958	Dow Finsterwald	1974	Lee Trevino	1990	Wayne Grady	2006	Tiger Woods
1942	Sam Snead	1959	Bob Rosburg	1975	Jack Nicklaus	1991	John Daly	2007	Tiger Woods
1944	Bob Hamilton	1960	Jay Hebert	1976	Dave Stockton	1992	Nick Price	2008	Padraig Harrington
1945	Byron Nelson	1961	Jerry Barber	1977	Lanny Wadkins	1993	Paul Azinger	2009	Y.E. Yang
1946	Ben Hogan	1962	Gary Player	1978	John Mahaffey	1994	Nick Price	2010	Martin Kaymer
1947	Jim Ferrier	1963	Jack Nicklaus	1979	David Graham	1995	Steve Elkington	2011	Keegan Bradley
1948	Ben Hogan	1964	Bob Nichols	1980	Jack Nicklaus	1996	Mark Brooks	2012	Rory McIlroy
1949	Sam Snead	1965	Dave Marr	1981	Larry Nelson	1997	Davis Love III	2013	Jason Dufner
1950	Chandler Harper	1966	Al Geiberger	1982	Ray Floyd	1998	Vijay Singh	2014	Rory McIlroy
1951	Sam Snead	1967	Don January	1983	Hal Sutton	1999	Tiger Woods	2015	Jason Day
1952	James Turnesa	1968	Julius Boros	1984	Lee Trevino	2000	Tiger Woods	2016	Jimmy Walker
1953	Walter Burkemo	1969	Ray Floyd	1985	Hubert Green	2001	David Toms	2017	Justin Thomas
1954	Melvin Harbert	1970	Dave Stockton	1986	Bob Tway	2002	Rich Beem	2018	Brooks Koepka
1955	Doug Ford	1971	Jack Nicklaus	1987	Larry Nelson	2003	Shaun Micheel	2019	Brooks Koepka
1956	Jack Burke	1972	Gary Player	1988	Jeff Sluman	2004	Vijay Singh	2020	Collin Morikawa

PGA Tour Byron Nelson Award, 1980-2020

Awarded to the player with the best scoring average (1980-87) or adjusted scoring average (1988-present) who has competed in a minimum of 50 official rounds on the PGA Tour.

Year	Winner	Average	Year	Winner	Average	Year	Winner	Average
1980	Lee Trevino	69.73	1994	Greg Norman	68.81	2008	Sergio García	69.12
1981	Tom Kite	69.80	1995	Greg Norman	69.06	2009	Tiger Woods	68.05
1982	Tom Kite	70.21	1996	Tom Lehman	69.32	2010	Matt Kuchar	69.61
1983	Raymond Floyd	70.61	1997	Nick Price	68.98	2011	Luke Donald	68.86
1984	Calvin Peete	70.56	1998	David Duval	69.13	2012	Rory McIlroy	68.87
1985	Don Pooley	70.36	1999	Tiger Woods	68.43	2013	Steve Stricker	68.95
1986	Scott Hoch	70.08	2000	Tiger Woods	67.79	2014	Rory McIlroy	68.83
1987	David Frost	70.09	2001	Tiger Woods	68.81	2015	Jordan Spieth	68.94
1988	Greg Norman	69.38	2002	Tiger Woods	68.56	2016	Dustin Johnson	69.17
1989	Payne Stewart	69.485[1]	2003	Tiger Woods	68.41	2017	Jordan Spieth	68.85
1990	Greg Norman	69.10	2004	Vijay Singh	68.84	2018	Dustin Johnson	68.70
1991	Fred Couples	69.59	2005	Tiger Woods	68.66	2019	Rory McIlroy	69.06
1992	Fred Couples	69.38	2006	Tiger Woods	68.11	2020	Webb Simpson	68.98
1993	Greg Norman	68.90	2007	Tiger Woods	67.79			

(1) Tie broken by more precise calculation.

Ryder Cup, 1927-2018

The Ryder Cup began in 1927 as a biennial team competition between U.S. and British pro male golfers. The British team expanded in 1973 to include players from Ireland and in 1979 to golfers from the rest of Europe. The 2018 Cup was held Sept. 28-30 at Le Golf National near Paris, France; the 2020 Cup was postponed due to the coronavirus pandemic and was expected to be held Sept. 21-26, 2021, at Whistling Straits Golf Course in Mosel, WI.

Year	Winner, score	Year	Winner, score	Year	Winner, score	Year	Winner, score
1927	U.S., 9½-2½	1957	Great Britain, 7½-4½	1979	U.S., 17-11	1999	U.S., 14½-13½
1929	Great Britain, 7-5	1959	U.S., 8½-3½	1981	U.S., 18½-9½	2002	Europe, 15½-12½
1931	U.S., 9-3	1961	U.S., 14½-9½	1983	U.S., 14½-13½	2004	Europe, 18½-9½
1933	Great Britain, 6½-5½	1963	U.S., 23-9	1985	Europe, 16½-11½	2006	Europe, 18½-9½
1935	U.S., 9-3	1965	U.S., 19½-12½	1987	Europe, 15-13	2008	U.S., 16½-11½
1937	U.S., 8-4	1967	U.S., 23½-8½	1989	Draw, 14-14	2010	Europe, 14½-13½
1947	U.S., 11-1	1969	Draw, 16-16	1991	U.S., 14½-13½	2012	Europe, 14½-13½
1949	U.S., 7-5	1971	U.S., 18½-13½	1993	U.S., 15-13	2014	Europe, 16½-11½
1951	U.S., 9½-2½	1973	U.S., 19-13	1995	Europe, 14½-13½	2016	U.S., 17-11
1953	U.S., 6½-5½	1975	U.S., 21-11	1997	Europe, 14½-13½	2018	Europe, 17½-10½
1955	U.S., 8-4	1977	U.S., 12½-7½				

Women's All-Time Leading Major Professional Championship Winners

Through Sept. 2020. * = Active in 2020 LPGA season.

Player	ANA Inspiration[1]	KPMG Women's PGA[2]	U.S. Women's Open	Women's British Open[3]	Titleholders[4]	Western Open[5]	Total
Patty Berg	—	—	1946	—	1937-39, '48, '53, '55, '57	1941, '43, '48, '51, '55, '57-'58	15
Mickey Wright	—	1958, '60-'61, '63	1958-59, '61, '64	—	1961-62	1962-63, '66	13
Louise Suggs	—	1957	1949, '52	—	1946, '54, '56, '59	1946-47, '49, '53	11
Annika Sorenstam	2001-02, '05	2003-05	1995-96, 2006	2003	—	—	10
Babe Zaharias	—	—	1948, '50, '54	—	1947, '50, '52	1940, '44-'45, '50	10
Betsy Rawls	—	1959, '69	1951, '53, '57, '60	—	—	1952, '59	8
Juli Inkster*	1984, '89	1999-2000	1999, 2002	1984	—	—	7
Inbee Park*	2013	2013-15	2008, '13	2015	—	—	7
Karrie Webb*	2000, '06	2001	2000-01	1999, 2002	—	—	7

(1) Formerly the Nabisco Dinah Shore (1982-99), the Nabisco Championship (2000-01), and the Kraft Nabisco Championship (2002-14); designated major in 1983. (2) Formerly the LPGA Championship (1955-2014). (3) In 2001, the British Open replaced the du Maurier Classic as the LPGA's fourth major; wins in column prior to 2001 are for the Peter Jackson (1979-82) or du Maurier (1983-2000) Classic. (4) Titleholders Championship was a major, 1937-72. (5) Western Open was a major, 1930-67.

Ladies Professional Golf Association Leading Money Winners, 1954-2019

Year	Player	Earnings	Year	Player	Earnings	Year	Player	Earnings
1954	Patty Berg	$16,011	1976	Judy Rankin	$150,734	1998	Annika Sorenstam	$1,092,748
1955	Patty Berg	16,492	1977	Judy Rankin	122,890	1999	Karrie Webb	1,591,959
1956	Marlene Hagge	20,235	1978	Nancy Lopez	189,814	2000	Karrie Webb	1,876,853
1957	Patty Berg	16,272	1979	Nancy Lopez	197,489	2001	Annika Sorenstam	2,105,868
1958	Beverly Hanson	12,639	1980	Beth Daniel	231,000	2002	Annika Sorenstam	2,863,904
1959	Betsy Rawls	26,774	1981	Beth Daniel	206,998	2003	Annika Sorenstam	2,029,506
1960	Louise Suggs	16,892	1982	JoAnne Carner	310,400	2004	Annika Sorenstam	2,544,707
1961	Mickey Wright	22,236	1983	JoAnne Carner	291,404	2005	Annika Sorenstam	2,588,240
1962	Mickey Wright	21,641	1984	Betsy King	266,771	2006	Lorena Ochoa	2,592,872
1963	Mickey Wright	31,269	1985	Nancy Lopez	416,472	2007	Lorena Ochoa	4,364,994
1964	Mickey Wright	29,800	1986	Pat Bradley	492,021	2008	Lorena Ochoa	2,763,193
1965	Kathy Whitworth	28,658	1987	Ayako Okamoto	466,034	2009	Jiyai Shin	1,807,334
1966	Kathy Whitworth	33,517	1988	Sherri Turner	350,851	2010	Na Yeon Choi	1,871,166
1967	Kathy Whitworth	32,937	1989	Betsy King	654,132	2011	Yani Tseng	2,921,713
1968	Kathy Whitworth	48,379	1990	Beth Daniel	863,578	2012	Inbee Park	2,287,080
1969	Carol Mann	49,152	1991	Pat Bradley	763,118	2013	Inbee Park	2,456,619
1970	Kathy Whitworth	30,235	1992	Dottie Mochrie	693,335	2014	Stacy Lewis	2,539,039
1971	Kathy Whitworth	41,181	1993	Betsy King	595,992	2015	Lydia Ko	2,800,802
1972	Kathy Whitworth	65,063	1994	Laura Davies	687,201	2016	Ariya Jutanugarn	2,550,947
1973	Kathy Whitworth	82,864	1995	Annika Sorenstam	666,533	2017	Sung Hyun Park	2,335,883
1974	JoAnne Carner	87,094	1996	Karrie Webb	1,002,000	2018	Ariya Jutanugarn	2,743,949
1975	Sandra Palmer	76,374	1997	Annika Sorenstam	1,236,789	2019	Jin Young Ko	2,773,894

Women's All-Time Leading LPGA Tournament Winners

Ranked by career tournament wins through Sept. 2020. * = Active LPGA player in 2020.

Player	Wins	Majors	Player	Wins	Majors	Player	Wins	Majors
Kathy Whitworth	88	6	JoAnne Carner	43	2	Betsy King	34	6
Mickey Wright	82	13	Sandra Haynie	42	4	Beth Daniel	33	1
Annika Sorenstam	72	10	Babe Didrikson			*Juli Inkster	31	7
Louise Suggs	61	11	Zaharias	41	10	Pat Bradley	31	6
Patty Berg	60	15	*Karrie Webb	41	7	Amy Alcott	29	5
Betsy Rawls	55	8	Carol Mann	38	2	Lorena Ochoa	27	2
Nancy Lopez	48	3	Patty Sheehan	35	6	Jane Blalock	27	0

ANA Inspiration Winners, 1983-2020

Event began in 1972 and was designated a major championship in 1983. Formerly the Colgate Dinah Shore (1972-81), the Nabisco Dinah Shore (1982-99), the Nabisco Championship (2000-01), and the Kraft Nabisco Championship (2002-14).

Year	Winner	Year	Winner	Year	Winner	Year	Winner	Year	Winner
1983	Amy Alcott	1991	Amy Alcott	1999	Dottie Pepper	2007	Morgan Pressel	2014	Lexi Thompson
1984	Juli Inkster	1992	Dottie Pepper	2000	Karrie Webb	2008	Lorena Ochoa	2015	Brittany Lincicome
1985	Alice Miller	1993	Helen Alfredsson	2001	Annika Sorenstam	2009	Brittany Lincicome	2016	Lydia Ko
1986	Pat Bradley	1994	Donna Andrews	2002	Annika Sorenstam	2010	Yani Tseng	2017	So Yeon Ryu
1987	Betsy King	1995	Nanci Bowen	2003	P. Meunier-Lebouc	2011	Stacy Lewis	2018	Pernilla Lindberg
1988	Amy Alcott	1996	Patty Sheehan	2004	Grace Park	2012	Sun Young Yoo	2019	Jin Young Ko
1989	Juli Inkster	1997	Betsy King	2005	Annika Sorenstam	2013	Inbee Park	2020	Mirim Lee
1990	Betsy King	1998	Pat Hurst	2006	Karrie Webb				

KPMG Women's PGA Championship Winners, 1955-2020

Formerly LPGA Championship (1955-2014).

Year	Winner	Year	Winner	Year	Winner	Year	Winner	Year	Winner
1955	Beverly Hanson	1969	Betsy Rawls	1982	Jan Stephenson	1995	Kelly Robbins	2008	Yani Tseng
1956	Marlene Hagge	1970	Shirley Englehorn	1983	Patty Sheehan	1996	Laura Davies	2009	Anna Nordqvist
1957	Louise Suggs	1971	Kathy Whitworth	1984	Patty Sheehan	1997	Christa Johnson	2010	Cristie Kerr
1958	Mickey Wright	1972	Kathy Ahern	1985	Nancy Lopez	1998	Se Ri Pak	2011	Yani Tseng
1959	Betsy Rawls	1973	Mary Mills	1986	Pat Bradley	1999	Juli Inkster	2012	Shanshan Feng
1960	Mickey Wright	1974	Sandra Haynie	1987	Jane Geddes	2000	Juli Inkster	2013	Inbee Park
1961	Mickey Wright	1975	Kathy Whitworth	1988	Sherri Turner	2001	Karrie Webb	2014	Inbee Park
1962	Judy Kimball	1976	Betty Burfeindt	1989	Nancy Lopez	2002	Se Ri Pak	2015	Inbee Park
1963	Mickey Wright	1977	Chako Higuchi	1990	Beth Daniel	2003	Annika Sorenstam	2016	Brooke Henderson
1964	Mary Mills	1978	Nancy Lopez	1991	Meg Mallon	2004	Annika Sorenstam	2017	Danielle Kang
1965	Sandra Haynie	1979	Donna Caponi	1992	Betsy King	2005	Annika Sorenstam	2018	Sung Hyun Park
1966	Gloria Ehret	1980	Sally Little	1993	Patty Sheehan	2006	Se Ri Pak	2019	Hannah Green
1967	Kathy Whitworth	1981	Donna Caponi	1994	Laura Davies	2007	Suzann Pettersen	2020	Sei Young Kim
1968	Sandra Post								

U.S. Women's Open Winners, 1946-2019

Year	Winner	Year	Winner	Year	Winner	Year	Winner	Year	Winner
1946	Patty Berg	1961	Mickey Wright	1976	JoAnne Carner	1991	Meg Mallon	2006	Annika Sorenstam
1947	Betty Jameson	1962	Murle Lindstrom	1977	Hollis Stacy	1992	Patty Sheehan	2007	Cristie Kerr
1948	Babe Zaharias	1963	Mary Mills	1978	Hollis Stacy	1993	Lauri Merten	2008	Inbee Park
1949	Louise Suggs	1964	Mickey Wright	1979	Jerilyn Britz	1994	Patty Sheehan	2009	Eun-Hee Ji
1950	Babe Zaharias	1965	Carol Mann	1980	Amy Alcott	1995	Annika Sorenstam	2010	Paula Creamer
1951	Betsy Rawls	1966	Sandra Spuzich	1981	Pat Bradley	1996	Annika Sorenstam	2011	So Yeon Ryu
1952	Louise Suggs	1967	Catherine Lacoste	1982	Janet Alex	1997	Alison Nicholas	2012	Na Yeon Choi
1953	Betsy Rawls	1968	Susie Berning	1983	Jan Stephenson	1998	Se Ri Pak	2013	Inbee Park
1954	Babe Zaharias	1969	Donna Caponi	1984	Hollis Stacy	1999	Juli Inkster	2014	Michelle Wie
1955	Fay Crocker	1970	Donna Caponi	1985	Kathy Baker	2000	Karrie Webb	2015	In Gee Chun
1956	Kathy Cornelius	1971	JoAnne Carner	1986	Jane Geddes	2001	Karrie Webb	2016	Brittany Lang
1957	Betsy Rawls	1972	Susie Berning	1987	Laura Davies	2002	Juli Inkster	2017	Sung Hyun Park
1958	Mickey Wright	1973	Susie Berning	1988	Liselotte Neumann	2003	Hilary Lunke	2018	Ariya Jutanugarn
1959	Mickey Wright	1974	Sandra Haynie	1989	Betsy King	2004	Meg Mallon	2019	Jeongeun Lee6
1960	Betsy Rawls	1975	Sandra Palmer	1990	Betsy King	2005	Birdie Kim		

AIG Women's British Open Winners, 1979-2020

First contested as the Ladies' British Open in 1976; became the LPGA's fourth major championship in 2001, replacing the du Maurier Classic. Winners listed are for the Peter Jackson (1979-82) and du Maurier (1983-2000) Classic.

Year	Winner	Year	Winner	Year	Winner	Year	Winner	Year	Winner
1979	Amy Alcott	1988	Sally Little	1997	Colleen Walker	2005	Jeong Jang	2013	Stacy Lewis
1980	Pat Bradley	1989	Tammie Green	1998	Brandie Burton	2006	Sherri Steinhauer	2014	Mo Martin
1981	Jan Stephenson	1990	Cathy Johnston	1999	Karrie Webb	2007	Lorena Ochoa	2015	Inbee Park
1982	Sandra Haynie	1991	Nancy Scranton	2000	Meg Mallon	2008	Jiyai Shin	2016	Ariya Jutanugarn
1983	Hollis Stacy	1992	Sherri Steinhauer	2001	Se Ri Pak	2009	Catriona Matthew	2017	In-Kyung Kim
1984	Juli Inkster	1993	Brandie Burton	2002	Karrie Webb	2010	Yani Tseng	2018	Georgia Hall
1985	Pat Bradley	1994	Martha Nause	2003	Annika Sorenstam	2011	Yani Tseng	2019	Hinako Shibuno
1986	Pat Bradley	1995	Jenny Lidback	2004	Karen Stupples	2012	Jiyai Shin	2020	Sophia Popov
1987	Jody Rosenthal	1996	Laura Davies						

Evian Championship, 2013-19

Began in 1994 as the Evian Masters; became the LPGA's fifth major tournament in 2013, when it was renamed the Evian Championship. The 2020 Evian Championship was canceled due to the coronavirus pandemic.

Year	Winner	Year	Winner	Year	Winner	Year	Winner
2013	Suzann Pettersen	2015	Lydia Ko	2017	Anna Nordqvist	2019	Jin Young Ko
2014	Hyo Joo Kim	2016	In Gee Chun	2018	Angela Stanford		

Solheim Cup, 1990-2019

The Solheim Cup began in 1990 as a biennial team competition between pro women golfers from the U.S. and Europe.

Year	Winner, score	Year	Winner, score	Year	Winner, score	Year	Winner, score
1990	U.S., 11½-4½	1998	U.S., 16-12	2005	U.S., 15½-12½	2013	Europe, 18-10
1992	Europe, 11½-6½	2000	Europe, 14½-11½	2007	U.S., 16-12	2015	U.S., 14½-13½
1994	U.S., 13-7	2002	U.S., 15½-12½	2009	U.S., 16-12	2017	U.S., 16½-11½
1996	U.S., 17-11	2003	Europe, 17½-10½	2011	Europe, 15-13	2019	Europe, 14½-13½

TENNIS

Australian Open Champions, 1969-2020
First contested 1905 for men, 1922 for women. Became an open championship in 1969.

Year	Men's Singles Champion	Final opponent	Year	Women's Singles Champion	Final opponent
1969	Rod Laver	Andrés Gimeno	1969	Margaret Smith Court	Billie Jean King
1970	Arthur Ashe	Dick Crealy	1970	Margaret Smith Court	Kerry Melville Reid
1971	Ken Rosewall	Arthur Ashe	1971	Margaret Smith Court	Evonne Goolagong
1972	Ken Rosewall	Mal Anderson	1972	Virginia Wade	Evonne Goolagong
1973	John Newcombe	Onny Parun	1973	Margaret Smith Court	Evonne Goolagong
1974	Jimmy Connors	Phil Dent	1974	Evonne Goolagong	Chris Evert
1975	John Newcombe	Jimmy Connors	1975	Evonne Goolagong	Martina Navratilova
1976	Mark Edmondson	John Newcombe	1976	Evonne Goolagong Cawley	Renata Tomanova
1977	Roscoe Tanner	Guillermo Vilas	1977	Kerry Reid	Dianne Balestrat
	Vitas Gerulaitis	John Lloyd		Evonne Goolagong Cawley	Helen Gourlay
1978	Guillermo Vilas	John Marks	1978	Chris O'Neil	Betsy Nagelsen
1979	Guillermo Vilas	John Sadri	1979	Barbara Jordan	Sharon Walsh
1980	Brian Teacher	Kim Warwick	1980	Hana Mandlikova	Wendy Turnbull
1981	Johan Kriek	Steve Denton	1981	Martina Navratilova	Chris Evert Lloyd
1982	Johan Kriek	Steve Denton	1982	Chris Evert Lloyd	Martina Navratilova
1983	Mats Wilander	Ivan Lendl	1983	Martina Navratilova	Kathy Jordan
1984	Mats Wilander	Kevin Curren	1984	Chris Evert Lloyd	Helena Sukova
1985	Stefan Edberg	Mats Wilander	1985	Martina Navratilova	Chris Evert Lloyd
1987	Stefan Edberg	Pat Cash	1987	Hana Mandlikova	Martina Navratilova
1988	Mats Wilander	Pat Cash	1988	Steffi Graf	Chris Evert
1989	Ivan Lendl	Miloslav Mecir	1989	Steffi Graf	Helena Sukova
1990	Ivan Lendl	Stefan Edberg	1990	Steffi Graf	Mary Joe Fernandez
1991	Boris Becker	Ivan Lendl	1991	Monica Seles	Jana Novotna
1992	Jim Courier	Stefan Edberg	1992	Monica Seles	Mary Joe Fernandez
1993	Jim Courier	Stefan Edberg	1993	Monica Seles	Steffi Graf
1994	Pete Sampras	Todd Martin	1994	Steffi Graf	Arantxa Sánchez Vicario
1995	Andre Agassi	Pete Sampras	1995	Mary Pierce	Arantxa Sánchez Vicario
1996	Boris Becker	Michael Chang	1996	Monica Seles	Anke Huber
1997	Pete Sampras	Carlos Moya	1997	Martina Hingis	Mary Pierce
1998	Petr Korda	Marcelo Rios	1998	Martina Hingis	Conchita Martínez
1999	Yevgeny Kafelnikov	Thomas Enqvist	1999	Martina Hingis	Amélie Mauresmo
2000	Andre Agassi	Yevgeny Kafelnikov	2000	Lindsay Davenport	Martina Hingis
2001	Andre Agassi	Arnaud Clement	2001	Jennifer Capriati	Martina Hingis
2002	Thomas Johansson	Marat Safin	2002	Jennifer Capriati	Martina Hingis
2003	Andre Agassi	Rainer Schuettler	2003	Serena Williams	Venus Williams
2004	Roger Federer	Marat Safin	2004	Justine Henin-Hardenne	Kim Clijsters
2005	Marat Safin	Lleyton Hewitt	2005	Serena Williams	Lindsay Davenport
2006	Roger Federer	Marcos Baghdatis	2006	Amélie Mauresmo	Justine Henin-Hardenne
2007	Roger Federer	Fernando Gonzalez	2007	Serena Williams	Maria Sharapova
2008	Novak Djokovic	Jo-Wilfried Tsonga	2008	Maria Sharapova	Ana Ivanovic
2009	Rafael Nadal	Roger Federer	2009	Serena Williams	Dinara Safina
2010	Roger Federer	Andy Murray	2010	Serena Williams	Justine Henin
2011	Novak Djokovic	Andy Murray	2011	Kim Clijsters	Li Na
2012	Novak Djokovic	Rafael Nadal	2012	Victoria Azarenka	Maria Sharapova
2013	Novak Djokovic	Andy Murray	2013	Victoria Azarenka	Li Na
2014	Stanislas Wawrinka	Rafael Nadal	2014	Li Na	Dominika Cibulkova
2015	Novak Djokovic	Andy Murray	2015	Serena Williams	Maria Sharapova
2016	Novak Djokovic	Andy Murray	2016	Angelique Kerber	Serena Williams
2017	Roger Federer	Rafael Nadal	2017	Serena Williams	Venus Williams
2018	Roger Federer	Marin Cilic	2018	Caroline Wozniacki	Simona Halep
2019	Novak Djokovic	Rafael Nadal	2019	Naomi Osaka	Petra Kvitova
2020	Novak Djokovic	Dominic Thiem	2020	Sofia Kenin	Garbiñe Muguruza

French Open (Roland Garros) Champions, 1968-2020
First contested 1891 for men, 1897 for women. Became an open championship in 1968.

Men's Singles

Year	Champion	Final opponent
1968	Ken Rosewall	Rod Laver
1969	Rod Laver	Ken Rosewall
1970	Jan Kodes	Zeljko Franulovic
1971	Jan Kodes	Ilie Nastase
1972	Andrés Gimeno	Patrick Proisy
1973	Ilie Nastase	Nikki Pilic
1974	Björn Borg	Manuel Orantes
1975	Björn Borg	Guillermo Vilas
1976	Adriano Panatta	Harold Solomon
1977	Guillermo Vilas	Brian Gottfried
1978	Björn Borg	Guillermo Vilas
1979	Björn Borg	Victor Pecci
1980	Björn Borg	Vitas Gerulaitis
1981	Björn Borg	Ivan Lendl
1982	Mats Wilander	Guillermo Vilas
1983	Yannick Noah	Mats Wilander
1984	Ivan Lendl	John McEnroe
1985	Mats Wilander	Ivan Lendl
1986	Ivan Lendl	Mikael Pernfors
1987	Ivan Lendl	Mats Wilander
1988	Mats Wilander	Henri Leconte
1989	Michael Chang	Stefan Edberg
1990	Andres Gomez	Andre Agassi
1991	Jim Courier	Andre Agassi
1992	Jim Courier	Petr Korda
1993	Sergi Bruguera	Jim Courier
1994	Sergi Bruguera	Alberto Berasategui
1995	Thomas Muster	Michael Chang
1996	Yevgeny Kafelnikov	Michael Stich
1997	Gustavo Kuerten	Sergi Bruguera
1998	Carlos Moya	Alex Corretja
1999	Andre Agassi	Andrei Medvedev
2000	Gustavo Kuerten	Magnus Norman
2001	Gustavo Kuerten	Alex Corretja
2002	Albert Costa	Juan Carlos Ferrero
2003	Juan Carlos Ferrero	Martin Verkerk
2004	Gaston Gaudio	Guillermo Coria
2005	Rafael Nadal	Mariano Puerta
2006	Rafael Nadal	Roger Federer
2007	Rafael Nadal	Roger Federer
2008	Rafael Nadal	Roger Federer
2009	Roger Federer	Robin Soderling
2010	Rafael Nadal	Robin Soderling
2011	Rafael Nadal	Roger Federer
2012	Rafael Nadal	Novak Djokovic
2013	Rafael Nadal	David Ferrer
2014	Rafael Nadal	Novak Djokovic
2015	Stan Wawrinka	Novak Djokovic
2016	Novak Djokovic	Andy Murray
2017	Rafael Nadal	Stan Wawrinka
2018	Rafael Nadal	Dominic Thiem
2019	Rafael Nadal	Dominic Thiem
2020	Rafael Nadal	Novak Djokovic

Women's Singles

Year	Champion	Final opponent
1968	Nancy Richey	Ann Jones
1969	Margaret Smith Court	Ann Jones
1970	Margaret Smith Court	Helga Niessen
1971	Evonne Goolagong	Helen Gourlay
1972	Billie Jean King	Evonne Goolagong
1973	Margaret Smith Court	Chris Evert
1974	Chris Evert	Olga Morozova
1975	Chris Evert	Martina Navratilova
1976	Sue Barker	Renata Tomanova
1977	Mima Jausovec	Florenta Mihai

Year	Champion	Final opponent	Year	Champion	Final opponent
1978	Virginia Ruzici	Mima Jausovec	2000	Mary Pierce	Conchita Martínez
1979	Chris Evert Lloyd	Wendy Turnbull	2001	Jennifer Capriati	Kim Clijsters
1980	Chris Evert Lloyd	Virginia Ruzici	2002	Serena Williams	Venus Williams
1981	Hana Mandlikova	Sylvia Hanika	2003	Justine Henin-Hardenne	Kim Clijsters
1982	Martina Navratilova	Andrea Jaeger	2004	Anastasia Myskina	Elena Dementieva
1983	Chris Evert Lloyd	Mima Jausovec	2005	Justine Henin-Hardenne	Mary Pierce
1984	Martina Navratilova	Chris Evert Lloyd	2006	Justine Henin-Hardenne	Svetlana Kuznetsova
1985	Chris Evert Lloyd	Martina Navratilova	2007	Justine Henin	Ana Ivanovic
1986	Chris Evert Lloyd	Martina Navratilova	2008	Ana Ivanovic	Dinara Safina
1987	Steffi Graf	Martina Navratilova	2009	Svetlana Kuznetsova	Dinara Safina
1988	Steffi Graf	Natalia Zvereva	2010	Francesca Schiavone	Samantha Stosur
1989	Arantxa Sánchez Vicario	Steffi Graf	2011	Li Na	Francesca Schiavone
1990	Monica Seles	Steffi Graf	2012	Maria Sharapova	Sara Errani
1991	Monica Seles	Arantxa Sánchez Vicario	2013	Serena Williams	Maria Sharapova
1992	Monica Seles	Steffi Graf	2014	Maria Sharapova	Simona Halep
1993	Steffi Graf	Mary Joe Fernandez	2015	Serena Williams	Lucie Safarova
1994	Arantxa Sánchez Vicario	Mary Pierce	2016	Garbiño Muguruza	Serena Williams
1995	Steffi Graf	Arantxa Sánchez Vicario	2017	Jelena Ostapenko	Simona Halep
1996	Steffi Graf	Arantxa Sánchez Vicario	2018	Simona Halep	Sloane Stephens
1997	Iva Majoli	Martina Hingis	2019	Ashleigh Barty	Marketa Vondrousova
1998	Arantxa Sánchez Vicario	Monica Seles	2020	Iga Swiatek	Sofia Kenin
1999	Steffi Graf	Martina Hingis			

Wimbledon Champions, 1925-2019

First contested 1877 for men, 1884 for women. Became an open championship in 1968. Not held 1940-45, 2020.

Men's Singles

Year	Champion	Final opponent	Year	Champion	Final opponent
			1996	Richard Krajicek	MaliVai "Mai" Washington
1925	René Lacoste	Jean Borotra	1997	Pete Sampras	Cedric Pioline
1926	Jean Borotra	Howard Kinsey	1998	Pete Sampras	Goran Ivanisevic
1927	Henri Cochet	Jean Borotra	1999	Pete Sampras	Andre Agassi
1928	René Lacoste	Henri Cochet	2000	Pete Sampras	Patrick Rafter
1929	Henri Cochet	Jean Borotra	2001	Goran Ivanisevic	Patrick Rafter
1930	Bill Tilden	Wilmer Allison	2002	Lleyton Hewitt	David Nalbandian
1931	Sidney B. Wood	Francis X. Shields	2003	Roger Federer	Mark Philippoussis
1932	Ellsworth Vines	Henry Austin	2004	Roger Federer	Andy Roddick
1933	Jack Crawford	Ellsworth Vines	2005	Roger Federer	Andy Roddick
1934	Fred Perry	Jack Crawford	2006	Roger Federer	Rafael Nadal
1935	Fred Perry	Gottfried von Cramm	2007	Roger Federer	Rafael Nadal
1936	Fred Perry	Gottfried von Cramm	2008	Rafael Nadal	Roger Federer
1937	Donald Budge	Gottfried von Cramm	2009	Roger Federer	Andy Roddick
1938	Donald Budge	Henry Austin	2010	Rafael Nadal	Tomas Berdych
1939	Bobby Riggs	Elwood Cooke	2011	Novak Djokovic	Rafael Nadal
1946	Yvon Petra	Geoff E. Brown	2012	Roger Federer	Andy Murray
1947	Jack Kramer	Tom P. Brown	2013	Andy Murray	Novak Djokovic
1948	Bob Falkenburg	John Bromwich	2014	Novak Djokovic	Roger Federer
1949	Ted Schroeder	Jaroslav Drobny	2015	Novak Djokovic	Roger Federer
1950	Budge Patty	Frank Sedgman	2016	Andy Murray	Milos Raonic
1951	Dick Savitt	Ken McGregor	2017	Roger Federer	Marin Cilic
1952	Frank Sedgman	Jaroslav Drobny	2018	Novak Djokovic	Kevin Anderson
1953	Vic Seixas	Kurt Nielsen	2019	Novak Djokovic	Roger Federer
1954	Jaroslav Drobny	Ken Rosewall			
1955	Tony Trabert	Kurt Nielsen		**Women's Singles**	
1956	Lew Hoad	Ken Rosewall	Year	Champion	Final opponent
1957	Lew Hoad	Ashley Cooper	1925	Suzanne Lenglen	Joan Fry
1958	Ashley Cooper	Neale Fraser	1926	Kathleen McKane Godfree	Lili de Alvarez
1959	Alex Olmedo	Rod Laver	1927	Helen Wills	Lili de Alvarez
1960	Neale Fraser	Rod Laver	1928	Helen Wills	Lili de Alvarez
1961	Rod Laver	Chuck McKinley	1929	Helen Wills	Helen H. Jacobs
1962	Rod Laver	Martin Mulligan	1930	Helen Wills Moody	Elizabeth Ryan
1963	Chuck McKinley	Fred Stolle	1931	Cilly Aussem	Hilde Krahwinkel
1964	Roy Emerson	Fred Stolle	1932	Helen Wills Moody	Helen H. Jacobs
1965	Roy Emerson	Fred Stolle	1933	Helen Wills Moody	Dorothy Round
1966	Manuel Santana	Dennis Ralston	1934	Dorothy Round	Helen H. Jacobs
1967	John Newcombe	Wilhelm Bungert	1935	Helen Wills Moody	Helen H. Jacobs
1968	Rod Laver	Tony Roche	1936	Helen H. Jacobs	Hilde Krahwinkel Sperling
1969	Rod Laver	John Newcombe	1937	Dorothy Round	Jadwiga Jedrzejowska
1970	John Newcombe	Ken Rosewall	1938	Helen Wills Moody	Helen H. Jacobs
1971	John Newcombe	Stan Smith	1939	Alice Marble	Kay Stammers
1972	Stan Smith	Ilie Nastase	1946	Pauline Betz	Louise Brough
1973	Jan Kodes	Alex Metreveli	1947	Margaret Osborne	Doris Hart
1974	Jimmy Connors	Ken Rosewall	1948	Louise Brough	Doris Hart
1975	Arthur Ashe	Jimmy Connors	1949	Louise Brough	Margaret Osborne duPont
1976	Björn Borg	Ilie Nastase	1950	Louise Brough	Margaret Osborne duPont
1977	Björn Borg	Jimmy Connors	1951	Doris Hart	Shirley Fry
1978	Björn Borg	Jimmy Connors	1952	Maureen Connolly	Louise Brough
1979	Björn Borg	Roscoe Tanner	1953	Maureen Connolly	Doris Hart
1980	Björn Borg	John McEnroe	1954	Maureen Connolly	Louise Brough
1981	John McEnroe	Björn Borg	1955	Louise Brough	Beverly Fleitz
1982	Jimmy Connors	John McEnroe	1956	Shirley Fry	Angela Buxton
1983	John McEnroe	Chris Lewis	1957	Althea Gibson	Darlene Hard
1984	John McEnroe	Jimmy Connors	1958	Althea Gibson	Angela Mortimer
1985	Boris Becker	Kevin Curren	1959	Maria Bueno	Darlene Hard
1986	Boris Becker	Ivan Lendl	1960	Maria Bueno	Sandra Reynolds
1987	Pat Cash	Ivan Lendl	1961	Angela Mortimer	Christine Truman
1988	Stefan Edberg	Boris Becker	1962	Karen Hantze-Susman	Vera Sukova
1989	Boris Becker	Stefan Edberg	1963	Margaret Smith	Billie Jean Moffitt
1990	Stefan Edberg	Boris Becker	1964	Maria Bueno	Margaret Smith
1991	Michael Stich	Boris Becker	1965	Margaret Smith	Maria Bueno
1992	Andre Agassi	Goran Ivanisevic	1966	Billie Jean King	Maria Bueno
1993	Pete Sampras	Jim Courier	1967	Billie Jean King	Ann Haydon Jones
1994	Pete Sampras	Goran Ivanisevic	1968	Billie Jean King	Judy Tegart
1995	Pete Sampras	Boris Becker	1969	Ann Haydon Jones	Billie Jean King
			1970	Margaret Smith Court	Billie Jean King

Year	Champion	Final opponent	Year	Champion	Final opponent
1971	Evonne Goolagong	Margaret Smith Court	1995	Steffi Graf	Arantxa Sánchez Vicario
1972	Billie Jean King	Evonne Goolagong	1996	Steffi Graf	Arantxa Sánchez Vicario
1973	Billie Jean King	Chris Evert	1997	Martina Hingis	Jana Novotna
1974	Chris Evert	Olga Morozova	1998	Jana Novotna	Nathalie Tauziat
1975	Billie Jean King	Evonne Goolagong Cawley	1999	Lindsay Davenport	Steffi Graf
1976	Chris Evert	Evonne Goolagong Cawley	2000	Venus Williams	Lindsay Davenport
1977	Virginia Wade	Betty Stove	2001	Venus Williams	Justine Henin
1978	Martina Navratilova	Chris Evert	2002	Serena Williams	Venus Williams
1979	Martina Navratilova	Chris Evert Lloyd	2003	Serena Williams	Venus Williams
1980	Evonne Goolagong Cawley	Chris Evert Lloyd	2004	Maria Sharapova	Serena Williams
1981	Chris Evert Lloyd	Hana Mandlikova	2005	Venus Williams	Lindsay Davenport
1982	Martina Navratilova	Chris Evert Lloyd	2006	Amélie Mauresmo	Justine Henin-Hardenne
1983	Martina Navratilova	Andrea Jaeger	2007	Venus Williams	Marion Bartoli
1984	Martina Navratilova	Chris Evert Lloyd	2008	Venus Williams	Serena Williams
1985	Martina Navratilova	Chris Evert Lloyd	2009	Serena Williams	Venus Williams
1986	Martina Navratilova	Hana Mandlikova	2010	Serena Williams	Vera Zvonareva
1987	Martina Navratilova	Steffi Graf	2011	Petra Kvitova	Maria Sharapova
1988	Steffi Graf	Martina Navratilova	2012	Serena Williams	Agnieszka Radwanska
1989	Steffi Graf	Martina Navratilova	2013	Marion Bartoli	Sabine Lisicki
1990	Martina Navratilova	Zina Garrison	2014	Petra Kvitova	Eugenie Bouchard
1991	Steffi Graf	Gabriela Sabatini	2015	Serena Williams	Garbiñe Muguruza
1992	Steffi Graf	Monica Seles	2016	Serena Williams	Angelique Kerber
1993	Steffi Graf	Jana Novotna	2017	Garbiñe Muguruza	Venus Williams
1994	Conchita Martínez	Martina Navratilova	2018	Angelique Kerber	Serena Williams
			2019	Simona Halep	Serena Williams

U.S. Open Champions, 1925-2020

First contested 1881 for men, 1887 for women. The former U.S. National Championship became an open championship in 1968.

Men's Singles

Year	Champion	Final opponent	Year	Champion	Final opponent
1925	Bill Tilden	William Johnston	1986	Ivan Lendl	Miloslav Mecir
1926	René Lacoste	Jean Borotra	1987	Ivan Lendl	Mats Wilander
1927	René Lacoste	Bill Tilden	1988	Mats Wilander	Ivan Lendl
1928	Henri Cochet	Francis Hunter	1989	Boris Becker	Ivan Lendl
1929	Bill Tilden	Francis Hunter	1990	Pete Sampras	Andre Agassi
1930	John Doeg	Francis X. Shields	1991	Stefan Edberg	Jim Courier
1931	Ellsworth Vines	George Lott	1992	Stefan Edberg	Pete Sampras
1932	Ellsworth Vines	Henri Cochet	1993	Pete Sampras	Cedric Pioline
1933	Fred Perry	John Crawford	1994	Andre Agassi	Michael Stich
1934	Fred Perry	Wilmer Allison	1995	Pete Sampras	Andre Agassi
1935	Wilmer Allison	Sidney Wood	1996	Pete Sampras	Michael Chang
1936	Fred Perry	Don Budge	1997	Patrick Rafter	Greg Rusedski
1937	Don Budge	Gottfried von Cramm	1998	Patrick Rafter	Mark Philippoussis
1938	Don Budge	C. Gene Mako	1999	Andre Agassi	Todd Martin
1939	Bobby Riggs	S. Welby Van Horn	2000	Marat Safin	Pete Sampras
1940	Don McNeill	Bobby Riggs	2001	Lleyton Hewitt	Pete Sampras
1941	Bobby Riggs	F. L. Kovacs	2002	Pete Sampras	Andre Agassi
1942	F. R. Schroeder Jr.	Frank Parker	2003	Andy Roddick	Juan Carlos Ferrero
1943	Joseph Hunt	Jack Kramer	2004	Roger Federer	Lleyton Hewitt
1944	Frank Parker	Bill Talbert	2005	Roger Federer	Andre Agassi
1945	Frank Parker	Bill Talbert	2006	Roger Federer	Andy Roddick
1946	Jack Kramer	Tom Brown Jr.	2007	Roger Federer	Novak Djokovic
1947	Jack Kramer	Frank Parker	2008	Roger Federer	Andy Murray
1948	Pancho Gonzales	Eric Sturgess	2009	Juan Martín del Potro	Roger Federer
1949	Pancho Gonzales	F. R. Schroeder Jr.	2010	Rafael Nadal	Novak Djokovic
1950	Arthur Larsen	Herbert Flam	2011	Novak Djokovic	Rafael Nadal
1951	Frank Sedgman	E. Victor Seixas Jr.	2012	Andy Murray	Novak Djokovic
1952	Frank Sedgman	Gardnar Mulloy	2013	Rafael Nadal	Novak Djokovic
1953	Tony Trabert	E. Victor Seixas Jr.	2014	Marin Cilic	Kei Nishikori
1954	E. Victor Seixas Jr.	Rex Hartwig	2015	Novak Djokovic	Roger Federer
1955	Tony Trabert	Ken Rosewall	2016	Stan Wawrinka	Novak Djokovic
1956	Ken Rosewall	Lewis Hoad	2017	Rafael Nadal	Kevin Anderson
1957	Malcolm Anderson	Ashley Cooper	2018	Novak Djokovic	Juan Martín del Potro
1958	Ashley Cooper	Malcolm Anderson	2019	Rafael Nadal	Daniil Medvedev
1959	Neale A. Fraser	Alejandro Olmedo	2020	Dominic Thiem	Alexander Zverev
1960	Neale A. Fraser	Rod Laver			

Women's Singles

Year	Champion	Final opponent
1961	Roy Emerson	Rod Laver
1962	Rod Laver	Roy Emerson
1963	Rafael Osuna	F. A. Froehling III
1964	Roy Emerson	Fred Stolle
1965	Manuel Santana	Cliff Drysdale
1966	Fred Stolle	John Newcombe
1967	John Newcombe	Clark Graebner
1968	Arthur Ashe	Tom Okker
1969	Rod Laver	Tony Roche
1970	Ken Rosewall	Tony Roche
1971	Stan Smith	Jan Kodes
1972	Ilie Nastase	Arthur Ashe
1973	John Newcombe	Jan Kodes
1974	Jimmy Connors	Ken Rosewall
1975	Manuel Orantes	Jimmy Connors
1976	Jimmy Connors	Björn Borg
1977	Guillermo Vilas	Jimmy Connors
1978	Jimmy Connors	Björn Borg
1979	John McEnroe	Vitas Gerulaitis
1980	John McEnroe	Björn Borg
1981	John McEnroe	Björn Borg
1982	Jimmy Connors	Ivan Lendl
1983	Jimmy Connors	Ivan Lendl
1984	John McEnroe	Ivan Lendl
1985	Ivan Lendl	John McEnroe

Year	Champion	Final opponent
1925	Helen Willis	Kathleen McKane
1926	Molla B. Mallory	Elizabeth Ryan
1927	Helen Wills	Betty Nuthall
1928	Helen Wills	Helen H. Jacobs
1929	Helen Wills	Phoebe Holcroft-Watson
1930	Betty Nuthall	Anna McCune Harper
1931	Helen Wills Moody	E. B. Whittingstall
1932	Helen H. Jacobs	Carolin A. Babcock
1933	Helen H. Jacobs	Helen Wills Moody
1934	Helen H. Jacobs	Sarah H. Palfrey
1935	Helen H. Jacobs	Sarah Palfrey Fabyan
1936	Alice Marble	Helen H. Jacobs
1937	Anita Lizana	Jadwiga Jedrzejowska
1938	Alice Marble	Nancye Wynne
1939	Alice Marble	Helen H. Jacobs
1940	Alice Marble	Helen H. Jacobs
1941	Sarah Palfrey Cooke	Pauline Betz
1942	Pauline Betz	Louise Brough
1943	Pauline Betz	Louise Brough
1944	Pauline Betz	Margaret Osborne
1945	Sarah Palfrey Cooke	Pauline Betz
1946	Pauline Betz	Patricia Canning
1947	Louise Brough	Margaret Osborne
1948	Margaret Osborne duPont	Louise Brough
1949	Margaret Osborne duPont	Doris Hart

Year	Champion	Final opponent	Year	Champion	Final opponent
1950	Margaret Osborne duPont	Doris Hart	1986	Martina Navratilova	Helena Sukova
1951	Maureen Connolly	Shirley Fry	1987	Martina Navratilova	Steffi Graf
1952	Maureen Connolly	Doris Hart	1988	Steffi Graf	Gabriela Sabatini
1953	Maureen Connolly	Doris Hart	1989	Steffi Graf	Martina Navratilova
1954	Doris Hart	Louise Brough	1990	Gabriela Sabatini	Steffi Graf
1955	Doris Hart	Patricia Ward	1991	Monica Seles	Martina Navratilova
1956	Shirley Fry	Althea Gibson	1992	Monica Seles	Arantxa Sánchez Vicario
1957	Althea Gibson	Louise Brough	1993	Steffi Graf	Helena Sukova
1958	Althea Gibson	Darlene Hard	1994	Arantxa Sánchez Vicario	Steffi Graf
1959	Maria Bueno	Christine Truman	1995	Steffi Graf	Monica Seles
1960	Darlene Hard	Maria Bueno	1996	Steffi Graf	Monica Seles
1961	Darlene Hard	Ann Haydon	1997	Martina Hingis	Venus Williams
1962	Margaret Smith	Darlene Hard	1998	Lindsay Davenport	Martina Hingis
1963	Maria Bueno	Margaret Smith	1999	Serena Williams	Martina Hingis
1964	Maria Bueno	Carole Caldwell Graebner	2000	Venus Williams	Lindsay Davenport
1965	Margaret Smith	Billie Jean Moffitt	2001	Venus Williams	Serena Williams
1966	Maria Bueno	Nancy Richey	2002	Serena Williams	Venus Williams
1967	Billie Jean King	Ann Haydon Jones	2003	Justine Henin-Hardenne	Kim Clijsters
1968	Virginia Wade	Billie Jean King	2004	Svetlana Kuznetsova	Elena Dementieva
1969	Margaret Smith Court	Nancy Richey	2005	Kim Clijsters	Mary Pierce
1970	Margaret Smith Court	Rosemary Casals	2006	Maria Sharapova	Justine Henin-Hardenne
1971	Billie Jean King	Rosemary Casals	2007	Justine Henin	Svetlana Kuznetsova
1972	Billie Jean King	Kerry Melville	2008	Serena Williams	Jelena Jankovic
1973	Margaret Smith Court	Evonne Goolagong	2009	Kim Clijsters	Caroline Wozniacki
1974	Billie Jean King	Evonne Goolagong	2010	Kim Clijsters	Vera Zvonareva
1975	Chris Evert	Evonne Goolagong Cawley	2011	Samantha Stosur	Serena Williams
1976	Chris Evert	Evonne Goolagong Cawley	2012	Serena Williams	Victoria Azarenka
1977	Chris Evert	Wendy Turnbull	2013	Serena Williams	Victoria Azarenka
1978	Chris Evert	Pam Shriver	2014	Serena Williams	Caroline Wozniacki
1979	Tracy Austin	Chris Evert Lloyd	2015	Flavia Pennetta	Roberta Vinci
1980	Chris Evert Lloyd	Hana Mandlikova	2016	Angelique Kerber	Karolina Pliskova
1981	Tracy Austin	Martina Navratilova	2017	Sloane Stephens	Madison Keys
1982	Chris Evert Lloyd	Hana Mandlikova	2018	Naomi Osaka	Serena Williams
1983	Martina Navratilova	Chris Evert Lloyd	2019	Bianca Andreescu	Serena Williams
1984	Martina Navratilova	Chris Evert Lloyd	2020	Naomi Osaka	Victoria Azarenka
1985	Hana Mandlikova	Martina Navratilova			

Davis Cup, 1955-2019

The Davis Cup began in 1900 as a competition between the U.S. and Great Britain and later expanded to include other countries.

Year	Result	Year	Result	Year	Result
1955	Australia 5, U.S. 0	1977	Australia 3, Italy 1	1999	Australia 3, France 2
1956	Australia 5, U.S. 0	1978	U.S. 4, Great Britain 1	2000	Spain 3, Australia 1
1957	Australia 3, U.S. 2	1979	U.S. 5, Italy 0	2001	France 3, Australia 2
1958	U.S. 3, Australia 2	1980	Czechoslovakia 4, Italy 1	2002	Russia 3, France 2
1959	Australia 3, U.S. 2	1981	U.S. 3, Argentina 1	2003	Australia 3, Spain 1
1960	Australia 4, Italy 1	1982	U.S. 4, France, 1	2004	Spain 3, U.S. 2
1961	Australia 5, Italy 0	1983	Australia 3, Sweden 2	2005	Croatia 3, Slovakia 2
1962	Australia 5, Mexico 0	1984	Sweden 4, U.S. 1	2006	Russia 3, Argentina 2
1963	U.S. 3, Australia 2	1985	Sweden 3, W. Germany 2	2007	U.S. 4, Russia 1
1964	Australia 3, U.S. 2	1986	Australia 3, Sweden 2	2008	Spain 3, Argentina 1
1965	Australia 4, Spain 1	1987	Sweden 5, India 0	2009	Spain 5, Czech Republic 0
1966	Australia 4, India 1	1988	W. Germany 4, Sweden 1	2010	Serbia 3, France 2
1967	Australia 4, Spain 1	1989	W. Germany 3, Sweden 2	2011	Spain 3, Argentina 1
1968	U.S. 4, Australia 1	1990	U.S. 3, Australia 2	2012	Czech Republic 3, Spain 2
1969	U.S. 5, Romania 0	1991	France 3, U.S. 1	2013	Czech Republic 3, Serbia 2
1970	U.S. 5, W. Germany 0	1992	U.S. 3, Switzerland 1	2014	Switzerland 3, France 1
1971	U.S. 3, Romania 2	1993	Germany 4, Australia 1	2015	Great Britain 3, Belgium 1
1972	U.S. 3, Romania 2	1994	Sweden 4, Russia 1	2016	Argentina 3, Croatia 2
1973	Australia 5, U.S. 0	1995	U.S. 3, Russia 2	2017	France 3, Belgium 2
1974	South Africa (default by India)	1996	France 3, Sweden 2	2018	Croatia 3, France 1
1975	Sweden 3, Czechoslovakia 2	1997	Sweden 5, U.S. 0	2019	Spain 2, Canada 0
1976	Italy 4, Chile 1	1998	Sweden 4, Italy 1		

Note: The challenge round format, which guaranteed the previous year's winner a spot in the finals at home, was eliminated in 1972.

All-Time Grand Slam Singles Title Leaders

Men	Australian Open	French Open[1]	Wimbledon	U.S. Open	Total
Roger Federer*	2004, '06-'07, '10, '17-'18	2009	2003-07, '09, '12, '17	2004-08	20
Rafael Nadal*	2009	2005-08, '10-'14, '17-'20	2008, '10	2010, '13, '17, '19	20
Novak Djokovic*	2008, '11-'13, '15-'16, '19, '20	2016	2011, '14-'15, '18-'19	2011, '15, '18	17
Pete Sampras	1994, '97	—	1993-95, 1997-2000	1990, '93, '95-'96, 2002	14
Roy Emerson	1961, '63-'67	1963, '67	1964-65	1961, '64	12
Björn Borg	—	1974-75, '78-'81	1976-80	—	11
Rod Laver	1960, '62, '69	1962, '69	1961-62, '68-'69	1962, '69	11
Bill Tilden	—	—	1920-21, '30	1920-25, '29	10
Andre Agassi	1995, 2000-01, '03	1999	1992	1994, '99	8
Jimmy Connors	1974	—	1974, '82	1974, '76, '78, '82-'83	8
Ivan Lendl	1989-90	1984, '86-'87	—	1985-87	8
Fred Perry	1934	1935	1934-36	1933-34, '36	8
Ken Rosewall	1953, '55, '71-'72	1953, '68	—	1956, '70	8

Women	Australian Open	French Open[1]	Wimbledon	U.S. Open	Total
Margaret Smith Court	1960-66, '69-'71, '73	1962, '64, '69-'70, '73	1963, '65, '70	1962, '65, '69-'70, '73	24
Serena Williams*	2003, '05, '07, '09-'10, '15, '17	2002, '13, '15	2002-03, '09-'10, '12, '15-'16	1999, 2002, '08, '12-'14	23
Steffi Graf	1988-90, '94	1987-88, '93, '95-'96, '99	1988-89, '91-'93, '95-'96	1988-89, '93, '95-'96	22
Helen Wills Moody	—	1928-30, '32	1927-30, '32-'33, '35, '38	1923-25, '27-'29, '31	19
Chris Evert	1982, '84	1974-75, '79-'80, '83, '85-'86	1974, '76, '81	1975-78, '80, '82	18
Martina Navratilova	1981, '83, '85	1982, '84	1978-79, '82-'87, '90	1983-84, '86-'87	18
Billie Jean King	1968	1972	1966-68, '72-'73, '75	1967, '71-'72, '74	12
Suzanne Lenglen	—	1920-23, '25-'26	1919-23, '25	—	9
Maureen Connolly	1953	1953-54	1952-54	1951-53	9
Monica Seles	1991-93, '96	1990-92	—	1991-92	

* = Player active in 2020. (1) Prior to 1925, French Open entry was limited to members of French clubs.

AUTO RACING

Indianapolis 500 Winners, 1911-2020

At Indianapolis Motor Speedway in Indianapolis, IN. Not held 1917-18, 1942-45. * = Race record.

Year	Driver(s), car[1]	Avg. mph	Year	Driver(s), car[1]	Avg. mph
1911	Ray Harroun, Marmon	74.602	1969	Mario Andretti, Hawk-Ford	156.867
1912	Joe Dawson, National	78.719	1970	Al Unser, P.J. Colt-Ford	155.749
1913	Jules Goux, Peugeot	75.933	1971	Al Unser, P.J. Colt-Ford	157.735
1914	René Thomas, Delage	82.474	1972	Mark Donohue, McLaren-Offy	162.962
1915	Ralph DePalma, Mercedes	89.840	1973	Gordon Johncock, Eagle-Offy	159.036
1916	Dario Resta, Peugeot	84.001	1974	Johnny Rutherford, McLaren-Offy	158.589
1919	Howdy Wilcox, Peugeot	88.050	1975	Bobby Unser, Eagle-Offy	149.213
1920	Gaston Chevrolet, Frontenac	88.618	1976	Johnny Rutherford, McLaren-Offy	148.725
1921	Tommy Milton, Frontenac	89.621	1977	A. J. Foyt, Coyote-Foyt	161.331
1922	Jimmy Murphy, Duesenberg-Miller	94.484	1978	Al Unser, Lola-Cosworth	161.363
1923	Tommy Milton, Miller	90.954	1979	Rick Mears, Penske-Cosworth	158.899
1924	L. L. Corum/Joe Boyer, Duesenberg	98.234	1980	Johnny Rutherford, Chaparral-Cosworth	142.862
1925	Peter DePaolo, Duesenberg	101.127	1981	Bobby Unser, Penske-Cosworth	139.184
1926	Frank Lockhart, Miller	95.904	1982	Gordon Johncock, Wildcat-Cosworth	162.029
1927	George Souders, Duesenberg	97.545	1983	Tom Sneva, March-Cosworth	162.117
1928	Louis Meyer, Miller	99.482	1984	Rick Mears, March-Cosworth	163.612
1929	Ray Keech, Miller	97.585	1985	Danny Sullivan, March-Cosworth	152.982
1930	Billy Arnold, Summers-Miller	100.448	1986	Bobby Rahal, March-Cosworth	170.722
1931	Louis Schneider, Stevens-Miller	96.629	1987	Al Unser, March-Cosworth	162.175
1932	Fred Frame, Wetteroth-Miller	104.144	1988	Rick Mears, Penske-Chevy V8	144.809
1933	Louis Meyer, Miller	104.162	1989	Emerson Fittipaldi, Penske-Chevy Indy V8	167.581
1934	Bill Cummings, Miller	104.863	1990	Arie Luyendyk, Lola-Chevy Indy V8	185.981
1935	Kelly Petillo, Wetteroth-Offy	106.240	1991	Rick Mears, Penske-Chevy Indy V8	176.457
1936	Louis Meyer, Stevens-Miller	109.069	1992	Al Unser Jr., Galmer-Chevy Indy V8A	134.477
1937	Wilbur Shaw, Shaw-Offy	113.580	1993	Emerson Fittipaldi, Penske-Chevy Indy V8C	157.207
1938	Floyd Roberts, Wetteroth-Miller	117.200	1994	Al Unser Jr., Penske-Mercedes Benz	160.872
1939	Wilbur Shaw, Maserati	115.035	1995	Jacques Villeneuve, Reynard-Ford Cosworth XB	153.616
1940	Wilbur Shaw, Maserati	114.277	1996	Buddy Lazier, Reynard-Ford Cosworth XB	147.956
1941	Floyd Davis/Mauri Rose, Wetteroth-Offy	115.117	1997	Arie Luyendyk, G Force-Aurora	145.827
1946	George Robson, Adams-Sparks	114.820	1998	Eddie Cheever Jr., Dallara-Aurora	145.155
1947	Mauri Rose, Deidt-Offy	116.338	1999	Kenny Brack, Dallara-Aurora	153.176
1948	Mauri Rose, Deidt-Offy	119.814	2000	Juan Pablo Montoya, G Force-Oldsmobile	167.607
1949	Bill Holland, Deidt-Offy	121.327	2001	Helio Castroneves, Dallara-Oldsmobile	141.574
1950	Johnnie Parsons, Kurtis-Offy	124.002	2002	Helio Castroneves, Dallara-Chevrolet	166.499
1951	Lee Wallard, Kurtis-Offy	126.244	2003	Gil de Ferran, G Force-Toyota	156.291
1952	Troy Ruttman, Kuzma-Offy	128.922	2004	Buddy Rice, G Force-Honda	138.518
1953	Bill Vukovich, KK500A-Offy	127.740	2005	Dan Wheldon, Dallara-Honda	157.603
1954	Bill Vukovich, KK500A-Offy	130.840	2006	Sam Hornish Jr., Dallara-Honda	157.085
1955	Bob Sweikert, KK500D-Offy	128.209	2007	Dario Franchitti, Dallara-Honda	151.774
1956	Pat Flaherty, Watson-Offy	128.490	2008	Scott Dixon, Dallara-Honda	143.567
1957	Sam Hanks, Salih-Offy	135.601	2009	Helio Castroneves, Dallara-Honda	150.318
1958	Jimmy Bryan, Salih-Offy	133.791	2010	Dario Franchitti, Dallara-Honda	161.623
1959	Rodger Ward, Watson-Offy	135.857	2011	Dan Wheldon, Dallara-Honda	170.265
1960	Jim Rathmann, Watson-Offy	138.767	2012	Dario Franchitti, Dallara-Honda	167.734
1961	A. J. Foyt, Trevis-Offy	139.130	2013	Tony Kanaan, Dallara-Chevrolet	187.433*
1962	Rodger Ward, Watson-Offy	140.293	2014	Ryan Hunter-Reay, Dallara-Honda	186.563
1963	Parnelli Jones, Watson-Offy	143.137	2015	Juan Pablo Montoya, Dallara-Chevrolet	161.341
1964	A. J. Foyt, Watson-Offy	147.350	2016	Alexander Rossi, Dallara-Honda	166.634
1965	Jim Clark, Lotus-Ford	150.686	2017	Takuma Sato, Dallara-Honda	155.395
1966	Graham Hill, Lola-Ford	144.317	2018	Will Power, Dallara-Chevrolet	166.935
1967	A. J. Foyt, Coyote-Ford	151.207	2019	Simon Pagenaud, Dallara-Chevrolet	175.794
1968	Bobby Unser, Eagle-Offy	152.882	2020	Takuma Sato, Dallara-Honda	157.724

Note: The race was less than 500 mi in the following years: 1916 (300 mi), 1926 (400 mi), 1950 (345 mi), 1973 (332.5 mi), 1975 (435 mi), 1976 (255 mi), 2004 (450 mi), 2007 (415 mi). (1) Chassis-engine.

IndyCar Series Champions, 1996-2019

A breakaway group of Championship Auto Racing Teams (CART) drivers began the Indy Racing League (IRL) in 1994; it awarded its first championship in 1996. Known as the IndyCar Series in 2003-11 and as IndyCar from 2011 on. Merged with Champ Car World Series, 2008, under the IndyCar name.

Year	Driver	Year	Driver	Year	Driver	Year	Driver	Year	Driver
1996	Scott Sharp; Buzz Calkins (tie)	2000	Buddy Lazier	2005	Dan Wheldon	2010	Dario Franchitti	2015	Scott Dixon
1997	Tony Stewart	2001	Sam Hornish Jr.	2006	Sam Hornish Jr.	2011	Dario Franchitti	2016	Simon Pagenaud
1998	Kenny Brack	2002	Sam Hornish Jr.	2007	Dario Franchitti	2012	Ryan Hunter-Reay	2017	Josef Newgarden
1999	Greg Ray	2003	Scott Dixon	2008	Scott Dixon	2013	Scott Dixon	2018	Scott Dixon
		2004	Tony Kanaan	2009	Dario Franchitti	2014	Will Power	2019	Josef Newgarden

Champ Car World Series Winners, 1959-2007

Known as U.S. Auto Club, 1959-78; Championship Auto Racing Teams (CART), 1979-2003; Champ Car World Series, 2004-07. The Vanderbilt Cup became the series championship trophy in 2000. Merged with Indy Racing League (now IndyCar) in 2008.

Year	Driver	Year	Driver	Year	Driver	Year	Driver	Year	Driver
1959	Rodger Ward	1969	Mario Andretti	1979	Rick Mears	1989	Emerson Fittipaldi	1999	Juan Montoya
1960	A. J. Foyt	1970	Al Unser	1980	Johnny Rutherford	1990	Al Unser Jr.	2000	Gil de Ferran
1961	A. J. Foyt	1971	Joe Leonard	1981	Rick Mears	1991	Michael Andretti	2001	Gil de Ferran
1962	Rodger Ward	1972	Joe Leonard	1982	Rick Mears	1992	Bobby Rahal	2002	Cristiano da Matta
1963	A. J. Foyt	1973	Roger McCluskey	1983	Al Unser	1993	Nigel Mansell	2003	Paul Tracy
1964	A. J. Foyt	1974	Bobby Unser	1984	Mario Andretti	1994	Al Unser Jr.	2004	Sébastien Bourdais
1965	Mario Andretti	1975	A. J. Foyt	1985	Al Unser	1995	Jacques Villeneuve	2005	Sébastien Bourdais
1966	Mario Andretti	1976	Gordon Johncock	1986	Bobby Rahal	1996	Jimmy Vasser	2006	Sébastien Bourdais
1967	A. J. Foyt	1977	Tom Sneva	1987	Bobby Rahal	1997	Alex Zanardi	2007	Sébastien Bourdais
1968	Bobby Unser	1978	Tom Sneva	1988	Danny Sullivan	1998	Alex Zanardi		

NASCAR Cup Series Champions, 1949-2019

Known as Strictly Stock, 1949; Grand National, 1950-70; Winston Cup, 1971-2003; Sprint Cup, 2004-16; Monster Energy NASCAR Cup, 2017-present.

Year	Driver	Year	Driver	Year	Driver	Year	Driver	Year	Driver
1949	Red Byron	1964	Richard Petty	1978	Cale Yarborough	1992	Alan Kulwicki	2006	Jimmie Johnson
1950	Bill Rexford	1965	Ned Jarrett	1979	Richard Petty	1993	Dale Earnhardt	2007	Jimmie Johnson
1951	Herb Thomas	1966	David Pearson	1980	Dale Earnhardt	1994	Dale Earnhardt	2008	Jimmie Johnson
1952	Tim Flock	1967	Richard Petty	1981	Darrell Waltrip	1995	Jeff Gordon	2009	Jimmie Johnson
1953	Herb Thomas	1968	David Pearson	1982	Darrell Waltrip	1996	Terry Labonte	2010	Jimmie Johnson
1954	Lee Petty	1969	David Pearson	1983	Bobby Allison	1997	Jeff Gordon	2011	Tony Stewart
1955	Tim Flock	1970	Bobby Isaac	1984	Terry Labonte	1998	Jeff Gordon	2012	Brad Keselowski
1956	Buck Baker	1971	Richard Petty	1985	Darrell Waltrip	1999	Dale Jarrett	2013	Jimmie Johnson
1957	Buck Baker	1972	Richard Petty	1986	Dale Earnhardt	2000	Bobby Labonte	2014	Kevin Harvick
1958	Lee Petty	1973	Benny Parsons	1987	Dale Earnhardt	2001	Jeff Gordon	2015	Kyle Busch
1959	Lee Petty	1974	Richard Petty	1988	Bill Elliott	2002	Tony Stewart	2016	Jimmie Johnson
1960	Rex White	1975	Richard Petty	1989	Rusty Wallace	2003	Matt Kenseth	2017	Martin Truex Jr.
1961	Ned Jarrett	1976	Cale Yarborough	1990	Dale Earnhardt	2004	Kurt Busch	2018	Joey Logano
1962	Joe Weatherly	1977	Cale Yarborough	1991	Dale Earnhardt	2005	Tony Stewart	2019	Kyle Busch
1963	Joe Weatherly								

NASCAR Cup Series Rookie of the Year, 1958-2019

Year	Driver	Year	Driver	Year	Driver	Year	Driver	Year	Driver
1958	Shorty Rollins	1971	Walter Ballard	1984	Rusty Wallace	1996	Johnny Benson	2008	Regan Smith
1959	Richard Petty	1972	Larry Smith	1985	Ken Schrader	1997	Mike Skinner	2009	Joey Logano
1960	David Pearson	1973	Lennie Pond	1986	Alan Kulwicki	1998	Kenny Irwin	2010	Kevin Conway
1961	Woodie Wilson	1974	Earl Ross	1987	Davey Allison	1999	Tony Stewart	2011	Andy Lally
1962	Tom Cox	1975	Bruce Hill	1988	Ken Bouchard	2000	Matt Kenseth	2012	Stephen Leicht
1963	Billy Wade	1976	Skip Manning	1989	Dick Trickle	2001	Kevin Harvick	2013	Ricky Stenhouse Jr.
1964	Doug Cooper	1977	Ricky Rudd	1990	Rob Moroso	2002	Ryan Newman	2014	Kyle Larson
1965	Sam McQuagg	1978	Ronnie Thomas	1991	Bobby Hamilton	2003	Jamie McMurray	2015	Brett Moffitt
1966	James Hylton	1979	Dale Earnhardt	1992	Jimmy Hensley	2004	Kasey Kahne	2016	Chase Elliott
1967	Donnie Allison	1980	Jody Ridley	1993	Jeff Gordon	2005	Kyle Busch	2017	Erik Jones
1968	Pete Hamilton	1981	Ron Bouchard	1994	Jeff Burton	2006	Denny Hamlin	2018	William Byron
1969	Dick Brooks	1982	Geoff Bodine	1995	Ricky Craven	2007	Juan Pablo Montoya	2019	Daniel Hemric
1970	Bill Dennis	1983	Sterling Marlin						

Daytona 500 Winners, 1959-2020

At Daytona International Speedway in Daytona Beach, FL.

Year	Driver, car	Avg. mph	Year	Driver, car	Avg. mph	Year	Driver, car	Avg. mph
1959	Lee Petty, Oldsmobile	135.521	1980	Buddy Baker, Oldsmobile	177.602	2001	Michael Waltrip, Chevrolet	161.783
1960	Junior Johnson, Chevrolet	124.740	1981	Richard Petty, Buick	169.651	2002	Ward Burton, Dodge	142.971
1961	Marvin Panch, Pontiac	149.601	1982	Bobby Allison, Buick	153.991	2003	Michael Waltrip, Chevrolet	133.870
1962	Fireball Roberts, Pontiac	152.529	1983	Cale Yarborough, Pontiac	155.979	2004	Dale Earnhardt Jr.,	
1963	Tiny Lund, Ford	151.566	1984	Cale Yarborough,			Chevrolet	156.345
1964	Richard Petty, Plymouth	154.334		Chevrolet	150.994	2005	Jeff Gordon, Chevrolet	135.173
1965	Fred Lorenzen, Ford	141.539	1985	Bill Elliott, Ford	172.265	2006	Jimmie Johnson, Chevrolet	142.667
1966	Richard Petty, Plymouth	160.627	1986	Geoff Bodine, Chevrolet	148.124	2007	Kevin Harvick, Chevrolet	149.335
1967	Mario Andretti, Ford	146.926	1987	Bill Elliott, Ford	176.263	2008	Ryan Newman, Dodge	152.672
1968	Cale Yarborough, Mercury	143.251	1988	Bobby Allison, Buick	137.531	2009	Matt Kenseth, Ford	132.816
1969	LeeRoy Yarbrough, Ford	157.950	1989	Darrell Waltrip, Chevrolet	148.466	2010	Jamie McMurray, Chevrolet	137.284
1970	Pete Hamilton, Plymouth	149.601	1990	Derrike Cope, Chevrolet	165.761	2011	Trevor Bayne, Ford	130.326
1971	Richard Petty, Plymouth	144.462	1991	Ernie Irvan, Chevrolet	148.148	2012	Matt Kenseth, Ford	140.256
1972	A. J. Foyt, Mercury	161.550	1992	Davey Allison, Ford	160.256	2013	Jimmie Johnson, Chevrolet	159.250
1973	Richard Petty, Dodge	157.205	1993	Dale Jarrett, Chevrolet	154.972	2014	Dale Earnhardt Jr.,	
1974	Richard Petty, Dodge	140.894	1994	Sterling Marlin, Chevrolet	156.931		Chevrolet	145.290
1975	Benny Parsons, Chevrolet	153.649	1995	Sterling Marlin, Chevrolet	141.710	2015	Joey Logano, Ford	161.939
1976	David Pearson, Mercury	152.181	1996	Dale Jarrett, Ford	154.308	2016	Denny Hamlin, Toyota	157.549
1977	Cale Yarborough,		1997	Jeff Gordon, Chevrolet	148.295	2017	Kurt Busch, Ford	143.187
	Chevrolet	153.218	1998	Dale Earnhardt, Chevrolet	172.712	2018	Austin Dillon, Chevrolet	150.545
1978	Bobby Allison, Ford	159.730	1999	Jeff Gordon, Chevrolet	161.551	2019	Denny Hamlin, Toyota	137.440
1979	Richard Petty, Oldsmobile	143.977	2000	Dale Jarrett, Ford	155.669	2020	Denny Hamlin, Toyota	141.110

Note: The race was not 500 mi in the following years: 1965 (332.5 mi), 1966 (495 mi), 1974 (450 mi), 2003 (272.5 mi), 2009 (380 mi), 2020 (522.5 mi).

NASCAR All-Star Race Winners, 1985-2020

At Charlotte Motor Speedway in Concord, NC, 1985-2019; Bristol Motor Speedway in Bristol, TN, 2020.

Year	Driver, car	Year	Driver, car	Year	Driver, car
1985	Darrell Waltrip, Chevrolet	1997	Jeff Gordon, Chevrolet	2009	Tony Stewart, Chevrolet
1986	Bill Elliott, Ford	1998	Mark Martin, Ford	2010	Kurt Busch, Dodge
1987	Dale Earnhardt, Chevrolet	1999	Terry Labonte, Chevrolet	2011	Carl Edwards, Ford
1988	Terry Labonte, Chevrolet	2000	Dale Earnhardt Jr., Chevrolet	2012	Jimmie Johnson, Chevrolet
1989	Rusty Wallace, Pontiac	2001	Jeff Gordon, Chevrolet	2013	Jimmie Johnson, Chevrolet
1990	Dale Earnhardt, Chevrolet	2002	Ryan Newman, Ford	2014	Jamie McMurray, Chevrolet
1991	Davey Allison, Ford	2003	Jimmie Johnson, Chevrolet	2015	Denny Hamlin, Toyota
1992	Davey Allison, Ford	2004	Matt Kenseth, Ford	2016	Joey Logano, Ford
1993	Dale Earnhardt, Chevrolet	2005	Mark Martin, Ford	2017	Kyle Busch, Toyota
1994	Geoff Bodine, Ford	2006	Jimmie Johnson, Chevrolet	2018	Kevin Harvick, Ford
1995	Jeff Gordon, Chevrolet	2007	Kevin Harvick, Chevrolet	2019	Kyle Larson, Chevrolet
1996	Michael Waltrip, Ford	2008	Kasey Kahne, Dodge	2020	Chase Elliott, Chevrolet

Coca-Cola 600 Winners, 1960-2020

At Charlotte Motor Speedway in Concord, NC. Known as the World 600, 1960-85. * = Rain-shortened.

Year	Driver, car	Avg. mph	Year	Driver, car	Avg. mph	Year	Driver, car	Avg. mph
1960	Joe Lee Johnson, Chevrolet	107.735	1979	Darrell Waltrip, Chevrolet	136.674	2000	Matt Kenseth, Ford	142.640
1961	David Pearson, Pontiac	111.633	1980	Benny Parsons, Chevrolet	119.265	2001	Jeff Burton, Ford	138.107
1962	Nelson Stacy, Ford	125.552	1981	Bobby Allison, Buick	129.326	2002	Mark Martin, Ford	137.729
1963	Fred Lorenzen, Ford	132.418	1982	Neil Bonnett, Ford	130.058	2003	Jimmie Johnson, Chevrolet	126.198*
1964	Jim Paschal, Plymouth	125.772	1983	Neil Bonnett, Chevrolet	140.707	2004	Jimmie Johnson, Chevrolet	142.763
1965	Fred Lorenzen, Ford	121.722	1984	Bobby Allison, Buick	129.233	2005	Jimmie Johnson, Chevrolet	114.698
1966	Marvin Panch, Plymouth	135.042	1985	Darrell Waltrip, Chevrolet	141.807	2006	Kasey Kahne, Dodge	128.840
1967	Jim Paschal, Plymouth	135.832	1986	Dale Earnhardt, Chevrolet	140.406	2007	Casey Mears, Chevrolet	130.222
1968	Buddy Baker, Dodge	104.207*	1987	Kyle Petty, Ford	131.483	2008	Kasey Kahne, Dodge	135.772
1969	LeeRoy Yarbrough, Mercury	134.361	1988	Darrell Waltrip, Chevrolet	124.460	2009	David Reutimann, Toyota	120.899*
1970	Donnie Allison, Ford	129.680	1989	Darrell Waltrip, Chevrolet	144.077	2010	Kurt Busch, Dodge	144.966
1971	Bobby Allison, Mercury	140.422	1990	Rusty Wallace, Pontiac	137.650	2011	Kevin Harvick, Chevrolet	132.414
1972	Buddy Baker, Dodge	142.255	1991	Davey Allison, Ford	138.951	2012	Kasey Kahne, Chevrolet	155.687
1973	Buddy Baker, Dodge	134.890	1992	Dale Earnhardt, Chevrolet	132.980	2013	Kevin Harvick, Chevrolet	130.521
1974	David Pearson, Mercury	135.720	1993	Dale Earnhardt, Chevrolet	145.504	2014	Jimmie Johnson, Chevrolet	145.484
1975	Richard Petty, Dodge	145.327	1994	Jeff Gordon, Chevrolet	139.445	2015	Carl Edwards, Ford	147.803
1976	David Pearson, Mercury	137.352	1995	Bobby Labonte, Chevrolet	151.952	2016	Martin Truex Jr., Toyota	160.655
1977	Richard Petty, Dodge	137.676	1996	Dale Jarrett, Ford	147.581	2017	Austin Dillon, Chevrolet	138.800
1978	Darrell Waltrip, Chevrolet	138.355	1997	Jeff Gordon, Chevrolet	136.745*	2018	Kyle Busch, Toyota	136.692
			1998	Jeff Gordon, Chevrolet	136.424	2019	Martin Truex Jr., Toyota	124.074
			1999	Jeff Burton, Ford	151.367	2020	Brad Keselowski, Ford	135.042

Brickyard 400 Winners, 1994-2020

At Indianapolis Motor Speedway in Indianapolis, IN.

Year	Driver, car	Avg. mph	Year	Driver, car	Avg. mph	Year	Driver, car	Avg. mph
1994	Jeff Gordon, Chevrolet	131.977	2003	Kevin Harvick, Chevrolet	134.554	2012	Jimmie Johnson, Chevrolet	137.680
1995	Dale Earnhardt, Chevrolet	155.206	2004	Jeff Gordon, Chevrolet	115.037	2013	Ryan Newman, Chevrolet	153.485
1996	Dale Jarrett, Ford	139.508	2005	Tony Stewart, Chevrolet	118.782	2014	Jeff Gordon, Chevrolet	150.297
1997	Ricky Rudd, Ford	130.814	2006	Jimmie Johnson, Chevrolet	137.182	2015	Kyle Busch, Toyota	131.656
1998	Jeff Gordon, Chevrolet	126.772	2007	Tony Stewart, Chevrolet	117.379	2016	Kyle Busch, Toyota	128.940
1999	Dale Jarrett, Ford	148.194	2008	Jimmie Johnson, Chevrolet	115.117	2017	Kasey Kahne, Chevrolet	114.384
2000	Bobby Labonte, Pontiac	155.912	2009	Jimmie Johnson, Chevrolet	145.882	2018	Brad Keselowski, Ford	128.629
2001	Jeff Gordon, Chevrolet	130.790	2010	Jamie McMurray, Chevrolet	136.054	2019	Kevin Harvick, Ford	119.443
2002	Bill Elliott, Dodge	125.033	2011	Paul Menard, Chevrolet	140.762	2020	Kevin Harvick, Ford	123.162

Bass Pro Shops Night Race Winners, 1961-2020

At Bristol Motor Speedway in Bristol, TN. * = Rain-shortened.

Year	Driver, car	Avg. mph	Year	Driver, car	Avg. mph	Year	Driver, car	Avg. mph
1961	Jack Smith, Pontiac	68.373	1981	Darrell Waltrip, Buick	84.723	2002	Jeff Gordon, Chevrolet	77.097
1962	Bobby Johns, Pontiac	73.320	1982	Darrell Waltrip, Buick	94.318	2003	Kurt Busch, Ford	77.421
1963	Fred Lorenzen, Ford	74.844	1983	Darrell Waltrip, Chevrolet	89.430*	2004	Dale Earnhardt Jr., Chevrolet	88.538
1964	Fred Lorenzen, Ford	78.044	1984	Terry Labonte, Chevrolet	85.365			
1965	Ned Jarrett, Ford	61.826	1985	Dale Earnhardt, Chevrolet	81.388	2005	Matt Kenseth, Ford	84.678
1966	Paul Goldsmith, Plymouth	77.963	1986	Dale Earnhardt, Chevrolet	86.934	2006	Matt Kenseth, Ford	90.025
1967	Richard Petty, Plymouth	78.705	1987	Dale Earnhardt, Chevrolet	90.373	2007	Carl Edwards, Ford	89.006
1968	David Pearson, Ford	76.310	1988	Dale Earnhardt, Chevrolet	78.775	2008	Carl Edwards, Ford	91.581
1969	David Pearson, Ford	79.737	1989	Darrell Waltrip, Chevrolet	85.554	2009	Kyle Busch, Toyota	84.820
1970	Bobby Allison, Dodge	84.880	1990	Ernie Irvan, Chevrolet	91.782	2010	Kyle Busch, Toyota	99.071
1971	Charlie Glotzbach, Chevrolet	101.074	1991	Alan Kulwicki, Ford	82.028	2011	Brad Keselowski, Dodge	96.753
			1992	Darrell Waltrip, Chevrolet	91.198	2012	Denny Hamlin, Toyota	84.402
1972	Bobby Allison, Chevrolet	92.735	1993	Mark Martin, Ford	88.172	2013	Matt Kenseth, Toyota	90.279
1973	Benny Parsons, Chevrolet	91.342	1994	Rusty Wallace, Ford	91.363	2014	Joey Logano, Ford	92.965
1974	Cale Yarborough, Chevrolet	75.430	1995	Terry Labonte, Chevrolet	81.979	2015	Joey Logano, Ford	96.890
1975	Richard Petty, Dodge	97.016	1996	Rusty Wallace, Ford	91.267	2016	Kevin Harvick, Chevrolet	77.968
1976	Cale Yarborough, Chevrolet	99.175	1997	Dale Jarrett, Ford	80.013	2017	Kyle Busch, Toyota	95.969
1977	Cale Yarborough, Chevrolet	79.726	1998	Mark Martin, Ford	86.949	2018	Kurt Busch, Ford	89.538
1978	Cale Yarborough, Olds.	88.628	1999	Dale Earnhardt, Chevrolet	91.276	2019	Denny Hamlin, Toyota	94.531
1979	Darrell Waltrip, Chevrolet	91.493	2000	Rusty Wallace, Ford	85.394	2020	Kevin Harvick, Ford	95.911
1980	Cale Yarborough, Chevrolet	86.973	2001	Tony Stewart, Pontiac	85.106			

Formula One World Drivers' Champions, 1950-2019

Awarded by the Fédération Internationale de l'Automobile (FIA); champions determined through a series of Grand Prix races.

Year	Driver, country	Year	Driver, country	Year	Driver, country
1950	Giuseppe "Nino" Farina, Italy	1974	Emerson Fittipaldi, Brazil	1997	Jacques Villeneuve, Canada
1951	Juan Manuel Fangio, Argentina	1975	Niki Lauda, Austria	1998	Mika Hakkinen, Finland
1952	Alberto Ascari, Italy	1976	James Hunt, England, UK	1999	Mika Hakkinen, Finland
1953	Alberto Ascari, Italy	1977	Niki Lauda, Austria	2000	Michael Schumacher, Germany
1954	Juan Manuel Fangio, Argentina	1978	Mario Andretti, United States	2001	Michael Schumacher, Germany
1955	Juan Manuel Fangio, Argentina	1979	Jody Scheckter, South Africa	2002	Michael Schumacher, Germany
1956	Juan Manuel Fangio, Argentina	1980	Alan Jones, Australia	2003	Michael Schumacher, Germany
1957	Juan Manuel Fangio, Argentina	1981	Nelson Piquet, Brazil	2004	Michael Schumacher, Germany
1958	Mike Hawthorn, England, UK	1982	Keke Rosberg, Finland	2005	Fernando Alonso, Spain
1959	Jack Brabham, Australia	1983	Nelson Piquet, Brazil	2006	Fernando Alonso, Spain
1960	Jack Brabham, Australia	1984	Niki Lauda, Austria	2007	Kimi Raikkonen, Finland
1961	Phil Hill, United States	1985	Alain Prost, France	2008	Lewis Hamilton, England, UK
1962	Graham Hill, England, UK	1986	Alain Prost, France	2009	Jenson Button, England, UK
1963	Jim Clark, Scotland, UK	1987	Nelson Piquet, Brazil	2010	Sebastian Vettel, Germany
1964	John Surtees, England, UK	1988	Ayrton Senna, Brazil	2011	Sebastian Vettel, Germany
1965	Jim Clark, Scotland, UK	1989	Alain Prost, France	2012	Sebastian Vettel, Germany
1966	Jack Brabham, Australia	1990	Ayrton Senna, Brazil	2013	Sebastian Vettel, Germany
1967	Denis Hulme, New Zealand	1991	Ayrton Senna, Brazil	2014	Lewis Hamilton, England, UK
1968	Graham Hill, England, UK	1992	Nigel Mansell, England, UK	2015	Lewis Hamilton, England, UK
1969	Jackie Stewart, Scotland, UK	1993	Alain Prost, France	2016	Nico Rosberg, Germany
1970	Jochen Rindt, Austria	1994	Michael Schumacher, Germany	2017	Lewis Hamilton, England, UK
1971	Jackie Stewart, Scotland, UK	1995	Michael Schumacher, Germany	2018	Lewis Hamilton, England, UK
1972	Emerson Fittipaldi, Brazil	1996	Damon Hill, England, UK	2019	Lewis Hamilton, England, UK
1973	Jackie Stewart, Scotland, UK				

BOXING

There are many boxing governing bodies, including the World Boxing Assn. (WBA; known as the National Boxing Assn. [NBA] until 1962), World Boxing Council (WBC), International Boxing Fed. (IBF), World Boxing Org., N. American Boxing Fed., and European Boxing Union. All have their own champions and divisions.

Boxing Champions by Class

Class (weight limit)	WBA Champion	WBC Champion	IBF Champion
Heavyweight (none)	Anthony Joshua, UK[1]	Tyson Fury, UK	Anthony Joshua, UK
	Manuel Charr, Germany		
Cruiserweight (200 lbs)	Arsen Goulamirian, France[1]	Ilunga Makabu, Dem. Rep. of	Mairis Briedis, Latvia
	Beibut Shumenov, Kazakhstan	the Congo	
Light Heavyweight (175 lbs)	Dmitry Bivol, Russia[1]	Artur Beterbiev, Russia	Artur Beterbiev, Russia
	Jean Pascal, Canada		
Super Middleweight (168 lbs)	Callum Smith, UK[1]	Vacant	Caleb Plant, U.S.
	Canelo Alvarez, Mexico		
Middleweight (160 lbs)	Canelo Alvarez, Mexico[1]	Jermall Charlo, U.S.	Gennady Golovkin, Kazakhstan
	Ryota Murata, Japan		
Super Welterweight/	Jermell Charlo, U.S.[1]	Jermell Charlo, U.S.	Jermell Charlo, U.S.
Jr. Middleweight (154 lbs)	Erislandy Lara, U.S.		
Welterweight (147 lbs)	Manny Pacquiao, Philippines[1]	Errol Spence Jr., U.S.	Errol Spence Jr., U.S.
Super Lightweight/	Josh Taylor, UK[1]	Jose Carlos Ramirez. U.S.	Josh Taylor, UK
Jr. Welterweight (140 lbs)	Mario Barrios, U.S.		
Lightweight (135 lbs)	Teofimo Lopez Jr., U.S.[1]	Devin Haney, U.S.	Teofimo Lopez Jr., U.S.
	Gervonta Davis, U.S.		
Super Featherweight/	Leo Santa Cruz, Mexico[1]	Miguel Berchelt, Mexico	Joseph Diaz Jr., U.S.
Jr. Lightweight (130 lbs)	Rene Alvarado, Nicaragua		
Featherweight (126 lbs)	Leo Santa Cruz, Mexico[1]	Gary Russell Jr., U.S.	Josh Warrington, UK
	Xu Can, China		
Super Bantamweight/	Murodjon Akhmadaliev, Uzbekistan[1]	Luis Nery, Mexico[1]	Murodjon Akhmadaliev, Uzbekistan
Jr. Featherweight (122 lbs)	Brandon Figueroa, U.S.		
Bantamweight (118 lbs)	Naoya Inoue, Japan[1]	Nordine Oubaali, France	Naoya Inoue, Japan
	Guillermo Rigondeaux, Cuba		
Super Flyweight/	Roman Gonzalez, Nicaragua[1]	Juan Francisco Estrada, Mexico	Jerwin Ancajas, Philippines
Jr. Bantamweight (115 lbs)	Joshua Franco, U.S.		
Flyweight (112 lbs)	Artem Dalakian, Ukraine	Julio Cesar Martinez, Mexico	Moruti Mthalane, South Africa
Light Flyweight/	Hiroto Kyoguchi, Japan[1]	Kenshiro Teraji, Japan	Felix Alvarado, Nicaragua
Jr. Flyweight (108 lbs)	Carlos Canizales, Venezuela		
Strawweight/	Knockout CP Freshmart,	Wanheng Menayothin, Thailand	Pedro Taduran, Philippines
Mini Flyweight (105 lbs)	Thailand[1]		

Note: As of Oct. 17, 2020. (1) Super champion.

Ring Champions by Years

* = Abandoned/relinquished the title or was stripped of it. IBF champions listed only for heavyweight division. International Boxing Hall of Fame inductees in *italics*. For years with multiple champions, boxers are listed according to date of earliest title bout.

Heavyweights

1882-92	*John L. Sullivan*[1]	1978-83	*Larry Holmes* (WBC*)[6]	1996-99	*Evander Holyfield* (WBA/IBF)
1892-97	*James J. Corbett*[2]	1979-80	John Tate (WBA)	1997-99	Lennox Lewis (WBC)
1897-99	*Bob Fitzsimmons*	1980-82	Mike Weaver (WBA)	1999-2001	Lennox Lewis (WBA*/WBC/IBF)
1899-1905	*James J. Jeffries*[3]	1982-83	Michael Dokes (WBA)	2000-01	*Evander Holyfield* (WBA)
1905-06	Marvin Hart	1983-84	Gerrie Coetzee (WBA)	2001-03	John Ruiz (WBA)
1906-08	*Tommy Burns*	1983-85	*Larry Holmes* (IBF)[6]	2001	Hasim Rahman (WBC/IBF)
1908-15	*Jack Johnson*	1984	Tim Witherspoon (WBC)	2001-02	Lennox Lewis (IBF*)
1915-19	Jess Willard	1984-86	Pinklon Thomas (WBC)	2001-04	Lennox Lewis (WBC)
1919-26	*Jack Dempsey*	1984-85	Greg Page (WBA)	2002-06	Chris Byrd (IBF)
1926-28	*Gene Tunney*[*]	1985-86	Tony Tubbs (WBA)	2003	Roy Jones Jr. (WBA*)
1928-30	Vacant	1985-87	*Michael Spinks* (IBF*)[8]	2004-05	John Ruiz (WBA)[7];
1930-32	*Max Schmeling*	1986	Tim Witherspoon (WBA);		*Vitali Klitschko* (WBC*)
1932-33	*Jack Sharkey*		Trevor Berbick (WBC)	2005-06	Hasim Rahman (WBC)
1933-34	*Primo Carnera*	1986-87	*Mike Tyson* (WBC); James	2005-07	Nicolai Valuev (WBA)
1934-35	*Max Baer*		"Bonecrusher" Smith (WBA)	2006-15	*Wladimir Klitschko* (IBF)
1935-37	*James J. Braddock*	1987	Tony Tucker (IBF)	2006-08	Oleg Maskaev (WBC)
1937-49	*Joe Louis*[*]	1987-90	*Mike Tyson* (WBA/WBC/IBF)	2007-08	Ruslan Chagaev (WBA)
1949-51	*Ezzard Charles*	1990	James "Buster" Douglas	2008	Samuel Peter (WBC)
1951-52	*Joe Walcott*		(WBA/WBC/IBF)	2008-09	Nikolai Valuev (WBA)
1952-56	*Rocky Marciano*[*]	1990-92	*Evander Holyfield*	2008-13	*Vitali Klitschko* (WBC*)
1956-59	*Floyd Patterson*		(WBA/WBC/IBF)	2009-11	David Haye (WBA)
1959-60	*Ingemar Johansson*	1992-93	*Riddick Bowe* (WBA/WBC*/IBF)	2011-15	*Wladimir Klitschko* (WBA)
1960-62	*Floyd Patterson*	1992-94	Lennox Lewis (WBC)	2014-15	Bermane Stiverne (WBC)
1962-64	*Sonny Liston*	1993-94	*Evander Holyfield* (WBA/IBF)	2015-20	Deontay Wilder (WBC)
1964-67	*Cassius Clay (Muhammad Ali)*[*4]	1994	Michael Moorer (WBA/IBF)	2015-16	Tyson Fury (WBA*)
1968-70	Jimmy Ellis[4]	1994-95	Oliver McCall (WBC);	2015	Tyson Fury (IBF*)
1970-73	*Joe Frazier*		*George Foreman* (WBA*/IBF*)	2016	Charles Martin (IBF)
1973-74	*George Foreman*	1995-96	Bruce Seldon (WBA);	2016-19	Anthony Joshua (IBF)
1974-78	*Muhammad Ali*		Frank Bruno (WBC)	2017-19	Anthony Joshua (WBA)
1978	Leon Spinks (WBA/WBC*)[5];	1995	Frans Botha (IBF*)[*]	2019	Andy Ruiz Jr. (WBA/IBF)
	Ken Norton (WBC)[5]	1996	*Mike Tyson* (WBA/WBC*)	2019	Anthony Joshua (WBA/IBF)
1978-79	*Muhammad Ali* (WBA*)[5]	1996-97	Michael Moorer (IBF)	2020	Tyson Fury (WBC)

(1) London Prize Ring (bare-knuckle champion. (2) First Marquis of Queensberry champion. (3) Jeffries vacated title (1905) and designated Marvin Hart and Jack Root as logical contenders. Hart def. Root in 12 rounds (1905); in turn was def. by Tommy Burns (1906), who claimed the title. Jack Johnson def. Burns (1908) and was recognized as champ. Johnson won the title by defeating Jeffries in the latter's attempted comeback (1910). (4) Title declared vacant by the WBA and others in 1967 after Ali refused military induction for religious reasons during the Vietnam War. Joe Frazier recognized as champ by six states, Mexico, and S. America. Jimmy Ellis won a tournament for the WBA title. (5) After Spinks def. Ali for the WBA title, the WBC recognized Ken Norton as champ. Ali def. Spinks in 1978 rematch for WBA title and retired in 1979. (6) Relinquished WBC title in Dec. 1983 to fight as champ of the new IBF. (7) James Toney def. Ruiz Apr. 30, 2005, to claim the title, but it was rescinded when Toney tested positive for steroids.

Light Heavyweights

Year	Champion
1903-05	Bob Fitzsimmons
1905-12	Philadelphia Jack O'Brien*
1912-16	Jack Dillon
1916-20	Battling Levinsky
1920-22	Georges Carpentier
1922-23	Battling Siki
1923-25	Mike McTigue
1925-26	Paul Berlenbach
1926-27	Jack Delaney*
1927-29	Tommy Loughran*
1930-34	Maxie Rosenbloom
1934-35	Bob Olin
1935-39	John Henry Lewis*
1939	Melio Bettina
1939-41	Billy Conn*
1941	Anton Christoforidis (NBA)
1941-48	Gus Lesnevich
1948-50	Freddie Mills
1950-52	Joey Maxim
1952-62	Archie Moore
1962-63	Harold Johnson
1963-65	Willie Pastrano
1965-66	José Torres
1966-68	Dick Tiger
1968-74	Bob Foster*
1974-77	John Conteh (WBC*)
1974-78	Victor Galindez (WBA)
1977-78	Miguel Cuello (WBC)
1978	Mate Parlov (WBC)
1978-79	Mike Rossman (WBA); Marvin Johnson (WBC)
1979	Victor Galindez (WBA)
1979-81	Matthew Saad Muhammad (WBC)
1979-80	Marvin Johnson (WBA)
1980-81	Eddie Mustafa Muhammad (WBA)
1981-85	Michael Spinks (WBA)
1981-83	Dwight Muhammad-Qawi Braxton (WBC)
1983-85	Michael Spinks (WBC*)
1985-86	J. B. Williamson (WBC)
1986-87	Marvin Johnson (WBA); Dennis Andries (WBC)
1987	Thomas Hearns (WBC*)
1987	Leslie Stewart (WBA)
1987-91	Virgil Hill (WBA)
1987-88	Don Lalonde (WBC)
1988	Sugar Ray Leonard (WBC*)
1989	Dennis Andries (WBC)
1989-90	Jeff Harding (WBC)
1990-91	Dennis Andries (WBC)
1991-92	Thomas Hearns (WBA)
1991-94	Jeff Harding (WBC)
1992	Iran Barkley (WBA*)
1992-97	Virgil Hill (WBA)
1994-95	Mike McCallum (WBC)
1995-96	Fabrice Tiozzo (WBC*)
1996-97	Roy Jones Jr. (WBC)
1997	Montell Griffin (WBC); Dariusz Michalczewski (WBA*); Roy Jones Jr. (WBC)
1997-98	Lou Del Valle (WBA)
1998-2003	Roy Jones Jr. (WBA*/WBC*)
2003	Mehdi Sahnoune (WBA); Silvio Branco (WBA); Antonio Tarver (WBC)
2003-04	Roy Jones Jr. (WBA/WBC*)
2004	Antonio Tarver (WBA/WBC*)
2004-06	Fabrice Tiozzo (WBA)
2005-07	Tomasz Adamek (WBC)
2006-07	Silvio Branco (WBA)
2007-08	Chad Dawson (WBC*)
2007	Stipe Drews (WBA); Danny Green (WBA)
2008-09	Hugo Hernan Garay (WBA); Adrian Diaconu (WBC)
2009-11	Jean Pascal (WBC)
2009-10	Gabriel Campillo (WBA)
2010-14	Beibut Shumenov (WBA)
2011-12	Bernard Hopkins (WBC)
2012-13	Chad Dawson (WBC)
2013-18	Adonis Stevenson (WBC)
2014	Bernard Hopkins (WBA)
2014-16	Sergey Kovalev (WBA)
2016-17	Andre Ward (WBA)
2017-	Dmitry Bivol (WBA)
2018-19	Oleksandr Gvozdyk (WBC)
2019-	Artur Beterbiev (WBC)

Middleweights

Year	Champion
1884-91	Jack "Nonpareil" Dempsey
1891-97	Bob Fitzsimmons*
1897-1907	Tommy Ryan*
1907-08	Stanley Ketchel; Billy Papke
1908-10	Stanley Ketchel
1911-13	Vacant
1913	Frank Klaus; George Chip
1914-17	Al McCoy
1917-20	Mike O'Dowd
1920-23	Johnny Wilson
1923-26	Harry Greb
1926	Theodore "Tiger" Flowers
1926-31	Mickey Walker*
1931-32	William "Gorilla" Jones (NBA)
1932-37	Marcel Thil
1938	Al Hostak (NBA); Solly Krieger (NBA)
1939-40	Al Hostak (NBA)
1940-47	Tony Zale
1947-48	Rocky Graziano
1948	Tony Zale; Marcel Cerdan
1949-51	Jake LaMotta
1951	"Sugar" Ray Robinson; Randy Turpin
1951-52	"Sugar" Ray Robinson*
1953-55	Carl "Bobo" Olson
1955-57	"Sugar" Ray Robinson
1957	Gene Fullmer; "Sugar" Ray Robinson
1957-58	Carmen Basilio
1958	"Sugar" Ray Robinson
1959	Gene Fullmer (NBA); "Sugar" Ray Robinson (NY)
1960	Gene Fullmer (NBA); Paul Pender (NY/MA)
1961	Gene Fullmer (NBA); Terry Downes (NY/MA/Europe)
1962	Gene Fullmer; Paul Pender (NY/MA*);
1963	Dick Tiger (NBA)
	Dick Tiger (universal)
1963-65	Joey Giardello
1965-66	Dick Tiger
1966-67	Emile Griffith
1967	Nino Benvenuti
1967-68	Emile Griffith
1968-70	Nino Benvenuti
1970-77	Carlos Monzon*
1977-78	Rodrigo Valdez
1978-79	Hugo Corro
1979-80	Vito Antuofermo
1980	Alan Minter
1980-87	"Marvelous" Marvin Hagler
1987	Sugar Ray Leonard (WBC*)
1987-89	Sumbu Kalambay (WBA)
1987-88	Thomas Hearns (WBC)
1988-89	Iran Barkley (WBC)
1989-90	Roberto Duran (WBC*)
1989-91	Mike McCallum (WBA*)
1990-93	Julian Jackson (WBC)
1992-93	Reggie Johnson (WBA)
1993-95	Gerald McClellan (WBC*)
1993-94	John David Jackson (WBA*)
1994-95	Jorge Castro (WBA)
1995	Julian Jackson (WBC)
1995-96	Quincy Taylor (WBC)
1996-98	Keith Holmes (WBC)
1996-97	William Joppy (WBA)
1997	Julio Cesar Green (WBA)
1998-2001	William Joppy (WBA)
1998-99	Hacine Cherifi (WBC)
1999-2001	Keith Holmes (WBC)
2001	Felix Trinidad (WBA)
2001-05	Bernard Hopkins (WBC/WBA)
2005-06	Jermain Taylor (WBA)
2005-07	Jermain Taylor (WBC)
2006-07	Javier Castillejo (WBA)[1]
2007-12	Felix Sturm (WBA)
2007-10	Kelly Pavlik (WBC)
2009-11	Sebastian Zbik (WBC)
2010	Sergio Martinez (WBC)
2011-12	Julio Cesar Chavez Jr. (WBC)
2012	Daniel Geale (WBA*)
2012-14	Sergio Martinez (WBC)
2012-18	Gennady Golovkin (WBA)
2014-15	Miguel Cotto (WBC)
2015-16	Canelo Alvarez (WBC*)
2016-18	Gennady Golovkin (WBC)
2018-19	Canelo Alvarez (WBA/WBC2)[2]
2019-	Canelo Alvarez (WBA)
2019-	Jermall Charlo (WBC)

(1) Castillejo lost title to Mariano Carrera Dec. 2, 2006, but regained it Feb. 23, 2007, after Carrera tested positive for steroids. (2) Canelo Alvarez was reclassified in 2019 as WBC Franchise Champion.

Welterweights

Year	Champion
1892-94	"Mysterious" Billy Smith
1894-96	Tommy Ryan
1896	Kid McCoy*
1900	Rube Ferns; Matty Matthews
1901	Rube Ferns
1901-04	Joe Walcott
1904-06	Dixie Kid; Joe Walcott
1906	William "Honey" Mellody
1907-11	Mike Sullivan
1911-15	Ted Lewis
1915-16	Ted Lewis
1916-17	Jack Britton
1917-19	Ted Lewis
1919-22	Jack Britton
1922-26	Mickey Walker
1926-27	Pete Latzo
1927-29	Joe Dundee
1929-30	Jackie Fields
1930	Jack Thompson; Tommy Freeman
1931	Tommy Freeman; Jack Thompson; Lou Brouillard
1932	Jackie Fields
1933	Young Corbett III; Jimmy McLarnin
1934	Barney Ross; Jimmy McLarnin
1935-38	Barney Ross
1938-40	Henry Armstrong
1940-41	Fritzie Zivic
1941-46	Fred Cochrane
1946	Marty Servo*
1946-51	"Sugar" Ray Robinson*[1]
1951	Johnny Bratton (NBA)
1951-54	Kid Gavilan
1954-55	Johnny Saxton
1955	Tony DeMarco
1955-56	Carmen Basilio
1956	Johnny Saxton
1956-57	Carmen Basilio*
1958	Virgil Akins
1958-60	Don Jordan
1960-61	Benny Paret
1961	Emile Griffith
1961-62	Benny Paret
1962-63	Emile Griffith
1963	Luis Rodriguez
1963-66	Emile Griffith*
1966-69	Curtis Cokes
1969-70	José Nápoles
1970-71	Billy Backus
1971-75	José Nápoles
1975-76	Angel Espada (WBA); John Stracey (WBC)
1976-79	Carlos Palomino (WBC)
1976-80	José "Pipino" Cuevas (WBA)
1979	Wilfred Benitez (WBC)
1979-80	Sugar Ray Leonard (WBC)
1980	Roberto Duran (WBC)
1980-81	Thomas Hearns (WBA)
1980-82	Sugar Ray Leonard (WBC*/WBA*)
1983-85	Donald Curry (WBA); Milton McCrory (WBC)
1985-86	Donald Curry (WBC)
1986-87	Lloyd Honeyghan (WBC)
1987	Mark Breland (WBA)
1987-88	Marlon Starling (WBA); Jorge Vaca (WBC)

1988-89	Tomas Molinares (WBA*);	2000	Oscar De La Hoya (WBC*)	2009	Shane Mosley (WBA)
	Lloyd Honeyghan (WBC)	2000-02	Shane Mosley (WBC)	2009-12	Vyacheslav Senchenko (WBA)
1989-90	Marlon Starling (WBC);	2001-02	Andrew Lewis (WBA)	2011	Victor Ortiz (WBC)
	Mark Breland (WBA)	2002-03	Vernon Forrest (WBC)	2011-15	Floyd Mayweather Jr. (WBC*)
1990-91	Maurice Blocker (WBC);	2002	Ricardo Mayorga (WBA)	2012-13	Paulie Malignaggi (WBA)
	Aaron Davis (WBA)	2003	Ricardo Mayorga (WBA/WBC)	2013	Adrien Broner (WBA);
1991-92	Meldrick Taylor (WBA)	2003-05	Cory Spinks (WBA/WBC)		Marcos Maidana (WBA)
1991	Simon Brown (WBC)	2005-06	Zab Judah (WBA/WBC)	2014-15	Floyd Mayweather Jr. (WBA*)
1991-93	Buddy McGirt (WBC)	2006	Carlos Baldomir (WBC)	2016-17	Danny Garcia (WBC)
1992-94	Crisanto España (WBC)		Ricky Hatton (WBA*)	2016-19	Keith Thurman (WBA)
1993-97	Pernell Whitaker (WBC)	2006-08	Floyd Mayweather Jr. (WBC);	2017-18	Keith Thurman (WBC*)
1994-98	Ike Quartey (WBA*)		Miguel Cotto (WBA)	2018-19	Shawn Porter (WBC)
1997-99	Oscar De La Hoya (WBC*)	2008	Antonio Margarito (WBA)	2019-	Manny Pacquiao (WBA)
1998-2000	James Page (WBA*)	2008-11	Andre Berto (WBA)	2019-	Errol Spence Jr. (WBC)
1999-2000	Felix Trinidad (WBC*)				

(1) Robinson gained the title by defeating Tommy Bell in an elimination agreed to by the New York Commission and the National Boxing Association. Both claimed Robinson waived his title when he won the middleweight crown from Jake LaMotta in 1951.

Lightweights

1899-1902	Frank Erne	1971-72	Pedro Carrasco (WBC)	1998-99	Jean-Baptiste Mendy (WBA);
1902-08	Joe Gans	1972	Mando Ramos (WBC)		Cesar Bazan (WBC)
1908-10	Oscar "Battling" Nelson	1972-79	Roberto Duran (WBA*)	1999-2000	Steve Johnston (WBC)
1910-12	Ad Wolgast	1972	Chango Carmona (WBC)	1999	Julien Lorcy (WBA);
1912-14	Willie Ritchie	1972-74	Rodolfo Gonzalez (WBC)		Stefano Zoff (WBA)
1914-17	Freddie Welsh	1974-76	Ishimatsu Suzuki (WBC)	1999-2000	Gilberto Serrano (WBA)
1917-25	Benny Leonard*	1976-78	Esteban De Jesus (WBC)	2000-01	Takanori Hatakeyama (WBA)
1925	Jimmy Goodrich;	1978	Roberto Duran (WBC)	2000-02	José Luis Castillo (WBC)
	Rocky Kansas	1979-81	Jim Watt (WBC)	2001	Julien Lorcy (WBA)
1926-30	Sammy Mandell	1979-80	Ernesto España (WBA)	2001-02	Raul Balbi (WBA)
1930	Al Singer; Tony Canzoneri	1980-81	Hilmer Kenty (WBA)	2002-03	Leonard Dorin (WBA*)
1930-33	Tony Canzoneri	1981	Sean O'Grady (WBA*);	2002-04	Floyd Mayweather Jr. (WBC*)
1933-35	Barney Ross*		Claude Noel (WBA)	2004	Lakva Sim (WBA)
1935-36	Tony Canzoneri	1981-83	Alexis Arguello (WBC*)	2004-05	José Luis Castillo (WBC)
1936-38	Lou Ambers	1981-82	Arturo Frias (WBA)	2004-08	Juan Diaz (WBA)
1938	Henry Armstrong	1982-84	Ray Mancini (WBA)	2005-06	Diego Corrales (WBC)
1939	Lou Ambers	1983-84	Edwin Rosario (WBC)	2006	Joel Casamayor (WBC*)
1940	Lew Jenkins	1984-86	Livingstone Bramble (WBA)	2006-08	David Diaz (WBC)
1941-43	Sammy Angott	1984-85	José Luis Ramírez (WBC)	2008-09	Nate Campbell (WBA*);
1944	Sammy Angott (NBA);	1985-86	Hector "Macho" Camacho		Manny Pacquiao (WBC*)
	Juan Zurita (NBA)		(WBC*)	2009-12	Juan Manuel Marquez (WBA*)
1945-51	Ike Williams	1986-87	Edwin Rosario (WBA)	2009-10	Edwin Valero (WBC)
	(NBA; later universal)	1987-88	Julio Cesar Chavez (WBA);	2010-11	Humberto Soto (WBC*)
1951-52	James Carter		José Luis Ramírez (WBC)	2011-12	Antonio DeMarco (WBC)
1952	Lauro Salas; James Carter	1988-89	Julio Cesar Chavez	2012-14	Adrien Broner (WBC*)
1953-54	James Carter		(WBA*/WBC*)	2013-15	Richard Abril (WBA*)
1954	Paddy De Marco; James Carter	1989-90	Edwin Rosario (WBA);	2014	Omar Figueroa (WBC*)
1955	James Carter; Bud Smith		Pernell Whitaker (WBC)	2014-15	Jorge Linares (WBC)
1956	Bud Smith; Joe Brown	1990	Juan Nazario (WBA)	2015	Darleys Perez (WBA)
1956-62	Joe Brown	1990-92	Pernell Whitaker (WBC*/WBA*)	2015-16	Anthony Crolla (WBA)
1962-65	Carlos Ortiz	1992	Joey Gamache (WBA)	2016-17	Dejan Zlaticanin (WBC)
1965	Ismael Laguna	1992-96	Miguel Angel Gonzalez (WBC*)	2016-18	Jorge Linares (WBA)
1965-68	Carlos Ortiz	1992-93	Tony Lopez (WBA)	2017-19	Mikey Garcia (WBC*)
1968-69	Carlos Teo Cruz	1993	Dingaan Thobela (WBA)	2018-20	Vasiliy Lomachenko (WBA)
1969-70	Mando Ramos	1993-98	Orzubek Nazarov (WBA)	2019-20	Vasiliy Lomachenko[1] (WBC)
1970	Ismael Laguna	1996-97	Jean-Baptiste Mendy (WBC)	2019-	Devin Haney (WBC)
1970-72	Ken Buchanan (WBA)	1997-98	Steve Johnston (WBC)	2020-	Teofimo Lopez Jr.[1] (WBA/WBC)

(1) WBC Franchise Champion.

Featherweights

1901-12	Abe Attell	1972	Clemente Sanchez (WBC*)	1996-98	Wilfredo Vasquez (WBA*)
1912-23	Johnny Kilbane	1972-74	Ernesto Marcel (WBA*)	1998	Freddie Norwood (WBA*)
1923	Eugene Criqui	1972-73	José Legrá (WBC)	1998-99	Antonio Cermeno (WBA)
1923-25	Johnny Dundee*	1973-74	Eder Jofre (WBC*)	1999	César Soto (WBC)
1925-27	Louis "Kid" Kaplan*	1974	Ruben Olivares (WBA)	1999-2000	Freddie Norwood (WBA)
1927-28	Benny Bass; Tony Canzoneri	1974-75	Bobby Chacon (WBC)	1999	Naseem Hamed (WBC)
1928-29	Andre Routis	1974-76	Alexis Arguello (WBA*)	2000-01	Guty Espadas Jr. (WBC)
1929-32	Battling Battalino*	1975	Ruben Olivares (WBC)	2000-03	Derrick Gainer (WBA)
1932-34	Tommy Paul (NBA)	1975-76	David Kotey (WBC)	2001-04	Erik Morales (WBC)[1]
1933-36	Freddie Miller	1976-80	Danny "Little Red"	2003-05	Juan Manuel Marquez (WBA*)
1936-37	Petey Sarron		Lopez (WBC)	2004-06	In-Jin Chi (WBC)
1937-38	Henry Armstrong*	1977	Rafael Ortega (WBA)	2005-13	Chris John (WBA)
1938-40	Joey Archibald	1977-78	Cecilio Lastra (WBA)	2006	Takashi Koshimoto (WBC);
1940-41	Harry Jeffra	1978-85	Eusebio Pedroza (WBA)		Rodolfo Lopez (WBC)
1941	Joey Archibald	1980-82	Salvador Sanchez (WBC)	2006-07	In-Jin Chi (WBC)
1941-42	Chalky Wright	1982-84	Juan LaPorte (WBC)	2007-08	Jorge Linares (WBC*)
1942-48	Willie Pep	1984	Wilfredo Gomez (WBC)	2008	Oscar Larios (WBC)
1948-49	Sandy Saddler	1984-88	Azumah Nelson (WBC*)	2009	Takahiro Ao (WBC)
1949-50	Willie Pep	1985-86	Barry McGuigan (WBA)	2009-10	Elio Rojas (WBC)
1950-57	Sandy Saddler*	1986-87	Steve Cruz (WBA)	2010-11	Hozumi Hasegawa (WBC)
1957-59	Hogan "Kid" Bassey	1987-91	Antonio Esparragoza (WBA)	2011-12	Jhonny Gonzalez (WBC)
1959-63	Davey Moore	1988-90	Jeff Fenech (WBC*)	2012-13	Daniel Ponce de León (WBC)
1963-64	Ultiminio "Sugar" Ramos	1990-91	Marcos Villasana (WBC)	2013	Abner Mares (WBC)
1964-67	Vicente Saldivar*	1991-93	Park Yung Kyun (WBA);	2013-15	Jhonny Gonzalez (WBC)
1968	Raul Rojas (WBA)		Paul Hodkinson (WBC)	2013-14	Simpiwe Vetyeka (WBA)
1968-69	José Legrá (WBC)	1993	Goyo Vargas (WBC)	2014	Nonito Donaire (WBA)
1968-71	Shozo Saijyo (WBA)	1993-95	Kevin Kelley (WBC)	2014-15	Nicholas Walters (WBC)
1969-70	Johnny Famechon (WBC)	1993-96	Eloy Rojas (WBA)	2015-	Gary Russell Jr. (WBC)
1970	Vicente Saldivar (WBC)	1995	Alejandro Gonzalez (WBC);	2015-16	Leo Santa Cruz (WBA)
1970-72	Kuniaki Shibata (WBC)		Manuel Medina (WBC)	2016-17	Carl Frampton (WBA)
1971-72	Antonio Gomez (WBA)	1995-99	Luisito Espinosa (WBC)	2017-	Leo Santa Cruz (WBA)

(1) Marco Antonio Barrera won unanimous decision over Morales, June 22, 2002, but refused WBC title. Morales regained WBC title with unanimous decision over Paulie Ayala, Nov. 16, 2002. Morales moved to Jr. Lightweight div. in 2004.

International Boxing Hall of Fame Inductees, 2020

Source: International Boxing Hall of Fame, 1 Hall of Fame Dr., Canastota, NY 13032. www.ibhof.com

Men's Modern: Bernard Hopkins (55-8-2, 32 KO, 2 NC); Juan Manuel Marquez (56-7-1, 40 KO); Shane Mosley (49-10-1, 41 KO). **Women's Modern:** Christy Martin (49-10-3, 31 KO); Lucia Rijker (17-0, 14 KO). **Old-Timer:** Frank Erne (30-6-11, 15 KO, 1 NC).

Women's Trailblazer: Barbara Buttrick (30-1-1). **Pioneer:** Paddy Ryan. **Non-Participant:** Lou DiBella, TV executive/promoter; Kathy Duva, promoter; Dan Goossen, promoter. **Observer:** Bernard Fernandez, journalist; Thomas Hauser, journalist.

Title-Changing Heavyweight Championship Bouts, 1889-2020

1889: July 8, John L. Sullivan def. Jake Kilrain, 75, Richburg, MS.
1892: Sept. 7, James J. Corbett def. John L. Sullivan, 21, New Orleans.
1897: Mar. 17, Bob Fitzsimmons def. James J. Corbett, 14, Carson City, NV.
1899: June 9, James J. Jeffries def. Bob Fitzsimmons, 11, Coney Island, NY. (Jeffries retired as champion in 1905.)
1905: July 3, Marvin Hart KOd Jack Root, 12, Reno, NV. (James J. Jeffries refereed, gave title to Hart. Jack O'Brien also claimed the title.)
1906: Feb. 23, Tommy Burns def. Marvin Hart, 20, Los Angeles.
1908: Dec. 26, Jack Johnson def. Tommy Burns, 14, Sydney, Australia. (Police halted contest.)
1915: Apr. 5, Jess Willard KOd Jack Johnson, 26, Havana, Cuba.
1919: July 4, Jack Dempsey KOd Jess Willard, Toledo, OH. (Willard failed to answer bell for 4th round.)
1926: Sept. 23, Gene Tunney def. Jack Dempsey, 10, Philadelphia. (Tunney retired as champion in 1928.)
1930: June 12, Max Schmeling def. Jack Sharkey on a foul, 4, New York City. (Resulted in the election of a successor to Gene Tunney.)
1932: June 21, Jack Sharkey def. Max Schmeling, 15, NYC.
1933: June 29, Primo Carnera KOd Jack Sharkey, 6, NYC.
1934: June 14, Max Baer KOd Primo Carnera, 11, NYC.
1935: June 13, James J. Braddock def. Max Baer, 15, NYC.
1937: June 22, Joe Louis KOd James J. Braddock, 8, Chicago. (Louis retired as champion in 1949.)
1949: June 22, Ezzard Charles def. Joe Walcott, 15, Chicago; NBA recognition only.
1951: July 18, Joe Walcott KOd Ezzard Charles, 7, Pittsburgh.
1952: Sept. 23, Rocky Marciano KOd Joe Walcott, 13, Philadelphia. (Marciano retired as champion in 1956.)
1956: Nov. 30, Floyd Patterson KOd Archie Moore, 5, Chicago.
1959: June 26, Ingemar Johansson KOd Floyd Patterson, 3, NYC.
1960: June 20, Floyd Patterson KOd Ingemar Johansson, 5, NYC.
1962: Sept. 25, Sonny Liston KOd Floyd Patterson, 1, Chicago.
1964: Feb. 25, Cassius Clay (Muhammad Ali) KOd Sonny Liston, 7, Miami Beach, FL. (Liston failed to answer bell for 7th round. In 1967, Ali was stripped of title for refusing military service.)
1970: Feb. 16, Joe Frazier KOd Jimmy Ellis, 5, NYC. (Frazier def. Ali, 15, NYC, on Mar. 8, 1971, in "Fight of the Century.")
1973: Jan. 22, George Foreman KOd Joe Frazier, 2, Kingston, Jamaica.
1974: Oct. 30, Muhammad Ali KOd George Foreman, 8, Kinshasa, Zaire (billed as the "Rumble in the Jungle").
1978: Feb. 15, Leon Spinks def. Muhammad Ali, 15, Las Vegas (WBC recognized Ken Norton as champion after Spinks refused to fight him before his rematch with Ali); June 9, (WBC) Larry Holmes def. Ken Norton, 15, Las Vegas; Sept. 15, (WBA) Muhammad Ali def. Leon Spinks, 15, New Orleans. (Ali retired as champion in 1979.)
1979: Oct. 20, (WBA) John Tate def. Gerrie Coetzee, 15, Pretoria, South Africa.
1980: Mar. 31, (WBA) Mike Weaver KOd John Tate, 15, Knoxville, TN.
1982: Dec. 10, (WBA) Michael Dokes KOd Mike Weaver, 1, Las Vegas.
1983: Sept. 23, (WBA) Gerrie Coetzee KOd Michael Dokes, 10, Richfield, OH; in Dec., Larry Holmes relinquished the WBC title and was named champion of the newly formed IBF.
1984: Mar. 9, (WBC) Tim Witherspoon def. Greg Page, 12, Las Vegas; Aug. 31, (WBC) Pinklon Thomas def. Tim Witherspoon, 12, Las Vegas; Dec. 1, (WBA) Greg Page KOd Gerrie Coetzee, 8, Sun City, Bophuthatswana, South Africa.
1985: Apr. 29, (WBA) Tony Tubbs def. Greg Page, 15, Buffalo, NY; Sept. 21, (IBF) Michael Spinks def. Larry Holmes, 15, Las Vegas. (Spinks relinquished title in Feb. 1987.)
1986: Jan. 17, (WBA) Tim Witherspoon def. Tony Tubbs, 15, Atlanta; Mar. 22, (WBC) Trevor Berbick def. Pinklon Thomas, 12, Las Vegas; Nov. 22, (WBC) Mike Tyson KOd Trevor Berbick, 2, Las Vegas; Dec. 12, (WBA) James "Bonecrusher" Smith KOd Tim Witherspoon, 1, NYC.
1987: Mar. 7, (WBA) Mike Tyson def. James "Bonecrusher" Smith, 12, Las Vegas; May 30, (IBF) Tony Tucker KOd James "Buster" Douglas, 10, Las Vegas; Aug. 1, (IBF) Mike Tyson def. Tony Tucker, 12, Las Vegas. (Tyson became undisputed champion.)
1990: Feb. 11, (WBA/WBC/IBF) James "Buster" Douglas KOd Mike Tyson, 10, Tokyo, Japan; Oct. 25,

(WBA/WBC/IBF) Evander Holyfield KOd James "Buster" Douglas, 3, Las Vegas.
1992: Nov. 13, (WBA/WBC/IBF) Riddick Bowe def. Evander Holyfield, 12, Las Vegas; in Dec., Lennox Lewis was named WBC champion after Bowe relinquished the WBC title rather than fight Lewis.
1993: Nov. 6, (WBA/IBF) Evander Holyfield def. Riddick Bowe, 12, Las Vegas.
1994: Apr. 22, (WBA/IBF) Michael Moorer def. Evander Holyfield, 12, Las Vegas; Sept. 24, (WBC) Oliver McCall KOd Lennox Lewis, 2, London, Eng.; Nov. 5, (WBA/IBF) George Foreman KOd Michael Moorer, 10, Las Vegas.
1995: In Mar., George Foreman was stripped of his WBA title for refusing to fight challenger Tony Tucker; in June, Foreman relinquished his IBF title rather than submit to a rematch with Axel Schulz; Apr. 8, (WBA) Bruce Seldon TKOd Tony Tucker, 7, Las Vegas; Sept. 2, (WBC) Frank Bruno def. Oliver McCall, 12, London, Eng.; Dec. 9, (IBF) Frans Botha def. Axel Schulz, 12, Stuttgart, Germany (Botha was subsequently stripped of title after testing positive for a steroid).
1996: Mar. 16, (WBC) Mike Tyson KOd Frank Bruno, 3, Las Vegas; June 22, (IBF) Michael Moorer def. Axel Schulz, 12, Dortmund, Germany; Sept. 7, (WBA) Mike Tyson KOd Bruce Seldon, 1, Las Vegas (Tyson was subsequently stripped of WBC title after refusing to fight Lennox Lewis); Nov. 9, (WBA) Evander Holyfield KOd Mike Tyson, 11, Las Vegas.
1997: Feb. 7, (WBC) Lennox Lewis TKOd Oliver McCall, 5, Las Vegas; Nov. 8, (IBF) Evander Holyfield def. Michael Moorer, 8, Las Vegas.
1999: Nov. 13, (IBF) Lennox Lewis def. Evander Holyfield, 12, Las Vegas. (Lewis became undisputed champion.)
2000: In Apr., Lennox Lewis was stripped of his WBA title after refusing to fight challenger John Ruiz; Aug. 12, (WBA) Evander Holyfield def. John Ruiz, 12, Las Vegas.
2001: Mar. 3, (WBA) John Ruiz def. Evander Holyfield, 12, Las Vegas; Apr. 22, (WBC/IBF) Hasim Rahman KOd Lennox Lewis, 5, Brakpan, South Africa; Nov. 17, (WBC/IBF) Lennox Lewis KOd Hasim Rahman, 4, Las Vegas.
2002: In Sept., Lennox Lewis relinquished his IBF title; Dec. 14, (IBF) Chris Byrd def. Evander Holyfield, 12, Atlantic City, NJ.
2003: Mar. 1, (WBA) Roy Jones Jr. def. John Ruiz, 12, Las Vegas.
2004: Feb. 20, (WBA) John Ruiz gained title when Roy Jones Jr. relinquished it; Apr. 24, (WBC) Vitali Klitschko TKOd Corrie Sanders, 8, Los Angeles, to win title vacated by retirement of Lennox Lewis in Feb.
2005: Apr. 30, (WBA) James Toney def. John Ruiz, 12, NYC (title was returned to Ruiz after Toney tested positive for steroids); Nov. 9, (WBC) Hasim Rahman gained title when Vitali Klitschko retired due to an injury; Dec. 17, (WBA) Nikolai Valuev def. John Ruiz, 12, Berlin, Germany.
2006: Apr. 22, (IBF) Wladimir Klitschko TKOd Chris Byrd, 7, Mannheim, Germany; Aug. 12, (WBC) Oleg Maskaev TKOd Hasim Rahman, 12, Las Vegas.
2007: Apr. 14, (WBA) Ruslan Chagaev def. Nikolai Valuev, 12, Stuttgart, Germany. (An injured Chagaev was named champion in recess, July 2008.)
2008: Mar. 8, (WBC) Samuel Peter TKOd Oleg Maskaev, 6, Cancún, Mexico; Aug. 30, (WBA) Nikolai Valuev def. John Ruiz, 12, Berlin, Germany; Oct. 11, (WBC) Vitali Klitschko TKOd Samuel Peter, 8, Berlin, Germany.
2009: Nov. 7, (WBA) David Haye def. Nikolai Valuev, 12, Nuremberg, Germany.
2011: July 2, (WBA) Wladimir Klitschko def. David Haye, 12, Hamburg, Germany.
2014: May 10, (WBC) Bermane Stiverne TKOd Chris Arreola, 6, Los Angeles, to win title vacated in Dec. 2013.
2015: Jan. 17, (WBC) Deontay Wilder def. Bermane Stiverne, 12, Las Vegas; Nov. 28 (WBA/IBF) Tyson Fury def. Wladimir Klitschko, 12, Dusseldorf, Germany; in Dec., Fury was stripped of IBF title for refusing to fight mandatory challenger Vyacheslav Glazkov. (Fury relinquished WBA title Oct. 2016.)
2016: Jan. 16, (IBF) Charles Martin TKOd Vyacheslav Glazkov, 3, Brooklyn, NY; Apr. 9, (IBF) Anthony Joshua KOd Charles Martin, 2, London, Eng., UK.
2017: Apr. 29, (WBA) Anthony Joshua TKOd Wladimir Klitschko, 11, London, Eng., UK.
2019: June 1, (WBA/IBF) Andy Ruiz Jr. TKOd Anthony Joshua, 7, NYC; Dec. 7, (WBA/IBF) Anthony Joshua def. Andy Ruiz Jr., 12, Diriyah, Saudi Arabia.
2020: Feb. 22, (WBC) Tyson Fury TKOd Deontay Wilder, 7, Las Vegas.

THOROUGHBRED RACING
Triple Crown Winners

The Kentucky Derby, Preakness Stakes, and Belmont Stakes make up the Triple Crown. Since 1920, colts have carried 126 lbs in Triple Crown events; fillies, 121 lbs.

Year	Horse	Jockey	Trainer	Year	Horse	Jockey	Trainer
1919	Sir Barton	J. Loftus	H. G. Bedwell	1948	Citation	E. Arcaro	H. A. Jones
1930	Gallant Fox	E. Sande	J. Fitzsimmons	1973	Secretariat	R. Turcotte	L. Laurin
1935	Omaha	W. Sanders	J. Fitzsimmons	1977	Seattle Slew	J. Cruguet	W. H. Turner Jr.
1937	War Admiral	C. Kurtsinger	G. Conway	1978	Affirmed	S. Cauthen	L. S. Barrera
1941	Whirlaway	E. Arcaro	B. A. Jones	2015	American Pharoah	V. Espinoza	B. Baffert
1943	Count Fleet	J. Longden	G. D. Cameron	2018	Justify	M. Smith	B. Baffert
1946	Assault	W. Mehrtens	M. Hirsch				

Kentucky Derby Winners, 1875-2020

Churchill Downs, Louisville, KY. Distance: 1¼ mi; 1½ mi until 1896. 3-year-olds. Best time: 1:59-2/5, Secretariat (1973); 2020 time: 2:00.61. (Until 2001, times were measured in fifths of a second.)

Year	Horse	Jockey	Year	Horse	Jockey	Year	Horse	Jockey
1875	Aristides	O. Lewis	1924	Black Gold	J. D. Mooney	1973	Secretariat	R. Turcotte
1876	Vagrant	R. Swim	1925	Flying Ebony	E. Sande	1974	Cannonade	A. Cordero
1877	Baden Baden	W. Walker	1926	Bubbling Over	A. Johnson	1975	Foolish Pleasure	J. Vasquez
1878	Day Star	J. Carter	1927	Whiskery	L. McAtee	1976	Bold Forbes	A. Cordero
1879	Lord Murphy	C. Schauer	1928	Reigh Count	C. Lang	1977	Seattle Slew	J. Cruguet
1880	Fonso	G. Lewis	1929	Clyde Van Dusen	L. McAtee	1978	Affirmed	S. Cauthen
1881	Hindoo	J. McLaughlin	1930	Gallant Fox	E. Sande	1979	Spectacular Bid	R. Franklin
1882	Apollo	B. Hurd	1931	Twenty Grand	C. Kurtsinger	1980	Genuine Risk[1]	J. Vasquez
1883	Leonatus	W. Donohue	1932	Burgoo King	E. James	1981	Pleasant Colony	J. Velasquez
1884	Buchanan	I. Murphy	1933	Brokers Tip	D. Meade	1982	Gato Del Sol	E. Delahoussaye
1885	Joe Cotton	E. Henderson	1934	Cavalcade	M. Garner	1983	Sunny's Halo	E. Delahoussaye
1886	Ben Ali	P. Duffy	1935	Omaha	W. Saunders	1984	Swale	L. Pincay
1887	Montrose	I. Lewis	1936	Bold Venture	I. Hanford	1985	Spend a Buck	A. Cordero
1888	Macbeth II	G. Covington	1937	War Admiral	C. Kurtsinger	1986	Ferdinand	W. Shoemaker
1889	Spokane	T. Kiley	1938	Lawrin	E. Arcaro	1987	Alysheba	C. McCarron
1890	Riley	I. Murphy	1939	Johnstown	J. Stout	1988	Winning Colors[1]	G. Stevens
1891	Kingman	I. Murphy	1940	Gallahadion	C. Bierman	1989	Sunday Silence	P. Valenzuela
1892	Azra	A. Clayton	1941	Whirlaway	E. Arcaro	1990	Unbridled	C. Perret
1893	Lookout	E. Kunze	1942	Shut Out	W. Wright	1991	Strike the Gold	C. Antley
1894	Chant	F. Goodale	1943	Count Fleet	J. Longden	1992	Lil E. Tee	P. Day
1895	Halma	J. Perkins	1944	Pensive	C. McCreary	1993	Sea Hero	J. Bailey
1896	Ben Brush	W. Simms	1945	Hoop Jr.	E. Arcaro	1994	Go for Gin	C. McCarron
1897	Typhoon II	F. Garner	1946	Assault	W. Mehrtens	1995	Thunder Gulch	G. Stevens
1898	Plaudit	W. Simms	1947	Jet Pilot	E. Guerin	1996	Grindstone	J. Bailey
1899	Manuel	F. Taral	1948	Citation	E. Arcaro	1997	Silver Charm	G. Stevens
1900	Lieut. Gibson	J. Boland	1949	Ponder	S. Brooks	1998	Real Quiet	K. Desormeaux
1901	His Eminence	J. Winkfield	1950	Middleground	W. Boland	1999	Charismatic	C. Antley
1902	Alan-a-Dale	J. Winkfield	1951	Count Turf	C. McCreary	2000	Fusaichi Pegasus	K. Desormeaux
1903	Judge Himes	H. Booker	1952	Hill Gail	E. Arcaro	2001	Monarchos	J. Chavez
1904	Elwood	F. Prior	1953	Dark Star	H. Moreno	2002	War Emblem	V. Espinoza
1905	Agile	J. Martin	1954	Determine	R. York	2003	Funny Cide	J. Santos
1906	Sir Huon	R. Troxler	1955	Swaps	W. Shoemaker	2004	Smarty Jones	S. Elliot
1907	Pink Star	A. Minder	1956	Needles	D. Erb	2005	Giacomo	M. Smith
1908	Stone Street	A. Pickens	1957	Iron Liege	W. Hartack	2006	Barbaro	E. Prado
1909	Wintergreen	V. Powers	1958	Tim Tam	I. Valenzuela	2007	Street Sense	C. Borel
1910	Donau	F. Herbert	1959	Tomy Lee	W. Shoemaker	2008	Big Brown	K. Desormeaux
1911	Meridian	G. Archibald	1960	Venetian Way	W. Hartack	2009	Mine That Bird	C. Borel
1912	Worth	C. Shilling	1961	Carry Back	J. Sellers	2010	Super Saver	C. Borel
1913	Donerail	R. Goose	1962	Decidedly	W. Hartack	2011	Animal Kingdom	J. Velazquez
1914	Old Rosebud	J. McCabe	1963	Chateaugay	B. Baeza	2012	I'll Have Another	M. Gutierrez
1915	Regret[1]	J. Notter	1964	Northern Dancer	W. Hartack	2013	Orb	J. Rosario
1916	George Smith	J. Loftus	1965	Lucky Debonair	W. Shoemaker	2014	California Chrome	V. Espinoza
1917	Omar Khayyam	C. Borel	1966	Kauai King	D. Brumfield	2015	American Pharoah	V. Espinoza
1918	Exterminator	W. Knapp	1967	Proud Clarion	R. Ussery	2016	Nyquist	M. Gutierrez
1919	Sir Barton	J. Loftus	1968	Forward Pass[2]	I. Valenzuela	2017	Always Dreaming	J. Velazquez
1920	Paul Jones	T. Rice	1969	Majestic Prince	W. Hartack	2018	Justify	M. Smith
1921	Behave Yourself	C. Thompson	1970	Dust Commander	M. Manganello	2019	Country House[3]	F. Prat
1922	Morvich	A. Johnson	1971	Canonero II	G. Avila	2020	Authentic	J. Velazquez
1923	Zev	E. Sande	1972	Riva Ridge	R. Turcotte			

Note: Two jockeys have won the Kentucky Derby five times: Eddie Arcaro and Bill Hartack. Willie Shoemaker won four times. (1) Regret, Genuine Risk, and Winning Colors are the only fillies to have won the Derby. (2) Dancer's Image came in first but was disqualified after tests disclosed that the horse had run with a prohibited painkilling drug in his system. All wagers were paid on Dancer's Image, but Forward Pass was awarded the first-place money. (3) Maximum Security came in first but was disqualified for interference following the race.

Fastest Winning Times for the Kentucky Derby

Until 2001, Kentucky Derby times were measured in fifths of a second.

Time	Horse	Jockey	Year	Time	Horse	Jockey	Year
1 min., 59-2/5 s.	Secretariat	Ron Turcotte	1973	2 min., 1.19 s.	Funny Cide	Jose Santos	2003
1 min., 59.97 s.	Monarchos	Jorge Chavez	2001	2 min., 1-1/5 s.	Thunder Gulch	Gary Stevens	1995
2 min.	Northern Dancer	Bill Hartack	1964		Affirmed	Steve Cauthen	1978
2 min., 1/5 s.	Spend a Buck	Angel Cordero Jr.	1985		Lucky Debonair	Bill Shoemaker	1965
2 min., 2/5 s.	Decidedly	Bill Hartack	1962	2 min., 1.31 s.	Nyquist	Mario Gutierrez	2016
2 min., 3/5 s.	Proud Clarion	Robert Ussery	1967	2 min., 1-2/5 s.	Barbaro	Edgar Prado	2006
2 min., 0.61 s.	Authentic	J. Velazquez	2020		Whirlaway	Eddie Arcaro	1941
2 min., 1 s.	Fusaichi Pegasus	Kent Desormeaux	2000	2 min., 1-3/5 s.	Bold Forbes	Angel Cordero Jr.	1976
	Grindstone	Jerry Bailey	1996		Hill Gail	Eddie Arcaro	1952
2 min., 1.13 s.	War Emblem	Victor Espinoza	2002		Middleground	William Boland	1950

Preakness Stakes Winners, 1873-2020

Pimlico Race Course, Baltimore, MD. Distance: 1-3/16 mi. 3-year-olds. * = Horses ran in two divisions. Best time: 1:53, Secretariat (1973); 2020 time: 1:53.28.

Year	Horse	Jockey	Year	Horse	Jockey	Year	Horse	Jockey
1873	Survivor	G. Barbee	1924	Nellie Morse	J. Merimee	1973	Secretariat	R. Turcotte
1874	Culpepper	M. Donohue	1925	Coventry	C. Kummer	1974	Little Current	M. Rivera
1875	Tom Ochiltree	L. Hughes	1926	Display	J. Malben	1975	Master Derby	D. McHargue
1876	Shirley	G. Barbee	1927	Bostonian	A. Abel	1976	Elocutionist	J. Lively
1877	Cloverbrook	C. Holloway	1928	Victorian	R. Workman	1977	Seattle Slew	J. Cruguet
1878	Duke of Magenta	C. Holloway	1929	Dr. Freeland	L. Schaefer	1978	Affirmed	S. Cauthen
1879	Harold	L. Hughes	1930	Gallant Fox	E. Sande	1979	Spectacular Bid	R. Franklin
1880	Grenada	L. Hughes	1931	Mate	G. Ellis	1980	Codex	A. Cordero
1881	Saunterer	W. Costello	1932	Burgoo King	E. James	1981	Pleasant Colony	J. Velasquez
1882	Vanguard	W. Costello	1933	Head Play	C. Kurtsinger	1982	Aloma's Ruler	J. Kaenel
1883	Jacobus	G. Barbee	1934	High Quest	R. Jones	1983	Deputed	
1884	Knight of Ellerslie	S. Fisher	1935	Omaha	W. Saunders		Testamony	D. Miller
1885	Tecumseh	J. McLaughlin	1936	Bold Venture	G. Woolf	1984	Gate Dancer	A. Cordero
1886	The Bard	S. Fisher	1937	War Admiral	C. Kurtsinger	1985	Tank's Prospect	P. Day
1887	Dunboyne	W. Donohue	1938	Dauber	M. Peters	1986	Snow Chief	A. Solis
1888	Refund	F. Littlefield	1939	Challedon	G. Seabo	1987	Alysheba	C. McCarron
1889	Buddhist	G. Anderson	1940	Bimelech	F. A. Smith	1988	Risen Star	E. Delahoussaye
1890	Montague	W. Martin	1941	Whirlaway	E. Arcaro	1989	Sunday Silence	P. Valenzuela
1894	Assignee	F. Taral	1942	Alsab	B. James	1990	Summer Squall	P. Day
1895	Belmar	F. Taral	1943	Count Fleet	J. Longden	1991	Hansel	J. Bailey
1896	Margrave	H. Griffin	1944	Pensive	C. McCreary	1992	Pine Bluff	C. McCarron
1897	Paul Kauvar	C. Thorpe	1945	Polynesian	W. D. Wright	1993	Prairie Bayou	M. Smith
1898	Sly Fox	W. Simms	1946	Assault	W. Mehrtens	1994	Tabasco Cat	P. Day
1899	Half Time	R. Clawson	1947	Faultless	D. Dodson	1995	Timber Country	P. Day
1900	Hindus	H. Spencer	1948	Citation	E. Arcaro	1996	Louis Quatorze	P. Day
1901	The Parader	F. Landry	1949	Capot	T. Atkinson	1997	Silver Charm	G. Stevens
1902	Old England	L. Jackson	1950	Hill Prince	E. Arcaro	1998	Real Quiet	K. Desormeaux
1903	Flocarline	W. Gannon	1951	Bold	E. Arcaro	1999	Charismatic	C. Antley
1904	Bryn Mawr	E. Hildebrand	1952	Blue Man	C. McCreary	2000	Red Bullet	J. Bailey
1905	Cairngorm	W. Davis	1953	Native Dancer	E. Guerin	2001	Point Given	G. Stevens
1906	Whimsical	W. Miller	1954	Hasty Road	J. Adams	2002	War Emblem	V. Espinoza
1907	Don Enrique	G. Mountain	1955	Nashua	E. Arcaro	2003	Funny Cide	J. Santos
1908	Royal Tourist	E. Dugan	1956	Fabius	W. Hartack	2004	Smarty Jones	S. Elliot
1909	Effendi	W. Doyle	1957	Bold Ruler	E. Arcaro	2005	Afleet Alex	J. Rose
1910	Layminster	R. Estep	1958	Tim Tam	I. Valenzuela	2006	Bernardini	J. Castellano
1911	Watervale	E. Dugan	1959	Royal Orbit	W. Harmatz	2007	Curlin	R. Albarado
1912	Colonel Holloway	C. Turner	1960	Bally Ache	R. Ussery	2008	Big Brown	K. Desormeaux
1913	Buskin	J. Butwell	1961	Carry Back	J. Sellers	2009	Rachel Alexandra	C. Borel
1914	Holiday	A. Schuttinger	1962	Greek Money	J. L. Rotz	2010	Lookin At Lucky	M. Garcia
1915	Rhine Maiden	D. Hoffman	1963	Candy Spots	W. Shoemaker	2011	Shackleford	J. Castanon
1916	Damrosch	L. McAtee	1964	Northern Dancer	W. Hartack	2012	I'll Have Another	M. Gutierrez
1917	Kalitan	E. Haynes	1965	Tom Rolfe	R. Turcotte	2013	Oxbow	G. Stevens
1918*	War Cloud	J. Loftus	1966	Kauai King	D. Brumfield	2014	California Chrome	V. Espinoza
	Jack Hare Jr.	C. Peak	1967	Damascus	W. Shoemaker	2015	American Pharoah	V. Espinoza
1919	Sir Barton	J. Loftus	1968	Forward Pass	I. Valenzuela	2016	Exaggerator	K. Desormeaux
1920	Man o' War	C. Kummer	1969	Majestic Prince	W. Hartack	2017	Cloud Computing	J. Castellano
1921	Broomspun	F. Coltiletti	1970	Personality	E. Belmonte	2018	Justify	M. Smith
1922	Pillory	L. Morris	1971	Canonero II	G. Avila	2019	War of Will	T. Gaffalione
1923	Vigil	B. Marinelli	1972	Bee Bee Bee	E. Nelson	2020	Swiss Skydiver	R. Albarado

Belmont Stakes Winners, 1867-2020

Belmont Park, Elmont, NY. Distance: 1½ mi (2020, 1-1/8 mi). 3-year-olds. Best time: 2:24, Secretariat (1973); 2020 time: 1:46.53.

Year	Horse	Jockey	Year	Horse	Jockey	Year	Horse	Jockey
1867	Ruthless	J. Gilpatrick	1899	Jean Bereaud	R. R. Clawson	1933	Hurryoff	M. Garner
1868	General Duke	R. Swim	1900	Ildrim	N. Turner	1934	Peace Chance	W. D. Wright
1869	Fenian	C. Miller	1901	Commando	H. Spencer	1935	Omaha	W. Saunders
1870	Kingfisher	W. Dick	1902	Masterman	J. Bullman	1936	Granville	J. Stout
1871	Harry Bassett	W. Miller	1903	Africander	J. Bullman	1937	War Admiral	C. Kurtsinger
1872	Joe Daniels	J. Rowe	1904	Delhi	G. Odom	1938	Pasteurized	J. Stout
1873	Springbok	J. Rowe	1905	Tanya	E. Hildebrand	1939	Johnstown	J. Stout
1874	Saxon	G. Barbee	1906	Burgomaster	L. Lyne	1940	Bimelech	F. A. Smith
1875	Calvin	R. Swim	1907	Peter Pan	G. Mountain	1941	Whirlaway	E. Arcaro
1876	Algerine	W. Donohue	1908	Colin	J. Notter	1942	Shut Out	E. Arcaro
1877	Cloverbrook	C. Holloway	1909	Joe Madden	E. Dugan	1943	Count Fleet	J. Longden
1878	Duke of Magenta	L. Hughes	1910	Sweep	J. Butwell	1944	Bounding Home	G. L. Smith
1879	Spendthrift	S. Evans	1913	Prince Eugene	R. Troxler	1945	Pavot	E. Arcaro
1880	Grenada	L. Hughes	1914	Luke McLuke	M. Buxton	1946	Assault	W. Mehrtens
1881	Saunterer	T. Costello	1915	The Finn	G. Byrne	1947	Phalanx	R. Donoso
1882	Forester	J. McLaughlin	1916	Friar Rock	E. Haynes	1948	Citation	E. Arcaro
1883	George Kinney	J. McLaughlin	1917	Hourless	J. Butwell	1949	Capot	T. Atkinson
1884	Panique	J. McLaughlin	1918	Johren	F. Robinson	1950	Middleground	W. Boland
1885	Tyrant	P. Duffy	1919	Sir Barton	J. Loftus	1951	Counterpoint	D. Gorman
1886	Inspector B	J. McLaughlin	1920	Man o' War	C. Kummer	1952	One Count	E. Arcaro
1887	Hanover	J. McLaughlin	1921	Grey Lag	E. Sande	1953	Native Dancer	E. Guerin
1888	Sir Dixon	J. McLaughlin	1922	Pillory	C. H. Miller	1954	High Gun	E. Guerin
1889	Eric	W. Hayward	1923	Zev	E. Sande	1955	Nashua	E. Arcaro
1890	Burlington	S. Barnes	1924	Mad Play	E. Sande	1956	Needles	D. Erb
1891	Foxford	E. Garrison	1925	American Flag	A. Johnson	1957	Gallant Man	W. Shoemaker
1892	Patron	W. Hayward	1926	Crusader	A. Johnson	1958	Cavan	P. Anderson
1893	Comanche	W. Simms	1927	Chance Shot	E. Sande	1959	Sword Dancer	W. Shoemaker
1894	Henry of Navarre	W. Simms	1928	Vito	C. Kummer	1960	Celtic Ash	W. Hartack
1895	Belmar	F. Taral	1929	Blue Larkspur	M. Garner	1961	Sherluck	B. Baeza
1896	Hastings	H. Griffin	1930	Gallant Fox	E. Sande	1962	Jaipur	W. Shoemaker
1897	Scottish Chieftain	J. Scherrer	1931	Twenty Grand	C. Kurtsinger	1963	Chateaugay	B. Baeza
1898	Bowling Brook	F. Littlefield	1932	Faireno	T. Malley	1964	Quadrangle	M. Ycaza

Year	Horse	Jockey	Year	Horse	Jockey	Year	Horse	Jockey
1965	Hail to All	J. Sellers	1984	Swale	L. Pincay	2003	Empire Maker	J. Bailey
1966	Amberoid	W. Boland	1985	Creme Fraiche	E. Maple	2004	Birdstone	E. Prado
1967	Damascus	W. Shoemaker	1986	Danzig Connection	C. McCarron	2005	Afleet Alex	J. Rose
1968	Stage Door Johnny	H. Gustines	1987	Bet Twice	C. Perret	2006	Jazil	F. Jara
1969	Arts and Letters	B. Baeza	1988	Risen Star	E. Delahoussaye	2007	Rags to Riches	J. Velazquez
1970	High Echelon	J. L. Rotz	1989	Easy Goer	P. Day	2008	Da' Tara	A. Garcia
1971	Pass Catcher	W. Blum	1990	Go and Go	M. Kinane	2009	Summer Bird	K. Desormeaux
1972	Riva Ridge	R. Turcotte	1991	Hansel	J. Bailey	2010	Drosselmeyer	M. Smith
1973	Secretariat	R. Turcotte	1992	A.P. Indy	E. Delahoussaye	2011	Ruler On Ice	J. Valdivia Jr.
1974	Little Current	M. Rivera	1993	Colonial Affair	J. Krone	2012	Union Rags	J. Velazquez
1975	Avatar	W. Shoemaker	1994	Tabasco Cat	P. Day	2013	Palace Malice	M. Smith
1976	Bold Forbes	A. Cordero	1995	Thunder Gulch	G. Stevens	2014	Tonalist	J. Rosario
1977	Seattle Slew	J. Cruguet	1996	Editor's Note	R. Douglas	2015	American Pharoah	V. Espinoza
1978	Affirmed	S. Cauthen	1997	Touch Gold	C. McCarron	2016	Creator	I. Ortiz Jr.
1979	Coastal	R. Hernandez	1998	Victory Gallop	G. Stevens	2017	Tapwrit	J. Ortiz
1980	Temperence Hill	E. Maple	1999	Lemon Drop Kid	J. Santos	2018	Justify	M. Smith
1981	Summing	G. Martens	2000	Commendable	P. Day	2019	Sir Winston	J. Rosario
1982	Conquistador Cielo	L. Pincay	2001	Point Given	G. Stevens	2020	Tiz the Law	M. Franco
1983	Caveat	L. Pincay	2002	Sarava	E. Prado			

Annual Leading Jockey by Earnings, 1957-2019

Total purses earned by all horses that jockey raced in year listed; does not reflect what jockey earned.

Year	Jockey	Earnings	Year	Jockey	Earnings	Year	Jockey	Earnings
1957	Bill Hartack	$3,060,501	1978	Darrel McHargue	$6,029,885	1999	Pat Day	$18,092,845
1958	Willie Shoemaker	2,961,693	1979	Laffit Pincay Jr.	8,193,535	2000	Pat Day	17,479,838
1959	Willie Shoemaker	2,843,133	1980	Chris McCarron	7,663,300	2001	Jerry D. Bailey	22,597,720
1960	Willie Shoemaker	2,123,961	1981	Chris McCarron	8,397,604	2002	Jerry D. Bailey	19,271,814
1961	Willie Shoemaker	2,690,819	1982	Angel Cordero Jr.	9,483,590	2003	Jerry D. Bailey	23,354,960
1962	Willie Shoemaker	2,916,844	1983	Angel Cordero Jr.	10,116,697	2004	John R. Velazquez	22,220,261
1963	Willie Shoemaker	2,526,925	1984	Chris McCarron	12,045,813	2005	John R. Velazquez	20,799,923
1964	Willie Shoemaker	2,649,553	1985	Laffit Pincay Jr.	13,353,299	2006	Garrett K. Gomez	20,122,592
1965	Braulio Baeza	2,582,702	1986	Jose Santos	11,329,297	2007	Garrett K. Gomez	22,800,074
1966	Braulio Baeza	2,951,022	1987	Jose Santos	12,375,433	2008	Garrett K. Gomez	23,344,351
1967	Braulio Baeza	3,088,888	1988	Jose Santos	14,877,298	2009	Garrett K. Gomez	18,536,105
1968	Braulio Baeza	2,835,108	1989	Jose Santos	13,838,389	2010	Ramon A. Dominguez	16,911,880
1969	Jorge Velasquez	2,542,315	1990	Gary Stevens	13,881,198	2011	Ramon A. Dominguez	20,267,032
1970	Laffit Pincay Jr.	2,626,526	1991	Chris McCarron	14,441,083	2012	Ramon A. Dominguez	25,584,852
1971	Laffit Pincay Jr.	3,784,377	1992	Kent Desormeaux	14,193,006	2013	Javier Castellano	26,214,007
1972	Laffit Pincay Jr.	3,225,827	1993	Mike Smith	14,024,815	2014	Javier Castellano	25,056,464
1973	Laffit Pincay Jr.	4,093,492	1994	Mike Smith	15,979,820	2015	Javier Castellano	28,120,809
1974	Laffit Pincay Jr.	4,251,060	1995	Jerry D. Bailey	16,311,876	2016	Javier Castellano	26,826,241
1975	Braulio Baeza	3,695,198	1996	Jerry D. Bailey	19,465,376	2017	José L. Ortiz	27,318,875
1976	Angel Cordero Jr.	4,709,500	1997	Jerry D. Bailey	18,320,743	2018	Irad Ortiz Jr.	27,727,039
1977	Steve Cauthen	6,151,750	1998	Gary Stevens	19,622,855	2019	Irad Ortiz Jr.	34,109,019

Breeders' Cup World Thoroughbred Championships, 1984-2019

The Breeders' Cup began in 1984 and through 2006, consisted of seven races at one track on one day. In 2007, it expanded to two days, with new races. In 2018, the 5½-furlong Juvenile Turf Sprint debuted and was won by Bulletin (jockey: J. Castellano); in 2019, Four Wheel Drive (I. Ortiz Jr.).

Classic
Distance: 1¼ mi.

Year	Horse	Jockey	Year	Horse	Jockey	Year	Horse	Jockey
1984	Wild Again	P. Day	1996	Alphabet Soup	C. McCarron	2008	Raven's Pass	F. Dettori
1985	Proud Truth	J. Velasquez	1997	Skip Away	M. Smith	2009	Zenyatta	M. Smith
1986	Skywalker	L. Pincay Jr.	1998	Awesome Again	P. Day	2010	Blame	G. Gomez
1987	Ferdinand	W. Shoemaker	1999	Cat Thief	P. Day	2011	Drosselmeyer	M. Smith
1988	Alysheba	C. McCarron	2000	Tiznow	C. McCarron	2012	Fort Larned	B. Hernandez
1989	Sunday Silence	C. McCarron	2001	Tiznow	C. McCarron	2013	Mucho Macho Man	G. Stevens
1990	Unbridled	P. Day	2002	Volponi	J. Santos	2014	Bayern	M. Garcia
1991	Black Tie Affair	J. Bailey	2003	Pleasantly Perfect	A. Solis	2015	American Pharoah	V. Espinoza
1992	A.P. Indy	E. Delahoussaye	2004	Ghostzapper	J. Castellano	2016	Arrogate	M. Smith
1993	Arcangues	J. Bailey	2005	Saint Liam	J. Bailey	2017	Gun Runner	F. Geroux
1994	Concern	J. Bailey	2006	Invasor	F. Jara	2018	Accelerate	J. Rosario
1995	Cigar	J. Bailey	2007	Curlin	R. Albarado	2019	Vino Rosso	I. Ortiz Jr.

Juvenile
Distance: 1-1/16 mi, 1986 and since 1988; 1 mi, 1984-85, 1987.

Year	Horse	Jockey	Year	Horse	Jockey	Year	Horse	Jockey
1984	Chief's Crown	D. MacBeth	1996	Boston Harbor	J. Bailey	2008	Midshipman	G. Gomez
1985	Tasso	L. Pincay Jr.	1997	Favorite Trick	P. Day	2009	Vale of York	A. Ajtebi
1986	Capote	L. Pincay Jr.	1998	Answer Lively	J. Bailey	2010	Uncle Mo	J. Velazquez
1987	Success Express	J. Santos	1999	Anees	G. Stevens	2011	Hansen	R. Dominguez
1988	Is It True	L. Pincay Jr.	2000	Macho Uno	J. Bailey	2012	Shanghai Bobby	R. Napravnik
1989	Rhythm	C. Perret	2001	Johannesburg	M. Kinane	2013	New Year's Day	M. Garcia
1990	Fly So Free	J. Santos	2002	Vindication	M. Smith	2014	Texas Red	K. Desormeaux
1991	Arazi	P. Valenzuela	2003	Action This Day	D. Flores	2015	Nyquist	M. Gutierrez
1992	Gilded Time	C. McCarron	2004	Wilko	F. Dettori	2016	Classic Empire	J. Leparoux
1993	Brocco	G. Stevens	2005	Stevie Wonderboy	G. Gomez	2017	Good Magic	J. Ortiz
1994	Timber Country	P. Day	2006	Street Sense	C. Borel	2018	Game Winner	J. Rosario
1995	Unbridled's Song	M. Smith	2007	War Pass	C. Velasquez	2019	Storm the Court	F. Prat

Filly and Mare Sprint
Distance: 6 furlongs, 2007; 7 furlongs since 2008.

Year	Horse	Jockey	Year	Horse	Jockey	Year	Horse	Jockey
2007	Maryfield	E. Trujillo	2012	Groupie Doll	R. Maragh	2016	Finest City	M. Smith
2008	Ventura	G. Gomez	2013	Groupie Doll	R. Maragh	2017	Bar of Gold	I. Ortiz Jr.
2009	Informed Decision	J. Leparoux	2014	Judy the Beauty	M. Smith	2018	Shamrock Rose	I. Ortiz Jr.
2010	Dubai Majesty	J. Theriot	2015	Wavell Avenue	J. Rosario	2019	Covfefe	J. Rosario
2011	Musical Romance	J. Leyva						

Juvenile Fillies

Distance: 1-1/16 mi, 1986 and since 1988; 1 mi, 1984-85, 1987. Outstandingly won the 1984 race by disqualification.

Year	Horse	Jockey	Year	Horse	Jockey	Year	Horse	Jockey
1984	Outstandingly	W. Guerra	1997	Countess Diana	S. Sellers	2009	She Be Wild	J. Leparoux
1985	Twilight Ridge	J. Velasquez	1998	Silverbulletday	G. Stevens	2010	Awesome Feather	J. Sanchez
1986	Brave Raj	P. Valenzuela	1999	Cash Run	J. Bailey	2011	My Miss Aurelia	C. Nakatani
1987	Epitome	P. Day	2000	Caressing	J. Velazquez	2012	Beholder	G. Gomez
1988	Open Mind	A. Cordero Jr.	2001	Tempera	D. Flores	2013	Ria Antonia	J. Castellano
1989	Go for Wand	R. Romero	2002	Storm Flag Flying	J. Velazquez	2014	Take Charge Brandi	V. Espinoza
1990	Meadow Star	J. Santos	2003	Halfbridled	J. Krone			
1991	Pleasant Stage	E. Delahoussaye	2004	Sweet Catomine	C. Nakatani	2015	Songbird	M. Smith
1992	Eliza	P. Valenzuela	2005	Folklore	E. Prado	2016	Champagne Room	M. Gutierrez
1993	Phone Chatter	L. Pincay Jr.	2006	Dreaming of Anna	R. Douglas	2017	Caledonia Road	M. Smith
1994	Flanders	P. Day	2007	Indian Blessing	G. Gomez	2018	Jaywalk	J. Rosario
1995	My Flag	J. Bailey	2008	Stardom Bound	M. Smith	2019	British Idiom	J. Castellano
1996	Storm Song	C. Perret						

Sprint

Distance: 6 furlongs.

Year	Horse	Jockey	Year	Horse	Jockey	Year	Horse	Jockey
1984	Eillo	C. Perret	1996	Lit de Justice	C. Nakatani	2008	Midnight Lute	G. Gomez
1985	Precisionist	C. McCarron	1997	Elmhurst	C. Nakatani	2009	Dancing in Silks	J. Rosario
1986	Smile	J. Vasquez	1998	Reraise	C. Nakatani	2010	Big Drama	E. Coa
1987	Very Subtle	P. Valenzuela	1999	Artax	J. Chaves	2011	Amazombie	M. Smith
1988	Gulch	A. Cordero Jr.	2000	Kona Gold	A. Solis	2012	Trinniberg	W. Martinez
1989	Dancing Spree	A. Cordero Jr.	2001	Squirtle Squirt	J. Bailey	2013	Secret Circle	M. Garcia
1990	Safely Kept	C. Perret	2002	Orientate	J. Bailey	2014	Work All Week	F. Geroux
1991	Sheikh Albadou	P. Eddery	2003	Cajun Beat	C. Velasquez	2015	Runhappy	E. Prado
1992	Thirty Slews	E. Delahoussaye	2004	Speightstown	J. Velazquez	2016	Drefong	M. Garcia
1993	Cardmania	E. Delahoussaye	2005	Silver Train	E. Prado	2017	Roy H	K. Desormeaux
1994	Cherokee Run	M. Smith	2006	Thor's Echo	C. Nakatani	2018	Roy H	P. Lopez
1995	Desert Stormer	K. Desormeaux	2007	Midnight Lute	G. Gomez	2019	Mitole	R. Santana Jr.

Mile

Year	Horse	Jockey	Year	Horse	Jockey	Year	Horse	Jockey
1984	Royal Heroine	F. Toro	1996	Da Hoss	G. Stevens	2008	Goldikova	O. Peslier
1985	Cozzene	W. Guerra	1997	Spinning World	C. Asmussen	2009	Goldikova	O. Peslier
1986	Last Tycoon	Y. St.-Martin	1998	Da Hoss	J. Velazquez	2010	Goldikova	O. Peslier
1987	Miesque	F. Head	1999	Silic	C. Nakatani	2011	Court Vision	R. Albarado
1988	Miesque	F. Head	2000	War Chant	G. Stevens	2012	Wise Dan	J. Velazquez
1989	Steinlen	J. Santos	2001	Val Royal	J. Valdivia Jr.	2013	Wise Dan	J. Lezcano
1990	Royal Academy	L. Piggott	2002	Domedriver	T. Thulliez	2014	Karakatonie	S. Pasquier
1991	Opening Verse	P. Valenzuela	2003	Six Perfections	J. Bailey	2015	Tepin	J. Leparoux
1992	Lure	M. Smith	2004	Singletary	D. Flores	2016	Tourist	J. Rosario
1993	Lure	M. Smith	2005	Artie Schiller	G. Gomez	2017	World Approval	J. Velazquez
1994	Barathea	F. Dettori	2006	Miesque's Approval	E. Castro	2018	Expert Eye	F. Dettori
1995	Ridgewood Pearl	J. Murtagh	2007	Kip Deville	C. Velasquez	2019	Uni	J. Rosario

Distaff

Distance: 1-1/8 mi since 1988; 1¼ mi, 1984-87; race known as Ladies' Classic, 2008-12.

Year	Horse	Jockey	Year	Horse	Jockey	Year	Horse	Jockey
1984	Princess Rooney	E. Delahoussaye	1996	Jewel Princess	C. Nakatani	2008	Zenyatta	M. Smith
1985	Life's Magic	A. Cordero Jr.	1997	Ajina	M. Smith	2009	Life Is Sweet	G. Gomez
1986	Lady's Secret	P. Day	1998	Escena	G. Stevens	2010	Unrivaled Belle	K. Desormeaux
1987	Sacahuista	R. Romero	1999	Beautiful Pleasure	J. Chaves	2011	Royal Delta	J. Lezcano
1988	Personal Ensign	R. Romero	2000	Spain	V. Espinoza	2012	Royal Delta	M. Smith
1989	Bayakoa	L. Pincay Jr.	2001	Unbridled Elaine	P. Day	2013	Beholder	G. Stevens
1990	Bayakoa	L. Pincay Jr.	2002	Azeri	M. Smith	2014	Untapable	R. Napravnik
1991	Dance Smartly	P. Day	2003	Adoration	P. Valenzuela	2015	Stopchargingmaria	J. Castellano
1992	Paseana	C. McCarron	2004	Ashado	J. Velazquez	2016	Beholder	G. Stevens
1993	Hollywood Wildcat	E. Delahoussaye	2005	Pleasant Home	C. Velasquez	2017	Forever Unbridled	J. Velazquez
1994	One Dreamer	G. Stevens	2006	Round Pond	E. Prado	2018	Monomoy Girl	F. Geroux
1995	Inside Information	M. Smith	2007	Ginger Punch	R. Bejarano	2019	Blue Prize	J. Bravo

Turf

Distance: 1½ mi.

Year	Horse	Jockey	Year	Horse	Jockey	Year	Horse	Jockey
1984	Lashkari	Y. St.-Martin	1996	Pilsudski	W. Swinburn	2008	Conduit	R. Moore
1985	Pebbles	P. Eddery	1997	Chief Bearhart	J. Santos	2009	Conduit	R. Moore
1986	Manila	J. Santos	1998	Buck's Boy	S. Sellers	2010	Dangerous Midge	F. Dettori
1987	Theatrical	P. Day	1999	Daylami	F. Dettori	2011	St Nicholas Abbey	J. O'Brien
1988	Great Communicator	R. Sibille	2000	Kalanisi	J. Murtagh	2012	Little Mike	R. Dominguez
			2001	Fantastic Light	F. Dettori	2013	Magician	R. Moore
1989	Prized	E. Delahoussaye	2002	High Chaparral	M. Kinane	2014	Main Sequence	J. Velazquez
1990	In the Wings	G. Stevens	2003	(tie) High Chaparral	M. Kinane	2015	Found	R. Moore
1991	Miss Alleged	E. Legrix		Johar	A. Solis	2016	Highland Reel	S. Heffernan
1992	Fraise	P. Valenzuela	2004	Better Talk Now	R. Dominguez	2017	Talismanic	M. Barzalona
1993	Kotashaan	K. Desormeaux	2005	Shirocco	C. Soumillon	2018	Enable	F. Dettori
1994	Tikkanen	M. Smith	2006	Red Rocks	F. Dettori	2019	Bricks and Mortar	I. Ortiz Jr.
1995	Northern Spur	C. McCarron	2007	English Channel	J. Velasquez			

Filly and Mare Turf

Distance: 1-3/8 mi, 1999-2000, 2004, 2006-07, 2010-11, 2018; 1¼ mi, 2001-03, 2005, 2008-09, 2012-14, 2016, 2019; 1-3/16 mi, 2015; 1-1/8 mi, 2017.

Year	Horse	Jockey	Year	Horse	Jockey	Year	Horse	Jockey
1999	Soaring Softly	J. Bailey	2006	Ouija Board	F. Dettori	2013	Dank	R. Moore
2000	Perfect Sting	J. Bailey	2007	Lahudood	A. Garcia	2014	Dayatthespa	J. Castellano
2001	Banks Hill	O. Peslier	2008	Forever Together	J. Leparoux	2015	Stephanie's Kitten	J. Velazquez
2002	Starine	J. Velazquez	2009	Midday	T. Queally	2016	Queen's Trust	F. Dettori
2003	Islington	K. Fallon	2010	Shared Account	E. Prado	2017	Wuheida	W. Buick
2004	Ouija Board	F. Dettori	2011	Perfect Shirl	J. Velazquez	2018	Sistercharlie	J. Velazquez
2005	Intercontinental	R. Bejarano	2012	Zagora	J. Castellano	2019	Iridessa	W. Lordan

Juvenile Turf

Distance: 1 mi.

Year	Horse	Jockey	Year	Horse	Jockey	Year	Horse	Jockey
2007	Nownownow	J. Leparoux	2012	George Vancouver	R. Moore	2016	Oscar Performance	J. Ortiz
2008	Donativum	F. Dettori	2013	Outstrip	M. Smith	2017	Mendelssohn	R. Moore
2009	Pounced	F. Dettori	2014	Hootenanny	F. Dettori	2018	Line of Duty	W. Buick
2010	Pluck	G. Gomez	2015	Hit It a Bomb	R. Moore	2019	Structor	J. Ortiz
2011	Wrote	R. Moore						

Dirt Mile

Year	Horse	Jockey	Year	Horse	Jockey	Year	Horse	Jockey
2007	Corinthian	K. Desormeaux	2012	Tapizar	C. Nakatani	2016	Tamarkuz	M. Smith
2008	Albertus Maximus	G. Gomez	2013	Goldencents	R. Bejarano	2017	Battle of Midway	F. Prat
2009	Furthest Land	J. Leparoux	2014	Goldencents	R. Bejarano	2018	City of Light	J. Castellano
2010	Dakota Phone	J. Rosario	2015	Liam's Map	J. Castellano	2019	Spun to Run	I. Ortiz Jr.
2011	Caleb's Posse	R. Maragh						

Turf Sprint

Distance: 6½ furlongs, 2008-09, 2012-14, 2016; 5 furlongs, 2010-11, 2017, 2019; 5½ furlongs, 2015, 2018.

Year	Horse	Jockey	Year	Horse	Jockey	Year	Horse	Jockey
2008	Desert Code	R. Migliore	2012	Mizdirection	M. Smith	2016	Obviously	F. Prat
2009	California Flag	J. Talamo	2013	Mizdirection	M. Smith	2017	Stormy Liberal	J. Rosario
2010	Chamberlain Bridge	J. Theriot	2014	Bobby's Kitten	J. Rosario	2018	Stormy Liberal	D. Van Dyke
2011	Regally Ready	C. Nakatani	2015	Mongolian Saturday	F. Geroux	2019	Belvoir Bay	J. Castellano

Juvenile Fillies Turf

Distance: 1 mi.

Year	Horse	Jockey	Year	Horse	Jockey	Year	Horse	Jockey
2008	Maram	J. Lezcano	2012	Flotilla	C. Lemaire	2016	New Money Honey	J. Castellano
2009	Tapitsfly	R. Albarado	2013	Chriselliam	R. Hughes	2017	Rushing Fall	J. Castellano
2010	More Than Real	G. Gomez	2014	Lady Eli	I. Ortiz Jr.	2018	Newspaperofrecord	I. Ortiz Jr.
2011	Stephanie's Kitten	J. Velazquez	2015	Catch a Glimpse	F. Geroux	2019	Sharing	M. Franco

Eclipse Awards, 2019

The Eclipse Awards, honoring the Horse of the Year and other champions of thoroughbred racing, began in 1971 and are sponsored by the *Daily Racing Form*, the National Thoroughbred Racing Association, and the National Turf Writers Assn.

Horse of the Year: Bricks and Mortar
Two-year-old male: Storm the Court
Two-year-old filly: British Idiom
Three-year-old male: Maximum Security
Three-year-old filly: Covfefe
Older dirt male: Vino Rosso

Older dirt female: Midnight Bisou
Male sprinter: Mitole
Female sprinter: Covfefe
Male turf horse: Bricks and Mortar
Female turf horse: Uni
Steeplechase horse: Winston C

Owner: Klaravich Stables Inc. and William H. Lawrence
Breeder: George Strawbridge Jr.
Jockey: Irad Ortiz Jr.
Apprentice jockey: Kazushi Kimura
Trainer: Chad Brown

HARNESS RACING
Harness Horse of the Year, 1947-2019
Chosen by the U.S. Trotting Assn. and the U.S. Harness Writers Assn.

Year	Horse	Year	Horse	Year	Horse	Year	Horse
1947	Victory Song	1966	Bret Hanover	1984	Fancy Crown	2002	Real Desire
1948	Rodney	1967	Nevele Pride	1985	Nihilator	2003	No Pan Intended
1949	Good Time	1968	Nevele Pride	1986	Forrest Skipper	2004	Rainbow Blue
1950	Proximity	1969	Nevele Pride	1987	Mack Lobell	2005	Rocknroll Hanover
1951	Pronto Don	1970	Fresh Yankee	1988	Mack Lobell	2006	Glidemaster
1952	Good Time	1971	Albatross	1989	Matt's Scooter	2007	Donato Hanover
1953	Hi Lo's Forbes	1972	Albatross	1990	Beach Towel	2008	Somebeachsomewhere
1954	Stenographer	1973	Sir Dalrae	1991	Precious Bunny	2009	Muscle Hill
1955	Scott Frost	1974	Delmonica Hanover	1992	Artsplace	2010	Rock N Roll Heaven
1956	Scott Frost	1975	Savoir	1993	Staying Together	2011	San Pail
1957	Torpid	1976	Keystone Ore	1994	Cam's Card Shark	2012	Chapter Seven
1958	Emily's Pride	1977	Green Speed	1995	CR Kay Suzie	2013	Bee a Magician
1959	Bye Bye Byrd	1978	Abercrombie	1996	Continental Victory	2014	JK She'salady
1960	Adios Butler	1979	Niatross	1997	Malabar Man	2015	Wiggle It Jiggleit
1961	Adios Butler	1980	Niatross	1998	Moni Maker	2016	Always B Miki
1962	Su Mac Lad	1981	Fan Hanover	1999	Moni Maker	2017	Hannelore Hanover
1963	Speedy Scot	1982	Cam Fella	2000	Gallo Blue Chip	2018	McWicked
1964	Bret Hanover	1983	Cam Fella	2001	Bunny Lake	2019	Shartin N
1965	Bret Hanover						

Hambletonian Winners (3-year-old trotters), 1965-2020

Year	Horse	Driver	Year	Horse	Driver	Year	Horse	Driver
1965	Egyptian Candor	D. Cameron	1984	Historic Freight	B. Webster	2003	Amigo Hall	M. Lachance
1966	Kerry Way	F. Ervin	1985	Prakas	B. O'Donnell	2004	Windsong's Legacy	T. Smedshammer
1967	Speedy Streak	D. Cameron	1986	Nuclear Kosmos	U. Thoresen	2005	Vivid Photo	R. Hammer
1968	Nevele Pride	S. Dancer	1987	Mack Lobell	J. Campbell	2006	Glidemaster	J. Campbell
1969	Lindy's Pride	H. Beissinger	1988	Armbro Goal	J. Campbell	2007	Donato Hanover	R. Pierce
1970	Timothy T	J. Simpson Sr.	1989	Park Avenue Joe	R. Waples	2008	Deweycheatumnhowe	R. Schnittker
1971	Speedy Crown	H. Beissinger	1990	Harmonious	J. Campbell	2009	Muscle Hill	B. Sears
1972	Super Bowl	S. Dancer	1991	Giant Victory	J. Moiseyev	2010	Muscle Massive	R. Pierce
1973	Flirth	R. Baldwin	1992	Alf Palema	M. McNicholl	2011	Broad Bahn	G. Brennan
1974	Christopher T	B. Haughton	1993	American Winner	R. Pierce	2012	Market Share	T. Tetrick
1975	Bonefish	S. Dancer	1994	Victory Dream	M. Lachance	2013	Royalty For Life	B. Sears
1976	Steve Lobell	B. Haughton	1995	Tagliabue	J. Campbell	2014	Trixton	J. Takter
1977	Green Speed	B. Haughton	1996	Continental Victory	M. Lachance	2015	Pinkman	B. Sears
1978	Speedy Somolli	H. Beissinger	1997	Malabar Man	M. Burroughs	2016	Marion Marauder	S. Zeron
1979	Legend Hanover	G. Sholty	1998	Muscles Yankee	J. Campbell	2017	Perfect Spirit	A. Svanstedt
1980	Burgomeister	B. Haughton	1999	Self Possessed	M. Lachance	2018	Atlanta	S. Zeron
1981	Shiaway St. Pat	R. Remmen	2000	Yankee Paco	T. Ritchie	2019	Forbidden Trade	B. McClure
1982	Speed Bowl	T. Haughton	2001	Scarlet Knight	S. Melander	2020	Ramona Hill	A. McCarthy
1983	Duenna	S. Dancer	2002	Chip Chip Hooray	E. Ledford			

BOWLING

Professional Bowlers Association Tournament of Champions, 1965-2020

Year	Winner	Year	Winner	Year	Winner	Year	Winner
1965	Billy Hardwick	1979	George Pappas	1992	Marc McDowell	2008	Michael Haugen Jr.
1966	Wayne Zahn	1980	Wayne Webb	1993	George Branham III	2009	Patrick Allen
1967	Jim Stefanich	1981	Steve Cook	1994	Norm Duke	2010	Kelly Kulick
1968	Dave Davis	1982	Mike Durbin	1996	Dave D'Entremont	2011	Mika Koivuniemi
1969	Jim Godman	1983	Joe Berardi	1997	John Gant	2012	Sean Rash
1970	Don Johnson	1984	Mike Durbin	1998	Bryan Goebel	2013	Pete Weber
1971	Johnny Petraglia	1985	Mark Williams	1999	Jason Couch	2014	Jason Belmonte
1972	Mike Durbin	1986	Marshall Holman	2000	Jason Couch	2015	Jason Belmonte
1973	Jim Godman	1987	Pete Weber	2002	Jason Couch	2016	Jesper Svensson
1974	Earl Anthony	1988	Mark Williams	2003	Patrick Healey Jr.	2017	E. J. Tackett
1975	Dave Davis	1989	Del Ballard Jr.	2005	Steve Jaros	2018	Matt O'Grady
1976	Marshall Holman	1990	Dave Ferraro	2006	Chris Barnes	2019	Jason Belmonte
1977	Mike Berlin	1991	David Ozio	2007	Tommy Jones	2020	Kris Prather
1978	Earl Anthony						

Note: No tournament held in 2001 or 2004.

Professional Bowlers Association Leading Money Winners, 1962-2019

Total winnings from tournaments only. For 2000-13, year shown is year the PBA season ended.

Year	Bowler	Earnings	Year	Bowler	Earnings	Year	Bowler	Earnings
1962	Don Carter	$49,972	1981	Earl Anthony	$164,735	2000	Norm Duke	$143,325
1963	Dick Weber	46,333	1982	Earl Anthony	134,760	2002	Parker Bohn III	245,200
1964	Bob Strampe	33,592	1983	Earl Anthony	135,605	2003	Walter Ray Williams Jr.	419,700
1965	Dick Weber	47,674	1984	Mark Roth	158,712	2004	Mika Koivuniemi	238,590
1966	Wayne Zahn	54,720	1985	Mike Aulby	201,200	2005	Patrick Allen	350,740
1967	Dave Davis	54,165	1986	Walter Ray Williams Jr.	145,550	2006	Tommy Jones	301,700
1968	Jim Stefanich	67,377	1987	Pete Weber	175,491	2007	Doug Kent	200,530
1969	Billy Hardwick	64,160	1988	Brian Voss	225,485	2008	Norm Duke	176,855
1970	Mike McGrath	52,049	1989	Mike Aulby	298,237	2009	Norm Duke	190,130
1971	Johnny Petraglia	85,065	1990	Amleto Monacelli	204,775	2010	Walter Ray Williams Jr.	152,670
1972	Don Johnson	56,648	1991	David Ozio	225,585	2011	Mika Koivuniemi	333,040
1973	Don McCune	69,000	1992	Marc McDowell	174,215	2012	Sean Rash	140,250
1974	Earl Anthony	99,585	1993	Walter Ray Williams Jr.	296,370	2013	Sean Rash	248,317
1975	Earl Anthony	107,585	1994	Norm Duke	273,753	2014	Jason Belmonte	163,778
1976	Earl Anthony	110,833	1995	Mike Aulby	219,792	2015	Jason Belmonte	178,542
1977	Mark Roth	105,583	1996	Walter Ray Williams Jr.	241,330	2016	E. J. Tackett	168,290
1978	Mark Roth	134,500	1997	Walter Ray Williams Jr.	240,544	2017	Jason Belmonte	238,912
1979	Mark Roth	124,517	1998	Walter Ray Williams Jr.	238,225	2018	Anthony Simonsen	115,975
1980	Wayne Webb	116,700	1999	Parker Bohn III	240,912	2019	Jason Belmonte	285,290

World Chess Champions, 1886-2020

Source: U.S. Chess Federation, International Chess Federation (FIDE)

Official world champions since the title was first used. World championship match scheduled to begin Dec. 2020 was postponed to 2021.

Years	Champion, country	Years	Champion, country
1886-94	Wilhelm Steinitz, Austria	1972-75	Bobby Fischer, U.S.[2]
1894-1921	Emanuel Lasker, Germany	1975-85	Anatoly Karpov, USSR
1921-27	Jose R. Capablanca, Cuba	1985-2000	Garry Kasparov, USSR/Russia[3,4]
1927-35	Alexander Alekhine, France	1993-99	Anatoly Karpov, Russia (FIDE)[3]
1935-37	Max Euwe, Netherlands	1999-2000	Alexander Khalifman, Russia (FIDE)
1937-46	Alexander Alekhine, France[1]	2000-02	Viswanathan Anand, India (FIDE)
1948-57	Mikhail Botvinnik, USSR	2000-06	Vladimir Kramnik, Russia (classical)[4]
1957-58	Vassily Smyslov, USSR	2002-04	Ruslan Ponomariov, Ukraine (FIDE)
1958-59	Mikhail Botvinnik, USSR	2004-05	Rustam Kasimdzhanov, Uzbekistan (FIDE)
1960-61	Mikhail Tal, USSR	2005-06	Veselin Topalov, Bulgaria (FIDE)[5]
1961-63	Mikhail Botvinnik, USSR	2006-07	Vladimir Kramnik, Russia[5]
1963-69	Tigran Petrosian, USSR	2007-13	Viswanathan Anand, India
1969-72	Boris Spassky, USSR	2013-	Magnus Carlsen, Norway

(1) After Alekhine died in 1946, the title was vacant until 1948, when Botvinnik won the first world championship event sanctioned by FIDE. (2) Defaulted championship after refusing to accept FIDE rules for a championship match, Apr. 1975. (3) Kasparov broke with FIDE, Feb. 26, 1993. FIDE stripped Kasparov of his FIDE title Mar. 23. Kasparov defeated Nigel Short (UK) in a world championship match played Sept.-Oct. 1993 under the auspices of the Professional Chess Association (PCA), a new organization the two founded. FIDE held a championship match between Anatoly Karpov (Russia) and Jan Timman (Netherlands), which Karpov won in Nov. 1993. The PCA folded in 1995, but Kasparov was still considered the "classical" world champion. (That is, he defended his title against challengers; FIDE matches are arranged differently.) (4) In Nov. 2000, Kramnik defeated Kasparov for the classical world championship title. (5) Kramnik, the classical world champion since 2000, unified the chess titles by defeating Topalov on Oct. 13, 2006, at a world championship match.

U.S. and World Figure Skating Championships, 1952-2020

U.S. Champions		Year	World Champions	
Men's winner	**Women's winner**		**Men's winner, country**	**Women's winner, country**
Dick Button	Tenley Albright	1952	Dick Button, U.S.	Jacqueline du Bief, France
Hayes Jenkins	Tenley Albright	1953	Hayes Jenkins, U.S.	Tenley Albright, U.S.
Hayes Jenkins	Tenley Albright	1954	Hayes Jenkins, U.S.	Gundi Busch, W. Germany
Hayes Jenkins	Tenley Albright	1955	Hayes Jenkins, U.S.	Tenley Albright, U.S.
Hayes Jenkins	Tenley Albright	1956	Hayes Jenkins, U.S.	Carol Heiss, U.S.
David Jenkins	Carol Heiss	1957	David Jenkins, U.S.	Carol Heiss, U.S.
David Jenkins	Carol Heiss	1958	David Jenkins, U.S.	Carol Heiss, U.S.
David Jenkins	Carol Heiss	1959	David Jenkins, U.S.	Carol Heiss, U.S.
David Jenkins	Carol Heiss	1960	Alain Giletti, France	Carol Heiss, U.S.
No competition[1]		1961	No competition[1]	No competition[1]
Bradley Lord	Laurence Owen	1962	Don Jackson, Canada	Sjoukje Dijkstra, Netherlands
Monty Hoyt	Barbara Roles Pursley	1963	Don McPherson, Canada	Sjoukje Dijkstra, Netherlands
Tommy Litz	Lorraine Hanlon	1964	Manfred Schnelldorfer, W. Germany	Sjoukje Dijkstra, Netherlands
Scott Allen	Peggy Fleming	1965	Alain Calmat, France	Petra Burka, Canada
Gary Visconti	Peggy Fleming	1966	Emmerich Danzer, Austria	Peggy Fleming, U.S.
Scott Allen	Peggy Fleming	1967	Emmerich Danzer, Austria	Peggy Fleming, U.S.
Gary Visconti	Peggy Fleming	1968	Emmerich Danzer, Austria	Peggy Fleming, U.S.
Tim Wood	Peggy Fleming	1969	Tim Wood, U.S.	Gabriele Seyfert, E. Germany
Tim Wood	Janet Lynn	1970	Tim Wood, U.S.	Gabriele Seyfert, E. Germany
Tim Wood	Janet Lynn	1971	Ondrej Nepela, Czechoslovakia	Beatrix Schuba, Austria
John Misha Petkevich	Janet Lynn	1972	Ondrej Nepela, Czechoslovakia	Beatrix Schuba, Austria
Ken Shelley	Janet Lynn	1973	Ondrej Nepela, Czechoslovakia	Karen Magnussen, Canada
Gordon McKellen Jr.	Janet Lynn	1974	Jan Hoffmann, E. Germany	Christine Errath, E. Germany
Gordon McKellen Jr.	Dorothy Hamill	1975	Sergei Volkov, USSR	Dianne de Leeuw, Neth.
Gordon McKellen Jr.	Dorothy Hamill	1976	John Curry, UK	Dorothy Hamill, U.S.
Terry Kubicka	Dorothy Hamill	1977	Vladimir Kovalev, USSR	Linda Fratianne, U.S.
Charles Tickner	Linda Fratianne	1978	Charles Tickner, U.S.	Anett Poetzsch, E. Germany
Charles Tickner	Linda Fratianne	1979	Vladimir Kovalev, USSR	Linda Fratianne, U.S.
Charles Tickner	Linda Fratianne	1980	Jan Hoffmann, E. Germany	Anett Poetzsch, E. Germany
Charles Tickner	Linda Fratianne	1981	Scott Hamilton, U.S.	Denise Biellmann, Switzerland
Scott Hamilton	Elaine Zayak	1982	Scott Hamilton, U.S.	Elaine Zayak, U.S.
Scott Hamilton	Rosalynn Sumners	1983	Scott Hamilton, U.S.	Rosalynn Sumners, U.S.
Scott Hamilton	Rosalynn Sumners	1984	Scott Hamilton, U.S.	Katarina Witt, E. Germany
Scott Hamilton	Rosalynn Sumners	1985	Aleksandr Fadeev, USSR	Katarina Witt, E. Germany
Brian Boitano	Tiffany Chin	1986	Brian Boitano, U.S.	Debi Thomas, U.S.
Brian Boitano	Debi Thomas	1987	Brian Orser, Canada	Katarina Witt, E. Germany
Brian Boitano	Jill Trenary	1988	Brian Boitano, U.S.	Katarina Witt, E. Germany
Brian Boitano	Debi Thomas	1989	Kurt Browning, Canada	Midori Ito, Japan
Christopher Bowman	Jill Trenary	1990	Kurt Browning, Canada	Jill Trenary, U.S.
Todd Eldredge	Jill Trenary	1991	Kurt Browning, Canada	Kristi Yamaguchi, U.S.
Todd Eldredge	Tonya Harding	1992	Viktor Petrenko, Ukraine	Kristi Yamaguchi, U.S.
Christopher Bowman	Kristi Yamaguchi	1993	Kurt Browning, Canada	Oksana Baiul, Ukraine
Scott Davis	Nancy Kerrigan	1994	Elvis Stojko, Canada	Yuka Sato, Japan
Scott Davis	Vacant[2]	1995	Elvis Stojko, Canada	Chen Lu, China
Todd Eldredge	Nicole Bobek	1996	Todd Eldredge, U.S.	Michelle Kwan, U.S.
Rudy Galindo	Michelle Kwan	1997	Elvis Stojko, Canada	Tara Lipinski, U.S.
Todd Eldredge	Tara Lipinski	1998	Alexei Yagudin, Russia	Michelle Kwan, U.S.
Todd Eldredge	Michelle Kwan	1999	Alexei Yagudin, Russia	Maria Butyrskaya, Russia
Michael Weiss	Michelle Kwan	2000	Alexei Yagudin, Russia	Michelle Kwan, U.S.
Michael Weiss	Michelle Kwan	2001	Yevgeny Plushenko, Russia	Michelle Kwan, U.S.
Timothy Goebel	Michelle Kwan	2002	Alexei Yagudin, Russia	Irina Slutskaya, Russia
Todd Eldredge	Michelle Kwan	2003	Yevgeny Plushenko, Russia	Michelle Kwan, U.S.
Michael Weiss	Michelle Kwan	2004	Yevgeny Plushenko, Russia	Shizuka Arakawa, Japan
Johnny Weir	Michelle Kwan	2005	Stéphane Lambiel, Switzerland	Irina Slutskaya, Russia
Johnny Weir	Michelle Kwan	2006	Stéphane Lambiel, Switzerland	Kimmie Meissner, U.S.
Johnny Weir	Sasha Cohen	2007	Brian Joubert, France	Miki Ando, Japan
Evan Lysacek	Kimmie Meissner	2008	Jeffrey Buttle, Canada	Mao Asada, Japan
Evan Lysacek	Mirai Nagasu	2009	Evan Lysacek, U.S.	Yuna Kim, South Korea
Jeremy Abbott	Alissa Czisny	2010	Daisuke Takahashi, Japan	Mao Asada, Japan
Jeremy Abbott	Rachael Flatt	2011	Patrick Chan, Canada	Miki Ando, Japan
Ryan Bradley	Alissa Czisny	2012	Patrick Chan, Canada	Carolina Kostner, Italy
Jeremy Abbott	Ashley Wagner	2013	Patrick Chan, Canada	Yuna Kim, South Korea
Max Aaron	Ashley Wagner	2014	Yuzuru Hanyu, Japan	Mao Asada, Japan
Jeremy Abbott	Gracie Gold	2015	Javier Fernández, Spain	Elizaveta Tuktamysheva, Russia
Jason Brown	Ashley Wagner	2016	Javier Fernández, Spain	Evgenia Medvedeva, Russia
Adam Rippon	Gracie Gold	2017	Yuzuru Hanyu, Japan	Evgenia Medvedeva, Russia
Nathan Chen	Karen Chen	2018	Nathan Chen, U.S.	Kaetlyn Osmond, Canada
Nathan Chen	Bradie Tennell	2019	Nathan Chen, U.S.	Alina Zagitova, Russia
Nathan Chen	Alysa Liu	2020[3]	No champion	No champion

(1) Competition canceled after 18-member U.S. team died in plane crash en route. (2) Tonya Harding was stripped of the title for her involvement in an attack on rival Nancy Kerrigan. (3) World championships canceled due to COVID-19 pandemic.

Alpine Skiing Men's World Cup Champions, 1967-2020

Year	Champion, country	Year	Champion, country	Year	Champion, country
1967	Jean Claude Killy, France	1985	Marc Girardelli, Luxembourg	2003	Stephan Eberharter, Austria
1968	Jean Claude Killy, France	1986	Marc Girardelli, Luxembourg	2004	Hermann Maier, Austria
1969	Karl Schranz, Austria	1987	Pirmin Zurbriggen, Switzerland	2005	Bode Miller, U.S.
1970	Karl Schranz, Austria	1988	Pirmin Zurbriggen, Switzerland	2006	Benjamin Raich, Austria
1971	Gustavo Thoeni, Italy	1989	Marc Girardelli, Luxembourg	2007	Aksel Lund Svindal, Norway
1972	Gustavo Thoeni, Italy	1990	Pirmin Zurbriggen, Switzerland	2008	Bode Miller, U.S.
1973	Gustavo Thoeni, Italy	1991	Marc Girardelli, Luxembourg	2009	Aksel Lund Svindal, Norway
1974	Piero Gros, Italy	1992	Paul Accola, Switzerland	2010	Carlo Janka, Switzerland
1975	Gustavo Thoeni, Italy	1993	Marc Girardelli, Luxembourg	2011	Ivica Kostelic, Croatia
1976	Ingemar Stenmark, Sweden	1994	Kjetil André Aamodt, Norway	2012	Marcel Hirscher, Austria
1977	Ingemar Stenmark, Sweden	1995	Alberto Tomba, Italy	2013	Marcel Hirscher, Austria
1978	Ingemar Stenmark, Sweden	1996	Lasse Kjus, Norway	2014	Marcel Hirscher, Austria
1979	Peter Luescher, Switzerland	1997	Luc Alphand, France	2015	Marcel Hirscher, Austria
1980	Andreas Wenzel, Liechtenstein	1998	Hermann Maier, Austria	2016	Marcel Hirscher, Austria
1981	Phil Mahre, U.S.	1999	Lasse Kjus, Norway	2017	Marcel Hirscher, Austria
1982	Phil Mahre, U.S.	2000	Hermann Maier, Austria	2018	Marcel Hirscher, Austria
1983	Phil Mahre, U.S.	2001	Hermann Maier, Austria	2019	Marcel Hirscher, Austria
1984	Pirmin Zurbriggen, Switzerland	2002	Stephan Eberharter, Austria	2020	Aleksander Aamodt Kilde, Norway

Alpine Skiing Women's World Cup Champions, 1967-2020

Year	Champion, country	Year	Champion, country	Year	Champion, country
1967	Nancy Greene, Canada	1985	Michela Figini, Switzerland	2003	Janica Kostelic, Croatia
1968	Nancy Greene, Canada	1986	Maria Walliser, Switzerland	2004	Anja Paerson, Sweden
1969	Gertrud Gabl, Austria	1987	Maria Walliser, Switzerland	2005	Anja Paerson, Sweden
1970	Michèle Jacot, France	1988	Michela Figini, Switzerland	2006	Janica Kostelic, Croatia
1971	Annemarie Proell, Austria	1989	Vreni Schneider, Switzerland	2007	Nicole Hosp, Austria
1972	Annemarie Proell, Austria	1990	Petra Kronberger, Austria	2008	Lindsey Vonn, U.S.
1973	Annemarie Proell, Austria	1991	Petra Kronberger, Austria	2009	Lindsey Vonn, U.S.
1974	Annemarie Proell, Austria	1992	Petra Kronberger, Austria	2010	Lindsey Vonn, U.S.
1975	Annemarie Proell, Austria	1993	Anita Wachter, Austria	2011	Maria Höfl-Riesch, Germany
1976	Rose Mittermaier, W. Germany	1994	Vreni Schneider, Switzerland	2012	Lindsey Vonn, U.S.
1977	Lise-Marie Morerod, Switzerland	1995	Vreni Schneider, Switzerland	2013	Tina Maze, Slovenia
1978	Hanni Wenzel, Liechtenstein	1996	Katja Seizinger, Germany	2014	Anna Fenninger, Austria
1979	Annemarie Moser-Proell, Austria	1997	Pernilla Wiberg, Sweden	2015	Anna Fenninger, Austria
1980	Hanni Wenzel, Liechtenstein	1998	Katja Seizinger, Germany	2016	Lara Gut, Switzerland
1981	Marie-Theres Nadig, Switzerland	1999	Alexandra Meissnitzer, Austria	2017	Mikaela Shiffrin, U.S.
1982	Erika Hess, Switzerland	2000	Renate Goetschl, Austria	2018	Mikaela Shiffrin, U.S.
1983	Tamara McKinney, U.S.	2001	Janica Kostelic, Croatia	2019	Mikaela Shiffrin, U.S.
1984	Erika Hess, Switzerland	2002	Michaela Dorfmeister, Austria	2020	Federica Brignone, Italy

Tour de France, 2020

Slovenian Tadej Pogacar won the 107th edition of the Tour de France Sept. 20, 2020, marking the first time that cycling's premiere race was won by a Slovenian cyclist. The 21-year-old Pogacar, the youngest Tour winner since 1904, also claimed the white jersey as the best rider under age 25 and the polka dot jersey as the race's best climber. Postponed from its June start because of the coronavirus pandemic, the first stage of the 2,164-mi (3,483-km) Tour de France began Aug. 29 in Nice, France. The 21st and final stage ended in Paris, where Pogacar claimed victory in 87 hr., 20 min., 5 sec., followed by his fellow countryman Primoz Roglic, 59 sec. back, and Australian Richie Porte, 3 min., 30 sec. out of first. Ireland's Sam Bennett claimed the green jersey as points leader.

The 2021 Tour de France is scheduled to be held June 26-July 18. Its route will take cyclists from Brest, France, to Paris.

Tour de France Winners, 1903-2020

The Tour de France was first held in 1903. Sixty cyclists began the 1,509-mi (2,428-km) race at Montgeron, a suburb of Paris, and 21 cyclists finished the six-stage race 17 days later in Paris. The race route changes every year. Race not held, 1915-18, 1940-46.

Year	Winner, country	Year	Winner, country	Year	Winner, country
1903	Maurice Garin, France	1950	Ferdi Kübler, Switzerland	1986	Greg LeMond, U.S.
1904	Henri Cornet, France	1951	Hugo Koblet, Switzerland	1987	Stephen Roche, Ireland
1905	Louis Trousselier, France	1952	Fausto Coppi, Italy	1988	Pedro Delgado, Spain
1906	René Pottier, France	1953	Louison Bobet, France	1989	Greg LeMond, U.S.
1907	Lucien Petit-Breton, France	1954	Louison Bobet, France	1990	Greg LeMond, U.S.
1908	Lucien Petit-Breton, France	1955	Louison Bobet, France	1991	Miguel Indurain, Spain
1909	François Faber, Luxembourg	1956	Roger Walkowiak, France	1992	Miguel Indurain, Spain
1910	Octave Lapize, France	1957	Jacques Anquetil, France	1993	Miguel Indurain, Spain
1911	Gustave Garrigou, France	1958	Charly Gaul, Luxembourg	1994	Miguel Indurain, Spain
1912	Odile Defraye, Belgium	1959	Federico Bahamontes, Spain	1995	Miguel Indurain, Spain
1913	Philippe Thys, Belgium	1960	Gastone Nencini, Italy	1996	Bjarne Riis, Denmark
1914	Philippe Thys, Belgium	1961	Jacques Anquetil, France	1997	Jan Ullrich, Germany
1919	Firmin Lambot, Belgium	1962	Jacques Anquetil, France	1998	Marco Pantani, Italy
1920	Philippe Thys, Belgium	1963	Jacques Anquetil, France	1999	Vacant[1]
1921	Léon Scieur, Belgium	1964	Jacques Anquetil, France	2000	Vacant[1]
1922	Firmin Lambot, Belgium	1965	Felice Gimondi, Italy	2001	Vacant[1]
1923	Henri Pélissier, France	1966	Lucien Aimar, France	2002	Vacant[1]
1924	Ottavio Bottecchia, Italy	1967	Roger Pingeon, France	2003	Vacant[1]
1925	Ottavio Bottecchia, Italy	1968	Jan Janssen, Netherlands	2004	Vacant[1]
1926	Lucien Buysse, Belgium	1969	Eddy Merckx, Belgium	2005	Vacant[1]
1927	Nicolas Frantz, Luxembourg	1970	Eddy Merckx, Belgium	2006	Óscar Pereiro, Spain[2]
1928	Nicolas Frantz, Luxembourg	1971	Eddy Merckx, Belgium	2007	Alberto Contador, Spain
1929	Maurice Dewaele, Belgium	1972	Eddy Merckx, Belgium	2008	Carlos Sastre, Spain
1930	André Leducq, France	1973	Luis Ocaña, Spain	2009	Alberto Contador, Spain
1931	Antonin Magne, France	1974	Eddy Merckx, Belgium	2010	Andy Schleck, Luxembourg[3]
1932	André Leducq, France	1975	Bernard Thévenet, France	2011	Cadel Evans, Australia
1933	Georges Speicher, France	1976	Lucien Van Impe, Belgium	2012	Bradley Wiggins, UK
1934	Antonin Magne, France	1977	Bernard Thévenet, France	2013	Chris Froome, UK
1935	Romain Maes, Belgium	1978	Bernard Hinault, France	2014	Vincenzo Nibali, Italy
1936	Sylvère Maes, Belgium	1979	Bernard Hinault, France	2015	Chris Froome, UK
1937	Roger Lapépie, France	1980	Joop Zoetemelk, Netherlands	2016	Chris Froome, UK
1938	Gino Bartali, Italy	1981	Bernard Hinault, France	2017	Chris Froome, UK
1939	Sylvère Maes, Belgium	1982	Bernard Hinault, France	2018	Geraint Thomas, UK
1947	Jean Robic, France	1983	Laurent Fignon, France	2019	Egan Bernal, Colombia
1948	Gino Bartali, Italy	1984	Laurent Fignon, France	2020	Tadej Pogacar, Slovenia
1949	Fausto Coppi, Italy	1985	Bernard Hinault, France		

(1) Lance Armstrong, U.S., was stripped of his seven Tour titles Oct. 22, 2012; Armstrong had dropped his fight against doping charges Aug. 23, 2012. (2) Floyd Landis, U.S., was stripped of the 2006 title, Sept. 20, 2007, for doping. Landis lost a final appeal of the ruling June 30, 2008. (3) Alberto Contador, Spain, was stripped of the 2010 title, Feb. 6, 2012, for doping.

Swimming World Records

Long course (50-m pools only) records, as of Sept. 2020. All times in minutes:seconds.

Men's Records

Freestyle

Distance	Record	Holder	Nationality	Location	Date
50 meters	0:20.91	César Cielo Filho	Brazil	São Paulo, Brazil	Dec. 18, 2009
100 meters	0:46.91	César Cielo Filho	Brazil	Rome, Italy	July 30, 2009
200 meters	1:42.00	Paul Biedermann	Germany	Rome, Italy	July 28, 2009
400 meters	3:40.07	Paul Biedermann	Germany	Rome, Italy	July 26, 2009
800 meters	7:32.12	Zhang Lin	China	Rome, Italy	July 29, 2009
1,500 meters	14:31.02	Sun Yang	China	London, England, UK	Aug. 4, 2012

Backstroke

50 meters	0:24.00	Kliment Kolesnikov	Russia	Glasgow, Scotland, UK	Aug. 4, 2018
100 meters	0:51.85	Ryan Murphy	U.S.	Rio de Janeiro, Brazil	Aug. 13, 2016
200 meters	1:51.92	Aaron Peirsol	U.S.	Rome, Italy	July 31, 2009

Breaststroke

50 meters	0:25.95	Adam Peaty	UK	Budapest, Hungary	July 25, 2017
100 meters	0:56.88	Adam Peaty	UK	Gwangju, South Korea	July 21, 2019
200 meters	2:06.12	Anton Chupkov	Russia	Gwangju, South Korea	July 26, 2019

Butterfly

50 meters	0:22.27	Andriy Govorov	Ukraine	Rome, Italy	July 1, 2018
100 meters	0:49.50	Caeleb Dressel	U.S.	Gwangju, South Korea	July 26, 2019
200 meters	1:50.73	Kristof Milak	Hungary	Gwangju, South Korea	July 24, 2019

Individual medley

200 meters	1:54.00	Ryan Lochte	U.S.	Shanghai, China	July 28, 2011
400 meters	4:03.84	Michael Phelps	U.S.	Beijing, China	Aug. 10, 2008

Freestyle relay

400 m (4×100)	3:08.24	Phelps, Weber-Gale, Jones, Lezak	U.S.	Beijing, China	Aug. 11, 2008
800 m (4×200)	6:58.55	Phelps, Berens, Walters, Lochte	U.S.	Rome, Italy	July 31, 2009

Medley relay

400 m (4×100)	3:27.28	Peirsol, Shanteau, Phelps, Walters	U.S.	Rome, Italy	Aug. 2, 2009

Women's Records

Freestyle

Distance	Record	Holder	Nationality	Location	Date
50 meters	0:23.67	Sarah Sjöström	Sweden	Budapest, Hungary	July 29, 2017
100 meters	0:51.71	Sarah Sjöström	Sweden	Budapest, Hungary	July 23, 2017
200 meters	1:52.98	Federica Pellegrini	Italy	Rome, Italy	July 29, 2009
400 meters	3:56.46	Katie Ledecky	U.S.	Rio de Janeiro, Brazil	Aug. 7, 2016
800 meters	8:04.79	Katie Ledecky	U.S.	Rio de Janeiro, Brazil	Aug. 12, 2016
1,500 meters	15:20.48	Katie Ledecky	U.S.	Indianapolis, IN	May 16, 2018

Backstroke

50 meters	0:26.98	Liu Xiang	China	Jakarta, Indonesia	Aug. 21, 2018
100 meters	0:57.57	Regan Smith	U.S.	Gwangju, South Korea	July 28, 2019
200 meters	2:03.35	Regan Smith	U.S.	Gwangju, South Korea	July 26, 2019

Breaststroke

50 meters	0:29.40	Lilly King	U.S.	Budapest, Hungary	July 30, 2017
100 meters	1:04.13	Lilly King	U.S.	Budapest, Hungary	July 25, 2017
200 meters	2:19.11	Rikke Pedersen	Denmark	Barcelona, Spain	Aug. 1, 2013

Butterfly

50 meters	0:24.43	Sarah Sjöström	Sweden	Boras, Sweden	July 5, 2014
100 meters	0:55.48	Sarah Sjöström	Sweden	Rio de Janeiro, Brazil	Aug. 7, 2016
200 meters	2:01.81	Liu Zige	China	Jinan, China	Oct. 21, 2009

Individual medley

200 meters	2:06.12	Katinka Hosszú	Hungary	Kazan, Russia	Aug. 3, 2015
400 meters	4:26.36	Katinka Hosszú	Hungary	Rio de Janeiro, Brazil	Aug. 6, 2016

Freestyle relay

400 m (4×100)	3:30.05	Jack, Campbell, McKeon, Campbell	Australia	Gold Coast, Australia	Apr. 5, 2018
800 m (4×200)	7:41.50	Titmus, Wilson, Throssell, McKeon	Australia	Gwangju, South Korea	July 25, 2019

Medley relay

400 m (4×100)	3:50.40	Smith, King, Dahlia, Manuel	U.S.	Gwangju, South Korea	July 28, 2019

World Track and Field Outdoor Records

The International Association of Athletics Federations (IAAF), the world body of track and field, recognizes only records in metric distances, except for the mile. As of Sept. 2020.

Men's Records

Running

Event	Record	Holder	Nationality	Location	Date
100 meters	9.58 s.	Usain Bolt	Jamaica	Berlin, Germany	Aug. 16, 2009
200 meters	19.19 s.	Usain Bolt	Jamaica	Berlin, Germany	Aug. 20, 2009
400 meters	43.03 s.	Wayde Van Niekerk	South Africa	Rio de Janeiro, Brazil	Aug. 14, 2016
800 meters	1 min., 40.91 s.	David Rudisha	Kenya	London, England, UK	Aug. 9, 2012
1,000 meters	2 min., 11.96 s.	Noah Ngeny	Kenya	Rieti, Italy	Sept. 5, 1999
1,500 meters	3 min., 26.00 s.	Hicham El Guerrouj	Morocco	Rome, Italy	July 14, 1998
1 mile	3 min., 43.13 s.	Hicham El Guerrouj	Morocco	Rome, Italy	July 7, 1999
2,000 meters	4 min., 44.79 s.	Hicham El Guerrouj	Morocco	Berlin, Germany	Sept. 7, 1999
3,000 meters	7 min., 20.67 s.	Daniel Komen	Kenya	Rieti, Italy	Sept. 1, 1996
3,000-meter stpl.	7 min., 53.63 s.	Saif Saaeed Shaheen	Qatar	Brussels, Belgium	Sept. 3, 2004
5,000 meters	12 min., 37.35 s.	Kenenisa Bekele	Ethiopia	Hengelo, Netherlands	May 31, 2004
10,000 meters	26 min., 17.53 s.	Kenenisa Bekele	Ethiopia	Brussels, Belgium	Aug. 26, 2005
20,000 meters	56 min., 26.00 s.	Haile Gebrselassie	Ethiopia	Ostrava, Czech Rep.	June 27, 2007
25,000 meters	1 hr., 12 min., 25.4 s.	Moses Mosop	Kenya	Eugene, OR	June 3, 2011
Marathon[1]	2 hr., 1 min., 39 s.	Eliud Kipchoge	Kenya	Berlin, Germany	Sept. 16, 2018
110-meter hurdles	12.80 s.	Aries Merritt	U.S.	Brussels, Belgium	Sept. 7, 2012
400-meter hurdles	46.78 s.	Kevin Young	U.S.	Barcelona, Spain	Aug. 6, 1992
400 m (4×100)	36.84 s.	Carter, Frater, Blake, Bolt	Jamaica	London, England, UK	Aug. 11, 2012
800 m (4×200)	1 min., 18.63 s.	Ashmeade, Weir, Brown, Blake	Jamaica	Nassau, The Bahamas	May 24, 2014
1,600 m (4×400)	2 min., 54.29 s.	Valmon, Watts, Reynolds, Johnson	U.S.	Stuttgart, Germany	Aug. 22, 1993
3,200 m (4×800)	7 min., 2.43 s.	Mutua, Yiampoy, Kombich, Bungei	Kenya	Brussels, Belgium	Aug. 25, 2006

Field Events

Event	Record	Holder	Nationality	Location	Date
High jump	2.45 m (8' ½")	Javier Sotomayor	Cuba	Salamanca, Spain	July 27, 1993
Long jump	8.95 m (29' 4½")	Mike Powell	U.S.	Tokyo, Japan	Aug. 30, 1991
Triple jump	18.29 m (60' ¼")	Jonathan Edwards	UK	Gothenburg, Sweden	Aug. 7, 1995
Pole vault	6.14 m (20' 1¾")	Sergey Bubka	Ukraine	Sestriere, Italy	July 31, 1994
Discus	74.08 m (243' 0")	Jürgen Schult	E. Germany	Neubrandenburg, E. Germany	June 6, 1986
Hammer	86.74 m (284' 7")	Yuriy Sedykh	USSR	Stuttgart, W. Germany	Aug. 30, 1986
Javelin	98.48 m (323' 1")	Jan Zelezný	Czech Rep.	Jena, W. Germany	May 25, 1996
Shot put	23.12 m (75' 10¼")	Randy Barnes	U.S.	Westwood, CA	May 20, 1990
Decathlon	9,126 pts.	Kevin Mayer	France	Talence, France	Sept. 16, 2018

(1) Eliud Kipchoge, Kenya, ran a marathon in 1:59:40.2 in Vienna, Austria, Oct. 12, 2019, but the run was ineligible for record consideration per IAAF guidelines.

Women's Records

Running

Event	Record	Holder	Nationality	Location	Date
100 meters	10.49 s.	Florence Griffith-Joyner	U.S.	Indianapolis, IN	July 16, 1988
200 meters	21.34 s.	Florence Griffith-Joyner	U.S.	Seoul, S. Korea	Sept. 29, 1988
400 meters	47.60 s.	Marita Koch	E. Germany	Canberra, Australia	Oct. 6, 1985
800 meters	1 min., 53.28 s.	Jarmila Kratochvílová	Czechoslovakia	Munich, W. Germany	July 26, 1983
1,000 meters	2 min., 28.98 s.	Svetlana Masterkova	Russia	Brussels, Belgium	Aug. 23, 1996
1,500 meters	3 min., 50.07 s.	Genzebe Dibaba	Ethiopia	Monaco	July 17, 2015
1 mile	4 min., 12.33 s.	Sifan Hassan	Netherlands	Monaco	July 12, 2019
2,000 meters	5 min., 25.36 s.	Sonia O'Sullivan	Ireland	Edinburgh, Scotland, UK	July 8, 1994
3,000 meters	8 min., 6.11 s.	Wang Junxia	China	Beijing, China	Sept. 13, 1993
3,000-meter stpl.	8 min., 44.32 s.	Beatrice Chepkoech	Kenya	Monaco	July 20, 2018
5,000 meters	14 min., 11.15 s.	Tirunesh Dibaba	Ethiopia	Oslo, Norway	June 6, 2008
10,000 meters	29 min., 17.45 s.	Almaz Ayana	Ethiopia	Rio de Janeiro, Brazil	Aug. 12, 2016
20,000 meters	1 hr., 5 min., 26.6 s.	Tegla Loroupe	Kenya	Borgholzhausen, Germany	Sept. 3, 2000
Marathon	2 hr., 14 min., 4 s.	Brigid Kosgei	Kenya	Chicago, IL	Oct. 13, 2019
100-meter hurdles	12.20 s.	Kendra Harrison	U.S.	London, England, UK	July 22, 2016
400-meter hurdles	52.16 s.	Dalilah Muhammad	U.S.	Doha, Qatar	Oct. 4, 2019
400 m (4×100)	40.82 s.	Madison, Felix, Knight, Jeter	U.S.	London, England, UK	Aug. 10, 2012
800 m (4×200)	1 min., 27.46 s.	Jenkins, Colander, Perry, Jones	U.S.	Philadelphia, PA	Apr. 29, 2000
1,600 m (4×400)	3 min., 15.17 s.	Ledovskaya, Nazarova, Pinigina, Bryzgina	USSR	Seoul, S. Korea	Oct. 1, 1988
3,200 m (4×800)	7 min., 50.17 s.	Olizarenko, Gurina, Borisova, Podyalovskaya	USSR	Moscow, Russia	Aug. 5, 1984

Field Events

Event	Record	Holder	Nationality	Location	Date
High jump	2.09 m (6' 10¼")	Stefka Kostadinova	Bulgaria	Rome, Italy	Aug. 30, 1987
Long jump	7.52 m (24' 8¼")	Galina Chistyakova	USSR	Leningrad, Russia	June 11, 1988
Triple jump	15.50 m (50' 10¼")	Inessa Kravets	Ukraine	Gothenburg, Sweden	Aug. 10, 1995
Pole vault	5.06 m (16' 7¾")	Yelena Isinbayeva	Russia	Zürich, Switzerland	Aug. 28, 2009
Discus	76.80 m (252' 0")	Gabriele Reinsch	E. Germany	Neubrandenburg, E. Germany	July 9, 1988
Hammer	82.98 m (272' 3")	Anita Włodarczyk	Poland	Warsaw, Poland	Aug. 28, 2016
Javelin	72.28 m (237' 1¾")	Barbora Spotáková	Czech Rep.	Stuttgart, Germany	Sept. 13, 2008
Shot put	22.63 m (74' 3")	Natalya Lisovskaya	USSR	Moscow, Russia	June 7, 1987
Heptathlon	7,291 pts.	Jackie Joyner-Kersee	U.S.	Seoul, S. Korea	Sept. 24, 1988

Iditarod Trail Sled Dog Race, 2020

Thomas Waerner won the 48th annual Iditarod Trail Sled Dog Race Mar. 18, 2020, becoming the third Norwegian musher to claim victory in the race to Nome, AK. He finished a 975-mi course on the northern route to Nome in 9 days, 10 hr., 37 min., and 47 sec. and was awarded a $51,607 prize and a new truck.

The 2021 race was scheduled to begin Mar. 6 in Anchorage and follow the 998-mi southern route.

Westminster Kennel Club Best-In-Show Dogs, 1985-2020

Year	Best-in-Show winner, breed	Year	Best-in-Show winner, breed
1985	Braeburn's Close Encounter, Scottish Terrier	2004	Darbydale's All Rise Pouch Cove, Newfoundland
1986	Marjetta National Acclaim, Pointer	2005	Kan-Point's VJK Autumn Roses, Pointer (German
1987	Covy Tucker Hill's Manhattan, German Shepherd Dog		Shorthaired)
1988	Great Elms Prince Charming II, Pomeranian	2006	Rocky Top's Sundance Kid, Bull Terrier (Colored)
1989	Royal Tudor's Wild As The Wind, Doberman Pinscher	2007	Felicity's Diamond Jim, Spaniel (English Springer)
1990	Wendessa Crown Prince, Pekingese	2008	K-Run's Park Me In First, Beagle (15 Inch)
1991	Whisperwind On A Carousel, Poodle (Standard)	2009	Clussexx Three D Grinchy Glee, Spaniel (Sussex)
1992	Registry's Lonesome Dove, Fox Terrier (Wire)	2010	Roundtown Mercedes Of Maryscot, Scottish Terrier
1993	Salilyn's Condor, Spaniel (English Springer)	2011	Foxcliffe Hickory Wind, Scottish Deerhound
1994	Chidley Willum The Conqueror, Norwich Terrier	2012	Palacegarden Malachy, Pekingese
1995	Gaelforce Post Script, Scottish Terrier	2013	Banana Joe V Tani Kazari, Affenpinscher
1996	Clussexx Country Sunrise, Spaniel (Clumber)	2014	Afterall Painting The Sky, Fox Terrier (Wire)
1997	Parsifal Di Casa Netzer, Standard Schnauzer	2015	Tashtins Lookin For Trouble, Beagle (15 Inch)
1998	Fairewood Frolic, Norwich Terrier	2016	Vjk-Myst Garbonita's California Journey, Pointer (German
1999	Loteki Supernatural Being, Papillon		Shorthaired)
2000	Salilyn 'N Erin's Shameless, Spaniel (English Springer)	2017	Lockenhaus' Rumor Has It V Kenlyn, German Shepherd
2001	Special Times Just Right, Bichon Frise		Dog
2002	Surrey Spice Girl, Poodle (Miniature)	2018	Belle Creek's All I Care About Is Love, Bichon Frise
2003	Torums Scarf Michael, Kerry Blue Terrier	2019	Kingarthur Van Foliny Home, Fox Terrier (Wire)
		2020	Stone Run Afternoon Tea, Poodle (Standard)

World Marathon Majors Winners, 2006-19

Marathoners are awarded points relative to their finish in each race in the series; number of races and time period encompassed by each series varies.

Series	Men's winner, country	Women's winner, country	Series	Men's winner, country	Women's winner, country
I: 2006-07	Robert K. Cheruiyot, Kenya	Gete Wami, Ethiopia	VII: 2012-13	Tsegaye Kebede, Ethiopia	Priscah Jeptoo, Kenya
			VIII: 2013-14	Wiison Kipsang, Kenya	Edna Kiplagat, Kenya*
II: 2007-08	Martin Lel, Kenya	Irina Mikitenko, Germany	IX: 2015-16	Eliud Kipchoge, Kenya	Mary Keitany, Kenya
III: 2008-09	Samuel Wanjiru, Kenya	Irina Mikitenko, Germany	X: 2016-17	Eliud Kipchoge, Kenya	Edna Kiplagat, Kenya*
IV: 2009-10	Samuel Wanjiru, Kenya	Irina Mikitenko, Germany*	XI: 2017-18	Eliud Kipchoge, Kenya	Mary Keitany, Kenya
V: 2010-11	Emmanuel Mutai, Kenya	Edna Kiplagat, Kenya*	XII: 2018-19	Eliud Kipchoge, Kenya	Brigid Kosgei, Kenya
VI: 2011-12	Geoffrey Mutai, Kenya	Mary Keitany, Kenya			

* = Winner adjusted following doping disqualifications.

Boston Marathon Winners, 1972-2019

All times in hour:minute:second format. * = Course record. The 2020 race was canceled due to the COVID-19 pandemic.

Men's winner, country	Time	Year	Women's winner, country	Time
Olavi Suomalainen, Finland	2:15:39	1972	Nina Kuscsik, U.S.	3:10:26
Jon Anderson, U.S.	2:16:03	1973	Jacqueline Hansen, U.S.	3:05:59
Neil Cusack, Ireland	2:13:39	1974	Michiko Gorman, U.S.	2:47:11
Bill Rodgers, U.S.	2:09:55	1975	Liane Winter, West Germany	2:42:24
Jack Fultz, U.S.	2:20:19	1976	Kim Merritt, U.S.	2:47:10
Jerome Drayton, Canada	2:14:46	1977	Michiko Gorman, U.S.	2:48:33
Bill Rodgers, U.S.	2:10:13	1978	Gayle S. Barron, U.S.	2:44:52
Bill Rodgers, U.S.	2:09:27	1979	Joan Benoit, U.S.	2:35:15
Bill Rodgers, U.S.	2:12:11	1980	Jacqueline Gareau, Canada	2:34:28
Toshihiko Seko, Japan	2:09:26	1981	Allison Roe, New Zealand	2:26:46
Alberto Salazar, U.S.	2:08:52	1982	Charlotte Teske, West Germany	2:29:33
Greg Meyer, U.S.	2:09:00	1983	Joan Benoit, U.S.	2:22:43
Geoff Smith, England, UK	2:10:34	1984	Lorraine Moller, New Zealand	2:29:28
Geoff Smith, England, UK	2:14:05	1985	Lisa Larsen Weidenbach, U.S.	2:34:06
Robert de Castella, Australia	2:07:51	1986	Ingrid Kristiansen, Norway	2:24:55
Toshihiko Seko, Japan	2:11:50	1987	Rosa Mota, Portugal	2:25:21
Ibrahim Hussein, Kenya	2:08:43	1988	Rosa Mota, Portugal	2:24:30
Abebe Mekonnen, Ethiopia	2:09:06	1989	Ingrid Kristiansen, Norway	2:24:33
Gelindo Bordin, Italy	2:08:19	1990	Rosa Mota, Portugal	2:25:24
Ibrahim Hussein, Kenya	2:11:06	1991	Wanda Panfil, Poland	2:24:18
Ibrahim Hussein, Kenya	2:08:14	1992	Olga Markova, Russia	2:23:43
Cosmas Ndeti, Kenya	2:09:33	1993	Olga Markova, Russia	2:25:27
Cosmas Ndeti, Kenya	2:07:15	1994	Uta Pippig, Germany	2:21:45
Cosmas Ndeti, Kenya	2:09:22	1995	Uta Pippig, Germany	2:25:11
Moses Tanui, Kenya	2:09:15	1996	Uta Pippig, Germany	2:27:12
Lameck Aguta, Kenya	2:10:34	1997	Fatuma Roba, Ethiopia	2:26:23
Moses Tanui, Kenya	2:07:34	1998	Fatuma Roba, Ethiopia	2:23:21
Joseh Chebet, Kenya	2:09:52	1999	Fatuma Roba, Ethiopia	2:23:25
Elijah Lagat, Kenya	2:09:47	2000	Catherine Ndereba, Kenya	2:26:11
Lee Bong-ju, South Korea	2:09:43	2001	Catherine Ndereba, Kenya	2:23:53
Rodgers Rop, Kenya	2:09:02	2002	Margaret Okayo, Kenya	2:20:43
Robert Kipkoech Cheruiyot, Kenya	2:10:11	2003	Svetlana Zakharova, Russia	2:25:20
Timothy Cherigat, Kenya	2:10:37	2004	Catherine Ndereba, Kenya	2:24:27
Hailu Negussie, Ethiopia	2:11:45	2005	Catherine Ndereba, Kenya	2:25:13
Robert Kipkoech Cheruiyot, Kenya	2:07:14	2006	Rita Jeptoo, Kenya	2:23:38
Robert Kipkoech Cheruiyot, Kenya	2:14:13	2007	Lidiya Grigoryeva, Russia	2:29:18
Robert Kipkoech Cheruiyot, Kenya	2:07:46	2008	Dire Tune, Ethiopia	2:25:25
Deriba Merga, Ethiopia	2:08:42	2009	Salina Kosgei, Kenya	2:32:16
Robert Kiprono Cheruiyot, Kenya	2:05:52	2010	Teyba Erkesso, Ethiopia	2:26:11
Geoffrey Mutai, Kenya	2:03:02*	2011	Caroline Kilel, Kenya	2:22:36
Wesley Korir, Kenya	2:12:40	2012	Sharon Cherop, Kenya	2:31:50
Lelisa Desisa, Ethiopia	2:10:22	2013	Rita Jeptoo, Kenya	2:26:25
Meb Keflezighi, U.S.	2:08:37	2014	Buzunesh Deba, Ethiopia[1]	2:19:59*
Lelisa Desisa, Ethiopia	2:09:17	2015	Caroline Rotich, Kenya	2:24:55
Lemi Berhanu Hayle, Ethiopia	2:12:45	2016	Atsede Baysa, Ethiopia	2:29:19
Geoffrey Kirui, Kenya	2:09:37	2017	Edna Kiplagat, Kenya	2:21:52
Yuki Kawauchi, Japan	2:15:58	2018	Desiree Linden, U.S.	2:39:54
Lawrence Cherono, Kenya	2:07:57	2019	Worknesh Degefa, Ethiopia	2:23:31

(1) Kenya's Rita Jeptoo was stripped of the victory in Dec. 2016 due to doping.

New York City Marathon Winners, 1970-2019

All times in hour:minute:second format. * = Course record. Race not held, 2012, 2020.

Men's winner, country	Time	Year	Women's winner, country	Time
Gary Muhrcke, U.S.	2:31:38	1970	No finisher	
Norman Higgins, U.S.	2:22:54	1971	—	
Sheldon Karlin, U.S.	2:27:52	1972	Beth Bonner, U.S.	2:55:22
Tom Fleming, U.S.	2:19:25	1973	Nina Kuscsik, U.S.	3:08:41
Norbert Sander, U.S.	2:26:30	1974	Nina Kuscsik, U.S.	2:57:07
Tom Fleming, U.S.	2:19:27	1975	Katherine Switzer, U.S.	3:07:29
Bill Rodgers, U.S.	2:10:10	1976	Kim Merritt, U.S.	2:46:14
Bill Rodgers, U.S.	2:11:28	1977	Miki Gorman, U.S.	2:39:11
Bill Rodgers, U.S.	2:12:12	1978	Miki Gorman, U.S.	2:43:10
Bill Rodgers, U.S.	2:11:42	1979	Grete Waitz, Norway	2:32:30
Alberto Salazar, U.S.	2:09:41	1980	Grete Waitz, Norway	2:27:33
Alberto Salazar, U.S.	2:08:13	1981	Allison Roe, New Zealand	2:25:42
Alberto Salazar, U.S.	2:09:29	1982	Grete Waitz, Norway	2:25:29
Rod Dixon, New Zealand	2:08:59	1983	Grete Waitz, Norway	2:27:14
Orlando Pizzolato, Italy	2:14:53	1984	Grete Waitz, Norway	2:27:00
Orlando Pizzolato, Italy	2:11:34	1985	Grete Waitz, Norway	2:29:30
Gianni Poli, Italy	2:11:06	1986	Grete Waitz, Norway	2:28:34
Ibrahim Hussein, Kenya	2:11:01	1987	Priscilla Welch, England, UK	2:28:06
Steve Jones, Wales, UK	2:08:20	1988	Grete Waitz, Norway	2:30:17
Juma Ikangaa, Tanzania	2:08:01	1989	Ingrid Kristiansen, Norway	2:25:30
Douglas Wakiihuri, Kenya	2:12:39	1990	Wanda Panfil, Poland	2:30:45
Salvador García, Mexico	2:09:28	1991	Liz McColgan, Scotland, UK	2:27:32
Willie Mtolo, South Africa	2:09:29	1992	Lisa Ondieki, Australia	2:24:40
Andres Espinosa, Mexico	2:10:04	1993	Uta Pippig, Germany	2:26:24
German Silva, Mexico	2:11:21	1994	Tegla Loroupe, Kenya	2:27:37
German Silva, Mexico	2:11:00	1995	Tegla Loroupe, Kenya	2:28:06
Giacomo Leone, Italy	2:09:54	1996	Anuta Catuna, Romania	2:28:43
John Kagwe, Kenya	2:08:12	1997	F. Rochat-Moser, Switzerland	2:28:43
John Kagwe, Kenya	2:08:45	1998	Franca Fiacconi, Italy	2:25:17
Joseph Chebet, Kenya	2:09:14	1999	Adriana Fernandez, Mexico	2:25:06
Abdelkader El Mouaziz, Morocco	2:10:09	2000	Ludmila Petrova, Russia	2:25:45
Tesfaye Jifar, Ethiopia	2:07:43	2001	Margaret Okayo, Kenya	2:24:21
Rodgers Rop, Kenya	2:08:07	2002	Joyce Chepchumba, Kenya	2:25:56
Martin Lel, Kenya	2:10:30	2003	Margaret Okayo, Kenya	2:22:31*
Hendrik Ramaala, South Africa	2:09:28	2004	Paula Radcliffe, England, UK	2:23:10
Paul Tergat, Kenya	2:09:30	2005	Jelena Prokopcuka, Latvia	2:24:41
Marilson Gomes dos Santos, Brazil	2:09:58	2006	Jelena Prokopcuka, Latvia	2:25:05
Martin Lel, Kenya	2:09:04	2007	Paula Radcliffe, England, UK	2:23:09
Marilson Gomes dos Santos, Brazil	2:08:43	2008	Paula Radcliffe, England, UK	2:23:56
Meb Keflezighi, U.S.	2:09:15	2009	Derartu Tulu, Ethiopia	2:28:52
Gebre Gebremariam, Ethiopia	2:08:14	2010	Edna Kiplagat, Kenya	2:28:20
Geoffrey Mutai, Kenya	2:05:06*	2011	Firehiwot Dado, Ethiopia	2:23:15
Geoffrey Mutai, Kenya	2:08:24	2013	Priscah Jeptoo, Kenya	2:25:07
Wilson Kipsang, Kenya	2:10:59	2014	Mary Keitany, Kenya	2:25:07
Stanley Biwott, Kenya	2:10:34	2015	Mary Keitany, Kenya	2:24:25
Ghirmay Ghebreslassie, Eritrea	2:07:51	2016	Mary Keitany, Kenya	2:24:26
Geoffrey Kamworor, Kenya	2:10:53	2017	Shalane Flanagan, U.S.	2:26:53
Lelisa Desisa, Ethiopia	2:05:59	2018	Mary Keitany, Kenya	2:22:48
Geoffrey Kamworor, Kenya	2:08:13	2019	Joyciline Jepkosgei, Kenya	2:22:38

Ironman Triathlon World Championships, 1978-2019

A 2.4-mi ocean swim, 112-mi bike ride, and 26.2-mi run in Kailua-Kona, HI. All times in hr.:min.:sec. * = Course record. The 2020 Ironman world championship was canceled due to the COVID-19 pandemic.

Men's winner, country	Time	Year	Women's winner, country	Time
Gordon Haller, U.S.	11:46:58	1978	No finisher	
Tom Warren, U.S.	11:15:56	1979	Lyn Lemaire, U.S.	12:55:00
Dave Scott, U.S.	9:24:33	1980	Robin Beck, U.S.	11:21:24
John Howard, U.S.	9:38:29	1981	Linda Sweeney, U.S.	12:00:32
Dave Scott, U.S.	9:08:23	1982	Julie Leach, U.S.	10:54:08
Dave Scott, U.S.	9:05:57	1983	Sylviane Puntous, Canada	10:43:36
Dave Scott, U.S.	8:54:20	1984	Sylviane Puntous, Canada	10:25:13
Scott Tinley, U.S.	8:50:54	1985	Joanne Ernst, U.S.	10:25:22
Dave Scott, U.S.	8:28:37	1986	Paula Newby-Fraser, Zimbabwe	9:49:14
Dave Scott, U.S.	8:34:13	1987	Erin Baker, New Zealand	9:35:25
Scott Molina, U.S.	8:31:00	1988	Paula Newby-Fraser, Zimbabwe	9:01:01
Mark Allen, U.S.	8:09:15	1989	Paula Newby-Fraser, Zimbabwe	9:00:56
Mark Allen, U.S.	8:28:17	1990	Erin Baker, New Zealand	9:13:42
Mark Allen, U.S.	8:18:32	1991	Paula Newby-Fraser, Zimbabwe	9:07:52
Mark Allen, U.S.	8:09:08	1992	Paula Newby-Fraser, Zimbabwe	8:55:28
Greg Welch, Australia	8:07:45	1993	Paula Newby-Fraser, Zimbabwe	8:58:23
Mark Allen, U.S.	8:20:27	1994	Paula Newby-Fraser, Zimbabwe	9:20:14
Luc Van Lierde, Belgium	8:20:34	1995	Karen Smyers, U.S.	9:16:46
Thomas Hellriegel, Germany	8:04:08	1996	Paula Newby-Fraser, Zimbabwe	9:06:49
Peter Reid, Canada	8:33:01	1997	Heather Fuhr, Canada	9:31:43
Luc Van Lierde, Belgium	8:24:20	1998	Natascha Badmann, Switzerland	9:24:16
Peter Reid, Canada	8:17:17	1999	Lori Bowden, Canada	9:13:02
Timothy Deboom, U.S.	8:21:01	2000	Natascha Badmann, Switzerland	9:26:16
Timothy Deboom, U.S.	8:31:18	2001	Natascha Badmann, Switzerland	9:28:37
Peter Reid, Canada	8:29:56	2002	Lori Bowden, Canada	9:07:54
Normann Stadler, Germany	8:22:35	2003	Natascha Badmann, Switzerland	9:11:55
Faris al-Sultan, Germany	8:33:29	2004	Natascha Badmann, Switzerland[1]	9:50:04
Normann Stadler, Germany	8:14:17	2005	Natascha Badmann, Switzerland	9:09:30
Chris McCormack, Australia	8:11:56	2006	Michellie Jones, Australia	9:18:31
Craig Alexander, Australia	8:15:34	2007	Chrissie Wellington, UK	9:08:45
Craig Alexander, Australia	8:17:45	2008	Chrissie Wellington, UK	9:06:23
Chris McCormack, Australia	8:20:21	2009	Chrissie Wellington, UK	8:54:02
Craig Alexander, Australia	8:10:37	2010	Mirinda Carfrae, Australia	8:58:36
Pete Jacobs, Australia	8:03:56	2011	Chrissie Wellington, UK	8:55:08
Frederik Van Lierde, Belgium	8:18:37	2012	Leanda Cave, U.S.	9:15:54
Sebastian Kienle, Germany	8:12:29	2013	Mirinda Carfrae, Australia	8:52:14
Jan Frodeno, Germany	8:14:18	2014	Mirinda Carfrae, Australia	9:00:55
Jan Frodeno, Germany	8:14:40	2015	Daniela Ryf, Switzerland	8:57:57
Patrick Lange, Germany	8:06:30	2016	Daniela Ryf, Switzerland	8:46:46
Patrick Lange, Germany	8:01:40	2017	Daniela Ryf, Switzerland	8:50:47
Jan Frodeno, Germany	7:52:39	2018	Daniela Ryf, Switzerland	8:26:18*
Jan Frodeno, Germany	7:51:13*	2019	Anne Haug, Germany	8:40:10

(1) First-place finisher Nina Kraft, Germany, admitted to using performance-enhancing drugs and was disqualified, Nov. 15, 2004.

James E. Sullivan Award Winners, 1930-2019

The James E. Sullivan Award, named after the former president of the Amateur Athletic Union (AAU), is given annually by the AAU to the amateur American athlete who "has done the most during the year to advance the cause of sportsmanship."

Year	Winner	Sport	Year	Winner	Sport	Year	Winner	Sport
1930	Bobby Jones	Golf	1964	Don Schollander	Swimming	1994	Dan Jansen	Speed skating
1931	Barney Berlinger	Track	1965	Bill Bradley	Basketball			
1932	Jim Bausch	Track	1966	Jim Ryun	Track	1995	Bruce Baumgartner	Wrestling
1933	Glenn Cunningham	Track	1967	Randy Matson	Track	1996	Michael Johnson	Track
1934	Bill Bonthron	Track	1968	Debbie Meyer	Swimming	1997	Peyton Manning	Football
1935	Lawson Little	Golf	1969	Bill Toomey	Track	1998	Chamique Holdsclaw	Basketball
1936	Glenn Morris	Track	1970	John Kinsella	Swimming	1999	Coco Miller and	
1937	Don Budge	Tennis	1971	Mark Spitz	Swimming		Kelly Miller	Basketball
1938	Don Lash	Track	1972	Frank Shorter	Track	2000	Rulon Gardner	Wrestling
1939	Joe Burk	Rowing	1973	Bill Walton	Basketball	2001	Michelle Kwan	Figure skating
1940	Greg Rice	Track	1974	Rick Wohlhuter	Track			
1941	Leslie MacMitchell	Track	1975	Tim Shaw	Swimming	2002	Sarah Hughes	Figure skating
1942	Cornelius Warmerdam	Track	1976	Bruce Jenner	Track			
1943	Gilbert Dodds	Track	1977	John Naber	Swimming	2003	Michael Phelps	Swimming
1944	Ann Curtis	Swimming	1978	Tracy Caulkins	Swimming	2004	Paul Hamm	Gymnastics
1945	Doc Blanchard	Football	1979	Kurt Thomas	Gymnastics	2005	J. J. Redick	Basketball
1946	Arnold Tucker	Football	1980	Eric Heiden	Speed skating	2006	Jessica Long	Swimming
1947	John Kelly Jr.	Rowing				2007	Tim Tebow	Football
1948	Robert Mathias	Track	1981	Carl Lewis	Track	2008	Shawn Johnson	Gymnastics
1949	Dick Button	Skating	1982	Mary Decker	Track	2009	Amy Palmiero-Winters	Ultra-marathon
1950	Fred Wilt	Track	1983	Edwin Moses	Track			
1951	Rev. Robert Richards	Track	1984	Greg Louganis	Diving	2010	Evan Lysacek	Figure skating
1952	Horace Ashenfelter	Track	1985	Joan Benoit Samuelson	Marathon			
1953	Dr. Sammy Lee	Diving				2011	Andrew Rodriguez	Football
1954	Mal Whitfield	Track	1986	Jackie Joyner-Kersee	Track	2012	Missy Franklin	Swimming
1955	Harrison Dillard	Track	1987	Jim Abbott	Baseball	2013	John Urschel	Football
1956	Patricia McCormick	Diving	1988	Florence Griffith Joyner	Track	2014	Ezekiel Elliott	Football
1957	Bobby Joe Morrow	Track	1989	Janet Evans	Swimming	2015	Keenan Reynolds	Football
1958	Glenn Davis	Track	1990	John Smith	Wrestling		Breanna Stewart	Basketball
1959	Parry O'Brien	Track	1991	Mike Powell	Track	2016	Lauren Carlini	Volleyball
1960	Rafer Johnson	Track	1992	Bonnie Blair	Speed skating	2017	Kyle Snyder	Wrestling
1961	Wilma Rudolph Ward	Track				2018	Kathryn Plummer	Volleyball
1962	James Beatty	Track	1993	Charlie Ward	Football, basketball	2019	Sabrina Ionescu	Basketball
1963	John Pennel	Track					Spencer Lee	Wrestling

America's Cup Yacht Race, 1851-2017

An approximately 60-mi-long yacht race around the Isle of Wight during the London Exposition of 1851 became known as the first America's Cup after the New York Yacht Club won the race (and its prize cup) with the ship *America*. Prior to 1983, all yachts were American unless otherwise noted.

Year	Result (score)	Year	Result (score)
1851	America	1964	Constellation defeated Sovereign, England (4-0)
1870	Magic defeated Cambria, England (1-0)	1967	Intrepid defeated Dame Pattie, Australia (4-0)
1871	Columbia (first three races) and Sappho (last two races) defeated Livonia, England (4-1)	1970	Intrepid defeated Gretel II, Australia (4-1)
1876	Madeline defeated Countess of Dufferin, Canada (2-0)	1974	Courageous defeated Southern Cross, Australia (4-0)
1881	Mischief defeated Atalanta, Canada (2-0)	1977	Courageous defeated Australia, Australia (4-0)
1885	Puritan defeated Genesta, England (2-0)	1980	Freedom defeated Australia, Australia (4-1)
1886	Mayflower defeated Galatea, England (2-0)	1983	Australia II, Australia, defeated Liberty, U.S. (4-3)
1887	Volunteer defeated Thistle, Scotland (2-0)	1987	Stars & Stripes, U.S., defeated Kookaburra III, Aust. (4-0)
1893	Vigilant defeated Valkyrie II, England (3-0)	1988	Stars & Stripes, U.S., defeated Il Moro di Venezia, Italy (4-1)
1895	Defender defeated Valkyrie III, England (3-0)	1992	America[3], U.S., defeated Il Moro di Venezia, Italy (4-1)
1899	Columbia defeated Shamrock, England (3-0)	1995	Team New Zealand, NZ, defeated Young America, U.S. (5-0)
1901	Columbia defeated Shamrock II, England (3-0)	2000	Team New Zealand, NZ, defeated Luna Rossa, Italy (5-0)
1903	Reliance defeated Shamrock III, England (3-0)	2003	Alinghi, Switzerland, defeated Team New Zealand, NZ (5-0)
1920	Resolute defeated Shamrock IV, England (3-2)	2007	Alinghi, Switzerland, defeated Emirates Team New Zealand, NZ (5-2)
1930	Enterprise defeated Shamrock V, England (4-0)	2010	BMW Oracle Racing, U.S., defeated Alinghi 5, Switzerland (2-0)
1934	Rainbow defeated Endeavour, England (4-2)	2013	Oracle Team USA, U.S., defeated Emirates Team New Zealand, NZ (9-8)
1937	Ranger defeated Endeavour II, England (4-0)		
1958	Columbia defeated Sceptre, England (4-0)	2017	Emirates Team New Zealand, NZ, defeated Oracle Team USA, U.S. (8-1)
1962	Weatherly defeated Gretel, Australia (4-1)		

Pro Rodeo Cowboys Association All-Around Champions, 1977-2019

Year	Winner, hometown	Earnings	Year	Winner, hometown	Earnings
1977	Tom Ferguson, Miami, OK	$76,730	1999	Fred Whitfield, Hockley, TX	$217,819
1978	Tom Ferguson, Miami, OK	103,734	2000	Joe Beaver, Huntsville, TX	225,396
1979	Tom Ferguson, Miami, OK	96,272	2001	Cody Ohl, Stephenville, TX	296,419
1980	Paul Tierney, Rapid City, SD	105,568	2002	Trevor Brazile, Anson, TX	273,997
1981	Jimmie Cooper, Monument, NM	105,862	2003	Trevor Brazile, Anson, TX	294,839
1982	Chris Lybbert, Coyote, CA	123,709	2004	Trevor Brazile, Decatur, TX	253,170
1983	Roy Cooper, Durant, OK	153,391	2005	Ryan Jarrett, Summerville, GA	263,665
1984	Dee Pickett, Caldwell, ID	122,618	2006	Trevor Brazile, Decatur, TX	329,924
1985	Lewis Feild, Elk Ridge, UT	130,347	2007	Trevor Brazile, Decatur, TX	425,115
1986	Lewis Feild, Elk Ridge, UT	166,042	2008	Trevor Brazile, Decatur, TX	419,868
1987	Lewis Feild, Elk Ridge, UT	144,335	2009	Trevor Brazile, Decatur, TX	346,779
1988	Dave Appleton, Arlington, TX	121,546	2010	Trevor Brazile, Decatur, TX	507,921
1989	Ty Murray, Odessa, TX	134,806	2011	Trevor Brazile, Decatur, TX	337,601
1990	Ty Murray, Stephenville, TX	213,772	2012	Trevor Brazile, Decatur, TX	298,626
1991	Ty Murray, Stephenville, TX	244,230	2013	Trevor Brazile, Decatur, TX	426,010
1992	Ty Murray, Stephenville, TX	225,992	2014	Trevor Brazile, Decatur, TX	494,369
1993	Ty Murray, Stephenville, TX	297,896	2015	Trevor Brazile, Decatur, TX	518,011
1994	Ty Murray, Stephenville, TX	246,170	2016	Junior Nogueira, Presidente Prudente, Brazil	231,728
1995	Joe Beaver, Huntsville, TX	141,753	2017	Tuf Cooper, Decatur, TX	341,560
1996	Joe Beaver, Huntsville, TX	166,103	2018	Trevor Brazile, Decatur, TX	335,680
1997	Dan Mortensen, Manhattan, MT	184,559	2019	Stetson Wright, Milford, UT	297,923
1998	Ty Murray, Stephenville, TX	264,673			

GENERAL INDEX

Note: Page numbers in boldface indicate key reference. Page numbers in italics indicate photo or illustration captions.

QUICK REFERENCE INDEX

For complete index, see pages 980-1007.

CONTENTS

2020 SPECIAL FEATURES AND YEAR IN REVIEW

THE WORLD ALMANAC AND BOOK OF FACTS 2021

Top 10 News Topics of 2020

1. New Coronavirus Causes Worldwide Pandemic. The worst global pandemic in over 100 years sickened tens of millions and caused about 1.2 mil deaths as of Nov. 1, 2020. The cause was a new coronavirus first detected in late 2019 in Wuhan, Hubei Province, China, where local officials may have initially tried to conceal the severity of the problem. The airborne virus causes the disease COVID-19, which principally affects the respiratory system but can cause damage to many other systems of the body. By early 2020, COVID-19 was spreading around the world. By Nov. 1, the World Health Organization confirmed 46 mil cases. As vaccine and therapeutic-drug research went on, social distancing became a major means of preventing virus transmission. Businesses, schools, and colleges closed for a time or operated at reduced capacity, and large gatherings were prohibited or discouraged. The volume of travel plunged, and major economies saw steep declines.

2. COVID-19 Has Devastating Impact on U.S. As of Nov. 1, the U.S. had more than 9.1 mil confirmed COVID-19 cases and over 230,000 deaths (both about 20% of the world totals), according to Johns Hopkins Univ.'s Coronavirus Resource Center. The virus causing COVID-19 reached the U.S. by mid-Jan. or possibly earlier. By Mar. 31, the country had about 189,000 cases, with the Northeast, and especially New York City, the hardest-hit area. Some hospitals were filled to capacity. State and local governments across the U.S. ordered, Mar.-Apr., nonessential businesses, schools, and recreational facilities to close. Although Congress, in Mar., passed more than $2 tril in relief legislation, the pandemic's impact on the economy was severe. The unemployment rate hit 14.7% in Apr., a jump of more than 10 points over Mar. Pres. Trump, who often publicly downplayed the severity of the epidemic, encouraged reopening of the economy. Quick reopenings may have contributed to severe spikes in cases across the Sunbelt during the summer, and upper Midwest, Plains, and Mountain states were especially hard hit in the fall. Trump, who announced Oct. 2 he had COVID-19 and was briefly hospitalized, often opposed guidance from the Centers for Disease Control and Prevention, issued Apr. 3, that people wear masks in public to impede virus transmission.

3. Biden Apparent Presidential Election Winner. Pending recounts and court challenges, former Vice Pres. Joe Biden (D) won the Nov. 3 presidential election, defeating incumbent Pres. Donald Trump (R). A key part of Biden's campaign strategy was capturing three traditionally Democratic states that Trump won in 2016—Wisconsin, Michigan, and Pennsylvania. As of Nov. 7, apparent victories in those states gave Biden at least 279 electoral votes, more than the 270 required for election. He also had narrow leads in traditionally Republican Arizona and Georgia. Biden's running mate, Kamala Harris, was set to become the first woman, first Black woman, and first Indian American to serve as vice president. Amid the COVID-19 epidemic, record numbers voted by mail, prolonging vote counting and prompting baseless fraud allegations from Trump. In the nationwide popular vote, Biden led by more than 4 mil as of Nov. 7. Republicans did better than expected in congressional races and looked likely to maintain their Senate majority narrowly (after a net loss of 1), with two races in Georgia headed for Jan. 2021 runoffs. Democrats' House of Representatives majority was reduced.

4. George Floyd's Death Sparks Black Lives Matter Protests. On May 25 in Minneapolis, George Floyd, a Black man, died after a police officer held his knee on Floyd's neck for almost 9 minutes. The officer was later charged with murder. Floyd's death touched off months of protests in thousands of U.S. cities (as well as around the world) against a pattern of racist behavior by police. Other incidents that inflamed tensions included the fatal shooting in her home of Breonna Taylor, Mar. 13 in Louisville, KY, by police executing a no-knock search warrant, as well as the shooting, Aug. 23 in Kenosha, WI, of Jacob Blake by a police officer responding to a domestic incident. Most of the Black Lives Matter demonstrations were peaceful, but violence, looting, and property destruction accompanied some protests. Right-wing counter-protesters also engaged in or provoked violence at times. Federal law enforcement officials were deployed in cities including Washington, DC, and Portland, OR, where they sometimes aggressively dispersed or detained peaceful protesters and heightened tensions.

5. Pres. Trump Acquitted of Impeachment Charges. The U.S. House of Representatives voted on party lines, Dec. 18, 2019, to impeach Pres. Donald Trump on charges of abuse of power and obstruction of Congress. Trump was the third president formally impeached, following Andrew Johnson (1868) and Bill Clinton (1998). The charges against Trump stemmed from a July 25, 2019, phone call between Trump and Ukraine's president, in which Trump appeared to make military aid to U.S. ally Ukraine contingent on Ukraine's investigating Trump's political rival Joe Biden. After a trial in the Republican-controlled Senate, Trump was acquitted on both charges, Feb. 5. All Republican senators voted for acquittal (except for Mitt Romney of Utah on abuse of power); all Democrats voted for conviction.

6. Supreme Court Appointment Cements Conservative Majority. Associate Justice Ruth Bader Ginsburg—a champion of equal rights, especially women's rights, during a 6-decade legal career, including 27 years on the Supreme Court—died Sept. 18. Pres. Trump, Sept. 26, nominated U.S. Appeals Court Judge Amy Coney Barrett to fill the Supreme Court seat, despite criticism that he should not fill the vacancy just weeks before the Nov. 3 presidential election. The Senate, Oct. 26, voted to confirm Barrett, 52-48; all Republicans voted in favor, except for Susan Collins of Maine, and all Democrats voted against. A strict constructionist, Barrett was expected to give the Court a 6-3 majority of conservative justices.

7. Continuing Conflict, Moves Toward Peace Occur in Middle East, SW Asia. Already high U.S.-Iranian tensions increased following the U.S assassination, Jan. 3, of Iranian Revolutionary Guard Gen. Qassem Soleimani, killed in a drone strike in Iraq. Iran responded with missile strikes on two Iraqi bases housing U.S. troops. Moving toward exiting Afghanistan after 19 years of war, the U.S., Feb. 29, signed an agreement with the Taliban to reduce and eventually withdraw all U.S. troops in exchange for a Taliban pledge to not support anti-U.S. terrorism. Although conflict between Taliban and Afghan-government forces remained at high levels in 2020, direct peace talks between the two sides began Sept. 12. Reducing its regional isolation, Israel signed U.S.-brokered agreements, Sept. 15, to normalize relations with the United Arab Emirates and Bahrain.

8. Climate Change Affects U.S. Wildfires and Hurricanes. A devastating fire season in the western U.S. and highly active Atlantic hurricane season resulted in part from climate change, in the view of most scientists. Hotter, drier conditions helped spark fires that became especially severe beginning in Aug. In California, about 4,150,000 acres had burned by Nov. 1, the highest yearly figure ever recorded. More than 1 mil acres had burned in Oregon, about 620,000 in Colorado, and over 500,000 in Washington. A record-high 11 hurricanes and other tropical storms that made landfall in the mainland U.S. as of Nov. 1. Warmer ocean waters likely contributed to the development of 28 named storms by Nov. 1, tying 2005's record 28 storms.

9. Off-Field Events Dominate Sports. The COVID-19 pandemic caused major changes for sports leagues and tournaments. The Tokyo Olympics were postponed from summer 2020 to summer 2021. The NCAA, Mar. 12, canceled its 2020 basketball tournaments. The NBA suspended its season as of Mar. 12; games resumed July 30 with all players isolated at a sports complex near Orlando, FL, and with no fans in attendance. Major League Baseball played a shortened 60-game regular season, with no fans at games and other safety protocols; still, some games were postponed because team members tested positive for COVID-19. On Sept. 10, the NFL season began as scheduled, but in the following weeks, some games were postponed because of positive COVID-19 tests. Players and sports organizations also responded to social justice issues. NASCAR announced, June 10, it would ban display of the Confederate battle flag at all of its events and venues. NBA, WNBA, MLB, and other players forced postponements of a number of games in Aug. following the police shooting of Jacob Blake, a Black man, in Kenosha, WI. The NBA and its Players Association announced agreement, Aug. 28, on several programs to promote voting rights and racial justice.

10. Britain Achieves Brexit. The United Kingdom officially left the European Union, Jan. 31, becoming the first EU member to do so. In 2016, Britons had narrowly voted in a referendum to leave the EU, leading to complex negotiations over the terms of separation. After Jan. 31, the UK entered a transition period, during which it continued to follow EU laws and rules, with a Dec. 31, 2020, deadline for the UK to reach a new trade pact with the EU. The withdrawal agreement called for Northern Ireland to remain in the EU customs union beyond 2020, to maintain an open border with EU member Ireland.

THE WORLD
AT A GLANCE

Number Ones

World's most populous country . . . . China, 1.39 billion population in 2020 *(p. 737)*
World's most populous urban area . . . . Tokyo, Japan, 37.4 million population in 2020 *(p. 736)*
World's wealthiest person . . . . American Jeff Bezos, $113.0 billion net worth as of Mar. 2020 *(p. 86)*
Most-visited U.S. social networking website . . . . Facebook, 223.2 million unique visitors in June 2020 *(p. 333)*
Most-used U.S. search engine . . . . Google, 12.1 billion searches (61.9% of all searches) in June 2020 *(p. 333)*
Most popular U.S. mobile app . . . . YouTube, 163.5 million users in June 2020 *(p. 333)*
U.S. airline that carried the most passengers . . . . Southwest Airlines, 162.7 million passengers in 2019 *(p. 126)*
World's busiest airport by passenger traffic . . . . . Hartsfield-Jackson Atlanta Intl. Airport, 110.5 million passengers in 2019 *(p. 126)*
World's most-visited amusement park . . . . . . Magic Kingdom at Walt Disney World, Florida, 20.96 million visitors in 2019 *(p. 128)*
Nations with the most days off work per year . . . . Austria and Malta, 38 days off *(p. 741)*
Most popular recording artist by digital singles . . . . Drake, 163.5 million units sold as of Aug. 2020 *(p. 289)*
Most popular YouTuber . . . . PewDiePie, 106.0 million U.S. subscribers as of Aug. 2020 *(p. 282)*
World's top-grossing movie . . . . *Avengers: Endgame*, $2.8 billion gross as of Sept. 2020 *(p. 279)*
Highest-rated prime-time TV show . . . . *NCIS*, watched in 9.5% of TV-owning households in 2019-20 *(p. 292)*
Highest-rated syndicated TV show . . . . *Judge Judy*, watched in 6.5% of TV-owning households in 2019-20 *(p. 292)*
Highest-rated basic cable TV show . . . . *Yellowstone*, watched in 2.1% of TV-owning households in 2019-20 *(p. 293)*
Highest-rated premium cable TV show . . . . *Real Time With Bill Maher*, watched in 1.3% of TV-owning households in 2019-20 *(p. 293)*

Surprising Facts

Prior to 2020, the highest number of weekly U.S. unemployment filings was just under 12.1 mil, set in Jan. 2010. Pandemic-related shutdowns created repeated weekly highs in 2020, peaking at 32.4 mil claims in late June. *(p. 130)*

In 2019, 45.6% of 12th graders said they had ever tried vaping nicotine, marijuana, or just flavoring, compared to 22.3% who had ever tried smoking cigarettes. *(p. 183)*

Of high school students who drove a car at least once in the 30 days before they were surveyed in 2019, 39.0% said they had texted or emailed while driving; 5.4% said they drove when they had been drinking alcohol. *(p. 205)*

20.4% of female high school students reported being bullied electronically (e.g., bullied via texting, Instagram, Facebook, or other social media) in 2019; the rate for high school boys was 10.9%. *(p. 417)*

In 1995, 67.0% of airline seats were filled by passengers during scheduled service. By 2019, that number had climbed to 84.6%. *(p. 125)*

Americans paid an average of 24.0% of their gross earnings in income tax and Social Security contributions in 2019; Germans and Belgians, who had some of the highest personal income tax rates, paid an average of 39.3%. *(p. 740)*

The U.S. divorce rate has declined fairly steadily since it peaked at 5.3 per 1,000 pop. in 1981; in 2018, it was 2.9. The U.S. marriage rate has been hovering around all-time lows of 6.8-6.9 per 1,000 pop. since 2009 and fell even lower, to 6.5, in 2018. *(p. 199)*

Employed U.S. women's earnings were equal to 70.7% of men's earnings in 2019. Women's earnings came closest to matching men's in the construction industry, where their earnings were 93.2% of men's, but women made up only 10.3% of construction industry employees. *(p. 135)*

U.S. workers saw their productivity and compensation grow at similar rates, 1948-79, with 108.1% and 93.2% growth, respectively. But in 1979-2018, those rates diverged, with 69.6% in productivity gains and just 14.8% in compensation growth. *(p. 135)*

The number of refugees in the world increased from 10.5 million in 2010 to 20.4 million in 2019. The number of internally displaced persons (IDPs) increased even more steeply, from 14.7 million in 2010 to a record-high 43.5 million in 2019. *(p. 742)*

In 1950, the U.S. produced 75.7% of the world's motor vehicles manufactured that year; by 2019, that number had dropped to 11.9% (up from a low of 9.5% in 2009). *(p. 117)*

Milestone Birthdays, 2021

100
Prince Philip, June 10

90
Robert Duvall, Jan. 5
James Earl Jones, Jan. 17
William Shatner, Mar. 22
Willie Mays, May 6
Olympia Dukakis, June 20
Rita Moreno, Dec. 11

80
Joan Baez, Jan. 9
Faye Dunaway, Jan. 14
Neil Diamond, Jan. 24
Dick Cheney, Jan. 30
Bob Dylan, May 24
Martha Stewart, Aug. 3
Jesse Jackson, Oct. 8
Paul Simon, Oct. 13
Art Garfunkel, Nov. 5

70
Rush Limbaugh, Jan. 12
Phil Collins, Jan. 30
Anjelica Huston, July 8
Michael Keaton, Sept. 5
Mark Hamill, Sept. 25
Sting, Oct. 2

60
Julia Louis-Dreyfus, Jan. 13
Wayne Gretzky, Jan. 26
Eddie Murphy, Apr. 3
George Clooney, May 6
Michael J. Fox, June 9
Ricky Gervais, June 25
Forest Whitaker, July 15
Woody Harrelson, July 23
Laurence Fishburne, July 30
Barack Obama, Aug. 4
Billy Ray Cyrus, Aug. 25
Nadia Comaneci, Nov. 12
Meg Ryan, Nov. 19

50
Mary J. Blige, Jan. 11
Regina King, Jan. 15
Kid Rock, Jan. 17
Alex Borstein, Feb. 15
Sean Astin, Feb. 25
Jon Hamm, Mar. 10
Ewan McGregor, Mar. 31
Sofia Coppola, May 14
Idina Menzel, May 30
Elon Musk, June 28
Missy Elliott, July 1
Sandra Oh, July 20
Amy Poehler, Sept. 16
Snoop Dogg, Oct. 20
Winona Ryder, Oct. 29

40
Jared Kushner, Jan. 10
Alicia Keys, Jan. 25
Elijah Wood, Jan. 28

Justin Timberlake, Jan. 31
Paris Hilton, Feb. 17
Kunal Nayyar, Apr. 30
Rami Malek, May 12
Natalie Portman, June 9
Chris Evans, June 13
Meghan Markle, Aug. 4
Roger Federer, Aug. 8
Beyoncé, Sept. 4
Jennifer Hudson, Sept. 12
Britney Spears, Dec. 2

30
Ed Sheeran, Feb. 17
Emily Ratajkowski, June 7
Mike Trout, Aug. 7
Lakeith Stanfield, Aug. 12

18
Greta Thunberg, Jan. 3
JoJo Siwa, May 19

STATISTICAL SPOTLIGHT

U.S. Support for Black Lives Matter, 2020

Source: Pew Research Center

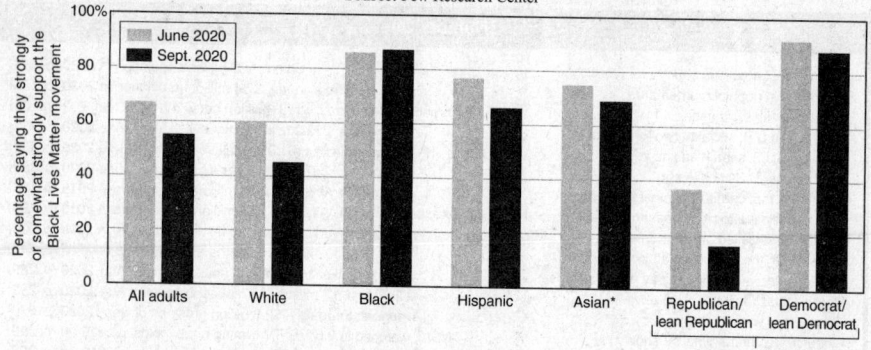

* = Interviewed in English only. **Note:** White, Black, and Asian adults include those who report being only one race and are not Hispanic. Hispanics are of any race.

Unemployment, Underemployment, and Gross Domestic Product, 1995-2020

Source: Current Population Survey, Bureau of Labor Statistics, U.S. Dept. of Labor; Bureau of Economic Analysis, U.S. Dept. of Commerce, via Federal Reserve Bank of St. Louis

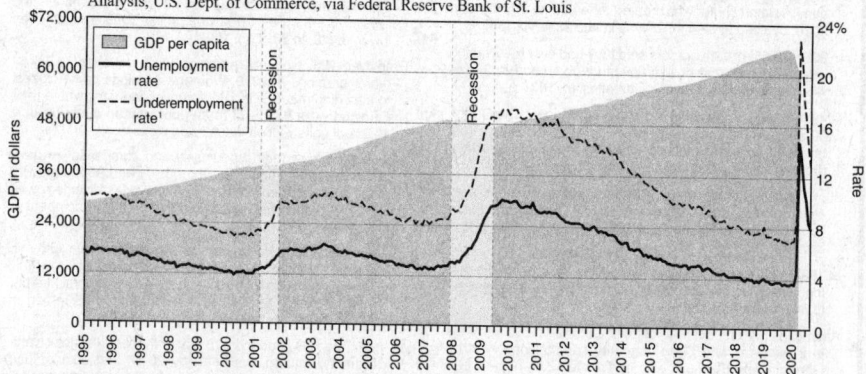

(1) Unemployment rate combined with a) those who currently are neither working nor looking for work but indicate that they want and are available for a job and have looked for work sometime in the past 12 months and b) those employed part time who want and are available for full-time work but have had to settle for a part-time schedule.

Total Cost of U.S. Elections, 1998-2020

Source: OpenSecrets.org, Center for Responsive Politics

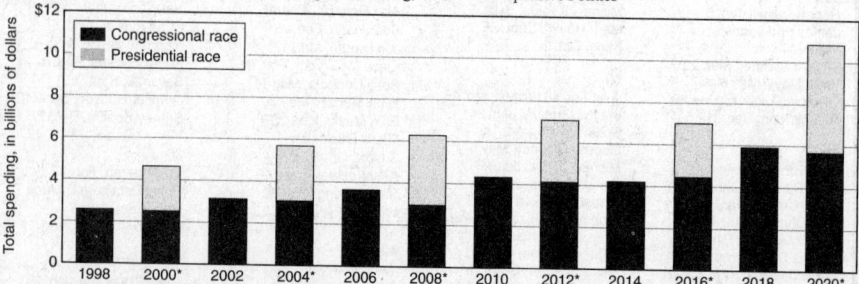

* = Presidential election year. **Note:** Includes all inflation-adjusted funds spent by candidates, political parties, independent interest groups, and political action committees (PACs) trying to influence federal elections; also includes PAC overhead expenses, 2014-20.

U.S. Weather Disasters and Costs, 1980-2020

Source: National Centers for Environmental Information, National Oceanic and Atmospheric Administration, U.S. Dept. of Commerce

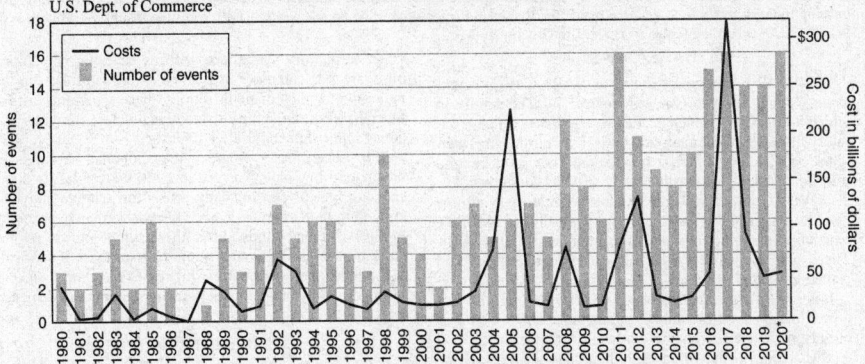

* = Compiled using preliminary data as of Oct. 7, 2020. **Note:** Disasters include drought, flooding, freeze, severe storm, tropical cyclone, wildfire, and winter storm events with losses exceeding $1 billion (previous years adjusted for inflation).

U.S. Political Knowledge and News Sources, 2020

Source: Pew Research Center

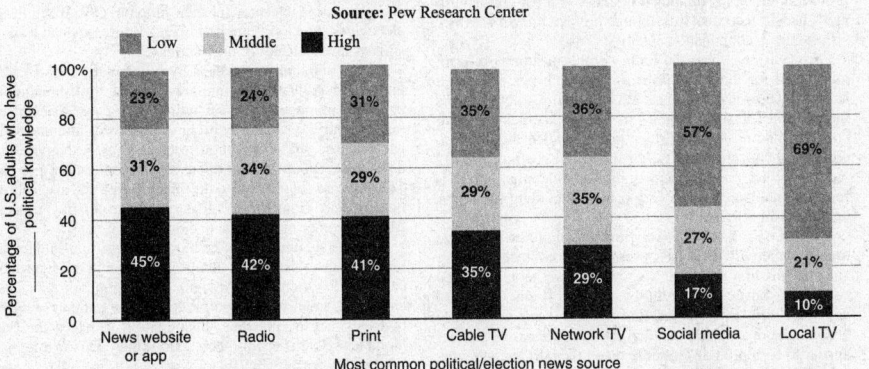

Note: Knowledge assessment based on index created from nine questions in Oct.-Nov. 2019. High political knowledge includes those who answered 8-9 questions correctly, middle knowledge includes those who answered 6-7 questions correctly, and low knowledge includes those who answered 5 or fewer questions correctly.

Refugees and Individuals Granted Asylum in the U.S., 1975-2020

Source: U.S. Dept. of Homeland Security, U.S. Dept. of Justice, U.S. Dept. of State

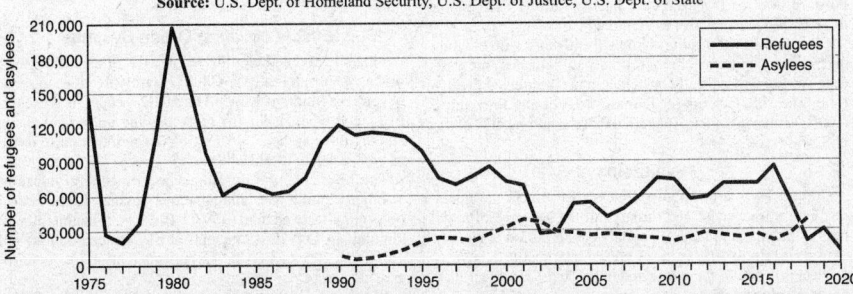

Note: Excludes Amerasians (children born in Cambodia, Korea, Laos, Thailand, or Vietnam after Dec. 31, 1950, and before Oct. 22, 1982, and fathered by a U.S. citizen) except in fiscal years 1989-91.

THE SCIENCE OF THE CORONAVIRUS PANDEMIC

The respiratory disease COVID-19, or Coronavirus disease 2019, was first identified in Wuhan, China, in Dec. 2019. Over the ensuing months it grew into a global pandemic that has infected 46 million people and caused 1.2 million deaths worldwide as of Nov. 1, 2020, according to the World Health Organization.

SARS-CoV-2

COVID-19 is caused by the virus SARS-CoV-2 (severe acute respiratory syndrome coronavirus 2). The family to which SARS-CoV-2 belongs, the coronaviruses, cause respiratory illnesses in mammals and birds. Four coronavirus subtypes circulate in the human population. They produce mild infections and are responsible for 15-30% of common colds.

COVID-19, along with severe acute respiratory syndrome (SARS) and Middle East respiratory syndrome (MERS), have made the jump from animals to humans more recently. These new coronavirus illnesses cause more serious and sometimes lethal infections.

It is not fully understood where COVID-19 originated or how it first entered the human population. SARS-CoV-2 is closely related to coronavirus strains in Chinese bats and to SARS-CoV-1, the coronavirus that causes SARS. However, part of SARS-CoV-2's genome more closely resembles sequences from coronaviruses that infect pangolins, scaly, anteater-like animals native to Africa and Southeast Asia. Different strains of coronaviruses sometimes recombine and exchange sequences. It is believed that SARS-CoV-2 was produced through recombination between a bat coronavirus and a pangolin coronavirus, though it is not known in which species this recombination occurred.

Coronaviruses, from the Latin *corona* meaning "crown," are named for the spike proteins that stick out from their surfaces. These spike proteins allow the virus to bind to and infect cells. The spike proteins of SARS-CoV-2 are specialized for binding a cell surface protein called angiotensin-converting enzyme 2 (ACE2, or the ACE2 receptor). ACE2 reduces blood pressure and regulates inflammation. It is found on human cells in many organs, including the lungs, heart, and digestive tract.

SARS-CoV-2 has a relatively low mutation rate compared to many other viruses. It has nevertheless continued to evolve since it was first detected. Six strains have been identified so far. The most common of these is the G strain. G evolved when the virus first entered Europe, and it has gone on to become the dominant strain across the Americas. G viruses appear to be more transmissible than other strains, allowing infections to spread 20% more quickly.

Fatality Rate

COVID-19's lethality depends on many factors, including the average age of those infected, their other health issues, and the level of medical care available in a given area. The infected fatality ratio (IFR), the fraction of infected individuals that die of a disease, cannot be determined directly. It must be inferred from the case fatality ratio (CFR), or the number of deaths relative to identified cases.

Since COVID-19 testing is limited, and those with obvious and severe symptoms are more likely to be tested, the case fatality ratio will typically be higher than the infected fatality ratio. The U.S. Centers for Disease Control and Prevention (CDC) estimated in late Aug. 2020 that the current IFR in the U.S. was 0.6%.

Symptoms

COVID-19 is a respiratory illness that affects the upper respiratory tract (nose and throat) and the lower respiratory tract (windpipe and lungs). The incubation period is usually 2-14 days. Up to 40% of cases are asymptomatic. The virus replicates inside of these infected individuals' cells, but they never develop an illness.

For those who do develop symptoms, COVID-19 typically first presents itself as a fever, sore throat, and dry cough.

Other respiratory symptoms, such as sneezing or a runny nose, are less common. In mild cases, which make up the majority of symptomatic infections, these symptoms last for several weeks, though most individuals clear the virus and are no longer infectious after 10 days.

More severe cases progress to pneumonia, shortness of breath, and low blood oxygen levels (hypoxemia). In some cases, oxygen levels drop dangerously low without individuals feeling short of breath. This is known as silent hypoxemia. In 20% of infected individuals, these symptoms are serious enough to require hospitalization. Half of these individuals experience acute respiratory distress syndrome (ARDS), severe difficulty breathing that usually requires supplemental oxygen.

Inflammation

Fluid in the lungs, or pulmonary edema, is a common feature of both mild and serious COVID-19 cases. On a CT scan, this fluid shows up as distinctive white or gray flecks known as ground-glass opacities. These can even be observed in asymptomatic individuals.

Infected individuals often also develop hypercoagulability, or an increased tendency for their blood to clot. When these clots block the blood supply to vital organs, they can lead to strokes, heart attacks, or organ failure.

These symptoms are caused by inflammation, part of an infected individual's own immune response. Inflammation is one of the immune system's first lines of response to an infection or injury. When tissue becomes inflamed, immune cells gather at the site of infection to clear away pathogens and dead cells. Blood vessels dilate and become more porous. This increases blood flow to the infected area and also causes fluid to leak from the blood into the surrounding tissues. Blood becomes more prone to clotting.

Clotting, dilated and leaky blood vessels, and inflammatory damage to tissues are all observed even in mild cases of COVID-19. Often, the first signs of inflammation look like chilblains, small reddish-purple lesions on patients' fingers or toes. They occur when inflammation damages the tiny blood vessels that supply these extremities. This feature has become known as "COVID toe."

Extreme or prolonged inflammation can cause severe health issues and lasting damage to tissues. In COVID-19, inflammation can continue to damage patients' tissues even after the virus itself is gone. Patients can experience autoinflammatory reactions, in which their immune systems attack their own tissues. In the most serious cases, this is believed to trigger severe autoinflammatory reactions that can cause multi-organ failure.

Effects on Other Organ Systems

Inflammation and clotting in COVID-19 can affect many organ systems. It is also possible for viral infections to spread beyond the respiratory tract. The ACE2 receptor is present on many cell types, including those making up the circulatory and digestive systems. SARS-CoV-2 can infect these tissues as well, causing localized damage.

The heart, kidneys, and brain are especially vulnerable to blood clotting and inflammation. Damage to the heart is observed after even mild COVID-19 cases. Inflammation and clotting put COVID-19 patients at risk of acute kidney failure. Some 20% of COVID-19 patients that go into intensive care need to be put on dialysis.

Blood clots in the brain can trigger strokes, leading to long-term brain damage. Inflammation can have a range of other effects on the nervous system. COVID-19 cases are often

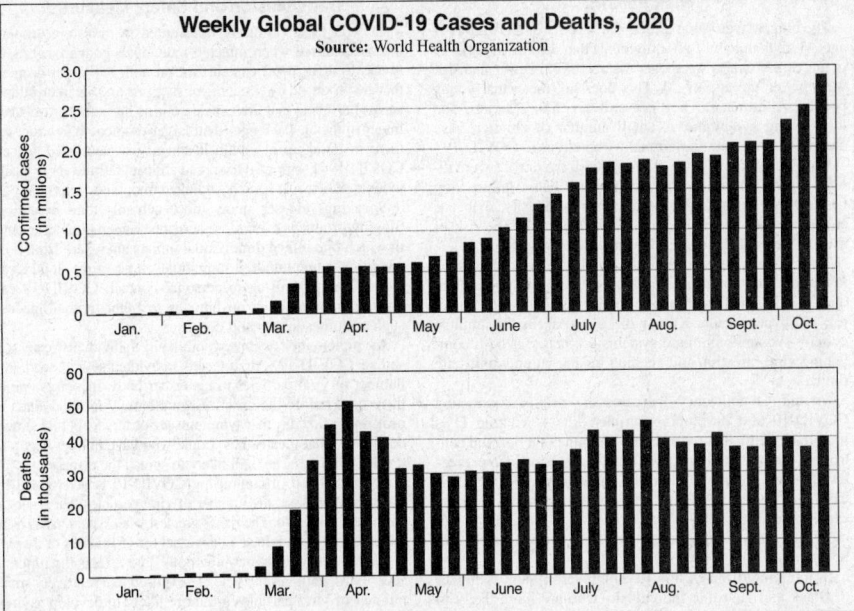

Weekly Global COVID-19 Cases and Deaths, 2020
Source: World Health Organization

accompanied by "head fog," confusion, and dizziness. In some cases, this inflammation can trigger severe autoimmune diseases such as acute disseminated encephalomyelinitis (ADEM) and Guillain-Barré syndrome. Neurons come under attack from the immune system. This results in lasting fatigue, weakness, paralysis, and other debilitating symptoms.

COVID-19 also infects the olfactory epithelium and olfactory bulb, the layers of cells in the nose that detect odors. In a majority of infected individuals, this results in a partial or complete loss of taste and smell. This is often the first COVID-19 symptom to develop, and it can serve as an early warning of the disease.

Infection of the digestive tract by COVID-19 can lead to gastrointestinal symptoms such as nausea, abdominal pain, and diarrhea. These occur in up to 60% of cases, and often begin before the onset of respiratory symptoms. A small number of infected individuals only experience gastrointestinal symptoms and never develop a cough or sore throat.

Long-Term Effects

The majority of individuals infected with SARS-CoV-2 clear their infections and are free of the virus within 10 days. However, a large percentage continue to report recurring or continuous symptoms even after testing negative for SARS-CoV-2. As COVID-19 is a new illness, it is not known how long these symptoms will persist.

Months after recovery, many formerly hospitalized individuals still report fatigue and shortness of breath. Troponin, a marker of damage to the heart muscle, is elevated after recovery from COVID-19. This is even observed following asymptomatic cases. The head fog and other neurological symptoms that infected individuals report often linger for months after recovery. Scarring and long-lasting damage to the lungs themselves seem to be relatively rare.

Immunity

As with most other infectious diseases, individuals who recover from COVID-19 develop an immunity to the virus.

They form antibodies and immune cells called memory T-cells that will recognize SARS-CoV-2 and prevent reinfection.

Immunity to coronaviruses does not tend to be long-lasting. For mild coronaviruses, it typically disappears within a year. In at least some individuals, immunity to COVID-19 may have an even shorter duration. A growing number of individuals have been reinfected with COVID-19 as few as three months after their initial recovery. In some of these cases, the second infection was more severe, resulting in at least one fatality.

T-cells produced in response to mild coronavirus infections may also cause partial immunity to COVID-19. These cross-reactive T-cells are not enough to prevent an infection but may reduce its severity.

Testing and Diagnosis

There are two types of COVID-19 tests. A viral test identifies active or recent infections. The test is administered via a nasopharyngeal swab, which gathers a sample from the back of the nose or throat. This sample is then analyzed for the presence of SARS-CoV-2's RNA or antigens. A positive result does not necessarily mean a person is still infectious. Viral material can be detected after the infection has been cleared.

The second type, an antibody test, is more useful for determining whether a person has had a COVID-19 infection sometime in the past. Antibodies continue to circulate in the bloodstream after the infection has been cleared and can be detected with a blood test. This is not a perfect indicator of whether a person has had a COVID-19 infection. The concentration of antibodies in the blood can decline to undetectable levels within 3 months of recovery.

In the absence of one of these tests, certain symptoms can be useful for distinguishing COVID-19 from other respiratory illnesses. These include ground-glass opacities, COVID toe, loss of taste and smell, and silent hypoxemia. While other diseases can cause these symptoms, they are particularly common in COVID-19.

Risk Factors

The biggest factor that affects the severity of COVID-19 is age. More than half of all individuals that died of COVID-19 in the United States were over the age of 75. Fewer than 1% were below the age of 30. This does not mean that young people are immune. They can still experience serious and long-lasting symptoms. A small number of children have died from severe autoinflammatory reactions to COVID-19.

Chronic kidney disease is a major risk factor for severe illness. It greatly increases the risk of acute kidney failure from COVID-19. Heart disease, hypertension, obesity, diabetes, and cancer all put individuals at elevated risk. The risk of severe illness is also higher for men than for women.

Those in at-risk groups tend to be less able to fight viral infections and more prone to inflammation. Chronic inflammation builds with age and is also elevated in obesity, diabetes, and hypertension. Kidney disease weakens the immune system. Women's immune systems are better at both combatting viral infection and keeping inflammation within safe limits.

Vitamin D deficiency increases the risk of contracting COVID-19 and developing serious illness. Vitamin D is important for maintaining healthy immune function and controlling chronic inflammation. It also causes cells to express fewer ACE2 receptors. This may make it harder for SARS-CoV-2 to infect cells. The skin produces vitamin D when exposed to ultraviolet light. Deficiency is extremely common, especially in cold areas that don't receive much sunlight.

In the United States, the risk of severe illness is higher in Black and Hispanic individuals, who are more likely to work in essential industries that preclude social distancing. They are also more likely to suffer from obesity, diabetes, and hypertension. Since people with darker skin tones produce less vitamin D, they are also more likely to have vitamin D deficiencies.

Transmission and Safety Measures

COVID-19 is primarily transmitted by moisture droplets that are emitted when infected individuals cough, sneeze, or speak. SARS-CoV-2 can survive on both the larger droplets that are produced by coughing or sneezing and the microscopic aerosol droplets that are exhaled during speech. Aerosols can linger in the air far longer than larger droplets. It is easier for them to build up in confined and poorly ventilated spaces. COVID-19 is estimated to spread almost 20 times more easily indoors. Few cases have been linked to outdoor activities.

Speaking releases many more aerosols than breathing. Singing produces even more aerosols. Superspreader events, in which one infected individual infects anywhere from dozens to over one hundred individuals at one time, tend to be indoor events with close personal contact. COVID-19 can also be transmitted from humans to other animal species, such as domestic cats and dogs.

Asymptomatic or presymptomatic individuals can still spread COVID-19. An infected individual's viral load, the number of viral particles in his or her body, increases one to three days before the onset of symptoms. Viral load tends to peak on the first day that symptoms are observed, before slowly declining. That means that people who have not yet begun to display symptoms are still likely to spread the disease.

The likelihood of contracting COVID-19 is determined by the infectious dose, the number of viral particles that a person has been exposed to. The risk is greatest when a person has been within 6 feet of an infected individual for 15 minutes or more.

Evidence suggests that infectious dose affects the illness's severity as well. People who are exposed to a relatively small number of viral particles are more likely to develop asymptomatic or mild infections.

Without social distancing precautions, one infected individual will, on average, infect 2.5 others. Social distancing and mask-wearing greatly reduce transmission. Staying at least 6 feet from other individuals reduces the risk of infec-

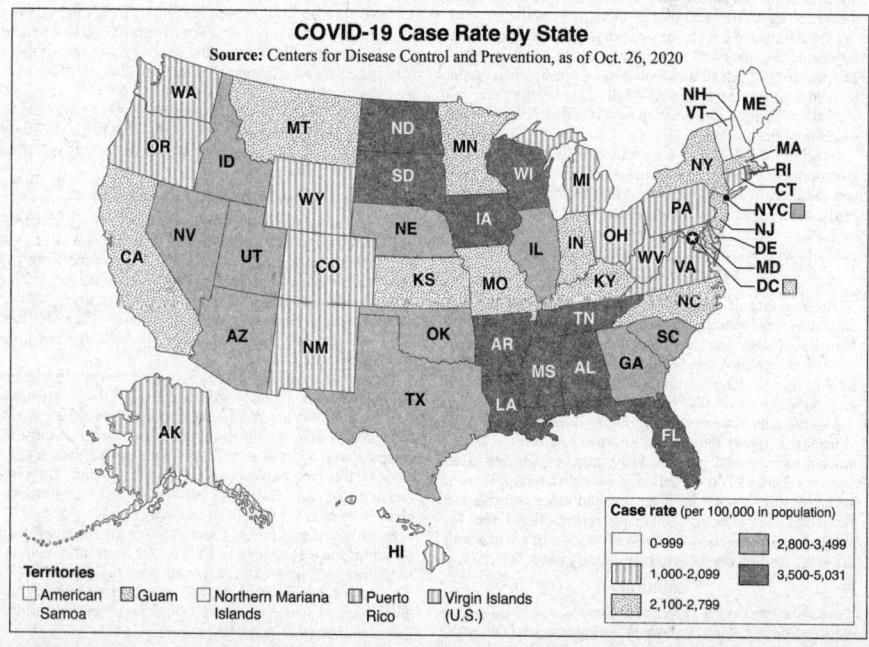

COVID-19 Case Rate by State
Source: Centers for Disease Control and Prevention, as of Oct. 26, 2020

Case rate (per 100,000 in population)
0-999
1,000-2,099
2,100-2,799
2,800-3,499
3,500-5,031

Territories
American Samoa   Guam   Northern Mariana Islands   Puerto Rico   Virgin Islands (U.S.)

tion. However, it is no guarantee against exposure to the virus, especially indoors.

Reusable cloth masks or surgical masks somewhat reduce the number of viral particles a wearer will inhale. However, their chief benefit is preventing infected individuals from transmitting the virus to others. They greatly reduce the amount of moisture that an infected wearer will exhale, and prevent droplets from carrying far. If everyone in a community wears a mask during face-to-face encounters, the risk of transmission is reduced many-fold.

The most effective masks are those with N95 filters or better. These block 95% of particles below 0.3 microns in diameter, about one-third the size of the smallest droplets that can transmit SARS-CoV-2.

Other Possible Transmission Routes

Objects contaminated with the virus (fomites) are a possible but unproven mode of transmission. SARS-CoV-2 can survive on some surfaces for days. There is a possibility that people could contract COVID-19 by touching contaminated objects and then touching their noses, mouths, or eyes. Transmission via fomites has never been conclusively documented in COVID-19. However, individuals are still advised to wash their hands or use alcohol-based hand sanitizers after spending time in public, and to avoid touching their faces.

SARS-CoV-2 particles have also been detected in feces. It is possible that the virus might be dispersed via plumbing systems, or in the plumes of water droplets that are created by a toilet flush. Several cases have been identified in which the virus appears to have infected multiple individuals in the same apartment complex by spreading through the plumbing system.

Pharmaceutical Treatments

Pharmaceutical treatments for COVID-19 are limited. Early studies suggested that the anti-malaria drug hydroxychloroquine could improve the odds of recovery in severe COVID-19 cases. However, additional research has failed to show any consistent benefit from hydroxychloroquine treatment.

The antiviral remdesivir prevents SARS-CoV-2 from copying its genome and replicating itself. Supplies of remdesivir, however, are limited. Dexamethasone, an anti-inflammatory corticosteroid drug, has proven effective in suppressing the inflammation that causes critical COVID-19 symptoms. The National Institutes of Health (NIH) recommends the use of both of these drugs in severe cases of COVID-19.

Other therapies are under investigation. The drug icatibant appears to be able to combat hypoxemia and pulmonary edema. Icatibant blocks the chemical signals that dilate blood vessels and cause them to become leaky. This stops fluid from entering the lungs.

Some antibodies, called neutralizing antibodies, bind to SARS-CoV-2's spike protein. This renders the virus unable to infect cells. Several neutralizing antibodies and antibody components are being developed as a potential line of treatment for COVID-19. None have been approved. However, an antibody cocktail developed by Regeneron Pharmaceuticals has been administered to Pres. Trump and a handful of other patients via a compassionate use exemption.

Medical Care

For mild cases, there's little to be done except ensuring that infected individuals get rest, stay isolated whenever possible, and remain hydrated and well-nourished. COVID-19 depletes electrolytes, especially potassium. Vitamin C, zinc, and vitamin D are all crucial for maintaining healthy immune function. It is important that infected individuals maintain adequate intakes of these nutrients. There is no evidence, however, that taking large doses of zinc or vitamin C exceeding those in a healthy diet can improve outcomes.

In more severe cases, the most important concern is to ensure that patients have sufficient oxygen. Simply putting patients on their bellies, or proning, makes it easier for them to breathe and improves their odds of survival. Proning causes fluid to shift to the front of the lungs, where they are narrowest. This reduces the amount of lung tissue that is obstructed by fluid, and makes it easier for the lungs to extract oxygen. If patients are still unable to breathe, they can be given supplemental oxygen or be put on mechanical ventilation.

COVID-19 Vaccines

Approximately 200 vaccines for COVID-19 are being developed in humans or animals. Once administered, a vaccine will cause the immune system to generate neutralizing antibodies against SARS-CoV-2 that will prevent viral infection. As immunity to COVID-19 is short-lasting, vaccines may need to be administered annually. Most of the vaccines currently in development must also be delivered in two doses to ensure an optimal immune response.

Vaccine Approval Process

Ordinarily, the testing and approval process for a new vaccine takes years. Usually, a vaccine must first be designed and tested on animals. If the results are encouraging, researchers must then seek government approval for three phases of clinical trials in humans. In phase I, the vaccine is tested on several dozen healthy individuals to make sure it is safe enough to warrant additional research. In phase II, it is tested on several hundred individuals to learn more about its side effects and determine whether it triggers potentially effective antibodies. In phase III, it is tested on several thousand people to identify additional side effects and determine whether it is effective at preventing infection.

The Food and Drug Administration or other national regulating body then reviews this data and decides whether to approve the vaccine. Each of these stages typically takes two years or more. It can take 15 years from the time the vaccine is designed to the time it reaches the market.

Accelerated Timetable

The development and testing timelines have been compressed for COVID-19. Advances in gene sequencing and vaccine development have made it easier to design vaccines. The first designs for a vaccine based on the spike protein were produced only two days after SARS-CoV-2's genome was released.

Multiple countries have also launched unprecedented efforts to fast-track testing, approval, and delivery of COVID-19 vaccines in a fraction of the usual time. In May 2020 the Trump administration announced a public-private partnership called Operation Warp Speed. Its goal was to deliver millions of doses of COVID-19 vaccines by Jan. 2021.

As of mid-Oct. 2020, 44 vaccines were currently in clinical trials, with 11 of those in phase III trials. Russia and China have both approved vaccines before phase III testing was complete. Russia has approved two vaccines following successful phase I and II trials. Its Sputnik V vaccine became the first COVID-19 vaccine to be approved in any country in Aug. 2020. A phase III trial of Sputnik V began in Sept. 2020. While the vaccine has been approved, it has not been administered on a large scale.

China has approved four vaccines for limited use among members of the armed forces and other essential personnel. The first of these vaccines, produced by the state-owned company Sinopharm, was approved in June 2020. The company announced in Sept. that it has vaccinated over 100,000 individuals.

These vaccines, and the others that have passed phase I and II trials, triggered immune responses in participants. Their immune systems generated antibodies and T-cells that bound to SARS-CoV-2 in the laboratory. Until phase III trials have concluded, and scientists compare the rate of infection in vaccinated individuals against that of an unvaccinated control group, it will remain unknown whether they actually protect participants from infection.

World COVID-19 Cases and Deaths

Source: World Health Organization
(as of Oct. 31, 2020)

Country/territory	Cases	Deaths
Afghanistan	41,334	1,533
Albania	20,634	502
Algeria	57,332	1,949
American Samoa	0	0
Andorra	4,665	75
Angola	10,558	279
Anguilla	3	0
Antigua and Barbuda	127	3
Argentina	1,143,800	30,442
Armenia	89,813	1,341
Aruba	4,472	37
Australia	27,582	907
Austria	101,443	1,079
Azerbaijan	54,174	718
The Bahamas	6,644	142
Bahrain	81,466	319
Bangladesh	406,364	5,905
Barbados	236	7
Belarus	97,499	977
Belgium	392,163	11,308
Belize	3,382	56
Benin	2,643	41
Bermuda	199	9
Bhutan	348	0
Bolivia	141,484	8,705
Bonaire, Sint, Eustatius and Saba	153	3
Bosnia and Herzegovina	43,174	1,125
Botswana	6,642	24
Brazil	5,494,376	158,969
Brunei	148	3
Bulgaria	51,041	1,254
Burkina Faso	2,477	67
Burundi	585	1
Cabo Verde	8,694	95
Cambodia	291	0
Cameroon	21,793	426
Canada	228,542	10,074
Cayman Islands	240	1
Central African Republic	4,866	62
Chad	1,483	98
Chile	508,571	14,158
China	91,893	4,746
Colombia	1,053,122	30,926
Comoros	530	7
Congo, Dem. Rep. of.	11,305	307
Congo Rep.	5,290	92
Cook Islands	0	0
Costa Rica	107,570	1,357
Côte d'Ivoire	20,628	124
Croatia	46,547	531
Cuba	6,801	128
Curaçao	944	1
Cyprus	4,217	25
Czechia	323,673	3,078
Denmark	45,225	719
Djibouti	5,559	61
Dominica	42	0
Dominican Republic	126,332	2,236
Ecuador	167,147	12,632
Egypt	107,385	6,258
El Salvador	33,445	971
Equatorial Guinea	5,083	83
Eritrea	463	0
Estonia	4,771	73
Eswatini	5,909	117
Ethiopia	95,789	1,464
Falkland Islands	13	0
Faroe Islands	494	0
Fiji	34	2
Finland	15,910	358
France	1,299,278	36,250
French Guiana	10,425	70
French Polynesia	7,262	29
Gabon	8,957	55
Gambia	3,666	119
Georgia	38,936	307
Germany	518,753	10,452
Ghana	48,055	320
Gibraltar	688	0
Greece	37,196	620
Greenland	17	0
Grenada	28	0
Guadeloupe	7,742	139
Guatemala	107,339	3,714
Guernsey	267	13
Guinea	12,020	71
Guinea-Bissau	2,413	41
Guyana	4,098	123
Haiti	9,054	232
Honduras	96,150	2,661
Hungary	71,413	1,699
Iceland	4,797	12
India	8,137,119	121,641
Indonesia	406,945	13,782
International conveyance (Diamond Princess)	741	13
Iran	604,952	34,478
Iraq	470,633	10,862
Ireland	61,059	1,908
Isle of Man	352	24
Israel	313,533	2,517
Italy	647,674	38,321
Jamaica	9,005	205
Japan	100,392	1,755
Jersey	569	32
Jordan	69,306	772
Kazakhstan	149,699	2,219
Kenya	53,797	981
Kiribati	0	0
Korea, North	0	0
Korea, South	26,511	464
Kosovo	19,285	668
Kuwait	125,337	773
Kyrgyzstan	58,878	1,145
Laos	24	0
Latvia	5,679	69
Lebanon	79,529	625
Lesotho	1,947	43
Liberia	1,426	82
Libya	60,628	847
Liechtenstein	523	2
Lithuania	13,823	157
Luxembourg	17,134	152
Madagascar	16,968	244
Malawi	5,923	184
Malaysia	30,889	249
Maldives	11,643	37
Mali	3,545	136
Malta	5,042	61
Marshall Islands	2	0
Martinique	3,818	31
Mauritania	7,663	163
Mauritius	441	10
Mayotte	4,366	44
Mexico	912,811	90,773
Micronesia	0	0
Moldova	75,201	1,766
Monaco	355	2
Mongolia	340	0
Montenegro	18,260	294
Montserrat	13	1
Morocco	215,294	3,625
Mozambique	12,777	91
Myanmar	51,496	1,219
Namibia	12,907	133
Nauru	0	0
Nepal	168,235	920
Netherlands	340,974	7,335
New Caledonia	28	0
New Zealand	1,601	25
Nicaragua	4,424	156
Niger	1,220	69
Nigeria	62,691	1,144
Niue	0	0
North Macedonia	30,488	982
Norway	19,563	282
Oman	114,434	1,208
Pakistan	332,186	6,795
Palau	0	0
Palestinian Territories	64,741	553
Panama	132,045	2,678
Papua New Guinea	589	7
Paraguay	62,050	1,373
Peru	897,594	34,362
Philippines	378,933	7,185
Pitcairn Islands	0	0
Poland	340,834	5,351
Portugal	137,272	2,468
Qatar	132,343	232
Réunion	5,659	22
Romania	235,586	6,867
Russia	1,618,116	27,990
Rwanda	5,134	35
St. Barthélemy	89	0
St. Helena	0	0
St. Kitts and Nevis	19	0
St. Lucia	76	0
St. Martin	591	9
St. Pierre and Miquelon	16	0
St. Vincent and the Grenadines	74	0

Country/territory	Cases	Deaths	Country/territory	Cases	Deaths
Samoa	0	0	Togo	2,296	55
San Marino	958	42	Tokelau	0	0
São Tomé and Príncipe	945	16	Tonga	0	0
Saudi Arabia	346,880	5,383	Trinidad and Tobago	5,636	107
Senegal	15,593	323	Tunisia	58,029	1,253
Serbia	45,137	814	Turkey	373,154	10,177
Seychelles	152	0	Turkmenistan	0	0
Sierra Leone	2,365	74	Turks and Caicos Islands	703	6
Singapore	58,003	28	Tuvalu	0	0
Sint Maarten	805	22	Uganda	12,410	110
Slovakia	55,091	212	Ukraine	387,481	7,196
Slovenia	32,510	225	United Arab Emirates	131,508	490
Solomon Islands	8	0	United Kingdom	989,749	46,229
Somalia	3,941	104	United States	8,852,730	227,178
South Africa	723,682	19,230	Uruguay	3,044	57
South Sudan	2,905	58	Uzbekistan	66,801	564
Spain	1,185,678	35,878	Vanuatu	0	0
Sri Lanka	10,424	19	Vatican City	26	0
Sudan	13,804	837	Venezuela	91,280	789
Suriname	5,197	111	Vietnam	1,177	35
Sweden	124,355	5,938	Virgin Islands (UK)	72	1
Switzerland	153,728	2,035	Wallis and Futuna	1	0
Syria	5,683	285	Yemen	2,066	600
Tajikistan	10,977	82	Zambia	16,415	349
Tanzania	509	21	Zimbabwe	8,362	242
Thailand	3,780	59	**World**	**45,428,731**	**1,185,721**
Timor-Leste	30	0			

United States COVID-19 Cases and Deaths

Source: U.S. Centers for Disease Control and Prevention
(as of Oct. 31, 2020)

	Cumulative total		Rate per 100,000 pop.	
State/territory	Cases	Deaths	Cases	Deaths
Alabama	190,496	2,932	3,897	59
Alaska	14,837	81	2,012	10
American Samoa	0	0	0	0
Arizona	244,045	5,934	3,403	82
Arkansas	110,874	1,900	3,679	63
California	916,918	17,571	2,318	44
Colorado	104,426	2,278	1,834	40
Connecticut	71,207	4,616	1,993	129
Delaware	24,951	708	2,580	73
District of Columbia	17,144	646	2,441	91
Florida	789,714	16,720	3,708	78
Georgia	358,225	7,955	3,405	75
Guam	4,628	79	2,792	47
Hawaii	14,933	215	1,051	15
Idaho	63,810	626	3,638	35
Illinois	408,660	9,994	3,207	78
Indiana	175,893	4,286	2,628	64
Iowa	125,025	1,706	3,961	54
Kansas	85,181	1,029	2,926	35
Kentucky	105,242	1,476	2,355	33
Louisiana	186,649	5,919	4,005	127
Maine	6,668	147	498	10
Maryland	145,281	4,147	2,404	68
Massachusetts	163,125	9,958	2,363	144
Michigan	193,388	7,665	1,936	76
Minnesota	145,465	2,491	2,592	44
Mississippi	120,160	3,334	4,023	111
Missouri	183,186	3,024	2,990	49
Montana	31,916	364	3,004	34
Nebraska	69,645	646	3,610	33
Nevada	99,786	1,777	3,288	58
New Hampshire	10,884	482	802	35
New Jersey	236,523	16,339	2,655	183
New Mexico	45,909	1,007	2,191	48
New York (excl. NYC)	242,921	9,259	2,180	83
New York City	266,051	24,001	3,168	285
North Carolina	271,830	4,332	2,618	41
North Dakota	43,916	524	5,778	68
Northern Mariana Islands	92	2	0	3
Ohio	212,782	5,291	1,820	45
Oklahoma	126,618	1,313	3,211	33
Oregon	44,388	675	1,059	16
Pennsylvania	205,517	8,784	1,605	68
Puerto Rico	66,128	822	2,070	25
Rhode Island	32,874	1,201	3,109	113
South Carolina	175,594	3,896	3,454	76
South Dakota	44,559	415	5,051	47
Tennessee	259,488	3,341	3,833	49
Texas	893,451	17,934	3,113	62
Utah	112,932	601	3,572	19
Vermont	2,155	58	344	9
Virgin Islands (U.S.)	1,362	21	1,301	20
Virginia	181,191	3,654	2,127	42
Washington	106,573	2,366	1,414	31
West Virginia	23,990	451	1,328	24
Wisconsin	232,062	2,029	3,992	34
Wyoming	13,028	87	2,255	15
United States	**9,024,298**	**229,109**	**2,727**	**69**

ELECTION, 2020

Former Vice Pres. Joe Biden (D) defeated Pres. Donald Trump (R) to win the White House, capping an extraordinarily divisive campaign set amid the ongoing coronavirus pandemic and concurrent economic distress. More than 100 mil ballots were cast prior to Election Day, Nov. 3, 2020, in either early in-person or mail-in and other absentee voting, shattering records. The winner of the election was, as forecast, unknown for days as a number of closely fought states—including Arizona, Georgia, Michigan, Nevada, North Carolina, Pennsylvania, and Wisconsin—worked to complete their ballot counting. Democrats maintained control of the House but lost seats to Republicans, while Republicans appeared likely to hold onto their majority in the Senate. As of Nov. 7, when the Associated Press and other news organizations projected Biden as the eventual winner of the electoral vote, the Democratic ticket, with Sen. Kamala Harris (CA) as Biden's running mate, was ahead in the popular vote, with 74.5 mil (50.5%) versus 70.3 mil (47.7%) for the Republican ticket, with Vice Pres. Mike Pence again as Trump's running mate. Trump's defeat was the first by an incumbent U.S. president since George H.W. Bush in 1992. Harris would be the first woman, first Black woman, and first Indian American elected as vice president.

Biden vs. Trump

While the volume of early voting and mail-in and absentee ballots may skew 2020 exit polling, preliminary estimates undertaken by Edison Research showed that white voters preferred Trump over Biden, 57%-42%, especially those without a college degree (64%-35%), a similar margin to the 2016 Trump-Hillary Clinton race. Biden won women's votes, 56%-43%, also in line with the previous presidential race. According to the estimates, 87% of Black voters and 67% of Hispanic voters cast ballots for Biden. Voters aged 18-29 favored Biden 62%-35% (up from 55% for Clinton in 2016), while those 65 years old or older voted for Trump 51%-48%. Independents went for Biden by a margin of 54%-40%, up from 42% for Clinton. While Trump again won the white evangelical Christian vote, 76%-23%, his support from this group fell from the 2016 race (down from 81%). Trump also lost support among those who had served in the military; winning their votes 61%-34% in 2016, his advantage over Biden slipped, 52%-45%.

Trump by early morning Nov. 4 had claimed election fraud by Democrats and that he had in fact won the presidency despite millions of ballots yet to be counted in key states. Later that day, Trump's campaign launched lawsuits to stop the counting of ballots in Pennsylvania and Michigan and to challenge ballot handling in Georgia. The campaign also sought a recount in Wisconsin, which Biden was projected to win. Biden spoke from Wilmington, DE, the afternoon of Nov. 4, projecting confidence in an eventual win while pledging that all votes would be counted.

In a public address from the White House, Trump the evening of Nov. 5 doubled down on his accusations of election fraud, asserting without evidence that ongoing tabulation of legal mail-in ballots in several close states was fraudulent. Legal challenges and recounts were possible and even probable in some close states, but by the morning of Nov. 7, Biden was the projected winner in both Pennsylvania and Nevada, giving him the necessary electoral votes to be named the winner.

Fall Campaign

National polls for the year leading up to the fall campaign showed Trump consistently trailing Biden. Though the president's approval ratings at the start of 2020 were among his highest up to that point, his backing slid among nearly every demographic subgroup as the coronavirus pandemic and economic disruption, including massive spikes in unemployment, accelerated in the U.S. from mid-Mar. Trump's law-and-order message condemning civil unrest arising from the mostly peaceful urban protests appeared to fail to gain much ground. The pandemic response and handling of the economy continued to lead polls of voters' concerns.

In Sept., advance copies of reporter Bob Woodward's book *Rage* made public Trump's remarks—supported by audio recordings of Woodward's interviews with Trump—revealing the president was aware in early Feb. of the serious nature of the coronavirus threat but opted to downplay it. The president throughout his campaign continued to repeatedly minimize or contradict messaging from health officials, including top infectious disease doctor Anthony Fauci, on the virus's severity and wearing of masks.

In deference to the pandemic and associated risks, Biden's campaign focused on small in-person events, virtual (online) campaigns, and drive-in rallies. Biden also outspent Trump's campaign on TV ads nearly 2-1 from early May on. In contrast, Trump staged frequent, large-scale rallies, at least 15 of which, Sept. 1-Oct. 6, violated CDC coronavirus guidelines, according to *USA Today*. Trump resumed these events upon restarting his campaign Oct. 12, 10 days after announcing he and first lady Melania Trump had contracted the virus.

Both Trump and Biden offered dire warnings for the future of the country if the other won the election. The first presidential debate, Sept. 29, seen by 73 mil TV viewers, was a chaotic clash, with Trump responsible for more than three-quarters of the evening's persistent interruptions. Trump tried to cast Biden as a career politician who had achieved little in over 47 years in elected office; he also notably refused to condemn white supremacy. Biden rebuffed his opponent's characterization of him as a "radical leftist," stating that he did not support the Green New Deal or defunding police. Biden also criticized Trump over a recent *NY Times* report that he paid just $750 in federal personal income taxes in both 2016 and 2017. The next scheduled debate was canceled after Trump refused a virtual format following his coronavirus diagnosis and treatment; each candidate instead appeared Oct. 15 in separate town hall meetings televised simultaneously on different networks.

The second and final presidential debate, Oct. 22, seen by 63 mil TV viewers after a record 48.5 mil Americans had already cast ballots, was more civil, likely due to organizers' ability to mute the microphone of the nonspeaking candidate during his opponent's opening answer. Trump said that the U.S. was "rounding the corner" on the pandemic despite surging cases and hospitalizations, while Biden strongly criticized the Trump administration's response to the pandemic and continuing attempts to repeal Obamacare and its guarantee of coverage for preexisting conditions. Trump said Biden would shut down the entire country over COVID-19, and attempted to tie Biden's stated goal of transitioning the country away from fossil fuels to slowing down economies in some key states. While post-debate fact-checkers found some of Biden's statements false or misleading, they found far more of Trump's remarks to be untrue.

In the final stretch of their campaigns, Trump and Biden barnstormed heavily in swing states. According to polls, Biden led in most swing states by a narrow margin. Over the final three days of the campaign, Trump held 14 rallies in seven states, including Florida, Iowa, Michigan, North Carolina, and Pennsylvania, where he held four events. Biden, meanwhile, held events in Michigan, Ohio, and Pennsylvania.

Election Security and Ballot Integrity

Concern over attempts to unduly influence the outcome of the 2020 election remained high in the wake of numerous investigations—among them Special Counsel Robert Mueller's Russia probe and that of a GOP-led Senate panel—concluding that Russia had carried out an expansive campaign to try to sway the 2016 race in favor of then-candidate Donald Trump, including hacking emails from Democratic contender Hillary Clinton and creating false or misleading Facebook posts that had reached up to 126 mil Americans.

In early Feb. 2020, FBI Dir. Christopher Wray branded Russia's disinformation efforts an "ongoing problem." The director of the Natl. Counterintelligence and Security Center in an Aug. 8 statement said that Russia, China, and Iran were all working to influence voting, with the last two nations favoring Joe Biden; most of the efforts, according to other U.S. officials, emanated from Russia. In late Oct., Dir. of Natl. Intelligence John Ratcliffe said Russia and Iran had accessed U.S. voter information and that Iran operatives had sent emails, purportedly from the far-right extremist group Proud Boys, that threatened recipients not voting for Trump in an apparent effort to damage Trump's campaign.

Tech companies made efforts to aid in disrupting meddling and preventing disinformation, compared to 2016. In July,

Balance of Power, 2020
(as of Nov. 7, 2020)

Party	Senate		House		Governors	
	Before	After	Before	After	Before	After
Dem.	45	46	232	215	24	23
Rep.	53	48	197	196	26	27
Ind.	2[1]	2[1]	1[2]	—	—	—

Note: Four Senate races and 24 House races were not yet called. (1) Both independent senators were expected to continue caucusing with the Democrats. (2) Ind./Libertarian.

Facebook announced it had removed nine networks of inauthentic accounts, including U.S.-based ones, highlighting the increasing threat of domestic misinformation efforts. Facebook Sept. 1 said it had removed 13 accounts associated with Peace Data, a fake news site run by the Russian disinformation hub Internet Research Agency, using content sourced from U.S. contributors. The *Washington Post* in mid-Sept. uncovered what it alleged was an Arizona-based pro-Trump "troll farm," prompting Facebook and Twitter to suspend numerous accounts. Microsoft Sept. 10 said it had detected mostly unsuccessful cyberattacks from Iran and China on individuals linked to the Biden campaign, along with some 200 targeted by Russian hackers.

Interference in 2020 also included direct attempts by pro-Russia elements to influence U.S. lawmakers and other officials. On Sept. 10, the Treasury Dept. sanctioned four people, including a Ukrainian parliamentarian/Russian agent, whom it said distributed packets detailing discredited allegations of corruption against Biden to Trump-allied Republican lawmakers. The *Washington Post* Oct. 15 reported U.S. intelligence officials had cautioned the White House in 2019 that Trump's personal attorney, Rudolph Giuliani, had been used by Russian agents in a disinformation campaign against Biden. The next day, the *NY Post* published an unverified report that Biden's son Hunter in 2015 arranged via email for then-Vice Pres. Biden to meet as an executive at the Ukrainian energy company Burisma, on whose board Hunter served. Giuliani claimed he obtained a copy of Hunter's laptop hard drive containing the email, which provided the foundation of the *NY Post*'s reporting. Trump repeated the influence-peddling allegation in the final presidential debate.

The White House itself was alleged by critics to have undermined election integrity through Trump's frequent and unfounded assertions that expansion of mail-in and absentee voting due to the coronavirus pandemic would lead to widespread fraud by Democrats and a "rigged election." According to U.S. intelligence analysts, Russian state-run media and proxy sites in mid-Aug. amplified Trump's claims. In some cases, Twitter appended disclaimers to Trump's tweets on voting and other topics; the platform had pledged in Sept. to take action on tweets that discouraged voting, preemptively declared an election victory before votes were counted, or contained misinformation regarding the voting process.

Trump in a Fox Business interview Aug. 13 said he was blocking additional funding to the U.S. Postal Service to inhibit its ability to process the additional ballots. He continued throughout the remainder of his campaign to make unsubstantiated claims of electoral fraud. Sowing potential voter intimidation, the president urged supporters during his first debate Sept. 29 with Biden to "go into the polls and watch very carefully." On multiple occasions, including in the final debate Oct. 22, Trump declined to commit to a peaceful transfer of power.

The U.S. Supreme Court the week before Election Day issued rulings related to GOP challenges of extension of mail-in ballot counting in three battleground states. The Court ruled that Wisconsin could not count ballots received after Election Day, but permitted counting in North Carolina of mail-in ballots postmarked by Nov. 3 but received up to nine days later. The Court declined to review before Election Day a Pennsylvania court decision allowing counting of ballots postmarked by Nov. 3 and received three days after, but left the door open to a post-election challenge. A federal judge Nov. 2 had ruled valid some 127,000 votes cast via "drive-through" voting sites in Democrat-heavy Harris County, TX, saying the plaintiffs lacked legal standing to challenge them.

Paths to Nomination

Pres. Trump officially announced his candidacy for reelection in June 2019 and encountered no serious opposition. He again chose Vice Pres. Mike Pence as his running mate.

Though Biden declined to run for president in 2016 following the 2015 death of his son Beau, he had high name recognition as Pres. Barack Obama's vice president and was the apparent choice of the party establishment before he formally announced his candidacy in an Apr. 25, 2019, video in which he cast himself as a moderate amid a primary race that eventually ballooned to 28 candidates. Nineteen candidates besides Biden made the cut in late June 2019 for the first of 11 Democratic debates, held on two nights. During the debate, then-candidate Sen. Kamala Harris challenged Biden over his resistance in the 1970s to federally imposed school desegregation busing, a program she said directly benefited her as a student.

Sen. Bernie Sanders (Ind., VT), runner-up in delegate votes for the 2016 Democratic nomination, was popular again with progressives, young voters, and others doubting Biden's ability to overcome Trump. Critical of international trade deals, economic inequality, and GOP environmental policies, Sanders criticized Biden for his support of the North American Free Trade Agreement in the 1990s, and along with fellow progressive candidate Sen. Elizabeth Warren (D, MA), faulted Biden for his ties to Wall Street donors.

When Biden announced he was running, the RealClearPolitics average of national polls put him ahead of Sanders, 29.3% to 23.0%, but Sanders and 38-year-old former South Bend, IN, Mayor Pete Buttigieg both easily bested Biden in the botched Iowa Democratic caucus, held Feb. 3, 2020. A single winner was unclear for weeks, but in final results announced Feb. 27, Buttigieg won 26.2% of support and the most delegates, with Sanders drawing 26.1% support, and 15.8% for Biden; Warren trailed Buttigieg by some eight points. Sanders won the Feb. 11 primary in his neighboring state of New Hampshire, again trouncing Biden, and barely edging out Buttigieg, the

Electoral Votes for President, 2020

Electoral votes based on the 2010 Census were in force beginning with the 2012 elections.

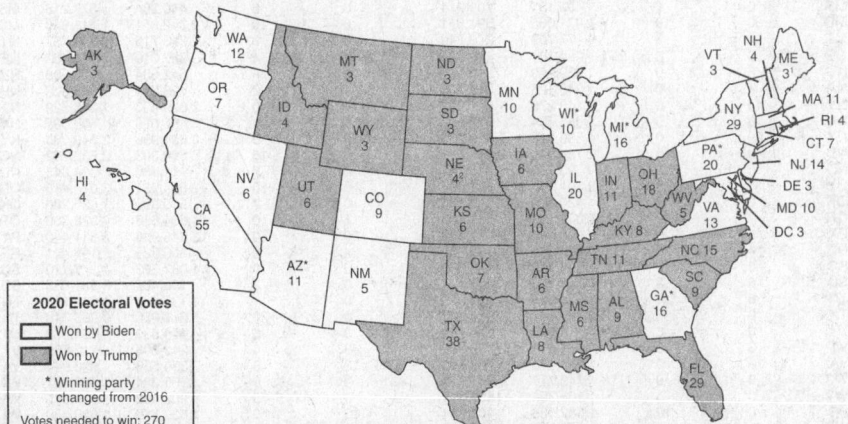

2020 Electoral Votes
- ☐ Won by Biden
- ▨ Won by Trump
- * Winning party changed from 2016

Votes needed to win: 270

Note: Three states (AK, GA, NC) had not yet been called for either candidate. Map reflects electoral forecast based on vote as of Nov. 7, 2020. (1) Trump was awarded one of Maine's four electoral votes. (2) Biden was awarded one of Nebraska's five electoral votes.

first openly gay contender to mount a serious campaign for the presidential nomination from a major party. Though Sanders led Biden again the following week in Nevada, where Buttigieg finished third, Biden easily captured South Carolina on Feb. 29 and steamrolled his way to the lead on Super Tuesday, Mar. 3, capturing wins in 10 state primaries, including in 7 Southern states, where he was aided by his popularity among Black voters.

Following a string of primary victories by Biden in eight more states, including delegate-rich Illinois and Florida, to just one by Sanders (North Dakota), the field by the end of Mar. narrowed to just these two candidates. Buttigieg and Sen. Amy Klobuchar (D, MN) suspended their campaigns, Mar. 1 and Mar. 2, respectively, followed two days later by former New York City Mayor Michael Bloomberg, who didn't enter the race until late Nov. 2019. Warren ended her campaign Mar. 5. Entrepreneur and political novice Andrew Yang, who gained attention with his proposal of a universal basic income for all Americans, withdrew in Feb. after winning just 1% of the Iowa caucus vote.

The Democratic candidates who withdrew from the race were united in endorsing Biden over Sanders. Vowing to participate in a one-on-one debate, Sanders challenged Biden during a Mar. 15 forum on issues that included income inequality and health care. After receiving just half as many votes as Biden in Wisconsin's primary, a contest he won in 2016, Sanders suspended his campaign Apr. 8 and the following week endorsed the former vice president.

As tallied by the Green Papers, Trump in the primaries earned some 18 mil votes, or 94% of all GOP primary votes cast. Biden earned nearly 52% of the Democratic vote, or just over 19 mil, while Sanders drew close to 10 mil, or 26%. Though Republican primary voter turnout was predictably much lower than in 2016, total Democratic voters nationwide exceeded their 2016 turnout by approximately 20% despite the ongoing coronavirus pandemic, which state elections officials addressed with additional early voting and absentee voting options.

At the Democratic National Convention, anchored in Milwaukee, WI, but meeting almost entirely virtually Aug. 17-20 due to the pandemic, Biden received 3,558 delegate votes (75% of the total) while Sanders drew 1,151 votes (24%). At the Republican National Convention, held Aug. 24-27, with operations headquartered in Charlotte, NC, and other events held remotely, Trump won votes from all 2,550 delegates.

Electoral and Popular Vote, 2016 and 2020

Source: 2020 results, © Associated Press; all rights reserved; preliminary as of Nov. 7, 2020. 2016 results, Federal Election Commission Three states (AK, GA, NC) had not yet been called by AP; 2020 electoral assignments reflect votes tallied Nov. 7, 2020.

	2016				2020				
	Electoral vote		Popular vote		Electoral vote		Popular vote		
State	Clinton	Trump	Clinton	Trump	Biden	Trump	Biden	Trump	State
AL	0	9	729,547	1,318,255	0	9	834,533	1,430,589	AL
AK	0	3	116,454	163,387	0	3	63,992	118,602	AK
AZ	0	11	1,161,167	1,252,401	11	0	1,626,943	1,606,370	AZ
AR	0	6	380,494	684,872	0	6	417,897	755,815	AR
CA	55	0	8,753,792	4,483,814	55	0	8,969,107	4,630,099	CA
CO	9	0	1,338,870	1,202,484	9	0	1,753,416	1,335,253	CO
CT	7	0	897,572	673,215	7	0	1,029,132	714,981	CT
DE	3	0	235,603	185,127	3	0	295,403	199,829	DE
DC	3	0	282,830	12,723	3	0	268,625	15,075	DC
FL	0	29	4,504,975	4,617,886	0	29	5,284,453	5,658,847	FL
GA	0	16	1,877,963	2,089,104	16	0	2,461,455	2,454,207	GA
HI	3	0	266,891	128,847	4	0	365,802	196,602	HI
ID	0	4	189,765	409,055	0	4	286,991	554,019	ID
IL	20	0	3,090,729	2,146,015	20	0	3,056,219	2,316,566	IL
IN	0	11	1,033,126	1,557,286	0	11	1,239,605	1,726,508	IN
IA	0	6	653,669	800,983	0	6	757,655	896,014	IA
KS	0	6	427,005	671,018	0	6	551,144	752,903	KS
KY	0	8	628,854	1,202,971	0	8	771,884	1,325,742	KY
LA	0	8	780,154	1,178,638	0	8	855,597	1,255,481	LA
ME	3	1	357,735	335,593	3	1	430,023	359,502	ME
MD	10	0	1,677,928	943,169	10	0	1,495,874	831,401	MD
MA	11	0	1,995,196	1,090,893	11	0	2,316,338	1,148,777	MA
MI	0	16	2,268,839	2,279,543	16	0	2,790,648	2,644,525	MI
MN	10	0	1,367,716	1,322,951	10	0	1,717,952	1,484,855	MN
MS	0	6	485,131	700,714	0	6	440,284	677,218	MS
MO	0	10	1,071,068	1,594,511	0	10	1,242,851	1,711,848	MO
MT	0	3	177,709	279,240	0	3	243,719	341,767	MT
NE	0	5	284,494	495,961	1	4	367,319	548,462	NE
NV	6	0	539,260	512,058	6	0	642,604	616,905	NV
NH	4	0	348,526	345,790	4	0	423,291	365,373	NH
NJ	14	0	2,148,278	1,601,933	14	0	2,029,493	1,385,529	NJ
NM	5	0	385,234	319,667	5	0	496,826	400,095	NM
NY	29	0	4,556,118	2,819,533	29	0	5,094,990	2,849,085	NY
NC	0	15	2,189,316	2,362,631	0	15	2,656,303	2,732,782	NC
ND	0	3	93,758	216,794	0	3	114,480	234,845	ND
OH	0	18	2,394,164	2,841,005	0	18	2,603,731	3,074,418	OH
OK	0	7	420,375	949,136	0	7	503,890	1,020,280	OK
OR	7	0	1,002,106	782,403	7	0	1,304,536	928,706	OR
PA	0	20	2,926,441	2,970,733	20	0	3,345,906	3,311,448	PA
RI	4	0	252,525	180,543	4	0	300,325	197,421	RI
SC	0	9	855,373	1,155,389	0	9	1,087,223	1,377,120	SC
SD	0	3	117,458	227,721	0	3	150,467	261,035	SD
TN	0	11	870,695	1,522,925	0	11	1,139,666	1,849,211	TN
TX	0	36	3,877,868	4,685,047	0	38	5,217,656	5,865,248	TX
UT	0	6	310,676	515,231	0	6	444,531	701,078	UT
VT	3	0	178,573	95,369	3	0	242,805	112,688	VT
VA	13	0	1,981,473	1,769,443	13	0	2,339,558	1,930,944	VA
WA	8	0	1,742,718	1,221,747	12	0	2,286,324	1,498,301	WA
WV	0	5	188,794	489,371	0	5	232,502	539,610	WV
WI	0	10	1,382,536	1,405,284	10	0	1,630,570	1,610,030	WI
WY	0	3	55,973	174,419	0	3	73,445	193,456	WY
Total	**227**	**304**	**65,853,514**	**62,984,828**	**306**	**232**	**74,488,666**	**70,337,285**	**Total**

Note: In 2016, 7 electors (1 from HI, 2 from TX, 4 from WA) voted for candidates to whom they were not pledged; their votes are not included here. Maine and Nebraska are the only two states with laws that allow electoral votes to be split between candidates.

Congressional Contests

Democrats had hopes of winning control of the Senate because Republicans had 23 seats to defend compared to Democrats' 12 seats. The Democrats needed a net gain of 3-4 seats (depending on the party of the vice president, who breaks tie votes) to win the majority. In the immediate post-election results, Democrats lost one seat and picked up only two from Republicans. Results in two bitterly fought Senate races in Georgia were pending, as no candidate appeared to have won the required 50% majority. Each seat would be decided in a runoff held in Jan. 2021.

Sen. Cory Gardner (R, CO), elected in the 2014 Republican wave, lost the seat to former two-term Gov. John Hickenlooper (D). Sen. Martha McSally (R), who lost a 2018 Senate race in Arizona to Kyrsten Sinema (D) but was appointed to the state's other seat in 2019 following the death of long-serving Sen. John McCain (R), lost to centrist Mark Kelly (D), a former astronaut. Alabama Sen. Doug Jones (D) was defeated by a 20+-point margin by former Auburn Univ. football coach Tommy Tuberville; Jones had won the traditionally GOP-held seat in a 2017 special election against scandal-ridden Roy Moore (R).

In other closely watched, highly funded races, incumbent Trump ally Sen. Lindsey Graham (R) defended his seat from a challenge by associate Democratic Party chair Jaime Harrison, who had raised a record $105 mil against $73 mil by Graham. In Kentucky, Senate Majority Leader Mitch McConnell (R) clinched reelection easily against his similarly well-funded opponent, Amy McGrath (D), a former fighter pilot. Maine Sen. Susan Collins (R), a long-serving, self-professed moderate who nonetheless mostly supported Trump, defeated her Democratic challenger Sara Gideon by more than 7 points. First-term Sen. Joni Ernst (R, IA) prevailed in a race that drew more than $230 mil. In the Senate's most expensive race (over $280 mil), Sen. Thom Tillis (R, NC) led against challenger Cal Cunningham (D), but the race remained too close to call.

Democrats' hopes to expand their control of the House not only failed to materialize, but the party instead lost representation. Though Republicans fell far short of the 21 new seats needed to win a majority, they did score key gains, picking up eight seats while losing just three to Democrats as of Nov. 7. (Some two dozen seats had not yet been called.) Republicans notably flipped seats in Florida (2), Iowa, New Mexico, Oklahoma, and South Carolina, all first won by Democrats in 2018.

Democrats won two North Carolina seats vacated by Republicans and redistricted by court order in 2020.

Statehouses and Ballot Issues

There were seven governorships currently held by Republicans and four by Democrats on 2020 ballots. Of these 11, Republicans won 8 and Democrats won 3. Incumbent Gov. Roy Cooper (D) held on to his post in closely watched North Carolina, defeating Lt. Gov. Dan Forest (R). Montana's governorship—vacated by term-limited Steve Bullock (D), who lost the state's 2020 Senate race—was easily won by U.S. Rep. Greg Gianforte (R). Heading into the election, Republicans held a majority in 59 state chambers to 39 by Democrats, and had "trifecta" control—the post of governor as well as both branches of government—in 21 states versus 15 by Democrats. As of Nov. 6, the GOP had 22 trifecta states to Democrats' 15. Most state legislatures were expected to begin redistricting their states in accordance with 2020 census results in 2021, making unified party control at the state level even more significant.

Voters weighed in on 121 measures on statewide ballots in 2020. California approved a measure—in the most expensive ballot-measure campaign in state history—repealing a controversial law prohibiting ride-share companies from classifying drivers as independent contractors. The state also rejected (56%-44%) a measure restoring affirmative action, banned since 1996, for admission to public universities/colleges and in state government hiring. Voters in Oregon agreed to legalize possession of small amounts of "hard" drugs (e.g., cocaine, heroin), making it the first state to do so. Oregon also legalized psychedelic mushrooms, and DC decriminalized their use. Four states—Arizona, Montana, New Jersey, and South Dakota—approved recreational marijuana use; South Dakotans and Mississippians approved medical marijuana. Florida voters by a wide margin agreed to a higher minimum wage. After years of legal action over alleged gerrymandering, Virginia voters widely approved a measure creating a bipartisan electoral redistricting commission.

Campaign Trail Quotes, 2020

"We have to restore America's soul, as I've said from the moment I announced. It is in jeopardy under this president of the United States."
—**Former Vice Pres. Joe Biden**, Jan. 14, in Democratic primary debate in Iowa.

"[M]aybe, just maybe, we should join the rest of the industrialized world, guarantee health care to all people as a human right, raise that minimum wage to a living wage of 15 bucks an hour, and have the guts to take on the fossil fuel industry."
—**Sen. Bernie Sanders** (I, VT), Feb. 19, at Democratic primary debate in Las Vegas.

"We can't be complacent or smug or sense that somehow it's so obvious that this president hasn't done a good job, because look, he won once."
—**Former Pres. Barack Obama**, at his first campaign event for Biden, June 23.

"Our nation is witnessing a merciless campaign to wipe out our history, defame our heroes … and indoctrinate our children. Angry mobs are trying to tear down statues of our founders … and unleash a wave of violent crime in our cities."
—**Pres. Donald Trump**, speaking at rally at Mount Rushmore, July 3.

"Joe Biden is a man for our times. Times that call for all of us to take off our partisan hats and put our nation first for ourselves and of course for our children."
—**Former Ohio Gov. John Kasich** (R), at Democratic National Convention, Aug. 17.

"We must elect a president who will bring … all of us together—Black, white, Latino, Asian, Indigenous—to achieve the future we collectively want."
—**Sen. Kamala Harris** (CA), vice-presidential nominee, at Democratic convention, Aug. 19.

"I'm just a regular kid, and in a short amount of time, Joe Biden made me feel more confident about something that's bothered me my whole life."
—**Brayden Harrington**, at Democratic convention, Aug. 20; Biden had bonded with the 13-year-old in New Hampshire over their common struggle to overcome stuttering.

"[I]t's now fashionable to say that America is racist. That is a lie. America is not a racist country."
—**Former UN ambassador and South Carolina Gov. Nikki Haley**, at Republican National Convention, Aug. 24.

"What they're doing is using COVID to steal an election. They're using COVID to defraud the American people, all of our people, of a fair and free election."
—**Pres. Trump**, at Republican convention, Aug. 24.

"I recognize that my dad's communication style is not to everyone's taste. And I know his tweets can feel a bit … unfiltered. But the results speak for themselves."
—**Ivanka Trump**, Pres. Trump's daughter and adviser, at Republican convention, Aug. 27.

"Joe Biden is not a savior of America's soul. He is the destroyer of America's jobs, and if given the chance, he will be the destroyer of American greatness."
—**Pres. Trump**, accepting renomination, at Republican convention, Aug. 27.

"Do I look like a radical socialist with a soft spot for rioters? … I want a safe America. Safe from COVID, safe from crime and looting, safe from racially motivated violence, safe from bad cops … safe from four more years of Donald Trump."
—**Vice Pres. Biden**, Aug. 31, speaking in Pittsburgh, after the GOP convention.

"If you give a climate arsonist four more years in the White House, why would anyone be surprised if we have more of America ablaze?"
—**Vice Pres. Biden** at speech in Wilmington, Sept. 14, faulting Trump for failing to address climate change and its contribution to the proliferation of forest fires.

"Will you shut up, man?"
—**Vice Pres. Biden** reacting to repeated interruptions by Trump at candidates' debate in Cleveland, Sept. 29.

"Simply put, it's a choice between a socialist nightmare and the American dream."
—**Pres. Trump**, in campaign speech video streamed from the White House Rose Garden, Oct. 14.

Profiles of Presidential Nominees, 2020

Republican Nominee for President: Donald Trump

Born: Donald John Trump, June 14, 1946, Queens, NY, to parents Frederick C. Trump, Mary (MacLeod) Trump. **Education:** Fordham Univ., 1964-66; BS, Wharton School of Finance, Univ. of Penn., 1968. **Career:** assumed control of family business, 1971; star and coproducer, NBC's *The Apprentice* and *Celebrity Apprentice*, 2004-15. **Net worth:** $2.5 bil (*Forbes* est., Sept. 2020). **Religion:** Nondenominational Christian. **Family:** married Ivana Marie Zelníčková (b. 1949), 1977; children: Donald Jr. (b. 1977), Ivanka (b. 1981), Eric (b. 1984); div. 1992; married Marla Maples (b. 1963), 1993; daughter: Tiffany (b. 1993); div. 1999; married Melania Knauss (b. 1970), 2005; son: Barron (b. 2006).

Donald Trump grew up in Queens, NY, the fourth of five children. His father made a small fortune developing apartment complexes in the city's outer boroughs. At age 13 Trump was sent to a military boarding school. After graduating from the Wharton School he advanced to leadership of his father's company and spearheaded its expansion in Manhattan and beyond. He later boosted its brand value through his reality TV series. The Trump Organization today has valuable assets around the world, along with heavy debts. As president he surrendered legal control of the organization, but not ownership, to his elder sons.

Trump explored running for president as a third-party candidate in 2000. During Obama's presidency he was a leading "birther," casting doubt that Pres. Barack Obama was born in the U.S and constitutionally eligible to be president. In 2016 he won the GOP presidential nomination, defeating a large field of rivals. Using often inflammatory rhetoric and making claims frequently found inaccurate—practices he continued in the White House—he portrayed himself as a skilled outsider who would create prosperity and put "America first." Surviving accusations of sexual misconduct and exposure of crude remarks about women, he defeated Sen. Hillary Clinton (D) in the 2016 general election.

Pres. Trump promoted building of a wall along the U.S.-Mexico border and tightened border enforcement; reports of children separated from parents drew criticism. He sought to end an Obama-era program protecting many undocumented immigrants ("dreamers") from deportation and banned entry of foreign nationals from a number of mostly Muslim-majority nations, citing security concerns. Opponents said such policies were motivated by racism or xenophobia. Trump withdrew the U.S. from the Trans-Pacific Partnership and imposed tariffs especially on Chinese imports. He also began a process to exit the 2016 Paris Agreement on climate change and roll back strict fuel efficiency mandates for vehicles, and moved to repeal Obama's Clean Power Plan.

Abroad, the administration withdrew from a 2015 multinational nuclear deal with Iran and supported rival Saudi Arabia in its intervention in the Yemen civil war. While making progress in defeating ISIS, the U.S. under Trump ordered some troop reductions in the Middle East, including a controversial withdrawal from northern Syria. The administration had close relations with the conservative Israeli government and helped to restore economic or diplomatic ties between Israel and several Arab countries in 2020. While accused of alienating European allies, Trump cultivated friendly relations with the leaders of China and Russia, and with North Korean dictator Kim Jong Un after a tense war of words and nuclear threats.

Trump demanded strong loyalty from subordinates and fired James Comey as FBI director amid an agency probe of Russian interference in the 2016 election. Though a final FBI report found Russian involvement, it did not decide whether Trump himself committed any crime. But charges that Trump had tried to use military aid as a means to pressure Ukraine into announcing a corruption investigation targeting political rival Joe Biden led to his impeachment by the Democrat-controlled House. He was acquitted by the GOP-controlled Senate in Feb. 2020.

Despite partial moves by the administration to restrict incoming travel from abroad, the coronavirus, by early 2020, entered and spread, leading to over 200,000 deaths by early fall. Shutdowns to prevent the virus's spread caused a huge economic contraction, wiping out strong gains, including historically low unemployment rates. Trump often minimized the pandemic threat and criticized countermeasures urged by government health experts, stressing a need for national economic recovery.

The death of a Black man in Minneapolis in May 2020, attributed to violence by a white police officer, fueled protracted widespread demonstrations against alleged systemic racist police brutality that elevated the issue of racial justice. Trump blamed Democrats for failing to react to instances of violence, looting, and destruction of property.

Trump won nomination for a second term without significant primary opposition, though some prominent Republicans came out against him. An *Atlantic* magazine article reported in Sept. 2020 that Trump privately showed scorn for military members. Journalist Bob Woodward, in a Sept. 2020 book, quoted Trump saying he deliberately downplayed the COVID-19 threat to prevent panic.

After the death of U.S. Supreme Court Associate Justice Ruth Bader Ginsburg, in Sept. 2020, Trump, who had previously appointed Neil Gorsuch and Brett Kavanaugh to the Court, took the opportunity to nominate Amy Coney Barrett.

The *NY Times*, in fall 2020, published articles reportedly based on leaked tax records, claiming Trump avoided paying personal federal income tax for years by claiming heavy business losses, and while president reaped profits from those who sought access and influence.

Weeks before the election, Trump himself, along with the first lady and a number of officials and staff, tested positive for the coronavirus; he was briefly hospitalized. As polls predicted a Biden victory, Trump cast doubt as to whether the Nov. election could be fairly conducted.

Republican Nominee for Vice President: Mike Pence

Born: Michael Richard Pence, June 7, 1959, Columbus, IN, to parents Edward J. Pence Jr., Nancy Jane (Cawley) Pence. **Education:** BA (history), Hanover College, 1981; J.D., Indiana Univ. School of Law, 1986. **Career:** attorney in private practice, 1986-91; pres., Indiana Policy Review Foundation, 1991-93; host, syndicated radio talk show, 1992-99, and morning TV talk show, 1995-99; U.S. representative (IN), 2001-13; chair, House Republican Conference, 2009-11; Indiana governor, 2013-17; U.S. vice president, 2017-present. **Net worth:** $1 mil (*Forbes* est. 2019). **Religion:** Evangelical Christian. **Family:** married Karen Pence (neé Batten) (b. 1957), 1985; children: Michael, Charlotte, Audrey.

One of six children born to an Irish Catholic family, Mike Pence grew up as an admirer of Pres. John F. Kennedy and volunteered for the county Democratic Party. In college he became a conservative and was introduced to evangelical Christianity, to which he later converted. He worked as an attorney and entered politics as a Republican precinct committeeman. He made unsuccessful runs for Congress in 1988 and 1990, later expressing regret that he had used attack ads in his campaign. He aired his political opinions as a radio and TV talk show host in Indiana.

Pence was elected to Congress in 2000 and reelected five times. He described himself as "a Christian, a conservative, and a Republican, in that order." Diverging from Pres. George W. Bush, he voted against the No Child Left Behind bill (2001), the Medicare prescription drug expansion (2003), and the bank bailout (2008). He failed in a 2006 challenge to Rep. John Boehner (OH) for the House speakership, but two years later was chosen as Republican conference chair.

Elected governor of Indiana in 2012, Pence signed into law tax and spending cuts that created a budget surplus. He also expanded a voucher program for nonpublic schools and signed legislation to remove Indiana from federal Common Core standards in favor of state-developed standards, though these ended up being similar. In 2015 he signed a broadly worded Religious Freedom Restoration Act; after backlash he approved an amendment designed to protect LGBT minorities from being denied services. In 2016 he signed a measure banning abortions for reasons of race, gender, or disability, but it was blocked in court.

Pence initially supported Sen. Ted Cruz (TX) for the 2016 GOP presidential nomination. In naming Pence as his choice for vice president Trump cited a need for party unity, while also praising his record as governor. As vice president, Pence fully supported Trump and his policies. He cast more than a dozen tie-breaking Senate votes, including the first-ever to confirm a cabinet appointee—charter school advocate Betsy De Vos as education secretary. As head of the administration's coronavirus task force he sometimes showed more deference to experts than Trump did, but he did not publicly criticize the president.

Democratic Nominee for President: Joe Biden

Born: Joseph Robinette Biden Jr., Nov. 20, 1942, Scranton, PA, to parents Joseph Robinette Biden Sr. and Catherine Eugenia (Finnegan) Biden. **Education:** BA, Univ. of Delaware, 1965; JD, Syracuse Univ., 1968. **Career:** attorney/public defender, Wilmington, DE, 1969-72; member, New Castle County Council, 1970-72; U.S. senator (DE), 1973-2009; chair, Senate Judiciary Committee, 1987-95; chair, Foreign Relations Committee, 2001-03, 2007-09; contender for Dem. presidential nomination, 1988, 2008; U.S. vice president, 2009-17. **Net worth:** $9 mil (Forbes est., Aug. 2019). **Religion:** Roman Catholic. **Family:** married Neilia Hunter (1942-72), 1966; children: Beau (1969-2015), Hunter (b. 1970), Naomi (1971-72); married Jill Tracy Biden (née Jacobs) (b. 1951), 1977; children: Ashley (b. 1981).

Biden was the oldest of four children in a working-class household. He went to law school, married as a student, and practiced law while becoming active in the Democratic Party. In Nov. 1972, at age 29, he won a U.S. Senate seat from Delaware, in an upset victory over the Republican incumbent. The following month, his wife and infant daughter were killed in a car crash, and their two sons seriously injured; Biden was sworn in to office at their hospital bedside. Five years later he married Jill Jacobs, a high school English teacher.

Biden won reelection six times. He famously commuted to work by Amtrak so he could be with his family in Delaware every night. As chairman of the Judiciary Committee he presided over contentious Supreme Court nomination hearings that ended in the defeat of Robert Bork's nomination (1987) and in Clarence Thomas's confirmation (1991). He won both acclaim and criticism for working with Republicans, including segregationists, to achieve his objectives, and for his lead role in passing a 1994 crime bill that banned assault weapons but also increased criminal penalties and swelled prison populations. He voted in 2002 for use of force in Iraq, but later criticized the Bush administration's Iraq war policy. In 2005 he supported a restrictive bankruptcy bill opposed by most Democrats.

Biden ran for the 1988 Democratic presidential nomination but withdrew, damaged by his use of a major part of another politician's speech without attribution. The following year he underwent two high-risk surgeries for brain aneurysms but made a full recovery. He ran again for the party's presidential nomination in 2008 but dropped out after a poor finish in the Iowa caucus. Obama subsequently selected him as his running mate.

As vice president Biden chaired a White House Task Force on Working Families, served as a liaison to Congress, and made frequent visits to Iraq. He worked closely with Obama and contributed advice that was sometimes contrarian—for example, he reportedly showed skepticism about plans for the 2011 raid that killed Osama bin Laden. He played a key role in negotiations to resolve the federal debt crisis that same year.

In 2015 Biden's son Beau, an Iraq war veteran, former attorney general of Delaware, and rising political star, died from brain cancer. He decided against a 2016 run for president, indicating that he still needed to recover from his bereavement. In Apr. 2019, Biden announced he was running for president. He lambasted Trump for having failed to condemn a 2017 white supremacist rally in Charlottesville, VA, and characterized the 2020 race as a battle for the "soul of this nation." Facing a wide field of rivals in the primaries, including strong progressive challengers, he overcame a slow start to win nomination. He restricted his search for a running mate to women, selecting Kamala Harris for reasons that included generational and racial diversity and overall compatibility.

Biden hoped to reverse Trump's immigration policies and deregulatory moves, and called for a $1.7-tril plan to help eliminate net greenhouse gas emissions by 2050. He advocated a public health care option similar to Medicare, rather than "Medicare for All." He favored increased spending on social programs but not "defunding" police. He supported repeal of GOP tax cuts and increases in top individual and corporate income tax rates. Biden opposed key Trump policies on Iran and Saudi Arabia, while advocating a continuing U.S. military presence in the Middle East. A Catholic in the liberal mode, he came to support same-sex marriage and pro-choice policies on abortion that included repeal of the Hyde amendment.

Critics made allegations of influence peddling abroad by Biden for his son Hunter, but Biden denied any impropriety. Biden was accused of acting over-familiarly toward women and girls, and in one instance, of sexual misconduct, which he denied. Long known for his effusive and empathetic personality, and for his loquaciousness and gaffes, he was portrayed by some critics as lacking in mental acuity, or as too old to take on the presidency. (He would be a record 78 years old at the Jan. 2021 inauguration.) A Dec. 2019 medical report by his physician pronounced him physically fit.

Democratic Nominee for Vice President: Kamala Harris

Born: Kamala Devi Harris, Oct. 20, 1964, Oakland, CA, to parents Donald Jasper Harris and Shyamala Gopalan. **Education:** BA, Howard University, 1986; J.D., Univ. of California, 1989. **Career:** deputy district attorney, Alameda County, CA, 1990-98; managing attorney, San Francisco District Attorney's Office, 1998-2000; chief, San Francisco City Attorney's Div. on Children and Families, 2000-04; San Francisco district attorney, 2004-11; CA attorney gen., 2011-16; U.S. senator (CA), 2017-present; contender for 2020 Dem. pres. nomination. **Net worth:** $6 mil (Forbes est., Aug. 2019). **Religion:** Southern Baptist. **Family:** married Douglas Emhoff (b. 1964), 2014; stepchildren: Ella and Cole.

Kamala Harris was born in California to a Jamaica-born Black economist father and India-born biomedical scientist mother. Her parents, both immigrants who met as student-activists at the Univ. of California at Berkeley, divorced when Kamala was seven years old. After law school Harris worked in the Alameda County District Attorney's Office, focusing on child sexual assault cases. The first Black woman to become San Francisco's DA and the first to be California attorney general, she won big settlements for homeowners against banks and for students against a for-profit education company. Her husband, Doug Emhoff, is an entertainment lawyer, and she is a stepmother to two adult children from his first marriage.

In 2016 Harris outpolled a large field of candidates in California's "top-two" nonpartisan primary and defeated U.S. Rep. Loretta Sanchez (D) in the general election to win a U.S. Senate seat and become the second-ever Black woman senator. She was noted for her aggressive questioning of Trump nominees, including Brett Kavanaugh in his Supreme Court confirmation hearing before the Judiciary Committee. Harris supported the Green New Deal and also introduced or co-sponsored legislation to increase the federal minimum wage, reform cash bail, and prevent religious employers from denying health care coverage for employees or claiming exemptions to civil rights.

In Jan. 2019, Harris announced her candidacy for the 2020 Democratic presidential nomination, and, in the first candidates' debate in June 2019, she confronted Biden for opposing school busing as a means of racial integration in the 1970s and 1980s, noting that she herself had been bused to school as a child. The criminal justice plan she released during her campaign included progressive policies she had opposed as a prosecutor. At the same time she dropped her support for "Medicare for All" in favor a more incremental approach. After a brief period in the top tier, her poll numbers fizzled, and she dropped out of the primary race in Dec. 2019.

After committing to choose a woman VP, Biden selected Harris as his running mate. She was the third woman candidate for vice president on a major-party ticket and the first Black woman and first Asian American woman.

Members of the 117th Congress: U.S. Senate

Source: © Associated Press; all rights reserved. 2020 results are preliminary as of Nov. 4-6, 2020.

48 Republicans, 46 Democrats, 2 independents (who caucus with Democrats); 4 seats undecided. Boldface denotes the 2020 election winner; italics denotes a race not yet called by the Associated Press. Because of the large number of absentee and mail-in ballots in 2020—as well as vast differences in states' counting procedures and timelines—final tallies may vary substantially from preliminary numbers shown here. * = Incumbent. Third-party or independent candidates receiving fewer than 50,000 votes are not necessarily listed.

Terms are for six years and end Jan. 3 of the year preceding the senator's name in the following table. Annual salary: $174,000; President Pro Tempore, Majority Leader, and Minority Leader: $193,400. To be eligible to serve in the Senate, a person must be at least 30 years old, a U.S. citizen for at least nine years, and a resident of the state from which elected.

D = Democrat; R = Republican; DFL = Dem.-Farmer-Labor; Ind. = Independent; LB = Libertarian.

Term ends	Senator/candidate (party); service from	2020 election results
Alabama		
2023	Richard Shelby (R); 1/6/1987	
2027	**Tommy Tuberville (R)**	**1,381,938**
	Doug Jones* (D); 1/3/2018	904,683
Alaska		
2023	Lisa Murkowski (R); 12/20/2002	
2027	*Dan Sullivan* (R); 1/6/2015*	*118,978*
	Al Gross (D)	*61,362*
Arizona		
2023[1]	**Mark Kelly (D)**	**1,601,546**
	Martha McSally* (R); 1/3/2019	1,500,939
2025	Kyrsten Sinema (D); 1/3/2019	
Arkansas		
2023	John Boozman (R); 1/5/2011	
2027	**Tom Cotton* (R); 1/6/2015**	**784,400**
	Ricky Harrington (LB)	392,392
California		
2023	Kamala Harris (D); 1/3/2017	
2025	Dianne Feinstein (D); 11/10/1992	
Colorado		
2023	Michael Bennet (D); 1/22/2009	
2027	**John Hickenlooper (D)**	**1,579,173**
	Cory Gardner* (R); 1/6/2015	1,299,505
Connecticut		
2023	Richard Blumenthal (D); 1/5/2011	
2025	Christopher S. Murphy (D); 1/3/2013	
Delaware		
2025	Thomas R. Carper (D); 1/3/2001	
2027	**Christopher Coons* (D); 11/15/2010**	**290,983**
	Lauren Witzke (R)	185,416
Florida		
2023	Marco Rubio (R); 1/5/2011	
2025	Rick Scott (R); 1/8/2019	
Georgia		
2023[2,3]	*Raphael Warnock (D)*	*1,602,858*
	Kelly Loeffler (R); 1/6/2020*	*1,266,966*
	Doug Collins (R)	*975,564*
	Deborah Jackson (D)	*320,105*
	Matt Lieberman (D)	*134,956*
	Tamara Johnson-Shealey (D)	*105,405*
	Jamesia James (D)	*93,074*
	Derrick Grayson (R)	*51,128*
2027[3]	*David Perdue* (R); 1/6/2015*	*2,449,502*
	Jon Ossoff (D)	*2,351,092*
	Shane Hazel (LB)	*113,768*
Hawaii		
2023	Brian Schatz (D); 12/26/2012	
2025	Mazie K. Hirono (D); 1/3/2013	
Idaho		
2023	Mike Crapo (R); 1/6/1999	
2027	**Jim Risch* (R); 1/6/2009**	**537,456**
	Paulette Jordan (D)	285,830
Illinois		
2023	Tammy Duckworth (D); 1/3/2017	
2027	**Richard J. Durbin* (D); 1/7/1997**	**2,724,808**
	Mark Curran (R)	2,133,699
	Danny Malouf (LB)	98,611
	Willie Wilson (Ind.)	64,569
Indiana		
2023	Todd C. Young (R); 1/3/2017	
2025	Mike Braun (R); 1/3/2019	
Iowa		
2023	Chuck Grassley (R); 1/5/1981	
2027	**Joni Ernst* (R); 1/6/2015**	**863,690**
	Theresa Greenfield (D)	753,314
Kansas		
2023	Jerry Moran (R); 1/5/2011	
2027	**Roger Marshall (R)**	**698,079**
	Barbara Bollier (D)	536,526
	Jason Buckley (LB)	63,662

Term ends	Senator/candidate (party); service from	2020 election results
Kentucky		
2023	Rand Paul (R); 1/5/2011	
2027	**Mitch McConnell* (R); 1/3/1985**	**1,222,749**
	Amy McGrath (D)	793,729
	Brad Barron (LB)	83,826
Louisiana		
2023	John Kennedy (R); 1/3/2017	
2027	**Bill Cassidy* (R); 1/6/2015**	**1,228,661**
	Adrian Perkins (D)	393,866
	Derrick Edwards (D)	229,698
	Antoine Pierce (D)	55,684
Maine		
2025	Angus King (Ind.); 1/3/2013	
2027	**Susan M. Collins* (R); 1/7/1997**	**409,900**
	Sara Gideon (D)	339,342
Maryland		
2023	Chris Van Hollen (D); 1/3/2017	
2025	Ben Cardin (D); 1/4/2007	
Massachusetts		
2025	Elizabeth A. Warren (D); 1/3/2013	
2027	**Edward Markey* (D); 7/16/2013**	**2,276,729**
	Kevin O'Connor (R)	1,144,477
Michigan		
2025	Debbie Stabenow (D); 1/3/2001	
2027	**Gary Peters* (D); 1/6/2015**	**2,722,724**
	John James (R)	2,636,667
	Valerie Willis (U.S. Taxpayers)	51,234
Minnesota		
2025	Amy Klobuchar (DFL); 1/4/2007	
2027	**Tina Smith* (DFL); 1/3/2018**	**1,546,501**
	Jason Lewis (R)	1,378,114
	Kevin O'Connor (Legal Marijuana Now)	187,197
	Oliver Steinberg (Grass Roots)	56,077
Mississippi		
2025	Roger F. Wicker (R); 12/31/2007	
2027	**Cindy Hyde-Smith* (R); 4/9/2018**	**606,224**
	Mike Espy (D)	463,826
Missouri		
2023	Roy Blunt (R); 1/5/2011	
2025	Josh Hawley (R); 1/3/2019	
Montana		
2025	Jon Tester (D); 1/4/2007	
2027	**Steve Daines* (R); 1/6/2015**	**320,392**
	Steve Bullock (D)	263,242
Nebraska		
2025	Deb Fischer (R); 1/3/2013	
2027	**Ben Sasse* (R); 1/6/2015**	**568,102**
	Chris Janicek (D)	217,905
	Gene Siadek (LB)	53,215
Nevada		
2023	Catherine Cortez Masto (D); 1/3/2017	
2025	Jacky Rosen (D); 1/3/2019	
New Hampshire		
2023	Maggie Hassan (D); 1/3/2017	
2027	**Jeanne Shaheen* (D); 1/6/2009**	**445,973**
	Corky Messner (R)	322,426
New Jersey		
2025	Robert Menendez (D); 1/18/2006	
2027	**Cory Booker* (D); 10/31/2013**	**1,723,102**
	Rikin Mehta (R)	1,079,469
New Mexico		
2025	Martin Heinrich (D); 1/3/2013	
2027	**Ben Ray Lujan (D)**	**463,195**
	Mark Ronchetti (R)	414,835

Term ends	Senator/candidate (party); service from	2020 election results
New York		
2023	Charles Schumer (D); 1/6/1999	
2025	Kirsten E. Gillibrand (D); 1/27/2009	
North Carolina		
2023	Richard Burr (R); 1/4/2005	
2027	*Thom Tillis* (R); 1/6/2015*	*2,640,381*
	Cal Cunningham (D)	*2,543,693*
	Shannon Bray (LB)	*167,968*
	Kevin Hayes (Constitution)	*66,668*
North Dakota		
2023	John Hoeven (R); 1/5/2011	
2025	Kevin Cramer (R); 1/3/2019	
Ohio		
2023	Rob Portman (R); 1/5/2011	
2025	Sherrod Brown (D); 1/4/2007	
Oklahoma		
2023	James Lankford (R); 1/6/2015	
2027	**James M. Inhofe* (R); 11/21/1994**	**977,813**
	Abby Broyles (D)	509,186
Oregon		
2023	Ron Wyden (D); 2/6/1996	
2027	**Jeff Merkley* (D); 1/6/2009**	**1,229,443**
	Jo Rae Perkins (R)	827,820
Pennsylvania		
2023	Pat Toomey (R); 1/5/2011	
2025	Bob Casey Jr. (D); 1/4/2007	
Rhode Island		
2025	Sheldon Whitehouse (D); 1/4/2007	
2027	**Jack Reed* (D); 1/7/1997**	**317,813**
	Allen Waters (R)	161,821
South Carolina		
2023	Tim Scott (R); 1/3/2013	
2027	**Lindsey Graham* (R); 1/7/2003**	**1,337,155**
	Jaime Harrison (D)	1,072,702
South Dakota		
2023	John Thune (R); 1/4/2005	

Term ends	Senator/candidate (party); service from	2020 election results
2027	**Mike Rounds* (R); 1/6/2015**	**257,842**
	Dan Ahlers (D)	121,603
Tennessee		
2025	Marsha Blackburn (R); 1/3/2019	
2027	**Bill Hagerty (R)**	**1,838,276**
	Marquita Bradshaw (D)	1,036,911
Texas		
2025	Ted Cruz (R); 1/3/2013	
2027	**John Cornyn* (R); 12/2/2002**	**5,904,784**
	Mary Hegar (D)	4,801,291
	Kerry McKennon (LB)	207,042
	David Collins (Green)	80,166
Utah		
2023	Mike Lee (R); 1/5/2011	
2025	Mitt Romney (R); 1/3/2019	
Vermont		
2023	Patrick Leahy (D); 1/3/1975	
2025	Bernie Sanders (Ind.); 1/4/2007	
Virginia		
2025	Timothy M. Kaine (D); 1/3/2013	
2027	**Mark Warner* (D); 1/6/2009**	**2,352,320**
	Daniel Gade (R)	1,873,087
Washington		
2023	Patty Murray (D); 1/3/1993	
2025	Maria Cantwell (D); 1/3/2001	
West Virginia		
2025	Joe Manchin III (D); 11/15/2010	
2027	**Shelley Moore Capito* (R); 1/6/2015**	**541,641**
	Paula Jean Swearengin (D)	207,210
Wisconsin		
2023	Ron Johnson (R); 1/5/2011	
2025	Tammy Baldwin (D); 1/3/2013	
Wyoming		
2025	John Barrasso (R); 6/22/2007	
2027	**Cynthia Lummis (R)**	**197,961**
	Merav Ben-David (D)	72,720

(1) Special election to fill the seat vacated by Sen. John McCain (R), who died in office Aug. 25, 2018. (2) Special election to fill the seat vacated by Sen. Johnny Isakson (R), who resigned effective Dec. 31, 2019. (3) A runoff between the top two vote-getters was scheduled for Jan. 5, 2021.

Members of the 117th Congress: U.S. House of Representatives

Source: © Associated Press; all rights reserved. 2020 results are preliminary as of Nov. 4-7, 2020.

215 Democrats, 196 Republicans; 24 seats undecided. Boldface denotes the 2020 election winner; italics denotes a race not yet called by the Associated Press. * = Incumbent. Third-party or independent candidates receiving fewer than 10,000 votes are not necessarily listed.

Terms are for two years ending on Jan. 3, 2023. Annual salary, $174,000; Majority Leader and Minority Leader, $193,400; Speaker of the House, $223,500. To be eligible to serve in the House, a person must be at least 25 years of age, a U.S. citizen for at least seven years, and a resident of the state from which elected.

D = Democrat; R = Republican; C = Conservative; DFL = Dem.-Farmer-Labor; Ind. = Independent; LB = Libertarian; NPA = No party affiliation; NPL = Nonpartisan League.

Dist.	Representative/candidate (party)	2020 election results
Alabama		
1	**Jerry Carl (R)**	**210,636**
	James Averhart (D)	115,592
2	**Barry Moore (R)**	**197,329**
	Phyllis Harvey-Hall (D)	104,592
3	**Mike Rogers* (R)**	**216,700**
	Adia Winfrey (D)	103,874
4	**Robert Aderholt* (R)**	**257,201**
	Rick Neighbors (D)	52,688
5	**Mo Brooks* (R)**	**Unopposed**
6	**Gary Palmer* (R)**	**Unopposed**
7	**Terri A. Sewell* (D)**	**Unopposed**
Alaska		
	Don Young* (R)	*119,999*
	Alyse Galvin (Ind./D)	*69,674*
Arizona		
1	*Tom O'Halleran* (D)*	*171,659*
	Tiffany Shedd (R)	*158,857*
2	**Ann Kirkpatrick* (D)**	**189,084**
	Brandon Martin (R)	142,830
3	**Raúl M. Grijalva* (D)**	**145,135**
	Daniel Wood (R)	77,408

Dist.	Representative/candidate (party)	2020 election results
4	**Paul A. Gosar* (R)**	**237,538**
	Delina DiSanto (D)	106,692
5	**Andy Biggs* (R)**	**198,148**
	Joan Greene (D)	153,397
6	**David Schweikert* (R)**	**214,474**
	Hiral Tipirneni (D)	196,828
7	**Ruben Gallego* (D)**	**127,645**
	Joshua Barnett (D)	37,569
8	**Debbie Lesko* (R)**	**197,431**
	Michael Muscato (D)	145,000
9	**Greg Stanton* (D)**	**178,556**
	Dave Giles (R)	102,322
Arkansas		
1	**Rick Crawford* (R)**	**Unopposed**
2	**French Hill* (R)**	**182,248**
	Joyce Elliott (D)	145,255
3	**Steve Womack* (R)**	**211,732**
	Celeste Williams (D)	103,966
	Michael Kalagias (LB)	12,832
4	**Bruce Westerman* (R)**	**188,125**
	William Hanson (D)	74,174

Dist.	Representative/candidate (party)	2020 election results
California		
1	**Doug LaMalfa* (R)**	**142,742**
	Audrey Denney (D)	116,985
2	**Jared Huffman* (D)**	**202,840**
	Dale Mensing (R)	57,274
3	**John Garamendi* (D)**	**123,527**
	Tamika Hamilton (R)	89,220
4	*Tom McClintock* (R)*	*188,244*
	Brynne Kennedy (D)	*160,983*
5	**Mike Thompson* (D)**	**193,191**
	Scott Giblin (R)	52,493
6	**Doris O. Matsui* (D)**	**107,316**
	Chris Bish (R)	34,150
7	**Ami Bera* (D)**	**116,437**
	Buzz Patterson (R)	74,436
8	*Jay Obernolte (R)*	*102,510*
	Christine Bubser (D)	*88,324*
9	**Jerry McNerney* (D)**	**96,487**
	Tony Amador (R)	60,318
10	**Josh Harder* (D)**	**107,081**
	Ted Howze (R)	74,492
11	**Mark DeSaulnier* (D)**	**178,219**
	Nisha Sharma (R)	58,338
12	**Nancy Pelosi* (D)**	**227,989**
	Shahid Buttar (D)	59,745
13	**Barbara Lee* (D)**	**160,901**
	Nikka Piterman (R)	15,882
14	**Jackie Speier* (D)**	**197,031**
	Ran Petel (R)	47,635
15	**Eric Swalwell* (D)**	**119,572**
	Alison Hayden (R)	44,752
16	**Jim Costa* (D)**	**92,921**
	Kevin Cookingham (R)	60,695
17	**Ro Khanna* (D)**	**125,258**
	Ritesh Tandon (R)	43,775
18	**Anna G. Eshoo* (D)**	**151,540**
	Rishi Kumar (R)	79,028
19	**Zoe Lofgren* (D)**	**135,927**
	Justin Aguilera (R)	47,511
20	**Jimmy Panetta* (D)**	**186,617**
	Jeff Gorman (R)	52,132
21	*David Valadao (R)*	*58,827*
	TJ Cox* (D)	*54,794*
22	**Devin Nunes* (R)**	**126,022**
	Phil Arballo (D)	109,596
23	**Kevin McCarthy* (R)**	**94,025**
	Kim Mangone (D)	68,949
24	**Salud Carbajal* (D)**	**169,061**
	Andy Caldwell (R)	104,016
25	*Mike Garcia* (R)*	*143,059*
	Christy Smith (D)	*142,794*
26	**Julia Brownley* (D)**	**167,047**
	Ronda Baldwin-Kennedy (R)	102,428
27	**Judy Chu* (D)**	**170,643**
	Johnny Nalbandian (R)	70,271
28	**Adam Schiff* (D)**	**194,417**
	Eric Early (R)	68,110
29	**Tony Cárdenas* (D)**	**86,173**
	Angelica Duenas (D)	62,988
30	**Brad Sherman* (D)**	**190,475**
	Mark Reed (R)	79,057
31	**Pete Aguilar* (D)**	**104,026**
	Agnes Gibboney (R)	60,389
32	**Grace Flores Napolitano* (D)**	**123,387**
	Joshua Scott (R)	63,380
33	**Ted Lieu* (D)**	**211,426**
	James Bradley (R)	95,130
34	*Jimmy Gomez* (D)*	*88,388*
	David Kim (D)	*78,910*
35	**Norma Torres* (D)**	**94,961**
	Mike Cargile (R)	40,000
36	**Raul Ruiz* (D)**	**93,477**
	Erin Cruz (R)	56,643
37	**Karen Bass* (D)**	**194,334**
	Errol Webber (R)	30,039
38	**Linda Sánchez* (D)**	**136,154**
	Michael Tolar (D)	46,642

Dist.	Representative/candidate (party)	2020 election results
39	*Young Kim (R)*	*146,297*
	Gil Cisneros* (D)	*143,800*
40	**Lucille Roybal-Allard* (D)**	**90,612**
	C. Antonio Delgado (R)	33,806
41	**Mark Takano* (D)**	**67,535**
	Aja Smith (R)	37,777
42	*Ken Calvert* (R)*	*86,834*
	William O'Mara (D)	*69,684*
43	**Maxine Waters* (D)**	**145,866**
	Joe Collins (R)	55,224
44	**Nanette Barragán* (D)**	**99,112**
	Analilia Joya (D)	43,902
45	**Katie Porter* (D)**	**191,827**
	Greg Raths (R)	161,324
46	**Lou Correa* (D)**	**122,752**
	James Waters (R)	56,919
47	**Alan Lowenthal* (D)**	**152,917**
	John Briscoe (R)	89,499
48	*Michelle Steel (R)*	*179,452*
	Harley Rouda* (D)	*174,678*
49	**Mike Levin* (D)**	**170,925**
	Brian Maryott (R)	141,569
50	**Darrell Issa (R)**	**159,864**
	Ammar Campa-Najjar (D)	139,973
51	**Juan Vargas* (D)**	**108,986**
	Juan M. Hidalgo Jr. (R)	46,581
52	**Scott Peters* (D)**	**200,919**
	Jim DeBello (R)	116,606
53	**Sara Jacobs (D)**	**153,993**
	Georgette Gomez (D)	104,867
Colorado		
1	**Diana DeGette* (D)**	**265,849**
	Shane Bolling (R)	80,257
2	**Joe Neguse* (D)**	**294,354**
	Charlie Winn (R)	167,791
	Thom Atkinson (LB)	11,575
3	**Lauren Boebert (R)**	**211,395**
	Diane Mitsch Bush (D)	188,752
4	**Ken Buck* (R)**	**262,781**
	Ike McCorkle (D)	162,289
5	**Doug Lamborn* (R)**	**218,272**
	Jillian Freeland (D)	144,825
	Ed Duffett (LB)	11,396
6	**Jason Crow* (D)**	**238,755**
	Steve House (R)	165,087
7	**Ed Perlmutter* (D)**	**244,262**
	Charles Stockham (R)	153,387
	Ken Biles (LB)	10,788
Connecticut		
1	**John B. Larson* (D)**	**172,742**
	Mary Fay (R)	95,494
2	**Joe Courtney* (D)**	**159,387**
	Justin Anderson (R)	104,304
3	**Rosa L. DeLauro* (D)**	**116,941**
	Margaret Streicker (R)	87,815
4	**Jim Himes* (D)**	**138,452**
	Jonathan Riddle (R)	93,227
5	**Jahana Hayes* (D)**	**166,231**
	David Sullivan (R)	128,938
Delaware		
	Lisa Blunt Rochester* (D)	**280,612**
	Lee Murphy (R)	195,708
Florida		
1	**Matt Gaetz* (R)**	**282,980**
	Phil Ehr (D)	148,948
2	**Neal Dunn* (R)**	**Unopposed**
3	**Kat Cammack (R)**	**222,873**
	Adam Christensen (D)	167,050
4	**John Rutherford* (R)**	**307,779**
	Donna Deegan (D)	195,652
5	**Al Lawson* (D)**	**218,483**
	Gary Adler (R)	117,199
6	**Michael Waltz* (R)**	**265,041**
	Clint Curtis (D)	172,064
7	**Stephanie Murphy* (D)**	**224,561**
	Leo Valentin (R)	175,526

Dist.	Representative/candidate (party)	2020 election results
8	**Bill Posey* (R)**	**281,869**
	Jim Kennedy (D)	177,531
9	**Darren Soto* (D)**	**240,285**
	William Olson (R)	188,622
10	**Val Demings* (D)**	**239,238**
	Vennia Francois (R)	136,790
11	**Daniel Webster* (R)**	**316,655**
	Dana Cottrell (D)	157,860
12	**Gus Bilirakis* (R)**	**284,680**
	Kimberly Walker (D)	167,989
13	**Charlie Crist* (D)**	**215,179**
	Anna Luna (R)	190,547
14	**Kathy Castor* (D)**	**223,227**
	Christine Quinn (R)	147,276
15	**Scott Franklin (R)**	**215,839**
	Alan Cohn (D)	173,700
16	**Vern Buchanan* (R)**	**268,129**
	Margaret Good (D)	214,697
17	**Greg Steube* (R)**	**266,180**
	Allen Ellison (D)	140,268
18	**Brian Mast* (R)**	**251,824**
	Pam Keith (D)	185,195
19	**Byron Donalds (R)**	**271,296**
	Cindy Banyai (D)	171,420
20	**Alcee Hastings* (D)**	**251,751**
	Greg Musselwhite (R)	68,164
21	**Lois Frankel* (D)**	**233,069**
	Laura Loomer (R)	154,666
22	**Ted Deutch* (D)**	**234,698**
	James Pruden (R)	165,745
23	**Debbie Wasserman Schultz* (D)**	**220,856**
	Carla Spalding (R)	158,631
24	**Frederica Wilson* (D)**	**218,655**
	Lavern Spicer (R)	59,016
	Christine Olivo (NPA)	11,685
25	**Mario Diaz-Balart* (R)**	**Unopposed**
26	**Carlos Gimenez (R)**	**177,141**
	Debbie Mucarsel-Powell* (D)	165,301
27	**Maria Elvira Salazar (R)**	**175,984**
	Donna Shalala* (D)	166,568

Georgia

Dist.	Representative/candidate (party)	2020 election results
1	**Earl L. "Buddy" Carter* (R)**	**179,215**
	Joyce Griggs (D)	116,188
2	**Sanford D. Bishop Jr.* (D)**	**154,745**
	Don Cole (R)	109,860
3	**Drew Ferguson* (R)**	**235,820**
	Val Almonord (D)	125,217
4	**Hank Johnson* (D)**	**271,673**
	Johsie Ezammudeen (R)	68,231
5	**Nikema Williams (D)**	**265,504**
	Angela Stanton-King (R)	46,591
6	**Lucy McBath* (D)**	**193,956**
	Karen Handel (R)	166,564
7	**Carolyn Bourdeaux (D).**	**187,187**
	Rich McCormick (R)	178,577
8	**Austin Scott* (R)**	**193,725**
	Lindsay Holliday (D)	102,919
9	**Andrew Clyde (R)**	**287,843**
	Devin Pandy (D)	76,293
10	**Jody Hice* (R)**	**230,871**
	Tabitha Johnson-Green (D)	139,033
11	**Barry Loudermilk* (R)**	**240,444**
	Dana Barrett (D)	153,051
12	**Rick Allen* (R).**	**180,401**
	Liz Johnson (D)	128,033
13	**David Scott* (D)**	**260,062**
	Becky Hites (R)	78,088
14	**Marjorie Greene (R)**	**227,128**
	Kevin Van Ausdal (D)	76,455

Hawaii

Dist.	Representative/candidate (party)	2020 election results
1	**Ed Case* (D)**	**183,053**
	Ron Curtis (R)	71,094
2	**Kaiali'i Kahele (D)**	**171,398**
	Joe Akana (R)	83,928

Idaho

Dist.	Representative/candidate (party)	2020 election results
1	**Russ Fulcher* (R)**	**310,737**
	Rudy Soto (D)	131,268
	Joe Evans (LB)	16,435
2	**Mike Simpson* (R)**	**250,678**
	Aaron Swisher (D)	124,151

Illinois

Dist.	Representative/candidate (party)	2020 election results
1	**Bobby L. Rush* (D)**	**195,418**
	Philanise White (R)	73,368
2	**Robin Kelly* (D)**	**188,086**
	Theresa Raborn (R)	57,761
3	**Marie Newman (D)**	**129,853**
	Mike Fricilone (R)	114,399
4	**Jesús "Chuy" García* (D).**	**148,795**
	Jesus Solorio (R)	30,030
5	**Mike Quigley* (D)**	**197,018**
	Tommy Hanson (R)	82,289
6	**Sean Casten* (D).**	**184,809**
	Jeanne Ives (R)	167,629
7	**Danny Davis* (D).**	**185,516**
	Craig Cameron (R)	30,696
	Tracy Jennings (Ind.)	14,310
8	**Raja Krishnamoorthi* (D).**	**146,495**
	Preston Nelson (LB)	60,130
9	**Jan Schakowsky* (D)**	**177,022**
	Sargis Sangari (R)	85,070
10	**Brad Schneider* (D)**	**139,196**
	Valerie Ramirez Mukherjee (R)	92,622
11	**Bill Foster* (D)**	**181,896**
	Rick Laib (R)	107,466
12	**Mike Bost* (R)**	**181,839**
	Raymond Lenzi (D)	115,468
13	**Rodney Davis* (R)**	**175,883**
	Betsy Dirksen Londrigan (D)	146,399
14	*Lauren Underwood* (D).*	*192,472*
	Jim Oberweis (R)	*191,383*
15	**Mary Miller (R).**	**230,835**
	Erika Weaver (D)	84,711
16	**Adam Kinzinger* (R)**	**213,503**
	Dani Brzozowski (D)	114,079
17	**Cheri Bustos* (D)**	**154,147**
	Esther Joy King (R)	142,621
18	**Darin LaHood* (R)**	**255,005**
	George Petrilli (D)	106,876

Indiana

Dist.	Representative/candidate (party)	2020 election results
1	**Frank Mrvan (D)**	**144,201**
	Mark Leyva (R)	101,065
2	**Jackie Walorski* (R)**	**158,718**
	Patricia Hackett (D)	86,428
3	**Jim Banks* (R)**	**207,864**
	Chip Coldiron (D)	90,048
4	**Jim Baird* (R)**	**223,648**
	Joe Mackey (D)	112,106
5	**Victoria Spartz (R)**	**208,053**
	Christina Hale (D)	190,898
	Kenneth Tucker (LB)	16,764
6	**Greg Pence* (R)**	**200,047**
	Jeannine Lake (D)	78,690
	Tom Ferkinhoff (LB)	10,280
7	**André Carson* (D)**	**125,789**
	Susan Smith (R)	80,107
8	**Larry Bucshon* (R)**	**176,982**
	Thomasina Marsili (D)	70,457
9	**Trey Hollingsworth* (R)**	**217,929**
	Andy Ruff (D)	124,623
	Tonya Millis (LB)	15,563

Iowa

Dist.	Representative/candidate (party)	2020 election results
1	**Ashley Hinson (R).**	**211,573**
	Abby Finkenauer* (D)	200,814
2	*Mariannette Miller-Meeks (R)*	*196,769*
	Rita Hart (D)	*196,487*
3	**Cindy Axne* (D)**	**218,968**
	David Young (R)	212,727
4	**Randy Feenstra (R).**	**236,852**
	J.D. Scholten (D)	144,344

Kansas

Dist.	Representative/candidate (party)	2020 election results
1	**Tracey Mann (R)**	**202,548**
	Kali Barnett (D)	80,326
2	**Jake LaTurner (R)**	**180,147**
	Michelle De La Isla (D)	130,758
	Robert Garrard (LB)	13,504

Dist.	Representative/candidate (party)	2020 election results
3	**Sharice Davids* (D)**	**210,404**
	Amanda Adkins (R)	172,485
	Steven Hohe (LB)	10,925
4	**Ron Estes* (R)**	**187,628**
	Laura Lombard (D)	101,197

Kentucky

Dist.	Representative/candidate (party)	2020 election results
1	**James Comer* (R)**	**245,438**
	James Rhodes (D)	81,299
2	**S. Brett Guthrie* (R)**	**253,168**
	Hank Linderman (D)	92,293
3	**John A. Yarmuth* (D)**	**221,005**
	Rhonda Palazzo (R)	134,187
4	**Thomas Massie* (R)**	**254,469**
	Alexandra Owensby (D)	123,344
5	**Harold Rogers* (R)**	**249,654**
	Matthew Best (D)	46,550
6	**Andy Barr* (R)**	**214,268**
	Josh Hicks (D)	149,739

Louisiana

Dist.	Representative/candidate (party)	2020 election results
1	**Steve Scalise* (R)**	**270,287**
	Lee Ann Dugas (D)	94,713
2	**Cedric Richmond* (D)**	**201,579**
	David Schilling (R)	47,564
	Glenn Harris (R)	33,651
	Sheldon Vincent (R)	15,560
	Belden "Noonie Man" Batiste (Ind.)	12,258
3	**Clay Higgins* (R)**	**230,473**
	Braylon Harris (D)	60,851
	Rob Anderson (D)	39,423
4	**Mike Johnson* (R)**	**185,174**
	Kenny Houston (D)	78,063
	Ryan Trundle (D)	23,791
	Ben Gibson (R)	19,320
5[1]	*Luke Letlow (R)*	*102,516*
	Lance Harris (R)	*51,229*
	Sandra Christophe (D)	*50,773*
	Martin Lemelle (D)	*32,168*
6	**Garret Graves* (R)**	**265,684**
	Dartanyon Williams (D)	95,531

Maine

Dist.	Representative/candidate (party)	2020 election results
1	**Chellie Pingree* (D)**	**260,747**
	Jay Allen (R)	162,257
2	**Jared Golden* (D)**	**192,324**
	Dale Crafts (R)	171,460

Maryland

Dist.	Representative/candidate (party)	2020 election results
1	**Andy Harris* (R)**	**212,118**
	Mia Mason (D)	103,888
2	**C.A. Dutch Ruppersberger* (D)**	**141,675**
	Johnny Salling (R)	73,176
3	**John P. Sarbanes* (D)**	**176,115**
	Charles Anthony (R)	76,839
4	**Anthony Brown* (D)**	**208,984**
	George McDermott (R)	50,494
5	**Steny Hoyer* (D)**	**198,200**
	Chris Palombi (R)	97,021
6	**David Trone* (D)**	**142,845**
	Neil Parrott (R)	111,297
7	**Kweisi Mfume* (D)**	**167,705**
	Kimberly Klacik (R)	67,482
8	**Jamie Raskin* (D)**	**176,895**
	Gregory Coll (R)	97,022

Massachusetts

Dist.	Representative/candidate (party)	2020 election results
1	**Richard E. Neal* (D)**	**Unopposed**
2	**James McGovern* (D)**	**244,116**
	Tracy Lovvorn (R)	129,316
3	**Lori Trahan* (D)**	**Unopposed**
4	**Jake Auchincloss (D)**	**242,104**
	Julie Hall (R)	154,498
5	**Katherine Clark* (D)**	**284,732**
	Caroline Colarusso (R)	99,767
6	**Seth Moulton* (D)**	**280,969**
	John Paul Moran (R)	148,600
7	**Ayanna Pressley* (D)**	**251,571**
	Roy Owens (Ind.)	36,650
8	**Stephen F. Lynch* (D)**	**299,429**
	Jonathan Lott (Ind.)	69,181
9	**Bill Keating* (D)**	**252,958**
	Helen Brady (R)	145,660

Michigan

Dist.	Representative/candidate (party)	2020 election results
1	**Jack Bergman* (R)**	**244,954**
	Dana Ferguson (D)	147,833
2	**Bill Huizenga* (R)**	**239,361**
	Bryan Berghoef (D)	154,211
3	**Peter Meijer (R)**	**213,147**
	Hillary Scholten (D)	188,654
4	**John Moolenaar* (R)**	**242,668**
	Jerry Hilliard (D)	120,829
5	**Daniel Kildee* (D)**	**192,917**
	Tim Kelly (R)	149,124
6	**Fred Upton* (R)**	**205,684**
	Jon Hoadley (D)	133,489
	Jeff DePoy (LB)	10,010
7	**Tim Walberg* (R)**	**227,514**
	Gretchen Driskell (D)	159,746
8	**Elissa Slotkin* (D)**	**222,121**
	Paul Junge (R)	204,788
9	**Andy Levin* (D)**	**231,829**
	Charles Langworthy (R)	153,677
10	**Lisa McClain (R)**	**271,413**
	Kimberly Bizon (D)	138,155
11	**Haley Stevens* (D)**	**226,076**
	Eric Esshaki (R)	215,362
12	**Debbie Dingell* (D)**	**233,365**
	Jeff Jones (R)	111,800
	Gary Walkowicz (Working Class)	10,537
13	**Rashida Tlaib* (D)**	**188,172**
	David Dudenhoefer (R)	48,128
14	**Brenda Lawrence* (D)**	**257,126**
	Robert Patrick (R)	62,178

Minnesota

Dist.	Representative/candidate (party)	2020 election results
1	**Jim Hagedorn* (R)**	**178,870**
	Dan Feehan (DFL)	167,683
	Bill Rood (Grass Roots)	21,402
2	**Angie Craig* (DFL)**	**203,640**
	Tyler Kistner (R)	194,245
	Adam Weeks (Legal Marijuana Now)	24,644
3	**Dean Phillips* (DFL)**	**243,747**
	Kendall Qualls (R)	194,245
4	**Betty McCollum* (DFL)**	**245,436**
	Gene Rechtzigel (R)	112,590
	Susan Sindt (Grass Roots)	29,453
5	**Ilhan Omar* (DFL)**	**252,939**
	Lacy Johnson (R)	101,470
	Michael Moore (Legal Marijuana Now)	37,295
6	**Tom Emmer* (R)**	**264,608**
	Tawnja Zahradka (DFL)	135,917
7	**Michelle Fischbach (R)**	**193,311**
	Collin C. Peterson* (DFL)	144,462
	Slater Johnson (Legal Marijuana Now)	17,648
8	**Pete Stauber* (R)**	**216,124**
	Quinn Nystrom (DFL)	143,406
	Judith Schwartzbacker (Grass Roots)	21,543

Mississippi

Dist.	Representative/candidate (party)	2020 election results
1	**Trent Kelly* (R)**	**201,134**
	Antonia Eliason (D)	84,733
2	**Bennie G. Thompson* (D)**	**157,075**
	Brian Flowers (R)	88,178
3	**Michael Guest* (R)**	**188,283**
	Dorothy Benford (D)	98,572
4	**Steven Palazzo* (R)**	**Unopposed**

Missouri

Dist.	Representative/candidate (party)	2020 election results
1	**Cori Bush (D)**	**245,520**
	Anthony Rogers (R)	59,156
2	**Ann Wagner* (R)**	**230,617**
	Jill Schupp (D)	201,520
	Martin Schulte (LB)	11,558
3	**Blaine Luetkemeyer* (R)**	**282,424**
	Megan Rezabek (D)	115,909
4	**Vicky Hartzler* (R)**	**245,064**
	Lindsey Simmons (D)	107,528
5	**Emanuel Cleaver* (D)**	**204,631**
	Ryan Derks (R)	135,396
6	**Sam Graves* (R)**	**258,895**
	Gena Ross (D)	118,753
7	**Billy Long* (R)**	**251,757**
	Teresa Montseny (D)	96,501
	Kevin Craig (LB)	15,401

Dist. Representative/candidate (party)	2020 election results
8 Jason Smith* (R)	253,646
Kathy Ellis (D)	70,504
Montana	
Matt Rosendale (R)	326,139
Kathleen Williams (D)	253,704
Nebraska	
1 Jeff Fortenberry* (R)	184,650
Kate Bolz (D)	116,941
2 Don Bacon* (R)	162,087
Kara Eastman (D)	146,992
3 Adrian Smith* (R)	223,302
Mark Elworth (D)	50,067
Dustin Hobbs (LB)	10,761
Nevada	
1 Dina Titus* (D)	109,391
Joyce Bentley (R)	61,767
2 Mark Amodei* (R)	198,322
Patricia Ackerman (D)	142,974
3 Susie Lee* (D)	184,681
Dan Rodimer (R)	172,377
4 Steven Horsford* (D)	141,737
Jim Marchant (R)	134,057
New Hampshire	
1 Chris Pappas* (D)	204,675
Matt Mowers (R)	184,279
2 Ann McLane Kuster* (D)	204,701
Steven Negron (R)	166,603
New Jersey	
1 Donald Norcross* (D)	161,993
Claire Gustafson (R)	88,367
2 Jeff Van Drew* (R)	174,187
Amy Kennedy (D)	155,173
3 Andy Kim* (D)	173,009
David Richter (R)	138,095
4 Chris Smith* (R)	151,651
Stephanie Schmid (D)	110,729
5 Josh Gottheimer* (D)	169,189
Frank Pallotta (R)	120,599
6 Frank Pallone Jr.* (D)	115,505
Christian Onuoha (R)	56,839
7 Tom Malinowski* (D)	148,081
Thomas Kean Jr. (R)	119,771
8 Albio Sires* (D)	119,084
Jason Mushnick (R)	33,453
9 Bill Pascrell Jr.* (D)	123,101
Billy Prempeh (R)	56,155
10 Donald Payne Jr.* (D)	161,805
Jennifer Zinone (R)	21,381
11 Mikie Sherrill* (D)	141,932
Rosemary Becchi (R)	100,161
12 Bonnie Watson Coleman* (D)	164,079
Mark Razzoli (R)	66,017
New Mexico	
1 Debra A. Haaland* (D)	185,196
Michelle Garcia Holmes (R)	133,695
2 Yvette Herrell (R)	141,227
Xochitl Torres Small* (D)	120,766
3 Teresa Leger Fernandez (D)	178,247
Alexis Johnson (R)	129,316
New York	
1 Lee Zeldin* (R)	176,317
Nancy Goroff (D)	111,188
2 Andrew Garbarino (R)	157,001
Jackie Gordon (D)	111,204
3 George Santos (R)	137,928
Thomas Suozzi* (D)	133,743
4 Kathleen Rice* (D)	147,580
Douglas Tuman (R)	134,243
5 Gregory W. Meeks* (D)	Unopposed
6 Grace Meng* (D)	106,131
Thomas Zmich (R)	63,324
7 Nydia Velázquez* (D)	142,815
Brian Kelly (R)	27,907
8 Hakeem S. Jeffries* (D)	175,140
Garfield Wallace (R)	36,873
9 Yvette D. Clarke* (D)	170,898
Constantine Jean-Pierre (R)	36,847
10 Jerrold Nadler* (D)	120,273
Cathy Bernstein (R)	52,842

Dist. Representative/candidate (party)	2020 election results
11 Nicole Malliotakis (R)	136,382
Max Rose* (D)	99,224
12 Carolyn Maloney* (D)	153,815
Carlos Santiago-Cano (R)	37,973
13 Adriano Espaillat* (D)	179,589
Lovelynn Gwinn (R)	16,787
14 Alexandria Ocasio-Cortez* (D)	105,455
John Cummings (R)	46,877
15 Ritchie Torres (D)	136,471
Patrick Delices (R)	18,198
16 Jamaal Bowman (D)	160,289
Patrick McManus (C)	32,831
17 Mondaire Jones (D)	134,845
Maureen McArdle Schulman (R)	98,634
18 Sean Patrick Maloney* (D)	134,682
Chele Chiavacci Farley (R)	127,118
19 Antonio Delgado* (D)	141,997
Kyle Van De Water (R)	134,608
20 Paul Tonko* (D)	164,664
Elizabeth Joy (R)	127,394
21 Elise Stefanik* (R)	167,935
Tedra Lynne Cobb (D)	92,596
22 Claudia Tenney (R)	136,679
Anthony J. Brindisi* (D)	106,944
23 Tom Reed* (R)	160,930
Tracy Mitrano (D)	91,331
24 John Katko* (R)	155,830
Dana Balter (D)	100,728
25 Joseph Morelle* (D)	133,287
George Mitris (R)	113,071
26 Brian Higgins* (D)	168,883
Ricky Donovan (R)	81,959
27 Chris Jacobs* (R)	203,977
Nathan D. McMurray (D)	109,422
North Carolina	
1 G. K. Butterfield* (D)	187,125
Sandy Smith (R)	158,530
2 Deborah Ross (D)	308,458
Alan Swain (R)	170,376
Jeff Matemu (LB)	10,568
3 Greg Murphy* (R)	227,462
Daryl Farrow (D)	131,011
4 David Price* (D)	328,933
Robert Thomas (R)	159,509
5 Virginia Foxx* (R)	255,767
David Brown (D)	118,444
6 Kathy Manning (D)	251,082
Lee Haywood (R)	152,195
7 David Rouzer* (R)	269,857
Christopher Ward (D)	176,654
8 Richard Hudson* (R)	201,181
Patricia Timmons-Goodson (D)	175,891
9 Dan Bishop* (R)	221,803
Cynthia Wallace (D)	177,355
10 Patrick T. McHenry* (R)	281,922
David Parker (D)	126,826
11 Madison Cawthorn (R)	243,898
Moe Davis (D)	189,516
12 Alma Adams* (D)	Unopposed
13 Ted Budd* (R)	263,270
Scott Huffman (D)	122,415
North Dakota	
Kelly Armstrong* (R)	244,460
Zach Raknerud (D-NPL)	97,603
Steven Peterson (LB)	11,980
Ohio	
1 Steve Chabot* (R)	193,637
Kate Schroder (D)	166,061
Kevin Kahn (LB)	13,042
2 Brad Wenstrup* (R)	225,271
Jaime Castle (D)	143,436
3 Joyce Beatty* (D)	217,332
Mark Richardson (R)	90,474
4 Jim Jordan* (R)	230,384
Shannon Freshour (D)	99,663
5 Bob Latta* (R)	251,713
Nick Rubando (D)	118,245
6 Bill Johnson* (R)	243,540
Shawna Roberts (D)	84,237

Dist.	Representative/candidate (party)	2020 election results
7	**Bob Gibbs* (R)**	**231,246**
	Quentin Potter (D)	100,027
	Brandon Lape (LB)	11,205
8	**Warren Davidson* (R)**	**241,503**
	Vanessa Enoch (D)	108,244
9	**Marcy Kaptur* (D)**	**184,367**
	Rob Weber (R)	108,085
10	**Mike Turner* (R)**	**208,347**
	Desiree Tims (D)	147,985
11	**Marcia L. Fudge* (D)**	**233,126**
	Laverne Gore (R)	58,139
12	**Troy Balderson* (R)**	**236,181**
	Alaina Shearer (D)	178,432
	John Stewart (LB)	12,495
13	**Tim Ryan* (D)**	**169,487**
	Christina Hagan (R)	145,275
14	**David Joyce* (R)**	**233,828**
	Hillary O'Connor Mueri (D)	155,515
15	**Steve Stivers* (R)**	**236,473**
	Joel Newby (D)	136,286
16	**Anthony Gonzalez* (R)**	**241,656**
	Aaron Godfrey (D)	141,212

Oklahoma

Dist.	Representative/candidate (party)	2020 election results
1	**Kevin Hern* (R)**	**213,251**
	Kojo Asamoa-Caesar (D)	109,455
	Evelyn Rogers (Ind.)	12,098
2	**Markwayne Mullin* (R)**	**216,234**
	Danyell Lanier (D)	63,403
3	**Frank Lucas* (R)**	**242,392**
	Zoe Midyett (D)	66,430
4	**Tom Cole* (R)**	**212,830**
	Mary Brannon (D)	90,350
	Bob White (D)	10,786
5	**Stephanie Bice (R)**	**158,044**
	Kendra Horn* (D)	145,541

Oregon

Dist.	Representative/candidate (party)	2020 election results
1	**Suzanne Bonamici* (D)**	**268,256**
	Christopher Christensen (R)	144,171
2	**Cliff Bentz (R)**	**269,310**
	Alex Spenser (D)	165,148
	Robert Werch (LB)	13,525
3	**Earl Blumenauer* (D)**	**329,946**
	Joanna Harbour (R)	94,600
4	**Peter DeFazio* (D)**	**236,073**
	Alek Skarlatos (R)	211,607
5	**Kurt Schrader (D)**	**223,982**
	Amy Ryan Courser (R)	192,511

Pennsylvania

Dist.	Representative/candidate (party)	2020 election results
1	**Brian Fitzpatrick* (R)**	**217,435**
	Christina Finello (D)	145,764
2	**Brendan Boyle* (D)**	**152,692**
	David Torres (R)	65,876
3	**Dwight Evans* (D)**	**258,479**
	Michael Harvey (R)	26,534
4	**Madeleine Dean* (D)**	**223,150**
	Kathy Barnette (R)	161,707
5	**Mary Gay Scanlon* (D)**	**205,666**
	Dasha Pruett (R)	123,801
6	**Chrissy Houlahan* (D)**	**182,793**
	John Emmons (R)	160,543
7	**Susan Wild* (D)**	**191,450**
	Lisa Scheller (R)	178,118
8	**Matt Cartwright* (D)**	**174,188**
	Jim Bognet (R)	162,502
9	**Dan Meuser* (R)**	**215,956**
	Gary Wegman (D)	100,966
10	**Scott Perry* (R)**	**204,864**
	Eugene DePasquale (D)	178,862
11	**Lloyd Smucker* (R)**	**221,147**
	Sarah E. Hammond (D)	109,043
12	**Fred Keller* (R)**	**230,328**
	Lee Griffin (D)	90,403
13	**John Joyce* (R)**	**240,351**
	Todd Rowley (D)	69,489
14	**Guy Reschenthaler* (R)**	**179,616**
	Bill Marx (D)	88,798
15	**Glenn Thompson* (R)**	**238,909**
	Robert Williams (D)	74,221
16	**Mike Kelly* (R)**	**179,119**
	Kristy Gnibus (D)	90,270
17	**Conor Lamb* (D)**	**216,094**
	Sean Parnell (R)	207,103

Dist.	Representative/candidate (party)	2020 election results
18	**Mike Doyle* (D)**	**210,482**
	Luke Negron (R)	104,892

Rhode Island

Dist.	Representative/candidate (party)	2020 election results
1	**David Cicilline* (D)**	**153,010**
	Frederick Wysocki (Ind.)	34,705
	Jeffrey Lemire (D)	27,740
2	**Jim Langevin* (D)**	**148,978**
	Robert Lancia (R)	107,981

South Carolina

Dist.	Representative/candidate (party)	2020 election results
1	**Nancy Mace (R)**	**206,307**
	Joe Cunningham* (D)	195,976
2	**Joe Wilson* (R)**	**201,837**
	Adair Boroughs (D)	153,902
3	**Jeff Duncan* (R)**	**236,796**
	Hosea Cleveland (D)	95,427
4	**William Timmons* (R)**	**220,505**
	Kim Nelson (D)	132,381
5	**Ralph Norman* (R)**	**217,469**
	Moe Brown (D)	144,888
6	**Jim Clyburn* (D)**	**194,992**
	John McCollum (R)	88,450
7	**Tom Rice* (R)**	**207,665**
	Melissa Watson (D)	122,458

South Dakota

Dist.	Representative/candidate (party)	2020 election results
	Dusty Johnson* (R)	**296,302**
	Randy Luallin (LB)	64,975

Tennessee

Dist.	Representative/candidate (party)	2020 election results
1	**Diana Harshbarger (R)**	**227,562**
	Blair Walsingham (D)	68,126
2	**Tim Burchett* (R)**	**238,446**
	Renee Hoyos (D)	109,298
3	**Chuck Fleischmann* (R)**	**215,318**
	Meg Gorman (D)	99,510
4	**Scott DesJarlais* (R)**	**223,593**
	Christopher Hale (D)	111,527
5	**Jim Cooper* (D)**	**Unopposed**
6	**John Rose* (R)**	**257,201**
	Christopher Finley (D)	83,652
7	**Mark Green* (R)**	**246,374**
	Kiran Sreepada (D)	94,372
8	**David Kustoff* (R)**	**226,609**
	Erika Stotts Pearson (D)	97,314
9	**Steve Cohen* (D)**	**187,258**
	Charlotte Bergmann (R)	48,688

Texas

Dist.	Representative/candidate (party)	2020 election results
1	**Louie Gohmert* (R)**	**218,385**
	Hank Gilbert (D)	82,359
2	**Dan Crenshaw* (R)**	**197,300**
	Sima Ladjevardian (D)	148,727
3	**Van Taylor* (R)**	**228,648**
	Lulu Seikaly (D)	177,221
4	**Pat Fallon (R)**	**255,039**
	Russell Foster (D)	77,262
5	**Lance Gooden* (R)**	**173,251**
	Carolyn Salter (D)	100,413
6	**Ron Wright* (R)**	**176,243**
	Stephen Daniel (D)	145,847
	Melanie Black (LB)	10,812
7	**Lizzie Fletcher* (D)**	**158,019**
	Wesley Hunt (R)	147,802
8	**Kevin Brady* (R)**	**276,960**
	Elizabeth Hernandez (D)	97,182
9	**Al Green* (D)**	**171,127**
	Johnny Teague (R)	48,991
10	**Michael T. McCaul* (R)**	**215,896**
	Mike Siegel (D)	186,350
11	**August Pfluger (R)**	**231,781**
	Jon Hogg (D)	53,198
12	**Kay Granger* (R)**	**229,265**
	Lisa Welch (D)	117,077
	Trey Holcomb (LB)	11,771
13	**Ronny Jackson (R)**	**214,593**
	Gus Trujillo (D)	48,737
14	**Randy Weber* (R)**	**189,691**
	Adrienne Bell (D)	117,862
15	**Vicente Gonzalez* (D)**	**115,005**
	Monica De La Cruz-Hernandez (R)	108,466
16	**Veronica Escobar* (D)**	**145,766**
	Irene Armendariz-Jackson (R)	80,762
17	**Pete Sessions* (R)**	**170,974**
	Rick Kennedy (D)	124,993

Dist.	Representative/candidate (party)	2020 election results
18	**Sheila Jackson Lee* (D)**	**180,125**
	Wendell Champion (R)	57,617
19	**Jodey Arrington* (R)**	**197,509**
	Tom Watson (D)	60,200
20	**Joaquin Castro* (D)**	**172,648**
	Mauro Garza (R)	88,171
21	**Chip Roy* (R)**	**233,766**
	Wendy Davis (D)	203,028
22	**Troy Nehls (R)**	**204,956**
	Sri Preston Kulkarni (D)	176,066
	Joseph LeBlanc (LB)	15,510
23	**Tony Gonzales (R)**	**147,496**
	Gina Ortiz Jones (D)	135,415
24	*Beth Van Duyne (R)*	*166,363*
	Candace Valenzuela (D)	*161,874*
25	**Roger Williams* (R)**	**219,053**
	Julie Oliver (D)	164,415
26	**Michael Burgess* (R)**	**260,160**
	Carol Iannuzzi (D)	159,605
27	**Michael Cloud* (R)**	**171,738**
	Ricardo De La Fuente (D)	95,021
28	**Henry Cuellar* (D)**	**103,784**
	Sandra Whitten (R)	79,409
29	**Sylvia Garcia* (D)**	**110,567**
	Jaimy Blanco (R)	42,527
30	**Eddie Bernice Johnson* (D)**	**204,324**
	Tre Pennie (R)	48,508
	Eric Williams (Ind.)	10,822
31	**John Carter* (R)**	**210,768**
	Donna Imam (D)	174,394
32	**Colin Allred* (D)**	**177,669**
	Genevieve Collins (R)	157,288
33	**Marc Veasey* (D)**	**103,351**
	Fabian Vasquez (R)	39,104
34	**Filemon Vela* (D)**	**109,891**
	Rey Gonzalez Jr. (R)	83,572
35	**Lloyd Doggett* (D)**	**174,429**
	Jenny Sharon (R)	80,016
36	**Brian Babin* (R)**	**221,754**
	Rashad Lewis (D)	72,920
Utah		
1	**Blake Moore (R)**	**172,656**
	Darren Parry (D)	80,506
2	**Chris Stewart* (R)**	**168,389**
	Kael Weston (D)	94,229
	J. Robert Latham (LB)	10,722
3	**John Curtis* (R)**	**182,019**
	Devin Thorpe (D)	72,924
4	*Ben McAdams (D)*	*138,747*
	Burgess Owens (R)	*138,342*
Vermont		
	Peter Welch* (D)	**238,778**
	Miriam Berry (R)	95,810
Virginia		
1	**Robert J. Wittman* (R)**	**246,433**
	Qasim Rashid (D)	172,244
2	**Elaine Luria* (D)**	**175,115**
	Scott Taylor (R)	159,990
3	**Bobby Scott* (D)**	**198,254**
	John Collick (R)	103,847
4	**A. Donald McEachin* (D)**	**232,144**
	Leon Benjamin (R)	148,638

Dist.	Representative/candidate (party)	2020 election results
5	**Robert Good (R)**	**210,320**
	Cameron Webb (D)	187,912
6	**Ben Cline* (R)**	**253,665**
	Nicholas Betts (D)	134,652
7	*Abigail Spanberger* (D)*	*224,727*
	Nick Freitas (R)	*219,983*
8	**Donald Beyer* (D)**	**293,235**
	Jeff Jordan (R)	93,907
9	**Morgan Griffith* (R)**	**Unopposed**
10	**Jennifer Wexton* (D)**	**261,919**
	Aliscia Andrews (R)	202,376
11	**Gerry Connolly* (D)**	**271,410**
	Manga Anantatmula (R)	107,359
Washington		
1	**Suzan DelBene* (D)**	**217,973**
	Jeffrey Beeler (R)	141,349
2	**Rick Larsen* (D)**	**220,866**
	Timothy Hazelo (R)	115,911
3	**Jaime Herrera Beutler* (R)**	**219,819**
	Carolyn Long (D)	172,951
4	**Dan Newhouse* (R)**	**128,953**
	Douglas McKinley (D)	68,381
5	**Cathy McMorris Rodgers* (R)**	**196,040**
	Dave Wilson (D)	133,444
6	**Derek Kilmer* (D)**	**217,737**
	Elizabeth Kreiselmaier (R)	135,528
7	**Pramila Jayapal* (D)**	**344,541**
	Craig Keller (R)	61,940
8	*Kim Schrier* (D)*	*202,378*
	Jesse Jensen (R)	*183,915*
9	**Adam Smith* (D)**	**221,871**
	Doug Basler (R)	70,167
10	**Marilyn Strickland (D)**	**136,002**
	Beth Doglio (D)	97,357
West Virginia		
1	**David McKinley* (R)**	**178,925**
	Natalie Cline (D)	80,195
2	**Alex Mooney* (R)**	**169,506**
	Cathy Kunkel (D)	98,990
3	**Carol Miller* (R)**	**160,292**
	Hilary Turner (D)	64,170
Wisconsin		
1	**Bryan Steil* (R)**	**238,257**
	Roger Polack (D)	163,154
2	**Mark Pocan* (D)**	**318,487**
	Peter Theron (R)	138,293
3	**Ron Kind* (D)**	**199,676**
	Derrick Van Orden (R)	188,681
4	**Gwen Moore* (D)**	**232,654**
	Tim Rogers (R)	70,768
5	**Scott Fitzgerald (R)**	**265,417**
	Tom Palzewicz (D)	175,872
6	**Glenn Grothman* (R)**	**238,858**
	Jessica King (D)	164,215
7	**Tom Tiffany* (R)**	**251,998**
	Tricia Zunker (D)	162,724
8	**Mike Gallagher* (R)**	**267,862**
	Amanda Stuck (D)	150,824
Wyoming		
	Liz Cheney* (R)	**185,602**
	Lynnette Grey Bull (D)	66,539
	Richard Brubaker (LB)	10,113

(1) A runoff between the top two vote recipients was scheduled for Dec. 5, 2020.

Nonvoting Members of Congress

Delegate/candidate (party)	2020 election results
American Samoa	
Aumua Amata Coleman Radewagen* (R)	**9,880**
Oreta Tufaga-Mapu Crichton (D)	1,704
Meleagi Suitonu-Chapman (D)	249
District of Columbia	
Eleanor Holmes Norton* (D)	**225,845**
Patrick Hynes (LB)	7,302
Barbara Washington Franklin (Ind.)	5,769
Guam	
Michael F.Q. San Nicolas* (D)	*13,000*
Robert Underwood (D)	*9,300*
William Castro (R)	*5,942*

Delegate/candidate (party)	2020 election results
Northern Mariana Islands	
Gregorio Kilili Camacho Sablan* (D)	**Unopposed**
Puerto Rico—Resident Commissioner	
(4-year term; begins Jan. 2021)	
Jennifer González-Colón* (New Progressive)	**461,401**
Aníbal Acevedo Vilá (Popular Democratic)	363,165
Zayira Jordán Conde (Citizen's Victory Movement)	150,437
Ada Norah Henriquez (Project Dignity)	91,795
Luis Roberto Piñero (PR Independence)	73,438
Virgin Islands	
Stacey E. Plaskett* (D)	**15,470**
Shekema M. George (Ind.)	1,992

Governors of the 50 States

27 Republicans, 23 Democrats. Boldface denotes the 2020 election winner. * = Incumbent. Third-party or independent candidates receiving fewer than 50,000 votes are not necessarily listed. Governors of states not holding elections in Nov. 2020 are shown for reference. Unless otherwise noted, terms are for four years—with the exception of two-year terms for governors of New Hampshire and Vermont—ending in Jan. of year listed. D = Democrat; R = Republican; DFL = Dem.-Farmer-Labor; LB = Libertarian.

Term expires	Governor	2020 election results
Alabama		
2023	Kay Ivey (R)	
Alaska		
Dec. 2022	Mike Dunleavy (R)	
Arizona		
2023	Doug Ducey (R)	
Arkansas		
2023	Asa Hutchinson (R)	
California		
2023	Gavin Newsom (D)	
Colorado		
2023	Jared Polis (D)	
Connecticut		
2023	Ned Lamont (D)	
Delaware		
2025	**John Carney* (D)**	292,151
	Julianne Murray (R)	189,714
Florida		
2023	Ron DeSantis (R)	
Georgia		
2023	Brian Kemp (R)	
Hawaii		
Dec. 2022	David Ige (D)	
Idaho		
2023	Brad Little (R)	
Illinois		
2023	JB Pritzker (D)	
Indiana		
2025	**Eric Holcomb* (R)**	1,512,884
	Woody Myers (D)	800,932
	Donald Rainwater (LB)	322,191
Iowa		
2023	Kim Reynolds (R)	
Kansas		
2023	Laura Kelly (D)	
Kentucky		
Dec. 2023	Andy Beshear (D)	
Louisiana		
2024	John Bel Edwards (D)	
Maine		
2023	Janet Mills (D)	
Maryland		
2023	Larry Hogan (R)	
Massachusetts		
2023	Charlie Baker (R)	
Michigan		
2023	Gretchen Whitmer (D)	
Minnesota		
2023	Tim Walz (DFL)	
Mississippi		
2024	Tate Reeves (R)	
Missouri		
2025	**Mike Parson* (R)**	1,713,152
	Nicole Galloway (D)	1,216,192
Montana		
2025	**Greg Gianforte (R)**	316,026
	Mike Cooney (D)	242,890
Nebraska		
2023	Pete Ricketts (R)	
Nevada		
2023	Steve Sisolak (D)	
New Hampshire		
2023	**Chris Sununu* (R)**	512,415
	Dan Feltes (D)	262,035
New Jersey		
2022	Phil Murphy (D)	
New Mexico		
2023	Michelle Lujan Grisham (D)	
New York		
2023	Andrew Cuomo (D)	
North Carolina		
2025	**Roy Cooper* (D)**	2,803,782
	Dan Forest (R)	2,563,258
	Steven DiFiore (LB)	58,818
North Dakota		
Dec. 2024	**Doug Burgum* (R)**	234,741
	Shelley Lenz (D)	90,445
Ohio		
2023	Mike DeWine (R)	
Oklahoma		
2023	Kevin Stitt (R)	
Oregon		
2023	Kate Brown (D)	
Pennsylvania		
2023	Tom Wolf (D)	
Rhode Island		
2023	Gina Raimondo (D)	
South Carolina		
2023	Henry McMaster (R)	
South Dakota		
2023	Kristi Noem (R)	
Tennessee		
2023	Bill Lee (R)	
Texas		
2023	Greg Abbott (R)	
Utah		
2025	**Spencer Cox (R)**	654,505
	Chris Peterson (D)	315,575
Vermont		
2023	**Phil Scott* (R)**	248,354
	David Zuckerman (D)	99,202
Virginia		
2022	Ralph Northam (D)	
Washington		
2025	**Jay Inslee* (D)**	1,964,176
	Loren Culp (R)	1,338,616
West Virginia		
2025	**Jim Justice* (R)**	492,743
	Ben Salango (D)	233,704
Wisconsin		
2023	Tony Evers (D)	
Wyoming		
2023	Mark Gordon (R)	

Governors of U.S. Commonwealths and Territories

Term expires	Governor/candidate	2020 election results
American Samoa		
2025	**Lemanu Palepoi Mauga**	7,154
	Gaoteote Palaie Tofau	2,594
	I'aulualo Fa'afetai Talia	1,461
	Nua Sao	652
Guam		
2023	Lou Leon Guerrero (D)	
Northern Mariana Islands		
2023	Ralph Anthony Deleon Guerrero Torres (R)	
Puerto Rico		
2025	**Pedro Pierluisi Urrutia (New Progressive)**	406,830
	Carlos Delgado Altieri (Popular Democratic)	389,896
	Alexandra Lúgaro (Citizen Victory Movement)	175,583
	Juan Dalmau Ramírez (PR Independence)	169,516
Virgin Islands		
2023	Albert Bryan (D)	

Presidential Election Results by State and County, 2020

Source: © Associated Press, all rights reserved. 2020 results preliminary as of Nov. 4-7, 2020. Because of the large number of absentee and mail-in ballots in 2020—as well as vast differences in states' counting procedures and timelines—final city, county, and statewide tallies may vary substantially from preliminary numbers shown here. Statewide totals may include votes from areas not listed separately. New England (CT, ME, MA, NH, RI, VT) results are for select cities and towns, not counties.

Alabama

County	2020		2016	
	Biden (D)	Trump (R)	Clinton (D)	Trump (R)
Autauga	7,450	19,764	5,936	18,172
Baldwin	24,344	83,055	18,458	72,883
Barbour	4,772	5,605	4,871	5,454
Bibb	1,982	7,508	1,874	6,738
Blount	2,627	24,595	2,156	22,859
Bullock	3,439	1,143	3,530	1,140
Butler	3,953	5,448	3,726	4,901
Calhoun	15,118	34,964	13,242	32,865
Chambers	6,356	8,748	5,784	7,843
Cherokee	1,619	10,562	1,547	8,953
Chilton	3,056	16,052	2,911	15,081
Choctaw	3,126	4,294	3,109	4,106
Clarke	5,730	7,310	5,749	7,140
Clay	1,262	5,589	1,237	5,245
Cleburne	672	6,472	684	5,764
Coffee	5,050	16,832	4,221	15,875
Colbert	7,057	17,311	7,312	16,746
Conecuh	2,951	3,435	3,080	3,420
Coosa	1,794	3,626	1,782	3,381
Covington	2,717	14,579	2,387	13,267
Crenshaw	1,700	4,864	1,664	4,513
Cullman	4,475	36,831	3,798	32,989
Dale	5,154	14,281	4,413	13,808
Dallas	12,228	5,523	12,836	5,789
De Kalb	4,271	24,744	3,622	21,405
Elmore	10,304	30,089	8,443	27,634
Escambia	4,894	10,844	4,605	9,935
Etowah	11,487	35,343	10,442	32,353
Fayette	1,390	7,295	1,362	6,712
Franklin	2,085	10,364	2,197	9,466
Geneva	1,592	10,844	1,525	9,994
Greene	3,880	875	4,013	838
Hale	4,687	3,190	4,775	3,173
Henry	2,589	6,593	2,292	5,632
Houston	12,738	32,384	10,664	30,728
Jackson	3,709	19,644	3,673	16,672
Jefferson	180,936	138,443	156,873	134,768
Lamar	978	6,168	1,036	5,823
Lauderdale	11,872	31,578	9,952	27,899
Lawrence	3,544	12,266	3,627	10,833
Lee	27,600	42,019	21,230	34,617
Limestone	13,510	34,337	9,468	29,067
Lowndes	4,968	1,835	4,883	1,751
Macon	7,084	1,539	7,566	1,431
Madison	86,885	102,395	62,822	89,520
Marengo	5,476	5,337	5,615	5,233
Marion	1,457	12,190	1,432	11,274
Marshall	5,880	33,094	4,917	29,233
Mobile	78,754	100,605	72,186	95,116
Monroe	4,418	6,126	4,332	5,795
Montgomery	64,065	33,122	58,916	34,003
Morgan	13,159	39,504	11,254	37,486
Perry	3,849	1,336	3,824	1,407
Pickens	4,017	5,590	3,972	5,456
Pike	5,613	8,020	5,056	7,693
Randolph	2,203	8,548	2,291	7,705
Russell	11,078	9,796	9,579	9,210
St. Clair	7,698	36,119	5,589	31,651
Shelby	33,036	79,428	22,977	73,020
Sumter	4,639	1,598	4,746	1,581
Talladega	13,092	22,210	12,121	20,614
Tallapoosa	5,815	14,905	5,519	13,594
Tuscaloosa	28,560	47,367	31,762	47,723
Walker	4,826	25,947	4,497	24,266
Washington	2,253	6,554	2,374	6,042
Wilcox	4,036	1,826	4,339	1,742
Winston	974	10,187	872	9,228
Totals	**834,533**	**1,430,589**	**729,547**	**1,318,255**

All candidates, 2020: Trump, R, 1,430,589; Biden, D, 834,533; Jorgensen, LB, 24,902.

Alaska

	2020		2016	
	Biden (D)	Trump (R)	Clinton (D)	Trump (R)
Totals	63,992	118,602	116,454	163,387

All candidates, 2020: Trump, R, 118,602; Biden, D, 63,992; Jorgensen, LB, 5,198; Ventura, Green, 1,524; Pierce, petitioning cand., 774; Blankenship, Const., 673; De La Fuente, Alliance, 207.

Arizona

County	2020		2016	
	Biden (D)	Trump (R)	Clinton (D)	Trump (R)
Apache	16,574	7,491	17,083	8,240
Cochise	21,980	31,265	17,450	28,092
Coconino	44,103	26,519	32,404	21,108
Gila	8,943	18,375	7,003	14,182
Graham	4,034	10,747	3,301	8,025
Greenlee	1,182	2,433	1,092	1,892
La Paz	2,050	4,542	1,575	4,003
Maricopa	1,023,516	977,495	702,907	747,361
Mohave	24,687	77,724	17,455	58,282
Navajo	23,217	27,417	16,459	20,577
Pima	295,049	197,183	224,661	167,428
Pinal	67,814	92,954	47,892	72,819
Santa Cruz	13,121	6,179	11,690	3,897
Yavapai	49,111	90,280	35,590	71,330
Yuma	31,562	35,766	24,605	25,165
Totals	**1,626,943**	**1,606,370**	**1,161,167**	**1,252,401**

All candidates, 2020: Biden, D, 1,626,943; Trump, R, 1,606,370; Jorgensen, LB, 49,182.

Arkansas

County	2020		2016	
	Biden (D)	Trump (R)	Clinton (D)	Trump (R)
Arkansas	1,813	4,301	1,939	3,826
Ashley	2,119	5,540	2,408	5,338
Baxter	4,625	15,810	4,169	14,682
Benton	41,894	73,605	28,005	60,871
Boone	3,061	13,644	2,926	12,235
Bradley	1,208	2,332	1,317	2,164
Calhoun	467	1,609	639	1,556
Carroll	2,735	6,754	3,342	6,786
Chicot	2,252	1,750	2,350	1,716
Clark	3,413	4,605	3,620	4,404
Clay	959	4,084	1,199	3,781
Cleburne	1,962	10,292	2,101	9,458
Cleveland	649	2,857	723	2,462
Columbia	2,781	5,469	3,140	5,456
Conway	2,593	5,672	2,656	4,849
Craighead	11,854	25,482	10,538	22,892
Crawford	4,936	18,566	4,488	16,686
Crittenden	8,325	7,244	8,410	6,964
Cross	1,759	4,928	1,999	4,584
Dallas	963	1,573	1,165	1,509
Desha	2,016	1,920	2,228	1,919
Drew	2,408	4,338	2,365	3,968
Faulkner	18,267	34,338	14,629	29,346
Franklin	1,298	5,664	1,376	5,039
Fulton	1,031	3,944	1,067	3,471
Garland	13,944	28,940	12,311	26,087
Grant	1,268	6,791	1,373	5,725
Greene	3,045	12,651	3,071	10,720
Hempstead	2,135	4,463	2,377	4,401
Hot Spring	3,053	9,178	3,149	8,172
Howard	1,333	3,358	1,351	3,157
Independence	2,798	11,232	2,881	9,936
Izard	1,019	4,615	1,113	4,042
Jackson	1,360	3,583	1,583	3,267
Jefferson	14,882	9,500	15,772	9,250
Johnson	2,262	6,867	2,427	6,091
Lafayette	820	1,730	1,032	1,758
Lawrence	1,080	4,569	1,263	4,064
Lee	1,423	1,286	1,735	1,229
Lincoln	1,031	2,725	1,252	2,455
Little River	1,226	3,714	1,397	3,605
Logan	1,544	6,438	1,715	5,746
Lonoke	6,684	22,884	5,664	19,958
Madison	1,555	5,630	1,588	4,928
Marion	1,526	5,767	1,434	5,336
Miller	4,184	11,817	4,273	11,294
Mississippi	4,542	7,262	5,670	7,061
Monroe	1,146	1,545	1,312	1,489
Montgomery	722	3,021	748	2,643
Nevada	1,076	2,133	1,157	2,000
Newton	0	0	699	2,875
Ouachita	3,395	5,253	4,321	5,351
Perry	1,005	3,466	1,049	3,008
Phillips	3,561	2,393	4,310	2,446

County	2020 Biden (D)	Trump (R)	2016 Clinton (D)	Trump (R)
Pike	643	3,514	685	3,150
Poinsett	1,388	5,852	1,880	5,502
Polk	1,242	7,018	1,212	6,618
Pope	5,747	18,041	5,000	16,256
Prairie	646	2,764	814	2,505
Pulaski	98,855	62,389	89,574	61,257
Randolph	1,203	5,327	1,425	4,509
St. Francis	3,571	3,221	4,031	3,195
Saline	16,042	39,519	13,256	35,863
Scott	364	1,790	602	2,731
Searcy	587	3,365	601	2,955
Sebastian	14,371	31,024	12,300	29,127
Sevier	1,116	3,884	1,075	3,282
Sharp	1,392	5,923	1,472	5,407
Stone	1,173	4,605	1,203	4,113
Union	5,559	10,446	5,855	10,456
Van Buren	1,566	5,962	1,549	5,382
Washington	43,327	47,229	33,366	41,476
White	5,909	24,057	5,170	21,077
Woodruff	849	1,543	1,118	1,347
Yell	1,275	5,205	1,480	4,608
Totals	**415,832**	**751,810**	**380,494**	**684,872**

All candidates, 2020: Trump, R, 751,810; Biden, D, 415,832; Jorgensen, LB, 13,001; West, Ind., 4,054; Hawkins, Green, 2,930; Collins, Ind., 2,778; Pierce, Ind., 2,122; Blankenship, Const., 2,076; Carroll, Amer. Solidarity, 1,698; Gammon, Ind., 1,450; Myers, other, 1,363; La Riva, Socialism/Liberation, 1,317; De La Fuente, Ind., 1,296.

California

County	2020 Biden (D)	Trump (R)	2016 Clinton (D)	Trump (R)
Alameda	300,278	59,832	514,842	95,922
Alpine	473	238	334	217
Amador	7,566	11,727	6,004	10,485
Butte	44,455	41,182	41,567	45,144
Calaveras	8,804	13,275	7,944	13,511
Colusa	1,861	2,296	2,661	3,551
Contra Costa	265,942	86,253	319,287	115,956
Del Norte	3,991	4,925	3,485	5,134
El Dorado	42,694	43,630	36,404	49,249
Fresno	147,683	123,941	141,341	124,049
Glenn	2,080	3,444	3,065	5,788
Humboldt	28,123	12,208	33,200	18,373
Imperial	13,247	6,171	32,667	12,704
Inyo	3,443	2,776	3,155	4,248
Kern	69,278	71,254	98,689	129,584
Kings	15,075	19,830	13,617	18,093
Lake	6,874	3,955	11,496	10,599
Lassen	2,150	5,379	2,224	7,574
Los Angeles	2,247,254	835,122	2,464,364	769,743
Madera	17,879	21,834	17,029	23,357
Marin	84,014	14,486	108,707	21,771
Mariposa	3,841	5,330	3,122	5,185
Mendocino	18,303	6,312	22,079	10,888
Merced	33,993	25,355	37,317	28,725
Modoc	1,063	2,675	877	2,696
Mono	3,807	2,364	2,773	2,111
Monterey	84,211	30,854	89,088	34,895
Napa	32,228	11,368	39,199	17,411
Nevada	17,861	11,697	26,053	23,365
Orange	686,230	560,732	609,961	507,148
Placer	81,572	74,784	73,509	95,138
Plumas	4,465	6,247	3,459	5,420
Riverside	236,290	186,331	373,695	333,243
Sacramento	219,638	112,260	326,023	189,789
San Benito	14,153	8,155	12,521	7,841
San Bernardino	267,253	197,789	340,833	271,240
San Diego	763,255	447,345	735,476	477,766
San Francisco	300,606	41,559	345,084	37,688
San Joaquin	86,114	53,611	121,124	88,936
San Luis Obispo	69,339	44,380	67,107	56,164
San Mateo	202,821	48,331	237,882	57,929
Santa Barbara	103,902	47,471	107,142	56,365
Santa Clara	386,292	116,570	511,684	144,826
Santa Cruz	100,045	22,142	95,249	22,438
Shasta	23,387	41,313	22,301	51,778
Sierra	710	1,106	601	1,048
Siskiyou	7,885	9,707	7,234	11,341
Solano	105,189	53,069	102,360	51,920
Sonoma	153,342	40,478	160,435	51,408
Stanislaus	72,651	62,194	81,647	78,494
Sutter	12,325	14,359	13,076	18,116
Tehama	6,543	11,777	6,809	15,494
Trinity	2,383	2,513	2,214	2,812
Tulare	46,559	53,034	47,585	58,299
Tuolumne	10,940	15,349	9,123	14,551
Ventura	202,000	123,161	194,402	132,323
Yolo	40,635	13,381	54,752	20,739
Yuba	7,800	10,574	7,910	13,170
Totals	**7,722,795**	**3,899,436**	**8,753,792**	**4,483,814**

All candidates, 2020: Biden, D, 7,722,795; Trump, R, 3,899,436; Jorgensen, LB, 107,131; Hawkins, Green, 47,878; De La Fuente, Amer. Ind., 33,873; La Riva, Peace/Freedom, 29,688.

Colorado

County	2020 Biden (D)	Trump (R)	2016 Clinton (D)	Trump (R)
Adams	126,003	87,787	96,558	80,082
Alamosa	3,624	3,676	3,189	3,046
Arapahoe	202,452	118,442	159,885	117,053
Archuleta	3,693	5,126	2,500	4,264
Baca	313	1,840	283	1,753
Bent	723	1,468	590	1,188
Boulder	137,134	32,229	132,334	41,396
Broomfield	26,869	14,281	19,731	14,367
Chaffee	7,112	6,180	4,888	5,391
Cheyenne	127	966	132	925
Clear Creek	3,495	2,618	2,729	2,575
Conejos	1,936	2,269	1,771	1,914
Costilla	1,279	713	1,125	588
Crowley	427	1,262	339	1,079
Custer	1,104	2,433	797	2,061
Delta	5,862	13,013	4,087	11,655
Denver	240,699	45,483	244,551	62,690
Dolores	332	1,080	242	944
Douglas	101,669	115,074	68,657	102,573
Eagle	18,095	9,685	14,099	8,990
El Paso	142,446	171,432	108,010	179,228
Elbert	4,310	12,878	3,134	11,705
Fremont	7,170	17,213	5,297	15,122
Garfield	14,647	13,805	11,271	13,132
Gilpin	2,199	1,815	1,634	1,566
Grand	3,827	3,602	3,358	4,494
Gunnison	6,976	3,599	5,128	3,289
Hinsdale	255	353	197	339
Huerfano	2,071	2,193	1,633	1,883
Jackson	173	680	171	629
Jefferson	216,289	146,639	160,776	138,177
Kiowa	98	795	91	728
Kit Carson	644	3,084	536	2,967
La Plata	2,287	1,492	15,525	12,587
Lake	20,310	14,106	1,616	1,270
Larimer	121,998	86,750	93,113	83,430
Las Animas	3,465	4,255	2,650	3,710
Lincoln	467	2,118	409	1,892
Logan	2,201	7,987	1,851	7,282
Mesa	30,106	53,344	21,729	49,779
Mineral	317	425	237	344
Moffat	1,186	5,627	874	5,305
Montezuma	5,802	9,267	3,973	7,853
Montrose	7,648	16,658	5,466	14,382
Morgan	3,741	9,407	3,151	8,145
Otero	3,415	5,479	2,943	4,928
Ouray	2,341	1,547	1,697	1,351
Park	4,786	6,864	3,421	6,135
Phillips	477	1,945	436	1,791
Pitkin	8,906	2,739	7,333	2,550
Prowers	1,438	3,977	1,186	3,531
Pueblo	41,554	38,231	35,875	36,265
Rio Blanco	534	2,884	436	2,791
Rio Grande	2,488	3,045	2,001	3,085
Routt	10,523	5,883	7,600	5,230
Saguache	1,857	1,389	1,417	1,147
San Juan	342	202	265	215
San Miguel	3,890	1,081	2,975	1,033
Sedgwick	297	1,120	267	1,015
Summit	12,535	5,275	9,557	5,100
Teller	5,224	11,158	3,603	9,745
Washington	363	2,537	296	2,299
Weld	59,926	83,939	46,519	76,651
Yuma	763	4,037	726	3,850
Totals	**1,645,240**	**1,239,099**	**1,338,870**	**1,202,484**

All candidates, 2020: Biden, D, 1,645,240; Trump, R, 1,239,099; Jorgensen, LB, 43,765; Hawkins, Green, 7,460; West, unaff., 6,433; Blankenship, Amer. Const., 4,538; Hammons, Unity, 2,381; Carroll, Amer. Solidarity, 2,149; Charles, unaff., 1,764; La Riva, Socialism/Liberation, 796; Kopitke, Ind. Amer., 675; McHugh, unaff., 550; De La Fuente, Alliance, 537; Collins, Prohib., 489; Pierce, unaff., 489; Jacob-Fambro, unaff., 386; Hunter, Progressive, 319; Huber, Approval Voting, 306; Kennedy, Socialist Workers, 291; Kishore, Soc. Equal., 162; Scott, unaff., 148.

Connecticut

City	2020 Biden (D)	Trump (R)	2016 Clinton (D)	Trump (R)
Bridgeport	21,742	6,452	32,035	6,596
Bristol	14,759	13,382	12,499	12,752
Danbury	18,174	12,449	16,084	11,626
East Hartford	14,787	5,524	13,180	5,213
Fairfield	22,859	12,048	18,041	12,112
Glastonbury	13,476	7,742	11,074	7,533
Greenwich	22,239	13,264	17,630	12,215
Hamden	21,839	7,685	18,962	7,790
Hartford	26,597	3,813	30,375	2,531
Manchester	18,038	8,051	15,109	8,358
Meriden	14,844	9,944	12,788	8,660
Middletown	15,508	7,611	12,959	7,126
Milford	17,107	13,145	13,598	13,383
New Britain	15,936	7,678	15,498	6,055
New Haven	21,957	4,898	35,933	4,540
Norwalk	30,595	24,384	24,414	12,324
Shelton	10,360	12,362	8,001	12,051
Southington	12,313	13,064	9,890	12,383
Stamford	32,477	16,074	34,148	16,222
Stratford	16,210	10,004	13,729	10,534
Wallingford	12,834	11,311	10,651	10,940
Waterbury	21,091	13,990	19,870	12,837
West Hartford	24,375	7,764	23,781	8,055
West Haven	14,245	8,126	12,477	7,774
Westport	12,775	4,184	10,655	4,169
Windsor	13,183	4,090	11,370	4,013
Other	542,828	453,607	442,821	435,423
Totals	**1,023,148**	**712,646**	**897,572**	**673,215**

All candidates, 2020: Biden, D, 1,023,148; Trump, R, 712,646; Jorgensen, LB, 19,630; Hawkins, Green, 7,163.

Delaware

County	2020 Biden (D)	Trump (R)	2016 Clinton (D)	Trump (R)
Kent	44,518	40,976	33,351	36,991
New Castle	194,238	87,685	162,919	85,525
Sussex	56,647	71,168	39,333	62,611
Totals	**295,403**	**199,829**	**235,603**	**185,127**

All candidates, 2020: Biden, D, 295,403; Trump, R, 199,829; Jorgensen, LB, 4,977; Hawkins, Green, 2,135.

District of Columbia

	2020 Biden (D)	Trump (R)	2016 Clinton (D)	Trump (R)
Totals	252,328	14,022	282,830	12,723

All candidates, 2020: Biden, D, 252,328; Trump, R, 14,022; Jorgensen, LB, 1,398; Hawkins, Green, 1,265; La Riva, Ind., 598; Pierce, Ind., 503.

Florida

County	2020 Biden (D)	Trump (R)	2016 Clinton (D)	Trump (R)
Alachua	89,527	50,891	75,820	46,834
Baker	2,037	11,911	2,112	10,294
Bay	25,538	65,993	21,797	62,194
Bradford	3,160	10,334	2,924	8,913
Brevard	148,403	207,700	119,679	181,848
Broward	617,689	332,960	553,320	260,951
Calhoun	1,206	5,269	1,241	4,655
Charlotte	42,240	73,202	33,445	60,218
Citrus	27,049	65,230	22,789	54,456
Clay	38,248	84,422	27,822	74,963
Collier	77,529	128,820	61,085	105,423
Columbia	8,900	23,819	7,601	20,368
De Soto	4,249	8,292	3,781	6,778
Dixie	1,364	6,757	1,270	5,822
Duval	250,942	232,846	205,704	211,672
Escambia	70,824	96,573	57,461	88,808
Flagler	28,124	42,991	22,026	33,850
Franklin	2,118	4,675	1,744	4,125
Gadsden	16,139	7,461	15,020	6,728
Gilchrist	1,700	7,893	1,458	6,740
Glades	1,384	3,781	1,271	2,996
Gulf	1,985	6,111	1,720	5,329
Hamilton	1,959	3,811	1,904	3,443
Hardee	2,291	6,120	2,149	5,242
Hendry	4,925	7,898	4,615	6,195
Hernando	37,446	70,321	31,795	58,970
Highlands	16,861	34,787	14,937	29,565
Hillsborough	374,714	326,158	307,896	266,870
Holmes	924	8,074	853	7,483
Indian River	37,801	58,797	29,043	48,620
Jackson	6,749	15,466	6,397	14,257
Jefferson	3,893	4,474	3,541	3,930

County	2020 Biden (D)	Trump (R)	2016 Clinton (D)	Trump (R)
Lafayette	507	3,126	518	2,809
Lake	83,273	125,687	62,838	102,188
Lee	156,957	232,075	124,908	191,551
Leon	103,364	57,384	92,068	53,821
Levy	6,189	16,721	5,101	13,775
Liberty	693	2,846	651	2,543
Madison	3,746	5,673	3,526	4,851
Manatee	89,534	124,541	71,224	101,944
Marion	74,802	127,744	62,041	107,833
Martin	36,873	61,133	30,185	53,204
Miami-Dade	617,201	532,409	624,146	333,999
Monroe	21,848	25,668	18,971	21,904
Nassau	15,542	42,502	10,869	34,266
Okaloosa	34,165	79,633	23,780	71,893
Okeechobee	4,380	11,460	3,959	9,356
Orange	394,602	245,162	329,894	195,216
Osceola	97,157	73,373	85,458	50,301
Palm Beach	429,856	332,760	374,673	272,402
Pasco	118,767	179,343	90,142	142,101
Pinellas	277,191	275,949	233,701	239,201
Polk	144,775	194,271	117,433	157,430
Putnam	10,512	25,496	10,094	22,138
St. Johns	63,808	110,886	43,099	88,684
St. Lucie	84,005	86,748	68,881	70,289
Santa Rosa	27,560	77,306	18,464	65,339
Sarasota	119,892	148,065	97,870	124,438
Seminole	132,213	125,035	105,914	109,443
Sumter	29,326	62,753	22,638	52,730
Suwannee	4,480	16,387	3,964	14,287
Taylor	2,288	7,725	2,152	6,930
Union	1,052	5,130	1,014	4,568
Volusia	130,395	173,544	109,091	143,007
Wakulla	5,346	12,868	4,348	10,512
Walton	10,333	32,924	6,876	25,756
Washington	2,344	9,869	2,264	8,637
Totals	**5,282,894**	**5,657,933**	**4,504,975**	**4,617,886**

All candidates, 2020: Trump, R, 5,657,933; Biden, D, 5,282,894; Jorgensen, LB, 70,001; Hawkins, Green, 13,696; La Riva, Socialism/Liberation, 6,711; De La Fuente, RF, 5,697; Blankenship, Const., 3,887.

Georgia

County	2020 Biden (D)	Trump (R)	2016 Clinton (D)	Trump (R)
Appling	1,779	6,526	1,434	5,494
Atkinson	825	2,300	697	1,878
Bacon	625	4,018	608	3,364
Baker	652	897	650	775
Baldwin	9,140	8,903	7,970	7,697
Banks	932	7,795	684	6,134
Barrow	10,453	26,804	6,580	21,108
Bartow	12,091	37,673	8,212	29,911
Ben Hill	2,392	4,110	2,101	3,739
Berrien	1,268	6,409	1,047	5,422
Bibb	43,234	26,506	36,787	24,043
Bleckley	1,311	4,328	1,101	3,719
Brantley	699	6,991	619	5,567
Brooks	2,790	4,260	2,528	3,701
Bryan	6,739	14,244	4,014	10,529
Bulloch	11,243	18,386	9,261	15,097
Burke	5,209	5,400	4,731	4,491
Butts	3,271	8,403	2,566	6,717
Calhoun	1,259	923	1,179	830
Camden	7,967	15,251	5,930	12,310
Candler	1,258	3,129	1,026	2,664
Carroll	16,238	37,476	12,464	30,029
Catoosa	6,932	25,167	4,771	20,876
Charlton	1,102	3,419	1,004	2,951
Chatham	78,181	53,191	62,290	45,688
Chattahoochee	667	880	594	751
Chattooga	1,854	8,064	1,613	6,462
Cherokee	42,683	99,474	25,231	80,649
Clarke	35,969	14,412	29,603	12,717
Clay	790	637	697	566
Clayton	94,365	15,671	78,220	12,645
Clinch	747	2,105	686	1,727
Cobb	221,234	164,965	160,121	152,912
Coffee	4,463	10,532	4,094	9,588
Colquitt	4,185	11,776	3,463	9,898
Columbia	29,115	49,952	18,887	43,085
Cook	2,059	4,900	1,753	4,176
Coweta	24,210	51,501	16,583	42,533
Crawford	1,615	4,428	1,421	3,635
Crisp	2,986	4,987	2,837	4,549
Dade	1,261	6,066	965	5,051
Dawson	2,486	13,393	1,448	9,900
Decatur	4,780	6,758	4,124	6,020
DeKalb	305,197	57,993	251,370	51,468

County	2020 Biden (D)	Trump (R)	2016 Clinton (D)	Trump (R)
Dodge	2,170	5,839	1,839	5,021
Dooly	1,911	2,159	1,872	1,951
Dougherty	24,540	10,446	23,311	10,232
Douglas	42,609	25,308	31,005	24,817
Early	2,437	2,719	2,168	2,552
Echols	167	1,256	156	1,007
Effingham	7,720	23,357	4,853	17,874
Elbert	2,879	6,226	2,539	5,292
Emanuel	2,884	6,551	2,435	5,335
Evans	1,324	2,888	1,130	2,404
Fannin	2,571	12,144	1,923	9,632
Fayette	31,863	36,316	23,284	35,048
Floyd	10,959	27,059	9,159	24,114
Forsyth	42,177	85,081	23,462	69,851
Franklin	1,593	9,069	1,243	7,054
Fulton	377,484	136,140	297,051	117,783
Gilmer	2,905	13,382	1,965	10,477
Glascock	155	1,403	138	1,235
Glynn	15,879	25,616	11,775	21,512
Gordon	4,384	19,405	3,181	15,191
Grady	3,608	7,027	3,013	6,053
Greene	4,088	7,068	3,199	5,490
Gwinnett	241,140	166,016	166,153	146,989
Habersham	3,559	16,616	2,483	13,190
Hall	25,002	64,105	16,180	51,733
Hancock	2,985	1,159	2,701	843
Haralson	1,792	12,331	1,475	9,585
Harris	5,457	14,319	4,086	11,936
Hart	3,157	9,464	2,585	7,286
Heard	824	4,516	743	3,370
Henry	73,276	48,187	50,057	45,724
Houston	32,232	41,534	22,553	35,430
Irwin	1,008	3,134	891	2,716
Jackson	7,642	29,497	4,491	21,784
Jasper	1,761	5,822	1,544	4,360
Jeff Davis	1,028	4,695	901	4,104
Jefferson	4,061	3,537	3,821	3,063
Jenkins	1,266	2,161	1,123	1,895
Johnson	1,222	2,850	1,136	2,519
Jones	4,888	9,965	3,961	8,305
Lamar	2,612	6,322	2,270	5,190
Lanier	1,019	2,509	806	1,984
Laurens	8,048	14,479	6,752	12,411
Lee	4,558	12,007	3,170	10,646
Liberty	13,051	7,944	9,556	6,134
Lincoln	1,432	3,175	1,273	2,759
Long	2,033	3,528	1,360	2,626
Lowndes	20,117	25,691	15,064	21,635
Lumpkin	3,122	12,160	2,220	9,619
Macon	2,857	1,783	2,705	1,540
Madison	3,365	11,146	2,425	9,201
Marion	1,311	2,275	1,213	1,921
McDuffie	4,168	6,169	3,699	5,432
McIntosh	2,612	4,016	2,303	3,487
Meriwether	4,287	6,524	3,804	5,222
Miller	749	2,066	623	1,891
Mitchell	3,995	4,935	3,493	4,279
Monroe	4,384	11,060	3,571	8,832
Montgomery	976	2,959	847	2,670
Morgan	3,355	8,228	2,663	6,559
Murray	2,302	12,943	1,800	10,341
Muscogee	49,425	30,018	39,851	26,976
Newton	29,781	23,867	21,943	20,913
Oconee	8,160	16,594	5,581	13,425
Oglethorpe	2,435	5,591	1,831	4,625
Paulding	29,658	54,460	18,025	44,662
Peach	5,920	6,502	5,100	5,413
Pickens	2,808	14,075	1,979	11,651
Pierce	1,099	7,899	903	6,302
Pike	1,503	9,124	1,240	7,278
Polk	3,658	13,589	2,867	11,014
Pulaski	1,217	2,805	1,104	2,437
Putnam	3,448	8,291	2,758	6,544
Quitman	497	604	461	575
Rabun	1,984	7,474	1,444	6,287
Randolph	1,671	1,391	1,598	1,271
Richmond	58,776	26,707	48,814	24,461
Rockdale	31,199	12,990	23,255	13,478
Schley	462	1,800	401	1,472
Screven	2,661	3,915	2,300	3,305
Seminole	1,251	2,607	1,189	2,345
Spalding	11,784	18,057	9,357	15,646

County	2020 Biden (D)	Trump (R)	2016 Clinton (D)	Trump (R)
Stephens	2,385	9,368	1,837	7,686
Stewart	1,182	801	1,222	805
Sumter	6,318	5,732	5,520	5,276
Talbot	2,113	1,390	2,002	1,196
Taliaferro	561	360	545	349
Tattnall	2,059	6,048	1,681	5,096
Taylor	1,387	2,418	1,296	2,064
Telfair	1,480	2,822	1,313	2,450
Terrell	2,376	2,004	2,267	1,874
Thomas	8,708	12,954	7,142	11,228
Tift	5,322	10,784	4,347	9,584
Toombs	2,939	7,872	2,338	6,615
Towns	1,550	6,384	1,210	5,383
Treutlen	952	2,101	862	1,809
Troup	11,542	18,097	9,713	15,750
Turner	1,410	2,349	1,246	2,095
Twiggs	2,040	2,368	1,971	2,035
Union	2,801	12,651	1,963	9,852
Upson	4,201	8,602	3,475	7,292
Walker	5,769	23,174	4,215	18,950
Walton	12,634	37,617	8,292	31,125
Ware	4,249	9,930	3,440	8,513
Warren	1,488	1,177	1,314	991
Washington	4,730	4,663	4,200	4,149
Wayne	2,687	9,987	2,041	8,153
Webster	639	748	473	630
Wheeler	688	1,583	646	1,421
White	2,411	12,222	1,674	9,761
Whitfield	10,670	25,636	7,937	21,537
Wilcox	862	2,403	852	2,096
Wilkes	2,159	2,823	1,848	2,572
Wilkinson	2,075	2,664	1,894	2,333
Worth	2,395	6,826	2,020	6,152
Totals	**2,461,455**	**2,454,207**	**1,877,963**	**2,089,104**

All candidates, 2020: Biden, D, 2,461,455; Trump, R, 2,454,207; Jorgensen, LB, 61,792.

Hawaii

County	2020 Biden (D)	Trump (R)	2016 Clinton (D)	Trump (R)
Hawaii	58,683	26,851	41,259	17,501
Honolulu	238,601	136,061	175,896	90,326
Kauai	21,217	11,579	16,456	7,574
Maui	47,301	22,111	33,480	13,446
Overseas	NA	NA	NA	NA
Totals	**365,802**	**196,602**	**266,891**	**128,847**

All candidates, 2020: Biden, D, 365,802; Trump, R, 196,602; Jorgensen, LB, 5,525; Hawkins, Green, 3,814; ; Pierce, Amer. Shop., 1,181; Blankenship, Const., 930.

Idaho

County	2020 Biden (D)	Trump (R)	2016 Clinton (D)	Trump (R)
Ada	120,539	130,699	75,677	93,752
Adams	591	1,941	415	1,556
Bannock	14,682	23,331	10,342	17,180
Bear Lake	350	2,814	255	2,203
Benewah	977	3,878	770	3,103
Bingham	4,124	15,295	2,924	10,007
Blaine	8,919	4,031	6,416	3,340
Boise	1,214	3,495	777	2,673
Bonner	8,310	18,369	5,819	13,343
Bonneville	14,254	37,805	8,930	26,699
Boundary	1,220	4,937	933	3,789
Butte	188	1,202	160	914
Camas	149	507	110	410
Canyon	25,881	61,759	16,883	47,222
Caribou	431	2,906	271	2,275
Cassia	1,464	7,907	1,036	5,949
Clark	41	264	44	203
Clearwater	877	3,453	704	2,852
Custer	603	2,089	427	1,777
Elmore	2,601	7,246	1,814	5,816
Franklin	657	5,845	385	3,901
Fremont	998	5,548	651	4,090
Gem	1,803	7,951	1,229	5,980
Gooding	1,256	4,659	930	3,743
Idaho	1,561	7,826	1,196	6,441

County	2020 Biden (D)	Trump (R)	2016 Clinton (D)	Trump (R)
Jefferson	1,658	12,099	976	8,436
Jerome	1,893	5,734	1,329	4,644
Kootenai	24,312	62,837	16,264	44,449
Latah	10,199	9,463	8,093	7,265
Lemhi	1,032	3,592	733	3,011
Lewis	349	1,489	270	1,202
Lincoln	414	1,469	360	1,184
Madison	2,666	13,559	1,201	8,941
Minidoka	1,550	6,265	1,167	4,887
Nez Perce	6,686	13,738	4,828	10,699
Oneida	249	2,148	184	1,531
Owyhee	816	3,819	591	3,052
Payette	2,161	8,862	1,507	6,489
Power	865	2,116	699	1,666
Shoshone	1,693	4,216	1,384	3,297
Teton	3,318	2,858	2,159	2,167
Twin Falls	9,391	25,897	6,233	19,828
Valley	2,976	3,947	1,913	2,906
Washington	1,073	4,154	776	3,283
Totals	286,991	554,019	189,765	409,055

All candidates, 2020: Trump, R, 554,019; Biden, D, 286,991; Jorgensen, LB, 16,401; West, Ind., 3,632; Pierce, Ind., 2,808; Blankenship, Const., 1,884; De La Fuente, Ind., 1,491.

Illinois

County	2020 Biden (D)	Trump (R)	2016 Clinton (D)	Trump (R)
Adams	8,569	24,131	7,676	22,790
Alexander	0	0	1,262	1,496
Bond	2,275	5,612	2,068	4,888
Boone	10,372	13,762	8,986	12,282
Brown	485	1,930	476	1,796
Bureau	6,545	10,296	6,029	9,281
Calhoun	674	2,043	739	1,721
Carroll	2,737	5,098	2,447	4434
Cass	1,615	3,624	1,621	3,216
Champaign	54,412	34,537	50,137	33,368
Christian	4,286	11,505	3,992	10,543
Clark	1,990	6,215	1,877	5,622
Clay	1,129	5,626	1,020	5,021
Clinton	4,459	14,264	3,945	12,412
Coles	7,997	13,981	7,309	13,003
Cook	1,264,254	456,943	1,611,946	453,287
Crawford	2,198	7,025	1,992	6,277
Cumberland	0	0	1,031	4,206
DeKalb	24,484	21,818	20,466	19,091
DeWitt	2,171	5,623	1,910	5,077
Douglas	2,327	6,221	1,949	5,698
DuPage	256,338	182,773	228,622	166,415
Edgar	1,869	6,169	1,793	5,645
Edwards	488	2,833	434	2,778
Effingham	3,700	14,983	3,083	13,635
Fayette	1,815	8,025	1,819	7,372
Ford	1,691	4,956	1,414	4,480
Franklin	2,080	8,912	4,727	13,116
Fulton	6,371	9,798	6,133	8,492
Gallatin	621	2,019	657	1,942
Greene	1,349	4,767	1,205	4,145
Grundy	9,445	16,372	8,065	13,454
Hamilton	821	3,429	802	3,206
Hancock	1,114	5,309	2,139	6,430
Hardin	0	0	420	1,653
Henderson	1,186	2,391	1,155	2,155
Henry	9,762	15,266	8,871	13,985
Iroquois	2,895	10,858	2,504	9,750
Jackson	3,749	7,066	11,634	10,843
Jasper	1,006	4,492	924	3,975
Jefferson	4,597	12,461	4,425	11,695
Jersey	2,956	8,699	2,679	7,748
Jo Daviess	5,097	7,161	4,462	6,121
Johnson	1,280	5,052	1,142	4,649
Kane	127,792	95,557	103,665	82,734
Kankakee	20,112	28,410	18,971	25,129
Kendall	31,394	28,515	24,884	24,961
Knox	10,421	11,818	10,083	10,737
Lake	144,674	105,416	171,095	109,767
LaSalle	21,491	29,482	19,543	26,689
Lawrence	1,414	4,849	1,290	4,521
Lee	6,368	9,584	5,528	8,612
Livingston	4,568	12,134	4,023	10,208
Logan	3,769	9,042	3,313	8,181
Macon	19,633	28,373	18,343	26,866
Macoupin	7,313	16,058	6,689	14,322

County	2020 Biden (D)	Trump (R)	2016 Clinton (D)	Trump (R)
Madison	56,845	75,272	50,587	70,490
Marion	4,396	12,540	4,369	11,859
Marshall	2,004	4,196	1,789	3,785
Mason	1,984	4,645	2,014	4,058
Massac	1,719	4,989	1,558	4,846
McDonough	4,973	7,009	5,288	6,795
McHenry	73,610	79,396	60,803	71,612
McLean	43,719	40,365	36,196	37,237
Menard	2,003	4,772	1,817	4,231
Mercer	3,212	5,328	3,071	4,807
Monroe	6,489	14,046	5,535	12,629
Montgomery	3,889	9,504	3,504	8,630
Morgan	5,020	9,903	4,696	9,076
Moultrie	1,645	4,938	1,481	4,455
Ogle	9,300	16,092	8,050	14,352
Peoria	42,600	37,612	38,060	35,633
Perry	2,609	7,305	2,462	6,855
Piatt	3,302	6,219	2,645	5,634
Pike	1,458	6,235	1,413	5,754
Pope	432	1,720	375	1,678
Pulaski	891	1,699	962	1,675
Putnam	1,309	1,978	1,147	1,767
Randolph	3,590	11,065	3,439	10,023
Richland	1,824	6,078	1,584	5,739
Rock Island	36,647	28,585	32,298	26,998
St. Clair	66,920	56,014	60,756	53,857
Saline	2,786	8,096	2,572	8,276
Sangamon	48,756	53,303	40,907	49,944
Schuyler	1,064	2,767	1,075	2,524
Scott	569	2,104	535	1,966
Shelby	2,488	9,396	2,288	8,229
Stark	814	2,000	751	1,778
Stephenson	8,756	12,253	7,768	11,083
Tazewell	24,486	42,194	20,685	38,707
Union	2,575	6,157	2,402	5,790
Vermilion	10,313	20,710	10,039	19,087
Wabash	1,248	4,228	1,151	4,047
Warren	3,087	4,671	2,987	4,275
Washington	1,639	6,110	1,448	5,571
Wayne	0	0	1,048	6,967
White	1,517	5,788	1,412	5,640
Whiteside	12,195	14,472	11,035	12,615
Will	174,226	149,695	151,927	132,720
Williamson	10,107	22,681	8,581	21,570
Winnebago	69,590	46,735	55,713	55,624
Woodford	4,664	11,764	5,092	13,207
Totals	2,885,428	2,255,912	3,090,729	2,146,015

All candidates, 2020: Biden, D, 2,885,428; Trump, R, 2,255,912; Jorgensen, LB, 57,820; Hawkins, Green, 25,942; Carroll, Amer. Solidarity, 7,803; La Riva, Socialism/Liberation, 6,778.

Indiana

County	2020 Biden (D)	Trump (R)	2016 Clinton (D)	Trump (R)
Adams	3,236	10,685	2,805	9,648
Allen	56,504	80,878	55,382	83,930
Bartholomew	12,934	22,409	9,841	20,640
Benton	1,009	3,007	860	2,579
Blackford	1,376	3,838	1,243	3,350
Boone	15,244	22,351	10,181	19,654
Brown	2,996	5,725	2,518	5,016
Carroll	2,224	7,086	1,892	6,273
Cass	4,301	10,551	3,759	9,701
Clark	23,088	33,656	18,808	30,035
Clay	2,549	9,498	2,306	8,531
Clinton	3,361	9,334	2,819	8,531
Crawford	1,296	3,370	1,323	3,015
Daviess	2,169	9,576	1,800	8,545
Dearborn	2,143	12,384	4,883	18,113
Decatur	2,436	9,570	2,121	8,490
DeKalb	4,966	14,237	3,942	12,054
Delaware	20,328	26,724	18,153	24,263
Dubois	6,292	15,032	5,329	13,365
Elkhart	25,413	46,311	20,740	41,867
Fayette	2,237	7,755	2,252	6,839
Floyd	17,397	22,906	13,945	21,432
Fountain	1,627	6,151	1,476	5,662
Franklin	2,137	9,691	1,969	8,669
Fulton	2,274	6,667	1,960	6,010
Gibson	4,027	11,817	3,721	11,081
Grant	8,015	18,543	7,010	17,008

County	2020 Biden (D)	2020 Trump (R)	2016 Clinton (D)	2016 Trump (R)
Greene	3,389	11,103	2,929	10,277
Hamilton	79,530	94,964	57,263	87,404
Hancock	12,821	28,816	8,904	25,074
Harrison	5,334	14,542	4,783	12,943
Hendricks	32,453	53,688	22,600	48,337
Henry	5,442	14,526	5,124	13,895
Howard	13,270	26,400	11,215	23,675
Huntington	4,254	13,147	3,506	11,649
Jackson	4,302	14,555	3,843	12,859
Jasper	3,798	11,383	3,329	9,382
Jay	1,926	6,361	1,889	5,697
Jefferson	4,735	9,659	4,326	8,546
Jennings	2,521	9,488	2,364	8,224
Johnson	24,729	51,209	17,318	45,456
Knox	4,067	11,654	3,772	11,077
Kosciusko	8,350	26,476	6,313	23,935
LaGrange	2,355	8,110	2,080	7,025
Lake	124,157	91,472	116,935	75,625
LaPorte	0	0	19,798	22,687
Lawrence	4,961	15,601	4,210	14,035
Madison	19,459	31,153	18,595	32,376
Marion	203,940	112,954	212,899	130,360
Marshall	5,712	13,841	4,798	12,288
Martin	1,011	4,029	881	3,697
Miami	3,235	10,925	2,766	9,975
Monroe	39,855	22,061	34,216	20,592
Montgomery	4,008	11,874	3,362	11,059
Morgan	7,777	27,510	6,040	23,674
Newton	1,509	4,942	1,404	4,077
Noble	4,660	14,195	3,904	12,198
Ohio	750	2,392	686	2,118
Orange	2,224	6,432	2,048	5,803
Owen	2,419	7,285	1,946	6,153
Parke	1,503	5,398	1,441	4,863
Perry	3,202	5,343	3,062	4,556
Pike	1,415	4,692	1,297	4,398
Porter	12,145	23,708	33,676	38,832
Posey	3,811	9,206	3,521	8,404
Pulaski	1,463	4,246	1,327	3,854
Putnam	3,946	12,278	3,356	10,637
Randolph	2,512	8,312	2,446	7,517
Ripley	2,773	11,260	2,471	9,806
Rush	1,754	6,035	1,525	5,292
St. Joseph	40,426	44,550	52,252	52,021
Scott	2,698	7,328	2,642	6,074
Shelby	5,023	14,568	4,247	12,718
Spencer	3,208	7,354	2,861	6,572
Starke	2,650	7,466	2,489	6,367
Steuben	4,509	11,322	3,744	10,133
Sullivan	2,153	6,687	2,113	6,138
Switzerland	964	3,133	930	2,558
Tippecanoe	34,719	34,273	27,282	30,768
Tipton	1,834	6,110	1,587	5,589
Union	736	2,687	715	2,445
Vanderburgh	15,690	19,730	28,530	40,496
Vermillion	2,171	5,114	2,081	4,513
Vigo	8,673	10,657	15,931	21,937
Wabash	3,494	10,762	3,018	9,821
Warren	974	3,401	839	2,898
Warrick	11,919	21,324	9,086	19,113
Washington	2,783	9,112	2,636	8,209
Wayne	0	0	8,322	16,028
Wells	2,928	10,855	2,586	10,005
White	2,868	7,353	2,590	6,893
Whitley	4,233	12,856	3,379	11,358
Totals	**1,059,709**	**1,569,619**	**1,033,126**	**1,557,286**

All candidates, 2020: Trump, R, 1,569,619; Biden, D, 1,059,709; Jorgensen, LB, 53,142.

Iowa

County	2020 Biden (D)	2020 Trump (R)	2016 Clinton (D)	2016 Trump (R)
Adair	1,197	2,917	1,133	2,461
Adams	590	1,528	565	1,395
Allamakee	2,575	4,733	2,421	4,093
Appanoose	1,889	4,508	1,814	4,033
Audubon	1,071	2,292	1,080	2,136
Benton	5,156	9,179	4,678	8,232
Black Hawk	35,621	29,623	32,233	27,476
Boone	6,293	8,676	5,541	7,484

County	2020 Biden (D)	2020 Trump (R)	2016 Clinton (D)	2016 Trump (R)
Bremer	5,954	8,287	5,356	7,208
Buchanan	4,167	6,418	3,970	5,510
Buena Vista	2,919	5,004	2,856	4,903
Butler	2,423	5,540	2,157	4,921
Calhoun	1,469	3,687	1,398	3,468
Carroll	3,444	7,720	3,309	6,638
Cass	2,201	4,968	1,951	4,761
Cedar	4,336	6,161	3,599	5,295
Cerro Gordo	10,941	12,435	9,862	11,621
Cherokee	1,934	4,489	1,679	4,192
Chickasaw	2,230	4,299	2,266	3,742
Clarke	1,466	3,140	1,465	2,713
Clay	2,653	6,126	2,249	5,877
Clayton	3,339	6,105	3,237	5,317
Clinton	10,806	13,349	10,095	11,276
Crawford	2,211	4,842	1,991	4,617
Dallas	26,771	27,882	15,701	19,339
Davis	1,013	3,030	977	2,723
Decatur	1,117	2,613	1,201	2,296
Delaware	3,152	6,653	2,957	5,694
Des Moines	8,887	10,589	8,212	9,529
Dickinson	3,660	7,432	3,056	6,753
Dubuque	25,601	27,153	22,850	23,460
Emmet	1,515	3,254	1,357	3,124
Fayette	3,833	6,139	3,689	5,620
Floyd	3,168	4,730	3,179	4,375
Franklin	1,614	3,408	1,493	3,163
Fremont	1,078	2,711	963	2,407
Greene	1,768	3,221	1,691	2,820
Grundy	2,194	4,911	1,856	4,527
Guthrie	1,985	4,272	1,732	3,628
Hamilton	2,842	4,956	2,726	4,463
Hancock	1,682	4,386	1,587	3,977
Hardin	2,971	5,842	2,787	5,254
Harrison	2,439	5,563	2,131	4,902
Henry	3,264	6,483	2,904	5,779
Howard	1,772	3,126	1,677	2,611
Humboldt	1,439	3,812	1,252	3,568
Ida	917	2,876	792	2,655
Iowa	3,532	5,984	3,084	5,205
Jackson	4,024	6,937	3,837	5,824
Jasper	7,813	12,480	7,109	10,560
Jefferson	4,314	4,442	3,710	3,748
Johnson	59,108	22,907	50,200	21,044
Jones	4,211	6,569	3,787	5,720
Keokuk	1,409	3,785	1,342	3,390
Kossuth	2,681	6,244	2,543	5,653
Lee	6,539	9,764	6,215	8,803
Linn	70,451	53,098	58,935	48,390
Louisa	1,726	3,498	1,648	3,069
Lucas	1,220	2,981	1,239	2,877
Lyon	1,065	5,703	920	5,192
Madison	3,126	6,486	2,678	5,360
Mahaska	2,879	8,256	2,619	7,432
Marion	6,170	12,657	5,482	10,962
Marshall	8,171	9,564	7,652	9,146
Mills	2,500	5,572	2,090	5,067
Mitchell	2,048	3,665	1,888	3,190
Monona	1,402	3,234	1,247	3,120
Monroe	1,078	2,974	1,056	2,638
Montgomery	1,583	3,653	1,314	3,436
Muscatine	9,320	10,791	8,368	9,584
O'Brien	1,567	5,857	1,315	5,752
Osceola	600	2,688	552	2,531
Page	2,081	5,314	1,807	4,893
Palo Alto	1,517	3,366	1,398	3,081
Plymouth	3,483	10,472	2,885	9,680
Pocahontas	932	2,825	963	2,702
Polk	146,173	106,752	119,804	93,492
Pottawattamie	18,570	26,241	15,355	24,447
Poweshiek	4,301	5,645	4,304	4,946
Ringgold	708	1,964	753	1,824
Sac	1,383	4,052	1,270	3,703
Scott	46,890	43,661	40,440	39,149
Shelby	1,951	4,688	1,662	4,362
Sioux	3,017	15,669	2,300	14,785
Story	28,975	20,200	25,709	19,458
Tama	3,573	5,299	3,196	4,971
Taylor	745	2,459	758	2,111
Union	2,049	4,000	1,922	3,525

County	2020 Biden (D)	2020 Trump (R)	2016 Clinton (D)	2016 Trump (R)
Van Buren	874	2,857	845	2,527
Wapello	5,818	9,504	5,594	8,715
Warren	12,537	17,738	10,411	14,814
Washington	4,558	6,966	3,943	6,173
Wayne	727	2,338	719	2,069
Webster	6,604	10,927	6,305	10,056
Winnebago	2,123	3,692	1,931	3,447
Winneshiek	5,616	6,234	5,254	5,344
Woodbury	18,683	25,700	16,210	24,727
Worth	1,593	2,732	1,530	2,453
Wright	1,995	4,135	1,896	3,800
Totals	**757,580**	**896,286**	**653,669**	**800,983**

All candidates, 2020: Trump, R, 896,286; Biden, D, 757,580; Jorgensen, LB, 19,546; West, no party, 3,202; Hawkins, Green, 3,067; Blankenship, Const., 1,704; De La Fuente, Alliance, 1,081; King, other, 550; Pierce, no party, 549.

Kansas

County	2020 Biden (D)	2020 Trump (R)	2016 Clinton (D)	2016 Trump (R)
Allen	1,544	4,140	1,433	3,651
Anderson	750	2,836	672	2,435
Atchison	2,311	4,817	1,989	4,049
Barber	284	1,992	286	1,850
Barton	2,277	8,419	1,839	7,888
Bourbon	1,504	4,906	1,336	4,424
Brown	1,086	3,202	863	2,906
Butler	8,938	22,187	6,573	19,073
Chase	341	1,114	316	969
Chautauqua	211	1,393	197	1,236
Cherokee	2,154	6,612	2,005	6,182
Cheyenne	219	1,139	181	1,173
Clark	142	880	120	825
Clay	883	3,128	677	2,891
Cloud	887	3,152	761	2,919
Coffey	926	3,403	727	3,050
Comanche	124	743	102	715
Cowley	4,168	9,438	3,551	8,270
Crawford	5,849	9,635	5,199	8,624
Decatur	208	1,230	178	1,210
Dickinson	2,036	7,036	1,609	6,029
Doniphan	672	2,919	587	2,606
Douglas	38,386	16,278	31,195	14,688
Edwards	266	1,126	212	1,037
Elk	191	1,130	160	1,048
Ellis	3,554	9,423	2,742	8,466
Ellsworth	639	2,102	521	1,969
Finney	4,037	7,027	3,195	6,350
Ford	2,873	5,701	2,149	5,114
Franklin	3,585	8,266	2,892	7,185
Geary	3,722	5,104	2,722	4,274
Gove	163	1,256	149	1,140
Graham	221	1,052	188	1,025
Grant	493	1,902	441	1,804
Gray	337	1,871	263	1,698
Greeley	76	537	83	534
Greenwood	562	2,397	485	2,160
Hamilton	134	683	121	705
Harper	301	1,903	393	1,996
Harvey	6,466	9,816	5,068	8,668
Haskell	260	1,100	245	1,040
Hodgeman	151	866	124	855
Jackson	1,836	4,406	1,512	3,939
Jefferson	3,099	6,170	2,518	5,213
Jewell	204	1,356	180	1,223
Johnson	176,030	149,796	129,852	137,490
Kearny	255	1,134	174	1,075
Kingman	742	3,098	599	2,530
Kiowa	152	956	114	900
Labette	2,526	5,539	2,291	5,335
Lane	114	757	106	718
Leavenworth	13,634	21,162	10,209	17,638
Lincoln	266	1,270	215	1,179
Linn	853	3,931	736	3,484
Logan	185	1,223	149	1,132
Lyon	5,815	7,332	4,649	6,552
Marion	1,433	4,327	1,204	4,003
Marshall	1,236	3,657	1,072	3,307
McPherson	3,596	9,225	3,226	8,549
Meade	261	1,507	210	1,415
Miami	5,130	12,109	3,991	10,003
Mitchell	547	2,451	477	2,308
Montgomery	3,051	9,580	2,637	8,679

County	2020 Biden (D)	2020 Trump (R)	2016 Clinton (D)	2016 Trump (R)
Morris	720	2,078	601	1,820
Morton	143	1,002	147	995
Nemaha	906	4,570	725	4,124
Neosho	1,716	4,774	1,501	4,431
Ness	147	1,312	162	1,228
Norton	360	1,975	281	1,840
Osage	2,091	5,589	1,753	4,826
Osborne	269	1,562	233	1,460
Ottawa	497	2,576	424	2,283
Pawnee	635	2,028	579	1,904
Phillips	373	2,855	300	2,233
Pottawatomie	3,254	9,236	2,225	7,612
Pratt	898	3,034	771	2,838
Rawlins	214	1,250	163	1,220
Reno	8,563	17,892	6,837	15,513
Republic	399	1,934	375	2,024
Rice	940	3,141	695	2,837
Riley	11,756	11,018	9,341	10,107
Rooks	328	2,278	275	2,031
Rush	290	1,425	233	1,197
Russell	582	2,747	461	2,574
Saline	7,910	15,175	6,317	13,828
Scott	290	1,989	236	1,865
Sedgwick	80,763	109,363	69,627	104,353
Seward	1,734	3,281	1,628	3,159
Shawnee	41,147	39,433	33,926	35,934
Sheridan	144	1,237	127	1,197
Sherman	385	2,220	347	2,089
Smith	327	1,732	297	1,661
Stafford	354	1,630	304	1,490
Stanton	147	607	115	492
Stevens	232	1,730	220	1,599
Sumner	2,547	7,991	2,076	6,984
Thomas	621	3,104	473	2,908
Trego	238	1,341	198	1,227
Wabaunsee	952	2,807	776	2,372
Wallace	43	759	46	721
Washington	458	2,315	387	2,194
Wichita	147	803	140	769
Wilson	700	3,090	594	2,788
Woodson	282	1,186	273	1,082
Wyandotte	35,195	18,337	30,146	15,806
Totals	**534,593**	**739,253**	**427,005**	**671,018**

All candidates, 2020: Trump, R, 739,253; Biden, D, 534,593; Jorgensen, LB, 28,402.

Kentucky

County	2020 Biden (D)	2020 Trump (R)	2016 Clinton (D)	2016 Trump (R)
Adair	1,391	7,275	1,323	6,637
Allen	1,626	7,571	1,349	6,466
Anderson	3,339	9,651	2,634	8,242
Ballard	825	3,355	816	3,161
Barren	5,116	14,646	4,275	13,483
Bath	1,573	3,986	1,361	3,082
Bell	1,789	8,139	1,720	7,764
Boone	19,589	43,840	15,026	39,082
Bourbon	3,292	6,185	2,791	5,569
Boyd	7,024	14,223	6,021	13,591
Boyle	5,001	8,682	4,281	8,040
Bracken	799	3,397	705	2,711
Breathitt	1,301	4,265	1,537	3,991
Breckinridge	2,350	7,699	1,960	6,484
Bullitt	10,126	30,338	8,255	26,210
Butler	1,078	4,960	947	4,428
Caldwell	1,432	4,905	1,260	4,507
Calloway	5,791	11,342	4,749	10,367
Campbell	19,339	28,465	14,658	25,050
Carlisle	463	2,159	432	2,094
Carroll	1,114	2,947	1,106	2,588
Carter	2,641	8,773	2,276	7,587
Casey	918	6,179	767	5,482
Christian	8,282	15,060	7,188	14,108
Clark	6,000	11,806	4,706	10,710
Clay	430	6,003	752	5,861
Clinton	603	4,280	547	3,809
Crittenden	730	3,449	617	3,290
Cumberland	508	2,769	459	2,502
Daviess	17,107	30,922	14,163	28,907
Edmonson	682	4,265	979	4,135
Elliott	707	2,240	740	2,000
Estill	1,354	5,098	1,108	4,236
Fayette	85,211	57,132	69,778	56,894
Fleming	1,470	5,532	1,348	4,722

County	2020 Biden (D)	Trump (R)	2016 Clinton (D)	Trump (R)
Floyd	3,855	12,211	4,015	11,993
Franklin	12,590	12,876	10,717	11,819
Fulton	791	1,605	774	1,549
Gallatin	813	2,947	749	2,443
Garrard	1,798	6,526	1,453	5,904
Grant	2,200	8,720	1,910	7,268
Graves	3,525	13,144	3,308	12,671
Grayson	2,395	9,445	1,959	8,219
Green	915	4,837	832	4,372
Greenup	4,855	13,038	4,146	11,546
Hancock	1,346	3,132	1,244	2,788
Hardin	17,811	29,678	13,944	26,971
Harlan	1,491	9,363	1,372	9,129
Harrison	2,398	6,331	2,031	5,435
Hart	1,897	6,329	1,730	5,320
Henderson	7,550	12,653	6,707	12,159
Henry	2,119	5,823	1,828	4,944
Hickman	458	1,714	449	1,657
Hopkins	5,421	15,726	4,310	15,277
Jackson	605	5,450	482	4,889
Jefferson	218,944	147,168	190,836	143,768
Jessamine	8,406	17,003	6,144	15,474
Johnson	1,607	8,446	1,250	8,043
Kenton	31,966	47,973	24,214	42,958
Knott	1,410	4,779	1,245	4,357
Knox	2,111	11,010	1,761	9,885
LaRue	1,502	5,685	1,278	4,799
Laurel	4,464	23,221	3,440	20,592
Lawrence	1,237	5,633	1,045	4,816
Lee	459	2,159	444	2,151
Leslie	446	4,318	400	4,015
Letcher	1,729	7,176	1,542	7,293
Lewis	821	4,983	785	4,363
Lincoln	2,247	8,484	1,865	7,338
Livingston	939	4,010	887	3,570
Logan	3,083	9,055	2,755	7,778
Lyon	1,092	3,099	1,045	2,789
Madison	15,549	27,336	11,793	23,431
Magoffin	1,213	4,168	1,172	3,824
Marion	2,719	6,110	2,679	5,122
Marshall	4,042	13,249	3,672	12,322
Martin	402	3,496	363	3,503
Mason	2,361	5,472	1,970	4,944
McCracken	10,582	21,399	9,134	20,774
McCreary	723	5,663	664	5,012
McLean	1,068	3,633	988	3,381
Meade	3,597	10,161	3,026	8,660
Menifee	743	2,302	700	2,010
Mercer	3,029	8,504	2,395	7,740
Metcalfe	973	3,957	976	3,491
Monroe	643	4,577	601	4,278
Montgomery	3,608	8,966	3,158	7,856
Morgan	1,172	4,297	1,006	3,628
Muhlenberg	3,539	10,493	3,272	9,393
Nelson	7,164	15,683	6,434	13,431
Nicholas	954	2,407	787	1,957
Ohio	2,403	8,577	2,080	7,942
Oldham	14,476	22,630	10,268	20,469
Owen	1,096	4,292	1,062	3,745
Owsley	215	1,652	256	1,474
Pendleton	1,321	5,514	1,164	4,604
Perry	2,350	8,118	2,136	8,158
Pike	4,855	20,272	4,280	19,747
Powell	1,281	3,966	1,272	3,513
Pulaski	5,660	25,437	4,208	22,902
Robertson	252	883	222	759
Rockcastle	1,133	6,576	915	5,609
Rowan	3,873	5,990	3,295	5,174
Russell	1,329	7,506	1,093	6,863
Scott	10,550	17,750	7,715	15,052
Shelby	7,520	14,631	6,276	13,196
Simpson	2,678	5,885	2,144	5,077
Spencer	2,522	8,726	1,921	7,196
Taylor	2,958	9,373	2,553	8,320
Todd	1,202	4,060	1,042	3,612
Trigg	1,788	5,486	1,587	4,931
Trimble	1,012	3,226	879	2,771
Union	1,527	4,961	1,331	4,701
Warren	21,595	31,388	16,966	28,673
Washington	1,619	4,456	1,420	4,013
Wayne	1,699	7,428	1,431	6,371
Webster	1,410	4,504	1,240	4,397
Whitley	2,548	12,564	2,067	11,312

County	2020 Biden (D)	Trump (R)	2016 Clinton (D)	Trump (R)
Wolfe	837	2,097	753	1,804
Woodford	6,510	8,348	4,958	7,697
Totals	750,597	1,315,455	628,854	1,202,971

All candidates, 2020: Trump, R, 1,315,455; Biden, D, 750,597; Jorgensen, LB, 26,459; West, Ind., 6,259; Pierce, Ind., 3,498.

Louisiana

Parish	2020 Biden (D)	Trump (R)	2016 Clinton (D)	Trump (R)
Acadia	5,443	22,596	5,638	21,162
Allen	2,108	7,574	2,106	6,867
Ascension	20,397	40,682	16,476	36,143
Assumption	3,833	7,271	3,931	6,714
Avoyelles	4,979	12,028	5,035	11,165
Beauregard	2,542	13,575	2,393	12,238
Bienville	3,066	3,891	3,129	3,756
Bossier	15,658	38,065	12,641	35,474
Caddo	54,993	47,927	53,483	49,006
Calcasieu	25,982	55,062	26,296	54,191
Caldwell	745	3,976	788	3,822
Cameron	324	3,670	323	3,256
Catahoula	1,269	3,541	1,322	3,479
Claiborne	2,731	3,770	2,717	3,585
Concordia	3,177	5,550	3,272	5,477
DeSoto	5,446	9,111	5,165	8,068
East Baton Rouge	115,533	88,396	102,828	84,660
East Carroll	1,900	1,080	1,838	1,059
East Feliciana	4,280	6,064	4,235	5,569
Evangeline	4,158	11,053	4,208	10,360
Franklin	2,658	6,970	2,506	6,514
Grant	1,157	8,117	1,181	7,408
Iberia	11,027	21,249	10,698	20,903
Iberville	8,514	7,893	8,324	7,320
Jackson	2,143	5,394	2,139	5,169
Jefferson	84,438	105,890	73,670	100,398
Jefferson Davis	3,208	11,423	3,080	10,775
Lafayette	39,685	72,518	32,726	68,195
Lafourche	8,668	36,020	8,423	31,959
LaSalle	574	6,348	605	5,836
Lincoln	7,559	11,311	7,107	10,761
Livingston	9,249	54,870	6,950	48,824
Madison	2,654	1,930	2,744	1,927
Morehouse	4,946	6,510	5,155	6,502
Natchitoches	6,896	9,358	7,144	8,968
Orleans	147,729	26,645	133,996	24,292
Ouachita	25,905	42,245	24,428	41,734
Plaquemines	3,413	7,411	3,347	6,900
Pointe Coupee	4,683	7,503	4,764	6,789
Rapides	19,472	38,346	18,322	36,816
Red River	1,644	2,413	1,938	2,391
Richland	3,225	6,607	3,157	6,287
Sabine	1,731	8,776	1,703	7,879
St. Bernard	6,151	11,178	4,960	10,237
St. Charles	9,800	18,233	8,559	16,621
St. Helena	3,346	2,714	3,353	2,497
St. James	6,509	5,954	6,418	5,456
St. John the Baptist	13,581	7,538	12,661	7,569
St. Landry	17,371	23,167	17,209	21,971
St. Martin	8,439	18,203	8,266	16,873
St. Mary	8,054	14,810	8,050	14,359
St. Tammany	37,744	99,665	27,717	90,915
Tangipahoa	18,883	37,799	10,070	33,959
Tensas	1,326	1,195	1,332	1,182
Terrebonne	11,198	34,339	10,665	31,902
Union	2,654	8,406	2,691	7,972
Vermilion	5,009	21,930	4,857	20,063
Vernon	2,897	14,104	2,665	13,471
Washington	5,970	13,307	5,692	12,556
Webster	6,172	11,829	6,260	11,542
West Baton Rouge	6,200	7,684	5,383	6,927
West Carroll	710	4,317	715	3,970
West Feliciana	2,298	3,863	2,248	3,390
Winn	1,543	4,617	1,644	4,608
Totals	855,597	1,255,481	780,154	1,178,638

All candidates, 2020: Trump, R, 1,255,481; Biden, D, 855,597; Jorgensen, LB, 21,636; West, other, 4,894; Carroll, Amer. Solidarity, 2,496; Simmons, other, 1,625; Boddie, other, 1,125; La Riva, Socialism/Liberation, 986; Blankenship, Const., 860; Pierce, other, 749; Hoefling, other, 668; Hammons, Unity, 662; Kennedy, Socialist Workers, 534.

Maine

City	2020 Biden (D)	Trump (R)	2016 Clinton (D)	Trump (R)
Auburn	6,471	5,406	5,296	5,325
Augusta	5,248	4,155	4,396	3,805
Bangor	8,575	5,498	8,155	6,001
Biddeford	7,019	3,703	5,505	3,729
Brunswick	9,708	3,729	7,992	3,647
Cape Elizabeth	5,349	1,462	4,480	1,593
Falmouth	6,147	2,672	4,877	2,633
Gorham	6,460	4,275	4,995	3,945
Kennebunk	5,368	2,682	4,224	2,648
Lewiston	9,578	7,206	8,222	7,336
Portland	33,784	6,483	28,534	6,789
Saco	7,794	4,497	5,902	4,067
Sanford	5,392	5,182	4,447	4,744
Scarborough	9,487	5,217	6,893	4,918
South Portland	12,075	3,781	9,919	3,950
Waterville	4,991	2,619	4,171	2,424
Westbrook	7,309	3,591	5,431	3,573
Windham	5,780	5,276	4,308	4,860
York	6,117	3,352	4,929	3,260
Other	263,168	274,396	225,059	256,346
Totals	425,820	355,182	357,735	335,593

All candidates, 2020: Biden, D, 425,820; Trump, R, 355,182; Jorgensen, LB, 13,997; Hawkins, Green, 8,127; De La Fuente, Alliance, 1,373.

Maryland

County	2020 Biden (D)	Trump (R)	2016 Clinton (D)	Trump (R)
Allegany	6,603	18,558	7,875	21,270
Anne Arundel	115,840	87,967	128,419	122,403
Baltimore	154,044	96,193	218,412	149,477
Calvert	17,137	21,852	18,225	26,176
Caroline	3,572	9,237	4,009	9,368
Carroll	29,135	54,176	26,567	58,215
Cecil	12,476	26,067	13,650	28,868
Charles	35,937	20,289	49,341	25,614
Dorchester	5,295	7,804	6,245	8,413
Frederick	62,152	56,602	56,522	59,522
Garrett	2,573	10,912	2,567	10,776
Harford	43,381	69,468	47,077	77,860
Howard	98,462	40,422	102,597	47,484
Kent	3,579	4,185	4,575	4,876
Montgomery	247,363	59,516	357,837	92,704
Prince George's	287,927	26,227	344,049	32,811
Queen Anne's	8,050	16,703	7,973	16,993
St. Mary's	17,417	25,885	17,534	28,663
Somerset	2,679	3,943	4,196	5,341
Talbot	9,046	9,662	8,653	10,724
Washington	21,178	34,142	21,129	40,998
Wicomico	16,913	20,364	18,050	22,198
Worcester	7,898	15,386	9,753	17,210
City				
Baltimore	147,371	17,731	202,673	25,205
Totals	1,356,028	753,291	1,677,928	943,169

All candidates, 2020: Biden, D, 1,356,028; Trump, R, 753,291; Jorgensen, LB, 21,437; Hawkins, Green, 10,219; Segal, Bread/Roses, 6,506.

Massachusetts

City	2020 Biden (D)	Trump (R)	2016 Clinton (D)	Trump (R)
Arlington	23,024	4,313	20,539	4,652
Barnstable	15,685	10,824	13,005	11,195
Boston	225,368	42,707	221,093	38,087
Brockton	28,087	8,402	25,593	8,801
Brookline	26,046	3,322	24,583	3,175
Cambridge	45,426	3,248	46,563	3,323
Fall River	17,379	13,409	17,467	10,850
Framingham	23,613	7,705	20,520	7,063
Haverhill	17,880	12,071	15,407	12,050
Lowell	24,492	12,054	23,555	10,584
Lynn	24,123	10,191	22,164	9,311
Medford	22,717	7,412	20,690	7,671
New Bedford	20,805	12,781	20,812	10,327
Newton	39,428	8,165	36,463	7,764
Peabody	16,826	12,688	14,395	12,036
Plymouth	20,780	14,349	15,602	14,309
Quincy	29,956	14,224	25,477	13,321
Somerville	35,392	4,153	33,740	4,128
Springfield	38,849	13,896	40,341	11,231
Waltham	19,847	7,624	17,355	7,592
Weymouth	19,254	12,293	15,398	11,983
Worcester	48,030	21,018	43,084	17,732
Other	1,519,501	880,314	1,240,325	853,265
Totals	2,302,508	1,137,747	1,995,196	1,090,893

All candidates, 2020: Biden, D, 2,302,508; Trump, R, 1,137,747; Jorgensen, LB, 45,472; Hawkins, Green, 18,011.

Michigan

County	2020 Biden (D)	Trump (R)	2016 Clinton (D)	Trump (R)
Alcona	2,142	4,848	1,732	4,201
Alger	2,053	3,014	1,663	2,585
Allegan	24,447	41,381	18,050	34,183
Alpena	6,000	10,686	4,877	9,090
Antrim	7,289	9,783	4,448	8,469
Arenac	2,773	5,928	2,384	4,950
Baraga	1,475	2,512	1,156	2,158
Barry	11,804	23,473	9,114	19,202
Bay	21,718	30,919	21,642	28,328
Benzie	5,480	6,600	4,108	5,539
Berrien	37,438	43,518	29,495	38,647
Branch	6,161	14,066	5,061	11,786
Calhoun	28,417	35,900	24,157	31,494
Cass	9,122	16,686	7,270	14,243
Charlevoix	6,939	9,841	5,137	8,674
Cheboygan	5,435	10,171	4,302	8,683
Chippewa	6,651	10,682	5,379	9,122
Clare	5,200	10,860	4,249	8,505
Clinton	21,963	25,095	16,492	21,636
Crawford	2,612	4,955	2,110	4,354
Delta	7,605	13,206	6,436	11,121
Dickinson	4,569	8,469	3,923	8,580
Eaton	31,297	31,797	24,938	27,609
Emmet	9,662	12,135	6,972	10,616
Genesee	120,082	99,199	102,751	84,175
Gladwin	4,524	9,893	3,794	8,124
Gogebic	3,573	4,600	2,925	4,018
Grand Traverse	28,682	30,502	20,965	27,413
Gratiot	6,693	12,104	5,666	9,880
Hillsdale	5,883	17,037	4,799	14,095
Houghton	7,755	10,380	6,018	8,475
Huron	5,349	11,949	4,579	10,692
Ingham	94,221	47,640	79,110	43,868
Ionia	10,899	20,655	8,352	16,635
Iosco	5,371	9,760	4,345	8,345
Iron	2,493	4,216	2,004	3,675
Isabella	14,072	14,815	11,404	12,338
Jackson	32,004	47,381	25,795	39,793
Kalamazoo	83,674	56,823	67,148	51,034
Kalkaska	3,003	7,436	2,280	6,116
Kent	186,753	165,318	138,683	148,180
Keweenaw	672	862	527	814
Lake	2,288	3,946	1,939	3,159
Lapeer	16,368	35,480	12,734	30,037
Leelanau	8,793	7,915	6,774	7,239
Lenawee	20,916	31,539	16,750	26,430
Livingston	48,218	76,980	34,384	65,680
Luce	842	2,109	681	1,756
Mackinac	2,589	4,258	2,085	3,744
Macomb	225,561	264,535	176,317	224,665
Manistee	6,107	8,321	4,979	6,915
Marquette	20,465	16,288	16,042	14,646
Mason	6,802	10,207	5,281	8,505
Mecosta	7,373	13,265	5,827	10,305
Menominee	4,314	8,120	3,539	6,702
Midland	20,513	27,706	15,635	23,846
Missaukee	1,967	6,648	1,565	5,386
Monroe	32,975	52,710	26,863	43,261
Montcalm	9,703	21,815	7,874	16,907
Montmorency	1,628	4,171	1,287	3,498
Muskegon	46,389	46,408	37,304	36,127
Newaygo	7,874	18,864	6,212	15,173
Oakland	433,982	325,916	343,070	289,203
Oceana	4,944	8,892	3,973	7,228
Ogemaw	3,475	8,253	3,030	6,827
Ontonagon	1,391	2,358	1,176	2,066
Osceola	3,214	8,928	2,705	7,336
Oscoda	1,342	3,466	1,044	2,843
Otsego	4,743	9,779	3,556	8,266
Ottawa	64,566	100,511	44,973	88,467
Presque Isle	2,912	5,343	2,400	4,488
Roscommon	5,166	9,470	4,287	8,141
Saginaw	51,068	50,784	44,396	45,469
St. Clair	31,363	59,184	24,553	49,051
St. Joseph	9,262	18,128	7,526	14,884
Sanilac	5,966	16,194	4,873	13,446
Schoolcraft	1,589	3,090	1,369	2,556
Shiawassee	15,371	23,154	12,546	19,230
Tuscola	8,713	20,310	7,429	17,102
Van Buren	16,800	21,591	13,258	17,890
Washtenaw	157,130	56,241	128,483	50,631
Wayne	587,074	264,149	519,444	228,993
Wexford	5,838	12,102	4,436	10,000
Totals	2,791,549	2,646,423	2,268,839	2,279,543

All candidates, 2020: Biden, D, 2,791,549; Trump, R, 2,646,423; Jorgensen, LB, 60,343; Hawkins, Green, 13,691; Blankenship, U.S. Taxpayers, 7,240; De La Fuente, Natural Law, 2,990.

Minnesota

County	2020 Biden (D)	Trump (R)	2016 Clinton (D)	Trump (R)
Aitkin	3,604	6,256	3,134	5,516
Anoka	99,358	103,763	75,500	93,339
Becker	6,560	12,415	5,208	10,880
Beltrami	11,423	12,181	8,688	10,783
Benton	7,278	14,373	5,640	12,872
Big Stone	1,052	1,862	921	1,608
Blue Earth	18,136	16,620	14,428	15,667
Brown	4,745	9,548	3,763	8,708
Carlton	10,094	9,787	8,460	8,160
Carver	30,736	33,972	21,508	29,056
Cass	3,248	5,559	4,949	9,982
Chippewa	2,227	4,247	1,978	3,764
Chisago	11,771	21,879	9,278	18,441
Clay	16,346	15,031	12,971	13,543
Clearwater	1,258	3,371	1,100	2,925
Cook	2,494	1,202	1,912	1,156
Cottonwood	1,816	4,060	1,678	3,679
Crow Wing	13,611	25,301	10,982	22,287
Dakota	144,885	108,834	110,483	99,583
Dodge	4,074	7,774	3,102	6,527
Douglas	7,762	15,395	6,227	13,966
Faribault	2,529	5,186	2,153	4,659
Fillmore	4,550	7,284	3,872	6,271
Freeborn	6,715	8,917	6,041	8,808
Goodhue	11,796	16,048	9,446	14,041
Grant	1,299	2,267	1,105	2,063
Hennepin	525,710	203,663	429,288	191,770
Houston	4,851	6,332	4,145	5,616
Hubbard	4,458	8,194	3,423	7,261
Isanti	7,008	16,316	5,657	13,635
Itasca	10,784	15,232	9,015	12,920
Jackson	1,744	3,945	1,492	3,609
Kanabec	2,773	6,276	2,327	5,230
Kandiyohi	8,434	14,433	7,266	12,785
Kittson	1,005	1,544	823	1,349
Koochiching	2,659	4,129	2,306	3,569
Lac Qui Parle	1,445	2,527	1,305	2,293
Lake	3,646	3,392	3,077	2,932
Lake of the Woods	671	1,699	553	1,540
Le Sueur	5,667	10,769	4,623	9,182
Lincoln	937	2,120	860	1,931
Lyon	4,624	7,975	3,825	7,256
Mahnomen	1,110	1,142	930	991
Marshall	1,293	3,716	1,225	3,208
Martin	3,304	7,476	2,733	7,062
McLeod	6,410	13,982	4,978	12,155
Meeker	3,865	9,351	3,191	8,104
Mille Lacs	3,071	9,089	3,710	8,340
Morrison	4,365	14,815	3,637	12,925
Mower	7,537	7,692	7,437	8,823
Murray	1,449	3,362	1,295	2,974
Nicollet	9,612	9,009	7,886	8,437
Nobles	2,928	5,598	2,733	5,299
Norman	1,400	1,951	1,264	1,699
Olmsted	49,397	39,618	36,268	35,668
Otter Tail	11,916	23,753	9,340	20,939
Pennington	2,567	4,532	2,147	4,000
Pine	5,416	10,256	4,580	8,191
Pipestone	1,305	3,552	1,127	3,338
Polk	5,435	9,857	4,712	8,979
Pope	2,478	4,413	2,106	3,793
Ramsey	211,211	77,271	177,738	70,894
Red Lake	689	1,450	540	1,141
Redwood	2,357	5,774	1,887	5,137
Renville	2,497	5,465	2,117	4,890
Rice	17,386	17,455	14,437	15,429
Rock	1,554	3,578	1,373	3,091
Roseau	2,180	6,053	1,856	5,451
St. Louis	67,579	49,052	57,771	44,630
Scott	40,006	45,840	28,502	39,948
Sherburne	14,249	32,951	13,293	31,053
Sibley	2,416	5,863	1,954	5,193
Stearns	31,433	50,232	25,576	47,617
Steele	7,794	12,472	6,241	11,198
Stevens	1,921	3,045	2,116	2,799
Swift	1,784	3,316	1,686	2,963
Todd	3,284	9,752	2,783	8,485
Traverse	662	1,173	630	1,049
Wabasha	4,691	8,149	3,866	6,989
Wadena	2,021	5,517	1,684	4,837
Waseca	3,493	6,621	2,838	5,967
Washington	89,036	73,693	67,086	64,428
Watonwan	1,985	3,100	1,814	2,768
Wilkin	1,027	2,333	893	2,129
Winona	13,210	13,133	11,366	12,122
Wright	27,763	51,076	20,334	43,274
Yellow Medicine	1,685	3,734	1,524	3,382
Totals	**1,694,554**	**1,462,940**	**1,367,716**	**1,322,951**

All candidates, 2020: Biden, D, 1,694,554; Trump, R, 1,462,940; Jorgensen, LB, 34,226; Hawkins, Green, 9,806; West, Ind., 7,820; Pierce, Ind., 5,571; De La Fuente, Alliance, 5,523; La Riva, Socialism/Liberation, 1,241; Kennedy, Socialist Workers, 682.

Mississippi

County	2020 Biden (D)	Trump (R)	2016 Clinton (D)	Trump (R)
Adams	6,914	5,222	7,757	5,874
Alcorn	2,741	12,689	2,684	11,819
Amite	2,114	3,781	2,697	4,289
Attala	2,644	4,177	3,242	4,897
Benton	1,661	2,553	1,719	2,251
Bolivar	7,203	4,260	9,046	4,590
Calhoun	1,878	4,592	1,910	4,390
Carroll	1,705	3,887	1,680	3,799
Chickasaw	2,904	3,488	3,649	4,127
Choctaw	1,170	2,971	1,218	2,788
Claiborne	3,676	589	3,708	540
Clarke	2,815	5,372	2,585	5,137
Clay	5,728	4,147	5,722	4,150
Coahoma	5,189	1,846	6,378	2,426
Copiah	5,227	5,407	6,741	6,103
Covington	2,658	5,083	3,276	5,435
DeSoto	23,237	38,257	20,591	43,089
Forrest	10,603	15,326	11,716	15,461
Franklin	1,476	2,894	1,502	2,721
George	1,208	9,602	1,027	8,696
Greene	952	4,740	974	4,335
Grenada	2,866	4,889	4,424	5,970
Hancock	3,095	13,999	3,344	13,811
Harrison	18,499	41,281	21,169	40,354
Hinds	59,192	21,242	67,594	25,275
Holmes	5,182	1,196	6,689	1,309
Humphreys	2,994	1,115	3,071	1,151
Issaquena	355	308	395	298
Itawamba	1,036	8,656	1,117	8,470
Jackson	12,061	32,563	14,657	33,629
Jasper	4,287	4,256	4,368	4,038
Jefferson	3,325	529	3,337	490
Jefferson Davis	3,557	2,513	3,720	2,466
Jones	7,017	19,130	7,791	20,133
Kemper	2,275	1,609	2,827	1,778
Lafayette	6,904	9,878	7,969	10,872
Lamar	5,821	17,700	5,190	18,751
Lauderdale	9,885	15,791	11,269	17,741
Lawrence	2,240	4,254	2,195	4,091
Leake	3,358	4,973	3,584	4,782
Lee	9,911	21,297	10,029	22,220
Leflore	5,444	2,623	7,787	3,212
Lincoln	3,978	10,107	4,458	10,550
Lowndes	10,010	11,918	11,819	13,271
Madison	18,931	26,188	20,343	28,265
Marion	3,421	7,783	3,677	7,836
Marshall	6,283	6,591	8,023	6,587
Monroe	4,565	9,677	5,524	10,167
Montgomery	1,507	2,236	2,115	2,818
Neshoba	3,247	8,311	2,715	7,679
Newton	2,542	6,037	2,756	6,548
Noxubee	2,867	1,057	4,347	1,200
Oktibbeha	8,243	7,617	8,859	8,576
Panola	5,798	6,756	7,431	7,449
Pearl River	0	0	3,604	17,782
Perry	1,340	4,426	1,220	4,135
Pike	7,328	7,106	8,043	8,009
Pontotoc	2,580	11,425	2,386	10,336

County	2020 Biden (D)	Trump (R)	2016 Clinton (D)	Trump (R)
Prentiss	1,808	7,596	2,067	7,648
Quitman	2,138	1,020	2,312	1,001
Rankin	13,496	39,025	14,110	47,178
Scott	3,575	5,688	4,268	6,122
Sharkey	1,132	575	1,479	692
Simpson	3,384	6,552	3,874	7,393
Smith	1,518	5,697	1,617	5,928
Stone	1,208	5,239	1,573	5,306
Sunflower	6,631	2,755	6,725	2,794
Tallahatchie	3,105	2,488	3,337	2,462
Tate	3,469	7,594	3,926	7,495
Tippah	1,583	7,119	1,842	7,240
Tishomingo	839	6,951	999	7,166
Tunica	2,525	912	2,667	853
Union	2,145	10,289	2,012	9,235
Walthall	2,236	3,426	2,790	4,056
Warren	7,625	8,481	9,284	9,767
Washington	6,218	4,114	11,380	5,244
Wayne	3,592	6,264	3,524	5,990
Webster	1,024	4,255	1,019	3,976
Wilkinson	2,730	1,311	2,857	1,318
Winston	4,009	5,084	3,850	4,910
Yalobusha	2,767	3,658	2,582	3,376
Yazoo	4,533	4,370	5,369	4,598
Totals	428,937	648,383	485,131	700,714

All candidates, 2020: Trump, R, 648,383; Biden, D, 428,937; Jorgensen, LB, 7,093; West, Ind., 3,300; Hawkins, Green, 1,303; Collins, Ind., 1,146; Blankenship, Amer. Const., 1,135; Carroll, Amer. Solidarity, 1,036; Pierce, Ind., 569.

Missouri

County	2020 Biden (D)	Trump (R)	2016 Clinton (D)	Trump (R)
Adair	3,705	6,391	3,500	6,030
Andrew	2,351	7,256	2,045	6,665
Atchison	564	2,199	541	2,060
Audrain	2,703	7,727	2,570	6,981
Barry	2,948	12,425	2,710	11,428
Barton	844	5,168	795	4,959
Bates	1,672	6,595	1,618	6,001
Benton	2,179	8,106	2,025	7,213
Bollinger	749	5,162	705	4,827
Boone	49,999	38,596	41,125	36,200
Buchanan	13,445	22,450	12,013	21,320
Butler	3,301	14,599	3,036	13,650
Caldwell	897	3,725	838	3,232
Callaway	5,868	14,812	4,989	13,057
Camden	5,640	18,825	4,768	16,944
Cape Girardeau	10,738	28,873	8,492	27,017
Carroll	785	3,706	745	3,480
Carter	418	2,451	436	2,324
Cass	19,035	37,172	14,846	33,098
Cedar	1,143	5,786	1,011	5,021
Chariton	916	3,109	888	2,950
Christian	11,126	34,904	8,508	30,946
Clark	678	2,672	724	2,458
Clay	59,519	64,583	45,304	57,476
Clinton	2,894	7,789	2,572	7,067
Cole	12,687	26,066	10,913	24,616
Cooper	2,249	6,272	1,932	5,624
Crawford	2,113	8,725	1,824	7,724
Dade	656	3,414	637	3,184
Dallas	1,380	6,620	1,272	5,895
Daviess	740	3,077	730	2,767
DeKalb	930	3,827	824	3,540
Dent	1,056	5,987	978	5,600
Douglas	1,012	5,896	984	5,486
Dunklin	2,200	8,135	2,360	8,026
Franklin	14,561	38,034	12,341	35,430
Gasconade	1,601	6,222	1,520	5,670
Gentry	613	2,580	605	2,304
Greene	53,307	81,312	42,728	78,035
Grundy	799	3,585	780	3,462
Harrison	597	3,198	574	2,965
Henry	2,615	8,019	2,357	7,075
Hickory	1,054	3,965	1,016	3,542

County	2020 Biden (D)	Trump (R)	2016 Clinton (D)	Trump (R)
Holt	338	1,976	347	1,926
Howard	1,412	3,552	1,283	3,277
Howell	3,214	15,174	2,881	13,893
Iron	945	3,596	933	3,173
Jackson	198,031	125,897	71,237	91,557
Jasper	13,539	37,714	10,572	35,070
Jefferson	37,507	77,021	31,568	69,036
Johnson	6,961	15,468	5,930	13,719
Knox	340	1,486	379	1,416
Laclede	2,779	13,755	2,553	12,881
Lafayette	4,470	12,262	4,053	10,988
Lawrence	3,214	14,421	2,901	13,089
Lewis	984	3,541	934	3,344
Lincoln	6,553	21,702	5,575	18,159
Linn	1,274	4,344	1,240	4,088
Livingston	1,409	5,266	1,265	4,879
Macon	1,661	6,075	1,548	5,798
Madison	1,017	4,581	1,005	4,102
Maries	814	3,890	794	3,561
Marion	3,201	9,910	2,994	9,419
McDonald	1,437	7,465	1,329	6,599
Mercer	222	1,541	216	1,486
Miller	2,038	10,175	1,750	9,285
Mississippi	1,178	3,537	1,458	3,600
Moniteau	1,307	5,738	1,237	5,347
Monroe	931	3,466	853	3,159
Montgomery	1,206	4,457	1,119	4,127
Morgan	1,924	7,439	1,768	6,760
New Madrid	1,748	5,447	1,933	5,270
Newton	5,793	22,090	4,990	20,553
Nodaway	2,849	6,855	2,529	6,380
Oregon	823	3,847	865	3,671
Osage	1,031	6,341	998	5,856
Ozark	752	4,064	724	3,639
Pemiscot	1,556	4,116	1,947	3,964
Perry	1,661	7,634	1,520	6,908
Pettis	4,776	13,835	4,324	12,810
Phelps	5,619	13,438	4,766	12,709
Pike	1,717	5,856	1,806	5,274
Platte	28,111	29,251	20,057	25,933
Polk	2,883	11,849	2,631	10,438
Pulaski	3,735	10,326	2,922	9,876
Putnam	361	1,984	353	1,936
Ralls	1,205	4,396	1,138	3,969
Randolph	2,485	8,018	2,283	7,529
Ray	3,107	8,328	3,090	7,104
Reynolds	529	2,733	540	2,406
Ripley	833	4,838	830	4,522
St. Charles	89,346	128,193	68,626	121,650
St. Clair	988	3,930	936	3,501
St. Francois	7,044	20,506	6,250	17,468
St. Louis Co.	322,802	196,808	286,704	202,434
Ste. Genevieve	2,713	6,627	2,542	5,496
Saline	2,903	6,447	2,789	5,977
Schuyler	373	1,606	354	1,505
Scotland	387	1,560	365	1,525
Scott	3,753	13,769	3,575	13,168
Shannon	706	3,164	776	2,966
Shelby	592	2,699	606	2,524
Stoddard	1,814	11,460	1,876	11,079
Stone	3,486	14,716	2,887	13,158
Sullivan	478	1,974	526	1,884
Taney	5,325	20,426	4,373	18,276
Texas	1,716	9,478	1,728	8,875
Vernon	1,902	7,135	1,707	6,533
Warren	4,769	13,222	3,915	11,111
Washington	1,804	8,046	1,926	7,048
Wayne	844	4,984	948	4,658
Webster	3,572	14,874	3,177	12,840
Worth	215	877	195	808
Wright	1,167	7,452	1,170	6,707
City				
Kansas City	106,470	26,166	97,735	24,654
St. Louis	108,385	21,185	104,235	20,832
Totals	1,242,851	1,711,848	1,071,068	1,594,511

All candidates, 2020: Trump, R, 1,711,848; Biden, D, 1,242,851; Jorgensen, LB, 40,932; Hawkins, Green, 8,219; Blankenship, Const., 3,894.

Montana

County	2020 Biden (D)	Trump (R)	2016 Clinton (D)	Trump (R)
Beaverhead	1,608	3,923	1,143	3,353
Big Horn	1,029	1,011	2,094	1,853
Blaine	1,589	1,469	1,202	1,268
Broadwater	830	3,139	573	2,348
Carbon	2,412	4,424	1,828	3,748
Carter	74	775	70	678
Cascade	15,384	23,199	12,175	19,632
Chouteau	988	1,888	732	1,679
Custer	1,510	4,204	1,176	3,657
Daniels	195	799	168	730
Dawson	962	3,758	787	3,320
Deer Lodge	2,562	2,184	2,058	1,763
Fallon	172	1,375	154	1,279
Fergus	1,491	4,830	1,202	4,269
Flathead	20,238	38,233	13,293	30,240
Gallatin	35,159	28,423	24,246	23,802
Garfield	41	764	34	653
Glacier	3,603	1,882	3,121	1,620
Golden Valley	78	414	71	365
Granite	638	1,419	472	1,192
Hill	2,972	3,952	2,371	3,478
Jefferson	2,625	5,345	1,998	4,177
Judith Basin	275	1,040	235	872
Lake	6,911	9,319	4,776	7,530
Lewis and Clark	19,741	21,407	14,478	16,895
Liberty	249	821	206	698
Lincoln	2,812	8,516	2,041	6,729
Madison	1,770	4,186	1,180	3,297
McCone	155	956	154	862
Meagher	258	833	193	729
Mineral	234	505	519	1,330
Missoula	41,737	24,488	31,543	22,250
Musselshell	413	2,423	332	1,967
Park	5,277	6,022	3,595	4,980
Petroleum	39	298	30	278
Phillips	414	1,936	318	1,723
Pondera	903	2,030	738	1,799
Powder River	154	970	127	884
Powell	752	2,347	551	2,029
Prairie	126	603	100	556
Ravalli	8,757	19,105	6,223	14,810
Richland	874	4,792	671	3,908
Roosevelt	1,902	1,991	1,560	1,797
Rosebud	1,199	2,485	987	2,253
Sanders	1,824	5,664	1,218	4,286
Sheridan	574	1,402	477	1,241
Silver Bow	10,442	7,790	8,619	6,376
Stillwater	1,155	4,430	908	3,661
Sweet Grass	549	1,840	402	1,595
Teton	1,007	2,608	808	2,170
Toole	467	1,596	402	1,497
Treasure	78	373	59	351
Valley	1,030	3,135	886	2,698
Wheatland	225	823	179	702
Wibaux	77	516	55	463
Yellowstone	28,523	45,564	22,171	40,920
Totals	**237,063**	**330,222**	**177,709**	**279,240**

All candidates, 2020: Trump, R, 330,222; Biden, D, 237,063; Jorgensen, LB, 14,359.

Nebraska

County	2020 Biden (D)	Trump (R)	2016 Clinton (D)	Trump (R)
Adams	4,171	9,993	3,302	9,287
Antelope	449	3,076	383	2,732
Arthur	21	260	17	244
Banner	43	362	19	357
Blaine	35	280	30	276
Boone	499	2,653	414	2,299
Box Butte	1,037	3,920	965	3,617
Boyd	135	1,006	128	983
Brown	190	1,468	153	1,385
Buffalo	6,292	16,473	4,763	14,569
Burt	1,061	2,560	930	2,367
Butler	869	3,526	691	3,079
Cass	4,364	9,296	3,484	8,452
Cedar	725	4,174	571	3,532
Chase	226	1,714	171	1,648
Cherry	367	2,838	317	2,623
Cheyenne	851	3,782	711	3,665
Clay	631	2,840	477	2,422
Colfax	1,024	2,635	859	2,171
Cuming	862	3,476	719	3,122
Custer	768	4,996	641	4,695
Dakota	2,696	3,869	2,314	3,616
Dawes	1,076	2,919	801	2,632
Dawson	2,484	6,487	2,136	5,984
Deuel	141	871	120	809
Dixon	651	2,335	556	2,041
Dodge	5,526	10,963	4,544	9,933
Douglas	141,140	112,354	113,798	108,077
Dundy	105	883	89	823
Fillmore	691	2,333	613	2,130
Franklin	276	1,434	250	1,347
Frontier	185	1,207	161	1,110
Furnas	397	2,155	304	1,921
Gage	3,373	7,397	2,935	6,380
Garden	161	1,016	153	869
Garfield	133	925	121	821
Gosper	215	893	166	794
Grant	20	373	20	367
Greeley	228	1,015	210	912
Hall	7,551	15,950	6,282	14,408
Hamilton	1,117	4,297	878	3,783
Harlan	282	1,615	254	1,496
Hayes	34	492	30	472
Hitchcock	174	1,260	161	1,232
Holt	678	4,717	531	4,354
Hooker	59	376	40	355
Howard	648	2,786	544	2,284
Jefferson	1,009	2,593	837	2,399
Johnson	646	1,517	563	1,355
Kearney	699	2,812	550	2,531
Keith	760	3,525	571	3,235
Keya Paha	49	476	40	460
Kimball	267	1,553	230	1,330
Knox	903	3,719	720	3,188
Lancaster	80,513	68,321	61,898	61,588
Lincoln	3,655	12,887	2,913	12,164
Logan	38	407	32	400
Loup	75	370	48	323
Madison	3,393	11,678	2,711	10,628
McPherson	17	274	14	257
Merrick	740	3,407	602	2,926
Morrill	386	2,113	284	1,802
Nance	358	1,430	281	1,261
Nemaha	911	2,396	785	2,116
Nuckolls	409	1,850	353	1,726
Otoe	2,481	5,609	2,025	4,860
Pawnee	322	1,069	279	974
Perkins	199	1,316	161	1,217
Phelps	749	4,131	572	3,849
Pierce	480	3,462	382	3,052
Platte	3,208	11,827	2,646	10,965
Polk	527	2,286	413	2,028
Red Willow	811	4,525	645	4,258
Richardson	981	2,981	818	2,769
Rock	84	741	70	687
Saline	1,737	3,458	1,733	3,004
Sarpy	40,020	49,796	28,033	45,143
Saunders	3,318	9,036	2,523	7,555
Scotts Bluff	4,133	10,810	3,207	10,076
Seward	2,430	6,424	1,875	5,454
Sheridan	340	2,292	287	2,211
Sherman	341	1,306	340	1,150
Sioux	72	640	81	616
Stanton	532	2,561	417	2,187
Thayer	619	2,285	499	2,051
Thomas	45	377	30	344
Thurston	1,107	1,164	919	1,043
Valley	410	1,892	339	1,780
Washington	3,547	8,533	2,623	7,424
Wayne	1,022	3,055	835	2,693
Webster	335	1,511	306	1,330

County	2020 Biden (D)	2020 Trump (R)	2016 Clinton (D)	2016 Trump (R)
Wheeler	59	437	62	377
York	1,619	5,296	1,186	4,700
Totals	**361,017**	**542,398**	**284,494**	**495,961**

All candidates, 2020: Trump, R, 542,398; Biden, D, 361,017; Jorgensen, LB, 19,402.

Nevada

County	2020 Biden (D)	2020 Trump (R)	2016 Clinton (D)	2016 Trump (R)
Churchill	2,966	9,088	2,210	7,830
Clark	465,835	385,037	402,227	320,057
Douglas	11,390	21,237	8,454	17,415
Elko	4,375	16,048	3,401	13,551
Esmeralda	72	389	65	329
Eureka	92	833	74	723
Humboldt	1,608	5,531	1,386	4,521
Lander	478	2,110	403	1,828
Lincoln	318	1,949	285	1,671
Lyon	8,264	20,302	6,146	16,005
Mineral	759	1,343	637	1,179
Nye	6,950	16,575	5,094	13,324
Pershing	525	1,668	430	1,403
Storey	899	1,905	752	1,616
Washoe	124,752	113,881	97,379	94,758
White Pine	836	3,238	707	2,723
City				
Carson City	12,485	15,771	9,610	13,125
Totals	**642,604**	**616,905**	**539,260**	**512,058**

All candidates, 2020: Biden, D, 642,604; Trump, R, 616,905; Jorgensen, LB, 12,814; None of these candidates, 12,308; Blankenship, Ind. Amer., 2,772.

New Hampshire

City	2020 Biden (D)	2020 Trump (R)	2016 Clinton (D)	2016 Trump (R)
Bedford	7,521	7,052	5,851	6,816
Concord	15,341	7,836	12,984	7,812
Derry	8,110	9,316	6,825	9,237
Dover	12,508	6,331	10,118	6,015
Durham	5,970	1,712	6,501	2,450
Exeter	6,820	3,321	5,514	3,286
Goffstown	4,967	5,040	4,146	5,009
Hanover	6,210	841	6,561	926
Hudson	6,632	7,744	5,306	7,220
Keene	8,950	3,758	7,932	3,831
Londonderry	7,738	7,905	5,968	7,338
Manchester	28,584	21,833	24,941	21,554
Merrimack	8,725	7,669	6,405	7,397
Nashua	26,316	17,699	22,690	17,476
Portsmouth	10,643	3,829	8,911	3,632
Rochester	8,132	8,367	6,267	7,789
Salem	7,638	9,969	6,068	9,312
Other	238,825	232,994	193,828	218,279
Totals	**419,630**	**363,216**	**346,816**	**345,379**

All candidates, 2020: Biden, D, 419,630; Trump, R, 363,216; Jorgensen, LB, 12,946.

New Jersey

County	2020 Biden (D)	2020 Trump (R)	2016 Clinton (D)	2016 Trump (R)
Atlantic	61,032	51,884	60,924	52,690
Bergen	224,702	144,224	231,211	175,529
Burlington	113,527	62,520	121,725	89,272
Camden	105,963	40,258	146,717	72,631
Cape May	21,159	27,756	18,750	28,446
Cumberland	11,911	6,744	27,771	24,453
Essex	206,048	56,149	240,837	63,176
Gloucester	76,925	69,839	66,870	67,544
Hudson	130,018	39,751	163,917	49,043
Hunterdon	27,539	24,961	28,898	38,712
Mercer	98,338	38,339	104,775	46,193
Middlesex	141,137	70,095	193,044	122,953
Monmouth	104,227	83,326	137,181	166,723
Morris	67,026	48,466	115,249	126,071
Ocean	99,722	166,644	87,150	179,079
Passaic	67,754	42,881	116,759	72,902
Salem	11,613	13,992	11,904	16,381
Somerset	87,411	51,400	85,689	65,505
Sussex	12,594	15,238	24,212	46,658
Union	88,984	32,422	147,414	68,114
Warren	16,038	18,232	17,281	29,858
Totals	**1,773,668**	**1,105,131**	**2,148,278**	**1,601,933**

All candidates, 2020: Biden, D, 1,773,668; Trump, R, 1,105,131; Jorgensen, LB, 15,907; Hawkins, Green, 7,586; Hammons, Unity, 1,806; Blankenship, Const., 1,629; La Riva, Socialism/Liberation, 1,588; De La Fuente, Alliance, 1,423.

New Mexico

County	2020 Biden (D)	2020 Trump (R)	2016 Clinton (D)	2016 Trump (R)
Bernalillo	192,042	115,674	143,417	94,698
Catron	580	1,672	427	1,464
Chaves	6,376	15,641	5,534	12,872
Cibola	4,668	3,946	3,741	3,195
Colfax	2,611	3,271	2,129	2,585
Curry	4,179	10,303	3,121	9,035
De Baca	230	653	193	620
Doña Ana	47,202	32,484	37,947	25,374
Eddy	5,343	17,356	5,033	13,147
Grant	7,538	6,528	6,276	5,288
Guadalupe	1,229	912	970	595
Harding	179	319	156	311
Hidalgo	812	1,105	784	910
Lea	3,990	16,370	3,930	12,495
Lincoln	3,139	6,872	2,331	5,896
Los Alamos	7,363	4,230	5,562	3,359
Luna	3,563	4,406	3,195	3,478
McKinley	17,684	7,597	13,576	5,104
Mora	1,744	902	1,536	665
Otero	8,235	14,343	6,124	11,887
Quay	1,165	2,623	1,017	2,212
Rio Arriba	10,896	5,390	9,592	3,599
Roosevelt	1,774	4,612	1,454	3,884
San Juan	17,991	32,807	12,865	27,946
San Miguel	7,822	3,406	7,285	2,313
Sandoval	39,895	33,836	27,707	25,905
Santa Fe	61,121	18,101	50,793	14,332
Sierra	2,213	3,516	1,612	3,010
Socorro	3,686	3,242	3,313	2,616
Taos	7,966	2,977	10,668	2,727
Torrance	2,314	4,732	1,785	3,714
Union	381	1,381	320	1,216
Valencia	14,051	17,245	10,841	13,215
Totals	**489,982**	**398,452**	**385,234**	**319,667**

All candidates, 2020: Biden, D, 489,982; Trump, R, 398,452; Jorgensen, LB, 12,318; Hawkins, Green, 4,302; Tittle, Const., 1,766; La Riva, Socialism/Liberation, 1,603.

New York

County	2020 Biden (D)	2020 Trump (R)	2016 Clinton (D)	2016 Trump (R)
Albany	73,189	45,570	83,071	47,808
Allegany	4,188	12,670	4,882	12,525
Bronx[1]	271,835	55,849	353,646	37,797
Broome	32,209	38,296	39,212	40,943
Cattaraugus	9,142	20,295	9,497	19,692
Cayuga	11,993	17,639	13,522	17,384
Chautauqua	16,200	31,247	19,091	31,594
Chemung	11,573	19,388	13,757	20,097
Chenango	5,126	11,736	6,775	11,921
Clinton	12,690	14,354	15,059	14,449
Columbia	14,148	12,883	15,284	13,756
Cortland	6,829	9,484	8,771	9,900
Delaware	6,420	11,952	6,627	11,942
Dutchess	56,395	59,415	62,261	61,797
Erie	174,286	204,516	215,456	188,303
Essex	6,970	7,953	7,762	7,958
Franklin	6,586	8,530	7,297	8,221
Fulton	4,542	12,983	6,496	13,462
Genesee	7,048	17,340	7,650	16,915
Greene	7,675	12,722	7,405	13,073
Hamilton	863	1,914	949	2,064
Herkimer	7,282	17,038	8,083	16,699
Jefferson	12,053	22,779	13,809	21,763
Kings (Brooklyn)[1]	514,133	174,731	640,553	141,044
Lewis	2,768	7,931	3,146	7,400
Livingston	9,150	16,575	10,697	17,290
Madison	10,417	16,553	11,667	15,936
Monroe	146,180	122,504	188,592	136,582
Montgomery	5,746	11,500	6,595	11,301
Nassau	280,115	286,633	332,154	292,025

County	2020 Biden (D)	Trump (R)	2016 Clinton (D)	Trump (R)
New York (Manhattan)[1]	377,605	65,001	579,013	64,930
Niagara	34,809	51,355	35,559	51,961
Oneida	26,205	48,213	33,743	51,437
Onondaga	93,850	78,994	112,337	83,649
Ontario	20,779	25,757	22,233	26,029
Orange	61,223	74,703	68,278	76,645
Orleans	4,082	11,173	4,470	10,936
Oswego	14,677	28,914	17,095	27,688
Otsego	9,138	12,682	10,451	13,308
Putnam	17,106	25,899	19,366	27,024
Queens[1]	412,393	181,225	517,220	149,341
Rensselaer	29,997	33,210	32,717	33,726
Richmond (Staten Island)[1]	67,223	110,094	74,143	101,437
Rockland	50,926	63,830	69,342	60,911
St. Lawrence	12,976	21,862	16,488	19,942
Saratoga	52,459	60,092	50,913	54,575
Schenectady	31,685	27,544	33,747	28,953
Schoharie	4,006	9,010	4,240	8,831
Schuyler	2,958	5,181	3,091	5,050
Seneca	5,076	7,582	5,697	7,236
Steuben	11,299	26,781	12,526	26,831
Suffolk	256,183	331,256	303,951	350,570
Sullivan	10,995	15,555	12,568	15,931
Tioga	7,063	13,990	7,526	13,260
Tompkins	21,643	8,522	28,890	10,371
Ulster	42,606	33,580	44,597	35,239
Warren	11,811	15,200	13,091	15,751
Washington	8,342	14,212	9,098	13,610
Wayne	12,799	23,734	13,473	23,380
Westchester	217,858	122,371	272,926	131,238
Wyoming	3,840	12,969	3,904	12,442
Yates	3,046	5,552	3,659	5,660
Totals	**3,664,409**	**2,869,023**	**4,556,118**	**2,819,533**

(1) Borough of New York City.
All candidates, 2020: Biden, D, 3,664,409; Trump, R, 2,869,023; Jorgensen, LB, 46,833; Hawkins, Green, 22,809; Pierce, Ind., 17,217.

North Carolina

County	2020 Biden (D)	Trump (R)	2016 Clinton (D)	Trump (R)
Alamance	38,186	45,490	29,833	38,815
Alexander	4,113	15,806	3,767	13,893
Alleghany	1,480	4,501	1,306	3,814
Anson	5,768	5,301	5,859	4,506
Ashe	4,149	11,368	3,500	9,412
Avery	2,171	7,092	1,689	6,298
Beaufort	9,575	16,352	8,764	14,543
Bertie	5,846	3,778	5,778	3,456
Bladen	7,281	9,623	7,058	8,550
Brunswick	32,984	55,373	23,282	42,720
Buncombe	95,881	61,983	75,452	55,716
Burke	12,985	30,814	11,251	26,238
Cabarrus	51,594	62,722	35,521	53,819
Caldwell	10,105	31,877	8,425	26,621
Camden	1,515	4,277	1,274	3,546
Carteret	11,999	29,886	9,939	26,569
Caswell	4,831	7,040	4,792	6,026
Catawba	25,420	56,203	21,216	48,324
Chatham	26,642	21,055	21,065	17,105
Cherokee	3,563	12,568	2,860	10,844
Chowan	3,232	4,458	2,992	4,014
Clay	1,685	5,074	1,367	4,437
Cleveland	16,879	33,664	14,964	28,479
Columbus	9,382	16,696	9,063	14,272
Craven	20,977	30,831	17,630	27,731
Cumberland	83,533	59,498	71,605	51,265
Currituck	4,151	11,566	2,913	9,163
Dare	9,855	13,844	7,222	11,460
Davidson	21,483	62,143	18,109	54,317
Davie	6,653	18,115	5,270	15,602
Duplin	8,676	13,703	8,283	12,217
Durham	142,770	31,827	121,250	28,350
Edgecombe	15,935	9,139	16,224	8,261
Forsyth	111,769	84,176	94,464	75,975
Franklin	15,776	20,748	12,874	16,368
Gaston	40,231	72,132	31,177	61,798
Gates	2,540	3,354	2,385	2,874
Graham	896	3,667	768	3,283
Granville	14,448	16,548	12,909	13,591
Greene	3,820	4,858	3,605	4,374
Guilford	171,538	106,384	149,248	98,062

County	2020 Biden (D)	Trump (R)	2016 Clinton (D)	Trump (R)
Halifax	15,382	9,973	15,748	9,031
Harnett	21,839	34,905	16,737	27,614
Haywood	13,095	22,698	10,473	18,929
Henderson	27,014	39,810	19,827	35,809
Hertford	7,077	3,470	6,910	3,099
Hoke	11,929	9,601	9,726	7,760
Hyde	1,035	1,408	965	1,288
Iredell	33,426	66,439	24,734	54,754
Jackson	9,522	11,263	7,713	9,870
Johnston	40,861	67,901	28,362	54,372
Jones	2,175	3,267	2,065	2,974
Lee	12,076	16,388	10,469	13,712
Lenoir	13,494	14,500	12,634	13,613
Lincoln	13,178	36,167	9,897	28,806
Macon	6,213	14,152	4,876	12,127
Madison	4,878	7,928	3,926	6,783
Martin	5,876	6,493	5,846	5,897
McDowell	5,807	16,839	4,667	14,568
Mecklenburg	375,503	178,066	294,562	155,518
Mitchell	1,852	7,041	1,596	6,282
Montgomery	4,305	8,363	4,150	7,130
Moore	20,547	36,459	16,329	30,490
Nash	25,702	25,653	23,235	23,319
New Hanover	64,876	62,420	50,979	55,344
Northampton	6,048	3,977	6,144	3,582
Onslow	23,474	45,016	17,514	37,122
Orange	63,097	19,993	59,923	18,557
Pamlico	2,699	4,815	2,448	4,258
Pasquotank	9,653	9,626	8,615	8,180
Pender	11,655	21,833	9,354	17,639
Perquimans	2,485	4,894	2,319	4,177
Person	8,416	13,104	7,833	11,185
Pitt	46,515	38,437	41,824	35,691
Polk	4,485	7,643	3,735	6,768
Randolph	15,506	56,589	13,194	49,430
Richmond	8,676	11,752	8,501	10,383
Robeson	17,998	25,927	19,016	20,762
Rockingham	15,766	30,955	14,228	26,830
Rowan	22,889	49,053	19,400	42,810
Rutherford	9,049	24,631	7,512	21,871
Sampson	10,606	17,132	10,547	14,838
Scotland	7,137	7,399	7,319	6,256
Stanly	8,037	25,297	7,094	21,964
Stokes	5,258	19,997	4,665	17,116
Surry	8,635	27,344	7,488	23,671
Swain	2,765	4,152	2,196	3,565
Transylvania	8,413	11,578	6,558	10,520
Tyrrell	757	1,043	720	975
Union	48,199	79,778	34,337	66,707
Vance	12,412	8,385	12,229	7,332
Wake	388,686	223,466	302,736	196,082
Warren	6,344	3,739	6,413	3,214
Washington	3,387	2,778	3,510	2,564
Watauga	16,925	14,332	14,138	13,697
Wayne	23,986	30,505	21,770	27,540
Wilkes	7,445	27,397	6,638	23,752
Wilson	20,579	19,437	19,663	17,531
Yadkin	3,744	15,861	3,160	13,880
Yancey	3,678	7,481	3,196	6,385
Totals	**2,655,383**	**2,732,084**	**2,189,316**	**2,362,631**

All candidates, 2020: Trump, R, 2,732,084; Biden, D, 2,655,383; Jorgensen, LB, 47,215; Hawkins, Green, 11,852; Blankenship, Const., 7,381.

North Dakota

County	2020 Biden (D)	Trump (R)	2016 Clinton (D)	Trump (R)
Adams	258	978	216	909
Barnes	1,800	3,532	1,597	3,160
Benson	817	1,090	842	929
Billings	72	539	59	495
Bottineau	819	2,563	736	2,494
Bowman	227	1,382	227	1,446
Burke	136	984	119	895
Burleigh	14,226	34,588	10,881	32,532
Cass	40,219	42,567	31,361	39,816
Cavalier	474	1,499	476	1,357
Dickey	602	1,732	554	1,667
Divide	265	899	245	867
Dunn	338	1,945	358	1,771
Eddy	382	851	355	791

County	2020 Biden (D)	Trump (R)	2016 Clinton (D)	Trump (R)
Emmons	237	1,735	215	1,677
Foster	369	1,338	347	1,241
Golden Valley	136	870	99	796
Grand Forks	12,856	16,963	10,851	16,340
Grant	207	1,132	185	1,108
Griggs	308	906	298	847
Hettinger	195	1,086	168	1,050
Kidder	221	1,206	179	1,111
LaMoure	526	1,633	502	1,481
Logan	125	923	114	888
McHenry	559	2,345	490	2,050
McIntosh	259	1,147	235	1,100
McKenzie	813	4,476	698	3,670
McLean	1,216	4,169	1,081	3,860
Mercer	703	3,850	621	3,759
Morton	3,865	12,234	3,080	11,336
Mountrail	1,251	2,806	1,220	2,582
Nelson	585	1,139	536	1,025
Oliver	127	917	119	830
Pembina	783	2,435	681	2,208
Pierce	497	1,583	431	1,437
Ramsey	1,636	3,570	1,505	3,217
Ransom	942	1,411	838	1,210
Renville	218	1,053	201	993
Richland	2,495	5,035	2,064	4,767
Rolette	2,475	1,253	2,099	1,217
Sargent	737	1,261	694	1,088
Sheridan	104	688	95	650
Sioux	804	257	758	260
Slope	44	379	43	362
Stark	2,490	12,091	1,753	9,755
Steele	392	649	361	538
Stutsman	2,670	6,981	2,498	6,718
Towner	317	828	305	733
Traill	1,491	2,519	1,241	2,265
Walsh	1,329	3,309	1,167	2,995
Ward	7,264	19,921	5,806	18,636
Wells	442	1,891	419	1,796
Williams	2,157	11,707	1,735	10,069
Totals	**114,480**	**234,845**	**93,758**	**216,794**

All candidates, 2020: Trump, R, 234,845; Biden, D, 114,480; Jorgensen, LB, 9,347.

Ohio

County	2020 Biden (D)	Trump (R)	2016 Clinton (D)	Trump (R)
Adams	2,130	9,660	2,326	8,659
Allen	13,611	32,052	13,294	30,487
Ashland	6,448	19,002	5,740	17,493
Ashtabula	16,207	26,225	15,577	23,318
Athens	14,047	10,386	16,370	11,354
Auglaize	4,583	20,451	3,980	18,658
Belmont	9,011	23,110	8,785	21,108
Brown	4,326	16,032	4,353	14,573
Butler	67,729	111,722	58,642	106,976
Carroll	3,206	10,525	3,154	9,254
Champaign	4,946	14,086	4,594	12,631
Clark	23,625	38,217	23,328	35,205
Clermont	33,505	73,077	26,715	67,518
Clinton	4,556	15,061	4,066	13,838
Columbiana	13,183	35,124	12,432	31,676
Coshocton	4,057	11,982	4,013	10,785
Crawford	4,831	15,043	4,625	13,611
Cuyahoga	402,315	195,089	398,271	184,211
Darke	4,668	21,569	4,470	20,012
Defiance	5,870	12,778	5,368	11,688
Delaware	56,961	65,163	40,872	57,568
Erie	17,142	21,724	16,057	19,648
Fairfield	30,634	49,714	24,881	44,314
Fayette	2,911	9,220	2,739	7,995
Franklin	391,584	203,154	351,198	199,331
Fulton	6,595	15,396	6,069	13,709
Gallia	2,911	10,289	2,628	9,822
Geauga	20,980	33,581	17,569	30,227
Greene	34,023	50,937	28,943	48,540

County	2020 Biden (D)	Trump (R)	2016 Clinton (D)	Trump (R)
Guernsey	4,498	13,077	4,359	11,445
Hamilton	238,101	173,015	215,719	173,665
Hancock	11,535	25,796	9,609	24,183
Hardin	3,025	9,698	2,920	8,717
Harrison	1,742	5,668	1,688	5,098
Henry	3,995	10,273	3,756	9,301
Highland	3,741	15,369	3,773	14,020
Hocking	3,836	9,554	3,775	8,497
Holmes	1,981	10,645	1,788	8,720
Huron	7,643	18,537	7,192	16,226
Jackson	3,193	10,804	3,226	9,949
Jefferson	9,823	22,309	9,675	21,117
Knox	8,433	21,825	8,171	19,131
Lake	54,337	71,615	46,397	64,255
Lawrence	7,353	19,759	6,974	18,689
Licking	32,324	57,965	27,376	51,241
Logan	4,990	17,625	4,647	15,957
Lorain	72,792	76,719	66,949	66,818
Lucas	111,989	79,628	110,833	75,698
Madison	5,558	13,445	4,779	11,631
Mahoning	56,346	58,601	57,381	53,616
Marion	8,089	18,526	7,928	16,961
Medina	39,326	63,451	32,182	54,810
Meigs	2,452	8,163	2,260	7,309
Mercer	3,981	19,145	3,384	17,506
Miami	15,420	40,531	13,120	37,079
Monroe	1,597	5,392	1,662	4,868
Montgomery	131,592	126,085	122,016	123,909
Morgan	1,703	4,932	1,736	4,431
Morrow	3,988	13,784	3,761	11,948
Muskingum	11,755	27,334	11,123	24,056
Noble	1,156	5,024	1,221	4,549
Ottawa	8,847	14,285	8,285	12,653
Paulding	2,172	6,927	2,093	6,500
Perry	4,006	11,959	4,138	10,228
Pickaway	7,167	20,059	6,529	17,076
Pike	3,051	8,872	3,539	7,902
Portage	34,935	45,034	32,397	39,971
Preble	4,435	16,697	4,325	15,446
Putnam	3,152	16,218	2,922	14,961
Richland	17,231	40,534	16,085	36,590
Ross	10,345	21,687	10,356	18,652
Sandusky	10,391	18,487	9,929	16,316
Scioto	8,876	21,926	9,132	20,550
Seneca	8,147	16,739	7,404	14,825
Shelby	4,399	19,988	4,243	18,590
Stark	74,336	108,610	68,146	98,388
Summit	148,151	122,023	134,256	112,026
Trumbull	43,534	53,756	43,014	49,024
Tuscarawas	12,643	29,519	12,188	26,918
Union	10,985	21,233	7,718	18,096
Van Wert	3,026	11,470	2,697	10,469
Vinton	1,306	4,525	1,351	3,883
Warren	45,040	85,069	33,730	77,643
Washington	9,114	21,798	8,026	20,514
Wayne	16,340	36,059	15,031	32,270
Williams	4,726	13,218	4,358	11,939
Wood	29,797	34,815	27,318	32,498
Wyandot	2,690	8,248	2,515	7,468
Totals	**2,603,731**	**3,074,418**	**2,394,164**	**2,841,005**

All candidates, 2020: Trump, R, 3,074,418; Biden, D, 2,603,731; Jorgensen, LB, 65,069; Hawkins, Ind., 18,032.

Oklahoma

County	2020 Biden (D)	Trump (R)	2016 Clinton (D)	Trump (R)
Adair	1,382	5,560	1,382	4,787
Alfalfa	231	1,978	216	1,933
Atoka	761	4,543	795	4,084
Beaver	190	1,964	176	1,993
Beckham	1,048	6,753	960	6,308
Blaine	688	3,133	711	2,884
Bryan	3,317	12,319	2,804	10,478
Caddo	2,666	7,006	2,420	6,482
Canadian	16,729	43,481	11,674	39,986
Carter	4,470	14,699	4,002	13,752
Cherokee	6,023	11,210	5,456	9,994

County	2020 Biden (D)	Trump (R)	2016 Clinton (D)	Trump (R)
Choctaw	1,081	4,696	1,067	4,206
Cimarron	70	966	71	963
Cleveland	49,754	66,569	38,829	62,538
Coal	373	2,091	411	1,898
Comanche	13,743	20,894	11,463	19,183
Cotton	393	2,117	424	2,054
Craig	1,217	4,686	1,252	4,283
Creek	6,570	23,269	5,841	21,575
Custer	2,365	8,051	2,104	7,826
Delaware	3,470	13,532	3,311	11,826
Dewey	213	2,121	222	1,965
Ellis	162	1,686	155	1,611
Garfield	4,915	16,956	4,397	16,009
Garvin	1,864	8,863	1,855	8,253
Grady	4,131	18,499	3,882	17,316
Grant	280	1,916	288	1,827
Greer	328	1,604	323	1,482
Harmon	177	747	225	715
Harper	136	1,324	134	1,318
Haskell	782	4,158	882	3,701
Hughes	919	3,875	961	3,388
Jackson	1,645	6,391	1,473	5,969
Jefferson	319	2,023	365	1,910
Johnston	736	3,431	786	3,093
Kay	4,037	12,829	3,738	12,172
Kingfisher	853	5,514	786	5,156
Kiowa	699	2,667	767	2,596
Latimer	762	3,435	797	3,100
Le Flore	3,296	15,199	3,250	13,362
Lincoln	2,607	11,996	2,430	10,854
Logan	5,452	15,596	4,248	13,633
Love	711	3,301	735	2,922
Major	320	3,082	310	2,948
Marshall	1,099	4,887	1,096	4,206
Mayes	3,580	12,743	3,423	11,555
McClain	3,581	15,264	2,894	13,169
McCurtain	1,856	9,478	1,802	8,656
McIntosh	2,024	6,152	2,123	5,505
Murray	1,156	4,610	1,087	4,175
Muskogee	8,013	16,495	7,977	15,043
Noble	1,000	3,816	901	3,715
Nowata	712	3,610	742	3,321
Okfuskee	889	3,046	943	2,800
Oklahoma	141,587	144,916	112,813	141,569
Okmulgee	4,352	9,651	4,385	8,944
Osage	5,998	14,107	5,597	12,577
Ottawa	2,684	8,545	2,584	7,631
Pawnee	1,362	5,256	1,344	4,729
Payne	10,881	17,778	8,788	16,651
Pittsburg	3,766	13,829	3,711	12,753
Pontotoc	4,116	10,784	3,637	10,431
Pottawatomie	7,274	20,224	6,015	17,848
Pushmataha	668	4,015	748	3,581
Roger Mills	168	1,626	151	1,547
Rogers	9,578	33,988	7,902	30,913
Seminole	2,150	6,008	2,071	5,613
Sequoyah	3,035	12,113	3,061	10,888
Stephens	3,151	15,552	3,086	14,182
Texas	894	4,504	858	4,621
Tillman	597	2,076	657	1,944
Tulsa	108,813	150,266	87,847	144,258
Wagoner	8,439	26,058	6,723	23,005
Washington	5,790	17,069	5,048	15,825
Washita	596	4,078	588	3,854
Woods	590	2,989	522	2,947
Woodward	1,005	6,607	873	6,347
Totals	**503,289**	**1,018,870**	**420,375**	**949,136**

All candidates, 2020: Trump, R, 1,018,870; Biden, D, 503,289; Jorgensen, LB, 24,686; West, Ind., 5,590; Simmons, Ind., 3,650; Pierce, Ind., 2,542.

Oregon

County	2020 Biden (D)	Trump (R)	2016 Clinton (D)	Trump (R)
Baker	2,332	7,316	1,797	6,218

County	2020 Biden (D)	Trump (R)	2016 Clinton (D)	Trump (R)
Benton	35,438	14,647	29,193	13,445
Clackamas	103,832	66,470	102,095	88,392
Clatsop	12,295	9,713	9,252	8,138
Columbia	13,535	16,779	10,167	13,217
Coos	14,024	21,488	10,448	17,865
Crook	3,715	11,103	2,637	8,511
Curry	6,003	8,403	4,300	7,212
Deschutes	64,102	54,183	42,444	45,692
Douglas	18,780	42,513	14,096	34,582
Gilliam	323	830	239	671
Grant	923	3,537	739	3,210
Harney	890	3,465	683	2,912
Hood River	8,530	3,858	6,510	3,272
Jackson	58,386	63,012	44,447	53,870
Jefferson	4,306	7,044	2,980	5,483
Josephine	17,608	30,205	13,453	26,923
Klamath	10,260	25,048	7,210	20,435
Lake	788	3,449	639	3,022
Lane	131,311	78,562	102,753	67,141
Lincoln	17,248	12,336	12,501	10,039
Linn	25,319	44,411	17,995	33,488
Malheur	3,202	8,101	2,246	7,194
Marion	68,086	63,188	57,788	63,377
Morrow	1,345	3,557	1,017	2,721
Multnomah	357,909	80,038	292,561	67,954
Polk	22,431	23,259	16,420	18,940
Sherman	257	914	202	732
Tillamook	7,956	8,306	5,768	6,538
Umatilla	10,499	21,002	7,673	17,059
Union	4,227	10,247	3,249	8,431
Wallowa	1,619	3,390	1,116	2,848
Wasco	6,467	6,965	4,781	5,833
Washington	184,356	84,560	153,251	83,197
Wheeler	216	710	155	591
Yamhill	25,296	27,494	19,301	23,250
Totals	**1,243,814**	**870,103**	**1,002,106**	**782,403**

All candidates, 2020: Biden, D, 1,243,814; Trump, R, 870,103; Jorgensen, LB, 35,412; Hawkins, Pacific Green, 10,414; Hunter, Progressive, 4,426.

Pennsylvania

County	2020 Biden (D)	Trump (R)	2016 Clinton (D)	Trump (R)
Adams	17,919	37,009	14,219	31,423
Allegheny	415,737	274,028	367,617	259,480
Armstrong	8,352	27,112	7,178	23,484
Beaver	37,389	53,886	32,531	48,167
Bedford	4,266	22,529	3,645	19,552
Berks	89,530	105,941	78,437	96,626
Blair	17,425	44,714	13,958	39,135
Bradford	7,978	21,514	6,369	18,141
Bucks	198,251	182,742	167,060	164,361
Butler	36,534	73,023	28,584	64,428
Cambria	21,614	47,885	18,867	42,258
Cameron	634	1,771	531	1,589
Carbon	10,990	21,607	8,936	18,743
Centre	39,718	36,042	37,088	35,274
Chester	179,065	126,844	141,682	116,114
Clarion	4,615	14,363	4,273	12,576
Clearfield	9,598	28,984	8,200	24,932
Clinton	5,406	11,668	4,744	10,022
Columbia	10,445	19,867	8,934	18,004
Crawford	12,584	27,990	10,971	24,987
Cumberland	61,168	76,149	47,085	69,076
Dauphin	77,387	65,129	64,706	60,863
Delaware	200,911	116,216	177,402	110,667
Elk	4,478	11,993	3,853	10,025
Erie	67,471	65,972	58,112	60,069
Fayette	19,486	39,956	17,946	34,590
Forest	715	1,864	626	1,683
Franklin	22,040	56,628	17,465	49,768
Fulton	1,068	6,660	912	5,694
Greene	4,882	12,436	4,482	10,849
Huntingdon	5,448	17,059	4,539	14,494
Indiana	12,475	27,832	11,528	24,888
Jefferson	4,498	17,928	3,650	15,192
Juniata	2,253	9,648	1,821	8,273
Lackawanna	61,124	51,501	51,983	48,384
Lancaster	112,536	156,938	91,093	137,914

County	2020 Biden (D)	Trump (R)	2016 Clinton (D)	Trump (R)
Lawrence	15,557	29,071	14,009	25,428
Lebanon	23,412	45,907	18,953	40,525
Lehigh	95,539	82,134	81,324	73,690
Luzerne	62,983	84,649	52,451	78,688
Lycoming	16,722	40,885	13,020	35,627
McKean	5,024	13,892	4,025	11,635
Mercer	20,426	35,282	18,733	31,544
Mifflin	4,560	16,532	3,877	14,094
Monroe	42,102	37,297	33,918	33,386
Montgomery	313,543	182,907	256,082	162,731
Montour	3,768	5,842	2,857	5,288
Northampton	84,145	82,830	66,272	71,736
Northumber-land	12,440	28,435	9,788	25,427
Perry	5,704	17,879	4,632	15,616
Philadelphia	558,264	126,253	584,025	108,748
Pike	12,878	18,979	9,256	16,056
Potter	1,686	7,117	1,302	6,251
Schuylkill	20,425	48,100	16,770	44,001
Snyder	4,848	13,816	4,002	11,725
Somerset	8,543	31,105	7,376	27,379
Sullivan	921	2,622	750	2,291
Susquehanna	6,084	14,879	5,123	12,891
Tioga	4,953	15,735	3,901	13,614
Union	7,377	12,342	6,180	10,622
Venango	7,475	18,286	6,309	16,021
Warren	5,987	14,020	5,145	12,477
Washington	44,712	71,375	36,322	61,386
Wayne	9,135	18,466	7,008	16,244
Westmoreland	70,738	128,304	59,669	116,522
Wyoming	4,642	9,819	3,811	8,837
York	85,323	143,260	68,524	128,528
Totals	**3,345,906**	**3,311,448**	**2,926,441**	**2,970,733**

All candidates, 2020: Biden, D, 3,345,906; Trump, R, 3,311,448; Jorgensen, LB, 77,286.

Rhode Island

City	2020 Biden (D)	Trump (R)	2016 Clinton (D)	Trump (R)
Barrington	7,513	2,812	6,153	2,898
Bristol	6,606	4,486	5,771	4,080
Coventry	8,882	10,285	7,032	9,199
Cranston	22,205	16,952	18,763	15,934
Cumberland	10,649	8,274	8,655	7,444
East Providence	14,394	7,788	11,904	7,134
Johnston	6,689	8,104	5,652	7,563
Lincoln	6,445	5,698	5,279	5,410
Newport	7,548	2,587	6,287	2,644
North Kingstown	9,992	6,524	7,793	6,147
North Providence	9,224	7,029	7,760	6,936
Pawtucket	17,280	6,869	15,574	6,221
Providence	44,686	9,959	45,053	7,682
Smithfield	5,449	5,658	4,402	5,254
South Kingstown	10,915	4,900	8,677	4,627
Warwick	25,112	19,210	20,038	18,338
West Warwick	7,079	6,390	5,540	5,724
Westerly	6,903	5,350	5,291	5,031
Woonsocket	7,077	6,155	6,346	5,442
Other	62,425	50,967	50,555	46,815
Totals	**297,073**	**195,997**	**252,525**	**180,523**

All candidates, 2020: Biden, D, 297,073; Trump, R, 195,997; Jorgensen, LB, 4,891; De La Fuente, Alliance; La Riva, Socialism/Liberation, 801; Carroll, Amer. Solidarity, 734.

South Carolina

County	2020 Biden (D)	Trump (R)	2016 Clinton (D)	Trump (R)
Abbeville	4,087	8,207	3,741	6,763
Aiken	32,257	51,554	25,455	46,025
Allendale	2,714	19	2,735	789
Anderson	27,055	67,286	21,097	56,232
Bamberg	4,003	2,413	3,898	2,204
Barnwell	4,717	5,487	4,400	4,889
Beaufort	36,176	48,229	32,138	42,922
Berkeley	45,126	57,285	30,705	44,587

County	2020 Biden (D)	Trump (R)	2016 Clinton (D)	Trump (R)
Calhoun	3,903	4,302	3,573	3,787
Charleston	121,084	92,952	89,299	75,443
Cherokee	6,980	18,040	6,092	15,167
Chester	6,941	8,657	6,579	7,265
Chesterfield	7,427	11,279	6,858	9,312
Clarendon	8,250	8,359	7,732	7,386
Colleton	8,568	10,396	7,627	9,091
Darlington	15,199	16,808	13,888	14,989
Dillon	6,435	6,578	5,834	5,637
Dorchester	26,067	36,734	24,055	34,987
Edgefield	4,953	8,183	4,491	6,842
Fairfield	7,369	4,619	6,945	4,027
Florence	30,792	32,304	26,710	29,573
Georgetown	15,787	20,431	13,310	17,389
Greenville	102,640	149,253	74,483	127,832
Greenwood	12,090	19,366	10,711	16,961
Hampton	5,310	3,893	5,170	3,488
Horry	40,863	104,075	39,410	89,288
Jasper	7,162	7,065	5,956	5,187
Kershaw	12,690	20,458	10,330	17,542
Lancaster	18,824	30,146	13,812	23,719
Laurens	10,141	19,969	8,889	16,816
Lee	5,308	2,997	5,199	2,803
Lexington	49,206	92,594	35,230	80,026
Marion	8,846	5,694	8,569	5,444
Marlboro	6,277	5,027	5,954	4,267
McCormick	2,685	2,958	2,479	2,652
Newberry	6,926	11,418	6,217	10,017
Oconee	10,396	29,641	7,998	24,178
Orangeburg	27,250	13,586	26,318	11,931
Pickens	13,625	42,759	10,354	36,236
Richland	130,491	57,603	108,000	52,469
Saluda	2,948	6,179	2,813	5,526
Spartanburg	52,592	92,562	39,997	76,277
Sumter	27,297	20,951	24,047	18,745
Union	4,934	8,182	4,729	7,061
Williamsburg	10,282	5,523	9,953	4,864
York	58,094	80,501	41,593	66,754
Totals	**1,052,767**	**1,352,522**	**855,373**	**1,155,389**

All candidates, 2020: Trump, R, 1,352,522; Biden, D, 1,052,767; Jorgensen, LB, 28,036; Hawkins, Green, 6,711; De La Fuente, Alliance, 1,787.

South Dakota

County	2020 Biden (D)	Trump (R)	2016 Clinton (D)	Trump (R)
Aurora	317	1,052	340	974
Beadle	2,107	4,808	1,912	4,455
Bennett	465	694	412	666
Bon Homme	721	2,235	704	2,105
Brookings	6,109	8,000	4,879	6,748
Brown	6,538	10,580	5,452	9,613
Brule	673	1,750	571	1,565
Buffalo	350	182	296	171
Butte	939	3,723	696	3,357
Campbell	117	747	105	704
Charles Mix	1,175	2,551	935	2,382
Clark	437	1,373	398	1,139
Clay	3,082	2,455	2,608	2,109
Codington	3,837	8,958	3,174	7,764
Corson	622	647	535	588
Custer	1,522	3,851	1,121	3,293
Davison	2,648	5,613	2,355	5,157
Day	1,052	1,869	974	1,627
Deuel	609	1,699	570	1,366
Dewey	1,131	790	888	723
Douglas	216	1,468	214	1,338
Edmunds	417	1,538	380	1,433
Fall River	1,053	2,876	821	2,511
Faulk	198	964	204	858
Grant	1,056	2,617	971	2,382
Gregory	455	1,772	391	1,600
Haakon	105	1,025	77	936
Hamlin	647	2,372	555	2,051
Hand	373	1,433	334	1,391
Hanson	557	1,793	424	1,497
Harding	49	748	38	695

County	2020 Biden (D)	2020 Trump (R)	2016 Clinton (D)	2016 Trump (R)
Hughes	2,953	5,519	2,450	5,174
Hutchinson	762	2,940	692	2,517
Hyde	136	564	125	543
Jackson	359	738	323	722
Jerauld	270	720	264	648
Jones	90	498	69	450
Kingsbury	819	1,903	703	1,680
Lake	2,068	3,681	2,314	4,038
Lawrence	4,537	8,753	3,356	7,411
Lincoln	11,981	19,616	8,076	15,499
Lyman	524	1,042	369	977
Marshall	858	1,287	754	1,056
McCook	769	2,068	623	1,794
McPherson	222	1,075	192	892
Meade	3,285	9,875	2,223	8,441
Mellette	298	449	238	402
Miner	320	787	281	706
Minnehaha	16,700	32,877	30,610	42,043
Moody	1,179	1,951	1,043	1,731
Oglala Lakota	2,824	297	2,510	241
Pennington	20,603	35,061	14,074	29,804
Perkins	239	1,401	188	1,333
Potter	227	1,139	215	1,071
Roberts	1,828	2,404	1,540	2,144
Sanborn	257	905	241	819
Spink	998	2,104	919	1,854
Stanley	421	1,203	329	1,148
Sully	185	726	137	679
Todd	1,963	532	1,505	487
Tripp	494	2,161	462	2,069
Turner	1,139	3,290	961	2,937
Union	2,729	5,949	2,227	5,290
Walworth	565	1,966	457	1,896
Yankton	4,016	6,581	3,301	5,659
Ziebach	481	404	353	368
Totals	**126,676**	**244,649**	**117,458**	**227,721**

All candidates, 2020: Trump, R, 244,649; Biden, D, 126,676; Jorgensen, LB, 10,254.

Tennessee

County	2020 Biden (D)	2020 Trump (R)	2016 Clinton (D)	2016 Trump (R)
Anderson	11,733	23,163	9,013	19,212
Bedford	4,443	14,317	3,395	11,486
Benton	1,526	5,661	1,474	4,716
Bledsoe	971	4,725	897	3,622
Blount	17,834	47,195	12,100	37,443
Bradley	9,849	35,194	7,070	29,768
Campbell	2,438	12,330	2,248	9,870
Cannon	1,261	5,190	1,127	4,007
Carroll	2,558	9,194	2,327	7,756
Carter	4,526	19,574	3,453	16,898
Cheatham	5,457	14,328	3,878	11,297
Chester	1,411	5,951	1,243	5,081
Claiborne	2,201	10,598	1,832	8,602
Clay	735	2,733	707	2,141
Cocke	2,524	12,128	1,981	9,791
Coffee	5,704	17,863	4,743	14,417
Crockett	1,382	4,673	1,303	3,982
Cumberland	6,728	25,167	5,202	20,413
Davidson	197,846	99,415	148,864	84,550
Decatur	1,341	4,473	894	3,588
DeKalb	1,747	6,663	1,569	5,171
Dickson	6,098	17,619	4,722	13,233
Dyer	3,157	11,766	2,816	10,180
Fayette	7,000	15,661	5,874	13,055
Fentress	1,210	7,403	1,100	6,038
Franklin	4,863	13,977	4,374	11,532
Gibson	5,764	16,245	5,258	13,786
Giles	3,298	9,783	2,917	7,970
Grainger	1,463	8,559	1,154	6,626
Greene	5,183	22,185	4,216	18,562
Grundy	985	4,795	999	3,636
Hamblen	5,497	18,789	4,075	15,857
Hamilton	75,360	91,991	55,316	78,733
Hancock	362	2,372	322	1,843
Hardeman	4,180	5,760	4,185	4,919
Hardin	1,774	9,556	1,622	8,012
Hawkins	4,069	20,372	3,507	16,648
Haywood	4,000	3,338	3,711	3,013
Henderson	2,092	9,797	1,800	8,138

County	2020 Biden (D)	2020 Trump (R)	2016 Clinton (D)	2016 Trump (R)
Henry	3,547	11,230	3,063	9,508
Hickman	2,130	7,577	1,824	5,695
Houston	869	2,715	866	2,182
Humphreys	2,017	6,115	1,967	4,930
Jackson	1,133	4,106	1,129	3,236
Jefferson	4,645	18,609	3,494	14,776
Johnson	1,242	6,466	988	5,410
Knox	91,097	124,339	62,878	105,767
Lake	526	1,492	577	1,357
Lauderdale	3,193	5,672	3,056	4,884
Lawrence	3,195	15,334	2,821	12,420
Lewis	1,068	4,473	890	3,585
Lincoln	2,909	12,258	2,554	10,398
Loudon	6,933	21,684	4,919	17,610
Macon	1,307	8,095	1,072	6,263
Madison	18,309	23,922	15,448	21,335
Marion	3,165	9,873	2,832	7,696
Marshall	3,603	11,029	2,852	8,184
Maury	14,326	30,908	10,038	23,799
McMinn	4,357	18,175	3,510	14,691
McNairy	1,943	9,085	1,848	7,841
Meigs	1,008	4,464	856	3,342
Monroe	3,760	16,742	3,186	13,374
Montgomery	32,426	42,156	21,699	32,341
Moore	573	2,888	496	2,325
Morgan	1,161	6,926	1,054	5,441
Obion	2,589	10,790	2,426	9,526
Overton	2,028	7,911	1,945	6,059
Perry	615	2,775	597	2,167
Pickett	524	2,373	536	2,021
Polk	1,492	6,792	1,252	5,097
Putnam	9,154	23,694	6,851	19,002
Rhea	2,363	11,031	1,942	8,660
Roane	6,034	19,195	4,837	15,880
Robertson	8,690	24,535	6,637	19,410
Rutherford	59,189	81,373	36,706	64,515
Scott	986	8,004	934	6,044
Sequatchie	1,295	5,846	1,053	4,441
Sevier	8,695	33,742	6,297	28,629
Shelby	245,208	129,543	208,992	116,344
Smith	1,798	7,124	1,689	5,494
Stewart	1,230	4,942	1,222	3,864
Sullivan	17,226	55,774	12,578	46,979
Sumner	27,630	63,404	18,161	50,129
Tipton	6,832	20,063	5,785	16,910
Trousdale	1,011	2,930	946	2,103
Unicoi	1,610	6,593	1,262	5,671
Union	1,248	6,777	1,012	5,053
Van Buren	544	2,337	539	1,820
Warren	4,126	12,323	3,535	9,514
Washington	18,214	40,120	13,024	34,252
Wayne	820	5,795	717	5,036
Weakley	3,011	10,382	2,772	9,008
White	2,134	9,587	1,845	7,671
Williamson	50,161	86,469	31,013	68,212
Wilson	22,197	50,149	14,385	39,406
Totals	**1,139,666**	**1,849,211**	**870,695**	**1,522,925**

All candidates, 2020: Trump, R, 1,849,211; Biden, D, 1,139,666; Jorgensen, LB, 29,815; West, Ind., 10,216; Blankenship, Ind., 5,340; Hawkins, Ind., 4,526; Kennedy, Ind., 2,582; La Riva, Ind., 2,292; De La Fuente, Ind., 1,833.

Texas

County	2020 Biden (D)	2020 Trump (R)	2016 Clinton (D)	2016 Trump (R)
Anderson	3,934	15,062	3,369	13,201
Andrews	849	4,937	836	3,927
Angelina	9,136	25,070	7,538	21,668
Aransas	2,896	9,210	2,465	7,740
Archer	446	4,300	394	3,786
Armstrong	75	1,035	70	924
Atascosa	5,865	12,020	4,651	8,618
Austin	2,931	11,282	2,320	9,637
Bailey	407	1,430	397	1,344
Bandera	2,503	10,050	1,726	8,163
Bastrop	15,452	20,486	10,569	16,328
Baylor	179	1,478	191	1,267
Bee	3,280	5,999	3,444	4,744
Bell	56,032	67,113	37,801	51,998
Bexar	440,823	303,871	319,550	240,333
Blanco	1,905	5,429	1,244	4,212
Borden	16	395	31	330

County	2020 Biden (D)	Trump (R)	2016 Clinton (D)	Trump (R)	County	2020 Biden (D)	Trump (R)	2016 Clinton (D)	Trump (R)
Bosque	1,552	7,446	1,278	6,339	Hansford	166	1,848	171	1,730
Bowie	10,692	27,053	8,838	24,924	Hardeman	241	1,330	249	1,207
Brazoria	61,780	89,939	43,200	72,791	Hardin	3,449	23,806	2,780	19,606
Brazos	35,242	47,456	23,121	38,738	Harris	911,913	699,771	707,914	545,955
Brewster	2,251	2,451	1,873	2,077	Harrison	7,812	21,318	7,151	18,749
Briscoe	77	639	91	625	Hartley	195	1,866	173	1,730
Brooks	1,470	998	1,937	613	Haskell	353	1,837	314	1,403
Brown	2,103	13,681	1,621	12,017	Hays	59,213	47,427	33,224	33,826
Burleson	1,786	6,740	1,491	5,316	Hemphill	206	1,486	181	1,462
Burnet	5,615	18,721	3,797	14,638	Henderson	7,048	28,816	5,669	23,650
Caldwell	6,536	7,975	4,795	6,691	Hidalgo	127,391	89,925	118,809	48,642
Calhoun	2,146	5,640	2,118	4,638	Hill	2,829	11,869	2,547	10,108
Callahan	734	6,006	569	4,865	Hockley	1,481	6,534	1,260	5,809
Cameron	63,732	48,834	59,402	29,472	Hood	5,605	26,243	4,008	21,382
Camp	1,392	3,626	1,260	3,201	Hopkins	3,043	12,713	2,510	10,707
Carson	289	2,747	249	2,620	Houston	2,312	7,050	1,978	6,205
Cass	2,777	10,979	2,391	9,726	Howard	2,017	7,899	1,770	6,637
Castro	466	1,601	526	1,414	Hudspeth	371	771	324	503
Chambers	3,997	17,343	2,948	13,339	Hunt	8,879	29,135	6,396	23,910
Cherokee	4,196	15,065	3,469	12,919	Hutchinson	957	7,659	854	7,042
Childress	305	1,928	253	1,802	Irion	120	759	90	660
Clay	614	5,064	536	4,377	Jack	331	3,415	314	2,973
Cochran	176	806	190	679	Jackson	1,018	5,116	904	4,266
Coke	215	1,565	140	1,265	Jasper	2,906	12,453	2,590	10,609
Coleman	450	3,638	388	3,177	Jeff Davis	501	783	422	695
Collin	227,868	250,194	140,624	201,014	Jefferson	46,022	47,535	42,443	42,862
Collingsworth	155	1,048	145	983	Jim Hogg	1,197	831	1,635	430
Colorado	2,403	3,653	1,987	6,325	Jim Wells	5,094	7,077	6,694	5,420
Comal	24,369	62,260	14,238	45,136	Johnson	16,418	54,523	10,988	44,382
Comanche	852	5,177	789	4,333	Jones	989	5,621	936	4,819
Concho	197	1,058	148	885	Karnes	1,220	3,959	1,145	2,965
Cooke	3,205	15,579	2,352	13,181	Kaufman	18,290	37,474	10,278	29,587
Coryell	7,542	15,397	5,064	12,225	Kendall	6,008	20,064	3,643	15,700
Cottle	113	543	92	506	Kenedy	65	127	99	84
Crane	241	1,247	299	1,049	Kent	47	411	59	360
Crockett	344	1,219	372	980	Kerr	6,510	20,858	4,681	17,727
Crosby	527	1,396	468	1,181	Kimble	284	1,987	206	1,697
Culberson	438	415	454	280	King	8	151	5	149
Dallam	196	1,386	222	1,261	Kinney	446	1,144	458	936
Dallas	597,407	306,572	461,080	262,945	Kleberg	5,359	5,557	4,716	4,367
Dawson	808	2,951	835	2,636	Knox	265	1,180	247	1,078
Deaf Smith	1,263	3,293	1,185	2,911	La Salle	1,052	1,335	1,129	872
Delta	403	2,157	400	1,836	Lamar	4,420	16,698	3,583	14,561
Denton	188,023	221,829	110,890	170,603	Lamb	835	3,513	771	3,111
DeWitt	1,494	6,567	1,163	5,519	Lampasas	2,134	8,070	1,483	6,385
Dickens	130	850	128	755	Lavaca	1,333	8,802	1,170	7,347
Dimmit	2,264	1,384	2,173	974	Lee	1,745	6,248	1,372	4,997
Donley	198	1,438	191	1,225	Leon	1,072	7,522	909	6,391
Duval	2,573	2,442	2,783	1,316	Liberty	5,779	23,288	4,862	18,892
Eastland	982	7,216	776	6,011	Limestone	2,213	6,786	1,778	5,796
Ector	11,310	32,586	10,249	25,020	Lipscomb	131	1,203	135	1,159
Edwards	166	893	303	746	Live Oak	819	4,198	742	3,464
El Paso	168,801	81,235	147,843	55,512	Llano	3,167	9,996	1,825	8,299
Ellis	27,513	56,651	16,253	44,941	Loving	4	60	4	58
Erath	2,914	13,669	2,160	11,210	Lubbock	39,757	78,560	28,023	65,651
Falls	1,899	4,177	1,684	3,441	Lynn	428	1,853	403	1,546
Fannin	2,638	12,150	2,132	9,548	Madison	1,084	4,165	881	3,351
Fayette	2,650	10,163	2,144	8,743	Marion	1,331	3,459	1,165	2,983
Fisher	352	1,448	403	1,265	Martin	288	1,857	266	1,455
Floyd	437	1,581	435	1,474	Mason	566	2,108	354	1,656
Foard	99	445	113	383	Matagorda	3,726	9,836	3,500	8,366
Fort Bend	188,155	153,011	134,686	117,291	Maverick	8,324	6,881	10,397	2,816
Franklin	803	4,153	665	3,585	McCulloch	490	2,898	482	2,552
Freestone	1,629	6,966	1,471	6,026	McLennan	36,550	59,432	27,063	48,260
Frio	2,421	2,812	2,444	1,856	McMullen	53	460	40	454
Gaines	572	5,323	597	3,907	Medina	6,731	15,599	4,634	12,085
Galveston	58,247	93,306	43,658	73,757	Menard	196	819	154	682
Garza	231	1,411	230	1,225	Midland	12,258	45,463	10,025	36,973
Gillespie	3,163	12,495	2,288	10,446	Milam	2,475	7,950	2,051	6,364
Glasscock	39	611	34	553	Mills	271	2,214	243	1,951
Goliad	872	3,081	973	2,620	Mitchell	397	2,169	354	1,780
Gonzales	1,894	5,568	1,571	4,587	Montague	1,097	8,613	885	7,526
Gray	820	6,812	701	6,500	Montgomery	74,255	193,224	45,835	150,314
Grayson	14,223	43,776	10,301	35,325	Moore	1,059	4,356	1,098	3,977
Gregg	14,657	32,352	11,677	28,764	Morris	1,664	3,841	1,425	3,446
Grimes	2,831	9,419	2,194	7,065	Motley	46	604	40	566
Guadalupe	28,706	47,423	18,391	36,632	Nacogdoches	8,989	17,359	6,846	14,771
Hale	2,271	7,162	2,101	6,366	Navarro	5,097	13,787	4,002	11,994
Hall	167	992	164	893	Newton	1,175	4,882	1,156	4,288
Hamilton	641	3,613	479	3,060	Nolan	1,161	4,127	1,029	3,552

County	2020 Biden (D)	Trump (R)	2016 Clinton (D)	Trump (R)
Nueces	60,749	64,467	49,198	50,766
Ochiltree	302	2,811	274	2,628
Oldham	81	917	78	850
Orange	6,354	29,170	5,735	25,513
Palo Pinto	2,177	10,170	1,708	8,284
Panola	2,057	9,322	1,835	8,445
Parker	12,789	61,584	8,344	46,473
Parmer	488	2,133	485	1,915
Pecos	1,378	3,213	1,554	2,468
Polk	5,353	18,496	4,187	15,176
Potter	9,867	22,732	7,657	19,630
Presidio	1,463	721	1,458	652
Rains	841	5,147	628	3,968
Randall	12,750	50,597	8,367	43,462
Reagan	172	942	167	709
Real	320	1,643	262	1,382
Red River	1,244	4,513	1,149	3,926
Reeves	1,394	2,249	1,659	1,417
Refugio	1,108	2,210	1,034	1,830
Roberts	17	529	20	524
Robertson	2,359	5,631	2,203	4,668
Rockwall	18,149	38,842	9,655	28,451
Runnels	531	3,682	453	3,250
Rusk	4,624	16,511	3,935	14,675
Sabine	662	4,767	614	3,998
San Augustine	979	3,005	910	2,622
San Jacinto	2,332	10,154	2,038	8,059
San Patricio	8,971	16,495	7,871	13,030
San Saba	287	2,308	293	2,025
Schleicher	211	939	208	821
Scurry	818	4,978	733	4,410
Shackelford	130	1,484	103	1,378
Shelby	2,058	7,962	1,758	7,179
Sherman	91	885	96	807
Smith	29,343	68,546	22,300	58,930
Somervell	768	4,099	541	3,206
Starr	9,099	8,224	9,289	2,224
Stephens	396	3,385	348	3,034
Sterling	51	584	70	549
Stonewall	116	615	135	555
Sutton	322	1,222	313	1,075
Swisher	478	1,842	462	1,671
Tarrant	397,174	399,342	288,392	345,921
Taylor	14,489	39,439	10,085	33,250
Terrell	119	334	140	288
Terry	757	2,809	753	2,459
Throckmorton	82	806	84	715
Titus	2,852	7,563	2,597	6,511
Tom Green	12,106	32,129	9,173	27,494
Travis	432,062	159,907	308,260	127,209
Trinity	1,323	5,579	1,154	4,737
Tyler	1,390	8,095	1,248	6,624
Upshur	2,869	15,775	2,380	13,209
Upton	169	1,176	286	1,007
Uvalde	4,066	6,160	3,867	4,835
Val Verde	6,401	7,839	6,964	5,890
Van Zandt	3,419	22,126	2,799	18,473
Victoria	10,271	23,244	8,866	21,275
Walker	7,875	15,368	6,091	12,884
Waller	8,130	14,206	5,748	10,531
Ward	761	3,238	783	2,547
Washington	4,254	12,949	3,382	10,945
Webb	12,827	8,576	42,307	12,947
Wharton	4,671	11,892	4,238	10,149
Wheeler	168	2,158	194	2,087
Wichita	11,355	30,036	8,770	27,631
Wilbarger	954	3,520	809	3,166
Willacy	3,097	2,437	3,422	1,547
Williamson	142,457	138,649	84,468	104,175
Wilson	6,350	18,457	4,790	13,998
Winkler	358	1,753	420	1,403
Wise	4,953	26,986	3,412	20,670
Wood	3,487	18,962	2,630	15,700
Yoakum	419	2,172	426	1,797
Young	1,036	7,112	876	6,601
Zapata	1,820	2,032	2,063	1,029
Zavala	2,864	1,490	2,636	694
Totals	5,166,253	5,828,268	3,877,868	4,685,047

All candidates, 2020: Trump, R, 5,828,268; Biden, D, 5,166,253; Jorgensen, LB, 124,653; Hawkins, Green, 32,917.

Utah

County	2020 Biden (D)	Trump (R)	2016 Clinton (D)	Trump (R)
Beaver	352	2,618	264	1,838
Box Elder	2,883	11,361	2,282	12,230
Cache	13,873	30,017	8,563	21,139
Carbon	2,306	6,255	1,717	5,275
Daggett	105	473	77	331
Davis	49,128	82,491	28,776	62,219
Duchesne	773	7,016	500	5,508
Emery	566	4,166	380	3,425
Garfield	513	2,149	358	1,606
Grand	2,733	2,168	1,960	1,975
Iron	4,033	14,474	2,450	11,561
Juab	638	5,069	442	2,827
Kane	1,005	2,777	741	2,265
Millard	529	4,267	431	3,860
Morgan	1,060	4,957	577	3,188
Piute	86	773	47	626
Rich	178	1,118	104	797
Salt Lake	182,476	128,592	175,863	138,043
San Juan	2,451	2,634	2,042	2,645
Sanpete	1,673	9,705	1,061	6,673
Sevier	1,032	8,427	695	6,740
Summit	11,733	6,122	10,503	7,333
Tooele	8,033	17,594	4,573	11,169
Uintah	1,601	12,777	995	9,810
Utah	58,001	132,618	28,522	102,182
Wasatch	5,762	9,953	3,063	6,115
Washington	18,840	59,618	10,288	42,650
Wayne	362	1,207	271	966
Weber	28,864	38,612	23,131	40,235
Totals	401,589	610,008	310,676	515,231

All candidates, 2020: Trump, R, 610,008; Biden, D, 401,589; Jorgensen, LB, 22,319; West, unaff., 4,344; Blankenship, Const., 3,556; Hawkins, Green, 2,913; Pierce, unaff., 1,548; McHugh, unaff., 1,344; La Riva, unaff., 673.

Vermont

City	2020 Biden (D)	Trump (R)	2016 Clinton (D)	Trump (R)
Barre Town	2,512	2,093	1,760	1,862
Bennington	4,369	2,473	3,361	1,949
Brattleboro	5,423	1,053	4,347	859
Burlington	19,238	2,292	14,519	2,082
Colchester	6,452	2,852	4,483	2,425
Essex	9,581	3,415	6,753	3,030
Hartford	4,516	1,574	3,190	1,303
Milton	3,344	2,612	2,260	2,085
Montpelier	4,576	468	3,698	492
Rutland City	4,679	3,026	3,495	2,734
Shelburne	4,358	953	3,390	941
S. Burlington	10,057	2,271	7,246	2,059
Williston	4,961	1,699	3,508	1,481
Other	158,739	85,909	116,563	72,067
Totals	242,805	112,688	178,573	95,369

All candidates, 2020: Biden, D, 242,805; Trump, R, 112,688; Jorgensen, LB, 3,573; Hawkins, Green, 1,303; West, Ind., 1,266; Paige, Ind., 1,157; LaFontaine, Ind., 850; Kennedy, Socialist Workers, 230; Duncan, Ind., 213; Blankenship, Const., 208; Carroll, Amer. Solidarity, 207; La Riva, Liberty Union, 171; Swing, other, 142; Collins, Prohib., 138; McCormic, other, 123; Pierce, unaff., 106; Segal, Bread/Roses, 65; Huber, Approval Voting, 62; Kopitke, Ind., 54; De La Fuente, Alliance, 48; Scalf, Ind., 31.

Virginia

City	2020 Biden (D)	Trump (R)	2016 Clinton (D)	Trump (R)
Accomack	6,824	8,822	6,740	8,583
Albemarle	41,812	20,566	33,345	19,259
Alleghany	2,221	5,842	2,166	4,874
Amelia	2,390	5,370	2,128	4,708
Amherst	5,367	10,783	5,057	9,719
Appomattox	2,403	6,688	2,023	5,715
Arlington	102,510	21,598	92,016	20,186
Augusta	10,699	30,539	8,177	26,163
Bath	644	1,826	603	1,548
Bedford	11,986	35,369	9,768	30,659
Bland	530	2,899	453	2,573
Botetourt	5,623	15,021	4,494	13,375
Brunswick	4,525	3,343	4,481	3,046
Buchanan	1,582	8,277	1,721	7,296
Buckingham	3,456	4,537	3,128	3,950
Campbell	7,965	21,033	6,664	19,551
Caroline	8,081	7,761	6,432	7,147
Carroll	2,795	12,594	2,559	10,663
Charles City	2,610	1,750	2,496	1,476
Charlotte	2,309	3,801	2,155	3,479
Chesterfield	111,094	98,541	81,074	85,045
Clarke	3,914	5,187	3,051	4,661

City	2020 Biden (D)	Trump (R)	2016 Clinton (D)	Trump (R)	City	2020 Biden (D)	Trump (R)	2016 Clinton (D)	Trump (R)
Craig	584	2,522	541	2,140	Covington	964	1,578	914	1,349
Culpeper	10,509	15,929	7,759	13,349	Danville	11,568	7,393	11,059	7,303
Cumberland	2,221	3,005	2,036	2,697	Emporia	1,611	754	1,530	789
Dickenson	1,501	5,746	1,335	4,932	Fairfax	9,048	3,962	7,367	3,702
Dinwiddie	6,194	8,679	5,765	7,447	Falls Church	7,077	1,472	5,819	1,324
Essex	3,029	3,070	2,542	2,657	Franklin	2,505	1,482	2,519	1,421
Fairfax	405,294	162,312	355,133	157,710	Fredericksburg	8,454	4,016	6,707	3,744
Fauquier	17,362	24,933	12,971	22,127	Galax	775	1,832	681	1,603
Floyd	2,970	6,189	2,300	5,293	Hampton	45,481	18,191	41,312	17,902
Fluvanna	7,289	8,071	5,760	7,025	Harrisonburg	10,868	5,514	10,212	6,262
Franklin	8,312	20,797	7,257	18,569	Hopewell	2,658	2,106	4,724	3,885
Frederick	16,021	30,126	11,932	26,083	Lexington	1,780	901	1,514	766
Giles	2,151	6,869	1,950	5,910	Lynchburg	23,394	27,966	14,792	17,982
Gloucester	6,884	14,803	5,404	13,096	Manassas	10,100	6,182	8,423	5,953
Goochland	6,623	9,882	4,889	8,384	Manassas Park	3,913	2,062	3,204	1,733
Grayson	1,529	6,503	1,407	5,592	Martinsville	3,741	2,164	3,533	2,149
Greene	4,089	6,819	2,924	5,945	Newport News	50,319	25,594	45,618	25,468
Greensville	2,618	1,911	2,558	1,737	Norfolk	52,846	19,995	57,023	21,552
Halifax	7,638	10,396	6,897	9,704	Norton	462	1,106	383	1,021
Hanover	25,003	44,121	19,382	39,630	Petersburg	12,293	1,573	12,021	1,451
Henrico	99,667	55,704	93,935	59,857	Poquoson	2,045	5,572	1,601	5,092
Henry	8,995	16,601	8,198	15,208	Portsmouth	30,447	12,634	28,497	12,795
Highland	416	1,089	371	958	Radford	3,330	2,773	2,925	2,638
Isle of Wight	9,346	13,661	7,881	12,204	Richmond	86,460	15,707	81,259	15,581
James City	23,172	20,407	19,105	21,306	Roanoke	25,929	15,356	22,286	14,789
King and Queen	1,581	2,444	1,468	2,099	Salem	5,143	7,676	4,202	7,226
King George	5,381	8,431	4,007	7,341	Staunton	6,886	5,642	5,333	5,133
King William	3,057	7,194	2,760	5,975	Suffolk	28,484	20,006	23,280	18,006
Lancaster	3,358	3,694	2,869	3,523	Virginia Beach	134,252	115,107	91,032	98,224
Lee	1,489	8,363	1,627	7,543	Waynesboro	4,918	5,474	3,764	4,801
Loudoun	135,806	81,107	100,795	69,949	Williamsburg	4,754	1,953	5,206	1,925
Louisa	8,205	13,244	6,212	10,528	Winchester	6,451	5,156	5,164	4,790
Lunenburg	2,395	3,525	2,227	3,204	**Totals**	**2,326,518**	**1,924,131**	**1,981,473**	**1,769,443**
Madison	2,684	5,294	2,203	4,419	All candidates, 2020: Biden, D, 2,326,518; Trump, R, 1,924,131;				
Mathews	1,822	3,895	1,563	3,517	Jorgensen, LB, 62,611.				
Mecklenburg	6,751	9,232	6,285	8,288					
Middlesex	2,482	4,181	2,108	3,670					
Montgomery	22,812	20,532	20,021	19,459	**Washington**				
Nelson	4,301	4,791	3,689	4,154	County	2020 Biden (D)	Trump (R)	2016 Clinton (D)	Trump (R)
New Kent	1,440	6,616	3,546	8,118	Adams	1,064	2,361	1,299	3,083
Northampton	3,643	2,947	3,255	2,686	Asotin	3,442	5,825	3,134	5,741
Northumberland	3,239	4,471	2,852	4,302	Benton	31,505	46,502	26,360	47,194
Nottoway	2,966	4,022	2,829	3,712	Chelan	15,454	16,975	13,032	18,114
Orange	7,921	12,373	5,957	10,521	Clallam	20,966	17,509	17,677	18,794
Page	2,982	9,316	2,514	7,831	Clark	118,803	94,984	92,757	92,441
Patrick	1,948	7,474	1,768	6,454	Columbia	644	1,699	526	1,497
Pittsylvania	10,027	23,637	9,199	21,554	Cowlitz	20,621	27,205	17,908	24,185
Powhatan	5,299	14,026	4,060	11,885	Douglas	6,727	11,241	4,918	9,603
Prince Edward	4,937	4,428	4,591	4,101	Ferry	1,415	2,669	1,098	2,202
Prince George	6,870	10,106	6,419	9,157	Franklin	11,176	15,813	8,886	13,206
Prince William	139,502	76,432	113,144	71,721	Garfield	350	962	279	851
Pulaski	4,882	12,066	4,172	10,322	Grant	7,543	14,101	7,810	18,518
Rappahannock	2,075	2,795	1,747	2,539	Gray's Harbor	14,043	14,174	12,020	14,067
Richmond	1,513	2,547	1,347	2,213	Island	26,762	20,151	20,960	18,465
Roanoke	21,218	33,758	17,200	31,408	Jefferson	14,831	5,163	12,656	6,037
Rockbridge	4,022	8,047	3,508	6,680	King	791,995	210,741	718,322	216,339
Rockingham	9,311	28,608	9,366	25,990	Kitsap	81,115	50,190	63,156	49,018
Russell	2,360	10,850	2,330	9,521	Kittitas	9,470	11,106	7,489	10,100
Scott	1,685	8,964	1,581	8,247	Klickitat	4,588	5,012	4,194	5,789
Shenandoah	6,763	16,390	5,273	14,094	Lewis	13,699	27,625	9,654	21,992
Smyth	2,989	10,941	2,665	9,750	Lincoln	1,587	4,466	1,244	4,108
Southampton	3,917	5,716	3,595	5,035	Mason	15,658	15,966	11,993	13,677
Spotsylvania	7,474	18,410	24,207	34,623	Okanogan	5,661	6,272	6,298	9,610
Stafford	39,657	37,308	27,908	33,868	Pacific	6,283	6,176	4,620	5,360
Surry	2,392	2,023	2,272	1,819	Pend Oreille	2,578	5,655	1,934	4,373
Sussex	2,822	2,217	2,879	2,055	Pierce	217,791	162,611	172,538	146,824
Tazewell	3,169	16,635	2,895	15,168	San Juan	9,066	2,654	7,172	2,688
Warren	6,564	14,033	5,169	11,773	Skagit	21,582	13,724	26,690	24,736
Washington	6,583	21,615	5,553	19,320	Skamania	2,798	3,151	2,232	2,928
Westmoreland	4,413	5,253	3,836	4,448	Snohomish	226,663	135,503	185,227	128,255
Wise	3,084	13,315	2,701	12,086	Spokane	122,188	126,675	93,767	113,435
Wythe	3,123	11,700	2,770	10,046	Stevens	4,783	8,652	5,767	15,161
York	17,410	20,087	12,999	18,837	Thurston	75,687	44,117	68,798	48,624
City					Wahkiakum	1,079	1,532	832	1,344
Alexandria	65,201	14,251	57,242	13,285	Walla Walla	8,289	8,246	9,694	13,651
Bristol	2,296	5,330	1,835	4,892	Whatcom	77,551	46,015	60,340	40,599
Buena Vista	825	1,860	693	1,430	Whitman	7,865	6,394	8,146	7,403
Charlottesville	20,198	3,046	17,901	2,960	Yakima	20,204	21,499	31,291	41,735
Colonial Heights	2,954	5,989	2,367	5,681	**Totals**	**2,023,526**	**1,221,386**	**1,742,718**	**1,221,747**

All candidates, 2020: Biden, D, 2,023,526; Trump, R, 1,221,386; Jorgensen, LB, 52,639; Hawkins, Green, 12,353; La Riva, Socialism/Liberation, 3,188; Kennedy, Socialist Workers, 1,772.

West Virginia

County	2020 Biden (D)	Trump (R)	2016 Clinton (D)	Trump (R)
Barbour	1,438	5,094	1,222	4,527
Berkeley	16,075	32,062	12,321	28,244
Boone	2,029	6,775	1,790	6,504
Braxton	1,453	4,115	1,321	3,537
Brooke	2,936	7,516	2,568	6,625
Cabell	14,733	21,440	11,447	19,850
Calhoun	563	2,346	456	2,035
Clay	640	2,661	568	2,300
Doddridge	432	2,592	362	2,358
Fayette	5,031	11,514	4,290	10,357
Gilmer	591	1,997	545	1,896
Grant	605	4,861	512	4,346
Greenbrier	4,641	10,898	3,765	9,556
Hampshire	1,919	7,829	1,580	6,692
Hancock	3,670	9,653	3,262	8,909
Hardy	1,371	4,827	1,155	4,274
Harrison	9,149	20,581	7,694	18,750
Jackson	3,197	10,025	2,663	9,020
Jefferson	11,831	14,813	9,518	13,204
Kanawha	34,131	46,086	28,263	43,850
Lewis	1,531	5,759	1,347	5,274
Lincoln	1,703	5,967	1,459	5,307
Logan	2,325	10,501	2,092	9,897
Marion	8,836	16,218	6,964	14,668
Marshall	3,348	10,137	2,918	9,666
Mason	2,511	8,422	2,081	7,654
McDowell	1,323	5,125	1,438	4,629
Mercer	5,522	19,185	4,704	17,404
Mineral	2,579	9,904	2,050	9,070
Mingo	1,385	8,521	1,370	7,911
Monongalia	20,064	20,656	14,699	18,432
Monroe	1,330	5,012	1,111	4,443
Morgan	1,945	6,157	1,573	5,732
Nicholas	2,206	8,221	1,840	7,251
Ohio	7,139	12,226	5,493	11,139
Pendleton	816	2,764	729	2,398
Pleasants	692	2,726	621	2,358
Pocahontas	1,039	2,876	928	2,496
Preston	3,147	11,143	2,470	9,538
Putnam	7,824	19,921	5,884	17,788
Raleigh	7,841	24,297	6,443	22,048
Randolph	3,353	8,655	2,735	7,629
Ritchie	585	3,637	496	3,405
Roane	1,451	4,199	1,222	3,781
Summers	1,444	4,068	1,190	3,455
Taylor	1,787	5,439	1,491	4,733
Tucker	933	2,833	751	2,565
Tyler	626	3,183	507	2,996
Upshur	2,247	7,721	1,766	7,005
Wayne	3,964	12,462	3,357	11,152
Webster	608	2,737	556	2,302
Wetzel	1,529	4,933	1,359	4,519
Wirt	461	2,103	386	1,911
Wood	10,816	26,963	8,400	25,434
Wyoming	1,149	7,254	1,062	6,547
Totals	**232,502**	**539,610**	**188,794**	**489,371**

All candidates, 2020: Trump, R, 539,610; Biden, D, 232,502; Jorgensen, LB, 10,462; Hawkins, Mountain, 2,547.

Wisconsin

County	2020 Biden (D)	Trump (R)	2016 Clinton (D)	Trump (R)
Adams	4,329	7,362	3,745	5,966
Ashland	4,794	3,845	4,226	3,303
Barron	9,194	15,803	7,889	13,614
Bayfield	6,155	4,617	4,953	4,124
Brown	65,509	75,865	53,382	67,210
Buffalo	2,859	4,834	2,525	4,048
Burnett	3,569	6,461	2,949	5,410
Calumet	12,115	18,142	9,642	15,367
Chippewa	14,001	21,316	11,887	17,916
Clark	4,520	10,001	4,221	8,652
Columbia	16,408	16,925	13,528	14,163
Crawford	3,953	4,620	3,419	3,836
Dane	260,157	78,789	217,697	71,275
Dodge	16,355	31,354	13,968	26,635
Door	10,044	9,752	8,014	8,580
Douglas	13,214	10,919	11,357	9,661
Dunn	9,909	13,176	9,034	11,486
Eau Claire	31,617	25,339	27,340	23,331
Florence	781	2,133	665	1,898
Fond du Lac	20,588	35,754	17,387	31,022
Forest	1,722	3,287	1,579	2,787
Grant	10,942	13,981	10,051	12,350
Green	10,850	10,165	9,122	8,693
Green Lake	3,344	7,165	2,693	6,216
Iowa	7,828	5,907	6,669	4,809
Iron	1,533	2,439	1,275	2,081
Jackson	4,255	5,789	3,818	4,906
Jefferson	19,904	27,209	16,569	23,417
Juneau	4,747	8,749	4,073	7,130
Kenosha	42,191	44,972	35,799	36,037
Kewaunee	3,977	7,927	3,627	6,618
La Crosse	37,817	28,661	32,406	26,378
Lafayette	3,647	4,820	3,288	3,977
Langlade	3,703	7,330	3,250	6,478
Lincoln	6,260	10,017	5,371	8,401
Manitowoc	16,815	26,944	14,538	23,244
Marathon	30,807	44,623	26,481	39,014
Marinette	7,363	15,303	6,409	13,122
Marquette	3,239	5,719	2,808	4,709
Menominee	1,303	278	1,002	267
Milwaukee	317,251	134,355	288,822	126,069
Monroe	8,432	13,775	7,052	11,356
Oconto	6,715	16,226	5,940	13,345
Oneida	10,105	13,671	8,109	12,132
Outagamie	47,659	58,379	38,068	49,879
Ozaukee	26,515	33,912	20,170	30,464
Pepin	1,489	2,584	1,344	2,206
Pierce	9,789	12,813	8,399	11,272
Polk	9,362	16,590	7,565	13,810
Portage	20,426	19,298	18,529	17,305
Price	3,132	5,394	2,667	4,559
Racine	50,154	54,475	42,641	46,681
Richland	3,995	4,877	3,569	4,013
Rock	46,649	37,133	39,339	31,493
Rusk	2,517	5,257	2,171	4,564
St. Croix	23,190	32,190	17,482	26,222
Sauk	18,103	17,489	14,690	14,799
Sawyer	4,494	5,883	3,503	5,185
Shawano	7,131	15,447	6,068	12,769
Sheboygan	27,109	37,624	23,000	32,514
Taylor	2,693	7,656	2,393	6,579
Trempealeau	6,283	8,828	5,636	7,366
Vernon	7,457	8,216	6,371	7,004
Vilas	5,903	9,261	4,770	8,166
Walworth	22,783	33,844	18,710	28,863
Washburn	3,867	6,332	3,282	5,436
Washington	26,647	60,235	20,852	51,740
Waukesha	103,867	159,633	79,224	142,543
Waupaca	9,699	18,948	8,451	16,209
Waushara	4,388	9,016	3,791	7,667
Winnebago	44,060	47,795	37,047	43,445
Wood	16,360	24,306	14,225	21,498
Totals	**1,630,542**	**1,609,734**	**1,382,536**	**1,405,284**

All candidates, 2020: Biden, D, 1,630,542; Trump, R, 1,609,734; Jorgensen, LB, 38,414; Carroll, Amer. Solidarity, 5,254; Blankenship, Const., 5,207.

Wyoming

County	2020 Biden (D)	Trump (R)	2016 Clinton (D)	Trump (R)
Albany	9,091	8,575	6,890	7,602
Big Horn	788	4,806	604	4,067
Campbell	1,935	16,973	1,324	15,778
Carbon	1,427	5,012	1,279	4,409
Converse	861	5,916	668	5,520
Crook	378	3,651	273	3,348
Fremont	5,519	12,007	4,200	11,167
Goshen	1,203	4,878	924	4,418
Hot Springs	482	1,999	400	1,939
Johnson	897	3,881	638	3,477
Laramie	15,181	27,814	11,573	24,847
Lincoln	1,509	8,673	1,105	6,779
Natrona	8,528	25,267	6,577	23,552
Niobrara	155	1,118	115	1,116
Park	3,404	12,802	2,535	11,115
Platte	890	3,898	719	3,437
Sheridan	4,043	11,843	2,927	10,266
Sublette	882	3,957	644	3,449
Sweetwater	3,822	12,197	3,231	12,154
Teton	9,848	4,341	7,314	3,921
Uinta	1,591	7,494	1,202	6,154
Washakie	651	3,245	532	2,911
Weston	360	3,107	299	3,033
Totals	**73,445**	**193,456**	**55,973**	**174,419**

All candidates, 2020: Trump, R, 193,456; Biden, D, 73,445; Jorgensen, LB, 5,765; Pierce, Ind., 2,224.

Nov. 1, 2019, to Oct. 31, 2020

The Chronology of Events reports the top National, International, and General news stories, month by month. Unless otherwise noted, COVID-19 case and death statistics throughout this section were per the World Health Organization.

November 2019

National

Job Numbers Grow Despite Auto Strike; Stock Indexes Achieve Multiple Closing Highs; Other Economic, Business News—The U.S. Labor Dept. reported Nov. 1 that the economy added 128,000 jobs in Oct. even as a General Motors strike that had shuttered production for nearly six weeks, beginning mid-Sept., continued through Oct. 25. With some 325,000 additional Americans seeking jobs, the unemployment rate ticked up to 3.6% from 3.5% in Sept. Wall Street saw the three major indexes achieve record high closings repeatedly in Nov.—the Dow Jones Industrial Average ended Nov. at 28,051.41, a 3.7% increase from Oct., while the S&P 500 finished the month at 3,140.98, up 3.4%. The Nasdaq Composite Index closed Nov. at 8,665.47, up 4.5%.

On Nov. 22, the Federal Communications Commission unanimously designated Chinese telecom tech companies Huawei and ZTE as national security risks, thereby blocking $8.5 bil in federal rural service funds. On Nov. 21, New York-based office space provider WeWork said it was laying off 2,400 employees, nearly one-fifth of its workforce; the move came less than two months after the company abandoned its IPO. Google announced Nov. 1 it was buying fitness tracker Fitbit for $2.1 bil; on Dec. 3, Google co-founders Sergey Brin and Larry Page announced they were leaving their posts at parent company Alphabet and leaving leadership to Google CEO Sundar Pichai.

Off-Year Elections Deliver Split Verdict—Republican Tate Reeves easily won the Mississippi governor's seat over Jim Hood (D), Nov. 5, and Democrats won narrowly in two gubernatorial races during the month. Incumbent Kentucky Gov. Matt Bevin (R) conceded a close Nov. 5 race to challenger Andy Beshear (D) only after a recanvass Nov. 14, while incumbent Louisiana Gov. John Bel Edwards (D) fended off GOP opponent Eddie Rispone, 51.3% to 48.7%, in the state's runoff election Nov. 16. Democrats in Virginia won a majority in the state's assembly Nov. 5, giving the party control of both chambers of government and the governorship for the first time since 1993.

House Impeachment Inquiry Begins Public Phase; Trump Adviser Convicted of Lying to Congress—The House's impeachment inquiry against Pres. Donald Trump began a new chapter Nov. 13 as witnesses began providing public testimony to the intelligence committee over allegations that Trump attempted to make nearly $400 mil in U.S. military aid to Ukraine contingent on Ukrainian Pres. Volodymyr Zelensky publicly announcing an investigation into unsubstantiated wrongdoing by former U.S. Vice Pres. Joe Biden. During more than 30 hours of testimony delivered over the course of two weeks, the witness most consequential to the charges against Trump appeared to be U.S. ambassador to Ukraine Gordon Sondland, who Nov. 20 affirmed his revised closed-door deposition and said that Trump's personal attorney, Rudy Giuliani, made a White House visit by Zelensky conditional on a Biden investigation, and that he "came to believe" the same was true regarding the promised military aid, which he communicated to a top Zelensky aide. Sondland said that Vice Pres. Mike Pence and Sec. of State Mike Pompeo, among other top officials, knew of the alleged "quid pro quo" scheme.

Acting ambassador to Ukraine Bill Taylor testified Nov. 13 that one of his staff overheard a phone call—on July 26, the day after Trump via phone urged Zelensky to investigate Biden—between Trump and Sondland during which Trump requested updates on the status of Ukraine's Biden investigation. Former U.S. ambassador to Ukraine Marie Yovanovitch, who was removed from her post in May, prior to the Zelensky call, testified to a coordinated effort by Giuliani and Ukrainian associates to push her out of her job. (During Yovanovitch's testimony, Pres. Trump posted comments critical of her to Twitter.) Army Lt. Col. Alexander Vindman, the National Security Council's Director of European Affairs, who was privy to the July 25 call between Zelensky and Trump, testified Nov. 19 to his belief that Trump's request for an investigation into Biden was "improper." In his Nov. 19 testimony, former special envoy to Ukraine Kurt Volker branded Trump's allegations of wrongdoing by Biden,

along with accusations of 2016 election meddling by Ukraine, as "conspiracy theory." Former National Security Adviser John Bolton and White House Chief of Staff Mick Mulvaney, proposed as potential witnesses, did not testify.

On Nov. 15, longtime Trump political adviser Roger Stone was convicted by a federal jury in Washington, DC, on all seven counts of witness tampering, lying to investigators, and obstruction of Congress. The charges stemmed from special counsel Robert Mueller's Russia election-interference probe. On Nov. 7, a New York state judge ordered Trump to pay $2 mil for improperly using the now-defunct Trump Foundation to promote his 2016 campaign and pay business debts.

Trump Gives Clemency to Three Charged With War Crimes—Pres. Donald Trump Nov. 15 granted clemency to three U.S. military personnel convicted or charged with war crimes despite opposition by top military officials, including Defense Sec. Mark Esper. The clemency orders cleared Army 1st Lt. Clint Lorance, serving a 19-year sentence for ordering his troops to fire on unarmed Afghan villagers, killing two; Army Maj. Mathew L. Golsteyn, facing trial for premeditated murder of an Afghan civilian he alleged was a Taliban bombmaker; and Navy SEAL Edward Gallagher, acquitted of murder in both Iraq and Afghanistan but convicted on a related, lesser charge.

International

Extremist Groups Target Military Posts in Mali, Niger—A series of attacks in late 2019 supported growing concerns about the spread of Islamist extremism in West Africa. Gunmen killed approximately 53 soldiers and one civilian at a military outpost in northern Mali's Menaka region, Nov. 1, in an attack claimed by the Sunni terrorist group Islamic State of Iraq and Syria (ISIS). A separate assault, for which ISIS also claimed responsibility, killed 30 Malian soldiers Nov. 18. In late Sept., an al-Qaeda-linked group had been blamed for twin attacks that killed 38 soldiers in central Mali. At least 71 soldiers died in a jihadist attack on a military base near the Mali border in Inates, Niger, Dec. 10. The Dec. raid, attributed to an Islamic State-affiliated group, was one of the deadliest ever in Niger.

U.S. Formalizes Climate Accord Withdrawal; Severe Flooding Hits Venice—In an announcement Nov. 4, Sec. of State Mike Pompeo formally initiated the process of withdrawing the U.S. from the landmark 2015-16 Paris Agreement on climate change, as promised by Pres. Trump in June 2017. Trump, who repeatedly voiced skepticism toward human-caused climate change and the scientific consensus around it, argued the accord disadvantaged the U.S.

On Nov. 12, the iconic Italian canal city of Venice suffered its worst flooding in 53 years, followed by two other major flood events within five days. At least two people were killed by the high water levels, which the city's mayor blamed on climate change.

Protests Oust Bolivian President—Facing military pressure, Bolivia's leftist Pres. Evo Morales resigned Nov. 10 following nearly three weeks of protests and counterprotests over his Oct. reelection, the same day that an Organization of American States (OAS) report recommended the election be held again due to widespread irregularities. Morales called for new elections, then abruptly stepped down and sought asylum in Mexico. The first indigenous Bolivian leader and a 14-year incumbent, Morales was popular with some Bolivians for his anti-poverty and economic policies, but a referendum on his running for a fourth term did not pass. (The courts cleared his candidacy nonetheless in 2017.) After the resignations of several ranking Morales allies, Second Senate Vice Pres Jeanine Áñez Chávez became acting president Nov. 12. In the aftermath, Morales supporters clashed with security forces; at least 33 people were killed between the Oct. 20 vote and Nov. 25 (30 of those after Áñez took office).

Demonstrations Rock Colombia, Chile—In Colombia's largest national strike since 1977, hundreds of thousands of protesters demonstrated Nov. 21 over rumored cuts to pensions and education funding. Though largely peaceful, violence between protesters and police occurred in multiple cities including Cali and the capital, Bogotá. As protests continued into Dec., activists also criticized the government's failure to implement its 2016 peace accord with FARC rebels.

Protests in Chile that began in mid-Oct. over subway fare increases continued in Nov. and Dec. as demonstrators voiced opposition to inequality and health care costs. Lawmakers in mid-Nov. agreed to hold a referendum in Apr. 2020 on replacing Chile's 1980 constitution. At least 29 people were killed in the unrest through 2019, and the UN in mid-Dec. accused Chilean police and security forces of abuses including torture, sexual violence, and use of unnecessary lethal force.

Clampdown on Iranian Protests Kills Up to 1,500—Iranian authorities suppressed nationwide protests that broke out Nov. 15 after the government unexpectedly increased fuel prices by as much as 300% and ordered rationing. While casualty estimates varied widely, the crackdown, which was reportedly ordered by Iran's Supreme Leader Ayatollah Ali Khamenei and included shooting unarmed protesters, killed some 1,500 people in less than two weeks, according to a Reuters dispatch that cited three Iranian ministers. (Amnesty International put the death toll at just over 300, Nov. 15-18; a U.S. official said more than 1,000 may have been killed by government forces.) The fuel price hikes were linked to efforts by the regime to address an economic crisis exacerbated by U.S. sanctions.

Authoritarian Family Returns to Office After Sri Lankan Election—Ultranationalist former Sri Lankan defense secretary Gotabaya Rajapaksa defeated the ruling party candidate Nov. 16 in a hard-fought election reflecting deep ethnic divisions lingering after the country's bloody 26-year civil war. Rajapaksa won in regions where Sinhalese Buddhists, who comprise some 70% of the population, predominate, and the final tally showed Rajapaksa winning 52%-42% over Sajith Premadasa in the polling, participated in by 83.7% of eligible voters. While many Sinhalese voters credited Gotabaya Rajapaksa and his brother, former Pres. Mahinda Rajapaksa (2005-15), with ending the fighting, Tamil political groups strongly opposed Gotabaya Rajapaksa, who was accused of brutal tactics including torture and extrajudicial killing in the war's later years.

Netanyahu Charged as Israel Government Stalemate Continues; U.S. Formally Recognizes West Bank Settlements—Israeli Prime Min. Benjamin Netanyahu—in the post for more than 13 years—was formally charged Nov. 21 with bribery, breach of trust, and fraud. The charges came after nearly three years of investigations related to allegations that Netanyahu and his wife, Sara Netanyahu, received over $260,000 of goods in exchange for political favors and that the couple gave favorable regulatory concessions to two media outlets in return for positive coverage. Netanyahu's rival, Benny Gantz of the Blue and White alliance, failed to form a government Nov. 20 ahead of the deadline established following Netanyahu's own inability to do so in Oct. Israel was moving toward an unprecedented third national election in less than a year (to be held in Mar. 2020, until which Netanyahu would continue as interim PM).

The Trump administration reversed decades of longstanding policy Nov. 18 when it declared that the U.S. does not regard Israeli settlements in the Palestinian-occupied West Bank as contravening international law.

Despite being charged while in office, a first for a sitting Israeli premier, the 70-year-old Netanyahu easily won his party's leadership race, held Dec. 26, with 72.5% support.

Pro-Democracy Candidates Win Big in Hong Kong Elections as Protests Continue—Pro-democracy candidates won 389 of 452 seats on Hong Kong's district council—up from just 124 of seats held previously—in Nov. 24 voting that was participated in by 71% of eligible voters. Pro-democracy demonstrations in Hong Kong continued for a fifth straight month, with the first protest-related death recorded when a university student died from injuries sustained in a Nov. 4 fall from a parking garage, where police and protesters were clashing. An elderly man was killed Nov. 14 by a brick thrown by a protester the previous day.

Iraq's Prime Minister Steps Down Amid Continuing Deadly Protests—Iraqi Prime Min. Adel Abdul Mahdi announced his resignation Nov. 29 following two months of recurring anti-government demonstrations during which at least 400 mostly unarmed protesters and bystanders were killed—according to UN and medical sources—by security forces and militias firing tear gas and live ammunition. Voicing opposition to government corruption, lack of opportunity, and Iranian influence in the country, protesters had blocked access to the main Iraqi port near Basra and set fire to Iranian consulates in centrally located Karbala and the southern city of Najaf.

General

Nine Killed in Mexico Ambush Blamed on Cartel—Gunmen killed three women and six children with dual U.S.-Mexican citizenship in attacks on the victims' vehicles about 70 mi. south of the U.S.-Mexico border at Douglas, AZ, Nov. 4. The victims—all members of the LeBaron family who belonged to an isolated Mormon offshoot community in Mexico—were traveling to a wedding; some children escaped and survived. Mexican officials said drug traffickers had mistaken the vehicles for those of a competing cartel, but that account was not confirmed.

CDC Finds Vaping Illness Link—The Centers for Disease Control and Prevention Nov. 8 announced what it believed was a strong link between Vitamin E acetate and a nationwide outbreak of vaping-related lung illnesses, with over 2,000 cases and at least 40 deaths. The additive (primarily used in THC vaping products) was confirmed by an agency official to be the cause of most of the deaths, which had risen to 54, Dec. 20.

Seattle Claims MLS Championship—The Seattle Sounders FC defeated Toronto FC, 3-1, at CenturyLink field in Seattle, WA, Nov. 10, winning the team's second Major League Soccer Cup. Seattle, which defeated Toronto in the 2016 final but lost the title to them a year later, scored the first goal in the 57th minute on a shot by right-back Kelvin Leerdam that deflected off an opponent. Midfielder Víctor Rodríguez and forward Raúl Ruidíaz added goals for Seattle in the 76th and 90th minutes, respectively, before Toronto striker Jozy Altidore scored on a header in the third minute of stoppage time. Rodríguez, who didn't enter the game until the 61st minute as a substitute, was named the Cup's MVP.

Francis Makes First Papal Visit to Japan—Pope Francis Nov. 23-26 visited Japan, where he called for the worldwide disarmament of nuclear weapons while speaking at Nagasaki and Hiroshima and for the abolition of nuclear power as he addressed survivors of the country's 2011 Fukushima Daiichi nuclear disaster. It was the first visit by a pope to Japan—where Catholics comprise less than 1% of the population—since Pope John Paul II traveled there in 1981.

December 2019
National

White House Tightens Food Stamp Eligibility, Approves Federal Parental Leave—The Trump administration Dec. 4 established a rule narrowing states' ability to waive employment requirements for adults receiving federal food stamp assistance. According to Agriculture Dept. officials, the move would deny eligibility for food benefits to roughly 688,000 work-eligible recipients without dependents while saving approx. $5.5 bil over five years. The move was sharply criticized by Democratic lawmakers and anti-poverty groups. Pres. Trump Dec. 20 signed a measure providing civilian federal employees with 12 weeks of paid parental leave—already available to military personnel—beginning in Oct. 2020.

California Utility PG&E Settles With Fire Victims; Boeing Halts 737 Max Production; Other Economic/Business News—Pacific Gas & Electric, in bankruptcy proceedings since early 2019, agreed Dec. 6 to pay $13.5 bil to victims of four 2015-18 northern California wildfires—including 2018's Camp Fire, the deadliest in the state's history with 85 civilian fatalities—blamed on faulty PG&E equipment. (The company also pleaded guilty to related manslaughter charges in Mar. 2020.) Boeing announced Dec. 16 it would temporarily stop production the next month of its 737 Max airliner, grounded globally since Mar. 2019 following two crashes that killed nearly 350 people in Indonesia and Ethiopia. The company fired CEO Dennis Muilenburg Dec. 23, two days after whistleblowers testifying before Congress alleged an unsafe culture of cost-cutting at Boeing, and of lax oversight by the FAA. Former Nissan chairman Carlos Ghosn, under house arrest in Japan for charges that included financial misconduct, attracted international attention after he fled Dec. 29 allegedly stowed in a musical instrument case on a private jet.

The Labor Dept. reported Dec. 6 that the U.S. economy added 266,000 jobs in Nov., far outpacing expectations amid indicators of a slowing global economy. Aided in part by the return of GM autoworkers sidelined during a six-week strike, the unemployment rate ticked back to Sept.'s 50-year-low rate of 3.5%. The Bureau of Economic Analysis's final estimate for the third quarter of 2019 reported real GDP increased by an annual rate of 2.1%, compared to 2.0% in the second quarter. On Wall Street, the Dow Jones Industrial Average ended Dec. at 28,538.44, a 1.7% increase from Nov., while the S&P 500 finished the month at 3,230.78, up 2.9%; the Nasdaq Composite Index closed Dec. at 8,972.60, up 3.5%. Over 2019, the S&P 500 and Nasdaq indices experienced their greatest annual gains since 2013, increasing by 28.9% and 35.2%, respectively, while the Dow gained 22.3%.

Saudi Arabia's state-owned oil giant Saudi Aramco raised $25.6 bil Dec. 5 in a record-setting IPO but fell short of expectations.

Watchdog Report Legitimizes FBI Russia Investigation, Critiques Wiretap Process—The Justice Dept.'s inspector general's office Dec. 9 released a report on the origins of the FBI's probe into Russian interference in the 2016 presidential election. The long-anticipated analysis concluded the agency was legally justified in launching an investigation in July 2016 into then-candidate Donald Trump's campaign and acted without political bias. Inspector Gen. Michael Horowitz's report also refuted accusations that the investigation was carried out to sabotage Trump and debunked the theory that the FBI "spied" on the campaign through undercover sources. The report detailed multiple errors with the agency's legal applications to wiretap former Trump campaign adviser Carter Page including "significant inaccuracies and omissions." Trump and his allies continued to insist—despite Horowitz's findings—that the FBI had engaged in a conspiracy aimed at his "overthrow," and Attorney Gen. William Barr, the head of the Justice Dept., released a statement disputing the FBI's "authorized purpose" to investigate.

House Impeaches Pres. Trump—A very divided House of Representatives voted almost completely along party lines Dec. 18 to impeach Pres. Donald Trump. The House action represented only the third time in U.S. history a president was charged with "high crimes and misdemeanors," after Pres. Andrew Johnson (1868) and Pres. Bill Clinton (1998). Accused of attempting to condition U.S. security assistance to Ukraine on that country publicly investigating his political rival, former Vice Pres. Joe Biden, Trump was impeached on two articles, abuse of power (by a 230-197 vote) and obstruction of Congress (229-198), without the support of any GOP lawmakers. Two Democrats, Rep. Collin Peterson (MN), and Jeff Van Drew (NJ), voted against both articles; Van Drew switched his party affiliation to Republican the next day. Ahead of the vote, lawmakers debated for some eight hours during which Democrats asserted it was the lawmakers' constitutional responsibility to impeach, while Republicans condemned the inquiry process itself as unfair. Public support for Trump's impeachment and removal declined slightly ahead of the House vote, according to a Gallup poll conducted Dec. 2-15, with 46% in favor of impeachment and removal compared to 52% in early Oct., shortly after the inquiry was first announced in late Sept.

Leading up to the House vote, the chamber's intelligence committee Dec. 3 released its report, based primarily on 17 witness interviews, including the public testimony of 12 current or former officials. The report claimed "overwhelming" evidence of misconduct by Trump along with an "unprecedented campaign" of defying subpoenas to impede the House's investigation. Republicans representing three House committees Dec. 2 released a separate report in defense of Trump, which ignored witness testimony and instead embraced debunked theories of Ukrainian interference in the 2016 election and corruption involving Biden and his son, Hunter. On the first day of hearings in the House Judiciary Committee, which later voted along party lines to authorize the impeachment articles, three legal scholars summoned by Democrats testified that Trump's efforts to pressure Ukraine clearly warranted impeachment, while a Republican legal-expert invitee said it did not.

For the remainder of Dec., House Speaker Nancy Pelosi (D, CA) refused to formally send the approved articles of impeachment to the Senate in an apparent effort to force Senate Major-

ity Leader Mitch McConnell (R, KY) to allow new testimony and evidence in the pending Senate trial, including potentially calling as witnesses Trump's chief of staff Mick Mulvaney and former national security adviser John Bolton. In a public statement, McConnell said that he was in "total coordination" with the White House, which some criticized as contradicting his role as a juror in the Senate trial.

International

NATO Summit Tainted by Hostility Between Trump, Allies—Tensions between U.S. Pres. Donald Trump and French Pres. Emmanuel Macron and other members of the international community dominated the 70th anniversary meeting of NATO member countries Dec. 3-4 near London, England, UK. Macron in an interview published in *The Economist* in Nov. said NATO was experiencing a "brain death"—exemplified by Trump's Oct. removal of troops from northern Syria, which allowed NATO member Turkey to proceed with widely condemned cross-border attacks against U.S.-allied Syrian Kurdish forces—and said NATO allies may no longer be able to depend on America for defense. Trump, in a pre-summit press conference, said Macron had been "very disrespectful" and continued to criticize other NATO member countries, especially Germany, for defense spending shortfalls. Nevertheless, the alliance's joint closing statement reaffirmed members' "mutual commitment" and highlighted recent threats posed by Russia and China.

Bombshell Afghanistan War Report Reveals Deliberate U.S. Deception—The *Washington Post* Dec. 9 published interviews and notes from confidential government reports concerning the U.S. war in Afghanistan that revealed that U.S. officials had intentionally misinformed the public during the 18-year conflict, concealing military failures, claiming fictional progress, and distorting evidence. The *Post* obtained the more than 2,000 pages of documents—which it dubbed the Afghanistan Papers—following a three-year legal effort under the Freedom of Information Act. Over 775,000 U.S. troops have been deployed to Afghanistan since 2001, of whom 2,300 were killed and 20,589 wounded in action.

Afghan officials announced Dec. 22 that incumbent Pres. Ashraf Ghani narrowly won reelection, with 50.6% of the first-round Sept. 28 vote, according to long-delayed preliminary results. The polling was marred by record-low turnout, accusations of fraud, and violence that killed at least 85 civilians during the campaign.

Ukraine, Russia Reach Cease-Fire in Donbass—Russian Pres. Vladimir Putin and Ukrainian Pres. Volodymyr Zelensky made a small but significant step toward achieving peace in war-torn eastern Ukraine Dec. 9 when they agreed to implement a cease-fire in the region known as Donbass, contested by pro-Russia separatists and the Ukrainian government, by the end of the month. Meeting for the first time, in talks mediated in Paris, France, by French Pres. Emmanuel Macron and German Chancellor Angela Merkel, the two leaders also agreed to swap all conflict-related prisoners and withdraw Ukrainian and Russian-backed forces from three additional areas by the end of Mar. 2020. Since 2014, fighting in Ukraine has killed more than 13,000 people and displaced some 1.4 mil.

Conservatives Increase Majority in UK Elections, Clear Way for Brexit—Britain's ruling Conservative Party won a definitive victory in parliamentary elections Dec. 12, delivering Prime Min. Boris Johnson a mandate to "get Brexit done," his oft-repeated campaign phrase. Achieving their largest majority since 1987, the Conservatives secured 365 of 650 seats in the House of Commons, up 48 from 2017, while the main opposition Labour Party won just 202, down 60, in polling participated in by 67.3% of eligible voters. Labour's Jeremy Corbyn said he would resign as leader in early 2020. The House of Commons Dec. 20 approved (358-234) Johnson's plan for the UK to leave the EU by the end of Jan., paving the way for its passage in the House of Lords.

On Dec. 13 Northern Ireland voters for the first time elected more Irish nationalist MPs than British Unionists.

Tentative U.S.-China Trade Deal Forestalls New Tariffs—Pres. Donald Trump Dec. 13 announced that the White House and China had agreed to a "phase one" deal aimed at easing the 21-month-old U.S.-China trade war, beginning with the suspension of tariffs on roughly $160 bil of Chinese imports set to take effect Dec. 15 and the halving of existing 15% duties on $120 bil in other products. (A 25% tariff on $250 bil in imports would remain as the U.S entered the second phase.) Though Trump said China had agreed to "many structural changes," he provided few details; an administration official said China had committed to purchasing some $200 bil in energy, farm, and manufactured products over two years. Trump and Chinese Vice Premier Liu He signed the deal at the White House Jan. 15.

UN Climate Talks Fail to Deliver Results, Expose Rift—The 2019 United Nations Climate Change Conference in Madrid, Spain, concluded Dec. 15 after two weeks of disappointment over pending withdrawal by the U.S. from the 2015 Paris climate accord and deep divisions between industrialized countries, quickly expanding economies such as Brazil and India, and vulnerable island nations. Negotiators were unable to devise rules for a carbon trading system, and major greenhouse gas emitters, led by the U.S., resisted developing a funding mechanism to aid poorer countries already grappling with climate change effects.

Five Sentenced to Death in Saudi Journalist's Killing—A Saudi court sentenced five people to death and three others to a combined 24 years in prison Dec. 23 for the killing of Saudi dissident journalist Jamal Khashoggi in 2018. The nearly year-long trial was criticized by human rights groups for what they called its total absence of transparency as well as the government's refusal to coordinate with independent inspectors. Saudi officials said the assassination was carried out by a rogue operation, disregarding the CIA's conclusion that Saudi Crown Prince Mohammed bin Salman had ordered the killing,

Somalia Suicide Bombing Kills Dozens—A suicide truck bomber detonated at a checkpoint in Somalia's capital, Mogadishu, Dec. 28, killing at least 90 people and injuring about 150. The attack was claimed by al-Qaeda affiliate al-Shabab. Earlier in the month, al-Shabab claimed a gun attack on a Mogadishu hotel that killed five people, including three civilians.

Iraqis Storm American Embassy in Baghdad Over Air Raid—Iraqi Shiite militia supporters reportedly numbering at least several dozen forced their way into the U.S. embassy compound in Baghdad Dec. 31, two days after U.S. airstrikes killed 25 members of the Iran-backed fighters Kataeb Hezbollah in Iraq. The assault ended without reported fatalities within hours; an estimated 6,000 protesters at the compound dispersed the next day. In response, Pres. Donald Trump ordered the deployment of roughly 650 additional troops to the Middle East.

Following nearly three months of anti-government protests that had resulted in the deaths of more than 450 Iraqis (mostly by the country's security forces), Iraqi Pres. Barham Salih Dec. 26 threatened to resign rather than name as prime minister the nominee of the parliament's largest, Iran-backed bloc, whom he said protesters demanding an independent PM would reject.

General

Saudi Trainee Kills Three at Florida Air Base; Anti-Semitic Attacks Befall NY, NJ—A Saudi air force trainee at Naval Air Station Pensacola, FL, fatally shot three U.S. Navy sailors Dec. 6. Armed with a handgun, the 21-year-old was killed by police following the attack, later classified by the Justice Dept. as terrorism. Four days later, two shooters killed three people at a kosher market in Jersey City, NJ, before they were killed in a four-hour standoff with police; preceding the attack, also investigated as a potential act of terrorism, the two men killed a police officer at a cemetery. On Dec. 28, a man stabbed and injured five people at a Hanukkah celebration in an Orthodox Jewish rabbi's residence in Monsey, NY. The attacker fled in his vehicle and was apprehended soon after.

Russia Barred From Global Sports for 4 Years—The World Anti-Doping Agency (WADA) banned Russia from most international athletic competitions through 2023—including the 2020 and 2022 Olympic Games and 2022 FIFA World Cup—over allegations of noncompliance by Russia's drug-monitoring body. Russian athletes without drug violations could continue to compete under a neutral flag.

Catastrophic Wildfires Decimate Australia; New Zealand Volcano Eruption Kills 21—Australian bushfires that began in Sept. continued to worsen across the continent and Tasmania in Dec., burning some 12.4 mil acres and killing at least 16 people by Dec. 31. The southeastern coastal states of Victoria and New South Wales were most affected. Bolstered by deforestation and prolonged drought, the blazes were thought to have killed upwards of 1 bil animals including threatened/endangered species; widely publicized images and videos of injured koalas and kangaroos helped spur donations. The ecological tragedy sparked protests within Australia over Prime Min. Scott Morrison's perceived lack of action on climate change, which was thought by most scientists to have exacerbated the bushfires.

A volcano erupted violently and unexpectedly on New Zealand's Whakaari/White Island Dec. 9, spewing ash and toxic gases that killed 21 people by the end of Jan. 2020. Nearly all of the remaining 26 people on the 800-acre tourist destination at the time of the eruption sustained burn injuries.

January 2020
National

Job Growth Slows in Dec.; Facebook Agrees to Illinois Privacy Violation Settlement—The Labor Dept. reported Jan. 10 that the economy added 145,000 jobs in Dec. For the year 2019, the economy added 2.1 mil jobs, 600,000 fewer than in 2018. Unemployment remained at a historic-low 3.5% as annual wages increased by 2.9% throughout 2019, down from 3.3% a year prior. On Wall Street, the Dow Jones Industrial Average ended Jan. at 28,256.03, a 1.0% decrease from Dec., while the S&P 500 finished the month at 3,225.52, down 0.2%; the Nasdaq Composite Index closed Jan. at 9,150.94, up 2.0%.

Facebook Jan. 29 agreed to pay $550 mil to settle a class-action lawsuit in Illinois alleging it violated the state's privacy law by collecting users' facial recognition data without their permission.

Trump Impeachment Trial Begins; Senate Rejects New Witnesses—For only the third time in history, the Senate commenced presidential impeachment trial proceedings, Jan. 16, the day after the House voted 228-193 to send articles of impeachment to the chamber. The articles charged Pres. Donald Trump with abuse of power and obstruction of Congress related to allegations that the president attempted to withhold military aid to Ukraine in exchange for that country's president announcing investigations into Trump's political rival former Vice Pres. Joe Biden and his son Hunter's business dealings in Ukraine. House Intelligence Committee Chair Adam Schiff (CA) and six other House Democrats—Jason Crow (CO), Val Demings (FL), Sylvia R. Garcia (TX), Hakeem Jeffries (NY), Zoe Lofgren (CA), Jerrold Nadler (NY)—managed the prosecution in the Senate. In opening statements Jan. 22, Schiff highlighted the necessity of holding the trial ahead of the impending 2020 election, saying "we cannot be assured that the vote will be fairly won." The managers' arguments focused on witnesses' testimony before the House during its three-month inquiry, including allegations of quid pro quo they argued were strongly supported by archived text messages and statements by current and former Trump administration officials.

Led by White House counsel Pat Cipollone, Trump's defense team (including legal professor and media figure Alan Dershowitz and former Pres. Bill Clinton impeachment prosecutor Kenneth Starr) opened its rebuttal Jan. 25, arguing that Democrats lacked direct evidence of wrongdoing. Charging Democrats with attempting to overturn the 2016 election results and steal the upcoming race, they maintained Trump had been legitimately concerned over possible meddling by Ukraine in the 2016 election, a theory which had been widely debunked. Senators questioned the defense team for 16 hours Jan. 29-30, with Sen. Mitt Romney (R, UT) and Lisa Murkowski (R, AK) asking if Trump's actions were impeachable if he was motivated by both public and private concerns. Dershowitz argued quid pro quo actions are not impeachable if the president is acting to get himself "elected in the public interest."

Despite a Jan. 26 *NY Times* report that former White House national security adviser John Bolton in his yet-to-be-published book said Trump told him he was making the Ukrainian aid contingent on an investigation announcement, the Senate Jan. 31 rejected (51-49, with GOP Sens. Romney and Susan Collins (ME) voting with Democrats) a measure to allow subpoenas to call new witnesses—including Bolton—and consider new evidence. In mid-Jan., the U.S. Government Accountability Office declared illegal the Trump administration's freezing of the Ukraine assistance.

Trump Signs Updated Free Trade Agreement With Mexico, Canada—Pres. Donald Trump signed a revised version of the 25-year-old North American Free Trade Agreement (NAFTA) Jan. 29, fulfilling a campaign pledge to overhaul it. Though the U.S.-Mexico-Canada Agreement (USMCA) retained most of NAFTA's framework, it boosted U.S. farmers' access to the Canadian dairy market, established new e-commerce guidelines, and increased mandates on North American-made parts and minimum wages for automakers. To gain Democratic support, the White House conceded to some of lawmakers' demands over labor, environmental regulations, and prescription drug enforcement. The Senate Jan. 16 approved the deal by an 89-10 vote, a month after the House (385-41, Dec. 19). Despite Trump's rare bipartisan victory, he declined to invite Democratic lawmakers to the signing. Mexico's Senate approved the pact in Dec. 2019; Canada ratified it in Mar. 2020.

International

U.S. Drone Kills Top Iranian Commander; Counterattack Injures 100+ U.S. Troops; Iran Downs Ukrainian Airliner—A controversial U.S. drone strike targeted and killed Iranian Islamic Revolutionary Guard Corps (IRGC) Major Gen. Qassem Soleimani near Iraq's Baghdad Intl. Airport, early morning Jan. 3. Pres. Donald Trump said the strike was ordered to stop a "major attack" planned by Soleimani and the IRGC, which the Trump administration in 2019 had designated a foreign terrorist organization. The strike killed nine others, including four more IRGC officers and an Iraqi militia leader. During three days of national mourning, hundreds of thousands of Iranians flooded the streets in Tehran; 50 were killed and 200 injured in a stampede Jan. 7 ahead of a burial ceremony in Kerman. That same day, Iran launched ballistic missiles at two Iraqi bases housing American troops. While no one was killed and other effects of the attacks were initially downplayed, U.S. defense officials in Feb. said the missile attacks had caused mild brain injuries to at least 109 U.S. personnel. Trump Jan. 8 announced further economic sanctions on Iran.

Ukraine Intl. Airlines Flight 752 crashed Jan. 8 shortly after departing Tehran's international airport, killing all 176 onboard, including 63 Canadians. Iran later that week admitted its military shot the jet down, saying it was mistaken for a cruise missile.

Though the White House had blamed Soleimani for attacks in recent months, including a Dec. 27 rocket attack near Kirkuk, Iraq, that killed a U.S. contractor and a Dec. 31 assault on the U.S. embassy in Baghdad, senior administration defense officials in the wake of Soleimani's death did not confirm Trump's claim that Soleimani had been targeting for attack four U.S. embassies. Democratic lawmakers were highly critical of the attack, saying his killing dangerously escalated already tense U.S.-Iranian relations and claiming the White House violated protocol by not consulting Congress ahead of the strike. Republican legislators largely supported the action; however, GOP Sens. Mike Lee (UT) and Rand Paul (KY) publicly voiced dissatisfaction with a classified Jan. 8 briefing meant to justify it. The House voted on party lines Jan. 9, 224-194, to limit Trump's war powers in Iran. The Soleimani strike also sparked demonstrations in Baghdad. Earlier in Jan., Iraq's parliament voted to eject U.S. troops, after which Pres. Trump threatened sanctions; U.S.-Iraq joint military operations resumed in Iraq Jan. 15.

Drone Attack Kills Over 100 Yemeni Soldiers—A missile and drone strike Jan. 18 on a military training camp in Yemen's central province of Marib killed at least 116 mostly government troops. The attack, blamed on Iran-backed Houthi rebels, targeted a mosque on the base and came amid a period of relative calm despite the country's ongoing civil war. Two days later,

pro-government forces staged assaults on rebels east of Marib, and Saudi-led airstrikes reportedly hit the rebel-controlled capital Sanaa and Saada province. Since 2015, fighting had killed more than 100,000 people, displaced roughly 3.6 mil, and left about 24 mil—80% of the population—aid-dependent in what the UN has called the "world's worst humanitarian crisis."

The White House announced Feb. 6 that Qasim al-Raymi, the leader of al-Qaeda in the Arabian Peninsula, was killed in a Jan. 2020 drone strike in Yemen.

Trump Reveals Middle East Peace Plan—Pres. Donald Trump announced his administration's long-anticipated Israeli-Palestinian peace plan Jan. 28, calling it a "realistic two-state solution." The proposal was immediately rejected by Palestinian Authority Pres. Mahmoud Abbas as strongly favoring Israel, an analysis shared by most international observers. In addition to moving the Palestinian capital to the outskirts of East Jerusalem, the proposal permitted Israel to annex most of its controversial West Bank settlements—viewed as illegal by most of the international community—while freezing any further settlement construction during negotiations. In exchange for ceding control of nearly 30% of the West Bank and dismantling Hamas and other militant groups, Palestinians under the plan would be granted new, mostly desert territory along the Egyptian border adjoining the Gaza Strip and provided an international investment fund totaling $50 bil over 10 years.

Engineered by Trump's son-in-law and senior adviser Jared Kushner, the plan was embraced at the announcement by acting Israeli Prime Min. Benjamin Netanyahu, who was formally indicted that same day by an Israeli court on charges of fraud, bribery, and breach of trust in three different cases.

Novel Coronavirus Kills Over 250 in China, Prompting Travel Restrictions and Emergency Declarations—The UN-affiliated World Health Organization (WHO) declared a global health emergency Jan. 30 amid an outbreak of a highly contagious and untreatable new coronavirus that was identified in Wuhan, Hubei province, China, in Dec. 2019 and had by the end of Jan. killed at least 258 people out of 11,000 confirmed cases, mostly in Hubei. The mild-to-severe respiratory illness, known as coronavirus disease 2019, or COVID-19, was caused by a virus named SARS-CoV-2, and by then was identified in approximately 100 people outside of China.

The U.S. Centers for Disease Control and Prevention (CDC) Jan. 21 announced the first confirmed COVID-19 case in the U.S., diagnosed in a person north of Seattle, who had recently traveled from Wuhan. Chinese health authorities Jan. 23 "sealed off" Wuhan and its population of 11 mil, and numerous countries restricted travel to and from China. Pres. Trump announced an executive order barring entry to the U.S. to the majority of foreign nationals who had traveled to China in the last two weeks, effective Feb. 2, and he declared a national public health emergency Jan. 31.

UK Officially Achieves Brexit; Trade Negotiations to Follow—Entering into an unknown future, the UK left the European Union at 11 p.m. on Jan. 31, three-and-a-half years after voters narrowly chose "Brexit" in a contentious referendum. In the wake of Prime Min. Boris Johnson's pro-Brexit Conservative Party's sweeping victory at the polls in Dec. 2019, the House of Commons Jan. 9 passed his withdrawal agreement bill (330-231) without the fractious debate that had characterized Brexit proceedings under former Prime Min. Theresa May. Parliament had rejected May's agreement three times, Jan.-Mar. 2019, primarily over border issues between Ireland and Northern Ireland. (Johnson's deal aligned Northern Ireland, which is part of the UK, with the EU for at least four years.) The House of Lords ratified it Jan. 22. Queen Elizabeth gave her symbolic assent the next day, ahead of the EU parliament's approval Jan. 29 (by a 621-49 vote). The UK commenced an 11-month transition period under which most EU laws regarding movement of people and goods continued; Johnson was tasked with negotiating a new trade agreement with the bloc.

General

Golden Globes Set Tone for Awards Season—The Hollywood Foreign Press Assn. awarded best drama film to the British war epic *1917* at the 77th Golden Globe Awards Jan. 5 in Beverly

Hills, CA. Among other major winners, 1960s-set epic *Once Upon a Time... in Hollywood* earned best comedy/musical film, and writer Quentin Tarantino took home best screenplay. In the TV categories, HBO's satirical *Succession* won best TV drama (with star Brian Cox taking best actor in a dramatic series) and BBC's *Fleabag* claimed best comedy series, with its star and creator Phoebe Waller-Bridge awarded best musical/comedy series actress.

Harry and Meghan Announce Retreat From Royal Family—Britain's Prince Harry—sixth in line to the monarchial throne—and wife Meghan Markle announced Jan. 8 via Instagram that they would "step back" from royal life, strive to become financially independent, and split their time between the UK, Canada, and the U.S. According to a royal statement released 10 days later, the couple, who married in 2018, would give up public funds and repay some $3 mil used to refurbish their home; their royal duties formally ended Mar. 31.

LSU Takes College Football Championship—The Louisiana State Univ. Tigers claimed their fourth national title, overwhelming the defending champion Clemson Univ. Tigers, 42-25, in the College Football Playoff (CFP) Championship game at Mercedes-Benz Superdome in New Orleans, LA, Jan. 13. Racking up three straight touchdowns, top-ranked LSU overcame a 10-point deficit in the second quarter to lead No. 3-seed Clemson 28-17 at halftime. LSU's Joe Burrow was named Offensive MVP with 31 of 49 pass completions for a CFP-record 463 yards. In Dec. 2019, Burrow won the Heisman Trophy, earning a record 90.7% of first-place votes.

Jeter, Walker Elected to Baseball Hall of Fame; MLB Penalizes Astros for Sign Stealing—The Baseball Writers' Assn. of America (BBWAA) elected NY Yankees shortstop Derek Jeter and Canadian slugger Larry Walker to the Baseball Hall of Fame Jan. 22. Jeter, who amassed 3,465 hits and five World Series rings, was elected in his first year on the ballot just one vote short of a unanimous decision. A five-time All-Star with 383 home runs over 17 seasons, Walker was selected in his final year of eligibility and was only the second player from Canada elected, as well as the first from the Colorado Rockies. On Dec. 8, the Modern Baseball Era Committee elected 8-time All-Star catcher Ted Simmons and baseball labor pioneer Marvin Miller.

Major League Baseball commissioner Rob Manfred Jan. 13 fined the Houston Astros organization $5 mil and suspended for one year the team's general manager Jeff Luhnow and manager A.J. Hinch for their roles in a scandal in which the team admitted it had used a center-field video camera at 2017 home games to steal signs. Manfred was criticized for not revoking the team's 2017 World Series title nor disciplining any Astros players. The Astros fired both Luhnow and Hinch immediately after Manfred's announcement of the penalties.

Kobe Bryant, Others Killed in L.A. Copter Crash—Former NBA star Kobe Bryant, his 13-year-old daughter Gianna, and seven others were killed in a helicopter crash in Calabasas, CA, Jan. 26. The fatal crash occurred in foggy conditions that violated certifications held by the company operating the helicopter. An outpouring of tributes to the 41-year-old Bryant followed from NBA figures, celebrities, and politicians, including Pres. Donald Trump and former Pres. Barack Obama.

Billie Eilish Wins Big at Grammy Awards—Eighteen-year-old breakout pop musician Billie Eilish swept the four major categories at the 62nd Grammy Awards ceremony held Jan. 26 at the Staples Center in Los Angeles. Eilish was the youngest artist ever to claim album of the year (*When We All Fall Asleep, Where Do We Go?*) and record and song of the year ("Bad Guy"). Singer Lizzo, nominated for the most awards at eight, won three, including best pop solo performance for "Truth Hurts."

February 2020
National

First Democratic Presidential Contests Deliver Mixed Results—Former Vice Pres. Joe Biden, the presumptive frontrunner for the 2020 Democratic presidential nomination, suffered a self-described "gut punch" Feb. 3, placing fourth with just 15.8% support in the Iowa caucus behind Massachusetts Sen. Elizabeth Warren (18.0%), Vermont Sen. Bernie Sanders (26.1%), and former South Bend, IN, Mayor Pete Buttigieg (26.2%). Iowa's new smartphone app-based reporting system was blamed for major delays in voting results; the Iowa Democratic Party failed to announce any official results by the morning of Feb. 4, and the outcome was not made public until late Feb. 9, less than two days before New Hampshire's Feb. 11 primary, which Sanders won with 25.6% of the vote. Close behind, Buttigieg achieved 24.3% support, followed by Minnesota Sen. Amy Klobuchar (19.7%), Warren (9.2%), and Biden (8.4%).

Sanders also came out on top with 46.8% of the vote in Nevada Feb. 22, easily leading Biden (20.2%), Buttigieg (14.3%), and Warren (9.7%). Rebounding Feb. 29 in the first primary in which Black voters constituted a majority, Biden captured South Carolina with 48.4% of the vote, versus 19.9% for Sanders. Buttigieg, who drew 8.2% in South Carolina, suspended his campaign Mar. 1 and endorsed Biden the next day. Not including Buttigieg, the Democratic field—at one point more than 20 candidates strong—had winnowed by the close of Feb. to six. Other prominent candidates who had dropped out by the end of the month included former Rep. Beto O'Rourke (TX), Nov. 1; Sen. Kamala Harris (CA), Dec. 3; Sen. Cory Booker (NJ), Jan. 13; and entrepreneur Andrew Yang (Feb. 11).

Trump Delivers State of the Union Address, Issues Contentious Pardons and Clemencies—In his third State of the Union Address before Congress, Feb. 4, Pres. Donald Trump ignored his ongoing impeachment trial and instead made an opening argument for his reelection in Nov. 2020. Extolling the domestic economy as "the best it has ever been," he also saluted his administration's recent renegotiation of the North American Free Trade Agreement and killing of Iranian military general Qassem Soleimani. Further illustrating the sharp partisan divide between the president and Democratic lawmakers, Trump would not shake the hand of House Speaker Nancy Pelosi (D, CA), who after the address conspicuously ripped up her copy of Trump's address.

The president Feb. 18 announced pardons or clemencies he was granting to 11 individuals, including junk bond trader Michael Milken, former NYC police commissioner Bernard Kerik, and former Illinois Gov. Rod Blagojevich.

Trump Impeachment Proceedings End in Senate Acquittal—The GOP-controlled Senate Feb. 5 voted against two articles of impeachment against Pres. Donald Trump Feb. 5, 52-48 and 53-47. Though the historic votes ending just the third-ever U.S. presidential impeachment trial predictably fell far short of the required two-thirds majority to convict, Sen. Mitt Romney (UT) was notably the only Republican to join all of the chamber's Democrats to vote for conviction on the first article of abuse of power, alleging Trump pressured Ukraine to investigate former Vice Pres. Joe Biden. All GOP lawmakers voted against the second article accusing the Trump of obstructing Congress.

In closing arguments delivered Feb. 3, lead House impeachment manager Rep. Adam Schiff (D, CA) implored senators to block a "runaway presidency," after which the president's defense team argued that Trump was blameless and should be judged instead by voters. Within days of his acquittal, Trump fired EU ambassador Gordon Sondland and Natl. Security Council European affairs director Lt. Col. Alexander Vindman, both of whom had testified against him in impeachment proceedings.

President's Interference in Adviser's Sentencing Draws Pushback—In a development that appeared to suggest White House exerting undue influence, the Justice Dept. Feb. 11 recommended a lesser punishment for former Trump adviser Roger Stone than initially requested by prosecutors after Trump via Twitter declared prosecutors' original sentencing proposals a "miscarriage of justice." After the Justice Dept.'s new recommendations were made public, all four prosecutors withdrew from Stone's case. On Feb. 20, Stone was sentenced by a federal judge to 40 months in prison, well under the 7-9 years initially recommended after his conviction on seven charges including witness tampering, obstruction, and lying to Congress.

Congress Acts to Restrict President's War Powers Against Iran—The Republican-controlled Senate Feb. 13 approved a resolution limiting Pres. Donald Trump's ability to carry out military action on Iran without congressional authorization. Passed 55-45 with the support of all Democrats and eight GOP lawmakers, the measure was in response to the administration's controversial Jan. 2020 drone strike that killed Iranian military commander Qassem Soleimani. The Democrat-led House passed the bill (227-186) on Mar. 11; Trump vetoed the measure May 6.

Stock Markets See Major Losses Amid Coronavirus Fears; T-Mobile-Sprint Merger Wins Approval; Other Business News—Reflecting rising investor uncertainty as the coronavirus pandemic worsened, Wall Street Feb. 28 concluded its worst week since the 2008 financial crisis. The Dow Jones Industrial Average suffered its worst-ever single-day drop Feb. 27, losing 1,190.95 points. The Dow ended Feb. at 25,409.36, down 10.1% from Jan., while the S&P 500 finished the month at 2,954.22, down 8.4%, and the Nasdaq Composite Index closed Feb. at 8,567.37, down 6.4%. The economy the previous month added 225,000 jobs as the unemployment rate edged up a tenth of a point to 3.6%, according to a U.S. Labor Dept. report released Feb. 7.

On Feb. 11, a federal district judge in New York approved cell-phone carrier T-Mobile's $26.5 bil deal to acquire rival Sprint, overruling antitrust objections. Initiating the largest banking deal in over a decade, Morgan Stanley agreed Feb. 20 to purchase E-Trade for $13 bil. The following day, banking giant Wells Fargo admitted fault and agreed to pay $3 bil to end investigations into its fraudulent creation of millions of unauthorized accounts under customers' names. Concluding a case closely monitored by legal observers, a jury Feb. 15 ordered German companies Bayer and BASF pay $265 mil to a Missouri farmer who said their herbicide, applied to neighboring fields, had damaged his crop.

The Boy Scouts of America, facing waning membership amid numerous lawsuits related to sexual abuse allegations, filed Feb. 18 for bankruptcy protection.

International

Coronavirus Deaths Spike in China as Fatalities Spread to Other Countries; Vice Pres. Pence Takes Lead on U.S. Coronavirus Task Force—The outbreak of the highly contagious and thus-far untreatable COVID-19—the disease caused by the new coronavirus first identified in Dec. 2019 in Wuhan, China—worsened substantially in Feb., killing over 1,000 mostly elderly and immunocompromised people in China by Feb. 11 and 2,870 by Feb. 29, according to Chinese government data. Li Wenliang, a Wuhan doctor who was targeted by Chinese officials for trying to sound the alarm on the "SARS-like" virus in Dec. 2019, died due to the virus on Feb. 7.

On Feb. 2, health authorities noted the first known COVID-19-related death outside of China, a Wuhan resident who had traveled to the Philippines. On Feb. 3, the UK-registered, U.S.-owned *Diamond Princess* cruise ship and its 3,700 passengers and crew were held off the port of Yokohama, Japan, after a disembarking passenger in Hong Kong tested positive. By the time all crew disembarked Mar. 1 following a quarantine, 700 aboard the ship had tested positive and at least 6 had died. In Italy, the site of Europe's largest outbreak with 21 deaths and nearly 900 cases by the end of Feb., authorities placed more than 50,000 people in the Lombardy region under "lockdown." The Iranian government Feb. 24 reported 12 deaths and 61 confirmed cases, though international observers theorized the outbreak was far more widespread there. Africa's first case was reported Feb. 14, in Egypt.

U.S. Centers for Disease Control and Prevention (CDC) officials Feb. 25 warned that an outbreak in the U.S. was inevitable, though Pres. Donald Trump the day prior tweeted that the virus "is very much under control." Trump Feb. 26 appointed Vice Pres. Mike Pence to head a coronavirus task force and branded criticism of his administration's response the "new hoax" at a rally in Charleston, SC, Feb. 28. Including 44 Americans diagnosed aboard the *Diamond Princess*, the U.S. by the end of Feb. reported 68 positive cases, including the first known U.S. COVID-19 fatality Feb. 29 of a man in the Seattle, WA, area not known to have traveled abroad. Washington Gov. Jay Inslee (D) declared a state of emergency that same day, four days after San Francisco Mayor London Breed.

As of Feb. 29, there were over 85,000 diagnosed cases and more than 2,900 deaths in at least 60 countries, but many nations still lagged in establishing comprehensive testing and contact-tracing protocols recommended by the World Health Org.

Sinn Féin Surges at Irish Polls—Nationalist party Sinn Féin caught Ireland's governing center-right Fine Gael party and Prime Min. Leo Varadkar by surprise in general elections Feb. 8, winning 37 seats in the country's 160-seat parliament, an increase of 15 seats for Sinn Féin and a 12-seat demotion for the ruling Fine Gael (35 seats). Though Sinn Féin, led by Mary Lou McDonald, won the highest percentage of first-preference votes (24.5%), center-right Fianna Fáil, led by Micheál Martin, won the most seats at 38, down from 45. The outcome marked a departure from nearly a century of Fine Gael-Fianna Fáil dominance and opened the door to three-way coalition rule.

South Sudanese Adversaries Strike Peace Deal—South Sudan's president Salva Kiir and rival leader Riek Machar succeeded Feb. 22 in forming a transitional unity government aimed at ending the conflict that had killed up to 400,000 people and displaced 2.2 mil since late 2013. The accord, which installed Machar as Kiir's deputy, was lauded as an important milestone despite two prior failed peace deals. Along with restarting the country's conflict-choked economy, difficult issues remained including preparing for elections to be held in three years, the first since independence in 2011.

U.S., Taliban Sign Peace Agreement; Afghanistan Announces Disputed Election Results—The U.S. and the Taliban militant group approved a historic deal Feb. 29 aimed at ending 18 years of conflict in Afghanistan. Signed in Doha, Qatar, the agreement called for the U.S. to reduce its forces in Afghanistan from 13,000 to 8,600 personnel after 135 days, and the remainder—along with those of its NATO allies and coalition partners—within 14 months. Critics noted multiple shortcomings in the agreement, including its failure to require the Taliban to formally renounce al-Qaeda and linking the U.S. troop pullout not to the success of required intra-country peace talks but to the Taliban honoring its anti-ISIS and anti-terrorism obligations. U.S. Rep. Liz Cheney (R, WY) and some 20 other GOP House colleagues Feb. 26 sent a letter to the administration warning that it should not depend on the Taliban to be a "reliable counterterrorism partner." Over 2,300 U.S. military personnel had been killed in Afghanistan—America's longest war—since the U.S. invaded in 2001, including two fatally shot Feb. 8 in an "insider attack" during joint U.S.-Afghan military exercises.

On Feb. 18, Afghanistan's Independent Electoral Commission after repeated delays declared incumbent Pres. Ashraf Ghani the victor of late-Sept. 2019 presidential elections, with 50.6% of the vote, to 39.5% for Chief Executive Abdullah Abdullah. The latter contested the results of the voting, which saw historically low turnout of roughly 20% of eligible voters. Ghani was sworn in Mar. 9, as Abdullah held his own inauguration, setting up a potential new crisis.

General

Kenin, Djokovic Win at Australian Open—American 21-year-old Sofia Kenin defeated Garbiñe Muguruza of Spain (4-6, 6-2, 6-2) in the women's singles final at Rod Laver Arena in Melbourne, Feb. 1, to win the Australian Open title and her first Grand Slam. The next night, defending men's singles champion Novak Djokovic of Serbia defeated Austria's Dominic Thiem (6-4, 4-6, 2-6, 6-3, 6-4) in a 3 hr., 59 min. match that won Djokovic his eighth Australian Open title.

Kansas City Claims First Super Bowl Win in Half Century; Other NFL News—The Kansas City Chiefs overcame the San Francisco 49ers, 31-20, at Hard Rock Stadium in Miami Gardens, FL, to win Super Bowl LIV on Feb. 2. Though the teams were tied 10-10 at halftime, the Chiefs trailed by 10 at the end of the third quarter before tallying three unanswered touchdowns. Kansas City QB Patrick Mahomes, at 24 the youngest quarterback ever to be named Super Bowl MVP, completed 26 of 42 passes for 286 yards and two touchdowns. The broadcast, which included a halftime show featuring Jennifer Lopez and Shakira, was watched by an average 102 mil viewers.

Three years after filing paperwork to relocate from Oakland, CA, the Raiders franchise Jan. 22 formally announced its renaming as the Las Vegas Raiders, to play at soon-to-be-finished Allegiant Stadium in Las Vegas, NV, beginning in 2020. After 20 seasons and six Super Bowl wins with the New England Patriots, 42-year-old quarterback Tom Brady Mar. 20 signed a two-year, $50-mil contract with the Tampa Bay Buccaneers.

South Korea's *Parasite* Wins Big at Academy Awards—The South Korean black comedy *Parasite* claimed four Oscar wins at the 92nd Academy Awards held Feb. 9 at the Dolby Theatre in Los Angeles. *Parasite* was the first-ever non-English-language film to capture the best picture prize and also claimed best director for Bong Joon-ho and best original screenplay for Bong and Han Jin-won. Joaquin Phoenix took home the best actor award for his portrayal of Batman's title nemesis in *Joker*, while Renée Zellweger won best actress for the biopic *Judy*. The second straight Oscars ceremony to lack a host drew an all-time-low 23.6 mil viewers.

Hamlin Takes Daytona 500—Denny Hamlin won his second consecutive Daytona 500 and third in five years in Daytona Beach, FL, Feb. 17 in the ninth lap of a chaotic double overtime. Postponed from the day prior due to rain after just 20 completed laps, the remainder was largely uneventful until a 19-car pileup on lap 184, followed by another collision. Leader Randy Newman was knocked out of contention in the final turn by challenger Ryan Blaney, allowing Hamlin to slingshot around Blaney and hold him off by just 0.014 seconds in a photo finish.

#MeToo Spark Weinstein Convicted of Rape and Sexual Abuse—Nearly two-and-a-half years after a flood of sexual misconduct accusations against movie producer Harvey Weinstein gave rise to the #MeToo movement, Weinstein was convicted Feb. 24 by a New York jury of sexual assault and third degree rape. Though he was acquitted of more serious charges that carried a potential life sentence, the 67-year-old was sentenced in Mar. to 23 years in prison; assault charges by two other women were pending in Los Angeles.

Wisconsin Brewery Shooting Kills Six—A gunman armed with two handguns fatally shot five employees at the Milwaukee, WI, campus of Molson Coors brewing, before killing himself, Feb. 26. The shooter, 51-year-old Anthony Ferrill, had been fired from his position as an electrician at the brewery.

March 2020
National

Democratic Presidential Primary Race Narrows to Biden, Sanders—Former Vice Pres. Joe Biden surged past Vermont Sen. Bernie Sanders in the race for the Democratic presidential nomination, winning 10 of 14 Super Tuesday primaries held Mar. 3 and eight more states by month's end. In Mar. 10 voting, Sanders claimed one state compared with Biden's five. Biden claimed all three contests held Mar. 17, cruising to victory in Arizona and delegate-rich Illinois and Florida. Former South Bend, IN, Mayor Pete Buttigieg suspended his race Mar. 1, followed by Sen. Amy Klobuchar (MN), Mar. 2; former New York City Mayor Michael Bloomberg, Mar. 4; Sen. Elizabeth Warren (MA), Mar. 5; and Rep. Tulsi Gabbard (HI), Mar. 19; all endorsed Joe Biden. On the GOP side, former Massachusetts Gov. Bill Weld ended his campaign Mar. 18 after Pres. Donald Trump gained sufficient delegates to win the nomination.

The worsening coronavirus pandemic caused several states to postpone voting and heavily impacted campaigning. The first one-on-one debate between Biden and Sanders, on Mar. 15, was held without an audience in CNN's Washington, DC, studio.

Trump Replaces Chief of Staff—Pres. Donald Trump Mar. 6 announced he was replacing acting White House chief of staff Mick Mulvaney with Rep. Mark Meadows (R, NC). In the position for 14 months, Mulvaney had reportedly lost Trump's confidence over his treatment of impeachment matters. Meadows became the president's fourth chief of staff upon his Mar. 30 resignation from the House.

Wall Street Plummets Over Pandemic; An Astounding 10 Million File Jobless Claims in Just Two Weeks—The coronavirus pandemic and related developments sent a shockwave through the financial world, inducing the worst monthly performance since 2008 for Wall Street's three major indices and causing the Dow Jones Industrial Average to close out the first three months of the year (ending Mar. 31) down 23.2%, its worst first quarter showing in history. Mar. saw multiple daily plunges for the Dow, including losing 2,013.7 points Mar. 9 amid a Russian-Saudi oil price war; 2,352 points Mar. 12, the day after the World Health Org. declared the virus a global pandemic; and a record 2,997.20 points Mar. 16 despite the Federal Reserve, Mar. 15, cutting its benchmark interest rate a full percentage point. The Dow ended Mar. at 21,917.16, a 13.7% decrease from Feb., while the S&P 500 finished the month at 2,584.59, down 12.5%, and the Nasdaq Composite Index closed Mar. at 7,700.10, a 10.1% decrease.

A record 3.3 mil Americans submitted claims for unemployment benefits Mar. 15-21, followed by 6.8 mil the next week. The Feb. monthly employment report, released Mar. 6, showed a strong 273,000 jobs added with an unemployment rate of 3.5%.

International

Coronavirus Infects 750,000+ Worldwide, With Over 36,000 Dead; Global Pandemic Declared—The director of the World Health Org. (WHO) Mar. 11 declared the novel coronavirus that causes the respiratory disease COVID-19 a global pandemic as incidences of cases rose sharply outside of China, where it was first reported in late Dec. 2019. At the time of the WHO's announcement, the UN agency had tallied 118,000 confirmed cases in more than 110 countries and territories, with 4,292 deaths. While at that point just four countries (China, Iran, Italy, and South Korea) accounted for over 90% of cases, by the end of Mar. the U.S. led all countries in reported cases, topping 140,000 cases (with nearly 2,400 deaths), with more than 750,000 cases and 36,400 deaths worldwide.

Chinese officials Mar. 23 recorded the country's fifth straight day without any new cases transmitted locally, evidence of the success of strict "social distancing" measures in place. After 62 days, most lockdown restrictions were officially lifted for Hubei province Mar. 25. (The city of Wuhan remained on lockdown until Apr. 8.) Beginning Mar. with nearly 80,000 confirmed cases and 2,873 deaths, China ended the month with under 2,600 additional new cases and 450 additional deaths.

Taking China's place as the pandemic's hotspot, Italy's confirmed caseload exploded in Mar. from 1,128 to 101,739, with confirmed deaths spiking to 11,591 from just 29 on Mar. 1, overwhelming hospitals with patients in need of acute care. Prime Min. Giuseppe Conte applied northern Italy's lockdown nationwide as of Mar. 9.

Confirmed cases in Iran, numbering 8,042 at the time of the WHO's pandemic declaration, reached nearly 42,000 Mar. 31, with 2,757 deaths. By late Mar., 300 Iranians also had reportedly died from drinking toxic methanol they mistakenly believed would protect them against the virus. Though South Korea reported over 7,750 cases Mar. 11 with 60 deaths, its caseload increased by just over 2,000 by the end of the month (with 162 total deaths), a result public health officials attributed to aggressive testing—widely available at mobile and drive-through centers—that reached 270,000 of roughly 50 mil residents by mid-Mar.

Pres. Donald Trump Mar. 11 delivered an Oval Office address on the pandemic, during which he announced a 30-day ban on some travel from Europe. Trump branded the coronavirus a "foreign virus," drawing post-speech criticism for appearing to stoke xenophobia. (The previous day, he retweeted a post that referred to it as the "China Virus," and called it the "Chinese Virus" in a tweet the next week, ignoring warnings that it could create backlash against Asian Americans.) On Mar. 13, as U.S. confirmed cases reached over 1,250 with 36 deaths, Trump declared the pandemic a national emergency.

The president's address and emergency declaration marked a change in course from downplaying the threat—including his Mar. 9 tweet describing COVID-19 as less dangerous than the common flu—and, in tandem with diminished availability of supplies such as hand sanitizer, disinfecting wipes, and toilet paper, coincided with several mainstream cultural developments that appeared to register the serious nature of the pandemic with the public. Well-known actors Tom Hanks and Rita Wilson announced Mar. 11 they had contracted the coronavirus in Australia and were initially hospitalized and then later quarantined; that same day, an NBA game between the Oklahoma City Thunder and Utah Jazz was abruptly canceled after pregame warmups when it was revealed that a Jazz player had tested positive for COVID-19.

On Mar. 8, Washington state officials announced a 17th death from the virus in King County, 16 of which were linked to a single nursing home in Kirkwood. The shocking mortality rate focused attention on the extreme vulnerability of residents in such facilities, and industry leaders recommended nursing homes end nonessential visits nationwide.

While larger gatherings had been prohibited earlier in many localities, state governors and local-level officials began blocking restaurants from serving dine-in customers, and also ordered gyms, casinos, and movie theaters closed. The White House Mar. 16 issued social-distancing guidelines designed to "flatten the curve," or slow rates of virus transmission to prevent hospitals from being overwhelmed by people requiring acute care. By Mar. 18, as U.S. COVID-19 cases exceeded 3,500, including 58 deaths, school closures in 39 states affected more than 41 mil students and their families. As confirmed cases exceeded 1,000 in California with 19 deaths, according to the state's Dept. of Public Health, Gov. Gavin Newsom (D) Mar. 19 announced the nation's first statewide stay-home order, advising residents to leave home only to carry out tasks essential to health and safety. New York, Illinois, and Oregon issued similar mandates the next day, and by the end of Mar., 308 mil people, or 94% of the U.S. population, in 42 states and additional municipalities were under similar orders.

Densely populated New York City and the surrounding region became the nation's COVID-19 epicenter in the latter part of Mar., with the area making up about 5% of cases worldwide and roughly one-third nationwide. The office of New York City Mayor Bill de Blasio cited 10,764 positive cases in the city as of Mar. 22, including 99 deaths and at least 1,800 hospitalized. New York Gov. Andrew Cuomo (D), who had been critical of the federal pandemic response, Mar. 24 said the state was in need of 30,000 ventilators in anticipation of a further spike in critical cases, and implored the federal government to release 20,000 ventilators from its reserves. On Mar. 31, the NYC mayor's office reported that positive cases had ballooned to 41,000+, including 1,096 total deaths, with some 8,500 currently hospitalized. Trump, who directed states not to rely on the federal government for additional ventilators, said during a Mar. 30 call with governors that test kits were not in short supply, in contrast to public statements by numerous state officials that testing shortages were a major obstacle to grasping the virus's spread. N-95 masks and other personal protective equipment (PPE) for medical personnel were also in short supply.

The pandemic's effect on the economy was stark, impacting all major industries and causing a record 3.3 mil Americans to apply for unemployment benefits Mar. 15-21 followed by more than double that number the next week. Congress passed and Trump, Mar. 27, signed into law a $2-tril economic aid bill aimed at blunting the downturn. The largest stimulus bill in U.S. history, it provided Americans with $300 bil in direct payments ($1,200 to most individuals making less than $75,000 in annual income, and $500 per child for families); infused unemployment insurance programs with an additional $260 bil, which helped cover nontraditional workers; and offered $500 bil to key industries, $350 bil in small business loans, and $150 bil in relief to state and local governments. The House passed the measure Mar. 27 by voice vote, after the Senate (96-0) on Mar. 25. Earlier legislative response measures included a bill Trump signed Mar. 18 addressing paid emergency sick leave, food assistance, and free coronavirus testing, and an $8.3-bil emergency spending bill signed by Trump Mar. 6 aimed to fight the virus's spread and fund vaccine development.

Diverging from public health experts—including Dr. Anthony Fauci, head of the National Institute of Allergy and Infectious Diseases—who advocated for greater testing as a precondition to loosening lockdowns, Trump repeatedly via Twitter and at daily coronavirus press briefings (held beginning Mar. 16) suggested the country could "reopen" by Easter (Apr. 12). Trump on Mar. 29 extended social-distancing guidelines through at least Apr. 30 amid reports of surging cases, including a same-day U.S. Centers for Disease Control and Prevention (CDC) tally of over 122,600 positive or presumptive U.S. cases and over 2,100 deaths. On Mar. 31, Trump warned Americans to prepare for "a very, very painful two weeks," and said up to 240,000 Americans might die from the virus even with current mitigation strategies.

Outside the U.S., Spain became a second "hotspot" in Europe, reporting over 7,300 deaths and nearly 85,200 total cases. Though the WHO tallied nearly 62,000 COVID-19 cases in Germany as of Mar. 31, the country saw far fewer deaths than Spain or Italy, with 583. France recorded more than 3,000 COVID-19 deaths and nearly 44,000 cases, roughly double that of the UK, where Prime Min. Boris Johnson himself tested positive for the virus in late Mar. Canada, whose border with the U.S. was closed to all nonessential travel beginning Mar. 18, reported its first COVID-19 death on Mar. 8; by Mar. 31, that number had increased to 66, with more than 6,300 total positive cases. South Africa led the continent in cases, with 1,326 by the end of the month. By Mar. 20, the WHO said it was working with researchers on at least 20 separate vaccines, some of which had already advanced to the clinical trial phase.

Winter and spring NCAA tournaments were canceled, the NBA and NHL seasons were suspended, MLB's Opening Day was postponed, and the 2020 Olympic Games in Tokyo, Japan, were rescheduled for July-Aug. 2021. Pope Francis announced he would hold Easter service in Apr. via livestream, and Saudi officials in late Mar. urged Muslims to delay Hajj pilgrimage plans, for which more than 2 mil travel to Mecca and Medina annually.

In Historic First, Trump Speaks With Taliban Leader; ICC Backs Investigation of U.S. War Crimes in Afghanistan—Three days after a U.S.-Taliban peace deal was signed, Pres. Donald Trump Mar. 3 spoke via phone with the group's co-founder in what marked the first known conversation between a U.S. president and a senior leader of the Taliban. In the 35-min. conversation, Abdul Ghani Baradar urged Trump to withdraw U.S. troops from Afghanistan. However, the Taliban was not yet willing to hold peace talks with the Afghan government, one requirement of U.S. troop withdrawal, until 5,000 Taliban prisoners were released.

On Mar. 5, International Criminal Court judges approved opening an investigation into crimes against humanity in Afghanistan allegedly committed by Afghan National Security Forces, the U.S. military and CIA, and the Taliban.

Russia, Turkey Agree to Truce in Syria's War-Torn Idlib—Russia and Turkey agreed Mar. 5 to a cease-fire deal in Syria's northwestern province of Idlib, the last holdout of Syrian rebels fighting the regime of Pres. Bashar al-Assad and target of a three-month-old Syrian offensive backed by Russian airstrikes that had displaced more than 950,000 people. Neighboring Turkey, which supported the rebels fighting the regime of Assad, in Feb. sent 7,000 troops to Idlib. On Feb. 27, Idlib airstrikes speculated to have been carried out by Russia killed 34 Turkish troops. Turkey two days later retaliated with a drone strike that killed 26 Syrian soldiers.

Boko Haram Unleashes Major Attacks on Military in Chad, Nigeria—The Nigeria-based Islamist terror group Boko Haram attacked military forces in neighboring Chad Mar. 23, killing at least 92 soldiers in what Chad's president Idriss Déby said was the militants' deadliest raid in his country. The attack occurred in the Lake Chad border region where forces from Chad, Niger, and Nigeria had engaged Boko Haram jointly for the past five years. That same day, the group ambushed a troop convoy in Nigeria's Yobe province, killing at least 47. Also on Mar. 23, militants ambushed and killed some 70 troops in the northeastern Nigerian state of Borno. Attacks from Boko Haram—which began in 2009—and Islamic State-West Africa Province (ISWAP) had killed at least 36,000 people in northeastern Nigeria and displaced about 3.3 mil in four Lake Chad nations.

U.S. Indicts Venezuelan President—The U.S. Justice Dept. Mar. 26 charged Venezuelan Pres. Nicolás Maduro and 14 current and former Venezuelan officials with drug trafficking, narco-terrorism, corruption, and other crimes. The action was the strongest yet taken against Venezuela's leadership by the U.S., which supported opposition leader and self-declared interim president Juan Guaidó over Maduro.

General

Major Australian Bushfires Extinguished—Officials in Australia's New South Wales (NSW) on Mar. 2 declared that the devastating bushfires that had burned in the state for more than 240 days, killing at least 34 people nationwide along with an estimated 480 mil to 1 bil animals, were at last fully extinguished. The fires charred some 42,000 sq mi—roughly the size of Virginia.

Tennessee Tornadoes Kill 25—A series of tornadoes hit central Tennessee late Mar. 2 through early Mar. 3, killing 25 people. Though at least seven tornadoes were reported in the state, the majority of the damage was caused by two—an EF-4 tornado that hit Cookeville in Putnam County and killed 19 people there, and an EF-3 tornado that initially struck north of downtown Nashville.

April 2020
National

U.S. Responds to Rampaging Coronavirus Pandemic—The U.S. Centers for Disease Control and Prevention (CDC) reversed itself Apr. 3, urging Americans to wear nonmedical face masks in public. Previously, the agency had recommended only those with symptoms wear masks to protect others. By Apr. 28, according to Johns Hopkins Univ. data, the U.S. was reporting nearly a million COVID-19 cases and over 55,000 fatalities. Though New York City remained the country's hotspot with over 164,000 cases and 18,231 deaths by the end of the month according to New York City Dept. of Health data, new confirmed cases in the city peaked on Apr. 6. Two NYC medical centers Apr. 30 revealed data suggesting the virus's spread in the city originated with travelers from Europe and the U.S.—not from Asia—as early as late Jan.

Ten other states by late Apr. reported caseloads of 25,000 or more, including Massachusetts (over 50,000) and New Jersey (over 100,000), the latter of which drew additional media attention after authorities discovered 17 bodies in a holding area of a nursing home, Andover Subacute and Rehabilitation Center, where at least 33 of 68 people who had died since the beginning of 2020 were confirmed to have been as a result of COVID-19.

In South Dakota, where Gov. Kristi Noem (R) had resisted issuing a stay-at-home order, Smithfield Foods' pork processing plant in Sioux Falls became a single-source hotspot, with 644 cases tied to the facility by Apr. 15. The company Apr. 12 announced the plant's indefinite closure and later that week shuttered two other plants. Pres. Donald Trump Apr. 28 granted the USDA more powers to keep meatpacking plants, 22 of which had closed throughout the Midwest, in production; some 3,300 workers had tested positive for COVID-19.

U.S. Navy aircraft carrier USS *Theodore Roosevelt* gained attention as another hotspot, with at least 585 of 4,860 crew testing positive; one sailor died Apr. 13 from the virus, 11 days after the navy fired the ship's captain, Brett Crozier, reportedly for sending an urgent email requesting immediate help outside of the normal chain of command.

Lawmakers, governors, and health officials urged the Trump administration to develop a national plan to supersede state and local coronavirus testing efforts, and the White House unveiled a blueprint requiring states create their own plans with federal "strategic direction and technical assistance." Facing persistent criticism that he had failed to act quickly enough to curb the virus, Pres. Trump Apr. 15 announced he was halting U.S. funding to the World Health Org. (WHO), saying that the UN agency had mismanaged its response and that it was covering up the severity of the coronavirus in China. The *Washington Post* Apr. 19 reported that U.S. scientists and experts working at WHO—some

from the CDC—had communicated to the White House the virus's spread beginning in late Dec., and in late Apr. that U.S. intelligence agencies had warned about the virus in over a dozen classified briefings in Jan. and Feb.

The president's public divergence from health officials broadened in late Mar. and Apr., as Trump alleged without evidence that the virus was created in a Wuhan lab and touted antimalarial drugs chloroquine and hydroxychloroquine for treatment even as the FDA issued warnings of serious side effects and statements on their lack of proven benefits for COVID-19 patients. Top infectious disease expert Dr. Anthony Fauci during an Apr. 22 briefing contradicted the president's theory that the virus might naturally disappear by fall, and in late Apr. said the country lacked the testing capacity to safely reopen. Trump Apr. 23 suggested researchers test whether directly injecting disinfectants such as bleach into the body of a COVID-19 patient would kill the virus, drawing widespread ridicule and warnings from the medical community not to ingest household cleaners. (Trump tried to explain his comment, saying he was being sarcastic.)

Florida Apr. 3 was the 34th state to require residents remain home for all but essential services, though states' definitions of "essential" varied. Pres. Trump, who did not extend federal social-distancing guidelines that expired Apr. 30, erroneously said Apr. 13 he had "total authority" to order governors to re-open. Though he assured governors they would be "calling the shots" three days later, Trump via Twitter encouraged resistance against lockdown orders. Anti-quarantine protests, reportedly organized or amplified by conservative groups, materialized in the latter half of Apr. in numerous states. In Michigan, where Gov. Gretchen Whitmer (D) extended a stay-at-home order through May 28, hundreds of protesters, some armed, attempted Apr. 30 to force their way into the state capitol's legislative chamber.

Confronting rapidly increasing unemployment claims on state funds and decreasing revenue, governors of a number of states took initial steps to reopen. Texas, whose residents were not under a stay-at-home order until Apr. 2, was the first to announce a phased reopening timeline, beginning with reintroducing curbside retail Apr. 24. Georgia Gov. Brian Kemp (R) set an aggressive reopening plan that permitted gyms, barbershops, and other businesses to reopen Apr. 24. Despite Kemp's orders, Atlanta Mayor Keisha Lance Bottoms asked city residents to remain at home, and many businesses there opted to remain closed as of May 1. Confirmed COVID-19 cases in Georgia surpassed 25,000 on Apr. 25, with 1,052 deaths, according to the state's health department data.

Trump Fires Inspector General Who Triggered Impeachment Proceedings; Other Personnel Changes—Trump Apr. 3 fired inspector general Michael Atkinson, who in his role as intelligence community watchdog relayed the whistleblower complaint to Congress that led to Trump's impeachment. On Apr. 7, Trump named campaign aide Kayleigh McEnany as press secretary to take the place of Stephanie Grisham, who notably did not hold a press briefing during her nine-month tenure. Trump Apr. 7 removed the acting Defense Dept. Inspector General, Glenn Fine, from his post as head of a committee monitoring $2 tril in coronavirus spending.

Biden Assumes Role of Apparent Democratic Presidential Nominee—Former Vice Pres. Joe Biden all but secured the Democratic nomination for president after Sen. Bernie Sanders (I, VT) suspended his campaign Apr. 8. Sanders, who was also runner-up for the 2016 nomination, lost out to Biden in Wisconsin's Apr. 7 primary by more than 30 points. (Though Wisconsin Gov. Tony Evers (D) Apr. 6 had ordered in-person voting postponed until June, the state's supreme court overruled him; the state was the first to conduct statewide in-person voting since COVID-19-related stay-at-home orders were put in place.) Biden also won mail-in voting held in Alaska, Wyoming, and Ohio in Apr., giving him 1,406 of 1,991 delegates needed to claim the nomination.

Trump Administration Loosens Obama-Era Environmental Regulations—The Environmental Protection Agency (EPA)

Apr. 16 effectively defanged a regulation mandating coal utility plants reduce emissions of the toxin mercury, one of several environmental policies established by former Pres. Barack Obama's administration and scaled back under the Trump administration. The Trump White House had decried such regulations as government overreach, despite pushback by some electric utilities, which had already invested in the necessary upgrades, and from environmental groups citing EPA's own analysis, which found it had diminished mercury's neurological impacts on children and prevented thousands of premature deaths.

On Mar. 31, the Trump administration had completed its rollback of Obama-era motor vehicle emissions standards, requiring just 1.5% yearly fuel efficiency improvements through 2026 instead of the 5% mandated under Obama. California and other states arguing for their right to set stricter-than-federal standards were expected to quickly file court challenges. The EPA said Mar. 26 it would stop enforcing a range of agency regulations due to the coronavirus pandemic and expected industries to comply "where reasonably practicable."

GOP-Led Senate Panel Backs Findings of Russian Meddling in 2016 Race—The Senate Intelligence Committee in a bipartisan report released Apr. 21 fully supported the U.S. intelligence community's analysis that Russia interfered in the 2016 election to help then-candidate Donald Trump win the presidency. The committee's conclusion, which described the 2017 intelligence assessment as politically unbiased, weakened frequent past allegations by Trump that former CIA Dir. John Brennan and Dir. of Natl. Intelligence James Clapper had used the intelligence community to undermine the election results. The committee also found that information in the "Steele Dossier," controversial for being initiated as opposition research by the campaign of Democratic presidential nominee Hillary Clinton, did not form the basis for the 2017 findings.

Coronavirus Lockdown Spurs Massive Spike in Unemployment Claims; Oil Prices Plummet; Stock Markets Rebound Despite Grim Economic News—The widening global coronavirus pandemic continued to bludgeon the U.S. economy, causing 3.8 mil more Americans to file first-time unemployment claims during the week ending Apr. 25. Since mid-Mar. an astonishing 30.3 mil—18.6% of the country's labor force—had filed for weekly unemployment benefits, with first-time claims peaking at 6.9 mil for the last week of Mar. According to Labor Dept. data released Apr. 3, the economy lost 701,000 jobs in Mar.—when stay-at-home and shutdown orders were first implemented in parts of the country—for the largest monthly decline in 11 years, as the unemployment rate, considered a lagging indicator of the developing crisis, rose to 4.4%.

Demand for gasoline plummeted, along with crude oil futures, which fell to $37.63 per barrel Apr. 20 despite OPEC nations reaching a deal to cut production. Major Bakken shale producer Whiting Petroleum Corp. and Diamond Offshore Drilling filed for bankruptcy protection Apr. 1 and Apr. 26, respectively. Rebounding from major Mar. losses, the Dow Jones Industrial Average ended Apr. at 24,345.72, an 11.1% jump from Mar., while the Nasdaq Composite Index closed Apr. at 8,889.55, a 15.4% increase, and the S&P 500 finished the month at 2,912.43, up 12.7%.

International

Coronavirus Infections Surge to 3 Million, Over 200,000 Dead; Countries Weigh Reopening; Other Global Pandemic Developments—Confirmed cases of the novel coronavirus causing the respiratory disease COVID-19 surpassed 3 mil worldwide by Apr. 27, leading to more than 200,000 deaths, with the U.S. grimly leading in both categories with nearly a million cases and over 55,000 fatalities according to data from Johns Hopkins Univ. Numerous countries began taking steps to ease mandatory lockdowns, which public health officials asserted had doubtless saved lives but took a major economic toll. According to UN data made public Apr. 7, workplaces accounting for more than 80% of the world's 3.3 bil-person workforce saw full or partial closures; Intl. Monetary Fund head Kristalina

Georgieva said Apr. 9 that the world was on the brink of the most severe economic crisis since the Great Depression.

Spain in early Apr. surpassed Italy for second-highest number of confirmed cases in the world, with nearly 213,000 by the end of the month and 24,275 deaths; Italy registered nearly 204,000 cases. In the UK, cases grew to more than 165,000 by Apr. 30. UK Prime Min. Boris Johnson was released from the hospital Apr. 12 after spending three nights in intensive care being treated for COVID-19. Germany, fifth-highest globally with over 159,000 cases Apr. 30, reported a relatively low number of deaths, with 6,288. After extending its lockdown for another month Apr. 13, France ended Apr., with more than 127,000 cases—including 668 of nearly 2,000 sailors on the aircraft carrier *Charles de Gaulle*—and 24,054 deaths. EU ministers agreed Apr. 9 on a nearly $600 bil loan package to member nation economies.

Brazil became the first Southern Hemisphere nation to exceed 1,000 coronavirus deaths, which spiked to 5,017 by the end of Apr., from among nearly 72,000 confirmed cases; Brazilian Pres. Jair Bolsonaro drew backlash for demanding that state governors lift lockdowns. Reported deaths from the virus in Mexico climbed from just 20 in Mar. to 1,569 by Apr. 30 (from among 16,752 confirmed cases), while Ecuador recorded over 880 deaths and nearly 24,700 cases by Apr. 30. Canada surpassed 50,000 cases, including 2,904 deaths, by Apr. 30. Japan's reported caseload grew by over 12,000 in Apr., to 14,088, with 415 deaths. On Apr. 17 officials in the city of Wuhan, ground zero for the pandemic, revised upwards the death toll there by 1,290—roughly 50%—to 3,869, which increased China's national count to 4,632.

New Zealand Prime Minister Jacinda Ardern, who had supported stringent social-distancing guidelines, announced Apr. 27 that the country had eliminated community transmission of the virus and allowed easing of lockdown measures.

Hungary's Leader Strengthens Rule Through Controversial Emergency Powers—In the wake of Hungary's parliament granting Prime Min. Viktor Orbán nearly unlimited powers in late Mar. to combat the coronavirus, Orbán by mid-Apr. carried out a number of actions criticized by civil rights groups. Actions with no seeming connection to maintaining public health included seizing opposition political party campaign funding for economic stimulus, moving to obfuscate key details of a Chinese-funded rail project, and removing hurdles to facilitate a construction deal resisted by the opposition parties. Critics also condemned a provision of the Mar. legislation permitting the government to prosecute and jail anyone spreading what it determined to be "fake news" obstructing its coronavirus response. On Apr. 17, the European Parliament passed a resolution denouncing Hungary's rule-by-decree. Though the Hungarian parliament voted June 16 to end the emergency powers, Orbán and his government were left with greater authority than before the crisis.

Cease-Fire Extended in Yemen as Separatists Declare Self-Rule in South—The Saudi-led coalition fighting Iran-aligned Houthi rebels in Yemen announced Apr. 24 that it was extending by one month its two-week unilateral cease-fire put in place to support coronavirus suppression efforts. The Houthis, who reportedly demanded the coalition lift sea and air blockades ahead of any truce, had rejected the previous cease-fire, and violence had continued between the two in multiple provinces. Complicating the six-year-old conflict in Yemen, Southern Transitional Council (STC) separatists backed by the United Arab Emirates (UAE), Saudi Arabia's key coalition partner, declared it was establishing an autonomous administration across southern provinces it controlled.

General

Deadly Tornadoes Strike South, SE U.S.—An outbreak of more than 140 tornadoes hit 10 southern states Apr. 12-13, killing at least 36 people. Mississippi reported at least 12 fatalities across six counties after an EF-4 twister tracked a 67-mi, 2.25-mi-wide path—the third largest tornado on record in the U.S.—nearly in parallel with a 1.1-mi-wide EF-3 that traveled 82 mi. South Carolina, hit by multiple EF-2 tornadoes, suffered nine deaths including five in rural Hampton County. Seven people were killed at two mobile home parks in northern Georgia.

On Apr. 22, tornadoes killed seven people in central Louisiana, south central Oklahoma, and eastern Texas. With 73 confirmed deaths thus far, the 2020 tornado season was the deadliest since 2011.

Shooter Disguised as Policeman Kills 22 in Canada's Deadliest Mass Shooting—A gunman in the Canadian province of Nova Scotia killed 22 people over 13 hours Apr. 18-19, eclipsing a 1989 shooting that killed 15 (including the shooter) in Montréal as the country's deadliest. Dressed as a police officer, the 51-year-old gunman, identified as Gabriel Wortman, carried out the attacks at 16 different locations north of Halifax and set at least five fires. Ultimately fatally shot by police, the shooter had reportedly assaulted his girlfriend, who escaped, just prior to his spree. In the aftermath, Canadian Prime Min. Justin Trudeau May 1 announced a ban on assault-style weapons.

May 2020
National

Coronavirus Deaths Pass 100,000 in U.S. as Many Shutdown Restrictions Ease—Remaining at the center of the global pandemic of the novel coronavirus causing the respiratory disease COVID-19, the U.S. May 27-28 became the first country to exceed the grim milestone of 100,000 deaths, from among some 1.7 mil confirmed cases, according to the Centers for Disease Control and Prevention (CDC). Though data remained incomplete, researchers increasingly noted the disproportionate degree to which nonwhite population groups were affected by the virus. A May 27 NPR analysis of data compiled by the Antiracist Research & Policy Center and the COVID Tracking Project revealed that the Black share of COVID-19 deaths was two times greater than their share of the national population.

The CDC May 14 provided states with consolidated reopening guidelines following the Trump administration's rejection of its draft recommendations. Connecticut May 20 became the final state to start lifting shutdown restrictions, though ProPublica analysis released in late May revealed only three states—Connecticut, Illinois, and New York—met all five of the CDC's criteria for beginning phased reopening.

Intergovernmental rifts over coronavirus response became increasingly public, including House testimony May 14 by former Biomedical Advanced Research and Development Authority Dir. Rick Bright—who had filed a whistleblower complaint—that his early warnings about medical personal protective equipment (PPE) supply shortages were disregarded and that he was fired for opposing fast-tracked use of the drug hydroxychloroquine as a COVID-19 treatment. Though the CDC in early Apr. had urged Americans to wear face masks to prevent virus spread, Trump himself did not do so publicly, and Trump trade adviser Peter Navarro May 17 on *Meet the Press* said the CDC had "let the country down." Individual incidents of backlash against mask use—in Flint, MI, a Family Dollar security guard was shot and killed May 1 after telling a customer that masks were required—were reported broadly.

The FDA May 1 granted an emergency use authorization for the antiviral drug remdesivir after it was shown in a National Institutes of Health clinical trial to increase recovery among patients with advanced COVID-19. Trump May 15 announced the White House's "Operation Warp Speed" initiative aimed at facilitating hundreds of millions of doses of a COVID-19 vaccine by the end of 2020.

Biden Denies Sexual Assault Allegations—Presumptive Democratic presidential nominee and former Vice Pres. Joe Biden in a statement published May 1 denied sexual assault allegations made against him by Tara Reade, who worked in the office of then-Sen. Biden (DE) for eight months in 1992-93. Reade said Biden assaulted her in a Capitol hallway, after which she filed a complaint with a congressional personnel office that did not explicitly allege assault or harassment. Biden called for the records of the complaint to be made public; however, the

secretary of the Office of the Senate said it could not legally disclose such records.

Justice Dept. Drops Charges Against Former Trump Adviser—Fueling allegations that Atty. Gen. William Barr was unduly serving the political interests of the White House, the Dept. of Justice sought May 7 to drop charges against Pres. Donald Trump's former national security adviser Michael Flynn, who had twice pleaded guilty to lying to the FBI about interactions he had with Russia's ambassador before taking office in 2017. In its request to the court, the Justice Dept. argued the FBI's interview with Flynn did not materially serve the department's overarching special counsel investigation into Russian meddling in the 2016 presidential election and possible collusion by Trump's campaign. Nearly 2,000 former DOJ officials signed an open letter in May calling for Barr's resignation and asking Congress to censure him.

Pandemic Economy Sheds Millions of Jobs, With Record-High Unemployment; Major Companies Declare Bankruptcy; Other Economic News—According to the monthly Labor Dept. report released May 8, the coronavirus pandemic pulled the national economy deeper into crisis in Apr., driving the loss of a staggering 20.5 mil jobs, the greatest monthly decline since record-keeping began in 1939. The unemployment rate more than tripled to 14.7%, the highest since the 1930s Great Depression; with furloughed workers included, the rate increased to 19.5%. Another 9.9 mil people were jobless but not tallied among the unemployed as they weren't actively seeking work. Nearly 40 mil Americans—roughly 25% of workers—filed unemployment claims over 10 weeks ending May 23.

On May 4, the U.S. Treasury Dept. said it planned to borrow $3 tril in the second quarter of the fiscal year—over five times the quarterly record, set during the 2008 financial crisis—to pay for coronavirus relief measures legislated by Congress. Citing plunging demand, a number of well-known U.S. companies filed for Chapter 11 bankruptcy: clothing retailer J. Crew, May 4; department stores Neiman Marcus, May 7, and J. C. Penney, May 15; and car rental giant Hertz, May 22.

Sen. Richard Burr (R, NC) stepped down as chair of the Senate Intelligence Committee May 15 as the FBI investigated insider trading allegations against Burr and his wife, who were accused of selling $1.7 mil in stock in early Feb. because of information Burr received at non-public COVID-19 briefings. Continuing Wall Street's rebound from a disastrous showing in Mar., the Dow Jones Industrial Average ended May at 25,383.11, a 4.3% jump from Apr., while the Nasdaq Composite Index closed May at 9,489.87, a 6.8% increase, and the S&P 500 finished the month at 3,044.31, up 4.5%.

Death of Black Minneapolis Man in Police Custody Sparks Fervent Protests—A white police officer in Minneapolis, MN, on May 25 kneeled for nearly 9 minutes on the neck of a prone Black man, 46-year-old George Floyd, resulting in Floyd's death. A widely circulated bystander's video showed Floyd repeatedly saying that he could not breathe before he appeared to lose consciousness. Results of both an independent autopsy and that of the Hennepin County Medical Examiner's office, released June 1, ruled Floyd's death a homicide. Minneapolis police officer Derek Chauvin, who had pinned Floyd to the ground with Chauvin's knee on Floyd's neck, and three other officers present who did not intervene, were fired May 26, and the city's police chief called for an FBI investigation into discrepancies between the police report and the bystander video. Surveillance video footage also appeared to disprove the police report's contention that Floyd resisted arrest. Chauvin was arrested May 29 and charged with murder.

Peaceful protests beginning May 27 later turned violent, with looting, multiple large-scale building fires, and a fatal shooting. Minneapolis Mayor Jacob Frey (D), who voiced his support for peaceful protests, declared a local emergency May 28, and Minnesota Gov. Tim Walz (D) deployed more than 500 National Guard troops. Protesters May 28 set fire to the city's 3rd precinct police station after police evacuated. (In neighboring St. Paul, dozens of fires were started and nearly 200 buildings looted May 28.) Demonstrations continued despite an 8 p.m. curfew, and Walz said protesters had overwhelmed the police and the National Guard. Via Twitter, Pres. Donald Trump called the video of Floyd's death "shocking," but criticized Frey's leadership and called the protesters "thugs." A follow-up post that said "when the looting starts, the shooting starts," prompted Twitter to add a warning that the message's content glorified violence, a violation of the site's terms of service. Declining Trump's offer for active-duty military to quell the unrest, Walz May 30 activated the state's full National Guard force.

According to the Minneapolis *Star Tribune*, about 1,500 buildings were damaged or burned completely May 27-30, largely on hard-hit Lake Street. Later estimated at more than $500 mil in property damages, the Floyd protests were reportedly the second most materially destructive episode of civil unrest in U.S. history behind the 1992 Los Angeles riots.

Protests in support of the Black Lives Matter movement occurred in at least 140 U.S. cities by the end of May, with curfews imposed in at least 25 cities; governors activating National Guard troops in 21 states; and police arresting nearly 1,400 people in 17 cities May 28-30, according to an Associated Press tally.

The protests also brought renewed attention to the police killing of Breonna Taylor—a Black woman in Louisville, KY, who was killed by police executing a "no-knock" search warrant in Mar.—and to the shooting death in Feb. of Ahmaud Arbery, a 25-year-old unarmed Black man in Brunswick, GA. In Arbery's case, local authorities initially seemed not to pursue an investigation, but a video allegedly showing father-and-son suspects Gregory McMichael and Travis McMichael trapping Arbery at gunpoint spread widely in May; both were charged with murder May 7. (William Bryan, who recorded the video from his pickup which he also used to strike Arbery, was charged May 21.)

International

World Coronavirus Infections Approach 6 Million, With 360,000 Dead; Cases in Brazil Surge; Other International Developments—Confirmed cases of the novel coronavirus causing the respiratory disease COVID-19 surpassed 5.9 mil worldwide by May 31, leading to more than 367,000 deaths. The U.S. led both categories, with over 1.7 mil cases and over 100,000 fatalities. Brazil, which had recorded over 465,000 positive cases (and nearly 28,000 deaths) by the end of May—up more than six-fold from Apr.— overtook Spain as the second-most-infected country.

Confirmed infections surged in Russia, to over 405,000 cases, third-highest globally, though it reported far fewer deaths proportionally (nearly 4,700) than Brazil. Known infections in the UK jumped more than 100,000 to 272,800—fourth highest—while deaths increased to 38,376, trailing only the U.S. In late May, Denmark and Norway announced they would welcome tourists from one another's countries beginning in mid-June but would continue to restrict travelers from lockdown-free Sweden, which reported 37,113 cases and 4,395 deaths by May 31, more than in Denmark and Norway combined.

Reported deaths in Mexico rose sharply from 1,569 in Apr. to 9,415 by May 31 (from among 84,627 confirmed cases), while known infections in Peru spiked to over 148,000 (including 4,230 deaths). Chile, which saw rioting over lockdown-induced food shortages in Santiago, neared 95,000 cases, including 997 deaths. Canada reported 89,741 infections and 6,996 deaths. Continuing to lead the African continent in infections, South Africa reported nearly 31,000 cases by May 31, including 643 deaths, while Iran led the Middle East with 148,950 cases and 7,734 deaths, and India recorded 182,143 cases and 5,164, the most in Southeast Asia.

New Zealand's Ministry of Health May 4 reported no new infections since the country adopted stringent lockdown restrictions Mar. 25.

Venezuelan Military Thwarts Coup Attempt—Venezuelan forces May 3 staved off an attempt to overthrow the country's authoritarian president, Nicolás Maduro, halting an armed marine incursion involving U.S. mercenaries. The approximately 60-person group left neighboring Colombia in two boats,

entering Venezuela near the northern port cities of La Guaira and Macuto about 20 mi. from the capital Caracas; Maduro's forces killed eight dissident Venezuelans in the subsequent skirmish and arrested 13, including two Americans, both former Green Berets. A third American, also a former Green Beret, 43-year-old Jordan Goudreau, claimed responsibility for the failed attack; the Associated Press reported he trained former Venezuelan soldiers at secret camps established in Colombia by former Venezuelan Major Gen. Cliver Alcalá, who had surrendered himself to U.S. authorities in late Mar. on drug charges. Venezuelan authorities claimed to have infiltrated Goudreau's group, and Maduro blamed the incident on the U.S.; Pres. Trump denied any U.S. military involvement.

Iraq Forms New Government After Months of Gridlock—After more than five months without a prime minister, Iraq May 7 named former intelligence head Mustafa al-Kadhimi to the post, vacated by Adel Abdul Mahdi in Nov. 2019 amid anti-government protests. Kadhimi, an independent candidate backed by several major blocs, was notably considered acceptable to both the U.S. and Iran. He had pledged to hold accountable those responsible for Iraqi protester deaths, which numbered over 650 in the last three months of 2019 according to the Iraqi War Crimes Documentation Center. Kadhimi and his new government faced widespread bureaucratic corruption as well as an economy hard-hit by both crashing oil prices and the pandemic.

Taliban Violence Surges Despite U.S. Peace Deal—The Taliban claimed responsibility for an attack on a military convoy in eastern Afghanistan's Laghman Province that reportedly killed 27 Afghan soldiers May 10, just one of hundreds of attacks the Sunni group was accused of perpetrating since signing the U.N.-backed peace deal with the U.S. in late Feb. (A UN provisional summary released May 19 reported an increase in civilian deaths in Apr. 2020 by the Taliban and Afghan forces of 25% and 38%, respectively, compared to Apr. 2019.) Despite the escalation in violence, in late May Taliban leaders publicly affirmed the group's commitment to the deal.

Opposition Afghan presidential candidate Abdullah Abdullah, who had disputed the outcome of 2019 elections, signed a power-sharing deal May 17 with incumbent president Ashraf Ghani. Abdullah was appointed to lead talks with the Taliban, a condition of the U.S. peace deal. Though the Taliban declared and observed a three-day cease-fire beginning May 24, the group was blamed for an attack May 28 on a checkpoint in Parwan that killed at least seven Afghan security personnel.

Israel Inaugurates Stalemate-Ending Unity Government—An Israeli unity government was sworn in May 17, ending a 508-day political impasse—the country's longest—that included three divisive elections and several rounds of failed negotiations. Approved 73-46 by Israel's Knesset, the unconventional government was to be headed for the first 18 months by conservative Likud party chair and longtime Prime Min. Benjamin Netanyahu, followed by his former rival, centrist Blue and White Alliance leader Benny Gantz. (Before taking the reins, Gantz was to serve as "alternative prime minister" and defense minister.) Netanyahu with the support of Gantz pledged to move forward with a controversial plan to annex roughly one-third of the West Bank.

The first sitting Israeli prime minister to stand trial, Netanyahu faced opening proceedings May 24 on charges of bribery, breach of trust, and fraud.

General

Astronomers Detect Closest Known Black Hole—The European Southern Observatory announced May 6 that a team of astronomers, along with scientists from other institutions, had detected a black hole about 1,000 light-years from Earth, the closest such phenomenon yet discovered. It was also notably the first black hole in a stellar system—the now triple-star system HR 6819—whose stars are visible to the naked eye.

Pakistan Air Disaster Kills Nearly 100—Pakistan International Airlines Flight 8303 bound for Karachi from Lahore crashed near Jinnah International Airport May 22, killing all but two of 91 passengers, all eight crew, and one person on the ground. In a preliminary report, Pakistan's investigators said the crew retracted the Airbus A320's landing gear during an aborted landing, causing the jet's engines to scrape the runway several times before the plane reascended. Damaged from the impact, both engines failed during a second landing attempt and the aircraft crashed less than a mile from the runway.

SpaceX Launches American Astronauts Into Orbit— SpaceX made history as the first privately funded company to send a human into orbit when its Falcon 9 rocket propeled the Crew Dragon craft May 30 from NASA's Kennedy Space Center in Florida with two NASA astronauts, docking at the International Space Station (ISS) 19 hours later. The launch also marked the first time since the final space shuttle mission in 2011 that NASA astronauts reached space via a U.S. vessel. (In the interim, they had reached the ISS in Russian spacecraft.)

June 2020
National

Anti-Racism Protests Spread Broadly; Protests Renew Calls for Removal of Racist Symbols—Spurred by the late-May death of George Floyd, a Black man in police custody in Minneapolis, MN, protests calling for racial justice continued to shake the U.S., drawing demonstrators to the streets of more than 2,000 cities and towns by June 9. Overnight curfews were in place in some 40 cities May 31-June 1 to quell the threat of violence emerging from the largely peaceful daytime protests. In Davenport, IA, two protesters were shot and killed, as a separate ambush on police injured an officer. Two bystanders in Cicero, IL, were killed by what police said were "outside agitators"; police in Las Vegas fatally shot an armed man wearing body armor, while separately an officer was shot and seriously injured; four police officers were shot amid rioting in St. Louis, MO; and police and National Guard forces who were allegedly fired upon in Louisville, KY, shot back at protesters, killing a Black restaurant owner.

Pres. Donald Trump in a June 1 phone call with state officials said that "weak" governors must "dominate" the streets and threatened to deploy active-duty troops without states' consent. Trump also drew widespread criticism for walking to a photo shoot staged June 1 in front of St. John's Church that was preceded by the use of tear gas and rubber bullets to clear a peaceful crowd of protesters at nearby Lafayette Square. A *Washington Post* poll conducted June 2-7 found 74% of Americans generally backed the protests. Outside the U.S., anti-racism events were held in solidarity with the U.S. movement and in protest of local incidents of police abuse, including large rallies in major European cities.

While the widespread protests continued, largely peacefully, throughout June, incidents of violence and lootings grabbed headlines. A Black retired police captain was killed June 2 in St. Louis while attempting to secure a pawnshop against looters. A 75-year-old white protester was hospitalized with a head injury June 4 after Buffalo, NY, police pushed him to the ground. On June 7, a KKK member was arrested in Henrico County, VA, after allegedly driving into protesters, as was a man in Seattle, who was also charged with shooting a protester. Atlanta protesters burned a Wendy's where a Black man, Rayshard Brooks, was fatally shot June 12 while fleeing arrest; Atlanta police officer Garrett Rolfe was charged with Brooks's murder. A gunman June 27 in Louisville fired at a demonstration against the killing of Breonna Taylor, killing one person. Tens of thousands gathered across the nation June 14 in support of two Black transgender women killed five days prior in Ohio and Pennsylvania. By June 22, police had arrested more than 14,000 people for protest-related offenses—mostly low-level offenses, such as curfew violations—in more than 49 cities nationwide, according to a *Washington Post* tally.

In Minneapolis, where charges against ex-officer Derek Chauvin for Floyd's death were formally upgraded June 3 to second-degree murder, and aiding and abetting chargers were filed against the other three officers present, the city council June 26 voted unanimously (12-0) to move forward with a plan

to abolish the city's police department. On June 16, Pres. Trump signed an executive order, which restricted but did not ban choke holds and expanded federal oversight of police.

The protests renewed calls for the removal of racist or racially charged symbols throughout the U.S. Mississippi Gov. Tate Reeves (R) June 30 signed a bill to create a new state flag minus the Confederate battle emblem that had featured prominently on the flag for 126 years. Earlier in the month, Bubba Wallace, the only full-time Black driver in NASCAR, successfully persuaded the league to ban the Confederate flag from its events.

Jobs Report Surprises; GDP Drops 5.0% in First Quarter; Other Business News—Defying expectations, the Labor Dept. reported June 5 that the U.S. economy added 2.5 mil jobs in May, with an unemployment rate of 13.3%, for the first month of reported job growth since Feb. Wall Street weathered a turbulent month involving multiple surges and plunges; the Dow Jones Industrial Average closed June 11 at a 1,861.82 point loss (–6.9%). The Dow finished June at 25,812.88, a 1.7% increase from May, while the Nasdaq closed the month at 10,058.77, a 6.0% increase, and the S&P 500 finished June at 3,100.29, up 1.8%. The Labor Dept. June 25 reported that close to 1.5 mil first-time unemployment claims the week prior brought the total new claims since mid-Mar. to 47.3 mil. The Bureau of Economic Analysis's revised figures, released June 25, showed that in the first quarter of 2020, real GDP contracted—an annual rate of –5.0%—compared to a 2.1% gain the previous quarter.

On June 8, oil giant BP announced it was slashing 15% of its global workforce by the end of the year—some 10,000 jobs—as low demand for oil appeared likely to continue. The Commerce Dept. confirmed June 15 that it was relaxing its prohibition against U.S. companies doing business with Chinese telecom giant Huawei. On June 16, California utility PG&E formally pleaded guilty in court to 84 counts of manslaughter in connection with the 2018 Camp Fire—the state's deadliest—which CEO Bill Johnson admitted the utility's faulty equipment started. The next week, Bayer, which acquired agricultural giant Monsanto in 2018, announced it would pay more than $10 bil to resolve most of the roughly 125,000 lawsuits alleging the herbicide Roundup causes cancer.

Coronavirus Hotspots Emerge in South, Western States— Remaining firmly at the center of the global coronavirus pandemic, the U.S. by June 13 surpassed 2 mil confirmed cases including nearly 114,000 deaths from among more than 7.5 mil worldwide, and saw large increases throughout the month in recently reopened southern and western states, even as cases declined sharply in former hotspot states such as Illinois, Michigan, New York, and Washington.

Texas continued its phased reopening but saw infections rise dramatically around Dallas, Houston, and San Antonio. Texas Gov. Greg Abbott (R) June 25 halted further reopening of the state and closed bars, known to be high-risk for transmission, June 26. Florida Gov. Ron DeSantis (R) took the same action after the state's health officials announced a record-shattering 8,492 daily confirmed cases for June 26 that contributed to a Johns Hopkins Univ. tally of a record 40,173 new U.S. cases that day. Though roughly 20 states by June 30 announced they were pausing or rolling back reopenings, Pres. Donald Trump repeatedly blamed the exploding case numbers on increased testing. Scientists debunked that claim by highlighting the rate of positive tests, which had reached an average of more than 21% in Arizona and 12% in Florida.

Health officials continued to urge Americans to wear face masks, even as Pres. Trump refused to wear one publicly. A number of states by June mandated mask-wearing; absent state requirements, many municipalities did so as well. Pres. Trump June 22 suspended entry to the U.S. of some foreign workers, which the White House said would aid the economy.

Supreme Court Issues Key Rulings on LGBTQ Rights, Immigration—The U.S. Supreme Court June 15 announced a landmark 6-3 ruling in *Bostock v. Clayton County, Georgia* that prohibited employers from discriminating against workers solely based on their identification as gay or transgender. Previously, 26 states were without explicit existing protections for LGBTQ workers. Writing for the majority, Associate Justice Neil Gorsuch said that such persons were protected under the spirit of the 1964 Civil Rights Act barring discrimination on the basis of sex. Gorsuch, a Trump appointee, was joined in the majority by Chief Justice John Roberts, as well as Associate Justices Ginsburg, Breyer, Sotomayor, and Kagan, the foursome typically described as the Court's liberal wing. Justices Alito, Thomas, and Kavanaugh dissented in the ruling.

Siding again with Ginsburg, Breyer, Sotomayor, and Kagan, Roberts June 18 authored the majority opinion in the Court's 5-4 decision in *Dept. of Homeland Security v. Regents of the Univ. of California*, halting the Trump administration's attempt to end the Deferred Action for Childhood Arrivals (DACA) program, which since 2012 had shielded from deportation roughly 700,000 undocumented so-called "Dreamers" brought to the U.S. as children. The opinion did not rule out future attempts to end DACA but declaimed the administration's justification.

Trump Tulsa Rally Draws Criticism, Low Turnout; Bolton Memoir Released; Biden Secures Democratic Nomination—Pres. Donald Trump held his first campaign rally in more than three months, June 20, in Tulsa, OK, amid the continuing coronavirus pandemic. Some 6,200 supporters attended the rally at the city's 19,200-seat BOK Center, well shy of the 1 mil RSVPs claimed by the Trump campaign. Neither social distancing nor masks were required, and those who attended signed waivers of Trump campaign liability for any illness. At least six campaign staffers working at the event tested positive for coronavirus prior to the rally. Speaking for nearly two hours, Trump blamed an "unhinged left-wing mob" for escalating nationwide anti-racism protests and told rally-goers he had instructed health officials to slow the pace of coronavirus testing to keep case counts lower.

Ex-White House national security adviser John Bolton's book, *The Room Where It Happened: A White House Memoir*, was released June 23, three days after a federal judge denied Trump's request to block it. Among other claims, Bolton said that Trump sought foreign reelection interference from China in addition to Ukraine.

Former Vice Pres. Joe Biden, the presumptive Democratic presidential nominee since Apr., June 5 passed the required threshold of 1,991 delegates, according to the Associated Press. According to FiveThirtyEight's national polling average, Biden at the end of June led Trump, 51.1% to 41.5%, in nationwide support.

Firing of Federal Attorney Sows Confusion—Calling into further question the independence of the federal Justice Dept., U.S. Atty. for the Southern District of New York Geoffrey Berman, whose office was investigating Pres. Donald Trump's personal attorney Rudy Giuliani, stepped down June 20 after Atty. Gen. William Barr told Berman that Trump had fired him at Barr's request. The matter gained attention the day prior when Barr unexpectedly announced Berman was leaving the post, after which Berman in a statement said he would not resign until the Senate confirmed his replacement. When questioned by reporters, Trump said he was "not involved," and that Berman's firing was "all up to the attorney general."

International

U.S.-Recognized Libya Government of National Accord (GNA) Retakes Tripoli from Rival Forces—Marking a potential new phase in Libya's six-year-old civil war, forces from the United Nations-backed, internationally recognized GNA announced June 4 that they had regained full control of Tripoli, Libya's capital, after recapturing the city's international airport from forces of the eastern-based Libyan National Army (LNA). Backed by Russia, the LNA under Gen. Khalifa Haftar had waged a 14-month offensive but pulled back from the capital's suburbs after facing military intervention by Turkey on the side of the GNA. The next day, the GNA announced the liberation of LNA's final western stronghold of Tarhuna, 40 mi southeast, along with two districts of the strategic coastal city of Sirte on June 6.

India-China Border Clash Kills 20 Indian Troops—Fighting June 15 between Indian and Chinese troops in a disputed region of the Himalayas bordering northern India and southwestern China left at least 20 Indian soldiers dead, 76 wounded, and unknown Chinese casualties. Said to be the first fatal border conflict between the two countries since 1975, the confrontation occurred in the Galwan Valley where they fought with fists and rocks; Chinese forces reportedly also used clubs spiked with nails or barbed wire. (A 1996 agreement, which the Indian Army said it would no longer follow, forbade either side's troops from using firearms there.)

Reports Surface of Russian Effort to Pay Bounties for U.S. Soldiers in Afghanistan—The *NY Times* June 26 reported that U.S. intelligence officials months earlier had concluded that a Russian intelligence unit had offered Taliban-linked militias money to kill coalition forces, including American soldiers, in Afghanistan in 2019, generating outrage against Russia and questions for the White House over its response. The report, which was confirmed by the *Washington Post*, drew immediate claims from Pres. Trump that he had not been apprised of the matter. Though the *Times* in a subsequent report revealed the intelligence had appeared in written form in the President's Daily Brief (PDB) in late Feb., Trump reportedly rarely read the PDB. Defense Sec. Mark Esper and Gen. Mark Milley, the chairman of the Joint Chiefs of Staff, on July 9 told the House Armed Services Committee that the intelligence concerning the alleged bounty program had not been verified.

Global COVID-19 Cases Pass 10 Million, With a Half-Million Deaths—The ongoing global coronavirus pandemic surpassed 10 mil confirmed infections worldwide by June 29 (including nearly 500,000 deaths). Though the U.S. remained the global hotspot with more than 2.5 mil cases by the end of the month, outbreaks in Latin America, Asia, and the Middle East contributed to the eruption in cases. Brazil, which had reported some 465,000 total cases at the close of May, nearly tripled that number by June 30 to more than 1.34 mil including 57,622 deaths. While Chile and Peru each recorded more than 275,000 cases, Mexico reported fewer total cases—less than 217,000—but ended the month with 26,648 confirmed deaths, nearly five times that of Chile. Canada reported over 103,000 total cases, including 8,522 deaths. In India, the number of confirmed cases jumped to nearly 567,000. Cases in Iran and Pakistan also surged by the close of June, with approx. 225,000 and 209,000, respectively, while South Africa continued to far outpace other African nations, with more than 144,000 cases and 2,529 deaths. The EU in late June confirmed it was barring entry to travelers from the U.S., Brazil, and Russia over those countries' high rates of the virus.

Beijing Approves Controversial New Security Law for Hong Kong—Imposing arguably the greatest change on Hong Kong since its return to Chinese rule in 1997, China's parliament June 30 unanimously approved widespread new security powers over the semi-autonomous region, the site of waves of large-scale pro-democracy demonstrations. Outlawing secession, subversion, and conspiring with foreign forces, the new security law was said to essentially criminalize protests and limit freedom of speech, a hallmark of the former UK colony. Over the next day, July 1, the 23rd anniversary of Hong Kong's handover, police arrested at least 370 demonstrators.

July 2020
National

Supreme Court Term Ends With Rulings on Presidential Power, Contraception, Native American Rights, "Faithless Electors"—The U.S. Supreme Court concluded its 2019-20 term July 9 with a 7-2 ruling in *Trump v. Vance* that rejected Pres. Donald Trump's assertion of total immunity from a subpoena issued by the Manhattan district attorney's office for Trump's financial records. Writing the majority opinion, Chief Justice John G. Roberts Jr. said, "No citizen, not even the President, is categorically above the common duty to produce evidence when called upon in a criminal proceeding." In a separate 7-2 decision in *Trump v. Mazars*, the Court that same day blocked congressional Democrats at least temporarily from accessing

Trump's financial records when it sent the case back to a lower federal circuit court to rule on the separation of powers debate. (The *Vance* case was also sent back to a lower court to allow the president's attorneys to submit further objections over the subpoena.)

The Court, July 8, in a 7-2 decision in *Little Sisters of the Poor v. Pennsylvania*, held that private employers and universities may opt out of the Affordable Care Act mandate requiring coverage of contraceptive care if they object on religious or moral grounds.

Voting with the liberal wing, Associate Justice Neil Gorsuch was the swing vote and authored the majority opinion in the Court's July 9 decision in *McGirt v. Oklahoma*, which ruled that most of eastern Oklahoma, home to 1.8 mil people, is Native American reservation land. The decision most directly meant that only federal authorities may pursue future major crime charges against Native Americans there. On July 6, the Court in *Chiafalo v. Washington* ruled, 9-0, that states may compel their Electoral College electors to vote for candidates to whom they pledged their support.

Trump Commutes Adviser's Sentence; Attorney General Testifies in Combative House Hearing—Pres. Donald Trump July 10 commuted the 40-month sentence of friend and former political adviser Roger Stone, stemming from the Dept. of Justice's Russia election-interference probe. Stone was convicted in Nov. 2019 on all seven charges including obstruction, threatening a witness, and lying to Congress.

Atty. Gen. William Barr testified before the House Judiciary Committee July 28 in a contentious oversight hearing lasting nearly five hours, during which he said he had not acted on Trump's behalf when he called for a lighter sentence for Stone, among other actions or inactions interpreted as the department's operating at the president's behest. Barr testified that his order to clear Washington, DC's Lafayette Square of racial-justice protesters in June 2020 was not tied to a photo op involving Trump, said federal agents had been sent to Portland, OR, to protect federal buildings and not to bolster Trump's reelection campaign, and disputed Democratic lawmakers' claims of systemic racism in police departments.

Federal Executions Resume After 17-Year Pause—The first federal execution since 2003 took place July 14, when federal officials in Terre Haute, IN, executed Daniel Lewis Lee, convicted of killing an Arkansas family of three in 1996, concluding an informal moratorium. Pres. Barack Obama in 2014 ordered a Justice Dept. review of lethal injection drugs following a mishandled execution in Oklahoma; the review was reportedly completed in 2019, and Atty. Gen. William Barr approved a single drug—pentobarbital—in place of a three-drug cocktail previously used. Two more federal executions took place within the week.

Federal Presence at Racial Justice Protests Draws Rebuke—Media attention to widespread protests against police brutality and systemic racism focused squarely on Oregon, which sued the federal government July 17, alleging it was detaining protesters in the state's largest city, Portland, without probable cause. (A judge rejected the suit a week later.) The Trump administration had deployed federal agents to the city in early July under an executive order aimed at protecting federal monuments and buildings. City officials, media, and demonstrators reported agents operating well away from the federal courthouse they were ostensibly protecting, and reports of protesters held in unmarked vehicles and use of overly aggressive tactics were widespread. On July 11, a U.S. Marshal shot a non-lethal impact munition at a peaceful protester, causing a head injury, and federal agents on July 18 broke the hand of a 53-year-old Navy veteran, whom they seemingly also tear-gassed without provocation as seen in video footage. (According to the U.S. attorney's office in Oregon, 28 federal agents were injured in Portland by July 22.)

Portland Mayor Ted Wheeler and Oregon Gov. Kate Brown (D) publicly opposed the federal presence, and Wheeler himself was tear-gassed July 22, even as some protesters criticized the mayor for local police's use of tear gas against the protests,

which Pres. Trump said had been hijacked by "anarchists who hate our Country." On July 18, a self-described "Wall of Moms" began positioning itself between protesters and federal agents, followed over succeeding days by a "Wall of Dads" and "Wall of Vets." Brown and Vice Pres. Mike Pence July 29 negotiated the removal of federal agents from downtown Portland.

Other demonstrations sparked by the deaths of Black citizens like George Floyd and Breonna Taylor continued throughout the U.S. In Seattle, where police July 1 cleared protesters' self-declared Capitol Hill Autonomous Zone, a protester was killed July 4 by a motorist later charged with homicide. The July 4 police shooting death of a man in a parked car in Phoenix, AZ, reignited protests there. An armed protester in Austin, TX, was fatally shot July 25 by a U.S. Army sergeant who had previously tweeted about striking back against protesters.

Defense Sec. Mark Esper July 17 effectively prohibited the display of the Confederate flag at all U.S. military bases. Amid pressure from sponsors, Washington Redskins owner Daniel Snyder agreed to change the NFL team name.

Coronavirus Surges in West and South as U.S. Cases Top 4 Million; Trump Administration Weighs in on Masks, School Reopenings; Other Developments—The U.S. July 23 surpassed 4 mil coronavirus cases and 143,000 deaths, according to Johns Hopkins Univ.'s COVID-19 tracker, even as a Centers for Disease Control and Prevention (CDC) study published July 21 in *JAMA* estimated the actual number of U.S. cases at 6-24 times higher than the confirmed count. Infection rates increased in 40 states, and cases and hospitalizations spiked across the South and West. California July 24 reported over 420,000 total cases, overtaking New York, and Florida moved into second place July 25, with 414,000 confirmed cases and almost 5,800 deaths. Numerous medical facilities struggled to keep pace; more than 700 military medical personnel were deployed in California and Texas. On July 5 the *NY Times* reported that an analysis of CDC data on nearly 1.5 mil COVID-19 patients showed that African Americans and Latinos were three times more likely to contract the virus than white counterparts.

White House coronavirus coordinator Dr. Deborah Birx in early July attributed the surge in cases to easing stay-home restrictions too early. Pres. Donald Trump formally moved to begin withdrawing the U.S. from the World Health Org., effective July 6, 2021, and rejected health officials' calls to issue a nationwide order requiring or encouraging Americans to wear face masks. (Trump did not himself wear a mask in public until July 11.) The president July 8 threatened (without apparent legal authority) to withhold federal funding from schools that did not provide in-person teaching in the fall, and also criticized CDC school reopening guidelines as "impractical." The CDC released updated reopening procedures July 23. By the end of July, 32 states and the District of Columbia had mask orders in place; Arizona and Florida notably did not, and Georgia Gov. Brian Kemp (R) in mid-July invalidated mask orders by 15 local governments in his state. According to an AP-NORC poll conducted July 16-20, just 32% of Americans supported Trump's coronavirus strategy.

With Congress's failure to pass a new coronavirus relief bill, the $600-per-week additional federal unemployment aid expired at the end of the month, impacting some 30 mil Americans. Moving closer to a vaccine, Pfizer and Moderna both announced the start of Phase 3 trails July 27.

GDP Takes Record Dive in Second Quarter; Economy Recovers 5 Million Jobs—Further revealing the devastating economic impact of the coronavirus pandemic, the Bureau of Economic Analysis July 30 released advance figures for the second quarter of 2020 (Apr.-June) showing that real GDP fell at an annual rate of 32.9%. The severe downturn far exceeded the previous quarterly record loss of 10.0% set in 1958 and was the worst since record-keeping began in 1947. The first quarter of 2020 also saw 4.8% loss.

The Labor Dept. reported July 2 that the unemployment rate in June fell to 11.1% from 13.3% as the economy added 4.8 mil jobs, many from reopening businesses no longer under shutdown orders. Wall Street stock indexes maintained an upward course as the Dow Jones Industrial Average finished July at 26,428.32, a 2.4% increase from June. The Nasdaq Composite Index, which achieved seven record-high closings during July, closed the month at 10,745.27, up 6.8%, and the S&P 500 finished July at 3,271.12, up 5.5%.

International

Unrest Rocks Ethiopia Following Killing of Activist Performer—Violent protests in Ethiopia were sparked by the murder in late June of prominent singer Hachalu Hundessa, leaving at least 239 people dead by July 11 and leading to the arrest of almost 5,000 people. The 34-year-old Hachalu, a member of the Oromo ethnic group, was an active advocate for the long marginalized people.

U.S. Accuses China of Stealing Trade Secrets, Shuts Chinese Consulate in Houston—Accusing China of intellectual property espionage, the Trump administration July 21 ordered the closure of its consulate in Houston, TX, after which China demanded the shuttering of the U.S. consulate in the Chinese city of Chengdu. On July 13, China announced economic sanctions on Sens. Ted Cruz (R, TX) and Marco Rubio (R, FL), and others in response to economic sanctions the U.S. imposed the previous week on Chinese political figures. U.S. Sec. of State Mike Pompeo July 13 declared illegal most of China's South China Sea maritime claims.

Ukraine, Separatists Forge Shaky Cease-Fire—A comprehensive cease-fire between Ukrainian government forces and Russia-backed separatists went into force July 27, five days after reaching an agreement—facilitated by Organization for Security and Cooperation in Europe (OSCE) negotiators—aimed at ending fighting in Ukraine's eastern Donetsk and Luhansk region that had killed over 13,000 people since 2014. While the cease-fire—a precondition for implementing a 2015 peace deal reached in Minsk, Belarus—was initially hailed as a breakthrough, the OSCE said it was violated more than 100 times hours after it went into effect.

Yemeni Separatists Revoke Self-Rule Declaration in Push to Reconcile Pro-Government Alliance—The United Arab Emirates-backed Southern Transitional Council (STC) in Yemen on July 29 rescinded a three-month-old declaration of self-rule in southern Yemen, paving the way for the separatist group to reunite with its former ally, the U.S.-Saudi-backed, UN-recognized government engaged in a nearly six-year-old power struggle with Iran-backed Houthi rebels. (Pushed out of the former capital Sanaa in 2015, the government based itself in the port city of Aden, which the STC seized in Aug. 2019.) Pressured by both the UAE and Saudi Arabia, the STC reportedly also pledged to implement a stalled power-sharing deal signed by the two sides nearly nine months earlier in Riyadh.

Global COVID-19 Cases Pass 17 Million, Almost 670,000 Deaths; EU Approves Recovery Plan—Worldwide total confirmed cases of coronavirus surpassed 17 mil by July 31 (including 668,910 deaths), nearly 7 mil more than reported at the end of June. The U.S. remained at the epicenter, adding over 1.8 mil cases to end July with nearly 4.4 mil cases (including 150,054 deaths). Brazil, whose president Jair Bolsonaro tested positive for the virus July 7, continued to trail only the U.S. in cases, almost doubling its count to 2.6 mil by July 31 (with 90,134 deaths). India recorded over 1.6 mil infections (and 35,747 deaths), the third-highest case count globally, followed in the region by Bangladesh and Indonesia. Russia, fourth overall and leading European nations, tallied nearly 840,000 cases (and 13,963 deaths). On July 21, European Union leaders agreed on a 750-bil-euro ($857 bil) economic recovery package.

South Africa reported more than 482,000 cases by July 31, more than 3.3 times the number from June. Iran continued to lead the Middle East, with over 300,000 cases, and 16,569 deaths. The Philippines added nearly 53,000 cases in July to surpass China and lead the region with over 89,000 cases total.

General

Myanmar Mining Disaster Kills 170+—A landslide at a poorly regulated jade mine in Myanmar's Kachin state killed at least 174 people and left dozens more missing, July 2. Weeks of monsoon rains loosened a 1,000-ft hill above the flooded Wai Khar mine, creating a 20-ft. wave of water and mud that engulfed the victims.

U.S. Sports Leagues Attempt Spectator-Free Relaunch—Major League Baseball's Opening Day July 23 kicked off the league's pandemic-shortened, 60-game season with teams playing in home ballparks without fans. Within four days, 11 Florida Marlins players and 2 coaches reportedly tested positive for COVID-19, throwing the restart in jeopardy; other positive tests and delayed games followed. On hiatus since Mar. 11, 22 of 30 NBA teams returned July 30 to wrap up regular-season games taking place in a so-called "bubble" near Orlando, FL, in which all teams and support staff were to be sequestered for the duration of their playoff eligibility.

The National Women's Soccer League had been the first major professional sports league both to restart and finish its season amid the pandemic, when it returned June 27 for an 8-team, 23-game tournament, the 2020 Challenge Cup, staged in Herriman and Sandy, UT. Houston Dash defeated Chicago Red Stars (2-0) in the final July 26. The WNBA tipped off its revised season—12 teams playing 22 games each in Bradenton, FL—on July 25. Major League Soccer returned July 8 with its "MLS Is Back Tournament" through Aug. 11 near Orlando.

Hurricane Hanna Causes Flooding in Texas, Deaths in Mexico—Coastal Texas faced sustained winds up to 90 mph and heavy rain from Hurricane Hanna, which made landfall as a Category 1 storm July 25 about 130 mi south of Corpus Christi, causing significant flooding. The storm by the end of the following day dumped over 15 in. of rain between Brownsville and Port Mansfield, TX. The border cities of Mission and McAllen further inland saw numerous water rescues, and four deaths were reported in northeastern Mexico.

U.S., China, UAE Launch Mars Probes—NASA July 30 launched its $2.4-bil unmanned Mars rover *Perseverance* from Cape Canaveral, FL, to begin a decade-long mission in the planet's 28-mi-wide Jezero Crater when it lands in Feb. 2021. The car-sized, nuclear-powered *Perseverance* was an upgrade from NASA's *Curiosity*, exploring Mars's Gale Crater since landing in 2012.

A week earlier, China launched Mars-bound probe *Tianwen-1*, consisting of a separate orbiter, lander, and 530-lb rover, marking China's first independent interplanetary expedition. It too was scheduled to reach the planet in seven months, after which it would orbit for 2-3 months before deploying its lander unit. On July 20, the United Arab Emirates launched its unmanned Mars probe *Hope*—the Arab world's maiden interplanetary spacecraft. It was expected to orbit Mars for some 690 days, gathering atmospheric data.

August 2020
National

Trump Orders TikTok Sale; Other Economic, Business News—Citing national security concerns, Pres. Donald Trump Aug. 6 issued executive orders mandating the Chinese parent companies of the apps TikTok and WeChat divest U.S. operations within 45 days. (The deadline for TikTok's owner was extended to Nov. 12; in Sept., Oracle beat out Microsoft to acquire TikTok's U.S. business.)

The U.S. Labor Dept. reported Aug. 7 that the U.S. added 1.8 mil jobs in July. The July unemployment rate fell to 10.2% from 11.1%; 28.3 mil were collecting unemployment benefits, which no longer included federal supplements passed as part of coronavirus relief. Wall Street indexes saw historic growth throughout the month as the S&P 500 recorded six consecutive late-month record-high closes, and the Nasdaq Composite Index topped 11,000 points for the first time. The Dow Jones Industrial Average finished Aug. at 28,430.05, a 7.6% increase from July, while the Nasdaq closed the month at 11,775.46, up 9.6%, and the S&P 500 ended Aug. at 3,500.31, up 7.0%.

Postal Service in Spotlight Amid Service Changes, Mail-In Voting Considerations—After repeating an unfounded claim that expanding mail-in voting would lead to widespread fraud in the upcoming Nov. election, Pres. Donald Trump in an interview on Fox Business Aug. 13 said he was blocking additional funding to the U.S. Postal Service to intentionally hobble its ability to process the expected flood of ballots. The USPS gained further national attention that same day after reports that recently installed Postmaster Gen. Louis DeJoy, a major Trump donor with no prior postal experience, was planning to remove from service nearly 700 mail-sorting machines, thus reducing 20% of its capacity, ahead of the election. By Aug. 18, at least 21 states sued in federal court, arguing the change would impair their ability to operate free and fair elections. Though DeJoy, Aug. 18, said he would suspend further cost-cutting changes until after the election, in a Senate hearing Aug. 21, he testified that USPS would not reinstall collection boxes and machines already removed from service. The House Aug. 22 voted 257-150 (with the support of 26 Republicans) to provide $25 bil in USPS funding and prohibit service changes until 2021; however, Majority Leader Mitch McConnell (R, KY) said the Senate would not take up the House bill.

Democratic Convention Nominates Biden, Harris; Republicans Renominate Trump, Pence—The rescheduled Democratic National Convention—technically anchored at the Wisconsin Center in Milwaukee, WI, but meeting almost entirely remotely due to the coronavirus pandemic Aug. 17-20—formally nominated former Vice Pres. Joe Biden for president and Sen. Kamala Harris (CA) for vice president. Biden had named Harris, a former 2020 presidential contender, his running mate Aug. 11, making her the first Black and South Asian American woman on a major political party's presidential ticket. The 77-year-old Biden formally accepted the nomination Aug. 20 in a 25-min. speech delivered from Wilmington, DE. Pledging to gain control of the coronavirus, restore the economy, address racial injustice and climate change, and protect the Affordable Care Act, Biden said he would unite the country and bring it out of its "season of darkness," without mentioning his incumbent opponent by name.

The Republican National Convention convened Aug. 24-27, with operations headquartered at the Charlotte Convention Center in Charlotte, NC, and other events held remotely. Pres. Donald Trump formally accepted the nomination in a 70-min. speech Aug. 27 in front of more than 1,500 guests gathered on the White House South Lawn, during which he promised to resurrect the U.S. economy and cast his opponent as being under the control of leftist elements. Highlighting the law-and-order theme that also dominated his 2016 campaign, Trump derided nationwide protests against police violence and said Biden would give "free rein to violent anarchists, agitators, and criminals."

White House senior adviser Kellyanne Conway, one of Trump's longest-serving aides, announced her resignation Aug. 23, effective at the end of the month.

Senate Intelligence Committee Releases Bipartisan Report on 2016 Campaign Interference; Other Developments—The GOP-led Senate Intelligence Committee Aug. 18 released the most detailed report to date on Russian interference in the 2016 presidential election on behalf of then-candidate Trump, with what appeared to be the most damning evidence thus far of potential collusion between the Trump campaign and Russian intelligence officials. Based on interviews with more than 200 witnesses and more than 1 mil documents, the 3-year investigation notably revealed that a Russian contact with whom Trump's then-campaign chair Paul Manafort had met frequently and shared campaign information was a Kremlin intelligence officer. The report also concluded Trump had communicated with adviser Roger Stone about WikiLeaks making public emails hacked by Russia from Democratic contender Hillary Clinton. Nevertheless, the committee's GOP members, including acting chair Marco Rubio (R, FL), said the report vindicated Trump and his campaign.

Wisconsin Police Shooting of Black Man Sparks Turmoil—Amid ongoing nationwide protests over racial justice, a white officer Aug. 23 in Kenosha, WI—called to the scene over a domestic incident—shot 29-year-old Black resident Jacob Blake seven times in the back at close range. A bystander caught the shooting on video, which spread widely via social media.

Within hours, hundreds of protesters marched to the city's public safety building, where they clashed with police; numerous vehicles were set ablaze in a nearby used car lot. Though daytime protests were peaceful over the next two days, unrest and property damage intensified after dark. Kenosha's fire chief reported at least 34 fires the night of Aug. 24. Gov. Tony Evers (D), who approved deployment of 125 National Guard troops that day, declared a state of emergency Aug. 25. That night, police fired tear gas and rubber bullets at protesters, and two people were fatally shot and one wounded by 17-year-old Illinois resident Kyle Rittenhouse, who was among other self-declared vigilantes and counterprotesters present. He was charged Aug. 30 with two counts of first-degree intentional homicide.

About 200 federal agents and some 1,000 National Guard troops had been deployed to Kenosha by Aug. 28. Pres. Donald Trump, who said Rittenhouse had been acting in self-defense, visited Kenosha Sept. 1 over the objections of local leaders. While Trump did not meet with Blake or his family, former Vice Pres. Biden, whose visit was also opposed by Evers, met with Blake's family and other community members Sept. 3. After Milwaukee Bucks players staged a strike in protest, the NBA postponed playoff games until Aug. 29; other major pro leagues also postponed games. Protests over Blake's death also occurred in Atlanta, Chicago, Detroit, Minneapolis, Los Angeles, New York City, Philadelphia, and Seattle.

Clashes between Trump supporters and Black Lives Matter and other activists in Portland, OR, turned deadly the night of Aug. 29 when a member of the right-wing group Patriot Prayer was fatally shot. Prior to the shooting, a caravan of some 600 vehicles driven by Patriot Prayer members and other supporters arrived downtown, where for more than 90 days, Portland demonstrators had protested racial injustice. The 48-year-old suspected shooter, Michael Reinoehl, who reportedly self-identified as a member of antifa, was himself shot dead by police who said they acted in self-defense while trying to apprehend Reinoehl.

U.S. Coronavirus Cases Top 6 Million—The U.S. reached 6 mil total COVID-19 cases including more than 183,200 deaths Aug. 31, up 1.5 mil from the end of July and accounting for roughly 25% of global cases, according to data from Johns Hopkins Univ. Though virus spread had slowed in some states, including Arizona, California, Florida, and Texas, by the end of Aug. a number of Midwestern states had reported sharp increases, with some outbreaks centered in college towns. Amid the continuing pandemic, many school districts, including Chicago Public Schools, opted to start their 2020-21 school years fully online.

Twitter Aug. 5 temporarily restricted the Trump campaign from tweeting after the campaign's account shared a video in which Trump falsely said children were "almost immune" to the virus. Attempting to replace the $600-per-week federal unemployment supplement received through July 31 by up to 30 mil Americans who lost jobs during the pandemic, Pres. Trump Aug. 8 signed an executive order offering a $300 weekly supplement using FEMA funds. However, as of Aug. 27, only five states were paying out the extra portion, as the order was considered legally dubious.

International

Massive Beirut Chemical Blast Kills Nearly 200—A massive warehouse explosion in the port of Lebanon's capital of Beirut Aug. 4 killed at least 190 people, injured more than 6,500, and left at least 300,000 homeless. Caused by the improper storage of some 2,700 tons of ammonium nitrate, the blast—which was followed by a number of smaller detonations—created a 140-meter crater; property damage was estimated at more than $10 bil. The explosion triggered accusations of negligence and corruption against the government, sparking protests in the city beginning Aug. 6. (Lebanon had already seen periodic protests since Oct. 2019 over its collapsing economy.) Prime Min. Hassan Diab and his cabinet resigned Aug. 10.

UAE, Bahrain Normalize Relations with Israel—The United Arab Emirates and Israel reached an agreement to normalize relations, according to a statement Aug. 13 by Pres. Donald Trump, who negotiated the accord between UAE Crown Prince

Sheikh Mohammed bin Zayed al Nahyan and Israeli Prime Min. Benjamin Netanyahu. Signed Sept. 15 at the White House, the deal would halt future annexation by Israel of parts of the Palestinian-occupied West Bank. The UAE followed Egypt (1979) and Jordan (1994) as the third nation in the Middle East to normalize relations with Israel; on Sept. 11, Trump announced Israel and Bahrain would normalize diplomatic relations.

Disputed Belarus Election Triggers Mass Unrest—Tens of thousands of Belarusians rejecting longtime authoritarian Pres. Aleksandr Lukashenko's reelection gathered Aug. 16 in the capital Minsk for the country's largest protests since independence from the Soviet Union. Though state media reported 80.2% support for Lukashenko in Aug. 9 voting to 9.9% for political newcomer Sviatlana Tsikhanouskaya, the election lacked independent observers and was widely said to be rigged in favor of Lukashenko, in power since 1994. At least 3,000 demonstrators were arrested Aug. 9 after protests began in about 20 cities nationwide. Police responded aggressively, and three protesters were killed by Aug. 12. On Aug. 11, the 37-year-old Tsikhanouskaya fled to Lithuania, citing fear for her family's safety; she had emerged as the consensus opposition candidate after her husband, dissident blogger Sergei Tikhanovsky, was jailed and blocked from running. Up to 100,000 people protested in Minsk, Aug. 23, and the European Union agreed later that week to sanction 20 Belarusian senior officials. Russian Pres. Vladimir Putin pledged military support for Lukashenko, who said new elections would be held only after adoption of a new referendum-approved constitution.

Malian President Steps Down After Military Mutiny—Mali's Pres. Ibrahim Boubacar Keita resigned and dissolved the government Aug. 19, the day after he and Prime Min. Boubou Cissé were seized by mutinying soldiers, who detained them at a military facility near the capital, Bamako. Though Keita won a second term in 2018, corruption, economic mismanagement, and a dispute over results of long-delayed parliamentary elections brought thousands of protesters into the streets beginning early June, demanding Keita's resignation. The coup, which reportedly left four people dead, was the second since 2012.

Global COVID-19 Cases Pass 25 Million; Europe Faces Second Wave—Worldwide total confirmed cases in the ongoing global coronavirus pandemic topped 25.1 mil (including 844,312 deaths) by Aug. 31, roughly 8 mil more than the World Health Org. reported at the end of the previous month. Though the U.S. remained firmly in the lead in total infections and deaths for the fifth straight month (5.9 mil cases; 180,689 deaths), it saw a more than 38% reduction nationally in new cases from the end of July. Brazil, however, in second place globally (4.4 mil cases; 133,119 deaths), experienced a nearly 72% surge in cases from the month prior, and India added almost 2 mil cases in Aug., a nearly 121% increase, for 3.6 mil cases.

What appeared to be a resurgence of the virus hit Europe in Aug., which health officials attributed to decreased adherence to social distancing and mask usage following reopenings. Infecting mostly younger people and resulting in relatively few new deaths, the wave nonetheless pushed total cases over the entire region to more than 4 mil by Aug. 30, up 17.5% from four weeks earlier. Spain saw cumulative cases over the same span increase by nearly 46%, to almost 459,000, while France reported over 272,000 total, a nearly 37% increase. In other developments, South Africa, fifth highest in world cases behind Russia (995,319 as of Aug. 31), India, Brazil, and the U.S., passed 500,000 cases on Aug. 2.

General

Destructive Derecho Blasts Iowa—A severe wind and thunderstorm complex known as a derecho barreled an approximately 700-mi-long path through the Midwest Aug. 10-11, most severely affecting the Cedar Rapids, IA, area, where it set a state record for non-tornado wind gusts of up to 140 mph. Along with damaging structures and downing power lines, some 14 mil acres of cropland in the state, valued at $6 bil, were lost. (The USDA estimated total crop acreage affected across the Midwest at 37.7 mil acres.) Three people were killed in Iowa and 1 in Indiana by

the derecho, which also spawned 15 tornadoes across northern Illinois and northwest Indiana.

Sato Takes Indy 500—Japan's Takuma Sato won the 104th Indy 500 at Indianapolis Motor Speedway Aug. 23, holding off 2008 victor Scott Dixon of New Zealand by just under 0.06 sec. The 2017 race winner, Sato first took the lead in the final quarter, after which he traded the top spot multiple times with Dixon—race lap leader with 111 of 200 circuits—before commanding the final 28 laps. Originally scheduled for May 24, the race was postponed and held without spectators due to the coronavirus pandemic.

"Unsurvivable" Hurricane Laura Strikes Louisiana—Powerful Category 4 Hurricane Laura struck coastal Louisiana Aug. 27 in sparsely populated Cameron Parish—about 35 mi. east of the Texas border—with gusts exceeding 150 mph, severely impacting the city of Lake Charles as it continued northward before being downgraded to a tropical storm. Reportedly the 10th most powerful Atlantic hurricane ever documented, Laura was responsible for at least 27 deaths in Louisiana—mostly due to carbon monoxide poisoning from generators and heat-related illnesses—by Sept. 9; 5 deaths were reported in Texas, and over 20 in Haiti and the Dominican Republic were killed. An early estimate by CoreLogic assessed damage from high winds at up to $12 bil.

September 2020
National

Slow Job Growth Continues; Fed Signals Freeze of Near-Zero Interest Rates; Other Economic News—The Labor Dept. reported Sept. 4 that the U.S. economy gained 1.4 mil jobs in Aug., still down some 11.5 mil jobs since Feb. Though the unemployment rate fell sharply to 8.4% in Aug. from 10.2% in July, all but one of the Federal Reserve's policymakers in projections released Sept. 16 said they favored maintaining near-zero interest rates through at least 2022.

In its third and final estimate released Sept. 30, the Bureau of Economic Analysis said that U.S. GDP plummeted at an annualized rate of 31.4% during the second quarter of 2020.

A federal court Sept. 27 temporarily blocked Pres. Donald Trump's ban on U.S. downloads of the Chinese-owned social-video app TikTok. Disney Sept. 29 announced it was laying off 28,000 theme-park employees, some two-thirds of whom were part-time workers. The Dow Jones Industrial Average finished Sept. at 27,781.70, a 2.3% decrease from Aug., while the Nasdaq Composite Index closed at 11,167.51, down 5.2%, and the S&P 500 ended Sept. at 3,363.00, a 3.9% drop from Aug.

Supreme Court's Ginsburg Dies, Prompting Political Battle—U.S. Supreme Court Justice Ruth Bader Ginsburg—the oldest member of the Court at 87—died Sept. 18 at her Washington, DC, home, leaving a contentious vacancy on the nation's highest court just 46 days prior to the 2020 presidential election. Confirmed in 1993, Ginsburg, the second woman to serve on the Court, was a staunch proponent of gender equality and became known in later years for searing, unambiguous dissents. She became the first woman as well as the first Jewish person to lie in state in the Capitol Sept. 25.

Within hours of Ginsburg's death, Senate Majority Leader Mitch McConnell (R, KY) pledged to hold a vote on her yet-unnamed successor. McConnell had cited proximity to a presidential election when refusing to hold hearings on then-Pres. Barack Obama's Mar. 2016 Court nominee, Merrick Garland. Pres. Donald Trump Sept. 26 announced the nomination of 48-year-old Amy Coney Barrett, whom he had appointed to the Chicago-based 7th U.S. Circuit Court of Appeals in 2017.

Video of Rochester Police Killing Triggers Protests; Grand Jury in Breonna Taylor Shooting Votes Against Most Charges—Protests began Sept. 2 following the release of a Mar. 2020 video showing Rochester, NY, police officers holding Daniel Prude, a Black man experiencing a mental-health crisis, face-down with a hood over his head in an act that resulted in Prude's death, which was ruled a homicide. The nights of Sept. 4 and 5, police fired tear gas and pepper balls at Rochester crowds after episodes of vandalism and violence; at least three officers were injured. A report released Sept. 3 by the Armed Conflict Location & Event Data Project (ACLED) found more than 93% of some 7,750 Black Lives Matter-affiliated demonstrations from May 26-Aug. 22, 2020, were peaceful.

A grand jury in Louisville, KY, Sept. 23 charged former police officer Brett Hankison with endangerment, related to his actions in the Mar. 2020 police shooting death of Breonna Taylor, a 26-year-old medical worker reportedly asleep in her Louisville, KY, residence at the time that police executed a botched "no-knock" warrant. Besides Hankison, who was fired in June, charges were considered but not filed against two other officers involved in the incident. Louisville erupted in protests in response to the grand jury announcement, and two police officers were shot. Louisville Sept. 15 had agreed to pay a $12-mil settlement to the Taylor family and institute police reforms.

U.S. Coronavirus Cases Top 7 Million; Schools Adjust Reopenings—The U.S. Sept. 25 surpassed 7 mil coronavirus cases (including 203,329 deaths), according to Johns Hopkins Univ.'s COVID-19 tracker. A Reuters analysis showed growing infection rates in 27 states, led by Wisconsin with a 111% increase. Cases in the Dakotas, Montana, Utah, West Virginia, and Wyoming surged by more than 50% in Sept. but fell in summer hotspots of California and Florida by 50% and 47%, respectively.

States and municipalities continued to grapple with reopening schools amid the pandemic, with many adopting a hybrid approach that blended on-campus and remote learning. According to *Education Week* data, 39 states as of Oct. 5 permitted individual districts to determine reopening; 7 states, including California, ordered schools partially closed; and 4 (Arkansas, Florida, Iowa, and Texas) ordered schools open daily. Chicago, Denver, and Los Angeles were among a number of the large cities whose public school systems offered remote learning only; nearly half of New York City's public school students opted for off-campus instruction.

Pres. Donald Trump Sept. 16 said that at least 100 mil doses of a vaccine would be available by the end of the year, hours after Centers for Disease Control and Prevention (CDC) Dir. Robert Redfield told a Senate panel that a vaccine would not be widely available until mid-2021 or later. The CDC, which had faced accusations of compromising its public health mission to defer to the Trump administration's wishes, Sept. 18 reversed widely criticized Aug. guidelines on testing recommendations for persons who had been in close contact with known infected persons.

NY Times **Report: Trump Paid No Federal Income Taxes for Over a Decade Due to Large Business Losses**—The *NY Times* Sept. 27 reported that two decades of income tax return data it obtained showed Pres. Donald Trump paid only $750 in federal income taxes in 2016 and 2017, and no federal income taxes for 11 of the previous 18 years due to large annual losses of "tens of millions." Also among the findings, the president deducted as business expenses costs typically considered personal, such as those for residences and aircraft used to travel between them. (Trump was also still under audit by the IRS over a $72.9 mil tax refund.) Trump declared the *Times* report "fake news." Though presidents were not legally required to make their personal finances public, since the mid-1970s, every president besides Pres. Trump had done so.

First Presidential Debate Proves Contentious; Other Campaign Developments—Six days after refusing during a White House press conference to pledge to peacefully transfer power should he lose in Nov., Pres. Trump Sept. 29 verbally tussled with former Vice Pres. Joe Biden in the first of three scheduled debates, moderated by Fox News's Chris Wallace at Case Western Reserve Univ. in Cleveland, OH. Persistently interrupting both Biden and Wallace, Trump during the chaotic 90 minutes notably did not condemn white supremacy and asked his backers "to go into the polls and watch very carefully" after repeating unsubstantiated claims of widespread voter fraud. Biden, who lambasted Trump as a "racist" and "clown," criticized the president's coronavirus response, lack of a health care plan, and policies on racial justice.

The reelection campaign of Pres. Trump also confronted a Sept. 3 report in *The Atlantic* that Trump had privately disparaged U.S. soldiers killed in combat. According to anonymous sources, Trump in 2018 canceled a visit to a French cemetery

containing remains of WWI soldiers, dismissing them as "losers" and "suckers." A week later, advance copies of reporter Bob Woodward's book *Rage* made public quotes from interviews with Trump—supported by audio recordings—showing the president in early Feb. was aware of the threat level of the coronavirus but preferred to downplay it.

Pres. Trump Sept. 13 held his first indoor rally since June, in Henderson, NV, defying state coronavirus guidelines before a tightly packed crowd. Throughout Sept., Trump held multiple campaign events that attracted thousands of supporters, 15 of which *USA Today* determined violated public health guidelines.

Record-Breaking Wildfires Ravage California, Oregon, Washington—Drought conditions and a historic heat wave contributed to California's worst-ever wildfire season, with over 8,100 fires scorching more than 3.9 mil acres through Sept. 30. Killing at least 31 people, including four firefighters, from Aug.-Sept., the fires included five of the state's six largest ever, including the record-shattering August Complex fire, ignited by lightning in mid-Aug., which by Oct. 5 had burned 1 mil acres in the Mendocino National Forest and surrounding land.

Oregon was hard-hit by fires in Sept. that increased the state's yearly total to roughly 1 mil acres burned, killed at least 10 people, and forced authorities to evacuate over 40,000 people. In Washington state, the Cold Springs Fire near Omak killed one person and along with another nearby fire burned roughly 415,000 acres. Pres. Donald Trump met Sept. 14 with California Gov. Gavin Newsom (D) and other state officials, where the president denied scientific consensus that climate change had played a key role in exacerbating the fires. Trump in Aug. and Sept. declared the fires in California and Oregon, respectively, major disasters, making federal aid available.

International

Japan's Parliament Approves New PM—Chief Cabinet Sec. Yoshihide Suga was elected Japan's prime minister Sept. 16 by a parliamentary vote, 462-314, replacing Shinzo Abe, who announced his resignation in Aug. as the country's longest serving PM (2012-20; 2006-07). Abe remained in parliament but was reportedly in ill health. Suga easily won the support of the ruling conservative Liberal Democratic Party and was expected to continue the economic policies of Abe ("Abenomics"), which included fiscal stimulus through increased government spending.

Global COVID-19 Cases Pass 33 Million, 1 Million Deaths—Worldwide total confirmed cases of coronavirus surpassed 33.4 mil by Sept. 30 (including 1 mil deaths), over 8 mil more than reported at the end of Aug. The U.S. remained the pandemic's epicenter, ending Sept. with nearly 7.1 mil cases (including 203,874 deaths). India, which finished Sept. with over 6.2 mil total cases and 97,497 deaths, moved ahead of Brazil for second-most cases. Brazil recorded nearly 900,000 more cases, tallying over 4.7 mil total (142,058 deaths), ahead of Russia, fourth overall and leading European nations with over 1.1 mil cases (20,722 deaths). France, Spain, and the UK, all of which saw a resurgence in cases in Aug., continued to report increasing numbers to varying degrees in Sept.

South Africa continued to far outpace the rest of Africa, ending Sept. with over 670,000 cases (16,667 deaths), while Iran led the Middle East with over 450,000 cases (25,986 deaths), and the Philippines, with over 310,000 cases total (including 5,448 deaths), had the most cases in the Western Pacific region.

General

Osaka, Thiem Take Tennis U.S. Open Titles—No. 4-seed Naomi Osaka of Japan defeated unranked Belarusian Victoria Azarenka (1-6, 6-3, 6-3) to win her second U.S. Open singles title Sept. 12. The next day, Austrian Dominic Thiem, the men's No. 2-seed, outlasted No. 5-seed Alexander Zverev of Germany in a grueling 4-hr. match (2-6, 4-6, 6-4, 6-3, 7-6) that brought Thiem his first Grand Slam title. Novak Djokovic of Serbia, the No. 1-seed, was disqualified Sept. 6 after a ball he appeared to smack in frustration hit a judge in the neck.

Scientists Find Possible Signs of Life in Venus's Clouds—Venus's toxic atmosphere contains phosphine, a gas generated biologically on Earth, according to a study published Sept. 14 in *Nature Astronomy* and led by a Cardiff Univ. scientist. Though the observation, detected by the James Clerk Maxwell Telescope in Hawaii and Chile's Atacama Large Millimeter Array, may signify life in Venus's clouds, the research team had not yet determined the source of the gas.

DeChambeau Triumphs at U.S. Open Golf Tournament—Bryson DeChambeau won the 120th U.S. Open Sept. 20 at Winged Foot Golf Club in Mamaroneck, NY. Capturing his first major career title, the 27-year-old began the final round two shots behind tournament novice Matthew Wolff but passed him on the fifth hole and finished six strokes ahead at 6-under-274.

Schitt's Creek, Succession, Watchmen Big Winners at Emmy Awards—Canadian comedy *Schitt's Creek* made history at the 72nd Primetime Emmy Awards held largely remotely Sept. 20, becoming the first series to sweep all four comedy acting awards in the same year. In its sixth and final season, the show claimed nine 2020 awards, including best comedy series. The HBO drama *Succession* won seven awards including best drama series and outstanding lead actor in a drama series (Jeremy Strong). HBO's graphic novel-based *Watchmen* earned 11 awards, including best actress in a limited series or movie for Regina King.

Slovenian Wins Tour de France—Tadej Pogacar of Slovenia won the 107th Tour de France Sept. 20, completing the grueling 2,164-mi, 21-stage race in 87 hr., 20 min., 5 sec., just 59 sec. ahead of fellow countryman Primoz Roglic. The first Slovenian winner and the youngest winner since 1904, the 21-year-old was the first ever to claim the race's yellow (winner), polka dot (best mountain rider), and white (best young rider) jerseys in the same year. Delayed for more than two months due to the pandemic, the race in its later stages entered coronavirus "red zones," forcing race officials to ban spectators from race starts, finishes, and some climbs.

Tampa Bay Lightning Win Stanley Cup—Capping a playoff tournament held in two different "bubble" cities due to the coronavirus pandemic, the Tampa Bay Lightning captured their second Stanley Cup Sept. 28, defeating the Dallas Stars (2-0) in Game 6 at Rogers Place in Edmonton, AB, Canada, one day after succumbing to the Stars (3-2) in double overtime. Lightning defenseman Victor Hedman won the Conn Smythe Trophy as MVP of the Stanley Cup playoffs, scoring 10 goals and 11 assists in 24 games.

October 2020
National

Trump Tests Positive for Coronavirus, Signals White House Outbreak—Pres. Donald Trump revealed via Twitter early morning Oct. 2 that he and first lady Melania Trump had tested positive for COVID-19. Trump was flown later that day to Walter Reed National Military Medical Center, where remained for about 72 hours before discharge. Though Trump's White House physician publicly presented an optimistic picture of Trump's health in press updates, he said the president had twice required supplemental oxygen. Trump resumed holding large rallies Oct. 12.

White House officials' refusal to disclose when Trump last tested negative for the virus brought questions about the possibility that he had knowingly infected others. An outbreak within the president's circle infected at least three dozen people by mid-Oct. Critics pointed to the Supreme Court nomination announcement ceremony held in the White House Rose Garden Sept. 26—attended by more than 150 mostly mask-less supporters—as evidence of Trump's lax stance on the virus. By the end of Oct., at least five aides to Vice Pres. Mike Pence also tested positive.

FBI Foils Plot to Kidnap Michigan Governor—Exposing the increasing threat of extremist groups, federal officials Oct. 8 charged six people over a failed attempt to kidnap Michigan Gov. Gretchen Whitmer (D). State charges were levied against seven others accused of planning to attack law enforcement and the state's capitol. According to authorities, the suspects, part of or working with the right-wing Wolverine Watchmen militia group, were attempting to foment civil war by seizing state officials including Whitmer, whom Pres. Donald Trump had repeatedly criticized. Whitmer faulted Trump's rhetoric—including his refusal to condemn white supremacist groups—for the scheme. The FBI said the plotters also discussed kidnapping Virginia Gov. Ralph Northam (D).

Trump, Biden Face Off in Competing Town Halls, Final Debate; Other Campaign Developments—The campaigns of Pres. Donald Trump (R) and former Vice Pres. Joe Biden (D) each made their final push to win voters, with Trump restarting his campaign following coronavirus treatment with a large rally near Orlando, FL, Oct. 12. The debate commission canceled the second scheduled debate between Trump and Biden after the president refused to participate in a virtual format. Trump and Biden instead held separate town hall meetings televised simultaneously Oct. 15 on different networks.

The candidates appeared together in their second one-on-one debate at Belmont Univ. in Nashville, TN, Oct. 22. Though it was a more civil encounter than their first debate, due likely in part to moderators' ability to mute each candidate's microphone while the other delivered opening answers at the beginning of each topic, the two sparred over differing visions of America. Trump said that the U.S. was "rounding the corner" on the COVID-19 pandemic and predicted vaccine availability within weeks. Biden forecast a "dark winter" due to Trump's pandemic response, and criticized Republicans' continued attempts to repeal Obamacare without a replacement plan.

Trump in the debate also repeated dubious, unproven allegations (first reported by the *NY Post* Oct. 14) that Biden's son Hunter in 2015 arranged via email for then-Vice Pres. Biden to meet an executive at the Ukrainian energy company Burisma, on whose board Hunter served. The *Washington Post* reported Oct. 15 that intelligence agencies had cautioned the White House in 2019 that Trump's personal attorney, Rudolph Giuliani—who had obtained the copy of Hunter Biden's hard drive used as evidence in the *NY Post* report's allegations—had been used by Russian agents in a disinformation campaign.

Vice Pres. Mike Pence (R) and Sen. Kamala Harris (D, CA), the Democratic nominee for vice president, squared off Oct. 7 in their only scheduled debate at the Univ. of Utah in Salt Lake City.

National polling averages by RealClearPolitics showed Americans favoring Biden over Trump leading up to Nov. 3 voting. The average Oct. 1 had Biden with 50.1% support, 7.2 points ahead of Trump; Biden continued to lead Trump, 51.3%-43.5%, as of Oct. 31.

U.S. Launches Anti-Trust Case Against Google; GDP Rebounds in Third Quarter; Other Economic News—The U.S. Dept. of Justice and 11 states sued Google Oct. 20, arguing the internet search goliath employed anti-competitive practices. Agency officials commenting on the case, the largest anti-trust suit against a tech company since *U.S. v. Microsoft* was filed in 1998, did not rule out calling for Google's breakup. The following day, the Justice Dept. announced OxyContin maker Purdue Pharma agreed to pay $8.3 bil to settle charges it defrauded federal agencies and paid kickbacks to doctors to boost opioid prescriptions that contributed to the addiction-related deaths of more than 450,000 Americans since 1999.

According to an Oct. 2 Labor Dept. report, the economy added 661,000 jobs in Sept., the fifth straight month of gains since 22 mil jobs were lost due to the COVID-19 pandemic in Mar-Apr. (The country was still down 10.7 mil jobs from Feb.) Though the unemployment rate for Sept. fell to 7.9%, analysts partially attributed the drop to fewer people looking for employment. The Trump administration Oct. 16 reported that the federal deficit had soared to $3.1 tril—more than twice the previous record. Preliminary figures released Oct. 29 by the Bureau of Economic Analysis showed that in the third quarter of 2020, real GDP grew by a record annual rate of 33.1%, compared to a 31.4% drop the previous quarter. Wall Street stocks tumbled in late Oct. amid investor concerns over the virus—the Dow Jones Industrial Average finished the month at 26,501.60, dropping 4.6% from Sept., while the Nasdaq Composite Index closed down 2.3% at 10,911.59, and the S&P 500 ended Oct. at 3,269.96, a 2.8% drop from Sept.

Senate Confirms Third Trump Supreme Court Nominee—The GOP-led Senate Oct. 26 confirmed 48-year-old Chicago federal appeals court judge Amy Coney Barrett to the U.S. Supreme Court, filling the seat vacated just 39 days earlier by the death of liberal Associate Justice Ruth Bader Ginsburg. With cases over voting issues and the future of Obamacare anticipated immediately, the conservative Barrett was swiftly approved by a narrow 52-48 vote along party lines with the exception of Maine Sen. Susan Collins (R), who voted against confirmation. Ahead of her confirmation and same-day swearing-in, Barrett during Senate Judiciary Committee testimony Oct. 12-14 did not volunteer opinions on key legal matters, including same-sex marriage, abortion, and climate change. Partially opposed to the confirmation on the grounds that Senate Republicans in 2016 refused to hold hearings for then-Pres. Barack Obama's nominee during an election year, some Democrats vowed to expand the number of Supreme Court justices.

Philadelphia Police Shooting Triggers Unrest—Evening protests erupted in Philadelphia Oct. 26 following the fatal shooting caught on video that day of 27-year-old Black man Walter Wallace Jr., fired upon by officers after he walked toward them with a knife. According to his family, who said they had called emergency services for an ambulance, not police intervention, Wallace was suffering from a mental health crisis at the time of the incident. Some protests became violent Oct. 26, and resulted in more than 90 arrests, including for looting and assault on police; 30 officers were reported injured including one struck by a vehicle. Protesters accused police of using excessive force, and a video taken Oct. 27 appeared to show officers breaking a car's windows, dragging its occupants out, and beating them. Twenty-three more officers were reported injured Oct. 27, and 81 more arrests made. Philadelphia Mayor Jim Kenney (D) called in National Guard troops the following day.

U.S. Coronavirus Cases Surge, Surpass 9 Million—The U.S. Oct. 30 topped 9 mil cases (including 229,686 deaths), according to Johns Hopkins Univ.'s COVID-19 tracker. That same day, the country recorded nearly 100,000 new cases, setting a record for daily infections. A Reuters analysis showed growing infection rates in 36 states for the two weeks ending Oct. 25 as the upper Midwest remained the epicenter of the "third wave." Pres. Trump at various times during the month continued to attribute the sharp increases—which also saw more than 20 states recording record 7-day averages—on increased testing alone, but health officials pointed to the overburdening of numerous hospitals by COVID-19 patients. A Dept. of Health and Human Services memo, obtained by ABC News Oct. 22, reported more than 80% of ICU beds full in roughly a quarter of U.S. hospitals. Congress failed to pass another round of economic stimulus to aid cash-strapped Americans and small businesses, much of which expired at the end of July.

International

Sudan Govt., Rebels Ink Peace Deal—Sudan's interim government and a rebel group coalition formally signed a landmark peace agreement Oct. 3 aimed at halting nearly two decades of civil war, which had killed some 300,000 people and displaced up to 3 mil. Signed in the South Sudan capital of Juba, the accord, which followed failed peace deals in 2006 and 2011, addressed power sharing, reparations, and rebel force dismantling, but was boycotted by the northern faction of the Sudan People's Liberation Movement (SPLM-N) and one other rebel group. On Sept. 3, transitional Prime Min. Abdalla Hamdok and the leader of the SPLM-N had approved a declaration on establishing secular government.

Sudanese officials Sept. 4 declared a three-month state of emergency after flooding killed about 100 people since late July, including in the hard-hit capital of Khartoum.

Voters Return Bolivia to Leftist Control—Luis Arce of Bolivia's Movement Toward Socialism (MAS) won presidential elections Oct. 18, less than one year after MAS's Evo Morales resigned over disputed allegations of voter fraud after being elected to his fourth term; Morales referred to the allegations as a coup and fled the country. Since his departure, Bolivia had been governed by a U.S.-backed, far-right caretaker government that instituted widely criticized tactics, including "national pacification," that reportedly killed at least 30 Morales supporters. Declared free and fair by international observers, the elections saw Arce receive 55% support to less than 29% for the centrist candidate and 14% for the conservative nominee; MAS also won a majority in both legislative chambers.

Dozens of Nigerians Killed in Police-Brutality Protests—At least 56 people were killed in widespread protests that began Oct. 8 in Nigeria against police brutality, according to Amnesty International, including 12 unarmed protesters whom security forces shot Oct. 19 at two different locations in Lagos. A prison in the city was also set on fire, and attacks on two similar facilities in Benin City led to the escape of nearly 2,000 inmates. The demonstrations were sparked by a video appearing to show members of a controversial anti-robbery police unit, known as SARS, shooting and killing a man and driving off in his car. SARS was long accused of torture and extortion and the unit was officially disbanded Oct. 11.

Global COVID-19 Cases Pass 45 Million, Spike in Europe—Worldwide total confirmed cases of coronavirus surpassed 45.4 mil (including more than 1.18 mil deaths) by Oct. 31, 12 mil more than reported at the end of Sept. At the epicenter, the U.S. ended Oct. with approximately 8.9 mil cases (including 227,178 deaths), while India recorded 8.1 mil total (121,641 deaths), and Brazil tallied close to 5.5 mil total cases (158,969 deaths). Cases in Russia spiked by over 440,000 from late Sept. to more than 1.6 mil (27,990 deaths) amid a second wave of the virus in Europe that saw total cases in France more than double in a month to 1.3 mil (36,250 deaths). At least a dozen European countries—including Belgium, France, Germany, Italy, and the UK—re-imposed lockdown restrictions. South Africa continued to outpace the rest of its continent with 720,000 total cases (19,230 deaths). Iran led the Middle East with over 604,000 cases (34,478 deaths); the Philippines, with nearly 380,000 cases (including 7,185 deaths), had the most cases in the Western Pacific region.

General

Swiatek and Nadal Take French Open Titles—Iga Swiatek of Poland stunned 4th-seeded American Sofia Kenin in straight sets (6-4, 6-1) to win the French Open women's singles title Oct. 10 at Roland Garros in Paris, France, making her, at No. 54, the lowest-ranked player to win the tournament. The next day, Spain's Rafael Nadal overcame Serbia's Novak Djokovic (6-0, 6-2, 7-5) to claim his 13th French Open singles title and match Roger Federer's record of 20 Grand Slam singles titles.

L.A. Lakers Win NBA Championship—The Los Angeles Lakers won Game 6, 106-93, over the Miami Heat at the ESPN Wide World of Sports Complex outside Orlando, FL, Oct. 11, to secure the franchise its 17th title. Capping a shortened season completed by 22 of 30 teams in a so-called Bubble due to the coronavirus pandemic, the win tied the Lakers with the Boston Celtics for most NBA championships. LeBron James, in his second season with the Lakers, averaged 29.8 points and 11.8 rebounds in the Finals and was named NBA Finals MVP for the fourth time.

U.S. Spacecraft Lands on Asteroid; NASA Finds Water Evidence on Moon—Marking a first for the U.S., a NASA spacecraft touched down on and collected rock samples Oct. 20 from asteroid Bennu some 200 mil mi from Earth. Launched in 2016, the van-sized OSIRIS-REx, which arrived at the 1,700-ft asteroid in Dec. 2018, was not set to return with the samples to Earth until 2023.

NASA Oct. 26 announced it had discovered water molecules on the surface of the sunlit side of the Earth's moon. Identified by the agency's Stratospheric Observatory for Infrared Astronomy (SOFIA), the detection of water was immediately celebrated for its potential to aid NASA in developing human settlement on the moon.

L.A. Dodgers Win World Series—The Los Angeles Dodgers won the World Series over the Tampa Bay Rays in a 3-1 Game 6 victory played Oct. 27 in front of a limited crowd at Globe Life Field in Arlington, TX, the neutral site of all of the Series games due to the coronavirus pandemic. It was the seventh title for the Dodgers franchise, which was appearing in its third Series in four years. With 2 home runs, 5 RBI, and a .400 batting average over 6 games, Corey Seager was named the World Series MVP. Drawing criticism, Dodgers third baseman Justin Turner rejoined the team to celebrate the win on the field after being removed mid-game due to testing positive for COVID-19.

OBITUARIES

For those whose deaths occurred Nov. 1, 2019-Oct. 31, 2020.

A

Adderley, Herb, 81, Hall of Fame cornerback for the Green Bay Packers and Dallas Cowboys; won three Super Bowls; Oct. 30, 2020.

Aiello, Danny, 86, actor known for his Academy Award-nominated performance in *Do the Right Thing* (1989); NJ, Dec. 12, 2019.

Anderson, Philip, 96, Nobel Prize-winning physicist whose work led to a greater understanding of electrical properties; Princeton, NJ, Mar. 29, 2020.

Aoyagi, Takuo, 84, Japanese engineer who pioneered pulse oximetry; Tokyo, Japan, Apr. 18, 2020.

Auberjonois, René, 79, Tony Award-winning actor known for TV roles in *Benson* (1980-86) and *Star Trek: Deep Space Nine* (1993-99); Los Angeles, CA, Dec. 8, 2019.

B

Beard, Peter, 82, photographer best known for wildlife images; Montauk, NY, Apr. 1, 2020.

Blanton, Thomas, 82, Ku Klux Klan member who in 2001 received four life sentences for his role in a 1963 church bombing that killed four Black girls in Birmingham, AL; Bessemer, AL, June 26, 2020.

Boseman, Chadwick, 43, actor best known for playing historic Black figures and a superhero in Marvel's *Black Panther* (2018); Los Angeles, CA, Aug. 28, 2020.

Bream, Julian, 87, British classical guitarist and lutenist; Wiltshire, Eng., UK, Aug. 14, 2020.

Brimley, Wilford, 85, character actor best known for *The Natural* (1984), *Cocoon* (1985), and TV commercials for Quaker Oats and diabetes supplies; St. George, UT, Aug. 1, 2020.

Brock, Lou, 81, Hall of Fame outfielder best known for base stealing; broke Ty Cobb's career steals record in 1977; St. Charles, MO, Sept. 6, 2020.

Brooker, Tony, 94, British mathematician and computer scientist who developed the Autocode programming language; Hexham, Eng., UK, Nov. 20, 2019.

Brown, Timothy Ray, 54, first person considered cured of HIV/AIDS, after undergoing an experimental bone marrow transplant in 2007; Palm Springs, CA, Sept. 29, 2020.

Bryant, Kobe, 41, 18-time NBA All-Star who won five NBA championships with the L.A. Lakers; Calabasas, CA, Jan. 26, 2020.

Burbidge, E. Margaret, 100, British-born astronomer and astrophysicist who presented evidence that chemical elements are formed inside stars; San Francisco, CA, Apr. 5, 2020.

Burgie, Irving, 95, Hall of Fame songwriter best known for "Day-O (The Banana Boat Song)," popularized by Harry Belafonte; Brooklyn, NY, Nov. 29, 2019.

Burson, Harold, 98, public relations agency head who assisted companies in crisis, such as Johnson & Johnson after the Tylenol cyanide poisonings (1982); Memphis, TN, Jan. 10, 2020.

Byars, Betsy, 91, Newbery Medal-winning children's writer known for *The Summer of the Swans* (1970) and *The Night Swimmers* (1980); Seneca, SC, Feb. 26, 2020.

C

Cain, Herman, 74, CEO of Godfather's Pizza (1986-96) who ran for the Republican presidential nomination in 2012; Atlanta, GA, July 30, 2020.

Caldwell, Zoe, 86, Tony Award-winning Australian-born actress best known for *The Prime of Miss Jean Brodie* (1968) and *Master Class* (1995-97); Pound Ridge, NY, Feb. 16, 2020.

Cancel Miranda, Rafael, 89, Puerto Rican nationalist who with others opened fire in the U.S. House of Representatives in 1954, wounding 5 congressmen; San Juan, PR, Mar. 2, 2020.

Cary, Diana Serra, 101, child actress from the silent-film era known as "Baby Peggy"; Gustine, CA, Feb. 24, 2020.

Chiang, Cecilia, 100, Chinese-born American restaurateur who championed authentic Chinese food in her San Francisco restaurant, the Mandarin; San Francisco, CA, Oct. 28, 2020.

Christo, 84, Bulgarian-born artist who with his wife, Jeanne-Claude, created large-scale outdoor installations, including *Wrapped Reichstag* (1995) in Berlin, Germany, and *The Gates* (2005) in New York City; New York, NY, May 31, 2020.

Clark, Mary Higgins, 92, author known as "Queen of Suspense," whose 56 books were bestsellers; Naples, FL, Jan. 31, 2020.

Clemente, Vera, 78, humanitarian and widow of Pittsburgh Pirates Hall of Famer Roberto Clemente, whose charitable legacy was extended through his wife's efforts; San Juan, PR, Nov. 16, 2019.

Coburn, Tom, 72, physician who served as U.S. rep. (R, OK, 1995-2001) and sen. (2005-15); known for blocking federal spending bills, earning him the nickname "Dr. No"; Tulsa, OK, Mar. 28, 2020.

Cole, Joanna, 75, children's writer best known for the Magic School Bus series; Sioux City, IA, July 12,2020.

Coleman, Daisy, 23, sexual abuse survivor and advocate who was the subject of documentary *Audrie & Daisy* (2016); CO, Aug. 4, 2020.

Connery, Sean, 90, Scottish actor best known as the original British secret agent James Bond in seven films (1962-83); Nassau, The Bahamas, Oct. 31, 2020.

Conway, John Horton, 82, British-born mathematician whose love of games caused him to create the Game of Life, a zero-player cellular automaton game in 1970; New Brunswick, NJ, Apr. 11, 2020.

Coulombe, Joe, 89, founder and CEO of the Trader Joe's (1967) grocery store chain, which embraced private label items; Pasadena, CA, Feb. 28, 2020.

Cross, Ben, 72, British actor best known for his portrayal of Olympic athlete Harold Abrahams in *Chariots of Fire* (1981); Vienna, Austria, Aug. 18, 2020.

Crouch, Stanley, 74, journalist and critic known for essays about Black culture and helping to found Jazz at Lincoln Center in 1987; Bronx, NY, Sept. 16, 2020.

Crowley, Mart, 84, playwright whose groundbreaking *The Boys in the Band* (1968) featured multiple realistic gay characters; New York, NY, Mar. 7, 2020.

Culp, Connie, 57, recipient of the first U.S. partial face transplant (2008); Cleveland, OH, July 29, 2020.

Cussler, Clive, 88, novelist and adventurer known for bestselling thrillers featuring Dirk Pitt, a marine engineer; Scottsdale, AZ, Feb. 24, 2020.

D

Daniels, Charlie, 83, Grammy Award-winning country singer-songwriter and fiddler best known for "The Devil Went Down to Georgia" (1979); Nashville, TN, July 6, 2020.

Dass, Ram, 88, countercultural spiritual leader known for the book *Be Here Now* (1971) and for encouraging experimentation with hallucinogens; Maui, HI, Dec. 22, 2019.

Davis, Mac, 78, singer-songwriter who crossed over from country to pop; best known for No. 1 "Baby Don't Get Hooked on Me" (1972); Nashville, TN, Sept. 29, 2020.

Davis, Willie, 85, Hall of Fame defensive end who won Super Bowls I and II with the Green Bay Packers; Santa Monica, CA, Apr. 15, 2020.

de Havilland, Olivia, 104, two-time Academy Award-winning actress best known as Melanie in *Gone with the Wind* (1939), as well as for *To Each His Own* (1946) and *The Heiress* (1949); Paris, France, July 26, 2020.

Dennehy, Brian, 81, Tony Award-winning actor known for powerful lead performances in *Death of a Salesman* (1999) and *Long Day's Journey Into Night* (2003); New Haven, CT, Apr. 15, 2020.

dePaola, Tomie, 85, children's book writer and illustrator whose best known for his "Strega Nona" series; Lebanon, NH, Mar. 30, 2020.

Diffie, Joe, 61, Grammy Award-winning country singer-songwriter known for "Home" (1990) and "Pickup Man" (1994); Nashville, TN, Mar. 29, 2020.

Dillard, Harrison, 96, four-time Olympic gold medal-winning track athlete; Cleveland, OH, Nov. 15, 2019.

Dobbins, Georgia, 78, singer-songwriter who performed with the Marvelettes and co-wrote "Please Mr. Postman" (1961); Wayne, MI, Sept. 18, 2020.

Dodson, Betty, 91, sex educator; New York, NY, Oct. 31, 2020.

Douglas, Kirk, 103, actor and producer best remembered for the title role in *Spartacus* (1960); Beverly Hills, CA, Feb. 5, 2020.

Downs, Hugh, 99, TV host known for NBC's morning show *Today* (1962-71) and the ABC newsmagazine *20/20* (1978-99); Scottsdale, AZ, July 1, 2020.

Drucker, Mort, 91, cartoonist with *Mad* magazine, providing caricatures of films and TV shows for more than 50 years; Woodbury, NY, Apr. 9, 2020.

Drury, James, 85, actor known for playing the title role in TV western *The Virginian* (1962-71); Houston, TX, Apr. 6, 2020.

DuBois, Ja'Net, 74?, actress and singer known for *Good Times* (1974-79) and for co-writing and performing *The Jeffersons* theme song, "Movin' on Up"; Glendale, CA, Feb. 17, 2020.

Duch (Kaing Guek Eav), 77, Cambodian prison commandant who oversaw the torture and murder of thousands under the Khmer Rouge regime; Phnom Penh, Cambodia, Sept. 2, 2020.

Dwyer, Jim, 63, Pulitzer Prize-winning newspaper journalist whose subject was New York City; also known for books about the World Trade Center attacks of 1993 and 2001; New York, NY, Oct. 8, 2020.

Dyson, Freeman, 96, British-born physicist and mathematician whose works covered quantum electrodynamics and speculation about extraterrestrial civilizations; Princeton, NJ, Feb. 28, 2020.

E

Ebbers, Bernard, 78, Canadian co-founder and CEO of WorldCom (1985-2002); convicted on charges related to the company's $11-bil accounting fraud; Brookhaven, MS, Feb. 2, 2020.

Evans, Harold, 92, British-American journalist who led *The Sunday Times* (1967-81) and Random House (1990-97); also known as spouse to writer-editor Tina Brown; New York, NY, Sept. 23, 2020.

F

Fabric, Bent, 95, Danish pianist and composer best known for popular instrumental song "Alley Cat" (1961); July 28, 2020.

Feightner, Edward, 100, U.S. Navy flying ace during World War II who also worked as a postwar test pilot; Coeur d'Alene, ID, Apr. 1, 2020.

Ferrell, Conchata, 77, actress best known as housekeeper Berta in sitcom *Two and a Half Men* (2003-15); Sherman Oaks, CA, Oct. 12, 2020.

Finkel, Howard, 69, WWE Hall of Fame pro wrestling ring announcer; Madison, CT, Apr. 16, 2020.

Ford, Whitey, 91, Hall of Fame NY Yankees pitcher, who was a six-time World Series champion and claimed a franchise-record 236 wins; Lake Success, NY, Oct. 8, 2020.

Frankland, William, 108, British allergist and immunologist who studied desensitizing patients to allergens and developed immunotherapies for hay fever; London, Eng., UK, Apr. 2, 2020.

Frates, Pete, 34, former college baseball player who popularized the viral "Ice Bucket Challenge" (2014), which raised over $100 mil for amyotrophic lateral sclerosis (Lou Gehrig's disease) research; Beverly, MA, Dec. 9, 2019.

Friedman, Bruce Jay, 90, novelist who became a successful screenwriter with the films *Stir Crazy* (1980) and *Splash* (1984); Brooklyn, NY, June 3, 2020.

Fry, Hayden, 90, Hall of Fame college football coach who had his greatest success at Iowa after coaching SMU and North Texas; Dallas, TX, Dec. 17, 2019.

G

Gaines, Ernest J., 86, novelist known for *The Autobiography of Miss Jane Pittman* (1971) and *A Lesson Before Dying* (1993); Oscar, LA, Nov. 5, 2019.

Gates, Bill, Sr., 94, attorney and philanthropist who helped found and lead the charitable efforts that eventually became the Bill & Melinda Gates Foundation; Hood Canal, WA, Sept. 14, 2020.

George, Phyllis, 70, first woman to host a national network sportscast, on CBS's *NFL Today* (1975-78, 1980-83); Lexington, KY, May 14, 2020.

Gibson, Bob, 84, Hall of Fame St. Louis Cardinals pitcher (1959-75); two-time winner of World Series MVP and Cy Young awards; Omaha, NE, Oct. 2, 2020.

Gilbert, Craig, 94, producer who created the groundbreaking "reality" TV documentary *An American Family* (1973); New York, NY, Apr. 10, 2020.

Ginsburg, Ruth Bader, 87, U.S. Supreme Court associate justice (1993-2020) known for her forceful dissents whose noteworthy legal career included many victories for gender equality; Washington, DC, Sept. 18, 2020.

Glaser, Milton, 91, graphic designer best known for the "I ♥ NY" campaign and co-founding *New York* magazine; New York, NY, June 26, 2020.

Glenn, Annie, 100, speech disorder activist who overcame stuttering after being thrust into public life as the wife of astronaut (later U.S. senator) John Glenn; St. Paul, MN, May 19, 2020.

Glickman, Harriet, 93, teacher who advocated for cartoonists, notably Charles Schulz, to include Black characters in comics; Sherman Oaks, CA, Mar. 27, 2020.

Goodacre, Glenna, 80, sculptor who designed the Sacagawea dollar obverse and the Vietnam Women's Memorial in Washington, DC; Santa Fe, NM, Apr. 13, 2020.

Grau, Shirley Ann, 91, Pulitzer Prize-winning author best known for *The Keepers of the House* (1964); Kenner, LA, Aug. 3, 2020.

Groom, Winston, 77, novelist best known for *Forrest Gump* (1986); Fairhope, AL, Sept. 17, 2020.

H

Hamill, Pete, 85, author and journalist known for his street-wise style in New York tabloids; Brooklyn, NY, Aug. 5, 2020.

Harris, Barbara, 89, first woman ordained a bishop in the Episcopal Church of the U.S. (1989); Lincoln, MA, Mar. 13, 2020.

Harwood, Ronald, 85, Academy Award-winning British screenwriter best known for *The Dresser* (1983) and *The Pianist* (2002); Sussex, Eng., UK, Sept. 8, 2020.

Hatcher, Richard G., 86, first Black mayor of Gary, IN (1968-88); Chicago, IL, Dec. 13, 2019.

Heinemann, Larry, 75, National Book Award-winning novelist known for work about the Vietnam War; Bryan, TX, Dec. 11, 2019.

Henry, Buck, 89, actor, writer, and director who wrote the screenplay for *The Graduate* (1967) and co-created the spy spoof *Get Smart* (1965-70); Los Angeles, CA, Jan. 8, 2020.

Herman, Jerry, 88, Tony Award-winning composer and lyricist known for *Hello, Dolly!* (1964), *Mame* (1966), and *La Cage aux Folles* (1983); Miami, FL, Dec. 26, 2019.

Hite, Shere, 77, sex educator and feminist whose controversial work challenged notions about the way women achieved sexual pleasure; London, Eng., UK, Sept. 9, 2020.

Holm, Ian, 88, Tony Award-winning British actor best known for *Chariots of Fire* (1981) and his portrayal of Bilbo Baggins in Peter Jackson's Tolkien films; London, Eng., UK, June 19, 2020.

Horn, Roy, 75, German-born entertainer who as half of the Las Vegas act Siegfried & Roy was known for magic involving exotic animals, until a 2003 tiger attack ended his career; Las Vegas, NV, May 8, 2020.

Hume, John, 83, Nobel Peace Prize-winning political leader who helped orchestrate the Good Friday Agreement (1998), bringing peace to Northern Ireland; Londonderry, N. Ire., UK, Aug. 3, 2020.

I

Imus, Don, 79, mercurial radio and TV host known for vitriol and attacks on a wide range of targets; College Station, TX, Dec. 27, 2019.

J

James, Clive, 80, Australian-born critic, writer, and TV host known for his wit; Cambridge, Eng., UK, Nov. 24, 2019.

Johnson, Junior (Robert Glenn Johnson Jr.), 88, Hall of Fame NASCAR driver; Charlotte, NC, Dec. 20, 2019.

Johnson, Katherine, 101, NASA mathematician who calculated trajectories for its first human space flights; Newport News, VA, Feb. 24, 2020.

Jones, Terry, 77, Welsh-born actor, director, and writer known as a founding member of irreverent troupe Monty Python; London, Eng., UK, Jan. 21, 2020.

K

Kahn, Roger, 92, writer best known for seminal baseball book *The Boys of Summer* (1972); Mamaroneck, NY, Feb. 6, 2020.

Kaline, Al, 85, Hall of Fame Detroit Tigers outfielder (1953-74) who was an 18-time All-Star; Bloomfield Hills, MI, Apr. 6, 2020.

Karina, Anna, 79, Danish-born actress known as the muse of French New Wave director Jean-Luc Godard in *A Woman Is a Woman* (1961) and *The Little Soldier* (1963); Paris, France, Dec. 14, 2019.

Kawasaki, Tomisaku, 95, Japanese pediatrician who identified Kawasaki disease (1967), an inflammatory illness in children's hearts; Tokyo, Japan, June 5, 2020.

Kendall, Donald, 99, PepsiCo CEO (1963-86) who challenged Coca-Cola and expanded the company into fast food; Greenwich, CT, Sept. 19, 2020.

Khan, Irrfan, 53, Indian-born actor who became a global star with *Slumdog Millionaire* (2008) and *Life of Pi* (2012); Mumbai, India, Apr. 29, 2020.

Knight, Shirley, 83, Tony and Emmy Award-winning character actress best known for Oscar-nominated role in *Sweet Bird of Youth* (1962); San Marcos, TX, Apr. 22, 2020.

Kramer, Larry, 84, playwright and HIV/AIDS activist who co-founded the Gay Men's Health Crisis (1981) and the more radical ACT UP (1987); his largely autobiographical play *The Normal Heart* (1985) was an account of the epidemic; New York, NY, May 27, 2020.

Kretzmar, Herbert, 95, South African-born English theater critic and lyricist who wrote the English lyrics for French musical *Les Misérables* (1985); London, Eng., UK, Oct. 14, 2020.

L

Larsen, Don, 90, MLB pitcher who, for the NY Yankees, pitched the only perfect World Series game (1956); Hayden Lake, ID, Jan. 1, 2020.

Laurer, George, 94, engineer who created the now-ubiquitous universal product code (UPC); Wendell, NC, Dec. 5, 2019.

Lee Kun-hee, 78, South Korean chairman of Samsung (1987-2008, 2010-20) who grew the company into a global technology giant; convicted and pardoned twice for corruption and tax evasion; Seoul, S. Korea, Oct. 25, 2020.

Lehrer, Jim, 85, journalist best known as anchor on *PBS NewsHour* (1975-2011); Washington, DC, Jan. 23, 2020.

Leibman, Ron, 82, Emmy and Tony Award-winning actor known for playing Roy Cohn in *Angels in America* (1993); New York, NY, Dec. 6, 2019.

Lewis, John, 80, U.S. rep. (D, GA, 1987-2020) and civil rights leader who helped plan the 1963 March on Washington and was badly beaten on "Bloody Sunday" (1965) in Selma, AL; Atlanta, GA, July 17, 2020.

Li Zhensheng, 79, Chinese photojournalist who captured the propaganda and brutality of China's Cultural Revolution; New York, June 2020.

Lipton, James, 93, creator and host of *Inside the Actors Studio* (1994-2018), in which writers, directors, and actors were the subjects of his in-depth interviews; New York, NY, Mar. 2, 2020.

Little Richard (Richard Penniman), 87, pioneering rock 'n' roll singer-songwriter known for hits "Tutti Frutti" (1955), "Long Tall Sally" (1956), and "Good Golly, Miss Molly" (1958); Tullahoma, TN, May 9, 2020.

Loengard, John, 85, *Life* magazine photographer best known for images of celebrities; New York, NY, May 24, 2020.

Lopez, Trini, 83, guitarist and singer known for his covers of "If I Had a Hammer" (1963) and "Lemon Tree" (1965); Rancho Mirage, CA, Aug. 11, 2020.

Lowery, Joseph, 98, minister and Black civil rights activist who helped organize the 1955 Montgomery bus boycott and led the Southern Christian Leadership Conference (1977-97); Atlanta, GA, Mar. 27, 2020.

Lynn, Vera, 103, British singer known for entertaining troops with hit songs "We'll Meet Again" (1939) and "(There'll Be Bluebirds Over) The White Cliffs of Dover" (1941); East Sussex, Eng., UK, June 18, 2020.

Lyon, Phyllis, 95, LGBT rights activist who with partner, Del Martin, became the first same-sex couple to marry legally in California (2008); San Francisco, CA, Apr. 9, 2020.

Lyon, Sue, 73, actress known for playing the title role in Stanley Kubrick's *Lolita* (1962); Los Angeles, CA, Dec. 26, 2019.

M

Mandel, Johnny, 94, Oscar and Grammy Award-winning composer best known for "Suicide Is Painless" (1970), the theme for both the film and TV series *M*A*S*H*; Ojai, CA, June 29, 2020.

Marsalis, Ellis, Jr., 85, jazz pianist and educator; patriarch of a family of prominent jazz musicians; New Orleans, LA, Apr. 1, 2020.

Martignetti, Anthony, 63, child actor in an iconic 1969 Prince spaghetti commercial seen racing home to his mother's calls of "Anthony! Anthony!"; West Roxbury, MA, Aug. 23, 2020.

Massie, Robert K., 90, Pulitzer Prize-winning historian known for works on the Romanov family, including *Nicholas and Alexandra* (1967); Irvington, NY, Dec. 2, 2019.

Mays, Lyle, 66, Grammy Award-winning jazz composer and pianist who performed with the Pat Metheny Group (1977-2010); Simi Valley, CA, Feb. 10, 2020.

Mayweather, Roger, 58, boxer who was a world champion in two weight classes and coached his champion nephew, Floyd Mayweather Jr.; Las Vegas, NV, Mar. 17, 2020.

McCain, Roberta, 108, oil heiress who was mother of Sen. John McCain (R, AZ); took an active role in her son's 2008 presidential campaign at the age of 96; Washington, DC, Oct. 12, 2020.

McNally, Terrence, 81, Tony Award-winning playwright known for *Kiss of the Spider Woman* (1993), *Love! Valour! Compassion!* (1995) and *Master Class* (1995); Sarasota, FL, Mar. 24, 2020.

Mehta, Sonny (Ajai Singh), 77, India-born editor and publishing executive; New York, NY, Dec. 30, 2019.

Menzel, Jirí, 82, Czech director best known for the Academy Award-winning *Closely Watched Trains* (1966); Prague, Czechia, Sept. 5, 2020.

Mercado, Walter, 87, Puerto Rican astrologer and TV personality known for flamboyant presence in daily Spanish-language horoscopes; San Juan, PR, Nov. 2, 2019.

Misaka, Wat(aru), 95, basketball player who in 1947 was the first non-white person and first person of Asian descent to play in the NBA (then the BAA); Salt Lake City, UT, Nov. 20, 2019.

Mitchell, Bobby, 84, Hall of Fame NFL receiver and activist who was the first Black player for Washington; Apr. 5, 2020.

Moi, Daniel arap, 95, president of Kenya (1978-2002) whose tenure included violence against opponents and human rights abuses; Nairobi, Kenya, Feb. 4, 2020.

Morgan, Joe, 77, Hall of Fame infielder and sportscaster who was a two-time National League MVP; Danville, CA, Oct. 11, 2020.

Morricone, Ennio, 91, Academy Award-winning Italian film composer best known for spaghetti western scores, including *The Good, the Bad and the Ugly* (1966); Rome, Italy, July 6, 2020.

Morrow, Bobby, 84, sprinter who won three gold medals at the 1956 Melbourne Olympics; San Benito, TX, May 30, 2020.

Mubarak, Hosni, 91, Egyptian president (1981-2011) whose autocratic rule ended during the 2011 Arab Spring uprising; Cairo, Egypt, Feb. 25, 2020.

Mueller, Lisel, 96, Pulitzer Prize-winning German-born American poet whose lyrical work was both whimsical and sad; Chicago, IL, Feb. 21, 2020.

N

Nash, Johnny, 80, singer-songwriter known for reggae-influenced No. 1 "I Can See Clearly Now" (1972); Houston, TX, Oct. 6, 2020.

O

O'Neil, Denny, 81, comic book writer known for *Green Lantern/Green Arrow* and *Batman* titles; Nyack, NY, June 11, 2020.

Osmond, Ken, 76, actor best known as troublemaker Eddie Haskell on TV sitcom *Leave It to Beaver* (1957-63); Los Angeles, CA, May 18, 2020.

P

Peart, Neil, 67, Canadian drummer and lyricist for prog-rock trio Rush; Santa Monica, CA, Jan. 7, 2020.

Penderecki, Krzysztof, 86, Grammy Award-winning Polish composer-conductor known for avant-garde compositions and works adapted for *The Exorcist* (1973) and *The Shining* (1980); Krakow, Poland, Mar. 29, 2020.

Pepper, Beverly, 97, sculptor known for her large-scale outdoor works; Todi, Italy, Feb. 5, 2020.

Perego, Maria, 95, Italian puppeteer who created the mouse Topo Gigio, popularized on Ed Sullivan's eponymous 1960s TV variety show; Milan, Italy, Nov. 7, 2019.

Perez de Cuellar, Javier, 100, Peruvian diplomat who served as UN sec.-gen. (1982-91); Lima, Peru, Mar. 4, 2020.

Philbin, Regis, 88, Emmy Award-winning TV host best known for live morning shows paired with Kathie Lee Gifford (1988-2000) and Kelly Ripa (2001-11) and assorted game shows; Greenwich, CT, July 24, 2020.

Pointer, Bonnie, 69, Grammy Award-winning singer with the Pointer Sisters; Los Angeles, June 8, 2020.

Portis, Charles, 86, novelist best known for western *True Grit* (1968); Little Rock, AR, Feb. 17, 2020.

Preston, Kelly, 57, actress best known as the hardhearted fiancée in *Jerry Maguire* (1996); Clearwater, FL, July 12, 2020.

Prine, John, 73, Grammy Award-winning singer-songwriter who wrote about everyday people and problems in such songs as "Angel From Montgomery" and "Paradise" (both 1971); Nashville, TN, Apr. 7, 2020.

R

Reddy, Helen, 78, Australian-born singer-songwriter whose No. 1 hit "I Am Woman" (1972) became an anthem for the women's movement; Los Angeles, CA, Sept. 29, 2020.

Redstone, Sumner, 97, media executive and owner of National Amusements, Inc., a movie theater chain and the parent company of ViacomCBS; Los Angeles, CA, Aug. 11, 2020.

Reidy, Carolyn, 71, president and CEO of Simon & Schuster; Southampton, NY, May 12, 2020.

Reiner, Carl, 98, Emmy Award-winning actor, director, and writer who created *The Dick Van Dyke Show* (1961-66), teamed with Mel Brooks on "2000 Year Old Man" comedy routines, and directed *The Jerk* (1979); Beverly Hills, CA, June 29, 2020.

Reynolds, Gene, 96, Emmy Award-winning actor-director-producer who co-created *M*A*S*H* (1972-83) and *Lou Grant* (1977-82); Burbank, CA, Feb. 3, 2020.

Richard, Henri, 84, Canadian Hall of Fame center for the Montréal Canadiens who played for a record 11 Stanley Cup-winning teams; Laval, QC, Canada, Mar. 6, 2020.

Rigg, Diana, 82, Tony Award-winning British actress known for roles in TV's *The Avengers* (1965-68) and *Game of Thrones* (2013-17); London, Eng., UK, Sept. 10, 2020.

Rivera, Naya, 33, actress and singer best known for *Glee* (2009-15); Ventura Co., CA, July 8, 2020.

Robbins, John, 86, physician and medical researcher known for developing a bacterial meningitis vaccine; New York, NY, Nov. 27, 2019.

Rogers, Kenny, 81, Hall of Fame singer-songwriter whose country hits—including "Lucille" (1977), "The Gambler" (1978), and "Lady" (1980)—crossed over into pop; sold more than 120 mil records; Sandy Springs, GA, Mar. 20, 2020.

Roy, Travis, 45, Boston Univ. ice hockey player whose 1995 career-ending injury left him a quadriplegic; became an advocate for spinal cord injury survivors; nr. Burlington, VT, Oct. 29, 2020.

Ruckelshaus, William, 87, founding Environmental Protection Agency administrator (1970-73; 1983-85); resigned as deputy attorney general in what became known as Pres. Richard Nixon's "Saturday Night Massacre" (1973); Medina, WA, Nov. 27, 2019.

S

Sayers, Gale, 77, Hall of Fame Chicago Bears halfback also known for his friendship, depicted in *Brian's Song* (1971), with teammate Brian Piccolo; Wakarusa, IN, Sept. 23, 2020.

Schlesinger, Adam, 52, Grammy and Emmy Award-winning songwriter-musician known for band Fountains of Wayne and for composing for film and TV, including *That Thing You Do* (1996) and *Crazy Ex-Girlfriend* (2015-19); Poughkeepsie, NY, Apr. 1, 2020.

Schumacher, Joel, 80, director known for "Brat Pack" film *St. Elmo's Fire* (1985) and *Batman Forever* (1995); New York, NY, June 22, 2020.

Seaver, Tom, 75, Hall of Fame pitcher (1967-86), mostly for the NY Mets, who helped the team win the 1969 World Series; Calistoga, CA, Aug. 31, 2020.

Segel, Joseph, 88, business executive who founded 22 companies, including the Franklin Mint and the QVC TV shopping network; Gladwyne, PA, Dec. 21, 2019.

Sessions, William, 90, FBI director (1987-93) fired by Pres. Clinton due to ethics charges; tenure also notable for violent standoffs; San Antonio, TX, June 12, 2020

Shane, Bob, 85, founding member of folk group the Kingston Trio, known for hit "Tom Dooley" (1958); Phoenix, AZ, Jan. 26, 2020.

Sheehy, Gail, 83, journalist and writer known for the bestseller *Passages* (1976); Southampton, NY, Aug. 24, 2020.

Shula, Don, 90, Hall of Fame football coach whose 33-season career included the most wins in NFL history (347) and the only perfect season (1972); Miami Lakes, FL, May 4, 2020.

Shur, Gerald, 86, lawyer for the U.S. Justice Dept. who created the U.S. Federal Witness Protection Program; Warminster, PA, Aug. 25, 2020.

Sloan, Jerry, 78, Hall of Fame basketball coach who led the Utah Jazz for 23 years; Salt Lake City, UT, May 22, 2020.

Smith, B. (Barbara), 70, Black model turned restaurateur known for lifestyle books and a syndicated TV series; Long Island, NY, Feb. 22, 2020.

Smith, Jean Kennedy, 92, diplomat who served as U.S. ambassador to Ireland (1993-98); New York, NY, June 17, 2020.

Spinney, Caroll, 85, Emmy Award-winning puppeteer who created and performed legendary *Sesame Street* characters Big Bird and Oscar the Grouch (1969-2018); Woodstock, CT, Dec. 8, 2019.

Stark, Pete, 88, U.S. rep. (D, CA, 1973-2013) who helped shape health care legislation; Harwood, MD, Jan. 24, 2020.

Stempel, Herb, 93, 1950s game-show contestant who admitted he had been coached on *Twenty-One* to allow his opponent to win; New York, NY, Apr. 7, 2020.

Stern, David, 77, NBA commissioner (1984-2014) who transformed the sport into an international industry; New York, NY, Jan. 1, 2020.

Stiller, Jerry, 92, actor who was half of a comedy duo with wife Anne Meara and had success in sitcoms *Seinfeld* (1993-98) and *King of Queens* (1998-2007); New York, NY, May 11, 2020.

Suleimani, Qassim, 62, Iranian major general who directed clandestine operations; killed in U.S. drone attack, Baghdad, Iraq, Jan. 3, 2020.

Sutton, Eddie, 84, Hall of Fame college basketball coach who took four schools to the NCAA Div. I championship tournament; Tulsa, OK, May 23, 2020.

T

Tesler, Larry, 74, computer science pioneer credited with creating and naming the "cut, copy, and paste" functions; Portola Valley, CA, Feb. 16, 2020.

Thompson, John, Jr., 78, Hall of Fame college basketball coach; with Georgetown, the first Black head coach to win an NCAA Div. I national championship (1984); Arlington, VA, Aug. 30, 2020.

Tolkien, Christopher, 95, British editor who organized and posthumously published works of his father, J. R. R. Tolkien, including *The Silmarillion* (1977); Draguignan, France, Jan. 16, 2020.

Triplett, Irene, 90, last living Civil War pensioner; cognitive impairments qualified her for a lifelong pension based on her father's service in the Confederate and Union armies; Wilkesboro, NC, May 31, 2020.

Tripp, Linda, 70, government worker who secretly recorded White House intern Monica Lewinsky talking about her relationship with Pres. Clinton, which helped lead to his impeachment; Apr. 8, 2020.

Turner, John, 91, Canadian prime minister (1984) who held the office for just 79 days when his Liberal Party was swept out of office; Toronto, ON, Can., Sept. 19, 2020.

U

Unseld, Wes, 74, Hall of Fame basketball player named NBA MVP and Rookie of the Year in his first year with the then-Baltimore Bullets (1968-69); June 2, 2020.

V

Van Halen, Eddie, 65, Dutch-born Grammy Award-winning guitarist, who co-founded the Rock & Roll Hall of Fame-inducted band Van Halen, best known for "Eruption" (1978) and "Jump" (1984); Santa Monica, CA, Oct. 6, 2020.

Vivian, C(ordy) T(indell), 95, minister and Black civil rights activist who led non-violent protests through sit-ins and Freedom Rides; Atlanta, GA, July 17, 2020.

Volcker, Paul, 92, economist who as the chair of the Federal Reserve (1979-87) helped curb inflation; New York, NY, Dec. 8, 2019.

von Sydow, Max, 90, Swedish-born actor known for collaborations with Ingmar Bergman in such films as *The Seventh Seal* (1957); Provence, France, Mar. 8, 2020.

W

Waggoner, Lyle, 84, actor best known for *The Carol Burnett Show* (1967-74) and *Wonder Woman* (1975-79); Westlake Village, CA, Mar. 17, 2020.

Walker, Jerry Jeff, 78, country singer-songwriter best known for writing "Mr. Bojangles" (1968); Austin, TX, Oct. 23, 2020.

Weber, Idelle, 88, artist known for black silhouettes on brightly colored backgrounds; Los Angeles, CA, Mar. 23, 2020.

Welch, Jack, 84, General Electric CEO (1981-2001) who streamlined the company with a bottom-line approach, which included massive layoffs; New York, NY, Mar. 1, 2020.

Willard, Fred, 86, comedic actor known for roles in *This Is Spinal Tap* (1984), *Waiting for Guffman* (1996), and *Best in Show* (2000); Los Angeles, CA, May 15, 2020.

Williams, Betty, 76, Nobel Peace Prize-winning Northern Irish activist who co-founded Community of Peace People, which sought a peaceful resolution to Northern Ireland's "Troubles"; Belfast, Northern Ireland, Mar. 17, 2020.

Williamson, Oliver E., 87, Nobel Prize-winning economist who studied the cost of transactions and decisions made by businesses; Oakland, CA, May 21, 2020.

Wilson, Larry, 82, Hall of Fame NFL defensive back for the St. Louis Cardinals (1960-72); Scottsdale, AZ, Sept. 17, 2020.

Withers, Bill, 81, Grammy Award-winning singer-songwriter known for "Ain't No Sunshine" (1971), "Lean on Me" (1972), and "Lovely Day" (1977); Los Angeles, CA, Mar. 30, 2020.

Wong-Staal, Flossie, 73, Chinese-born American virologist and molecular biologist who helped determine that HIV was the cause of AIDS; La Jolla, CA, July 8, 2020.

Wood, Vicki, 101, race car driver who was the first woman to race in NASCAR in the 1950s; Troy, MI, June 5, 2020.

Wood, Willie, 83, Hall of Fame defensive back for the Green Bay Packers (1960-71) whose interception in Super Bowl I helped win the first title; Washington, DC, Feb. 3, 2020.

Wright, Mickey, 85, Hall of Fame pro golfer who had 82 career wins on the LPGA tour, including 13 major tournaments; Port St. Lucie, FL, Feb. 17, 2020.

Wuorinen, Charles, 81, Pulitzer Prize-winning composer who created an opera based on Annie Proulx's "Brokeback Mountain"; New York, NY, Mar. 11, 2020.

Wurtzel, Elizabeth, 52, writer whose memoir *Prozac Nation* (1994) opened a conversation about clinical depression; New York, NY, Jan. 7, 2020.

CONGRESS

116th Congress: Key Information

The 116th Congress convened Jan. 3, 2019, with Republicans maintaining control of the Senate (53-45, 2 ind.) and Democrats leading the House for the first time in eight years (235-199, 1 vacancy). As of Mar. 7, 2019, a record 131 women were serving, of whom 25 were in the Senate and 106 (including 3 nonvoting delegates and Puerto Rico's Resident Commissioner) were in the House. For the fifth consecutive cycle, the 116th Congress also made record minority representation, including five Hispanic lawmakers serving in the Senate and 45 (including 2 nonvoting delegates and the resident commissioner) in the House. The Senate membership also included three Black senators and three senators of Asian, South Asian, or Pacific Islander heritage. The House had 55 Black members (including 2 nonvoting delegates); 17 Asian/South Asian/Pac. Isl. Americans (including 3 nonvoting delegates); and 4 American Indians. Three lawmakers died during the 116th Congress: 12-term Rep. Walter B. Jones (R, NC), on Feb. 10, 2019; 12-term Rep. Elijah Cummings (D, MD), on Oct. 17, 2019; and 17-term Rep. John Lewis (D, GA), on July 17, 2020. Five-term Michigan Rep. Justin Amash left the Republican party in July 2019 and officially changed his affiliation to the Libertarian Party on May 1, 2020.

Leadership. In the House, where the party balance had shifted, former Minority Leader Nancy Pelosi (D, CA) was elected Speaker (220-15); Steny Hoyer (D, MD) became Majority Leader. Kevin McCarthy (R, CA), became Minority Leader. James Clyburn (D, SC) became Majority Whip, and Steve Scalise (R, LA) took the Minority Whip position.

In the Senate, Majority Leader Mitch McConnell (R, KY), Minority Leader Charles Schumer (D, NY), and Minority Whip Richard Durbin (D, IL) all retained their positions. John Thune (R, SD) became Majority Whip.

Ethics. After hearings on election fraud and misconduct by operatives working for Mark Harris, the Republican candidate for North Carolina's 9th district in 2018, the State Board of Elections Feb. 21, 2019, ordered a new election held Sept. 10, 2019.

Three lawmakers from the 116th Congress, all from the House, resigned amid separate allegations of wrongdoing. Accused of insider trading and lying to the FBI, 4-term Rep. Chris Collins (R, NY) stepped down Sept. 30; he pleaded guilty the next day and was sentenced in early 2020 to 26 months in federal prison. On Jan. 13, 2020, Duncan Hunter (R, CA) resigned after pleading guilty the month before to misusing campaign funds on personal expenses. He was sentenced in Mar. 2020 to 11 months in prison. First-term Rep. Katie Hill (D, CA) resigned effective Nov. 3, 2019, after admitting she had an inappropriate relationship with a campaign staffer in violation of congressional rules adopted in 2018.

For Further Information. Detailed legislative information can be accessed at www.congress.gov

Major Actions of the 116th Congress

Major actions taken by the 116th Congress through Oct. 27, 2020. Laws are identified by their Public Law (PL) number.

9/11 Victim Care. The Never Forget the Heroes: James Zadroga, Ray Pfeifer, and Luis Alvarez Permanent Authorization of the September 11th Victim Compensation Fund Act permanently renews funds for medical care for victims of physical harm from the 9/11 attacks, including first responders and others exposed to toxic chemicals who later became ill. Extends the deadline for filing claims from Dec. 2020 to Oct. 2090. Passed by the House (as amended) July 12, 402-12; passed by the Senate, July 23, 97-2; signed by Pres. Trump, July 29, 2019 (PL 116-34).

Presidential Impeachment. On Nov. 13, 2019, the House Intelligence Committee initiated public impeachment hearings against Pres. Donald Trump over his dealings with Ukraine. By a nearly party-line vote Dec. 18, the House impeached Trump on two charges, abuse of power (230-197) and obstruction of Congress (229-198). The Senate Feb. 5, 2020, acquitted Trump of both charges along party lines (52-48; 53-47), with only Sen. Mitt Romney (R, UT) breaking rank to vote guilty on the abuse of power charge.

Military Authority. Passed following the Jan. 2020 White House-directed fatal strike against Iranian Gen. Qassem Soleimani, the Iran War Powers Resolution (Sen. Jt. Res. 68) would prohibit the president from using U.S. military force against Iran without a congressional declaration of war or other authorization, unless to defend the U.S. from imminent attack. Passed by the Senate, Feb. 13, 55-45; passed by the House, Mar. 11, 227-186; vetoed by Trump, May 6, 2020.

Trade Regulations. The United States-Mexico-Canada Agreement Implementation Act revises the 1994 North American Free Trade Agreement. Among changes, it increases to 75% from 62.5% the minimum portion of a car's components made in Mexico, U.S., or Canada to avoid tariffs; grants U.S. increased access to the Canadian dairy market; extends copyright protection duration; and establishes e-commerce trade rules including prohibiting duties on digital products. Passed by the House, Dec. 19, 2019, 385-41; passed by the Senate Jan. 16, 2020, 89-10; signed by Pres. Trump, Jan. 29, 2020 (PL 116-113).

Coronavirus Response. The Families First Coronavirus Response Act delivers assistance in response to the global coronavirus pandemic. Requires most employers with fewer than 500 employees to provide 2 weeks emergency paid sick leave; funds free coronavirus testing and an expansion of food stamps and unemployment benefits. Passed by the House, Mar. 14 (as amended), 363-40; passed by the Senate, Mar. 18, 90-8; signed by Pres. Trump, Mar. 18, 2020 (PL 116-127). Follows first major COVID-19-related legislation, the Coronavirus Preparedness and Response Supplemental Appropriations Act, 2020, which funded vaccine research, public health agencies, and medical supplies. Passed by the House, Mar. 4, 415-2; passed by the Senate, Mar. 5, 96-1; signed by Pres. Trump, Mar. 6, 2020 (PL 116-123).

Pandemic Financial Aid. The Coronavirus Aid, Relief, and Economic Security Act (CARES Act) provides financial aid to Americans and the U.S. economy amid the COVID-19 pandemic. The $2.2-trillion package, the largest emergency aid package in U.S. history, provides assistance including checks for up to $1,200 to most adults (and $500 per child); $600 per week in expanded unemployment benefits for 4 months, in addition to state unemployment insurance; $500 bil in loans to distressed companies (including $29 bil to airlines); $349 bil for low-interest loans to small businesses to help retain and pay employees through the Paycheck Protection Program (PPP); $100 bil to hospitals; and $150 bil to state, territory, and tribal governments. Passed by the Senate, Mar. 25, 96-0; passed by the House, Mar. 27, by voice vote; signed by Pres. Trump, Mar. 27, 2020 (PL 116-136). In Apr. 2020, the Paycheck Protection Program and Health Care Enhancement Act appropriated $484 bil to supplement CARES Act programs and replenish others, including $321 bil for PPP. Passed by the Senate (as amended), Apr. 21, by voice vote; passed by the House (as amended), Apr. 23, 388-5; signed by Pres. Trump, Apr. 24, 2020 (PL 116-139).

Leadership of Selected Congressional Committees

Congressional leadership as of Oct. 2020.

House

Appropriations: Nita Lowey (D, NY)
Armed Services: Adam Smith (D, WA)
Budget: John Yarmuth (D, KY)
Education and Labor: Bobby Scott (D, VA)
Energy and Commerce: Frank Pallone Jr. (D, NJ)
Ethics: Ted Deutch (D, FL)
Financial Services: Maxine Waters (D, CA)
Foreign Affairs: Eliot L. Engel (D, NY)
Intelligence: Adam Schiff (D, CA)
Judiciary: Jerrold Nadler (D, NY)
Natural Resources: Raúl M. Grijalva (D, AZ)
Oversight and Reform: Carolyn B. Maloney (D, NY)
Transportation and Infrastructure: Peter A. DeFazio (D, OR)
Ways and Means: Richard Neal (D, MA)

Senate

Appropriations: Richard Shelby (R, AL)
Armed Services: James M. Inhofe (R, OK)
Banking, Housing, and Urban Affairs: Mike Crapo (R, ID)
Budget: Michael B. Enzi (R, WY)
Commerce, Science, and Transportation: Roger Wicker (R, MS)
Energy and Natural Resources: Lisa Murkowski (R, AK)
Environment and Public Works: John Barrasso (R, WY)
Ethics: James Lankford (R, OK)
Finance: Chuck Grassley (R, IA)
Foreign Relations: James E. Risch (R, ID)
Health, Education, Labor, and Pensions: Lamar Alexander (R, TN)
Intelligence: Marco Rubio (R, FL)
Judiciary: Lindsey Graham (R, SC)

Joint Committees

Economic: Sen. Mike Lee (R, UT), Rep. Don Beyer (D, VA)
Taxation: Sen. Chuck Grassley (R, IA), Rep. Richard Neal (D, MA)

U.S. SUPREME COURT

The U.S. Supreme Court's 2019-20 term began Oct. 7, 2019, and concluded July 9, 2020. The justices decided 61 cases (53 of which carried signed opinions; *per curiam* opinions, which do not identify an author, typically resolve straightforward cases without any oral arguments). Chief Justice John G. Roberts Jr. presided over his 15th full term. The eight associate justices in Oct. 2019, by order of seniority, were Clarence Thomas, Ruth Bader Ginsburg, Stephen G. Breyer, Samuel A. Alito Jr., Sonia Sotomayor, Elena Kagan, Neil M. Gorsuch, and Brett M. Kavanaugh. Both Gorsuch and Kavanaugh were nominated by Pres. Donald Trump and confirmed after the GOP-controlled Senate extended the "nuclear option" to allow confirmation to the Supreme Court by a simple majority vote.

Associate Justice Amy Coney Barrett was sworn in Oct. 26, 2020, replacing Associate Justice Ginsburg, who died Sept. 18, 2020.

Notable Supreme Court Decisions, 2019-20

Note: The columns on the right provide information on how each justice voted. Gray shading indicates a justice who was part of the majority. MO = justice authored majority opinion; CDO = justice authored opinion concurring in part and dissenting in part; CO = justice authored concurring opinion; COJ = justice authored opinion concurring in judgment but not its reasoning; COP = justice authored opinion concurring in part of the judgment; DO = justice authored dissenting opinion.

Elections

In *Chiafalo v. Washington*, July 6, the Court ruled unanimously that a state could require presidential electors to vote in the Electoral College for the candidate who won the most votes in the state. The justices found that while the framers of the Constitution might have envisioned that electors would be free agents, they never required this, and the Electoral College had swiftly become a mechanism for tallying popular votes by states.

Case	Kagan	Sotomayor	Breyer	Ginsburg	Roberts	Thomas	Alito	Gorsuch	Kavanaugh
Chiafalo v. Washington	MO					COJ			

Executive Powers

On June 29 the Supreme Court, overruling lower courts, 5-4, found that Congress violated the separation of powers when it created the federal Consumer Financial Protection Bureau with a single director whom a president could fire only for "inefficiency, neglect of duty, or malfeasance in office." The Court held that the director could be fired at will by the president. The case was *Seila Law v. CFPB*.

On July 9, ruling 7-2 in *Trump v. Vance*, the Court rejected Pres. Trump's claim of presidential immunity, finding that a New York grand jury operating in secret could subpoena his tax returns and other records to investigate potential crimes, though objections could still be raised based on other grounds, including scope and relevance.

In a 7-2 ruling on *Trump v. Mazars USA*, July 9, the Court overturned lower court rulings that had upheld House committees' subpoenas of the president's financial and banking records, holding that Congress can do so only when the requests are narrowly focused and needed for framing legislation. It sent the cases at issue back to lower courts to determine whether they fit those limits.

Case	Kagan	Sotomayor	Breyer	Ginsburg	Roberts	Thomas	Alito	Gorsuch	Kavanaugh
Seila Law v. CFPB	COP				MO	CDO			
Trump v. Vance					MO	DO	DO		COJ
Trump v. Mazars USA					MO	DO	DO		

Immigration

In *Dept. of Homeland Security v. Regents of the Univ. of California*, the Court found, 5-4, June 18, that the Trump administration had failed to provide the needed reasoned justification for ending the Obama-era Deferred Action for Childhood Arrivals (DACA) program, and thus could not immediately end it. The decision enabled some 700,000 immigrants ("Dreamers") who entered the U.S. as children to obtain work permits and temporarily avoid deportation.

Case	Kagan	Sotomayor	Breyer	Ginsburg	Roberts	Thomas	Alito	Gorsuch	Kavanaugh
DHS v. Regents		CDO			MO	CDO	CDO		CDO

LGBTQ Rights

The Court June 15 ruled, 6-3, in *Bostock v. Clayton County*, that gay and transgender employees were protected from discrimination in the workplace, since discrimination based on sexual orientation or gender is prohibited under the wording of 1964 civil rights legislation barring discrimination based on sex.

Case	Kagan	Sotomayor	Breyer	Ginsburg	Roberts	Thomas	Alito	Gorsuch	Kavanaugh
Bostock v. Clayton County							DO	MO	DO

Native American Rights

In a 5-4 ruling in *McGirt v. Oklahoma*, July 9, the Court found that since Congress never revoked treaties establishing a reservation for the Creek Nation in eastern Oklahoma, only the federal government, not the state, has jurisdiction to prosecute serious crimes committed there by Native Americans.

Case	Kagan	Sotomayor	Breyer	Ginsburg	Roberts	Thomas	Alito	Gorsuch	Kavanaugh
McGirt v. Oklahoma					DO	DO		MO	

Religious Rights

In a 5-4 decision in *Espinoza v. Montana Dept. of Revenue*, the Court, June 30, ruled that the state could not exclude church schools from a state-sponsored scholarship program available to students in other private schools, on the basis that it would constitute unconstitutional discrimination against religion.

In *Our Lady of Guadalupe School v. Morrissey-Berru*, a decision involving the cases of two lay Catholic-school teachers in California, the Court found, 7-2, June 8, that based on the 1st Amendment right of free exercise of religion, federal anti-discrimination laws cannot be applied to decisions of a religiously affiliated school in hiring and firing employees for positions viewed as vital to its religious mission.

Case	Kagan	Sotomayor	Breyer	Ginsburg	Roberts	Thomas	Alito	Gorsuch	Kavanaugh
Espinoza v. Montana Dept. of Revenue		DO	DO	DO	MO	CO	CO	CO	
Our Lady of Guadalupe School v. Morrissey-Berru		DO				CO	MO		

Reproductive Rights

In a 5-4 ruling June 29, in *June Medical Services v. Russo*, the Supreme Court found that a Louisiana law requiring doctors performing abortions to have admitting privileges at a nearby hospital would severely reduce access to abortion, and thus impose an unconstitutional "undue burden" on women seeking abortions. Chief Justice Roberts concurred on the basis of precedent established under a 2016 decision involving a similar Texas law.

On July 8, the Court found that the Trump administration could exempt employers who cite religious or moral objections from the part of the Affordable Care Act that requires employers to offer or allow health insurance covering contraceptives for employees. The 7-2 vote, in *Little Sisters of the Poor v. Pennsylvania*, overturned a circuit court decision immediately blocking the exemption, but returned the case to that court to examine whether the exemption was "arbitrary and capricious."

Case	Kagan	Sotomayor	Breyer	Ginsburg	Roberts	Thomas	Alito	Gorsuch	Kavanaugh
June Medical Services v. Russo			MO		COJ	DO	DO	DO	DO
Little Sisters of the Poor v. Pennsylvania	COJ		DO			MO	CO		

NOTABLE QUOTES, 2020

National News

"We have it totally under control. It's one person coming in from China, and we have it under control. It's going to be just fine."
—**Pres. Donald Trump**, Jan. 22, shortly after the first confirmed U.S. case of COVID-19 was reported.

"What they are asking you to do is to throw out a successful president on the eve of an election, with no basis and in violation of the Constitution. It would ... weaken ... forever all of our democratic institutions."
—**Trump attorney Pat Cipollone**, at Senate impeachment trial, Jan. 28.

"We must say enough — enough! He has betrayed our national security, and he will do so again. He has compromised our elections, and he will do so again. ... Truth matters little to him. What's right matters even less, and decency matters not at all."
—**Rep. Adam Schiff** (D, CA), addressing the Senate in closing argument as lead impeachment trial manager, Feb 3.

"You just breathe the air and that's how it's passed. And so that's a very tricky one. ... It's also more deadly than even your strenuous flu."
—**Pres. Trump**, Feb. 7, in interview with journalist Bob Woodward, unpublished until Sept., referring to COVID-19.

"We're going to be pretty soon at only five people. And we could be at just one or two people over the next short period of time. So we've had very good luck."
—**Pres. Trump**, Feb. 26, at a White House news conference, discussing the first reported cases of COVID-19 in the U.S.

"I like this stuff. I really get it. People are surprised that I understand it. Every one of these doctors said, 'How do you know so much about this?'"
—**Pres. Trump**, while touring U.S. Centers for Disease Control and Prevention, Mar. 6.

"I can't jump in front of the microphone and push him down."
—**Dr. Anthony Fauci**, director, Natl. Institute of Allergy and Infectious Diseases, referring to Pres. Trump's coronavirus briefing statements, in interview with *Science* magazine published Mar. 22.

"The president of the United States calls the shots. ... When somebody's the president of the United States, the authority is total."
—**Pres. Trump** at news briefing, Apr. 13, when asked what constitutional provision gave him the power to override states on reopening from pandemic-response shutdowns.

"It has been an absolute chaotic disaster."
—**Former Pres. Barack Obama**, speaking about the Trump administration's response to the COVID-19 pandemic, in a May 8 call with former members of his administration.

"Please. Please. I can't breathe, officer. ... I cannot breathe. I cannot breathe."
—**George Floyd**, in video recorded by bystander; a Black man, Floyd died May 25 after a white Minneapolis police officer restrained him by compressing his neck for eight minutes.

"These THUGS are dishonoring the memory of George Floyd, and I won't let that happen. ... Any difficulty and we will assume control but, when the looting starts, the shooting starts. Thank you!"
—**Pres. Trump** May 29 in a tweet flagged by Twitter as violating its rule against "glorifying violence."

"I'm 100 percent with people who are protesting for justice, but is this justice?"
—**Francisco Araujo**, owner of a Bronx jewelry store targeted by looters June 1.

"I am asking you, is that what a Black man's life is worth? Twenty dollars?"
—**Philonise Floyd**, testifying before a House Judiciary Committee hearing, June 10, into the death of his brother, George Floyd, who died in the process of his arrest over a complaint he had passed a counterfeit $20 bill.

"I believe, for the most part, you can trust respected medical authorities. I believe I'm one of them, so I think you can trust me."
—**Dr. Anthony Fauci** during a Georgetown Institute of Politics and Public Service event, July 14.

"Why should I go to that cemetery? It's filled with losers."
—**Pres. Trump**, when he skipped a 2018 scheduled visit to a cemetery in France where American war dead were buried; this alleged quote, which came from anonymous sources, was reported in *The Atlantic* magazine, Sept. 3.

"I'm the leader of the country, I can't be jumping up and down and scaring people."
—**Pres. Trump** speaking to Sean Hannity on Fox News, Sept. 9.

"The debate is over around climate change. Just come to the state of California. Observe it with your own eyes."
—**California Gov. Gavin Newsom** (D), Sept. 11, as he toured a portion of the millions of acres devastated by wildfires in Western states.

"My most fervent wish is that I will not be replaced until a new president is installed."
—**U.S. Supreme Court Associate Justice Ruth Bader Ginsburg**, shortly before her death on Sept. 18.

"Well, we're going to have to see what happens."
—**Pres. Trump**, Sept. 23, when asked whether he'd commit to a peaceful transition of power after the election.

"Don't be afraid of Covid. Don't let it dominate your life."
—**Pres. Trump**, in Oct. 5 tweet, announcing he planned to leave Walter Reed Medical Center after his 3-night stay for COVID-19 treatments.

"I can't characterize the facts in a hypothetical situation, and I can't apply the law to a hypothetical set of facts."
—**U.S. Supreme Court nominee Amy Coney Barrett**, Oct. 13, during confirmation hearings, in response to question from Sen. Amy Klobuchar (D, MN) about voter intimidation.

Around the World

"[T]his letter serves as a warning and reprimand over your illegally spreading untruthful information online. ... We want you to calm down and reflect on your actions, and solemnly warn you: If you ... continue the illegal activity, you will be punished per the law!"
—**Wuhan (China) Public Security Bureau**, in Jan. 3 letter, which Dr. Li Wenliang was forced to sign after being detained for alerting others to COVID-19. He later died of the virus.

"These f------ hairdressers who go into houses to cut women's hair, what the f--- are they for? Do you understand that the coffin will be closed? Who's going to see you with your hair fixed in the coffin?"
—**Antonio Tutolo**, mayor of Lucera, Italy, as reported in Euronews, Mar. 24, as the coronavirus pandemic swept through Italy.

"I'm sorry, some people will die, they will die, that's life. You can't stop a car factory because of traffic deaths."
—**Brazilian Pres. Jair Bolsonaro**, Mar. 27 in TV interview, referring to coronavirus casualties.

"I want to express my deepest regrets for the wounds of the past."
—**King Philippe** of Belgium in a letter June 30 to the president of the Democratic Republic of the Congo, a former colony that suffered atrocities under Belgian rule.

"Putin, Drink Some Tea."
—**Translation of a Russian protest sign**, following the apparent poisoning of Pres. Vladimir Putin's most prominent critic, Alexei Navalny, after he had tea in an airport cafe, Aug. 20.

"Kill all you see, whether children or adults."
—**Myanmar military command** given to Pvt. Zaw Naing Tun's battalion, as he reported in a video confessing involvement in a reported 2017 massacre of an estimated 6,700 Rohingya Muslim villagers; he and another soldier were brought, Sept. 7, into custody of the International Criminal Court in The Hague.

People and Culture

"It brings me great sadness that it has come to this."
—**UK's Prince Harry**, at a Jan. 19 event, referring to his and his wife Meghan Markle's decision to step back from royal duties.

"Bikes are like the new toilet paper."
—**Eric Attayi**, owner of a cycling store in Houston, TX, who saw a pandemic-fueled consumer demand for bikes revitalize his business; as quoted by CNN, June 2.

"No one really thinks that these statues are teaching anybody history. The bubonic plague was a major event in history—we don't go around and put up statues of rats."
—**Trevor Noah**, referring to statues of Confederate figures, June 8 on *The Daily Show with Trevor Noah*.

"If we don't carry on, he just ain't in good trouble for nothing."
—**Rev. Dr. Jacquelyn Lancaster-Denson**, a leader of the African Methodist Episcopal Church in Alabama, paying tribute to the late U.S. Rep. John Lewis (D, GA), July 26.

"Homosexual people have the right to be in a family. They are children of God. ... What we have to have is a civil union law—that way they are legally covered."
—**Pope Francis**, in two separate past statements, the first referring specifically to parental acceptance; as quoted in a documentary clip widely publicized Oct. 21.

The Elephant IS the Room

Over a 138-year history, Lucy, a 65-foot-high elephant-shaped building in Margate, NJ, has been a real estate office, a tavern, a private residence, and since 1976, a national historic landmark. On Mar. 5, 2020, though, Lucy was posted on Airbnb for three one-night stays; reservations were snapped up in a matter of seconds. The visits, scheduled for later in Mar., were delayed until Sept. after Lucy was closed due to COVID-19 restrictions.

Meggan Haig, a resident of nearby Dennis Township, was one of six guests to snag a night in the replica pachyderm. Haig remembered seeing Lucy every summer during family road trips to Atlantic City, so she set an alarm on her phone to ensure she'd be ready to book the last night as soon as its availability came online. Another lucky winner, Doris Perkins, grew up on the Jersey Shore, where she knew Lucy as a landmark she had gone by dozens of times. But prior to her overnight stay, Perkins had never been inside, even for the docent-led tour (something that 132,000 others do each year).

Eat More Frites

With people eating at home more during 2020 coronavirus lockdowns, the world's supply of potatoes—not all potatoes, just the longer, thinner varieties used to make french fries—quickly outstripped demand. (Consumption of other types of potatoes skyrocketed as people reached for potato chips, hash browns, tater tots, and other comfort foods during the pandemic.) Potato growers in Belgium, Canada, France, Germany, the Netherlands, and the U.S. saw demand plummet.

But as french-fryable potatoes started to pile up and go bad in Apr., Romain Cools, secretary general of Belgium's potato processing association Belgapom, tried to clear the glut by appealing to Belgians' national pride. Many Belgians claim the country invented fries (or *frites*, as they're known in Belgium), but U.S. soldiers stationed in French-speaking parts of the country during World War I mistakenly called them french fries. Statistics show that Belgians typically eat fries only once a week; Cools urged them to double their consumption.

Sending Out an SOS

It turns out that scrawling a call for help in the sand actually works. Three sailors from Micronesia found themselves marooned on tiny Pikelot Island in late July after their 23-foot boat ran out of fuel. They wrote "SOS" in giant letters in the sand, and three days after they were reported missing on July 31, a U.S. Air Force plane on patrol spotted their plea.

"We turned to avoid some rain showers and that's when we looked down and saw an island, so we decide to check it out and that's when we saw SOS and a boat right next to it on the beach," said Lt. Col. Jason Palmeira-Yen, the U.S. Air Force pilot. Palmeira-Yen relayed the discovery to the nearby Royal Australian Navy ship HMAS *Canberra*, which sent helicopters to check for survivors. The helicopter crew found the mariners in good condition and delivered food and water. A U.S. Coast Guard crew dropped a radio onto the island so the stranded mariners could communicate with the Micronesian ship FSS *Independence*, which picked them up on Aug. 3 and delivered them safely home.

It wasn't the first time a message seen from above proved lifesaving in the South Pacific. In 2016, three shipwreck survivors swam two miles to the equally remote island of Fanadik, where they wrote HELP in the sand. A U.S. Navy aircraft spotted the sign and sent a ship to pick them up.

Brother, Can You Spare a Dime?
Or a Quarter? Or a Nickel?

Of all the problems COVID-19 has caused, a lack of spare change is one few people anticipated. Initially, the shortage resulted from COVID protocols at the U.S. Mint, which reduced its production of new coins to keep employees safe. But Americans staying home and buying things online with credit cards instead of in stores with cash had an even greater impact on the change supply. The Federal Reserve in July 2020 assembled a U.S. Coin Task Force to deal with the problem, and by Sept., the mint said it planned to produce more coins in 2020 than it had in nearly two decades. The additional production was intended to compensate for all the pennies, nickels, dimes, and quarters gathering dust in people's piggy banks, change jars, and couch cushions during the pandemic.

The coin shortage had an outsize effect on businesses like laundromats and automated car washes that traffic heavily in quarters. The owners of The Laundry Room in San Diego, CA, told the *San Diego Union Tribune* that they removed their change machine because so many people were coming into the store and taking all of their quarters offsite, forcing employees to dispense change only by hand to laundry customers. In July, the Kroger grocery chain announced that it would no longer issue coins as change on purchases. Customers could opt to have the remainder cents applied to loyalty cards or round up their purchases to the next dollar and donate the difference to local food banks.

Not So Great Scot!

If you're looking for information about Scotland, you might not want to trust Wikipedia. In Aug. 2020, a Reddit poster with the username Ultach reported that nearly half of the entries on the Scots-language version of Wikipedia had been written or edited by a single contributor—one who doesn't actually speak the Scots language or understand Scots grammar. The articles were apparently simply written in English, changed a bit with the help of an online Scots dictionary, but then augmented with intentional misspellings to sound like a spoken Scottish accent. "I think this person has possibly done more damage to the Scots language than anyone else in history," Ultach wrote on Reddit.

The editor in question was identified as a North Carolina teenager with the username AmaryllisGardner. As an admin of the Scots Wikipedia site, he had almost unfettered access to what went on (and stayed on) its pages. He responded to the revelations by admitting on Wikipedia that he had been contributing faux-Scots articles since he was 12 years old, "thinking I was doing good." Initially, AmaryllisGardner was honest about his deception. An entry on the Canada goose, for example, included the caveat "The 'Scots' that wis uised in this airticle wis written bi a body that's mither tongue isna Scots. Please impruive this airticle gin ye can," according to *The Guardian*. But he stopped including the warning.

There was much discussion about what should happen to the Scots Wikipedia site, but little resolution. As of Oct. 2020, Scots Wikipedia pages merely carried the following disclaimer: "Followin recent revelations, Scots Wikipedia is presently reviewin its airticles for muckle leid inaccuracies." It was unclear whether the notice had been written by an actual speaker of Scots, or some other user doing an impression.

They Point the Way, Sometimes Hilariously

While air travel was significantly down during the pandemic (in Mar.-Aug. 2020, the number of U.S. passengers boarding airplanes totaled just over 102 mil, less than a quarter of the volume of that period in 2019), when pilots do fly across the country, they can't just follow step-by-step directions on Google Maps. To keep planes safe distances from one another, the FAA assigns each aircraft a route, with specific markers along the way known as waypoints. Each waypoint has a unique five-letter name, and it turns out that the folks who named them were a bit more irreverent than you might expect.

In the skies near Detroit, for example, you'll find waypoints named WONDR and MOTWN. Boston's airspace includes waypoints named CELTS and BOSOX; Chicago's has KUBBS. A Eurythmics fan in St. Louis appears to have named the waypoints ANNII and LENXX, while Kansas City's culinary reputation extends to the air, with waypoints named SPICY, BARBQ, SMOKE, and RIBBS.

Because it is so large, Texas has hundreds of waypoints, including several referencing the state's fondness for football, including QTRBK and TCHDN. Santa Rosa, CA, residence of *Peanuts* creator Charles Schulz, features a waypoint named for SNUPY.

Perhaps the most endearing combination of names is seen by pilots heading into Portsmouth, NH, from the northwest. It's unofficially known as the Looney Tunes approach: ITAWT, ITAWA, PUDYE, TTATT, IDEED.

HISTORICAL ANNIVERSARIES

1921 — 100 Years Ago

British-supported Persian Cossack Brigade leader Reza Khan effects coup d'état, seizing control of Tehran in Feb.

Warren G. Harding is sworn in as president Mar. 4, becoming the first president to travel to his inauguration in an automobile.

USSR's New Economic Policy is proclaimed Mar. 21, a partial retreat from the full nationalization of the country's industries.

The Emergency Quota Act, aimed at sharply curbing immigration using a quota system, is signed into law May 19; the act strongly favored immigrants seeking entry from northern European countries.

Up to 300 are killed as "Black Wall Street"—the Greenwood District in Tulsa, OK—is looted and burned by white rioters, May 31-June 1.

Pres. Harding signs a joint congressional resolution declaring post-World War peace with Germany, Austria, and Hungary July 2.

Italian-born anarchists Nicola Sacco and Bartolomeo Vanzetti are convicted July 14 of killing two men in a Massachusetts armed robbery and sentenced to death.

Adolf Hitler July 29 is made chairman of upstart National Socialist German Workers' (Nazi) Party.

Following a plebiscite, Faisal is made king of British Mandate of Iraq Aug. 23.

Arlington National Cemetery's Tomb of the Unknown Soldier is dedicated Nov. 11.

Limitation of Armaments Conference begins in Washington, DC, Nov. 12, resulting in a 1922 agreement in which parties agreed to outlaw poison gas and restrict submarine attacks.

Art. Georges Braque's *Guitar and Still Life on a Mantelpiece*, Max Ernst's *The Elephant Celebes*, Pablo Picasso's *Three Musicians*.

Film. *The Four Horsemen of the Apocalypse* and *The Sheik* launch Rudolph Valentino into stardom. *The Kid* starring Charlie Chaplin and Jackie Coogan.

Health and medicine. Canadian physician Frederick Banting and American colleague Charles Best, working in the lab of John Macleod, isolate the hormone insulin.

Literature. John Dos Passos's *Three Soldiers*, Langston Hughes's "The Negro Speaks of Rivers," Booth Tarkington's *Alice Adams*, W. B. Yeats's *Michael Robartes and the Dancer*, including "Easter, 1916."

Music. Carl Nielsen's *Moderen*, Sergei Prokofiev's *Piano Concerto No. 3*.

Nonfiction. Hendrik van Loon's *The Story of Mankind*, Zitkala-Sa's *American Indian Stories*.

Pop music. "Ain't We Got Fun" by Richard A. Whiting, Raymond Egan, and Gus Kahn; "All By Myself" by Irving Berlin; "April Showers" performed by Al Jolson.

Science and technology. General Motors engineer Thomas Midgley Jr. discovers the anti-knock properties of tetraethyl lead as a gasoline additive.

Sports. Babe Ruth hits a record 59 home runs for the NY Yankees. MLB commissioner Kenesaw Mountain Landis bans eight Chicago White Sox players from the sport for conspiring with gamblers to throw the 1919 World Series, one day after the players were acquitted of related charges.

Theater. *Shuffle Along* is first major financially successful Broadway production with black writers and cast. Eugene O'Neill's *Anna Christie*.

Miscellaneous. Future Pres. Franklin Roosevelt's walking ability is permanently compromised by a bout with poliomyelitis. White Castle burger chain is founded in Wichita, KS.

1971 — 50 Years Ago

Military officer Idi Amin assumes the presidency of Uganda in a coup d'état Jan. 25.

Charles Manson and three of his cult followers are found guilty Jan. 25 of first-degree murder in 1969 slaying of actress Sharon Tate and six others.

A major earthquake affects California's San Fernando Valley Feb. 9, killing 65.

A court-martial jury Mar. 29 convicts Army Lt. William Calley in murder of 22 unarmed South Vietnamese civilians at My Lai in 1968.

Pres. Richard Nixon, Apr. 14, eases the 20-year-old U.S. trade embargo with the People's Republic of China, which Nov. 15 is seated at the UN, displacing the Republic of China (Taiwan).

Vietnam Veterans Against the War protests Apr. 19-23 in Washington, DC, followed by a massive public demonstration on the Mall Apr. 24 attended by an estimated 200,000 people.

New York Times June 13 publishes first of classified "Pentagon Papers," a secret Defense Dept. study on U.S. involvement in Vietnam. The U.S. Supreme Court, 6-3, upholds the press's right to publish the documents June 30.

Pres. Nixon June 17 declares drug abuse "public enemy number one in the United States."

The 26th Amendment to the U.S. Constitution is ratified July 1, lowering the minimum federal voting age to 18 from 21.

In a TV address to the nation, Pres. Nixon announces Aug. 15 that the U.S. will no longer exchange foreign governments' dollars for gold and institutes a 90-day wage and price freeze.

Inmates at Attica prison in New York Sept. 9 take control of a portion of the facility, demanding better conditions; 43 inmates and hostages were killed, mostly as state forces regained control in a violent offensive Sept. 13.

Military conflict between West Pakistan (now Pakistan) and East Pakistan (Bangladesh) ends with West Pakistan's surrender Dec. 16 and independence for Bangladesh.

U.S. bombers launch massive airstrikes Dec. 26 in North Vietnam in retaliation for alleged violations of agreements reached prior to a 1968 bombing halt.

Art. David Hockney's *Mr and Mrs Clark and Percy*, Fritz Koenig's *The Sphere* (orig. *Grosse Kugelkaryatide N.Y.*).

Film. Mike Nichols's *Carnal Knowledge*, *Dirty Harry* starring Clint Eastwood, *Fiddler on the Roof*, *The French Connection* starring Gene Hackman, *Harold and Maude*, *Klute* starring Jane Fonda, Peter Bogdanovich's *The Last Picture Show*, *Shaft*, Melvin Van Peebles's *Sweet Sweetback's Baadasssss Song*, *Willy Wonka & the Chocolate Factory* starring Gene Wilder.

Health and medicine. World Health Org. declares smallpox eradicated throughout the Americas. Infamous "Stanford Prison Experiment" is conducted.

Literature. Maya Angelou's *Just Give Me a Cool Drink of Water 'fore I Diiie*, Ernest J. Gaines's *The Autobiography of Miss Jane Pittman*, Ursula K. Le Guin's *The Lathe of Heaven*, V. S. Naipaul's *In a Free State*, Robert C. O'Brien's *Mrs. Frisby and the Rats of NIMH*, Dr. Seuss's *The Lorax*, Wallace Stegner's *Angle of Repose*, Gay Talese's *Honor Thy Father*, John Updike's *Rabbit Redux*.

Music. Leonard Bernstein's *Mass* is premiered at opening of the Kennedy Center in Washington, DC. Steve Reich's *Drumming*, Dmitri Shostakovich's *Symphony No. 15*, Karlheinz Stockhausen's *Sternklang* and *Trans*.

Nonfiction. Boston Women's Health Collective publishes *Our Bodies, Our Selves*. Jane Goodall's *In the Shadow of Man*, Joseph P. Lash's *Eleanor and Franklin*, B. F. Skinner's *Beyond Freedom and Dignity*.

Pop music. Bee Gees' "How Can You Mend A Broken Heart," Marvin Gaye's *What's Going On*, Al Green's "Tired of Being Alone," Carole King's *Tapestry*, Led Zeppelin IV, John Lennon's "Imagine," Joni Mitchell's *Blue*, Dolly Parton's *Coat of Many Colors*, Rolling Stones' *Sticky Fingers* feat. "Brown Sugar," Rod Stewart's "Maggie May," The Temptations' "Just My Imagination," Three Dog Night's "Joy to the World," The Who's *Who's Next*, Bill Withers's "Ain't No Sunshine."

Science and technology. First email is sent by Ray Tomlinson, who also introduces the use of the "@" sign to address the message. Intel engineer Ted Hoff invents the computer microprocessor. Soviet Union launches *Salyut*, the first ever space station, into orbit.

Sports. Satchel Paige is the first Negro League player voted into Baseball's Hall of Fame. Joe Frazier defeats Muhammad Ali in "Fight of the Century."

Television. Norman Lear's *All in the Family* debuts and wins its first Emmy Award. *Masterpiece Theatre, Sonny and Cher Comedy Hour*, and *Soul Train* air first episodes.

Theater. *Sleuth* and *Company* win Tony Awards; *Jesus Christ Superstar* premieres on Broadway.

Miscellaneous. Walt Disney World opens in Florida. A man who became known in the press as D. B. Cooper hijacks a plane and parachutes away with $200,000 in ransom money; the crime was never solved.

1996 — 25 Years Ago

U.S. Senate ratifies the U.S.'s START II arms reduction treaty with Russia Jan. 26.

Federal authorities Apr. 3 arrest Theodore Kaczynski, the domestic terrorist known as the "Unabomber," at his remote cabin in Montana.

Pres. Bill Clinton signs into law, Apr. 9, a line-item veto bill.

A mass shooting Apr. 28-29 in Port Arthur, Tasmania, kills 35 and leads to major reforms to Australian gun laws.

Arkansas Gov. Jim Guy Tucker and two other Clinton associates are convicted May 28 in Whitewater case.

The antigovernment Montana Freemen surrender to federal authorities June 13 after an 81-day armed standoff near Jordan, MT.

Likud leader Benjamin Netanyahu takes office as prime minister of Israel June 18.

A truck bomb explodes June 25 at Khobar Towers, a U.S. Air Force housing complex in Saudi Arabia, killing 19 U.S. service personnel.

TWA Flight 800 crashes into Atlantic minutes after takeoff from JFK Airport in New York July 17, killing all 230 aboard.

A pipe bomb is detonated July 27 at Centennial Olympic Park in Atlanta, GA, as the city hosts the Summer Olympic Games; one person is killed.

Russia and Chechen rebels agree to a cease-fire, Aug. 13.

Pres. Clinton signs major welfare reform, Aug. 22, and Defense of Marriage Act (DOMA), Sept. 21, into law.

The Taliban militia captures Kabul Sept. 27 and forms a fundamentalist government in Afghanistan, based in sharia law.

Pres. Clinton is reelected Nov. 5 over Sen. Bob Dole (R, KS).

Two planes collide near Delhi, India, Nov. 12, killing 349 in world's deadliest midair collision.

Art. Julie Mehretu's *Untitled (two)* and *Map Paint (white)*, Chris Ofili's *The Holy Virgin Mary*.

Film. *The Birdcage*; *The English Patient*; Joel and Ethan Coen's *Fargo*, *First Wives Club* starring Goldie Hawn, Diane Keaton, and Bette Midler; *Independence Day* starring Will Smith; *Jerry Maguire*; *Mission: Impossible* starring Tom Cruise; Wes Craven's *Scream*; *Trainspotting*; *Twister*; Christopher Guest's *Waiting for Guffman*.

Health and medicine. Pfizer patents sildenafil, later marketed as Viagra. UNAIDS launches to coordinate the global efforts to prevent HIV/AIDS.

Literature. Oprah Winfrey introduces her book club with Jacquelyn Mitchard's *The Deep End of the Ocean*. Helen Fielding's *Bridget Jones's Diary*, Stephen King's *The Green Mile*, George R. R. Martin's *A Game of Thrones*, Joyce Carol Oates's *We Were the Mulvaneys*, Chuck Palahniuk's *Fight Club*, David Foster Wallace's *Infinite Jest*.

Music. Peter Maxwell Davies's *Symphony No. 6*, Philip Glass's *Les Enfants Terribles*.

Nonfiction. Stephen Ambrose's *Undaunted Courage*, Gabriel García Márquez's *News of a Kidnapping*, Richard Kluger's *Ashes to Ashes*.

Pop music. Rapper Tupac Shakur is fatally shot in Las Vegas. Bone Thugs-n-Harmony's "Tha Crossroads," Tracy Chapman's "Give Me One Reason," Celine Dion's "Because You Loved Me" and "It's All Coming Back to Me Now," Fugees' *The Score*, Jay-Z's *Reasonable Doubt*, Los del Rio's "Macarena (Bayside Boys remix)," Spice Girls' "Wannabe," Shania Twain's "You Win My Love" and "No One Needs to Know."

Science and technology. Scientists at CERN in Switzerland announce they have synthesized particles of antimatter. Dolly the sheep, the first mammal cloned from an adult cell, is born. Nintendo 64 gaming system launches in U.S.

Sports. Chicago Bulls win then-NBA-record 72 regular season games and the NBA Finals. Andre Agassi wins Olympic gold in singles tennis. NY Yankees win first World Series since 1978, defeating Atlanta in six games.

Television. MSNBC and Fox News Channel launch. *Frasier* and *ER* win Emmy Awards; *Judge Judy* debuts. Tickle Me Elmo, based on a *Sesame Street* character, is blockbuster new toy.

Theater. Restoration of the Globe Theatre is completed in London. *Master Class* and *Rent* win Tony Awards. Eve Ensler's *The Vagina Monologues* debuts Off-Broadway.

Miscellaneous. Eight people die in a blizzard on descent from Mt. Everest. UK royals Charles and Diana formally divorce after a four-year separation.

WORLD ALMANAC EDITORS' PICKS
2020 Time Capsule

The editors of *The World Almanac* have selected the following items as representative of the year 2020.

- Prince Harry and Meghan Markle's Jan. 8, 2020, Instagram post announcing they would be stepping back from their "senior" roles in the British royal family.
- The results of the votes in the U.S. Senate acquitting Donald Trump of both impeachment charges, Feb. 5, 2020.
- A variety of coronavirus preventatives and other essential home supplies that became scarce as the COVID-19 pandemic spread in the U.S. from early 2020 on: face masks, gloves, sanitizers, disinfectant spray, hand soap and sanitizer, and toilet paper.
- A Nintendo Switch gaming device loaded with *Animal Crossing*, along with subscriptions to every streaming service from Apple TV to YouTube, helping to keep those stuck inside during COVID-19 lockdowns entertained.
- The bystander video of the death of Minneapolis resident George Floyd, taken May 25, 2020, invigorating a protest movement in favor of racial justice.

- A helmet worn by players on the NFL's Washington Football Team, which announced July 13, 2020, that they would no longer use the "Redskins" name and logo.
- Cardboard fan photo cutouts, which many teams used to create the illusion of filled seats as many sports leagues came back from suspended or delayed seasons in July 2020.
- A check representing $600 in supplemental weekly benefits, which until July 31, 2020, provided financial relief to many Americans who had lost their employment due to COVID-19-related shutdowns.
- U.S. Supreme Court Justice Ruth Bader Ginsburg's trademark lace jabot; the jurist died Sept. 18, 2020.
- LeBron James's fourth championship ring—and fourth Finals MVP trophy—earned with the L.A. Lakers in the NBA Finals in the league's "bubble" Oct. 11, 2020.
- A sample mail-in ballot for the Nov. 3, 2020, general election.

ECONOMICS

U.S. Gross Domestic Product, 1930-2019
Source: Bureau of Economic Analysis, U.S. Dept. of Commerce
(in billions of current dollars)

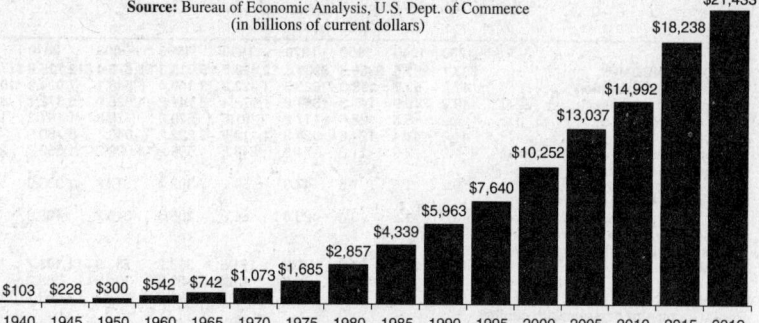

1930	1935	1940	1945	1950	1960	1965	1970	1975	1980	1985	1990	1995	2000	2005	2010	2015	2019
$92	$74	$103	$228	$300	$542	$742	$1,073	$1,685	$2,857	$4,339	$5,963	$7,640	$10,252	$13,037	$14,992	$18,238	$21,433

Tracking the U.S. Economy, 1960-2019
Source: Bureau of Economic Analysis, U.S. Dept. of Commerce
(in billions of current dollars, revised)

	1960	1970	1980	1990	2000	2010	2018	2019
Gross domestic product	$542.4	$1,073.3	$2,857.3	$5,963.1	$10,252.3	$14,992.1	$20,611.9	$21,433.2
Gross national product	545.5	1,079.7	2,891.5	5,997.8	10,287.4	15,187.8	20,896.6	21,702.9
Less: Consumption of fixed capital. . . .	67.9	136.8	428.4	888.5	1,511.2	2,390.9	3,265.0	3,420.9
Equals: Net national product	477.6	942.9	2,463.1	5,109.3	8,776.1	12,796.8	17,631.6	18,281.9
Less: Statistical discrepancy	−1.3	5.3	44.4	95.5	−96.3	60.0	−58.0	12.8
Equals: National income	478.9	937.5	2,418.6	5,013.8	8,872.4	12,736.8	17,689.6	18,269.1
Less: Corporate profits with inventory valuation and capital consumption adjustments	54.7	86.2	223.6	417.7	786.6	1,728.7	2,243.0	2,250.5
Less: Taxes on production and imports less subsidies[1].	43.4	86.6	190.5	398.0	662.7	1,007.3	1,381.5	1,417.5
Less: Contributions for government social insurance	16.4	46.4	166.2	410.1	705.8	983.7	1,360.4	1,418.8
Less: Net interest and miscellaneous payments on assets.	10.3	39.5	182.2	433.4	541.1	465.2	619.1	573.4
Less: Business current transfer payments (net).	1.7	4.4	14.0	39.2	85.2	127.9	156.6	158.0
Less: Current surplus of government enterprises	0.5	−1.0	−4.5	3.7	11.5	−20.1	−5.8	−7.6
Plus: Personal income receipts on assets	44.5	114.9	396.9	1,005.3	1,485.7	1,782.3	2,946.7	2,967.9
Plus: Personal current transfer receipts	25.7	74.7	280.1	596.9	1,087.3	2,325.2	2,970.3	3,125.2
Equals: Personal income.	422.1	865.0	2,323.6	4,913.8	8,652.6	12,551.6	17,851.8	18,551.5
Addenda:								
Gross domestic income	543.7	1,068.0	2,812.9	5,867.6	10,348.6	14,932.1	20,669.9	21,420.4
Gross national income	546.8	1,074.4	2,847.1	5,902.3	10,383.7	15,127.8	20,954.6	21,690.0

Note: Numbers may not add up to totals due to rounding. (1) Subsidies are included net of the current surplus of government enterprises.

U.S. Gross Domestic Product, 2005-19
Source: Bureau of Economic Analysis, U.S. Dept. of Commerce

	Billions of current dollars				Billions of constant (2012) dollars			
	2005	2010	2018	2019	2005	2010	2018	2019
Gross domestic product	$13,036.6	$14,992.1	$20,611.9	$21,433.2	$14,912.5	$15,598.8	$18,687.8	$19,091.7
Personal consumption expenditures	8,747.1	10,185.8	13,993.3	14,544.6	10,075.9	10,643.0	12,928.1	13,240.2
Goods.	3,082.9	3,317.8	4,371.9	4,512.2	3,384.7	3,485.7	4,590.2	4,760.5
Durable goods	1,128.6	1,049.0	1,481.6	1,534.4	1,004.9	1,027.3	1,692.7	1,774.6
Nondurable goods	1,954.3	2,268.9	2,890.3	2,977.9	2,383.4	2,461.3	2,910.3	3,001.5
Services	5,664.2	6,868.0	9,621.4	10,032.4	6,689.5	7,157.4	8,367.1	8,520.5
Gross private domestic investment.	2,534.7	2,165.5	3,632.9	3,751.2	2,670.6	2,216.5	3,384.9	3,442.6
Fixed investment	2,477.2	2,111.6	3,575.1	3,702.1	2,618.7	2,164.2	3,310.4	3,371.7
Nonresidential	1,621.0	1,735.0	2,776.7	2,895.0	1,716.4	1,781.0	2,698.9	2,776.8
Structures	353.0	379.8	631.4	650.2	466.1	412.8	551.1	547.7
Equipment	794.9	777.0	1,213.4	1,241.0	760.0	781.2	1,242.2	1,267.7
Intellectual property products	473.1	578.2	931.8	1,003.8	493.1	588.1	910.2	968.2
Residential	856.2	376.6	798.5	807.1	885.4	383.0	612.0	601.5
Change in inventories.	57.5	53.9	57.7	49.1	63.7	57.3	53.4	48.5
Net exports of goods and services	−721.2	−513.9	−609.5	−610.5	−887.8	−565.9	−877.7	−917.6
Exports.	1,305.2	1,846.3	2,528.7	2,514.8	1,533.2	1,977.9	2,549.5	2,546.6
Goods	921.9	1,272.4	1,663.9	1,636.7	1,085.4	1,368.7	1,784.3	1,782.5
Services	383.3	573.8	864.8	878.0	447.6	609.2	768.7	767.6
Imports	2,026.4	2,360.2	3,138.2	3,125.2	2,421.0	2,543.8	3,427.2	3,464.2
Goods	1,715.5	1,944.8	2,565.6	2,525.6	2,062.3	2,112.7	2,909.4	2,923.4
Services	311.0	415.4	572.6	599.6	358.6	430.8	523.7	543.1
Government consumption expenditures and gross investment.	2,476.0	3,154.6	3,595.2	3,747.9	3,015.5	3,307.2	3,229.8	3,303.9
Federal	947.5	1,297.9	1,339.4	1,419.2	1,099.1	1,346.1	1,227.8	1,277.2
National defense	609.4	828.0	794.3	852.4	708.6	861.3	739.1	780.2
Nondefense	338.0	469.9	545.1	566.7	390.6	484.8	488.4	497.1
State and local	1,528.5	1,856.7	2,255.7	2,328.7	1,920.1	1,961.3	2,000.2	2,025.5

U.S. National Income by Type, 1930-2019

Source: Bureau of Economic Analysis, U.S. Dept. of Commerce

(in billions of current dollars)

	1930	1940	1950	1970	1980	1990	2000	2010	2018	2019
NATIONAL INCOME[1]	$83.1	$91.5	$266.6	$937.5	$2,418.6	$5,013.8	$8,872.4	$12,736.8	$17,689.6	$18,269.1
Employee compensation	47.2	52.7	158.3	623.3	1,622.2	3,340.4	5,848.1	7,924.9	10,950.1	11,432.4
Wages and salaries	46.2	49.9	147.3	551.6	1,373.4	2,741.2	4,825.9	6,372.1	8,894.2	9,309.3
Government	5.2	8.5	22.6	117.2	261.5	519.0	779.8	1,191.2	1,402.5	1,450.8
Other	41.0	41.4	124.6	434.3	1,112.0	2,222.2	4,046.1	5,180.9	7,491.7	7,858.5
Supplements to wages and salaries	1.0	2.9	11.0	71.8	248.8	599.2	1,022.2	1,552.9	2,055.9	2,123.1
Employer contributions for employee pension and insurance funds	0.9	1.5	7.6	47.9	159.9	392.7	677.0	1,083.9	1,430.7	1,474.0
Employer contributions for government social insurance	0.0	1.4	3.4	23.8	88.9	206.5	345.2	469.0	625.2	649.1
Proprietors' income with inventory valuation and capital consumption adjustments	10.9	12.2	37.5	77.8	171.6	353.2	753.9	1,108.7	1,585.9	1,657.7
Farm	3.9	4.1	12.9	12.9	11.7	32.2	31.5	39.0	43.0	49.7
Nonfarm	7.0	8.2	24.6	64.9	159.9	321.0	722.4	1,069.7	1,542.9	1,608.0
Rental income of persons with capital consumption adjustments	5.4	3.8	8.8	20.7	19.0	28.2	183.5	394.2	759.3	787.1
Corporate profits with inventory valuation and capital consumption adjustments	7.5	9.9	36.1	86.2	223.6	417.7	786.6	1,728.7	2,243.0	2,250.5
Taxes on corporate income	0.8	2.8	17.7	31.3	75.5	121.8	233.4	272.3	282.9	298.7
Profits after tax with inventory valuation and capital consumption adjustments	6.7	7.0	18.3	55.0	148.1	295.9	553.1	1,456.5	1,960.1	1,951.8
Net dividends	5.5	4.0	9.0	27.8	75.8	192.7	410.2	643.2	1,390.1	1,360.8
Undistributed profits with inventory valuation and capital consumption adjustments	1.2	3.0	9.3	27.2	72.3	103.2	142.9	813.3	570.0	591.0
Net interest and miscellaneous payments	4.8	3.3	3.1	39.5	182.2	433.4	541.1	465.2	619.1	573.4

Note: Numbers may not add up to totals because of rounding and incomplete enumeration. (1) National income is the aggregate of labor and property earnings that arise in the production of goods and services. It is the sum of employee compensation, proprietors' income, rental income, adjusted corporate profits, and net interest. It measures the total factor costs of goods and services produced by the economy. Income is measured before deduction of taxes. Total national income figures include adjustments not itemized.

U.S. National Income by Industry, 2000-19

Source: Bureau of Economic Analysis, U.S. Dept. of Commerce

(in billions of current dollars)

	2000	2005	2010	2015	2017	2018	2019
National income without capital consumption adjustment	$8,780.9	$11,293.2	$12,668.1	$15,705.8	$16,583.6	$17,236.5	$17,916.4
Domestic industries	8,745.9	11,215.3	12,472.4	15,485.4	16,291.3	16,951.8	17,646.8
Private industries	7,702.7	9,853.4	10,821.5	13,668.9	14,385.7	14,968.2	15,595.6
Agriculture, forestry, fishing, and hunting	72.3	97.0	118.3	154.7	140.9	137.3	140.0
Mining	91.4	176.0	183.6	155.5	157.4	185.7	180.2
Utilities	140.4	161.8	181.9	176.8	172.7	194.1	205.5
Construction	473.7	650.9	533.3	749.1	845.7	885.1	929.1
Manufacturing	1,244.1	1,335.4	1,345.8	1,693.2	1,610.2	1,675.5	1,696.2
Durable goods	758.8	763.7	750.2	981.9	967.3	990.7	1,014.6
Nondurable goods	485.2	571.7	595.6	711.3	642.9	684.8	681.6
Wholesale trade	568.3	684.1	726.7	938.0	938.9	950.6	1,000.1
Retail trade	665.0	857.1	862.7	1,070.7	1,104.4	1,127.3	1,183.3
Transportation and warehousing	270.3	335.1	383.3	504.2	536.8	554.9	595.9
Information	315.2	438.8	456.0	597.2	628.6	642.9	665.0
Finance, insurance, real estate, rental, and leasing	1,462.3	1,915.6	2,126.5	2,709.5	2,943.2	3,048.5	3,147.9
Professional and business services[1]	1,087.1	1,438.2	1,735.2	2,218.7	2,396.1	2,536.6	2,687.2
Educational services, health care, and social assistance	689.5	987.2	1,302.7	1,559.1	1,686.3	1,749.7	1,829.5
Arts, entertainment, recreation, accommodation, and food services	340.2	439.5	494.3	680.2	741.8	772.9	807.2
Other services, except government	283.2	336.8	371.3	462.0	482.8	507.2	528.5
Government	1,043.2	1,361.9	1,650.8	1,816.5	1,905.5	1,983.6	2,051.2
Rest of the world	35.0	78.0	195.7	220.4	292.3	284.7	269.6

Note: Estimates based on the 2012 North American Industry Classification System (NAICS). (1) Consists of professional, scientific, and technical services; management of companies and enterprises; and administrative and waste management services.

Consumer Price Index

The Consumer Price Index (CPI) is a measure of the change in prices over time of one or more kinds of basic consumer goods and services. The overall CPI is based on the price of food, clothing, shelter, and fuels; transportation fares; charges for doctors' and dentists' services; drug prices; and the cost of other goods and services bought for day-to-day living. Since Jan. 1988, the base period for comparison has been 1982-84, which equals 100.0. The price of apparel, entertainment and recreation, and education and communication have not risen significantly, while the cost of medical care has more than quadrupled since 1982-84. The Consumer Price Index for all urban consumers (CPI-U) covers about 87% of the total U.S. population. The Bureau of Labor Statistics also publishes a separate Consumer Price Index for urban wage earners and clerical workers (CPI-W), which covers about 32% of the total U.S. population.

Distribution of U.S. Total Personal Income, 1930-2019

Source: Bureau of Economic Analysis, U.S. Dept. of Commerce
(in billions of current dollars, except for per capita figures)

Year	Personal income	Personal current taxes	Disposable personal income	Personal outlays	Personal savings	Savings as % of income[1]	Disposable personal income per capita Current dollars	Disposable personal income per capita Constant (2012) dollars
1930	$76.5	$1.6	$75.0	$71.6	$3.3	4.5%	$609.0	$6,822.0
1940	79.4	1.7	77.7	72.4	5.3	6.8	588.0	7,942.0
1950	233.7	18.9	214.8	194.8	20.0	9.3	1,416.0	10,666.0
1960	422.1	46.1	376.1	338.2	37.9	10.1	2,080.0	12,629.0
1970	865.0	103.1	762.0	664.4	97.6	12.8	3,715.0	17,734.0
1980	2,323.6	299.5	2,024.1	1,800.1	224.1	11.1	8,888.0	21,542.0
1990	4,913.8	594.7	4,319.1	3,958.0	361.1	8.4	17,264.0	27,250.0
2000	8,652.6	1,236.3	7,416.3	7,060.2	356.1	4.8	26,262.0	33,568.0
2005	10,598.2	1,212.5	9,385.8	9,095.7	290.1	3.1	31,710.0	36,526.0
2010	12,551.6	1,237.6	11,314.0	10,573.6	740.3	6.5	36,523.0	38,162.0
2015	15,724.2	1,939.9	13,784.3	12,745.6	1,038.7	7.5	42,953.0	41,684.0
2016	16,160.7	1,957.9	14,202.8	13,227.8	975.0	6.9	43,946.0	42,207.0
2017	16,948.6	2,046.7	14,901.9	13,830.9	1,071.0	7.2	45,821.0	43,234.0
2018	17,851.8	2,085.3	15,766.5	14,529.2	1,237.3	7.8	48,223.0	44,553.0
2019	18,551.5	2,202.9	16,348.6	15,117.4	1,231.2	7.5	49,763.0	45,301.0

Note: Personal income minus current taxes equals disposable income; disposable income minus outlays equals savings. Figures may not add up to totals because of rounding. (1) Personal savings as a percentage of disposable personal income.

U.S. Consumer Price Index, 1915-2019

Source: Bureau of Labor Statistics, U.S. Dept. of Labor

Excluding 2009, prices as measured by the U.S. Consumer Price Index have risen steadily since World War II. What cost $1.00 in 1982-84 cost about $0.10 in 1913, $0.18 in 1945, and $2.56 in 2019.

(Annual averages of monthly figures, for all urban consumers. **1982-84 = 100**.)

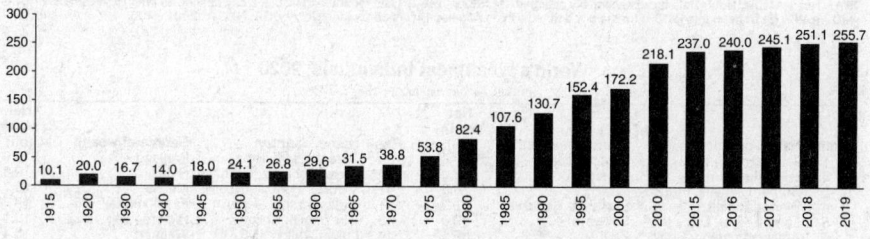

Year	Value
1915	10.1
1920	20.0
1925	16.7
1930	14.0
1935	18.0
1940	24.1
1945	26.8
1950	29.6
1955	31.5
1960	38.8
1965	53.8
1970	82.4
1975	107.6
1980	130.7
1985	152.4
1990	172.2
1995	218.1
2000	237.0
2005	240.0
2010	245.1
2015	251.1
2016	255.7

U.S. Consumer Price Index by Major Group, 1915-2019

Source: Bureau of Labor Statistics, U.S. Dept. of Labor
For all urban consumers. **1982-84 = 100**, unless otherwise noted.

Year	All items	Apparel	Food & beverages	Housing	Transportation	Medical care	Entertainment & recreation[1]	Educ. & communication[1]	Other goods & services
1915	10.1	15.3	—	—	—	—	—	—	—
1920	20.0	43.1	—	—	—	—	—	—	—
1930	16.7	24.2	—	—	—	—	—	—	—
1940	14.0	21.8	—	—	14.2	10.4	—	—	—
1945	18.0	31.4	—	—	15.9	11.9	—	—	—
1950	24.1	40.3	—	—	22.7	15.1	—	—	—
1955	26.8	42.9	—	—	25.8	18.2	—	—	—
1960	29.6	45.7	—	—	29.8	22.3	—	—	—
1965	31.5	47.8	—	—	31.9	25.2	—	—	—
1970	38.8	59.2	40.1	36.4	37.5	34.0	—	—	40.9
1975	53.8	72.5	60.2	50.7	50.1	47.5	—	—	53.9
1980	82.4	90.9	86.7	81.1	83.1	74.9	—	—	75.2
1985	107.6	105.0	105.6	107.7	106.4	113.5	—	—	114.5
1990	130.7	124.1	132.1	128.5	120.5	162.8	—	—	159.0
1995	152.4	132.0	148.9	148.5	139.1	220.5	94.5	92.2	206.9
2000	172.2	129.6	168.4	169.6	153.3	260.8	103.3	102.5	271.1
2005	195.3	119.5	191.2	195.7	173.9	323.2	109.4	113.7	313.4
2010	218.1	119.5	220.0	216.3	193.4	388.4	113.3	129.9	381.3
2015	237.0	125.9	246.8	238.1	199.1	446.8	115.9	138.2	414.9
2016	240.0	126.0	247.7	244.0	194.9	463.7	117.0	139.1	423.1
2017	245.1	125.6	249.8	251.2	201.6	475.3	118.5	136.5	432.6
2018	251.1	125.2	253.3	258.5	210.7	484.7	119.1	136.8	442.3
2019	255.7	124.1	258.0	266.0	210.1	498.4	120.6	137.8	451.3

— = Comparable data not available. (1) Dec. 1997 = 100. Entertainment was reclassified as Recreation in 1997. Data is not seasonally adjusted.

Consumer Price Indexes by Region and Major Cities, 1990-2019

Source: Bureau of Labor Statistics, U.S. Dept. of Labor
For all urban consumers; % change not annualized. 1982-84 = 100, unless otherwise noted.

Region and city	1990	1995	2000	2005	2010	2015	2017	2018	2019
U.S. city average	130.7	152.4	172.2	195.3	218.1	237.0	245.1	251.1	255.7
Northeast urban	136.3	159.1	179.4	207.5	233.9	252.2	259.5	265.1	269.4
Boston-Cambridge-Newton, MA-NH.	138.9	158.6	183.6	216.4	237.4	256.7	267.0	275.8	281.1
New York-Newark-Jersey City, NY-NJ-PA	138.5	162.2	182.5	212.7	240.9	260.6	268.5	273.6	278.2
Philadelphia-Camden-Wilmington, PA-NJ-DE-MD.	135.8	158.7	176.5	204.2	227.7	243.9	248.4	251.6	256.6
Pittsburgh, PA.	126.2	149.2	168.0	189.8	215.4	240.6	250.1	NA	NA
Midwest urban	127.4	148.4	168.3	188.4	208.0	224.2	229.9	234.3	237.8
Chicago-Naperville-Elgin, IL-IN-WI.	131.7	153.3	173.8	194.3	212.9	227.8	233.6	237.7	241.2
Cincinnati-Hamilton, OH-KY-IN.	126.5	146.2	164.8	181.6	204.7	223.3	229.9	NA	NA
Cleveland-Akron, OH	129.0	147.9	168.0	187.9	204.6	220.5	223.4	NA	NA
Detroit-Warren-Dearborn, MI	128.6	148.6	169.8	190.8	205.1	218.7	226.9	232.3	235.3
Kansas City, MO-KS.	126.0	145.3	166.6	185.3	205.4	222.3	228.2	NA	NA
Milwaukee-Racine, WI	126.2	151.0	168.6	185.2	209.6	226.6	232.4	NA	NA
Minneapolis-St. Paul-Bloomington, MN-WI.	127.0	147.0	170.1	193.1	211.7	230.6	239.2	245.0	250.1
St. Louis, MO-IL	128.1	145.2	163.1	186.2	203.2	219.3	224.7	228.9	231.2
South urban	127.9	149.0	167.2	188.3	211.3	230.1	237.5	242.7	246.3
Atlanta-Sandy Springs-Roswell, GA	131.7	150.9	170.6	188.9	205.5	221.6	232.9	238.6	243.7
Dallas-Fort Worth-Arlington, TX	125.1	144.9	164.7	184.7	201.6	217.5	226.1	232.8	237.7
Houston-The Woodlands-Sugar Land, TX	120.6	139.8	154.2	175.6	194.2	213.0	220.7	225.9	228.8
Miami-Fort Lauderdale-W. Palm Beach, FL	128.0	148.9	167.8	194.3	223.1	245.4	256.7	265.1	269.8
Tampa-St. Petersburg-Clearwater, FL[1]	111.7	129.7	145.7	168.5	193.5	211.6	219.5	224.3	228.1
Washington-Arlington-Alexandria, DC-MD-VA-WV[2]	135.6	141.2	107.6	124.3	142.2	250.7	256.2	261.4	264.8
West urban	131.5	153.5	174.8	198.9	221.2	243.0	254.7	263.3	270.4
Urban Alaska.	118.6	138.9	150.9	171.8	195.1	216.9	218.9	225.5	228.7
Denver-Aurora-Lakewood, CO	120.9	147.9	173.2	190.9	212.4	240.0	255.0	262.0	267.0
Urban Hawaii	138.1	168.1	176.3	197.8	234.9	260.2	272.0	277.1	281.6
Los Angeles-Long Beach-Anaheim, CA[3]	135.9	154.6	171.6	201.8	225.9	244.6	256.2	266.0	274.1
Phoenix-Mesa-Scottsdale, AZ[4]	NA	NA	NA	108.3	118.2	128.0	133.3	138.9	142.9
Portland-Salem, OR-WA.	127.4	153.2	178.0	196.0	218.3	244.2	259.8	NA	NA
San Diego-Carlsbad, CA.	138.4	156.8	182.8	220.6	245.5	269.4	283.0	292.5	299.4
San Francisco-Oakland-Hayward, CA	132.1	151.6	180.2	202.7	227.5	258.6	274.9	285.6	295.0
Seattle-Tacoma-Bellevue, WA	126.8	152.3	179.2	200.2	226.7	249.4	262.7	271.1	278.0

NA = Not available. **Note:** Data is not seasonally adjusted. (1) 1987 = 100. (2) Data for 2000-10 is for the city defined as Washington-Baltimore, DC-MD-VA-WV. (3) Data prior to 2018 is for the city defined as Los Angeles-Riverside-Orange County, CA. (4) Dec. 2001 = 100.

World's Wealthiest Individuals, 2020

Source: *Forbes* magazine, Mar. 3, 2020

Rank	Name, country	Source of wealth	Net worth (bil)	Rank	Name, country	Source of wealth	Net worth (bil)
1.	Jeff Bezos, U.S.	Amazon.com.	$113.0	39.	Joseph Safra, Brazil	Banking.	$19.9
2.	Bill Gates, U.S.	Microsoft.	98.0	40.	Dieter Schwarz, Germany	Retail.	19.8
3.	Bernard Arnault, France	LVMH.	76.0	41.	Vladimir Potanin, Russia	Metals.	19.7
4.	Warren Buffett, U.S.	Berkshire Hathaway	67.5		Tadashi Yanai, Japan	Fashion retail.	19.7
5.	Larry Ellison, U.S.	Software.	59.0	43.	Qin Yinglin, China	Pig breeding.	18.5
6.	Amancio Ortega, Spain	Zara.	55.1	44.	Lukas Walton, U.S.	Walmart.	18.4
7.	Mark Zuckerberg, U.S.	Facebook.	54.7	45.	Vladimir Lisin, Russia	Steel, transport.	18.1
8.	Jim Walton, U.S.	Walmart.	54.6	46.	Ray Dalio, U.S.	Hedge funds.	18.0
9.	Alice Walton, U.S.	Walmart.	54.4	47.	Takemitsu Takizaki, Japan	Sensors.	17.4
10.	Rob Walton, U.S.	Walmart.	54.1	48.	Leonid Mikhelson, Russia	Gas, chemicals.	17.1
11.	Steve Ballmer, U.S.	Microsoft.	52.7		Alain Wertheimer, France	Chanel.	17.1
12.	Carlos Slim Helú, Mexico	Telecom.	52.1		Gerard Wertheimer, France.	Chanel.	17.1
13.	Larry Page, U.S.	Google.	50.9				
14.	Sergey Brin, U.S.	Google.	49.1	51.	Theo Albrecht Jr., Germany	Aldi, Trader Joe's.	17.0
15.	Françoise Bettencourt Meyers, France	L'Oreal.	48.9		Len Blavatnik, U.S.	Diversified.	17.0
					William Lei Ding, China.	Online games.	17.0
16.	Michael Bloomberg, U.S.	Bloomberg LP.	48.0	54.	Susanne Klatten, Germany	BMW, pharmaceuticals	16.8
17.	Jack Ma, China	Ali Baba e-commerce	38.8		Alexey Mordashov, Russia	Steel, investments.	16.8
18.	Charles Koch, U.S.	Koch Industries.	38.2	56.	Masayoshi Son, Japan	Internet, telecom.	16.6
	Julia Koch, U.S.	Koch Industries.	38.2	57.	Colin Zheng Huang, China	E-commerce.	16.5
20.	Ma Huateng, China.	Internet media.	38.1		Dietrich Mateschitz, Austria	Red Bull	16.5
21.	Mukesh Ambani, India	Petrochemicals, oil & gas.	36.8	59.	Joseph Lau, Hong Kong	Real estate	16.4
					Laurene Powell Jobs, U.S.	Apple, Disney	16.4
22.	Mackenzie Scott, U.S.	Amazon.com.	36.0	61.	Zhang Yiming, China	Software.	16.2
23.	Beate Heister & Karl Albrecht Jr., Germany	Supermarkets.	33.3	62.	Leonardo Del Vecchio, Italy	Eyeglasses.	16.1
24.	David Thomson, Canada	Media.	31.6	63.	Donald Bren, U.S.	Real estate	15.5
25.	Phil Knight, U.S.	Nike.	29.5	64.	Stephen Schwarzman, U.S.	Investments.	15.4
26.	Lee Shau Kee, Hong Kong	Real estate.	28.1	65.	Vagit Alekperov, Russia	Oil	15.2
					Lee Man Tat, Hong Kong	Food	15.2
27.	François Pinault, France	Luxury goods.	27.0		Wang Wei, China	Package delivery.	15.2
28.	Sheldon Adelson, U.S.	Casinos.	26.8	68.	Petr Kellner, Czechia	Finance, telecom.	14.9
	Jacqueline Mars, U.S.	Candy, pet food.	24.7		Rupert Murdoch, U.S.	Newspapers, TV	14.9
	John Mars, U.S.	Candy, pet food.	24.7	70.	Leonard Lauder, U.S.	Estée Lauder	14.6
31.	Elon Musk, U.S.	Tesla, SpaceX.	24.6		Zhong Huijuan, China	Pharmaceuticals.	14.6
32.	Giovanni Ferrero, Italy.	Nutella, chocolates	24.5	72.	Gennady Timchenko, Russia.	Oil, gas.	14.4
33.	Michael Dell, U.S.	Dell computers.	22.9				
34.	Hui Ka Yan, China.	Real estate.	21.8	73.	Thomas Peterffy, U.S.	Discount brokerage.	14.3
35.	Li Ka-Shing, Hong Kong	Diversified.	21.7	74.	Klaus-Michael Kuehne, Germany	Shipping.	14.2
36.	He Xiangjian, China	Home appliances.	21.6				
	Jim Simons, U.S.	Hedge funds.	21.6	75.	Lee Kun-Hee, South Korea	Samsung	14.1
38.	Yang Huiyan, China	Real estate.	20.3				

Median Income by Race, Hispanic Origin, and Sex, 1948-2019

Source: Current Population Survey, U.S. Census Bureau, U.S. Dept. of Commerce

Race, Hispanic origin, and year		Male			Female		
		Number with income (thous.)	Median income Current dollars	2019 dollars	Number with income (thous.)	Median income Current dollars	2019 dollars
All races	2019	116,561	$44,310	$44,310	118,731	$29,407	$29,407
	2018	115,219	41,615	42,369	116,920	27,079	27,570
	2010	105,191	32,205	37,844	107,220	20,775	24,413
	2000	98,504	28,343	42,195	101,704	16,063	23,913
	1990	88,220	20,293	38,607	92,245	10,070	19,158
	1980	78,661	12,530	37,117	80,826	4,920	14,574
	1970	65,008	6,670	39,300	51,647	2,237	13,180
	1960	55,172	4,080	30,908	36,526	1,261	9,553
	1950	47,585	2,570	23,891	24,651	953	8,859
	1948	47,370	2,396	22,274	22,725	1,009	9,380
White	2019	92,667	46,471	46,471	91,860	29,879	29,879
	2018	91,817	43,413	44,200	90,779	27,344	27,839
	2010	86,368	34,374	40,393	85,486	20,896	24,555
	2000	83,372	29,797	44,360	84,123	16,079	23,937
	1990	76,480	21,170	40,275	78,566	10,317	19,628
	1980	69,420	13,328	39,481	70,573	4,947	14,654
	1970	58,447	7,011	41,309	45,288	2,266	13,351
	1960	49,788	4,296	32,544	32,001	1,352	10,242
	1950	NA	2,709	25,184	NA	1,060	9,854
	1948	NA	2,510	23,334	NA	1,133	10,533
White, not Hispanic	2019	75,344	50,565	50,565	76,539	31,338	31,338
	2018	74,815	47,817	48,683	76,078	29,468	30,002
	2010	72,723	37,154	43,659	73,995	21,715	25,517
	2000	72,530	31,508	46,907	75,206	16,665	24,810
	1990	69,987	21,958	41,775	72,939	10,581	20,130
	1980	65,564	13,681	40,526	67,084	4,980	14,752
Black	2019	14,138	31,151	31,151	16,718	26,974	26,974
	2018	13,722	31,102	31,666	16,375	25,264	25,722
	2010	11,433	23,086	27,128	14,212	19,548	22,971
	2000	9,905	21,343	31,774	12,461	15,881	23,643
	1990	8,820	12,868	24,481	10,687	8,328	15,844
	1980	7,387	8,009	23,725	8,596	4,580	13,567
	1970	5,844	4,157	24,493	5,844	2,063	12,155
	1960	5,384	2,260	17,121	4,525	837	6,341
	1950	NA	1,471	13,675	NA	474	4,406
	1948	NA	1,363	12,671	NA	492	4,574
Asian	2019	7,501	52,055	52,055	7,876	32,327	32,327
	2018	7,365	51,070	51,995	7,495	31,062	31,625
	2010	5,406	35,121	41,270	5,604	23,552	27,676
	2000	4,303	30,833	45,902	4,192	17,356	25,838
	1990	2,235	19,394	36,897	2,333	11,086	21,091
Hispanic	2019	19,352	32,285	32,285	17,395	23,420	23,420
	2018	18,981	31,417	31,986	16,667	21,687	22,080
	2010	15,106	22,420	26,346	12,947	16,292	19,145
	2000	11,343	19,498	29,027	9,431	12,248	18,234
	1990	6,767	13,470	25,626	5,903	7,532	14,329
	1980	3,996	9,659	28,612	3,617	4,405	13,049

NA = Not available. **Note:** Income for persons 15 years of age and over beginning in Mar. 1980; 14 years of age and over as of Mar. of the following year for previous years. Beginning in 2010, totals for Black and Asian include those who identified themselves as being that race in combination with some other race; totals for white are for those who identified as white alone. Before 2010, Asian category includes Pacific Islanders. Hispanic persons may be of any race.

Consumer Credit Outstanding, 2010-19

Source: Federal Reserve System
(in billions of dollars, not seasonally adjusted)

	2010	2018	2019		2010	2018	2019
TOTAL	$2,647.2	$3,998.1	$4,180.6	Finance companies	$81.5	$23.7	$21.9
Major holders				Credit unions	36.3	62.6	67.8
Depository institutions	1,185.5	1,687.4	1,774.0	Nonfinancial business	25.5	21.4	21.4
Finance companies	705.0	534.4	537.6	Nonrevolving	1,807.8	2,943.6	3,086.4
Credit unions	226.5	469.2	482.4	Depository institutions	520.8	740.5	790.8
Federal government[1]	363.8	1,236.3	1,319.2	Finance companies	623.5	510.7	515.8
Nonprofit and				Credit unions	190.1	406.6	414.7
educational institutions[2] . . .	71.3	31.3	27.7	Federal government[1]	363.8	1,236.3	1,319.2
Nonfinancial business	44.8	39.6	39.6	Nonprofit and			
Major types of credit, by holder				educational institutions[2] . . .	71.3	31.3	27.7
Revolving	839.4	1,054.6	1,094.2	Nonfinancial business	19.3	18.2	18.2
Depository institutions	664.7	946.8	983.1				

(1) Includes student loans originated by the Dept. of Education under the Federal Direct Loan Program and the Perkins Loan Program, as well as Federal Family Education Program loans that the government purchased under the Ensuring Continued Access to Student Loans Act. (2) Includes student loans originated under the Federal Family Education Loan Program and held by educational institutions and nonprofit organizations.

Poverty Thresholds by Family Size, 1980-2019

Source: U.S. Census Bureau, U.S. Dept. of Commerce

	1980	1990	2000	2010	2019		1980	1990	2000	2010	2019
1 person	$4,190	$6,652	$8,791	$11,137	$13,011	3 people	$6,565	$10,419	$13,740	$17,373	$20,335
Under age 65....	4,290	6,800	8,959	11,344	13,300	4 people	8,414	13,359	17,604	22,315	26,172
Age 65 or older ..	3,949	6,268	8,259	10,458	12,261	5 people	9,966	15,792	20,815	26,442	31,021
2 people	5,363	8,509	11,235	14,216	16,521	6 people	11,269	17,839	23,533	29,904	35,129
Householder						7 people	12,761	20,241	26,750	34,019	40,016
under age 65 ..	5,537	8,794	11,589	14,676	17,196	8 people	14,199	22,582	29,701	37,953	44,461
Householder age						9 or more people ..	16,896	26,848	35,150	45,224	52,875
65 or older.....	4,983	7,905	10,418	13,194	15,468						

Note: Weighted averages; not used for computing poverty data.

Persons Below Poverty Level by Race and Hispanic Origin, 1960-2019

Source: U.S. Census Bureau, U.S. Dept. of Commerce

	Number below poverty level (mil)					% of subgroup below poverty level					Avg. income cutoff, family of 4 at poverty level[4]
Year	All races[1]	Asian[2]	White	Black[2]	Hispanic[3]	All races[1]	Asian[2]	White	Black[2]	Hispanic[3]	
1960	39.9	NA	28.3	NA	NA	22.2%	NA	17.8%	NA	NA	$3,022
1970	25.4	NA	17.5	7.5	NA	12.6	NA	9.9	33.5%	NA	3,968
1980	29.3	NA	19.7	8.6	3.5	13.0	NA	10.2	32.5	25.7%	8,414
1990	33.6	0.9	22.3	9.8	6.0	13.5	12.2%	10.7	31.9	28.1	13,359
1995	36.4	1.4	24.4	9.9	8.6	13.8	14.6	11.2	29.3	30.3	15,569
2000	31.6	1.3	21.6	8.0	7.7	11.3	9.9	9.5	22.5	21.5	17,604
2005	37.0	1.5	24.9	9.5	9.4	12.6	10.9	10.6	24.7	21.8	19,971
2010	46.3	2.1	31.1	11.6	13.5	15.1	12.0	13.0	27.4	26.5	22,315
2012	46.5	2.1	30.8	11.8	13.6	15.0	11.4	12.7	27.1	25.6	23,492
2013	46.3	2.4	31.3	11.2	13.4	14.8	12.5	12.9	25.3	24.7	23,834
2014	46.7	2.3	31.1	11.6	13.1	14.8	11.5	12.7	26.0	23.6	24,230
2015	43.1	2.2	28.6	10.8	12.1	13.5	11.1	11.6	23.9	21.4	24,257
2016	40.6	2.1	27.1	10.0	11.1	12.7	9.9	11.0	21.8	19.4	24,563
2017	39.6	2.1	26.0	10.1	10.8	12.3	9.6	10.5	21.7	18.3	25,093
2018	38.1	2.2	24.9	9.7	10.5	11.8	9.8	10.1	20.7	17.6	25,701
2019	34.0	1.6	22.5	8.8	9.5	10.5	7.1	9.1	18.7	15.7	26,172

NA = Not available. **Note:** Because of a change in the definition of poverty, data prior to 1980 are not directly comparable to data since 1980. (1) Includes other races not shown separately. (2) Beginning in 2002, numbers include those who identified themselves as being Asian or Black in combination with some other race. For 1990-2000, Asian includes Pacific Islanders. (3) Persons of Hispanic origin may be of any race. (4) Figures for 1960-80 for nonfarm families only.

Families Below Poverty Level by Status, Race, and Sex, 1980-2019

Source: U.S. Census Bureau, U.S. Dept. of Commerce
(numbers in thousands)

	All families			Married-couple families			Male householder, no spouse present			Female householder, no spouse present		
		Below poverty level			Below poverty level			Below poverty level			Below poverty level	
Year and race	Total	Number	Percent	Total	Number	Percent	Total	Number	Percent	Total	Number	Percent
All races												
1980	60,309	6,217	10.3%	49,294	3,032	6.2%	1,933	213	11.0%	9,082	2,972	32.7%
1990	66,322	7,098	10.7	52,147	2,981	5.7	2,907	349	12.0	11,268	3,768	33.4
2000	73,778	6,400	8.7	56,598	2,637	4.7	4,277	485	11.3	12,903	3,278	25.4
2010	79,559	9,400	11.8	58,667	3,681	6.3	5,649	892	15.8	15,243	4,827	31.7
2015	82,199	8,589	10.4	60,258	3,245	5.4	6,311	939	14.9	15,630	4,404	28.2
2018	83,508	7,504	9.0	61,971	2,938	4.7	6,485	824	12.7	15,052	3,742	24.9
2019	83,698	6,554	7.8	62,355	2,507	4.0	6,506	746	11.5	14,838	3,300	22.2
White[1]												
1980	52,710	4,195	8.0	44,860	2,437	5.4	1,584	149	9.4	6,266	1,609	25.7
1990	56,803	4,622	8.1	47,014	2,386	5.1	2,277	226	9.9	7,512	2,010	26.8
2000	61,330	4,333	7.1	49,473	2,181	4.4	3,283	332	10.1	8,574	1,820	21.2
2010	63,976	6,305	9.9	50,016	2,921	5.8	4,176	563	13.5	9,784	2,822	28.8
2015	65,272	5,743	8.8	50,588	2,539	5.0	4,643	610	13.1	10,042	2,594	25.8
2018	66,132	5,004	7.6	51,643	2,258	4.4	4,744	492	10.4	9,745	2,253	23.1
2019	66,102	4,323	6.5	51,853	1,936	3.7	4,734	477	10.1	9,514	1,909	20.1
Black[1]												
1980	6,317	1,826	28.9	3,392	474	14.0	291	52	17.7	2,634	1,301	49.4
1990	7,471	2,193	29.3	3,569	448	12.6	472	97	20.6	3,430	1,648	48.1
2000	8,731	1,686	19.3	4,214	266	6.3	732	120	16.3	3,785	1,300	34.3
2010	9,982	2,403	24.1	4,473	407	9.1	979	257	26.3	4,531	1,738	38.4
2015	10,342	2,175	21.0	4,670	369	7.9	1,099	256	23.3	4,573	1,551	33.9
2018	10,333	1,830	17.7	4,966	358	7.2	1,140	235	20.6	4,227	1,237	29.3
2019	10,529	1,689	16.0	5,084	319	6.3	1,113	189	16.9	4,332	1,181	27.3
Hispanic[2]												
1980	3,235	751	23.2	2,365	363	15.3	164	26	16.0	706	362	51.3
1990	4,981	1,244	25.0	3,454	605	17.5	341	66	19.4	1,186	573	48.3
2000	8,017	1,540	19.2	5,426	772	14.2	765	104	13.6	1,826	664	36.4
2010	11,284	2,739	24.3	7,065	1,221	17.3	1,241	248	20.0	2,978	1,270	42.6
2015	12,761	2,502	19.6	8,003	1,077	13.5	1,473	259	17.6	3,284	1,166	35.5
2018	13,279	2,057	15.5	8,445	855	10.1	1,584	200	12.6	3,250	1,002	30.8
2019	13,172	1,833	13.9	8,350	781	9.4	1,529	171	11.2	3,292	881	26.8

Note: The Census Bureau revised race categories in 2002, so data after 2002 are not directly comparable with data for previous years. (1) Beginning in 2010, totals for white include only those who identified themselves as white alone; totals for Black include those who identified themselves as Black alone or in combination with some other race. (2) Persons of Hispanic origin may be of any race.

Poverty Rates by State, 1990-2019

Source: U.S. Census Bureau, U.S. Dept. of Commerce

The poverty rate is the proportion of the population with income below the government's official poverty level, which is the same nationwide but is adjusted each year for inflation.

State	1990	2000	2010	2018	2019	State	1990	2000	2010	2018	2019
Alabama	19.2%	13.3%	17.2%	16.0%	12.9%	Montana	16.3%	14.1%	14.5%	10.3%	9.7%
Alaska	11.4	7.6	12.5	13.1	10.2	Nebraska	10.3	8.6	10.2	10.5	8.7
Arizona	13.7	11.7	18.8	12.8	9.9	Nevada	9.8	8.8	16.6	13.0	10.4
Arkansas	19.6	16.5	15.3	15.9	14.1	New Hampshire	6.3	4.5	6.5	6.1	3.7
California	13.9	12.7	16.3	11.9	10.1	New Mexico	20.9	17.5	18.3	16.6	15.3
Colorado	13.7	9.8	12.3	9.1	9.3	New Jersey	9.2	7.3	11.1	8.2	6.3
Connecticut	6.0	7.7	8.6	10.2	8.3	New York	14.3	13.9	16.0	11.1	12.5
Delaware	6.9	8.4	12.2	7.4	6.5	North Carolina	13.0	12.5	17.4	13.1	12.7
Dist. of Columbia	21.1	15.2	19.5	14.7	12.5	North Dakota	13.7	10.4	12.6	9.7	8.1
Florida	14.4	11.0	16.0	13.7	11.5	Ohio	11.5	10.0	15.4	11.9	12.4
Georgia	15.8	12.1	18.8	14.8	12.1	Oklahoma	15.6	14.9	16.3	13.4	10.8
Hawaii	11.0	8.9	12.4	9.2	8.4	Oregon	9.2	10.9	14.3	9.7	8.1
Idaho	14.9	12.5	13.8	11.5	7.1	Pennsylvania	11.0	8.6	12.2	11.8	8.7
Illinois	13.7	10.7	14.1	10.3	9.3	Rhode Island	7.5	10.2	14.0	8.9	9.2
Indiana	13.0	8.5	16.3	11.6	10.1	South Carolina	16.2	11.1	16.9	12.8	15.1
Iowa	10.4	8.3	10.3	8.9	9.5	South Dakota	13.3	10.7	13.6	10.6	10.6
Kansas	10.3	8.0	14.5	7.5	9.5	Tennessee	16.9	13.5	16.7	12.0	13.1
Kentucky	17.3	12.6	17.7	15.7	13.6	Texas	15.9	15.5	18.4	13.7	11.1
Louisiana	23.6	17.2	21.5	19.0	17.9	Utah	8.2	7.6	10.0	6.9	7.3
Maine	13.1	10.1	12.6	11.6	10.4	Vermont	10.9	10.0	10.8	9.7	8.6
Maryland	9.9	7.4	10.9	8.0	7.0	Virginia	11.1	8.3	10.7	9.8	8.8
Massachusetts	10.7	9.8	10.9	8.7	7.5	Washington	8.9	10.8	11.6	8.6	7.0
Michigan	14.3	9.9	15.7	10.5	10.2	West Virginia	18.1	14.7	16.8	15.9	13.9
Minnesota	12.0	5.7	10.8	7.9	5.7	Wisconsin	9.3	9.3	10.1	8.6	8.4
Mississippi	25.7	14.9	22.5	19.6	19.2	Wyoming	11.0	10.8	9.6	9.5	9.2
Missouri	13.4	9.2	15.0	12.4	9.4	**United States**	**13.5**	**11.3**	**15.1**	**11.8**	**10.5**

Income Inequality in the U.S., 1970-2019

Source: U.S. Census Bureau, U.S. Dept. of Commerce

Top earners' share of income has grown considerably over the past half century. In 1970, the richest 5% of Americans earned 16.6% percent of all income while the share earned by the poorest 20% was 4.1%. By 2019, the top 5% took home 23.0% of income and the poorest 20% earned just 3.1% of the total. The middle class's share declined from 17.4% to 14.1% over the same period.

Income group	Income in 2019[1]	Percentage of income earned by each quintile										
		1970	1975	1980	1985	1990	1995	2000	2005	2010	2015	2018	2019
Lowest 20%	$15,286	4.1%	4.3%	4.2%	3.9%	3.8%	3.7%	3.6%	3.4%	3.3%	3.1%	3.1%	3.1%
Second quintile	40,652	10.8	10.4	10.2	9.8	9.6	9.1	8.9	8.6	8.5	8.2	8.3	8.3
Middle 20%	68,938	17.4	17.0	16.8	16.2	15.9	15.2	14.8	14.6	14.6	14.3	14.1	14.1
Fourth quintile	111,112	24.5	24.7	24.7	24.4	24.0	23.3	23.0	23.0	23.4	23.2	22.6	22.7
Highest 20%	254,449	43.3	43.6	44.1	45.6	46.6	48.7	49.8	50.4	50.3	51.1	52.0	51.9
Top 5%	451,122	16.6	16.5	16.5	17.6	18.5	21.0	22.1	22.2	21.3	22.1	23.1	23.0

(1) Mean household income in 2019.

Temporary Assistance for Needy Families (TANF), 1997-2018

Source: Office of Family Assistance, Admin. for Children and Families, U.S. Dept. of Health and Human Services

Year	Total TANF expenditures (mil)	Average number of monthly cash beneficiaries			Year	Total TANF expenditures (mil)	Average number of monthly cash beneficiaries		
		Families	Recipients	Children			Families	Recipients	Children
1997	$19,010.2	3,936,610	10,935,125	NA	2009	$30,577.8	1,847,152	4,364,979	3,280,150
2000	24,780.7	2,229,315	5,833,043	4,303,943	2010	33,255.5	1,847,152	4,364,979	3,280,150
2001	25,667.4	2,087,646	5,335,891	3,968,499	2011	30,264.1	1,921,243	4,599,846	3,435,218
2002	25,414.4	2,038,373	5,067,963	3,791,560	2012	28,867.3	1,876,426	4,476,476	3,351,971
2003	26,340.0	2,009,666	4,900,889	3,693,056	2013	29,147.1	1,751,067	4,102,491	3,091,076
2004	25,821.2	1,965,960	4,722,588	3,581,448	2014	29,350.9	1,652,996	3,894,213	2,934,582
2005	25,580.1	1,901,810	4,495,175	3,428,885	2015	29,295.9	1,333,707	4,176,387	2,370,198
2006	25,593.8	1,789,460	4,179,295	3,207,216	2016	28,321.2	1,206,820	3,886,868	2,144,955
2007	26,922.0	1,697,432	3,957,330	3,047,043	2017	28,701.0	1,095,368	3,650,293	1,943,028
2008	28,129.7	1,726,799	4,041,292	3,084,413	2018	28,719.7	1,004,923	3,234,514	1,785,278

NA = Not available.

Adults Receiving TANF Funds by Employment Status, 2018

Source: Office of Family Assistance, Admin. for Children and Families, U.S. Dept. of Health and Human Services

State	Adults	Employed	State	Adults	Employed	State	Adults	Employed	State	Adults	Employed
AL	3,621	43.0%	IL	2,421	81.6%	NE	1,456	64.4%	SC	2,350	39.7%
AK	2,417	36.4	IN	1,146	27.8	NV	6,242	42.9	SD	508	16.8
AZ	2,615	16.1	IA	4,879	39.2	NH	1,495	29.5	TN	10,572	25.6
AR	1,683	26.5	KS	2,299	25.9	NJ	6,016	16.2	TX	7,224	26.5
CA	183,263	27.8	KY	5,460	34.8	NM	6,423	27.8	UT	1,683	18.4
CO	10,652	60.3	LA	2,543	13.6	NY	54,183	30.7	VT	1,228	17.4
CT	5,460	26.2	ME	2,149	30.9	NC	2,830	10.8	Virgin Isls.	142	2.8
DE	1,013	26.5	MD	10,230	14.0	ND	408	47.8	VA	7,227	28.8
DC	3,176	39.0	MA	17,527	13.9	OH	9,470	27.2	WA	14,558	20.0
FL	9,657	11.6	MI	4,759	37.2	OK	1,846	13.0	WV	1,721	23.3
GA	2,049	16.9	MN	9,515	44.3	OR	9,575	7.8	WI	5,228	27.1
Guam	174	8.5	MS	1,773	19.1	PA	30,039	25.2	WY	297	25.6
HI	3,694	33.7	MO	4,637	19.4	Puerto Rico	5,569	1.4	**U.S. total**	**492,385**	**27.3**
ID	69	10.3	MT	2,499	34.8	RI	2,716	9.7			

TANF = Temporary Assistance for Needy Families.

Selected Personal Consumption Expenditures in the U.S., 1990-2019

Source: Bureau of Economic Analysis, U.S. Dept. of Commerce
(in billions of dollars)

	1990	2000	2010	2015	2017	2018	2019
Personal consumption expenditures	$3,809.0	$6,762.1	$10,185.8	$12,297.5	$13,340.4	$13,993.3	$14,544.6
GOODS	1,491.3	2,453.2	3,317.8	3,923.0	4,172.3	4,371.9	4,512.2
Durable goods	497.1	912.6	1,049.0	1,307.6	1,410.7	1,481.6	1,534.4
Motor vehicles and parts	205.1	363.2	344.5	475.3	503.6	523.2	521.8
New motor vehicles	134.7	210.7	182.3	276.9	282.1	287.3	284.9
Net purchases of used motor vehicles	42.2	110.7	105.6	128.6	148.6	161.0	158.5
Motor vehicle parts and accessories	28.3	41.8	56.6	69.8	72.9	74.9	78.4
Furnishings, durable household equipment	120.9	208.1	240.9	294.2	324.7	343.3	357.4
Furniture and furnishings	69.2	121.7	140.5	177.3	199.7	213.4	223.7
Household appliances	23.7	34.1	44.1	52.7	55.4	57.3	58.5
Glassware, tableware, and household utensils	18.4	35.3	36.4	37.1	39.6	41.0	43.0
Recreational goods and vehicles	105.6	230.9	298.6	336.5	374.2	399.0	433.4
Video, audio, photo, and info-processing equip.	56.1	127.7	182.8	194.2	216.2	233.6	256.3
Sporting equipment, guns, ammunition	19.9	39.1	52.8	66.3	71.9	75.1	79.9
Sports and recreational vehicles	16.6	34.9	35.8	52.0	60.0	62.8	68.0
Recreational books	10.9	24.4	22.6	18.5	20.1	21.3	22.4
Other durable goods	65.5	110.4	165.0	201.6	208.1	216.0	221.7
Jewelry and watches	30.3	49.1	60.9	73.1	72.4	75.3	76.7
Therapeutic appliances and equipment	18.4	32.2	52.4	61.7	66.1	69.0	72.4
Nondurable goods	994.2	1,540.6	2,268.9	2,615.4	2,761.6	2,890.3	2,977.9
Food and beverages purchased for off-premises consumption	391.2	540.6	786.9	921.0	970.2	998.8	1,025.7
Food and nonalcoholic beverages	341.2	463.1	678.6	794.9	833.6	856.0	878.1
Alcoholic beverages	49.3	77.1	107.9	125.4	136.1	142.3	147.2
Clothing and footwear	195.2	280.8	316.6	368.7	380.0	394.2	403.5
Women's and girls' clothing	94.5	132.7	149.2	171.8	177.1	183.2	186.2
Men's and boys' clothing	57.4	85.9	83.7	98.0	100.0	103.2	105.7
Children's and infants' clothing	8.1	11.4	18.0	18.2	18.4	18.8	18.9
Other clothing materials and footwear	35.3	50.8	65.8	80.8	84.5	89.0	92.6
Gasoline and other energy goods	124.2	184.5	336.7	309.4	309.0	349.2	335.4
Other nondurable goods	283.6	534.7	828.7	1,016.3	1,102.5	1,148.0	1,213.3
Pharmaceutical and other medical products	59.1	159.0	326.1	445.8	491.9	511.6	548.6
Recreational items	50.9	91.9	129.9	159.0	170.5	175.5	183.2
Household supplies	54.2	86.7	108.2	126.5	135.6	141.0	146.9
Personal care products	39.3	68.5	106.0	125.2	132.3	137.2	142.6
Tobacco	41.0	68.5	97.9	94.0	97.3	99.0	99.8
Magazines, newspapers, and stationery	36.5	56.6	52.2	58.5	67.9	73.4	80.8
SERVICES	2,317.7	4,309.0	6,868.0	8,374.5	9,168.1	9,621.4	10,032.4
Housing and utilities	696.5	1,198.6	1,903.9	2,257.9	2,459.5	2,570.2	2,681.2
Housing	570.6	1,010.5	1,604.0	1,940.6	2,133.3	2,224.1	2,330.6
Rental of tenant-occupied nonfarm housing	150.8	227.9	372.6	516.6	575.3	592.7	621.7
Imputed rental of owner-occupied nonfarm housing	412.8	768.9	1,214.2	1,405.0	1,538.3	1,610.7	1,687.2
Household utilities	125.9	188.1	299.9	317.3	326.2	346.1	350.6
Water supply and sanitation	27.1	50.4	78.5	91.6	100.3	104.4	108.0
Electricity	71.8	98.4	166.8	177.6	177.6	189.0	189.4
Natural gas	27.0	39.3	54.6	48.1	48.3	52.7	53.2
Health care	506.2	918.4	1,699.6	2,057.3	2,248.3	2,345.0	2,450.8
Outpatient services	232.1	436.6	774.6	926.7	1,020.9	1,066.6	1,104.2
Physician services	134.8	229.2	410.5	488.9	538.0	558.8	572.0
Dental services	32.4	63.6	104.5	116.3	126.6	131.8	134.8
Paramedical services	64.9	143.8	259.6	321.4	356.2	376.0	397.4
Hospitals	228.8	393.9	769.9	957.6	1,043.8	1,091.4	1,156.5
Nursing homes	45.3	87.9	155.1	173.1	183.7	187.1	190.1
Transportation services	126.4	261.3	305.2	398.7	440.3	466.7	483.4
Motor vehicle services	87.2	174.4	201.0	255.9	285.7	298.5	306.0
Motor vehicle maintenance and repair	73.9	112.5	136.7	163.3	179.9	187.9	192.3
Public transportation	39.2	86.9	104.2	142.7	154.7	168.2	177.4
Recreation services	121.8	254.4	403.7	491.7	538.5	561.8	580.4
Membership clubs, sports centers, parks, theaters, museums	49.7	91.9	140.1	177.7	198.0	208.9	218.2
Audio-video, photographic, and information processing equipment services	37.9	70.1	106.4	134.1	140.9	143.4	145.4
Gambling	23.7	67.6	109.4	125.7	135.9	141.8	147.0
Food services and accommodations	262.7	408.8	635.7	832.9	913.7	961.2	999.5
Purchased meals and beverages	228.3	344.9	521.8	677.5	746.7	788.3	820.7
Accommodations	27.6	55.0	98.6	136.4	145.9	150.9	156.3
Financial services and insurance	230.8	543.0	754.4	957.3	1,052.4	1,119.5	1,176.1
Financial services	119.0	336.7	465.5	605.7	665.1	704.2	733.4
Insurance	111.7	206.3	289.0	351.6	387.3	415.3	442.7
Other services	297.5	566.5	871.1	1,007.2	1,098.6	1,158.2	1,221.8
Telecommunication services	60.7	126.4	147.6	152.9	152.0	157.1	161.1
Internet access	0.1	12.0	40.5	65.2	71.2	71.9	75.2
Higher education	34.7	76.8	155.0	173.6	181.6	185.6	192.4
Nursery, elementary, and secondary schools	14.8	24.1	35.6	41.4	46.5	48.9	51.3
Commercial and vocational schools	11.1	24.3	39.9	47.3	51.7	53.7	56.0
Professional and other services	67.7	113.0	158.9	180.2	195.4	198.1	204.0
Personal care and clothing services	44.5	80.4	115.8	141.4	154.2	167.3	175.2
Social services and religious activities	41.2	81.1	139.0	171.5	193.0	203.2	212.4
Household maintenance	25.4	49.2	61.6	79.4	82.6	90.9	95.2

Note: Subtotals may not add up to totals due to rounding or incomplete enumeration.

Leading U.S. Businesses, 2019

Source: *Fortune* magazine, June 2020

(ranked by 2019 revenues, in millions of dollars)

Industry/company (rank)	Revenues
Advertising, Marketing	
Omnicom Group (211)	$14,954
Interpublic Group (308)	10,221
Aerospace & Defense	
Raytheon Technologies (39)	$77,046
Boeing (40)	76,559
Lockheed Martin (57)	59,812
General Dynamics (83)	39,350
Northrop Grumman (96)	33,841
Raytheon (108)	29,176
Howmet Aerospace (226)	14,192
Textron (236)	13,630
L3Harris Technologies (250)	12,856
Huntington Ingalls Industries (357)	8,899
Spirit AeroSystems Holdings (406)	7,863
Airlines	
Delta Air Lines (68)	$47,007
American Airlines Group (70)	45,768
United Airlines Holdings (76)	43,259
Southwest Airlines (141)	22,428
Alaska Air Group (360)	8,781
JetBlue Airways (394)	8,094
Apparel	
TJX (80)	$41,717
Nike (85)	39,117
Gap (199)	16,383
Ross Stores (202)	16,039
VF (233)	13,871
L Brands (248)	12,914
PVH (322)	9,909
Foot Locker (397)	8,005
Burlington Stores (424)	7,286
Hanesbrands (436)	6,967
Ralph Lauren (469)	6,313
Ascena Retail Group (473)	6,243
Tapestry (485)	6,027
Levi Strauss (495)	5,763
Automotive Retailing, Services	
Penske Automotive Group (136)	$23,179
AutoNation (154)	21,336
CarMax (173)	19,146
Lithia Motors (252)	12,673
Group 1 Automotive (264)	12,044
Sonic Automotive (301)	10,454
Hertz Global Holdings (326)	9,779
Avis Budget Group (345)	9,172
Asbury Automotive Group (428)	7,210
Rush Enterprises (492)	5,810
Beverages	
Coca-Cola (88)	$37,266
Keurig Dr Pepper (288)	11,120
Molson Coors Beverage (320)	10,579
Constellation Brands (392)	8,116
Building Materials, Glass	
Builders FirstSource (425)	$7,280
Owens Corning (431)	7,160
Chemicals	
Dow (78)	$42,951
3M (103)	32,136
DuPont (152)	21,512
Sherwin-Williams (180)	17,901
PPG Industries (209)	15,146
Ecolab (213)	14,906
Eastman Chemical (343)	9,273
Air Products & Chemicals (355)	8,919
Mosaic (356)	8,906
Huntsman (382)	8,342
Westlake Chemical (391)	8,118
Celanese (470)	6,297
Olin (481)	6,110
Commercial Banks	
JPMorgan Chase (17)	$142,422
Bank of America (25)	113,589
Wells Fargo (30)	103,915
Citigroup (31)	103,449
Goldman Sachs Group (60)	53,922
Morgan Stanley (61)	53,823
Capital One Financial (97)	33,766
U.S. Bancorp (113)	27,325
PNC Financial Services Group (151)	21,624
Bank of New York Mellon (159)	20,822
Truist Financial (217)	$14,664
Discover Financial Services (231)	13,989
State Street (244)	13,131
Fifth Third Bancorp (325)	9,790
Citizens Financial Group (395)	8,066
KeyCorp (411)	7,694
M&T Bank (438)	6,941
Northern Trust (440)	6,895
Regions Financial (446)	6,755
Huntington Bancshares (500)	5,655
Computer Software	
Microsoft (21)	$125,843
Oracle (82)	39,506
salesforce.com (190)	17,098
Adobe (285)	11,171
Intuit (445)	6,784
Computers, Office Equipment	
Apple (4)	$260,174
Dell Technologies (34)	92,154
HP (58)	58,756
Hewlett Packard Enterprise (109)	29,135
Western Digital (198)	16,569
Xerox Holdings (347)	9,145
NCR (439)	6,915
NetApp (478)	6,146
Construction, Farm Machinery	
Caterpillar (62)	$53,800
Deere (84)	39,258
Paccar (118)	25,600
Navistar International (284)	11,251
AGCO (350)	9,041
Oshkosh (377)	8,382
Diversified Financials	
Fannie Mae (24)	$120,304
Freddie Mac (41)	75,125
American Express (67)	47,020
StoneX (100)	32,897
Synchrony Financial (170)	19,461
Marsh & McLennan (195)	16,652
Ameriprise Financial (245)	13,103
Ally Financial (273)	11,618
Icahn Enterprises (352)	8,992
Voya Financial (353)	8,942
Blackstone Group (420)	7,338
Arthur J. Gallagher (429)	7,195
Diversified Outsourcing Services	
Aramark (200)	$16,227
Automatic Data Processing (227)	14,175
Cintas (441)	6,892
ABM Industries (462)	6,499
Electronics, Electrical Equipment	
Honeywell International (92)	$36,709
Whirlpool (162)	20,419
Corning (277)	11,503
Rockwell Automation (452)	6,695
Energy	
World Fuel Services (91)	$36,819
Vistra Energy (270)	11,809
Calpine (319)	10,072
NRG Energy (324)	9,871
Cheniere Energy (329)	9,730
UGI (423)	7,320
Engineering, Construction	
AECOM (163)	$20,173
Fluor (181)	17,817
Jacobs Engineering Group (206)	15,463
Quanta Services (261)	12,112
Peter Kiewit Sons' (307)	10,283
EMCOR Group (344)	9,175
MasTec (430)	7,183
Entertainment	
Walt Disney (49)	$69,570
ViacomCBS (111)	27,812
Netflix (164)	20,156
Live Nation Entertainment (275)	11,548
Fox (280)	11,389
Discovery (287)	11,144
Liberty Media (306)	10,292
Activision Blizzard (463)	6,489
Equipment Leasing	
United Rentals (340)	$9,351
Financial Data Services	
Visa (137)	$22,977
PayPal Holdings (182)	17,772
Mastercard (191)	16,883
Fidelity National Information Services (303)	10,333
Fiserv (311)	10,187
S&P Global (451)	6,699
Alliance Data Systems (456)	6,581
Food Consumer Products	
PepsiCo (51)	$67,161
Mondelez International (117)	25,868
Kraft Heinz (122)	24,977
General Mills (192)	16,865
Land O'Lakes (232)	13,888
Kellogg (237)	13,578
Campbell Soup (322)	9,909
Conagra Brands (334)	9,538
Hormel Foods (337)	9,497
Hershey (398)	7,986
J.M. Smucker (407)	7,838
Dean Foods (421)	7,329
Post Holdings (499)	5,681
Food & Drug Stores	
Walgreens Boots Alliance (19)	$136,866
Kroger (23)	122,286
Albertsons (55)	60,535
Publix Super Markets (87)	38,463
Rite Aid (150)	21,674
Food Production	
Archer Daniels Midland (54)	$64,656
Tyson Foods (79)	42,405
CHS (105)	31,901
Corteva (234)	13,846
Andersons (390)	8,170
Seaboard (444)	6,840
Ingredion (475)	6,209
Food Services	
Starbucks (114)	$26,509
McDonald's (156)	21,077
Yum China Holdings (361)	8,776
Darden Restaurants (372)	8,510
Forest & Paper Products	
Weyerhaeuser (457)	$6,554
General Merchandisers	
Walmart (1)	$523,964
Costco Wholesale (14)	152,703
Target (37)	78,112
Macy's (120)	25,331
Kohl's (165)	19,974
Nordstrom (205)	15,524
BJ's Wholesale Club (243)	13,191
J.C. Penney (286)	11,167
Dillard's (468)	6,343
Health Care: Insurance & Managed Care	
UnitedHealth Group (7)	$242,155
Anthem (29)	104,213
Centene (42)	74,639
Humana (52)	64,888
Molina Healthcare (193)	16,829
Magellan Health (432)	7,159
Health Care: Medical Facilities	
HCA Healthcare (65)	$51,336
Tenet Healthcare (174)	18,479
DaVita (230)	14,102
Community Health Systems (241)	13,210
Universal Health Services (281)	11,378
Health Care: Pharmacy & Other Services	
CVS Health (5)	$256,776
Cigna (13)	153,566
Laboratory Corp. of America (274)	11,555
IQVIA Holdings (290)	11,088
Quest Diagnostics (410)	7,726
Cerner (498)	5,693
Home Equipment, Furnishings	
Stanley Black & Decker (220)	$14,442
Newell Brands (316)	10,083
Mohawk Industries (321)	9,971

Industry/company (rank)	Revenues
Masco (384)	$8,235
Fortune Brands Home & Security (494)	5,765
Homebuilders	
Lennar (147)	$22,260
D.R. Horton (183)	17,593
PulteGroup (309)	10,213
NVR (417)	7,428
Toll Brothers (426)	7,224
Hotels, Casinos, Resorts	
Marriott International (157)	$20,972
Las Vegas Sands (235)	13,739
MGM Resorts International (249)	12,900
Hilton Worldwide Holdings (338)	9,452
Caesars Holdings (363)	8,742
Wynn Resorts (454)	6,611
Household & Personal Products	
Procter & Gamble (50)	$67,684
Kimberly-Clark (175)	18,450
Colgate-Palmolive (203)	15,693
Estée Lauder (215)	14,863
Coty (366)	8,649
Clorox (474)	6,214
Industrial Machinery	
General Electric (33)	$95,214
Cummins (132)	23,571
Emerson Electric (176)	18,372
Parker-Hannifin (224)	14,320
Illinois Tool Works (229)	14,109
Westinghouse Air Brake (388)	8,200
Fortive (422)	7,326
Dover (433)	7,136
Information Technology Services	
IBM (38)	$77,147
DXC Technology (155)	21,184
CDW (178)	18,032
Cognizant Technology Solutions (194)	16,783
Leidos Holdings (289)	11,094
Insight Enterprises (409)	7,731
Booz Allen Hamilton Holding (450)	6,704
Science Applications Intl. (466)	6,379
Insurance: Life, Health (Mutual)	
New York Life Insurance (73)	$44,117
TIAA (81)	40,454
Massachusetts Mutual Life Insurance (89)	37,253
Northwestern Mutual (102)	32,294
Guardian Life Ins. Co. of America (238)	13,477
Thrivent Financial for Lutherans (368)	8,612
Western & Southern Financial Group (401)	7,921
Insurance: Life, Health (Stock)	
MetLife (45)	$69,620
Prudential Financial (53)	64,807
Aflac (146)	22,307
Lincoln National (188)	17,258
Principal Financial (201)	16,222
Reinsurance Group of America (225)	14,300
Unum Group (266)	11,999
Pacific Life (269)	11,847
Mutual of Omaha Insurance (300)	10,456
Equitable Holdings (333)	9,591
Genworth Financial (364)	8,681
Securian Financial Group (455)	6,601
Brighthouse Financial (457)	6,554
Insurance: Property & Casualty (Mutual)	
State Farm Insurance (36)	$79,395
Nationwide (74)	43,982
Farmers Insurance Exchange (255)	12,593
Auto-Owners Insurance (320)	10,007
Erie Insurance Group (376)	8,443
Insurance: Property & Casualty (Stock)	
Berkshire Hathaway (6)	$254,616
AIG (66)	49,746
Allstate (72)	44,675
Liberty Mutual Insurance Group (77)	43,228
Progressive (86)	39,022
USAA (94)	35,617
Travelers (106)	31,581
Hartford Financial Services Group (160)	20,740
Loews (212)	14,931
American Family Insurance Group (254)	12,633
Assurant (315)	10,087
Markel (335)	$9,526
Alleghany (351)	9,041
Fidelity National Financial (375)	8,469
American Financial Group (383)	8,237
Cincinnati Financial (400)	7,924
W.R. Berkley (402)	7,902
Old Republic International (427)	7,214
FM Global (447)	6,743
First American Financial (476)	6,202
Internet Services & Retailing	
Amazon.com (2)	$280,522
Alphabet (11)	161,857
Facebook (46)	70,697
Booking Holdings (210)	15,066
Uber Technologies (228)	14,147
Qurate Retail Group (239)	13,458
Expedia Group (263)	12,067
eBay (295)	10,800
Wayfair (348)	9,127
Mail, Package, & Freight Delivery	
United Parcel Service (43)	$74,094
FedEx (47)	69,693
Medical Products & Equipment	
Abbott Laboratories (104)	$31,904
Danaher (161)	20,521
Becton Dickinson (187)	17,290
Stryker (214)	14,884
Baxter International (282)	11,362
Boston Scientific (296)	10,735
Zimmer Biomet Holdings (399)	7,982
Metals	
Nucor (139)	$22,589
United States Steel (247)	12,937
Reliance Steel & Aluminum (291)	10,974
Steel Dynamics (299)	10,465
Alcoa (302)	10,433
AK Steel Holding (467)	6,359
Commercial Metals (491)	5,829
Mining, Crude Oil Production	
ConocoPhillips (93)	$36,670
Occidental Petroleum (148)	21,971
EOG Resources (186)	17,380
Freeport-McMoRan (221)	14,402
Newmont (328)	9,740
Pioneer Natural Resources (341)	9,304
Chesapeake Energy (373)	8,489
Devon Energy (419)	7,372
Ovintiv (449)	6,726
Hess (461)	6,510
Apache (465)	6,411
Motor Vehicles & Parts	
Ford Motor (12)	$155,900
General Motors (18)	137,237
Tesla (124)	24,578
Lear (166)	19,810
Tenneco (185)	17,450
Goodyear Tire & Rubber (216)	14,745
BorgWarner (312)	10,168
Dana (367)	8,620
Autoliv (369)	8,548
Thor Industries (404)	7,865
American Axle & Manufacturing (460)	6,531
Network & Other Communications Equipment	
Cisco Systems (63)	$51,904
CommScope Holding (381)	8,345
Amphenol (386)	8,225
Motorola Solutions (403)	7,887
Oil & Gas Equipment, Services	
Baker Hughes (129)	$23,838
Halliburton (142)	22,408
National Oilwell Varco (374)	8,479
Packaging, Containers	
International Paper (144)	$22,376
WestRock (177)	18,289
Crown Holdings (272)	11,665
Ball (279)	11,474
Berry Global Group (358)	8,878
Avery Dennison (435)	7,070
Packaging Corp. of America (437)	6,964
O-I Glass (453)	6,691
Graphic Packaging Holding (477)	6,160
Petroleum Refining	
Exxon Mobil (3)	$264,938
Chevron (15)	146,516
Marathon Petroleum (22)	124,813
Phillips 66 (27)	109,559
Valero Energy (32)	$102,729
PBF Energy (125)	24,508
HollyFrontier (184)	17,487
Delek US Holdings (342)	9,298
Pharmaceuticals	
Johnson & Johnson (35)	$82,059
Pfizer (64)	51,750
Merck (69)	46,840
AbbVie (99)	33,266
Bristol-Myers Squibb (115)	26,145
Amgen (135)	23,362
Gilead Sciences (140)	22,449
Eli Lilly (145)	22,320
Biogen (223)	14,378
Regeneron Pharmaceuticals (405)	7,863
Zoetis (472)	6,260
Pipelines	
Energy Transfer (59)	$54,213
Plains GP Holdings (98)	33,669
Enterprise Products Partners (101)	32,789
NGL Energy Partners (127)	24,088
Kinder Morgan (242)	13,209
Oneok (313)	10,164
Targa Resources (365)	8,671
Williams (387)	8,201
DCP Midstream (413)	7,625
EnLink Midstream (483)	6,053
Publishing, Printing	
News Corp. (318)	$10,074
R.R. Donnelley & Sons (471)	6,276
Railroads	
Union Pacific (149)	$21,708
CSX (267)	11,937
Norfolk Southern (283)	11,296
Real Estate	
CBRE Group (128)	$23,894
Jones Lang LaSalle (179)	17,983
American Tower (414)	7,580
Realogy Holdings (490)	5,870
Crown Castle International (496)	5,763
Simon Property Group (497)	5,755
Scientific, Photographic, & Control Equipment	
Thermo Fisher Scientific (119)	$25,542
Avantor (484)	6,040
Securities	
BlackRock (219)	$14,539
Charles Schwab (271)	11,785
Edward Jones (336)	9,526
KKR (349)	9,120
Raymond James Financial (396)	8,023
Intercontinental Exchange (459)	6,547
TD Ameritrade Holding (486)	6,016
Franklin Resources (493)	5,775
Semiconductors & Other Electronic Components	
Intel (45)	$71,965
Jabil (121)	25,282
Qualcomm (126)	24,273
Micron Technology (134)	23,406
Broadcom (138)	22,597
Applied Materials (218)	14,608
Texas Instruments (222)	14,383
Nvidia (292)	10,918
Lam Research (331)	9,654
Sanmina (385)	8,234
Advanced Micro Devices (448)	6,731
Analog Devices (487)	5,991
Specialty Retailers: Other	
Home Depot (26)	$110,225
Lowe's (75)	72,148
Best Buy (75)	43,638
Dollar General (112)	27,754
Dollar Tree (131)	23,611
Murphy USA (262)	12,101
Bed Bath & Beyond (265)	12,029
AutoZone (268)	11,864
ODP (297)	10,647
O'Reilly Automotive (314)	10,150
Advance Auto Parts (330)	9,709
Dick's Sporting Goods (362)	8,751
Casey's General Stores (378)	8,365
Tractor Supply (380)	8,352
Ulta Beauty (418)	7,398
GameStop (464)	6,466
TravelCenters of America (480)	6,117
Williams-Sonoma (489)	5,898

Industry/company (rank)	Revenues
Telecommunications	
AT&T (9)	$181,193
Verizon Communications (20)	131,868
Comcast (28)	108,942
Charter Communications (71)	45,764
CenturyLink (143)	22,401
DISH Network (251)	12,808
Altice USA (327)	9,761
Frontier Communications (393)	8,107
Temporary Help	
ManpowerGroup (158)	$20,864
Robert Half International (482)	6,074
Tobacco	
Philip Morris International (107)	$29,805
Altria Group (167)	19,796
Transportation Equipment	
Polaris (442)	$6,863
Transportation & Logistics	
XPO Logistics (196)	$16,648
C.H. Robinson Worldwide (208)	15,310
Expeditors International of Washington (389)	8,175
Trucking, Truck Leasing	
J.B. Hunt Transport Services (346)	$9,165
Ryder System (354)	8,926
Utilities: Gas & Electric	
Exelon (95)	$34,438
Duke Energy (123)	24,658
Southern (153)	$21,419
NextEra Energy (172)	19,204
PG&E (189)	17,129
Dominion Energy (197)	16,572
American Electric Power (204)	15,561
DTE Energy (253)	12,669
Consolidated Edison (256)	12,574
Sempra Energy (258)	12,443
Edison International (259)	12,347
CenterPoint Energy (260)	12,301
Xcel Energy (276)	11,529
Entergy (293)	10,879
FirstEnergy (294)	10,850
AES (310)	10,189
Public Service Enterprise Group (317)	10,076
Eversource Energy (371)	8,527
PPL (408)	7,769
WEC Energy Group (416)	7,523
CMS Energy (443)	6,845
Ameren (488)	5,910
Waste Management	
Waste Management (207)	$15,455
Republic Services (305)	10,299
Wholesalers: Diversified	
Genuine Parts (171)	$19,392
Global Partners (246)	13,082
LKQ (257)	12,506
W.W. Grainger (278)	$11,486
Univar Solutions (339)	9,444
WESCO International (379)	8,359
Veritiv (412)	7,659
Graybar Electric (415)	7,524
Beacon Roofing Supply (434)	7,105
HD Supply Holdings (478)	6,146
Wholesalers: Electronics & Office Equipment	
Tech Data (90)	$36,998
Arrow Electronics (110)	28,917
Synnex (130)	23,757
Avnet (169)	19,519
Anixter International (359)	8,846
Wholesalers: Food & Grocery	
Sysco (56)	$60,114
US Foods Holding (116)	25,939
United Natural Foods (133)	23,481
Performance Food Group (168)	19,744
Core-Mark Holding (240)	13,329
SpartanNash (370)	8,536
Wholesalers: Health Care	
McKesson (8)	$214,319
AmerisourceBergen (10)	179,589
Cardinal Health (16)	145,534
Henry Schein (304)	10,305
Owens & Minor (332)	9,650

World's Largest Companies, 2019

Source: *Fortune* magazine, July 2020
(ranked by 2019 revenues, in millions of dollars)

Rank	Company (2018 rank), country	Revenue
1.	Walmart (1), U.S.	$523,964
2.	Sinopec Group (2), China	407,009
3.	State Grid (5), China	383,906
4.	China National Petroleum (4), China	379,130
5.	Royal Dutch Shell (3), Netherlands	352,106
6.	Saudi Aramco (6), Saudi Arabia	329,784
7.	Volkswagen (9), Germany	282,760
8.	BP (7), UK	282,616
9.	Amazon.com (13), U.S.	280,522
10.	Toyota Motor (10), Japan	275,288
11.	Exxon Mobil (8), U.S.	264,938
12.	Apple (11), U.S.	260,174
13.	CVS Health (19), U.S.	256,776
14.	Berkshire Hathaway (12), U.S.	254,616
15.	UnitedHealth Group (14), U.S.	242,155
16.	McKesson (17), U.S.	231,051
17.	Glencore (16), Switzerland	215,111
18.	China State Construction Engineering (21), China	205,839
19.	Samsung Electronics (15), South Korea	197,705
20.	Daimler (18), Germany	193,346
21.	Ping An Insurance (29), China	184,280
22.	AT&T (25), U.S.	181,193
23.	AmerisourceBergen (27), U.S.	179,589
24.	Industrial & Commercial Bank of China (26), China	177,069
25.	Total (20), France	176,249
26.	Hon Hai Precision Industry (23), Taiwan	172,869
27.	Trafigura Group (22), Singapore	171,474
28.	EXOR Group (24), Netherlands	162,754
29.	Alphabet (37), U.S.	161,857
30.	China Construction Bank (31), China	158,884
31.	Ford Motor (30), U.S.	155,900
32.	Cigna (209), U.S.	153,566
33.	Costco Wholesale (35), U.S.	152,703
34.	AXA (46), France	148,984
35.	Agricultural Bank of China (36), China	147,313
36.	Chevron (28), U.S.	146,516
37.	Cardinal Health (38), U.S.	145,534
38.	JPMorgan Chase (41), U.S.	142,422
39.	Honda Motor (34), Japan	137,332
40.	General Motors (32), U.S.	137,237
41.	Walgreens Boots Alliance (40), U.S.	136,866
42.	Mitsubishi (33), Japan	135,940
43.	Bank of China (44), China	135,091
44.	Verizon Communications (43), U.S.	131,868
45.	China Life Insurance (51), China	131,244
46.	Allianz (45), Germany	130,359
47.	Microsoft (60), U.S.	125,843
48.	Marathon Petroleum (72), U.S.	124,813
49.	Huawei Investment & Holding (61), China	124,316
50.	China Railway Engineering Group (55), China	123,324
51.	Kroger (47), U.S.	$122,286
52.	SAIC Motor (39), China	122,071
53.	Fannie Mae (49), U.S.	120,304
54.	China Railway Construction (59), China	120,302
55.	Gazprom (42), Russia	118,009
56.	BMW Group (53), Germany	116,638
57.	Lukoil (50), Russia	114,621
58.	Bank of America (58), U.S.	113,589
59.	Home Depot (62), U.S.	110,225
60.	Japan Post Holdings (52), Japan	109,915
61.	Phillips 66 (54), U.S.	109,559
62.	Nippon Telegraph & Telephone (64), Japan	109,448
63.	Comcast (75), U.S.	108,942
64.	China National Offshore Oil (63), China	108,687
65.	China Mobile Communications (56), China	108,527
66.	Assicurazioni Generali (92), Italy	105,921
67.	Crédit Agricole (91), France	104,972
68.	Anthem (79), U.S.	104,213
69.	Wells Fargo (69), U.S.	103,915
70.	Citigroup (71), U.S.	103,449
71.	Valero Energy (57), U.S.	102,729
72.	Itochu (65), Japan	100,522
73.	HSBC Holdings (99), UK	98,673
74.	Siemens (70), Germany	97,937
75.	Pacific Construction Group (97), China	97,536
76.	Rosneft Oil (86), Russia	96,313
77.	General Electric (48), U.S.	95,214
78.	China Communications Construction (93), China	95,096
79.	China Resources (80), China	94,758
80.	Prudential (372), UK	93,736
81.	Dell Technologies (84), U.S.	92,154
82.	Nestlé (76), Switzerland	92,107
83.	Nissan Motor (66), Japan	90,863
84.	Hyundai Motor (94), South Korea	90,740
85.	Legal & General Group, UK	90,615
86.	Deutsche Telekom (90), Germany	90,135
87.	Enel (89), Italy	89,907
88.	Aviva, UK	89,647
89.	China FAW Group (87), China	89,417
90.	China Post Group (101), China	89,347
91.	Amer International Group (119), China	88,862
92.	China Minmetals (112), China	88,357
93.	Banco Santander (85), Spain	88,257
94.	SoftBank Group (98), Japan	87,440
95.	Bosch Group (77), Germany	86,990
96.	Reliance Industries (106), India	86,270
97.	SK Holdings (73), South Korea	86,163
98.	Carrefour (81), France	85,905
99.	BNP Paribas (104), France	85,058
100.	Dongfeng Motor (82), China	84,049

Top U.S. Franchises, 2020

Source: *Entrepreneur* magazine

Rank	Company (2019 rank)	Type of business	U.S. locations	Startup costs[1]
1.	Dunkin' (2)	Coffee, doughnuts, baked goods	9,499	$396,000-1.6 mil
2.	Taco Bell (4)	Mexican food	6,161	$526,000-3.0 mil
3.	McDonald's (1)	Burgers, chicken, salads, beverages	13,226	$1.3 mil-2.2 mil
4.	Sonic Drive-In (3)	Burgers, hot dogs, chicken sandwiches	3,231	$1.2 mil-3.5 mil
5.	The UPS Store (5)	Postal, business, and printing centers	4,819	$138,000-470,000
6.	Ace Hardware (13)	Hardware and home improvement stores	4,386	$286,000-2.1 mil
7.	Planet Fitness (7)	Fitness clubs	1,740	$1.1 mil-4.2 mil
8.	Jersey Mike's Subs (9)	Subs	1,520	$237,000-767,000
9.	Culver's (6)	Frozen custard, specialty burgers	709	$2.0 mil-4.7 mil
10.	Pizza Hut LLC (16)	Pizza, pasta, wings	6,087	$357,000-2.2 mil
11.	7-Eleven Inc. (10)	Convenience stores	7,206	$47,000-1.2 mil
12.	Kumon Math & Reading Centers (14)	Supplemental education	1,565	$74,000-157,000
13.	Baskin-Robbins (12)	Ice cream, frozen yogurt, frozen beverages	2,524	$94,000-402,000
14.	Smoothie King (22)	Smoothies, healthful snacks, health products	908[2]	$264,000-844,000
15.	Great Clips (8)	Hair salons	4,216	$147,000-282,000
16.	Dairy Queen (21)	Ice cream, burgers, chicken	4,364[2]	$1.1 mil-1.8 mil
17.	Budget Blinds LLC (35)	Window coverings, window film, rugs	1,141	$125,000-254,000
18.	Tropical Smoothie Cafe (65)	Smoothies, salads, wraps, sandwiches	840	$199,000-544,000
19.	HomeVestors of America Inc. (30)	Home buying, repair, and selling	1,122	$96,000-426,000
20.	Palm Beach Tan (86)	Tanning	319	$624,000-927,000
21.	uBreakiFix (29)	Electronics repairs	467	$55,000-236,000
22.	Anytime Fitness (20)	Fitness centers	2,405	$98,000-524,000
23.	Jimmy John's Gourmet Sandwiches (11)	Sandwiches	2,703	$314,000-556,000
24.	KFC US LLC (23)	Chicken	3,980[2]	$1.4 mil-2.8 mil
25.	Arby's (43)	Sandwiches, fries, shakes	2,170	$629,000-2.2 mil

Note: Franchises are ranked by a combination of factors, including financial strength and stability, growth rate, number of locations, startup costs, and whether the company provides financing. (1) Does not include franchise fees, which vary. (2) As of 2019.

Small Businesses in the U.S. Economy, 1977-2018

Source: Business Dynamics Statistics, U.S. Census Bureau; Small Business Administration

Year	Total businesses	Small businesses	Small businesses as % of private nonfarm GDP	Total employed	Small business employees	% employed by small business
1977	3,432,013	3,421,875	52.0%	66,091,813	34,519,673	52.2%
1980	3,608,883	3,597,797	51.0	74,749,926	39,441,701	52.8
1985	3,977,854	3,965,106	50.0	80,896,890	44,020,000	54.4
1990	4,312,888	4,297,295	51.0	92,553,401	49,405,250	53.4
1995	4,617,160	4,600,494	50.0	98,485,465	52,017,989	52.8
2000	4,840,136	4,821,350	50.3	112,607,042	56,925,603	50.6
2005	5,141,900	5,123,273	46.3	115,140,083	59,011,437	51.3
2006	5,185,814	5,166,701	46.1	118,614,800	60,480,334	51.0
2007	5,253,216	5,232,786	46.2	119,627,021	60,201,946	50.3
2008	5,204,140	5,184,058	45.8	119,780,685	59,688,492	49.8
2009	5,030,089	5,010,001	46.0	113,333,976	56,056,768	49.5
2010	4,956,460	4,937,934	44.6	110,792,627	54,863,184	49.5
2011	4,915,209	4,896,614	NA	112,121,688	54,908,981	49.0
2012	4,991,078	4,971,340	NA	114,761,137	56,024,730	48.8
2013	5,025,673	5,005,505	NA	117,194,376	56,678,331	48.4
2014	5,060,326	5,039,793	NA	119,102,910	57,525,365	48.3
2015	5,108,544	5,087,860	NA	121,637,451	58,583,432	48.2
2016	5,168,809	5,147,852	NA	124,231,335	59,672,952	48.0
2017	5,265,087	5,243,126	NA	127,308,658	61,566,492	48.4
2018	5,287,128	5,266,095	NA	129,840,639	61,791,302	47.6

NA = Not available. **Note:** Small businesses are firms employing fewer than 500 people. Figures include only businesses with paid employees.

Denominations of U.S. Currency

Since 1969 the largest denomination of U.S. currency that has been issued is the $100 bill. As larger-denomination bills reach the Federal Reserve Bank, they are removed from circulation. Because some discontinued currency is expected to be in the hands of holders for many years, the description of the various denominations below is continued.

Note	Portrait	Embellishment on back	Note	Portrait	Embellishment on back
$1	George Washington	Great Seal of U.S.	$500[1]	William McKinley	Ornate denominational marking
2	Thomas Jefferson	Signers of Declaration	1,000[2]	Grover Cleveland	Ornate denominational marking
5	Abraham Lincoln	Lincoln Memorial	5,000	James Madison	Washington resigning as Army commander
10	Alexander Hamilton	U.S. Treasury			
20	Andrew Jackson	White House	10,000	Salmon Chase	Embarkation of the Pilgrims
50	Ulysses S. Grant	U.S. Capitol	100,000[3]	Woodrow Wilson	Ornate denominational marking
100	Benjamin Franklin	Independence Hall			

(1) John Marshall appeared on the earliest version of the $500 bill. (2) Alexander Hamilton appeared on the earliest version of the $1,000 bill, but these were discontinued to avoid confusion with the $10 bill. (3) For use only in transactions between Federal Reserve System and Treasury Department.

The U.S. $1 Bill

Plate position: Shows where on the 32-note plate this bill was printed.

Serial number: Each bill has its own.

Federal Reserve Bank number: Shows which district issued the bill.

Federal Reserve seal: The name of the Federal Reserve Bank that issued the bill is printed in the seal. The letter also tells you which bank distributed the bill. Here are the number and letter codes for the 12 Federal Reserve Banks:

1/A: Boston
2/B: New York
3/C: Philadelphia
4/D: Cleveland
5/E: Richmond
6/F: Atlanta
7/G: Chicago
8/H: St. Louis
9/I: Minneapolis
10/J: Kansas City
11/K: Dallas
12/L: San Francisco

Treasurer of the U.S. signature

Series indicator: Year note's design was first used.

Secretary of the Treasury signature

Treasury Department seal: The balancing scales represent justice. The pointed stripe across the middle has 13 stars for the original 13 colonies. The key represents authority.

Plate serial number: Shows which printing plate was used for the face of the bill.

Plate serial number: Shows which plate was used for the back.

Front of the Great Seal of the United States: The bald eagle is the national bird. The shield has 13 stripes for the 13 original colonies. The eagle holds 13 arrows (symbol of war) and an olive branch with 13 olives and leaves (symbol of peace). Above the eagle is the motto "E Pluribus Unum," Latin for "out of many, one," and a constellation of 13 stars.

Reverse of the Great Seal of the United States: The pyramid symbolizes something that endures for ages. The eye, known as the Eye of Providence, probably comes from an ancient Egyptian symbol. The pyramid has 13 levels; at its base are the Roman numerals for 1776, the year of American independence. "Annuit Coeptis" is Latin for "God has favored our undertaking." "Novus Ordo Seclorum" is Latin for "a new order of the ages." Both phrases are from the works of the Roman poet Virgil.

U.S. Currency and Coin

Source: Bureau of the Fiscal Service, U.S. Dept. of the Treasury

Total Money in Circulation, 1955-2020

Date	Dollars (mil)	Per capita[1]	Date	Dollars (mil)	Per capita[1]	Date	Dollars (mil)	Per capita[1]
June 30, 1955	$30,229	$183	Sept. 30, 1990	$278,903	$1,105	June 30, 2015	$1,368,622	$4,260
June 30, 1960	32,064	177	Sept. 30, 1995	409,272	1,553	June 30, 2016	1,463,923	4,520
June 30, 1965	39,719	204	Sept. 30, 2000	568,614	2,061	June 30, 2017	1,561,808	4,800
June 30, 1970	54,351	265	Sept. 30, 2005	766,487	2,578	June 30, 2018	1,666,817	5,081
June 30, 1975	81,196	380	June 30, 2010	945,138	3,051	June 30, 2019	1,742,978	5,294
Sept. 30, 1980	129,916	581	June 30, 2013	1,193,771	3,774	June 30, 2020	1,969,957	5,970
Sept. 30, 1985	187,337	782	June 30, 2014	1,282,431	4,027			

(1) Based on U.S. Census Bureau population estimates.

Money in Circulation by Denomination, 2020

Denomination	Amount in circulation	Denomination	Amount in circulation	Denomination	Amount in circulation
$1	$12,932,747,433	$50	$106,204,656,800	$10,000	$3,450,000
$2	2,677,277,412	$100	1,532,669,088,200	Fractional notes[1]	600
$5	15,929,707,650	$500	141,749,000	Total currency	$1,921,723,098,695
$10	22,229,420,920	$1,000	165,146,000	Total coins	$48,233,712,654
$20	228,768,089,680	$5,000	1,765,000	Total currency and coins	$1,969,956,811,349

(1) Represents the value of certain partial denominations not presented for redemption.

U.S. Budget Receipts and Outlays, 1789-1940

Source: U.S. Dept. of the Treasury
(in thousands of dollars; annual statements for years ending June 30, unless otherwise noted)

Yearly average	Receipts	Outlays	Yearly average	Receipts	Outlays	Yearly average	Receipts	Outlays
1789-1800[1]	$5,717	$5,776	1866-1870	$447,301	$377,642	1906-1910	$628,507	$639,178
1801-1810[2]	13,056	9,086	1871-1875	336,830	287,460	1911-1915	710,227	720,252
1811-1820[2]	21,032	23,943	1876-1880	288,124	255,598	1916-1920	3,483,652	8,065,333
1821-1830[2]	21,928	16,162	1881-1885	366,961	257,691	1921-1925	4,306,673	3,578,989
1831-1840[2]	30,461	24,495	1886-1890	375,448	279,134	1926-1930	4,069,138	3,182,807
1841-1850[2]	28,545	34,097	1891-1895	352,891	363,599	1931-1935	2,770,973	5,214,874
1851-1860	60,237	60,163	1896-1900	434,877	457,451	1936-1940	4,960,614	10,192,367
1861-1865	160,907	683,785	1901-1905	559,481	535,559			

(1) Average for period Mar. 4, 1789, to Dec. 31, 1800. (2) Years 1801-42 end Dec. 31; average for 1841-50 is for the period Jan. 1, 1841, to June 30, 1850.

U.S. Budget Receipts and Outlays, Fiscal Years 2000-19

Source: Congressional Budget Office; *Budget of the U.S. Government*, Office of Mgmt. and Budget, Exec. Office of the President

A $236-bil government surplus in 2000 ballooned into a $1.4-tril deficit by 2009. The deficit was reduced by nearly $1 tril, 2009-15, but it began rising again in 2016 and was close to $1 tril again by 2019.

(in millions of current dollars; numbers may not add up to totals because of independent rounding or omitted subcategories, including some subcategories with negative values)

Function and subfunction	2000	2005	2010	2015	2018	2019
NET RECEIPTS	**$2,025,191**	**$2,153,611**	**$2,162,706**	**$3,249,890**	**$3,329,907**	**$3,464,161**
Individual income taxes	1,004,462	927,222	898,549	1,540,802	1,683,538	1,717,857
Corporation income taxes	207,289	278,282	191,437	343,797	204,733	230,245
Social insurance and retirement receipts	652,852	794,125	864,814	1,065,257	1,170,701	1,243,372
Employment and general retirement	620,451	747,664	815,894	1,010,427	1,121,155	1,197,393
Old-age and survivors insurance (off-budget)	411,677	493,646	539,996	658,543	691,215	770,282
Disability insurance (off-budget)	68,907	83,830	91,691	111,829	163,532	144,021
Hospital insurance	135,529	166,068	180,068	234,189	260,659	277,572
Railroad retirement/pension fund (trust funds)	2,688	2,284	2,285	3,336	3,353	3,259
Railroad social security equivalent account	1,650	1,836	1,854	2,530	2,396	2,259
Unemployment insurance	27,640	42,002	44,823	51,178	45,042	41,193
Other retirement	4,761	4,459	4,097	3,652	4,504	4,786
Excise taxes	68,865	73,094	66,909	98,279	94,986	99,452
Federal funds	22,692	22,547	18,256	37,759	30,067	34,927
Alcohol	8,140	8,111	9,229	9,639	10,057	9,992
Tobacco	7,221	7,920	17,160	14,453	12,861	12,457
Telephone	5,670	6,047	993	607	512	436
Transportation fuels	819	−770	−11,000	−3,394	−1,459	−3,623
Trust funds	46,173	50,547	48,653	60,520	64,919	64,525
Transportation	34,972	37,892	34,992	40,813	42,613	44,119
Airport and airway	9,739	10,314	10,612	14,268	15,793	15,976
Black lung disability	518	610	595	552	384	217
Inland waterway	101	91	74	98	115	117
Oil spill liability	182	—	476	496	503	156
Aquatic resources	342	429	580	574	562	574
Leaking underground storage tank	184	189	169	179	223	226
Tobacco assessments	—	899	937	49	3	—
Vaccine injury compensation	133	123	218	275	309	280
Other receipts	91,723	80,888	140,997	201,755	175,949	173,235
OUTLAYS	**1,788,950**	**2,471,957**	**3,457,079**	**3,691,850**	**4,109,044**	**4,448,316**
National defense	294,363	495,294	693,485	589,659	631,130	686,003
Department of Defense—Military	281,029	474,071	666,703	562,499	600,683	653,986
Military personnel	75,950	127,463	155,690	145,206	145,827	156,267
Operation and maintenance	105,812	188,118	275,988	247,239	256,657	271,699
Procurement	51,696	82,294	133,603	101,342	112,669	124,699
Research, development, test, and evaluation	37,602	65,694	76,990	64,124	76,976	89,280
Military construction	5,109	5,331	21,169	8,132	6,706	7,412
Family housing	3,413	3,720	3,173	1,198	1,155	1,166
Atomic energy defense activities	12,138	18,031	19,308	18,692	20,919	22,767
Defense-related activities	1,196	3,192	7,474	8,468	9,528	9,250
International affairs	17,213	34,565	45,195	52,040	48,996	52,739
International development and humanitarian assistance	6,516	17,696	19,014	24,087	25,102	26,270
International security assistance	6,387	7,895	11,363	12,907	11,417	11,227
Conduct of foreign affairs	4,708	9,148	13,557	13,246	11,958	12,644
Foreign information and exchange activities	817	1,129	1,485	1,531	1,641	1,671
International financial programs	−1,215	−1,303	−224	269	−1,122	927
General science, space, and technology	18,594	23,597	30,100	29,412	31,534	32,410
General science and basic research	6,167	8,819	11,730	11,719	12,426	12,939
Space flight, research, and supporting activities	12,427	14,778	18,370	17,693	19,108	19,471
Energy	−761	440	11,618	6,841	2,169	5,041
Energy supply	−1,818	−929	5,801	4,710	1,444	4,110
Energy conservation	666	883	4,997	1,187	1,094	1,086
Emergency energy preparedness	162	162	199	449	−878	−743
Energy information, policy, and regulation	229	324	621	495	509	588
Natural resources and environment	25,003	27,983	43,667	36,033	39,140	37,844
Water resources	5,078	5,724	11,662	7,760	6,008	7,793
Conservation and land management	6,762	6,226	10,783	10,519	13,408	11,108
Recreational resources	2,540	2,990	3,911	3,501	3,988	3,894
Pollution control and abatement	7,395	8,065	10,841	7,240	8,028	8,188
Agriculture	36,458	26,565	21,356	18,500	21,789	38,257
Farm income stabilization	33,442	22,043	16,478	13,424	16,718	32,892
Agricultural research and services	3,016	4,522	4,878	5,076	5,071	5,365
Commerce and housing credit	3,207	7,566	−82,316	−37,905	−9,470	−25,715
Mortgage credit	−3,335	−862	35,840	−35,658	−7,432	−43,544
Postal service	2,129	−1,223	−682	−1,610	−1,407	−1,048
Deposit insurance	−3,053	−1,371	−32,033	−12,812	−15,850	−8,035
Transportation	46,853	67,894	91,972	89,533	92,785	97,116
Ground transportation	31,697	42,317	60,784	59,126	61,868	63,079
Air transportation	10,571	18,807	21,431	20,033	20,213	22,609
Water transportation	4,394	6,439	9,351	9,994	10,195	11,010
Community and regional development	10,623	26,262	23,894	20,669	42,159	26,876
Community development	5,480	5,861	9,901	7,817	7,067	6,321
Area and regional development	2,538	2,745	3,249	3,861	2,842	3,369
Disaster relief and insurance	2,605	17,656	10,744	8,991	32,250	17,186
Education, training, employment, and social services	53,764	97,555	128,598	122,035	95,503	136,752
Elementary, secondary, and vocational education	20,578	38,271	73,261	40,022	39,474	41,406
Higher education	10,115	31,442	20,908	51,315	24,610	63,107
Research and general education aids	2,543	3,124	3,631	3,493	3,601	3,748

Function and subfunction	2000	2005	2010	2015	2018	2019
Training and employment	$6,777	$6,852	$9,854	$7,103	$6,759	$6,650
Social services	12,557	16,251	19,179	18,303	19,141	19,913
Health	**154,504**	**250,568**	**369,068**	**482,257**	**551,219**	**584,816**
Health care services	136,201	219,559	330,710	446,368	511,574	542,197
Health research and training	15,979	28,050	34,214	31,426	35,468	37,690
Consumer and occupational health and safety	2,324	2,939	4,144	4,463	4,177	4,929
Medicare	**197,113**	**298,638**	**451,636**	**546,202**	**588,706**	**650,996**
Income security	**253,724**	**345,847**	**622,210**	**508,800**	**495,289**	**514,787**
General retirement and disability insurance (excl. social security)	5,189	6,976	6,564	7,805	6,284	3,693
Federal employee retirement and disability	77,152	93,351	119,867	139,123	140,685	149,619
Unemployment compensation	23,012	35,435	160,145	34,978	30,948	29,900
Housing assistance	28,949	37,899	58,651	47,823	49,499	50,552
Food and nutrition assistance	32,483	50,833	95,110	104,797	98,065	93,587
Social security	**409,423**	**523,305**	**706,737**	**887,753**	**987,791**	**1,044,409**
Veterans benefits and services	**46,989**	**70,120**	**108,384**	**159,781**	**178,895**	**199,843**
Income security for veterans	24,907	35,767	49,163	76,403	85,574	101,105
Veterans education, training, and rehabilitation	1,285	2,790	8,089	13,383	12,401	13,094
Hospital and medical care for veterans	19,516	28,754	45,714	61,893	73,941	80,321
Veterans housing	364	860	540	743	−1,295	−3,111
Administration of justice	**28,499**	**40,019**	**54,383**	**51,906**	**60,418**	**65,740**
Federal law enforcement activities	12,121	19,912	28,713	26,937	31,333	34,156
Federal litigative and judicial activities	7,762	10,658	14,494	14,717	16,974	17,279
Federal correctional activities	3,707	4,845	6,327	7,049	6,821	7,091
Criminal justice assistance	4,909	4,604	4,849	3,203	5,290	7,214
General government	**13,013**	**16,997**	**23,014**	**20,956**	**23,885**	**23,436**
Legislative functions	2,227	3,460	4,100	3,751	4,089	4,328
Executive direction and management	456	569	528	510	492	481
Central fiscal operations	8,285	9,515	11,906	11,096	11,480	12,144
General property and records management	−32	472	1,194	−490	−199	−873
Central personnel management	184	101	338	81	−26	285
General purpose fiscal assistance	2,084	3,333	5,082	7,266	7,368	7,661
Deductions for offsetting receipts	−2,383	−2,841	−1,721	−4,786	−1,845	−2,877
Net interest	**222,949**	**183,986**	**196,194**	**223,181**	**324,975**	**375,158**
Undistributed offsetting receipts	**−42,581**	**−65,224**	**−82,116**	**−115,803**	**−97,869**	**−98,192**
TOTAL SURPLUS/DEFICIT	**236,241**	**−318,346**	**−1,294,373**	**−441,960**	**−779,137**	**−984,155**

— = Not available.

Federal Receipts, Outlays, and Surpluses or Deficits, 1901-2020

Source: *Budget of the U.S. Government, Fiscal Year 2021*, Office of Management and Budget, Exec. Office of the President

(in millions of current dollars)

Fiscal year	Receipts	Outlays	Surplus or deficit (−)	Fiscal year	Receipts	Outlays	Surplus or deficit (−)	Fiscal year	Receipts	Outlays	Surplus or deficit (−)
1901	$588	$525	**$63**	1941	$8,712	$13,653	−$4,941	1981	$599,272	$678,241	−$78,968
1902	562	485	**77**	1942	14,634	35,137	−20,503	1982	617,766	745,743	−127,977
1903	562	517	**45**	1943	24,001	78,555	−54,554	1983	600,562	808,364	−207,802
1904	541	584	−43	1944	43,747	91,304	−47,557	1984	666,438	851,805	−185,367
1905	544	567	−23	1945	45,159	92,712	−47,553	1985	734,037	946,344	−212,308
1906	595	570	**25**	1946	39,296	55,232	−15,936	1986	769,155	990,382	−221,227
1907	666	579	**87**	1947	38,514	34,496	**4,018**	1987	854,288	1,004,017	−149,730
1908	602	659	−57	1948	41,560	29,764	**11,796**	1988	909,238	1,064,416	−155,178
1909	604	694	−89	1949	39,415	38,835	**580**	1989	991,104	1,143,743	−152,639
1910	676	694	−18	1950	39,443	42,562	−3,119	1990	1,031,958	1,252,993	−221,036
1911	702	691	**11**	1951	51,616	45,514	**6,102**	1991	1,054,988	1,324,226	−269,238
1912	693	690	**3**	1952	66,167	67,686	−1,519	1992	1,091,208	1,381,529	−290,321
1913	714	715	—	1953	69,608	76,101	−6,493	1993	1,154,334	1,409,386	−255,051
1914	725	726	—	1954	69,701	70,855	−1,154	1994	1,258,566	1,461,752	−203,186
1915	683	746	−63	1955	65,451	68,444	−2,993	1995	1,351,790	1,515,742	−163,952
1916	761	713	**48**	1956	74,587	70,640	**3,947**	1996	1,453,053	1,560,484	−107,431
1917	1,101	1,954	−853	1957	79,990	76,578	**3,412**	1997	1,579,232	1,601,116	−21,884
1918	3,645	12,677	−9,032	1958	79,636	82,405	−2,769	1998	1,721,728	1,652,458	**69,270**
1919	5,130	18,493	−13,363	1959	79,249	92,098	−12,849	1999	1,827,452	1,701,842	**125,610**
1920	6,649	6,358	**291**	1960	92,492	92,191	**301**	2000	2,025,191	1,788,950	**236,241**
1921	5,571	5,062	**509**	1961	94,388	97,723	−3,335	2001	1,991,082	1,862,846	**128,236**
1922	4,026	3,289	**736**	1962	99,676	106,821	−7,146	2002	1,853,136	2,010,894	−157,758
1923	3,853	3,140	**713**	1963	106,560	111,316	−4,756	2003	1,782,314	2,159,899	−377,585
1924	3,871	2,908	**963**	1964	112,613	118,528	−5,915	2004	1,880,114	2,292,841	−412,727
1925	3,641	2,924	**717**	1965	116,817	118,228	−1,411	2005	2,153,611	2,471,957	−318,346
1926	3,795	2,930	**865**	1966	130,835	134,532	−3,698	2006	2,406,869	2,655,050	−248,181
1927	4,013	2,857	**1,155**	1967	148,822	157,464	−8,643	2007	2,567,985	2,728,686	−160,701
1928	3,900	2,961	**939**	1968	152,973	178,134	−25,161	2008	2,523,991	2,982,544	−458,553
1929	3,862	3,127	**734**	1969	186,882	183,640	**3,242**	2009	2,104,989	3,517,677	−1,412,688
1930	4,058	3,320	**738**	1970	192,807	195,649	−2,842	2010	2,162,706	3,457,079	−1,294,373
1931	3,116	3,577	−462	1971	187,139	210,172	−23,033	2011	2,303,466	3,603,065	−1,299,599
1932	1,924	4,659	−2,735	1972	207,309	230,681	−23,373	2012	2,449,990	3,526,563	−1,076,573
1933	1,997	4,598	−2,602	1973	230,799	245,707	−14,908	2013	2,775,106	3,454,881	−679,775
1934	2,955	6,541	−3,586	1974	263,224	269,359	−6,135	2014	3,021,491	3,506,284	−484,793
1935	3,609	6,412	−2,803	1975	279,090	332,332	−53,242	2015	3,249,890	3,691,850	−441,960
1936	3,923	8,228	−4,304	1976	298,060	371,792	−73,732	2016	3,267,965	3,852,616	−584,651
1937	5,387	7,580	−2,193	1977	355,559	409,218	−53,659	2017	3,316,184	3,981,630	−665,446
1938	6,751	6,840	−89	1978	399,561	458,746	−59,185	2018	3,329,907	4,109,044	−779,137
1939	6,295	9,141	−2,846	1979	463,302	504,028	−40,726	2019	3,464,161	4,448,316	−984,155
1940	6,548	9,468	−2,920	1980	517,112	590,941	−73,830	2020[1]	3,706,327	4,789,746	−1,083,419

— = $500,000 or less. Figures in **bold** denote annual surplus. **Note:** Budget figures prior to 1933 are based on administrative budget concepts under unified budget concepts. Through 1976, fiscal year ends June 30; after 1976, fiscal year ends Sept. 30. Surplus or deficit column may not equal difference between figures because of rounding. (1) Estimate as of Mar. 2020.

Public Debt of the U.S., 1946-2026

Source: *Budget of the U.S. Government, Fiscal Year 2021*, Office of Management and Budget, Exec. Office of the President

Year	Debt held by public — Current dollars (bil)	Debt held by public — FY2018 dollars (bil)	As % of GDP	Interest on public debt as % of — Total federal outlays	GDP
1946	$241.9	$2,602.8	106.1%	7.6%	1.8%
1950	219.0	1,904.1	78.6	11.4	1.7
1955	226.6	1,731.7	55.8	7.6	1.3
1960	236.8	1,603.9	44.3	8.5	1.5
1965	260.8	1,655.1	36.8	8.1	1.4
1970	283.2	1,497.9	27.1	7.9	1.5
1975	394.7	1,537.8	24.6	7.5	1.6
1980	711.9	1,928.5	25.5	10.6	2.2
1985	1,507.3	3,111.9	35.3	16.2	3.6
1990	2,411.6	4,277.8	40.9	16.2	3.4
1995	3,604.4	5,639.2	47.7	15.8	3.2
2000	3,409.8	4,916.0	33.7	13.0	2.3
2005	4,592.2	5,925.1	35.8	7.7	1.5
2010	$9,018.9	$10,540.4	60.8%	6.6%	1.5%
2015	13,116.7	14,048.7	72.5	7.1	1.4
2016	14,167.6	15,041.1	76.4	7.4	1.5
2017	14,665.4	15,298.4	76.0	7.8	1.6
2018	15,749.6	16,054.3	77.4	9.0	1.8
2019	16,800.7	16,800.7	79.2	9.5	2.0
2020[1]	17,881.2	17,535.5	80.5	9.0	1.9
2021[1]	18,912.1	18,183.1	81.0	9.0	1.9
2022[1]	19,890.7	18,746.5	81.0	9.1	1.9
2023[1]	20,688.3	19,115.1	80.2	9.5	1.9
2024[1]	21,283.7	19,277.3	78.5	10.0	1.9
2025[1]	21,848.3	19,399.4	76.7	10.3	2.0
2026[1]	22,361.9	19,463.3	74.8	10.7	2.0

Note: As of end of fiscal year. Through 1976, the fiscal year ended June 30. For 1977 on, the fiscal year ended Sept. 30. (1) Estimate.

State Finances: Revenues, Taxes, Expenditures, and Debt, 2018

Source: U.S. Census Bureau, U.S. Dept. of Commerce

(in thousands of dollars)

State	Total revenue	Revenues — General revenue	Revenues — Intergovernmental revenue	Taxes	Total expenditure	Debt at end of fiscal year
Alabama	$34,406,835	$28,250,965	$10,303,451	$11,055,577	$33,899,390	$9,856,082
Alaska	9,919,282	8,152,092	3,457,365	1,641,733	11,979,183	5,889,417
Arizona	45,167,570	38,133,225	16,011,205	16,212,105	41,145,292	13,703,759
Arkansas	25,425,732	21,402,327	7,877,352	9,843,173	22,520,209	6,832,598
California	412,385,628	320,249,459	103,018,851	175,016,884	375,092,304	148,027,188
Colorado	42,389,685	30,878,620	9,402,733	14,802,263	37,449,374	17,853,552
Connecticut	35,139,473	30,490,255	7,440,296	19,082,263	28,070,663	40,287,423
Delaware	10,484,729	9,275,531	2,619,277	4,219,572	9,991,686	5,127,188
Florida	110,235,411	91,783,197	28,298,587	45,961,204	96,821,778	27,593,512
Georgia	55,479,427	45,135,668	15,295,883	23,428,056	51,558,184	13,305,788
Hawaii	16,150,841	14,078,337	3,013,717	7,714,451	13,654,476	9,870,931
Idaho	11,958,060	9,155,174	2,819,674	4,845,431	10,431,120	3,439,046
Illinois	92,717,937	72,948,065	22,429,882	39,857,069	92,468,099	67,495,522
Indiana	45,089,558	40,546,768	15,075,489	19,397,879	41,636,298	22,026,355
Iowa	28,867,827	24,072,068	6,075,843	10,088,480	23,877,036	6,270,052
Kansas	21,877,508	19,078,088	4,072,601	9,546,790	19,572,429	6,136,579
Kentucky	34,510,574	29,299,781	11,970,566	12,059,970	35,312,518	14,617,245
Louisiana	37,294,923	29,227,226	13,648,190	11,357,686	35,118,216	18,155,260
Maine	10,657,988	8,814,837	3,012,515	4,410,632	9,236,942	4,759,978
Maryland	48,040,253	42,101,136	13,023,465	22,427,037	46,183,945	27,998,569
Massachusetts	68,541,549	58,094,512	17,101,109	29,654,803	67,366,110	78,620,996
Michigan	81,630,737	66,231,312	21,365,685	30,508,361	76,289,557	33,563,347
Minnesota	56,306,765	44,475,950	11,742,550	26,697,469	49,584,827	16,600,028
Mississippi	23,421,200	19,137,029	8,271,815	7,890,571	21,832,564	7,252,112
Missouri	39,804,179	30,919,843	11,947,706	13,027,504	34,992,860	17,854,734
Montana	9,239,440	7,021,451	3,124,693	2,944,827	7,805,481	2,739,404
Nebraska	12,347,188	10,470,221	3,264,232	5,393,093	11,123,881	2,056,773
Nevada	21,771,811	16,087,532	5,454,068	9,157,036	17,414,692	3,435,955
New Hampshire	9,734,653	7,566,526	2,799,206	2,920,888	8,907,923	7,739,271
New Jersey	80,619,851	66,129,799	18,014,349	35,365,046	78,906,750	65,574,574
New Mexico	20,973,043	17,627,371	7,534,520	5,671,904	21,468,456	7,268,214
New York	223,525,982	175,700,469	64,587,716	88,541,099	213,163,460	147,960,540
North Carolina	67,302,674	56,343,509	18,704,775	27,855,070	60,929,395	15,354,553
North Dakota	8,880,056	7,746,544	1,742,138	4,205,184	7,216,315	3,040,855
Ohio	101,023,062	68,842,609	24,388,743	29,130,040	89,026,066	31,622,762
Oklahoma	26,986,320	22,075,260	7,100,962	9,563,830	25,314,521	8,910,608
Oregon	43,875,212	32,138,083	10,470,949	12,644,869	39,369,778	14,285,969
Pennsylvania	108,605,542	87,715,628	29,418,893	40,709,545	102,651,514	49,064,189
Rhode Island	9,904,803	8,406,086	2,868,687	3,483,100	9,471,982	9,093,878
South Carolina	35,446,262	28,177,916	9,916,827	10,550,096	35,002,566	14,571,479
South Dakota	5,614,951	4,409,773	1,499,310	1,917,548	5,243,258	3,739,690
Tennessee	35,851,416	30,234,945	11,826,420	14,269,061	33,738,083	6,289,301
Texas	171,756,387	137,622,906	47,201,933	60,328,843	150,890,074	51,529,919
Utah	24,322,339	18,687,798	4,724,208	8,038,690	21,887,604	7,355,005
Vermont	6,976,132	6,346,252	2,091,212	3,284,231	7,021,342	3,580,807
Virginia	62,586,631	50,882,334	10,957,750	23,489,398	56,366,947	29,074,498
Washington	68,160,975	50,923,984	14,446,364	26,574,889	57,994,626	33,926,356
West Virginia	15,551,414	12,970,565	4,846,089	5,417,673	15,359,180	8,610,296
Wisconsin	54,526,374	36,278,147	9,494,180	18,742,929	42,177,837	22,812,370
Wyoming	7,505,169	5,602,117	2,363,993	1,837,401	6,168,848	832,440
United States	2,630,991,367	2,097,939,270	688,138,024	1,022,783,253	2,410,705,638	1,173,606,967

Note: Figures may not add up to totals because of rounding.

State and Local Government Receipts and Current Expenditures, 1960-2019

Source: Bureau of Economic Analysis, U.S. Dept. of Commerce
(in billions of current dollars; as of July 2020)

	1960	1970	1980	1990	2000	2010	2015	2018	2019
Current receipts	$44.2	$119.1	$335.9	$730.1	$1,304.1	$1,994.4	$2,373.2	$2,643.2	$2,742.9
Current tax receipts	37.0	91.3	230.0	519.1	893.2	1,306.4	1,598.4	1,810.3	1,877.1
Personal current taxes	4.2	14.2	48.9	122.6	236.7	294.1	407.4	467.8	489.9
Income taxes	2.5	10.9	42.6	109.6	217.4	265.8	374.5	429.9	451.0
Other	1.7	3.3	6.3	13.0	19.4	28.3	32.9	37.9	38.9
Taxes on production and imports	31.5	73.3	166.7	374.1	621.3	966.3	1,134.8	1,282.0	1,317.7
Sales taxes	5.3	17.0	53.6	125.6	221.4	295.1	374.2	421.2	434.8
Excise taxes	6.8	14.7	29.2	58.7	95.5	154.8	181.3	205.1	208.4
Property taxes	16.2	36.7	68.8	161.5	254.7	438.6	490.4	549.2	564.0
Other	3.1	5.0	15.0	28.2	49.8	77.8	89.0	106.6	110.5
Taxes on corporate income	1.2	3.7	14.5	22.5	35.2	46.1	56.2	60.5	69.5
Contributions for government social insurance	0.5	1.1	3.6	10.0	10.8	17.8	19.2	21.0	21.7
Income receipts on assets	1.3	5.2	26.3	68.5	94.2	83.5	82.0	94.6	96.8
Interest receipts	1.0	4.3	23.1	64.1	86.6	69.0	65.4	77.1	78.4
Dividends	—	—	0.1	0.2	1.4	3.0	5.4	6.0	6.6
Rents and royalties	0.3	0.8	3.1	4.2	6.3	11.4	11.2	11.5	11.8
Current transfer receipts	4.3	20.1	76.9	126.4	299.7	604.4	675.5	722.5	753.0
Federal grants-in-aid	3.8	18.3	69.7	104.4	233.1	505.2	533.1	582.6	608.1
From business (net)	0.2	0.6	2.5	7.1	28.6	40.3	65.9	54.3	55.7
From persons	0.3	1.2	4.7	14.9	38.0	58.8	75.9	84.2	87.8
Current surplus of government enterprises	1.2	1.4	−0.8	6.1	6.1	−17.7	−2.0	−5.2	−5.7
Current expenditures	41.7	117.6	341.8	766.3	1,344.8	2,301.8	2,588.9	2,856.8	2,950.7
Consumption expenditures	33.5	90.4	249.0	544.0	961.7	1,509.5	1,653.5	1,847.8	1,897.8
Government social benefit payments to persons	4.6	16.1	51.2	127.7	271.4	523.9	665.3	727.2	754.6
Interest payments	3.6	11.1	41.2	94.3	111.1	266.9	269.7	281.3	297.7
Subsidies	0.0	0.0	0.4	0.4	0.5	1.6	0.5	0.6	0.6
Net state and local government saving	2.5	1.4	−5.9	−36.2	−40.6	−307.5	−215.8	−213.7	−207.7
Social insurance funds	0.0	0.2	1.3	2.0	2.0	0.9	3.7	6.4	6.7
Other	2.5	1.3	−7.2	−38.2	−42.6	−308.4	−219.5	−220.1	−214.5
Addenda:									
Total receipts	47.2	125.3	354.5	755.1	1,348.3	2,071.3	2,443.0	2,715.3	2,816.7
Current receipts	44.2	119.1	335.9	730.1	1,304.1	1,994.4	2,373.2	2,643.2	2,742.9
Capital transfer receipts	3.0	6.2	18.6	25.0	44.2	76.9	69.8	72.2	73.8
Total expenditures	52.1	137.1	376.6	837.6	1,468.2	2,447.7	2,705.4	3,000.7	3,105.0
Current expenditures	41.7	117.6	341.8	766.3	1,344.8	2,301.8	2,588.9	2,856.8	2,950.7
Gross government investment	14.1	29.3	65.7	132.2	231.5	347.3	356.0	407.9	431.0
Net purchases of nonproduced assets	0.9	1.1	2.2	5.7	8.6	12.0	11.9	16.2	16.8
Less: Consumption of fixed capital	4.5	10.9	33.1	66.6	116.6	213.4	251.4	280.3	293.5
Net lending or net borrowing (−)	−4.9	−11.8	−22.1	−82.5	−119.9	−376.4	−262.4	−285.3	−288.3

— = Not applicable.

Federal Deposit Insurance Corporation (FDIC)

The Federal Deposit Insurance Corporation (FDIC) was created by Congress during the height of the Depression to maintain stability and public confidence in the nation's banking system. It covered depositors for up to $2,500 in case of bank failure in 1934; the limit today is 100 times that much, or $250,000. In its unique role as deposit insurer of banks and savings associations, and in cooperation with other federal and state regulatory agencies, the FDIC seeks to promote the safety and soundness of insured depository institutions in the U.S. financial system.

The quarterly premiums on deposit insurance are paid by the banks rather than by consumers. The amount of the premium is based on the institution's balance of insured deposits for the preceding quarter and the institution's risk to the insurance fund. In 2009, Congress permanently increased the limit that the FDIC may borrow from the U.S. Treasury from $30 bil to $100 bil.

U.S. Banks, 1935-2020

Source: Summary of Deposits, Federal Deposit Insurance Corp. (FDIC)
Comprises all FDIC-insured commercial and savings banks, including savings and loan institutions (S&Ls).

	Number of banks					Deposits (in mil dollars)				
		Commercial banks[2]			Savings banks, total		Commercial banks[2]			Savings banks, total
Year	All banks[1]	National charter	State charter	Non-members		All deposits[1]	National charter	State charter	Non-members	
1935[3]	15,295	5,386	1,001	7,735	1,173	$45,102	$24,802	$13,653	$5,669	$978
1940	15,772	5,144	1,342	6,956	2,330	67,494	35,787	20,642	7,040	4,025
1950	16,500	4,958	1,912	6,576	3,054	171,963	84,941	41,602	19,726	25,694
1960	17,549	4,530	1,641	6,955	4,423	310,262	120,242	65,487	34,369	90,164
1970	18,205	4,621	1,147	7,743	4,694	686,901	285,436	101,512	95,566	204,367
1980	18,763	4,425	997	9,013	4,328	1,832,716	656,752	191,183	344,311	640,470
1990	15,158	3,979	1,009	7,355	2,815	3,637,292	1,558,915	397,797	693,438	987,142
1995	12,289	2,941	995	6,230	2,082	3,214,687	1,337,105	439,430	696,108	735,856
2000	10,119	2,302	996	5,180	1,622	4,003,744	1,792,773	707,562	793,275	706,461
2005	8,855	1,864	906	4,779	1,293	5,933,742	2,946,589	765,673	1,191,977	1,023,620
2010	7,821	1,427	836	4,413	1,135	7,676,878	4,305,697	1,002,425	1,464,022	891,159
2015	6,358	1,027	816	3,629	876	10,657,721	6,393,433	1,573,880	1,823,558	823,906
2016	6,068	962	794	3,482	820	11,280,518	6,786,952	1,713,434	1,873,530	867,643
2017	5,797	897	783	3,331	776	11,859,860	7,153,816	1,776,419	1,949,135	933,174
2018	5,551	850	763	3,219	709	12,307,919	7,420,588	1,910,259	2,006,686	924,864
2019	5,313	798	746	3,086	673	12,813,124	7,688,213	2,038,003	2,121,389	924,330
2020	5,076	779	702	2,949	636	15,588,514	9,615,139	2,179,210	2,696,156	1,054,195

Note: Figures are for the end of the year shown through 1990 and for June 30 thereafter. (1) Includes U.S. branches of foreign banks not listed separately. (2) Nonmembers are banks that are not members of the Federal Reserve System; national charter and state charter institutions are Federal Reserve members. (3) Figures for 1935 do not include S&Ls, the data for which are not available.

U.S. Bank Failures, 1934-2020

Source: Federal Deposit Insurance Corp. (FDIC)

Covers all FDIC-insured commercial and savings banks, including savings and loan institutions (S&Ls) 1980 and after. As of Oct. 10, 2020.

Year	Closed or assisted	Year	Closed or assisted	Year	Closed or assisted	Year	Closed or assisted	Year	Closed or assisted
1934	9	1970-79	79	1990	382	2001	4	2012	51
1935	25	1980	22	1991	271	2002	11	2013	24
1936	69	1981	40	1992	181	2003	3	2014	18
1937	75	1982	119	1993	50	2004	4	2015	8
1938	74	1983	99	1994	15	2005	0	2016	5
1939	60	1984	106	1995	8	2006	0	2017	8
1940	43	1985	180	1996	6	2007	3	2018	0
1941	15	1986	204	1997	1	2008	30	2019	4
1942	20	1987	262	1998	3	2009	148	2020	2
1943-49	21	1988	470	1999	8	2010	157	**Total,**	
1950-59	28	1989	534	2000	7	2011	92	**1934-2020**	**4,102**
1960-69	44								

Largest U.S. Bank Holding Companies, 2020

Source: National Information Center, Federal Financial Institutions Examination Council
(ranked by total assets, in millions of dollars; as of Mar. 31, 2020)

Rank	Institution, location	Assets	Rank	Institution, location	Assets
1.	JPMorgan Chase & Co., New York, NY	$3,139,431	20.	BNP Paribas USA, Inc., New York, NY	$183,085
2.	Bank of America Corp., Charlotte, NC	2,619,954	21.	Ally Financial Inc., Detroit, MI	182,527
3.	Citigroup Inc., New York, NY	2,219,770	22.	Barclays U.S. LLC, New York, NY	179,955
4.	Wells Fargo & Company, San Francisco, CA	1,981,349	23.	United Services Automobile Association, San Antonio, TX	178,003
5.	Goldman Sachs Group, Inc., New York, NY	1,089,759			
6.	Morgan Stanley, New York, NY	947,795	24.	Citizens Financial Group, Inc., Providence, RI	176,981
7.	U.S. Bancorp, Minneapolis, MN	542,909	25.	State Farm Mutual Automobile Insurance Company, Bloomington, IL	166,299
8.	Truist Financial Corp., Charlotte, NC	506,229			
9.	Bank of New York Mellon Corp., New York, NY	468,155	26.	MUFG Americas Holdings Corp., New York, NY	165,696
10.	TD Group U.S. Holdings LLC, Wilmington, DE	447,269	27.	UBS Americas Holding LLC, New York, NY	163,249
11.	PNC Financial Services Group, Inc., Pittsburgh, PA	445,568	28.	Northern Trust Corp., Chicago, IL	161,709
12.	Capital One Financial Corp., McLean, VA.	396,878	29.	KeyCorp, Cleveland, OH.	157,003
13.	Charles Schwab Corp., San Francisco, CA	370,779	30.	Santander Holdings USA, Inc., Boston, MA	152,145
14.	State Street Corp., Boston, MA	362,528	31.	Ameriprise Financial, Inc. Minneapolis, MN	145,691
15.	Teachers Insurance & Annuity Association of America, New York, NY.	315,996	32.	RBC US Group Holdings LLC, Toronto, Canada	137,944
16.	HSBC North America Holdings Inc., New York, NY	297,536	33.	Regions Financial Corp., Birmingham, AL	133,638
17.	BMO Financial Corp., Wilmington, DE	187,756	34.	Credit Suisse Holdings (USA), Inc., New York, NY	131,778
18.	American Express Co., New York, NY	186,054	35.	M&T Bank Corp., Buffalo, NY	124,578
19.	Fifth Third Bancorp, Cincinnati, OH	185,391	36.	DB USA Corp., New York, NY	117,159

Note: Includes foreign-owned banks with a strong presence in the U.S.

Status of Top Recipients of Treasury Department "Bailout" Funds, 2020

Source: ProPublica

Since Oct. 2008, the federal government has spent $634 bil to bail out 985 institutions severely affected by the financial crisis. As of Aug. 12, 2020, the government had recouped $390 bil in loans and $353 bil in dividends, interest, and other returns, leading to an overall profit of more than $110 bil. Disbursements to some companies currently appear as losses, but may ultimately turn a profit; those investments are listed in *italics*. Companies that failed to repay the government and never will are listed in **bold italics**.
(in billions of dollars, ranked by amount disbursed; as of Oct. 23, 2020)

Recipient	Disbursed	Repaid[1]	Net profit or amount outstanding	Recipient	Disbursed	Repaid[1]	Net profit or amount outstanding
Fannie Mae	$119.8	$181.3	$61.5	BB&T	$3.1	$3.3	$0.2
Freddie Mac	71.6	119.7	48.0	Bank of New York Mellon	3.0	3.2	0.2
AIG	67.8	72.9	5.0	KeyCorp	2.5	2.9	0.4
General Motors	50.7	39.4	−11.3	*CalHFA Mortgage Assistance Corporation*	2.4	0.0	−2.4
Bank of America	45.0	49.6	4.6				
Citigroup	45.0	58.4	13.4	***CIT Group***	2.3	—	−2.3
JPMorgan Chase	25.0	26.7	1.7	*Bank of America subsidiaries (incl. Countrywide)*	2.3	0.0	−2.3
Wells Fargo	25.0	27.3	2.3				
GMAC (now Ally Financial)	16.3	19.3	3.1	Comerica Incorporated	2.3	2.6	0.3
Chrysler	10.7	9.5	−1.2	State Street	2.0	2.1	0.1
Goldman Sachs	10.0	11.4	1.4	*RLJ Western Asset Public/ Private Master Fund, L.P.*	1.9	2.3	0.5
Morgan Stanley	10.0	11.3	1.3				
PNC Financial Services	7.6	8.3	0.7	*Invesco Legacy Securities Master Fund, L.P.*	1.7	2.3	0.6
U.S. Bancorp	6.6	6.9	0.3				
SunTrust	4.9	5.4	0.5	Marshall & Ilsley	1.7	1.9	0.2
Ocwen Financial Corp.	4.8	0.0	−4.8	Oaktree PPIP Fund, L.P.	1.7	2.0	0.3
Capital One Financial Corp.	3.6	3.8	0.3	*Select Portfolio Servicing*	1.6	0.0	−1.6
Regions Financial Corp.	3.5	4.1	0.6	Blackrock PPIF, L.P.	1.6	2.0	0.4
Wellington Management Legacy Securities PPIF Master Fund, LP	3.4	4.2	0.7	Northern Trust	1.6	1.7	0.1
				Nationstar Mortgage, LLC dba Mr. Cooper.	1.5	0.0	−1.5
Fifth Third Bancorp	3.4	4.0	0.6	Chrysler Financial Services	1.5	1.5	—
Hartford Financial Services.	3.4	4.2	0.8	*Marathon Legacy Securities Public–Private Investment Partnership, L.P.*	1.4	1.8	0.4
American Express	3.4	3.8	0.4				
AG GECC PPIP Master Fund, L.P.	3.4	4.3	0.9	Zions Bancorp	1.4	1.7	0.3
				Huntington Bancshares	1.4	1.6	0.2
Wells Fargo Bank, NA.	3.3	0.0	−3.3	Discover Financial Services	1.2	1.5	0.2
JPMorgan Chase subsidiaries	3.2	0.0	−3.2	*Florida Housing Finance Corporation.*	1.1	0.0	−1.1
AllianceBernstein Legacy Securities Master Fund, L.P.	3.2	3.8	0.6				

— = less than $0.1 bil. **Note:** Total includes other disbursements not shown. Figures may not add up to totals due to rounding. (1) Amounts repaid include principal, dividends, interest, warrants, and other proceeds.

Federal Reserve System

The Federal Reserve System is the central bank for the U.S. The system was established on Dec. 23, 1913, originally to give the country an elastic currency, provide facilities for discounting commercial paper, and improve the supervision of banking. Since then, the system's responsibilities have been broadened. Over the years, stability and growth of the economy, a high level of employment, stability in the purchasing power of the dollar, and reasonable balance in transactions with other countries have come to be recognized as primary objectives of governmental economic policy.

The Federal Reserve System consists of three key entities: the Board of Governors, 12 District Reserve Banks and their branches, and the Federal Open Market Committee. Several advisory councils help the board meet its varied responsibilities.

The hub of the system is the seven-member **Board of Governors** in Washington, DC. The members of the board are appointed by the president and confirmed by the Senate to 14-year terms. The president also appoints the chairman and vice chairman of the board from among the board members for four-year terms. As of Oct. 2020, the board members were Jerome H. Powell, chair; Richard H. Clarida, vice chair; Randal K. Quarles, vice chair for supervision; Michelle W. Bowman; and Lael Brainard. Two seats were vacant.

The 12 **Federal Reserve Banks** and their branch offices serve as the decentralized portion of the system, carrying out day-to-day operations such as circulating currency and coin and providing fiscal agency functions and payments mechanism services. The 12 Reserve Banks are located in Boston, New York, Philadelphia, Cleveland, Richmond, Atlanta, Chicago, St. Louis, Minneapolis, Kansas City, Dallas, and San Francisco.

The system's principal function is monetary policy, which it controls using three tools: reserve requirements, the discount rate, and open market operations.

Uniform **reserve requirements**, set by the board, are applied to the transaction accounts and nonpersonal time deposits of all depository institutions. Responsibility for setting the **discount rate** (the interest rate at which depository institutions can borrow money from the Reserve Banks) is shared by the Board of Governors and the Reserve Banks. Changes in the discount rate are recommended by the individual boards of directors of the Reserve Banks and are subject to approval by the Board of Governors.

The most important tool of monetary policy is **open market operations**, or the purchase and sale of government securities. Responsibility for influencing the cost and availability of money and credit through the purchase and sale of government securities lies with the **Federal Open Market Committee** (FOMC), which comprises the seven members of the Board of Governors, the president of the Federal Reserve Bank of New York, and four other Federal Reserve Bank presidents, who each serve one-year terms on a rotating basis. The committee bases its decisions on economic and financial developments and outlook, setting yearly growth objectives for key measures of money supply and credit. The decisions of the committee are carried out by the domestic trading desk of the Federal Reserve Bank of New York.

A Federal Advisory Council of banking industry representatives meets with the Federal Reserve Board four times a year to discuss business and financial conditions, as well as to make recommendations.

Website: www.federalreserve.gov

Federal Reserve Board Benchmark Interest Rates, 1955-2020

The interest rate that the Federal Reserve charges its member banks to borrow money overnight, the discount rate, was divided into two categories in 2003: primary credit, for banks in sound financial condition, and secondary credit, for banks that do not qualify for primary credit. The secondary credit rate is ½ a percentage point higher than the primary credit rate shown here for Jan. 9, 2003, and thereafter. Banks typically raise or lower the rates they extend to customers in accordance with changes in these rates.

Effective date	Rate	Effective date	Rate	Effective date	Rate	Effective date	Rate	Effective date	Rate
1955		**1971**		**1980 (cont.)**		**1995**		**2006**	
Jan. 3	1½	Jan. 8	5¼	Sept. 26	11	Feb. 1	5	Jan. 31	5½
Apr. 15	1¾	Jan. 22	5	Nov. 17	12	**1996**		Mar. 28	5¾
Aug. 5	2	Feb. 19	4¾	Dec. 5	13	Jan. 31	5	May 10	6
Sept. 9	2¼	July 16	5	**1981**		**1998**		June 29	6¼
Nov. 18	2½	Nov. 19	4¾	May 5	14	Oct. 15	4¾	**2007**	
1956		Dec. 17	4½	Nov. 2	13	Nov. 17	4½	Aug. 17	5¾
Apr. 13	2¾	**1973**		Dec. 4	12	**1999**		Sept. 18	5¼
Aug. 24	3	Jan. 15	5	**1982**		Aug. 24	4¾	Nov. 1	5
1957		Feb. 26	5½	July 20	11½	Nov. 16	5	Dec. 12	4¾
Aug. 23	3½	May 4	5¾	Aug. 2	11	**2000**		**2008**	
Nov. 15	3	May 11	6	Aug. 16	10	Feb. 2	5¼	Jan. 22	4
1958		June 11	6½	Aug. 27	10	Mar. 21	5½	Jan. 30	3½
Jan. 24	2¾	July 2	7	Oct. 12	9½	May 16	6	Mar. 17	3¼
Mar. 7	2¼	Aug. 14	7½	Dec. 15	8½	**2001**		Mar. 18	2½
Apr. 18	1¾	**1974**		**1984**		Jan. 3	5¾	Apr. 30	2¼
Sept. 12	2	Apr. 25	8	Apr. 9	9	Jan. 31	5	Oct. 8	1¾
Nov. 7	2½	Dec. 9	7¾	Nov. 21	8½	Mar. 20	4½	Oct. 29	1¼
1959		**1975**		Dec. 24	8	Apr. 18	4	Dec. 16	½
Mar. 6	3	Jan. 10	7¼	**1985**		May 15	3½	**2010**	
May 29	3½	Feb. 5	6¾	May 20	7½	June 27	3¼	Feb. 19	¾
Sept. 11	4	Mar. 19	6¼	**1986**		Aug. 21	3	**2015**	
1960		May 16	6	Mar. 7	7	Sept. 17	2½	Dec. 17	1
June 10	3½	**1976**		Apr. 21	6½	Oct. 2	2	**2016**	
Aug. 12	3	Jan. 19	5½	July 11	6	Dec. 11	1¼	Dec. 15	1¼
1963		Nov. 22	5¼	Aug. 21	5½	**2002**		**2017**	
July 17	3½	**1977**		**1987**		Nov. 6	¾	Mar. 16	1½
1964		Aug. 31	5¾	Sept. 4	6	**2003**		June 15	1¾
Nov. 24	4	Oct. 26	6	**1988**		Jan. 9	2¼	Dec. 14	2
1965		**1978**		Aug. 9	6½	June 25	2	**2018**	
Dec. 6	4½	Jan. 9	6½	**1989**		**2004**		Mar. 22	2¼
1967		May 11	7	Feb. 24	7	June 30	2¼	June 14	2½
Apr. 7	4	July 3	7¼	**1990**		Aug. 10	2½	Sept. 27	2¾
Nov. 20	4½	Aug. 21	7¾	Dec. 18	6½	Sept. 21	2¾	Dec. 20	3
1968		Sept. 22	8	**1991**		Nov. 10	3	**2019**	
Mar. 22	5	Oct. 16	8½	Apr. 30	5½	Dec. 14	3¼	Aug. 1	2¾
Apr. 19	5½	Nov. 1	9½	Sept. 13	5	**2005**		Sept. 19	2½
Aug. 30	5¼	**1979**		Nov. 6	4½	Feb. 2	3½	Oct. 31	2¼
Dec. 18	5½	July 20	10	Dec. 20	3½	Mar. 22	3¾	**2020**	
1969		Aug. 17	10½	**1992**		May 3	4	Mar. 4	1¾
Apr. 4	6	Sept. 19	11	July 2	3	June 30	4¼	Mar. 16	¼
1970		Oct. 8	12	**1994**		Aug. 9	4½		
Nov. 13	5¾	**1980**		May 17	3½	Sept. 20	4¾		
Dec. 4	5½	Feb. 15	13	Aug. 16	4	Nov. 1	5		
		May 30	12	Nov. 15	4¾	Dec. 13	5¼		
		June 13	11						
		July 28	10						

S&P 500 Index, 1965-2020
Source: S&P Dow Jones Indices
(as of Oct. 10, 2020)

Year	Highest close		Lowest close		Year	Highest close		Lowest close	
1965	Nov. 15	92.63	June 28	81.60	2009	Dec. 28	1,127.78	Mar. 9	676.53
1970	Jan. 5	93.46	May 26	69.29	2010	Dec. 29	1,259.78	July 2	1,022.58
1975	July 15	95.61	Jan. 8	70.04	2011	Apr. 29	1,363.61	Oct. 3	1,099.23
1980	Nov. 28	140.52	Mar. 27	98.22	2012	Sept. 14	1,465.77	Jan. 3	1,277.06
1985	Dec. 16	212.02	Jan. 4	163.68	2013	Dec. 31	1,848.36	Jan. 8	1,457.15
1990	July 16	368.95	Oct. 11	295.46	2014	Dec. 29	2,090.57	Feb. 3	1,741.89
1995	Dec. 13	621.69	Jan. 3	459.11	2015	May 21	2,130.82	Aug. 25	1,867.61
2000	Mar. 24	1,527.46	Dec. 20	1,264.74	2016	Dec. 13	2,271.72	Feb. 11	1,829.08
2005	Dec. 14	1,272.74	Apr. 20	1,137.50	2017	Dec. 18	2,690.16	Jan. 3	2,257.83
2006	Dec. 15	1,427.09	June 13	1,223.69	2018	Sept. 20	2,930.75	Dec. 24	2,351.10
2007	Oct. 9	1,565.15	Mar. 5	1,374.12	2019	Dec. 27	3,240.02	Jan. 3	2,447.89
2006	Jan. 2	1,447.16	Nov. 20	752.44	2020	Sept. 2	3,580.84	Mar. 23	2,237.40

U.S. Holdings of Foreign Securities, 2005-18
Source: *U.S. Portfolio Holdings of Foreign Securities*, U.S. Dept. of the Treasury
(in billions of dollars; countries within each region ranked by 2018 holdings)

Country	2005	2010	2015	2017	2018	Country	2005	2010	2015	2017	2018
Europe	$2,297	$3,154	$4,472	$5,459	$4,875	Latin America					
United Kingdom	815	1,001	1,240	1,473	1,360	and Caribbean	$739	$1,064	$1,959	$2,708	$2,561
France	274	366	474	605	563	Cayman Islands[1]	249	366	1,217	1,767	1,742
Ireland	75	132	498	495	503	Bermuda[1]	187	160	217	263	236
Switzerland	196	327	420	506	458	Brazil	90	235	116	182	169
Netherlands	192	233	404	538	456	Mexico	86	109	148	163	146
Germany	217	299	378	494	402	Curaçao[2]	47	83	70	73	36
Sweden	75	122	138	172	144	British Virgin					
Luxembourg	46	100	128	146	139	Islands[1]	8	16	63	67	65
Spain	70	87	115	158	139	Asia	940	1,342	1,817	2,585	2,275
Italy[1]	79	66	107	140	115	Japan	531	519	822	1,132	1,010
Jersey[1]	19	42	92	123	101	South Korea	119	148	171	263	213
Denmark	25	49	90	110	84	India	33	91	130	194	176
Canada	419	695	705	996	981	Hong Kong	46	135	136	164	171
Australia	128	323	296	355	333	China	28	102	108	162	159
Africa	46	99	104	178	148	Taiwan	58	95	108	178	158
South Africa	34	78	63	115	91	Singapore	36	64	99	171	89
Israel	44	64	80	66	65	Total	4,609	6,763	9,455	12,409	11,297

Note: Totals include countries not shown. (1) Not included in UK totals though it is a territory/dependency. (2) Figures are for Netherlands Antilles prior to 2013.

Record One-Day Gains and Losses of the Dow Jones Industrial Average
Source: S&P Dow Jones Indices
(ranked by largest one-day losses and gains for two terms; as of Oct. 10, 2020)

Greatest % gains

Rank	Date	Close	Net chg.	% chg.
1.	3/15/1933	62.10	8.26	15.34%
2.	10/6/1931	99.34	12.86	14.87
3.	10/30/1929	258.47	28.40	12.34
4.	3/24/2020	20,704.91	2,112.98	11.37
5.	9/21/1932	75.16	7.67	11.36

Greatest point gains

Rank	Date	Close	Net chg.	% chg.
1.	3/24/2020	20,704.91	2,112.98	11.37%
2.	3/13/2020	23,185.62	1,985.00	9.36
3.	4/6/2020	22,679.99	1,627.46	7.73
4.	3/26/2020	22,552.17	1,351.62	6.38
5.	3/2/2020	26,703.32	1,293.97	5.09

Greatest % losses

Rank	Date	Close	Net chg.	% chg.
1.	12/12/1914	54.62	−16.80	−23.52%
2.	10/19/1987	1,738.74	−508.00	−22.61
3.	3/16/2020	20,188.52	−2,997.10	−12.93
4.	10/28/1929	260.64	−38.33	−12.82
5.	10/29/1929	230.07	−30.57	−11.73

Greatest point losses

Rank	Date	Close	Net chg.	% chg.
1.	3/16/2020	20,188.52	−2,997.10	−12.93%
2.	3/12/2020	21,200.62	−2,352.60	−9.99
3.	3/9/2020	23,851.02	−2,013.76	−7.79
4.	6/11/2020	25,128.17	−1,861.82	−6.90
5.	3/11/2020	23,553.22	−1,464.95	−5.86

Dow Jones Industrial Average, 1965-2020
Source: S&P Dow Jones Indices
(as of Oct. 10, 2020)

Year	Highest close		Lowest close		Year	Highest close		Lowest close	
1965	Dec. 31	969.26	June 28	840.59	2005	Mar. 4	10,940.50	Apr. 20	10,012.36
1970	Dec. 29	842.00	May 6	631.16	2006	Dec. 27	12,510.57	Jan. 20	10,667.39
1975	July 15	881.81	Jan. 2	632.04	2007	Oct. 9	14,164.53	Mar. 5	12,050.41
1980	Nov. 20	1,000.17	Apr. 21	759.13	2008	Jan. 3	13,056.72	Nov. 20	7,552.29
1985	Dec. 16	1,553.10	Jan. 4	1,184.96	2009	Dec. 30	10,548.51	Mar. 9	6,547.05
1990	July 16	2,999.75	Oct. 11	2,365.10	2010	Dec. 29	11,585.38	July 2	9,686.48
1995	Dec. 13	5,216.47	Jan. 30	3,832.08	2011	Apr. 29	12,810.54	Oct. 3	10,655.30
1996	Dec. 27	6,560.91	Jan. 10	5,032.94	2012	Oct. 5	13,610.15	June 4	12,101.46
1997	Aug. 6	8,259.31	Apr. 11	6,391.69	2013	Dec. 31	16,576.66	Jan. 8	13,328.85
1998	Nov. 23	9,374.27	Aug. 31	7,539.07	2014	Dec. 26	18,053.71	Feb. 3	15,372.80
1999	Dec. 31	11,497.12	Jan. 22	9,120.67	2015	May 19	18,312.39	Aug. 25	15,666.44
2000	Jan. 14	11,722.98	Mar. 7	9,796.03	2016	Dec. 20	19,974.62	Feb. 11	15,660.18
2001	May 21	11,337.92	Sept. 21	8,235.81	2017	Dec. 28	24,837.51	Jan. 19	19,732.40
2002	Mar. 19	10,635.25	Oct. 9	7,286.27	2018	Oct. 3	26,828.39	Dec. 24	21,792.20
2003	Dec. 31	10,453.90	Mar. 11	7,524.06	2019	Dec. 27	28,645.26	Jan. 3	22,686.22
2004	Dec. 28	10,854.54	Oct. 25	9,749.99	2020	Feb. 12	29,551.42	Mar. 23	18,591.93

Milestones of the Dow Jones Industrial Average
(as of Oct. 10, 2020)

First close over—		First close over—		First close over—		First close over—	
100	Jan. 12, 1906	3,500	May 19, 1993	9,000	Apr. 6, 1998	16,000	Nov. 21, 2013	23,000	Oct. 17, 2017
500	Mar. 12, 1956	4,000	Feb. 23, 1995	10,000	Mar. 29, 1999	17,000	July 3, 2014	24,000	Nov. 30, 2017
1,000	Nov. 14, 1972	4,500	June 16, 1995	11,000	May 3, 1999	18,000	Dec. 23, 2014	25,000	Jan. 4, 2018
1,500	Dec. 11, 1985	5,000	Nov. 21, 1995	12,000	Oct. 19, 2006	19,000	Nov. 22, 2016	26,000	Jan. 16, 2018
2,000	Jan. 8, 1987	6,000	Oct. 14, 1996	13,000	Apr. 25, 2007	20,000	Jan. 25, 2017	27,000	July 11, 2019
2,500	July 17, 1987	7,000	Feb. 13, 1997	14,000	July 19, 2007	21,000	Mar. 1, 2017	28,000	Nov. 15, 2019
3,000	Apr. 17, 1991	8,000	July 16, 1997	15,000	June 27, 2013	22,000	Aug. 2, 2017	29,000	Jan. 15, 2020

Components of the Dow Jones Averages
(as of Oct. 10, 2020)

Dow Jones Industrial Average

- 3M Co. (MMM)
- American Express Co. (AXP)
- Amgen (AMGN)
- Apple Inc. (AAPL)
- Boeing Co. (BA)
- Caterpillar Inc. (CAT)
- Chevron Corp. (CVX)
- Cisco Systems Inc. (CSCO)
- Coca-Cola Co. (KO)
- Dow Inc. (DOW)
- Goldman Sachs Group Inc. (GS)

- Home Depot Inc. (HD)
- Honeywell International (HON)
- Intel Corp. (INTC)
- International Business Machines Corp. (IBM)
- Johnson & Johnson (JNJ)
- JPMorgan Chase & Co. (JPM)
- McDonald's Corp. (MCD)
- Merck & Co. Inc. (MRK)
- Microsoft Corp. (MSFT)

- Nike Inc. (NKE)
- Procter & Gamble Co. (PG)
- Salesforce.com (CRM)
- Travelers Companies Inc. (TRV)
- UnitedHealth Group Inc. (UNH)
- Verizon Communications Inc. (VZ)
- Visa Inc. (V)
- Walgreens Boots Alliance (WBA)
- Walmart Inc. (WMT)
- Walt Disney Co. (DIS)

Dow Jones Utility Average

- AES Corp. (AES)
- American Electric Power Co. Inc. (AEP)
- American Water Works Co. Inc. (AWK)
- CenterPoint Energy Inc. (CNP)
- Consolidated Edison Inc. (ED)

- Dominion Energy Inc. (D)
- Duke Energy Corp. (DUK)
- Edison International (EIX)
- Exelon Corp. (EXC)
- FirstEnergy Corp. (FE)
- NextEra Energy Inc. (NEE)

- NiSource Inc. (NI)
- PG&E Corp. (PCG)
- Public Service Enterprise Group Inc. (PEG)
- Southern Co. (SO)

Dow Jones Transportation Average

- Alaska Air Group Inc. (ALK)
- American Airlines Group Inc. (AAL)
- Avis Budget Group Inc. (CAR)
- C.H. Robinson Worldwide Inc. (CHRW)
- CSX Corp. (CSX)
- Delta Air Lines Inc. (DAL)
- Expeditors International of Washington Inc. (EXPD)

- FedEx Corp. (FDX)
- J.B. Hunt Transport Services Inc. (JBHT)
- JetBlue Airways Corp. (JBLU)
- Kansas City Southern (KSU)
- Kirby Corp. (KEX)
- Landstar System Inc. (LSTR)

- Matson Inc. (MATX)
- Norfolk Southern Corp. (NSC)
- Ryder System Inc. (R)
- Southwest Airlines Co. (LUV)
- Union Pacific Corp. (UNP)
- United Airlines Holdings Inc. (UAL)
- United Parcel Service Inc. (UPS)

Record One-Day Gains and Losses of the Nasdaq Composite Index
Source: Nasdaq, Inc.
(ranked by largest one-day losses and gains for two terms; as of Oct. 10, 2020)

Greatest point gains			Greatest % gains			Greatest point losses			Greatest % losses		
Rank	Date	Change	Rank	Date	% change	Rank	Date	Change	Rank	Date	% change
1.	3/13/2020	673.07	1.	1/3/2001	14.17%	1.	3/16/2020	−970.28	1.	3/16/2020	−12.32%
2.	3/24/2020	557.18	2.	10/13/2008	11.81	2.	3/12/2020	−750.24	2.	10/19/1987	−11.35
3.	4/6/2020	540.15	3.	12/5/2000	10.48	3.	3/9/2020	−624.94	3.	4/14/2000	−9.67
4.	3/17/2020	430.18	4.	10/28/2008	9.53	4.	9/3/2020	−598.34	4.	3/12/2020	−9.43
5.	3/26/2020	413.24	5.	3/13/2020	9.35	5.	6/11/2020	−527.61	5.	9/29/2008	−9.14
6.	3/10/2020	393.57	6.	4/5/2001	8.92	6.	9/8/2020	−465.44	6.	10/20/1987	−9.00
7.	3/2/2020	384.79	7.	4/18/2001	8.12	7.	2/27/2020	−414.29	7.	10/26/1987	−9.00
8.	12/26/2018	361.43	8.	3/24/2020	8.12	8.	3/11/2020	−392.20	8.	12/1/2008	−8.95
9.	3/4/2020	333.99	9.	5/30/2000	7.94	9.	4/14/2000	−355.49	9.	8/31/1998	−8.56
10.	1/3/2001	324.83	10.	10/13/2000	7.87	10.	2/24/2020	−355.31	10.	10/15/2008	−8.47

Nasdaq Composite Index Closing Prices, 1971-2020
Source: Nasdaq, Inc.; as of Oct. 10, 2020

Year	High	Low	Year	High	Low	Year	High	Low	Year	High	Low
1971	114.12	99.68	1984	288.41	223.91	1997	1,748.62	1,194.39	2009	2,167.70	1,265.52
1972	135.15	113.65	1985	325.53	245.82	1998	2,200.63	1,357.09	2010	2,671.48	2,091.79
1973	136.84	88.67	1986	411.21	322.14	1999	4,090.61	2,193.13	2011	2,873.54	2,335.83
1974	96.53	54.87	1987	456.27	288.49	2000	5,048.62	2,332.78	2012	3,183.95	2,648.36
1975	88.00	60.70	1988	397.54	329.00	2001	2,892.36	1,387.06	2013	4,176.59	3,091.81
1976	97.88	78.06	1989	487.60	376.87	2002	2,059.38	1,114.11	2014	4,806.91	3,996.96
1977	105.05	93.66	1990	470.30	322.93	2003	2,009.88	1,271.47	2015	5,218.86	4,506.49
1978	139.25	99.09	1991	586.35	352.85	2004	2,178.00	1,752.00	2016	5,487.44	4,266.84
1979	152.29	117.84	1992	676.95	545.85	2005	2,273.37	1,904.18	2017	6,965.36	5,429.09
1980	208.29	124.09	1993	790.56	645.02	2006	2,465.98	2,020.39	2018	8,109.69	6,192.92
1981	223.96	170.80	1994	803.93	691.23	2007	2,811.61	2,340.68	2019	9,022.39	6,463.50
1982	241.63	158.92	1995	1,072.82	740.53	2008	2,609.63	1,505.90	2020	12,056.44	6,860.67
1983	329.11	229.88	1996	1,328.45	978.17						

Average Yields of Treasury, Corporate, and State and Local Bonds, 1977-2020

Source: Office of Market Finance, U.S. Dept. of the Treasury; Federal Reserve System

Year	Treasury 30-year bonds[1]	New Aa corporate bonds[2]	State and local bonds[3]	Year	Treasury 30-year bonds[1]	New Aa corporate bonds[2]	State and local bonds[3]	Year	Treasury 30-year bonds[1]	New Aa corporate bonds[2]	State and local bonds[3]
1977	7.75%	8.02%	5.68%	1992	7.67%	8.14%	6.44%	2007	4.84%	5.56%	4.40%
1978	8.49	8.73	6.03	1993	6.59	7.22	5.59	2008	4.28	5.63	4.85
1979	9.28	9.63	6.52	1994	7.37	7.96	6.19	2009	4.08	5.31	4.62
1980	11.27	11.94	8.55	1995	6.88	7.59	5.95	2010	4.25	4.94	4.30
1981	13.45	14.17	11.34	1996	6.71	7.37	5.76	2011	3.91	4.64	4.50
1982	12.76	13.79	11.64	1997	6.61	7.26	5.52	2012	2.92	3.67	3.73
1983	11.18	12.04	9.51	1998	5.58	6.53	5.09	2013	3.45	4.24	4.26
1984	12.41	12.71	10.10	1999	5.87	7.04	5.43	2014	3.34	4.16	4.24
1985	10.79	11.37	9.11	2000	5.94	7.62	5.71	2015	2.84	3.89	3.65
1986	7.78	9.02	7.34	2001	5.49	7.08	5.15	2016	2.59	3.67	3.14
1987	8.59	9.38	7.65	2002	5.43	6.49	5.04	2017	2.89	3.74	NA
1988	8.96	9.71	7.68	2003	4.96	5.67	4.75	2018	3.11	3.93	NA
1989	8.45	9.26	7.23	2004	5.04	5.63	4.68	2019	2.58	3.39	NA
1990	8.61	9.32	7.27	2005	4.64	5.24	4.40	2020[4]	1.49	2.44	NA
1991	8.14	8.77	6.92	2006	4.91	5.59	4.40				

NA = Not available. (1) On Feb. 18, 2002, the U.S. Treasury discontinued the 30-year constant maturity yield and reintroduced it on Feb. 9, 2006; rates in the interim are for 20-year yields. (2) Treasury series based on 3-week moving average of reoffering yields of new corporate bonds rated Aa by Moody's Investors Service with an original maturity of at least 20 years. Treasury discontinued yield index after Jan. 31, 2003. Rates thereafter are for Moody's seasoned Aaa corporate bonds as listed by Federal Reserve. (3) Index of new reoffering yields on 20-year general obligations rated Aa by Moody's Investors Service; discontinued by Treasury Jan. 31, 2003; rates thereafter are from Bond Buyer Index of general obligation, 20 years to maturity, mixed quality state and local bonds. (4) Rates are for June 2020.

Ownership of U.S. Treasury Securities, 1990-2019

Source: *Treasury Bulletin, Sept. 2020*, Financial Management Service, U.S. Dept. of the Treasury

In 1990, just over 14% of U.S. treasury securities were held by foreign and international investors. By 2019, the total public debt had more than sextupled, while the portion held by investors outside the U.S. had more than doubled, to 29%.

(in billions of dollars)

	1990	1995	2000	2005	2010	2015	2017	2018	2019
Total public debt	$3,365	$4,989	$5,662	$8,170	$14,025	$18,922	$20,493	$21,974	$23,201
Federal Reserve and intra-governmental holdings	1,060	1,681	2,782	4,200	5,656	7,711	8,132	8,095	8,360
Total privately held	2,305	3,308	2,880	3,971	8,369	11,211	12,361	13,879	14,842
Depository institutions	207	315	261	129	319	547	638	772	938
U.S. savings bonds	126	185	185	205	188	172	160	156	151
Private pension funds[1]	130	142	182	184	207	505	432	671	732
Pension funds of state and local governments	145	192	206	154	154	175	289	373	383
Insurance companies	138	242	117	202	248	307	373	204	215
Mutual funds	163	287	338	254	722	1,318	1,798	2,023	2,351
State and local governments	411	290	246	512	596	681	733	691	712
Foreign and international	487	835	1,201	2,034	4,436	6,146	6,211	6,270	6,691
Other investors[2]	500	821	145	295	1,500	1,360	1,727	2,720	2,669

(1) Includes securities held by the Federal Employees Retirement System Thrift Savings Plan "G Fund." (2) Includes individuals, government-sponsored enterprises, brokers and dealers, bank personal trusts and estates, corporate and noncorporate businesses, and other investors.

Financial Assets of U.S. Families, 1989-2016

Source: Survey of Consumer Finances (triennial), Federal Reserve System

Category	1989	1992	1995	1998	2001	2004	2007	2010	2013	2016
Median net worth (thous.)	$47.2	$61.3	$66.4	$78.0	$106.1	$107.2	$126.4	$77.3	$83.7	$97.3
Average net worth (thous.)	183.7	230.5	244.8	307.4	487.0	517.1	584.6	498.8	551.3	692.1
				Percent of families holding asset						
Any asset	NA	NA	96.3%	96.8%	96.7%	97.9%	97.7%	97.4%	97.9%	99.4%
Any financial asset	88.4%	90.7%	91.0	92.9	93.1	93.8	93.9	94.0	94.5	98.5
Transaction accounts	85.1	87.5	87.0	90.5	90.9	91.3	92.1	92.5	93.2	98.0
Certificates of deposit	19.4	16.6	14.3	15.3	15.7	12.7	16.1	12.2	7.8	6.5
Savings bonds	23.8	22.7	22.8	19.3	16.7	17.6	14.9	12.0	10.0	8.6
Bonds	5.3	4.7	3.1	3.0	3.0	1.8	1.6	1.6	1.4	1.2
Stocks	16.2	17.8	15.2	19.2	21.3	20.7	17.9	15.1	13.8	13.9
Pooled investment funds (mutual funds)	7.1	11.2	12.3	16.5	17.7	15.0	11.4	8.7	8.2	10.0
Retirement accounts	35.4	39.3	45.2	48.8	52.2	49.7	52.6	50.4	49.2	52.1
Cash value life insurance	34.7	35.3	32.0	29.6	28.0	24.2	23.0	19.7	19.2	19.4
Other managed assets	3.5	4.3	3.9	5.9	6.6	7.3	5.8	5.7	5.2	5.5
Other	13.4	11.4	11.1	9.4	9.3	10.0	9.3	8.0	6.9	8.1
Any nonfinancial asset	89.1	91.3	90.9	89.9	90.7	92.5	92.0	91.3	91.0	90.8
Vehicles	83.6	86.4	84.1	82.8	84.8	86.3	87.0	86.7	86.3	85.2
Primary residence	63.8	63.8	64.7	66.2	67.7	69.1	68.6	67.3	65.2	63.7
Other residential property	20.0	20.0	11.8	12.8	11.3	12.5	13.7	14.3	13.2	13.8
Equity in nonresidential property	NA	NA	9.4	8.6	8.3	8.3	8.1	7.7	7.2	6.2
Business equity	13.2	14.9	11.1	11.5	11.8	11.5	12.0	13.3	11.7	13.0
Other	11.9	8.5	9.0	8.5	7.6	7.8	7.2	7.0	7.3	6.5

NA = Not available.

Characteristics of Mutual Fund Investors, 2019

Source: *Investment Company Fact Book 2020*, Investment Company Institute

Median age of head of household	51	Married or living with a partner	68%
Median annual household income	$100,000	Four-year college degree or more	54%
Median household financial assets	$250,000	Hold more than half their financial assets in	
Median mutual fund assets	$150,000	mutual funds	67%
Median number of funds owned	4	Own Individual Retirement Accounts (IRAs)	65%
Employed	77%	Own defined contribution retirement plan accounts	84%

Total Assets and New Cash Flow of Mutual Funds by Type, 2000-19

Source: *Investment Company Fact Book 2020*, Investment Company Institute

Sector	2000	2005	2010	2015	2016	2017	2018	2019
				Total net assets (year-end, in mil)				
Consumer.........	$1,042	$1,405	$3,113	$9,514	$8,962	$8,946	$7,925	$9,354
Financial..........	16,087	11,837	6,286	10,222	12,025	14,099	10,600	10,816
Health............	45,921	45,398	32,507	124,538	93,121	104,465	101,961	116,209
Natural resources...	2,885	11,972	22,714	28,988	39,256	37,720	29,472	28,880
Precious metals	1,143	7,003	23,065	4,487	6,882	7,277	3,780	5,368
Real estate........	11,675	59,158	55,120	101,459	105,701	111,353	94,209	115,884
Tech./telecom......	103,853	34,366	30,738	47,088	46,956	62,450	57,421	80,264
Utilities	22,908	28,390	33,332	32,516	38,543	35,539	29,000	32,202
Other sectors	3,917	3,189	4,597	7,006	8,014	9,727	6,633	7,722
				New net cash flow[1] (annual, in mil)				
Consumer.........	−$122	−$209	$101	$2,235	−$913	−$1,481	−$429	−$657
Financial..........	−534	−1,586	−626	978	49	208	−1,311	−2,471
Health............	9,256	836	−2,407	11,007	−17,602	−8,496	−4,071	−10,306
Natural resources...	248	3,471	1,493	−688	3,053	−2,489	−2,972	−3,811
Precious metals	−214	1,027	2,330	−37	325	−108	−505	87
Real estate........	339	3,000	1,746	−4,552	−771	−6,603	−11,439	−3,267
Tech./telecom......	43,837	−8,541	−1,391	288	−3,953	−932	−2,858	−1,659
Utilities	1,201	3,311	−848	−2,585	−1,155	−5,234	−4,043	−2,446
Other sectors	−187	121	724	−1,510	154	74	−1,411	−461

(1) Dollar value of new sales minus redemptions combined with net exchanges.

Mutual Fund Ownership, 1940-2019

Source: *Investment Company Fact Book 2020*, Investment Company Institute

Year	Mutual funds	Mutual fund accounts (thous.)	Total net assets (bil)	Households owning mutual funds		Exchange-traded funds (ETFs)	
				Number (thous.)	Percent of all households	Number of funds	Total net assets (bil)
1940	68	296	$0.45	NA	NA	NA	NA
1950	98	939	2.53	NA	NA	NA	NA
1960	161	4,898	17.03	NA	NA	NA	NA
1970	361	10,690	47.62	NA	NA	NA	NA
1980	564	12,088	134.76	4,600	5.7%	NA	NA
1990	3,078	61,948	1,064.34	23,400	25.1	NA	NA
2000	8,134	244,705	6,955.94	48,600	45.7	80	$65.59
2005	7,967	277,713	8,888.70	50,300	44.4	204	300.82
2006	8,106	288,596	10,395.24	49,900	43.6	359	422.55
2007	8,019	292,555	11,995.19	50,600	43.6	629	608.42
2008	8,022	264,599	9,618.69	52,500	45.0	728	531.29
2009	7,651	269,224	11,108.97	50,400	43.0	797	777.13
2010	7,546	291,299	11,831.06	53,200	45.3	923	991.99
2011	7,581	279,715	11,630.37	52,900	44.1	1,135	1,048.14
2012	7,596	257,074	13,053.59	53,800	44.4	1,195	1,337.12
2013	7,721	264,848	15,048.93	56,700	46.3	1,295	1,674.71
2014	7,934	NA	15,876.62	53,200	43.3	1,412	1,974.55
2015	8,121	NA	15,657.87	53,600	43.0	1,597	2,100.68
2016	8,073	NA	16,353.46	54,900	43.6	1,718	2,524.55
2017	7,966	NA	18,764.91	56,200	44.5	1,837	3,401.04
2018	8,094	NA	17,709.73	57,200	44.8	1,990	3,371.16
2019	7,945	NA	21,291.52	59,700	46.4	2,096	4,396.21

NA = Not available. **Note:** Does not include data for funds that invest primarily in other mutual funds. Mutual fund accounts data include both individual and omnibus accounts.

World's Leading Gold Producers, 1980-2019

Source: *Mineral Commodity Summaries 2020*, U.S. Geological Survey, U.S. Dept. of the Interior
(ranked by 2019 production; in thousands of troy ounces)

Country	1980	1990	2000	2005	2010	2014	2015	2016	2017	2018	2019[1]
China	225	3,215	5,787	7,234	11,092	14,468	14,468	14,564	13,696	12,892	13,503
Australia	548	7,845	9,530	8,423	8,391	8,809	8,938	9,324	9,677	10,127	10,610
Russia[2].........	8,300	9,710	4,598	5,279	6,173	7,941	8,102	8,134	8,681	9,999	9,967
United States	970	9,452	11,349	8,231	7,427	6,752	6,880	7,137	7,620	7,266	6,430
Canada........	1,627	5,433	5,022	3,844	2,926	4,887	4,919	5,305	5,273	5,884	5,787
Indonesia	60	360	4,006	4,200	3,858	2,218	3,119	2,572	2,411	4,340	5,144
Ghana..........	353	540	2,318	2,149	2,637	2,926	2,829	2,540	4,115	4,083	4,180
Peru	134	293	4,263	6,682	5,273	4,501	4,662	4,919	4,855	4,598	4,180
Mexico	196	311	848	976	2,347	3,794	4,340	3,569	4,051	3,762	3,537
Kazakhstan......	NA	NA	NA	NA	NA	NA	NA	2,218	2,733	3,215	3,215
Uzbekistan	NA	NA	2,733	2,894	2,894	3,215	3,279	3,279	3,344	3,344	3,215
South Africa	21,669	19,451	13,767	9,474	6,076	4,887	4,662	4,662	4,405	3,762	2,894
Brazil..........	NA	NA	NA	NA	1,865	2,572	2,604	2,733	2,572	2,733	2,733
Argentina	NA	NA	NA	NA	NA	NA	NA	NA	NA	2,315	2,315
Papua New Guinea	NA	NA	NA	NA	2,186	1,704	1,929	1,993	2,058	2,154	2,251
World[3]	39,197	70,089	82,949	79,412	82,306	96,131	99,667	99,989	103,847	106,097	106,097

NA = Not available. **Note:** One metric ton is equal to 32,150.7 troy ounces. (1) Estimated. (2) Figures for 1980-90 refer to the former USSR. Includes gold recovered as a byproduct but excludes secondary production. (3) Includes countries not shown here.

Gold Owned by the U.S., 2020

Source: *Status Report of U.S. Treasury-Owned Gold,* Bureau of the Fiscal Service, U.S. Dept. of the Treasury
(as of Aug. 31, 2020; numbers may not add to totals due to rounding)

	Fine troy ounces	Book value		Fine troy ounces	Book value
Total Treasury-owned gold	261,498,926	$11,041,059,958	**Held by the Federal Reserve**		
Gold bullion................	258,641,878	10,920,429,099	**Bank**...................	13,452,811	$568,007,257
Gold coins, blanks,			Gold bullion...............	13,378,981	564,890,013
miscellaneous.............	2,857,048	120,630,859	Federal Reserve Banks–		
Held by the U.S. Mint	248,046,116	10,473,052,701	NY vault.................	13,376,988	564,805,851
Denver, CO, deep storage	43,853,707	1,851,599,996	Federal Reserve Banks–display	1,993	84,162
Fort Knox, KY, deep storage ...	147,341,858	6,221,097,413	Gold coins.................	73,830	3,117,244
West Point, NY, deep storage ...	54,067,331	2,282,841,677	Federal Reserve Banks–		
Gold coins, blanks,			NY vault.................	73,452	3,101,308
miscellaneous.............	2,783,219	117,513,615	Federal Reserve Banks–display	377	15,936

Prices of Precious Metals, 1990-2019

Source: *Mineral Commodity Summaries 2020,* U.S. Geological Survey, U.S. Dept. of the Interior

	Dollars per troy ounce					Dollars per pound			
Year	Platinum[1]	Palladium[1]	Rhodium[1]	Gold	Silver	Copper[2]	Lead[3]	Tin[4]	Zinc[5]
1990	$467	NA	NA	$385	$4.82	$1.23	$0.46	$3.86	$0.75
1995	425	$153	$463	386	5.15	1.38	0.42	4.16	0.56
2000	549	692	1,990	280	5.00	0.88	0.44	3.70	0.56
2001	533	611	1,600	272	4.39	0.77	0.44	3.15	0.44
2002	543	340	839	311	4.62	0.76	0.44	2.92	0.39
2003	694	203	530	365	4.91	0.85	0.44	3.40	0.41
2004	849	233	983	411	6.69	1.34	0.55	5.47	0.52
2005	900	204	2,060	446	7.34	1.74	0.61	4.83	0.67
2006	1,144	323	4,561	606	11.57	3.15	0.77	5.65	1.59
2007	1,308	357	6,203	699	13.41	3.28	1.24	8.99	1.54
2008	1,578	355	6,534	874	15.00	3.19	1.20	11.29	0.89
2009	1,208	266	1,591	975	14.69	2.41	0.87	8.37	0.78
2010	1,616	531	2,459	1,228	20.20	3.48	1.09	12.40	1.02
2011	1,725	739	2,204	1,572	35.28	4.06	1.22	15.75	1.06
2012	1,555	649	1,275	1,673	31.22	3.67	1.14	12.83	0.96
2013	1,490	730	1,069	1,415	23.87	3.40	1.10	13.52	0.96
2014	1,388	810	1,174	1,269	19.09	3.18	1.06	10.23	1.07
2015	1,056	695	955	1,163	15.72	2.56	0.91	7.56	0.96
2016	990	617	697	1,252	17.20	2.25	0.94	8.39	1.01
2017	951	874	1,113	1,261	17.07	2.85	1.15	9.37	1.39
2018	883	1,036	2,225	1,272	15.75	2.99	1.11	9.36	1.41
2019[E]	850	1,500	3,300	1,400	16.20	2.80	1.00	8.60	1.25

E = Estimated. (1) Average annual dealer prices. (2) U.S. producer price for cathode copper. (3) North American producer price through 2012; North American market price thereafter. (4) *Platts Metals Week* composite price through 2013, New York dealer prices thereafter. (5) *Platts Metals Week* price for North American special high grade zinc except for 1990, which shows average price for high grade zinc.

Top Brands in Selected Categories, 2018-20

Source: Information Resources, Inc., a Chicago-based marketing research company

Data, for the 52-week periods ending Aug. 9, 2019, and 2020, represent "Total U.S. Multi-Outlet Sales," which includes grocery, drug, mass market, and select club, military, and dollar retailers. Brands are ranked by 2019-20 sales. Percent change represents dollar sales change in 2019-20 over same period in 2018-19; market share is for 2019-20.

Product	Sales (mil) 2018-19	2019-20	% change	Market share	Product	Sales (mil) 2018-19	2019-20	% change	Market share
Beer, domestic, total ..	$12,929	$15,009	16.1%		Kellogg's Frosted				
Bud Light..........	1,815	1,846	1.7	12.30%	Flakes	$403	$438	8.7%	4.89%
Michelob Ultra......	975	1,172	20.3	7.81	Gen. Mills Cinnamon				
Coors Light	998	1,061	6.3	7.07	Toast Crunch......	389	433	11.5	4.83
Miller Lite..........	914	992	8.5	6.61	Post Honey Bunches				
Budweiser..........	636	658	3.5	4.39	of Oats..........	389	413	6.2	4.60
Bottled water, total ..	$8,736	$9,280	6.2%						
Private label[1]........	2,705	2,992	10.6	32.25%	**Chocolate candy[2], total..**	$4,884	$5,226	7.0%	
Aquafina	649	705	8.6	7.60	M&M's	815	895	9.8	17.12%
Dasani	683	695	1.8	7.49	Hershey's	395	469	18.8	8.97
Nestlé Pure Life	641	612	–4.5	6.59	Reese's	300	355	18.4	6.79
Poland Spring	519	508	–2.2	5.47	Lindt Lindor	191	213	11.7	4.08
Cat food (dry), total ...	$2,400	$2,448	2.0%		Mars	215	211	–1.7	4.05
Private label[1]........	216	211	–2.5	8.61%	**Coffee (ground), total..**	$3,913	$4,075	4.2%	
Purina Kit & Kaboodle	200	209	4.1	8.52	Folgers	1,014	1,005	–0.9	24.67%
Meow Mix Original					Starbucks...........	461	527	14.3	12.92
Choice	201	202	0.8	8.27	Private label[1]........	415	425	2.3	10.42
Purina Cat Chow					Maxwell House	458	415	–9.3	10.19
Complete	111	155	40.0	6.34	Dunkin' Donuts	300	321	6.9	7.87
Meow Mix Tender					**Cookies, total ....**	$8,066	$8,691	7.7%	
Centers	100	121	21.0	4.96	Private label[1]........	1,379	1,419	3.0	16.33%
Cereal (ready-to-eat), total ..	$8,385	$8,973	7.0%		Nabisco Oreo	719	857	19.2	9.86
Private label[1]........	570	575	1.0	6.41%	Nabisco Chips Ahoy!	611	682	11.7	7.85
Gen. Mills Honey Nut									
Cheerios	454	525	15.7	5.86					

Product	Sales (mil) 2018-19	Sales (mil) 2019-20	% change	Market share
BelVita	$354	$373	5.4%	4.29%
Nabisco Oreo Double Stuf	297	351	18.2	4.04
Disposable diapers, total	**$3,724**	**$3,654**	**−1.9%**	
Private label[1]	703	680	−3.2	18.61%
Pampers Swaddlers	568	549	−3.3	15.03
Luvs Ultra Leak-guards	459	412	−10.2	11.28
Huggies Little Movers Disney Baby	354	393	10.9	10.74
Huggies Snug & Dry Disney Baby	320	249	−22.4	6.80
Dog food (dry), total	**$5,362**	**$5,417**	**1.0%**	
Private label[1]	752	689	−8.3	12.72%
Pedigree	632	638	0.9	11.78
Purina Dog Chow	476	523	9.8	9.65
Purina One Smart Blend	408	460	12.7	8.48
Iams Proactive Health	306	305	−0.6	5.62
Ice cream, total	**$5,507**	**$6,152**	**11.7%**	
Private label[1]	1,056	1,229	16.5	19.98%
Blue Bell	511	592	15.7	9.62
Häagen-Dazs	497	538	8.3	8.74
Ben & Jerry's	437	530	21.2	8.61
Breyers	369	407	10.1	6.61
Pasta, total	**$1,878**	**$2,260**	**20.4%**	
Barilla	587	704	19.8	31.14%
Private label[1]	528	615	16.4	27.19
Ronzoni	103	126	22.5	5.57
Mueller's	65	77	18.8	3.41
De Cecco	55	74	34.1	3.28
Potato chips, total	**$5,937**	**$6,449**	**8.6%**	
Lay's	1,702	1,924	13.0	29.83%
Ruffles	736	821	11.6	12.73
Pringles	630	675	7.1	10.47
Private label[1]	521	558	7.0	8.65
Wavy Lay's	462	359	−22.3	5.57

Product	Sales (mil) 2018-19	Sales (mil) 2019-20	% change	Market share
Salsa, total	**$1,193**	**$1,383**	**15.9%**	
Tostitos	471	552	17.2	39.93%
Private label[1]	158	178	12.5	12.89
Pace	134	154	14.6	11.13
Herdez	86	102	19.1	7.38
Chi-Chi's	43	52	19.6	3.75
Soft drinks (regular), total	**$13,733**	**$14,911**	**8.6%**	
Coca-Cola	3,353	3,684	9.9	24.71%
Pepsi	1,900	2,023	6.5	13.57
Dr Pepper	1,341	1,550	15.6	10.40
Mountain Dew	1,353	1,431	5.8	9.60
Sprite	1,209	1,352	11.8	9.07
Soft drinks (low-calorie), total	**$5,712**	**$6,370**	**11.5%**	
Diet Coke	1,477	1,576	6.7	24.73%
Diet Pepsi	880	947	7.6	14.86
Coca-Cola Zero	646	765	18.4	12.01
Diet Dr Pepper	524	602	14.9	9.44
Diet Mountain Dew	522	542	3.8	8.50
Toilet tissue, total	**$8,915**	**$10,418**	**16.8%**	
Private label[1]	2,196	2,724	24.0	26.15%
Angel Soft	1,186	1,414	19.2	13.57
Charmin Ultra Strong	1,014	1,186	17.0	11.39
Charmin Ultra Soft	1,064	1,149	8.0	11.03
Scott	950	1,045	10.0	10.03
Toothpaste, total	**$2,953**	**$3,115**	**5.5%**	
Crest 3D White	238	287	20.6	9.21%
Sensodyne Pronamel	202	214	6.1	6.87
Colgate Total	101	212	110.0	6.80
Sensodyne	153	162	5.6	5.19
Colgate	147	157	7.3	5.05
Yogurt, total	**$6,311**	**$6,465**	**2.4%**	
Chobani	906	1,000	10.4	15.47%
Private label[1]	554	588	6.1	9.09
Dannon Light & Fit	592	585	−1.0	9.06
Yoplait Original	465	488	5.2	7.56
Dannon Activia	354	351	−1.0	5.43

Note: Total category sales include other brands not listed here. (1) "Private label" represents the aggregated sales figures for store-branded products in that category. (2) Boxes, bags, or bars of 3.5 ounces or more.

Who Owns What: Familiar Consumer Products and Services

The following is a partial list of well-known consumer brands with their (U.S.) parent companies as of Sept. 2020. Among brands not listed are many whose parent companies have the same or a similar name (e.g., Colgate is owned by Colgate-Palmolive Co.).

ABC broadcasting: Walt Disney
Ace bandages: 3M
Advil: GlaxoSmithKline
Ajax cleanser: Colgate-Palmolive
Amana appliances: Whirlpool
American Girl: Mattel
Aquafina water: PepsiCo
Arm & Hammer: Church & Dwight
Band-Aid bandages: Johnson & Johnson
Barbie dolls: Mattel
Ben & Jerry's ice cream: Unilever
Benadryl: Johnson & Johnson
Betty Crocker products: General Mills
Bounty paper towels: Procter & Gamble
Braun appliances: Procter & Gamble
Brita water systems: Clorox
Cadbury chocolates: Mondelēz International
Calphalon cookware: Newell Rubbermaid
Canada Dry ginger ale: Keurig Dr Pepper
Cascade dishwasher detergent: Procter & Gamble
ChapStick: GlaxoSmithKline
Charmin toilet tissue: Procter & Gamble
Cheer detergent: Procter & Gamble
Chips Ahoy!: Mondelēz International
Claritin allergy products: Bayer
Contadina tomatoes: Del Monte
Crest toothpaste: Procter & Gamble
Crisco shortening: J.M. Smucker
Dairy Queen: Berkshire Hathaway
Dasani water: Coca-Cola
Depends adult diapers: Kimberly-Clark
Doritos chips: PepsiCo
Dove soap: Unilever
Dreyer's ice cream: Nestlé
Elmer's glue: Newell Rubbermaid

ESPN networks: Walt Disney
Febreze: Procter & Gamble
Fisher-Price toys: Mattel
Folgers coffee: J.M. Smucker
Frito-Lay's snacks: PepsiCo
Fruit of the Loom apparel: Berkshire Hathaway
Gatorade sports drinks: PepsiCo
GEICO auto insurance: Berkshire Hathaway
Gerber baby food: Nestlé
Gillette: Procter & Gamble
Glad products: Clorox
Glade air fresheners: S.C. Johnson
Green Giant vegetables: General Mills
Grey Poupon mustard: Kraft Heinz
Halls cough drops: Mondelēz International
Head & Shoulders shampoo: Procter & Gamble
Healthy Choice meals: ConAgra
Hebrew National meats: ConAgra
Hellmann's mayonnaise: Unilever
Hidden Valley Salad dressings: Clorox
Hill's Science Diet Pet Foods: Colgate-Palmolive
Hillshire Farm: Tyson Foods
Hot Pockets: Nestlé
Hot Wheels/Matchbox cars: Mattel
Hunt's tomatoes: ConAgra
Iams pet food: Mars
Irish Spring soap: Colgate-Palmolive
Ivory soap: Procter & Gamble
Jell-O: Kraft Heinz
Jennie-O turkey: Hormel
Jif peanut butter: J.M. Smucker
Jimmy Dean sausages: Tyson Foods
Jolly Rancher candy: Hershey
Keebler cookies: Ferrero

KFC restaurants: Yum! Brands
Kibbles 'n Bits pet food: J.M. Smucker
Kingsford charcoal: Clorox
KitchenAid appliances: Whirlpool
Kiwi shoe products: S.C. Johnson
Kleenex: Kimberly-Clark
Knorr soups: Unilever
Kool-Aid: Kraft Heinz
Lifesavers candies: Mars
Lipton tea: Unilever
Listerine mouthwash: Johnson & Johnson
Maxwell House coffee: Kraft Heinz
Maytag appliances: Whirlpool
Milk-Bone dog snacks: J.M. Smucker
Minute Maid juices: Coca-Cola
Mr. Clean: Procter & Gamble
Monopoly board game: Hasbro
Mott's applesauce: Keurig Dr Pepper
Mountain Dew soda: PepsiCo
Neosporin: Johnson & Johnson
Neutrogena soap: Johnson & Johnson
9Lives cat food: J.M. Smucker
o.b. tampons: Edgewell Personal Care
OFF! insect repellents: S.C. Johnson
Olay: Procter & Gamble
Old Navy clothing: Gap
Old Spice: Procter & Gamble
Oral-B toothbrushes: Procter & Gamble
Ore-Ida potatoes: Kraft Heinz
Oreo cookies: Mondelēz International
Oscar Mayer meats: Kraft Heinz
Pampers diapers: Procter & Gamble
Pantene shampoo: Procter & Gamble
Paper Mate pens: Newell Rubbermaid
Pepperidge Farm prods.: Campbell Soup
Pepto-Bismol: Procter & Gamble

Perrier water: Nestlé
Philadelphia cream cheese: Kraft Heinz
Pine-Sol cleaner: Clorox
Pizza Hut restaurants: Yum! Brands
Planters nuts: Kraft Heinz
Popsicle frozen treats: Unilever
Post-it notes: 3M
Prego pasta sauce: Campbell Soup
Pringles snacks: Kellogg Co.
Purina pet foods: Nestlé
Q-tips: Unilever
Quaker Oats: PepsiCo
Raid insecticide: S.C. Johnson
Reese's candy: Hershey
Rice-A-Roni: PepsiCo
Right Guard deodorant: Henkel

Ritz crackers: Mondelēz International
Robitussin: GlaxoSmithKline
Rogaine hair treatment: Johnson & Johnson
Roundup herbicide: Bayer
Saran wrap: S.C. Johnson
Schick razors: Edgewell Personal Care
Scope mouthwash: Procter & Gamble
Scotch tape: 3M
Skippy peanut butter: Hormel
Splenda artificial sweetener: Heartland
   Food Products Group
Sprite soda: Coca-Cola
Taco Bell restaurants: Yum! Brands
Tampax tampons: Procter & Gamble
Tide detergent: Procter & Gamble
Timberland apparel: VF Corp.

Trident gum: Mondelēz International
Trojan condoms: Church & Dwight
Tropicana juice: PepsiCo
Tylenol: Johnson & Johnson
Uncle Ben's Rice: Mars
Vaseline: GlaxoSmithKline
V8 vegetable juice: Campbell Soup
Velveeta cheese products: Kraft Heinz
Viagra: GlaxoSmithKline
Vicks cold medicines: Procter & Gamble
Visine eye drops: Johnson & Johnson
Windex cleaning products: S.C. Johnson
Wrigley's candy and gum: Mars
Xanax: GlaxoSmithKline
Yoplait yogurt: General Mills
Ziploc storage bags: S.C. Johnson

U.S. Home Ownership Rates by Selected Characteristics 1970-2020
Source: U.S. Census Bureau, U.S. Dept. of Commerce

	1970	1980	1990	1995	2000	2005	2010	2015	2019	2020
Region										
Northeast	58.2%	60.8%	62.2%	62.3%	63.4%	64.7%	64.2%	60.2%	61.2%	62.4%
Midwest	69.3	69.4	67.4	68.5	72.2	73.4	70.8	68.4	68.0	69.2
South	66.3	68.6	65.8	66.5	69.2	70.4	69.1	64.9	66.0	67.6
West	59.4	60.2	57.3	59.8	61.9	63.8	61.4	58.5	59.3	60.1
Age										
Under 35 years	—	—	—	38.7	40.2	42.8	39.0	34.8	36.4	37.3
35-44 years	—	—	—	65.1	67.5	68.7	65.6	58.0	59.4	61.5
45-54 years	—	—	—	75.2	76.7	76.3	73.6	69.9	70.1	70.3
55-64 years	—	—	—	79.9	80.3	81.3	78.7	75.4	74.8	76.3
65+ years	—	—	—	78.1	80.3	80.3	80.4	78.5	78.0	78.7
Race/ethnicity[1]										
White	—	—	—	70.2	73.7	75.6	74.4	71.6	73.1	73.7
Black	—	—	—	42.6	46.7	48.0	46.2	43.0	40.6	44.0
Hispanic	—	—	—	42.2	45.4	49.2	47.8	45.4	46.6	48.9
Other	—	—	—	47.6	54.4	58.0	55.7	52.6	55.0	56.0
Income[2]										
Median family income or greater	—	—	—	79.5	81.8	84.0	81.9	78.3	78.2	78.8
Less than median family income	—	—	—	48.6	50.8	52.7	51.9	48.6	50.0	51.8
Total U.S.	64.0	65.5	63.7	64.7	67.2	68.6	66.9	63.4	64.1	65.3

Note: Figures are for 2nd quarter of year shown, except in 2020, which shows 1st-quarter data (COVID-19 impaired completion of the survey for 2nd quarter). Not seasonally adjusted. (1) Hispanic householders may be of any race. "Other" includes householders self-identifying as Asian, Native Hawaiian/Pacific Islander, and American Indian/Alaska Native, as well as combinations of two or more races/ethnicities. (2) Due to a change in survey methodology, data from 2010 and later are not directly comparable with prior years.

U.S. Housing Affordability, 1990-2020
Source: National Association of REALTORS®

Year[1]	Median-priced existing home	Avg. mortgage rate[2]	Monthly principal & interest payment	Payment as % of median monthly income	Year[1]	Median-priced existing home	Avg. mortgage rate[2]	Monthly principal & interest payment	Payment as % of median monthly income
1990	$92,000	10.04%	$648	22.0%	2015	$223,900	4.03%	$858	15.1%
1995	110,500	7.85	639	18.9	2016	235,500	3.88	886	15.0
2000	139,000	8.03	818	19.3	2017	248,800	4.20	973	15.8
2005	219,000	5.91	1,040	22.4	2018	261,600	4.72	1,088	17.1
2008	196,600	6.15	958	18.1	2019	274,600	4.04	1,054	16.0
2009	172,100	5.14	751	14.8	2020	298,600	3.22	1,036	15.3
2010	173,100	4.89	734	14.5					

(1) 2020 figures are for June, the latest available. All other figures are annual averages. (2) All figures assume a down payment of 20% of the home price. Based on effective rate on loans closed on existing homes for the period shown.

S&P/Case-Shiller National Home Price Index, 1975-2020
Source: S&P Dow Jones Indices

This index compares the median price of existing U.S. homes over time. The baseline for comparison is Jan. 2000; all numbers before or after reflect home prices in relation to it. For example, the May 2020 index of 218.9 means that home prices were more than double what they were 20 years earlier, while the Jan. 1975 index of 25.2 means prices then were 25.2% of what they were in 2000.

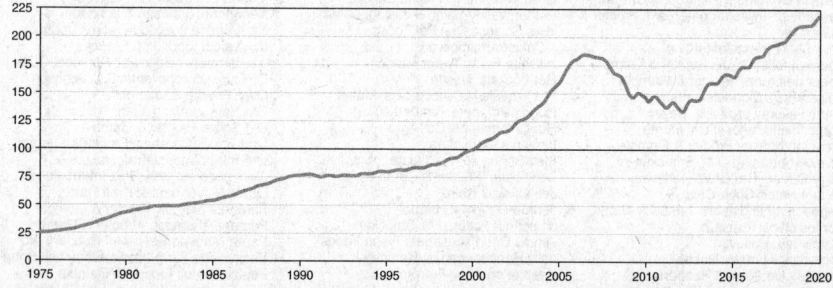

Median Price of Existing Single-Family Homes, by Metropolitan Area, 2010-20

Source: National Association of REALTORS®

Median prices are in thousands of dollars and based on all transactions within time period shown.

Metropolitan area	2010	2019	2020[1]	Metropolitan area	2010	2019	2020[1]
Akron, OH.	$108.9	$155.0	$165.2	Los Angeles-Long Beach-Glendale, CA	$323.3	$611.2	$581.7
Albany-Schenectady-Troy, NY.	195.7	218.8	227.5	Louisville/Jefferson County, KY-IN	134.6	192.7	208.1
Albuquerque, NM	178.7	225.0	238.7	Madison, WI	217.7	299.2	329.5
Allentown-Bethlehem-Easton, PA-NJ	224.0	207.2	230.4	Manchester-Nashua, NH	232.0	317.4	352.1
Amarillo, TX	124.7	165.1	185.9	Memphis, TN-MS-AR	120.2	188.7	220.0
Anaheim-Santa Ana-Irvine, CA.	546.4	825.0	859.0	Miami-Fort Lauderdale-West Palm			
Atlanta-Sandy Springs-Marietta, GA.	114.8	233.2	250.5	Beach, FL	201.9	360.0	379.0
Atlantic City-Hammonton, NJ	226.4	210.2	229.5	Milwaukee-Waukesha-West Allis, WI	205.9	268.4	290.7
Austin-Round Rock, TX	193.6	329.2	355.0	Minneapolis-St. Paul-Bloomington,			
Baltimore-Columbia-Towson, MD	246.1	299.4	324.7	MN-WI.	170.6	288.6	309.2
Barnstable Town, MA	326.0	430.0	455.3	Mobile, AL.	121.0	152.6	163.7
Baton Rouge, LA	169.6	216.4	224.6	Montgomery, AL	129.0	152.8	171.3
Beaumont-Port Arthur, TX	125.1	168.7	176.6	Nashville-Davidson-Murfreesboro-			
Birmingham-Hoover, AL	143.0	221.6	246.9	Franklin, TN.	153.8	275.0	293.4
Bismarck, ND	163.4	250.7	257.8	New Haven-Milford, CT.	231.0	237.4	256.9
Bloomington, IL.	157.9	158.7	169.8	New Orleans-Metairie, LA	159.7	222.0	234.2
Boise City-Nampa, ID.	136.2	294.2	332.8	New York-Newark-Jersey City,			
Boston-Cambridge-Newton, MA-NH.	357.3	491.9	549.0	NY-NJ-PA	393.7	423.9	439.7
Boulder, CO	358.1	618.6	606.7	North Port-Sarasota-Bradenton, FL	164.6	304.8	318.0
Bridgeport-Stamford-Norwalk, CT	408.6	445.6	494.6	Norwich-New London, CT	204.7	234.9	248.9
Buffalo-Cheektowaga-Niagara Falls, NY	121.2	160.9	169.9	Oklahoma City, OK.	145.7	158.9	170.2
Burlington-South Burlington, VT	261.2	308.3	333.0	Omaha-Council Bluffs, NE-IA	137.3	200.7	218.4
Canton-Massillon, OH.	90.9	139.4	153.9	Orlando-Kissimmee-Sanford, FL	134.7	276.0	296.0
Cape Coral-Fort Myers, FL	88.9	258.7	265.2	Palm Bay-Melbourne-Titusville, FL	103.0	238.9	255.0
Cedar Rapids, IA	144.7	165.6	175.9	Pensacola-Ferry Pass-Brent, FL.	141.0	219.9	232.0
Champaign-Urbana, IL	141.9	157.1	171.2	Peoria, IL	116.9	120.7	129.6
Charleston-North Charleston, SC.	200.5	293.5	302.4	Philadelphia-Camden-Wilmington,			
Charleston, WV.	129.1	137.6	141.8	PA-NJ-DE-MD.	214.9	246.2	264.8
Charlotte-Concord-Gastonia, NC-SC	143.3	258.6	286.9	Phoenix-Mesa-Scottsdale, AZ.	139.2	287.1	314.7
Chattanooga, TN-GA	121.4	193.2	213.5	Pittsfield, MA.	195.5	223.2	219.8
Chicago-Naperville-Elgin, IL-IN-WI.	191.4	265.1	282.9	Portland-South Portland, ME	NA	308.5	336.1
Cincinnati, OH-KY-IN	128.0	185.6	203.5	Portland-Vancouver-Hillsboro, OR-WA	237.3	409.3	435.6
Cleveland-Elyria, OH	114.5	164.1	177.3	Providence-Warwick, RI-MA.	228.5	311.1	335.9
Colorado Springs, CO	195.5	320.5	353.4	Raleigh, NC	190.4	291.5	313.3
Columbia, MO.	146.3	206.4	221.9	Reading, PA	153.3	173.8	186.0
Columbia, SC	142.6	185.0	199.1	Reno, NV	179.5	393.9	408.1
Columbus, OH	136.4	216.6	240.4	Richmond, VA.	NA	264.0	300.0
Corpus Christi, TX	135.1	201.1	220.6	Riverside-San Bernardino-Ontario, CA	179.3	378.5	400.0
Cumberland, MD-WV	100.3	106.7	123.3	Rochester, NY	118.9	154.2	165.7
Dallas-Fort Worth-Arlington, TX	143.8	268.6	280.9	Rockford, IL	106.9	128.3	136.7
Davenport-Moline-Rock Island, IA-IL	112.2	135.4	143.3	Sacramento-Roseville-Arden-			
Dayton, OH.	103.6	157.8	175.6	Arcade, CA	184.2	380.0	405.0
Deltona-Daytona Beach-Ormond				St. Louis, MO-IL	131.1	187.5	203.5
Beach, FL	115.6	225.0	237.6	Salem, OR	173.5	310.7	336.5
Denver-Aurora-Lakewood, CO	232.4	462.1	478.4	Salt Lake City, UT.	206.5	355.2	381.9
Des Moines-West Des Moines, IA	150.9	214.5	226.0	San Antonio-New Braunfels, TX	151.0	236.6	247.3
Detroit-Warren-Dearborn, MI	NA	195.8	215.3	San Diego-Carlsbad, CA	385.7	645.0	670.0
Dover, DE	193.3	218.2	232.7	San Francisco-Oakland-Hayward, CA	525.6	988.0	1,050.0
Durham-Chapel Hill, NC	158.3	295.9	317.7	San Jose-Sunnyvale-Santa Clara, CA	595.0	1,265.0	1,380.0
El Paso, TX	134.3	164.4	171.1	Seattle-Tacoma-Bellevue, WA	295.7	524.7	574.1
Erie, PA.	107.7	125.3	130.6	Shreveport-Bossier City, LA	156.6	176.4	162.3
Eugene, OR	196.3	308.6	338.6	Sioux Falls, SD	143.3	221.4	236.7
Fargo, ND-MN.	146.4	221.0	229.6	Spartanburg, SC.	118.2	183.8	199.0
Gainesville, FL	161.6	240.0	250.0	Spokane-Spokane Valley, WA.	172.0	265.3	296.9
Gary-Hammond, IN	122.9	183.6	191.8	Springfield, IL	124.0	141.8	153.8
Grand Rapids-Wyoming, MI	91.5	210.5	226.3	Springfield, MA	190.0	229.0	247.5
Green Bay, WI.	130.4	189.4	200.3	Springfield, MO.	109.1	154.6	164.5
Greensboro-High Point, NC	129.8	176.2	198.1	Syracuse, NY	125.1	146.5	154.1
Greenville-Anderson-Mauldin, SC	145.3	223.3	236.8	Tallahassee, FL	152.8	227.0	240.0
Gulfport-Biloxi-Pascagoula, MS	125.0	151.7	165.1	Tampa-St. Petersburg-Clearwater, FL.	134.2	245.0	265.0
Hartford-W. Hartford-E. Hartford, CT	235.8	237.3	253.9	Toledo, OH	81.5	131.0	141.6
Honolulu, HI	607.6	802.5	815.7	Topeka, KS	107.2	135.7	147.8
Houston-The Woodlands-Sugar				Trenton, NJ	250.7	276.3	292.5
Land, TX	155.0	245.8	256.3	Tucson, AZ	156.6	238.9	250.7
Indianapolis-Carmel-Anderson, IN	123.3	200.1	225.3	Tulsa, OK	132.3	173.2	188.6
Jackson, MS.	133.2	179.3	197.2	Virginia Beach-Norfolk-Newport			
Jacksonville, FL	137.7	225.7	271.3	News, VA-NC	205.0	235.0	260.0
Kansas City, MO-KS	141.6	219.4	237.8	Washington-Arlington-Alexandria,			
Knoxville, TN.	140.9	205.2	218.9	DC-VA-MD-WV	325.3	440.9	472.1
Lansing-East Lansing, MI	84.4	159.5	174.1	Wichita, KS.	118.7	158.2	174.1
Las Vegas-Henderson-Paradise, NV	138.0	306.0	317.8	Wilmington, NC.	NA	264.7	279.1
Lexington-Fayette, KY.	143.2	180.0	199.1	Winston-Salem, NC	134.7	177.3	198.8
Lincoln, NE	139.0	198.4	215.3	Worcester, MA-CT	223.3	288.1	314.7
Little Rock-N. Little Rock-Conway, AR.	132.5	152.5	164.9				

NA = Not available. (1) Preliminary figures for second quarter, 2020.

Characteristics of American Housing Units, 2011-17

Source: *American Housing Survey, 2017*, U.S. Census Bureau, U.S. Dept. of Commerce

Characteristic	2011 Number of homes (thous.)	2011 % of all homes	2017 Number of homes (thous.)	2017 % of all homes
Total housing units ..	114,833	100.0%	137,400	100.0%
Units in structure				
1, detached........	73,866	64.3	84,830	61.7
1, attached	6,660	5.8	10,040	7.3
2-4..............	8,973	7.8	9,744	7.1
5-9..............	5,463	4.8	6,645	4.8
10-19.............	5,031	4.4	6,180	4.5
20-49.............	3,702	3.2	4,903	3.6
50 or more.........	4,124	3.6	6,593	4.8
Manufactured/mobile home or trailer......	7,013	6.1	8,397	6.1
Condominiums	7,404	6.4	8,746	6.4
Year built				
2016-17..........	NA	NA	1,007	0.7
2010-15..........	NA	NA	5,772	4.2
2005-09..........	6,999	6.1	9,046	6.6
2000-04..........	8,093	7.1	10,520	7.7
1995-99..........	7,917	6.9	10,000	7.3
1990-94..........	6,134	5.3	7,271	5.3
1985-89..........	7,757	6.8	10,120	7.4
1980-84..........	6,676	5.8	8,851	6.4
1970-79..........	21,492	18.7	20,460	14.9
1960-69..........	13,593	11.8	14,290	10.4
1950-59..........	11,815	10.3	14,250	10.4
1940-49..........	6,617	5.8	6,617	4.8
1930-39..........	4,830	4.2	4,205	3.1
1920-29..........	4,624	4.0	5,409	3.9
1919 or earlier......	7,653	6.7	9,575	7.0
Median year built	*1974*	*NA*	*1977*	*NA*
Square footage of unit				
Less than 500	3,133	2.7	3,409	2.5
500-749...........	7,687	6.7	9,527	6.9
750-999...........	12,791	11.1	16,510	12.0
1,000-1,499........	26,444	23.0	31,570	23.0
1,500-1,999........	21,349	18.6	24,340	17.7
2,000-2,499........	14,207	12.4	15,670	11.4
2,500-2,999........	7,347	6.4	8,352	6.1
3,000-3,999........	7,005	6.1	7,875	5.7
4,000 or more	4,525	3.9	3,926	2.9
Median square footage	*1,500*	*NA*	*1,473*	*NA*
Number of bedrooms				
None	914	0.8	1,188	0.9
1	11,999	10.4	16,000	11.6
2	28,641	24.9%	35,770	26.0%
3	48,713	42.4	54,550	39.7
4 or more........	24,565	21.4	29,900	21.8
Number of complete bathrooms				
1	39,264	34.2	46,500	33.8
1-1/2	15,123	13.2	16,070	11.7
2	59,941[1]	52.2[1]	41,630	30.3
2-1/2	NA	NA	17,320	12.6
3 or more.........	NA	NA	15,543	11.3
Mortgage characteristics				
None, owned free and clear	25,853	34.0	31,380	40.5
One regular mortgage only	43,065	56.6	40,100	51.7
Two or more regular mortgages	6,700	8.8	1,898	2.4
Median outstanding loan amount......	*$120,000*	*NA*	*$126,000*	*NA*
Lot size				
Less than 1/8 acre ..	13,225	15.6	14,700	14.7
1/8-1/4 acre.......	21,897	25.8	33,400	33.5
1/4-1/2 acre.......	15,914	18.8	19,930	20.0
1/2-1 acre	10,152	12.0	9,455	9.5
1-5 acres.........	16,927	20.0	15,160	15.2
5-10 acres........	2,729	3.2	3,079	3.1
10+ acres........	3,946	4.7	4,028	4.0
Equipment				
Washing machine ..	95,514	83.2	110,500	80.4
Clothes dryer......	93,034	81.0	108,700	79.1
Dishwasher........	76,885	67.0	95,690	69.6
Central air conditioning	75,456	65.7	93,840	68.3
Main heating fuel[2]				
Piped gas	57,889	50.6	58,750	43.2
Electricity	40,029	35.0	60,290	44.4
Fuel oil...........	8,060	7.0	6,605	4.9
Bottled gas	5,474	4.8	6,513	4.8

NA = Not applicable/not available. (1) Figure is for 2 or more bathrooms. (2) Not all heating fuels are shown here.

Fair Market Rents for Select Metropolitan Areas, 2021

Source: *Fair Market Rents FY 2021*, U.S. Dept. of Housing and Urban Development (HUD)

Metropolitan area	0	1	2	3	4
Atlanta, GA	$1,016	$1,040	$1,185	$1,491	$1,823
Austin, TX	1,059	1,212	1,434	1,848	2,207
Baltimore, MD........	917	1,115	1,384	1,793	2,053
Birmingham, AL	817	871	1,002	1,303	1,409
Boston, MA..........	1,742	1,924	2,336	2,906	3,168
Buffalo, NY	743	772	920	1,144	1,284
Charlotte, NC	987	1,010	1,151	1,518	1,956
Chicago, IL	1,012	1,122	1,299	1,649	1,969
Cincinnati, OH	604	698	916	1,244	1,425
Cleveland, OH	599	705	865	1,137	1,188
Columbus, OH	717	827	1,031	1,298	1,468
Dallas, TX...........	1,029	1,134	1,352	1,746	2,309
Denver, CO..........	1,179	1,304	1,605	2,186	2,486
Detroit, MI..........	697	821	1,049	1,344	1,458
Hartford, CT	889	1,091	1,347	1,675	1,958
Honolulu, HI	1,433	1,577	2,073	2,967	3,589
Houston, TX	893	968	1,157	1,551	1,977
Indianapolis, IN......	678	781	946	1,248	1,455
Jacksonville, FL	746	921	1,113	1,455	1,852
Kansas City, MO......	731	857	1,021	1,364	1,552
Las Vegas, NV	780	937	1,143	1,636	1,977
Los Angeles, CA......	1,369	1,605	2,058	2,735	2,982
Louisville, KY	649	760	918	1,229	1,408
Memphis, TN	686	784	911	1,228	1,412
Miami, FL...........	1,057	1,231	1,551	2,068	2,483
Milwaukee, WI.......	$663	$803	$973	$1,242	$1,362
Minneapolis, MN......	898	1,054	1,308	1,838	2,156
Nashville, TN	998	1,031	1,197	1,539	1,930
New Orleans, LA	765	899	1,061	1,371	1,583
New York, NY	1,760	1,801	2,053	2,598	2,784
Oklahoma City, OK....	705	738	918	1,238	1,488
Orlando, FL..........	1,055	1,140	1,321	1,713	2,057
Philadelphia, PA	900	1,040	1,260	1,567	1,796
Phoenix, AZ	933	1,032	1,251	1,765	2,010
Pittsburgh, PA	714	772	940	1,206	1,321
Portland, OR........	1,245	1,331	1,536	2,193	2,657
Providence, RI	848	955	1,148	1,428	1,714
Richmond, VA	993	1,020	1,163	1,538	1,840
Riverside, CA	955	1,106	1,390	1,917	2,369
Sacramento, CA	1,060	1,188	1,495	2,140	2,588
St. Louis, MO	671	731	938	1,224	1,440
Salt Lake City, UT.....	829	1,001	1,204	1,690	1,892
San Antonio, TX	761	912	1,114	1,446	1,793
San Diego, CA	1,478	1,642	2,124	2,987	3,677
San Francisco, CA ...	2,350	2,923	3,553	4,567	4,970
San Jose, CA	2,228	2,558	3,051	3,984	4,593
San Juan, PR	436	477	556	740	909
Seattle, WA	1,523	1,599	1,906	2,694	3,172
Tampa, FL..........	989	1,040	1,271	1,651	2,028
Washington, DC	1,513	1,548	1,765	2,263	2,742

Note: Figures are projections made in the previous fiscal year. Metropolitan areas include adjacent cities not shown here. Fair market rents are primarily used by HUD to determine payment standard amounts for the Housing Choice Voucher program.

TRADE

U.S. Trade in Goods With Selected Countries and Major Areas, 2019

Source: U.S. Census Bureau and U.S. Bureau of Economic Analysis, U.S. Dept. of Commerce; *World Development Indicators 2019*, The World Bank

Weighted mean tariff rate is the average of tariffs applied to all products weighted by the product's share of the country's imports. A low tariff on a heavily imported product, therefore, has more impact on the weighted mean tariff rate than a high tariff on a product that is rarely imported. Weighted mean tariff rates in 2019 were generally based on 2018 trade data.

(trade in millions of dollars; top 25 countries as ranked by amount of total trade in goods with U.S.)

Rank	Country	Total trade with U.S.	U.S. exports to (rank)	U.S. imports from (rank)	U.S. trade balance with (rank[1])	Weighted mean tariff rate
1.	Mexico	$614,541	$256,570 (2)	$357,971 (2)	–$101,401 (2)	1.2%
2.	Canada	612,061	292,633 (1)	319,428 (3)	–26,795 (9)	1.5
3.	China[2]	558,099	106,447 (3)	451,651 (1)	–345,204 (1)	3.8
4.	Japan	217,942	74,377 (4)	143,566 (4)	–69,189 (3)	2.5
5.	Germany	187,620	60,112 (6)	127,507 (5)	–67,395 (4)	1.8
6.	South Korea	134,009	56,539 (7)	77,470 (6)	–20,931 (13)	5.1
7.	United Kingdom	132,297	69,078 (5)	63,219 (8)	5,858 (227)	1.8
8.	France	95,311	37,718 (10)	57,593 (11)	–19,875 (15)	1.8
9.	India	91,981	34,288 (12)	57,694 (10)	–23,406 (11)	5.8
10.	Taiwan	85,547	31,294 (13)	54,253 (13)	–22,959 (12)	NA
11.	Italy	81,103	23,839 (17)	57,264 (12)	–33,424 (7)	1.8
12.	Netherlands	80,827	51,108 (8)	29,719 (18)	21,389 (233)	1.8
13.	Vietnam	77,490	10,861 (27)	66,630 (7)	–55,770 (5)	2.7
14.	Brazil	73,697	42,853 (9)	30,844 (17)	12,009 (229)	8.6
15.	Ireland	70,953	9,058 (31)	61,895 (9)	–52,836 (6)	1.8
16.	Switzerland	62,540	17,896 (19)	44,644 (14)	–26,749 (10)	1.7
17.	Singapore	57,616	31,218 (14)	26,398 (19)	4,820 (225)	0.1
18.	Belgium	54,891	34,726 (11)	20,165 (21)	14,561 (230)	1.8
19.	Malaysia	53,758	13,192 (26)	40,567 (15)	–27,375 (8)	4.0
20.	Thailand	46,746	13,299 (25)	33,447 (16)	–20,148 (14)	3.5
21.	Australia	36,835	25,990 (16)	10,845 (31)	15,146 (231)	0.9
22.	Hong Kong	35,517	30,783 (15)	4,735 (50)	26,048 (234)	0.0
23.	Israel	33,912	14,405 (24)	19,508 (23)	–5,103 (22)	1.9
24.	Spain	31,994	15,208 (21)	16,787 (24)	–1,579 (36)	1.8
25.	Colombia	28,913	14,747 (22)	14,166 (25)	580 (198)	4.4
Major area/group						
North America	$1,226,602	$549,203	$677,399	–$128,195	
Europe	985,978	381,656	604,321	–222,665	
Euro Area	653,102	247,303	405,799	–158,495	
EU	851,934	336,726	515,208	–178,482	
Africa	56,936	26,722	30,214	–3,491	
OECD	2,620,103	1,105,337	1,514,765	–409,428	
Pacific Rim Countries	1,237,856	391,117	846,739	–455,622	
Asia-Near East	117,826	65,883	51,943	13,940	
Asia-South	111,721	40,545	71,176	–30,631	
ASEAN	292,444	86,109	206,334	–120,225	
APEC	2,657,995	995,088	1,662,908	–667,820	
South/Central America	270,485	161,624	108,861	52,763	
Twenty Latin Amer. Reps.	862,413	400,566	461,848	–61,282	
Latin Amer. Free Trade Association	793,275	358,818	434,457	–75,639	
CAFTA-DR	58,561	32,685	25,876	6,809	
Central Amer. Common Market	43,813	23,491	20,323	3,168	
NATO Allies	1,379,777	621,879	757,898	–136,019	
OPEC	96,958	51,318	45,640	5,678	
WORLD TOTAL	4,140,692	1,643,161	2,497,532	–854,371	

NA = Not available. **Note:** Figures shown are on Census Bureau basis and are not seasonally adjusted. Figures may not equal totals due to rounding. Country grouping data reflect groups at the time of reporting. Rankings include territories as well as nations. (1) Rank by size of U.S. trade deficit. (2) Not incl. Hong Kong and Macau.

Countries With Highest and Lowest Mean Tariff Rates, 2019

Source: *World Development Indicators 2019*, The World Bank

	HIGHEST TARIFF RATES			LOWEST TARIFF RATES	
Rank	Country	Weighted mean tariff rate	Rank	Country	Weighted mean tariff rate
1.	Palau	29.9%	1.	Brunei	0.0%
2.	St. Kitts and Nevis	21.1		Hong Kong	0.0
3.	Bermuda	20.9		Macau	0.0
4.	The Bahamas	18.6		Libya	0.0
5.	Solomon Islands	18.5	5.	Singapore	0.1
6.	Benin	17.8	6.	Chile	0.5
7.	Djibouti	17.6	7.	Georgia	0.7
8.	Gabon	16.9		Eswatini	0.7
9.	Cayman Islands	16.7	9.	Peru	0.8
10.	Central African Republic	16.4	10.	Albania	0.9
	Chad	16.4		Australia	0.9
12.	Fiji	16.1		Mauritius	0.9
13.	Equatorial Guinea	15.6		Namibia	0.9
14.	Guinea-Bissau	15.5	14.	Botswana	1.1
15.	Iran	15.2	15.	Mexico	1.2
16.	Barbados	14.2	16.	Guatemala	1.4
	Syria	14.2		Lesotho	1.4
18.	Togo	13.4		New Zealand	1.4
19.	Antigua and Barbuda	12.7	19.	Belarus	1.5
	Cameroon	12.7		Canada	1.5
	The Gambia	12.7		Laos	1.5
			22.	Iceland	1.6

U.S. Exports and Imports by Principal Commodities, 2019

Source: U.S. Census Bureau and U.S. Bureau of Economic Analysis, U.S. Dept. of Commerce

(in millions of dollars)

Item	Exports	Imports	Item	Exports	Imports
Total[1]	**$1,643,161**	**$2,497,531**	Fertilizers	3,101	6,555
Manufactured goods	**1,125,554**	**2,158,690**	Plastics in primary forms	35,517	15,627
Agricultural commodities	**136,642**	**131,183**	Plastics in nonprimary forms	13,369	11,607
			Chemical materials and products	34,085	17,831
Food and live animals	**100,343**	**115,916**	**Manufactured goods by material.** ..	**103,834**	**257,399**
Live animals other than fish	977	3,009	Leather and leather manufactures ...	775	1,275
Meat and preparations	19,226	9,681	Rubber manufactures.............	9,360	22,656
Dairy products and birds...........	5,108	2,332	Cork and wood manufactures.......	1,935	10,997
Fish and preparations.............	4,912	21,907	Paper and paperboard	14,726	17,064
Cereals and preparations	20,971	10,997	Textile yarn, fabrics...............	11,945	29,975
Vegetables and fruits	22,496	37,651	Nonmetallic mineral manufactures ...	11,742	43,322
Sugar, preparations, and honey	1,882	4,686	Iron and steel	12,124	31,821
Coffee, tea, cocoa, and spices	2,994	13,429	Nonferrous metals	15,117	42,297
Feeding stuff for animals...........	11,903	3,320	Manufactures of metals	26,110	57,991
Miscellaneous edible products	9,874	8,906	**Machinery and transport**		
Beverages and tobacco	**5,921**	**27,661**	**equipment**	**507,604**	**1,058,554**
Beverages......................	4,978	25,519	Power-generating machinery	36,425	78,329
Tobacco and manufactures........	943	2,142	Specialized industrial machinery	45,251	56,980
Crude materials except fuels	**74,045**	**34,288**	Metalworking machinery...........	4,814	11,108
Hides, skins, and furskins (raw)	1,048	46	General industrial machinery.......	60,793	107,525
Oil seeds and oleaginous fruits	20,735	977	Office machinery.................	17,710	125,745
Crude rubber	2,216	3,120	Telecommunications equipment	19,612	152,633
Cork and wood	6,126	7,375	Electrical machinery..............	79,291	186,750
Pulp and waste paper.............	8,322	3,424	Road vehicles...................	120,066	300,662
Textile fibers including waste	7,966	1,318	Transport equipment..............	123,642	38,821
Crude fertilizers	2,687	3,031	**Miscellaneous manufactured**		
Metalliferous ores and metal scrap...	21,592	9,017	**articles**	**126,715**	**405,375**
Crude animal and vegetable materials	3,352	5,980	Prefabricated buildings	2,399	13,309
Mineral fuels and lubricants	**197,836**	**200,900**	Furniture	5,969	50,611
Coal, coke, and briquettes	10,169	918	Travel goods...................	668	10,673
Petroleum products and preparations	156,553	189,075	Apparel and clothing accessories....	3,217	92,417
Gas, natural and manufactured	30,679	9,012	Footwear......................	1,133	27,091
Electric current	436	1,895	Scientific and controlling equipment..	51,205	64,501
Animal and vegetable oils	**2,498**	**6,086**	Photographic equipment	6,573	15,079
Animal oil and fat	813	339	Miscellaneous manufactured		
Fixed vegetable fats and oil, crude ...	1,455	5,492	articles	55,552	131,694
Animal or vegetable fats, processed..	230	255	**Miscellaneous commodities**	**64,632**	**123,520**
Chemicals and related products...	**209,235**	**267,834**	Special transactions	10,340	93,711
Organic chemicals	36,010	49,305	Coin, including gold coin...........	196	902
Inorganic chemicals	10,731	11,816	Coin, other than gold	21	21
Dyeing, tanning, and coloring			Gold, nonmonetary..............	18,232	10,060
materials.....................	7,209	4,302	Low value estimate...............	35,843	18,827
Medicinal and pharmaceutical			**Re-exports**......................	**250,497**	**NA**
products	52,429	134,186	Agricultural commodities	4,782	NA
Essential oil and reinoids	16,783	16,605	Manufactured goods..............	239,780	NA

NA = Not applicable. **Note:** Numbers may not add up to totals due to rounding. (1) Total on Census Bureau basis; includes re-exports.

Trends in U.S. Foreign Trade, 1790-2019

Source: U.S. Census Bureau and U.S. Bureau of Economic Analysis, U.S. Dept. of Commerce

In 1790, U.S. exports and imports combined came to $43 mil, and there was a $3 mil trade deficit. The trade balance was positive for much of the 20th century, but the U.S. has had a trade deficit in every year since 1975.

(in millions of dollars)

Year	Exports	Imports	Trade balance	Year	Exports	Imports	Trade balance	Year	Exports	Imports	Trade balance
1790	$20	$23	−$3	1895	$808	$732	$76	2000	$1,082,963	$1,452,650	−$369,686
1795	48	70	−22	1900	1,394	850	545	2001	1,015,366	1,375,739	−360,373
1800	71	91	−20	1905	1,519	1,118	401	2002	986,095	1,406,762	−420,666
1805	96	121	−25	1910	1,745	1,557	188	2003	1,028,186	1,524,429	−496,243
1810	67	85	−19	1915	2,769	1,674	1,094	2004	1,168,120	1,778,958	−610,838
1815	53	113	−60	1920	8,228	5,278	2,950	2005	1,291,503	2,008,045	−716,542
1820	70	74	−5	1925	4,910	4,227	683	2006	1,463,991	2,227,523	−763,533
1825	91	90	1	1930	3,843	3,061	782	2007	1,660,815	2,371,811	−710,997
1830	72	63	9	1935	2,283	2,047	235	2008	1,849,586	2,561,936	−712,350
1835	115	137	−22	1940	4,021	2,625	1,396	2009	1,592,792	1,987,563	−394,771
1840	124	98	25	1945	9,806	4,159	5,646	2010	1,872,320	2,375,407	−503,087
1845	106	113	−7	1950	9,997	8,954	1,043	2011	2,143,552	2,698,074	−554,522
1850	144	174	−29	1955	14,298	11,566	2,732	2012	2,247,453	2,773,359	−525,906
1855	219	258	−39	1960	25,939	22,433	3,508	2013	2,313,237	2,760,066	−446,829
1860	334	354	−20	1965	35,285	30,621	4,664	2014	2,392,268	2,876,412	−484,144
1865	166	239	−73	1970	56,640	54,385	2,255	2015	2,279,743	2,771,004	−491,261
1870	393	436	−43	1975	132,585	120,181	12,403	2016	2,237,923	2,719,092	−481,169
1875	513	533	−20	1980	271,835	291,242	−19,407	2017	2,387,391	2,901,181	−513,791
1880	836	668	168	1985	289,071	410,951	−121,879	2018	2,539,383	3,119,320	−579,937
1885	742	578	165	1990	535,234	616,098	−80,865	2019	2,528,262	3,105,127	−576,865
1890	858	789	69	1895	794,387	890,771	−96,384				

Note: Figures shown using balance of payments basis.

World Trade Organization (WTO)

The World Trade Organization is an international body that seeks to promote free trade by eliminating barriers to trade. Founded in 1995, the WTO had grown to 164 member countries as of Oct. 2020, with 24 others, including Belarus, Iran, and Vatican City, granted observer status. International intergovernmental organizations, such as the International Monetary Fund and the World Bank, may also be granted observer status. With the exception of Vatican City, observers must start accession negotiations within five years of becoming observers.

U.S. Trade in Goods and Services, 2019

Source: U.S. Census Bureau and U.S. Bureau of Economic Analysis, U.S. Dept. of Commerce
(top countries as ranked by amount of total trade with U.S.; in millions of dollars)

Country and category	Food and live animals	Beverages and tobacco	Crude materials, except fuels	Mineral fuels, lubricants	Chemicals	Manu- factured goods	Machinery and transport equip- ment	Misc. manu- factured articles	Commo- dities and transac- tions[1]	Total[2]
Canada										
U.S. exports to	$21,974	$2,360	$6,809	$24,632	$32,186	$32,940	$133,087	$28,318	$9,912	$292,633
U.S. imports from	23,471	1,161	11,750	90,339	26,575	38,817	92,725	16,275	23,717	326,818
Trade balance	−1,497	1,199	−4,941	−65,707	5,611	−5,877	40,361	12,043	−13,804	−34,185
Mexico										
U.S. exports to	15,507	368	7,454	34,376	27,839	31,520	112,440	19,031	7,543	256,568
U.S. imports from	24,707	6,586	2,037	13,395	7,286	23,067	234,159	37,727	12,031	361,174
Trade balance	−9,199	−6,218	5,417	20,981	20,552	8,454	−121,719	−18,696	−4,488	−104,604
China										
U.S. exports to	4,735	95	15,101	3,772	16,890	5,356	47,742	11,574	1,158	106,448
U.S. imports from	4,751	101	1,953	298	17,449	53,063	236,939	148,596	8,654	471,856
Trade balance	−16	−6	13,148	3,474	−559	−47,708	−189,197	−137,022	−7,496	−365,410
Japan										
U.S. exports to	10,843	335	4,204	9,242	11,711	3,774	22,916	9,990	1,328	74,376
U.S. imports from	854	193	708	1,289	12,238	9,546	106,211	11,470	4,336	146,902
Trade balance	9,990	142	3,496	7,953	−527	−5,772	−83,295	−1,479	−3,008	−72,524
Germany										
U.S. exports to	1,201	145	1,508	755	10,115	4,191	31,152	8,138	2,875	60,112
U.S. imports from	1,582	403	1,597	335	27,555	11,424	66,446	12,848	7,704	129,912
Trade balance	−381	−258	−89	420	−17,439	−7,233	−35,294	−4,710	−4,829	−69,799
South Korea										
U.S. exports to	6,716	147	2,932	13,052	8,096	2,390	17,266	4,756	860	56,538
U.S. imports from	771	192	498	4,416	7,159	9,448	50,765	5,185	1,496	79,933
Trade balance	5,945	−45	2,434	8,636	937	−7,058	−33,498	−429	−636	−23,394
United Kingdom										
U.S. exports to	1,074	410	2,465	7,400	7,010	4,292	23,521	8,883	13,963	69,076
U.S. imports from	782	2,235	570	4,070	10,278	3,547	27,841	7,592	7,350	64,279
Trade balance	292	−1,825	1,895	3,330	−3,268	745	−4,320	1,291	6,613	4,797

Note: Figures for exports are "free alongside ship" values; figures for imports are "cost, insurance, and freight" values. Neither is directly comparable with the Census Bureau basis shown in other tables in this section. Trade balance is with U.S. and may not sum from export/import numbers due to rounding. Total includes categories not shown here. (1) Not classified elsewhere. (2) Total includes animal and vegetable oils, fats, and waxes, not shown separately.

Exchange Rates for Foreign Currencies, 1970-2019

Source: Federal Reserve Board

One U.S. dollar was worth the following amounts in each country's national currency; exchange rates are annual averages.

Country (currency)	1970	1980	1990	2000	2010	2015	2016	2017	2018	2019
Australia (dollar)	0.90	0.88	1.28	1.72	1.09	1.33	1.34	1.30	1.34	1.44
Austria (schilling; euro)	25.88	12.95	11.37	1.08	0.75	0.90	0.90	0.89	0.85	0.89
Belgium (franc; euro)	49.68	29.24	33.42	1.08	0.75	0.90	0.90	0.89	0.85	0.89
Brazil (real)	NA	NA	NA	1.83	1.76	3.34	3.48	3.19	3.65	3.94
Canada (dollar)	1.01	1.17	1.17	1.49	1.03	1.28	1.32	1.30	1.30	1.33
China (yuan)	NA	NA	4.79	8.28	6.77	6.28	6.64	6.76	6.61	6.91
Denmark (krone)	7.49	5.63	6.19	8.10	5.63	6.73	6.73	6.60	6.31	6.67
France (franc; euro)	5.52	4.22	5.45	1.08	0.75	0.90	0.90	0.89	0.85	0.89
Germany[1] (mark; euro)	3.65	1.82	1.62	1.08	0.75	0.90	0.90	0.89	0.85	0.89
Greece (drachma; euro)	30.00	42.62	158.51	365.92	0.75	0.90	0.90	0.89	0.85	0.89
Hong Kong (dollar)	NA	NA	7.79	7.79	7.77	7.75	7.76	7.79	7.84	7.84
India (rupee)	7.58	7.89	17.50	45.00	45.65	64.11	67.16	65.07	68.37	70.38
Ireland (pound; euro)	2.40	2.06	1.66	1.08	0.75	0.90	0.90	0.89	0.85	0.89
Italy (lira; euro)	623.00	856.00	1,198.00	1.08	0.75	0.90	0.90	0.89	0.85	0.89
Japan (yen)	357.60	226.63	144.79	107.80	87.78	121.05	108.66	112.10	110.40	109.02
Malaysia (ringgit)	3.09	2.18	2.71	3.80	3.22	3.90	4.14	4.30	4.03	4.14
Mexico (peso[2])	NA	NA	NA	9.46	12.62	15.87	18.67	18.88	19.22	19.25
Netherlands (guilder; euro)	3.60	2.0	1.82	1.08	0.75	0.90	0.90	0.89	0.85	0.89
Norway (krone)	7.14	4.94	6.26	8.81	6.05	8.07	8.39	8.27	8.13	8.80
Portugal (escudo; euro)	28.75	50.08	142.55	1.08	0.75	0.90	0.90	0.89	0.85	0.89
Singapore (dollar)	3.08	2.14	1.81	1.73	1.36	1.37	1.38	1.38	1.35	1.36
South Korea (won)	310.57	607.43	707.76	1,130.90	1,155.74	1,130.96	1,159.34	1,129.04	1,099.29	1,165.80
Spain (peseta; euro)	69.72	71.76	101.93	1.08	0.75	0.90	0.90	0.89	0.85	0.89
Sweden (krona)	5.17	4.23	5.92	9.17	7.20	8.44	8.55	8.54	8.69	9.46
Switzerland (franc)	4.32	1.68	1.39	1.69	1.04	0.96	0.98	0.98	0.98	0.99
Taiwan (dollar)	NA	NA	26.92	31.26	31.50	31.74	32.23	30.40	30.13	30.91
Thailand (baht)	21.00	20.48	25.58	40.21	31.70	34.24	35.26	33.91	32.30	31.04
United Kingdom (pound)	0.42	0.43	0.56	0.66	0.65	0.65	0.74	0.78	0.75	0.78

NA = Not available. **Note:** The euro, the European Union's single currency, replaced the national currencies in the EU nations shown above. Since 1999 (or 2001 in the case of Greece), the euro has been fixed at the following conversion rates: 13.7603 Austrian schillings, 40.3399 Belgian francs, 6.55957 French francs, 1.95583 German marks, 340.750 Greek drachmas, 0.787564 Irish pounds, 1,936.27 Italian lire, 2.20371 Netherlands guilders, 200.482 Portuguese escudos, and 166.386 Spanish pesetas. (1) West Germany before 1991. (2) Mexico re-based its currency in 1993; earlier values are not comparable.

Top U.S. Trading Partners, 1985-2019

Source: U.S. Census Bureau, U.S. Dept. of Commerce
(in millions of dollars; top five countries as ranked by amount of total trade with U.S. in 2019)

Country/category	1985	1990	1995	2000	2005	2010	2015	2017	2018	2019
Mexico										
U.S. exports to	$13,635	$28,279	$46,292	$111,349	$120,248	$163,665	$236,460	$243,609	$265,945	$265,570
U.S. imports from	19,132	30,157	62,100	135,926	170,109	229,986	296,433	312,667	344272	357,971
Trade balance........	−5,497	−1,878	−15,808	−24,577	−49,861	−66,321	−59,973	−69,058	−78327	−101,401
Canada										
U.S. exports to	47,251	83,674	127,226	178,941	211,899	249,257	280,855	282,774	299,732	292,633
U.S. imports from	69,006	91,380	144,370	230,838	290,384	277,637	296,305	299,065	318,521	319,428
Trade balance........	−21,755	−7,706	−17,144	−51,897	−78,486	−28,380	−15,450	−16,292	−18,790	−26,795
China										
U.S. exports	3,856	4,806	11,754	16,185	41,192	91,911	115,873	129,997	120,289	106,447
U.S. imports from	3,862	15,237	45,543	100,018	243,470	364,953	483,202	505,165	539,243	451,651
Trade balance........	−6	−10,431	−33,790	−83,833	−202,278	−273,042	−367,328	−375,168	−418954	−345,204
Japan										
U.S. exports to	22,631	48,580	64,343	64,924	54,681	60,472	62,388	67,603	75,149	74,377
U.S. imports from	68,783	89,684	123,479	146,479	138,004	120,552	131,446	136,411	142,242	143,566
Trade balance........	−46,152	−41,105	−59,137	−81,555	−83,323	−60,080	−69,058	−68,808	−67,093	−69,189
Germany										
U.S. exports to	9,050	18,760	22,394	29,448	34,184	48,155	49,979	53,965	57,758	60,112
U.S. imports from	20,239	28,162	36,844	58,513	84,751	82,450	124,888	117,539	125,784	127,507
Trade balance........	−11,189	−9,402	−14,450	−29,065	−50,567	−34,295	−74,909	−63,574	−68,026	−67,395

Note: Figures shown are on Census Bureau basis.

Busiest U.S. Ports, 2018

Source: U.S. Army Corps of Engineers, Dept. of the Army, U.S. Dept. of Defense
(figures in millions of short tons; ranked by total tonnage handled)

Rank	Port	Domestic	Foreign	Total	Rank	Port	Domestic	Foreign	Total
1.	South Louisiana, LA	134.0	141.5	275.5	26.	Seattle, WA	5.6	20.4	26.0
2.	Houston, TX	77.8	191.1	268.9	27.	Valdez, AK	25.6	0.2	25.8
3.	New York, NY-NJ........	46.7	93.6	140.3	28.	Freeport, TX	4.5	20.9	25.4
4.	Beaumont, TX..........	38.4	61.8	100.2	29.	Port Everglades, FL	13.4	11.6	25.0
5.	Corpus Christi, TX	24.2	69.2	93.5	30.	Charleston, SC.........	2.0	22.8	24.8
6.	New Orleans, LA	49.5	43.8	93.3	31.	Portland, OR...........	7.6	15.7	23.2
7.	Long Beach, CA	10.3	76.2	86.5	32.	Tacoma, WA	3.2	19.6	22.8
8.	Baton Rouge, LA	47.2	35.1	82.2	33.	Pittsburgh, PA	21.6	0.0	21.6
9.	Virginia, VA	4.6	67.2	71.8	34.	Oakland, CA	2.0	17.4	19.4
10.	Los Angeles, CA.......	8.0	59.8	67.8	35.	Jacksonville, FL	8.3	9.7	18.0
11.	Mobile, AL............	22.1	36.5	58.6	36.	Two Harbors, MN	13.4	3.8	17.2
12.	Lake Charles, LA	27.8	29.1	56.9	37.	Chicago, IL	15.2	1.7	16.9
13.	Plaquemines, LA	31.1	25.7	56.9	38.	Boston, MA	5.2	11.0	16.2
14.	Baltimore, MD..........	7.3	37.5	44.8	39.	Paulsboro, NJ	4.7	11.5	16.1
15.	Texas City, TX..........	17.2	25.5	42.7	40.	Kalama, WA	1.0	14.8	15.8
16.	Savannah, GA	1.1	40.1	41.3	41.	Honolulu, HI	13.7	1.4	15.2
17.	Port Arthur, TX	10.9	29.0	39.9	42.	Detroit, MI	11.5	3.3	14.8
18.	Cincinnati-N. Kentucky,				43.	Longview, WA	1.2	12.5	13.7
	OH-KY.	38.5	0.0	38.5	44.	Marcus Hook, PA	7.0	5.2	12.2
19.	St. Louis, MO-IL	37.4	0.0	37.4	45.	Indiana Harbor, IN	11.7	0.2	11.9
20.	Duluth-Superior, MN-WI ..	26.8	8.3	35.1	46.	Cleveland, OH	10.1	1.7	11.8
21.	Huntington-Tristate, WV ..	34.2	0.0	34.2	47.	San Juan, PR	4.9	6.8	11.7
22.	Tampa, FL.............	18.8	12.2	31.0	48.	Memphis, TN	11.1	0.0	11.1
23.	Pascagoula, MS	9.8	17.5	27.4	49.	Anacortes, WA	7.9	3.1	11.0
24.	Richmond, CA	8.9	18.4	27.3	50.	Vancouver, WA	1.3	9.3	10.5
25.	Philadelphia, PA	10.5	16.2	26.7					

World's Busiest Ports, 2014-18

Source: *Review of Maritime Transport, 2019*, United Nations Conference on Trade and Development
(ranked by throughput volume in 2018 as measured in thousands of twenty-ft equivalent units (TEUs))

Rank	Port	Volume (TEUs)					Percent change			
		2014	2015	2016	2017	2018	2014-15	2015-16	2016-17	2017-18
1.	Shanghai, China	35,290	36,537	37,133	40,230	42,010	3.5%	1.6%	8.3%	4.4%
2.	Singapore	33,869	30,962	30,904	33,670	36,600	−8.6	−0.2	9.0	8.7
3.	Ningbo-Zhoushan, China	19,450	20,593	21,560	24,610	26,350	5.9	4.7	14.1	6.9
4.	Shenzhen, China	24,040	24,204	23,979	25,210	25,740	0.7	−0.9	5.1	2.1
5.	Guangzhou, China	16,610	17,457	18,858	20,370	21,920	5.1	8.0	8.0	7.6
6.	Busan, South Korea	18,683	19,296	19,850	21,400	21,660	3.3	2.9	7.8	5.5
7.	Hong Kong, China	22,200	20,114	19,813	20,760	19,600	−9.4	−1.5	4.8	−5.6
8.	Qingdao, China	16,580	17,465	18,010	18,260	19,320	5.3	3.1	1.4	5.5
9.	Tianjin, China	14,060	14,109	14,490	15,210	16,000	0.4	2.7	5.0	6.2
10.	Dubai, United Arab Emirates ..	15,200	15,592	14,772	15,440	14,950	2.6	−5.3	4.5	−2.9
11.	Rotterdam, Netherlands	12,298	12,235	12,385	13,600	14,510	−0.5	1.2	9.8	5.7
12.	Port Klang, Malaysia	10,946	11,891	13,170	12,060	12,030	8.6	10.8	−8.4	0.4
13.	Antwerp, Belgium	8,978	9,650	10,037	10,450	11,100	7.5	4.0	4.1	6.2
14.	Xiamen, China	8,572	9,179	9,614	10,380	10,700	7.1	4.7	8.0	3.1
15.	Kaohsiung, Taiwan	10,593	10,264	10,465	10,240	10,450	−3.1	2.0	−2.2	1.8
16.	Dalian, China	10,130	9,449	9,614	9,710	9,770	−6.7	1.7	1.0	0.6
17.	Los Angeles, CA, U.S.	8,340	8,160	8,857	9,340	9,460	−2.2	8.5	5.5	1.3
18.	Tanjung Pelepas, Malaysia ...	8,500	8,799	8,281	8,330	8,790	3.5	−5.9	0.6	6.4
19.	Hamburg, Germany	9,720	8,825	8,910	9,600	8,780	−9.2	1.0	7.7	−0.2
20.	Long Beach, CA, U.S........	NA	NA	NA	NA	8,070	NA	NA	NA	3.7

NA = Not available. **Note:** A TEU is the size of a typical shipping container.

Value of Freight Shipments by Transportation Mode, 2012-18

Source: *Freight Analysis Framework 2019*, U.S. Dept. of Transportation

(value in billions of 2012 dollars)

Mode of transportation	2012 Total	2012 Domestic	2012 Exports	2012 Imports	2018 Total	2018 Domestic	2018 Exports	2018 Imports
Truck	$12,216	$10,251	$884	$1,081	$12,975	$10,784	$910	$1,281
Rail	722	411	137	174	782	434	143	205
Water	430	270	73	87	546	300	154	92
Air[1]	673	135	284	254	593	140	219	234
Multiple modes and mail	2,121	1,746	97	278	2,265	1,794	114	357
Pipeline	1,325	1,150	53	122	1,533	1,387	44	102
Other and unknown	40	1	17	22	97	1	74	22
Total	17,729	13,965	1,545	2,219	18,908	14,838	1,658	2,412

Note: Imports and exports that pass through the U.S. from a foreign origin to a foreign destination by any mode not included. All truck, rail, water, and pipeline movements that involve more than one mode, including exports and imports that change mode at international gateways, are included in multiple modes and mail to avoid double counting.

Merchant Fleets of the World, 2019

Source: *Review of Maritime Transport, 2019*, United Nations Conference on Trade and Development
(ranked by dead-weight tonnage under flag of registration as of Jan. 1, 2019)

Flag of registration	Number of ships	Percent of total world ships	Dead-weight tonnage	Percent of total world tonnage	Average vessel size (dead-weight tons)	Tonnage change, 2018-19
1. Panama	7,860	8.16%	333,337	16.87%	44,930	-0.57%
2. Marshall Islands	3,537	3.67	245,763	12.43	69,878	3.23
3. Liberia	3,496	3.63	243,129	12.30	69,704	7.98
4. Hong Kong (China)	2,701	2.80	198,747	10.06	75,083	8.17
5. Singapore	3,433	3.57	129,581	6.56	39,785	1.16
6. Malta	2,172	2.26	110,682	5.60	51,890	1.39
7. China	5,589	5.80	91,905	4.65	19,646	8.16
8. The Bahamas	1,401	1.45	77,844	3.94	56,449	1.26
9. Greece	1,308	1.36	69,101	3.50	64,339	-4.28
10. Japan	5,017	5.21	39,034	1.97	10,263	4.23
11. Cyprus	1,039	1.08	34,588	1.75	34,110	-1.36
12. Isle of Man	392	0.41	27,923	1.41	71,232	2.28
13. Indonesia	9,879	10.26	23,880	1.21	4,674	5.54
14. Denmark	566	0.59	22,444	1.14	41,717	15.86
15. Norway	611	0.63	19,758	1.00	32,550	1.08
16. Madeira	465	0.48	19,107	0.97	41,179	-1.14
17. India	1,731	1.80	17,354	0.88	10,633	-6.41
18. United Kingdom	1,031	1.07	17,041	0.86	19,930	1.64
19. Italy	1,353	1.41	13,409	0.68	12,015	-11.82
20. Saudi Arabia	374	0.39	13,128	0.66	45,583	-2.97
21. South Korea	1,880	1.95	13,029	0.66	7,915	-6.65
22. United States	3,671	3.81	11,810	0.60	6,373	-1.03
23. Belgium	201	0.21	10,471	0.53	60,180	18.88
24. Malaysia	1,748	1.82	10,162	0.51	7,202	1.45
25. Russia	2,739	2.84	9,132	0.46	3,416	5.05
26. Bermuda	148	0.15	9,088	0.46	62,245	-15.62
27. Germany	609	0.63	8,470	0.43	16,607	-16.74
28. Vietnam	1,868	1.94	8,469	0.43	4,844	3.27
29. Antigua and Barbuda	780	0.81	7,501	0.38	9,715	-13.88
30. Turkey	1,234	1.28	7,489	0.38	7,866	-5.76
31. Netherlands	1,217	1.26	7,192	0.36	7,016	-1.78
32. Cayman Islands	170	0.18	6,743	0.34	42,678	8.76
33. France	94	0.10	6,231	0.32	66,287	3.91
34. Taiwan	389	0.40	5,751	0.29	19,105	19.35
35. Thailand	825	0.86	732	0.29	8,367	-8.66
World total	96,295	100.00	1,976,491	100.00	25,024	2.61

Note: World total includes flags of registration not shown.

U.S. International Transactions, 1970-2019

Source: U.S. Bureau of Economic Analysis, U.S. Dept. of Commerce
(in millions of dollars)

CURRENT ACCOUNT	1970	1980	1990	2000	2010	2015	2018	2019
Exports of goods and services and income payments (credits)	$68,388	$344,440	$712,128	$1,469,648	$2,623,991	$3,207,288	$3,792,867	$3,805,938
Goods	42,469	224,250	387,401	784,940	1,290,279	1,511,381	1,676,950	1,652,437
Services	14,171	47,585	147,833	290,381	562,759	755,310	862,433	875,825
Primary income receipts	11,748	72,605	176,894	356,706	680,169	810,073	1,108,472	1,135,691
Imports of goods and services and income payments (debits)	66,055	342,124	791,097	1,873,098	3,055,256	3,615,053	4,242,560	4,286,163
Goods	39,866	249,750	498,438	1,231,722	1,938,950	2,273,249	2,557,251	2,516,767
Services	14,519	41,492	117,660	216,115	409,313	491,966	562,069	588,359
Primary income payments	5,514	42,533	148,345	338,637	511,948	606,464	857,298	899,347
Secondary income payments (current transfers)[1]	6,156	8,349	26,654	86,624	195,045	243,372	265,943	281,689
CAPITAL ACCOUNT								
Capital transfer receipts, other credits	NA	NA	0	35	0	0	3,286	67
Capital transfer payments, other debits	NA	NA	7,220	36	157	42	7,482	6,311
Net U.S. acquisition of financial assets[2]	9,336	86,968	103,985	587,682	958,703	202,208	358,971	440,751
Net U.S. incurrence of liabilities[2]	7,226	62,036	162,109	1,066,074	1,391,042	501,121	758,291	797,960
Balance on current account	2,331	2,318	-78,969	-403,450	-431,265	-407,764	-449,693	-480,226
Balance on capital account	NA	NA	-7,221	-1	-157	-42	-4,196	-6,244
Net lending (+) or net borrowing (−) from financial-acct. transactions[3]	2,331	2,318	-86,190	-403,451	-431,422	-407,807	-419,724	-395,549

NA = Not available or applicable. (1) Includes U.S. government and private transfers, such as U.S. government grants and pensions, fines and penalties, withholding taxes, personal transfers (remittances), insurance-related transfers, and other current transfers. (2) Excludes financial derivatives. (3) Net lending means that U.S. residents are net suppliers of funds to foreign residents, and net borrowing means the opposite. Net lending or net borrowing can be computed from current- and capital-account transactions or from financial-account transactions.

U.S. International Direct Investments, 1990-2019
Source: U.S. Bureau of Economic Analysis, U.S. Dept. of Commerce
(in millions of dollars)

	U.S. direct investment abroad					Foreign direct investment in U.S.				
	1990	2000	2010	2018	2019	1990	2000	2010	2018	2019
All countries[1]	$430,521	$1,316,247	$3,741,910	$5,801,025	$5,959,592	$394,911	$1,256,867	$2,280,044	$4,127,175	$4,458,362
Canada	69,508	132,472	295,206	368,498	402,255	29,544	114,309	192,463	442,802	495,720
Europe[1]	**214,739**	**687,320**	**2,034,559**	**3,475,989**	**3,571,710**	**247,320**	**887,014**	**1,659,774**	**2,794,561**	**2,871,431**
Austria	1,113	2,872	11,485	6,740	7,643	625	3,007	4,532	12,392	13,964
Belgium	9,464	17,973	43,975	61,271	63,157	3,900	14,787	69,565	64,661	65,918
Czechia	NA	1,228	5,268	4,515	4,815	NA	NA	65	NA	NA
Denmark	1,726	5,270	11,802	9,498	8,992	819	4,025	7,772	20,654	23,870
Finland	544	1,342	1,597	3,268	3,745	1,504	8,875	4,943	14,464	14,826
France	19,164	42,628	78,320	68,035	83,826	18,650	125,740	189,763	268,169	282,226
Germany	27,609	55,508	103,319	137,148	148,259	28,232	122,412	203,077	328,124	372,879
Greece	282	795	1,775	1,399	938	94	659	-41	NA	NA
Hungary	NA	1,920	4,237	6,597	6,114	NA	5,287	39,266	NA	NA
Ireland	5,894	35,903	158,851	410,636	354,940	1,340	25,523	24,097	265,004	225,517
Italy	14,063	23,484	27,137	33,080	34,900	1,524	6,576	20,142	30,749	32,811
Luxembourg	1,697	27,849	272,206	726,121	766,099	2,195	58,930	170,309	312,976	297,052
Netherlands	19,120	115,429	514,689	810,238	860,528	64,671	138,894	234,408	462,303	487,079
Norway	4,209	4,379	28,541	26,145	25,556	773	2,665	10,478	26,007	24,221
Poland	NA	3,884	13,152	11,744	10,403	29	57	4,386	NA	NA
Portugal	897	2,664	2,612	2,513	2,425	-19	-68	204	NA	NA
Russia	NA	1,147	10,040	14,071	14,439	NA	118	5,689	NA	NA
Spain	7,868	21,236	52,390	35,425	40,793	792	5,068	43,095	83,379	86,796
Sweden	1,787	25,959	23,275	41,024	38,787	5,484	21,991	38,780	49,546	52,683
Switzerland	25,099	55,377	119,891	253,253	228,968	17,674	64,719	180,642	295,783	300,393
Turkey	522	1,826	4,155	3,903	3,333	20	188	749	NA	NA
UK	72,707	230,762	501,247	796,564	851,414	98,676	277,613	400,435	496,622	505,088
Latin America[1]	**71,413**	**266,576**	**752,788**	**948,789**	**911,869**	**20,168**	**53,691**	**62,130**	**153,638**	**193,786**
Argentina	2,531	17,488	11,747	9,522	10,698	420	364	464	NA	NA
The Bahamas	4,004	NA	NA	NA	NA	1,535	1,254	1,753	646	1,089
Barbados	252	2,141	7,524	39,802	45,382	191	1,560	706	NA	NA
Bermuda	20,169	60,114	265,524	333,843	262,418	1,550	18,336	365	28,018	56,279
Brazil	14,384	36,717	66,963	79,032	81,731	377	882	1,357	2,514	4,617
Chile	1,896	10,052	30,747	25,986	25,084	5	24	391	NA	NA
Colombia	1,677	3,693	6,181	8,055	8,264	55	2	382	NA	NA
Costa Rica	251	1,716	1,827	1,597	1,521	-2	2	-48	NA	NA
Curaçao[2]	-4,501	NA	NA	NA	NA	12,974	3,807	2,819	1,335	1,182
Dominican Rep.	529	1,143	1,432	2,162	2,604	0	79	-142	NA	NA
Ecuador	280	832	1,283	722	619	6	29	77	NA	NA
Honduras	262	399	936	850	1,281	8	-3	7	NA	NA
Mexico	10,313	39,352	85,751	95,873	100,888	575	7,462	10,970	21,050	21,526
Panama	9,289	30,758	5,156	5,075	5,272	4,188	3,819	952	2,789	2,965
Peru	599	3,130	7,196	5,765	7,470	NA	-13	182	NA	NA
UK isls. in Caribbean	5,929	33,451	191,680	282,937	300,505	-2,979	15,191	38,477	83,555	90,554
Venezuela	1,087	10,531	10,255	2,185	2,228	496	792	3,122	1,673	1,705
Africa[1]	**3,650**	**11,891**	**54,816**	**44,378**	**43,193**	**505**	**2,700**	**2,265**	**5,652**	**9,823**
Egypt	1,231	1,998	12,599	10,781	11,000	1	-4	-277	NA	NA
Nigeria	-401	470	5,058	4,501	5,469	-17	NA	23	NA	NA
South Africa	775	3,562	6,017	7,313	7,812	10	704	699	4,013	4,061
Middle East[1]	**3,959**	**10,863**	**34,431**	**75,240**	**75,205**	**4,425**	**6,506**	**16,808**	**29,329**	**29,076**
Israel	746	3,735	9,464	27,715	28,543	640	3,012	8,714	13,982	14,566
Saudi Arabia	1,899	3,661	7,436	10,884	10,826	1,811	NA	NA	6,912	6,220
UAE	409	683	4,935	17,437	17,153	99	64	747	5,530	5,099
Asia and Pacific[1]	**64,718**	**207,125**	**570,111**	**888,133**	**955,361**	**92,948**	**192,647**	**346,605**	**701,193**	**858,527**
Australia	15,110	34,838	125,421	163,999	162,400	6,542	18,775	35,632	63,070	80,974
China	354	11,140	58,996	109,332	116,203	NA	277	3,300	33,543	37,685
Hong Kong	6,055	27,447	41,264	79,797	81,883	1,511	1,493	4,440	13,159	14,110
India	372	2,379	24,666	42,444	45,883	NA	96	4,102	5,127	5,009
Indonesia	3,207	8,904	10,558	10,240	12,151	25	16	138	NA	NA
Japan	22,599	57,091	113,523	113,254	131,793	83,091	159,690	255,012	493,763	619,259
Korea, South	2,695	8,968	26,233	39,021	39,105	-1,009	3,110	15,746	56,612	61,822
Malaysia	1,466	7,910	11,791	10,867	10,849	56	310	338	1,218	981
New Zealand	3,156	4,271	6,724	11,667	12,018	157	395	584	2,107	2,550
Philippines	1,355	3,638	5,399	6,922	6,940	77	47	103	NA	NA
Singapore	3,975	24,133	102,778	254,670	287,951	1,289	5,087	21,517	18,267	21,060
Taiwan	2,226	7,836	22,188	16,562	17,353	836	3,174	4,642	10,512	11,099
Thailand	1,790	5,824	12,999	16,952	17,738	150	132	158	NA	NA

NA = Not available. **Note:** On a historical cost basis for comparison purposes. Direct investment in all industries. Book value of foreign direct investors' equity in, and net outstanding loans to, their U.S. affiliates. A U.S. affiliate is a U.S. business enterprise in which a single foreign direct investor owns at least 10% of the voting securities, or the equivalent. (1) Totals and subtotals include countries or territories not shown in table. (2) Curaçao figures before 2010 are for the entire Netherlands Antilles, a confederation that ended in 2010.

TRANSPORTATION AND TRAVEL

Top Motor Vehicle Producing Nations, 2019

Source: International Organization of Motor Vehicle Manufacturers (OICA)
(in thousands of units; ranked by total production)

Nation	Total motor vehicles	Cars	Commercial vehicles[1]	% change, 2018-19[2]	Nation	Total motor vehicles	Cars	Commercial vehicles[1]	% change, 2018-19[2]
China[3]	25,721	21,360	4,360	−7.5%	Poland	650	435	215	−1.5%
U.S.	10,880	2,513	8,367	−3.7	South Africa	632	349	283	3.5
Japan	9,684	8,329	1,356	−0.5	Malaysia	572	534	38	1.2
Germany. . . .	4,661	4,661	0	−9.0	Hungary	498	498	0	7.6
India	4,516	3,623	893	−12.2	Romania	490	490	0	2.9
Mexico	3,987	1,383	2,604	−2.8	Morocco	395	360	35	−1.8
South Korea	3,951	3,613	338	−1.9	Portugal	346	282	64	17.4
Brazil.	2,945	2,448	496	2.2	Argentina . . .	315	108	206	−32.5
Spain	2,822	2,248	574	0.1	Belgium.	286	247	39	−7.4
France	2,202	1,675	527	−2.9	Uzbekistan . .	271	271	0	22.9
Thailand	2,014	795	1,218	−7.1	Taiwan	251	190	62	−0.8
Canada.	1,917	461	1,455	−5.4	Slovenia	199	199	0	−4.9
Russia.	1,720	1,524	196	−2.8	Austria	179	158	21	8.8
Turkey.	1,461	983	479	−5.7	Finland	115	115	0	2.5
Czechia.	1,434	1,428	6	−0.6	Serbia	35	35	0	−37.8
UK.	1,381	1,303	78	−13.9	Egypt	19	19	0	0.0
Indonesia . . .	1,287	1,046	241	−4.2	Ukraine	7	6	1	9.7
Slovakia	1,100	1,100	0	0.6	Others	1,109	1,048	60	NA
Italy.	915	542	373	−13.8	**NAFTA**	**16,783**	**4,357**	**12,427**	**−3.7**
Iran	821	770	51	−25.0	**Total**	**91,787**	**67,149**	**24,638**	**−5.2**

NA = Not applicable. NAFTA = North American Free Trade Agreement. **Note:** Numbers may not add up to totals due to rounding. (1) Includes light commercial vehicles, heavy trucks, coaches, and buses. (2) Percent change in number of total motor vehicles. (3) Not including Taiwan.

World Motor Vehicle Production, 1950-2019

Source: For 1950-90, American Automobile Manufacturers Assn.; 2000-12, Automotive News Data Center and R.L. Polk; 2013-19, OICA
(in thousands of units)

Year	U.S.	Canada	Europe[1]	Japan	Other	World total	U.S. % of world total
1950	8,006	388	1,991	32	160	10,577	75.7%
1960	7,905	398	6,837	482	866	16,488	47.9
1970	8,284	1,160	13,049	5,289	1,637	29,419	28.2
1980	8,010	1,324	15,496	11,043	2,692	38,565	20.8
1990	9,783	1,928	18,866	13,487	4,496	48,554	20.1
2000	12,832	2,952	17,678	10,145	16,098	59,704	21.5
2005	12,018	2,665	20,855	10,800	20,691	67,892	17.7
2007	10,611	2,602	22,858	11,596	26,019	74,647	14.2
2008	8,503	2,046	21,608	10,969	31,224	67,602	12.6
2009	5,591	1,476	17,075	7,648	32,374	59,096	9.5
2010	7,632	2,074	19,371	9,197	35,036	73,311	10.4
2011	8,462	2,127	20,709	7,901	36,828	76,027	11.1
2012	10,142	2,454	22,324	9,448	36,714	81,082	12.5
2013	11,066	2,380	19,923	9,630	44,508	87,507	12.6
2014	11,661	2,394	20,430	9,775	45,536	89,776	12.9
2015	12,100	2,283	21,096	9,278	46,024	90,781	13.3
2016	12,198	2,370	21,700	9,205	49,504	94,977	12.8
2017	11,190	2,200	22,161	9,694	52,058	97,303	11.5
2018	10,986	2,000	21,273	9,201	48,079	91,539	12.0
2019	10,880	1,917	21,312	9,684	47,994	91,787	11.9

Note: Data may not be fully comparable across all years because they are derived from different sources. Number of units may not add up to totals due to rounding. (1) Prior to 2004, numbers exclude Eastern European production.

Passenger Cars Imported Into the U.S. by Country of Origin, 1970-2019

Source: U.S. Census Bureau, U.S. Dept. of Commerce
(in number of units)

Year	Mexico	Japan	Canada	S. Korea	Germany[1]	UK	Italy	Sweden	France	Total[2]
1970	NA	381,338	692,783	NA	674,945	76,257	42,523	57,844	37,114	2,013,420
1975	0	695,573	733,766	NA	370,012	67,106	102,344	51,993	15,647	2,074,653
1980	1	1,991,502	594,770	NA	338,711	32,517	46,899	61,496	47,386	3,116,448
1985	13,647	2,527,467	1,144,805	NA	473,110	24,474	8,689	142,640	42,882	4,397,679
1990	215,986	1,867,794	1,220,221	201,475	245,286	27,271	11,045	93,084	1,976	3,944,602
1995	462,800	1,114,360	1,552,691	131,718	204,932	42,450	1,031	82,593	14	3,624,428
2000	933,948	1,837,631	2,138,825	568,153	491,704	81,079	3,129	86,707	28,024	6,326,013
2005	693,149	1,832,534	1,967,985	730,500	547,191	184,716	5,377	93,736	412	6,564,844
2010	902,565	1,569,220	1,741,493	515,601	506,053	96,689	4,298	38,749	4,153	5,668,111
2011	953,514	1,421,750	1,835,819	587,574	537,158	95,742	5,372	26,884	3,580	5,673,139
2012	1,052,212	1,723,014	2,094,793	705,089	629,579	114,073	11,767	24,653	10,949	6,590,863
2013	1,127,375	1,722,119	2,009,140	759,964	657,832	115,326	14,289	21,617	12,694	6,682,557
2014	1,290,183	1,714,368	2,022,449	895,141	624,891	105,135	21,607	26,443	25,292	6,813,003
2015	1,438,840	1,609,709	1,969,502	1,065,972	639,879	134,413	132,340	37,789	28,034	7,420,613
2016	1,417,616	1,614,368	2,010,907	1,001,021	555,577	199,611	133,002	47,868	16,497	7,482,316
2017	1,724,526	1,731,889	1,850,765	929,530	502,059	217,341	159,802	58,492	9,801	7,660,401
2018	1,934,416	1,730,944	1,641,550	831,164	458,830	235,773	153,850	43,359	5,091	7,554,168
2019	2,018,683	1,733,158	1,558,586	916,610	414,815	213,528	102,642	60,147	2,413	7,507,929

NA = Not available. **Note:** Includes new and used cars. Excludes cars assembled in U.S. foreign trade zones. (1) Figures prior to 1991 are for West Germany. (2) Includes units imported from countries not shown in table.

Passenger Car Production in U.S. Plants, 2017-19

Source: Wards Intelligence
(in number of units)

	2019	2018	2017		2019	2018	2017
FCA TOTAL[1]	—	—	531	**HYUNDAI TOTAL**	198,593	233,987	269,919
Dodge Viper	—	—	531	Hyundai Elantra	123,761	147,018	131,753
FORD TOTAL	120,242	264,199	396,736	Hyundai Sonata	74,832	86,969	138,166
Ford C-Max	—	3,685	19,672	**KIA TOTAL**	98,387	90,799	96,444
Ford Focus	—	86,862	179,110	Kia Optima	98,387	90,799	96,444
Ford Mustang	99,174	108,540	120,780	**MERCEDES TOTAL**	26,176	46,378	53,628
Ford Taurus	7,269	46,733	51,375	Mercedes C-Class	26,176	46,378	53,628
Lincoln Continental	13,799	18,379	25,799	**NISSAN TOTAL**	272,383	286,064	340,554
GENERAL MOTORS TOTAL	253,837	446,208	490,629	Nissan Altima	225,934	219,600	261,872
Buick LaCrosse	2,038	11,312	12,208	Nissan Leaf	16,022	23,903	8,719
Cadillac ATS	176	8,608	13,335	Nissan Maxima	30,427	42,561	69,963
Cadillac CT5	3,166	—	—	**SUBARU TOTAL**	106,410	116,612	158,484
Cadillac CT6	10,147	9,137	9,914	Subaru Impreza	73,461	76,417	109,038
Cadillac CTS	5,186	11,185	8,929	Subaru Legacy	32,949	40,195	49,446
Chevrolet Camaro	41,858	56,205	59,869	**TESLA TOTAL**	333,707	204,820	53,846
Chevrolet Corvette	14,651	21,137	21,999	Tesla Model 3	301,479	152,977	2,685
Chevrolet Cruze	18,637	121,168	131,617	Tesla Model S	32,228	51,843	51,161
Chevrolet Impala	18,605	16,139	14,747	**TOYOTA TOTAL**	601,823	566,332	584,421
Chevrolet Malibu	123,451	148,226	161,816	Lexus ES	51,660	43,680	41,657
Chevrolet Sonic	12,694	20,278	34,324	Toyota Avalon	32,892	34,896	39,635
Chevrolet Volt	3,228	22,813	21,871	Toyota Camry	359,782	351,648	339,297
HONDA TOTAL	448,385	476,569	526,818	Toyota Corolla	157,489	136,108	163,832
Acura ILX	18,134	11,877	9,808	**VOLKSWAGEN TOTAL**	8,501	46,939	61,206
Acura NSX	228	433	925	Volkswagen Passat	8,501	46,939	61,206
Acura TLX	24,114	30,170	42,080	**VOLVO TOTAL**	43,267	6,257	—
Honda Accord	274,247	337,471	327,425	Volvo 60	43,267	6,257	—
Honda Civic	111,519	72,882	146,580				
Honda Insight	20,143	23,736	—	**TOTAL CARS**	2,511,711	2,785,164	3,033,216

— = No production. (1) Fiat Chrysler Automobiles, or FCA, was formed in 2014 when Fiat acquired the remaining shares of Chrysler Group that it did not already own.

Domestic and Imported Retail Car Sales in the U.S., 1980-2019

Source: Wards Intelligence
(in number of units)

	Cars			Light trucks			All vehicles		
Year	Domestic[1]	Imports	Total cars	Domestic[1]	Imports	Total light trucks	Domestic[1]	Imports	Total vehicles
1980	6,579,778	2,369,457	8,949,235	1,750,735	478,887	2,229,622	8,330,513	2,848,344	11,178,857
1985	8,204,670	2,774,517	10,979,187	3,629,080	832,186	4,461,266	12,109,999	3,615,292	15,725,291
1988	7,539,925	3,003,692	10,543,617	4,199,643	710,661	4,910,304	12,050,990	3,737,363	15,788,353
1989	7,095,484	2,680,419	9,775,903	4,113,441	641,387	4,754,828	11,500,770	3,341,877	14,842,647
1990	6,916,860	2,384,346	9,301,206	3,956,756	611,941	4,568,697	11,133,504	3,013,865	14,147,369
1991	6,161,573	2,023,406	8,184,979	3,605,633	538,008	4,143,641	9,975,798	2,573,725	12,549,523
1992	6,285,916	1,927,197	8,213,113	4,247,097	408,003	4,655,100	10,767,685	2,349,759	13,117,444
1993	6,741,667	1,776,192	8,517,859	5,000,482	377,639	5,378,121	12,029,051	2,169,803	14,198,854
1994	7,255,303	1,735,214	8,990,517	5,658,302	409,759	6,068,061	13,251,198	2,160,176	15,411,374
1995	7,113,902	1,506,257	8,620,159	5,705,708	402,181	6,107,889	13,192,861	1,923,464	15,116,325
1996	7,206,349	1,272,196	8,478,545	6,179,881	438,757	6,618,638	13,732,379	1,723,733	15,456,112
1997	6,862,175	1,355,305	8,217,480	6,324,758	579,483	6,904,241	13,549,251	1,948,609	15,497,860
1998	6,705,208	1,379,781	8,084,989	6,802,016	656,002	7,458,018	13,913,028	2,054,259	15,967,287
1999	6,918,781	1,718,927	8,637,708	7,480,607	775,223	8,255,830	14,901,266	2,513,462	17,414,728
2000	6,761,603	2,016,120	8,777,723	7,719,707	852,325	8,572,032	14,922,648	2,889,025	17,811,673
2001	6,254,371	2,097,629	8,352,000	7,789,089	981,280	8,770,369	14,372,624	3,099,754	17,472,378
2002	5,816,671	2,225,584	8,042,255	7,707,738	1,066,375	8,774,113	13,829,568	3,309,084	17,138,652
2003	5,472,500	2,083,051	7,555,551	7,856,322	1,227,180	9,083,502	13,638,351	3,329,091	16,967,442
2004	5,333,496	2,149,059	7,482,555	8,138,107	1,246,258	9,384,365	13,880,251	3,418,322	17,298,573
2005	5,473,450	2,186,533	7,659,983	8,072,456	1,215,315	9,287,771	14,020,528	3,423,801	17,444,329
2006	5,416,828	2,344,764	7,761,592	7,396,058	1,346,750	8,742,808	13,334,843	3,714,138	17,048,981
2007	5,197,271	2,365,063	7,562,334	7,138,803	1,388,085	8,526,888	12,687,016	3,773,299	16,460,315
2008	4,490,863	2,278,271	6,769,134	5,329,165	1,096,469	6,425,634	10,107,753	3,385,439	13,493,192
2009	3,558,283	1,843,282	5,401,565	4,116,550	884,242	5,000,792	7,867,766	2,734,277	10,602,043
2010	3,791,499	1,844,240	5,635,739	5,020,441	898,644	5,919,085	9,020,088	2,752,438	11,772,526
2011	4,145,964	1,946,897	6,092,861	5,666,512	982,443	6,648,955	10,108,762	2,939,624	13,048,386
2012	5,119,844	2,125,325	7,245,169	6,127,314	1,060,720	7,188,034	11,581,776	3,197,708	14,779,484
2013	5,433,158	2,153,176	7,586,334	6,704,449	1,239,268	7,943,767	12,479,306	3,403,406	15,882,712
2014	5,609,878	2,098,122	7,708,000	7,384,280	1,359,910	8,744,190	13,388,628	3,471,215	16,859,843
2015	5,595,123	1,921,703	7,516,826	8,097,387	1,782,078	9,879,465	14,127,526	3,718,098	17,845,624
2016	5,145,575	1,727,154	6,872,729	8,436,243	2,155,805	10,592,048	13,969,117	3,896,656	17,865,773
2017	4,592,965	1,487,984	6,080,949	8,651,782	2,403,628	11,055,410	13,644,445	3,906,956	17,551,401
2018	4,086,889	1,216,691	5,303,580	9,159,021	2,750,945	11,909,966	13,716,683	3,984,719	17,701,402
2019	3,543,923	1,171,082	4,715,005	9,622,843	2,615,064	12,237,907	13,678,041	3,801,963	17,480,004

Note: Vehicles are cars and light trucks belonging to gross vehicle weight (GVW) classes 1-3 (under 14,001 lbs). (1) Includes the U.S., Canada, and Mexico.

U.S. Vehicle Sales, 1980-2019
Source: Wards Intelligence; in millions

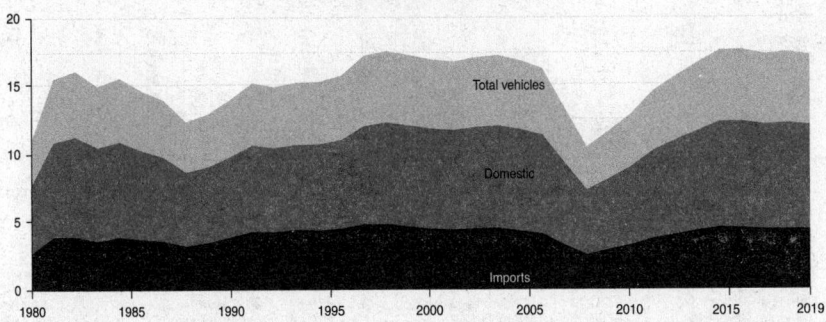

Note: Vehicles are cars and light trucks belonging to gross vehicle weight (GVW) classes 1-3 (under 14,001 lbs). Domestic sales include the U.S., Canada, and Mexico.

U.S. Sales of Hybrid and Electric Vehicles, 2000-19
Source: Wards Intelligence; in number of units sold

Power type	2000	2005	2010	2013	2014	2015	2016	2017	2018	2019
Hybrid car	9,350	151,253	231,819	468,005	416,944	350,753	276,995	252,366	217,459	230,676
Hybrid light truck	0	54,575	42,286	20,023	26,872	22,606	64,797	111,363	120,690	168,768
Total hybrid	**9,350**	**205,828**	**274,105**	**488,028**	**443,816**	**373,359**	**341,792**	**363,729**	**338,149**	**399,444**
Electric car	463	0	326	47,424	67,067	72,313	64,307	62,208	167,737	184,728
Electric light truck	0	0	0	1,096	1,184	61	16,067	40,172	39,325	49,094
Total electric	**463**	**0**	**326**	**48,520**	**68,251**	**72,374**	**80,374**	**102,380**	**207,062**	**233,822**
Fuel cell car	0	6	17	10	2	74	1,042	2,285	2,324	1,822
Fuel cell light truck	0	0	0	0	50	34	40	28	44	267
Total fuel cell	**0**	**6**	**17**	**10**	**52**	**108**	**1,082**	**2,313**	**2,368**	**2,089**
Plug-in hybrid car	0	0	326	49,043	55,341	41,739	60,972	76,420	95,279	58,576
Plug-in hybrid light truck	0	0	0	0	100	2,076	10,357	14,607	28,604	27,215
Total plug-in hybrid	**0**	**0**	**326**	**49,043**	**55,441**	**43,815**	**71,329**	**91,027**	**123,883**	**85,791**

Top-Selling Passenger Cars in the U.S., 2016-19
Source: Wards Intelligence; ranked by number of vehicles sold

Car	2019 sales	Car	2019 sales	Car	2019 sales
1. Toyota Camry	336,978	8. Ford Fusion	166,045	15. Kia Forte	95,609
2. Honda Civic	325,650	9. Tesla Model 3	142,774	16. Hyundai Sonata	87,466
3. Toyota Corolla	304,850	10. Chevrolet Malibu	131,917	17. Ford Mustang	72,489
4. Honda Accord	267,567	11. Volkswagen Jetta	100,453	18. Toyota Prius	68,442
5. Nissan Altima	209,183	12. Kia Soul	98,033	19. Nissan Versa	66,596
6. Nissan Sentra	184,618	13. Dodge Charger	96,935	20. Subaru Impreza	66,415
7. Hyundai Elantra	175,094	14. Kia Optima	96,623		

Car	2018 sales	Car	2017 sales	Car	2016 sales
1. Toyota Camry	343,439	1. Toyota Camry	387,081	1. Toyota Camry	388,618
2. Honda Civic	325,760	2. Honda Civic	377,286	2. Honda Civic	366,927
3. Honda Accord	291,071	3. Honda Accord	322,655	3. Toyota Corolla	360,483
4. Toyota Corolla	285,865	4. Toyota Corolla	308,695	4. Honda Accord	345,225
5. Nissan Sentra	213,046	5. Nissan Sentra	254,996	5. Nissan Altima	307,380
6. Nissan Altima	209,146	6. Nissan Sentra	218,451	6. Ford Fusion	265,840
7. Hyundai Elantra	200,415	7. Ford Fusion	209,623	7. Chevrolet Malibu	227,881
8. Ford Fusion	173,600	8. Hyundai Elantra	198,210	8. Nissan Sentra	214,709
9. Chevrolet Malibu	144,542	9. Chevrolet Malibu	185,857	9. Hyundai Elantra	208,319
10. Chevrolet Cruze	142,617	10. Chevrolet Cruze	184,751	10. Hyundai Sonata	199,416

U.S. Retail Car Sales by Vehicle Size, 1985-2019
Source: Wards Intelligence; as a percent of total U.S. sales

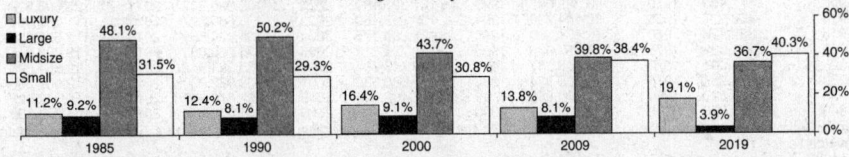

U.S. Light Truck Sales by Type, 1985-2019
Source: Wards Intelligence; as percent of total U.S. sales

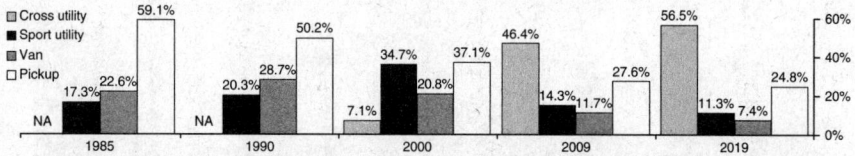

NA = Not applicable. **Note:** Comm. chassis sales (not shown) were 1.0% (for 1985), 0.8% (1990), 0.2% (2000), 0.1% (2009), 0.02% (2019).

Top-Selling Light Trucks in the U.S., 2017-19
Source: Wards Intelligence; ranked by number of vehicles sold

Truck	2019 sales	Truck	2018 sales	Truck	2017 sales
1. Ford F-Series	833,378	1. Ford F-Series	844,448	1. Ford F-Series	834,445
2. Ram Ram Pickup	617,227	2. Chevrolet Silverado	585,575	2. Chevrolet Silverado	585,864
3. Chevrolet Silverado	570,608	3. Ram Pickup	521,046	3. Ram Pickup	483,520
4. Toyota RAV4	448,071	4. Toyota RAV4	427,170	4. Toyota RAV4	407,594
5. Honda CR-V	384,168	5. Nissan Rogue	412,110	5. Nissan Rogue	403,465
6. Nissan Rogue	350,447	6. Honda CR-V	379,013	6. Honda CR-V	377,895
7. Chevrolet Equinox	346,048	7. Chevrolet Equinox	332,618	7. Ford Escape	308,296
8. Toyota Tacoma	248,801	8. Ford Escape	272,228	8. Chevrolet Equinox	290,458
9. Jeep Grand Cherokee	242,969	9. Ford Explorer	261,571	9. Ford Explorer	271,131
10. Ford Escape	241,388	10. Toyota Tacoma	245,659	10. Jeep Grand Cherokee	240,696

Most Popular Colors by Vehicle Type, 2019
Source: Axalta Coating Systems; for 2019 model year in North America

Luxury cars/SUVs		Intermediate cars/CUVs		Compact/sports cars		Light trucks	
Color	Percent	Color	Percent	Color	Percent	Color	Percent
Black/effect black	28%	White/pearl white	31%	White/pearl white	23%	White/pearl white	31%
White/pearl white	25	Gray	17	Gray	19	Black/effect black	20
Gray	16	Black/effect black	16	Black/effect black	17	Gray	16
Blue	10	Silver	13	Blue	14	Silver	11
Silver	9	Blue	9	Silver	12	Blue	9
Red	6	Red	8	Red	10	Red	9
Brown/beige	3	Brown/beige	2	Green	1	Brown/beige	3
Green	2	Green	1	Yellow/gold	1	Green	1
Yellow/gold	<1	Yellow/gold	1	Brown/beige	<1	Yellow/gold	<1
Other	1	Other	2	Other	3	Other	<1

U.S. Light-Duty Vehicle Fuel Efficiency, 1975-2019
Source: Natl. Vehicle and Fuel Emissions Laboratory, Office of Transportation and Air Quality, U.S. Environmental Protection Agency

Cars and light-duty trucks (SUVs, minivans, passenger vans, and pickup trucks) showed significant fuel-efficiency improvements from 1975 through 1987, when the fuel economy for both combined reached a high of 22 miles per gallon (mpg). The fuel economy value mainly declined, 1988-2004, but since 2005, fuel economy has generally increased, reaching a new all-time high of 25.5 mpg in 2019.

Year[1]	Cars (mpg)	Light-duty trucks (mpg)	All light-duty vehicles (mpg)	Year[1]	Cars (mpg)	Light-duty trucks (mpg)	All light-duty vehicles (mpg)
1975	13.5	11.6	13.1	2008	23.9	17.8	21.0
1980	20.0	15.8	19.2	2009	25.0	18.5	22.4
1985	23.0	17.5	21.3	2010	25.7	18.8	22.6
1990	23.3	17.4	21.2	2011	25.4	19.1	22.3
1995	23.3	17.0	20.5	2012	26.9	19.3	23.6
2000	22.5	16.8	19.8	2013	27.6	19.8	24.2
2002	22.8	16.5	19.5	2014	27.6	20.3	24.1
2003	23.0	16.7	19.6	2015	28.2	21.1	24.6
2004	22.9	16.5	19.3	2016	28.5	21.2	24.7
2005	23.1	16.9	19.9	2017	29.2	21.4	24.9
2006	23.0	17.2	20.1	2018	29.9	21.9	25.1
2007	23.7	17.4	20.6	2019[2]	29.9	22.3	25.5

Note: Adjusted mpg composite values (city and highway fuel efficiency combined in a 55%/45% ratio) are used for all vehicles and are intended to reflect real-world use. (1) Because of changes in methodology, mpg figures prior to 1986 are not entirely comparable with later values. (2) Preliminary.

Registered Cars in the U.S., 1900-2018
Source: Office of Highway Policy Information, Federal Highway Administration, U.S. Dept. of Transportation
(number of automobiles for public and private use)

Year	Reg. cars	Year	Reg. cars	Year	Reg. cars	Year	Reg. cars	Year	Reg. cars
1900	8,000	1945	25,796,985	1990	133,700,497	2001	137,633,467	2010	130,892,240
1905	77,400	1950	40,339,077	1993	127,327,189	2002	135,920,677	2011	125,656,528
1910	458,377	1955	52,144,739	1994	127,883,469	2003	135,669,897	2012	111,289,906
1915	2,332,426	1960	61,671,390	1995	128,386,775	2004	136,430,651	2013	113,676,345
1920	8,131,522	1965	75,257,588	1996	129,728,311	2005	136,568,083	2014	113,898,845
1925	17,481,001	1970	89,243,557	1997	129,748,704	2006	135,399,945	2015	112,864,228
1930	23,034,753	1975	106,705,934	1998	131,838,538	2007	135,932,930	2016	112,961,266
1935	22,567,827	1980	121,600,843	1999	132,432,044	2008	137,079,843	2017	111,177,029
1940	27,465,826	1985	127,885,193	2000	133,621,420	2009	134,879,600	2018	111,242,132

Note: There were no publicly owned vehicles before 1925; statistics also exclude military vehicles for all years. Alaska and Hawaii data included since 1960.

Licensed Drivers by Age and Sex, 1980-2018

Source: Office of Highway Policy Information, Federal Highway Administration, U.S. Dept. of Transportation
(numbers in thousands)

Age (years)	1980 Total	1990 Total	2000 Total	2010 Male	2010 Female	2010 Total	2018 Male	2018 Female	2018 Total	% total drivers
Under 16	93	43	27	199	198	398	21	22	43	0.0%
16	1,823	1,443	1,470	608	605	1,213	525	541	1,066	0.5
17	2,790	2,132	2,331	1,025	1,004	2,028	989	987	1,976	0.9
18	3,247	2,595	2,839	1,408	1,323	2,731	1,340	1,290	2,630	1.2
19	3,542	3,037	3,077	1,641	1,546	3,187	1,556	1,485	3,040	1.3
19 and under	11,496	9,249	9,744	4,880	4,676	9,556	4,431	4,324	8,756	3.8
20	3,636	3,229	3,140	1,744	1,682	3,426	1,658	1,590	3,249	1.4
21	3,733	3,249	3,172	1,756	1,717	3,474	1,706	1,649	3,355	1.5
22	3,811	3,262	3,182	1,757	1,725	3,483	1,775	1,731	3,506	1.5
23	3,938	3,398	3,247	1,767	1,748	3,515	1,842	1,803	3,645	1.6
24	3,915	3,758	3,225	1,792	1,779	3,571	1,895	1,869	3,764	1.7
20-24	19,032	16,897	15,966	8,817	8,651	17,469	8,876	8,643	17,519	7.7
25-29	18,925	19,895	17,586	9,179	9,253	18,431	10,099	10,088	20,186	8.9
30-34	17,369	20,578	19,155	8,934	8,915	17,849	9,953	10,026	19,979	8.8
35-39	13,696	19,055	21,059	9,079	9,082	18,161	9,725	9,877	19,603	8.6
40-44	11,134	16,905	21,093	9,613	9,565	19,178	8,956	9,087	18,043	7.9
45-49	10,076	13,020	19,154	10,381	10,433	20,814	9,550	9,648	19,198	8.4
50-54	10,090	10,484	16,868	10,241	10,388	20,628	9,665	9,779	19,445	8.5
55-59	9,770	9,438	12,760	9,127	9,313	18,440	10,134	10,405	20,539	9.0
60-64	8,232	9,235	9,915	7,847	8,011	15,858	9,328	9,713	19,042	8.4
65-69	6,580	8,375	8,386	5,652	5,816	11,468	7,759	8,183	15,942	7.0
70-74	NA	NA	7,468	4,029	4,202	8,231	5,963	6,289	12,252	5.4
75-79	NA	NA	5,911	2,966	3,192	6,158	3,878	4,176	8,054	3.5
80-84	NA	NA	3,511	2,090	2,373	4,464	2,315	2,621	4,936	2.2
85 and over	NA	NA	2,050	1,541	1,870	3,411	1,847	2,218	4,065	1.8
Total	145,295	167,015	190,625	104,374	105,740	210,115	112,480	115,079	227,558	100.0

NA = Not available. **Note:** Numbers may not add up to totals due to rounding.

Mobile Device Handheld Phone and Texting Laws for Drivers, 2020

Source: Insurance Institute for Highway Safety; as of Aug. 2020

State	Handheld ban	Texting ban	Enforcement	State	Handheld ban	Texting ban	Enforcement	State	Handheld ban	Texting ban	Enforcement
AL	No[1]	Yes	P	KY	No[5]	Yes	P	ND	No[5]	Yes	P
AK	No	Yes	P	LA	No[5,6,7]	Yes	P[8]	OH	No[5]	Yes	S[11]
AZ	Yes	Yes	P[2]	ME	Yes	Yes	P	OK	No[6]	Yes	P
AR	No[3]	Yes	P	MD	Yes	Yes	P	OR	Yes	Yes	P
CA	Yes	Yes	P[4]	MA	Yes	Yes	P	PA	No	Yes	P
CO	No[5]	Yes	P	MI	No[6]	Yes	P	RI	Yes	Yes	P
CT	Yes	Yes	P	MN	Yes	Yes	P	SC	No	Yes	P
DE	Yes	Yes	P	MS	No	Yes	P	SD	Yes	Yes	P[12]
DC	Yes	Yes	P	MO	No	No[9]	P	TN	Yes	Yes	P
FL	No	Yes	P	MT	No	No	NA	TX	No[5]	Yes	P
GA	Yes	Yes	P	NE	No[10]	Yes	S	UT	No[5]	Yes	P
HI	Yes	Yes	P	NV	Yes	Yes	P	VT	Yes	Yes	P
ID	Yes	Yes	P	NH	Yes	Yes	P	VA	No[13]	Yes	P[4]
IL	Yes	Yes	P	NJ	Yes	Yes	P	WA	Yes	Yes	P
IN	Yes	Yes	P	NM	No[6]	Yes	P	WV	Yes	Yes	P
IA	No[6]	Yes	P	NY	Yes	Yes	P	WI	No[6]	Yes	P
KS	No[6]	Yes	P	NC	No[5]	Yes	P	WY	No	Yes	P

NA = Not applicable. P = Officer may stop vehicle for violation (primary); S = Officer may issue citation only when vehicle is stopped for another moving violation (secondary). **Note:** Laws shown for licensed passenger car drivers. Different laws and regulations apply to school bus, municipal transit, and other mass transit operators. Different laws may apply in school zones, construction zones, or other such areas. (1) Yes for 16-year-old drivers and for 17-year-old drivers who have held an intermediate license for fewer than 6 months. (2) Primary after Jan. 1, 2021; until then, officer may only issue a warning. Secondary for learner's permit holders and intermediate license holders during the first 6 months after licensing. (3) Yes for drivers under 21 years of age. (4) Secondary for cellphone use by young drivers. (5) Yes for drivers under 18. (6) Yes for learner's permit and intermediate license holders. (7) Yes for drivers in the year after getting their first license. (8) Secondary for cellphone use by novice drivers age 18 and older. (9) Yes for drivers 21 and younger. (10) Yes for learner's permit and intermediate license holders under 18. (11) Primary for drivers younger than 18. (12) Secondary for learner's permit and intermediate license holders. (13) Yes for all drivers as of Jan. 1, 2021.

Selected Motor Vehicle Statistics

Source: Federal Highway Admin., U.S. Dept. of Transportation; Insurance Inst. for Highway Safety; American Petroleum Inst. Driver's license age requirements, state gas tax, and safety belt use laws (incl. laws passed, but not in effect) as of 2020. Other figures are for 2018.

STATE	Driver's license age requirements		Gas taxes (cents/ gal)[6]	Safety belt use law[7]	Licensed drivers		Reg. motor vehicles per 1,000 pop.	Fuel use per reg. motor vehicle (gal)	Annual miles driven		
	Learner's permit	Regular[1]			Per 1,000 resident pop.	Per reg. motor vehicle			Per gal used	Per reg. vehicle	Per lic. driver
Alabama	15	17	45.6	P(a)	818	0.77	1,084	689	19.50	13,427	17,796
Alaska	14	16y, 6m	32.2	P	727	0.69	1,090	535	12.75	6,828	10,237
Arizona	15y, 6m	16y, 6m	37.4	S	737	0.92	810	673	16.92	11,392	12,516
Arkansas	14	18	43.2	P	712	0.77	935	785	16.59	13,019	17,095
California	15y, 6m	17	80.9	P	684	0.89	784	607	18.53	11,243	12,900
Colorado	15	17	40.4	S	745	0.80	940	583	17.28	10,073	12,711
Connecticut	16	18[2,3,4]	54.2	P	729	0.91	806	630	17.42	10,971	12,126
Delaware	16	17[2]	41.4	P	813	0.78	1,043	602	16.78	10,094	12,943
Dist. of Columbia	16	18[4]	41.9	P	751	1.72	501	383	27.36	10,487	6,993
Florida	15	18	60.7	P	722	0.89	821	639	19.85	12,678	14,433
Georgia	15	18[2]	50.6	P	681	0.86	809	751	20.57	15,443	18,337
Hawaii	15y, 6m	17[2]	64.7	P	668	0.76	892	411	20.90	8,590	11,479
Idaho	14y, 6m	16[2]	51.4	S	714	0.67	1,072	610	15.45	9,421	14,139
Illinois	15	18[2]	70.4	P	684	0.83	831	613	16.63	10,195	12,387
Indiana	15	18	66.0	P	686	0.74	925	717	18.37	13,169	17,765
Iowa	14	17[2]	48.9	P	716	0.62	1,170	650	13.87	9,015	14,725
Kansas	14	16y, 6m	42.4	P(a)	738	0.81	922	678	17.69	11,993	14,976
Kentucky	16	17[2]	44.4	P	679	0.71	978	705	16.09	11,342	16,337
Louisiana	15	17	38.4	P	735	0.90	834	742	17.37	12,881	14,610
Maine	15	16y, 9m[2]	48.4	P	777	0.94	841	766	17.15	13,134	14,207
Maryland	15y, 9m	18[2]	54.7	P(a)	729	1.07	696	783	18.16	14,216	13,561
Massachusetts	16	18[2]	44.9	S	716	0.98	733	646	20.41	13,192	13,504
Michigan	14y, 9m	17[2]	60.4	P	716	0.86	839	704	17.34	12,209	14,314
Minnesota	15	16y, 6m[2]	47.0	P	604	0.63	963	665	16.81	11,183	17,823
Mississippi	15	16y, 6m	37.2	P	689	1.00	692	1,170	16.84	19,700	19,791
Missouri	15	17y, 11m	35.8	S(b)	697	0.78	898	664	20.98	13,930	17,926
Montana	14y, 6m	16[2]	51.2	S	759	0.44	1,737	446	15.43	6,882	15,752
Nebraska	15	17	52.5	S	736	0.74	1,017	710	15.07	10,694	14,768
Nevada	15y, 6m	18[2]	52.2	S	654	0.80	829	642	17.55	11,263	14,278
New Hampshire	15y, 6m	18[2]	42.2	None	856	0.87	993	624	16.41	10,233	11,859
New Jersey	16	18	59.8	P(a)	712	1.06	680	789	16.23	12,805	12,225
New Mexico	15	16y, 6m[2]	37.3	P	696	0.81	871	887	16.86	14,959	18,711
New York	16	17[2]	61.5	P	624	1.07	588	649	16.57	10,757	10,128
North Carolina	15	16y, 6m[2]	54.8	P(a)	723	0.93	791	745	19.81	14,753	16,130
North Dakota	14	16[2]	41.4	S	739	0.64	1,184	857	12.77	10,951	17,558
Ohio	15y, 6m	18[2]	56.9	S	687	0.74	934	632	16.60	10,489	14,251
Oklahoma	15y, 6m	16y, 6m	38.4	P	635	0.68	938	794	15.48	12,282	18,142
Oregon	15	17[2,3]	57.2	P	699	0.76	941	553	16.91	9,346	12,573
Pennsylvania	16	17	77.1	S(b)	702	0.85	838	607	15.69	9,518	11,356
Rhode Island	16	17y, 6m[2]	53.4	P	716	0.88	825	549	16.73	9,181	10,580
South Carolina	15	16y, 6m	43.2	P	756	0.90	877	829	15.37	12,743	14,769
South Dakota	14	16[5]	48.4	P	724	0.51	1,439	577	13.27	7,657	15,224
Tennessee	15	17	45.8	P	801	0.97	852	781	18.05	14,092	14,997
Texas	15	18	38.4	P	605	0.79	773	929	13.68	12,712	16,237
Utah	15	17[2]	49.5	P	642	0.87	751	738	18.32	13,515	15,793
Vermont	15	16y, 6m[2]	48.6	S	902	0.93	989	584	20.29	11,855	13,005
Virginia	15y, 6m	18[2]	47.8	S	696	0.79	893	689	16.29	11,222	14,393
Washington	15	17[2]	67.8	P	784	0.85	949	516	16.89	8,720	10,553
West Virginia	15	17	54.1	P	630	0.69	938	805	14.26	11,482	17,107
Wisconsin	15y, 6m	16y, 9m[2]	51.3	P	738	0.77	978	641	18.08	11,593	15,364
Wyoming	15	16y, 6m[2]	42.4	S	726	0.51	1,449	866	14.40	12,471	24,898
U.S. AVERAGE			54.8		696	0.84	836	690	17.17	11,843	14,240

Note: Most states have graduated licensing systems that phase in full driving privileges. During the learner's stage, driving generally is not permitted without adult supervision. In an intermediate stage, young licensees may be allowed to drive unsupervised under certain conditions. (1) Min. age at which all restrictions may be lifted on private passenger car operation. (2) Applicants under a specified age (typically between 17 and 19) must complete driver education. (3) Home training (CT) or more hours of supervised driving (OR) may be substituted for driver ed. (4) Learner's stage mandatory for all license applicants regardless of age. (5) Driver education required as of 1/1/21. (6) Some values rounded. Includes 18.4 cents per gallon in federal excise taxes. (7) P = Officer may stop vehicle for violation (primary); S = Officer may issue seat belt citation only when vehicle is stopped for another moving violation (secondary). (a) Secondary enforcement for rear seat occupants; (b) Primary enforcement for children under a specified age.

COVID-19 Effect on U.S. Air Travel, 2020
Source: Transportation Security Admin. (TSA); U.S. Travel Assn.

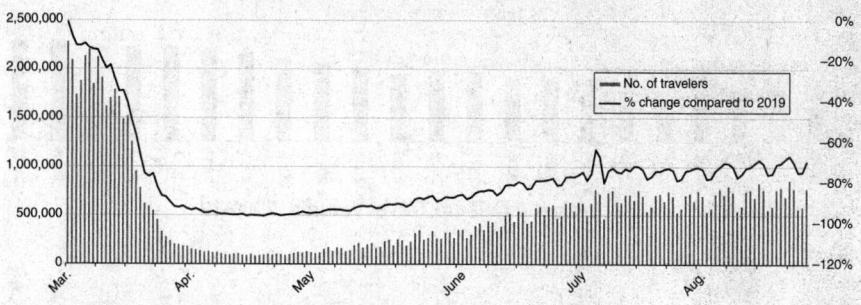

Note: Travelers are those who went through TSA checkpoint screening.

International Tourism Receipts, 2000-19
Source: World Tourism Organization (UNWTO), © UNWTO
(in billions of U.S. dollars; ranked by most recent figures available)

Rank	Country	2000	2005	2010	2015	2018	2019*
1.	U.S.	$100.2	$101.5	$137.0	$206.9	$214.7	$214.1
2.	Spain	30.9	49.7	58.8	56.6	81.5	79.7
3.	France....	33.0	44.0	57.1	58.3	66.0	63.8
4.	Thailand ...	7.5	9.6	20.1	44.9	56.4	60.5
5.	UK........	22.2	32.1	34.7	45.5	48.6	50.4
6.	Italy......	27.5	35.4	38.8	39.4	49.3	49.6
7.	Japan	3.4	6.6	13.2	25.0	42.1	46.1
8.	Australia ...	9.4	18.4	32.6	34.2	45.0	45.7
9.	Germany...	18.7	29.2	34.7	36.9	43.0	41.6
10.	Macau.....	3.2	6.9	22.3	31.0	40.7	39.5
11.	China[1]....	16.2	29.3	45.8	45.0	40.4	35.8
12.	India	3.5	7.5	14.5	21.0	28.6	30.0
13.	Turkey.....	7.6	19.2	22.6	26.6	25.2	29.8
14.	Hong Kong	5.9	10.3	22.2	36.2	36.9	29.0
15.	Canada....	$10.8	$13.7	$15.8	$16.5	$26.4	$27.0
16.	Mexico	8.3	11.8	12.0	17.7	22.5	24.6
17.	Austria	9.8	16.1	18.6	18.2	23.1	22.9
18.	South Korea	6.8	5.8	10.3	15.2	18.6	21.6
19.	United Arab Emirates	1.1	3.2	8.6	17.5	21.4	NA
20.	Portugal ...	5.2	7.7	10.1	12.7	20.1	20.6
21.	Greece	9.2	13.3	12.7	15.7	19.0	20.4
22.	Singapore ..	5.1	6.2	14.2	16.6	20.4	20.1
23.	Malaysia ...	5.0	8.8	18.1	17.6	19.6	19.8
24.	Netherlands	7.2	9.1	11.7	13.2	17.8	18.5
25.	Switzerland	6.6	10.0	14.7	16.4	17.0	17.1
	World	495	704	979	1,217	1,457	1,478

NA = Not available. * = Provisional. (1) Not including Hong Kong and Macau.

International Tourist Arrivals by Country of Destination, 2000-19
Source: World Tourism Organization (UNWTO), © UNWTO
(visitors in millions; ranked by most recent figures available)

Rank	Country	2000	2005	2010	2015	2018	2019*	% change, 2018-19
1.	France.....	77.2	75.0	77.6	84.5	89.4	NA	NA
2.	Spain	46.4	55.9	52.7	68.2	82.8	83.7	1.1%
3.	U.S........	51.2	49.2	60.0	77.5	79.7	79.3	−0.6
4.	China[1]....	31.2	46.8	55.7	56.9	62.9	65.7	4.5
5.	Italy......	41.2	36.5	43.6	50.7	61.6	64.5	4.8
6.	Turkey.....	9.6	24.2	31.4	39.5	45.8	51.2	11.9
7.	Mexico	20.6	21.9	23.3	32.1	41.3	45.0	9.0
8.	Thailand ...	9.6	11.6	15.9	29.9	38.2	39.8	4.2
9.	Germany...	19.0	21.5	26.9	35.0	38.9	39.6	1.8
10.	UK	23.2	28.0	28.3	34.4	36.3	37.5	3.2
11.	Japan	4.8	6.7	8.6	19.7	31.2	32.2	3.2
12.	Austria	18.0	20.0	22.0	26.7	30.8	31.9	3.5
13.	Greece	13.1	14.8	15.0	23.6	30.1	31.3	4.1
14.	Malaysia ...	10.2	16.4	24.6	25.7	25.8	26.1	1.0%
15.	Portugal ...	5.7	10.6	6.8	10.1	22.8	24.6	7.9
16.	Russia.....	21.2	22.2	22.3	26.9	24.6	24.4	−0.5
17.	Hong Kong	8.8	14.8	20.1	26.7	29.3	23.8	−18.8
18.	Canada....	19.6	18.8	16.2	18.0	21.1	22.1	4.8
19.	Poland.....	17.4	15.2	NA	16.7	19.6	21.2	7.8
20.	Netherlands	10.0	10.0	10.9	15.0	18.8	20.1	7.2
21.	Macau.....	5.2	9.0	11.9	14.3	18.5	18.6	0.8
22.	Vietnam ...	2.1	3.5	5.0	7.9	15.5	18.0	16.2
23.	India	2.6	3.9	5.8	13.3	17.4	17.9	2.8
24.	South Korea	5.3	6.0	8.8	13.2	15.3	17.5	14.0
25.	Croatia	5.3	7.7	9.0	12.7	16.6	17.4	4.3
	World	674	809	956	1,333	1,409	1,460	3.6

NA = Not available or not applicable. * = Provisional. (1) Not including Hong Kong and Macau.

World Tourism Receipts, 1990-2019
Source: World Tourism Organization (UNWTO), © UNWTO
(in billions of U.S. dollars)

Year	Receipts[1]	Year	Receipts[1]	Year	Receipts[1]	Year	Receipts[1]	Year	Receipts[1]	Year	Receipts[1]
1990	$271	1999	$475	2004	$652	2008	$968	2012	$1,110	2016	$1,239
1995	415	2000	495	2005	704	2009	881	2013	1,197	2017	1,347
1996	449	2001	481	2006	766	2010	979	2014	1,252	2018	1,457
1997	449	2002	501	2007	883	2011	1,073	2015	1,217	2019	1,478*
1998	457	2003	549								

* = Provisional. (1) Total of all transactions made by or on behalf of visitors for the duration of their visit. Does not include receipts from international passenger transport contracted from companies outside a traveler's country of residence.

International Travel to the U.S., 1990-2019
Source: National Travel and Tourism Office, Intl. Trade Admin., U.S. Dept. of Commerce
(number of visitors in millions)

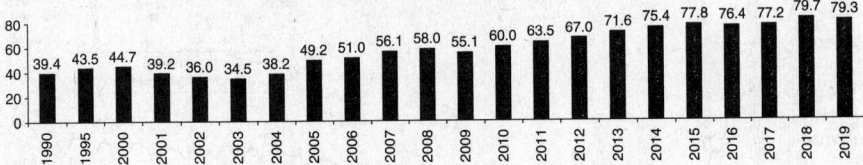

U.S. Domestic Leisure Travel Volume, 2000-19
Source: U.S. Travel Assn.
(in billions of person-trips of 50 mi or more, one-way)

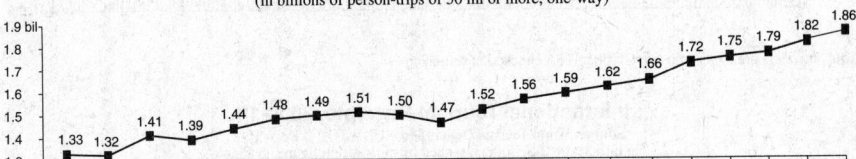

Note: Method of collecting travel data has been revised; data for earlier years have been adjusted to maintain comparability.

Top 10 U.S. States by Traveler Spending, 2018
Source: U.S. Travel Assn.
(domestic and international traveler spending within state, in billions of dollars)

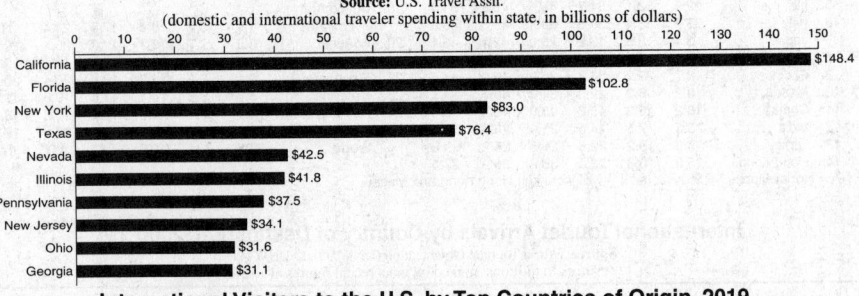

State	Spending
California	$148.4
Florida	$102.8
New York	$83.0
Texas	$76.4
Nevada	$42.5
Illinois	$41.8
Pennsylvania	$37.5
New Jersey	$34.1
Ohio	$31.6
Georgia	$31.1

International Visitors to the U.S. by Top Countries of Origin, 2019
Source: National Travel and Tourism Office, Intl. Trade Admin., U.S. Dept. of Commerce
(ranked by number of visitors)

Country of origin	Visitors	Expenditures (mil)	Expenditures per visitor	Country of origin	Visitors	Expenditures (mil)	Expenditures per visitor
1. Canada	20,723,322	$22,605	$1,091	12. Italy	1,086,026	$4,327	$3,984
2. Mexico	18,139,599	20,233	1,115	13. Colombia	944,013	NA	NA
3. United Kingdom	4,779,997	16,332	3,417	14. Spain[2]	876,248	2,911	3,322
4. Japan	3,752,980	16,030	4,271	15. Argentina	854,442	4,421	5,174
5. China[1]	2,829,970	33,533	11,849	16. Netherlands	727,229	2,813	3,868
6. South Korea	2,298,279	9,599	4,177	17. Ireland[2]	530,802	2,093	3,943
7. Brazil	2,104,617	11,338	5,387	18. Taiwan	499,520	2,228	4,460
8. Germany	2,063,767	8,314	4,029	19. Dominican			
9. France	1,843,782	6,469	3,509	Republic	488,703	NA	NA
10. India	1,473,517	16,456	11,168	20. Switzerland[2]	463,139	2,474	5,342
11. Australia	1,319,238	8,344	6,325	All countries	79,256,267	254,229	3,208

NA = Not available. Note: Expenditures include passenger fares. (1) Not including Hong Kong, Macau, and Taiwan. (2) Data is for 2018.

Traveler Spending in the U.S., 1987-2019
Source: National Travel and Tourism Office, Intl. Trade Admin., U.S. Dept. of Commerce; U.S. Travel Assn.
(in billions of dollars by origin of traveler)

Year	Domestic	International	Year	Domestic	International	Year	Domestic	International
1987	$235	$31	2000	$503	$82	2010	$644	$104
1990	291	43	2001	484	72	2011	694	119
1992	306	55	2002	478	67	2012	728	127
1993	323	58	2003	496	65	2013	751	135
1994	340	58	2004	532	75	2014	792	136
1995	360	63	2005	572	82	2015	814	157
1996	385	70	2006	610	86	2016	837	156
1997	406	73	2007	641	97	2017	882	156
1998	425	71	2008	662	110	2018	933	156
1999	458	75	2009	606	94	2019	972	155

Characteristics of U.S. Travelers Visiting Overseas Destinations, 2018

Source: Survey of Intl. Air Travelers, National Travel and Tourism Office, Intl. Trade Admin., U.S. Dept. of Commerce

			% of travelers
Total U.S. resident travelers	41,774,000	Leisure/recreational activities[1]	
Males (adults)	47%	Sightseeing	82%
Females (adults)	53%	Shopping	73
Avg. age of males (yrs.)	46.2	Small towns/countryside	45
Avg. age of females (yrs.)	44.8	Historical locations	42
Median annual household income	$100,000	Guided tours	40
Used prepaid package	12%	Fine dining	38
Visited only one country	82%	Art galleries/museums	36
Advanced trip decision (median days)	90	Cultural/ethnic heritage sights	33
Mean number of persons in travel party	1.6	National parks/monuments	32
Median number of nights	10	Nightclubbing	21
		Water sports	17
	% of travelers	Concert/play/musical	12
Main purpose of trip		Amusement/theme parks	10
Vacation/holiday	57%	Camping/hiking	8
Visit friends/relatives	26	Environmental/ecological excursions	8
Business	8	Casino/gambling	7
Education	4	Sporting event	6
Convention/conference/trade show	2	Hunting/fishing	3
Religion/pilgrimage	2	Golfing/tennis	3
Health treatment	1	Snow sports	1

(1) Percentages based on multiple responses.

U.S. Resident Travel Abroad, 1997-2017

Source: National Travel and Tourism Office, Intl. Trade Admin., U.S. Dept. of Commerce
(numbers in thousands)

Region/country[1]	2017	2000	1997	Region/country[1]	2017	2000	1997
Total outbound[2]	87,703	61,326	52,735	Caribbean	8,930	3,867	NA
Mexico	35,050	19,285	17,909	Dominican Republic	2,721	779	195
Canada	14,326	15,188	13,401	Jamaica	1,571	886	1,341
				Asia	6,899	4,914	NA
Overseas subtotal[3]	38,327	26,853	21,634	China[4]	1,380	644	476
Europe	14,488	13,373	NA	Japan	1,150	1,262	1,082
United Kingdom	3,756	4,189	3,570	India	1,111	457	368
France	2,645	2,927	2,098	Central America	2,760	886	NA
Italy	2,338	2,148	1,471	Costa Rica	1,073	NA	303
Germany	2,185	2,309	1,796	South America	2,491	2,095	NA
Spain	1,648	1,262	714	Middle East	1,840	1,370	NA
Ireland	1,150	725	411	Africa	1,035	483	NA
Netherlands	1,111	1,101	822	Oceania	767	1,047	NA

NA = Not available. **Note:** Visits of one or more nights. Visitation estimates for Canada and Mexico include all modes of transportation used. Estimates for all other countries are available only for air travel to that country and are based upon data from the airlines that voluntarily provided it. (1) Only individual countries that received more than 1 mil visitors in 2017 are shown. Region figures include U.S. resident travelers to all countries in region. (2) To Canada, Mexico, and overseas. (3) To all countries except Canada and Mexico. (4) Not including Hong Kong, Macau, and Taiwan.

U.S. Commercial Airline Safety, 1985-2018

Source: National Transportation Safety Board; Federal Aviation Administration, U.S. Dept. of Transportation

Year	Departures (mil)	Fatal accidents	Fatalities[1]	Rate of fatal accidents[2]	Year	Departures (mil)	Fatal accidents	Fatalities[1]	Rate of fatal accidents[2]
1985	6.1	4	197	0.066	2008	10.3	0	0	—
1990	7.8	4	11	0.051	2009	9.6	1	50	0.010
1995	8.1	1	160	0.012	2010	9.5	0	0	—
2000	11.1	2	89	0.018	2011	9.4	0	0	—
2001[3]	10.6	6	531	0.019	2012	9.2	0	0	—
2002	10.3	0	0	—	2013	9.3	0	0	—
2003	10.2	2	22	0.020	2014	9.0	0	0	—
2004	10.8	1	13	0.009	2015	9.0	0	0	—
2005	10.9	3	22	0.027	2016	9.1	0	0	—
2006	10.6	2	50	0.019	2017	9.1	0	0	—
2007	10.7	0	0	—	2018*	9.4	1	1	0.011

— = Not applicable. * = Preliminary. **Note:** Statistics are for scheduled commercial carriers. (1) Includes deaths that occurred on the ground as a result of an accident, except for fatalities resulting from the Sept. 11, 2001, terrorist attacks. (2) Per 100,000 departures. (3) The Sept. 11, 2001, terrorist attacks have been included among the number of fatal accidents but have been excluded when calculating the fatal accident rate.

U.S. Airline Statistics, 1995-2019

Source: Airlines for America

	1995	2000	2005	2010	2015	2016	2017	2018	2019
Passengers enplaned (mil)[1]	547.8	666.1	738.6	720.5	798.2	824.0	849.4	889.0	926.7
Revenue passenger miles (bil)[1,2]	540.7	692.8	779.0	798.0	902.2	933.5	964.3	1,011.5	1,055.6
Available seat miles (bil)[1,3]	807.1	957.0	1,003.4	972.6	1,077.0	1,119.0	1,154.9	1,208.2	1,247.1
Cargo revenue ton miles (mil)[1,2]	16,921	23,888	28,039	27,885	27,062	27,536	29,684	30,638	30,221
% of seating utilized[1]	67.0%	72.4%	77.6%	82.1%	83.8%	83.4%	83.5%	83.7%	84.6%
Passenger revenue (mil)[4]	$70,132	$94,307	$94,340	$104,431	$126,880	$125,213	$130,705	$139,005	$145,013
Net profit (mil)[4]	$2,001	$2,238	–$28,647	$2,245	$24,794	$14,224	$15,666	$11,775	$14,870
Total employment (thous.)[5]	595.6	739.6	619.6	564.4	605.3	660.9	697.2	717.6	741.2

(1) Scheduled service only. (2) One fare-paying passenger or one ton of revenue cargo transported one mile. (3) One seat transported one mile. (4) Passenger carriers only. (5) Figures are of the sum of full-time and part-time employees.

Top 25 U.S. Passenger Airlines, 2019

Source: Airlines for America

In 2019, 99.6% of all passengers enplaned flew on the top 25 U.S. passenger airlines.
(in millions; ranked by number of passengers enplaned in scheduled service in 2019)

	Airline	Passengers		Airline	Passengers		Airline	Passengers		Airline	Passengers
1.	Southwest Airlines	162.7	8.	Spirit Airlines	33.9	15.	Allegiant Air	14.9	21.	GoJet Airlines LLC	4.6
2.	Delta Air Lines	162.5	9.	Frontier Airlines	22.7	16.	Hawaiian Airlines	11.5	22.	Air Wisconsin	
3.	American Airlines	155.8	10.	Republic Airlines	18.8	17.	Horizon Air	7.8		Airlines	4.1
4.	United Air Lines	116.3	11.	Endeavor Air	15.1	18.	Compass Airlines	6.3	23.	Sun Country	3.5
5.	JetBlue Airways	42.8	12.	PSA Airlines	15.1	19.	ExpressJet		24.	Trans States	
6.	SkyWest Airlines	42.3	13.	Mesa Airlines	15.0		Airlines	6.0		Airlines	3.0
7.	Alaska Airlines	35.5	14.	Envoy Air	15.0	20.	Piedmont Airlines	5.0	25.	Commutair	2.4

Note: Includes domestic and international passengers on U.S. airlines.

Top North American Airports by Passenger Traffic, 2019

Source: *2019 World Annual Traffic Report*, Airports Council Intl.

City/airport name (airport code)	Total passengers[1]
1. Hartsfield-Jackson Atlanta Intl. (ATL)	110,531,300
2. Los Angeles Intl. (LAX)	88,068,013
3. Chicago O'Hare Intl. (ORD)	84,649,115
4. Dallas/Ft. Worth Intl. (DFW)	75,066,956
5. Denver Intl. (DEN)	69,015,703
6. New York John F. Kennedy Intl. (JFK)	62,551,072
7. San Francisco Intl. (SFO)	57,418,574
8. Seattle-Tacoma Intl. (SEA)	51,829,239
9. Las Vegas McCarran Intl. (LAS)	51,691,066
10. Orlando Intl. (MCO)	50,613,072
11. Toronto Pearson Intl. (YYZ)	50,496,804
12. Charlotte Douglas Intl. (CLT)	50,168,783
13. Newark Liberty Intl. (EWR)	46,336,452
14. Phoenix Sky Harbor Intl. (PHX)	46,287,790
15. Miami Intl. (MIA)	45,924,466
16. Houston George Bush Intercontinental (IAH)	45,276,595
17. Boston Logan Intl. (BOS)	42,587,664
18. Minneapolis/St. Paul Intl. (MSP)	39,555,035
19. Detroit Metropolitan Wayne County (DTW)	36,769,279
20. Ft. Lauderdale-Hollywood Intl. (FLL)	36,747,622

Top World Airports by Passenger Traffic, 2019

Source: *2019 World Annual Traffic Report*, Airports Council Intl.

City/airport name (country; airport code)	Total passengers[1]
1. Beijing Capital Intl. (China; PEK)	100,011,438
2. Dubai Intl. (United Arab Emirates; DXB)	86,396,757
3. Tokyo Haneda Intl. (Japan; HND)	85,505,054
4. London Heathrow (UK; LHR)	80,888,305
5. Shanghai Pudong Intl. (China; PVG)	76,153,455
6. Paris Charles de Gaulle (France; CDG)	76,150,009
7. Guangzhou Baiyun Intl. (China; CAN)	73,394,810
8. Amsterdam Schiphol (Netherlands; AMS)	71,706,999
9. Hong Kong Intl. (China; HKG)	71,415,245
10. Seoul Incheon Intl. (South Korea; ICN)	71,204,153
11. Frankfurt (Germany; FRA)	70,556,072
12. Delhi Indira Gandhi Intl. (India; DEL)	68,490,731
13. Singapore Changi (Singapore; SIN)	68,283,000
14. Bangkok Suvarnabhumi Intl. (Thailand; BKK)	65,421,844
15. Kuala Lumpur KL Intl. (Malaysia; KUL)	62,336,469
16. Adolfo Suárez Madrid-Barajas (Spain; MAD)	61,707,469
17. Chengdu Shuangliu Intl. (China; CTU)	55,858,552
18. Jakarta Soekarno-Hatta Intl. (Indonesia; CGK)	54,496,625
19. Shenzhen Baoan Intl. (China; SZX)	52,931,925
20. Barcelona-El Prat (Spain; BCN)	52,663,623

Note: World list excludes North American airports and airports that do not participate in Airports Council Intl.'s Airport Traffic Statistics collection. (1) Arriving and departing passengers and direct transit passengers counted once.

Busiest Amtrak Stations, 2019

Source: Amtrak; ranked by total ridership

(in thous.)

Station	Tickets from	Tickets to	Total ridership	Station	Tickets from	Tickets to	Total ridership
New York (Penn Sta.), NY	5,414	5,398	10,811	Boston (Back Bay Sta.), MA	361	359	720
Washington, DC	2,599	2,608	5,207	Wilmington, DE	354	351	705
Philadelphia (30th Street Sta.), PA	2,260	2,243	4,503	Seattle (King Street Sta.), WA	345	337	682
Chicago (Union Sta.), IL	1,664	1,668	3,332	San Diego (Downtown), CA	330	323	653
Boston (South Sta.), MA	819	766	1,585	Milwaukee (Downtown), WI	323	317	640
Los Angeles, CA	706	707	1,413	Emeryville, CA	291	295	586
Sacramento, CA	565	536	1,101	Portland (Union Sta.), OR	289	296	585
Baltimore (Penn Sta.), MD	523	520	1,044	Lancaster, PA	289	289	577
Albany-Rensselaer, NY	405	402	807	Harrisburg, PA	261	260	521
New Haven (Union Sta.), CT	395	384	779	Route 128 (Westwood), MA	234	230	464
Providence (Amtrak), RI	370	397	767	Boston (North Sta.), MA	235	224	459
BWI Airport Sta., MD	366	385	751	Trenton, NJ	222	217	440
Newark (Penn Sta.), NJ	367	365	731				

U.S. Public Transportation Usage, 1996-2018

Source: Federal Transit Administration, U.S. Dept. of Transportation

Public transportation usage is measured in unlinked passenger trips (UPT), which counts the number of passengers who board public transportation vehicles each time they board.

(in millions)

	Number of passengers by year					Number of passengers by mode of transportation			
Year	**UPT**	**Year**	**UPT**	**Year**	**UPT**		**2009 UPT**	**2018 UPT**	**% change, 2009-18**
1996	7,565	2004	8,937	2012	10,472	**Mode**			
1997	7,982	2005	9,175	2013	10,528	Bus	5,260	4,622	−13.8%
1998	8,115	2006	9,379	2014	10,633	Heavy rail[1]	3,490	3,724	6.3
1999	8,522	2007	10,054	2015	10,496	Commuter rail[2]	464	501	7.3
2000	8,720	2008	10,367	2016	10,369	Light rail[3]	464	487	4.8
2001	9,008	2009	10,252	2017	10,063	Other	220	268	17.9
2002	9,059	2010	10,082	2018	9,863	Demand response[4]	93	111	16.2
2003	8,876	2011	10,209			Vanpool	25	34	26.2

(1) An electric railway with the ability to carry a heavy volume of passengers and characterized by high-speed and rapid-acceleration passenger rail cars operating singly or in multi-car trains on fixed rails. (2) An electric- or diesel-propelled railway for urban passenger travel that operates between a central city and outlying areas. (3) An electric railway that operates singly on fixed rails and is powered by overhead electric lines. (4) Includes passenger cars, vans, or small buses dispatched by request to pick up passengers and transport them to their destinations.

Public Spending on Transportation Infrastructure, 1960-2017

Source: *Public Spending on Transportation and Water Infrastructure, 1956 to 2017*, Congressional Budget Office

Year	Federal spending[1]			State and local spending[2]		
	Highways	Mass transit and rail	Aviation	Highways	Mass transit and rail	Aviation
1960	60.33%	0.20%	11.59%	61.45%	6.47%	2.70%
1970	55.81	1.89	17.30	59.98	7.47	4.42
1980	32.83	19.45	12.68	51.99	9.84	4.20
1990	42.17	12.69	20.92	43.15	13.25	4.92
2000	46.61	11.38	19.16	41.84	13.77	6.55
2005	45.03	14.00	20.42	40.27	14.86	6.30
2010	45.13	15.79	16.69	37.09	15.10	6.68
2015	46.73	15.71	17.36	38.10	71.01	5.86
2016	47.32	16.94	17.00	38.40	16.84	5.71
2017	46.59	17.30	17.05	38.31	16.83	5.94
PERCENT CHANGE						
1960-2017	−22.77	8,550.00	47.11	−37.66	160.12	120.00
2000-17	−0.04	52.02	−11.01	−8.44	22.22	−9.31

Note: State and local spending is net of federal grants and loan subsidies. (1) Figures represent percentage of total federal infrastructure spending for the year, including categories not shown. (2) Figures represent percentage of total state and local infrastructure spending for the year, including categories not shown.

Top Travel Websites, 2020

Source: Comscore, Inc.; ranked by number of visitors

Rank	Website	Visitors[1]	Rank	Website	Visitors[1]
1.	TripAdvisor Inc.	55,918	12.	BigGlobalTravel.com	11,509
2.	Expedia Group	34,666	13.	USA TODAY Travel	10,549
3.	Uber	32,097	14.	Travel + Leisure Group	10,196
4.	Priceline.com Inc.	30,186	15.	MSN Travel	9,246
5.	CNN Travel	19,604	16.	Disney Parks & Experiences	8,337
6.	Airbnb sites	18,372	17.	American Airlines	7,270
7.	OnlyInYourState.com	18,250	18.	Kayak.com Network	6,453
8.	Southwest Airlines Co.	12,838	19.	Enterprise Rent-A-Car Company	6,370
9.	Mediavine Travel	12,128	20.	Marriott	5,789
10.	CafeMedia Travel	11,990	**Total travel audience[2]**		188,383
11.	Lyft, Inc.	11,864			

(1) Number of unique visitors, in thousands, who visited website at least once in June 2020. (2) Audience comprises all desktop users older than 2 years of age and all mobile users older than 18.

Record-Breaking Roller Coasters

Source: Roller Coaster DataBase; World Almanac research; as of Aug. 2020

Steel-Tracked Roller Coasters

Fastest

Fastest	Roller coaster	Theme park, location
149.1 mph	Formula Rossa	Ferrari World Abu Dhabi, United Arab Emirates
128	Kingda Ka	Six Flags Great Adventure, Jackson, NJ
120	Top Thrill Dragster	Cedar Point, Sandusky, OH
111.8	Red Force	Ferrari Land, Salou, Spain
111.8	Do-Dodonpa	Fuji-Q Highland, Fujiyoshida, Japan

Tallest

456 ft	Kingda Ka	Six Flags Great Adventure, Jackson, NJ
420	Top Thrill Dragster	Cedar Point, Sandusky, OH
415	Superman: Escape From Krypton	Six Flags Magic Mountain, Valencia, CA
367.3	Red Force	Ferrari Land, Salou, Spain
325	Fury 325	Carowinds, Charlotte, NC

Largest drop

418 ft	Kingda Ka	Six Flags Great Adventure, Jackson, NJ
400	Top Thrill Dragster	Cedar Point, Sandusky, OH
328.1	Superman: Escape From Krypton	Six Flags Magic Mountain, Valencia, CA
320	Fury 325	Carowinds, Charlotte, NC
306.8	Steel Dragon 2000	Nagashima Spa Land, Mie, Japan

Longest

8,133.2 ft.	Steel Dragon 2000	Nagashima Spa Land, Mie, Japan
7,442	The Ultimate	Lightwater Valley, Ripon, UK
6,708.7	Fujiyama	Fuji-Q Highland, Fujiyoshida, Japan
6,602	Fury 325	Carowinds, Charlotte, NC
6,595	Millennium Force	Cedar Point, Sandusky, OH

Wood-Tracked Roller Coasters

Fastest

Fastest	Roller coaster	Theme park, location
73 mph	Lightning Rod	Dollywood, Pigeon Forge, TN
72	Goliath	Six Flags Great America, Gurnee, IL
71.5	Wildfire	Kolmården Wildlife Park, Norrköping, Sweden
70	El Toro	Six Flags Great Adventure, Jackson, NJ
68.4	Colossos - Kampf der Giganten	Heide Park Resort, Soltau, Germany

Tallest

183.8 ft.	Wildfire	Kolmården Wildlife Park, Norrköping, Sweden
183.8	T Express	Everland, Yongin-si, S. Korea
181	El Toro	Six Flags Great Adventure, Jackson, NJ
165	Goliath	Six Flags Great America, Gurnee, IL
164	Colossos - Kampf der Giganten	Heide Park Resort, Soltau, Germany

Largest drop

180 ft	Goliath	Six Flags Great America, Gurnee, IL
176	El Toro	Six Flags Great Adventure, Jackson, NJ
165	Lightning Rod	Dollywood, Pigeon Forge, TN
162	Outlaw Run	Silver Dollar City, Branson, MO
160.8	Wildfire	Kolmården Wildlife Park, Norrköping, Sweden

Longest

7,359 ft.	The Beast	Kings Island, Mason, OH
6,442	The Voyage	Holiday World, Santa Claus, IN
5,383.8	T Express	Everland, Yongin-si, S. Korea
5,383	Shivering Timbers	Michigan's Adventure, Muskegon, MI
5,249.3	Jupiter	Kijima Kogen, Beppu, Japan

Most Visited Amusement/Theme Parks, 2019

Source: Themed Entertainment Association
(visitors in thousands)

	North America			World	
Rank	Park, location	Visitors	Rank	Park, location	Visitors
1.	Magic Kingdom[1], Lake Buena Vista, FL.	20,963	1.	Tokyo Disneyland, Tokyo, Japan.	17,910
2.	Disneyland, Anaheim, CA.	18,666	2.	Tokyo DisneySea, Tokyo, Japan.	14,650
3.	Disney's Animal Kingdom[1], Lake Buena		3.	Universal Studios Japan, Osaka, Japan.	14,500
	Vista, FL	13,888	4.	Chimelong Ocean Kingdom, Hengqin, China. . .	11,736
4.	Epcot[1], Lake Buena Vista, FL.	12,444	5.	Shanghai Disneyland, Shanghai, China.	11,210
5.	Disney's Hollywood Studios[1], Lake Buena		6.	Disneyland Park at Disneyland Paris,	
	Vista, FL	11,483		Marne-la-Vallée, France	9,745
6.	Universal Studios Florida[2], Orlando, FL.	10,922	7.	Everland, Seoul, South Korea	6,606
7.	Islands of Adventure[2], Orlando, FL.	10,375	8.	Lotte World, Seoul, South Korea.	5,953
8.	Disney California Adventure, Anaheim, CA.	9,861	9.	Nagashima Spa Land, Kuwana, Japan	5,950
9.	Universal Studios Hollywood, Universal City, CA . .	9,147	10.	Europa-Park, Rust, Germany	5,750
10.	SeaWorld Orlando, Orlando, FL.	4,640			

Note: World list excludes North American parks. (1) Located at Walt Disney World. (2) Located at Universal Orlando.

Passports, Foreign Travel, and Regulations for Air Travel

Source: Bureau of Consular Affairs, U.S. Dept. of State; Centers for Disease Control and Prevention (CDC), U.S. Dept. of Health and Human Services; World Health Organization (WHO); Transportation Security Administration (TSA), U.S. Dept. of Homeland Security

Passports, Visas

Passports are issued by the Dept. of State to U.S. citizens and nationals to provide documentation for foreign travel. As of Oct. 2020, the fees for a new passport book and passport card for persons ages 16 and over total $175; provided certain criteria are met, these can be renewed for $140. For a passport book alone, fees are $145 for a new passport and $110 for passport renewal.

In 2008, the U.S. government began issuing passport cards. Travelers arriving by land or sea from Canada, Mexico, the Caribbean, and Bermuda may present a passport card to enter the U.S. Passport cards may not be used for air travel, however. The fees for a new passport card for persons ages 16 and over total $65 ($30 to renew).

In response to the COVID-19 pandemic, the State Dept. significantly reduced passport operations in Mar. 2020. Agency service was restricted to emergency cases, routine processing was delayed, and expedited service was suspended. As states reopened, agencies began resuming operations in phases. As of early Oct. 2020, 9 agencies were in phase one (limited staff on-site), 15 agencies were in phase two (most staff off-site), and 3 were in phase 3, with all remaining staff returning to work on-site.

A U.S. passport is often sufficient for U.S. citizens to gain admission for a limited stay in another country. Some countries also require an entry visa. Each country has its own specific guidelines concerning length and purpose of visit, among other considerations. Visitors may need to provide proof of sufficient funds for their intended stay, onward/return tickets, and/or at least six months remaining validity on their U.S. passports.

All persons traveling by air outside of the U.S. (excluding direct travel to and from a U.S. territory) are required to present a passport or other valid document upon reentering the U.S.

For up-to-date passport and international travel information, visit the State Dept.'s Consular Affairs website (travel. state.gov) or call the National Passport Information Center at 1-877-4USA-PPT (1-877-487-2778).

COVID-19 Impact on Foreign Travel

The COVID-19 pandemic had a devastating effect on international travel in 2020. Travel challenges included mandatory quarantines, travel restrictions, and closed borders. Because countries were affected differently, the U.S. State Dept. urged travelers to check the travel advisory for their destination before traveling, found at travel.state.gov.

Summary of TSA Regulations

Airplane carry-ons. TSA promotes the liquids (or "3-1-1") rule regarding carry-on items. Containers with liquids, gels, aerosols, creams, or pastes must hold **3.4** oz (100 mL) or less; these containers should be packed inside a single **1**-quart, clear plastic, resealable bag; and this **1** bag must go through checkpoint security. Exceptions to the liquids rule include medication, baby formula and food, and breast milk. Travelers must declare any exceptions at security.

Security checkpoint identification. Adult travelers (18 years of age and over) must present a photo ID. Acceptable documents include a U.S. passport or passport card; foreign government-issued passport; state-issued driver's license; permanent resident card; or U.S. military ID, among others. Starting Oct. 1, 2021, travelers using a state-issued driver's license must have the enhanced version or one that is compliant with the REAL ID Act.

Screening process. Travelers may wear loose fitting or religious garments (incl. head coverings) through security. They may be subject to additional screening if clothing could conceal prohibited items. Travelers may request a private area if selected for personal screening. Travelers will be screened by someone of the same gender.

As of Oct. 2020, travelers were expected to follow all safety precautions related to the COVID-19 pandemic while traveling, including the wearing of face masks.

Disability-related permitted carry-on items:

- Wheelchairs, mobility scooters
- Crutches, canes, and walkers
- Portable oxygen concentrators (not permitted by all airlines)
- Medications and associated supplies
- Service animals

Permitted carry-on items:

- Disposable and electric razors (blades not allowed)
- Eye drops and contact lens solution (amounts less than 3.4 oz allowed)
- Strollers, baby carriers, child car seats
- Beverages (any size) purchased after security screening

Prohibited carry-on items:

- Knives (except for plastic or round-bladed butter knives), incl. pocket knives and knives that are religious objects
- Baseball bats, golf clubs, hiking poles, hockey sticks
- Firearms or realistic firearm replicas, ammunition
- Screwdrivers, wrenches, pliers, and other tools more than 7 in. in length; hammers
- Lighter fluid
- Self-defense sprays

For complete travel information, visit www.tsa.gov/travel

EMPLOYMENT

Employment and Unemployment in the U.S., 1900-2019

Source: Bureau of Labor Statistics, U.S. Dept. of Labor

(civilian labor force, persons 16 years of age and older unless otherwise noted; annual averages, in thousands)

Year	Employed	Unemployed Number	Rate	Year	Employed	Unemployed Number	Rate	Year	Employed	Unemployed Number	Rate
1900[1]	26,956	1,420	5.0%	1992	118,492	9,613	7.5%	2006	144,427	7,001	4.6%
1910[1]	34,599	2,150	5.9	1993	120,259	8,940	6.9	2007	146,047	7,078	4.6
1920[1]	39,208	2,132	5.2	1994	123,060	7,996	6.1	2008	145,362	8,924	5.8
1930[1]	44,183	4,340	8.9	1995	124,900	7,404	5.6	2009	139,877	14,265	9.3
1940[1]	47,520	8,120	14.6	1996	126,708	7,236	5.4	2010	139,064	14,825	9.6
1950	58,918	3,288	5.3	1997	129,558	6,739	4.9	2011	139,869	13,747	8.9
1960	65,778	3,852	5.5	1998	131,463	6,210	4.5	2012	142,469	12,506	8.1
1965	71,088	3,366	4.5	1999	133,488	5,880	4.2	2013	143,929	11,460	7.4
1970	78,678	4,093	4.9	2000	136,891	5,692	4.0	2014	146,305	9,617	6.2
1975	85,846	7,929	8.5	2001	136,933	6,801	4.7	2015	148,834	8,296	5.3
1980	99,303	7,637	7.1	2002	136,485	8,378	5.8	2016	151,436	7,751	4.9
1985	107,150	8,312	7.2	2003	137,736	8,774	6.0	2017	153,337	6,982	4.4
1990	118,793	7,047	5.6	2004	139,252	8,149	5.5	2018	155,761	6,314	3.9
1991	117,718	8,628	6.8	2005	141,730	7,591	5.1	2019	157,538	6,001	3.7

Note: Because of revisions in population controls, data for a given year may not be strictly comparable to other years. **Other unemployment rates (1905-55)**, persons 14 years of age and older: 1905, 4.3%; 1915, 8.5%; 1925, 3.2%; 1935, 20.3%; 1936, 16.9%; 1937, 14.3%; 1938, 19.0%; 1939, 17.2%; 1945, 1.9%; 1955, 4.4%. (1) Persons 14 years of age and older.

Unemployment Rate and Benefits Data by State, 2019

Source: Employment and Training Admin., U.S. Dept. of Labor; state programs only

State/ terr.	Unemployment rate	Monetarily eligible claimants	Number of first payments	Number of final payments	Initial claims	Benefits paid	Average weekly benefit	Employers subject to state law
AL	3.0%	79,270	47,624	14,762	130,732	$140,529,875	$226.56	91,906
AK	6.1	30,817	18,346	7,162	47,831	84,094,016	267.05	18,408
AZ	4.7	115,142	58,871	21,714	201,756	190,393,511	232.62	139,376
AR	3.5	62,364	38,062	12,127	97,223	88,266,798	265.31	71,652
CA	4.0	870,396	874,839	414,702	2,104,960	4,753,851,674	334.84	1,454,112
CO	2.8	83,012	62,219	24,414	97,461	368,791,773	449.23	184,043
CT	3.7	122,919	101,323	28,593	179,833	547,044,231	398.64	105,393
DE	3.8	22,401	14,047	4,143	32,255	61,145,619	272.12	32,288
DC	5.5	24,201	19,192	7,184	27,345	98,486,803	358.79	35,872
FL	3.1	213,785	140,211	73,524	307,701	319,824,449	250.97	567,485
GA	3.4	184,780	126,211	42,916	291,962	289,562,838	303.17	249,138
HI	2.7	26,365	20,010	5,486	62,207	145,645,257	528.80	33,243
ID	2.9	36,596	26,372	7,884	58,694	78,106,908	339.29	58,460
IL	4.0	292,675	269,867	82,222	503,579	1,583,350,500	398.69	332,614
IN	3.3	100,507	64,647	12,752	144,582	218,362,249	297.29	132,181
IA	2.7	99,575	78,695	17,244	154,324	372,671,629	410.17	80,314
KS	3.2	56,549	30,352	12,311	86,200	94,805,660	385.81	75,318
KY	4.3	92,363	43,592	13,894	141,973	269,318,808	359.56	95,816
LA	4.8	65,550	37,179	11,927	97,846	148,733,877	214.70	101,571
ME	3.0	23,494	18,096	4,704	34,208	71,946,032	345.08	43,438
MD	3.6	110,331	67,635	22,919	155,703	376,937,195	351.94	148,953
MA	2.9	192,771	161,854	52,192	283,710	1,289,851,482	535.73	232,562
MI	4.1	270,407	214,998	62,764	389,373	763,935,687	322.89	218,121
MN	3.2	147,118	110,205	33,383	197,885	694,476,024	469.42	137,665
MS	5.4	39,858	23,030	5,114	61,929	58,392,677	211.24	56,808
MO	3.3	114,664	70,638	23,921	185,494	229,645,951	265.97	166,250
MT	3.5	30,154	21,474	6,880	46,998	92,302,536	378.21	42,890
NE	3.0	28,447	15,826	3,403	40,993	62,281,394	347.67	58,965
NV	3.9	78,965	54,076	18,234	119,251	275,275,747	364.20	74,307
NH	2.5	17,365	11,104	1,771	24,437	44,310,786	334.52	43,871
NJ	3.6	296,643	249,007	100,136	496,839	1,767,804,256	460.71	240,248
NM	4.9	32,149	22,804	8,671	43,819	111,891,160	341.31	49,465
NY	4.0	516,463	374,954	112,370	817,103	1,945,106,701	363.24	526,496
NC	3.9	129,278	73,728	34,575	160,377	178,491,631	267.51	231,149
ND	2.4	19,778	14,554	5,461	23,538	79,373,951	460.82	25,246
OH	4.1	226,777	158,217	36,836	342,335	763,024,840	377.84	229,727
OK	3.3	73,741	42,617	15,298	96,794	220,574,018	386.15	90,216
OR	3.7	125,191	79,439	23,676	218,958	500,820,298	413.86	135,132
PA	4.4	376,113	316,041	80,256	745,029	1,637,726,656	393.94	308,831
PR	8.3	52,231	42,305	19,453	65,475	101,141,398	143.02	52,192
RI	3.6	34,578	27,114	7,494	55,693	141,885,026	367.82	35,440
SC	2.8	87,880	46,714	18,706	121,966	149,227,812	262.56	117,544
SD	3.3	9,320	5,511	769	11,596	25,274,362	345.60	28,631
TN	3.4	92,324	60,829	15,588	130,338	186,354,550	240.17	129,372
TX	3.5	521,080	363,357	134,451	697,486	1,929,916,786	417.86	563,356
UT	2.6	44,811	28,781	7,480	57,254	132,842,114	424.48	86,890
VT	2.4	16,859	13,900	2,033	27,852	57,415,893	381.54	23,220
VA	2.8	108,554	79,417	21,336	136,243	257,082,780	315.42	227,005
VI	NA	1,408	1,250	671	1,730	6,565,161	385.38	3,960
WA	4.3	192,780	125,470	37,765	341,259	902,546,238	476.33	244,108
WV	4.9	51,852	41,111	9,675	57,912	176,644,350	323.72	36,299
WI	3.3	136,888	108,010	15,454	291,484	367,790,416	325.10	146,036
WY	3.6	11,913	9,609	2,092	17,527	43,848,588	395.33	22,888
U.S.	**3.7**	**6,791,452**	**5,125,334**	**1,760,492**	**11,267,052**	**25,495,690,970**	**368.97**	**8,636,471**

NA = Not available.

Weekly Unemployment Insurance Claims, 2000-20
Source: Employment and Training Admin., U.S. Dept. of Labor

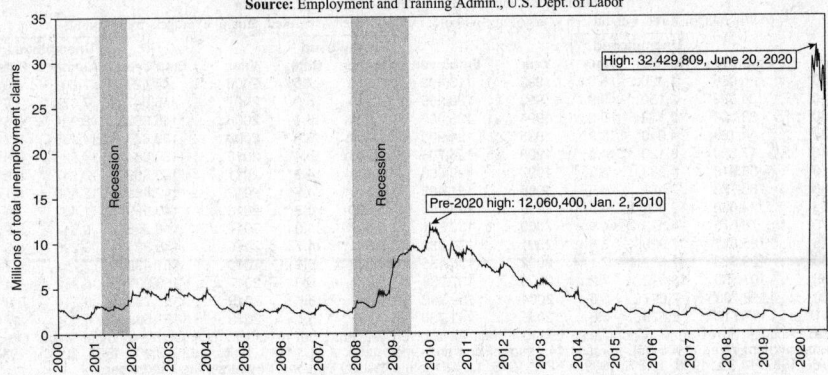

High: 32,429,809, June 20, 2020

Pre-2020 high: 12,060,400, Jan. 2, 2010

Note: Total includes state programs, programs for federal employees and ex-service members, extended and emergency programs, short-time compensation, Pandemic Unemployment Assistance, and Pandemic Emergency Unemployment Compensation.

U.S. Unemployment Duration by Industry and Occupation, 2019
Source: Bureau of Labor Statistics, U.S. Dept. of Labor

	Number of unemployed persons (thous.)					Weeks of unemployment	
Occupation	Total	Less than 5 weeks	5 to 14 weeks	15 to 26 weeks	27 weeks and over	Average (mean) duration	Median duration
Management, professional, and related	1,310	436	388	181	306	22.6	9.5
Management, business, and financial operations	499	153	138	77	132	23.0	11.1
Professional and related	811	283	250	104	174	22.4	8.8
Service	1,255	465	364	181	245	20.0	8.6
Sales and office	1,274	422	375	193	283	22.6	9.9
Sales and related	614	210	176	84	144	22.3	9.6
Office and administrative support	659	212	200	109	139	22.9	10.1
Natural resources, construction, and maintenance	703	266	216	100	121	17.8	8.2
Farming, fishing, and forestry	123	44	38	22	18	15.0	8.5
Construction and extraction	452	183	139	59	72	16.3	7.5
Installation, maintenance, and repair	129	39	38	19	31	26.1	10.4
Production, transportation, and material moving	847	296	259	121	171	21.5	8.9
Production	350	126	109	51	65	19.6	8.6
Transportation and material moving	497	170	150	70	107	22.9	9.2
Industry[1]							
Agriculture and related industries	133	45	45	22	21	16.1	8.7
Mining, quarrying, and oil and gas extraction	25	11	7	3	4	—	—
Construction	442	174	138	54	76	17.3	7.8
Manufacturing	476	158	147	73	99	20.9	9.6
Wholesale and retail trade	813	263	251	120	178	22.4	9.7
Transportation and utilities	271	95	69	39	69	26.2	9.6
Information	93	26	27	15	25	27.8	11.2
Financial activities	222	61	67	35	58	25.1	11.8
Professional and business services	671	215	195	107	153	21.2	10.1
Education and health services	850	311	279	107	152	19.2	8.1
Leisure and hospitality	773	303	223	111	137	18.7	8.0
Other services	218	78	54	33	53	24.0	9.7
Public administration	138	39	37	26	36	27.6	12.2
No previous work experience	591	196	182	81	132	24.8	9.4
Total unemployed[2]	**6,001**	**2,086**	**1,789**	**860**	**1,266**	**21.6**	**9.1**

— = Not available. **Note:** Persons 16 years of age and older. (1) Includes wage and salary workers only. (2) Includes persons whose last job was in the U.S. Armed Forces.

U.S. Displaced Workers, 2020
Source: Bureau of Labor Statistics, U.S. Dept. of Labor

	Number (thous.)	Reason for job loss (% distrib.)		
		Plant or company closed down or moved	Insufficient work	Position or shift abolished
Total displaced workers	2,672	40.6%	23.2%	36.2%
Age: 20 to 24 years	63	NA	NA	NA
25 to 54 years	1,676	42.6	23.2	34.2
55 to 64 years	702	33.2	24.7	42.1
65 years and over	232	43.8	19.5	36.7
Sex: Men	1,466	40.2	25.7	34.2
Women	1,206	41.0	20.3	38.7
Race: White	2,162	40.7	23.0	36.3
Black	335	47.3	21.4	31.3
Asian	110	13.8	24.4	61.8
Hispanic or Latino	461	50.6	27.5	22.0

NA = Not available. **Note:** As of Jan. 2020. Displaced workers are persons age 20 or older who lost or left jobs they had held for at least three years. Workers in this table were displaced between Jan. 2017 and Dec. 2019. Hispanic or Latino persons may be of any race.

U.S. Unemployment Rates by Selected Characteristics, 1995-2020

Source: Bureau of Labor Statistics, U.S. Dept. of Labor

	1995	2000	2005	2010	2015	2017	2018	2019 Jan.	2019 June	2019 Yr.	2020 Jan.	2020 June
Total (all civilian workers)	5.6%	4.0%	5.1%	9.6%	5.3%	4.4%	3.9%	4.4%	3.8%	3.7%	4.0%	11.1%
Men, 20 years and older	4.8	3.3	4.4	9.8	4.9	4.0	3.6	4.4	3.2	3.4	3.9	10.2
Women, 20 years and older	4.9	3.6	4.6	8.0	4.8	4.0	3.5	3.7	3.5	3.3	3.4	11.2
Both sexes, 16 to 19 years	17.3	13.1	16.6	25.9	16.9	14.0	12.9	13.7	15.0	12.7	13.0	29.1
White	4.9	3.5	4.4	8.7	4.6	3.8	3.5	4.0	3.5	3.3	3.5	10.1
Black	10.4	7.6	10.0	16.0	9.6	7.5	6.5	7.4	6.1	6.1	6.6	15.4
Asian	—	3.6	4.0	7.5	3.8	3.4	3.0	3.2	2.3	2.7	3.2	13.8
Hispanic or Latino (any race)	9.3	5.7	6.0	12.5	6.6	5.1	4.7	5.6	4.4	4.3	5.1	14.5
Married men, spouse present[1]	3.3	—	—	6.8	2.8	2.4	2.0	2.1	1.8	1.8	1.7	6.9
Married women, spouse present[1]	3.9	—	—	5.9	3.1	2.7	2.4	2.4	2.3	2.2	2.1	8.9
Women who maintain families, spouse absent	8.0	5.9	7.8	12.3	7.4	6.2	5.4	5.4	5.1	5.0	5.4	13.1
Occupation												
Management, professional, and related	2.4	1.8	2.3	4.7	2.5	2.2	2.1	2.5	2.4	2.0	2.2	6.5
Service	7.5	5.2	6.4	10.3	6.7	5.4	4.8	5.5	4.2	4.4	4.7	18.8
Sales and office	5.0	3.8	4.8	9.0	5.1	4.1	3.8	4.4	3.8	3.7	4.0	11.8
Natural resources, constr., and maintenance	—	5.3	6.5	16.1	7.2	6.0	5.1	7.0	4.0	4.7	6.3	10.6
Production, transp., and material moving	—	5.1	6.5	12.8	6.3	5.4	4.5	4.6	4.2	4.3	4.7	13.2
Industry												
Nonagricultural private wage and salary workers	5.8	4.1	5.2	9.9	5.1	4.2	3.7	4.2	3.5	3.5	3.8	11.7
Mining	5.2	4.4	3.1	9.4	8.6	4.1	3.4	5.3	3.2	3.2	1.9	17.8
Construction	11.5	6.2	7.4	20.6	7.3	6.0	5.1	6.4	4.0	4.5	5.4	10.1
Manufacturing	4.9	3.5	4.9	10.6	4.3	3.6	3.3	3.3	2.8	3.0	3.4	9.1
Durable goods	4.4	3.2	4.6	11.2	4.1	3.7	3.0	3.3	2.8	2.7	3.2	9.2
Nondurable goods	5.7	4.0	5.3	9.6	4.6	3.5	3.8	3.4	2.8	3.3	3.7	8.9
Wholesale and retail trade	6.5	4.3	5.4	9.5	5.5	4.6	4.3	4.8	3.9	4.1	4.7	11.2
Transportation and utilities	4.5	3.4	4.1	8.4	4.4	4.1	3.4	3.6	3.7	3.5	3.0	12.9
Information	—	3.2	5.0	9.7	3.9	4.5	3.7	4.7	2.7	3.5	2.3	12.0
Financial activities	3.3	2.4	2.9	6.9	2.6	2.4	2.2	2.4	2.0	2.1	2.5	5.1
Professional and business services	—	4.8	6.2	10.8	5.6	4.5	3.9	4.9	3.6	3.6	4.1	8.6
Education and health services	—	2.5	3.4	5.8	3.6	3.0	2.6	2.6	3.0	2.5	2.4	8.6
Leisure and hospitality	—	6.6	7.8	12.2	7.9	6.1	5.7	6.4	4.9	5.2	5.9	28.9
Other services	8.4	3.9	4.8	8.5	5.2	3.8	3.3	3.9	3.0	3.2	3.7	14.5
Agriculture and related private wage and salary workers	11.1	9.0	8.3	13.9	9.4	7.2	7.2	14.1	5.9	7.4	12.5	5.4
Government workers	2.9	2.1	2.6	4.4	2.7	2.5	2.3	2.6	3.3	2.3	2.1	7.3
Self-employed and unpaid family workers	—	2.1	2.7	5.9	3.9	3.2	2.8	3.7	2.3	2.7	3.6	8.1

— = Not available. Note: All monthly rates are unadjusted, except for married men and women, which are seasonally adjusted. (1) Refers to persons in opposite-sex married couples only.

U.S. Workers by Industry and Type, 2009, 2019

Source: Bureau of Labor Statistics, U.S. Dept. of Labor

(in thousands)

Industry	2009 Total employed	2009 Private industry workers	2009 Govt. workers	2009 Self-employed workers	2019 Total employed	2019 Private industry workers[1]	2019 Govt. workers	2019 Self-employed workers[2]
Mining[3]	707	688	1	18	750	732	4	14
Construction	9,702	7,528	465	1,701	11,373	9,302	395	1,671
Manufacturing	14,202	13,757	114	324	15,741	15,363	109	264
Durable goods	8,927	8,630	96	197	9,970	9,710	90	166
Nondurable goods	5,275	5,127	18	127	5,771	5,653	19	98
Wholesale and retail trade	19,684	18,599	108	963	19,742	18,898	77	762
Wholesale trade	3,808	3,623	13	170	3,525	3,403	9	113
Retail trade	15,877	14,976	94	793	16,217	15,494	68	649
Transportation and utilities	7,245	5,382	1,457	402	8,991	7,100	1,336	550
Transportation and warehousing	6,012	4,482	1,123	402	7,614	6,030	1,029	550
Utilities	1,233	900	334	—	1,377	1,070	307	—
Information	3,239	2,895	199	145	2,766	2,448	178	139
Financial activities	9,622	8,735	215	667	10,765	9,872	211	678
Finance and insurance	6,826	6,431	131	262	7,464	7,121	125	216
Real estate and rental and leasing	2,796	2,304	84	405	3,301	2,751	85	462
Professional and business services	15,008	12,581	420	1,996	19,606	17,157	458	1,982
Professional and technical services	9,159	7,814	231	1,110	12,808	11,364	263	1,176
Management, administrative, and waste services	5,849	4,767	189	886	6,799	5,792	195	806
Education and health services	31,819	19,835	10,877	1,102	35,894	24,301	10,556	1,034
Educational services	13,188	3,863	9,106	219	14,193	5,020	8,923	250
Health care and social assistance	18,632	15,972	1,772	883	21,701	19,281	1,633	784
Hospitals	6,265	5,432	823	10	7,425	6,656	755	14
Health services, except hospitals	9,213	8,367	464	378	10,846	10,037	392	416
Social assistance	3,154	2,173	484	494	3,430	2,588	487	354
Leisure and hospitality	12,736	11,677	415	636	14,643	13,552	398	683
Arts, entertainment, and recreation	3,018	2,246	367	404	3,444	2,649	335	459
Accommodation and food services	9,717	9,431	48	232	11,200	10,903	63	224
Other services	6,935	5,859	32	1,039	7,617	6,561	30	1,022
Other services, except private households	6,152	5,076	32	1,039	6,796	5,740	30	1,022
Private households	783	783	—	—	821	821	—	—
Public administration	6,875	—	6,875	—	7,225	—	7,225	—

— = No data or data that do not meet publication criteria. (1) Includes self-employed workers whose businesses are incorporated. (2) Unincorporated. (3) Includes quarrying and oil and gas extraction.

Persons Not in the U.S. Labor Force, 2019

Source: Bureau of Labor Statistics, U.S. Dept. of Labor

The Labor Dept.'s unemployment rate, based on its household survey, shows the number of people out of work as a percentage of adults age 16 and older in the labor force. That rate excludes the millions of adults considered to be not in the labor force.

(in thousands)

	Number	Age in years			Sex	
		16 to 24	25 to 54	55 and over	Men	Women
Total not in the labor force	95,636	16,656	22,102	56,879	38,667	56,970
Do not want a job now[1]	90,593	15,153	20,023	55,417	36,252	54,341
Want a job[1]	5,043	1,503	2,078	1,462	2,415	2,629
Did not search for work in previous year	3,084	883	1,157	1,045	1,430	1,654
Searched in previous year but not						
previous four weeks[2]	1,959	620	921	418	984	975
Not available to work now	556	229	252	75	242	314
Available to work now	1,403	391	669	343	742	661
Reason not currently looking[3]						
Discouraged over job prospects[4]........	382	86	193	103	239	143
Reasons other than discouragement.....	1,021	306	476	240	503	519
Family responsibilities	156	21	103	32	44	112
In school or training	146	116	27	4	76	70
Ill health or disability	135	14	63	58	73	63
Other[5]......................	584	155	283	147	310	274

(1) Includes some persons who are not asked if they want a job. (2) Persons who had a job in the prior 12 months must have searched since the end of that job to be considered unemployed. (3) Of those available to work now. (4) Includes believing no work is available, not being able to find work, lacking necessary schooling or training, thought of as too young or old by employers, and other types of discrimination. (5) Includes those who did not actively look for work in the prior four weeks for such reasons as child-care and transportation problems, as well as a small number for which reason for nonparticipation was not ascertained.

U.S. Small Business Employment by Industry, 2017

Source: U.S. Small Business Administration

Industry	Small business employment	Total private employment	% small business employment
Health care and social assistance	8,984,159	20,241,438	44.4%
Accommodation and food services........................	8,542,661	14,088,211	60.6
Retail trade...................................	5,526,296	15,705,808	35.2
Construction................................	5,373,702	6,533,061	82.3
Professional, scientific, and technical services...............	5,190,980	8,905,549	58.3
Manufacturing................................	5,039,772	11,721,785	43.0
Other services (excl. public administration)	4,697,878	5,534,978	84.9
Administrative, support, and waste management.............	3,754,463	11,897,056	31.6
Wholesale trade..............................	3,413,157	6,115,476	55.8
Finance and insurance	1,909,993	6,408,168	29.8
Transportation and warehousing	1,685,388	4,866,282	34.6
Educational services	1,645,962	3,688,541	44.6
Real estate, rental and leasing...................	1,451,546	2,148,006	67.6
Arts, entertainment, and recreation	1,428,531	2,368,928	60.3
Information	984,379	3,507,966	28.1
Management of companies and enterprises	423,295	3,462,498	12.2
Mining, quarrying, and oil and gas extraction............	244,367	578,098	42.3
Agriculture, forestry, and fishing and hunting	136,591	164,046	83.3
Utilities	111,747	644,703	17.3
Industries not classified	11,214	11,214	100.0
Total employed	**60,556,081**	**128,591,812**	**47.1**

Note: A small business is defined here as a firm employing fewer than 500 employees.

U.S. Occupations Projected to Grow Most, 2019-29

Source: Employment Projections Program, Bureau of Labor Statistics, U.S. Dept. of Labor

(ranked by greatest positive change in number of jobs; numbers in thousands)

Occupation	Employment		Change, 2019-29		Median annual wage, 2019
	2019	2029	Number	Percent	
Total, all occupations..................	162,795.6	168,834.7	6,039.2	3.7	$39,810
Home health and personal care aides	3,439.7	4,599.2	1,159.5	33.7	25,280
Fast food and counter workers.........................	4,047.7	4,508.6	460.9	11.4	22,740
Cooks, restaurant	1,417.3	1,744.6	327.3	23.1	27,790
Software developers and software quality assurance analysts and					
testers	1,469.2	1,785.2	316.0	21.5	107,510
Registered nurses................................	3,096.7	3,318.7	221.9	7.2	73,300
General and operations managers.....................	2,486.4	2,630.2	143.8	5.8	100,780
Medical assistants	725.2	864.4	139.2	19.2	34,800
Medical and health services managers	422.3	555.5	133.2	31.5	100,980
Market research analysts and marketing specialists	738.1	868.4	130.3	17.7	63,790
Laborers and freight, stock, and material movers, hand.........	2,986.0	3,111.7	125.7	4.2	29,510
Landscaping and groundskeeping workers	1,188.0	1,307.9	119.9	10.1	30,440
Nursing assistants	1,528.5	1,645.5	116.9	7.6	29,660
Nurse practitioners	211.3	322.0	110.7	52.4	109,820
Financial managers	697.9	806.0	108.1	15.5	129,890
Janitors and cleaners, except maids and housekeeping cleaners	2,374.2	2,479.8	105.6	4.4	27,430
Waiters and waitresses............................	2,613.8	2,711.4	97.6	3.7	22,890
Passenger vehicle drivers, except bus drivers, transit and intercity	853.3	947.8	94.4	11.1	31,340
Management analysts	876.3	970.2	93.8	10.7	85,260
Project management specialists and business operations					
specialists, all other..........................	1,361.8	1,441.6	79.8	5.9	73,570
Substance abuse, behavioral disorder, and mental health counselors	319.4	398.4	79.0	24.7	46,240
Construction laborers	1,398.0	1,473.4	75.4	5.4	36,860
Social and human service assistants	425.6	497.1	71.5	16.8	35,060
Animal caretakers................................	300.7	369.5	68.8	22.9	24,780

Note: BLS projections do not yet include impacts of the COVID-19 pandemic.

U.S. Occupations Projected to Decline Most, 2019-29

Source: Employment Projections Program, Bureau of Labor Statistics, U.S. Dept. of Labor
(ranked by greatest negative change in number of jobs; numbers in thousands)

Occupation	Employment 2019	Employment 2029	Change, 2019-29 Number	Change, 2019-29 Percent	Median annual wage, 2019
Total, all occupations	162,795.6	168,834.7	6,039.2	3.7%	$39,810
Cashiers	3,600.9	3,335.5	−265.3	−7.4	23,650
Secretaries and administrative assistants[1]	2,250.2	2,022.6	−227.5	−10.1	37,690
Miscellaneous assemblers and fabricators	1,389.1	1,211.5	−177.6	−12.8	32,350
Office clerks, general	3,126.3	2,970.4	−155.9	−5.0	34,040
Executive secretaries and executive administrative assistants	593.4	472.4	−121.1	−20.4	60,890
Inspectors, testers, sorters, samplers, and weighers	590.1	489.6	−100.4	−17.0	39,140
Bookkeeping, accounting, and auditing clerks	1,673.6	1,578.2	−95.4	−5.7	41,230
First-line supervisors of retail sales workers	1,476.4	1,395.3	−81.2	−5.5	40,350
Cooks, fast food	534.0	462.3	−71.6	−13.4	23,510
Tellers	449.0	380.4	−68.6	−15.3	31,230
Farmers, ranchers, and other agricultural managers	952.3	890.6	−61.6	−6.5	71,160
Shipping, receiving, and inventory clerks	710.4	648.8	−61.5	−8.7	34,190
Customer service representatives	3,018.8	2,959.8	−59.0	−2.0	34,710
First-line supervisors of office and administrative support workers	1,552.4	1,505.7	−46.7	−3.0	56,620
Postal service mail carriers	326.6	282.5	−44.1	−13.5	51,310

Note: BLS projections do not include impacts of COVID-19 pandemic. (1) Excl. legal, medical, executive.

Projected Employment by Typical Entry-Level Education, 2019-29

Source: Employment Projections Program, Bureau of Labor Statistics, U.S. Dept. of Labor

Typical entry-level education	Employment, 2019 Number (thous.)	Employment, 2019 Percent distribution	% change in employment, 2019-29	Median annual wage, 2019
Total, all occupations	162,795.6	100.0%	3.7%	$39,810
Doctoral or professional degree	4,412.8	2.7	5.9	107,660
Master's degree	2,633.9	1.6	15.0	76,180
Bachelor's degree	36,864.2	22.6	6.4	75,440
Associate's degree	3,601.6	2.2	6.2	54,940
Postsecondary nondegree award	10,093.2	6.2	5.6	39,940
Some college, no degree	4,085.0	2.5	−0.1	36,790
High school diploma or equivalent	62,410.0	38.3	1.5	37,930
No formal educational credential	38,694.8	23.8	3.3	25,700

Note: The occupational employment and growth rates shown in this table include projected growth in all jobs from 2019-29, not just entry-level jobs. Entry-level education reflects 2019 requirements—BLS does not project educational requirements. BLS projections do not include impacts of COVID-19 pandemic.

Highest Average Weekly Wages by County, 2019

Source: Bureau of Labor Statistics, U.S. Dept. of Labor

County	Avg. weekly wage	% change, 2018-19	County	Avg. weekly wage	% change, 2018-19
Santa Clara, CA	$2,825	5.6%	Fairfield, CT	$1,756	2.7%
San Mateo, CA	2,622	8.2	Fairfax, VA	1,735	3.3
San Francisco, CA	2,523	2.3	Middlesex, MA	1,724	4.3
New York, NY	2,502	4.3	Morris, NJ	1,691	4.3
Suffolk, MA	2,146	3.9	Alexandria City, VA	1,645	1.7
Washington, DC	1,992	2.5	Somerset, NJ	1,628	0.1
Arlington, VA	1,963	4.7	Alameda, CA	1,577	3.5
King, WA	1,818	7.8			

Note: Figures shown are for the 4th quarter, from among the 355 largest U.S. counties, which comprise 73.7% of total covered workers. Cameron County, TX, recorded the lowest average weekly earnings among the largest counties, with an average of $701. It was followed by Hidalgo, TX ($705); Horry, SC ($721); Webb, TX ($750); Osceola, FL ($788); Harrison, MS ($789); Lake, FL ($793); El Paso, TX ($798); Marion, FL ($810); and Mahoning, OH ($817). Data include all workers covered by state and federal unemployment insurance programs.

Fatal Occupational Injuries, 2018

Source: Census of Fatal Occupational Injuries, Bureau of Labor Statistics, U.S. Dept. of Labor

Event or exposure	Fatalities Number	%	Event or exposure	Fatalities Number	%
Total	5,250	100%	Nonroadway incident involving motorized land vehicle	225	4%
Violence and other injuries by persons or animals	828	16	Nonroadway noncollision incident	164	3
Intentional injury by person	757	14	Jack-knifed or overturned, nonroadway...	105	2
Homicides	453	9	Fire or explosion	115	2
Shooting by other person—intentional....	351	7	Fall, slip, trip	791	15
Stabbing, cutting, slashing, piercing	44	1	Fall on same level	154	3
Suicides	304	6	Fall to lower level	615	12
Transportation incidents	2,080	40	Fall from collapsing structure or equipment	50	1
Aircraft incidents	133	3	Fall through surface or existing opening	83	2
Rail vehicle incidents	48	1	Exposure to harmful substances or environments	621	12
Pedestrian vehicular incident	325	6	Exposure to electricity	160	3
Pedestrian struck by vehicle in work zone ..	58	1	Exposure to temperature extremes	60	1
Water vehicle incident	58	1	Exposure to other harmful substances	355	7
Roadway incident involving motorized land vehicle	1,276	24	Nonmedical use of drugs or alcohol, unintentional overdose	305	6
Roadway collision with other vehicle	677	13	Inhalation of harmful substance	42	1
Roadway collision moving in same direction	183	3	Contact with objects and equipment	786	15
Roadway collision moving in opposite directions, oncoming	243	5	Struck by object or equipment	566	11
Roadway collision moving perpendicularly	141	3	Struck by powered vehicle, nontransport	215	4
Roadway collision with object other than vehicle	373	7	Struck by falling object or equipment	278	5
Vehicle struck object or animal on side of roadway	345	7	Caught in or compressed by equipment or objects	137	3
Roadway noncollision incident	222	4	Caught in running equipment or machinery	106	2
Jack-knifed or overturned, roadway	170	3	Struck, caught, or crushed in collapsing structure, equipment, or material	73	1

Note: Category totals may include subcategories not shown. Percentages show incidence rate per total fatalities.

U.S. Occupational Injuries and Illnesses Involving Days Away From Work, 2018
Source: Bureau of Labor Statistics, U.S. Dept. of Labor

Characteristic	Illnesses/ injuries[2]	Percent of days-away-from-work cases[1] involving—							Median days away from work
		1 day	2 days	3-5 days	6-10 days	11-20 days	21-30 days	31 days or more	
Total	**900,380**	**13.8%**	**10.8%**	**17.6%**	**12.0%**	**10.6%**	**6.0%**	**29.2%**	**8**
Male	541,330	13.3	10.4	17.0	12.0	10.8	6.3	30.1	9
Female	353,440	14.5	11.5	18.6	11.8	10.4	5.6	27.8	7
Age									
14-15 years	250	60.0	16.0	8.0	—	8.0	—	—	1
16-19 years	25,780	20.8	13.8	22.6	13.8	13.5	3.6	11.9	5
20-24 years	88,840	17.7	14.4	20.0	14.5	10.9	5.2	17.4	5
25-34 years	191,650	16.4	12.2	19.8	12.1	10.6	5.2	23.6	6
35-44 years	174,020	13.7	11.6	18.4	11.2	10.0	6.3	28.9	8
45-54 years	193,650	12.0	9.2	16.3	11.8	9.9	6.2	34.6	11
55-64 years	168,520	10.4	8.2	14.6	11.2	11.4	7.0	37.2	15
65 years and over	42,550	9.8	9.4	14.2	11.9	11.4	7.9	35.4	14
Age group not reported	15,100	16.4	11.8	16.8	12.0	9.4	4.7	29.0	7
Occupation(s)									
Management, business, financial	29,000	18.3	11.3	17.1	9.7	10.6	7.3	25.6	7
Computer, engineering, science	5,860	17.2	13.3	17.4	18.4	8.2	6.0	19.5	6
Education, legal, community service, arts, media	25,100	19.0	13.6	20.8	11.6	9.2	4.4	21.4	5
Health-care practitioners, technical	50,810	15.2	12.1	19.6	13.1	10.4	5.5	24.1	6
Service	213,440	15.0	12.6	20.1	12.3	10.9	5.9	23.3	6
Sales and related	59,610	14.1	9.9	19.3	11.7	10.7	4.6	29.8	8
Office and administrative support	64,800	12.5	10.8	16.4	11.0	11.6	6.3	31.4	10
Farming, fishing, forestry	15,390	14.5	10.2	22.4	12.5	11.4	5.2	23.9	7
Construction, extraction	73,630	13.3	9.3	15.2	11.6	11.2	7.3	32.1	11
Installation, maintenance, repair	79,380	13.8	10.6	15.3	10.6	10.4	7.5	31.7	10
Production	98,140	15.9	10.6	17.5	11.3	11.0	5.4	28.4	7
Transportation, material moving	184,470	9.6	8.9	15.4	12.9	9.9	6.1	37.2	13

— = Data do not meet publication guidelines or may be too small to be displayed. **Note:** Because of rounding and data exclusion of nonclassifiable responses, data may not sum to the totals. (1) Cases include those that resulted in days away from work, some of which also included job transfer or restriction. (2) Number of nonfatal occupational injuries and illnesses involving days away from work for private industry workers.

Federal Minimum Hourly Wage Rates
Source: Bureau of Labor Statistics, U.S. Dept. of Labor; as of May 2020

Effective date	Minimum wage	% avg. earnings[1]	In 2020 dollars	Effective date	Minimum wage	% avg. earnings[1]	In 2020 dollars
Oct. 24, 1938	$0.25	40%	$4.58	Jan. 1, 1978	$2.65	43%	$10.87
Oct. 24, 1939	0.30	48	5.49	Jan. 1, 1979	2.90	43	10.89
Oct. 24, 1945	0.40	39	5.67	Jan. 1, 1980	3.10	43	10.22
Jan. 25, 1950	0.75	52	8.18	Jan. 1, 1981	3.35	42	9.87
Mar. 1, 1956	1.00	51	9.57	Apr. 1, 1990	3.80	35	7.56
Sept. 3, 1961	1.15	50	9.83	Apr. 1, 1991	4.25	38	8.06
Sept. 3, 1963	1.25	51	10.44	Oct. 1, 1996	4.75	37	7.69
Feb. 1, 1967	1.40	49	10.91	Sept. 1, 1997	5.15	39	8.19
Feb. 1, 1968	1.60	53	12.00	July 24, 2007	5.85	34	7.20
May 1, 1974	2.00	45	10.55	July 24, 2008	6.55	37	7.63
Jan. 1, 1975	2.10	43	10.33	July 24, 2009	7.25	40	8.63
Jan. 1, 1976	2.30	44	10.61				

Note: Before 1961, the minimum wage applied primarily to employees engaged in, or producing goods for, interstate commerce. The 1961 amendments extended coverage primarily to employees in large retail and service enterprises and to local transit, construction, and gas station employees. The 1966 and subsequent amendments extended coverage to farm workers; government employees; workers in various retail and service trades; and certain domestic workers. Starting in 1978, minimum wage applied equally to all covered, nonexempt workers. Exceptions apply to certain workers with disabilities, full-time students, persons under age 20 in their first 90 days of employment, tipped employees, and student-learners. (1) Percent of gross hourly earnings of production workers in manufacturing.

Civilian Employment of the Federal Government, 1940-2021
Source: U.S. Office of Personnel Management; Office of Management and Budget
(numbers in thousands)

Year	Total executive branch	Dept. of Defense	Civilian agencies/depts.									
			Total employees	Agricul- ture	HHS, Education, Social Sec.[1]	Homeland Sec.	Interior	Justice	Transpor- tation	Treasury	Veterans Affairs	Other
1940	699	256	443	98	9	18	46	11	NA	45	40	176
1945	3,370	2,635	736	82	11	20	45	19	NA	84	65	409
1950	1,439	753	686	84	13	20	66	20	NA	76	188	219
1955	1,860	1,187	673	86	40	21	54	24	NA	65	178	206
1960	1,808	1,047	761	99	62	21	56	24	NA	62	172	265
1965	1,901	1,034	867	113	87	21	71	27	NA	74	167	307
1970	2,203	1,219	983	118	112	23	75	33	62	84	169	308
1975	2,149	1,042	1,107	121	147	31	80	47	69	101	213	297
1980	2,161	960	1,201	129	163	40	77	48	66	102	228	346
1985	2,112	1,029	1,084	107	137	39	72	51	55	106	221	294
1990	2,174	1,006	1,168	111	122	48	71	66	59	130	214	347
1995	1,970	822	1,148	104	129	54	72	82	57	129	228	292
2000	1,814	660	1,153	95	128	67	67	95	57	113	203	328
2005	1,830	653	1,177	100	128	143	70	103	56	110	222	244
2010	2,128	741	1,386	96	137	173	71	113	57	112	285	342
2015	2,042	725	1,317	86	139	179	64	114	54	95	335	251
2019	2,085	742	1,344	81	138	192	62	112	53	88	376	242
2020[2]	2,206	775	1,431	85	141	197	62	116	55	90	390	294
2021[2]	2,172	774	1,399	84	142	193	61	118	55	102	405	240

NA = Not available. HHS = Health and Human Services. **Note:** End-of-fiscal-year count; U.S. Postal Service excluded. All years are not directly comparable, as 1940-80 is civilian employment of full-time permanent, temporary, part-time, and intermittent employees; 1985-2021 is full-time equivalent employees. (1) Estimated, 1940-50. (2) Estimated.

Unemployment Rates and Earnings by Education, 2019

Source: Bureau of Labor Statistics, U.S. Dept. of Labor

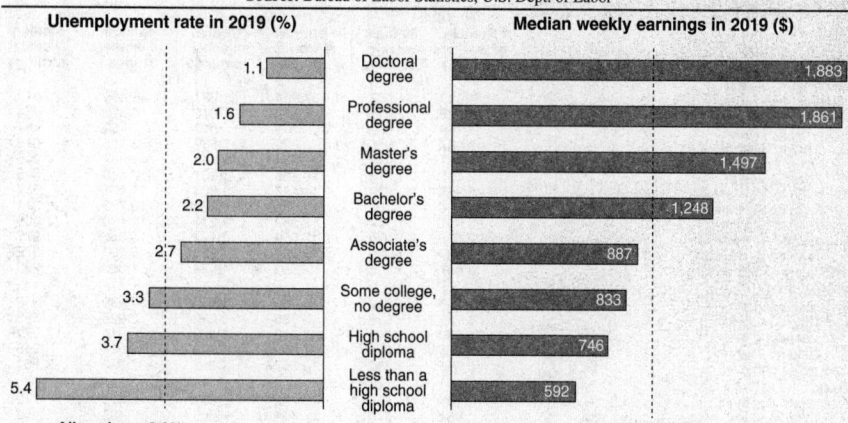

Unemployment rate in 2019 (%) | **Median weekly earnings in 2019 ($)**

Education	Unemployment rate (%)	Median weekly earnings ($)
Doctoral degree	1.1	1,883
Professional degree	1.6	1,861
Master's degree	2.0	1,497
Bachelor's degree	2.2	1,248
Associate's degree	2.7	887
Some college, no degree	3.3	833
High school diploma	3.7	746
Less than a high school diploma	5.4	592

All workers: 3.0%   **All workers: $969**

Note: Data for persons age 25 and over. Earnings are for full-time wage and salary workers.

Median Earnings by Industry and Sex, 2019

Source: American Community Survey, U.S. Census Bureau, U.S. Dept. of Commerce

Industry	Employed			Median earnings			Women's as % of men's
	Total	% men	% women	Total	Men	Women	
Total	158,758,794	52.3%	47.7%	$39,777	$45,893	$32,436	70.7%
Agriculture, forestry, fishing and hunting, and mining . . .	2,731,387	79.0	21.0	37,613	41,484	25,362	61.1
Construction	11,036,894	89.7	10.3	41,870	42,098	39,222	93.2
Manufacturing	15,770,698	70.5	29.5	48,406	52,026	37,694	72.5
Wholesale trade	4,013,368	70.3	29.7	48,553	51,407	40,630	79.0
Retail trade	17,216,634	51.1	48.9	25,452	30,592	21,415	70.0
Transportation and warehousing, and utilities	8,938,005	74.8	25.2	45,009	48,997	35,741	72.9
Information	2,959,616	59.2	40.8	57,106	65,475	46,552	71.1
Finance and insurance, and real estate, and rental and leasing	10,297,770	46.6	53.4	55,117	70,291	47,374	67.4
Professional, scientific, and management, and administrative, and waste management services	18,764,289	57.1	42.9	50,719	60,302	41,214	68.3
Educational services, and health care and social assistance	36,971,212	25.7	74.3	40,089	49,817	36,818	73.9
Arts, entertainment, and recreation, and accommodation and food services	15,334,575	48.3	51.7	19,530	21,993	16,801	76.4
Other services, except public administration	7,584,054	46.1	53.9	27,544	35,778	22,083	61.7
Public administration	7,140,292	54.5	45.5	57,982	66,032	50,132	75.9

Note: For the civilian employed population 16 years of age and over including workers not employed full-time.

Net Productivity and Workers' Hourly Compensation, 1948-2018

Source: Economic Policy Institute (EPI), based on U.S. Bureau of Economic Analysis and U.S. Bureau of Labor Statistics data

This graph shows the cumulative percent change since 1948 in net productivity and hourly compensation in the U.S. Net productivity is the growth of goods and services produced minus depreciation per hour worked. Hourly compensation is average wages and benefits for private-sector production and nonsupervisory workers, who make up around 80% of private payroll employment.

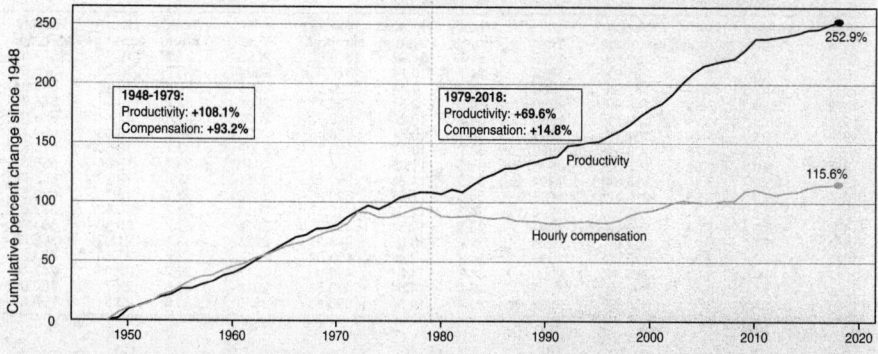

1948-1979:
Productivity: +108.1%
Compensation: +93.2%

1979-2018:
Productivity: +69.6%
Compensation: +14.8%

Productivity — 252.9%
Hourly compensation — 115.6%

U.S. Median Weekly Earnings, 2020

Source: Bureau of Labor Statistics, U.S. Dept. of Labor

AGE, RACE, AND ETHNICITY	Total		Men		Women	
	Number of workers (thous.)	Median weekly earnings	Number of workers (thous.)	Median weekly earnings	Number of workers (thous.)	Median weekly earnings
All workers, by age						
16 years and over....................	104,487	$1,002	57,994	$1,087	46,493	$913
16 to 24 years.....................	8,426	617	4,600	640	3,826	594
16 to 19 years....................	1,169	506	701	518	469	481
20 to 24 years....................	7,257	640	3,899	662	3,358	610
25 years and over....................	96,061	1,047	53,394	1,147	42,667	955
25 to 54 years.....................	73,435	1,040	40,835	1,137	32,600	949
25 to 34 years....................	25,958	918	14,487	963	11,471	867
35 to 44 years....................	24,526	1,135	13,798	1,239	10,728	1,011
45 to 54 years....................	22,951	1,144	12,550	1,271	10,400	1,005
55 years and over....................	22,626	1,073	12,559	1,191	10,066	977
55 to 64 years....................	18,169	1,090	9,966	1,220	8,203	972
65 years and over....................	4,457	1,018	2,593	1,034	1,863	998
White						
16 years and over....................	81,005	1,018	46,066	1,116	34,939	930
16 to 24 years.....................	6,715	616	3,786	639	2,928	593
25 years and over....................	74,290	1,069	42,280	1,173	32,010	971
25 to 54 years.....................	55,936	1,058	31,918	1,154	24,018	968
55 years and over....................	18,355	1,117	10,362	1,242	7,993	981
Black						
16 years and over....................	13,109	806	6,298	831	6,811	779
16 to 24 years.....................	959	579	474	606	485	552
25 years and over....................	12,149	840	5,824	871	6,325	810
25 to 54 years.....................	9,590	819	4,575	865	5,015	777
55 years and over....................	2,559	948	1,249	905	1,311	969
Asian						
16 years and over....................	6,827	1,336	3,771	1,479	3,056	1,141
16 to 24 years.....................	328	781	164	745	164	795
25 years and over....................	6,499	1,366	3,607	1,519	2,892	1,157
25 to 54 years.....................	5,319	1,427	2,926	1,564	2,393	1,221
55 years and over....................	1,180	1,035	681	1,105	499	985
Hispanic[1]						
16 years and over....................	18,077	786	10,884	843	7,193	717
16 to 24 years.....................	1,881	582	996	594	885	570
25 years and over....................	16,196	824	9,888	886	6,308	748
25 to 54 years.....................	13,443	834	8,226	894	5,217	750
55 years and over....................	2,753	771	1,662	819	1,091	741
OCCUPATION						
Management, professional, and related.........	48,871	1,356	23,825	1,606	25,046	1,168
Management, business, and financial.........	20,791	1,442	11,080	1,665	9,711	1,270
Professional and related....................	28,079	1,290	12,744	1,554	15,335	1,130
Service.............................	12,189	625	6,128	704	6,061	584
Sales and office.....................	19,857	819	7,752	962	12,105	755
Sales and related......................	8,167	918	4,489	1,069	3,678	709
Office and administrative support............	11,690	784	3,263	828	8,427	767
Natural resources, construction, and maintenance	9,862	906	9,382	917	480	676
Farming, fishing, and forestry................	860	601	655	621	205	530
Construction and extraction................	5,120	901	4,963	903	157	810
Installation, maintenance, and repair..........	3,882	1,002	3,763	1,004	119	766
Production, transportation, and material moving...	13,708	761	10,908	814	2,799	604
Production...........................	6,352	794	4,779	864	1,572	641
Transportation and material moving..........	7,356	731	6,129	774	1,227	563

Note: Not seasonally adjusted; figures are median usual weekly earnings of full-time wage and salary workers for second quarter 2020. Total includes races not shown here. (1) May be of any race.

Average Hours and Earnings of U.S. Production Workers, 1969-2019

Source: Bureau of Labor Statistics, U.S. Dept. of Labor

(annual averages)

Year	Weekly hours	Hourly earnings	Weekly earnings	Year	Weekly hours	Hourly earnings	Weekly earnings	Year	Weekly hours	Hourly earnings	Weekly earnings
1969....	37.5	$3.22	$120.80	1986....	34.7	$8.92	$309.69	2003....	33.7	$15.36	$517.68
1970....	37.0	3.41	125.91	1987....	34.7	9.14	317.33	2004....	33.7	15.68	528.65
1971....	36.7	3.63	133.35	1988....	34.6	9.44	326.50	2005....	33.8	16.12	543.94
1972....	36.9	3.91	143.99	1989....	34.5	9.81	338.42	2006....	33.9	16.74	566.94
1973....	36.9	4.14	152.71	1990....	34.5	10.20	349.63	2007....	33.8	17.41	589.09
1974....	36.4	4.44	161.76	1991....	34.1	10.51	358.46	2008....	33.6	18.06	607.10
1975....	36.0	4.74	170.45	1992....	34.2	10.77	368.17	2009....	33.1	18.60	615.82
1976....	36.0	5.06	182.36	1993....	34.3	11.05	378.74	2010....	33.4	19.04	636.02
1977....	35.9	5.44	195.34	1994....	34.5	11.34	391.17	2011....	33.6	19.43	652.72
1978....	35.8	5.88	210.17	1995....	34.3	11.65	399.93	2012....	33.7	19.73	665.54
1979....	35.6	6.34	225.46	1996....	34.3	12.04	413.17	2013....	33.7	20.13	677.62
1980....	35.2	6.84	240.83	1997....	34.5	12.51	431.75	2014....	33.7	20.60	694.74
1981....	35.2	7.43	261.29	1998....	34.5	13.01	448.36	2015....	33.7	21.03	708.70
1982....	34.7	7.86	272.98	1999....	34.3	13.48	463.09	2016....	33.6	21.53	723.20
1983....	34.9	8.20	286.34	2000....	34.3	14.01	480.90	2017....	33.7	22.05	742.48
1984....	35.1	8.49	298.08	2001....	33.9	14.54	493.53	2018....	33.8	22.71	766.99
1985....	34.9	8.73	304.37	2002....	33.9	14.96	506.48	2019....	33.6	23.51	790.67

Note: Data refer to production workers in mining, logging, and manufacturing; construction workers; and nonsupervisory workers in the service industries.

Elderly in U.S. Labor Force, 1890-2019

Source: U.S. Census Bureau, U.S. Dept. of Commerce

(percent of persons age 65 and older who participated in the labor force; 1910 figures not available)

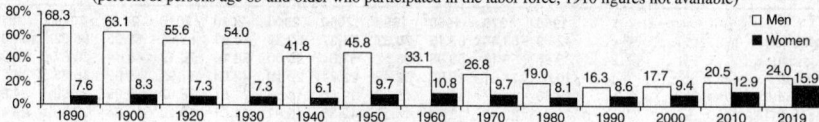

U.S. Union Membership, 1930-2019

Source: Bureau of Labor Statistics, U.S. Dept. of Labor

(numbers in thousands)

Year	Total employed[1]	% in union	Union members[2]	Year	Total employed[1]	% in union	Union members[2]	Year	Total employed[1]	% in union	Union members[2]
1930	29,424	11.6%	3,401	1975	76,945	25.5%	19,611	2011	125,187	11.8%	14,764
1935	27,053	13.2	3,584	1980	90,564	21.9	19,843	2012	127,577	11.3	14,366
1940	32,376	26.9	8,717	1985	94,521	18.0	16,996	2013	129,110	11.3	14,528
1945	40,394	35.5	14,322	1990	103,905	16.1	16,740	2014	131,431	11.1	14,576
1950	45,222	31.5	14,267	1995	110,038	14.9	16,360	2015	133,743	11.1	14,795
1955	50,675	33.2	16,802	2000	120,786	13.5	16,258	2016	136,101	10.7	14,555
1960	54,234	31.4	17,049	2005	125,889	12.5	15,685	2017	137,890	10.7	14,817
1965	60,815	28.4	17,299	2009	124,490	12.3	15,327	2018	140,099	10.5	14,744
1970	70,920	27.3	19,381	2010	124,073	11.9	14,715	2019	141,737	10.3	14,574

(1) Prior to 1985, total labor force figure, which includes unemployed persons. From 1985 on, does not include self-employed workers. (2) From 1930 to 1980, includes dues-paying members of traditional trade unions, regardless of employment status; after 1980, includes employed only. From 1985 on, includes members of employee associations similar to a union.

Median Weekly Earnings of U.S. Workers by Union Affiliation, 2000, 2019

Source: Bureau of Labor Statistics, U.S. Dept. of Labor

Sex and age	2000				2019			
	Total	Union members[1]	Represented by unions[2]	Non-union	Total	Union members[1]	Represented by unions[2]	Non-union
Total, 16 years and older	**$576**	**$696**	**$691**	**$542**	**$917**	**$1,095**	**$1,082**	**$892**
16 to 24 years	361	437	436	355	581	692	684	575
25 years and older	611	709	705	592	969	1,121	1,110	944
25 to 34 years	550	627	624	529	846	980	970	827
35 to 44 years	631	716	712	614	1,035	1,203	1,196	1,007
45 to 54 years	671	755	752	639	1,033	1,174	1,160	1,008
55 to 64 years	617	727	723	592	1,017	1,136	1,132	999
65 years and older	442	577	565	422	936	1,006	1,016	920
Men, 16 years and older	**646**	**739**	**737**	**620**	**1,007**	**1,147**	**1,139**	**986**
16 to 24 years	376	458	457	370	607	710	703	602
25 years and older	700	753	752	682	1,070	1,172	1,165	1,048
25 to 34 years	603	678	675	591	897	1,008	998	883
35 to 44 years	731	776	774	718	1,149	1,243	1,242	1,131
45 to 54 years	777	801	799	769	1,169	1,271	1,254	1,156
55 to 64 years	738	755	757	729	1,166	1,199	1,200	1,159
65 years and older	537	613	613	514	1,066	1,069	1,079	1,064
Women, 16 years and older	**491**	**616**	**613**	**472**	**821**	**1,018**	**1,004**	**792**
16 to 24 years	342	406	405	339	540	656	652	534
25 years and older	515	627	623	497	865	1,043	1,026	837
25 to 34 years	493	579	578	483	788	944	932	767
35 to 44 years	520	605	604	506	920	1,140	1,129	890
45 to 54 years	565	697	692	522	904	1,086	1,066	878
55 to 64 years	505	659	647	481	880	1,031	1,016	855
65 years and older	378	485	484	365	815	949	961	784

Note: Data refer to the sole or principal job of full-time wage and salary workers. Excludes self-employed workers regardless of whether or not their businesses are incorporated. (1) Includes members of an employee association similar to a union. (2) Includes members of a labor union as well as those whose jobs are covered by a union or an employee-association contract.

Work Stoppages (Strikes and Lockouts) in the U.S., 1950-2019

Source: Bureau of Labor Statistics, U.S. Dept. of Labor; involving 1,000 workers or more

Year	No.	Workers (thous.)	Days idle (thous.)	Year	No.	Workers (thous.)	Days idle (thous.)	Year	No.	Workers (thous.)	Days idle (thous.)
1950	424	1,698	30,390	1988	40	118	4,381	2004	17	171	3,344
1955	363	2,055	21,180	1989	51	452	16,996	2005	22	100	1,736
1960	222	896	13,260	1990	44	185	5,926	2006	20	70	2,688
1965	268	999	15,140	1991	40	392	4,584	2007	21	189	1,265
1970	381	2,468	52,761	1992	35	364	3,989	2008	15	72	1,954
1975	235	965	17,563	1993	35	182	3,981	2009	5	13	124
1978	219	1,006	23,774	1994	45	322	5,021	2010	11	45	302
1979	235	1,021	20,409	1995	31	192	5,771	2011	19	113	1,020
1980	187	795	20,844	1996	37	273	4,889	2012	19	148	1,131
1981	145	729	16,908	1997	29	339	4,497	2013	15	55	290
1982	96	656	9,061	1998	34	387	5,116	2014	11	34	200
1983	81	909	17,461	1999	17	73	1,996	2015	12	47	740
1984	62	376	8,499	2000	39	394	20,419	2016	15	99	1,543
1985	54	324	7,079	2001	29	99	1,151	2017	7	25	440
1986	69	533	11,861	2002	19	46	660	2018	20	485	2,815
1987	46	174	4,481	2003	14	129	4,091	2019	25	426	3,244

Note: Numbers cover stoppages that began in the year indicated. Workers are counted more than once if they are involved in more than one stoppage during the year. For work stoppages ongoing at the end of a calendar year, days idle include only the days for the calendar year.

ENERGY

U.S. Energy Overview, 1960-2019

Source: *Monthly Energy Review*, July 2020, Energy Information Administration (EIA), U.S. Dept. of Energy; in quadrillion Btu

	1960	1970	1980	1990	2000	2005	2010	2015	2017	2018	2019
Production	42.79	63.46	67.15	70.67	71.27	69.38	74.91	88.25	88.05	95.62	101.05
Fossil fuels	39.86	59.15	58.98	58.52	57.31	55.00	58.16	70.19	68.44	75.67	80.95
Coal[1]	10.82	14.61	18.60	22.49	22.74	23.19	22.04	17.95	15.63	15.36	14.27
Natural gas (dry)	12.66	21.67	19.91	18.33	19.66	18.56	21.81	28.07	28.29	31.69	34.90E
Crude oil[2]	14.94	20.40	18.25	15.57	12.36	10.97	11.61	19.70	19.54	22.89	25.44E
Natural gas plant liquids (NGPL)	1.45	2.48	2.23	2.14	2.55	2.28	2.71	4.48	4.99	5.73	6.34
Nuclear electric power	0.01	0.24	2.74	6.10	7.86	8.16	8.43	8.34	8.42	8.44	8.46
Renewable energy	2.93	4.07	5.43	6.04	6.10	6.22	8.31	9.73	11.20	11.51	11.64
Conventional hydroelectric power[3]	1.61	2.63	2.90	3.05	2.81	2.70	2.54	2.32	2.77	2.66	2.49
Biomass[4]	1.32	1.43	2.48	2.74	3.01	3.10	4.55	4.99	5.10	5.24	5.16
Geothermal energy	—	0.01	0.05	0.17	0.16	0.18	0.21	0.21	0.21	0.21	0.21
Solar	NA	NA	NA	0.06	0.06	0.06	0.09	0.43	0.78	0.92	1.04
Wind	NA	NA	NA	0.03	0.06	0.18	0.92	1.78	2.34	2.48	2.73
Imports	4.19	8.34	15.80	18.82	28.87	34.66	29.87	23.79	25.46	24.83	22.80
Coal	0.01	—	0.03	0.07	0.31	0.76	0.48	0.26	0.17	0.12	0.14
Natural gas	0.16	0.85	1.01	1.55	3.87	4.45	3.83	2.79	3.11	2.96	2.81
Petroleum[5]	4.00	7.47	14.66	17.12	24.42	29.20	25.36	20.41	21.87	21.50	19.58
Crude oil[2]	2.20	2.81	11.20	12.77	19.78	22.09	20.14	16.30	17.60	17.19	15.07
Petroleum products[6]	1.80	4.66	3.46	4.35	4.64	7.11	5.22	4.11	4.28	4.31	4.51
Biomass[7]	NA	NA	NA	NA	(s)	0.01	—	0.08	0.08	0.05	0.07
Electricity	0.02	0.02	0.09	0.06	0.17	0.15	0.15	0.26	0.22	0.20	0.20
Exports	1.48	2.63	3.70	4.75	3.96	4.46	8.18	12.90	17.95	21.21	23.52
Coal	1.02	1.94	2.42	2.77	1.53	1.27	2.10	1.85	2.39	2.81	2.31
Natural gas	0.01	0.07	0.05	0.09	0.25	0.74	1.15	1.80	3.18	3.64	4.70
Petroleum[5]	0.43	0.55	1.16	1.82	2.11	2.34	4.78	9.12	12.11	14.43	16.18
Crude oil[2]	0.02	0.03	0.61	0.23	0.11	0.07	0.09	0.96	2.42	4.28	6.20
Petroleum products[6]	0.41	0.52	0.55	1.59	2.00	2.28	4.69	8.15	9.68	10.16	9.98
Biomass[8]	NA	NA	NA	NA	NA	—	0.05	0.08	0.21	0.25	0.24
Electricity	—	0.01	0.01	0.06	0.05	0.07	0.07	0.03	0.03	0.05	0.07
Consumption	45.04	67.82	78.02	84.43	98.70	100.10	97.52	97.38	97.60	101.09	100.17
Fossil fuels	42.09	63.50	69.78	72.28	84.62	85.62	80.73	79.09	77.92	81.20	80.11
Coal	9.84	12.27	15.42	19.17	22.58	22.80	20.83	15.55	13.84	13.25	11.32
Natural gas[9]	12.39	21.80	20.24	19.60	23.82	22.57	24.58	28.19	28.06	31.09	32.10
Petroleum[10]	19.87	29.50	34.16	33.50	38.15	40.22	35.32	35.37	36.05	36.88	36.72
Nuclear electric power	0.01	0.24	2.74	6.10	7.86	8.16	8.43	8.34	8.42	8.44	8.46
Renewable energy	2.93	4.07	5.43	6.04	6.10	6.23	8.27	9.72	11.08	11.30	11.46
Conventional hydroelectric power[3]	1.61	2.63	2.90	3.05	2.81	2.70	2.54	2.32	2.77	2.66	2.49
Biomass[4]	1.32	1.43	2.48	2.74	3.01	3.11	4.51	4.98	4.98	5.03	4.99
Geothermal energy	—	0.01	0.05	0.17	0.16	0.18	0.21	0.21	0.21	0.21	0.21
Solar	NA	NA	NA	0.06	0.06	0.06	0.09	0.43	0.78	0.92	1.04
Wind	NA	NA	NA	0.03	0.06	0.18	0.92	1.78	2.34	2.48	2.73

NA = Not available. — = Less than 0.005 quadrillion Btu. (s) = Less than 0.5 trillion Btu. E = Estimate. **Note:** Numbers may not add up to totals because of rounding. (1) Incl. waste coal supplied beginning in 1989 and refuse recovery beginning in 2001. (2) Incl. lease condensate. (3) Starting in 1990, pumped storage was removed and expanded coverage of industrial use of hydroelectric power was included. (4) Category known as "wood, waste, and alcohol" for years prior to 2000. Includes wood, waste, and alcohol fuels (ethanol blended into motor gasoline. Ethanol is included in both Petroleum and Biomass categories but is only counted once in totals. (5) Imports incl. crude oil for the Strategic Petroleum Reserve, which began in 1977. Imports/exports excl. biofuels. (6) Incl. unfinished oils, natural gasoline, and gasoline blending components; excl. biofuels. (7) Fuel ethanol (minus denaturant) and biodiesel. (8) Beginning in 2001, incl. biodiesel; beginning in 2010, also incl. ethanol (minus denaturant); beginning in 2016, also incl. wood and wood-derived fuels. (9) Excl. supplemental gaseous fuels. (10) Petroleum products supplied; excl. biofuels that have been blended with petroleum.

U.S. Energy Consumption by Source, 1949-2019

Source: *Monthly Energy Review*, July 2020, Energy Information Administration (EIA), U.S. Dept. of Energy

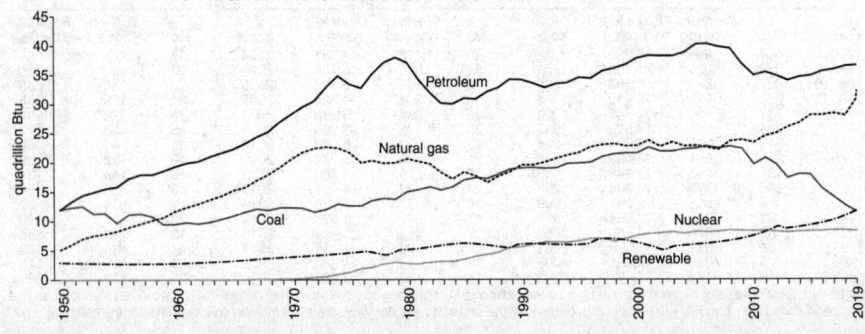

World's Largest Energy Producers and Consumers, 1980-2017

Source: Energy Information Administration (EIA), U.S. Dept. of Energy

(primary energy in quadrillion Btu; ranked by 2017 data as of July 30, 2020)

Production	1980	1990	2000	2010	2012	2013	2014	2015	2016	2017
1. China	19.54	31.88	41.26	97.03	110.99	113.40	114.79	114.30	107.12	112.02
2. United States	67.15	70.67	71.27	74.91	79.23	81.84	87.71	88.25	84.27	88.15
3. Russia..........	NA	NA	42.65	54.32	56.04	57.32	57.07	57.88	59.19	61.57
4. Saudi Arabia.....	22.43	15.92	21.59	25.43	27.87	27.52	27.52	28.55	29.41	28.81
5. Canada.........	10.15	13.15	17.78	18.30	19.12	19.93	20.81	20.92	21.18	21.89
6. Iran	3.94	7.65	10.40	14.61	13.63	13.05	13.90	14.48	17.01	18.21
7. India	2.83	6.16	8.66	13.86	15.27	15.16	15.73	16.15	17.12	17.68
8. Australia	3.41	6.49	9.50	12.68	13.23	14.12	15.12	15.25	15.94	16.55
9. Indonesia	4.22	5.27	7.40	11.39	13.14	14.86	14.43	14.35	14.39	14.24
10. Brazil.........	1.98	4.03	6.62	10.14	10.37	10.31	10.81	11.16	11.63	11.22
11. Qatar..........	1.20	1.14	2.83	8.04	9.85	10.18	10.01	10.09	10.14	10.13
12. United Arab Emirates	3.89	5.51	6.77	7.71	9.00	9.04	9.23	9.73	9.98	9.89
13. Norway	2.93	5.80	10.30	9.46	9.48	8.98	9.13	9.53	9.64	9.82
14. Iraq...........	5.45	4.54	5.62	5.21	6.44	6.60	7.24	8.67	9.56	9.55
15. Kazakhstan......	NA	NA	3.94	7.12	7.44	7.53	7.54	7.54	7.36	8.05
16. Algeria	2.80	4.75	6.19	6.93	7.00	6.51	6.56	6.70	6.91	6.78
17. Kuwait.........	3.99	2.79	5.03	5.63	6.52	6.56	6.50	6.79	7.07	6.70
18. Mexico	5.71	7.64	9.38	8.85	8.70	8.61	8.38	7.69	7.34	6.67
19. Venezuela.......	5.77	6.31	9.36	7.26	7.58	7.54	7.35	7.44	6.87	6.24
20. Nigeria	4.49	4.07	5.18	6.38	7.00	6.50	6.79	6.45	5.70	5.95
21. South Africa	2.55	3.96	5.23	5.84	5.92	5.89	6.03	5.81	5.90	5.93
22. United Kingdom ..	8.71	9.00	11.16	6.35	4.97	4.68	4.70	5.17	5.21	5.27
23. Colombia	0.66	1.92	3.01	4.42	5.23	5.31	5.35	5.32	5.18	5.13
24. France.........	2.35	4.27	5.04	5.20	5.22	5.31	5.40	5.38	5.09	4.87
25. Germany........	NA	NA	4.91	4.98	4.97	4.96	4.95	5.00	4.80	4.77

Consumption	1980	1990	2000	2010	2012	2013	2014	2015	2016	2017
1. China	19.83	31.05	42.94	109.36	129.41	135.04	136.90	137.28	137.42	139.44
2. United States	78.02	84.43	98.70	97.52	94.38	97.12	98.28	97.38	97.33	97.60
3. Russia..........	NA	NA	26.73	30.73	31.83	31.40	31.67	31.41	31.16	32.83
4. India	3.75	7.46	12.57	21.70	25.11	25.71	27.31	28.38	29.48	30.48
5. Japan	15.66	18.96	22.21	21.62	20.41	20.56	20.14	19.73	19.68	19.62
6. Canada.........	9.54	10.77	12.78	13.81	14.30	14.72	14.83	14.78	14.66	15.14
7. Germany........	NA	NA	13.82	14.04	13.61	13.99	13.56	13.72	13.84	14.01
8. Brazil..........	3.97	6.17	8.71	11.72	12.45	12.82	13.14	12.95	12.53	12.59
9. South Korea	1.88	4.07	8.11	10.86	11.51	11.49	11.61	11.93	12.29	12.36
10. Iran	1.60	3.01	5.14	9.22	9.78	10.02	10.64	10.78	11.17	11.60
11. Saudi Arabia.....	1.65	3.34	5.10	8.81	9.79	9.79	10.36	10.65	10.46	11.00
12. France.........	8.64	9.23	10.92	11.00	10.73	10.84	10.40	10.44	10.31	10.32
13. United Kingdom ..	9.00	9.29	9.90	9.19	8.75	8.73	8.27	8.35	8.29	8.29
14. Mexico	3.80	4.72	6.49	7.52	7.70	7.76	7.65	7.77	7.94	7.91
15. Indonesia	1.16	2.31	4.18	6.24	6.33	6.49	6.62	7.01	7.08	7.16
16. Italy	6.19	6.73	7.58	7.68	7.24	6.92	6.70	6.77	6.72	6.79
17. Turkey.........	1.00	1.94	3.19	4.51	5.06	5.09	5.21	5.75	5.97	6.43
18. Australia	2.79	3.75	4.68	5.52	5.68	5.69	5.64	5.75	5.92	6.07
19. Spain	3.18	4.01	5.52	6.20	5.80	5.67	5.60	5.60	5.74	5.73
20. South Africa	2.64	3.84	4.64	5.66	5.65	5.69	5.64	5.63	5.63	5.68
21. Thailand	0.50	1.25	2.56	4.42	4.80	5.10	5.08	5.15	5.31	5.46
22. Taiwan	1.09	2.02	3.59	4.64	4.54	4.57	4.69	4.69	4.79	4.67
23. United Arab Emirates	0.28	1.23	2.09	3.63	3.99	4.16	4.24	4.65	4.72	4.67
24. Poland.........	4.16	3.71	3.35	3.96	3.98	3.93	3.90	4.00	4.13	4.37
25. Egypt	0.71	1.42	2.01	3.50	3.78	3.74	3.73	3.73	3.77	4.01

NA = Not applicable or not available.

Average U.S. Gasoline Prices, 1976-2020

Source: *Monthly Energy Review*, July 2020; *Short-Term Energy Outlook*, July 2020; Energy Information Administration (EIA), U.S. Dept. of Energy

(in dollars per gallon, including taxes; constant dollars is price in July 2020 dollars)

	Current dollars		Constant dollars, unleaded		Current dollars		Constant dollars, unleaded
Year	Unleaded regular	Diesel	regular[1]	Year	Unleaded regular	Diesel	regular[1]
1976	$0.61	NA	$2.77	2006	$2.59	$2.71	$3.29
1980	1.25	NA	3.89	2007	2.80	2.89	3.48
1985	1.20	NA	2.79	2008	3.27	3.80	3.89
1990	1.16	NA	2.22	2009	2.35	2.47	2.82
1995	1.15	$1.11	1.87	2010	2.79	2.99	3.28
1996	1.23	1.24	1.97	2011	3.53	3.84	4.03
1997	1.23	1.20	1.92	2012	3.64	3.97	4.06
1998	1.06	1.04	1.62	2013	3.53	3.92	3.87
1999	1.17	1.12	1.76	2014	3.37	3.83	3.65
2000	1.51	1.49	2.22	2015	2.45	2.71	2.63
2001	1.46	1.40	2.07	2016	2.14	2.30	2.30
2002	1.36	1.32	1.92	2017	2.41	2.65	2.53
2003	1.59	1.51	2.18	2018	2.74	3.18	2.79
2004	1.88	1.81	2.52	2019	2.64	3.06	2.62
2005	2.30	2.40	2.99	2020	2.08[2]	2.41[2]	2.11[3]

NA = Not applicable. (1) Base prices vary slightly from unleaded regular column at left. (2) June 2020 figure. (3) Forecast.

Energy Consumption by State, 2018

Source: State Energy Data System, Energy Information Administration (EIA), U.S. Dept. of Energy

Total Consumption					Consumption per Capita				
Rank, state	**Btu (tril)**	**Rank, state**	**Btu (tril)**		**Rank, state**	**Btu (mil)**	**Rank, state**	**Btu (mil)**	
1. Texas	14,258.8	27. Massachusetts	1,458.6		1. Wyoming	967.1	27. Missouri	301.8	
2. California	7,966.6	28. Maryland	1,361.2		2. Louisiana	944.9	28. Delaware	300.7	
3. Louisiana	4,403.2	29. Mississippi	1,192.7		3. North Dakota	871.9	29. Maine	295.2	
4. Florida	4,281.3	30. Kansas	1,134.5		4. Alaska	829.5	30. Michigan	289.9	
5. Illinois	4,012.0	31. Arkansas	1,119.7		5. Iowa	513.3	31. Virginia	282.5	
6. Pennsylvania	3,961.6	32. Oregon	1,012.2		6. Texas	498.1	32. Washington	276.3	
7. New York	3,854.2	33. Nebraska	914.6		7. Nebraska	474.9	33. Georgia	273.6	
8. Ohio	3,755.9	34. Utah	835.1		8. West Virginia	461.6	34. Colorado	265.9	
9. Michigan	2,894.2	35. West Virginia	832.9		9. South Dakota	451.6	35. Utah	264.8	
10. Georgia	2,876.1	36. Connecticut	753.0		10. Oklahoma	433.1	36. New Jersey	252.2	
11. Indiana	2,837.6	37. Nevada	727.2		11. Indiana	423.8	37. North Carolina	252.0	
12. North Carolina	2,616.1	38. New Mexico	702.8		12. Montana	410.3	38. District of Columbia	248.8	
13. Virginia	2,401.2	39. North Dakota	661.0		13. Mississippi	400.1	39. Oregon	242.1	
14. Tennessee	2,255.9	40. Alaska	609.8		14. Alabama	399.9	40. Nevada	240.2	
15. New Jersey	2,240.7	41. Wyoming	558.6		15. Kentucky	390.9	41. New Hampshire	239.9	
16. Washington	2,078.7	42. Idaho	553.3		16. Kansas	389.7	42. Maryland	225.5	
17. Alabama	1,954.8	43. Montana	435.2		17. Arkansas	372.0	43. Vermont	222.9	
18. Minnesota	1,913.9	44. South Dakota	396.8		18. Minnesota	341.4	44. Massachusetts	211.9	
19. Wisconsin	1,885.9	45. Maine	395.3		19. New Mexico	335.8	45. Connecticut	210.8	
20. Missouri	1,847.8	46. New Hampshire	324.7		20. Tennessee	333.1	46. Arizona	207.9	
21. Kentucky	1,743.9	47. Hawaii	292.9		21. South Carolina	328.8	47. Hawaii	206.2	
22. Oklahoma	1,706.5	48. Delaware	290.3		22. Wisconsin	324.7	48. California	201.9	
23. South Carolina	1,671.8	49. Rhode Island	197.4		23. Ohio	321.7	49. Florida	201.5	
24. Iowa	1,616.1	50. Dist. of Columbia	174.5		24. Idaho	316.1	50. New York	197.3	
25. Colorado	1,513.3	51. Vermont	139.2		25. Illinois	315.3	51. Rhode Island	186.5	
26. Arizona	1,487.8	**United States**	**101,083.6**		26. Pennsylvania	309.5	**United States**	**309.4**	

(1) Includes −25.6 trillion Btu of net imports of coal coke that are not allocated to the states.

U.S. Production of Crude Oil by State, 1990-2019

Source: *Petroleum Supply Annual 2019*, Energy Information Administration (EIA), U.S. Dept. of Energy

Oil production in North Dakota more than quadrupled between 2010 and 2019 through the use of hydraulic fracturing, or fracking, a process by which water, sand, and chemicals are injected at high pressure to create fractures in shale rock, releasing the oil or natural gas within. Fracking accounted for just 2% of U.S. oil production in 2000 but grew to 63% by 2019.

(in thousands of barrels; ranked by 2019 production)

Rank, state	1990	2000	2010	2019	Rank, state	1990	2000	2010	2019
1. Texas	678,478	443,397	426,755	1,850,105	18. Michigan	19,676	7,907	6,980	5,125
2. North Dakota	36,717	32,719	112,535	512,287	19. Alabama	18,538	10,457	7,155	4,816
3. New Mexico	67,250	67,198	65,569	339,821	20. Arkansas	10,386	7,154	5,733	4,657
4. Oklahoma	112,273	69,976	70,196	211,856	21. Kentucky	5,409	3,465	2,519	2,505
5. Colorado	30,453	18,481	33,053	187,550	22. Nebraska	5,889	2,957	2,331	1,951
6. Alaska	647,309	355,199	218,904	169,947	23. Florida	5,675	4,626	1,777	1,784
7. California	320,868	271,132	200,370	161,496	24. Indiana	3,000	2,098	1,835	1,579
8. Wyoming	103,856	60,726	53,890	101,653	25. South Dakota	1,648	1,170	1,607	1,162
9. Louisiana	147,582	105,425	67,590	43,875	26. Nevada	4,011	621	426	261
10. Utah	27,604	15,636	24,663	37,440	27. New York	415	210	381	221
11. Kansas	55,428	34,463	40,468	33,056	28. Tennessee	506	346	257	201
12. Ohio	10,008	6,575	4,772	28,048	29. Missouri	146	94	146	82
13. Montana	19,810	15,428	25,332	22,993	30. Idaho	NA	NA	0	22
14. Mississippi	27,034	19,844	23,981	17,100	31. Arizona	121	59	37	7
15. West Virginia	2,143	1,400	1,842	16,506	32. Virginia	16	9	12	4
16. Illinois	19,954	12,206	9,067	8,243	Federal offshore	299,835	558,242	588,335	691,851
17. Pennsylvania	2,641	1,500	3,238	6,324	U.S. total	2,684,687	2,130,707	2,001,756	4,464,530

Note: One barrel is equal to 42 U.S. gallons.

Dry Shale Gas Production in the U.S., 2000-20

Source: Energy Information Administration (EIA), U.S. Dept. of Energy

(production in billions of cubic ft per day; ranked by 2020 production)

Site name (primary location)	2000	2005	2010	2014	2015	2016	2017	2018	2019	2020
Marcellus (PA, WV, OH, NY)	0.00	0.00	0.45	11.80	15.01	16.17	16.51	18.42	21.48	23.67
Permian (TX, NM)	0.56	0.58	0.88	2.28	2.79	3.40	4.29	5.69	8.62	11.32
Haynesville (LA, TX)	0.14	0.10	2.42	4.14	3.86	3.74	3.79	5.59	8.02	9.49
Utica (OH, PA, WV)	0.00	0.00	0.00	0.68	2.02	3.65	4.24	6.02	6.95	7.48
Eagle Ford (TX)	0.00	0.00	0.12	3.64	4.75	4.59	3.88	4.07	4.21	4.53
Woodford (OK)	0.01	0.02	0.98	1.59	1.98	2.43	2.47	2.75	3.12	2.98
Niobrara-Codell (CO, WY)	0.26	0.36	0.54	0.83	1.24	1.59	1.64	1.86	2.31	2.87
Mississippian (OK)	0.71	0.78	0.65	0.97	1.29	1.33	1.44	2.24	2.78	2.77
Barnett (TX)	0.13	0.97	4.13	4.36	3.93	3.32	2.92	2.57	2.45	2.24
Bakken (ND, MT)	0.01	0.02	0.11	0.61	0.93	1.11	1.06	1.37	1.80	2.01
Fayetteville (AR)	0.00	0.00	1.81	2.77	2.64	2.24	1.76	1.41	1.32	1.20
Other U.S. shale locations	1.81	1.40	1.62	1.97	2.03	2.07	1.86	2.25	2.50	2.45
Total	**3.63**	**4.23**	**13.72**	**35.63**	**42.46**	**45.65**	**45.86**	**54.25**	**65.56**	**72.99**

— = Less than 100 million cubic feet per day. **Note:** Figures are monthly averages of production per day estimates as of Jan. 1 of year shown. Numbers may not add up to totals because of rounding.

U.S. Petroleum Trade, 1950-2019

Source: *Monthly Energy Review*, July 2020, Energy Information Administration (EIA), U.S. Dept. of Energy
(in thousands of barrels per day; average for the year)

Year	Imports from Persian Gulf[1]	Total imports	Total exports	Net imports[2]	Petroleum products supplied[3]	Year	Imports from Persian Gulf[1]	Total imports	Total exports	Net imports[2]	Petroleum products supplied[3]
1950.....	NA	850	305	545	6,458	2005.....	2,334	13,714	1,165	12,549	20,802
1955.....	NA	1,248	368	880	8,455	2010.....	1,711	11,793	2,353	9,441	19,180
1960.....	326	1,815	202	1,613	9,797	2011.....	1,861	11,436	2,986	8,450	18,887
1965.....	359	2,468	187	2,281	11,512	2012.....	2,156	10,598	3,205	7,393	18,487
1970.....	184	3,419	259	3,161	14,697	2013.....	2,009	9,859	3,621	6,237	18,967
1975.....	1,165	6,056	209	5,846	16,322	2014.....	1,875	9,241	4,176	5,065	19,100
1980.....	1,519	6,909	544	6,365	17,056	2015.....	1,507	9,449	4,738	4,711	19,534
1985.....	311	5,067	781	4,286	15,726	2016.....	1,766	10,055	5,261	4,795	19,687
1990.....	1,966	8,018	857	7,161	16,988	2017.....	1,746	10,144	6,376	3,768	19,958
1995.....	1,573	8,835	949	7,886	17,725	2018.....	1,578	9,943	7,601	2,341	20,504
2000.....	2,488	11,459	1,040	10,419	19,701	2019.....	962	9,093	8,499	594	20,464

NA = Not available. **Note:** U.S. exports include shipments to U.S. territories; imports include receipts from U.S. territories. Numbers may not add up to totals because of rounding. (1) Bahrain, Iran, Iraq, Kuwait, Qatar, Saudi Arabia, United Arab Emirates, and the Neutral Zone between Kuwait and Saudi Arabia. (2) Total imports minus total exports. (3) Includes domestic production and imports minus change in stocks, refinery imports, and exports.

World Fossil Fuel Reserves

Source: International Energy Statistics Database, Energy Information Administration (EIA), U.S. Dept. of Energy

	Crude oil (bil barrels), 2020	Natural gas (tril cu ft), 2020	Coal (mil short tons), 2017		Crude oil (bil barrels), 2020	Natural gas (tril cu ft), 2020	Coal (mil short tons), 2017
North America...	220.9[1]	555.3[1]	262,247	**Middle East**	803.2	2,839.1	1,326
Canada	167.9	71.3	7,255	Bahrain	0.1	6.8	0
Greenland	0.0	0.0	202	Iran	155.6	1,197.1	1,326
Mexico.........	5.8	6.4	1,335	Iraq	145.0	131.7	0
United States...	47.1[1]	474.8[1]	253,455	Israel	0.0	6.2	0
Central & South				Kuwait	101.5	63.0	0
America	330.6	270.7	15,450	Oman..........	5.4	31.2	0
Argentina......	2.4	13.1	551	Qatar..........	25.2	842.1	0
Bolivia	0.2	10.7	1	Saudi Arabia ...	267.0	320.3	0
Brazil.........	13.2	13.0	7,271	Syria	2.5	8.5	0
Chile	0.2	3.5	1,302	UAE..........	97.8	215.1	0
Colombia......	2.0	3.8	5,380	Yemen.........	3.0	16.9	0
Cuba	0.1	2.5	0	**Africa**	125.8	624.1	38,470
Ecuador.......	8.3	0.4	26	Algeria........	12.2	159.1	65
Peru..........	1.0	12.9	112	Angola........	8.2	13.5	0
Trinidad &				Congo, Dem.			
Tobago.......	0.2	10.5	0	Rep. of	3.0	0.0	97
Venezuela	302.8	200.4	806	Congo Rep.....	0.2	10.1	0
Europe	13.8	86.2	109,422	Egypt.........	3.3	63.0	18
Albania	0.2	0.2	575	Eswatini			
Bosnia & Herz.	0.0	0.0	2,496	(Swaziland) ...	0.0	0.0	159
Bulgaria	0.0	0.2	2,608	Libya	48.4	53.1	0
Czechia	0.0	0.1	4,007	Mozambique ...	0.0	100.0	1,975
Germany	0.1	1.0	37,533	Namibia	0.0	2.2	0
Greece........	0.0	0.0	3,170	Nigeria........	37.0	200.4	379
Hungary.......	0.0	0.2	3,207	South Africa....	0.0	NA	34,723
Kosovo	0.0	0.0	1,724	Sudan	5.0	3.0	0
Montenegro	0.0	0.0	157	Tanzania	0.0	0.2	297
Netherlands....	0.1	6.9	548	Zambia	0.0	0.0	50
North Macedonia	0.0	0.0	366	Zimbabwe	0.0	0.0	553
Norway	8.2	57.3	1	**Asia & Oceania ..**	46.3[1]	614.0	471,033
Poland........	0.1	3.2	29,904	Afghanistan....	0.0	1.8	73
Romania	0.6	3.7	321	Australia	2.4	113.5	159,634
Serbia	0.1	1.7	8,283	Bangladesh....	0.0	4.5	323
Slovakia.......	0.0	0.5	149	Brunei	1.1	9.2	0
Slovenia.......	0.0	0.0	409	China.........	26.2	223.0	153,022
Spain.........	0.2	0.1	1,308	India..........	4.4	47.3	111,191
Turkey	0.4	0.1	12,515	Indonesia......	3.2	96.1	24,937
United Kingdom.	2.7	6.4	77	Japan.........	0.0	0.7	340
Eurasia.	118.9	2,273.0	246,288	Korea, North ...	0.0	0.0	661
Armenia.......	0.0	0.0	180	Korea, South ...	NA	0.3	359
Azerbaijan	7.0	45.0	0	Laos..........	0.0	0.0	554
Belarus	0.2	0.1	0	Malaysia	3.6	41.8	198
Georgia.......	0.0	0.3	222	Mongolia	NA	0.0	2,778
Kazakhstan	30.0	85.0	28,225	Myanmar......	0.1	22.5	7
Kyrgyzstan.....	0.0	0.2	1,070	New Zealand ...	0.0	1.0	8,350
Russia........	80.0	1,688.2	176,771	Pakistan........	0.3	11.3	3,377
Tajikistan	0.0	0.2	413	Philippines.....	0.1	3.5	348
Turkmenistan ...	0.6	350.0	0	Thailand.......	0.3	6.1	1,172
Ukraine	0.4	39.0	37,892	Vietnam.......	4.4	24.7	3,704
Uzbekistan.....	0.6	65.0	1,516	**World**	1,659.2[1]	7,176.9[1]	1,144,237

NA = Not available. **Note:** Regional and world totals may include countries not shown. Proved reserves only. Some countries omitted for lack of appreciable reserves. (1) As of 2019, the latest year available.

U.S. Crude Oil Imports by Selected Countries, 1975-2019

Source: Energy Information Administration (EIA), U.S. Dept. of Energy

The United States' dependence on foreign oil continues to decline as a consequence of increased U.S. production of crude oil, natural gas, and domestic biofuels like ethanol and biodiesel. Imports stood at just 6.8 mil barrels a day in 2019, down from more than 10.1 mil barrels per day in 2005. Since 2004, Canada has been the largest supplier of U.S. oil. In 2019, it was responsible for about 56% of all U.S. oil imports, more than twice as much as those from all OPEC countries combined. Since 1995, sanctions have prohibited the U.S. from importing oil from Iran.

(in thousands of barrels per day; ranked by 2019 imports)

Country	1975	1980	1985	1990	1995	2000	2005	2010	2015	2018	2019
Canada	600	199	468	643	1,040	1,348	1,633	1,970	3,169	3,707	3,810
Mexico	70	507	715	689	1,027	1,313	1,556	1,152	688	665	600
*Saudi Arabia	701	1,250	132	1,195	1,260	1,523	1,445	1,082	1,052	870	500
*Iraq	2	28	46	514	0	620	527	415	229	518	331
Colombia	0	0	0	140	207	318	156	338	373	295	318
*Ecuador[1]	0	0	0	0	96	125	276	210	225	176	199
*Nigeria	746	841	280	784	621	875	1,077	983	54	175	186
Russia[2]	0	0	0	1	14	7	199	269	38	73	132
Brazil	0	1	0	0	0	5	94	255	190	126	121
*Venezuela	395	156	306	666	1,151	1,223	1,241	912	776	506	81
United Kingdom	0	173	278	155	341	291	224	120	11	57	64
*Libya	223	548	0	0	0	0	0	44	43	3	60
Norway	12	144	31	96	258	302	119	25	9	53	47
Trinidad and Tobago	115	115	98	76	62	56	64	45	7	7	46
*Kuwait	4	27	4	79	213	263	227	195	204	78	45
*Angola[3]	71	37	104	236	360	295	456	383	124	90	33
Kazakhstan	NA	NA	NA	NA	NA	NA	12	18	NA	22	33
Brunei	NA	NA	NA	NA	NA	21	14	NA	NA	15	32
Argentina	NA	NA	NA	NA	44	53	56	29	18	23	30
Ghana	NA	NA	NA	NA	NA	NA	NA	NA	NA	11	24
*Algeria	264	456	84	63	27	1	228	328	3	79	19
*Congo Republic[4]	NA	NA	NA	NA	NA	20	42	25	70	9	15
Denmark	NA	NA	NA	NA	NA	7	NA	NA	NA	7	13
Egypt	NA	NA	NA	NA	32	4	4	7	1	22	13
*Equatorial Guinea[5]	NA	NA	NA	NA	NA	6	68	50	5	19	9
Cameroon	NA	NA	NA	NA	2	4	3	50	NA	3	9
Guatemala	NA	NA	NA	NA	8	18	11	11	8	7	7
Chad	NA	NA	NA	NA	NA	NA	74	18	72	20	5
*United Arab Emirates	117	172	35	9	5	3	9	2	2	5	3
South Sudan	NA	NA	NA	NA	NA	NA	NA	NA	NA	1	3
Belize	NA	NA	NA	NA	NA	NA	NA	2	1	1	1
Netherlands	4	0	0	0	0	1	NA	NA	NA	NA	1
Peru	NA	NA	NA	NA	21	4	4	14	6	1	1
Spain	NA	NA	NA	NA	1	NA	NA	NA	NA	NA	1
Non-OPEC countries	NA	NA	NA	NA	3,660	4,526	5,310	4,661	4,690	5,186	5,314
OPEC countries	3,211	3,864	1,312	3,514	3,570	4,544	4,816	4,553	2,673	2,583	1,481
Persian Gulf countries[6]	1,121	1,508	244	1,801	1,479	2,409	2,207	1,694	1,487	1,472	879
TOTAL	4,105	5,263	3,201	5,894	7,230	9,071	10,126	9,213	7,363	7,768	6,795

* = OPEC member, as of 2019. NA = Not available. **Note:** Subtotals and totals include countries not shown here. For years of OPEC membership, see footnotes on individual countries. (1) Ecuador suspended its OPEC membership Dec. 1992, rejoined in Oct. 2007, and again withdrew in Jan. 2020. Imports from Ecuador in 1993-2007 appear in non-OPEC totals, and imports from Ecuador in 2008-19 appear in OPEC totals. (2) May include oil from USSR states before 1992. (3) Angola became a member of OPEC as of 2007 and is not included in OPEC totals from before that year. (4) Congo Republic joined OPEC in June 2018 and is not included in OPEC totals before that year. (5) Equatorial Guinea joined OPEC in May 2017 and is not included in OPEC totals from before that year. (6) Bahrain, Iran, Iraq, Kuwait, Qatar, Saudi Arabia, and United Arab Emirates.

U.S. Coal Production and Consumption, 1950-2019

Source: *Monthly Energy Review*, July 2020; *Annual Coal Report 2018*; Energy Information Administration (EIA); U.S. Dept. of Energy

(in thousand short tons)

Year	Coal production[1]			Coal consumption				
	Surface mining	Underground mining	Total production	Residential[2]	Commercial	Industrial	Electric power[3]	Total consumption
1950	139,388	421,000	560,388	51,562	63,021	224,637	91,871	494,102
1960	141,745	292,584	434,329	24,159	16,789	177,402	176,685	398,081
1970	272,131	340,530	612,661	9,024	7,090	186,637	320,182	523,231
1975	361,174	293,467	654,641	2,823	6,587	147,244	405,962	562,640
1980	492,192	337,508	829,700	1,355	5,097	127,004	569,274	702,730
1985	532,838	350,800	883,638	1,711	6,068	116,429	693,841	818,049
1990	604,529	424,546	1,029,076	1,345	5,379	115,207	782,567	904,498
1995	636,725	396,249	1,032,974	755	5,052	106,067	850,230	962,104
2000	699,953	373,659	1,073,612	454	3,673	94,147	985,821	1,084,095
2005	762,887	368,612	1,131,498	378	4,342	83,774	1,037,485	1,125,978
2010	747,214	337,155	1,084,368	NA	3,081	70,381	975,052	1,048,514
2015	590,119	306,821	896,941	NA	1,503	58,167	738,444	798,115
2016	476,258	252,106	728,364	NA	1,183	51,333	678,554	731,071
2017	501,480	273,129	774,609	NA	1,061	50,801	664,993	716,856
2018	480,080	275,361	756,167	NA	972	49,917	637,217	688,105
2019	NA	NA	NA	NA	876	47,053	539,415	587,344

NA = Not available. (1) A small amount of refuse recovery has been included in coal production figures since 2001. (2) Beginning in 2008, residential coal consumption data no longer collected by the EIA. (3) Electricity-only and combined-heat-and-power (CHP) plants whose primary business is to sell electricity or electricity and heat to the public. Through 1988, data are for electric utilities only; beginning in 1989, data are for electric utilities and independent power producers.

World Nuclear Power Summary, 2019

Source: *Nuclear Power Reactors in the World*, International Atomic Energy Agency (IAEA); as of Dec. 31, 2019

Country	Reactors in operation No. of units	Reactors in operation Total MW(e)	Reactors under construction[1] No. of units	Reactors under construction[1] Total MW(e)	Nuclear electricity supplied in 2019 TW(e).h[2]	Nuclear electricity supplied in 2019 % of nation's total	Total operating experience[3] Years	Total operating experience[3] Months
Argentina	3	1,641	1	25	7.9	5.9%	88	2
Armenia	1	375	0	—	2.0	27.8	45	8
Belgium	7	5,930	0	—	41.4	47.6	303	7
Brazil	2	1,884	1	1,340	15.2	2.7	57	3
Bulgaria	2	2,006	0	—	15.9	37.5	167	3
Canada	19	13,554	0	—	94.9	14.9	769	6
China	48	45,518	11	10,564	330.1	4.9	370	1
Czechia	6	3,932	0	—	28.6	35.2	170	10
Finland	4	2,794	1	1,600	22.9	34.7	163	4
France	58	63,130	1	1,630	382.4	70.6	2,280	4
Germany	6	8,113	0	—	NA	NA	846	7
Hungary	4	1,902	0	—	15.4	49.2	138	2
India	22	6,255	7	4,824	40.7	3.2	526	11
Iran	1	915	1	974	5.9	1.8	8	4
Japan	33	31,679	2	2,653	65.7	7.5	1,899	6
Korea, South	24	23,172	5	5,360	138.8	26.2	572	2
Mexico	2	1,552	0	—	10.9	4.5	55	11
Netherlands	1	482	0	—	3.7	3.1	75	0
Pakistan	5	1,318	2	2,028	9.1	6.6	82	5
Romania	2	1,300	0	—	10.4	18.5	35	11
Russia	38	28,437	4	4,525	195.5	19.7	1,334	5
Slovakia	4	1,814	2	880	14.3	53.9	172	7
Slovenia	1	688	0	—	5.5	37.0	38	3
South Africa	2	1,860	0	—	13.6	6.7	70	3
Spain	7	7,121	0	—	55.9	21.4	343	1
Sweden	7	7,740	0	—	64.4	34.0	467	0
Switzerland	4	2,960	0	—	25.4	23.9	224	11
Taiwan	4	3,844	2	2,600	31.1	13.4	228	8
Ukraine	15	13,107	2	2,070	78.1	53.9	518	6
United Kingdom	15	8,923	2	3,260	51.0	15.6	1,619	7
United States	96	98,152	2	2,234	809.4	19.7	4,505	8
TOTAL	**443**	**392,098**	**54**	**57,441**	**2,586.2**	**—**	**18,329**	**10**

— = Not applicable. NA = Not available. MW(e) = Megawatt electricity. (1) Bangladesh, Belarus, Turkey, and United Arab Emirates have reactors under construction, which are included in totals but not listed separately. (2) 1 terawatt-hour [TW(e).h] = 10⁶ megawatt-hour [MW(e).h]. For an average power plant, 1 TW(e).h = 0.39 megaton of coal equivalent (input) and 0.23 megaton of oil equivalent (input). (3) Total includes shutdown plants for countries not listed here: Italy (80 years, 8 months), Kazakhstan (25 years, 10 months), and Lithuania (43 years, 6 months).

Nuclear Reliance by Nation, 2019

Source: Power Reactor Information System (PRIS), International Atomic Energy Agency (IAEA)
(nuclear electricity generation as % of total electricity generated within country)

Rank	Country	Nuclear share	Rank	Country	Nuclear share	Rank	Country	Nuclear share	Rank	Country	Nuclear share
1.	France	70.6%	9.	Finland	34.7%	17.	Romania	18.5%	24.	Argentina	5.9%
2.	Slovakia	53.9	10.	Sweden	34.0	18.	United Kingdom	15.6	25.	China	4.9
3.	Ukraine	53.9	11.	Armenia	27.8	19.	Canada	14.9	26.	Mexico	4.5
4.	Hungary	49.2	12.	South Korea	26.2	20.	Taiwan	13.4	27.	India	3.2
5.	Belgium	47.6	13.	Switzerland	23.9	21.	Japan	7.5	28.	Netherlands	3.1
6.	Bulgaria	37.5	14.	Spain	21.4	22.	South Africa	6.7	29.	Brazil	2.7
7.	Slovenia	37.0	15.	Russia	19.7	23.	Pakistan	6.6	30.	Iran	1.8
8.	Czechia	35.2	16.	United States	19.7						

U.S. Nuclear Generation, 1957-2019

Source: *Monthly Energy Review*, July 2020, Energy Information Administration (EIA), U.S. Dept. of Energy

Years	Total operable units[1]	Net summer capacity (mil kW)[2]	Nuclear electricity generation (mil net kWh)	Nuclear share of electricity net generation	Capacity factor[3]	Years	Total operable units[1]	Net summer capacity (mil kW)[2]	Nuclear electricity generation (mil net kWh)	Nuclear share of electricity net generation	Capacity factor[3]
1957	1	0.055	10	—	NA	2005	104	99.988	781,986	19.3%	89.3%
1958	1	0.055	165	—	NA	2006	104	100.334	787,219	19.4	89.6
1959	2	0.055	188	—	NA	2007	104	100.266	806,425	19.4	91.8
1960	3	0.411	518	0.1%	NA	2008	104	100.755	806,208	19.6	91.1
1965	13	0.793	3,657	0.3	NA	2009	104	101.004	798,855	20.2	90.3
1970	20	7.004	21,804	1.4	NA	2010	104	101.167	806,968	19.6	91.1
1975	57	37.267	172,505	9.0	55.9%	2011	104	101.419	790,204	19.3	89.1
1980	71	51.810	251,116	11.0	56.3	2012	104	101.885	769,331	19.0	86.1
1985	96	79.397	383,691	15.5	58.0	2013	100	99.240	789,016	19.4	89.9
1990	112	99.624	576,862	19.0	66.0	2014	99	98.569	797,166	19.5	91.7
1995	109	99.515	673,402	20.1	77.4	2015	99	98.672	797,178	19.6	92.3
2000	104	97.860	753,893	19.8	88.1	2016	99	99.565	805,694	19.8	92.3
2002	104	98.657	780,064	20.2	90.3	2017	99	99.629	804,950	20.0	92.3
2003	104	99.209	763,733	19.7	87.9	2018	98	99.433	807,084	19.3	92.5
2004	104	99.628	788,528	19.9	90.1	2019	96	98.070E	809,409	19.7	93.5

NA = Not available. — = Less than 0.05%. E = Estimate. (1) Total of nuclear generating units holding full-power licenses, or equivalent permission to operate. (2) The maximum output that generating equipment can supply to system load, as demonstrated by a multi-hour test, at the time of summer peak demand (June 1 through Sept. 30). (3) Beginning in 2008, capacity factor data calculated using a new methodology.

U.S. Nuclear Reactors Generating the Most Electricity, 2019

Source: Energy Information Administration (EIA), U.S. Dept. of Energy

(in megawatt hours)

Rank	Reactor, location	Electricity generated	Capacity[1]	Rank	Reactor, location	Electricity generated	Capacity[1]
1.	Peach Bottom-2, Delta, PA	11,533,439	107.6%	14.	Browns Ferry-3, Athens, AL	10,313,855	93.5%
2.	South Texas-1, Bay City, TX	11,490,063	102.5	15.	Braidwood-2, Braceville, IL	10,264,818	101.5
3.	Palo Verde-2, Wintersburg, AZ	11,435,511	99.3	16.	Vogtle-1, Waynesboro, GA	10,256,484	101.8
4.	Nine Mile Point-2, Scriba, NY	11,217,193	99.1	17.	Catawba-1, York, SC	10,249,745	100.9
5.	Susquehanna-1, Salem Township, PA	11,072,672	101.4	18.	Limerick-1, Limerick, PA	10,084,182	102.8
				19.	LaSalle-1, Marseilles, IL	10,026,816	101.2
6.	Grand Gulf-1, Port Gibson, NS	11,032,514	89.9	20.	Braidwood-1, Braceville, IL	9,986,322	96.4
7.	Seabrook-1, Seabrook, NH	10,906,923	99.6	21.	Palo Verde-3, Wintersburg, AZ	9,969,689	86.7
8.	Peach Bottom-3, Delta, PA	10,760,946	100.1	22.	Salem-2, Hancocks Bridge, NJ	9,966,009	98.2
9.	Browns Ferry-1, Athens, AL	10,757,301	97.8	23.	Fermi-2, nr. Toledo, OH	9,886,260	98.9
10.	Palo Verde-1, Wintersburg, AZ	10,515,168	91.6	24.	Sequoyah-2, Soddy-Daisy, TN	9,874,983	100.1
11.	South Texas-2, Bay City, TX	10,503,234	93.7	25.	Comanche Peak-2, Glen Rose, TX	9,863,180	94.2
12.	Byron-1, Byron, IL	10,459,123	102.6				
13.	McGuire-2, Huntersville, NC	10,316,393	101.7				

(1) The ratio of power generated to the maximum potential generation expressed as a percentage.

Renewable Energy Sources

Source: U.S. Dept. of Energy

Concern over the environmental impact of burning fossil fuels has helped spur interest in alternative fuels that are less polluting. And because the supply of fossil fuels is finite and diminishing, there is interest in "renewable" sources that do not deplete existing supplies. However, renewable energy sources still make up only a small share of U.S. domestic energy production (about 11.5% in 2019). The main reason for this is their relatively higher cost (in some cases two to four times that of power obtained from traditional fuels). The following are the major renewable energy sources available.

Biomass is plant- and animal-derived material usable as an energy source. It includes wood and wood processing waste; agricultural crops and waste materials; food, yard, and wood waste in garbage; and animal manure and human sewage. As of 2020, biomass was the most common renewable energy source in the U.S. Biomass such as wood can be burned to produce heat and generate electricity. Agricultural crops can be burned as a fuel or converted to liquid biofuels such as ethanol and biodiesel; these are usually blended with petroleum fuels but can also be used on their own. Second-generation biofuels made from other materials are in development, but the process has been slow. While biomass fuels provide some benefits to the environment, such as reduced waste in landfills, they still produce carbon dioxide and other pollutants.

Geothermal energy is generated from heat inside the Earth. This form of energy is both clean and renewable. The technology has caught on in countries with substantial geothermal activity such as Iceland, where it accounts for approximately two-thirds of primary energy use. In the U.S., the best sources for geothermal power are in the West, Alaska, and in Hawaii, where geothermal energy resources are close to the Earth's surface. Drilling wells and testing the temperature deep underground is the most reliable method for locating geothermal reservoirs, which are largely undetectable above ground.

Hydrogen is the most abundant element in the universe. It does not naturally occur on Earth as a pure gas or liquid but is always combined with other elements (such as oxygen, to form water, or carbon, to form methane). If hydrogen is to be used for energy, it must be separated from these other elements. The two most common methods for producing hydrogen are steam reforming and electrolysis (water splitting).

NASA began using liquid hydrogen in the 1950s as a rocket fuel and used hydrogen fuel cells to power electrical systems on spacecraft. Fuel cells produce electricity by combining hydrogen and oxygen atoms, resulting in an electrical current. Hydrogen use in vehicles is a major focus of fuel cell research and development, and several vehicle manufacturers have begun making light-duty hydrogen fuel cell electric vehicles available in regions where hydrogen fueling stations have been built.

Hydropower, or hydroelectric power, is generated by water flowing through turbines. Along with biomass fuels and wind power, it is one of the most common renewable energy sources in the U.S. today by amount of energy produced. A dam on a river is a common hydropower producer. No harmful greenhouse gases are produced, but the dams needed to generate power can harm river ecosystems. Researchers are working on technologies to maximize use of hydropower and reduce adverse environmental effects.

Ocean energy can be generated in two ways. Thermal ocean energy uses heat that the ocean absorbs from the sun to power generators, sometimes producing drinkable desalinated water as a byproduct. Mechanical ocean energy is generated by the movement of tides and waves through turbines. In both cases, power generation is not very efficient with current technology. New methods of capturing this energy are under development. Mechanical ocean energy requires the building of large dams or breakwater-type structures called tidal barrages, which could harm coastal ecosystems.

Solar energy is generated using heat and light from the sun. Solar energy is increasingly used to generate electricity. Photovoltaic (PV) cells, also called solar cells, are made of semi-conducting materials that can directly convert sunlight to electricity without producing any harmful waste. Arrays of mirrors can concentrate the sun's rays onto PV panels, making solar collectors more efficient. Solar thermal systems can use sunlight to heat water. According to the Dept. of Energy, homes incorporating solar heating designs can save 50% or more on heating bills. Solar energy is limited by its dependence on a range of factors, including location, time of year, and weather, as well as the efficiency of solar batteries.

Wind energy uses wind turbines to produce energy. It is one of the most common renewable energy sources in the U.S. today. Wind turbines typically are perched on towers 100 ft tall or higher; they are often placed in large groups ("farms"), which are sometimes located offshore. Farmers and homeowners sometimes use stand-alone turbines to generate supplemental electricity. Tax credits for wind energy producers and government incentives for homeowners have lowered the price of wind power. But some object to wind farms because of their appearance or the noise the turbines make. Wind power raises few other environmental problems, but the turbines can pose a danger to birds. In addition, because weather is involved, consistent energy generation can be a challenge.

CRIME

Crime in the U.S., 1990-2018

Source: *Crime in the United States, 2018*, Federal Bureau of Investigation (FBI), U.S. Dept. of Justice; Natl. Archive of Criminal Justice Data

Reported offenses are classified as **violent crimes** if they involve force or the threat of force: murder and nonnegligent manslaughter, rape, robbery, and aggravated assault. The following offenses are considered **property crimes**: burglary, larceny-theft, motor vehicle theft, and arson (excluded from this table because of insufficient data to make estimates).

Year(s)	Violent crime					Property crime			
	All violent crimes	Murder and nonnegligent manslaughter	Rape[1]	Robbery	Aggravated assault[2]	All property crimes	Burglary	Larceny-theft[3]	Motor vehicle theft
NUMBER OF OFFENSES									
1990	1,820,127	23,438	102,555	639,271	1,054,863	12,655,486	3,073,909	7,945,670	1,635,907
1995	1,798,792	21,606	97,470	580,509	1,099,207	12,063,935	2,593,784	7,997,710	1,472,441
2000	1,425,486	15,586	90,178	408,016	911,706	10,182,584	2,050,992	6,971,590	1,160,002
2005	1,390,745	16,740	94,347	417,438	862,220	10,174,754	2,155,448	6,783,447	1,235,859
2008	1,394,461	16,465	90,750	443,563	843,683	9,774,152	2,228,887	6,586,206	959,059
2010	1,251,248	14,722	85,593	369,089	781,844	9,112,625	2,168,459	6,204,601	739,565
2013	1,168,298	14,319	82,109	345,093	726,777	8,651,892	1,932,139	6,019,465	700,288
2014	1,153,022	14,164	84,864	322,905	731,089	8,209,010	1,713,153	5,809,054	686,803
2015	1,199,310	15,883	91,261	328,109	764,057	8,024,115	1,587,564	5,723,488	713,063
2016	1,250,162	17,413	96,970	332,797	802,982	7,928,530	1,516,405	5,644,835	767,290
2017	1,247,917	17,294	99,708	320,596	810,319	7,682,988	1,397,045	5,513,000	772,943
2018	1,206,836	16,214	101,151	282,061	807,410	7,196,045	1,230,149	5,217,055	748,841
PERCENT CHANGE: NUMBER OF OFFENSES									
2017-18	–3.3%	–6.2%	1.4%	–12.0%	–0.4%	–6.3%	–11.9%	–5.4%	–3.1%
2014-18	4.7	14.5	19.2	–12.6	10.4	–12.3	–28.2	–10.2	9.0
2009-18	–9.0	5.3	13.3	–31.0	–0.6	–22.9	–44.2	–17.7	–5.9
CRIME RATE PER 100,000 RESIDENTS									
1990	729.6	9.4	41.1	256.3	422.9	5,073.1	1,232.2	3,185.1	655.8
1995	684.5	8.2	37.1	220.9	418.3	4,590.5	987.0	3,043.2	560.3
2000	506.5	5.5	32.0	145.0	324.0	3,618.3	728.8	2,477.3	412.2
2005	469.0	5.6	31.8	140.8	290.8	3,431.5	726.9	2,287.8	416.8
2008	458.6	5.4	29.8	145.9	277.5	3,214.6	733.0	2,166.1	315.4
2010	404.5	4.8	27.7	119.3	252.8	2,945.9	701.0	2,005.8	239.1
2013	369.1	4.5	25.9	109.0	229.6	2,733.6	610.5	1,901.9	221.3
2014	361.6	4.4	26.6	101.3	229.2	2,574.1	537.2	1,821.5	215.4
2015	373.7	4.9	28.4	102.2	238.1	2,500.5	494.7	1,783.6	222.2
2016	386.6	5.4	30.0	102.9	248.3	2,451.6	468.9	1,745.4	237.3
2017	383.8	5.3	30.7	98.6	249.2	2,362.9	429.7	1,695.5	237.7
2018	368.9	5.0	30.9	86.2	246.8	2,199.5	376.0	1,594.6	228.9
PERCENT CHANGE: CRIME RATE PER 100,000 RESIDENTS									
2017-18	–3.9%	–6.8%	0.8%	–12.6%	–1.0%	–6.9%	–12.5%	–6.0%	–3.7%
2014-18	2.0	11.6	16.2	–14.9	7.7	–14.6	–30.0	–12.5	6.3
2009-18	–14.6	–1.2	6.4	–35.2	–6.8	–27.7	–47.6	–22.8	–11.7

(1) In 2013, the FBI began collecting rape data under a revised definition. For comparison purposes, this table presents data under the legacy definition of rape: "carnal knowledge of a female forcibly and against her will." That definition does not include statutory rape, other types of sexual offenses, or attacks with male victims. (2) Attack or attempted attack upon another with the intent of doing serious bodily harm; usually accompanied by the use of a weapon or other means likely to produce death or great bodily harm. (3) The unlawful taking of another's property not involving force or fraud (e.g., theft of motor vehicle parts, shoplifting). Excludes crimes such as embezzlement and check fraud.

Violent Crime Rates in the U.S., 1970-2018

Source: *Crime in the United States, 2018*, Federal Bureau of Investigation (FBI), U.S. Dept. of Justice; Natl. Archive of Criminal Justice Data

After rising during much of the 1970s and 1980s, the violent crime rate dropped sharply, from a historic high of 758.2 reported offenses per 100,000 population in 1991 to less than half that in 2018 (368.9). The rates of aggravated assault and robbery decreased even more precipitously over that same time period. The Uniform Crime Reporting Program began collecting rape data under a revised definition in 2013, but the data here uses the legacy definition of rape to allow for comparison.

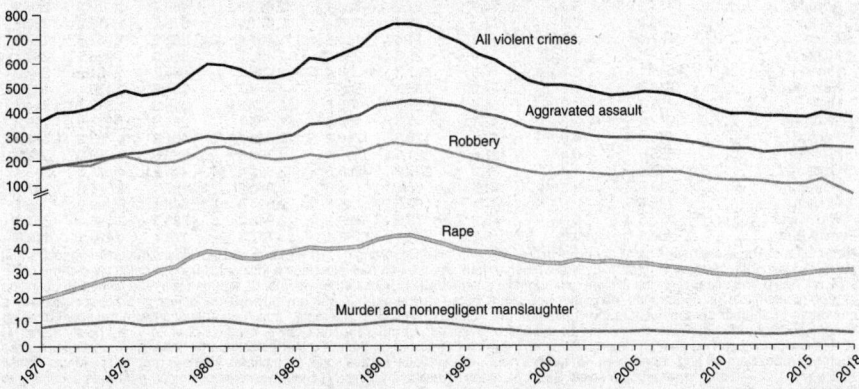

U.S. Crime Rates by Region and State, 2018

Source: *Crime in the United States, 2018*, Federal Bureau of Investigation (FBI), U.S. Dept. of Justice
(per 100,000 population, based on U.S. Census Bureau provisional estimates as of July 1)

| Area | Violent crime | | | | | Property crime[1] | | | |
	All violent crimes	Murder and nonnegligent manslaughter	Rape[2]	Robbery	Aggravated assault[3]	All property crimes	Burglary	Larceny-theft[4]	Motor vehicle theft
Total U.S.	380.6	5.0	42.6	86.2	246.8	2,199.5	376.0	1,594.6	228.9
Northeast	292.7	3.4	31.2	74.6	183.5	1,435.4	192.7	1,145.2	97.5
New England	255.8	2.0	33.6	50.1	170.0	1,400.1	206.3	1,076.5	117.3
Connecticut	207.4	2.3	23.5	61.4	120.2	1,681.0	222.5	1,251.8	206.7
Maine	112.1	1.8	33.3	17.0	60.0	1,357.8	202.7	1,097.1	58.1
Massachusetts	338.1	2.0	34.9	60.0	241.2	1,263.3	200.8	966.8	95.7
New Hampshire	173.2	1.5	39.4	26.5	105.8	1,248.5	136.2	1,048.2	64.1
Rhode Island	219.1	1.5	45.5	42.9	129.2	1,660.9	265.8	1,250.3	144.8
Vermont	172.0	1.6	45.8	11.2	113.4	1,283.1	234.2	1,008.5	40.4
Middle Atlantic	305.9	4.0	30.3	83.4	188.4	1,448.2	187.8	1,170.0	90.4
New Jersey	208.1	3.2	16.0	71.4	117.4	1,404.9	215.9	1,065.1	123.9
New York	350.5	2.9	33.6	93.1	220.9	1,440.5	159.3	1,214.0	67.2
Pennsylvania	306.0	6.1	35.0	76.9	188.0	1,489.9	211.6	1,175.9	102.4
Midwest	361.4	5.2	49.2	73.6	233.4	2,016.7	345.4	1,478.7	192.6
East North Central	366.2	5.6	50.0	82.0	228.7	1,923.1	337.3	1,413.5	172.4
Illinois	404.1	6.9	46.0	111.5	239.7	1,932.8	306.7	1,472.3	153.8
Indiana	382.3	6.5	35.4	88.7	251.6	2,179.3	377.6	1,572.7	229.1
Michigan	449.4	5.5	76.9	56.6	310.3	1,653.5	316.6	1,162.3	174.6
Ohio	279.9	4.8	45.3	78.6	151.2	2,177.1	412.2	1,594.6	170.3
Wisconsin	295.4	3.0	38.7	60.0	193.7	1,559.9	242.5	1,168.9	148.5
West North Central	350.8	4.5	47.5	55.2	243.7	2,222.0	363.2	1,621.9	236.9
Iowa[5]	250.1	1.7	30.9	29.5	187.9	1,691.5	352.6	1,190.4	148.5
Kansas	439.0	3.9	53.8	53.0	328.3	2,633.9	430.6	1,933.9	269.4
Minnesota	220.4	1.9	43.9	52.5	122.2	1,993.8	288.4	1,524.8	180.5
Missouri	502.1	9.9	47.5	84.8	359.8	2,647.1	444.9	1,878.8	323.4
Nebraska	284.8	2.3	63.9	39.2	179.4	2,079.9	271.9	1,555.3	252.6
North Dakota	280.6	2.4	52.2	20.8	205.2	2,040.2	358.4	1,448.3	233.5
South Dakota	404.7	1.4	69.6	29.7	304.0	1,728.7	291.4	1,264.5	172.7
South	403.9	6.0	40.7	85.6	271.5	2,433.3	440.0	1,771.0	222.2
South Atlantic	370.5	6.0	34.4	83.1	247.0	2,317.6	388.6	1,734.0	195.0
Delaware	423.6	5.0	34.9	89.5	294.2	2,324.4	326.5	1,845.3	152.6
District of Columbia[6]	995.9	22.8	64.1	343.8	565.3	4,373.8	254.5	3,750.1	369.1
Florida	384.9	5.2	39.6	79.3	260.8	2,281.8	337.7	1,750.8	193.3
Georgia	326.6	6.1	25.2	78.7	216.6	2,573.7	431.3	1,907.0	235.4
Maryland	468.7	8.1	32.8	160.8	267.0	2,033.3	312.6	1,519.8	200.9
North Carolina[7]	377.6	6.0	25.4	81.1	265.1	2,494.1	599.9	1,724.4	169.8
South Carolina	488.3	7.7	47.9	69.9	362.8	3,017.6	579.7	2,156.0	281.9
Virginia	200.0	4.6	34.3	42.3	118.7	1,665.8	182.8	1,356.4	126.5
West Virginia	289.9	3.7	36.1	31.7	218.5	1,485.6	296.5	1,049.6	139.5
East South Central	440.0	6.8	36.9	80.1	316.1	2,555.6	523.2	1,780.6	251.7
Alabama	519.6	7.8	40.8	83.4	387.6	2,817.2	590.1	1,958.9	268.3
Kentucky	211.9	5.5	38.2	55.0	113.2	1,962.6	384.7	1,348.2	229.6
Mississippi	234.4	5.7	18.0	53.4	157.2	2,403.0	697.8	1,561.2	144.0
Tennessee	623.7	7.4	41.7	106.2	468.5	2,825.4	489.4	2,034.1	301.9
West South Central	440.8	5.6	52.8	92.3	290.1	2,562.7	483.9	1,826.4	252.4
Arkansas	543.6	7.2	72.9	52.9	410.7	2,913.0	636.8	2,040.2	236.0
Louisiana	537.5	11.4	44.7	98.0	383.4	3,276.0	668.1	2,360.4	247.6
Oklahoma	466.1	5.2	58.3	70.8	331.8	2,875.0	681.1	1,856.8	337.0
Texas	410.9	4.6	51.2	98.4	256.6	2,367.2	410.8	1,713.1	243.2
West	423.2	4.1	48.0	106.6	264.5	2,535.4	432.3	1,737.2	365.8
Mountain	438.3	4.4	60.0	76.6	297.2	2,555.4	433.5	1,811.5	310.4
Arizona	474.9	5.1	50.7	91.0	328.1	2,676.8	439.7	1,970.3	266.9
Colorado	397.2	3.7	71.5	66.7	255.4	2,671.6	375.2	1,915.9	380.5
Idaho	227.1	2.0	45.1	11.4	168.6	1,461.4	281.6	1,067.8	112.0
Montana	374.1	3.2	51.9	25.3	293.7	2,496.3	306.6	1,926.5	263.2
Nevada	541.1	6.7	76.8	127.3	330.4	2,438.2	584.7	1,461.2	392.3
New Mexico	856.6	8.0	64.6	135.1	648.9	3,419.7	767.8	2,166.1	485.8
Utah	233.1	1.9	55.5	39.1	136.6	2,377.5	315.3	1,817.7	244.5
Wyoming	212.2	2.3	42.1	17.3	150.6	1,785.1	264.0	1,375.9	145.2
Pacific	416.3	4.0	42.5	120.3	249.5	2,526.2	431.8	1,703.1	391.2
Alaska	885.0	6.4	161.6	121.5	595.4	3,300.5	539.6	2,219.0	541.9
California	447.4	4.4	39.2	137.3	266.5	2,380.4	416.2	1,571.8	392.4
Hawaii	248.6	2.5	44.0	66.6	135.5	2,870.3	396.4	2,076.2	397.7
Oregon	285.5	2.0	47.1	60.8	175.6	2,894.0	389.1	2,109.9	395.1
Washington	311.5	3.1	45.3	73.9	189.1	2,946.2	533.5	2,045.4	367.3
Puerto Rico	200.8	20.0	6.2	71.1	103.6	777.8	171.7	490.1	116.0

Note: Offense totals are based on all agencies in the Uniform Crime Reporting (UCR) Program and include estimates for agencies that submitted less than 12 months of data. Only the most serious offense in a multiple-offense incident is used in calculating crime rates. (1) Excludes arson because of insufficient data to make estimates. (2) Unless otherwise noted, figures estimated using FBI definition of rape (revised 2013): "penetration, no matter how slight, of the vagina or anus with any body part or object, or oral penetration by a sex organ of another person, without the consent of the victim." (3) Attack or attempted attack upon another with the intent of doing serious bodily harm; usually accompanied by the use of a weapon or other means likely to produce death or great bodily harm. (4) The unlawful taking of another's property not involving force or fraud (e.g., theft of motor vehicle parts, shoplifting). Excludes crimes such as embezzlement and check fraud. (5) Limited data were available for this state. (6) Includes offenses reported by Metro Transit Police and DC Fire and Emergency Medical Services Arson Investigation Unit. (7) State agencies submitted rape data according to the legacy definition of rape.

Crime Rates in the Largest U.S. Metropolitan Areas, 2018

Source: *Crime in the United States, 2018,* Federal Bureau of Investigation (FBI), U.S. Dept. of Justice
(per 100,000 estimated population as of July 1)

Data includes metropolitan statistical areas (MSAs) with sufficient law enforcement agency participation and 12 months of data from the principal city/cities.

Metropolitan statistical area (MSA)	MSA pop. (mil)	Violent crime					Property crimes[3]
		Total	Murder[1]	Rape[2]	Robbery	Aggravated assault	
Atlanta-Sandy Springs-Alpharetta, GA	6.0	320.7	5.7	26.1	94.1	194.7	2,575.0
Austin-Round Rock-Georgetown, TX	2.2	291.4	2.4	60.9	58.9	169.2	2,319.6
Baltimore-Columbia-Towson, MD	2.8	720.8	13.3	38.3	258.4	410.8	2,470.6
Boston-Cambridge-Newton, MA-NH.	4.9	284.4	1.9	29.5	54.4	198.6	1,167.3
Charlotte-Concord-Gastonia, NC-SC	2.6	426.9	5.2	27.6	101.3	292.7	2,739.7
Chicago-Naperville-Elgin, IL-IN-WI.	9.5	NA	8.0	40.3	NA	NA	NA
Cincinnati, OH-KY-IN.	2.2	225.2	3.9	39.5	67.4	114.4	2,060.7
Cleveland-Elyria, OH[4]	2.1	NA	7.2	43.2	174.2	NA	2,110.7
Columbus, OH M.S.A.	2.1	282.4	6.1	59.2	109.2	108.0	2,552.0
Dallas-Fort Worth-Arlington, TX	7.5	351.0	4.4	45.1	103.6	197.9	2,232.7
Denver-Aurora-Lakewood, CO[4]	2.9	413.9	4.6	72.7	93.1	243.6	NA
Detroit-Warren-Dearborn, MI	4.3	535.1	8.0	60.5	82.2	384.4	NA
Houston-The Woodlands-Sugar Land, TX	7.0	NA	6.3	44.1	176.7	NA	2,604.7
Indianapolis-Carmel-Anderson, IN	2.0	641.5	9.3	46.3	166.8	419.1	2,643.8
Las Vegas-Henderson-Paradise, NV	2.2	NA	7.6	82.9	151.4	NA	2,670.8
Los Angeles-Long Beach-Anaheim, CA	13.3	494.8	4.6	41.0	162.7	286.4	2,246.9
Miami-Fort Lauderdale-Pompano Beach, FL	6.2	427.7	6.2	33.8	116.3	271.4	2,781.1
Minneapolis-St. Paul-Bloomington, MN-WI.	3.6	253.4	1.9	45.9	73.0	132.6	2,160.5
New York-Newark-Jersey City, NY-NJ-PA[4]	20.3	332.9	2.8	19.8	107.5	202.8	1,335.6
Orlando-Kissimmee-Sanford, FL	2.6	442.9	5.4	49.9	93.2	294.4	2,452.5
Philadelphia-Camden-Wilmington, PA-NJ-DE-MD	6.1	409.0	8.9	32.3	131.9	235.9	1,953.8
Phoenix-Mesa-Chandler, AZ.	4.9	446.2	4.6	49.5	98.2	294.0	2,608.7
Pittsburgh, PA	2.3	274.6	5.5	25.8	58.8	184.5	1,413.1
Portland-Vancouver-Hillsboro, OR-WA	2.5	299.1	1.9	55.5	70.7	171.0	2,870.0
Riverside-San Bernardino-Ontario, CA.	4.6	390.3	4.8	32.2	115.5	237.9	2,445.4
Sacramento-Roseville-Folsom, CA	2.3	375.3	3.7	29.2	105.3	237.1	2,161.4
St. Louis, MO-IL	2.8	455.1	12.9	41.9	93.3	307.1	NA
San Antonio-New Braunfels, TX	2.5	NA	5.4	72.2	80.3	NA	3,091.6
San Diego-Chula Vista-Carlsbad, CA	3.3	341.1	2.5	34.7	88.9	214.9	1,694.3
San Francisco-Oakland-Berkeley, CA.	4.7	472.7	4.1	38.3	217.6	212.6	3,283.5
San Jose-Sunnyvale-Santa Clara, CA	2.0	314.2	1.6	43.3	106.4	162.8	2,296.4
San Juan-Bayamon-Caguas, Puerto Rico.	2.0	224.6	24.6	5.9	95.4	98.7	911.7
Seattle-Tacoma-Bellevue, WA.	3.9	359.0	3.3	38.5	105.5	210.2	3,331.3
Tampa-St. Petersburg-Clearwater, FL	3.1	306.4	3.8	38.5	55.0	209.1	1,855.0
Washington-Arlington-Alexandria, DC-VA-MD-WV	6.3	264.8	5.0	31.8	84.3	143.7	1,656.8

NA = Not available because FBI determined agency data were over- or underreported or that agency did not follow reporting guidelines. (1) Data in category includes nonnegligent manslaughter. (2) Data submitted using both the revised and legacy definitions of rape. (3) Includes burglary, larceny-theft, and motor vehicle theft but not arson because of insufficient data to make estimates. (4) Data are for 2017.

Criminal Victimization, 2014-18

Source: *Criminal Victimization, 2018,* Bureau of Justice Statistics (BJS), U.S. Dept. of Justice

A crime committed against an individual or single household—whether threatened, attempted, or completed—counts as one **victimization.** Because more than one person may be victimized during a criminal incident, the number of victimizations may be greater than the number of personal crime incidents. **Victimization rates** measure the frequency with which victimizations occurred per 1,000 persons age 12 or older or per 1,000 households.

Crime type	Number				Rate			
	2014	2015	2016	2018	2014	2015	2016	2018
Violent crime[1]	5,359,570	5,006,620	5,353,820	6,385,520	20.1	18.6	19.7	23.2
Rape/sexual assault	284,350	431,840	298,410	734,630	1.1	1.6	1.1	2.7
Robbery	664,210	578,580	458,810	573,100	2.5	2.1	1.7	2.1
Assault	4,411,010	3,996,200	4,596,600	5,077,790	16.5	14.8	16.9	18.4
Aggravated assault	1,092,090	816,760	1,040,580	1,058,040	4.1	3.0	3.8	3.8
Simple assault	3,318,920	3,179,440	3,556,020	4,019,750	12.4	11.8	13.1	14.6
Violent crime excluding simple assault[2]	2,040,650	1,827,170	1,797,790	2,365,770	7.7	6.8	6.6	8.6
Selected characteristics of violent crime								
Domestic violence[3]	1,109,880	1,094,660	1,068,120	1,333,050	4.2	4.1	3.9	4.8
Intimate partner violence[4]	634,610	806,050	597,200	847,230	2.4	3.0	2.2	3.1
Stranger violence	2,166,130	1,821,310	2,082,410	2,493,750	8.1	6.8	7.7	9.1
Violent crime involving injury	1,375,950	1,303,290	1,220,640	1,449,530	5.2	4.8	4.5	5.3
Violent crime involving a weapon	1,306,900	977,840	1,203,200	1,329,700	4.9	3.6	4.4	4.8
Property crime	15,288,470	14,611,040	15,815,310	13,502,840	118.1	110.7	118.6	108.2
Burglary/trespassing[5]	2,993,480	2,904,570	3,160,450	2,639,620	23.1	22.0	23.7	21.1
Burglary[6]	2,051,570	1,888,720	2,071,660	1,724,720	15.8	14.3	15.5	13.8
Trespassing	941,910	1,015,850	1,088,800	914,910	7.3	7.7	8.2	7.3
Motor-vehicle theft	534,370	564,160	618,330	534,010	4.1	4.3	4.6	4.3
Other theft[7]	11,760,620	11,142,310	12,036,530	10,329,210	90.8	84.4	90.3	82.7

Note: Details may not add up to totals due to rounding. Because of survey changes, the number of property crimes in 2017 and 2018 should not be compared with that number in other years. (1) Does not include murder because data are based on interviews with victims. (2) Includes rape or sexual assault, robbery, and aggravated assault. Category formerly called serious violent crime. (3) Victimization by intimate partners or family members. (4) Victimization by current or former spouses, boyfriends, or girlfriends. (5) Formerly household burglary. Includes unlawful or forcible entry or attempted entry of places, such as a permanent (or other type of) residence (e.g., hotel room) or some other structure (e.g., garage), whether or not the offender stole anything. Does not include trespassing on land. (6) Includes only crimes where the offender committed or attempted a theft. (7) Includes other unlawful taking or attempted taking of property or cash without personal contact with victim.

Prison Population by State, 2000-18

Source: National Prisoner Statistics Program, Bureau of Justice Statistics (BJS), U.S. Dept. of Justice

As of Dec. 31, 2018, 1,465,158 prisoners were under the jurisdiction, or legal authority, of state (87.7%) or federal (12.3%) correctional authorities, a 9.3% decrease from a peak U.S. prison population of 1,615,487 in 2009. Jails, which are locally operated, typically hold persons awaiting trial or sentencing as well as those sentenced to one year or less.

Jurisdiction	2000	2017	2018	% change, 2017-18	Jurisdiction	2000	2017	2018	% change, 2017-18
U.S. total[1]	1,394,231	1,489,189	1,465,158	−1.6%	Mississippi	20,241	19,103	19,275	0.9%
Federal[2,3]	145,416	183,058	179,898	−1.7	Missouri	27,543	32,601	30,369	−6.8
State[1]	1,248,815	1,306,131	1,285,260	−1.6	Montana	3,105	3,698	3,765	—
Alabama	26,406	27,608	26,841	−2.8	Nebraska	3,895	5,313	5,491	3.4
Alaska[4]	4,173	4,399	4,380	−0.4	Nevada	10,063	13,721	13,641	−0.6
Arizona	26,510	42,030	42,005	−0.1	New Hampshire[1]	2,257	2,750	2,745	—
Arkansas	11,915	18,070	17,799	−1.5	New Jersey	29,784	19,585	19,362	−1.1
California	163,001	131,039	128,625	−1.8	New Mexico[1]	5,342	7,276	7,030	—
Colorado	16,833	19,946	20,372	2.1	New York	70,199	49,461	46,636	−5.7
Connecticut[4]	18,355	14,040	13,681	−2.6	North Carolina	31,266	36,394	34,899	−4.1
Delaware[4]	6,921	6,443	6,067	−5.8	North Dakota[1]	1,076	1,723	1,695	—
Dist. of Columbia[3]	10,352	—	—	—	Ohio	45,833	51,478	50,431	−2.0
Florida	71,319	98,504	97,538	−1.0	Oklahoma	23,181	28,143	27,709	−1.5
Georgia	44,232	53,667	53,647	0.0	Oregon[1]	10,580	15,218	15,268	—
Hawaii[4]	5,053	5,630	5,375	−4.5	Pennsylvania	36,847	48,333	47,239	−2.3
Idaho	5,535	8,579	8,664	1.0	Rhode Island[4]	3,286	2,861	2,767	−3.3
Illinois	45,281	41,427	39,965	−3.5	South Carolina	21,778	19,906	19,033	−4.4
Indiana	20,125	26,024	26,877	3.3	South Dakota	2,616	3,970	3,948	−0.6
Iowa	7,955	9,024	9,419	4.4	Tennessee	22,166	28,980	26,321	−9.2
Kansas	8,344	10,015	10,218	2.0	Texas	166,719	162,523	163,628	0.7
Kentucky	14,919	23,543	23,431	−0.5	Utah	5,637	6,219	6,648	—
Louisiana	35,207	33,739	32,397	−4.0	Vermont[4]	1,697	1,546	1,659	7.3
Maine	1,679	2,404	2,425	0.9	Virginia	30,168	37,158	36,660	−1.3
Maryland	23,538	19,367	18,856	−2.6	Washington	14,915	19,656	19,523	−0.7
Massachusetts	10,722	9,133	8,692	−4.8	West Virginia	3,856	7,092	6,775	−4.5
Michigan	47,718	39,666	38,761	−2.3	Wisconsin	20,754	23,945	24,064	0.5
Minnesota	6,238	10,708	10,101	−5.7	Wyoming	1,680	2,473	2,543	2.8

— = Not available or not applicable. (1) Includes BJS-imputed counts for states that did not submit prisoner data: New Hampshire, Oregon (2018), New Mexico, North Dakota (2017). (2) Includes adult prisoners held in nonsecure community-corrections facilities and adults and juveniles held in privately operated facilities. (3) DC has not operated a prison system since year-end 2001. 2000 figure includes jail and prison population. Felons sentenced under DC's criminal code are currently housed in federal facilities. (4) Prisons and jails form one integrated system. Data include total jail and prison populations.

Death Penalty by State, 1930-2018

Source: *Capital Punishment, 2017*, National Prisoner Statistics Program, Bureau of Justice Statistics (BJS), U.S. Dept. of Justice

In 2017, eight states executed 23 inmates while 2,703 prisoners remained under sentence of death at year's end, according to the most recent data available from the BJS. The death row population has decreased every year since 2000, but the demographic composition has changed little: as of year-end 2017, 55.8% of prisoners were white and 41.8% were Black.

At year-end 2018, 30 states and the federal government authorized the death penalty. Of the 20 states without the death penalty, Alaska, Hawaii, Maine, Michigan, Minnesota, North Dakota, Rhode Island, and Wisconsin are not shown here; they did not execute anyone after 1930. More recently, capital punishment was abolished in New Mexico (for crimes after July 1, 2009), Illinois (on July 1, 2011), Connecticut (in 2012), Maryland (for offenses after May 2, 2013), and New Hampshire (for offenses after May 30, 2019). State supreme courts have struck down the death penalty as unconstitutional in Delaware (2016) and Washington (2018). Governors have issued moratoriums on executions in Oregon (2011), Colorado (2013), Pennsylvania (2015), and California (2019). Nebraska voters, in a 2016 referendum, overturned their state's ban on capital punishment. The federal government was set to resume executions Dec. 9, 2019, after a nearly 17-year hiatus.

All death penalty states authorized lethal injection as their primary method of execution in 2018. Some states also permitted execution by electrocution, lethal gas, hanging, firing squad, and nitrogen hypoxia.

Jurisdiction	Prisoners under sentence of death, year-end 2017[1]	Executions[2,3] 2017	Executions[2,3] 1930-2017	Executions[2,3] 1977-2017	Jurisdiction	Prisoners under sentence of death, year-end 2017[1]	Executions[2,3] 2017	Executions[2,3] 1930-2017	Executions[2,3] 1977-2017
U.S. total	2,703	23	5,324	1,465	Missouri	24	1	150	88
Federal[1]	59	0	36	3	Montana	2	0	9	3
State	2,644	23	5,288	1,462	Nebraska	11	0	7	3
Alabama	182	3	196	61	Nevada	83	0	41	12
Arizona	120	0	75	37	New Hampshire	1	0	1	0
Arkansas	29	4	149	31	New Jersey	—	—	74	0
California	742	0	305	13	New Mexico[3]	2	0	9	1
Colorado	3	0	48	1	New York	0	—	329	0
Connecticut	—	—	22	1	North Carolina	143	0	306	43
Delaware[3]	1	—	28	16	Ohio	138	2	227	55
Dist. of Columbia	—	—	40	0	Oklahoma	46	0	172	112
Florida	349	3	265	95	Oregon	30	0	21	2
Georgia	55	1	436	70	Pennsylvania	154	0	155	3
Idaho	9	0	6	3	South Carolina	35	0	205	43
Illinois	—	—	102	12	South Dakota	3	0	4	3
Indiana	10	0	61	20	Tennessee	60	0	99	6
Iowa	—	—	18	0	Texas	234	7	842	545
Kansas	10	0	15	0	Utah	9	0	20	7
Kentucky	32	0	106	3	Vermont	—	—	4	0
Louisiana	71	0	161	28	Virginia	2	0	205	113
Maryland	—	—	73	5	Washington	8	0	52	5
Massachusetts	—	—	27	0	West Virginia	—	—	40	0
Mississippi	45	0	175	21	Wyoming	0	0	9	1

— = Not available or applicable. (1) Excludes persons held under Armed Forces jurisdiction with a military death sentence for murder. (2) Does not include 160 executions carried out by military authorities between 1930 and 1961. (3) Prisoners awaiting execution at year-end 2017 were resentenced to life in prison in Delaware (2018) and New Mexico (2019).

U.S. Prison Population, 1925-2018

Source: National Prisoner Statistics Program, Bureau of Justice Statistics (BJS), U.S. Dept. of Justice

As recently as 1970, the U.S. had fewer than 200,000 people behind bars nationwide, or less than 1 in 1,000 residents. That number rose steadily from the 1970s on, reaching an all-time high of more than 1.62 mil prisoners in 2009. The imprisonment rate has declined since its high of 506 prisoners per 100,000 residents in 2008.

Year	Prisoners	Imprison-ment rate	Year	Prisoners	Imprison-ment rate	Year	Prisoners	Imprison-ment rate
1925	91,669	79	1980	329,821	138	2013	1,576,950	479
1930	129,453	104	1990	773,919	295	2014	1,562,319	472
1940	173,706	131	1995	1,125,874	411	2015	1,526,603	459
1950	166,165	109	2000	1,394,231	470	2016	1,508,129	450
1960	212,953	117	2005	1,525,910	492	2017	1,489,189	441
1970	196,441	96	2010	1,613,803	500	2018	1,465,158	431

Note: Imprisonment rate is per 100,000 U.S. residents of all ages based on U.S. Census Bureau pop. ests. Since 1971, the rate is of prisoners sentenced to more than one year. Data for 1940-70 include all adult felons serving sentences in state and federal institutions. In 1977, the BJS began to include persons under state jurisdiction but not in a state's physical custody, such as persons in private prisons, local jails, and other facilities. Figures may not be directly comparable over time.

Prison Situation Under Correctional Authorities' Jurisdiction, 2018

Source: *Prisoners in 2018*, National Prisoner Statistics Program, Bureau of Justice Statistics (BJS), U.S. Dept. of Justice

Largest prison populations		% increase in prison population, 2017-18		Imprisonment rate of sentenced prisoners		Prison population as % of maximum estimated capacity	
Jurisdiction	Number	Jurisdiction	% change[1]	Jurisdiction	Rate[2]	Jurisdiction	% max. capacity[3]
U.S. total	1,465,158	U.S. total	−1.61%	U.S. total	431	U.S. total	NA
Federal[4]	179,898	Federal[4]	−1.73	Federal[4]	50	Federal	112.1%
State	1,285,260	State	−1.60	State	381	State	NA
1. Texas	163,628	1. Vermont[6]	7.31	1. Louisiana	695	1. Nebraska	130.4
2. California	128,625	2. Iowa	4.38	2. Oklahoma	693	2. Iowa	123.4
3. Florida	97,538	3. Nebraska	3.35	3. Mississippi	626	3. New Mexico	114.7
4. Georgia	53,647	4. Indiana	3.28	4. Arkansas	589	4. Idaho[7]	110.7
5. Ohio	50,431	5. Wyoming	2.83	5. Arizona	559	5. Colorado	109.1
6. Pennsylvania	47,239	6. Colorado	2.14	6. Texas	549	6. Washington	103.8
7. New York	46,636	7. Kansas	2.03	7. Kentucky	523	7. Oklahoma	101.8
8. Arizona	42,005	8. Idaho	0.99	8. Georgia	501	8. Virginia	101.3
9. Illinois	39,965	9. Mississippi	0.90	9. Missouri	495	9. Arizona[7]	101.2
10. Michigan	38,761	10. Maine	0.87	10. Florida	454	10. Wisconsin	100.8
11. Virginia	36,660	11. Texas	0.68	11. Nevada	445	11. Delaware	100.3
12. North Carolina	34,899	12. Wisconsin	0.50	12. Idaho	444	12. Hawaii	100.0
13. Louisiana	32,397	13. Georgia	−0.04	13. South Dakota	444	13. Kansas	99.6
14. Missouri	30,369	14. Arizona	−0.06	14. Wyoming	441	14. Minnesota	98.0
15. Oklahoma[5]	27,709	15. Alaska[6]	−0.43	15. Ohio	431	15. Florida	97.8
16. Indiana	26,877	16. Kentucky	−0.48	16. Virginia	429	16. Missouri	96.9
17. Alabama	26,841	17. South Dakota	−0.55	17. Alabama	418	17. Arkansas	96.6
18. Tennessee	26,321	18. Nevada	−0.58	18. Delaware[6]	410	18. California	96.4
19. Wisconsin	24,064	19. Washington	−0.68	19. Indiana	400	19. Kentucky	96.1
20. Kentucky	23,431	20. Florida	−0.98	20. Wisconsin	391	20. Montana	95.9

NA = Not applicable. Note: Jurisdiction refers to the legal authority of state or federal correctional officials over a prisoner, regardless of where the prisoner is held, at year end. Sentenced felons from DC were the responsibility of the Federal Bureau of Prisons. New Hampshire and Oregon (2018) and New Mexico and North Dakota (2017) did not submit prisoner data for one or both years. BJS imputed counts are included in state and U.S. totals. (1) Rankings do not incl. Montana and Utah, which changed reporting methodology; New Hampshire; or Oregon. (2) Prisoners sentenced to more than one year per 100,000 U.S. residents based on U.S. Census Bureau pop. ests. (3) Based on custody counts, not jurisdiction population, excl. inmates held in local jails, other states, or private facilities unless otherwise stated. As % of rated, operational, or design capacity. Some states define capacity differently from BJS. Connecticut and Ohio do not report capacity data. (4) Incl. adult prisoners held in nonsecure community corrections facilities and adults and juveniles held in privately operated facilities. (5) Incl. persons awaiting transfer in county jails to be moved to state prison. (6) Prisons and jails form one integrated system. Data include total jail and prison populations. (7) Incl. prisoners in private facilities.

Imprisonment Rate by Gender, Race, Hispanic Origin, and Age, 2018

Source: *Prisoners in 2018*, Bureau of Justice Statistics (BJS), U.S. Dept. of Justice

(number of prisoners with a sentence of more than one year, under the jurisdiction of state or federal correctional officials, per 100,000 U.S. residents in each group)

Age	All prisoners	Male					Female				
		Total	White	Black	Hispanic	Other[1]	Total	White	Black	Hispanic	Other[1]
Total[2]	431	810	392	2,272	1,018	1,215	63	49	88	65	113
18-19	121	226	64	811	213	216	11	7	24	11	14
20-24	570	1,039	377	3,011	1,213	1,245	77	53	126	84	121
25-29	945	1,700	745	4,325	2,052	2,160	158	129	197	158	240
30-34	1,019	1,834	917	4,712	2,247	2,588	185	160	213	186	288
35-39	1,022	1,872	956	5,008	2,251	2,738	170	146	199	160	278
40-44	855	1,595	808	4,430	1,894	2,408	125	108	164	112	197
45-49	698	1,313	699	3,605	1,563	2,058	97	82	133	87	161
50-54	562	1,067	570	3,013	1,262	1,779	72	55	116	68	125
55-59	392	763	408	2,213	1,000	1,319	41	31	71	40	92
60-64	235	470	247	1,366	708	860	20	14	34	23	45
65 or older	80	173	101	468	317	359	5	4	9	6	15

Note: Resident population estimates are from the U.S. Census Bureau. Includes imputed counts for states that did not submit prisoner data. Hispanics may be of any race. White, Black, and other exclude persons of Hispanic or Latino origin. (1) Includes Asians, Native Hawaiians, other Pacific Islanders, American Indians, Alaska Natives, and persons of two or more races. (2) Persons of all ages, including those under 18.

Prisoners and Incarceration Rates in Selected Countries, 2005-18

Source: UN Survey on Crime Trends and Operations of Criminal Justice Systems, United Nations (UN) Office on Drugs and Crime

The U.S. prison population is the largest of any nation, and its incarceration rate is the world's highest. The following table ranks countries with the largest prison population and the most persons incarcerated per 100,000 population. Excludes non-criminals held for administrative purposes (e.g., pending immigration status investigation).

Country	Number of prisoners				Country	Incarceration rates			
	2018	2017	2010	2005		2018	2017	2010	2005
U.S.........	—	2,153,600	2,279,100	2,200,400	U.S...............	—	662.5	737.5	745.9
China	—	—	1,646,593	1,558,511	El Salvador	617.4	621.8	398.8	207.0
Brazil........	720,888	700,489	513,954	361,402	Turkmenistan	—	528.9	520.9	283.1
Russia.......	563,166	602,176	819,280	823,444	Thailand	527.6	538.9	313.8	248.1
India	—	—	368,998	358,368	Rwanda	—	509.1	547.9	—
Thailand	366,316	372,979	210,855	162,293	Bahamas, The	460.6	—	360.0	891.4
Turkey......	264,842	233,415	120,194	55,966	St. Vincent and the				
Indonesia	256,051	232,081	117,863	97,691	Grenadines	426.4	426.4	962.0	333.9
Iran	240,000	230,000	—	134,384	St. Kitts and Nevis. ...	—	423.1	575.5	—
Mexico	196,322	201,903	188,013	208,272	Palau	422.2	483.3	—	485.0
Philippines ...	194,658	—	95,390	—	Grenada	414.4	398.2	413.2	225.7
South Africa ...	164,129	158,111	163,312	157,402	Panama	396.5	393.4	344.3	368.2
Vietnam	—	130,002	—	88,414	Seychelles	393.8	440.6	474.7	182.0
Colombia	—	114,750	84,444	66,829	Russia.............	386.4	413.8	571.0	573.1
Ethiopia......	—	—	104,467	—	Maldives	—	373.4	226.8	—
Myanmar.....	92,000	79,668	—	—	Belize	—	344.9	721.1	485.9
Peru	90,934	85,811	45,464	33,010	Belarus	344.4	363.6	420.6	427.5
Argentina	—	85,283	59,227	55,423	Brazil..............	344.2	337.0	262.6	194.2
Morocco	83,757	83,102	64,877	50,933	Nicaragua	323.5	—	116.6	101.8
Pakistan	83,718	83,718	75,586	89,370	Turkey.............	321.6	287.8	166.2	82.4
Bangladesh...	83,350	88,424	69,650	72,268	Antigua and Barbuda..	317.7	321.1	335.2	239.5
UK[1]........	81,904	84,441	84,004	75,121	Eswatini	304.0	—	—	258.7
Poland.......	72,818	74,480	82,372	84,875	Uruguay	297.0	322.3	259.0	187.0
Nigeria......	71,522	75,772	47,072	39,006	Barbados	296.2	309.4	322.7	361.2
France.......	—	68,974	60,544	55,302	Iran	293.4	285.1	—	192.6
					St. Lucia	—	291.2	302.3	308.6

— = Not available. **Note:** Use caution when making comparisons because of differences in each country's legal definitions and methods of offense counting and reporting. (1) England and Wales.

Law Enforcement Officers and Civilian Employees, 2018-19

Source: *Crime in the United States, 2018* and *Law Enforcement Officers Killed and Assaulted, 2018 and 2019*; Federal Bureau of Investigation (FBI); U.S. Dept. of Justice

As of Oct. 31, 2018, 13,497 city, county, state, college and university, and tribal agencies around the country collectively employed 975,305 full-time law enforcement workers. About 70% of these employees were sworn officers. The FBI defines a law enforcement officer as a person who ordinarily carries a firearm and badge, has full arrest powers, and is paid from government funds specifically dedicated to sworn law enforcement personnel. Civilians (e.g., clerks, radio dispatchers, correctional officers) made up the remainder.

Altogether, they provided service to an estimated 288 mil people around the country, meaning there were 3.4 full-time law enforcement employees and 2.4 sworn officers per 1,000 residents.

The great majority of officers (87.4%) were men, while women made up 60.3% of civilian employees. The most populous state, California, employed the greatest number of full-time law enforcement workers (120,041). Washington

DC, had the highest rate, with 7.3 full-time law enforcement employees per 1,000 residents, followed by New Jersey (4.7) and New York (4.5).

Nationwide, 48 law enforcement officers were killed feloniously (that is, willfully and intentionally by the offender) in the line of duty in 2019, compared to 55 officers in 2018 and a 10-year high of 72 in 2011. Of the 48 officers, 15 were killed while performing investigative or enforcement activities; 44 were killed by firearms. On average, the officers were 40 years of age and had served in law enforcement for 13 years when killed. An additional 41 officers were killed accidentally in 2019 while on the job; of those deaths, 19 in auto crashes. In 2018, the most recent year for which such data was available, 58,866 officers were reported to have been assaulted in the line of duty, 31.0% of them while responding to disturbance calls such as family quarrels.

Sentenced State Prisoners by Offense and Selected Characteristics, 2017

Source: *Prisoners in 2018*, Bureau of Justice Statistics (BJS), U.S. Dept. of Justice

	All prisoners[1]	Male	Female	White[2]	Black[2]	Hispanic
Total number of sentenced prisoners........	1,273,674	1,179,900	93,800	394,800	409,600	274,300
	Percent of total or subset of prisoners by most serious offense					
Violent	55.7%	57.1%	37.8%	47.8%	61.1%	60.8%
Murder and nonnegligent manslaughter	14.3	14.5	11.9	10.7	17.0	15.5
Manslaughter	1.5	1.4	2.7	1.4	0.9	1.1
Rape or sexual assault	13.1	13.9	2.5	16.6	8.4	14.3
Robbery	12.8	13.2	7.8	7.1	19.2	12.5
Aggravated or simple assault	10.8	10.9	8.7	9.1	12.1	13.5
Other................................	3.2	3.2	4.1	3.0	3.4	3.8
Property.............................	16.8	16.2	25.0	22.5	13.6	12.0
Burglary.............................	9.1	9.2	7.1	11.1	8.4	7.0
Larceny-theft..........................	3.0	2.6	7.0	4.6	2.4	2.0
Motor vehicle theft......................	0.8	0.8	1.0	1.0	0.6	1.0
Fraud...............................	2.0	1.6	7.0	2.8	1.2	1.0
Other................................	2.0	1.9	3.0	3.0	1.1	1.1
Drug[3]	14.4	13.6	25.4	15.9	12.9	13.5
Public order[4]........................	12.4	12.5	10.8	13.0	12.1	13.2
Other or unspecified[5].................	0.7	0.6	1.0	0.8	0.4	0.4

Note: Estimates based on prisoners with a sentence of more than one year under the jurisdiction, or legal authority, of state correctional officials. Details may not add up to totals due to rounding and missing offense data. Hispanics may be of any race. (1) Includes race categories not shown here and persons of two or more races. (2) Excludes persons of Hispanic or Latino origin. (3) Includes possession, trafficking, and other drug offenses. (4) Includes weapons, driving under the influence, and court offenses; commercialized vice, morals, and decency offenses; liquor-law violations; probation and parole violations; and other public-order offenses. (5) Includes juvenile offenses and other unspecified offense categories.

Arrests by Race and Hispanic Origin, 2018

Source: *Crime in the United States, 2018,* Federal Bureau of Investigation (FBI), U.S. Dept. of Justice

Each instance in which a person is arrested, cited, or summoned for an offense is counted as one arrest. Arrest data therefore do not show the number of individuals arrested but the number of times persons were arrested, as an individual may be arrested multiple times in one year. Arrest estimates are based on statistics from law enforcement agencies that reported 12 months of arrest data.

Offense charged	Total[2]	White	Black/ African Amer.	Amer. Indian/ Alaska Native	Asian	Native Hawaiian/ other Pacific Isl.	Hispanic origin Total[2]	Hispanic/ Latino
Total arrests	7,710,900	69.0%	27.4%	2.1%	1.2%	0.2%	6,343,684	18.8%
Violent crime	392,562	58.7	37.4	2.0	1.6	0.4	334,028	25.0
Murder and nonnegligent manslaughter...	8,957	44.1	53.3	1.2	1.0	0.3	7,050	20.9
Rape[3]	18,776	68.1	28.6	1.4	1.5	0.3	15,316	26.7
Robbery	66,789	43.5	54.2	1.0	1.0	0.4	57,048	22.5
Aggravated assault	298,040	61.9	33.7	2.3	1.7	0.4	254,614	25.6
Property crime	880,473	66.9	30.1	1.7	1.1	0.2	716,254	16.3
Burglary	134,542	68.1	29.4	1.2	1.1	0.2	114,027	20.3
Larceny-theft	669,983	66.9	30.0	1.8	1.1	0.2	540,174	14.5
Motor vehicle theft	69,002	64.5	32.3	1.7	1.2	0.3	56,263	25.6
Arson	6,946	71.1	25.1	2.0	1.5	0.4	5,790	18.2
Other assaults[4]	794,787	64.4	32.0	2.0	1.3	0.3	654,150	19.1
Forgery and counterfeiting	37,724	66.6	30.8	0.9	1.5	0.2	31,565	16.8
Fraud	89,610	65.4	31.7	1.6	1.2	0.2	74,521	12.9
Embezzlement	11,174	62.0	35.4	1.1	1.4	0.1	9,252	12.9
Stolen property; buying, receiving, possessing	69,874	63.2	33.9	1.3	1.2	0.5	57,379	19.7
Vandalism	134,794	67.6	28.8	2.2	1.2	0.2	112,716	19.1
Weapons; carrying, possessing, etc.	126,332	54.4	43.3	0.9	1.1	0.3	100,312	23.6
Prostitution and commercialized vice	23,502	55.0	38.8	0.4	5.6	0.3	21,484	20.4
Sex offenses (except rape and prostitution)	35,157	72.1	23.9	1.7	2.1	0.2	28,928	25.6
Drug abuse violations	1,234,178	70.6	27.0	1.1	1.1	0.2	1,044,789	20.3
Gambling	2,465	40.6	48.6	0.4	8.3	2.1	1,390	24.5
Offenses against the family and children	64,357	67.4	28.8	2.9	0.8	0.1	51,589	11.6
Driving under the influence	736,644	81.2	14.8	1.8	1.9	0.3	604,136	24.4
Liquor laws	128,453	78.4	14.6	5.4	1.5	0.1	102,624	15.6
Drunkenness	251,490	76.8	15.0	6.9	1.1	0.2	233,325	22.5
Disorderly conduct	248,716	63.7	31.4	3.9	0.8	0.1	186,261	13.2
Vagrancy	18,048	71.0	24.7	2.7	1.4	0.1	16,649	15.4
All other offenses (except traffic)	2,413,408	69.1	27.5	2.3	1.0	0.2	1,947,281	16.3
Suspicion	432	54.9	29.9	15.0	0.2	0.0	390	3.8
Curfew and loitering law violations	16,720	56.0	41.0	1.6	1.1	0.3	14,661	20.7

(1) Percentages may not add up to 100 because of rounding. (2) Not all agencies provide data by ethnicity so total arrests by race will not equal total arrests by Hispanic origin. Hispanic or Latino persons may be of any race. (3) Aggregate totals based on both the legacy and revised Uniform Crime Reporting definition of rape. (4) Assaults in which no dangerous weapons were used and the victim did not sustain serious injury (e.g., stalking).

Foreign Nationals Removed From the U.S. by Criminal Status and Nationality, 2010-18

Source: *Immigration Enforcement Actions: 2018,* Office of Immigration Statistics, U.S. Dept. of Homeland Security

(countries ranked by total foreign nationals removed in 2018)

Country of nationality	2010 Total removed	% criminal[1]	2014 Total removed	% criminal[1]	2015 Total removed	% criminal[1]	2016 Total removed	% criminal[1]	2017 Total removed	% criminal[1]	2018 Total removed	% criminal[1]
Total	382,461	44.7%	405,239	41.8%	325,668	37.1%	332,227	34.7%	288,093	38.2%	337,287	44.3%
Mexico	275,572	47.1	265,235	46.5	233,562	37.2	236,713	34.5	185,103	40.2	217,919	42.0
Guatemala	29,403	32.0	54,405	25.2	33,379	31.5	33,886	31.3	33,050	33.6	49,149	40.3
Honduras	24,652	42.3	40,877	34.4	20,298	42.2	22,015	39.0	22,163	41.9	28,452	44.8
El Salvador	20,017	42.0	26,671	33.6	21,899	33.0	20,264	33.2	18,449	35.2	14,877	47.1
Colombia	2,327	53.7	1,375	63.7	1,596	49.8	2,086	36.6	2,059	31.1	2,631	86.5
Brazil	3,248	15.3	980	28.7	1,016	28.3	1,501	22.0	1,724	23.6	2,131	55.7
Dominican Republic	3,413	67.2	2,072	79.2	1,883	80.8	1,979	75.0	2,031	74.6	1,869	80.3
Venezuela	406	33.5	172	45.9	206	29.6	701	7.8	1,085	7.5	1,456	87.9
Ecuador	2,346	29.5	1,569	36.4	1,430	34.1	1,427	32.6	1,397	36.3	1,427	62.2
Jamaica	1,491	78.3	1,043	80.0	868	73.8	1,081	57.4	1,110	61.1	1,095	91.4
All other countries	19,586	36.2	10,840	48.3	9,531	41.9	10,574	37.1	19,922	24.0	16,281	62.9

Note: Fiscal year (Oct. 1-Sept. 30) data. Excludes criminals removed by Customs and Border Protection. (1) Persons with a prior criminal conviction.

Gun Violence Incidents and Deaths, 2016-20

Source: Gun Violence Archive

The Gun Violence Archive is an independent data collection and research group with no affiliation with any advocacy organization. Since 2013, it has maintained an online archive of gun violence incidents, which it collects daily from more than 7,500 media, law enforcement, government, and commercial sources.

(number of actual deaths, injuries, or incidents verified as of Sept. 4, 2020; 2020 data are for partial year)

	2016	2017	2018	2019	2020		2016	2017	2018	2019	2020
Total gun violence incidents	56,637	59,597	55,261	NA	NA	Home invasions	2,568	2,564	2,096	NA	NA
						Defensive uses	2,001	2,110	1,897	1,590	957
Deaths[1]	15,117	15,699	14,834	15,404	12,258	Unintentional shootings	2,224	2,061	1,686	1,891	1,483
Injuries	30,654	31,258	28,406	30,125	25,195	**Officer-involved incidents**					
Children killed or injured	672	733	667	695	660	Officer shot or killed	302	303	280	371	280
Teens killed or injured	3,146	3,258	2,886	3,114	2,588	Subject-suspect shot or killed	2,029	2,156	2,188	2,077	1,550
Mass shootings[2]	382	346	337	418	422						

NA = Not available. **Note:** Children are age 11 or under; teens are age 12-17. Table does not include deaths from suicide unless otherwise noted. (1) In 2019-20, includes homicide, murder, unintentional shootings, and defensive gun use. (2) Four or more people shot and/or killed in a single event, not including the shooter.

Hate Crimes by Offense Type and Bias Motivation, 2018

Source: *Hate Crime Statistics, 2018*, Federal Bureau of Investigation (FBI), U.S. Dept. of Justice

Hate crimes are defined as crimes motivated in whole or in part by the offender's bias against a characteristic such as race, ethnicity, or religion. The Hate Crime Statistics Act of 1990 led to the collection of hate crime data as part of the FBI's Uniform Crime Reporting (UCR) program. Not all agencies that participate in the UCR program submit hate crime data, so the data presented is not representative of the nation as a whole.

Bias motivation	Total offenses	Crimes against persons				Crimes against property					Crimes against society[3]
		Aggravated assault	Simple assault	Intimidation	Other[1]	Robbery	Burglary	Larceny-theft	Destruction/ damage/ vandalism	Other[2]	
Total	8,496	1,026	1,895	2,560	85	132	131	330	1,876	172	289
Single-bias incidents	8,327	1,017	1,882	2,468	85	131	129	325	1,830	171	289
Race/ethnicity/ancestry	4,954	659	1,121	1,627	38	68	76	195	854	92	224
Anti-white	1,001	114	250	289	18	15	24	79	91	29	92
Anti-Black or African American	2,325	323	486	908	8	14	24	22	474	16	50
Anti-American Indian or Alaska Native	204	6	30	11	5	2	8	49	14	22	57
Anti-Asian, Native Hawaiian, other Pac. Isl.	197	23	52	67	0	4	2	8	33	3	5
Anti-multiple races, group	166	7	16	60	0	1	3	5	68	2	4
Anti-Arab	100	18	17	37	0	2	2	4	8	3	9
Anti-Hispanic or Latino	644	129	197	190	5	23	8	8	73	8	3
Anti-other race/ethnicity/ancestry	317	39	73	65	2	7	5	20	93	9	4
Religion	1,550	63	161	406	23	12	25	50	723	48	39
Anti-Jewish	896	24	65	243	19	5	2	3	522	11	2
Anti-Catholic	59	3	3	11	0	0	2	3	24	9	4
Anti-Protestant	38	4	4	3	0	0	0	7	15	3	2
Anti-Islamic (Muslim)	225	14	53	102	0	4	2	3	44	2	1
Anti-other religion[4]	276	17	32	36	4	3	17	31	91	20	25
Anti-multiple religions, group	50	1	3	11	0	0	2	2	24	2	5
Anti-atheism/agnosticism/etc.	6	0	1	0	0	0	0	1	3	1	0
Sexual orientation	1,404	245	468	356	11	32	18	44	214	11	5
Anti-gay (male)	839	160	297	198	6	23	10	15	125	4	1
Anti-lesbian	171	28	44	63	2	2	3	2	23	2	2
Anti-lesbian, gay, bisexual, or transgender (mixed group)	353	53	119	84	1	7	4	21	60	3	1
Anti-heterosexual	20	2	5	5	1	0	0	3	2	2	0
Anti-bisexual	21	2	3	6	1	0	1	3	4	0	1
Gender	58	5	13	20	5	2	0	3	5	3	2
Anti-male	26	5	5	6	3	2	0	1	1	2	1
Anti-female	32	0	8	14	2	0	0	2	4	1	1
Gender identity	184	29	64	40	2	14	3	4	22	2	4
Anti-transgender	157	26	56	37	1	14	2	2	15	2	2
Anti-gender non-conforming	27	3	8	3	1	0	1	2	7	0	2
Disability	177	16	55	19	6	3	7	29	12	15	15
Anti-physical	67	4	22	7	2	2	1	13	6	4	6
Anti-mental	110	12	33	12	4	1	6	16	6	11	9
Multiple-bias incidents[5]	169	9	13	92	0	1	2	5	46	1	0

(1) Includes murder, nonnegligent manslaughter, rape (revised definition only), and additional offenses not shown here in detail. (2) Includes arson, motor vehicle theft, and additional offenses not shown here in detail. (3) Includes drug or narcotic offenses, gambling and prostitution offenses, weapon law violations, and animal cruelty offenses where society as a whole is considered the victim. (4) Includes offenses against religions not shown. (5) Incidents in which one or more offense types are motivated by two or more biases.

Federal Sentence Length by Type of Crime, 2019

Source: *2019 Sourcebook of Federal Sentencing Statistics*, U.S. Sentencing Commission

Data based on court documentation for federal cases involving felonies and misdemeanors (excluding petty misdemeanors) in which the offender was sentenced in fiscal year 2019 (Oct. 1, 2018-Sept. 30, 2019). Excludes cases where data was missing or incomplete.

Type of crime[1]	Mean months	Median months	Number of cases	Type of crime[1]	Mean months	Median months	Number of cases
Total	43	18	75,809	Fraud/theft/embezzlement	22	12	6,212
Administration of justice	12	8	694	Immigration	9	6	29,225
Antitrust	6	4	20	Individual rights[2]	31	6	64
Arson	76	60	68	Kidnapping	171	120	96
Assault	65	36	766	Manslaughter	70	60	74
Bribery/corruption	22	12	340	Money laundering	61	33	1,174
Burglary/trespass	16	14	63	Murder	255	240	373
Child pornography	103	84	1,367	National defense	43	24	188
Commercialized vice	24	20	90	Obscenity/other sex offenses	20	18	389
Drug possession	2	0	485	Prison offenses	11	8	621
Drug trafficking	76	60	19,811	Robbery	109	92	1,825
Environmental	4	0	165	Sexual abuse	205	180	1,165
Extortion/racketeering	32	27	182	Stalking/harassing	29	24	222
Firearms	50	38	8,378	Tax	16	12	547
Food and drug	9	0	48	Other[3]	3	0	881
Forgery/counter/copyright	15	12	276				

(1) Applicable offense with the highest sentencing range. (2) For example, obstructing an election or registration and intercepting communications or eavesdropping among other individual-rights offenses. (3) Includes interference with a flight crew and evading reporting or recordkeeping requirements involving chemicals among other offenses not within any of the other categories.

American Deaths in Terrorist Attacks, 1995-2017

Source: Global Terrorism Database, National Consortium for the Study of Terrorism and Responses to Terrorism (START)

Year	Total attacks in U.S.	Total fatalities in U.S.	U.S. fatalities in U.S.	U.S. fatalities worldwide	Year	Total attacks in U.S.	Total fatalities in U.S.	U.S. fatalities in U.S.	U.S. fatalities worldwide
1995	60	178	177	195	2007	8	0	0	1
1996	35	2	2	36	2008	18	2	2	14
1997	40	2	1	14	2009	11	18	18	19
1998	31	4	3	135	2010	17	4	4	6
1999	53	20	20	25	2011	10	0	0	3
2000	32	0	0	36	2012	20	7	6	12
2001	41	3,008	2,913	2,915	2013	20	23	21	29
2002	33	4	0	30	2014	29	26	26	41
2003	32	0	0	17	2015	38	54	53	68
2004	9	0	0	5	2016	64	68	59	79
2005	21	0	0	3	2017	65	95	84	99
2006	6	1	1	4	Total	694	3,516	3,390	3,786

Note: Number of fatalities includes those of perpetrators. Fatalities worldwide do not include deaths in Afghanistan and Iraq.

Notable Terrorist Incidents Worldwide Since 1971

Source: U.S. Dept. of State; *Facts On File World News Digest*; World Almanac research

Selected noteworthy incidents, excluding most assassinations, kidnappings, and military targets. Does not include all incidents in Iraq or Afghanistan, 2001-present; see also Chronology of the Year's Events.

1971—Mar. 1: Senate wing of U.S. Capitol Building in Wash., DC, bombed by Weather Underground; no deaths.

1972—July 21: "Bloody Friday." Provisional IRA exploded 20+ bombs across Belfast, N. Ireland; 9 killed, hundreds injured. **Sept. 5:** Palestinian group Black September killed 2 Israeli athletes and seized 9 others at Olympic Village in Munich, W. Germany, during Summer Olympics; 9 hostages, 5 militants, 1 Ger. officer died in botched rescue.

1973—Dec. 17: Palestinian gunmen attacked Rome airport and bombed plane on tarmac; hijacked Lufthansa plane with 5 Italian hostages to Athens, Greece, then to Kuwait; 31 killed in all.

1974—June 17: Houses of Parliament in London, England, bombed by Provisional IRA; 11 injured.

1975—Jan. 27: Puerto Rican FALN nationalists bombed Fraunces Tavern in New York City; 4 killed, 53 injured. **Jan. 29:** U.S. State Dept. building in Wash., DC, bombed by Weather Underground; no deaths.

1976—June 27: Palestinian and Baader-Meinhof militants forced Air France jet to land in Entebbe, Uganda. Israeli army rescued 103 hostages from airport terminal in battle with terrorists and Ugandan troops, July 3-4; 32 killed in all.

1978—Mar. 11: Palestinian militants shot civilians and hijacked bus with hostages from Haifa to Tel Aviv, Israel. Bus exploded during firefight with police at a roadblock; 38 killed.

1979—Nov. 4: Iranian radicals seized U.S. embassy in Tehran, taking 66 Americans hostage. 52 were held until Jan. 20, 1981. **Nov. 20:** Around 200 Islamic fundamentalists opposed to the Saudi monarchy seized Grand Mosque in Mecca, Saudi Arabia, and held hundreds of pilgrims hostage. Saudi forces retook mosque Dec. 4; about 270 died.

1980—Feb. 27: Members of leftist guerrilla group April 19 Movement (M-19) seized Dominican Republic embassy in Bogota, Colombia; 80 hostages taken, 18 held until Apr. 27.

1983—Apr. 18: Hezbollah suicide truck bomb at U.S. embassy in Beirut, Lebanon, killed 63. **Oct. 9:** N. Korean agents ambushed a S. Korean govt. delegation in Rangoon, Burma, killing 21. **Oct. 23:** Hezbollah suicide truck bombings of U.S. and French military bases, Beirut, Lebanon; 242 Americans, 58 French killed.

1984—Sept. 20: U.S. embassy annex nr. Beirut, Lebanon, bombed, killing approx. 20. **Sept. 20:** In worst bioterrorism attack in U.S. history, members of Rajneesh cult contaminated an Oregon salsa bar with salmonella, sickening 751.

1985—Apr. 12: Bomb blast at restaurant nr. U.S. air base in Torrejon, Spain; 18 killed. **June 14:** Hezbollah members hijacked TWA Flight 847 with 153 passengers and crew to Beirut, Lebanon; 39 held for 17 days, 1 U.S. Navy sailor killed. **June 23:** Air India Flight 182 destroyed by bomb off coast of Ireland; 329 killed. Blamed on Sikh terrorists. **Oct. 7:** Four Palestinians hijacked Italian cruise ship *Achille Lauro*; 1 passenger killed. **Nov. 23:** EgyptAir Flight 648 from Athens, Greece, to Cairo hijacked to Malta by Palestinian group Abu Nidal; 60 killed in rescue. **Dec. 27:** Palestinian militants opened fire at El-Al (Isr.) airline counters at Rome and Vienna airports; 19 killed.

1986—Apr. 5: Nightclub in Berlin, W. Germany, bombed; 3 killed, incl. 2 U.S. service personnel, 200+ hurt. 3 Libyan embassy workers in Germany convicted.

1987—Apr. 17: Bomb in Sri Lankan capital killed 100+; blamed on Tamil rebels who, 4 days later, attacked Sinhalese travelers on highway, killing 127. **June 19:** Basque group ETA bombed supermarket garage in Barcelona, Spain; 21 killed. **Nov. 29:** Bomb planted by N. Korean agents exploded on Korean Air Lines Flight 858 over Indian Ocean; 115 killed.

1988—Dec. 21: Pan Am Flight 103 exploded over Lockerbie, Scotland, killing all 259 aboard and 11 on ground; Libya took responsibility for bombing in Aug. 2003.

1989—Sept. 19: French UTA Flight 722 from Congo Republic to Paris destroyed by bomb in midair over Niger; 170 killed.

1992—Mar. 17: Israeli embassy in Buenos Aires, Argentina, bombed; 28 killed, 200+ injured. Hezbollah suspected.

1993—Feb. 26: Truck bomb exploded in World Trade Center garage in New York City; 6 killed. Blast later linked to al-Qaeda. **Mar. 12-19:** At least 11 bombs ripped through Bombay and Calcutta, India; 300+ killed.

1994—Feb. 25: U.S.-born Israeli settler Baruch Goldstein opened fire in mosque in Hebron, West Bank; about 30 Muslim worshippers killed. **July 18:** Buenos Aires, Argentina, Jewish center bombed; 87 killed. Blamed on Hezbollah.

1995—Mar. 20: Twelve killed and over 5,000 injured when Japanese cult members released sarin nerve gas in Tokyo subway cars. **Apr. 19:** Murrah Federal Building in Oklahoma City bombed, killing 168. Timothy McVeigh and Terry Nichols convicted. McVeigh executed in 2001; Nichols sentenced to life in prison. **Nov. 13:** U.S. military compound in Riyadh, Saudi Arabia, bombed by Islamic Movement of Change; 7 killed.

1996—Jan. 31: Tamil Tigers drove explosives-laden truck into Central Bank in Colombo, Sri Lanka; 90 killed. **June 25:** Fuel truck exploded outside Khobar Towers, U.S. military complex in Dhahran, Saudi Arabia; killed 19. **July 27:** Bomb exploded in Atlanta, GA, during Olympic Games; killed 2, injured 100+. Extremist Eric Robert Rudolph sentenced to life in prison, 2005. **Dec. 3:** Bomb exploded on subway in Paris; 4 killed, 86 injured. Algerian Islamic extremist group suspected.

1997—Nov. 17: Gamaa al-Islamiya militants killed 58 tourists and 4 Egyptians in Valley of the Kings nr. Luxor, Egypt.

1998—Aug. 7: U.S. embassies in Nairobi, Kenya, and Dar-es-Salaam, Tanzania, bombed; 257 people killed. Al-Qaeda claimed responsibility. **Aug. 15:** IRA car bomb outside courthouse in Omagh, N. Ireland, killed 29. **Oct. 18:** National Liberation Army of Colombia blew up Ocensa oil pipeline; about 71 killed.

1999—Sept. 9-16: Three buildings bombed in Moscow and Volgodonsk, Russia; about 300 killed. Chechen rebels blamed.

2000—Oct. 12: Small boat assisting in docking of USS *Cole* exploded alongside it in Aden, Yemen; 17 U.S. sailors killed. Blamed on al-Qaeda.

2001—Sept. 11: 19 al-Qaeda terrorists hijacked 4 U.S. domestic flights, including 2 planes that crashed into New York City's World Trade Center towers and 1 into Pentagon. Total dead minus hijackers: 2,977; deadliest terrorist attack yet on U.S. soil. **Sept.-Nov. 7:** Letters tainted with deadly anthrax bacteria mailed through U.S. postal system killed 5, sickened 17; investigation concluded in 2010 that government-employed microbiologist Bruce Ivins, who committed suicide in 2008, was responsible.

2002—**Mar. 27:** Suicide bombing at hotel in Netanya, Israel, during Passover celebration; 27 killed. **Oct. 12:** Resort in Bali, Indonesia, bombed; 202 dead. Jemaah Islamiah blamed. **Oct. 23:** Chechen guerrillas seized theater in Moscow, held 700+ hostages. Russian authorities gassed theater; most guerrillas and about 128 hostages killed. **Dec. 27:** Chechen rebels plowed truck bomb into pro-Russian govt. headquarters in Grozny, Chechnya; 80 killed, 152 injured.

2003—**May 12-13:** Al-Qaeda militants detonated car bombs at 3 residential complexes used by Westerners in Riyadh, Saudi Arabia; 34 killed. **May 16:** Five explosions in Casablanca, Morocco; 44 killed. Blamed on al-Qaeda. **Aug. 19:** UN headquarters in Baghdad bombed by truck; 22 killed, incl. UN envoy to Iraq. **Aug. 25:** 2 bombs exploded in taxis in Mumbai, India; 46 killed. Islamic militants suspected. **Nov. 15:** Two synagogues in Istanbul, Turkey, bombed; 25 killed. **Nov. 20:** British consulate and offices of HSBC bombed in Istanbul, Turkey; 27 killed. Blamed on al-Qaeda. **Dec. 5:** Suicide bombing on commuter train in Yessentuki, Russia; 44 killed. Blamed on Chechen rebels.

2004—**Feb. 6:** Bomb exploded in Moscow subway; 39 killed, 130 injured. Chechen rebels blamed. **Mar. 11:** Al-Qaeda cell bombed 4 commuter trains during morning rush hour in Madrid, Spain; 191 killed, about 1,200 injured. **May 29:** Al-Qaeda militants stormed foreigner compound in Khobar, Saudi Arabia, taking hostages; 22 killed. **Aug. 24:** Chechen suicide bombers caused crash of two Russian passenger planes in diff. parts of Russia; 90 killed. **Sept. 1:** Chechen militants seized school in Beslan, in North Ossetia, Russia; held 1,000+ hostage for 3 days before Russian troops stormed school. About 330 killed, incl. 27 hostage-takers.

2005—**July 7:** Four bombs exploded on 3 separate subways and 1 bus in London, Eng.; 52 killed, about 700 injured. **July 23:** Three car bombs explode nr. Sharm el-Sheik, Egypt, resorts; about 90 killed. **Nov. 9:** 3 suicide bombings targeted hotels in Amman, Jordan; killed 56. Al-Qaeda in Iraq took responsibility.

2006—**July 11:** 8 explosions struck 7 different trains and 1 station of public commuter rail system in Mumbai, India; 207 killed. Lashkar-e-Qahhar (Army of Terror) claimed responsibility.

2007—**Feb. 19:** Train traveling between New Delhi and border with Pakistan caught fire, 68 killed; Indian ministers blamed Muslim militants for trying to disrupt peace talks between India and Pakistan. **Dec. 11:** Two coordinated car bombs went off outside govt. building and UN office building in Algiers, Algeria; 41 killed, incl. 17 UN employees, 170 wounded.

2008—**Sept. 20:** Suicide bomber in truck set off explosion outside of Marriott Hotel in Islamabad, Pakistan; 53 killed, 271 wounded. **Nov. 26-29:** Series of attacks and bombings on luxury hotels and high-profile targets in Mumbai, India; 171 killed, 300 injured.

2009—**Feb. 20:** Suicide bomber targeted Shiite funeral in Dera Ismail Khan, Pakistan; 30 killed. **Nov. 5:** U.S. Army major opened fire on Fort Hood (TX) military base, killing 13 and wounding 30+. **Dec. 25:** A Nigerian man failed to blow up a flight from Amsterdam to Detroit with bomb hidden in his underpants.

2010—**Jan. 1:** Taliban suicide bomber killed more than 100 on playground in NW Pakistan. **Mar. 29:** Two female Chechen separatists detonated suicide bombs at two landmark Moscow subway stations, killing at least 40. **July 9:** Suicide bombers targeted tribal elders in Mohmand, Pakistan, killing more than 100. **July 11:** Several bombs claimed by al-Shabab exploded simultaneously in Kampala, Uganda, killing more than 70 people who had gathered to watch the World Cup final broadcast.

2011—**Jan. 24:** Suicide bomber killed 35 in Moscow's Domodedovo Airport, location chosen to maximize deaths of foreigners. **July 22:** Anders Behring Breivik, right-wing Norwegian extremist, set off a bomb in van outside govt. buildings in Oslo, then massacred dozens of young people at a summer camp on Tyrifjorden Lake, bringing death toll to 77.

2012—**Jan. 21:** Series of attacks by Islamist extremist group Boko Haram killed more than 185 in Kano, Nigeria. **May 21:** Suicide bomber claimed by al-Qaeda in the Arabian Peninsula (AQAP) killed more than 100 soldiers during military

parade rehearsal nr. Yemeni presidential palace. **Aug. 5:** White supremacist fatally shot 6 worshippers at a Sikh temple before killing himself, Oak Creek, WI. **Sept. 11:** Terrorists stormed U.S. embassy in Benghazi, Libya, killing 4 Americans, including U.S. Amb. J. Christopher Stevens.

2013—**Apr. 15:** Two bombs exploded nr. Boston Marathon finish line, killing 3 and injuring 264; 4-day search ended in death of suspect Tamerlan Tsarnaev and capture of his brother, Dzhokhar, a naturalized Chechen immigrant. **Sept. 21:** Al-Shabab, a Somali militant group, killed up to 70 people and wounded at least 175 at a Nairobi, Kenya, shopping mall.

2014—**Apr.-May:** Islamist extremist group Boko Haram kidnapped more than 250 girls from schools in Nigeria; killed more than 150 villagers in Gamboru. **Dec. 15:** Nine Taliban gunmen attacked military-affiliated school in Peshawar, Pakistan, executing about 150, including 132 children.

2015—**Jan. 7:** Gunmen stormed Paris offices of *Charlie Hebdo*, a satirical newspaper, killing 12. Two days later, French police killed suspects, brothers who identified themselves as belonging to AQAP. **Mar. 18:** Gunmen killed 21 tourists and a police officer at Tunisia's National Bardo Museum. Several terrorist groups claimed credit. **Apr. 2:** Al-Shabab militants killed 147 students at Kenya's Garissa Univ. after separating Christian and Muslim students. **June 17:** Lone white-supremacist gunman killed 9, incl. a state senator, in a historically Black church in Charleston, SC. **Oct. 31:** Terrorists downed a Russian charter flight shortly after takeoff from Egyptian resort, killing all 224 onboard. Egyptian affiliate of the Sunni extremist group the Islamic State in Iraq and Syria (ISIS) said it smuggled a soda-can bomb onto plane. **Nov. 13:** Series of coordinated suicide bombings and other attacks by ISIS on Paris cafes, a soccer stadium, and a concert hall killed 137 (incl. 7 attackers); wounded 350+. **Dec. 2:** A heavily armed married couple opened fire on the husband's coworkers at a holiday party for San Bernardino (CA) County Health Dept., killing 14, wounding 21.

2016—**Mar. 22:** Three explosions in Brussels, two at the airport and one at a busy subway station, killed 35 people (incl. 3 bombers) and injured 300+. ISIS claimed credit; investigators linked perpetrators to 2015 Paris attacks. **June 12:** Lone gunman killed 49 people and wounded 53 at a gay nightclub in Orlando, FL. **July 7:** A heavily armed man shot and killed five police officers and wounded seven other officers and two civilians in downtown Dallas, TX, during peaceful protest. **July 14:** Tunisian-born man drove rented truck into Bastille Day crowds in Nice, France, killing 86 and injuring 400+. **Dec. 19:** Tunisian man on Germany's terror watch list drove hijacked truck through outdoor market in Berlin, killing 12; 56+ injured.

2017—**May 22:** Suicide bomber detonated in entrance hall of Manchester, England, arena as fans left a concert by U.S. singer Ariana Grande, killing 22; 800 injured. ISIS claimed responsibility. **June 3:** Three assailants in a van hit pedestrians on London Bridge before exiting vehicle and attacking people with knives; 8 killed and 48+ injured. **Aug. 18:** A Moroccan man killed 2 and injured 8 with a knife in Turku, Finland; country's first terror attack. **Oct. 14:** Two truck bombs detonated in Mogadishu, Somalia, leaving 512 dead, 300+ injured. Blamed on al-Shabab. **Nov. 24:** Attack on Sufi mosque in Bir al-Abed, Egypt, by extremists affiliated with ISIS, killed 311 people and injured 100+ others.

2018—**Oct. 27:** Man opened fire inside of Tree of Life Congregation synagogue in Pittsburgh, PA, killing 11 worshippers.

2019—**Mar. 15:** Australian gunman attacked two mosques in Christchurch, New Zealand, killing 51. **Apr. 21:** Nine Muslim extremists with alleged links to Islamic State staged suicide bombings in churches and hotels on Easter Sunday in Sri Lanka, killing more than 250. **Aug. 3:** Gunman killed 23 and injured 20+ at Walmart store in El Paso, TX; claimed to be targeting Hispanics. **Aug. 18:** Suicide bomber killed at least 80 people and injured 180+ at a wedding party in Kabul, Afghanistan. ISIS claimed responsibility. **Dec. 28:** Al-Shabab claimed credit for truck bombing at a Mogadishu, Somalia, police checkpoint that killed 85.

Notable Assassinations Since 1865

1865—**Apr. 14:** U.S. Pres. Abraham Lincoln shot by John Wilkes Booth, well-known actor with Confederate sympathies, at Ford's Theater in Washington, DC; died Apr. 15.

1881—**Mar. 13:** Alexander II of Russia. **July 2:** U.S. Pres. James A. Garfield shot by Charles J. Guiteau, disappointed office seeker, in Washington, DC; died Sept. 19.

1894—**June 24:** French Pres. Sadi Carnot by Sante Caserio, Italian anarchist, in Lyon.

1898—**Sept. 10:** Empress Elizabeth of Austria stabbed by Luigi Luccheni, Italian anarchist.

1900—**July 29:** Umberto I, king of Italy, by an anarchist.

1901—**Sept. 6:** U.S. Pres. William McKinley shot by Leon Czolgosz, anarchist, in Buffalo, NY; died Sept. 14.

1908—**Feb. 1:** King Carlos I of Portugal and his son Luís Filipe, in Lisbon.

1913—**Feb. 23:** Mexican Pres. Francisco I. Madero and Vice Pres. José María Pino Suárez. **Mar. 18:** King George of Greece, by an anarchist.

1914—**June 28:** Archduke Franz Ferdinand of Austria-Hungary and his wife shot by Gavrilo Princip, Serb nationalist, in Sarajevo, Bosnia.

1916—**Dec. 30:** Grigory Rasputin, Russian mystic and court figure, by group of aristocrats.

1918—**July 12:** Grand Duke Michael of Russia, at Perm. **July 16:** Nicholas II, former (abdicated) czar of Russia; his wife, Czarina Alexandra; their son, Czarevitch Alexis; their daughters, Grand Duchesses Olga, Tatiana, Marie, Anastasia; and 4 members of household executed by Bolsheviks at Ekaterinburg.

1920—**May 20:** Mexican Pres. Gen. Venustiano Carranza, in Tlaxcalantongo.

1922—Aug. 22: Michael Collins, Irish revolutionary, in West Cork. **Dec. 16:** Polish Pres. Gabriel Narutowicz in Warsaw.
1923—July 20: Gen. Francisco "Pancho" Villa, ex-rebel leader, in Parral, Mexico.
1928—July 17: Gen. Alvaro Obregon, president-elect of Mexico, in San Angel.
1932—May 6: French Pres. Paul Doumer shot by Russian émigré, Pavel Gorgulov, in Paris.
1934—July 25: Austrian Chancellor Engelbert Dollfuss by Nazis, in Vienna.
1935—Sept. 8: Sen. Huey P. Long, former Louisiana governor, shot by Dr. Carl Austin Weiss, son-in-law of political opponent, in Baton Rouge; died Sept. 10.
1940—Aug. 20: Leon Trotsky (Lev Bronstein), exiled Soviet commissar of war, fatally wounded with ice ax by Soviet agent nr. Mexico City.
1948—Jan. 30: Leader of movement for Indian independence Mohandas K. Gandhi (Mahatma) shot by Hindu fanatic in New Delhi. **Sept. 17:** Count Folke Bernadotte, UN mediator for Palestine, by Jewish extremists in Jerusalem.
1951—July 20: Jordanian King Abdullah ibn Hussein. **Oct. 16:** Prime Min. Liaquat Ali Khan of Pakistan shot, in Rawalpindi.
1956—Sept. 21: Pres. Anastasio Somoza of Nicaragua shot in Leon by a young poet; died Sept. 29.
1957—July 26: Guatemalan Pres. Carlos Castillo Armas, in Guatemala City by one of his guards.
1958—July 14: King Faisal of Iraq, Crown Prince Abdullah, and **July 15,** Prem. Nuri as-Said, by rebels in Baghdad.
1959—Sept. 25: Prime Min. Solomon Bandaranaike of Ceylon (Sri Lanka), by Buddhist monk in Colombo.
1961—Jan. 17: First elected prime min. of Dem. Rep. of the Congo, Patrice Lumumba, in Katanga Prov. by political rivals. **May 30:** Dominican dictator Rafael Trujillo, nr. Ciudad Trujillo.
1963—June 12: Medgar Evers, NAACP's Mississippi field secretary, shot by Byron De La Beckwith in Jackson, MS. **Nov. 2:** Pres. Ngo Dinh Diem of South Vietnam and his brother, Ngo Dinh Nhu, in military coup. **Nov. 22:** U.S. Pres. John F. Kennedy shot while riding in motorcade through downtown Dallas, TX; accused gunman Lee Harvey Oswald murdered by nightclub owner Jack Ruby while awaiting trial.
1965—Jan. 21: Iranian Prem. Hassan Ali Mansour, in Tehran. **Feb. 21:** Malcolm X, Black nationalist leader, shot by 3 men linked to Nation of Islam at New York City rally.
1966—Sept. 6: Prime Min. Hendrik F. Verwoerd of South Africa stabbed to death in parliament at Cape Town.
1968—Apr. 4: Rev. Martin Luther King Jr. fatally shot in Memphis, TN; James Earl Ray convicted of crime. **June 5:** Sen. Robert F. Kennedy (D, NY) shot in Los Angeles; died June 6. Sirhan Sirhan convicted of crime.
1971—Nov. 28: Jordanian Prime Min. Wasfi Tal by Palestinian guerrillas, in Cairo, Egypt.
1973—Mar. 2: U.S. Amb. Cleo A. Noel Jr., U.S. Charge d'Affaires George C. Moore, and Belgian Charge d'Affaires Guy Eid by Palestinian guerrillas, in Khartoum, Sudan. **Dec. 20:** Spanish Prem. Luis Carrero Blanco in car bombing by Basque separatist group ETA, in Madrid.
1974—Aug. 19: U.S. Amb. to Cyprus, Rodger P. Davies, by sniper's bullet in Nicosia.
1975—Feb. 11: Pres. Richard Ratsimandrava of Madagascar shot in Antananarivo. **Mar. 25:** Saudi Arabian King Faisal shot by nephew Prince Musad Abdel Aziz, in Riyadh. **Aug. 15:** Bangladesh Pres. Sheik Mujibur Rahman killed in coup.
1976—Feb. 13: Nigerian head of state, Gen. Murtala Ramat Mohammed, by self-styled young revolutionaries.
1977—Mar. 16: Kamal Jumblatt, Lebanese Druze chieftain, shot nr. Beirut. **Mar. 18:** Rep. of the Congo Pres. Marien Ngouabi shot in Brazzaville.
1978—May 9: Former Italian Prem. Aldo Moro killed by Red Brigades terrorists who had abducted him Mar. 16 in Rome and held him hostage. **July 9:** Former Iraqi Prem. Abdul Razzak al-Naif shot in London.
1979—Aug. 27: Lord Mountbatten, WWII hero, and 2 others when a bomb exploded on his fishing boat off coast of Co. Sligo, Ireland. IRA claimed responsibility. **Oct. 26:** S. Korean Pres. Park Chung Hee and 6 bodyguards fatally shot by Kim Jae Kyu, head of S. Korean intelligence agency.
1980—Apr. 12: Liberian Pres. William R. Tolbert, in military coup. **Sept. 17:** Former Nicaraguan Pres. Anastasio Somoza Debayle shot in Paraguay.
1981—Oct. 6: Egyptian Pres. Anwar al-Sadat shot by commandos while reviewing military parade in Cairo; 7 others killed.
1982—Sept. 14: Lebanese Pres.-elect Bashir Gemayel killed by bomb in east Beirut.
1983—Aug. 21: Philippine opposition leader Benigno Aquino Jr. shot at Manila Intl. Airport.
1984—Oct. 31: Indian Prime Min. Indira Gandhi shot by 2 Sikh bodyguards in New Delhi.
1986—Feb. 28: Swedish Prime Min. Olof Palme shot on Stockholm street; case officially closed in June 2020, when a

Swedish prosecutor identified the assassin as Stig Engström, who died in 2000.
1987—June 1: Lebanese Prem. Rashid Karami killed when bomb exploded aboard helicopter.
1988—Apr. 16: PLO military chief Khalil Wazir (Abu Jihad) gunned down by Israeli commandos in Tunisia.
1989—Aug. 18: Colombian pres. candidate Luis Carlos Galán killed by Medellín cartel drug traffickers at campaign rally in Bogotá. **Nov. 22:** Lebanese Pres. Rene Moawad killed when bomb exploded next to his motorcade.
1990—Mar. 22: Colombian pres. candidate Bernardo Jaramillo Ossa shot at airport in Bogotá.
1991—May 21: Former Indian Prime Min. Rajiv Gandhi killed by bomb during election rally in Madras.
1992—June 29: Algerian Pres. Mohamed Boudiaf shot in Annaba.
1993—May 1: Sri Lankan Pres. Ranasinghe Premadasa killed by suicide bomber in Colombo.
1994—Apr. 6: Burundian Pres. Cyprien Ntaryamira and Rwandan Pres. Juvénal Habyarimana killed with 8 others when their plane was shot down, precipitating Rwandan genocide.
1995—Nov. 4: Israeli Prime Min. Yitzhak Rabin shot by Jewish extremist at peace rally in Tel Aviv.
1996—Oct. 2: Andrei Lukanov, former Bulgarian prime min., shot outside of Sofia home.
1998—Apr. 26: Guatemalan Roman Catholic Bishop Juan José Gerardi Conedera, human rights champion, beaten to death in Guatemala City.
1999—Apr. 9: Niger Pres. Ibrahim Bare Mainassara killed by dissident soldiers. **Oct. 27:** Armenian Prime Min. Vazgen Sarkissian, with 7 others, shot during session of parliament.
2001—Jan. 16: Dem. Rep. of Congo Pres. Laurent Kabila shot to death by bodyguard at pres. palace in Kinshasa. **June 1:** Nepal's King Birendra, Queen Aiswarya, and 7 other royals fatally shot by Crown Prince Dipendra, who then killed self.
2002—July 6: Afghan Vice Pres. Haji Abdul Qadir shot outside his office in Kabul.
2003—Mar. 12: Serbian Prime Min. Zoran Djindjic shot by paramilitary snipers outside govt. headquarters in Belgrade.
2004—Feb. 13: Former Chechen Pres. Zelimkhan Yandarbiyev killed after car exploded in Qatar. **Mar. 22:** Sheik Ahmed Yassin, spiritual leader of Hamas, by Israeli missile attack in Gaza City. **May 9:** Chechen Pres. Akhmad Kadyrov by bomb at WWII memorial service in Grozny. **Nov. 2:** Filmmaker Theo van Gogh, critic of Islam and great-grandnephew of painter Vincent van Gogh, shot and stabbed by Muslim militant in Amsterdam.
2005—Jan. 4: Baghdad Gov. Ali al-Haidari gunned down by insurgents in Baghdad, Iraq.
2007—Aug. 2: Oakland Post editor Chauncey Bailey, who was investigating financial status of Your Black Muslim Bakery, shot in Oakland, CA. **Dec. 27:** Benazir Bhutto, former Pakistani prime min. and first female elected leader of a Muslim state, by bomb and gunman later linked to then-Pres. Pervez Musharraf.
2008—Feb. 12: Imad Mughniyeh, top Hezbollah commander and reputed mastermind of the 1983 bombing of U.S. embassy in Beirut, by car bomb in Damascus, Syria. Mughniyeh had been on FBI's Most Wanted Terrorist list. **Oct. 23:** Ivo Pukanic, editor-in-chief of Croatian political newspaper Nacional, killed in Zagreb when bomb exploded in his car.
2009—Mar. 2: Guinea-Bissau's longtime Pres. João Bernardo Vieira shot by army troops outside his home in Bissau. **May 31:** Dr. George Tiller, one of the few doctors in the U.S. to perform abortions late in pregnancy, shot to death in his Wichita, KS, church by anti-abortion extremist.
2011—Sept. 20: Burhanuddin Rabbani, leader of Afghanistan's High Peace Council and a former pres., killed in his Kabul home by assassin with explosives hidden in his turban.
2012—Jan. 11: Iranian nuclear scientist Mostafa Ahmadi Roshan killed by car bomb.
2014—Sept. 1: U.S. airstrikes killed Ahmed Abdi Godane, leader of Somalia-based Islamist militant group al-Shabab.
2015—Feb. 27: Boris Y. Nemtsov, Russian opposition leader and former first deputy prime minister, shot near Red Square.
2016—June 16: UK Labour MP Jo Cox shot and stabbed in West Yorkshire by far-right assailant. **Dec. 20:** Turkish police officer shot Russian ambassador to Turkey, Andrei Karlov, in Ankara. Apparently motivated by Russian military involvement in Syria, the attack was caught on widely distributed video.
2017—Feb. 13: Kim Jong Nam, half-brother to N. Korean leader Kim Jong Un, killed in chemical nerve agent attack at Kuala Lumpur airport. Two women, charged in attack by Malaysian authorities, blamed coercion by N. Korean agents.
2018—Feb. 21: Slovak journalist Ján Kuciak and fiancée shot dead in their home. **Oct. 2:** Saudi journalist Jamal Khashoggi, a U.S. resident, murdered inside Saudi consulate in Istanbul, Turkey; U.S., other intelligence agencies pointed to Saudi crown prince Mohammed bin Salman's involvement.
2020—Jan. 3: Iranian Gen. Qassem Soleimani, killed by U.S. air strike in Baghdad.

MILITARY AFFAIRS

Chairmen of the Joint Chiefs of Staff, 1949-2020

Chairman	Service	Chairman	Service
Gen. of the Army Omar N. Bradley, USA	8/16/1949-8/15/1953	Adm. William J. Crowe Jr., USN	10/1/1985-9/30/1989
Adm. Arthur W. Radford, USN	8/15/1953-8/15/1957	Gen. Colin L. Powell, USA	10/1/1989-9/30/1993
Gen. Nathan F. Twining, USAF	8/15/1957-9/30/1960	Gen. John M. Shalikashvili, USA	10/25/1993-9/30/1997
Gen. Lyman L. Lemnitzer, USA	10/1/1960-9/30/1962	Gen. Henry H. Shelton, USA	10/1/1997-9/30/2001
Gen. Maxwell D. Taylor, USA	10/1/1962-7/1/1964	Gen. Richard B. Myers, USAF	10/1/2001-9/30/2005
Gen. Earle G. Wheeler, USA	7/3/1964-7/2/1970	Gen. Peter Pace, USMC	10/1/2005-9/30/2007
Adm. Thomas H. Moorer, USN	7/2/1970-7/1/1974	Adm. Michael G. Mullen, USN	10/1/2007-9/30/2011
Gen. George S. Brown, USAF	7/1/1974-6/20/1978	Gen. Martin E. Dempsey, USA	10/1/2011-9/30/2015
Gen. David C. Jones, USAF	6/21/1978-6/18/1982	Gen. Joseph F. Dunford Jr., USMC	10/1/2015-9/30/2019
Gen. John W. Vessey Jr., USA	6/18/1982-9/30/1985	Gen. Mark A. Milley, USA	10/1/2019-

Chief Commanding Officers of the U.S. Military

Chairman, Joint Chiefs of Staff: Gen. Mark A. Milley (USA). **Vice Chairman:** Gen. John E. Hyten (USAF)

Date of rank is date when the individual achieved his or her current rank. While serving in any of these positions, or as commander of a unified or specified combatant command, basic pay is $16,441.80 per month. Officers below hold positions listed as of Sept. 21, 2020.

Army

Chief of Staff (CSA)	Date of rank
McConville, James C.	Aug. 9, 2019

Other Generals	
Abrams, Robert B.	Aug. 10, 2015
Clarke, Richard D.	Mar. 29, 2019
Daly, Edward M.	July 2, 2020
Dickinson, James H.	Aug. 20, 2020
Funk, Paul E., II	June 21, 2019
Garrett, Michael X.	Mar. 21, 2019
Hokanson, Daniel R.	Aug. 3, 2020
LaCamera, Paul J.	Nov. 18, 2019
Lyons, Stephen R.	Aug. 24, 2018
Martin, Joseph M.	July 26, 2019
Miller, Austin S.	Sept. 2, 2018
Milley, Mark A.	Aug. 14, 2014
Murray, John M.	Aug. 24, 2018
Nakasone, Paul M.	May 4, 2018
Perna, Gustave F.	Sept. 30, 2016
Townsend, Stephen J.	Mar. 2, 2018

Marine Corps

Commandant of the Marine Corps (CMC)	Date of rank
Berger, David H.	July 11, 2019

Other Generals	
McKenzie, Kenneth F., Jr.	Mar. 28, 2019
Thomas, Gary L.	Oct. 2, 2018

Coast Guard

Commandant, with rank of Admiral	Date of rank
Schultz, Karl L.	June 1, 2018

Vice Commandant, with rank of Admiral

Ray, Charles W.	May 24, 2018

Air Force

Chief of Staff (CSAF or AF/CC)	Date of rank
Brown, Charles Q., Jr.	July 26, 2018

Other Generals	
Bunch, Arnold W., Jr.	May 31, 2019
Harrigian, Jeffrey L.	May 1, 2019
Hyten, John E.	Aug. 15, 2014
Kelly, Mark D.	Aug. 28, 2020
Ray, Timothy M.	Aug. 21, 2018
Raymond, John W.	Oct. 25, 2016
Van Ovost, Jacqueline D.	Aug. 20, 2020
VanHerck, Glen D.	Aug. 20, 2020
Wilsbach, Kenneth S.	July 8, 2020
Wilson, Stephen W.	July 22, 2016
Wolters, Tod D.	Aug. 11, 2016

Navy

Chief of Naval Operations (CNO)	Date of rank
Gilday, Michael (surface warfare)	Aug. 22, 2019

Other Admirals	
Aquilino, John C. (aviator)	May 17, 2018
Burke, Robert P. (submariner)	June 10, 2019
Caldwell, James F., Jr. (submariner)	Aug. 14, 2015
Davidson, Philip S. (surface warfare)	Dec. 19, 2014
Faller, Craig S. (surface warfare)	Nov. 26, 2018
Grady, Christopher W. (surface warfare)	May 4, 2018
Lescher, William K. (aviator)	May 29, 2020
Richard, Charles A. (submariner)	Nov. 18, 2019

Commanders of the Unified Combatant Commands

U.S. European Command, Stuttgart-Vaihingen, Germany:
Gen. Tod D. Wolters (USAF)

U.S. Indo-Pacific Command, Honolulu, Hawaii:
Adm. Philip S. Davidson (USN)

U.S. Special Operations Command, MacDill AFB, Florida:
Gen. Richard D. Clarke (U.S. Army)

U.S. Transportation Command, Scott AFB, Illinois:
Gen. Stephen R. Lyons (U.S. Army)

U.S. Central Command, MacDill AFB, Florida:
Gen. Kenneth F. McKenzie Jr. (USMC)

U.S. Southern Command, Doral, Florida:
Adm. Craig S. Faller (USN)

U.S. Northern Command, Peterson AFB, Colorado:
Gen. Glen D. VanHerck (USAF)

U.S. Strategic Command, Offutt AFB, Nebraska:
Adm. Charles A. Richard (USN)

U.S. Africa Command, Kelley Barracks, Stuttgart, Germany:
Gen. Stephen J. Townsend (U.S. Army)

U.S. Cyber Command, Fort George G. Meade, Maryland:
Gen. Paul M. Nakasone (U.S. Army)

U.S. Space Command, Peterson AFB, Colorado:
Gen. James H. Dickinson (U.S. Army)

North Atlantic Treaty Organization (NATO) International Commands

NATO Headquarters: Chairman, NATO Military Committee:
Air Chief Marshal Stuart Peach (British Armed Forces)
ACO Operational Level Commands:
Joint Force Command Brunssum (JFC Brunssum):
Gen. Jörg Vollmer (German Army), Commander
Joint Force Command Naples (JFC Naples):
Adm. Robert P. Burke (USN), Commander

Strategic Commands:
Allied Command Operations (ACO): Gen. Tod D. Wolters (USAF), Supreme Allied Commander, Europe
Allied Command Transformation (ACT): Gen. André Lanata (French Air Force), Supreme Allied Commander Transformation

Directors of the Central Intelligence Agency, 1946-2020

In 1942, Pres. Franklin D. Roosevelt established the Office of Strategic Services (OSS); it was disbanded in 1945. In 1946, Pres. Harry Truman established the Central Intelligence Group (CIG) to operate under the National Intelligence Authority (NIA). A 1947 law replaced the NIA with the National Security Council (NSC) and the CIG with the Central Intelligence Agency (CIA).

Director	Served	Appointed by President	Director	Served	Appointed by President
Adm. Sidney W. Souers	1946	Truman	William H. Webster	1987-1991	Reagan
Gen. Hoyt S. Vandenberg	1946-1947	Truman	Robert M. Gates	1991-1993	Bush, G. H. W.
Adm. Roscoe H. Hillenkoetter	1947-1950	Truman	R. James Woolsey	1993-1995	Clinton
Gen. Walter Bedell Smith	1950-1953	Truman	John M. Deutch	1995-1996	Clinton
Allen W. Dulles	1953-1961	Eisenhower	George J. Tenet	1997-2004	Clinton
John A. McCone	1961-1965	Kennedy	Porter Goss	2004-2006	Bush, G. W.
Adm. William F. Raborn Jr.	1965-1966	Johnson, L. B.	Gen. Michael V. Hayden	2006-2009	Bush, G. W.
Richard Helms	1966-1973	Johnson, L. B.	Leon E. Panetta	2009-2011	Obama
James R. Schlesinger	1973	Nixon	Gen. David H. Petraeus	2011-2012	Obama
William E. Colby	1973-1976	Nixon	John O. Brennan	2013-2017	Obama
George H. W. Bush	1976-1977	Ford	Michael R. Pompeo	2017-2018	Trump
Adm. Stansfield Turner	1977-1981	Carter	Gina Haspel	2018-	Trump
William J. Casey	1981-1987	Reagan			

U.S. Military Personnel Strength on Active Duty Worldwide, 2020
Source: U.S. Dept. of Defense
(as of Mar. 31, 2020)

Area	Personnel	Area	Personnel	Area	Personnel
TOTAL WORLDWIDE[1]	1,363,816	Regional total[2]	758	Saudi Arabia	346
U.S., TERRITORIES, AND		**FORMER SOVIET UNION**		United Arab Emirates	2,502
SPEC. LOCATIONS		Regional total[2]	197	**Regional total**[2,3]	10,273
Regional total[2]	1,195,221	**EAST ASIA AND PACIFIC**		**EUROPE**	
OTHER WESTERN		Australia	296	Belgium	1,142
HEMISPHERE		British Indian Ocean Territory	245	Germany	34,674
Bahamas, The	66	Japan	55,165	Greece	400
Brazil	51	Korea, South	26,184	Greenland	147
Canada	136	Philippines	196	Hungary	75
Colombia	67	Singapore	213	Italy	12,353
Cuba (Guantánamo)	813	Thailand	111	Netherlands	398
El Salvador	52	**Regional total**[2]	82,690	Norway	669
Honduras	380	**NORTH AFRICA, NEAR EAST, AND**		Poland	175
Mexico	75	**SOUTH ASIA**		Portugal	249
Regional total[2]	1,976	Bahrain	4,074	Romania	125
SUB-SAHARAN AFRICA		Egypt	294	Spain	3,227
Djibouti	120	Israel	98	Turkey	1,702
Kenya	47	Jordan	116	United Kingdom	9,394
Somalia	45	Kuwait	2,018	**Regional total**[2]	65,144
South Africa	47	Qatar	562		

(1) Includes undistributed/other personnel. (2) Most countries and areas with fewer than 100 assigned U.S. military members not listed; regional totals include personnel stationed in countries and areas not shown. (3) Does not include troops deployed to Afghanistan/Iraq/Syria.

U.S. Military Personnel on Active Duty in U.S. States/Territories, 2020
Source: U.S. Dept. of Defense
(as of Mar. 31, 2020)

State/area	Active personnel	Reserve personnel	State/area	Active personnel	Reserve personnel	State/area	Active personnel	Reserve personnel
Alabama	8,730	19,102	Maryland	29,233	19,020	South Dakota	3,451	4,687
Alaska	19,760	4,709	Massachusetts	3,766	14,797	Tennessee	2,467	18,014
Arizona	20,181	15,394	Michigan	2,064	15,325	Texas	121,088	55,635
Arkansas	3,886	10,813	Minnesota	662	18,827	Utah	4,631	11,912
California	162,456	56,944	Mississippi	12,322	16,012	Vermont	168	3,402
Colorado	36,372	13,881	Missouri	17,062	19,477	Virginia	128,957	25,953
Connecticut	6,389	6,839	Montana	3,373	4,251	Washington	61,201	18,039
Delaware	3,619	5,124	Nebraska	6,244	6,001	West Virginia	187	7,807
District of			Nevada	11,777	7,854	Wisconsin	1,097	14,476
Columbia	9,969	4,344	New Hampshire	1,024	4,159	Wyoming	3,202	3,004
Florida	67,429	37,705	New Jersey	7,952	17,601	Unknown[1]	5,857	0
Georgia	68,450	27,773	New Mexico	12,677	5,064	**U.S. total**	1,188,860	783,504
Hawaii	42,797	9,586	New York	19,985	29,063	American Samoa	3	292
Idaho	3,669	5,533	North Carolina	100,936	21,095	Guam	6,183	2,599
Illinois	20,951	24,533	North Dakota	7,501	4,430	Northern Mariana		
Indiana	1,049	17,923	Ohio	7,048	28,116	Islands	2	81
Iowa	265	11,123	Oklahoma	21,455	13,077	Puerto Rico	158	11,507
Kansas	22,004	10,042	Oregon	1,553	9,421	U.S. Virgin		
Kentucky	32,103	12,430	Pennsylvania	2,576	29,003	Islands	10	687
Louisiana	15,731	17,025	Rhode Island	3,635	4,298	Wake Island	5	0
Maine	852	3,557	South Carolina	37,047	17,666	**Territorial total**	6,361	15,166

Note: Armed Forces (AF) Europe and AF Pacific—deployed primarily at sea or not at fixed-duty stations (1,646 reserve)—are not shown. (1) includes undistributed/other personnel.

U.S. Army Personnel on Active Duty, 1940-2020
Source: Dept. of the Army, U.S. Dept. of Defense
(as of midyear, except where noted)

Date	Total strength[1]	Commissioned officers			Warrant officers[3]		Enlisted personnel		
		Total	Male	Female[2]	Male	Female	Total	Male	Female
1940	267,767	17,563	16,624	939	763	—	249,441	249,441	—
1942	3,074,184	203,137	190,662	12,475	3,285	—	2,867,762	2,867,762	—
1943	6,993,102	557,657	521,435	36,222	21,919	—	6,413,526	6,358,200	55,325
1944	7,992,868	740,077	692,351	47,726	36,893	10	7,215,888	7,144,601	71,287
1945	8,266,373	835,403	772,511	62,892	56,216	44	7,374,710	7,283,930	90,780
1946	1,889,690	257,300	240,658	16,642	9,826	18	1,622,546	1,605,847	16,699
1950	591,487	67,784	63,375	4,409	4,760	22	518,921	512,370	6,551
1955	1,107,606	111,347	106,196	5,151	10,552	48	985,659	977,943	7,716
1960	871,348	91,056	86,832	4,224	10,141	39	770,112	761,833	8,279
1965	967,049	101,812	98,029	3,783	10,285	23	854,929	846,409	8,520
1970	1,319,735	143,704	138,469	5,235	23,005	13	1,153,013	1,141,537	11,476
1975	781,316	89,756	85,184	4,572	13,214	22	678,324	640,621	37,703
1980 (Sept. 30)	772,661	85,339	77,843	7,496	13,265	113	673,944	612,593	61,351
1990 (Mar. 31)	746,220	91,330	79,520	11,810	15,177	470	639,713	567,015	72,698
2000	471,633	66,344	56,391	9,953	10,608	781	393,900	333,947	59,953
2005 (Sept. 30)	492,728	69,114	57,675	11,499	11,506	976	406,923	346,194	57,354
2010 (Sept. 30)	566,045	78,588	64,952	13,636	14,106	1,434	467,248	406,871	60,377
2015 (Dec. 31)	482,264	78,586	64,223	14,363	13,577	1,421	384,301	331,620	52,681
2017	466,990	77,040	62,735	14,305	13,088	1,361	372,082	319,313	52,769
2018	468,331	77,850	63,184	14,666	12,987	1,378	372,667	319,270	53,397
2019	472,209	78,883	63,733	15,150	12,905	1,395	375,600	321,500	54,100
2020	476,306	78,739	63,388	15,351	12,818	1,433	379,993	323,683	56,310

— = Not applicable. **Note:** Represents strength of active Army, including Philippine Scouts (1940-46), ret. Regular Army personnel on extended active duty, and National Guard and Reserve personnel on extended active duty; excl. those (e.g., U.S. Military Academy cadets, contract surgeons, and National Guard and Reserve personnel) not on extended active duty. (1) Includes categories not listed, e.g., West Point cadets. Data for 1940-46 include personnel in the Army Air Forces and its predecessors (Air Service and Air Corps). (2) Includes Army Nurse Corps for all years, Women's Army Corps (1942-78), and Medical Specialists Corps (1949 and after). (3) Act of Congress approved Apr. 27, 1926, directed the appointment as warrant officers of field clerks still in active service. Includes flight officers as follows: 1943, 5,700; 1944, 13,615; 1945, 31,117; 1946, 2,580.

U.S. Navy Personnel on Active Duty, 1940-2020

Source: U.S. Dept. of Defense
(as of midyear, except where noted)

Year	Officers	Nurses[1]	Enlisted	Officer candidates[1]	Total[2]	Year	Officers	Nurses[1]	Enlisted	Officer candidates[1]	Total[2]
1940	13,162	442	144,824	2,569	160,997	2011	53,620	—	270,425	—	328,648
1945	320,293	11,086	2,988,207	61,231	3,380,817	2012	53,799	—	262,975	—	321,300
1950	42,687	1,964	331,860	5,037	381,538	2013	54,062	—	263,647	—	322,242
1960	67,456	2,103	544,040	4,385	617,984	2014	54,852	—	265,622	—	323,792
1970	78,488	2,273	605,899	6,000	692,660	2015	54,770	—	268,408	—	326,504
1980	63,100	—	464,100	—	527,200	2016	54,973	—	271,100	—	330,556
1990 (Sept.)	74,429	—	530,133	—	604,562	2017	55,047	—	264,404	—	323,938
1995 (May)	61,075	—	402,626	—	463,701	2018	55,401	—	268,340	—	328,244
2000 (Oct.)	53,698	—	320,212	—	373,910	2019	55,475	—	275,474	—	335,444
2005	54,039	—	305,368	—	363,858	2020	56,248	—	279,147	—	339,782
2010	53,071	—	273,609	—	330,065						

— = Not applicable. (1) Starting in 1980, "Nurses" are included with "Officers," and "Officer candidates" are included with "Enlisted." (2) May include categories not shown, e.g., midshipmen.

U.S. Air Force Personnel on Active Duty, 1918-2020

Source: U.S. Dept. of Defense
(as of midyear)

Year[1]	Total	Year[1]	Total	Year[1]	Total	Year[1]	Total	Year[1]	Total	Year[1]	Total
1918	195,023	1943	2,197,114	1980	557,969	2003	373,116	2009	333,423	2015	312,195
1920	9,050	1944	2,372,292	1990	535,233	2004	379,887	2010	337,505	2016	315,786
1930	13,531	1945	2,282,259	1995	400,051	2005	358,705	2011	333,729	2017	322,559
1940	51,165	1950	411,277	2000	357,777	2006	352,620	2012	333,487	2018	325,222
1941	152,125	1960	814,213	2001	351,935	2007	340,596	2013	333,506	2019	331,332
1942	764,415	1970	791,078	2002	369,721	2008	328,771	2014	328,791	2020	333,559

(1) Prior to 1950, data are for U.S. Army Air Corps and Air Service of the Signal Corps.

U.S. Marine Corps Personnel on Active Duty, 1940-2020

Source: U.S. Dept. of Defense
(as of midyear)

Year	Officers	Enlisted	Total	Year	Officers	Enlisted	Total	Year	Officers	Enlisted	Total
1940	1,800	26,545	28,345	1995	18,017	153,929	171,946	2014	21,507	169,327	190,834
1945	37,067	437,613	474,680	2000	17,897	154,744	172,641	2015	21,144	163,144	184,587
1950	7,254	67,025	74,279	2005	19,118	159,113	178,231	2016	20,827	162,543	183,370
1960	16,203	154,418	170,621	2010	21,680	179,446	201,126	2017	21,296	163,234	184,530
1970	24,941	234,796	259,737	2011	22,281	178,546	200,827	2018	21,582	163,637	185,219
1980	18,198	170,271	188,469	2012	22,380	174,748	197,128	2019	21,769	165,045	186,814
1990	19,958	176,694	196,652	2013	22,045	173,048	195,093	2020	21,941	160,788	182,729

U.S. Coast Guard Personnel on Active Duty, 1970-2020

Source: U.S. Dept. of Defense
(as of midyear, except where noted)

Year	Officers	Cadets	Enlisted	Total	Year	Officers	Cadets	Enlisted	Total
1970	5,512	653	31,524	37,689	2012 (Mar.)	8,316	988	33,758	43,062
1980	6,463	877	32,041	39,381	2013 (Jan.)	8,376	1,010	32,971	42,357
1985	6,775	733	31,087	38,595	2014	8,572	676	31,233	40,481
1990	6,475	820	29,860	37,308	2015	8,550	623	30,896	40,069
1995	7,489	841	28,401	36,731	2016	8,550	623	30,896	40,069
2000	7,154	863	27,695	35,712	2017	8,483	623	32,015	41,121
2005	7,908	1,006	31,900	40,814	2018	8,578	807	32,719	42,104
2010	8,678	744	33,713	43,135	2019	8,361	809	32,406	41,576
2011	8,659	1,053	33,615	43,327	2020	8,925	1,086[1]	31,787	41,798

(1) As of July 15, 2020.

Women in the U.S. Armed Forces

Source: U.S. Dept. of Defense; U.S. Census Bureau, U.S. Dept. of Commerce; U.S. Coast Guard, U.S. Dept. of Homeland Security
Women in the Army, Navy, Air Force, Marines, and Coast Guard are fully integrated with male personnel. All enlisted jobs were opened to women when the draft ended June 30, 1973. Admission to service academies began in 1976. Under rules instituted in 1993, women began to fly combat aircraft and serve aboard warships. By the mid-1990s, 80% of all jobs and more than 90% of all career fields had been opened to women. A woman first achieved the rank of four-star general in 2009. In 2010, the Navy removed its ban on women serving on submarine crews. The Pentagon in 2013 lifted its ban on women serving in direct ground combat units. In Aug. 2015, the first two women graduated from the Army's Ranger School. In Sept. 2017, the first female Marine graduated the Infantry Officer Course.

Women Active Duty Troops, 2020

Service	% women
Army	15.5%
Navy	20.4
Marines	9.0
Air Force	21.1
Coast Guard	15.4

Women on Active Duty, All DOD[1] Services, 1973-2020

Year	% women	Year	% women
1973	2.5%	2010	14.5%
1981	8.9	2015	15.6
1987	10.2	2017	16.3
1993	11.6	2018	16.6
2000	14.4	2019	17.0
2005	14.6	2020	17.3

Women Veterans by Period of Service, 2020

Period of service	% of women vets[2]
Gulf War era[3]	65.3%
Vietnam era	12.7
Korean War	1.5
World War II	0.8
Peacetime only	21.0

Note: Numbers on active duty are as of June 30 in 2020 and Sept. 30 in previous years. (1) Does not include Coast Guard. (2) Some women served in multiple periods. (3) Includes women who served both pre- and post-9/11 but not in peacetime only.

Average Age and Length of Service of Active Enlisted Personnel, 1973-2018

Source: U.S. Dept. of Defense

Year	Avg. age	Avg. months of service	Year	Avg. age	Avg. months of service	Year	Avg. age	Avg. months of service
1973	25.0	69.8	1989	26.4	78.0	2004	27.0	82.6
1974	25.0	69.6	1990	26.7	81.8	2005	27.1	83.2
1975	24.9	68.2	1991	27.0	84.8	2006	27.1	82.0
1976	24.9	67.6	1992	27.1	86.4	2007	27.1	81.0
1977	24.9	66.5	1992	27.1	86.4	2008	27.1	80.3
1978	25.0	67.3	1993	27.2	87.7	2009	27.2	80.4
1979	25.1	67.7	1994	27.3	89.6	2010	27.3	80.9
1980	25.0	66.5	1995	27.4	89.3	2011	27.4	81.1
1981	25.1	67.1	1996	27.4	89.6	2012	27.4	NA
1982	25.4	68.6	1997	27.4	89.2	2013	27.3	NA
1983	25.6	70.0	1998	27.3	88.4	2014	27.3	NA
1984	25.7	71.1	1999	27.3	87.3	2015	27.2	NA
1985	25.8	72.3	2000	27.1	85.5	2016	27.1	NA
1986	25.9	73.1	2001	27.0	84.4	2017	27.0	NA
1987	26.1	74.8	2002	27.1	84.1	2018	26.9	NA
1988	26.3	76.7	2003	27.0	83.3			

NA = Not available.

Monthly Military Pay Scale, 2020

Source: U.S. Dept. of Defense

(effective Jan. 1, 2020; salaries rounded to nearest dollar)

	Cumulative years of service													
	<2	2	3	4	6	8	10	12	14	16	18	20	22	24	26
Commissioned officers															
O-10	NA	NA	NA	NA	NA	NA	NA	NA	NA	NA	NA	16,442	16,442	16,442	16,442
O-9	NA	NA	NA	NA	NA	NA	NA	NA	NA	NA	NA	15,546	15,771	16,094	16,442
O-8	11,000	11,360	11,600	11,666	11,965	12,463	12,579	13,052	13,188	13,596	14,186	14,730	15,093	15,093	15,093
O-7	9,140	9,565	9,761	9,917	10,200	10,480	10,803	11,125	11,448	12,463	13,320	13,320	13,320	13,320	13,388
O-6	6,931	7,615	8,114	8,114	8,145	8,495	8,541	8,541	9,026	9,884	10,388	10,891	11,177	11,468	12,030
O-5	5,778	6,509	6,959	7,044	7,326	7,494	7,864	8,135	8,486	9,023	9,278	9,530	9,817	9,817	9,817
O-4	4,985	5,771	6,156	6,242	6,599	6,983	7,460	7,832	8,090	8,238	8,324	8,324	8,324	8,324	8,324
O-3	4,383	4,969	5,363	5,847	6,128	6,435	6,634	6,961	7,131	7,131	7,131	7,131	7,131	7,131	7,131
O-2	3,788	4,313	4,968	5,136	5,241	5,241	5,241	5,241	5,241	5,241	5,241	5,241	5,241	5,241	5,241
O-1	3,287	3,422	4,136	4,136	4,136	4,136	4,136	4,136	4,136	4,136	4,136	4,136	4,136	4,136	4,136

Commisioned officers with over 4 years of active duty service as enlisted member or warrant officer

	<2	2	3	4	6	8	10	12	14	16	18	20	22	24	26
O-3E	NA	NA	NA	5,847	6,128	6,435	6,634	6,961	7,236	7,395	7,611	7,611	7,611	7,611	7,611
O-2E	NA	NA	NA	5,136	5,241	5,408	5,690	5,908	6,070	6,070	6,070	6,070	6,070	6,070	6,070
O-1E	NA	NA	NA	4,136	4,417	4,580	4,747	4,911	5,136	5,136	5,136	5,136	5,136	5,136	5,136

Warrant officers

	<2	2	3	4	6	8	10	12	14	16	18	20	22	24	26
W-5	NA	NA	NA	NA	NA	NA	NA	NA	NA	NA	NA	8,055	8,463	8,768	9,104
W-4	4,530	4,873	5,012	5,150	5,387	5,622	5,859	6,216	6,529	6,827	7,071	7,309	7,658	7,945	8,273
W-3	4,137	4,309	4,486	4,544	4,729	5,094	5,473	5,652	5,859	6,072	6,455	6,714	6,868	7,033	7,257
W-2	3,661	4,007	4,113	4,187	4,424	4,793	4,976	5,156	5,376	5,548	5,704	5,890	6,013	6,110	6,110
W-1	3,213	3,559	3,652	3,848	4,081	4,423	4,583	4,807	5,027	5,200	5,359	5,552	5,552	5,552	5,552

Enlisted members

	<2	2	3	4	6	8	10	12	14	16	18	20	22	24	26
E-9	NA	NA	NA	NA	NA	NA	5,473	5,597	5,753	5,937	6,123	6,419	6,671	6,935	7,340
E-8	NA	NA	NA	NA	NA	4,480	4,678	4,801	4,948	5,107	5,395	5,540	5,788	5,926	6,264
E-7	3,114	3,399	3,530	3,701	3,836	4,067	4,198	4,429	4,622	4,753	4,892	4,946	5,129	5,226	5,597
E-6	2,694	2,964	3,095	3,222	3,355	3,653	3,770	3,995	4,064	4,114	4,172	4,172	4,172	4,172	4,172
E-5	2,468	2,634	2,761	2,891	3,095	3,306	3,481	3,502	3,502	3,502	3,502	3,502	3,502	3,502	3,502
E-4	2,263	2,378	2,507	2,635	2,747	2,747	2,747	2,747	2,747	2,747	2,747	2,747	2,747	2,747	2,747
E-3	2,043	2,171	2,303	2,303	2,303	2,303	2,303	2,303	2,303	2,303	2,303	2,303	2,303	2,303	2,303
E-2	1,943	1,943	1,943	1,943	1,943	1,943	1,943	1,943	1,943	1,943	1,943	1,943	1,943	1,943	1,943
E-1[1]	1,733	1,733	1,733	1,733	1,733	1,733	1,733	1,733	1,733	1,733	1,733	1,733	1,733	1,733	1,733

NA = Not applicable. **Note:** Basic pay rate for Academy cadets/midshipmen and ROTC members/applicants is $1,151. See Dept. of Defense Financial Management Regulations for details on pay-scale limitations and eligibility requirements. **Over 30 years**—O-10: $16,442; O-9: $16,442; O-8: $15,471; O-7: $13,656; O-6: $12,270; W-5: $9,560; W-4: $8,438; E-9: $7,706; E-8: $6,390. **Over 34 years**— O-10: $16,442; O-9: $16,442; O-8: $15,857; W-5: $10,037; E-9: $8,092. **Over 38 years**—O-10: $16,442; O-9: $16,442; W-5: $10,540; E-9: $8,498. (1) Applicable to E-1 with 4 months of active duty. Basic pay for an E-1 with less than 4 months of active duty is $1,602.

U.S. Veteran Population, 2020

Source: U.S. Dept. of Veterans Affairs

(projected population, in thousands, as of Sept. 30)

Period of service	Vet. pop.	Period of service	Vet. pop.
Total peacetime veterans[1]	4,341	**Total Vietnam War era**[3]	6,258
Service between Vietnam War era and Gulf War era	2,951	Vietnam War era with no other wartime service....	5,754
Service between Korean War and Vietnam War era	1,334	Vietnam War era with service in Korea	96
Service between WWII and Korean War	53	Vietnam War era with service in Korea and WWII ..	8
Pre-WWII service	2	Total Gulf War era[3]	8,051
Total wartime veterans[2]	15,201	Gulf War era pre-9/11 with service in Vietnam era..	276
Total World War II[3]	326	Gulf War era pre-9/11, post-9/11, and with service	
WWII only	299	in Vietnam War era	64
Total Korean War[3]	1,096	Gulf War era pre-9/11	2,738
Korean War with no other wartime service	974	Gulf War era pre-9/11 and post-9/11	1,548
Korean War with service in WWII	18	Gulf War era post-9/11	3,366
		TOTAL VETERANS IN CIVILIAN LIFE	**19,542**

Note: Figures are for U.S. veterans worldwide. Includes those who served on active duty in Army, Navy, Air Force, Marines, Coast Guard, uniformed Public Health Service and NOAA, and reservists called to federal active duty. Excludes those dishonorably discharged, those whose only active duty was training, and those currently on active duty. (1) Veterans with both wartime and peacetime service are counted only as "wartime veterans." (2) Veterans serving in more than one period are counted only once in total. (3) Total includes veterans who also served in other periods.

African American Service in U.S. Wars

Source: U.S. Dept. of Defense; U.S. Census Bureau, U.S. Dept. of Commerce

American Revolution. About 5,000 served in the Continental Army, mostly in integrated units, some in all-black combat units.

Civil War. Some 180,000 served in 163 units of the Union Army's U.S. Colored Troops, and 200,000 worked in service units—10% of the Union Army in all; about 37,000 died, 31,000 wounded.

World War I. 350,000-400,000 served in the armed forces, 100,000 in France. Some 40,000 fought.

World War II. Some 1 mil served in the armed forces—8% of all troops—mostly in Army service units; all-black fighter and bomber Army Air Force units and infantry divisions gave distinguished service.

Korean War. More than 600,000 served in the military; 3,075 lost their lives in combat. By 1954, armed forces were completely desegregated.

Vietnam War. 274,937 served in the armed forces (1965-74)—9.8% of all troops; 7,243 were killed in combat.

Persian Gulf War. About 104,000 served in the Kuwaiti theater—20% of all U.S. troops; 66 died in combat.

Operation Enduring Freedom/Freedom's Sentinel. 203 military deaths and 1,457 wounded in Afghanistan and elsewhere.

Operation Iraqi Freedom/Operation New Dawn/Operation Inherent Resolve. 463 military deaths and 2,793 wounded.

Outlays for Individual Payments to Veterans, 1940-2021

Source: White House Office of Management and Budget
(in millions of dollars)

Year	Total	Compensation	Pensions	Hospital, medical	Education	Insurance & burial	Year	Total	Compensation	Pensions	Hospital, medical	Education	Insurance & burial
1940	$574	$244	$185	$69	—	$76	2008	$84,463	$36,266	$3,790	$39,409	$3,634	$1,364
1950	8,613	1,533	476	764	$2,739	3,101	2009	94,985	40,490	4,161	44,637	4,328	1,369
1960	5,300	2,049	1,263	931	392	665	2010	106,454	43,498	4,359	48,506	8,773	1,318
1970	8,883	2,980	2,255	1,798	1,002	848	2011	122,524	52,780	4,664	52,681	11,112	1,287
1980	21,153	7,446	3,585	6,513	2,421	1,188	2012	119,544	50,058	4,537	52,972	10,734	1,243
1990	28,801	10,735	3,594	12,281	791	1,400	2013	134,083	59,393	5,173	55,067	13,220	1,230
2000	46,835	20,777	2,969	20,090	1,636	1,363	2014	143,412	64,360	5,251	58,906	13,729	1,166
2001	46,187	18,587	2,760	21,730	1,763	1,347	2015	153,506	69,725	5,299	63,652	13,605	1,225
2002	52,621	22,429	3,166	23,465	2,241	1,320	2016	167,046	79,907	5,824	65,810	14,579	926
2003	57,407	24,705	3,229	25,568	2,574	1,331	2017	167,399	79,839	5,505	67,949	13,520	586
2004	62,567	26,307	3,334	28,556	2,978	1,392	2018	170,949	79,986	4,796	72,899	12,703	565
2005	69,824	30,888	3,663	30,650	3,254	1,369	2019	194,241	95,599	4,940	79,661	13,433	608
2006	71,139	31,000	3,547	31,888	3,354	1,350	2020*	209,413	106,141	4,807	82,851	14,649	965
2007	73,726	31,064	3,376	34,485	3,456	1,345	2021*	228,660	114,049	4,911	93,755	15,048	897

— = Not available. * = Estimate. **Note:** Compensation is service-connected; pension is not.

Veterans Health Administration Characteristics, 2002-15

Source: U.S. Dept. of Veterans Affairs

Fiscal year	Total enrollees[1] (mil)	Outpatient visits[2] (mil)	Inpatient admissions (thous.)	Fiscal year	Total enrollees[1] (mil)	Outpatient visits[2] (mil)	Inpatient admissions (thous.)
2002	6.8	46.5	564.7	2009	8.1	74.9	662.0
2003	7.1	49.8	567.3	2010	8.3	80.2	682.3
2004	7.3	54.0	589.8	2011	8.6	79.8	692.1
2005	7.7	57.5	585.8	2012	8.8	83.6	703.5
2006	7.9	59.1	568.9	2013	8.9	86.4	694.7
2007	7.8	62.3	589.0	2014	9.1	92.4	707.4
2008	7.8	67.7	641.4	2015	9.0	95.2	699.1

(1) Includes non-enrolled veteran patients. (2) Includes fee visits.

Employment Status of Veterans With Service-Connected Disabilities, 2019

Source: Bureau of Labor Statistics, U.S. Dept. of Labor; as of Aug. 2019

Veteran status, presence of disability, and period of service	Employed (thous.)			Unemployed (thous.)			Unemployment rate (%)			Not in labor force (thous.)		
	Total	Men	Women	Total	Men	Women	Total	Men	Women	Total	Men	Women
Total veterans	8,664	7,660	1,005	353	309	43	3.9%	3.9%	4.1%	9,759	8,921	838
With service-connected disability	2,144	1,894	249	109	102	7	4.8	5.1	2.7	2,489	2,185	305
Without service-connected disability	6,260	5,535	725	243	207	36	3.7	3.6	4.8	7,027	6,508	519
Gulf War era, total	5,596	4,841	755	236	205	32	4.1	4.1	4.0	1,587	1,140	446
With service-connected disability	1,698	1,471	227	84	78	6	4.7	5.0	2.6	777	555	223
Without service-connected disability	3,688	3,191	497	153	127	26	4.0	3.8	4.9	773	558	215
Gulf War era II	3,356	2,897	458	164	143	21	4.7	4.7	4.4	891	596	295
With service-connected disability	1,230	1,080	150	72	66	6	5.5	5.7	3.8	490	329	161
Without service-connected disability	1,998	1,712	286	92	77	15	4.4	4.3	5.0	373	248	125
Gulf War era I	2,240	1,943	297	72	62	10	3.1	3.1	3.4	695	544	152
With service-connected disability	468	391	77	12	12	NA	2.5	3.0	NA	287	225	62
Without service-connected disability	1,690	1,479	211	60	50	10	3.4	3.3	4.7	400	310	90
WWII, Korean War, and Vietnam era	1,225	1,187	38	44	36	8	3.5	2.9	NA	5,893	5,692	201
With service-connected disability	213	209	4	13	12	0	5.6	5.5	NA	1,315	1,270	45
Without service-connected disability	1,006	972	34	31	24	8	3.0	2.4	NA	4,420	4,266	155
Other service periods	1,843	1,632	211	72	69	4	3.8	4.0	1.7	2,279	2,089	191
With service-connected disability	232	215	18	12	12	1	5.1	5.2	NA	396	360	37
Without service-connected disability	1,566	1,373	194	59	56	3	3.6	3.9	1.6	1,833	1,684	149

NA = Not available. **Note:** Veterans in survey were on active duty in the U.S. Armed Forces during these periods of service: Gulf War era II (Sept. 2001-present), Gulf War era I (Aug. 1990-Aug. 2001), Vietnam era (Aug. 1964-Apr. 1975), Korean War (July 1950-Jan. 1955), World War II (Dec. 1941-Dec. 1946), and other service periods. Veterans who served in more than one wartime period only. A service-connected disability is a health condition or impairment caused or made worse by military service.

Nations With Largest Armed Forces, 2020

Source: *The Military Balance 2020*, International Institute for Strategic Studies, published by Routledge Journals, Taylor & Francis, UK
(ranked by active-duty troop strength as of 2020; all other data as of Nov. 2019 unless otherwise noted)

Rank	Country	Active troops (thous.)	Reserve troops (thous.)	Defense expend. (mil)	Tanks (MBT) (army only)	Cruisers/ frigates/ destroyers	Sub-marines	Combat aircraft (air force only) FGA	FTR
1.	China	2,035	510	$181,135	5,850	1C/52F/28D*	59	794+	759
2.	India	1,456	1,155	60,543	3,565+	13F/13D*	17	498	62
3.	United States	1,380	849	684,568	2,389	24C/19F/67D*	67	969	271
4.	North Korea	1,280	600	—	3,500+	2F	73	30	401+
5.	Russia	900	2,000	48,206	2,800	4C/15F/13D*	49	444	180
6.	Pakistan	654	0	10,314	2,433	9F	8	203	153
7.	Iran	610	350	17,428	1,513+	0	19	87	184+
8.	South Korea	599	3,100	39,764	2,221	3C/17F/6D	22	309	174
9.	Vietnam	482	5,000	5,214	1,379	4F	8	72	0
10.	Egypt	439	479	3,351	2,480	9F/1D	6	319	62
11.	Myanmar	406	0	2,060	185+	5F	0	5	63
12.	Indonesia	396	400	7,429	103	11F	4	40	9
13.	Brazil	367	1,340	27,467	393	8F/2D	5	48	46
14.	Thailand	361	200	7,103	360	9F*	0	11	78
15.	Turkey	355	379	8,103	2,379	20F	12	283	27
16.	Colombia	293	35	10,451	0	4F	4	22	0
17.	Sri Lanka	255	6	1,668	62	0	0	1	5
18.	Japan	247	56	48,590	617	2C/11F/34D*	21	137	201
19.	Mexico	236	82	5,085	0	0	0	0	0
20.	Saudi Arabia	227	0	78,400	880	4F/3D	0	207	81
21.	Ukraine	209	900	3,831	854	1F	0	14	71
22.	France	204	39	52,268	222	11F/11D*	9	166	41
23.	Eritrea	202	120	78[1]	270	0	0	2	8
24.	Morocco	196	150	3,633	602	5F/1D	0	49	22
25.	Iraq	193	0	20,471	391+	0	0	36	0
26.	South Sudan	185	0	70	80+	0	0	0	0
27.	Germany	181	29	48,548	245	7F/8D	6	0	140
28.	Afghanistan	181	0	1,906	20	0	0	0	0
29.	Israel	170	465	19,273	490	0	5	266	58
30.	Syria	169	0	—	0	0	0	118	64

— = Not available. * = Navy with aircraft carrier(s), as follows: China 1, France 1, India 1, Italy 2, Japan 4, Russia 1, Thailand 1, U.S. 11.
FGA = Fighter, ground attack. FTR = Fighter. MBT = Main battle tank. (1) As of 2013.

U.S. Anti-Terrorism Overseas Contingency Operations (OCO), 2008-20

Source: U.S. Dept. of Defense

(fiscal-year enacted funding, in billions; annual average troop levels, in thousands)

	2008	2009	2010	2011	2012	2013	2014	2015	2016	2017	2018	2019	2020
Total: OCO designated funding	$187	$146	$163	$159	$115	$82	$85	$63	$59	$82	$83	$69	$71[1]
Op. Inherent Resolve[2]........	148	94	62	45	10	3	1	5	5	14	13	14	7
Op. Freedom's Sentinel[3]......	39	52	101	114	105	79	84	54	44	46	47	45	17[3]
European Deterrence Initiative/non-war..........	NA	NA	NA	NA	NA	NA	NA	2	2	4	6	7	6
Base requirements	NA	NA	NA	NA	NA	NA	NA	2	8	18	17	2	5
Total: OCO troop levels	187	185	180	145	99	63	37	13	14	14	24	26	22*
Op. Inherent Resolve[2]........	154	141	96	47	9	0	0	3	4	6	6	11	7
Op. Freedom's Sentinel[3]......	33	44	84	98	90	63	37	10	10	8	18	16	15

NA = Not applicable. * = Requested. (1) Total includes $36 bil of in-theater and U.S. stateside costs attributed to individual operations for previous years and excludes funding associated with border security and hurricane reconstruction efforts. (2) Includes Operations Iraqi Freedom, New Dawn, Inherent Resolve, and other activities in Iraq and Syria. (3) Includes Operations Enduring Freedom and Freedom's Sentinel, both in Afghanistan.

Conventional Arms Transfer Agreements With the World by Supplier, 2010-19

Source: Stockholm International Peace Research Institute (SIPRI); as of Mar. 9, 2020

(SIPRI trend-indicator values [TIVs] in millions of current U.S. dollars; ranked by 2010-19 totals)

Supplier	2010	2011	2012	2013	2014	2015	2016	2017	2018	2019	Total, 2010-19
United States	$8,033	$8,988	$9,074	$7,508	$9,608	$9,963	$9,855	$12,050	$10,414	$10,752	$96,244
Russia...........	6,275	8,730	8,261	7,986	5,527	5,990	6,841	6,015	6,506	4,718	66,848
France...........	866	1,731	1,010	1,468	1,627	1,995	2,041	2,367	1,773	3,368	18,245
Germany.........	2,664	1,317	747	779	1,788	1,766	2,514	1,982	1,071	1,185	15,814
China	1,478	1,277	1,540	2,080	1,226	1,799	2,372	1,346	1,140	1,423	15,683
United Kingdom ...	1,157	1,055	929	1,608	1,651	1,179	1,376	1,225	699	972	11,850
Spain	263	1,429	546	728	1,050	1,163	471	820	1,025	1,061	8,555
Italy.............	539	947	747	862	671	676	618	793	555	491	6,900
Israel............	637	538	455	420	393	720	1,392	1,195	655	369	6,774
Netherlands	371	546	858	374	631	461	471	1,048	438	285	5,484
Ukraine..........	485	570	1,501	674	622	343	486	307	195	91	5,274
All others.......	3,003	2,978	2,501	2,645	2,229	2,550	2,830	2,396	2,694	2,479	26,305
All suppliers	25,771	30,106	28,169	27,132	27,023	28,605	31,267	31,544	27,165	27,194	283,976

Note: SIPRI data on arms transfers relate to actual deliveries of major conventional weapons, using TIV. TIV is based on the known unit production costs of a core set of weapons and is intended to represent the transfer of military resources rather than the financial value of the transfer. A weapon that has been in service in another armed force is valued at 40% of a new weapon. A significantly refurbished or modified used weapon is valued at 66% of that of a new weapon. Figures may not add to totals due to rounding.

U.S. Foreign Military Financing, 2010-17

Source: Defense Security Cooperation Agency, U.S. Dept. of Defense

Listed are grants extended to foreign governments in a fiscal year to pay for military equipment and services. May be from the U.S. Dept. of Defense (DOD) or, for specific countries, negotiated directly with U.S. commercial suppliers with DOD approval.

(in thousands of U.S. dollars)

	2010	2015	2017		2010	2015	2017
Western Hemisphere	$89,720	$48,550	$74,897	**Europe**	$151,696	$146,150	$170,080
Colombia	55,000	27,000	38,525	Bosnia and			
Costa Rica	325	1,200	7,000	Herzegovina	4,000	4,000	4,000
Guatemala	1,375	1,000	2,427	Bulgaria	9,000	5,000	7,450
Honduras	1,514	3,100	5,000	Croatia	2,500	3,500	3,000
Mexico	5,250	4,675	5,000	Czech Republic	6,000	2,127	3,000
Panama	1,800	1,800	4,375	Estonia	2,500	1,600	20,000
Near East and				Georgia	16,000	30,000	37,000
South Asia	4,666,797	4,886,776	4,668,408	Latvia	2,500	2,535	10,000
Bahrain	19,000	7,500	0	Lithuania	2,700	2,400	19,680
Egypt	1,300,000	1,300,000	195,000	Moldova	750	11,250	12,750
Iraq	0	0	107,378	Poland	47,000	9,000	8,150
Israel	2,775,000	3,100,000	3,760,000	Romania	12,999	5,400	8,350
Jordan	300,000	385,000	470,000	Ukraine	11,000	47,000	14,000
Lebanon	0	84,117	132,330	**Africa**	45,370	52,950	129,500
Oman	8,847	4,000	0	Chad	500	0	4,090
Pakistan	248,000	0	0	Djibouti	2,000	710	500
East Asia and				Kenya	1,500	1,810	4,200
Pacific	59,100	77,250	93,600	Liberia	6,000	2,500	2,500
Indonesia	20,000	14,000	14,000	Morocco	9,000	12,000	10,000
Mongolia	4,500	2,000	2,600	Niger	0	500	6,535
Philippines	29,000	50,000	50,250	Tunisia	18,000	30,000	95,000
Vietnam	2,000	10,750	26,750	**World total**	5,015,952	5,211,901	5,144,253

Note: Regional subtotals include countries not listed.

Leading Defense Contract Recipients, 2019

Source: U.S. Dept. of Defense; Federal Procurement Data System, U.S. General Services Administration

Listed are the 50 companies or organizations receiving the largest dollar volume of prime contract awards from the U.S. Dept. of Defense during fiscal year 2019 (Oct. 1, 2018-Sept. 30, 2019).

Rank	Recipient	Funds awarded	Rank	Recipient	Funds awarded
1.	Lockheed Martin Corp.	$47,073,503,160	26.	Science Applications International Corp.	$1,809,842,141
2.	The Boeing Co.	26,317,459,542	27.	Bell Boeing Joint Project Office.	1,724,170,323
3.	General Dynamics Corp.	16,504,393,195	28.	Textron Inc.	1,707,289,088
4.	Raytheon Co.	15,013,250,768	29.	United Launch Alliance L.L.C.	1,695,877,793
5.	Northrop Grumman Corp.	14,182,732,150	30.	Southwest Valley Constructors Co.	1,645,275,200
6.	United Technologies Corp.	9,262,915,698	31.	Leonardo S.p.A.	1,494,915,228
7.	Humana Inc.	6,723,695,162	32.	CACI International Inc.	1,490,293,935
8.	Huntington Ingalls Industries, Inc.	6,637,043,094	33.	Austal USA.	1,414,323,693
9.	BAE Systems PLC	6,157,554,472	34.	Perspecta Inc.	1,376,683,754
10.	L3Harris Technologies, Inc.	6,145,463,543	35.	Sierra Nevada Corp.	1,340,920,259
11.	General Atomic Technologies Corp.	3,341,138,608	36.	Jacobs Engineering Group Inc.	1,317,337,748
12.	Analytic Services Inc.	3,325,445,284	37.	Honeywell International Inc.	1,309,408,158
13.	General Electric Co.	3,304,744,119	38.	Sullivan Land Services Ltd.	1,299,213,563
14.	Atlantic Diving Supply, Inc.	3,064,660,687	39.	Massachusetts Institute of Tech.	1,110,237,077
15.	Centene Corp.	3,023,585,699	40.	Vectrus, Inc.	1,080,241,271
16.	Leidos Holdings, Inc.	3,013,705,511	41.	Johns Hopkins University	1,043,868,519
17.	Oshkosh Corp.	2,863,076,286	42.	The Aerospace Corp.	1,011,229,673
18.	McKesson Corp.	2,720,562,307	43.	FedEx Corp.	960,467,423
19.	Fluor Corp.	2,538,732,049	44.	Rolls-Royce Holdings plc	923,731,909
20.	AmerisourceBergen Corp.	2,360,611,692	45.	M1 Support Services, L.P.	903,632,975
21.	KBR Inc.	2,219,616,365	46.	The MITRE Corp.	869,271,958
22.	Bechtel Group, Inc.	2,180,116,349	47.	L-3 Communications Vertex Aerospace LLC	819,689,032
23.	Booz Allen Hamilton Holding Corp.	2,075,204,411	48.	MacAndrews & Forbes Holdings Inc.	809,557,497
24.	AECOM	1,909,090,473	49.	Patriot Team	729,824,763
25.	Cerberus Capital Management, L.P.	1,866,569,588	50.	Alion Science and Tech. Corp.	688,545,373

U.S. Military Awards in Selected Wars and Conflicts

Source: U.S. Army Human Resources Command, U.S. Dept. of Defense; Congressional Medal of Honor Society

Award	Civil War	WWI	WWII	Korea	Vietnam	Gulf War	Afghanistan[1]	Iraq[2]
Medal of Honor	1,523	132	473	146	263	0	18	7
Distinguished Service Cross	NA	6,428	4,710	734	1,066	0	29	18
Silver Star	NA	NA	73,654	10,061	21,634	75	411	376
Legion of Merit	NA	NA	20,273	NA	10,356	158	245	185
Distinguished Flying Cross	NA	NA	126,318	NA	21,697	108	61	121
Soldier's Medal	NA	NA	12,485	581	5,402	43	210	117
Bronze Star (total)	NA	NA	395,408	30,359	719,971	28,857	73,000	115,927
Purple Heart	NA	NA	NA	NA	220,527	504	9,468	22,626
Air Medal (total)	NA	NA	1,166,471	0	1,039,125	6,399	20,447	23,531
Army Commendation (total)	NA	NA	0	0	837,040	81,979	193,167	411,123

NA = Not available or applicable. **Note:** Numbers for the individual decorations shown here represent only those awards that were properly processed and reported to Dept. of the Army Headquarters. The actual number of individual decorations awarded under combat conditions, when award approval authority is delegated to field commanders, cannot be stated with absolute certainty. Numbers here reflect the current statistics recorded by the Military Awards Branch, as of Aug. 18, 2020, unless noted, except for MOH, which was reported by the Congressional Medal of Honor Society as of Aug. 7, 2020. (1) Operation Enduring Freedom and Operation Freedom's Sentinel. May include awards for actions related to operations but occurring outside of Afghanistan. As of Dec. 10, 2019. (2) Operation Iraqi Freedom, Operation New Dawn, and Operation Inherent Resolve. May include awards for actions related to operations but occurring in other nations, including Syria. As of Dec. 10, 2019.

Medal of Honor

Source: Congressional Medal of Honor Society; U.S. Army, U.S. Dept. of Defense
(as of Aug. 31, 2020)

The Medal of Honor is the highest military award for individual bravery in the U.S. On Dec. 21, 1861, Pres. Abraham Lincoln signed a bill to create the Navy Medal of Honor. Lincoln, on July 14, 1862, approved a resolution providing for the presentation of Medals of Honor to enlisted men of the Army and Voluntary Forces. The law was amended on Mar. 3, 1863, so that officers as well as enlisted men were eligible. The first Army Medals of Honor were awarded on Mar. 25, 1863; the first Navy medals went to sailors and Marines on Apr. 3, 1863.

The Medal of Honor is awarded in the name of Congress to a person who, while a member of the armed forces, distinguishes himself or herself conspicuously by gallantry and intrepidity at the risk of life above and beyond the call of duty while engaged in an action against any enemy of the U.S.; while engaged in military operations involving conflict with an opposing foreign force; or while serving with friendly foreign forces engaged in

an armed conflict against an opposing armed force in which the U.S. is not a belligerent party.

The deed performed must have been one of personal bravery or self-sacrifice so conspicuous as to clearly distinguish the individual above his or her comrades and must have involved risk of life. Incontestable proof of the performance of service is required, and each recommendation for award of this decoration is considered on the standard of extraordinary merit.

Prior to World War I, the 2,625 Army Medal of Honor awards up to that time were reviewed to determine which met new stringent criteria. The Army removed 911 names from the list, most of them former members of a Civil War volunteer infantry group who had been induced to extend their enlistments when they were promised the medal. However, the medal was restored to Dr. Mary Walker in 1977 and to Buffalo Bill Cody and seven other scouts in 1989.

Medal of Honor Recipients From Recent Conflicts

Honoree	Rank[1]	Branch of service	Date of action	Date of award
Somalia Campaign				
Gordon, Gary I.*	Master Sgt.	U.S. Army	10/3/1993	5/23/1994
Shughart, Randall D.*	Sgt. First Class	U.S. Army	10/3/1993	5/23/1994
War in Iraq				
Atkins, Travis W.*	Staff Sgt.	U.S. Army	6/1/2007	3/27/2019
Bellavia, David G.	Staff Sgt.	U.S. Army	11/10/2004	6/25/2019
Dunham, Jason L.*	Corporal	USMC	4/14/2004	1/11/2007
McGinnis, Ross A.*	Pvt. First Class/Specialist*	U.S. Army	12/4/2006	6/5/2008
Monsoor, Michael A.*	Petty Officer Second Class	U.S. Navy	9/29/2006	4/8/2008
Payne, Thomas P.	Sgt. Major	U.S. Army	10/22/2015	9/11/2020
Smith, Paul R.*	Sgt. First Class	U.S. Army	4/4/2003	4/5/2005
War in Afghanistan				
Byers, Edward C., Jr.	Senior Chief	U.S. Navy	12/8-9/2012	2/29/2016
Carpenter, William Kyle	Lance Cpl.	USMC	11/21/2010	6/19/2014
Carter, Ty M.	Staff Sgt.	U.S. Army	10/3/2009	8/26/2013
Chapman, John A.*	Technical Sgt.	USAF	3/4/2002	8/22/2018
Giunta, Salvatore A.	Staff Sgt.	U.S. Army	10/25/2007	11/16/2010
Groberg, Florent A.	Capt.	U.S. Army	8/8/2012	11/12/2015
Meyer, Dakota	Sgt.	USMC	9/8/2009	9/15/2011
Miller, Robert J.*	Staff Sgt.	U.S. Army	1/25/2008	10/6/2010
Monti, Jared C.*	Sgt. First Class	U.S. Army	6/21/2006	9/17/2009
Murphy, Michael P.*	Lt.	U.S. Navy	6/28/2005	10/22/2007
Petry, Leroy A.	Sgt. First Class	U.S. Army	5/26/2008	7/12/2011
Pitts, Ryan M.	Staff Sgt.	U.S. Army	7/13/2008	7/21/2014
Romesha, Clinton L.	Staff Sgt.	U.S. Army	10/3/2009	2/11/2013
Shurer, Ronald J., II	Staff Sgt.	U.S. Army	4/6/2008	10/1/2018
Slabinski, Britt K.	Master Chief	U.S. Navy	3/4/2002	5/24/2018
Swenson, William D.	Capt.	U.S. Army	9/8/2009	10/15/2013
White, Kyle J.	Sgt.	U.S. Army	11/9/2007	5/13/2014
Williams, Matthew O.	Master Sgt.	U.S. Army	4/6/2008	10/30/2019

* = Awarded posthumously. (1) Rank at date of award.

Other Selected Awards

Source: The Institute of Heraldry, U.S. Army; Navy Department Awards Web Service; Air Force Personnel Center

Distinguished Service Cross

Established July 9, 1918, on recommendation of Gen. John J. "Black Jack" Pershing, and awarded for extraordinary heroism not justifying the award of a Medal of Honor. The act or acts of heroism must have been so notable and have involved risk of life so extraordinary as to set the individual apart from his or her comrades. The Navy Cross and Air Force Cross are equivalent.

Silver Star

Third-highest military combat honor. An earlier version of this award, the Citation Star, was established by Congress on July 19, 1918, and retroactively awarded to soldiers for "gallantry in action," back to the Spanish-American War. The Silver Star medal replaced the Citation Star in 1932 and is awarded for gallantry in action which, while of a lesser degree than that required for award of the Distinguished Service Cross, must nevertheless have been performed with marked distinction.

Distinguished Flying Cross

Established by Congress July 2, 1926, and awarded for heroism or extraordinary achievement while participating in aerial flight. Awards are made only to recognize single acts of heroism or extraordinary achievement, not sustained operational activities against an armed enemy. Initial awards were given to persons who made record-breaking long-distance and endurance flights or who set altitude records.

Soldier's Medal

Established by Congress July 2, 1926, to recognize acts of heroism not involving actual conflict with an enemy. The same degree of heroism is required as for the award of the Distinguished Flying Cross. The performance must have involved

personal hazard or danger and the voluntary risk of life under conditions not involving conflict with an armed enemy. Awards are not made solely on the basis of having saved a life.

Bronze Star

Established by executive order Feb. 4, 1944, largely to raise the morale of ground troops in WWII, on the recommendation of Gen. George C. Marshall. It is awarded to any person who, while serving in any capacity in or with the U.S. military, distinguishes himself or herself by heroic or meritorious achievement or service not involving participation in aerial flight.

Purple Heart

The original Purple Heart, designated as the Badge of Military Merit, was established by Gen. George Washington on Aug. 7, 1782. Following the American Revolution, the badge fell into disuse until 1932, the 200th anniversary of Washington's birth. During WWII, the Order of the Purple Heart was awarded for both wounds received in action and for meritorious service. Following the introduction of the Legion of Merit, the Purple Heart was awarded only for combat wounds. Today, it is awarded to any armed forces member who, while serving with the U.S. Armed Services, has been wounded or killed, or who has died or may hereafter die after being wounded in action against an enemy of the U.S. or in an armed conflict in which the U.S. or friendly foreign forces are engaged; as the result of an act of any hostile foreign force; as a result of an international terrorist attack against the U.S. or a friendly foreign nation; or as a result of military operations outside the U.S. as part of a peacekeeping force. Wounds must be inflicted directly by enemy action, including while held as a prisoner of war or while being taken captive.

U.S. Army, Navy, Air Force, Marine Corps, and Coast Guard Insignia

Source: Dept. of the Army, Dept. of the Navy, Dept. of the Air Force, U.S. Dept. of Defense; U.S. Coast Guard, U.S. Dept. of Homeland Security

Army

General of the Armies—Gen. John J. Pershing (1860-1948), the only person to have held this rank while living, was authorized to prescribe his own insignia but never wore in excess of four stars. Congress established the rank in 1799 to be bestowed on George Washington; Washington was finally promoted to the rank by joint resolution of Congress, approved by Pres. Gerald Ford, Oct. 19, 1976.

General of the Army—Five silver stars fastened together in a circle and the coat of arms of the U.S. in gold color metal with shield and crest enameled. Reserved for wartime use only.

Rank	Insignia
General of the Army*	Five silver stars
General	Four silver stars
Lieutenant General	Three silver stars
Major General	Two silver stars
Brigadier General	One silver star
Colonel	Silver eagle
Lieutenant Colonel	Silver oak leaf
Major	Gold oak leaf
Captain	Two silver bars
First Lieutenant	One silver bar
Second Lieutenant	One gold bar

Warrant Officers

Grade Five—Silver bar with enamel black line.
Grade Four—Silver bar with 4 enamel black squares.
Grade Three—Silver bar with 3 enamel black squares.
Grade Two—Silver bar with 2 enamel black squares.
Grade One—Silver bar with 1 enamel black square.

Noncommissioned Officers

Sergeant Major of the Army (E-9)—Three chevrons above 3 arcs, with a U.S. coat of arms centered on the chevrons, flanked by 2 stars—1 star on each side of the eagle. Also distinctive red-and-white shield collar insignia.

Command Sergeant Major (E-9)—Three chevrons above 3 arcs with a 5-pointed star with a wreath around the star between the chevrons and arcs.

Sergeant Major (E-9)—Three chevrons above 3 arcs with a 5-pointed star between the chevrons and arcs.

First Sergeant (E-8)—Three chevrons above 3 arcs with a lozenge between the chevrons and arcs.

Master Sergeant (E-8)—Three chevrons above 3 arcs.
Sergeant First Class (E-7)—Three chevrons above 2 arcs.
Staff Sergeant (E-6)—Three chevrons above 1 arc.
Sergeant (E-5)—Three chevrons.
Corporal (E-4)—Two chevrons.

Specialists

Specialist (E-4)—Eagle device only.

Other Enlisted

Private First Class (E-3)—One chevron above 1 arc.
Private (E-2)—One chevron.
Private (E-1)—None.
*Rank reserved for wartime use only.

Air Force

Insignia for Air Force officers are identical to those of the Army. Insignia for enlisted personnel are worn on both sleeves and consist of 1 star and an appropriate number of rockers. Chevrons appear above 5 rockers for the top three noncommissioned officer ranks, as follows (in ascending order): Master Sergeant, 1 chevron; Senior Master Sergeant, 2 chevrons; Chief Master Sergeant, 3 chevrons. The insignia of the Chief Master Sergeant of the Air Force has 3 chevrons and a wreath around the star design, while the Command Chief Master Sergeant insignia features an additional star. General of the Air Force is reserved for wartime use only.

Navy

The following stripes are worn on the lower sleeves of the Service Dress Blue uniform. They are of gold embroidery.

Rank	Insignia
Fleet Admiral*	1 two inch with 4 one-half inch
Admiral	1 two inch with 3 one-half inch
Vice Admiral	1 two inch with 2 one-half inch
Rear Admiral (upper half)	1 two inch with 1 one-half inch
Rear Admiral (lower half)	1 two inch
Captain	4 one-half inch
Commander	3 one-half inch
Lieutenant Commander	2 one-half inch with 1 one-quarter inch between
Lieutenant	2 one-half inch
Lieutenant (jr. grade)	1 one-half inch with 1 one-quarter inch above
Ensign	1 one-half inch
Warrant Officer W-5	½" stripe under ⅛" blue strip with 1 break
Warrant Officer W-4	½" stripe with 1 break
Warrant Officer W-3	½" stripe with 2 breaks, 2" apart
Warrant Officer W-2	½" stripe with 3 breaks, 2" apart

Enlisted personnel (noncommissioned petty officers)—Rating badge worn on the upper left sleeve consisting of a spread eagle, appropriate number of chevrons, and centered specialty mark.

* = Rank reserved for wartime use only.

Marine Corps

Marine Corps' distinctive cap and collar ornament is the Marine Corps emblem—a combination of the American eagle, a globe, and an anchor. Marine Corps and Army officer insignia are similar. Marine Corps enlisted insignia, although basically similar to the Army's, feature crossed rifles beneath the chevrons. Marine Corps enlisted rank insignia are as follows:

Sergeant Major of the Marine Corps (E-9)—Same as Sergeant Major (below) but with Marine Corps emblem in the center with a 5-pointed star on both sides of the emblem.

Sergeant Major (E-9)—Three chevrons above 4 rockers with a 5-pointed star in the center.

Master Gunnery Sergeant (E-9)—Three chevrons above 4 rockers with a bursting bomb insignia in the center.

First Sergeant (E-8)—Three chevrons above 3 rockers with a diamond in the middle.

Master Sergeant (E-8)—Three chevrons above 3 rockers with crossed rifles in the middle.

Gunnery Sergeant (E-7)—Three chevrons above 2 rockers with crossed rifles in the middle.

Staff Sergeant (E-6)—Three chevrons above 1 rocker with crossed rifles in the middle.

Sergeant (E-5)—Three chevrons above crossed rifles.
Corporal (E-4)—Two chevrons above crossed rifles.
Lance Corporal (E-3)—One chevron above crossed rifles.
Private First Class (E-2)—One chevron.
Private (E-1)—None.

Coast Guard

Coast Guard insignia follow Navy custom, with certain minor changes such as the officer cap insignia. The Coast Guard shield is worn on both sleeves of officers and on the right sleeve of all enlisted personnel.

Federal Service Academies

U.S. Military Academy, West Point, NY. Founded 1802. Awards B.S. degree and Army commission for a 5-year service obligation. **Website:** www.usma.edu

U.S. Naval Academy, Annapolis, MD. Founded 1845. Awards B.S. degree and Navy or Marine Corps commission for a 5-year service obligation. **Website:** www.usna.edu

U.S. Air Force Academy, Colorado Springs, CO. Founded 1954. Awards B.S. degree and Air Force commission for a 6-year service obligation. **Website:** www.usafa.af.mil

U.S. Coast Guard Academy, New London, CT. Founded 1876. Awards B.S. degree and Coast Guard commission for a 5-year service obligation. **Website:** www.cga.edu

U.S. Merchant Marine Academy, Kings Point, NY. Founded 1943. Awards B.S. degree; a license as a deck, engineer, or dual officer; and a U.S. Naval Reserve commission. Service obligations vary according to options taken by the graduate. **Website:** www.usmma.edu

Casualties in Principal Wars of the U.S.

Source: U.S. Dept. of Defense; U.S. Coast Guard, U.S. Dept. of Homeland Security

Data prior to World War I are based on incomplete records in many cases. Casualty data are confined to dead and wounded personnel and, therefore, exclude personnel captured or missing in action who were subsequently returned to military control.

	Branch of service	Number serving	CASUALTIES Battle deaths	Other deaths	Wounds not mortal[1]	Total[2]
Revolutionary War 1775-83	Total	184,000 to 250,000[13]	4,435	—	6,188	10,623
War of 1812 1812-15	Total	286,730[14]	2,260	—	4,505	6,765
	Army	—	1,950	—	4,000	5,950
	Navy	—	265	—	439	704
	Marines	—	45	—	66	111
Mexican War 1846-48	Total	78,718[14]	1,733	11,550	4,152	17,435
	Army	—	1,721	11,550	4,102	17,373
	Navy	—	1	—	3	4
	Marines	—	11	—	47	58
	Coast Guard[8]	71 off.	—	—	—	—
Civil War 1861-65 Union forces[3]	Total	2,213,363	140,414	224,097	281,881	646,392
	Army	2,128,948[14]	138,154	221,374	280,040	639,568
	Navy	84,415	2,112	2,411	1,710	6,233
	Marines	(in Navy total)	148	312	131	591
	Coast Guard[8]	219 off.	1	—	—	1
Confederate forces (estimate)[3]	Total	600,000 to 1.5 mil	74,524	59,297	—	133,821
Spanish-American War 1898	Total	306,760	385	2,061	1,662	4,108
	Army[9]	280,564	369	2,061	1,594	4,024
	Navy	22,875	10	—	47	57
	Marines	3,321	6	—	21	27
	Coast Guard[8]	660	0	—	—	—
World War I Apr. 6, 1917-Nov. 11, 1918	Total	4,734,991	53,402	63,114	204,002	320,518
	Army[10]	4,057,101	50,510	55,868	193,663	300,041
	Navy	599,051	431	6,856	819	8,106
	Marines	78,839	2,461	390	9,520	12,371
	Coast Guard	8,835	30	81	—	111
World War II[4] Dec. 7, 1941-Dec. 31, 1946	Total	16,112,566	291,557	113,842	670,846	1,076,245
	Army[11]	11,260,000	234,874	83,400	565,861	884,135
	Navy[12]	4,183,466	36,950	25,664	37,778	100,392
	Marines	669,100	19,733	4,778	67,207	91,718
	Coast Guard	241,093	574	1,343	—	1,917
Korean War[5] June 25, 1950-July 27, 1953	Total	5,720,000	33,739	2,835	103,284	139,858
	Army	2,834,000	27,731	2,125	77,596	107,452
	Navy	1,177,000	503	154	1,576	2,233
	Marines	424,000	4,267	242	23,744	28,253
	Air Force	1,285,000	1,238	314	368	1,920
	Coast Guard	44,143	—	—	—	—
Vietnam War[6] Aug. 4, 1964-Jan. 27, 1973	Total	8,744,000	47,434	10,786	153,303	211,523
	Army	4,368,000	30,963	7,261	96,802	135,026
	Navy	1,842,000	1,631	935	4,178	6,744
	Marines	794,000	13,095	1,749	51,392	66,236
	Air Force	1,740,000	1,745	841	931	3,517
	Coast Guard	8,000	7	2	60	69
Persian Gulf War. 1991	Total	2,225,000	147	235	467	849
	Army	782,000	98	126	354	578
	Navy	669,000	5	50	12	67
	Marines	213,000	24	44	92	160
	Air Force	561,000	20	15	9	44
	Coast Guard	400	—	—	—	—
Iraq War[7] Mar. 19, 2003-Dec. 15, 2011	Total	269,363[15]	3,520	973	32,293	36,786
	Army	99,664[15]	2,574	727	22,543	25,844
	Navy	61,018[15]	64	49	672	785
	Marines	66,166[15]	852	171	8,625	9,648
	Air Force	42,515[15]	29	26	452	507
	Coast Guard	1,250[15]	1	—	1	2

— = Not available. Off. = Officers. **Note:** As of Aug. 2020, there were 1,845 battle deaths, 503 non-hostile deaths, and 20,149 wounded in Op. Enduring Freedom (Oct. 7, 2001-Dec. 31, 2014), mostly in Afghanistan and the Persian Gulf area; 64 battle deaths, 29 non-hostile deaths, and 572 wounded in Operation Freedom's Sentinel (Jan. 1, 2015-) in Afghanistan; 21 battle deaths, 76 non-hostile deaths, and 231 wounded in Operation Inherent Resolve (Aug. 8, 2014-) against ISIS in Iraq and Syria. (1) Marine Corps data for Iraq War, World War II, Spanish-American War, and prior wars represent the number of individuals wounded, whereas all other data in this column represent the total number (incidence) of wounds. (2) Totals for all branches do not include categories for which no data are listed. (3) From the final report of the Provost Marshal General, 1863-66. Authoritative statistics for the Confederate forces are not available. In addition, an estimated 26,000-31,000 Confederate personnel died in Union prisons. New estimates published in *Civil War History* in 2012 recalculated the death toll for both sides and determined that it was 20% higher than previously thought, at 750,000. (4) Data are for Dec. 1, 1941, through Dec. 31, 1946, when hostilities were officially terminated by presidential proclamation; few battle deaths or wounds not mortal were incurred after Japanese acceptance of Allied peace terms on Aug. 14, 1945. Numbers serving Dec. 1, 1941-Aug. 31, 1945: Total—14,903,213; Army—10,420,000; Navy—3,883,520; Marine Corps—599,693. (5) As a result of an ongoing Dept. of Defense review of available Korean War casualty record information, updates have been made to previously reported figures for battle deaths and other deaths. (6) Number serving Aug. 5, 1964-Jan. 27, 1973 (date of cease-fire). Includes casualties incurred in Mayaguez incident. Wounds not mortal exclude 150,341 persons not requiring hospital care. (7) Military deaths during the invasion phase, which ended Apr. 30, 2003, totaled 115 combat-related and 23 other. (8) Then known as the U.S. Revenue Cutter Services, predecessor to the U.S. Coast Guard. (9) Number serving Apr. 21-Aug. 13, 1898, while dead and wounded data are for May 1-Aug. 31, 1898. Active hostilities ceased on Aug. 13, 1898, but the U.S. and Spain did not exchange ratifications of the treaty of peace until Apr. 11, 1899. (10) Includes Army Air Forces battle deaths and wounds not mortal, as well as casualties suffered by American forces in northern Russia to Aug. 25, 1919, and in Siberia to Apr. 1, 1920. Other deaths cover Apr. 1, 1917-Dec. 31, 1918. (11) Includes Army Air Forces. (12) Battle deaths and wounds not mortal include casualties incurred in Oct. 1941 due to hostile action. (13) Estimated. (14) As reported by Commissioner of Pensions in his Annual Report for Fiscal Year 1903. (15) Number serving as of Mar. 31, 2003, i.e., does not include numbers of troops deployed since then.

Timeline of Major Wars Since 1066

Norman Conquest 1066-71	William I, duke of Normandy, landed on the English coast near Hastings on Sept. 28, 1066, and defeated Harold II, Saxon king of England, at Battle of Hastings Oct. 14. William crowned king Dec. 25 in Westminster Abbey. Most revolts were suppressed by 1071. **Conquest linked England's interests with those of the continent and led to its rise as a powerful monarchy.**
Crusades 1095-1270/1291	Military expeditions undertaken by **Western European Christians**, usually at the behest of the **papacy**, to recover **Jerusalem** and other Biblical places of pilgrimage from **Muslim** control. In the long term, stimulated trade and flow of ideas between East and West. Pope Urban II called Nov. 27, 1095, for the **First Crusade**; Crusaders took Jerusalem on July 15, 1099, massacred inhabitants, and founded four temporary states: Antioch, Edessa, Jerusalem, and Tripoli. The failed **Second Crusade** was prompted by Muslims' capture of Edessa in 1144. Jerusalem was captured by Ayyubid sultan Saladin on Oct. 2, 1187, leading to the **Third Crusade**, which involved the Holy Roman emperor, Frederick I (Barbarossa); the French king, Philip II (Augustus); and the English king, Richard I (Lion-Heart) but did not lead to a Crusader victory. The **Fourth Crusade** sacked Constantinople on Apr. 13, 1204. The **Fifth Crusade** began with capture of Damietta in Egypt (1219) but failed at Cairo. A **Sixth Crusade** led to the Treaty of Jaffa in 1229, giving Jerusalem to the Crusaders until 1244, when its seizure by the Khwarezmians led to the launch of a **Seventh Crusade**. The last crusade abruptly ended when its leader, French King Louis IX, died in 1270. The last major Crusader stronghold, Acre, was lost on May 18, 1291.
Hundred Years War 1337-1453	Series of armed conflicts over rival claims to the French throne, broken by a number of truces and peace treaties. Edward III declared self king of France in 1338 and invaded, with victories at Crécy (1346) and Poitiers (1356). **Treaty of Brétigny** signed May 8, 1360, but French king Charles V renewed fighting in 1369. Truce from 1396 until **Henry V** of England invaded in 1415 and **defeated French army at Agincourt**, capturing land north of Loire River, including Paris. **Treaty of Troyes** in 1420 made Henry VI heir of both thrones. The siege of French stronghold Orléans, lifted in 1429 with help from **Joan of Arc**, turned tide in favor of French, who won last battle (1453). **War ended English claims to France, paved way for French absolute monarchy.**
Wars of the Roses 1455-85	Series of dynastic civil wars for the throne in England fought by the **rival houses of Lancaster and York.** Richard, third duke of York, in conflict with the Lancastrian King **Henry VI**, won victories at St. Albans (1455) and Northampton (1460); Richard died at Battle of Wakefield on Dec. 30, 1460, before coronation, leaving his son to become King Edward IV. Henry VI imprisoned in Tower of London, 1465. Edward died in 1483; his brother became **Richard III** after usurping throne from Edward V, nephew. Henry Tudor defeated Richard III at the Battle of Bosworth Field (1485). As Henry VII, he married Edward IV's daughter Elizabeth, 1486, **uniting the houses.**
Thirty Years' War 1618-48	A series of religious and political conflicts involving **most countries of Western Europe**; majority of fighting in Germany, devastating it. Protestants stormed Habsburg palace in the "Defenestration of Prague" (May 23, 1618). Major conflicts included defeat of King Christian IV of Denmark and Norway by Catholic League (1626); victories by Lutheran King Gustav II Adolph of Sweden at Breitenfeld (1631) and Lützen (1632). France, under cardinal and statesman **Richelieu**, chief minister of King Louis XIII, declared war on the Habsburgs in May 1635; defeated Austro-Bavarian army (Aug. 3, 1645), leading to Truce of Ulm. **Peace of Westphalia** signed at Münster on Oct. 24, 1648, bringing peace by recognizing the rulers' sovereignty within their lands and their right to determine the religious beliefs of their subjects.
English Civil Wars 1638-60	Series of conflicts between followers of King Charles (Cavaliers) and of Parliament (Roundheads), over divine right of king versus Parliament's right to control national finances. Presbyterian Scots, allied with Parliament, rioted and in 1640 occupied the northern counties of England. **Oliver Cromwell**, second in command of Parliament's New Model Army, destroyed the king's army at Battle of Naseby (June 14, 1645); first civil war ended May 1646 when Charles surrendered to the Scots. Charles later allied with Scots but was defeated by Cromwell at Preston Aug. 17-19, 1648, and executed Jan. 30, 1649. Parliament abolished monarchy and House of Lords. Cromwell suppressed Irish and Scottish rebellions, was briefly succeeded by son Richard after death (1658). **Charles II restored to the throne** by the "Long Parliament," May 1660.
War of the Spanish Succession 1701-14	War fought by the Grand Alliance (originally England, Netherlands, Denmark, and Austria; later also Portugal), against coalition of France, Spain, and a number of small Italian and German principalities to preserve balance of power after death of Spanish king Charles II. Opened with invasion of Italy, via Venice, by an Austrian army under Prince Eugène of Savoy in May 1701. French forced to withdraw from Netherlands and Italy in 1706 and were finally defeated in 1709 in bloodiest battle of the war at French village of Malplaquet. Treaties of Rastatt and Baden signed in 1714; **Austria given control of Spanish Netherlands, and peace settled between Austria and France.**
War of the Austrian Succession 1740-48	Conflict over rival claims for the **hereditary dominions of the Habsburg family**, following death (1740) of Charles VI, Holy Roman emperor and archduke of Austria. An alliance of Bavaria, France, Spain, Sardinia, Prussia, and Saxony fought against Austria, allied with Holland and Great Britain. King Frederick the Great of Prussia captured Silesia from Austria in the First (1740-42) and Second (1744-45) Silesian Wars. British king George II decided French army at Battle of Dettingen am Main (June 27, 1743). French conquered Austrian Netherlands (1745-46). Treaty of Aix-la-Chapelle Oct. 18, 1748, **restored most original borders; Prussia became significant force.**
Seven Years' War 1756-63	Worldwide conflicts fought for **control of Germany and for supremacy in colonial N America and India**. French defeated British Gen. Edward Braddock in Battle of Monongahela in 1754, leading to formal declaration of **French-Indian War**, May 1756. Frederick II of Prussia invaded Saxony on Aug. 29, 1756; defeated French at Rossbach (1757), Austrians at Leuthen (1757), Russians at Zorndorf (1758). By 1760, British conquered French Canada. Peter III of Russia signed armistice with Prussia, 1762. Treaty of Paris signed Feb. 10, 1763; Peace of Hubertusburg Feb. 15, 1763, between Prussia and Austria. **England emerged as leading world naval power.**
American Revolution 1775-83	Conflict between Great Britain and 13 British colonies in eastern N America. George Washington took command of the Continental Army, July 3, 1775, and King George III declared colonies traitors on Aug. 23. **Declaration of Independence of colonies adopted July 4, 1776.** France recognized the colonies' independence Feb. 6, 1778, followed by Spain on June 21, 1779; both pledged support. French fleet drove British fleet under Adm. Thomas Graves from Chesapeake Bay on Sept. 5, 1781. French and Americans laid siege to Yorktown, VA, Sept. 28-Oct. 19, forcing British Gen. Cornwallis to surrender. **Treaty of Paris** (Sept. 3, 1783) recognized U.S. independence.
Wars of French Revolution and Napoleonic Wars 1792-1815	Large-scale wars fought between France and two multinational coalitions. France declared war on the Austrian part of the Holy Roman Empire, Apr. 20, 1792. Newly created French Republic declared war on monarchs of Britain and Holland, Feb. 1, 1793, and of Spain, Mar. 7. **Napoleon Bonaparte** defeated Austria in War I (1796-97), captured Egypt from Britain (1798-99; Battle of the Pyramids, July 21, 1798), and became First Consul after coup d'état of Nov. 9-10, 1799. French Grande Armée later swept through Europe using innovative and aggressive tactics. French navy decisively defeated by British under Adm. Horatio Nelson at **Trafalgar** (Oct. 21, 1805), but Napoleon defeated Austro-Russian forces at Austerlitz (Dec. 2) and controlled most of Europe except Russia and Great Britain by 1808. France suffered its first major defeat by Austria at Aspern-Essling, May 21-22, 1809. **Napoleon invaded Russia**, captured Moscow Sept. 14, 1812, but fled the bitter Russian winter and abandoned Germany after defeat at Leipzig, Oct. 16-19, 1813. Paris captured by Allied armies Mar. 30-31, 1814. Napoleon exiled to Elba May 4 but returned for "Hundred Days" reign, Mar. 20-June 28, 1815; **final defeat at Waterloo** by British and Prussian troops (June 18). The **Bourbon monarchy was restored under Louis XVIII**, and Britain, Prussia, Russia, and Austria maintained European peace.

Crimean War 1853-56	Conflict between **Russia** and coalition of **Great Britain, France, Sardinia, and Turkey for influence over Balkans** and the straits between the Black Sea and Mediterranean. Russia destroyed Turkish fleet at Sinope on Nov. 30, 1853. Britain and France declared war in Mar. 1854 and with Turkish troops defeated Russians at Battle of Alma River, Sept. 20. Lord Lucan of Britain prevented Russia from capturing Balaklava on Oct. 25 ("Charge of the Light Brigade" led by Lord Cardigan). Siege of Sevastopol ended when Russia evacuated Sept. 8, 1855. Treaty of Paris signed Mar. 30, 1856; **curbed Russian expansion and loosened European power alignments.**
American Civil War 1861-65	Conflict between the U.S. (the Union) and 11 secessionist Southern states (the Confederate States of America). Union garrison at Fort Sumter in harbor of Charleston, SC, surrendered to Brig. Gen. P.G.T. Beauregard (Apr. 12-13, 1861). Under Beauregard, 22,000 Confederates repelled 35,000 Union troops under Gen. Irvin McDowell along Bull Run stream near Manassas, VA (July 21). The *Merrimack* (renamed *Virginia*) battled the *Monitor* Mar. 9, 1862. In **Battle of Antietam,** MD (Sept. 17), some 12,000 Northerners and 12,700 Southerners were killed or wounded. Pres. Abraham Lincoln announced **Emancipation Proclamation** Sept. 22. Confederate Gen. Robert E. Lee's 75,000 forces battled 88,000 Union troops under Gen. George Meade at **Gettysburg,** PA, July 1-3, 1863; Lee's army forced across the Potomac R. Lee surrendered to Ulysses S. Grant at **Appomattox Court House** in Virginia (Apr. 9, 1865). **The Union was preserved and slavery subsequently abolished.**
Franco-Prussian War 1870-71	German states led by Prussia defeated France, seizing Alsace and part of Lorraine. French defeated in several major battles, culminating at **Sedan** Sept. 1, 1870, when Prussian forces decisively defeated the French army and captured emperor Napoleon III. Prussian king William I was made emperor of unified Germany, Jan 18, 1871. **France surrendered** Jan. 28. Final treaty signed May 10; set the stage for later **German imperialistic expansion.**
Spanish-American War 1898	War waged by the U.S. to **liberate Cuba from Spanish rule.** A mysterious explosion, blamed on Spain by American newspapers, sank the U.S. battleship *Maine* in Havana's harbor (Feb. 15, 1898), killing 260. The U.S. called for Spain's withdrawal from Cuba, and Spain declared war (Apr. 24). William Rufus Shafter led 17,000 U.S. troops from Daiquirí to Santiago de Cuba, taking **San Juan Hill** with help of the Rough Riders under Teddy Roosevelt. Santiago de Cuba surrendered July 17. The Treaty of Paris (Dec. 10, 1898) provided for the **independence of Cuba** and the cession by Spain to the U.S. of **Puerto Rico, Guam, and for a $20 mil payment, the Philippine Islands.**
World War I 1914-18	Local European war that grew into a global war involving 32 nations; the Allies and the Associated Powers—28 nations including Great Britain, France, Russia, Italy, and the U.S.—versus the Central Powers of Germany, Austria-Hungary, Turkey, and Bulgaria. Archduke Francis Ferdinand of Austria assassinated in Sarajevo, Bosnia (June 28, 1914). Germany invaded France through Belgium; advance on Paris halted by the French under Gen. Joseph Jacques Césaire Joffre at the **First Battle of the Marne,** Sept. 5-12. Germany checked the Russian army at the Battle of Tannenberg, Aug. 26-30. The British suffered 57,470 casualties (19,240 dead) in the opening day of the **First Battle of the Somme** (July 1-Nov. 18, 1916), first of 12 battles that forced Germany back to Hindenburg Line. **U.S. declared war on Germany Apr. 6, 1917.** Russian involvement ended when Bolshevik party seized power on Nov. 7; signed armistice Dec. 15. German offensive halted by U.S. and French troops at **Second Battle of the Marne** (July 15-Aug. 5, 1918), turning point of the war. Allied counteroffensive broke the fortified defensive Hindenburg Line, and an armistice was signed Nov. 11.
World War II 1939-45	Global military conflict stemming from European unrest after World War I and Japan's aggressive expansion into Asia and the Pacific. **War in Europe:** Nazi-Soviet nonaggression pact (Aug. 23, 1939) freed Germany and the Soviet Union to attack Poland in Sept. **Britain and France declared war on Germany** Sept. 3. German forces raced through Europe (Apr.-June 1940), captured Paris June 14. **Italy declared war on France and Britain** June 10. German-Italian campaigns won the Balkans and N Africa by June 1941. U.S. entered war Dec. 1941. Three million Axis troops invaded Russia June 22, 1941, but Russian counterthrusts stopped the German advance (**Stalingrad,** Aug. 20, 1942-Feb. 2, 1943), and Allies took N Africa (Nov. 8, 1942-May 13, 1943), Italy (July 10, 1943-May 2, 1945). Normandy invaded on **D-Day,** June 6, 1944; Paris liberated Aug. 25. Leaders at Yalta Conference (Feb. 4-11, 1945) discussed defeat and division of Germany into four. Adolf Hitler committed suicide Apr. 30. **Germany surrendered unconditionally** May 7. **War in the Pacific:** Japan invaded China (July 7, 1937), joined alliance with Germany and Italy (Sept. 27, 1940), and signed nonaggression pact with Russia (Apr. 13, 1941); attacked Hawaii's Pearl Harbor, Dec. 7, 1941; U.S. declared war on Japan Dec. 8. **Battle of Midway** (June 4-7, 1942) repulsed Japanese advance. Marines landed on Guadalcanal Aug. 7. Navy defeated Japanese fleet at **Leyte Gulf,** Oct. 23-26, 1944. B-29 bombing raids on Japan began in Nov. Marines invaded Iwo Jima (Feb. 19-Mar. 16, 1945) with heavy casualties, then Okinawa (Apr. 1-June 21). **U.S. atom bombs dropped** on Hiroshima (Aug. 6) and Nagasaki (Aug. 9) and Soviet invasion of Manchuria (Aug. 8) **forced Japan to agree, on Aug. 14, to surrender;** formal surrender Sept. 2.
Korean War 1950-53	Military struggle fought on the Korean Peninsula between the Democratic Peoples' Republic of Korea (N Korea) and the Republic of Korea (S Korea) that developed into an international war involving China allied with N Korea against the U.S. and other nations under the UN flag. DPRK army crossed the 38th parallel and invaded S Korea (June 25, 1950), entering Seoul (June 26). Amphibious assault launched at **Inchon** by Gen. Douglas MacArthur (Sept. 15) helped U.S. forces rout DPRK close to Yalu River by Nov. 24. The Chinese, in counterattack, retook Seoul (Jan. 4, 1951) but were forced back to the 38th parallel by Apr. 22. Armistice was signed (July 27, 1953) by the UN, DPRK, and China, but not ROK, **leaving the peninsula partitioned at about the 38th parallel.**
Vietnam War 1959-75	Struggle primarily in S Vietnam that widened into a war between S Vietnam supported mainly by the U.S. and N Vietnam supported by the USSR and China. Viet Minh, led by Communist leader Ho Chi Minh, formed the Democratic Republic of Vietnam (Sept. 2, 1945). Colonial power France withdrew after fortress at Dien Bien Phu fell (May 8, 1954). Pres. John F. Kennedy pledged U.S. commitment to S Vietnamese independence Dec. 14, 1961. USS *Maddox* destroyer damaged in **Gulf of Tonkin** (Aug. 2, 1964), prompting Congress to increase involvement. Regular bombing of N Vietnam began (Feb. 24, 1965), and the first U.S. combat ground forces arrived (Mar. 6). N Vietnamese Army siege of **Khe Sanh** (Jan. 21-Apr. 7, 1968) and the **"Tet" offensive** (Jan. 30) aimed to cause insurrection in the S. **My Lai Massacre** by U.S. soldiers of civilians (Mar. 16, 1968) created scandal, fueled U.S. disaffection with war. U.S. forces peaked at 543,400 in Apr. 1969. NVA **"Easter Offensive"** (Mar. 30, 1972) rebuffed, and U.S. responded with aerial bombings in May and Dec. U.S. withdrew after cease-fire, Jan. 1973. **NVA offensive captured Saigon, Apr. 30, 1975,** and unified Vietnam under Communist rule.
Persian Gulf Wars 1991, 2003-10	Conflicts fought principally between Iraq and the U.S. concerning Iraq's influence in the Middle East and its development of weapons of mass destruction. **First Gulf War:** Iraq under dictator Saddam Hussein invaded Kuwait Aug. 2, 1990, and annexed it; UN Security Council ordered Iraqi forces to withdraw by Jan. 15, 1991. Beginning Jan. 17, a U.S.-led multinational force (**Operation Desert Storm**) bombed military targets in Iraq and Kuwait. A coordinated air-land offensive (**Operation Desert Sabre,** begun Feb. 24) retook Kuwait City Feb. 26, and permanent cease-fire was signed on Apr. 6. Iraq was ordered to pay reparations to Kuwait, reveal locations of biological and chemical weapons, and eliminate weapons of mass destruction. **Second Gulf War:** The U.S. and UK mistakenly asserted that Iraq was still producing WMDs and posed an imminent threat. The UN passed Resolution 1441, Nov. 8, 2002, warning Iraq of "serious consequences" if it failed to cooperate fully and unconditionally with UN weapons inspectors. Iraq rejected a Mar. 17, 2003, U.S. ultimatum demanding Hussein and his sons leave Iraq. U.S. launched **Operation Iraqi Freedom**, Mar 19, 2003, with support from UK and other allies, but without full UN Security Council support. Baghdad fell Apr. 9, and major combat operations declared over May 1. Hussein was captured Dec. 13, 2003, but guerrilla opposition to U.S. troops and insurgent violence continued. U.S. combat operations in Iraq formally ended Aug. 31, 2010.

FOOD AND AGRICULTURE

Number and Acreage of Farms by State, 2000, 2019

Source: National Agricultural Statistics Service, U.S. Dept. of Agriculture

State	No. of farms (thous.) 2019	2000	Acreage in farms (mil) 2019	2000	Acreage per farm 2019	2000	State	No. of farms (thous.) 2019	2000	Acreage in farms (mil) 2019	2000	Acreage per farm 2019	2000
AL	38.8	47.0	8.3	9.0	214	191	NE	45.7	46.1	44.9	46.1	982	887
AK	1.1	0.6	0.9	0.9	810	1,569	NV	3.4	3.1	6.1	6.4	1,821	2,065
AZ	19.0	10.7	26.2	26.9	1,379	2,518	NH	4.1	3.3	0.4	0.4	105	133
AR	42.3	48.0	14.0	14.6	331	304	NJ	9.9	9.7	0.8	0.8	76	86
CA	69.9	83.1	24.3	28.0	348	337	NM	24.8	18.0	40.0	44.9	1,613	2,494
CO	38.7	30.0	31.8	31.6	822	1,060	NY	33.4	37.5	6.9	7.7	207	205
CT	5.5	4.2	0.4	0.4	69	86	NC	46.2	55.5	8.4	9.2	182	166
DE	2.3	2.6	0.5	0.6	230	215	ND	26.1	30.8	39.3	39.4	1,506	1,279
FL	47.4	44.0	9.7	10.4	205	238	OH	77.8	79.0	13.6	14.8	175	187
GA	41.5	49.1	10.2	10.9	246	223	OK	77.3	84.5	34.4	33.8	445	401
HI	7.3	5.5	1.1	1.4	151	251	OR	37.2	40.0	15.8	17.3	425	433
ID	24.6	24.5	11.5	11.9	467	486	PA	52.7	59.0	7.3	7.7	139	130
IL	71.4	77.0	27.0	27.5	378	357	RI	1.1	0.8	0.1	0.1	55	75
IN	56.0	63.4	14.9	15.2	266	240	SC	24.6	24.2	4.8	4.9	195	203
IA	85.3	94.0	30.6	32.5	359	346	SD	29.6	32.4	43.2	44.0	1,459	1,358
KS	58.5	64.5	45.7	47.5	781	736	TN	69.7	88.0	10.8	11.8	155	134
KY	74.8	90.0	12.9	13.7	172	152	TX	247.0	228.3	126.5	130.9	512	573
LA	27.4	29.0	8.0	8.0	292	277	UT	17.8	15.5	10.7	11.6	601	747
ME	7.6	7.1	1.3	1.4	171	190	VT	6.8	6.6	1.2	1.3	176	192
MD	12.4	12.4	2.0	2.1	161	172	VA	42.4	48.5	7.8	8.7	184	180
MA	7.2	6.1	0.5	0.5	69	89	WA	35.6	37.0	14.6	15.6	410	420
MI	47.0	53.0	9.8	10.2	209	192	WV	22.9	20.8	3.5	3.6	153	173
MN	68.0	81.0	25.5	27.9	375	344	WI	64.9	77.5	14.3	16.0	220	206
MS	34.5	42.0	10.4	11.2	301	266	WY	12.0	9.2	29.0	34.5	2,417	3,750
MO	95.2	109.0	27.6	30.2	290	277	U.S.	2,023.4	2,166.8	897.4	945.1	444	436
MT	26.8	27.8	58.0	59.3	2,164	2,133							

Supplemental Nutrition Assistance Program (SNAP), 1969-2019

Source: Food and Nutrition Service (FNS), U.S. Dept. of Agriculture

Fiscal year	Avg. participation (thous.)	Avg. monthly benefit per person	Total benefits (mil)	All other costs (mil)[1]	Total costs (mil)	Fiscal year	Avg. participation (thous.)	Avg. monthly benefit per person	Total benefits (mil)	All other costs (mil)[1]	Total costs (mil)
1969	2,878	$6.63	$228.8	$21.7	$250.5	2006	26,549	$94.75	$30,187.4	$2,715.7	$32,903.1
1970	4,340	10.55	549.7	27.2	576.9	2007	26,316	96.18	30,373.3	2,800.3	33,173.5
1975	17,064	21.40	4,385.5	233.2	4,618.7	2008	28,223	102.19	34,608.4	3,031.3	37,639.6
1980	21,082	34.47	8,720.9	485.6	9,206.5	2009	33,490	125.31	50,359.9	3,260.0	53,619.9
1985	19,899	44.99	10,743.6	959.6	11,703.2	2010	40,302	133.79	64,702.2	3,581.3	68,283.5
1990	20,049	58.78	14,142.8	1,304.5	15,447.3	2011	44,709	133.85	71,810.9	3,875.6	75,686.5
1995	26,619	71.27	22,764.1	1,856.3	24,620.4	2012	46,609	133.41	74,619.3	3,791.8	78,411.1
1999	18,183	72.27	15,769.4	2,051.5	17,820.9	2013	47,636	133.07	76,066.3	3,792.7	79,859.0
2000	17,194	72.62	14,983.3	2,070.7	17,054.0	2014	46,664	125.01	69,998.8	4,061.5	74,060.3
2001	17,318	74.81	15,547.4	2,242.0	17,789.4	2015	45,767	126.81	69,645.1	4,301.0	73,946.2
2002	19,096	79.67	18,256.2	2,380.8	20,637.0	2016	44,220	125.40	66,539.3	4,374.3	70,913.6
2003	21,250	83.94	21,404.3	2,412.0	23,816.3	2017	42,233	125.71	63,711.1	4,463.6	68,174.6
2004	23,811	86.16	24,618.9	2,480.1	27,099.0	2018[2]	39,431	124.68	58,996.5	4,524.5	63,521.0
2005	25,628	92.89	28,567.9	2,504.1	31,072.0	2019[2]	34,474	129.95	53,758.2	4,717.0	58,475.2

(1) Includes the federal share of state administrative expenses, nutrition education, and employment and training programs, in addition to other federal costs (e.g., benefit and retailer redemption and monitoring, payment accuracy, EBT [electronic benefit transfer] systems, program evaluation and modernization, program access, health and nutrition pilot projects). (2) Excludes North Carolina.

U.S. Federal Food Assistance Programs, 1990-2019

Source: Food and Nutrition Service (FNS), U.S. Dept. of Agriculture

(in millions of dollars; for fiscal years ending on Sept. 30)

Program	1990	1995	2000	2005	2010	2015	2017	2018	2019
Supplemental Nutrition Assistance Program (SNAP)[1]	$15,491	$24,620	$17,054	$31,073	$68,284	$73,946	$68,175	$65,452	$60,357
Puerto Rico nutrition assistance[2]	937	1,131	1,268	1,495	2,001	1,951	1,949	1,920	1,924
Natl. school lunch[3]	3,834	5,160	6,149	8,031	10,880	13,003	13,644	13,823	14,199
School breakfast[3,4]	596	1,048	1,393	1,927	2,859	3,892	4,252	4,396	4,546
WIC (Women, Infants, and Children)[5]	2,122	3,440	3,982	4,994	6,690	6,241	5,706	5,463	5,225
Summer food service[6]	164	237	267	267	359	488	483	473	481
Child and adult care[7]	813	1,464	1,683	2,111	2,638	3,307	3,537	3,622	3,735
Special milk[4]	19	17	15	16	12	11	8	8	7
Nutrition for the elderly (NSIP)[8]	142	148	137	4	3	3	3	3	3
Food distrib. to Indian reserv.[9]	66	65	76	76	95	120	122	126	135
Commodity supplemental food[9]	85	99	98	156	165	193	206	230	257
Food distrib. to charitable insts.[10]	104	64	2	4	1	0	0	0	0
Emergency food assistance (TEFAP)[11]	334	135	225	373	631	525	660	630	764
Total[12]	24,707	37,628	32,349	50,527	94,618	103,680	98,745	96,146	91,633

Note: 2019 data are preliminary. All data subject to revision by the FNS. (1) Formerly known as the Food Stamp Program. Includes benefits and admin. expenses. (2) Provides benefits analogous to SNAP. (3) Nine-month averages (summer months excluded). (4) Cash payments based on federal reimbursement rates to states. (5) Includes food benefits, nutrition services and admin. funds, Farmers' Market Nutrition Program, infrastructure, breastfeeding promotion and peer counseling, program evaluation, and technical assistance. (6) Includes cash payments, commodity costs, and admin. costs for services similar to natl. school lunch and breakfast programs. (7) Includes cash payments, entitlement and bonus commodities, cash-in-lieu of commodities, sponsor admin. costs, start-up costs, and audits. (8) For 2003 and on, Nutrition Services Incentive Program administered by the Agency on Aging, Dept. of Health and Human Services; FNS costs limited to value of commodities distributed. (9) Includes cost of commodity distrib. and admin. expenses. (10) Includes summer camps. (11) Includes cost of commodities to hunger relief orgs. (e.g., food banks, soup kitchens) and admin. expenses. (12) Does not include federal share of state admin. costs for some programs shown.

U.S. Cost of Food, 2020

Source: Center for Nutrition Policy and Promotion (CNPP), U.S. Dept. of Agriculture (USDA)

Age-gender group	Weekly cost				Monthly cost			
	Thrifty plan	Low-cost plan	Mod.-cost plan	Liberal plan	Thrifty plan	Low-cost plan	Mod.-cost plan	Liberal plan
Individual child[1]								
1 year	$22.90	$30.80	$34.90	$42.20	$99.10	$133.70	$151.20	$183.00
2-3 years	25.00	32.30	38.50	47.00	108.40	140.00	167.00	203.60
4-5 years	26.40	33.10	41.40	49.80	114.40	143.20	179.30	215.70
6-8 years	33.90	48.20	56.60	66.30	147.00	208.80	245.20	287.40
9-11 years	38.00	49.90	65.30	76.10	164.90	216.10	283.10	329.90
Individual male[1]								
12-13 years	40.80	58.40	72.80	85.60	177.00	253.10	315.60	370.80
14-18 years	42.00	59.20	75.00	87.20	182.10	256.30	324.80	377.90
19-50 years	45.10	58.70	73.40	90.20	195.30	254.30	318.20	390.70
51-70 years	41.10	55.40	69.50	83.50	178.20	239.80	301.30	361.70
71+ years	41.30	54.50	67.80	83.60	178.70	236.20	293.80	362.10
Individual female[1]								
12-13 years	40.30	49.80	60.30	74.30	174.60	215.80	261.20	321.80
14-18 years	39.90	49.90	59.80	73.90	172.80	216.20	259.20	320.30
19-50 years	40.00	50.80	62.40	79.40	173.10	220.20	270.40	344.20
51-70 years	39.70	49.50	61.50	74.30	172.20	214.30	266.40	322.00
71+ years	38.70	48.90	60.90	73.10	167.70	211.90	263.80	316.90
2-person family[2]								
19-50 years	93.50	120.50	149.40	186.60	405.20	522.00	647.50	808.40
51-70 years	89.00	115.30	144.10	173.60	385.50	499.60	624.50	752.00
4-person family[3] with 2 children ages—								
2-3 and 4-5 years	136.40	174.90	215.80	266.40	591.20	757.80	934.90	1,154.20
6-8 and 9-11 years	157.00	207.60	257.80	312.10	680.30	899.50	1,116.90	1,352.20

Note: As of June 2020. The official USDA food plans represent a nutritious diet at four different cost levels. The nutritional bases are the 1997-2005 Dietary Reference Intakes, 2005 Dietary Guidelines for Americans, and 2005 MyPyramid food intake recommendations. In addition to cost, differences among plans are in specific foods and quantities of foods. Another basis of the food plans is that all meals and snacks are prepared at home. For specific foods and quantities, see *Thrifty Food Plan, 2006* and *The Low-Cost, Moderate-Cost, and Liberal Food Plans, 2007* from the CNPP. All four plans are based on 2001-02 data and updated to current dollars using the consumer price index for specific food items. All costs are rounded to nearest 10 cents. (1) The costs given are for individuals in 4-person families. (2) Male and female. (3) Defined as a couple (male and female), 19-50 years old, and two children.

U.S. Household Food Security by Selected Characteristics, 2019

Source: Economic Research Service, U.S. Dept. of Agriculture

(in thousands of households)

	Total[1]	Food secure		With low food security		With very low food security	
		No.	%	No.	%	No.	%
All households	129,621	115,959	89.5%	8,340	6.4%	5,322	4.1%
Household composition							
With children under 18 years old	37,614	32,480	86.4	3,677	9.7	1,457	3.9
With children under 6 years old	16,115	13,783	85.5	1,736	10.8	596	3.7
Married-couple families	24,382	22,543	92.5	1,494	6.1	345	1.4
Female head, no spouse	9,349	6,663	71.3	1,790	19.1	896	9.6
Male head, no spouse	3,311	2,802	84.6	313	9.5	196	5.9
Other household with child[2]	572	472	82.5	NA	NA	NA	NA
With no children under 18 years old	92,007	83,479	90.7	4,663	5.1	3,865	4.2
More than one adult	54,420	50,762	93.3	2,185	4.0	1,473	2.7
Women living alone	20,886	18,161	87.0	1,386	6.6	1,339	6.4
Men living alone	16,701	14,556	87.2	1,092	6.5	1,053	6.3
With elderly	40,220	37,318	92.8	1,842	4.6	1,060	2.6
Elderly living alone	15,329	13,996	91.3	801	5.2	532	3.5
Race/ethnicity of households							
White, non-Hispanic	85,196	78,438	92.1	3,966	4.6	2,792	3.3
Black, non-Hispanic	16,504	13,356	80.9	1,891	11.5	1,257	7.6
Other, non-Hispanic	9,886	8,949	90.5	546	5.5	391	4.0
Hispanic[3]	18,035	15,216	84.4	1,937	10.7	882	4.9
Area of residence[4]							
Inside metropolitan area	111,547	100,071	89.7	6,990	6.3	4,486	4.0
In principal cities[5]	38,411	33,662	87.6	2,875	7.5	1,874	4.9
Not in principal cities	55,517	50,923	91.7	2,867	5.2	1,727	3.1
Outside metropolitan area	18,073	15,887	87.9	1,350	7.5	836	4.6

NA = Not reported. **Note:** Low food security households report food acquisition problems and reduced diet quality but typically few, if any, indications of reduced food intake. The very low food security category identifies households in which the food intake of one or more members was reduced and eating patterns disrupted because of insufficient money and resources for food. (1) Totals exclude households of unknown food security status. Exclusions represented 0.2% of all households in 2019. (2) Households with children in complex living arrangements, e.g., children of other relatives or unrelated roommate or boarder. (3) Hispanics may be of any race. (4) Based on 2013 Office of Management and Budget delineations of metropolitan areas. (5) Households within incorporated areas of the largest cities in each metropolitan area. Residence in or out of principal cities unknown for about 16% of households in metropolitan statistical areas.

Recent Food Insufficiency for U.S. Households, 2020

Source: U.S. Census Bureau Household Pulse Survey, Week 12

Select characteristics	Total[1]	Households with food insufficiency in the last 7 days, July 16-21, 2020			
		% with enough food, but not always the types wanted	% reporting "sometimes not enough to eat"	% reporting "often not enough to eat"	% that did not report
Total............................	115,585,275	69.2%	20.6%	4.7%	5.4%
Reason for recent food insufficiency[2]					
Couldn't afford to buy more food.....	58,575,199	59.3	32.7	8.0	—
Couldn't get out to buy food.........	15,247,539	69.7	23.8	6.4	—
Afraid to go or didn't want to go out to buy food......................	31,498,692	80.8	16.8	2.4	—
Couldn't get groceries or meals delivered	6,193,639	69.4	23.9	6.7	—
The stores didn't have the food I wanted.....................	35,108,077	87.4	10.6	2.0	—
Received free groceries or meal in last 7 days.........................	15,625,694	61.4	29.3		
Did not receive free groceries/meal	92,895,450	74.2	20.2	4.3	1.3
Provider of free groceries or free meal[2]					
School or other programs aimed at children	6,819,663	66.9	29.5	2.9	0.7
Food pantry or food bank	6,188,379	56.6	30.8	12.1	0.5
Home-delivered meal service	560,014	62.4	33.8	1.8	2.0
Religious organization..............	3,577,678	49.1	41.3	8.9	0.7
Shelter or soup kitchen.............	289,823	49.8	28.4	18.8	3.0
Other community program	2,398,724	61.3	21.2	16.8	0.7
Family, friends, or neighbors	4,383,229	58.7	31.8	9.4	0.1
Confidence in being able to afford food in next 4 weeks					
Not at all confident	23,143,118	40.5	42.3	16.5	0.7
Somewhat confident................	42,464,640	74.7	22.0	2.4	0.8
Moderately confident...............	26,413,146	87.7	11.1	0.5	0.7
Very confident	11,256,782	93.7	2.6	0.9	2.8
Did not report	12,307,590	42.2	12.3	2.8	42.7

— = Not available. (1) Includes "Did not report." (2) Totals may not add to 100 as the question allowed for multiple categories to be marked.

U.S. Annual Per Capita Consumption of Selected Foods, 1970-2017

Source: Economic Research Service, U.S. Dept. of Agriculture; Distilled Spirits Council of the U.S.; Beer Institute; Wine Institute

(fruits and vegetables in pounds, beverages in gallons)

	1970	1990	2017	% change, 1970-2017		1970	1990	2017	% change, 1970-2017
Fresh fruit	100.6	117.3	142.7	41.8%	Fresh vegetables	154.4	176.4	202.6	31.3%
Apples...............	17.2	19.8	17.8	3.5	Broccoli..............	0.5	3.4	7.1	1,236.5
Avocados	0.5	1.4	7.5	1,568.8	Carrots	6.0	8.3	7.4	23.2
Bananas	17.4	24.3	28.7	65.3	Cucumbers	2.8	4.7	7.4	163.6
Grapes	2.9	7.9	8.3	183.0	Garlic	0.4	1.4	3.0	581.7
Oranges	16.1	12.6	8.0	−50.1	Lettuce head..........	22.4	27.7	15.2	−32.0
Peaches/nectarines	5.8	5.5	2.7	−53.0	Onions	10.1	15.1	25.1	147.1
Strawberries	1.7	3.2	8.4	381.7	Potatoes	61.8	46.7	34.4	−44.4
					Tomatoes	12.1	15.5	20.5	68.4
Canned vegetables....	100.7	110.3	84.8	−15.8	**Beverages**				
Sweet corn	14.3	10.9	5.1	−64.6	Orange juice..........	3.6	3.6	2.5	−31.8
Tomatoes	62.1	75.3	57.9	−6.8	Coffee...............	33.4	26.8	26.2[2]	−21.5[2]
Frozen vegetables	43.7	66.7	72.8	66.6	Beer	18.5	23.9	19.0	2.7
Broccoli..............	1.0	2.2	2.4	140.0	Wine	1.3	2.1	2.9	124.4
Carrots	1.4	2.3	2.4	71.4	**Sweeteners**	119.1	132.3	127.3	6.8
Green peas...........	1.9	2.2	1.3	−31.6	Sugar (refined)	101.8	64.4	69.3	−31.9
Potatoes	28.5	46.4	51.9	82.1	Honey...............	1.0	0.7	1.4	42.3
Sweet corn	5.7	8.6	8.1	42.1	High fructose corn syrup	0.5	49.6	39.8	7,166.8

Note: All figures are rounded; percent change is calculated based on unrounded original data. Per capita consumption based on total population. Alcoholic beverage consumption would be higher if based on legal drinking age population. (1) As of 2015. (2) Percent change as of 1970-2015.

U.S. Meat Production and Consumption, 1940-2020

Source: Economic Research Service, U.S. Dept. of Agriculture

(in millions of pounds)

Year	Beef		Veal		Lamb and mutton		Pork		All red meats[1]		All poultry[2]	
	Prod.	Cons.	Prod.	Cons.	Prod.	Cons.	Prod.	Cons.	Prod.	Cons.	Prod.	Cons.
1940	7,175	7,257	981	981	876	873	10,044	9,701	19,076	18,812	NA	NA
1950	9,534	9,825	1,230	1,206	597	602	10,714	10,612	22,075	22,279	3,174	3,097
1960	14,753	15,490	1,109	1,118	768	856	13,905	14,057	30,535	31,521	6,310	6,168
1970	21,684	23,451	588	613	551	669	14,699	14,957	37,522	39,689	10,193	9,981
1980	21,643	23,560	400	420	318	351	16,617	16,838	38,978	41,170	14,173	13,525
1990	22,743	24,030	327	325	363	397	15,354	16,025	38,787	40,778	23,468	22,152
2000	26,888	27,338	225	225	234	354	18,952	18,643	46,299	46,560	36,073	30,508
2010	26,412	26,392	145	150	168	317	22,437	19,072	49,180	45,931	43,058	35,201
2015	23,760	24,771	88	88	155	357	24,517	20,656	48,520	45,872	45,769	38,785
2016	25,221	25,673	81	73	155	381	24,941	20,891	50,388	47,019	47,225	39,577
2017	26,187	26,492	80	78	150	396	25,584	21,035	51,991	48,000	48,118	40,236
2018	26,872	26,762	80	89	158	415	26,315	21,491	53,417	48,757	49,018	40,975
2019	27,155	27,272	79	81	153	421	27,638	22,188	55,015	49,963	50,251	42,081
2020*	26,934	27,121	NA	NA	NA	NA	28,536	21,990	55,682	49,597	50,862	42,686

NA = Not available. * = July projection. (1) Includes beef, veal, lamb and mutton, and pork. May not add up to totals because of rounding. (2) Includes broilers, turkeys, and mature chicken.

Estimated Calorie Requirements

Source: *2015-2020 Dietary Guidelines for Americans*, U.S. Dept. of Agriculture and U.S. Dept. of Health and Human Services
Estimated amount of calories, rounded to the nearest 200, needed to maintain energy balance by sex, for various age groups and levels of physical activity. In adults, calorie needs generally decrease with age.

	Age (years)	Sedentary[1]	Moderately active[2]	Active[3]		Age (years)	Sedentary[1]	Moderately active[2]	Active[3]
Female[4]	2-3	1,000	1,000-1,200	1,000-1,400	Male	2-3	1,000	1,000-1,400	1,000-1,400
	4-8	1,200-1,400	1,400-1,600	1,400-1,800		4-8	1,200-1,400	1,400-1,600	1,600-2,000
	9-13	1,400-1,600	1,600-2,000	1,800-2,200		9-13	1,600-2,000	1,800-2,200	2,000-2,600
	14-18	1,800	2,000	2,400		14-18	2,000-2,400	2,400-2,800	2,800-3,200
	19-30	1,800-2,000	2,000-2,200	2,400		19-30	2,400-2,600	2,600-2,800	3,000
	31-50	1,800	2,000	2,200		31-50	2,200-2,400	2,400-2,600	2,800-3,000
	51+	1,600	1,800	2,000-2,200		51+	2,000-2,200	2,200-2,400	2,400-2,800

Note: Based on Estimated Energy Requirements (EER) equations, using reference heights and weights. The reference man is 5 ft 10 in. tall and weighs 154 lbs. The reference woman is 5 ft 4 in. tall and weighs 126 lbs. (1) Engaging only in the light activities associated with ordinary day-to-day life. (2) Includes physical activity equivalent to walking 1.5-3 mi per day at 3-4 mph. (3) Includes physical activity equivalent to walking more than 3 mi per day at 3-4 mph. (4) Excludes women who are pregnant or breastfeeding.

Top 10 Calorie Sources in American Diets

Source: National Health and Nutrition Examination Survey, 2005-06, National Center for Health Statistics, CDC, U.S. Dept. of Health and Human Services

Rank	All Americans (ages 2+)	Rank	Children and adolescents (ages 2-18)	Rank	All adults (ages 19+)
1.	Grain-based desserts	1.	Grain-based desserts	1.	Grain-based desserts
2.	Yeast breads	2.	Pizza	2.	Yeast breads
3.	Chicken dishes	3.	Soda/energy/sports drinks	3.	Chicken dishes
4.	Soda/energy/sports drinks	4.	Yeast breads	4.	Soda/energy/sports drinks
5.	Pizza	5.	Chicken dishes	5.	Alcoholic beverages
6.	Alcoholic beverages	6.	Pasta dishes	6.	Pizza
7.	Pasta dishes	7.	Reduced-fat milk	7.	Tortillas, burritos, tacos
8.	Tortillas, burritos, tacos	8.	Dairy desserts	8.	Pasta dishes
9.	Beef dishes	9.	Potato/corn/other chips	9.	Beef dishes
10.	Dairy desserts	10.	Ready-to-eat cereals	10.	Dairy desserts

Note: Data are drawn from analyses of usual dietary intakes conducted by the Natl. Cancer Institute. Foods and beverages consumed were divided into 97 categories and ranked according to calorie contribution to the diet. Average total daily calorie intake was 2,157 overall, 2,027 for children and adolescents (ages 2-18), and 2,199 for adults (ages 19+).

Understanding Food Components

Water dissolves and transports other nutrients throughout the body, aiding in the processes of digestion, absorption, circulation, and excretion. It helps regulate body temperature.

Macronutrients

Carbohydrates, of which starches and sugars are the major types, are the most important source of energy for the body. The digestive system changes carbohydrates into glucose, which the body uses for energy for cells, tissues, and organs. The body stores extra sugar in the liver and muscles. Best sources: grains, legumes, vegetables, fruits.

Fats provide energy by furnishing calories to the body. They also help the body absorb vitamins A, D, E, and K. Best sources of polyunsaturated and monounsaturated fats: olive, canola, and peanut oils; nuts and nut butters; olives; avocado. Sources of saturated fats: meats, cheeses, butter, cream, egg yolks, lard.

Fiber is the portion of plant foods that our bodies cannot digest. There are two basic types: insoluble and soluble. Insoluble fibers help move food materials through the digestive tract; soluble fibers tend to slow them down. Both types absorb water, thus preventing constipation. Soluble fibers may also be helpful in reducing blood cholesterol levels. Best sources: beans, bran, fruits, whole grains, vegetables.

Proteins, composed of amino acids, are essential to good nutrition. They build, maintain, and repair the body. Proteins from animal sources (eggs, meat, fish, milk) supply adequate amounts of all indispensable amino acids and are thus called complete. Proteins from plants, legumes, nuts, seeds, and vegetables can be combined to complete protein needs.

Vitamins

Vitamin A promotes good eyesight; helps keep skin and mucous membranes resistant to infection. Best sources: liver, sweet potatoes, carrots, kale, cantaloupe, fortified milk.

Vitamin B_1 (thiamin) is essential to energy metabolism and the growth, development, and function of cells. Best sources: whole grains, fortified bread and cereal, pork, fish, seeds.

Vitamin B_2 (riboflavin) is essential to growth, red blood cell production, and energy metabolism. Best sources: eggs, dairy products, organ meats, lean meats, bread products, fortified cereal, green vegetables.

Vitamin B_6 (pyridoxine and related compounds) is important in making antibodies, maintaining normal nerve function, and protein metabolism. Best sources: fish, organ meats, potatoes, noncitrus fruits, chickpeas.

Vitamin B_{12} (cobalamin) is needed to form red blood cells. Best sources: beef liver, clams, meat, fish, poultry, eggs.

Folate (vitamin B_9; folic acid is a synthetic form used in supplements and fortified foods) is required for making DNA and other genetic material and for cell division. Best sources: liver, dark green leafy vegetables, enriched and whole-grain breads, fortified cereals.

Niacin (vitamin B_3) helps turn food into energy and is important for cell development and function. Best sources: poultry, nuts, fish.

Other B vitamins include biotin and pantothenic acid.

Vitamin C (ascorbic acid) is needed to make collagen, a protein necessary for the formation of skin, ligaments, and bones as well as wound healing; also acts as an antioxidant. Best sources: citrus fruits, broccoli, Brussels sprouts, potatoes, tomatoes, red and green peppers.

Vitamin D is important for bone development. Best sources: sunlight, fortified dairy products, tuna, salmon.

Vitamin E is an antioxidant and enhances immune function. Best sources: vegetable oils, nuts, seeds, green leafy vegetables.

Vitamin K is necessary for formation of prothrombin, which helps blood to clot. Best dietary sources: green leafy vegetables, plant oils. Also made by intestinal bacteria.

Minerals

Calcium works with phosphorus to build and maintain bones and teeth. Best sources: dairy, leafy green vegetables.

Iron is a component of hemoglobin, which transports oxygen within blood, and myoglobin, which supplies oxygen to the muscles. Best sources: lean meats, beans, green leafy vegetables, seafood, whole grains, fortified cereal.

Phosphorus is present in every cell of the body, and its primary function is the development of bones and teeth. Best sources: cheese, milk, meats, poultry, fish.

Other minerals include chloride, chromium, copper, fluoride, iodine, magnesium, manganese, molybdenum, potassium, selenium, sodium, zinc.

Understanding Food Label Claims

Source: Center for Food Safety and Applied Nutrition, U.S. Food and Drug Admin. (FDA), U.S. Dept. of Health and Human Services; Food Safety and Inspection Service, Agricultural Marketing Service, U.S. Dept. of Agriculture (USDA)

Nutrition Packaging Terms

Manufacturers can make certain claims on processed food labels only if they meet the definitions specified here.

SUGAR. Sugar free: less than 0.5 g per serving; **No added sugars; Without added sugars:** no sugars or sugar-containing ingredients added during processing; must state if food is not "low calorie" or "reduced calorie"; **Unsweetened; No added sweeteners:** factual statements; **Reduced sugar:** at least 25% less sugar per serving than reference food.

FAT. Fat free: less than 0.5 g of total fat per serving; **Saturated fat free:** less than 0.5 g of saturated fat and less than 0.5 g of trans fatty acids per serving; **Low fat:** 3 g or less of total fat per serving (and per 50 g if the serving size is small, i.e., 30 g or less, 2 tbs or less); **Low saturated fat:** 1 g or less per serving and not more than 15% of calories from saturated fat; **Reduced fat; Less fat:** at least 25% less total fat per serving than reference food.

FIBER. High fiber: 20% or more of the daily value per serving; **Good source of fiber:** 10%-19% of the daily value per serving; **More fiber; Added fiber:** 10% or more of the daily value per serving than reference food.

SODIUM. Sodium free: less than 5 mg per serving; **Low sodium:** 140 mg or less per serving (and per 50 g if the serving size is small, i.e., 30 g or less, 2 tbs or less); **Very low sodium:** 35 mg or less per serving (and per 50 g if the serving size is small); **Reduced sodium; Less sodium:** at least 25% less per serving than reference food.

CALORIES. Calorie free: less than 5 calories per serving; **Low calorie:** 40 calories or less per serving (and per 50 g if the serving size is small, i.e., 30 g or less, 2 tbs or less); **Reduced calories; Fewer calories:** at least 25% fewer calories per serving than reference food.

CHOLESTEROL. Cholesterol claims are only permitted when food contains 2 g or less saturated fat per serving. **Cholesterol free:** less than 2 mg of cholesterol; **Low cholesterol:** 20 mg or less of cholesterol (and per 50 g of food if the serving size is small, i.e., 30 g or less, 2 tbs or less); **Reduced cholesterol; Less cholesterol:** at least 25% less per serving than reference food.

Other Packaging Terms

The FDA allows food producers and marketers to use language on their packaging that advertises the health benefits and production methods of their products. Products marked "certified" have been formally evaluated by a USDA National Organic Program-authorized certifying agent. Below are some common packaging terms and their meanings.

Organic: Organic operations must demonstrate that their practices foster cycling of resources, promote ecological balance, and conserve biodiversity. Before a product can be labeled organic, a farm or business must pass a site inspection by a USDA-accredited certifying agent. Organic foods must be produced without ionizing radiation, sewage sludge, synthetic fertilizers, prohibited pesticides, and genetic engineering.

Foods that contain all organic ingredients may advertise "100 percent certified organic" on the "principal display panel" (generally the front of the packaging) along with the USDA organic seal. Foods with at least 95% organic ingredients may be called "organic" and may place the official seal on their packaging. Products with at least 70% organic ingredients may display "made with organic—" but may not use the organic seal. Products with less than 70% organic ingredients may not make any organic claims on the principal display panel but may list organic ingredients on the information panel.

Natural: Product contains no artificial ingredient or added color and is only minimally processed (i.e., does not fundamentally alter the product).

Free range or **free roaming:** Producers must demonstrate that poultry has been allowed access to the outside.

Fresh poultry: Whole poultry and cuts that have never been below 26°F.

Frozen poultry: Temperature of raw, frozen poultry is 0°F or below.

Gluten free: Products with a gluten limit of 20 parts per million.

Halal and **Zabiah Halal:** Produced in federally inspected meat packing plants and handled in accordance with Islamic law and under Islamic authority.

Kosher: Meat and poultry products prepared under rabbinical supervision.

No hormones: Hormones are not allowed in the raising of hogs or poultry, so those products may not make this claim. If sufficient documentation is provided to the USDA, this term may appear on packages of beef.

No antibiotics: Claim may be made on a package (red meat and poultry) if sufficient documentation is provided to the USDA showing that the animals were raised without antibiotics.

Dietary Guidelines for Americans, 2015-20: Key Recommendations

Source: *2015-2020 Dietary Guidelines for Americans,* U.S. Dept. of Agriculture and U.S. Dept. of Health and Human Services

The federal government revises its dietary guidelines every five years. The most recent edition aims to help Americans establish a healthy eating pattern that meets nutrient needs over time at an appropriate calorie level. All foods and beverages consumed should be accounted for.

Healthy eating patterns include a variety from the following food groups:

- **Vegetables** from the five subgroups: dark green, red and orange, legumes (beans and peas), starchy, and other.
- **Fruits,** especially whole fruits.
- **Grains,** at least half of which should be whole grains. Choose refined grains that are enriched.
- Fat-free or low-fat **dairy,** including milk, yogurt, and cheese. Those who cannot or choose not to consume dairy should eat foods, such as fortified soy beverages, that provide the same nutrients.
- A variety of **protein foods,** including seafood, lean meats and poultry, eggs, nuts, seeds, and soy products. Legumes (beans and peas) can be considered vegetables or proteins but should be counted in one group only.
- **Oils,** such as corn oil and olive oil, are fats that are usually liquid at room temperature because of their higher percentage of unsaturated fatty acids. Oils should replace solid fats where possible.
- Potassium, dietary fiber, calcium, and vitamin D are among the nutrients underconsumed in American diets, which affects public health. The underconsumption of iron by young children and women who could become or are pregnant is also of concern.

Dietary components to limit:

- Less than 2,300 mg per day of **sodium.** Adults with prehypertension and hypertension may benefit from consuming less than 1,500 mg of sodium per day.
- Less than 10% of daily calories from **saturated fats;** replace with monounsaturated and polyunsaturated fats.
- Less than 10% of daily calories from **added sugars.**
- As little as possible of **trans fats** and **dietary cholesterol.**
- **Alcohol** in moderation, if at all—up to one drink per day for women and two drinks per day for men.

U.S. Annual Per Capita Consumption of Meat and Dairy, 1910-2017

Source: Economic Research Service, U.S. Dept. of Agriculture

(in pounds per capita per year, unless otherwise noted)

Meat	1910	1930	1950	1970	1990	2000	2010	2015	2016	2017	% change, 1910-2017
Beef	48.5	33.7	44.6	79.8	63.9	64.5	56.7	51.4	52.9	54.3	11.9%
Chicken	11.0	11.1	14.3	27.4	42.5	54.2	58.0	62.6	63.2	64.1	483.7
Fish/shellfish	11.2	10.2	11.9	11.7	14.9	15.2	15.8	15.5	14.9	16.1	43.7
Pork	38.2	41.1	43.0	48.5	46.4	47.8	44.4	46.3	46.6	46.7	22.1
Total red meat[1]	96.0	83.6	95.8	132.5	112.2	113.7	102.0	98.6	100.5	102.0	6.3
Dairy											
Butter	18.4	17.6	10.9	5.4	4.3	4.5	4.9	5.6	5.7	5.7	−69.0
Cheese, American	2.8	3.2	5.5	7.0	11.1	12.7	13.3	14.0	14.4	15.1	446.9
Cheese, other	1.5	1.5	2.2	4.4	13.5	16.9	19.4	21.1	22.1	21.9	1,347.2
Ice cream	1.9	9.3	16.4	16.7	15.4	16.1	14.0	12.9	12.9	12.8	559.0
Milk, skim/lower fat (gallons)	7.1	5.0	2.9	5.8	15.2	14.6	14.8	12.5	12.0	11.4	61.6
Milk, whole (gallons)	25.2	28.2	34.3	25.5	10.5	8.2	5.7	5.5	5.8	5.9	−76.5

(1) Includes beef, veal, lamb, and pork.

Characteristics of Organic Farms in the U.S., 2017

Source: National Agricultural Statistics Service, U.S. Dept. of Agriculture

Total farms/acreage	All farms	Farms with certified organic sales — Organic less than 50% of total sales	Farms with certified organic sales — Organic 50% or more of total sales	Farms with organic sales, exempt from certification[1]
Farms (number)	2,042,220	4,301	11,650	2,215
Land in farms (acres)	900,217,576	4,082,741	4,912,949	112,809
Average size of farms (acres)	441	949	422	51
Market value of ag. prod. sold/govt. payments				
Total (thous.)	$397,466,269	$8,473,343	$6,744,349	$23,698
Average per farm	$194,625	$1,970,087	$578,914	$10,699
Total sales (thous.)	$388,522,695	$8,435,721	$6,696,211	$22,534
Value of crops[2] (thous.)	$193,546,699	$7,119,268	$3,777,059	$16,957
Value of livestock, poultry, and their products (thous.)	$194,975,996	$1,316,453	$2,919,152	$5,577
Government payments (thous.)	$8,943,574	$37,622	$48,137	$1,164
Land use (acres)				
Total cropland	396,433,817	2,882,881	2,764,555	34,397
Harvested cropland	320,041,858	2,391,939	2,044,553	20,094
Permanent pasture and rangeland	400,771,178	866,997	1,458,601	30,713
Irrigated land	58,013,907	1,272,583	738,351	5,521
Type of farming (no. of farms)				
Oilseed and grain	325,033	695	1,700	18
Vegetable and melon	45,165	531	2,320	573
Fruit and tree nut	95,441	680	2,204	507
Greenhouse, nursery, floriculture	45,477	307	470	300
Tobacco	3,757	69	83	—
Cotton	8,815	26	12	—
Sugarcane, hay, and all other crop farming	443,402	615	1,148	375
Beef cattle ranching and farming	641,496	385	335	98
Cattle feedlots	13,379	49	34	—
Dairy cattle and milk production	37,750	368	2,372	4
Hog and pig	23,048	67	28	32
Poultry and egg production	44,260	260	764	105
Sheep and goat	92,974	105	57	84
Aquaculture[3] and other animal production[4]	222,223	144	123	119

(—) = Not available. (1) Normally less than $5,000 in sales. (2) Including nursery and greenhouse crops. (3) Primarily engaged in the farm raising of finfish, shellfish, or any other kind of animal aquaculture. (4) Primarily engaged in raising animals and insects (except cattle, hogs and pigs, poultry, sheep and goats, and aquaculture) for sale or product production, primarily engaged in one of the following: bees, horses and other equine, rabbits and other fur-bearing animals, etc. and producing products such as honey and other bee products.

Livestock on Farms in the U.S., 1900-2020

Source: National Agricultural Statistics Service, U.S. Dept. of Agriculture

(in thousands as of Jan. 1, unless otherwise noted)

Year	All cattle[1]	Milk cows	Sheep and lambs	Hogs and pigs[2]	Year	All cattle[1]	Milk cows	Sheep and lambs	Hogs and pigs[2]
1900	59,739	16,544	48,105	51,055	2000	98,199	9,183	7,036	59,335
1910	58,993	19,450	50,239	48,072	2005	95,018	9,004	6,135	60,975
1920	70,400	21,455	40,743	60,159	2009	94,721	9,332	5,747	66,768
1930	61,003	23,032	51,565	55,705	2010	93,881	9,086	5,620	65,327
1940	68,309	24,940	52,107	61,165	2011	100,000	9,200	5,480	64,625
1950	77,963	23,853	29,826	58,937	2012	90,769	9,230	5,365	66,361
1960	96,236	19,527	33,170	59,026	2013	89,300	9,218	5,335	66,373
1965	109,000	16,981	25,127	56,106	2014	88,526	9,208	5,245	64,775
1970	112,369	12,091	20,423	57,046	2015	89,143	9,307	5,280	66,145
1975	132,028	11,220	14,515	54,693	2016	91,918	9,310	5,300	68,919
1980	111,242	10,758	12,699	67,318	2017	93,705	9,346	5,250	71,545
1985	109,582	10,777	10,716	54,073	2018	94,298	9,432	5,265	73,145
1990	95,816	10,015	11,358	53,788	2019	94,805	9,353	5,230	74,550
1995	102,785	9,482	8,886	57,150	2020	94,413	9,335	5,200	78,658

(1) For 1970 and on, includes milk cows and heifers that have calved. (2) As of Dec. 1 of preceding year.

Production of Principal U.S. Crops, 1990-2019

Source: National Agricultural Statistics Service, U.S. Dept. of Agriculture

Year	Corn for grain (1,000 bu)	Oats (1,000 bu)	Barley (1,000 bu)	Sorghum for grain (1,000 bu)	All wheat (1,000 bu)	Rye (1,000 bu)	Canola (1,000 lb)	Cotton (upland) (1,000 b)	Cottonseed (1,000 t)
1990	7,934,028	357,654	422,196	573,303	2,729,778	10,176	NA	15,505.4	5,968.5
1995	7,373,876	162,027	359,562	460,373	2,182,591	10,064	548,447	17,532.2	6,848.7
2000	9,915,051	149,545	318,728	470,526	2,232,460	8,386	1,998,310	16,799.2	6,435.6
2005	11,114,082	114,878	211,896	392,933	2,104,690	7,537	1,580,985	23,259.7	8,172.1
2009	13,091,862	93,081	227,323	382,983	2,218,061	6,993	1,464,780	11,787.6	4,148.8
2010	12,446,865	81,190	180,268	345,625	2,206,916	7,431	2,447,628	17,600.0	6,098.1
2011	12,359,612	53,649	155,780	214,443	1,999,347	6,326	1,528,010	14,722.0	5,370.0
2012	10,755,111	61,486	218,990	247,742	2,252,307	6,542	2,391,610	16,534.0	5,666.0
2013	13,828,964	64,642	216,745	392,331	2,134,979	7,626	2,210,505	12,275.0	4,203.0
2014	14,215,532	70,232	181,542	432,575	2,026,310	7,189	2,512,645	15,753.0	5,125.0
2015	13,601,964	89,535	218,187	596,751	2,061,939	11,616	2,878,470	12,455.0	4,043.0
2016	15,148,038	64,770	199,914	480,261	2,308,723	13,451	3,086,340	16,601.0	5,369.0
2017	14,609,407	49,585	143,258	361,871	1,740,910	10,252	3,055,410	20,223.0	6,422.0
2018	14,340,369	56,130	153,527	364,986	1,885,156	8,432	3,615,440	17,566.0	5,631.0
2019	13,691,561	53,148	169,566	341,160	1,920,139	10,622	3,402,000	19,380.0	6,232.0

Year	Tobacco (1,000 lb)	All hay (1,000 t)	Beans, dry edible (1,000 cwt)	Peas, dry edible (1,000 cwt)	Peanuts[1] (1,000 lb)	Soybeans[2] (1,000 bu)	Potatoes (1,000 cwt)	Sweet potatoes (1,000 cwt)
1990	1,626,380	146,212	32,379	2,372	3,602,770	1,925,947	402,110	12,594
1995	1,268,538	154,166	30,812	4,765	4,247,455	2,176,814	443,606	12,906
2000	1,052,999	151,921	26,409	3,474	3,265,505	2,757,810	513,621	13,794
2005	645,015	151,017	26,772	14,003	4,869,860	3,063,237	423,926	15,730
2009	822,581	147,700	25,427	17,137	3,691,650	3,359,011	432,601	19,469
2010	718,190	145,624	31,801	14,221	4,156,840	3,329,181	404,273	23,845
2011	598,252	131,216	19,890	5,625	3,658,590	3,093,524	429,647	26,964
2012	762,709	117,072	31,925	11,002	6,753,880	3,042,044	464,970	26,482
2013	723,579	135,002	24,576	15,620	4,173,170	3,357,984	434,652	24,785
2014	876,415	139,923	28,910	17,155	5,188,665	3,927,090	442,170	29,584
2015	719,171	134,502	30,057	18,283	6,001,357	3,926,339	441,205	31,016
2016	628,720	134,995	28,703	27,762	5,581,570	4,296,086	441,411	31,546
2017	710,161	128,207	35,961	14,195	7,115,410	4,411,633	450,921	35,646
2018	533,241	123,600	37,745	15,929	5,495,935	4,428,150	450,020	27,378
2019	467,956	128,864	20,811	22,346	5,496,087	3,558,281	422,890	31,973

Year	Rice (1,000 t)	Sugarcane (1,000 t)	Sugar beets (1,000 t)	Pecans[3] (1,000 lb)	Apples (1,000 t)	Grapes (1,000 t)	Peaches (1,000 t)	Oranges[4] (1,000 bx)	Grapefruit[4] (1,000 bx)
1990	156,088	28,136	27,513	205,000	4,828	5,660	1,121	184,415	49,300
1995	173,871	30,944	27,954	268,000	5,293	5,922	1,150	263,605	71,050
2000	190,872	36,114	32,541	209,850	5,291	7,688	1,276	299,760	66,980
2005	223,235	26,606	27,433	280,250	4,853	7,814	1,185	216,500	25,640
2009	219,850	30,432	29,783	302,020	4,853	7,307	1,104	210,709	32,025
2010	243,104	27,360	32,034	293,740	4,646	7,471	1,150	192,835	30,400
2011	184,941	29,224	28,896	269,700	4,713	7,448	1,072	204,949	30,360
2012	199,939	32,227	35,224	302,300	4,496	7,531	968	206,119	27,650
2013	189,953	30,761	32,789	266,330	5,216	8,632	904	189,893	28,950
2014	222,215	30,424	31,285	264,150	5,907	7,884	853	155,977	25,200
2015	193,148	32,122	35,371	254,290	5,023	7,621	847	146,602	21,950
2016	224,145	32,118	36,920	268,770	5,689	7,697	796	141,891	19,400
2017	178,228	33,238	35,317	304,850	5,777	7,384	701	118,520	16,960
2018	223,833	34,542	33,282	240,930	5,120	7,596	652	91,130	12,480
2019	184,675	31,798	28,600	255,600	5,509	6,871	682	124,050	13,810

b = bale; bu = bushel; bx = box; cwt = hundred weight; lb = pound; t = ton. **Note:** Some 2019 figures are preliminary estimates. (1) Harvested for nuts. (2) Harvested for beans. (3) Utilized production only. (4) Crop year ending in year cited.

Animal Products: Average Prices Received by U.S. Farmers, 1940-2019

Source: National Agricultural Statistics Service, U.S. Dept. of Agriculture

Figures represent dollars per 100 lb for veal calves, beef cattle, hogs, lambs, milk (wholesale), and sheep; dollars per head for milk cows; cents per lb for broilers, chickens, turkeys, and wool; and cents per dozen for eggs. Weighted calendar year prices for livestock and livestock products other than wool. For 1943-63, wool prices were weighted on marketing year basis. The marketing year was changed in 1964 from a calendar year to a Dec.-Nov. basis for broilers, chickens, eggs, and hogs.

Year	Broilers	Calves (veal)	Cattle (beef)	Chickens (excl. broilers)	Eggs	Hogs	Lambs[1]	Milk	Milk cows	Sheep[1]	Turkeys	Wool
1940	17.3	8.83	7.56	13.0	18.0	5.39	8.10	1.82	61	3.95	15.2	28.4
1950	27.4	26.30	23.30	22.2	36.3	18.00	25.10	3.89	198	11.60	32.8	62.1
1960	16.9	22.90	20.40	12.2	36.1	15.30	17.90	4.21	223	5.61	25.4	42.0
1970	13.6	34.50	27.10	9.1	39.1	22.70	26.40	5.71	332	7.51	22.6	35.4
1980	27.7	76.80	62.40	11.0	56.3	38.00	63.60	13.05	1,190	21.30	41.3	88.1
1990	32.6	95.60	74.60	9.3	70.9	53.70	55.50	13.74	1,160	23.20	39.4	80.0
2000	33.6	104.00	68.60	5.7	61.8	42.30	79.80	12.40	1,340	34.30	40.7	33.0
2005	43.6	135.00	89.70	6.5	54.0	50.20	110.00	15.19	1,770	45.10	44.9	71.0
2008	45.8	110.00	89.10	6.6	109.0	47.00	99.60	18.45	1,950	27.20	56.5	99.0
2009	45.7	105.00	80.30	7.2	81.7	41.60	99.60	12.93	1,390	32.50	50.0	79.0
2010	48.2	117.00	92.20	8.1	85.7	54.10	125.00	16.35	1,330	49.70	61.5	115.0
2011	46.6	142.00	113.00	8.7	95.6	65.30	NA	20.25	1,420	NA	68.2	167.0
2012	50.0	168.00	122.00	8.8	101.1	64.20	NA	18.56	1,430	NA	72.1	153.0
2013	60.6	181.00	125.00	9.5	107.2	67.20	NA	20.12	1,380	NA	66.5	145.0

Year	Broilers	Calves (veal)	Cattle (beef)	Chickens (excl. broilers)	Eggs	Hogs	Lambs[1]	Milk	Milk cows	Sheep[1]	Turkeys	Wool
2014	63.7	261.00	152.00	10.1	122.1	76.50	NA	24.07	1,830	NA	73.5	146.0
2015	53.8	247.00	147.00	10.3	168.0	55.30	NA	17.21	1,990	NA	81.1	145.0
2016	47.8	158.00	119.00	8.1	76.3	49.30	NA	16.34	1,760	NA	82.6	145.0
2017	54.4	168.00	120.00	4.7	85.6	53.10	NA	17.69	1,620	NA	64.6	147.0
2018	55.9	170.00	115.00	4.8	116.1	50.20	NA	16.28	1,360	NA	51.0	175.0
2019	48.6	159.00	116.00	3.7	81.6	51.40	NA	18.63	1,200	NA	57.9	189.0

NA = Not available. (1) Prices not calculated after 2010.

Crops: Average Prices Received by U.S. Farmers, 1940-2019

Source: National Agricultural Statistics Service, U.S. Dept. of Agriculture

Figures represent cents per lb for apples, cotton, and peanuts; dollars per bushel for barley, corn, oats, soybeans, and wheat; dollars per 100 lb for potatoes, rice, and sorghum; and dollars per ton for cottonseed and baled hay. Weighted crop year prices. The marketing year is described as follows: apples, June-May; barley, hay, oats, potatoes, and wheat, July-June; cotton, cottonseed, peanuts, and rice, Aug.-July; soybeans, Sept.-Aug.; and corn and sorghum grain, Oct.-Sept.

Year	Apples	Barley	Corn	Cotton-seed	Cotton (upland)*	Hay	Oats	Peanuts	Pota-toes	Rice	Sor-ghum	Soy-beans	Wheat
1940	NA	0.39	0.62	21.70	9.8	9.78	0.30	3.7	0.85	1.80	0.87	0.89	0.67
1950	NA	1.19	1.52	86.60	39.9	21.10	0.79	10.9	1.50	5.09	1.88	2.47	2.00
1960	2.7	0.84	1.00	42.50	30.1	21.70	0.60	10.0	2.00	4.55	1.49	2.13	1.74
1970	6.5	0.97	1.33	56.40	21.9	26.10	0.62	12.8	2.21	5.17	2.04	2.85	1.33
1980	12.1	2.86	3.11	129.00	74.4	71.00	1.79	25.1	6.55	12.80	5.25	7.57	3.91
1990	20.9	2.14	2.28	121.00	67.1	80.60	1.14	34.7	6.08	6.68	3.79	5.74	2.61
2000	17.8	2.11	1.85	105.00	49.8	84.60	1.10	27.4	5.08	5.61	3.37	4.54	2.62
2005	24.4	2.53	2.00	96.00	47.7	98.20	1.63	17.3	7.06	7.65	3.33	5.66	3.42
2008	23.2	5.37	4.06	223.00	47.8	152.00	3.15	23.0	9.09	16.80	5.72	9.97	6.78
2009	23.1	4.66	3.55	158.00	62.9	108.00	2.02	21.7	8.25	14.40	5.75	9.59	4.87
2010	25.1	3.86	5.18	161.00	81.5	114.00	2.52	22.5	9.20	12.70	8.96	11.30	5.70
2011	30.3	5.35	6.22	260.00	88.3	178.00	3.49	31.8	9.41	14.50	10.70	12.50	7.24
2012	37.1	6.43	6.89	252.00	72.5	191.00	3.89	30.1	8.63	15.10	11.30	14.40	7.77
2013	30.3	6.06	4.46	246.00	77.9	176.00	3.75	24.9	9.71	16.30	7.64	13.00	6.87
2014	25.7	5.30	3.70	194.00	61.3	172.00	3.21	22.0	8.88	13.40	7.20	10.10	5.99
2015	33.6	5.52	3.61	227.00	61.2	145.00	2.12	19.3	8.76	12.20	5.91	8.95	4.89
2016	31.6	4.96	3.36	195.00	68.0	129.00	2.06	19.7	9.08	10.40	4.98	9.47	3.89
2017	32.1	4.47	3.36	142.00	68.6	142.00	2.59	22.9	9.17	12.90	5.75	9.33	4.72
2018	29.9	4.62	3.61	155.00	70.3	166.00	2.66	21.5	8.90	12.60	5.82	8.48	5.16
2019[1]	25.8	4.60	3.85	159.00	60.3	165.00	2.95	20.1	9.79	13.00	6.00	8.75	4.55

* = Beginning in 1964, 480-lb net weight bales. NA = Not available. (1) Preliminary.

World Meat Production, 2000, 2018

Source: UN Food and Agriculture Organization; in thousands of metric tons; ranked by top producers in 2018

Top beef producers

Rank	Country	2000	2018
1.	U.S.	12,017	12,219
2.	Brazil	6,579	9,900
3.	China[1]	5,131	6,441
4.	Argentina	2,718	3,066
5.	India	2,242	2,610
6.	Australia	1,988	2,219
7.	Mexico	1,409	1,981
8.	Pakistan	886	1,934
9.	Russia	1,898	1,608
10.	France	1,528	1,436
11.	Canada	1,263	1,231
12.	Germany	1,304	1,123
13.	Turkey	359	1,004
14.	South Africa	582	1,003
15.	Uzbekistan	390	922
16.	UK	705	922
17.	Colombia	745	886
18.	Italy	1,153	809
19.	Egypt	570	721
20.	New Zealand	587	677
21.	Spain	651	669
22.	Kenya	257	652
23.	Ireland	577	638
24.	Poland	349	595
25.	Uruguay	453	590
	Africa	4,331	7,081
	Asia	13,041	18,506
	Central America	1,766	2,536
	Europe	11,771	10,642
	North America	13,280	13,451
	Oceania	2,591	2,912
	South America	11,846	16,251
	World total	58,850	71,601

Top pork producers

Rank	Country	2000	2018
1.	China[1]	39,660	54,037
2.	U.S.	8,597	11,943
3.	Germany	3,982	5,370
4.	Spain	2,905	4,530
5.	Vietnam	1,418	3,816
6.	Brazil	2,600	3,788
7.	Russia	1,578	3,744
8.	France	2,312	2,166
9.	Canada	1,640	2,142
10.	Poland	1,923	2,136
11.	Philippines	1,213	1,873
12.	Denmark	1,625	1,583
13.	Mexico	1,030	1,503
14.	Italy	1,479	1,471
15.	Netherlands	1,623	1,461
16.	South Korea	916	1,325
17.	Japan	1,256	1,284
18.	Belgium	1,042	1,073
19.	Myanmar	118	1,063
20.	Thailand	693	999
21.	UK	899	927
22.	Taiwan	921	829
23.	Ukraine	676	703
24.	Argentina	214	621
25.	Chile	261	521
	Africa	784	1,588
	Asia	47,959	66,726
	Central America	1,140	1,708
	Europe	25,283	29,665
	North America	10,237	14,085
	Oceania	488	568
	South America	3,774	6,168
	World total	89,873	120,881

Top poultry producers

Rank	Country	2000	2018
1.	U.S.	16,575	22,298
2.	China[1]	11,890	19,395
3.	Brazil	6,125	15,498
4.	Russia	775	4,543
5.	India	904	3,616
6.	Mexico	1,869	3,377
7.	Indonesia	818	2,588
8.	Japan	1,195	2,250
9.	Turkey	668	2,229
10.	Iran	815	2,199
11.	Argentina	1,000	2,115
12.	UK	1,513	1,939
13.	Myanmar	244	1,896
14.	Malaysia	714	1,873
15.	France	2,148	1,786
16.	Thailand	1,149	1,780
17.	South Africa	821	1,762
18.	Poland	589	1,711
19.	Spain	990	1,622
20.	Colombia	504	1,593
21.	Peru	510	1,582
22.	Germany	790	1,571
23.	Canada	1,065	1,474
24.	Pakistan	332	1,396
25.	Philippines	557	1,380
	Africa	2,957	6,081
	Asia	22,907	46,469
	Central America	2,371	4,450
	Europe	11,824	21,191
	North America	17,640	23,773
	Oceania	767	1,515
	South America	9,697	23,186
	World total	68,639	127,298

(1) Not including Hong Kong or Macau.

World Corn, Rice, and Wheat Production, 2000, 2018

Source: UN Food and Agriculture Organization; in millions of metric tons; ranked by top producers in 2018

	Top corn producers				Top rice producers				Top wheat producers		
Rank	Country	2000	2018	Rank	Country	2000	2018	Rank	Country	2000	2018
1.	U.S.	251.9	392.5	1.	China	187.9	212.1	1.	China	99.6	131.4
2.	China	106.0	257.2	2.	India	127.5	172.6	2.	India	76.4	99.7
3.	Brazil	32.3	82.3	3.	Indonesia	51.9	83.0	3.	Russia	34.5	72.1
4.	Argentina	16.8	43.5	4.	Bangladesh	37.6	56.4	4.	U.S.	60.6	51.3
5.	Ukraine	3.8	35.8	5.	Vietnam	32.5	44.0	5.	France	37.4	35.8
6.	Indonesia	9.7	30.3	6.	Thailand	25.8	32.2	6.	Canada	26.5	31.8
7.	India	12.0	27.8	7.	Myanmar	21.0	25.4	7.	Pakistan	21.1	25.1
8.	Mexico	17.6	27.2	8.	Philippines	12.4	19.1	8.	Ukraine	10.2	24.7
9.	Romania	4.9	18.7	9.	Brazil	11.1	11.7	9.	Australia	22.1	20.9
10.	Canada	7.0	13.9	10.	Pakistan	7.2	10.8	10.	Germany	21.6	20.3
11.	France	16.0	12.7	11.	Cambodia	4.0	10.6	11.	Turkey	21.0	20.0
12.	South Africa	11.4	12.5	12.	U.S.	8.7	10.2	12.	Argentina	15.5	18.5
13.	Russia	1.5	11.4	13.	Japan	11.9	9.7	13.	Iran	8.1	14.5
14.	Nigeria	4.1	10.2	14.	Nigeria	3.3	6.8	14.	Kazakhstan	9.1	13.9
15.	Hungary	5.0	8.0	15.	South Korea	7.2	5.2	15.	UK	16.7	13.6
16.	Philippines	4.5	7.8	16.	Nepal	4.2	5.2	16.	Romania	4.4	10.1
17.	Ethiopia	2.7	7.4	17.	Egypt	6.0	4.9	17.	Poland	8.5	9.8
18.	Egypt	6.5	7.3	18.	Madagascar	2.5	4.0	18.	Egypt	6.6	8.8
19.	Serbia	NA	7.0	19.	Sri Lanka	2.9	3.9	19.	Spain	7.3	8.0
20.	Pakistan	1.6	6.3	20.	Laos	2.2	3.6	20.	Morocco	1.4	7.3
21.	Italy	10.1	6.2	21.	Peru	1.9	3.6	21.	Italy	7.5	6.9
22.	Tanzania	2.0	6.0	22.	Colombia	2.2	3.3	22.	Bulgaria	2.8	5.8
23.	Turkey	2.3	5.7	23.	Mali	0.7	3.2	23.	Brazil	1.7	5.4
24.	Paraguay	0.6	5.3	24.	Tanzania	0.8	3.0	24.	Uzbekistan	3.7	5.4
25.	Thailand	4.5	5.0	25.	Malaysia	2.1	2.7	25.	Hungary	3.7	5.2
	Africa	43.8	78.9		Africa	17.5	33.2		Africa	14.3	29.3
	Asia	149.1	361.6		Asia	545.2	705.4		Asia	254.7	328.2
	Central America	20.3	31.1		Central America	1.3	1.2		Central America	3.5	2.9
	Europe	63.1	128.6		Europe	3.2	4.0		Europe	183.4	242.1
	North America	258.8	406.3		North America	8.7	10.2		North America	87.2	83.1
	Oceania	0.6	0.6		Oceania	1.1	0.6		Oceania	22.4	21.3
	South America	55.8	139.9		South America	20.5	26.1		South America	19.6	27.1
	World total	**592.0**	**1,147.6**		**World total**	**598.7**	**782.0**		**World total**	**585.0**	**734.0**

NA = Not applicable.

Value of U.S. Agricultural Exports and Imports, 1978-2019

Source: Economic Research Service, U.S. Dept. of Agriculture
(in billions of dollars, unless otherwise noted)

Year[1]	Agric. trade surplus	Agric. exports	% of all exports	Agric. imports	% of all imports	Year[1]	Agric. trade surplus	Agric. exports	% of all exports	Agric. imports	% of all imports
1978	$13.4	$27.3	21%	$13.9	8%	2002	$12.4	$53.3	8%	$41.0	4%
1980	23.2	40.5	19	17.3	7	2003	10.3	56.0	9	45.7	4
1985	11.5	31.2	15	19.7	6	2004	9.7	62.4	9	52.7	4
1987	7.2	27.9	12	20.7	5	2005	4.8	62.5	8	57.7	4
1988	14.3	35.3	12	21.0	5	2006	4.6	68.6	8	64.0	3
1989	18.1	39.7	12	21.6	5	2007	12.2	82.2	8	70.1	4
1990	16.6	39.5	11	22.9	5	2008	35.6	114.9	10	79.3	4
1991	16.4	39.3	10	22.9	5	2009	22.9	96.3	10	73.4	5
1992	18.3	43.1	10	24.8	5	2010	29.6	108.5	10	79.0	4
1993	17.7	42.9	10	25.1	4	2011	43.0	137.5	11	94.5	4
1994	19.2	46.2	10	27.0	4	2012	32.5	135.9	10	103.4	5
1995	26.0	56.3	10	30.3	4	2013	37.3	141.1	10	103.9	5
1996	26.8	60.3	10	33.5	4	2014	43.1	152.3	11	109.3	5
1997	21.7	57.3	9	35.7	4	2015	25.5	139.8	11	114.2	5
1998	16.8	53.7	8	36.8	4	2016	16.6	129.6	11	113.0	5
1999	11.8	49.1	8	37.3	4	2017	21.1	140.2	11	119.1	5
2000	11.9	50.8	7	38.9	3	2018	15.9	143.4	10	127.5	5
2001	13.7	52.7	8	39.0	3	2019	4.6	135.5	NA	130.8	NA

NA = Not available. (1) Fiscal year (Oct.-Sept.).

Crop Consumption Per Capita in Selected Nations, 1980-2017

Source: UN Food and Agriculture Organization
(in kilograms per capita per year, unless otherwise noted)

Country	Corn				Rice				Wheat			
	1980	1990	2014	2017	1980	1990	2014	2017	1980	1990	2014	2017
Afghanistan	33	24	2	1	20	17	19	20	162	140	155	155
Argentina	6	5	11	12	2	6	13	12	115	114	105	105
Australia	2	4	5	5	8	8	14	16	81	70	77	76
Bangladesh	0	0	1	1	144	159	267	268	29	21	18	18
Brazil	22	22	29	29	39	41	46	48	50	44	54	49
Canada	4	3	16	19	3	6	14	13	76	78	76	84
China	5	4	7	8	76	81	122	122	58	77	63	63
Congo Republic	5	3	4	3	2	5	26	31	33	33	40	42
Cuba	0	0	29	34	51	47	98	74	78	74	57	60
Egypt	49	57	62	61	26	31	55	53	129	151	148	146
France	2	13	11	11	4	4	7	8	95	92	110	111
Germany	3	6	13	10	2	2	5	5	69	67	86	88
India	8	8	7	8	64	78	99	103	45	41	60	62
Indonesia	24	29	36	42	125	131	207	208	10	9	26	27
Iran	1	1	3	3	30	30	41	43	154	164	156	164
Iraq	0	3	0	1	31	37	56	46	144	185	134	132

Country	Corn 1980	1990	2014	2017	Rice 1980	1990	2014	2017	Wheat 1980	1990	2014	2017
Israel	12	23	16	15	6	8	15	17	138	124	109	102
Italy	5	3	4	4	5	5	5	9	174	149	147	146
Japan	15	19	14	13	73	65	84	82	44	44	45	44
Kenya	114	88	80	79	2	2	19	20	20	23	37	37
Korea, North	43	56	44	41	71	70	111	111	32	22	22	21
Korea, South	2	13	13	15	138	97	124	120	49	48	51	52
Mexico	118	124	127	127	5	4	9	9	42	42	36	34
New Zealand	1	3	5	4	2	4	10	11	78	69	85	93
Nigeria	6	33	33	35	15	21	47	46	16	3	26	18
Pakistan	7	6	13	13	23	14	17	17	114	128	109	105
Philippines	22	19	20	21	97	94	174	181	17	20	24	28
Russia	NA	NA	1	1	NA	NA	8	8	NA	NA	132	129
Saudi Arabia	11	13	26	25	33	18	52	51	88	104	95	96
South Africa	120	108	101	103	4	8	25	25	56	56	58	57
Thailand	5	5	5	5	137	114	180	178	4	4	11	12
Turkey	8	21	23	20	3	6	15	16	210	223	153	144
Ukraine	NA	NA	14	13	NA	NA	4	4	NA	NA	90	123
United Arab Emirates	1	1	1	1	43	34	57	57	63	65	105	102
UK	3	3	3	3	2	2	8	8	82	82	100	100
U.S.	8	13	12	12	4	7	11	11	70	81	81	81
Venezuela	55	54	54	58	21	13	37	33	50	51	48	47
Vietnam	7	7	12	11	128	133	217	218	17	3	10	11
Africa	38	41	46	47	15	17	36	36	45	47	50	49
Asia	8	9	10	11	77	82	116	117	53	60	62	63
Central America	107	113	111	111	8	7	16	16	38	38	35	34
Europe	4	5	7	7	5	4	6	7	118	117	109	110
North America	7	12	13	13	4	7	11	11	71	81	80	81
Oceania	2	4	4	4	9	10	17	19	79	69	76	77
South America	22	23	29	30	29	32	42	44	58	53	59	58
World per capita consumption	13	15	19	20	50	54	81	81	64	68	65	66

NA = Not available or not applicable. **Note:** All figures are rounded. Data for 2014 and 2017 are not directly comparable to earlier years because of a change in methodology.

Meat Consumption Per Capita in Selected Nations, 1980-2017

Source: UN Food and Agriculture Organization
(in kilograms per capita per year, unless otherwise noted)

Country	Beef 1980	1990	2014	2017	Pork 1980	1990	2014	2017	Poultry 1980	1990	2014	2017
Afghanistan	5	7	4	3	NA	NA	0	0	1	1	2	2
Argentina	85	64	54	54	9	4	10	11	11	11	37	42
Australia	53	47	35	36	15	18	25	26	21	24	47	48
Bangladesh	1	1	1	1	0	0	0	0	1	1	1	2
Brazil	22	28	39	37	8	7	12	14	10	14	44	48
Canada	40	36	28	18	35	28	23	24	22	28	37	39
China	0	1	5	6	12	20	39	38	2	3	13	13
Congo Republic	4	1	3	3	1	2	2	6	2	5	13	22
Cuba	15	13	6	7	5	10	18	19	9	12	17	24
Egypt	7	8	12	11	1	0	0	0	4	4	12	13
France	33	33	24	23	37	34	33	33	16	21	24	23
Germany	23	22	14	15	60	60	53	50	10	11	18	19
India	2	2	1	1	0	0	0	0	0	0	2	2
Indonesia	2	2	2	2	1	3	1	1	1	3	6	7
Iran	6	6	4	5	0	0	0	0	6	7	26	28
Iraq	5	7	3	3	0	0	0	0	9	11	14	15
Israel	13	14	25	27	2	2	2	1	35	39	67	67
Italy	26	27	19	16	25	32	37	44	18	20	18	19
Japan	5	8	9	9	13	15	20	21	10	14	18	19
Kenya	12	9	9	11	0	0	0	0	2	1	1	1
Korea, North	2	2	1	1	10	11	4	5	2	3	2	2
Korea, South	3	6	14	16	8	13	33	38	2	6	16	17
Mexico	11	14	14	14	18	9	15	17	6	10	30	33
New Zealand	57	39	24	21	12	14	24	24	10	17	34	35
Nigeria	5	2	2	2	1	1	1	1	2	2	1	1
Pakistan	5	6	8	9	0	0	0	NA	1	1	5	6
Philippines	3	2	4	5	9	12	17	18	5	4	13	14
Russia	NA	NA	16	14	NA	NA	24	27	NA	NA	29	31
Saudi Arabia	6	4	5	4	NA	NA	NA	0	24	29	44	43
South Africa	20	17	17	17	3	4	4	4	8	15	35	36
Thailand	6	6	2	2	6	9	13	12	7	9	14	13
Turkey	3	7	12	13	0	0	0	0	6	8	19	21
Ukraine	NA	NA	9	7	NA	NA	17	17	NA	NA	23	23
United Arab Emirates	14	13	8	7	NA	NA	NA	NA	43	39	43	43
UK	23	21	17	18	26	25	23	25	14	19	28	32
U.S.	47	43	37	37	33	28	28	30	26	39	51	56
Venezuela	22	18	25	15	6	5	7	4	17	13	39	20
Vietnam	2	2	12	13	5	10	36	38	2	2	13	12
Africa	7	6	6	6	1	1	1	1	2	3	6	6
Asia	2	3	4	5	6	9	16	15	2	3	9	10
Central America	10	12	13	13	14	8	12	14	6	9	28	30
Europe	23	25	15	14	32	35	34	36	12	15	23	25
North America	47	43	37	35	33	28	27	29	26	38	50	54
Oceania	50	43	31	31	14	17	24	24	18	22	43	44
South America	28	27	32	30	7	6	11	12	9	12	37	38
World per capita consumption	11	10	9	9	12	13	16	16	6	8	15	15

NA = Not available or not applicable. **Note:** All figures are rounded. Data for 2014 and 2017 are not directly comparable to earlier years because of a change in methodology.

World Capture of Fish, Crustaceans, and Mollusks, 2008-17

Source: UN Food and Agriculture Organization
(in thousands of metric tons; ranked by 2017 captures)

Country	2008	2010	2015	2016	2017	Country	2008	2010	2015	2016	2017
China	14,791	14,807	16,386	15,788	15,373	Chile	3,555	2,680	1,786	1,497	1,919
Indonesia	5,000	5,386	6,690	6,542	6,689	Philippines . . .	2,489	2,500	2,151	2,025	1,887
India	4,099	4,689	4,843	5,062	5,428	Bangladesh. . .	1,558	1,727	1,624	1,675	1,801
U.S.	4,367	4,312	5,040	4,903	5,036	Mexico	1,582	1,527	1,467	1,511	1,629
Russia.	3,384	4,070	4,457	4,759	4,869	Thailand	1,873	1,811	1,501	1,531	1,479
Peru	7,395	4,302	4,824	3,797	4,157	Malaysia	1,398	1,433	1,492	1,580	1,470
Vietnam	2,055	2,250	2,906	3,128	3,278	Morocco	997	1,136	1,365	1,447	1,377
Japan	4,337	4,091	3,395	3,193	3,204	South Korea . .	1,957	1,722	1,650	1,365	1,358
Norway	2,431	2,680	2,294	2,034	2,368	Iceland	1,284	1,061	1,319	1,067	1,163
Myanmar.	1,907	1,961	1,970	2,072	2,150	Spain	923	975	973	909	954

World Aquaculture Production, 2008-17

Source: UN Food and Agriculture Organization; ranked by 2017 production volume

Country	Metric tons (thous.)					Value (mil)				
	2008	2010	2015	2016	2017	2008	2010	2015	2016	2017
China	32,730	35,513	43,748	45,816	46,824	$57,069	$70,830	$126,350	$135,190	$140,076
India	3,851	3,786	5,260	5,700	6,180	6,076	7,073	10,366	10,528	12,294
Indonesia	1,690	2,305	4,342	4,901	6,150	2,814	4,894	7,900	9,826	11,913
Vietnam	2,462	2,683	3,462	3,570	3,821	4,606	5,980	8,885	9,139	9,714
Bangladesh.	1,006	1,309	2,060	2,204	2,333	1,766	2,840	5,150	5,621	5,905
Egypt	694	920	1,175	1,371	1,452	1,251	1,679	1,830	1,767	1,377
Norway	848	1,020	1,381	1,326	1,308	3,139	5,081	5,811	7,624	7,857
Chile	843	701	1,046	1,035	1,203	4,503	3,753	6,834	7,868	10,371
Myanmar.	675	851	997	1,018	1,049	817	956	1,645	1,992	1,750
Thailand	1,331	1,286	920	881	890	2,346	2,813	2,321	2,460	2,703
Philippines	741	745	782	796	822	1,576	1,562	1,869	1,791	1,834
Japan	730	718	705	677	615	3,343	4,083	3,567	3,842	3,676
Brazil.	331	411	575	590	595	851	1,307	1,220	1,251	1,462
South Korea	474	476	479	508	545	1,287	1,481	1,719	1,745	2,668
Ecuador	173	273	426	451	465	768	1,250	2,303	2,339	2,408
U.S.	501	497	426	445	440	984	1,023	1,150	1,243	1,212
Iran	155	220	346	398	413	447	638	1,029	1,193	1,274
Spain	250	252	290	284	311	657	519	508	561	581
Nigeria	143	201	317	307	296	410	576	904	876	849
Taiwan	324	310	313	255	282	1,069	1,116	1,205	1,020	1,162
World total[1]	52,915	57,743	72,773	76,426	80,134	106,766	131,264	206,234	222,705	237,550

Note: Does not include production of aquatic plants or marine mammals. (1) Includes nations not shown.

U.S. Commercial Landings of Fish and Shellfish, 1990-2018

Source: Natl. Marine Fisheries Service, Natl. Oceanic and Atmospheric Admin., U.S. Dept. of Commerce

Year	Landings for human food		Landings for industrial purposes[1]		Total	
	Weight (mil lbs)	Value (mil)	Weight (mil lbs)	Value (mil)	Weight (mil lbs)	Value (mil)
1990	7,041	$3,366	2,363	$156	9,404	$3,522
1995	7,667	3,625	2,121	145	9,788	3,770
2000	6,912	3,398	2,157	152	9,069	3,550
2005	7,997	3,825	1,710	117	9,707	3,933
2007	7,490	4,015	1,819	177	9,309	4,192
2008	6,633	4,231	1,692	152	8,325	4,383
2009	6,198	3,733	1,833	158	8,031	3,891
2010	6,526	4,356	1,705	164	8,231	4,520
2011	7,909	5,108	1,949	181	9,858	5,289
2012	7,477	4,923	2,157	180	9,634	5,103
2013	8,043	5,268	1,827	198	9,870	5,466
2014	7,828	5,256	1,658	192	9,486	5,448
2015	7,750	4,972	1,968	231	9,718	5,203
2016	7,484	5,007	2,088	305	9,572	5,312
2017	8,228	5,187	1,688	234	9,916	5,421
2018[2]	7,500	5,322	1,885	249	9,385	5,571

Note: Does not include products of aquaculture, except oysters and clams. Landings reported in round (live) weight for all items except univale and bivalve mollusks (e.g., clams, oysters, scallops), which are reported in weight of meats (excluding the shell). (1) Processed into meal, oil, solubles, and shell products or used as bait or animal food. (2) Preliminary.

U.S. Domestic Landings by Region, 2005, 2018

Source: Natl. Marine Fisheries Service, Natl. Oceanic and Atmospheric Admin., U.S. Dept. of Commerce

Region	2005		2018[1]	
	Weight (thous. lbs)	Value (thous.)	Weight (thous. lbs)	Value (thous.)
New England	684,090	$971,663	571,709	$1,394,365
Middle Atlantic[2].	199,937	221,505	627,913	473,233
Chesapeake[2]	508,953	218,933	NA	NA
South Atlantic.	122,422	125,117	109,102	179,308
Gulf.	1,196,355	620,987	1,540,948	887,357
Pacific Coast (incl. Alaska)	6,950,647	1,700,927	6,487,258	2,500,309
Great Lakes[3].	16,732	12,434	12,944	17,716
Hawaii.	28,139	70,811	35,494	119,116
Total	9,707,275	3,942,376	9,385,368	5,571,404

NA = Not available. **Note:** Landings reported in round (live) weight for all items except univale and bivalve mollusks (e.g., clams, oysters, scallops), which are reported in weight of meats (excluding the shell). (1) Preliminary. (2) Chesapeake Region states (Maryland and Virginia) included with Middle Atlantic in 2018. (3) Data for the Great Lakes states lag by one year (i.e., figures are for 2004 and 2017).

HEALTH

U.S. Health Expenditures, 1960-2018

Source: Office of the Actuary, Centers for Medicare & Medicaid Services, U.S. Dept. of Health and Human Services

Type of expenditure	1960	1970	1980	1990	2000	2010	2017	2018
				Amount in billions				
NATIONAL HEALTH EXPENDITURES....	$27.2	$74.6	$255.3	$721.4	$1,369.2	$2,593.2	$3,487.3	$3,649.4
				Percent distribution				
Health consumption expenditures	90.8%	89.9%	92.2%	93.4%	93.9%	94.5%	95.2%	95.2%
Personal health care................	85.5	84.6	85.0	85.3	84.8	84.5	84.7	84.3
Hospital care....................	33.0	36.4	39.4	34.7	30.3	31.7	32.7	32.7
Professional services	29.1	26.5	25.3	28.7	28.3	26.5	26.5	26.4
Physician and clinical services	20.4	19.2	18.7	22.0	21.0	19.8	20.0	19.9
Other professional services.......	1.4	1.0	1.4	2.4	2.7	2.7	2.8	2.8
Dental services	7.3	6.3	5.2	4.4	4.5	4.1	3.7	3.7
Other health, residential, personal care	1.6	1.7	3.3	3.3	4.7	5.0	5.3	5.3
Home health care[1]...............	0.2	0.3	0.9	1.7	2.4	2.8	2.8	2.8
Nursing care facilities and continuing care retirement communities[1]	3.0	5.4	6.0	6.2	6.2	5.4	4.8	4.6
Retail outlet sales of medical products..	18.5	14.2	10.1	10.6	13.0	13.1	12.7	12.5
Prescription drugs	9.8	7.4	4.7	5.6	8.8	9.6	9.4	9.2
Durable medical equipment	2.7	2.3	1.6	1.9	1.8	1.5	1.5	1.5
Other nondurable medical products..	6.0	4.5	3.8	3.1	2.3	2.0	1.8	1.8
Government administration[2]..........	0.2	1.0	1.1	1.0	1.2	1.2	1.3	1.3
Net cost of health insurance	3.7	2.5	3.6	4.4	4.7	5.9	6.5	7.1
Government public health activities	1.4	1.8	2.5	2.8	3.1	2.9	2.6	2.6
Investment..........................	9.2	10.1	7.8	6.6	6.1	5.5	4.8	4.8
Research[3].........................	2.6	2.6	2.1	1.8	1.9	1.9	1.4	1.4
Structures and equipment............	6.7	7.5	5.7	4.8	4.2	3.6	3.4	3.3
			Average annual percent change from previous year shown					
NATIONAL HEALTH EXPENDITURES....	—	10.6%	13.1%	10.9%	6.6%	6.6%	4.3%	4.6%
Health consumption expenditures	—	10.5	13.4	11.1	6.7	6.7	4.4	4.7
Personal health care................	—	10.5	13.2	11.0	6.6	6.6	4.4	4.1
Hospital care....................	—	11.7	14.0	9.6	5.2	7.1	4.8	4.5
Professional services..............	—	9.6	12.6	12.4	6.4	5.9	4.3	4.4
Physician and clinical services	—	9.9	12.8	12.7	6.2	5.9	4.5	4.1
Other professional services.......	—	6.3	17.0	17.4	7.8	6.7	4.9	6.5
Dental services	—	9.0	11.0	9.0	7.0	5.5	2.9	4.6
Other health, residential, personal care	—	11.5	20.5	11.0	10.4	7.3	5.1	4.6
Home health care[1]...............	—	14.5	26.9	18.1	9.9	8.3	4.4	5.2
Nursing care facilities and continuing care retirement communities[1]	—	17.4	14.2	11.4	6.6	5.2	2.4	1.4
Retail outlet sales of medical products..	—	7.7	9.4	11.4	8.8	6.7	3.9	2.9
Prescription drugs	—	7.5	8.2	12.8	11.6	7.5	4.0	2.5
Durable medical equipment	—	9.0	8.8	13.0	6.2	4.7	4.0	4.7
Other nondurable medical products..	—	7.4	11.4	8.6	3.5	5.0	3.2	3.6
Government administration[2]..........	—	30.0	14.1	10.0	9.0	5.9	5.8	6.0
Net cost of health insurance	—	6.4	17.2	13.0	7.4	9.1	5.9	13.2
Government public health activities	—	13.8	16.9	12.0	8.0	5.8	2.7	2.4
Investment..........................	—	11.6	10.2	9.1	5.8	5.5	2.4	3.6
Research[3].........................	—	10.9	10.8	8.9	7.2	6.8	0.3	5.0
Structures and equipment............	—	11.9	10.0	9.2	5.3	4.9	3.4	3.0

— = Not applicable. **Note:** Numbers may not add up to totals due to rounding. (1) In freestanding facilities only. Additional services of this type provided in hospital-based facilities are counted as hospital care. (2) Incl. all administrative costs (e.g., employee salaries) associated with insuring individuals enrolled in federally managed health insurance programs. (3) Research and development expenditures of drug companies and other mfrs. and providers of med. equip. and supplies are included in the expenditure class in which a product falls instead of here.

Health Coverage for Persons Under 65, 1984-2018

Source: National Health Interview Survey, National Center for Health Statistics, CDC, U.S. Dept. of Health and Human Services
(percent of population)

	Private insurance				Medicaid[1]				Uninsured[2]			
	1984	2000	2010	2018	1984	2000	2010	2018	1984	2000	2010	2018
Total......................	76.8%	71.5%	61.7%	65.3%	6.8%	9.5%	16.9%	19.4%	14.5%	17.0%	18.2%	11.0%
Age												
Under 18 years.............	72.6	66.6	54.1	54.5	11.9	19.6	36.4	36.3	13.9	12.6	7.8	5.2
18-44 years................	76.5	70.5	60.0	66.6	5.1	5.6	10.9	14.9	17.1	22.4	27.1	15.4
45-64 years................	83.3	78.7	71.3	72.8	3.4	4.5	6.8	10.5	9.6	12.6	15.7	10.2
Race and Hispanic origin												
White only, non-Hispanic	82.4	79.5	72.0	74.9	3.7	6.1	11.0	12.8	11.9	12.5	13.7	7.8
Black only, non-Hispanic......	58.2	56.0	45.1	52.4	20.7	21.0	30.0	30.5	19.7	19.5	20.7	12.1
Hispanic or Latino, any race ...	55.7	47.8	36.8	45.4	13.3	15.5	28.6	31.3	29.5	35.6	32.0	20.1
Percent of poverty level												
Below 100%................	32.2	25.2	16.0	17.0	33.0	38.4	50.8	59.0	33.9	34.2	30.3	19.7
100%-199%................	70.3	50.1	34.8	34.2	5.3	16.2	28.5	41.4	21.8	31.0	32.4	18.8
200%-399%[3]..............	89.3	78.1	70.7	82.3	0.8	4.0	8.4	6.7	7.6	15.4	17.4	7.2
400% or more	95.4	91.9	89.9	NA	0.2	0.9	2.0	NA	3.2	5.9	5.6	NA
Geographic region												
Northeast.................	80.5	76.3	68.2	70.3	8.6	10.6	17.9	20.3	10.2	12.2	12.4	6.3
Midwest..................	80.6	74.8	66.7	70.6	7.4	8.0	17.3	16.8	11.3	12.3	14.1	9.5
South....................	74.3	66.8	57.5	61.2	5.1	9.4	16.0	18.2	17.7	20.5	21.9	15.0
West....................	71.9	66.5	58.9	63.4	7.0	10.4	17.1	22.9	18.2	20.7	20.6	9.7

NA = Not available. **Note:** Data based on household interviews of a sample of the civilian noninstitutionalized population. Totals incl. groups not shown separately. Because of questionnaire redesign, data for 1984 are not strictly comparable with data for later years. (1) Incl. persons who had some other state-sponsored health plan such as Children's Health Insurance Program (CHIP). (2) Incl. persons who had only Indian Health Service coverage or had only a private plan that paid for one type of service (e.g., accidents, dental care). (3) 200% or greater in 2018.

Spending on Health in the 50 Most Populous Countries, 2017

Source: Global Health Expenditure Database, World Health Organization (WHO)

Country	As % of GDP[1]	Per capita[1]	Country	As % of GDP[1]	Per capita[1]	Country	As % of GDP[1]	Per capita[1]	Country	As % of GDP[1]	Per capita[1]
Afghanistan...	11.8%	$67	France......	11.3%	$4,380	Morocco	5.2%	$161	Sudan.......	6.3%	$194
Algeria	6.4	258	Germany.....	11.2	5,033	Mozambique..	4.9	21	Tanzania.....	3.6	34
Angola	2.8	114	Ghana.......	3.3	67	Myanmar.....	4.6	58	Thailand	3.7	247
Argentina ...	9.1	1,325	India	3.5	69	Nepal	5.6	48	Turkey	4.2	445
Bangladesh...	2.3	36	Indonesia ...	3.0	115	Nigeria	3.8	74	Uganda......	6.3	39
Brazil........	9.5	929	Iran	8.7	475	Pakistan	2.9	45	Ukraine	7.0	177
Canada	10.6	4,755	Iraq	4.2	210	Peru	5.0	333	UK..........	9.6	3,859
China	5.2	441	Italy.........	8.8	2,840	Philippines ...	4.4	133	U.S..........	17.1	10,246
Colombia ...	7.2	459	Japan........	10.9	4,169	Poland.......	6.5	907	Uzbekistan ...	6.4	99
Congo, Dem.			Kenya	4.8	77	Russia.......	5.3	586	Venezuela....	1.2	94
Rep. of the..	4.0	19	Korea, South..	7.6	2,283	Saudi Arabia[2]	5.8	1,166	Vietnam	5.5	130
Egypt	5.3	106	Malaysia	3.8	374	South Africa ..	8.1	499	Yemen[3]......	4.2	72
Ethiopia......	3.5	25	Mexico	5.5	495	Spain	8.9	2,506	World[4]	6.3	884

(1) At average exchange rate. (2) As of 2016. (3) As of 2015. (4) Includes other nations not shown.

Population Not Covered by Health Insurance by State, 1990-2019

Source: American Community Survey and Current Population Survey, U.S. Census Bureau, U.S. Dept. of Commerce
(numbers in thousands)

	1990 No. not covered	1990 % pop. not covered	2000 No. not covered	2000 % pop. not covered	2019 No. not covered	2019 % pop. not covered		1990 No. not covered	1990 % pop. not covered	2000 No. not covered	2000 % pop. not covered	2019 No. not covered	2019 % pop. not covered
AL	710	17.4%	547	12.5%	469	9.7%	MT	115	14.0%	144	16.1%	87	8.3%
AK	77	15.4	108	17.4	86	12.2	NE	138	8.5	134	7.9	158	8.3
AZ	547	15.5	853	16.4	809	11.3	NV	201	16.5	321	15.7	348	11.4
AR	421	17.4	373	14.1	271	9.1	NH	107	9.9	97	7.9	84	6.3
CA	5,683	19.1	5,956	17.5	3,002	7.7	NJ	773	10.0	857	10.2	692	7.9
CO	495	14.7	559	12.9	453	8.0	NM	339	22.2	415	23.0	205	10.0
CT	226	6.9	300	8.9	207	5.9	NY	2,176	12.1	2,730	14.5	1,007	5.2
DE	96	13.9	66	8.5	63	6.6	NC	883	13.8	964	12.1	1,157	11.3
DC	109	19.2	71	12.8	25	3.6	ND	40	6.3	61	9.8	51	6.9
FL	2,376	18.0	2,591	16.2	2,784	13.2	OH	1,123	10.3	1,101	9.8	758	6.6
GA	971	15.3	1,126	13.9	1,398	13.4	OK	574	18.6	587	17.4	553	14.3
HI	81	7.3	95	7.9	56	4.1	OR	360	12.4	398	11.6	299	7.2
ID	159	15.2	198	15.4	191	10.8	PA	1,218	10.1	915	7.6	726	5.8
IL	1,272	10.9	1,474	12.0	923	7.4	RI	105	11.1	71	6.9	43	4.1
IN	587	10.7	608	10.1	578	8.7	SC	550	16.2	426	10.7	548	10.9
IA	225	8.1	233	8.1	156	5.0	SD	81	11.6	80	10.8	88	10.1
KS	272	10.8	256	9.6	262	9.2	TN	673	13.7	603	10.7	682	10.2
KY	480	13.2	509	12.7	283	6.5	TX	3,569	21.1	4,555	22.0	5,234	18.4
LA	797	19.7	736	16.8	404	8.9	UT	156	9.0	243	10.8	307	9.7
ME	139	11.2	131	10.4	107	8.1	VT	54	9.5	44	7.4	28	4.5
MD	601	12.7	473	9.0	357	6.0	VA	996	15.7	670	9.6	658	7.9
MA	530	9.1	450	7.1	204	3.0	WA	557	11.4	767	13.1	496	6.6
MI	865	9.4	767	7.8	571	5.8	WV	249	13.8	239	13.4	118	6.7
MN	389	8.9	393	8.0	273	4.9	WI	321	6.7	378	7.1	329	5.7
MS	531	19.9	368	13.2	377	13.0	WY	58	12.5	71	14.7	70	12.3
MO	665	12.7	474	8.6	604	10.0	U.S.	34,719	13.9	36,586	13.1	29,639	9.2

Persons Not Covered by Health Insurance by Selected Characteristics, 2019

Source: Annual Social and Economic Supplement, Current Population Survey, U.S. Census Bureau, U.S. Dept. of Commerce
(numbers without health insurance coverage for entire calendar year, in thousands)

Characteristic	Number not covered	Percent	Characteristic	Number not covered	Percent
Total..........................	26,111	8.0%	**Household income**		
Race and Hispanic origin[1]			Less than $25,000	4,914	13.1%
White...................	19,381	7.8	$25,000 to less than $50,000....	7,185	12.8
White, not Hispanic	10,187	5.2	$50,000 to less than $75,000....	5,500	10.4
Black....................	4,118	9.6	$75,000 to less than $100,000 ..	3,211	7.5
Asian...................	1,240	6.2	$100,000 to less than $125,000 ..	2,234	6.3
Hispanic (any race)............	10,122	16.7	$125,000 to less than $150,000 ..	981	4.1
Age			$150,000 or more..............	2,086	2.7
Under 65 years	25,517	9.5	**Work experience**[4]		
Under 19 years[2]	3,994	5.2	All workers	16,059	10.2
19 to 64 years	21,523	11.1	Full-time, year-round	10,091	8.9
19 to 25 years[3]............	4,202	14.2	Less than full-time, year-round..	5,968	13.4
26 to 34 years	5,379	13.3	Did not work at least one week...	6,476	12.2
35 to 44 years	4,716	11.4	**Marital status**[5]		
45 to 64 years	7,227	8.8	Married...................	7,629	7.6
65 years and over............	594	1.1	Widowed..................	447	13.5
Nativity			Divorced..................	2,196	12.0
Native-born	18,134	6.5	Separated.................	724	19.0
Foreign-born	7,977	17.8	Never married..............	10,528	15.7
Naturalized citizen	1,977	8.7			
Not a citizen	6,000	27.1			

(1) Numbers are for one race alone unless otherwise noted. (2) Eligible for Medicaid/Children's Health Insurance Program. (3) May be eligible to be a dependent on a parent's health insurance. (4) Aged 15 to 64 years only. (5) Aged 19 to 64 years only.

Health Insurance Marketplace Plan Enrollment by Selected Characteristics

Source: Centers for Medicare & Medicaid Services (CMS), U.S. Dept. of Health and Human Services
(cumulative enrollment-related activity for Nov. 1-Dec. 21, 2019; exact dates vary for state-based exchanges)

	Marketplace total		Federal marketplace[1]		State marketplaces[2]	
	Number	Percent	Number	Percent	Number	Percent
Number who have selected a plan	11,409,447	100.0%	8,286,871	100.0%	3,122,576	100.0%
Under 18 years of age	1,016,313	8.9	789,317	9.5	226,996	7.3
18 to 25 years of age	1,127,053	9.9	837,701	10.1	289,352	9.3
26 to 34 years of age	1,801,041	15.8	1,250,826	15.1	550,215	17.6
35 to 44 years of age	1,827,996	16.0	1,326,983	16.0	501,013	16.0
45 to 54 years of age	2,251,860	19.7	1,633,271	19.7	618,589	19.8
55 to 64 years of age	3,234,445	28.3	2,337,856	28.2	896,589	28.7
65 years of age and older................	150,725	1.3	110,917	1.3	39,808	1.3
Number receiving financial assistance[3]	9,617,901	84.3	7,221,736	87.1	2,396,165	76.7
With advance premium tax credits	9,593,360	84.1	7,205,225	86.9	2,388,135	76.5
With cost-sharing reductions.............	5,563,299	48.8	4,332,303	52.3	1,230,996	39.4

Note: Figures may not add up to totals due to rounding. (1) For the 38 states using HealthCare.gov, the federally facilitated marketplace. (2) For the 12 states and the Dist. of Columbia that have implemented their own exchanges. (3) Advance premium tax credit (APTC) only, cost-sharing reduction (CSR) only, or both APTC and CSR.

Health Insurance Marketplace Average Monthly Premiums, 2020

Source: Centers for Medicare & Medicaid Services, U.S. Dept. of Health and Human Services
For the 2020 open enrollment period, 38 states used HealthCare.gov, the eligibility and enrollment platform run by the federal government. Twelve states and the Dist. of Columbia ran their own exchanges (state-based exchanges, or SBEs).
(based on enrollment-related activity for Nov. 1-Dec. 21, 2019; exact dates vary for state-based exchanges)

State	Avg. premium after tax credits	Avg. premium before tax credits	Avg. tax credits	Avg. % reduction in premium after tax credits	State	Avg. premium after tax credits	Avg. premium before tax credits	Avg. tax credits	Avg. % reduction in premium after tax credits
Alabama	$130	$691	$625	81.2%	Nebraska	$107	$765	$711	86.0%
Alaska.	187	739	671	74.7	Nevada[2]	NA	NA	NA	NA
Arizona	220	589	472	62.6	New Hampshire. .	238	529	418	55.0
Arkansas[1]	197	522	383	62.3	New Jersey[1]	241	554	419	56.5
California[2]	185	569	445	67.5	New Mexico[1]	195	476	374	59.0
Colorado[2]	205	478	368	57.1	New York[2]	226	643	345	64.9
Connecticut[2]	244	684	638	64.3	North Carolina . .	116	660	606	82.4
Delaware	192	668	572	71.3	North Dakota . . .	184	453	323	59.4
Dist. of Columbia[2]	505	534	422	5.4	Ohio	230	522	389	55.9
Florida	98	597	533	83.6	Oklahoma	108	644	594	83.2
Georgia.	133	566	495	76.5	Oregon[1]	231	558	456	58.6
Hawaii.	223	632	523	64.7	Pennsylvania[1] . . .	213	648	517	67.1
Idaho[2]	NA	NA	NA	NA	Rhode Island[2] . . .	180	435	326	58.6
Illinois	224	636	500	64.8	South Carolina . .	124	613	543	79.8
Indiana	270	544	399	50.4	South Dakota . . .	136	687	602	80.2
Iowa	111	823	809	86.5	Tennessee	145	641	580	77.4
Kansas	171	638	547	73.2	Texas	115	532	470	78.4
Kentucky[1]	185	594	509	68.9	Utah	93	425	368	78.1
Louisiana	190	677	564	71.9	Vermont[2].	448	1,034	738	56.7
Maine	176	642	552	72.6	Virginia	174	641	556	72.9
Maryland[2].	178	498	443	64.3	Washington[2]	283	528	408	46.4
Massachusetts[2]. .	198	398	263	50.3	West Virginia. . . .	285	992	819	71.3
Michigan.	176	480	366	63.3	Wisconsin	173	657	569	73.7
Minnesota[2]	285	444	292	35.8	Wyoming.	128	967	923	86.8
Mississippi	82	608	559	86.5	**Total**				
Missouri	158	634	564	75.1	**HealthCare.gov**	**145**	**595**	**517**	**75.6**
Montana	173	572	486	69.8					

NA = Not available (not reported). (1) State-based exchange using the HealthCare.gov platform for eligibility determinations, enrollments, and related functions. (2) State-based exchange.

Health Care Visits by Selected Characteristics, 1997-2017

Source: *Health, United States, 2018*, National Center for Health Statistics, CDC, U.S. Dept. of Health and Human Services

Characteristic	Zero visits			1-3 visits			4-9 visits			10 or more visits		
	1997	2010	2017	1997	2010	2017	1997	2010	2017	1997	2010	2017
						Percent distribution						
All persons[1].	16.5%	15.6%	14.0%	46.2%	45.4%	50.4%	23.6%	25.8%	23.2%	13.7%	13.2%	12.4%
Age												
Under 6 years	5.0	3.7	5.0	44.9	48.9	54.0	37.0	36.8	34.1	13.0	10.6	7.0
6-17 years	15.3	10.4	8.5	58.7	59.1	65.5	19.3	23.6	19.9	6.8	6.9	6.2
18-44 years	21.7	24.2	21.5	46.7	43.9	49.2	19.0	20.6	18.3	12.6	11.3	11.1
45-64 years	16.9	14.8	12.7	42.9	42.8	46.7	24.7	26.1	24.9	15.5	16.4	15.7
65-74 years	9.8	6.3	6.4	36.9	36.1	40.5	31.6	35.7	33.5	21.6	21.9	19.6
75 years and over	7.7	4.1	4.4	31.8	31.0	32.6	33.8	38.0	35.3	26.6	27.0	27.6
Sex												
Male	21.3	20.4	17.6	47.1	46.4	51.9	20.6	22.7	20.9	11.0	10.5	9.7
Female.	11.8	10.9	10.5	45.4	44.4	49.0	26.5	28.8	25.6	16.3	15.9	15.0
Health insurance status[2]												
Insured continuously	14.1	12.1	11.9	49.2	48.6	53.8	23.6	26.2	22.7	13.0	13.0	11.6
Uninsured, up to 12 mos. . .	18.9	18.5	20.9	46.0	47.8	48.8	20.8	22.0	20.3	14.4	11.6	10.1
Uninsured 12+ mos.	39.0	43.8	47.9	41.4	39.7	40.1	13.2	12.6	8.5	6.4	3.9	3.5

Note: Totals include visits to hospital emergency departments, doctor offices, and clinics as well as home visits by a health care professional. (1) Includes persons of unknown health insurance status. (2) In 12 months prior to interview, for persons under age 65 only.

Reasons Given by Patients for Physician Office Visits, 2016

Source: National Ambulatory Medical Care Survey, National Center for Health Statistics, Centers for Disease Control and Prevention, U.S. Dept. of Health and Human Services

Rank	Primary reason	Number of visits (thous.)	% of all visits	Rank	Primary reason	Number of visits (thous.)	% of all visits
1.	Progress visit, not otherwise specified	127,535	14.4%	11.	Hypertension	11,406	1.3%
2.	General medical examination	72,132	8.2	12.	Knee symptoms	10,581	1.2
3.	Prenatal examination, routine	22,477	2.5	13.	Preoperative visit	10,129	1.1
4.	Postoperative visit	18,636	2.1	14.	Symptoms referable to throat	10,056	1.1
5.	Medication, other and unspecified kinds	17,283	2.0	15.	For other and unspecified test results	9,786	1.1
6.	Cough	16,417	1.9	16.	Vision dysfunctions	9,666	1.1
7.	Well-baby examination	15,865	1.8	17.	Fever	8,836	1.0
8.	Medical counseling, not otherwise specified	13,485	1.5	18.	Other special examination	8,739	1.0
				19.	Diabetes mellitus	8,512	1.0
9.	Skin rash	13,374	1.5	20.	Earache or ear infection	8,507	1.0
10.	Gynecological examination	11,743	1.3		All other reasons	458,559	51.9
					All visits	883,725	100.0

Note: Based on nationally representative sample survey of visits to nonfederal office-based patient care physicians. Numbers may not add to totals because of rounding.

Visits to Physician Offices and Hospital Outpatient and Emergency Departments, 1995-2015

Source: National Ambulatory Medical Care Survey and National Hospital Ambulatory Medical Care Survey, National Center for Health Statistics, Centers for Disease Control and Prevention, U.S. Dept. of Health and Human Services

(number of visits per 100 persons)

Sex and age	All places[1] 1995	2000	2011	Physician offices[2] 1995	2000	2010	2015	Hospital outpatient depts. 1995	2000	2011	Hospital emergency depts. 1995	2000	2010	2015
Total	334	374	400	271	304	325	297	26	31	40	37	40	43	44
Male	290	325	354	232	261	283	252	21	26	32	37	38	40	40
Under 18	273	302	372	209	231	262	203	25	29	37	40	41	43	44
18-44	190	203	208	139	148	151	122	14	17	20	37	38	38	39
45-54	275	316	322	229	260	265	251	20	26	34	26	30	35	36
55-64	351	428	430	300	367	396	378	26	32	45	25	30	32	31
65-74	508	614	655	445	539	597	560	20	38	52	34	36	37	34
75 and over	711	771	869	616	670	760	799	34	42	49	61	59	60	60
Female	377	420	444	309	345	367	342	31	35	48	37	41	47	48
Under 18	277	285	341	217	221	252	204	25	29	38	35	35	37	43
18-44	336	377	393	265	298	323	285	31	33	47	40	46	57	57
45-54	400	451	459	339	384	372	411	32	36	53	29	31	40	39
55-64	446	529	520	382	453	469	424	38	45	54	26	31	31	33
65-74	603	692	707	534	609	647	607	36	46	60	32	37	40	38
75 and over	666	763	790	571	645	685	736	34	49	61	61	69	66	61

(1) Incl. visits to physician offices and hospital outpatient and emergency departments. Prior to 2006, visits to community health centers were not included in survey. (2) 2010 data incl. visits to community health centers.

Most Frequently Mentioned Drugs at Office Visits, 2016

Source: National Ambulatory Medical Care Survey, National Center for Health Statistics, Centers for Disease Control and Prevention, U.S. Dept. of Health and Human Services

Rank	Therapeutic drug category[1]	No. of mentions (thous.)	% of total[2]	Rank	Therapeutic drug category[1]	No. of mentions (thous.)	% of total[2]
1.	Analgesics[3]	327,162	11.1%	11.	Beta-adrenergic blocking agents	90,004	3.1%
2.	Antihyperlipidemic agents	131,431	4.5	12.	Diuretics	84,872	2.9
3.	Dermatological agents	123,825	4.2	13.	Proton pump inhibitors	82,065	2.8
4.	Vitamins	121,093	4.1	14.	Vitamin and mineral combinations	80,402	2.7
5.	Antidepressants	118,752	4.0	15.	Immunostimulants	74,457	2.5
6.	Bronchodilators	107,253	3.7	16.	Antihistamines	70,656	2.4
7.	Antiplatelet agents	101,466	3.5	17.	Ophthalmic preparations	65,903	2.2
8.	Anxiolytics, sedatives, and hypnotics	100,564	3.4	18.	ACE[4] inhibitors	60,984	2.1
9.	Antidiabetic agents	100,365	3.4	19.	Adrenal cortical steroids	54,364	1.9
10.	Anticonvulsants	94,067	3.2	20.	Calcium channel blocking agents	51,114	1.7

Note: A mention is documentation in a patient's record of a drug provided, prescribed, or continued at a visit to a nonfederal office-based patient care physician. (1) Based on the Multum Lexicon second-level therapeutic drug category. (2) Based on an estimated 2,935,894,000 drug mentions at office visits in 2016. (3) Incl. narcotic and nonnarcotic analgesics and nonsteroidal anti-inflammatory drugs. (4) Angiotensin-converting enzyme.

U.S. Organ Transplants

Source: Organ Procurement and Transplantation Network (OPTN), United Network for Organ Sharing (UNOS)

Waiting List, July 2020			Transplants Performed, 2019		
Type of transplant	Candidates	% of total	Type of transplant	Number	% of total
All organs	109,889	100.0%	All organs	39,719	100.0%
Kidney	92,756	84.4	Kidney	23,401	58.9
Liver	12,346	11.2	Liver	8,896	22.4
Heart	3,497	3.2	Heart	3,552	8.9
Kidney-pancreas	1,721	1.6	Lung	2,714	6.8
Lung	1,070	1.0	Kidney-pancreas	872	2.2
Pancreas	886	0.8	Pancreas	143	0.4
Intestine	250	0.2	Intestine	81	0.2
Heart-lung	51	0.05	Heart-lung	45	0.1

Note: Waiting list as of July 14, 2020; numbers may not add up to total because of patients waiting for multiple organs. Total transplants performed include organs not shown separately.

Illicit Drug Use Among Persons Age 12 or Older, 2002-19

Source: National Survey on Drug Use and Health, SAMHSA, U.S. Dept. of Health and Human Services

Of all those age 12 or older who used an illicit drug in the past month in 2019, approximately 2.2 mil were adolescents aged 12-17 (making 8.7% of that age group current drug users). About 8.4 mil current users were young adults aged 18-25 (or 24.9% of that age group).

(numbers in thousands)

Substance	2002 No.	%	2005 No.	%	2010 No.	%	2014 No.	%	2018 No.	%	2019 No.	%
Used in lifetime												
Illicit drugs[1]	—	—	—	—	—	—	—	—	134,791	49.2	138,027	50.2
Marijuana	94,946	40.4	97,545	40.1	106,612	42.0	117,213	44.2	123,935	45.3	127,139	46.2
Cocaine	33,910	14.4	33,673	13.8	37,361	14.7	39,200	14.8	40,194	14.7	41,445	15.1
Crack	8,402	3.6	7,928	3.3	9,208	3.6	9,424	3.6	9,177	3.4	9,375	3.4
Heroin	3,668	1.6	3,534	1.5	4,144	1.6	4,813	1.8	5,108	1.9	5,696	2.1
Hallucinogens	—	—	—	—	—	—	—	—	43,255	15.8	44,087	16.0
LSD	24,516	10.4	22,433	9.2	23,375	9.2	25,035	9.4	27,339	10.0	27,528	10.0
PCP	7,418	3.2	6,603	2.7	6,255	2.5	6,388	2.4	6,085	2.2	5,516	2.0
Inhalants	—	—	—	—	—	—	—	—	24,783	9.1	25,090	9.1
Methamphetamine	—	—	—	—	—	—	—	—	14,892	5.4	16,013	5.8
Used in past year												
Illicit drugs[1]	—	—	—	—	—	—	—	—	53,182	19.4	57,203	20.8
Marijuana	25,755	11.0	25,375	10.4	29,301	11.6	35,124	13.2	43,486	15.9	48,242	17.5
Cocaine	5,902	2.5	5,523	2.3	4,533	1.8	4,553	1.7	5,529	2.0	5,468	2.0
Crack	1,554	0.7	1,381	0.6	885	0.3	773	0.3	757	0.3	778	0.3
Heroin	404	0.2	379	0.2	621	0.2	914	0.3	808	0.3	745	0.3
Hallucinogens	—	—	—	—	—	—	—	—	5,595	2.0	6,010	2.2
LSD	999	0.4	563	0.2	881	0.3	1,290	0.5	2,319	0.8	2,470	0.9
PCP	235	0.1	164	0.1	96	0.0	90	0.0	71	0.0	73	0.0
Inhalants	—	—	—	—	—	—	—	—	2,003	0.7	2,142	0.8
Methamphetamine	—	—	—	—	—	—	—	—	1,867	0.7	1,999	0.7
Misuse of psychotherapeutics[2]	—	—	—	—	—	—	—	—	16,882	6.2	16,304	5.9
Opioids[3]	—	—	—	—	—	—	—	—	10,250	3.7	10,065	3.7
Used in past month												
Illicit drugs[1]	—	—	—	—	—	—	—	—	31,918	11.7	35,803	13.0
Marijuana	14,584	6.2	14,626	6.0	17,409	6.9	22,188	8.4	27,667	10.1	31,606	11.5
Cocaine	2,020	0.9	2,397	1.0	1,472	0.6	1,530	0.6	1,949	0.7	1,998	0.7
Crack	567	0.2	682	0.3	378	0.1	354	0.1	436	0.2	378	0.1
Heroin	166	0.1	136	0.1	239	0.1	435	0.2	354	0.1	431	0.2
Hallucinogens	—	—	—	—	—	—	—	—	1,630	0.6	1,915	0.7
LSD	112	0.0	104	0.0	155	0.0	287	0.1	458	0.2	580	0.2
PCP	58	0.0	48	0.0	36	0.0	*	*	34	0.0	*	*
Inhalants	—	—	—	—	—	—	—	—	612	0.2	807	0.3
Methamphetamine	—	—	—	—	—	—	—	—	1,001	0.4	1,173	0.4
Misuse of psychotherapeutics[2]	—	—	—	—	—	—	—	—	5,424	2.0	5,337	1.9
Opioids[3]	—	—	—	—	—	—	—	—	3,042	1.1	3,101	1.1

— = Not comparable due to methodological changes or not reported due to measurement issues. * = Low precision. **Note:** Misuse is defined as use in any way not directed by a doctor, including use without a prescription or use in greater amounts, more often, or for a longer period of time. (1) Includes marijuana, cocaine (including crack), heroin, hallucinogens, inhalants, methamphetamine, the misuse of psychotherapeutics, and opioids. (2) Includes four categories of prescription drugs (pain relievers, stimulants, tranquilizers, sedatives) but not over-the-counter drugs. (3) Includes the misuse of prescription opioid pain relievers and the use of heroin.

Lifetime Prevalence of Drug Use in 12th Graders, 1975-2019

Source: Monitoring the Future study, Univ. of Michigan Inst. for Social Research; Natl. Inst. on Drug Abuse, Natl. Insts. of Health

(percent who have ever used)

Drug	1975	1980	1985	1990	1995	2000	2005	2010	2015	2016	2017	2018	2019	2018-19 change
Any illicit drug[1]	55.2%	65.4%	60.6%	47.9%	48.4%	54.0%	50.4%	48.2%	48.9%	48.3%	48.9%	47.8%	47.4%	−0.4%
Marijuana/hashish	47.3	60.3	54.2	40.7	41.7	48.8	44.8	43.8	44.7	44.5	45.0	43.6	43.7	0.1
Inhalants[2]	—	17.3	18.1	18.5	17.4	14.2	11.4	9.0	5.7	5.0	4.9	4.4	5.3	0.9
Nitrites	—	11.1	7.9	2.1	1.5	0.8	1.1	—	—	—	—	—	—	—
Hallucinogens[3]	—	15.6	12.1	9.7	12.7	13.0	8.8	8.6	6.4	6.7	6.7	6.6	6.9	0.3
LSD	11.3	9.3	7.5	8.7	11.7	11.1	3.5	4.0	4.3	4.9	5.0	5.1	5.6	0.5
PCP	—	9.6	4.9	2.8	2.7	3.4	2.4	1.8	—	—	—	—	—	—
MDMA (Ecstasy, Molly)	—	—	—	—	—	11.0	5.4	7.3	5.9	4.9	4.9	4.1	3.3	−0.7
Cocaine	9.0	15.7	17.3	9.4	6.0	8.6	8.0	5.5	4.0	3.7	4.2	3.9	3.8	−0.1
Crack	—	—	—	3.5	3.0	3.9	3.5	2.4	1.7	1.4	1.7	1.5	1.7	0.1
Heroin	2.2	1.1	1.2	1.3	1.6	2.4	1.5	1.6	0.8	0.7	0.7	0.8	0.6	−0.2
Narcotics other than heroin[4]	9.0	9.8	10.2	8.3	7.2	10.6	12.8	13.0	8.4	7.8	6.8	6.0	5.3	−0.8
Amphetamines[4]	22.3	26.4	26.2	17.5	15.3	15.6	13.1	11.1	10.8	10.0	9.2	8.6	7.7	−1.0
Methamphetamine	—	—	—	—	—	—	7.9	4.5	2.3	1.0	1.2	1.1	0.7	0.1
Crystal meth	—	—	—	2.7	3.9	4.0	4.0	1.8	1.2	1.4	1.5	1.1	1.3	0.1
Sedatives (barbiturates)[4]	18.2	14.9	11.8	7.5	7.4	9.2	10.5	7.5	5.9	5.2	4.5	4.2	4.2	0.0
Methaqualone[4]	8.1	9.5	6.7	2.3	1.2	0.8	1.3	0.4	—	—	—	—	—	—
Tranquilizers[4]	17.0	15.2	11.9	7.2	7.1	8.9	9.9	8.5	6.9	7.6	7.5	6.6	6.1	−0.5
Alcohol	90.4	93.2	92.2	89.5	80.7	80.3	75.1	71.0	64.0	61.2	61.5	58.5	58.5	0.0
Cigarettes	73.6	71.0	68.8	64.4	64.2	62.5	50.0	42.2	31.1	28.3	26.6	23.8	22.3	−1.5
Smokeless tobacco	—	—	—	—	30.9	23.1	17.5	17.6	13.2	14.2	11.0	10.1	9.8	−0.3
Any vaping[5]	—	—	—	—	—	—	—	—	35.5	33.8	35.8	42.5	45.6	3.0
Steroids[4]	—	—	—	2.9	2.3	2.5	2.6	2.0	2.3	1.6	1.6	1.6	1.6	0.0

— = Not available. **Note:** Because of changes to question wording, some data may not be directly comparable across years. (1) Includes marijuana, LSD, other hallucinogens, crack, cocaine other than crack, or heroin; or any use of narcotics other than heroin, amphetamines, sedatives (barbiturates), or tranquilizers not under a doctor's orders. (2) Not adjusted for underreporting of amyl and butyl nitrites. (3) Not adjusted for underreporting of PCP. (4) Includes only drug use not under a doctor's orders. (5) Includes vaping of nicotine, marijuana, or just flavoring.

Cigarette Use in the U.S., 1985-2019

Source: National Survey on Drug Use and Health, Substance Abuse and Mental Health Services Admin. (SAMHSA), U.S. Dept. of Health and Human Services

(percentage of persons age 12 or older, unless otherwise noted, reporting use in the month prior to the survey)

	1985	2000	2005	2010	2015	2018	2019		1985	2000	2005	2010	2015	2018	2019
Total	38.7	24.9	24.9	23.0	19.4	17.2	16.7	**Race/Hispanic origin**							
								White, not Hispanic	38.9	25.9	26.0	24.3	20.7	18.7	18.0
Sex								Black, not Hispanic	38.0	23.3	24.5	22.6	21.3	17.9	18.7
Male	43.4	26.9	27.4	25.4	21.8	19.1	18.6	Hispanic, any race	40.0	20.7	22.1	20.1	15.3	12.5	12.2
Female	34.5	23.1	22.5	20.7	17.1	15.3	14.9	**Education[2]**							
								Non-HS graduate	37.3	32.4	34.8	34.3	28.1	25.2	26.5
Age								HS graduate	37.0	31.1	31.8	29.6	27.4	25.5	24.9
12-17 years	29.4	13.4	10.8	8.4	4.2	2.7	2.3	Some college	32.6	27.7	28.1	25.8	23.5	20.5	20.2
18-25 years	47.4	38.3	39.0	34.3	26.7	17.1	17.5	College graduate	23.0	13.9	13.8	12.8	9.6	8.8	8.0
26 years or older[1]	45.7	24.2	24.3	22.8	20.0	18.5	18.2								

HS = High school. **Note:** Because of methodological changes in 2002 and 2015, data may not be comparable across years. (1) Persons age 26 to 34 only in 1985. (2) Persons age 18 or older.

Daily Use of Cigarettes by 8th, 10th, and 12th Graders, 1995-2019

Source: Monitoring the Future study, Univ. of Michigan Inst. for Social Research; Natl. Inst. on Drug Abuse, Natl. Insts. of Health

(percent who smoked daily in last 30 days)

	8th grade				% change, 2005-19	10th grade				% change, 2005-19	12th grade				% change, 2005-19
	1995	2000	2005	2019		1995	2000	2005	2019		1995	2000	2005	2019	
Total	9.3	7.4	4.0	0.8	−80.0%	16.3	14.0	7.5	1.3	−82.7%	21.6	20.6	13.6	2.4	−82.4%
Gender															
Male	9.2	7.0	3.9	0.6	−84.6	16.3	13.7	7.2	1.5	−79.2	21.7	20.9	14.6	2.8	−80.8
Female	9.2	7.5	4.0	0.9	−77.5	16.1	14.1	7.7	1.2	−84.4	20.8	19.7	11.9	1.6	−86.6
College plans															
None/ under 4 yrs.	22.5	21.7	14.4	2.8	−80.6	32.7	28.8	19.2	3.6	−81.3	33.7	31.7	24.9	5.6	−77.5
Complete 4 yrs.	7.5	5.6	2.9	0.5	−82.8	13.3	11.6	5.9	0.9	−84.7	17.4	16.6	10.5	1.3	−87.6
Region															
Northeast	9.2	6.9	3.2	0.4	−87.5	15.8	14.1	7.6	0.4	−94.7	22.5	22.8	13.3	1.8	−86.5
Midwest	11.0	9.0	4.8	0.6	−87.5	17.6	16.3	8.6	1.6	−81.4	25.7	23.6	16.3	2.2	−86.5
South	9.4	7.8	5.0	0.8	−84.0	19.3	15.7	8.8	1.5	−83.0	21.7	19.4	15.4	2.7	−82.5
West	7.0	4.9	2.4	1.2	−50.0	9.4	7.8	4.0	1.3	−67.5	14.5	16.9	7.6	2.4	−68.4
Parental education[1]															
Some HS/less	15.8	13.1	7.8	1.1	−85.9	20.0	18.9	9.9	1.5	−84.8	21.3	22.8	11.7	2.9	−75.2
Some/completed HS	11.3	11.3	6.3	1.3	−79.4	21.6	17.6	11.1	2.5	−77.5	24.6	22.9	18.3	3.4	−81.4
Completed HS/ some coll.	9.4	6.7	4.3	0.6	−86.0	17.0	14.2	7.9	1.5	−81.0	21.6	21.2	14.4	2.4	−83.3
Some/completed coll.	7.2	3.9	2.2	0.4	−81.8	12.6	11.5	5.2	0.4	−92.3	19.7	18.6	11.7	1.2	−89.7
Completed coll./higher	5.7	4.1	1.4	0.7	−50.0	10.3	9.8	4.4	0.8	−81.8	18.5	15.2	8.1	1.1	−86.4
Race/ethnicity[2]															
White	10.5	9.0	4.6	0.7	−84.8	17.6	17.7	9.1	1.9	−79.1	23.9	25.7	17.1	3.5	−79.5
Black	2.8	3.2	2.1	0.5	−76.2	4.7	5.2	3.9	0.8	−79.5	6.1	8.0	5.6	1.8	−67.9
Hispanic	9.2	7.1	3.1	0.6	−80.6	9.9	8.8	5.9	1.1	−81.4	11.6	15.7	7.7	1.9	−75.3

Coll. = college; HS = high school. **Note:** Figures may not add up to totals because of rounding. (1) Avg. highest level of education attained by respondent's mother and father. (2) For each of these groups, data for the specified year and previous year have been combined to increase sample size and thus provide more stable estimates.

Tobacco Use by High School and Middle School Students, 2019

Source: National Youth Tobacco Survey, Centers for Disease Control and Prevention (CDC), U.S. Dept. of Health and Human Services

Between 2011 and 2019, current use—defined as use on one or more days in the past 30 days—of cigarettes, cigars, and smokeless tobacco declined significantly among high school or middle school students. The use of electronic cigarettes (e-cigarettes), however, increased from 1.5% among high school students and 0.6% among middle school students in 2011 to 27.5% and 10.5%, respectively, in 2019. Since 2014, e-cigarettes have been the most commonly used tobacco product among students in grades 6 through 12.

Tobacco product	High school students using tobacco				Middle school students using tobacco			
	Female	Male	All students	Estimated no. of users[1]	Female	Male	All students	Estimated no. of users[1]
E-cigarettes	27.4	27.6	27.5	4,110,000	10.8	10.2	10.5	1,240,000
Cigars	6.2	9.0	7.6	1,140,000	2.0	2.7	2.3	270,000
Cigarettes	4.1	7.3	5.8	860,000	2.5	2.1	2.3	270,000
Smokeless tobacco	1.8	7.5	4.8	720,000	—	2.7	1.8	210,000
Hookahs	3.2	3.6	3.4	500,000	1.8	1.3	1.6	180,000
Pipe tobacco	—	1.5	1.1	160,000	—	—	—	—
Any tobacco product[2]	30.6	31.8	31.2	4,690,000	12.4	12.5	12.5	1,470,000
Any combustible tobacco[3]	10.2	13.6	12.0	1,800,000	4.9	4.6	4.8	560,000
2+ tobacco products	8.0	13.4	10.8	1,620,000	3.7	4.2	4.0	470,000

— = Not available. (1) Rounded down to nearest 10,000. (2) Includes e-cigarettes, cigarettes, cigars, smokeless tobacco, hookahs, pipe tobacco, and/or bidis, which is not shown separately here. (3) Does not include e-cigarettes and smokeless tobacco (i.e., chewing or dissolvable tobacco, snuff, dip, snus).

Alcohol Use by 8th and 12th Graders, 1980-2019

Source: Monitoring the Future study, Univ. of Michigan Inst. for Social Research; Natl. Inst. on Drug Abuse, Natl. Insts. of Health

	1980	1990	1995	2000	2005	2010	2013	2015	2018	2019	% change, 2018-19
Alcohol use[1]			Percent using in the 30 days before the survey								
All 8th graders	—	—	24.6%	22.4%	17.1%	13.8%	10.2%	9.7%	8.2%	7.9%	−0.2%
Male	—	—	25.0	22.5	16.2	13.2	9.3	9.1	7.4	7.3	0.0
Female	—	—	24.0	22.0	17.9	14.3	11.2	9.9	9.1	8.3	−0.8
White...........	—	—	25.4	24.7	17.9	13.9	9.5	8.9	7.3	8.0	0.8
Black...........	—	—	18.7	16.0	14.9	11.8	9.7	8.2	6.0	4.9	−1.1
Hispanic	—	—	32.4	26.7	20.6	18.1	14.3	10.4	9.8	9.6	−0.3
All 12th graders ...	72.0%	57.1%	51.3	50.0	47.0	41.2	39.2	35.3	30.2	29.3	−0.9
Male	77.4	61.3	55.7	54.0	50.7	44.2	41.8	36.0	30.4	29.8	−0.7
Female	66.8	52.3	47.0	46.1	43.8	37.9	36.3	35.0	30.1	28.5	−1.5
White...........	75.4	63.8	54.5	55.1	52.3	45.4	43.6	40.9	38.0	34.9	−3.2
Black...........	47.6	35.8	35.2	30.0	29.0	31.4	28.4	24.0	21.2	19.4	−1.9
Hispanic	63.6	49.1	48.7	51.2	43.3	40.1	39.0	36.3	26.4	24.4	−2.0
Heavy alcohol use[2]			Percent heavily using in the two weeks before the survey								
All 8th graders	—	—	12.3%	11.7%	8.4%	7.2%	5.1%	4.6%	3.7%	3.8%	0.2%
Male	—	—	12.5	11.7	8.2	6.5	4.5	4.6	3.3	3.5	0.2
Female	—	—	12.1	11.3	8.6	7.8	5.7	4.6	3.9	4.0	0.1
White...........	—	—	12.1	13.0	9.0	7.1	4.2	4.0	2.9	3.4	0.5
Black...........	—	—	8.3	7.3	6.1	5.3	4.5	4.1	2.6	1.9	−0.8
Hispanic	—	—	18.4	16.0	12.1	10.8	7.8	5.4	5.2	5.3	0.1
All 12th graders ...	41.2%	32.2%	29.8	30.0	27.1	23.2	22.1	17.2	13.8	14.4	0.6
Male	52.1	39.1	36.9	36.7	32.6	28.0	26.1	19.3	15.9	16.1	0.2
Female	30.5	24.4	23.0	23.5	21.6	18.4	18.1	14.9	11.9	12.4	0.5
White...........	44.3	36.6	32.3	34.6	32.5	27.6	25.6	21.2	19.4	17.6	−1.8
Black...........	17.7	14.4	14.9	11.5	11.3	13.1	12.5	9.8	7.4	6.7	−0.7
Hispanic	33.1	25.6	26.6	31.0	23.9	22.1	22.4	18.5	11.7	10.8	−0.9

— = Not available. **Note:** To derive percentages for each race/ethnicity subgroup, data for the specified year and previous year have been combined to increase sample size and thus provide more stable estimates. (1) In 1993, the alcohol question was changed slightly to indicate that a "drink" is defined as "more than a few sips." (2) Five or more drinks in a row (binge drinking) on one or more occasions.

Acquired Immune Deficiency Syndrome (AIDS)

Source: Centers for Disease Control and Prevention (CDC), U.S. Dept. of Health and Human Services

AIDS (Acquired Immune Deficiency Syndrome) is caused by the human immunodeficiency virus (HIV). HIV disables or kills crucial immune cells known as CD4 cells (also called T cells, or T-lymphocyte or T-helper cells), progressively destroying the body's ability to fight disease.

HIV is commonly spread through unprotected sexual contact with an infected partner's semen or vaginal fluids. It is also spread through contact with infected blood. Modern screening techniques make HIV transmission through transfusions or organ/tissue transplants, rare, but HIV can spread among intravenous drug users who share syringes and similar equipment. A woman can also transmit HIV to her child during pregnancy or delivery or through breastfeeding. With treatment, a woman can reduce her transmission rate from about 25% to less than 1%. There is no evidence HIV can spread through saliva or casual contact such as shaking hands or the sharing of food utensils, towels and bedding, or toilet seats.

About two-thirds of people experience flu-like symptoms within a few weeks of being infected with HIV. After the acute HIV infection stage, the infection enters a stage of chronic infection, also referred to as asymptomatic HIV infection or clinical latency. Even though a person may not have any symptoms, the HIV continues to multiply, infect, and kill CD4 cells, which signal other immune cells to perform their functions.

The term AIDS applies to the final (third) stage of HIV infection. According to the official case definition issued by the CDC, an HIV-infected person 6 years of age or older with fewer than 200 CD4 cells per cubic millimeter of blood can be said to have AIDS. (Healthy adults usually have 500-1,600 T cells per cu mm.) An HIV-infected person, regardless of T cell count, can also be diagnosed with AIDS after developing one of 20+ opportunistic illnesses, such as invasive cervical cancer, lymphoma, or recurrent pneumonia, that can occur when the immune system is severely weakened.

Months or years prior to the onset of AIDS, people may experience such symptoms as swollen glands, lack of energy, fevers and sweats, and memory loss or other neurologic disorders. Children with AIDS may have delayed development or fail to thrive.

HIV is primarily detected by testing blood for the presence of antibodies (disease-fighting proteins of the immune system) to HIV. HIV antibodies can be detected within 3-12 weeks of exposure. Combination HIV tests that look for both HIV antibodies and parts of the virus called antigens can detect an infection in 18-90 days. A nucleic acid test can detect the presence of HIV in blood 10-33 days after exposure, but the test is expensive and not used in routine screening.

In 1987, the U.S. Food and Drug Administration approved a drug called zidovudine (commonly known as AZT) for the treatment of HIV. Since then, the FDA has approved approximately 45 drugs and drug combinations (fixed doses of two or more medications in a single pill) to treat people living with HIV/AIDS. These drugs are grouped into classes: nucleoside reverse transcriptase inhibitors (NRTIs), non-nucleoside reverse transcriptase inhibitors (NNRTIs), protease inhibitors (PIs), fusion inhibitors, CCR5 antagonists, integrase inhibitors (INSTIs), and post-attachment inhibitors (PAIs). Each class of drug attacks the virus at a different point in its life cycle. Patients generally take three different HIV medicines from at least two different classes as part of antiretroviral therapy (ART), which extends the period between HIV infection and the development of serious illness.

Without a vaccine or cure for AIDS, the best way to prevent HIV infection is to avoid activities that carry a risk. The CDC recommends abstinence, mutual monogamy with an uninfected partner, limiting the number of sexual partners, never sharing needles, and using condoms correctly and consistently. People who do not have HIV but are at high risk of exposure can take medication daily to prevent HIV infection, called pre-exposure prophylaxis (PrEP). Daily PrEP reduces the risk of getting HIV from sex by more than 90% and from injection drug use by more than 70%. Post-exposure prophylaxis (PEP) is the emergency use of HIV medicines after a single high-risk event. PEP must be started within 72 hours of exposure to HIV, and it is not always effective.

New AIDS Diagnoses in the U.S., by Transmission Category, 1985-2018

Source: *HIV Surveillance Report, 2018 (Preliminary)*; National Center for HIV/AIDS, Viral Hepatitis, STD, and TB Prevention; CDC

Transmission category	All years[1]	1985	1990	2000	2005	2010	2015	2017	2018
All males 13 years of age and older	987,349	7,504	36,193	28,643	25,545	20,583	14,074	13,420	12,884
Male-to-male sexual contact	611,167	5,348	23,658	15,796	15,690	14,022	10,112	9,730	9,473
Injection drug use	183,449	1,103	6,923	6,118	3,665	1,926	975	938	894
Male-to-male sexual contact and injection drug use	90,787	661	2,943	2,728	2,373	1,458	853	792	717
Heterosexual contact[2]	90,209	32	715	3,819	3,681	3,067	2,039	1,890	1,716
Other[3]	11,738	—	—	182	138	110	95	70	84
All females 13 years of age and older	257,646	524	4,547	10,070	9,235	6,889	4,514	4,268	4,106
Injection drug use	91,516	287	2,347	3,472	2,493	1,392	801	744	730
Heterosexual contact[2]	159,946	119	1,538	6,466	6,616	5,370	3,630	3,438	3,295
Other[3]	6,184	—	—	132	126	128	83	86	81
All children, under 13 years of age	9,581	—	—	132	55	23	40	34	42
Perinatal	8,701	—	—	—	—	—	31	27	30
Other[3]	880	—	—	—	—	—	9	7	12

— = Not available. **Note:** Table shows number of persons diagnosed with an HIV infection at stage 3 (AIDS). The definition of AIDS cases has expanded over time. Data for 2018 are preliminary. (1) Includes diagnoses for years not shown, from the beginning of the epidemic (1981) through 2018. (2) Heterosexual contact with a person known to have or be at high risk for HIV infection. (3) Includes hemophilia, blood transfusion, perinatal exposure (for persons 13 and older), and risk factor not reported or not identified.

New HIV Diagnoses in the U.S., 2014-18

Source: *HIV Surveillance Report, 2018 (Updated)*; National Center for HIV/AIDS, Viral Hepatitis, STD, and TB Prevention; CDC

Characteristic	Number of diagnoses					Diagnoses per 100,000 resident pop.				
	2014	2015	2016	2017	2018	2014	2015	2016	2017	2018
All persons	40,187	39,959	39,698	38,456	37,515	12.6	12.5	12.3	11.8	11.5
Gender										
Male	31,972	31,948	31,523	30,535	29,794	—	—	—	—	—
Female	7,657	7,416	7,526	7,326	7,109	—	—	—	—	—
Transgender female	523	555	617	549	553	—	—	—	—	—
Transgender male	27	30	20	33	47	—	—	—	—	—
Additional gender identity[1]	8	10	12	13	12	—	—	—	—	—
Age at diagnosis										
Under 13 years	182	142	129	105	87	0.3	0.3	0.2	0.2	0.2
13-14 years	33	26	26	27	20	0.4	0.3	0.3	0.3	0.2
15-19 years	1,742	1,758	1,715	1,767	1,704	8.3	8.3	8.1	8.4	8.1
20-24 years	7,372	7,286	6,920	6,479	6,093	32.2	32.1	31.0	29.4	27.9
25-29 years	7,206	7,594	7,962	7,727	7,690	32.8	33.9	34.7	33.1	32.6
30-34 years	5,419	5,452	5,648	5,649	5,665	25.2	25.2	25.9	25.7	25.6
35-39 years	4,227	4,255	4,231	4,283	4,215	21.3	20.9	20.4	20.2	19.5
40-44 years	3,779	3,406	3,266	2,984	2,981	18.4	16.9	16.6	15.2	15.1
45-49 years	3,619	3,310	3,097	2,952	2,818	17.4	15.9	14.8	14.1	13.6
50-54 years	2,885	2,998	2,875	2,652	2,476	12.8	13.5	13.2	12.4	11.9
55-59 years	1,923	1,883	1,894	1,877	1,849	9.0	8.7	8.6	8.5	8.4
60-64 years	969	999	1,081	1,083	1,039	5.2	5.3	5.6	5.4	5.1
65 years and over	831	850	854	871	878	1.8	1.8	1.7	1.7	1.7
Race/ethnicity										
Not Hispanic/Latino										
Amer. Ind./Alaska Native	178	180	220	208	186	7.6	7.6	9.2	8.7	7.7
Asian	904	930	953	943	876	5.4	5.4	5.4	5.2	4.7
Black	17,286	17,229	17,090	16,518	16,047	43.8	43.2	42.5	40.7	39.2
Native Hawaiian/Pac. Isl.	42	69	40	53	66	7.7	12.4	7.1	9.2	11.3
White	10,449	10,252	9,995	9,820	9,572	5.3	5.2	5.1	5.0	4.8
Multiple races	1,638	1,488	1,364	1,125	948	25.7	22.7	20.2	16.2	13.3
Hispanic/Latino, any race	9,690	9,811	10,036	9,789	9,820	17.6	17.4	17.4	16.7	16.4

— = Not available because of lack of denominator data. **Note:** Data shown are for the 50 states and DC. They are estimates of the min. number of persons for whom HIV infection, regardless of stage of the disease, has been diagnosed and reported to the CDC as of Dec. 31, 2019. Sums of subpopulations may not equal totals. (1) Includes, e.g., bigender, gender queer, and two-spirit.

U.S. Deaths of Persons With HIV Ever Classified as AIDS, 1981-2017

Source: *HIV Surveillance Report, 2018 (Preliminary)*; National Center for HIV/AIDS, Viral Hepatitis, STD, and TB Prevention; CDC

Age at death	Number	% of total	Transmission category	Number	% of total
Under 13 years	4,951	0.7%	Male adult or adolescent	576,918	80.8%
13-14 years	293	0.04	Male-to-male sexual contact	333,600	46.7
15-19 years	1,305	0.2	Injection drug use	136,501	19.1
20-24 years	10,212	1.4	Male-to-male sexual contact and		
25-29 years	47,924	6.7	injection drug use	56,031	7.8
30-34 years	103,122	14.4	Heterosexual contact[2]	41,407	5.8
35-39 years	129,907	18.2	Perinatal	532	0.1
40-44 years	124,900	17.5	Other[3]	8,847	1.2
45-49 years	100,822	14.1	Female adult or adolescent	132,016	18.5
50-54 years	74,498	10.4	Injection drug use	61,264	8.6
55-59 years	50,581	7.1	Heterosexual contact[2]	66,386	9.3
60-64 years	31,658	4.4	Perinatal	671	0.1
65 years and over	33,712	4.7	Other[3]	3,695	0.5
Race/ethnicity			Child (<13 yrs at death)	4,951	0.7
American Indian/Alaska Native	2,019	0.3	Perinatal	4,495	0.6
Asian[1]	3,664	0.5	Other[3]	456	0.1
Black/African American	294,697	41.3	**Region of residence**		
Hispanic/Latino (any race)	110,311	15.5	Northeast	216,845	30.4
Native Hawaiian/other Pac. Islander	384	0.1	Midwest	76,857	10.8
White	285,638	40.0	South	283,496	39.7
Multiple races	17,129	2.4	West	136,687	19.1
			Total[4]	713,885	100.0

Note: Deaths of persons with diagnosed HIV infection may be due to any cause. Number of deaths are cumulative from the beginning of the epidemic, in 1981. Figures are estimated and calculated independently, so they may not add up to totals. (1) Includes Asian/Pacific Islander legacy cases. (2) Heterosexual contact with a person known to have or to be at high risk for HIV infection. (3) Includes hemophilia, blood transfusion, and risk factor not reported or not identified. (4) Includes persons of unknown race/ethnicity.

Allergies and Asthma

Source: Asthma and Allergy Foundation of America (AAFA), Centers for Disease Control and Prevention (CDC)

An estimated one in six Americans suffers from allergies each year. People with allergies have immune systems that overreact to a normally harmless substance, called an allergen. Common allergens include plant pollens, dust mites, or animal dander; plants such as poison ivy; certain drugs, such as penicillin; and foods such as eggs, milk, wheat, nuts, or seafood.

The tendency to develop allergies is usually inherited. Though allergies typically manifest in childhood, they can show up at any age. Food allergies and eczema (inflamed or irritated skin) are common allergies among infants. Older children and adults may develop allergic rhinitis, or hay fever, in reaction to an inhaled allergen. Allergic rhinitis symptoms include nasal congestion, runny nose, and sneezing.

People with allergies should avoid contact with an allergen, if feasible. Medications, such as antihistamines and nasal corticosteroids, may be used to decrease an allergic reaction. Other effective allergy treatments include decongestants, eye drops, and ointments. Allergy shots, a form of immunotherapy, aims to desensitize a patient to an allergen through gradual exposure to increasingly higher doses of it. People at risk of anaphylaxis—a severe, whole-body allergic reaction that occurs rapidly—should have access to emergency medication, such as injectable epinephrine.

Some allergy sufferers also have asthma. About 24.8 mil Americans in 2018 had a current diagnosis of asthma, which can develop at any age. Asthma is a chronic inflammation disease affecting the passageways that carry air into and out of the lungs. During an asthma attack, these airways become inflamed and fill with mucus. A person may experience wheezing, difficulty breathing, tightening of the chest, and coughing. Exposure to an allergen can set off an attack. Asthma can become life-threatening if not controlled in its early stages. The following symptoms may be indicative of an emergency: the patient shows no improvement minutes after initial treatment; struggles to breathe while hunched over with chest and neck pulled in; has trouble walking or talking; and develops gray or blue lips or fingernails.

Tobacco smoke, cold air, and expressing strong emotion can also trigger an asthma attack, as can respiratory infections and physical exercise. An accurate diagnosis by a physician is important. Although there is no cure for asthma or allergies, they can be controlled through lifestyle changes and quick-relief and long-term medications.

Website: www.aafa.org

Persons With Asthma, 2018

Source: National Health Interview Survey, NCHS, CDC, U.S. Dept. of Health and Human Services

Characteristic	Number (thous.)	Percent
Total	24,753	7.7%
Child (under age 18)	5,530	7.5
Adult	19,223	7.7
Age		
0-4 years	744	3.8
5-14 years	3,552	8.6
15-19 years	2,204	11.0
20-24 years	1,741	8.1
25-34 years	2,895	6.5
35-64 years	9,588	7.7
65+ years	4,029	7.8
Sex		
Males	9,786	6.2
Under age 18	3,122	8.3
Age 18 and over	6,665	5.5
Females	14,967	9.1
Under age 18	2,408	6.7
Age 18 and over	12,559	9.8
Race/ethnicity[1]		
White non-Hispanic	15,496	8.0
Black non-Hispanic	4,159	10.7
Hispanic (any race)	3,747	6.5
Puerto Rican	781	14.0
Mexican	1,916	5.4

Note: Includes only those with a current diagnosis of asthma. Numbers may not add up to totals due to rounding. (1) Data are for 2016-18.

Alzheimer's Disease

Source: Alzheimer's Association

Alzheimer's disease is a degenerative brain disease in which nerve cells deteriorate and die. It is the most common cause of dementia. Early symptoms include forgetting newly learned information and apathy or depression. As the disease advances, a person may exhibit disorientation and behavior changes; confusion about events, time, and place; and suspicion towards family, friends, and caregivers.

The rate of the disease's progression varies, with changes to the brain possibly beginning 20 or more years before symptoms occur in a stage researchers call preclinical Alzheimer's disease. In the next stage—mild cognitive impairment (MCI) due to Alzheimer's disease—a person can still perform everyday activities without significant trouble. A person may remain independent with assistance early in the disease's third stage, dementia due to Alzheimer's disease. Ultimately, however, an individual loses the ability to perform basic bodily functions, such as walking or swallowing, making him or her susceptible to infections of the lungs, urinary tract, and other organs. The average length of time from diagnosis of Alzheimer's dementia until death is 4-8 years for those age 65 and older.

Within the U.S. population, about 10% of persons age 65 and older and 32% of those age 85 and older have Alzheimer's dementia. Almost two-thirds of Americans with Alzheimer's are women. Alzheimer's dementia is also more prevalent in the older Black and Hispanic/Latino populations than in the older white population.

Diagnosis involves a comprehensive evaluation that may include a complete health history, physical examination, neurological and mental status assessments, and other tests. Depression, drug interactions, nutritional imbalances, and excessive alcohol consumption can cause symptoms that look similar to dementia. Parkinson's disease, frontotemporal lobar degeneration, and cerebrovascular disease can also cause dementia. Scientists are researching possible biological markers for Alzheimer's disease, the way high blood pressure can be measured to determine a person's heart disease risk.

Treatments for cognitive and behavioral symptoms are available, and clinical trials are ongoing for ways to prevent Alzheimer's or to slow its course. The FDA has approved five drugs that temporarily improve symptoms, but their effectiveness varies. Age is the greatest risk factor for Alzheimer's disease. Having the e4 form of the APOE (apolipoprotein E) gene and a family history of the disease are also risk factors. Staying physically and mentally active and socially connected may be associated with a lower risk for the disease.

An estimated 5.8 mil Americans were living with Alzheimer's dementia in 2020. The U.S. cost in 2020 of diagnosing, treating, and providing long-term care for persons with Alzheimer's or other dementias was an estimated $305 bil. The unpaid care that family members, friends, and others provided persons with Alzheimer's or other dementias was valued at around $244 bil in 2019.

Website: www.alz.org

Warning Signs of Alzheimer's Disease

- Memory loss that disrupts daily life
- Challenges in planning or solving problems
- Difficulty completing familiar tasks at home, at work, or at leisure
- Confusion with time or place
- Trouble understanding visual images and spatial relationships
- New problems with words in speaking or writing
- Misplacing things and losing the ability to retrace steps
- Decreased or poor judgment
- Withdrawal from work or social activities
- Changes in mood and personality

Arthritis

Source: Arthritis Foundation; Centers for Disease Control and Prevention (CDC), U.S. Dept. of Health and Human Services

The term arthritis refers to more than 100 different diseases that cause pain, aching, stiffness, and swelling in or around the joints. An estimated 54.4 mil U.S. adults (22.7% of that population) reported having doctor-diagnosed arthritis in 2013-15. Some researchers who looked at the data suggest 92.1 mil is a more accurate estimate of the number of Americans age 18 or older who have doctor-diagnosed arthritis or symptoms consistent with such a diagnosis. The cause of most types of arthritis is unknown; scientists are studying the role of genetics, lifestyle, and environment.

Of the three most prevalent forms of arthritis, **osteoarthritis** (OA) is the most common, affecting approximately 30.8 mil Americans. With OA, also called degenerative arthritis, protective cartilage at a joint breaks down. When the bones of the joint thus rub together, pain and stiffness may result. The most commonly affected joints are in the lower back, hips, knees, hands, and feet.

Fibromyalgia, another common arthritis condition, affects about 4 mil Americans, the majority of whom are women ages 40-75. People suffering from fibromyalgia experience widespread pain, abnormal pain processing, sleep disturbance, and psychological distress. Other symptoms include tingling or numbness in hands and feet and problems with thinking and memory.

Rheumatoid arthritis (RA) is an autoimmune disease that affects an estimated 1.5 mil in the U.S. It is one of the most serious and disabling forms of arthritis, which women experience at 2-3 times the rate of men. With RA, the body's immune system attacks healthy cells in the joints, causing inflammation that can lead to cartilage and bone damage.

Other forms of arthritis and related conditions include lupus, gout, scleroderma, and Sjögren's syndrome. To diagnose arthritis, a doctor will record a patient's symptoms and look for any swelling or limited movement during a physical. Other signs of arthritis include rashes, mouth sores, and dry eyes. A doctor may test a patient's blood, urine, or joint fluid or take joint X-rays.

Medications that relieve pain and swelling, such as analgesics and anti-inflammatory drugs, can be used to treat arthritis. Regular physical activity, in particular low-impact sports like walking or swimming, can improve mood and ease pain. Maintaining a healthy weight puts less stress on joints. Surgery to replace a joint is an option if OA gets to be too severe.

Website: www.arthritis.org

Attention Deficit Hyperactivity Disorder (ADHD)

Source: Centers for Disease Control and Prevention; Natl. Institute of Mental Health; Children and Adults with Attention-Deficit/Hyperactivity Disorder (CHADD)

Attention deficit hyperactivity disorder, or ADHD, is one of the most common neurodevelopmental disorders of childhood, when it is usually first diagnosed. Individuals with ADHD may have trouble paying attention and controlling impulsive behaviors.

Signs and Symptoms of ADHD

- Daydreaming a lot
- Forgetting or losing things frequently
- Squirming or fidgeting
- Talking too much
- Making careless mistakes or taking unnecessary risks
- Having a hard time resisting temptation
- Having trouble taking turns
- Having difficulty getting along with others

ADHD may manifest in one of three ways. A person who is **predominantly inattentive** is easily distracted or forgets details of daily routines. Someone who is **predominantly hyperactive-impulsive** may feel restless and impulsive. In the third type, **combined presentation**, an individual displays symptoms of both inattentiveness and hyperactivity-impulsivity. The cause of ADHD is unknown, but current research shows that genetics plays a significant role. Scientists are also looking into possible risk factors such as alcohol, tobacco, or drug use during pregnancy and low birth weight.

According to a 2016 survey, about 9.4% of American children age 2-17 have ever been diagnosed with ADHD. In addition, two out of three children (63.8%) with a current diagnosis of ADHD had at least one co-occurring condition, including oppositional defiant disorder, conduct disorder, anxiety or depression, or an autism spectrum disorder. Boys are more likely to be diagnosed with ADHD than girls. About one-third of children with ADHD will continue to have it as adults.

In most cases, ADHD is treated with a combination of medication and behavior therapy. Stimulants are the most widely used medication. Nonstimulants do not work as quickly as stimulants but have fewer side effects and can last up to 24 hours.

Breast Cancer

Source: American Cancer Society, Inc.; National Cancer Institute, National Institutes of Health

In 2020, an estimated 276,480 women and 2,620 men in the U.S. will be newly diagnosed with breast cancer, and about 42,170 women and 520 men will die from it. More than 3.5 mil women live with a history of breast cancer, but mortality rates have been declining, especially among younger women, probably because of earlier detection and improved treatment.

The risk for breast cancer is higher for women and increases with age. It is higher for women with a personal or family history of cancer (particularly breast cancer), a longer menstrual history (menstrual periods that started early and ended later in life), recent use of hormonal birth control, use of menopausal hormone therapy, and in those who have no children or had no live birth until after age 30. Other risk factors include alcohol consumption, physical inactivity, and being overweight or obese. About 5%-10% of breast cancers are probably due to inherited mutations, the most common being those in the BRCA1 and BRCA2. Most women who develop breast cancer have no family history of it.

Breast cancer often manifests first as a new lump or mass. Other symptoms include swelling, distortion, tenderness, skin irritation, redness, scaliness, or nipple abnormalities, such as ulceration, retraction, or spontaneous discharge.

Studies show that early detection increases survival and treatment options. Although most detected breast lumps are noncancerous, any suspicious lump should be biopsied.

Treatment for breast cancer may involve breast-conserving surgery (removal of the tumor and surrounding tissue), mastectomy (surgical removal of the breast), radiation, chemotherapy, hormone therapy, and/or targeted therapy. The five-year relative survival rate for female invasive breast cancer patients has improved from 74.8% in 1975-77 to 91.4% in 2010-16; for women diagnosed with localized breast cancer (cancer that has not spread to lymph nodes or other locations outside the breast), survival is 100.0%.

Website: www.cancer.org

Prostate Cancer

Source: Prostate Cancer Foundation; American Cancer Society, Inc.; National Cancer Institute, National Institutes of Health

The prostate is a male gland located between the bladder and scrotum that secretes seminal fluid. Among men in the U.S., prostate cancer is the most commonly diagnosed non-skin cancer and the second-most common cause, after lung and bronchus cancer, of cancer deaths. In 2020, an estimated 191,930 men will be newly diagnosed with prostate cancer, and about 33,330 will die from the disease. More than 3.1 mil men in the U.S. are living with a history of prostate cancer today.

The most identifiable risk factors for prostate cancer are age, family history, and African ancestry. The median age at diagnosis is 66, and the chances of developing the disease rise dramatically with age. Black men in the U.S. and Caribbean have the world's highest documented incidence rate of prostate cancer. The cause for this disparity remains unclear.

Usually, the disease has no symptoms in its early stages. As the disease advances, a man may experience weak or interrupted urine flow; inability to urinate or difficulty starting or stopping the urine flow; the need to urinate frequently, especially at night; blood in the urine; or pain or burning with urination. Advanced prostate cancer commonly spreads to the bones, causing pain in areas such as the hips, spine, or ribs.

The American Cancer Society recommends that once they reach 50, men at average risk of prostate cancer should speak with their health care provider about the benefits and limitations of prostate-specific antigen (PSA) testing. An increased PSA level may indicate a higher chance of having prostate cancer, but older age and the use of certain medications, among other factors, can raise or lower PSA levels. Black men or those with a family history of the disease (a close relative who was diagnosed before age 65) should be aware of their screening options beginning at age 45. Men with more than one close relative with prostate cancer should discuss screening at 40. The U.S. Preventive Services Task Force recommends that men ages 55-69 screen for prostate cancer. It advises against routine screening with a PSA in men age 70 and older. Because prostate cancer is slow-growing, testing is not likely to help men with a life expectancy of less than 10 years. Men under 40 seldom get prostate cancer.

Prostate cancer treatment may include surgery, radiation, hormonal therapy, chemotherapy, or some combination. If caught early on, while tumor cells are localized within the prostate, the five-year relative survival rate approaches 100%.

Websites: www.pcf.org; www.cancer.org

Skin Cancer

Source: American Cancer Society, Inc; National Cancer Institute, National Institutes of Health

Skin cancer—the most common cancer diagnosed in the U.S.—is generally divided into the following types: **basal and squamous cell skin cancers** (or nonmelanomas) and **melanomas**. Invasive melanoma accounts for only about 1% of all skin cancers but the majority of skin cancer deaths. Risk factors include heavy exposure to UV light, multiple moles (more than 50), fair skin, family or personal history of skin cancers, a history of sunburns, and occupational exposure to certain compounds.

Melanomas generally look like abnormal moles on the surface of the skin. Abnormal moles differ from regular skin cells and may be a sign of skin cancer. An irregular mole should be examined by a doctor as soon as possible.

If caught early, melanoma is highly curable. In 2010-16, the five-year relative survival rate for melanoma at the localized stage was 99.0%; at the regional stage, 66.2%; and 27.3% at the distant stage.

Treatment may include simple removal of the melanoma; amputation if the cancer is found on a finger or toe; or chemotherapy, immunotherapy, and/or radiation if the melanoma has spread to other parts of the body.

Warning Signs of Abnormal Moles

- **Asymmetry:** one half does not match the other half
- **Border:** edges are irregular, ragged, notched, or blurred
- **Color:** not uniform; may be shades of brown or black, and patches of pink, red, blue, or white
- **Diameter:** moles wider than ¼ inch are abnormal (however, melanomas can be smaller)
- **Evolving:** mole changes size, shape, or color over time

Website: www.cancer.org

Cancer Risk Factors

Source: American Cancer Society, Inc., www.cancer.org; National Cancer Institute, National Institutes of Health

Alcohol: Alcohol consumption increases the risk of cancers of the mouth, pharynx, larynx, esophagus, liver, colorectum, breast, and possibly pancreas. Alcohol consumption combined with tobacco use increases the risk of cancers of the mouth, pharynx, larynx, and esophagus far more than either drinking or smoking alone.

Diet and physical activity: Overweight and obesity are associated with increased risk for developing many cancers, including cancers of the breast in postmenopausal women, colorectum, kidney, pancreas, and esophagus. Overweight and obesity may also be associated with increased risk of fatal prostate cancer, non-Hodgkin lymphoma, and male breast cancer. It's not yet known for certain how diet, nutrition intake, and the amount and distribution of body fat factor into the development of certain cancers.

Environmental hazards: Exposure to certain substances, called carcinogens, can increase the risk of various cancers. Carcinogens like arsenic or radon may occur naturally, or they may be manufactured, like vinyl chloride. The risk of lung cancer from asbestos exposure is greatly increased among smokers.

Estrogen: Menopausal hormone therapy (MHT, formerly called hormone replacement therapy) without the use of progestin can increase the risk of endometrial and ovarian cancer. Combining progestin with estrogen MHT may help minimize that risk. Studies, however, suggest that use of MHT increases the risk of breast cancer. The benefits and risks of the use of estrogen should be discussed carefully with one's doctor.

HPV infection: Although most HPV infections do not cause cancer, almost all cervical cancers are caused by a persistent HPV infection. Persistent HPV infections also cause about 90% of anal cancers, and 60%-75% of oropharyngeal,

vaginal, vulvar, and penile cancers. The Centers for Disease Control and Prevention (CDC) estimates that most people in the U.S. will acquire HPV at some point in their lives. It recommends routine vaccination at age 11-12, although the current vaccine only protects against certain types of HPV.

Radiation: Excessive exposure to ionizing radiation can increase cancer risk. Medical and dental X-rays are adjusted to deliver the lowest dose possible without sacrificing image quality. Excessive radon exposure in the home may increase lung cancer risk, especially in cigarette smokers.

Smokeless tobacco: Use of chewing tobacco, snuff, snus, and other tobacco products that are not smoked increase the risk of oral, esophageal, and pancreatic cancers.

Smoking: Smoking is responsible for about 30% of cancer deaths and about 80% of lung cancer deaths in the U.S. Exposure to secondhand smoke is also responsible for lung cancer cases in adults who have never smoked. Cigarette smoking also increases the risk of the following cancers: larynx, oral cavity and pharynx, esophagus, stomach, pancreas, uterine cervix, kidney, bladder, stomach, colorectum, and acute myeloid leukemia. While electronic cigarettes (e-cigarettes) generally have lower carcinogen levels than combustible tobacco products, the long-term risks of use are not yet clear. Adolescents and young adults who use e-cigarettes may also be more likely to begin using combustible tobacco products according to early research.

Sunlight: Many of the 5.4 mil skin cancers diagnosed annually in the U.S. could have been prevented by protection from the sun's rays and avoiding indoor tanning. Epidemiological evidence shows that sun exposure is a major factor in the development of melanoma and that incidence rates are increasing.

Screening Guidelines for Early Detection of Cancer

Cancer site	Population	Test or procedure	Frequency
Breast	Women, age 40+	Mammography	The American Cancer Society no longer recommends regular breast self-exams or clinical breast exams; research has not found that they reduce the risk of dying from breast cancer. Women should be familiar with how their breasts look and feel and report any changes to a health care professional. For women at average risk (e.g., lack of strong family history of breast cancer), at age 40: begin annual mammography if desired; for ages 45-54: annual mammograms; for ages 55+: mammograms yearly or every two years for those in good health with a life expectancy of 10 or more years. Women at high risk for breast cancer, such as a BRCA1 or BRCA2 gene mutation, should get an MRI and mammogram yearly.
Cervix	Women, ages 21+	Pap test, HPV test	All women should begin screening at age 21. For ages 21-29: Pap test every 3 years; HPV testing only after an abnormal test result. For ages 30-65, preferably a Pap test combined with an HPV test (co-testing) every 5 years. Another option is to get a Pap test alone every 3 years. For ages 65+: women who have had regular screenings with normal results in the previous 10 years should no longer be tested; women with a history of serious cervical precancers should continue to be tested for at least 20 years after diagnosis. Women who have had a total hysterectomy for reasons unrelated to cervical cancer should not be screened. Women should not be screened annually by any method at any age.
Colorectal	Men and women, ages 45-75 or 50-75	Guaiac-based fecal occult blood test (gFOBT) or fecal immunochemical test (FIT) or	The U.S. Preventive Services Task Force (USPSTF) recommends screening beginning at age 50, though the American Cancer Society recommends starting at age 45. Annual, for people with average risk. Testing at home with adherence to instructions for collection and number of samples is recommended. An FOBT or FIT done with a stool sample collected during a digital rectal examination in a health care setting is not sufficient for screening.
		Stool DNA test (MT-sDNA), or	Every 3 years, starting at age 45 or 50.
		Flexible sigmoidoscopy (FSIG), or	Every 5 years, starting at age 45 or 50. Can be performed every 10 years if an FIT is done yearly.
		CT, or virtual, colonography, or	Every 5 years, starting at age 45 or 50.
		Colonoscopy	Every 10 years, starting at age 45 or 50. A colonoscopy should also be done if any of the above tests is positive.
Endometrial	Women, at menopause		Women at average risk should be informed about risks and symptoms of endometrial cancer and encouraged to report any unexpected bleeding or discharge to their physician.
Lung	Current or former smokers, ages 55-74	Low-dose CT scan (LDCT)	Apparently healthy patients with a history of heavy smoking (at least one pack per day over 30 years, or two packs per day over 15 years, etc.), whether they currently smoke or have quit within the past 15 years, should discuss with a clinician the potential benefits, limitations, and harms associated with lung-cancer screening. The USPSTF recommends screening continue up to age 81.
Prostate	Men, age 40+	Digital rectal examination (DRE) and prostate-specific antigen test (PSA)	Men with an average risk and an expected life span of 10+ years should talk with their health care provider at age 50 about whether the benefits of screening surpass the risks. African Americans—who have a higher rate of prostate cancer—and men with a first-degree relative diagnosed with prostate cancer before age 65 should have this talk at age 45. Men with more than one first-degree relative diagnosed at an early age should have the talk at age 40. The USPSTF advises against routine screening with a PSA in men age 70 and older.

New U.S. Cancer Cases and Deaths for Leading Sites, 2020

Source: *Cancer Facts & Figures 2020*, American Cancer Society

The following estimates exclude basal cell and squamous cell skin cancers, also referred to as nonmelanoma skin cancers, and in situ carcinomas (i.e., noninvasive cancers) except of the urinary bladder. In 2020, an estimated 48,530 cases of carcinoma in situ of the female breast and 95,710 cases of melanoma in situ are expected to be diagnosed. An est. 5.4 mil cases of basal cell and squamous cell skin cancer were diagnosed among 3.3 mil people in 2012 according to the most recent study available.

Estimated New Cases

Both sexes		Male		Female	
Breast	279,100	Prostate	191,930	Breast	276,480
Lung and bronchus	228,820	Lung and bronchus	116,300	Lung and bronchus	112,520
Prostate	191,930	Colon and rectum	78,300	Colon and rectum	69,650
Colon and rectum	147,950	Urinary bladder	62,100	Uterine corpus	65,620
Melanoma of the skin	100,350	Melanoma of the skin	60,190	Thyroid	40,170
Urinary bladder	81,400	Kidney and renal pelvis	45,520	Melanoma of the skin	40,160
Non-Hodgkin lymphoma	77,240	Non-Hodgkin lymphoma	42,380	Non-Hodgkin lymphoma	34,860
Kidney and renal pelvis	73,750	Oral cavity and pharynx	38,380	Kidney and renal pelvis	28,230
Uterine corpus	65,620	Leukemia	35,470	Pancreas	27,200
Leukemia	60,530	Pancreas	30,400	Leukemia	25,060
All sites	1,806,590	All sites	893,660	All sites	912,930

Estimated Deaths

Both sexes		Male		Female	
Lung and bronchus	135,720	Lung and bronchus	72,500	Lung and bronchus	63,220
Colon and rectum	53,200	Prostate	33,330	Breast	42,170
Pancreas	47,050	Colon and rectum	28,630	Colon and rectum	24,570
Breast	42,690	Pancreas	24,640	Pancreas	22,410
Prostate	33,330	Liver and intrahepatic bile duct	20,020	Ovary	13,940
Liver and intrahepatic bile duct	30,160	Leukemia	13,420	Uterine corpus	12,590
Leukemia	23,100	Esophagus	13,100	Liver and intrahepatic bile duct	10,140
Non-Hodgkin lymphoma	19,940	Urinary bladder	13,050	Leukemia	9,680
Brain and other nervous system	18,020	Non-Hodgkin lymphoma	11,460	Non-Hodgkin lymphoma	8,480
Urinary bladder	17,980	Brain and other nervous system	10,190	Brain and other nervous system	7,830
All sites	606,520	All sites	321,160	All sites	285,360

U.S. Cancer Survival Rates by Year of Diagnosis, 1960-2016

Source: SEER (Surveillance, Epidemiology, and End Results) Cancer Statistics Review 1975-2017, National Cancer Institute, National Institutes of Health

	All races			White			Black		
Year of diagnosis	% total	% male	% female	% total	% male	% female	% total	% male	% female
1960-63	—	—	—	39.0%	—	—	27.0%	—	—
1970-73	—	—	—	43.0	—	—	31.0	—	—
1975-77	48.9%	41.7%	55.9%	49.8	42.7%	56.5%	39.1	32.7%	46.3%
1978-80	49.0	43.1	54.9	50.0	44.3	55.6	39.0	33.3	45.6
1981-83	50.2	45.2	55.1	51.3	46.5	56.0	38.8	34.2	44.4
1984-86	52.4	47.1	57.6	53.6	48.6	58.6	40.2	35.5	45.5
1987-89	55.3	51.1	59.6	56.7	52.8	60.6	43.0	38.9	47.7
1990-92	59.9	59.1	60.9	61.4	60.8	62.1	47.9	47.7	48.2
1993-95	61.3	60.9	61.8	62.4	62.1	62.8	52.9	54.6	50.7
1996-98	63.3	63.0	63.6	64.4	64.1	64.7	55.4	58.1	52.2
1999-2001	66.0	66.3	65.7	67.2	67.6	66.8	58.2	61.3	54.4
2002-04	67.1	67.7	66.5	68.4	69.0	67.7	59.8	63.5	55.5
2005-09	68.9	69.5	68.3	70.0	70.6	69.5	62.6	65.9	58.8
2010-16	69.5	68.6	70.5	70.5	69.5	71.5	64.1	66.1	62.1

— = Statistic could not be calculated. **Note:** The geographic areas of surveillance may vary for different years. Rates are five-year relative (estimated) survival rates for all invasive cancer sites; based on follow-up of patients into 2017.

U.S. Cancer Survival Rates by Age at Diagnosis, 2010-16

Source: SEER (Surveillance, Epidemiology, and End Results) Cancer Statistics Review, 1975-2017, National Cancer Institute, National Institutes of Health

	All races			White			Black		
Age at diagnosis	% total	% male	% female	% total	% male	% female	% total	% male	% female
Under age 45	83.3%	79.4%	85.8%	84.6%	80.9%	87.0%	74.1%	69.2%	76.9%
Ages 45-54	75.3	69.7	79.6	76.0	70.0	80.7	68.6	67.5	69.6
Ages 55-64	70.1	68.6	71.9	70.9	69.0	73.1	63.8	65.5	61.4
Under age 65	74.3	70.6	77.7	75.1	71.1	78.8	67.0	66.5	67.6
Ages 65-74	67.4	68.8	65.6	67.7	68.7	66.4	62.5	66.8	56.7
Ages 65 and over	60.1	62.4	57.5	60.4	62.2	58.3	55.8	61.2	49.8
Ages 75 and over	50.8	52.8	49.0	51.5	52.9	50.1	44.4	48.7	41.1

Note: Rates are five-year relative (estimated) survival rates for all invasive cancer sites; based on follow-up of patients into 2017.

Depression

Source: Substance Abuse and Mental Health Services Admin. and National Institutes of Health, U.S. Dept. of Health and Human Services

Depression is a serious illness that affects thoughts, feelings, and the ability to function in everyday life. It is one of the most common mental disorders in the U.S., affecting all age groups. In 2018, an estimated 17.7 mil adults age 18 and older (or 7.2% of the adult population) in the U.S. had at least one major depressive episode. Over the same 12-month period, 13.8% of persons aged 18–25 years experienced at least one major depressive episode versus 4.5% of those 50 or older. More women (9.0%) than men (5.3%) reported at least one major depressive episode in 2018.

Available treatments can alleviate symptoms. But many depressed people—and those around them—still fail to realize that they have an illness or could benefit from medical help.

Symptoms and Types of Depression

- Persistent sad, anxious, or "empty" feelings
- Feelings of hopelessness or pessimism
- Feelings of guilt, worthlessness, or helplessness
- Irritability, restlessness
- Loss of interest in activities or hobbies once pleasurable, including sex
- Fatigue and decreased energy
- Difficulty concentrating, remembering, or making decisions
- Insomnia, early-morning wakefulness, or excessive sleeping
- Appetite and/or weight changes
- Thoughts of death or suicide, or suicide attempts
- Aches or pains, headaches, cramps, or digestive problems that do not ease even with treatment

A diagnosis of **major depressive disorder** (or **clinical depression**) is made if an individual reports experiencing five or more of these symptoms in the same two-week period.

Bipolar disorder (or **manic-depressive illness**), while distinct from depression, is characterized by periods of depression alternating with episodes of mania, when a person experiences a an abnormally elevated mood, less need for sleep, increased talkativeness, racing thoughts, distractibility,

agitation, and engaging in risky activities (e.g., spending a lot of money, reckless sex). Depression in women who are pregnant or who recently gave birth; psychotic depression, where a person also suffers some psychosis; and seasonal affective disorder are some other forms of depression.

Treatments for Depression

Depression can be treated by medication, psychotherapy, or a combination of the two. Antidepressants influence the functioning of certain neurotransmitters in the brain. The most popular antidepressants are selective serotonin reuptake inhibitors (SSRIs). Serotonin and norepinephrine reuptake inhibitors (SNRIs) and bupropion are also commonly prescribed as they have fewer side effects than drugs from older classes, such as tricyclics, tetracyclics, and monoamine oxidase inhibitors (MAOIs). Some people respond better, however, to the older antidepressants.

Research has shown that certain types of psychotherapy, particularly cognitive-behavioral therapy (CBT) and interpersonal therapy (IPT), can help relieve depression. CBT helps patients change the negative thinking and behaving patterns often associated with depression. IPT focuses patients on working through personal relationships that may contribute to depression. Studies of adults have shown that a combination of psychotherapy and antidepressant medication is most effective in treating moderate-to-severe depression.

Electroconvulsive therapy (ECT) has been found effective in treating some cases of severe depression, particularly those that have not responded to other treatment. ECT involves producing a seizure in the brain of a patient under general anesthesia by applying electrical stimulation through electrodes placed on the scalp. Memory loss and other cognitive problems, though common side effects, are typically short-lived. Other types of treatment involving brain stimulation are currently being studied.

Website: www.nimh.nih.gov

Diabetes

Source: American Diabetes Association; Centers for Disease Control and Prevention (CDC), U.S. Dept. of Health and Human Services

Diabetes is a chronic disease in which the body does not produce or properly use the hormone **insulin**. Insulin is needed to convert sugar, starches, and other foods into energy. Both genetics and environment appear to play roles in the onset of diabetes. This disease, which has no cure, was the seventh leading cause of death in the U.S. in 2018, with 84,946 deaths. In 2018, an est. 25.3 mil Americans (6.8% of the population) had diagnosed diabetes. Diagnosed diabetes in the U.S. cost an estimated $327 bil in direct medical costs and in reduced productivity in 2017.

The American Diabetes Association supports studies proving that detection at an earlier stage and modest lifestyle changes, such as eating better and exercising more, will help prevent or delay complications.

There are two major types of diabetes:

Type 1 (formerly known as insulin-dependent or juvenile diabetes). The body does not produce insulin; the disease is usually diagnosed in children and young adults. People with type 1 diabetes must take daily insulin to stay alive.

Type 2 (formerly known as non-insulin dependent or adult-onset diabetes). The body does not produce enough or cannot properly use insulin. It is the most common form of the disease (90%-95% of all diabetes cases) and often begins later in life.

Prediabetes

In 2018, 88 mil Americans age 18 and older (or 1 in 3 adults) had prediabetes, the state that occurs when a person's blood glucose levels are higher than normal but not high enough for a diagnosis of diabetes. People with prediabetes are at increased risk of developing type 2 diabetes unless lifestyle changes are made.

Complications From Diabetes

People often have diabetes for many years before it is diagnosed. During that time, serious complications may develop. Potential complications include the following:

Diabetic eye disease. High blood glucose can damage blood vessels to the eyes. In 2018, about 24.6% of adults age 18 and older with diagnosed diabetes had some visual impairment. Diabetic retinopathy is the most common cause of vision loss among those with diabetes. People with diabetes are also more likely to develop glaucoma or cataracts.

Kidney disease. One in three adults with diabetes may have chronic kidney disease. In 2016, 58,183 people with diagnosed diabetes (191.5 per 100,000 of the total diabetic population) had end-stage renal disease.

Amputations. Diabetes is the most frequent cause for non-traumatic lower-limb amputations. About 1 per 1,000 adults age 18 and older with diabetes were hospitalized in 2016 for amputation below the knee; the rate was 0.4 per 1,000 for amputation above the knee and 1.1 for amputation of the foot.

Heart disease and stroke. Among adults age 35 and older with diabetes, 30.1% had heart disease or a stroke in 2018.

Common Diabetes Symptoms

- Frequent urination
- Thirst
- Hunger
- Fatigue
- Blurry vision
- Cuts and bruises that are slow to heal
- Weight loss, nausea, vomiting (type 1)
- Tingling or numbness in hands or feet (type 2)

Gestational Diabetes

Gestational diabetes is a form of diabetes that develops during or is first diagnosed during pregnancy. Hormones released during pregnancy can cause insulin resistance, allowing blood glucose levels to rise. Usually there are no symptoms, or the symptoms are mild. Because gestational diabetes usually starts around the 24th week, pregnant women should receive a glucose tolerance test between the 24th and 28th week of pregnancy. Diet and exercise can help keep blood glucose levels within normal limits. Treatment may also include daily blood glucose testing and insulin injections. Women with gestational diabetes tend to have larger babies at birth, which can complicate delivery. Glucose levels usually return to normal after delivery, but the odds of recurrence in future pregnancies and development of type 2 diabetes later in life increase. Around 8.6 per 100 hospital deliveries among females ages 15-44 years in 2016 involved gestational diabetes.

Website: www.diabetes.org

Eating Disorders

Source: National Institute of Mental Health (NIMH), National Institutes of Health, U.S. Dept. of Health and Human Services

Eating disorders are medical illnesses that involve serious disturbances in eating behavior, usually in the forms of extreme and unhealthy reduction of food intake or severe overeating. The main types are anorexia nervosa, bulimia nervosa, and binge-eating disorder. Though these disorders can develop at any age, they usually appear in adolescence or early adulthood. Their exact cause is not yet known, but a combination of genetics and behavioral, psychological, and social factors may be responsible. Eating disorders often occur with other illnesses such as depression, substance abuse, and anxiety disorders. If not treated, eating disorders can lead to serious complications, including heart conditions and kidney failure, which may result in death.

Anorexia nervosa affects an estimated 0.6% of the U.S. adult population and three times as many women as men. It has the highest mortality rate of any mental disorder in the U.S. Symptoms include resistance to maintaining weight at minimally healthy levels, intense fear of gaining weight, exaggerated importance of body weight or shape in one's self image, and infrequent or absent menstrual periods. Anorexics see themselves as overweight even when they are dangerously thin. In response, they avoid food and take other extreme measures to lose weight, such as exercising compulsively or purging by means of vomiting or laxatives and enemas. While some anorexics fully recover after a single episode, others may relapse frequently or experience chronic deterioration.

Bulimia nervosa affects an estimated 1.0% of the U.S. adult population. It is five times more prevalent in women than men. It is characterized by recurrent uncontrolled binge-eating episodes followed by what is believed to be compensatory behavior to prevent weight gain, such as self-induced vomiting, use of laxatives or diuretics, exercising excessively, or fasting. Persons with bulimia can weigh within the normal range for their age and height, but they still fear gaining weight and are intensely dissatisfied with their bodies. They often perform their behaviors in secret, feeling shame when they binge and relief when they purge.

Binge-eating disorder affects an estimated 2.8% of the U.S. adult population, with women twice as likely than men to have it. As with bulimia, a binge-eating disorder involves episodes of excessive eating during which the sufferer may feel a complete lack of control. But individuals with this disorder do not compensate by purging, exercising, or fasting. Many are thus overweight or obese, and the shame they feel can lead to further binge-eating.

Early diagnosis and a comprehensive treatment program are essential to recovery. Some patients may need immediate hospitalization. For anorexia, treatment usually follows three established steps: weight restoration, usually in an inpatient hospital setting; treatment of any accompanying psychological disturbances, including the use of medications; and achieving long-term remission or recovery by reducing or eliminating negative thoughts and behaviors.

Heart and Blood Vessel Disease

Source: American Heart Assn.; American Stroke Assn.; Natl. Ctr. for Chronic Disease Prevention and Health Promotion, Centers for Disease Control and Prevention; Natl. Heart, Blood, and Lung Inst., Natl. Insts. of Health (NIH), U.S. Dept. of Health and Human Services

Warning Signs of Heart Attack

- Discomfort in chest. Most heart attacks involve discomfort, such as pressure, squeezing, or pain, in the center of the chest that lasts more than a few minutes or occurs intermittently. Most common symptom in men and women.
- Discomfort in other upper body areas, including one or both arms, the back, neck, jaw, or stomach.
- Shortness of breath, with or without chest discomfort.
- Breaking out in a cold sweat, nausea, or lightheadedness, among other signs.

While chest discomfort is the most common symptom of a heart attack, women are more likely to experience the other symptoms, such as abdominal pain, shortness of breath, dizziness, fainting, and extreme fatigue, without having any chest pain. The American Heart Association advises calling 911 at onset of symptoms so that emergency medical services can begin treatment on the way to the hospital.

Warning Signs of Stroke

- Face drooping or weakness on one side
- Arm weakness
- Speech difficulty, including slurring
- Time to call 911
  Other stroke symptoms, which may appear separately or in combination with F.A.S.T.:
- Sudden numbness or weakness of the face, arm, or leg, especially on one side of the body
- Sudden confusion or trouble speaking or comprehending
- Sudden vision difficulty in one or both eyes
- Sudden trouble walking, dizziness, or loss of coordination
- Sudden severe headache with no known cause

If someone has one or more stroke symptoms lasting more than a few minutes, call 911 or the emergency medical service number immediately so an ambulance, ideally one with advanced life support, can be sent. Prompt treatment of a stroke can prevent death or lessen the long-term effects.

Major Modifiable Risk Factors

Major risk factors for heart and blood vessel (cardiovascular) disease that can't be changed include age, gender, and heredity. People 65 years of age or older are more likely to die of coronary heart disease. Men are at greater risk, as well as African Americans and those with a family history of heart disease. Major risk factors that can be modified include the following:

High blood pressure. High blood pressure, or hypertension, increases the risk of stroke, heart attack, kidney failure, and congestive heart failure. It affects men and women of all races, ethnic origins, and ages. But obesity, physical inactivity, and an unhealthy diet can contribute to this often symptomless disease. Everyone 3 years of age and older should have a blood pressure reading at least once a year.

A blood pressure reading consists of two measurements written one above the other, such as 122/78 mmHg (millimeters of mercury). The upper number (systolic pressure) represents the amount of pressure in the arteries when the heart contracts (beats) and pushes blood through the circulatory system. The lower number (diastolic pressure) represents the pressure in the arteries between beats, when the heart is resting. According to guidelines revised in 2017, a blood pressure reading below 120/80 is considered normal, while a reading of 130/80 or higher indicates hypertension, of which there are two stages:

Stage 1 is 130-139 (systolic) over 80-89 (diastolic);
Stage 2 is 140+ (systolic) over 90+ (diastolic).
The diagnosis can be based on either the systolic or the diastolic reading. Any reading higher than 180/120 is a hypertensive crisis that must be addressed by a doctor immediately.

High blood pressure usually cannot be cured, but it can be controlled in a variety of ways, including through diet, exercise, quitting smoking (where applicable), and medication. Treatment should be at the direction and under the supervision of a physician.

High blood cholesterol. Cholesterol is a waxy fat-like substance produced by the liver and found in all cells of the body. Dietary cholesterol exists in animal foods. Excess levels of cholesterol increase the risk of heart disease. High cholesterol in itself usually does not cause symptoms, so many people are unaware that they have a problem.

There are two major kinds of cholesterol: LDL (low-density lipoprotein), often called "bad" cholesterol, can build up on the inside walls of blood vessels, narrowing them. HDL (high-density lipoprotein), known as "good" cholesterol, helps reduce that risk.

NIH guidelines classify healthy total cholesterol levels (determined by a blood test) as less than 170 mg/dL for those age 19 or younger and 125 to 200 mg/dL for persons age 20 or older. LDL levels of less than 100 mg/dL are considered healthy. Healthy levels of HDL are more than 45 mg/dL for those age 19 or younger, 40 mg/dL or higher for men ages 20+, and 50 mg/dL or higher for women ages 20+. More than 12% of adults age 20 and over had a total cholesterol level higher than 240 mg/dL in 2015-16.

As with high blood pressure, high blood cholesterol can be controlled with lifestyle changes and medication and should be treated by a physician.

Triglycerides, another form of fat in the blood, can also raise the risk of heart disease. Levels that are borderline high (150-199 mg/dL), high (200-499 mg/dL), or very high (500 mg/dL or more) may need treatment.

Diabetes. Even with glucose levels under control, at least 68% of people age 65 or older with diabetes mellitus die of some form of heart disease; 16% die of stroke.

Tobacco smoke. Cigarette smokers and nonsmokers exposed to secondhand smoke are more likely to develop coronary heart disease (CHD).

Obesity. People with excess body fat, especially around the waist (more than 40 in. for men, more than 35 in. for women), are more likely to develop heart and blood vessel disease even without any other risk factors.

Physical inactivity. A sedentary lifestyle is a risk factor for CHD. The risk increase is comparable to that observed for high blood cholesterol, high blood pressure, or cigarette smoking.

Women and Cardiovascular Disease

Heart disease was the number one cause of death for women in the United States in 2017, accounting for 21.8% of all female deaths. (Stroke was the fourth leading cause, at 6.2%.) Because heart disease was long viewed as a "man's" disease, many of the major cardiovascular studies were conducted only on men. Researchers are now trying to understand the influence of gender on cardiovascular disease risk and prevention.

One problem in **diagnosis** is that women tend to have heart attacks later in life than men, so symptoms may be masked by other age-related diseases such as arthritis or osteoporosis. Even certain diagnostic tests and procedures such as the exercise stress test may not be as accurate in women, with the result that the disease process leading to heart attack or stroke may not be detected early on, with potentially serious consequences.
Website: www.heart.org

Common Infectious Diseases

Source: Centers for Disease Control and Prevention (CDC), U.S. Dept. of Health and Human Services; World Health Organization

State and local officials, in connection with the CDC, monitor certain diseases in the interests of public health. Some diseases must be confirmed in a laboratory while others may be diagnosed based on epidemiologic data (e.g., exposure to a foodborne pathogen linked to confirmed cases of illness in other patients). Statistics may thus appear uneven because of different reporting methods for each disease. This list is meant to be used for reference purposes only and not as a diagnostic tool.

Chickenpox

(Varicella-zoster virus, or VZV) Highly contagious disease commonly associated with children that can be especially serious in babies, adults, pregnant women, and people with weakened immune systems. A person who has had chickenpox may develop shingles later in life if the virus reactivates. **Transmission:** direct contact with rash or through the air when an infected person coughs or sneezes. **Symptoms:** blister-like rash that can last up to 7 days, fever. **Vaccine:** available since 1995. **Treatment:** for relief of symptoms; antivirals only for those at risk of complications. **Annual U.S. cases:** before 1995, about 4 mil, mostly children; in 2018, 8,201 cases, 6 deaths reported.

Chlamydia

(*Chlamydia trachomatis*) One of the most widely spread sexually transmitted diseases (STDs), and the most common condition reported to the CDC of the diseases that it tracks. **Transmission:** sexually transmitted. A mother can pass an infection to her baby during delivery. **Symptoms:** Most of those infected show no symptoms. In women, abnormal vaginal discharge, infection of the cervix and urinary tract; can cause pelvic inflammatory disease. In men, infection of urinary tract and pain and swelling in one or both testicles; can also infect the throat, rectum, and eyes. **Treatment:** curable with antibiotics. **Annual U.S. cases:** 1,758,668 in 2018.

Common cold

(More than 200 different viruses, rhinoviruses being most common) An upper respiratory viral infection. **Transmission:** touching one's nose, eyes, or mouth after touching something contaminated by the virus; inhalation of airborne virus. **Symptoms:** irritated nose or scratchy throat, sneezing and watery green or yellow nasal discharge, coughing, muscle aches, headaches, postnasal drip (mucus dripping down throat). **Treatment:** no cure. Over-the-counter remedies can relieve symptoms. **Annual U.S. cases:** about 1 bil.

Gonorrhea

(*Neisseria gonorrhoeae*) Very common bacterial STD. **Transmission:** sexually transmitted. Can pass from mother to infant during delivery. **Symptoms:** pain or burning during urination. In men, white, yellow, or green discharge from urethra; in women, increased vaginal discharge, vaginal bleeding between periods. Many men and most women do not present symptoms. **Treatment:** curable with antibiotics, although bacteria has become increasingly resistant. **Annual U.S. cases:** 583,405 in 2018.

Hepatitis

A viral disease that causes inflammation of the liver. In the U.S., five forms are common: A, B, C, D, and E. Forms A, B, and C are the most common. HBV and HCV can cause chronic disease. **Symptoms:** all forms have generally similar symptoms including jaundice, fatigue, abdominal pain, loss of appetite, nausea, mild flu-like symptoms. Many cases cause no symptoms. In extreme cases, infected persons may develop end-stage liver disease.

Hepatitis A (*Hepatovirus picornaviridae*). **Transmission:** consuming food or water contaminated with feces from infected persons. **Vaccine:** effective. (In developing countries, older children and adults may generally be immune after having been infected when young.) **Treatment:** disease usually resolves on its own; alcohol consumption should be avoided. **Annual U.S. cases:** 12,474 acute (i.e., newly acquired) in 2018.

Hepatitis B (*Orthohepadnavirus hepadnaviridae*). **Transmission:** unsterilized needle sharing; contaminated blood transfusions; sexual contact; infants during childbirth. **Vaccine:** highly effective. **Treatment:** for chronic cases, drug treatment is necessary. For acute cases, disease usually resolves itself. **Annual U.S. cases:** 3,322 acute, 23 perinatal (pregnant woman to child) in 2018.

Hepatitis C (*Hepacivirus flavinviridae*). **Transmission:** unsterilized needle sharing; contaminated blood transfusions;

sexual contact; infants during childbirth. **Vaccine:** none. **Treatment:** chronic cases treated with drugs, which can eliminate the virus in more than 90% of patients. For acute cases, the CDC recommends monitoring by a doctor and starting treatment if the infection becomes chronic. **Annual U.S. cases:** 4,768 acute in 2018.

HPV

(More than 200 related human papillomaviruses) Most common sexually transmitted infection in U.S.; causes virtually all cases of cervical cancer, over 90% of anal cancers. **Transmission:** sexually transmitted. **Symptoms:** most of those infected have no symptoms though in some cases, low-risk HPVs result in genital warts and precancerous bumps on anus, cervix or vulva, or penis. High-risk HPVs can persist for years and lead to cell changes that become cancerous, possibly producing symptoms. **Vaccine:** recommended at ages 11 or 12. **Treatment:** while there is no cure, a healthy immune system can usually fight off HPV on its own. Women age 21 and older should be regularly screened for cervical cancer. **Annual U.S. cases:** est. 14 mil new cases; approximately 79 mil currently infected with HPV.

Influenza

(Various influenza viruses) Highly contagious viral respiratory infection. **Transmission:** airborne; contact with face after touching infected surface. **Symptoms:** chills, fatigue, fever, headaches, sore throat, sinus congestion, coughing. ("Stomach flu" is not influenza.) **Vaccine:** yearly vaccinations recommended; available as injection or nasal spray. **Treatment:** antiviral drugs; disease normally runs its course in a matter of days. **Annual U.S. cases:** est. 35.5 mil illnesses, 490,600 hospitalizations, and 34,200 deaths from influenza during the 2018-19 influenza season. Adults 65 years of age and older made up 57% of all those hospitalized and 74.8% of deaths from influenza.

Lyme disease

(*Borrelia burgdorferi*) Bacterial inflammatory disease, first identified 1975 in Old Lyme, CT. Concentrated in New England, the mid-Atlantic and upper Midwest U.S., usually in areas with large deer populations. Also on the West Coast, particularly Northern California. **Transmission:** bite from infected blacklegged (or deer) tick. Mice and deer are most common tick hosts. **Symptoms:** mimic those of other diseases. Flu-like symptoms: fatigue, stiff neck, joints. A roughly circular rash may appear at site of tick bite and expand to look like a bull's eye. **Treatment:** antibiotics in early stages; anti-inflammatory drugs to relieve symptoms. Without treatment, long-term complications (some fatal) involving joints, heart, and nervous system. **Annual U.S. cases:** from 9,465 reported cases in 1991—the first year the CDC began collecting Lyme disease data—to 33,666 cases (23,558 confirmed; 10,108 probable) in 2018. The CDC estimates up to 300,000 people are diagnosed with Lyme disease each year.

Malaria

(*Plasmodium* parasite) Mosquito-borne disease that mostly occurs in tropical and subtropical regions. **Transmission:** bite from infected *Anopheles* mosquito. **Symptoms:** high fever, shaking chills, heavy sweating, headaches, fatigue, enlarged spleen. If left untreated, organ damage and death. **Treatment:** antimalarial drugs, such as doxycycline, for treatment and prevention. **Annual cases:** 1,748 confirmed in 2018, 1,650 (provisional) in 2019 in the U.S.; est. 228 mil cases and 405,000 deaths worldwide in 2018, with 20 African countries and India accounting for almost 85% of the global malaria burden.

Measles

(*Rubeola* virus) Declared eliminated in the U.S. in 2000; spreads mostly via unvaccinated travelers from abroad. **Transmission:** airborne transmission. The virus can survive for up to two hours in the air where an infected person has coughed or sneezed. **Symptoms:** itchy and raised rash, cough, watery eyes, high fever. Complications include ear infections, pneumonia, brain swelling, premature birth, or even death. **Vaccine:** highly effective. **Treatment:** no specific treatment; relief of symptoms. **Annual U.S. cases:** 375 in 2018. 1,282 cases (preliminary) were confirmed in 2019.

Mumps

(Mumps virus) Acute and contagious viral infection. **Transmission:** direct contact with mucus or saliva of infected persons. **Symptoms:** headaches, fever, loss of appetite may precede painful, visible swelling of the salivary glands under one or both ears. In severe cases, inflammation of testes, pancreas, ovaries; brain swelling; deafness. **Vaccine:** MMR (measles, mumps, and rubella) vaccine is effective. **Treatment:** no specific treatment; symptoms may be relieved by applying cold or warm compress to swollen glands. **Annual U.S. cases:** 2,515 in 2018; 3,486 (provisional) in 2019.

Peptic ulcer

(Most from *Helicobacter pylori* [*H. pylori*] bacteria; also long-term use of aspirin or other anti-inflammatory drugs) Weakening of the stomach or duodenum's protective mucous coating, allowing stomach acid and bacteria to irritate the lining and cause a sore. **Transmission:** *H. pylori* may be transmitted through food and water; possibly through close contact between infected persons. **Symptoms:** indigestion; bloating; dull, transient abdominal pain or discomfort; nausea; vomiting. **Treatment:** antibiotics, drugs to reduce stomach acid. **Annual U.S. cases:** 4-6 mil people.

Pertussis or Whooping cough

(*Bordetella pertussis*) Upper respiratory bacterial infection. **Transmission:** airborne transmission by infected persons; highly contagious. **Symptoms:** initially, mild cold-like symptoms, fever, difficulty breathing; later, violent coughing with characteristic "whooping" sound when patient tries to breathe between coughs, vomiting. Many babies, instead of coughing, may stop breathing and turn blue. **Vaccine:** available as part of Tdap (tetanus, diphtheria, pertussis) combination vaccine. **Treatment:** antibiotics in early cases; otherwise, disease must run its course. **Annual U.S. cases:** 15,609 in 2018; 15,662 (provisional) in 2019.

Salmonella or Salmonellosis

(*Salmonella*) Bacterial infection. **Transmission:** eating foods contaminated by feces carrying the bacteria or eating undercooked meats or raw eggs contaminated by bacteria. Contact with infected domestic animals. **Symptoms:** fever, diarrhea, abdominal cramps. **Treatment:** no standard treatment. Runs its course in 4-7 days. Antibiotics in severe cases. **Annual U.S. cases:** 60,999 lab-confirmed infections in 2018.

Shigellosis

(Four species of *Shigella* bacteria) Diarrheal disease. **Transmission:** swallowing water or consuming food contaminated by infected feces. **Symptoms:** sometimes bloody diarrhea, fever, stomach pain usually lasting 5-7 days, to 4+ weeks. **Treatment:** replacement of fluids and salts to prevent dehydration. Antibiotics in severe cases. Antidiarrheal medi-

cines may make illness worse. **Annual U.S. cases:** 16,333 in 2018; 16,383 (provisional) in 2019.

Syphilis

(*Treponema pallidum*) Bacterial infection that can cause significant health problems if left untreated. **Transmission:** sexually transmitted; pregnant women can transmit during fetal development or at birth. **Symptoms:** primary stage: painless sore, called a chancre, where bacteria entered the body; usually heals in 3-6 weeks with or without treatment. Without treatment, disease enters secondary stage: skin rash as chancre is healing or weeks after it has healed. Without treatment, enters latent stage (no visible symptoms). Very rarely, can move into tertiary stage 10-30 years after infection and cause death. Syphilis can spread to the brain and nervous system (neurosyphilis) or eyes (ocular syphilis) at any stage; symptoms include fever, fatigue, dementia, vision changes. **Treatment:** antibiotics, though reinfection is possible. **Annual U.S. cases:** 115,045 (35,063 primary and secondary) in 2018.

Tetanus or Lockjaw

(*Clostridium tetani*) Bacterial infection. **Transmission:** bacteria commonly found in soil entering body through broken skin. **Symptoms:** muscle stiffness and spasms or "locking" of muscles of the jaw, neck, and limbs; seizures, fever. Breathing difficulties may lead to death in 1-2 of every 10 cases. **Vaccine:** four forms of immunization. **Treatment:** tetanus immune globulin to fight infection, drugs to control spasms. **Annual U.S. cases:** 23 in 2018; 18 (provisional) in 2019.

Tuberculosis

(*Mycobacterium tuberculosis*) Bacterial infection that primarily affects the lungs. **Transmission:** airborne transmission by persons with TB disease. **Symptoms:** no symptoms in person with latent TB infection. Person with TB disease may have weight loss, fever, cough with discharge (sometimes with bloody sputum) lasting 3 or more weeks, night sweats. **Vaccine/treatment:** BCG (bacille Calmette-Guérin) vaccine for children where TB is prevalent. Not recommended for use in the U.S. because of low infection risk and variable effectiveness in adults. Antibiotics to treat TB disease or to prevent latent infection from becoming active. **Annual U.S. cases:** 9,025 in 2018; 8,920 (provisional) in 2019.

Yellow fever

(Yellow fever virus, in *flavivirus* genus) Viral infection endemic in tropical areas of Africa and Central and South America. **Transmission:** bite from virus-carrying mosquito. **Symptoms:** head and, body aches, nausea and vomiting, fatigue; more severely, fever, jaundice (yellowing skin), organ failure, coma, and death. Most infected people exhibit no symptoms or only mild symptoms. **Vaccine:** safe and effective, conferring lifetime immunity to most who receive it. **Treatment:** symptoms treated until disease runs its course. **Annual cases:** none in the U.S. in 2018 or 2019; est. 84,000-170,000 severe cases and 29,000-60,000 deaths worldwide in 2013.

U.S. Vaccine-Preventable Diseases, 1950-2018

Source: Centers for Disease Control and Prevention (CDC), U.S. Dept. of Health and Human Services

Year	Diphtheria		Tetanus		Pertussis		Polio (paralytic)		Measles		Mumps		Rubella	
	Cases	Deaths	Cases	Deaths	Cases	Deaths	Cases	Deaths	Cases	Deaths	Cases	Deaths	Cases	Deaths
1950	5,796	410	486	336	120,718	1,118	33,300[1]	1,904	319,124	468	NR	NA	NR	NA
1960	918	69	368	231	14,809	118	2,525	230	441,703	380	NR	42	NR	12
1970	435	30	148	79	4,249	12	31	7	47,351	89	104,953	16	56,552	31
1980	3	1	95	28	1,730	11	9	2	13,506	11	8,576	2	3,904	1
1990	4	1	64	11	4,570	12	6	0	27,786	64	5,292	1	1,125	8
2000	1	0	35	5	7,867	12	0	0	86	1	338	2	176	0
2005	0	0	27	1	25,616	31	1[2]	0	66	NA	314	0	11	0
2007	0	0	28	5	10,454	9	0	0	43	0	800	0	11	
2008	0	0	19	3	13,278	6	0	0	140	0	454	2	16	0
2009	0	0	18	6	16,858	1	1[2]	0	71	2	1,991	2	3	2
2010	0	0	26	3	27,550	5	0	0	63	2	2,612	1	5	2
2011	0	0	36	6	18,719	1	0	0	220	0	404	0	4	1
2012	1	0	37	4	48,277	4	0	0	55	2	229	0	9	0
2013	0	0	26	3	28,639	2	1[2]	0	187	0	584	1	9	0
2014	1	0	25	1	32,971	7	0	0	667	0	1,223	0	6	0
2015	0	NA	29	NA	20,762	NA	0	NA	188	NA	1,329	NA	5	NA
2016	0	NA	34	NA	17,972	NA	0	NA	85	NA	6,369	NA	1	NA
2017	0	NA	33	NA	18,975	NA	0	NA	120	NA	6,109	NA	7	NA
2018	1	NA	23	NA	15,609	NA	0	NA	375	NA	2,515	NA	4	NA

NA = Not applicable or available. NR = Not nationally reportable. (1) Incl. non-paralytic reported cases. (2) Vaccine-associated/derived paralytic polio.

Effectiveness of the Seasonal Flu Vaccine, 2004-20

Source: National Center for Immunization and Respiratory Diseases, Centers for Disease Control and Prevention (CDC)
The CDC conducts studies to determine how effective each season's flu vaccine was in preventing the flu among a nationwide sample of patients.

Flu season	Vaccine effectiveness	Flu season	Vaccine effectiveness	Flu season	Vaccine effectiveness
2004-05	10%	2010-11	60%	2015-16	48%
2005-06	21	2011-12	47	2016-17	40
2006-07	52	2012-13	49	2017-18	38
2007-08	37	2013-14	52	2018-19	29
2008-09	41	2014-15	19	2019-20*	39
2009-10	56				

* = Preliminary.

Weight Guidelines for Adults

Source: National Center for Health Statistics, CDC, U.S. Dept. of Health and Human Services

Clinical guidelines on the identification, evaluation, and treatment of overweight and obesity in adults were released in 1998 by the National Heart, Lung, and Blood Institute (NHLBI) in cooperation with the National Institute of Diabetes and Digestive and Kidney Diseases (NIDDK). The guidelines define overweight and obese in terms of **body mass index (BMI)**. BMI, based on a person's weight and height, can be an indicator of total body fat. A BMI of 18.5-24.9 is considered normal weight while 25.0-29.9 is said to indicate **overweight**; a BMI of 30.0 or higher indicates **obesity**. BMI can be calculated at www.nhlbi.nih.gov/health/educational/lose_wt/BMI/bmicalc.htm.

Waist circumference should be evaluated along with BMI. Men with a waist circumference of more than 40 inches and non-pregnant women with a waist circumference of more than 35 inches may be at increased risk for disease because of excess abdominal fat. BMI and waist circumference are screening tools, not diagnostics. A health-care provider should also perform other assessments to evaluate risk and diagnose disease, taking into consideration such factors as blood pressure, cholesterol levels, and family medical history.

The National Center for Health Statistics notes that 42.4% of American adults (ages 20 and over) in 2017-18 and 18.5% of youth (ages 2-19) in 2015-16 were obese. The prevalence of obesity has increased over time, from 30.5% of adults and 13.9% of youth in 1999-2000 to its current levels. Among all age groups, obesity was more prevalent in the non-Hispanic Black and Hispanic population than among non-Hispanic whites and non-Hispanic Asians.

A high prevalence of overweight and obesity is a public health concern because higher body weights increase a person's risk of developing type 2 diabetes, hypertension, dyslipidemia, cardiovascular disease, stroke, gallbladder disease, sleep and respiratory problems, osteoarthritis, and certain cancers.

Adults Meeting U.S. Fitness Guidelines, 1998-2017

Source: National Health Interview Survey, National Center for Health Statistics, CDC, U.S. Dept. of Health and Human Services

Characteristic	% meeting aerobic activity guidelines					% meeting muscle-strengthening guidelines				
	1998	2000	2005	2010	2017	1998	2000	2005	2010	2017
Sex and age										
Male, 18-44 years	51.5%	53.6%	50.0%	59.0%	65.7%	27.2%	26.3%	28.7%	35.6%	39.7%
Male, 45-54 years	44.3	45.2	42.6	50.7	57.2	18.8	18.0	19.2	24.8	28.6
Male, 55-64 years	38.3	38.9	38.4	46.0	52.4	12.9	13.8	15.7	22.9	23.4
Male, 65-74 years	38.5	41.8	38.3	40.7	50.1	12.0	12.2	14.5	20.6	22.7
Male, 75 years and over	26.1	30.7	28.6	32.3	34.9	9.5	10.1	12.4	14.5	16.9
Female, 18-44 years	40.0	42.0	43.1	48.5	55.4	17.9	17.9	19.8	22.1	26.8
Female, 45-54 years	36.1	39.1	38.1	44.7	50.9	13.7	16.1	19.8	20.4	22.8
Female, 55-64 years	32.5	33.5	34.1	38.6	45.9	10.3	12.4	15.9	17.5	20.4
Female, 65-74 years	26.2	32.6	30.2	31.8	41.4	7.8	10.5	13.3	15.6	19.6
Female, 75 years and over	14.0	16.8	18.8	18.3	26.0	5.7	6.7	6.7	10.8	12.0
Race or Hispanic origin[1]										
White, not Hispanic	43.1	45.7	45.7	51.5	58.6	18.7	19.3	22.5	26.3	30.0
Black, not Hispanic	30.4	31.7	29.1	37.3	44.6	15.6	16.0	15.7	21.6	24.7
Amer. Indian or AK Native	39.7	29.7	41.6	42.0	54.3	18.2	13.9	20.5	16.7	27.6
Asian	37.1	41.7	37.5	44.2	51.5	17.2	17.2	16.9	21.9	25.8
Two or more races	—	43.9	41.1	50.2	57.0	—	22.2	23.6	30.4	30.5
Hispanic or Latino	29.1	30.8	28.5	36.2	45.0	12.7	11.9	12.9	18.1	22.5
Geographic region										
Northeast	39.6	45.3	43.3	46.9	53.5	17.5	20.0	21.6	24.3	29.1
Midwest	42.0	43.5	43.5	46.1	55.5	18.2	19.3	21.9	24.7	29.7
South	35.3	37.3	36.5	45.0	50.8	15.0	15.1	17.6	22.0	24.7
West	46.7	46.9	44.4	52.0	58.7	22.3	19.7	21.3	27.5	30.0
Total, 18 years and over	40.0	42.2	41.1	47.3	54.1	17.7	18.0	20.2	24.4	27.8

— = Not available. **Note:** Measures of physical activity reflect the federal 2008 Physical Activity Guidelines for Americans, which recommend that for substantial health benefits, adults each week perform at least 150 min. of moderate-intensity, 75 min. of vigorous-intensity, or an equivalent combination of moderate- and vigorous-intensity aerobic activity. Aerobic activity should be performed in episodes of at least 10 min., preferably spread throughout the week. The guidelines also recommend that adults perform muscle-strengthening activities that are moderate or high intensity and involve all major muscle groups on two or more days a week. (1) Persons reporting only one race, unless otherwise noted. Persons of Hispanic origin may be of any race.

Obesity Among Adults in the U.S., 2018

Source: National Health Interview Survey, National Center for Health Statistics, CDC, U.S. Dept. of Health and Human Services

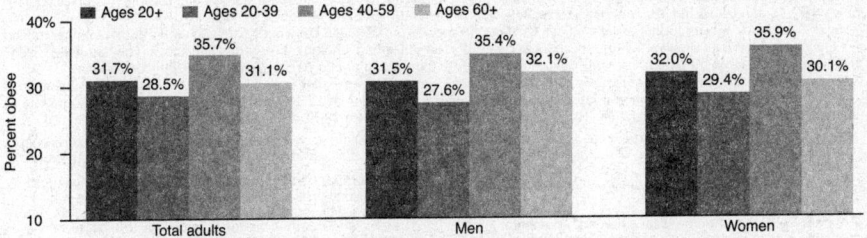

Overweight and Obesity Among U.S. Adults, 1960-2018

Source: National Health and Nutrition Examination Survey, NCHS, CDC, U.S. Dept. of Health and Human Services
(as percent of adults age 20-74 in 1960-80 and age 20 and over for all other years shown here)

Survey period	Total			Men			Women		
	Overweight	Obesity	Severe obesity	Overweight	Obesity	Severe obesity	Overweight	Obesity	Severe obesity
1960-62	31.5%	13.4%	0.9%	38.7%	10.7%	0.3%	24.7%	15.8%	1.4%
1971-74	32.7	14.5	1.3	41.7	12.1	0.6	24.3	16.6	2.0
1976-80	32.1	15.0	1.4	39.9	12.7	0.4	24.9	17.0	2.2
1988-94	33.1	22.9	2.8	40.7	20.2	1.7	25.9	25.4	3.9
1999-2000	34.0	30.5	4.7	39.7	27.5	3.1	28.6	33.4	6.2
2001-02	35.1	30.5	5.1	42.2	27.7	3.6	28.2	33.2	6.5
2003-04	34.1	32.2	4.8	39.7	31.1	2.8	28.6	33.2	6.9
2005-06	32.6	34.3	5.9	39.9	33.3	4.2	25.5	35.3	7.4
2007-08	34.3	33.7	5.7	40.1	32.2	4.2	28.6	35.4	7.3
2009-10	33.0	35.7	6.3	38.4	35.5	4.4	27.9	35.8	8.1
2011-12	33.6	34.9	6.4	37.8	33.5	4.4	29.7	36.1	8.3
2013-14	32.5	37.7	7.7	38.7	35.0	5.5	26.5	40.4	9.9
2015-16	31.6	39.6	7.7	36.5	37.9	5.6	26.9	41.1	9.7
2017-18	NA	42.4	9.2	NA	43.0	6.9	NA	41.9	11.5

NA = Not available. **Note:** Overweight is body mass index (BMI) of 25 or greater but less than 30; obesity is BMI greater than or equal to 30; extreme obesity is BMI greater than or equal to 40. Does not include pregnant women.

Obesity Among Children and Adolescents in the U.S., 1988-2016

Source: National Health and Nutrition Examination Survey, NCHS, CDC, U.S. Dept. of Health and Human Services
(percent of population)

Age/sex/poverty level	1988-94	1999-2002	2003-06	2005-08	2007-10	2009-12	2011-14	2013-16
2-5 years								
Both sexes	7.2%	10.3%	12.5%	10.5%	11.1%	10.2%	8.9%	11.6%
Boys	6.2	10.0	12.8	9.8	11.9	12.0	9.2	11.5
Girls	8.2	10.6	12.2	11.2	10.2	8.4	8.6	11.7
Percent of poverty level[1]								
Below 100%	9.7	10.9	14.3	12.3	13.2	12.3	11.6	13.5
100%-199%	7.3	13.8*	12.7	10.0	11.8	11.6	10.2	12.6
200%-399%	5.6	7.6*	11.9	11.6	13.9	11.0	7.7*	10.4
400% or more	—	—	10.0*	—	5.8*	5.0*	—	8.2
6-11 years								
Both sexes	11.3	15.9	17.0	17.4	18.8	17.9	17.5	17.9
Boys	11.6	16.9	18.0	18.7	20.7	18.3	17.6	19.6
Girls	11.0	14.7	15.8	16.0	16.9	17.4	17.5	16.1
Percent of poverty level[1]								
Below 100%	11.4	19.1	22.0	21.5	22.2	24.6	21.5	20.8
100%-199%	11.1	16.4	19.2	22.2	20.7	18.5	20.4	20.8
200%-399%	11.7	15.3	16.7	16.8	18.9	15.8	15.7	17.1
400% or more	—	12.9*	9.2*	9.5*	12.5*	12.2*	12.2*	12.2
12-19 years								
Both sexes	10.5	16.0	17.6	17.9	18.2	19.4	20.5	20.6
Boys	11.3	16.7	18.2	18.2	18.7	19.4	20.0	20.1	20.0
Girls	9.7	15.3	16.8	17.0	16.9	18.9	21.0	21.2
Percent of poverty level[1]								
Below 100%	15.8	19.8	19.3	23.1	24.3	23.2	22.4	25.7
100%-199%	11.2	15.1	18.4	19.8	20.1	22.5	25.7	24.3
200%-399%	9.4	15.7	16.3	17.2	16.3	17.9	19.7	19.3
400% or more	—	13.9	12.6	14.0	14.0	13.8	13.7*	13.7

* = Estimate is considered unreliable. — = Estimate not given as it is considered unreliable. **Note:** Obesity is defined as body mass index (BMI) at or above the sex- and age-specific 95th percentile of the 2000 CDC growth charts. (1) Ratio of family's household income to contemporary federal poverty guidelines.

Basic First Aid

Source: Courtesy of the American National Red Cross, www.redcross.org. All rights reserved in all countries.

Note: This information is not intended to be a substitute for formal training. It is recommended that you contact your local American Red Cross chapter to sign up for a First Aid/CPR/AED (automated external defibrillator) course. Similar courses are also offered by organizations like the American Heart Association and National Safety Council.

In an emergency, it is important to get medical assistance as soon as possible, but knowing what to do until a doctor or other trained person gets to the scene can save a life, especially in cases of severe bleeding, choking, poisoning, and shock. The "Stop the Bleed" initiative provides free training in bleeding control techniques to the general public. **Website:** www.bleedingcontrol.org

People with special medical problems, such as diabetes, cardiovascular disease, epilepsy, or allergies, are urged to wear some sort of emblem identifying the problem as a safeguard against receiving medication that might be harmful or even fatal. Emblems can be purchased from MedicAlert Foundation, 101 Lander Ave., Turlock, CA 95380; (800) 432-5378; www.medicalert.org

Allergic reaction and anaphylaxis: If you know the person has a severe allergy or is having difficulty breathing, call 911 or the local emergency number. Have the person use any medication they might carry to use in an emergency, such as epinephrine.

Animal bite: Call 911 or the local emergency number if the wound is bleeding seriously or if the animal was wild or a stray or you suspect it of having rabies. Control any bleeding. Wash minor wounds with soap under running water and apply antibiotic ointment and a dressing. In the U.S., people most commonly get rabies through contact with a bat, which may not leave a noticeable bite mark. When possible, proper authorities should test the animal for rabies.

Bleeding: Use a barrier between your hand and the wound to help prevent infection. Cover wound with a sterile dressing. Apply direct pressure until bleeding stops. Cover compress with a bandage. Call 911 or the local emergency number if bleeding is severe.

Burn: Check for life-threatening conditions. If the burn is mild, with skin unbroken and no blisters, flush with cold running water for at least 10 minutes (at least 15 minutes if the burn was caused by a chemical). Gently wash with soap and water and pat dry. Apply a thin layer of antibiotic ointment and then a loose, sterile dry dressing to prevent infection. If the burn is severe, call 911 or the local emergency number. Care for shock (see separate entry). Keep the person from getting chilled or overheated until advanced medical assistance arrives. Do not try to clean a severe burn or break blisters.

Chemical in eye: Call 911 or the local emergency number. Turn the person's head to the side so that the affected eye is lower than the unaffected eye. Flush the affected eye with large amounts of water for at least 20 minutes.

Choking: See **First Aid for Choking** below.

Convulsions (seizures): Remove nearby objects that might cause injury. Protect the person's head by placing a thin folded towel or item of clothing under it. Roll them on one side to drain fluids from the mouth. Do not place anything between the person's teeth. Stay with the person until they are fully conscious. If convulsions last for longer than 5 minutes or the person has a health condition like diabetes or is pregnant, call 911 or the local emergency number.

Cut (minor): Use a clean barrier between your hand and the wound to prevent infection. Apply direct pressure for a few minutes to control any bleeding. Wash the wound thoroughly with soap and water and apply a thin layer of antibiotic ointment or a microthin film dressing. Cover the wound with a sterile dressing and a bandage.

Diabetic emergency: A person experiencing a diabetic emergency might have a headache or even appear intoxicated, slurring their speech and moving with difficulty. Offer the person some form of sugar only if they are conscious and able to swallow. Call 911 if the person is unresponsive.

Foreign object in eye: If an object is embedded in someone's eye, do not remove it. If the object is not embedded, have the person blink several times. If the object doesn't come out, gently flush the eye with saline solution or water. Do not rub the eye. Seek medical attention if the foreign object remains.

Frostbite: Handle the frostbitten area gently. Do not rub. If there is no danger of the affected area refreezing, soak it in warm water (not warmer than 105°F), without allowing it to touch the side of the water container, until normal color returns and it feels warm. Loosely bandage the area with dry, sterile dressings. Put cotton or gauze between any frostbitten fingers or toes. Do not break any blisters. Call 911 or seek emergency help as soon as possible.

Heart attack and stroke: See **Heart and Blood Vessel Disease** earlier in chapter.

Heat stroke: Remove the person from the heat. Loosen any tight clothing. Immerse person in cold water until they become alert. If a large enough source of water is not available, drench the person with cold water and fan constantly. If the person is conscious, have them slowly drink some cool water. Call 911 if the person's condition does not improve.

Hypothermia: Call 911 or the local emergency number. For mild hypothermia, cover all exposed skin. Replace wet clothes with something dry. If the person is alert, give them simple carbohydrates to eat and warm, nonalcoholic, decaffeinated liquids to drink. Apply heat pads or other heat sources if available but do not place against bare skin.

Loss of limb: Call 911 or the local emergency number and care for any life-threatening conditions. If a limb is severed, properly protect it for possible reattachment. After the victim is cared for, the limb should be wrapped in sterile gauze and placed in a plastic bag. Place bag in a larger bag or container of an ice and water slurry, not ice alone. Be sure the limb accompanies the victim to the hospital.

Poisoning: Care for any life-threatening conditions. Call the National Capital Poison Center (800-222-1222), 911, or the local emergency number. Do not give the person any food or drink or induce vomiting unless specified to do so by medical professionals. In cases of **alcohol poisoning**, place the person in a position that keeps their airway clear. In cases of **carbon monoxide poisoning**, remove the person from the area if you can do so safely. In some states, the public can receive training to administer naloxone as a nasal spray or autoinjectable to reverse an **opioid overdose**.

Shock (injury-related): Monitor breathing and consciousness. Have the person lie down and keep them as comfortable as possible. Do not give the person anything to eat or drink as it increases the risk of vomiting or aspiration. If the weather is cold or damp, place blankets or extra clothing over and under the person; if the weather is hot, provide shade.

Snakebite: Call 911 or the local emergency number immediately if you're not sure whether or not the snake was venomous. Do not wait for symptoms to appear. Gently wash the injury with soap and water and keep the area below the level of the heart. Have the person remain still if possible. Do not cut, suck at, or apply a tourniquet or ice to a snakebite. Applying an elastic roller bandage may help slow the spread of venom.

Sprains and strains: Splint any injured bone or joint that the person cannot use.

Sting from bee or wasp: If possible, remove the stinger by scraping it away with your finger or a plastic card (like a credit card) or using tweezers. If you use tweezers, grasp the stinger, not the venom sac. Wash the area with soap and water and cover it with a bandage. Apply cold to the area to reduce swelling and pain. Call 911 or the local emergency number immediately if the wound does not stop swelling, the person collapses, or they are known to be allergic to the sting.

Tick bite: Promptly remove any ticks to lower the chance of infection. Use tweezers to grasp it at its head as close to the skin as possible. Pull it slowly and steadily out. Do not use a match or petroleum jelly to remove an embedded tick. Wash and dress the bite area.

Unconsciousness: Call 911 or the local emergency number immediately. Do not move the person if a spinal injury is suspected.

First Aid for Choking

The recommended first aid for a conscious choking victim who is unable to speak, cough, or breathe is to deliver a series of five blows to the back followed by five thrusts to the abdomen. Have another person call 911 or the local emergency number. Obtain consent from the victim to treat them. Apply the back blows by leaning the victim forward and striking between the shoulder blades with the heel of your hand. If the victim is still choking, stand or kneel behind the victim and wrap your arms around their waist. Make a fist with one hand and place the thumb side against the middle of the person's abdomen, just above the navel and well below the lower tip of the breastbone. Grasp your fist in your other hand and quickly thrust upwards into the abdomen. Continue back blows and abdominal thrusts until the object is dislodged, and the person can breathe or cough forcefully, or the person loses consciousness.

VITAL STATISTICS

Births and Deaths in the U.S., 1960-2019

Source: National Center for Health Statistics (NCHS), CDC, U.S. Dept. of Health and Human Services

Year	BIRTHS Total number	Rate	DEATHS Total number	Rate	Year	BIRTHS Total number	Rate	DEATHS Total number	Rate
1960	4,257,850	23.7	1,711,982	9.5	2008	4,247,694	14.0	2,471,984	8.1
1970	3,731,386	18.4	1,921,031	9.5	2009	4,130,665	13.5	2,437,163	7.9
1980	3,612,258	15.9	1,989,841	8.8	2010	3,999,386	13.0	2,468,435	8.0
1990	4,092,994	16.7	2,148,463	8.6	2011	3,953,590	12.7	2,515,458	8.1
2000	4,058,814	14.4	2,403,351	8.5	2012	3,952,841	12.6	2,543,279	8.1
2001	4,025,933	14.1	2,416,425	8.5	2013	3,932,181	12.4	2,596,993	8.2
2002	4,021,726	13.9	2,443,387	8.5	2014	3,988,076	12.5	2,626,418	8.2
2003	4,089,950	14.1	2,448,288	8.4	2015	3,978,497	12.4	2,712,630	8.4
2004	4,112,052	14.0	2,397,615	8.2	2016	3,945,875	12.2	2,744,248	8.5
2005	4,138,349	14.0	2,448,017	8.3	2017	3,855,500	11.8	2,813,503	8.6
2006	4,265,555	14.2	2,426,264	8.1	2018	3,791,712	11.6	2,839,205	8.7
2007	4,316,233	14.3	2,423,712	8.0	2019[1]	3,745,540	11.4[2]	2,855,000	8.7[2]

Note: Rates are per 1,000 population; population counts are enumerated as of Apr. 1 for decennial census years and estimated as of July 1 for all other years. Beginning in 1970, statistics exclude births and deaths among nonresidents of the U.S. (1) Provisional. (2) Not directly comparable to previous years due to difference in calculation.

Marriage and Divorce Rates in the U.S., 1920-2018

Source: National Center for Health Statistics (NCHS), CDC, U.S. Dept. of Health and Human Services

(Per 1,000 total population. Rates for 2000-18 may exclude data and populations from nonreporting states. Some data are provisional.)

The U.S. marriage rate dipped during the Depression and peaked sharply just after World War II; the trend after that has been more gradual. The divorce rate generally rose from the 1920s through 1981, when it peaked at 5.3 per 1,000 population, before declining somewhat. The graph below shows marriage and divorce rates since 1920.

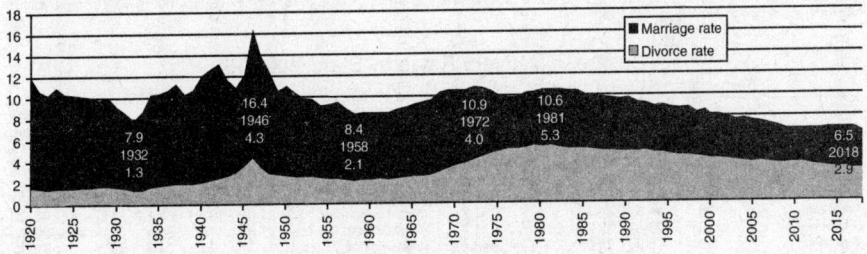

U.S. Median Age at First Marriage, 1890-2019

Source: U.S. Census Bureau, U.S. Dept. of Commerce

Year[1]	Men	Women	Year[1]	Men	Women	Year[1]	Men	Women	Year[1]	Men	Women
1890	26.1	22.0	1950	22.8	20.3	1990	26.1	23.9	2014	29.3	27.0
1900	25.9	21.9	1960	22.8	20.3	1995	26.9	24.5	2015	29.2	27.1
1910	25.1	21.6	1970	23.2	20.8	2000	26.8	25.1	2016	29.5	27.4
1920	24.6	21.2	1975	23.5	21.1	2005	27.1	25.3	2017	29.5	27.4
1930	24.3	21.3	1980	24.7	22.0	2010	28.2	26.1	2018	29.8	27.8
1940	24.3	21.5	1985	25.5	23.3	2013	29.0	26.6	2019[2]	29.8	28.0

(1) Figures for 1947 and on are based on Current Population Survey data; earlier figures based on decennial censuses. (2) Starting in 2019, estimates for marriages include same-sex married couples.

Divorce Rates by State, 2018

Source: National Center for Health Statistics (NCHS), CDC, U.S. Dept. of Health and Human Services

(per 1,000 population, estimated as of July 1)

State	Divorce rate	State	Divorce rate	State	Divorce rate
Alabama	3.7	Louisiana	1.7	Ohio	2.9
Alaska	3.7	Maine	3.2	Oklahoma	3.8
Arizona	3.0	Maryland	2.4	Oregon	3.4
Arkansas	4.1	Massachusetts	2.1	Pennsylvania	2.6
California	NA	Michigan	2.8	Rhode Island	2.9
Colorado	3.3	Minnesota	NA	South Carolina	2.5
Connecticut	2.9	Mississippi	2.7	South Dakota	2.6
Delaware	2.8	Missouri	3.0	Tennessee	3.5
District of Columbia	2.5	Montana	3.0	Texas	2.6
Florida	3.6	Nebraska	2.9	Utah	3.8
Georgia	2.5	Nevada	4.4	Vermont	3.1
Hawaii	NA	New Hampshire	3.1	Virginia	3.1
Idaho	3.8	New Jersey	2.7	Washington	3.3
Illinois	1.5	New Mexico	NA	West Virginia	3.3
Indiana	NA	New York	2.8	Wisconsin	2.5
Iowa	2.2	North Carolina	3.1	Wyoming	3.8
Kansas	2.3	North Dakota	2.6	**United States**	**2.9**
Kentucky	3.5				

NA = Not available. **Note:** Rates based on provisional counts of divorce including annulments and, for certain areas, divorce petitions filed or legal separations.

Birth Rates and Fertility Rates by Age of Mother, 1950-2019

Source: National Center for Health Statistics (NCHS), CDC, U.S. Dept. of Health and Human Services

Live births per 1,000 women by age of mother

Year	Birth rate[1]	Fertility rate[2]	10-14 years	15-19 years	15-17 years	18-19 years	20-24 years	25-29 years	30-34 years	35-39 years	40-44 years	45-49 years[3]
1950	24.1	106.2	1.0	81.6	40.7	132.7	196.6	166.1	103.7	52.9	15.1	1.2
1960	23.7	118.0	0.8	89.1	43.9	166.7	258.1	197.4	112.7	56.2	15.5	0.9
1970	18.4	87.9	1.2	68.3	38.8	114.7	167.8	145.1	73.3	31.7	8.1	0.5
1980	15.9	68.4	1.1	53.0	32.5	82.1	115.1	112.9	61.9	19.8	3.9	0.2
1990	16.7	70.9	1.4	59.9	37.5	88.6	116.5	120.2	80.8	31.7	5.5	0.2
2000	14.4	65.9	0.9	47.7	26.9	78.1	109.7	113.5	91.2	39.7	8.0	0.5
2005	14.0	66.7	0.7	40.5	21.4	69.9	102.2	115.5	95.8	46.3	9.1	0.6
2006	14.2	68.5	0.6	41.9	22.0	73.0	105.9	116.7	97.7	47.3	9.4	0.6
2007	14.3	69.5	0.6	42.5	22.1	73.9	106.3	117.5	99.9	47.5	9.5	0.6
2008	14.0	68.6	0.6	41.5	21.7	70.6	103.0	115.1	99.3	46.9	9.8	0.7
2009	13.5	66.2	0.5	37.9	19.6	64.0	96.2	111.5	97.5	46.1	10.0	0.7
2010	13.0	64.1	0.4	34.2	17.3	58.2	90.0	108.3	96.5	45.9	10.2	0.7
2011	12.7	63.2	0.4	31.3	15.4	54.1	85.3	107.2	96.5	47.2	10.3	0.7
2012	12.6	63.0	0.4	29.4	14.1	51.4	83.1	106.5	97.3	48.3	10.4	0.7
2013	12.4	62.5	0.3	26.5	12.3	47.1	80.7	105.5	98.0	49.3	10.4	0.8
2014	12.5	62.9	0.3	24.2	10.9	43.8	79.0	105.8	100.8	51.0	10.6	0.8
2015	12.4	62.5	0.2	22.3	9.9	40.7	76.8	104.3	101.5	51.8	11.0	0.8
2016	12.2	62.0	0.2	20.3	8.8	37.5	73.8	102.1	102.7	52.7	11.4	0.9
2017	11.8	60.2	0.2	18.8	7.9	35.1	71.0	98.0	100.3	52.3	11.6	0.9
2018	11.6	59.1	0.2	17.4	7.2	32.3	68.0	95.3	99.7	52.6	11.8	0.9
2019[4]	11.4[5]	58.2	0.2	16.6	6.7	31.1	66.6	93.7	98.3	52.7	12.0	0.9

(1) Live births per 1,000 population. (2) Live births per 1,000 women 15-44 years of age. (3) Beginning in 1997, rate computed by relating the number of births to women age 45 and over to women 45-49 years of age. (4) Provisional. (5) Not directly comparable to previous years due to difference in calculation.

Cesarean Delivery Rates by State, 2000-19

Source: National Center for Health Statistics (NCHS), CDC, U.S. Dept. of Health and Human Services

State	2000	2010	2013	2019[1]	Percent change, 2000-19	State	2000	2010	2013	2019[1]	Percent change, 2000-19
Alabama	26.3%	35.3%	35.8%	34.6%	31.6%	Montana	19.0%	30.3%	29.7%	28.5%	50.0%
Alaska	17.0	21.5	24.0	21.7	27.6	Nebraska	22.5	31.1	30.3	29.1	29.3
Arizona	18.6	27.0	27.4	27.8	49.5	Nevada	21.7	34.8	34.9	32.8	51.2
Arkansas	26.3	34.8	34.4	34.5	31.2	New Hampshire	21.0	30.4	30.1	31.6	50.5
California	23.4	33.0	33.2	30.8	31.6	New Jersey	27.3	38.4	38.4	33.8	23.8
Colorado	18.3	25.9	26.0	26.8	46.4	New Mexico	17.1	22.8	24.3	26.5	55.0
Connecticut	21.6	35.1	34.8	34.7	60.6	New York	24.6	34.5	34.3	33.2	35.0
Delaware	24.8	33.9	31.5	31.5	27.0	North Carolina	23.0	30.8	30.4	29.1	26.5
District of Columbia	22.6	33.0	34.2	31.9	41.2	North Dakota	20.6	27.7	28.6	26.5	28.6
Florida	24.9	37.8	37.7	36.5	46.6	Ohio	20.0	30.7	31.1	31.0	55.0
Georgia	22.5	33.8	34.2	34.3	52.4	Oklahoma	21.0	34.7	33.8	32.1	52.9
Hawaii	14.6	27.2	25.2	26.8	83.6	Oregon	19.4	29.4	28.0	28.0	44.3
Idaho	18.3	24.8	24.9	24.0	31.1	Pennsylvania	21.7	31.3	31.3	30.2	39.2
Illinois	20.9	31.1	31.7	30.6	46.4	Rhode Island	21.9	33.0	31.3	32.0	46.1
Indiana	21.5	30.3	30.5	29.3	36.3	South Carolina	25.2	35.0	35.0	33.2	31.7
Iowa	20.8	30.3	30.8	29.6	42.3	South Dakota	22.8	26.6	25.5	24.5	7.5
Kansas	22.2	30.5	30.2	29.7	33.8	Tennessee	24.8	34.2	33.4	31.8	28.2
Kentucky	23.6	35.4	36.6	33.7	42.8	Texas	24.7	35.1	35.2	34.8	40.9
Louisiana	26.6	39.6	38.9	36.6	37.6	Utah	16.8	23.1	22.4	23.1	37.5
Maine	22.8	29.8	30.0	30.3	32.9	Vermont	17.3	27.5	27.3	25.7	48.6
Maryland	24.1	34.5	35.1	33.0	36.9	Virginia	23.1	34.3	33.7	32.0	38.5
Massachusetts	23.3	33.0	31.5	31.4	34.8	Washington	20.6	29.5	28.3	27.8	35.0
Michigan	21.9	32.6	32.6	32.1	46.6	West Virginia	25.4	36.0	35.9	34.6	36.2
Minnesota	19.4	27.1	26.9	27.6	42.3	Wisconsin	17.5	26.0	26.2	26.7	52.6
Mississippi	28.2	37.0	38.5	38.5	36.5	Wyoming	19.4	27.9	28.9	26.3	35.6
Missouri	22.3	31.9	31.1	30.1	35.0	**United States**	**22.8**	**32.7**	**32.7**	**31.7**	**39.0**

Note: The cesarean rate is the percentage of all live births by cesarean delivery. (1) Provisional.

Infertility and Use of Infertility Services, by Age and Type of Service, 2015-17

Source: National Survey of Family Growth, National Center for Health Statistics (NCHS), U.S. Dept. of Health and Human Services

A special tabulation in 2015-17 found that for all women 15-49 years of age, 12.7% had ever received any infertility services and 13.1% had impaired fecundity; and for married women 15-49 years of age, 8.8% were infertile and 16.2% had impaired fecundity.

Age	% of all women who have impaired fecundity[1] 0 births	1 or more births	% of all women who have ever received any infertility service 0 births	1 or more births
15-29 years	9.4%	11.7%	2.7%	10.3%
30-39 years	24.1	11.5	13.8	18.3
40-49 years	33.9	13.3	20.5	19.7
Total 15-49 years	14.2	12.3	6.3	17.3

Type of infertility service	% of women[2]
Medical help to get pregnant	9.5%
Advice	6.7
Tests on woman or man	5.8
Any medical help to prevent miscarriage	5.1
Ovulation drugs	4.3
Artificial insemination	2.0
Surgery to treatment on blocked tubes	0.8
Assisted Reproductive Technology	0.6

(1) Not surgically sterile, and for whom it is difficult or impossible to get pregnant or carry a pregnancy to term. (2) Age 15-49 years.

Numbers of Multiple Births in the U.S., 1990-2018

Source: National Center for Health Statistics (NCHS), CDC, U.S. Dept. of Health and Human Services

Year	Twins	Triplets	Quad-ruplets	Quin-tuplets[1]	Year	Twins	Triplets	Quad-ruplets	Quin-tuplets[1]
1990	93,865	2,830	185	13	2010	132,562	5,153	313	37
1995	96,736	4,551	365	57	2011	131,269	5,137	239	41
2000	118,916	6,742	506	77	2012	131,024	4,598	276	45
2004	132,219	6,750	439	86	2013	132,324	4,364	270	66
2005	133,122	6,208	418	68	2014	135,336	4,233	246	47
2006	137,085	6,118	355	67	2015	133,155	3,871	228	24
2007	138,961	5,967	369	91	2016	131,723	3,755	217	31
2008	138,660	5,877	345	46	2017	128,310	3,675	193	49
2009	137,217	5,905	355	80	2018	123,536	3,400	115	10

(1) Quintuplets and other multiple births of five or more.

Origin Countries for U.S. Foreign Adoptions, 2000-19

Source: Annual Report on Intercountry Adoption, Bureau of Consular Affairs, U.S. Dept. of State; Office of Immigration Statistics, U.S. Dept. of Homeland Security

(ranked by fiscal year 2019 adoptions)

Country	2019	2018	2017	2016	2015	2014	2013	2012	2011	2010	2005	2000
China[1]	819	1,475	1,905	2,231	2,354	2,040	2,306	2,697	2,589	3,401	7,906	5,053
Ukraine	298	248	215	303	303	521	438	395	632	445	821	659
Colombia	244	229	181	131	153	172	159	195	216	235	291	246
India	241	302	221	194	138	136	119	159	228	243	323	503
South Korea	166	206	276	260	318	370	138	627	736	863	1,630	1,794
Bulgaria	134	134	147	201	185	183	159	125	75	40	30	214
Haiti	130	196	227	178	143	464	388	154	33	1,332	234	131
Nigeria	116	173	176	121	154	130	183	197	148	189	65	4
Philippines	94	105	111	156	150	172	178	125	230	214	271	173
Liberia	51	30	20	10	8	16	12	34	29	48	183	25
Total[3]	2,971	4,059	4,714	5,372	5,648	6,441	7,094	8,668	9,320	11,059[2]	22,710	18,120

(1) Not incl. adoptions from Hong Kong. (2) Does not reflect approx. 1,090 Haitian children admitted as part of the Special Humanitarian Parole following the 2010 earthquake in Haiti. (3) Includes countries not shown.

Leading Causes of Infant Death in the U.S., 2018

Source: National Vital Statistics System, National Center for Health Statistics (NCHS), CDC, U.S. Dept. of Health and Human Services

Cause of death	Number	Percent of total deaths	Mortality rate[1]
Congenital malformations, deformations, and chromosomal abnormalities	4,473	20.8%	118.0
Disorders related to short gestation and low birth weight, not elsewhere classified	3,679	17.1	97.0
Newborn affected by maternal complications of pregnancy	1,358	6.3	35.8
Sudden infant death syndrome	1,334	6.2	35.2
Accidents (unintentional injuries)	1,168	5.4	30.8
Newborn affected by complications of placenta, cord, and membranes	724	3.4	19.1
Bacterial sepsis[2] of newborn	579	2.7	15.3
Diseases of the circulatory system	428	2.0	11.3
Respiratory distress of newborn	390	1.8	10.3
Neonatal hemorrhage	375	1.7	9.9
All other causes	6,959	32.4	—
All causes	21,467	100.0	566.2

— = Not available. (1) Deaths of infants under 1 year of age per 100,000 live births. (2) Toxic condition resulting from the spread of bacteria.

Nonmarital Childbearing in the U.S., 1970-2018

Source: National Center for Health Statistics (NCHS), CDC, U.S. Dept. of Health and Human Services

	1970	1975	1980	1985	1990	1995	2000	2005	2010	2015	2017	2018
Live births to unmarried mothers (thous.)	399	448	666	828	1,165	1,254	1,347	1,527	1,633	1,602	1,534	1,503
Race/Hispanic origin of mother	Percent of live births to unmarried women											
All races and origins	10.7%	14.3%	18.4%	22.0%	28.0%	32.2%	33.2%	36.9%	40.8%	40.3%	39.8%	39.6%
White	5.5	7.1	11.2	14.7	20.4	25.3	27.1	31.7	35.9	35.8	28.4	28.2
Black	37.5	49.5	56.1	61.2	66.5	69.9	68.5	69.3	72.1	70.1	69.4	69.4
American Indian or Alaska Native	22.4	32.7	39.2	46.8	53.6	57.2	58.4	63.5	65.6	65.8	69.2	68.2
Asian or Pacific Islander[1]	—	—	7.3	9.5	13.2	16.3	14.8	16.2	17.0	16.4	13.1	13.2
Hispanic origin (select states)[2,3]	—	—	23.6	29.5	36.7	40.8	42.7	48.0	53.4	53.0	52.1	51.8
Maternal age	Percent distribution of live births to unmarried women											
Under 20 years	50.1%	52.1%	40.8%	33.8%	30.9%	30.9%	28.0%	23.1%	20.1%	12.9%	11.4%	10.9%
20-24 years	31.8	29.9	35.6	36.3	34.7	34.5	37.4	38.3	36.8	35.0	32.8	31.9
25 years and over	18.1	18.0	23.5	29.9	34.4	34.7	34.6	38.7	43.1	52.1	55.8	57.2
Race/Hispanic origin of mother	Live births per 1,000 unmarried women 15-44 years of age[4]											
All races and origins	26.4	24.5	29.4	32.8	43.8	44.3	44.0	47.2	47.5	43.4	41.0	40.1
White[5]	13.9	12.4	18.1	22.5	32.9	37.0	38.2	43.2	44.5	40.4	29.2	28.8
Black[5]	95.5	84.2	81.1	77.0	90.5	74.5	70.5	67.2	65.3	59.6	57.5	56.4
Hispanic origin (select states)[2,3]	—	—	—	—	89.6	88.7	87.2	96.2	80.6	67.4	62.5	59.5

— = Not available. (1) For 2017-18, data is for Asian and Native Hawaiian or Other Pacific Islander combined. (2) Hispanic origin data prior to 1995 is not directly comparable with data for more recent years due to differences in reporting area. (3) Hispanics may be of any race. (4) Rates computed by dividing births to unmarried mothers, regardless of mother's age, by the pop. of unmarried women 15-44 years of age. (5) For 1970 and 1975, birth rates are by race of child.

Number, Ratio, and Rate of Legal Abortions in U.S., 1970-2016

Source: *Abortion Surveillance—United States, 2016*, Centers for Disease Control and Prevention, U.S. Dept. of Health and Human Services

Year	Legal abortions	Ratio[1]	Rate[2]	Year	Legal abortions	Ratio[1]	Rate[2]	Year	Legal abortions	Ratio[1]	Rate[2]
1970	193,491	52	5	1997	1,186,039	306	20	2007	827,609	226	16
1971	485,816	137	11	1998	884,273	270	17	2008	825,564	229	16
1972	586,760	180	13	1999	861,789	261	17	2009	789,217	224	15
1973	615,831	196	14	2000	857,475	251	16	2010	765,651	225	14
1974	763,476	242	17	2001	853,485	249	16	2011	730,322	217	14
1975	854,853	272	18	2002	854,122	250	16	2012	699,202	208	13
1980	1,297,606	359	25	2003	848,163	245	16	2013	664,435	198	12
1990	1,429,247	344	24	2004	839,226	241	16	2014	652,639	192	12
1995	1,210,883	311	20	2005	820,151	235	16	2015	638,169	188	12
1996	1,225,937	315	21	2006	852,385	233	16	2016	623,471	186	12

Note: After 1998, reporting area varies. (1) Number of abortions per 1,000 live births. (2) Number of abortions per 1,000 women aged 15-44 years.

Reported U.S. Abortions by Age, Race, and Marital Status, 2016

Source: *Abortion Surveillance—United States, 2016*, Centers for Disease Control and Prevention, U.S. Dept. of Health and Human Services

Characteristic	White No.	%	Black No.	%	Other No.	%	Total, all races No.	%
Age[1]								
Under 15 years.	262	0.2%	341	0.3%	50	0.2%	653	0.3%
15-19 years.	10,920	9.8	9,611	8.9	2,187	8.8	22,718	9.3
20-24 years.	33,888	30.3	34,199	31.8	6,783	27.3	74,870	30.6
25-29 years.	30,691	27.4	33,013	30.7	6,581	26.5	70,285	28.8
30-34 years.	19,870	17.8	18,568	17.3	4,863	19.6	43,301	17.7
35-39 years.	11,970	10.7	9,329	8.7	3,107	12.5	24,406	10.0
40 years and over.	4,247	3.8	2,578	2.4	1,282	5.2	8,107	3.3
Total.	**111,848**	**100.0**	**107,639**	**100.0**	**24,853**	**100.0**	**244,340**	**100.0**
Marital status[2]								
Married.	16,369	16.0	7,225	7.2	6,080	27.2	29,674	13.2
Unmarried.	86,170	84.0	92,525	92.8	16,277	72.8	194,972	86.8
Total.	**102,539**	**100.0**	**99,750**	**100.0**	**22,357**	**100.0**	**224,646**	**100.0**

Note: The CDC requests data annually from the central health agencies of 52 reporting areas (all states, DC, and NYC). Reporting is voluntary. Data exclude areas that did not report, did not report by characteristic, or did not meet reporting standards. (1) Data from 32 reporting areas; excludes 20 (AZ, CA, CO, CT, DC, FL, IL, KY, MD, MA, NV, NH, NM, NY, NYC, PA, TX, UT, WA, WY). (2) Data from 31 reporting areas; excludes 21 (AZ, CA, CO, DC, FL, HI, IL, MD, MA, NV, NH, NM, NY, NYC, OH, PA, TX, UT, WA, WI, WY).

Adult LGBT and Transgender Population by State

Source: The Williams Institute, UCLA School of Law

(Adult population self-identifying as LGBT and/or transgender as a percentage of overall population.)

State	LGBT, 2017	Transgender, 2016	State	LGBT, 2017	Transgender, 2016	State	LGBT, 2017	Transgender, 2016
Alabama	3.1%	0.6%	Kentucky	3.4%	0.5%	North Dakota	2.7%	0.3%
Alaska.	3.7	0.5	Louisiana	3.9	0.6	Ohio	4.3	0.5
Arizona	4.5	0.6	Maine	4.9	0.5	Oklahoma	3.8	0.6
Arkansas.	3.3	0.6	Maryland.	4.2	0.5	Oregon	5.6	0.7
California	5.3	0.8	Massachusetts	5.4	0.6	Pennsylvania. . .	4.1	0.4
Colorado.	4.6	0.5	Michigan	4.0	0.4	Rhode Island .	4.5	0.5
Connecticut. . .	3.9	0.4	Minnesota	4.1	0.6	South Carolina	3.5	0.6
Delaware.	4.5	0.6	Mississippi . . .	3.5	0.6	South Dakota .	3.0	0.3
District of			Missouri	3.8	0.5	Tennessee . . .	3.5	0.6
Columbia. . .	9.8	2.8	Montana	2.9	0.3	Texas	4.1	0.7
Florida	4.6	0.7	Nebraska	3.8	0.4	Utah	3.7	0.4
Georgia.	4.5	0.8	Nevada	5.5	0.6	Vermont	5.2	0.6
Hawaii.	4.6	0.8	New			Virginia	3.9	0.6
Idaho.	2.8	0.4	Hampshire. .	4.7	0.4	Washington. . .	5.2	0.6
Illinois	4.3	0.5	New Jersey . . .	4.1	0.4	West Virginia. . .	4.0	0.4
Indiana	4.5	0.6	New Mexico . .	4.5	0.8	Wisconsin	3.8	0.4
Iowa	3.6	0.3	New York.	5.1	0.5	Wyoming	3.3	0.3
Kansas	3.3	0.4	North Carolina	4.0	0.6	**United States**	**4.5**	**0.6**

Sexual Orientation and Gender Identity by Age Group, 2019

Source: *Accelerating Acceptance 2020*, a national survey among U.S. adults conducted by research firm Cint on behalf of GLAAD

(percent of survey respondents)

Sexual orientation	Age 18-34	35-51	52-71	72+	Gender identity	Age 18-34	35-51	52-71	72+
Strictly straight/heterosexual	76%	88%	90%	96%	Cisgender.	84%	89%	92%	94%
Non-heterosexual	24	12	10	4	Non-cisgender	16	11	8	6
Bisexual	15	5	3	—	Transgender	3	3	1	—
Gay or lesbian	3	3	3	2	Gender fluid	3	3	2	1
Pansexual.	3	2	1	—	Bigender.	3	2	—	—
Queer.	—	1	1	—	Genderqueer	1	1	1	1
Asexual	2	—	—	—	Agender	1	—	1	—
Unsure or questioning	1	1	1	2	Unsure or questioning . . .	5	2	3	4

— = Less than 0.5%. NA = Not available. **Note:** Asexual: not experiencing sexual attraction; bi-gender: identifying equally as both genders; bisexual: experiencing sexual attraction to more than one gender; cisgender: strictly identifying with the sex assigned at birth; gay/lesbian: experiencing sexual attraction to the same gender; gender fluid: identifying as male, female, and/or outside the binary at different times; genderqueer: identifying outside of, or beyond, the binary of female and male; pansexual: experiencing sexual attraction to people of all gender identities; queer: experiencing sexual attraction in a way that does not fit into the dominant norms; transgender: identifying with a gender that does not correspond to the sex assigned at birth.

Sexual Orientation Among U.S. Adults, 2018

Source: *National Health Interview Survey, 2018*, National Center for Health Statistics (NCHS), U.S. Dept. of Health and Human Services

	Gay or lesbian[1]		Straight[2]		Bisexual	
	Number (thous.)	% of group	Number (thous.)	% of group	Number (thous.)	% of group
Total	3,955	1.6%	233,360	97.0%	3,143	1.3%
Sex						
Men.	2,250	1.9	113,250	97.3	895	0.8
Women	1,705	1.4	120,109	96.8	2,248	1.8
Age						
18-44 years.	2,113	1.9	105,755	95.8	2,550	2.3
45-64 years.	1,484	1.8	78,338	97.6	475	0.6
65 years and older	358	0.7	49,267	99.0	118	0.2

Note: Percent distributions may not equal 100 due to rounding. (1) Response option provided was "gay" for men and "gay or lesbian" for women. (2) Response option provided was "straight, that is, not gay" for men and "straight, that is, not gay or lesbian" for women.

Sexual Behavior With Opposite-Sex and Same-Sex Partners, 2011-13

Source: National Survey of Family Growth, National Center for Health Statistics (NCHS), U.S. Dept. of Health and Human Services

		Percent of selected pop. at left who have had any—				
Characteristic	Number (thous.)	Opposite-sex sexual contact[1]	Vaginal intercourse with opposite-sex partner	Oral sex with opposite-sex partner	Anal sex with opposite-sex partner	Same-sex sexual contact[2]
All women aged 18-44	55,271	95.3%	94.2%	86.2%	35.9%	17.4%
Age						
18-24 years.	14,269	85.6	81.7	77.3	28.4	19.4
25-34 years.	20,790	98.3	98.0	89.8	39.0	20.0
35-44 years.	20,212	99.1	99.1	88.7	38.0	13.1
Marital/cohabiting status						
Currently married	23,191	100.0	100.0	91.2	37.5	10.9
Currently cohabiting	9,032	100.0	100.0	90.3	42.2	23.9
Never married, not cohabiting.	17,499	85.2	81.5	76.4	27.8	20.1
Formerly married, not cohabiting . . .	5,549	100.0	100.0	89.0	44.4	25.0
All men aged 18-44.	54,685	93.5	92.0	87.4	42.3	6.2
Age						
18-24 years.	14,718	83.5	79.9	77.6	29.3	6.6
25-34 years.	20,453	95.6	94.6	90.1	49.3	6.0
35-44 years.	19,514	98.9	98.5	92.0	44.8	6.0
Marital/cohabiting status						
Currently married	21,298	100.0	100.0	93.4	45.4	3.9
Currently cohabiting	8,157	100.0	100.0	94.7	57.0	5.4
Never married, not cohabiting.	21,793	83.7	79.9	77.4	30.8	8.9
Formerly married, not cohabiting . . .	3,438	100.0	100.0	97.3	60.4	5.2

Note: Totals include those of other or multiple race and origin groups not shown separately. (1) Includes vaginal, oral, or anal sex. (2) For women, includes oral sex or any sexual experience with same-sex (female) partners. For men, includes oral or anal sex with male partners.

Contraceptive Use in the U.S., 2002-17

Source: National Survey of Family Growth, National Center for Health Statistics (NCHS), U.S. Dept. of Health and Human Services

Method	2002	2006-10	2011-15	2002	2006-10	2011-15	2015-17
		Ever used[1]			Currently using[2]		
Any method of contraception	98.2%	99.1%	99.3%	61.9%	62.2%	61.6%	64.9%
Male condom	89.7	93.4	95.0	14.7	10.2	9.2	8.7
Pill.	82.3	81.9	79.3	19.2	17.1	15.9	12.6
Withdrawal	56.1	59.6	64.8	5.4	3.2	3.9	3.9
3-month injectable (Depo-Provera).	16.8	23.2	25.4	3.3	2.3	2.6	2.1
Female sterilization.	20.7	19.5	17.1	16.7	16.5	14.3	18.6
Calendar rhythm method	16.2	18.1	15.9	NA	NA	NA	1.3
Male sterilization.	13.0	13.3	11.4	6.3	6.2	4.5	5.9
Emergency contraception.	4.2	10.8	20.0	NA	NA	NA	NA
Contraceptive patch	0.9	10.4	10.6	NA	NA	NA	1.2
Intrauterine device (IUD).	5.8	7.7	15.0	1.3	3.5	6.8	7.9
Not currently using contraception[3]	NA	NA	NA	38.1	37.8	38.4	35.1

NA = Not available/not applicable. (1) Among women ages 15-44 who have ever had intercourse. (2) Percentage of women ages 15-44 using specified contraception in month of interview. Women could be using more than one method. Women are classified here according to the one most effective contraceptive method they are using. Additional methods women may be using are not shown. (3) Currently pregnant or postpartum, trying to get pregnant, not having sex, etc.

Child Care Arrangements of Young Children, 2016

Source: *Digest of Education Statistics*, National Center for Education Statistics, U.S. Dept. of Education

Child's characteristic	Pop. under 6 years old (thous.)	% in center-based programs[1]	Hours per week in nonparental care[2]	Parental care only	Center-based care	Non-relative's home	Non-relative in child's home	Relative	Multiple arrange-ments[3]
					Type of care (% distrib.)				
Total	**21,362**	**35.9%**	**30.6**	**40.3%**	**29.4%**	**6.9%**	**3.2%**	**18.5%**	**1.8%**
Age									
Under 1 year	4,724	13.2	33.0	52.6	10.7	8.0	3.7	23.2	1.6
1-2 years	8,552	24.7	30.8	46.0	21.4	7.9	3.5	19.9	1.3
3-5 years	8,087	60.9	29.5	27.1	48.7	5.1	2.5	14.4	2.3
Race/ethnicity[4]									
White	10,731	38.5	30.5	37.8	31.4	8.5	3.9	16.4	2.0
Black	2,837	40.3	33.5	32.5	31.6	6.6	2.2	24.9	2.3
Hispanic	5,418	28.3	28.1	48.5	23.1	4.9	2.3	19.7	1.5
Asian/Pacific Islander	1,009	36.1	30.0	43.2	30.9	2.3	3.5	19.6	NA
Two or more races	1,235	37.3	33.6	39.2	33.7	6.9	2.1	17.7	NA

NA = Not applicable. **Note:** Detail may not sum to totals because of rounding and because children in multiple care arrangements are included under the category in which the child spent the most time. (1) Includes day care centers, Head Start programs, preschools, prekindergartens, and other early childhood programs. (2) Mean hours per week per child, among preschool children enrolled in any type of nonparental care arrangement. For children with more than one arrangement, the hours of each weekly arrangement were summed to calculate the total amount of time in child care per week. (3) Children who spent an equal number of hours per week in multiple nonparental care arrangements. (4) Race categories exclude persons of Hispanic ethnicity (Hispanic persons can be of any race).

Sexual Activity of U.S. High School Students, 2019

Source: *Youth Risk Behavior Surveillance—United States, 2019*, Centers for Disease Control and Prevention, U.S. Dept. of Health and Human Services

(percent of selected population to have engaged in activity)

Race/ethnicity	Ever had sexual intercourse Female	Male	Total	First sexual intercourse before age 13 Female	Male	Total	Currently sexually active[1] Female	Male	Total	Condom use during last sexual intercourse[2] Female	Male	Total
White, non-Hispanic	39.2%	36.7%	38.0%	1.5%	2.2%	1.9%	29.9%	25.2%	27.5%	51.6%	60.9%	55.8%
Black, non-Hispanic	34.0	50.1	42.3	2.8	10.8	6.9	25.4	32.4	29.0	44.5	51.8	48.2
Hispanic, any race	40.3	43.6	41.8	3.5	4.2	3.8	30.3	29.2	29.7	50.9	62.3	56.2
Grade												
9	16.7	21.6	19.2	3.0	4.4	3.7	10.8	12.5	11.7	51.8	69.0	61.3
10	31.8	35.4	33.6	2.5	3.9	3.2	24.3	22.0	23.1	47.8	64.2	55.4
11	46.6	46.6	46.5	1.5	4.6	3.0	35.9	32.7	34.3	52.3	60.7	56.3
12	56.8	56.3	56.7	1.3	2.6	2.0	43.8	40.6	42.3	47.8	53.4	50.3
Sexual identity												
Heterosexual (straight)	36.8	39.7	38.4	1.2	3.5	2.4	28.5	26.7	27.6	52.6	60.7	56.6
Gay, lesbian, or bisexual	46.7	40.0	44.9	5.7	7.8	6.1	32.2	25.8	30.3	39.0	51.6	41.3
Not sure	24.8	25.2	25.0	4.0	7.5	5.6	18.4	14.8	17.4	41.0	—	47.3
Sex of sexual contacts[3]												
Opposite sex only	75.5	76.3	75.9	2.4	6.0	4.4	57.7	52.0	54.6	52.2	60.2	56.3
Same sex only or both sexes	73.3	78.4	74.4	9.6	21.5	12.2	53.4	49.6	52.6	44.5	52.5	46.5
All students	**37.6**	**39.2**	**38.4**	**2.1**	**3.9**	**3.0**	**28.4**	**26.3**	**27.4**	**49.6**	**60.0**	**54.3**

NA = Not available. (1) Sexual intercourse with at least 1 person during the 3 months before the survey. (2) Among the 27.1% of students who were currently sexually active. (3) Students who had no sexual contact are excluded from the analyses by sex of sexual contacts.

Sexual Violence Against U.S. High School Students, 2019

Source: *Youth Risk Behavior Surveillance—United States, 2019*, CDC, U.S. Dept. of Health and Human Services

(as percent of selected population)

Race/ethnicity	Ever physically forced to have sexual intercourse[1] Female	Male	Total	Experienced sexual violence by anyone[2] Female	Male	Total	Experienced sexual dating violence[3] Female	Male	Total
White, non-Hispanic	11.5%	2.8%	7.1%	16.3%	4.4%	10.2%	12.7%	3.5%	8.1%
Black, non-Hispanic	9.9	4.8	7.2	14.4	6.8	10.3	8.2	4.3	6.2
Hispanic, any race	11.8	4.0	8.0	18.4	5.8	12.2	13.2	3.6	8.7
Grade									
9	8.1	2.3	5.1	14.2	3.6	8.7	12.8	3.6	8.0
10	10.3	2.9	6.6	15.3	5.0	10.1	11.6	3.4	7.6
11	13.1	4.7	8.9	18.3	5.7	11.9	13.6	3.2	8.4
12	14.0	3.4	8.7	18.5	6.2	12.3	12.3	4.7	8.6
Sexual identity									
Heterosexual (straight)	9.2	2.5	5.5	14.9	4.2	9.0	11.3	2.9	6.7
Gay, lesbian, or bisexual	21.0	15.6	19.4	23.6	15.7	21.5	18.2	10.3	16.4
Not sure	14.7	8.2	12.8	17.5	12.6	16.2	15.1	13.1	15.0
Total	**11.4**	**3.4**	**7.3**	**16.6**	**5.2**	**10.8**	**12.6**	**3.8**	**8.2**

(1) When they did not want to. (2) Being forced to do "sexual things" (e.g., kissing, touching, or being physically forced to have sexual intercourse) they did not want to do by anyone, one or more times during the 12 months before the survey. (3) Being forced to do "sexual things" they did not want to do by someone they were dating or going out with, one or more times, among the 66.2% of students who dated or went out with someone during the 12 months before the survey.

Risky Vehicular Behaviors by U.S. High School Students, 2019

Source: *Youth Risk Behavior Surveillance—United States, 2019*, Centers for Disease Control and Prevention, U.S. Dept. of Health and Human Services

(percent of selected population to have engaged in activity)

Race/ethnicity	Rarely or never wore a seat belt[1]			Rode with a driver who had been drinking alcohol[2]			Drove when drinking alcohol[3]			Texted or emailed while driving[4]		
	Female	Male	Total	Female	Male	Total	Female	Male	Total	Female	Male	Total
White, non-Hispanic ...	3.5	6.0%	4.8%	16.0%	14.1%	15.1%	3.3%	6.7%	5.1%	45.3%	42.5%	43.9%
Black, non-Hispanic ...	10.7	12.2	11.6	13.8	17.4	15.9	1.9	5.7	4.1	25.1	32.8	29.5
Hispanic, any race ...	7.2	7.7	7.5	22.0	19.4	20.8	5.2	8.0	6.6	32.2	38.0	35.2
Grade												
9	5.8	8.1	7.0	18.7	14.2	16.5	1.6	4.2	3.0	12.6	20.8	17.2
10	5.7	8.3	7.1	17.7	15.7	16.9	2.1	5.1	3.7	21.6	23.0	22.4
11	5.5	6.8	6.2	17.3	14.4	16.0	3.5	6.8	5.1	41.5	41.9	41.8
12	4.6	6.1	5.4	15.7	18.1	17.0	5.2	10.2	7.8	58.6	60.2	59.5
Total	5.6	7.4	6.5	17.5	15.6	16.7	3.6	7.0	5.4	38.4	39.6	39.0

(1) When riding in a car driven by someone else. (2) In a car or other vehicle, one or more times during the 30 days before the survey. (3) Among the 59.9% of students who had driven a car or other vehicle one or more times during the 30 days before the survey. (4) Among the 60.1% of students who had driven a car or other vehicle on at least one day during the 30 days before the survey.

U.S. Motor Vehicle Crashes, 2018

Source: National Safety Council (NSC) website: injuryfacts.nsc.org; Natl. Highway Traffic Safety Admin. (NHTSA)

An estimated 39,404 people in the U.S. were killed in motor vehicle crashes in 2018, down 2.1% from the total for 2017. The number of licensed drivers (227.5 mil) and vehicle miles driven (3.24 tril) increased in 2018; the death rate per 100 mil vehicle miles decreased 2% to 1.22.

Motor vehicle deaths per 10,000 registered vehicles was 1.42 in 2018. In comparison, the death rate was 1.48 in 2017 and 1.55 in 2008, which represents an 8% decrease over 10 years. The number of fatalities per 100,000 population declined 8% between 2008 and 2018 and declined 3% from 2017-2018.

In 2018, male drivers were involved in about 6.8 mil crashes, whereas female drivers were in 5.2 mil. Male drivers were involved in 72% of fatal crashes, or about 37,062, compared with 13,269 incidents involving female drivers.

In 2018, 10,511 motor vehicle traffic fatalities (29%) involved an alcohol-impaired (blood alcohol concentration of 0.08% or greater) driver or motorcycle operator.

Seat belt use was 90.7% in 2019. The least likely seat belt users were occupants of pickup trucks (86%) and those traveling in light traffic (84%). In 2018, the most recent year for which data was available, 47% of passenger vehicle occupants killed in traffic crashes were unrestrained.

Crashes	Deaths	Injuries
All motor vehicle crashes	39,404	4,500,000
Collision between motor vehicles	16,600	3,550,000
Collision with fixed object	10,500	557,000
Collision with pedestrian	7,700	150,000
Noncollision accidents (e.g., rollovers)	3,300	120,000
Collision with pedalcycle	1,100	100,000
Collision with railroad train	127	1,000
Collision with animal or animal-drawn vehicle	100	22,000

Note: NSC numbers are rounded and preliminary.

U.S. Passenger Deaths and Death Rates, 1999-2018

Source: National Safety Council website: injuryfacts.nsc.org

Year	Light duty vehicles[1]		Vans, SUVs, pickup trucks[1]		Buses[2]		Railroad passenger trains		Scheduled airlines[3]	
	Deaths	Rate[4]	Deaths	Rate[4]	Deaths	Rate[4]	Deaths	Rate[4]	Deaths	Rate[4]
1999	20,851	0.84	11,295	0.76	40	0.07	14	0.10	23	0.005
2000	20,689	0.81	11,545	0.76	3	0.01	4	0.03	94	0.02
2004	19,183	0.71	12,678	0.75	27	0.05	3	0.02	13	0.002
2005	18,509	0.68	13,043	0.76	43	0.07	16	0.10	20	0.003
2006	17,792	0.66	12,723	0.72	15	0.02	2	0.01	51	0.01
2007	29,075	0.66	NA	NA	18	0.03	5	0.03	0	0.00
2008	25,457	0.59	NA	NA	50	0.08	24	0.12	0	0.00
2009	23,441	0.53	NA	NA	21	0.04	3	0.02	49	0.01
2010	22,271	0.50	NA	NA	28	0.05	3	0.02	0	0.00
2011	21,315	0.48	NA	NA	36	0.06	6	0.03	0	0.00
2012	21,773	0.49	NA	NA	25	0.04	5	0.02	0	0.00
2013	21,218	0.47	NA	NA	36	0.06	6	0.03	5	0.001
2014	21,039	0.46	NA	NA	28	0.04	4	0.02	0	0.00
2015	22,362	0.49	NA	NA	28	0.04	15	0.07	1	<0.001
2016	23,776	0.50	NA	NA	47	0.07	2	0.01	6	0.001
2017	23,656	0.49	NA	NA	27	0.04	9	0.04	0	0.00
2018	22,692	0.47	NA	NA	20	0.03	5	0.03	1	<0.001

NA = Not available. (1) From 2007 on, light duty vehicles include passenger cars and vans, SUVs, pickup trucks, and other light trucks, which were classified separately in previous years. Drivers of light duty vehicles (except taxis) are considered passengers. Includes taxi passengers. (2) Excludes school buses. (3) Excludes charter, cargo, and on-demand services and deaths due to suicide/sabotage. (4) Deaths per 100 mil passenger miles.

Related Factors in Fatal Crashes, 1995-2018
Source: National Highway Traffic Safety Admin. (NHTSA)

Factor	2018 Number	2018 %	2010 Number	2010 %	2005 Number	2005 %	1995 Number	1995 %
Driving too fast for conditions or in excess of posted speed limit.	8,596	16.7%	9,532	21.4%	11,803	20.0%	11,656	20.8%
Under the influence of alcohol, drugs, or medication	5,175	10.1	7,052	15.9	7,441	12.6	—	—
Failure to keep in proper lane	3,706	7.2	7,436	16.7	16,551	28.0	15,873	28.3
Failure to yield right of way	3,579	7.0	3,196	7.2	4,306	6.3	4,868	8.7
Operating vehicle in a careless manner[1]	2,797	5.4	—	—	2,712	4.6	2,850	5.1
Distracted (phone, talking, eating, object, etc.)[2]	2,688	5.2	2,912	6.6	3,415	5.8	3,323	5.9
Failure to obey traffic signs, signals, or officer	1,990	3.9	1,912	4.3	2,354	4.0	3,189	5.7
Operating vehicle in erratic, reckless, or negligent manner[1]	1,955	3.8	2,438	5.5	—	—	—	—
Overcorrecting/oversteering	1,617	3.1	2,034	4.6	2,319	3.9	1,328	2.4
Vision obscured (rain, snow, glare, etc.)	1,540	3.0	1,426	3.2	1,496	2.5	1,309	2.3
Driving wrong way on one-way or on wrong side of road	1,243	2.4	1,356	3.1	858	1.5	1,387	2.5
Drowsy, asleep, fatigued, ill, or blackout	1,221	2.4	1,218	2.7	1,552	2.6	1,816	3.2
Swerving or avoiding due to wind, slippery surface, etc.	1,176	2.3	1,687	3.8	2,301	3.9	1,926	3.4
Making improper turn	635	1.2	970	2.2	1,590	2.7	1,253	2.2
Other factors	5,505	10.7	5,971	13.4	9,304	15.7	9,096	16.2
None reported.	9,167	17.8	13,521	30.4	21,265	36.0	20,443	36.4
Unknown.	16,012	31.1	3,408	7.7	1,187	2.0	990	1.8
Total drivers	**51,490**	**100.0**	**44,440**	**100.0**	**59,104**	**100.0**	**56,155**	**100.0**

— = Not available or not applicable. Note: For each year, the sum of the numbers and percentages is greater than total drivers as more than one factor may be present for the same driver. (1) In 1995 and 2005, the two categories were combined; "careless" not mentioned in factor in 2010. (2) "Inattentive (talking, eating, etc.)" in 1995, 2005.

U.S. Death Rates for Suicide at Selected Ages, 1960-2017
Source: *Health, United States, 2018*, National Center for Health Statistics (NCHS), CDC, U.S. Dept. of Health and Human Services
(deaths per 100,000 resident population)

Age	2017 Both sexes	2017 Male	2017 Female	2000 Both sexes	2000 Male	2000 Female	1980 Both sexes	1980 Male	1980 Female	1960 Both sexes	1960 Male	1960 Female
15-24 years.	14.5	22.7	5.8	10.2	17.1	3.0	12.3	20.2	4.3	5.2	8.2	2.2
25-44 years.	17.7	27.5	7.8	13.4	21.3	5.4	15.6	24.0	7.7	12.2	17.9	6.6
45-64 years.	19.6	30.1	9.7	13.5	21.3	6.2	15.9	23.7	8.9	22.0	34.4	10.2
65 years and older	16.8	31.4	5.2	15.2	31.1	4.0	17.6	35.0	6.1	24.5	44.0	8.4
All ages[1]	**14.0**	**22.4**	**6.1**	**10.4**	**17.7**	**4.0**	**12.2**	**19.9**	**5.7**	**12.5**	**20.0**	**5.6**

(1) Incl. ages not shown separately here.

Leading Causes of Death in the U.S., 2018
Source: National Vital Statistics System, National Center for Health Statistics, CDC, U.S. Dept. of Health and Human Services

Cause of death	Number	% of total deaths	Death rate[1]	Cause of death	Number	% of total deaths	Death rate[1]
All causes	2,839,205	100.0%	723.6	6. Alzheimer's disease	122,019	4.3%	30.5
1. Heart disease	655,381	23.1	163.6	7. Diabetes	84,946	3.0	21.4
2. Cancer	599,274	21.1	149.1	8. Influenza and pneumonia	59,120	2.1	14.9
3. Accidents (unintentional injuries)	167,127	5.9	48.0	9. Kidney disease	51,386	1.8	12.9
4. Chronic lower respiratory diseases	159,486	5.6	39.7	10. Suicide	48,344	1.7	14.2
5. Stroke	147,810	5.2	37.1	All other causes (residual)	744,312	26.2	—

— = Not applicable. (1) Per 100,000 U.S. population.

Overdose Deaths From Selected Drugs in the U.S., 1999-2018
Source: National Center on Health Statistics (NCHS), CDC WONDER, U.S. Dept. of Health and Human Services

	1999	2000	2005	2010	2012	2015	2016	2017	2018	Percent change 1999-2018	Percent change 2017-18
Total overdose deaths	16,849	17,415	29,813	38,329	41,502	52,404	63,632	70,237	67,367	299.8%	-4.1%
Female	5,591	5,852	11,089	15,323	16,390	19,447	22,074	23,685	22,426	301.1	-5.3
Male	11,258	11,563	18,724	23,006	25,112	32,957	41,558	46,552	44,941	299.2	-3.5
Any opioid	8,048	8,407	14,917	21,088	23,164	33,091	42,249	47,600	46,802	481.5	-1.7
Female	2,057	2,264	5,161	7,733	8,431	11,420	13,751	15,263	14,724	615.8	-3.5
Male	5,991	6,143	9,756	13,355	14,733	21,671	28,498	32,337	32,078	435.4	-0.8
Prescription opioids	3,442	3,785	9,612	14,583	14,240	15,281	17,087	17,029	14,975	335.1	-12.1
Other synthetic narcotics[1]	730	782	1,742	3,007	2,628	9,580	19,413	28,466	31,335	4,192.5	10.1
Heroin.	1,960	1,842	2,009	3,036	5,925	12,989	15,469	15,482	14,996	665.1	-3.1
Cocaine	3,822	3,544	6,208	4,183	4,404	6,784	10,375	13,942	14,666	283.7	5.2
Benzodiazepines	1,135	1,298	3,084	6,497	6,524	8,791	10,684	11,537	10,724	844.8	-7.0
Psychostimulants[2]	547	578	1,608	1,854	2,635	5,716	7,542	10,333	12,676	2,217.4	22.7
Antidepressants	1,749	1,798	2,861	3,889	4,259	4,894	4,812	5,269	5,064	189.5	-3.9

Note: Numbers include all deaths with underlying causes of drug poisoning, regardless of intent. (1) Synthetic narcotics other than methadone. This category is dominated by fentanyl-related overdoses. (2) This category, "Psychostimulants with abuse potential" is dominated by methamphetamine-related overdoses.

Drug-Induced Deaths in the U.S., 2018

Source: National Center on Health Statistics (NCHS), CDC WONDER, U.S. Dept. of Health and Human Services

Numbers include deaths from poisoning and medical conditions caused by use of legal or illegal drugs regardless of intent (accident, suicide, homicide, or undetermined).

State	Number	Rate[1]	State	Number	Rate[1]	State	Number	Rate[1]	State	Number	Rate[1]
Alabama.....	895	18.3	Illinois........	2,770	21.7	Montana.....	138	13.0	Rhode Island..	328	31.0
Alaska.....	119	16.1	Indiana......	1,684	25.2	Nebraska....	171	8.9	South Carolina	1,195	23.5
Arizona......	1,784	24.9	Iowa........	304	9.6	Nevada......	712	23.5	South Dakota..	59	6.7
Arkansas.....	475	15.8	Kansas......	371	12.7	New Hampshire	472	34.8	Tennessee ...	1,950	28.8
California ...	5,771	14.6	Kentucky.....	1,407	31.5	New Jersey...	2,980	33.5	Texas	3,163	11.0
Colorado.....	1,038	18.2	Louisiana	1,186	25.5	New Mexico ...	562	26.8	Utah	676	21.4
Connecticut...	1,105	30.9	Maine	364	27.2	New York.....	3,904	20.0	Vermont	161	25.7
Delaware.....	409	42.3	Maryland.....	2,385	39.5	North Carolina	2,340	22.5	Virginia	1,502	17.6
District of			Massachusetts	2,391	34.6	North Dakota..	76	10.0	Washington...	1,319	17.5
Columbia...	266	37.9	Michigan.....	2,840	28.4	Ohio	4,153	35.5	West Virginia..	926	51.3
Florida......	4,928	23.1	Minnesota.....	736	13.1	Oklahoma....	739	18.7	Wisconsin...	1,108	19.1
Georgia......	1,500	14.3	Mississippi ...	334	11.2	Oregon	678	16.2	Wyoming	67	11.6
Hawaii......	237	16.7	Missouri	1,660	27.1	Pennsylvania..	4,535	35.4	**U.S.**	**71,147**	**21.7**
Idaho........	274	15.6									

(1) Number of deaths due to drug-induced causes per 100,000 population.

Principal Types of Accidental Deaths in the U.S., 1970-2018

Source: National Safety Council website: injuryfacts.nsc.org; National Center for Health Statistics, U.S. Dept. of Health and Human Services

Year[1]	Total[2]	Motor vehicle	Falls	Poisoning	Choking: Inhalation of food, object	Drowning	Fires, flames, smoke	Mechanical suffocation	Firearms
1970	114,638	54,633	16,926	5,299	2,753	7,860	6,718	NA	2,406
1980	105,718	53,172	13,294	4,331	3,249	7,257	5,822	NA	1,955
1985	93,457	45,901	12,001	5,170	3,551	5,316	4,938	NA	1,649
1990	91,983	46,814	12,313	5,803	3,303	4,685	4,175	NA	1,416
1995	93,320	43,363	13,986	9,072	3,185	4,350	3,761	NA	1,225
2000	97,900	43,354	13,322	12,757	4,313	3,482	3,377	1,335	776
2005	117,809	45,343	19,656	23,617	4,386	3,582	3,197	1,514	789
2010	120,859	35,332	26,009	33,041	4,570	3,782	2,782	1,595	606
2012	127,792	36,415	28,756	36,332	4,634	3,551	2,464	1,604	548
2013	130,557	35,369	30,208	38,851	4,864	3,391	2,760	1,737	505
2014	135,928	35,398	31,959	42,032	4,816	3,406	2,701	1,764	461
2015	146,571	37,757	33,381	47,478	5,051	3,602	2,646	1,863	489
2016	161,374	40,327	34,673	58,335	4,829	3,789	2,730	1,781	495
2017	169,936	40,231	36,338	64,795	5,216	3,709	2,812	1,730	486
2018	167,127	39,404	37,455	62,399	5,084	3,710	2,972	1,617	458
Deaths per 100,000 population									
1970	56.2	26.8	8.3	2.6	1.4	3.9	3.3	NA	1.2
1980	46.5	23.4	5.9	1.9	1.4	3.2	2.6	NA	0.9
1985	39.3	19.3	5.0	2.2	1.5	2.2	2.1	NA	0.7
1990	36.9	18.8	4.9	2.3	1.3	1.9	1.7	NA	0.6
1995	35.5	16.5	5.3	3.4	1.2	1.7	1.4	NA	0.5
2000	35.6	15.7	4.8	4.6	1.6	1.3	1.2	0.5	0.3
2005	39.7	15.3	6.6	8.0	1.5	1.2	1.1	0.5	0.3
2010	39.0	11.4	8.4	10.7	1.5	1.2	0.9	0.5	0.2
2012	40.7	11.6	9.2	11.6	1.5	1.1	0.8	0.5	0.2
2013	41.3	11.2	9.6	12.3	1.5	1.1	0.9	0.5	0.2
2014	42.6	11.1	10.0	13.2	1.5	1.1	0.8	0.6	0.1
2015	45.6	11.7	10.4	14.8	1.6	1.1	0.8	0.6	0.2
2016	49.9	12.5	10.7	18.1	1.5	1.2	0.8	0.6	0.2
2017	52.2	12.4	11.2	19.9	1.6	1.1	0.9	0.5	0.2
2018	51.1	12.0	11.4	19.1	1.6	1.1	0.9	0.5	0.1

NA = Not available. **Note:** All figures include on-the-job deaths. (1) Data after 1999 are not comparable with earlier data because of classification changes. (2) Total incl. other accidental deaths not shown in detail here.

Deaths in the U.S. Involving Firearms by Age and Sex, 2018

Source: National Safety Council website: injuryfacts.nsc.org

Type and sex	All ages	Under 5	5-14	15-24	25-44	45-54	55-64	65-74	75 or older
Total firearms deaths	**39,740**	**98**	**437**	**7,411**	**14,127**	**5,323**	**5,353**	**3,662**	**3,328**
Male	33,955	67	308	6,524	12,039	4,329	4,474	3,149	3,064
Female	5,785	31	129	887	2,088	994	879	513	264
Preventable/accidental......	**458**	**30**	**24**	**129**	**125**	**45**	**51**	**34**	**20**
Male	413	26	19	120	114	41	44	32	17
Female	45	4	5	9	11	4	7	2	3
Suicide..................	**24,432**	**0**	**203**	**2,995**	**6,651**	**3,787**	**4,421**	**3,237**	**3,138**
Male	21,101	0	159	2,650	5,633	3,103	3,739	2,863	2,954
Female	3,331	0	44	345	1,018	684	682	374	184
Assault..................	**13,958**	**60**	**191**	**4,107**	**6,917**	**1,382**	**802**	**347**	**151**
Male	11,641	34	113	3,594	5,899	1,091	620	214	75
Female	2,317	26	78	513	1,018	291	182	133	76
Legal intervention..........	**539**	**0**	**0**	**87**	**308**	**67**	**55**	**18**	**4**
Male	516	0	0	83	297	63	52	17	4
Female	23	0	0	4	11	4	3	1	0
Undetermined[1]	**353**	**8**	**19**	**93**	**126**	**42**	**24**	**26**	**15**
Male	284	7	17	77	96	31	19	23	14
Female	69	1	2	16	30	11	5	3	1

(1) The intention of the death (unintentional/preventable, suicide, or homicide) could not be determined.

U.S. Infant Mortality Rates by Race and Sex, 1960-2018

Source: National Center for Health Statistics (NCHS), CDC, U.S. Dept. of Health and Human Services
(deaths of infants under 1 year old per 1,000 live births)

Year	All races[1]			White[2]			Black[2]		
	Both sexes	Male	Female	Both sexes	Male	Female	Both sexes	Male	Female
1960	26.0	29.3	22.6	22.9	26.0	19.6	44.3	49.1	39.4
1970	20.0	22.4	17.5	17.8	20.0	15.4	32.7	36.2	29.0
1980	12.6	13.9	11.2	10.9	12.1	9.5	22.2	24.2	20.2
1990	9.2	10.3	8.1	7.6	8.5	6.6	18.0	19.6	16.3
2000	6.9	7.6	6.2	5.7	6.3	5.1	14.1	15.5	12.7
2002	7.0	7.6	6.3	5.9	6.5	5.1	14.3	15.4	13.2
2003	6.8	7.6	6.1	5.7	6.4	5.0	14.2	15.7	12.6
2004	6.8	7.5	6.1	5.7	6.3	5.1	14.2	15.7	12.7
2005	6.9	7.6	6.2	5.7	6.7	4.8	14.3	15.8	12.8
2006	6.7	7.3	6.0	5.6	6.2	5.0	13.8	15.0	12.5
2007	6.8	7.4	6.1	5.6	6.2	5.0	13.8	15.0	12.4
2008	6.6	7.2	6.0	5.5	6.0	5.0	13.1	14.4	11.9
2009	6.4	7.0	5.8	5.3	5.8	4.7	13.1	14.6	11.5
2010	6.1	6.7	5.6	5.1	5.5	4.6	12.0	13.1	10.9
2011	6.1	6.6	5.5	5.1	5.5	4.6	12.0	13.1	10.8
2012	6.0	6.5	5.4	5.0	5.4	4.5	11.6	12.8	10.4
2013	6.0	6.5	5.4	5.0	5.5	4.4	11.6	12.5	10.7
2014	5.8	6.3	5.3	4.8	5.3	4.3	11.4	12.3	10.4
2015	5.9	6.4	5.4	4.8	5.3	4.4	11.7	12.8	10.7
2016	5.9	6.4	5.3	4.8	5.2	4.3	11.8	12.7	10.8
2017	5.8	6.3	5.2	4.7	5.1	4.1	11.0	12.6	10.3
2018	5.7	6.3	5.1	4.6	5.1	4.2	10.8	12.0	9.4

Note: Number of live births is tabulated according to mother's race (1980 and on) or parents' race (before 1980) stated on birth certificate. (1) Incl. races not shown. (2) Non-Hispanic.

Years of Life Expected at Birth in U.S., 1900-2017

Source: National Center for Health Statistics (NCHS), CDC, U.S. Dept. of Health and Human Services

Year	All races[1]			White[2]			Black[2,3]		
	Both sexes	Male	Female	Both sexes	Male	Female	Both sexes	Male	Female
1900[4]	47.3	46.3	48.3	47.6	46.6	48.7	33.0	32.5	33.5
1910[4]	50.0	48.4	51.8	50.3	48.6	52.0	35.6	33.8	37.5
1920[4]	54.1	53.6	54.6	54.9	54.4	55.6	45.3	45.5	45.2
1930	59.7	58.1	61.6	61.4	59.7	63.5	48.1	47.3	49.2
1940	62.9	60.8	65.2	64.2	62.1	66.6	53.1	51.5	54.9
1950	68.2	65.6	71.1	69.1	66.5	72.2	60.8	59.1	62.9
1960	69.7	66.6	73.1	70.6	67.4	74.1	63.6	61.1	66.3
1970	70.8	67.1	74.7	71.7	68.0	75.6	64.1	60.0	68.3
1980	73.7	70.0	77.4	74.4	70.7	78.1	68.1	63.8	72.5
1990	75.4	71.8	78.8	76.1	72.7	79.4	69.1	64.5	73.6
2000	76.8	74.1	79.3	77.3	74.7	79.9	71.8	68.2	75.1
2010	78.7	76.2	81.0	78.8	76.4	81.1	74.7	71.5	77.7
2011	78.7	76.3	81.1	78.7	76.4	81.1	75.0	71.8	77.8
2012	78.8	76.4	81.2	78.9	76.5	81.2	75.1	71.9	78.1
2013	78.8	76.4	81.2	78.8	76.5	81.2	75.1	71.9	78.1
2014	78.9	76.5	81.3	78.8	76.5	81.2	75.3	72.2	78.2
2015	78.7	76.3	81.1	78.7	76.3	81.1	75.1	71.9	78.1
2016	78.7	76.2	81.1	78.6	76.2	81.0	74.9	71.6	78.0
2017	78.6	76.1	81.1	78.5	76.1	81.0	74.9	71.5	78.1

(1) Includes races not shown. (2) Non-Hispanic beginning in 2010. (3) Data for 1900-60 are for the "nonwhite" pop. (4) Data prior to 1930 does not include all states.

U.S. Life Expectancy at Selected Ages, 2017

Source: National Center for Health Statistics (NCHS), CDC, U.S. Dept. of Health and Human Services

Exact age in years	All races[1]			White[2]			Black[2]		
	Both sexes	Male	Female	Both sexes	Male	Female	Both sexes	Male	Female
0	78.6	76.1	81.1	78.5	76.1	81.0	74.9	71.5	78.1
1	78.1	75.6	80.5	77.9	75.5	80.3	74.7	71.4	77.9
5	74.1	71.7	76.6	74.0	71.6	76.4	70.8	67.5	74.0
10	69.2	66.7	71.6	69.0	66.6	71.4	65.9	62.5	69.0
15	64.2	61.8	66.7	64.0	61.7	66.4	61.0	57.6	64.1
20	59.4	57.0	61.8	59.2	56.9	61.5	56.2	53.0	59.2
25	54.7	52.4	56.9	54.5	52.2	56.7	51.6	48.5	54.4
30	50.0	47.8	52.1	49.8	47.7	51.9	47.0	44.1	49.6
35	45.3	43.2	47.3	45.2	43.2	47.2	42.5	39.7	44.9
40	40.7	38.7	42.6	40.6	38.6	42.5	38.0	35.3	40.3
45	36.1	34.2	37.9	36.0	34.2	37.8	33.6	31.0	35.8
50	31.6	29.8	33.4	31.6	29.8	33.3	29.3	26.9	31.4
55	27.4	25.6	28.9	27.3	25.6	28.8	25.2	23.0	27.2
60	23.3	21.7	24.7	23.2	21.7	24.6	21.5	19.4	23.3
65	19.4	18.0	20.6	19.3	18.0	20.5	18.1	16.2	19.5
70	15.7	14.5	16.7	15.6	14.5	16.6	14.9	13.3	16.0
75	12.3	11.3	13.0	12.2	11.2	12.9	11.9	10.6	12.7
80	9.2	8.4	9.8	9.1	8.3	9.7	9.2	8.1	9.8
85	6.6	5.9	7.0	6.5	5.9	6.9	6.9	6.1	7.3
90	4.5	4.1	4.8	4.5	4.0	4.7	5.0	4.5	5.2
95	3.1	2.8	3.2	3.0	2.7	3.2	3.6	3.3	3.7
100	2.2	2.0	2.2	2.1	1.9	2.2	2.7	2.5	2.7

(1) Includes races not shown. (2) Non-Hispanic.

NOTED PERSONALITIES

Widely Known Americans of the Present

Political leaders, journalists, other prominent living persons. As of Oct. 2020. Excludes most who fall in categories listed elsewhere in Noted Personalities, such as Writers of the Present and Entertainment Personalities of the Present. Includes some figures who are active in American life but are not U.S. citizens.

Stacey Abrams, b 12/9/1973 (Madison, WI), former GA House minority leader (D).

Sheldon Adelson, b 8/4/1933 (Dorchester, MA), Las Vegas Sands founder, CEO.

Madeleine K. Albright, b 5/15/1937 (Prague, Czech.), former sec. of state.

Edwin "Buzz" Aldrin, b 1/20/1930 (Montclair, NJ), former astronaut, second person to walk on the Moon.

Samuel A. Alito Jr., b 4/1/1950 (Trenton, NJ), U.S. Supreme Court justice.

Marin Alsop, b 10/16/1956 (New York, NY), Baltimore Symphony musical dir.

Christiane Amanpour, b 1/12/1958 (London, Eng., UK), TV journalist.

Marc Andreessen, b 7/9/1971 (New Lisbon, IA), co-author of web browser Mosaic, cofounder of Netscape.

David Axelrod, b 2/22/1955 (New York, NY), political strategist; former sr. adviser to Pres. Obama.

F. Lee Bailey, b 6/10/1933 (Waltham, MA), attorney.

James Baker, b 4/28/1930 (Houston, TX), former sec. of state.

Robert Ballard, b 6/30/1942 (Wichita, KS), oceanographer; found wreck of the *Titanic.*

Steve Ballmer, b 3/24/1956 (Detroit, MI), former Microsoft CEO; L.A. Clippers owner.

Steve Bannon, b 11/27/1953 (Norfolk, VA), former chief strategist to Pres. Trump, Breitbart News exec.

Mike Barnicle, b 8/24/1944 (Fitchburg, MA), columnist.

William Barr, b 5/23/1950 (New York, NY), U.S. atty. gen. (1991-93, 2019-).

Mary Barra, b 12/24/1961 (Waterford, MI), General Motors CEO.

Amy Coney Barrett, b 1/28/1972 (New Orleans, LA), U.S. Supreme Court nominee.

Dave Barry, b 7/3/1947 (Armonk, NY), humorist.

Glenn Beck, b 2/10/1964 (Mount Vernon, WA), political commentator.

Michael Bennet, b 11/28/1964 (New Delhi, India), U.S. sen. (D, CO), 2020 pres. contender.

Chris Berman, b 5/10/1955 (Greenwich, CT), sportscaster.

Ben Bernanke, b 12/13/1953 (Augusta, GA), former Federal Reserve chair.

Carl Bernstein, b 2/14/1944 (Washington, DC), journalist; with Bob Woodward cracked Watergate scandal.

Jeff Bezos, b 1/12/1964 (Albuquerque, NM), founder and CEO of Amazon.

Jill Biden, b 6/5/1951 (Hammonton, NJ), professor, wife of former U.S. vice pres. Joe Biden.

Joseph R. Biden Jr., b 11/20/1942 (Scranton, PA), former U.S. vice pres., sen. (D, DE); 2020 pres. nominee.

Deborah Birx, b 4/4/1956 (Baltimore, MD), physician, White House coronavirus response coordinator.

Wolf Blitzer, b 3/22/1948 (Augsburg, Germany), TV journalist.

Michael R. Bloomberg, b 2/14/1942 (Brighton, MA), former NYC mayor, financial information/media entrepreneur.

Charles M. Blow, b 8/11/1970 (Gibsland, LA), columnist.

Cory Booker, b 4/27/1969 (Washington, DC), U.S. sen. (D, NJ), former Newark mayor; 2020 pres. contender.

Andy Borowitz, b 1/4/1958 (Cleveland, OH), humorist.

Donna Brazile, b 12/15/1959 (Kenner, LA), political analyst.

Stephen Breyer, b 8/15/1938 (San Francisco, CA), U.S. Supreme Court justice.

Sergey Brin, b 8/21/1973 (Moscow, Russia), cofounder of Google.

Tom Brokaw, b 2/6/1940 (Webster, SD), TV journalist, retired anchor.

David Brooks, b 8/11/1961 (Toronto, ON, Can.), columnist, political commentator.

Aaron Brown, b 11/10/1948 (Hopkins, MN), broadcast journalist.

Jerry (Edmund G.) Brown Jr., b 4/7/1938 (San Francisco, CA), CA gov. (D, 1975-83, 2011-19); former pres. candidate.

Frank Bruni, b 10/31/1964 (White Plains, NY), columnist.

Pat Buchanan, b 11/2/1938 (Washington, DC), journalist, former pres. candidate (R).

Warren Buffett, b 8/30/1930 (Omaha, NE), investor, leading philanthropist.

Lonnie Bunch III, b 11/18/1952 (Newark, NJ), Smithsonian Institution sec.

Tarana Burke, b 9/12/1973 (New York, NY), activist who started #metoo movement.

Barbara Bush, b 11/25/1981 (Dallas, TX), daughter of former pres. George W. Bush.

George W. Bush, b 7/6/1946 (New Haven, CT), 43rd U.S. president.

Jeb Bush, b 2/11/1953 (Midland, TX), former FL gov. (R); 2016 pres. contender.

Laura Bush, b 11/4/1946 (Midland, TX), former first lady.

Pete Buttigieg, b 1/19/1982 (South Bend, IN), former South Bend mayor; 2020 pres. contender (D).

Gretchen Carlson, b 6/21/1966 (Anoka, MN), TV journalist.

Tucker Carlson, b 5/16/1969 (San Francisco, CA), TV commentator.

Jimmy Carter, b 10/1/1924 (Plains, GA), 39th U.S. president; 2002 Nobel Peace Prize winner.

Rosalynn Carter, b 8/18/1927 (Plains, GA), former first lady.

Joaquin Castro, b 9/16/1974 (San Antonio, TX), U.S. rep. (D, TX).

Julián Castro, b 9/16/1974 (San Antonio, TX), fmr. housing and urban dev. sec.; 2020 pres. contender (D).

Dick Cheney, b 1/30/1941 (Lincoln, NE), former U.S. vice president.

Lynne Cheney, b 8/14/1941 (Casper, WY), political commentator, wife of former U.S. vice pres. Dick Cheney.

Brian Chesky, b 8/29/1981 (Niskayuna, NY), Airbnb founder, CEO.

Judy Chicago, b 7/20/1939 (Chicago, IL), artist.

Dale Chihuly, b 9/20/1941 (Tacoma, WA), glass sculptor.

Noam Chomsky, b 12/7/1928 (Philadelphia, PA), linguist, activist.

Chris Christie, b 9/6/1962 (Newark, NJ), former NJ gov. (R); 2016 pres. contender.

Connie Chung, b 8/20/1946 (Washington, DC), former TV journalist.

Bill Clinton, b 8/19/1946 (Hope, AR), 42nd U.S. president.

Chelsea Clinton, b 2/27/1980 (Little Rock, AR), daughter of former pres. Bill Clinton and Hillary Clinton.

Hillary Rodham Clinton, b 10/26/1947 (Chicago, IL), former sec. of state, U.S. sen. (D, NY), first lady; 2016 presidential nominee.

Kate Clinton, b 11/9/1947 (Buffalo, NY), political humorist.

Jim Clyburn, b 7/21/1940 (Sumter, SC), House majority whip (D, MD).

Michael Cohen, b 8/25/1966 (Lawrence, NY), former atty. to Pres. Trump.

Kenneth Cole, b 3/23/1954 (Brooklyn, NY), fashion designer.

Gail Collins, b 11/25/1945 (Cincinnati, OH), newspaper columnist, writer.

Jason Collins, b 12/2/1978 (Northridge, CA), first openly gay active NBA player.

James Comey, b 12/14/1960 (Yonkers, NY), former FBI director.

Kellyanne Conway, b 1/20/1967 (Camden, NJ), counselor to Pres. Trump.

Tim Cook, b 11/1/1960 (Robertdale, AZ), CEO of Apple Inc.

Anderson Cooper, b 6/3/1967 (New York, NY), TV news anchor.

Bob Costas, b 3/22/1952 (Astoria, Queens, NY), TV sports journalist.

Ann Coulter, b 12/8/1961 (New Canaan, CT), political commentator, author.

Katie Couric, b 1/7/1957 (Arlington, VA), TV and online journalist.

Candy Crowley, b 12/12/1948 (Kalamazoo, MI), TV journalist.

Ted Cruz, b 12/22/1970 (Calgary, AB, Can.), U.S. sen. (R, TX); 2016 pres. contender.

Mark Cuban, b 7/31/1958 (Pittsburgh, PA), entrepreneur, Dallas Mavericks owner.

Andrew Cuomo, b 12/6/1957 (New York, NY), NY gov. (D); former state atty. gen.

Chris Cuomo, b 8/9/1970 (Queens, NY), TV journalist.

Ann Curry, b 11/19/1956 (Guam), TV journalist.

Bill de Blasio, b 5/8/1961 (New York, NY), NYC mayor (D); 2020 pres. contender.

Michael Dell, b 2/23/1965 (Houston, TX), founder and CEO of tech giant Dell.

Alan Dershowitz, b 9/1/1938 (Brooklyn, NY), attorney, political commentator.

Betsy DeVos, b 1/8/1958 (Holland, MI), education sec., philanthropist.

José Díaz-Balart, b 11/7/1960 (Fort Lauderdale, FL), TV journalist.

Barry Diller, b 2/2/1942 (San Francisco, CA), media exec.

Jamie Dimon, b 3/13/1956 (New York, NY), chair, CEO of JPMorgan Chase.

Lou Dobbs, b 9/24/1945 (Childress, TX), TV journalist.

James Dobson, b 4/21/1936 (Shreveport, LA), evangelical Christian leader.

Timothy Dolan, b 2/6/1950 (St. Louis, MO), Rom. Cath. cardinal, archbishop of NY.

Robert Dole, b 7/22/1923 (Russell, KS), former U.S. Senate majority leader (R, KS), 1996 pres. nominee.

Jack Dorsey, b 11/19/1976 (St. Louis, MO), Twitter cofounder.

Maureen Dowd, b 1/14/1952 (Washington, DC), columnist.

Elizabeth Drew, b 11/16/1935 (Cincinnati, OH), journalist.

Matt Drudge, b 10/27/1966 (Takoma Park, MD), Drudge Report founder/editor.

Michael S. Dukakis, b 11/3/1933 (Brookline, MA), former MA gov. (D), 1988 pres. nominee.

David Duke, b 7/1/1950 (Tulsa, OK), white nationalist activist; politician.

Dick Durbin, b 11/21/1944 (East St. Louis, IL), U.S. Senate minority whip (D, IL).

Sylvia Earle, b 8/30/1935 (Gibbstown, NJ), marine biologist.

Marian Wright Edelman, b 6/6/1939 (Bennettsville, SC), Children's Defense Fund founder.

Michael Eisner, b 3/7/1942 (Mt. Kisco, NY), former Disney Co. CEO.

Lawrence J. Ellison, b 8/17/1944 (New York, NY), Oracle Corp. cofounder.

Rahm Emanuel, b 11/29/1959 (Chicago, IL), fmr. Chicago mayor, Obama chief of staff, U.S. rep. (D, IL).

Myrlie Evers-Williams, b 3/17/1933 (Vicksburg, MS), civil rights activist.

Louis Farrakhan, b 5/11/1933 (Roxbury, MA), Nation of Islam leader.

Ronan Farrow, b 12/19/1987 (New York, NY), investigative journalist.

Anthony Fauci, b 12/24/1940 (New York, NY), physician, National Institute of Allergy and Infectious Diseases dir.

Michael Flynn, b 12/1/1958 (Middletown, RI), U.S. Army gen. (ret.); briefly Pres. Trump's natl. security adviser.

Larry Flynt, b 11/1/1942 (Lakeville, KY), publisher.

Steve (Malcolm) Forbes Jr., b 7/18/1947 (Morristown, NJ), publisher, former pres. contender.

Christine Blasey Ford, b 11/28/1966 (Potomac, MD), professor; complainant against U.S. Supreme Court justice Brett Kavanaugh.

Tom Ford, b 8/27/1961 (Austin, TX), fashion designer, director.

Thomas Friedman, b 7/20/1953 (Minneapolis, MN), columnist, author.

Tulsi Gabbard, b 4/12/1981 (Leloaloa, Amer. Samoa), U.S. rep (D, HI); 2020 pres. contender.

Bill Gates, b 10/28/1955 (Seattle, WA), software pioneer; Microsoft exec.

Henry Louis Gates Jr., b 9/16/1950 (Keyser, WV), African American studies scholar.

Melinda Gates, b 8/15/1964 (Dallas, TX), philanthropist.

David Geffen, b 2/21/1943 (Brooklyn, NY), entertainment exec.

Charles Gibson, b 3/4/1943 (Evanston, IL), TV journalist.

Gabrielle Giffords, b 6/8/1970 (Tucson, AZ), former U.S. rep. (D, AZ); shot in 2011 assassination attempt.

Kirsten Gillibrand, b 12/9/1966 (Albany, NY), U.S. sen. (D, NY); 2020 pres. contender.

Newt Gingrich, b 6/17/1943 (Harrisburg, PA), former House speaker (R, GA); 2012 pres. contender.

Rudolph Giuliani, b 5/28/1944 (Brooklyn, NY), atty. for Pres. Trump, former NYC mayor (R).

Ira Glass, b 3/3/1959 (Baltimore, MD), radio host.

Roger Goodell, b 2/19/1959 (Jamestown, NY), NFL commissioner.

Ellen Goodman, b 4/11/1941 (Newton, MA), columnist.

Doris Kearns Goodwin, b 1/4/1943 (Brooklyn, NY), historian, TV commentator.

Berry Gordy, b 11/28/1929 (Detroit, MI), Motown record label founder.

Al Gore Jr., b 3/31/1948 (Washington, DC), former U.S. sen. (D, TN), vice pres., 2000 pres. nominee.

Lindsey Graham, b 7/9/1955 (Central, SC), U.S. sen. (R, SC); 2016 pres. contender.

Temple Grandin, b 8/29/1947 (Boston, MA), animal behavioral scientist, autism activist.

Chuck Grassley, b 9/17/1933 (New Hartford, IA), U.S. sen. (R, IA) and Senate pres. pro tempore.

Jeff Greenfield, b 6/10/1943 (New York, NY), TV journalist.

Alan Greenspan, b 3/6/1926 (New York, NY), former Federal Reserve chair.

Savannah Guthrie, b 12/27/1971 (Melbourne, Vic., Australia), TV journalist.

Jenna Bush Hager, b 11/25/1981 (Dallas, TX), daughter of former pres. George W. Bush; TV personality.

Nikki Haley, b 1/20/1972 (Bamberg, SC), fmr. U.S. ambassador to UN, SC gov. (R).

Carla Hall, b 5/12/1964 (Nashville, TN), chef, TV personality.

Nikole Hannah-Jones, b 4/9/1976 (Waterloo, IA), journalist.

Sean Hannity, b 12/30/1961 (New York, NY), radio and TV host, author, political commentator.

Kamala Harris, b 10/20/1964 (Oakland, CA), U.S. sen. (D, CA); 2020 vice-pres. nominee.

Reed Hastings, b 10/8/1960 (Boston, MA), founder, CEO Netflix, Inc.

Carla Hayden, b 8/10/1952 (Tallahassee, FL), librarian of U.S. Congress.

John Hickenlooper, b 2/7/1952 (Narbeth, PA), former CO gov. (D); 2020 pres. contender; 2020 sen. nominee.

Tommy Hilfiger, b 3/24/1951 (Elmira, NY), fashion designer.

Anita Hill, b 7/30/1956 (Morris, OK), legal scholar; complainant against U.S. Supreme Court justice Clarence Thomas.

Paris Hilton, b 2/17/1981 (New York, NY), heiress, actress.

Perez Hilton, b 3/23/1978 (Miami, FL), gossip columnist.

James P. Hoffa, b 5/19/1941 (Detroit, MI), Teamsters Union head.

Larry Hogan, b 5/25/1956 (Washington, DC), MD gov. (R).

Eric Holder Jr., b 1/21/1951 (Bronx, NY), former U.S. atty. gen.

Lester Holt, b 3/8/1959 (San Francisco, CA), TV journalist.

David Horowitz, b 1/10/1939 (New York, NY), consumer advocate, columnist, author.

Steny H. Hoyer, b 6/14/1939 (New York, NY), House majority leader (D, MD).

Mike Huckabee, b 8/24/1955 (Hope, AR), former AR gov. (R), TV host, pres. contender (2008, '16).

Dolores Huerta, b 4/10/1930 (Dawson, NM), labor activist.

Arianna Huffington, b 7/15/1950 (Athens, Greece), political commentator.

H. Wayne Huizenga, b 12/29/1939 (Evergreen Park, IL), entrepreneur, sports exec.

Brit Hume, b 6/22/1943 (Washington, DC), TV journalist.

Carl Icahn, b 2/16/1936 (Brooklyn, NY), financier.

Bob Iger, b 2/10/1951 (Oceanside, NY), Walt Disney Co. CEO.

Jay Inslee, b 2/9/1951 (Seattle, WA), WA gov. (D); 2020 pres. contender.

Jesse Jackson, b 10/8/1941 (Greenville, SC), civil rights leader, former pres. contender (D).

Marc Jacobs, b 4/9/1964 (New York, NY), fashion designer.

Jasper Johns, b 5/15/1930 (Augusta, GA), painter, printmaker.

Robert L. Johnson, b 4/8/1946 (Hickory, MS), Black Entertainment Television co-founder.

Sheila Johnson, b 1/25/1949 (PA), Black Entertainment Television co-founder.

Alex Jones, b 2/11/1974 (Dallas, TX), InfoWars creator, radio host.

Cleve Jones, b 10/11/1954 (W. Lafayette, IN), AIDS and LGBTQ rights activist.

Vernon E. Jordan Jr., b 8/15/1935 (Atlanta, GA), attorney, former pres. adviser.

Colin Kaepernick, b 11/3/1987 (Milwaukee, WI), football player, activist.

Elena Kagan, b 4/28/1960 (New York, NY), U.S. Supreme Court justice.

Tim Kaine, b 2/26/1958 (St. Paul, MN), U.S. sen. (D, VA). 2016 vice-pres. nominee.

Travis Kalanick, b 8/6/1976 (Los Angeles, CA), Uber cofounder and former CEO.

Donna Karan, b 10/2/1948 (Forest Hills, Queens, NY), fashion designer.

John Kasich, b 5/13/1952 (McKees Rocks, PA), fmr. OH gov. (R); 2016 pres. contender.

Jeffrey Katzenberg, b 12/21/1950 (New York, NY), entertainment exec.

Brett Kavanaugh, b 2/12/1965 (Washington, DC), U.S. Supreme Court justice.

Garrison Keillor, b 8/7/1942 (Anoka, MN), author, broadcaster.

John F. Kelly, b 5/11/1950 (Boston, MA), former Trump White House chief of staff; U.S. Marine gen. (ret.).

Mark Kelly, b 2/21/1964 (Orange, NJ), former NASA shuttle commander; 2020 U.S. sen. (D, AZ) nominee.

Megyn Kelly, b 11/18/1970 (Syracuse, NY), TV commentator, host.

Anthony M. Kennedy, b 7/23/1936 (Sacramento, CA), former U.S. Supreme Court justice.

John Kerry, b 12/11/1943 (Aurora, CO), former sec. of state, U.S. sen. (D, MA); 2004 pres. nominee.

Gayle King, b 12/28/1954 (Chevy Chase, MD), TV and magazine journalist.

Larry King, b 11/19/1933 (Brooklyn, NY), TV talk-show host.

Henry Kissinger, b 5/27/1923 (Furth, Germany), former sec. of state.

Calvin Klein, b 11/19/1942 (Bronx, NY), fashion designer.

Amy Klobuchar, b 5/25/1960 (Plymouth, MN), U.S. sen. (D, MN); 2020 pres. contender.

Philip H. Knight, b 2/24/1938 (Portland, OR), founder and chair emeritus of Nike.

Charles G. Koch, b 5/3/1940 (Wichita, KS), Koch Industries exec.; philanthropist.

Sarah Koenig, b 7/9/1969 (New York, NY), radio journalist.

Jeff Koons, b 1/21/1955 (York, PA), artist.

Ted Koppel, b 2/8/1940 (Lancashire, Eng., UK), former TV journalist.

Michael Kors, b 8/9/1959 (Merrick, NY), fashion designer.

Hoda Kotb, b 8/9/1964 (Norman, OK), TV journalist.

Nicholas D. Kristof, b 4/27/1959 (Chicago, IL), columnist, author.

William Kristol, b 12/23/1952 (New York, NY), editor, columnist.

Steve Kroft, b 8/22/1945 (Kokomo, IN), TV journalist.

Paul Krugman, b 2/28/1953 (Albany, NY), economist, columnist.

Jared Kushner, b 1/10/1981 (Livingston, NJ), Trump senior adviser; real estate developer.

Brian Lamb, b 10/9/1941 (Lafayette, IN), cable TV exec., founder.

Wayne LaPierre Jr., b 11/8/1949 (Schenectady, NY), National Rifle Assn. exec. VP.

Matt Lauer, b 12/30/1957 (New York, NY), TV journalist.

Ralph Lauren, b 10/14/1939 (Bronx, NY), fashion designer.

Norman Lear, b 7/27/1922 (New Haven, CT), TV producer, political activist.

Annie Leibovitz, b 10/2/1949 (Waterbury, CT), photographer.

Monica Lewinsky, b 7/23/1973 (San Francisco, CA), former White House intern.

Rush Limbaugh, b 1/12/1951 (Cape Girardeau, MO), radio talk-show host.

Shannon Lucid, b 1/14/1943 (Shanghai, China), NASA scientist, astronaut.

Loretta Lynch, b 5/21/1959 (Greensboro, NC), former U.S. atty. gen.

Rachel Maddow, b 4/1/1973 (Castro Valley, CA), TV/radio host, political commentator.

Bernie Madoff, b 4/29/1938 (Queens, NY), financier who swindled investors; sentenced to 150 years in prison.

Michelle Malkin, b 10/20/1980 (Philadelphia, PA), political commentator.

Rob Manfred, b 9/28/1958 (Rome, NY), MLB commissioner.

Chelsea Manning, b 12/17/1987 (Crescent, OK), Army pvt. convicted on espionage charges.

Ruth Marcus, b 5/15/1958 (Philadelphia, PA), columnist.

Meghan Markle (Duchess of Sussex), b 8/4/1981 (Los Angeles, CA), wife of UK's Prince Harry, actress.

Chris Matthews, b 12/17/1945 (Philadelphia, PA), TV journalist.

James Mattis, b 9/8/1950 (Pullman, WA), fmr. defense sec.; U.S. Marine gen. (ret.).

Peter Max, b 10/19/1937 (Berlin, Germany), artist.

Marissa Mayer, b 5/30/1975 (Wausau, WI), former Yahoo CEO.

Kevin McCarthy, b 1/26/1965 (Bakersfield, CA), U.S. rep. (R, CA), House minority leader.

Mitch McConnell, b 2/20/1942 (Tuscumbia, AL), U.S. sen. majority leader (R, KY).

David McCullough, b 7/7/1933 (Pittsburgh, PA), historian, biographer.

Ronna Romney McDaniel, b 1973 (Austin, TX), Rep. Natl. Committee chair.

Kayleigh McEnany, b 4/18/1988 (Tampa, FL), White House press secretary.

Dr. Phil McGraw, b 9/1/1950 (Vinita, OK), talk-show host, motivational speaker, author.

Mark Meadows, b 7/28/1959 (Verdun, France), White House Chief of Staff; fmr. U.S. rep. (R, NC).

Lorne Michaels, b 11/17/44 (Toronto, ON, Canada), creator and producer of *Saturday Night Live*.

Kate Michelman, b 8/4/1942 (NJ), activist.

George Mitchell, b 8/20/1933 (Waterville, ME), former U.S. Sen. majority leader (D, ME), diplomat, Disney Co. chair.

Steven Mnuchin, b 12/21/1962 (New York, NY), Treasury sec.

Walter Mondale, b 1/5/1928 (Ceylon, MN), former vice pres., U.S. sen. (D, MN), 1984 pres. nominee.

Michael Moore, b 4/23/1954 (Davison, MI), activist, documentary filmmaker, author.

Bill Moyers, b 6/5/1934 (Hugo, OK), TV journalist, author.

Robert S. Mueller III, b 8/7/1944 (New York, NY), special counsel who investigated Russian interference in 2016 U.S. elections; former FBI director.

David Muir, b 11/8/1973 (Syracuse, NY), TV news anchor.

Mick Mulvaney, b 7/21/1967 (Alexandria, VA), fmr. acting White House Chief of Staff, Office of Management and Budget dir.

Rupert Murdoch, b 3/11/1931 (Melbourne, Vic., Austral.), media exec.

Bobby Murphy, b 7/19/1988 (Berkeley, CA), Snapchat cofounder.

Elon Musk, b 6/28/1971 (Pretoria, S. Afr.), SpaceX and Tesla CEO.

Satya Nadella, b 8/19/1967 (Hyderabad, India), Microsoft CEO.

Ralph Nader, b 2/27/1934 (Winsted, CT), consumer advocate, independent pres. cand. (1996, 2000, '04, '08).

Craig Newmark, b 12/6/1952 (Morristown, NJ), founder of Craigslist.com.

Gavin Newsom, b 10/10/1967 (San Francisco, CA), CA gov. (D).

Peggy Noonan, b 9/7/1950 (Brooklyn, NY), columnist, speechwriter.

Oliver North, b 10/7/1943 (San Antonio, TX), former NRA pres.; Natl. Sec. Council aide, figure in Iran-contra scandal.

Eleanor Holmes Norton, b 6/13/1937 (Washington, DC), DC delegate to U.S. House (D).

Barack Obama, b 8/4/1961 (Honolulu, HI), 44th U.S. president, former U.S. sen. (D, IL).

Michelle Obama, b 1/17/1964 (Chicago, IL), former first lady, lawyer.

Soledad O'Brien, b 9/19/1966 (Smithtown, NY), TV journalist.

Alexandria Ocasio-Cortez, b 10/13/1989 (Bronx, NY), U.S. rep. (D, NY).

Sandra Day O'Connor, b 3/26/1930 (El Paso, TX), former Supreme Court justice.

Keith Olbermann, b 1/27/1959 (New York, NY), political commentator, former ESPN/MSNBC host.

Todd Oldham, b 11/22/1961 (Corpus Christi, TX), fashion designer.

Ilhan Omar, b 10/4/1981 (Mogadishu, Somalia), U.S. rep. (D, MN).

Bill O'Reilly, b 9/10/1949 (New York, NY), TV personality.

Suze Orman, b 5/5/1951 (Chicago, IL), financial adviser, TV host.

Beto O'Rourke, b 9/26/1972 (El Paso, TX), former U.S. rep. (D, TX); 2020 pres. contender.

Joel Osteen, b 3/5/1963 (Houston, TX), televangelist, author.

Michael Ovitz, b 12/14/1946 (Encino, CA), entertainment exec.

Candace Owens, b 4/29/1989 (Stamford, CT), political activist.

Clarence Page, b 6/2/1947 (Dayton, OH), journalist, TV commentator.

Lawrence Page, b 3/26/1973 (East Lansing, MI), cofounder of Google.

Camille Paglia, b 4/2/1947 (Endicott, NY), scholar, author.

Sarah Palin, b 2/11/1964 (Sandpoint, ID), former AK gov. (R), 2008 vice-pres. nominee.

Leon E. Panetta, b 6/28/1938 (Monterey, CA), former sec. of defense, CIA director, Obama chief of staff, U.S. rep. (D, CA).

Sean Parker, b 12/3/1979 (Herndon, VA), cofounder of Napster, Facebook.

Rand Paul, b 1/7/1963 (Pittsburgh, PA), U.S. sen. (R, KY); 2016 pres. contender.

Jane Pauley, b 10/31/1950 (Indianapolis, IN), TV journalist.

Nancy Pelosi, b 3/26/1940 (Baltimore, MD), U.S. Speaker of the House (D, CA).

Karen Pence, b 1/1/1957 (Indianapolis, IN), wife of U.S. vice pres. Mike Pence.

Mike Pence, b 6/7/1959 (Columbus, IN), U.S. vice pres., former IN gov. (R).

Tom Perez, b 10/7/1961 (Buffalo, NY), Dem. Natl. Committee chair; former sec. of labor.

David Petraeus, b 11/7/1952 (Cornwall-on-Hudson, NY), former CIA director, CENTCOM cmdr.

Alexandra Petri, b 3/15/1988 (WI), columnist.

Mike Pompeo, b 12/30/1963 (Orange, CA), sec. of state; former CIA director.

Colin Powell, b 4/5/1937 (New York, NY), former sec. of state, natl. security adviser, Joint Chiefs of Staff chair.

Jerome Powell, b 2/4/1953 (Washington, DC), Federal Reserve chair.

Reince Priebus, b 3/18/1972 (Kenosha, WI), former White House chief of staff, Rep. Natl. Committee chair.

Dan Quayle, b 2/4/1947 (Indianapolis, IN), former U.S. vice pres., U.S. sen. (R, IN).

Anna Quindlen, b 7/8/1953 (Philadelphia, PA), author, columnist.

Martha Raddatz, b 1953 (Idaho Falls, ID), TV journalist.

Jorge Ramos, b 3/15/1958 (Mexico City, Mex.), TV journalist.

Dan Rather, b 10/31/1931 (Wharton, TX), TV journalist, retired anchor.

Robert Redfield, b 7/15/1951, Centers for Disease Control and Prevention dir.

Ralph Reed Jr., b 6/24/1961 (Portsmouth, VA), political adviser.

Robert B. Reich, b 6/24/1946 (Scranton, PA), economist, author, former labor sec.

Condoleezza Rice, b 11/14/1954 (Birmingham, AL), former sec. of state, natl. security adviser.

Frank Rich, b 6/2/1949 (Washington, DC), essayist, columnist.

John G. Roberts, b 1/27/1955 (Buffalo, NY), U.S. Supreme Court chief justice.

Robin Roberts, b 11/23/1960 (Tuskegee, AL), *Good Morning America* co-host.

Pat Robertson, b 3/22/1930 (Lexington, VA), religious broadcasting exec., former pres. contender (R).

Eugene Robinson, b 3/12/1954 (Orangeburg, SC), columnist.

V. Gene Robinson, b 5/29/1947 (Lexington, KY), first openly gay Episcopal bishop (retired).

Al Roker, b 8/20/1954 (Queens, NY), TV weather person.

Mitt Romney, b 3/12/1947 (Detroit, MI), U.S. sen. (R, UT); 2012 pres. nominee, former MA gov.

Charlie Rose, b 1/5/1942 (Henderson, NC), TV journalist.

Rod Rosenstein, b 1/13/65 (Philadelphia, PA), fmr. U.S. deputy atty. gen.

Karl Rove, b 12/25/1950 (Denver, CO), former adviser to Pres. G. W. Bush, political commentator.

Marco Rubio, b 5/28/1971 (Miami, FL), U.S. sen. (R, FL); 2016 pres. contender.

Donald Rumsfeld, b 7/9/1932 (Chicago, IL), former sec. of defense.

Edward Ruscha, b 12/16/1937 (Omaha, NE), artist.

Paul Ryan, b 1/29/1970 (Janesville, WI), 2012 vice-pres. nominee, former U.S. rep. (R, WI) and House Speaker.

Sheryl Sandberg, b 8/28/1969 (Washington, DC), Facebook exec.; author.

Bernie Sanders, b 9/8/1941 (New York, NY), U.S. sen. (I, VT); 2016 and 2020 Dem. pres. contender.

Sarah Huckabee Sanders, b 8/13/1982 (Hope, AR), TV commentator; fmr. White House press sec.

Mark Sanford, b 5/28/1960 (Ft. Lauderdale, FL), fmr. SC gov., U.S. rep. (R); 2020 pres. contender.

Diane Sawyer, b 12/22/1945 (Glasgow, KY), TV journalist.

Stephen Scalise, b 10/6/1965 (New Orleans, LA), U.S. rep. (R, LA), House minority whip.

Bob Schieffer, b 2/25/1937 (Austin, TX), TV journalist.

Caroline Kennedy Schlossberg, b 11/27/1957 (New York, NY), author, daughter of Pres. Kennedy.

Eric Schmidt, b 4/27/1955 (Washington, DC), former Google CEO.

Charles Schumer, b 11/23/1950 (Brooklyn, NY), U.S. sen. minority leader (D, NY).

Arnold Schwarzenegger, b 7/30/1947 (Thal, Styria, Austria), actor, former CA gov. (R).

Willard Scott, b 3/7/1934 (Alexandria, VA), former TV weather person.

Richard Serra, b 11/2/1939 (San Francisco, CA), sculptor.

Jeff Sessions, b 12/24/1946 (Selma, AL), fmr. U.S. atty. gen., U.S. sen. (R, AL).

Al Sharpton, b 10/3/1954 (Brooklyn, NY), activist, civil rights leader, TV personality.

Amy Sherald, b 8/30/1973 (Columbus, GA), artist.

Will Shortz, b 8/26/1952 (Crawfordsville, IN), puzzle editor.

Maria Shriver, b 11/6/1955 (Chicago, IL), TV journalist, former CA first lady.

George P. Shultz, b 12/13/1920 (New York, NY), economist; former sec. of state.

Michelangelo Signorile, b 12/19/1960 (Brooklyn, NY), journalist, author.

Adam Silver, b 4/25/1962 (Rye, NY), NBA commissioner.

Nate Silver, b 1/13/1978 (E. Lansing, MI), statistician.

Russell Simmons, b 10/4/1957 (Queens, NY), music producer.

O. J. Simpson, b 7/9/1947 (San Francisco, CA), former NFL star, murder defendant.

Harry Smith, b 8/21/1951 (Lansing, IL), TV journalist.

Edward Snowden, b 6/21/1983 (Elizabeth City, NC), computer specialist accused of leaking classified information about U.S. and UK govt. surveillance.

George Soros, b 8/12/1930 (Budapest, Hung.), financier, philanthropist.

Sonia Sotomayor, b 6/25/1954 (Bronx, NY), U.S. Supreme Court justice.

Evan Spiegel, b 6/4/1990 (Los Angeles, CA), Snapchat cofounder.

Steven Spielberg, b 12/18/1946 (Cincinnati, OH), movie director, producer.

Lesley Stahl, b 12/16/1941 (Swampscott, MA), TV journalist.

Shelby Steele, b 1/1/1946 (Chicago, IL), scholar, critic.

Ben Stein, b 11/25/1944 (Washington, DC), attorney, columnist, TV personality.

Gloria Steinem, b 3/25/1934 (Toledo, OH), author, feminist.

Frank Stella, b 5/12/1936 (Malden, MA), painter.

George Stephanopoulos, b 2/10/1961 (Fall River, MA), TV journalist, *Good Morning America* co-host; former pres. adviser.

Howard Stern, b 1/12/1954 (Jackson Heights, NY), radio host.

Martha Stewart, b 8/3/1941 (Nutley, NJ), homemaking adviser, entrepreneur, TV personality.

Biz Stone, b 3/10/1974 (Boston, MA), cofounder of Twitter.

Roger Stone, b 8/27/1952 (Norwalk, CT), political consultant.

Chesley Sullenberger III, b 1/23/1951 (Denison, TX), pilot who safely landed a passenger jet in the Hudson River.

Andrew Sullivan, b 8/10/1963 (S. Godstone, Eng., UK), political commentator.

A(rthur) G(regg) Sulzberger, b 8/5/1980 (Washington, DC), *NY Times* publisher.

Arthur Ochs Sulzberger Jr., b 9/22/1951 (Mt. Kisco, NY), NY Times Co. chairman.

Lawrence H. Summers, b 11/30/1954 (New Haven, CT), economist; former Natl. Economic Council dir., Harvard Univ. pres., sec. of treasury.

Jake Tapper, b 3/12/1969 (New York, NY), TV journalist.

Marc A. Thiessen, 1/13/1967, columnist.

Clarence Thomas, b 6/23/1948 (Savannah, GA), U.S. Supreme Court justice.

John Thune, b 1/7/1961 (Pierre, SD), U.S. Sen. majority whip (R, SD).

Rex Tillerson, b 3/23/1952 (Wichita Falls, KS), former sec. of state, ExxonMobil CEO.

Joseph Tobin, b 5/3/1952 (Detroit, MI), Rom. Cath. cardinal, archbishop of Newark, NJ.

Chuck Todd, b 4/8/1972 (Miami, FL), TV journalist, *Meet the Press* moderator.

Richard Trumka, b 7/24/1949 (Waynesburg, PA), pres. of AFL-CIO.

Donald Trump, b 6/14/1946 (Jamaica, Queens, NY), 45th U.S. president; real estate exec., TV personality.

Ivanka Trump, b 10/30/1981 (New York, NY), daughter of and adviser to Pres. Trump.

Melania Trump, b 4/26/1970 (Novo Mesto, [now] Slovenia), first lady, former model.

Ted Turner, b 11/19/1938 (Cincinnati, OH), TV exec., philanthropist.

Neil deGrasse Tyson, b 10/5/1958 (New York, NY), astrophysicist, director of NYC's Hayden Planetarium, author, TV host.

Hamdi Ulukaya, b 10/26/1972 (Erzincan, Turkey), Chobani CEO.

Urvashi Vaid, b 10/8/1958 (New Delhi, India), LGBTQ rights activist.

Greta Van Susteren, b 6/11/1954 (Appleton, WI), attorney, TV journalist.

Jesse Ventura, b 7/15/1951 (Minneapolis, MN), former wrestler, MN gov. (I).

Meredith Vieira, b 12/30/1953 (Providence, RI), TV journalist/host.

Diane von Fürstenberg, b 12/31/1946 (Brussels, Belgium), fashion designer.

Jimmy Wales, b 8/8/1966 (Huntsville, AL), cofounder of Wikipedia.

Barbara Walters, b 9/25/1929 (Boston, MA), TV journalist.

Alexander Wang, b 5/17/1984 (San Francisco, CA), fashion designer.

Vera Wang, b 6/27/1949 (New York, NY), fashion designer.

Elizabeth Warren, b 6/22/1949 (Oklahoma City, OK), U.S. sen. (D, MA); 2020 pres. contender.

Maxine Waters, b 8/15/1938 (St. Louis, MO), U.S. rep. (D, CA).

James Watson, b 4/6/1928 (Chicago, IL), biochemist, DNA pioneer.

Andrew Weil, b 6/8/1942 (Philadelphia, PA), health adviser.

Harvey Weinstein, b 3/19/1952 (Flushing, Queens, NY), movie exec.; convicted in 2020 on rape and sexual abuse charges.

Bill Weld, b 7/31/1945 (Smithtown, NY), fmr. MA gov. (R); 2020 pres. contender.

Jann Wenner, b 1/7/1946 (New York, NY), founder of *Rolling Stone*.

Cornel West, b 6/23/1953 (Tulsa, OK), academic, critic.

Ruth Westheimer, b 6/4/1928 (Frankfurt am Main, Germany), human sexuality expert.

Kehinde Wiley, b 2/28/1977 (Los Angeles, CA), artist.

George Will, b 5/4/1941 (Champaign, IL), journalist, author.

Brian Williams, b 5/5/1959 (Ridgewood, NJ), TV journalist.

Evan Williams, b 3/31/1972 (Clarks, NE), Twitter cofounder.

Jody Williams, b 10/9/1950 (Brattleboro, VT), peace activist, 1997 Nobel Peace Prize winner.

Marianne Williamson, b 7/8/1952 (Houston, TX), activist and author; 2020 pres. contender (D).

Oprah Winfrey, b 1/29/1954 (Kosciusko, MS), TV and media personality, entrepreneur, actress.

Anna Wintour, b 11/3/1949 (London, Eng., UK), *Vogue* editor.

Susan Wojcicki, b 7/5/1968 (Santa Clara, CA), CEO of YouTube.

Judy Woodruff, b 11/20/1946 (Tulsa, OK), TV journalist.

Bob Woodward, b 3/26/1943 (Geneva, IL), journalist; with Carl Bernstein cracked Watergate scandal.

Steve Wozniak, b 8/11/1950 (Sunnyvale, CA), inventor, cofounder of Apple.

Steve Wynn, b 1/27/1942 (New Haven, CT), casino developer.

Andrew Yang, b 1/13/1975 (Schenectady, NY), Venture for America founder; 2020 pres. contender (D).

Chuck Yeager, b 2/13/1923 (Myra, WV), test pilot, first to break sound barrier.

Janet Yellen, b 8/13/1946 (New York, NY), former Federal Reserve chair.

Mark Zuckerberg, b 5/14/1984 (Dobbs Ferry, NY), founder of Facebook.

Mortimer Zuckerman, b 6/4/1937 (Montréal, QC, Can.), publisher, columnist.

Widely Known World Personalities of the Present

Living non-Americans only. Generally excludes current heads of state or government (see Nations of the World) and excludes most others covered elsewhere, such as in Widely Known Americans, Writers, and Entertainment or Sports Personalities.

Mahmoud Abbas (Abu Mazen), b 3/26/1935 (Safed, Palestine [now Israel]), president of the Palestinian National Authority.

Gerry Adams, b 10/6/1948 (Belfast, N. Ireland, UK), fmr. Sinn Fein leader.

Mahmoud Ahmadinejad, b 10/28/1956 (Garmsar, Iran), former Iranian pres.

Ai Weiwei, b 1957 (Beijing, China), visual artist, activist.

Akihito, b 12/23/1933 (Tokyo, Jpn.), Japanese emperor emeritus.

Albert II, b 6/6/1934 (Brussels, Belgium), former king of Belgium (1993-2013).

Prince Andrew (Duke of York), b 2/19/1960 (London, Eng., UK), second son of Queen Elizabeth II.

Princess Anne (Princess Royal), b 8/15/1950 (London, Eng., UK), daughter of Queen Elizabeth II.

Oscar Arias Sánchez, b 9/13/1941 (Heredia, Costa Rica), former Costa Rican pres., 1987 Nobel Peace Prize laureate.

Giorgio Armani, b 7/30/1934 (Piacenza, Italy), fashion designer.

Hanan Ashrawi, b 10/8/1946 (Nablus, Israel), Palestinian activist.

Julian Assange, b 7/3/1971 (Townsville, Qld., Austral.), founder of WikiLeaks media org.

Ban Ki-moon, b 6/13/1944 (Umsong, [now] South Korea), former UN sec.-gen.

Ehud Barak, b 2/12/1942 (Mishmar Ha-Sharon Kibbutz, Israel), former Israeli min. of defense, prime min.

Beatrix, b 1/31/1938 (Baarn, Netherlands), former Dutch queen (1980-2013).

Jocelyn Bell Burnell, b 7/15/1943 (Belfast, N. Ire.), astrophysicist.

Benedict XVI (Joseph Ratzinger), b 4/16/1927 (Marktl am Inn, Germany), pope emeritus of Rom. Cath. Church, elected 2005, resigned 2013.

Tim Berners-Lee, b 6/8/1955 (London, Eng., UK), World Wide Web inventor.

Tony Blair, b 5/6/1953 (Edinburgh, Scot., UK), former British prime min.

Hans Blix, b 6/28/1928 (Uppsala, Swed.), former UN weapons inspector.

Bono (Paul David Hewson), b 5/20/1960 (Glasnevin, Dublin, Ire.), musician, social activist, philanthropist.

Fernando Botero, b 4/19/1932 (Medellín, Colombia), artist.

Richard Branson, b 7/18/1950 (S. London, Eng., UK), British Virgin Records and Airways founder.

Gordon Brown, b 2/20/1951 (Glasgow, Scot., UK), former British prime min.

Tina Brown, b 11/21/1953 (Maidenhead, Eng., UK), journalist, author.

Gisele Bündchen, b 7/20/1980 (Horizontina, Rio Grande do Sul, Braz.), model.

Mark Burnett, b 7/17/1960 (Myland, Eng., UK), reality TV producer.

Rhonda Byrne, b 3/12/1951 (Australia), author, TV writer and producer.

David Cameron, b 10/9/1966 (London, Eng., UK), former British prime min.

Kim Campbell, b 3/10/1947 (Port Alberni, BC, Can.), former Canadian prime min.

Pierre Cardin, b 7/7/1922 (San Biaggio di Callalta, Italy), fashion designer.

Magnus Carlsen, b 11/30/1990 (Tonsberg, Norway), world chess champion.

Princess Caroline, b 1/23/1957 (Monte Carlo, Monaco), Monaco royal (eldest daughter of Prince Rainier and Princess Grace).

Raúl Castro Ruz, b 6/3/1931 (Birán, Cuba), former pres. of Cuba.

Catherine (Kate) Middleton (Duchess of Cambridge), b 1/9/1982 (Reading, Eng., UK), wife of Prince William.

Prince Charles (of Wales), b 11/14/1948 (London, Eng., UK), eldest son of Queen Elizabeth II; heir to British throne.

Princess Charlotte Elizabeth Diana (of Cambridge), b 5/2/2015 (London, Eng., UK), daughter of Prince William and Catherine.

Chen Guangcheng, b 11/12/1971 (Dongshigu, China), civil rights activist.

Yao Chen, b 10/5/1979 (Nanping, Fujian, China), actress, microblogger.

Deepak Chopra, b 1946 (New Delhi, India), writer, alternative medicine advocate.

Jean Chrétien, b 1/11/1934 (Shawinigan, QC, Can.), former Canadian prime min.

Joe (Charles Joseph) Clark, b 6/5/1939 (High River, AB, Can.), former Canadian prime min.

King Constantine II, b 6/2/1940 (Psychiko, Greece), former king of Greece.

Simon Cowell, b 10/7/1959 (Brighton, East Sussex, Eng., UK), music exec., TV producer, former *American Idol* host.

Dalai Lama, 14th (Tenzin Gyatso), b 7/6/1935 (Taktser, Amdo, Tibet), Buddhist leader; 1989 Nobel Peace Prize winner.

Richard Dawkins, b 3/26/1941 (Nairobi, Kenya), ethologist, evolutionary biologist, author.

F. W. (Frederik Willem) de Klerk, b 3/18/1936 (Johannesburg, S. Afr.), former S. African pres.; 1993 Nobel Peace Prize winner.

Shirin Ebadi, b 6/21/1947 (Hamadan, Iran), human rights activist, 2003 Nobel Peace Prize winner.

Prince Edward (Earl of Essex), b 3/10/1964 (London, Eng., UK), third son of Queen Elizabeth II.

Daniel Ek, b 2/21/1983 (Stockholm, Sweden), Spotify cofounder/CEO.

Mohamed ElBaradei, b 6/17/1942 (Cairo, Egypt), former director general of the International Atomic Energy Agency (IAEA); 2005 Nobel Peace Prize winner.

Francis (Jorge Mario Bergoglio), b 12/17/1936 (Buenos Aires, Argentina), pope of Roman Catholic Church.

Fumihito, Prince Akishino, b 11/30/1965 (Tokyo, Jpn.), crown prince of Japan.

John Galliano, b 11/28/1960 (Gibraltar, UK), fashion designer.

Prince George Alexander Louis (of Cambridge), b 7/22/2013 (London, Eng., UK), son of Prince William and Catherine.

Wael Ghonim, b 12/23/1980 (Cairo, Egypt), computer engineer and internet activist.

Valery Giscard d'Estaing, b 2/2/1926 (Koblenz, Ger.), former French pres.

Jane Goodall, b 4/3/1934 (London, Eng., UK), anthropologist, primatologist.

Mikhail Gorbachev, b 3/2/1931 (Privolnoye, USSR), former Soviet pres.; 1990 Nobel Peace Prize winner.

Juan Guaidó, b 7/28/1983 (La Guaira, Venezuela), Venezuelan opposition leader.

António Guterres, b 4/30/1949 (Lisbon, Portugal), UN sec.-gen.

Jürgen Habermas, b 6/18/1929 (Dusseldorf, Ger.), philosopher.

Stephen Harper, b 4/30/1959 (Toronto, ON, Can.), former Canadian prime min.

Prince Henry (Harry) (Duke of Sussex), b 9/15/1984 (London, Eng., UK), son of Prince Charles and Diana.

Damien Hirst, b 6/7/1965 (Bristol, Eng., UK), artist.

David Hockney, b 7/9/1937 (Bradford, Eng., UK), artist.

Hu Jintao, b 12/21/1942 (Shanghai, China), former pres. of China.

Jiang Zemin, b 8/17/1926 (Yangzhou, Jiangsu Prov., China), former pres. of China.

Juan Carlos I, b 1/5/1938 (Rome, Italy), former king of Spain (1975-2014).

Hamid Karzai, b 12/24/1957 (Kandahar, Afghanistan), former pres. of Afghanistan.

Garry Kasparov, b 4/13/1963 (Baku, Azerbaijan, USSR), former world chess champion; Russian pro-democracy leader.

Ayatollah Ali Khamenei, b 7/17/1939 (Mashhad, Iran), Supreme Leader, cleric; former president of Iran.

Marie Kondo, b 10/9/1984 (Tokyo, Japan), organizing specialist.

Hans Küng, b 3/19/1928 (Sursee, Switz.), Rom. Cath. theologian.

Christine Lagarde, b 1/1/1956 (Paris, Fr.), European Central Bank pres.

Carrie Lam, b 5/13/1957 (Wan Chai, Hong Kong), chief executive of Hong Kong.

Richard Leakey, b 12/19/1944 (Nairobi, Kenya), anthropologist, paleontologist, conservationist.

Jean-Marie Le Pen, b 6/20/1928 (La Trinité-sur-Mer, Fr.), French right-wing politician.

Marine Le Pen, b 8/5/1968 (Neuilly-sur-Seine, Fr.), head of France's National Front.

Tzipi Livni, b 7/5/1958 (Tel Aviv, Isr.), attorney, Israeli politician.

Prince Louis Arthur Charles (of Cambridge), b 4/23/2018 (London, Eng., UK), son of Prince William and Catherine.

John Major, b 3/29/1943 (Wimbledon, Eng., UK), former British prime min.

Nouri al-Maliki, b 7/1/1950 (Iraq), former prime min. of Iraq.

Imelda Marcos, b 7/2/1929 (Manila, Philip.), former first lady of the Philippines.

Paul Martin, b 8/28/1938 (Windsor, ON, Can.), former prime min. of Canada.

Empress Masako, b 12/9/1963 (Tokyo, Jpn.), empress of Japan.

Theresa May, b 10/1/1956 (Eastbourne, Eng., UK), former British prime min.

Stella McCartney, b 9/13/1971 (London, Eng., UK), fashion designer.

Dmitry Medvedev, b 9/14/1965 (Leningrad, Soviet Union [now Russia]), prime min. of Russia, fmr. president.

Rigoberta Menchú, b 1/9/1959 (Aldea Chimel, Guatemala), human rights activist, 1992 Nobel Peace Prize winner.

Angela Merkel, b 7/17/1954 (Hamburg, Ger.), first woman chancellor of Germany.

Jean-Marie Messier, b 12/13/1956 (Grenoble, Fr.), former CEO of Vivendi Universal.

Michiko, b 10/20/1934 (Tokyo, Japan), empress emerita of Japan.

Kate Moss, b 1/16/1974 (Addiscombe, Surrey, Eng., UK), model.

Archie Harrison Mountbatten-Windsor, b 5/6/2019 (London, Eng., UK), son of Prince Harry and Meghan Markle.

Brian Mulroney, b 3/20/1939 (Baie-Corneau, QC, Can.), former Canadian prime min.

Renhō Murata, b 11/28/1968 (Tokyo, Japan), first woman leader of Japan's Democratic Party.

Hassan Nasrallah, b 8/31/1960 (Qarantina, Lebanon), sec.-gen. of Hezbollah.

Queen Noor (Lisa Halaby), b 8/23/1951 (Washington, DC), American-born widow of Jordan's King Hussein.

Ehud Olmert, b 9/30/1945 (Binyamina, Palestine), former prime min. of Israel.

Daniel Ortega Saavedra, b 11/11/1945 (La Libertad, Nicar.), Nicaraguan pres., Sandinista leader.

Camilla Parker-Bowles (Duchess of Cornwall), b 7/17/1947 (London, Eng., UK), wife of Prince Charles.

Prince Philip (Duke of Edinburgh), b 6/10/1921 (Corfu, Greece), husband of Queen Elizabeth II.

Ren Zhengfei, b 10/25/1944 (Guizhou, China), founder and CEO of Huawei Technologies.

Gerhard Richter, b 2/9/1932 (Dresden, Ger.), artist.

Mary Robinson, b 5/21/1944 (Ballina, Co. Mayo, Ire.), former Irish pres., former UN High Commissioner for Human Rights.

Arundhati Roy, b 11/24/1961 (Shillong, Meghalaya, India), author, political activist.

Ségolène Royal, b 9/22/1953 (Dakar, Senegal), French socialist politician.

Muqtada al-Sadr, b 8/4/1974 (Najaf, Iraq), extremist Shiite cleric.

Mohammad bin Salman, b 8/31/1985 (Riyadh, Saudi Arabia), Saudi crown prince.

Nicolas Sarkozy, b 1/28/1955 (Paris, France), former French pres.

Gerhard Schröder, b 4/7/1944 (Mossenburg, Ger.), former German chancellor.

Nawaz Sharif, b 12/25/1949 (Lahore, Pakistan), former Pakistan prime min.

Ayatollah Ali al-Sistani, b 8/4/1930 (Mashhad, Iran), major Iraqi Shiite religious leader.

Carlos Slim Helú, b 1/28/1940 (Mexico City, Mex.), founder of Grupo Carso; former chair of Telmex, América Móvil.

Princess Stephanie, b 2/1/1965 (Monte Carlo, Monaco), youngest child of Prince Rainier and Princess Grace.

Dominique Strauss-Kahn, b 4/25/1949 (Neuilly-sur-Seine, France), former Intl. Monetary Fund managing dir.

Aung San Suu Kyi, b 6/19/1945 (Rangoon, Myanmar), political activist, 1991 Nobel Peace Prize winner; de facto Myanmar govt. leader.

Valentina Tereshkova, b 3/6/1937 (Maslennikovo, Russia, USSR), first woman in space.

Greta Thunberg, b 1/3/2003 (Swed.), environmental activist.

Desmond Tutu, b 10/7/1931 (Klerksdorp, Transvaal, S. Afr.), former S. African archbishop; 1984 Nobel Peace Prize winner.

Ursula von der Leyen, b 10/8/1958 (Brussels, Belg.), first woman European Commission pres.

Lech Walesa, b 9/29/1943 (Popowo, Pol.), Solidarity leader, former pres. of Poland; 1983 Nobel Peace Prize winner.

Justin Welby, b 1/6/1956 (London, Eng., UK), archbishop of Canterbury.

Prince William (Duke of Cambridge), b 6/21/1982 (London, Eng., UK), eldest son of Prince Charles and Diana; 2nd in line to British throne.

Rowan Williams, b 6/14/1950 (Ystradgynlais, Wales, UK), former archbishop of Canterbury.

Malala Yousafzai, b 7/12/1997 (Mingora, Pakistan), activist for girls' education, 2014 Nobel Peace Prize winner.

Muhammad Yunus, b 6/28/1940 (Chittagong, Bangladesh), economist, 2006 Nobel Peace Prize winner.

Mohammad Javad Zarif, b 1/8/1960 (Tehran, Iran), Irani minister of foreign affairs.

Ayman al-Zawahiri, b 6/19/1951 (Cairo, Egypt), reputed high-ranking al-Qaeda leader.

Architects

Alvar Aalto, 1898-1976, Säynätsalo Town Hall, Vuoksenniska Church, Finland.

Max Abramovitz, 1908-2004, Avery Fisher Hall, New York, NY; U.S. Steel Tower (Bldg.), Pittsburgh, PA.

Tadao Ando, b 1941, Modern Art Museum, Ft. Worth, TX; Stone Hill Center, MA.

Michael Arad, b 1969, Natl. 9/11 Memorial, New York, NY.

Henry Bacon, 1866-1924, Lincoln Memorial, Washington, DC.

Benjamin Banneker, 1731-1806, African American inventor, astronomer, mathematician; helped design and lay out Washington, DC.

Pietro Belluschi, 1899-1994, Juilliard School, Lincoln Center, Pan Am Bldg. (now MetLife Bldg.) with Walter Gropius, New York, NY.

Marcel Breuer, 1902-81, Whitney Museum of American Art (now Met Breuer) (with Hamilton Smith), New York, NY.

Filippo Brunelleschi, 1377-1446, Santa Maria del Fiore Cathedral, Florence, Italy.

Charles Bulfinch, 1763-1844, State House, Boston, MA; Capitol (part), Wash., DC.

Gordon Bunshaft, 1909-90, Lever House, New York, NY; Hirshhorn Museum, Washington, DC.

Daniel H. Burnham, 1846-1912, Union Station, Washington, DC; Flatiron Bldg., New York, NY.

Irwin Chanin, 1892-1988, theaters, skyscrapers. New York, NY.

David Childs, b 1941, Washington Mall Master Plan/Constitution Gardens, Washington, DC; One World Trade Center, New York, NY.

Lucio Costa, 1902-98, master plan for city of Brasilia, Brazil (with Oscar Niemeyer).

Ralph Adams Cram, 1863-1942, Cath. of St. John the Divine, New York, NY; U.S. Military Acad. (part), West Point, NY.

Gustave Eiffel, 1832-1923, Eiffel Tower, Paris.

Norman Foster, b 1935, Commerzbank Headquarters, Frankfurt-am-Main, Ger.; London Millennium Bridge, 30 St. Mary Axe ("The Gherkin"), London, Eng., UK.

James Ingo Freed, 1930-2005, Holocaust Memorial Museum, Washington, DC; Jacob K. Javits Center, New York, NY.

R. Buckminster Fuller, 1895-1983, U.S. Pavilion (geodesic domes), Expo 67, Montréal, QC, Can.

Antoni Gaudí, 1852-1926, Basilica and Expiatory Temple of the Sagrada Familia, Barcelona, Spain.

Frank O. Gehry, b 1929, Guggenheim Museum, Bilbao, Spain; Walt Disney Concert Hall, Los Angeles, CA.

Cass Gilbert, 1859-1934, Custom House, Woolworth Bldg., New York, NY; Supreme Court Bldg., Washington, DC.

Bertram G. Goodhue, 1869-1924, Capitol, Lincoln, NE; St. Thomas's Church, St. Bartholomew's Church, New York, NY.

Michael Graves, 1934-2015, Portland Bldg., Portland, OR; Humana Bldg., Louisville, KY.

Walter Gropius, 1883-1969, Pan Am Bldg. (now MetLife Bldg.) (with Pietro Belluschi), New York, NY.

Zaha Hadid, 1950-2016, Rosenthal Center for Contemporary Art, Cincinnati, OH; London Aquatics Centre, Eng., UK.

Lawrence Halprin, 1916-2009, Ghirardelli Sq., San Francisco, CA; Nicollet Mall, Minneapolis, MN; FDR Memorial, Wash., DC.

Peter Harrison, 1716-75, Touro Synagogue, Redwood Library, Newport, RI.

Wallace K. Harrison, 1895-1981, Metropolitan Opera House, Lincoln Center, New York, NY.

Thomas Hastings, 1860-1929, NY Public Library (with John Carrère), Frick Mansion, New York, NY.

James Hoban, 1762-1831, White House, Washington, DC.

Raymond Hood, 1881-1934, Rockefeller Center (part), Daily News Bldg., New York, NY; Tribune Tower, Chicago, IL.

Richard M. Hunt, 1827-95, Metropolitan Museum (part), New York, NY; Biltmore Estate, Asheville, NC.

Arata Isozaki, b 1931, Museum of Contemporary Art, Los Angeles, CA.

Toyo Ito, b 1941, Sendai Mediatheque, Sendai, Japan; Tower of Winds, Yokohama, Japan.

Helmut Jahn, b 1940, United Airlines Terminal, O'Hare Airport, Chicago, IL.

William Le Baron Jenney, 1832-1907, Home Insurance Bldg. (demolished 1931), Chicago, IL.

Philip C. Johnson, 1906-2005, AT&T Bldg. (now 550 Madison Ave.), New York, NY; Transco (now Williams) Tower, Houston, TX.

Albert Kahn, 1869-1942, General Motors Bldg. (now Cadillac Place), Detroit, MI.

Louis Kahn, 1901-74, Salk Laboratory, La Jolla, CA; Yale Art Gallery, New Haven, CT.

Rem Koolhaas, b 1944, Seattle Central Library, Seattle, WA.

Christopher Grant LaFarge, 1862-1938, Roman Catholic Chapel, West Point, NY.

Benjamin H. Latrobe, 1764-1820, Capitol (part), Washington, DC; State Capitol Bldg., Richmond, VA.

Le Corbusier (Charles-Edouard Jeanneret), 1887-1965, Salvation Army Hostel, Swiss Dormitory, Paris, France; master plan for cities of Algiers and Buenos Aires.

William Lescaze, 1896-1969, Philadelphia Savings Fund Society, PA; Borg-Warner Bldg., Chicago, IL.

Daniel Libeskind, b 1946, developed master plan for the rebuilding of World Trade Center site, New York, NY.

Maya Lin, b 1959, Vietnam Veterans Mem., Washington, DC.

Charles Rennie Mackintosh, 1868-1928, Glasgow School of Art; Hill House, Helensburgh, Scot., UK.

Bernard R. Maybeck, 1862-1957, Hearst Hall, Univ. of CA, Berkeley; First Church of Christ Scientist, Berkeley, CA.

Charles F. McKim, 1847-1909, Boston Public Library; Columbia Univ. (part), New York, NY.

Charles M. McKim, 1920-2017, KUHT-TV Transmitter Bldg., Lutheran Church of the Redeemer, Houston, TX.

Richard Meier, b 1934, Getty Center, Los Angeles, CA; High Museum of Art, Atlanta, GA.

Ludwig Mies van der Rohe, 1886-1969, Seagram Bldg. (with Philip C. Johnson), New York, NY; National Gallery, Berlin, Ger.

Robert Mills, 1781-1855, Washington Monument, Washington, DC.

Charles Moore, 1925-93, Sea Ranch, nr. San Francisco, CA; Piazza d'Italia, New Orleans, LA.

Julia Morgan, 1872-1957, Hearst Castle, San Simeon, CA.

John Nash, 1752-1835, Buckingham Palace, London, Eng., UK.

Richard J. Neutra, 1892-1970, Orange Co. Courthouse, Santa Ana, CA.

Oscar Niemeyer, 1907-2012, government buildings, Brasilia Palace Hotel, Brasilia, Braz.

Gyo Obata, b 1923, Natl. Air and Space Museum, Smithsonian Inst., Washington, DC; Dallas-Ft. Worth Airport, TX.

Frederick L. Olmsted, 1822-1903, Central Park, New York, NY; Fairmount Park, Philadelphia, PA.

I(eoh) M(ing) Pei, 1917-2019, East Wing, Natl. Gallery of Art, Washington, DC; Pyramid, The Louvre, Paris, Fr.; Rock & Roll Hall of Fame and Museum, Cleveland, OH.

Cesar Pelli, 1926-2019, World Financial Center, Carnegie Hall Tower, New York, NY; Petronas Twin Towers, Malaysia.

William Pereira, 1909-85, Cape Canaveral, FL; Transamerica Pyramid, San Francisco.

Renzo Piano, b 1937, Pompidou Centre, Paris, Fr.; New York Times Bldg., New York, NY; The Shard, London, Eng., UK.

John Russell Pope, 1874-1937, National Gallery, Jefferson Memorial, Wash., DC.

John Portman, 1924-2017, Peachtree Center, Atlanta, GA.

George Browne Post, 1837-1913, NY Stock Exchange, New York, NY; Capitol, Madison, WI.

James Renwick Jr., 1818-95, Grace Church, St. Patrick's Cathedral, New York, NY; Smithsonian Institution (Castle), Washington, DC.

Henry H. Richardson, 1838-86, Trinity Church, Boston, MA.

Kevin Roche, 1922-2019, Oakland Museum, Oakland, CA; Fine Arts Center, Univ. of Massachusetts, Amherst, MA.

James Gamble Rogers, 1867-1947, Columbia-Presbyterian Medical Ctr., New York, NY; Northwestern Univ., Evanston, IL.

John Wellborn Root, 1887-1963, Palmolive Bldg., Chicago, IL; Hotel Statler (now Capital Hilton), Washington, DC.

Paul Rudolph, 1918-97, Jewitt Art Center, Wellesley College, MA; Art & Architecture Bldg., Yale Univ., New Haven, CT.

Eero Saarinen, 1910-61, Gateway to the West Arch, St. Louis, MO; TWA Flight Center, JFK Airport, New York, NY.

Kazuyo Sejima, b 1956, 21st Century Museum of Contemporary Art (with Ryue Nishizawa), Kanazawa, Japan.

Kodja Mimar Sinan, 1489-1588, chief court architect of Ottoman dynasty.

Louis Skidmore, 1897-1962, Atomic Energy Commission town site, Oak Ridge, TN; Terrace Plaza Hotel, Cincinnati, OH.

Norma Merrick Sklarek, 1928-2012, Terminal One, Los Angeles International Airport, CA.

Clarence S. Stein, 1882-1975, Temple Emanu-El, New York, NY.

Edward Durell Stone, 1902-78, interior of Radio City Music Hall, Museum of Modern Art, New York, NY.

Louis H. Sullivan, 1856-1924, Auditorium Bldg., Chicago, IL.

Kenzo Tange, 1913-2005, Hiroshima Peace Park, 1964 Tokyo Olympic stadiums, Japan.

Richard Upjohn, 1802-78, Trinity Church, New York, NY.

Max O. Urbahn, 1912-95, Vehicle Assembly Bldg., Cape Canaveral, FL.

Joern Utzon, 1918-2008, Sydney Opera House, NSW, Australia.

William Van Alen, 1883-1954, Chrysler Building, New York, NY.

Calvert Vaux, 1824-95, Central Park, New York, NY; Prospect Park, Brooklyn, NY.

Robert Venturi, 1925-2018, Gordon Wu Hall, Princeton, NJ; Mielparque Nikko Kirifuri Resort, Japan.

Ralph T. Walker, 1889-1973, NY Telephone (now Verizon) Bldg., Irving Trust Bldg. (now 1 Wall St.), New York, NY.

Wang Shu, b 1963, Ningbo Museum, China.

Roland A. Wank, 1898-1970, Cincinnati Union Terminal, OH; head architect, 1933-44, Tennessee Valley Authority.

Stanford White, 1853-1906, Washington Arch in Washington Square Park, first Madison Square Garden, New York, NY.

Christopher Wren, 1632-1723, St. Paul's Cathedral, London, Eng., UK.

Frank Lloyd Wright, 1867-1959, Imperial Hotel, Tokyo, Japan; Guggenheim Museum, New York, NY; Kaufmann "Fallingwater" house, Mill Run, PA; Taliesin West, Scottsdale, AZ.

Thomas Wright, b 1957, Burj Al Arab hotel, Dubai, UAE.

William Wurster, 1895-1973, Ghirardelli Sq., San Francisco, CA.

Minoru Yamasaki, 1912-86, World Trade Center (destroyed 2001), New York, NY.

Artists, Photographers, and Sculptors of the Past

Artists are painters unless otherwise indicated.

Berenice Abbott, 1898-1991, (U.S.) photographer. Documentary of New York City, *Changing New York* (1939).

Ansel Easton Adams, 1902-84, (U.S.) photographer. Landscapes of the American Southwest.

Washington Allston, 1779-1843, (U.S.) landscapist. *Belshazzar's Feast*.

Albrecht Altdorfer, 1480-1538, (Ger.) landscapist.

Fra Angelico, c. 1400-55, (It.) Renaissance muralist. *Madonna of the Linen Drapers' Guild*.

Diane Arbus, 1923-71, (U.S.) photographer. Disturbing images.

Alexsandr Archipenko, 1887-1964, (U.S.) sculptor. *Boxing Match, Medranos*.

Jean Arp, 1887-1966, (Fr.) sculptor and painter. Founder of Dada movement.

Richard Artschwager, 1923-2013, (U.S.) painter and sculptor. *Table With Pink Tablecloth*.

Eugène Atget, 1856-1927, (Fr.) photographer. Paris life.

John James Audubon, 1785-1851, (U.S.) *Birds of America*.

Richard Avedon, 1923-2004, (U.S.) fashion and celebrity photographer.

Hans Baldung-Grien, 1484-1545, (Ger.) *Todentanz*.

Ernst Barlach, 1870-1938, (Ger.) Expressionist sculptor. *Man Drawing a Sword*.

Frédéric-Auguste Bartholdi, 1834-1904, (Fr.) sculptor. *Liberty Enlightening the World* (Statue of Liberty).

Fra Bartolommeo, 1472-1517, (It.) *Vision of St. Bernard*.

Romare Bearden, 1911-88, (U.S.) collage and other media. *The Visitation*.

Aubrey Beardsley, 1872-98, (Br.) illustrator. *Salome, Lysistrata, Morte d'Arthur, Volpone*.

Cecil Beaton, 1904-80, (Br.) fashion and celebrity photographer.

Max Beckmann, 1884-1950, (Ger.) Expressionist. *The Descent From the Cross*.

Gentile Bellini, 1426-1507, (It.) Renaissance. *Procession in St. Mark's Square*.

Giovanni Bellini, 1428-1516, (It.) Renaissance. *St. Francis in Ecstasy*.

Jacopo Bellini, 1400-70, (It.) Renaissance. *Crucifixion*.

George Wesley Bellows, 1882-1925, (U.S.) sports artist, portraitist, landscapist. *Stag at Sharkey's, Edith Clavell*.

Thomas Hart Benton, 1889-1975, (U.S.) American regionalist. *Threshing Wheat, Arts of the West*.

Ruth Bernhard, 1905-2006, (Ger.-U.S.) photographer. Black-and-white studies of female nudes.

Gianlorenzo Bernini, 1598-1680, (It.) Baroque sculptor. *The Assumption.*

Albert Bierstadt, 1830-1902, (U.S.) landscapist. *The Rocky Mountains, Mount Corcoran.*

George Caleb Bingham, 1811-79, (U.S.) American frontier. *Fur Traders Descending the Missouri.*

William Blake, 1757-1827, (Br.) engraver. *Book of Job, Songs of Innocence, Songs of Experience.*

Rosa Bonheur, 1822-99, (Fr.) Realist. *The Horse Fair.*

Pierre Bonnard, 1867-1947, (Fr.) Intimist. *The Breakfast Room, Girl in a Straw Hat.*

Gutzon Borglum, 1867-1941, (U.S.) sculptor. Mt. Rushmore Memorial.

Hieronymus Bosch, 1450-1516, (Flem.) religious allegories. *The Crowning With Thorns.*

Sandro Botticelli, 1444-1510, (It.) Renaissance. *Birth of Venus, Adoration of the Magi, Guiliano de' Medici.*

Louise Bourgeois, 1911-2010, (Fr.) sculptor. *Maman.*

Margaret Bourke-White, 1904-71, (U.S.) photographer, photojournalist. WWII, USSR, rural South during the Depression.

Mathew Brady, c. 1823-96, (U.S.) photographer. Civil War.

Constantin Brancusi, 1876-1957, (Romania-Fr.) Nonobjective sculptor. *Flying Turtle, The Kiss.*

Georges Braque, 1882-1963, (Fr.) Cubist. *Violin and Palette.*

Pieter Bruegel the Elder, c. 1525-69, (Flem.) Renaissance. *The Peasant Dance, Hunters in the Snow, Magpie on the Gallows.*

Pieter Bruegel the Younger, 1564-1638, (Flem.) Baroque. *Village Fair, The Crucifixion.*

Edward Burne-Jones, 1833-98, (Br.) Pre-Raphaelite artist-craftsman. *The Mirror of Venus.*

Alexander Calder, 1898-1976, (U.S.) sculptor. *Lobster Trap and Fish Tail.*

Julia Margaret Cameron, 1815-79, (Br.) photographer, prominent portraitist.

Robert Capa (Endre Friedmann), 1913-54, (Hung.-U.S.) photographer, war photojournalist. Invasion of Normandy.

Michelangelo Merisi da Caravaggio, 1573-1610, (It.) Baroque. *The Supper at Emmaus.*

Emily Carr, 1871-1945, (Can.) landscapist. *Blunden Harbour, Big Raven, Rushing Sea of Undergrowth.*

Carlo Carrà, 1881-1966, (It.) Metaphysical school. *Lot's Daughters, The Enchanted Room.*

Leonora Carrington, 1917-2011, (Br.) Surrealist. *The Inn of the Dawn Horse (Self-Portrait).*

Henri Cartier-Bresson, 1908-2004, (Fr.) photographer. *Imagenes à la sauvette.*

Mary Cassatt, 1844-1926, (U.S.) Impressionist. *The Cup of Tea, Woman Bathing, The Boating Party.*

George Catlin, 1796-1872, (U.S.) American Indian life. *Gallery of Indians, Buffalo Dance.*

Benvenuto Cellini, 1500-71, (It.) Mannerist sculptor, goldsmith. *Perseus and Medusa.*

Paul Cézanne, 1839-1906, (Fr.) Post-Impressionist. *Card Players, Mont-Sainte-Victoire With Large Pine Trees.*

Marc Chagall, 1887-1985, (Russ.) Jewish life and folklore. *I and the Village, The Praying Jew.*

John Chamberlain, 1927-2011, (U.S.) sculptor of automobile metal.

Jean Simeon Chardin, 1699-1779, (Fr.) still lifes. *The Kiss, The Grace.*

Giorgio de Chirico, 1888-1978, (It.) founded the Metaphysical school. *Enigma of an Autumn Night.*

Christo (Javacheff), 1935-2020, (Bulg.), large-scale environmental installation artist with wife Jeanne-Claude. *The Gates, Surrounded Islands.*

Frederick Church, 1826-1900, (U.S.) Hudson River school. *Niagara, Andes of Ecuador.*

Giovanni Cimabue, 1240-1302, (It.) Byzantine mosaicist. *Madonna Enthroned With St. Francis.*

Claude (Lorrain) (Claude Gellée), 1600-82, (Fr.) Ideal-landscapist. *The Enchanted Castle.*

Thomas Cole, 1801-48, (U.S.) Hudson River school. *The Ox-Bow, In the Catskills.*

John Constable, 1776-1837, (Br.) landscapist. *Salisbury Cathedral From the Bishop's Grounds.*

John Singleton Copley, 1738-1815, (U.S.) portraitist. *Samuel Adams, Watson and the Shark.*

Lovis Corinth, 1858-1925, (Ger.) Expressionist. *Apocalypse.*

Jean-Baptiste-Camille Corot, 1796-1875, (Fr.) landscapist. *Souvenir de Mortefontaine, Pastorale.*

Correggio, 1494-1534, (It.) Renaissance muralist. *Mystic Marriages of St. Catherine.*

Gustave Courbet, 1819-77, (Fr.) Realist. *The Artist's Studio.*

Lucas Cranach the Elder, 1472-1553, (Ger.) Protestant Reformation portraitist. *Luther.*

Bill Cunningham, 1929-2016, (U.S.) fashion photographer.

Imogen Cunningham, 1883-1976, (U.S.) photographer, portraitist. Plants.

Nathaniel Currier, 1813-88, and **James M. Ives**, 1824-95, (both U.S.) lithographers. *A Midnight Race on the Mississippi, American Forest Scene—Maple Sugaring.*

John Steuart Curry, 1897-1946, (U.S.) Americana, murals. *Baptism in Kansas.*

Edward S. Curtis, 1868-1952, (U.S.) photographer. *The North American Indian.*

Louis Daguerre, 1787-1851, (Fr.) photographer. Invented daguerreotype process.

Salvador Dalí, 1904-89, (Sp.) Surrealist. *Persistence of Memory, The Crucifixion.*

Honoré Daumier, 1808-79, (Fr.) caricaturist. *The Third-Class Carriage.*

Jacques-Louis David, 1748-1825, (Fr.) Neoclassicist. *The Oath of the Horatii.*

Arthur Davies, 1862-1928, (U.S.) Romantic landscapist. *Unicorns, Leda and the Dioscuri.*

Edgar Degas, 1834-1917, (Fr.) Realist/ Impressionist. *The Ballet Class.*

Willem de Kooning, 1904-97, (Neth.-U.S.) Abstract Expressionist. *Excavation, Woman I, Door to the River.*

Eugène Delacroix, 1798-1863, (Fr.) Romantic. *Massacre at Chios, Liberty Leading the People.*

Paul Delaroche, 1797-1856, (Fr.) historical themes. *Children of Edward IV.*

Luca Della Robbia, 1400-82, (It.) Renaissance terra-cotta. *Cantoria (singing gallery),* Florence cathedral.

Donatello, 1386-1466, (It.) Renaissance sculptor. *David, Gattamelata.*

Aaron Douglas, 1899-79, (U.S.) Harlem Renaissance illustrator and muralist.

Jean Dubuffet, 1902-85, (Fr.) painter, sculptor, printmaker. *Group of Four Trees.*

Marcel Duchamp, 1887-1968, (Fr.) Dadaist. *Nude Descending a Staircase, No. 2.*

Raoul Dufy, 1877-1953, (Fr.) Fauvist. *Chateau and Horses.*

Asher Brown Durand, 1796-1886, (U.S.) Hudson River school. *Kindred Spirits.*

Albrecht Dürer, 1471-1528, (Ger.) Renaissance painter, engraver, woodcuts. *St. Jerome in His Study, Melencolia I.*

Anthony van Dyck, 1599-1641, (Flem.) Baroque portraitist. *Portrait of Charles I Hunting.*

Thomas Eakins, 1844-1916, (U.S.) Realist. *The Gross Clinic.*

Alfred Eisenstaedt, 1898-1995, (Ger.-U.S.) photographer, photojournalist. Famous photo, V-J Day, Aug. 14, 1945.

Peter Henry Emerson, 1856-1936, (Br.) photographer. Promoted photography as an independent art form.

Jacob Epstein, 1880-1959, (Br.) religious and allegorical sculptor. *Genesis, Ecce Homo.*

Erté (Romain de Tiertoff), 1892-1990, (Fr.) painter, fashion and stage designer.

Walker Evans, 1903-75, (U.S.) photographer. Documented Great Depression.

Jan van Eyck, c. 1390-1441, (Flem.) naturalistic panels. *Adoration of the Lamb.*

Horst Faas, 1933-2012, (Ger.) Vietnam War photographer.

Roger Fenton, 1819-69, (Br.) photographer. Crimean War.

Anselm Feuerbach, 1829-80, (Ger.) Romantic Classicist. *Judgment of Paris, Iphigenia.*

John Bernard Flannagan, 1895-1942, (U.S.) animal sculptor. *Triumph of the Egg.*

Jean-Honoré Fragonard, 1732-1806, (Fr.) Rococo. *The Swing.*

Robert Frank, 1924-2019, (Switz.-U.S.) photographer. *The Americans.*

Helen Frankenthaler, 1928-2011, (U.S.) Abstract Expressionist. *Mountains and Sea.*

Daniel Chester French, 1850-1931, (U.S.) sculptor. *The Minute Man of Concord;* seated *Lincoln,* Lincoln Memorial, Washington, DC.

Lucian Freud, 1922-2011, (Ger.-Br.) portraitist. *Girl With Roses.*

Caspar David Friedrich, 1774-1840, (Ger.) Romantic landscapist. *Man and Woman Gazing at the Moon.*

Thomas Gainsborough, 1727-88, (Br.) portraitist. *The Blue Boy, The Watering Place, The Parish Clerk.*

Alexander Gardner, 1821-82, (U.S.) photographer. Civil War, railroad construction, Great Plains Indians.

Paul Gauguin, 1848-1903, (Fr.) Post-Impressionist. *The Tahitians, Spirit of the Dead Watching.*

Lorenzo Ghiberti, 1378-1455, (It.) Renaissance sculptor. "Gates of Paradise" baptistery doors, Florence, It.

Alberto Giacometti, 1901-66, (Switz.) attenuated sculptures of solitary figures. *Man Pointing.*

Giorgione, c. 1477-1510, (It.) Renaissance. *The Tempest.*

Giotto di Bondone, 1267-1337, (It.) Renaissance. *Presentation of Christ in the Temple.*

François Girardon, 1628-1715, (Fr.) Baroque sculptor of classical themes. *Apollo Tended by the Nymphs.*

Milton Glaser, 1929-2020, (U.S.) graphic designer. I ♥ NY logo.

Edward Gorey, 1925-2000, (U.S.) illustrator. *The Doubtful Guest.*

Arshile Gorky, 1905-48, (U.S.) Surrealist. *The Liver Is the Cock's Comb.*

Francisco de Goya y Lucientes, 1746-1828, (Sp.) painter, printmaker. *The Naked Maja, The Disasters of War* (etchings).

El Greco (Domenikos Theotokopoulos), 1541-1614, (Gr.-Sp.) painter, sculptor. *View of Toledo, Assumption of the Virgin.*

Horatio Greenough, 1805-52, (U.S.) Neoclassical sculptor.

Matthias Grünewald, 1480-1528, (Ger.) mystical religious themes. *The Resurrection.*

Frans Hals, c. 1580-1666, (Neth.) portraitist. *Laughing Cavalier, Gypsy Girl.*

Richard Hamilton, 1922-2011, (Br.) Pop Art. *Just What Is It That Makes Today's Homes So Different, So Appealing?*

Austin Hansen, 1910-96, (U.S.) photographer. Harlem, NY, life.

Keith Haring, 1958-90, (U.S.) painter, muralist. *Crack is Wack.*

Childe Hassam, 1859-1935, (U.S.) Impressionist. *Southwest Wind, July 14 Rue Daunon.*

Edward Hicks, 1780-1849, (U.S.) folk. *The Peaceable Kingdom.*

Lewis Wickes Hine, 1874-1940, (U.S.) photographer. Studies of immigrants, children in industry.

Hans Hofmann, 1880-1966, (U.S.) early Abstract Expressionist. *Spring, The Gate.*

William Hogarth, 1697-1764, (Br.) caricaturist. *The Rake's Progress.*

Katsushika Hokusai, 1760-1849, (Jpn.) printmaker. *Crabs.*

Hans Holbein the Elder, 1460-1524, (Ger.) late Gothic. *Presentation of Christ in the Temple.*

Hans Holbein the Younger, 1497-1543, (Ger.) portraitist. *Henry VIII, The French Ambassadors.*

Winslow Homer, 1836-1910, (U.S.) naturalist, marine themes. *Marine Coast, High Cliff.*

Edward Hopper, 1882-1967, (U.S.) realistic urban scenes. *Nighthawks, House by the Railroad.*

Horst P. Horst, 1906-99, (Ger.) fashion, celebrity photographer.

Jean-Auguste-Dominique Ingres, 1780-1867, (Fr.) Classicist. *Valpincon Bather.*

George Inness, 1825-94, (U.S.) luminous landscapist. *Delaware Water Gap.*

William Henry Jackson, 1843-1942, (U.S.) photographer. American West, building of Union Pacific Railroad.

Jeanne-Claude (Javacheff), 1935-2009, (Moroc.), large-scale environmental installation artist with husband Christo. *The Gates, Surrounded Islands.*

Frances Benjamin Johnston, 1864-1952, (U.S.) photographer. Historic homes.

Donald Judd, 1928-94, (U.S.) sculptor, major Minimalist.

Frida Kahlo, 1907-54, (Mex.) folkloric stylist. *Self-Portrait With Monkey.*

Wassily Kandinsky, 1866-1944, (Russ.) Abstractionist. *Capricious Forms, Improvisation 28 (second version).*

Ellsworth Kelly, 1923-2015, (U.S.) painter, sculptor. *Red Blue Green.*

Paul Klee, 1879-1940, (Switz.) Abstractionist. *Twittering Machine, Pastoral, Death and Fire.*

Gustav Klimt, 1862-1918, (Austria) cofounder of Vienna Secession Movement. *The Kiss.*

Oskar Kokoschka, 1886-1980, (Austria) Expressionist. *View of Prague, Harbor of Marseilles.*

Käthe Kollwitz, 1867-1945, (Ger.) printmaker, social justice themes. *The Peasant War.*

Gaston Lachaise, 1882-1935, (U.S.) figurative sculptor. *Standing Woman.*

John La Farge, 1835-1910, (U.S.) muralist. *Red and White Peonies, The Ascension.*

Edwin (Henry) Landseer, 1802-73, (Br.) painter, sculptor. *Shoeing, Rout of Comus.*

Dorothea Lange, 1895-1965, (U.S.) photographer. Great Depression, migrant farm workers.

Fernand Léger, 1881-1955, (Fr.) Machine art. *The Cyclists.*

Saul Leiter, 1923-2013, (U.S.) photographer.

Leonardo da Vinci, 1452-1519, (It.) Renaissance. *Mona Lisa, Last Supper, The Annunciation.*

Emanuel Leutze, 1816-68, (U.S.) historical themes. *Washington Crossing the Delaware.*

Edmonia Lewis, 1844?-1907, (U.S.) sculptor. *The Death of Cleopatra.*

Roy Lichtenstein, 1923-97, (U.S.) Pop Art.

Jacques Lipchitz, 1891-1973, (Fr.) Cubist sculptor. *Harpist.*

Filippino Lippi, 1457-1504, (It.) Renaissance. *Adoration of the Magi.*

Fra Filippo Lippi, 1406-69, (It.) Renaissance. *Coronation of the Virgin, Madonna and Child With Angels.*

Morris Louis, 1912-62, (U.S.) Abstract Expressionist. *Signa, Stripes, Alpha-Phi.*

René Magritte, 1898-1967, (Belg.) Surrealist. *The Descent of Man, The Betrayal of Images.*

Aristide Maillol, 1861-1944, (Fr.) sculptor. *L'Harmonie.*

Édouard Manet, 1832-83, (Fr.) forerunner of Impressionism. *Luncheon on the Grass, Olympia.*

Andrea Mantegna, 1431-1506, (It.) Renaissance frescoes. *Triumph of Caesar.*

Robert Mapplethorpe, 1946-89, (U.S.) photographer.

Franz Marc, 1880-1916, (Ger.) Expressionist. *Blue Horses.*

John Marin, 1870-1953, (U.S.) Expressionist seascapes. *Maine Island.*

Reginald Marsh, 1898-1954, (U.S.) satire. *Tattoo and Haircut.*

Agnes Martin, 1912-2004, (U.S.) abstract artist. *Night Sea.*

Masaccio, 1401-28, (It.) Renaissance. *The Tribute Money.*

Henri Matisse, 1869-1954, (Fr.) Fauvist. *Woman With the Hat.*

John McCracken, 1934-2011, (U.S.) Minimalist sculptor.

Michelangelo Buonarroti, 1475-1564, (It.) Renaissance. *Pietà, David, Moses, The Last Judgment*, Sistine Chapel ceiling.

Jean-Francois Millet, 1814-75, (Fr.) peasants. *The Gleaners, The Man With a Hoe.*

Joan Miró, 1893-1983, (Sp.) exuberant colors, playful images. *Catalan landscape, Dutch Interior.*

Amedeo Modigliani, 1884-1920, (It.) figurative paintings, sculptures. *Reclining Nude.*

Piet Mondrian, 1872-1944, (Neth.) Abstractionist. *Composition With Red, Yellow and Blue.*

Claude Monet, 1840-1926, (Fr.) Impressionist. *The Bridge at Argenteuil, Haystacks, Bridge Over a Pond of Water Lillies.*

Henry Moore, 1898-1986, (Br.) sculptor of large-scale, abstract works. *Reclining Figure* (several).

Gustave Moreau, 1826-98, (Fr.) Symbolist. *The Apparition (Dance of Salome).*

James Wilson Morrice, 1865-1924, (Can.) landscapist. *The Ferry, Quebec, Venice, Looking Over the Lagoon.*

William Morris, 1834-96, (Br.) decorative artist, leader of Arts and Crafts movement.

Grandma Moses (Anna Mary Robertson Moses), 1860-1961, (U.S.) folk. *Out for the Christmas Tree, Catching the Thanksgiving Turkey.*

Samuel Morse, 1791-1872, (U.S.) portraitist. *Gallery of the Louvre.*

Edvard Munch, 1863-1944, (Nor.) Expressionist. *The Cry.*

Bartolome Murillo, 1618-82, (Sp.) Baroque religious artist. *Vision of St. Anthony, The Two Trinities.*

Elizabeth Murray, 1940-2007, (U.S.) abstract colors. *Kitchen Party.*

Eadweard Muybridge, 1830-1904, (Br.-U.S.) photographer. Studies of motion, *Animal Locomotion.*

Nadar (Gaspar-Félix Tournachon), 1820-1910, (Fr.) photographer, caricaturist, portraitist. Invented photo-essay.

LeRoy Neiman, 1921-2012, (U.S.) sports expressionist painter.

Arnold Newman, 1918-2006, (U.S.) portrait photographer.

Barnett Newman, 1905-70, (U.S.) Abstract Expressionist. *Stations of the Cross.*

Isamu Noguchi, 1904-88, (U.S.) abstract sculptor, designer. *Kouros, BirdC(MU)*, sculptural gardens.

Kenneth Noland, 1924-2010, (U.S.) Color Field, abstract.

Georgia O'Keeffe, 1887-1986, (U.S.) Southwest motifs. *Cow's Skull: Red, White, and Blue; The Shelton With Sunspots.*

José Clemente Orozco, 1883-1949, (Mex.) frescoes. *House of Tears, Pre-Columbian Golden Age.*

Timothy H. O'Sullivan, 1840-82, (U.S.) Civil War photographer.

Gordon Parks, 1912-2006, (U.S.) African American photographer, filmmaker. *Life* photographer, 1948-68.

Charles Willson Peale, 1741-1827, (U.S.) Amer. Revolutionary portraitist. *The Staircase Group*, U.S. presidents.

Rembrandt Peale, 1778-1860, (U.S.) portraitist. *Thomas Jefferson.*

Irving Penn, 1917-2009, (U.S.) portraitist, fashion photographer.

Pietro Perugino, 1446-1523, (It.) Renaissance. *Delivery of the Keys to St. Peter.*

Pablo Picasso, 1881-1973, (Sp.) painter, sculptor. *Guernica, Dove, Head of a Woman, Head of a Bull, Metamorphosis.*

Piero della Francesca, c. 1415-92, (It.) Renaissance. *Duke of Urbino, Flagellation of Christ.*

Camille Pissarro, 1830-1903, (Fr.) Impressionist. *Boulevard des Italiens, Morning, Sunlight; Bather in the Woods.*

Jackson Pollock, 1912-56, (U.S.) Abstract Expressionist. *Autumn Rhythm.*

Nicolas Poussin, 1594-1665, (Fr.) Baroque pictorial classicism. *St. John on Patmos.*

Maurice B. Prendergast, c. 1860-1924, (U.S.) Postimpressionist watercolorist. *Umbrellas in the Rain.*

Pierre-Paul Prud'hon, 1758-1823, (Fr.) Romanticist. *Crime Pursued by Vengeance and Justice.*

Pierre Cecile Puvis de Chavannes, 1824-98, (Fr.) muralist. *The Poor Fisherman.*

Raphael Sanzio, 1483-1520, (It.) Renaissance. *Disputa, School of Athens, Sistine Madonna.*

Robert Rauschenberg, 1925-2008, (U.S.) printmaker. *Combine, Bed, Revolvers, Outpost.*

Man Ray (Emmanuel Radnitsky), 1890-1976, (U.S.) Dadaist and Surrealist. *Observing Time, The Lovers, Marquis de Sade.*

Odilon Redon, 1840-1916, (Fr.) Symbolist painter, lithographer. *In the Dream, Vase of Flowers.*

Rembrandt van Rijn, 1606-69, (Neth.) painter, printmaker. *The Bridal Couple, The Night Watch.*

Frederic Remington, 1861-1909, (U.S.) painter, sculptor. Portrayer of the American West, *Bronco Buster.*

Pierre-Auguste Renoir, 1841-1919, (Fr.) Impressionist. *The Luncheon of the Boating Party, Dance in the Country.*

Joshua Reynolds, 1723-92, (Br.) portraitist. *Mrs. Siddons as the Tragic Muse.*

Herb Ritts, 1952-2002, (U.S.) photographer. Nudes, celebrities.

Diego Rivera, 1886-1957, (Mex.) frescoes. *The Fecund Earth.*

Larry Rivers, 1923-2002, (U.S.) painter, sculptor, often realistic. Dutch Masters series.

Henry Peach Robinson, 1830-1901, (Br.) a leader of "high art" photography.

Norman Rockwell, 1894-1978, (U.S.) painter, illustrator. *Saturday Evening Post* covers.

Auguste Rodin, 1840-1917, (Fr.) sculptor. *The Thinker.*

Milton Rogovin, 1909-2011, (U.S.) documentary photographer.

Willy Ronis, 1910-2009, (Fr.) photographer. Postwar Paris.

Joe Rosenthal, 1911-2006, (U.S.) photojournalist. Photographed six Marines raising the U.S. flag over Iwo Jima in WWII.

Mark Rothko, 1903-70, (U.S.) Abstract Expressionist. *Light, Earth and Blue.*

Georges Rouault, 1871-1958, (Fr.) Expressionist. *Three Judges.*

Henri Rousseau, 1844-1910, (Fr.) primitive exotic themes. *The Snake Charmer.*

Theodore Rousseau, 1812-67, (Switz.-Fr.) landscapist. *Under the Birches, Evening.*

Peter Paul Rubens, 1577-1640, (Flem.) Baroque. *Mystic Marriage of St. Catherine.*

Jacob van Ruisdael, c. 1628-82, (Neth.) landscapist. *Jewish Cemetery.*

Charles M. Russell, 1866-1926, (U.S.) Western life.

Salomon van Ruysdael, c. 1600-70, (Neth.) landscapist. *River With Ferry-Boat.*

Albert Pinkham Ryder, 1847-1917, (U.S.) seascapes. *Toilers of the Sea.*

Augustus Saint-Gaudens, 1848-1907, (U.S.) memorial statues. *Farragut, Mrs. Henry Adams (Grief).*

Niki de Saint Phalle, 1930-2002, (Fr.) paintings, sculptures, prints, large public installations.

Andrea Sansovino, 1460-1529, (It.) Renaissance sculptor. *Baptism of Christ.*

Jacopo Sansovino, 1486-1570, (It.) Renaissance sculptor. *St. John the Baptist.*

John Singer Sargent, 1856-1925, (U.S.) Edwardian society portraitist. *The Wyndham Sisters, Madame X.*

Andrea del Sarto, 1486-1530, (It.) frescoes. *Madonna of the Harpies.*

George Segal, 1924-2000, (U.S.) sculptor. Life-sized figures realistically depicting daily life.

Georges Seurat, 1859-91, (Fr.) Pointillist. *Sunday Afternoon on the Island of La Grande Jatte.*

Gino Severini, 1883-1966, (It.) Futurist and Cubist. *Dynamic Hieroglyph of the Bal Tabarin.*

Ben Shahn, 1898-1969, (U.S.) social and political themes. *Sacco and Vanzetti* series, *Seurat's Lunch, Handball.*

Charles Sheeler, 1883-1965, (U.S.) abstractionist.

David Alfaro Siqueiros, 1896-1974, (Mex.) political muralist. *March of Humanity.*

David Smith, 1906-65, (U.S.) welded metal sculpture. *Hudson River Landscape, Zig, Cubi* series.

Edward Steichen, 1879-1973, (U.S.) photographer. Credited with transforming photography into an art form.

Alfred Stieglitz, 1864-1946, (U.S.) photographer, editor. Helped create acceptance of photography as art.

Paul Strand, 1890-1976, (U.S.) photographer. People, nature, landscapes.

Gilbert Stuart, 1755-1828, (U.S.) portraitist. George Washington, Thomas Jefferson, James Madison.

Thomas Sully, 1783-1872, (U.S.) portraitist. *The Passage of the Delaware.*

William Henry Fox Talbot, 1800-77, (Br.) photographer. *Pencil of Nature,* early photographically illustrated book.

George Tames, 1919-94, (U.S.) photographer. Presidents, political leaders.

Yves Tanguy, 1900-55, (Fr.) Surrealist. *Mama, Papa Is Wounded!*

Giovanni Battista Tiepolo, 1696-1770, (It.) Rococo frescoes. *The Crucifixion.*

Louis Comfort Tiffany, 1848-1933, (U.S.) stained glass, decorative arts.

Jacopo Tintoretto, 1518-94, (It.) Mannerist. *The Last Supper.*

Titian (Tiziano Vecellio), c. 1488-1576, (It.) Renaissance. *Venus and the Lute Player, The Bacchanal.*

Jose Rey Toledo, 1916-94, (U.S.) Native American life. Tribal dances.

George Tooker, 1920-2011, (U.S.) Magic Realist. *Subway.*

Henri de Toulouse-Lautrec, 1864-1901, (Fr.) Postimpressionist. *At the Moulin Rouge.*

John Trumbull, 1756-1843, (U.S.) historical themes. *The Declaration of Independence.*

Deborah Turbeville, 1937-2013, (U.S.) fashion photographer.

J(oseph) M(allord) W(illiam) Turner, 1775-1851, (Br.) Romantic landscapist. *Snow Storm.*

Cy Twombly, 1928-2011, (U.S.) painter and sculptor. *Leda and the Swan.*

Paolo Uccello, 1397-1475, (It.) Gothic-Renaissance. *The Rout of San Romano.*

Maurice Utrillo, 1883-1955, (Fr.) Impressionist. *Sacré-Coeur de Montmartre.*

Vincent van Gogh, 1853-90, (Neth.) *The Starry Night, L'Arlesienne, Bedroom at Arles, Self-Portrait.*

John Vanderlyn, 1775-1852, (U.S.) Neoclassicist. *Ariadne Asleep on the Island of Naxos.*

Diego Velázquez, 1599-1660, (Sp.) Baroque. *Las Meninas, Portrait of Juan de Pareja.*

Jan Vermeer, 1632-75, (Neth.) interior genre subjects. *Young Woman With a Water Jug.*

Paolo Veronese, 1528-88, (It.) Venetian painter. *The Temptation of St. Anthony.*

Andrea del Verrocchio, 1435-88, (It.) sculptor. *Colleoni.*

Maurice de Vlaminck, 1876-1958, (Fr.) Fauvist landscapist, *Red Trees.*

Andy Warhol, 1928-87, (U.S.) Pop Art. *Campbell's Soup Cans, Marilyn Diptych.*

Antoine Watteau, 1684-1721, (Fr.) Rococo "scenes of gallantry." *The Embarkation for Cythera.*

George Frederic Watts, 1817-1904, (Br.) painter and sculptor. Grandiose allegorical themes. *Hope.*

Benjamin West, 1738-1820, (U.S.) realistic historical themes. *Death of General Wolfe.*

Edward Weston, 1886-1958, (U.S.) photographer. Landscapes of American West.

James Abbott McNeill Whistler, 1834-1903, (U.S.) *Arrangement in Grey and Black No. 1* (*Portrait of the Artist's Mother*).

Archibald M. Willard, 1836-1918, (U.S.) murals. *The Spirit of '76.*

Grant Wood, 1891-1942, (U.S.) Midwestern regionalist. *American Gothic, Daughters of Revolution.*

Andrew Wyeth, 1917-2009, (U.S.), regionalist. *Christina's World.*

Ossip Zadkine, 1890-1967, (Russ.) School of Paris sculptor. *The Destroyed City, Musicians, Christ.*

Business Leaders and Philanthropists of the Past

Giovanni Agnelli, 1921-2003, (It.) industrialist; principal shareholder of Fiat.

Karl Albrecht, 1920-2014, and **Theo Albrecht,** 1922-2010, (both Ger.) cofounders of Aldi supermarkets.

Paul Allen, 1953-2018, (U.S.) Microsoft cofounder; philanthropist.

Walter Annenberg, 1908-2002, (U.S.) publisher, founder of *TV Guide,* philanthropist.

Elizabeth Arden (F. N. Graham), 1884-1966, (U.S.) Canadian-born founder of cosmetics empire.

Philip D. Armour, 1832-1901, (U.S.) industrialist; streamlined meatpacking.

Brooke Astor, 1902-2007, (U.S.) philanthropist; pres. of Vincent Astor Foundation.

John Jacob Astor, 1763-1848, (U.S.) German-born fur trader, banker, real estate magnate; at death, richest in U.S.

Francis W. Ayer, 1848-1923, (U.S.) ad industry pioneer.

August Belmont, 1816-90, (U.S.) German-born financier.

Liliane Bettencourt, 1922-2017, (Fr.) L'Oreal heiress, philanthropist.

James B. (Diamond Jim) Brady, 1856-1917, (U.S.) financier, philanthropist, legendary bon vivant.

Adolphus Busch, 1839-1913, (U.S.) German-born brewery founder.

Asa Candler, 1851-1929, (U.S.) founded Coca-Cola Co.

Andrew Carnegie, 1835-1919, (U.S.) Scottish-born industrialist, philanthropist; founded Carnegie Steel Co.

Tom Carvel, 1908-89, (Gr.-U.S.) founded ice cream chain.

William Colgate, 1783-1857, (Br.-U.S.) businessman, philanthropist; founded soap-making empire.

Jay Cooke, 1821-1905, (U.S.) financier.

Peter Cooper, 1791-1883, (U.S.) industrialist, inventor, philanthropist; founded Cooper Union college (1859).

Ezra Cornell, 1807-74, (U.S.) businessman, philanthropist; headed Western Union.

Erastus Corning, 1794-1872, (U.S.) financier; headed New York Central Railroad.

Charles Crocker, 1822-88, (U.S.) railroad builder, financier.

Samuel Cunard, 1787-1865, (Can.) pioneered transatlantic steam navigation.

Marcus Daly, 1841-1900, (U.S.) Irish-born copper magnate.

W. Edwards Deming, 1900-93, (U.S.) quality-control expert who revolutionized Japanese manufacturing.

Walt Disney, 1901-66, (U.S.) pioneer in cinema animation; built entertainment empire.

Herbert H. Dow, 1866-1930, (U.S.) founder of chemical co.

Anthony Drexel, 1826-93, (U.S.) banker, philanthropist, university founder.

James Duke, 1856-1925, (U.S.) founded American Tobacco, Duke Univ.

Eleuthere I. du Pont, 1771-1834, (Fr.-U.S.) gunpowder manufacturer.

Thomas C. Durant, 1820-85, (U.S.) railroad official, financier.

William C. Durant, 1861-1947, (U.S.) industrialist; formed General Motors.

George Eastman, 1854-1932, (U.S.) inventor; manufacturer of photographic equipment.

Marshall Field, 1834-1906, (U.S.) founded Chicago's largest department store.

Harvey Firestone, 1868-1938, (U.S.) founded tire company.

Avery Fisher, 1906-94, (U.S.) industrialist, philanthropist; founded Fisher Electronics.

Henry M. Flagler, 1830-1913, (U.S.) financier; helped form Standard Oil, developed FL as resort state.

Malcolm Forbes, 1919-90, (U.S.) magazine publisher.

Henry Ford, 1863-1947, (U.S.) automaker; developed first popular low-priced car.

Henry Ford II, 1917-87, (U.S.) headed auto company founded by grandfather.

Henry C. Frick, 1849-1919, (U.S.) steel and coke magnate; had prominent role in development of U.S. Steel.

Jakob Fugger (Jakob the Rich), 1459-1525, (Ger.) headed leading banking, trading house in 16th-cent. Europe.

Alfred C. Fuller, 1885-1973, (U.S.) Canadian-born businessman; founded brush company.

Elbert H. Gary, 1846-1927, (U.S.) chaired board of U.S. Steel, 1903-27.

Jean Paul Getty, 1892-1976, (U.S.) founded oil empire.

Amadeo Giannini, 1870-1949, (U.S.) founded Bank of America.

Stephen Girard, 1750-1831, (U.S.) French-born financier, philanthropist.

Leonard H. Goldenson, 1905-99, (U.S.) turned ABC into major TV network.

Jay Gould, 1836-92, (U.S.) railroad magnate, financier.

Hetty Green, 1834-1916, (U.S.) financier nicknamed "witch of Wall St."

William Gregg, 1800-67, (U.S.) launched textile industry in the South.

Meyer Guggenheim, 1828-1905, (U.S.) Swiss-born merchant, philanthropist; built merchandising, mining empires.

Armand Hammer, 1898-1990, (U.S.) headed Occidental Petroleum.

Elliot Handler, 1916-2011, (U.S.) cofounder of Mattel; introduced the Barbie doll.

Edward H. Harriman, 1848-1909, (U.S.) railroad magnate; headed Union Pacific.

Hugh Hefner, 1926-2017, (U.S.) founded Playboy Enterprises.

Henry J. Heinz, 1844-1919, (U.S.) founded food empire.

Harry, 1909-97, and **Leona Helmsley,** 1920-2007, (both U.S.) real estate magnates, philanthropists.

Milton Snavely Hershey, 1857-1945, (U.S.) chocolate co. founder, philanthropist.

James J. Hill, 1838-1916, (U.S.) Canadian-born railroad magnate, financier; founded Great Northern Railway.

Conrad N. Hilton, 1888-1979, (U.S.) hotel chain founder.

Howard Hughes, 1905-76, (U.S.) industrialist, aviator, filmmaker.

H. L. Hunt, 1889-1974, (U.S.) oil magnate.

Collis P. Huntington, 1821-1900, (U.S.) railroad magnate.

Henry E. Huntington, 1850-1927, (U.S.) railroad builder, philanthropist.

Lee Iacocca, 1924-2019, (U.S.) auto executive (Ford, Chrysler).

Walter L. Jacobs, 1898-1985, (U.S.) founder of the first rental car agency.

Steve Jobs, 1955-2011, (U.S.) Apple cofounder and exec.; Pixar exec.

Howard Johnson, 1896-1972, (U.S.) founded restaurants.

John H. Johnson, 1918-2005, (U.S.) publisher of *Ebony* and *Jet.*

Samuel Curtis Johnson, 1928-2004, (U.S.) headed S.C. Johnson & Sons.

Henry J. Kaiser, 1882-1967, (U.S.) industrialist; built empire in steel, aluminum.

Ingvar Kamprad, 1926-2018, (Swed.) Ikea founder.

Minor C. Keith, 1848-1929, (U.S.) railroad magnate; founded United Fruit Co.

Will K. Kellogg, 1860-1951, (U.S.) businessman, philanthropist; founded breakfast food co.

Kirk Kerkorian, 1917-2015, (U.S.) private equity magnate; real estate developer.

Richard King, 1825-85, (U.S.) cattle farmer; founded King Ranch in Texas.

John W. Kluge, 1914-2010, (Ger.-U.S.) Metromedia chair; philanthropist.

William S. Knudsen, 1879-1948, (U.S.) Danish-born auto industry executive.

David Koch, 1940-2019, (U.S.) businessman, chemical engineer, political activist.

Samuel H. Kress, 1863-1955, (U.S.) businessman, art collector, philanthropist; founded "dime store" chain.

Ray A. Kroc, 1902-84, (U.S.) oversaw vast expansion of McDonald's.

Alfred Krupp, 1812-87, (Ger.) armaments magnate.

Estée Lauder, 1908-2004, (U.S.) cofounder of Estée Lauder companies.

Kenneth L. Lay, 1942-2006, (U.S.) former CEO of Enron; indicted on fraud charges.

William Levitt, 1907-94, (U.S.) industrialist; "suburb maker."

Thomas Lipton, 1850-1931, (Scot.) merchant; tea empire.

James McGill, 1744-1813, (Scot.-Can.) funded Montréal's McGill Univ.

Andrew W. Mellon, 1855-1937, (U.S.) financier, industrialist, philanthropist.

Charles E. Merrill, 1885-1956, (U.S.) financier; developed firm of Merrill Lynch.

J(ohn) P(ierpont) Morgan, 1837-1913, (U.S.) most powerful figure in finance and industry at turn of 20th cent.

Akio Morita, 1921-99, (Jpn.) cofounded Sony Corp.

Malcolm Muir, 1885-1979, (U.S.) created *Business Week;* led *Newsweek,* 1937-61.

Roy Neuberger, 1903-2010, (U.S.) financier, art patron.

Samuel Newhouse, 1895-1979, (U.S.) publishing and broadcasting magnate.
Jean Nidetch, 1923-2015, (U.S.) Weight Watchers cofounder.
Aristotle Onassis, 1906-75, (Gr.) shipping magnate.
William S. Paley, 1901-90, (U.S.) built CBS communications empire.
Frederick D. Patterson, 1901-88, (U.S.) founder of United Negro College Fund, 1944.
George Peabody, 1795-1869, (U.S.) merchant, financier, philanthropist.
James C. Penney, 1875-1971, (U.S.) businessman; developed department store.
Frank Perdue, 1920-2005, (U.S.) founder of Perdue Farms, chicken-processing co.
Ross Perot, 1930-2019, (U.S.) computer services pioneer, philanthropist; 2-time pres. candidate (Ind.)
William C. Procter, 1862-1934, (U.S.) headed soap co.
Sumner Redstone, 1923-2020, (U.S.) National Amusements owner, incl. subsidiaries Viacom, CBS.
David Rockefeller, 1915-2017, (U.S.) banker, philanthropist.
John D. Rockefeller, 1839-1937, (U.S.) industrialist; established Standard Oil.
John D. Rockefeller Jr., 1874-1960, (U.S.) philanthropist; provided land for UN.
Laurance S. Rockefeller, 1910-2004, (U.S.) philanthropist, conservationist.
Meyer A. Rothschild, 1743-1812, (Ger.) founded international banking house.

Thomas Fortune Ryan, 1851-1928, (U.S.) financier; a founder of American Tobacco.
Edmond J. Safra, 1932-99, (U.S.) banker.
David Sarnoff, 1891-1971, (U.S.) broadcasting pioneer; established first radio network, NBC.
Richard Sears, 1863-1914, (U.S.) founded mail-order co.
Werner von Siemens, 1816-92, (Ger.) industrialist, inventor.
Alfred P. Sloan, 1875-1966, (U.S.) industrialist, philanthropist; headed GM.
A. Leland Stanford, 1824-93, (U.S.) railroad official, philanthropist; founded university.
Frank Stanton, 1908-2006, (U.S.) president of CBS network, 1946-71.
Nathan Straus, 1848-1931, (U.S.) German-born merchant, philanthropist; headed Macy's dept. stores.
Levi Strauss, c. 1829-1902, (U.S.) pants manufacturer.
Clement Studebaker, 1831-1901, (U.S.) wagon, carriage maker.
Gustavus Swift, 1839-1903, (U.S.) pioneer meatpacker.
Gerard Swope, 1872-1957, (U.S.) industrialist, economist; headed General Electric.
Dave Thomas, 1932-2002, (U.S.) Wendy's restaurant chain founder.
James Walter Thompson, 1847-1928, (U.S.) ad exec., founder of ad agency.
Alice Tully, 1902-93, (U.S.) arts patron.
Theodore N. Vail, 1845-1920, (U.S.) organized Bell Telephone, led AT&T.
Cornelius Vanderbilt, 1794-1877, (U.S.) financier; established steamship, railroad empires.

Lillian Vernon, 1927-2015, (Ger.-U.S.) catalog merchant, philanthropist.
Henry Villard, 1835-1900, (U.S.) German-born railroad executive, financier.
Charles R. Walgreen, 1873-1939, (U.S.) founded drugstore chain.
Madame C. J. Walker, 1867-1919, (U.S.) African American hair care entrepreneur, philanthropist.
DeWitt, 1889-1981, and **Lila Wallace**, 1889-1964, (both U.S.) cofounders of *Reader's Digest* magazine.
Sam Walton, 1918-92, (U.S.) Walmart founder.
John Wanamaker, 1838-1922, (U.S.) department-store merchandising pioneer.
Aaron Montgomery Ward, 1843-1913, (U.S.) established first mail-order firm.
Thomas J. Watson, 1874-1956, (U.S.) IBM head, 1914-56.
Jack Welch, 1935-2020, (U.S.) General Electric CEO.
George Westinghouse, 1846-1914, (U.S) inventor, manufacturer; organized Westinghouse Electric Co., 1886.
John Hay Whitney, 1905-82, (U.S.) publisher, sportsman, philanthropist.
Chuck Williams, 1915-2015, (U.S.) Williams-Sonoma founder.
Charles E. Wilson, 1890-1961, (U.S.) auto exec., public official.
Frank W. Woolworth, 1852-1919, (U.S.) created five-and-dime chain.
William Wrigley Jr., 1861-1932, (U.S.) founded Wrigley chewing gum co.

American Cartoonists

Reviewed by Lucy Shelton Caswell, Professor and Curator, Cartoon Research Library, Ohio State University.

Scott Adams, b 1957, Dilbert.
Charles Addams, 1912-88, macabre cartoons.
Brad Anderson, 1924-2015, Marmaduke.
Sergio Aragonés, b 1937, (Span.-Mex.) *Mad* magazine.
Peter Arno, 1904-68, *The New Yorker*.
Tex Avery, 1908-80, animator; Bugs Bunny, Porky Pig.
George Baker, 1915-75, The Sad Sack.
Carl Barks, 1901-2000, Donald Duck comic books.
Alison Bechdel, b 1960, graphic novelist.
C. C. Beck, 1910-89, Captain Marvel.
Dave Berg, 1920-2002, *Mad* magazine.
Jim Berry, 1932-2015, Berry's World.
Herb Block (Herblock), 1909-2001, political cartoonist.
George Booth, b 1926, *The New Yorker*.
Loren Bouchard, b 1969, Bob's Burgers.
Berkeley Breathed, b 1957, Bloom County.
Dik Browne, 1917-89, Hi & Lois, Hagar the Horrible.
Marjorie Buell, 1904-93, Little Lulu.
Ernie Bushmiller, 1905-82, Nancy.
Milton Caniff, 1907-88, Terry & the Pirates, Steve Canyon.
Al Capp, 1909-79, Li'l Abner.
Roz Chast, b 1954, *The New Yorker*.
Gene Colan, 1926-2011, Daredevil.
Paul Conrad, 1924-2010, political cartoonist.
Roy Crane, 1901-77, Captain Easy, Buz Sawyer.
R(obert) Crumb, b 1943, underground cartoonist.
Shamus Culhane, 1908-96, animator.
Jay N. "Ding" Darling, 1876-1962, political cartoonist.
Jack Davis, 1924-2016, *Mad* magazine.
Jim Davis, b 1945, Garfield.
Billy DeBeck, 1890-1942, Barney Google.
Rudolph Dirks, 1877-1968, The Katzenjammer Kids.
Walt Disney, 1901-66, produced animated cartoons; Mickey Mouse, Donald Duck.
Steve Ditko, 1927-2018, Spider-Man.
Mort Drucker, 1929-2020, *Mad* magazine.
Will Eisner, 1917-2005, The Spirit.
Jules Feiffer, b 1929, political cartoonist.
Bud Fisher, 1885-1954, Mutt & Jeff.
Ham Fisher, 1900-55, Joe Palooka.
Max Fleischer, 1883-1972, Betty Boop.
Hal Foster, 1892-1982, Tarzan, Prince Valiant.
Fontaine Fox, 1884-1964, Toonerville Folks.
Isadore "Friz" Freleng, 1905-95, animator; Yosemite Sam, Porky Pig, Sylvester and Tweety Bird.
Rube Goldberg, 1883-1970, Boob McNutt.
Chester Gould, 1900-85, Dick Tracy.
Harold Gray, 1894-1968, Little Orphan Annie.
Matt Groening, b 1954, Life in Hell, The Simpsons.
Cathy Guisewite, b 1950, Cathy.

Bill Hanna, 1910-2001, and **Joe Barbera**, 1911-2006, animators; Tom & Jerry, Yogi Bear, Flintstones.
Oliver Harrington, 1912-95, Bootsie.
Johnny Hart, 1931-2007, B.C., Wizard of Id.
Alfred Harvey, 1913-94, created Casper the Friendly Ghost.
Jimmy Hatlo, 1898-1963, Little Iodine.
John Held Jr., 1889-1958, Jazz Age.
George Herriman, 1881-1944, Krazy Kat.
Harry Hershfield, 1885-1974, Abie the Agent.
Stephen Hillenburg, 1961-2018, SpongeBob SquarePants.
Al Hirschfeld, 1903-2003, *NY Times* theater caricaturist.
Burne Hogarth, 1911-96, Tarzan.
Helen Hokinson, 1900-49, *The New Yorker*.
Nicole Hollander, b 1939, Sylvia.
Al Jaffee, b 1921, *Mad* magazine.
Lynn Johnston, b 1947, (Can.) For Better or For Worse.
Oliver Johnston, 1912-2008, Disney animator.
Chuck Jones, 1912-2002, animator; Bugs Bunny, Porky Pig; created Road Runner, Wile E. Coyote.
Mike Judge, b 1962, Beavis and Butt-Head, King of the Hill.
Bob Kane, 1916-98, Batman.
Bil Keane, 1922-2011, The Family Circus.
Walt Kelly, 1913-73, Pogo.
Hank Ketcham, 1920-2001, Dennis the Menace.
Ted Key, 1912-2008, Hazel.
Frank King, 1883-1969, Gasoline Alley.
Jack Kirby, 1917-94, Fantastic Four, The Incredible Hulk.
Rollin Kirby, 1875-1952, political cartoonist.
B(ernard) Kliban, 1935-90, cat books.
Edward Koren, b 1935, *The New Yorker*.
John Kricfalusi, b 1955, Ren & Stimpy.
Joe Kubert, 1926-2012, Sgt. Rock.
Harvey Kurtzman, 1921-93, *Mad* magazine.
Walter Lantz, 1900-94, Woody Woodpecker.
Gary Larson, b 1950, The Far Side.
Mell Lazarus, 1927-2016, Momma.
Stan Lee, 1922-2018, Marvel Comics.
David Levine, 1926-2009, *NY Review of Books* caricatures.
Seth MacFarlane, b 1973, Family Guy.
Jeff MacNelly, 1947-2000, political cartoonist; Shoe.
Doug Marlette, 1949-2007, political cartoonist; Kudzu.
Don Martin, 1931-2000, *Mad* magazine.
Bill Mauldin, 1921-2003, political cartoonist.
Winsor McCay, 1872-1934, Little Nemo.
John T. McCutcheon, 1870-1949, political cartoonist.
Patrick McDonnell, b 1956, Mutts.
Dwayne McDuffie, 1962-2011, Justice League.
Aaron McGruder, b 1974, The Boondocks.

George McManus, 1884-1954, Bringing Up Father.
Dale Messick, 1906-2005, Brenda Starr.
Wiley Miller, b 1951, Non Sequitur.
Norman Mingo, 1896-1980, Alfred E. Neuman.
Bob Montana, 1920-75, Archie.
Dick Moores, 1909-86, Gasoline Alley.
Willard Mullin, 1902-78, sports cartoonist; Dodgers' "Brooklyn Bum," "Mets Kid."
Randall Munroe, b 1984, xkcd.
Russell Myers, b 1938, Broom Hilda.
Thomas Nast, 1840-1902, political cartoonist; Republican elephant, Democratic donkey.
Pat Oliphant, b 1935, political cartoonist.
Frederick Burr Opper, 1857-1937, Happy Hooligan.
Richard Outcault, 1863-1928, Yellow Kid, Buster Brown.
Brant Parker, 1920-2007, Wizard of Id.
Trey Parker, b 1969, South Park co-creator.
Harvey Pekar, 1939-2010, American Splendor.
Mike Peters, b 1943, Mother Goose & Grimm.
George Price, 1901-95, *The New Yorker*.
Antonio Prohias, 1921-98, Spy vs. Spy.
Alex Raymond, 1909-56, Flash Gordon, Jungle Jim.
Forrest (Bud) Sagendorf, 1915-94, Popeye.
Art Sansom, 1920-91, The Born Loser.
Charles Schulz, 1922-2000, Peanuts.
Elzie C. Segar, 1894-1938, Popeye.
Marie Severin, 1929-2018, Marvel Comics.
Joe Shuster, 1914-92, and **Jerry Siegel**, 1914-96, Superman.
Sidney Smith, 1887-1935, The Gumps.
Otto Soglow, 1900-75, Little King.
Art Spiegelman, b 1948, Raw, Maus.
William Steig, 1907-2003, *The New Yorker*.
Matt Stone, b 1971, South Park co-creator.
James Swinnerton, 1875-1974, Little Jimmy, Canyon Kiddies.
Paul Szep, b 1941, political cartoonist.
Paul Terry, 1887-1971, animator of Mighty Mouse.
Bob Thaves, 1924-2006, Frank and Ernest.
James Thurber, 1894-61, *The New Yorker*.
Garry Trudeau, b 1948, Doonesbury.
Jim Unger, 1937-2012, Herman.
Mort Walker, 1923-2018, Beetle Bailey.
Bill Watterson, b 1958, Calvin and Hobbes.
Russ Westover, 1887-1966, Tillie the Toiler.
Signe Wilkinson, b 1950, political cartoonist.
Frank Willard, 1893-1958, Moon Mullins.
J. R. Williams, 1888-1957, The Willets Family, Out Our Way.
Gahan Wilson, 1930-2019, *The New Yorker*.
Tom Wilson, 1931-2011, Ziggy.
Art Young, 1866-1943, political cartoonist.
Chic Young, 1901-73, Blondie.

Economists, Educators, Historians, and Social Scientists of the Past

For psychologists, see Scientists of the Past.

Brooks Adams, 1848-1927, (U.S.) historian, political theoretician; *The Law of Civilization and Decay.*

Henry Adams, 1838-1918, (U.S.) historian, autobiographer; *The Education of Henry Adams.*

Stephen Ambrose, 1936-2002, (U.S.) historian; *Eisenhower.*

Hannah Arendt, 1906-75, (Ger.) political philosopher; *The Origins of Totalitarianism.*

Francis Bacon, 1561-1626, (Eng.) philosopher, essayist, statesman; championed observation and induction.

George Bancroft, 1800-91, (U.S.) historian; 10-volume *History of the United States.*

Jack Barbash, 1910-94, (U.S.) labor economist; helped create the AFL-CIO.

Henry Barnard, 1811-1900, (U.S.) public school reformer.

Charles A. Beard, 1874-1948, (U.S.) historian; *The Economic Basis of Politics.*

(St.) Bede (the Venerable), c. 673-735, (Br.) scholar, historian; *Ecclesiastical History of the English People.*

Daniel Bell, 1919-2011, (U.S.) sociologist; *The End of Ideology.*

Ruth Benedict, 1887-1948, (U.S.) anthropologist; studied Indian tribes of the Southwest.

Isaiah Berlin, 1909-97, (Br.) philosopher, historian; *The Age of Enlightenment.*

Leonard Bloomfield, 1887-1949, (U.S.) linguist; *Language.*

Franz Boas, 1858-1942, (U.S.) German-born anthropologist; studied American Indians.

Van Wyck Brooks, 1886-1963, (U.S.) historian; critic of New England culture, especially literature.

Edmund Burke, 1729-97, (Ire.) British parliamentarian and political philosopher; *Reflections on the Revolution in France.*

James MacGregor Burns, 1918-2014, (U.S.) historian, political scientist.

Nicholas Murray Butler, 1862-1947, (U.S.) educator; headed Columbia Univ., 1902-45; 1931 Nobel Peace Prize winner.

Joseph Campbell, 1904-87, (U.S.) author, editor, teacher; wrote books on mythology, folklore.

Thomas Carlyle, 1795-1881, (Scot.) historian, critic; *Sartor Resartus, Past and Present, The French Revolution.*

(Charles) Bruce Catton, 1899-1978, (U.S.) historian; *A Stillness at Appomattox.*

Edward Channing, 1856-1931, (U.S.) historian; 6-volume *History of the United States.*

Henry Steele Commager, 1902-98, (U.S.) historian, educator; *The Growth of the American Republic.*

John R. Commons, 1862-1945, (U.S.) economist, labor historian; *Legal Foundations of Capitalism.*

James B. Conant, 1893-1978, (U.S.) educator, diplomat; *The American High School Today.*

Benedetto Croce, 1866-1952, (It.) philosopher, statesman, historian; *Philosophy of the Spirit.*

Bernard A. De Voto, 1897-1955, (U.S.) historian; wrote trilogy on American West, edited Mark Twain manuscripts.

Melvil Dewey, 1851-1931, (U.S.) devised decimal system of library-book classification.

Donald Herbert Donald, 1920-2009, (U.S.) Pulitzer Prize-winning Civil War and Lincoln historian.

St. Clair Drake, 1911-90, (U.S.) sociologist, Black studies pioneer; *Black Metropolis* (1945), with Horace R. Cayton.

W(illiam) E(dward) B(urghardt) Du Bois, 1868-1963, (U.S.) historian, sociologist; NAACP founder, 1909.

Will(iam), 1885-1981, (U.S.) and **Ariel Durant**, 1898-1981, (Ukraine) historians; *The Story of Civilization.*

Émile Durkheim, 1858-1917, (Fr.) a founder of modern sociology; *The Rules of Sociological Method.*

Charles Eliot, 1834-1926, (U.S.) educator, Harvard president.

Friedrich Engels, 1820-95, (Ger.) political writer; with Karl Marx wrote the *Communist Manifesto.*

Irving Fisher, 1867-1947, (U.S.) economist; contributed to the development of modern monetary theory.

John Fiske, 1842-1901, (U.S.) historian and lecturer; popularized Darwinian theory of evolution.

Charles Fourier, 1772-1837, (Fr.) utopian socialist.

John Hope Franklin, 1915-2009, (U.S.) historian; *From Slavery to Freedom: A History of African Americans.*

James George Frazer, 1854-1941, (Br.) anthropologist; studied myth in religion; *The Golden Bough.*

Milton Friedman, 1912-2006, (U.S.) economist; advocate for free markets.

Paul Fussell, 1924-2012, (U.S.) literary historian; *The Great War and Modern Memory.*

John Kenneth Galbraith, 1908-2006, (Can.-U.S.) economist, author, professor, former amb. to India.

Peter Gay, 1923-2015, (Ger.-U.S.) cultural historian; *The Enlightenment: An Interpretation.*

Giovanni Gentile, 1875-1944, (It.) philosopher, educator; reformed Italian educational system.

Henry George, 1839-97, (U.S.) economist, reformer; led single-tax movement.

Edward Gibbon, 1737-94, (Br.) historian; *The History of the Decline and Fall of the Roman Empire.*

Horace Greeley, 1928-2013, (U.S.) Rom. Cath. priest; sociologist.

Francesco Guicciardini, 1483-1540, (It.) historian; *Storia d'Italia,* principal historical work of the 16th cent.

Thomas Hobbes, 1588-1679, (Eng.) philosopher, political theorist; *Leviathan.*

Richard Hofstadter, 1916-70, (U.S.) historian; *The Age of Reform.*

Charles Hamilton Houston, 1895-1950, (U.S.) African-American lawyer, Howard Univ. instructor; champion of minority rights.

Samuel Huntington, 1927-2008, (U.S.), political scientist, Harvard University professor; *The Clash of Civilizations.*

Alfred Kahn, 1917-2010, (U.S.) economist; deregulated the U.S. airline industry.

John Keegan, 1934-2012, (Br.) war historian; *The Face of Battle.*

George F. Kennan, 1904-2005, (U.S.) diplomat, historian; main architect of U.S. Cold War "containment" strategy.

John Maynard Keynes, 1883-1946, (Br.) economist; principal advocate of deficit spending.

Alfred Kinsey, 1894-1956, (U.S.) zoologist; pioneering human sex researcher.

Russell Kirk, 1918-94, (U.S.), social philosopher; *The Conservative Mind.*

Alfred L. Kroeber, 1876-1960, (U.S.) cultural anthropologist; studied Indians of North and South America.

Elisabeth Kubler-Ross, 1926-2004, (Switz.) psychiatrist, author; *On Death and Dying.*

Christopher Lasch, 1932-94, (U.S.) social critic, historian; *The Culture of Narcissism.*

James L. Laughlin, 1850-1933, (U.S.) economist; helped establish Federal Reserve System.

Margaret Leech, 1893-1974, (U.S.) historian; *Reveille in Washington, 1860-1865.*

Lucien Lévy-Bruhl, 1857-1939, (Fr.) philosopher; studied the psychology of primitive societies; *Primitive Mentality.*

John Locke, 1632-1704, (Eng.) philosopher, political theorist; *Two Treatises of Government.*

Thomas B. Macaulay, 1800-59, (Br.) historian, statesman.

Niccolò Machiavelli, 1469-1527, (It.) writer, statesman; *The Prince.*

Bronislaw Malinowski, 1884-1942, (Pol.) considered the father of social anthropology.

Thomas R. Malthus, 1766-1834, (Br.) economist; *Essay on the Principle of Population.*

Horace Mann, 1796-1859, (U.S.) pioneered modern public school system.

Karl Mannheim, 1893-1947, (Hung.) sociologist, historian; *Ideology and Utopia.*

Harriet Martineau, 1802-76, (Eng.) writer, feminist; *Society in America.*

Karl Marx, 1818-83, (Ger.) political theorist, proponent of Communism; *Communist Manifesto, Das Kapital.*

Benjamin Mays, 1895-1984, (U.S.) minister, educator, civil rights leader; headed Morehouse College, 1940-67.

Giuseppe Mazzini, 1805-72, (It.) political philosopher.

William H. McGuffey, 1800-73, (U.S.) his *Reader* was a mainstay of 19th-cent. U.S. public education.

George H. Mead, 1863-1931, (U.S.) philosopher, social psychologist.

Margaret Mead, 1901-78, (U.S.) cultural anthropologist; popularized field; *Coming of Age in Samoa.*

Alexander Meiklejohn, 1872-1964, (U.S.) Br.-born educator; championed academic freedom and experimental curricula.

James Mill, 1773-1836, (Scot.) philosopher, historian, economist; a proponent of utilitarianism.

John Stuart Mill, 1806-73, (Eng.) philosopher, economist; *Utilitarianism.* Eldest son of James Mill.

Perry G. Miller, 1905-63, (U.S.) historian; interpreted 17th-cent. New England.

Theodor Mommsen, 1817-1903, (Ger.) historian; *The History of Rome.*

Ashley Montagu, 1905-99, (Eng.) anthropologist; *The Natural Superiority of Women.*

Charles-Louis Montesquieu, 1689-1755, (Fr.) social philosopher; *The Spirit of Laws.*

Maria Montessori, 1870-1952, (It.) educator, physician; started Montessori method of student self-motivation.

Samuel Eliot Morison, 1887-1976, (U.S.) historian; chronicled voyages of early explorers.

Edmund Morris, 1940-2019, (Br.-U.S.) historian, presidential biographer (T. Roosevelt, Reagan).

Lewis Mumford, 1895-1990, (U.S.) sociologist, critic; *The Culture of Cities.*

Gunnar Myrdal, 1898-1987, (Swed.) economist, social scientist; *Asian Drama: An Inquiry Into the Poverty of Nations.*

Allan Nevins, 1890-1971, (U.S.) historian, biographer; *The Ordeal of the Union.*

José Ortega y Gasset, 1883-1955, (Sp.) philosopher; advocated control by elite; *The Revolt of the Masses.*

Elinor Ostrom, 1933-2012, (U.S.) political economist.

Robert Owen, 1771-1858, (Br.) political philosopher, reformer; pioneer in cooperative movement.

Thomas Paine, 1737-1809, (Br.-U.S.) political theorist, writer; *Common Sense.*

Vilfredo Pareto, 1848-1923, (It.) economist, sociologist.

Francis Parkman, 1823-93, (U.S.) historian; *France and England in North America.*

Elizabeth P. Peabody, 1804-94, (U.S.) education pioneer; founded first kindergarten in U.S., 1860.

William Prescott, 1796-1859, (U.S.) early American historian; *The Conquest of Peru.*

Pierre Joseph Proudhon, 1809-65, (Fr.) social theorist; father of anarchism; *The Philosophy of Property.*

François Quesnay, 1694-1774, (Fr.) economic theorist.

Robert V. Remini, 1921-2013, (U.S.) historian; *The Life of Andrew Jackson*.

David Ricardo, 1772-1823, (Br.) economic theorist; advocated free international trade.

David Riesman, 1909-2002, (U.S.) sociologist; co-author, *The Lonely Crowd*.

Jacqueline de Romilly, 1913-2010, (Fr.) scholar of Greek civilization and language.

Theodore Roszak, 1933-2011, (U.S.) historian; *The Making of a Counter Culture*.

Jean-Jacques Rousseau, 1712-78, (Fr.) social philosopher; the father of romantic sensibility; *Confessions*.

Paul Samuelson, 1915-2009, (U.S.) economist, famed for modern mathematical approach to economics.

Edward Sapir, 1884-1939, (Ger.-U.S.) anthropologist; studied ethnology and linguistics of American Indian groups.

Ferdinand de Saussure, 1857-1913, (Switz.) a founder of modern linguistics.

Arthur Schlesinger Jr., 1917-2007, (U.S.) historian, author; *The Imperial Presidency*.

Joseph Schumpeter, 1883-1950, (Czech.-U.S.) economist, sociologist.

Elizabeth Seton, 1774-1821, (U.S.) nun; established parochial school education in U.S., first native-born American saint.

Georg Simmel, 1858-1918, (Ger.) sociologist, philosopher; helped establish German sociology.

Robert Sklar, 1936-2011, (U.S.) film scholar.

Adam Smith, 1723-90, (Br.) economist; advocated laissez-faire economy, free trade; *The Wealth of Nations*.

Jared Sparks, 1789-1866, (U.S.) historian, educator, editor; *The Library of American Biography*.

Oswald Spengler, 1880-1936, (Ger.) philosopher, historian; *The Decline of the West*.

Leo Steinberg, 1920-2011, (Russ.-U.S.) art historian.

William G. Sumner, 1840-1910, (U.S.) social scientist, economist; laissez-faire economy, Social Darwinism.

Hippolyte Taine, 1828-93, (Fr.) historian, basis of naturalistic school; *The Origins of Contemporary France*.

A(lan) J(ohn) P(ercivale) Taylor, 1906-90, (Br.) historian; *The Origins of the Second World War*.

Nikolaas Tinbergen, 1907-88, (Neth.-Br.) ethologist; pioneer in study of animal behavior.

Alexis de Tocqueville, 1805-59, (Fr.) political scientist, historian; *Democracy in America*.

Francis E. Townsend, 1867-1960, (U.S.) led old-age pension movement, 1933.

Arnold Toynbee, 1889-1975, (Br.) historian; *A Study of History*, sweeping analysis of hist. of civilizations.

George Trevelyan, 1876-1962, (Br.) historian, statesman; favored "literary" over "scientific" history; *History of England*.

Henri Troyat, 1911-2007, (Russ.-Fr.), biographies of major figures in Russian history.

Frederick J. Turner, 1861-1932, (U.S.) historian, educator; *The Frontier in American History*.

Thorstein B. Veblen, 1857-1929, (U.S.) economist, social philosopher; *The Theory of the Leisure Class*.

Giovanni Vico, 1668-1744, (It.) historian, biographer; regarded by many as first modern historian; *New Science*.

Izaak Walton, 1593-1683, (Eng.) biographer; political-philosophical study of fishing, *The Compleat Angler*.

Booker T. Washington, 1856-1915, (U.S.) founder, 1881, and first pres. of Tuskegee Institute; *Up From Slavery*.

Sidney J., 1859-1947, and **Beatrice Webb**, 1858-1943, (both Br.) leading figures in Fabian Society and Labor Party.

Max Weber, 1864-1920, (Ger.) sociologist; *The Protestant Ethic and the Spirit of Capitalism*.

Walter White, 1893-1955, (U.S.) exec. sec., NAACP, 1931-55.

Roy Wilkins, 1901-81, (U.S.) exec. director, NAACP, 1955-77.

Emma Hart Willard, 1787-1870, (U.S.) pioneered higher education for women.

James Q. Wilson, 1931-2012, (U.S.) political scientist; co-authored broken windows theory.

Carter G. Woodson, 1875-1950, (U.S.) historian; founded Assn. for the Study of Negro Life and History.

C. Vann Woodward, 1908-99, (U.S.) historian; *The Strange Career of Jim Crow*.

Howard Zinn, 1922-2010, (U.S.) historian; *A People's History of the United States*.

American Journalists of the Past

Reviewed by Dean Mills, Dean, Missouri School of Journalism.

See also Business Leaders and Philanthropists, American Cartoonists, and Writers of the Past.

Franklin P. Adams (F.P.A.), 1881-1960, humorist; wrote column "The Conning Tower."

Roger Ailes, 1940-2017, Fox News cofounder and CEO.

Joseph W. Alsop, 1910-89, and **Stewart Alsop**, 1914-74, Washington-based political analysts, columnists.

Jack Anderson, 1922-2006, muckraking Washington, DC, syndicated columnist.

Brooks Atkinson, 1894-1984, theater critic.

Robert L. Bartley, 1937-2003, editorial-page editor for *Wall Street Journal*.

Jessie Tarbox Beals, 1870-1942, photojournalist.

James Gordon Bennett, 1795-1872, editor and publisher; founded *NY Herald*.

James Gordon Bennett Jr., 1841-1918, succeeded father, financed expeditions, founded afternoon paper.

Nellie Bly (Elizabeth Cochrane), 1864?-1922, pioneer woman journalist, investigative reporter; noted for series on trip around the world.

Elias Boudinot, c. 1803-39, founding editor of first Native American newspaper in U.S., *Cherokee Phoenix* (1828-34).

Benjamin Bradlee, 1921-2014, (U.S.) *Washington Post* exec. editor.

Ed Bradley, 1941-2006, TV journalist (*60 Minutes*).

Andrew Breitbart, 1969-2012, conservative commentator and blogger.

Jimmy Breslin, 1928-2017, *NY Daily News* columnist.

David Brinkley, 1920-2003, co-anchor of NBC's *Huntley-Brinkley Report*, host of ABC's *This Week With David Brinkley*.

Arthur Brisbane, 1864-1936, editor; helped introduce "yellow journalism" with sensational, simply written articles.

David Broder, 1929-2011, political journalist for *Washington Post*.

Joyce Brothers, 1927-2013, psychologist, columnist.

Heywood Broun, 1888-1939, author, columnist; founded American Newspaper Guild.

Helen Gurley Brown, 1922-2012, author; editor-in-chief of *Cosmopolitan* magazine (1965-97).

Art Buchwald, 1925-2007, journalist, humorist, syndicated columnist.

William F. Buckley Jr., 1925-2008, columnist and commentator; founder of *National Review*.

Herb Caen, 1916-97, longtime columnist for *San Francisco Chronicle* and *Examiner*.

John Campbell, 1653-1728, published *Boston News-Letter*, first continuing newspaper in the American colonies.

Jimmy Cannon, 1909-73, syndicated sports columnist.

John Chancellor, 1927-96, NBC reporter, anchor.

Harry Chandler, 1864-1944, *L.A. Times* publisher (1917-41).

Otis Chandler, 1928-2006, *Los Angeles Times* publisher (1960-80).

Marquis Childs, 1903-90, reporter and columnist for *St. Louis Post-Dispatch* and United Feature syndicate.

Craig Claiborne, 1920-2000, *NY Times* food editor and critic; key in internationalizing American tastes.

Alexander Cockburn, 1941-2012, left-wing journalist.

Charles Collingwood, 1917-85, CBS news correspondent.

Alistair Cooke, 1908-2004, Brit. journalist, TV narrator; naturalized American citizen, "Letter From America" series.

Howard Cosell, 1920-95, TV and radio sportscaster.

Gardner Cowles, 1861-1946, founded newspaper chain.

Judith Crist, 1922-2012, film critic.

Walter Cronkite, 1916-2009, CBS evening news anchor, TV journalist.

Evelyn Cunningham, 1916-2010, African-American civil rights reporter.

Cyrus Curtis, 1850-1933, publisher of *Saturday Evening Post*, *Ladies' Home Journal*, *Country Gentleman*.

John Charles Daly, 1914-91, war correspondent, TV journalist; Voice of America head.

Charles Anderson Dana, 1819-97, editor, publisher; made *NY Sun* famous for its news reporting.

Elmer (Holmes) Davis, 1890-1958, *NY Times* editorial writer, radio commentator.

Richard Harding Davis, 1864-1916, war correspondent, travel writer, fiction writer.

Benjamin Day, 1810-89, published *NY Sun* beginning in 1833, introducing penny press to the U.S.

Dorothy Dix (Elizabeth Meriwether Gilmer), 1861-1951, reporter; pioneer of the advice column genre.

Finley Peter Dunne, 1867-1936, humorist, social critic; wrote "Mr. Dooley" columns.

Roger Ebert, 1942-2013, film critic.

Mary Baker Eddy, 1821-1910, founded Christian Science movement and *Christian Science Monitor*.

Rowland Evans Jr., 1921-2001, Washington columnist.

Fanny Fern (Sara Willis Parton), 1811-72, newspaper columnist, author.

Marshall Field III, 1893-1956, retail magnate; *Chicago Sun* founder.

Doris Fleeson, 1901-70, war correspondent, columnist.

Benjamin Franklin, 1706-90, publisher of *Poor Richard's Almanack*.

James Franklin, 1697-1735, printer, pioneer journalist; publisher of *New England Courant* and *Rhode Island Gazette*.

Fred W. Friendly, 1915-98, radio, TV reporter, producer, executive; collaborator with Edward R. Murrow.

Margaret Fuller, 1810-50, social reformer, transcendentalist, critic and foreign correspondent for *NY Tribune*.

Frank E. Gannett, 1876-1957, founded newspaper chain.

Mary Ellen Garber, 1916-2008, sports journalist.

William Lloyd Garrison, 1805-79, abolitionist; publisher of *The Liberator*.

Jack Germond, 1928-2013, political reporter.

Edwin Lawrence Godkin, 1831-1902, founder of *The Nation*, editor of *NY Evening Post*.

Katharine Graham, 1917-2001, *Washington Post* publisher.

Sheilah Graham, 1904-89, Hollywood gossip columnist.

Horace Greeley, 1811-72, editor, politician; founded *NY Tribune*.

Meg Greenfield, 1930-99, *Newsweek* columnist, *Washington Post* editorial page editor.

Gilbert Hovey Grosvenor, 1875-1966, longtime editor of *National Geographic* magazine.

John Gunther, 1901-70, *Chicago Daily News* foreign correspondent, author.

David Halberstam, 1934-2007, journalist, sports reporter, author; *The Best and the Brightest*, *Summer of '49*.

Sarah Josepha Buell Hale, 1788-1879, first female magazine editor; *Ladies' Magazine*, later *Godey's Lady's Book*.

Pete Hamill, 1935-2020, NY tabloid journalist.

Paul Harvey, 1918-2009, radio broadcaster and commentator.

William Randolph Hearst, 1863-1951, founder of Hearst newspaper chain; one of the pioneers of yellow journalism.

Gabriel Heatter, 1890-1972, radio commentator.

John Hersey, 1914-98, foreign correspondent for *Time*, Life, and *The New Yorker*; author.

Marguerite Higgins, 1920-66, reporter, war correspondent.

Christopher Hitchens, 1949-2011, columnist and literary critic.

Hedda Hopper, 1885-1966, Hollywood gossip columnist.

Tony Horwitz, 1958-2019, author and journalist.

Roy Howard, 1883-1964, editor, executive; Scripps-Howard papers and United Press (later United Press International).

Chet (Chester Robert) Huntley, 1911-74, co-anchor of NBC's *Huntley-Brinkley Report*.

Ada Louise Huxtable, 1921-2013, architecture critic.

Gwen Ifill, 1955-2016, TV journalist.

Ralph Ingersoll, 1900-85, editor; *Fortune, Time, Life* exec.

Molly Ivins, 1944-2007, author, syndicated political columnist.

Peter Jennings, 1938-2005, ABC correspondent, anchor.

Pauline Kael, 1919-2001, film critic.

H. V. (Hans von) Kaltenborn, 1878-1965, radio commentator, reporter.

Murray Kempton, 1917-97, reporter, columnist for magazines and newspapers, including *NY Post*.

Dorothy Kilgallen, 1913-65, crime reporter, columnist.

James J. Kilpatrick, 1920-2010, political columnist, author and television personality.

John S. Knight, 1894-1981, editor, publisher; founded Knight newspaper group, which merged into Knight-Ridder.

Joseph Kraft, 1942-86, foreign policy columnist.

Irving Kristol, 1920-2009, columnist, commentator.

Arthur Krock, 1886-1974, *NY Times* political writer, Washington bureau chief.

Charles Kuralt, 1934-97, TV anchor; host of CBS "On the Road" featuring stories about life in the U.S.

Ann Landers (Eppie Lederer), 1918-2002, advice columnist.

David Lawrence, 1888-1973, reporter, columnist, publisher; founded *U.S. News & World Report*.

Jim Lehrer, 1934-2020, television journalist.

Frank Leslie, 1821-80, engraver, publisher of newspapers and magazines, notably *Leslie's Illustrated Newspaper*.

Anthony Lewis, 1927-2013, legal journalist.

Alexander Liberman, 1912-99, editorial director for Condé Nast magazines.

A(bbott) J(oseph) Liebling, 1904-63, foreign correspondent, critic; principally with *The New Yorker*.

Walter Lippmann, 1889-1974, political analyst, social critic, columnist, author.

Peter Lisagor, 1915-76, Washington bureau chief, *Chicago Daily News*; broadcast commentator.

David Ross Locke, 1833-88, humorist, satirist under pseudonym P.V. Nasby; owned *Toledo (Ohio) Blade*.

Elijah Parish Lovejoy, 1802-37, abolitionist editor in St. Louis and in Alton, IL; killed by proslavery mob.

Clare Booth Luce, 1903-87, war correspondent for *Life*, diplomat, playwright.

Henry R. Luce, 1898-1967, founded *Time, Fortune, Life, Sports Illustrated*.

Dwight Macdonald, 1906-82, reporter, social critic.

Don Marquis, 1878-1937, humor columnist for *NY Sun* and *NY Tribune*; wrote "Archy and Mehitabel" stories.

Nancy Hicks Maynard, 1946-2008, African American publisher, journalist.

Robert Maynard, 1937-97, first African-American editor and then owner of major U.S. paper, the *Oakland Tribune*.

C(harles) K(enny) McClatchy, 1858-1936, founder of McClatchy newspaper chain.

Sarah McClendon, 1910-2003, veteran White House correspondent.

Samuel McClure, 1857-1949, founder (1893) of *McClure's Magazine*, famous for its investigative reporting.

Anne O'Hare McCormick, 1889-1954, foreign correspondent; first woman on *NY Times* editorial board.

Robert R. McCormick, 1880-1955, editor, publisher, executive of *Chicago Tribune* and *NY Daily News*.

Ralph McGill, 1893-1969, crusading editor, publisher of *Atlanta Constitution*.

Mary McGrory, 1918-2004, Washington columnist.

O(scar) O(dd) McIntyre, 1884-1938, feature writer, syndicated columnist on everyday life in New York City.

John McLaughlin, 1927-2016, TV journalist.

Joseph Medill, 1823-99, longtime editor of the *Chicago Tribune*.

H(enry) L(ouis) Mencken, 1880-1956, reporter, editor, columnist with *Baltimore Sun* papers; anti-establishment viewpoint.

Edwin Meredith, 1876-1928, founder of magazine company.

Frank A. Munsey, 1854-1925, owner, editor, and publisher of newspapers and magazines, including *Munsey's Magazine*.

Edward R. Murrow, 1908-65, broadcast reporter, exec.; reported from Britain in WWII; hosted *See It Now, Person to Person*.

Allen Neuharth, 1924-2013, *USA Today* founder.

Edwin Newman, 1919-2010, NBC news correspondent.

Louella Parsons, 1881-1972, Hollywood gossip columnist.

Ethel L. Payne, 1911-91, African American civil rights reporter.

Daniel Pearl, 1963-2002, American journalist; kidnapped and murdered in Pakistan.

Drew (Andrew Russell) Pearson, 1897-1969, investigative reporter, columnist.

(James) Westbrook Pegler, 1894-1969, reporter, columnist.

Shirley Povich, 1905-98, sports columnist.

Joseph Pulitzer, 1847-1911, *NY World* publisher; founded Columbia Journalism School, Pulitzer Prizes.

Joseph Pulitzer II, 1885-1955, longtime *St. Louis Post-Dispatch* editor, publisher; built it into major paper.

Ernie Pyle, 1900-45, reporter, war correspondent; killed in WWII.

William Raspberry, 1935-2012, public affairs columnist.

Henry Raymond, 1820-69, cofounder, editor, *NY Times*.

Harry Reasoner, 1923-91, ABC and CBS news reporter, anchor.

John Reed, 1887-1920, reporter; foreign correspondent famous for coverage of Bolshevik Revolution; buried at the Kremlin.

Whitelaw Reid, 1837-1912, longtime editor, *NY Tribune*.

James Reston, 1909-95, *NY Times* political reporter, columnist.

Frank Reynolds, 1923-83, ABC reporter, anchor.

(Henry) Grantland Rice, 1880-1954, sportswriter.

Jacob Riis, 1849-1914, reporter, photographer; exposed slum conditions in *How the Other Half Lives*.

Cokie Roberts, 1943-2019, broadcast journalist.

Max Robinson, 1939-88, first African American to anchor network news (ABC), 1978.

Andy Rooney, 1919-2011, radio and TV commentator (*60 Minutes*).

A. M. Rosenthal, 1922-2006, reporter, editor for *NY Times*, 1943-99.

Harold Ross, 1892-1951, founder, editor, *The New Yorker*.

Carl T. Rowan, 1925-2000, reporter, columnist, author.

Mike Royko, 1932-97, Chicago newspaper columnist; wrote *Boss*, biography of Mayor Richard J. Daley (1902-76).

Louis Rukeyser, 1933-2006, TV journalist, financial analyst; hosted *Wall Street Week* on public television.

(Alfred) Damon Runyon, 1884-1946, sportswriter, columnist; stories collected in *Guys and Dolls*.

Tim Russert, 1950-2008, TV journalist; moderator of *Meet the Press* (NBC).

John B. Russwurm, 1799-1851, cofounded (1827) nation's first Black newspaper, *Freedom's Journal*, in New York, NY.

Morley Safer, 1931-2016, TV journalist (*60 Minutes*).

William Safire, 1929-2009, Pulitzer Prize-winning columnist, *NY Times*.

Adela Rogers St. Johns, 1894-1988, reporter, sportswriter for Hearst newspapers.

Pierre Salinger, 1925-2004, press sec. under Pres. Kennedy and Johnson, foreign correspondent.

Harrison Salisbury, 1908-93, reporter, foreign correspondent; Soviet specialist.

Andrew Sarris, 1928-2012, film critic, *Village Voice*.

Daniel Schorr, 1916-2010, broadcast and print journalist.

E(dward) W(illis) Scripps, 1854-1926, founded first large U.S. newspaper chain, pioneered syndication.

Eric Sevareid, 1912-92, war correspondent, radio newscaster, CBS commentator.

Anthony Shadid, 1968-2012, foreign correspondent.

Randy Shilts, 1951-94, journalist; author of *And the Band Played On*.

William L. Shirer, 1904-93, broadcaster, foreign correspondent; wrote *The Rise and Fall of the Third Reich*.

Howard K. Smith, 1914-2002, ABC news reporter, anchor.

Liz Smith, 1923-2017, gossip columnist.

Red (Walter) Smith, 1905-82, sportswriter.

Edgar P. Snow, 1905-71, correspondent; expert on Chinese Communist movement.

Tony Snow, 1955-2008, columnist, radio/TV journalist, White House press sec.

Tom Snyder, 1936-2007, television journalist.

Lawrence Spivak, 1900-94, co-creator, moderator, producer of *Meet the Press*.

(Joseph) Lincoln Steffens, 1866-1936, muckraking journalist.

I(sidor) F(einstein) Stone, 1907-89, one-man editor of *I. F. Stone's Weekly*.

Arthur Hays Sulzberger, 1891-1968, longtime publisher of *NY Times*, 1935-61.

Arthur Ochs "Punch" Sulzberger, 1926-2012, longtime publisher of *NY Times*, 1963-92.

C(yrus) L(eo) Sulzberger, 1912-93, *NY Times* foreign correspondent, columnist.

David Susskind, 1920-87, TV producer, public affairs talk-show host (*Open End*).

John Cameron Swayze, 1906-95, early TV newscaster (NBC).

Herbert Bayard Swope, 1882-1958, war correspondent, editor of *NY World*.

Ida Tarbell, 1857-1944, muckraking journalist.

Helen Thomas, 1920-2013, White House correspondent, 1959-2010.

Isaiah Thomas, 1750-1831, printer, publisher; cofounder of revolutionary journal, *Massachusetts Spy*.

Lowell Thomas, 1892-1981, radio newscaster, world traveler.

Dorothy Thompson, 1894-1961, foreign correspondent, columnist, radio commentator.

Hunter S. Thompson, 1937-2005, political journalist, author; *Fear and Loathing on the Campaign Trail* (1972).

Kenneth Thompson, 1923-2006, Canadian media magnate; owned Toronto *Globe and Mail* newspaper.

Abigail Van Buren (Pauline Phllips), 1918-2013, advice columnist.

Mike Wallace, 1918-2012, TV journalist (*60 Minutes*).

Ida Bell Wells-Barnett, 1862-1931, African-American reporter, editor, anti-lynching crusader.

William Allen White, 1868-1944, newspaper editor, publisher.

Tom Wicker, 1926-2011, *NY Times* political reporter, columnist.

Walter Winchell, 1897-1972, reporter, columnist, broadcaster of celebrity news.

John Peter Zenger, 1697-1746, printer, journalist; acquitted in precedent-setting libel suit (1735).

Military and Naval Leaders of the Past

Reviewed by Alan C. Aimone, U.S. Military Academy Library.

Alexander the Great, 356-323 BCE, (Maced.) conquered Persia and much of the world known to Europeans.

Harold Alexander, 1891-1969, (Br.) led Allied invasion of Italy, 1943, WWII.

Ethan Allen, 1738-89, (U.S.) headed Green Mountain Boys; captured Ft. Ticonderoga, 1775, Amer. Rev.

Edmund Allenby, 1861-1936, (Br.) in Boer War, WWI; led Egyptian expeditionary force, 1917-18.

Benedict Arnold, 1741-1801, (U.S.) victorious at Saratoga; tried to betray West Point to British, Amer. Rev.

Henry "Hap" Arnold, 1886-1950, (U.S.) commanded Army Air Force in WWII.

Ashurnasirpal II, 884-859 BCE, (Assyria) king; began Assyrian conquest of Middle East.

John Barry, 1745-1803, (U.S.) won numerous sea battles during Amer. Rev.

Pierre Beauregard, 1818-93, (U.S.) Confed. general; ordered bombardment of Ft. Sumter that began Civil War.

Belisarius, c. 505-565, (Byzant.) won remarkable victories for Byzantine emperor Justinian I.

Black Hawk, 1767-1838, (Amer. Ind.) Sauk war chief.

Gebhard von Blücher, 1742-1819, (Ger.) helped defeat Napoleon at Waterloo.

Simón Bolívar, 1783-1830, (Venez.) S. Amer. revolutionary who liberated much of the continent from Spanish rule.

Edward Braddock, 1695-1755, (Br.) commanded forces in French and Indian War.

Omar N. Bradley, 1893-1981, (U.S.) headed U.S. ground troops in Normandy invasion, 1944, WWII.

John Burgoyne, 1722-92, (Br.) general; defeated at Saratoga, Amer. Rev.

Julius Caesar, 100-44 BCE, (Rom.) general and politician; conquered northern Gaul, overthrew Roman Republic.

Charlemagne, 742-814, (Fr.) king of the Franks, Holy Roman Emperor; conquered most of Western Europe.

Claire Lee Chennault, 1893-1958, (U.S.) headed Flying Tigers in WWII.

El Cid (Rodrigo Díaz de Vivar), 1040-99, (Sp.) renowned knight; captured Valencia (1094), hero of "Song of Cid" epic.

Mark W. Clark, 1896-1984, (U.S.) helped plan N African invasion in WWII; commander of UN forces, Korean War.

Karl von Clausewitz, 1780-1831, (Prus.) military theorist.

Lucius D. Clay, 1897-1978, (U.S.) led Berlin airlift, 1948-49.

Henry Clinton, 1738-95, (Br.) commander of forces in Amer. Rev., 1778-81.

Cochise, c. 1815-74, (Amer. Ind.) chief of Chiricahua band of Apache Indians in Southwest U.S.

Charles Cornwallis, 1738-1805, (Br.) victorious at Brandywine, 1777; surrendered at Yorktown, Amer. Rev.

Hernán Cortés, 1485-1547, (Sp.) led Spanish conquistadors in the defeat of the Aztec empire, 1519-28.

Crazy Horse, 1849-77, (Amer. Ind.) Sioux war chief victorious at Battle of the Little Bighorn.

George Armstrong Custer, 1839-76, (U.S.) army officer defeated and killed at Battle of the Little Bighorn.

Benjamin O. Davis Jr., 1912-2002, (U.S.) leader of WWII Black aviators; first African American general in U.S. Air Force.

Benjamin O. Davis Sr., 1877-1970, (U.S.) first African American general in U.S. Army, 1940.

Moshe Dayan, 1915-81, (Isr.) directed campaigns in the 1967, 1973 Arab-Israeli wars.

Stephen Decatur, 1779-1820, (U.S.) naval hero of Barbary wars, War of 1812.

Anton Denikin, 1872-1947, (Russ.) led White forces in Russian civil war.

George Dewey, 1837-1917, (U.S.) destroyed Spanish fleet at Manila, 1898, Span.-Amer. War.

Karl Doenitz, 1891-1980, (Ger.) submarine cmdr. in chief and naval cmdr., WWII; last pres. of Third Reich.

Jimmy Doolittle, 1896-1993, (U.S.) led 1942 air raid on Tokyo and other Japanese cities in WWII.

Hugh Dowding, 1882-1970, (Br.) headed RAF Fighter Command, 1936-40, WWII.

Jubal Early, 1816-94, (U.S.) Confed. general; led raid on Washington, DC, 1864, Civil War.

Dwight D. Eisenhower, 1890-1969, (U.S.) commanded Allied forces in Europe, WWII.

Erich von Falkenhayn, 1861-1922, (Ger.) minister of war, general, commander at Verdun in WWI.

David Farragut, 1801-70, (U.S.) Union admiral; captured New Orleans, Mobile Bay, Civil War.

John Arbuthnot Fisher, 1841-1920, (Br.) WWI admiral; naval reformer.

Ferdinand Foch, 1851-1929, (Fr.) headed victorious Allied armies, 1918, WWI.

Nathan Bedford Forrest, 1821-77, (U.S.) Confed. general; led raids against Union supply lines, Civil War.

Frederick the Great, 1712-86, (Prus.) led Prussia in Seven Years' War.

Horatio Gates, 1728-1806, (U.S.) commanded army at Saratoga, Amer. Rev.

Genghis Khan, 1162-1227, (Mongol) unified Mongol tribes, subjugated much of Asia, 1206-21.

Geronimo, 1829-1909, (Amer. Ind.) leader of Chiricahua band of Apache Indians.

Vo Nguyen Giap, 1911?-2013, (Viet.) commanded People's Army of Vietnam against U.S.

Charles G. Gordon, 1833-85, (Br.) led forces in China, Crimean War; killed at Khartoum, Sudan.

Ulysses S. Grant, 1822-85, (U.S.) headed Union army, Civil War, 1864-65; forced Robert E. Lee's surrender, 1865.

Nathanael Greene, 1742-86, (U.S.) defeated British in Southern campaign, 1780-81, Amer. Rev.

Heinz Guderian, 1888-1954, (Ger.) tank theorist; led panzer tank forces in Poland, France, Russia, WWII.

Gustavus Adolphus, 1594-1632, (Swed.) king, military tactician, reformer; led forces in Thirty Years' War.

Douglas Haig, 1861-1928, (Br.) led British armies in France, 1915-18, WWI.

William F. Halsey, 1882-1959, (U.S.) defeated Japanese fleet at Leyte Gulf, 1944, WWII.

Hannibal, 247-183 BCE, (Carthage) invaded Rome, crossing Alps, in Second Punic War, 218-201 BCE.

Arthur Travers Harris, 1895-1984, (Br.) led Britain's WWII bomber command.

Paul von Hindenburg, 1847-1934, (Ger.) chief of general staff, WWI; second pres. of Weimar Republic.

Richard Howe, 1726-99, (Br.) commanded navy in Amer. Rev., 1776-78; June 1 victory against French, 1794.

William Howe, 1729-1814, (Br.) commanded forces in Amer. Rev., 1776-78.

Isaac Hull, 1773-1843, (U.S.) sunk British frigate *Guerriere*, War of 1812.

Thomas "Stonewall" Jackson, 1824-63, (U.S.) Confed. general; led Shenandoah Valley campaign, Civil War.

Daniel James Jr., 1920-78, (U.S.) first Black 4-star general, 1975; commander, N. American Air Defense Command.

Joseph Joffre, 1852-1931, (Fr.) headed Allied armies; won Battle of the Marne, 1914, WWI.

John Paul Jones, 1747-92, (U.S.) commanded *Bonhomme Richard* in victory over *Serapis*, Amer. Rev., 1779.

Chief Joseph, c. 1840-1904, (Amer. Ind.) chief of the Nez Percé; forced by U.S. army to retreat and surrender.

Stephen Kearny, 1794-1848, (U.S.) headed Army of the West in Mexican War.

Albert Kesselring, 1885-1960, (Ger.) field marshal who led the defense of Italy in WWII.

Ernest J. King, 1878-1956, (U.S.) key WWII naval strategist.

Horatio H. Kitchener, 1850-1916, (Br.) led forces in Boer War, victorious at Khartoum, organized army in WWI.

Henry Knox, 1750-1806, (U.S.) general in Amer. Rev.; first sec. of war under U.S. Constitution.

Lavrenti Kornilov, 1870-1918, (Russ.) commander-in-chief, 1917; led counterrevolutionary march on Petrograd.

Thaddeus Kosciuszko, 1746-1817, (Pol.) aided Amer. Rev.

Walter Krueger, 1881-1967, (U.S.) led Sixth Army in WWII in Southwest Pacific.

Mikhail Kutuzov, 1745-1813, (Russ.) fought at Borodino, Napol. Wars, 1812; abandoned Moscow, forced French retreat.

Marquis de Lafayette, 1757-1834, (Fr.) fought in, secured French aid for Amer. Rev.

T(homas) E. Lawrence (of Arabia), 1888-1935, (Br.) organized revolt of Arabs against Turks in WWI.

William Daniel Leahy, 1875-1959, (U.S.) chief of staff to Pres. Roosevelt in WWII, Fleet Admiral.

Henry (Light-Horse Harry) Lee, 1756-1818, (U.S.) cavalry officer in Amer. Rev.

Robert E. Lee, 1807-70, (U.S.) Confed. general; defeated at Gettysburg, Civil War; surrendered to Grant, 1865.

Curtis LeMay, 1906-90, (U.S.) Air Force cmdr. in WWII, Korean War, Vietnam War.

Lyman Lemnitzer, 1899-1988, (U.S.) WWII hero; later general, chairman of Joint Chiefs of Staff.

James Longstreet, 1821-1904, (U.S.) aided Lee at Gettysburg, Civil War.

Erich Ludendorff, 1865-1937, (Ger.) general; victor at Tannenberg, WWI.

Douglas MacArthur, 1880-1964, (U.S.) commanded forces in SW Pacific in WWII; headed occupation forces in Japan, 1945-51; UN commander in Korean War.

Carl Gustaf Mannerheim, 1867-1951, (Fin.) army officer and pres. of Finland, 1944-46.

Erich von Manstein, 1887-1973, (Ger.) served WWI, WWII; planned invasion of France (1940); convicted of war crimes.

Francis Marion, 1733-95, (U.S.) led guerrilla actions in South Carolina during Amer. Rev.

Duke of Marlborough, 1650-1722, (Br.) led forces against Louis XIV in War of the Spanish Succession.

George C. Marshall, 1880-1959, (U.S.) chief of staff in WWII; authored Marshall Plan.

Maurice, Count of Nassau, 1567-1625, (Neth.) military innovator; led forces in Thirty Years' War.

George B. McClellan, 1826-85, (U.S.) Union general; commanded Army of the Potomac, 1861-62, Civil War.

George Meade, 1815-72, (U.S.) commanded Union forces at Gettysburg, Civil War.

Doris "Dorie" Miller, 1919-43, (U.S.) Navy hero of Pearl Harbor attack; first African American awarded Navy Cross.

Billy Mitchell, 1879-1936, (U.S.) WWI air-power advocate; court-martialed for insubordination, later vindicated.

Helmuth von Moltke, 1800-91, (U.S.) victorious in Austro-Prussian, Franco-Prussian wars.

Louis de Montcalm, 1712-59, (Fr.) headed troops in Canada, French and Indian War; defeated at Quebec, 1759.

Bernard Law Montgomery, 1887-1976, (Br.) stopped German offensive at Alamein, 1942, WWII; helped plan Normandy invasion.

Daniel Morgan, 1736-1802, (U.S.) victorious at Cowpens, 1781, Amer. Rev.

Louis Mountbatten, 1900-79, (Br.) Supreme Allied Commander of SE Asia, 1943-46, WWII.

Joachim Murat, 1767-1815, (Fr.) led cavalry at Marengo, Austerlitz, and Jena, Napoleonic Wars.

Napoleon Bonaparte, 1769-1821, (Fr.) defeated Russia and Austria at Austerlitz, 1805; invaded Russia, 1812; defeated at Waterloo, 1815.

Horatio Nelson, 1758-1805, (Br.) naval cmdr.; destroyed French fleet at Trafalgar.

Michel Ney, 1769-1815, (Fr.) commanded forces in Switz., Austria, Russ., Napoleonic Wars; defeated at Waterloo.

Chester Nimitz, 1885-1966, (U.S.) cmdr. of naval forces in Pacific in WWII.

Osceola, 1804-38, (Amer. Ind.) war leader of Seminole people of Florida.

George S. Patton, 1885-1945, (U.S.) led assault on Sicily, 1943, Third Army invasion of Europe, WWII.

Oliver Perry, 1785-1819, (U.S.) won Battle of Lake Erie in War of 1812.

John Pershing, 1860-1948, (U.S.) commanded Mexican border campaign, 1916; Amer. Expeditionary Force, WWI.

Henri Philippe Pétain, 1856-1951, (Fr.) defended Verdun, 1916; headed Vichy government in WWII.

George E. Pickett, 1825-75, (U.S.) Confed. general famed for "charge" at Gettysburg, Civil War.

Pontiac, 1720?-69, (Amer. Ind.) Ottawa war chief.

Charles Portal, 1893-1971, (Br.) chief of staff, Royal Air Force, 1940-45; led in Battle of Britain.

Manfred Freiherr von Richthofen (Red Baron), 1892-1918, (Ger.) WWI flying ace, led elite fighter squadron.

Hyman Rickover, 1900-86, (U.S.) father of nuclear navy.

Matthew Bunker Ridgway, 1895-1993, (U.S.) commanded Allied ground forces in Korean War.

Erwin Rommel, 1891-1944, (Ger.) headed Afrika Korps, WWII.

Gerd von Rundstedt, 1875-1953, (Ger.) supreme cmdr. in West, 1942-45, WWII.

Saladin, 1138-93, (Kurdish Muslim) recaptured Jerusalem from Crusaders.

Aleksandr Samsonov, 1859-1914, (Russ.) led invasion of E Prussia, WWI; defeated at Tannenberg, 1914.

Antonio López de Santa Anna, 1794-1876, (Mex.) defeated Texans at the Alamo; defeated in Mexican War.

Maurice, Count of Saxe, 1696-1750, (Fr.) general, noted tactician; War of Austrian Succession, War of Pol. Succession.

H. Norman Schwarzkopf, 1934-2012, (U.S.) army general; led Persian Gulf War, 1991.

Scipio Africanus the Elder, 234?-183 BCE, (Roman) hero of Second Punic War; defeated Hannibal, invaded N Africa.

Winfield Scott, 1786-1866, (U.S.) hero of War of 1812; headed forces in Mexican War, took Mexico City.

Philip Sheridan, 1831-88, (U.S.) Union cavalry officer; headed Army of the Shenandoah, 1864-65, Civil War.

William T. Sherman, 1820-91, (U.S.) Union general; sacked Atlanta during "march to the sea," 1864, Civil War.

Sitting Bull, c. 1831-90, (Amer. Ind.) Hunkpapa Lakota chief victorious at Battle of the Little Bighorn.

Carl Spaatz, 1891-1974, (U.S.) directed strategic bombing against Germany, later Japan, in WWII.

Raymond Spruance, 1886-1969, (U.S.) victorious at Battle of Midway Island, 1942, WWII.

Joseph W. Stilwell, 1883-1946, (U.S.) headed forces in the China, Burma, India theater in WWII.

J.E.B. Stuart, 1833-64, (U.S.) Confed. cavalry commander, Civil War.

Sun Tzu, 6th? cent. BCE, (China) general; author of *The Art of War*.

Aleksandr Suvorov, 1729-1800, (Russ.) commanded Allied Russian and Austrian armies, Russo-Turkish War.

Tamerlane, 1336-1405, (Turkoman Mongol) conqueror; established empire from India to Mediterranean Sea.

Tecumseh, 1768-1813, (Amer. Ind.) Shawnee chief; led Indian confederation opposing colonists.

George H. Thomas, 1816-70, (U.S.) saved Union army at Chattanooga, 1863; won at Nashville, 1864, Civil War.

Semyon Timoshenko, 1895-1970, (USSR) defended Moscow, Stalingrad, WWII; led winter offensive, 1942-43.

Alfred von Tirpitz, 1849-1930, (Ger.) responsible for submarine blockade in WWI.

Henri de la Tour d'Auvergne, Viscount of Turenne, 1611-75, (Fr.) marshal; Thirty Years' War, Fronde, War of Devolution.

Sebastien Le Prestre de Vauban, 1633-1707, (Fr.) innovative military engineer, theorist.

Jonathan M. Wainwright, 1883-1953, (U.S.) forced to surrender on Corregidor, Philippines, 1942, WWII.

George Washington, 1732-99, (U.S.) led Continental army, 1775-83, Amer. Rev.

Archibald Wavell, 1883-1950, (Br.) commanded forces in N and E Africa, SE Asia in WWII.

Anthony Wayne, 1745-96, (U.S.) captured Stony Point, NY, 1779, Amer. Rev.

Duke of Wellington, 1769-1852, (Br.) defeated Napoleon at Waterloo, 1815.

William Westmoreland, 1914-2005, (U.S.) commanded forces in Vietnam, 1964-68.

William I (The Conqueror), 1027-87, (Br.) victor, Battle of Hastings, 1066; became first Norman king of England.

James Wolfe, 1727-59, (Br.) captured Quebec from French, 1759, French and Indian War.

Isoroku Yamamoto, 1884-1943, (Jpn.) cmdr. in chief of Japanese fleet; naval planner before and during WWII.

Georgi Zhukov, 1895-1974, (Russ.) defended Moscow, 1941; led assault on Berlin, 1945, WWII.

Philosophers and Religious Figures of the Past

Excludes biblical figures and popes (see Religion chapter). For Greeks and Romans, see also Historical Figures chapter.

Lyman Abbott, 1835-1922, (U.S.) clergyman, reformer; advocate of Christian Socialism.

Pierre Abelard, 1079-1142, (Fr.) philosopher, theologian, teacher; used dialectic method to support Christian beliefs.

Felix Adler, 1851-1933, (U.S.) German-born founder of the Ethical Culture Soc.

Mortimer Adler, 1902-2001, (U.S.) philosopher; helped create "Great Books" program.

(St.) Anselm, c. 1033-1109, (It.) philosopher-theologian, church leader; "ontological argument" for God's existence.

(St.) Thomas Aquinas, 1225-74, (It.) preeminent medieval philosopher-theologian; *Summa Theologica*.

Aristotle, 384-322 BCE, (Gr.) pioneering wide-ranging philosopher, logician, ethician, naturalist.

(St.) Augustine, 354-430, (N Africa) philosopher, theologian, bishop; *Confessions*, *City of God*, *On the Trinity*.

J. L. Austin, 1911-60, (Br.) ordinary-language philosopher.

Averroes (Ibn Rushd), 1126-98, (Sp.) Islamic philosopher, physician.

Avicenna (Ibn Sina), 980-1037, (Iran) Islamic philosopher, scientist.

A(lfred) J(ules) Ayer, 1910-89, (Br.) philosopher, logical positivist; *Language, Truth, and Logic*.

Roger Bacon, c. 1214-94, (Eng.) philosopher, scientist.

Bahá'u'lláh (Mirza Husayn Ali), 1817-92, (Pers.) founder of Bahá'í faith.

Karl Barth, 1886-1968, (Switz.) theologian; a leading force in 20th-cent. Protestantism.

Thomas à Becket, 1118-70, (Eng.) archbishop of Canterbury; opposed Henry II, murdered by king's men.

(St.) Benedict, c. 480-547, (It.) founded the Benedictine order.

Jeremy Bentham, 1748-1832, (Br.) philosopher, reformer; enunciated utilitarianism.

Henri Bergson, 1859-1941, (Fr.) philosopher of evolution.

George Berkeley, 1685-1753, (Ire.) idealist philosopher, bishop.

John Biddle, 1615-62, (Eng.) founder of English Unitarianism.

Jakob Boehme, 1575-1624, (Ger.) theosophist, mystic.

Dietrich Bonhoeffer, 1906-45, (Ger.) Lutheran theologian, pastor; executed as opponent of Nazis.

William Brewster, 1567-1644, (Eng.) *Mayflower* passenger, Plymouth Colony leader.

Emil Brunner, 1889-1966, (Switz.) Protestant theologian.

Giordano Bruno, 1548-1600, (It.) philosopher, pantheist.

Martin Buber, 1878-1965, (Ger.) Jewish philosopher, theologian; *I and Thou*.

Buddha (Siddhartha Gautama), c. 563-c. 483 BCE, (India) philosopher; founded Buddhism.

John Calvin, 1509-64, (Fr.) theologian; a key figure in the Protestant Reformation.

Rudolph Carnap, 1891-1970, (U.S.) German-born analytic philosopher; a founder of logical positivism.

William Ellery Channing, 1780-1842, (U.S.) clergyman; early spokesman for Unitarianism.

Auguste Comte, 1798-1857, (Fr.) philosopher; originated positivism.

Confucius, 551-479 BCE, (China) founder of Confucianism.

John Cotton, 1584-1652, (Eng.) Puritan theologian.

Thomas Cranmer, 1489-1556, (Eng.) Anglican churchman; wrote much of *Book of Common Prayer*.

Jacques Derrida, 1930-2004, (Fr.) deconstructionist philosopher.

René Descartes, 1596-1650, (Fr.) philosopher, mathematician; "father of modern philosophy"; *Discourse on Method*, *Meditations on First Philosophy*.

John Dewey, 1859-1952, (U.S.) philosopher, educator; instrumentalist theory of knowledge, progressive education.

Denis Diderot, 1713-84, (Fr.) philosopher, encyclopedist.

John Duns Scotus, c. 1266-1308, (Scot.) Franciscan philosopher, theologian.

Mary Baker Eddy, 1821-1910, (U.S.) founder of Christian Science; *Science and Health*.

Jonathan Edwards, 1703-58, (U.S.) preacher, theologian; "Sinners in the Hands of an Angry God."

(Desiderius) Erasmus, c. 1466-1536, (Neth.) Renaissance humanist; *On the Freedom of the Will*.

Jerry Falwell, 1933-2007, (U.S.) TV evangelist, religious commentator.

Johann Fichte, 1762-1814, (Ger.) idealist philosopher.

Michel Foucault, 1926-84, (Fr.) structuralist philosopher, historian.

George Fox, 1624-91, (Br.) founder of Society of Friends (Quakers).

(St.) Francis of Assisi, 1182-1226, (It.) espoused voluntary poverty, founded Franciscans order.

al-Ghazali, 1058-1111, (Iran) Islamic philosopher.

Billy Graham, 1918-2018, (U.S.) evangelist, adviser to presidents.

Billy James Hargis, 1925-2004, (U.S.) anti-Communist televangelist; founder of the Church of the Christian Crusade.

Georg W. F. Hegel, 1770-1831, (Ger.) idealist philosopher; *Phenomenology of Mind*.

Martin Heidegger, 1889-1976, (Ger.) existentialist philosopher; affected many fields; *Being and Time*.

Johann G. Herder, 1744-1803, (Ger.) philosopher, cultural historian; a founder of German Romanticism.

Thomas Hobbes, 1588-1679, (Eng.) philosopher, political theorist; *Leviathan.*

David Hume, 1711-76, (Scot.) empiricist philosopher; *Enquiry Concerning Human Understanding.*

Jan Hus, 1369-1415, (Czech.) religious reformer.

Edmund Husserl, 1859-1938, (Ger.) philosopher; founded the phenomenological movement.

Thomas Huxley, 1825-95, (Br.) philosopher, educator.

William Ralph Inge, 1860-1954, (Br.) theologian; explored mystic aspects of Christianity.

William James, 1842-1910, (U.S.) philosopher, psychologist, pragmatist; studied religious experience.

Karl Jaspers, 1883-1969, (Ger.) existentialist philosopher.

Joan of Arc, 1412-31, (Fr.) national heroine, a patron saint of France; key figure in the Hundred Years War.

Immanuel Kant, 1724-1804, (Ger.) philosopher; founder of modern critical philosophy; *Critique of Pure Reason.*

Thomas à Kempis, c. 1380-1471, (Ger.) monk, devotional writer; *Imitation of Christ* attributed to him.

Soren Kierkegaard, 1813-55, (Den.) religious philosopher, pre-existentialist; *Either/Or, The Sickness Unto Death.*

John Knox, 1505-72, (Scot.) leader of Protestant Reformation in Scotland.

Lao-Tzu, 604-531 BCE, (China) philosopher; considered the founder of the Taoist religion.

Gottfried von Leibniz, 1646-1716, (Ger.) rationalist philosopher, logician, mathematician.

John Locke, 1632-1704, (Eng.) political theorist, empiricist philosopher; *Essay Concerning Human Understanding.*

(St.) Ignatius Loyola, 1491-1556, (Sp.) founder of the Jesuits; *Spiritual Exercises.*

Martin Luther, 1483-1546, (Ger.) leader of the Protestant Reformation; founded Lutheran church.

Jean-Francois Lyotard, 1924-98, (Fr.) postmodern philosopher, lecturer; *The Post-Modern Condition.*

Maimonides, 1135-1204, (Sp.) major Jewish philosopher.

Gabriel Marcel, 1889-1973, (Fr.) Rom. Cath. existentialist philosopher, dramatist.

Jacques Maritain, 1882-1973, (Fr.) neo-Thomist philosopher.

Cotton Mather, 1663-1728, (U.S.) defender of orthodox Puritanism; founded Yale, 1701.

Aimee Semple McPherson, 1890-1944, (Can.-U.S.) Pentecostal evangelist.

Philipp Melanchthon, 1497-1560, (Ger.) theologian, humanist; an important voice in the Reformation.

Maurice Merleau-Ponty, 1908-61, (Fr.) existentialist philosopher; *Phenomenology of Perception.*

Thomas Merton, 1915-68, (U.S.) Trappist monk, spiritual writer; *The Seven Storey Mountain.*

Dwight Moody, 1837-99, (U.S.) evangelist.

Rev. Sun Myung Moon, 1920-2012, (N. Kor.) Unification Church founder.

G(eorge) E(dward) Moore, 1873-1958, (Br.) philosopher; *Principia Ethica,* "A Defense of Common Sense."

Muhammad, c. 570-632, (Arab.) prophet of Islam.

Elijah Muhammad, 1897-1975, (U.S.) founder of Black Muslim group, Nation of Islam.

Heinrich Muhlenberg, 1711-87, (Ger.) organized the Lutheran Church in America.

John H. Newman, 1801-90, (Br.) Rom. Cath. convert, cardinal; led Oxford Movement; *Apologia pro Vita Sua.*

Reinhold Niebuhr, 1892-1971, (U.S.) Protestant theologian.

Richard Niebuhr, 1894-1962, (U.S.) Protestant theologian.

Friedrich Nietzsche, 1844-1900, (Ger.) philosopher; *The Birth of Tragedy, Beyond Good and Evil, Thus Spake Zarathustra.*

Robert Nozick, 1938-2002, (U.S.) political philosopher; *Anarchy, State, and Utopia.*

Blaise Pascal, 1623-62, (Fr.) philosopher, mathematician; *Pensées* (Thoughts).

(St.) Patrick, c. 389-c. 461, (Br.) brought Christianity to Ireland.

Norman Vincent Peale, 1898-1993, (U.S.) minister, author; *The Power of Positive Thinking.*

C(harles) S. Peirce, 1839-1914, (U.S.) philosopher, logician; originated concept of pragmatism, 1878.

Plato, c. 428-347 BCE, (Gr.) philosopher; wrote Socratic dialogues; argued for immortality of soul, indep. reality of ideas or forms; *Republic, Meno, Phaedo, Apology.*

Plotinus, 205-70, (Rom.) a founder of neo-Platonism; *Enneads.*

W(illard) V(an) O(rman) Quine, 1908-2001, (U.S.) philosopher, logician; "On What There Is."

John Rawls, 1922-2002, (U.S.) political philosopher; *A Theory of Justice.*

Oral Roberts, 1918-2009, (U.S.) televangelist, university founder.

Moishe Rosen, 1932-2010, (U.S.) Jews for Jesus founder.

Josiah Royce, 1855-1916, (U.S.) idealist philosopher.

Bertrand Russell, 1872-1970, (Br.) philosopher, logician; one of the founders of modern logic; prolific popular writer.

Charles T. Russell, 1852-1916, (U.S.) founder of Jehovah's Witnesses.

Gilbert Ryle, 1900-76, (Br.) analytic philosopher; *The Concept of Mind.*

George Santayana, 1863-1952, (U.S.) philosopher, writer, critic; *The Sense of Beauty, The Realms of Being.*

Jean-Paul Sartre, 1905-80, (Fr.) philosopher, novelist, playwright; *Nausea, No Exit, Being and Nothingness.*

Friedrich von Schelling, 1775-1854, (Ger.) philosopher of romantic movement.

Friedrich Schleiermacher, 1768-1834, (Ger.) theologian; a founder of modern Protestant theology.

Arthur Schopenhauer, 1788-1860, (Ger.) philosopher; *The World as Will and Idea.*

Robert Schuller, 1926-2015, (U.S.) evangelist; Crystal Cathedral founder.

Albert Schweitzer, 1875-1965, (Ger.) theologian, social philosopher, medical missionary.

Joseph Smith, 1805-44, (U.S.) founded Latter-Day Saints (Mormon) movement, 1830.

Socrates, 469-399 BCE, (Gr.) philosopher immortalized by Plato.

Herbert Spencer, 1820-1903, (Br.) philosopher of evolution.

Herbert Spiegel, 1914-2009, (U.S.) psychiatrist who popularized hypnosis.

Baruch de Spinoza, 1632-77, (Neth.) rationalist philosopher; *Ethics.*

John Stott, 1921-2011, (Br.) evangelical Anglican cleric.

Billy Sunday, 1862-1935, (U.S.) evangelist.

Daisetz Teitaro Suzuki, 1870-1966, (Jpn.) Buddhist scholar.

Emanuel Swedenborg, 1688-1772, (Swed.) philosopher, mystic; *Principia.*

Pierre Teilhard de Chardin, 1881-1955, (Fr.) Jesuit priest, paleontologist, philosopher-theologian; *The Divine Milieu.*

(St.) Therese of Lisieux, 1873-97, (Fr.) Carmelite nun ("Little Flower"), revered for everyday sanctity; *The Story of a Soul.*

Paul Tillich, 1886-1965, (U.S.) German-born philosopher, theologian; brought depth psychology to Protestantism.

John Wesley, 1703-91, (Br.) theologian, evangelist; founded Methodism.

Alfred North Whitehead, 1861-1947, (Br.) philosopher, mathematician; *Process and Reality.*

William of Occam, c. 1285-c. 1349, (Eng.) medieval scholastic philosopher, nominalist.

Roger Williams, c. 1603-83, (U.S.) clergyman; championed religious freedom and separation of church and state.

Ludwig Wittgenstein, 1889-1951, (Austria) philosopher; major influence on contemporary language philosophy; *Tractatus Logico-Philosophicus, Philosophical Investigations.*

John Woolman, 1720-72, (U.S.) Quaker social reformer, abolitionist, writer; *The Journal.*

John Wycliffe, 1320-84, (Eng.) theologian, reformer.

(St.) Francis Xavier, 1506-52, (Sp.) Jesuit missionary; "Apostle of the Indies."

Brigham Young, 1801-77, (U.S.) Mormon leader after Joseph Smith's death; colonized Utah.

Huldrych Zwingli, 1484-1531, (Switz.) theologian; led Swiss Protestant Reformation.

Political Leaders of the Past

U.S. presidents, vice presidents, Supreme Court justices, and signers of the Declaration of Independence listed elsewhere. See also Historical Figures.

Abu Bakr, 573-634, (Arab.) Muslim leader, first caliph, chosen successor to Muhammad.

Dean Acheson, 1893-1971, (U.S.) sec. of state; architect of Cold War foreign policy.

Samuel Adams, 1722-1803, (U.S.) patriot; Boston Tea Party firebrand.

Konrad Adenauer, 1876-1967, (Ger.) first West German chancellor.

Emilio Aguinaldo, 1869-1964, (Philip.) revolutionary; fought against Spain and the U.S.

Akbar, 1542-1605, Mogul emperor of India.

Carl Albert, 1908-2000, (U.S.) House rep. (D, OK), Speaker, 1971-76.

Salvador Allende Gossens, 1908-73, (Chile) Marxist pres., 1970-73; ousted and died in coup.

Idi Amin, 1925-2003, (Uganda) Ugandan ruler, 1971-79; blamed for hundreds of thousands of deaths.

Kofi Annan, 1938-2018, (Ghana) UN sec.-gen.

Corazon Aquino, 1933-2009, (Philip.) pres. of the Philippines, 1986-92.

Yasir Arafat, 1929-2004, (Egypt) leader of the Palestine Liberation Organization (PLO).

Herbert H. Asquith, 1852-1928, (Br.) Liberal prime min.; instituted major social reforms.

Hafez al Assad, 1930-2000, (Syr.) pres. of Syria, 1970-2000.

Atahualpa, 1500?-33, (Inca) last ruling chief of Incan empire (in present-day Peru).

Kemal Atatürk, 1881-1938, (Turk.) founded modern Turkey.

Clement Attlee, 1883-1967, (Br.) Labour leader, prime min.; enacted natl. health service; nationalized many industries.

Stephen F. Austin, 1793-1836, (U.S.) led Texas colonization.

Mikhail Bakunin, 1814-76, (Russ.) revolutionary; leading exponent of anarchism.

Arthur J. Balfour, 1848-1930, (Br.) foreign sec. under Lloyd George; issued Balfour Declaration backing Zionism.

Bernard M. Baruch, 1870-1965, (U.S.) financier, govt. adviser.

Fulgencio Batista y Zaldívar, 1901-73, (Cuba) Cuban pres., 1940-44, 1952-59; overthrown by Castro.

Menachem Begin, 1913-92, (Isr.) Israeli prime min.; shared 1978 Nobel Peace Prize.

Ahmed Ben Bella, 1918-2012, (Alg.) first Algerian pres., 1963-65.

Eduard Benes, 1884-1948, (Czech.) pres. during interwar and post-WWII eras.

David Ben-Gurion, 1886-1973, (Isr.) first prime min. of Israel, 1948-53, 1955-63.

Thomas Hart Benton, 1782-1858, (U.S.) MO senator; championed agrarian interests and westward expansion.

Ernest Bevin, 1881-1951, (Br.) Labour party leader, foreign minister; helped lay foundation for NATO.

King Bhumibol Adulyadej, 1927-2016, (Thai.) monarch, 1946-2016.

Benazir Bhutto, 1953-2007, (Pak.) Pakistan prime min.; first elected woman leader of a majority-Muslim country.

Otto von Bismarck, 1815-98, (Ger.) statesman known as the Iron Chancellor; uniter of Germany, 1870.

Black Kettle, 1803?-68, (Amer. Ind.) Cheyenne peace chief.

James G. Blaine, 1830-93, (U.S.) Republican politician, diplomat; influential in Pan-American movement.

Léon Blum, 1872-1950, (Fr.) socialist leader, writer; headed first Popular Front government.

William E. Borah, 1865-1940, (U.S.) isolationist senator (R, ID); helped block U.S. membership in League of Nations.

Cesare Borgia, 1476-1507, (It.) soldier, politician; Italian Renaissance figure who partly inspired Machiavelli's *The Prince*.

P. W. Botha, 1916-2006, (S. Afr.) S. African president, prime min.

Boutros Boutros-Ghali, 1922-2016, (Egypt), UN sec.-gen.

Willy Brandt, 1913-92, (Ger.) statesman, chancellor of West Germany, 1969-74; promoted East/West peace, *Ostpolitik*.

Joseph Brant, 1742-1807, (Amer. Ind.) Mohawk chief.

Leonid Brezhnev, 1906-82, (USSR) Soviet leader, 1964-82.

Aristide Briand, 1862-1932, (Fr.) foreign min.; chief architect of Locarno Pact and anti-war Kellogg-Briand Pact.

William Jennings Bryan, 1860-1925, (U.S.) Democratic, populist leader, orator; three times lost races for presidency.

Ralph Bunche, 1904-71, (U.S.) first Black person to win the Nobel Peace Prize, 1950; undersecretary of the UN, 1950.

Robert Byrd, 1917-2010, (U.S.) longest serving U.S. senator (D, WV), 1959-2010.

John C. Calhoun, 1782-1850, (U.S.) political leader; champion of states' rights and a symbol of the Old South.

James Callaghan (Baron Callaghan), 1912-2005, (Br.) Labour party politician, prime min., 1976-79.

Robert Castlereagh, 1769-1822, (Br.) foreign sec.; guided Grand Alliance against Napoleon.

Fidel Castro, 1926-2016, (Cuba) prime min./pres., 1959-2008; led Communist revolution.

Camillo Benso Cavour, 1810-61, (It.) statesman; largely responsible for uniting Italy under the House of Savoy.

Nicolae Ceausescu, 1918-89, (Rom.) Communist leader, head of state, 1967-89; executed.

Neville Chamberlain, 1869-1940, (Br.) Conservative prime min. whose appeasement of Hitler led to Munich Pact.

Hugo Chávez, 1954-2013, (Venez.) socialist Venezuelan pres., 1999-2013.

Chiang Kai-shek, 1887-1975, (China) Nationalist Chinese pres. whose govt. was driven from mainland to Taiwan.

Madame Chiang Kai-shek (Mayling Soong), 1898-2003, (China) highly influential wife of Nationalist Chinese leader Chiang Kai-shek.

Jacques Chirac, 1932-2019, (Fr.) pres. of France, 1995-2007.

Shirley Chisholm, 1924-2005, (U.S.) first Black woman elected to U.S. house (1968, D, NY); pres. contender, 1972.

Winston Churchill, 1874-1965, (Br.) prime min., soldier, author; guided Britain through WWII.

Galeazzo Ciano, 1903-44, (It.) Fascist foreign minister; helped create Rome-Berlin Axis; executed by Benito Mussolini.

Henry Clay, 1777-1852, (U.S.) "The Great Compromiser"; one of the most influential pre-Civil War political leaders.

Georges Clemenceau, 1841-1929, (Fr.) twice prem.; Woodrow Wilson's antagonist at Paris Peace Conference after WWI.

DeWitt Clinton, 1769-1828, (U.S.) political leader; promoted Erie Canal.

Robert Clive, 1725-74, (Br.) first administrator of Bengal; laid foundation for British Empire in India.

Jean Baptiste Colbert, 1619-83, (Fr.) statesman; influential under Louis XIV; created the French navy.

David Crockett, 1786-1836, (U.S.) frontiersman, congressman; died defending the Alamo.

Oliver Cromwell, 1599-1658, (Br.) Lord Protector of England; led parliamentary forces during Civil War.

Mario Cuomo, 1932-2015, NY governor (D), 1983-94.

Curzon of Kedleston, 1859-1925, (Br.) viceroy of India, foreign sec.; major force in post-WWI world.

Édouard Daladier, 1884-1970, (Fr.) Radical Socialist politician; arrested by Vichy government, interned by Germans.

Richard J. Daley, 1902-76, (U.S.) Chicago mayor, 1955-76.

Georges Danton, 1759-94, (Fr.) leading French Rev. figure.

Jefferson Davis, 1808-89, (U.S.) pres. of the Confederacy.

Charles G. Dawes, 1865-1951, (U.S.) statesman, banker; advanced plan to stabilize post-WWI German finances.

Alcide De Gasperi, 1881-1954, (It.) prime min.; founder of Christian Democratic party.

Charles De Gaulle, 1890-1970, (Fr.) general, statesman; first pres. of the Fifth Republic.

Deng Xiaoping, 1904-97, (China) "paramount leader" of China; backed economic modernization.

Eamon De Valera, 1882-1975, (Ire.-U.S.) statesman; led fight for Irish independence.

Thomas E. Dewey, 1902-71, (U.S.) NY governor (R); twice lost in try for presidency.

Ngo Dinh Diem, 1901-63, (Viet.) South Vietnamese pres.; assassinated in government takeover.

John Dingell Jr., 1926-2019, (U.S.) longest-serving U.S. rep (D, MI), 1955-2015.

Benjamin Disraeli, 1804-81, (Br.) prime min.; considered founder of modern Conservative party.

Anatoly Dobrynin, 1919-2010, (Russ.) diplomat and Soviet amb. to U.S. (1962-86).

Engelbert Dollfuss, 1892-1934, (Austria) chancellor; assassinated by Nazis.

Andrea Doria, 1466-1560, (It.) Genoese admiral, statesman; called "Father of Peace" and "Liberator of Genoa."

Stephen A. Douglas, 1813-61, (U.S.) Democratic leader, orator; ran against Lincoln for IL sen. seat, presidency.

Alexander Dubcek, 1921-92, (Czech.) statesman whose attempted liberalization was crushed, 1968.

John Foster Dulles, 1888-1959, (U.S.) sec. of state under Eisenhower; Cold War policy maker.

Friedrich Ebert, 1871-1925, (Ger.) Social Democratic movement leader; first pres., Weimar Republic, 1919-25.

Anthony Eden, 1897-1977, (Br.) foreign sec., prime min. during Suez invasion of 1956.

Ludwig Erhard, 1897-1977, (Ger.) economist, West German chancellor; led nation's economic rise after WWII.

King Fahd, 1923-2005, (Saudi Arabia) monarch from 1982 but inactive after 1995 stroke; encouraged U.S. relations.

Geraldine Ferraro, 1935-2011, (U.S.) U.S. rep. (D, NY), first woman vice-pres. nominee (1984).

João Baptista de Figueiredo, 1918-99, (Braz.) pres. of Brazil; restored nation's democracy after military rule.

Hamilton Fish, 1808-93, (U.S.) sec. of state; successfully mediated disputes with Great Britain, Latin America.

James V. Forrestal, 1892-1949, (U.S.) sec. of navy, first sec. of defense.

Francisco Franco, 1892-1975, (Sp.) leader of rebel forces during Spanish Civil War, longtime ruler of Spain.

Benjamin Franklin, 1706-90, (U.S.) printer, publisher, author, inventor, scientist, diplomat.

Louis de Frontenac, 1620-98, (Fr.) governor of New France (Canada).

J. William Fulbright, 1905-95, (U.S.) U.S. senator (D, AR); leading figure in U.S. foreign policy during Cold War years.

Hugh Gaitskell, 1906-63, (Br.) Labour party leader; major force in reversing its stand for unilateral disarmament.

Albert Gallatin, 1761-1849, (U.S.) sec. of treasury; instrumental in negotiating end of War of 1812.

Léon Gambetta, 1838-82, (Fr.) statesman, politician; one of the founders of the Third Republic.

Indira Gandhi, 1917-84, (India) daughter of Jawaharlal Nehru; prime min. of India, 1966-77, 1980-84; assassinated.

Mohandas K. Gandhi, 1869-1948, (India) political leader, ascetic; led movement against British rule; assassinated.

Giuseppe Garibaldi, 1807-82, (It.) patriot, soldier; a leader in the Risorgimento, Italian unification movement.

Ruth Bader Ginsburg, 1933-2020, (U.S.) U.S. Supreme Court justice (1993-2020).

William E. Gladstone, 1809-98, (Br.) prime min.; dominant force of Liberal party, 1868-94.

Paul Joseph Goebbels, 1897-1945, (Ger.) Nazi propagandist; master of mass psychology.

Barry Goldwater, 1909-98, (U.S.) conservative U.S. senator (R, AZ), 1964 pres. nominee.

Klement Gottwald, 1896-1953, (Czech.) Communist leader.

Haile Selassie (Tafari Makonnen), 1892-1975, (Ethiopia) emperor of Ethiopia.

Alexander Hamilton, 1755-1804, (U.S.) first treasury sec.; champion of strong central government.

Dag Hammarskjöld, 1905-61, (Swed.) statesman; UN sec.-general.

King Hassan II, 1929-99, (Moroc.) ruler of Morocco, 1962-99.

Vaclav Havel, 1936-2011, (Czech.) first president of Czech Republic, 1989-92.

John Hay, 1838-1905, (U.S.) sec. of state; primarily associated with Open Door Policy toward China.

Edward Heath, 1916-2005, (Br.) Conservative prime min., 1970-74; promoted European unity.

Patrick Henry, 1736-99, (U.S.) major Revolutionary War figure, orator.

Édouard Herriot, 1872-1957, (Fr.) Radical Socialist leader; twice prem., pres. of National Assembly.

Theodor Herzl, 1860-1904, (Hung.) founded modern Zionism.

Heinrich Himmler, 1900-45, (Ger.) head of Nazi SS and Gestapo.

Paul von Hindenburg, 1847-1934, (Ger.) field marshal, WWI; second pres. of Weimar Republic, 1925-34.

Adolf Hitler, 1889-1945, (Ger.) dictator; built Nazism, launched WWII, presided over the Holocaust.

Ho Chi Minh, 1890-1969, (Viet.) N. Vietnamese pres., Communist leader.

Harry L. Hopkins, 1890-1946, (U.S.) New Deal administrator; closest adviser to Franklin D. Roosevelt during WWII.

Edward M. House, 1858-1938, (U.S.) diplomat; confidential adviser to Woodrow Wilson.

Samuel Houston, 1793-1863, (U.S.) leader of struggle for Texas independence.

Cordell Hull, 1871-1955, (U.S.) sec. of state, 1933-44; initiated reciprocal trade to lower tariffs, helped organize UN.

John Hume, 1937-2020, (N. Ire.) nationalist party leader; 1998 Nobel Peace Prize winner.

Hubert H. Humphrey, 1911-78, (U.S.) U.S. senator (D, MN), vice pres., pres. nominee (1968).

King Hussein, 1935-99, (Jordan) peacemaker; ruler of Jordan, 1952-99.

Saddam Hussein, 1937-2006, (Iraq) Iraqi ruler; put to death for crimes against humanity.

Muhammad Ali Jinnah, 1876-1948, (Pak.) founder, first gov.-gen. of Pakistan.

Barbara Jordan, 1936-96, (U.S.) U.S. rep. (D, TX), orator, educator; first Black woman to win a seat in the TX state senate, 1966.

Benito Juarez, 1806-72, (Mex.) rallied his country against foreign threats; sought to create democratic, federal republic.

Betty Mae Tiger Jumper, 1923-2011, (Amer. Ind.) first woman Seminole chief.

Constantine Karamanlis, 1907-98, (Gr.) Greek prime min.; restored democracy, later president.

Frank B. Kellogg, 1856-1937, (U.S.) sec. of state; negotiated Kellogg-Briand Pact to outlaw war.

Edward M. Kennedy, 1932-2009, (U.S.) senator (D, MA); championed progressive causes.

Robert F. Kennedy, 1925-68, (U.S.) attorney general, U.S. sen. (D, NY); assassinated while seeking presidency.

Aleksandr Kerensky, 1881-1970, (Russ.) headed provisional government after Feb. 1917 revolution.

Ayatollah Ruhollah Khomeini, 1900-89, (Iran), religious-political leader; spearheaded overthrow of Shah, 1979.

Nikita Khrushchev, 1894-1971, (USSR) prem., first sec. of Communist party; initiated de-Stalinization.

Kim Dae-jung, 1925-2009, (Korea) S. Korean dissident, opposition leader, pres.; 2000 Nobel Peace Prize winner.

Kim Il Sung, 1912-94, (Korea) N. Korean dictator, 1948-94.

Kim Jong Il, 1942-2011, (Korea) N. Korean dictator, 1994-2011.

Edward I. Koch, 1924-2013, (U.S.) New York City mayor, 1978-89.

Helmut Kohl, 1930-2017, (Ger.) chancellor, 1982-98; reunified Germany.

Lajos Kossuth, 1802-94, (Hung.) principal figure in 1848 Hungarian revolution.

Pyotr Kropotkin, 1842-1921, (Russ.) anarchist; championed the peasants but opposed Bolshevism.

Kublai Khan, c. 1215-94, (Mongol) emperor; founder of Yuan dynasty in China.

Béla Kun, 1886-c. 1939, (Hung.) member of Third Communist International; tried to foment worldwide revolution.

Robert M. LaFollette, 1855-1925, (U.S.) Wisconsin public official; leader of progressive movement.

Fiorello La Guardia, 1882-1947, (U.S.) New York City reform mayor, 1933-45.

Pierre Laval, 1883-1945, (Fr.) politician, Vichy foreign min.; executed for treason.

Andrew Bonar Law, 1858-1923, (Can.) Conservative party politician, British prime min.; led opposition to Irish home rule.

Vladimir Ilyich Lenin (Ulyanov), 1870-1924, (Russ.) revolutionary; founded Bolshevism; Soviet leader, 1917-24.

Ferdinand de Lesseps, 1805-94, (Fr.) diplomat, engineer; conceived idea of Suez Canal.

René Lévesque, 1922-87, (Can.) prem. of Quebec, 1976-85; led unsuccessful separatist campaign.

Trygve Lie, 1896-1968, (Nor.) first UN sec.-gen.

Maxim Litvinov, 1876-1951, (Pol.-Russ.) revolutionary, commissar of foreign affairs; favored cooperation with West.

David Lloyd George, 1863-1945, (Br.) Liberal party prime min.; laid foundations for modern welfare state.

Henry Cabot Lodge, 1850-1924, (U.S.) U.S. senator (R, MA); led opposition to participation in League of Nations.

Huey P. Long, 1893-1935, (U.S.) Louisiana political demagogue, governor, U.S. senator (D); assassinated.

Rosa Luxemburg, 1871-1919, (Ger.) revolutionary; leader of the German Social Democratic party and Spartacus party.

J. Ramsay MacDonald, 1866-1937, (Br.) first Labour party prime min. of Great Britain.

Harold Macmillan, 1895-1986, (Br.) prime min. of Great Britain, 1957-63.

Makarios III, 1913-77, (Cyprus) Greek Orthodox archbishop; first pres. of Cyprus.

Nelson Mandela, 1918-2013, (S. Afr.) antiapartheid leader; first Black pres. of S. Africa, 1994-99.

Wilma Mankiller, 1945-2010, (Amer. Ind.) first female chief of the Cherokee Nation.

Mao Zedong, 1893-1976, (China) chief Chinese Marxist theorist, revolutionary, political leader; led revolution establishing his nation as Communist state.

Jean Paul Marat, 1743-93, (Fr.) revolutionary, politician; identified with radical Jacobins; assassinated.

Thurgood Marshall, 1908-93, (U.S.) first Black U.S. solicitor general, 1965; first Black justice of U.S. Supreme Court, 1967-91.

José Martí, 1853-95, (Cuba) patriot, poet; independence leader.

Jan Masaryk, 1886-1948, (Czech.) foreign min.; died under mysterious circumstances, allegedly by suicide, following Communist coup.

Thomas G. Masaryk, 1850-1937, (Czech.) statesman, philosopher; first pres. of Czechoslovakia.

Jules Mazarin, 1602-61, (Fr.) cardinal, statesman; prime min. under Louis XIII and queen regent Anne of Austria.

Giuseppe Mazzini, 1805-72, (It.) reformer dedicated to Risorgimento movement for renewal of Italy.

Tom Mboya, 1930-69, (Kenya) political leader; instrumental in securing independence for Kenya.

John McCain, 1936-2018, (U.S.) U.S. sen. (R, AZ), 2008 pres. nominee.

Eugene McCarthy, 1916-2005, (U.S.) political leader, author; 1968 Dem. presidential contender.

Joseph R. McCarthy, 1908-57, (U.S.) senator (R, WI); extremist in searching out alleged Communists and pro-Communists.

Cosimo I de' Medici, 1519-74, (It.) Duke of Florence, grand duke of Tuscany.

Lorenzo de' Medici (the Magnificent), 1449-92, (It.) merchant prince; a towering figure in Italian Renaissance.

Catherine de Médicis, 1519-89, (Fr.) queen consort of Henry II, regent of France; influential in Catholic-Huguenot wars.

Golda Meir, 1898-1978, (Ukr.-Isr.) a founder of the state of Israel; prime min., 1969-74.

Klemens W. N. L. Metternich, 1773-1859, (Austria) statesman; arbiter of post-Napoleonic Europe.

Slobodan Milosevic, 1941-2006, (Serb./Yugo.) former Yugoslav pres.; tried for genocide, crimes against humanity.

François Mitterrand, 1916-96, (Fr.) pres. of France, 1981-95.

Mobutu Sese Seko, 1930-97, (Zaire) longtime ruler of Zaire (now Dem. Rep. of Congo), 1965-97; exiled after rebellion.

Guy Mollet, 1905-75, (Fr.) socialist politician, resistance leader.

Henry Morgenthau Jr., 1891-1967, (U.S.) sec. of treasury; fundraiser for New Deal and U.S. WWII activities.

Gouverneur Morris, 1752-1816, (U.S.) statesman, diplomat, financial expert; helped plan decimal coinage.

Mohammed Morsi, 1951-2019, (Egypt) first democratically elected pres. of Egypt, 2012; deposed 2013.

Daniel Patrick Moynihan, 1927-2003, (U.S.) senator (D, NY), diplomat, social scientist, author.

Hosni Mubarak, 1928-2020, (Egy.) Egyptian president deposed in 2011 uprising.

Robert Mugabe, 1924-2019, (Zimb.) prime min. and pres. of Zimbabwe.

Benito Mussolini, 1883-1945, (It.) leader of the Italian fascist state; assassinated.

Imre Nagy, c. 1896-1958, (Hung.) Communist prem.; assassinated after Soviets crushed 1956 uprising.

Gamal Abdel Nasser, 1918-70, (Egypt) leader of Arab unification; second Egyptian pres.

Jawaharlal Nehru, 1889-1964, (India) prime min.; guided India through its early years of independence.

Kwame Nkrumah, 1909-72, (Ghana) first prime min., 1957-60; pres., 1960-66, of Ghana.

Manuel Noriega, 1934-2017, (Pan.) dictator, 1983-89; military officer, CIA informant.

Frederick North, 1732-92, (Br.) prime min.; his policies led to loss of American colonies.

Julius K. Nyerere, 1922-99, (Tanz.) founding father; first pres., 1962-85, of Tanzania.

Daniel O'Connell, 1775-1847, (Ire.) nationalist political leader; known as The Liberator.

Omar, c. 581-644, (Arab.) Muslim leader; second caliph, led Islam to become an imperial power.

Thomas P. (Tip) O'Neill Jr., 1912-94, (U.S.) U.S. rep. (D, MA), speaker of the House, 1977-86.

Ignace Paderewski, 1860-1941, (Pol.) statesman, pianist, composer, briefly prime min.; ardent patriot.

Ian Paisley, 1926-2014, (Ire.) Unionist Party leader who agreed to power sharing in N. Ireland.

Viscount Palmerston, 1784-1865, (Br.) Whig-Liberal prime min.; foreign min.; embodied British nationalism.

Andreas George Papandreou, 1919-96, (Gr.) leftist politician; served as prem., 1981-89, 1993-96.

Georgios Papandreou, 1888-1968, (Gr.) Republican politician; served three times as prime min.

Franz von Papen, 1879-1969, (Ger.) politician; major role in overthrow of Weimar Republic and rise of Hitler.

Charles Stewart Parnell, 1846-91, (Ire.) nationalist leader; "uncrowned king of Ireland."

Lester Pearson, 1897-1972, (Can.) diplomat, Liberal party leader, prime min.

Robert Peel, 1788-1850, (Br.) reformist prime min.; founder of Conservative party.

Shimon Peres, 1922-2016, (Bela.-Isr.) Israel prime min., 1984-86, 1995-96; president, 2007-14.

Javier Pérez de Cuéllar, 1920-2020 (Per.) UN sec.-gen.

Frances Perkins, 1882-1965, (U.S.) first female cabinet member (sec. of labor).

Eva (Evita) Perón, 1919-52, (Arg.) highly influential second wife of Juan Perón.

Juan Perón, 1895-1974, (Arg.) dynamic pres. of Argentina, 1946-55, 1973-74.

Joseph Pilsudski, 1867-1935, (Pol.) statesman; instrumental in reestablishing Polish state in the 20th cent.

Charles Pinckney, 1757-1824, (U.S.) founding father; his Pinckney plan largely incorporated into Constitution.

Christian Pineau, 1905-95, (Fr.) leader of French Resistance during WWII; foreign min., 1956-58.

Augusto Pinochet (Ugarte), 1915-2006, (Chile) former Chilean ruler; indicted for human rights abuses while in office.

William Pitt the Elder, 1708-78, (Br.) statesman; the "Great Commoner," transformed Britain into imperial power.

William Pitt the Younger, 1759-1806, (Br.) prime min. during French Revolutionary wars.

Georgi Plekhanov, 1857-1918, (Russ.) revolutionary, social philosopher; called "father of Russian Marxism."

Raymond Poincaré, 1860-1934, (Fr.) French pres.; advocated harsh punishment of Germany after WWI.

Pol Pot, 1925-98, (Camb.) leader of Khmer Rouge; ruled Cambodia, 1975-79; responsible for mass deaths.

Georges Pompidou, 1911-74, (Fr.) Gaullist political leader; pres., 1969-74.

Grigori Potemkin, 1739-91, (Russ.) field marshal; favorite of empress Catherine II.

Adam Clayton Powell Jr., 1908-72, (U.S.) civil rights leader; U.S. rep. (D, NY), 1945-69.

Muammar al-Qaddafi, 1942-2011, (Libya) Libyan ruler, 1969-2011.

Yitzhak Rabin, 1922-95, (Isr.) military, political leader; prime min. of Israel, 1974-77, 1992-95; assassinated.

Joseph H. Rainey, 1832-87, (U.S.) first Black person elected to U.S. House (1869), from SC.

Edmund Randolph, 1753-1813, (U.S.) attorney; prominent in drafting, ratification of Constitution.

John Randolph, 1773-1833, (U.S.) Southern planter; strong advocate of states' rights.

Jeannette Rankin, 1880-1973, (U.S.) pacifist; first woman member of U.S. Congress (R, MT).

Walt(h)er Rathenau, 1867-1922, (Ger.) industrialist, statesman.

Sam Rayburn, 1882-1961, (U.S.) U.S. rep. (D, TX) for 47 years, House speaker for 17.

Red Cloud, 1822?-1909, (Amer. Ind.) leader of the Oglala Lakota.

Janet Reno, 1938-2016, (U.S.) first woman attorney general.

Hiram R. Revels, 1822-1901, (U.S.) first African American U.S. senator (R); elected in MS, served 1870-71.

Paul Reynaud, 1878-1966, (Fr.) statesman; prem. in 1940 at time of France's defeat by Germany.

Syngman Rhee, 1875-1965, (Korea) first pres. of S. Korea.

Cecil Rhodes, 1853-1902, (Br.) imperialist, industrial magnate; established Rhodes scholarships in his will.

Ann Richards, 1933-2006, (U.S.) former TX gov. (D).

Cardinal de Richelieu, 1585-1642, (Fr.) statesman, known as "red eminence"; chief minister to Louis XIII.

Maximilien Robespierre, 1758-94, (Fr.) leading figure in French Revolution and Reign of Terror.

Eleanor Roosevelt, 1884-1962, (U.S.) influential first lady, humanitarian, UN diplomat.

Elihu Root, 1845-1937, (U.S.) lawyer, statesman, diplomat; leading Republican supporter of the League of Nations.

John Ross, 1790-1866, (Amer. Ind.) longest-serving principal chief of Cherokee Nation (1828-66).

Dean Rusk, 1909-95, (U.S.) statesman; sec. of state, 1961-69.

John Russell, 1792-1878, (Br.) Liberal prime min. during the Irish potato famine.

Anwar al-Sadat, 1918-81, (Egypt) pres., 1970-81; promoted peace with Israel; Nobel laureate; assassinated.

António de Oliveira Salazar, 1889-1970, (Port.) longtime dictator of Portugal.

José de San Martín, 1778-1850, ([now] Arg.) S. Amer. revolutionary; protector of Peru.

Eisaku Sato, 1901-75, (Jpn.) prime min.; presided over Japan's post-WWII emergence as major world power.

Abdul Aziz Ibn Saud, c. 1880-1953, (Saudi Arabia) king of Saudi Arabia, 1932-53.

Helmut Schmidt, 1918-2015, (Ger.) German chancellor, 1974-82.

Robert Schuman, 1886-1963, (Fr.) statesman; founded European Coal and Steel Community.

Carl Schurz, 1829-1906, (Ger.-U.S.) political leader, journalist, orator, reformer.

Kurt Schuschnigg, 1897-1977, (Austria) chancellor; unsuccessful in stopping Austria's annexation by Germany.

William H. Seward, 1801-72, (U.S.) antislavery activist; as U.S. sec. of state purchased Alaska.

Carlo Sforza, 1872-1952, (It.) foreign min., anti-Fascist.

Yitzhak Shamir, 1915-2012, (Russ.-Isr.) prime min. of Israel, 1983-84, 1986-92.

Ariel Sharon, 1928-2014, (Isr.) prime min. of Israel, 2001-06.

Eduard Shevardnadze, 1928-2014, (Geo.) Georgian pres., 1995-2003.

Norodom Sihanouk, 1922-2012, (Camb.) king of Cambodia, 1941-55, 1993-2004.

Sitting Bull, c. 1831-90, (Amer. Ind.) Hunkpapa Lakota leader; defeated Custer at Battle of the Little Bighorn.

Alfred E. Smith, 1873-1944, (U.S.) NY Democratic governor; first Roman Catholic to run for president (1928).

Margaret Chase Smith, 1897-1995, (U.S.) U.S. rep., senator (R, ME); first woman elected to both houses of Congress.

Jan C. Smuts, 1870-1950, (S. Afr.) statesman, philosopher, soldier, prime min.

Paul Henri Spaak, 1899-1972, (Belg.) statesman, socialist leader.

Joseph Stalin, 1879-1953, (USSR) Soviet dictator, 1924-53; instituted forced collectivization, massive purges, and labor camps, causing millions of deaths.

Edwin M. Stanton, 1814-69, (U.S.) sec. of war, 1862-68.

Alexander Stephens, 1812-83, (U.S.) vice pres. of the Confederacy.

Edward R. Stettinius Jr., 1900-49, (U.S.) industrialist; sec. of state who coordinated aid to WWII allies.

Adlai E. Stevenson, 1900-65, (U.S.) Democratic leader, diplomat, governor (IL), presidential nominee (1952, '56).

Henry L. Stimson, 1867-1950, (U.S.) statesman; served in five administrations, foreign policy adviser in 1930s and 1940s.

Carl Stokes, 1927-96, (U.S.) first Black mayor of a major American city (Cleveland, 1967-72).

Suharto, 1921-2008, (Indon.) former longtime Indonesian ruler.

Sukarno, 1901-70, (Indon.) dictatorial first pres. of the Indonesian republic.

Sun Yat-sen, 1866-1925, (China) revolutionary; leader of Kuomintang political party, regarded as father of modern China.

Robert A. Taft, 1889-1953, (U.S.) conservative Senate leader (OH); called "Mr. Republican."

Charles de Talleyrand, 1754-1838, (Fr.) statesman, diplomat; the major force of the Congress of Vienna of 1814-15.

U Thant, 1909-74, (Burma) statesman, UN sec.-general.

Margaret Thatcher, 1925-2013, (Br.) conservative British prime min., 1979-90; first woman UK prime min.

Norman M. Thomas, 1884-1968, (U.S.) social reformer; six times Socialist party presidential candidate.

Josip Broz Tito, 1892-1980, (Yugo.) pres. of Yugoslavia, 1953-80; WWII guerrilla chief, postwar rival of Stalin.

Palmiro Togliatti, 1893-1964, (It.) major Italian Communist leader.

Hideki Tojo, 1885-1948, (Jpn.) statesman, soldier; prime min. during most of WWII.

François Toussaint L'Ouverture, c. 1744-1803, (Haiti) patriot, martyr; thwarted French colonial aims.

Leon Trotsky, 1879-1940, (Russ.) revolutionary; founded Red Army, expelled from party in conflict with Stalin; assassinated.

Pierre Elliott Trudeau, 1919-2000, (Can.) longtime liberal prime min. of Canada, 1968-79, 1980-84; achieved native Canadian constitution.

Rafael L. Trujillo Molina, 1891-1961, (Dom. Rep.) dictator of Dominican Republic, 1930-61; assassinated.

Moise K. Tshombe, 1919-69, (Congo) pres. of secessionist Katanga prov., prem. of Congo (now Dem. Rep. of the Congo).

William M. Tweed, 1823-78, (U.S.) political boss of Tammany Hall, New York City's Democratic political machine.

Walter Ulbricht, 1893-1973, (Ger.) Communist leader of German Democratic Republic.

Arthur H. Vandenberg, 1884-1951, (U.S.) senator (R, MI); proponent of bipartisan anti-Communist foreign policy.

Eleutherios Venizelos, 1864-1936, (Gr.) most prominent Greek statesman of early 20th cent.

Hendrik F. Verwoerd, 1901-66, (S. Afr.) prime min.; rigorously applied apartheid policy despite protest.

Kurt Waldheim, 1918-2007, (Austria) UN sec.-gen., Austrian pres.

George Wallace, 1919-98, (U.S.) former segregationist governor of Alabama, pres. candidate.

Robert Walpole, 1676-1745, (Br.) statesman; generally considered Britain's first prime min.

Nancy Ward (Nan'yehi), 1738?-1824?, (Amer. Ind.) Cherokee peace leader.

Robert C. Weaver, 1907-97, (U.S.) first African American appointed to cabinet; sec. of Housing and Urban Development.

Daniel Webster, 1782-1852, (U.S.) orator, politician; advocate of business interests during Jacksonian agrarianism.

Caspar Weinberger, 1917-2006, (U.S.) business exec.; former defense sec., other cabinet posts.

Chaim Weizmann, 1874-1952, (Russ.-Isr.) Zionist leader, scientist; first Israeli pres.

Kevin White, 1929-2012, (U.S.) Boston mayor, 1967-84.

Wendell L. Willkie, 1892-1944, (U.S.) Republican who tried to unseat Franklin D. Roosevelt when he ran for his third term.

Harold Wilson, 1916-95, (Br.) Labour party leader; prime min., 1964-70, 1974-76.

Boris Yeltsin, 1931-2007, (Russ.) first freely elected pres. of post-Soviet Russia.

Emiliano Zapata, c. 1879-1919, (Mex.) revolutionary; major influence on modern Mexico.

Todor Zhivkov, 1911-98, (Bulg.) Communist ruler of Bulgaria from 1954 until ousted in a 1989 coup.

Zhou Enlai, 1898-1976, (China) diplomat, prime min.; a leading figure of the Chinese Communist party.

Scientists of the Past

Revised by Peter Barker, Prof. and Chair, Dept. of the History of Science, Univ. of Oklahoma.

For pre-modern scientists, see also Philosophers and Religious Figures of the Past and the Historical Figures chapter.

Albertus Magnus, c. 1200-80, (Ger.) theologian, philosopher; helped found medieval study of natural science.

Alhazen (Ibn al-Haytham), c. 965-c. 1040, (Arab.) mathematician, astronomer, optical theorist.

Andre-Marie Ampère, 1775-1836, (Fr.) mathematician, chemist; founder of electrodynamics.

Mary Anning, 1799-1847, (Br.) paleontologist.

Neil Armstrong, 1930-2012, (U.S.) astronaut; first man to walk on the Moon.

John V. Atanasoff, 1903-95, (U.S.) physicist; co-invented Atanasoff-Berry electronic digital computer (1939-41).

Amedeo Avogadro, 1776-1856, (It.) chemist, physicist; proposed that equal volumes of gas contain equal numbers of molecules, permitting determination of molecular weights.

John Bardeen, 1908-91, (U.S.) double Nobel laureate in physics (transistor, 1956; superconductivity, 1972).

A. H. Becquerel, 1852-1908, (Fr.) physicist; discovered radioactivity in uranium (1896).

Alexander Graham Bell, 1847-1922, (U.S.) inventor; first to patent and commercially exploit the telephone (1876).

Daniel Bernoulli, 1700-82, (Switz.) mathematician; developed fluid dynamics and kinetic theory of gases.

Clifford Berry, 1918-63, (U.S.) collaborated with John V. Atanasoff on the ABC electronic digital computer (1939-41).

Jöns Jakob Berzelius, 1779-1848, (Swed.) chemist; developed modern chemical symbols and formulas.

Henry Bessemer, 1813-98, (Br.) engineer; invented Bessemer steel-making process.

Hans Bethe, 1906-2005, (Ger.-U.S.) physicist; won Nobel Prize in 1967 for describing how stars generate energy.

Bruno Bettelheim, 1903-90, (Austria-U.S.) psychoanalyst; studied disturbed children; *Uses of Enchantment* (1976).

Louis Blériot, 1872-1936, (Fr.) engineer; monoplane pioneer.

Franz Boas, 1858-1942, (Ger.-U.S.) founded modern anthropology; studied Pacific Coast tribes.

Niels Bohr, 1885-1962, (Den.) atomic and nuclear physicist; founded quantum mechanics.

Norman Borlaug, 1914-2009, (U.S.) plant pathologist and geneticist; father of "green" (agricultural) revolution.

Max Born, 1882-1970, (Ger.) atomic and nuclear physicist; helped develop quantum mechanics.

Satyendranath Bose, 1894-1974, (India) physicist; forerunner of modern quantum theory for integral-spin particles.

Louis de Broglie, 1892-1987, (Fr.) physicist; proposed quantum wave-particle duality.

Robert Bunsen, 1811-99, (Ger.) chemist; pioneered spectroscopic analysis; discovered rubidium, caesium.

Luther Burbank, 1849-1926, (U.S.) naturalist; developed plant breeding into a modern science.

Vannevar Bush, 1890-1974, (U.S.) electrical engineer; developed differential analyzer, an early analogue computer; led WWII Office of Scientific Res. and Dev.

Marvin Camras, 1916-95, (U.S.) inventor, electrical engineer; invented magnetic tape recording.

Alexis Carrel, 1873-1944, (Fr.) surgeon, biologist; developed methods of suturing blood vessels, transplanting organs.

Rachel Carson, 1907-64, (U.S.) marine biologist, environmentalist; *Silent Spring* (1962).

George Washington Carver, 1864-1943, (U.S.) chemist and botanist; promoted alternative crops.

James Chadwick, 1891-1974, (Br.) physicist; discovered the neutron (1932); led Brit. team on Manhattan Project in U.S.

Eugenie Clark, 1922-2015, (U.S.) ichthyologist and oceanographer.

Albert Claude, 1898-1983, (Belg.-U.S.) a founder of modern cell biology; determined role of mitochondria.

Samuel Cohen, 1921-2010, (U.S.) physicist who invented the neutron bomb.

Barry Commoner, 1917-2012, (U.S.) biologist; noted environmentalist.

Nicolaus Copernicus, 1473-1543, (Pol.) first modern astronomer to propose Sun as center of the planets' motions.

Jacques Yves Cousteau, 1910-97, (Fr.) oceanographer; co-inventor, with Emile Gagnan (Fr.), of the Aqualung (1943).

Seymour Cray, 1925-96, (U.S.) computer industry pioneer; developed supercomputers.

Francis Crick, 1916-2004, (Br.) biophysicist; co-discoverer of genetic code; shared 1962 Nobel Prize in Physiology/Medicine.

Marie, 1867-1934, (Pol.-Fr.) and **Pierre Curie**, 1859-1906, (Fr.) physical chemists; pioneer investigators of radioactivity; discovered radium and polonium (1898).

Gottlieb Daimler, 1834-1900, (Ger.) engineer, inventor; pioneer automobile manufacturer.

John Dalton, 1766-1844, (Br.) chemist, physicist; formulated atomic theory, made first table of atomic weights.

Charles Darwin, 1809-82, (Br.) naturalist; established theory of organic evolution; *Origin of Species* (1859).

Lee De Forest, 1873-1961, (U.S.) inventor of triode; pioneer in wireless telegraphy, sound pictures, television.

Pierre-Gilles de Gennes, 1932-2007, (Fr.) physicist whose research aided development of liquid-crystal display (LCD); awarded 1991 Nobel Prize for Physics.

Max Delbrück, 1906-81, (Fr.-Ger.-U.S.) a founder of molecular biology.

Rudolf Diesel, 1858-1913, (Ger.) mechanical engineer; patented Diesel engine (1892).

Theodosius Dobzhansky, 1900-75, (Russ.-U.S.) biologist; reconciled genetics and natural selection.

Christian Doppler, 1803-53, (Austria) physicist; showed change in wave frequency caused by motion of source, now known as Doppler effect.

J. Presper Eckert Jr., 1919-95, (U.S.) co-inventor, with John W. Mauchly, of the ENIAC computer (1943-45).

Thomas A. Edison, 1847-1931, (U.S.) inventor; held more than 1,000 patents, including incandescent electric lamp.

Robert Edwards, 1925-2013, (Br.) physiologist; pioneered in vitro fertilization.

Paul Ehrlich, 1854-1915, (Ger.) medical researcher in immunology and bacteriology; pioneered antitoxin production.

Albert Einstein, 1879-1955, (Ger.-U.S.) theoretical physicist; founded relativity theory.

John F. Enders, 1897-1985, (U.S.) virologist; helped discover vaccines against polio, measles, mumps, and chicken pox.

Erik Erikson, 1902-94, (U.S.) psychoanalyst, author; theory of developmental stages of life; *Childhood and Society* (1950).

Leonhard Euler, 1707-83, (Switz.) mathematician, physicist; pioneer of calculus, revived ideas of Fermat.

Gabriel Fahrenheit, 1686-1736, (Ger.) physicist; improved thermometers and introduced Fahrenheit temperature scale.

Michael Faraday, 1791-1867, (Br.) chemist, physicist; discovered electrical induction and invented dynamo (1831).

Philo T. Farnsworth, 1906-71, (U.S.) inventor; built first television system (San Francisco, 1928).

Pierre de Fermat, 1601-65, (Fr.) mathematician; founded modern theory of numbers.

Enrico Fermi, 1901-54, (It.-U.S.) nuclear physicist; demonstrated first controlled chain reaction (Chicago, 1942).

Richard Feynman, 1918-88, (U.S.) theoretical physicist, author; founder of Quantum Electrodynamics (QED).

Alexander Fleming, 1881-1955, (Br.) bacteriologist; discovered penicillin (1928).

Dian Fossey, 1932-85, (U.S.) primatologist.

Jean B. J. Fourier, 1768-1830, (Fr.) introduced Fourier Series, method of analysis in math and physics.

Sigmund Freud, 1856-1939, (Austria) psychiatrist; founder of psychoanalysis; *Interpretation of Dreams* (1901).

Erich Fromm, 1900-80, (U.S.) psychoanalyst; *Man for Himself* (1947).

Galileo Galilei, 1564-1642, (It.) physicist; used telescope to vindicate Copernicus, founded modern science of motion.

Carl Friedrich Gauss, 1777-1855, (Ger.) mathematician; completed work of Fermat and Euler in number theory.

Josiah W. Gibbs, 1839-1903, (U.S.) theoretical physicist, chemist; founded chemical thermodynamics.

John Glenn, 1921-2016, (U.S.) astronaut, first American to orbit Earth (1962).

Robert H. Goddard, 1882-1945, (U.S.) physicist; invented liquid fuel rocket (1926).

George W. Goethals, 1858-1928, (U.S.) chief engineer who completed Panama Canal (1907-14).

William C. Gorgas, 1854-1920, (U.S.) physician; pioneer in prevention of yellow fever and malaria.

Stephen Jay Gould, 1941-2002, (U.S.) paleontologist, evolutionary biologist, writer.

Ernst Haeckel, 1834-1919, (Ger.) zoologist, evolutionist; early Darwinist, introduced concept of "ecology."

Otto Hahn, 1879-1968, (Ger.) chemist; with Lise Meitner discovered nuclear fission (1938).

Edmund Halley, 1656-1742, (Br.) astronomer; predicted return of 1682 comet (Halley's Comet) in 1759.

William Harvey, 1578-1657, (Br.) physician, anatomist; discovered circulation of the blood (1628).

Stephen Hawking, 1942-2018, (Br.) physicist; explored gravity, black holes; *A Brief History of Time* (1988).

Werner Heisenberg, 1901-76, (Ger.) physicist; developed matrix mechanics and uncertainty principle (1927).

Hermann von Helmholtz, 1821-94, (Ger.) physicist, physiologist; formulated principle of conservation of energy.

Caroline Herschel, 1750-1848, (Ger.-Br.) astronomer.

William Herschel, 1738-1822, (Ger.-Br.) astronomer; discovered Uranus (1781).

Heinrich Hertz, 1857-94, (Ger.) physicist; discovered radio waves and photoelectric effect (1886-87).

David Hilbert, 1862-1943, (Ger.) mathematician; contributed to algebra, calculus, and foundational studies (formalism).

Albert Hofmann, 1906-2008, (Switz.) chemist; inventor of LSD.

Edwin P. Hubble, 1889-1953, (U.S.) astronomer; discovered observational evidence of expanding universe.

Alexander von Humboldt, 1769-1859, (Ger.) naturalist; explored Central, S. America, ideated ecology.

Edward Jenner, 1749-1823, (Br.) physician; pioneered vaccination, introduced term "virus."

Katherine Johnson, 1918-2020, (U.S.) NASA mathematician.

James Joule, 1818-89, (Br.) physicist; found relation between heat and mechanical energy (conservation of energy).

Carl Jung, 1875-1961, (Switz.) psychiatrist; founder of analytical psychology.

Ernest Everett Just, 1883-1941, (U.S.) marine biologist; studied egg development; *Biology of Cell Surfaces* (1941).

Johannes Kepler, 1571-1630, (Ger.) astronomer; discovered laws of planetary motion.

Al-Khwarizmi, early 9th cent., (Arab.) mathematician; regarded as founder of algebra.

Robert Koch, 1843-1910, (Ger.) bacteriologist; isolated bacterial causes of tuberculosis and other diseases.

Georges Köhler, 1946-95, (Ger.) immunologist; with César Milstein, developed monoclonal antibody technique.

Willem Kolff, 1911-2009, (Neth.-U.S.) physician, biomedical engineer; developed first practical kidney dialysis machine; considered the "father of artificial organs."

Jacques Lacan, 1901-81, (Fr.) influential psychoanalyst.

Joseph Lagrange, 1736-1813, (Fr.) geometer, astronomer; showed that gravity of Earth and Moon cancel, creating stable points in space around them.

Jean B. Lamarck, 1744-1829, (Fr.) naturalist; forerunner of Darwin in evolutionary theory.

Pierre Simon de Laplace, 1749-1827, (Fr.) astronomer, physicist; proposed nebular origin for solar system.

Lewis H. Latimer, 1848-1928, (U.S.) African American scientist; associate of Edison; supervised installation of first electric street lighting in New York City.

Antoine Lavoisier, 1743-94, (Fr.) a founder of modern chemistry.

Ernest O. Lawrence, 1901-58, (U.S.) physicist; invented the cyclotron.

Louis, 1903-72, and **Mary Leakey**, 1913-96, (both Br.) early hominid paleoanthropologists; discovered remains in Africa.

Anton van Leeuwenhoek, 1632-1723, (Neth.) founder of microscopy.

Jerome Lejeune, 1927-94, (Fr.) geneticist; discovered chromosomal cause of Down syndrome (1959).

Claude Lévi-Strauss, 1908-2009, (Belg.-Fr.) cultural anthropologist, sociologist, philosopher.

Kurt Lewin, 1890-1947, (Ger.-U.S.) social psychologist; studied human motivation and group dynamics.

Justus von Liebig, 1803-73, (Ger.) founded quantitative chemistry.

Joseph Lister, 1827-1912, (Br.) physician; pioneered antiseptic surgery.

Hendrik Lorentz, 1853-1928, (Neth.) physicist; developed electron theory of matter, contributed to relativity theory.

Konrad Lorenz, 1903-89, (Austria) ethologist; pioneer in study of animal behavior.

Bernard Lovell, 1913-2012, (Br.) physicist and radio astronomer.

Percival Lowell, 1855-1916, (U.S.) astronomer; predicted the existence of Pluto.

Louis, 1864-1948, and **Auguste Lumière**, 1862-1954, (both Fr.) invented cinematograph, made first motion picture (1895).

Theodore H. Maiman, 1927-2007, (U.S.) physicist; invented the first workable laser, which he displayed in 1960.

Guglielmo Marconi, 1874-1937, (It.) physicist; developed wireless telegraphy.

John W. Mauchly, 1907-80, (U.S.) co-inventor, with J. Presper Eckert Jr., of computer ENIAC (1943-45).

James Clerk Maxwell, 1831-79, (Br.) physicist; unified electricity and magnetism, electromagnetic theory of light.

Maria Goeppert Mayer, 1906-72, (Ger.-U.S.) physicist; developed shell model of atomic nuclei.

Barbara McClintock, 1902-92, (U.S.) geneticist; showed that some genetic elements are mobile.

Lise Meitner, 1878-1968, (Austria) co-discoverer, with Otto Hahn, of nuclear fission (1938).

Gregor J. Mendel, 1822-84, (Austria) botanist, monk; his experiments became the foundation of modern genetics.

Dmitri Mendeleyev, 1834-1907, (Russ.) chemist; established Periodic Table of the Elements.

Bruce R. Merrifield, 1921-2006, (U.S.) chemist; discovered how to synthesize proteins quickly and efficiently.

Franz Mesmer, 1734-1815, (Ger.) physician; introduced hypnotherapy.

Albert A. Michelson, 1852-1931, (U.S.) physicist; invented interferometer.

Robert A. Millikan, 1868-1953, (U.S.) physicist; measured electronic charge.

Thomas Hunt Morgan, 1866-1945, (U.S.) geneticist, embryologist; established role of chromosomes in heredity.

John F. Nash Jr., 1928-2015, (U.S.) mathematician; Nobel Prize winner (1994) in economics for work on game theory.

Isaac Newton, 1642-1727, (Br.) natural philosopher; discovered laws of gravitation, motion; with Gottfried Wilhelm von Leibniz, founded calculus.

Robert N. Noyce, 1927-90, (U.S.) invented microchip.

J. Robert Oppenheimer, 1904-67, (U.S.) physicist; scientific director of Manhattan Project.

Wilhelm Ostwald, 1853-1932, (Ger.) chemist, philosopher; main founder of modern physical chemistry.

Louis Pasteur, 1822-95, (Fr.) chemist; showed that germs cause disease and fermentation; originated pasteurization.

Linus C. Pauling, 1901-94, (U.S.) chemist; studied chemical bonds; campaigned for nuclear disarmament.

Jean Piaget, 1896-1980, (Switz.) psychologist; four-stage theory of intellectual development in children.

Max Planck, 1858-1947, (Ger.) physicist; introduced quantum hypothesis (1900).

Jules Henri Poincaré, 1854-1912, (Fr.) mathematician; founded algebraic topology, many other discoveries.

Walter S. Reed, 1851-1902, (U.S.) Army physician; proved mosquitoes transmit yellow fever.

Theodor Reik, 1888-1969, (Austria-U.S.) psychoanalyst; major Freudian disciple.

Sally Ride, 1951-2012, (U.S.) astronaut; 1st U.S. woman in space.

Bernhard Riemann, 1826-66, (Ger.) mathematician; developed non-Euclidean geometry used by Einstein.

Norbert Rillieux, 1806-94, (U.S.) African American inventor of a vacuum pan evaporator (1846); revolutionized sugar-refining industry.

Wilhelm Roentgen, 1845-1923, (Ger.) physicist; discovered X-rays (1895).

Carl Rogers, 1902-87, (U.S.) psychotherapist, author; originated nondirective therapy.

Ernest Rutherford, 1871-1937, (Br.) physicist; pioneer investigator of radioactivity, identified the atomic nucleus.

Albert B. Sabin, 1906-93, (Russ.-U.S.) developed oral polio live-virus vaccine.

Carl Sagan, 1934-96, (U.S.) astronomer, author.

Jonas Salk, 1914-95, (U.S.) developed first successful polio vaccine, widely used in U.S. after 1955.

Allan Sandage, 1926-2010, (U.S.) astronomer; refined the Hubble Constant, a measure of the universe's expansion.

Frederick Sanger, 1918-2013, (Br.) biochemist; detailed molecular structure of insulin.

Giovanni Schiaparelli, 1835-1910, (It.) astronomer; reported canals on Mars.

Erwin Schrödinger, 1887-1961, (Austria) physicist; developed wave equation for quantum systems.

Glenn T. Seaborg, 1912-99, (U.S.) chemist; Nobel Prize winner (1951); co-discoverer of plutonium.

Harlow Shapley, 1885-1972, (U.S.) astronomer; mapped galactic clusters and position of Sun in Milky Way Galaxy.

Norman E. Shumway, 1923-2006, (U.S.) surgeon; performed world's first successful heart-lung transplant.

B. F. Skinner, 1904-90, (U.S.) psychologist; leading advocate of behaviorism.

Richard E. Smalley, 1943-2005, (U.S.) chemist; with three other scientists, discovered buckminsterfullerenes, a previously unknown class of carbon molecules.

Roger W. Sperry, 1913-94, (U.S.) neurobiologist; established different functions of right and left sides of brain.

Benjamin Spock, 1903-98, (U.S.) pediatrician, child care expert; *Common Sense Book of Baby and Child Care.*

Charles P. Steinmetz, 1865-1923, (Ger.-U.S.) electrical engineer; developed basic ideas on alternating current.

Ernst Stuhlinger, 1913-2008, (Ger.) rocket scientist; electric propulsion for NASA in early space age.

Leo Szilard, 1898-1964, (Hung.-U.S.) physicist; helped on Manhattan Project, later opposed nuclear weapons.

Edward Teller, 1908-2003, (Hung.-U.S.) physicist; aided on Manhattan Project, had key role in development of H-bomb.

Nikola Tesla, 1856-1943, (Serb.-U.S.) invented electrical devices including AC dynamos, transformers, and motors.

William Thomson (Lord Kelvin), 1824-1907, (Br.) physicist; aided in success of transatlantic telegraph cable (1865); proposed Kelvin absolute temperature scale.

Alan Turing, 1912-54, (Br.) mathematician; helped develop basis for computers.

James Van Allen, 1914-2006, (U.S.) physicist; discovered the presence of radiation belts around Earth (Van Allen belts).

Rudolf Virchow, 1821-1902, (Ger.) pathologist; pioneered the modern theory that diseases affect the body through cells.

Alessandro Volta, 1745-1827, (It.) physicist; electricity pioneer.

Wernher von Braun, 1912-77, (Ger.-U.S.) aerospace engineer; developed rockets for warfare and space exploration.

John von Neumann, 1903-57, (Hung.-U.S.) mathematician; originated game theory; basic design for modern computers.

Alfred Russell Wallace, 1823-1913, (Br.) naturalist; proposed concept of evolution independently of Darwin.

John B. Watson, 1878-1958, (U.S.) psychologist; a founder of behaviorism.

James E. Watt, 1736-1819, (Br.) mechanical engineer, inventor; invented modern steam engine (1765).

Alfred L. Wegener, 1880-1930, (Ger.) meteorologist, geophysicist; postulated continental drift.

Norbert Wiener, 1894-1964, (U.S.) mathematician; founder of cybernetics.

Daniel Hale Williams, 1858-1931, (U.S.) African American surgeon; performed one of first two open-heart operations (1893).

Sewall Wright, 1889-1988, (U.S.) evolutionary theorist; helped found population genetics.

Wilhelm Wundt, 1832-1920, (Ger.) founder of experimental psychology.

Qian Xuesen, 1911-2009, (China) rocket scientist; helped found Jet Propulsion Lab, father of China's space program.

Rosalyn Yalow, 1921-2011, (U.S.) physicist; co-developer of radioimmunoassay.

Ferdinand von Zeppelin, 1838-1917, (Ger.) soldier, aeronaut, airship designer.

Social Reformers, Activists, and Humanitarians of the Past

Ralph David Abernathy, 1926-90, (U.S.) Black civil rights activist; pres., 1968, Southern Christian Leadership Conf.

Jane Addams, 1860-1935, (U.S.) cofounder of Hull House; won Nobel Peace Prize, 1931.

Susan B. Anthony, 1820-1906, (U.S.) a leader in temperance, antislavery, and woman suffrage movements.

Dennis Banks, 1937-2017, (Amer. Ind.) civil rights activist.

Thomas Barnardo, 1845-1905, (Br.) social reformer; pioneer in care of destitute children.

Clara Barton, 1821-1912, (U.S.) organized American Red Cross.

Daisy Bates, 1914-99, (U.S.) Black civil rights leader who fought for integration; advocate for the "Little Rock 9" during Arkansas desegregation crisis in 1957.

Henry Ward Beecher, 1813-87, (U.S.) clergyman, abolitionist.

Peter Benenson, 1921-2005, (Br.) activist; founded Amnesty International, 1961.

Mary McLeod Bethune, 1875-1955, (U.S.) Black educator, civil rights activist; adviser to FDR and Truman; founder, pres., Bethune-Cookman College.

Elizabeth Blackwell, 1821-1910, (Br.) first female physician in the U.S.

Amelia Bloomer, 1818-94, (U.S.) suffragette, social reformer.

Julian Bond, 1940-2015, (U.S.) civil rights leader, NAACP chair, 1998-2015.

Yelena Bonner, 1923-2011, (Russ.) human rights activist in former Soviet Union.

William Booth, 1829-1912, (Br.) founded Salvation Army.

James Brady, 1940-2014, (U.S.) gun control advocate; Reagan press sec.

John Brown, 1800-59, (U.S.) abolitionist who led murder of five pro-slavery men; hanged.

Linda Brown, 1943-2018, (U.S.) civil rights activist; daughter of *Brown v. Board of Education* (1954) plaintiff.

Frances Xavier (Mother) Cabrini, 1850-1917, (It.-U.S.) nun; founded charitable institutions; first American canonized as a saint, 1946.

Stokely Carmichael (Kwame Ture), 1941-98, (Trinidad-U.S.) Black power activist; major proponent of Pan-Africanism; prime min. of Black Panthers.

Carrie Chapman Catt, 1859-1947, (U.S.) suffragette.

Cesar Chavez, 1927-93, (U.S.) labor leader; helped establish United Farm Workers of America.

Eldridge Cleaver, 1935-98, (U.S.) revolutionary social critic; former minister of information for Black Panthers; *Soul on Ice.*

Clarence Darrow, 1857-1938, (U.S.) lawyer; defender of underdog, opponent of capital punishment.

Ossie Davis, 1917-2005, (U.S.) Black civil rights activist, actor, director.

Dorothy Day, 1897-1980, (U.S.) founder of Catholic Worker movement.

Eugene V. Debs, 1855-1926, (U.S.) labor leader; led Pullman Strike, 1894; four-time Socialist presidential candidate.

Vine Deloria Jr., 1933-2005, (U.S.) Native American activist, author; *Custer Died for Your Sins.*

Dorothea Dix, 1802-87, (U.S.) crusader for mentally ill.

Thomas Dooley, 1927-61, (U.S.) "jungle doctor"; noted for efforts to supply medical aid to developing countries.

Marjory Stoneman Douglas, 1890-1998, (U.S.) writer, environmentalist; campaigned to save Florida Everglades.

Frederick Douglass, 1817-95, (U.S.) author, editor, orator, diplomat; edited abolitionist weekly *The North Star.*

Andrea Dworkin, 1946-2005, (U.S.) radical feminist, antipornography crusader.

Medgar Evers, 1925-63, (U.S.) Black civil rights leader; campaigned to register Black voters; assassinated.

James Farmer, 1920-99, (U.S.) Black civil rights leader; founded Congress of Racial Equality (CORE).

Betty Friedan, 1921-2006, (U.S.) author, feminist; *The Feminine Mystique.*

Millard Fuller, 1935-2009, (U.S.) founder of Habitat for Humanity.

William Lloyd Garrison, 1805-79, (U.S.) abolitionist.

Miep Gies, 1909-2010, (Neth.) protector of Anne Frank and her family during WWII.

Emma Goldman, 1869-1940, (Russ.-U.S.) published anarchist *Mother Earth;* birth-control advocate.

Samuel Gompers, 1850-1924, (U.S.) labor leader; first pres. of the American Federation of Labor (AFL).

Juliette Gordon Low, 1860-1927, (U.S.) Girl Scouts founder.

Prince Hall, 1735-1807, (U.S.) activist; founded Black Freemasonry; served in American Revolutionary War.

Michael Harrington, 1928-89, (U.S.) exposed poverty in affluent U.S. in *The Other America,* 1963.

Dorothy Height, 1912-2010, (U.S.) civil rights activist; pres. of the National Council of Negro Women, 1957-97.

Sidney Hillman, 1887-1946, (Lith.-U.S.) labor leader; helped organize CIO.

Benjamin Hooks, 1925-2010, (U.S.) civil rights activist; exec. dir. NAACP, 1977-92.

Samuel G. Howe, 1801-76, (U.S.) social reformer; changed public attitudes toward the blind, deaf, mentally challenged.

Marsha P. Johnson, 1945-92, (U.S.) LGBT rights activist.

Franklin Kameny, 1925-2011, (U.S.) gay rights activist.

Helen Keller, 1880-1968, (U.S.) crusader for better treatment for the disabled; deaf and blind herself.

Jack Kevorkian 1928-2011, (U.S.) pathologist; assisted-suicide activist.

Coretta Scott King, 1927-2006, (U.S.) Black civil rights leader; wife of Rev. Martin Luther King Jr.

Rev. Martin Luther King Jr., 1929-68, (U.S.) civil rights leader; led 1955-56 Montgomery, AL, boycott; founder, pres., Southern Christian Leadership Conference, 1957; Nobel peace laureate, 1964; assassinated.

Larry Kramer, 1935-2020, (U.S.) HIV/AIDS activist.

Maggie Kuhn, 1905-95, (U.S.) founded Gray Panthers, 1970.

William Kunstler, 1919-95, (U.S.) civil liberties attorney.

John Lewis, 1940-2020, (U.S.) U.S. rep. (D, GA), Black civil rights activist.

John L. Lewis, 1880-1969, (U.S.) labor leader; headed United Mine Workers, 1920-60.

Belva Lockwood, 1830-1917, (U.S.) lawyer; first woman to argue before U.S. Supreme Court.

Almena Lomax, 1915-2011, (U.S.) civil rights activist; journalist who founded *The Los Angeles Tribune.*

Rev. Joseph Lowery, 1921-2020, (U.S.) Black civil rights activist.

Clara Luper, 1923-2011, (U.S.) civil rights activist.

Wangari Maathai, 1940-2011, (Kenya) environmental activist; 2004 Nobel Peace Prize winner.

Robert Macauley, 1923-2010, (U.S.) founder of AmeriCares.

Malcolm X (Little), 1925-65, (U.S.) Black Muslim, Black nationalist leader; promoted Black pride; assassinated.

Russell Means, 1939-2012, (Amer. Ind.) civil rights activist.

Karl Menninger, 1893-1990, (U.S.) with brother **William Menninger** (1899-1966), founded Menninger Clinic and Menninger Foundation.

Harvey Milk, 1930-78, (U.S.) LGBT rights activist; assassinated.

Kate Millett, 1934-2017, (U.S.) writer, feminist; *Sexual Politics.*

Lucretia Mott, 1793-1880, (U.S.) reformer, pioneer feminist.

Philip Murray, 1886-1952, (U.S.) Scottish-born labor leader.

Huey P. Newton, 1942-89, (U.S.) co-founded Black Panther Party, 1966.

Florence Nightingale, 1820-1910, (Br.) founder of modern nursing.

Emmeline Pankhurst, 1858-1928, (Br.) suffragette.

Rosa Parks, 1913-2005, (U.S.) Black civil rights activist; her actions sparked 1955-56 Montgomery, AL, bus boycott.

A. Philip Randolph, 1889-1979, (U.S.) organized Brotherhood of Sleeping Car Porters, 1925; an organizer of 1941 and 1963 March on Washington movements.

Walter Reuther, 1907-70, (U.S.) labor leader; headed United Auto Workers.

Jacob Riis, 1849-1914, (Den.-U.S.) crusader for urban reforms.

Sylvia Rivera, 1951-2002, (U.S.) LGBT rights activist.

Paul Robeson, 1898-1976, (U.S.) actor, singer, Black civil rights activist.

Bayard Rustin, 1910-87, (U.S.) Black and LGBT civil rights activist; an organizer of the 1963 March on Washington.

Margaret Sanger, 1883-1966, (U.S.) social reformer; pioneered the birth-control movement.

Phyllis Schlafly, 1924-2016, (U.S.) anti-Equal Rights Amendment activist.

Earl of Shaftesbury (A. A. Cooper), 1801-85, (Br.) social reformer.

Eunice Kennedy Shriver, 1921-2009, (U.S.) cofounder of Special Olympics for athletes with intellectual disabilities.

Sargent Shriver, 1915-2011, (U.S.) founding director of Peace Corps; founder of Job Corps, Head Start.

Fred Shuttlesworth, 1922-2011, (U.S.) civil rights activist.

Albertina Sisulu, 1918-2011, (S. Africa) anti-apartheid activist.

Elizabeth Cady Stanton, 1815-1902, (U.S.) woman suffrage pioneer.

Lucy Stone, 1818-93, (U.S.) feminist, abolitionist.

Mother Teresa of Calcutta, 1910-97, (Alban.) nun; founded order to care for sick, dying poor; 1979 Nobel Peace Prize winner; canonized 2016.

Willard Townsend, 1895-1957, (U.S.) organized the United Transport Service Employees (Red Caps), 1935.

Sojourner Truth (Isabella Baumfree), 1797-1883, (U.S.) preacher, abolitionist; worked for Black educ. opportunity.

Harriet Tubman, 1823-1913, (U.S.) prominent figure in the Underground Railroad; nurse, spy for Union Army in the Civil War.

Nat Turner, 1800-31, (U.S.) slave who led the most significant of more than 200 slave revolts in U.S., in Southampton, VA; hanged.

Philip Vera Cruz, 1905-94, (Philip.-U.S.) helped found the United Farm Workers Union.

Rev. C(ordy) T(indell) Vivian, 1924-2020, (U.S.) Black civil rights activist.

Edgar Wayburn, 1906-2010, (U.S.) conservationist; Sierra Club pres.

Elie Wiesel, 1928-2016, (Rom.-U.S.) Holocaust survivor, author, and activist; 1986 Nobel Peace Prize winner.

William Wilberforce, 1759-1833, (Br.) social reformer; prominent in struggle to abolish slave trade.

Frances E. Willard, 1839-98, (U.S.) temperance, women's rights leader.

Betty Williams, 1944-2020, (N. Ire.) peace activist; 1976 Nobel Peace Prize winner.

Edith Windsor, 1929-2007, (U.S.) LGBT civil rights activist.

Mary Wollstonecraft, 1759-97, (Br.) *Vindication of the Rights of Women.*

Victoria Woodhull, 1838-1927, (U.S.) suffragist, first woman to run for president (1872).

Sports Personalities of the Past and Present

Henry (Hank) Aaron, b 1934, Milwaukee-Atlanta outfielder; hit then-record 755 home runs, record 2,297 RBI.

Kareem Abdul-Jabbar, b 1947, Milwaukee, L.A. Lakers center; MVP 6 times; all-time leading NBA scorer, 38,387 pts.

Andre Agassi, b 1970, tennis player; 8 Grand Slam singles titles.

Troy Aikman, b 1966, quarterback; led Dallas Cowboys to Super Bowl wins in 1993-94, '96; Super Bowl MVP, 1993.

Ben Ainslie, b 1977, (Br.) most decorated Olympic sailor; gold, 2000, '04, '08, '12; silver, 1996.

Michelle Akers, b 1966, soccer player; led U.S. to victory in World Cup (1991, '99).

Grover Cleveland "Pete" Alexander, 1887-1950, pitcher; won 373 NL games; pitched 16 shutouts, 1916.

Muhammad Ali, 1942-2016, 3-time heavyweight champion, activist.

Fernando Alonso, b 1981, (Sp.) Formula 1 racer; youngest ever to win a World Grand Prix championship, 2005; defended title, 2006.

Morten Andersen, b 1960, (Den.) NFL kicker, career leader in games played (382).

Sparky Anderson, 1934-2010, first manager to win World Series in the NL (Cincinnati, 1975-76) and AL (Detroit, 1984).

Mario Andretti, b 1940, (It.) race-car driver; won Daytona 500 (1967), Indy 500 (1969); Formula 1 world title (1978).

Earl Anthony, 1938-2001, bowler; 6 PBA Championships (1973-75, '81-'83), 43 career PBA tournaments.

Eddie Arcaro, 1916-97, only jockey to win racing's Triple Crown twice, 1941, '48; rode to 4,779 wins in his career.

Lance Armstrong, b 1971, cyclist; record 7-time winner of Tour de France (1999-2005); stripped of victories in 2012 for use of performance-enhancing drugs.

Arthur Ashe, 1943-93, tennis player; first Black man to win U.S. Open (1968), Austral. Open (1970), Wimbledon (1975).

Evelyn Ashford, b 1957, sprinter; won 100m gold (1984) and silver (1988); member of 5 U.S. Olympic teams.

Red Auerbach, 1917-2006, coached Boston to 9 NBA titles.

Geno Auriemma, b 1954, (It.) UConn women's basketball coach; record 11 NCAA women's basketball titles.

Tracy Austin, b 1962, tennis player; youngest to win U.S. Open (age 16 in 1979).

Ernie Banks, 1931-2015, Chicago Cubs slugger; hit 512 NL homers; twice MVP.

Roger Bannister, 1929-2018, (Br.) physician; ran 1st sub-4-min. mile, May 6, 1954 (3 min., 59.4 sec.).

Charles Barkley, b 1963, NBA MVP, 1993; 4th player ever to surpass 20,000 pts., 10,000 rebounds, 4,000 assists.

Rick Barry, b 1944, NBA scoring leader, 1967; ABA scoring leader, 1969.

Sammy Baugh, 1914-2008, Washington Redskins quarterback, punter, defensive back.

Elgin Baylor, b 1934, L.A. Lakers forward; 11-time all-star.

Bob Beamon, b 1946, Olympic long jump gold medalist, 1968; world record jump of 29 ft 2½ in. stood until 1991.

Boris Becker, b 1967, (Ger.) tennis player; 6 Grand Slam singles titles.

David Beckham, b 1975, (Br.) soccer midfielder; joined L.A. Galaxy, 2007-12, with record-breaking $250-mil contract.

Bill Belichick, b 1952, NFL coach; led New England to 6 Super Bowl wins; best all-time post-season coaching record.

Jean Béliveau, 1931-2014, (Can.) Montréal Canadiens center; scored 507 career goals; twice MVP.

Johnny Bench, b 1947, Cincinnati Reds catcher; twice MVP; led league in home runs twice, RBIs 3 times.

Patty Berg, 1918-2006, won a record 15 LPGA majors.

Chris Berman, b 1955, sportscaster.

Yogi Berra, 1925-2015, NY Yankees catcher (1946-63); 3-time MVP.

Abebe Bikila, 1932-73, (Eth.) runner; won consecutive Olympic marathon gold medals in 1960 (barefoot), '64.

Simone Biles, b 1997, gymnast; won 4 Olympic gold medals, including all-around and team (2016); record 25 world championship medals.

Matt Biondi, b 1965, swimmer; won 5 golds, 1988 Olympics.

Larry Bird, b 1956, Boston Celtics forward (1979-92); NBA MVP, 1984-86; 1998 coach of the year with Indiana Pacers.

Bonnie Blair, b 1964, speed skater; won 5 individual gold medals in 3 Olympics (1988, '92, '94).

George Blanda, 1927-2010, quarterback, kicker; 26 years as active player, scored 2,002 career points.

Fanny Blankers-Koen, 1918-2004, (Neth.) track and field athlete; won 4 Olympic gold medals (1948).

Wade Boggs, b 1958, AL batting champ, 1983, '85-'88; reached 3,000 career hits, 1999 (3,010).

Usain Bolt, b 1986, (Jam.) Olympic sprinter, gold medalist, 2008, '12, '16; world record for men's 100-m, 200-m runs.

Barry Bonds, b 1964, outfielder; hit record 73 homers, 2001; record 7-time NL MVP; 1st all-time in HRs (762); indicted in steroid scandal, 2007.

Björn Borg, b 1956, (Swed.) tennis player; 11 Grand Slam singles titles.

Ray Bourque, b 1960, (Can.) leads NHL defensemen in career goals, assists, points; 5-time Norris Trophy winner.

Bill Bradley, b 1943, led NY Knicks to 2 NBA titles (1970, '73); U.S. senator (NJ), 1979-97.

Donald Bradman, 1908-2001, (Austral.) widely regarded as greatest cricketer ever; set several batting records.

Terry Bradshaw, b 1948, quarterback; led Pittsburgh to 4 Super Bowl wins, 1975-76, '79-'80; NFL MVP, 1978.

Tom Brady, b 1977, quarterback; led New England to 6 Super Bowl titles; 4-time Super Bowl MVP; 3-time NFL MVP.

Drew Brees, b 1979, New Orleans Saints quarterback; Super Bowl MVP, 2010.

Christine Brennan, b 1958, sports journalist for *USA Today*, radio and TV commentator specializing in figure skating.

George Brett, b 1953, Kansas City Royals infielder; led AL in batting, 1976, '80, '90; MVP, 1980.

Lou Brock, 1939-2020, St. Louis Cardinals outfielder; stole NL single-season record 118 bases, 1974; led NL 8 times.

Jim Brown, b 1936, Cleveland fullback; 12,312 career yds; 3-time NFL MVP.

Paul Brown, 1908-91, football team owner, coach; led eponymous Cleveland Browns to 3 NFL championships.

Bob Bryan, b 1978, tennis player; won 16 Grand Slam doubles titles; Olympic gold, 2012.

Mike Bryan, b 1978, tennis player; won 18 Grand Slam doubles titles; Olympic gold, 2012.

Kobe Bryant, 1978-2020, NBA guard; won 3 titles with Lakers (2000-02); leading NBA scorer, 2006, '07; NBA MVP, 2008; NBA Finals MVP, 2010; Olympic gold medal winner (2008, '12).

Paul "Bear" Bryant, 1913-83, college football coach with 323 wins; led Alabama to 6 national titles (1961, '64-'65, '73, '78-'79).

Sergei Bubka, b 1963, (Ukr.) pole vaulter; first to clear 20 ft; gold medal, 1988 Olympics.

Don Budge, 1915-2000, won numerous amateur and pro tennis titles; Grand Slam, 1938.

Reggie Bush, b 1985, NFL running back; helped USC to 2 national titles (2003-04; '04 vacated).

Dick Butkus, b 1942, Chicago Bears linebacker; NFL defensive player of the year (1969-70).

Dick Button, b 1929, figure skater; won 1948, '52 Olympic gold medals; world titleholder, 1948-52.

Miguel Cabrera, b 1983, (Venez.) 11-time MLB All-Star; won AL triple crown (2012); AL MVP 2012, '13.

Walter Camp, 1859-1925, Yale football player, coach, athletic director; established many rules for modern football.

Roy Campanella, 1921-93, Brooklyn Dodgers catcher (1948-57); 3-time NL MVP.

Earl Campbell, b 1955, NFL running back; MVP 1978-79.

Jose Canseco, b 1964, outfielder; led Oakland A's to the World Series, 1988; wrote book about steroids in baseball, 2005.

Eric Cantona, b 1966, (Fr.) soccer forward; Manchester United (1992-97).

Rod Carew, b 1945, AL infielder; 7 batting titles, 1977 MVP.

Steve Carlton, b 1944, NL pitcher; won 20 games 6 times, 4-time Cy Young winner; 4,136 career strikeouts.

Pete Carroll, b 1951, football coach; NCAA champion (2003, '04); won Super Bowl XLVIII.

Billy Casper, 1931-2015, PGA Player of the Year 2 times; U.S. Open champ twice.

Tamika Catchings, b 1979, basketball forward, WNBA MVP, 2011; 4-time Olympic gold medalist.

Tracy Caulkins, b 1963, swimmer; 3-time Olympic gold medalist.

Wilt Chamberlain, 1936-99, center; 7-time NBA leading scorer, 4-time MVP; scored 100 pts. in a game, 1962.

Nathan Chen, b 1999, figure skater, U.S. champion, 2017-20; world champion, 2018-19.

Bobby Clarke, b 1949, (Can.) Philadelphia Flyers center; led team to 2 Stanley Cup championships; 3-time MVP.

Roger Clemens, b 1962, pitcher; 1986 AL MVP; only 7-time Cy Young winner; 354 wins, 4,672 Ks (3rd all-time); accused of lying to Congress about steroids, 2010.

Roberto Clemente, 1934-72, Pittsburgh Pirates outfielder; won 4 batting titles; MVP, 1966; 3,000 career hits; killed in plane crash on aid mission.

Kim Clijsters, b 1983, (Belg.) tennis player; 4 Grand Slam singles titles.

Ty Cobb, 1886-1961, Detroit Tigers outfielder; record .367 lifetime batting average, 12 batting titles.

Sebastian Coe, b 1956, (Br.) runner; won Olympic 1,500m gold medal and 800m silver medal in both 1980, '84.

Nadia Comaneci, b 1961, (Rom.) gymnast; won 3 gold medals, achieved 7 perfect scores, 1976 Olympics; 9 Olympic medals overall.

Maureen Connolly, 1934-69, tennis player; 9 Grand Slam singles titles.

Jimmy Connors, b 1952, tennis player; 8 Grand Slam singles titles.

Alberto Contador, b 1982, (Sp.) cyclist; won Tour de France 2007, '09; stripped of 2010 title because of doping offense.

Cynthia Cooper, b 1963, WNBA player; 4-time finals MVP; 2-time league MVP.

James J. Corbett, 1866-1933, heavyweight champion, 1892-97; credited with being the first "scientific" boxer.

Angel Cordero Jr., b 1942, jockey; leading money winner, 1976, '82-'83; rode 3 Kentucky Derby winners.

Margaret Smith Court, b 1942, (Austral.) tennis player; won 24 Grand Slam singles titles (11 in Open Era).

Bob Cousy, b 1928, Boston guard; 6 NBA titles, 1957 MVP.

Sidney Crosby, b 1987, (Can.) hockey player; Art Ross, Hart Trophies (2007, '14), Olympic gold medal (2010, '14).

Mark Cuban, b 1958, Dallas Mavericks owner; known for outspokenness.

Stephen Curry, b 1988, NBA point guard; NBA MVP, 2015, '16.

Bjoern Daehlie, b 1967, (Nor.) cross-country skier; 8 Olympic gold medals.

Al Davis, 1929-2011, Oakland Raiders owner, former coach.

Oscar De La Hoya, b 1973, won IBF lightweight (1995); WBC super lightweight (1996); welterweight (1997-99, 2000) titles.

Donna de Varona, b 1947, swimmer; won 2 Olympic golds, 1964; 1st female sportscaster at a major network, 1965.

Dizzy Dean, 1910-74, pitcher; St. Louis Cardinals' "Gashouse Gang" in the '30s.

Mary Decker Slaney, b 1958, runner; has held 6 separate American records from the 800m to 10,000m.

Frank Deford, 1938-2017, writer for *Sports Illustrated*; author, commentator.

Jack Dempsey, 1895-1983, heavyweight champ, 1919-26.

Gail Devers, b 1966, Olympic 100m gold medalist (1992, '96).

Joe DiMaggio, 1914-99, NY Yankees outfielder; hit safely in record 56 consecutive games, 1941; AL MVP 3 times.

Novak Djokovic, b 1987, (Serb.) tennis player; 17 Grand Slam singles titles.

Landon Donovan, b 1982, soccer forward.

Tony Dorsett, b 1954, Heisman winner who led the Dallas Cowboys to an NFL title in his rookie year, 1977.

Gabrielle Douglas, b 1995, gymnast; Olympic gold in all-around (2012), team (2012, '16).

Tim Duncan, b 1976, San Antonio center; 3-time NBA Finals MVP; NBA MVP, 2002, '03.

Margaret Osborne duPont, 1918-2012, tennis player; 6-time Grand Slam singles champion.

Roberto Duran, b 1951, (Pan.) boxer; held titles at 3 weights; lost 1980 "no mas" fight to Sugar Ray Leonard.

Kevin Durant, b 1988, NBA forward; NBA MVP, 2014; Finals MVP, 2017, '18; Olympic gold medalist, 2012, '16.

Leo Durocher, 1905-91, manager; won 3 NL pennants (Brooklyn, 1941; NY Giants, 1951, '54), 1954 World Series.

Dale Earnhardt Jr., b 1974, stock car racer; Daytona 500 winner (2004, '14).

Dale Earnhardt Sr., 1951-2001, 7-time NASCAR Winston Cup champ; died in a last-lap crash at 2001 Daytona 500.

Ashton Eaton, b 1988, Olympic decathlon gold medalist, 2012, '16.

Stefan Edberg, b 1966, (Swed.) tennis player; 6 Grand Slam singles titles.

Gertrude Ederle, 1905-2003, first woman to swim English Channel; broke existing men's record, 1926.

Teresa Edwards, b 1964, 5-time basketball Olympian; gold medalist, 1984, '88, '96, 2000; bronze medalist, 1992.

Hicham El Guerrouj, b 1974, (Morocco) runner; holds world records in mile (3:43.13) and 1,500m (3:26); won gold medals in 1,500m and 5,000m, 2004 Olympics.

John Elway, b 1960, quarterback; led Denver Broncos to 2 Super Bowl wins, 1998-99; NFL MVP, 1987; Super Bowl MVP, 1999.

Roy Emerson, b 1936, (Austral.) tennis player; 12 Grand Slam singles titles.

Julius "Dr. J" Erving, b 1950, 3-time ABA MVP, 1981 NBA MVP.

Phil Esposito, b 1942, (Can.) NHL scoring leader 5 times.

Janet Evans, b 1971, 4 Olympic swimming golds, 1988, '92.

Lee Evans, b 1947, Olympic 400m gold medalist in 1968 with 43.86-sec. world record not broken until 1988.

Chris Evert, b 1954, tennis player; 18 Grand Slam singles titles.

Ray Ewry, 1873-1937, track and field athlete; won 8 Olympic gold medals (1900, '04, '08).

Nick Faldo, b 1957, (Br.) golfer; won Masters, British Open 3 times each.

Juan Manuel Fangio, 1911-95 (Arg.), 5-time World Grand Prix driving champ (1951, '54-'57).

Marshall Faulk, b 1973, 2000 NFL MVP; scored then-record 26 TDs, 2001; 3-time Off. Player of the Year (1999-2001).

Brett Favre, b 1969, quarterback; led Green Bay to Super Bowl win, 1997; 3-time NFL MVP.

Roger Federer, b 1981, (Switz.) tennis player; 20 Grand Slam singles titles (1st all-time).

Bob Feller, 1918-2010, Cleveland Indians pitcher; won 266 games; pitched 3 no-hitters, 12 one-hitters.

Rollie Fingers, b 1946, pitcher; 341 career saves; AL MVP, Cy Young, 1981; World Series MVP, 1974.

Peggy Fleming, b 1948, world figure skating champion, 1966-68; Olympic gold, 1968 Olympics.

Whitey Ford, 1928-2020, NY Yankees pitcher; won 10 World Series games.

George Foreman, b 1949, heavyweight champion, 1973-74, '94-'95; at 45, oldest to win a heavyweight title; gold medalist, 1968 Olympics.

Dick Fosbury, b 1947, high jumper; won 1968 Olympic gold medal; developed the "Fosbury Flop."

Jimmie Foxx, 1907-67, Red Sox, Athletics slugger; MVP 3 times; triple crown, 1933.

A. J. Foyt, b 1935, won Indy 500 4 times; U.S. Auto Club champ 7 times.

Dario Franchitti, b 1973, (Scot.) 3-time Indy 500 winner, 2007, '10, '12.

Missy Franklin, b 1995, swimmer; 5-time Olympic gold medalist (2012, '16).

Joe Frazier, 1944-2011, heavyweight champion, 1970-73; gold medalist, 1964 Olympics.

Walt Frazier, b 1945, guard for NY Knicks' NBA championship teams (1970, '73).

Chris Froome, b 1985, (Kenya) 4-time Tour de France winner (2013, '15-'17).

Peter Gammons, b 1945, sportswriter, broadcaster.

Lou Gehrig, 1903-41, NY Yankees 1st baseman; MVP, 1927, '36; triple crown, 1934; played 2,130 straight games (1925-39).

Althea Gibson, 1927-2003, tennis player; first Black woman to compete and win at Wimbledon, U.S. Open; 5 Grand Slam singles titles.

Bob Gibson, 1935-2020, St. Louis Cardinals pitcher; won Cy Young twice; struck out 3,117 batters.

Josh Gibson, 1911-47, Negro Leagues catcher; hit as many as 84 season home runs and 800 in career.

Marc Girardelli, b 1963, (Lux.) skier; won 5 World Cup titles.

Raúl González, b 1977, (Sp.) soccer player; led Real Madrid to 3 Champions League titles (1998, 2000, '02).

Jeff Gordon, b 1971, race-car driver; youngest to win NASCAR title 4 times (1995, '97-'98, 2001).

Steffi Graf, b 1969, (Ger.) tennis player; 22 Grand Slam singles titles (3rd all-time).

Otto Graham, 1921-2003, Cleveland quarterback; 4-time all-pro.

Red Grange, 1903-91, All-American at Univ. of Illinois, 1923-25; played for Chicago Bears, 1925-35.

"Mean" Joe Greene, b 1946, Pittsburgh Steelers lineman; twice NFL outstanding defensive player.

Wayne Gretzky, b 1961, (Can.) top scorer in NHL history with record 894 goals, 1,963 assists, 2,857 pts.; MVP, 1980-87, '89.

Bob Griese, b 1945, All-Pro quarterback; led Miami Dolphins to 17-0 season, 1972, 2 Super Bowl titles, 1973-74.

Ken Griffey Jr., b 1969, outfielder; led AL in homers 1994, '97-'99; 1997 AL MVP; 10 gold gloves.

Archie Griffin, b 1954, Ohio State running back; only 2-time winner of the Heisman Trophy (1974-75).

Florence Griffith Joyner, 1959-98, sprinter; won 3 gold medals at 1988 Olympics; world and Olympic record for 100m.

Lefty Grove, 1900-75, pitcher; won 300 AL games.

Janet Guthrie, b 1938, 1st woman to drive in Indy 500 (1977).

Tony Gwynn, 1960-2014, 8-time NL batting champ; 3,141 career hits.

Walter Hagen, 1892-1969, golfer; 5 PGA, 4 British Open titles.

Mika Hakkinen, b 1968, (Fin.) Formula One racing driver; Formula One champion, 1998-99.

George Halas, 1895-1983, founder/player/coach of Chicago Bears; won 6 NFL championships as coach.

Roy Halladay, 1977-2017, pitcher; Cy Young, 2003, '10; perfect game, 2010.

Scott Hamilton, b 1958, U.S. and world figure skating champion, 1981-84; Olympic gold medalist, 1984.

Mia Hamm, b 1972, soccer player; led U.S. teams to World Cup victories (1991, '99) and Olympic gold (1996, 2004).

Yuzuru Hanyu, b 1994, (Jpn.) figure skater; Olympic gold medalist, 2014, '18.

James Harden, b 1989, shooting guard for Houston Rockets; NBA MVP, 2018.

Franco Harris, b 1950, running back; 4 Super Bowls with Steelers (1975-76, '79-'80); 1,000+ season yds 8 times.

Marvin Harrison, b 1972, Indianapolis Colts wide receiver; 143 single-season receptions, 2002.

Bill Hartack, 1932-2007, jockey; rode 5 Kentucky Derby winners.

Dominik Hasek, b 1965, (Czech.) NHL goaltender; 6 Vezina Trophies; NHL MVP, 1997-98.

John Havlicek, 1940-2019, Boston Celtics forward; scored 26,395 career pts.

Elvin Hayes, b 1945, 12-time NBA All-Star; scored 27,313 career pts.

Eric Heiden, b 1958, speed skater; won 5 Olympic golds, 1980.

Rickey Henderson, b 1958, outfielder; 1990 AL MVP; record 130 stolen bases, 1982; all-time leader in steals, runs.

Sonja Henie, 1912-69, (Nor.) world champion figure skater, 1927-36; Olympic gold medalist, 1928, '32, '36.

Martina Hingis, b 1980, (Switz.) 5 Grand Slam singles titles; youngest number-one player (16 yrs., 6 mos.), 1997.

Ben Hogan, 1912-97, golfer; won 4 U.S. Open titles, 2 PGA Championships, 2 Masters.

Larry Holmes, b 1949, World Heavyweight Champion, 1978-85.

Evander Holyfield, b 1962, 4-time heavyweight champion.

Rogers Hornsby, 1896-1963, NL 2nd baseman; batted record .424, 1924; twice won triple crown.

Paul Hornung, b 1935, Green Bay running back, kicker; Heisman Trophy winner.

Gordie Howe, 1928-2016, (Can.) hockey forward; NHL MVP 6 times; scored 801 goals in 26 NHL seasons.

Carl Hubbell, 1903-88, NY Giants pitcher; 20-game winner 5 consecutive seasons, 1933-37.

Bobby Hull, b 1939, (Can.) NHL all-star 10 times; MVP, 1965-66.

Brett Hull, b 1964, (Can.) St. Louis Blues forward; led NHL in goals, 1990-92; MVP, 1991.

Catfish Hunter, 1946-99, pitched perfect game, 1968; 20-game winner 5 times.

Don Hutson, 1913-97, Packers receiver; caught 99 TD passes; 2-time NFL MVP.

Juli Inkster, b 1960, golfer; won 7 career LPGA major titles.

Bo Jackson, b 1962, NFL running back (1987-90) and MLB outfielder (1986-91, '93-'94); 1985 Heisman Trophy winner.

Phil Jackson, b 1945, won 11 NBA titles as coach of Bulls and Lakers; 1970, '73 title as player with NY Knicks.

Reggie Jackson, b 1946, slugger; led AL in home runs 4 times; MVP, 1973; hit 5 World Series home runs, 1977.

"Shoeless" Joe Jackson, 1889-1951, outfielder; .356 career batting average; one of the "Black Sox" banned for allegedly throwing 1919 World Series.

Jaromír Jágr, b 1972, (Czech.) hockey player; NHL MVP, 1999; 5 Art Ross Trophies.

LeBron James, b 1984, NBA forward; 4-time NBA MVP; 4 NBA titles, 4-time Finals MVP.

Ron Jaworski, b 1951, NFL quarterback (1974-89), analyst.

Sally Jenkins, b 1960, sports journalist and writer for *Washington Post*.

Caitlyn (fmr. Bruce) Jenner, b 1949, Olympic decathlon gold medalist, 1976; came out as transgender woman, 2015.

Lynn Jennings, b 1960, runner; 3-time World, 9-time U.S. cross country champ; bronze (10,000m), 1992 Olympics.

Derek Jeter, b 1974, shortstop; led NY Yankees to 5 World Series titles; World Series MVP, 2000.

Earvin "Magic" Johnson, b 1959, 3-time NBA MVP; 5 NBA titles; 3-time Finals MVP.

Jack Johnson, 1878-1946, heavyweight champion, 1908-15.

Jimmie Johnson, b 1975, 7-time NASCAR Series champ.

Michael Johnson, b 1967, sprinter; 4-time Olympic gold medalist (1992, '96, 2000); longtime world and Olympic record-holder.

Randy Johnson, b 1963, MLB pitcher with 4,875 strikeouts (2nd all-time), perfect game, 2004; 5-time Cy Young winner.

Walter Johnson, 1887-1946, Washington Senators pitcher; won 417 games; record 110 shutouts.

Bobby Jones, 1902-71, won golf's Grand Slam, 1930; U.S. amateur champ 5 times, U.S. Open champ 4 times.

Cobi Jones, b 1970, soccer player; most U.S. national team appearances with 164.

David "Deacon" Jones, 1938-2013, 5-time All-Pro with L.A. Rams (1965-69); "sack" specialist credited with inventing the term.

Marion Jones, b 1975, multi-event Olympic medalist; stripped of medals in 2007 after admitting use of PEDs.

Roy Jones Jr., b 1969, light heavyweight champ, 1999-2004.

Michael Jordan, b 1963, guard; 10-time leading NBA scorer; 5-time MVP; 6-time Finals MVP.

Jackie Joyner-Kersee, b 1962, Olympic gold medalist in heptathlon (1988, '92), long jump (1988).

Dorothy Kamenshek, 1925-2010, 4 All-American Girls Baseball League titles, 1940s.

Mary Keitany, b 1982, (Ken.) distance runner; 4-time NYC marathon winner.

Clayton Kershaw, b 1988, pitcher; NL Cy Young winner (2011, '13, '14).

Harmon Killebrew, 1936-2011, Minnesota Twins slugger; led AL in home runs 6 times; 573 career home runs.

Jean Claude Killy, b 1943, (Fr.) skier; 3 Olympic golds, 1968.

Ralph Kiner, 1922-2014, Pittsburgh Pirates slugger; led NL in home runs 7 consecutive years, 1946-52.

Billie Jean King, b 1943, 12 Grand Slam singles titles (8 in Open Era); beat Bobby Riggs, 1973.

Peter King, b 1957, sportswriter.

Bob Knight, b 1940, NCAA basketball coach; led Indiana to men's title in 1976, '81, '87.

Brooks Koepka, b 1990, golfer; won U.S. Open, 2017-18; PGA championship, 2018-19.

Olga Korbut, b 1955, (Belarus) gymnast; 4 Olympic gold medals, 1972, '76.

Sandy Koufax, b 1935, 3-time Cy Young winner; lowest ERA in NL, 1962-66; pitched 4 no-hitters, 1 perfect game.

Jack Kramer, 1921-2009, world's number one tennis player, 1946-53; first at Wimbledon to compete in shorts.

Ingrid Kristiansen, b 1956, (Nor.) only runner to have held simultaneous world records in 5,000m, 10,000m, and marathon.

Julie Krone, b 1963, winningest female jockey; first woman to ride a winner in a Triple Crown race (Belmont, 1993).

Mike Krzyzewski, b 1947, basketball coach; 5 NCAA championships with Duke; led 3 Olympic gold medal teams (2008, '12, '16).

Michelle Kwan, b 1980, figure skater; 9 U.S., 5 World titles; silver medalist at 1998 Olympics, bronze in 2002.

Guy Lafleur, b 1951, (Can.) 3-time NHL scoring leader; 1977-78 MVP.

Alexi Lalas, b 1970, soccer player; first modern-era American to play in Italian League Serie A.

Kenesaw Mountain Landis, 1866-1944, 1st commissioner of baseball (1920-44); banned the 8 "Black Sox" involved in fixing 1919 World Series.

Tom Landry, 1924-2000, Dallas Cowboys head coach, 1960-88; won 2 Super Bowls (1972, '78); 270 career wins.

Dick "Night Train" Lane, 1928-2002, defensive back; NFL season record 14 interceptions (1952).

Don Larsen, 1929-2020, as NY Yankee, pitched only World Series perfect game, Oct. 8, 1956—2-0 win over Brooklyn.

Rod Laver, b 1938, (Austral.) tennis player; 11-time Grand Slam singles champ. (5 in Open era).

Katie Ledecky, b 1997, swimmer; Olympic medalist, incl. 5 gold (2012, '16).

Mario Lemieux, b 1965, (Can.) 6-time NHL leading scorer; 3-time MVP; playoff MVP, 1991-92.

Greg Lemond, b 1961, cyclist; 3-time Tour de France winner (1986, '89-'90); first American to win the event.

Ivan Lendl, b 1960, (Czech.) tennis player; 8 Grand Slam singles titles.

Sugar Ray Leonard, b 1956, boxer; held titles in 5 different weight classes.

Lisa Leslie, b 1972, L.A. Sparks center; 3-time WNBA MVP.

Carl Lewis, b 1961, track and field athlete; won 9 Olympic gold medals in sprinting and long jump.

Lennox Lewis, b 1965, (Br.) heavyweight champ, 1994, 1997-2004; Olympic gold medalist, 1988.

Ray Lewis, b 1975, linebacker for the Baltimore Ravens; Super Bowl MVP, 2001.

Tara Lipinski, b 1982, youngest figure skater to win world championships, 1997, and Winter Olympic gold, 1998.

Carli Lloyd, b 1982, soccer midfielder; Olympic gold medalist (2008, '12); World Cup champion (2015, '19).

Ryan Lochte, b 1984, swimmer; 12-time Olympic medalist, incl. 6 gold (2004, '08, '12, '16).

Vince Lombardi, 1913-70, Green Bay Packers coach; led team to 5 NFL championships, 2 Super Bowl victories.

Nancy Lopez, b 1957, golfer; 4-time LPGA Player of the Year; 3-time winner of the LPGA Championship.

Greg Louganis, b 1960, won Olympic gold medals in both springboard and platform diving, 1984, '88.

Joe Louis, 1914-81, heavyweight champion, 1937-49.

Sid Luckman, 1916-98, Chicago Bears quarterback; led team to 4 NFL championships; MVP, 1943.

Connie Mack, 1862-1956, Philadelphia Athletics manager, 1901-50; won 9 pennants, 5 championships.

John Madden, b 1936, won Super Bowl as coach of Oakland Raiders (1977); former NFL TV analyst.

Greg Maddux, b 1966, pitcher; won 4 Cy Young awards, 1992-95; 355 career wins.

Karl Malone, b 1963, Utah Jazz, L.A. Lakers forward; MVP, 1997, '99; 14-time All-Star; 36,928 career pts. (2nd all-time).

Moses Malone, 1955-2015, NBA center; 3-time MVP.

Eli Manning, b 1981, NY Giants quarterback; Super Bowl MVP, 2008, '12.

Peyton Manning, b 1976, quarterback; record 5 NFL MVP awards; Super Bowl MVP, 2007; single-season passing yards record (5,477), 2013.

Mickey Mantle, 1931-95, NY Yankees outfielder; triple crown, 1956; 18 World Series home runs; MVP 3 times.

Diego Maradona, b 1960, (Arg.) soccer player; led Argentina to World Cup, 1986.

Pete Maravich, 1947-88, guard; scored NCAA record 44.2 ppg during collegiate career; led NBA in scoring, 1977.

Rocky Marciano, 1923-69, heavyweight champion, 1952-56; retired undefeated.

Dan Marino, b 1961, Miami quarterback; NFL MVP, 1984; 5-time passing yards leader.

Roger Maris, 1934-85, NY Yankees outfielder; hit AL record 61 home runs, 1961, record held 37 years; MVP, 1960-61.

Marta (Marta Vieira da Silva), b 1986, (Braz.) soccer forward; FIFA World Player of the Year a record 6 times.

Eddie Mathews, 1931-2001, Milwaukee-Atlanta Braves 3rd baseman; hit 512 career home runs.

Christy Mathewson, 1880-1925, pitcher; won 373 games.

Bob Mathias, 1930-2006, decathlon gold, 1948, '52 Olympics.

Misty May-Treanor, b 1977, beach volleyball player; 3-time Olympic gold medalist with Kerri Walsh Jennings (2004, '08, '12).

Willie Mays, b 1931, NY-S.F. Giants center fielder; hit 660 home runs, led NL 4 times; had 3,283 hits; twice MVP.

Willie McCovey, 1938-2018, S.F. Giants slugger; hit 521 home runs; led NL 3 times; MVP, 1969.

John McEnroe, b 1959, tennis player; 7 Grand Slam singles titles.

John McGraw, 1873-1934, NY Giants manager; led team to 10 pennants, 3 championships.

Conor McGregor, b 1988, (Ire.) mixed martial artist.

Mark McGwire, b 1963, hit then-record 70 home runs in 1998; 583 career home runs; admitted PED use, 2010.

Rory McIlroy, b 1989, (N. Ire.) golfer; won U.S. Open, 2011; PGA Championship, 2012, '14; British Open, 2014.

Tamara McKinney, b 1962, 1st U.S. skier to win overall Alpine World Cup championship (1983).

Andrea Mead Lawrence, 1932-2009, skier; first woman to win 2 Olympic gold medals in alpine skiing at one Olympics (1952).

Lionel Messi, b 1987, (Arg.) forward for FC Barcelona; FIFA World Player of the Year, 2009-10.

Mark Messier, b 1961, (Can.) center; NHL MVP, 1990, '92; Conn Smythe Trophy, 1984.

Debbie Meyer, b 1952, 1st swimmer to win 3 individual Olympic golds (1968).

Al Michaels, b 1944, *NBC Sunday Night Football* announcer.

Phil Mickelson, b 1970, golfer; 5 career major titles.

George Mikan, 1924-2005, Minn. Lakers center; considered the best basketball player of first half of 20th cent.

Stan Mikita, 1940-2018, (Czech.) Chicago Blackhawks center; led NHL in scoring 4 times; MVP twice.

Billy Mills, b 1938, runner; upset winner of the 1964 Olympic 10,000m; only American man ever to win the event.

Joe Montana, b 1956, S.F. 49ers quarterback; 3-time Super Bowl MVP.

Archie Moore, 1913-98, light-heavyweight champ, 1952-62.

Howie Morenz, 1902-37, (Can.) Montréal Canadiens forward; considered best hockey player of first half of 20th cent.

Edwin Moses, b 1955, undefeated in 122 consecutive 400m hurdles races, 1977-87; Olympic gold medalist, 1976, '84.

Shirley Muldowney, b 1940, 1st woman to race Natl. Hot Rod Assn. Top Fuel dragsters; 3-time NHRA points champ.

Andy Murray, b 1987, (Br.) tennis player; 3-time Grand Slam singles champion; Olympic gold medal in men's singles (2012, '16).

Eddie Murray, b 1956, 3rd MLB player with both 3,000+ hits and 500+ home runs.

Stan Musial, 1920-2013, St. Louis Cardinals hitter who won 7 NL batting titles; MVP 3 times.

Rafael Nadal, b 1986, (Sp.) tennis player; 20-time Grand Slam singles champion; Olympic gold medal in men's singles (2008).

Bronko Nagurski, 1908-90, (Can.) Chicago Bears fullback and tackle; gained more than 4,000 yds rushing.

Joe Namath, b 1943, Jets quarterback; 1969 Super Bowl MVP.

Rosie Napravnik, b 1988, jockey.

Steve Nash, b 1974, (Can.) Phoenix Suns point guard; NBA MVP, 2005, '06.

Martina Navratilova, b 1956, (Czech.) tennis player; won 18 Grand Slam singles titles.

Byron Nelson, 1912-2006, won 11 consecutive golf tournaments in 1945; twice Masters and PGA titlist.

Ernie Nevers, 1903-76, Stanford fullback; early pro football star.

Paula Newby-Fraser, b 1962, ([now] Zimbabwe) 8-time Ironman Triathlon world champ.

John Newcombe, b 1944, (Austral.) tennis player; 7 Grand Slam singles and 17 Grand Slam men's doubles titles.

Neymar (Neymar da Silva Santos Júnior), b 1992, (Braz.) soccer forward; led Brazil to Olympic gold, 2016.

Jack Nicklaus, b 1940, PGA Player of the Year, 1967, '72; leading money winner 8 times; won 18 majors (6 Masters).

Chuck Noll, 1932-2014, Pittsburgh Steelers coach; won 4 Super Bowls.

Dirk Nowitzki, b 1978, (Ger.) NBA forward; led Mavericks to NBA title, 2011; NBA MVP, 2007.

Paavo Nurmi, 1897-1973, (Fin.) distance runner; won 9 Olympic gold medals, 1920, '24, '28.

Lorena Ochoa, b 1981, (Mex.) LPGA Player of the Year, 2006-09, money leader 2006-08.

Al Oerter, 1936-2007, discus thrower; won gold medal at 4 consecutive Olympics, 1956, '60, '64, '68.

Apolo Ohno, b 1982, short-track speed skater; most decorated U.S. Winter Olympic athlete with 2 gold, 2 silver, 4 bronze (2002, '06, '10).

Hakeem Olajuwon, b 1963, (Nigeria) Houston center; NBA MVP, 1994; playoff MVP, 1994-95; career blocked shots leader (3,830).

Barney Oldfield, 1878-1946, pioneer auto racer; was first to drive a car 60 mph, 1903.

Shaquille O'Neal, b 1972, center; led L.A. Lakers to NBA titles, 2000-02, and Miami Heat to NBA title, 2006; Finals MVP 2000-02; NBA MVP 2000.

Bobby Orr, b 1948, (Can.) Boston Bruins defenseman; 8-time Norris Trophy winner; led NHL in scoring twice, assists 5 times.

Naomi Osaka, b 1997, (Jpn.) tennis player; won U.S. Open (2018, 2020), Austral. Open (2019).

Mel Ott, 1909-58, NY Giants right fielder; hit 511 home runs; led NL 6 times.

Alexander Ovechkin, b 1985, (Russ.) hockey player; NHL MVP, 2008, '09, '13.

Jesse Owens, 1913-80, track-and-field athlete; 4 1936 Olympic golds.

Terrell Owens, b 1973, NFL wide receiver.

Satchel Paige, 1906-82, pitcher; starred in Negro Leagues, 1924-48; entered major leagues at age 42.

Arnold Palmer, 1929-2016, golf's first $1 mil winner; won 4 Masters, 2 British Opens.

Jim Palmer, b 1945, Baltimore Orioles pitcher; won Cy Young award 3 times; 20-game winner 8 times.

Inbee Park, b 1988, (S. Kor.) golfer; 2nd woman ever to win first 3 majors of season (2013).

Candace Parker, b 1986, L.A. Sparks forward; WNBA MVP (2008, '13); Olympic gold medalist (2008, '12).

Joe Paterno, 1926-2012, Penn St. football coach; national title winner, 1982, '86; most wins in NCAA Div. I coaching history (409); legacy complicated by child sex abuse scandal at Penn St.

Danica Patrick, b 1982, race car driver; 1st woman to lead Indy 500 and to win NASCAR Sprint Cup series pole.

Floyd Patterson, 1935-2006, 2-time heavyweight champion; first to ever regain the title after losing it.

Walter Payton, 1954-99, Chicago Bears running back; 2nd most rushing yards in NFL history; top NFC rusher, 1976-80.

Pelé (Edson Arantes do Nascimento), b 1940, (Braz.) soccer player; led Brazil to 3 World Cups (1958, '62, '70); scored 1,281 goals.

Bob Pettit, b 1932, first NBA player to score 20,000 pts.; twice NBA scoring leader.

Richard Petty, b 1937, NASCAR national champ 7 times; 7-time Daytona 500 winner.

Michael Phelps, b 1985, Olympic swimmer; record-holder, most Olympic medals (28) and gold medals (23) won by a single athlete.

Oscar Pistorius, b 1986, (S. Afr.) sprinter; 1st double-leg amputee to compete in Olympics, 2012; convicted (2015) of murder in girlfriend's death.

Jacques Plante, 1929-86, (Can.) NHL goaltender; 7 Vezina trophies; first goalie to wear mask in a game.

Gary Player, b 1935, (S. Afr.) golfer; won 3 Masters, 3 British Opens, 2 PGA Championships, and U.S. Open.

Mike Powell, b 1963, track-and-field athlete; holds world record for long jump (29 ft 4.5 in.).

Steve Prefontaine, 1951-75, runner; 1st to win 4 NCAA titles in same event (5,000m, 1970-73).

Kirby Puckett, 1960-2006, Minnesota center fielder with .318 career avg; World Series titles, 1987, '91.

Albert Pujols, b 1980, MLB slugger; NL MVP, 2005, '08-'09.

Paula Radcliffe, b 1973, British runner; fmr. marathon world record holder.

Manny Ramirez, b 1972, (Dom. Rep.) outfielder; 2004 World Series MVP; suspended for violating MLB performance-enhancing drug policy, 2009, '11.

Megan Rapinoe, b 1985, soccer forward; World Cup champion (2015, '19); won Golden Boot, Golden Ball (2019).

Willis Reed, b 1942, NY Knicks center; MVP, 1970; playoff MVP, 1970, '73.

Mary Lou Retton, b 1968, gymnast; won all-around gold medal at 1984 Olympics; also won 2 silvers, 2 bronzes.

Jerry Rice, b 1962, receiver; 1989 Super Bowl MVP; NFL record for career touchdowns (208), receptions (1,549).

Maurice Richard, 1921-2000, (Can.) Montréal Canadiens forward; scored 544 regular season goals, 82 playoff goals.

Branch Rickey, 1881-1965, MLB exec. helped break baseball's color barrier, 1947; initiated farm system, 1919.

Cal Ripken Jr., b 1960, Baltimore shortstop; AL MVP, 1983, '91; most consecutive games played (2,632).

Mariano Rivera, b 1969, (Pan.) relief pitcher; helped NY Yankees to 5 World Series titles; World Series MVP, 1999; all-time MLB leader in regular season and postseason saves.

Oscar Robertson, b 1938, NBA guard; averaged career 25.7 pts. per game; MVP, 1964.

Brooks Robinson, b 1937, Baltimore Orioles 3rd baseman; played in 4 World Series; MVP, 1964; 16 gold gloves.

Frank Robinson, 1935-2019, MVP in both NL and AL; triple crown, 1966; 586 career home runs; first Black manager in majors.

Jackie Robinson, 1919-72, broke baseball's color barrier with Brooklyn Dodgers, 1947; NL MVP, 1949.

Sugar Ray Robinson, 1921-89, boxer; middleweight champion 5 times; welterweight champion, 1946-51.

Knute Rockne, 1888-1931, Notre Dame football coach, 1918-31; revolutionized game by stressing forward pass.

Aaron Rodgers, b 1983, Green Bay quarterback; led Packers to victory in Super Bowl XLV; Super Bowl MVP, 2011; NFL MVP, 2011, '14.

Bill Rodgers, b 1947, runner; won Boston and New York City marathons 4 times each between 1975 and 1980.

Alex Rodriguez, b 1975, MLB infielder; 3-time AL MVP; 14-time All Star; admitted steroid use 2001-03; suspended 162 games for PED use, 2013-14.

Juan "Chi Chi" Rodriguez, b 1935, champion golfer; 8 PGA tour wins, 22 Champions tour wins.

Ben Roethlisberger, b 1982, Pittsburgh Steelers quarterback; youngest QB to win Super Bowl, 2005.

Ronaldinho (Ronaldo de Assis Moreira), b 1980, (Braz.) soccer midfielder; FIFA World Player of the Year, 2004, '05.

Ronaldo (Ronaldo Luiz Nazario de Lima), b 1976, (Braz.) soccer forward; led Brazil to 2002 World Cup title; 3-time FIFA world player of the year.

Cristiano Ronaldo, b 1985, (Port.) soccer forward; FIFA player of the year, 2008; UEFA career scoring leader (130).

Art Rooney, 1901-88, NFL owner; bought Pittsburgh Pirates in 1933, renamed Steelers, 1940.

Pete Rose, b 1941, won 3 NL batting titles; hit in 44 consecutive games, 1978; most career hits, 4,256; banned for gambling, 1989; admitted betting on his team, 2004.

Ken Rosewall, b 1934, (Austral.) tennis player; 8 Grand Slam singles titles.

Ronda Rousey, b 1987, judoka and mixed martial arts fighter.

Patrick Roy, b 1965, (Can.) Montréal-Colorado goalie; only 3-time NHL playoffs MVP, 1986, '93, 2001.

Wilma Rudolph, 1940-94, sprinter; won 3 1960 Olympic golds.

Adolph Rupp, 1901-77, NCAA basketball coach; led Kentucky to 4 national titles, 1948-49, '51, '58.

Bill Russell, b 1934, Boston Celtics center; led team to 11 NBA titles; MVP 5 times; first Black coach of major pro sports team.

Babe Ruth, 1895-1948, NY Yankees outfielder; hit 60 home runs, 1927, 714 lifetime (3rd all-time); led AL 12 times.

Johnny Rutherford, b 1938, auto racer; won 3 Indy 500s.

Nolan Ryan, b 1947, pitcher; holds season (383), career (5,714) strikeout records; won 324 games (7 no-hitters).

Pete Sampras, b 1971, tennis player; 14 Grand Slam singles wins.

Joan Benoit Samuelson, b 1957, won 1st Olympic women's marathon (1984), Boston Marathon (1979, '83).

Barry Sanders, b 1968, running back; won Heisman Trophy, 1988; NFL MVP, 1997.

Deion Sanders, b 1967, NFL cornerback (1989-2000, '04-'05) and MLB outfielder (1989-95, '97, 2005).

Gale Sayers, 1943-2020, Chicago running back; twice led NFL in rushing.

Mike Schmidt, b 1949, Phillies 3rd baseman; led NL in home runs 8 times; 548 lifetime; 3-time NL MVP.

Michael Schumacher, b 1969, (Ger.) race-car driver; 7-time Formula 1 world champ (1994-95, 2000-04).

Tom Seaver, 1944-2020, pitcher; won NL Cy Young award 3 times; won 311 major league games.

Monica Seles, b 1973, (Yugo.) tennis player; won 9 Grand Slam singles titles; stabbed on court by spectator, 1993.

Maria Sharapova, b 1987, (Russ.) tennis player; 5 Grand Slam singles titles.

Patty Sheehan, b 1956, golfer; 3 LPGA Championships (1983-84, '93).

Willie Shoemaker, 1931-2003, jockey; rode 4 Kentucky Derby, 5 Belmont Stakes winners.

Frank Shorter, b 1947, runner; only American to win men's Olympic marathon (1972) since 1908; silver medalist (1976).

Don Shula, 1930-2020, all-time winningest NFL coach (347 games).

Bill Simmons, b 1969, columnist; podcast, TV host; Grantland and theringer.com founder.

O. J. Simpson, b 1947, running back; rushed for 2,003 yds, 1973; AFC leading rusher 4 times; acquitted of murder, 1995; found guilty of robbery and kidnapping, imprisoned 2008-17.

Dean Smith, 1931-2015, basketball coach; 879 Division I wins; led North Carolina to 2 NCAA titles (1982, '93).

Emmitt Smith, b 1969, running back; NFL and Super Bowl MVP, 1993; rushed for career record 18,355 yds.

Conn Smythe, 1895-1980, (Can.) won 7 Stanley Cups as Toronto GM (1929-61); playoff MVP award named in his honor.

Sam Snead, 1912-2002, PGA and Masters champ 3 times each; record 82 PGA tournament victories.

Annika Sorenstam, b 1970, (Swed.) golfer; set LPGA 18-hole record of 59 (–13); won 10 LPGA majors, including career Grand Slam.

Sammy Sosa, b 1968, (Dom. Rep.) MLB slugger; NL MVP, 1998; 1st to hit 60+ HR 3 times (1998-99, 2001).

Warren Spahn, 1921-2003, pitcher; won 363 NL games; 20-game winner 13 times; Cy Young winner, 1957.

Tris Speaker, 1888-1958, AL outfielder; batted .345 over 22 seasons; hit record 792 career doubles.

Jordan Spieth, b 1993, golfer; won Masters, 2015; U.S. Open, 2015; British Open, 2017.

Mark Spitz, b 1950, swimmer; won 7 golds at 1972 Olympics.

Amos Alonzo Stagg, 1862-1965, football innovator; Univ. of Chicago football coach for 41 years, 5 undefeated seasons.

Bart Starr, 1934-2019, Green Bay Packers quarterback; led team to 5 NFL titles, 2 Super Bowl victories.

Roger Staubach, b 1942, Dallas Cowboys quarterback; 2-time Super Bowl champ.

George Steinbrenner, 1930-2010, NY Yankees owner.

Casey Stengel, 1890-1975, managed Yankees to 10 pennants, 7 World Series wins between 1949 and 1960.

Jackie Stewart, b 1939, (Scot.) auto racer; 27 Grand Prix wins.

John Stockton, b 1962, Utah Jazz guard; NBA career leader in assists, steals; block assists leader, 1988-96.

Picabo Street, b 1971, skier; 2-time World Cup downhill champion (1995-96); Olympic super G gold medalist, 1998.

Louise Suggs, 1923-2015, golfer; U.S. Women's Open champ, 1949, '52; 11 major victories.

John L. Sullivan, 1858-1918, last bareknuckle heavyweight champion, 1882-92.

Pat Summerall, 1930-2013, NFL kicker, radio and TV sportscaster who announced 26 Super Bowls.

Pat Summitt, 1952-2016, women's basketball coach; led Tennessee to 8 NCAA titles; 1,098 career wins.

Ichiro Suzuki, b 1973, (Jpn.) outfielder; AL MVP, 2001; single-season hits record (262), 2004; career (Japan-U.S.) hits leader since 2013; 3,000th U.S. hit, 2016.

Sheryl Swoopes, b 1971, guard/forward; 1st 3-time WNBA MVP (2000, '02, '05); Olympic gold medalist (1996, 2000, '04).

Fran Tarkenton, b 1940, Minnesota NY Giants quarterback; 342 career TD passes; 1975 Player of the Year.

Diana Taurasi, b 1982, WNBA guard; 4-time Olympic gold medalist; WNBA MVP, 2009.

Lawrence Taylor, b 1959, linebacker; led NY Giants to 2 Super Bowl titles; played in 10 Pro Bowls.

Daley Thompson, b 1958, (Br.) decathlete; Olympic gold medalist in 1980, '84.

Jenny Thompson, b 1973, swimmer; 12 Olympic medals (8 gold) in 1992, '96, 2000, '04.

Bobby Thomson, 1923-2010, MLB utility player known for pennant-clinching "Shot Heard 'Round the World" for the NY Giants, 1951.

Jim Thorpe, 1888-1953, football All-American, 1911-12; won pentathlon and decathlon, 1912 Olympics.

Bill Tilden, 1893-1953, tennis player; won 7 U.S. Open titles, 3 Wimbledon.

Y. A. Tittle, 1926-2017, NY Giants quarterback; MVP, 1961, '63.

Alberto Tomba, b 1966, (It.) alpine skier; 5 Olympic medals (3 golds, 2 silver) in 1988, '92, '94.

LaDainian "L.T." Tomlinson, b 1979, running back; NFL single-season record for rushing touchdowns (28).

Joe Torre, b 1940, MLB player, manager; NL MVP, 1971; won 4 World Series in 5 years as NY Yankees manager.

Lee Trevino, b 1939, golfer; 6-time PGA major winner.

Bryan Trottier, b 1956, (Can.) Islanders, Penguins center for 6 Stanley Cup champs.

Mike Trout, b 1991, MLB outfielder; 3-time AL MVP, 2014, '16, '19.

Gene Tunney, 1897-1978, heavyweight champion, 1926-28.

Mike Tyson, b 1966, undisputed heavyweight champ, 1987-90; at 20, youngest to win a heavyweight title (WBC, 1986).

Wyomia Tyus, b 1945, Olympic 100m gold medalist, 1964, '68.

Johnny Unitas, 1933-2002, Baltimore Colts quarterback; passed for more than 40,000 yds; MVP, 1957, '67.

Al Unser, b 1939, Indy 500 winner 4 times.

Bobby Unser, b 1934, Indy 500 winner 3 times.

Norm Van Brocklin, 1926-83, quarterback; passed for game record 554 yds, 1951; MVP, 1960.

Amy Van Dyken, b 1973, swimmer; first American woman to win 4 gold medals in one Olympics (1996).

Justin Verlander, b 1983, pitcher; won AL MVP, 2011, and Cy Young, 2011, '19.

Michael Vick, b 1980, quarterback; suspended and convicted (2007) of illegal dog fighting, gambling activities.

Lasse Viren, b 1949, (Fin.) runner; Olympic 5,000m and 10,000m gold medalist in 1972, '76.

Lindsey Vonn, b 1984, skier; Olympic gold, 2010; 4 overall World Cup titles 2008-10, '12.

Dwyane Wade, b 1982, guard; led Miami Heat to NBA title, 2006, '12-'13; finals MVP, 2006; NBA scoring title, 2009.

Honus Wagner, 1874-1955, Pittsburgh Pirates shortstop; 8 NL batting titles.

Grete Waitz, 1953-2011, (Nor.) distance runner; 9-time winner of the New York City Marathon (1978-80, '82-'86, '88).

"Jersey" Joe Walcott, 1914-94, boxer; became heavyweight champion at age 37, 1951-52.

Kerri Walsh Jennings, b 1978, beach volleyball player; 3-time Olympic gold medalist with Misty May-Treanor (2004, '08, '12).

Bill Walton, b 1952, center; led Portland Trail Blazers to 1977 NBA title; MVP, 1978; TV commentator.

Abby Wambach, b 1980, soccer player; 2 gold medals in Olympics (2004, '12).

Kurt Warner, b 1971, quarterback; NFL MVP, 1999, 2001; Super Bowl MVP, 2000.

Gerry "Bubba" Watson, b 1978, golfer; won Masters, 2012, '14.

Tom Watson, b 1949, golfer; 6-time PGA Player of the Year; won 5 British Opens, 2 Masters, U.S. Open.

Stan Wawrinka, b 1985, (Switz.) tennis player; won Austral. Open (2014), French Open (2015), U.S. Open (2016).

Karrie Webb, b 1974, (Austral.) golfer; youngest woman (26 yrs., 6 mos.) to win career Grand Slam, 1999-2001.

Johnny Weissmuller, 1903-84, swimmer; won 52 national championships, 5 Olympic gold medals.

Jerry West, b 1938, L.A. Lakers guard; career averaged 27 pts. per game.

Dan Wheldon, 1978-2011, (Br.) race-car driver; 2-time Indy 500 winner (2005, '11).

Byron "Whizzer" White, 1917-2002, running back; led NCAA in scoring and rushing at Colorado, 1937; led NFL in rushing twice, 1938, '40; Supreme Court justice, 1962-93.

Shaun White, b 1986, snowboarder/skateboarder; Olympic gold medalist in half-pipe (2006, '10, '18).

Kathy Whitworth, b 1939, 7-time LPGA Player of the Year; 88 tour wins, most on LPGA or PGA tour.

Michelle Wie, b 1989, golfer; in 2002 became youngest-ever qualifier for LPGA event; turned pro at age 15.

Bradley Wiggins, b 1980, (Br.) cyclist; Tour de France winner, 2012; 8 Olympic medals (5 gold) over 5 Games.

Michael Wilbon, b 1958, commentator/analyst for ESPN.

Lenny Wilkens, b 1937, 3rd winningest coach in NBA history; Hall of Fame player and coach.

Serena Williams, b 1981, tennis player; 23-time Grand Slam singles champion; Olympic gold medals in singles (2012) and doubles (2000, '08, '12) with sister Venus.

Ted Williams, 1918-2002, Boston Red Sox outfielder; won 6 batting titles, 2 triple crowns; hit .406 in 1941.

Venus Williams, b 1980, tennis player; 7-time Grand Slam singles champion; Olympic gold medals in singles (2000) and doubles with sister Serena (2000, '08, '12).

Helen Wills Moody, 1905-98, tennis player; won U.S. Open 7 times, Wimbledon 8 times.

Katarina Witt, b 1965, (Ger.) figure skater; won Olympic gold medal, 1984, '88; world champ, 1984-85, '87-'88.

John Wooden, 1910-2010, UCLA basketball coach; 10 NCAA titles.

Tiger Woods, b 1975, golfer; youngest to win career Grand Slam, at age 24 (1997-2000); 15 career major titles.

Mickey Wright, 1935-2020, golfer; won LPGA and U.S. Open championship 4 times; 82 career wins, including 13 majors.

Eric Wynalda, b 1969, soccer player; scored 1st goal in major league soccer history (1996).

Kristi Yamaguchi, b 1971, figure skater; won national, world, Olympic titles, in 1992.

Yao Ming, b 1980, (China) center for Houston Rockets; 8-time NBA All-Star.

Carl Yastrzemski, b 1939, Boston Red Sox slugger; won 3 batting titles; triple crown, 1967.

Cy Young, 1867-1955, pitcher; won record 511 games.

Steve Young, b 1961, 49ers quarterback; NFL MVP, 1992, '94; 3 Super Bowl titles, Super Bowl MVP, 1995.

Babe Didrikson Zaharias, 1911-56, all-around athlete; 3 track-and-field medals (2 golds), 1932 Olympics; won 10 golf majors; also played baseball; 6-time AP Female Athlete of the Year.

Emil Zátopek, 1922-2000, (Czech.) runner; won 3 gold medals at 1952 Olympics (5,000m, 10,000m, marathon).

Zinedine Zidane, b 1972, (Fr.) soccer midfielder; led France to 1998 World Cup title; named top player in 2006; 3-time FIFA world player of the year (1998, 2000, '03).

Writers of the Present

Name	Birthplace	Birthdate
Chimamanda Ngozi Adichie	Enugu, Nigeria	9/15/1977
Mitch Albom	Passaic, NJ	5/23/1958
Elizabeth Alexander	New York, NY	5/30/1962
Sherman Alexie	Wellpinit, WA.	10/7/1966
Isabel Allende	Lima, Peru	8/2/1942
Dorothy Allison	Greenville, SC.	4/11/1949
Martin Amis	Oxford, England, UK.	8/25/1949
Piers Anthony	Oxford, England, UK.	8/6/1934
Jeffrey Archer	Somerset, England, UK.	4/15/1940
Margaret Atwood	Ottawa, ON, Canada.	11/18/1939
David Auburn	Chicago, IL	11/30/1969
Jean Auel	Chicago, IL	2/18/1936
Paul Auster	Newark, NJ	2/3/1947
Alan Ayckbourn	Hampstead, England, UK	4/12/1939
Fredrik Backman	Stockholm, Sweden	6/2/1981
Nicholson Baker	New York, NY	1/7/1957
David Baldacci	Richmond, VA	8/5/1960
Russell Banks	Newton, MA	3/28/1940
Sebastian Barry	Dublin, Ireland.	7/5/1955
John Barth	Cambridge, MD	5/27/1930
Ann Beattie	Washington, DC	9/8/1947
Alan Bennett	Leeds, England, UK	5/9/1934
John Berendt	Syracuse, NY	12/5/1939
Elizabeth Berg	St. Paul, MN	12/2/1948
Judy Blume	Elizabeth, NJ	2/12/1938
T. Coraghessan Boyle	Peekskill, NY.	12/2/1948
Barbara Taylor Bradford	Leeds, England, UK	5/10/1933
Christopher Bram	Buffalo, NY	2/22/1952
Geraldine Brooks	Sydney, NSW, Australia	9/14/1955
Dan Brown	Exeter, NH	6/22/1964
Rita Mae Brown	Hanover, PA	11/28/1944
Christopher Buckley	New York, NY	9/28/1952
James Lee Burke	Houston, TX	12/5/1936
Augusten Burroughs	Pittsburgh, PA.	10/23/1965
Robert Olen Butler	Granite City, IL	1/20/1945
A. S. Byatt	Sheffield, England, UK	8/24/1936
Ethan Canin	Ann Arbor, MI	7/19/1960
Peter Carey	Bacchus-Marsh, Vic., Australia	5/7/1943
Robert A. Caro	New York, NY	10/30/1935
Caleb Carr	New York, NY	8/2/1955
Michael Chabon	Washington, DC	5/24/1963
Tracy Chevalier	Washington, DC	10/19/1962
Lee Child	Coventry, England, UK	10/29/1954
Sandra Cisneros	Chicago, IL	12/20/1954
Beverly Cleary	McMinnville, OR	4/12/1916
Ta-Nehisi Coates	Baltimore, MD.	9/30/1975
Harlan Coben	Newark, NJ	1/4/1962
Paulo Coelho	Rio de Janeiro, Brazil	8/24/1947
J(ohn) M(axwell) Coetzee	Capetown, South Africa	2/9/1940
Billy Collins	New York, NY	3/22/1941
Suzanne Collins	Hartford, CT	8/10/1962
Robin Cook	New York, NY	5/4/1940
Patricia Cornwell	Miami, FL	6/9/1956
Michael Cunningham	Cincinnati, OH	11/6/1952
Don DeLillo	Bronx, NY	11/20/1936
Nelson DeMille	Jamaica, Queens, NY	8/23/1943
Junot Díaz	Santo Domingo, Dominican Republic	12/31/1968
Joan Didion	Sacramento, CA	12/5/1934
Annie Dillard	Pittsburgh, PA.	4/30/1945
Anthony Doerr	Cleveland, OH	10/27/1973
Emma Donoghue	Dublin, Ireland.	10/24/1969
Rita Dove	Akron, OH.	8/28/1952
Roddy Doyle	Dublin, Ireland.	5/8/1958
Carol Ann Duffy	Glasgow, Scotland, UK.	12/23/1955
Jennifer Egan	Chicago, IL	9/7/1962
Dave Eggers	Boston, MA	3/12/1970
Bret Easton Ellis	Los Angeles, CA.	3/7/1964
James Ellroy	Los Angeles, CA.	3/4/1948
Louise Erdrich	Little Falls, MN	6/7/1954
Laura Esquivel	Mexico City, Mexico	9/30/1950
Jeffrey Eugenides	Detroit, MI.	3/8/1960
Janet Evanovich	South River, NJ.	4/22/1943
Lawrence Ferlinghetti	Yonkers, NY	3/24/1919
Helen Fielding	Morley, Yorkshire, Eng., UK.	2/19/1958
Fannie Flagg	Birmingham, AL	9/21/1944
Gillian Flynn	Kansas City, MO.	2/24/1971
Jonathan Safran Foer	Washington, DC	2/21/1977
Ken Follett	Cardiff, Wales, UK.	6/5/1949
Richard Ford	Jackson, MS.	2/16/1944
Frederick Forsyth	Ashford, England, UK.	8/25/1938
Jonathan Franzen	Western Springs, IL	8/17/1959
Michael Frayn	London, England, UK.	9/8/1933
Charles Frazier	Asheville, NC	11/4/1950
Neil Gaiman	Portchester, England, UK.	11/10/1960
Roxane Gay	Omaha, NE.	10/15/1974
Malcolm Gladwell	Fareham, Hampshire, Eng., UK	9/3/1963
Robert Goddard	Fareham, Hampshire, Eng., UK	11/13/1954
Gail Godwin	Birmingham, AL	6/18/1937
Mary Gordon	Far Rockaway, NY	12/8/1949
John Green	Indianapolis, IN.	8/24/1977
Andrew Sean Greer	Washington, DC	11/21/1970
John Grisham	Jonesboro, AR	2/8/1955
John Guare	New York, NY	2/5/1938
David Handler	Los Angeles, CA.	9/14/1952
Paul Harding	Wenham, MA	12/19/1967
David Hare	St. Leonards, Sussex, Eng., UK	6/5/1947
Robert Hass	San Francisco, CA	3/1/1941
Paula Hawkins	Harare, Zimbabwe	8/28/1972
Mark Helprin	New York, NY	6/28/1947
Carl Hiaasen	Plantation, FL	3/12/1953
Laura Hillenbrand	Fairfax, VA.	5/15/1967
S. E. Hinton	Tulsa, OK	7/22/1948
Alice Hoffman	New York, NY	3/16/1952
Alan Hollinghurst	Stroud, Gloucestershire, England, UK.	5/26/1954
Khaled Hosseini	Kabul, Afghanistan	3/4/1965
John Irving	Exeter, NH	3/2/1942
Walter Isaacson	New Orleans, LA	5/20/1952
Kazuo Ishiguro	Nagasaki, Japan.	11/8/1954
John Jakes	Chicago, IL	3/31/1932
E. L. James	London, England, UK.	7/3/1963
Elfriede Jelinek	Müzzuschlag, Austria	10/20/1946
N. K. Jemisin	Iowa City, IA	9/19/1972
Ha Jin	Liaoning, China.	2/21/1956
Adam Johnson	South Dakota	7/12/1967
Edward P. Jones	Washington, DC	10/5/1950
Erica Jong	New York, NY	3/26/1942
Sebastian Junger	Boston, MA.	1/17/1962
Jan Karon	Lenoir, NC.	3/14/1937
Garrison Keillor	Anoka, MN	8/7/1942
Thomas Keneally	Sydney, NSW, Australia	10/7/1935
William Kennedy	Albany, NY	1/16/1928
Sue Monk Kidd	Sylvester, GA	8/12/1948
Jamaica Kincaid	St. John's, Antigua and Barbuda.	5/25/1949
Stephen King	Portland, ME.	9/21/1947
Barbara Kingsolver	Annapolis, MD	4/8/1955
Maxine Hong Kingston	Stockton, CA.	10/27/1940
Dean Koontz	Everett, PA	7/9/1945
Ted Kooser	Ames, IA.	4/25/1939
Jon Krakauer	Brookline, MA.	4/12/1954
Milan Kundera	Brno, Czechoslovakia.	4/1/1929
Tony Kushner	New York, NY	7/16/1956
Jhumpa Lahiri	London, England, UK.	7/11/1967
Erik Larson	Brooklyn, NY.	1/3/1954
John le Carré	Poole, England, UK	10/19/1931
Jean Marie Gustave Le Clézio	Nice, France	4/13/1940
David Leavitt	Pittsburgh, PA.	6/23/1961
Jonathan Lethem	Brooklyn, NY.	2/19/1964
David Lodge	South London, England, UK.	1/28/1935
Alison Lurie	Chicago, IL	9/3/1926
Gregory Maguire	Albany, NY	6/9/1954
David Malouf	Brisbane, Qld., Australia.	3/20/1934
Thomas Mallon	Glen Cove, NY	11/2/1951
David Mamet	Chicago, IL	11/30/1947
Hilary Mantel	Derbyshire, England, UK	7/6/1952
Yann Martel	Salamanca, Spain	6/25/1963
George R. R. Martin	Bayonne, NJ	9/20/1948
Bobbie Ann Mason	nr. Mayfield, KY.	5/1/1940
Armistead Maupin	Washington, DC	4/13/1944
Colum McCann	Dublin, Ireland.	2/28/1965
Cormac McCarthy	Providence, RI	7/20/1933
David McCullough	Pittsburgh, PA.	7/7/1933
Alice McDermott	Brooklyn, NY.	6/27/1953
Ian McEwan	Aldershot, England, UK	6/21/1948
Thomas McGuane	Wyandotte, MI.	12/11/1939
Jay McInerney	Hartford, CT	1/13/1955
Terry McMillan	Port Huron, MI	10/18/1951
Larry McMurtry	Wichita Falls, TX	6/3/1936
John McPhee	Princeton, NJ	3/8/1931
Stephenie Meyer	Hartford, CT	12/24/1973
Steven Millhauser	New York, NY	8/3/1943
Walter Mosley	Los Angeles, CA.	1/12/1952
Andrew Motion	London, England, UK	10/26/1952
Jojo Moyes	Maidstone, England, UK.	8/4/1969
Herta Müller	Nitzkydorf, Banat, Romania	8/17/1953
Alice Munro	Wingham, ON, Canada.	7/10/1931
Haruki Murakami	Kyoto, Japan.	1/12/1949
Celeste Ng	Pittsburgh, PA.	7/30/1980
Viet Thanh Nguyen	Buon Me Thuot, Vietnam	3/13/1971
Lynn Nottage	Brooklyn, NY.	11/2/1964
Joyce Carol Oates	Lockport, NY.	6/16/1938
Edna O'Brien	Tuamgraney, Ireland.	12/15/1930
Tim O'Brien	Austin, MN	10/1/1946
Kenzaburō Ōe	Uchiko, Japan.	1/31/1935
Michael Ondaatje	Colombo, Sri Lanka	9/12/1943
Cynthia Ozick	New York, NY	4/17/1928
Orhan Pamuk	Istanbul, Turkey.	6/7/1952

Name	Birthplace	Birthdate	Name	Birthplace	Birthdate
Suzan-Lori Parks	Fort Knox, KY	5/10/1963	John Patrick Shanley	Bronx, NY	10/13/1950
Ann Patchett	Los Angeles, CA	12/2/1963	Lionel Shriver	Gastonia, NC	5/18/1957
James Patterson	Newburgh, NY	3/22/1947	Jane Smiley	Los Angeles, CA	9/26/1949
Jodi Picoult	New York, NY	5/19/1966	Zadie Smith	London, Eng., UK	10/25/1975
Marge Piercy	Detroit, MI	3/31/1936	Wole Soyinka	Abeokuta, Nigeria	7/13/1934
Robert Pinsky	Long Branch, NJ	10/20/1940	Nicholas Sparks	Omaha, NE	12/31/1965
Michael Pollan	New York, NY	2/6/1955	Danielle Steel	New York, NY	8/14/1947
Richard Powers	Evanston, IL	6/18/1957	R(obert) L(awrence)		
Richard Price	Bronx, NY	10/12/1949	Stine	Columbus, OH	10/8/1943
E. Annie Proulx	Norwich, CT	8/22/1935	Kathryn Stockett	Jackson, MS	5/17/1969
Philip Pullman	Norwich, England, UK	10/19/1946	Tom Stoppard	Zlin, Czechoslovakia	7/3/1937
Thomas Pynchon	Glen Cove, NY	5/8/1937	Elizabeth Strout	Portland, ME	1/6/1956
David Rabe	Dubuque, IA	3/10/1940	Amy Tan	Oakland, CA	2/19/1952
Ishmael Reed	Chattanooga, TN	2/22/1938	Donna Tartt	Greenwood, MS	12/23/1963
Anne Rice	New Orleans, LA	10/4/1941	Paul Theroux	Medford, MA	4/10/1941
Mary Roach	Etna, NH	3/20/1959	Calvin Trillin	Kansas City, MO	12/5/1935
Nora Roberts	Silver Spring, MD	10/10/1950	Scott F. Turow	Chicago, IL	4/12/1949
Marilynne Robinson	Sandpoint, IL	11/26/1943	Anne Tyler	Minneapolis, MN	10/25/1941
Veronica Roth	New York, NY	8/19/1988	Mario Vargas Llosa	Arequipa, Peru	3/28/1936
J. K. Rowling	Chipping Sodbury, Eng., UK	7/31/1965	Paula Vogel	Washington, DC	11/16/1951
Norman Rush	San Francisco, CA	10/24/1933	Sarah Vowell	Muskogee, OK	12/27/1969
Salman Rushdie	Bombay, India	6/19/1947	Alice Walker	Eatonton, GA	2/9/1944
Richard Russo	Johnstown, NY	7/15/1949	Joseph Wambaugh	East Pittsburgh, PA	1/22/1937
George Saunders	Amarillo, TX	12/2/1958	Jesmyn Ward	DeLisle, MS	4/1/1977
Alice Sebold	Madison, WI	9/6/1963	Edmund White	Cincinnati, OH	1/13/1940
David Sedaris	Johnson City, NY	12/26/1956	Colson Whitehead	New York, NY	11/6/1969
Vikram Seth	Calcutta, India	6/20/1952	Tobias Wolff	Birmingham, AL	6/19/1945

Writers of the Past

See also Journalists, and Greeks and Romans in Historical Figures chapter.

Chinua Achebe, 1930-2013, (Nigeria) novelist. *Things Fall Apart.*

Alice Adams, 1926-99, (U.S.) novelist, short-story writer. *Superior Woman.*

Richard Adams, 1920-2016, (Br.) novelist. *Watership Down.*

James Agee, 1909-55, (U.S.) novelist. *A Death in the Family.*

S(hmuel) Y(osef) Agnon, 1888-1970, (Isr.) Hebrew novelist. *Only Yesterday.*

Conrad Aiken, 1889-1973, (U.S.) poet, critic. *Ushant.*

Anna Akhmatova, 1889-1966, (Russ.) poet. *Requiem.*

Edward Albee, 1928-2016, (U.S.) playwright. *Who's Afraid of Virginia Woolf?*

Louisa May Alcott, 1832-88, (U.S.) novelist. *Little Women.*

Sholom Aleichem, 1859-1916, (Russ.) Yiddish writer. *Tevye's Daughters, The Old Country.*

Vicente Aleixandre, 1898-1984, (Sp.) poet. *La destrucción o el amor, Dialogos del conocimiento.*

Horatio Alger, 1832-99, (U.S.) "rags-to-riches" books.

Jorge Amado, 1912-2001, (Brazil) novelist. *Dona Flor and Her Two Husbands, The Violent Land.*

Eric Ambler, 1909-98, (Br.) suspense novelist. *A Coffin for Dimitrios.*

Kingsley Amis, 1922-95, (Br.) novelist, critic. *Lucky Jim.*

Hans Christian Andersen, 1805-75, (Den.) author of fairy tales. *The Ugly Duckling.*

Maxwell Anderson, 1888-1959, (U.S.) playwright. *What Price Glory?, High Tor, Winterset, Key Largo.*

Sherwood Anderson, 1876-1941, (U.S.) short-story writer. "Death in the Woods," *Winesburg, Ohio.*

Maya Angelou, 1928-2014, (U.S.) poet, memoirist. *I Know Why the Caged Bird Sings.*

Reinaldo Arenas, 1943-90, (Cuba) short-story writer, novelist. *Before Night Falls.*

Ludovico Ariosto, 1474-1533, (It.) novelist. *Orlando Furioso.*

Matthew Arnold, 1822-88, (Br.) poet, critic. "Thrysis," "Dover Beach," "Culture and Anarchy."

John Ashbery, 1927-2007, (U.S.) poet. *Self-Portrait in a Convex Mirror.*

Isaac Asimov, 1920-92, (U.S.) versatile writer, espec. of science fiction. *I Robot.*

Miguel Angel Asturias, 1899-1974, (Guat.) novelist. *El Señor Presidente.*

Louis Auchincloss, 1917-2010, (U.S.) novelist, memoirist, short-story writer. *The Rector of Justin.*

W(ystan) H(ugh) Auden, 1907-73, (Br.) poet, playwright, literary critic. "The Age of Anxiety."

Jane Austen, 1775-1817, (Br.) novelist. *Pride and Prejudice, Sense and Sensibility, Emma, Mansfield Park.*

Ba Jin (Li Yaotang), 1904-2005, (China) novelist of pre-revolutionary China.

Isaac Babel, 1894-1941, (Russ.) short-story writer, playwright. *Odessa Tales, Red Cavalry.*

Russell Baker, 1925-2019, (U.S.) columnist, essayist. *Growing Up.*

James Baldwin, 1924-87, (U.S.) author, playwright. *The Fire Next Time, Blues for Mister Charlie.*

Honoré de Balzac, 1799-1850, (Fr.) novelist. *Le Père Goriot, Cousine Bette, Eugénie Grandet.*

James M. Barrie, 1860-1937, (Br.) playwright, novelist. *Peter Pan, Dear Brutus, What Every Woman Knows.*

Charles Baudelaire, 1821-67, (Fr.) poet. *Les Fleurs du Mal.*

L(yman) Frank Baum, 1856-1919, (U.S.) *Wizard of Oz* series.

Simone de Beauvoir, 1908-86, (Fr.) novelist, essayist. *The Second Sex, Memoirs of a Dutiful Daughter.*

Samuel Beckett, 1906-89, (Ire.) novelist, playwright. *Waiting for Godot, Endgame* (plays); *Murphy, Watt, Molloy* (novels).

Brendan Behan, 1923-64, (Ire.) playwright. *The Quare Fellow, The Hostage, Borstal Boy.*

Saul Bellow, 1915-2005, (U.S.) novelist. *The Adventures of Augie March, Humboldt's Gift.*

Robert Benchley, 1889-1945, (U.S.) humorist.

Stephen Vincent Benét, 1898-1943, (U.S.) poet, novelist. *John Brown's Body.*

Jan Berenstain, 1923-2012, and **Stan Berenstain**, 1923-2005, (both U.S.) co-writers and illustrators of Berenstain Bears series of children's books.

Thomas Berger, 1924-2014, (U.S.) novelist. *Little Big Man.*

John Berryman, 1914-72, (U.S.) poet. *Homage to Mistress Bradstreet.*

Ambrose Bierce, 1842-1914, (U.S.) short-story writer, journalist. *In the Midst of Life, The Devil's Dictionary.*

Maeve Binchy, 1940-2012, (Ire.) novelist, short-story writer. *Circle of Friends, Tara Road.*

Elizabeth Bishop, 1911-79, (U.S.) poet. *North and South—A Cold Spring.*

William Blake, 1757-1827, (Br.) poet, artist. *Songs of Innocence, Songs of Experience.*

Aleksandr Blok, 1880-1921, (Russ.) poet. "The Twelve," "The Scythians."

Harold Bloom, 1930-2019, (U.S.) literary critic. *The Anxiety of Influence.*

Enid Blyton, 1897-1968, (Br.) children's writer. *Famous Five* series.

Giovanni Boccaccio, 1313-75, (It.) poet. *Decameron.*

Heinrich Böll, 1917-85, (Ger.) novelist, short-story writer. *Group Portrait With Lady.*

Jorge Luis Borges, 1900-86, (Arg.) short-story writer, poet, essayist. *Labyrinths.*

James Boswell, 1740-95, (Scot.) biographer. *The Life of Samuel Johnson.*

Pierre Boulle, 1913-94, (Fr.) novelist. *The Bridge Over the River Kwai, Planet of the Apes.*

Paul Bowles, 1910-99, (U.S.) novelist, short-story writer. *The Sheltering Sky.*

Ray Bradbury, 1920-2012, (U.S.) novelist, short-story writer. *Fahrenheit 451, The Martian Chronicles.*

Anne Bradstreet, c. 1612-72, (U.S.) poet. *The Tenth Muse Lately Sprung Up in America.*

Bertolt Brecht, 1898-1956, (Ger.) dramatist, poet. *The Threepenny Opera, Mother Courage and Her Children.*

Joseph Brodsky, 1940-96, (Russ.-U.S.) poet. *A Part of Speech, Less Than One, To Urania.*

Charlotte Brontë, 1816-55, (Br.) novelist. *Jane Eyre.*

Emily Brontë, 1818-48, (Br.) novelist. *Wuthering Heights.*

Sterling A. Brown, 1901-89, (U.S.) poet, literature professor. *Southern Road.*

William Wells Brown, 1815-84, (U.S.) writer, memoirist; first novel by an African American, *Clotel*, 1853.

Elizabeth Barrett Browning, 1806-61, (Br.) poet. *Sonnets From the Portuguese, Aurora Leigh.*

Robert Browning, 1812-89, (Br.) poet. "My Last Duchess," "Fra Lippo Lippi," *The Ring and the Book.*

Pearl S. Buck, 1892-1973, (U.S.) novelist. *The Good Earth.*

Charles Bukowski, 1920-94, (U.S.) novelist, poet. *Ham on Rye, Women.*

Mikhail Bulgakov, 1891-1940, (Russ.) novelist, playwright. *The Heart of a Dog, The Master and Margarita.*

John Bunyan, 1628-88, (Br.) writer. *Pilgrim's Progress*.

Anthony Burgess, 1917-93, (Br.) author. *A Clockwork Orange*.

Frances Hodgson Burnett, 1849-1924, (Br.-U.S.) novelist. *The Secret Garden*.

Robert Burns, 1759-96, (Scot.) poet. "Flow Gently, Sweet Afton," "My Heart's in the Highlands," "Auld Lang Syne."

Edgar Rice Burroughs, 1875-1950, (U.S.) writer; created Tarzan, John Carter.

William S. Burroughs, 1914-97, (U.S.) novelist. *Naked Lunch*.

Octavia Butler, 1947-2006, (U.S.) science-fiction writer. *Kindred*.

George Gordon, Lord Byron, 1788-1824, (Br.) poet. *Don Juan, Childe Harold, Manfred, Cain*.

Pedro Calderon de la Barca, 1600-81, (Sp.) playwright. *Life Is a Dream*.

Hortense Calisher, 1911-2009, (U.S.) novelist, short-story writer. *False Entry*.

Italo Calvino, 1923-85, (It.) novelist, short-story writer. *If on a Winter's Night a Traveler*.

Luís Vaz de Camões, 1524?-80 (Port.) poet. *The Lusiads*.

Albert Camus, 1913-60, (Fr.) writer. *The Stranger, The Fall*.

Elias Canetti, 1905-94, (Bulg.) novelist, essayist. *Auto-Da-Fe*.

Karel Čapek, 1890-1938, (Czech.) playwright, novelist, essayist. *R.U.R. (Rossum's Universal Robots)*.

Truman Capote, 1924-84, (U.S.) author. *Other Voices, Other Rooms; Breakfast at Tiffany's; In Cold Blood*.

Lewis Carroll (Charles Dodgson), 1832-98, (Br.) writer, mathematician. *Alice's Adventures in Wonderland*.

Barbara Cartland 1901-2000, (Br.) romance novelist.

Giacomo Casanova, 1725-98, (It.) adventurer, memoirist.

Willa Cather, 1873-1947, (U.S.) novelist. *O Pioneers!, My Ántonia, Death Comes for the Archbishop*.

Constantine Cavafy, 1863-1933, (Gr.) poet. "Ithaka," "Sensual Pleasures."

Camilo Jose Cela, 1916-2001, (Sp.) novelist. *The Family of Pascual Duarte, The Hive*.

Miguel de Cervantes Saavedra, 1547-1616, (Sp.) novelist, dramatist, poet. *Don Quixote*.

Raymond Chandler, 1888-1959, (U.S.) writer of detective fiction. Philip Marlowe series.

Geoffrey Chaucer, c. 1340-1400, (Br.) poet. *The Canterbury Tales, Troilus and Criseyde*.

John Cheever, 1912-82, (U.S.) novelist, short-story writer. *The Wapshot Scandal*, "The Country Husband."

Anton Chekhov, 1860-1904, (Russ.) short-story writer, dramatist. *Uncle Vanya, The Cherry Orchard, The Three Sisters*.

Charles Waddell Chesnutt, 1858-1932, (U.S.) author known for his short stories. *The Conjure Woman*.

G(ilbert) K(eith) Chesterton, 1874-1936, (Br.) critic, novelist, relig. apologist. Father Brown series of mysteries.

Kate Chopin, 1851-1904, (U.S.) writer. *The Awakening*.

Agatha Christie, 1890-1976, (Br.) mystery writer; created Miss Marple, Hercule Poirot. *Murder on the Orient Express, Murder of Roger Ackroyd*.

Tom Clancy, 1947-2013, novelist. *The Hunt for Red October*.

Mary Higgins Clark, 1927-2020, (U.S.) novelist. *Where Are the Children?*

Arthur C. Clarke, 1917-2008, (Br.) science-fiction writer. *2001: A Space Odyssey*.

James Clavell, 1924-94, (Br.-U.S.) novelist. *Shogun, King Rat*.

Jean Cocteau, 1889-1963, (Fr.) writer, visual artist, filmmaker. *The Beauty and the Beast, Les Enfants Terribles*.

Samuel Taylor Coleridge, 1772-1834, (Br.) poet, critic. "Kubla Khan," "The Rime of the Ancient Mariner."

(Sidonie) Colette, 1873-1954, (Fr.) novelist. *Claudine, Gigi*.

Wilkie Collins, 1824-89, (Br.) novelist. *The Moonstone*.

Evan S. Connell, 1924-2013, (Br.) novelist, short-story writer. *Mrs. Bridge*.

Joseph Conrad, 1857-1924, (Br.) novelist. *Lord Jim, Heart of Darkness, The Secret Agent*.

Pat Conroy, 1945-2016, (U.S.) novelist. *The Prince of Tides, The Great Santini*.

James Fenimore Cooper, 1789-1851, (U.S.) novelist. *Leatherstocking Tales, The Last of the Mohicans*.

Pierre Corneille, 1606-84, (Fr.) dramatist. *Medée, Le Cid*.

Hart Crane, 1899-1932, (U.S.) poet. "The Bridge."

Stephen Crane, 1871-1900, (U.S.) novelist, short-story writer. *The Red Badge of Courage*, "The Open Boat."

Harry Crews, 1935-2012, (U.S.) novelist. *A Feast of Snakes*.

Michael Crichton, 1942-2008, (U.S.) writer. *The Andromeda Strain, Jurassic Park*.

Countee Cullen, 1903-46, (U.S.) poet, prominent in the Harlem Renaissance of the 1920s. *The Black Christ*.

E. E. Cummings, 1894-1962, (U.S.) poet. *Tulips and Chimneys*.

Roald Dahl, 1916-90, (Br.-U.S.) writer. *Charlie and the Chocolate Factory, James and the Giant Peach*.

Gabriele D'Annunzio, 1863-1938, (It.) poet, novelist, dramatist. *The Child of Pleasure, The Intruder, The Victim*.

Dante Alighieri, 1265-1321, (It.) poet. *The Divine Comedy*.

Robertson Davies, 1913-95, (Can.) novelist, playwright, essayist. Salterton, Deptford, and Cornish trilogies.

Daniel Defoe, 1660-1731, (Br.) writer. *Robinson Crusoe, Moll Flanders, Journal of the Plague Year*.

Philip K. Dick, 1928-82, (U.S.) science-fiction writer. *Do Androids Dream of Electric Sheep?*

Charles Dickens, 1812-70, (Br.) novelist. *David Copperfield, Oliver Twist, Great Expectations, A Tale of Two Cities*.

James Dickey, 1923-97, (U.S.) poet, novelist. *Deliverance*.

Emily Dickinson, 1830-86, (U.S.) poet. "Because I could not stop for Death …," "Success is counted sweetest …"

Isak Dinesen (Karen Blixen), 1885-1962, (Den.) author. *Out of Africa, Seven Gothic Tales, Winter's Tales*.

E(dgar) L(awrence) Doctorow, 1931-2015, (U.S.) novelist. *Ragtime, Billy Bathgate*.

John Donne, 1573-1631, (Br.) poet. *Songs and Sonnets*.

José Donoso, 1924-96, (Chile) surreal novelist and short-story writer. *The Obscene Bird of Night*.

John Dos Passos, 1896-1970, (U.S.) novelist. *U.S.A.*

Fyodor Dostoyevsky, 1821-81, (Russ.) novelist. *Crime and Punishment, The Brothers Karamazov, The Possessed*.

Arthur Conan Doyle, 1859-1930, (Br.) novelist. Sherlock Holmes mystery stories.

Theodore Dreiser, 1871-1945, (U.S.) novelist. *An American Tragedy, Sister Carrie*.

John Dryden, 1631-1700, (Br.) poet, dramatist, critic. *All for Love, Mac Flecknoe, Absalom and Achitophel*.

Alexandre Dumas (père), 1802-70, (Fr.) novelist, dramatist. *The Three Musketeers, The Count of Monte Cristo*.

Alexandre Dumas (fils), 1824-95, (Fr.) dramatist, novelist. *La Dame aux Camélias, Le Demi-Monde*.

Paul Laurence Dunbar, 1872-1906, (U.S.) poet, novelist. *Lyrics of Lowly Life*.

Lawrence Durrell, 1912-90, (Br.) novelist, poet. *Alexandria Quartet*.

Umberto Eco, 1932-2016, (It.) novelist. *The Name of the Rose*.

Ilya G. Ehrenburg, 1891-1967, (Russ.) writer. *The Thaw*.

George Eliot (Mary Ann or Marian Evans), 1819-80, (Br.) novelist. *Silas Marner, Middlemarch*.

T(homas) S(tearns) Eliot, 1888-1965, (Br.) poet, critic. *The Waste Land*, "The Love Song of J. Alfred Prufrock."

Stanley Elkin, 1930-95, (U.S.) novelist, short-story writer. *George Mills*.

Ralph Ellison, 1914-94, (U.S.) writer. *Invisible Man*.

Ralph Waldo Emerson, 1803-82, (U.S.) poet, essayist. "Brahma," "Nature," "The Over-Soul," "Self-Reliance."

James T. Farrell, 1904-79, (U.S.) novelist. *Studs Lonigan*.

Howard Fast, 1914-2003, (U.S.) novelist. *Spartacus, The Immigrants*.

William Faulkner, 1897-1962, (U.S.) novelist. *Sanctuary; Light in August; The Sound and the Fury; Absalom, Absalom!*

Edna Ferber, 1887-1968, (U.S.) novelist, short-story writer, playwright. *So Big, Cimarron, Show Boat*.

Henry Fielding, 1707-54, (Br.) novelist. *Tom Jones*.

F(rancis) Scott Fitzgerald, 1896-1940, (U.S.) short-story writer, novelist. *The Great Gatsby, Tender Is the Night*.

Gustave Flaubert, 1821-80, (Fr.) novelist. *Madame Bovary*.

Ian Fleming, 1908-64, (Br.) novelist. James Bond spy thrillers. *Dr. No, Goldfinger*.

Horton Foote, 1916-2009, (U.S.) playwright, screenwriter. *The Trip to Bountiful*.

Ford Madox Ford, 1873-1939, (Br.) novelist, critic, poet. *The Good Soldier*.

C(ecil) S(cott) Forester, 1899-1966, (Br.) writer. Horatio Hornblower books.

E(dward) M(organ) Forster, 1879-1970, (Br.) novelist. *A Passage to India, Howards End*.

Anatole France, 1844-1924, (Fr.) writer. *Penguin Island, My Friend's Book, The Crime of Sylvestre Bonnard*.

Dick Francis, 1920-2010, (Br.) crime novelist.

Marilyn French, 1929-2009, (U.S.) novelist. *The Women's Room*.

Brian Friel, 1929-2015, (N. Ire.) playwright. *Dancing at Lughnasa*.

Robert Frost, 1874-1963, (U.S.) poet. "Birches," "Fire and Ice," "Stopping by Woods on a Snowy Evening."

Carlos Fuentes, 1928-2012, (Pan.) novelist, essayist. *The Old Gringo*.

William Gaddis, 1922-98, (U.S.) novelist. *The Recognitions*.

Ernest J. Gaines, 1933-2019, (U.S.) novelist. *The Autobiography of Miss Jane Pittman*.

John Galsworthy, 1867-1933, (Br.) novelist, dramatist. *The Forsyte Saga*.

Federico García Lorca, 1898-1936, (Sp.) poet, dramatist. *Blood Wedding*.

Gabriel García Márquez, 1927-2014, (Col.) novelist. *One Hundred Years of Solitude*.

Erle Stanley Gardner, 1889-1970, (U.S.) mystery writer; created Perry Mason.

Jean Genet, 1911-86, (Fr.) playwright, novelist. *The Maids*.

Kahlil Gibran, 1883-1931, (Leban.-U.S.) mystical novelist, essayist, poet. *The Prophet*.

André Gide, 1869-1951, (Fr.) writer. *The Immoralist, The Pastoral Symphony, Strait Is the Gate*.

Allen Ginsberg, 1926-97, (U.S.) Beat poet. "Howl."

Jean Giraudoux, 1882-1944, (Fr.) novelist, dramatist. *Electra, The Madwoman of Chaillot, Ondine, Tiger at the Gate*.

Johann Wolfgang von Goethe, 1749-1832, (Ger.) poet, dramatist, novelist. *Faust, Sorrows of Young Werther*.

Nikolai Gogol, 1809-52, (Russ.) short-story writer, dramatist, novelist. *Dead Souls, The Inspector General*.

William Golding, 1911-93, (Br.) novelist. *Lord of the Flies*.

William Goldman, 1931-2018, (U.S.) novelist, screenwriter. *The Marathon Man, The Princess Bride*.

Oliver Goldsmith, 1728-74, (Br.-Ire.) dramatist, novelist. *The Vicar of Wakefield, She Stoops to Conquer.*

Nadine Gordimer, 1923-2014, (S. Afr.) novelist. *Burger's Daughter.*

Maxim Gorky, 1868-1936, (Russ.) dramatist, novelist. *The Lower Depths.*

Sue Grafton, 1940-2017, (U.S.) crime novelist; created Kinsey Millhone "alphabet mysteries."

Günter Grass, 1927-2015, (Ger.) novelist, poet. *The Tin Drum.*

Shirley Ann Grau, 1929-2020, (U.S.) novelist. *The Keepers of The House.*

Robert Graves, 1895-1985, (Br.) poet, classical scholar, novelist. *I, Claudius; The White Goddess.*

Thomas Gray, 1716-71, (Br.) poet. "Elegy Written in a Country Churchyard," "The Progress of Poesy."

Julien Green, 1900-98, (U.S.-Fr.) expatriate American novelist. *Moira, Each Man in His Darkness.*

Graham Greene, 1904-91, (Br.) novelist. *The Power and the Glory, The Heart of the Matter, The Ministry of Fear.*

Zane Grey, 1872-1939, (U.S.) writer of Western stories.

Jakob Grimm, 1785-1863, philologist, folklorist; with brother **Wilhelm Grimm**, 1786-1859, (both Ger.) collected *Grimm's Fairy Tales.*

Alex Haley, 1921-92, (U.S.) author. *Roots.*

Dashiell Hammett, 1894-1961, (U.S.) detective-story writer; created Sam Spade. *The Maltese Falcon.*

Jupiter Hammon, c. 1720-1800, (U.S.) poet; first African American to have his works published, 1761.

Knut Hamsun, 1859-1952, (Nor.) novelist. *Hunger.*

Lorraine Hansberry, 1930-65, (U.S.) playwright. *A Raisin in the Sun.*

Thomas Hardy, 1840-1928, (Br.) novelist, poet. *The Return of the Native, Tess of the D'Urbervilles, Jude the Obscure.*

E. Lynn Harris, 1955-2009, (U.S.) novelist. *Invisible Life, Basketball Jones.*

Joel Chandler Harris, 1848-1908, (U.S.) writer. *Uncle Remus* stories.

Jim Harrison, 1937-2016, (U.S.) novelist and essayist. *Legends of the Fall.*

Moss Hart, 1904-61, (U.S.) playwright. *Once in a Lifetime, You Can't Take It With You, The Man Who Came to Dinner.*

Bret Harte, 1836-1902, (U.S.) short-story writer, poet. *The Luck of Roaring Camp.*

Jaroslav Hasek, 1883-1923, (Czech.) writer, playwright. *The Good Soldier Schweik.*

Vaclav Havel, 1936-2011, (Czech.) essayist, poet, playwright. *The Power of the Powerless.*

John Hawkes, 1925-98, (U.S.) experimental fiction writer. *The Goose on the Grave, Blood Oranges.*

Nathaniel Hawthorne, 1804-64, (U.S.) novelist, short-story writer. *The Scarlet Letter,* "Young Goodman Brown."

Seamus Heaney, 1939-2013, (Ire.) poet. *Death of a Naturalist.*

Heinrich Heine, 1797-1856, (Ger.) poet. *Book of Songs.*

Robert Heinlein, 1907-88, (U.S.) science-fiction writer. *Stranger in a Strange Land.*

Joseph Heller, 1923-99, (U.S.) novelist. *Catch-22.*

Lillian Hellman, 1905-84, (U.S.) playwright, memoirist. *The Little Foxes, An Unfinished Woman* (autobiography).

Ernest Hemingway, 1899-1961, (U.S.) novelist, short-story writer. *A Farewell to Arms, For Whom the Bell Tolls.*

O. Henry (W.S. Porter), 1862-1910, (U.S.) short-story writer. "The Gift of the Magi."

George Herbert, 1593-1633, (Br.) poet. "The Altar," "Easter Wings."

Zbigniew Herbert, 1924-98, (Pol.) poet. "Apollo and Marsyas."

Robert Herrick, 1591-1674, (Br.) poet. "To the Virgins to Make Much of Time."

John Hersey, 1914-93, (U.S.) novelist, journalist. *Hiroshima, A Bell for Adano.*

Hermann Hesse, 1877-1962, (Ger.) novelist, poet. *Death and the Lover, Steppenwolf, Siddhartha.*

Georgette Heyer, 1902-74, (Br.) Regency romance novelist.

Oscar Hijuelos, 1951-2013, (U.S.) novelist. *The Mambo Kings Play Songs of Love.*

Tony Hillerman, 1925-2008, (U.S.) novelist. *Dance Hall of the Dead.*

James Hilton, 1900-54, (Br.) novelist. *Lost Horizon.*

Chester Himes, 1909-84, (U.S.) novelist. *Cotton Comes to Harlem.*

Oliver Wendell Holmes, 1809-94, (U.S.) poet, novelist. *The Autocrat of the Breakfast-Table.*

Gerard Manley Hopkins, 1844-89, (Br.) poet. "Pied Beauty," "God's Grandeur."

A(lfred) E. Housman, 1859-1936, (Br.) poet. *A Shropshire Lad.*

William Dean Howells, 1837-1920, (U.S.) novelist, critic. *The Rise of Silas Lapham.*

Langston Hughes, 1902-67, (U.S.) poet, lyric writer, author; a major influence in 1920s Harlem Renaissance

Ted Hughes, 1930-98, (Br.) British poet laureate, 1984-98. *Crow.*

Victor Hugo, 1802-85, (Fr.) poet, dramatist, novelist. *Notre Dame de Paris, Les Misérables.*

Zora Neale Hurston, 1891-1960, (U.S.) novelist, folklorist. *Their Eyes Were Watching God, Mules and Men.*

Aldous Huxley, 1894-1963, (Br.) writer. *Brave New World.*

Henrik Ibsen, 1828-1906, (Nor.) dramatist, poet. *A Doll's House, Ghosts, The Wild Duck, Hedda Gabler.*

William Inge, 1913-73, (U.S.) playwright. *Picnic; Bus Stop.*

Eugene Ionesco, 1910-94, (Fr.) surrealist dramatist. *The Bald Soprano, The Chairs.*

Washington Irving, 1783-1859, (U.S.) writer. "Rip Van Winkle," "The Legend of Sleepy Hollow."

Christopher Isherwood, 1904-86, (Br.) novelist, playwright. *The Berlin Stories.*

Shirley Jackson, 1916-65, (U.S.) short-story writer. "The Lottery."

Henry James, 1843-1916, (U.S.) novelist, short-story writer, critic. *The Portrait of a Lady, The Ambassadors, Daisy Miller.*

P(hyllis) D(orothy) James, 1920-2014, (Br.) mystery novelist.

Robinson Jeffers, 1887-1962, (U.S.) poet, dramatist. *Tamar and Other Poems, Medea.*

James Weldon Johnson, 1871-1938, (U.S.) poet, novelist, diplomat; lyricist for *Lift Every Voice and Sing.*

Samuel Johnson, 1709-84, (Br.) author, scholar, critic. *Dictionary of the English Language, Vanity of Human Wishes.*

Ben Jonson, 1572-1637, (Br.) dramatist, poet. *Volpone.*

James Joyce, 1882-1941, (Ire.) writer. *Ulysses, Dubliners, A Portrait of the Artist as a Young Man, Finnegans Wake.*

Ernst Junger, 1895-1998, (Ger.) novelist, essayist. *The Peace, On the Marble Cliff.*

Franz Kafka, 1883-1924, (Austria-Hung./Czech.) novelist, short-story writer. *The Trial, The Castle,* "The Metamorphosis."

George S. Kaufman, 1889-1961, (U.S.) playwright. *The Man Who Came to Dinner, You Can't Take It With You.*

Yasunari Kawabata, 1899-1972, (Jpn.) novelist. *The Sound of the Mountains.*

Nikos Kazantzakis, 1883-1957, (Gr.) novelist. *Zorba the Greek, A Greek Passion.*

Alfred Kazin, 1915-98 (U.S.) author, critic. *On Native Grounds.*

John Keats, 1795-1821, (Br.) poet. "Ode on a Grecian Urn," "Ode to a Nightingale," "La Belle Dame Sans Merci."

Jack Kerouac, 1922-69, (U.S.) author, Beat novelist. *On the Road, The Dharma Bums,* "Mexico City Blues."

Joyce Kilmer, 1886-1918, (U.S.) poet. "Trees."

Galway Kinnell, 1927-2014, (U.S.) poet.

Rudyard Kipling, 1865-1936, (Br.) author, poet. "The White Man's Burden," "Gunga Din," *The Jungle Book.*

Larry Kramer, 1935-2020, (U.S.) playwright. *The Normal Heart.*

Judith Krantz, 1928-2019, (U.S.) novelist. *Scruples.*

Maxine Kumin, 1925-2014, (U.S.) poet, author. *Up Country: Poems of New England.*

Jean de la Fontaine, 1621-95, (Fr.) poet. *Fables choisies* (Selected Fables).

Pär Lagerkvist, 1891-1974, (Swed.) poet, dramatist, novelist. *Barabbas, The Sybil.*

Selma Lagerlöf, 1858-1940, (Swed.) novelist. *Jerusalem, The Ring of the Lowenskolds.*

Alphonse de Lamartine, 1790-1869, (Fr.) poet, novelist, statesman. *Méditations poétiques.*

Charles Lamb, 1775-1834, (Br.) essayist. *Specimens of English Dramatic Poets, Essays of Elia.*

Louis L'Amour, 1908-88, (U.S.) Western author, screenwriter. *Hondo, The Cherokee Trail.*

Giuseppe di Lampedusa, 1896-1957, (It.) novelist. *The Leopard.*

William Langland, c. 1332-1400, (Br.) poet. *Piers Plowman.*

Ring Lardner, 1885-1933, (U.S.) short-story writer, humorist.

Steig Larsson, 1954-2004, (Swed.) novelist. *The Girl With the Dragon Tattoo.*

Arthur Laurents, 1917-2011, (U.S.) playwright and director. *West Side Story.*

D(avid) H(erbert) Lawrence, 1885-1930, (Br.) novelist. *Sons and Lovers, Women in Love, Lady Chatterley's Lover.*

Halldór Laxness, 1902-98, (Iceland) novelist. *Iceland's Bell.*

Harper Lee, 1926-2016, (U.S.) novelist. *To Kill a Mockingbird.*

Ursula K. Le Guin, 1929-2018, (U.S.) science-fiction writer. *The Left Hand of Darkness.*

Madeleine L'Engle, 1918-2007, (U.S.) young-adult novelist. *A Wrinkle in Time.*

Elmore Leonard, 1925-2013, (U.S.) novelist. *Get Shorty.*

Mikhail Lermontov, 1814-41, (Russ.) novelist, poet. "Demon," *Hero of Our Time.*

Alain-René Lesage, 1668-1747, (Fr.) novelist. *Gil Blas de Santillane.*

Doris Lessing, 1919-2013, (Br.) writer. *The Golden Notebook.*

Gotthold Lessing, 1729-81, (Ger.) dramatist, philosopher, critic. *Miss Sara Sampson, Minna von Barnhelm.*

Ira Levin, 1929-2007, (U.S.) novelist, playwright. *Deathtrap, Rosemary's Baby.*

C(live) S(taples) Lewis, 1898-1963, (Br.) critic, novelist, religious writer. *Allegory of Love; The Lion, the Witch and the Wardrobe; Out of the Silent Planet.*

Sinclair Lewis, 1885-1951, (U.S.) novelist. *Babbitt, Main Street, Dodsworth.*

Li Po, 701-762, (China) poet. "Song Before Drinking," "She Spins Silk."

Vachel Lindsay, 1879-1931, (U.S.) poet. *General William Booth Enters Into Heaven, The Congo.*

Hugh Lofting, 1886-1947, (Br.) writer. Dr. Doolittle series.

Jack London, 1876-1916, (U.S.) novelist, journalist. *Call of the Wild, The Sea-Wolf, White Fang.*

Henry Wadsworth Longfellow, 1807-82, (U.S.) poet. *Evangeline, The Song of Hiawatha.*

Lope de Vega, 1562-1635, (Sp.) playwright. *Noche de San Juan, Maestro de Danzar.*

H(oward) P(hillips) Lovecraft, 1890-1937, (U.S.) novelist, short-story writer. "At the Mountains of Madness."

Amy Lowell, 1874-1925, (U.S.) poet, critic. "Lilacs."

James Russell Lowell, 1819-91, (U.S.) poet, editor. *Poems, The Biglow Papers.*

Robert Lowell, 1917-77, (U.S.) poet. "Lord Weary's Castle."

Joaquim Maria Machado de Assis, 1839-1908, (Brazil) novelist, poet. *The Posthumous Memoirs of Bras Cubas.*

Archibald MacLeish, 1892-1982, (U.S.) poet. *Conquistador.*

Naguib Mahfouz, 1911-2006, (Egypt) novelist; first Arabic-language writer to win the Nobel Prize for Literature. *Cairo Trilogy.*

Norman Mailer, 1923-2007, (U.S.) novelist, essayist, journalist. *The Naked and the Dead.*

Bernard Malamud, 1914-86, (U.S.) short-story writer, novelist. "The Magic Barrel," *The Assistant, The Fixer.*

Stéphane Mallarmé, 1842-98, (Fr.) poet. *Poésies.*

Thomas Malory, c. 1410-71, (Br.) writer. *Morte d'Arthur.*

Andre Malraux, 1901-76, (Fr.) novelist. *Man's Fate.*

Osip Mandelstam, 1891-1938, (Russ.) poet. *Stone, Tristia.*

Thomas Mann, 1875-1955, (Ger.) novelist, essayist. *Buddenbrooks, The Magic Mountain,* "Death in Venice."

Katherine Mansfield, 1888-1923, (Br.) short-story writer. "Bliss."

Christopher Marlowe, 1564-93, (Br.) dramatist, poet. *Tamburlaine the Great, Dr. Faustus, The Jew of Malta.*

Andrew Marvell, 1621-78, (Br.) poet. "To His Coy Mistress."

John Masefield, 1878-1967, (Br.) poet. "Sea Fever," "Cargoes," *Salt Water Ballads.*

Edgar Lee Masters, 1869-1950, (U.S.) poet, biographer. *Spoon River Anthology.*

Peter Matthiessen, 1927-2014, (U.S.) novelist. *The Snow Leopard.*

W(illiam) Somerset Maugham, 1874-1965, (Br.) author. *Of Human Bondage, The Moon and Sixpence.*

Guy de Maupassant, 1850-93, (Fr.) novelist, short-story writer. "A Life," "Bel-Ami," "The Necklace."

François Mauriac, 1885-1970, (Fr.) novelist, dramatist. *Viper's Tangle, The Kiss to the Leper.*

Vladimir Mayakovsky, 1893-1930, (Russ.) poet, dramatist. *The Cloud in Trousers.*

Mary McCarthy, 1912-89, (U.S.) critic, novelist, memoirist. *Memories of a Catholic Girlhood.*

Frank McCourt, 1930-2009, (U.S.) memoirist. *Angela's Ashes, 'Tis.*

Carson McCullers, 1917-67, (U.S.) novelist. *The Heart Is a Lonely Hunter, Member of the Wedding.*

Colleen McCullough, 1937-2015, (Austral.) novelist. *The Thorn Birds.*

Terrence McNally, 1939-2020, (U.S.) playwright. *Love! Valour! Compassion!*

Herman Melville, 1819-91, (U.S.) novelist, poet. *Moby-Dick, Typee, Billy Budd, Omoo.*

George Meredith, 1828-1909, (Br.) novelist, poet. *The Ordeal of Richard Feverel, The Egoist.*

Prosper Mérimée, 1803-70, (Fr.) author. *Carmen.*

James Merrill, 1926-95, (U.S.) poet. *Divine Comedies.*

W(illiam) S(tanley) Merwin, 1927-2019, (U.S.) poet. *The Lice.*

James Michener, 1907-97, (U.S.) novelist. *Tales of the South Pacific.*

Edna St. Vincent Millay, 1892-1950, (U.S.) poet. *The Harp Weaver and Other Poems.*

Arthur Miller, 1915-2005, (U.S.) playwright. *The Crucible, After the Fall, Death of a Salesman.*

Henry Miller, 1891-1980, (U.S.) novelist. *Tropic of Cancer.*

A(lan) A(lexander) Milne, 1882-1956, (Br.) author. *Winnie-the-Pooh.*

Czeslaw Milosz, 1911-2004, (Pol.) essayist, poet. "Esse," "Encounter."

John Milton, 1608-74, (Br.) poet, writer. *Paradise Lost, Comus, Lycidas, Areopagitica.*

Mishima Yukio (Hiraoka Kimitake) 1925-70, (Jpn.) writer. *Confessions of a Mask.*

Gabriela Mistral, 1889-1957, (Chile) poet. *Sonnets of Death.*

Margaret Mitchell, 1900-49, (U.S.) novelist. *Gone With the Wind.*

Jean Baptiste Molière, 1622-73, (Fr.) dramatist. *Tartuffe, Le Misanthrope, Le Bourgeois Gentilhomme.*

Ferenc Molnár, 1878-1952, (Hung.) dramatist, novelist. *Liliom, The Guardsman, The Swan.*

Michel de Montaigne, 1533-92, (Fr.) essayist. *Essais.*

Eugenio Montale, 1896-1981, (It.) poet.

Brian Moore, 1921-99, (Ire.-U.S.) novelist. *The Lonely Passion of Judith Hearne.*

Clement C. Moore, 1779-1863, (U.S.) poet, educator. "A Visit From Saint Nicholas."

Marianne Moore, 1887-1972, (U.S.) poet.

Alberto Moravia, 1907-90, (It.) novelist, short-story writer. *The Time of Indifference.*

Thomas More, 1478-1535, (Br.) writer, statesman, saint. *Utopia.*

Wright Morris, 1910-98, (U.S.) novelist. *My Uncle Dudley.*

Toni Morrison, 1931-2019, (U.S.) novelist. *Song of Solomon, Beloved.*

Bharati Mukherjee, 1940-2017, (India-U.S.) novelist, short-story writer. *Jasmine.*

Murasaki Shikibu, c. 978-1026, (Jpn.) novelist. *The Tale of Genji.*

Iris Murdoch, 1919-99, (Br.) novelist, philosopher. *The Sea, the Sea.*

Alfred de Musset, 1810-57, (Fr.) poet, dramatist. *La Confession d'un Enfant du Siècle.*

Vladimir Nabokov, 1899-1977, (Russ.-U.S.) novelist. *Lolita, Pale Fire.*

V. S. Naipaul, 1932-2018, (Trinidad) novelist, travel writer. *A House for Mr. Biswas.*

R. K. Narayan, 1906-2001, (India) novelist. *The Guide.*

Ogden Nash, 1902-71, (U.S.) poet of light verse.

Irène Némirovsky, 1903-42, (Ukraine) novelist. *David Golder, Suite Française.*

Pablo Neruda, 1904-73, (Chile) poet. *Twenty Love Poems and One Song of Despair, Toward the Splendid City.*

Patrick O'Brian, 1914-2000, (Br.) historical novelist. *Master and Commander, Blue at the Mizzen.*

Sean O'Casey, 1884-1964, (Ire.) dramatist. *Juno and the Paycock, The Plough and the Stars.*

Flannery O'Connor, 1925-64, (U.S.) novelist, short-story writer. *Wise Blood,* "A Good Man Is Hard to Find."

Frank O'Connor (Michael Donovan), 1903-66, (Ire.) short-story writer. "Guests of a Nation."

Clifford Odets, 1906-63, (U.S.) playwright. *Waiting for Lefty, Awake and Sing, Golden Boy, The Country Girl.*

John O'Hara, 1905-70, (U.S.) novelist, short-story writer. *From the Terrace, Appointment in Samarra, Pal Joey.*

Omar Khayyam, c. 1028-1122, (Per.) poet. *Rubaiyat.*

Eugene O'Neill, 1888-1953, (U.S.) playwright. *Emperor Jones, Anna Christie, Long Day's Journey Into Night.*

George Orwell (Eric Arthur Blair), 1903-50, (Br.) novelist, essayist. *Animal Farm, Nineteen Eighty-Four.*

John Osborne, 1929-95, (Br.) dramatist, novelist. *Look Back in Anger, The Entertainer.*

Wilfred Owen, 1893-1918, (Br.) poet. "Dulce et Décorum Est."

Grace Paley, 1922-2007, (U.S.) short-story writer, poet. *The Little Disturbances of Man.*

Dorothy Parker, 1893-1967, (U.S.) short-story writer, poet. *Enough Rope, Laments for the Living.*

Robert B. Parker, 1932-2010, (U.S.) crime novelist. "Spenser" novels.

Boris Pasternak, 1890-1960, (Russ.) poet, novelist. *Doctor Zhivago.*

Alan Paton, 1903-88, (S. Africa) novelist. *Cry, the Beloved Country.*

Octavio Paz, 1914-98, (Mex.) poet, essayist. *The Labyrinth of Solitude, They Shall Not Pass!, The Sun Stone.*

Samuel Pepys, 1633-1703, (Br.) public official, diarist.

S(idney) J(oseph) Perelman, 1904-79, (U.S.) humorist. *The Road to Miltown, Under the Spreading Atrophy.*

Charles Perrault, 1628-1703, (Fr.) writer. *Tales From Mother Goose (Sleeping Beauty, Cinderella).*

Petrarch (Francesco Petrarca), 1304-74, (It.) poet. *Africa, Trionfi, Canzoniere.*

Harold Pinter, 1930-2008, (Br.) playwright. *The Birthday Party, The Caretaker, The Homecoming.*

Luigi Pirandello, 1867-1936, (It.) novelist, dramatist. *Six Characters in Search of an Author.*

Sylvia Plath, 1932-63, (U.S.) author, poet. *The Bell Jar, The Colossus.*

Edgar Allan Poe, 1809-49, (U.S.) poet, short-story writer, critic. "Annabel Lee," "The Raven," "The Purloined Letter."

Alexander Pope, 1688-1744, (Br.) poet. *The Rape of the Lock, The Dunciad, An Essay on Man.*

Katherine Anne Porter, 1890-1980, (U.S.) novelist, short-story writer. *Ship of Fools.*

Chaim Potok, 1929-2002, (U.S.) novelist. *The Chosen.*

Ezra Pound, 1885-1972, (U.S.) poet. *Cantos.*

Anthony Powell, 1905-2000, (Br.) novelist. *A Dance to the Music of Time* series.

Terry Pratchett, 1948-2015, (Br.) fantasy novelist. *Discworld* series.

Reynolds Price, 1933-2011, (U.S.) novelist, short-story writer, poet. *A Long and Happy Life.*

J(ohn) B(oynton) Priestley, 1894-1984, (Br.) novelist, dramatist. *The Good Companions.*

Marcel Proust, 1871-1922, (Fr.) novelist. *Remembrance of Things Past.*

Aleksandr Pushkin, 1799-1837, (Russ.) poet, novelist. *Boris Godunov, Eugene Onegin.*

Mario Puzo, 1920-99, (U.S.) novelist. *The Godfather.*

François Rabelais, 1495-1553, (Fr.) writer. *Gargantua.*

Jean Racine, 1639-99, (Fr.) dramatist. *Andromaque, Phèdre, Bérénice, Britannicus.*

David Rakoff, 1964-2012, (Can.-U.S.) essayist. *Fraud, Don't Get Too Comfortable.*

Ayn Rand, 1905-82, (Russ.-U.S.) novelist, moral theorist. *The Fountainhead, Atlas Shrugged.*

Terence Rattigan, 1911-77, (Br.) playwright. *Separate Tables, The Browning Version.*

Erich Maria Remarque, 1898-1970, (Ger.-U.S.) novelist. *All Quiet on the Western Front.*

Mary Renault, 1905-83, (Br.) novelist. *The Last of the Wine.*

Ruth Rendell, 1930-2015, (Br.) novelist. Chief Inspector Reginald Wexford mysteries.

Adrienne Rich, 1929-2012, (U.S.) poet. *Diving Into the Wreck: Poems, 1971-1972.*

Samuel Richardson, 1689-1761, (Br.) novelist. *Pamela; or Virtue Rewarded.*

Rainer Maria Rilke, 1875-1926, (Ger.) poet. *Life and Songs, Duino Elegies, Poems From the Book of Hours.*

Arthur Rimbaud, 1854-91, (Fr.) poet. *A Season in Hell.*

Harold Robbins, 1916-97, (U.S.) novelist. *The Carpetbaggers.*

Edwin Arlington Robinson, 1869-1935, (U.S.) poet. "Richard Cory," "Miniver Cheevy," *Merlin.*

Theodore Roethke, 1908-63, (U.S.) poet. *Open House, The Waking, The Far Field.*

Romain Rolland, 1866-1944, (Fr.) novelist, biographer. *Jean-Christophe.*

Pierre de Ronsard, 1524-85, (Fr.) poet. *Sonnets pour Hélène, La Franciade.*

Christina Rossetti, 1830-94, (Br.) poet. "When I Am Dead, My Dearest."

Dante Gabriel Rossetti, 1828-82, (Br.) poet, painter. "The Blessed Damozel."

YEAR *in* PICTURES

RELIEF NEEDED Local food banks and pantries saw a surge in demand in spring 2020, as family resources were stretched thin amid the coronavirus pandemic and related shutdowns.

ESSENTIAL WORK In spite of lockdown measures to prevent COVID-19 spread in spring 2020, millions of workers continued to perform essential jobs.

HOME SCHOOLING Educators, children, and parents confronted a new normal, after schoolwork for many moved online as schools closed to impede the spread of COVID-19 beginning in Mar. 2020.

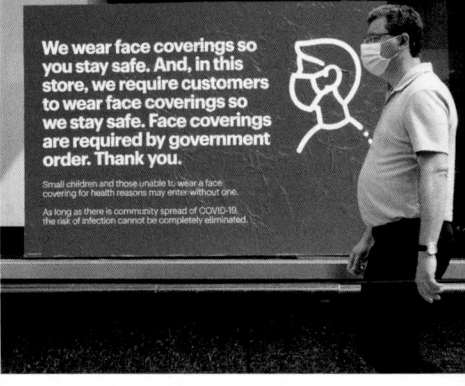

We wear face coverings so you stay safe. And, in this store, we require customers to wear face coverings so we stay safe. Face coverings are required by government order. Thank you.

Small children and those unable to wear a face covering for health reasons may enter without one.

As long as there is community spread of COVID-19, the risk of infection cannot be completely eliminated.

A NEW NORMAL By Apr. 2020, local public health officials and the CDC encouraged mask-wearing to prevent the spread of the coronavirus.

OPEN UP Protesters voiced demands beginning in Apr. 2020 for an end to COVID-19-related shutdown measures, such as business and church closures.

BEARING WITNESS The May 25, 2020, death of George Floyd after a white police officer kneeled on his neck transfomed the Minneapolis resident into a symbol of racial injustice and the need for change.

FORCE TO RECKON WITH The use of federal agents in response to ongoing protests against racial inequality in Portland, OR, drew criticism in July 2020, including from Portland's mayor and the state's governor.

BLACK LIVES MATTER Spurred by the deaths of George Floyd, Breonna Taylor, and other Black men and women in dealings with police, mostly peaceful protests peaked nationwide in June 2020, calling for an end to systemic racism, especially in policing.

NATIONAL

HISTORIC TICKET Sen. Kamala Harris (CA) made her first appearance as part of former Vice Pres. Joe Biden's Democratic ticket Aug. 12, 2020, in Delaware; Harris was the first Black woman to be nominated on the presidential ticket for a major party.

VERDICT IN The U.S. Senate Feb. 5, 2020, formally acquitted Pres. Trump on two articles of impeachment related to his dealings with Ukraine.

HOME FREE
Pres. Trump July 10, 2020, commuted the sentence of longtime political operative Roger Stone, who had been convicted on seven felony charges related to obstructing a congressional inquiry into the 2016 presidential campaign.

PANDEMIC AT THE WHITE HOUSE On Oct. 2, 2020, the world learned that Pres. Donald Trump had tested positive for COVID-19, along with the first lady and many others in their orbit.

SNAIL MAIL With millions of Americans expected to vote by mail in Nov. 2020 elections, mail slowdowns and policy changes at the USPS became a major concern by late summer.

MAKE HISTORY Confederate statues and monuments were targeted for protest as symbols of systemic racism during ongoing protests in summer 2020; many states and municipalities ordered statues dismantled or removed.

SUPREME TRANSITION The Sept. 18, 2020, death of long-serving U.S. Supreme Court Associate Justice Ruth Bader Ginsburg sparked tributes and speculation over the confirmation battle to follow.

WESTERN BLAZES Multiple wildfires ravaged parts of California, Oregon, and Washington in a record-setting fire season that began in late summer 2020, as scientists called worsening fire trends a symptom of climate change.

WORLD

GROUND ZERO A deadly new coronavirus emerged first in China in late 2019, and the country responded with extreme lockdown and other measures, even as a global pandemic had already been sparked.

MISSION ACCOMPLISHED More than three years after UK voters chose "Brexit" in a referendum, the UK officially left the EU on Jan. 31, 2020.

ECO DISASTER Australian wildfires that began in late 2019 and stretched into 2020 killed some 1.25 bil animals and scorched 46 mil acres by Mar. 2020.

TARGETED STRIKE A U.S. drone attack in Baghdad, Iraq, killed Iranian Gen. Qassem Soleimani on Jan. 3, 2020.

DISSENT IN RUSSIA Protesters in Khabarovsk rallied in support of the region's former governor, arrested July 9, 2020, even as reforms passed that would allow Russian Pres. Vladimir Putin to stay in power until 2036.

NEW IRAQ LEADERSHIP Months of anti-government protests in Iraq forced the appointment of a new prime minister, Mustafa al-Kadhimi, May 7, 2020.

STRANGE BEDFELLOWS After a long stalemate that included three separate elections, Israeli political rivals Benjamin Netanyahu and Benny Gantz were sworn in May 17, 2020, having agreed to form an unconventional, power-sharing government.

HONG KONG CRACKDOWN China's parliament June 30, 2020, unanimously passed a controversial new security law for Hong Kong, the site of months of major pro-democracy protests.

AVOIDABLE DISASTER A major explosion Aug. 4, 2020, in Beirut, Lebanon, killed some 200 people and injured more than 6,000 others; investigators blamed faulty storage of tons of explosive ammonium nitrate at a portside warehouse.

GRIM DEATH TOLL Behind the United States, Brazil led the world in COVID-19 deaths, according to WHO data, by Sept. 2020.

VOICE VOTE Daily demonstrations in Minsk, Belarus, challenged the result of elections held Aug. 9, 2020, in which Pres. Aleksandr Lukashenko was reelected with 80 percent of the vote.

END OF AN ERA Prime Min. Shinzo Abe, Japan's longest-serving prime minister, announced Aug. 28, 2020, that he would resign over health concerns.

Edmond Rostand, 1868-1918, (Fr.) poet, dramatist. *Cyrano de Bergerac.*
Philip Roth, 1933-2018, (U.S.) novelist. *Portnoy's Complaint.*
Damon Runyon, 1880-1946, (U.S.) short-story writer, journalist. *Guys and Dolls, Blue Plate Special.*
John Ruskin, 1819-1900, (Br.) critic, social theorist. *Modern Painters, The Seven Lamps of Architecture.*
Oliver Sacks, 1933-2015, (Br.) neurologist, writer. *The Man Who Mistook His Wife for a Hat.*
François de Saint-Exupéry, 1900-44, (Fr.) writer. *Wind, Sand and Stars; The Little Prince.*
Saki (or H[ector] H[ugh] Munro), 1870-1916, (Br.) writer. *The Chronicles of Clovis.*
J. D. Salinger, 1919-2010, (U.S.) novelist. *The Catcher in the Rye.*
George Sand (Amandine Lucie Aurore Dupin), 1804-76, (Fr.) novelist. *Indiana, Consuelo.*
Carl Sandburg, 1878-1967, (U.S.) poet. *The People, Yes; Chicago Poems; Smoke and Steel; Harvest Poems.*
José Saramago, 1922-2010, (Port.) novelist. *Blindness.*
William Saroyan, 1908-81, (U.S.) playwright, novelist. *The Time of Your Life, The Human Comedy.*
Nathalie Sarraute, 1900-99, (Fr.) Nouveau Roman novelist. *Tropismes.*
May Sarton, 1914-95, (Belg.-U.S.) poet, novelist. *Encounter in April, Anger.*
Dorothy L. Sayers, 1893-1957, (Br.) mystery writer; created Lord Peter Wimsey.
Richard Scarry, 1920-94, (U.S.) author of children's books. *Richard Scarry's Best Story Book Ever.*
Friedrich von Schiller, 1759-1805, (Ger.) dramatist, poet, historian. *Don Carlos, Maria Stuart, Wilhelm Tell.*
Walter Scott, 1771-1832, (Scot.) novelist, poet. *Ivanhoe.*
Gil Scott-Heron, 1949-2011, (U.S.) poet. "The Revolution Will Not Be Televised."
Jaroslav Seifert, 1902-86, (Czech.) poet.
Maurice Sendak, 1928-2012, (U.S.) children's book author and illustrator. *Where the Wild Things Are.*
Dr. Seuss (Theodor Seuss Geisel), 1904-91, (U.S.) children's book author and illustrator. *The Cat in the Hat.*
William Shakespeare, 1564-1616, (Br.) dramatist, poet. *Romeo and Juliet, Hamlet, King Lear, Julius Caesar,* sonnets.
Karl Shapiro, 1913-2000, (U.S.) poet. "Elegy for a Dead Soldier."
George Bernard Shaw, 1856-1950, (Ire.-Br.) playwright, critic. *St. Joan, Pygmalion, Major Barbara, Man and Superman.*
Sidney Sheldon, 1917-2007, (U.S.) screenwriter, novelist. *Rage of Angels, Memories of Midnight.*
Mary Wollstonecraft Shelley, 1797-1851, (Br.) novelist, feminist. *Frankenstein, The Last Man.*
Percy Bysshe Shelley, 1792-1822, (Br.) poet. *Prometheus Unbound, Adonais,* "Ode to the West Wind," "To a Skylark."
Sam Shepard, 1943-2017, (U.S.) playwright. *Buried Child, True West.*
Richard B. Sheridan, 1751-1816, (Br.) dramatist. *The Rivals, School for Scandal.*
Robert Sherwood, 1896-1955, (U.S.) playwright, biographer. *The Petrified Forest, Abe Lincoln in Illinois.*
Mikhail Sholokhov, 1906-84, (Russ.) writer. *The Silent Don.*
Anne Rivers Siddons, 1936-2019, (U.S.) novelist. *Peachtree Road.*
Shel Silverstein, 1932-99, (U.S.) poet, writer. *The Giving Tree, Where the Sidewalk Ends.*
Georges Simenon (Georges Sims), 1903-89, (Belg.-Fr.) mystery writer; created Inspector Maigret.
Neil Simon, 1927-2018, (U.S.) playwright. *The Odd Couple, Brighton Beach Memoirs.*
Upton Sinclair, 1878-1968, (U.S.) novelist. *The Jungle.*

Isaac Bashevis Singer, 1904-91, (Pol.-U.S.) novelist, short-story writer, in Yiddish. *The Magician of Lublin.*
C(harles) P(ercy) Snow, 1905-80, (Br.) novelist, scientist. *Strangers and Brothers, Corridors of Power.*
Aleksandr Solzhenitsyn, 1918-2008, (Russ.) novelist, dramatist. *One Day in the Life of Ivan Denisovich.*
Susan Sontag, 1933-2004, (U.S.) critic, essayist, novelist. *Notes on Camp, The Volcano Lover, In America.*
Stephen Spender, 1909-95, (Br.) poet, critic, novelist. *Twenty Poems,* "Elegy for Margaret."
Edmund Spenser, 1552-99, (Br.) poet. *The Faerie Queene.*
Mickey Spillane, 1918-2006, (U.S.) novelist; Mike Hammer detective novels. *The Killing Man.*
Johanna Spyri, 1827-1901, (Switz.) children's author. *Heidi.*
Christina Stead, 1903-83, (Austral.) novelist, short-story writer. *The Man Who Loved Children.*
Richard Steele, 1672-1729, (Br.) essayist, playwright; began the *Tatler* and *Spectator. The Conscious Lovers.*
Gertrude Stein, 1874-1946, (U.S.) writer. *Three Lives.*
John Steinbeck, 1902-68, (U.S.) novelist. *The Grapes of Wrath, Of Mice and Men, The Winter of Our Discontent.*
Stendhal (Marie Henri Beyle), 1783-1842, (Fr.) novelist. *The Red and the Black, The Charterhouse of Parma.*
Laurence Sterne, 1713-68, (Br.) novelist. *Tristram Shandy.*
Wallace Stevens, 1879-1955, (U.S.) poet. *Harmonium, The Man With the Blue Guitar, Notes Toward a Supreme Fiction.*
Robert Louis Stevenson, 1850-94, (Br.) novelist, poet, essayist. *Treasure Island, A Child's Garden of Verses.*
Mary Stewart, 1916-2014, (Br.) novelist. *Merlin* trilogy.
Bram Stoker, 1847-1912, (Br.) writer. *Dracula.*
Rex Stout, 1886-1975, (U.S.) mystery writer; created Nero Wolfe.
Harriet Beecher Stowe, 1811-96, (U.S.) novelist. *Uncle Tom's Cabin.*
Lytton Strachey, 1880-1932, (Br.) biographer, critic. *Eminent Victorians, Queen Victoria, Elizabeth and Essex.*
Mark Strand, 1934-2014, (Can.-U.S.) poet. *Blizzard of One.*
August Strindberg, 1849-1912, (Swed.) dramatist, novelist. *The Father, Miss Julie, The Creditors.*
William Styron, 1925-2006, (U.S.) novelist, essayist. *The Confessions of Nat Turner, Sophie's Choice, Darkness Visible: A Memoir of Madness.*
Jonathan Swift, 1667-1745, (Br.) satirist, poet. *Gulliver's Travels,* "A Modest Proposal."
Algernon C. Swinburne, 1837-1909, (Br.) poet, dramatist. *Atalanta in Calydon.*
John M. Synge, 1871-1909, (Ire.) poet, dramatist. *Riders to the Sea, The Playboy of the Western World.*
Wislawa Szymborska, 1923-2012, (Pol.) poet. "Cat in an Empty Apartment."
Rabindranath Tagore, 1861-1941, (India) author, poet. *Sadhana, The Realization of Life, Gitanjali.*
Booth Tarkington, 1869-1946, (U.S.) novelist. *The Magnificent Ambersons.*
Peter Taylor, 1917-94, (U.S.) novelist. *A Summons to Memphis.*
Sara Teasdale, 1884-1933, (U.S.) poet. *Helen of Troy and Other Poems, Rivers to the Sea.*
Alfred, Lord Tennyson, 1809-92, (Br.) poet. *Idylls of the King, In Memoriam,* "The Charge of the Light Brigade."
William Makepeace Thackeray, 1811-63, (Br.) novelist. *Vanity Fair, Henry Esmond, Pendennis.*
Dylan Thomas, 1914-53, (Wales) poet. *Under Milk Wood, A Child's Christmas in Wales.*
Hunter S. Thompson, 1937-2005, (U.S.) author, journalist. *Hell's Angels, Fear and Loathing in Las Vegas.*

Henry David Thoreau, 1817-62, (U.S.) writer, philosopher, naturalist. *Walden,* "Civil Disobedience."
James Thurber, 1894-1961, (U.S.) humorist. "The Secret Life of Walter Mitty," *My Life and Hard Times.*
J(ohn) R(onald) R(euel) Tolkien, 1892-1973, (Br.) writer. *The Hobbit, Lord of the Rings* trilogy.
Leo Tolstoy, 1828-1910, (Russ.) novelist, short-story writer. *War and Peace, Anna Karenina,* "The Death of Ivan Ilyich."
Lionel Trilling, 1905-75, (U.S.) critic, author. *The Liberal Imagination.*
Anthony Trollope, 1815-82, (Br.) novelist. *The Warden, Barchester Towers,* the Palliser novels.
Ivan Turgenev, 1818-83, (Russ.) novelist, short-story writer. *Fathers and Sons, First Love, A Month in the Country.*
Amos Tutuola, 1920-97, (Nigeria) novelist. *The Palm-Wine Drunkard, My Life in the Bush of Ghosts.*
Mark Twain (Samuel Clemens), 1835-1910, (U.S.) novelist, humorist. *The Adventures of Huckleberry Finn.*
Sigrid Undset, 1881-1949, (Nor.) novelist. *Kristin Lavransdatter.*
John Updike, 1932-2009, (U.S.) novelist, literary critic. *Rabbit Is Rich, The Witches of Eastwick.*
Paul Valéry, 1871-1945, (Fr.) poet, critic. *La Jeune Parque, The Graveyard by the Sea.*
Paul Verlaine, 1844-96, (Fr.) Symbolist poet. *Songs Without Words.*
Jules Verne, 1828-1905, (Fr.) novelist. *Twenty Thousand Leagues Under the Sea.*
Gore Vidal, 1925-2012, (U.S.) novelist. *The City and the Pillar.*
François Villon, 1431-c. 1463, (Fr.) poet. *The Lays, The Grand Testament.*
Voltaire (F. M. Arouet), 1694-1778, (Fr.) writer of "philosophical romances"; philosopher, historian. *Candide.*
Kurt Vonnegut Jr., 1922-2007, (U.S.) novelist, essayist. *Cat's Cradle, Slaughterhouse-Five, Breakfast of Champions.*
Derek Walcott, 1930-2016, (St. Lucia) poet. "Omeros."
David Foster Wallace, 1962-2008, (U.S.) novelist, essayist. *Infinite Jest, A Supposedly Fun Thing I'll Never Do Again.*
Robert Penn Warren, 1905-89, (U.S.) novelist, poet, critic. *All the King's Men.*
Wendy Wasserstein, 1950-2006, (U.S.) playwright. *The Heidi Chronicles.*
Evelyn Waugh, 1903-66, (Br.) novelist. *The Loved One, Brideshead Revisited, A Handful of Dust.*
H(erbert) G(eorge) Wells, 1866-1946, (Br.) novelist. *The Time Machine, The Invisible Man, The War of the Worlds.*
Eudora Welty, 1909-2001, (U.S.) Southern short-story writer, novelist. "Why I Live at the P.O.," "The Ponder Heart."
Rebecca West, 1893-1983, (Br.) novelist, critic, journalist. *Black Lamb and Grey Falcon.*
Edith Wharton, 1862-1937, (U.S.) novelist. *The Age of Innocence, The House of Mirth, Ethan Frome.*
Phillis Wheatley, c. 1753-84, (U.S.) poet; 2nd American woman and first Black woman to be published, 1770.
E(lwyn) B(rooks) White, 1899-1985, (U.S.) essayist, novelist. *Charlotte's Web, Stuart Little.*
Patrick White, 1912-90, (Austral.) novelist. *The Tree of Man.*
T(erence) H(anbury) White, 1906-64, (Br.) author. *The Once and Future King, A Book of Beasts.*
Walt Whitman, 1819-92, (U.S.) poet. *Leaves of Grass.*
John Greenleaf Whittier, 1807-92, (U.S.) poet, journalist. *Snow-Bound.*
Elie Wiesel, 1928-2016, (Rom.) memoirist, novelist. *Night.*
Oscar Wilde, 1854-1900, (Ire.) novelist, playwright. *The Picture of Dorian Gray, The Importance of Being Earnest.*
Laura Ingalls Wilder, 1867-1957, (U.S.) novelist. *Little House on the Prairie* series of children's books.

Thornton Wilder, 1897-1975, (U.S.) playwright. *Our Town*, *The Skin of Our Teeth*, *The Matchmaker*.

Tennessee Williams, 1911-83, (U.S.) playwright. *A Streetcar Named Desire*, *Cat on a Hot Tin Roof*, *The Glass Menagerie*.

William Carlos Williams, 1883-1963, (U.S.) poet, physician. *The Tempers*, *Al Que Quiere! Paterson*, "This Is Just to Say."

Edmund Wilson, 1895-1972, (U.S.) critic, novelist. *Axel's Castle*, *To the Finland Station*.

Lanford Wilson, 1937-2011, (U.S.) playwright. *Talley's Folly*, *Fifth of July*.

P(elham) G(renville) Wodehouse, 1881-1975, (Br.-U.S.) humorist. Jeeves novels, *Anything Goes*.

Thomas Wolfe, 1900-38, (U.S.) novelist, journalist. *Look Homeward, Angel*; *You Can't Go Home Again*.

Tom Wolfe, 1930-2018, (U.S.) novelist, journalist. *Bonfire of the Vanities*, *The Right Stuff*.

Virginia Woolf, 1882-1941, (Br.) novelist, essayist. *Mrs. Dalloway*, *To the Lighthouse*, *A Room of One's Own*.

William Wordsworth, 1770-1850, (Br.) poet. "Tintern Abbey," "Ode: Intimations of Immortality," *The Prelude*.

Herman Wouk, 1915-2019, (U.S.) novelist. *The Caine Mutiny*.

Richard Wright, 1908-60, (U.S.) novelist, short-story writer. *Native Son*, *Black Boy*, *Uncle Tom's Children*.

Elinor Wylie, 1885-1928, (U.S.) poet. *Nets to Catch the Wind*.

William Butler Yeats, 1865-1939, (Ire.) poet, playwright. "The Second Coming," *The Wild Swans at Coole*.

Frank Yerby, 1916-91, (U.S.) first best-selling African American novelist. *The Foxes of Harrow*.

Yevgeny Yevtushenko, 1933-2017, (Russ.) poet. "Babi Yar."

Émile Zola, 1840-1902, (Fr.) novelist. *Nana*, *Thérèse Raquin*.

Poets Laureate

In England, Henry III (1216-72) reportedly had a Versificator Regis, or King's Poet, paid 100 shillings per year. Other poets said to have filled the role of poet laureate include Geoffrey Chaucer (d 1400), Edmund Spenser (d 1599), Ben Jonson (d 1637), and William d'Avenant (d 1668). The first official English poet laureate was John Dryden, appointed 1668, for life. Then came Thomas Shadwell, in 1689; Nahum Tate, 1692; Nicholas Rowe, 1715; Rev. Laurence Eusden, 1718; Colley Cibber, 1730; William Whitehead, 1757; Rev. Thomas Warton, 1785; Henry James Pye, 1790; Robert Southey, 1813; William Wordsworth, 1843; Alfred, Lord Tennyson, 1850; Alfred Austin, 1896; Robert Bridges, 1913; John Masefield, 1930; C. Day Lewis, 1968; John Betjeman,

1972; Ted Hughes, 1984; Andrew Motion, 1999; Carol Ann Duffy, 2009; and Simon Armitage, 2019.

In the U.S., appointment is by the Librarian of Congress to a term of one year, which may be renewed: Robert Penn Warren, appointed 1986; Richard Wilbur, 1987; Howard Nemerov, 1988; Mark Strand, 1990; Joseph Brodsky, 1991; Mona Van Duyn, 1992; Rita Dove, 1993; Robert Hass, 1995; Robert Pinsky, 1997; Stanley Kunitz, 2000; Billy Collins, 2001; Louise Glück, 2003; Ted Kooser, 2004; Donald Hall, 2006; Charles Simic, 2007; Kay Ryan, 2008; W. S. Merwin, 2010; Philip Levine, 2011; Natasha Trethewey, 2012; Charles Wright, 2014; Juan Felipe Herrera, 2015; Tracy K. Smith, 2017; Joy Harjo, 2019.

Composers of Classical and Avant-Garde Music

John Adams, b 1947, (U.S.) *Nixon in China*, *The Death of Klinghoffer*.

Milton Babbitt, 1916-2011, (U.S.) serial and electronic music.

Carl Philipp Emanuel Bach, 1714-88, (Ger.) cantatas, passions, numerous keyboard and instrumental works.

Johann Christian Bach, 1735-82, (Ger.) concertos, operas, sonatas. Known as the "English" Bach.

Johann Sebastian Bach, 1685-1750, (Ger.) *St. Matthew Passion*, *The Well-Tempered Clavier*.

Samuel Barber, 1910-81, (U.S.) *Adagio for Strings*, *Vanessa*.

Béla Bartók, 1881-1945, (Hung.) *Concerto for Orchestra*, *The Miraculous Mandarin*.

Amy Beach (Mrs. H. H. A. Beach), 1867-1944, (U.S.) *The Year's at the Spring*, *Fireflies*, *The Chambered Nautilus*.

Ludwig van Beethoven, 1770-1827, (Ger.) concertos (*Emperor*), sonatas (*Moonlight*, *Pathétique*), 9 symphonies.

Vincenzo Bellini, 1801-35, (It.) *I Puritani*, *La Sonnambula*, *Norma*.

Alban Berg, 1885-1935, (Austria) *Wozzeck*, *Lulu*.

Hector Berlioz, 1803-69, (Fr.) *Damnation of Faust*, *Symphonie Fantastique*, *Requiem*.

Leonard Bernstein, 1918-90, (U.S.) *Chichester Psalms*, *Jeremiah Symphony*, *Mass*.

Georges Bizet, 1838-75, (Fr.) *Carmen*, *Pearl Fishers*.

Ernest Bloch, 1880-1959, (Switz.-U.S.) *Macbeth* (opera), *Schelomo*, *Voice in the Wilderness*.

Luigi Boccherini, 1743-1805, (It.) chamber music and guitar pieces.

Alexander Borodin, 1833-87, (Russ.) *Prince Igor*, *In the Steppes of Central Asia*, *Polovtzian Dances*.

Pierre Boulez, 1925-2016, (Fr.) *Le Visage nuptial*, *Éclat/Multiples*, *Domaines*.

Johannes Brahms, 1833-97, (Ger.) *Liebeslieder Waltzes*, *Academic Festival Overture*, chamber music, 4 symphonies.

Henry Brant, 1913-2008, (Can.) spatial music.

Benjamin Britten, 1913-76, (Br.) *Peter Grimes*, *Turn of the Screw*, *A Ceremony of Carols*, *War Requiem*.

Anton Bruckner, 1824-96, (Austria) 9 symphonies.

Dietrich Buxtehude, 1637-1707, (Den.) organ works, vocal music.

William Byrd, 1543-1623, (Br.) masses, motets.

John Cage, 1912-92, (U.S.) *Winter Music*, *Fontana Mix*.

Elliott Carter, 1908-2012, (U.S.) *Second String Quartet*, *Third String Quartet*.

Emmanuel Chabrier, 1841-94, (Fr.) *Le Roi Malgré Lui*, *España*.

Gustave Charpentier, 1860-1956, (Fr.) *Louise*.

Frédéric Chopin, 1810-49, (Pol.) mazurkas, waltzes, etudes, nocturnes, polonaises, sonatas.

Aaron Copland, 1900-90, (U.S.) *Appalachian Spring*, *Fanfare for the Common Man*, *Lincoln Portrait*.

John Corigliano, b 1938, (U.S.) *Symphony No.2*.

Paul Creston, 1906-85, (U.S.) *Walt Whitman*.

Claude Debussy, 1862-1918, (Fr.) *Pelleas et Melisande*, *La Mer*, *Prelude to the Afternoon of a Faun*.

David Del Tredici, b 1937, (U.S.) *Child Alice*, *In Memory of a Summer Day*.

Gaetano Donizetti, 1797-1848, (It.) *Elixir of Love*, *Lucia di Lammermoor*, *Daughter of the Regiment*.

Paul Dukas, 1865-1935, (Fr.) *Sorcerer's Apprentice*.

Antonín Dvořák, 1841-1904, (Czech.) *Songs My Mother Taught Me*, *Symphony in E Minor (From the New World)*.

Edward Elgar, 1857-1934, (Br.) *Enigma Variations*, *Pomp and Circumstance*.

Manuel de Falla, 1876-1946, (Sp.) *El Amor Brujo*, *La Vida Breve*, *The Three-Cornered Hat*.

Gabriel Fauré, 1845-1924, (Fr.) *Requiem*, *Elègie for Cello and Piano*.

Cesar Franck, 1822-90, (Belg.) *Symphony in D minor*, *Violin Sonata*.

George Gershwin, 1898-1937, (U.S.) *Rhapsody in Blue*, *An American in Paris*, *Porgy and Bess*.

Philip Glass, b 1937, (U.S.) *Einstein on the Beach*, *The Voyage*.

Mikhail Glinka, 1804-57, (Russ.) *A Life for the Tsar*, *Ruslan and Ludmilla*.

Christoph W. Gluck, 1714-87, (Ger.) *Alceste*, *Iphigène en Tauride*.

Henryk Gorecki, 1933-2010, (Pol.) Symphony no. 3 (*Symphony of Sorrowing Songs*).

Charles Gounod, 1818-93, (Fr.) *Faust*, *Romeo and Juliet*.

Percy Grainger, 1882-1961, (Austral.) *Country Gardens*.

Edvard Grieg, 1843-1907, (Nor.) *Peer Gynt Suite*, *Concerto in A minor for piano*.

George Frideric Handel, 1685-1759, (Ger.-Br.) *Messiah*, *Water Music*.

Howard Hanson, 1896-1981, (U.S.) Symphonies No. 1 (Nordic) and No. 2 (Romantic).

Roy Harris, 1898-1979, (U.S.) symphonies.

(Franz) Joseph Haydn, 1732-1809, (Austria) symphonies (*Clock*, *London*, *Toy*), chamber music, oratorios.

Hildegard von Bingen, 1098-1179, (Ger.) *Ordo virtutum*.

Paul Hindemith, 1895-1963, (U.S.) *Mathis der Maler*.

Gustav Holst, 1874-1934, (Br.) *The Planets*.

Arthur Honegger, 1892-1955, (Fr.) *Judith*, *Le Roi David*, *Pacific 231*.

Alan Hovhaness, 1911-2000, (U.S.) symphonies, *Magnificat*.

Engelbert Humperdinck, 1854-1921, (Ger.) *Hansel and Gretel*.

Charles Ives, 1874-1954, (U.S.) *Concord Sonata*, symphonies.

Aram Khachaturian, 1903-78, (Russ.) ballets, piano pieces, *Sabre Dance*.

Zoltán Kodaly, 1882-1967, (Hung.) *Háry János*, *Psalmus Hungaricus*.

Fritz Kreisler, 1875-1962, (Austria) *Caprice Viennois*, *Tambourin Chinois*.

Edouard Lalo, 1823-92, (Fr.) *Symphonie Espagnole*.

David Lang, b 1957, (U.S.) *The Little Match Girl Passion*.

Morten Lauridsen, b 1943, (U.S.) *Lux Aeterna*.

Ruggero Leoncavallo, 1857-1919, (It.) *Pagliacci*.

György Ligeti, 1923-2006, (Rom.) *Atmosphères*, *Requiem*.

Franz Liszt, 1811-86, (Hung.) 20 Hungarian rhapsodies, symphonic poems.

Edward MacDowell, 1861-1908, (U.S.) *To a Wild Rose*.

Gustav Mahler, 1860-1911, (Austria) *Das Lied von der Erde*; 9 complete symphonies.

Pietro Mascagni, 1863-1945, (It.) *Cavalleria Rusticana*.

Jules Massenet, 1842-1912, (Fr.) *Manon, Le Cid, Thaïs.*
Felix Mendelssohn, 1809-47, (Ger.) *A Midsummer Night's Dream, Songs Without Words,* violin concerto.
Gian Carlo Menotti, 1911-2007, (It.-U.S.) *The Medium, The Consul, Amahl and the Night Visitors.*
Olivier Messiaen, 1908-1992, (Fr.) *Apparition de l'Église Éternelle.*
Claudio Monteverdi, 1567-1643, (It.) opera, masses, madrigals.
Wolfgang Amadeus Mozart, 1756-91, (Austria) chamber music, concertos, operas (*Magic Flute, Marriage of Figaro*), 41 symphonies.
Modest Mussorgsky, 1839-81, (Russ.) *Boris Godunov, Pictures at an Exhibition.*
Carl Nielsen, 1865-1931, (Den.) *Saul og David.*
Jacques Offenbach, 1819-80, (Fr.) *Tales of Hoffmann.*
Carl Orff, 1895-1982, (Ger.) *Carmina Burana.*
Johann Pachelbel, 1653-1706, (Ger.) Canon and Fugue in D major.
Ignacy Paderewski, 1860-1941, (Pol.) Minuet in G.
Niccolò Paganini, 1782-1840, (It.) Caprices for violin solo.
Giovanni Palestrina, c. 1525-94, (It.) masses, madrigals.
Arvo Pärt, b 1935, (Eston.) sacred music. *Fratres, Cantus in memoriam Benjamin Britten, Tabula Rasa.*
Krzysztof Penderecki, 1933-2020, (Pol.) *Psalmus, Polymorphia, De natura sonoris.*
Francis Poulenc, 1899-1963, (Fr.) *Dialogues des Carmélites.*
Mel Powell, 1923-98, (U.S.) *Duplicates: A Concerto for Two Pianos and Orchestra, Cantilena Concertante.*
Sergei Prokofiev, 1891-1953, (Russ.) *Classical Symphony, Love for Three Oranges, Peter and the Wolf.*

Giacomo Puccini, 1858-1924, (It.) *La Boheme, Manon Lescaut, Tosca, Madama Butterfly.*
Henry Purcell, 1659-95, (Br.) *Dido and Aeneas.*
Sergei Rachmaninoff, 1873-1943, (Russ.) concertos, preludes (Prelude in C sharp minor), symphonies.
Maurice Ravel, 1875-1937, (Fr.) *Bolèro, Daphnis et Chloè,* Piano Concerto in D for Left Hand Alone.
Steve Reich, b 1936, (U.S.) *Double Sextet, Three Tales.*
Nikolai Rimsky-Korsakov, 1844-1908, (Russ.) *Golden Cockerel, Scheherazade, Flight of the Bumblebee.*
Gioachino Rossini, 1792-1868, (It.) *Barber of Seville, Otello, William Tell.*
John Rutter, b 1945, (Br.) *Magnificat, Requiem.*
Camille Saint-Saëns, 1835-1921, (Fr.) *Carnival of Animals (The Swan), Samson and Delilah, Danse Macabre.*
Alessandro Scarlatti, 1660-1725, (It.) cantatas, oratorios, operas.
Domenico Scarlatti, 1685-1757, (It.) harpsichord works.
Alfred Schnittke, 1934-98 (Russ.-Ger.) *Life With an Idiot.*
Arnold Schoenberg, 1874-1951, (Austria) *Pelleas and Melisande, Pierrot Lunaire, Verklärte Nacht.*
Franz Schubert, 1797-1828, (Austria) chamber music (*Trout Quintet*), lieder, symphonies ("Unfinished").
Robert Schumann, 1810-56, (Ger.) *Die Frauenliebe und Leben, Träumerei.*
Dmitri Shostakovich, 1906-75, (Russ.) symphonies, *Lady Macbeth of the District Mzensk.*
Jean Sibelius, 1865-1957, (Fin.) *Finlandia.*
Bedrich Smetana, 1824-84, (Czech.) *The Bartered Bride.*

Karlheinz Stockhausen, 1928-2008, (Ger.) *Kontra-Punkte, Kontakte for Electronic Instruments.*
Richard Strauss, 1864-1949, (Ger.) *Salome, Elektra, Der Rosenkavalier, Thus Spake Zarathustra.*
Igor Stravinsky, 1882-1971, (Russ.) *Noah and the Flood, The Rake's Progress, The Rite of Spring.*
Toru Takemitsu, 1930-96, (Jpn.) *Requiem for Strings, Dorian Horizon.*
Thomas Tallis, c. 1505-85, (Br.) anthems, motets.
Peter I. Tchaikovsky, 1840-93, (Russ.) *Nutcracker, Swan Lake, The Sleeping Beauty.*
Georg Philipp Telemann, 1681-1767, (Ger.) church music, orchestral suites, chamber music.
Virgil Thomson, 1896-1989, (U.S.) opera, film music, *Four Saints in Three Acts.*
Dmitri Tiomkin, 1894-1979, (Russ.-U.S.) film scores, including *High Noon.*
Michael Tippett, 1905-98, (Br.) *A Child of Our Time, The Midsummer Marriage, The Knot Garden.*
Michael Torke, b 1961, (U.S.) *Bright Blue Music, Ecstatic Orange.*
Eric Whitacre, b 1970, (U.S.) *Cloudburst.*
Ralph Vaughan Williams, 1872-1958, (Br.) *Fantasia on a Theme by Thomas Tallis,* symphonies, vocal music.
Giuseppe Verdi, 1813-1901, (It.) *Aida, Rigoletto, Don Carlo, Il Trovatore, La Traviata, Falstaff, Macbeth.*
Heitor Villa-Lobos, 1887-1959, (Braz.) *Bachianas Brasileiras.*
Antonio Vivaldi, 1678-1741, (It.) Concerto grossos (*The Four Seasons*).
Richard Wagner, 1813-83, (Ger.) *Rienzi, Tannhäuser, Lohengrin, Tristan and Isolde.*
William Walton, 1902-83, (Br.) *Façade, Belshazzar's Feast.*
Carl Maria von Weber, 1786-1826, (Ger.) *Der Freischutz.*

Composers of Operettas, Musicals, and Popular Music

Richard Adler, 1921-2012, (U.S.) *Pajama Game; Damn Yankees.*
Milton Ager, 1893-1979, (U.S.) "I Wonder What's Become of Sally"; "Hard-Hearted Hannah"; "Ain't She Sweet?"
Leroy Anderson, 1908-75, (U.S.) "Sleigh Ride"; "Blue Tango"; "Syncopated Clock."
Paul Anka, b 1941, (Can.) "My Way"; *Tonight Show* theme.
Harold Arlen, 1905-86, (U.S.) "Stormy Weather"; "Over the Rainbow"; "Blues in the Night"; "That Old Black Magic."
Burt Bacharach, b 1928, (U.S.) "Raindrops Keep Fallin' on My Head"; "Walk on By"; "What the World Needs Now Is Love."
Ernest Ball, 1878-1927, (U.S.) "Mother Machree"; "When Irish Eyes Are Smiling."
John Barry, 1933-2011, (U.S.) *Born Free; Lion in Winter; Out of Africa.*
Irving Berlin, 1888-1989, (U.S.) *Annie Get Your Gun; Call Me Madam;* "God Bless America"; "White Christmas."
Alan Bergman, b 1925, and **Marilyn Bergman**, b 1929, (both U.S.) "The Way We Were"; "You Don't Bring Me Flowers."
Leonard Bernstein, 1918-90, (U.S.) *On the Town; Wonderful Town; Candide; West Side Story.*
Eubie Blake, 1883-1983, (U.S.) *Shuffle Along;* "I'm Just Wild About Harry."
Jerry Bock, 1928-2010, (U.S.) *Mr. Wonderful; Fiorello!; Fiddler on the Roof; The Rothschilds.*
Carrie Jacobs Bond, 1862-1946, (U.S.) "I Love You Truly."
Nacio Herb Brown, 1896-1964, (U.S.) "Singing in the Rain"; "You Were Meant for Me"; "All I Do Is Dream of You."
Hoagy Carmichael, 1899-1981, (U.S.) "Stardust"; "Georgia on My Mind"; "Old Buttermilk Sky."
James Cleveland, 1931-91, (U.S.) composer, musician, singer; first Black gospel artist to appear at Carnegie Hall.

George M. Cohan, 1878-1942, (U.S.) "Give My Regards to Broadway"; "You're a Grand Old Flag"; "Over There."
Cy Coleman, 1929-2004, (U.S.) *Sweet Charity;* "Witchcraft."
John Frederick Coots, 1895-1985, (U.S.) "Santa Claus Is Coming to Town"; "You Go to My Head"; "For All We Know."
Noël Coward, 1899-1973, (Br.) *Bitter Sweet;* "Mad Dogs and Englishmen"; "Mad About the Boy."
Neil Diamond, b 1941, (U.S.) "I'm a Believer"; "Sweet Caroline."
Walter Donaldson, 1893-1947, (U.S.) "My Buddy"; "Carolina in the Morning"; "Makin' Whoopee."
Vernon Duke, 1903-69, (U.S.) "April in Paris."
Bob Dylan, b 1941, (U.S.) "Blowin' in the Wind"; "Like a Rolling Stone."
Gus Edwards, 1879-1945, (U.S.) "School Days"; "By the Light of the Silvery Moon"; "In My Merry Oldsmobile."
Sherman Edwards, 1919-81, (U.S.) "See You in September"; "Wonderful! Wonderful!"
Duke Ellington, 1899-1974, (U.S.) "Sophisticated Lady"; "Satin Doll"; "It Don't Mean a Thing"; "Solitude."
Sammy Fain, 1902-89, (U.S.) "I'll Be Seeing You"; "Love Is a Many-Splendored Thing."
Fred Fisher, 1875-1942, (U.S.) "Peg O' My Heart"; "Chicago."
Stephen Collins Foster, 1826-64, (U.S.) "My Old Kentucky Home"; "Old Folks at Home"; "Beautiful Dreamer."
Rudolf Friml, 1879-1972, (Czech.-U.S.) *The Firefly; Rose Marie; Vagabond King; Bird of Paradise.*
John Gay, 1685-1732, (Br.) *The Beggar's Opera.*
George Gershwin, 1898-1937, (U.S.) "Someone to Watch Over Me"; "I've Got a Crush on You"; "Embraceable You."

João Gilberto, 1931-2019, (Brazil) bossa nova pioneer.
Morton Gould, 1913-96, (U.S.) "Fall River Suite"; "Holocaust Suite"; "Spirituals for Orchestra"; "Stringmusic."
Ferde Grofe, 1892-1972, (U.S.) "Grand Canyon Suite."
Marvin Hamlisch, 1944-2012, (U.S.) "The Way We Were"; "Nobody Does It Better"; *A Chorus Line.*
Ray Henderson, 1896-1970, (U.S.) *George White's Scandals;* "That Old Gang of Mine"; "Five Foot Two, Eyes of Blue."
Victor Herbert, 1859-1924, (Ire.-U.S.) *Mlle. Modiste; Babes in Toyland; The Red Mill; Naughty Marietta; Sweethearts.*
Jerry Herman, 1931-2019, (U.S.) *Hello, Dolly!; Mame.*
Brian Holland, b 1941, **Lamont Dozier**, b 1941, and **Eddie Holland**, b 1939, (all U.S.) "Heat Wave"; "Stop! In the Name of Love"; "Baby, I Need Your Loving."
Rupert Holmes, b 1947, (Br.-U.S.) *The Mystery of Edwin Drood; Curtains.*
James Horner, 1953-2015, (U.S.) *Titanic;* "Somewhere Out There"; "My Heart Will Go On."
Antonio Carlos Jobim, 1927-94, (Brazil) "The Girl From Ipanema"; "Desafinado"; "One Note Samba."
Billy Joel (William Martin), b 1949, (U.S.) "Just the Way You Are"; "Honesty"; "Piano Man."
Elton John, b 1947, (Br.) *The Lion King;* "Candle in the Wind"; "Your Song."
Scott Joplin, 1868-1917, (U.S.) "Maple Leaf Rag; *Treemonisha.*
John Kander, b 1927, (U.S.) *Cabaret; Chicago; Funny Lady.*
Jerome Kern, 1885-1945, (U.S.) *Sally; Sunny; Show Boat.*
Carole King, b 1942, (U.S.) "Will You Love Me Tomorrow?"; "Natural Woman"; "One Fine Day"; "Up on the Roof."
Burton Lane, 1912-97, (U.S.) *Finian's Rainbow.*

Jonathan Larson, 1960-96, (U.S.) *tick, tick… BOOM!*; *Rent*.

Franz Lehar, 1870-1948, (Hung.) *Merry Widow*.

Jerry Leiber, 1933-2011, and **Mike Stoller**, b 1933, (both U.S.) "Hound Dog"; "Searchin'"; "Yakety Yak"; "Love Me Tender."

Mitch Leigh, 1928-2014, (U.S.) *Man of La Mancha*.

John Lennon, 1940-80, and **Paul McCartney**, b 1942, (both Br.) "I Want to Hold Your Hand"; "She Loves You."

Jay Livingston, 1915-2001, (U.S.) "Mona Lisa"; "Que Sera, Sera."

Andrew Lloyd Webber, b 1948, (Br.) *Jesus Christ Superstar*; *Evita*; *Cats*; *The Phantom of the Opera*.

Frank Loesser, 1910-69, (U.S.) *Guys and Dolls*; *Where's Charley?*; *The Most Happy Fella*; *How to Succeed in Business…*.

Frederick Loewe, 1901-88, (Austria-U.S.) *Brigadoon*; *Paint Your Wagon*; *My Fair Lady*; *Camelot*.

Robert Lopez, b 1975, (U.S.) *Avenue Q*; *The Book of Mormon*; *Frozen*.

Henry Mancini, 1924-94, (U.S.) "Moon River"; "Days of Wine and Roses"; "Pink Panther Theme."

Barry Mann, b 1939, and **Cynthia Weil**, b 1937, (both U.S.) "You've Lost That Loving Feeling."

Hugh Martin, 1914-2011, (U.S.) "Have Yourself a Merry Little Christmas"; "The Trolley Song."

Jimmy McHugh, 1894-1969, (U.S.) "Don't Blame Me"; "I'm in the Mood for Love"; "I Feel a Song Coming On."

Alan Menken, b 1949, (U.S.) *Little Shop of Horrors*; *Beauty and the Beast*.

Joseph Meyer, 1894-1987, (U.S.) "If You Knew Susie"; "California, Here I Come"; "Crazy Rhythm."

Lin-Manuel Miranda, b 1980, (U.S.) *In the Heights*; *Hamilton*.

Ennio Morricone, 1928-2020, (It.) *The Good, the Bad and the Ugly*; *The Untouchables*.

Willie Nelson, b 1933, (U.S.) "Crazy"; "On the Road Again."

Chauncey Olcott, 1858-1932, (U.S.) "Mother Machree."

Jerome "Doc" Pomus, 1925-91, (U.S.) "Save the Last Dance for Me"; "A Teenager in Love."

Cole Porter, 1891-1964, (U.S.) *Anything Goes*; *Kiss Me Kate*; *Can Can*; *Silk Stockings*.

Smokey Robinson, b 1940, (U.S.) "Shop Around"; "My Guy"; "My Girl"; "Get Ready."

Richard Rodgers, 1902-79, (U.S.) *Oklahoma!*; *Carousel*; *South Pacific*; *The King and I*; *The Sound of Music*.

Sigmund Romberg, 1887-1951, (Hung.) *Maytime*; *The Student Prince*; *Desert Song*; *Blossom Time*.

Harold Rome, 1908-93, (U.S.) *Pins and Needles*; *Call Me Mister*; *Wish You Were Here*; *Fanny*; *Destry Rides Again*.

Vincent Rose, 1880-1944, (U.S.) "Avalon"; "Whispering"; "Blueberry Hill."

Harry Ruby, 1895-1974, (U.S.) "Three Little Words"; "Who's Sorry Now?"

Arthur Schwartz, 1900-84, (U.S.) *The Band Wagon*; "Dancing in the Dark"; "By Myself"; "That's Entertainment."

Steven Schwartz, b 1948, (U.S.) *Godspell*; *Pippin*; *Wicked*.

Neil Sedaka, b 1939, (U.S.) "Breaking Up Is Hard to Do."

Marc Shaiman, b 1959, (U.S.) *Hairspray*.

Paul Simon, b 1942, (U.S.) "Sounds of Silence"; "I Am a Rock"; "Mrs. Robinson"; "Bridge Over Troubled Waters."

Stephen Sondheim, b 1930, (U.S.) *A Little Night Music*; *Company*; *Sweeney Todd*; *Sunday in the Park With George*.

John Philip Sousa, 1854-1932, (U.S.) *El Capitan*; "Stars and Stripes Forever."

Oskar Straus, 1870-1954, (Austria) *Chocolate Soldier*.

Johann Strauss, 1825-99, (Austria) *Gypsy Baron*; *Die Fledermaus*; waltzes: *Blue Danube*; *Artist's Life*.

Charles Strouse, b 1928, (U.S.) *Bye Bye, Birdie*; *Annie*.

Jule Styne, 1905-94, (Br.-U.S.) *Gentlemen Prefer Blondes*; *Bells Are Ringing*; *Gypsy*; *Funny Girl*.

Arthur S. Sullivan, 1842-1900, (Br.) *H.M.S. Pinafore*; *Pirates of Penzance*; *The Mikado*.

Deems Taylor, 1885-1966, (U.S.) *Peter Ibbetson*.

Jeanine Tesori, b 1971, (U.S.) *Fun Home*; *Shrek the Musical*.

Harry Tobias, 1905-94, (U.S.) *I'll Keep the Lovelight Burning*.

Egbert von Alstyne, 1882-1951, (U.S.) "In the Shade of the Old Apple Tree"; "Memories"; "Pretty Baby."

Jimmy Van Heusen, 1913-90, (U.S.) "Moonlight Becomes You"; "Swinging on a Star"; "All the Way"; "Love and Marriage."

Albert von Tilzer, 1878-1956, (U.S.) "I'll Be With You in Apple Blossom Time"; "Take Me Out to the Ball Game."

Harry von Tilzer, 1872-1946, (U.S.) "Only a Bird in a Gilded Cage"; "Wait 'til the Sun Shines, Nellie."

Fats Waller, 1904-43, (U.S.) "Honeysuckle Rose"; "Ain't Misbehavin'."

Harry Warren, 1893-1981, (U.S.) "You're My Everything"; "We're in the Money"; "I Only Have Eyes for You."

Jimmy Webb, b 1946, (U.S.) "Up, Up and Away"; "By the Time I Get to Phoenix"; "Didn't We?"; "Wichita Lineman."

Kurt Weill, 1900-50, (Ger.-U.S.) *Threepenny Opera*; *Lady in the Dark*; *Knickerbocker Holiday*; *One Touch of Venus*.

Percy Wenrich, 1887-1952, (U.S.) "When You Wore a Tulip"; "Moonlight Bay"; "Put On Your Old Gray Bonnet."

Richard A. Whiting, 1891-1938, (U.S.) "Till We Meet Again"; "Sleepytime Gal"; "Beyond the Blue Horizon"; "My Ideal."

Frank Wildhorn, b 1959, (U.S.) *Jekyll and Hyde*; *Victor/Victoria*; *The Civil War*.

John Williams, b 1932, (U.S.) *Jaws*; *E.T.*; *Star Wars* series; *Raiders of the Lost Ark* series.

Meredith Willson, 1902-84, (U.S.) *The Music Man*.

Stevie Wonder, b 1950, (U.S.) "You Are the Sunshine of My Life"; "Signed, Sealed, Delivered, I'm Yours."

Vincent Youmans, 1898-1946, (U.S.) *Two Little Girls in Blue*; *Wildflower*; *No, No, Nanette*; *Hit the Deck*; *Rainbow*; *Smiles*.

Lyricists

Howard Ashman, 1950-91, (U.S.) *Little Shop of Horrors*; *The Little Mermaid*.

Johnny Burke, 1908-84, (U.S.) "Misty"; "Imagination."

Irving Caesar, 1895-1996, (U.S.) "Swanee"; "Tea for Two"; "Just a Gigolo."

Sammy Cahn, 1913-93, (U.S.) "High Hopes"; "Love and Marriage"; "The Second Time Around"; "It's Magic."

Leonard Cohen, 1934-2016, (Can.) "Suzanne"; "Hallelujah."

Betty Comden, 1917-2006, and **Adolph Green**, 1915-2002, (both U.S.) "The Party's Over"; "New York, New York."

Hal David, 1921-2012, (U.S.) "What the World Needs Now Is Love."

Buddy De Sylva, 1895-1950, (U.S.) "When Day Is Done"; "Look for the Silver Lining"; "April Showers."

Howard Dietz, 1896-1983, (U.S.) "Dancing in the Dark"; "That's Entertainment."

Al Dubin, 1891-1945, (U.S.) "Tiptoe Through the Tulips"; "Lullaby of Broadway."

Fred Ebb, 1936-2004, (U.S.) *Cabaret*; *Zorba*; *Woman of the Year*; *Chicago*.

Ray Evans, 1915-2007, (U.S.) "Mona Lisa"; "Que Sera, Sera."

Dorothy Fields, 1905-74, (U.S.) "On the Sunny Side of the Street"; "Don't Blame Me"; "The Way You Look Tonight."

Ira Gershwin, 1896-1983, (U.S.) "The Man I Love"; "S'Wonderful"; "Embraceable You."

William S. Gilbert, 1836-1911, (Br.) *H.M.S. Pinafore*; *Pirates of Penzance*.

Gerry Goffin, 1939-2014, (U.S.) "Will You Love Me Tomorrow"; "Take Good Care of My Baby"; "Up on the Roof."

Mack Gordon, 1905-59, (Pol.-U.S.) "You'll Never Know"; "The More I See You"; "Chattanooga Choo-Choo."

Oscar Hammerstein II, 1895-1960, (U.S.) *Show Boat*; *Oklahoma!*; *Carousel*.

E.Y. (Yip) Harburg, 1898-1981, (U.S.) "Brother, Can You Spare a Dime"; "April in Paris"; "Over the Rainbow."

Sheldon Harnick, b 1924, (U.S.) *Fiddler on the Roof*; *She Loves Me*.

Lorenz Hart, 1895-1943, (U.S.) "Isn't It Romantic"; "Blue Moon"; "Lover"; "Manhattan"; "My Funny Valentine."

DuBose Heyward, 1885-1940, (U.S.) "Summertime."

Gus Kahn, 1886-1941, (U.S.) "Memories"; "Ain't We Got Fun."

Alan J. Lerner, 1918-86, (U.S.) *Brigadoon*; *My Fair Lady*; *Camelot*; *Gigi*; *On a Clear Day You Can See Forever*.

Johnny Mercer, 1909-76, (U.S.) "Blues in the Night"; "Come Rain or Come Shine"; "Laura"; "That Old Black Magic."

Bob Merrill, 1921-98, (U.S.) "People"; "(How Much Is That) Doggie in the Window."

Jack Norworth, 1879-1959, (U.S.) "Take Me Out to the Ball Game"; "Shine On Harvest Moon."

Mitchell Parish, 1901-93, (U.S.) "Stardust"; "Stairway to the Stars."

Andy Razaf, 1895-1973, (U.S.) "Honeysuckle Rose"; "Ain't Misbehavin."

Tim Rice, b 1944, (Br.) *Jesus Christ Superstar*; *Evita*; *The Lion King*.

Leo Robin, 1900-84, (U.S.) "Thanks for the Memory"; "Diamonds Are a Girl's Best Friend."

Robert Sherman, 1925-2012, (U.S.) *Mary Poppins*; *The Jungle Book*.

Bernie Taupin, b 1947 (Br.) "Rocket Man"; "Your Song."

Paul Francis Webster, 1907-84, (U.S.) "Secret Love"; "The Shadow of Your Smile"; "Love Is a Many-Splendored Thing."

Jack Yellen, 1892-1991, (U.S.) "Ain't She Sweet"; "Happy Days Are Here Again."

Blues and Jazz Artists of the Past

Julian "Cannonball" Adderley, 1928-75, alto sax.

Nat Adderley, 1931-2000, cornet.

Henry "Red" Allen, 1908-67, trumpet.

Mose Allison, 1927-2016, piano.

Louis "Satchmo" Armstrong, 1901-71, trumpet, singer, bandleader.

Albert Ayler, 1936-70, tenor sax, alto sax.

Mildred Bailey, 1907-51, singer.

Chet Baker, 1929-88, trumpet, singer.

Ray Barretto, 1930-2006, conga drummer.

William "Count" Basie, 1904-84, bandleader, piano, composer.

Sidney Bechet, 1897-1959, soprano sax, clarinet.

Bix Beiderbecke, 1903-31, cornet, composer, piano.

Rowland "Bunny" Berigan, 1908-42, trumpet.

Barney Bigard, 1906-80, clarinet.

Eubie Blake, 1883?-1983, composer, piano.

Art Blakey, 1919-90, drums, bandleader.

Jimmy Blanton, 1921-42, bass.

Charles "Buddy" Bolden, 1877-1931, cornet, pioneer bandleader.

Lester Bowie, 1941-99, trumpet, composer, bandleader.

Michael Brecker, 1949-2007, saxophone.

Big Bill Broonzy, 1893-1958, blues singer, guitar.

Clarence "Gatemouth" Brown, 1924-2005, guitar, singer.

Clifford Brown, 1930-56, trumpet.

Ray Brown, 1926-2002, bass.

Dave Brubeck, 1920-2012, piano, bandleader.

Don Byas, 1912-72, tenor sax.

Charlie Byrd, 1925-99, guitar; popularized bossa nova.
Cab Calloway, 1907-94, bandleader, singer.
Harry Carney, 1910-74, baritone sax, clarinet.
Benny Carter, 1907-2003, alto sax.
Betty Carter, 1930-98, jazz singer.
Sidney "Big Sid" Catlett, 1910-51, drums.
Adolphus Anthony "Doc" Cheatham, 1905-97, trumpet.
Don Cherry, 1936-95, trumpet.
Charlie Christian, 1916-42, guitar.
Kenny "Klook" Clarke, 1914-85, drums.
Buck Clayton, 1911-91, trumpet.
Al Cohn, 1925-88, tenor sax.
Nat "King" Cole, 1919-65, piano, singer.
William "Cozy" Cole, 1909-81, drums.
Ornette Coleman, 1930-2015, alto sax, composer.
Alice Coltrane, 1937-2007, piano, composer.
John Coltrane, 1926-67, tenor sax, soprano sax, composer.
Eddie Condon, 1905-73, guitar, bandleader.
Tadd Dameron, 1917-65, piano, composer.
Eddie "Lockjaw" Davis, 1921-86, tenor sax.
Miles Davis, 1926-91, trumpet, composer.
Wild Bill Davison, 1906-89, cornet.
Blossom Dearie, 1924-2009, singer.
Paul Desmond, 1924-77, alto sax.
Vic Dickenson, 1906-84, trombone.
Willie Dixon, 1915-92, composer, bass.
Johnny Dodds, 1892-1940, clarinet.
Warren "Baby" Dodds, 1898-1959, drums.
Eric Dolphy, 1928-64, alto sax, bass clarinet, flute.
Jimmy Dorsey, 1904-57, alto sax, bandleader.
Tommy Dorsey, 1905-56, trombone, bandleader.
Billy Eckstine, 1914-93, singer, bandleader.
Harry "Sweets" Edison, 1915-99, trumpet.
David "Honeyboy" Edwards, 1915-2011, guitar, singer.
Roy Eldridge, 1911-89, trumpet, singer.
Duke Ellington, 1899-1974, piano, bandleader, composer.
Bill Evans, 1929-80, piano.
Gil Evans, 1912-88, composer, arranger, piano.
Art Farmer, 1928-99, trumpet, flugelhorn.
Maynard Ferguson, 1926-2006, trumpet, bandleader.
Ella Fitzgerald, 1917-96, singer.
Tommy Flanagan, 1930-2001, piano.
Pete Fountain, 1930-2016, clarinetist.
Erroll Garner, 1921-77, piano, composer.
Stan Getz, 1927-91, tenor sax.
Dizzy Gillespie, 1917-93, trumpet, composer, singer.
Jimmy Giuffre, 1921-2008, clarinetist, composer.
Benny Goodman, 1909-86, clarinet, bandleader.
Dexter Gordon, 1923-90, tenor sax.
Stéphane Grappelli, 1908-97, violin.
Bobby Hackett, 1915-76, trumpet, cornet.
Lionel Hampton, 1908-2002, vibraphone, bandleader.
W. C. Handy, 1873-1958, composer.
Jimmy Harrison, 1900-31, trombone.
Coleman Hawkins, 1904-69, tenor sax.
Percy Heath, 1923-2005, bass.
Fletcher Henderson, 1898-1952, bandleader, arranger.
Woody Herman, 1913-87, clarinet, alto sax, bandleader.
Jay C. Higginbotham, 1906-73, trombone.
Ruiz Hilton, 1952-2006, piano, composer.
Earl "Fatha" Hines, 1903-83, piano.
Milt Hinton, 1910-2000, bass.
Al Hirt, 1922-99, trumpet.
Johnny Hodges, 1906-70, alto sax.
Billie Holiday, 1915-59, singer.
John Lee Hooker, 1917-2001, blues guitar, singer.
Sam "Lightnin'" Hopkins, 1912-82, blues singer, guitar.

Shirley Horn, 1934-2005, piano, singer.
Howlin' Wolf (Chester Burnett), 1910-76, blues singer, harmonica, guitar.
Alberta Hunter, 1895-1984, singer.
Mahalia Jackson, 1911-72, gospel singer.
Milt Jackson, 1923-99, vibraphone.
Elmore James, 1918-63, blues singer, guitar.
Etta James, 1938-2012, blues singer.
Al Jarreau, 1940-2017, jazz singer.
"Blind" Lemon Jefferson, 1897-1929, blues singer, guitar.
J. J. Johnson, 1924-2001, trombone.
James P. Johnson, 1891-1955, piano, composer.
Robert Johnson, 1912-38, blues singer, guitar.
William "Bunk" Johnson, 1879-1949, composer.
Elvin Jones, 1927-2004, drums.
Jo Jones, 1911-85, drums.
Philly Joe Jones, 1923-85, drums.
Thad Jones, 1923-86, cornet, bandleader, composer.
Scott Joplin, 1868-1917, ragtime composer.
Louis Jordan, 1908-75, singer, alto sax.
Stan Kenton, 1911-79, bandleader, composer, piano.
Barney Kessel, 1923-2004, guitar.
Albert King, 1923-92, blues guitar.
B. B. King, 1925-2015, blues guitar, singer.
John Kirby, 1908-52, bandleader, bass.
Rahsaan Roland Kirk, 1936-77, saxophone, composer.
Gene Krupa, 1909-73, drums, bandleader.
Scott LaFaro, 1936-61, bass.
Lead Belly (Huddie Ledbetter), 1888-1949, folk and blues singer, guitar.
Peggy Lee, 1920-2002, singer.
John Lewis, 1920-2001, piano, Modern Jazz Quartet founder.
Mel Lewis, 1929-90, drums, bandleader.
Jimmie Lunceford, 1902-47, bandleader.
Machito (Frank Grillo), 1908-84, Latin percussion, singer, bandleader.
Shelly Manne, 1920-84, drums, bandleader.
Ellis Marsalis Jr., 1934-2020, piano.
Jackie McLean, 1931-2006, saxophone, composer.
Jimmy McPartland, 1907-91, trumpet.
Marian McPartland, 1918-2013, pianist.
Carmen McRae, 1920-94, singer.
Glenn Miller, 1904-44, trombone, bandleader.
Charles Mingus, 1922-79, bass, composer, bandleader.
Thelonious Monk, 1917-82, piano, composer.
Wes Montgomery, 1925-68, guitar.
James Moody, 1925-2010, saxophone.
Ferdinand "Jelly Roll" Morton, 1885-1941, composer, piano.
Bennie Moten, 1894-1935, piano, bandleader.
Gerry Mulligan, 1927-96, baritone sax, composer.
Theodore "Fats" Navarro, 1923-50, trumpet.
Red Nichols, 1905-65, cornet, bandleader.
Red Norvo, 1908-99, vibraphone, xylophone, bandleader.
Anita O'Day, 1919-2006, singer.
Arturo "Chico" O'Farrill, 1921-2001, Latin composer, arranger.
King Oliver, 1885-1938, cornet, bandleader.
Sy Oliver, 1910-88, arranger, composer.
Edward "Kid" Ory, 1886-1973, trombone, bandleader.
Johnny Otis, 1921-2012, blues singer.
Oran "Hot Lips" Page, 1908-54, trumpet, singer.
Charlie "Bird" Parker, 1920-55, alto sax, composer.
Joe Pass, 1929-94, guitar.
Jaco Pastorius, 1951-87, bass guitarist.
Art Pepper, 1925-82, alto sax.
Pinetop Perkins, 1913-2011, piano.

Oscar Peterson, 1925-2007, piano.
Oscar Pettiford, 1922-60, bass.
Earl "Bud" Powell, 1924-66, piano.
Chano Pozo, 1915-48, percussionist, singer.
Louis Prima, 1911-78, singer, bandleader.
Tito Puente, 1923-2000, Latin percussion, bandleader.
Gertrude "Ma" Rainey, 1886-1939, blues singer.
Lou Rawls, 1933-2006, singer.
Dewey Redman, 1931-2006, tenor sax.
Don Redman (Robert Rodney Chudnick), 1900-64, composer, arranger.
Django Reinhardt, 1910-53, guitar.
Buddy Rich, 1917-87, drums.
Max Roach, 1924-2007, drums, composer.
Red Rodney (Robert Chudnick), 1927-94, trumpet.
Jimmy Rowles, 1918-96, piano.
Jimmy Rushing, 1903-72, blues and jazz singer.
Charles "Pee Wee" Russell, 1906-69, clarinet.
Artie Shaw, 1910-2004, swing-era bandleader, clarinet.
George Shearing, 1919-2011, piano.
Nina Simone (Eunice Waymon), 1933-2003, singer.
John "Zoot" Sims, 1925-85, tenor sax.
Zutty Singleton, 1898-1975, drums.
Bessie Smith, 1894-1937, blues singer.
Clarence "Pinetop" Smith, 1904-29, piano, singer, boogie woogie pioneer.
Willie "The Lion" Smith, 1897-1973, piano, composer.
Francis "Muggsy" Spanier, 1906-67, cornet.
Edward "Sonny" Stitt, 1924-82, tenor sax, alto sax.
Billy Strayhorn, 1915-67, composer, piano, Duke Ellington collaborator.
Sun Ra (Herman Blount), 1915?-93, bandleader, piano, composer.
Art Tatum, 1910-56, piano.
Art Taylor, 1929-95, drums.
Billy Taylor, 1921-2010, piano.
Jack Teagarden, 1905-64, trombone, singer.
Clark Terry, 1920-2015, trumpet.
Mel Tormé, 1925-99, singer ("The Velvet Fog").
Dave Tough, 1908-48, drums.
Lennie Tristano, 1919-78, piano, composer.
Joe Turner, 1911-85, blues singer.
Sarah Vaughan, 1924-90, singer.
Joe Venuti, 1903-78, violin.
Aaron "T-Bone" Walker, 1910-75, blues guitar.
Thomas "Fats" Waller, 1904-43, piano, singer, composer.
Dinah Washington (Ruth Jones), 1924-63, singer.
Grover Washington Jr., 1943-99, pop-jazz sax, composer.
Ethel Waters, 1896-1977, jazz and blues singer.
Muddy Waters (McKinley Morganfield), 1915-83, blues singer, songwriter.
Julius Watkins, 1921-77, French horn.
William "Chick" Webb, 1902-39, bandleader, drums.
Ben Webster, 1909-73, tenor sax.
Junior Wells (Amos Blackmore), 1934-98, blues singer, harmonica.
Paul Whiteman, 1890-1967, bandleader.
Margaret Whiting, 1924-2011, singer.
Charles "Cootie" Williams, 1910-85, trumpet, bandleader.
Joe Williams, 1918-99, singer.
Mary Lou Williams, 1910-81, piano, composer.
Tony Williams, 1945-97, drums.
John Lee "Sonny Boy" Williamson, 1914-48, blues singer, harmonica.
Sonny Boy Williamson (Aleck "Rice" Miller), 1900?-65, blues singer, harmonica.
Teddy Wilson, 1912-86, piano.
Kai Winding, 1922-83, trombone.
Jimmy Yancey, 1894-1951, piano.
Lester "Pres" Young, 1909-59, tenor sax.

Country Music Artists of the Past and Present
* = Inducted into Country Music Hall of Fame (Nashville, TN) as performer between 1961 and 2020.

*Roy Acuff, 1903-92, singer, songwriter; "Wabash Cannon Ball."

*Alabama (Jeff Cook, b 1949; Teddy Gentry, b 1952; Mark Herndon, b 1955; Randy Owen, b 1949); "Feels So Right."

Jason Aldean, b 1977, singer; "Don't You Wanna Stay."

*James "Whispering Bill" Anderson, b 1937, singer, songwriter; "Make Mine Night Time."

*Eddy Arnold, 1918-2008, singer, guitarist, known as the Tennessee Plowboy.

*Chet Atkins, 1924-2001, guitarist, composer, producer; helped create the "Nashville sound."

*Gene Autry, 1907-98, singing movie cowboy; "Back in the Saddle Again."

Clint Black, b 1962, singer, songwriter; "Killin' Time."

*Garth Brooks, b 1962, singer, songwriter; "Friends in Low Places."

*Brooks & Dunn (Kix Brooks, b 1955; Ronnie Dunn, b 1953); "Hard Workin' Man."

Luke Bryan, b 1976, singer, songwriter; "Someone Else Calling You Baby."

*Boudleaux, 1920-87, and Felice Bryant, 1925-2003, songwriting team; "Hey Joe."

*Glen Campbell, 1936-2017, singer, guitarist; "Gentle on My Mind."

Mary Chapin Carpenter, b 1958, singer, songwriter; "I Feel Lucky."

*Carter Family (original members A. P., 1891-1960; "Mother" Maybelle, 1909-78; Sara, 1898-1979); "Wildwood Flower."

*Johnny Cash, 1932-2003, singer, songwriter; "I Walk the Line," "Ring of Fire," "Folsom Prison Blues."

Kenny Chesney, b 1968, guitarist, singer, songwriter; "You Had Me From Hello."

The Chicks (fmr. Dixie Chicks) (Natalie Maines b 1974; Emily Erwin Robison, b 1972; Martie Seidel, b 1969); Wide Open Spaces.

*Roy Clark, 1933-2018, guitarist, banjoist, singer, co-host of Hee Haw; "Yesterday, When I Was Young."

*Patsy Cline, 1932-63, singer; "Walkin' After Midnight," "Crazy," "Sweet Dreams."

Luke Combs, b 1990, singer, songwriter; "Beautiful Crazy."

Billy Ray Cyrus, b 1961, singer, songwriter; "Achy Breaky Heart."

*Charlie Daniels, 1936-2020, guitarist, fiddler; "The Devil Went Down to Georgia."

*Jimmy Dean, 1928-2010, singer; "Big Bad John."

John Denver, 1943-97, singer, songwriter; "Rocky Mountain High."

Dale Evans, 1912-2001, singer, actress, married Roy Rogers.

Sara Evans, b 1971, singer, songwriter; "Born to Fly."

*Flatt & Scruggs (Lester Flatt, 1914-79; Earl Scruggs, 1924-2012), guitar-banjo duo and soloists; "Foggy Mountain Breakdown."

*Red Foley, 1910-68, singer; "Chattanoogie Shoe Shine Boy."

*Tennessee Ernie Ford, 1919-91, singer, TV host; "Sixteen Tons."

*William "Lefty" Frizzell, 1928-75, singer, guitarist; "Long Black Veil."

*Vince Gill, b 1957, singer, songwriter; "When I Call Your Name."

*Merle Haggard, 1937-2016, singer, songwriter; "Okie From Muskogee."

*Emmylou Harris, b 1947, singer, songwriter, folk-country crossover artist; "If I Could Only Win Your Love."

Hunter Hayes, b 1991, singer; "Wanted."

Faith Hill, b 1967, singer, songwriter; "Breathe."

*Alan Jackson, b 1958, singer, songwriter; "Where Were You (When the World Stopped Turning)."

*Waylon Jennings, 1937-2002, singer, songwriter, outlaw country pioneer; "Luckenbach, Texas."

*George Jones, 1931-2013, singer; "He Stopped Loving Her Today."

The Judds (Naomi, b 1946; Wynonna, b 1964), mother-daughter duo; Wynonna also a solo act.

Toby Keith, b 1961, singer, songwriter, guitarist; "Should've Been a Cowboy."

Alison Krauss, b 1971, bluegrass fiddler, singer, bandleader; "When You Say Nothing at All."

*Kris Kristofferson, b 1936, singer, songwriter, actor; "Me and Bobby McGee."

Lady A (fmr. Lady Antebellum) (Dave Haywood, b 1982; Charles Kelley, b 1981; Hillary Scott, b 1984); Need You Now.

Miranda Lambert, b 1983, singer, guitarist; "The House That Built Me."

*Louvin Brothers (Charlie, 1927-2011; Ira, 1924-65), singers; "If I Could Only Win Your Love."

Patty Loveless, b 1957, singer, songwriter; "How Can I Help You Say Goodbye."

Lyle Lovett, b 1957, singer, songwriter, bandleader, actor; "Cowboy Man."

*Loretta Lynn, b 1932, singer; "Coal Miner's Daughter."

*Barbara Mandrell, b 1948, singer; "I Was Country When Country Wasn't Cool."

Kathy Mattea, b 1959, singer, songwriter; "Eighteen Wheels and a Dozen Roses."

Martina McBride, b 1966, singer, songwriter; "Independence Day."

*Reba McEntire, b 1955, singer, songwriter, actress; "Whoever's in New England."

Tim McGraw, b 1967, singer; "It's Your Love," "I Like It, I Love It."

*Roger Miller, 1936-92, singer, songwriter; "King of the Road."

*Ronnie Milsap, b 1943, singer, songwriter; "There's No Gettin' Over Me."

*Bill Monroe, 1911-96, singer, songwriter, mandolin player, "father of bluegrass music"; "Mule Skinner Blues."

Anne Murray, b 1945, singer; "You Needed Me."

Kacey Musgraves, b 1988, singer, songwriter; "Space Cowboy."

*Willie Nelson, b 1933, singer, songwriter, actor; "On the Road Again."

Mark O'Connor, b 1961, fiddler, country-classical crossover composer.

*Buck Owens, 1929-2006, singer, guitarist; "Act Naturally."

Brad Paisley, b 1972, singer, songwriter; "Whiskey Lullaby," "When I Get Where I'm Going."

*Dolly Parton, b 1946, singer, songwriter, actress; "Here You Come Again," "9 to 5."

Johnny Paycheck (Don Lytle), 1938-2003, singer, guitarist; "Take This Job and Shove It."

*Minnie Pearl, 1912-96, comedian, Grand Ole Opry star.

Kellie Pickler, b 1986, singer, songwriter.

*Ray Price, 1926-2013, country singer, guitarist, songwriter; "Crazy Arms."

*Charley Pride, b 1938, singer, first African American country star; "Kiss an Angel Good Mornin'."

John Prine, 1946-2020, singer, songwriter; "Angel From Montgomery."

Eddie Rabbit, 1941-98, singer, songwriter; "I Love a Rainy Night."

Rascal Flatts (Jay DeMarcus, b 1971; Gary LeVox, b 1970; Joe Don Rooney, b 1975); "Life Is a Highway"; "Rewind."

*Jim Reeves, 1923-64, singer, songwriter; "Four Walls."

Charlie Rich, 1932-95, singer, called the "Silver Fox"; "The Most Beautiful Girl."

LeAnn Rimes, b 1982, singer; Blue.

*Tex Ritter, 1905-74, singer, songwriter; "Jingle, Jangle, Jingle."

*Marty Robbins, 1925-82, singer, songwriter; "A White Sport Coat and a Pink Carnation."

*Jimmie Rodgers, 1897-1933, singer, songwriter; "T for Texas."

*Kenny Rogers, 1938-2020, singer, songwriter; "The Gambler."

*Roy Rogers (Leonard Slye), 1911-98, singer, actor, "King of the Cowboys," sang with Sons of the Pioneers.

*Fred Rose, 1898-1954, songwriter, singer, producer; "Blue Eyes Cryin' in the Rain."

Blake Shelton, b 1976, singer; "Home."

*Ricky Skaggs, b 1954, singer, songwriter, bandleader; "Don't Cheat in Our Hometown."

Ralph Stanley, 1927-2016, singer, banjo player; "Man of Constant Sorrow."

Chris Stapleton, b 1978, singer, songwriter; Traveller.

*George Strait, b 1952, singer, bandleader; "Ace in the Hole."

Sugarland (Kristian Bush b 1970; Jennifer Nettles, b 1974); "Stay."

Taylor Swift, b 1989, singer, songwriter; "You Belong With Me."

*Lonnie "Mel" Tillis, 1932-2017, singer, songwriter, bandleader; "I Ain't Never."

*Merle Travis, 1917-83, singer, guitarist, songwriter; "Divorce Me C.O.D."

*Randy Travis, b 1959, singer, songwriter; "Forever and Ever, Amen."

*Ernest Tubb, 1914-84, singer, songwriter, guitarist; "Walking the Floor Over You."

Josh Turner, b 1977, singer; "Why Don't We Just Dance."

Shania Twain, b 1965, singer, songwriter; "You're Still the One."

*Conway Twitty, 1933-93, singer, songwriter; "Hello Darlin'."

Carrie Underwood, b 1983, singer, songwriter; American Idol winner.

Keith Urban, b 1967, guitarist, singer, songwriter; "Somebody Like You."

*Porter Wagoner, 1927-2007, singer, songwriter, guitarist; "Soul of a Convict."

*Kitty Wells (Ellen Deason), 1919-2012, singer, songwriter; "It Wasn't God Who Made Honky-Tonk Angels."

*Dottie West, 1932-91, singer, songwriter; "Here Comes My Baby."

*Hank Williams Jr., b 1949, singer, songwriter; "Bocephus"; "All My Rowdy Friends (Have Settled Down)."

*Hank Williams Sr., 1923-53, singer, songwriter; "Your Cheatin' Heart."

*Bob Wills, 1905-75, Western Swing fiddler, singer, bandleader, songwriter; "New San Antonio Rose."

Lee Ann Womack, b 1966, singer, songwriter; "I Hope You Dance."

*Tammy Wynette, 1942-98, singer; "Stand By Your Man."

Trisha Yearwood, b 1964, singer, songwriter; "How Do I Live."

Dwight Yoakam, b 1957, singer, songwriter, actor; "Ain't That Lonely Yet."

Zac Brown Band (Coy Bowles, b 1979; Zac Brown, b 1978; Clay Cook, Jimmy De Martini, Chris Fryar, b 1970; John Driskell Hopkins, b 1971); "Chicken Fried."

Dance Figures of the Past

Alvin Ailey, 1931-89, (U.S.) modern dancer, choreographer; melded modern dance and Afro-Caribbean techniques.

Alicia Alonso, 1920-2019, (Cuba) ballerina, founder of National Ballet of Cuba.

Frederick Ashton, 1904-88, (Br.) choreographer; director of Great Britain's Royal Ballet, 1963-70.

Fred Astaire, 1899-1987, dancer, actor; teamed with dancer/actress **Ginger Rogers**, 1911-95, (both U.S.) in movie musicals.

George Balanchine, 1904-83, (Russ.-U.S.) ballet choreographer, teacher; most influential exponent of neoclassical style; founded, with Lincoln Kirstein, School of American Ballet and New York City Ballet.

Pina Bausch, 1940-2009, (Ger.) modern dance choreographer influencing the Tanztheater style of dance.

Carlo Blasis, 1795-1878, (It.) ballet dancer, choreographer, writer; his teaching methods are standards of classical dance.

August Bournonville, 1805-79, (Den.) ballet dancer, choreographer, teacher; exuberant, light style.

Fernando Bujones, 1955-2005, (Cuba-U.S.) ballet dancer.

Gisella Caccialanza, 1914-98, (U.S.) ballerina; charter member of Balanchine's American Ballet.

Irene, 1893-1969, (U.S.) and **Vernon Castle**, 1887-1918, (Br.) husband-and-wife ballroom dancers.

Enrico Cecchetti, 1850-1928, (It.) ballet dancer, leading dancer of Russia's Imperial Ballet; his technique was basis for Britain's Imperial Soc. of Teachers of Dancing.

Gower, 1921-80, dancer, choreographer, director; with wife **Marge Champion**, b 1923, (both U.S.) choreographed, danced in Broadway musicals and films.

John Cranko, 1927-73, (S. Afr.) choreographer; created narrative ballets based on literary works.

Merce Cunningham, 1919-2009, (U.S.) dancer, choreographer of avant-garde dance.

Alexandra Danilova, 1903-97, (Russ.) ballerina; noted teacher at the School of American Ballet.

Agnes de Mille, 1905-93, (U.S.) ballerina, choreographer; known for using American themes, she choreographed the ballet *Rodeo* and the musical *Oklahoma!*

Dame Ninette De Valois, 1898-2001, (Br.) choreographer, founding director of London's Royal Ballet; *The Rake's Progress*.

Sergei Diaghilev, 1872-1929, (Russ.) impresario; formed Les Ballet Russes; saw ballet as art unifying dance, drama, music, and decor.

Isadora Duncan, 1877-1927, (U.S.) expressive dancer who united free movement with serious music; one of the founders of modern dance.

Katherine Dunham, 1910-2006, (U.S.) dancer, choreographer; internationally known for African, Caribbean, and African American dance forms.

Fanny Elssler, 1810-84, (Austria) ballerina of the Romantic era; known for dramatic skill, sensual style.

Michel Fokine, 1880-1942, (Russ.) ballet dancer, choreographer, teacher; rejected strict classicism in favor of dramatically expressive style.

Margot Fonteyn, 1919-91, (Br.) prima ballerina, Royal Ballet of Great Britain; famed performance partner of Rudolf Nureyev.

Bob Fosse, 1927-87, (U.S.) jazz dancer, choreographer, director; Broadway musicals and film.

Serge Golovine, 1924-98, (Fr.) ballet dancer with Grand Ballet du Marquis de Cuevas, choreographer.

Martha Graham, 1894-1991, (U.S.) modern dancer, choreographer; created and codified her own dramatic technique.

Melissa Hayden, 1923-2006, (Can.) ballet dancer.

Martha Hill, 1900-95, (U.S.) educator; leading figure in modern dance; founded American Dance Festival.

Gregory Hines, 1946-2003, (U.S.) tap-dance innovator; master of improvisation.

Doris Humphrey, 1895-1958, (U.S.) modern dancer, choreographer, writer, teacher.

Michael Jackson, 1958-2009, (U.S.) singer and dancer who perfected the "moonwalk."

Robert Joffrey, 1930-88, ballet dancer, choreographer; cofounded with **Gerald Arpino**, 1928-2008, (both U.S.) the Joffrey Ballet.

Kurt Jooss, 1901-79, (Ger.) choreographer, teacher; created expressionist works using modern and classical techniques.

Tamara Karsavina, 1885-1978, (Russ.) prima ballerina of Russia's Imperial Ballet and Diaghilev's Ballets Russes; partner of Nijinsky.

Nora Kaye, 1920-87, (U.S.) ballerina with Metropolitan Opera Ballet and Ballet Theater (now American Ballet Theatre).

Gene Kelly, 1912-96, (U.S.) dancer, actor in movie musicals.

Michael Kidd, 1915-2003, (U.S.) dancer, film and theater choreographer.

Lincoln Kirstein, 1907-96 (U.S.) brought ballet as an art form to U.S.; founded, with George Balanchine, School of American Ballet and New York City Ballet.

Serge Lifar, 1905-86, (Russ.-Fr.) prem. danseur, choreographer; director of dance at Paris Opera, 1930-45, 1947-58.

José Limón, 1908-72, (Mex.-U.S.) modern dancer, choreographer, teacher; developed technique based on Humphrey.

Catherine Littlefield, 1908-51, (U.S.) ballerina, choreographer, teacher; pioneer of American ballet.

Kenneth MacMillan, 1929-92, (Br.) dancer, choreographer; directed Royal Ballet of Great Britain, 1970-77.

Dame Alicia Markova, 1910-2004, (Br.) ballerina known for title role in *Giselle*; helped popularize ballet in U.S. and Britain.

Léonide Massine, 1896-1979, (Russ.-U.S.) ballet dancer, choreographer; known for his "symphonic ballet."

Arthur Mitchell, 1934-2018, (U.S.) dancer, choreographer; cofounded Dance Theatre of Harlem.

Fayard Nicholas, 1914-2006, tap dancer, choreographer, actor; together with brother **Harold Nicholas**, 1921-2000, (both U.S.) formed the Nicholas Brothers.

Vaslav Nijinsky, 1890-50, (Russ.) prem. danseur, choreographer; leading member of Diaghilev's Ballets Russes; his ballets were revolutionary for their time.

Alwin Nikolais, 1910-93, (U.S.) modern choreographer; created dance theater utilizing mixed media effects.

Jean-George Noverre, 1727-1810, (Fr.) ballet choreographer, teacher, writer; "Shakespeare of the Dance."

Rudolf Nureyev, 1938-93, (Russ.) prem. danseur, choreographer; leading male dancer of his generation; director of dance at Paris Opera, 1983-89.

Ruth Page, 1899-1991, (U.S.) ballerina, choreographer; danced, directed ballet at Chicago Lyric Opera.

Anna Pavlova, 1881-1931, (Russ.) prima ballerina; toured with her own company to world acclaim.

Marius Petipa, 1818-1910, (Fr.) ballet dancer, choreographer; ballet master of the Imperial Ballet; established Russian classicism as leading style of late 19th cent.

Roland Petit, 1924-2011, (Fr.) dancer, choreographer; founder of Les Ballets de Paris.

Pearl Primus, 1919-95, (Trinidad-U.S.) modern dancer, choreographer, scholar; combined African, Caribbean, and African American styles.

Jerome Robbins, 1918-98, (U.S.) choreographer, director, dancer; *The King and I*, *West Side Story*, *Fiddler on the Roof*.

Bill "Bojangles" Robinson, 1878-1949, (U.S.) famed tap dancer; called "King of Tapology" on stage and screen.

Ruth St. Denis, 1877-1968, (U.S.) influential interpretive dancer, choreographer, teacher.

Ted Shawn, 1891-1972, (U.S.) modern dancer, choreographer; formed dance company and school with Ruth St. Denis; established Jacob's Pillow Dance Festival.

Marie Taglioni, 1804-84, (It.) ballerina, teacher; in title role of *La Sylphide* established image of the ethereal ballerina.

Maria Tallchief, 1925-2013, (U.S.) prima ballerina, 1st of Amer. Indian descent.

Paul Taylor, 1930-2018, (U.S.) dancer, choreographer, teacher.

Glen Tetley, 1926-2007, (U.S.) dancer, choreographer, ballet director; fused elements of modern dance with ballet.

Antony Tudor, 1908-87, (Br.) choreographer, teacher; exponent of the "psychological ballet."

Galina Ulanova, 1910-98, (Russ.) revered ballerina with Bolshoi Ballet.

Agrippina Vaganova, 1879-1951, (Russ.) ballet teacher, director called "queen of variations"; codified Soviet ballet technique.

Mary Wigman, 1886-1973, (Ger.) modern dancer, choreographer, teacher; influenced European expressionist dance.

Opera Singers of the Past

Licia Albanese, 1909-2014, (It.) soprano.
Frances Alda, 1879-1952, (N.Z.) soprano.
Pasquale Amato, 1878-1942, (It.) baritone.
Marian Anderson, 1897-1993, (U.S.) contralto.
Charles Anthony, 1929-2012, (U.S.) tenor.
Jussi Björling, 1911-60, (Swed.) tenor.
Lucrezia Bori, 1887-1960, (It.) soprano.
Montserrat Caballé, 1933-2018, (Sp.) soprano.
Maria Callas, 1923-77, (U.S.) soprano.
Emma Calvé, 1858-1942, (Fr.) soprano.
Enrico Caruso, 1873-1921, (It.) tenor.
Feodor Chaliapin, 1873-1938, (Russ.) bass.

Lili Chookasian, 1921-2012, (U.S.) contralto.
Boris Christoff, 1914-93, (Bulg.) bass.
Franco Corelli, 1921-2003, (It.) tenor.
Hughes Cuenod, 1902-2010, (Switz.) tenor.
Victoria De Los Angeles, 1923-2005, (Sp.) soprano.
Giuseppe De Luca, 1876-1950, (It.) baritone.
Fernando De Lucia, 1860-1925, (It.) tenor.
Edouard De Reszke, 1853-1917, (Pol.) bass.
Jean De Reszke, 1850-1925, (Pol.) tenor.
Emmy Destinn, 1878-1930, (Czech.) soprano.

Mattiwilda Dobbs, 1925-2015, (U.S.) coloratura soprano.
Emma Eames, 1865-1952, (U.S.) soprano.
(Carlo Broschi) Farinelli, 1705-82, (It.) castrato.
Geraldine Farrar, 1882-1967, (U.S.) soprano.
Eileen Farrell, 1920-2002, (U.S.) soprano.
Kathleen Ferrier, 1912-53, (Eng.) contralto.
Dietrich Fischer-Dieskau, 1925-2012, (Ger.) baritone.
Kirsten Flagstad, 1895-1962, (Nor.) soprano.

Olive Fremstad, 1871-1951, (Swed.-U.S.) soprano.
Amelita Galli-Curci, 1882-1963, (It.) soprano.
Mary Garden, 1874-1967, (Br.) soprano.
Nicolai Gedda, 1925-2017, (Swed.) tenor.
Nicolai Ghiaurov, 1929-2004, (Bulg.) bass.
Beniamino Gigli, 1890-1957, (It.) tenor.
Tito Gobbi, 1913-84, (It.) baritone.
Giulia Grisi, 1811-69, (It.) soprano.
Frieda Hempel, 1885-1955, (Ger.) soprano.
Jerome Hines, 1921-2003, (U.S.) bass.
Hans Hotter, 1909-2003, (Ger.) bass-baritone.
Maria Jeritza, 1887-1982, (Czech.) soprano.
Sena Jurinac, 1921-2011, (Yugo.) soprano.
Alexander Kipnis, 1891-1978, (Russ.-U.S.) bass.
Dorothy Kirsten, 1910-92, (U.S.) soprano.
Alfredo Kraus, 1927-99, (Sp.) tenor.
Luigi Lablache, 1794-1858, (It.) bass.
Lilli Lehmann, 1848-1929, (Ger.) soprano.
Lotte Lehmann, 1888-1976, (Ger.-U.S.) soprano.
Jenny Lind, 1820-87, (Swed.) soprano.
Cornell MacNeil, 1922-2011, (U.S.) baritone.
Maria Malibran, 1808-36, (Sp.) mezzo-soprano.
Giovanni Martinelli, 1885-1969, (It.) tenor.
John McCormack, 1884-1945, (Ire.) tenor.
Nellie Melba, 1861-1931, (Austral.) soprano.
Lauritz Melchior, 1890-1973, (Den.) tenor.
Robert Merrill, 1919-2004, (U.S.) baritone.

Zinka Milanov, 1906-89, (Yugo.) soprano.
Patrice Munsel, 1925-2015, (U.S.) coloratura soprano.
Patricia Neway, 1919-2012, (U.S.) soprano.
Birgit Nilsson, 1918-2005, (Swed.) soprano.
Lillian Nordica, 1857-1914, (U.S.) soprano.
Jessye Norman, 1945-2019, (U.S.) soprano.
Magda Olivero, 1910-2014, (It.) soprano.
Giuditta Pasta, 1797-1865, (It.) soprano.
Adelina Patti, 1843-1919, (It.) soprano.
Luciano Pavarotti, 1935-2007, (It.) tenor.
Peter Pears, 1910-86, (Eng.) tenor.
Jan Peerce, 1904-84, (U.S.) tenor.
Roberta Peters, 1930-2017, (U.S.) soprano.
Ezio Pinza, 1892-1957, (It.) bass.
Lily Pons, 1898-1976, (Fr.) soprano.
Rosa Ponselle, 1897-1981, (U.S.) soprano.
Hermann Prey, 1929-98, (Ger.) baritone.
Margaret Price, 1941-2011, (Br.) soprano.
Regina Resnik, 1922-2013, (U.S.) soprano turned mezzo-soprano.
Elisabeth Rethberg, 1894-1976, (Ger.) soprano.
Giovanni Battista Rubini, 1794-1854, (It.) tenor.
Leonie Rysanek, 1926-98, (Austria) soprano.
Dorothy Sarnoff, 1914-2008, (U.S.) soprano.
Bidú Sayão, 1902-99, (Braz.) soprano.
Friedrich Schorr, 1888-1953, (Hung.) bass-baritone.
Elisabeth Schwarzkopf, 1915-2006, (Ger.) soprano.

Marcella Sembrich, 1858-1935, (Pol.) soprano.
Cesare Siepi, 1923-2010, (It.) bass.
Beverly Sills, 1929-2007, (U.S.) soprano.
Elisabeth Söderström, 1927-2009, (Swed.) soprano.
Eleanor Steber, 1914-90, (U.S.) soprano.
Risë Stevens, 1913-2013, (U.S.) mezzo-soprano.
Joan Sutherland, 1926-2010, (Austral.) soprano.
Ferruccio Tagliavini, 1913-95, (It.) tenor.
Renata Tebaldi, 1922-2004 (It.) soprano.
Luisa Tetrazzini, 1871-1940, (It.) soprano.
Lawrence Tibbett, 1896-1960, (U.S.) baritone.
Giorgio Tozzi, 1923-2011, (U.S.) bass-baritone.
Tatiana Troyanos, 1938-93, (U.S.) mezzo-soprano.
Richard Tucker, 1913-75, (U.S.) tenor.
Shirley Verrett, 1931-2010, (U.S.) mezzo-soprano.
Pauline Viardot, 1821-1910, (Fr.) mezzo-soprano.
Jon Vickers, 1926-2015, (Can.) tenor.
William Warfield, 1920-2002, (U.S.) bass-baritone.
Leonard Warren, 1911-60, (U.S.) baritone.
Ljuba Welitsch, 1913-96, (Bulg.) soprano.
Camilla Williams, 1919-2012, (U.S.) soprano.
Wolfgang Windgassen, 1914-74, (Ger.) tenor.

Rock 'n' Roll, Rhythm and Blues, and Rap Artists

Titles in quotation marks are singles; others are albums. * = Inducted into Rock & Roll Hall of Fame as performer between 1986 and 2020; year is in parentheses.

*ABBA (2010): "Dancing Queen"
Paula Abdul: "Straight Up"
*AC/DC (2003): "Back in Black"
Bryan Adams: "Cuts Like a Knife"
Adele: "Rolling in the Deep"
*Aerosmith (2001): "Sweet Emotion"
Christina Aguilera: "What a Girl Wants"
Alice in Chains: "Heaven Beside You"
*The Allman Brothers Band (1995): "Ramblin' Man"
*The Animals (1994): "House of the Rising Sun"
Paul Anka: "Lonely Boy"
Fiona Apple: "Criminal"
Frankie Avalon: "Venus"
Iggy Azalea: "Fancy"
The B-52s: "Love Shack"
Bachman Turner Overdrive: "Takin' Care of Business"
Backstreet Boys: "I Want It That Way"
Bad Company: "Can't Get Enough"
Erykah Badu: "On and On"
*Joan Baez (2017): "The Night They Drove Old Dixie Down"
*La Vern Baker (1991): "I Cried a Tear"
*Hank Ballard[1] and the Midnighters (1990): "Work With Me, Annie"
*The Band (1994): "The Weight"
Barenaked Ladies: "One Week"
*The Beach Boys (1988): "Good Vibrations"
*Beastie Boys (2012): "(You Gotta) Fight for Your Right (to Party)"
*The Beatles (1988): Sgt. Pepper's Lonely Hearts Club Band
Beck: "Loser"
*Jeff Beck (2009): "Escape"
*The Bee Gees (1997): "Stayin' Alive"
Pat Benatar: "Hit Me With Your Best Shot"
*Chuck Berry (1986): "Johnny B. Goode"
Beyoncé: "Crazy in Love"
The Big Bopper: "Chantilly Lace"
Björk: "Human Behavior"
The Black Crowes: "Hard to Handle"
Black Eyed Peas: Elephunk
*Black Sabbath (2006): "Paranoid"
*Bobby "Blue" Bland (1992): "Turn On Your Love Light"
Mary J. Blige: My Life
Blind Faith: "Can't Find My Way Home"
Blink-182: "All the Small Things"
*Blondie (2006): "Heart of Glass"
Blood, Sweat, and Tears: "Spinning Wheel"
Blues Traveler: "Run-Around"
Gary "U.S." Bonds: "Quarter to Three"
*Bon Jovi (2018): "Livin' on a Prayer"
*Booker T. and the M.G.'s (1992): "Green Onions"
Boston: "More Than a Feeling"

*David Bowie (1996): "Space Oddity"
Boyz II Men: "I'll Make Love to You"
Toni Braxton: "Un-Break My Heart"
Chris Brown: "Kiss Kiss"
*James Brown (1986): "Papa's Got a Brand New Bag"
*Ruth Brown (1993): "Lucky Lips"
*Jackson Browne (2004): "Doctor My Eyes"
*Buffalo Springfield (1997): "For What It's Worth"
Jimmy Buffett: "Margaritaville"
*Solomon Burke (2001): "Over and Over (Huggin' and Lovin')"
*The Paul Butterfield Blues Band (2015): "Born in Chicago"
*The Byrds (1991): "Turn! Turn! Turn!"
Cardi B: "Bodak Yellow"
Mariah Carey: "Always Be My Baby"
The Carpenters: "(They Long to Be) Close to You"
*The Cars (2018): "Shake It Up"
*Johnny Cash (1992): "I Walk the Line"
*Ray Charles (1986): "Georgia on My Mind"
*Cheap Trick (2016): "Surrender"
Chubby Checker: "The Twist"
*Chicago (2016): "Saturday in the Park"
*Eric Clapton (2000): "Layla"
Kelly Clarkson: "Since U Been Gone"
*The Clash (2003): "Rock the Casbah"
*Jimmy Cliff (2010): "I Can See Clearly Now"
*The Coasters (1987): "Yakety Yak"
*Eddie Cochran (1987): "Summertime Blues"
Joe Cocker: "With a Little Help From My Friends"
*Leonard Cohen (2008): "Suzanne"
Coldplay: "Clocks"
Collective Soul: "The World I Know"
Phil Collins: "Against All Odds"
*Sam Cooke (1986): "You Send Me"
Coolio: "Gangsta's Paradise"
*Alice Cooper (2011): "School's Out"
*Elvis Costello and the Attractions (2003): "Alison"
Counting Crows: "Mr. Jones"
*Cream (1993): "Sunshine of Your Love"
Creed: "Arms Wide Open"
*Creedence Clearwater Revival (1993): "Proud Mary"
*Crosby, Stills and Nash (1997): "Suite: Judy Blue Eyes"
Sheryl Crow: "All I Want to Do"
The Crystals: "Da Doo Ron Ron"
*The Cure (2019): "Boys Don't Cry"
Daft Punk: "Get Lucky"
Danny and the Juniors: "At the Hop"
*Bobby Darin (1990): "Splish Splash"

Daughtry: "It's Not Over"
*The Dave Clark Five (2008): "Glad All Over"
Dave Matthews Band: "Don't Drink the Water"
*Miles Davis (2006): Bitches Brew
Spencer Davis Group: "Gimme Some Lovin'"
*Deep Purple (2016): "Smoke on the Water"
*Def Leppard (2019): "Photograph"
*The Dells (2004): "Oh, What a Night"
*Depeche Mode (2020): "Strange Love"
Destiny's Child: "Survivor"
*Neil Diamond (2011): "Cracklin' Rosie"
*Bo Diddley (1987): "Who Do You Love?
*Dion[1] and the Belmonts (1989): "A Teenager in Love"
Celine Dion: "Because You Loved Me"
*Dire Straits (2018): "Money for Nothing"
DMX: "What's My Name"
*Fats Domino (1986): "Blueberry Hill"
*Donovan (2012): "Mellow Yellow"
*The Doobie Brothers (2020): "What a Fool Believes"
*The Doors (1993): "Light My Fire"
Dr. Dre: "Nothin' But a 'G' Thang"
*Dr. John (2011): "Right Place, Wrong Time"
Drake: "Hotline Bling"
*The Drifters (1988): "Save the Last Dance for Me"
Duran Duran: "Hungry Like the Wolf"
*Bob Dylan (1988): "Like a Rolling Stone"
*The Eagles (1998): "Hotel California"
*Earth, Wind, and Fire (2000): "Shining Star"
*Duane Eddy (1994): "Rebel-Rouser"
*Electric Light Orchestra (2017): "Don't Bring Me Down"
Missy Elliott: "Sock It 2 Me"
Eminem: "The Real Slim Shady"
En Vogue: "Hold On"
The Eurythmics: "Sweet Dreams (Are Made of This)"
Everclear: "Father Of Mine"
*The Everly Brothers (1986): "Wake Up, Little Susie"
50 Cent (Curtis Jackson): Get Rich or Die Tryin'
The Five Satins: "In the Still of the Night"
Roberta Flack: "The First Time Ever I Saw Your Face"
*The Flamingos (2001): "I Only Have Eyes for You"
*Fleetwood Mac (1998): Rumours
The Foo Fighters: "I'll Stick Around"
Foreigner: "Double Vision"
*The Four Seasons (1990): "Sherry"
*The Four Tops (1990): "I Can't Help Myself (Sugar Pie, Honey Bunch)"

*Aretha Franklin (1987): "Respect"
fun.: "We Are Young"
Nelly Furtado: "I'm Like a Bird"
*Peter Gabriel (2014): "Shock the Monkey"
*Gamble (Kenny) and Huff (Leon) (2008):
   "If You Don't Know Me by Now"
*Marvin Gaye (1987): "I Heard It Through
   the Grapevine"
*Genesis (2010): "No Reply at All"
Goo Goo Dolls: "Iris"
Grand Funk Railroad: "We're an American
   Band"
*Grandmaster Flash and the Furious Five
   (2007): "The Message"
*The Grateful Dead (1994): "Uncle John's
   Band"
*Al Green (1995): "Let's Stay Together"
*Green Day (2015): "Boulevard of Broken
   Dreams"
The Guess Who: "American Woman"
*Guns N' Roses (2012): "Sweet Child o'
   Mine"
*Buddy Guy (2005): A Man and His Blues
*Bill Haley[1] and His Comets (1987):
   "Rock Around the Clock"
*Hall (Darryl) and Oates (John) (2014):
   "Kiss on My List"
*George Harrison (2004): "My Sweet Lord"
*Isaac Hayes (2002): "Theme From 'Shaft'"
*Heart (2013): "Barracuda"
*Jimi Hendrix (1992): "Purple Haze"
Lauryn Hill: "Doo-Wop (That Thing)"
*The Hollies (2010): "Long Cool Woman
   (In a Black Dress)"
*Buddy Holly (1986): "Peggy Sue"
*John Lee Hooker (1991): "Boogie Chillen"
Hootie and the Blowfish: Cracked Rear
   View
*Whitney Houston (2020): "I Will Always
   Love You"
*The Impressions (1991): "For Your Pre-
   cious Love"
Indigo Girls: "Closer to Fine"
INXS: "Need You Tonight"
*The Isley Brothers (1992): "It's Your Thing"
Ja Rule: Venni, Vetti, Vecci
*The Jackson Five (1997): "ABC"
*Janet Jackson (2019): Rhythm Nation
*Michael Jackson (2001): Thriller
*Etta James (1993): "At Last"
Tommy James and the Shondells: "Crim-
   son and Clover"
Jane's Addiction: "Jane Says"
Jay and the Americans: "This Magic Moment"
Jay Z: "99 Problems"
*Jefferson Airplane (1996): "White Rabbit"
Jethro Tull: Aqualung
*Joan Jett and the Blackhearts (2015):
   "I Love Rock 'n' Roll"
Jewel: "You Were Meant for Me"
*Billy Joel (1999): "Piano Man"
*Elton John (1994): "Candle in the Wind"
*Little Willie John (1996): "Sleep"
Norah Jones: Come Away With Me
*Janis Joplin (1995): "Me and Bobby McGee"
*Journey (2017): "Don't Stop Believin'"
K.C. and the Sunshine Band: "Get Down
   Tonight"
R. Kelly: "I Can't Sleep Baby (If I)"
Alicia Keys: "Fallin'"
Kid Rock: "Cowboy"
*B. B. King (1987): "The Thrill Is Gone"
Carole King: Tapestry
*The Kinks (1990): "You Really Got Me"
*Kiss (2014): "Rock 'n' Roll All Night"
*Gladys Knight and the Pips (1996): "Mid-
   night Train to Georgia"
Korn: "Blind"
Lenny Kravitz: "Are You Gonna Go My Way?"
Lady Gaga: "Poker Face"
Kendrick Lamar: DAMN.
*Led Zeppelin (1995): "Stairway to Heaven"
*Brenda Lee (2002): "I'm Sorry"
John Legend: "Ordinary People"
*John Lennon (1994): "Imagine"
*Jerry Lee Lewis (1986): "Whole Lotta
   Shakin' Going On"
Lil' Kim: "No Matter What They Say"
Lil Wayne: Tha Block Is Hot
Limp Bizkit: "Break Stuff"
Linkin Park: "One Step Closer"
*Little Anthony and the Imperials (2009):
   "Tears on My Pillow"
*Little Richard (1986): "Tutti Frutti"
*Little Walter (2008): "Juke"
Lizzo: "Truth Hurts"

LL Cool J: "Mama Said Knock You Out"
Jennifer Lopez: "Love Don't Cost a Thing"
*Darlene Love (2011): "He's a Rebel"
*The Lovin' Spoonful (2000): "Summer in
   the City"
Ludacris: "Money Maker"
*Frankie Lymon and the Teenagers
   (1993): "Why Do Fools Fall in Love?"
*Lynyrd Skynyrd (2006): "Free Bird"
*Madonna (2008): "Material Girl"
*The Mamas and the Papas (1998):
   "Monday, Monday"
Marilyn Manson: "Beautiful People"
*Bob Marley (1994): Exodus
Maroon 5: "Moves Like Jagger"
Bruno Mars: "Just the Way You Are"
*Martha and the Vandellas (1995):
   "Dancin' in the Streets"
The Marvelettes: "Please, Mr. Postman"
Matchbox 20: "Push"
John Mayer: "Daughters"
*Curtis Mayfield (1999): "Superfly"
*Paul McCartney (1999): "Band on the Run"
Don McLean: "American Pie"
*Clyde McPhatter (1987): "A Lover's
   Question"
Meat Loaf: "Paradise by the Dashboard Light"
Megan Thee Stallion: "Savage"
*John (Cougar) Mellencamp (2008): "Jack
   and Diane"
Men at Work: "Who Can It Be Now?"
*Metallica (2009): "Enter Sandman"
George Michael: "Faith"
*Steve Miller (2016): "Take the Money and
   Run"
Nicki Minaj: Pink Friday
*Joni Mitchell (1997): Blue
Moby: "Bodyrock"
Janelle Monáe: "Make Me Feel"
The Monkees: "I'm a Believer"
*Moody Blues (2018): "Nights in White Satin"
*The Moonglows (2000): "Blue Velvet"
Alanis Morissette: "Ironic"
*Van Morrison (1993): "Brown-Eyed Girl"
Mötley Crüe: "Live Wire"
Motörhead: "Ace of Spades"
Jason Mraz: "I'm Yours"
Mumford & Sons: "Little Lion Man"
Nelly: Country Grammar
*Ricky Nelson (1987): "Hello, Mary Lou"
*Stevie Nicks (2019): "Edge of Seventeen"
*Nine Inch Nails (2020): "Closer"
*Nirvana (2014): Nevermind
No Doubt: Rock Steady
*The Notorious B.I.G. (2020): "Mo Money
   Mo Problems"
NSYNC: "Bye, Bye, Bye"
Ted Nugent: "Stranglehold"
*N.W.A. (2016): "Straight Outta Compton"
*The O'Jays (2005): "Back Stabbers"
One Direction: "What Makes You Beautiful"
*Roy Orbison (1987): "Oh, Pretty Woman"
Ozzy Osbourne: "Crazy Train"
OutKast: Speakerboxxx/The Love Below
*Parliament/Funkadelic (1997): "One
   Nation Under a Groove"
*Pearl Jam (2017): Ten
*Carl Perkins (1987): "Blue Suede Shoes"
Katy Perry: "Firework"
Peter, Paul, and Mary: "Leaving on a Jet
   Plane"
Liz Phair: Exile in Guyville
Phish: "Sample in a Jar"
*Wilson Pickett (1991): "Land of 1,000
   Dances"
Pink: Missundaztood
*Pink Floyd (1996): The Wall
*Gene Pitney (2002): "Only Love Can
   Break a Heart"
*The Platters (1990): "The Great Pretender"
The Pointer Sisters: "I'm So Excited"
*The Police (2003): "Every Breath You Take"
Iggy Pop: "Lust for Life"
*Elvis Presley (1986): "Love Me Tender"
*The Pretenders (2005): "Back on the
   Chain Gang"
*Lloyd Price (1998): "Stagger Lee"
*Prince (2004): "Purple Rain"
*Public Enemy (2013): "Fight the Power"
Puff Daddy and the Family: No Way Out
*Queen (2001): "Bohemian Rhapsody"
*Radiohead (2019): OK Computer
Rage Against the Machine: "Bulls on
   Parade"
*Bonnie Raitt (2000): "Something to Talk
   About"

*The Ramones (2002): "I Wanna Be Sedated"
*Red Hot Chili Peppers (2012): "Under the
   Bridge"
*Otis Redding (1989): "(Sittin' on) The Dock
   of the Bay"
*Jimmy Reed (1991): "Ain't That Loving
   You, Baby?"
*Lou Reed (2015): "Walk on the Wild Side"
*R.E.M. (2007): "Losing My Religion"
REO Speedwagon: "Can't Fight This Feeling"
Busta Rhymes: "What's It Gonna Be?"
*The Righteous Brothers (2003): "You've
   Lost That Lovin' Feelin'"
Rihanna: "Umbrella"
Johnny Rivers: "Poor Side of Town"
*Smokey Robinson[1] and the Miracles
   (1987): "Shop Around"
*The Rolling Stones (1989): "Satisfaction"
*The Ronettes (2007): "Be My Baby"
*Linda Ronstadt (2014): "You're No Good"
Diana Ross: "I'm Coming Out"
*Roxy Music (2019): "Love Is the Drug"
*Run-DMC (2009): "Raisin' Hell"
*Rush (2013): "Tom Sawyer"
Sade: "Smooth Operator"
Salt-N-Pepa: "Shoop"
*Sam and Dave (1992): "Soul Man"
*Santana (1998): "Black Magic Woman"
Seal: "Kiss From a Rose"
Neil Sedaka: "Breaking Up Is Hard to Do"
*Bob Seger (2004): "Old Time Rock & Roll"
*Sex Pistols (2006): "Anarchy in the UK"
Shakira: "Whenever, Wherever"
*Tupac Shakur (2017): "How Do U Want It"
*Del Shannon (1999): "Runaway"
Ed Sheeran: "Thinking Out Loud"
*The Shirelles (1996): "Soldier Boy"
Carly Simon: "You're So Vain"
*Paul Simon (2001): "50 Ways to Leave
   Your Lover"
*Simon and Garfunkel (1990): "Bridge
   Over Troubled Water"
*Nina Simone (2018): "Mississippi
   Goddamn"
*Percy Sledge (2005): "When a Man Loves
   a Woman"
*Sly and the Family Stone (1993): "Every-
   day People"
Smashing Pumpkins: "Today"
*Patti Smith (2007): "Because the Night"
Sam Smith: "Stay With Me"
Will Smith: "Gettin' Jiggy With It"
The Smiths: "This Charming Man"
Snoop Dogg (a.k.a. Snoop Lion,
   Snoopzilla): "Gin and Juice"
Sonic Youth: "Bull in the Heather"
Soundgarden: "Black Hole Sun"
Britney Spears: "Hit Me Baby One More
   Time"
Spice Girls: "Wannabe"
*Dusty Springfield (1999): "I Only Want to
   Be With You"
*Bruce Springsteen (1999): "Born to Run"
*Staple Singers (1999): "I'll Take You There"
*Steely Dan (2001): "Rikki Don't Lose That
   Number"
Gwen Stefani: "Hollaback Girl"
Steppenwolf: "Born to Be Wild"
*Cat Stevens (2014): "Wild World"
*Rod Stewart (1994): "Maggie Mae"
Sting: "If You Love Somebody, Set Them
   Free"
Stone Temple Pilots: "Plush"
*The Stooges (2010): "I Wanna Be Your Dog"
Styx: "Come Sail Away"
The Sugar Hill Gang: "Rapper's Delight"
*Donna Summer (2013): "Bad Girls"
*The Supremes (1988): "Stop! In the Name
   of Love"
Talking Heads (2002): "Once in a Lifetime"
*James Taylor (2001): "You've Got a Friend"
*The Temptations (1989): "My Girl"
Robin Thicke: "Blurred Lines"
Three Dog Night: "Joy to the World"
Justin Timberlake: "SexyBack"
TLC: "Waterfalls"
Traffic (2004): Traffic
*T. Rex (2020): "Bang a Gong (Get It On)"
*Big Joe Turner (1987): "Shake, Rattle & Roll"
*Ike and Tina Turner (1991): "Proud Mary"
The Turtles: "Happy Together"
*U2 (2005): "With or Without You"
Usher: "You Make Me Wanna"
*Ritchie Valens (2001): "La Bamba"
*Van Halen (2007): "Running With the Devil"
*Stevie Ray Vaughan & Double Trouble
   (2015): "Change It"

*The Velvet Underground (1996): "Sweet Jane"
*The Ventures (2008): "Walk, Don't Run"
*Gene Vincent (1998): "Be-Bop-A-Lula"
*Tom Waits (2011): "Downtown Train"
The Wallflowers: "One Headlight"
Dionne Warwick: "I Say a Little Prayer"
*Muddy Waters (1987): "I Can't Be Satisfied"
Mary Wells: "My Guy"
Kanye West: "Gold Digger"

The White Stripes: "Seven Nation Army"
Whitesnake: "Here I Go Again"
*The Who (1990): Tommy
Pharrell Williams: "Happy"
*Jackie Wilson (1987): "That's Why"
*Bill Withers (2015): "Lean on Me"
*Bobby Womack (2009): "Lookin' for a Love"
*Stevie Wonder (1989): "You Are the Sunshine of My Life"

Wu-Tang Clan: "Protect Ya Neck"
*The Yardbirds (1992): "For Your Love"
*Yes (2017): "Owner of a Lonely Heart"
*Neil Young (1995): "Down by the River"
*The Young Rascals/The Rascals (1997): "Good Lovin'"
*Frank Zappa[1]/Mothers of Invention (1995): Hot Rats
*The Zombies (2019): "She's Not There"
*ZZ Top (2004): "Legs"

(1) Only individual performer is in Rock and Roll Hall of Fame.

Entertainment Personalities of the Present

Living actors, musicians, dancers, singers, producers, directors, and radio-TV performers.

Name	Birthplace	Birthdate
Abdul, Paula	San Fernando, CA	6/19/1962
Abraham, F. Murray	Pittsburgh, PA	10/24/1939
Abrams, J(effrey) J(acob)	New York, NY	6/27/1966
Adams, Amy	Vicenza, Italy	8/20/1974
Adams, Bryan	Kingston, ON, Canada	11/5/1959
Adams, Yolanda	Houston, TX	8/27/1961
Adele	London, England, UK	5/5/1988
Adjani, Isabelle	Paris, France	6/27/1955
Ad-Rock	South Orange, NJ	10/31/1966
Aduba, Uzo	Boston, MA	2/10/1981
Affleck, Ben	Berkeley, CA	8/15/1972
Affleck, Casey	Falmouth, MA	8/12/1975
Aghdashloo, Shohreh	Tehran, Iran	5/11/1952
Aguilera, Christina	Staten Island, NY	12/18/1980
Ahmed, Riz	Wembley, Eng., UK	12/1/1982
Aiken, Clay	Raleigh, NC	11/30/1978
Aimée, Anouk	Paris, France	4/27/1932
Alba, Jessica	Pomona, CA	4/28/1981
Alberghetti, Anna Maria	Pesaro, Italy	5/15/1936
Albert, Marv	Brooklyn, NY	6/12/1941
Alda, Alan	New York, NY	1/28/1936
Alexander, Jane	Boston, MA	10/28/1939
Alexander, Jason	Newark, NJ	9/23/1959
Ali, Mahershala	Oakland, CA	2/16/1974
Allen, Debbie	Houston, TX	1/16/1950
Allen, Joan	Rochelle, IL	8/20/1956
Allen, Karen	Carrollton, IL	10/5/1951
Allen, Tim	Denver, CO	6/13/1953
Allen, Woody	Bronx, NY	12/1/1935
Alley, Kirstie	Wichita, KS	1/12/1951
Alpert, Herb	Los Angeles, CA	3/31/1935
Almodóvar, Pedro	Calzada de Calatrava, Spain	9/24/1949
Ambrose, Lauren	New Haven, CT	2/20/1978
Ames, Ed	Malden, MA	7/9/1927
Amos, John	Newark, NJ	12/27/1939
Amos, Tori	Newton, NC	8/22/1963
Anderson, Anthony	Los Angeles, CA	8/15/1970
Anderson, Gillian	Chicago, IL	8/9/1968
Anderson, Ian	Dunfermline, Scotland, UK	8/10/1947
Anderson, Loni	St. Paul, MN	8/5/1945
Anderson, Louie	St. Paul, MN	3/24/1953
Anderson, Melissa Sue	Berkeley, CA	9/26/1962
Anderson, Pamela	Ladysmith, BC, Canada	7/1/1967
Anderson, Richard Dean	Minneapolis, MN	1/23/1950
Anderson, Wes	Houston, TX	5/1/1969
André 3000	Atlanta, GA	5/27/1975
Andress, Ursula	Bern, Switzerland	3/19/1936
Andrews, Julie	Walton-on-Thames, Surrey, England, UK	10/1/1935
Andrews, Naveen	London, England, UK	1/17/1969
Aniston, Jennifer	Sherman Oaks, CA	2/11/1969
Anka, Paul	Ottawa, ON, Canada	7/30/1941
Ann-Margret	Stockholm, Sweden	4/28/1941
Ansari, Aziz	Columbia, SC	2/23/1983
Anthony, Marc	New York, NY	9/16/1968
Apatow, Judd	Syosset, NY	12/6/1967
Apple, Fiona	New York, NY	9/13/1977
Applegate, Christina	Los Angeles, CA	11/25/1971
Archer, Anne	Los Angeles, CA	8/24/1947
Arkin, Adam	Brooklyn, NY	8/19/1956
Arkin, Alan	New York, NY	3/26/1934
Armisen, Fred	Hattiesburg, MS	12/4/1966
Arnaz, Desi, Jr.	Hollywood, CA	1/19/1953
Arnaz, Lucie	Hollywood, CA	7/17/1951
Arnett, Will	Toronto, ON, Canada	5/4/1970
Arnold, Tom	Ottumwa, IA	3/6/1959
Arquette, David	Winchester, VA	9/8/1971
Arquette, Patricia	Chicago, IL	4/8/1968
Arquette, Rosanna	New York, NY	8/10/1959
Ashanti (Douglas)	Glen Cove, NY	10/13/1980
Ashley, Elizabeth	Ocala, FL	8/30/1939
Asner, Ed	Kansas City, KS	11/15/1929
Assante, Armand	New York, NY	10/4/1949

Name	Birthplace	Birthdate
Astin, John	Baltimore, MD	3/30/1930
Astin, Sean	Santa Monica, CA	2/25/1971
Atkins, Eileen	London, England, UK	6/16/1934
Atkinson, Rowan	Newcastle upon Tyne, Eng., UK	1/6/1955
Austin, Patti	New York, NY	8/10/1948
Avalon, Frankie	Philadelphia, PA	9/18/1940
Awkwafina	Stony Brook, NY	6/2/1988
Aykroyd, Dan	Ottawa, ON, Canada	7/1/1952
Azalea, Iggy	Sydney, NSW, Australia	6/7/1990
Azaria, Hank	Forest Hills, Queens, NY	4/25/1964
Babyface	Indianapolis, IN	4/10/1959
Baccarin, Morena	Rio de Janeiro, Brazil	6/2/1979
Bacon, Kevin	Philadelphia, PA	7/8/1958
Badalucco, Michael	Brooklyn, NY	12/20/1954
Bader, Diedrich	Alexandria, VA	12/24/1966
Badu, Erykah	Dallas, TX	2/26/1971
Baez, Joan	Staten Island, NY	1/9/1941
Baio, Scott	Brooklyn, NY	9/22/1960
Baker, Anita	Toledo, OH	1/26/1958
Baker, Carroll	Johnstown, PA	5/28/1931
Baker, Diane	Hollywood, CA	2/25/1938
Baker, Joe Don	Groesbeck, TX	2/12/1936
Baker, Kathy	Midland, TX	6/8/1950
Baker, Simon	Launceston, Tas., Australia	7/30/1969
Bakula, Scott	St. Louis, MO	10/9/1954
Baldwin, Alec	Massapequa, NY	4/3/1958
Baldwin, Daniel	Massapequa, NY	10/5/1960
Baldwin, Stephen	Massapequa, NY	5/12/1966
Baldwin, William	Massapequa, NY	2/21/1963
Bale, Christian	Pembrokeshire, Wales, UK	1/30/1974
Balfe, Caitriona	Dublin, Ireland	10/4/1979
Ballas, Mark	Houston, TX	5/24/1986
Bana, Eric	Melbourne, Vic., Australia	8/9/1968
Banderas, Antonio	Málaga, Spain	8/10/1960
Banks, Elizabeth	Pittsfield, MA	2/10/1974
Banks, Jonathan	Washington, DC	1/31/1947
Banks, Tyra	Los Angeles, CA	12/4/1973
Baranski, Christine	Buffalo, NY	5/2/1952
Barbeau, Adrienne	Sacramento, CA	6/11/1945
Bardem, Javier	Las Palmas, Canary Islands, Spain	3/1/1969
Bardot, Brigitte	Paris, France	9/28/1934
Barker, Bob	Darrington, WA	12/12/1923
Barkin, Ellen	Bronx, NY	4/16/1955
Barrie, Barbara	Chicago, IL	5/23/1931
Barrino, Fantasia	High Point, NC	6/30/1984
Barrymore, Drew	Los Angeles, CA	2/22/1975
Bartoli, Cecilia	Rome, Italy	6/4/1966
Barton, Misha	London, England, UK	1/24/1986
Baryshnikov, Mikhail	Riga, Latvia	1/28/1948
Basinger, Kim	Athens, GA	12/8/1953
Bass, Lance	Laurel, MS	5/4/1979
Bassett, Angela	New York, NY	8/16/1958
Bassey, Shirley	Cardiff, Wales, UK	1/8/1937
Bateman, Jason	Rye, NY	1/14/1969
Bateman, Justine	Rye, NY	2/19/1966
Bates, Kathy	Memphis, TN	6/28/1948
Batt, Bryan	New Orleans, LA	3/1/1963
Battle, Kathleen	Portsmouth, OH	8/13/1948
Baxter, Meredith	South Pasadena, CA	6/21/1947
Bean, Sean	Sheffield, England, UK	4/17/1959
Beatty, Ned	Louisville, KY	7/6/1937
Beatty, Warren	Richmond, VA	3/30/1937
Beauvais, Garcelle	St. Marc, Haiti	11/26/1966
Beck	Los Angeles, CA	7/8/1970
Beck, Jeff	Wallington, Surrey, Eng., UK	6/24/1944
Beckham, Victoria	Hertfordshire, England, UK	4/17/1974
Beckinsale, Kate	London, England, UK	7/26/1973
Bedelia, Bonnie	New York, NY	3/25/1948
Bee, Samantha	Toronto, ON, Canada	10/25/1969
Begley, Ed, Jr.	Los Angeles, CA	9/16/1949
Behar, Joy	Brooklyn, NY	10/7/1942

Name	Birthplace	Birthdate
Belafonte, Harry	New York, NY	3/1/1927
Bell, Kristen	Huntington Woods, MI	7/18/1980
Bello, Maria.	Norristown, PA.	4/18/1967
Belmondo, Jean-Paul	Neuilly-sur-Seine, France	4/9/1933
Belushi, Jim	Chicago, IL	6/15/1954
Belzer, Richard	Bridgeport, CT.	8/4/1944
Benanti, Laura	Kinnelon, NJ	7/15/1979
Benatar, Pat	Brooklyn, NY	1/10/1953
Benedict, Dirk	Helena, MT	3/1/1945
Benigni, Roberto	Misericordia, Italy.	10/27/1952
Bening, Annette	Topeka, KS	5/29/1958
Benjamin, Richard	New York, NY	5/22/1938
Bennett, Alan	Leeds, England, UK.	5/9/1934
Bennett, Tony	Astoria, Queens, NY	8/3/1926
Benson, George	Pittsburgh, PA	3/22/1943
Benson, Robby	Dallas, TX	1/21/1956
Berenger, Tom	Chicago, IL	5/31/1950
Bergen, Candice	Beverly Hills, CA	5/9/1946
Bergeron, Tom	Haverhill, MA.	5/6/1955
Bernard, Crystal	Garland, TX.	9/30/1961
Bernhard, Sandra	Flint, MI	6/6/1955
Bernsen, Corbin	North Hollywood, CA	9/7/1954
Berry, Halle.	Cleveland, OH.	8/14/1966
Bertinelli, Valerie	Wilmington, DE	4/23/1960
Best, Eve	London, England, UK	7/31/1971
Bettany, Paul.	London, England, UK	5/27/1971
Bialik, Mayim	San Diego, CA.	12/12/1975
Bichir, Demián	Mexico City, Mexico.	8/1/1963
Bieber, Justin	Stratford, ON, Canada	3/1/1994
Biel, Jessica	Ely, MN	3/3/1982
Big Boi	Savannah, GA	2/1/1975
Bigelow, Kathryn.	San Carlos, CA	11/27/1951
Biggs, Jason	Pompton Plains, NJ	5/12/1978
Bilson, Rachel	Los Angeles, CA	8/25/1981
Binoche, Juliette	Paris, France	3/9/1964
Birch, Thora	Beverly Hills, CA	3/11/1982
Birney, David.	Washington, DC	4/23/1939
Bisset, Jacqueline.	Weybridge, England, UK	9/13/1944
Björk (Gudmundsdottir)	Reykjavik, Iceland	11/21/1965
Black, Clint	Long Branch, NJ	2/4/1962
Black, Jack	Santa Monica, CA	8/28/1969
Black, Lewis	Washington, DC	8/30/1948
Blades, Ruben	Panama City, Panama	7/16/1948
Blair, Linda	St. Louis, MO.	1/22/1959
Blake, Robert	Nutley, NJ	9/18/1933
Blanchett, Cate	Melbourne, Vic., Australia	5/14/1969
Bledel, Alexis	Houston, TX	9/16/1981
Bledsoe, Tempestt	Chicago, IL	8/1/1973
Bleeth, Yasmine	New York, NY	6/14/1968
Blethyn, Brenda	Ramsgate, Kent, Eng., UK	2/20/1946
Blige, Mary J.	Bronx, NY	1/11/1971
Bloom, Claire	London, England, UK	2/15/1931
Bloom, Orlando	Canterbury, England, UK	1/13/1977
Bloom, Rachel	Manhattan Beach, CA	4/3/1987
Blunt, Emily.	London, England, UK	2/23/1983
Blyth, Ann	Mt. Kisco, NY.	8/16/1928
Bocelli, Andrea	Lajatico, Italy	9/22/1958
Bogdanovich, Peter	Kingston, NY	7/30/1939
Bogosian, Eric	Woburn, MA	4/24/1953
Bolton, Michael	New Haven, CT	2/26/1953
Bomer, Matt	Spring, TX	10/11/1977
Bon Jovi, Jon	Sayreville, NJ.	3/2/1962
Bonaduce, Danny	Broomall, PA	8/13/1959
Bonet, Lisa	San Francisco, CA.	11/16/1967
Bonham Carter, Helena.	London, England, UK	5/26/1966
Bonneville, Hugh.	London, England, UK	11/10/1963
Bono	Dublin, Ireland	5/10/1960
Boone, Debby	Hackensack, NJ.	9/22/1956
Boone, Pat	Jacksonville, FL.	6/1/1934
Boreanaz, David	Buffalo, NY	5/16/1969
Borstein, Alex	Chicago, IL	2/15/1971
Bostwick, Barry	San Mateo, CA	2/24/1945
Bosworth, Kate	Los Angeles, CA	1/2/1983
Bottoms, Timothy	Santa Barbara, CA.	8/30/1951
Bow Wow	Columbus, OH.	3/9/1987
Bowen, Julie	Baltimore, MD	3/3/1970
Bowles, Peter	London, England, UK	10/16/1936
Boxleitner, Bruce	Elgin, IL.	5/12/1950
Boy George	Bexleyheath, England, UK	6/14/1961
Boyle, Danny	Manchester, England, UK	10/20/1956
Boyle, Lara Flynn	Davenport, IA	3/24/1970
Boyle, Susan.	Blackburn, Scotland, UK	4/1/1961
Bracco, Lorraine	Brooklyn, NY	10/2/1955
Brady, Wayne	Orlando, FL.	6/2/1972
Braff, Zach	South Orange, NJ	4/6/1975
Branagh, Kenneth.	Belfast, N. Ireland, UK	12/10/1960
Brand, Russell	Grays, Essex, UK	6/4/1975
Brandauer, Klaus Maria	Steiermark, Austria	6/22/1944
Brandy (Norwood)	McComb, MS.	2/11/1979
Bratt, Benjamin	San Francisco, CA.	12/16/1963
Braugher, Andre	Chicago, IL	7/1/1962
Braxton, Toni	Severn, MD	10/7/1966
Bremner, Ewen	Edinburgh, Scotland, UK	1/23/1972
Brendon, Nicholas	Los Angeles, CA	4/12/1971
Brenneman, Amy	Glastonbury, CT.	6/22/1964
Bridges, Beau	Los Angeles, CA	12/9/1941
Bridges, Jeff	Los Angeles, CA	12/4/1949
Brightman, Sarah	Berkhamsted, England, UK	8/14/1960
Brinkley, Christie.	Monroe, MI	2/2/1954
Britton, Connie	Boston, MA	3/6/1967
Broadbent, Jim	Lincolnshire, England, UK	5/24/1949
Broderick, Matthew	New York, NY	3/21/1962
Brody, Adam	San Diego, CA.	12/15/1979
Brody, Adrien	New York, NY	4/14/1973
Brolin, James	Los Angeles, CA	7/18/1940
Brolin, Josh	Los Angeles, CA	2/12/1968
Brooks, Albert	Beverly Hills, CA	7/22/1947
Brooks, Garth	Tulsa, OK	2/7/1962
Brooks, James L.	North Bergen, NJ.	5/9/1940
Brooks, Mel.	Brooklyn, NY.	6/28/1926
Brosnahan, Rachel	Milwaukee, WI	12/15/1990
Brosnan, Pierce	Navan, Co. Meath, Ireland	5/16/1953
Brown, Blair	Washington, DC	4/23/1946
Brown, Bobby	Roxbury, MA	2/5/1969
Brown, Bryan	Panania, NSW, Australia	6/23/1947
Brown, Chris	Tappahannock, VA.	5/5/1989
Brown, Foxy	Brooklyn, NY.	9/6/1979
Brown, Millie Bobby	Marbella, Spain	2/19/2004
Brown, Sterling K.	St. Louis, MO.	4/5/1976
Browne, Jackson	Heidelberg, Germany.	10/9/1948
Bruckheimer, Jerry	Detroit, MI	9/21/1943
Bryan, Luke	Leesburg, GA	7/17/1976
Bryson, Peabo	Greenville, SC	4/13/1951
Bublé, Michael	Burnaby, BC, Canada	9/9/1975
Buckley, Betty	Big Spring, TX	7/3/1947
Buffett, Jimmy	Pascagoula, MS	12/25/1946
Bujold, Geneviève	Montréal, QC, Canada.	7/1/1942
Bullock, Sandra	Arlington, VA	7/26/1964
Bumbry, Grace	St. Louis, MO.	1/4/1937
Bündchen, Gisele	Horizontina, Brazil	7/20/1980
Burgess, Tituss	Athens, GA	2/21/1979
Burghoff, Gary	Bristol, CT.	5/24/1943
Burke, Cheryl	San Francisco, CA.	5/3/1984
Burke, Delta	Orlando, FL.	7/30/1956
Burnett, Carol	San Antonio, TX.	4/26/1933
Burns, Edward	Woodside, Queens, NY	1/29/1968
Burns, Ken	New York, NY	7/29/1953
Burrell, Ty	Grants Pass, OR	8/22/1967
Burstyn, Ellen	Detroit, MI	12/7/1932
Burton, LeVar	Landstuhl, Germany	2/16/1957
Burton, Tim	Burbank, CA	8/25/1958
Buscemi, Steve	Brooklyn, NY.	12/13/1957
Busey, Gary	Goose Creek, TX.	6/29/1944
Busfield, Timothy	Lansing, MI	6/12/1957
Butler, Brett	Montgomery, AL	1/30/1958
Butler, Dan	Fort Wayne, IN.	12/2/1954
Butler, Gerard	Glasgow, Scotland, UK	11/13/1969
Butz, Norbert Leo	St. Louis, MO.	1/30/1967
Buzzi, Ruth	Westerly, RI	7/24/1936
Bynes, Amanda	Thousand Oaks, CA	4/3/1986
Byrne, David	Dumbarton, Scotland, UK	5/14/1952
Byrne, Gabriel	Dublin, Ireland.	5/12/1950
Byrne, Rose	Sydney, NSW, Australia	7/24/1979
Caan, James	Bronx, NY	3/26/1940
Cage, Nicolas	Long Beach, CA	1/7/1964
Cain, Dean	Mt. Clemens, MI	7/31/1966
Caine, Michael	London, England, UK	3/14/1933
Callies, Sarah Wayne	LaGrange, IL.	6/1/1977
Callow, Simon.	London, England, UK	6/15/1949
Cameron, James	Kapuskasing, ON, Canada	8/16/1954
Cameron, Kirk.	Panorama City, CA	10/12/1970
Campbell, Bruce	Royal Oak, MI	6/22/1958
Campbell, Naomi	South London, Eng., UK	5/22/1970
Campbell, Neve	Guelph, ON, Canada	10/3/1973
Campion, Jane	Waikanae, New Zealand	4/30/1954
Cannavale, Bobby	Union City, NJ	5/3/1971
Cannon, Dyan	Tacoma, WA	1/4/1937
Cannon, Nick	San Diego, CA.	10/8/1980
Caplan, Lizzy	Los Angeles, CA	6/30/1982
Capshaw, Kate	Ft. Worth, TX	11/3/1953
Cara, Irene	New York, NY	3/18/1959
Cardellini, Linda	Redwood City, CA	6/25/1975
Cardi B	New York, NY	10/11/1992
Cardinale, Claudia	Tunis, Tunisia.	4/15/1938
Carell, Steve	Concord, MA	8/16/1962
Carey, Drew	Cleveland, OH.	5/23/1958
Carey, Mariah	Huntington, NY	3/27/1970
Cariou, Len	St. Boniface, MB, Canada	9/30/1939
Carlton, Vanessa	Milford, PA.	8/16/1980
Carmen, Eric.	Cleveland, OH.	8/11/1949
Caron, Leslie.	Boulogne, France	7/1/1931
Carpenter, John	Carthage, NY	1/16/1948
Carpenter, Mary Chapin	Princeton, NJ.	2/21/1958
Carr, Vikki	El Paso, TX.	7/19/1941
Carreras, Jose	Barcelona, Spain.	12/5/1946
Carrere, Tia	Honolulu, HI	1/2/1967
Carrey, Jim	Newmarket, ON, Canada.	1/17/1962
Carroll, Pat	Shreveport, LA	5/5/1927

Name	Birthplace	Birthdate
Carter, Jim	Harrogate, Yorkshire, England, UK	8/19/1948
Carter, Lynda	Phoenix, AZ.	7/24/1951
Carter, Nick.	Jamestown, NY.	1/28/1980
Carter, Ron.	Ferndale, MI	5/4/1937
Cartwright, Nancy.	Kettering, OH.	10/25/1957
Caruso, David.	Forest Hills, Queens, NY. .	1/17/1956
Carvey, Dana	Missoula, MT.	6/2/1955
Cash, Rosanne.	Memphis, TN.	5/24/1955
Castellaneta, Dan.	Chicago, IL.	10/29/1957
Castle-Hughes, Keisha.	Donnybrook, WA, Australia	3/24/1990
Cates, Phoebe.	New York, NY.	7/16/1963
Cattrall, Kim.	Liverpool, England, UK.	8/21/1956
Cavanagh, Tom.	Ottawa, ON, Canada.	10/26/1963
Cavett, Dick.	Gibbon, NE.	11/19/1936
Caviezel, Jim.	Mount Vernon, WA.	9/26/1968
Cavill, Henry.	Jersey, Channel Isls., UK.	5/5/1983
Cedric the Entertainer.	Jefferson City, MO.	4/24/1964
Cera, Michael.	Brampton, ON, Canada.	6/7/1988
Chalamet, Timothée.	New York, NY.	12/27/1995
Chalke, Sarah.	Ottawa, ON, Canada.	8/27/1976
Chamberlain, Richard.	Beverly Hills, CA.	3/31/1934
Chambers, Justin.	Springfield, OH.	7/11/1970
Chan, Jackie.	Hong Kong	4/7/1954
Chance the Rapper.	Chicago, IL	4/16/1993
Chandler, Kyle	Buffalo, NY	9/17/1965
Channing, Stockard.	New York, NY	2/13/1944
Chaplin, Geraldine.	Santa Monica, CA	7/31/1944
Chapman, Tracy.	Cleveland, OH.	3/30/1964
Chappelle, Dave.	Washington, DC	8/24/1973
Charles, Josh.	Baltimore, MD	9/15/1971
Charo.	Murcia, Spain	1/15/1951?
Chase, Chevy.	New York, NY	10/8/1943
Chasez, JC (Joshua).	Washington, DC	8/8/1976
Chastain, Jessica.	Sacramento, CA	3/29/1977
Cheadle, Don.	Kansas City, MO	11/29/1964
Checker, Chubby.	Spring Gulley, SC	10/3/1941
Chen, Julie.	New York, NY	1/6/1970
Chenoweth, Kristin.	Broken Arrow, OK.	7/24/1968
Cher.	El Centro, CA.	5/20/1946
Chesney, Kenny.	Lutrelle, TN	3/26/1968
Chianese, Dominic.	Bronx, NY.	2/24/1931
Chiba, Sonny.	Fukuoka, Kyushu, Japan. .	1/23/1939
Chiklis, Michael.	Lowell, MA.	8/30/1963
Chlumsky, Anna.	Chicago, IL	12/3/1980
Chmerkovskiy, Maksim.	Odessa, Ukraine	1/17/1980
Cho, Margaret.	San Francisco, CA.	12/5/1968
Chong, Thomas	Edmonton, AB, Canada. .	5/24/1938
Chopra, Priyanka	Jamshedpur, India	7/18/1982
Chow Yun-Fat.	Lamma Island, Hong Kong.	5/18/1955
Christensen, Hayden	Vancouver, BC, Canada. .	4/19/1981
Christie, Julie	Chukua, Assam, India	4/14/1940
Chuck D	Roosevelt, NY	8/1/1960
Church, Charlotte	Llandaff, Cardiff, Wales, UK	2/21/1986
Church, Thomas Haden	El Paso, TX.	6/17/1960
Clapton, Eric.	Ripley, Surrey, Eng., UK. .	3/30/1945
Clark, Petula.	Epson, Surrey, Eng., UK. .	11/15/1932
Clarke, Emilia.	London, Eng., UK	10/23/1986
Clarkson, Kelly.	Burleson, TX	4/24/1982
Clarkson, Patricia.	New Orleans, LA.	12/29/1959
Clay, Andrew Dice.	Brooklyn, NY.	9/29/1957
Cleese, John.	Weston-super-Mare, Eng., UK	10/27/1939
Clooney, George.	Lexington, KY.	5/6/1961
Close, Glenn.	Greenwich, CT	3/19/1947
Coen, Ethan.	St. Louis Park, MN.	9/21/1957
Coen, Joel.	St. Louis Park, MN.	11/29/1954
Cohen, Andy.	St. Louis, MO.	6/2/1968
Cohen, Sacha Baron	London, England, UK.	10/13/1971
Colbert, Stephen.	Washington, DC	5/13/1964
Cole, Gary	Park Ridge, IL.	9/20/1956
Coleman, Dabney.	Austin, TX.	1/3/1932
Colfer, Chris	Fresno, CA.	5/27/1990
Collette, Toni.	Blacktown, NSW, Australia.	11/1/1972
Collins, Joan.	London, England, UK.	5/23/1933
Collins, Judy.	Seattle, WA.	5/1/1939
Collins, Pauline.	Exmouth, England, UK	9/3/1940
Collins, Phil.	London, England, UK	1/30/1951
Collins, Stephen.	Des Moines, IA	10/1/1947
Colman, Olivia.	Norfolk, Eng., UK.	1/30/1974
Columbus, Chris	Spangler, PA	9/10/1958
Colvin, Shawn.	Vermillion, SD	1/10/1956
Combs, Sean	New York, NY	11/4/1969
Comer, Jodie	Liverpool, Eng., UK	3/11/1993
Connelly, Jennifer	Round Top, NY	12/12/1970
Connery, Sean	Edinburgh, Scotland, UK. .	8/25/1930
Connick, Harry, Jr.	New Orleans, LA.	9/11/1967
Connolly, Kevin	Patchogue, NY	3/5/1974
Conroy, Frances	Monroe, GA.	11/13/1953
Constantine, Michael	Reading, PA.	5/22/1927
Conti, Tom	Paisley, Scotland, UK.	11/22/1941
Coogler, Ryan	Oakland, CA	5/23/1986
Coolidge, Rita	Nashville, TN.	5/1/1945
Coolio	Compton, CA.	8/1/1963
Coon, Carrie	Copley, OH.	1/24/1981

Name	Birthplace	Birthdate
Cooper, Alice	Detroit, MI	2/4/1948
Cooper, Bradley	Philadelphia, PA	1/5/1975
Cooper, Chris	Kansas City, MO	7/9/1951
Copeland, Misty	Kansas City, MO	9/10/1982
Copperfield, David	Metuchen, NJ	9/16/1956
Coppola, Francis Ford	Detroit, MI	4/7/1939
Coppola, Sofia	New York, NY	5/14/1971
Corbett, John	Wheeling, WV	5/9/1961
Corbin, Barry	Lamesa, TX.	10/16/1940
Corden, James	Hillingdon, England, UK. .	8/22/1978
Corea, Chick	Chelsea, MA	6/12/1941
Corgan, Billy	Elk Grove, IL	3/17/1967
Corwin, Jeff.	Norwell, MA.	7/11/1967
Cosby, Bill.	Philadelphia, PA	7/12/1937
Cosgrove, Miranda	Los Angeles, CA	5/14/1993
Costas, Bob	Astoria, Queens, NY	3/22/1952
Costello, Elvis	London, England, UK	8/25/1954
Costner, Kevin	Compton, CA.	1/18/1955
Cotillard, Marion	Paris, France	9/30/1975
Cowell, Simon.	London, England, UK	10/7/1959
Cox, Brian.	Dundee, Scotland, UK. .	6/1/1946
Cox, Courteney.	Birmingham, AL.	6/15/1964
Cox, Laverne	Mobile, AL.	5/29/1972
Cox, Ronny.	Cloudcroft, NM.	7/23/1938
Coyote, Peter	New York, NY	10/10/1941
Craig, Daniel.	Chester, England, UK. .	3/2/1968
Cranston, Bryan	San Fernando Valley, CA. .	3/7/1956
Crawford, Cindy	DeKalb, IL.	2/20/1966
Crawford, Michael	Salisbury, England, UK. .	1/19/1942
Criss, Darren.	San Francisco, CA.	2/5/1987
Cromwell, James	Los Angeles, CA	1/27/1940
Crosby, David	Los Angeles, CA	8/14/1941
Cross, Marcia	Marlborough, MA.	3/25/1962
Crow, Sheryl	Kennett, MO	2/11/1962
Crowe, Cameron	Palm Springs, CA	7/13/1957
Crowe, Russell	Wellington, New Zealand. .	4/7/1964
Crudup, Billy	Manhasset, NY	7/8/1948
Cruise, Tom	Syracuse, NY	7/3/1962
Cruz, Penelope	Madrid, Spain	4/28/1974
Cryer, Jon	New York, NY	4/16/1965
Crystal, Billy	Long Beach, NY	3/14/1948
Cuarón, Alfonso	Mexico City, Mexico	11/28/1961
Culkin, Macaulay	New York, NY	8/26/1980
Cullum, John.	Knoxville, TN	3/2/1930
Cumberbatch, Benedict.	London, England, UK	7/19/1976
Cumming, Alan	Aberfeldy, Perthshire, Scotland, UK	1/27/1965
Cuoco, Kaley	Camarillo, CA	11/30/1985
Curry, Tim	Grappenhall, Cheshire, England, UK	4/19/1946
Curtin, Jane	Cambridge, MA	9/6/1947
Curtis, Jamie Lee	Los Angeles, CA	11/22/1958
Cusack, Joan	New York, NY	10/11/1962
Cusack, John	Evanston, IL	6/28/1966
Cyrus, Billy Ray	Flatwoods, KY	8/25/1961
Cyrus, Miley	Nashville, TN.	11/23/1992
Dafoe, Willem	Appleton, WI	7/22/1955
Dahl, Arlene	Minneapolis, MN	8/11/1925
Dale, Jim.	Rothwell, England, UK.	8/15/1935
Dalton, Timothy.	Colwyn Bay, Wales, UK. .	3/21/1946
Daltrey, Roger	London, England, UK.	3/1/1944
Daly, Carson	Santa Monica, CA	6/22/1973
Daly, Timothy	New York, NY	3/1/1956
Daly, Tyne	Madison, WI	2/21/1946
Damon, Matt	Cambridge, MA	10/8/1970
Dane, Eric.	San Francisco, CA.	11/9/1972
Danes, Claire	New York, NY	4/12/1979
D'Angelo	Richmond, VA	2/11/1974
D'Angelo, Beverly	Columbus, OH.	11/15/1954
Daniels, Anthony.	Salisbury, England, UK. .	2/21/1946
Daniels, Jeff	Athens, GA	2/19/1955
Daniels, Lee	Philadelphia, PA	12/24/1959
Daniels, William	Brooklyn, NY.	3/31/1927
Danner, Blythe	Rosemont, PA	2/3/1943
Danson, Ted	San Diego, CA.	12/29/1947
Danza, Tony	Brooklyn, NY.	4/21/1951
Darby, Kim	Hollywood, CA.	7/8/1948
Daughtry, Chris.	Roanoke Rapids, NC. . . .	12/26/1979
David, Larry	Brooklyn, NY.	7/2/1947
Davidson, John.	Pittsburgh, PA.	12/13/1941
Davis, Clifton.	Chicago, IL.	10/4/1945
Davis, Geena	Wareham, MA.	1/21/1956
Davis, Hope	Englewood, NJ	3/23/1964
Davis, Judy	Perth, WA, Australia. .	4/23/1955
Davis, Kristin.	Boulder, CO.	2/24/1965
Davis, Viola	Saint Matthews, SC. .	8/11/1965
Dawber, Pam	Farmington Hills, MI. . . .	10/18/1951
Dawson, Rosario	New York, NY	5/9/1979
Day-Lewis, Daniel	London, England, UK	4/29/1957
De Mornay, Rebecca	Santa Rosa, CA.	8/29/1962
De Niro, Robert.	New York, NY	8/17/1943
De Rossi, Portia	Melbourne, Vic., Australia.	1/31/1973
DeGeneres, Ellen	Metairie, LA.	1/26/1958
DeGraw, Gavin	Middletown, NY.	2/4/1977

Name	Birthplace	Birthdate
Fonda, Jane	New York, NY	12/21/1937
Ford, Faith	Alexandria, LA	9/14/1964
Ford, Harrison	Chicago, IL	7/13/1942
Forte, Will	Alameda Co., CA	6/17/1970
Foster, Jodie	Los Angeles, CA	11/19/1962
Foster, Sutton	Statesboro, GA	3/18/1975
Fox, Jorja	New York, NY	7/7/1968
Fox, Matthew	Abington, PA	7/14/1966
Fox, Megan	Rockwood, TN	5/16/1986
Fox, Michael J.	Edmonton, AB, Canada	6/9/1961
Fox, Vivica A.	South Bend, IN	7/30/1964
Foxworth, Robert	Houston, TX	11/1/1941
Foxworthy, Jeff	Atlanta, GA	9/6/1958
Foxx, Jamie	Terrell, TX	12/13/1967
Foy, Claire	Stockport, England, UK	4/16/1984
Frampton, Peter	Kent, England, UK	4/22/1950
Francis, Connie	Newark, NJ	12/12/1938
Franco, Dave	Palo Alto, CA	6/12/1985
Franco, James	Palo Alto, CA	4/19/1978
Franken, Al	New York, NY	5/21/1951
Franz, Dennis	Maywood, IL	10/28/1944
Fraser, Brendan	Indianapolis, IN	12/3/1968
Freeman, Martin	Aldershot, Hampshire, Eng., UK	9/8/1971
Freeman, Morgan	Memphis, TN	6/1/1937
French, Dawn	Holyhead, Wales, UK	10/11/1957
Fricker, Brenda	Dublin, Ireland	2/17/1945
Friedkin, William	Chicago, IL	8/29/1939
Froggatt, Joanne	Littlebeck, North Yorkshire, England, UK	8/21/1980
Fry, Stephen	London, England, UK	8/24/1957
Fuentes, Daisy	Havana, Cuba	11/17/1966
Fuller, Robert	Troy, NY	7/29/1933
Furlong, Edward	Pasadena, CA	8/2/1977
Furtado, Nelly	Victoria, BC, Canada	12/2/1978
Gabriel, Peter	Surrey, England, UK	2/13/1950
Gaines, Boyd	Atlanta, GA	5/11/1953
Galecki, Johnny	Bree, Belgium	4/30/1975
Galifianakis, Zach	Wilkesboro, NC	10/1/1969
Gallagher, Peter	Armonk, NY	8/19/1955
Gallo, Vincent	Buffalo, NY	4/11/1961
Galway, James	Belfast, N. Ireland, UK	12/8/1939
Garber, Victor	London, ON, Canada	3/16/1949
Garcia, Andy	Havana, Cuba	4/12/1956
Garfield, Andrew	Los Angeles, CA	8/20/1983
Garfunkel, Art	Forest Hills, Queens, NY	11/5/1941
Garlin, Jeff	Chicago, IL	6/5/1962
Garner, Jennifer	Houston, TX	4/17/1972
Garner, Julia	Bronx, NY	2/1/1994
Garofalo, Janeane	Newton, NJ	9/28/1964
Garr, Teri	Lakewood, OH.	12/11/1944
Garrett, Brad	Woodland Hills, CA	4/14/1960
Garth, Jennie	Urbana, IL	4/3/1972
Gatlin, Larry	Seminole, TX.	5/2/1948
Gayle, Crystal	Paintsville, KY	1/9/1951
Gaynor, Mitzi	Chicago, IL	9/4/1931
Geary, Anthony	Coalville, UT	5/29/1947
Gellar, Sarah Michelle	New York, NY	4/14/1977
Gere, Richard	Philadelphia, PA	8/31/1949
Gervais, Ricky	Reading, England, UK	6/25/1961
Gerwig, Greta	Sacramento, CA	8/4/1983
Giamatti, Paul	New Haven, CT	6/6/1967
Giannini, Giancarlo	La Spezia, Italy	8/1/1942
Gibb, Barry	Isle of Man, England, UK.	9/1/1946
Gibbons, Leeza	Hartsville, SC	3/26/1957
Gibbs, Marla	Chicago, IL	6/14/1931
Gibson, Debbie	Brooklyn, NY	8/31/1970
Gibson, Mel	Peekskill, NY	1/3/1956
Gibson, Thomas	Charleston, SC	7/3/1962
Gifford, Kathie Lee	Neuilly-sur-Seine, France	8/16/1953
Gilbert, Melissa	Los Angeles, CA	5/8/1964
Gilbert, Sara	Santa Monica, CA	1/29/1975
Gilberto, Astrud	Salvador, Brazil	3/30/1940
Gill, Vince	Norman, OK	4/12/1957
Gillette, Anita	Baltimore, MD	8/16/1936
Gilley, Mickey	Natchez, MS	3/9/1936
Gilliam, Terry	Minneapolis, MN	11/22/1940
Gilmour, David	Cambridge, England, UK	3/6/1946
Gilpin, Peri	Waco, TX	5/27/1961
Givens, Robin	New York, NY	11/27/1964
Glaser, Paul Michael	Cambridge, MA	3/25/1943
Gleeson, Brendan	Belfast, N. Ireland, UK	3/29/1955?
Glenn, Scott	Pittsburgh, PA	1/26/1941
Gless, Sharon	Los Angeles, CA	5/31/1943
Glover, Crispin	New York, NY	4/20/1964
Glover, Danny	San Francisco, CA	7/22/1947
Glover, Donald	Edwards Air Force Base, CA	9/25/1983
Glover, Julian	London, England, UK	3/27/1935
Glover, Savion	Newark, NJ	11/19/1973
Godard, Jean-Luc	Paris, France	12/3/1930
Goldberg, Whoopi	New York, NY	11/13/1955
Goldblum, Jeff	Pittsburgh, PA	10/22/1952
Goldthwait, Bobcat	Syracuse, NY	5/26/1962
Goldwyn, Tony	Los Angeles, CA	5/20/1960
Gomez, Selena	Grand Prairie, TX	7/22/1992
Gooding, Cuba, Jr.	Bronx, NY	1/2/1968

Name	Birthplace	Birthdate
Goodman, John	Affton, MO	6/20/1952
Goodman, Len	London, England, UK	4/25/1944
Gordon-Levitt, Joseph	Los Angeles, CA	2/17/1981
Gosling, Ryan	London, ON, Canada	11/12/1980
Gosselaar, Mark-Paul	Panorama City, CA	3/1/1974
Gossett, Louis, Jr.	Brooklyn, NY	5/27/1936
Gottfried, Gilbert	Brooklyn, NY	2/28/1955
Gould, Elliott	Brooklyn, NY	8/29/1938
Grace, Topher	New York, NY	7/12/1978
Graham, Heather	Milwaukee, WI	1/29/1970
Graham, Lauren	Honolulu, HI	3/16/1967
Grammer, Kelsey	St. Thomas, U.S. Virgin Isls.	2/21/1955
Grande, Ariana	Boca Raton, FL	6/26/1993
Grant, Amy	Augusta, GA	11/25/1960
Grant, Hugh	London, England, UK	9/9/1960
Grant, Lee	Bronx, NY	10/31/1925
Gray, Linda	Santa Monica, CA	9/12/1940
Gray, Macy	Canton, OH.	9/6/1969
Green, Al	Forrest City, AR	4/13/1946
Green, Cee Lo	Atlanta, GA	5/30/1974
Green, Seth	Philadelphia, PA	2/8/1974
Green, Tom	Pembroke, ON, Canada	7/30/1971
Greene, Graham	Six Nations Reserve, ON, Canada	6/22/1952
Greene, Shecky	Chicago, IL	4/8/1926
Greenfield, Max	Dobbs Ferry, NY	9/4/1980
Greenwood, Bruce	Noranda, QC, Canada	8/12/1956
Gregory, Cynthia	Los Angeles, CA	7/8/1946
Grenier, Adrian	Santa Fe, NM	7/10/1976
Grey, Jennifer	New York, NY	3/26/1960
Grey, Joel	Cleveland, OH	4/11/1932
Grier, David Alan.	Detroit, MI	6/30/1955
Grier, Pam	Winston-Salem, NC	5/26/1949
Griffin, Kathy	Oak Park, IL	11/4/1961
Griffith, Melanie	New York, NY	8/9/1957
Griffiths, Rachel	Melbourne, Vic., Australia	12/18/1968
Grint, Rupert	Walton-at-Stone, Hertfordshire, Eng., UK	8/24/1988
Groban, Josh	Los Angeles, CA	2/27/1981
Grodin, Charles	Pittsburgh, PA	4/21/1935
Groff, Jonathan	Lancaster, PA	3/26/1985
Grohl, Dave	Warren, OH.	1/14/1969
Gross, Michael	Chicago, IL	6/21/1947
Guest, Christopher	New York, NY	2/5/1948
Gumbel, Bryant	New Orleans, LA	9/29/1948
Gumbel, Greg	New Orleans, LA	5/3/1946
Gunn, Anna	Santa Fe, NM	8/11/1968
Gunn, Tim	Washington, DC	7/29/1953
Guthrie, Arlo	Brooklyn, NY	7/10/1947
Guttenberg, Steve	Brooklyn, NY	8/24/1958
Guy, Buddy	Lettsworth, LA.	7/30/1936
Guy, Jasmine	Boston, MA	3/10/1964
Gyllenhaal, Jake	Los Angeles, CA	12/19/1980
Gyllenhaal, Maggie	New York, NY	11/16/1977
Hackman, Gene	San Bernardino, CA	1/30/1930
Haddish, Tiffany	Los Angeles, CA	12/3/1979
Hader, Bill	Tulsa, OK	6/7/1978
Hagerty, Julie	Cincinnati, OH	6/15/1955
Hale, Tony	West Point, NY	9/30/1970
Hall, Anthony Michael	West Roxbury, MA	4/14/1968
Hall, Arsenio	Cleveland, OH	2/12/1955
Hall, Daryl	Pottstown, PA	10/11/1946
Hall, Deidre	Milwaukee, WI.	10/31/1947
Hall, Michael C.	Raleigh, NC	2/1/1971
Hall, Tamron	Luling, TX	9/16/1970
Hall, Tom T.	Olive Hill, KY.	5/25/1936
Halliwell, Geri	Watford, England, UK	8/6/1972
Hamill, Mark	Oakland, CA	9/25/1951
Hamilton, George	Memphis, TN	8/12/1939
Hamilton, Linda	Salisbury, MD	9/26/1956
Hamlin, Harry	Pasadena, CA.	10/30/1951
Hamm, Jon	St. Louis, MO	3/10/1971
Hammer, Armie	Los Angeles, CA	8/28/1986
Hammer (M.C.)	Oakland, CA.	3/30/1963
Hammond, Darrell	Melbourne, FL	10/8/1955
Hancock, Herbie	Chicago, IL.	4/12/1940
Handler, Chelsea	Livingston, NJ	2/25/1975
Hanks, Colin	Sacramento, CA	11/24/1977
Hanks, Tom	Concord, CA	7/9/1956
Hannah, Daryl	Chicago, IL.	12/3/1960
Hannigan, Alyson	Washington, DC	3/24/1974
Hanson, Isaac	Tulsa, OK	11/17/1980
Hanson, Taylor	Tulsa, OK	3/14/1983
Hanson, Zac	Tulsa, OK	10/22/1985
Harden, Marcia Gay	La Jolla, CA	8/14/1959
Hardy, Tom	London, England, UK	9/15/1977
Harewood, Dorian	Dayton, OH.	8/6/1950
Hargitay, Mariska	Los Angeles, CA	1/23/1964
Harington, Kit	London, Eng., UK	12/26/1986
Harmon, Angie	Highland Park, TX.	8/10/1972
Harmon, Mark	Burbank, CA	9/2/1951
Harper, Ben	Claremont, CA	10/28/1969
Harper, Tess	Mammoth Spring, AR	8/15/1950
Harrelson, Woody	Midland, TX.	7/23/1961
Harris, Ed	Tenafly, NJ	11/28/1950
Harris, Emmylou	Birmingham, AL	4/2/1947

Name	Birthplace	Birthdate
Harris, Jared	London, Eng., UK	8/24/1961
Harris, Neil Patrick	Albuquerque, NM	6/15/1973
Harris, Rosemary	Ashby, England, UK	9/19/1927?
Harris, Steve	Chicago, IL	12/3/1965
Harrison, Gregory	Avalon, CA	5/31/1950
Harry, Deborah	Miami, FL	7/1/1945
Hart, Kevin	Philadelphia, PA	7/3/1980
Hart, Mary	Madison, SD	11/8/1950
Hart, Melissa Joan	Smithtown, NY	4/18/1976
Hartley, Mariette	New York, NY	6/21/1940
Hartman, David	Pawtucket, RI	5/19/1935
Hartman Black, Lisa	Houston, TX	6/1/1956
Hartnett, Josh	San Francisco, CA	7/21/1978
Harvey, P. J.	Yeovil, Somerset, Eng., UK	10/9/1969
Harvey, Steve	Welch, WV	1/17/1956
Hasselbeck, Elisabeth	Cranston, RI	5/28/1977
Hasselhoff, David	Baltimore, MD	7/17/1952
Hatcher, Teri	Sunnyvale, CA	12/8/1964
Hatfield, Juliana	Wiscasset, ME	7/27/1967
Hathaway, Anne	Brooklyn, NY	11/12/1982
Hawke, Ethan	Austin, TX	11/6/1970
Hawn, Goldie	Washington, DC	11/21/1945
Hayek, Salma	Coatzacoalcos, Mexico	9/2/1966
Hayes, Hunter	Breaux Bridge, LA	9/9/1991
Hayes, Sean	Glen Ellyn, IL	6/26/1970
Hays, Robert	Bethesda, MD	7/24/1947
Haysbert, Dennis	San Mateo, CA	6/2/1955
Head, Anthony	Camden Town, Eng., UK	2/20/1954
Headey, Lena	Hamilton, Bermuda	10/3/1973
Hearn, George	St. Louis, MO	6/18/1934
Heaton, Patricia	Bay Village, OH	3/4/1958
Heche, Anne	Aurora, OH	5/25/1969
Heder, Jon	Fort Collins, CO	10/26/1977
Hedges, Lucas	New York, NY	12/12/1996
Hedren, Tippi	New Ulm, MN	1/19/1930
Heigl, Katherine	Washington, DC	11/24/1978
Helberg, Simon	Los Angeles, CA	12/9/1980
Helfgott, David	Melbourne, Vic., Australia	5/19/1947
Helgenberger, Marg	Fremont, NE	11/16/1958
Helms, Ed	Atlanta, GA	1/24/1974
Hemingway, Mariel	Mill Valley, CA	11/22/1961
Hemsworth, Chris	Melbourne, Vic., Australia	8/11/1983
Hemsworth, Liam	Melbourne, Vic., Australia	1/13/1990
Hemsworth, Luke	Melbourne, Vic., Australia	11/5/1980
Hendricks, Christina	Knoxville, TN	5/3/1975
Henley, Don	Gilmer, TX	7/22/1947
Henner, Marilu	Chicago, IL	4/6/1952
Hennessy, Jill	Edmonton, AB, Canada	11/25/1968
Henson, Taraji P.	Washington, DC	9/11/1970
Herman, Pee-Wee	Peekskill, NY.	8/27/1952
Hershey, Barbara	Hollywood, CA	2/5/1948
Hesseman, Howard	Lebanon, OR	2/27/1940
Hetfield, James	Downey, CA	8/3/1963
Hewitt, Jennifer Love	Waco, TX	2/21/1979
Hicks, Catherine	Scottsdale, AZ.	8/6/1951
Hiddleston, Tom	London, England, UK	2/9/1981
Higgins, John Michael	Boston, MA.	2/12/1963
Hightower, Chelsie	Las Vegas, NV	7/21/1989
Hill, Dulé	Orange, NJ	-5/3/1975
Hill, Faith	Jackson, MS	9/21/1967
Hill, Jonah	Los Angeles, CA	12/20/1983
Hill, Lauryn	South Orange, NJ	5/26/1975
Hines, Cheryl	Miami Beach, FL	9/21/1965
Hirsch, Emile	Palms, CA	3/13/1985
Hirsch, Judd	Bronx, NY	3/15/1935
Hodgman, John	Cambridge, MA.	6/3/1971
Hoffman, Dustin	Los Angeles, CA	8/8/1937
Hogan, Hulk	Augusta, GA	8/11/1953
Hogan, Paul	Lightning Ridge, NSW, Australia	10/8/1939
Holbrook, Hal	Cleveland, OH	2/17/1925
Holliday, Polly	Jasper, AL.	7/2/1937
Holloway, Josh	San Jose, CA	7/20/1969
Holly, Lauren	Bristol, PA	10/28/1963
Holmes, Katie	Toledo, OH	12/18/1978
Hopkins, Anthony	Port Talbot, South Wales, UK	12/31/1937
Hopkins, Bo	Greenville, SC	2/2/1942
Hopkins, Telma	Louisville, KY.	10/28/1948
Horne, Marilyn	Bradford, PA	1/16/1934
Hornsby, Bruce	Williamsburg, VA	11/23/1954
Horsley, Lee	Muleshoe, TX	5/15/1955
Hough, Derek	Salt Lake City, UT	5/17/1985
Hough, Julianne	Salt Lake City, UT	7/20/1988
Hounsou, Djimon	Cotonou, Benin	4/24/1964
Howard, Clint	Burbank, CA	4/20/1959
Howard, Ron	Duncan, OK.	3/11/1954
Howard, Terrence	Chicago, IL	3/11/1969
Howell, C. Thomas	Van Nuys, CA	12/7/1966
Howes, Sally Ann	St. John's Wood, London, England, UK	7/20/1930
Hudgens, Vanessa	Salinas, CA	12/14/1988
Hudson, Jennifer	Chicago, IL	9/12/1981
Hudson, Kate	Los Angeles, CA	4/19/1979
Huffman, Felicity	Bedford, NY.	12/9/1962
Hughley, D. L.	Los Angeles, CA	3/6/1963
Hulce, Tom	Detroit, MI	12/6/1953
Humperdinck, Engelbert	Madras, India.	5/2/1936
Humphries, Barry	Melbourne, Vic., Australia.	2/17/1934
Hunt, Bonnie	Chicago, IL	9/22/1964
Hunt, Helen	Culver City, CA	6/15/1963
Hunt, Linda	Morristown, NJ	4/2/1945
Hunter, Holly	Conyers, GA	3/20/1958
Hurley, Elizabeth	Hampshire, England, UK	6/10/1965
Hurt, Mary Beth	Marshalltown, IA	9/26/1948
Hurt, William	Washington, DC	3/20/1950
Huston, Anjelica	Santa Monica, CA	7/8/1951
Hutcherson, Josh	Union, KY	10/12/1992
Hutton, Lauren	Charleston, SC	11/17/1943
Hutton, Timothy	Malibu, CA.	8/16/1960
Ian, Janis	Bronx, NY	4/7/1951
Ice Cube	Los Angeles, CA	6/15/1969
Ice-T	Newark, NJ	2/16/1958
Idle, Eric	S. Shields, England, UK..	3/29/1943
Idol, Billy	Middlesex, England, UK	11/30/1955
Iglesias, Enrique	Madrid, Spain	5/8/1975
Iglesias, Julio	Madrid, Spain	9/23/1943
Iler, Robert	New York, NY	3/2/1985
Iman	Mogadishu, Somalia	7/25/1955
Imbruglia, Natalie	Sydney, NSW, Australia	2/4/1975
Imperioli, Michael	Mount Vernon, NY	3/26/1966
Iñárritu, Alejandro G.	Mexico City, Mexico	8/15/1963
Innes, Laura	Pontiac, MI	8/16/1957?
Ireland, Kathy	Glendale, CA.	3/20/1963
Irons, Jeremy	Cowes, Isle of Wight, Eng., UK	9/19/1948
Irving, Amy	Palo Alto, CA	9/10/1953
Irwin, Bill	Santa Monica, CA	4/11/1950
Isaac, Oscar	Guatemala.	1/5/1980
Ivanek, Željko	Ljubljana, Yugo. (Slovenia)	8/15/1957
Ivey, Judith	El Paso, TX	9/4/1951
Ivory, James	Berkeley, CA	6/7/1928
Izzard, Eddie	Aden, Yemen.	2/7/1962
Ja Rule	Hollis, Queens, NY	2/29/1976
Jackée (Harry)	Winston-Salem, NC	8/14/1956
Jackman, Hugh	Sydney, NSW, Australia	10/12/1968
Jackson, Cheyenne	Newport, WA	7/12/1975
Jackson, Glenda	Birkenhead, England, UK.	5/9/1936
Jackson, Janet	Gary, IN.	5/16/1966
Jackson, Jermaine	Gary, IN.	12/11/1954
Jackson, Jonathan	Orlando, FL.	5/11/1982
Jackson, Joshua	Vancouver, BC, Canada.	6/11/1978
Jackson, Kate	Birmingham, AL.	10/29/1948
Jackson, La Toya	Gary, IN.	5/29/1956
Jackson, Peter	Wellington, New Zealand.	10/31/1961
Jackson, Samuel L.	Washington, DC	12/21/1948
Jacobi, Derek	London, England, UK	10/22/1938
Jagger, Mick	Dartford, England, UK	7/26/1943
James, Kevin	Mineola, NY.	4/26/1965
Jamison, Judith	Philadelphia, PA	5/10/1943
Janis, Conrad	New York, NY	2/11/1928
Janney, Allison	Dayton, OH	11/19/1959
Janssen, Famke	Amsterdam, Netherlands.	11/5/1965
Jardine, Al	Lima, OH.	9/3/1942
Jarmusch, Jim	Akron, OH	1/22/1953
Jarrett, Keith	Allentown, PA	5/8/1945
Jay-Z	Brooklyn, NY	12/4/1969
Jenkins, Barry	Miami, FL	11/19/1979
Jenkins, Richard	DeKalb, IL	5/4/1947
Jenner, Caitlyn	Mount Kisco, NY	10/28/1949
Jenner, Kendall	Los Angeles, CA	9/3/1995
Jenner, Kris	San Diego, CA	11/5/1955
Jenner, Kylie	Los Angeles, CA	8/10/1997
Jepsen, Carly Rae	Mission, BC, Canada.	11/21/1985
Jett, Joan	Philadelphia, PA	9/22/1958
Jewel (Kilcher)	Payson, UT	5/23/1974
Jewison, Norman	Toronto, ON, Canada.	7/21/1926
Jillette, Penn	Greenfield, MA	3/5/1955
Jillian, Ann	Cambridge, MA	1/29/1950
Joel, Billy	Bronx, NY	5/9/1949
Johansson, Scarlett	New York, NY	11/22/1984
John, Elton	Pinner, Middlesex, Eng., UK	3/25/1947
Johns, Glynis	Durban, South Africa	10/5/1923
Johnson, Beverly	Buffalo, NY	10/13/1952
Johnson, Don	Flatt Creek, MO.	12/15/1949
Johnson, Dwayne "The Rock"	Hayward, CA	5/2/1972
Johnston, Bruce	Los Angeles, CA	6/24/1942
Johnston, Kristen	Washington, DC	9/20/1967
Jolie, Angelina	Los Angeles, CA	6/4/1975
Jonas, Joe	Casa Grande, AZ.	8/15/1989
Jonas, Kevin	Teaneck, NJ	11/5/1987
Jonas, Nick	Dallas, TX	9/16/1992
Jones, Angus T.	Austin, TX	10/8/1993
Jones, Bill T.	Bunnell, FL	2/15/1952
Jones, Cherry	Paris, TN	11/21/1956

Name	Birthplace	Birthdate	Name	Birthplace	Birthdate
Jones, Gemma	London, England, UK	12/4/1942	Krasinski, John	Newton, MA.	10/20/1979
Jones, Grace	Spanish Town, Jamaica	5/19/1948	Krause, Peter	Alexandria, MN	8/12/1965
Jones, Jack	Hollywood, CA	1/14/1938	Kressley, Carson	Allentown, PA	11/11/1969
Jones, James Earl	Arkabutla, MS	1/17/1931	Kretschmann, Thomas	Dessau, E. Germany	9/8/1962
Jones, John Paul	Sidcup, England, UK	1/3/1946	Kristofferson, Kris	Brownsville, TX	6/22/1936
Jones, January	Sioux Falls, SD	1/5/1978	Kudrow, Lisa	Encino, CA	7/30/1963
Jones, Leslie	Memphis, TN	9/7/1967	Kunis, Mila	Kiev, Ukraine	8/14/1983
Jones, Mick	London, England, UK	6/26/1955	Kurtz, Swoosie	Omaha, NE	9/6/1944
Jones, Norah	New York, NY	3/30/1979	Kutcher, Ashton	Cedar Rapids, IA	2/7/1978
Jones, Quincy	Chicago, IL	3/14/1933	Kwan, Nancy	Hong Kong	5/19/1939
Jones, Shirley	Charleroi, PA	3/31/1934	LaBelle, Patti	Philadelphia, PA	5/24/1944
Jones, Star	Badin, NC	3/24/1962	LaBeouf, Shia	Los Angeles, CA	6/11/1986
Jones, Tom	Pontypridd, Wales, UK	6/7/1940	Lachey, Nick	Harlan, KY.	11/9/1973
Jones, Tommy Lee	San Saba, TX	9/15/1946	Ladd, Cheryl	Huron, SD	7/12/1951
Jonze, Spike	Rockville, MD	10/22/1969	Ladd, Diane	Meridian, MS.	11/29/1932
Jordan, Michael B.	Santa Ana, CA	2/9/1987	Lady Gaga	New York, NY	3/28/1986
Jovovich, Milla	Kiev, Ukraine	12/17/1975	Lagasse, Emeril	Fall River, MA	10/15/1959
Judd, Ashley	Granada Hills, CA	4/19/1968	Lahti, Christine	Birmingham, MI.	4/4/1950
Judd, Naomi	Ashland, KY	1/11/1946	Laine, Cleo	Southall, England, UK	10/28/1927
Judd, Wynonna	Ashland, KY	5/30/1964	Lake, Ricki	Hastings-on-Hudson, NY.	9/21/1968
Kaczmarek, Jane	Milwaukee, WI	12/21/1955	Lamar, Kendrick	Compton, CA.	6/17/1987
Kaling, Mindy	Cambridge, MA	6/24/1979	Lamas, Lorenzo	Santa Monica, CA	1/20/1958
Kaluuya, Daniel	London, Eng., UK	2/24/1989	Lambert, Adam	Indianapolis, IN	1/29/1982
Kanaly, Steve	Burbank, CA	3/14/1946	Lambert, Christopher	Great Neck, NY	3/29/1957
Kane, Carol	Cleveland, OH	6/18/1952	Lambert, Miranda	Longview, TX.	11/10/1983
Kaplan, Gabe	Brooklyn, NY	3/31/1945	Landis, John	Chicago, IL	8/3/1950
Kardashian, Khloe	Los Angeles, CA	6/27/1984	Lane, Diane	New York, NY	1/22/1965
Kardashian, Kim	Los Angeles, CA	10/21/1980	Lane, Nathan	Jersey City, NJ.	2/3/1956
Kardashian, Kourtney	Los Angeles, CA	4/18/1979	lang, k.d.	Consort, AB, Canada	11/2/1961
Karn, Richard	Seattle, WA	2/17/1956	Lang, Stephen	Jamaica Estates, Queens,	
Katic, Stana	Hamilton, ON, Canada	4/26/1978		NY	7/11/1952
Kattan, Chris	Sherman Oaks, CA	10/19/1970	Lange, Jessica	Cloquet, MN	4/20/1949
Kaufmann, Jonas	Munich, Germany	1/10/1969	Langella, Frank	Bayonne, NJ	1/1/1938
Kavner, Julie	Burbank, CA	9/7/1951	Lansbury, Angela	London, England, UK	10/16/1925
Kaye, Judy	Phoenix, AZ.	12/11/1948	LaPaglia, Anthony	Adelaide, SA, Australia	1/31/1959
Kazan, Lainie	New York, NY	5/15/1940	Larroquette, John	New Orleans, LA	11/25/1947
Keach, Stacy	Savannah, GA	6/2/1941	Larson, Brie	Sacramento, CA	10/1/1989
Keaton, Diane	Santa Ana, CA	1/5/1946	LaSalle, Eriq	Hartford, CT	6/23/1962
Keaton, Michael	Coraopolis, PA.	9/5/1951	Lauper, Cyndi	Ozone Park, Queens, NY	6/22/1953
Keener, Catherine	Miami, FL	3/23/1959	Laurie, Hugh	Oxford, England, UK	6/11/1959
Keillor, Garrison	Anoka, MN	8/7/1942	Laurie, Piper	Detroit, MI	1/22/1932
Keitel, Harvey	Brooklyn, NY	5/13/1939	Lautner, Taylor	Grand Rapids, MI	2/11/1992
Keith, David	Knoxville, TN	5/8/1954	Lavigne, Avril	Belleville, ON, Canada.	9/27/1984
Keith, Penelope	Sutton, Surrey, Eng., UK	4/2/1940	Lavin, Linda	Portland, ME	10/15/1937
Kellerman, Sally	Long Beach, CA	6/2/1937	Law, Jude	London, England, UK	12/29/1972
Kelly, Minka	Los Angeles, CA	6/24/1980	Lawless, Lucy	Mount Albert, New Zealand	3/29/1968
Kelly, R(obert)	Chicago, IL	1/8/1967	Lawrence, Carol	Melrose Park, IL	9/5/1934
Kemper, Ellie	Kansas City, MO	5/2/1980	Lawrence, Jennifer	Louisville, KY.	8/15/1990
Kendrick, Anna	Portland, ME	8/9/1985	Lawrence, Joey	Montgomery, PA	4/20/1976
Kennedy, Jamie	Upper Darby, PA	5/25/1970	Lawrence, Martin	Frankfurt, Germany	4/16/1965
Kenny G	Seattle, WA	6/5/1956	Lawrence, Steve	Brooklyn, NY	7/8/1935
Kent, Allegra	Santa Monica, CA	8/11/1937	Lawrence, Vicki	Inglewood, CA.	3/26/1949
Keoghan, Phil	Christchurch, New Zealand	5/31/1967	Leachman, Cloris	Des Moines, IA	4/30/1926
Kerns, Joanna	San Francisco, CA.	2/12/1953	Lear, Norman	New Haven, CT.	7/27/1922
Kesha	Los Angeles, CA	3/1/1987	Learned, Michael	Washington, DC	4/9/1939
Key, Keegan-Michael	Southfield, MI	3/22/1971	Leary, Denis	Worcester, MA.	8/18/1957
Keys, Alicia	New York, NY	1/25/1981	LeBlanc, Matt	Newton, MA.	7/25/1967
Khaled, DJ	New Orleans, LA	11/26/1975	LeBon, Simon	Bushey, England, UK.	10/27/1958
Khalifa, Wiz.	Minot, ND	9/8/1987	Lee, Ang	Pingtung, Taiwan	10/23/1954
Khan, Chaka	Great Lakes, IL	3/23/1953	Lee, Brenda	Lithonia, GA	12/11/1944
Kid Rock	Romeo, MI.	1/17/1971	Lee, Jason	Huntington Beach, CA.	4/25/1970
Kidman, Nicole	Honolulu, HI	6/20/1967	Lee, Michele	Los Angeles, CA	6/24/1942
Kilborn, Craig	Kansas City, KS.	8/24/1962	Lee, Spike	Atlanta, GA	3/20/1957
Kilmer, Val	Los Angeles, CA	12/31/1959	Leeves, Jane	Ilford, England, UK	4/18/1961
Kim, Daniel Dae	Pusan, South Korea.	8/4/1968	Legend, John	Springfield, OH	12/28/1978
Kimmel, Jimmy	Brooklyn, NY	11/13/1967	Leguizamo, John	Bogotá, Colombia	7/22/1964
King, Carole	Brooklyn, NY	2/9/1942	Leigh, Jennifer Jason	Hollywood, CA.	2/5/1962
King, Gayle	Chevy Chase, MD	12/28/1954?	Leighton, Laura	Iowa City, IA	7/24/1968
King, Larry	Brooklyn, NY	11/19/1933	Lennox, Annie	Aberdeen, Scotland, UK	12/25/1954
King, Perry	Alliance, OH	4/30/1948	Leno, Jay	New Rochelle, NY	4/28/1950
King, Regina	Los Angeles, CA	1/15/1971	Leo, Melissa	New York, NY	9/14/1960
Kingsley, Ben	Scarborough, England, UK	12/31/1943	Leonard, Robert Sean	Westwood, NJ.	2/28/1969
Kingston, Alex.	London, England, UK	3/11/1963	Leoni, Tea	New York, NY	2/25/1966
Kinnear, Greg	Logansport, IN.	6/17/1963	Leto, Jared	Bossier City, LA.	12/26/1971
Kinney, Kathy	Stevens Point, WI	11/3/1954	Letterman, David	Indianapolis, IN	4/12/1947
Kinski, Nastassja	Berlin, W. Germany	1/24/1960	Levin, Harvey	Los Angeles, CA	9/2/1960
Kirkland, Gelsey	Bethlehem, PA.	12/29/1952	Levine, Adam	Los Angeles, CA	3/18/1979
Kirkpatrick, Chris	Clarion, PA	10/17/1971	Levine, James	Cincinnati, OH.	6/23/1943
Kirshner, Mia.	Toronto, ON, Canada.	1/25/1975	Levine, Ted	Bellaire, OH.	5/29/1957
Kitsch, Taylor	Kelowna, BC, Canada	4/8/1981	Levinson, Barry.	Baltimore, MD	4/6/1942
Klein, Robert.	Bronx, NY	2/8/1942	Levy, Daniel	Toronto, ON, Canada.	8/9/1983
Kline, Kevin.	St. Louis, MO.	10/24/1947	Levy, Eugene	Hamilton, ON, Canada.	12/17/1946
Klum, Heidi	Bergish-Gladbach, Germany	6/1/1973	Lewis, Damian	London, Eng., UK	2/11/1971
Knight, Gladys	Atlanta, GA	5/28/1944	Lewis, Huey	New York, NY	7/5/1950
Knight, T. R.	Minneapolis, MN	3/26/1973	Lewis, Jason	Newport Beach, CA.	6/25/1971
Knight, Wayne.	New York, NY	8/7/1955	Lewis, Jerry Lee	Ferriday, LA.	9/29/1935
Knightley, Keira	Teddington, England, UK.	3/26/1985	Lewis, Juliette	Los Angeles, CA	6/21/1973
Knopfler, Mark	Glasgow, Scotland, UK	8/12/1949	Lewis, Leona	London, England, UK	4/3/1985
Knowles, Beyoncé	Houston, TX	9/4/1981	Lewis, Richard	Brooklyn, NY	6/29/1947
Knoxville, Johnny	Knoxville, TN.	3/11/1971	Li, Jet	Beijing, China	4/26/1963
Kopell, Bernie	Brooklyn, NY	6/21/1933	Light, Judith	Trenton, NJ.	2/9/1949
Kotto, Yaphet	New York, NY	11/15/1937	Lightfoot, Gordon	Orillia, ON, Canada	11/17/1938
Krakowski, Jane	Parsippany, NJ.	10/11/1968	Lil' Kim	Brooklyn, NY.	7/11/1975

Name	Birthplace	Birthdate
Lil Nas X	Lithia Springs, GA	4/9/1999
Lil' Romeo	New Orleans, LA	8/19/1989
Lil Wayne	New Orleans, LA	9/27/1982
Lilly, Evangeline	Fort Saskatchewan, AB, Can.	8/3/1979
Lincoln, Andrew	London, England, UK	9/14/1973
Linden, Hal	Bronx, NY	3/20/1931
Ling, Lisa	Sacramento, CA	8/30/1973
Linn-Baker, Mark	St. Louis, MO.	6/17/1954
Linney, Laura	New York, NY	2/5/1964
Liotta, Ray	Newark, NJ	12/18/1954
Lithgow, John	Rochester, NY	10/19/1945
Little, Rich	Ottawa, ON, Canada	11/26/1938
Littrell, Brian	Lexington, KY	2/20/1975
Liu, Lucy	Jackson Heights, Queens, NY	12/2/1968
Lively, Blake	Tarzana, CA	8/25/1987
LL Cool J	St. Albans, Queens, NY	1/14/1968
Lloyd, Christopher	Stamford, CT	10/22/1938
Lloyd Webber, Andrew	London, England, UK	3/22/1948
Lockhart, June	New York, NY	6/25/1925
Locklear, Heather	Westwood, CA.	9/25/1961
Loggins, Kenny	Everett, WA	1/7/1948
Lohan, Lindsay	New York, NY	7/2/1986
Lollobrigida, Gina	Subiaco, Italy	7/4/1927
Lonergan, Kenneth	New York, NY	10/16/1962
Long, Nia	Brooklyn, NY	10/30/1970
Long, Shelley	Ft. Wayne, IN.	8/23/1949
Longoria, Eva	Corpus Christi, TX	3/15/1975
Lopez, George	Mission Hills, CA	4/23/1961
Lopez, Jennifer	Bronx, NY	7/24/1969
Lopez, Mario	San Diego, CA	10/10/1973
Lorde	Takapuna, New Zealand	11/7/1996
Loren, Sophia	Rome, Italy	9/20/1934
Louis C.K.	Washington, DC	9/12/1967
Louis-Dreyfus, Julia	New York, NY	1/13/1961
Lovato, Demi	Albuquerque, NM.	8/20/1992
Love, Courtney	San Francisco, CA.	7/9/1964
Love, Mike	Baldwin Hills, CA	3/15/1941
Loveless, Patty	Pikeville, KY	1/4/1957
Lovett, Lyle	Klein, TX	11/1/1957
Lovitz, Jon	Tarzana, CA.	7/21/1957
Lowe, Rob	Charlottesville, VA	3/17/1964
Lucas, George	Modesto, CA	5/14/1944
Lucci, Susan	Scarsdale, NY	12/23/1946
Luckinbill, Laurence	Ft. Smith, AR	11/21/1934
Ludacris	Champaign, IL	9/11/1977
Ludwig, Christa	Berlin, Germany	3/16/1924
Luhrmann, Baz	Sydney, NSW, Australia	9/17/1962
LuPone, Patti	Northport, NY	4/21/1949
Lynch, David	Missoula, MT.	1/20/1946
Lynch, Jane	Dolton, IL.	7/14/1960
Lynn, Loretta	Butcher Hollow, KY	4/14/1932
Lynne, Shelby	Quantico, VA	10/22/1968
Lyonne, Natasha	New York, NY	4/4/1979
Ma, Yo-Yo	Paris, France	10/7/1955
Macchio, Ralph	Huntington, NY	11/4/1961
MacDonald, Kelly	Glasgow, Scotland, UK	2/23/1976
MacDowell, Andie	Gaffney, SC	4/21/1958
MacFarlane, Seth	Kent, CT	10/26/1973
MacGowan, Shane	Tunbridge, Kent, Eng., UK	12/25/1957
MacGraw, Ali	Pound Ridge, NY	4/1/1939
Macklemore	Seattle, WA	6/19/1983
MacLachlan, Kyle	Yakima, WA.	2/22/1959
MacLaine, Shirley	Richmond, VA	4/24/1934
MacLeod, Gavin	Mt. Kisco, NY.	2/28/1931
MacNicol, Peter	Dallas, TX	4/10/1954
MacPherson, Elle	Sydney, NSW, Australia	3/29/1964
Macy, William H.	Miami, FL	3/13/1950
Madden, John	Austin, MN.	4/10/1936
Madden, Richard	Elderslie, Scot., UK	6/18/1986
Madigan, Amy	Chicago, IL	9/11/1950
Madonna (Ciccone)	Bay City, MI	8/16/1958
Madsen, Michael	Chicago, IL	9/25/1959
Maguire, Tobey	Santa Monica, CA	6/27/1975
Maher, Bill	New York, NY	1/20/1956
Majors, Lee	Wyandotte, MI	4/23/1939
Makarova, Natalia	Leningrad, Russia	11/21/1940
Malek, Rami	Los Angeles, CA	5/12/1981
Malick, Terrence	Ottawa, IL	11/30/1943
Malick, Wendie	Buffalo, NY	12/13/1950
Malina, Joshua	New York, NY	1/17/1966
Malkovich, John	Christopher, IL	12/9/1953
Mamet, David	Chicago, IL	11/30/1947
Manchester, Melissa	Bronx, NY	2/15/1951
Mandel, Howie	Toronto, ON, Canada.	11/29/1955
Mandrell, Barbara	Houston, TX	12/25/1948
Mangione, Chuck	Rochester, NY	11/29/1940
Manheim, Camryn	Caldwell, NJ	3/8/1961
Manilow, Barry	Brooklyn, NY	6/17/1943
Mann, Aimee	Richmond, VA	8/9/1960
Manoff, Dinah	New York, NY	1/25/1958
Manson, Marilyn	Canton, OH	1/5/1969

Name	Birthplace	Birthdate
Mantegna, Joe	Chicago, IL	11/13/1947
Mantello, Joe	Rockford, IL.	12/27/1962
Mara, Kate	Bedford, NY.	2/27/1983
Mara, Rooney	Bedford, NY.	4/17/1985
Margulies, Julianna.	Spring Valley, NY.	6/8/1966
Marie, Constance	Hollywood, CA.	9/9/1965
Marin, Cheech	Los Angeles, CA	7/13/1946
Marinaro, Ed.	New York, NY	3/31/1950
Mars, Bruno	Honolulu, HI	10/8/1985
Marsalis, Branford.	Breaux Bridge, LA	8/26/1960
Marsalis, Wynton	New Orleans, LA	10/18/1961
Marsh, Jean	London, England, UK	7/1/1934
Marshall, Peter	Huntington, WV	3/30/1926
Martin, Chris	Devon, England, UK	3/2/1977
Martin, Jesse L.	Rocky Mount, VA	1/18/1969
Martin, Kellie.	Riverside, CA.	10/16/1975
Martin, Ricky	San Juan, Puerto Rico.	12/24/1971
Martin, Steve	Waco, TX.	8/14/1945
Martindale, Margo.	Jacksonville, TX.	7/18/1951
Martins, Peter	Copenhagen, Denmark	10/27/1946
Maslany, Tatiana	Regina, SK, Canada	9/22/1985
Mason, Jackie.	Sheboygan, WI	6/9/1931
Mason, Marsha	St. Louis, MO.	4/3/1942
Masterson, Mary Stuart	New York, NY	6/28/1966
Mastrantonio, Mary Elizabeth.	Lombard, IL.	11/17/1958
Masur, Richard	New York, NY	11/20/1948
Mathers, Jerry.	Sioux City, IA.	6/2/1948
Matheson, Tim	Glendale, CA.	12/31/1947
Mathis, Johnny	Gilmer, TX.	9/30/1935
Matlin, Marlee	Morton Grove, IL	8/24/1965
Matthews, Dave	Johannesburg, South Africa	1/9/1967
May, Elaine	Philadelphia, PA	4/21/1932
Mayer, John	Bridgeport, CT.	10/16/1977
Mays, Jayma	Bristol, TN	7/16/1979
Mazar, Debi	Jamaica, Queens, NY	8/13/1964
McAdams, Rachel.	London, ON, Canada.	11/17/1978
McArdle, Andrea	Abington, PA	11/5/1963
McAvoy, James	Glasgow, Scotland, UK	4/21/1979
McBride, Patricia	Teaneck, NJ	8/23/1942
McCallum, David.	Glasgow, Scotland, UK	9/19/1933
McCarthy, Andrew	Westfield, NJ	11/29/1962
McCarthy, Jenny	Chicago, IL	11/1/1972
McCarthy, Melissa	Plainfield, IL.	8/26/1970
McCartney, Paul	Liverpool, England, UK	6/18/1942
McCarver, Tim	Memphis, TN.	10/16/1941
McConaughey, Matthew	Uvalde, TX.	11/4/1969
McCoo, Marilyn	Jersey City, NJ.	9/30/1943
McCormack, Eric	Toronto, ON, Canada.	4/18/1963
McCormack, Mary	Plainsfield, NJ	2/8/1969
McCrane, Paul	Philadelphia, PA	1/19/1961
McDaniel, James	Washington, DC	3/25/1958
McDermott, Dylan	Waterbury, CT	10/26/1961
McDiarmid, Ian	Carnoustie, Tayside, Scot., UK	4/17/1944?
McDonald, Audra	Berlin, Germany	7/3/1970
McDonnell, Mary	Wilkes-Barre, PA	4/28/1952
McDormand, Frances.	Chicago, IL	6/23/1957
McDowell, Malcolm.	Leeds, England, UK.	6/13/1943
McEntire, Reba.	McAlester, OK.	3/28/1955
McFerrin, Bobby	New York, NY	3/11/1950
McGillis, Kelly	Newport Beach, CA.	7/9/1957
McGovern, Elizabeth	Evanston, IL	7/18/1961
McGovern, Maureen	Youngstown, OH	7/27/1949
McGraw, Tim.	Delhi, LA	5/1/1967
McGregor, Ewan.	Crieff, Scotland, UK	3/31/1971
McHale, Joel.	Rome, Italy	11/20/1971
McHale, Kevin.	Plano, TX.	6/14/1988
McKean, Michael	New York, NY	10/17/1947
McKechnie, Donna	Pontiac, MI	11/16/1942
McKellen, Ian	Burnley, England, UK.	5/25/1939
McKenzie, Ben	Austin, TX	9/12/1978
McKidd, Kevin.	Elgin, Scotland, UK	8/9/1973
McKinnon, Kate	Sea Cliff, NY	1/6/1984
McLachlan, Sarah.	Halifax, NS, Canada	1/28/1968
McLean, A. J.	West Palm Beach, FL	1/9/1978
McNichol, Kristy	Los Angeles, CA	9/11/1962
McRaney, Gerald	Collins, MS	8/19/1947
McQueen, Steven	London, England, UK	10/9/1969
McQueen, Steven R.	Los Angeles, CA	7/13/1988
McShane, Ian	Blackburn, England, UK.	9/29/1942
Meat Loaf	Dallas, TX	9/27/1947
Meester, Leighton	Marco Island, FL	4/9/1986
Mehta, Zubin.	Bombay, India	4/29/1936
Mellencamp, John.	Seymour, IN	10/7/1951
Meloni, Christopher	Washington, DC	4/2/1961
Mendes, Sam	Redding, England, UK.	8/1/1965
Mendes, Sergio	Niteroi, Brazil.	2/11/1941
Mendes, Shawn	Toronto, ON, Canada.	8/8/1998
Menzel, Idina	Syosset, NY.	5/30/1971
Menzies, Tobias	London, England, UK	3/7/1974
Merchant, Natalie	Jamestown, NY.	10/26/1963
Merkerson, S. Epatha	Saginaw, MI.	11/28/1952

Name	Birthplace	Birthdate
Messing, Debra	Brooklyn, NY	8/15/1968
Metcalf, Laurie	Carbondale, IL	6/16/1955
Meyers, Seth	Bedford, NH.	12/28/1973
Michaels, Al	Brooklyn, NY	11/12/1944
Michaels, Bret.	Butler, PA	3/15/1963
Michaels, Lorne	Toronto, ON, Canada	11/17/1944
Michele, Lea	Bronx, NY	8/29/1986
Midler, Bette	Honolulu, HI	12/1/1945
Midori (Goto)	Osaka, Japan	10/25/1971
Miguel, Luis	San Juan, PR	4/19/1970
Mike D	Brooklyn, NY	11/20/1965
Milano, Alyssa	Brooklyn, NY	12/19/1972
Miles, Sarah	Ingatestone, England, UK	12/31/1941
Miles, Vera	nr. Boise City, OK.	8/23/1930
Miller, Dennis	Pittsburgh, PA	11/3/1953
Miller, Jonny Lee	Kingston Upon Thames, England, UK	11/15/1972
Miller, Penelope Ann.	Santa Monica, CA	1/13/1964
Mills, Donna	Chicago, IL	12/11/1943
Mills, Hayley	London, England, UK	4/18/1946
Milnes, Sherrill	Downers Grove, IL.	1/10/1935
Milsap, Ronnie	Robinsville, NC	1/16/1943
Mimieux, Yvette.	Hollywood, CA.	1/8/1942
Minaj, Nicki	St. James, Trinidad and Tobago.	12/8/1982
Ming-Na (Wen)	Coloane Island, Macao	11/20/1963
Minhaj, Hasan.	Davis, CA	9/23/1985
Minnelli, Liza.	Los Angeles, CA	3/12/1946
Minogue, Kylie	Melbourne, Vic., Australia.	5/28/1968
Miranda, Lin-Manuel	New York, NY	1/16/1980
Mirren, Helen	London, England, UK	7/26/1945
Mitchell, Brian Stokes	Seattle, WA	10/31/1957
Mitchell, Elizabeth.	Los Angeles, CA	3/27/1970
Mitchell, Jerry	Paw Paw, MI	1/15/1960
Mitchell, Joni.	Fort McLeod, AB, Canada	11/7/1943
Moby	New York, NY	9/11/1965
Modine, Matthew	Loma Linda, CA.	3/22/1959
Molina, Alfred	London, England, UK	5/24/1953
Moll, Richard.	Pasadena, CA	1/13/1943
Moloney, Janel	Woodland Hills, CA	10/3/1969
Monáe, Janelle	Kansas City, KS.	12/1/1985
Monaghan, Dominic	Berlin, Germany	12/8/1976
Monica (Arnold)	College Park, GA.	10/24/1980
Mo'Nique	Woodlawn, MD	12/11/1967
Moore, Demi	Roswell, NM	11/11/1962
Moore, Julianne	Fort Bragg, NC	12/3/1960
Moore, Mandy.	Nashua, NH.	4/10/1984
Moore, Melba	New York, NY	10/29/1945
Moore, Michael	Flint, MI.	4/23/1954
Moore, Terry	Los Angeles, CA	1/7/1929
Morales, Esai	Brooklyn, NY	10/1/1962
Moranis, Rick	Toronto, ON, Canada.	4/18/1953
Moreno, Rita	Humacao, Puerto Rico.	12/11/1931
Morgan, Jeffrey Dean	Seattle, WA	4/22/1966
Morgan, Piers	Guildford, Surrey, UK.	3/30/1965
Morgan, Tracy	Bronx, NY	11/10/1968
Moriarty, Michael	Detroit, MI	4/5/1941
Morris, Garrett	New Orleans, LA	2/1/1937
Morissette, Alanis	Ottawa, ON, Canada	6/1/1974
Morrison, Matthew	Fort Ord, CA	10/30/1978
Morrison, Van	Belfast, N. Ireland, UK	8/31/1945
Morrissey (Steven Patrick)	Manchester, England, UK.	5/22/1959
Morrow, Rob	New Rochelle, NY	9/21/1962
Morse, David.	Beverly, MA	10/11/1953
Morse, Robert.	Newton, MA.	5/18/1931
Mortensen, Viggo	New York, NY	10/20/1958
Mortimer, Emily.	London, England, UK	12/1/1971
Morton, Joe.	New York, NY	10/18/1947
Morton, Samantha	Nottingham, England, UK	5/13/1977
Moses, William	Los Angeles, CA	11/17/1959
Moss, Carrie-Anne	Vancouver, BC, Canada.	8/21/1967
Moss, Elisabeth	Los Angeles, CA	7/24/1982
Moss, Kate	Croydon, Surrey, Eng., UK	1/16/1974
Moyer, Stephen.	Brentwood, UK	10/11/1969
Moynahan, Bridget	Binghamton, NY	4/28/1971
Mueller-Stahl, Armin	Tilsit, E. Prussia.	12/17/1930
Mulaney, John.	Chicago, IL	8/26/1982
Muldaur, Diana	Brooklyn, NY	8/19/1938
Mulgrew, Kate	Dubuque, IA	4/29/1955
Mull, Martin.	Chicago, IL	8/18/1943
Mullally, Megan	Los Angeles, CA	11/12/1958
Mullan, Peter.	Peterhead, Scotland, UK .	11/2/1959
Mulligan, Carey.	London, England, UK	5/28/1985
Mulroney, Dermot	Alexandria, VA.	10/31/1963
Muniz, Frankie	Wood-Ridge, NJ	12/5/1985
Murphy, Ben	Jonesboro, AR.	3/6/1942
Murphy, Donna	Corona, Queens, NY	3/7/1958
Murphy, Eddie.	Brooklyn, NY	4/3/1961
Murphy, Michael	Los Angeles, CA	5/5/1938
Murphy, Ryan	Indianapolis, IN	11/30/1965
Murray, Anne.	Springhill, NS, Canada	6/20/1945
Murray, Bill	Wilmette, IL	9/21/1950
Murray, Don	Hollywood, CA	7/31/1929

Name	Birthplace	Birthdate
Musburger, Brent	Portland, OR	5/26/1939
Muti, Riccardo.	Naples, Italy.	7/28/1941
Myers, Mike	Scarborough, ON, Canada	5/25/1963
Nagra, Parminder	Leicester, England, UK	10/5/1975
Nanjiani, Kumail	Karachi, Pakistan.	2/21/1978
Nash, Graham	Blackpool, England, UK..	2/2/1942
Nash, Niecy	Palmdale, CA.	2/23/1970
Naughton, James	Middletown, CT	12/6/1945
Navarro, Dave	Santa Monica, CA	6/7/1967
Nealon, Kevin	St. Louis, MO.	11/18/1953
Neeson, Liam	Ballymena, N. Ireland, UK	6/7/1952
Neill, Sam	Ulster, N. Ireland, UK	9/14/1947
Nelligan, Kate	London, ON, Canada.	3/16/1951
Nelly	Austin, TX	11/2/1974
Nelson, Craig T.	Spokane, WA.	4/4/1944
Nelson, Judd.	Portland, ME	11/28/1959
Nelson, Tracy	Santa Monica, CA	10/25/1963
Nelson, Willie	Abbott, TX	4/30/1933
Nero, Peter	Brooklyn, NY	5/22/1934
Nesmith, Michael	Houston, TX	12/30/1942
Neuwirth, Bebe	Newark, NJ	12/31/1958
Neville, Aaron	New Orleans, LA	1/24/1941
Newhart, Bob	Oak Park, IL	9/5/1929
Newman, Randy	New Orleans, LA	11/28/1943
Newton, Thandie	London, England, UK	11/6/1972
Newton, Wayne.	Norfolk, VA	4/3/1942
Newton-John, Olivia	Cambridge, England, UK.	9/26/1948
Nicholas, Denise	Detroit, MI	7/12/1944
Nicholson, Jack	Neptune, NJ	4/22/1937
Nicks, Stevie	Phoenix, AZ.	5/26/1948
Nighy, Bill	Caterham, Surrey, Eng., UK	12/12/1949
Nixon, Cynthia	New York, NY	4/9/1966
Noah, Trevor	Soweto, South Africa	2/20/1984
Noble, John.	Port Pirie, S. Austral., Australia.	8/20/1948
Nolan, Christopher	London, England, UK	7/30/1970
Nolte, Nick	Omaha, NE.	2/8/1941
Noone, Peter.	Manchester, England, UK..	11/5/1947
Norris, Chuck	Ryan, OK.	3/10/1940
Northam, Jeremy	Cambridge, England, UK..	12/1/1961
Norton, Edward.	Boston, MA.	8/18/1969
Noth, Christopher	Madison, WI	11/13/1954
Novak, Kim	Chicago, IL	2/13/1933
Nuyen, France	Marseilles, France	7/31/1939
Nyong'o, Lupita.	Mexico City, Mexico	3/1/1983
Oates, John	New York, NY	4/7/1949
O'Brien, Conan	Brookline, MA	4/18/1963
O'Brien, Margaret	San Diego, CA.	1/15/1937
Ocean, Billy	Fyzabad, Trinidad and Tobago.	1/21/1950
Ocean, Frank	Long Beach, CA	10/28/1987
O'Connor, Sinead	Glenageary, Ireland.	12/8/1966
Odenkirk, Bob.	Berwyn, IL.	10/22/1962
O'Donnell, Chris	Winnetka, IL	6/26/1970
O'Donnell, Rosie.	Commack, NY	3/21/1962
Offerman, Nick	Joliet, IL.	6/26/1970
O'Grady, Gail	Detroit, MI	1/23/1963
Oh, Sandra	Nepean, ON, Canada	7/20/1971
O'Hara, Catherine.	Toronto, ON, Canada.	3/4/1954
O'Hare, Denis	Kansas City, MO	1/17/1962
Oka, Masi	Tokyo, Japan.	12/27/1974
Oldman, Gary	South London, Eng., UK .	3/21/1958
Olin, Ken	Chicago, IL	7/30/1954
Olin, Lena	Stockholm, Sweden.	3/22/1955
Oliver, Jamie	Clavering, England, UK ..	5/27/1975
Oliver, John.	Birmingham, England, UK	4/23/1977
Olmos, Edward James	E. Los Angeles, CA	2/24/1947
Olsen, Ashley	Sherman Oaks, CA	6/13/1986
Olsen, Mary-Kate	Sherman Oaks, CA	6/13/1986
Olson, Nancy	Milwaukee, WI	7/14/1928
Olyphant, Timothy	Honolulu, HI	5/20/1968
O'Malley, Mike	Boston, MA	10/31/1966
O'Neal, Ryan	Los Angeles, CA	4/20/1941
O'Neal, Tatum	Los Angeles, CA	11/5/1963
O'Neill, Ed.	Youngstown, OH	4/12/1946
Ontkean, Michael	Vancouver, BC, Canada.	1/24/1946
O'Quinn, Terry	Newbury, MI	7/15/1952
Orlando, Tony	New York, NY	4/3/1944
Ormond, Julia	Epsom, England, UK	1/4/1965
Osbourne, Jack	London, England, UK	11/8/1985
Osbourne, Kelly	London, England, UK	10/27/1984
Osbourne, Ozzy	Birmingham, England, UK	12/3/1948
Osbourne, Sharon	London, England, UK	10/9/1952
Osment, Haley Joel	Los Angeles, CA	4/10/1988
Osmond, Donny	Ogden, UT	12/9/1957
Osmond, Marie.	Ogden, UT	10/13/1959
Oswalt, Patton.	Portsmouth, VA	1/27/1969
O'Toole, Annette	Houston, TX	4/1/1951
Owen, Clive	Keresley, England, UK ..	10/3/1964
Oyelowo, David.	Oxford, England, UK ..	4/1/1976
Oz, Frank	Herford, England, UK..	5/25/1944
Ozawa, Seiji	Shenyang, China.	9/1/1935
Pacino, Al	New York, NY	4/25/1940

Name	Birthplace	Birthdate
Packer, Billy	Wellsville, NY	2/25/1940
Page, Ellen	Halifax, NS, Canada	2/21/1987
Page, Jimmy	Heston, England, UK	1/9/1944
Paget, Debra	Denver, CO	8/19/1933
Paige, Janis	Tacoma, WA	9/16/1922
Paisley, Brad	Glen Dale, WV	10/28/1972
Palin, Michael	Sheffield, England, UK	5/5/1943
Palmer, Geoffrey	London, England, UK	6/4/1927
Palminteri, Chazz	Bronx, NY	5/15/1951
Paltrow, Gwyneth	Los Angeles, CA	9/27/1972
Panettiere, Hayden	Palisades, NY	8/21/1989
Panjabi, Archie	Edgware, England, UK	5/31/1972
Pantoliano, Joe	Hoboken, NJ	9/12/1951
Papas, Irene	Chiliomodi, Greece	9/3/1926
Paquin, Anna	Winnipeg, MB, Canada	7/24/1982
Parker, Jameson	Baltimore, MD	11/18/1947
Parker, Mary-Louise	Fort Jackson, SC	8/2/1964
Parker, Sarah Jessica	Nelsonville, OH	3/25/1965
Parsons, Estelle	Marblehead, MA	11/20/1927
Parsons, Jim	Houston, TX	3/24/1973
Parton, Dolly	Sevierville, TN	1/19/1946
Pasdar, Adrian	Pittsfield, MA	4/30/1965
Patinkin, Mandy	Chicago, IL	11/30/1952
Patric, Jason	Flushing, Queens, NY	6/17/1966
Pattinson, Robert	London, England, UK	5/13/1986
Patton, Will	Charleston, SC	6/14/1954
Paul, Aaron	Emmett, ID	8/27/1979
Paul, Adrian	London, England, UK	5/29/1959
Paulson, Sarah	Tampa, FL	12/17/1975
Pearce, Guy	Ely, England, UK	10/5/1967
Peele, Jordan	New York, NY	2/21/1979
Peet, Amanda	New York, NY	1/11/1972
Penn, Kal	Montclair, NJ	4/23/1977
Penn, Sean	Burbank, CA	8/17/1960
Pepper, Barry	Campbell River, BC, Can.	4/4/1970
Perez, Rosie	Brooklyn, NY	9/6/1964
Perkins, Elizabeth	Flushing, Queens, NY	11/18/1960
Perlman, Itzhak	Tel Aviv, Israel	8/31/1945
Perlman, Rhea	Brooklyn, NY	3/31/1948
Perlman, Ron	New York, NY	4/13/1950
Perrine, Valerie	Galveston, TX	9/3/1943
Perry, Katy	Santa Barbara, CA	10/25/1984
Perry, Matthew	Williamstown, MA	8/19/1969
Perry, Tyler	New Orleans, LA	9/13/1969
Persoff, Nehemiah	Jerusalem, Israel	8/2/1919
Pesci, Joe	Newark, NJ	2/9/1943
Peters, Bernadette	Ozone Park, Queens, NY.	2/28/1948
Peters, Evan	St. Louis, MO	1/20/1987
Petersen, Wolfgang	Emden, Germany	3/14/1941
Petty, Lori	Chattanooga, TN	3/23/1963
Pfeiffer, Michelle	Santa Ana, CA	4/29/1958
Phair, Liz	New Haven, CT	4/17/1967
Phillippe, Ryan	New Castle, DE	9/10/1974
Phillips, Lou Diamond	Subic Bay, Philippines	2/17/1962
Phillips, Mackenzie	Alexandria, VA	11/10/1959
Phillips, Michelle	Long Beach, CA	6/4/1944
Phillips, Sian	Bettws, Wales, UK	5/14/1934
Phoenix, Joaquin	San Juan, Puerto Rico	10/28/1974
Pierce, David Hyde	Albany, NY.	4/3/1959
Pike, Rosamund	London, England, UK	1/27/1979
Pinchot, Bronson	New York, NY	5/20/1959
Pink	Doylestown, PA	9/8/1979
Pinkett Smith, Jada	Baltimore, MD	9/18/1971
Pirner, Dave	Green Bay, WI	4/16/1964
Piscopo, Joe	Passaic, NJ	6/17/1951
Pitbull	Miami, FL	1/15/1981
Pitt, Brad	Shawnee, OK	12/18/1963
Piven, Jeremy	New York, NY	7/26/1965
Plant, Robert	W. Bromwich, England, UK	8/20/1948
Plimpton, Martha	New York, NY	11/16/1970
Plowright, Joan	Brigg, England, UK	10/28/1929
Plummer, Amanda	New York, NY	3/23/1957
Plummer, Christopher	Toronto, ON, Canada	12/13/1927
Poehler, Amy	Newton, MA.	9/16/1971
Poitier, Sidney	Miami, FL	2/20/1927
Polanski, Roman	Paris, France	8/18/1933
Pompeo, Ellen	Everett, MA	11/10/1969
Pop, Iggy	Muskegon, MI	4/21/1947
Porter, Billy	Pittsburgh, PA	9/21/1969
Portman, Natalie	Jerusalem, Israel	6/9/1981
Posey, Parker	Baltimore, MD	11/8/1968
Post, Markie	Palo Alto, CA	11/4/1950
Potente, Franka	Dulmen bei Munster, Germany	7/22/1974
Potts, Annie	Nashville, TN.	10/28/1952
Povich, Maury	Washington, DC	1/17/1939
Powell, Jane	Portland, OR	4/1/1929
Powers, Stefanie	Hollywood, CA	11/2/1942
Pratt, Chris	Virginia, MN.	6/21/1979
Prentiss, Paula	San Antonio, TX	3/4/1939
Prepon, Laura	Watchung, NJ	3/7/1980
Presley, Priscilla	Brooklyn, NY	5/24/1945

Name	Birthplace	Birthdate
Pressly, Jaime	Kinston, NC	7/30/1977
Price, Leontyne	Laurel, MS.	2/10/1927
Price, Molly	North Plainfield, NJ	12/15/1966
Pride, Charley	Sledge, MS	3/18/1938
Priestley, Jason	Vancouver, BC, Canada	8/28/1969
Prince, Faith	Augusta, GA	8/5/1957
Principal, Victoria	Fukuoka, Japan	1/3/1950
Probst, Jeff	Wichita, KS	11/4/1962
Proctor, Emily	Raleigh, NC	10/8/1968
Pryce, Jonathan	Holywell, N. Wales, UK	6/1/1947
Puck, Wolfgang	St. Veit, Austria	1/8/1949
Pulliam, Keshia Knight	Newark, NJ	4/9/1979
Pullman, Bill	Hornell, NY	12/17/1953
Purcell, Sarah	Richmond, IN	10/8/1948
Purefoy, James	Taunton, England, UK	6/3/1964
Quaid, Dennis	Houston, TX	4/9/1954
Quaid, Randy	Houston, TX	10/1/1950
Queen Latifah	Newark, NJ	3/18/1970
Quinn, Aidan	Chicago, IL	3/8/1959
Quinn, Colin	Brooklyn, NY	6/6/1959
Quinn, Martha	Albany, NY.	5/11/1959
Quinto, Zachary	Pittsburgh, PA	6/2/1977
Rachins, Alan	Cambridge, MA	10/3/1942
Radcliffe, Daniel	London, England, UK	7/23/1989
Radnor, Josh	Columbus, OH.	7/29/1974
Raffi (Cavoukian)	Cairo, Egypt.	7/8/1948
Rainbow, Randy	Plantation, FL	7/6/1981
Raitt, Bonnie	Burbank, CA	11/8/1949
Ramey, Samuel	Colby, KS.	3/28/1942
Ramirez, Efren	Los Angeles, CA	10/2/1973
Ramirez, Sara	Mazatlan, Mexico.	8/31/1975
Rampling, Charlotte	Sturmer, MA	2/5/1946
Ramsay, Gordon	Elderslie, Scotland, UK	11/8/1966
Rancic, Giuliana	Naples, Italy.	8/17/1975
Randolph, Joyce	Detroit, MI	10/21/1924
Raphael, Sally Jessy	Easton, PA.	2/25/1935
Rashad, Phylicia	Houston, TX	6/19/1948
Ratzenberger, John	Bridgeport, CT.	4/6/1947
Raver, Kim	New York, NY	3/15/1969
Ray, Rachael	Glen Falls, NY	8/25/1968
Redford, Robert	Santa Monica, CA	8/18/1936
Redgrave, Vanessa	London, England, UK	1/30/1937
Redmayne, Eddie	London, England, UK	1/6/1982
Reed, Rex	Ft. Worth, TX	10/2/1938
Reeves, Keanu	Beirut, Lebanon	9/2/1964
Reeves, Martha	Eufaula, AL	7/18/1941
Regalbuto, Joe	New York, NY	8/24/1949
Reid, Tara	Wyckoff, NJ	11/8/1975
Reid, Tim	Norfolk, VA	12/19/1944
Reid, Vernon	London, England, UK	8/22/1958
Reilly, John C.	Chicago, IL	5/24/1965
Reiner, Rob.	Bronx, NY	3/6/1947
Reinhold, Judge	Wilmington, DE	5/21/1957
Reinking, Ann	Seattle, WA	11/10/1949
Reiser, Paul	New York, NY	3/30/1957
Reitman, Ivan	Komarno, Czechoslovakia	10/26/1946
Remini, Leah	Brooklyn, NY	6/15/1970
Renner, Jeremy	Modesto, CA	1/7/1971
Reynolds, Ryan	Vancouver, BC, Canada.	10/23/1976
Reznor, Trent	Mercer, PA.	5/17/1965
Rhames, Ving	New York, NY	5/12/1959
Rhimes, Shonda	Chicago, IL	1/13/1970
Rhymes, Busta	Brooklyn, NY	5/20/1972
Rhys, Matthew	Cardiff, Wales, UK	11/4/1974
Rhys Meyers, Jonathan	Dublin, Ireland.	7/27/1977
Ribisi, Giovanni	Los Angeles, CA	12/17/1974
Ricci, Christina	Santa Monica, CA	2/12/1980
Richards, Denise	Downers Grove, IL	2/17/1971
Richards, Keith	Dartford, Kent, Eng., UK	12/18/1943
Richards, Michael	Culver City, CA	7/24/1949
Richardson, Kevin	Lexington, KY	10/3/1971
Richardson, Miranda	Lancashire, England, UK.	3/3/1958
Richardson, Patricia	Bethesda, MD	2/23/1951
Richie, Lionel	Tuskegee, AL	6/20/1949
Richie, Nicole	Berkeley, CA	9/21/1981
Richter, Andy	Grand Rapids, MI	10/28/1966
Riegert, Peter	New York, NY	4/11/1947
Rihanna	St. Michael, Barbados	2/20/1988
Riley, Amber	Long Beach, CA	2/15/1986
Rimes, LeAnn	Jackson, MS	8/28/1982
Ringwald, Molly	Roseville, CA	2/18/1968
Ripa, Kelly	Stratford, NJ	10/2/1970
Rivera, Chita	Washington, DC	1/23/1933
Rivera, Geraldo	New York, NY	7/4/1943
Robbie, Margot	Dalby, Qld., Australia	7/2/1990
Robbins, Tim	W. Covina, CA	10/16/1958
Roberts, Eric	Biloxi, MS	4/18/1956
Roberts, Julia	Smyrna, GA.	10/28/1967
Roberts, Tony	New York, NY	10/22/1939
Robinson, Smokey	Detroit, MI	2/19/1940
Rock, Chris	Andrews, SC	2/7/1965
Rockwell, Sam	Daly City, CA	11/5/1968

Name	Birthplace	Birthdate
Rodgers, Jimmie	Camas, WA	9/18/1933
Rodriguez, Michelle	Bexar County, TX	7/12/1978
Rogan, Joe	Newark, NJ	8/11/1967
Rogen, Seth	Vancouver, BC, Canada	4/15/1982
Rogers, Mimi	Coral Gables, FL	1/27/1956
Rohm, Elisabeth	Dusseldorf, Germany	4/28/1973
Rollins, Henry	Washington, DC	2/13/1961
Rollins, Sonny	New York, NY	9/7/1930
Romano, Ray	Forest Hills, Queens, NY	12/21/1957
Romijn, Rebecca	Berkeley, CA	11/6/1972
Ronan, Saoirse	New York, NY	4/12/1994
Ronson, Mark	London, England, UK	9/4/1975
Ronstadt, Linda	Tucson, AZ	7/15/1946
Root, Stephen	Sarasota, FL	11/17/1951
Rose, Axl	Lafayette, IN	2/6/1962
Roseanne	Salt Lake City, UT	11/3/1952
Ross, Charlotte	Winnetka, IL	1/21/1968
Ross, Diana	Detroit, MI	3/26/1944
Ross, Katharine	Hollywood, CA	1/29/1940
Ross, Marion	Albert Lea, MN	10/25/1928
Ross, Tracee Ellis	Los Angeles, CA	10/29/1972
Rossdale, Gavin	London, England, UK	10/30/1965
Rossellini, Isabella	Rome, Italy	6/18/1952
Rossum, Emmy	New York, NY	9/12/1986
Roth, David Lee	Bloomington, IN	10/10/1955
Roth, Tim	London, England, UK	5/14/1961
Rotten, Johnny	London, England, UK	1/31/1956
Roundtree, Richard	New Rochelle, NY	7/9/1942
Rourke, Mickey	Schenectady, NY	9/16/1952
Routh, Brandon	Des Moines, IA	10/9/1979
Routledge, Patricia	Birkenhead, England, UK	2/17/1929
Rowan, Kelly	Ottawa, ON, Canada	10/26/1965
Rowlands, Gena	Cambria, WI	6/19/1930
Rubinstein, John	Beverly Hills, CA	12/8/1946
Rudd, Paul	Passaic, NJ	4/6/1969
Rudner, Rita	Miami, FL	9/17/1955?
Rudolph, Maya	Gainesville, FL	7/27/1972
Ruehl, Mercedes	Jackson Heights, Queens, NY	2/28/1948
Ruffalo, Mark	Kenosha, WI	11/22/1967
RuPaul	San Diego, CA	11/17/1960
Rupp, Debra Jo	Glendale, CA	2/24/1951
Rush, Barbara	Denver, CO	1/4/1927
Rush, Geoffrey	Toowoomba, Qld., Australia	7/6/1951
Russell, Keri	Fountain Valley, CA	3/23/1976
Russell, Kurt	Springfield, MA	3/17/1951
Russell, Mark	Buffalo, NY	8/23/1932
Russell, Theresa	San Diego, CA	3/20/1957
Russo, Rene	Burbank, CA	2/17/1954
Ruttan, Susan	Oregon City, OR	9/16/1950
Ryan, Meg	Fairfield, CT	11/19/1961
Ryan, Roz	Detroit, MI	7/7/1951
Rydell, Bobby	Philadelphia, PA	4/26/1942
Ryder, Winona	Winona, MN	10/29/1971
Rylance, Mark	Ashford, England, UK	1/18/1960
Sabato, Antonio, Jr.	Rome, Italy	2/29/1972
Sade (Adu)	Ibadan, Nigeria	1/16/1959
Sagal, Katey	Hollywood, CA	1/19/1954
Saget, Bob	Philadelphia, PA	5/17/1956
Sagnier, Ludivine	La Celle-St.-Cloud, France	7/3/1979
Sahl, Mort	Montréal, QC, Canada	5/11/1927
Saint, Eva Marie	Newark, NJ	7/4/1924
St. James, Susan	Hollywood, CA	8/14/1946
St. John, Jill	Los Angeles, CA	8/19/1940
St. Patrick, Mathew	Philadelphia, PA	3/17/1968
Sajak, Pat	Chicago, IL	10/26/1946
Saldana, Zoë	Passaic, NJ	6/19/1978
Salonga, Lea	Manila, Philippines	2/22/1971
Samberg, Andy	Berkeley, CA	8/18/1978
Samms, Emma	London, England, UK	8/28/1960
San Giacomo, Laura	Hoboken, NJ	11/14/1962
Sandler, Adam	Brooklyn, NY	9/9/1966
Sands, Julian	West Yorkshire, Eng., UK	1/15/1958
Santana, Carlos	Autlan, Mexico	7/20/1947
Sara, Mia	Brooklyn, NY	6/19/1967
Sarandon, Susan	New York, NY	10/4/1946
Sartain, Gailard	Tulsa, OK	9/18/1946
Savage, Ben	Highland Park, IL	9/13/1980
Savage, Fred	Highland Park, IL	7/9/1976
Sawa, Devon	Vancouver, BC, Canada	9/7/1978
Sayles, John	Schenectady, NY	9/28/1950
Scacchi, Greta	Milan, Italy	2/18/1960
Scaggs, Boz	Canton, OH	6/8/1944
Scales, Prunella	Sutton Abinger, Eng., UK	6/22/1932
Scalia, Jack	Brooklyn, NY	11/10/1951
Schiff, Richard	Bethesda, MD	5/27/1955
Schiffer, Claudia	Rheinbach, Germany	8/25/1970
Schneider, John	Mt. Kisco, NY	4/8/1960
Schneider, Rob	San Francisco, CA	10/31/1963
Schreiber, Liev	San Francisco, CA	10/4/1967
Schroder, Rick	Staten Island, NY	4/13/1970
Schumer, Amy	New York, NY	6/1/1981
Schwarzenegger, Arnold	Thal, Austria	7/30/1947
Schwimmer, David	Astoria, Queens, NY	11/2/1966
Sciorra, Annabella	Wethersfield, CT	3/24/1964
Scolari, Peter	New Rochelle, NY	9/12/1954
Scorsese, Martin	Flushing, Queens, NY	11/17/1942
Scott, Ridley	South Shields, England, UK	11/30/1937
Scott, Seann William	Cottage Grove, MN	10/3/1976
Scott Thomas, Kristin	Redruth, England, UK	5/24/1960
Scotto, Renata	Savona, Italy	2/24/1934
Scully, Vin	Bronx, NY	11/29/1927
Seacrest, Ryan	Atlanta, GA	12/24/1974
Seagal, Steven	Lansing, MI	4/10/1951
Secor, Kyle	Tacoma, WA	5/31/1957
Sedaka, Neil	Brooklyn, NY	3/13/1939
Sedgwick, Kyra	New York, NY	8/19/1965
Segal, George	Great Neck, NY	2/13/1934
Segel, Jason	Los Angeles, CA	1/18/1980
Seidelman, Susan	Abington, PA	12/11/1952
Seinfeld, Jerry	Brooklyn, NY	4/29/1954
Sellecca, Connie	Bronx, NY	5/25/1955
Selleck, Tom	Detroit, MI	1/29/1945
Severinsen, Doc	Arlington, OR.	7/7/1927
Sevigny, Chloë	Springfield, MA	11/18/1974
Sewell, Rufus	Twickenham, Middlesex, England, UK	10/29/1967
Seyfried, Amanda	Allentown, PA	12/3/1985
Seymour, Jane	Hillingdon, England, UK	2/15/1951
Shackelford, Ted	Oklahoma City, OK	6/23/1946
Shaffer, Paul	Thunder Bay, ON, Canada	11/28/1949
Shakira (Mebarak Ripoll)	Barranquilla, Colombia	2/2/1977
Shalhoub, Tony	Green Bay, WI	10/9/1953
Shannon, Molly	Shaker Heights, OH.	9/16/1964
Shatner, William	Montréal, QC, Canada	3/22/1931
Shaughnessy, Charles	London, England, UK	2/9/1955
Shaver, Helen	St. Thomas, ON, Canada	2/24/1951
Shaw, Fiona	Cork, Ireland	7/10/1958
Shawkat, Alia	Riverside, CA.	4/18/1989
Shea, John	North Conway, NH	4/14/1949
Shearer, Harry	Los Angeles, CA	12/23/1943
Sheedy, Ally	New York, NY	6/13/1962
Sheen, Charlie	Los Angeles, CA	9/3/1965
Sheen, Martin	Dayton, OH	8/3/1940
Sheen, Michael	Newport, Wales, UK	2/5/1969
Sheeran, Ed	Hebden Bridge, West Yorkshire, Eng., UK	2/17/1991
Sheindlin, Judy	Brooklyn, NY	10/21/1942
Shelton, Blake	Ada, OK	6/18/1976
Shepherd, Cybill	Memphis, TN	2/18/1950
Shepherd, Sherri	Chicago, IL	4/22/1967
Sheridan, Nicollette	Worthing, England, UK	11/21/1963
Shields, Brooke	New York, NY	5/31/1965
Shire, Talia	Lake Success, NY	4/25/1946
Short, Martin	Hamilton, ON, Canada	3/26/1950
Shortz, Will	Crawfordsville, IN.	8/26/1952
Show, Grant	Detroit, MI	2/27/1962
Shue, Andrew	South Orange, NJ	2/20/1967
Shue, Elisabeth	Wilmington, DE	10/6/1963
Shyamalan, M. Night	Pondicherry, India	8/6/1970
Sidibe, Gabourey	Brooklyn, NY	5/6/1983
Sigler, Jamie-Lynn	Jericho, NY	5/15/1981
Sikking, James B.	Los Angeles, CA	3/5/1934
Silverman, Jonathan	Beverly Hills, CA	8/5/1966
Silverman, Sarah	Bedford, NH.	12/1/1970
Silverstone, Alicia	San Francisco, CA.	10/4/1976
Simmons, Gene	Haifa, Israel	8/25/1049
Simmons, Henry	Stamford, CT	7/1/1970
Simmons, Richard	New Orleans, LA	7/12/1948
Simon, Carly	New York, NY	6/25/1945
Simon, Paul	Newark, NJ	10/13/1941
Simpson, Ashlee	Waco, TX.	10/3/1984
Simpson, Jessica	Abilene, TX	7/10/1980
Sinatra, Nancy	Jersey City, NJ.	6/8/1940
Sinbad	Benton Harbor, MI	11/10/1956
Sinise, Gary	Blue Island, IL	3/17/1955
Sirico, Tony	Brooklyn, NY	7/29/1942
Sisto, Jeremy	Grass Valley, CA	10/6/1974
Sizemore, Tom	Detroit, MI	9/29/1961
Skarsgard, Alexander	Stockholm, Sweden	8/25/1976
Skarsgard, Stellan	Gothenburg, Sweden	6/13/1951
Skerritt, Tom	Detroit, MI	8/25/1933
Slater, Christian	New York, NY	8/18/1969
Slater, Helen	Massapequa, NY.	12/15/1963
Slattery, John	Boston, MA	8/13/1962
Slezak, Erika	Hollywood, CA.	8/5/1946
Slick, Grace	Evanston, IL	10/30/1939
Smirnoff, Karina	Kharkiv, Ukraine	1/2/1978
Smirnoff, Yakov	Odessa, Ukraine	1/24/1951
Smith, Allison	New York, NY	12/9/1969
Smith, Jaclyn	Houston, TX	10/26/1945

Name	Birthplace	Birthdate
Smith, Jaden	Malibu, CA	7/8/1998
Smith, Kevin	Red Bank, NJ	8/2/1970
Smith, Maggie	Ilford, England, UK	12/28/1934
Smith, Patti	Chicago, IL	12/30/1946
Smith, Robert	Blackpool, England, UK	4/21/1959
Smith, Sam	London, England, UK	5/19/1992
Smith, Will	Philadelphia, PA	9/25/1968
Smith, Willow	Los Angeles, CA	10/31/2000
Smits, Jimmy	Brooklyn, NY	7/9/1955
Smothers, Dick	Governor's Island, NY	11/20/1938
Smothers, Tom	Governor's Island, NY	2/2/1937
Smulders, Cobie	Vancouver, BC, Canada	4/3/1982
Snipes, Wesley	Orlando, FL	7/31/1962
Snooki (Nicole Polizzi)	Santiago, Chile	11/23/1987
Snoop Dogg	Long Beach, CA	10/20/1971
Soderbergh, Steven	Atlanta, GA	1/14/1963
Soloway, Jill	Chicago, IL	9/26/1965
Somerhalder, Ian	Covington, LA	12/8/1978
Somers, Suzanne	San Bruno, CA	10/16/1946
Sommer, Elke	Berlin, Germany	11/5/1940
Sorbo, Kevin	Mound, MN	9/24/1958
Sorvino, Mira	Tenafly, NJ	9/28/1967
Sorvino, Paul	Brooklyn, NY	4/13/1939
Soul, David	Chicago, IL	8/28/1943
Spacek, Sissy	Quitman, TX	12/25/1949
Spacey, Kevin	South Orange, NJ	7/26/1959
Spade, David	Birmingham, MI	7/22/1964
Spader, James	Boston, MA	2/7/1960
Spalding, Esperanza	Portland, OR	10/18/1984
Spano, Joe	San Francisco, CA	7/7/1946
Spears, Britney	Kentwood, LA	12/2/1981
Spears, Jamie-Lynn	McComb, MS	4/4/1991
Spector, Phil	Bronx, NY	12/26/1940
Spelling, Tori	Los Angeles, CA	5/16/1973
Spencer, Octavia	Montgomery, AL	5/25/1972
Spielberg, Steven	Cincinnati, OH	12/18/1946
Spiner, Brent	Houston, TX	2/2/1949
Springer, Jerry	London, England, UK	2/13/1944
Springfield, Rick	Sydney, NSW, Australia	8/23/1949
Springsteen, Bruce	Long Branch, NJ	9/23/1949
Spurlock, Morgan	Parksburg, WV	11/7/1970
Stahl, Nick	Harlingen, TX	12/5/1979
Stallone, Sylvester	New York, NY	7/6/1946
Stamos, John	Cypress, CA	8/19/1963
Stamp, Terence	Stepney, England, UK	7/22/1938
Stapleton, Chris	Lexington, KY	4/15/1978
Starr, Ringo	Liverpool, England, UK	7/7/1940
Statham, Jason	Shirebrook, England, UK	7/26/1967
Steenburgen, Mary	Newport, AR	2/8/1953
Stefani, Gwen	Fullterton, CA	10/3/1969
Stein, Ben	Washington, DC	11/25/1944
Stern, Daniel	Bethesda, MD	8/28/1957
Stern, Howard	Roosevelt, NY	1/12/1954
Sternhagen, Frances	Washington, DC	1/13/1930
Stevens, Andrew	Memphis, TN	6/10/1955
Stevens, Cat (Yusef Islam)	London, England, UK	7/21/1948
Stevens, Connie	Brooklyn, NY	8/8/1938
Stevens, Stella	Yazoo City, MS	10/1/1936
Stevenson, Parker	Philadelphia, PA	6/4/1952
Stewart, French	Albuquerque, NM	2/20/1964
Stewart, Jon	New York, NY	11/28/1962
Stewart, Kristen	Los Angeles, CA	4/9/1990
Stewart, Patrick	Mirfield, England, UK	7/13/1940
Stewart, Rod	London, England, UK	1/10/1945
Stiles, Julia	New York, NY	3/28/1981
Stiller, Ben	New York, NY	11/30/1965
Stills, Stephen	Dallas, TX	1/3/1945
Sting	Newcastle upon Tyne, England, UK	10/2/1951
Stipe, Michael	Decatur, GA	1/4/1960
Stockwell, Dean	North Hollywood, CA	3/5/1936
Stoltz, Eric	Whittier, CA	9/30/1961
Stone, Dee Wallace	Kansas City, KS	12/14/1948
Stone, Emma	Scottsdale, AZ	11/6/1988
Stone, Oliver	New York, NY	9/15/1946
Stone, Sharon	Meadville, PA	3/10/1958
Stonestreet, Eric	Kansas City, KS	9/9/1971
Stookey, Paul	Baltimore, MD	12/30/1937
Storch, Larry	New York, NY	1/8/1923
Stowe, Madeleine	Eagle Rock, CA	8/18/1958
Strahan, Michael	Houston, TX	11/21/1971
Strait, George	Pearsall, TX	5/18/1952
Strasser, Robin	New York, NY	5/7/1945
Strathairn, David	San Francisco, CA	1/26/1949
Strauss, Peter	Croton-on-Hudson, NY	2/20/1947
Streep, Meryl	Summit, NJ	6/22/1949
Streisand, Barbra	Brooklyn, NY	4/24/1942
Stringfield, Sherry	Colorado Springs, CO	6/24/1967
Stroman, Susan	Wilmington, DE	10/17/1954
Struthers, Sally	Portland, OR	7/28/1948

Name	Birthplace	Birthdate
Styles, Harry	Holmes Chapel, Cheshire, Eng., UK	2/1/1994
Suchet, David	London, England, UK	5/2/1946
Sudeikis, Jason	Fairfax, VA	9/18/1975
Sullivan, Susan	New York, NY	11/18/1942
Sunjata, Daniel	Evanston, IL	12/30/1971
Sutherland, Donald	St. John, NB, Canada	7/17/1934
Sutherland, Kiefer	London, England, UK	12/21/1966
Suvari, Mena	Newport, RI	2/9/1979
Swank, Hilary	Lincoln, NE	7/30/1974
Swift, Taylor	Wyomissing, PA	12/13/1989
Swinton, Tilda	London, England, UK	11/5/1960
Swit, Loretta	Passaic, NJ	11/4/1937
Sykes, Wanda	Portsmouth, VA	3/7/1964
Szmanda, Eric	Milwaukee, WI	7/24/1975
T, Mr.	Chicago, IL	5/21/1952
Takei, George	Los Angeles, CA	4/20/1937
Tamblyn, Amber	Santa Monica, CA	5/14/1983
Tamblyn, Russ	Los Angeles, CA	12/30/1934
Tambor, Jeffrey	San Francisco, CA	7/8/1944
Tarantino, Quentin	Knoxville, TN	3/27/1963
Tatum, Channing	Cullman, AL	4/26/1980
Tautou, Audrey	Beaumont, France	8/9/1976?
Taylor, Buck	Hollywood, CA	5/13/1938
Taylor, James	Boston, MA	3/12/1948
Taylor, Lili	Glencoe, IL	2/20/1967
Taymor, Julie	Newton, MA	12/15/1952
Te Kanawa, Kiri	Gisborne, New Zealand	3/6/1944
Teigen, Chrissy	Delta, Utah	11/30/1985
Teller	Philadelphia, PA	2/14/1948
Tennant, David	Bathgate, West Lothian, Scotland, UK	4/18/1971
Tennant, Victoria	London, England, UK	9/30/1950
Tennille, Toni	Montgomery, AL	5/8/1940
Tesh, John	Garden City, NY	7/9/1952
Tharp, Twyla	Portland, IN	7/1/1941
The Weeknd	Toronto, ON, Canada	2/16/1990
Theron, Charlize	Benoni, South Africa	8/7/1975
Thicke, Robin	Los Angeles, CA	3/10/1977
Thiessen, Tiffani	Long Beach, CA	1/23/1974
Thomas, Jonathan Taylor	Bethlehem, PA	9/8/1981
Thomas, Marlo	Deerfield, MI	11/21/1937
Thomas, Michael Tilson	Hollywood, CA	12/21/1944
Thomas, Philip Michael	Columbus, OH	5/26/1949
Thomas, Richard	New York, NY	6/13/1951
Thomas, Sean Patrick	Wilmington, DE	12/17/1970
Thompson, Emma	London, England, UK	4/15/1959
Thompson, Jack	Sydney, NSW, Australia	8/31/1940
Thompson, Kenan	Atlanta, GA	5/10/1978
Thompson, Lea	Rochester, MN	5/31/1961
Thorne-Smith, Courtney	San Francisco, CA	11/8/1967
Thornton, Billy Bob	Hot Springs, AR	8/4/1955
Thurman, Uma	Boston, MA	4/29/1970
Tiegs, Cheryl	Breckenridge, MN	9/25/1947
Tierney, Maura	Boston, MA	2/3/1965
Tilly, Jennifer	Harbor City, CA	9/16/1958
Tilly, Meg	Long Beach, CA	2/14/1960
Timberlake, Justin	Memphis, TN	1/31/1981
Tisdale, Ashley	West Deal, NJ	7/2/1985
Tomei, Marisa	Brooklyn, NY	12/4/1964
Tomlin, Lily	Detroit, MI	9/1/1939
Tonioli, Bruno	Ferrara, Italy	11/25/1955
Tovey, Russell	Billericay, Essex, Eng., UK	11/14/1981
Townsend, Robert	Chicago, IL	2/6/1957
Townsend, Peter	Chiswick, England, UK	5/19/1945
Travanti, Daniel J.	Kenosha, WI	3/7/1940
Travis, Nancy	Astoria, Queens, NY	9/21/1961
Travis, Randy	Marshville, NC	5/4/1959
Travolta, John	Englewood, NJ	2/18/1954
Trebek, Alex	Sudbury, ON, Canada	7/22/1940
Tripplehorn, Jean	Tulsa, OK	6/10/1963
Tritt, Travis	Marietta, GA	2/9/1963
Tucci, Stanley	Peekskill, NY	1/11/1960
Tucker, Chris	Decatur, GA	8/31/1972
Tucker, Michael	Baltimore, MD	2/6/1944
Tucker, Tanya	Seminole, TX	10/10/1958
Tune, Tommy	Wichita Falls, TX	2/28/1939
Turlington, Christy	Walnut Creek, CA	1/2/1969
Turner, Janine	Lincoln, NE	12/6/1962
Turner, Kathleen	Springfield, MO	6/19/1954
Turner, Sophie	Northampton, Eng., UK	2/21/1996
Turner, Tina	Nutbush, TN	11/26/1939
Turturro, John	Brooklyn, NY	2/28/1957
Tveit, Aaron	Middletown, NY	10/21/1983
Twain, Shania	Windsor, ON, Canada	8/28/1965
Twiggy (Lawson)	London, England, UK	9/19/1949
Tyler, Liv	New York, NY	7/1/1977
Tyler, Steven	Yonkers, NY	3/26/1948
Tyson, Cicely	New York, NY	12/19/1924
Uecker, Bob	Milwaukee, WI	1/26/1934
Uggams, Leslie	New York, NY	5/25/1943
Ullman, Tracey	Slough, England, UK	12/30/1959

Name	Birthplace	Birthdate
Ullmann, Liv	Tokyo, Japan	12/16/1938
Ulrich, Skeet	Lynchburg, VA	1/20/1970
Underwood, Blair	Tacoma, WA	8/25/1964
Underwood, Carrie	Muskogee, OK	3/10/1983
Urban, Keith	Whangarei, North Island, New Zealand	10/26/1967
Urie, Michael	Dallas, TX	8/8/1980
Usher (Raymond IV)	Dallas, TX	10/14/1978
Vaccaro, Brenda	Brooklyn, NY	11/18/1939
Valley, Mark	Ogdensburg, NY	12/24/1964
Valli, Frankie	Newark, NJ	5/3/1934
Van Ark, Joan	New York, NY	6/16/1943
Van Damme, Jean-Claude	Brussels, Belgium	10/18/1960
Van Der Beek, James	Cheshire, CT	3/8/1977
Van Doren, Mamie	Rowena, SD	2/6/1931
Van Dyke, Dick	West Plains, MO	12/13/1925
Van Peebles, Mario	Mexico City, Mexico	1/15/1957
Van Sant, Gus	Louisville, KY	7/24/1952
Van Zandt, Steven	Winthrop, MA	11/22/1950
VanCamp, Emily	Port Perry, ON, Canada	5/12/1986
Vance, Courtney B.	Detroit, MI	3/12/1960
Vardalos, Nia	Winnipeg, MB, Canada	9/24/1962
Vaughn, Vince	Minneapolis, MN	3/28/1970
Vedder, Eddie	Evanston, IL	12/23/1964
Ventimiglia, Milo	Anaheim, CA	7/8/1977
Vereen, Ben	Miami, FL	10/10/1946
Vergara, Sofia	Barranquilla, Colombia	7/10/1972
Vieira, Meredith	Providence, RI	12/30/1953
Vikander, Alicia	Gothenburg, Sweden	10/3/1988
Villella, Edward	Long Island, NY	10/1/1936
Vinton, Bobby	Canonsburg, PA	4/16/1935
Visnjic, Goran	Sibenik, Yugo. (Croatia)	9/9/1972
Vitale, Dick	East Rutherford, NJ	6/9/1939
Voight, Jon	Yonkers, NY	12/29/1938
Von Stade, Frederica	Somerville, NJ	6/1/1945
Von Trier, Lars	Copenhagen, Denmark	4/30/1956
Wagner, Jack	Washington, MO	10/3/1959
Wagner, Lindsay	Los Angeles, CA	6/22/1949
Wagner, Robert	Detroit, MI	2/10/1930
Wahl, Ken	Chicago, IL	10/31/1954
Wahlberg, Donnie	Dorchester, MA	8/17/1969
Wahlberg, Mark	Dorchester, MA	6/5/1971
Waits, Tom	Pomona, CA	12/7/1949
Walden, Robert	New York, NY	9/25/1943
Walken, Christopher	Astoria, Queens, NY	3/31/1943
Waller-Bridge, Phoebe	London, England, UK	7/14/1985
Wallis, Quvenzhané	Houma, LA	8/23/2008
Walsh, Kate	San Jose, CA	10/13/1967
Walter, Jessica	Brooklyn, NY	1/31/1941
Waltz, Christoph	Vienna, Austria	10/4/1956
Warburton, Patrick	Paterson, NJ	11/14/1964
Ward, Fred	San Diego, CA	12/30/1942
Ward, Sela	Meridian, MS	7/11/1956
Warfield, Marsha	Chicago, IL	3/5/1954
Warner, Malcolm-Jamal	Jersey City, NJ	8/18/1970
Warren, Lesley Ann	New York, NY	8/16/1946
Warwick, Dionne	East Orange, NJ	12/12/1940
Washington, Denzel	Mt. Vernon, NY	12/28/1954
Washington, Isaiah	Houston, TX	8/3/1963
Washington, Kerry	Bronx, NY	1/31/1977
Wasikowska, Mia	Canberra, Australia	10/14/1989
Watanabe, Ken	Koide, Niigata, Japan	10/21/1959
Waters, John	Baltimore, MD	4/22/1946
Waters, Roger	Great Bookham, Eng., UK	9/6/1943
Waterston, Sam	Cambridge, MA	11/15/1940
Watson, Emily	London, England, UK	1/14/1967
Watson, Emma	Paris, France	4/15/1990
Watts, Naomi	Shoreham, England, UK	9/28/1968
Wayans, Damon	New York, NY	9/4/1960
Wayans, Keenen Ivory	Brooklyn, NY	6/8/1958
Wayans, Marlon	New York, NY	7/23/1972
Wayans, Shawn	New York, NY	1/19/1971
Weathers, Carl	New Orleans, LA	1/14/1948
Weaver, Sigourney	New York, NY	10/8/1949
Weir, Peter	Sydney, NSW, Australia	8/21/1944
Weisz, Rachel	London, England, UK	3/7/1971
Welch, Raquel	Chicago, IL	9/5/1940
Weld, Tuesday	New York, NY	8/27/1943
Weller, Peter	Stevens Point, WI	6/24/1947
Welling, Tom	Putnam Valley, NY	4/26/1977
Wendt, George	Chicago, IL	10/17/1948
Wentz, Pete	Wilmette, IL	6/5/1979
West, Dominic	Sheffield, Eng., UK	10/15/1969
West, Kanye	Atlanta, GA	6/8/1977
West, Shane	Baton Rouge, LA	6/10/1978
Wettig, Patricia	Cincinnati, OH	12/4/1951
Whalley, Joanne	Manchester, England, UK	8/25/1964
Wheaton, Wil	Burbank, CA	7/29/1972
Whishaw, Ben	Clifton, Eng., UK	10/14/1980
Whitaker, Forest	Longview, TX	7/15/1961
White, Betty	Oak Park, IL	1/17/1922
White, Jack	Detroit, MI	7/9/1975
White, Jaleel	Pasadena, CA	11/27/1976
White, Vanna	N. Myrtle Beach, SC	2/18/1957
Whitford, Bradley	Madison, WI	10/10/1959
Whittaker, Jodie	Skelmanthorpe, West Yorkshire, England, UK	6/17/1982
Wiest, Dianne	Kansas City, MO	3/28/1948
Wiig, Kristen	Canandaigua, NY	8/22/1973
Wilde, Olivia	New York, NY	3/10/1984
Wilkinson, Tom	Leeds, England, UK	12/12/1948
Williams, Armstrong	Marion, SC	2/5/1959
Williams, Barry	Santa Monica, CA	9/30/1954
Williams, Billy Dee	New York, NY	4/6/1937
Williams, Cindy	Van Nuys, CA	8/22/1947
Williams, Hal	Columbus, OH	12/14/1938
Williams, Hank, Jr.	Shreveport, LA	5/26/1949
Williams, JoBeth	Houston, TX	12/6/1948
Williams, Lucinda	Lake Charles, LA	1/26/1953
Williams, Maisie	Bristol, Eng., UK	4/15/1997
Williams, Michael Kenneth	Brooklyn, NY	11/22/1966
Williams, Michelle	Kalispell, MT	9/9/1980
Williams, Montel	Baltimore, MD	7/3/1956
Williams, Paul	Omaha, NE	9/19/1940
Williams, Pharrell	Virginia Beach, VA	4/5/1973
Williams, Treat	Rowayton, CT	12/1/1951
Williams, Vanessa	Millwood, NY	3/18/1963
Williams-Paisley, Kimberly	Rye, NY	9/14/1971
Williamson, Kevin	New Bern, NC	3/14/1965
Willis, Bruce	Idar-Oberstein, W. Germany	3/19/1955
Wilmore, Larry	Los Angeles, CA	10/30/1961
Wilson, Brian	Inglewood, CA	6/20/1942
Wilson, Cassandra	Jackson, MS	12/4/1955
Wilson, Chandra	Houston, TX	8/27/1969
Wilson, Demond	Valdosta, GA	10/13/1946
Wilson, Luke	Dallas, TX	9/21/1971
Wilson, Owen	Dallas, TX	11/18/1968
Wilson, Rainn	Seattle, WA	1/20/1966
Wilson, Rebel	Sydney, NSW, Australia	2/3/1980
Winfrey, Oprah	Kosciusko, MS	1/29/1954
Winger, Debra	Cleveland, OH	5/16/1955
Winkler, Henry	New York, NY	10/30/1945
Winningham, Mare	Phoenix, AZ	5/16/1959
Winslet, Kate	Reading, England, UK	10/5/1975
Winwood, Steve	Birmingham, England, UK	5/12/1948
Withers, Jane	Atlanta, GA	4/12/1926
Witherspoon, Reese	New Orleans, LA	3/22/1976
Witt, Alicia	Worcester, MA	8/21/1975
Wolf, Scott	Boston, MA	6/4/1968
Wonder, Stevie	Saginaw, MI	5/13/1950
Wong, B. D.	San Francisco, CA	10/24/1962
Wong, Faye	Beijing, China	8/8/1969
Woo, John	Guangzhou, China	5/1/1946
Wood, Elijah	Cedar Rapids, IA	1/28/1981
Wood, Evan Rachel	Raleigh, NC	9/7/1987
Woodard, Alfre	Tulsa, OK	11/8/1952
Woodley, Shailene	Simi Valley, CA	11/15/1991
Woods, James	Vernal, UT	4/18/1947
Woodward, Joanne	Thomasville, GA	2/27/1930
Wopat, Tom	Lodi, WI	9/9/1951
Worthington, Sam	Godalming, Surrey, Eng., UK	8/2/1976
Wright, Jeffrey	Washington, DC	12/7/1965
Wright, Robin	Dallas, TX	4/8/1966
Wright, Steven	New York, NY	12/6/1955
Wu, Constance	Richmond, VA	3/22/1982
Wyle, Noah	Hollywood, CA	6/4/1971
Wyman, Bill	London, England, UK	10/24/1936
Yankovic, Weird Al	Lynwood, CA	10/23/1959
Yanni (Chrysomallis)	Kalamata, Greece	11/14/1954
Yarrow, Peter	New York, NY	5/31/1938
Yearwood, Trisha	Monticello, GA	9/19/1964
Yeoh, Michelle	Ipoh, Malaysia	8/6/1962
Yoakam, Dwight	Pikesville, KY	10/23/1956
York, Michael	Fulmer, England, UK	3/27/1942
Young, Burt	New York, NY	4/30/1940
Young, Neil	Toronto, ON, Canada	11/12/1945
Young, Sean	Louisville, KY	11/20/1959
Zane, Billy	Chicago, IL	2/24/1966
Zellweger, Renée	Katy, TX	4/25/1969
Zemeckis, Robert	Chicago, IL	5/14/1952
Zendaya	Oakland, CA	9/1/1996
Zerbe, Anthony	Long Beach, CA	5/20/1936
Zeta-Jones, Catherine	Swansea, Wales, UK	9/25/1969
Zhang Ziyi	Beijing, China	2/9/1979
Zimbalist, Stephanie	New York, NY	10/8/1956
Zimmer, Constance	Seattle, WA	10/11/1970
Zimmer, Kim	Grand Rapids, MI	2/2/1955
Zukerman, Pinchas	Tel Aviv, Israel	7/16/1948
Zuniga, Daphne	Berkeley, CA	10/28/1962

Entertainment Personalities of the Past

See also other lists for some deceased entertainers not included here.

Name	Born	Died	Name	Born	Died	Name	Born	Died
Aaliyah (Haughton)	1979	2001	Barrymore, Lionel	1878	1954	Boyd, Stephen	1928	1977
Abbado, Claudio	1933	2014	Barrymore, Maurice	1848	1905	Boyd, William	1898	1972
Abbott, Bud	1895	1974	Barthelmess, Richard	1895	1963	Boyer, Charles	1899	1978
Abbott, George	1887	1995	Bartholomew, Freddie	1924	1992	Boyle, Peter	1935	2006
Acuff, Roy	1903	1992	Barty, Billy	1924	2000	Bracken, Eddie	1915	2002
Adams, Don	1923	2005	Basehart, Richard	1914	1984	Brady, Alice	1892	1939
Adams, Edie	1927	2008	Basie, Count	1904	1984	Brando, Marlon	1924	2004
Adams, Joey	1911	1999	Bates, Alan	1934	2003	Branigan, Laura	1957	2004
Adams, Maude	1872	1953	Bavier, Frances	1902	1989	Brazzi, Rossano	1916	1994
Adler, Jacob P.	1855	1926	Baxter, Anne	1923	1985	Brennan, Eileen	1932	2013
Adler, Stella	1902	1992	Baxter, Warner	1889	1951	Brennan, Walter	1894	1974
Adoree, Renee	1898	1933	Beaumont, Hugh	1909	1982	Brenner, David	1936	2014
Agar, John	1921	2002	Beavers, Louise	1902	1962	Brent, George	1904	1979
Aherne, Brian	1902	1986	Beery, Noah, Jr.	1913	1994	Brett, Jeremy	1935	1995
Aiello, Danny	1933	2019	Beery, Noah, Sr.	1884	1946	Brewer, Teresa	1931	2007
Ailey, Alvin	1931	1989	Beery, Wallace	1885	1949	Brice, Fanny	1891	1951
Akins, Claude	1918	1994	Begley, Ed	1901	1970	Bridges, Lloyd	1913	1998
Albert, Eddie	1906	2005	Bel Geddes, Barbara	1922	2005	Brimley, Wilford	1934	2020
Albertson, Jack	1907	1981	Bell, Art	1945	2018	Broderick, Helen	1891	1959
Alda, Robert	1914	1986	Bellamy, Ralph	1904	1991	Bronson, Charles	1921	2003
Allen, Fred	1894	1956	Belushi, John	1949	1982	Brooks, Foster	1912	2001
Allen, Gracie	1906	1964	Benaderet, Bea	1906	1968	Brooks, Louise	1906	1985
Allen, Mel	1913	1996	Bendix, William	1906	1964	Brown, Clarence	1890	1987
Allen, Peter	1944	1992	Bennett, Constance	1904	1965	Brown, James	1933	2006
Allen, Steve	1921	2000	Bennett, Joan	1910	1990	Brown, Joe E.	1892	1973
Allgood, Sara	1883	1950	Bennett, Michael	1943	1987	Brown, Johnny Mack	1904	1974
Allman, Gregg	1947	2017	Benny, Jack	1894	1974	Brown, Les	1912	2001
Allyson, June	1917	2006	Berg, Gertrude	1899	1966	Browne, Roscoe Lee	1925	2007
Altman, Robert	1925	2006	Bergen, Edgar	1903	1978	Browning, Tod	1882	1962
Ameche, Don	1908	1993	Bergen, Polly	1930	2014	Brubeck, Dave	1920	2012
Ames, Leon	1903	1993	Bergman, Ingmar	1918	2007	Bruce, Lenny	1925	1966
Amsterdam, Morey	1908	1996	Bergman, Ingrid	1915	1982	Bruce, Nigel	1895	1953
Anderson, G. M. "Bronco Billy"	1882	1971	Berkeley, Busby	1895	1976	Bruce, Virginia	1910	1982
Anderson, Harry	1952	2018	Berle, Milton	1908	2002	Brynner, Yul	1915	1985
Anderson, Judith	1897	1992	Berlin, Irving	1888	1989	Buchanan, Edgar	1903	1979
Anderson, Marian	1897	1993	Berman, Shelley	1925	2017	Buñuel, Luis	1900	1983
Anderson, Richard	1926	2017	Bernardi, Herschel	1923	1986	Buono, Victor	1938	1982
Andersson, Bibi	1935	2019	Bernhardt, Sarah	1844	1923	Burke, Billie	1885	1970
Andre the Giant	1946	1993	Bernstein, Leonard	1918	1990	Burnette, Smiley	1911	1967
Andrews, Dana	1909	1992	Berry, Chuck	1926	2017	Burns, George	1896	1996
Andrews, Laverne	1913	1967	Berry, Ken	1933	2018	Burr, Raymond	1917	1993
Andrews, Maxene	1916	1995	Bertolucci, Bernardo	1941	2018	Burton, Richard	1925	1984
Andrews, Patty	1918	2013	Bessell, Ted	1939	1996	Busch, Mae	1897	1946
Angeli, Pier	1932	1971	Bickford, Charles	1889	1967	Bushman, Francis X.	1883	1966
Antonioni, Michelangelo	1912	2007	Big Bopper, The	1930	1959	Buttons, Red	1919	2006
Arbuckle, Fatty (Roscoe)	1887	1933	Bikel, Theodore	1924	2015	Byington, Spring	1893	1971
Archerd, Army	1922	2009	Billingsley, Barbara	1915	2010	Caballé, Montserrat	1933	2018
Arden, Eve	1908	1990	Bing, Rudolf	1902	1997	Cabot, Bruce	1904	1972
Arlen, Richard	1900	1976	Bishop, Joey	1918	2007	Cabot, Sebastian	1918	1977
Arliss, George	1868	1946	Bitzer, Billy	1872	1944	Caesar, Sid	1922	2014
Armstrong, Louis	1901	1971	Bixby, Bill	1934	1993	Cagney, James	1899	1986
Arnaz, Desi	1917	1986	Black, Karen	1939	2013	Caldwell, Sarah	1924	2006
Arness, James	1923	2011	Blackstone, Harry, Jr.	1934	1997	Caldwell, Zoe	1933	2020
Arnold, Eddy	1918	2008	Blackstone, Harry, Sr.	1885	1965	Calhern, Louis	1895	1956
Arnold, Edward	1890	1956	Blaine, Vivian	1921	1995	Calhoun, Rory	1922	1999
Arquette, Cliff	1905	1974	Blake, Amanda	1931	1989	Callas, Charlie	1927	2011
Arthur, Beatrice	1922	2009	Blake, Eubie	1887	1983	Callas, Maria	1923	1977
Arthur, Jean	1900	1991	Blanc, Mel	1908	1989	Calloway, Cab	1907	1994
Arzner, Dorothy	1897	1979	Blocker, Dan	1928	1972	Cambridge, Godfrey	1933	1976
Ashcroft, Peggy	1907	1991	Blondell, Joan	1909	1979	Campanella, Joseph	1924	2018
Astaire, Fred	1899	1987	Blondin, Charles	1824	1897	Campbell, Glen	1936	2017
Astor, Mary	1906	1987	Blyden, Larry	1925	1975	Campbell, Mrs. Patrick	1865	1940
Atkins, Chet	1924	2001	Bogarde, Dirk	1921	1999	Candy, John	1950	1994
Attenborough, Richard	1923	2014	Bogart, Humphrey	1899	1957	Canova, Judy	1916	1983
Atwill, Lionel	1885	1946	Boland, Mary	1880	1965	Cantinflas	1911	1993
Auberjonois, René	1940	2019	Boles, John	1895	1969	Cantor, Eddie	1892	1964
Autry, Gene	1907	1998	Bolger, Ray	1904	1987	Capra, Frank	1897	1991
Avildsen, John	1935	2017	Bologna, Joseph	1934	2017	Carey, Harry	1878	1947
Ayres, Lew	1908	1996	Bond, Ward	1903	1960	Carey, Harry, Jr.	1921	2012
Aznavour, Charles	1924	2018	Bondi, Beulah	1888	1981	Carlin, George	1937	2008
Bacall, Lauren	1924	2014	Bono, Sonny	1935	1998	Carlisle Hart, Kitty	1910	2007
Backus, Jim	1913	1989	Boone, Richard	1917	1981	Carney, Art	1918	2003
Bailey, Pearl	1918	1990	Booth, Edwin	1833	1893	Carpenter, Karen	1950	1983
Bain, Conrad	1923	2013	Booth, John Wilkes	1838	1865	Carradine, David	1936	2009
Bainter, Fay	1892	1968	Booth, Junius Brutus	1796	1852	Carradine, John	1906	1988
Baker, Josephine	1906	1975	Booth, Shirley	1898	1992	Carrillo, Leo	1880	1961
Balanchine, George	1904	1983	Borge, Victor	1909	2000	Carroll, Diahann	1935	2019
Ball, Lucille	1911	1989	Borgnine, Ernest	1917	2012	Carroll, Leo G.	1892	1972
Ballard, Kaye	1925	2019	Borzage, Frank	1893	1962	Carroll, Madeleine	1906	1987
Balsam, Martin	1919	1996	Bosco, Philip	1930	2018	Carson, Jack	1910	1963
Bancroft, Anne	1931	2005	Boseman, Chadwick	1976	2020	Carson, Johnny	1925	2005
Bankhead, Tallulah	1902	1968	Bosley, Tom	1927	2010	Carter, Benny	1907	2003
Bara, Theda	1885?	1955	Bourdain, Anthony	1956	2018	Carter, Dixie	1939	2010
Barnum, Phineas T.	1810	1891	Bow, Clara	1905	1965	Carter, Jack	1923	2015
Barrett, Syd	1946	2006	Bowes, Maj. Edward	1874	1946	Carter, Nell	1948	2003
Barry, Gene	1919	2009	Bowie, David	1947	2016	Caruso, Enrico	1873	1921
Barrymore, Ethel	1879	1959	Bowman, Lee	1914	1979	Casals, Pablo	1876	1973
Barrymore, John	1882	1942	Boxcar Willie	1931	1999	Cash, Johnny	1932	2003

Name	Born	Died
Cash, June Carter	1929	2003
Cass, Peggy	1924	1999
Cassavetes, John	1929	1989
Cassidy, David	1950	2017
Cassidy, Jack	1927	1976
Castle, Irene	1893	1969
Castle, Vernon	1887	1918
Champion, Gower	1919	1980
Chandler, Jeff	1918	1961
Chaney, Lon	1883	1930
Chaney, Lon, Jr.	1905	1973
Channing, Carol	1921	2019
Chapin, Harry	1942	1981
Chaplin, Charles	1889	1977
Chapman, Graham	1941	1989
Charisse, Cyd	1922	2008
Charles, Ray	1930	2004
Chase, Ilka	1905	1978
Chatterton, Ruth	1893	1961
Cherrill, Virginia	1908	1996
Chevalier, Maurice	1888	1972
Child, Julia	1912	2004
Christopher, William	1932	2016
Cimino, Michael	1939	2016
Clair, René	1898	1981
Clark, Dick	1929	2012
Clark, Roy	1933	2018
Clayburgh, Jill	1944	2010
Clayton, Jan	1917	1983
Clemons, Clarence	1942	2011
Cliburn, Van	1934	2013
Clift, Montgomery	1920	1966
Cline, Patsy	1932	1963
Clooney, Rosemary	1928	2002
Cobain, Kurt	1967	1994
Cobb, Lee J.	1911	1976
Coburn, Charles	1877	1961
Coburn, James	1928	2002
Coca, Imogene	1908	2001
Cocker, Joe	1944	2014
Coco, James	1930	1987
Cody, Buffalo Bill	1846	1917
Cody, Iron Eyes	1907	1999
Cohan, George M.	1878	1942
Cohen, Leonard	1934	2016
Cohen, Myron	1902	1986
Colbert, Claudette	1903	1996
Cole, Nat "King"	1919	1965
Cole, Natalie	1950	2015
Coleman, Gary	1968	2010
Coleman, Ornette	1930	2015
Collins, Gary	1938	2012
Collins, Ray	1890	1965
Colman, Ronald	1891	1958
Columbo, Russ	1908	1934
Comden, Betty	1917	2006
Como, Perry	1912	2001
Conklin, Chester	1888	1971
Conniff, Ray	1916	2002
Connors, Chuck	1921	1992
Connors, Mike	1925	2017
Conrad, Robert	1935	2020
Conrad, William	1920	1994
Conried, Hans	1917	1982
Conte, Richard	1911	1975
Convy, Bert	1933	1991
Conway, Tim	1933	2019
Coogan, Jackie	1914	1984
Cook, Barbara	1927	2017
Cook, Elisha, Jr.	1904	1995
Cooke, Alistair	1908	2004
Cooke, Sam	1931	1964
Cooper, Gary	1901	1961
Cooper, Gladys	1888	1971
Cooper, Jackie	1922	2011
Copland, Aaron	1900	1990
Corby, Ellen	1913	1999
Corelli, Franco	1921	2003
Corey, Jeff	1914	2002
Corio, Ann	1914	1999
Corley, Pat	1930	2006
Cornelius, Don	1936	2012
Cornell, Chris	1964	2017
Cornell, Katharine	1893	1974
Correll, Charles	1890	1972
Costello, Dolores	1905	1979
Costello, Lou	1906	1959
Cotten, Joseph	1905	1994
Coward, Noel	1899	1973
Cox, Wally	1924	1973
Crabbe, Buster	1908	1983
Crain, Jeanne	1925	2003
Crane, Bob	1928	1978
Craven, Wes	1939	2015
Crawford, Broderick	1911	1986
Crawford, Joan	1904	1977
Crenna, Richard	1926	2003
Crews, Laura Hope	1880	1942
Crisp, Donald	1880	1974
Crisp, Quentin	1908	1999
Croce, Jim	1942	1973
Cronyn, Hume	1911	2003
Crosby, Bing	1903	1977
Cross, Ben	1947	2020
Crothers, Scatman	1910	1986
Cruz, Celia	1925	2003
Cugat, Xavier	1900	1990
Cukor, George	1899	1983
Cullen, Bill	1920	1990
Culp, Robert	1930	2010
Cummings, Constance	1910	2005
Cummings, Robert	1908	1990
Curtis, Tony	1925	2010
Curtiz, Michael	1888	1962
Cushing, Peter	1913	1994
Da Silva, Howard	1909	1986
Dailey, Dan	1915	1978
Damone, Vic	1928	2018
Dandridge, Dorothy	1923	1965
Dangerfield, Rodney	1921	2004
Daniell, Henry	1894	1963
Daniels, Bebe	1901	1971
Daniels, Charlie	1936	2020
Darin, Bobby	1936	1973
Darnell, Linda	1923	1965
Darwell, Jane	1879	1967
Davenport, Harry	1866	1949
Davies, Marion	1897	1961
Davis, Ann B.	1926	2014
Davis, Bette	1908	1989
Davis, Joan	1907	1961
Davis, Mac	1942	2020
Davis, Ossie	1917	2005
Davis, Sammy, Jr.	1925	1990
Dawson, Richard	1932	2012
Day, Dennis	1917	1988
Day, Doris	1922	2019
Day, Laraine	1920	2007
De Carlo, Yvonne	1922	2007
De Havilland, Olivia	1916	2020
De Laurentiis, Dino	1919	2010
de Mille, Agnes	1905	1993
De Mille, Cecil B.	1881	1959
De Wilde, Brandon	1942	1972
De Wolfe, Billy	1907	1974
Dean, James	1931	1955
Dean, Jimmy	1928	2010
Dearie, Blossom	1924	2009
Dee, Frances	1907	2004
Dee, Ruby	1922	2014
Dee, Sandra	1942	2005
Defore, Don	1917	1993
DeFranco, Buddy	1923	2014
DeHaven, Gloria	1925	2016
Dekker, Albert	1905	1968
Del Rio, Dolores	1905	1983
DeLuise, Dom	1933	2009
Demarest, William	1892	1983
Demme, Jonathan	1944	2017
Dennehy, Brian	1938	2020
Dennis, Sandy	1937	1992
Denny, Reginald	1891	1967
Denver, Bob	1935	2005
Denver, John	1943	1997
Derek, John	1926	1998
DeSica, Vittorio	1901	1974
Devine, Andy	1905	1977
Dewhurst, Colleen	1924	1991
Diamond, Selma	1920	1985
Diddley, Bo	1928	2008
Dietrich, Marlene	1901	1992
Diller, Phyllis	1917	2012
Disney, Walt	1901	1966
Dix, Richard	1894	1949
Dmytryk, Edward	1908	1999
Dobson, Kevin	1943	2020
Domino, Fats	1928	2017
Donahue, Troy	1936	2001
Donat, Robert	1905	1958
Donen, Stanley	1924	2019
Donlevy, Brian	1901	1972
Dors, Diana	1931	1984
Dorsey, Jimmy	1904	1957
Dorsey, Tommy	1905	1956
Dotrice, Roy	1923	2017
Douglas, Kirk	1916	2020
Douglas, Melvyn	1901	1981
Dove, Billie	1900	1998
Downey, Morton, Jr.	1933	2001
Downs, Hugh	1921	2020
Doyle, David	1929	1997
Drake, Alfred	1914	1992
Draper, Ruth	1884	1956
Dressler, Marie	1869	1934
Drew, Ellen	1915	2003
Drew, Mrs. John	1820	1897
Duchin, Eddy	1909	1951
Duff, Howard	1917	1990
Duggan, Andrew	1923	1988
Duke, Patty	1946	2016
Dumbrille, Douglass	1890	1974
Dumont, Margaret	1889	1965
Duncan, Isadora	1878	1927
Duncan, Michael Clarke	1957	2012
Dunham, Katherine	1910	2006
Dunn, James	1905	1967
Dunne, Irene	1898	1990
Dunnock, Mildred	1901	1991
Durante, Jimmy	1893	1980
Durbin, Deanna	1921	2013
Durning, Charles	1923	2012
Duryea, Dan	1907	1968
Duse, Eleanora	1858	1924
Dvorak, Ann	1912	1979
Dysart, Richard	1929	2015
Eagels, Jeanne	1894	1929
Ebert, Roger	1942	2013
Ebsen, Buddy	1908	2003
Eckstine, Billy	1914	1993
Eddy, Nelson	1901	1967
Edelman, Herb	1933	1996
Edwards, Blake	1922	2010
Edwards, Cliff	1895	1971
Edwards, Ralph	1913	2005
Edwards, Vince	1928	1996
Egan, Richard	1923	1987
Eisenstein, Sergei	1898	1948
Ekberg, Anita	1931	2015
Elam, Jack	1916	2003
Ellington, Duke	1899	1974
Elliot, Cass	1941	1974
Elliott, Bob	1923	2016
Elliott, Denholm	1922	1992
Elman, Mischa	1891	1967
Ephron, Nora	1941	2012
Evans, Dale	1912	2001
Evans, Edith	1888	1976
Evans, Maurice	1901	1989
Evans, Robert	1930	2019
Everett, Chad	1937	2012
Everly, Phil	1939	2014
Ewell, Tom	1909	1994
Fabray, Nanette	1920	2018
Fairbanks, Douglas	1883	1939
Fairbanks, Douglas, Jr.	1909	2000
Falk, Peter	1927	2011
Farentino, James	1938	2012
Farina, Dennis	1944	2013
Farley, Chris	1964	1997
Farmer, Frances	1913	1970
Farnsworth, Richard	1920	2000
Farnum, Dustin	1874	1929
Farnum, William	1876	1953
Farrar, Geraldine	1882	1967
Farrell, Charles	1901	1990
Farrell, Eileen	1920	2002
Fassbinder, Rainer Werner	1946	1982
Fawcett, Farrah	1947	2009
Faye, Alice	1915	1998
Fazenda, Louise	1895	1962
Feld, Fritz	1900	1993
Feldman, Marty	1933	1982
Fell, Norman	1924	1998
Fellini, Federico	1920	1993
Fenneman, George	1919	1997
Ferrer, Jose	1912	1992
Ferrer, Mel	1917	2008

Name	Born	Died	Name	Born	Died	Name	Born	Died
Fetchit, Stepin	1898	1985	Gilbert, Billy	1894	1971	Hartman, Phil	1948	1998
Fiedler, Arthur	1894	1979	Gilbert, John	1895	1936	Harvey, Laurence	1928	1973
Fiedler, John	1925	2005	Gilford, Jack	1907	1990	Harvey, Paul	1918	2009
Fields, Gracie	1898	1979	Gillespie, Dizzy	1917	1993	Harwell, Ernie	1918	2010
Fields, Totie	1930	1978	Gillette, William	1853	1937	Hatfield, Bobby	1940	2003
Fields, W. C.	1879	1946	Gingold, Hermione	1897	1987	Hauer, Rutger	1944	2019
Finch, Peter	1916	1977	Gish, Dorothy	1898	1968	Havens, Richie	1941	2013
Fine, Larry	1902	1975	Gish, Lillian	1893	1993	Havoc, June	1912	2010
Finney, Albert	1936	2019	Gleason, Jackie	1916	1987	Hawkins, Jack	1910	1973
Fisher, Carrie	1956	2016	Gleason, James	1886	1959	Hawkins, Screamin' Jay	1929	2000
Fisher, Eddie	1928	2010	Gluck, Alma	1884	1938	Hawks, Howard	1896	1977
Fiske, Minnie Maddern	1865	1932	Gobel, George	1919	1991	Hawthorne, Nigel	1929	2001
Fitzgerald, Barry	1888	1961	Goddard, Paulette	1905?	1990	Hayakawa, Sessue	1890	1973
Fitzgerald, Ella	1917	1996	Godfrey, Arthur	1903	1983	Hayden, Sterling	1916	1986
Fitzgerald, Geraldine	1913	2005	Godunov, Alexander	1949	1995	Hayes, Gabby	1885	1969
Fleming, Art	1924	1995	Goldwyn, Samuel	1882	1974	Hayes, Helen	1900	1993
Fleming, Victor	1889	1949	Goodman, Benny	1909	1986	Hayes, Isaac	1942	2008
Flynn, Errol	1909	1959	Gorcey, Leo	1917	1969	Haymes, Dick	1917	1980
Flynn, Joe	1925	1974	Gordon, Gale	1906	1995	Hayward, Leland	1902	1971
Foch, Nina	1924	2008	Gordon, Ruth	1896	1985	Hayward, Louis	1909	1985
Fogelberg, Dan	1951	2007	Gorme, Eydie	1932	2013	Hayward, Susan	1917	1975
Foley, Red	1910	1968	Gorshin, Frank	1934	2005	Hayworth, Rita	1918	1987
Fonda, Henry	1905	1982	Gosden, Freeman	1899	1982	Head, Edith	1897	1981
Fonda, Peter	1940	2019	Gottschalk, Louis	1829	1869	Healy, Ted	1896	1937
Fontaine, Joan	1917	2013	Gould, Glenn	1932	1982	Heard, John	1945	2017
Fontanne, Lynn	1887	1983	Gould, Harold	1923	2010	Heckart, Eileen	1919	2001
Fonteyn, Margot	1919	1991	Gould, Morton	1913	1996	Heflin, Van	1910	1971
Ford, Glenn	1916	2006	Goulet, Robert	1933	2007	Heifetz, Jascha	1901	1987
Ford, John	1894	1973	Grable, Betty	1916	1973	Held, Anna	1873	1918
Ford, Paul	1901	1976	Graham, Martha	1894	1991	Helm, Levon	1940	2012
Ford, Tennessee Ernie	1919	1991	Graham, Virginia	1912	1998	Helmond, Katherine	1929	2019
Forman, Milos	1932	2018	Grahame, Gloria	1925	1981	Hemingway, Margaux	1955	1996
Forrest, Edwin	1806	1872	Granger, Farley	1925	2011	Hemsley, Sherman	1938	2012
Forrest, Helen	1917	1999	Granger, Stewart	1913	1993	Henderson, Florence	1934	2016
Forsythe, John	1918	2010	Grant, Cary	1904	1986	Henderson, Skitch	1918	2005
Fosse, Bob	1927	1987	Granville, Bonita	1923	1988	Hendrix, Jimi	1942	1970
Foster, Preston	1901	1970	Grapewin, Charley	1869	1956	Henie, Sonja	1912	1969
Foxx, Redd	1922	1991	Graves, Peter	1926	2010	Henreid, Paul	1908	1992
Foy, Eddie	1856	1928	Gray, Dolores	1924	2002	Henry, Buck	1930	2020
Franchi, Sergio	1926	1990	Gray, Spalding	1941	2004	Henson, Jim	1936	1990
Franciosa, Anthony	1928	2006	Grayson, Kathryn	1922	2010	Hepburn, Audrey	1929	1993
Francis, Anne	1930	2011	Greco, Jose	1918	2000	Hepburn, Katharine	1907	2003
Francis, Arlene	1907	2001	Green, Adolph	1915	2002	Herrmann, Edward	1943	2014
Francis, Kay	1905	1968	Greene, Lorne	1915	1987	Hersholt, Jean	1886	1956
Franciscus, James	1934	1991	Greenstreet, Sydney	1879	1954	Heston, Charlton	1923	2008
Frankenheimer, John	1930	2002	Greenwood, Charlotte	1890	1978	Hickey, William	1928	1997
Franklin, Aretha	1942	2018	Gregory, Dick	1932	2017	Hickson, Joan	1906	1998
Franklin, Bonnie	1944	2013	Gregory, James	1911	2002	Hildegarde	1906	2005
Frawley, William	1887	1966	Griffin, Merv	1925	2007	Hill, Arthur	1922	2006
Freed, Alan	1921	1965	Griffith, Andy	1926	2012	Hill, Benny	1925	1992
Freeman, Al, Jr.	1934	2012	Griffith, D. W.	1874	1948	Hill, George Roy	1921	2002
Freeman, Mona	1926	2014	Griffith, Hugh	1912	1980	Hiller, Wendy	1912	2003
French, Victor	1934	1989	Griffiths, Richard	1947	2013	Hillerman, John	1932	2017
Friganza, Trixie	1870	1955	Grimes, Tammy	1934	2016	Hines, Gregory	1946	2003
Froman, Jane	1907	1980	Grizzard, George	1928	2007	Hingle, Pat	1924	2009
Frost, David	1939	2013	Guardino, Harry	1925	1995	Hirt, Al	1922	1999
Funicello, Annette	1942	2013	Guillaume, Robert	1927	2017	Hitchcock, Alfred	1899	1980
Funt, Allen	1914	1999	Guinness, Alec	1914	2000	Ho, Don	1930	2007
Furness, Betty	1916	1994	Guthrie, Woody	1912	1967	Hodiak, John	1914	1955
Gabin, Jean	1904	1976	Guy-Blaché, Alice	1873	1968	Hoffman, Philip Seymour	1967	2014
Gable, Clark	1901	1960	Gwenn, Edmund	1875	1959	Holden, William	1918	1981
Gabor, Eva	1920	1995	Gwynne, Fred	1926	1993	Holder, Geoffrey	1930	2014
Gabor, Zsa Zsa	1917	2016	Hackett, Buddy	1924	2003	Holiday, Billie	1915	1959
Gandolfini, James	1961	2013	Hackett, Joan	1934	1983	Holliday, Judy	1921	1965
Garagiola, Joe	1926	2016	Hagen, Jean	1923	1977	Holloway, Sterling	1905	1992
Garbo, Greta	1905	1990	Hagen, Uta	1919	2004	Holly, Buddy	1936	1959
Garcia, Jerry	1942	1995	Haggard, Merle	1937	2016	Holm, Celeste	1919	2012
Gardenia, Vincent	1922	1992	Hagman, Larry	1931	2012	Holm, Ian	1931	2020
Gardner, Ava	1922	1990	Haines, William	1900	1973	Holt, Jack	1888	1951
Garfield, John	1913	1952	Hale, Alan, Jr.	1918	1990	Holt, Tim	1918	1973
Garland, Beverly	1926	2008	Hale, Alan, Sr.	1892	1950	Homolka, Oscar	1898	1978
Garland, Judy	1922	1969	Hale, Barbara	1922	2017	Hooker, John Lee	1917	2001
Garner, James	1928	2014	Haley, Bill	1925	1981	Hope, Bob	1903	2003
Garrett, Betty	1919	2011	Haley, Jack	1899	1979	Hopkins, Miriam	1902	1972
Garson, Greer	1904	1996	Hall, Huntz	1919	1999	Hopper, Dennis	1936	2010
Gassman, Vittorio	1922	2000	Hall, Jon	1915	1979	Hopper, DeWolf	1858	1935
Gavin, John	1931	2018	Hall, Monty	1921	2017	Hopper, Hedda	1885	1966
Gaye, Marvin	1939	1984	Hamilton, Margaret	1902	1985	Horowitz, Vladimir	1904	1989
Gaynor, Janet	1906	1984	Hammerstein, Oscar	1847	1919	Horne, Lena	1917	2010
Gazzara, Ben	1930	2012	Hammerstein, Oscar, II	1895	1960	Horton, Edward Everett	1886	1970
Gebel-Williams, Gunther	1934	2001	Hampton, Lionel	1908	2002	Hoskins, Bob	1942	2014
Geer, Will	1902	1978	Hardwicke, Cedric	1893	1964	Houdini, Harry	1874	1926
Gershwin, George	1898	1937	Hardy, Oliver	1892	1957	Houseman, John	1902	1988
Getty, Estelle	1923	2008	Harlow, Jean	1911	1937	Houston, Whitney	1963	2012
Ghostley, Alice	1926	2007	Harper, Valerie	1939	2019	Howard (Horwitz), Curly	1903	1952
Gibb, Andy	1958	1988	Harrington, Pat, Jr.	1929	2016	Howard, Ken	1944	2016
Gibb, Maurice	1949	2003	Harris, Julie	1925	2013	Howard, Leslie	1890	1943
Gibb, Robin	1949	2012	Harris, Phil	1904	1995	Howard (Horwitz), Moe	1897	1975
Gibson, Henry	1935	2009	Harris, Richard	1930	2002	Howard (Horwitz), Shemp	1895	1955
Gibson, Hoot	1892	1962	Harrison, George	1943	2001	Howard, Trevor	1916	1988
Gielgud, John	1904	2000	Harrison, Rex	1908	1990	Hudson, Rock	1925	1985
Gifford, Frank	1930	2015	Hart, William S.	1864	1946	Hughes, Bernard	1915	2006

Name	Born	Died	Name	Born	Died	Name	Born	Died
Mature, Victor	1913	1999	Morton, Jelly Roll	1885	1941	Pangborn, Franklin	1894	1958
Maxwell, Marilyn	1921	1972	Mostel, Zero	1915	1977	Pardo, Don	1918	2014
Mayer, Louis B.	1885	1957	Mowbray, Alan	1897	1969	Parker, Alan	1944	2020
Mayfield, Curtis	1942	1999	Mulhare, Edward	1923	1997	Parker, Eleanor	1922	2013
Mayo, Virginia	1920	2005	Mulligan, Gerry	1927	1996	Parker, Fess	1925	2010
Mazursky, Paul	1930	2014	Mulligan, Richard	1932	2000	Parker, Jean	1915	2005
MCA (Adam Yauch)	1964	2012	Muni, Paul	1895	1967	Parks, Bert	1914	1992
McCambridge, Mercedes	1916	2004	Murnau, F. W.	1888	1931	Parks, Larry	1914	1975
McCarey, Leo	1898	1969	Murphy, Audie	1924	1971	Pasternack, Josef A.	1881	1940
McCarthy, Kevin	1914	2010	Murphy, Brittany	1977	2009	Pastor, Tony (vaudevillian)	1837	1908
McCartney, Linda	1941	1998	Murphy, George	1902	1992	Pastor, Tony (bandleader)	1907	1969
McClanahan, Rue	1934	2010	Murray, Arthur	1895	1991	Patrick, Gail	1911	1980
McClure, Doug	1935	1995	Murray, Kathryn	1906	1999	Patti, Adelina	1843	1919
McCormack, John	1884	1945	Murray, Mae	1889	1965	Patti, Carlotta	1840	1889
McCrea, Joel	1905	1990	Nabors, Jim	1930	2017	Paul, Les	1915	2009
McDaniel, Hattie	1895	1952	Nagel, Conrad	1897	1970	Pavarotti, Luciano	1935	2007
McDowall, Roddy	1928	1998	Naish, J. Carroll	1900	1973	Pavlova, Anna	1885	1931
McFarland, Spanky (George)	1928	1993	Naldi, Nita	1898	1961	Paxton, Bill	1955	2017
McGoohan, Patrick	1928	2009	Nance, Jack	1943	1996	Paycheck, Johnny	1938	2003
McGuire, Al	1931	2001	Natwick, Mildred	1908	1994	Payne, John	1912	1989
McGuire, Dorothy	1916	2001	Nazimova, Alla	1879	1945	Pearl, Minnie	1912	1996
McHugh, Frank	1898	1981	Neal, Patricia	1926	2010	Peck, Gregory	1916	2003
McIntire, John	1907	1991	Negri, Pola	1897	1987	Peckinpah, Sam	1925	1984
McLaglen, Victor	1886	1959	Nelson, David	1936	2011	Pendergrass, Teddy	1950	2010
McMahon, Ed	1923	2009	Nelson, Ed	1928	2014	Penn, Arthur	1922	2010
McPartland, Marian	1918	2013	Nelson, Harriet (Hilliard)	1909	1994	Penner, Joe	1905	1941
McQueen, Butterfly	1911	1995	Nelson, Ozzie	1906	1975	Peppard, George	1928	1994
McQueen, Steve	1930	1980	Nelson, Rick	1940	1985	Perkins, Anthony	1932	1992
Meader, Vaughn	1936	2004	Nesbit, Evelyn	1884	1967	Perkins, Carl	1932	1998
Meadows, Audrey	1924	1996	Nettleton, Lois	1927	2008	Perkins, Marlin	1905	1986
Meadows, Jayne	1919	2015	Newley, Anthony	1931	1999	Perry, Luke	1965	2019
Meara, Anne	1929	2015	Newman, Edwin	1919	2010	Peters, Brock	1927	2005
Meek, Donald	1880	1946	Newman, Paul	1925	2008	Peters, Jean	1926	2000
Méliès, Georges	1861	1938	Nicholas, Fayard	1914	2006	Peters, Roberta	1930	2017
Menjou, Adolphe	1890	1963	Nicholas, Harold	1924	2000	Peterson, Oscar	1925	2007
Menuhin, Yehudi	1916	1999	Nichols, Mike	1931	2014	Petty, Tom	1950	2017
Mercer, Marian	1935	2011	Nielsen, Leslie	1926	2010	Philbin, Regis	1931	2020
Mercouri, Melina	1925	1994	Nijinsky, Vaslav	1890	1950	Phillips, John	1935	2001
Mercury, Freddie	1946	1991	Nilsson, Anna Q.	1888	1974	Phoenix, River	1970	1993
Meredith, Burgess	1909	1997	Nimoy, Leonard	1931	2015	Piaf, Edith	1915	1963
Merman, Ethel	1908	1984	Niven, David	1910	1983	Pickens, Slim	1919	1983
Merrick, David	1911	2000	Nolan, Lloyd	1902	1985	Pickett, Wilson	1941	2006
Merrill, Dina	1925	2017	Norman, Jessye	1945	2019	Pickford, Mary	1892	1979
Merrill, Gary	1915	1990	Normand, Mabel	1894	1930	Pidgeon, Walter	1897	1984
Michael, George	1963	2016	North, Sheree	1933	2005	Pinza, Ezio	1892	1957
Mifune, Toshiro	1920	1997	Notorious B.I.G.	1972	1997	Pitney, Gene	1941	2006
Milland, Ray	1905	1986	Novarro, Ramon	1899	1968	Pitts, Zasu	1898	1963
Miller, Ann	1923	2004	Nureyev, Rudolf	1938	1993	Plato, Dana	1964	1999
Miller, Glenn	1904	1944	Oakie, Jack	1903	1978	Pleasence, Donald	1919	1995
Miller, Marilyn	1898	1936	Oakley, Annie	1860	1926	Pleshette, Suzanne	1937	2008
Miller, Mitch	1911	2010	Oates, Warren	1928	1982	Pollack, Sydney	1934	2008
Miller, Roger	1936	1992	Oberon, Merle	1911	1979	Pons, Lily	1904	1976
Mills, John	1908	2005	O'Brien, Edmond	1915	1985	Ponselle, Rosa	1897	1981
Milner, Martin	1931	2015	O'Brien, George	1900	1985	Ponti, Carlo	1912	2007
Mineo, Sal	1939	1976	O'Brien, Pat	1899	1983	Porter, Edwin S.	1870	1941
Minghella, Anthony	1954	2008	O'Connell, Arthur	1908	1981	Postlethwaite, Pete	1946	2011
Mingus, Charles	1922	1979	O'Connell, Helen	1921	1993	Poston, Tom	1921	2007
Minnelli, Vincente	1903	1986	O'Connor, Carroll	1924	2001	Powell, Dick	1904	1963
Miranda, Carmen	1909	1955	O'Connor, Donald	1925	2003	Powell, Eleanor	1912	1982
Mitchell, Thomas	1892	1962	O'Connor, Una	1880	1959	Powell, William	1892	1984
Mitchum, Robert	1917	1997	Odetta (Holmes)	1930	2008	Power, Tyrone	1914	1958
Mix, Tom	1880	1940	O'Hara, Maureen	1920	2015	Preminger, Otto	1905	1986
Moffat, Donald	1930	2018	O'Herlihy, Daniel	1919	2005	Presley, Elvis	1935	1977
Molinaro, Al	1919	2015	O'Keefe, Dennis	1908	1968	Preston, Billy	1946	2006
Monroe, Marilyn	1926	1962	Oland, Warner	1880	1938	Preston, Robert	1918	1987
Monroe, Vaughn	1911	1973	Olcott, Chauncey	1860	1932	Previn, Andre	1929	2019
Montalban, Ricardo	1920	2009	Oliveira, Manoel de	1908	2015	Price, Ray	1926	2013
Montand, Yves	1921	1991	Oliver, Edna May	1883	1942	Price, Vincent	1911	1993
Monteith, Cory	1982	2013	Olivier, Laurence	1907	1989	Prima, Louis	1911	1978
Montgomery, Elizabeth	1933	1995	Olsen, Merlin	1940	2010	Prince	1958	2016
Montgomery, George	1916	2000	O'Neal, Ron	1937	2004	Prince, Hal	1928	2019
Montgomery, Robert	1904	1981	O'Neill, James	1849	1920	Prinze, Freddie	1954	1977
Moody, Ron	1924	2015	Ophüls, Max	1902	1957	Prosky, Robert	1930	2008
Moore, Clayton	1914	1999	Orbach, Jerry	1935	2004	Provine, Dorothy	1937	2010
Moore, Colleen	1900	1988	Orbison, Roy	1936	1988	Prowse, Juliet	1936	1996
Moore, Dudley	1935	2002	Ormandy, Eugene	1899	1985	Pryor, Richard	1940	2005
Moore, Garry	1915	1993	O'Shea, Milo	1926	2013	Puente, Tito	1923	2000
Moore, Grace	1898	1947	O'Sullivan, Maureen	1911	1998	Pyle, Denver	1920	1997
Moore, Mary Tyler	1936	2017	O'Toole, Peter	1932	2013	Quayle, Anthony	1913	1989
Moore, Roger	1927	2017	Ouspenskaya, Maria	1876	1949	Questel, Mae	1908	1998
Moorehead, Agnes	1906	1974	Owen, Reginald	1887	1972	Quinn, Anthony	1915	2001
Moreau, Jeanne	1928	2017	Owens, Buck	1929	2006	Quintero, José	1924	1999
Morgan, Dennis	1910	1994	Paar, Jack	1918	2004	Rabb, Ellis	1930	1998
Morgan, Frank	1890	1949	Paderewski, Ignace	1860	1941	Rabbit, Eddie	1941	1998
Morgan, Harry	1915	2011	Page, Bettie	1923	2008	Radner, Gilda	1946	1989
Morgan, Helen	1900	1941	Page, Geraldine	1924	1987	Rae, Charlotte	1926	2018
Morgan, Henry	1915	1994	Page, Patti	1927	2013	Rafferty, Gerry	1947	2011
Morita, Pat	1932	2005	Pakula, Alan	1928	1998	Raft, George	1895	1980
Morley, Robert	1908	1992	Palance, Jack	1919	2006	Rainer, Luise	1910	2014
Morris, Chester	1901	1970	Paliette, Eugene	1889	1954	Rains, Claude	1889	1967
Morris, Greg	1934	1996	Palmer, Betsy	1926	2015	Raitt, John	1917	2005
Morrison, Jim	1943	1971	Palmer, Lilli	1914	1986	Ralston, Esther	1902	1994
Morrow, Vic	1929	1982	Palmer, Robert	1949	2003	Ramis, Harold	1944	2014

Name	Born	Died	Name	Born	Died	Name	Born	Died
Ramone, Dee Dee	1952	2002	Rose Marie	1923	2017	Silvers, Phil	1912	1985
Ramone, Joey	1951	2001	Rose, Billy	1899	1966	Sim, Alastair	1900	1976
Ramone, Johnny	1948	2004	Rossellini, Roberto	1906	1977	Simmons, Jean	1929	2010
Ramone, Tommy	1949	2014	Rostropovich, Mstislav	1927	2007	Simone, Nina	1933	2003
Rampal, Jean-Pierre	1922	2000	Rowan, Dan	1922	1987	Sinatra, Frank	1915	1998
Randall, Tony	1920	2004	Rubinstein, Artur	1887	1982	Sinclair, Madge	1938	1995
Randolph, John	1915	2004	Rubenstein, Zelda	1933	2010	Singleton, John	1968	2019
Rathbone, Basil	1892	1967	Ruggles, Charles	1886	1970	Singleton, Penny	1908	2003
Ratoff, Gregory	1897	1960	Russell, Harold	1914	2002	Sirk, Douglas	1900	1987
Rawls, Lou	1933	2006	Russell, Jane	1921	2011	Siskel, Gene	1946	1999
Ray, Aldo	1926	1991	Russell, Ken	1927	2011	Sjostrom, Victor	1879	1960
Ray, Johnnie	1927	1990	Russell, Leon	1942	2016	Skelton, Red	1913	1997
Ray, Nicholas	1911	1979	Russell, Lillian	1861	1922	Skinner, Otis	1858	1942
Rayburn, Gene	1917	1999	Russell, Nipsey	1923	2005	Sledge, Percy	1940	2015
Raye, Martha	1916	1994	Russell, Rosalind	1911	1976	Smith, Alexis	1921	1993
Raymond, Gene	1908	1998	Rutherford, Ann	1917	2012	Smith, Bessie	1894?	1937
Reagan, Ronald	1911	2004	Rutherford, Margaret	1892	1972	Smith, Buffalo Bob	1917	1998
Redding, Otis	1941	1967	Ryan, Irene	1903	1973	Smith, C. Aubrey	1863	1948
Reddy, Helen	1941	2020	Ryan, Robert	1909	1973	Smith, Elliott	1969	2003
Redgrave, Corin	1939	2010	Sabu (Dastagir)	1924	1963	Smith, Kate	1907	1986
Redgrave, Lynn	1943	2010	St. Cyr, Lili	1917	1999	Smith, Keely	1928	2017
Redgrave, Michael	1908	1985	St. Denis, Ruth	1877	1968	Snodgress, Carrie	1946	2004
Reed, Donna	1921	1986	Sakall, S. Z.	1883	1955	Snow, Hank	1914	1999
Reed, Lou	1942	2013	Saks, Gene	1921	2015	Snyder, Tom	1936	2007
Reed, Oliver	1938	1999	Sale (Chic), Charles	1885	1936	Solti, George	1912	1997
Reed, Robert	1932	1992	Sales, Soupy	1926	2009	Sondergaard, Gale	1899	1985
Rees, Roger	1944	2015	Sanders, George	1906	1972	Sothern, Ann	1909	2001
Reese, Della	1931	2017	Sanford, Isabel	1917	2004	Sousa, John Philip	1854	1932
Reeve, Christopher	1952	2004	Sargent, Dick	1933	1994	Spelling, Aaron	1923	2006
Reeves, George	1914	1959	Sarrazin, Michael	1940	2011	Spencer, John	1946	2005
Reeves, Steve	1926	2000	Savalas, Telly	1922	1994	Sperber, Wendie Jo	1958	2005
Reid, Wallace	1891	1923	Saxon, John	1936	2020	Springfield, Dusty	1939	1999
Reilly, Charles Nelson	1931	2007	Schallert, William	1922	2016	Stack, Robert	1919	2003
Reiner, Carl	1922	2020	Scheider, Roy	1935	2008	Stafford, Jo	1917	2008
Reinhardt, Max	1873	1943	Schell, Maria	1926	2005	Stander, Lionel	1908	1994
Remick, Lee	1935	1991	Schell, Maximilian	1930	2014	Stang, Arnold	1918	2009
Renaldo, Duncan	1904	1980	Schenkel, Chris	1923	2005	Stanley, Kim	1925	2001
Rennie, Michael	1909	1971	Schiavelli, Vincent	1948	2005	Stanton, Harry Dean	1926	2017
Renoir, Jean	1894	1979	Schildkraut, Joseph	1896	1964	Stanwyck, Barbara	1907	1990
Rettig, Tommy	1941	1996	Schlesinger, John	1926	2003	Stapleton, Jean	1923	2013
Reynolds, Burt	1936	2018	Schnabel, Artur	1882	1951	Stapleton, Maureen	1925	2006
Reynolds, Debbie	1932	2016	Schneider, Maria	1952	2011	Steiger, Rod	1925	2002
Rich, Charlie	1932	1995	Schneider, Romy	1938	1982	Sterling, Jan	1921	2004
Richardson, Ian	1934	2007	Schwartzkopf, Elizabeth	1915	2006	Stern, Isaac	1920	2001
Richardson, Natasha	1963	2009	Scofield, Paul	1922	2008	Stevens, Craig	1918	2000
Richardson, Ralph	1902	1983	Scott, George C.	1927	1999	Stevens, George	1904	1975
Rickles, Don	1926	2017	Scott, Gordon	1926	2007	Stevens, Inger	1934	1970
Rickman, Alan	1946	2016	Scott, Hazel	1920	1981	Stevens, Mark	1916	1994
Riddle, Nelson	1921	1985	Scott, Lizabeth	1922	2015	Stevens, Risë	1913	2013
Riefenstahl, Leni	1902	2003	Scott, Martha	1914	2003	Stevenson, McLean	1929	1996
Rigg, Diana	1938	2020	Scott, Randolph	1898	1987	Stewart, James	1908	1997
Ripperton, Minnie	1947	1979	Scott, Stuart	1965	2015	Stickney, Dorothy	1896	1998
Ritchard, Cyril	1898	1977	Scott, Zachary	1914	1965	Stiers, David Ogden	1942	2018
Ritter, John	1948	2003	Scott-Heron, Gil	1949	2011	Stiller, Jerry	1927	2020
Ritter, Tex	1905	1974	Scott-Siddons, Mrs.	1843	1896	Stokowski, Leopold	1882	1977
Ritter, Thelma	1905	1969	Seberg, Jean	1938	1979	Stone, Lewis	1879	1953
Ritz, Al	1901	1965	Seeger, Pete	1919	2014	Stone, Milburn	1904	1980
Ritz, Harry	1906	1986	Seeley, Blossom	1892	1974	Storm, Gale	1922	2009
Ritz, Jimmy	1903	1985	Segovia, Andres	1893	1987	Straight, Beatrice	1918	2001
Rivers, Joan	1933	2014	Seldes, Marian	1928	2014	Strasberg, Lee	1901	1982
Roach, Hal	1892	1992	Selena (Quintanilla)	1971	1995	Strasberg, Susan	1938	1999
Roach, Max	1924	2007	Sellers, Peter	1925	1980	Stritch, Elaine	1925	2014
Robards, Jason	1922	2000	Selznick, David O.	1902	1965	Strummer, Joe	1952	2002
Robbins, Jerome	1918	1998	Sennett, Mack	1880	1960	Stuart, Gloria	1910	2010
Robbins, Marty	1925	1982	Señor Wences	1896	1999	Stuarti, Enzo	1919	2005
Roberts, Doris	1925	2016	Serling, Rod	1924	1975	Sturges, Preston	1898	1959
Roberts, Pernell	1928	2010	Shakur, Tupac	1971	1996	Sullavan, Margaret	1911	1960
Roberts, Rachel	1927	1980	Shandling, Garry	1949	2016	Sullivan, Barry	1912	1994
Robertson, Cliff	1925	2011	Shankar, Ravi	1920	2012	Sullivan, Ed	1902	1974
Robertson, Dale	1923	2013	Sharif, Omar	1932	2015	Sumac, Yma	1922	2008
Robeson, Paul	1898	1976	Shaw, Artie	1910	2004	Summer, Donna	1948	2012
Robinson, Bill	1878	1949	Shaw, Robert (actor)	1927	1978	Summerville, Slim	1892	1946
Robinson, Edward G.	1893	1973	Shaw, Robert (conductor)	1916	1999	Sutherland, Joan	1926	2010
Robson, Flora	1902	1984	Shawn, Ted	1891	1972	Swanson, Gloria	1899	1983
Roche, Eugene	1928	2004	Shearer, Moira	1926	2006	Swayze, Patrick	1952	2009
Rochester (Eddie Anderson)	1905	1977	Shearer, Norma	1902	1983	Sweet, Blanche	1896	1986
Roddenberry, Gene	1921	1991	Shearing, George	1919	2011	Switzer, Carl "Alfalfa"	1927	1959
Rodgers, Jimmie	1897	1933	Shelley, Carole	1939	2018	Talbot, Lyle	1902	1996
Rogers, Buddy	1904	1999	Shepard, Sam	1943	2017	Tallchief, Maria	1925	2013
Rogers, Fred	1928	2003	Sheppard, Bob	1910	2010	Talmadge, Constance	1900	1973
Rogers, Ginger	1911	1995	Sheridan, Ann	1915	1967	Talmadge, Norma	1893	1957
Rogers, Kenny	1938	2020	Shore, Dinah	1917	1994	Tamiroff, Akim	1899	1972
Rogers, Roy	1911	1998	Short, Bobby	1924	2005	Tandy, Jessica	1909	1994
Rogers, Wayne	1933	2015	Shubert, Lee	1875	1953	Tanguay, Eva	1878	1947
Rogers, Will	1879	1935	Shull, Richard B.	1929	1999	Tati, Jacques	1908	1982
Rohmer, Éric	1920	2010	Siddons, Sarah	1755	1831	Taylor, Billy	1921	2010
Roland, Gilbert	1905	1994	Sidney, Sylvia	1910	1999	Taylor, Dub	1907	1994
Rolle, Esther	1920	1998	Siegel, Don	1912	1991	Taylor, Elizabeth	1932	2011
Rollins, Howard	1950	1996	Signoret, Simone	1921	1985	Taylor, Estelle	1899	1958
Roman, Ruth	1924	1999	Sills, Beverly	1929	2007	Taylor, Laurette	1887	1946
Romero, Cesar	1907	1994	Silver, Ron	1946	2009	Taylor, Paul	1930	2018
Rooney, Mickey	1920	2014	Silverheels, Jay	1912	1980	Taylor, Rip	1931	2019

Name	Born	Died	Name	Born	Died	Name	Born	Died
Taylor, Robert	1911	1969	Vidor, King	1894	1982	Willard, Fred	1939	2020
Taylor, Rod	1930	2015	Vigoda, Abe	1921	2016	Williams, Andy	1927	2012
Temple Black, Shirley	1928	2014	Villechaize, Herve	1943	1993	Williams, Bert	1874	1922
Terry, Ellen	1847	1928	Vincent, Gene	1935	1971	Williams, Esther	1921	2013
Thalberg, Irving	1899	1936	Vincent, Jan-Michael	1944	2019	Williams, Guy	1924	1989
Thaw, John	1942	2002	Von Stroheim, Erich	1885	1957	Williams, Hank, Sr.	1923	1953
Thaxter, Phyllis	1919	2012	Von Sydow, Max	1929	2020	Williams, Robin	1951	2014
Thicke, Alan	1947	2016	Von Zell, Harry	1906	1981	Williamson, Nicol	1936	2011
Thigpen, Lynne	1948	2003	Wain, Bea	1917	2017	Wills, Bob	1905	1975
Thomas, Danny	1912	1991	Waite, Ralph	1928	2014	Wills, Chill	1902	1978
Thomas, Jay	1948	2017	Walker, Clint	1927	2018	Wilson, Carl	1946	1998
Thompson, Sada	1927	2011	Walker, Junior	1942	1995	Wilson, Dennis	1944	1983
Thorndike, Sybil	1882	1976	Walker, Nancy	1922	1992	Wilson, Dooley	1894	1953
Thulin, Ingrid	1926	2004	Walker, Paul	1973	2013	Wilson, Elizabeth	1921	2015
Tierney, Gene	1920	1991	Walker, Robert	1918	1951	Wilson, Flip	1933	1998
Tillis, Mel	1932	2017	Wallace, Marcia	1942	2013	Wilson, Jackie	1934	1984
Tiny Tim	1932	1996	Wallach, Eli	1915	2014	Wilson, Marie	1917	1972
Todd, Michael	1909	1958	Wallenda, Karl	1905	1978	Wilson, Nancy	1937	2018
Todd, Richard	1919	2009	Walsh, J. T.	1943	1998	Windom, William	1923	2012
Tomlinson, David	1917	2000	Walsh, Raoul	1887	1980	Winehouse, Amy	1983	2011
Tone, Franchot	1905	1968	Walston, Ray	1914	2001	Winfield, Paul	1941	2004
Tork, Peter	1942	2019	Walter, Bruno	1876	1962	Winter, Johnny	1944	2014
Torme, Mel	1925	1999	Ward, Simon	1941	2012	Winters, Jonathan	1925	2013
Torn, Rip	1931	2019	Warden, Jack	1920	2006	Winters, Shelley	1920	2006
Toscanini, Arturo	1867	1957	Waring, Fred	1900	1984	Wise, Robert	1914	2005
Tracy, Lee	1898	1968	Warner, H. B.	1876	1958	Wiseman, Joseph	1918	2009
Tracy, Spencer	1900	1967	Warrick, Ruth	1915	2005	Withers, Bill	1938	2020
Travers, Henry	1874	1965	Washington, Dinah	1924	1963	Wolfman Jack	1938	1995
Travers, Mary	1936	2009	Waters, Ethel	1896	1977	Wong, Anna May	1907	1961
Treacher, Arthur	1894	1975	Waters, Muddy	1913?	1983	Wood, Ed	1924	1978
Tree, Herbert Beerbohm	1853	1917	Waxman, Al	1935	2001	Wood, Natalie	1938	1981
Trevor, Claire	1909	2000	Wayne, David	1914	1995	Wood, Peggy	1892	1978
Truffaut, Francois	1932	1984	Wayne, John	1907	1979	Wood, Sam	1884	1949
Tucker, Forrest	1919	1986	Weaver, Dennis	1924	2006	Woodward, Edward	1930	2009
Tucker, Richard	1913	1975	Weaver, Fritz	1926	2016	Wooley, Sheb	1921	2003
Tucker, Sophie	1884	1966	Webb, Clifton	1891	1966	Woolley, Monty	1888	1963
Turner, Big Joe	1911	1985	Webb, Jack	1920	1982	Worth, Irene	1916	2002
Turner, Ike	1931	2008	Weems, Ted	1901	1963	Wray, Fay	1907	2004
Turner, Lana	1920?	1995	Weiland, Scott	1967	2015	Wright, Teresa	1918	2005
Turpin, Ben	1869	1940	Weissmuller, Johnny	1904	1984	Wyatt, Jane	1910	2006
Twitty, Conway	1933	1993	Welk, Lawrence	1903	1992	Wyler, William	1902	1981
Urich, Robert	1946	2002	Welles, Orson	1915	1985	Wyman, Jane	1917	2007
Ustinov, Peter	1921	2004	Wellman, William	1896	1975	Wynette, Tammy	1942	1998
Valens, Ritchie	1941	1959	Wells, Kitty	1919	2012	Wynn, Ed.	1886	1966
Valentino, Rudolph	1895	1926	Werner, Oskar	1922	1984	Wynn, Keenan	1916	1986
Vallee, Rudy	1901	1986	West, Adam	1928	2017	York, Dick	1928	1992
Van, Bobby	1928	1980	West, Mae	1893	1980	York, Susannah	1939	2011
Van Cleef, Lee	1925	1989	Weston, Jack	1924	1996	Young, Alan	1919	2016
Van Fleet, Jo	1922	1996	Whale, James	1889	1957	Young, Clara Kimball	1890	1960
Van Halen, Eddie	1955	2020	White, Barry	1944	2003	Young, Gig	1913	1978
Van Patten, Dick	1928	2015	White, Jesse	1919	1997	Young, Loretta	1913	2000
Vance, Vivian	1912	1979	White, Pearl	1889	1938	Young, Robert	1907	1998
Vandross, Luther	1951	2005	Whiteman, Paul	1891	1967	Young, Roland	1887	1953
Varney, Jim	1949	2000	Whiting, Margaret	1924	2011	Youngman, Henny	1906	1998
Vaughan, Sarah	1924	1990	Whitmore, James	1921	2009	Zanuck, Darryl F.	1902	1979
Vaughn, Robert	1932	2016	Whitty, May	1865	1948	Zappa, Frank	1940	1993
Veidt, Conrad	1893	1943	Wickes, Mary	1910	1995	Zeffirelli, Franco	1923	2019
Velez, Lupe	1908	1944	Widmark, Richard	1914	2008	Zevon, Warren	1947	2003
Vera-Ellen (Rohe)	1926	1981	Wilde, Cornel	1915	1989	Ziegfeld, Florenz	1869	1932
Verdon, Gwen	1925	2000	Wilder, Billy	1906	2002	Zimbalist, Efrem, Jr.	1918	2014
Verrett, Shirley	1931	2010	Wilder, Gene	1933	2016	Zinneman, Fred	1907	1997
Vicious, Sid	1957	1979	Wilding, Michael	1912	1979	Zukor, Adolph	1873	1976
Vickers, Jon	1926	2015						

Original Names of Selected Entertainers

Adele: Adele Laurie Blue Adkins
Ad-Rock: Adam Horovitz
Clay Aiken: Clayton Grissom
Alan Alda: Alphonso D'Abruzzo
Jason Alexander: Jay Greenspan
Woody Allen: Allen Konigsberg
André 3000: Andre Benjamin
Julie Andrews: Julia Wells
Criss Angel: Christopher Sarantakos
Beatrice Arthur: Bernice Frankel
Fred Astaire: Frederick Austerlitz
Awkwafina: Nora Lum
Babyface: Kenneth Edmonds
Lauren Bacall: Betty Joan Perske
Erykah Badu: Erica Wright
Eric Bana: Eric Banadinovich
Anne Bancroft: Anna Maria Italiano
Theda Bara: Theodosia Goodman
Beck: Bek David Campbell
Pat Benatar: Patricia Andrejewski
Tony Bennett: Anthony Benedetto
Jack Benny: Benjamin Kubelsky
Milton Berle: Mendel Berlinger
Irving Berlin: Israel Baline

Sarah Bernhardt: Henriette-Rosine Bernard
Jello Biafra: Eric Reed Boucher
Big Boi: Antwan Patton
The Big Bopper: Jiles Perry "J.P." Richardson
Robert Blake: Michael James Vijencio Gubitosi
Jon Bon Jovi: John Francis Bongiovi
Bono: Paul Hewson
David Bowie: David Robert Jones
Boy George: George Alan O'Dowd
Fanny Brice: Fanny Borach
Charles Bronson: Charles Buchinski
Albert Brooks: Albert Einstein
Mel Brooks: Melvin Kaminsky
Foxy Brown: Inga Marchand
George Burns: Nathan Birnbaum
Ellen Burstyn: Edna Gilhooley
Richard Burton: Richard Jenkins
Red Buttons: Aaron Chwatt
Nicolas Cage: Nicholas Coppola
Michael Caine: Maurice Micklewhite
Maria Callas: Maria Kalogeropoulos
Cardi B: Belcalis Marlenis Almánza
Jackie Chan: Chan Kwong-Sung

Cyd Charisse: Tula Finklea
Ray Charles: Ray Charles Robinson
Charo: María Rosario Pilar Martínez Molina Baeza
Chubby Checker: Ernest Evans
Cher: Cherilyn Sarkisian
Chuck D: Carlton Ridenhour
Patsy Cline: Virginia Patterson Hensley
Claudette Colbert: Lily Chauchoin
Coolio: Artis Leon Ivey Jr.
Alice Cooper: Vincent Furnier
David Copperfield: David Kotkin
Howard Cosell: Howard Cohen
Elvis Costello: Declan McManus
Lou Costello: Louis Cristillo
Peter Coyote: Peter Cohon
Joan Crawford: Lucille LeSueur
Quentin Crisp: Denis Pratt
Tom Cruise: Thomas Cruise Mapother IV
Tony Curtis: Bernard Schwartz
Miley Cyrus: Destiny Hope Cyrus
D'Angelo: Michael D'Angelo Archer
Rodney Dangerfield: Jacob Cohen
Bobby Darin: Walden Robert Cassotto

Doris Day: Doris von Kappelhoff
Yvonne De Carlo: Peggy Middleton
Portia de Rossi: Amanda Lee Rogers
Sandra Dee: Alexandra Zuck
John Denver: Henry John Deutschendorf Jr.
Bo Derek: Mary Cathleen Collins
Danny DeVito: Daniel Michaeli
Angie Dickinson: Angeline Brown
Bo Diddley: Elias Bates
Vin Diesel: Mark Vincent
Phyllis Diller: Phyllis Driver
Divine: Harris Glenn Milstead
DMX: Earl Simmons
Troy Donahue: Merle Johnson Jr.
Kirk Douglas: Issur Danielovitch
Drake: Aubrey Drake Graham
Bob Dylan: Robert Zimmerman
Barbara Eden: Barbara Huffman
Elvira: Cassandra Peterson
Eminem: Marshall Mathers
Enya: Eithne Ni Bhraonain
Dale Evans: Frances Smith
Chad Everett: Raymon Cramton
Fabian: Fabian Anthony Forte
Fabolous: John David Jackson
Douglas Fairbanks: Douglas Ullman
Morgan Fairchild: Patsy McClenny
Jamie Farr: Jameel Farah
Fergie: Stacy Ferguson
Stepin Fetchit: Lincoln Perry
W. C. Fields: William Claude Dukenfield
50 Cent: Curtis Jackson
Flavor Flav: William Drayton
Joan Fontaine: Joan de Havilland
Jodie Foster: Alicia Christian Foster
Jamie Foxx: Eric Bishop
Redd Foxx: John Sanford
Arlene Francis: Arlene Kazanjian
Connie Francis: Concetta Franconero
Greta Garbo: Greta Gustafsson
Judy Garland: Frances Gumm
James Garner: James Bumgarner
Crystal Gayle: Brenda Gail Webb
George Gershwin: Jacob Gershowitz
Kathie Lee Gifford: Kathie Epstein
Whoopi Goldberg: Caryn Johnson
Cary Grant: Archibald Leach
Lee Grant: Lyova Rosenthal
Robert Guillaume: Robert Williams
Buddy Hackett: Leonard Hacker
Hammer: Stanley Kirk Burrell
Jean Harlow: Harlean Carpenter
Helen Hayes: Helen Brown
Susan Hayward: Edythe Marrener
Rita Hayworth: Margarita Cansino
Pee-Wee Herman: Paul Reubenfeld
Charlton Heston: John Charles Carter
Perez Hilton: Mario Lavandeira Jr.
Hulk Hogan: Terry Gene Bollea
Billie Holiday: Eleanora Fagan
Judy Holliday: Judith Tuvim
Bob Hope: Leslie Townes Hope
Harry Houdini: Erik Weisz
Howlin' Wolf: Chester Burnett
Rock Hudson: Roy Scherer Jr. (later Fitzgerald)
Engelbert Humperdinck: Arnold Dorsey
Kim Hunter: Janet Cole
Ice Cube: O'Shea Jackson
Ice-T: Tracy Morrow
Billy Idol: William Broad
Etta James: Jamesetta Hawkins
Ja Rule: Jeffrey Atkins
Jay-Z: Shawn Carter
Elton John: Reginald Dwight
Al Jolson: Asa Yoelson
Jennifer Jones: Phylis Isley
Tom Jones: Thomas Woodward
Spike Jonze: Adam Spiegel
Wynonna Judd: Christina Ciminella
Boris Karloff: William Henry Pratt

Diane Keaton: Diane Hall
Michael Keaton: Michael Douglas
Kesha: Kesha Rose Sebert
Alicia Keys: Alicia Augello Cook
Chaka Khan: Yvette Stevens
Kid Rock: Robert Ritchie
Carole King: Carole Klein
Larry King: Larry Zeiger
Ben Kingsley: Krishna Banji
Ted Knight: Tadewurz Wladziu Konopka
Cheryl Ladd: Cheryl Stoppelmoor
Lady Gaga: Stefani Germanotta
Veronica Lake: Constance Ockleman
Kendrick Lamar: Kendrick Lamar Duckworth
Hedy Lamarr: Hedwig Kiesler
Dorothy Lamour: Mary Leta Dorothy Slaton
Michael Landon: Eugene Orowitz
Mario Lanza: Alfredo Cocozza
Queen Latifah: Dana Owens
Stan Laurel: Arthur Jefferson
Brenda Lee: Brenda Mae Tarpley
Gypsy Rose Lee: Rose Louise Hovick
Peggy Lee: Norma Egstrom
Janet Leigh: Jeanette Morrison
Vivien Leigh: Vivian Hartley
Huey Lewis: Hugh Cregg
Jerry Lewis: Joseph Levitch
Lil' Kim: Kimberly Denise Jones
Little Richard: Richard Penniman
LL Cool J: James Todd Smith
Carole Lombard: Jane Peters
Lorde: Ella Yelich-O'Connor
Sophia Loren: Sophia Scicolone
Peter Lorre: Laszlo Lowenstein
Louis C.K.: Louis Szekely
Myrna Loy: Myrna Williams
Bela Lugosi: Bela Ferenc Blasko
Moms Mabley: Loretta Mary Aiken
Macklemore: Ben Haggerty
Shirley MacLaine: Shirley Beaty
Elle Macpherson: Eleanor Gow
Madonna: Madonna Louise Veronica Ciccone
Lee Majors: Harvey Lee Yeary
Karl Malden: Mladen Sekulovich
Barry Manilow: Barry Alan Pincus
Jayne Mansfield: Vera Jane Palmer
Marilyn Manson: Brian Warner
Bruno Mars: Peter Gene Hernandez
Dean Martin: Dino Crocetti
Ricky Martin: Enrique Jose Martin Morales
MCA: Adam Yauch
Meat Loaf: Marvin Lee Aday
Freddie Mercury: Farrokh Bulsara
Ethel Merman: Ethel Zimmermann
George Michael: Georgios Panayiotou
Mike D: Michael Diamond
Nicki Minaj: Onika Tanya Maraj
Helen Mirren: Ilynea Lydia Mironoff
Joni Mitchell: Roberta Joan Anderson
Moby: Richard Melville Hall
Mo'Nique: Monique Imes
Marilyn Monroe: Norma Jean Mortenson (later Baker)
Yves Montand: Ivo Livi
Demi Moore: Demetria Guynes
Rita Moreno: Rosita Alverio
Harry Morgan: Harry Bratsburg
Morrissey: Steven Patrick Morrissey
Mr. T: Lawrence Tureaud
Paul Muni: Mehilem Weisenfreund
Nelly: Cornell Haynes Jr.
Mike Nichols: Michael Igor Peschowsky
Chuck Norris: Carlos Ray Norris
Notorious B.I.G.: Christopher Wallace
Hugh O'Brian: Hugh Krampke
Maureen O'Hara: Maureen FitzSimons
Jack Palance: Vladimir Palanuik
Minnie Pearl: Sarah Ophelia Cannon
Katy Perry: Kathryn Hudson

Bernadette Peters: Bernadette Lazzara
Joaquin Phoenix: Joaquin Bottom
Edith Piaf: Edith Gassion
Slim Pickens: Louis Lindley
Mary Pickford: Gladys Smith
Pink: Alecia Moore
Pitbull: Armando Christian Pérez
Iggy Pop: James Newell Osterberg
Natalie Portman: Natalie Hershlag
Prince: Prince Rogers Nelson
Dee Dee Ramone: Douglas Colvin
Joey Ramone: Jeffrey Hyman
Johnny Ramone: John Cummings
Tommy Ramone: Tom Erdelyi
Tony Randall: Leonard Rosenberg
Della Reese: Delloreese Patricia Early
Busta Rhymes: Trevor Smith Jr.
Joan Rivers: Joan Sandra Molinsky
Edward G. Robinson: Emmanuel Goldenberg
The Rock: Dwayne Johnson
Ginger Rogers: Virginia McMath
Roy Rogers: Leonard Franklin Slye
Mickey Rooney: Joe Yule Jr.
Johnny Rotten: John Lydon
Lillian Russell: Helen Leonard
Meg Ryan: Margaret Hyra
Winona Ryder: Winona Horowitz
Sade: Helen Folsade Abu
Soupy Sales: Milton Supman
Susan Sarandon: Susan Tomaling
Seal: Seal Henry Olusegun Olumide Adeola Samuel
Jane Seymour: Joyce Frankenberg
Omar Sharif: Michael Shalhoub
Charlie Sheen: Carlos Irwin Estevez
Martin Sheen: Ramon Estevez
Talia Shire: Talia Coppola
Beverly Sills: Belle Silverman
Phil Silvers: Philip Silversmith
Gene Simmons: Chaim Witz
Sinbad: David Adkins
Anna Nicole Smith: Vickie Lynn Hogan
Snoop Dogg: Calvin Broadus
Barbara Stanwyck: Ruby Stevens
Jean Stapleton: Jeanne Murray
Ringo Starr: Richard Starkey
Cat Stevens: Stephen Demetre Georgiou
Connie Stevens: Concetta Ingolia
Jon Stewart: Jonathan Stuart Leibowitz
Sting: Gordon Sumner
Joe Strummer: John Graham Mellor
Donna Summer: La Donna Gaines
Rip Taylor: Charles Elmer Taylor Jr.
Robert Taylor: Spangler Brugh
The Weeknd: Abel Makkonen Tesfaye
Danny Thomas: Muzyad Yakhoob (later Amos Jacobs)
Tiny Tim: Herbert Khaury
Rip Torn: Elmore Rual Torn Jr.
Randy Travis: Randy Traywick
Tina Turner: Annie Mae Bullock
Shania Twain: Eilleen Regina Edwards
Twiggy: Lesley Hornby
Conway Twitty: Harold Lloyd Jenkins
Steven Tyler: Stephen Tallarico
Rudolph Valentino: Rudolpho D'Antonguolla
Frankie Valli: Frank Castelluccio
Eddie Vedder: Edward Louis Seversen III
Sid Vicious: John Simon Ritchie
John Wayne: Marion Morrison
Raquel Welch: Raquel Tejada
Gene Wilder: Jerome Silberman
Shelley Winters: Shirley Schrift
Stevie Wonder: Stevland Morris
Jane Wyman: Sarah Jane Mayfield
Loretta Young: Gretchen Michaels Young
Buckwheat Zydeco: Stanley Dural Jr.

ARTS AND MEDIA

Worldwide Top-Grossing American Movies, 2000-20

Source: Box Office Mojo

Year	Title	Gross (mil)	Year	Title	Gross (mil)
2000	Mission: Impossible II	$546.4	2010	Toy Story 3	$1,067.0
2001	Harry Potter and the Sorcerer's Stone	974.8	2011	Harry Potter and the Deathly Hallows: Part 2	1,341.5
2002	The Lord of the Rings: The Two Towers	923.3	2012	The Avengers	1,518.8
2003	The Lord of the Rings: The Return of the King	1,140.7	2013	Frozen	1,280.8
2004	Shrek 2	928.8	2014	Transformers: Age of Extinction	1,104.1
2005	Harry Potter and the Goblet of Fire	896.0	2015	Star Wars: Episode VII—The Force Awakens	2,068.2
2006	Pirates of the Caribbean: Dead Man's Chest	1,066.2	2016	Captain America: Civil War	1,153.3
2007	Pirates of the Caribbean: At World's End	961.0	2017	Star Wars: Episode VIII—The Last Jedi	1,332.5
2008	The Dark Knight	1,003.0	2018	Avengers: Infinity War	2,048.4
2009	Avatar	2,744.3	2019	Avengers: Endgame	2,797.8
			2020	The Eight Hundred	425.6

Note: Box-office grosses worldwide through Sept. 22, 2020.

All-Time Top-Grossing American Movies

Source: Comscore, Inc.

Rank	Title (original release date)	Gross (mil)	Rank	Title (original release date)	Gross (mil)
1.	Star Wars: Episode VII—The Force Awakens (2015)	$936.7	26.	The Hunger Games: Catching Fire (2013)	$424.7
2.	Avengers: Endgame (2019)	858.4	27.	Pirates of the Caribbean: Dead Man's Chest (2006)	423.3
3.	Avatar (2009)	760.5	28.	Jurassic World: Fallen Kingdom (2018)	417.7
4.	Black Panther (2018)	700.1	29.	Toy Story 3 (2010)	415.0
5.	Avengers: Infinity War (2018)	678.8	30.	Wonder Woman (2017)	412.6
6.	Jurassic World (2015)	652.3	31.	Iron Man 3 (2013)	409.0
7.	The Avengers (2012)	623.4	32.	Captain America: Civil War (2016)	408.1
8.	Star Wars: Episode VIII—The Last Jedi (2017)	620.2	33.	The Hunger Games (2012)	408.0
9.	Incredibles 2 (2018)	608.6	34.	Jumanji: Welcome to the Jungle (2017)	404.5
10.	Titanic (1997)	600.8	35.	Spider-Man (2002)	403.7
11.	The Lion King (2019)	543.6	36.	Jurassic Park (1993)	402.5
12.	The Dark Knight (2008)	533.3	37.	Transformers: Revenge of the Fallen (2009)	402.1
13.	Rogue One: A Star Wars Story (2016)	532.2	38.	Frozen (2013)	400.7
14.	Star Wars: Episode IX—The Rise of Skywalker	515.2	39.	Spider-Man: Far From Home (2019)	390.5
15.	Beauty and the Beast (2017)	504.0	40.	Guardians of the Galaxy Vol. 2 (2017)	389.8
16.	Finding Dory (2016)	486.3	41.	Harry Potter and the Deathly Hallows: Part 2 (2011)	381.2
17.	Frozen 2 (2019)	477.4	42.	Star Wars: Episode III—Revenge of the Sith (2005)	380.3
18.	Star Wars: Episode I—The Phantom Menace (1999)	474.5	43.	Lord of the Rings: The Return of the King (2003)	377.0
19.	Star Wars: Episode IV—A New Hope (1977)	461.0	44.	Spider-Man 2 (2004)	373.4
20.	Avengers: Age of Ultron (2015)	459.0	45.	The Passion of the Christ (2004)	370.3
21.	The Dark Knight Rises (2012)	448.1	46.	The Secret Life of Pets (2016)	368.4
22.	Shrek 2 (2004)	436.7	47.	Despicable Me 2 (2013)	368.1
23.	E.T. the Extra-Terrestrial (1982)	435.0	48.	The Jungle Book (2016)	364.0
24.	Toy Story 4 (2019)	434.8	49.	Deadpool (2016)	363.1
25.	Captain Marvel (2019)	426.8	50.	Inside Out (2015)	356.5

Note: Box-office grosses in the U.S. and Canada through Aug. 31, 2020, in absolute dollars. Rising ticket prices favor newer films. Revenues from re-releases are included.

Top-Grossing American Movies (Adjusted Lifetime Gross)

Source: Box Office Mojo

Rank	Title (original release date)	Adj. gross (mil)	Rank	Title (original release date)	Adj. gross (mil)
1.	Gone with the Wind (1939)	$1,895.4	24.	Fantasia (1940)	$778.1
2.	Star Wars: Episode IV—A New Hope (1977)	1,669.0	25.	The Godfather (1972)	739.5
3.	The Sound of Music (1965)	1,335.1	26.	Forrest Gump (1994)	736.8
4.	E.T. the Extra-Terrestrial (1982)	1,329.2	27.	Mary Poppins (1964)	732.6
5.	Titanic (1997)	1,270.1	28.	Grease (1978)	722.4
6.	The Ten Commandments (1956)	1,227.5	29.	The Avengers (2012)	720.4
7.	Jaws (1975)	1,200.8	30.	Jurassic World (2015)	719.5
8.	Doctor Zhivago (1965)	1,163.1	31.	Black Panther (2018)	715.0
9.	The Exorcist (1973)	1,036.3	32.	Thunderball (1965)	700.9
10.	Snow White and the Seven Dwarfs (1937)	1,021.3	33.	The Dark Knight (2008)	698.1
11.	Star Wars: Episode VII—The Force Awakens (2015)	1,013.0	34.	The Jungle Book (1967)	690.4
12.	101 Dalmatians (1961)	936.2	35.	Sleeping Beauty (1959)	681.0
13.	Star Wars: Episode V—The Empire Strikes Back (1980)	919.9	36.	Avengers: Infinity War (2018)	678.6
14.	Ben-Hur (1959)	918.7	37.	Ghostbusters (1984)	667.8
15.	Avatar (2009)	911.8	38.	Shrek 2 (2004)	665.7
16.	Avengers: Endgame (2019)	892.7	39.	Spider-Man (2002)	661.8
17.	Star Wars: Episode VI—Return of the Jedi (1983)	881.3	40.	Butch Cassidy and the Sundance Kid (1969)	661.1
18.	Jurassic Park (1993)	859.6	41.	Love Story (1970)	656.0
19.	Star Wars: Episode I—The Phantom Menace (1999)	846.2	42.	Independence Day (1996)	649.0
20.	The Lion King (1994)	835.3	43.	Home Alone (1990)	634.7
21.	The Sting (1973)	835.3	44.	Star Wars: Episode VIII—The Last Jedi (2017)	633.4
22.	Raiders of the Lost Ark (1981)	829.7	45.	Pinocchio (1940)	631.6
23.	The Graduate (1967)	801.9	46.	Cleopatra (1963)	629.5
			47.	Beverly Hills Cop (1984)	629.2
			48.	Goldfinger (1964)	621.2
			49.	Incredibles 2 (2018)	621.2
			50.	Airport (1970)	619.5

Note: Adjusted lifetime gross is in 2020 dollars, as of Aug. 13, 2020, and adjusts for ticket price inflation using estimated number of tickets sold.

50 Top-Grossing Movies, 2019

Source: Comscore, Inc.

Rank	Title	Gross (mil)	Rank	Title	Gross (mil)
1.	Avengers: Endgame	$858.4	26.	The Upside	$108.3
2.	The Lion King	543.6	27.	Ford v Ferrari	107.2
3.	Toy Story 4	434.0	28.	The Lego Movie 2: The Second Part	105.8
4.	Frozen 2	430.1	29.	Hustlers	105.0
5.	Captain Marvel	426.8	30.	The Addams Family	99.5
6.	Star Wars: The Rise of Skywalker	390.7	31.	Downton Abbey	96.9
7.	Spider-Man: Far From Home	390.5	32.	Rocketman	96.4
8.	Aladdin	355.6	33.	Alita: Battle Angel	85.7
9.	Joker	333.8	34.	Good Boys	83.1
10.	IT Chapter Two	211.6	35.	Spider-Man: Into the Spider-Verse	82.1
11.	Jumanji: The Next Level	192.1	36.	Men in Black International	80.0
12.	Us	175.1	37.	Annabelle Comes Home	74.2
13.	Fast & Furious Presents: Hobbs & Shaw	174.0	38.	Yesterday	73.3
14.	John Wick: Chapter 3 - Parabellum	171.0	39.	Tyler Perry's A Madea Family Funeral	73.3
15.	How to Train Your Dragon: The Hidden World	160.8	40.	Zombieland: Double Tap	72.9
16.	The Secret Life of Pets 2	157.9	41.	Angel Has Fallen	69.0
17.	Pokémon Detective Pikachu	144.1	42.	Scary Stories to Tell in the Dark	68.9
18.	Once Upon a Time...in Hollywood	141.1	43.	Mary Poppins Returns	66.0
19.	Shazam!	140.4	44.	Dark Phoenix	65.8
20.	Aquaman	136.0	45.	Terminator: Dark Fate	62.3
21.	Knives Out	115.7	46.	Abominable	60.7
22.	Dumbo	114.8	47.	Dora and the Lost City of Gold	60.5
23.	Maleficent: Mistress of Evil	113.3	48.	Escape Room	57.0
24.	Glass	111.0	49.	A Beautiful Day in the Neighborhood	56.7
25.	Godzilla: King of the Monsters	110.5	50.	Midway	56.3

Note: Box-office grosses in the U.S. and Canada, Jan. 1-Dec. 31, 2019; some films had 2018 release dates.

National Film Registry, 2019

Source: National Film Registry, Library of Congress

The National Film Registry adds 25 "culturally, historically, or aesthetically significant" American films annually.

Amadeus (1984)	Fog of War (2003)	Old Yeller (1957)
Becky Sharp (1935)	Gaslight (1944)	The Phenix City Story (1955)
Before Stonewall (1984)	George Washington Carver at Tuskegee	Platoon (1986)
Body and Soul (1925)	Institute (1937)	Purple Rain (1984)
Boys Don't Cry (1999)	Girlfriends (1978)	Real Women Have Curves (2002)
Clerks (1994)	I Am Somebody (1970)	She's Gotta Have It (1986)
Coal Miner's Daughter (1980)	The Last Waltz (1978)	Sleeping Beauty (1959)
Emigrants Landing at Ellis Island (1903)	My Name Is Oona (1969)	Zoot Suit (1981)
Employees Entrance (1933)	A New Leaf (1971)	

Best American Movies of All Time

Source: American Film Institute

First unveiled in 1998 based on ballots sent to 1,500 individuals, mostly from the film world, in 1997. Updated in 2007 (the version shown here) to include newly eligible films and reflect shifting cultural perspectives. Criteria for judging included historical significance, cultural impact, critical recognition and awards, and popularity. The year each film was first released is in parentheses.

1. Citizen Kane (1941)
2. The Godfather (1972)
3. Casablanca (1942)
4. Raging Bull (1980)
5. Singin' in the Rain (1952)
6. Gone With the Wind (1939)
7. Lawrence of Arabia (1962)
8. Schindler's List (1993)
9. Vertigo (1958)
10. The Wizard of Oz (1939)
11. City Lights (1931)
12. The Searchers (1956)
13. Star Wars (1977)
14. Psycho (1960)
15. 2001: A Space Odyssey (1968)
16. Sunset Boulevard (1950)
17. The Graduate (1967)
18. The General (1927)
19. On the Waterfront (1954)
20. It's a Wonderful Life (1946)
21. Chinatown (1974)
22. Some Like It Hot (1959)
23. The Grapes of Wrath (1940)
24. E.T. the Extra-Terrestrial (1982)
25. To Kill a Mockingbird (1962)
26. Mr. Smith Goes to Washington (1939)
27. High Noon (1952)
28. All About Eve (1950)
29. Double Indemnity (1944)
30. Apocalypse Now (1979)
31. The Maltese Falcon (1941)
32. The Godfather Part II (1974)
33. One Flew Over the Cuckoo's Nest (1975)
34. Snow White and the Seven Dwarfs (1937)
35. Annie Hall (1977)
36. The Bridge on the River Kwai (1957)
37. The Best Years of Our Lives (1946)
38. The Treasure of the Sierra Madre (1948)
39. Dr. Strangelove (1964)
40. The Sound of Music (1965)
41. King Kong (1933)
42. Bonnie and Clyde (1967)
43. Midnight Cowboy (1969)
44. The Philadelphia Story (1940)
45. Shane (1953)
46. It Happened One Night (1934)
47. A Streetcar Named Desire (1951)
48. Rear Window (1954)
49. Intolerance (1916)
50. The Lord of the Rings: The Fellowship of the Ring (2001)
51. West Side Story (1961)
52. Taxi Driver (1976)
53. The Deer Hunter (1978)
54. M*A*S*H (1970)
55. North by Northwest (1959)
56. Jaws (1975)
57. Rocky (1976)
58. The Gold Rush (1925)
59. Nashville (1975)
60. Duck Soup (1933)
61. Sullivan's Travels (1941)
62. American Graffiti (1973)
63. Cabaret (1972)
64. Network (1976)
65. The African Queen (1951)
66. Raiders of the Lost Ark (1981)
67. Who's Afraid of Virginia Woolf? (1966)
68. Unforgiven (1992)
69. Tootsie (1982)
70. A Clockwork Orange (1971)
71. Saving Private Ryan (1998)
72. The Shawshank Redemption (1994)
73. Butch Cassidy and the Sundance Kid (1969)
74. The Silence of the Lambs (1991)
75. In the Heat of the Night (1967)

Movie Theaters, 1946-2019

Source: Motion Picture Association of America (MPAA); Comscore, Inc.

Year	Box office (mil)	Admissions (mil)	Admissions per week (mil)	Screens	Avg. ticket price	Films produced	Films released
1946	$1,692.0	4,067.3	78.2	NA	$0.42	NA	400
1950	1,379.0	3,017.5	58.0	NA	0.46	NA	483
1955	1,204.0	2,072.3	39.9	NA	0.58	NA	319
1960	984.4	1,304.5	25.1	NA	0.76	NA	248
1965	1,041.8	1,031.5	19.8	NA	1.01	NA	279
1970	1,429.2	920.6	17.7	NA	1.55	279	306
1975	2,114.8	1,032.8	19.9	15,030	2.03	258	233
1980	2,748.5	1,021.5	19.6	17,590	2.69	214	233
1985	3,749.4	1,056.1	20.3	21,147	3.55	264	470
1990	5,021.8	1,188.6	22.9	23,689	4.22	346	410
1995	5,269.0	1,211.0	23.3	27,805	4.35	631	411
2000	7,468.0	1,383.0	26.6	37,396	5.39	683	475
2005	8,832.0	1,376.0	26.5	38,852	6.41	920	507
2010	10,741.0	1,341.0	25.8	39,547	7.89	795	563
2011	10,186.1	1,285.0	24.7	39,641	7.93	818	609
2012	10,774.5	1,358.0	26.0	39,918	7.96	476[1]	678
2013	10,919.7	1,340.0	25.8	42,814	8.13	455[1]	658
2014	10,329.0	1,267.6	24.4	41,518	8.17	482[1]	706
2015	11,081.2	1,321.0	25.4	42,552	8.43	495[1]	707
2016	11,573.4	1,315.0	25.3	42,659	8.65	511[1]	732
2017	11,072.7	1,240.0	23.8	43,216	8.97	549[1]	785
2018	11,852.1	1,304.0	25.1	43,459	9.11	576[1]	765
2019	11,375.3	1,242.0	23.9	43,681	9.16	601[1,2]	835

NA = Not available. (1) Non-MPAA members with est. budget under $1 mil were not tracked. (2) 2019 was the first year Netflix was counted as a member studio.

Digital Movie Sales and Rentals, 2019

Source: Comscore Dynamic Studio Share and Digital Download Essentials Industry Services

U.S. and Canadian home entertainment spending totaled $25.2 bil in 2019. Spending on physical formats fell to $4.7 bil from $9.1 bil in 2015, but digital spending increased from $8.9 bil in 2015 to $20.5 bil in 2019.

Top Digital Sales, 2019

Rank	Movie	Rank	Movie
1.	Avengers: Endgame	12.	Toy Story 4
2.	Aquaman (2018)	13.	How to Train Your Dragon: The Hidden World
3.	Spider-Man: Into the Spider-Verse (2018)	14.	Shazam!
4.	A Star Is Born (2018)	15.	Fantastic Beasts: The Crimes of Grindelwald (2018)
5.	Captain Marvel		
6.	Spider-Man: Far From Home	16.	The Lion King (2019 remake)
7.	Bohemian Rhapsody (2018)	17.	The Secret Life of Pets 2
8.	Aladdin (2019 remake)	18.	Fast & Furious Presents: Hobbs & Shaw
9.	Ralph Breaks the Internet (2018)	19.	Pokémon Detective Pikachu
10.	Joker	20.	Godzilla: King of the Monsters
11.	John Wick: Chapter 3 - Parabellum		

Top Digital Rentals, 2019

Rank	Movie	Rank	Movie
1.	Bohemian Rhapsody (2018)	11.	Creed II (2018)
2.	A Star Is Born (2018)	12.	John Wick: Chapter 3 - Parabellum
3.	Aquaman (2018)	13.	Spider-Man: Far From Home
4.	Captain Marvel		
5.	Green Book (2018)	14.	Aladdin (2019 remake)
6.	Instant Family (2018)	15.	The Mule (2018)
7.	Spider-Man: Into the Spider-Verse (2018)	16.	Shazam!
8.	Avengers: Endgame	17.	Dr. Seuss' The Grinch
9.	Ralph Breaks the Internet (2018)	18.	Venom (2018)
		19.	Bumblebee (2018)
10.	Night School (2018)	20.	BlacKkKlansman (2018)

Note: Includes electronic sell-through (EST), video-on-demand (VOD), and subscription streaming (paid subscribers only). Movies released in 2019 unless otherwise noted.

Film and TV Content Ratings

The Motion Picture Association of America (MPAA) established a ratings system in 1968. It was revised in 1984 and in 1990. The MPAA, Natl. Cable Television Assn., and Natl. Assn. of Broadcasters developed the TV ratings system in 1997, in accordance with the Telecommunications Act of 1996; it was implemented in Oct. 1997.

Film Ratings

G: General Audience. All ages admitted. Does not contain themes, language, nudity, sex, or violence that the MPAA ratings board believes would offend parents whose younger children see the film. Does not necessarily denote a certificate of approval nor children's movie. No nudity, sex scenes, or drug use depicted.

PG: Parental Guidance Suggested. Some material may not be suited for children. The MPAA ratings board recommends that parents determine whether the content of the film is appropriate for their children. The film may contain more mature themes, some profanity, violence, or brief nudity. No drug use depicted.

PG-13: Parents Strongly Cautioned. Some material may be inappropriate for children under 13. Any movie depicting drug use or more than brief nudity is automatically rated at least PG-13. Violence is permitted, though it is generally not both realistic or extreme and persistent violence. The single use of one sexually-derived expletive rates a PG-13; more than one use requires at least an R rating.

R: Restricted. Under 17 requires accompanying parent or adult guardian. Movies given R ratings contain some adult material, defined as adult themes or activity, hard language, intense or persistent violence, sexually-oriented nudity, or drug abuse.

NC-17: No One 17 and Under Admitted. These films that most parents would consider too adult for children under 17. An NC-17 rating does not mean the film is obscene or pornographic. The rating can be based on violence, sex, aberrational behavior, drug abuse, or any other element.

TV Ratings

TV-Y: All Children. Program designed to be acceptable for children of all ages. Its themes and elements are designed for a very young audience.

TV-Y7: Directed to Older Children. Program designed for children ages 7 and older, and more appropriate for those who have the skills to distinguish between make-believe and reality. May include mild fantasy/comedic violence. Programs with more than mild fantasy violence are denoted TV-Y7-FV.

TV-G: General Audience. Program not necessarily designed for children, but most parents would find it suitable for all ages. Little or no violence, no strong language, and little or no sexual dialogue or situations.

TV-PG: Parental Guidance Suggested. Program might contain material that parents would consider inappropriate for children, such as an adult theme or one or more of the following: suggestive dialogue (D), infrequent coarse language (L), some sexual situations (S), or moderate violence (V).

TV-14: Parents Strongly Cautioned. Program contains material that many parents would consider inappropriate for children under 14, such as one or more of the following: intensely suggestive dialogue (D), strong coarse language (L), intense sexual situations (S), or intense violence (V).

TV-MA: Mature Audience Only. Program specifically designed for adults and may be unsuitable for children under 17. Contains one or more of the following: crude indecent language (L), explicit sexual activity (S), or graphic violence (V).

Most Popular YouTubers, 2020

Source: SocialBlade

Rank	Name	Subscribers (mil)	Rank	Name	Subscribers (mil)	Rank	Name	Subscribers (mil)
1.	PewDiePie	106.0	19.	Billie Eilish	32.8	35.	Selena Gomez	26.1
2.	Cocomelon - Nursery		20.	LooLoo Kids - Nursery		36.	Boram Tube Vlog	25.9
	Rhymes	90.4		Rhymes and		37.	RihannaVEVO	25.7
3.	5-Minute Crafts	67.7		Children's Songs	32.6	38.	BST Kids - Nursery	
4.	WWE	64.3	21.	JustinBieberVEVO	32.6		Rhymes & Songs	25.5
5.	Kids Diana Show	60.7	22.	Little Baby Bum -		39.	EminemVEVO	25.5
6.	Like Nastya	58.7		Nursery Rhymes &		40.	The Tonight Show	
7.	Dude Perfect	52.7		Kids Songs	32.0		Starring Jimmy	
8.	Vlad and Niki	49.6	23.	Maroon 5	31.5		Fallon	25.4
9.	Marshmello	47.6	24.	Like Nastya Show	31.2	41.	KatyPerryVEVO	25.4
10.	EminemMusic	43.8	25.	SonyMusicIndiaVEVO	31.0	42.	Baby Doli - ToyPudding	25.2
11.	Ariana Grande	42.6	26.	YouTube	30.6	43.	Smosh	25.1
12.	Movieclips	42.2	27.	Trap Nation	29.0	44.	Toys and Colors	24.7
13.	MrBeast	40.6	28.	Luis Fonsi	27.9	45.	The Late Late Show	
14.	Taylor Swift	39.3	29.	Bruno Mars	27.9		With James Corden	24.4
15.	Katy Perry	37.9	30.	XXXTENTACION	27.0	46.	Ultra Music	24.2
16.	TheEllenShow	37.6	31.	TaylorSwiftVEVO	26.6	47.	WORLDSTARHIPHOP	24.0
17.	Pinkfong! Kids' Songs		32.	Markiplier	26.4	48.	Ninja	24.0
	& Stories	37.0	33.	TEDx Talks	26.3	49.	Maluma	24.0
18.	BRIGHT SIDE	35.9	34.	Ryan's World	26.2	50.	ImagineDragons	22.9

Note: Ranked by channel subscribers as of Aug. 13, 2020.

Most Popular Podcasts, 2020

Source: Podtrac

Rank	Podcast	Publisher	Rank	Podcast	Publisher
1.	The Daily	New York Times	12.	Fresh Air	NPR
2.	NPR News Now	NPR	13.	Wait Wait ... Don't Tell Me!	NPR
3.	Up First	NPR	14.	TED Talks Daily	TED
4.	Call Her Daddy	Barstool Sports	15.	RadioLab	WNYC Studios
5.	The Ben Shapiro Show	Daily Wire	16.	CNN News Briefing	WarnerMedia
6.	Stuff You Should Know	iHeartRadio	17.	NPR Politics	NPR
7.	This American Life	This American Life/Serial	18.	Hidden Brain	NPR
8.	Dateline NBC	NBC News	19.	TED Radio Hour	NPR
9.	Pardon My Take	Barstool Sports	20.	The Dan Bongino Show	Cumulus Media/
10.	Planet Money	NPR			Westwood One
11.	Serial	This American Life/Serial			

Note: Rankings based on U.S. unique monthly audience for July 2020.

Top-Selling Video Games, 2019

Source: The NPD Group/Retail Tracking Service

The U.S. video game industry generated $41.52 bil in revenue in 2019: $6.075 bil on hardware, including peripherals, and $35.44 bil on software, including in-game purchases and subscriptions. Spending was down 3% from $42.82 bil in 2018. Ranked by combined sales of game in physical/digital formats unless noted.

Rank	Game (console)	Rank	Game (console)
1.	Call of Duty: Modern Warfare (PC, PS4, XBO)	12.	Kingdom Hearts III (PS4, XBO)
2.	Grand Theft Auto V (PC, PS3/4/5, X360, XBO, XBSX)	13.	Mario Kart 8: Deluxe* (Switch)
3.	Madden NFL 20 (PC, PS4, XBO)	14.	Minecraft: PlayStation 4 Edition (Android, GVR, iOS, PC,
4.	NBA 2K20 (Android, iOS, PC, PS4, Stadia, Switch, XBO)		PS4, Switch, XBO)
5.	Mortal Kombat 11 (PC, PS4, Stadia, Switch, XBO)	15.	Tom Clancy's The Division 2 (PC, PS4, Stadia, XBO)
6.	Star Wars Jedi: Fallen Order (PC, PS4, XBO)	16.	Spider-Man (PS4)
7.	NBA 2K19 (Android, iOS, PC, PS4, Switch, XBO)	17.	FIFA 20 (PC, PS4, Stadia, Switch, XBO)
8.	Borderlands 3 (Mac, PC, PS4, Stadia, XBO)	18.	Resident Evil 2 (PC, PS4, XBO)
9.	Tom Clancy's Rainbow Six: Siege (PC, PS4/5 XBO, XBSX)	19.	Anthem (PC, PS4, XBO)
10.	Super Smash Bros. Ultimate* (Switch)	20.	Call of Duty: Black Ops 4 (PC, PS4, XBO)
11.	Red Dead Redemption II (PC, PS4, Stadia, XBO)		

* = Digital sales on Nintendo eShop not included. **Note:** Includes bundled, collector's, or game-of-the-year editions, except those bundled with hardware. GVR = Gear VR; PC = personal computer; PS = PlayStation; X360 = Microsoft Xbox 360; XBO = Microsoft Xbox One; XBSX = Microsoft Xbox Series X.

Opera: Most Produced Works, 2019-20

Source: OPERA America

Work, composer	Productions	Work, composer	Productions	Work, composer	Productions
La bohème, Giacomo Puccini	12	The Marriage of Figaro, Wolfgang		Pagliacci, Ruggero Leoncavallo	6
Madama Butterfly, Giacomo		Amadeus Mozart	9	Gianni Schicchi, Giacomo Puccini	5
Puccini	11	Hansel and Gretel, Engelbert		La Cenerentola, Gioachino Rossini	5
Amahl and the Night Visitors, Gian		Humperdinck	8	La traviata, Giuseppe Verdi	5
Carlo Menotti	10	Tosca, Giacomo Puccini	8	Rigoletto, Guiseppe Verdi	5
The Barber of Seville, Gioachino		Don Giovanni, Wolfgang Amadeus			
Rossini	10	Mozart	7		

Note: Scheduled productions of a given work (not individual performances) during the 2019-20 season (generally Sept.-Aug., cut short in Mar. 2020, by the COVID-19 pandemic) by members of OPERA America and Opera.ca.

Longest-Running Broadway Shows

Source: The Broadway League

Rank	Title (run)[1]	Performances[2]	Rank	Title (run)[1]	Performances[2]	Rank	Title (run)[1]	Performances[2]
1.	*The Phantom of the Opera (1988-)	13,370	16.	Grease (1972-80)	3,388	31.	Abie's Irish Rose (1922-27)	2,327
2.	*Chicago (revival) (1996-)	9,692	17.	Fiddler on the Roof (1964-72)	3,242	32.	Oklahoma! (1943-48)	2,212
3.	*The Lion King (1997-)	9,302	18.	Life With Father (1939-47)	3,224	33.	Smokey Joe's Café (1995-2000)	2,036
4.	Cats (1982-2000)	7,485	19.	Tobacco Road (1933-41)	3,182	34.	Pippin (1972-77)	1,944
5.	*Wicked (2003-)	6,836	20.	Hello, Dolly! (1964-70)	2,844	35.	South Pacific (1949-54)	1,925
6.	Les Misérables (1987-2003)	6,680	21.	My Fair Lady (1956-62)	2,717	36.	The Magic Show (1974-78)	1,920
7.	A Chorus Line (1975-90)	6,137	22.	Hairspray (2002-09)	2,642	37.	*Hamilton (2015-)	1,919
8.	Oh! Calcutta! (revival) (1976-89)	5,959	23.	Mary Poppins (2006-13)	2,619	38.	Aida (2000-04)	1,852
9.	Mamma Mia! (2001-15)	5,758	24.	Avenue Q (2003-09)	2,534	39.	Gemini (1977-81)	1,819
10.	Beauty and the Beast (1994-2007)	5,462	25.	*Aladdin (2014-)	2,506	40.	Deathtrap (1978-82)	1,793
11.	Rent (1996-2008)	5,123	26.	Kinky Boots (2013-19)	2,505	41.	Harvey (1944-49)	1,775
12.	Jersey Boys (2005-17)	4,642	27.	The Producers (2001-07)	2,502	42.	Dancin' (1978-82)	1,774
13.	Miss Saigon (1991-2001)	4,092	28.	Beautiful: The Carole King Musical (2014-19)	2,416	43.	La Cage aux Folles (1983-87)	1,761
14.	*The Book of Mormon (2011-)	3,748	29.	Cabaret (revival) (1998-2004)	2,377	44.	Hair (1968-72)	1,750
15.	42nd Street (1980-89)	3,486		Annie (1977-83)	2,377	45.	The Wiz (1975-79)	1,672
			30.	Rock of Ages (2009-15)	2,328	46.	Born Yesterday (1946-49)	1,642
				Man of La Mancha (1965-71)	2,328	47.	Crazy For You (1992-96)	1,622
						48.	Ain't Misbehavin' (1978-82)	1,604

* = Still running as of Mar. 12, 2020. (1) Unless noted, listings reflect a play's first run on Broadway. (2) Number of performances through Mar. 12, 2020, when Broadway was shut down as a result of the COVID-19 pandemic.

Broadway Season Statistics, 1959-2019

Source: The Broadway League

Season	Gross (mil $)	Attendance (mil)	Playing weeks	New productions	Avg. ticket price	Season	Gross (mil $)	Attendance (mil)	Playing weeks	New productions	Avg. ticket price
1959-1960	$46	7.9	1,156	58	$5.82	2007-2008	$938	12.3	1,560	36	$76.45
1964-1965	51	8.2	1,250	67	6.20	2008-2009	943	12.2	1,548	43	77.61
1969-1970	53	7.1	1,047	62	7.46	2009-2010	1,020	11.9	1,464	39	85.79
1974-1975	57	6.6	1,101	54	8.64	2010-2011	1,081	12.5	1,588	42	86.27
1979-1980	146	9.6	1,540	61	15.21	2011-2012	1,139	12.3	1,522	41	92.38
1984-1985	209	7.3	1,078	33	28.47	2012-2013	1,139	11.6	1,430	46	98.42
1989-1990	282	8.0	1,070	39	35.07	2013-2014	1,269	12.2	1,496	44*	103.88
1994-1995	406	9.0	1,120	33	44.91	2014-2015	1,365	13.1	1,626	37	104.18
1999-2000	603	11.4	1,460	37	52.99	2015-2016	1,373	13.3	1,648	39	103.11
2004-2005	769	11.5	1,494	39	66.70	2016-2017	1,449	13.3	1,580	45**	109.21
2005-2006	862	12.0	1,501	39	71.83	2017-2018	1,697	13.8	1,624	33	123.07
2006-2007	939	12.3	1,509	35	76.28	2018-2019	1,829	14.8	1,737	38	123.87

* = Includes one return engagement. ** = Includes two return engagements. **Note:** Broadway shut down Mar. 12, 2020, due to the COVID-19 pandemic. Data was not released for its shortened season.

Notable U.S. Museums

This unofficial list of some of the largest museums in the U.S., by budget, was compiled with the assistance of the American Association of Museums (AAM). Zoos, aquariums, arboretums, botanical gardens, and planetariums may be AAM members but are not included here. * = Not yet open as of Sept. 2020; expected debut date in parentheses.

Museum	City	State
*Academy Museum of Motion Pictures (2021)	Los Angeles	CA
American Museum of Natural History	New York	NY
Amon Carter Museum of Western Art	Ft. Worth	TX
The Art Institute of Chicago	Chicago	IL
Boston Children's Museum	Boston	MA
Brooklyn Museum of Art	Brooklyn	NY
Busch-Reisinger Museum	Cambridge	MA
California Academy of Sciences	San Francisco	CA
California Science Center	Los Angeles	CA
Carnegie Museums of Pittsburgh	Pittsburgh	PA
Children's Museum of Indianapolis	Indianapolis	IN
Cincinnati Art Museum	Cincinnati	OH
Cincinnati Museum Center	Cincinnati	OH
Cleveland Museum of Art	Cleveland	OH
Colonial Williamsburg	Williamsburg	VA
Corning Museum of Glass	Corning	NY
Crystal Bridges Museum of American Art	Bentonville	AR
Dallas Museum of Art	Dallas	TX
Denver Art Museum	Denver	CO
Denver Museum of Nature and Science	Denver	CO
Detroit Institute of Arts	Detroit	MI
Exploratorium	San Francisco	CA
The Field Museum	Chicago	IL
Fine Arts Museums of San Francisco	San Francisco	CA
Franklin Institute	Philadelphia	PA
The Frick Collection	New York	NY
J. Paul Getty Museum	Los Angeles	CA
Solomon R. Guggenheim Museum of Art	New York	NY
Harvard University Art Museums	Cambridge	MA
Henry F. DuPont Winterthur Museum	Winterthur	DE
Henry Ford Museum/Greenfield Village	Dearborn	MI
High Museum of Art	Atlanta	GA
Houston Museum of Natural Science	Houston	TX
Jamestown-Yorktown Foundation	Williamsburg	VA
Jewish Museum	New York	NY
L.A. County Museum of Art	Los Angeles	CA
Liberty Science Center, Liberty State Park	Jersey City	NJ
Maryland Science Center	Baltimore	MD
Mashantucket Pequot Museum and Research Center	Mashantucket	CT
Metropolitan Museum of Art	New York	NY
Milwaukee Public Museum	Milwaukee	WI
Minneapolis Institute of Arts	Minneapolis	MN
Museum of African American History	Detroit	MI
*Museum of the American Arts and Crafts Movement (2020/2021)	St. Petersburg	FL
Museum of the American West	Los Angeles	CA
Museum of Contemporary Art	Los Angeles	CA
Museum of Fine Arts	Boston	MA
Museum of Fine Arts	Houston	TX

Museum	City	State
Museum of Modern Art	New York	NY
Museum of New Mexico	Santa Fe	NM
Museum of Science	Boston	MA
Museum of Science and Industry	Chicago	IL
Musical Instrument Museum	Phoenix	AZ
Mystic Seaport Museum	Mystic	CT
National Air and Space Museum	Washington	DC
National Baseball Hall of Fame and Museum, Inc.	Cooperstown	NY
National Civil Rights Museum	Memphis	TN
National Constitution Center	Philadelphia	PA
National Gallery of Art	Washington	DC
National Museum of African American History and Culture	Washington	DC
National Museum of American History	Washington	DC
National Museum of the American Indian	Washington	DC
National Museum of Natural History	Washington	DC
National 9/11 Memorial & Museum	New York	NY
National World War II Museum	New Orleans	LA

Museum	City	State
Nelson-Atkins Museum of Art	Kansas City	MO
New-York Historical Society	New York	NY
New York State Museum	Albany	NY
Peabody Essex Museum	Salem	MA
Philadelphia Museum of Art	Philadelphia	PA
Rock and Roll Hall of Fame and Museum, Inc.	Cleveland	OH
St. Louis Science Center	St. Louis	MO
San Diego Museum of Art	San Diego	CA
San Francisco Museum of Modern Art	San Francisco	CA
Science Museum of Minnesota	St. Paul	MN
Toledo Museum of Art	Toledo	OH
U.S. Holocaust Memorial Museum	Washington	DC
Univ. of Pennsylvania Museum of Archaeology and Anthropology	Philadelphia	PA
Virginia Museum of Fine Arts	Richmond	VA
Wadsworth Atheneum	Hartford	CT
Walker Art Center	Minneapolis	MN
Whitney Museum of American Art	New York	NY

Characteristics of Public Libraries by State, 2017
Source: Public Libraries Survey, Institute of Museum and Library Services

State	Libraries[1]	Operating revenue[2] (thous.)	Library visits		Circulation[3]		Internet use[4]	
			Total (thous.)	Per capita	Total (thous.)	Per capita	Total (thous.)	Per capita
AL	218	$106,891	14,578	3.2	19,919	4.3	3,730	0.8
AK	61	37,968	3,364	5.2	4,680	7.3	604	0.9
AZ	90	191,756	24,589	3.5	45,352	6.6	5,577	0.8
AR	60	83,910	10,358	3.9	13,900	5.3	1,527	0.6
CA	184	1,556,766	151,059	3.8	208,171	5.3	27,220	0.7
CO	113	346,164	31,976	5.9	62,439	11.5	6,491	1.2
CT	181	197,276	20,036	5.9	24,804	7.6	3,893	1.2
DE	21	26,415	4,118	4.3	5,546	5.8	569	0.6
DC	1	58,024	3,593	5.2	4,293	6.2	906	1.3
FL	81	605,424	66,753	3.3	99,660	4.9	12,530	0.6
GA	63	200,917	28,816	2.7	35,453	3.4	12,184	1.2
HI	1	38,093	4,135	2.9	5,906	4.1	820	0.6
ID	102	58,541	8,029	5.6	15,618	11.0	1,589	1.1
IL	622	840,167	66,175	5.7	107,710	9.3	11,618	1.0
IN	236	354,219	31,849	5.2	70,761	11.6	6,035	1.0
IA	535	131,392	17,233	5.6	25,213	8.3	2,799	0.9
KS	319	140,029	13,734	5.5	24,534	9.8	2,553	1.0
KY	119	189,776	17,909	4.0	29,539	6.7	4,215	1.0
LA	67	262,498	17,211	3.7	21,469	4.6	4,941	1.1
ME	228	46,778	6,673	5.8	8,467	7.3	914	0.8
MD	24	297,796	26,090	4.4	56,357	9.5	5,609	1.0
MA	368	317,778	40,456	6.0	54,673	8.1	5,767	0.9
MI	397	439,913	46,053	4.7	77,583	7.9	8,841	0.9
MN	137	231,197	23,357	4.2	48,990	8.9	4,507	0.8
MS	52	50,264	8,582	2.9	7,189	2.4	2,187	0.7
MO	148	261,839	26,129	4.8	51,981	9.5	4,891	0.9
MT	82	28,950	4,215	4.3	5,973	6.0	1,154	1.2
NE	235	61,341	7,726	4.9	12,395	7.9	1,783	1.1
NV	22	97,173	9,685	3.3	18,414	6.2	2,656	0.9
NH	222	63,025	7,016	5.3	10,425	7.9	713	0.5
NJ	286	488,715	41,874	4.8	51,596	6.0	8,105	0.9
NM	87	52,689	7,019	4.7	9,321	6.2	1,751	1.2
NY	756	1,426,595	100,012	5.2	127,223	6.6	17,701	0.9
NC	81	236,263	32,621	3.2	49,231	4.9	5,939	0.6
ND	74	20,837	2,159	3.2	3,592	5.3	495	0.7
OH	251	831,491	71,896	6.3	170,443	14.9	15,131	1.3
OK	119	127,435	13,491	4.2	23,661	7.3	3,388	1.1
OR	131	234,530	20,260	5.7	54,031	15.2	3,143	0.9
PA	453	369,883	42,252	3.4	61,830	5.0	6,073	0.5
RI	48	52,318	5,669	5.4	6,049	5.7	972	0.9
SC	42	144,795	14,568	3.1	23,924	5.1	3,508	0.8
SD	111	26,970	3,700	4.7	5,929	7.6	1,011	1.3
TN	186	129,398	19,397	3.0	26,992	4.2	4,483	0.7
TX	540	557,088	70,302	2.8	117,268	4.6	13,754	0.5
UT	74	113,395	15,327	5.1	33,801	11.4	2,452	0.8
VT	162	24,573	3,585	6.2	3,932	7.4	558	1.0
VA	92	295,619	34,563	4.2	65,985	7.9	6,893	0.8
WA	62	447,306	37,988	5.3	84,405	11.7	7,476	1.0
WV	97	41,817	5,231	2.8	6,510	3.5	818	0.4
WI	381	254,140	30,877	5.3	55,712	9.6	4,816	0.8
WY	23	38,405	3,367	5.8	4,691	8.0	661	1.1
U.S.	**9,045**	**13,236,542**	**1,317,654**	**4.2**	**2,163,539**	**6.9**	**257,953**	**0.8**

(1) Includes central libraries only. (2) Some operating revenues may be estimated. (3) The total annual circulation of all library materials of all types, including renewals. (4) Total number of sessions accessing the internet using the library's devices.

Top 25 Public Libraries in the U.S by Holdings, 2016

Source: American Library Association (ALA)

Rank	Library name	Print materials	Electronic books	Audio and video	Total holdings
1.	New York Public Library, The Branch Libraries, NY	21,935,221	1,788,493	1,547,509	25,271,223
2.	Public Library of Cincinnati and Hamilton County, OH	4,936,677	5,889,477	895,276	11,721,430
3.	Boston Public Library, MA	7,997,591	95,927	103,492	8,197,010
4.	Los Angeles Public Library, CA	5,922,133	171,493	641,935	6,735,561
5.	Chicago Public Library, IL	5,451,914	46,195	451,142	5,949,251
6.	County of Los Angeles Public Library, CA	4,734,248	40,403	1,005,192	5,779,843
7.	Queens Borough Public Library, NY	4,972,997	85,829	611,737	5,670,563
8.	San Diego Public Library, CA	4,715,696	96,457	460,626	5,272,779
9.	Dallas Public Library, TX	4,563,199	68,076	524,372	5,155,647
10.	Hennepin County Library, MN	4,366,003	253,743	275,566	4,895,312
11.	Dayton Metro Library, OH	871,785	3,670,432	177,457	4,719,674
12.	Detroit Public Library, MI	4,083,856	6,517	303,820	4,394,193
13.	King County Library System, WA	3,091,198	232,684	643,990	3,967,872
14.	Cleveland Public Library, OH	3,219,589	373,194	353,633	3,946,416
15.	Cuyahoga County Public Library, OH	1,551,993	1,376,514	732,757	3,661,264
16.	Brooklyn Public Library, NY	3,175,967	131,448	353,117	3,660,532
17.	Miami-Dade Public Library System, FL	3,160,588	156,845	308,720	3,626,153
18.	Allen County Public Library, IN	3,048,427	220,412	299,603	3,568,442
19.	Hawaii State Public Library System, HI	2,967,198	58,452	377,927	3,403,577
20.	City of St. Louis Municipal Library District, MO	2,894,428	222,614	164,338	3,281,380
21.	Broward County Libraries Division, FL	2,408,899	92,815	692,631	3,194,345
22.	San Francisco Public Library, CA	2,618,747	159,602	343,910	3,122,259
23.	Houston Public Library, TX	2,597,505	217,319	269,809	3,084,633
24.	Las Vegas-Clark County Library District, NV	2,246,053	109,257	685,709	3,041,019
25.	Atlanta Fulton Public Library System, GA	2,619,417	232,772	99,225	2,951,414

Most Challenged Books, 2019

Source: Office for Intellectual Freedom, American Library Association (ALA)

A challenge is a formal, written complaint filed with a library or school requesting that materials be removed because of content or appropriateness. The common reasons given for challenges follow each book's title and author.

1. *George*, Alex Gino. LGBTQIA+ character, "creating confusion."
2. *Beyond Magenta: Transgender Teens Speak Out*, Susan Kuklin. LGBTQIA+ content.
3. *A Day in the Life of Marlon Bundo*, Jill Twiss. LGBTQIA+ characters, political/religious viewpoints.
4. *Sex is a Funny Word*, Cory Silverberg. LGBTQIA+ content.
5. *Prince & Knight*, Daniel Haack. Gay marriage and LGBTQIA+ content, "potential to cause confusion."
6. *I Am Jazz*, Jessica Herthel and Jazz Jennings. LGBTQIA+ character, "sensitive, controversial, and politically charged" topic.
7. *The Handmaid's Tale*, Margaret Atwood. Profanity and sexual overtones.
8. *Drama*, RainaTelgemeier. LGBTQIA+ content.
9. Harry Potter series, J.K. Rowling. Magic and witchcraft.
10. *And Tango Makes Three*, Peter Parnell and Justin Richards. LGBTQIA+ content.

Best-Selling U.S. Magazines, 2020

Source: Alliance for Audited Media (AAM)

General magazines, exclusive of comics; also excludes magazines that failed to file reports to AAM. Based on total average paid and verified circulation during the six months ending June 30, 2020; ranked by paid circulation size.

Publication	Paid circ.	Publication	Paid circ.	Publication	Paid circ.
1. AARP The Magazine	23,608,221	17. Us Weekly	1,959,748	34. Women's Health	1,331,841
2. AARP The Bulletin	22,669,110	18. Sports Illustrated	1,866,026	35. HGTV Magazine	1,303,944
3. American Main Street Publications	9,545,242	19. EatingWell	1,808,536	36. Magnolia Journal	1,268,000
		20. Food Network Magazine	1,766,813	37. The New Yorker	1,258,096
4. Better Homes and Gardens	7,649,079	21. American Legion Magazine	1,744,955	38. Vogue	1,218,279
5. Good Housekeeping	4,014,028	22. In Style	1,717,502	39. Vanity Fair	1,218,077
6. People	3,502,833	23. Taste of Home	1,711,487	40. Golf Magazine	1,216,133
7. Southern Living	2,820,399	24. American Rifleman	1,706,688	41. Allure	1,179,721
8. Reader's Digest	2,677,027	25. Texas Co-op Power	1,686,418	42. The Family Handyman	1,169,250
9. Shape	2,530,783	26. Golf Digest	1,627,353	43. Airbnb	1,163,466
10. Cosmopolitan	2,461,192	27. Time	1,617,447	44. Country Living	1,154,718
11. Woman's Day	2,452,766	28. Smithsonian	1,615,265	45. Car and Driver	1,113,121
12. O, The Oprah Magazine	2,275,959	29. Men's Health	1,581,074	46. TV Guide Magazine	1,100,682
13. National Geographic	2,129,477	30. Bon Appétit	1,528,041	47. Guideposts	1,080,729
14. Martha Stewart Living	2,072,270	31. Entertainment Weekly	1,515,115	48. Essence	1,070,039
15. Parents	2,054,329	32. Allrecipes	1,457,735	49. Elle	1,061,272
16. Real Simple	2,002,498	33. Health	1,362,072	50. Popular Mechanics	1,020,815

Note: As of Aug.15, 2020, Game Informer Magazine, which regularly ranked in the top 10, had not reported its 2020 circulation.

Best-Selling Digital Replica U.S. Magazines, 2020

Source: Alliance for Audited Media (AAM)

General magazines, exclusive of comics; also excludes magazines that failed to file reports to AAM. Based on total average paid and verified circulation during the six months ending June 30, 2020; ranked by paid circulation size.

Publication	Paid circ.	Publication	Paid circ.	Publication	Paid circ.
1. Us Weekly	744,351	18. Wired	142,425	35. The Knot	96,585
2. Star Magazine	489,491	19. National Geographic	142,208	36. Entrepreneur	95,223
3. Men's Journal	436,384	20. Men's Health	140,056	37. Popular Mechanics	95,180
4. Better Homes and		21. Real Simple	138,385	38. Outside	93,298
Gardens	396,270	22. EatingWell	136,582	39. Golf Digest	89,706
5. OK! Weekly	310,132	23. In Touch Weekly	135,158	40. Reader's Digest	88,747
6. Woman's World	301,515	24. Entertainment Weekly	131,672	41. ABA Journal	88,241
7. First for Women	296,409	25. Allrecipes	127,754	42. Southern Living	87,683
8. Cosmopolitan	246,985	26. Backpacker	116,118	43. Woman's Day	82,819
9. The New Yorker	241,909	27. Health	115,426	44. Marie Claire	80,734
10. People	234,184	28. Good Housekeeping	113,462	45. Economist (North	
11. Shape	211,476	29. Food Network Magazine	104,836	America)	80,578
12. O, The Oprah Magazine	198,245	30. HGTV Magazine	103,297	46. Elle	80,078
13. Parents	185,904	31. Fortune (North America)	101,452	47. Bridal Guide	79,537
14. Martha Stewart Living	171,287	32. Clean Eating	99,759	48. Esquire	78,520
15. Women's Health	170,671	33. Time	98,589	49. Birds & Blooms	78,089
16. The Atlantic	163,218	34. Vanity Fair	96,777	50. Popular Science	75,718
17. In Style	158,897				

Note: As of Aug.15, 2020, Game Informer Magazine, which regularly ranked in the top 10, had not reported its 2020 circulation.

Some Notable New Books, 2020

Source: Reference and User Services Association, American Library Association (ALA)

Fiction

Trust Exercise, Susan Choi
The Water Dancer, Ta-Nehisi Coates
The Innocents, Michael Crummey
Dominicana, Angie Cruz
Everything Inside: Stories, Edwidge Danticat
Girl, Woman, Other, Bernardine Evaristo
Sabrina & Corina: Stories, Kali Fajardo-Anstine
The Topeka School, Ben Lerner
Lost Children Archive, Valeria Luiselli
Lanny, Max Porter
Normal People, Sally Rooney
Don't Skip Out on Me, Willy Vlautin
On Earth We're Briefly Gorgeous, Ocean Vuong
The Nickel Boys, Colson Whitehead

Poetry

The Tradition, Jericho Brown
Deaf Republic: Poems, Ilya Kaminsky

Nonfiction

Elderhood: Redefining Aging, Transforming Medicine, Reimagining Life, Louise Aronson
Yellow House, Sarah M. Broom
Thick: And Other Essays, Tressie McMillan Cottom
A Good Provider Is One Who Leaves: One Family and Migration in the 21st Century, Jason DeParle
Mama's Last Hug: Animal Emotions and What They Tell Us About Themselves, Frans De Waal
Midnight in Chernobyl: The Untold Story of the World's Greatest Nuclear Disaster, Adam Higginbotham
Say Nothing: A True Story of Murder and Memory in Northern Ireland, Patrick Radden Keefe
Underland: A Deep Time Journey, Robert Macfarlane
Late Migrations: A Natural History of Love and Loss, Margaret Renkl
The Uninhabitable Earth: Life After Warming, David Wallace-Wells
The Impeachers: The Trial of Andrew Johnson and the Dream of a Just Nation, Brenda Wineapple

Best-Selling Books, 2019

Source: NPD BookScan

Hardcover Fiction

1. Where the Crawdads Sing, Delia Owens
2. The Guardians, John Grisham
3. The Institute, Stephen King
4. The Testaments, Margaret Atwood
5. The Silent Patient, Alex Michaelides
6. The Water Dancer, Ta-Nehisi Coates
7. The Boy, The Mole, The Fox and The Horse, Charlie Mackesy
8. Blue Moon, Lee Child
9. Strange Planet, Nathan W. Pyle
10. The Dutch House, Ann Pachett

Hardcover Nonfiction

1. Becoming, Michelle Obama
2. Educated: A Memoir, Tara Westover
3. Girl, Wash Your Face: Stop Believing the Lies About Who You Are So You Can Become Who You Were Meant to Be, Rachel Hollis
4. Girl, Stop Apologizing: A Shame-Free Plan for Embracing and Achieving Your Goals, Rachel Hollis
5. The Pioneer Woman Cooks: The New Frontier: 112 Fantastic Favorites for Everyday Eating, Ree Drummond
6. Talking to Strangers: What We Should Know About the People We Don't Know, Malcolm Gladwell
7. It's Not Supposed to Be This Way: Finding Unexpected Strength When Disappointments Leave You Shattered, Lysa TerKeurst
8. The Pioneers: The Heroic Story of the Settlers Who Brought the American Ideal West, David McCullough
9. Me: Elton John Official Biography, Elton John
10. Guinness World Records 2020

Trade Paperback

1. The Tattooist of Auschwitz, Heather Morris
2. You Are a Badass: How to Stop Doubting Your Greatness and Start Living an Awesome Life, Jen Sincero
3. The 5 Love Languages: The Secret to Love That Lasts, Dr. Gary Chapman

4. The Woman in the Window, A. J. Finn
5. Before We Were Yours, Lisa Wingate
6. Eleanor Oliphant Is Completely Fine, Gail Honeymoon
7. The Four Agreements: A Practical Guide to Personal Freedom, Don Miguel Ruiz
8. Little Fires Everywhere, Celeste Ng
9. The Overstory, Richard Powers
10. Sapiens: A Brief History of Humankind, Yuval Noah Harari

Mass Market Fiction

1. The Reckoning, John Grisham
2. Doctor Sleep, Stephen King
3. The House Next Door, James Patterson
4. Silent Night, Danielle Steel
5. Wyoming Heart, Diana Palmer
6. Sea of Greed, Clive Cussler
7. You Don't Own Me, Mary Higgins Clark
8. The 13-Minute Murder, James Patterson
9. Tom Clancy Oath of Office, Marc Cameron
10. Running Scared, Lisa Jackson

Children's and Young Adult Hardcover

1. Dog Man: For Whom the Ball Rolls (Dog Man #7), Dav Pilkey
2. Wrecking Ball (Diary of a Wimpy Kid #14), Jeff Kinney
3. Diary of an Awesome Friendly Kid: Rowley Jefferson's Journal, Jeff Kinney
4. Dog Man: Fetch-22 (Dog Man #8), Dav Pilkey
5. Harry Potter and the Goblet of Fire: The Illustrated Edition (Harry Potter, Book 4), J. K. Rowling and Jim Kay
6. 5-Minute Frozen (5-Minute Stories), Disney Book Group
7. The Tyrant's Tomb (The Trials of Apollo, Book 4), Rick Riordan
8. Tales From a Not-So-Best Friend Forever (Dork Diaries 14), Rachel Renée Russell
9. The Pigeon HAS to Go to School!, Mo Willems
10. The Good Egg (Bad Seed Series, Book 2 of 3), Jory John and Pete Oswald

Note: Hardcover bestsellers include 2018 and 2019 releases. Trade paperback bestsellers are for overall 2019 sales of paperback editions for titles first published in any year. Mass market fiction and children's and young adult bestsellers include frontlist/2019 releases only.

U.S. Daily Newspapers, 2018

Source: *Editor & Publisher International Data Book*
(ranked by circulation as of Sept. 30, 2018)

Rank	Newspaper	Circulation	Rank	Newspaper	Circulation
1.	McLean (VA) *USA Today*	2,081,202	26.	San Diego (CA) *Union-Tribune*	153,132
2.	New York (NY) *Wall Street Journal*	1,111,167	27.	Milwaukee (WI) *Journal Sentinel*	152,944
3.	New York (NY) *Times*	513,776	28.	Honolulu (HI) *Star-Advertiser*	151,585
4.	Los Angeles (CA) *Times*	452,793	29.	Washington (DC) *Post Express*	150,634
5.	New York (NY) *Post*	425,365	30.	Kansas City (MO) *Star*	143,327
6.	Chicago (IL) *Tribune*	419,864	31.	Portland (OR) *Oregonian*	143,220
7.	Washington (DC) *Post*	349,586	32.	San Jose (CA) *Mercury News*	141,005
8.	Melville (NY) *Newsday*	309,047	33.	Sacramento (CA) *Bee*	140,167
9.	Denver (CO) *Post*	285,027	34.	Atlanta (GA) *Journal-Constitution*	139,864
10.	Minneapolis (MN) *Star Tribune*	278,013	35.	Rockaway (NJ) *Herald News*	138,904
11.	New York (NY) *Daily News*	271,163	36.	St. Louis (MO) *Post-Dispatch*	135,705
12.	Houston (TX) *Chronicle*	225,120	37.	Chicago (IL) *Sun-Times*	134,874
13.	Boston (MA) *Globe*	224,286	38.	Las Vegas (NV) *Sun*	127,648
14.	Dallas (TX) *Morning News*	223,553	39.	Woodland Park (NJ) *Record*	125,038
15.	St. Petersburg (FL) *Tampa Bay Times*	219,920	40.	Little Rock (AR) *Democrat-Gazette*	124,041
16.	Philadelphia (PA) *Inquirer and Daily News*	203,986	41.	Orlando (FL) *Sentinel*	121,799
17.	Seattle (WA) *Times*	185,749	42.	Buffalo (NY) *News*	119,226
18.	New York (NY) *amNewYork*	184,583	43.	Santa Ana (CA) *Orange County Register*	116,250
19.	Phoenix (AZ) *Republic*	183,849	44.	Columbia (MO) *Daily Tribune*	114,672
20.	Cleveland (OH) *Plain Dealer*	179,224	45.	Walnut Creek (CA) *East Bay Times*	113,068
21.	San Francisco (CA) *Chronicle*	170,471	46.	Indianapolis (IN) *Star*	109,121
22.	St. Paul (MN) *Pioneer Press*	165,768	47.	Greensburg (PA) *Tribune-Review*	108,810
23.	Newark (NJ) *Star-Ledger*	161,963	48.	Louisville (KY) *Courier-Journal*	108,363
24.	Detroit (MI) *Free Press*	156,321	49.	Hartford (CT) *Courant*	107,410
25.	Pittsburgh (PA) *Post-Gazette*	153,738	50.	Norfolk (VA) *Virginian-Pilot*	106,913

Note: Excludes newspapers for which no average weekday circulation number was available.

Paid U.S. Newspaper Circulation, 1940-2019

Source: *Editor & Publisher International Data Book*
(circulation figures in thousands, as of Sept. 30, 2019)

Year	Number of daily newspapers			Circulation of daily newspapers			Sunday newspapers	
	Morning	Evening	Total	Morning	Evening	Total	Number	Circulation
1940	380	1,498	1,878	16,114	25,018	41,132	525	32,371
1950	322	1,450	1,772	21,266	32,563	53,829	549	46,582
1960	312	1,459	1,763	24,029	34,853	58,882	563	47,699
1970	334	1,429	1,748	25,934	36,174	62,108	586	49,217
1980	387	1,388	1,745	29,414	32,787	62,202	736	54,676
1990	559	1,084	1,611	41,311	21,017	62,328	863	62,635
2000	766	727	1,480	46,772	9,000	55,773	917	59,421
2005	817	645	1,452	46,122	7,222	53,345	914	55,270
2006	833	614	1,437	45,441	6,888	52,329	907	53,179
2007	867	565	1,422	44,548	6,194	50,742	907	51,246
2008	872	546	1,408	42,758	5,840	48,598	902	49,115
2009	869	528	1,397	40,796	5,482	46,278	919	46,850
2011	931	451	1,382	40,321	4,100	44,421	900	48,510
2012	985	442	1,427	38,723	4,709	43,432	981	48,821
2013	980	444	1,395	36,795	3,737	40,712	934	43,292
2014	953	402	1,331	36,765	3,655	40,420	923	42,751
2015	972	389	1,350	31,620	3,280	34,900	904	40,013
2016	939	369	1,286	30,357	3,063	33,419	869	37,998
2017	947	356	1,277	26,190	2,995	29,185	857	33,160
2018	902	352	1,254	22,570	3,170	25,740	840	29,316

Note: Data for 2010 was not available.

Canadian Daily Newspapers, 2019

Source: *Editor & Publisher International Data Book*
(ranked by circulation as of Sept. 30, 2019)

Rank	Newspaper	Circulation	Rank	Newspaper	Circulation
1.	Toronto (ON) *Globe and Mail*	311,702	6.	Saint John's (MB) *Winnipeg Free Press*	91,452
2.	Montréal (QC) *Le Journal de Montréal*	158,423	7.	Toronto (ON) *Sun*	86,462
3.	Toronto (ON) *National Post*	125,674	8.	Ottawa (ON) *Citizen*	81,103
4.	Toronto (ON) *Star*	119,943	9.	Québec City (QC) *Le Journal de Québec*	76,585
5.	Vancouver (BC) *Sun*	99,079	10.	Vancouver (BC) *Province*	75,637

Top Newspaper Websites, 2020

Source: Comscore, Inc.
(ranked by number of visitors, in thousands)

Rank	Website	Visitors[1]	Rank	Website	Visitors[1]
1.	USA Today Network	147,399	11.	McClatchy Company	47,778
2.	New York Times Digital	113,959	12.	REACH Group	41,508
3.	WashingtonPost.com	101,635	13.	News UK Sites	37,175
4.	NY Post Network	87,208	14.	MediaNews Group, Inc.	36,596
5.	Mail Online/Daily Mail	83,175	15.	Prisa	27,571
6.	Tribune Publishing	63,622	16.	WashingtonTimes.com	18,792
7.	Hearst Newspapers	60,184	17.	Berkshire Hathaway Media Group	18,208
8.	The Guardian	59,969	18.	Lee Enterprises, Inc.	14,958
9.	NantMedia Holdings	49,059	19.	Boston Globe Media Sites	14,016
10.	TheHill.com	47,854	20.	Bizjournals Digital Network	13,874

(1) Number of persons age 2 and older, in thousands, who visited the media property (including website/apps) at least once from any U.S. location in June 2020. Mobile visitors under age 18 are not measured.

Top News/Information Websites, 2020

Source: Comscore, Inc.

(ranked by number of visitors, in thousands)

Rank Website	Visitors[1]	Rank Website	Visitors[1]
1. Yahoo-HuffPost News Network	171,699	11. WashingtonPost.com	101,635
2. NBC News Digital	166,417	12. Nexstar Broadcast	96,147
3. CNN Network	164,467	13. ABC News Digital	91,193
4. The Weather Company	154,248	14. CBS News	90,017
5. Microsoft News	147,958	15. CNET	88,897
6. USA Today Network	147,399	16. NYPost Network	87,208
7. New York Times Digital	113,959	17. Future Plc	85,979
8. Forbes Digital	113,743	18. Mail Online/Daily Mail	83,175
9. Fox News Digital Network	111,870	19. Dow Jones & Company	81,718
10. Insider Inc.	111,519	20. Tegna	76,036

(1) Number of persons age 2 and older, in thousands, who visited the media property (including website/apps) at least once from any U.S. location in June 2020. Mobile visitors under age 18 are not measured.

National Recording Registry, 2019

Source: Library of Congress

Each year since 2002, the National Recording Registry at the Library of Congress adds 25 recordings showcasing the "range and diversity of American recorded sound heritage."

"Whispering," Paul Whiteman and His Orchestra (1920)
"Protesta per Sacco e Vanzetti," Compagnia Columbia; "Sacco e Vanzetti," Raoul Romito (1927)
"La Chicharronera," Narciso Martinez and Santiago Almeida (1936)
"The Bathysphere" episode, *Arch Oboler's Plays* (Nov. 18, 1939)
"Me and My Chauffeur Blues," Memphis Minnie (1941)
"The 1951 National League Tiebreaker: New York Giants vs. Brooklyn Dodgers," Russ Hodges, announcer (Oct. 3, 1951)
Puccini's "Tosca," Maria Callas, Giuseppe di Stefano, Angelo Mercuriali, Tito Gobbi, Melchiorre Luise, Dario Caselli, Victor de Sabata (1953)
"Hello Muddah, Hello Fadduh," Allan Sherman (1963)
WGBH broadcast of the Boston Symphony on the day of the John F. Kennedy assassination, Boston Symphony Orchestra (1963)
Fiddler on the Roof, Original Broadway Cast (1964)
"Make the World Go Away," Eddy Arnold (1965)
Hiromi Lorraine Sakata Collection of Afghan Traditional Music (1966-67; 1971-73)

"Wichita Lineman," Glen Campbell (1968)
Dusty in Memphis, Dusty Springfield (1969)
Mister Rogers Sings 21 Favorite Songs From Mister Rogers' Neighborhood, Fred Rogers (1973)
Cheap Trick at Budokan, Cheap Trick (1978)
Holst: Suite No. 1 in E-Flat, Suite No. 2 in F / Handel: Music for the Royal Fireworks / Bach: Fantasia in G (Special Edition Audiophile Pressing album), Frederick Fennell and the Cleveland Symphonic Winds (1978)
"Y.M.C.A.," Village People (1978)
A Feather on the Breath of God, Gothic Voices (1982)
Private Dancer, Tina Turner (1984)
Ven Conmigo, Selena (1990)
The Chronic, Dr. Dre (1992)
"I Will Always Love You," Whitney Houston (1992)
Concert in the Garden, Maria Schneider Orchestra (2004)
Percussion Concerto, Colin Currie (2008)

U.S. Commercial Radio Stations by Format, 2010-20

Source: Inside Radio (www.insideradio.com)

(as of July 2020; ranked by 2020 numbers)

Format	2010	2011	2012	2013	2014	2015	2016	2017	2018	2019	2020
1. Country	1,997	1,987	2,020	2,042	2,053	2,112	2,126	2,121	2,143	2,157	2,147
2. News/Talk	1,437	1,455	1,503	1,453	1,409	1,360	1,355	1,330	1,296	1,268	1,241
3. Classic Hits	637	657	657	678	754	805	881	965	1,001	1,046	1,081
4. Spanish	806	818	816	835	844	862	878	858	865	867	886
5. Sports	665	670	692	740	788	788	780	752	726	702	687
6. Top 40	495	523	559	573	577	579	583	594	595	591	582
7. Adult Contemporary	634	607	597	605	597	609	608	592	581	575	567
8. Classic Rock	481	477	477	486	486	486	492	519	522	548	558
9. Hot AC	417	435	420	428	465	462	464	451	452	447	471
10. Religion (Teaching, Variety)	322	332	342	336	324	318	318	332	351	365	392
11. Rock	294	301	295	299	302	304	304	291	285	289	291
12. Oldies	637	628	597	566	476	413	343	293	295	278	262
13. Contemporary Christian	166	166	171	172	157	168	173	193	172	195	201
14. Black Gospel	235	225	214	212	211	218	213	206	198	198	182
15. Urban Adult Contemporary	159	155	152	158	167	166	163	170	170	164	168
Total stations	**11,306**	**11,355**	**11,434**	**11,402**	**11,386**	**11,314**	**11,386**	**11,412**	**11,365**	**11,297**	**11,215**

Note: Totals include stations that are changing or did not report format, as well as formats not listed here.

Top-Selling Albums of All Time

Source: Recording Industry Assn. of America (RIAA)

Sales figures represent RIAA multi-platinum certifications; albums ranked by latest sales certification. As of Aug. 15, 2020.

Rank	Title, artist	Unit sales (mil)	Rank	Title, artist	Unit sales (mil)
1.	*Their Greatest Hits (1971-1975)*, Eagles	38.0	16.	*Boston*, Boston	17.0
2.	*Thriller*, Michael Jackson	33.0	17.	*Greatest Hits*, Elton John	17.0
3.	*Hotel California*, Eagles	26.0	18.	*The Beatles 1967-1970*, The Beatles	17.0
4.	*Back in Black*, AC/DC	25.0	19.	*Jagged Little Pill*, Alanis Morissette	16.0
5.	*The Beatles*, The Beatles	24.0	20.	*Saturday Night Fever* (soundtrack), Bee Gees	16.0
6.	*Greatest Hits Volume I & Volume II*, Billy Joel	23.0	21.	*Physical Graffiti*, Led Zeppelin	16.0
7.	*Led Zeppelin IV*, Led Zeppelin	23.0	22.	*Metallica*, Metallica	16.0
8.	*The Wall*, Pink Floyd	23.0	23.	*Legend*, Bob Marley and the Wailers	15.0
9.	*Double Live*, Garth Brooks	21.0	24.	*Born in the U.S.A.*, Bruce Springsteen	15.0
10.	*Cracked Rear View*, Hootie & the Blowfish	21.0	25.	*Greatest Hits*, Journey	15.0
11.	*Rumours*, Fleetwood Mac	20.0	26.	*Dark Side of the Moon*, Pink Floyd	15.0
12.	*Come on Over*, Shania Twain	20.0	27.	*Supernatural*, Santana	15.0
13.	*Appetite for Destruction*, Guns N' Roses	18.0	28.	*The Beatles 1962-1966*, The Beatles	15.0
14.	*The Bodyguard* (soundtrack), Whitney Houston	18.0	29.	*21*, Adele	14.0
15.	*No Fences*, Garth Brooks	18.0	30.	*Backstreet Boys*, Backstreet Boys	14.0

Top-Selling Musical Artists by Digital Sales

Source: Recording Industry Assn. of America (RIAA)

Units represent digital singles certified as sold, including streaming-equivalent, as of Aug. 15, 2020.

Artist	Units (mil)	Artist	Units (mil)	Artist	Units (mil)	Artist	Units (mil)
Drake	163.5	Post Malone	52.0	Blake Shelton	34.0	Panic! At the Disco	29.5
Rihanna	128.0	Flo Rida	51.5	XXXTentacion	34.0	Travis Scott	29.5
Taylor Swift	126.5	Future	50.0	Jason Derulo	33.5	J. Cole	29.0
Eminem	107.5	Carrie Underwood	44.5	Lil Wayne	33.0	Queen	29.0
Katy Perry	103.0	Florida Georgia Line	44.0	Mariah Carey	33.0	Tim McGraw	29.0
Justin Bieber	86.0	Twenty One Pilots	43.0	DJ Khaled	32.5	Big Sean	28.5
Kanye West	77.0	Michael Jackson	42.0	Halsey	32.5	Meghan Trainor	28.5
Lady Gaga	77.0	Kendrick Lamar	41.0	Imagine Dragons	32.0	Thomas Rhett	28.0
Maroon 5	76.0	Billie Eilish	40.0	Adele	31.5	Eric Church	27.5
The Weeknd	73.0	Cardi B	37.0	Keith Urban	30.5	Shawn Mendes	26.5
Bruno Mars	69.5	Sam Smith	37.0	Lil Uzi Vert	30.5	Beyoncé	26.0
Chris Brown	69.5	The Chainsmokers	37.0	Nicki Minaj	30.5	Fall Out Boy	26.0
Ed Sheeran	68.0	Kesha	35.5	Kenny Chesney	30.0	Miley Cyrus	26.0
Luke Bryan	61.0	Khalid	35.5	Linkin Park	30.0	Rae Sremmurd	26.0
Ariana Grande	52.5	Wiz Khalifa	34.5	Jason Aldean	29.5	Zac Brown Band	26.0

Top Musical Artists All-Time by Album Sales

Source: Recording Industry Assn. of America (RIAA)

Certified album sales in millions, including streaming equivalent where applicable, as of Aug. 14, 2020.

Artist	Certified sales (mil)	Artist	Certified sales (mil)	Artist	Certified sales (mil)
The Beatles	183.0	Metallica	63.0	Alan Jackson	43.5
Garth Brooks	157.0	Whitney Houston	59.0	Santana	43.5
Elvis Presley	139.0	Van Halen	56.5	Reba McEntire	41.0
Eagles	120.0	Fleetwood Mac	54.5	Eric Clapton	40.0
Led Zeppelin	111.5	U2	51.0	Chicago	38.5
Billy Joel	84.5	Celine Dion	50.0	Simon & Garfunkel	38.5
Michael Jackson	84.0	Neil Diamond	49.5	Foreigner	38.0
Elton John	79.0	Journey	48.0	Rod Stewart	38.0
AC/DC	75.0	Kenny G	48.0	Tim McGraw	37.5
Pink Floyd	75.0	Shania Twain	48.0	Backstreet Boys	37.0
George Strait	69.0	Kenny Rogers	47.5	2Pac	36.5
Barbra Streisand	68.5	Alabama	46.5	Bob Dylan	36.0
Aerosmith	66.5	Eminem	46.5	Def Leppard	35.5
The Rolling Stones	66.5	Taylor Swift	45.0	Queen	35.0
Bruce Springsteen	65.5	Bob Seger & the Silver Bullet Band	44.5	Bon Jovi	34.5
Madonna	64.5	Guns N' Roses	44.5	Britney Spears	34.5
Mariah Carey	64.5			Dave Matthews Band	34.5

Multi-Platinum Awards for Recorded Music, 2019-20

Source: Recording Industry Assn. of America (RIAA)

To be certified platinum, an **album** must sell 1 mil units (LPs, CDs, or digital) with a manufacturer's dollar volume of at least $2 mil based on one-third of the suggested retail list price for each copy sold. To achieve multi-platinum status, an album must reach minimum total sales of at least 2 mil units with a manufacturer's dollar volume of at least $4 mil based on one-third of the list price. RIAA began including streaming in their award formulas in 2018; 1,500 streams count as the equivalent of 10 track sales or 1 album sale. **Digital singles** must sell 2 mil to achieve a multi-platinum award. For digital singles award formulas, 150 streams equal one download sold.

Awards listed here are for albums and digital singles (released Sept. 2018-Aug. 15, 2020) that were certified Sept. 2019-Aug. 15, 2020. Number in parentheses represents millions sold. Alphabetized by artist name.

Albums

A Star Is Born soundtrack, Lady Gaga & Bradley Cooper (2)
Thank You, Next, Ariana Grande (2)
When We All Fall Asleep, Where Do We Go? Billie Eilish (3)
Lover, Taylor Swift (2)

Digital Singles

"Look Back at It" (3), "Swervin" (3), A Boogie wit da Hoodie
"I Hope" (2), Gabby Barrett
"Intentions" (2), Justin Bieber feat. Quavo
"hot girl bummer" (2), Blackbear
"The Git Up" (2), Blanco Brown
"Envy Me" (2), Calboy
"Money" (4), Cardi B
"Please Me" (3), Cardi B and Bruno Mars
"This Feeling" (2), The Chainsmokers
"Middle Child" (5), J. Cole
"Suge" (2), DaBaby
"10,000 Hours" (3), Dan + Shay & Justin Bieber
"Falling" (2), Trevor Daniel
"Heartless" (2), Diplo feat. Morgan Wallen
"Taki Taki" (3), DJ Snake feat. Selena Gomez, Ozuna & Cardi B
"Bad Guy" (6), "Bury A Friend" (3), "Everything I Wanted" (2), "When the Party's Over" (4), Billie Eilish
"Life Is Good" (6), Future feat. Drake
"Fine China" (2), Future and Juice World
"Shallow" (4), Lady Gaga & Bradley Cooper
"7 Rings" (5), "Break Up with Your Girlfriend, I'm Bored" (3), "Thank You, Next" (5), Ariana Grande
"Wake Up in the Sky" (3), Gucci Mane feat. Bruno Mars & Kodak Black
"Without Me" (7), Halsey
"Slow Dancing in the Dark" (2), Joji
"Sucker" (3), Jonas Brothers
"Robbery" (2), Juice Wrld
"Better" (3), "Talk" (4), Khalid
"Zeze" (4), Kodak Black feat. Travis Scott and Offset
"Pure Cocaine" (3), "Woah" (3), Lil Baby
"Close Friends" (4), "Drip Too Hard" (7), Lil Baby and Gunna
"Never Recover" (2), Lil Baby and Gunna feat. Drake
"Panini" (5), Lil Nas X
"Old Town Road" (12), Lil Nax X feat. Billy Ray Cyrus
"Ransom" (2), Lil Tecca
"F.N" (2), Lil Tjay
"Don't Start Now" (2), Dua Lipa
"Sunflower" (8), Post Malone feat. Swae Lee
"Memories" (2), Maroon 5
"Going Bad" (5), Meek Mill feat. Drake
"Pure Water" (3), Mustard feat. Migos
"Ballin'" (3), Mustard & Robby Richh
"Shotta Flow" (2), NLE Choppa
"Pop Out" (4), Polo G feat. Lil Tjay
"The Box" (7), Roddy Richh
"High Fashion" (2), Roddy Richh feat. Mustard
"My Type" (2), Saweetie
"I Don't Care" (2), Ed Sheeran & Justin Bieber
"God's Country" (3), Blake Shelton
"Faucet Failure" (2), Ski Mask the Slump God
"Dancing With a Stranger" (3), Sam Smith & Normani
"Adore You" (2), "Watermelon Sugar" (2), Harry Styles
"Dance Monkey" (3), Tones and I
"A Lot" (2), 21 Savage
"Earfquake" (2), Tyler, the Creator
"Girls Need Love" (2), Summer Walker
"Heart On Ice" (2), Rod Wave
"I Love It" (2), Kanye West & Lil Pump
"Worth It" (2), YK Osiris
"Suicidal" (2), YNW Melly
"Mixed Personalities" (2), YNW Melly feat. Kanye West
"Put a Date on It" (2), Yo Gotti feat. Lil Baby
"The London" (3), Young Thug feat. J. Cole & Travis Scott
"Roxanne" (3), Arizona Zervas

Top-Grossing North American Concert Tours, 1985-2019

Source: Pollstar

Rank Artist (year)	Total gross[1]	Cities/ shows	Rank Artist (year)	Total gross[1]	Cities/ shows
1. Taylor Swift (2018)	$277.3	27/40	15. Guns N' Roses (2016)	$130.8	24/31
2. Taylor Swift (2015)	199.4	41/62	16. One Direction (2014)	127.2	21/31
3. The Rolling Stones (2019)	177.8	14/16	17. U2 (2009)	123.0	16/20
4. U2 (2017)	176.1	26/30	18. Bruce Springsteen & The E Street Band (2016)	122.4	42/48
5. Beyoncé (2016)	169.4	30/32			
6. Jay-Z and Beyoncé (2018)	166.4	24/30	19. The Rolling Stones (1994)	121.2	43/60
7. Eagles (2018)	166.0	45/53	20. Kenny Chesney (2015)	116.4	56/59
8. The Rolling Stones (2005)	162.0	38/42	21. Bruce Springsteen & The E Street		
9. Elton John (2019)	157.4	57/81	Band (2003)	115.9	30/47
10. U2 (2011)	156.0	21/25	22. Garth Brooks (2015)	114.9	23/120
11. U2 (2005)	138.9	43/78	23. Kenny Chesney (2018)	114.4	40/42
12. The Rolling Stones (2006)	138.5	35/39	24. Taylor Swift (2013)	112.7	47/66
13. Madonna (2012)	133.7	31/45	25. Bruno Mars (2017)	112.4	50/67
14. The Police (2007)	133.2	41/54			

(1) In millions. Not adjusted for inflation.

Music Sales by Format and Value, 1990-2019

Source: Recording Industry Assn. of America

(in millions, net after returns)

	1990	1995	2000	2005	2010	2015	2017	2018	2019	% change, 2018-19
Physical units shipped	865.7	1,112.7	1,079.2	748.8	267.7	135.0	105.7	70.5	67.3	-4.5%
Dollar value	$7,541.1	12,320.3	14,323.7	11,195.0	3,663.7	1,862.2	1,495.5	1,154.8	1,148.3	-0.6
Compact discs (CDs)	286.5	722.9	942.5	705.4	253.0	117.1	87.7	52.0	46.5	-10.6
Dollar value	$3,451.6	9,377.4	13,214.5	10,520.2	3,389.4	1,445.0	1,057.3	698.4	614.5	-12.0
LPs/EPs	11.7	2.2	2.2	1.0	4.2	13.7	15.6	16.7	19.1	14.4
Dollar value	$86.5	25.1	27.7	14.2	88.9	333.4	388.5	419.2	497.6	18.7
Music videos	9.2	12.6	18.2	33.8	9.1	3.1	1.9	1.4	1.3	-7.1
Dollar value	$172.3	220.3	281.9	602.2	177.6	70.4	38.6	27.6	27.7	0.4
Other physical[1]	558.3	375.0	116.3	8.6	1.4	1.1	0.6	0.5	0.4	-20.0
Dollar value	$3,830.7	2,697.5	799.6	58.4	7.8	13.4	11.0	9.6	8.5	-11.5
Digital formats: number downloaded	—	—	—	553.1	1,471.8	1,120.5	636.9	461.7	385.9	-16.4
Digital formats: dollar value	—	—	—	$925.3	2,699.8	2,314.3	1,404.5	1,039.1	855.7	-17.6
Albums downloaded	—	—	—	13.6	85.8	106.8	66.4	49.7	40.2	-19.1
Dollar value	—	—	—	$135.7	872.1	1,064.4	668.5	499.7	394.5	-21.0
Singles downloaded	—	—	—	366.9	1,177.4	986.3	553.5	399.8	335.3	-16.1
Dollar value	—	—	—	$363.3	1,336.4	1,185.2	678.5	490.4	414.8	-15.4
Ringtones and ringbacks	—	—	—	170.0	188.5	21.9	14.3	10.0	8.6	-14.0
Dollar value	—	—	—	$421.6	448.0	54.6	35.5	24.9	21.4	-14.1
Other digital downloads[2]	—	—	—	2.6	20.1	5.5	2.7	2.2	1.8	-18.2
Dollar value	—	—	—	$4.7	43.0	10.1	5.1	4.2	3.5	-16.7
Other digital licensing	—	—	—	—	—	—	16.9	24.1	25.0	3.7
Subscription and streaming dollar value	—	—	—	$169.6	461.6	2,331.3	5,664.5	7,366.8	8,831.3	19.9
Subscription formats[3]	—	—	—	1.3	1.5	10.8	35.3	46.9	60.4	28.8
Dollar value	—	—	—	$149.2	212.4	1,156.7	3,500.5	4,656.0	5,934.4	27.5
Limited tier paid subscriptions	—	—	—	—	—	—	591.6	747.1	829.5	11.0
SoundExchange distribution[4]	—	—	—	$20.4	249.2	802.6	652.0	952.8	908.2	-4.7
On-demand streaming (ad supported)[5]	—	—	—	—	372.0	658.6	759.5	908.1	19.6	
Other ad-supported streaming[6]	—	—	—	—	—	—	261.8	251.4	251.1	-0.1
Synchronization royalties[7]	—	—	—	—	$188.7	202.9	232.1	285.5	276.3	-3.2
Total physical and digital[8]	865.7	1,112.7	1,079.2	1,301.9	1,739.5	1,255.5	742.6	532.3	453.3	-14.8
Total value physical and digital	$7,541.1	12,320.3	14,323.7	12,289.9	7,013.8	6,710.8	8,796.6	9,846.1	11,111.6	12.9

— = Not available or not applicable. (1) Includes CD singles, cassettes, vinyl singles, DVD audio, and SACD. (2) Includes kiosk and music video downloads. (3) Streaming, tethered, and other paid subscription services not operating under statutory licenses. Subscription volume is annual average number of subscriptions (excluding limited tier). (4) Estimated payments to performers/copyright holders for digital radio services under statutory licenses. (5) Ad-supported audio and music video services not operating under statutory licenses. (6) Revenues from services paid directly that are not distributed by SoundExchange or included in other streaming categories. (7) Includes fees and royalties from sound recordings used in other media. (8) Units total includes physical and downloaded albums and singles but not streaming, subscriptions, or royalties.

Top Basic Cable TV Networks, 2019

Source: Kagan, a media research group within S&P Global Market Intelligence

Rank	Network (year began)	Subscribers (mil)	Rank	Network (year began)	Subscribers (mil)
1.	C-SPAN (1979)	91.0	11.	AMC (1984)	87.1
2.	Food Network (1993)	89.2	12.	Disney Channel (1983)	87.0
3.	TBS (1976)	88.9	13.	Cartoon Network (1992) / Adult Swim (2001)	87.0
4.	USA (1980)	88.5	14.	National Geographic Channel (2001)	86.9
5.	CNN (1980)	88.4	15.	HLN (1982)	86.7
6.	HGTV (1994)	88.3	16.	A&E (1994)	86.4
7.	TNT (1988)	88.2	17.	E! (1987)	86.3
8.	FX (1994)	87.5	18.	Freeform (1977)	86.1
9.	Discovery Channel (1985)	87.4	19.	Lifetime Television (1994)	86.0
10.	History (1995)	87.1	20.	Syfy (1992)	86.0

U.S. Television Owners, 2020

Source: Nielsen Media Research, July 2020

Of the 120.6 mil U.S. households that owned at least one TV in 2020—

71.6% had 2 or more TV sets	0.3% had a VCR	68.3% received basic cable
16.2% had 4 or more TV sets	55.9% had a DVD player	38.7% received premium cable
40.6% had a video game console	50.5% had a DVR	82.1% had a PC with internet access

U.S. Households With Cable Television, 1980-2020
Source: Nielsen Media Research

Year[1]	Subscribers[2] (mil)	As % of households with TVs	Year[1]	Subscribers[2] (mil)	As % of households with TVs	Year[1]	Subscribers[2] (mil)	As % of households with TVs
1980	17.7	22.6%	2002	87.8	83.8%	2012	103.6	90.3%
1985	38.7	45.3	2003	88.4	82.9	2013	103.3	90.5
1990	53.9	58.6	2004	92.4	85.3	2014	103.7	89.6
1990	62.1	65.1	2005	94.0	85.7	2015	100.2	86.0
1996	63.6	66.3	2006	95.0	86.2	2016	97.8	84.0
1997	65.1	67.2	2007	94.5	83.8	2017	96.0	81.0
1998	65.9	67.2	2008	99.7	88.2	2018	92.8	77.6
1999	76.4	76.9	2009	103.0	89.7	2019	88.4	73.7
2000	78.6	77.9	2010	104.1	90.6	2020	82.3	68.3
2001	81.5	79.8	2011	104.8	90.4			

(1) After 1998, figures include wired-cable households as well as households that receive TV programming via alternate delivery systems (including satellite receivers, SMATV, and MMDS). (2) Households that subscribe to basic cable service.

Selected Reality TV Show Winners, 2000-20
Numbers in parentheses represent the season, edition, or cycle of the show. As of Sept. 2020.

The Amazing Race. Debuted Aug. 2001 on CBS. Rob Frisbee & Brennan Swain (1); Chris Luca & Alex Boylan (2); Flo Pesenti & Zach Behr (3); Reichen Lehmkuhl & Chip Arndt (4); Chip & Kim McAllister (5); Freddy Holliday & Kendra Bentley (6); Uchenna & Joyce Agu (7); The Linz Family (8); B. J. Averell & Tyler MacNiven (9); Tyler Denk & James Branaman (10); Eric Sanchez & Danielle Turner (All Stars, 11); TK Erwin & Rachel Morales (12); Nick & Starr Spangler (13); Tammy & Victor Jih (14); Meghan Rickey & Cheyne Whitney (15); Dan & Jordan Pious (16); Natalie Strand & Katherine Chang (17); LaKisha & Jennifer Hoffman (18); Ernie Halvorsen & Cindy Chiang (19); Rachel Brown & Dave Brown Jr. (20); Josh Kilmer-Purcell & Brent Ridge (21); Bates & Anthony Battaglia (22); Jason Case & Amy Diaz (23); David & Connor O'Leary (All Stars, 24); Amy DeJong & Maya Warren (25); Laura Pierson & Tyler Adams (26); Kelsey Gerckens & Joey Buttitta (27); Dana Borriello & Matt Steffanina (28); Brooke Camhi & Scott Flanary (29); Jessica Graf & Cody Nickson (30); Colin Guinn & Christie Woods (31).

American Idol. Debuted July 2002 on FOX. Kelly Clarkson (1); Ruben Studdard (2); Fantasia Barrino (3); Carrie Underwood (4); Taylor Hicks (5); Jordin Sparks (6); David Cook (7); Kris Allen (8); Lee DeWyze (9); Scotty McCreery (10); Phillip Phillips (11); Candice Glover (12); Caleb Johnson (13); Nick Fradiani (14); Trent Harmon (15); Maddie Poppe (16); Laine Hardy (17); Just Sam (18).

America's Got Talent. Debuted June 2006 on NBC. Bianca Ryan (1); Terry Fator (2); Neil E. Boyd (3); Kevin Skinner (4); Michael Grimm (5); Landau Eugene Murphy Jr. (6); Olate Dogs (7); Kenichi Ebina (8); Mat Franco (9); Paul Zerdin (10); Grace VanderWaal (11); Darci Lynne Farmer (12); Shin Lim (13); Kodi Lee (14); Brandon Leake (15).

The Apprentice. Debuted Jan. 2004 on NBC. Bill Rancic (1); Kelly Perdew (2); Kendra Todd (3); Randal Pinkett (4); Sean Yazbeck (5); Stefanie Schaeffer (6); Brandy Kuentzel (7). *Celebrity Apprentice:* Piers Morgan (1); Joan Rivers (2); Bret Michaels (3); John Rich (4); Arsenio Hall (5); Trace Adkins (All Stars, 6); Leeza Gibbons (7); Matt Iseman (8).

The Bachelor. Debuted Mar. 2002 on ABC. Alex Michel chose Amanda Marsh (1); Aaron Buerge, Helene Eksterowicz (2); Andrew Firestone, Jen Schefft (3); Bob Guiney, Estella Gardinier (4); Jesse Palmer, Jessica Bowlin (5); Byron Velvick, Mary Delgado (6); Charlie O'Connell, Sarah Brice (7); Travis Stork, Sarah Stone (8); Lorenzo Borghese, Jennifer Wilson (9); Andy Baldwin, Tessa Horst (10); Brad Womack, no one (11); Matt Grant, Shayne Lamas (12); Jason Mesnick, Melissa Rycroft (13); Jake Pavelka, Vienna Girardi (14); Brad Womack, Emily Maynard (15); Ben Flajnik, Courtney Robertson (16); Sean Lowe, Catherine Giudici (17); Juan Pablo Galavis, Nikki Ferrell (18); Chris Soules, Whitney Bischoff (19); Ben Higgins, Lauren Bushnell (20); Nick Viall, Vanessa Grimaldi (21); Arie Luyendyk Jr., Becca Kufrin (22); Colton Underwood, Cassie Randolph (23); Peter Weber, Hannah Ann Sluss (24).

The Bachelorette. Debuted Jan. 2003 on ABC. Trista Rehn chose Ryan Sutter (1); Meredith Phillips, Ian McKee (2); Jen Schefft, Jerry Ferris (3); DeAnna Pappas, Jesse Csincsak (4); Jillian Harris, Ed Swiderski (5); Ali Fedotowsky, Roberto Martinez (6); Ashley Hebert, J. P. Rosenbaum (7); Emily Maynard, Jef Holm (8); Desiree Hartsock, Chris Siegfried (9); Andi Dorfman, Josh Murray (10); Kaitlyn Bristowe, Shawn Booth (11); JoJo Fletcher, Jordan Rodgers (12); Rachel Lindsay, Bryan Abasolo (13); Becca Kufrin, Garrett Yrigoyen (14); Hannah Brown, Jed Wyatt (15).

Big Brother. Debuted July 2000 on CBS. Eddie McGee (1); Will Kirby (2); Lisa Donahue (3); Jun Song (4); Drew Daniel (5); Maggie Ausburn (6); Mike Malinto (7); Dick Donato (8); Adam Jasinski (9); Dan Gheesling (10); Jordan Lloyd (11); Hayden Moss (12); Rachel Reilly (13); Ian Terry (14); Andy Herren (15); Derrick Levasseur (16); Steve Moses (17); Nicole Franzel (18); Josh Martinez (19); Kaycee Clark (20); Jackson Michie (21).

Dancing With the Stars. Debuted June 2005 on ABC. Kelly Monaco & Alex Mazo (1); Drew Lachey & Cheryl Burke (2); Emmitt Smith & Cheryl Burke (3); Apolo Anton Ohno & Julianne Hough (4); Helio Castroneves & Julianne Hough (5); Kristi Yamaguchi & Mark Ballas (6); Brooke Burke & Derek Hough (7); Shawn Johnson & Mark Ballas (8); Donny Osmond & Kym Johnson (9); Nicole Scherzinger & Derek Hough (10); Jennifer Grey & Derek Hough (11); Hines Ward & Kym Johnson (12); J.R. Martinez & Karina Smirnoff (13); Donald Driver & Peta Murgatroyd (14); Melissa Rycroft & Tony Dovolani (All Stars, 15); Kellie Pickler & Derek Hough (16); Amber Riley & Derek Hough (17); Meryl Davis & Maksim Chmerkovskiy (18); Alfonso Ribeiro & Witney Carson (19); Rumer Willis & Val Chmerkovskiy (20); Bindi Irwin & Derek Hough (21); Nyle DiMarco & Peta Murgatroyd (22); Laurie Hernandez & Val Chmerkovskiy (23); Rashad Jennings & Emma Slater (24); Jordan Fisher & Lindsay Arnold (25); Adam Rippon & Jenna Johnson (26); Bobby Bones & Sharna Burgess (27); Hannah Brown & Alan Bersten (28).

Project Runway. Debuted Dec. 2004 on Bravo. Jay McCarroll (1); Chloe Dao (2); Jeffrey Sebelia (3); Christian Siriano (4); Leanne Marshall (5); Irina Shabayeva (6); Seth Aaron Henderson (7); Gretchen Jones (8); Anya Ayoung-Chee (9); Dmitry Sholokhov (10); Michelle Lesniak Franklin (11); Dom Streater (12); Sean Kelly (13); Ashley Nell Tipton (14); Erin Robertson (15); Kentaro Kameyama (16); Sebastian Grey (17); Geoffrey Mac (18). *All-Stars:* Mondo Guerra (1); Anthony Ryan Auld (2); Seth Aaron Henderson (3); Dmitry Sholokhov (4); Dom Streater (5); Anthony Williams (6); Michelle Lesniak (7).

RuPaul's Drag Race. Debuted Feb. 2009 on Logo. Bebe Zahara Benet (1); Tyra Sanchez (2); Raja (3); Sharon Needles (4); Jinkx Monsoon (5); Bianca Del Rio (6); Violet Chachki (7); Bob the Drag Queen (8); Sasha Velour (9); Aquaria (10); Yvie Oddly (11); Jaida Essence Hall (12). *All Stars:* Chad Michaels (1); Alaska (2); Trixie Mattel (3); Monét X Change, Trinity The Tuck (4); Shea Couleé (5).

So You Think You Can Dance. Debuted July 2005 on FOX. Nick Lazzarini (1); Benji Schwimmer (2); Sabra Johnson (3); Joshua Allen (4); Jeanine Mason (5); Russell Ferguson (6); Lauren Froderman (7); Melanie Moore (8); Eliana Girard & Chehon Wespi-Tschopp (9); DuShaunt "Fik-Shun" Stegall & Amy Yakima (10); Ricky Ubeda (11); Gaby Diaz (12); Leon "Kida" Burns (13); Lex Ishimoto (14); Hannahlei Cabanilla (15); Bailey Munoz (16).

Survivor. Debuted May 2000 on CBS. Richard Hatch (1); Tina Wesson (2); Ethan Zohn (3); Vecepia Towery (4); Brian Heidik (5); Jenna Morasca (6); Sandra Diaz-Twine (7); Amber Brkich (8); Chris Daugherty (9); Tom Westman (10); Danni Boatwright (11); Aras Baskauskas (12); Yul Kwon (13); Earl Cole (14); Todd Herzog (15); Parvati Shallow (16); Robert Crowley (17); James "JT" Thomas (18); Natalie White (19); Sandra Diaz-Twine (20); Jud Birza (21); Rob Mariano (22); Sophie Clarke (23); Kim Spradlin (24); Denise Stapley (25); John Cochran (26); Tyson Apostol (27); Tony Vlachos (28); Natalie Anderson (29); Mike Holloway (30); Jeremy Collins (31); Michele Fitzgerald (32); Adam Klein (33); Sarah Lacina (34); Ben Driebergen (35); Wendell Holland (36); Nick Wilson (37); Chris Underwood (38); Tommy Sheehan (39); Tony Vlachos (40).

Top Chef. Debuted Mar. 2006 on Bravo. Harold Dieterle (1); Ilan Hall (2); Hung Huynh (3); Stephanie Izard (4); Hosea Rosenberg (5); Michael Voltaggio (6); Kevin Sbraga (7); Richard Blais (8); Paul Qui (9); Kristen Kish (10); Nicholas Elmi (11); Mei Lin (12); Jeremy Ford (13); Brooke Williamson (14); Joseph Flamm (15); Kelsey Barnard Clark (16); Melissa King (17). *Top Chef Masters:* Rick Bayless (1); Marcus Samuelsson (2); Floyd Cardoz (3); Chris Cosentino (4); Douglas Keane (5).

The Voice. Debuted Apr. 2011 on NBC. Javier Colon (1); Jermaine Paul (2); Cassadee Pope (3); Danielle Bradbery (4); Tessanne Chin (5); Josh Kaufman (6); Craig Wayne Boyd (7); Sawyer Fredericks (8); Jordan Smith (9); Alisan Porter (10); Sundance Head (11); Chris Blue (12); Chloe Kohanski (13); Brynn Cartelli (14); Chevel Shepherd (15); Maelyn Jarmon (16); Jake Hoot (17); Todd Tilghman (18).

Average U.S. Television Viewing Time, 2019-20

Source: Nielsen Media Research; viewing time given in hours:minutes

Group	Age	Total per week	M-F 7-10 AM	M-F 10 AM-4 PM	M-Sun. 8-11 PM	M-F 11:30 PM-1 AM	Sat. 7 AM-1 PM	Sun. 1-7 PM
Men	18+	28:30	1:47	4:12	6:28	1:15	0:54	1:36
	18-24	8:19	0:22	1:08	1:57	0:26	0:13	0:32
	25-54	20:54	1:09	2:40	4:56	1:03	0:39	1:15
	55+	45:46	3:07	7:22	10:05	1:48	1:27	2:26
Women	18+	32:57	2:11	5:26	7:15	1:27	0:59	1:35
	18-24	9:33	0:25	1:29	2:14	0:29	0:14	0:29
	25-54	24:37	1:33	3:42	5:33	1:12	0:45	1:14
	55+	49:42	3:28	8:40	10:45	2:02	1:30	2:19
Children	2-11	12:25	0:49	2:10	2:29	0:24	0:32	0:43
Teens	12-17	8:00	0:21	1:01	1:55	0:22	0:15	0:29
All viewers[1]		26:37	1:43	4:11	5:55	1:09	0:50	1:23

Note: For viewing period Sept. 23, 2019-May 31, 2020. Includes DVR playback. (1) Ages 2+.

Highest-Rated Prime-Time Television Programs, 2019-20

Source: Nielsen Media Research

Data are for regularly scheduled network programs Sept. 23, 2019-May 31, 2020 (unless otherwise noted). Ranked by average audience percentages, or ratings, which are estimates of the percentage of all TV-owning households watching a particular program live or on DVR within seven days of broadcast. Audience share percentages are estimates of the percentage of those watching TV at a certain time that are tuned in to a particular program.

Rank	Program, network	Avg. audience	Audience share	Rank	Program, network	Avg. audience	Audience share
1.	NCIS, CBS	9.5%	18.1%	27.	Survivor[3], CBS	5.4%	10.6%
2.	FBI, CBS	7.9	15.2	28.	America's Got Talent:		
3.	Blue Bloods, CBS	7.6	16.7		The Champions[4], NBC	5.3	10.2
4.	This Is Us, NBC	7.5	14.5	29.	Dancing With the Stars[5], ABC	5.2	9.6
5.	Chicago Fire, NBC	7.4	14.3	30.	Criminal Minds, CBS	5.2	10.6
6.	Chicago Med, NBC	7.2	13.8	31.	The Rookie, ABC	5.1	11.0
7.	Chicago P.D., NBC	7.2	15.5	32.	All Rise, CBS	5.0	9.5
8.	Young Sheldon, CBS	7.0	13.9	33.	The Bachelor[6], ABC	5.0	9.7
9.	The Good Doctor, ABC	7.0	15.0	34.	Tommy, CBS	5.0	11.0
10.	America's Got Talent[1]-Tuesday, NBC	7.0	14.7	35.	American Idol[7]-Monday, ABC	5.0	9.3
11.	Bull, CBS	6.8	14.4	36.	A Million Little Things, ABC	5.0	10.4
12.	60 Minutes, CBS	6.5	12.8	37.	The Conners, ABC	5.0	9.7
13.	FBI: Most Wanted, CBS	6.5	14.0	38.	Seal Team, CBS	4.9	9.7
14.	New Amsterdam, NBC	6.4	13.8	39.	Manifest, NBC	4.9	10.6
15.	911, FOX	6.4	11.9	40.	American Idol[7], ABC	4.9	9.6
16.	The Voice[2], NBC	6.2	11.8	41.	Bob Hearts Abishola, CBS	4.8	9.0
17.	Grey's Anatomy, ABC	6.2	12.2	42.	The Neighborhood, CBS	4.8	9.2
18.	NCIS: New Orleans, CBS	6.1	13.2	43.	God Friended Me, CBS	4.8	9.1
19.	The Masked Singer[3], FOX	6.0	11.9	44.	MacGyver, CBS	4.7	9.7
20.	Hawaii Five-0, CBS	6.0	12.6	45.	S.W.A.T., CBS	4.6	10.1
21.	The Voice[2]-Tuesday, NBC	5.9	11.6	46.	The Unicorn, CBS	4.5	8.7
22.	NCIS: Los Angeles, CBS	5.6	11.0	47.	Madam Secretary, CBS	4.4	10.4
23.	911: Lone Star, FOX	5.6	10.8	48.	Modern Family, ABC	4.4	8.4
24.	Magnum, P.I., CBS	5.5	11.5	49.	The Resident, FOX	4.4	8.3
25.	Station 19, ABC	5.5	10.9	50.	Man With a Plan, CBS	4.3	8.6
26.	Mom, CBS	5.5	10.6				

(1) May 26, 2020-Sept. 23, 2020. (2) Sept. 23-Dec. 17, 2019. (3) Sept. 25-Dec. 18, 2019. (4) Jan. 6-Feb. 17, 2020. (5) Sept. 16-Nov. 25, 2019. (6) Jan. 6-Mar. 10, 2020. (7) Feb. 16-May 17, 2020.

Highest-Rated Syndicated Programs, 2019-20

Source: Nielsen Media Research

Average audience percentages, or ratings, are estimates of the percentage of all TV-owning households watching a program live or on DVR within seven days of broadcast, Sept. 18, 2019-Aug. 18, 2020.

Rank	Program	Avg. audience	Rank	Program	Avg. audience
1.	Judge Judy	6.5%	14.	Hot Bench	2.1%
2.	Jeopardy	6.2	15.	Family Feud (weekend)	2.1
3.	Family Feud	6.1	16.	Live With Kelly and Ryan	2.0
4.	Wheel of Fortune	5.8	17.	Modern Family (weekend)	1.8
5.	Litton's Weekend Adventure	4.4	18.	Jeopardy (weekend)	1.8
6.	Dateline Weekly	3.5	19.	The Ellen DeGeneres Show	1.7
7.	Christopher Kimball's Milk Street	3.2	20.	The Big Bang Theory (weekend)	1.6
8.	The Big Bang Theory	3.1	21.	Access Hollywood (weekend)	1.6
9.	Inside Edition	2.7	22.	Relationship Court	1.5
10.	Entertainment Tonight	2.7	23.	Modern Family	1.5
11.	Wheel of Fortune (weekend)	2.3	24.	Law & Order: Special Victims Unit (weekend)	1.5
12.	Dr. Phil Show	2.3	25.	America's Test Kitchen	1.5
13.	Last Man Standing	2.1			

Highest-Rated Basic Cable Programs, 2019-20

Source: Nielsen Media Research

Data are for regularly scheduled basic cable programs Sept. 18, 2019-Aug. 18, 2020; excludes children's series, miniseries, movies, and news events. Average audience percentages, or ratings, are estimates of the percentage of all TV-owning households watching a program live or on DVR within seven days of broadcast.

Rank	Program, channel	Avg. audience	Rank	Program, channel	Avg. audience
1.	Yellowstone, Paramount	2.1%	16.	Rick and Morty, Adult Swim	1.1%
2.	The Walking Dead, AMC	1.7	17.	90 Day Fiancé, TLC	1.1
3.	The Curse of Oak Island, History	1.5	18.	The Rachel Maddow Show, MSNBC	1.0
4.	90 Day Fiancé: Before the 90 Days, TLC	1.4	19.	Special Report With Bret Baier, Fox News Channel	1.0
5.	Hannity, Fox News Channel	1.3	20.	My Feet Are Killing Me, TLC	1.0
6.	90 Day Fiancé: Happily Ever After?, TLC	1.3	21.	Good Witch, Hallmark	1.0
7.	Tucker Carlson Tonight, Fox News Channel	1.3	22.	Sister Wives, TLC	0.9
8.	90 Day Fiancé: The Other Way, TLC	1.3	23.	Better Call Saul, AMC	0.9
9.	Dr. Pimple Popper, TLC	1.2	24.	The Real Housewives of Atlanta, Bravo	0.9
10.	The Five, Fox News Channel	1.1	25.	Below Deck Mediterranean, Bravo	0.9
11.	The Ingraham Angle, Fox News Channel	1.1	26.	The Greg Gutfeld Show, Fox News Channel	0.9
12.	When Calls the Heart, Hallmark	1.1	27.	Gold Rush: Parker's Trail, Discovery	0.9
13.	American Horror Story, FX	1.1	28.	The Secret of Skinwalker Ranch, History	0.9
14.	Celebrity IOU, HGTV	1.1	29.	Mayans M.C., FX	0.9
15.	Gold Rush, Discovery	1.1	30.	Below Deck, Bravo	0.9

Highest-Rated Premium Cable Programs, 2019-20

Source: Nielsen Media Research

Average audience percentages, or ratings, are estimates of the percentage of all TV-owning households watching a program live or on DVR within seven days of broadcast, Sept. 18, 2019-Aug. 18, 2020.

Highest-Rated Series

Rank	Program, channel	Avg. audience
1.	Real Time With Bill Maher, HBO	1.3%
2.	Last Week Tonight With John Oliver, HBO	1.2
3.	Power, Starz	1.1
4.	Shameless, Showtime	1.1
5.	Perry Mason, HBO	1.1
6.	Ray Donovan, Showtime	1.0
7.	The Outsider, HBO	1.0
8.	Homeland, Showtime	1.0
9.	Westworld, HBO	0.9
10.	Watchmen, HBO	0.9
11.	Curb Your Enthusiasm, HBO	0.8
12.	Outlander, Starz	0.8
13.	Billions, Showtime	0.8
14.	Ballers, HBO	0.8
15.	Succession, HBO	0.7

Highest-Rated Movies

Rank	Program, channel	Avg. audience
1.	Joker, HBO	1.0%
2.	Fast & Furious Presents: Hobbs & Shaw, HBO	0.9
3.	John Wick: Chapter 3 - Parabellum, HBO	0.9
4.	Ford v Ferrari, HBO	0.9
5.	X-Men: Dark Phoenix, HBO	0.9
6.	Bad Education, HBO	0.8
7.	Midway, HBO	0.8
8.	Shazam!, HBO	0.7
9.	Godzilla: King of the Monsters, HBO	0.7
10.	Ad Astra, HBO	0.7
11.	Doctor Sleep, HBO	0.7
12.	Alita: Battle Angel, HBO	0.7
13.	Glass, HBO	0.7
14.	The Kitchen, HBO	0.6
15.	Anna, HBO	0.6

All-Time Most Watched Television Programs

Source: Nielsen Media Research, Jan. 1961-Aug. 2020

Estimates exclude unsponsored or joint network telecasts (e.g., presidential addresses) and programs under 30 minutes long. Ranked by number of TV-owning households tuned in to the program (avg. audience). (Rating is percentage of all TV-owning households tuned in.)

Rank	Program	Telecast date	Network	Rating	Avg. audience (thous.)
1.	Super Bowl XLIX	2/1/2015	NBC	48.1%	55,948
2.	Super Bowl 50	2/7/2016	CBS	47.1	54,775
3.	Super Bowl XLVIII	2/2/2014	FOX	47.1	54,585
4.	Super Bowl LI	2/5/2017	FOX	45.8	54,180
5.	Super Bowl XLVI	2/5/2012	NBC	47.0	53,910
6.	Super Bowl XLV	2/6/2011	FOX	46.1	53,435
7.	Super Bowl XLVII	2/3/2013	CBS	46.7	53,363
8.	Super Bowl LII	2/4/2018	NBC	43.5	52,017
9.	Super Bowl XLIV	2/7/2010	CBS	45.2	51,873
10.	Super Bowl XLVII Delay	2/3/2013	CBS	44.5	50,861
11.	Super Bowl LIV	2/2/2020	FOX	42.1	50,726
12.	M*A*S*H (last episode)	2/28/1983	CBS	60.2	50,150
13.	Super Bowl LIII	2/3/2019	CBS	41.4	49,595
14.	Super Bowl XLII	2/3/2008	FOX	43.2	48,721
15.	Super Bowl XLIII	2/1/2009	NBC	42.0	48,139
16.	Super Bowl XLI	2/4/2007	CBS	42.7	47,535
17.	Super Bowl XL	2/5/2006	ABC	41.6	45,869
18.	XVII Winter Olympics (Women's figure skating)	2/23/1994	CBS	48.5	45,690
19.	Super Bowl XXXIX	2/6/2005	FOX	41.1	45,080
20.	Super Bowl XXXVIII	2/1/2004	CBS	41.4	44,910
21.	Super Bowl XXX	1/28/1996	NBC	46.0	44,150
22.	Super Bowl XXXII	1/25/1998	NBC	44.5	43,630
23.	Super Bowl XXXIV	1/30/2000	ABC	43.3	43,620
24.	Super Bowl XXXVII	1/26/2003	ABC	40.7	43,430
25.	Super Bowl XXVIII	1/30/1994	NBC	45.5	42,860
26.	Super Bowl XXXVI	2/3/2002	FOX	40.4	42,660
27.	Cheers (last episode)	5/20/1993	NBC	45.5	42,360
28.	Super Bowl XXXI	1/26/1997	FOX	43.3	42,000
29.	Super Bowl XXVII	1/31/1993	NBC	45.1	41,990
30.	XVII Winter Olympics (Women's figure skating)	2/25/1994	CBS	44.1	41,540
31.	Super Bowl XX	1/26/1986	NBC	48.3	41,490
32.	Dallas ("Who Shot J.R.?" episode)	11/21/1980	CBS	53.3	41,470

Highest-Rated Television Programs by Season, 1950-2020

Source: Nielsen Media Research; regular series programs (excl. sports), Sept.-May season

Rating is percentage of all TV-owning households tuned in to the program. Data prior to 1988-89 exclude Alaska and Hawaii.

Season	Program	Rating	TV-owning households (thous.)	Season	Program	Rating	TV-owning households (thous.)
1950-51	Texaco Star Theatre	61.6%	10,320	1985-86	The Cosby Show	33.8	85,900
1951-52	Godfrey's Talent Scouts	53.8	15,300	1986-87	The Cosby Show	34.9%	87,400
1952-53	I Love Lucy	67.3	20,400	1987-88	The Cosby Show	27.8	88,600
1953-54	I Love Lucy	58.8	26,000	1988-89	Roseanne	25.5	90,400
1954-55	I Love Lucy	49.3	30,700	1989-90	Roseanne	23.4	92,100
1955-56	$64,000 Question	47.5	34,900	1990-91	Cheers	21.6	93,100
1956-57	I Love Lucy	43.7	38,900	1991-92	60 Minutes	21.7	92,100
1957-58	Gunsmoke	43.1	41,920	1992-93	60 Minutes	21.6	93,100
1958-59	Gunsmoke	39.6	43,950	1993-94	Home Improvement	21.9	94,200
1959-60	Gunsmoke	40.3	45,750	1994-95	Seinfeld	20.5	95,400
1960-61	Gunsmoke	37.3	47,200	1995-96	E.R.	22.0	95,900
1961-62	Wagon Train	32.1	48,555	1996-97	E.R.	21.2	97,000
1962-63	Beverly Hillbillies	36.0	50,300	1997-98	Seinfeld	22.0	98,000
1963-64	Beverly Hillbillies	39.1	51,600	1998-99	E.R.	17.8	99,400
1964-65	Bonanza	36.3	52,700	1999-2000	Who Wants to Be a Millionaire	18.6	100,800
1965-66	Bonanza	31.8	53,850	2000-01	Survivor II	17.4	102,200
1966-67	Bonanza	29.1	55,130	2001-02	Friends	15.3	105,500
1967-68	The Andy Griffith Show	27.6	56,670	2002-03	CSI	16.3	106,700
1968-69	Rowan & Martin's Laugh-In	31.8	58,250	2003-04	CSI	15.9	108,400
1969-70	Rowan & Martin's Laugh-In	26.3	58,500	2004-05	CSI	16.5	106,900
1970-71	Marcus Welby, M.D.	29.6	60,100	2005-06	American Idol-Tuesday	17.6	110,200
1971-72	All in the Family	34.0	62,100	2006-07	American Idol-Tuesday	17.3	112,800
1972-73	All in the Family	33.3	64,800	2007-08	American Idol-Tuesday	15.5	113,050
1973-74	All in the Family	31.2	66,200	2008-09	American Idol-Wednesday	14.4	114,900
1974-75	All in the Family	30.2	68,500	2009-10	American Idol-Tuesday	13.7	114,900
1975-76	All in the Family	30.1	69,600	2010-11	American Idol-Wednesday	14.5	115,900
1976-77	Happy Days	31.5	71,200	2011-12	NCIS	12.3	114,700
1977-78	Laverne & Shirley	31.6	72,900	2012-13	NCIS	13.5	114,200
1978-79	Laverne & Shirley	30.5	74,500	2013-14	NCIS	12.6	115,800
1979-80	60 Minutes	28.2	76,300	2014-15	The Big Bang Theory	11.6	116,400
1980-81	Dallas	31.2	79,900	2015-16	NCIS	12.8	116,400
1981-82	Dallas	28.4	81,500	2016-17	The Big Bang Theory	11.5	118,400
1982-83	60 Minutes	25.5	83,300	2017-18	The Big Bang Theory	11.3	119,600
1983-84	Dallas	25.7	83,800	2018-19	The Big Bang Theory	10.9	119,900
1984-85	Dynasty	25.0	84,900	2019-20	NCIS	9.5	120,600

All-Time Highest-Rated Television Programs

Source: Nielsen Media Research, Jan. 1961-Aug. 2020

Estimates exclude unsponsored or joint network telecasts (e.g., presidential addresses) and programs under 30 minutes long. Ranked by rating (percentage of all TV-owning households tuned in to the program). Average audience is number of TV-owning households tuned in.

Rank	Program	Telecast date	Network	Rating	Avg. audience (thous.)
1.	M*A*S*H (last episode)	2/28/1983	CBS	60.2%	50,150
2.	Dallas ("Who Shot J.R.?" episode)	11/21/1980	CBS	53.3	41,470
3.	Roots-Pt. 8	1/30/1977	ABC	51.1	36,380
4.	Super Bowl XVI	1/24/1982	CBS	49.1	40,020
5.	Super Bowl XVII	1/30/1983	NBC	48.6	40,480
6.	XVII Winter Olympics (Women's figure skating)	2/23/1994	CBS	48.5	45,690
7.	Super Bowl XX	1/26/1986	NBC	48.3	41,490
8.	Super Bowl XLIX	2/1/2015	NBC	48.1	55,948
9.	Gone With the Wind-Pt. 1	11/7/1976	NBC	47.7	33,960
10.	Gone With the Wind-Pt. 2	11/8/1976	NBC	47.4	33,750
11.	Super Bowl XII	1/15/1978	CBS	47.2	34,410
12.	Super Bowl XLVIII	2/2/2014	FOX	47.1	54,585
12.	Super Bowl XIII	1/21/1979	NBC	47.1	35,090
12.	Super Bowl 50	2/7/2016	CBS	47.1	54,775
15.	Super Bowl XLVI	2/5/2012	NBC	47.0	53,910
16.	Super Bowl XLVII	2/3/2013	CBS	46.7	53,363
17.	Bob Hope Christmas Show	1/15/1970	NBC	46.6	27,260
18.	Super Bowl XVIII	1/22/1984	CBS	46.4	38,880
18.	Super Bowl XIX	1/20/1985	ABC	46.4	39,390
20.	Super Bowl XIV	1/20/1980	CBS	46.3	35,330
21.	Super Bowl XLV	2/6/2011	FOX	46.1	53,435
22.	Super Bowl XXX	1/28/1996	NBC	46.0	44,150
22.	ABC Sunday Night Movie (The Day After)	11/20/1983	ABC	46.0	38,550
24.	Roots-Pt. 6	1/28/1977	ABC	45.9	32,680
24.	The Fugitive (last episode)	8/29/1967	ABC	45.9	25,700
26.	Super Bowl LI	2/5/2017	FOX	45.8	54,180
26.	Super Bowl XXI	1/25/1987	CBS	45.8	40,030
28.	Roots-Pt. 5	1/27/1977	ABC	45.7	32,540
29.	Super Bowl XXVIII	1/30/1994	NBC	45.5	42,860
30.	Cheers (last episode)	5/20/1993	NBC	45.5	42,360
31.	The Ed Sullivan Show (first live U.S. TV appearance of The Beatles)	2/9/1964	CBS	45.3	23,240

AWARDS — MEDALS — PRIZES

Alfred B. Nobel Prizes, 1901-2020

Alfred B. Nobel (1833-96) bequeathed $9 mil, the interest on which was to be distributed yearly to those judged to have most benefited humankind in chemistry, literature, promotion of peace, physics, and physiology or medicine. Prizes were first awarded in 1901. The prize in economics, funded by Sweden's central bank, was first awarded in 1969. Each prize is now worth 9 mil Swedish kronor (about $1.0 mil). If year is omitted, no award was given. The Royal Swedish Academy selects prize winners for chemistry, economics, and physics; the Nobel Assembly at Karolinska Institutet, physiology or medicine; the Swedish Academy, literature; and the Norwegian Nobel Committee, the peace prize. Winners sharing a prize are generally listed in alphabetical order, except when the awarding body has given a larger proportion of a shared prize to one or more recipients.

Physics

1901 Wilhelm C. Röntgen, Ger.
1902 Hendrik A. Lorentz,
Pieter Zeeman, Neth.
1903 Antoine Henri Becquerel, Pierre
Curie, Fr.; Marie Curie, Pol.-Fr.
1904 Lord Rayleigh (John W. Strutt), UK
1905 Philipp E. A. von Lenard, Ger.
1906 Joseph J. Thomson, UK
1907 Albert A. Michelson, U.S.
1908 Gabriel Lippmann, Fr.
1909 Carl F. Braun, Ger.;
Guglielmo Marconi, Ital.
1910 Johannes D. van der Waals, Neth.
1911 Wilhelm Wien, Ger.
1912 Nils G. Dalén, Swed.
1913 Heike Kamerlingh Onnes, Neth.
1914 Max von Laue, Ger.
1915 William H. Bragg,
William L. Bragg, UK
1917 Charles G. Barkla, UK
1918 Max K. E. L. Planck, Ger.
1919 Johannes Stark, Ger.
1920 Charles E. Guillaume, Fr.-Switz.
1921 Albert Einstein, Ger.-U.S.
1922 Niels Bohr, Den.
1923 Robert A. Millikan, U.S.
1924 Karl M. G. Siegbahn, Swed.
1925 James Franck, Gustav Hertz, Ger.
1926 Jean B. Perrin, Fr.
1927 Arthur H. Compton, U.S.;
Charles T. R. Wilson, UK
1928 Owen W. Richardson, UK
1929 Prince Louis-Victor de Broglie, Fr.
1930 Chandrasekhara V. Raman, India
1932 Werner Heisenberg, Ger.
1933 Paul A. M. Dirac, UK;
Erwin Schrödinger, Austria
1935 James Chadwick, UK
1936 Carl D. Anderson, U.S.;
Victor F. Hess, Austria
1937 Clinton J. Davisson, U.S.;
George P. Thomson, UK
1938 Enrico Fermi, Ital.-U.S.
1939 Ernest O. Lawrence, U.S.
1943 Otto Stern, U.S.
1944 Isidor Isaac Rabi, U.S.
1945 Wolfgang Pauli, U.S.-Austria
1946 Percy W. Bridgman, U.S.
1947 Edward V. Appleton, UK
1948 Patrick M. S. Blackett, UK
1949 Hideki Yukawa, Jpn.
1950 Cecil F. Powell, UK
1951 John D. Cockcroft, UK;
Ernest T. S. Walton, Ire.
1952 Felix Bloch, Edward M. Purcell, U.S.
1953 Frits Zernike, Neth.
1954 Max Born, UK; Walter Bothe, Ger.
1955 Polykarp Kusch,
Willis E. Lamb, U.S.
1956 John Bardeen, Walter H. Brattain,
William Shockley, U.S.
1957 Tsung-Dao Lee, Chen Ning Yang,
U.S.-China

1958 Pavel Cherenkov, Il'ja Frank,
Igor Y. Tamm, USSR
1959 Owen Chamberlain,
Emilio G. Segre, U.S.
1960 Donald A. Glaser, U.S.
1961 Robert Hofstadter, U.S.;
Rudolf L. Mossbauer, Ger.
1962 Lev D. Landau, USSR
1963 Maria Goeppert-Mayer,
Eugene P. Wigner, U.S.;
J. Hans D. Jensen, Ger.
1964 Nicolay G. Basov,
Aleksandr M. Prokhorov, USSR;
Charles H. Townes, U.S.
1965 Sin-Itiro Tomonaga, Jpn.;
Julian S. Schwinger,
Richard P. Feynman, U.S.
1966 Alfred Kastler, Fr.
1967 Hans A. Bethe, U.S.
1968 Luis W. Alvarez, U.S.
1969 Murray Gell-Mann, U.S.
1970 Hannes Alfvén, Swed.;
Louis Néel, Fr.
1971 Dennis Gabor, UK
1972 John Bardeen, Leon N. Cooper,
John R. Schrieffer, U.S.
1973 Brian D. Josephson, UK;
Leo Esaki, Jpn.; Ivar Giaever, U.S.
1974 Antony Hewish, Martin Ryle, UK
1975 Aage Bohr, Den.;
Ben Mottelson, U.S.-Den.;
Leo James Rainwater, U.S.
1976 Burton Richter,
Samuel C. C. Ting, U.S.
1977 Philip W. Anderson,
John H. van Vleck, U.S.;
Nevill F. Mott, UK
1978 Pyotr Kapitsa, USSR; Arno Penzias,
Robert Wilson, U.S.
1979 Sheldon L. Glashow,
Steven Weinberg, U.S.;
Abdus Salam, Pakistan
1980 James W. Cronin, Val L. Fitch, U.S.
1981 Nicolaas Bloembergen,
Arthur Schawlow, U.S.;
Kai M. Siegbahn, Swed.
1982 Kenneth G. Wilson, U.S.
1983 Subramanyan Chandrasekhar,
William A. Fowler, U.S.
1984 Carlo Rubbia, Ital.;
Simon van der Meer, Neth.
1985 Klaus von Klitzing, Ger.
1986 Ernest Ruska, Gerd Binnig, Ger.;
Heinrich Rohrer, Switz.
1987 J. Georg Bednorz, Ger.;
K. Alex Müller, Switz.
1988 Leon M. Lederman, Melvin
Schwartz, Jack Steinberger, U.S.
1989 Norman F. Ramsey, U.S.;
Hans G. Dehmelt, Ger.-U.S.;
Wolfgang Paul, Ger.
1990 Jerome I. Friedman, Henry W.
Kendall, U.S.; Richard E. Taylor, Can.

1991 Pierre-Gilles de Gennes, Fr.
1992 Georges Charpak, Pol.-Fr.
1993 Russell A. Hulse,
Joseph H. Taylor, U.S.
1994 Bertram N. Brockhouse, Can.;
Clifford G. Shull, U.S.
1995 Martin Perl, Frederick Reines, U.S.
1996 David M. Lee, Douglas D. Osheroff,
Robert C. Richardson, U.S.
1997 Steven Chu, William D. Phillips, U.S.;
Claude Cohen-Tannoudji, Fr.
1998 Robert B. Laughlin, U.S.;
Horst L. Störmer, Ger.-U.S;
Daniel C. Tsui, China-U.S.
1999 Gerardus 't Hooft,
Martinus J. G. Veltman, Neth.
2000 Jack S. Kilby, U.S.;
Herbert Kroemer, Ger.-U.S.;
Zhores I. Alferov, Russ.
2001 Eric A. Cornell, Carl E. Wieman,
U.S.; Wolfgang Ketterle, Ger.
2002 Raymond Davis Jr.,
Riccardo Giacconi, U.S.;
Masatoshi Koshiba, Jpn.
2003 Alexei A. Abrikosov,
Vitaly L. Ginzburg, Russ.;
Anthony J. Leggett, UK
2004 David J. Gross, H. David Politzer,
Frank Wilczek, U.S.
2005 Roy J. Glauber, John L. Hall, U.S.;
Theodor W. Hänsch, Ger.
2006 John C. Mather,
George F. Smoot, U.S.
2007 Albert Fert, Fr.; Peter Grünberg, Ger.
2008 Yoichiro Nambu, U.S.;
Makoto Kobayashi,
Toshihide Maskawa, Jpn.
2009 Charles K. Kao, U.S.-UK;
Willard S. Boyle, U.S.-Can.;
George E. Smith, U.S.
2010 Andre Geim, Russ.-Neth.;
Konstantin Novoselov, Russ.-UK
2011 Saul Perlmutter, Adam G. Riess,
U.S.; Brian P. Schmidt, Austral.-U.S.
2012 Serge Haroche, Fr.;
David J. Wineland, U.S.
2013 François Englert, Belg.;
Peter W. Higgs, UK
2014 Isamu Akasaki, Hiroshi Amano, Jpn.;
Shuji Nakamura, Jpn.-U.S.
2015 Takaaki Kajita, Jpn.;
Arthur B. McDonald, Can.
2016 David J. Thouless, UK-U.S.;
F. Duncan M. Haldane,
J. Michael Kosterlitz, UK-U.S.
2017 Rainer Weiss, Ger.-U.S.; Barry C.
Barish, Kip S. Thorne, U.S.
2018 Arthur Ashkin, U.S.; Gérard
Mourou, Fr.; Donna Strickland, Can.
2019 James Peebles, Can.-U.S.;
Michel Mayor, Didier Queloz, Switz.
2020 Roger Penrose, UK;
Reinhard Genzel, Ger.;
Andrea Ghez, U.S.

Chemistry

1901	Jacobus H. van 't Hoff, Neth.
1902	Emil Fischer, Ger.
1903	Svante A. Arrhenius, Swed.
1904	William Ramsay, UK
1905	Adolf von Baeyer, Ger.
1906	Henri Moissan, Fr.
1907	Eduard Buchner, Ger.
1908	Ernest Rutherford, UK
1909	Wilhelm Ostwald, Ger.
1910	Otto Wallach, Ger.
1911	Marie Curie, Pol.-Fr.
1912	Victor Grignard, Paul Sabatier, Fr.
1913	Alfred Werner, Switz.
1914	Theodore W. Richards, U.S.
1915	Richard M. Willstätter, Ger.
1918	Fritz Haber, Ger.
1920	Walther H. Nernst, Ger.
1921	Frederick Soddy, UK
1922	Francis W. Aston, UK
1923	Fritz Pregl, Austria
1925	Richard A. Zsigmondy, Ger.
1926	Theodor Svedberg, Swed.
1927	Heinrich O. Wieland, Ger.
1928	Adolf O. R. Windaus, Ger.
1929	Arthur Harden, UK; Hans von Euler-Chelpin, Swed.
1930	Hans Fischer, Ger.
1931	Friedrich Bergius, Carl Bosch, Ger.
1932	Irving Langmuir, U.S.
1934	Harold C. Urey, U.S.
1935	Frédéric Joliot, Irène Joliot-Curie, Fr.
1936	Peter J. W. Debye, Neth.
1937	Walter N. Haworth, UK; Paul Karrer, Switz.
1938	Richard Kuhn, Ger.
1939	Adolf F. J. Butenandt, Ger.; Leopold Ruzicka, Switz.
1943	George de Hevesy, Hung.
1944	Otto Hahn, Ger.
1945	Artturi I. Virtanen, Fin.
1946	James B. Sumner, John H. Northrop, Wendell M. Stanley, U.S.
1947	Robert Robinson, UK
1948	Arne W. K. Tiselius, Swed.
1949	William F. Giauque, U.S.
1950	Kurt Alder, Otto P. H. Diels, Ger.
1951	Edwin M. McMillan, Glenn T. Seaborg, U.S.
1952	Archer J. P. Martin, Richard L. M. Synge, UK
1953	Hermann Staudinger, Ger.
1954	Linus C. Pauling, U.S.
1955	Vincent du Vigneaud, U.S.
1956	Cyril N. Hinshelwood, U.K.; Nikolay N. Semenov, USSR
1957	Lord (Alexander R.) Todd, UK
1958	Frederick Sanger, UK
1959	Jaroslav Heyrovsky, Czech.
1960	Willard F. Libby, U.S.
1961	Melvin Calvin, U.S.
1962	John C. Kendrew, Max F. Perutz, UK
1963	Giulio Natta, Ital.; Karl Ziegler, Ger.
1964	Dorothy C. Hodgkin, UK
1965	Robert B. Woodward, U.S.
1966	Robert S. Mulliken, U.S.
1967	Manfred Eigen, Ger.; Ronald G. W. Norrish, George Porter, UK
1968	Lars Onsanger, U.S.
1969	Derek H. R. Barton, UK; Odd Hassel, Nor.
1970	Luis F. Leloir, Arg.
1971	Gerhard Herzberg, Can.
1972	Christian B. Anfinsen, Stanford Moore, William H. Stein, U.S.
1973	Ernst Otto Fischer, Ger.; Geoffrey Wilkinson, UK
1974	Paul J. Flory, U.S.
1975	John Cornforth, Austral.-UK; Vladimir Prelog, Bosnia-Switz.
1976	William N. Lipscomb, U.S.
1977	Ilya Prigogine, Belg.
1978	Peter Mitchell, UK
1979	Herbert C. Brown, U.S.; Georg Wittig, Ger.
1980	Paul Berg, Walter Gilbert, U.S.; Frederick Sanger, UK
1981	Kenichi Fukui, Jpn.; Roald Hoffmann, U.S.
1982	Aaron Klug, UK-Lith.
1983	Henry Taube, Can.
1984	Robert Bruce Merrifield, U.S.
1985	Herbert A. Hauptman, Jerome Karle, U.S.
1986	Dudley Herschbach, Yuan T. Lee, U.S.; John C. Polanyi, Can.
1987	Donald J. Cram, Charles J. Pedersen, U.S.; Jean-Marie Lehn, Fr.
1988	Johann Deisenhofer, Robert Huber, Hartmut Michel, Ger.
1989	Sidney Altman, Thomas R. Cech, U.S.
1990	Elias James Corey, U.S.
1991	Richard R. Ernst, Switz.
1992	Rudolph A. Marcus, Can.-U.S.
1993	Kary B. Mullis, U.S.; Michael Smith, UK-Can.
1994	George A. Olah, U.S.
1995	Paul Crutzen, Neth.; Mario Molina, Mex.-U.S.; Sherwood Rowland, U.S.
1996	Robert F. Curl Jr., Richard E. Smalley, U.S.; Harold W. Kroto, UK
1997	Paul D. Boyer, U.S.; John E. Walker, UK; Jens C. Skou, Den.
1998	Walter Kohn, U.S.; John A. Pople, UK
1999	Ahmed H. Zewail, U.S.
2000	Alan J. Heeger, U.S.; Alan G. MacDiarmid, N.Z.-U.S.; Hideki Shirakawa, Jpn.
2001	K. Barry Sharpless, William S. Knowles, U.S.; Ryoji Noyori, Jpn.
2002	John B. Fenn, U.S.; Koichi Tanaka, Jpn.; Kurt Wüthrich, Switz.
2003	Peter Agre, Roderick MacKinnon, U.S.
2004	Aaron Ciechanover, Avram Hershko, Isr.; Irwin Rose, U.S.
2005	Yves Chauvin, Fr.; Robert H. Grubbs, Richard R. Schrock, U.S.
2006	Roger D. Kornberg, U.S.
2007	Gerhard Ertl, Ger.
2008	Martin Chalfie, Osamu Shimomura, Roger Y. Tsien, U.S.
2009	Venkatraman Ramakrishnan, UK; Thomas A. Steitz, U.S.; Ada E. Yonath, Isr.
2010	Richard F. Heck, U.S.; Ei-ichi Negishi, Jpn.-U.S.; Akira Suzuki, Jpn.
2011	Dan Shechtman, Isr.
2012	Brian K. Kobilka, Robert J. Lefkowitz, U.S.
2013	Martin Karplus, Austria-U.S.; Michael Levitt, S. Afr.-U.S.; Arieh Warshel, Isr.-U.S.
2014	Eric Betzig, William E. Moerner, U.S.; Stefan W. Hell, Ger.
2015	Tomas Lindahl, Swed.-UK; Paul Modrich, U.S.; Aziz Sancar, Turk.-U.S.
2016	Bernard L. Feringa, Neth.; Jean-Pierre Sauvage, France; J. Fraser Stoddart, UK-U.S.
2017	Jacques Dubochet, Switz.; Joachim Frank, Ger.-U.S.; Richard Henderson, UK
2018	Frances H. Arnold, George P. Smith, U.S.; Gregory P. Winter, UK
2019	John B. Goodenough, Ger.-U.S.; M. Stanley Whittingham, UK-U.S.; Akira Yoshino, Jpn.
2020	Emmanuelle Charpentier, France; Jennifer Doudna, U.S.

Physiology or Medicine

1901	Emil A. von Behring, Ger.
1902	Ronald Ross, UK
1903	Niels R. Finsen, Den.
1904	Ivan P. Pavlov, Russ.
1905	Robert Koch, Ger.
1906	Camillo Golgi, Ital.; Santiago Ramón y Cajal, Spain
1907	Charles L. A. Laveran, Fr.
1908	Paul Ehrlich, Ger.; Ilya Mechnikov, Fr.
1909	Emil T. Kocher, Switz.
1910	Albrecht Kossel, Ger.
1911	Allvar Gullstrand, Swed.
1912	Alexis Carrel, Fr.
1913	Charles R. Richet, Fr.
1914	Robert Bárány, Austria
1919	Jules Bordet, Belg.
1920	Schack A. S. Krogh, Den.
1922	Archibald V. Hill, UK; Otto F. Meyerhof, Ger.
1923	Frederick G. Banting, Can.; John J. R. Macleod, UK
1924	Willem Einthoven, Neth.
1926	Johannes A. G. Fibiger, Den.
1927	Julius Wagner-Jauregg, Austria
1928	Charles J. H. Nicolle, Fr.
1929	Christiaan Eijkman, Neth.; Frederick G. Hopkins, UK
1930	Karl Landsteiner, U.S.
1931	Otto H. Warburg, Ger.
1932	Edgar D. Adrian, Charles S. Sherrington, UK
1933	Thomas H. Morgan, U.S.
1934	George R. Minot, William P. Murphy, G. H. Whipple, U.S.
1935	Hans Spemann, Ger.
1936	Henry H. Dale, UK; Otto Loewi, U.S.
1937	Albert Szent-Gyorgyi, Hung.-U.S.
1938	Corneille J. F. Heymans, Belg.
1939	Gerhard Domagk, Ger.
1943	Henrik C. P. Dam, Den.; Edward A. Doisy, U.S.
1944	Joseph Erlanger, Herbert S. Gasser, U.S.
1945	Ernst B. Chain, Alexander Fleming, Howard W. Florey, UK
1946	Hermann J. Muller, U.S.
1947	Carl F. Cori, Gerty T. Cori, U.S.; Bernardo A. Houssay, Arg.
1948	Paul H. Müller, Switz.
1949	Walter R. Hess, Switz.; Antonio Egas Moniz, Port.
1950	Philip S. Hench, Edward C. Kendall, U.S.; Tadeus Reichstein, Switz.
1951	Max Theiler, U.S.
1952	Selman A. Waksman, U.S.
1953	Hans A. Krebs, UK; Fritz A. Lipmann, U.S.
1954	John F. Enders, Frederick C. Robbins, Thomas H. Weller, U.S.
1955	Alex H. T. Theorell, Swed.
1956	André F. Cournand, Dickinson W. Richards, U.S.; Werner Forssmann, Ger.
1957	Daniel Bovet, Ital.
1958	George W. Beadle, Edward L. Tatum, Joshua Lederberg, U.S.
1959	Arthur Kornberg, Severo Ochoa, U.S.
1960	Frank Macfarlane Burnet, Austral.; Peter B. Medawar, UK
1961	Georg von Békésy, U.S.
1962	Francis H. C. Crick, Maurice H. F. Wilkins, UK; James D. Watson, U.S.
1963	John C. Eccles, Austral.; Alan L. Hodgkin, Andrew F. Huxley, UK
1964	Konrad E. Bloch, U.S.; Feodor Lynen, Ger.
1965	François Jacob, André Lwoff, Jacques Monod, Fr.
1966	Charles B. Huggins, Peyton Rous, U.S.
1967	Ragnar Granit, Swed.; Haldan Keffer Hartline, George Wald, U.S.
1968	Robert W. Holley, H. Gobind Khorana, Marshall W. Nirenberg, U.S.
1969	Max Delbrück, Alfred D. Hershey, Salvador Luria, U.S.
1970	Julius Axelrod, U.S.; Bernard Katz, UK; Ulf von Euler, Swed.
1971	Earl W. Sutherland Jr., U.S.
1972	Gerald M. Edelman, U.S.; Rodney R. Porter, UK

1973 Konrad Lorenz, Austria;
Nikolaas Tinbergen, UK;
Karl von Frisch, Ger.
1974 Albert Claude, Lux.-U.S.;
Christian de Duve, Belg.;
George Emil Palade, Rom.-U.S.
1975 David Baltimore, Howard Temin,
U.S.; Renato Dulbecco, Ital.-U.S.
1976 Baruch S. Blumberg,
Daniel Carleton Gajdusek, U.S.
1977 Rosalyn S. Yalow,
Roger Guillemin,
Andrew V. Schally, U.S.
1978 Werner Arber, Switz.;
Daniel Nathans,
Hamilton O. Smith, U.S.
1979 Allan M. Cormack, U.S.;
Godfrey N. Hounsfield, UK
1980 Baruj Benacerraf, George Snell,
U.S.; Jean Dausset, Fr.
1981 Roger W. Sperry, David H. Hubel,
Torsten N. Wiesel, U.S.
1982 Sune K. Bergström,
Bengt I. Samuelsson, Swed.;
John R. Vane, UK
1983 Barbara McClintock, U.S.
1984 Niels K. Jerne, UK-Den.;
Georges J. F. Köhler, Ger.;
César Milstein, UK-Arg.
1985 Michael S. Brown,
Joseph L. Goldstein, U.S.
1986 Stanley Cohen, U.S.;
Rita Levi-Montalcini, Ital.-U.S.
1987 Susumu Tonegawa, Jpn.

1988 James W. Black, UK;
Gertrude B. Elion,
George H. Hitchings, U.S.
1989 J. Michael Bishop,
Harold E. Varmus, U.S.
1990 Joseph E. Murray,
E. Donnall Thomas, U.S.
1991 Edwin Neher, Bert Sakmann, Ger.
1992 Edmond H. Fisher,
Edwin G. Krebs, U.S.
1993 Richard J. Roberts, UK;
Phillip A. Sharp, U.S.
1994 Alfred G. Gilman,
Martin Rodbell, U.S.
1995 Edward B. Lewis,
Eric F. Wieschaus, U.S.;
Christiane Nüsslein-Volhard, Ger.
1996 Peter C. Doherty, Austral.;
Rolf M. Zinkernagel, Switz.
1997 Stanley B. Prusiner, U.S.
1998 Robert F. Furchgott,
Louis J. Ignarro, Ferid Murad, U.S.
1999 Günter Blobel, U.S.
2000 Arvid Carlsson, Swed.;
Paul Greengard, U.S.;
Eric R. Kandel, Austria-U.S.
2001 Leland H. Hartwell, U.S.;
R. Timothy (Tim) Hunt,
Paul M. Nurse, UK
2002 Sydney Brenner, John E. Sulston,
UK; H. Robert Horvitz, U.S.
2003 Paul C. Lauterbur, U.S.;
Peter Mansfield, UK
2004 Richard Axel, Linda B. Buck, U.S.

2005 Barry J. Marshall,
J. Robin Warren, Austral.
2006 Andrew Z. Fire, Craig C. Mello, U.S.
2007 Mario R. Capecchi,
Oliver Smithies, U.S.;
Martin J. Evans, UK
2008 Harald zur Hausen, Ger.;
Françoise Barré-Sinoussi,
Luc Montagnier, Fr.
2009 Elizabeth H. Blackburn,
Carol W. Greider,
Jack W. Szostak, U.S.
2010 Robert G. Edwards, UK
2011 Bruce A. Beutler, U.S.;
Jules A. Hoffmann, Fr.;
Ralph M. Steinman, Can.-U.S.
2012 John B. Gurdon, UK;
Shinya Yamanaka, Jpn.-U.S.
2013 James E. Rothman,
Randy W. Schekman, U.S.;
Thomas C. Südhof, Ger.-U.S.
2014 John O'Keefe, U.S.-UK; May-Britt
Moser, Edvard I. Moser, Nor.
2015 William C. Campbell, Ire.-U.S.;
Satoshi Omura, Jpn.;
Youyou Tu, China
2016 Yoshinori Ohsumi, Jpn.
2017 Jeffrey C. Hall, Michael Rosbash,
Michael W. Young, U.S.
2018 James P. Allison, U.S.;
Tasuku Honjo, Jpn.
2019 William G. Kaelin Jr.,
Gregg L. Semenza, U.S.;
Peter J. Ratcliffe, UK
2020 Harvey J. Alter,
Charles M. Rice, U.S.;
Michael Houghton, UK

Literature

1901 Rene F. A. Sully Prudhomme, Fr.
1902 Theodor Mommsen, Ger.
1903 Bjørnstjerne Bjørnson, Nor.
1904 José Echegaray y Eizaguirre, Spain;
Frédéric Mistral, Fr.
1905 Henryk Sienkiewicz, Pol.
1906 Giosuè Carducci, Ital.
1907 Rudyard Kipling, UK
1908 Rudolf C. Eucken, Ger.
1909 Selma Lagerlöf, Swed.
1910 Paul J. L. Heyse, Ger.
1911 Maurice Maeterlinck, Belg.
1912 Gerhart Hauptmann, Ger.
1913 Rabindranath Tagore, India
1915 Romain Rolland, Fr.
1916 Verner von Heidenstam, Swed.
1917 Karl A. Gjellerup,
Henrik Pontoppidan, Den.
1919 Carl F. G. Spitteler, Switz.
1920 Knut Hamsun, Nor.
1921 Anatole France, Fr.
1922 Jacinto Benavente, Spain
1923 William Butler Yeats, Ire.
1924 Wladyslaw S. Reymont, Pol.
1925 George Bernard Shaw, Ire.-UK
1926 Grazia Deledda, Ital.
1927 Henri Bergson, Fr.
1928 Sigrid Undset, Nor.
1929 Thomas Mann, Ger.
1930 Sinclair Lewis, U.S.
1931 Erik A. Karlfeldt, Swed.
1932 John Galsworthy, UK
1933 Ivan A. Bunin, USSR
1934 Luigi Pirandello, Ital.
1936 Eugene O'Neill, U.S.
1937 Roger Martin du Gard, Fr.
1938 Pearl S. Buck, U.S.
1939 Frans E. Sillanpää, Fin.
1944 Johannes V. Jensen, Den.

1945 Gabriela Mistral, Chile
1946 Hermann Hesse, Ger.-Switz.
1947 André Gide, Fr.
1948 T. S. Eliot, UK
1949 William Faulkner, U.S.
1950 Bertrand Russell, UK
1951 Pär F. Lagerkvist, Swed.
1952 François Mauriac, Fr.
1953 Winston Churchill, UK
1954 Ernest Hemingway, U.S.
1955 Halldór K. Laxness, Ice.
1956 Juan Ramón Jiménez, Spain
1957 Albert Camus, Fr.
1958 Boris L. Pasternak, USSR
(declined)
1959 Salvatore Quasimodo, Ital.
1960 Saint-John Perse, Fr.
1961 Ivo Andric, Yugo.
1962 John Steinbeck, U.S.
1963 Giorgos Seferis, Greece
1964 Jean-Paul Sartre, Fr. (declined)
1965 Mikhail Sholokhov, USSR
1966 Shmuel Yosef Agnon, Isr.;
Nelly Sachs, Swed.
1967 Miguel Angel Asturias, Guat.
1968 Yasunari Kawabata, Jpn.
1969 Samuel Beckett, Ire.
1970 Aleksandr I. Solzhenitsyn, USSR
1971 Pablo Neruda, Chile
1972 Heinrich Böll, Ger.
1973 Patrick White, Austral.
1974 Eyvind Johnson,
Harry Edmund Martinson, Swed.
1975 Eugenio Montale, Ital.
1976 Saul Bellow, U.S.
1977 Vicente Aleixandre, Spain
1978 Isaac Bashevis Singer, U.S.
1979 Odysseus Elytis, Greece
1980 Czeslaw Milosz, Pol.-U.S.

1981 Elias Canetti, Bulg.-UK
1982 Gabriel García Márquez, Colombia
1983 William Golding, UK
1984 Jaroslav Siefert, Czech.
1985 Claude Simon, Fr.
1986 Wole Soyinka, Nigeria
1987 Joseph Brodsky, USSR-U.S.
1988 Naguib Mahfouz, Egypt
1989 Camilo José Cela, Spain
1990 Octavio Paz, Mex.
1991 Nadine Gordimer, S. Afr.
1992 Derek Walcott, St. Lucia
1993 Toni Morrison, U.S.
1994 Kenzaburō Oe, Jpn.
1995 Seamus Heaney, Ire.
1996 Wislawa Szymborska, Pol.
1997 Dario Fo, Ital.
1998 José Saramago, Por.
1999 Günter Grass, Ger.
2000 Gao Xingjian, China-Fr.
2001 V. S. Naipaul, UK
2002 Imre Kertész, Hung.
2003 J. M. Coetzee, S. Afr.
2004 Elfriede Jelinek, Austria
2005 Harold Pinter, UK
2006 Orhan Pamuk, Turk.
2007 Doris Lessing, UK
2008 Jean-Marie Gustave Le Clézio, Fr.
2009 Herta Müller, Ger.
2010 Mario Vargas Llosa, Peru
2011 Tomas Tranströmer, Swed.
2012 Mo Yan, China
2013 Alice Munro, Can.
2014 Patrick Modiano, Fr.
2015 Svetlana Alexievich, Belarus
2016 Bob Dylan, U.S.
2017 Kazuo Ishiguro, Jpn.-UK
2018 Olga Tokarczuk, Pol.
2019 Peter Handke, Austria
2020 Louise Glück, U.S.

Peace

1901 Jean H. Dunant, Switz.;
Frédéric Passy, Fr.
1902 Élie Ducommun,
Charles A. Gobat, Switz.
1903 William R. Cremer, UK
1904 Institute of International Law, Belg.
1905 Baroness Bertha von Suttner,
Austria
1906 Theodore Roosevelt, U.S.
1907 Ernesto T. Moneta, Ital.;
Louis Renault, Fr.
1908 Klas P. Arnoldson, Swed.;
Fredrik Bajer, Den.

1909 Auguste M. F. Beernaert, Belg.;
Paul H. B. B. d'Estournelles
de Constant, Fr.
1910 Permanent Intl. Peace Bureau
1911 Tobias M. C. Asser, Neth.;
Alfred H. Fried, Austria
1912 Elihu Root, U.S.
1913 Henri La Fontaine, Belg.
1917 Intl. Committee of the Red Cross
1919 Woodrow Wilson, U.S.
1920 Léon V. A. Bourgeois, Fr.
1921 Karl H. Branting, Swed.;
Christian L. Lange, Nor.

1922 Fridtjof Nansen, Nor.
1925 Austen Chamberlain, UK;
Charles G. Dawes, U.S.
1926 Aristide Briand, Fr.;
Gustav Stresemann, Ger.
1927 Ferdinand E. Buisson, Fr.;
Ludwig Quidde, Ger.
1929 Frank B. Kellogg, U.S.
1930 Nathan Söderblom, Swed.
1931 Jane Addams,
Nicholas Murray Butler, U.S.
1933 Norman Angell, UK
1934 Arthur Henderson, UK

1935 Carl von Ossietzky, Ger.	1975 Andrei Sakharov, USSR	1998 John Hume, David Trimble, N. Ire.
1936 Carlos Saavedra Lamas, Arg.	1976 Mairead Corrigan,	1999 Médecins Sans Frontières
1937 Lord Robert Cecil, UK	Betty Williams, N. Ire.	(Doctors Without Borders), Fr.
1938 Nansen Intl. Office for Refugees	1977 Amnesty International, UK	2000 Kim Dae Jung, S. Kor.
1944 Intl. Committee of the Red Cross	1978 Anwar al-Sadat, Egypt;	2001 UN; Kofi Annan, Ghana
1945 Cordell Hull, U.S.	Menachem Begin, Isr.	2002 Jimmy Carter, U.S.
1946 Emily G. Balch, John R. Mott, U.S.	1979 Mother Teresa of Calcutta,	2003 Shirin Ebadi, Iran
1947 Friends Service Council, UK; Amer.	Alb.-India	2004 Wangari Maathai, Kenya
Friends Service Committee, U.S.	1980 Adolfo Pérez Esquivel, Arg.	2005 Mohamed ElBaradei, Egypt;
1949 Lord John Boyd Orr of Brechin, UK	1981 Office of UN High Commissioner	Intl. Atomic Energy Agency, Austria
1950 Ralph J. Bunche, U.S.	for Refugees	2006 Muhammad Yunus,
1951 Léon Jouhaux, Fr.	1982 Alfonso García Robles, Mex.;	Grameen Bank, Bangl.
1952 Albert Schweitzer, Fr.	Alva Myrdal, Swed.	2007 Intergovernmental Panel on Climate
1953 George C. Marshall, U.S.	1983 Lech Walesa, Pol.	Change, Switz.;
1954 Office of UN High Commissioner	1984 Bishop Desmond Tutu, S. Afr.	Albert Arnold Gore Jr., U.S.
for Refugees	1985 Intl. Physicians for the Prevention	2008 Martti Ahtisaari, Fin.
1957 Lester B. Pearson, Can.	of Nuclear War, U.S.	2009 Barack H. Obama, U.S.
1958 Georges Pire, Belg.	1986 Elie Wiesel, Rom.-U.S.	2010 Liu Xiaobo, China
1959 Philip J. Noel-Baker, UK	1987 Oscar Arias Sánchez, Costa Rica	2011 Leymah Gbowee,
1960 Albert J. Lutuli, S. Afr.	1988 UN Peacekeeping Forces	Ellen Johnson Sirleaf, Liberia;
1961 Dag Hammarskjöld, Swed.	1989 Dalai Lama (Tenzin Gyatso), Tibet	Tawakkol Karman, Yemen
1962 Linus C. Pauling, U.S.	1990 Mikhail S. Gorbachev, USSR	2012 European Union
1963 Intl. Committee of the Red Cross,	1991 Aung San Suu Kyi, Burma	2013 Organization for the Prohibition of
League of Red Cross Societies	1992 Rigoberta Menchú Tum, Guat.	Chemical Weapons (OPCW)
1964 Martin Luther King Jr., U.S.	1993 Frederik W. de Klerk,	2014 Kailash Satyarthi, India;
1965 UN Children's Fund (UNICEF)	Nelson Mandela, S. Afr.	Malala Yousafzai, Pakistan
1968 René Cassin, Fr.	1994 Yasser Arafat, Pal.; Shimon Peres,	2015 National Dialogue Quartet, Tunisia
1969 Intl. Labor Organization, Switz.	Yitzhak Rabin, Isr.	2016 Juan Manuel Santos, Colombia
1970 Norman E. Borlaug, U.S.	1995 Joseph Rotblat, Pol.-UK;	2017 Intl. Campaign to Abolish Nuclear
1971 Willy Brandt, Ger.	Pugwash Conferences, Can.	Weapons
1973 Henry Kissinger, U.S.;	1996 Bishop Carlos Ximenes Belo,	2018 Denis Mukwege, Congo;
Le Duc Tho, N. Viet. (Tho declined)	José Ramos-Horta, Timor-Leste	Nadia Murad, Iraq
1974 Seán MacBride, Ire.;	1997 Jody Williams, U.S.;	2019 Abiy Ahmed, Ethiopia
Eisaku Sato, Jpn.	Intl. Campaign to Ban Landmines	2020 World Food Programme

Nobel Memorial Prize in Economic Sciences

1969 Ragnar Frisch, Nor.;	1990 Harry M. Markowitz, Merton H.	2006 Edmund S. Phelps, U.S.
Jan Tinbergen, Neth.	Miller, William F. Sharpe, U.S.	2007 Leonid Hurwicz, Eric S. Maskin,
1970 Paul A. Samuelson, U.S.	1991 Ronald H. Coase, UK-U.S.	Roger B. Myerson, U.S.
1971 Simon Kuznets, U.S.	1992 Gary S. Becker, U.S.	2008 Paul Krugman, U.S.
1972 Kenneth J. Arrow, U.S.;	1993 Robert W. Fogel,	2009 Elinor Ostrom,
John R. Hicks, UK	Douglass C. North, U.S.	Oliver E. Williamson, U.S.
1973 Wassily Leontief, U.S.	1994 John C. Harsanyi, John F. Nash,	2010 Peter A. Diamond, Dale T.
1974 Gunnar Myrdal, Swed.;	U.S.; Reinhard Selten, Ger.	Mortensen, U.S.; Christopher A.
Friedrich A. von Hayek, Austria	1995 Robert E. Lucas Jr., U.S.	Pissarides, Cyprus-UK
1975 Leonid Kantorovich, USSR;	1996 James A. Mirrlees, UK;	2011 Thomas J. Sargent,
Tjalling C. Koopmans, Neth.-U.S.	William Vickrey, Can.-U.S.	Christopher A. Sims, U.S.
1976 Milton Friedman, U.S.	1997 Robert C. Merton, U.S.;	2012 Alvin E. Roth, Lloyd S. Shapley, U.S.
1977 James E. Meade, UK;	Myron S. Scholes, Can.-U.S.	2013 Eugene F. Fama, Lars Peter
Bertil Ohlin, Swed.	1998 Amartya Sen, India	Hansen, Robert J. Shiller, U.S.
1978 Herbert A. Simon, U.S.	1999 Robert A. Mundell, Can.	2014 Jean Tirole, Fr.
1979 Arthur Lewis, UK;	2000 James J. Heckman,	2015 Angus Deaton, UK-U.S.
Theodore W. Schultz, U.S.	Daniel L. McFadden, U.S.	2016 Oliver Hart, U.S.;
1980 Lawrence R. Klein, U.S.	2001 George A. Akerlof, A. Michael	Bengt Holmström, Fin.-U.S.
1981 James Tobin, U.S.	Spence, Joseph E. Stiglitz, U.S.	2017 Richard H. Thaler, U.S.
1982 George J. Stigler, U.S.	2002 Daniel Kahneman, U.S.-Isr.;	2018 William D. Nordhaus,
1983 Gerard Debreu, Fr.-U.S.	Vernon L. Smith, U.S.	Paul M. Romer, U.S.
1984 Richard Stone, UK	2003 Robert F. Engle, U.S.;	2019 Abhijit Banerjee, India-U.S.;
1985 Franco Modigliani, Ital.-U.S.	Clive W. J. Granger, UK	Esther Duflo, Fr.-U.S.;
1986 James M. Buchanan, U.S.	2004 Finn E. Kydland, Nor.;	Michael Kremer, U.S.
1987 Robert M. Solow, U.S.	Edward C. Prescott, U.S.	2020 Paul R. Milgrom,
1988 Maurice Allais, Fr.	2005 Robert J. Aumann, Isr.-U.S.;	Robert B. Wilson, U.S.
1989 Trygve Haavelmo, Nor.	Thomas C. Schelling, U.S.	

Pulitzer Prizes in Journalism, Letters, and Music, 1917-2020

Endowed by Joseph Pulitzer (1847-1911), publisher of the *New York World*, in a bequest to Columbia Univ. and awarded annually, in years shown, for work published the previous year. Prizes are currently $10,000 in each category except Public Service (in Journalism), for which a gold medal is given. The prize board began considering submissions from online-only publications in 2009.

Pulitzer Prizes in Journalism, 2020

Public Service: *Anchorage Daily News* with ProPublica, for a series revealing that one-third of Alaska's villages had no police protection, spurring funding and legislative changes.

Breaking News Reporting: Louisville, KY's *Courier-Journal*, for covering hundreds of last-minute pardons by Kentucky's governor.

Investigative Reporting: Brian M. Rosenthal, *NY Times*, for an exposé of New York City's taxi industry that showed how lenders profited from predatory loans.

Explanatory Reporting: *Washington Post* staff, for series clearly illustrating the dire effects of extreme temperatures on the planet.

Local Reporting: *Baltimore Sun* staff, for exposing an undisclosed financial relationship between the city's mayor and the public hospital system she helped to oversee.

National Reporting: Dominic Gates, Steve Miletich, Mike Baker, and Lewis Kamb, *Seattle Times*, for stories that exposed design flaws in the Boeing 737 MAX; T. Christian Miller, Megan Rose, and Robert Faturechi, ProPublica, for investigation into the U.S. Navy's 7th Fleet after a series of deadly accidents.

International Reporting: *NY Times* staff, for series exposing the predations of Vladimir Putin's regime.

Feature Writing: Ben Taub, *The New Yorker*, for his account of a man who was kidnapped, tortured, and deprived of liberty for over a decade at the Guantánamo Bay detention facility.

Commentary: Nikole Hannah-Jones, *NY Times*, for an essay for the groundbreaking "1619 Project," which seeks to place the enslavement of Africans at the center of America's story.

Criticism: Christopher Knight, *L.A. Times*, for extraordinary community service by a critic, applying his expertise and enterprise to critique a proposed overhaul of the L.A. County Museum of Art.

Editorial Writing: Jeffery Gerritt, *Palestine (TX) Herald-Press*, for editorials that exposed how pre-trial inmates died in a small Texas county jail and took on the local judicial establishment.

Editorial Cartooning: Barry Blitt, *The New Yorker*, for work that skewers Trump White House personalities and policies.

Breaking News Photography: Reuters staff, for images of Hong Kong protests.

Feature Photography: Channi Anand, Mukhtar Khan, and Dar Yasin, Associated Press, for images of life in the contested territory of Kashmir as India revoked its independence.

Audio Reporting: *This American Life* staff, with Molly O'Toole, *L.A. Times*, and Emily Green, freelancer, *Vice News*, for "The Out Crowd."

Pulitzer Prizes in Letters, 1918-2020

Other Pulitzer Prize Winners, 2020: Biography/autobiography: Benjamin Moser, *Sontag: Her Life and Work*. History (U.S.): W. Caleb McDaniel, *Sweet Taste of Liberty: A True Story of Slavery and Restitution in America*. Poetry: Jericho Brown, *The Tradition*.

Fiction

1918 Ernest Poole, *His Family*
1919 Booth Tarkington, *The Magnificent Ambersons*
1921 Edith Wharton, *The Age of Innocence*
1922 Booth Tarkington, *Alice Adams*
1923 Willa Cather, *One of Ours*
1924 Margaret Wilson, *The Able McLaughlins*
1925 Edna Ferber, *So Big*
1926 Sinclair Lewis, *Arrowsmith* (refused)
1927 Louis Bromfield, *Early Autumn*
1928 Thornton Wilder, *The Bridge of San Luis Rey*
1929 Julia Peterkin, *Scarlet Sister Mary*
1930 Oliver La Farge, *Laughing Boy*
1931 Margaret Ayer Barnes, *Years of Grace*
1932 Pearl S. Buck, *The Good Earth*
1933 T. S. Stribling, *The Store*
1934 Caroline Miller, *Lamb in His Bosom*
1935 Josephine W. Johnson, *Now in November*
1936 Harold L. Davis, *Honey in the Horn*
1937 Margaret Mitchell, *Gone With the Wind*
1938 John P. Marquand, *The Late George Apley*
1939 Marjorie Kinnan Rawlings, *The Yearling*
1940 John Steinbeck, *The Grapes of Wrath*
1942 Ellen Glasgow, *In This Our Life*
1943 Upton Sinclair, *Dragon's Teeth*
1944 Martin Flavin, *Journey in the Dark*
1945 John Hersey, *A Bell for Adano*
1947 Robert Penn Warren, *All the King's Men*
1948 James A. Michener, *Tales of the South Pacific*
1949 James Gould Cozzens, *Guard of Honor*
1950 A. B. Guthrie Jr., *The Way West*
1951 Conrad Richter, *The Town*
1952 Herman Wouk, *The Caine Mutiny*
1953 Ernest Hemingway, *The Old Man and the Sea*
1955 William Faulkner, *A Fable*
1956 MacKinlay Kantor, *Andersonville*
1958 James Agee, *A Death in the Family*
1959 Robert Lewis Taylor, *The Travels of Jaimie McPheeters*
1960 Allen Drury, *Advise and Consent*
1961 Harper Lee, *To Kill a Mockingbird*
1962 Edwin O'Connor, *The Edge of Sadness*
1963 William Faulkner, *The Reivers*
1965 Shirley Ann Grau, *The Keepers of the House*
1966 Katherine Anne Porter, *Collected Stories*
1967 Bernard Malamud, *The Fixer*
1968 William Styron, *The Confessions of Nat Turner*
1969 N. Scott Momaday, *House Made of Dawn*
1970 Jean Stafford, *Collected Stories*
1972 Wallace Stegner, *Angle of Repose*
1973 Eudora Welty, *The Optimist's Daughter*
1975 Michael Shaara, *The Killer Angels*
1976 Saul Bellow, *Humboldt's Gift*
1978 James Alan McPherson, *Elbow Room*
1979 John Cheever, *The Stories of John Cheever*
1980 Norman Mailer, *The Executioner's Song*
1981 John Kennedy Toole, *A Confederacy of Dunces*
1982 John Updike, *Rabbit Is Rich*
1983 Alice Walker, *The Color Purple*
1984 William Kennedy, *Ironweed*
1985 Alison Lurie, *Foreign Affairs*
1986 Larry McMurtry, *Lonesome Dove*
1987 Peter Taylor, *A Summons to Memphis*
1988 Toni Morrison, *Beloved*
1989 Anne Tyler, *Breathing Lessons*
1990 Oscar Hijuelos, *The Mambo Kings Play Songs of Love*
1991 John Updike, *Rabbit at Rest*
1992 Jane Smiley, *A Thousand Acres*
1993 Robert Olen Butler, *A Good Scent From a Strange Mountain*
1994 E. Annie Proulx, *The Shipping News*
1995 Carol Shields, *The Stone Diaries*
1996 Richard Ford, *Independence Day*
1997 Steven Millhauser, *Martin Dressler: The Tale of an American Dreamer*
1998 Philip Roth, *American Pastoral*
1999 Michael Cunningham, *The Hours*
2000 Jhumpa Lahiri, *Interpreter of Maladies*
2001 Michael Chabon, *The Amazing Adventures of Kavalier & Clay*
2002 Richard Russo, *Empire Falls*
2003 Jeffrey Eugenides, *Middlesex*
2004 Edward P. Jones, *The Known World*
2005 Marilynne Robinson, *Gilead*
2006 Geraldine Brooks, *March*

2007 Cormac McCarthy, *The Road*
2008 Junot Díaz, *The Brief Wondrous Life of Oscar Wao*
2009 Elizabeth Strout, *Olive Kitteridge*
2010 Paul Harding, *Tinkers*
2011 Jennifer Egan, *A Visit From the Goon Squad*
2013 Adam Johnson, *The Orphan Master's Son*
2014 Donna Tartt, *The Goldfinch*
2015 Anthony Doerr, *All the Light We Cannot See*
2016 Viet Thanh Nguyen, *The Sympathizer*
2017 Colson Whitehead, *The Underground Railroad*
2018 Andrew Sean Greer, *Less*
2019 Richard Powers, *The Overstory*
2020 Colson Whitehead, *The Nickel Boys*

Drama

1918 Jesse Lynch Williams, *Why Marry?*
1920 Eugene O'Neill, *Beyond the Horizon*
1921 Zona Gale, *Miss Lulu Bett*
1922 Eugene O'Neill, *Anna Christie*
1923 Owen Davis, *Icebound*
1924 Hatcher Hughes, *Hell-Bent Fer Heaven*
1925 Sidney Howard, *They Knew What They Wanted*
1926 George Kelly, *Craig's Wife*
1927 Paul Green, *In Abraham's Bosom*
1928 Eugene O'Neill, *Strange Interlude*
1929 Elmer Rice, *Street Scene*
1930 Marc Connelly, *The Green Pastures*
1931 Susan Glaspell, *Alison's House*
1932 George S. Kaufman, Morrie Ryskind, and Ira Gershwin, *Of Thee I Sing*
1933 Maxwell Anderson, *Both Your Houses*
1934 Sidney Kingsley, *Men in White*
1935 Zoe Akins, *The Old Maid*
1936 Robert E. Sherwood, *Idiot's Delight*
1937 George S. Kaufman and Moss Hart, *You Can't Take It With You*
1938 Thornton Wilder, *Our Town*
1939 Robert E. Sherwood, *Abe Lincoln in Illinois*
1940 William Saroyan, *The Time of Your Life*
1941 Robert E. Sherwood, *There Shall Be No Night*
1943 Thornton Wilder, *The Skin of Our Teeth*
1945 Mary Chase, *Harvey*
1946 Russel Crouse and Howard Lindsay, *State of the Union*
1948 Tennessee Williams, *A Streetcar Named Desire*
1949 Arthur Miller, *Death of a Salesman*
1950 Richard Rodgers, Oscar Hammerstein II, and Joshua Logan, *South Pacific*
1952 Joseph Kramm, *The Shrike*
1953 William Inge, *Picnic*
1954 John Patrick, *The Teahouse of the August Moon*
1955 Tennessee Williams, *Cat on a Hot Tin Roof*
1956 Frances Goodrich and Albert Hackett, *The Diary of Anne Frank*
1957 Eugene O'Neill, *Long Day's Journey Into Night*
1958 Ketti Frings, *Look Homeward, Angel*
1959 Archibald MacLeish, *J.B.*
1960 George Abbott, Jerome Weidman, Sheldon Harnick, and Jerry Bock, *Fiorello!*
1961 Tad Mosel, *All the Way Home*
1962 Frank Loesser and Abe Burrows, *How to Succeed in Business Without Really Trying*
1965 Frank D. Gilroy, *The Subject Was Roses*
1967 Edward Albee, *A Delicate Balance*
1969 Howard Sackler, *The Great White Hope*
1970 Charles Gordone, *No Place to Be Somebody*
1971 Paul Zindel, *The Effect of Gamma Rays on Man-in-the-Moon Marigolds*
1973 Jason Miller, *That Championship Season*
1975 Edward Albee, *Seascape*
1976 Michael Bennett, James Kirkwood, Nicholas Dante, Marvin Hamlisch, and Edward Kleban, *A Chorus Line*
1977 Michael Cristofer, *The Shadow Box*
1978 Donald L. Coburn, *The Gin Game*
1979 Sam Shepard, *Buried Child*
1980 Lanford Wilson, *Talley's Folly*
1981 Beth Henley, *Crimes of the Heart*
1982 Charles Fuller, *A Soldier's Play*
1983 Marsha Norman, *'night, Mother*
1984 David Mamet, *Glengarry Glen Ross*
1985 Stephen Sondheim and James Lapine, *Sunday in the Park With George*
1987 August Wilson, *Fences*
1988 Alfred Uhry, *Driving Miss Daisy*

1989 Wendy Wasserstein, *The Heidi Chronicles*
1990 August Wilson, *The Piano Lesson*
1991 Neil Simon, *Lost in Yonkers*
1992 Robert Schenkkan, *The Kentucky Cycle*
1993 Tony Kushner, *Angels in America: Millennium Approaches*
1994 Edward Albee, *Three Tall Women*
1995 Horton Foote, *The Young Man From Atlanta*
1996 Jonathan Larson, *Rent*
1998 Paula Vogel, *How I Learned to Drive*
1999 Margaret Edson, *Wit*
2000 Donald Margulies, *Dinner With Friends*
2001 David Auburn, *Proof*
2002 Suzan-Lori Parks, *Topdog/Underdog*
2003 Nilo Cruz, *Anna in the Tropics*
2004 Doug Wright, *I Am My Own Wife*
2005 John Patrick Shanley, *Doubt, a parable*
2007 David Lindsay-Abaire, *Rabbit Hole*
2008 Tracy Letts, *August: Osage County*
2009 Lynn Nottage, *Ruined*
2010 Tom Kitt and Brian Yorkey, *Next to Normal*
2011 Bruce Norris, *Clybourne Park*
2012 Quiara Alegría Hudes, *Water by the Spoonful*
2013 Ayad Akhtar, *Disgraced*
2014 Annie Baker, *The Flick*
2015 Stephen Adly Guirgis, *Between Riverside and Crazy*
2016 Lin-Manuel Miranda, *Hamilton*
2017 Lynn Nottage, *Sweat*
2018 Martyna Majok, *Cost of Living*
2019 Jackie Sibblies Drury, *Fairview*
2020 Michael R. Jackson, *A Strange Loop*

General Nonfiction

1962 Theodore H. White, *The Making of the President 1960*
1963 Barbara W. Tuchman, *The Guns of August*
1964 Richard Hofstadter, *Anti-Intellectualism in American Life*
1965 Howard Mumford Jones, *O Strange New World*
1966 Edwin Way Teale, *Wandering Through Winter*
1967 David Brion Davis, *The Problem of Slavery in Western Culture*
1968 Will and Ariel Durant, *Rousseau and Revolution*
1969 Norman Mailer, *The Armies of the Night*; Rene Jules Dubos, *So Human an Animal: How We Are Shaped by Surroundings and Events*
1970 Eric H. Erikson, *Gandhi's Truth*
1971 John Toland, *The Rising Sun*
1972 Barbara W. Tuchman, *Stilwell and the American Experience in China, 1911-1945*
1973 Frances FitzGerald, *Fire in the Lake: The Vietnamese and the Americans in Vietnam*; Robert Coles, *Children of Crisis, Vols. II and III*
1974 Ernest Becker, *The Denial of Death*
1975 Annie Dillard, *Pilgrim at Tinker Creek*
1976 Robert N. Butler, *Why Survive? Being Old in America*
1977 William W. Warner, *Beautiful Swimmers*
1978 Carl Sagan, *The Dragons of Eden*
1979 Edward O. Wilson, *On Human Nature*
1980 Douglas R. Hofstadter, *Gödel, Escher, Bach: An Eternal Golden Braid*
1981 Carl E. Schorske, *Fin-de-Siècle Vienna: Politics and Culture*
1982 Tracy Kidder, *The Soul of a New Machine*
1983 Susan Sheehan, *Is There No Place on Earth for Me?*
1984 Paul Starr, *Social Transformation of American Medicine*
1985 Studs Terkel, *The Good War*
1986 Joseph Lelyveld, *Move Your Shadow*; J. Anthony Lukas, *Common Ground*
1987 David K. Shipler, *Arab and Jew: Wounded Spirits in a Promised Land*
1988 Richard Rhodes, *The Making of the Atomic Bomb*
1989 Neil Sheehan, *A Bright Shining Lie: John Paul Vann and America in Vietnam*

1990 Dale Maharidge and Michael Williamson, *And Their Children After Them*
1991 Bert Holldobler and Edward O. Wilson, *The Ants*
1992 Daniel Yergin, *The Prize: The Epic Quest for Oil, Money, and Power*
1993 Garry Wills, *Lincoln at Gettysburg*
1994 David Remnick, *Lenin's Tomb: The Last Days of the Soviet Empire*
1995 Jonathan Weiner, *The Beak of the Finch: A Story of Evolution in Our Time*
1996 Tina Rosenberg, *The Haunted Land: Facing Europe's Ghosts After Communism*
1997 Richard Kluger, *Ashes to Ashes: America's Hundred-Year Cigarette War, the Public Health, and the Unabashed Triumph of Philip Morris*
1998 Jared Diamond, *Guns, Germs, and Steel: The Fates of Human Societies*
1999 John McPhee, *Annals of the Former World*
2000 John W. Dower, *Embracing Defeat: Japan in the Wake of World War II*
2001 Herbert P. Bix, *Hirohito and the Making of Modern Japan*
2002 Diane McWhorter, *Carry Me Home: Birmingham, Alabama: The Climactic Battle of the Civil Rights Revolution*
2003 Samantha Power, *A Problem From Hell: America and the Age of Genocide*
2004 Anne Applebaum, *Gulag: A History*
2005 Steve Coll, *Ghost Wars*
2006 Caroline Elkins, *Imperial Reckoning: The Untold Story of Britain's Gulag in Kenya*
2007 Lawrence Wright, *The Looming Tower: Al-Qaeda and the Road to 9/11*
2008 Saul Friedländer, *The Years of Extermination: Nazi Germany and the Jews, 1939-1945*
2009 Douglas A. Blackmon, *Slavery by Another Name: The Re-Enslavement of Black Americans From the Civil War to World War II*
2010 David E. Hoffman, *The Dead Hand: The Untold Story of the Cold War Arms Race and Its Dangerous Legacy*
2011 Siddhartha Mukherjee, *The Emperor of All Maladies: A Biography of Cancer*
2012 Stephen Greenblatt, *The Swerve: How the World Became Modern*
2013 Gilbert King, *Devil in the Grove: Thurgood Marshall, the Groveland Boys, and the Dawn of a New America*
2014 Dan Fagin, *Toms River: A Story of Science and Salvation*
2015 Elizabeth Kolbert, *The Sixth Extinction: An Unnatural History*
2016 Joby Warrick, *Black Flags: The Rise of ISIS*
2017 Matthew Desmond, *Evicted: Poverty and Profit in the American City*
2018 James Forman Jr., *Locking up Our Own: Crime and Punishment in Black America*
2019 Eliza Griswold, *Amity and Prosperity: One Family and the Fracturing of America*
2020 Greg Grandin, *The End of the Myth: From the Frontier to the Border Wall in the Mind of America*; Anne Boyer, *The Undying: Pain, Vulnerability, Mortality, Medicine, Art, Time, Dreams, Data, Exhaustion, Cancer, and Care*

Special Citation in Letters

1944 Richard Rodgers and Oscar Hammerstein II, for *Oklahoma!*
1957 Kenneth Roberts, for his historical novels
1960 *The Armada*, by Garrett Mattingly
1961 *American Heritage Picture History of the Civil War*
1973 *George Washington, Vols. I-IV*, by James Thomas Flexner
1977 Alex Haley, for *Roots*
1978 E. B. White
1984 Theodor Seuss Geisel (Dr. Seuss)
1992 Art Spiegelman, for *Maus*
2006 Edmund S. Morgan
2007 Ray Bradbury

Pulitzer Prizes in Music, 1943-2020

1943 William Schuman, *Secular Cantata No. 2, A Free Song*
1944 Howard Hanson, *Symphony No. 4, Op. 34*
1945 Aaron Copland, *Appalachian Spring*
1946 Leo Sowerby, *The Canticle of the Sun*
1947 Charles Ives, *Symphony No. 3*
1948 Walter Piston, *Symphony No. 3*
1949 Virgil Thomson, *Louisiana Story*
1950 Gian-Carlo Menotti, *The Consul*
1951 Douglas Moore, *Giants in the Earth*
1952 Gail Kubik, *Symphony Concertante*
1954 Quincy Porter, *Concerto for Two Pianos and Orchestra*
1955 Gian-Carlo Menotti, *The Saint of Bleecker Street*
1956 Ernest Toch, *Symphony No. 3*
1957 Norman Dello Joio, *Meditations on Ecclesiastes*

1958 Samuel Barber, *Vanessa*
1959 John LaMontaine, *Concerto for Piano and Orchestra*
1960 Elliott Carter, *Second String Quartet*
1961 Walter Piston, *Symphony No. 7*
1962 Robert Ward, *The Crucible*
1963 Samuel Barber, *Piano Concerto No. 1*
1966 Leslie Bassett, *Variations for Orchestra*
1967 Leon Kirchner, *Quartet No. 3*
1968 George Crumb, *Echoes of Time and the River*
1969 Karel Husa, *String Quartet No. 3*
1970 Charles Wuorinen, *Time's Encomium*
1971 Mario Davidovsky, *Synchronisms No. 6*
1972 Jacob Druckman, *Windows*
1973 Elliott Carter, *String Quartet No. 3*

1974 Donald Martino, *Notturno*
1975 Dominick Argento, *From the Diary of Virginia Woolf*
1976 Ned Rorem, *Air Music*
1977 Richard Wernick, *Visions of Terror and Wonder*
1978 Michael Colgrass, *Deja Vu for Percussion and Orchestra*
1979 Joseph Schwantner, *Aftertones of Infinity*
1980 David Del Tredici, *In Memory of a Summer Day*
1982 Roger Sessions, *Concerto for Orchestra*
1983 Ellen Taaffe Zwilich, *Symphony No. 1*
1984 Bernard Rands, *Canti del Sole*
1985 Stephen Albert, *Symphony, RiverRun*
1986 George Perle, *Wind Quintet IV*
1987 John Harbison, *The Flight Into Egypt*
1988 William Bolcom, *12 New Etudes for Piano*
1989 Roger Reynolds, *Whispers Out of Time*
1990 Mel Powell, *Duplicates: A Concerto for Two Pianos and Orchestra*
1991 Shulamit Ran, *Symphony*
1992 Wayne Peterson, *The Face of the Night, The Heart[2] of the Dark*
1993 Christopher Rouse, *Trombone Concerto*
1994 Gunther Schuller, *Of Reminiscences and Reflections*
1995 Morton Gould, *Stringmusic*
1996 George Walker, *Lilacs for Voice and Orchestra*
1997 Wynton Marsalis, *Blood on the Fields*
1998 Aaron Jay Kernis, *String Quartet No. 2 (musica instrumentalis)*
1999 Melinda Wagner, *Concerto for Flute, Strings, and Percussion*
2000 Lewis Spratlan, *Life is a Dream, Opera in Three Acts: Act II, Concert Version*
2001 John Corigliano, *Symphony No. 2 for String Orchestra*
2002 Henry Brant, *Ice Field*

2003 John Adams, *On the Transmigration of Souls*
2004 Paul Moravec, *Tempest Fantasy*
2005 Steven Stucky, *Second Concerto for Orchestra*
2006 Yehudi Wyner, *Piano Concerto: "Chiavi in Mano"*
2007 Ornette Coleman, *Sound Grammar*
2008 David Lang, *The Little Match Girl Passion*
2009 Steve Reich, *Double Sextet*
2010 Jennifer Higdon, *Violin Concerto*
2011 Zhou Long, *Madame White Snake*
2012 Kevin Puts, *Silent Night: Opera in Two Acts*
2013 Caroline Shaw, *Partita for 8 Voices*
2014 John Luther Adams, *Become Ocean*
2015 Julia Wolfe, *Anthracite Fields*
2016 Henry Threadgill, *In for a Penny, In for a Pound*
2017 Du Yun, *Angel's Bone*
2018 Kendrick Lamar, *DAMN.*
2019 Ellen Reid, *p r i s m*
2020 Anthony Davis, *The Central Park Five*

Special Citation in Music

1974 Roger Sessions
1976 Scott Joplin
1982 Milton Babbitt
1985 William Schuman
1998 George Gershwin
1999 Edward Kennedy "Duke" Ellington
2006 Thelonious Monk
2007 John Coltrane
2008 Bob Dylan
2010 Hank Williams
2019 Aretha Franklin

Booker Prize for Fiction, 1969-2019

The Booker Prize for fiction, established in 1968 and named the Man Booker Prize, 2002-18, is £50,000, awarded annually to the author of the best new full-length novel written in English. Award-winning authors were required to be a citizen of the UK, the Commonwealth, or Ireland until 2014, the first year in which all English-language novels published in Britain were considered.

Year Author, book

1969 P. H. Newby, *Something to Answer For*
1970 Bernice Rubens, *The Elected Member*
1971 V. S. Naipaul, *In a Free State*
1972 John Berger, *G*
1973 J. G. Farrell, *The Siege of Krishnapur*
1974 Nadine Gordimer, *The Conservationist*; Stanley Middleton, *Holiday*
1975 Ruth Prawer Jhabvala, *Heat and Dust*
1976 David Storey, *Saville*
1977 Paul Scott, *Staying On*
1978 Iris Murdoch, *The Sea, the Sea*
1979 Penelope Fitzgerald, *Offshore*
1980 William Golding, *Rites of Passage*
1981 Salman Rushdie, *Midnight's Children[1]*
1982 Thomas Keneally, *Schindler's Ark*
1983 J. M. Coetzee, *Life and Times of Michael K*
1984 Anita Brookner, *Hotel du Lac*
1985 Keri Hulme, *The Bone People*
1986 Kingsley Amis, *The Old Devils*
1987 Penelope Lively, *Moon Tiger*
1988 Peter Carey, *Oscar and Lucinda*
1989 Kazuo Ishiguro, *The Remains of the Day*
1990 A. S. Byatt, *Possession*
1991 Ben Okri, *The Famished Road*
1992 Michael Ondaatje, *The English Patient[2]*; Barry Unsworth, *Sacred Hunger*
1993 Roddy Doyle, *Paddy Clarke Ha Ha Ha*

Year Author, book

1994 James Kelman, *How Late It Was, How Late*
1995 Pat Barker, *The Ghost Road*
1996 Graham Swift, *Last Orders*
1997 Arundhati Roy, *The God of Small Things*
1998 Ian McEwan, *Amsterdam*
1999 J. M. Coetzee, *Disgrace*
2000 Margaret Atwood, *The Blind Assassin*
2001 Peter Carey, *True History of the Kelly Gang*
2002 Yann Martel, *Life of Pi*
2003 DBC Pierre, *Vernon God Little*
2004 Alan Hollinghurst, *The Line of Beauty*
2005 John Banville, *The Sea*
2006 Kiran Desai, *The Inheritance of Loss*
2007 Anne Enright, *The Gathering*
2008 Aravind Adiga, *The White Tiger*
2009 Hilary Mantel, *Wolf Hall*
2010 Howard Jacobson, *The Finkler Question*
2011 Julian Barnes, *The Sense of an Ending*
2012 Hilary Mantel, *Bring up the Bodies*
2013 Eleanor Catton, *The Luminaries*
2014 Richard Flanagan, *The Narrow Road to the Deep North*
2015 Marlon James, *A Brief History of Seven Killings*
2016 Paul Beatty, *The Sellout*
2017 George Saunders, *Lincoln in the Bardo*
2018 Anna Burns, *Milkman*
2019 Margaret Atwood, *The Testaments*; Bernardine Evaristo, *Girl, Woman, Other*

(1) Rushdie's *Midnight's Children* also won the Booker of Bookers prize in 1993 and the Best of the Booker prize in 2008.
(2) Ondaatje's *The English Patient* also won the Golden Man Booker prize in 2018.

Newbery Medal, 1922-2020

The Newbery Medal is awarded annually by the Association for Library Service to Children, a division of the American Library Association, to the most distinguished contribution to American children's literature published in the previous year.

Year Book, author

1922 *The Story of Mankind*, Hendrik Willem van Loon
1923 *The Voyages of Dr. Dolittle*, Hugh Lofting
1924 *The Dark Frigate*, Charles Boardman Hawes
1925 *Tales From Silver Lands*, Charles J. Finger
1926 *Shen of the Sea*, Arthur Bowie Chrisman
1927 *Smoky, the Cowhorse*, Will James
1928 *Gay-Neck: The Story of a Pigeon*, Dhan Gopal Mukerji
1929 *The Trumpeter of Krakow*, Eric P. Kelly
1930 *Hitty, Her First Hundred Years*, Rachel Field
1931 *The Cat Who Went to Heaven*, Elizabeth Coatsworth
1932 *Waterless Mountain*, Laura Adams Armer
1933 *Young Fu of the Upper Yangtze*, Elizabeth Foreman Lewis
1934 *Invincible Louisa*, Cornelia Meigs
1935 *Dobry*, Monica Shannon

Year Book, author

1936 *Caddie Woodlawn*, Carol Ryrie Brink
1937 *Roller Skates*, Ruth Sawyer
1938 *The White Stag*, Kate Seredy
1939 *Thimble Summer*, Elizabeth Enright
1940 *Daniel Boone*, James Daugherty
1941 *Call It Courage*, Armstrong Sperry
1942 *The Matchlock Gun*, Walter D. Edmonds
1943 *Adam of the Road*, Elizabeth Janet Gray
1944 *Johnny Tremain*, Esther Forbes
1945 *Rabbit Hill*, Robert Lawson
1946 *Strawberry Girl*, Lois Lenski
1947 *Miss Hickory*, Carolyn Sherwin Bailey
1948 *The Twenty-One Balloons*, William Pène du Bois
1949 *King of the Wind*, Marguerite Henry

Year	Book, author
1950	*The Door in the Wall*, Marguerite de Angeli
1951	*Amos Fortune, Free Man*, Elizabeth Yates
1952	*Ginger Pye*, Eleanor Estes
1953	*Secret of the Andes*, Ann Nolan Clark
1954	*… And Now Miguel*, Joseph Krumgold
1955	*The Wheel on the School*, Meindert DeJong
1956	*Carry On, Mr. Bowditch*, Jean Lee Latham
1957	*Miracles on Maple Hill*, Virginia Sorensen
1958	*Rifles for Watie*, Harold Keith
1959	*The Witch of Blackbird Pond*, Elizabeth George Speare
1960	*Onion John*, Joseph Krumgold
1961	*Island of the Blue Dolphins*, Scott O'Dell
1962	*The Bronze Bow*, Elizabeth George Speare
1963	*A Wrinkle in Time*, Madeleine L'Engle
1964	*It's Like This, Cat*, Emily Cheney Neville
1965	*Shadow of a Bull*, Maia Wojciechowska
1966	*I, Juan de Pareja*, Elizabeth Borton de Trevino
1967	*Up a Road Slowly*, Irene Hunt
1968	*From the Mixed-Up Files of Mrs. Basil E. Frankweiler*, E. L. Konigsburg
1969	*The High King*, Lloyd Alexander
1970	*Sounder*, William H. Armstrong
1971	*The Summer of the Swans*, Betsy Byars
1972	*Mrs. Frisby and the Rats of NIMH*, Robert C. O'Brien
1973	*Julie of the Wolves*, Jean Craighead George
1974	*The Slave Dancer*, Paula Fox
1975	*M. C. Higgins, the Great*, Virginia Hamilton
1976	*The Grey King*, Susan Cooper
1977	*Roll of Thunder, Hear My Cry*, Mildred D. Taylor
1978	*Bridge to Terabithia*, Katherine Paterson
1979	*The Westing Game*, Ellen Raskin
1980	*A Gathering of Days*, Joan Blos
1981	*Jacob Have I Loved*, Katherine Paterson
1982	*A Visit to William Blake's Inn: Poems for Innocent and Experienced Travelers*, Nancy Willard
1983	*Dicey's Song*, Cynthia Voigt
1984	*Dear Mr. Henshaw*, Beverly Cleary
1985	*The Hero and the Crown*, Robin McKinley

Year	Book, author
1986	*Sarah, Plain and Tall*, Patricia MacLachlan
1987	*The Whipping Boy*, Sid Fleischman
1988	*Lincoln: A Photobiography*, Russell Freedman
1989	*Joyful Noise: Poems for Two Voices*, Paul Fleischman
1990	*Number the Stars*, Lois Lowry
1991	*Maniac Magee*, Jerry Spinelli
1992	*Shiloh*, Phyllis Reynolds Naylor
1993	*Missing May*, Cynthia Rylant
1994	*The Giver*, Lois Lowry
1995	*Walk Two Moons*, Sharon Creech
1996	*The Midwife's Apprentice*, Karen Cushman
1997	*The View From Saturday*, E. L. Konigsburg
1998	*Out of the Dust*, Karen Hesse
1999	*Holes*, Louis Sachar
2000	*Bud, Not Buddy*, Christopher Paul Curtis
2001	*A Year Down Yonder*, Richard Peck
2002	*A Single Shard*, Linda Sue Park
2003	*Crispin: The Cross of Lead*, Avi
2004	*The Tale of Despereaux*, Kate DiCamillo
2005	*Kira-Kira*, Cynthia Kadohata
2006	*Criss Cross*, Lynne Rae Perkins
2007	*The Higher Power of Lucky*, Susan Patron
2008	*Good Masters! Sweet Ladies! Voices From a Medieval Village*, Laura Amy Schlitz
2009	*The Graveyard Book*, Neil Gaiman
2010	*When You Reach Me*, Rebecca Stead
2011	*Moon Over Manifest*, Clare Vanderpool
2012	*Dead End in Norvelt*, Jack Gantos
2013	*The One and Only Ivan*, Katherine Applegate
2014	*Flora & Ulysses: The Illuminated Adventures*, Kate DiCamillo
2015	*The Crossover*, Kwame Alexander
2016	*Last Stop on Market Street*, Matt de la Peña
2017	*The Girl Who Drank the Moon*, Kelly Barnhill
2018	*Hello, Universe*, Erin Entrada Kelly
2019	*Merci Suárez Changes Gears*, Meg Medina
2020	*New Kid*, Jerry Craft

Caldecott Medal, 1938-2020

The Caldecott Medal is awarded annually by the Association for Library Service to Children, a division of the American Library Association, to the illustrator of the most distinguished American picture book for children.

Year	Book, illustrator
1938	*Animals of the Bible*, Dorothy P. Lathrop
1939	*Mei Li*, Thomas Handforth
1940	*Abraham Lincoln*, Ingri and Edgar Parin d'Aulaire
1941	*They Were Strong and Good*, Robert Lawson
1942	*Make Way for Ducklings*, Robert McCloskey
1943	*The Little House*, Virginia Lee Burton
1944	*Many Moons*, Louis Slobodkin
1945	*Prayer for a Child*, Elizabeth Orton Jones
1946	*The Rooster Crows*, Maude and Miska Petersham
1947	*The Little Island*, Leonard Weisgard
1948	*White Snow, Bright Snow*, Roger Duvoisin
1949	*The Big Snow*, Berta and Elmer Hader
1950	*Song of the Swallows*, Leo Politi
1951	*The Egg Tree*, Katherine Milhous
1952	*Finders Keepers*, Nicolas, pseud. (Nicholas Mordvinoff)
1953	*The Biggest Bear*, Lynd Ward
1954	*Madeline's Rescue*, Ludwig Bemelmans
1955	*Cinderella, or the Little Glass Slipper*, Marcia Brown
1956	*Frog Went A-Courtin'*, Feodor Rojankovsky
1957	*A Tree Is Nice*, Marc Simont
1958	*Time of Wonder*, Robert McCloskey
1959	*Chanticleer and the Fox*, Barbara Cooney
1960	*Nine Days to Christmas*, Marie Hall Ets
1961	*Baboushka and the Three Kings*, Nicolas Sidjakov
1962	*Once a Mouse*, Marcia Brown
1963	*The Snowy Day*, Ezra Jack Keats
1964	*Where the Wild Things Are*, Maurice Sendak
1965	*May I Bring a Friend?*, Beni Montresor
1966	*Always Room for One More*, Nonny Hogrogian
1967	*Sam, Bangs, and Moonshine*, Evaline Ness
1968	*Drummer Hoff*, Ed Emberley
1969	*The Fool of the World and the Flying Ship*, Uri Shulevitz
1970	*Sylvester and the Magic Pebble*, William Steig
1971	*A Story A Story*, Gail E. Haley
1972	*One Fine Day*, Nonny Hogrogian
1973	*The Funny Little Woman*, Blair Lent
1974	*Duffy and the Devil*, Margot Zemach
1975	*Arrow to the Sun*, Gerald McDermott
1976	*Why Mosquitoes Buzz in People's Ears*, Leo and Diane Dillon
1977	*Ashanti to Zulu: African Traditions*, Leo and Diane Dillon
1978	*Noah's Ark*, Peter Spier
1979	*The Girl Who Loved Wild Horses*, Paul Goble
1980	*Ox-Cart Man*, Barbara Cooney
1981	*Fables*, Arnold Lobel

Year	Book, illustrator
1982	*Jumanji*, Chris Van Allsburg
1983	*Shadow*, Marcia Brown
1984	*The Glorious Flight: Across the Channel With Louis Bleriot*, Alice and Martin Provensen
1985	*Saint George and the Dragon*, Trina Schart Hyman
1986	*The Polar Express*, Chris Van Allsburg
1987	*Hey, Al*, Richard Egielski
1988	*Owl Moon*, John Schoenherr
1989	*Song and Dance Man*, Stephen Grammell
1990	*Lon Po Po: A Red-Riding Hood Story From China*, Ed Young
1991	*Black and White*, David Macaulay
1992	*Tuesday*, David Wiesner
1993	*Mirette on the High Wire*, Emily Arnold McCully
1994	*Grandfather's Journey*, Allen Say
1995	*Smoky Night*, David Diaz
1996	*Officer Buckle and Gloria*, Peggy Rathmann
1997	*Golem*, David Wisniewski
1998	*Rapunzel*, Paul O. Zelinsky
1999	*Snowflake Bentley*, Mary Azarian
2000	*Joseph Had a Little Overcoat*, Simms Taback
2001	*So You Want to Be President?*, David Small
2002	*The Three Pigs*, David Wiesner
2003	*My Friend Rabbit*, Eric Rohmann
2004	*The Man Who Walked Between the Towers*, Mordicai Gerstein
2005	*Kitten's First Full Moon*, Kevin Henkes
2006	*The Hello, Goodbye Window*, Chris Raschka
2007	*Flotsam*, David Wiesner
2008	*The Invention of Hugo Cabret*, Brian Selznick
2009	*The House in the Night*, Beth Krommes
2010	*The Lion & the Mouse*, Jerry Pinkney
2011	*A Sick Day for Amos McGee*, Erin E. Stead
2012	*A Ball for Daisy*, Chris Raschka
2013	*This Is Not My Hat*, Jon Klassen
2014	*Locomotive*, Brian Floca
2015	*The Adventures of Beekle: The Unimaginary Friend*, Dan Santat
2016	*Finding Winnie: The True Story of the World's Most Famous Bear*, Sophie Blackall
2017	*Radiant Child: The Story of Young Artist Jean-Michel Basquiat*, Javaka Steptoe
2018	*Wolf in the Snow*, Matthew Cordell
2019	*Hello Lighthouse*, Sophie Blackall
2020	*The Undefeated*, Kadir Nelson

National Book Awards, 1950-2019

The National Book Awards (known as American Book Awards 1980-86) are administered by the National Book Foundation and have been given annually since 1950. The $10,000 prizes are awarded for works published in the U.S. In some years, multiple awards were given for nonfiction in various categories; in such cases, the history and biography (if any) or biography winner is listed. Selected additional awards in nonfiction are listed in footnotes.

Other National Book Awards, 2019: Poetry: Arthur Sze, *Sight Lines*. Translated Literature: Ottilie Mulzet, László Krasznahorkai, *Baron Wenckheim's Homecoming*. Young People's Literature: Martin W. Sandler, *1919 The Year That Changed America*. Distinguished Contribution to American Letters: Edmund White. Literarian Award: Oren Teicher.

Fiction

Year	Author, book	Year	Author, book
1950	Nelson Algren, *The Man With the Golden Arm*	1985	Don DeLillo, *White Noise*
1951	William Faulkner, *The Collected Stories*	1986	E. L. Doctorow, *World's Fair*
1952	James Jones, *From Here to Eternity*	1987	Larry Heinemann, *Paco's Story*
1953	Ralph Ellison, *Invisible Man*	1988	Pete Dexter, *Paris Trout*
1954	Saul Bellow, *The Adventures of Augie March*	1989	John Casey, *Spartina*
1955	William Faulkner, *A Fable*	1990	Charles Johnson, *Middle Passage*
1956	John O'Hara, *Ten North Frederick*	1991	Norman Rush, *Mating*
1957	Wright Morris, *The Field of Vision*	1992	Cormac McCarthy, *All the Pretty Horses*
1958	John Cheever, *The Wapshot Chronicle*	1993	E. Annie Proulx, *The Shipping News*
1959	Bernard Malamud, *The Magic Barrel*	1994	William Gaddis, *A Frolic of His Own*
1960	Philip Roth, *Goodbye, Columbus*	1995	Philip Roth, *Sabbath's Theater*
1961	Conrad Richter, *The Waters of Kronos*	1996	Andrea Barrett, *Ship Fever and Other Stories*
1962	Walker Percy, *The Moviegoer*	1997	Charles Frazier, *Cold Mountain*
1963	J. F. Powers, *Morte d'Urban*	1998	Alice McDermott, *Charming Billy*
1964	John Updike, *The Centaur*	1999	Ha Jin, *Waiting*
1965	Saul Bellow, *Herzog*	2000	Susan Sontag, *In America*
1966	Katherine Anne Porter, *The Collected Stories*	2001	Jonathan Franzen, *The Corrections*
1967	Bernard Malamud, *The Fixer*	2002	Julia Glass, *Three Junes*
1968	Thornton Wilder, *The Eighth Day*	2003	Shirley Hazzard, *The Great Fire*
1969	Jerzy Kosinski, *Steps*	2004	Lily Tuck, *The News From Paraguay*
1970	Joyce Carol Oates, *Them*	2005	William T. Vollmann, *Europe Central*
1971	Saul Bellow, *Mr. Sammler's Planet*	2006	Richard Powers, *The Echo Maker*
1972	Flannery O'Connor, *The Complete Stories*	2007	Denis Johnson, *Tree of Smoke*
1973	John Barth, *Chimera*	2008	Peter Matthiessen, *Shadow Country*
1974	Thomas Pynchon, *Gravity's Rainbow*	2009	Colum McCann, *Let the Great World Spin*
1974	Isaac Bashevis Singer, *A Crown of Feathers*	2010	Jaimy Gordon, *Lord of Misrule*
1975	Robert Stone, *Dog Soldiers*	2011	Jesmyn Ward, *Salvage the Bones*
1976	William Gaddis, *JR*	2012	Louise Erdrich, *The Round House*
1977	Wallace Stegner, *The Spectator Bird*	2013	James McBride, *The Good Lord Bird*
1978	Mary Lee Settle, *Blood Ties*	2014	Phil Klay, *Redeployment*
1979	Tim O'Brien, *Going After Cacciato*	2015	Adam Johnson, *Fortune Smiles: Stories*
1980	William Styron, *Sophie's Choice*	2016	Colson Whitehead, *The Underground Railroad*
1981	Wright Morris, *Plains Song*	2017	Jesmyn Ward, *Sing, Unburied, Sing*
1982	John Updike, *Rabbit Is Rich*	2018	Sigrid Nunez, *The Friend*
1983	Alice Walker, *The Color Purple*	2019	Susan Choi, *Trust Exercise*
1984	Ellen Gilchrist, *Victory Over Japan*		

Nonfiction

Year	Author, book	Year	Author, book
1950	Ralph L. Rusk, *Ralph Waldo Emerson*	1975	Richard B. Sewall, *The Life of Emily Dickinson*[6]
1951	Newton Arvin, *Herman Melville*	1976	David Brion Davis, *The Problem of Slavery in the Age of Revolution, 1770-1823*
1952	Rachel Carson, *The Sea Around Us*		
1953	Bernard A. De Voto, *The Course of an Empire*	1977	W. A. Swanberg, *Norman Thomas: The Last Idealist*[7]
1954	Bruce Catton, *A Stillness at Appomattox*	1978	W. Jackson Bate, *Samuel Johnson*
1955	Joseph Wood Krutch, *The Measure of Man*	1979	Arthur M. Schlesinger Jr., *Robert Kennedy and His Times*
1956	Herbert Kubly, *An American in Italy*		
1957	George F. Kennan, *Russia Leaves the War*	1980	Tom Wolfe, *The Right Stuff*
1958	Catherine Drinker Bowen, *The Lion and the Throne*	1981	Maxine Hong Kingston, *China Men*
1959	J. Christopher Herold, *Mistress to an Age: A Life of Madame De Stael*	1982	Tracy Kidder, *The Soul of a New Machine*
		1983	Fox Butterfield, *China: Alive in the Bitter Sea*
1960	Richard Ellmann, *James Joyce*	1984	Robert V. Remini, *Andrew Jackson and the Course of American Democracy, 1833-1845*
1961	William L. Shirer, *The Rise and Fall of the Third Reich*		
1962	Lewis Mumford, *The City in History: Its Origins, Its Transformations, and Its Prospects*	1985	J. Anthony Lukas, *Common Ground: A Turbulent Decade in the Lives of Three American Families*
		1986	Barry Lopez, *Arctic Dreams*
1963	Leon Edel, *Henry James, Vol. II: The Conquest of London* and *Vol. III: The Middle Years*	1987	Richard Rhodes, *The Making of the Atom Bomb*
		1988	Neil Sheehan, *A Bright Shining Lie: John Paul Vann and America in Vietnam*
1964	William H. McNeill, *The Rise of the West: A History of the Human Community*		
		1989	Thomas L. Friedman, *From Beirut to Jerusalem*
1965	Louis Fisher, *The Life of Lenin*	1990	Ron Chernow, *The House of Morgan: An American Banking Dynasty and the Rise of Modern Finance*
1966	Arthur M. Schlesinger Jr., *A Thousand Days: John F. Kennedy in the White House*		
		1991	Orlando Patterson, *Freedom*
1967	Peter Gay, *The Enlightenment, An Interpretation, Vol. I: The Rise of Modern Paganism*	1992	Paul Monette, *Becoming a Man: Half a Life Story*
		1993	Gore Vidal, *United States: Essays 1952-1992*
1968	George F. Kennan, *Memoirs: 1925-1950*[1]	1994	Sherwin B. Nuland, *How We Die: Reflections on Life's Final Chapter*
1969	Winthrop D. Jordan, *White Over Black: American Attitudes Toward the Negro, 1550-1812*[2]		
		1995	Tina Rosenberg, *The Haunted Land: Facing Europe's Ghosts After Communism*
1970	T. Harry Williams, *Huey Long*[3]		
1971	James MacGregor Burns, *Roosevelt: The Soldier of Freedom*	1996	James Carroll, *An American Requiem: God, My Father, and the War That Came Between Us*
1972	Joseph P. Lash, *Eleanor and Franklin: The Story of Their Relationship, Based on Eleanor Roosevelt's Private Papers*	1997	Joseph J. Ellis, *American Sphinx: The Character of Thomas Jefferson*
		1998	Edward Ball, *Slaves in the Family*
1973	James Thomas Flexner, *George Washington, Vol. IV: Anguish and Farewell, 1793-1799*[4]	1999	John W. Dower, *Embracing Defeat: Japan in the Wake of World War II*
1974	John Clive, *Macaulay: The Shaping of the Historian*; Douglas Day, *Malcolm Lowry: A Biography*[5]	2000	Nathaniel Philbrick, *In the Heart of the Sea: The Tragedy of the Whaleship Essex*

Year	Author, book
2001	Andrew Solomon, *The Noonday Demon: An Atlas of Depression*
2002	Robert A. Caro, *Master of the Senate: The Years of Lyndon Johnson*
2003	Carlos Eire, *Waiting for Snow in Havana: Confessions of a Cuban Boy*
2004	Kevin Boyle, *Arc of Justice: A Saga of Race, Civil Rights, and Murder in the Jazz Age*
2005	Joan Didion, *The Year of Magical Thinking*
2006	Timothy Egan, *The Worst Hard Time: The Untold Story of Those Who Survived the Great American Dust Bowl*
2007	Tim Weiner, *Legacy of Ashes: The History of the CIA*
2008	Annette Gordon-Reed, *The Hemingses of Monticello: An American Family*
2009	T. J. Stiles, *The First Tycoon: The Epic Life of Cornelius Vanderbilt*
2010	Patti Smith, *Just Kids*
2011	Stephen Greenblatt, *The Swerve: How the World Became Modern*
2012	Katherine Boo, *Behind the Beautiful Forevers: Life, Death, and Hope in a Mumbai Undercity*
2013	George Packer, *The Unwinding: An Inner History of the New America*
2014	Evan Osnos, *Age of Ambition: Chasing Fortune, Truth, and Faith in the New China*
2015	Ta-Nehisi Coates, *Between the World and Me*
2016	Ibram X. Kendi, *Stamped From the Beginning: The Definitive History of Racist Ideas in America*
2017	Masha Gessen, *The Future Is History: How Totalitarianism Reclaimed Russia*
2018	Jeffrey C. Stewart, *The New Negro: The Life of Alain Locke*
2019	Sarah M. Broom, *The Yellow House*

(1) Science, Philosophy, & Religion: Jonathan Kozol, *Death at an Early Age*. (2) Arts & Letters: Norman Mailer, *The Armies of the Night: History as a Novel, the Novel as History*. (3) Arts & Letters: Lillian Hellman, *An Unfinished Woman: A Memoir*. (4) Contemp. Affairs: Frances FitzGerald, *Fire in the Lake: The Vietnamese and the Americans in Vietnam*. (5) Arts & Letters: Pauline Kael, *Deeper Into the Movies*. (6) Arts & Letters: Roger Shattuck, *Marcel Proust*; Lewis Thomas, *The Lives of a Cell: Notes of a Biology Watcher*. (7) Contemp. Thought: Bruno Bettelheim, *The Uses of Enchantment: The Meaning and Importance of Fairy Tales*.

Journalism Awards, 2020

National Magazine Awards, by American Society of Magazine Editors and Columbia Univ. Graduate School of Journalism, honoring excellence in print and on digital platforms. General Excellence: News, Sports, and Entertainment: *NY Times Magazine*; Literature, Science, and Politics: *Quanta*; Service and Lifestyle: *Bon Appétit*; Special Interest: *Hollywood Reporter*. Design: *Bon Appétit*. Photography: *National Geographic*. Feature Design: *National Geographic*. Feature Photography: *National Geographic*. Website: *The Marshall Project*. Digital Innovation: *The Marshall Project* in partnership with *The Guardian*. Social Media: *National Geographic*. Podcasting: *NY Times Magazine*, "1619." Video: *Bon Appétit* with Condé Nast Entertainment. ASME Award for Fiction: *The Paris Review*. Columns and Commentary: *Catapult*. Essays and Criticism: *Poetry*. Feature Writing: *NY Times Magazine*. Leisure Interests: *Bon Appétit*. Personal Service: *Audubon*. Profile Writing: *The Georgia Review*. Public Interest: *NY Times Magazine* in partnership with ProPublica. Single-Topic Issue: *Washington Post Magazine*.

George Foster Peabody Awards, by Univ. of Georgia, awarded to the best in electronic media. Career achievement: Cicely Tyson. Institutional awards: *Frontline*, *The Simpsons*. Other awards are listed alphabetically by media outlet. *Fleabag*, Amazon. *In the Dark: The Path Home*, APM Reports. *Threshold: The Refuge*, Auricle. *Dickinson*, Apple TV+. *Have You Heard George's Podcast?* BBC Sounds. *Apollo 11*, *The Hidden Workforce: Undocumented in America*, CNN. *Chernobyl*, *Succession*, *True Justice: Bryan Stevenson's Fight for Equality*, *Watchmen*, HBO. *Ramy*, Hulu. *Surviving R. Kelly*, Lifetime. *American Betrayal*, NBC/MSNBC. *A Different Kind of Force: Policing Mental Illness*, NBC News. *The Edge of Democracy*, *Stranger Things*, *Unbelievable*, *When They See Us*, Netflix. *Long Island Divided*, Newsday. *David Makes Man*, OWN. *For Sama*, Independent Lens: Hale County This Morning, This Evening; POV: *The Distant Barking of Dogs*, *Inventing Tomorrow*, *Midnight Traveler*, *The Silence of Others*; PBS. *Molly of Denali*, PBS Kids. *Unwarranted*, WBBM (Chicago). *Dolly Parton's America*, WNYC.

Scripps Howard Awards, by Scripps Howard Foundation. Breaking News: *Washington Post*, Broadcast, Local Coverage: WFAA (Dallas). Broadcast, Natl./Intl. Coverage: *Frontline* (PBS). Business/Financial Reporting: *Seattle Times*. Community Journalism: *Anchorage Daily News* and ProPublica. Distinguished Service to the First Amendment: *The Post and Courier* (Charleston, SC). Environmental Reporting: *Oregonian*/Oregon Live. Human Interest Storytelling: *Washington Post*. Innovation: Newsy. Investigative Reporting: *Washington Post*. Multimedia: Vox. Opinion: Kyle Whitmire, Alabama Media Group. Visual Journalism: Rodrigo Abd, Associated Press. Radio/Podcast: The Public's Radio (Rhode Island). Topic of the Year (Impact of Climate Change on Communities): NPR and Univ. of Maryland Howard Center for Investigative Journalism.

Miscellaneous Book Awards, 2020

Coretta Scott King Awards, by American Library Assn., for African American authors and illustrators of outstanding books for children and young adults. Author: Jerry Craft, *New Kid*. Illustrator: Kadir Nelson, *The Undefeated* (written by Kwame Alexander). New talent, author: Alicia D. Williams, *Genesis Begins Again*. New talent, illustrator: April Harrison, *What Is Given From the Heart* (written by Patricia C. McKissack).

Costa Book Awards. Book of the Year (formerly Whitbread Award): *The Volunteer*, Jack Fairweather.

Edgar Awards, by Mystery Writers of America. Novel: *The Stranger Diaries*, Elly Griffiths. First Novel: *Miracle Creek*, Angie Kim. Paperback Original: *The Hotel Neversink*, Adam O'Fallon Price. Fact Crime: *The Less People Know About Us: A Mystery of Betrayal, Family Secrets, and Stolen Identity*, Axton Betz-Hamilton. Critical/Biographical: *Hitchcock and the Censors*, John Billheimer. Short Story: "One of These Nights," *Cutting Edge: New Stories of Mystery and Crime by Women Writers*, Livia Llewellyn. Juvenile: *Me and Sam-Sam Handle the Apocalypse*, Susan Vaught. Young Adult: *Catfishing on CatNet*, Naomi Kritzer. TV Episode: "Season 5, Episode 4," *Line of Duty*, Jed Mercurio. Robert L. Fish Memorial Award: "There's a Riot Goin' On," *Milwaukee Noir*, Derrick Harriell. Grand Master: Barbara Neely. Raven Award: Left Coast Crime. Ellery Queen Award: Kelley Ragland, Minotaur Books. Mary Higgins Clark Award: *The Night Visitors*, Carol Goodman. G.P. Putnam's Sons Sue Grafton Memorial Award: *Borrowed Time*, Tracy Clark.

Golden Kite Awards, by the Society of Children's Book Writers and Illustrators. Middle Grade Fiction: *The Bridge Home*, Padma Venkatraman. Nonfiction (younger readers): *Mario and the Hole in the Sky*, Elizabeth Rusch. Nonfiction (older readers): *Torpedoed*, Deborah Heiligman. Young Adult Fiction: *Lovely War*, Julie Berry. Picture Book Text: *A Green Place to Be*, Ashley Benham Yazdani. Picture Book Illustration: *Clever Little Witch*, Hyewon Yum. Sid Fleischman Humor Award: *Pie in the Sky*, Remy Lai.

Hugo Awards. Novel: *A Memory Called Empire*, Arkady Martine. Novella: *This Is How You Lose the Time War*, Amal El-Mohtar and Max Gladstone. Novelette: "Emergency Skin," N.K. Jemisin. Short Story: "As the Last I May Know," S. L. Huang. Related Work: "2019 John W. Campbell Award Acceptance Speech," Jeannette Ng. Series: *The Expanse*, James S. A. Corey. Graphic Story: *LaGuardia*, Nnedi Okorafor, art by Tana Ford. Dramatic Presentation, long form: *Good Omens*, Neil Gaiman. Dramatic Presentation, short form: "The Answer," *The Good Place*, Daniel Schofield.

National Book Critics Circle Awards. Fiction: Edwidge Danticat, *Everything Inside*. Nonfiction: Patrick Radden Keefe, *Say Nothing: A True Story of Murder and Memory in Northern Ireland*. Autobiography: Chanel Miller, *Know My Name: A Memoir*. Biography: Josh Levin, *The Queen: The Forgotten Life Behind an American Myth*. Criticism: Saidiya Hartman, *Wayward Lives, Beautiful Experiments: Intimate Histories of Social Upheaval*. Poetry: Morgan Parker, *Magical Negro: Poems*. John Leonard Prize: Sarah M. Broom, *The Yellow House*. Ivan Sandrof Lifetime Achievement Award: Naomi Shihab Nye. Nona Balakian Citation for Excellence in Reviewing: Katy Waldman.

Nebula Awards, by the Science Fiction and Fantasy Writers of America. Novel: *A Song for a New Day*, Sarah Pinsker. Novella: *This Is How You Lose the Time War*, Amal El-Mohtar and Max Gladstone. Novelette: "Carpe Glitter," Cat Rambo. Short Story: "Give the Family My Love," A. T. Greenblatt. Ray Bradbury Award: "Hard Times," *Good Omens*, Neil Gaiman. Andre Norton Award: *Riverland*, Fran Wilde.

Printz Award, for young adult literature: *Dig*, A.S. King.

Spingarn Medal, 1915-2019

The Spingarn Medal has been awarded annually in most years since 1915 by the National Assn. for the Advancement of Colored People for outstanding achievement by an African American.

1915 Ernest E. Just	**1942** A. Philip Randolph	**1967** Edward W. Brooke	**1993** Dorothy I. Height
1916 Charles Young	**1943** William H. Hastie	**1968** Sammy Davis Jr.	**1994** Maya Angelou
1917 Harry T. Burleigh	**1944** Charles Drew	**1969** Clarence M. Mitchell Jr.	**1995** John Hope Franklin
1918 William S. Braithwaite	**1945** Paul Robeson	**1970** Jacob Lawrence	**1996** A. Leon Higginbotham Jr.
1919 Archibald H. Grimké	**1946** Thurgood Marshall	**1971** Leon H. Sullivan	**1997** Carl T. Rowan
1920 W. E. B. Du Bois	**1947** Dr. Percy L. Julian	**1972** Gordon Parks	**1998** Myrlie Evers-Williams
1921 Charles S. Gilpin	**1948** Channing H. Tobias	**1973** Wilson C. Riles	**1999** Earl G. Graves Sr.
1922 Mary B. Talbert	**1949** Ralph J. Bunche	**1974** Damon Keith	**2000** Oprah Winfrey
1923 George W. Carver	**1950** Charles H. Houston	**1976** Henry (Hank) Aaron	**2001** Vernon E. Jordan Jr.
1924 Roland Hayes	**1951** Mabel K. Staupers	**1977** Alvin Ailey	**2002** John Lewis
1925 James W. Johnson	**1952** Harry T. Moore	**1977** Alex Haley	**2003** Constance Baker Motley
1926 Carter G. Woodson	**1953** Paul R. Williams	**1979** Andrew Young	**2004** Robert L. Carter
1927 Anthony Overton	**1954** Theodore K. Lawless	**1979** Rosa L. Parks	**2005** Oliver W. Hill
1928 Charles W. Chesnutt	**1955** Carl Murphy	**1980** Dr. Rayford W. Logan	**2006** Dr. Benjamin S. Carson
1929 Mordecai W. Johnson	**1956** Jack R. Robinson	**1981** Coleman Young	**2007** John Conyers Jr.
1930 Henry A. Hunt	**1957** Martin Luther King Jr.	**1982** Dr. Benjamin E. Mays	**2008** Ruby Dee
1931 Richard B. Harrison	**1958** Daisy Bates and the	**1983** Lena Horne	**2009** Julian Bond
1932 Robert R. Moton	Little Rock Nine	**1985** Thomas Bradley	**2010** Cicely Tyson
1933 Max Yergan	**1959** Duke Ellington	**1985** Bill Cosby	**2011** Frankie Muse Freeman
1934 William T. B. Williams	**1960** Langston Hughes	**1986** Dr. Benjamin L. Hooks	**2012** Harry Belafonte
1935 Mary McLeod Bethune	**1961** Kenneth B. Clark	**1987** Percy E. Sutton	**2013** Jessye Norman
1936 John Hope	**1962** Robert C. Weaver	**1988** Frederick D. Patterson	**2014** Quincy Jones
1937 Walter White	**1963** Medgar W. Evers	**1989** Jesse Jackson	**2015** Sidney Poitier
1939 Marian Anderson	**1964** Roy Wilkins	**1990** L. Douglas Wilder	**2016** Nathaniel R. Jones
1940 Louis T. Wright	**1965** Leontyne Price	**1991** Gen. Colin L. Powell	**2018** Willie L. Brown Jr.
1941 Richard Wright	**1966** John H. Johnson	**1992** Barbara Jordan	**2019** Patrick Gaspard

Miss America Winners, 1921-2020

Year	Winner, hometown	Year	Winner, hometown
1921	Margaret Gorman, Washington, DC	1975	Shirley Cothran, Denton, Texas
1922-23	Mary Campbell, Columbus, Ohio	1976	Tawney Elaine Godin, Saratoga Springs, New York
1924	Ruth Malcolmson, Philadelphia, Pennsylvania	1977	Dorothy Kathleen Benham, Edina, Minnesota
1925	Fay Lamphier, Oakland, California	1978	Susan Perkins, Columbus, Ohio
1926	Norma Smallwood, Tulsa, Oklahoma	1979	Kylene Barker, Roanoke, Virginia
1927	Lois Delander, Joliet, Illinois	1980	Cheryl Prewitt, Ackerman, Mississippi
1933	Marion Bergeron, West Haven, Connecticut	1981	Susan Powell, Elk City, Oklahoma
1935	Henrietta Leaver, Pittsburgh, Pennsylvania	1982	Elizabeth Ward, Russellville, Arkansas
1936	Rose Coyle, Philadelphia, Pennsylvania	1983	Debra Maffett, Anaheim, California
1937	Bette Cooper, Bertrand Island, New Jersey	1984[1]	Suzette Charles, Mays Landing, New Jersey
1938	Marilyn Meseke, Marion, Ohio	1985	Sharlene Wells, Salt Lake City, Utah
1939	Patricia Donnelly, Detroit, Michigan	1986	Susan Akin, Meridian, Mississippi
1940	Frances Marie Burke, Philadelphia, Pennsylvania	1987	Kellye Cash, Memphis, Tennessee
1941	Rosemary LaPlanche, Los Angeles, California	1988	Kaye Lani Rae Rafko, Monroe, Michigan
1942	Jo-Caroll Dennison, Tyler, Texas	1989	Gretchen Carlson, Anoka, Minnesota
1943	Jean Bartel, Los Angeles, California	1990	Debbye Turner, Columbia, Missouri
1944	Venus Ramey, Washington, DC	1991	Marjorie Vincent, Oak Park, Illinois
1945	Bess Myerson, New York, New York	1992	Carolyn Suzanne Sapp, Honolulu, Hawaii
1946	Marilyn Buferd, Los Angeles, California	1993	Leanza Cornett, Jacksonville, Florida
1947	Barbara Walker, Memphis, Tennessee	1994	Kimberly Aiken, Columbia, South Carolina
1948	BeBe Shopp, Hopkins, Minnesota	1995	Heather Whitestone, Birmingham, Alabama
1949	Jacque Mercer, Litchfield, Arizona	1996	Shawntel Smith, Muldrow, Oklahoma
1951	Yolande Betbeze, Mobile, Alabama	1997	Tara Dawn Holland, Overland Park, Kansas
1952	Coleen Kay Hutchins, Salt Lake City, Utah	1998	Kate Shindle, Evanston, Illinois
1953	Neva Jane Langley, Macon, Georgia	1999	Nicole Johnson, Roanoke, Virginia
1954	Evelyn Margaret Ay, Ephrata, Pennsylvania	2000	Heather Renee French, Maysville, Kentucky
1955	Lee Meriwether, San Francisco, California	2001	Angela Perez Baraquio, Honolulu, Hawaii
1956	Sharon Ritchie, Denver, Colorado	2002	Katie Harman, Gresham, Oregon
1957	Marian McKnight, Manning, South Carolina	2003	Erika Harold, Urbana, Illinois
1958	Marilyn Van Derbur, Denver, Colorado	2004	Ericka Dunlap, Orlando, Florida
1959	Mary Ann Mobley, Brandon, Mississippi	2005	Deidre Downs, Birmingham, Alabama
1960	Lynda Lee Mead, Natchez, Mississippi	2006	Jennifer Berry, Tulsa, Oklahoma
1961	Nancy Fleming, Montague, Michigan	2007	Lauren Nelson, Lawton, Oklahoma
1962	Maria Fletcher, Asheville, North Carolina	2008	Kirsten Haglund, Farmington Hills, Michigan
1963	Jacquelyn Mayer, Sandusky, Ohio	2009	Katie Stam, Seymour, Indiana
1964	Donna Axum, El Dorado, Arkansas	2010	Caressa Cameron, Fredricksburg, Virginia
1965	Vonda Kay Van Dyke, Phoenix, Arizona	2011	Teresa Scanlan, Gering, Nebraska
1966	Deborah Irene Bryant, Overland Park, Kansas	2012	Laura Kaeppeler, Kenosha, Wisconsin
1967	Jane Anne Jayroe, Laverne, Oklahoma	2013	Mallory Hytes Hagen, Brooklyn, New York
1968	Debra Dene Barnes, Moran, Kansas	2014	Nina Davuluri, Syracuse, New York
1969	Judith Anne Ford, Belvidere, Illinois	2015	Kira Kazantsev, New York, New York
1970	Pamela Anne Eldred, Birmingham, Michigan	2016	Betty Cantrell, Warner Robins, Georgia
1971	Phyllis Ann George, Denton, Texas	2017	Savvy Shields, Fayetteville, Arkansas
1972	Laurie Lea Schaefer, Bexley, Ohio	2018	Cara Mund, Bismarck, North Dakota
1973	Terry Anne Meeuwsen, DePere, Wisconsin	2019	Nia Franklin, Brooklyn, New York
1974	Rebecca Ann King, Denver, Colorado	2020	Camille Schrier, Richmond, Virginia

Note: Since the 1950 pageant, winners have been crowned Miss America of the following year (e.g., Miss America 1951 competed in 1950). (1) Miss New York, Vanessa Williams, resigned July 23, 1984.

Tony (Antoinette Perry) Awards, 2019

Play: *The Ferryman*
Musical: *Hadestown*
Book of a musical: *Tootsie*, Robert Horn
Original score: *Hadestown*, Anaïs Mitchell
Play revival: *The Boys in the Band*
Musical revival: *Rodgers & Hammerstein's Oklahoma!*
Actor, play: Bryan Cranston, *Network*
Actress, play: Elaine May, *The Waverly Gallery*
Actor, musical: Santino Fontana, *Tootsie*
Actress, musical: Stephanie J. Block, *The Cher Show*
Featured actor, play: Bertie Carvel, *Ink*
Featured actress, play: Celia Keenan-Bolger, *To Kill a Mockingbird*
Featured actor, musical: André De Shields, *Hadestown*
Featured actress, musical: Ali Stroker, *Rodgers & Hammerstein's Oklahoma!*
Direction, play: Sam Mendes, *The Ferryman*
Direction, musical: Rachel Chavkin, *Hadestown*
Choreography: Sergio Trujillo, *Ain't Too Proud—The Life and Times of the Temptations*

Orchestrations: Michael Chorney and Todd Sickafoose, *Hadestown*
Costume design, play: Rob Howell, *The Ferryman*
Costume design, musical: Bob Mackie, *The Cher Show*
Lighting design, play: Neil Austin, *Ink*
Lighting design, musical: Bradley King, *Hadestown*
Scenic design, play: Rob Howell, *The Ferryman*
Scenic design, musical: Rachel Hauck, *Hadestown*
Sound design, play: Fitz Patton, *Choir Boy*
Sound design, musical: Nevin Steinberg and Jessica Paz, *Hadestown*
Regional theatre: TheatreWorks Silicon Valley, Palo Alto, CA
Special Tony Award: Marin Mazzie, Sonny Tilders and Creature Technology Company, Jason Michael Webb
Special Tony Award, lifetime achievement: Rosemary Harris, Terrence McNally, Harold Wheeler
Isabelle Stevenson Award: Judith Light
Tony Honors for Excellence in the Theatre: Broadway Inspirational Voices (Michael McElroy, Founder); Peter Entin; FDNY Engine 54, Ladder 4, Battalion 9; Joseph Blakely Forbes

Tony Awards, 1948-2019

Year	Play	Musical	Year	Play	Musical
1948	*Mister Roberts*	No award	1984	*The Real Thing*	*La Cage aux Folles*
1949	*Death of a Salesman*	*Kiss Me Kate*	1985	*Biloxi Blues*	*Big River*
1950	*The Cocktail Party*	*South Pacific*	1986	*I'm Not Rappaport*	*The Mystery of Edwin Drood*
1951	*The Rose Tattoo*	*Guys and Dolls*	1987	*Fences*	*Les Misérables*
1952	*The Fourposter*	*The King and I*	1988	*M. Butterfly*	*Phantom of the Opera*
1953	*The Crucible*	*Wonderful Town*	1989	*The Heidi Chronicles*	*Jerome Robbins' Broadway*
1954	*The Teahouse of the August Moon*	*Kismet*	1990	*The Grapes of Wrath*	*City of Angels*
1955	*The Desperate Hours*	*The Pajama Game*	1991	*Lost in Yonkers*	*The Will Rogers Follies*
1956	*The Diary of Anne Frank*	*Damn Yankees*	1992	*Dancing at Lughnasa*	*Crazy for You*
1957	*Long Day's Journey Into Night*	*My Fair Lady*	1993	*Angels in America: Millennium Approaches*	*Kiss of the Spider Woman*
1958	*Sunrise at Campobello*	*The Music Man*	1994	*Angels in America: Perestroika*	*Passion*
1959	*J.B.*	*Redhead*	1995	*Love! Valour! Compassion!*	*Sunset Boulevard*
1960	*The Miracle Worker*	*Fiorello!* and *The Sound of Music*	1996	*Master Class*	*Rent*
1961	*Becket*	*Bye, Bye Birdie*	1997	*The Last Night of Ballyhoo*	*Titanic*
1962	*A Man for All Seasons*	*How to Succeed in Business Without Really Trying*	1998	*Art*	*The Lion King*
1963	*Who's Afraid of Virginia Woolf?*	*A Funny Thing Happened on the Way to the Forum*	1999	*Side Man*	*Fosse*
1964	*Luther*	*Hello, Dolly!*	2000	*Copenhagen*	*Contact*
1965	*The Subject Was Roses*	*Fiddler on the Roof*	2001	*Proof*	*The Producers*
1966	*Marat/Sade*	*Man of La Mancha*	2002	*Edward Albee's The Goat or Who Is Sylvia?*	*Thoroughly Modern Millie*
1967	*The Homecoming*	*Cabaret*	2003	*Take Me Out*	*Hairspray*
1968	*Rosencrantz and Guildenstern Are Dead*	*Hallelujah, Baby!*	2004	*I Am My Own Wife*	*Avenue Q*
1969	*The Great White Hope*	*1776*	2005	*Doubt*	*Monty Python's Spamalot*
1970	*Borstal Boy*	*Applause*	2006	*The History Boys*	*Jersey Boys*
1971	*Sleuth*	*Company*	2007	*The Coast of Utopia*	*Spring Awakening*
1972	*Sticks and Bones*	*Two Gentlemen of Verona*	2008	*August: Osage County*	*In the Heights*
1973	*That Championship Season*	*A Little Night Music*	2009	*God of Carnage*	*Billy Elliot, The Musical*
1974	*The River Niger*	*Raisin*	2010	*Red*	*Memphis*
1975	*Equus*	*The Wiz*	2011	*War Horse*	*The Book of Mormon*
1976	*Travesties*	*A Chorus Line*	2012	*Clybourne Park*	*Once*
1977	*The Shadow Box*	*Annie*	2013	*Vanya and Sonia and Masha and Spike*	*Kinky Boots*
1978	*Da*	*Ain't Misbehavin'*	2014	*All the Way*	*A Gentleman's Guide to Love & Murder*
1979	*The Elephant Man*	*Sweeney Todd*	2015	*The Curious Incident of the Dog in the Night-Time*	*Fun Home*
1980	*Children of a Lesser God*	*Evita*	2016	*The Humans*	*Hamilton*
1981	*Amadeus*	*42nd Street*	2017	*Oslo*	*Dear Evan Hansen*
1982	*The Life and Adventures of Nicholas Nickelby*	*Nine*	2018	*Harry Potter and the Cursed Child, Parts One and Two*	*The Band's Visit*
1983	*Torch Song Trilogy*	*Cats*	2019	*The Ferryman*	*Hadestown*

Selected Prime-Time Emmy Awards, 2020

Drama series: *Succession*, HBO
Comedy series: *Schitt's Creek*, Pop
Limited series: *Watchmen*, HBO
TV movie: *Bad Education*, HBO
Variety talk series: *Last Week Tonight With John Oliver*, HBO
Variety sketch series: *Saturday Night Live*, NBC
Lead actor, drama: Jeremy Strong, *Succession*, HBO
Lead actress, drama: Zendaya, *Euphoria*, HBO
Lead actor, comedy: Eugene Levy, *Schitt's Creek*, Pop
Lead actress, comedy: Catherine O'Hara, *Schitt's Creek*, Pop

Lead actor, limited series: Mark Ruffalo, *I Know This Much Is True*, HBO
Lead actress, limited series: Regina King, *Watchmen*, HBO
Sup. actor, drama: Billy Crudup, *The Morning Show*, Apple TV+
Sup. actress, drama: Julia Garner, *Ozark*, Netflix
Sup. actor, comedy: Daniel Levy, *Schitt's Creek*, Pop
Sup. actress, comedy: Annie Murphy, *Schitt's Creek*, Pop
Sup. actor, limited series: Yahya Abdul-Mateen II, *Watchmen*, HBO
Sup. actress, limited series: Uzo Aduba, *Mrs. America*, FX
Reality-competition program: *RuPaul's Drag Race*, VH1

Prime-Time Emmy Awards, 1952-2020

The Academy of Television Arts and Sciences presented the first Emmy Awards in 1949. Through the years, award categories have changed, but since 1952, the Academy has given out an outstanding comedy and drama award annually.

Year	Comedy	Drama	Year	Comedy	Drama
1952	*Red Skelton Show*, NBC	*Studio One*, CBS	1983	*Cheers*, NBC	*Hill Street Blues*, NBC
1953	*I Love Lucy*, CBS	*Robert Montgomery Presents*, NBC	1984	*Cheers*, NBC	*Hill Street Blues*, NBC
1954	*I Love Lucy*, CBS	*The U.S. Steel Hour*, ABC	1985	*The Cosby Show*, NBC	*Cagney & Lacey*, CBS
1955	*Make Room for Daddy*, ABC	*The U.S. Steel Hour*, ABC	1986	*Golden Girls*, NBC	*Cagney & Lacey*, CBS
1956	*Phil Silvers Show*, CBS	*Producers' Showcase*, NBC	1987	*Golden Girls*, NBC	*L.A. Law*, NBC
1957	*Phil Silvers Show*, CBS	"Requiem for a Heavyweight," CBS[1]	1988	*The Wonder Years*, ABC	*thirtysomething*, ABC
1958	*Phil Silvers Show*, CBS	*Gunsmoke*, CBS	1989	*Cheers*, NBC	*L.A. Law*, NBC
1959[2]	*Jack Benny Show*, CBS	2 awards[3]	1990	*Murphy Brown*, CBS	*L.A. Law*, NBC
1960	*Art Carney Special*, NBC	*Playhouse 90*, CBS	1991	*Cheers*, NBC	*L.A. Law*, NBC
1961	*Jack Benny Show*, CBS	*Hallmark Hall of Fame: Macbeth*, NBC	1992	*Murphy Brown*, CBS	*Northern Exposure*, CBS
			1993	*Seinfeld*, NBC	*Picket Fences*, CBS
1962	*Bob Newhart Show*, CBS	*The Defenders*, CBS	1994	*Frasier*, NBC	*Picket Fences*, CBS
1963	*Dick Van Dyke Show*, CBS	*The Defenders*, CBS	1995	*Frasier*, NBC	*NYPD Blue*, ABC
1964	*Dick Van Dyke Show*, CBS	*The Defenders*, CBS	1996	*Frasier*, NBC	*ER*, NBC
1965	*Dick Van Dyke Show*, CBS	*Hallmark Hall of Fame: The Magnificent Yankee*, NBC	1997	*Frasier*, NBC	*Law & Order*, NBC
			1998	*Frasier*, NBC	*The Practice*, ABC
1966	*Dick Van Dyke Show*, CBS	*The Fugitive*, ABC	1999	*Ally McBeal*, FOX	*The Practice*, ABC
1967	*The Monkees*, NBC	*Mission: Impossible*, CBS	2000	*Will & Grace*, NBC	*The West Wing*, NBC
1968	*Get Smart*, NBC	*Mission: Impossible*, CBS	2001	*Sex and the City*, HBO	*The West Wing*, NBC
1969	*Get Smart*, NBC	*NET Playhouse*, NET	2002	*Friends*, NBC	*The West Wing*, NBC
1970	*My World and Welcome to It*, NBC	*Marcus Welby, M.D.*, ABC	2003	*Everybody Loves Raymond*, CBS	*The West Wing*, NBC
1971	*All in the Family*, CBS	*The Bold Ones: The Senator*, NBC	2004	*Arrested Development*, FOX	*The Sopranos*, HBO
			2005	*Everybody Loves Raymond*, CBS	*Lost*, ABC
1972	*All in the Family*, CBS	*Masterpiece Theatre: Elizabeth R*, PBS	2006	*The Office*, NBC	*24*, FOX
1973	*All in the Family*, CBS	*The Waltons*, CBS	2007	*30 Rock*, NBC	*The Sopranos*, HBO
1974	*M*A*S*H*, CBS	*Masterpiece Theatre: Upstairs, Downstairs*; PBS	2008	*30 Rock*, NBC	*Mad Men*, AMC
1975	*Mary Tyler Moore Show*, CBS	*Masterpiece Theatre: Upstairs, Downstairs*; PBS	2009	*30 Rock*, NBC	*Mad Men*, AMC
			2010	*Modern Family*, ABC	*Mad Men*, AMC
1976	*Mary Tyler Moore Show*, CBS	*Police Story*, NBC	2011	*Modern Family*, ABC	*Mad Men*, AMC
1977	*Mary Tyler Moore Show*, CBS	*Masterpiece Theatre: Upstairs, Downstairs*; PBS	2012	*Modern Family*, ABC	*Homeland*, Showtime
1978	*All in the Family*, CBS	*The Rockford Files*, NBC	2013	*Modern Family*, ABC	*Breaking Bad*, AMC
1979	*Taxi*, ABC	*Lou Grant*, CBS	2014	*Modern Family*, ABC	*Breaking Bad*, AMC
1980	*Taxi*, ABC	*Lou Grant*, CBS	2015	*Veep*, HBO	*Game of Thrones*, HBO
1981	*Taxi*, ABC	*Hill Street Blues*, NBC	2016	*Veep*, HBO	*Game of Thrones*, HBO
1982	*Barney Miller*, ABC	*Hill Street Blues*, NBC	2017	*Veep*, HBO	*The Handmaid's Tale*, Hulu
			2018	*The Marvelous Mrs. Maisel*, Amazon	*Game of Thrones*, HBO
			2019	*Fleabag*, Amazon	*Game of Thrones*, HBO
			2020	*Schitt's Creek*, Pop	*Succession*, HBO

(1) Best single program of the year; shown on *Playhouse 90*, which was named best new series. (2) Beginning in 1959, Emmys were awarded for work in the season encompassing the previous and current year. (3) *Playhouse 90* (CBS) was best dramatic series of one hour or longer, *Alcoa-Goodyear Theatre* (NBC) of less than one hour.

Selected Daytime Emmy Awards, 2020

Children's or family viewing program: *Ghostwriter*, Apple TV+
Children's series (animated): *The Dragon Prince*, Netflix
Children's series (preschool): *Sesame Street*, HBO
Culinary program: *Giada Entertains*, Food Network
Drama series: *The Young and the Restless*, CBS, and *The Bay*, Amazon
Entertainment news program: *Entertainment Tonight*, synd.
Game show: *Jeopardy!*, synd.
Legal/courtroom program: *The People's Court*, synd.
Morning program: *Today Show*, NBC
Talk show, entertainment: *The Ellen DeGeneres Show*, synd.
Talk show, informative: *The View*, ABC
Travel/adventure program: *The Zimmern List*, Travel Channel
Young adult program: *Trinkets*, Netflix

Lead actress: Heather Tom, *The Bold and the Beautiful*, CBS
Lead actor: Jason Thompson, *The Young and the Restless*, CBS
Supp. actress: Tamara Braun, *General Hospital*, ABC
Supp. actor: Bryton James, *The Young and the Restless*, CBS
Young performer: Olivia Rose Keegan, *Days of Our Lives*, NBC
Culinary host: Giada De Laurentiis, *Giada Entertains*, Food Network
Game show host: Alex Trebek, *Jeopardy!*, synd.
Talk show host, entertainment: Kelly Clarkson, *The Kelly Clarkson Show*, synd.
Talk show host, informative: Tamron Hall, *Tamron Hall*, synd.
Directing team: *General Hospital*, ABC
Writing team: *The Bold and the Beautiful*, CBS

Golden Globe Awards, 2020

The Hollywood Foreign Press Association (then the Hollywood Foreign Press Correspondents Association) presented its first awards for achievement in film in 1944; TV in 1955. **Cecil B. deMille Award:** Tom Hanks. **Carol Burnett Award:** Ellen DeGeneres.

Film

Drama: *1917*
Comedy/musical: *Once Upon a Time...in Hollywood*
Actress, drama: Renée Zellweger, *Judy*
Actor, drama: Joaquin Phoenix, *Joker*
Actress, comedy/musical: Awkwafina, *The Farewell*
Actor, comedy/musical: Taron Egerton, *Rocketman*
Supporting actress: Laura Dern, *Marriage Story*
Supporting actor: Brad Pitt, *Once Upon a Time...in Hollywood*
Director: Sam Mendes, *1917*
Screenplay: Quentin Tarantino, *Once Upon a Time...in Hollywood*
Animated film: *Missing Link*
Foreign-language film: *Parasite*, South Korea
Original score: Hildur Gudnadóttir, *Joker*
Original song: "(I'm Gonna) Love Me Again," *Rocketman*, Elton John, Bernie Taupin

Television

Series, drama: *Succession*, HBO
Series, comedy/musical: *Fleabag*, Amazon
Limited series or made-for-TV movie: *Chernobyl*, HBO
Actress, drama: Olivia Colman, *The Crown*, Netflix
Actor, drama: Brian Cox, *Succession*, HBO
Actress, comedy/musical: Phoebe Waller-Bridge, *Fleabag*, Amazon
Actor, comedy/musical: Ramy Youssef, *Ramy*, Hulu
Actress, limited series/TV movie: Michelle Williams, *Fosse/Verdon*, FX
Actor, limited series/TV movie: Russell Crowe, *The Loudest Voice*, Showtime
Supporting actress: Patricia Arquette, *The Act*, Hulu
Supporting actor: Stellan Skarsgard, *Chernobyl*, HBO

Academy Awards (Oscars), 1927-2019

Year	Picture	Actor	Actress	Supporting actor[1]	Supporting actress[1]	Director
1927 -28	Wings	Emil Jannings The Way of All Flesh	Janet Gaynor Seventh Heaven	NA	NA	Frank Borzage Seventh Heaven; Lewis Milestone Two Arabian Knights
1928 -29	Broadway Melody	Warner Baxter In Old Arizona	Mary Pickford Coquette	NA	NA	Frank Lloyd The Divine Lady
1929 -30	All Quiet on the Western Front	George Arliss Disraeli	Norma Shearer The Divorcee	NA	NA	Lewis Milestone All Quiet on the Western Front
1930 -31	Cimarron	Lionel Barrymore Free Soul	Marie Dressler Min and Bill	NA	NA	Norman Taurog Skippy
1931 -32	Grand Hotel	Fredric March Dr. Jekyll and Mr. Hyde; Wallace Beery The Champ	Helen Hayes The Sin of Madelon Claudet	NA	NA	Frank Borzage Bad Girl
1932 -33	Cavalcade	Charles Laughton The Private Life of Henry VIII	Katharine Hepburn Morning Glory	NA	NA	Frank Lloyd Cavalcade
1934	It Happened One Night	Clark Gable It Happened One Night	Claudette Colbert It Happened One Night	NA	NA	Frank Capra It Happened One Night
1935	Mutiny on the Bounty	Victor McLaglen The Informer	Bette Davis Dangerous	NA	NA	John Ford The Informer
1936	The Great Ziegfeld	Paul Muni The Story of Louis Pasteur	Luise Rainer The Great Ziegfeld	Walter Brennan Come and Get It	Gale Sondergaard Anthony Adverse	Frank Capra Mr. Deeds Goes to Town
1937	The Life of Emile Zola	Spencer Tracy Captains Courageous	Luise Rainer The Good Earth	Joseph Schildkraut The Life of Emile Zola	Alice Brady In Old Chicago	Leo McCarey The Awful Truth
1938	You Can't Take It With You	Spencer Tracy Boys Town	Bette Davis Jezebel	Walter Brennan Kentucky	Fay Bainter Jezebel	Frank Capra You Can't Take It With You
1939	Gone With the Wind	Robert Donat Goodbye, Mr. Chips	Vivien Leigh Gone With the Wind	Thomas Mitchell Stage Coach	Hattie McDaniel Gone With the Wind	Victor Fleming Gone With the Wind
1940	Rebecca	James Stewart The Philadelphia Story	Ginger Rogers Kitty Foyle	Walter Brennan The Westerner	Jane Darwell The Grapes of Wrath	John Ford The Grapes of Wrath
1941	How Green Was My Valley	Gary Cooper Sergeant York	Joan Fontaine Suspicion	Donald Crisp How Green Was My Valley	Mary Astor The Great Lie	John Ford How Green Was My Valley
1942	Mrs. Miniver	James Cagney Yankee Doodle Dandy	Greer Garson Mrs. Miniver	Van Heflin Johnny Eager	Teresa Wright Mrs. Miniver	William Wyler Mrs. Miniver
1943	Casablanca	Paul Lukas Watch on the Rhine	Jennifer Jones The Song of Bernadette	Charles Coburn The More the Merrier	Katina Paxinou For Whom the Bell Tolls	Michael Curtiz Casablanca
1944	Going My Way	Bing Crosby Going My Way	Ingrid Bergman Gaslight	Barry Fitzgerald Going My Way	Ethel Barrymore None But the Lonely Heart	Leo McCarey Going My Way
1945	The Lost Weekend	Ray Milland The Lost Weekend	Joan Crawford Mildred Pierce	James Dunn A Tree Grows in Brooklyn	Anne Revere National Velvet	Billy Wilder The Lost Weekend
1946	The Best Years of Our Lives	Fredric March The Best Years of Our Lives	Olivia de Havilland To Each His Own	Harold Russell The Best Years of Our Lives	Anne Baxter The Razor's Edge	William Wyler The Best Years of Our Lives
1947	Gentleman's Agreement	Ronald Colman A Double Life	Loretta Young The Farmer's Daughter	Edmund Gwenn Miracle on 34th Street	Celeste Holm Gentleman's Agreement	Elia Kazan Gentleman's Agreement
1948	Hamlet	Laurence Olivier Hamlet	Jane Wyman Johnny Belinda	Walter Huston The Treasure of the Sierra Madre	Claire Trevor Key Largo	John Huston The Treasure of the Sierra Madre
1949	All the King's Men	Broderick Crawford All the King's Men	Olivia de Havilland The Heiress	Dean Jagger Twelve O'Clock High	Mercedes McCambridge All the King's Men	Joseph L. Mankiewicz Letter to Three Wives
1950	All About Eve	José Ferrer Cyrano de Bergerac	Judy Holliday Born Yesterday	George Sanders All About Eve	Josephine Hull Harvey	Joseph L. Mankiewicz All About Eve
1951	An American in Paris	Humphrey Bogart The African Queen	Vivien Leigh A Streetcar Named Desire	Karl Malden A Streetcar Named Desire	Kim Hunter A Streetcar Named Desire	George Stevens A Place in the Sun
1952	The Greatest Show on Earth	Gary Cooper High Noon	Shirley Booth Come Back, Little Sheba	Anthony Quinn Viva Zapata!	Gloria Grahame The Bad and the Beautiful	John Ford The Quiet Man
1953	From Here to Eternity	William Holden Stalag 17	Audrey Hepburn Roman Holiday	Frank Sinatra From Here to Eternity	Donna Reed From Here to Eternity	Fred Zinnemann From Here to Eternity

Year	Picture	Actor	Actress	Supporting actor[1]	Supporting actress[1]	Director
1954	On the Waterfront	Marlon Brando On the Waterfront	Grace Kelly The Country Girl	Edmond O'Brien, The Barefoot Contessa	Eva Marie Saint On the Waterfront	Elia Kazan On the Waterfront
1955	Marty	Ernest Borgnine Marty	Anna Magnani The Rose Tattoo	Jack Lemmon Mister Roberts	Jo Van Fleet East of Eden	Delbert Mann Marty
1956	Around the World in 80 Days	Yul Brynner The King and I	Ingrid Bergman Anastasia	Anthony Quinn Lust for Life	Dorothy Malone Written on the Wind	George Stevens Giant
1957	The Bridge on the River Kwai	Alec Guinness The Bridge on the River Kwai	Joanne Woodward The Three Faces of Eve	Red Buttons Sayonara	Miyoshi Umeki Sayonara	David Lean The Bridge on the River Kwai
1958	Gigi	David Niven Separate Tables	Susan Hayward I Want to Live	Burl Ives The Big Country	Wendy Hiller Separate Tables	Vincente Minnelli Gigi
1959	Ben-Hur	Charlton Heston Ben-Hur	Simone Signoret Room at the Top	Hugh Griffith Ben-Hur	Shelley Winters Diary of Anne Frank	William Wyler Ben-Hur
1960	The Apartment	Burt Lancaster Elmer Gantry	Elizabeth Taylor Butterfield 8	Peter Ustinov Spartacus	Shirley Jones Elmer Gantry	Billy Wilder The Apartment
1961	West Side Story	Maximilian Schell Judgment at Nuremberg	Sophia Loren Two Women	George Chakiris West Side Story	Rita Moreno West Side Story	Jerome Robbins and Robert Wise West Side Story
1962	Lawrence of Arabia	Gregory Peck To Kill a Mockingbird	Anne Bancroft The Miracle Worker	Ed Begley Sweet Bird of Youth	Patty Duke The Miracle Worker	David Lean Lawrence of Arabia
1963	Tom Jones	Sidney Poitier Lilies of the Field	Patricia Neal Hud	Melvyn Douglas Hud	Margaret Rutherford The V.I.P.s	Tony Richardson Tom Jones
1964	My Fair Lady	Rex Harrison My Fair Lady	Julie Andrews Mary Poppins	Peter Ustinov Topkapi	Lila Kedrova Zorba the Greek	George Cukor My Fair Lady
1965	The Sound of Music	Lee Marvin Cat Ballou	Julie Christie Darling	Martin Balsam A Thousand Clowns	Shelley Winters A Patch of Blue	Robert Wise The Sound of Music
1966	A Man for All Seasons	Paul Scofield A Man for All Seasons	Elizabeth Taylor Who's Afraid of Virginia Woolf?	Walter Matthau The Fortune Cookie	Sandy Dennis Who's Afraid of Virginia Woolf?	Fred Zinnemann A Man for All Seasons
1967	In the Heat of the Night	Rod Steiger In the Heat of the Night	Katharine Hepburn Guess Who's Coming to Dinner	George Kennedy Cool Hand Luke	Estelle Parsons Bonnie and Clyde	Mike Nichols The Graduate
1968	Oliver!	Cliff Robertson Charly	Katharine Hepburn The Lion in Winter; Barbra Streisand Funny Girl	Jack Albertson The Subject Was Roses	Ruth Gordon Rosemary's Baby	Carol Reed Oliver!
1969	Midnight Cowboy	John Wayne True Grit	Maggie Smith The Prime of Miss Jean Brodie	Gig Young They Shoot Horses, Don't They?	Goldie Hawn Cactus Flower	John Schlesinger Midnight Cowboy
1970	Patton	George C. Scott Patton (refused)	Glenda Jackson Women in Love	John Mills Ryan's Daughter	Helen Hayes Airport	Franklin Schaffner Patton
1971	The French Connection	Gene Hackman The French Connection	Jane Fonda Klute	Ben Johnson The Last Picture Show	Cloris Leachman The Last Picture Show	William Friedkin The French Connection
1972	The Godfather	Marlon Brando The Godfather (refused)	Liza Minnelli Cabaret	Joel Grey Cabaret	Eileen Heckart Butterflies Are Free	Bob Fosse Cabaret
1973	The Sting	Jack Lemmon Save the Tiger	Glenda Jackson A Touch of Class	John Houseman The Paper Chase	Tatum O'Neal Paper Moon	George Roy Hill The Sting
1974	The Godfather Part II	Art Carney Harry and Tonto	Ellen Burstyn Alice Doesn't Live Here Anymore	Robert DeNiro The Godfather Part II	Ingrid Bergman Murder on the Orient Express	Francis Ford Coppola The Godfather Part II
1975	One Flew Over the Cuckoo's Nest	Jack Nicholson One Flew Over the Cuckoo's Nest	Louise Fletcher One Flew Over the Cuckoo's Nest	George Burns The Sunshine Boys	Lee Grant Shampoo	Milos Forman One Flew Over the Cuckoo's Nest
1976	Rocky	Peter Finch Network	Faye Dunaway Network	Jason Robards, All the President's Men	Beatrice Straight Network	John G. Avildsen Rocky
1977	Annie Hall	Richard Dreyfuss The Goodbye Girl	Diane Keaton Annie Hall	Jason Robards Julia	Vanessa Redgrave Julia	Woody Allen Annie Hall
1978	The Deer Hunter	Jon Voight Coming Home	Jane Fonda Coming Home	Christopher Walken The Deer Hunter	Maggie Smith California Suite	Michael Cimino The Deer Hunter
1979	Kramer vs. Kramer	Dustin Hoffman Kramer vs. Kramer	Sally Field Norma Rae	Melvyn Douglas Being There	Meryl Streep Kramer vs. Kramer	Robert Benton Kramer vs. Kramer
1980	Ordinary People	Robert DeNiro Raging Bull	Sissy Spacek Coal Miner's Daughter	Timothy Hutton Ordinary People	Mary Steenburgen Melvin and Howard	Robert Redford Ordinary People
1981	Chariots of Fire	Henry Fonda On Golden Pond	Katharine Hepburn On Golden Pond	John Gielgud Arthur	Maureen Stapleton Reds	Warren Beatty Reds
1982	Gandhi	Ben Kingsley Gandhi	Meryl Streep Sophie's Choice	Louis Gossett Jr. An Officer and a Gentleman	Jessica Lange Tootsie	Richard Attenborough Gandhi
1983	Terms of Endearment	Robert Duvall Tender Mercies	Shirley MacLaine Terms of Endearment	Jack Nicholson Terms of Endearment	Linda Hunt The Year of Living Dangerously	James L. Brooks Terms of Endearment
1984	Amadeus	F. Murray Abraham Amadeus	Sally Field Places in the Heart	Haing S. Ngor The Killing Fields	Peggy Ashcroft A Passage to India	Milos Forman Amadeus
1985	Out of Africa	William Hurt Kiss of the Spider Woman	Geraldine Page The Trip to Bountiful	Don Ameche Cocoon	Anjelica Huston Prizzi's Honor	Sydney Pollack Out of Africa
1986	Platoon	Paul Newman The Color of Money	Marlee Matlin Children of a Lesser God	Michael Caine Hannah and Her Sisters	Dianne Wiest Hannah and Her Sisters	Oliver Stone Platoon

Year	Picture	Actor	Actress	Supporting actor[1]	Supporting actress[1]	Director
1987	The Last Emperor	Michael Douglas Wall Street	Cher Moonstruck	Sean Connery The Untouchables	Olympia Dukakis Moonstruck	Bernardo Bertolucci The Last Emperor
1988	Rain Man	Dustin Hoffman Rain Man	Jodie Foster The Accused	Kevin Kline A Fish Called Wanda	Geena Davis The Accidental Tourist	Barry Levinson Rain Man
1989	Driving Miss Daisy	Daniel Day-Lewis My Left Foot	Jessica Tandy Driving Miss Daisy	Denzel Washington Glory	Brenda Fricker My Left Foot	Oliver Stone, Born on the Fourth of July
1990	Dances With Wolves	Jeremy Irons Reversal of Fortune	Kathy Bates Misery	Joe Pesci Goodfellas	Whoopi Goldberg Ghost	Kevin Costner Dances With Wolves
1991	The Silence of the Lambs	Anthony Hopkins The Silence of the Lambs	Jodie Foster The Silence of the Lambs	Jack Palance City Slickers	Mercedes Ruehl The Fisher King	Jonathan Demme The Silence of the Lambs
1992	Unforgiven	Al Pacino Scent of a Woman	Emma Thompson Howards End	Gene Hackman Unforgiven	Marisa Tomei My Cousin Vinny	Clint Eastwood Unforgiven
1993	Schindler's List	Tom Hanks Philadelphia	Holly Hunter The Piano	Tommy Lee Jones The Fugitive	Anna Paquin The Piano	Steven Spielberg Schindler's List
1994	Forrest Gump	Tom Hanks Forrest Gump	Jessica Lange Blue Sky	Martin Landau Ed Wood	Dianne Wiest, Bullets Over Broadway	Robert Zemeckis Forrest Gump
1995	Braveheart	Nicolas Cage Leaving Las Vegas	Susan Sarandon Dead Man Walking	Kevin Spacey The Usual Suspects	Mira Sorvino Mighty Aphrodite	Mel Gibson Braveheart
1996	The English Patient	Geoffrey Rush Shine	Frances McDormand Fargo	Cuba Gooding Jr. Jerry Maguire	Juliette Binoche The English Patient	Anthony Minghella The English Patient
1997	Titanic	Jack Nicholson As Good As It Gets	Helen Hunt As Good As It Gets	Robin Williams Good Will Hunting	Kim Basinger L.A. Confidential	James Cameron Titanic
1998	Shakespeare in Love	Roberto Benigni Life Is Beautiful	Gwyneth Paltrow Shakespeare in Love	James Coburn Affliction	Judi Dench Shakespeare in Love	Steven Spielberg Saving Private Ryan
1999	American Beauty	Kevin Spacey American Beauty	Hilary Swank Boys Don't Cry	Michael Caine, The Cider House Rules	Angelina Jolie Girl, Interrupted	Sam Mendes American Beauty
2000	Gladiator	Russell Crowe Gladiator	Julia Roberts Erin Brockovich	Benicio Del Toro Traffic	Marcia Gay Harden Pollock	Steven Soderbergh Traffic
2001	A Beautiful Mind	Denzel Washington Training Day	Halle Berry Monster's Ball	Jim Broadbent Iris	Jennifer Connelly A Beautiful Mind	Ron Howard A Beautiful Mind
2002	Chicago	Adrien Brody The Pianist	Nicole Kidman The Hours	Chris Cooper Adaptation	Catherine Zeta-Jones, Chicago	Roman Polanski The Pianist
2003	The Lord of the Rings: The Return of the King	Sean Penn Mystic River	Charlize Theron Monster	Tim Robbins Mystic River	Renée Zellweger Cold Mountain	Peter Jackson The Lord of the Rings: The Return of the King
2004	Million Dollar Baby	Jamie Foxx Ray	Hilary Swank Million Dollar Baby	Morgan Freeman Million Dollar Baby	Cate Blanchett The Aviator	Clint Eastwood Million Dollar Baby
2005	Crash	Philip Seymour Hoffman Capote	Reese Witherspoon Walk the Line	George Clooney Syriana	Rachel Weisz The Constant Gardener	Ang Lee Brokeback Mountain
2006	The Departed	Forest Whitaker, The Last King of Scotland	Helen Mirren The Queen	Alan Arkin Little Miss Sunshine	Jennifer Hudson Dreamgirls	Martin Scorsese The Departed
2007	No Country for Old Men	Daniel Day-Lewis There Will Be Blood	Marion Cotillard La Vie en Rose	Javier Bardem No Country for Old Men	Tilda Swinton Michael Clayton	Joel Coen and Ethan Coen, No Country for Old Men
2008	Slumdog Millionaire	Sean Penn Milk	Kate Winslet The Reader	Heath Ledger The Dark Knight	Penelope Cruz, Vicky Cristina Barcelona	Danny Boyle Slumdog Millionaire
2009	The Hurt Locker	Jeff Bridges Crazy Heart	Sandra Bullock The Blind Side	Christoph Waltz Inglourious Basterds	Mo'Nique Precious	Kathryn Bigelow The Hurt Locker
2010	The King's Speech	Colin Firth The King's Speech	Natalie Portman Black Swan	Christian Bale The Fighter	Melissa Leo The Fighter	Tom Hooper The King's Speech
2011	The Artist	Jean Dujardin The Artist	Meryl Streep The Iron Lady	Christopher Plummer, Beginners	Octavia Spencer The Help	Michel Hazanavicius The Artist
2012	Argo	Daniel Day-Lewis Lincoln	Jennifer Lawrence Silver Linings Playbook	Christoph Waltz Django Unchained	Anne Hathaway Les Misérables	Ang Lee Life of Pi
2013	12 Years a Slave	Matthew McConaughey Dallas Buyers Club	Cate Blanchett Blue Jasmine	Jared Leto Dallas Buyers Club	Lupita Nyong'o 12 Years a Slave	Alfonso Cuarón Gravity
2014	Birdman	Eddie Redmayne The Theory of Everything	Julianne Moore Still Alice	J. K. Simmons Whiplash	Patricia Arquette Boyhood	Alejandro G. Iñárritu Birdman
2015	Spotlight	Leonardo DiCaprio The Revenant	Brie Larson Room	Mark Rylance Bridge of Spies	Alicia Vikander The Danish Girl	Alejandro G. Iñárritu The Revenant
2016	Moonlight	Casey Affleck Manchester by the Sea	Emma Stone La La Land	Mahershala Ali Moonlight	Viola Davis Fences	Damien Chazelle La La Land
2017	The Shape of Water	Gary Oldman Darkest Hour	Frances McDormand Three Billboards Outside Ebbing, Missouri	Sam Rockwell Three Billboards Outside Ebbing, Missouri	Allison Janney I, Tonya	Guillermo del Toro The Shape of Water
2018	Green Book	Rami Malek Bohemian Rhapsody	Olivia Colman The Favourite	Mahershala Ali Green Book	Regina King If Beale Street Could Talk	Alfonso Cuarón Roma
2019	Parasite	Joaquin Phoenix Joker	Renée Zellweger Judy	Brad Pitt Once Upon a Time... in Hollywood	Laura Dern Marriage Story	Bong Joon-ho Parasite

NA = Not applicable. (1) Award not given until 1936.

Other Academy Award Winners, 2019

Animated film: Toy Story 4
Cinematography: 1917
Costume design: Little Women
Documentary feature: American Factory
Film editing: Ford v Ferrari
International feature film: Parasite, South Korea
Makeup and hairstyling: Bombshell
Original score: Joker, Hildur Gudnadóttir
Original song: "(I'm Gonna) Love Me Again," Rocketman, Elton John and Bernie Taupin

Production design: Once Upon a Time...in Hollywood
Short films: Hair Love (animated), Learning to Skateboard in a Warzone (If You're a Girl) (documentary), The Neighbors' Window (live action)
Sound editing: Ford v Ferrari
Sound mixing: 1917
Visual effects: 1917
Writing (adapted screenplay): Jojo Rabbit, Taika Waititi
Writing (original screenplay): Parasite, Bong Joon-ho

Other Film Awards, 2020

British Academy of Film and Television Awards (BAFTAs)

Awarded in 2020 to films released in the UK in 2019.
Best film: 1917
Outstanding British film: 1917
Director: Sam Mendes, 1917
Original screenplay: Parasite, Han Jin Won, Bong Joon Ho
Adapted screenplay: Jojo Rabbit, Taika Waititi
Animated film: Klaus
Documentary: For Sama
Film not in the English language: Parasite
Actor: Joaquin Phoenix, Joker
Actress: Renée Zellweger, Judy
Supporting actor: Brad Pitt, Once Upon a Time…in Hollywood
Supporting actress: Laura Dern, Marriage Story

Directors Guild of America Awards

Feature film: Sam Mendes, 1917
First-time feature film: Alma Har'el, Honey Boy
Documentary: Steven Bognar, Julia Reichert, American Factory
TV movie/limited series: Johan Renck, Chernobyl
TV series (drama): Nicole Kassell, Watchmen, "It's Summer and We're Running Out of Ice"
TV series (comedy): Bill Hader, Barry, "ronny/lily"

Screen Actors Guild Awards

Motion picture cast: Parasite
Female actor in a lead role: Renée Zellweger, Judy
Male actor in a lead role: Joaquin Phoenix, Joker
Female actor in a supporting role: Laura Dern, Marriage Story
Male actor in a supporting role: Brad Pitt, Once Upon a Time… in Hollywood

Drama series ensemble: The Crown
Female actor in a drama series: Jennifer Aniston, The Morning Show
Male actor in a drama series: Peter Dinklage, Game of Thrones
Comedy series ensemble: The Marvelous Mrs. Maisel
Female actor in a comedy series: Phoebe Waller-Bridge, Fleabag
Male actor in a comedy series: Tony Shalhoub, The Marvelous Mrs. Maisel
Female actor in a TV movie/limited series: Michelle Williams, Fosse/Verdon
Male actor in a TV movie/limited series: Sam Rockwell, Fosse/Verdon

Sundance Film Festival Awards

U.S. Grand Jury Prize: Minari (drama); Boys State (doc.)
World Cinema Grand Jury Prize: Yalda, a Night for Forgiveness, Iran/France/Ger./Switz./Lux. (drama); Epicentro, Austria/France/U.S. (doc.)
U.S. Audience Award: Minari (drama); Crip Camp (doc.)
World Cinema Audience Award: Sin Señas Particulares (Identifying Features), Mex./Spain (drama); The Reason I Jump, UK (doc.)
NEXT Audience Award: I Carry You With Me
U.S. Directing: Radha Blank, The 40-Year-Old Version (drama); Garrett Bradley, Time (doc.)
World Cinema Directing: Maïmouna Doucouré, Cuties, France (drama); Iryna Tsilyk, The Earth Is Blue as an Orange, Ukr./Lith. (doc.)
Waldo Salt Screenwriting Award: Edson Oda, Nine Days
Alfred P. Sloan Feature Prize: Tesla

Academy of Country Music Awards, 2020

Entertainer: Thomas Rhett, Carrie Underwood
Male artist: Luke Combs
Female artist: Maren Morris
Duo: Dan + Shay
Group: Old Dominion

Album: What You See Is What You Get, Luke Combs
Single: "God's Country," Blake Shelton
Song: "One Man Band," Old Dominion
Video: "Remember You Young," Thomas Rhett

Music event: "Fooled Around and Fell in Love," Miranda Lambert feat. Maren Morris, Ashley McBryde, Tenille Townes, Caylee Hammack, Elle King
New female artist: Tenille Townes
New male artist: Riley Green
Songwriter: Hillary Lindsey

Selected Grammy Awards, 2019

Source: The Recording Academy
For albums released Oct. 1, 2018-Aug. 31, 2019, awarded in Jan. 2020.

Record of the year (single): "Bad Guy," Billie Eilish
Album of the year: When We All Fall Asleep, Where Do We Go? Billie Eilish
Song of the year: "Bad Guy," Billie Eilish (Billie Eilish O'Connell, Finneas O'Connell, songwriters)
New artist: Billie Eilish
Pop performance, solo: "Truth Hurts," Lizzo
Pop performance, duo/group: "Old Town Road," Lil Nas X feat. Billy Ray Cyrus
Pop album, traditional vocal: Look Now, Elvis Costello & The Imposters
Pop album, vocal: When We All Fall Asleep, Where Do We Go? Billie Eilish
Dance recording: "Got to Keep On," The Chemical Brothers
Dance/electronic album: No Geography, The Chemical Brothers
Contemporary instrumental album: Mettavolution, Rodrigo y Gabriela
Rock performance: "This Land," Gary Clark Jr.
Metal performance: "7empest," Tool
Rock song: "This Land," Gary Clark Jr. (Gary Clark Jr., songwriter)
Rock album: Social Cues, Cage The Elephant
Alternative music album: Father of the Bride, Vampire Weekend
R&B performance: "Come Home," Anderson Paak feat. André 3000
R&B performance, traditional: "Jerome," Lizzo
R&B song: "Say So," PJ Morton feat. JoJo (PJ Morton, songwriter)
R&B album: Ventura, Anderson Paak
Urban contemporary album: Cuz I Love You (Deluxe), Lizzo
Rap performance: "Racks in the Middle," Nipsey Hussle feat. Roddy Ricch & Hit-Boy
Rap/sung performance: "Higher," DJ Khaled feat. Nipsey Hussle & John Legend
Rap song: "A Lot," 21 Savage feat. J. Cole (Jermaine Cole, Dacoury Natche, 21 Savage, Anthony White, songwriters)

Rap album: Igor, Tyler, The Creator
Country performance, solo: "Ride Me Back Home," Willie Nelson
Country performance, duo/group: "Speechless," Dan + Shay
Country song: "Bring My Flowers Now," Tanya Tucker (Brandi Carlile, Phil Hanseroth, Tim Hanseroth, Tanya Tucker, songwriters)
Country album: While I'm Livin', Tanya Tucker
Jazz album, instrumental: Finding Gabriel, Brad Mehldau
Jazz album, vocal: 12 Little Spells, Esperanza Spalding
Americana album: Oklahoma, Keb' Mo'
Bluegrass album: Tall Fiddler, Michael Cleveland
Blues album, traditional: Tall, Dark & Handsome, Delbert McClinton & Self-Made Men + Dana
Contemporary Christian album: Burn The Ships, For King & Country
Folk album: Patty Griffin, Patty Griffin
Gospel album: Long Live Love, Kirk Franklin
Latin rock/urban/alternative album: El Mal Querer, Rosalía
Latin pop album: #Eldisco, Alejandro Sanz
New age album: Wings, Peter Kater
Comedy album: Sticks & Stones, Dave Chappelle
Spoken word album: Becoming, Michelle Obama
Soundtrack album, compilation: A Star Is Born, Lady Gaga & Bradley Cooper (Paul "DJWS" Blair, Bradley Cooper, Lady Gaga, Nick Monson, Lukas Nelson, Mark Nilan Jr., Benjamin Rice, compilation producers)
Soundtrack album, score: Chernobyl, Hildur Gudnadóttir
Song, visual media: "I'll Never Love Again," A Star Is Born, Lady Gaga and Bradley Cooper (Natalie Hemby, Lady Gaga, Hillary Lindsey & Aaron Raitiere, songwriters)
Music video: "Old Town Road (Official Movie)," Lil Nas X & Billy Ray Cyrus
Music film: Homecoming, Beyoncé

Grammy Awards, 1958-2019

Record of the Year (single)	Year	Album of the Year
Domenico Modugno, "Nel Blu Dipinto Di Blu (Volare)"	1958	Henry Mancini, *The Music From Peter Gunn*
Bobby Darin, "Mack the Knife"	1959	Frank Sinatra, *Come Dance With Me*
Percy Faith, "Theme From a Summer Place"	1960	Bob Newhart, *Button Down Mind*
Henry Mancini, "Moon River"	1961	Judy Garland, *Judy at Carnegie Hall*
Tony Bennett, "I Left My Heart in San Francisco"	1962	Vaughn Meader, *The First Family*
Henry Mancini, "The Days of Wine and Roses"	1963	Barbra Streisand, *The Barbra Streisand Album*
Stan Getz and Astrud Gilberto, "The Girl From Ipanema"	1964	Stan Getz and João Gilberto, *Getz/Gilberto*
Herb Alpert, "A Taste of Honey"	1965	Frank Sinatra, *September of My Years*
Frank Sinatra, "Strangers in the Night"	1966	Frank Sinatra, *A Man and His Music*
5th Dimension, "Up, Up and Away"	1967	The Beatles, *Sgt. Pepper's Lonely Hearts Club Band*
Simon and Garfunkel, "Mrs. Robinson"	1968	Glen Campbell, *By the Time I Get to Phoenix*
5th Dimension, "Aquarius/Let the Sunshine In"	1969	Blood, Sweat & Tears, *Blood, Sweat & Tears*
Simon and Garfunkel, "Bridge Over Troubled Water"	1970	Simon and Garfunkel, *Bridge Over Troubled Water*
Carole King, "It's Too Late"	1971	Carole King, *Tapestry*
Roberta Flack, "The First Time Ever I Saw Your Face"	1972	George Harrison and Friends, *The Concert for Bangla Desh*
Roberta Flack, "Killing Me Softly With His Song"	1973	Stevie Wonder, *Innervisions*
Olivia Newton-John, "I Honestly Love You"	1974	Stevie Wonder, *Fulfillingness' First Finale*
Captain & Tennille, "Love Will Keep Us Together"	1975	Paul Simon, *Still Crazy After All These Years*
George Benson, "This Masquerade"	1976	Stevie Wonder, *Songs in the Key of Life*
Eagles, "Hotel California"	1977	Fleetwood Mac, *Rumours*
Billy Joel, "Just the Way You Are"	1978	Bee Gees, *Saturday Night Fever*
The Doobie Brothers, "What a Fool Believes"	1979	Billy Joel, *52nd Street*
Christopher Cross, "Sailing"	1980	Christopher Cross, *Christopher Cross*
Kim Carnes, "Bette Davis Eyes"	1981	John Lennon and Yoko Ono, *Double Fantasy*
Toto, "Rosanna"	1982	Toto, *Toto IV*
Michael Jackson, "Beat It"	1983	Michael Jackson, *Thriller*
Tina Turner, "What's Love Got to Do With It"	1984	Lionel Richie, *Can't Slow Down*
USA for Africa, "We Are the World"	1985	Phil Collins, *No Jacket Required*
Steve Winwood, "Higher Love"	1986	Paul Simon, *Graceland*
Paul Simon, "Graceland"	1987	U2, *The Joshua Tree*
Bobby McFerrin, "Don't Worry, Be Happy"	1988	George Michael, *Faith*
Bette Midler, "Wind Beneath My Wings"	1989	Bonnie Raitt, *Nick of Time*
Phil Collins, "Another Day in Paradise"	1990	Quincy Jones, *Back on the Block*
Natalie Cole, with Nat "King" Cole, "Unforgettable"	1991	Natalie Cole, with Nat "King" Cole, *Unforgettable*
Eric Clapton, "Tears in Heaven"	1992	Eric Clapton, *Unplugged*
Whitney Houston, "I Will Always Love You"	1993	Whitney Houston, *The Bodyguard*
Sheryl Crow, "All I Wanna Do"	1994	Tony Bennett, *MTV Unplugged*
Seal, "Kiss From a Rose"	1995	Alanis Morissette, *Jagged Little Pill*
Eric Clapton, "Change the World"	1996	Celine Dion, *Falling Into You*
Shawn Colvin, "Sunny Came Home"	1997	Bob Dylan, *Time Out of Mind*
Celine Dion, "My Heart Will Go On"	1998	Lauryn Hill, *The Miseducation of Lauryn Hill*
Santana feat. Rob Thomas, "Smooth"	1999	Santana, *Supernatural*
U2, "Beautiful Day"	2000	Steely Dan, *Two Against Nature*
U2, "Walk On"	2001	Various artists, *O Brother, Where Art Thou?*
Norah Jones, "Don't Know Why"	2002	Norah Jones, *Come Away With Me*
Coldplay, "Clocks"	2003	OutKast, *Speakerboxxx/The Love Below*
Ray Charles and Norah Jones, "Here We Go Again"	2004	Ray Charles and various artists, *Genius Loves Company*
Green Day, "Boulevard of Broken Dreams"	2005	U2, *How to Dismantle an Atomic Bomb*
Dixie Chicks, "Not Ready to Make Nice"	2006	Dixie Chicks, *Taking the Long Way*
Amy Winehouse, "Rehab"	2007	Herbie Hancock, *River: The Joni Letters*
Robert Plant and Alison Krauss, "Please Read the Letter"	2008	Robert Plant and Alison Krauss, *Raising Sand*
Kings of Leon, "Use Somebody"	2009	Taylor Swift, *Fearless*
Lady Antebellum, "Need You Now"	2010	Arcade Fire, *The Suburbs*
Adele, "Rolling in the Deep"	2011	Adele, *21*
Gotye, "Somebody That I Used to Know"	2012	Mumford & Sons, *Babel*
Daft Punk feat. Pharrell Williams and Nile Rodgers, "Get Lucky"	2013	Daft Punk, *Random Access Memories*
Sam Smith, "Stay With Me"	2014	Beck, *Morning Phase*
Mark Ronson feat. Bruno Mars, "Uptown Funk"	2015	Taylor Swift, *1989*
Adele, "Hello"	2016	Adele, *25*
Bruno Mars, "24K Magic"	2017	Bruno Mars, *24K Magic*
Childish Gambino, "This Is America"	2018	Kacey Musgraves, *Golden Hour*
Billie Eilish, "Bad Guy"	2019	Billie Eilish, *When We All Fall Asleep, Where Do We Go?*

MTV Video Music Awards, 2020

Video of the year: "Blinding Lights," The Weeknd
Artist of the year: Lady Gaga
Song of the year: "Rain on Me," Lady Gaga with Ariana Grande
Best new artist: Doja Cat
MTV Tricon Award: Lady Gaga
Best collaboration: "Rain on Me," Lady Gaga with Ariana Grande
Best group: BTS
Best music video from home: "Stuck With U," Ariana Grande and Justin Bieber
Best quarantine performance: *MTV Unplugged at Home*, CNCO
Video for good: "I Can't Breathe," H.E.R.
Everyday heroes: Frontline Medical Workers
Best alternative: "Bloody Valentine," Machine Gun Kelly

Best hip-hop: "Savage," Megan Thee Stallion
Best K-pop: "On," BTS
Best Latin: "Qué Pena," Maluma feat. J Balvin
Best pop: "On," BTS
Best rock: "Orphans," Coldplay
Best R&B: "Blinding Lights," The Weeknd
Art direction: "Mother's Daughter," Miley Cyrus
Choreography: "On," BTS
Cinematography: "Rain on Me," Lady Gaga with Ariana Grande
Direction: "The Man," Taylor Swift
Editing: "Mother's Daughter," Miley Cyrus
Visual effects: "Physical," Dua Lipa

SCIENCE

Science and Technology News

The following were some of the developments in science and technology in the previous year, as of Sept. 2020.

Falling Body Temperature

The conventional average normal temperature of the human body was established in 1851, when the German physician Carl Reinhold August Wunderlich concluded it was 37°C (98.6°F), based on temperatures taken from some 25,000 patients. In early Jan. 2020, however, a new analysis suggested that the average body temperature had actually fallen by about 0.03°C (0.05°F) per decade in the past 157 years. The study, published in *eLife*, found that men born in the early 19th century had temperatures 0.59°C (1.06°F) higher than men today. Women born in the 1890s were about 0.32°C (0.58°F) warmer than those born in the 2000s. Researchers analyzed three large sets of temperatures going back to American Civil War veterans (measured 1860–1940). The downward trend remained even when the researchers took into account improved measurement technology and uncertainty about the carefulness with which the Civil War veterans' data were collected. The study noted several possible causes of the drop in body temperature. The most plausible, they suggested, was a decline in inflammation, a side effect of falling infectious disease rates.

Xenobots: Living Robots

A paper in the Jan. 28, 2020, issue of the *Proceedings of the National Academy of Sciences* reported the creation of the first living robots. The tiny "xenobots," less than 1 mm (0.04 in) wide, consisted of cells taken from embryos of the African clawed frog (*Xenopus laevis*). The researchers, with the help of artificial intelligence, applied an algorithm that imitated natural selection—that is, the action of evolution in nature. The algorithm tested random combinations of hundreds of cells to see which cell configuration, or design, might be able to produce a desired behavior, including movement, object manipulation, and object transport. The testing was done in a virtual environment with simulated heart and skin cells. Using the designs that seemed most promising, the researchers then built agglomerations of actual live cells, and found that often the resulting xenobots could indeed perform simple behaviors. Since they were made of living cells, the xenobots could also heal themselves if injured. They could remain alive for several days, feeding on the fuel already present in the embryonic frog cells. With further development, xenobots might someday be used for cleaning toxic materials, delivering medications within the body, or even performing internal surgery, after which they would die and biodegrade.

Of course, it remains to be seen what sorts of further development may be feasible, practical, or desirable. Can, or should, xenobots be equipped with sensory cells, or a nervous system, or the ability to reproduce? Ethical, legal, and even philosophical questions will need to be answered. One of the paper's authors commented, "People will ask: is it a robot, is it a machine, is it an animal? What this is really telling us is that we need to have better definitions of all these things."

Graphene From Garbage; Other Material News

Graphene is an extraordinary material. Stronger than steel and able to conduct electricity and heat better than copper, it comes in a one-atom-thick sheet of carbon atoms arrayed in a chicken-wire-like pattern. It has uses in electronics, high-strength plastic, and elsewhere. Unfortunately, making a high-quality form of it has been an expensive process resulting in just tiny amounts of the substance. In the Jan. 30, 2020, issue of the journal *Nature*, however, scientists reported development of an inexpensive method for producing graphene in large amounts, potentially from almost any carbon-containing solid matter, such as discarded food or old tires. The so-called "flash graphene" technique sends a high-voltage electric current through carbon powder, heating it to some 2,800°C (5,000°F) and breaking the bonds between carbon atoms, transforming the carbon into graphene as new bonds form. The process produces a bright flash of light—hence its name.

Other advances in materials reported in 2020 included a novel fabric that appeared to be as strong as Kevlar or Twaron but provided far superior thermal resistance—a quality potentially useful for astronauts, firefighters, and soldiers. The new fabric was reported online in the journal *Matter* in late June. The following month, progress in developing a virtually uncuttable

material was announced in *Scientific Reports*. The lightweight metallic material, called Proteus, contains ceramic grains that create extreme resistance to cutting tools.

Oldest Ancestor of Animals Like Us

Most animals are bilaterians (at least in the embryo stage), with a morphology (form and structure) that includes a head and a back end, connected by a continuous gut, or digestive tract; they have a bilaterally symmetrical body. The fossil record of such creatures stretches hundreds of millions of years, back to simple wormlike species. A report in the Apr. 7, 2020, issue of the *Proceedings of the National Academy of Sciences* described the oldest such animal yet found, represented by fossils of more than 100 tiny organisms found in Australia. The fossils, along with traces of burrows in the enclosing rock, dated from some 555 million years ago, in the Ediacaran period, which saw the appearance of the first nonmicroscopic multicellular creatures. The newly found species was dubbed *Ikaria wariootia*. (*Ikara* means "meeting place" in the indigenous language where the fossils were found; a creek in the area has the name Warioota.) The creatures measured roughly 2-7 mm (0.08-0.28 in) long and about 1-2.5 mm (0.04-0.1 in) wide—no bigger than a grain of rice. Analysis of the fossils with a 3D-laser scanner, along with other evidence, indicated that the animals had a mouth and an anus and made their burrows by wiggling through the earth. The researchers wrote: "*Ikaria* was likely able to detect organic matter buried in well-oxygenated environments as well as potentially toxic conditions, suggesting rudimentary sensory abilities. Combined, these features suggest that, despite the simple morphology that can be directly observed in fossil specimens of *Ikaria*, this organism was remarkably complex."

Enormous Mayan Structure

A study published in the June 25, 2020, issue of *Nature* described a previously unknown, colossal structure—a huge artificial plateau—discovered through the use of the archaeology-revolutionizing technology lidar ("light detection and ranging") and excavations at a site called Aguada Fénix in Mexico's Tabasco State. The plateau measures 1,400-m (about 4,600 ft) long and 10-15-m (33-49 ft) high, and has nine causeways, or roads, and multiple structures, including a 4-m (13 ft) tall pyramid. The complex, built by the early Mayans between 1000 and 800 BCE, is far larger than all other known Mayan pyramids and ceremonial plateaus. (Structures from the so-called classic period of Mayan civilization, which began some ten centuries later, were notably smaller.) The lead author of the *Nature* study speculated that building the artificial platform would have taken 5,000 people more than six years of full-time work.

Used from an airplane or drone, lidar scans Earth's surface with a pulsed laser, and the reflected signals can be used to construct a model of the terrain, which, after digital processing removes vegetation, may reveal the existence of archaeologically important features that might otherwise escape detection.

One Big Hot Volcano

Pūhāhonu ("turtle surfacing for air"), once called Gardner Pinnacles—two islets of the Hawaiian chain located nearly 1,000 km (600 mi) northwest of Honolulu—reach a maximum height of only 52 m (170 ft) above sea level. But these small dots in the Pacific Ocean are actually the tips of the largest volcano on Earth, according to a study in the July 15, 2020, issue of *Earth and Planetary Science Letters*. Using sonar and gravity detectors, researchers found that Pūhāhonu volcano contains about 150,000 cu km (36,000 cu mi) of rock, twice the size of Hawaii's Mauna Loa, which at some 74,000 cu km (18,000 cu mi) had been considered the world's biggest volcano. Both Pūhāhonu and Mauna Loa are shield volcanoes, but unlike Mauna Loa, Pūhāhonu, thought to have been formed roughly 14 million years ago, is no longer active. Most of Pūhāhonu's immense volcanic mass lies today below the level of the ocean floor; the volcano's great weight has caused the underlying crust of the Earth to sag. Seeking a possible explanation for the gargantuan amount of liquid magma that welled up from the mantle below the crust to form Pūhāhonu, the researchers analyzed samples of olivine (a mineral commonly found in rock formed from magma) from the volcano. The samples' composition suggested that the magma rising from the mantle reached temperatures as high as 1,700°C (3,000°F)—the hottest magma on record.

Science Glossary

This glossary covers some concepts that come up frequently in the news, in biology, chemistry, geology, and physics.

Biology

Amino acid: one of about 20 similar small molecules that are the building blocks of proteins.

Antibiotic: a substance produced by or derived from a bacterium, fungus, or other organism that battles infections and diseases caused by microorganisms, especially bacteria; it works by killing the microorganism or halting its growth.

Archaeon (plural, archaea): one of a group of single-celled microorganisms; archaea are prokaryotes, like bacteria, but they share some similarities with eukaryotes.

Autoimmunity: a condition in which an individual's immune system reacts against his or her own tissues; leads to diseases such as lupus, some forms of diabetes, inflammatory bowel disease, and rheumatoid arthritis.

Bacterium (plural, bacteria): one of a large, varied class of microscopic and simple, single-celled organisms. Bacteria live almost everywhere; some forms cause disease, while others are useful in digestion and other natural processes.

Biodiversity (biological diversity): richness of variety of life-forms—including plants, animals, and other types—in a given environment.

Cell: the smallest unit of life capable of living independently, or with other cells; usually bounded by a membrane. May include a nucleus and other specialized parts.

Cholesterol: a fatty substance in animal tissues. It is produced by the liver in humans; is found in foods such as butter, eggs, and meat; and is an essential body constituent.

Chromosome: one of the rod-like structures in cell nuclei that carry genetic material (DNA).

Cloning: the process of copying a particular piece of DNA to allow it to be sequenced, studied, or used in some other way; can also refer to producing a complete copy of an organism.

CRISPR (Clustered Regularly Interspaced Short Palindromic Repeats): a segment of DNA in prokaryotes that helps defend against virus attacks; it contains short genetic sequences that, coupled with a special enzyme, permit recognition and cleavage of like sequences in invading viruses. Term is also applied to a technology based on this approach that provides relatively precise targeting of specific bits of genetic code for such purposes as genetic modification or diagnosis.

DNA (deoxyribonucleic acid): a usually double-stranded molecule that carries genetic information, which determines the form and functioning of all known living things.

Ecosystem: an interdependent community of living organisms and their climatic and geographical habitat.

Enzyme: a protein that promotes a particular chemical reaction in the body.

Estrogen: one of a group of hormones that promote development of female secondary sex characteristics and the growth and health of the female reproductive system; males also produce small amounts of estrogen.

Eukaryote: any of the group of single- or multi-celled organisms whose cells have distinct nuclei.

Evolution: the process of gradual change that can occur in a species as it adapts to its environment; natural selection is the process by which evolution occurs.

Gene: a portion of a DNA molecule that provides the blueprint for the assembly of a protein.

Gene pool: the collection and total diversity of genes in an interbreeding population.

Gene therapy: a treatment in which scientists try to implant functioning genes into a person's cells so the genes can produce proteins that the person lacks or that help the person fight disease.

Genetic sequencing: the process of finding the order of subunits in a gene or the order of all an organism's genes.

Genome: the complete set of an organism's genetic material.

Hormone: a substance secreted in one part of an organism that regulates the functioning of other tissues or organs.

Meiosis: the process of cell division that results in gametes (sperm or egg cells), all of which contain half the number of chromosomes as their precursor.

Metabolism: the sum total of the body's chemical processes providing energy for vital functions and enabling new material to be synthesized.

Mitosis: the process by which a cell divides its nucleus and other cell materials into two duplicate daughter cells with the same DNA.

Neuron or **nerve cell:** any of the cells in the nervous system that send electrical and chemical messages to other cells.

Nucleus (plural, nuclei): the center of an atom; or the portion of a eukaryotic cell that contains most of the cell's genetic material. (In most eukaryotic cells, some DNA is also found in the cell's "powerhouses"—tiny components called **mitochondria** that lie outside the nucleus and supply chemical energy.)

Organism: a living entity, capable of growth, metabolism, and usually reproduction.

Phenotype: the observable properties and characteristics of an organism arising at least in part from its genetic makeup.

Pheromone: a chemical secreted by an organism to influence the behavior of other members of its species.

Placebo effect: a phenomenon in which patients show improvements even though they have taken a medically inactive substance, called a placebo.

Prokaryote: a single-celled organism that does not have a distinct nucleus, such as a bacterium or archaeon.

Protein: a complex molecule made up of one or more chains of amino acids; essential to the structure and function of all cells.

RNA (ribonucleic acid): a complex molecule similar to the genetic material DNA but usually single-stranded; several forms of RNA translate the genetic code of DNA and use that code to assemble proteins for structural and biological functions in the body. RNA also serves as the genetic material of some viruses.

Species: a population of organisms that breed with each other in nature and produce fertile offspring; other definitions of species exist to accommodate the diversity of life on Earth.

Stem cell: a cell that can develop into other types of cells; for instance, stem cells in bone marrow can differentiate into different types of blood cells.

Steroid: a type of chemical substance with a certain molecular structure. Some steroids are hormones that can suppress immune response or influence stress reaction, blood pressure, or sexual development.

Testosterone: a steroid hormone that stimulates the development and maintenance of male sexual characteristics and the production of sperm; women also produce small amounts of testosterone.

Virus: a microscopic, often disease-causing, agent made of genetic material surrounded by a protein shell; can only reproduce inside a living cell. There also exist "subviral" infectious agents, such as **viroids** (which consist of a short, circular strand of RNA without a protein coat) and **prions** (consisting of protein material).

Chemistry

Acid: a class of compounds that contrasts with bases. Acids taste sour, turn litmus red/pink, and often produce hydrogen gas in contact with some metals. Acids donate protons (hydrogen atoms minus the electron) in chemical reactions.

Base: a substance that yields hydroxyl ions (OH-) when dissolved in water; any of a class of compounds whose aqueous solutions taste bitter, feel slippery, turn litmus blue, and react with acids to form salts; also known as **alkaline**.

Carbon fiber: an extremely strong, thin fiber made by pyrolyzing (decomposing by heat) synthetic fibers, such as rayon, until charred; used to make high-strength composites.

Chlorofluorocarbon (CFC): one of a group of industrial chemicals that contain chlorine, fluorine, and carbon and can damage Earth's ozone layer.

Element: a substance that cannot be chemically decomposed into simpler substances; all the atoms of an element have the same number of protons.

Isotope: an atom of a chemical element with the same number of protons in its nucleus as other atoms of that element, but with a different number of neutrons.

Molecule: the basic unit of a chemical compound, composed of two or more atoms bound together.

Noble gases or **inert gases:** a group of gases including helium, neon, argon, krypton, xenon, and radon that are not reactive except in rare and limited instances.

Osmosis: the transfer of a fluid across a semipermeable membrane, usually from an area of higher concentration to one of lower concentration.

Polymer: a huge molecule containing hundreds or thousands of smaller molecules arranged in repeating units.

Salt: a neutral compound produced by the reaction of an acid and a base.

Geology

Anthropocene: a proposed epoch of geologic time marked by a significant influence of human activity on the environment. Suggested starting points include the mid-20th century (when extensive testing of nuclear and thermonuclear bombs began) and the Industrial Revolution of the 19th century.

Fault, tectonic: a crack or break in Earth's crust, often due to the slippage of tectonic plates past or over one another; usually geologically unstable.

Igneous: a type of rock formed by solidification from a molten state, especially from molten magma.

Magma: hot liquid rock material under Earth's surface, from which igneous rock is formed by cooling.

Metamorphic: in geology, the name given to rocks or minerals that have recrystallized under the influence of heat and pressure since their original formation.

Pangaea: a single supercontinent that scientists believe began to break apart at least 200 million years ago to form the current continents.

Plate tectonics: theory that Earth's lithosphere—the uppermost layer that includes the crust—is made up of many separate rigid plates of rock that float on top of hot semi-liquid rock.

Sedimentary: a type of rock formed by the buildup of material at the bottoms of bodies of water.

Physics

Absolute zero: the theoretical temperature at which all motion within a molecule stops, corresponding to −273.15°C (−459.67°F).

Antimatter: matter that consists of antiparticles, such as antiprotons, that have an opposite charge from normal particles; when matter meets antimatter, both are destroyed, and their combined mass is converted to energy. Antimatter is created in certain radioactive decay processes but appears to be present in only small amounts in the universe.

Atom: the basic unit of a chemical element.

Atomic mass: the total mass of an atom of a given element; atoms of the same element with different atomic masses (different numbers of neutrons but not protons) are called **isotopes**.

Atomic number: the number of protons in an atom of a given element of the periodic table; the characteristic that sets atoms of different elements apart.

Axion: a hypothetical subatomic particle with low mass and energy that has been proposed to exist because of the properties of the strong nuclear force. Axions have been suggested as a candidate for dark matter and also as a possible explanation for the imbalance between matter and antimatter in the universe.

Bose-Einstein condensate (BEC): a "super-atom" comprising thousands of atoms super-cooled to within a few hundred millionths of a degree of absolute zero and thus condensed into the lowest energy state. Atoms bound in the BEC behave synchronously, giving the BEC wavelike properties.

Boson: one of the two primary categories of particles in the Standard Model; bosons include the Higgs boson and force-carrying particles such as photons, gluons, and the W and Z particles.

Dark energy: a mysterious, undefined energy leading to a repulsive force pervading all of space-time; proposed by cosmologists as counteracting gravity and accelerating the expansion of the universe; predicted to make up 68.3% of the universe's composition.

Dark matter: hypothetical, invisible matter that some scientists believe makes up 26.8% of the universe (dark matter and ordinary matter together make up 31.7% of the universe). Its existence was proposed to account for otherwise inexplicable gravitational forces observed in space.

Doppler effect: a change in the frequency of sound, light, or radio waves caused by the motion of the source emitting the waves or the motion of the person or instrument perceiving the waves.

Electron: negatively charged particle that (along with its positively charged counterpart, the **positron**) is the least massive electrically charged fundamental particle; one of six **leptons**.

Energy: capacity to perform work. Energy can take various forms, such as potential energy, kinetic energy, and chemical energy.

Entropy: a measure of disorder in a system.

Fermion: any one of a number of matter particles including electrons, protons, neutrons, neutrinos, leptons, and quarks; one of the two primary categories of particles in the Standard Model, the other being bosons.

Field: the existence of physical effects such as forces (gravitational, electric, etc.) is visualized and described mathematically by physicists in terms of fields, which show the strength and direction of a force at a given position.

Fission: a nuclear reaction that occurs when the nuclei of large, unstable atoms break apart, releasing large amounts of energy.

Fluorescence: luminescence that is caused by the absorption of radiation at one wavelength followed by an almost immediate re-radiation, usually at a different wavelength, that stops almost immediately when the causative radiation stops.

Force: in classical physics, something that causes acceleration in a body; can be thought of as a push or pull.

Fusion: a nuclear reaction occurring when atomic nuclei collide at high temperatures and combine to form one heavier atomic nucleus, releasing enormous energy in the process.

Gravity: an attractive force between any two objects or particles, proportional to the mass (or energy) of the objects; strength of the force decreases with greater distance; the only fundamental force still unaccounted for by the Standard Model.

Half-life: the time it takes for half of a given amount of a radioactive element to decay.

Hertz (Hz): a measure of frequency, or how many times a given event occurs per second; applied to sound waves, electrical current, and microchip clock speeds.

Higgs boson: a boson associated with a field accounting for the existence of mass in many particles.

Laser: light consisting of a cascade of photons all having the same wavelength; stands for Light Amplification by Stimulated Emission of Radiation.

Light-emitting diode (LED): a semiconductor that emits light when an electrical current is passed through it. The color of the light depends on the material used in making the diode.

Neutrino: a tiny fundamental particle, or fermion, with no electrical charge and very small mass that moves very quickly through the universe; comes in three varieties, or flavors, called electron, muon, and tau.

Neutron: a neutral particle, made up of quarks, found in the nuclei of atoms (except the most common isotope of hydrogen).

Particle accelerator: a machine that accelerates charged particles to extremely high speeds around a circular track or along a straight line. Accelerators are used in scientific research, manufacturing, and medical diagnosis and therapy. Those used to study fundamental physics can be enormous—the Large Hadron Collider in Switzerland has a circumference of 16.8 mi (27 km).

Phosphorescence: luminescence that is caused by the absorption of radiation at one wavelength followed by a delayed re-radiation, usually at a different wavelength, that continues for a time after the causative radiation stops.

Photon: the elementary unit, or quantum, of electromagnetic radiation, such as light. It has no mass or electrical charge and is one of the fundamental force-carrying particles described by the Standard Model.

Plasma: a high-energy state of matter different from solid, liquid, or gas in which atomic nuclei and the electrons orbiting them separate from each other.

Proton: a positively charged subatomic particle, made up of quarks, found in the nuclei of atoms.

Quantum: a natural unit of some physically measurable property, such as energy or electrical charge.

Quark: a fundamental matter particle classed as a fermion; there are six different varieties, or flavors, of quarks grouped in pairs: up and down, charm and strange, top and bottom. Each flavor has a corresponding antiquark. Quarks combine to form such particles as neutrons and protons. Quark-antiquark combinations form the composite particles known as mesons.

Radiation: energy emitted as rays or particles. Radiation includes heat, light, ultraviolet rays, gamma rays, X-rays, cosmic rays, alpha particles, and beta particles.

Relativity, general theory of: a theory of space-time proposed by Albert Einstein in 1915; it links gravity to the curvature of space-time.

Relativity, special theory of: Albert Einstein's theory of space and time: all laws of physics are valid in all uniformly moving frames of reference, and the speed of light in a vacuum is always the same, so long as the source and the observer are moving uniformly (not accelerating).

Standard Model: prevailing theory of the interaction of subatomic particles. Particles are either fermions—such as electrons, neutrinos, and quarks—or bosons—such as Higgs bosons, gluons, W or Z bosons, and photons; successfully explains three of the four elementary forces acting on particles (strong, weak, electromagnetic) but thus far has not incorporated gravity.

String theory: a theory that seeks to unify quantum mechanics and general relativity, positing that the basic constituents of matter can best be understood not as pointlike particles but as tiny oscillating "strings."

Subatomic particle: a particle that makes up an atom; includes electrons (elementary particles) and neutrons and protons (composite particles).

Superconductivity: the property of certain materials, usually metals and chemically complex ceramics, to conduct electricity without resistance, generally at very cold temperatures.

Thermodynamics: the branch of physics that describes how energy, heat, and temperature flow in physical systems.

Ultraviolet radiation: a form of light, invisible to the human eye, that has a shorter wavelength and greater energy than visible light but a longer wavelength and less energy than X-rays.

Virtual particle: subatomic particle that rapidly pop into and out of existence and can exert real forces; usually occur in particle-antiparticle pairs and are rapidly annihilated.

Mohs Scale of Hardness

Hardness is the ability of a solid substance to resist abrasion or deformation on its surface. Soft minerals scratch more easily than hard ones. For example, a diamond will scratch graphite because graphite is softer. In 1812, German mineralogist Frederich Mohs (1773-1839) created the arbitrary scale shown below to measure relative hardness using 10 minerals that were readily available at that time. The numbers in the Mohs scale are arranged in order of increasing hardness. An item's hardness is obtained by determining which mineral in the Mohs scale can scratch it.

Mohs scale

1 . . . . Talc	6 . . . . . Orthoclase feldspar		
2 . . . . . . Gypsum	7 . . . . . . Quartz		
3 . . . . . . Calcite	8 . . . . . . Topaz		
4 . . . . . . Fluorite	9 . . . . . Corundum		
5 . . . . . . Apatite	10 . . . . . Diamond		

Selected items and their relative hardness

2.5 . . . . . .Fingernail	5.5 . . . . .Steel knife blade
2.5-3 . . . .Gold, silver	6-7 . . . . .Glass
3 . . . . . .Copper penny	6.5 . . . . .Iron pyrite
4-4.5 . . . . .Platinum	7+. . . . . .Hardened steel file
4-5 . . . . . .Iron	

Chemical Elements, Atomic Numbers, Year Discovered

Source: International Union of Pure and Applied Chemistry (IUPAC)

See Periodic Table of the Elements on the following page for atomic weights.

Element	Symbol	Atomic number	Year discov.	Element	Symbol	Atomic number	Year discov.	Element	Symbol	Atomic number	Year discov.
Actinium	Ac	89	1899	Gold	Au	79	BCE	Potassium	K	19	1807
Aluminum	Al	13	1825	Hafnium	Hf	72	1923	Praseodymium	Pr	59	1885
Americium	Am	95	1944	Hassium	Hs	108	1984	Promethium	Pm	61	1945
Antimony	Sb	51	1450	Helium	He	2	1868	Protactinium	Pa	91	1917
Argon	Ar	18	1894	Holmium	Ho	67	1878	Radium	Ra	88	1898
Arsenic	As	33	13th cent.	Hydrogen	H	1	1766	Radon	Rn	86	1900
Astatine	At	85	1940	Indium	In	49	1863	Rhenium	Re	75	1925
Barium	Ba	56	1808	Iodine	I	53	1811	Rhodium	Rh	45	1803
Berkelium	Bk	97	1949	Iridium	Ir	77	1804	Roentgenium	Rg	111	1995
Beryllium	Be	4	1798	Iron	Fe	26	BCE	Rubidium	Rb	37	1861
Bismuth	Bi	83	15th cent.	Krypton	Kr	36	1898	Ruthenium	Ru	44	1845
Bohrium	Bh	107	1981	Lanthanum	La	57	1839	Rutherfordium	Rf	104	1969
Boron	B	5	1808	Lawrencium	Lr	103	1961	Samarium	Sm	62	1879
Bromine	Br	35	1826	Lead	Pb	82	BCE	Scandium	Sc	21	1879
Cadmium	Cd	48	1817	Lithium	Li	3	1817	Seaborgium	Sg	106	1974
Calcium	Ca	20	1808	Livermorium	Lv	116	2000	Selenium	Se	34	1817
Californium	Cf	98	1950	Lutetium	Lu	71	1907	Silicon	Si	14	1823
Carbon	C	6	BCE	Magnesium	Mg	12	1829	Silver	Ag	47	BCE
Cerium	Ce	58	1803	Manganese	Mn	25	1774	Sodium	Na	11	1807
Cesium	Cs	55	1860	Meitnerium	Mt	109	1982	Strontium	Sr	38	1790
Chlorine	Cl	17	1774	Mendelevium	Md	101	1955	Sulfur	S	16	BCE
Chromium	Cr	24	1797	Mercury	Hg	80	BCE	Tantalum	Ta	73	1802
Cobalt	Co	27	1735	Molybdenum	Mo	42	1782	Technetium	Tc	43	1937
Copernicium	Cn	112	1996	Moscovium	Mc	115	2004	Tellurium	Te	52	1782
Copper	Cu	29	BCE	Neodymium	Nd	60	1885	Tennessine	Ts	117	2010
Curium	Cm	96	1944	Neon	Ne	10	1898	Terbium	Tb	65	1843
Darmstadtium	Ds	110	1995	Neptunium	Np	93	1940	Thallium	Tl	81	1861
Dubnium (Hahnium)[1]	Db (Ha)	105	1970	Nickel	Ni	28	1751	Thorium	Th	90	1828
Dysprosium	Dy	66	1886	Nihonium	Nh	113	2004	Thulium	Tm	69	1879
Einsteinium	Es	99	1952	Niobium[2]	Nb	41	1801	Tin	Sn	50	BCE
Erbium	Er	68	1843	Nitrogen	N	7	1772	Titanium	Ti	22	1791
Europium	Eu	63	1901	Nobelium	No	102	1958	Tungsten (Wolfram)	W	74	1783
Fermium	Fm	100	1953	Oganesson	Og	118	2006	Uranium	U	92	1789
Flerovium	Fl	114	1999	Osmium	Os	76	1804	Vanadium	V	23	1830
Fluorine	F	9	1771	Oxygen	O	8	1774	Xenon	Xe	54	1898
Francium	Fr	87	1939	Palladium	Pd	46	1803	Ytterbium	Yb	70	1878
Gadolinium	Gd	64	1886	Phosphorus	P	15	1669	Yttrium	Y	39	1794
Gallium	Ga	31	1875	Platinum	Pt	78	1735	Zinc	Zn	30	BCE
Germanium	Ge	32	1886	Plutonium	Pu	94	1941	Zirconium	Zr	40	1789
				Polonium	Po	84	1898				

(1) The name Dubnium (Db) was approved by IUPAC for element 105, but the name Hahnium (Ha) was used in most of the scientific literature before 1998 and is still sometimes used in the U.S. (2) Formerly Columbium.

Periodic Table of the Elements

Source: Los Alamos National Laboratory Chemistry Division; International Union of Pure and Applied Chemistry (IUPAC)

Shaded elements are commonly regarded as metals.

atomic number — 14 28.06-28.09
name — Silicon
Si — symbol
atomic weight[1]

1																	2
H 1.008 Hydrogen																	**He** 4.003 Helium
3 **Li** 6.938-6.997 Lithium	4 **Be** 9.012 Beryllium											5 **B** 10.81-10.82 Boron	6 **C** 12.017 Carbon	7 **N** 14.01 Nitrogen	8 **O** 16.00 Oxygen	9 **F** 19.00 Fluorine	10 **Ne** 20.18 Neon
11 **Na** 22.99 Sodium	12 **Mg** 24.30-24.31 Magnesium											13 **Al** 26.98 Aluminum	14 **Si** 28.06-28.09 Silicon	15 **P** 30.97 Phosphorus	16 **S** 32.06-32.08 Sulfur	17 **Cl** 35.45-35.46 Chlorine	18 **Ar** 39.80-39.96 Argon
19 **K** 39.10 Potassium	20 **Ca** 40.08 Calcium	21 **Sc** 44.96 Scandium	22 **Ti** 47.87 Titanium	23 **V** 50.94 Vanadium	24 **Cr** 52.00 Chromium	25 **Mn** 54.94 Manganese	26 **Fe** 55.85 Iron	27 **Co** 58.93 Cobalt	28 **Ni** 58.69 Nickel	29 **Cu** 63.55 Copper	30 **Zn** 65.38 Zinc	31 **Ga** 69.72 Gallium	32 **Ge** 72.63 Germanium	33 **As** 74.92 Arsenic	34 **Se** 78.97 Selenium	35 **Br** 79.90-79.91 Bromine	36 **Kr** 83.80 Krypton
37 **Rb** 85.47 Rubidium	38 **Sr** 87.62 Strontium	39 **Y** 88.91 Yttrium	40 **Zr** 91.22 Zirconium	41 **Nb** 92.91 Niobium	42 **Mo** 95.95 Molybdenum	43 **Tc** [98]* Technetium	44 **Ru** 101.1 Ruthenium	45 **Rh** 102.9 Rhodium	46 **Pd** 106.4 Palladium	47 **Ag** 107.9 Silver	48 **Cd** 112.4 Cadmium	49 **In** 114.8 Indium	50 **Sn** 118.7 Tin	51 **Sb** 121.8 Antimony	52 **Te** 127.6 Tellurium	53 **I** 126.9 Iodine	54 **Xe** 131.3 Xenon
55 **Cs** 132.9 Cesium	56 **Ba** 137.3 Barium	57-71 Lanthanoids	72 **Hf** 178.5 Hafnium	73 **Ta** 180.9 Tantalum	74 **W** 183.8 Tungsten	75 **Re** 186.2 Rhenium	76 **Os** 190.2 Osmium	77 **Ir** 192.2 Iridium	78 **Pt** 195.1 Platinum	79 **Au** 197.0 Gold	80 **Hg** 200.6 Mercury	81 **Tl** 204.4 Thallium	82 **Pb** 207.2 Lead	83 **Bi** 209.0* Bismuth	84 **Po** [209]* Polonium	85 **At** [210]* Astatine	86 **Rn** [222]* Radon
87 **Fr** [223]* Francium	88 **Ra** [226]* Radium	89-103 Actinoids	104 **Rf** [265]* Rutherfordium	105 **Db** [270]* Dubnium	106 **Sg** [269]* Seaborgium	107 **Bh** [270]* Bohrium	108 **Hs** [270]* Hassium	109 **Mt** [278]* Meitnerium	110 **Ds** [281]* Darmstadtium	111 **Rg** [281]* Roentgenium	112 **Cn** [285]* Copernicium	113 **Nh** [286]* Nihonium	114 **Fl** [289]* Flerovium	115 **Mc** [289]* Moscovium	116 **Lv** [293]* Livermorium	117 **Ts** [293]* Tennessine	118 **Og** [294]* Oganesson

Lanthanoid series

57 **La** 138.9 Lanthanum	58 **Ce** 140.1 Cerium	59 **Pr** 140.9 Praseodymium	60 **Nd** 144.2 Neodymium	61 **Pm** [145]* Promethium	62 **Sm** 150.4 Samarium	63 **Eu** 152.0 Europium	64 **Gd** 157.3 Gadolinium	65 **Tb** 158.9 Terbium	66 **Dy** 162.5 Dysprosium	67 **Ho** 164.9 Holmium	68 **Er** 167.3 Erbium	69 **Tm** 168.9 Thulium	70 **Yb** 173.1 Ytterbium	71 **Lu** 175.0 Lutetium

Actinoid series

89 **Ac** [227]* Actinium	90 **Th** 232.0* Thorium	91 **Pa** 231.0* Protactinium	92 **U** 238.0* Uranium	93 **Np** [237]* Neptunium	94 **Pu** [244]* Plutonium	95 **Am** [243]* Americium	96 **Cm** [247]* Curium	97 **Bk** [247]* Berkelium	98 **Cf** [251]* Californium	99 **Es** [252]* Einsteinium	100 **Fm** [257]* Fermium	101 **Md** [258]* Mendelevium	102 **No** [259]* Nobelium	103 **Lr** [262]* Lawrencium

Note: Atomic weight shown is a weighted average of the atomic masses of normally found isotopes. A value enclosed in brackets, e.g. [209], indicates the mass number of the longest-lived isotope of the element. However, four such elements (Bi, Th, Pa, and U) do have a characteristic terrestrial isotopic composition, and for these an atomic weight is tabulated. (1) For elements having two or more stable isotopes with a notable variation in atomic-weight values, a range is shown. * = Element has no stable nuclides.

Basic Laws of Physics

Newton's Laws of Motion

1. An object in motion moves at a constant velocity in a straight line unless acted upon by a force. Likewise, an object at rest will stay at rest. These two properties are known as inertia.

2. The acceleration of an object is proportional to the force acting on it and inversely proportional to the mass of the object. Force (F) equals mass (m) times acceleration (a):

$$F = ma$$

3. For every action, there is an equal and opposite reaction. For example, if a force of one ton pushes down on an object, the object pushes up with an equal force. As per the second law, the amount of movement (acceleration) produced in the object will depend on the object's mass.

Law of Gravity

In common usage, gravity refers to the gravitational force between planets and objects on or near them. But in scientific parlance, gravitation is one of four basic forces controlling the interactions of matter. (The others are the strong and weak forces, which act on the subatomic level, and the electromagnetic force.) The gravitational force (F) between objects is proportional to the product of their masses (m_1 and m_2) and inversely proportional to the square of the distance (d) between them. G represents the gravitational constant in Newton's law of gravity, a fixed ratio of approximately 6.67408×10^{-11} newton m^2/kg^2.

The basic law of gravity is:

$$F = G \frac{m_1 m_2}{d^2}$$

Near Earth's surface, Earth's gravitational force pulls objects downward at a constant acceleration of 9.8 m/s^2 (g). This allows calculation of the vertical velocity (v) of an object with an initial vertical velocity of v_0 in free fall at a given point in time (t) and calculation of the distance (d) of an object from Earth at any given time with a given initial velocity (v_0) and a known initial height (a) via the following equations (here, the effects of air resistance are ignored, and downward velocities and directions are negative):

$$v = v_0 - g t$$
$$d = -\tfrac{1}{2}g(t^2) + v_0 t + a$$

Assuming that height is measured in feet and speeds in feet per second, the maximum height (H) reached by an object with a positive (upward) initial velocity is expressed as:

$$H = a + \frac{v_0^2}{64}$$

For motion not near Earth's surface, more complicated equations are required. Also, if the object's upward velocity is very great, the object may escape Earth's gravity. Even near Earth's surface, there are slight complications. Gravity is lessened by the centrifugal force of the Earth's rotation. At the poles, where centrifugal force is absent, acceleration due to gravity is greater.

Gravity is weaker on a mountaintop than at sea level because the mountaintop is farther from Earth's center.

Conservation Laws

In physics, laws of conservation state that in a closed system, where neither mass nor energy is added or subtracted, certain measurable quantities remain constant.

Conservation of Mass: Mass is neither created nor destroyed within a closed system except when converted from or to energy.

Conservation of Momentum: All moving objects have momentum, and in a closed system, total momentum is always conserved. Linear momentum is the product of the mass of an object and its velocity. In the following equation, M and V represent the initial total mass and velocity of objects within a closed system. After a collision between those objects, the mass and velocity of individual objects may change (for example, one object breaks into smaller pieces, each traveling at a different velocity), but the product of the total mass and velocity in the system after the collision (mv) will remain the same.

$$MV = mv$$

Any object moving in a circle has another kind of momentum—angular momentum. This is because circular motion requires acceleration toward the center of the circle. The amount of acceleration depends on the speed of the object and the square of the radius of the circle. (Angular momentum is the product of this speed, the mass of the object, and the square of the radius.)

Conservation of Energy: The total amount of energy in a closed system will not change except when converted from or to mass.

Conservation of Mass-Energy: Although mass and energy can be converted into one another, the total amount of mass and energy together must be conserved. This is reflected in Einstein's famous equation, where m is mass, E is energy, and c is the speed of light in a vacuum (which is constant):

$$E = mc^2$$

Relativistic mass can describe how mass increases with velocity. The following equation—where m is the mass of a moving object, m_0 is the object's mass when not moving, v is the object's velocity in relation to a stationary observer, and c is the speed of light—shows the relationship:

$$m = \frac{m_0}{\sqrt{1 - \dfrac{v^2}{c^2}}}$$

The theory that no object can travel faster than the speed of light is based on this equation. As an object approaches c, so much energy is converted to mass that it no longer accelerates.

Laws of Thermodynamics

1. Heat is a form of energy. Within a closed system energy must be conserved except in nuclear reactions or other extreme conditions. It is neither created nor destroyed.

2. Within a self-sustaining system, heat can never go from an area of low temperature to an area of high temperature, for that would require added energy. Without added energy, disorder, or entropy, can only increase.

3. Absolute zero cannot be attained by any procedure in a finite number of steps. Although it can be approached asymptotically, it can never be reached.

Laws of Current Electricity

Electric current generally represents the flow of electrons through a conductor. The rate at which electrons flow can be measured in amperes, defined as the number of electrons (measured in a unit called the coulomb, equal to about 6.24 quintillion or 6.24×10^{18} electrons) moving past a particular point every second. One ampere is equal to 1 coulomb of charge passing each second. Like water, electrons tend to move from areas of high pressure to low pressure. The difference between these two pressures, known as potential difference, is measured in volts.

Certain substances, such as copper and carbon, allow electric currents to pass more readily than others—that is, they have greater conductivity. Resistance to conductivity is measured in ohms.

Ohm's Law: Electric current is directly proportional to the potential difference and inversely proportional to the total resistance of the circuit. I is electric current (measured in amperes), V is the potential difference (measured in volts), and R is resistance (measured in ohms):

$$I = \frac{V}{R}$$

Law of Electric Power: Electric power (P), measured in watts, represents the rate at which electricity is converted into some other form of energy (such as light, in the case of a lightbulb). For a direct-current circuit, P is the product of current and potential difference:

$$P = IV$$

Two Basic Laws of Quantum Physics

1. Heisenberg's uncertainty principle: Certain pairs of observable quantities like energy and time or position and momentum cannot be measured with complete accuracy simultaneously. Also known as the indeterminacy principle.

2. Pauli's exclusion principle: Two electrons in an atom cannot simultaneously occupy the same quantum or energy state. This has since been shown to be true also for other types of the subatomic particles known as fermions.

Breaking the Sound Barrier; Speed of Sound

The prefix **Mach** is used to describe supersonic speed. It was named for Ernst Mach (1838-1916), a Czech-born Austrian physicist. Mach may be defined as the ratio of the velocity of an object to the velocity of sound in a particular medium. A plane moving at the speed of sound moves at Mach 1. At twice the speed of sound, it moves at Mach 2.

When a plane passes the sound barrier—that is, flies faster than the speed at which sound travels—people in the area, though not the people on the plane, hear what seem to be thunderclaps. These sounds are sometimes called sonic booms.

Sound is produced by vibrations of an object. It is transmitted by the alternating increase and decrease in pressure that radiates outward from a source through a material medium of molecules, like waves spreading out on a pond after a rock has been tossed in.

The **frequency of sound** is determined by the number of times the vibrating waves undulate per second. It is measured in cycles per second. The slower the cycle of waves, the lower the frequency. As the frequency increases, the sound becomes higher in pitch. The human ear is sensitive to frequencies between 20 and 20,000 vibrations per second, although this range varies among individuals and decreases with age.

Intensity, or loudness, is the strength of the pressure of these radiating waves and is measured in decibels (dB).

The **speed of sound** varies depending on temperature and the medium through which it travels. It moves faster in water than in air, for example. At sea level and a temperature of 59°F (15°C), the speed of sound is approximately 761 mph, or 1,100 ft per sec.

Light and Colors of the Spectrum

Light, a form of electromagnetic radiation similar to radiant heat, radio waves, and X-rays, is emitted from a source in straight lines and spreads in area as it travels. For emission from a point source, light per unit area diminishes in proportion to the square of the distance.

The English mathematician and physicist Isaac Newton (1642-1727) described light as an **emission of particles**; the Dutch astronomer, mathematician, and physicist Christiaan Huygens (1629-95) and others developed the theory that light travels in a **wave motion**. It is now believed that these two theories are essentially complementary. The development of quantum theory has led to results where light acts like a series of particles in some experiments and like a wave in others.

The first relatively accurate measurement of the **speed of light** was made by French physicist Armand Hippolyte Louis Fizeau (1819-96). Today the speed of light is known precisely as 299,792.458 km per sec (or 186,282.397 mi/sec) in a vacuum. In water the speed of light is about 25% less, and in glass, 33% less.

Color sensations are produced through the excitation of the retina of the eye by light vibrating at different frequencies. The different colors of the visible spectrum may be seen by viewing light refracted by passage through a prism, which separates light into its component wavelengths.

Customarily, the basic colors are taken to be the six monochromatic (single) colors that occupy relatively large areas of the spectrum: red, orange, yellow, green, blue, and violet. So-called primary colors can be combined to produce the sensation of other colors. However, scientists disagree about how many and what primary colors to recognize. The color sensation of **black** is due to complete lack of stimulation of the retina, that of **white** to complete stimulation.

Infrared and **ultraviolet rays**, which are below the red (long) end and above the violet (short) end of the visible spectrum, respectively, are invisible to the naked human eye. Heat is the principal effect of infrared rays, and chemical action that of ultraviolet rays. Some animals can see infrared or ultraviolet light.

Life Cycles of Selected Animals

Information reviewed by Ronald M. Nowak, author of *Walker's Mammals of the World* (6th ed., Johns Hopkins University Press, 1999). Average longevity figures supplied by Ronald T. Reuther. These apply to animals in captivity; the potential life span of animals is rarely attained in nature. Figures on gestation and incubation are averages based on estimates.

Animal	Gestation (days)	Average longevity (yrs.)	Maximum longevity (yrs.-mos.)	Animal	Gestation (days)	Average longevity (yrs.)	Maximum longevity (yrs.-mos.)
Ass	365	12	47	Leopard	98	12	23
Baboon	187	20	45	Lion	100	15	30
Bear (black)	219	18	36-10	Monkey (rhesus)	166	15	37
Bear (grizzly)	225	25	50	Moose	240	12	27
Bear (polar)	240	20	45	Mouse (domestic white)	19	3	6
Beaver	105	5	50	Mouse (meadow)	21	3	4
Bison	285	15	40	Opossum (American)	13	1	5
Camel	406	12	50	Pig (domestic)	112	10	27
Cat (domestic)	63	12	38	Puma	90	12	20
Chimpanzee	230	20	60	Rabbit (domestic)	31	5	18-10
Chipmunk	31	6	10	Rhinoceros (black)	450	15	45-10
Cow	284	15	30	Rhinoceros (white)	480	20	50
Deer (white-tailed)	201	8	20	Sea lion (California)	350	12	34
Dog (domestic)	61	12	21	Sheep (domestic)	154	12	23
Elephant (African)	660	35	70	Squirrel (gray)	44	10	23-6
Elephant (Asian)	645	40	77	Tiger	105	16	26-3
Elk	250	15	26-8	Wolf (maned)	63	5	15-8
Fox (red)	52	7	14	Zebra (Grant's)	365	15	50
Giraffe	457	10	36-2				
Goat (domestic)	151	8	18	**Animal**			**Incubation time (days)**
Gorilla	258	20	54	Chicken			21
Guinea pig	68	4	8	Duck			30
Cow	284	15	30	Goose			30
Hippopotamus	238	41	61	Pigeon			18
Horse	330	20	50	Turkey			26
Kangaroo (gray)	36	7	24				

Geologic Time Scale

Our understanding of Earth's ancient history is largely a result of geoscientists' study of climate, rock strata, ice samples, mineral deposits, and fossils from around the world; clues to the planet's origin have also been found through the study of extraterrestrial bodies. Geologists divide Earth's history into the following units (MYA = million years ago):

PRECAMBRIAN TIME (4,600-541 MYA)

HADEAN EON (4,600-4,000 MYA) Earth initially has no continents, oceans, or life; surface conditions are defined by intense volcanic activity and widespread meteorite impact. Oldest known minerals and rocks, many of meteoric origin, date to this eon, which may also have seen the first appearance of life.

ARCHEAN EON (4,000-2,500 MYA) Earth's surface cools and water vapor in atmosphere condenses to form early oceans, which define small protocontinents; there is substantial evidence for the existence of single-celled organisms, bacteria and archaea, in these oceans.

PROTEROZOIC EON (2,500-541 MYA) Protocontinents merge into larger landmasses as Earth's crust continues to shift. Atmospheric oxygen levels increase, and first known multicellular life appears. Later, soft-bodied marine animals emerge.

PHANEROZOIC EON (541 MYA-present)

Paleozoic Era (541-252 MYA)

Cambrian Period (541-485 MYA). The supercontinent known as Gondwana, or Gondwanaland, dominates the Southern Hemisphere. Seas experience an explosion of invertebrate animal life, including thousands of species of trilobites; the first known vertebrates appear. There is no life on land.

Ordovician Period (485-444 MYA). Gondwanaland extends from South Pole to tropic regions; Northern Hemisphere is mostly open ocean. Average global temperatures are warmer than in the current era. First primitive land plants, early ancestors of starfish and mollusks, and first armored, jawless fishes appear. The period ends in mass extinction of a majority of species, possibly a result of a global drop in sea level due to glaciation.

Silurian Period (444-419 MYA). South Pole remains covered by supercontinent, but precursors of present-day N America, Europe, and Asia coalesce around the equator and middle latitudes. Appearance of first known vascular land plants, first freshwater fish, first jawed fish, first coral reefs, and first air-breathing animals (certain eurypterids, also called sea scorpions, largest known arthropods).

Devonian Period (419-359 MYA). Collisions between Gondwanaland and ancestral landmasses of N America and Eurasia produce mountains visible today as northern Appalachians. Newly-formed ozone layer offers protection from sun's rays, allowing first air-breathing spiders and mites to appear on dry land. Fish with fins and scales and first amphibians emerge. Late Devonian mass extinction.

Carboniferous Period (359-299 MYA). Precursors of modern N America and Northern Europe lie in tropical latitudes N of the equator; warm and humid conditions there facilitate spread of lush forests and peat swamps that later form most of the world's coal and limestone. Later period sees emergence of first true conifers, Lepidodendrales ("scale trees") as tall as 100 ft, and first true reptiles.

Permian Period (299-252 MYA). All major landmasses collide to form the supercontinent Pangaea, surrounded by the world ocean Panthalassa. Gradual warming through much of the Permian allows for initial flourishing of species, including dinosaur precursors (up to 10 ft long) and marine species in shallow inland seas. The period ended with the largest of Earth's five mass extinctions. As much as 95% of all marine species and most land species went extinct in the event, which was likely caused by increased greenhouse gases in atmosphere.

Mesozoic Era (252-66 MYA)

Triassic Period (252-201 MYA). Pangaea separates into supercontinents of Laurasia and Gondwana; subtropical conditions extend as far N as present-day Wyoming and New England. Emergence of icthyosaurs and plesiosaurs (large marine reptiles), several species of dinosaurs (up to 15 ft long), first true mammals, and first insects to undergo metamorphosis from larva to pupa to adult. Triassic-Jurassic mass extinction.

Jurassic Period (201-145 MYA). N American continent drifts westward, opening Gulf of Mexico; rift forms between S America and Africa. Warm, moist climate contributes to flourishing of coral reefs and temperate and subtropical forests. Appearance of first angiosperms (flowering plants), pterosaurs (winged reptiles), the earliest known birds (offshoots of a dinosaur group), and huge dinosaurs such as the carnivorous *Allosaurus* and herbivorous *Apatosaurus*.

Cretaceous Period (145-66 MYA). African continental plate drifts N, creating roots of European Alps; gap between S America and Africa broadens; western movement of N America drives formation of Sierra Nevada and Rocky Mountains, turning the western interior of continent into a vast swamp. Later, sea levels rise and cover about one-third of Earth's present land area. The global climate is warm and mild. The period ends in a mass extinction of plant and animal species (including dinosaurs). Likely causes include an asteroid impact and increased volcanic activity.

Cenozoic Era (66 MYA-present)

Paleogene Period (66-23 MYA)
- Paleocene Epoch (66-56 MYA). Australia begins to separate from Antarctica; N America and Greenland begin to spread apart. Mammalian life predominates, including early marsupials, insectivores, creodonts (carnivorous relatives of cats and dogs), and primitive hoofed mammals.
- Eocene Epoch (56-33.9 MYA). Australia drifts farther from Antarctica; the Indian subcontinent becomes welded to Asia, and tectonic forces drive the upheaval of the Alpine-Himalayan system. Climate in N America and Europe is subtropical and moist, with temperate forests as far N as Greenland and Siberia. Ancestors of modern horses, elephants, rhinoceroses, camels, bats, primates, and squirrel-like rodents emerge; earliest known marine mammals appear in later Eocene.
- Oligocene Epoch (33.9-23 MYA). San Andreas fault develops between N American and Pacific plates. Mammalian species continue to diversify, producing modern horse and multiple rodent, camel, and rhinoceros-like species, as well as first known species of great ape. Long-term cooling trend begins that would later cause Pleistocene ice ages.

Neogene Period (23-2.6 MYA)
- Miocene Epoch (23-5.3 MYA). Crustal plate collisions continue to drive uplift of Alps, Himalayas, and Cordilleran Ranges in Americas; eroded sediment is deposited in shallow marine basins, forming reservoirs for oil fields of California, Romania, and Caspian Sea. Ocean currents prevent Antarctica from receiving warmer waters, fostering growth of Antarctic ice sheet. Northern forests become grassy prairies. Large apes related to the orangutan live in Asia and southern Europe. Oldest hominin fossils from Africa date to this epoch.
- Pliocene Epoch (5.3-2.6 MYA). Alps continue to rise in Europe, and subduction of the Pacific tectonic plate elevates the Sierra Nevada and volcanic Cascade Range. Climate becomes cooler and drier, driving formation of permanent Arctic ice cap. Rapid primate evolution produces *Australopithecus*, an early direct ancestor of modern humans (*Homo sapiens*).

Quarternary Period (2.6 MYA-present)
- Pleistocene Epoch (2.6 MYA-11,700 years ago). Glacier ice covers as much as 25% or more of Earth's land surface, carving numerous present-day features including the Great Lakes; increased rainfall in lower latitudes allows plant and animal life to flourish in northern and eastern Africa. Late Pleistocene brings worldwide extinction of many large mammals, including the mastodon, saber-toothed tiger, and ground sloth. Evidence of Neanderthals, Denisovans, and the small archaic humans *Homo floresiensis* and *Homo luzonensis* dates from the latter part of the Pleistocene.
- Holocene Epoch (11,700 years ago-present). Melting ice caused sea levels to rise 100 ft or more in early Holocene, covering large areas of land and extending continental shelf of N America. Humans proliferate, and civilization begins.

Biological Classification

In biology, classification is the identification, naming, and grouping of organisms into a formal system. The two fields that are most directly concerned with classification are taxonomy and systematics. Although they overlap, taxonomy is more concerned with nomenclature (naming) and with constructing hierarchical systems, and systematics with uncovering evolutionary relationships. Two kingdoms of living forms, Plantae and Animalia, have been recognized since Aristotle established the first taxonomy in the 4th century BCE. Plants and animals are examples of eukaryotes; their cells have nuclei bound by membranes. Two other kingdoms of eukaryotes that have been identified are Protista (mostly one-celled organisms) and Fungi. Single-celled bacteria and archaea lack such nuclei. They are referred to as prokaryotes (or procaryotes) and are commonly placed in separate kingdoms. The seven basic categories of classification (from most general to most specific) are kingdom, phylum (or division), class, order, family, genus, and species. (In addition, many scientists group all eukaryotes in a single "domain," and treat bacteria and archaea as two other domains.) Below are two examples of classification:

ZOOLOGICAL HIERARCHY

Kingdom	Phylum	Class	Order	Family	Genus	Species name	Common name
Animalia	Chordata	Mammalia	Primates	Hominidae	*Homo*	*Homo sapiens*	Human

BOTANICAL HIERARCHY

Kingdom	Division*	Class	Order	Family	Genus	Species name	Common name
Plantae	Magnoliophyta	Magnoliopsida	Magnoliales	Magnoliaceae	*Magnolia*	*M. virginiana*	Sweet bay

*In botany, the division is generally used in place of the phylum.

Selected Endangered Animal Species

Source: Fish and Wildlife Service, U.S. Dept. of the Interior

Common name	Scientific name	Range where endangered
Albatross, Amsterdam	Diomedia amsterdamensis	Amsterdam Island, Indian Ocean
Antelope, giant sable	Hippotragus niger variani	Angola
Armadillo, giant	Priodontes maximus	Venezuela and Guyana to Argentina
Bandicoot, desert	Perameles eremiana	Australia
Bat, gray	Myotis grisescens	Central, southeastern U.S.
Bear, Mexican grizzly	Ursus arctos	Mexico
Bobcat, Mexican	Lynx rufus escuinapae	Mexico
Bumble bee, rusty patched	Bombus affinis	Canada; Eastern, midwestern U.S.
Camel, Bactrian	Camelus bactrianus	Mongolia, China
Caribou, woodland	Rangifer tarandus caribou	Canada, U.S. (ID, WA)
Cheetah	Acinonyx jubatus	Africa to India
Chimpanzee, pygmy	Pan paniscus	Dem. Rep. of the Congo
Condor, California	Gymnogyps californianus	U.S. (AZ, CA, NV, UT), Mexico (Baja California)
Crane, whooping	Grus americana	Canada, central U.S.
Crocodile, American	Crocodylus acutus	Caribbean (except for FL pop.); Central, S America
Dolphin, Chinese river	Lipotes vexillifer	China
Duck, Hawaiian	Anas wyvilliana	U.S. (HI)
Elephant, Asian	Elephas maximus	South-central and southeastern Asia
Fox, northern swift	Vulpes velox hebes	Canada
Frog, mountain yellow-legged	Rana muscosa	U.S. (CA)
Gorilla	Gorilla gorilla	Central and western Africa
Hyena, brown	Parahyaena brunnea	Southern Africa
Impala, black-faced	Aepyceros melampus petersi	Angola, Namibia
Kangaroo, Tasmanian forester	Macropus giganteus tasmaniensis	Australia (Tasmania)
Leopard	Panthera pardus	Central and Southern Africa, Asia
Monkey, spider	Ateles geoffroyi frontatus	Central America
Ocelot	Leopardus pardalis	U.S. (AZ, TX), Mexico; Central, S America
Orangutan	Pongo pygmaeus	Indonesia
Ostrich, West African	Struthio camelus spatzi	Western Sahara
Otter, marine	Lontra felina	Peru south to Straits of Magellan
Panda, giant	Ailuropoda melanoleuca	China
Panther, Florida	Puma concolor coryi	U.S. (FL)
Parrot, imperial	Amazona imperialis	Dominica
Penguin, Galapagos	Spheniscus mendiculus	Ecuador (Galapagos Islands)
Rhinoceros, black	Diceros bicornis	Sub-Saharan Africa
Salamander, Chinese giant	Andrias davidianus	China
Salmon, sockeye	Oncorhynchus nerka	U.S. (OR, WA)
Sea lion, Steller (Western pop.)	Eumetopias jubatus	U.S. (AK), Russia
Squirrel, Carolina northern flying	Glaucomys sabrinus coloratus	U.S. (NC, TN, VA)
Tiger	Panthera tigris	Asia
Tortoise, Galapagos	Geochelone nigra	Ecuador (Galapagos Islands)
Whale, gray (Western North Pacific pop.)	Eschrichtius robustus	NW Pacific Ocean
Wolf, red	Canis rufus	U.S. (FL)
Woodpecker, ivory-billed	Campephilus principalis	U.S. (AR)
Yak, wild	Bos mutus	China (Tibet), India
Zebra, mountain	Equus zebra zebra	South Africa

Status of Endangered and Threatened Species, 2020

Source: Fish and Wildlife Service, U.S. Dept. of the Interior; as of July 2020

Group	Endangered		Threatened		Total species[1]	U.S. species with active recovery plans
	U.S.	Foreign	U.S.	Foreign		
Mammals	68	260	28	23	379	56
Birds	77	217	22	21	337	87
Fishes	94	26	75	10	205	105
Reptiles	16	71	29	24	140	40
Clams	76	2	15	0	93	72
Insects	75	4	13	0	92	46
Snails	40	1	12	1	54	33
Amphibians	21	8	15	1	45	24
Crustaceans	24	0	4	0	28	19
Corals	0	3	7	15	25	0
Arachnids	12	5	0	0	17	12
Annelid worms	0	0	0	0	0	0
Flatworms and Roundworms	0	0	0	0	0	0
Hydroids	0	0	0	0	0	0
Millipedes	0	0	0	0	0	0
Sponges	0	0	0	0	0	0
Animal subtotals	**503**	**597**	**220**	**95**	**1,415**	**494**
Plant subtotals	**772**	**1**	**171**	**2**	**946**	**723**
Grand total	**1,275**	**598**	**391**	**97**	**2,361**	**1,217**

(1) 22 animal species are counted more than once in this table, primarily because these animals have distinct population segments, each with its own individual listing status. The U.S. species tallied more than once as endangered or threatened are Atlantic sturgeon, bearded seal, California tiger salamander, Chinook salmon, chum salmon, coho salmon, gray wolf, mountain yellow-legged frog, roseate tern, piping plover, sockeye salmon, and steelhead. The foreign species counted more than once are argali, broad-snouted caiman, humpback whale, leopard, scalloped hammerhead shark, and vicuña. Green sea turtles and loggerhead sea turtles appear on both the U.S. and foreign lists.

Major Venomous Animals

Snakes

Asian pit viper—2 ft to 5 ft long; throughout Asia; reactions and mortality vary, but most bites cause tissue damage; mortality generally low.

Australian brown snake—4 ft to 7 ft long; very slow onset of cardiac or respiratory distress; moderate mortality, but because death can be sudden and unexpected, it is the most dangerous of the Australian snakes; antivenom.

Barba amarilla or fer-de-lance—up to 7 ft long; from tropical Mexico to Brazil; severe tissue damage common; moderate mortality; antivenom.

Black mamba—up to 14 ft long; southern and central Africa; rapid onset of dizziness, difficulty breathing, erratic heartbeat; mortality high, nears 100% without antivenom.

Boomslang—less than 6 ft long; African savannahs; rapid onset of nausea and dizziness, often followed by slight recovery and then sudden death from internal hemorrhaging; bites rare, mortality high; antivenom.

Bushmaster—up to 12 ft long; tropical forests of Central and S America; few bites occur, but mortality high.

Common, or Asian, cobra—4 ft to 8 ft long; throughout S Asia; considerable tissue damage, sometimes paralysis; mortality probably not more than 10%; antivenom.

Copperhead—less than 4 ft long; New England to Texas; pain and swelling; very seldom fatal; antivenom seldom needed.

Coral snake—2 ft to 5 ft long; in Americas S of Canada; bite may be painless; slow onset of paralysis, impaired breathing; mortalities rare but high without antivenom and mechanical respiration.

Cottonmouth water moccasin—up to 5 ft long; wetlands of southern U.S. from Virginia to Texas; rapid onset of severe pain, swelling, tissue destruction can be extensive; mortality low; antivenom.

Death adder—less than 3 ft long; Australia; rapid onset of faintness, cardiac and respiratory distress; at least 50% mortality without antivenom.

Desert horned viper—up to 2 ft long; dry areas of Africa and western Asia; swelling and tissue damage; mortality low; antivenom.

European viper—1 ft to 3 ft long; throughout Europe; bleeding and tissue damage; mortality low; antivenom.

Gaboon viper—more than 6 ft long; S of the Sahara; massive tissue damage, internal bleeding; few recorded bites.

King cobra—up to 16 ft long; throughout S Asia; rapid swelling, dizziness, loss of consciousness, difficulty breathing, erratic heartbeat; mortality varies with amount of venom involved, but most bites involve nonfatal amounts; antivenom.

Krait—up to 5 ft long; SE Asia; rapid onset of sleepiness, numbness; up to 50% mortality even with use of antivenom.

Puff adder—up to 5 ft long, thick; S of the Sahara, throughout the Middle East; rapid large swelling, great pain, dizziness; moderate mortality, often from internal bleeding; antivenom.

Rattlesnake—2 ft to 6 ft long; throughout Western Hemisphere; rapid onset of severe pain, swelling; mortality low, but amputation of affected digits is sometimes necessary; antivenom. Mojave rattler may produce temporary paralysis.

Ringhals, or spitting, cobra—5 ft to 7 ft long; southern Africa; squirts venom through holes in front of fangs as a defense; venom severely irritating and can cause blindness.

Russell's viper or tic-polonga—more than 5 ft long; throughout Asia; internal bleeding; bite reports common; moderate mortality rate; antivenom.

Saw-scaled, or carpet, viper—up to 2 ft long; dry areas from India to Africa; severe bleeding, fever; high mortality, causes more human fatalities than any other snake; antivenom.

Sea snake—3 ft to 10 ft long; throughout Pacific, Indian Oceans except NE Pacific; almost painless bite; variety of muscle pain, paralysis; mortality low, many bites not envenomed; some antivenoms.

Sharp-nosed pit viper or hundred-pace snake—up to 5 ft long; S Vietnam, Taiwan, and China; the most toxic of Asian pit vipers; very rapid onset of swelling and tissue damage, internal bleeding; moderate mortality; antivenom.

Taipan—up to 11 ft long; Australia and New Guinea; rapid paralysis with severe breathing difficulty; mortality nears 100% without antivenom.

Tiger snake—2 ft to 6 ft long; southern Australia; pain, numbness, mental disturbances with rapid paralysis; may be deadliest of all land snakes; but antivenom is quite effective.

Yellow, or cape, cobra—7 ft long; southern Africa; most toxic venom of any cobra; rapid onset of swelling, breathing and cardiac difficulties; mortality is high without treatment; antivenom.

Note: Not all bites by venomous snakes are actually envenomed. Any animal bite, however, carries the danger of tetanus, and anyone suffering a venomous snake bite should seek medical attention. Antivenoms do not cure; they are only an aid in the treatment of bites. Mortality rates above are for envenomed bites: low mortality, c. 2% or less; moderate, 2%-5%; high, 5%-15%.

Lizards

Gila monster—up to 24 in. long, with heavy body and tail; high desert in SW U.S. and northern Mexico; immediate severe pain, transient low blood pressure; no recent mortality.

Mexican beaded lizard—similar to Gila monster; W coast of Mexico; reaction and mortality similar to Gila monster.

Insects

Ants, bees, hornets, wasps—global distribution; usual reaction is piercing pain in area of sting, though many people suffer allergic reactions (swelling, rashes); not directly fatal, except in cases of massive multiple stings, and a few may die within minutes from severe sensitivity to the venom (anaphylactic shock).

Spiders, scorpions

Black widow—small, round-bodied with red hourglass marking; the widow and its relatives are found in tropical and temperate zones; severe musculoskeletal pain, weakness, breathing difficulty, convulsions, which may be more serious in small children; low mortality; antivenom. The **redback** spider of Australia has the hourglass marking on its back, rather than on its front, but otherwise looks almost identical to the black widow.

Brown recluse, or fiddleback, spider—small, oblong body; throughout U.S.; pain with later ulceration, which may last months, at place of bite; fever, nausea, and stomach cramps in severe cases; very low mortality.

Funnel web spider—several varieties, often large; Australia; slow onset of breathing, circulation difficulties; low mortality; antivenom.

Scorpion—crablike body with stinger in tail, various sizes; many varieties throughout tropical and subtropical areas; severe pain spreading from the wound, numbness, severe agitation, cramps, and even respiratory failure; low mortality, usually in children; antivenoms.

Tarantula—large, hairy spider; worldwide; the American tarantula, and probably all other tarantulas, are harmless to humans, though their bite may cause some pain and swelling.

Sea life

Cone-shell—mollusk in small shell; S Pacific and Indian Oceans; shoots barbs into victims; paralysis; low mortality.

Octopus—global distribution, usually in warm waters; rapid onset of paralysis with breathing difficulty; all varieties produce venom, but only a few can cause death.

Portuguese man-of-war—jellyfish-like siphonophore with tentacles up to 100 ft long; in most warm water areas; immediate severe pain; not directly fatal, though shock may cause death in rare cases.

Sea wasp or box jellyfish—tentacles up to 30 ft long; S Pacific; very rapid onset of circulatory problems; high mortality because of speed of toxic reaction; antivenom.

Stingray—several varieties of differing sizes; tropical and temperate seas and some freshwater; severe pain, rapid onset of nausea, vomiting, breathing difficulties; wound area may ulcerate, gangrene may occur; seldom fatal.

Stonefish—brownish fish that lies motionless on bottom of shallow waters; S Pacific and Indian Oceans; extraordinary pain, rapid paralysis; low mortality; antivenom, warm water relieves pain.

Speeds of Selected Animals

Source: *Natural History* magazine. © American Museum of Natural History

Animal	Speed (mph)	Animal	Speed (mph)	Animal	Speed (mph)
Cheetah	70	Mongolian wild ass	40	Human	27.89
Pronghorn antelope	61	Greyhound	39.35	Elephant	25
Wildebeest	50	Whippet	35.50	Black mamba snake	20
Lion	50	Rabbit (domestic)	35	Six-lined race runner (lizard)	18
Thomson's gazelle	50	Mule deer	35	Wild turkey	15
Quarterhorse	47.5	Jackal	35	Squirrel	12
Elk	45	Reindeer	32	Pig (domestic)	11
Cape hunting dog	45	Giraffe	32	Chicken	9
Coyote	43	White-tailed deer	30	Spider (*Tegenaria atrica*)	1.17
Gray fox	42	Warthog	30	Giant tortoise	0.17
Hyena	40	Grizzly bear	30	Three-toed sloth	0.15
Zebra	40	Cat (domestic)	30	Garden snail	0.03

Note: Most of these measurements are for maximum speeds over approximate quarter-mile distances. Exceptions are the lion and elephant, whose speeds were clocked in the act of charging; the whippet, which was timed over a 200-yd course; the cheetah, timed over a 100-yd distance; a human, timed over a 15-yd segment of a 100-yd run; and the black mamba, six-lined race runner, spider, giant tortoise, three-toed sloth, and garden snail, which were measured over various small distances.

Most Popular Breeds of Cats, 2019

Source: The Cat Fanciers' Association
(ranked by total registrations)

Rank	Breed	Rank	Breed	Rank	Breed	Rank	Breed	Rank	Breed
1.	Ragdoll	10.	Scottish Fold	20.	Selkirk Rex	29.	Bombay	37.	Lykoi
2.	Exotic	11.	Oriental	21.	Tonkinese	30.	Manx	38.	Korat
3.	British Shorthair	12.	Siamese	22.	American Curl	31.	Colorpoint	39.	Burmilla
4.	Persian	13.	Cornish Rex	23.	Ocicat		Shorthair	40.	Havana Brown
5.	Maine Coon	14.	Russian Blue	24.	Ragamuffin	32.	Turkish Angora	41.	Khao Manee
6.	Devon Rex	15.	Norwegian Forest	25.	Somali	33.	Balinese	42.	American Bobtail
7.	American	16.	Bengal	26.	Japanese Bobtail	34.	Chartreux	43.	Turkish Van
	Shorthair	17.	Siberian	27.	Egyptian Mau	35.	Toybob	44.	American Wirehair
8.	Abyssinian	18.	Birman	28.	Singapura	36.	European Burmese	45.	La Perm
9.	Sphynx	19.	Burmese						

Most Popular American Kennel Club Dog Breed Registrations, 2016-19

Source: American Kennel Club (AKC)
(ranked by 2019 registrations)

Breed	Rank				Breed	Rank			
	2019	2018	2017	2016		2019	2018	2017	2016
Labrador Retrievers	1	1	1	1	Cavalier King Charles				
German Shepherds	2	2	2	2	Spaniels	16	18	19	19
Golden Retrievers	3	3	3	3	Great Danes	17	16	14	14
French Bulldogs	4	4	4	6	Miniature Schnauzers	18	19	18	17
Bulldogs	5	5	5	4	Doberman Pinschers	19	17	16	15
Poodles	6	7	7	7	Shih Tzu	20	20	20	20
Beagles	7	6	6	5	Boston Terriers	21	21	21	21
Rottweilers	8	8	8	8	Havanese	22	24	23	23
German Shorthaired					Bernese Mountain Dogs	23	22	25	27
Pointers	9	9	10	11	Pomeranians	24	23	22	22
Pembroke Welsh Corgis	10	13	15	18	Shetland Sheepdogs	25	25	24	24
Dachshunds	11	12	13	13	Brittanys	26	26	26	25
Yorkshire Terriers	12	10	9	9	English Springer Spaniels	27	27	27	26
Australian Shepherds	13	15	17	16	Cocker Spaniels	28	30	29	29
Boxers	14	11	11	10	Miniature American				
Siberian Huskies	15	14	12	12	Shepherds	29	34	35	36
					Cane Corso	30	32	37	40

Dog Breeds by Type

Source: American Kennel Club (AKC)

As of mid-2020, the AKC recognized 195 registered breeds and used the following seven groups to classify them, according to functions and other distinctive traits.

Herding Group: Australian Cattle Dog, Australian Shepherd, Bearded Collie, Beauceron, Belgian Malinois, Belgian Sheepdog, Belgian Tervuren, Bergamasco Sheepdog, Berger Picard, Border Collie, Bouvier des Flandres, Briard, Canaan Dog, Cardigan Welsh Corgi, Collie, Entlebucher Mountain Dog, Finnish Lapphund, German Shepherd Dog, Icelandic Sheepdog, Miniature American Shepherd, Norwegian Buhund, Old English Sheepdog, Pembroke Welsh Corgi, Polish Lowland Sheepdog, Puli, Pumi, Pyrenean Shepherd, Shetland Sheepdog, Spanish Water Dog, Swedish Vallhund.

Hound Group: Afghan Hound, American English Coonhound, American Foxhound, Azawakh, Basenji, Basset Hound, Beagle, Black and Tan Coonhound, Bloodhound, Bluetick Coonhound, Borzoi, Cirneco dell'Etna, Dachshund, English Foxhound, Grand Basset Griffon Vendéen, Greyhound, Harrier, Ibizan Hound, Irish Wolfhound, Norwegian Elkhound, Otterhound, Petit Basset Griffon Vendéen, Pharaoh Hound, Plott Hound, Portuguese Podengo Pequeno, Redbone Coonhound, Rhodesian Ridgeback, Saluki, Scottish Deerhound, Sloughi, Treeing Walker Coonhound, Whippet.

Non-Sporting Group: American Eskimo Dog, Bichon Frise, Boston Terrier, Bulldog, Chinese Shar-Pei, Chow Chow, Coton de Tulear, Dalmatian, Finnish Spitz, French Bulldog, Keeshond, Lhasa Apso, Löwchen, Norwegian Lundehund, Poodle (standard and miniature), Schipperke, Shiba Inu, Tibetan Spaniel, Tibetan Terrier, Xoloitzcuintli.

Sporting Group: American Water Spaniel, Barbet, Boykin Spaniel, Brittany, Chesapeake Bay Retriever, Clumber Spaniel, Cocker Spaniel, Curly-Coated Retriever, English Cocker Spaniel, English Setter, English Springer Spaniel, Field Spaniel, Flat-Coated Retriever, German Shorthaired Pointer, German Wirehaired Pointer, Golden Retriever, Gordon Setter, Irish Red and White Setter, Irish Setter, Irish Water Spaniel, Labrador Retriever, Lagotto Romagnolo, Nederlandse Kooikerhondje, Nova Scotia Duck Tolling Retriever, Pointer, Spinone Italiano, Sussex Spaniel, Vizsla, Weimaraner, Welsh Springer Spaniel, Wirehaired Pointing Griffon, Wirehaired Vizsla.

Terrier Group: Airedale Terrier, American Hairless Terrier, American Staffordshire Terrier, Australian Terrier, Bedlington Terrier, Border Terrier, Bull Terrier, Cairn Terrier, Cesky Terrier, Dandie Dinmont Terrier, Glen of Imaal Terrier, Irish Terrier, Kerry Blue Terrier, Lakeland Terrier, Manchester Terrier (standard), Miniature Bull Terrier, Miniature Schnauzer, Norfolk Terrier, Norwich Terrier, Parson Russell Terrier, Rat Terrier, Russell Terrier, Scottish Terrier, Sealyham Terrier, Skye Terrier, Smooth Fox Terrier, Soft Coated Wheaten Terrier, Staffordshire Bull Terrier, Welsh Terrier, West Highland White Terrier, Wire Fox Terrier.

Toy Group: Affenpinscher, Brussels Griffon, Cavalier King Charles Spaniel, Chihuahua, Chinese Crested, English Toy Spaniel, Havanese, Italian Greyhound, Japanese Chin, Maltese, Manchester Terrier (toy), Miniature Pinscher, Papillon, Pekingese, Pomeranian, Poodle (toy), Pug, Shih Tzu, Silky Terrier, Toy Fox Terrier, Yorkshire Terrier.

Working Group: Akita, Alaskan Malamute, Anatolian Shepherd Dog, Bernese Mountain Dog, Black Russian Terrier, Boerboel, Boxer, Bullmastiff, Cane Corso, Chinook, Doberman Pinscher, Dogo Argentino, Dogue de Bordeaux, German Pinscher, Giant Schnauzer, Great Dane, Great Pyrenees, Greater Swiss Mountain Dog, Komondor, Kuvasz, Leonberger, Mastiff, Neapolitan Mastiff, Newfoundland, Portuguese Water Dog, Rottweiler, Saint Bernard, Samoyed, Siberian Husky, Standard Schnauzer, Tibetan Mastiff.

Discoveries and Innovations: Biology, Chemistry, Medicine, Physics

Discovery	Date	Discoverer(s)	Nationality
Acetylene gas	1862	Berthelot	French
ACTH	1927	Evans, Long	U.S.
Adrenaline	1901	Takamine	Japanese
Aluminum, electrolytic process	1886	Hall	U.S.
Aluminum, isolated	1825	Oersted	Danish
Anesthesia, ether	1842	Long	U.S.
Anesthesia, local	1885	Koller	Austrian
Anesthesia, spinal	1898	Bier	German
Aniline dye	1856	Perkin	English
Anti-rabies	1885	Pasteur	French
Antiseptic surgery	1867	Lister	English
Antitoxin, diphtheria	1891	Von Behring	German
Argyrol	1897	Bayer	German
Arsphenamine	1910	Ehrlich	German
Aspirin	1853	Gerhardt	French
Atabrine	1932	Mietzsch, et al.	German
Atomic numbers	1913	Moseley	English
Atomic theory	1803	Dalton	English
Atomic time clock	1948	Lyons	U.S.
Atom-smashing theory	1919	Rutherford	English
Bacitracin	1943	Johnson, Meleneyi	U.S.
Bacteria, description	1676	Leeuwenhoek	Dutch
Bacterial genome, synthetic	2010	Venter	U.S.
Bleaching powder	1798	Tennant	English
Blood, circulation	1628	Harvey	English
Bordeaux mixture	1885	Millardet	French
Bromine from the sea	1826	Balard	French
Calcium carbide	1888	Wilson	U.S.
Calculus	1670	Newton	English
Camphor synthetic	1896	Haller	French
Canning (food)	1804	Appert	French
Carbon oxides	1925	Fisher	German
Chemotherapy	1909	Ehrlich	German
Chloramphenicol	1947	Burkholder	U.S.
Chlorine	1774	Scheele	Swedish
Chloroform	1831	Guthrie	U.S.
Chlortetracycline	1948	Duggen	U.S.
Classification of plants and animals	1735	Linnaeus	Swedish
Cloning, DNA	1973	Boyer, Cohen	U.S.
Cloning, mammal	1996	Wilmut, et al.	Scottish
Cocaine	1860	Niermann	German
Combustion explained	1777	Lavoisier	French
Conditioned reflex	1914	Pavlov	Russian
Cortisone	1936	Kendall	U.S.
Cortisone, synthesis	1946	Sarett	U.S.
Cosmic rays	1910	Gockel	Swiss
Cyclotron	1930	Lawrence	U.S.

Discovery	Date	Discoverer(s)	Nationality
DDT (not applied as insecticide until 1939)	1874	Zeidler	German
Denisovan humans (DNA analysis)	2010	Krause, et al.	German
		Pääbo	Swedish
Deuterium	1932	Urey, Brickwedde, Murphy	U.S.
DNA (as carrier of heredity)	1943	Avery, MacLeod, McCarty	U.S.
DNA (structure)	1953	Crick, Wilkins	English
		Watson	U.S.
Electric resistance, law of	1827	Ohm	German
Electric waves	1888	Hertz	German
Electrolysis	1852	Faraday	English
Electromagnetism	1819	Oersted	Danish
Electron	1897	Thomson, J.	English
Electron diffraction	1936	Thomson, G.	English
		Davisson	U.S.
Electroshock treatment	1938	Cerletti, Bini	Italian
Erythromycin	1952	McGuire	U.S.
Evolution, natural selection	1858	Darwin	English
Falling bodies, law of	1590	Galileo	Italian
Gases, law of combining volumes	1808	Gay-Lussac	French
Geometry, analytic	1619	Descartes	French
Gold, cyanide process for extraction	1887	MacArthur, R.Forrest, W. Forrest	Scottish
Gravitation, law	1687	Newton	English
Gravitational waves (detection)	2015	LIGO	U.S.-Intl.
Higgs boson	2012	CERN	International
HIV (human immunodeficiency virus)	1984	Montagnier	French
		Gallo	U.S.
Holograph	1948	Gabor	Hung.-British
Homo floresiensis ("hobbit" humans)	2003	Morwood, et al.	New Zea.
Human genome sequence (first draft)	2001	Human Genome Project, Celera Genomics Corp.	U.S.-Intl.
In vitro fertilization	1978	Steptoe, Edwards	English
Indigo, synthesis of	1880	Baeyer	German
Induction, electric	1830	Henry	U.S.
Insulin	1922	Banting, Best	Canadian
		Macleod	Scottish
Intelligence testing	1905	Binet, Simon	French
Isotopes, theory	1912	Soddy	English
Laser	1957	Gould	U.S.
Light, velocity	1675	Roemer	Danish

Discovery	Date	Discoverer(s)	Nationality
Light, wave theory	1690	Huygens	Dutch
Lithography	1796	Senefelder	Bohemian
Logarithms	1614	Napier	Scottish
LSD-25	1943	Hoffman	Swiss
Mendelian laws	1866	Mendel	Austrian
Mercator projection (map)	1568	Mercator (Kremer)	Flemish
Methanol	1661	Boyle	Irish
Milk condensation	1853	Borden	U.S.
Molecular hypothesis	1811	Avogadro	Italian
Motion, laws of	1687	Newton	English
Neomycin	1949	Waksman, Lechevalier	U.S.
Neutrino	1956	Reines, Cowan	U.S.
Neutron	1932	Chadwick	English
Nitric acid	1648	Glauber	German
Nitric oxide	1772	Priestley	English
Nitroglycerin	1846	Sobrero	Italian
Oil cracking process	1891	Dewar	U.S.
Oxygen	1774	Priestley	English
Oxytetracycline	1950	Finlay, et al.	U.S.
Ozone	1840	Schonbein	German
Paper, sulfite process	1867	Tilghman	U.S.
Paper, wood pulp, sulfate process	1884	Dahl	German
Penicillin	1928	Fleming	Scottish
Penicillin, practical use	1941	Florey, Chain	English
Periodic law and table of elements	1869	Mendeleyev	Russian
Physostigmine synthesis	1935	Julian	U.S.
Pill, birth-control	1954	Pincus, Rock	U.S.
Planetary motion, laws	1609	Kepler	German
Plutonium fission	1940	Kennedy, Wahl, Seaborg, Segre	U.S.
Polymyxin	1947	Ainsworth	English
Positron	1932	Anderson	U.S.
Proton	1919	Rutherford	New Zea.
Psychoanalysis	1900	Freud	Austrian
Pulsars	1967	Bell	English
Quantum theory	1900	Planck	German
Quasars	1963	Matthews, Sandage	U.S.
Quinine synthetic	1946	Woodward, Doering	U.S.
Radioactivity	1896	Becquerel	French
Radiocarbon dating	1947	Libby	U.S.
Radium	1898	Curie, Pierre	French
		Curie, Marie	Pol.-Fr.
Relativity theory	1905	Einstein	German
Reserpine	1949	Jal Vakil	Indian
Schick test	1913	Schick	U.S.

Discovery	Date	Discoverer(s)	Nationality
Silicon	1823	Berzelius	Swedish
Smallpox eradication	1979	World Health Org.	UN
Streptomycin	1944	Waksman, et al.	U.S.
Sulfanilamide	1935	Bovet, Trefouel	French
Sulfanilamide theory	1908	Gelmo	German
Sulfapyridine	1938	Ewins, Phelps	English
Sulfathiazole	1939	Fosbinder, Walter	U.S.
Sulfuric acid	1831	Phillips	English
Sulfuric acid, lead	1746	Roebuck	English
Superconductivity	1911	Onnes	Dutch
Superconductivity theory	1957	Bardeen, Cooper, Schreiffer	U.S.
Superconductors, high-temp.	1986	Bednorz, Muller	Ger., Swiss
Syphilis test	1906	Wassermann	German
Transplant, face	2005	Devauchelle, Dubernard	French
Transplant, heart	1967	Barnard	S. African
Tuberculin	1890	Koch	German
Uranium fission, atomic reactor	1942	Fermi, Szilard	U.S.
Uranium fission theory	1939	Hahn, Meitner, Strassmann	German
		Bohr	Danish
		Fermi	Italian
		Einstein, Pegram, Wheeler	U.S.
Vaccine, Ebola	2016	Public Health Agency of Canada	Canadian
Vaccine, measles	1963	Enders	U.S.
Vaccine, MMR	1971	Hilleman	U.S.
Vaccine, meningitis (first conjugate)	1987	Gordon, et al., Connaught Labs	U.S.
Vaccine, polio	1954	Salk	U.S.
Vaccine, polio, oral	1960	Sabin	U.S.
Vaccine, rabies	1885	Pasteur	French
Vaccine, smallpox	1796	Jenner	English
Vaccine, typhus	1909	Nicolle	French
Vaccine, varicella	1974	Takahashi	Japanese
Van Allen belts, radiation	1958	Van Allen	U.S.
Vitamin A	1913	McCollum, Davis	U.S.
Vitamin B	1916	McCollum	U.S.
Vitamin C	1928	Szent-Gyorgyi	Hungarian
		King	U.S.
Vitamin D	1922	McCollum	U.S.
Xerography	1938	Carlson	U.S.
X-ray	1895	Roentgen	German

Inventions

Invention	Date	Inventor(s)	Nationality
Adding machine	1642	Pascal	French
Adding machine	1885	Burroughs	U.S.
Aerosol spray	1926	Rotheim	Norwegian
Air brake	1869	Westinghouse	U.S.
Air conditioning	1902	Carrier	U.S.
Air pump	1654	Guericke	German
Airbag	1952	Hetrick	U.S.
Airplane, automatic pilot	1912	Sperry	U.S.
Airplane, experimental	1896	Langley	U.S.
Airplane, hydro	1911	Curtiss	U.S.
Airplane jet engine	1939	Ohain	German
Airplane with motor	1903	Wright Bros.	U.S.
Airship	1852	Giffard	French
Aqua-Lung	1943	Cousteau, Gagnan	French
Arc welder	1919	Thomson	U.S.
Aspartame	1965	Schlatter	U.S.
ATM (automated cash-dispensing machine)	1967	Shepherd-Barron	Scottish
Autogyro	1920	de la Cierva	Spanish
Automobile, diff. gear	1885	Benz	German
Automobile, electric	1892	Morrison	U.S.
Automobile, exp'mtl	1864	Marcus	Austrian
Automobile, gasoline	1889	Daimler	German
Automobile, gasoline	1892	Duryea	U.S.
Automobile magneto	1897	Bosch	German
Automobile muffler	1904	Pope	U.S.
Automobile self-starter	1911	Kettering	U.S.
Bakelite	1907	Baekeland	Belg., U.S.
Bar code	1952	Woodland, Silver	U.S.
Barometer	1643	Torricelli	Italian
Bicycle, electric	1895	Bolton	U.S.
Bicycle, modern	1885	Starley	English
Bifocal lens	1780	Franklin	U.S.
Bottle machine	1895	Owens	U.S.
Bluetooth	1994	Haartsen	Dutch

Invention	Date	Inventor(s)	Nationality
Braille printing	1829	Braille	French
Brassiere, modern	1913	Jacob	U.S
Bubble gum	1928	Diemer	U.S.
Burner, gas	1855	Bunsen	German
Calculator, electronic pocket	1972	Merryman, Van Tassel	U.S.
Calculator, mechanical	1623	Schickard	German
Camera, digital	1977	Lloyd, Sasson	U.S.
Camera, Kodak	1888	Eastman, Walker	U.S.
Camera, Polaroid Land	1948	Land	U.S.
Can, pop-top	1959	Fraze	U.S.
Car coupler	1873	Janney	U.S.
Carburetor, gasoline	1893	Maybach	German
Carding machine	1797	Whittemore	U.S.
Carpet sweeper	1876	Bissell	U.S.
Cash register	1879	Ritty	U.S.
Cassette, audio	1963	Philips Co.	Dutch
Cassette, videotape	1969	Sony	Japanese
CAT, or CT, scan	1973	Hounsfield	English
Cathode-ray tube	1897	Braun	German
Cellophane	1908	Brandenberger	Swiss
Celluloid	1870	Hyatt	U.S.
Cement, Portland	1824	Aspdin	English
Chronometer	1735	Harrison	English
Circuit breaker	1925	Hilliard	U.S.
Circuit, integrated	1959	Kilby, Noyce, Texas Instr.	U.S.
Clock, pendulum	1657	Huygens	Dutch
Coaxial cable system	1929	Affel, Espensched.	U.S.
Coca-Cola	1885	Pemberton	U.S.
Coffeemaker, auto drip	1963	Bunn Corp.	U.S.
Compressed air rock drill	1871	Ingersoll	U.S.
Comptometer	1887	Felt	U.S.
Computer, electronic	1942	Atanasoff, Berry	U.S.

Invention	Date	Inventor(s)	Nationality
Computer, laptop	1987	Sinclair	English
Computer, large-scale automatic digital	1943	Aiken, et al.	U.S.
Computer, mini	1960	Digital Corp.	U.S.
Condenser microphone (telephone)	1916	Wente	U.S.
Contact lens, corneal	1948	Tuohy	U.S.
Contraceptive, oral	1954	Pincus, Rock.	U.S.
Corn, hybrid	1917	Jones	U.S.
Cotton gin	1793	Whitney.	U.S.
Cream separator	1878	DeLaval	Swedish
Cultivator, disc	1878	Mallon.	U.S.
Cyclotron	1931	Lawrence	U.S.
Cystoscope	1878	Nitze	German
Diapers, disposable	1950	Donovan.	U.S.
Diesel engine	1895	Diesel.	German
Disc, compact	1972	RCA	U.S.
Disc player, compact	1979	Sony, Philips Co.	Japanese, Dutch
Dishwasher	1893	Cochrane	U.S.
Disk, floppy	1970	IBM	U.S.
Disk, video	1972	Philips Co.	Dutch
Drone (unmanned aircraft, remotely controlled)	1916	Low	English
Dynamite	1866	Nobel	Swedish
Dynamo, contin. current	1871	Gramme	Belgian
Electric battery	1800	Volta	Italian
Electric fan	1882	Wheeler	U.S.
Electrocardiograph	1903	Einthoven	Dutch
Electroencephalograph.	1929	Berger	German
Electromagnet	1824	Sturgeon	English
Electron microscope	1931	Ruska, Knoll	German
Electron spectrometer	1944	Deutsch, Elliott, Evans	U.S.
Electron tube multigrid	1913	Langmuir.	U.S.
Electronic cigarette (nicotine-based)	2003	Hon (Han)	Chinese
Electronic paper (e-ink)	1974	Sheridon	U.S.
Electroplating	1805	Brugnatelli.	Italian
Electrostatic generator	1929	Van de Graaff	U.S.
Elevator brake	1852	Otis	U.S.
Elevator, push button	1922	Larson	U.S.
Engine, automatic transmission	1910	Fottinger	German
Engine, coal-gas 4-cycle.	1876	Otto	German
Engine, compression ignition	1883	Daimler	German
Engine, electric ignition.	1883	Benz	German
Engine, gas, compound	1926	Eickemeyer	U.S.
Engine, gasoline	1872	Brayton	U.S.
Engine, gasoline	1889	Daimler	German
Engine, jet.	1930	Whittle	English
Engine, steam, piston	1705	Newcomen	English
Engine, steam, piston	1769	Watt	Scottish
Engraving, half-tone	1852	Talbot	English
Ferris wheel	1893	Ferris	U.S.
Fiber optic wire	1970	Keck, Maurer, Schultz	U.S.
Fiber optics	1955	Kapany	English
Fiberglass	1938	Owens-Corning.	U.S.
Filament, tungsten	1913	Coolidge	U.S.
Flanged rail	1831	Stevens.	U.S.
Flatiron, electric	1882	Seely.	U.S.
Food, frozen	1923	Birdseye	U.S.
Freon	1930	Midgley, et al.	U.S.
Furnace (for steel)	1858	Siemens	German
Galvanometer	1820	Sweigger	German
Garbage bag, polyethylene	1950	Wasylyk	Canadian
Gas discharge tube	1922	Hull	U.S.
Gas lighting	1792	Murdoch	Scottish
Gas mantle	1885	Welsbach	Austrian
Gasoline, cracked	1913	Burton.	U.S.
Gasoline, high octane.	1930	Ipatieff.	Russian
Gasoline (lead ethyl).	1922	Midgley.	U.S.
Geiger counter	1913	Geiger.	German
Geodesic dome	1948	Fuller.	U.S.
Glass, laminated safety	1909	Benedictus	French
Glider	1853	Cayley.	English
Google search software	1996	Brin, Page.	U.S.
Gun, breechloader	1811	Thornton.	U.S.
Gun, Browning	1897	Browning.	U.S.
Gun, magazine	1875	Hotchkiss	U.S.
Gun, silencer	1908	Maxim, H. P.	U.S.
Guncotton (nitrocellulose)	1847	Schoenbein.	German
Gyrocompass	1911	Sperry.	U.S.
Gyroscope	1852	Foucault	French
Hard drive, computer	1955	Johnson	U.S.
Harvester-thresher	1818	Lane	U.S.
Heart, artificial	1982	Jarvik	U.S.
Helicopter	1939	Sikorsky	U.S.
Hovercraft	1955	Cockerell.	English
Hydrometer	1768	Baume	French
Iron lung	1928	Drinker, Slaw	U.S.
Jet Ski	1973	Jacobsen	U.S.
Kaleidoscope	1817	Brewster	Scottish
Kevlar	1965	Kwolek, Blades.	U.S.
Kidney dialysis machine	1941	Kolff	Dutch
Kinetoscope	1889	Edison.	U.S.
Lamp, arc	1847	Staite	English
Lamp, fluorescent	1938	General Electric, Westinghouse.	U.S.
Lamp, incandescent	1879	Edison.	U.S.
Lamp, incand., gas	1913	Langmuir.	U.S.
Lamp, klieg	1911	Kliegl, A. and J.	U.S.
Lamp, mercury vapor	1912	Hewitt	U.S.
Lamp, miner's safety	1816	Davy	English
Lamp, neon	1909	Claude	French
Lathe, turret	1845	Fitch	U.S.
Launderette	1934	Cantrell	U.S.
Lens, achromatic	1758	Dollond	English
Lens, fused bifocal	1908	Borsch	U.S.
Leyden jar (condenser).	1745	von Kleist	German
Lightning rod	1752	Franklin.	U.S.
Linoleum	1860	Walton	English
Linotype	1884	Mergenthaler	U.S.
Linux	1991	Torvalds	Finnish
Liquid Paper	c.1951	Graham.	U.S.
Lock, cylinder	1851	Yale	U.S.
Locomotive, electric	1851	Vail	U.S.
Locomotive, exp'mtl	1802	Trevithick	English
Locomotive, exp'mtl	1812	Fenton, et al.	English
Locomotive, exp'mtl	1814	Stephenson	English
Locomotive, 1st U.S.	1830	Cooper.	U.S.
Locomotive, practical	1829	Stephenson	English
Loom, power	1785	Cartwright.	English
Loudspeaker, dynamic	1924	Rice, Kellogg	U.S.
Machine gun	1862	Gatling	U.S.
Machine gun, improved	1872	Hotchkiss	U.S.
Machine gun (Maxim)	1883	Maxim, H. S.	U.S.-Eng.
Magnet, electro	1828	Henry	U.S.
Magnetic Resonance Imaging (MRI)	1971	Damadian	U.S.
Maser	1953	Townes.	U.S.
Mason jar	1858	Mason.	U.S.
Match, friction	1827	Walker	English
Mercerized textiles	1843	Mercer	English
Meter, induction	1888	Shallenberger.	U.S.
Metronome	1816	Malzel.	German
Microcomputer	1973	Truong, et al.	French
Micrometer	1636	Gascoigne	English
Microphone	1877	Berliner.	U.S.
Microprocessor	1971	Intel Corp.	U.S.
Microscope, compound	1590	Janssen	Dutch
Microscope, electronic	1931	Knoll, Ruska	German
Microscope, field ion	1951	Mueller	German
Microwave oven	1947	Spencer	U.S.
Monitor, warship	1861	Ericsson	U.S.
Monotype	1887	Lanston	U.S.
Motor, AC	1892	Tesla.	U.S.
Motor, DC	1837	Davenport.	U.S.
Motor, induction	1887	Tesla.	U.S.
Motorcycle	1885	Daimler	German
Mouse, computer	1967	Engelbart	U.S.
Movie machine	1894	Jenkins.	U.S.
Movie, panoramic	1952	Waller	U.S.
Movie, talking	1927	Warner Bros.	U.S.
Mower, lawn	1831	Budding, Ferrabee	English
Mowing machine	1822	Bailey	U.S.
Neoprene	1930	Carothers	U.S.
Nylon	1937	Carothers, DuPont.	U.S.
Oil cracking furnace	1891	Gavriloy	Russian
Oil filled power cable	1921	Emanueli.	Italian
Oleomargarine	1869	Mege-Mouries.	French
Ophthalmoscope	1851	Helmholtz	German
Pacemaker	1952	Zoll	U.S.
Pacemaker, implantable cardiac	1958	Greatbatch	U.S.
Paper	105	Ts'ai	Chinese
Paper clip	1900	Waaler	Norwegian
Paper machine	1809	Dickinson	U.S.
Parachute	1785	Blanchard	French
Pen, ballpoint	1888	Loud	U.S.
Pen, fountain	1884	Waterman	U.S.
Pen, steel	1780	Harrison	English

Invention	Date	Inventor(s)	Nationality
Pendulum	1583	Galileo	Italian
Percussion cap	1807	Forsythe	Scottish
Phonograph	1877	Edison	U.S.
Photo, color	1892	Ives	U.S.
Photo film, celluloid	1893	Reichenbach	U.S.
Photo film, transparent	1884	Eastman, Goodwin	U.S.
Photocopier	1938	Carlson	U.S.
Photoelectric cell	1895	Elster	German
Photographic paper	1835	Talbot	English
Photography	1816	Niepce	French
Photography	1835	Daguerre	French
Photography	1835	Talbot	English
Photophone	1880	Bell	U.S.-Scot.
Phototelegraphy	1925	Bell Labs.	U.S.
Piano	1709	Cristofori	Italian
Piano, player	1863	Fourneaux	French
Pin, safety	1849	Hunt	U.S.
Pistol (revolver)	1836	Colt	U.S.
Plow, cast iron	1785	Ransome	English
Plow, disc	1896	Hardy	U.S.
Pneumatic hammer	1890	King	U.S.
Post-it note	1980	Fry, Silver	U.S.
Powder, smokeless	1884	Vieille	French
Printing press, rotary	1845	Hoe	U.S.
Printing press, web	1865	Bullock	U.S.
Propeller, screw	1804	Stevens	U.S.
Propeller, screw	1837	Ericsson	Swedish
Punch card accounting	1889	Hollerith	U.S.
Radar	1940	Watson-Watt	Scottish
Radio amplifier	1906	De Forest	U.S.
Radio beacon	1928	Donovan	U.S.
Radio crystal oscillator	1918	Nicolson	U.S.
Radio FM, 2-path	1933	Armstrong	U.S.
Radio, magnetic detector	1902	Marconi	Italian
Radio receiver, cascade tuning	1913	Alexanderson	U.S.
Radio receiver, heterodyne	1913	Fessenden	Canadian
Radio, signals	1895	Marconi	Italian
Radio transmitter triode modulation	1914	Alexanderson	U.S.
Radio tube diode	1904	Fleming	English
Radio tube oscillator	1915	De Forest	U.S.
Radio tube triode	1906	De Forest	U.S.
Rayon (acetate)	1895	Cross	English
Rayon (cuprammonium)	1890	Despeissis	French
Rayon (nitrocellulose)	1884	Chardonnet	French
Razor, electric	1928	Schick	U.S.
Razor, safety	1895	Gillette	U.S.
Reading machine for the blind	1976	Kurzweil	U.S.
Reaper	1834	McCormick	U.S.
Record, cylinder	1887	Bell, Tainter	U.S.
Record, disc	1887	Berliner	U.S.
Record, long playing	1947	Goldmark	U.S.
Record, wax cylinder	1888	Edison	U.S.
Refrigerator car	1868	David	U.S.
Remote control	1898	Tesla	U.S.
Resin, synthetic	1931	Hill	English
Richter scale	1935	Richter	U.S.
Rifle, repeating	1860	Henry	U.S.
Rocket, liquid fuel	1926	Goddard	U.S.
Rollerblades	1980	Olson	U.S.
Rubber, vulcanized	1839	Goodyear	U.S.
Saccharin	1879	Remsen, Fahlberg	U.S.
Saw, circular	1777	Miller	English
Scotch tape	1930	Drew	U.S.
Seat belt	1959	Volvo	Swedish
Segway human transporter	2001	Kamen	U.S.
Seismograph	1880	Milne, Ewing, Gray	Eng.-Scot.
Sewing machine	1790	Saint	English
Shoe-lasting machine	1883	Matzeliger	U.S.
Shoe-sewing machine	1860	McKay	U.S.
Shrapnel shell	1784	Shrapnel	English
Shuttle, flying	1733	Kay	English
Skates, in-line	1759	Merlin	Belgian
Sleeping-car	1865	Pullman	U.S.
Slide rule	1620	Oughtred	English
Slinky	1943	James	U.S.
Smoke detector	1969	Smith, House	U.S.
Soap, hardwater	1928	Bertsch	German
Spectroscope	1859	Kirchoff, Bunsen	German
Spectroscope (mass)	1918	Dempster	U.S.
Spinning jenny	c.1764	Hargreaves	English
Spinning mule	1779	Crompton	English
Steam car	1770	Cugnot	French
Steam turbine	1884	Parsons	English
Steamboat, exp'mtl	1778	Jouffroy	French
Steamboat, exp'mtl	1785	Fitch	U.S.
Steamboat, exp'mtl	1787	Rumsey	U.S.
Steamboat, exp'mtl	1803	Fulton	U.S.
Steamboat, exp'mtl	1804	Stevens	U.S.
Steamboat, practical	1802	Symington	Scottish
Steamboat, practical	1807	Fulton	U.S.
Steel alloy, high-speed	1901	Taylor, White	U.S.
Steel (converter)	1856	Bessemer	English
Steel, manganese	1884	Hadfield	English
Steel, stainless	1916	Brearley	English
Stereoscope	1838	Wheatstone	English
Stethoscope	1819	Laennec	French
Stethoscope, binaural	1840	Cammann	U.S.
Stock ticker	1870	Edison	U.S.
Storage battery, rechargeable	1859	Plante	French
Stove, electric	1896	Hadaway	U.S.
Submarine	1891	Holland	U.S.
Submarine, even keel	1894	Lake	U.S.
Submarine, torpedo	1776	Bushnell	U.S.
Synthesizer	1964	Moog	U.S.
Tank, military	1914	Swinton	English
Tape recorder, magnetic	1899	Poulsen	Danish
Taser	1974	Cover	U.S.
Teflon	1938	Du Pont	U.S.
Telegraph, magnetic	1837	Morse	U.S.
Telegraph, quadruplex	1864	Edison	U.S.
Telegraph, railroad	1887	Woods	U.S.
Telegraph, wireless high frequency	1895	Marconi	Italian
Telephone[1]	1871	Meucci	U.S.-Italian
Telephone[1]	1876	Bell	U.S.-Scot.
Telephone amplifier	1912	De Forest	U.S.
Telephone answering machine (1st practical)	1954	Hashimoto	Japanese
Telephone, automatic	1891	Strowger	U.S.
Telephone, cellular	1947	Bell Labs.	U.S.
Telephone, cordless[2]	1950	Gross	U.S.
Telephone, radio	1900	Poulsen / Fessenden	Danish / Canadian
Telephone, radio	1906	De Forest	U.S.
Telephone, radio, long distance	1915	AT&T	U.S.
Telephone, recording	1898	Poulsen	Danish
Telescope	1608	Lippershey	Dutch
Telescope	1609	Galileo	Italian
Telescope, astronomical	1611	Kepler	German
Telescope, reflecting	1668	Newton	English
Teletype	1928	Morkrum, Kleinschmidt	U.S.
Television, color	1928	Baird	Scottish
Television, electronic	1927	Farnsworth	U.S.
Television, iconoscope	1923	Zworykin	U.S.
Television, mech. scanner	1923	Baird	Scottish
Tesla coil	1891	Tesla	U.S.
Thermometer	1593	Galileo	Italian
Thermometer	1730	Reaumur	French
Thermometer, mercury	1714	Fahrenheit	German
3D printing (stereolithography)	1984	Hull	U.S.
Time recorder	1890	Bundy	U.S.
Tire, double-tube	1845	Thomson	Scottish
Tire, pneumatic	1888	Dunlop	Scottish
Toaster, automatic	1921	Strite	U.S.
Toilet, flush	1589	Harington	English
Torpedo, marine	1804	Fulton	U.S.
Tractor, crawler	1904	Holt	U.S.
Transformer, AC	1885	Stanley	U.S.
Transistor	1947	Shockley, Brattain, Bardeen	U.S.
Trolley car, electric	1884-87	Van DePoele, Sprague	U.S.
Tungsten, ductile	1912	Coolidge	U.S.
Tupperware®	1945	Tupper	U.S.
Turbine, gas	1849	Bourdin	French
Turbine, hydraulic	1849	Francis	U.S.
Turbine, steam	1884	Parsons	English
Type, movable	1447	Gutenberg	German
Typewriter	1867	Sholes, Soule, Glidden	U.S.
Universal Serial Bus (USB)	1994	Bhatt, et al.	U.S.
Vacuum cleaner, electric	1907	Spangler	U.S.
Vacuum evaporating pan	1846	Rillieux	U.S.
Velcro	1948	de Mestral	Swiss

Invention	Date	Inventor(s)	Nationality
Video game ("Pong")	1972	Bushnell	U.S.
Video home system (VHS)	1975	Matsushita, JVC	Japanese
Vinyl	1926	Semon	U.S.
Washer, electric	1901	Fisher	U.S.
Welding, atomic hydrogen	1924	Langmuir, Palmer	U.S.
Welding, electric	1877	Thomson	U.S.
Wheelchair, multiterrain	1986	Twitchell	U.S.
Wheelchair, stair-climbing	1962	Blanco	U.S.

Invention	Date	Inventor(s)	Nationality
Wiki software	1995	Cunningham	U.S.
Wind tunnel	1912	Eiffel	French
Windshield wiper	1903	Anderson	U.S.
Wire, barbed	1874	Glidden	U.S.
World Wide Web	1989	Berners-Lee	English
Wrench, double-acting	1913	Owen	U.S.
X-ray tube	1913	Coolidge	U.S.
Zamboni	1949	Zamboni	U.S.
Zeppelin	1900	Zeppelin	German
Zipper, early model	1893	Judson	U.S.
Zipper, improved	1913	Sundback	Canadian

(1) While Alexander Graham Bell has traditionally been credited with invention of the telephone, which he patented, Antonio Meucci developed a working model before Bell. (2) Al Gross held a number of important early patents in the field of wireless communication; other people were also involved in the development of practical cordless telephones.

U.S. Patents by Field of Technology, 2000-18

Source: World Intellectual Property Organization statistics database
(ranked by number of utility patents, or patents for inventions, for the top 20 fields in 2018, as of Apr. 2020)

Field	2000	2005	2010	2014	2015	2016	2017	2018	% change 2000-18
Computer technology	12,149	14,284	33,521	51,575	46,920	47,210	46,132	43,280	256.24%
Digital communication	3,625	5,278	9,390	19,642	23,398	25,726	27,631	27,294	652.94
Electrical machinery, apparatus, energy	9,537	9,293	14,228	17,323	18,633	20,170	21,778	21,147	121.74
Semiconductors	9,160	9,990	14,286	17,975	18,419	19,080	19,115	17,578	91.90
Medical technology	8,033	6,100	10,144	16,486	16,131	16,773	18,088	17,484	117.65
Audio-visual technology	7,913	8,161	12,202	17,094	15,949	15,895	16,386	15,480	95.63
Measurement	6,885	7,587	10,748	12,030	12,278	13,105	14,467	13,965	102.83
Transport	7,217	6,392	6,793	9,322	11,083	11,625	12,946	13,055	80.89
Telecommunications	5,867	6,364	10,955	14,243	12,752	11,692	12,188	11,308	92.74
Optics	7,510	8,314	10,825	11,124	11,656	11,643	11,620	11,103	47.84
Engines, pumps, turbines	4,144	4,269	4,162	6,045	6,300	6,432	7,467	7,837	89.12
Control	2,735	2,685	4,457	5,769	5,670	5,897	7,050	7,465	172.94
Mechanical elements	4,890	3,795	4,342	6,612	6,928	6,823	7,517	7,226	47.77
Pharmaceuticals	3,997	2,833	5,122	7,365	6,909	6,652	7,224	6,993	74.96
Civil engineering	4,420	3,484	4,754	6,193	6,435	6,597	6,904	6,981	57.94
Other special machines	4,955	3,612	4,626	5,986	6,135	6,490	6,954	6,959	40.44
Furniture, games	4,952	3,593	5,048	6,278	5,914	5,968	6,373	6,095	23.08
Biotechnology	3,872	2,810	3,991	5,299	5,433	5,748	6,030	6,034	55.84
Organic fine chemistry	4,724	3,200	5,257	7,162	7,066	6,333	6,174	5,665	19.92
Handling	4,403	3,140	4,383	5,673	5,168	5,201	5,571	5,553	26.12

Patent Offices Granting Most Utility Patents, 2000-18

Source: World Intellectual Property Organization statistics database
(ranked by 2018 figures; as of April 2020)

National or regional office	2000	2005	2010	2014	2015	2016	2017	2018
China	13,058	53,305	135,110	233,228	359,316	404,208	420,144	432,147
United States	157,496	143,806	219,614	300,678	298,407	303,049	318,829	307,759
Japan	125,880	122,944	222,693	227,142	189,358	203,087	199,577	194,525
European Patent Office	27,523	53,258	58,108	64,608	68,431	95,956	105,645	127,603
South Korea	34,956	73,512	68,843	129,786	101,873	108,875	120,662	119,012
Russia	17,592	23,390	30,322	33,950	34,706	33,536	34,254	35,774
Canada	12,125	15,516	19,120	23,749	22,201	26,424	24,099	23,499
Australia	13,548	10,979	14,557	19,304	23,098	23,744	22,742	17,065
Germany	14,707	17,063	13,678	15,030	14,795	15,652	15,653	16,367
India	1,263	4,320	7,138	6,153	6,022	8,248	12,387	13,908
France	11,274	11,473	9,899	11,889	12,699	12,374	11,865	12,249
Brazil	NA	2,439	3,251	2,749	3,411	4,195	5,450	9,966
Hong Kong	2,737	6,518	5,353	5,932	5,963	5,698	6,671	9,651
Mexico	5,527	8,098	9,399	9,819	9,338	8,652	8,510	8,921
Italy	5,285	5,534	16,106	7,795	7,153	6,429	4,855	6,424
Indonesia	NA	NA	NA	NA	1,911	3,005	2,309	6,374
United Kingdom	8,253	10,159	5,594	4,986	5,464	5,602	6,311	5,982
Singapore	5,090	7,530	4,442	5,538	7,054	7,341	6,217	5,172
South Africa	3,399	1,831	5,331	5,065	4,499	4,255	5,535	4,746
Malaysia	405	2,508	2,160	2,705	2,877	3,324	5,063	4,287
World	517,600	633,100	914,800	1,167,400	1,233,700	1,345,800	1,397,900	1,422,800

NA = Not available.

U.S. Utility Patents, 1790-2019

Source: U.S. Patent and Trademark Office, U.S. Dept. of Commerce

Year	Patent applications	Patents granted	Year	Patent applications	Patents granted	Year	Patent applications	Patents granted
1790	NA	3	2000	295,926	157,494	2010	490,226	219,614
1810	NA	223	2001	326,508	166,035	2011	503,582	224,505
1830	NA	544	2002	334,445	167,331	2012	542,815	253,155
1850	2,193	884	2003	342,441	169,023	2013	571,612	277,835
1870	19,171	12,157	2004	356,943	164,290	2014	578,802	300,677
1890	39,884	25,308	2005	390,733	143,806	2015	589,410	298,408
1910	63,293	35,130	2006	425,967	173,772	2016	605,571	303,049
1930	89,554	45,226	2007	456,154	157,282	2017	606,956	318,828
1950	67,264	43,039	2008	456,321	157,772	2018	597,141	307,759
1970	103,175	64,429	2009	456,106	167,349	2019	621,453	354,430
1990	164,558	90,365						

NA = Not available.

TECHNOLOGY

Computer Milestones

1623: German mathematician Wilhelm Schickard developed the first mechanical calculator, capable of adding, subtracting, multiplying, and dividing.

1642: French mathematician Blaise Pascal built the first of more than four dozen copies of an adding and subtracting machine that he invented.

1801: French inventor Joseph Marie Jacquard demonstrated a new control system for looms. He "programmed" the loom, communicating desired weaving operations to the machine via patterns of holes in paper cards.

1833-71: British mathematician and scientist Charles Babbage used the Jacquard punch-card system in his design for a sophisticated, programmable "Analytical Engine" that foreshadowed basic features of today's computers. Babbage's concept was beyond the capabilities of the technology of his time, and the machine remained unfinished at his death in 1871.

1889: American engineer Herman Hollerith patented an electromechanical punch-card tabulating system that facilitated the handling of large amounts of statistical data and quickly found use in censuses in the U.S. and other countries.

1911: Hollerith's Tabulating Machine Company merged with two other enterprises to form the Computing-Tabulating-Recording Company, which was renamed the International Business Machines Corporation (IBM) in 1924.

1941: German engineer Konrad Züse completed the Z3, the first fully functional digital computer to be controlled by a program; the Z3 was not electronic—it was based on electrical switches called relays.

1942: Iowa State Coll. physicist John Vincent Atanasoff and assistant Clifford Berry completed a working model of the first fully electronic computer using vacuum tubes, which could operate much more quickly than relays; the rudimentary machine was not programmable.

1943: IBM and Harvard professor Howard Aiken completed the first large-scale automatic digital computer, the Mark I, a relay-based machine 55-ft long and 8-ft high. British scientists built their first Colossus machine, an electronic computer for breaking German codes during World War II.

1946: ENIAC (Electronic Numerical Integrator and Computer), a 30-ton room-sized electronic computer with more than 18,000 vacuum tubes, was completed by physicist John Mauchly and engineer J. Presper Eckert at the Univ. of Pennsylvania for the U.S. Army. ENIAC could be programmed to do different tasks, but cables had to be plugged in, and switches had to be set by hand.

1951: Eckert and Mauchly's UNIVAC (Universal Automatic Computer) became the first commercially available computer in the U.S. Its first customer was the Census Bureau. CBS-TV used a UNIVAC in 1952 to predict presidential election results.

1959: COBOL, a computer programming language designed for business use, first appeared, based on programming language innovations of American mathematician Grace Hopper.

1967: American computer pioneer Doug Engelbart applied for a patent on the mouse.

1969-71: The powerful Unix operating system was developed at Bell Laboratories; later versions became widely used on large computers and formed the basis for the Macintosh OS X operating system (introduced in 2001).

1971: Intel released the 4004, the first commercial microprocessor (an entire computer processing unit on a chip).

1973: The Alto computer, developed at Xerox's Palo Alto Research Center, became operational, implementing many features of modern commercial personal computers, including a graphical user interface (GUI) featuring windows, icons, and pointers that could be manipulated by a mouse.

1975: The first widely marketed personal computer (PC), the MITS Altair 8800, was introduced in kit form, with no keyboard, video display, or printer, for under $400. Microsoft was founded by Americans Bill Gates and Paul Allen.

1976: The first word-processing program for personal computers, Electric Pencil, was written. Apple Computer Company was founded by Americans Steven Jobs and Stephen Wozniak.

1977: Apple introduced the Apple II; capable of displaying text and graphics in color, the machine enjoyed phenomenal success.

1981: IBM unveiled its Personal Computer (IBM 5150), which used an operating system from Microsoft known as MS-DOS (Disk Operating System).

1984: Apple introduced the first Macintosh. The easy-to-use Macintosh came with a proprietary operating system and was the first popular computer to have a GUI and a mouse.

1990: Microsoft released Windows 3.0, the first workable version of its own GUI. Adobe released the first commercial version of the image-editing software Photoshop.

1991: The Unix-like Linux operating system was invented by Helsinki Univ. student Linus Torvalds and made available for free.

1996: The Palm Pilot, the first widely successful handheld computer and personal information manager, arrived.

1997: The IBM supercomputer Deep Blue beat Russian world chess champion Garry Kasparov in a 6-game match, 2-1, with 3 draws.

2002: The total number of personal computers, including desktop and laptop machines of all types, shipped by manufacturers since 1975 reached 1 bil.

2007: Amazon launched the Kindle, a hardware/software system for displaying books electronically.

2008: Google released the Linux-based Android operating system for mobile devices.

2010: Apple released the iPad tablet computer and sold more than 3 mil devices in the first 80 days.

2012: Microsoft released Windows 8, featuring enhanced support for touchscreens and an interface with a grid of tiles displaying actively updated content and apps.

2015: Microsoft released Windows 10, promising faster startup and improved security, along with features like a personal digital assistant and a new web browser, Microsoft Edge.

2016: Univ. of Maryland scientists developed the first reprogrammable quantum computer; it used lasers to manipulate its five qubits, or bits of quantum information.

2020: Apple became the world's first company to achieve a stock market value of $2 tril; it was also the first to $1 tril in 2018.

World's Fastest Supercomputers, 2020

Source: Top500.org, as of midyear 2020

Rank	Name	Location	Manufacturer/vendor	Processors (cores)	Top speed[1]
1.	Supercomputer Fugaku	RIKEN Center for Computational Science, Japan	Fujitsu	7,299,072	415.53
2.	Summit	Oak Ridge National Laboratory, TN, U.S.	IBM	2,414,592	148.60
3.	Sierra	Lawrence Livermore National Laboratory, CA, U.S.	IBM	1,572,480	94.64
4.	Sunway TaihuLight	National Supercomputing Center, Wuxi, China.	NRCPC[2]	10,649,600	93.01
5.	Tianhe-2A (Milky Way-2A)	National Supercomputing Center, Guangzhou, China	NUDT[3]	4,981,760	61.44
6.	HPC5	Eni S.p.A., Italy	Dell EMC	669,760	35.45
7.	Selene	Nvidia, Santa Clara, CA, U.S.	Nvidia	272,800	27.58
8.	Frontera	Texas Advanced Computing Center/Univ. of Texas, U.S.	Dell EMC	448,448	23.52
9.	Marconi-100	CINECA consortium, Italy	IBM	347,776	21.64
10.	Piz Daint	Swiss National Supercomputing Centre, Switzerland	Cray	387,872	21.23

Note: The 500 fastest supercomputers use a version of the Linux operating system. (1) Top speed, in petaflops, achieved as measured according to the Linpack Benchmark. 1 petaflop = 1 quadrillion floating-point operations per sec. (2) NRCPC = National Research Center of Parallel Computer Engineering and Technology. (3) NUDT = National University of Defense Technology.

U.S. Sales and Household Penetration of Selected Hardware, 2017-19

Source: Consumer Technology Association (fmr. Consumer Electronics Association)
(factory sales to dealers in thousands of units and millions of dollars; percent of all households for Jan. of year shown)

Hardware	2017 Units	2017 Sales	2017 %	2018 Units	2018 Sales	2018 %	2019 Unit	2019 Sales	2019 %
Smartphones	167,924	$69,026	80%	169,412	$78,798	87%	162,588	$76,449	91%
Laptop/notebook/netbook PCs[1]	48,778	28,318	69	50,011	31,069	72	52,698	33,038	75
Tablet computers	51,688	14,454	62	44,565	11,141	64	39,544	9,095	65
Digital cameras.................	5,489	2,191	53	5,372	2,246	55	5,019	2,246	55
Desktop computers[1,2]...........	16,745	9,746	51	16,410	9,567	48	16,755	9,802	53
Streaming media players	16,920	1,050	36	18,612	1,005	45	19,915	946	51
E-readers	5,923	430	30	5,361	393	29	4,790	346	27
Smart watches	12,120	3,091	12	18,887	4,533	18	21,699	5,817	23
Camcorders	460	115	23	337	85	NA	282	73	NA

NA = Not available. **Note:** Based on sales data tracking and consumer surveys conducted by CEA/CTA. (1) Includes commercial and consumer shipments. (2) Includes all-in-one computers.

Households With a Computer by Region and Development Level, 2005-19

Source: ITU World Telecommunication/ICT Indicators Database

	2005	2009	2010	2011	2012	2013	2014	2015	2016	2017	2018	2019*
Africa	3.7%	5.2%	5.8%	6.2%	6.5%	7.1%	7.5%	8.0%	8.7%	9.6%	10.1%	10.7%
Arab States	15.4	27.0	29.6	33.4	35.3	39.0	42.3	44.0	46.6	48.5	51.0	51.9
Asia & Pacific	20.7	27.3	29.0	30.5	32.4	34.6	36.2	37.8	39.2	40.7	42.2	43.5
Commonwealth of Independent States...	18.1	42.1	48.0	53.9	59.5	61.9	64.0	65.5	67.4	67.4	66.3	66.3
Europe	48.8	64.9	68.0	70.8	73.0	75.2	75.7	76.0	76.8	77.1	77.5	78.0
The Americas	41.0	49.4	51.3	54.2	57.4	61.1	62.4	63.7	64.7	64.8	65.0	65.7
Developed countries................	55.3	68.9	71.1	72.9	75.4	78.6	78.9	79.8	80.7	81.2	81.6	82.3
Developing countries	15.6	22.6	24.7	26.8	28.8	30.8	32.5	33.9	35.2	36.3	37.5	38.5
Least developed countries	1.4	3.0	3.5	4.2	4.9	5.7	6.2	6.9	7.8	8.8	9.2	9.5
World	**27.3**	**35.4**	**37.3**	**39.2**	**41.3**	**43.5**	**44.8**	**45.9**	**47.1**	**47.9**	**48.8**	**49.7**

* = Estimated.

About the Internet

The internet is not owned or funded by any one institution, organization, or government. It has no CEO and is not a commercial service. Its development is guided by the Internet Society (ISOC), a nonprofit formed in 1992. The Internet Society helps fund the Internet Engineering Task Force (IETF), which deals with short-term issues of standards and the internet's architecture. The Internet Architecture Board (IAB), a committee of the IETF, oversees the latter's work and appoints the chair of the Internet Research Task Force (IRTF). The IAB and IRTF focus on long-term issues.

Major Historical Highlights

1969: ARPANET, an experimental four-computer network, was established by the Advanced Research Projects Agency (ARPA) of the U.S. Defense Dept. Two years later, ARPANET linked about 23 computers ("hosts") at 15 sites, including MIT and Harvard.

1971: Engineer Bob Thomas created Creeper, generally considered the first worm, a virus able to self-replicate over a network.

1976: British evolutionary biologist Richard Dawkins coined the term "meme," referring to an idea or a behavior that persists and may spread "virally."

1978: The first spam, or junk email, was sent over ARPANET.

1982: Author William Gibson coined the term "cyberspace" in the story "Burning Chrome."

1983: The set of communications rules (protocol) known as TCP/IP became the main networking protocol of ARPANET. Its adoption was tantamount to the birth of the internet. The military portion of ARPANET was moved onto MILNET.

1986: The U.S. National Science Foundation (NSF) launched NSFNET, the first large-scale network using internet technology.

1988: Internet Relay Chat (IRC) was developed by Finnish student Jarkko Oikarinen, enabling people to communicate via the internet in "real time."

1988: A worm crafted by Cornell U. computer science graduate student Robert Morris Jr. infected thousands of computers, shutting many down and causing millions of dollars of damage—the first known case of large-scale damage caused by a computer virus spread via the internet.

1989: Massachusetts-based The World—the first commercial internet service provider supplying dial-up access—debuted.

1989-90: English scientist Tim Berners-Lee invented the World Wide Web. Created as an environment in which scientists at the European Center for Nuclear Research in Switzerland could share information, it gradually evolved into a medium with text, graphics, audio, animation, and video.

1990: ARPANET was disbanded.

1991: NSFNET was opened to commercial traffic. Berners-Lee introduced the first browser, or software for accessing the web.

1993: The National Center for Supercomputing Applications (U.S.) released versions of Mosaic, the first web browser able to present both text and images on a single page.

1993: A coffee pot at England's Cambridge Univ. became the subject of the first live streaming (and the first webcam).

1994: Netscape Communications released the Netscape Navigator browser.

1995: Microsoft released its Internet Explorer browser. It initially failed to make a dent in Netscape's dominance of the browser market, but Internet Explorer surpassed Netscape by 1999.

1995: Amazon and AuctionWeb (now eBay) began operating online.

1997: The initial version of the WiFi network protocol was released.

1998: Under a contract with the U.S. Dept. of Commerce, the nonprofit Internet Corporation for Assigned Names and Numbers (ICANN) took over the management of assigning domain names and internet protocol (IP) addresses.

1999: Release of the free Napster file-sharing service enabled users to easily exchange files containing music or other content without regard to copyright restrictions.

2000: Estonia became the first country to pass a law declaring internet access a fundamental human right of its citizens.

2004: A group of Harvard students founded social network TheFacebook (later just Facebook).

2004: The Mozilla Foundation released the first official version of the open-source browser Mozilla Firefox.

2006: The microblogging and social networking service Twitter was introduced.

2008: Google introduced its Chrome browser. By 2012, Chrome ranked as the most widely used browser in the world, according to StatCounter.com.

2009: The software for Bitcoin, the world's first "cryptocurrency," was released. It relied on cryptography and a complex decentralized public ledger to secure transactions.

2011: ICANN decided to allow the use of almost any characters in any language for the names of generic top-level domains.

2012: The number of Facebook users surpassed 1 bil.

2014: The number of internet hosts (websites) passed 1 bil.

2014: Estonia became the first country in the world to offer noncitizens "e-residency"—a government-issued transnational digital identity.

2016: The leak of more than 11.5 mil documents from Panamanian law firm Mossack Fonseca, which said it was the victim of a hack, exposed large-scale offshore tax evasion.

2016: Global internet traffic surpassed 1 zettabyte (1 tril giga-bytes), according to networking giant Cisco.

2017: The number of Facebook users surpassed 2 bil.

2018: Amid growing concern over the misuse of individuals' personal data, the European Union's General Data Protection Regulation (GDPR) went into effect, providing strong safeguards governing personal data held by any organization worldwide that conducts business in Europe.

2018: By year's end the proportion of the world's population using the internet had passed the 50% mark, according to the Intl. Telecommunications Union.

Safety and Security on the Internet

Common sense dictates some basic security rules:

- Avoid using the same password for multiple websites. A password manager can generate passwords and then save them.

- Do not give out your phone number, address, credit card number, or other personal information unless needed for a transaction at a site you trust.

- If you feel someone is being threatening or dangerous, inform your internet service provider.

- Use protective firewall, antivirus, and antispyware software to guard your system against attacks by hackers.

- Be careful about opening email and file attachments from unknown correspondents.

- To avoid falling victim to **phishing**—which uses a forged email message, purportedly from a respectable organization, to elicit personal data—do not click on hyperlinks in emails from companies with which you do business. Phishing emails typically contain a link leading to a fabricated website resembling the site of the ostensible sender. If you want to visit a company's website, open your browser and manually enter the site's address.

- Users of so-called **peer-to-peer** (P2P) file-sharing networks or protocols should open up only part of their computer system, not their entire hard drive, to sharing.

- When manufacturers provide **patches** to solve security flaws or other problems with operating systems, web browsers, or other software, it is usually advisable to install these fixes. If a fix is not available for a serious security problem, consider switching to an alternative program.

Internet Addresses

The fundamental part of an address on the internet is called the domain. The final part of a domain name, known as the **top-level domain (TLD)**, is its most basic part. For example, .com is the top-level domain of *The World Almanac*'s web address (www.worldalmanac.com). So-called generic top-level domains (gTLDs) consist of three or more letters. Domain names with two letters are generally for countries or regions. Country-code TLDs (ccTLDs) are usually managed by an organization within a certain country.

Worst Data Breaches, 2010-20

Source: Upguard, Inc., as of mid-2020

(ranked by total number of exposed data records)

Rank	Company	Year	Records exposed (mil)	Rank	Company	Year	Records exposed (mil)
1.	Yahoo	2013	3,000	6.	Yahoo	2014	500
2.	Aadhaar	2018	1,100	7.	Marriott/Starwood	2018	500
3.	First American Financial Corp.	2019	885	8.	FriendFinder	2016	412
4.	Verifications.io	2019	763	9.	MySpace	2013	360
5.	Facebook	2019	540	10.	Exactis	2018	340

Leading Types of U.S. Internet Crime, Victims, and Losses, 2019

Source: Internet Crime Complaint Center, Federal Bureau of Investigation

Rank	Type of crime	Victims	Rank	Type of crime	Losses
1.	Phishing/vishing/smishing/pharming	114,702	1.	Business email compromise/email account compromise	$1,776,549,688
2.	Nonpayment/nondelivery	61,832	2.	Confidence fraud/romance	475,014,032
3.	Extortion	43,101	3.	Spoofing	300,478,433
4.	Personal data breach	38,218	4.	Investment	222,186,195
5.	Spoofing	25,789	5.	Real estate/rental	221,365,911
6.	Business email compromise/email account compromise	23,775	6.	Nonpayment/nondelivery	196,563,497
7.	Confidence fraud/romance	19,473	7.	Identity theft	160,305,789
8.	Identity theft	16,053	8.	Government impersonation	124,292,606
9.	Harassment/threats of violence	15,502	9.	Personal data breach	120,102,501
10.	Overpayment[1]	15,395	10.	Credit card fraud	111,491,163
11.	Advanced fee	14,607	11.	Extortion	107,498,956
12.	Employment	14,493	12.	Advanced fee	100,602,297
13.	Credit card fraud	14,378	13.	Other	66,223,160
14.	Government impersonation	13,873	14.	Phishing/vishing/smishing/pharming	57,836,379
15.	Tech support	13,633	15.	Overpayment[1]	55,820,212

(1) In overpayment, the scammer typically makes a payment via fake check or credit card for more than the agreed upon amount, and then asks that the victim return the excess amount by wire or other form of direct payment.

Fixed Broadband Penetration in Selected Countries, 2003-19

Source: Organisation for Economic Cooperation and Development (OECD)

(nonmobile broadband subscriptions per 100 inhabitants, for fourth quarter of given year; ranked by 2019 figures)

Country	2003	2005	2007	2009	2011	2013	2015	2017	2019
France	5.89	15.03	24.38	30.54	34.80	37.80	40.35	42.88	44.12
Germany	5.59	12.98	23.74	31.03	33.92	35.49	37.59	40.21	42.21
Canada	15.06	20.76	27.26	30.60	32.84	34.46	36.73	38.10	40.85
United Kingdom	5.37	16.31	25.59	29.48	32.75	35.50	37.88	39.44	40.14
United States	9.59	16.38	23.22	26.04	28.30	30.35	31.84	33.25	34.65
Japan	10.90	18.15	22.46	24.72	27.28	28.11	29.66	31.16	32.49
Italy	4.17	11.77	17.06	20.28	22.51	23.09	24.69	27.31	28.94

Note: Includes internet connections with speeds greater than 256 kilobits per second (256 kbps).

Nations With Highest Percentage of Population Using the Internet, 2000-18

Source: © International Telecommunication Union; ranked by 2017 figures

Rank	Nation	2000	2005	2010	2012	2014	2015	2016	2017	2018
1.	Kuwait..............	6.73%	25.93%	61.40%	70.45%	78.70%	72.00%	78.37%	100.00%	99.60%
2.	Iceland	44.47	87.00	93.39	96.21	98.16	98.20	98.24	98.26	99.01
3.	Liechtenstein	36.52	63.37	80.00	89.41	95.21	96.64	98.09	98.10	NA
4.	Qatar................	4.86	24.73	69.00	69.30	91.49	92.88	95.12	97.39	99.65
5.	Luxembourg	22.89	70.00	90.62	91.95	94.67	96.38	98.14	97.36	97.06
6.	Denmark.............	39.17	82.74	88.72	92.26	95.99	96.33	96.97	97.10	97.64
7.	Monaco.............	42.18	55.46	75.00	87.00	92.40	93.36	95.21	97.05	NA
8.	Norway	52.00	81.99	93.39	94.65	96.30	96.81	97.30	96.36	96.49
9.	Bahrain.............	6.15	21.30	55.00	88.00	90.50	93.48	98.00	95.88	98.64
10.	Sweden.............	45.69	84.83	90.00	93.18	92.52	90.61	89.65	95.51	92.14
11.	South Korea	44.70	73.50	83.70	84.07	87.56	89.90	92.84	95.07	95.90
12.	Brunei.............	9.00	36.47	53.00	60.27	68.77	71.20	90.00	94.87	94.60
13.	United Arab Emirates ..	23.63	40.00	68.00	85.00	90.40	90.50	90.60	94.82	98.45
14.	United Kingdom	26.82	70.00	85.00	87.48	91.61	92.00	94.78	94.62	94.90
15.	Netherlands	43.98	81.00	90.72	92.86	91.67	91.72	90.41	93.20	94.71
16.	Taiwan	28.10	58.01	71.50	75.99	78.04	78.04	79.75	92.78	NA
17.	Andorra.............	10.54	37.61	81.00	86.43	95.90	96.91	97.93	91.57	NA
18.	Canada.............	51.30	71.66	80.30	83.00	87.12	90.00	91.16	91.00	NA
19.	New Zealand	47.38	62.72	80.46	81.64	85.50	88.22	88.47	90.81	NA
20.	Switzerland..........	47.10	70.10	83.90	85.20	87.40	87.48	89.13	89.69	NA
21.	Estonia	28.58	61.45	74.10	78.39	84.24	88.41	87.24	88.10	89.36
22.	Austria	33.73	58.00	75.17	80.03	81.00	83.94	84.32	87.94	87.71
23.	Belgium.............	29.43	55.82	75.00	80.72	85.00	85.05	86.52	87.68	88.66
24.	Finland	37.25	74.48	86.89	89.88	86.53	86.42	87.70	87.47	88.89
25.	United States	43.08	67.97	71.69	74.70	73.00	74.55	85.54	87.27	NA

NA = Not available.

Nations With the Most Internet Users

Source: *The World Factbook*, Central Intelligence Agency (CIA), reported estimates as of mid-2020

Rank	Nation	Internet users[1]	% of worldwide users	Rank	Nation	Internet users[1]	% of worldwide users
1.	China	730,723,960	17.82%	14.	Vietnam	49,741,000	1.21%
2.	India	374,328,160	9.13	15.	Nigeria	47,759,904	1.16
3.	United States	246,809,221	6.02	16.	Turkey	46,838,412	1.14
4.	Brazil	122,841,218	3.00	17.	South Korea	44,153,000	1.08
5.	Japan	116,565,962	2.84	18.	Spain	39,123,384	0.95
6.	Russia	108,772,470	2.65	19.	Egypt	39,097,468	0.95
7.	Mexico	73,334,032	1.79	20.	Italy.............	38,025,661	0.93
8.	Germany..........	72,365,643	1.77	21.	Thailand	32,398,778	0.79
9.	Iran..............	67,600,000	1.65	22.	Canada...........	31,770,034	0.77
10.	Indonesia	65,525,226	1.60	23.	Pakistan	31,338,715	0.76
11.	United Kingdom	61,064,454	1.49	24.	Argentina	30,786,889	0.75
12.	France	57,226,585	1.40	25.	South Africa	29,322,380	0.72
13.	Philippines	56,956,436	1.39		World total	4,100,000,000	100.00%

(1) Estimated number of individuals who can access the internet at home, via any device type (computer or mobile) and connection.

Most-Visited World Websites, 2020

Source: Comscore, Inc.

Some websites represent an aggregation of commonly owned domain names; examples of popular domains within a group added in parentheses by World Almanac editors.

Rank	Website	Visitors[1]	Rank	Website	Visitors[1]
1.	Google sites (YouTube, Blogger)	1,553,131	11.	Qihoo.com sites	383,157
2.	Facebook (Instagram)...................	1,237,084	12.	Baidu.com Inc.	371,879
3.	Microsoft sites (Bing, Xbox Live)..........	1,085,231	13.	Times Internet Limited	357,596
4.	Amazon sites (Zappos, Audible, IMDb)......	838,430	14.	Sohu.com Inc..........................	355,770
5.	Alibaba.com Corp.	744,519	15.	Samsung Group	355,047
6.	Tencent Inc. (QQ)	705,870	16.	Xiaomi sites	346,259
7.	Bytedance Inc. (TikTok)	650,308	17.	Apple Inc.	344,930
8.	Verizon Media (AOL, HuffPost, Yahoo, Tumblr)	577,506	18.	PayPal...............................	340,973
9.	Wikimedia Foundation sites (Wikipedia).....	517,386	19.	Pinterest	333,972
10.	Twitter	445,412	20.	The Walt Disney Company...............	330,506

(1) Number of persons, in thousands, who visited a website at least once in June 2020.

Top Web Browsers Worldwide, 2009-20

Source: StatCounter Global Stats, gs.statcounter.com
(ranked by 2020 figures)

Browser	% of browser market					
	2009	2012	2015	2018	2019	2020
Chrome.......	3.01	33.81	55.39	67.60	71.05	69.55
Firefox........	30.50	23.73	17.24	11.23	9.52	8.61
Safari........	3.02	7.12	4.70	5.01	5.41	8.36
Edge (2020) ...	—	—	—	—	—	4.12
Internet Explorer	60.11	32.04	18.86	6.97	5.00	2.76
Opera	2.64	1.72	1.91	2.48	2.44	2.43
Edge (Legacy)..	—	—	0.05	4.19	4.60	1.93

— = Not available. **Note:** Percent of desktop (and laptop) computer users accessing the web via a particular browser, for July of year shown.

Top Operating Systems Worldwide, 2009-20

Source: StatCounter Global Stats, gs.statcounter.com
(ranked by 2020 figures)

Operating system	% of OS market					
	2009	2012	2015	2018	2019	2020
Android...........	0.02	3.29	25.62	42.26	39.91	39.06
Windows..........	93.85	79.14	50.85	35.93	35.12	36.05
iOS..............	0.36	5.16	11.37	12.82	13.85	14.22
OS X.............	4.07	6.16	4.90	5.39	5.94	7.91
Unknown..........	0.37	0.55	2.28	1.94	3.33	1.30
Linux............	0.76	0.75	1.12	0.77	0.77	0.87
Chrome OS........	—	—	0.15	0.22	0.24	0.31

— = Not available. **Note:** Percent of users accessing the web with a particular operating system (OS), for July of year shown. Includes desktop, laptop, tablet, and mobile devices' operating systems.

U.S. Internet Use by Selected Characteristics, 2013-19
Source: Pew Research Center

	% who are users			% who are users			% who are users	
	2013	2019		2013	2019		2013	2019
All adults	84%	90%	**Race/ethnicity**			**Annual household income**		
Gender			White, non-Hispanic. . .	85%	92%	Less than $30,000 . . .	72%	82%
Male	84	90	Black, non-Hispanic. . .	79	85	$30,000-$49,999	86	93
Female	84	91	Hispanic	80	86	$50,000-$74,999	93	97
Age			**Education**			$75,000 or more	97	98
18-29	97	100	No high school diploma	54	71	**Geography**		
30-49	92	97	High school graduate. .	75	84	Urban	86	91
50-64	81	88	Some college	92	95	Suburban	85	94
65+	56	73	College graduate.	96	98	Rural	78	85

Note: Percent of U.S. adults, age 18 and over, who use the internet, email, or access the internet via a mobile device. Data for each year based on a pooled analysis of all surveys conducted during that year. Hispanic data includes only those surveys incorporating Spanish-language interviews.

Most-Visited U.S. Websites, 2020
Source: Comscore, Inc.; Comscore qSearch

Some websites represent an aggregation of commonly owned domain names; examples of popular domains within a group as of June 2020 added in parentheses by World Almanac editors.

All U.S. Sites

Rank	Website	Visitors[1]
1.	Google sites (YouTube, Blogger)	259,872
2.	Facebook (Instagram)	223,214
3.	Microsoft sites (Bing, Xbox Live).	222,156
4.	Verizon Media (AOL, HuffPost, Yahoo, Tumblr)	210,877
5.	Amazon sites	208,590
6.	WarnerMedia	192,065
7.	Comcast NBCUniversal	188,490
8.	CBS Interactive (CNET, ZDNet)	175,698
9.	Apple Inc.	167,754
10.	Hearst.	164,217
11.	The Walt Disney Company (ABC, ESPN).	161,010
12.	CafeMedia	155,326
13.	The Weather Company.	154,248
14.	PayPal.	148,530
15.	USA TODAY Network	147,399

Blog Sites

Rank	Website	Visitors[1]
1.	CafeMedia	155,326
2.	Blogger	40,009
3.	Fexy	22,775
4.	Wordpress.com.	20,748
5.	Vulture.com.	18,137

Search and Navigation

Rank	Website	Searches (mil)	% of searches
1.	Google sites	12,064	61.9%
2.	Microsoft sites (Bing)	5,045	25.9
3.	Verizon Media (AOL, Yahoo).	2,222	11.4
4.	Ask Network	153	0.8

Email

Rank	Website	Visitors[1]
1.	Google (Gmail).	170,399
2.	Verizon Media (AOL Mail, Yahoo Mail)	70,258
3.	Outlook (Outlook.com)	41,795
4.	Samsung Email (mobile app)	27,006
5.	Outlook Web.	19,949

Social Networking Sites

Rank	Website	Visitors[1]
1.	Facebook	223,214
2.	Twitter.	125,437
3.	Pinterest	106,020
4.	Snapchat	76,192
5.	Reddit	74,972
6.	Bytedance Inc.	68,583
7.	LinkedIn	64,166
8.	Blogger	40,009
9.	Google Duo (mobile app)	30,980
10.	Change.org.	29,340

Video Sites

Rank	Website	Visitors[2]
1.	Google sites (YouTube).	155,627
2.	Facebook	48,806
3.	Verizon Media	46,832
4.	Amazon sites	40,380
5.	WarnerMedia	39,105
6.	Microsoft sites	37,083
7.	BroadbandTV	34,841
8.	CBS Interactive.	34,728
9.	The Walt Disney Company	34,204
10.	Comcast NBCUniversal	33,105

Note: Search and navigation data are for desktop computer users only for searches from the properties' core search engines (as opposed to searches within, for example, YouTube or Gmail). (1) Number of persons, in thousands, who visited the media property (including website/apps) at least once from any U.S. location in June 2020. Mobile users under age 18 are not measured. (2) Number of persons, in thousands, who visited the media property from a desktop in June 2020. Excludes advertisement videos.

Most Popular U.S. Mobile Apps, 2020
Source: Comscore, Inc.

Rank	App	Users[1]	Reach[2]	Rank	App	Users[1]	Reach[2]
1.	YouTube	163,491	76.6%	11.	Pandora Radio	87,499	41.0%
2.	Facebook	159,517	74.8	12.	Apple News	71,333	33.4
3.	Gmail	118,565	55.6	13.	Google Drive	66,631	31.2
4.	Google Search	117,700	55.2	14.	Google Photos	66,302	31.1
5.	Google Maps	116,470	54.6	15.	Spotify	60,589	28.4
6.	Facebook Messenger	103,439	48.5	16.	Snapchat	59,789	28.0
7.	Amazon Mobile	95,191	44.6	17.	Netflix	57,495	27.0
8.	Google Play	87,993	41.2	18.	Pinterest	55,342	25.9
9.	The Weather Channel	87,800	41.2	19.	Apple Maps	44,811	21.0
10.	Instagram	87,631	41.1	20.	Tik Tok (including Musical.ly) . . .	43,783	20.5

(1) Number, in thousands, of U.S. mobile users age 18 or over who used the app at least once in June 2020. (2) Percentage of total U.S. mobile users age 18 or over in June 2020.

U.S. Fixed Broadband Internet Connections by Technology, 2013-17

Source: Federal Communications Commission
(internet connections in thousands, as of Dec. of given year)

Connection type	2013	2014	2015	2016	2017
aDSL (asymmetric digital subscription line)	18,540	18,557	20,744	21,042	19,257
sDSL (symmetric digital subscription line)	36	28	20	20	17
Other wireline[1]	308	308	330	328	370
Cable modem	50,236	53,853	58,423	62,855	65,905
Fiber optic[2]	7,486	8,974	10,383	11,953	13,870
Satellite	1,181	1,558	1,744	1,609	1,563
Fixed wireless	388	594	712	954	1,054
Total	**78,175**	**83,872**	**92,356**	**98,761**	**102,035**

Note: Numbers may not add up to totals due to rounding. Includes connections with transmission speeds of at least 3 megabits per second (3 mbps) downstream (internet to user) and 768 kilobits per second (768 kbps) upstream (user to internet). (1) Includes power line. (2) Fiber to the premises (FTTP).

U.S. Time Spent Online, 2002-18

Source: The 2018 Digital Future Report, Center for the Digital Future at USC Annenberg

	2002	2005	2007	2008	2009	2010	2012	2013	2014	2015	2016	2018
Weekly time online[1]	11.1	13.3	15.3	17.3	19.0	18.3	20.4	20.5	21.5	23.5	23.6	22.5
Weekly time online, at home[1]	6.8	7.8	10.0	10.1	10.6	12.3	14.1	14.1	16.1	17.2	17.6	17.8
Weekly time online, at work[2]	5.5	5.6	7.4	8.3	9.0	9.2	9.2	10.4	10.2	10.9	10.1	10.7
Weekly time online, at school[3]	NA	NA	2.3	2.5	3.1	4.1	4.0	5.7	6.5	6.9	7.9	6.8
% who said communication technology made the world a better place[4]	66%	65%	57%	58%	56%	57%	55%	55%	58%	51%	52%	48%

NA = Not available. (1) Average number of active-use hours per week among internet users. (2) Average number of active-use hours per week among internet users who access the internet at work. (3) Average number of active-use hours per week at school among internet users who are students. (4) Among internet users age 16 and older.

U.S. Internet Use by Race and Ethnicity, 2003-19

Source: U.S. Census Bureau survey for National Telecommunications and Information Administration, U.S. Dept. of Commerce
(number in thousands of civilian individuals, age 3 and older)

Survey date	Total U.S.[1]		White, non-Hispanic		African American, non-Hispanic		Asian American, non-Hispanic		American Indian or Alaska Native, non-Hispanic		Hispanic	
	Number	% with internet use	Number	% with internet use	Number	% with internet use	Number	% with internet use	Number	% with internet use	Number	% with internet use
Oct. 2003	161,636	58.7%	122,243	65.1%	14,898	45.2%	7,043	63.0%	676	48.1%	14,038	37.2%
Oct. 2007	177,987	62.4	130,432	68.9	17,223	50.1	8,686	68.4	793	47.1	17,760	41.6
Oct. 2009	197,941	68.4	141,213	74.3	20,848	59.5	9,243	72.3	1,017	54.9	22,186	49.3
Oct. 2010	209,472	71.7	145,989	76.7	22,389	63.7	9,949	74.2	1,094	62.5	26,246	56.6
July 2011	204,596	69.7	142,827	75.0	21,287	60.2	10,010	73.6	1,142	59.7	25,648	54.4
Oct. 2012	222,038	74.7	149,231	79.1	24,290	68.3	11,643	78.4	1,350	62.5	30,960	62.1
July 2013	213,708	71.4	142,313	75.4	22,996	64.0	11,739	75.3	1,424	61.5	30,771	61.0
July 2015	226,747	74.6	147,408	78.0	25,025	67.8	12,919	77.4	1,423	70.2	34,772	65.8
Nov. 2017	240,270	77.7	151,594	80.2	27,949	73.4	13,993	79.4	1,497	62.7	39,826	72.1
Nov. 2019	248,526	79.4	154,232	81.8	28,814	74.7	14,774	78.3	1,850	73.8	43,129	74.8

(1) Includes other race categories not shown.

Media Purchases by U.S. Internet Users, 2012-18

Source: The 2018 Digital Future Report, Center for the Digital Future at USC Annenberg
(average monthly online purchases per internet user; ranked by 2018 figures)

Item	2012	2013	2014	2015	2016	2018
Streaming movies	2.0	2.9	4.0	3.8	3.9	4.9
Individual digital songs	1.5	1.4	1.7	1.3	1.2	0.8
E-books	0.6	0.5	0.5	0.5	0.5	0.6
Online movies as digital downloads	0.1	0.1	0.6	0.3	0.3	0.4
Online newspapers	0.1	0.1	0.1	0.1	0.1	0.2
Online magazines	0.1	0.1	0.1	0.1	0.2	0.1

Frequency of Selected Internet Activities in the U.S., 2018

Source: The 2018 Digital Future Report, Center for the Digital Future at USC Annenberg
(as % of all internet users age 12 and older)

Online activity	Several times a day	Daily	Weekly	Monthly	Less than monthly	Never
Check email	52%	31%	8%	2%	3%	4%
Visit social networking sites	32	28	12	5	7	16
Send direct message/chat	27	29	15	6	12	12
Download or listen to music	20	22	19	9	15	16
Download or watch videos	16	24	21	10	13	17
Look for news	14	35	21	8	12	10
Play games	14	20	16	7	12	32
Find or check a fact	13	24	30	13	12	8
Look up a definition	7	17	31	19	18	8
Listen to online radio	6	15	14	9	17	39
Post on discussion boards	6	10	12	10	22	40
Participate in distance learning for work/degree	2	5	5	6	17	66

Telecommunications Milestones

1753: Scottish surgeon Charles Morrison proposed using 26 electric lines, one for each letter of the alphabet, to make an electric telegraph. A letter would be indicated by charging the corresponding line, causing movement of a light object at the receiving end. Swiss scientist Georges-Louis Lesage built such a 26-line "electrostatic" system in 1774.

1837: In England, Charles Wheatstone and William Fothergill Cooke patented an electromagnetic telegraph. To indicate letters, their system used the magnetic field generated by a current to deflect compass needles. In 1839, they built the first commercial electric telegraph along a 13-mi (21-km) route.

1837: American inventor Samuel Morse filed a provisional patent application for a different type of electric telegraph that indicated letters by making marks of various lengths on paper. In 1844, he completed a 30-mi telegraph line from Washington, DC, to Baltimore, MD.

1866: The first successful transatlantic telegraph cable was laid.

1876: Alexander Graham Bell applied for a U.S. patent on the telephone. In his first successful experiment, on Mar. 10, he used the device to call his assistant.

1901: Italian inventor Guglielmo Marconi successfully transmitted the first transatlantic radio signal—from Cornwall, England, to Newfoundland, Canada.

1927: Commercial transatlantic telephone service (via radio) began between New York and London.

1946: The first commercial mobile phone service was launched, in St. Louis, MO.

1947: U.S. scientists invented the transistor, thereby giving birth to a revolution in telecommunications and electronics.

1948: U.S. mathematician/engineer Claude Shannon's epochal paper "A Mathematical Theory of Communication" laid the foundation for modern information theory. Its treatment of such crucial concepts as data compression and error detection and correction opened the way to digital communication.

1951: The mayors of Englewood, NJ, and Alameda, CA, made the first customer-dialed long-distance telephone call, facilitated by the introduction of area codes.

1956: The first transoceanic telephone cable went into service.

1962: NASA launched the world's first active communications satellite, AT&T's *Telstar 1*.

1978: Trials were conducted in Chicago and Newark, NJ, on a cellular approach to mobile telephony. This divided a region into a multitude of small overlapping areas, or cells, and made possible a significant increase in quality of calls and quantity of callers. Callers could be switched from one cell to another as they moved about.

1983: The first commercial cellular system in the U.S. went into operation in Chicago. A similar system was also launched in the Baltimore, MD-Washington, DC, area.

1984: As a result of a 1982 antitrust settlement with the U.S. government, AT&T, which handled most telephone service in the U.S., was broken up into several separate entities.

1994: The first smartphone, IBM's Simon Personal Communicator, went on the market. A bricklike touchscreen device, it combined a cellular phone with such features as an address book, calendar, calculator, email and faxing capability, and games.

2007: Apple released the iPhone, inaugurating an era of multifunctional smartphones.

2012: By late in the year more than 1 bil smartphones of all types were in use worldwide.

2016: Users of Facebook's messaging app Messenger passed the 1 bil mark.

2016: Total sales of Apple's iPhone reached 1 bil units.

2019: Telecommunications carriers began launching commercial "5G" (fifth generation) super-fast cellular networks, with the first large-scale deployments taking place in South Korea and the U.S.

Global Communications Technology Developments, 2001-19

Source: ITU World Telecommunication/Information and Communication Technology (ICT) Indicators Database
(per 100 inhabitants; 2019 data are estimated)

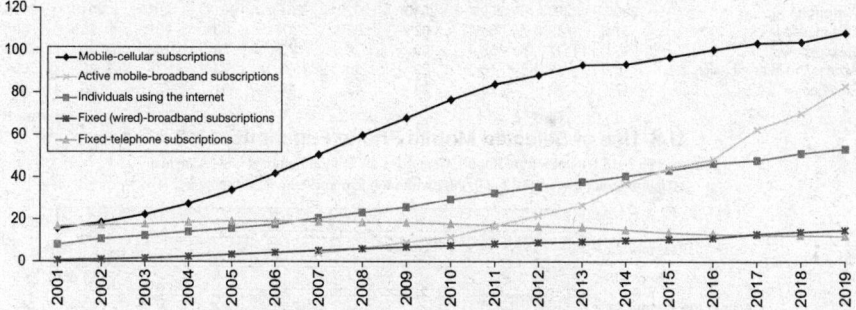

Nations With the Most Cellphone Use, 2018

Source: © International Telecommunication Union, estimated; ranked by countries with most cellphone subscriptions

Rank	Country	Subscriptions (thous.)	Per 100 pop.	Rank	Country	Subscriptions (thous.)	Per 100 pop.
1.	China	1,641,147	114.95	14.	Germany	107,500	129.32
2.	India	1,176,022	86.94	15.	Egypt	93,784	95.29
3.	United States	404,577	123.69	16.	Iran	88,722	108.46
4.	Indonesia	320,770	119.84	17.	South Africa	88,567	153.25
5.	Russia	229,431	157.43	18.	Italy	83,342	137.47
6.	Brazil	207,047	98.84	19.	Turkey	80,118	97.30
7.	Japan	177,067	139.20	20.	United Kingdom	78,924	117.55
8.	Nigeria	172,731	88.18	21.	France	70,455	108.41
9.	Bangladesh	156,989	97.28	22.	South Korea	66,356	129.67
10.	Pakistan	153,987	72.56	23.	Colombia	64,514	129.91
11.	Vietnam	140,639	147.20	24.	Myanmar	61,144	113.84
12.	Thailand	125,098	180.18	25.	Argentina	58,598	132.09
13.	Mexico	117,367	93.01		World	8,160,000	107.00

U.S. Wireless Industry, 1985-2018

Source: CTIA Semi-Annual Industry Survey, used with permission of CTIA. As of Dec. of year shown.

Year	Est. total subscribers	Total service revenues (thous.)	Cellphone antennas	Avg. monthly revenue per subscriber unit	Avg. local call length (min.)
1985	340,213	$482,428	913	NA	NA
1987	1,230,855	1,151,519	2,305	NA	2.33
1989	3,508,944	3,340,595	4,169	NA	2.48
1991	7,557,148	5,708,522	7,847	NA	2.38
1993	16,009,461	10,892,175	12,824	$76.55	2.41
1995	33,785,661	19,081,239	22,663	59.43	2.15
1997	55,312,293	27,485,633	51,600	49.39	2.31
1999	86,047,003	40,018,489	81,698	46.39	2.38
2000	109,478,031	52,466,020	104,288	48.55	2.56
2001	128,374,512	65,316,235	127,540	49.79	2.74
2003	158,721,981	87,624,093	162,986	51.55	3.07
2004	182,140,362	102,121,210	175,725	52.54	3.05
2005	207,896,198	113,538,221	183,689	50.65	3.00
2006	233,040,781	125,456,825	195,613	49.07	3.03
2007	255,395,599	138,869,304	213,299	49.26	NA
2008	270,333,881	148,084,170	242,130	48.87	2.27
2009	285,646,191	152,551,854	247,081	47.97	1.81
2010	296,285,629	159,929,649	253,086	47.53	1.79
2012	326,475,248	185,013,935	301,779	48.99	1.80
2013	335,652,171	189,192,812	304,360	48.79	NA
2014	355,445,472	187,848,447	298,055	46.64	NA
2015	377,921,241	191,949,025	307,626	44.65	NA
2016	395,881,497	188,524,256	308,334	41.50	NA
2017	400,205,829	179,091,135	323,448	38.66	NA
2018	421,793,010	182,779,484	349,344	37.85	NA

NA = Not available. **Note:** Survey conducted annually beginning 2013.

U.S. Use of Selected Mobile Phone Functions, 2007-18

Source: The 2018 Digital Future Report, Center for the Digital Future at USC Annenberg
(as % of internet users age 12 and older with mobile phones; ranked by percent use in 2018)

Function	2007	2008	2009	2010	2012	2013	2014	2015	2016	2018
Text message	31%	45%	54%	62%	82%	77%	83%	87%	93%	89%
Take pictures	33	47	52	60	79	70	76	83	89	88
Access the internet daily	8	13	18	23	59	59	73	79	82	85
Play games	17	22	20	23	43	43	51	54	58	56

U.S. Use of Selected Mobile Phone Functions, 2018

Source: The 2018 Digital Future Report, Center for the Digital Future at USC Annenberg
(% of internet users age 12 and older with mobile phone who used function)

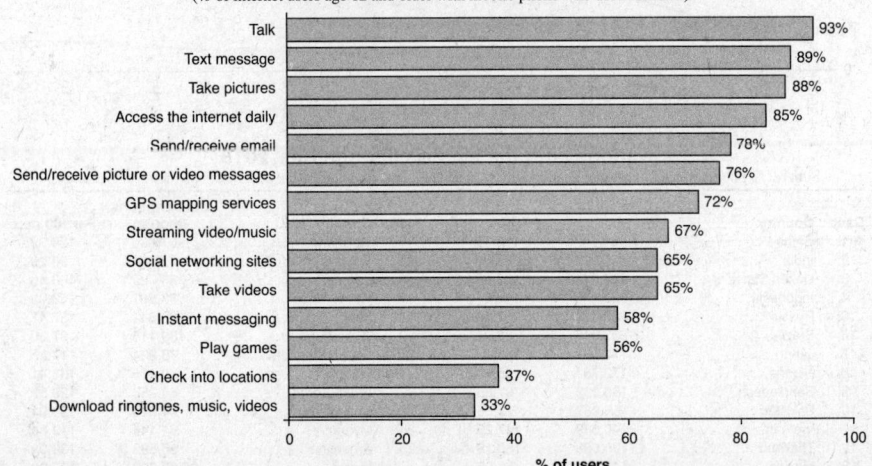

Function	%
Talk	93%
Text message	89%
Take pictures	88%
Access the internet daily	85%
Send/receive email	78%
Send/receive picture or video messages	76%
GPS mapping services	72%
Streaming video/music	67%
Social networking sites	65%
Take videos	65%
Instant messaging	58%
Play games	56%
Check into locations	37%
Download ringtones, music, videos	33%

% of users

ENVIRONMENT

U.S. Greenhouse Gas Emissions From Human Activities, 1990-2018

Source: U.S. Environmental Protection Agency

Gas and major source(s)	1990	2005	2014	2015	2016	2017	2018	% change, 1990-2018
Carbon dioxide (CO_2)	5,128.3	6,131.9	5,561.7	5,412.4	5,292.3	5,253.6	5,424.9	5.8%
Fossil fuel combustion	4,740.0	5,740.7	5,184.8	5,031.8	4,942.4	4,892.2	5,031.8	6.2
Methane (CH_4)	774.4	679.6	639.0	638.5	624.2	630.3	634.5	-18.1
Enteric fermentation[1]	164.2	168.9	164.2	166.5	171.8	175.4	177.6	8.2
Natural gas systems	183.3	158.1	141.1	141.9	135.8	139.3	140.0	-23.6
Landfills	179.6	131.3	112.6	111.3	108.0	107.7	110.6	-38.4
Manure management	37.1	51.6	54.3	57.9	59.6	59.9	61.7	66.3
Nitrous oxide (N_2O)	434.6	432.6	449.3	443.8	426.1	421.3	434.5	-0.0
Agricultural soil management	315.9	313.0	349.2	348.1	329.8	327.4	338.2	7.1
Hydrofluorocarbons (HFCs), etc.[2]	99.6	147.7	178.9	181.7	181.5	183.0	182.7	83.4
Total U.S. emissions	**6,437.0**	**7,391.8**	**6,829.0**	**6,676.4**	**6,524.1**	**6,488.2**	**6,676.6**	**3.7**
Net U.S. emissions[3]	**5,583.6**	**6,577.1**	**6,106.0**	**5,900.8**	**5,735.1**	**5,724.3**	**5,903.2**	**5.7**

Note: Emissions given in terms of equivalent emissions of carbon dioxide (CO_2), using units of million metric tons of carbon dioxide equivalent (MMT CO_2 eq.). (1) Digestive process of ruminant animals, such as cattle and sheep, producing methane as a byproduct. (2) Includes HFCs, PFCs (perfluorocarbons), SF_6 (sulfur hexafluoride), and NF_3 (nitrogen trifluoride). (3) Total emissions minus the net sum of all emissions (i.e., sources) of greenhouse gases to the atmosphere plus removals of CO_2 (i.e., sinks or negative emissions) from the atmosphere.

U.S. Greenhouse Gas Emissions, 2018
Source: U.S. Environmental Protection Agency

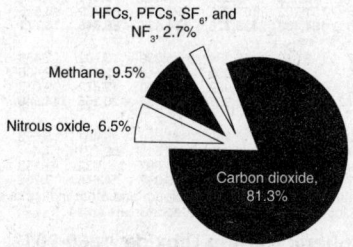

HFCs, PFCs, SF_6, and NF_3, 2.7%
Methane, 9.5%
Nitrous oxide, 6.5%
Carbon dioxide, 81.3%

World Carbon Dioxide Emissions From the Use of Fossil Fuels, 2017
Source: U.S. Energy Information Administration

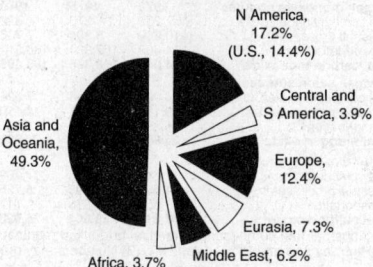

N America, 17.2% (U.S., 14.4%)
Central and S America, 3.9%
Europe, 12.4%
Eurasia, 7.3%
Middle East, 6.2%
Africa, 3.7%
Asia and Oceania, 49.3%

HFC = hydrofluorocarbon; PFC = perfluorocarbon; SF_6 = sulfur hexafluoride; NF_3 = nitrogen trifluoride. **Note:** Emissions sources are independently rounded; percentages may not add up to 100.

Top 20 Nations Producing Carbon Dioxide Emissions, 1980-2017

Source: Energy Information Administration, U.S. Dept. of Energy

(in million metric tons of carbon dioxide emitted from the consumption of energy; ranked by 2017 totals)

Country	1980	1990	2000	2005	2010	2015	2016	2017	% change, 1980-2017	% change, 1990-2017
China	1,665	2,667	3,523	6,106	8,779	10,512	10,502	10,419	525.9%	290.7%
U.S.	4,751	5,039	5,862	5,991	5,586	5,267	5,175	5,133	8.1	1.9
India	275	559	924	1,171	1,606	2,180	2,237	2,312	739.9	313.8
Russia[1]	3,562	4,343	1,539	1,597	1,736	1,742	1,690	1,782	-50.0	-59.0
Japan	911	1,113	1,200	1,252	1,122	1,139	1,139	1,117	22.6	0.4
Germany[2]	828	726	821	822	839	830	835	821	-0.8	13.1
Iran	119	216	322	452	568	641	631	676	468.3	213.9
South Korea	146	251	428	482	570	627	611	637	337.0	153.6
Saudi Arabia	177	208	291	405	502	625	611	631	256.6	202.8
Canada	412	413	545	589	539	569	541	558	35.5	35.1
Indonesia	85	158	268	317	423	509	500	531	525.9	237.0
Brazil	186	244	355	380	474	623	522	530	184.2	117.5
South Africa	230	331	396	448	481	476	474	477	107.3	43.8
Turkey	70	139	205	232	299	379	396	449	538.7	223.7
France	537	407	410	423	456	413	411	417	-22.4	2.4
Australia	192	247	345	370	384	399	408	416	116.5	68.6
UK	591	549	574	591	524	452	475	416	-29.6	-24.2
Mexico	214	243	386	424	397	414	411	406	89.8	67.2
Italy	399	434	446	473	446	385	383	376	-6.0	-13.5
Thailand	34	84	158	237	280	337	344	349	939.1	316.8
World[3]	**19,286**	**22,717**	**24,368**	**28,875**	**32,521**	**35,505**	**35,281**	**35,545**	**84.3**	**56.5**

(1) Numbers for 1980-90 are for the former Soviet Union. (2) Numbers for 1980-90 are for former West Germany. (3) Includes nations not listed.

Atmospheric Concentration of Carbon Dioxide, 1744-2019

Source: Carbon Dioxide Information Analysis Center, U.S. Dept. of Energy; Earth System Research Laboratory, Natl. Oceanic and Atmospheric Admin., U.S. Dept. of Commerce

Year[1]	CO_2 in ppm	Year[1]	CO_2 in ppm	Year[1]	CO_2 in ppm	Year[1]	CO_2 in ppm	Year[1]	CO_2 in ppm
1744	277	1878	290	1960	317	2005	380	2015	401
1791	280	1903	295	1970	326	2010	390	2016	404
1816	284	1915	301	1980	339	2012	394	2017	407
1843	287	1927	306	1990	354	2013	397	2018	409
1869	289	1943	308	2000	370	2014	399	2019	411

ppm = Parts per million. (1) Measurements for 1744-1943 were derived from a 200-m-deep ice core sample drilled near Siple Station in Antarctica in 1983-84. Measurements for 1960-2019 were taken directly from the atmosphere at Mauna Loa Observatory in Hawaii.

Emissions of Principal Air Pollutants in the U.S., 1970-2019

Source: Office of Air Quality Planning and Standards, U.S. Environmental Protection Agency; in million tons

Pollutant	1970	1975	1980	1985	1990	1995	2000	2005	2010	2019
Carbon monoxide	204.0	188.4	185.4	176.8	154.2	126.8	114.5	88.5	73.8	64.2
Nitrogen oxides[1]	26.9	26.4	27.1	25.8	25.5	25.0	22.6	20.4	14.8	9.0
Particulate matter[2]										
PM10	13.0	7.6	7.0	41.3	27.8	25.8	23.7	21.3	20.8	17.1
PM2.5	NA	NA	NA	NA	7.6	6.9	7.3	5.6	6.0	5.7
Sulfur dioxide	31.2	28.0	25.9	23.3	23.1	18.6	16.3	14.5	7.7	2.2
Volatile org. compounds[1]	34.7	30.8	31.1	27.4	24.1	22.0	17.5	17.8	17.8	16.9
Ammonia	NA	NA	NA	NA	4.3	4.7	4.9	3.9	4.3	4.3
Total[3]	309.8	281.2	276.5	294.6	266.6	229.8	206.8	172.0	145.2	119.4

NA = Not available. (1) Ozone, a major air pollutant and the primary constituent of smog, is not emitted directly to the air but is formed by sunlight acting on emissions of nitrogen oxides and volatile organic compounds. (2) PM10 = particulates 10 microns or smaller in diameter. PM2.5 = particulates 2.5 microns or smaller in diameter. (3) Totals are rounded, as are components of totals.

Sources of Air Pollutants in the U.S., 1970-2019

Source: Office of Air Quality Planning and Standards, U.S. Environmental Protection Agency; in thousand tons

Carbon monoxide sources	1970	1975	1980	1985	1990	1995	2000	2005	2010	2019
Fuel combustion, elec. util.	237	276	322	291	363	372	484	643	766	588
Industrial processes[1]	10,610	8,304	7,700	5,894	5,572	5,631	3,628	3,074	2,807	2,497
Transportation[2]	174,602	167,884	160,512	153,216	131,702	107,755	92,239	64,729	43,596	28,445
Total carbon monoxide[3]	**204,042**	**188,398**	**185,408**	**176,845**	**154,188**	**126,778**	**114,467**	**88,546**	**73,771**	**64,188**
Nitrogen oxide sources										
Fuel combustion, elec. util.	4,900	5,694	7,024	6,127	6,663	6,384	5,330	3,792	2,458	996
Industrial processes[1]	5,100	4,546	4,110	4,009	3,831	3,909	3,518	2,783	2,406	2,083
Transportation[2]	15,276	15,029	14,846	14,508	13,373	12,989	12,560	12,612	9,017	4,880
Total nitrogen oxide[3]	**26,882**	**26,378**	**27,080**	**25,757**	**25,527**	**24,955**	**22,598**	**20,355**	**14,846**	**8,950**
Sulfur dioxide sources										
Fuel combustion, elec. util.	17,398	18,268	17,469	16,272	15,909	12,080	11,396	10,404	5,696	1,017
Industrial processes[1]	11,661	7,993	6,725	5,597	5,402	4,945	3,515	2,721	1,447	813
Transportation[2]	551	635	717	809	874	741	697	682	158	50
Total sulfur dioxide[3]	**31,218**	**28,044**	**25,926**	**23,307**	**23,077**	**18,619**	**16,347**	**14,546**	**7,732**	**2,168**

(1) Industrial fuel combustion, chemical and allied manufacturing, metals processing, and petroleum and other industrial sectors. (2) Highway and off-highway vehicles. (3) Numbers may not add up to totals because not all categories are listed.

Average Global Temperature and Atmospheric Carbon Dioxide, 1880-2019

Source: Goddard Institute for Space Studies, National Aeronautics and Space Administration, via Earth Policy Institute; National Centers for Environmental Information, National Oceanic and Atmospheric Admin. (NOAA), U.S. Dept. of Commerce

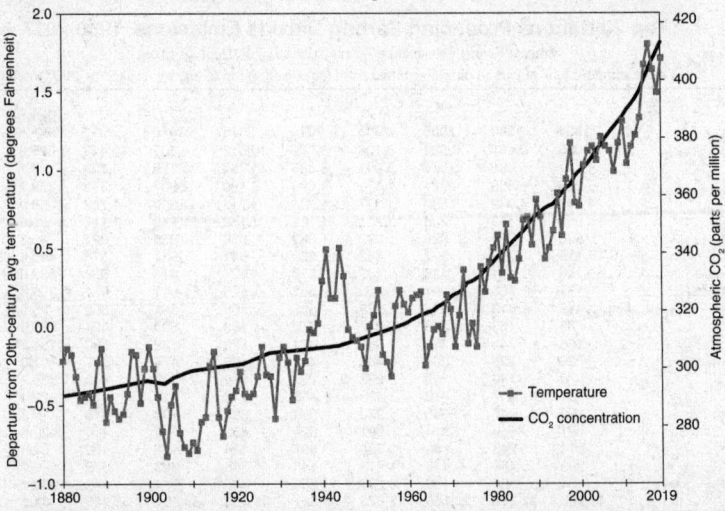

Note: NOAA uses temperature anomalies (departures from the reference value of 20th-century average temperature) rather than absolute temperatures to report average global temperatures.

Air Pollution in Selected World Cities, 2017-19

Source: IQAir

Particulate matter refers to extremely small particles and liquid droplets in the air that come from vehicle exhaust, burning of fuels, dust, cooking, tobacco smoke, and chemical reactions in the atmosphere. Particulates 2.5 microns or less in diameter (PM2.5) are capable of reaching deep into the respiratory tract and can cause or worsen heart and lung diseases. The World Health Org. (WHO) estimated that ambient (outdoor) air pollution caused 4.2 mil premature deaths worldwide in 2016 due to exposure to PM2.5. Data in this table show the annual average PM2.5 concentration measured in $\mu g/m^3$. WHO standards for acceptable air quality are annual mean concentrations of 10.0 or less.

City, country	PM2.5 level ($\mu g/m^3$)			City, country	PM2.5 level ($\mu g/m^3$)		
	2019	2018	2017		2019	2018	2017
Addis Ababa, Ethiopia	20.1	27.1	26.9	Montréal, QC, Canada	10.0	7.0	6.8
Amsterdam, Netherlands	10.7	11.5	12.2	Moscow, Russia	10.0	10.1	8.4
Bangkok, Thailand	22.8	25.2	27.6	Mumbai, India	45.3	58.6	54.2
Beijing, China	42.1	50.9	58.8	Naples, Italy	22.8	13.8	16.7
Berlin, Germany	9.7	11.7	8.5	New York, NY, U.S.	7.0	7.0	6.8
Bogota, Colombia	13.1	13.9	15.7	Oslo, Norway	7.5	8.2	7.4
Chicago, IL, U.S.	12.8	9.4	6.7	Paris, France	14.7	15.6	15.4
Delhi, India	98.6	113.5	108.2	Prague, Czech Republic	11.5	17.4	15.6
Dhaka, Bangladesh	83.3	97.1	79.7	Santiago, Chile	27.7	29.4	23.1
Dubai, United Arab Emirates	40.9	55.3	NA	São Paulo, Brazil	15.3	16.2	16.0
Hong Kong, China	20.3	20.2	21.8	Seoul, South Korea	24.8	23.3	25.2
Johannesburg, South Africa	25.3	NA	NA	Shanghai, China	35.4	36.0	38.9
Kolkata, India	59.8	85.4	76.7	Sofia, Bulgaria	26.8	28.2	20.8
Lima, Peru	23.7	28.0	27.7	Sydney, Australia	10.1	7.6	7.1
London, England, UK	11.4	12.0	12.7	Tehran, Iran	25.9	26.1	34.0
Los Angeles, CA, U.S.	12.7	14.4	16.1	Tokyo, Japan	11.7	13.1	13.0
Madrid, Spain	9.2	10.0	9.9	Toronto, ON, Canada	7.4	7.8	7.5
Mexico City, Mexico	20.5	19.7	20.4	Warsaw, Poland	17.3	24.2	26.7
Milan, Italy	23.3	22.1	27.8				

NA = Not available.

Air Quality Changes in Selected Cities During COVID-19 Lockdown, 2020

Source: IQAir

Air quality is measured using many factors, including particulate matter (PM). PM of 2.5 microns or less in diameter (PM2.5) can penetrate and lodge inside the lungs, contributing to the risk of developing cardiovascular and respiratory diseases and lung cancer. As entire urban areas and regions were locked down in response to the coronavirus pandemic in 2020, many cities experienced a dramatic reduction in air pollution. This table shows the level of PM2.5 during 3-week lockdowns compared to the same time periods in 2019 and 2016-19.

City	Dates[1]	Avg. PM2.5 ($\mu g/m^3$)	% change in PM2.5[2]	
			Vs. 2019	Vs. 2016-19 avg.
Delhi, India	3/23-4/13	32.8	−60%	−55%
London, England, UK	3/23-4/13	16.2	−9	6
Los Angeles, CA, U.S.	3/23-4/13	5.5	−31	−51
Madrid, Spain	3/23-4/13	6.4	−11	2
Mumbai, India	3/23-4/13	28.8	−34	−43
New York, NY, U.S.	3/23-4/13	4.4	−25	−29
Rome, Italy	3/9-3/30	16.7	30	NA
São Paulo, Brazil	3/23-4/13	10.1	−32	−26[3]
Seoul, South Korea	2/26-3/18	24.1	−54	−32
Wuhan, China	2/3-2/24	35.1	−44	−50

NA = Not available. (1) Dates reflect either the period when the most stringent lockdown measures were in place or, during longer lockdowns such as in Wuhan, coincide with the peak of daily reported COVID-19 cases. (2) Comparisons use same dates as shown at left, for respective years/averages. (3) Data based on a 3-year average, 2017-19.

Municipal Solid Waste, 2017

Source: U.S. Environmental Protection Agency

In 2017, Americans generated about 268 mil tons of refuse collected as municipal solid waste (MSW). Of that MSW, paper represented 25.0%; food 15.2%; plastics 13.2%; yard trimmings 13.1%; rubber, leather, and textiles 9.7%; metals 9.4%; wood 6.7%; glass 4.2%; and other material 3.5%. About 35.2%, or 94 mil tons, was recycled or composted; nearly half of recycled/composted materials consisted of paper and paperboard.

Municipal Solid Waste Generation, 1960-2017

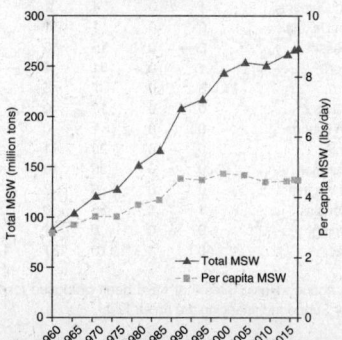

Municipal Solid Waste Recycling and Composting, 1960-2017

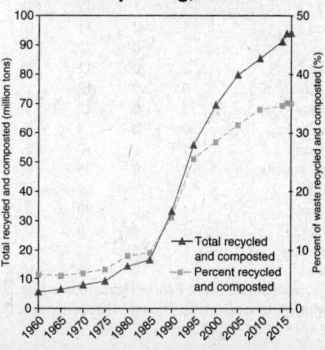

Air Quality of Selected U.S. Urban Areas, 1980-2019

Source: Office of Air Quality Planning and Standards, U.S. Environmental Protection Agency

Data indicate the number of days metropolitan statistical areas or corresponding core-based statistical areas failed to meet acceptable air-quality standards based on monitoring of six common pollutants.

Urban area	1980	1990	2000	2005	2010	2015	2016	2017	2018	2019
Atlanta-Sandy Springs-Roswell, GA	32	62	48	17	7	2	4	0	0	1
Bakersfield, CA	73	91	109	79	40	29	14	24	27	7
Baltimore-Columbia-Towson, MD	64	29	17	20	20	1	5	2	0	0
Baton Rouge, LA	27	30	35	22	3	2	0	0	1	0
Boston-Cambridge-Newton, MA-NH	27	8	2	8	1	1	0	0	0	0
Chicago-Naperville-Elgin, IL-IN-WI	96	47	10	26	2	3	5	2	6	1
Cincinnati, OH-KY-IN	80	53	14	22	4	1	0	0	2	0
Cleveland-Elyria, OH	37	19	9	21	5	1	5	0	0	0
Dallas-Fort Worth-Arlington, TX	43	26	35	40	5	5	1	0	9	1
Denver-Aurora-Lakewood, CO	28	3	1	2	2	2	4	1	8	2
Detroit-Warren-Dearborn, MI	48	16	5	18	2	1	0	1	2	0
Fresno, CA	89	55	106	45	22	24	25	27	19	2
Houston-The Woodlands-Sugar Land, TX	82	57	53	44	17	15	1	3	9	5
Indianapolis-Carmel-Anderson, IN	59	11	21	8	1	1	0	0	1	0
Kansas City, MO-KS	57	6	12	17	0	0	0	0	1	0
Las Vegas-Henderson-Paradise, NV	25	10	1	9	0	1	1	1	1	0
Los Angeles-Long Beach-Anaheim, CA	203	146	66	61	15	38	25	46	20	29
Memphis, TN-MS-AR	73	22	23	14	2	0	1	1	1	0
Miami-Fort Lauderdale-West Palm Beach, FL	19	2	1	1	0	0	1	0	0	0
Minneapolis-St. Paul-Bloomington, MN-WI	67	15	1	7	0	0	1	0	0	1
Nashville-Davidson—Murfreesboro—Franklin, TN	69	70	18	6	1	0	0	0	1	0
New Orleans-Metairie, LA	11	4	13	3	19	0	0	0	0	0
New York-Newark-Jersey City, NY-NJ-PA	90	45	18	22	12	3	2	2	3	0
Philadelphia-Camden-Wilmington, PA-NJ-DE-MD	90	39	20	26	12	2	2	2	3	0
Phoenix-Mesa-Scottsdale, AZ	113	29	19	11	2	3	7	12	11	5
Pittsburgh, PA	121	93	30	33	18	2	1	1	1	4
Riverside-San Bernardino-Ontario, CA	170	154	114	93	71	51	67	78	65	66
Sacramento-Roseville—Arden-Arcade, CA	53	42	42	42	9	6	16	3	23	0
Salt Lake City, UT	77	45	13	8	7	2	5	1	2	0
San Francisco-Oakland-Hayward, CA	11	6	4	2	1	0	2	8	12	2
Seattle-Tacoma-Bellevue, WA	35	8	5	1	0	3	1	11	7	0
Tucson, AZ	50	1	0	2	0	0	0	0	0	0
Washington-Arlington-Alexandria, DC-VA-MD-WV	53	23	12	18	13	1	0	0	1	1
Winston-Salem, NC	0	7	18	3	3	0	0	0	0	0

Hazardous Waste Sites in the U.S., 2020

Source: National Priorities List, U.S. Environmental Protection Agency; as of Apr. 2020

State/territory	Proposed Gen.	Proposed Fed.	Final Gen.	Final Fed.	Total	State/territory	Proposed Gen.	Proposed Fed.	Final Gen.	Final Fed.	Total
Alabama	2	0	9	3	14	Nebraska	0	0	16	1	17
Alaska	0	0	1	5	6	Nevada	1	0	1	0	2
Arizona	0	0	7	2	9	New Hampshire	1	0	19	1	21
Arkansas	0	0	9	0	9	New Jersey	1	0	108	6	115
California	2	0	73	24	99	New Mexico	0	0	15	1	16
Colorado	1	0	17	3	21	New York	1	0	81	4	86
Connecticut	1	0	12	1	14	North Carolina	0	0	36	2	38
Delaware	2	0	14	1	17	North Dakota	0	0	0	0	0
District of Columbia	0	0	0	1	1	Ohio	4	1	35	3	43
Florida	1	0	47	6	54	Oklahoma	2	0	7	1	10
Georgia	1	0	14	2	17	Oregon	1	0	11	2	14
Guam	0	0	1	1	2	Pennsylvania	2	0	85	6	93
Hawaii	0	0	1	2	3	Puerto Rico	0	0	18	1	19
Idaho	3	0	4	2	0	Rhode Island	0	0	10	2	12
Illinois	3	1	42	4	50	South Carolina	1	0	24	2	27
Indiana	1	0	41	0	42	South Dakota	0	0	1	1	2
Iowa	1	0	10	1	12	Tennessee	0	0	15	3	18
Kansas	2	0	11	1	14	Texas	1	0	51	4	56
Kentucky	0	0	12	1	13	Utah	3	0	7	5	15
Louisiana	3	0	12	1	16	Vermont	0	0	12	0	12
Maine	0	0	9	3	12	Virgin Islands	0	0	1	0	1
Maryland	1	0	10	10	21	Virginia	0	0	20	11	31
Massachusetts	1	0	25	6	32	Washington	0	0	35	13	48
Michigan	1	1	65	0	67	West Virginia	0	0	8	2	10
Minnesota	1	0	23	2	26	Wisconsin	1	0	36	0	37
Mississippi	1	0	9	0	10	Wyoming	0	0	0	1	1
Missouri	0	0	31	3	34	**Total**	**48**	**3**	**1,178**	**157**	**1,386**
Montana	1	0	17	0	18						

Gen. = Non-federal sites; Fed. = Hazardous waste produced by federal agency. **Note:** Sites that have been proposed for federal Superfund financing are listed under Proposed; sites that have qualified for Superfund financing are under Final.

Renewable Water Resources, 2017

Source: Food and Agriculture Organization (FAO), United Nations

Globally, water supplies are abundant, but they are unevenly distributed among and within countries. In some areas, water withdrawals are so high, relative to supply, that surface water supplies are shrinking, and groundwater reserves are being depleted faster than they can be replenished by precipitation. According to the FAO, the U.S. (including Alaska and Hawaii) has 8,685 cubic meters per capita and 2,818 cubic kilometers of internal renewable water resources total.

The tables below take into account only countries for which data are available, draw upon studies done over a number of years, and use 2017 population data. Numbers represent each country's internal resources. Countries ranked by per capita figures.

Countries With Greatest Internal Water Resources

Country	Cubic m per capita	Total cubic km
Iceland	507,463	170.0
Guyana	309,808	241.0
Suriname	175,719	99.0
Papua New Guinea	97,079	801.0
Bhutan	96,582	78.0
Gabon	80,988	164.0
Canada	77,818	2,850.0
Solomon Islands	73,123	44.7
Norway	72,008	382.0
New Zealand	69,486	327.0

Countries With Lowest Internal Water Resources

Country	Cubic m per capita	Total cubic km
Kuwait	0.0	0.0
Bahrain	2.679	0.004
Egypt	10.25	1.0
United Arab Emirates	15.96	0.15
Qatar	21.22	0.056
Maldives	68.76	0.03
Jordan	70.29	0.682
Saudi Arabia	72.86	2.4
Yemen	74.34	2.1
Israel	90.12	0.75

Top Countries by Forest Area, 1990-2017

Source: Food and Agriculture Organization, United Nations

(in square kilometers; ranked by 2017 area)

Country	Forest area, 1990	Forest area, 2017	% change, 1990-2017	% of land area covered by forest in 2017
Russia	NA	8,149,305	NA	49.8%
Brazil	5,467,050	4,935,380	-9.7%	59.0
Canada	3,482,730	3,470,690	-0.3	38.7
U.S.	3,024,500	3,100,950	2.5	33.9
China	1,571,406	2,083,213	32.6	22.2
Congo, Dem. Rep. of	1,603,630	1,525,780	-4.9	67.3
Australia	1,285,410	1,247,510	-2.9	16.2
Indonesia	1,185,450	910,100	-23.2	48.5
Peru	779,210	739,730	-5.1	57.8
India	639,390	706,820	10.5	23.8
Mexico	697,600	660,400	-5.3	34.0
Colombia	644,170	585,017	-9.2	52.7
Angola	609,760	578,560	-5.1	46.4
Bolivia	627,950	547,640	-12.8	50.6
Zambia	528,000	486,350	-7.9	65.4
Venezuela	520,260	466,830	-10.3	52.9
Tanzania	559,200	460,600	-17.6	52.0
Mozambique	433,780	379,400	-12.5	48.2
Papua New Guinea	336,270	335,590	-0.2	74.1
Myanmar	392,180	290,410	-25.9	44.5
Sweden	280,630	280,730	0.0	68.9
Argentina	347,930	271,120	-22.1	9.9%
Japan	249,500	249,580	0.0	68.5
Gabon	220,000	230,000	4.5	89.3
Congo Rep.	227,260	223,340	-1.7	65.4
Finland	218,750	222,180	1.6	73.1
Malaysia	223,760	221,950	-0.8	67.6
Central African Republic	225,600	221,700	-1.7	35.6
Sudan	NA	192,099	NA	NA
Cameroon	243,160	188,160	-22.6	39.8
Laos	176,449	187,614	6.3	81.3
Spain	138,095	184,179	33.4	36.9
Chile	152,630	177,350	16.2	23.9
France	144,360	169,890	17.7	31.0
Guyana	166,600	165,260	-0.8	84.0
Thailand	140,050	163,990	17.1	32.1
Suriname	154,300	153,320	-0.6	98.3
Paraguay	211,570	153,230	-27.6	38.6
Vietnam	93,630	147,730	57.8	47.6
Zimbabwe	221,640	140,620	-36.6	36.4
World	41,282,695	39,991,336	-3.1	30.8

NA = Not available.

Largest Trees in the U.S.

Source: American Forests

Nearly 900 native and naturalized species of trees grow in the U.S. The trunk of the world's largest known living tree, the General Sherman giant sequoia in California, weighs almost 1,400 tons—about as much as 15 adult blue whales. To determine the country's largest trees (or "national champions"), American Forests uses a point system whereby trunk circumference, or girth at 4.5 ft above ground level (in inches) + height (in feet) + ¼ average crown spread (in feet) = total points. As of May 27, 2020.

Tree type	Girth at 4.5 ft (in.)	Height (ft)	Crown spread (ft)	Total points	Location
Giant sequoia (Gen. Sherman tree)	1,020	274	107	1,321	Sequoia National Park, CA
Coast redwood	950	321	75	1,290	Jedediah Smith Redwoods State Park, CA
Sitka spruce	740	191	80	951	Olympic National Park, WA
Western redcedar	746	164	48	922	WA
Coast Douglas-fir	581	294	66	891	Lake Quinault, WA
Port-orford-cedar	522	242	35	773	Coos, OR
Bluegum Eucalyptus	586	141	126	759	Petrolia, CA
Common baldcypress	626	91	87	739	Cat Island National Wildlife Refuge, LA
Monterey cypress	588	102	111	718	Pescadero, CA
Fremont cottonwood	560	102	161	702	Yavapai, AZ

METEOROLOGY

National Weather Service Watches and Warnings

Source: National Weather Service, National Oceanic and Atmospheric Admin. (NOAA), U.S. Dept. of Commerce; *Glossary of Meteorology*, American Meteorological Society

The National Weather Service issues watches, warnings, and advisories for specific geographic areas to alert people to the possibility or imminent arrival of severe weather or of flooding. Often the weather hazard is a convective storm (a storm involving upward and downward movement of heat and moisture). A severe thunderstorm or tornado watch is issued when a severe convective storm, covering a relatively small geographic area or moving in a narrow path, is sufficiently intense to threaten life and property. Excessive localized convective rains are not classified as severe storms but are often the product of severe local storms. Such rainfall may result in phenomena, such as flash floods, that threaten life and property. Lightning occurs with all thunderstorms and, along with flash floods, is a leading cause of storm deaths and injuries.

Cyclone: Atmospheric circulation of winds rotating counterclockwise in the Northern Hemisphere and clockwise in the Southern Hemisphere. Tornadoes, hurricanes/typhoons, and the lows shown on weather maps are all examples of cyclones. Cyclones are usually accompanied by precipitation or stormy weather.

Severe thunderstorm: Thunderstorm (a local storm produced by a cumulonimbus cloud) that produces a tornado, winds of at least 50 knots (58 mph), and/or hail at least 1 in. in diameter. A severe thunderstorm watch indicates conditions are favorable for the development of a severe thunderstorm within 4 to 8 hours. A severe thunderstorm warning indicates a severe thunderstorm has been sighted by radar or reported by a spotter.

Tornado: Violently rotating column of air that extends from the base of a thunderstorm to the ground. On a local scale, it is the most destructive of all atmospheric phenomena. A tornado path can exceed 1 mi wide and 50 mi long and is generally less than 1.25 mi in diameter. The average forward speed is 30 mph, and wind speeds can reach 300 mph. A rotating column of air over water is called a **waterspout.**

Tropical storm: Cyclone that develops over tropical or subtropical waters with 1-min. sustained surface winds between 34 and 63 knots (39-73 mph). A tropical storm watch is issued when tropical storm conditions pose a threat to specified coastal areas within 48 hours. A tropical storm warning is issued when such conditions are expected in a specified coastal area within 36 hours.

Hurricane: Tropical cyclone having 1-min. sustained surface winds of 64 knots (74 mph) or more. (In the western North Pacific Ocean, west of the International Date Line, such storms are known as **typhoons.**) The hurricane-force winds form a circle or oval, sometimes as wide as 300 mi in diameter. In the lower latitudes, hurricanes usually move W or NW at 10-15 mph. When the center approaches 25° to 30° N, the direction of motion often changes to the NE, with increased forward speed. In the Atlantic, hurricane season is June 1-Nov. 30. Hurricane season is May 15-Nov. 30 in the eastern Pacific.

A hurricane warning is issued when a hurricane is forecast for an area within 36 hours.

Winter storm and **blizzard:** A winter storm watch is issued when there is a potential for heavy snow or significant ice accumulations, usually at least 24-36 hours in advance. A winter storm warning is issued when a winter storm is producing or is forecast to produce heavy snow or significant ice accumulations. A blizzard warning is issued for winter storm conditions in which winds are 35 mph or more, there is sufficient falling and/or blowing snow to frequently reduce visibility to less than ¼ mi, and the conditions are expected to prevail for at least 3 hours.

River flooding: Occurs when rains, sometimes coupled with melting snow, quickly fill river basins with an excess of water. Torrential rains from decaying hurricanes or tropical systems are also a major cause. **Coastal flooding:** Tropical storm and hurricane winds or intense offshore low-pressure systems can drive ocean water inland. Coastal floods can also be produced by sea waves called **tsunamis**, produced by earthquakes or underwater volcanic eruptions or landslides. **Flash flooding:** Usually due to copious amounts of rain falling in a short time. Ice can also cause flash flooding. When ice accumulates at natural or artificial obstructions, it can stop the flow of water. The resulting buildup of water can lead to flooding upstream. If the jam suddenly gives way, a flash flood can happen downstream. Flash flooding typically occurs within 6 hours of the causative event.

Flash floods account for the majority of flood deaths in the U.S. and are the leading cause of deaths associated with thunderstorms. Urbanization significantly increases runoff because less rain is absorbed by the terrain, making flash flooding in urban areas extremely dangerous. Streets can become swift-moving rivers, and basements can fill with water.

A flood watch indicates flooding or flash flooding is possible within a designated area. A flood warning indicates flooding is in progress, imminent, or highly likely.

National Weather Service Marine Warnings and Advisories

Primary sources of dissemination are mobile apps and push notifications, commercial radio, TV, U.S. Coast Guard radio, and National Oceanic and Atmospheric Admin. (NOAA) VHF radio broadcasts. The NOAA Weather Radio All Hazards (NWR) network broadcasts on seven frequencies between 162.40 and 162.55 MHz. These broadcasts can usually be received within about 40 mi of the transmission site using a special radio receiver. The following are examples of the warnings and advisories that may be addressed to mariners.

Small craft advisory: Alerts mariners to sustained weather and/or sea conditions, present or forecast, potentially hazardous to small boats, including winds 20-33 knots (23-38 mph) and/or dangerous wave conditions. The advisory is also issued when sea or lake ice exists that could be hazardous to small boats. Criteria vary depending on region and type of marine environment.

Special marine warning: Indicates potentially hazardous weather conditions not covered by existing marine warnings.

The conditions are usually of short duration (2 hr. or less) and involve wind speeds of 34 knots (39 mph) or more, and/or hail at least ¾ in. in diameter or waterspouts.

Gale warning: Indicates winds of 34-47 knots (39-54 mph) not directly associated with a tropical storm are forecast for the area.

Storm warning: Indicates winds 48-63 knots (55-73 mph) not directly associated with a tropical storm are forecast for the area.

Hurricane and Tornado Classifications

Source: National Weather Service, NOAA, U.S. Dept. of Commerce

The Saffir-Simpson Hurricane Wind Scale, created by Herbert Saffir and expanded upon by Robert Simpson, rates a hurricane's intensity from 1 to 5. The scale, updated in 2012, provides examples of the type of damage and impacts associated with winds of the indicated intensity. The Fujita (or F) Scale was created by T. Theodore Fujita in 1971 to classify tornadoes. The Enhanced Fujita Scale, an update, was implemented in the U.S. in 2007. It uses 3-sec. gusts estimated at the point of damage based on a judgment of eight levels of damage to 28 indicators.

Saffir-Simpson Hurricane Wind Scale			Enhanced Fujita Scale (Tornadoes)	
Category	Wind speed[1]	Summary of damage	Rank	3-sec. gust
1	74-95 mph	Very dangerous winds will produce some damage.	EF-0	65-85 mph
2	96-110 mph	Extremely dangerous winds will cause extensive damage.	EF-1	86-110 mph
3	111-129 mph	Devastating damage will occur.	EF-2	111-135 mph
4	130-156 mph	Catastrophic damage will occur.	EF-3	136-165 mph
5	157 mph or higher	Catastrophic damage will occur.	EF-4	166-200 mph
(1) 1-min. sustained winds.			EF-5	Over 200 mph

Monthly Normal Mean Temperatures, Precipitation in U.S. Cities

Source: National Climatic Data Center, NESDIS, NOAA, U.S. Dept. of Commerce

Normals are averages covering a 30-year period. The temperature and precipitation normals given here are based on records for 1981-2010. Temperatures listed below represent means of the normal daily maximum and normal daily minimum temperatures for each month. For stations that did not have continuous records from the same site for the entire 30 years, the means have been adjusted to the record at the present site. (*) = City station. Other figures are for airport stations. T = Temperature in Fahrenheit; P = Precipitation in inches.

	Jan.		Feb.		Mar.		Apr.		May		June		July		Aug.		Sept.		Oct.		Nov.		Dec.	
Station	T	P	T	P	T	P	T	P	T	P	T	P	T	P	T	P	T	P	T	P	T	P	T	P
Albany, NY	23	2.6	26	2.2	35	3.2	48	3.2	58	3.6	67	3.8	72	4.1	70	3.5	62	3.3	50	3.7	40	3.3	29	2.9
Albuquerque, NM	36	0.4	41	0.5	48	0.5	56	0.6	66	0.5	75	0.7	78	1.5	76	1.6	69	1.1	58	1.0	45	0.6	36	0.5
Anchorage, AK	17	0.7	20	0.7	27	0.6	37	0.5	48	0.7	55	1.0	59	1.8	57	3.3	49	3.0	35	2.0	22	1.2	19	1.1
Asheville, NC	37	3.7	40	3.8	47	3.8	55	3.3	63	3.7	71	4.7	74	4.3	73	4.4	66	3.8	56	2.9	47	3.7	39	3.6
Atlanta, GA	43	4.2	47	4.7	54	4.8	62	3.4	70	3.7	77	4.0	80	5.3	79	3.9	74	4.5	63	3.4	54	4.1	45	3.9
Atlantic City, NJ	33	3.2	35	2.9	42	4.2	52	3.6	61	3.4	71	3.1	76	3.7	74	4.1	67	3.2	56	3.4	47	3.3	37	3.7
Baltimore, MD	33	3.1	36	2.9	44	3.9	54	3.2	54	4.0	72	3.5	77	4.1	75	3.3	68	4.0	56	3.3	47	3.3	37	3.4
Barrow, AK	−13	0.1	−14	0.1	−13	0.1	2	0.2	21	0.2	36	0.3	41	1.0	39	1.1	32	0.1	17	0.4	−2	0.2	−8	0.1
Birmingham, AL	44	4.8	48	4.5	55	5.2	63	4.4	71	5.0	78	4.4	81	4.8	81	3.9	75	3.9	64	3.4	54	4.9	46	4.5
Bismarck, ND	13	0.4	18	0.5	30	0.9	44	1.3	56	2.4	65	3.2	71	2.9	70	2.3	59	1.6	45	1.3	29	0.7	16	0.5
Boise, ID	31	1.2	37	1.0	45	1.4	51	1.2	59	1.4	68	0.7	76	0.3	75	0.2	65	0.6	53	0.8	40	1.4	31	1.6
Boston, MA	29	3.4	32	3.3	38	4.3	48	3.7	58	3.5	68	3.7	73	3.4	72	3.4	65	3.4	54	3.9	45	4.0	35	3.8
Buffalo, NY	25	3.2	26	2.5	34	2.9	46	3.0	57	3.5	66	3.7	71	3.2	70	3.3	62	3.9	51	3.5	41	4.0	30	3.9
Burlington, VT	19	2.1	22	1.8	31	2.2	45	2.8	56	3.5	66	3.7	71	4.2	69	3.9	61	3.6	48	3.6	38	3.1	26	2.4
Caribou, ME	10	2.7	14	2.2	25	2.5	39	2.7	52	3.3	61	3.5	66	4.1	64	3.8	55	3.3	43	3.5	32	3.6	18	3.3
Charleston, SC	48	3.7	52	3.0	58	3.7	65	2.9	73	3.0	79	5.7	82	6.5	81	7.2	76	6.1	67	3.8	59	2.4	51	3.1
Charleston, WV	34	3.0	38	3.2	46	3.9	56	3.2	64	4.8	72	4.3	75	4.9	74	3.7	67	3.3	57	2.7	47	3.7	37	3.3
Chicago, IL	24	1.7	28	1.8	38	2.5	49	3.4	59	3.7	69	3.5	74	3.7	72	4.9	65	3.2	53	3.2	40	3.2	28	2.3
Cleveland, OH	28	2.7	31	2.3	38	2.9	50	3.5	60	3.7	69	3.4	74	3.5	72	3.5	65	3.8	54	3.1	44	3.6	32	3.1
Columbus, OH	30	2.7	33	2.3	42	3.0	53	3.4	63	4.2	72	4.0	75	4.8	74	3.3	67	2.8	55	2.6	44	3.2	34	3.0
Dallas-Ft. Worth, TX	46	2.1	50	2.7	58	3.5	66	3.1	74	4.9	81	3.8	85	2.2	86	1.9	78	2.6	68	4.2	57	2.7	47	2.6
Denver, CO	31	0.4	33	0.3	40	0.9	47	1.7	57	2.2	67	2.0	74	3.0	73	1.6	63	1.0	51	1.0	38	0.6	30	0.3
Des Moines, IA	23	1.0	27	1.3	39	2.3	52	3.9	62	4.7	72	4.9	76	4.5	74	4.1	66	3.1	53	2.6	39	2.2	26	1.4
Detroit, MI	26	2.0	28	2.0	37	2.3	49	2.9	60	3.4	69	3.5	74	3.4	72	3.0	64	3.3	52	2.5	42	2.8	30	2.4
Dodge City, KS	32	0.6	36	0.7	44	1.6	54	1.8	64	2.9	74	3.2	80	3.1	78	2.8	69	1.7	57	1.7	43	0.8	33	0.8
Duluth, MN	10	1.0	15	0.8	26	1.5	40	2.4	51	3.2	60	4.2	66	3.9	64	3.7	56	4.1	43	2.9	29	2.1	15	1.2
Fairbanks, AK	−8	0.6	−1	0.4	11	0.3	33	0.3	49	0.6	60	1.4	63	2.2	56	1.9	45	1.1	24	0.8	3	0.7	−4	0.6
Fresno, CA	47	2.2	52	2.0	57	2.0	62	1.0	70	0.4	77	0.2	83	0.0	82	0.0	76	0.2	66	0.6	54	1.1	47	1.8
Galveston, TX*	53	3.7	55	3.0	61	2.9	68	2.2	76	3.0	82	4.8	84	3.9	84	3.4	80	5.4	73	4.2	64	3.4	56	3.4
Grand Rapids, MI	24	2.1	27	1.8	36	2.4	48	3.4	59	4.0	68	3.8	73	3.8	71	3.6	63	4.3	51	3.3	40	3.5	29	2.5
Helena, MT	23	0.4	28	0.3	36	0.6	45	1.0	54	1.9	62	2.1	70	1.2	68	1.2	58	1.1	46	0.7	33	0.5	22	0.4
Honolulu, HI	73	2.3	73	2.0	75	2.0	76	0.6	78	0.6	80	0.3	81	0.5	82	0.6	82	0.7	80	1.8	78	2.4	75	3.2
Houston, TX	53	3.4	56	3.2	63	3.4	70	3.3	77	5.1	82	5.9	84	3.8	85	3.8	80	4.1	72	5.7	62	4.3	54	3.7
Huron, SD	17	0.5	22	0.6	33	1.5	47	2.3	58	3.1	68	3.9	74	2.9	72	2.4	62	2.5	48	1.8	33	0.9	19	0.5
Indianapolis, IN	28	2.7	32	2.3	42	3.6	53	3.8	63	5.1	72	4.3	75	4.6	74	3.1	67	3.1	55	3.1	44	3.7	32	3.2
Jackson, MS	46	5.0	50	4.8	57	5.0	64	5.0	72	4.4	79	4.1	82	4.8	81	4.2	76	3.0	65	3.9	56	4.8	48	5.2
Jacksonville, FL	53	3.3	56	3.2	62	4.0	67	2.6	74	2.5	80	6.5	82	6.6	82	6.8	78	8.2	70	3.9	62	2.1	55	2.8
Juneau, AK	28	5.4	30	4.1	34	3.8	41	2.9	49	3.4	55	3.2	57	4.6	56	5.7	50	8.6	42	8.6	33	6.0	30	5.8
Kansas City, MO	29	1.1	34	1.5	44	2.4	55	3.7	65	5.2	74	5.2	78	4.5	77	3.9	68	4.6	56	3.2	44	2.2	32	1.5
Knoxville, TN	38	4.3	42	4.3	50	4.3	59	4.0	67	4.5	75	3.8	78	5.1	78	3.3	71	3.2	60	2.5	50	4.0	41	4.5
Lander, WY	22	0.4	25	0.6	36	1.2	44	1.9	53	2.2	63	1.3	71	0.8	70	0.6	59	1.1	46	1.3	31	0.9	21	0.6
Lexington, KY	33	3.2	37	3.2	46	4.1	55	3.6	64	5.3	73	4.4	76	4.7	75	3.3	68	2.9	57	3.1	46	3.5	36	3.9
Little Rock, AR	41	3.6	45	3.7	53	4.7	62	5.1	71	4.9	79	3.7	83	3.3	83	2.6	75	3.2	64	4.9	53	5.3	43	5.0
Los Angeles, CA*	58	3.1	59	3.8	61	2.4	63	0.9	66	0.3	69	0.1	73	0.0	74	0.0	73	0.2	69	0.7	62	1.0	58	2.3
Louisville, KY	35	3.2	39	3.2	48	4.2	58	4.0	67	5.3	76	3.8	79	4.2	78	3.3	71	3.1	60	3.2	49	3.6	38	3.8
Marquette, MI*	19	1.8	21	1.3	29	2.0	40	2.5	51	2.5	60	2.7	67	2.8	67	2.6	59	3.2	47	3.1	35	2.6	24	2.0
Memphis, TN	41	4.0	46	4.4	54	5.2	63	5.5	72	5.3	80	3.6	83	4.6	82	2.9	75	3.1	64	4.0	53	5.5	44	5.7
Miami, FL	68	1.6	70	2.3	73	3.0	76	3.1	80	5.3	83	9.7	84	6.5	84	8.9	83	9.9	80	6.3	75	3.3	71	2.0
Milwaukee, WI	22	1.8	26	1.7	35	2.3	46	3.6	56	3.4	66	3.9	72	3.7	71	4.0	63	3.2	51	2.7	39	2.7	27	2.0
Minneapolis, MN	16	0.9	21	0.8	33	1.9	48	2.7	59	3.4	69	4.2	74	4.0	71	4.3	62	3.1	49	2.4	34	1.8	20	1.2
Mobile, AL	50	5.7	54	5.1	60	6.1	66	4.8	74	5.1	80	6.1	82	7.2	82	7.0	78	5.1	68	3.7	60	5.1	52	5.1
Moline, IL	23	1.5	27	1.6	39	2.9	51	3.6	62	4.3	72	4.5	75	4.3	74	4.5	65	3.1	53	3.0	40	2.6	27	2.2
Nashua, NH	24	3.7	27	3.2	35	4.3	46	4.0	57	2.9	66	4.3	71	3.7	70	4.5	62	3.4	50	4.7	40	4.1	30	3.7
Nashville, TN	38	3.8	42	3.9	50	4.1	59	4.0	68	5.5	76	4.1	79	3.6	79	3.2	72	3.4	60	3.0	50	4.3	40	4.2
New Orleans, LA	53	5.2	57	5.3	63	4.6	69	4.6	77	4.6	82	8.1	83	5.9	83	6.0	80	5.1	71	3.6	63	4.5	56	5.3
New York, NY*	33	3.7	35	3.1	43	4.4	53	4.5	62	4.2	71	4.4	77	4.6	75	4.4	68	4.3	57	4.4	48	4.0	38	4.0
Newark, NJ	32	3.5	35	2.9	42	4.2	53	4.2	63	4.1	72	4.0	77	4.8	76	3.7	68	3.8	57	3.6	47	3.7	37	3.8
Norfolk, VA	40	3.4	43	3.1	49	3.7	58	3.4	67	3.4	75	4.3	80	5.1	78	5.5	72	4.8	62	3.4	53	3.2	44	3.3
Oklahoma City, OK	39	1.4	44	1.6	52	3.1	61	3.1	70	4.7	78	4.9	83	2.9	82	3.3	74	4.1	63	3.7	51	2.0	41	1.9
Omaha, NE	24	0.7	28	0.9	40	2.0	52	3.0	62	4.8	72	4.2	77	3.8	75	3.8	66	2.7	53	2.2	39	1.6	26	1.0
Philadelphia, PA	33	3.0	36	2.7	44	3.8	54	3.6	64	3.7	73	3.4	78	4.4	77	3.5	69	3.8	58	3.2	48	3.0	38	3.6
Phoenix, AZ	56	0.9	60	0.9	65	1.0	73	0.3	82	0.1	91	0.0	95	1.1	94	1.0	88	0.6	77	0.6	64	0.7	55	0.9
Pittsburgh, PA	29	2.7	32	2.7	40	3.1	52	3.2	61	4.2	69	4.0	73	3.8	72	3.5	65	3.4	53	2.5	43	3.4	33	2.9
Portland, ME	22	3.4	26	3.3	34	4.2	44	4.3	54	4.0	63	3.8	69	3.6	68	3.1	60	3.7	49	4.9	39	4.9	29	4.0
Portland, OR	41	4.9	44	3.7	48	3.7	52	2.7	58	2.5	64	1.7	69	0.7	70	0.7	65	1.5	55	3.0	47	5.6	40	5.5
Providence, RI	29	3.9	32	3.3	39	5.0	49	4.4	59	3.6	68	3.6	74	3.3	72	3.6	65	3.9	54	3.9	45	4.5	34	4.2
Raleigh, NC	41	3.5	45	3.2	52	4.1	60	2.9	68	3.3	76	3.5	80	4.7	79	4.3	72	4.4	61	3.3	52	3.1	44	3.1
Rapid City, SD	25	0.3	27	0.4	35	0.9	45	1.8	55	3.2	65	2.5	73	1.9	72	1.6	61	1.3	48	1.4	35	0.5	25	0.4
Reno, NV	36	1.0	40	1.0	46	0.8	51	0.5	60	0.5	68	0.5	75	0.2	73	0.2	65	0.4	54	0.5	43	0.8	35	1.0
Richmond, VA	38	3.0	41	2.8	49	4.0	58	3.3	66	3.8	75	3.9	79	4.5	78	4.7	71	4.1	60	3.0	50	3.2	41	3.3
St. Louis, MO	32	2.4	36	2.2	46	3.3	57	3.7	67	4.7	76	4.3	80	4.1	79	3.0	70	3.1	59	3.3	47	3.9	35	2.8
Salt Lake City, UT	30	1.3	34	1.3	44	1.8	51	2.0	60	2.0	70	1.0	79	0.6	77	0.7	66	1.2	53	1.5	40	1.5	30	1.4
San Antonio, TX	52	1.8	56	1.8	62	2.3	69	2.1	77	4.0	82	4.1	85	2.7	85	2.1	80	3.0	71	4.1	61	2.3	53	1.9
San Diego, CA	57	2.0	58	2.3	59	1.8	62	0.8	64	0.1	66	0.1	70	0.0	72	0.0	71	0.2	67	0.6	61	1.0	57	1.5
San Francisco, CA	50	4.2	53	4.1	55	3.0	57	1.3	60	0.5	62	0.1	64	0.0	65	0.0	65	0.2	62	1.0	56	2.4	51	4.0
San Juan, PR	78	3.8	78	2.4	79	2.0	80	4.7	82	5.9	83	4.4	83	5.1	84	5.5	84	5.8	83	5.6	81	6.4	79	5.0
Santa Fe, NM	32	0.6	36	0.5	43	0.8	50	0.7	60	0.9	69	1.1	73	1.8	71	2.6	64	1.6	53	1.4	40	0.7	31	0.8
Savannah, GA	50	3.7	53	2.8	59	3.7	66	3.1	73	3.0	80	6.0	83	5.6	82	6.6	77	4.6	68	3.7	59	2.4	52	3.0
Seattle, WA	42	5.6	43	3.5	47	3.7	50	2.7	56	1.9	61	1.6	66	0.7	66	0.9	61	1.5	53	3.5	45	6.6	41	5.4
Spokane, WA	30	1.8	33	1.3	40	1.6	47	1.3	55	1.6	62	1.3	70	0.6	69	0.6	60	0.7	48	1.2	36	2.3	27	2.3
Springfield, MO	33	2.5	37	2.5	46	3.6	56	4.3	65	5.1	73	4.9	78	3.7	78	3.6	69	4.6	58	3.6	46	4.2	35	3.0
Tampa, FL	61	2.2	63	2.8	67	3.0	72	2.0	78	2.1	82	6.7	83	7.1	83	7.8	82	6.3	76	2.3	69	1.6	63	2.5
Washington, DC	36	2.8	39	2.6	47	3.5	57	3.1	66	4.0	75	3.8	80	3.7	78	2.9	71	3.7	60	3.4	50	3.2	40	3.1
Wilmington, DE	32	3.0	35	2.7	43	3.9	53	3.5	63	4.0	72	3.9	77	4.6	75	3.2	68	4.3	56	3.4	47	3.1	37	3.5
Windsor Locks, CT	26	3.2	30	2.9	38	3.6	49	3.7	60	4.4	69	4.4	74	4.2	72	3.9	64	3.9	52	4.4	42	3.9	32	3.4

Normal High and Low Temperatures, Precipitation in U.S. Cities

Source: National Climatic Data Center, NESDIS, NOAA, U.S. Dept. of Commerce

The normal temperatures and precipitation data given here are based on records for the period 1981-2010. The extreme temperatures are based on records from the time of each station's installation. (*) = City station. Other figures are for airport stations.

| | | NORMAL TEMPERATURE (°F) | | | | EXTREME | | AVG. ANNUAL |
| | | January | | July | | TEMPERATURE (°F) | | PRECIPITATION |
State	Station	Max.	Min.	Max.	Min.	Highest	Lowest	(in.)
Alabama	Mobile	61	40	91	73	105	3	66.15
Alaska	Anchorage	23	11	65	52	85	−34	16.58
Alaska	Barrow	−7	−20	47	35	79	−56	4.53
Alaska	Juneau	33	24	64	50	90	−22	62.27
Arizona	Phoenix	67	46	106	78	122	17	8.03
Arkansas	North Little Rock	50	33	92	73	111	−6	50.03
California	Los Angeles	65	49	74	64	110	23	12.82
California	San Francisco	56	44	72	55	106	20	20.65
Colorado	Denver	44	17	89	59	105	−19	14.92
Connecticut	Windsor Locks	35	18	85	63	102	−26	45.85
Delaware	Wilmington	40	25	86	68	103	11	43.08
District of Columbia	Washington–Reagan	43	29	88	71	105	−5	39.74
Florida	Jacksonville	65	41	92	73	105	7	52.39
Florida	Miami	76	60	91	77	98	30	61.90
Georgia	Atlanta	52	34	89	71	105	−8	49.71
Georgia	Savannah	60	39	92	73	105	3	47.96
Hawaii	Honolulu	80	66	88	75	95	53	17.10
Idaho	Boise	38	25	91	60	111	−25	11.73
Illinois	Chicago	31	17	84	64	104	−27	36.89
Indiana	Indianapolis	36	21	85	66	104	−27	42.44
Iowa	Des Moines	31	14	86	67	108	−26	36.01
Kansas	Dodge City	44	20	93	66	110	−21	21.60
Kentucky	Lexington	41	25	86	66	103	−21	45.17
Kentucky	Louisville	43	27	89	70	106	−22	44.91
Louisiana	New Orleans	62	45	91	75	102	11	62.66
Maine	Caribou	20	1	76	55	96	−41	38.49
Maine	Portland	31	13	79	59	103	−39	47.25
Maryland	Baltimore	41	24	87	67	105	−7	41.88
Massachusetts	Boston	36	22	81	65	102	−12	43.77
Michigan	Detroit	32	19	83	64	104	−21	33.47
Michigan	Grand Rapids	31	18	83	62	100	−22	38.27
Michigan	Sault Ste. Marie	23	8	76	54	98	−36	32.95
Minnesota	Duluth	19	2	76	55	97	−39	30.96
Minnesota	Minneapolis	24	8	83	64	105	−34	30.61
Mississippi	Jackson	56	35	92	72	107	2	54.14
Missouri	Kansas City	38	20	88	68	109	−23	38.86
Missouri	St. Louis	40	24	89	71	107	−18	40.96
Montana	Helena	33	13	86	54	105	−42	11.22
Nebraska	Omaha	33	14	87	66	114	−23	30.62
Nevada	Reno	46	25	92	58	108	−16	7.40
New Hampshire	Concord	31	10	82	58	102	−37	40.61
New Jersey	Atlantic City	42	25	86	67	106	−11	41.75
New Mexico	Albuquerque	47	26	90	66	107	−17	9.45
New York	Albany	31	15	82	61	100	−28	39.35
New York	Buffalo	31	19	80	62	99	−20	40.48
New York	New York–Central Park*	38	27	84	69	106	−15	49.94
North Carolina	Raleigh	51	31	90	70	105	−9	43.34
North Dakota	Bismarck	23	2	85	57	112	−44	17.85
Ohio	Cleveland	34	22	84	64	104	−20	39.14
Ohio	Columbus	37	23	85	66	102	−22	39.31
Oklahoma	Oklahoma City	50	29	94	72	110	−8	36.52
Oregon	Portland	47	36	81	58	107	−3	36.03
Pennsylvania	Philadelphia	40	26	87	69	104	−7	41.53
Pennsylvania	Pittsburgh	36	21	83	63	103	−22	38.19
Puerto Rico	San Juan	83	72	89	78	98	60	56.35
Rhode Island	Providence	37	21	83	64	104	−13	47.18
South Carolina	Charleston	59	38	91	73	105	6	51.03
South Dakota	Huron	27	7	86	61	112	−41	22.90
South Dakota	Rapid City	37	13	87	58	111	−31	16.29
Tennessee	Memphis	50	33	92	74	108	−13	53.68
Tennessee	Nashville	47	28	89	68	107	−17	47.25
Texas	Dallas-Fort Worth	56	36	96	75	113	−1	36.14
Texas	Houston	63	43	94	75	109	7	49.77
Utah	Salt Lake City	37	22	93	65	107	−30	16.10
Vermont	Burlington	27	10	81	60	101	−30	36.82
Virginia	Norfolk	48	33	87	72	105	−3	46.53
Virginia	Richmond	47	28	90	69	105	−12	43.60
Washington	Seattle-Tacoma	47	37	76	56	103	0	37.49
Washington	Spokane	34	25	83	56	108	−25	16.56
West Virginia	Charleston	43	26	85	66	104	−16	44.03
Wisconsin	Milwaukee	29	16	80	64	103	−26	34.76
Wyoming	Lander	33	10	87	56	101	−37	12.66

Mean annual snowfall (in.), selected cities: Based on climate normals 1981-2010: Albany, NY, 59.1; Anchorage, AK, 74.5; Boston, MA, 43.8; Burlington, VT, 81.2; Lander, WY, 91.4; Sault Ste. Marie, MI, 123.4.

Wettest spot: Mt. Waialeale in Kauai, HI, may be the rainiest place in the U.S. It has a recorded average annual rainfall of 460 in.

Temperature extremes: The highest temperature ever recorded under standard conditions in the U.S. was 134°F in Death Valley, CA, on July 10, 1913. The record low in the U.S. was −80°F at Prospect Creek, AK, Jan. 23, 1971.

Annual Climatological Data for U.S. Cities, 2019

Source: National Climatic Data Center, NESDIS, NOAA, U.S. Dept. of Commerce

| Station | Elev. (ft) | TEMPERATURE (°F) | | | | PRECIPITATION | | | Snowfall[1] | | | FASTEST WIND[2] | | NO. OF DAYS | |
		Highest	Date	Lowest	Date	Total (in.)	Greatest in 24 hrs. (in.)	Date	Total snowfall (in.)	Greatest in 24 hrs. (in.)	Date	MPH	Date	Prec. 0.01 in. or more	Snow, sleet 1 in. or more
Albany, NY	281	95	7/20	-8	2/1	—	—	—	71.9	13.3	12/1	47	2/25	—	—
Albuquerque, NM	5,308	100	7/20+	7	1/3	8.78	1.06	7/25	10.6	3.6	2/22	53	3/8	54	3
Anchorage, AK	222	90	7/4	-2	1/7+	14.56	0.88	9/17-18	58.1	8.4	11/16	36	8/18	125	20
Asheville, NC	2,174	91	10/3+	11	1/21	57.25	5.29	4/19	T	T	12/11+	40	12/17	125	0
Atlanta, GA	974	100	8/13	22	1/21	43.74	4.19	6/7-8	0.0	0.0	—	44	6/23	119	0
Atlantic City, NJ	117	100	7/21	6	2/2	44.84	2.55	7/11	13.5	4.6	1/13	43	4/15	138	5
Baltimore, MD	196	100	7/21+	5	1/31	38.13	1.85	3/21-22	16.9	4.8	1/13	40	2/25	127	5
Barrow, AK	38	73	6/20	-37	2/14	10.12	0.57	8/13-14	—	—	—	40	2/8	130	—
Birmingham, AL	630	101	10/3	18	11/13	52.55	3.31	10/30-31	T	T	3/25	39	7/7	122	0
Bismarck, ND	1,654	94	8/6	-33	1/30	29.58	21.00	2/3	84.7	9.5	3/9	52	8/6	125	23
Boise, ID	2,861	102	7/22	10	2/22	14.54	0.83	5/28	16.9	3.6	2/20	37	9/8	100	5
Boston, MA	180	98	7/21	5	1/31+	50.38	2.43	4/22-23	38.7	9.9	3/4	55	10/17	155	13
Buffalo, NY	717	90	7/10	-4	2/1	47.82	2.14	9/11	119.9	17.2	1/25	49	2/24	177	30
Burlington, VT	348	94	7/20	-16	1/22	43.47	3.30	10/31	100.3	15.6	1/20	36	4/18	169	28
Caribou, ME	626	91	7/5	-19	2/18	41.54	1.70	10/23	154.5	16.9	1/20	37	11/1	158	34
Charleston, SC	48	101	5/29+	27	1/30	49.45	4.47	9/4-5	0.0	0.0	—	52	9/5	102	0
Cheyenne, WY	6,128	95	9/2	-16	3/4	18.03	5.96	11/25-26	102.1	14.0	3/13	53	2/3	116	27
Chicago, IL	658	95	7/20	-23	1/30	49.54	2.47	9/27-28	45.7	5.4	4/14	46	6/30	151	14
Cleveland, OH	805	95	7/20	-3	1/30	39.98	1.62	6/20	36.8	6.2	1/19	48	2/24	163	12
Columbus, OH	812	94	10/2+	-4	1/31+	43.94	2.66	6/19-20	30.0	4.2	2/1	45	4/14	137	9
Dallas-Ft. Worth, TX	562	102	8/26+	21	3/5+	34.52	3.31	4/23-24	T	T	4/13	60	3/13	84	0
Denver, CO	5,382	101	7/19	-11	2/7	15.51	1.12	5/20-21	68.9	8.5	11/26	60	3/13	90	25
Des Moines, IA	971	96	7/19	-20	1/30	49.35	3.92	10/1-2	54.4	5.4	2/17	46	1/28	132	16
Detroit, MI	631	89	7/15+	-31	1/31	34.34	1.72	12/1	129.6	14.5	11/30	43	4/11	149	31
Duluth, MN	1,429	89	6/29	-44	1/12	16.40	1.60	8/2-3	69.7	5.3	2/12	30	4/3	121	26
Fairbanks, AK	464	89	6/29	-44	1/12	12.40	0.82	5/15-16	0.0	0.0	—	40	4/9	60	0
Fresno, CA	375	108	8/16	32	2/6	12.46	1.25	5/23	T	T	—	44	7/20	177	25
Grand Rapids, MI	788	92	7/20	-10	1/31	51.37	2.56	9/22	84.8	5.5	11/11	43	10/22	109	26
Helena, MT	3,867	96	8/5+	-30	3/4	16.50	1.38	7/8-9	65.2	4.6	2/25	39	2/10	85	—
Honolulu, HI	18	95	8/31	61	3/2	16.61	5.01	6/25-26	—	—	—	39	5/9	119	0
Houston, TX	107	103	8/13	30	11/13	51.93	9.39	9/18-19	T	T	6/28	39	5/9	125	21
Huron, SD	1,284	99	6/29	-30	1/30	37.30	3.71	8/2	79.2	10.0	4/11	55	7/13	125	0
Indianapolis, IN	797	94	6/30	-11	1/30	47.16	4.01	6/15-16	28.9	6.9	1/12	47	8/20	134	8
Jackson, MS	296	101	7/10	22	11/13	64.16	4.55	10/14-15	T	—	—	36	4/13	123	—
Jacksonville, FL	34	100	5/27	30	1/31	46.33	3.30	11/14-15	0.0	0.0	—	40	6/4	123	0
Kansas City, MO	1,008	97	7/20+	-6	1/30	53.21	3.51	6/22-23	26.4	3.8	2/15	45	5/21	116	9
Knoxville, TN	982	97	9/13+	14	1/21	64.29	5.08	2/23	3.8	1.8	1/29	47	5/18	130	2
Las Vegas, NV	2,091	113	8/5	28	1/2	6.87	1.11	2/14	0.8	0.5	2/20	39	10/10	36	0
Lexington, KY	984	100	9/10	2	1/31	56.04	2.63	11/30	10.5	2.1	1/12	44	3/14	132	6
Los Angeles, CA	185	97	10/24+	38	1/30	21.55	2.19	2/13-14	—	—	—	21	12/26	44	—
Louisville, KY	484	99	9/10	3	1/30	53.31	3.02	11/29-30	12.0	2.1	1/12	44	6/23	130	7
Marquette, MI	1,415	88	7/10	-26	12/28+	45.77	3.02	11/27	213.0	16.5	2/12	—	—	179	54
Memphis, TN	286	100	9/16	17	11/13	73.65	4.36	10/6-7	0.2	0.2	1/19	48	6/19	120	0
Miami, FL	29	98	7/2	46	1/21	67.15	3.73	6/7-8	—	—	—	31	6/28	155	—
Milwaukee, WI	680	94	7/10	-23	1/31	46.01	2.46	10/1-2	63.7	8.3	2/12	37	5/19	147	16
Minneapolis, MN	874	95	7/19	-28	1/30	43.17	2.02	7/1	91.7	9.1	2/20	38	4/11	134	23
Mobile, AL	212	100	9/18	26	11/13	64.70	3.83	7/12-13	T	T	1/20	48	6/28	122	0
Moline, IL	607	97	7/20	-33	1/31	49.59	2.68	4/28-29	54.3	6.9	1/12	44	5/21	142	18
Nashville, TN	574	99	10/3+	16	1/31	64.27	4.05	2/6-7	0.7	0.4	11/11	41	6/26	126	0
New Orleans, LA	7	99	9/8+	34	11/13	62.53	6.24	10/25	—	—	—	48	10/26	109	—
New York, NY	161	93	10/2	2	12/31	47.33	1.83	10/16	16.3	4.0	3/2	—	—	143	6
Norfolk, VA	69	100	7/22+	20	1/22+	46.18	2.93	8/7	T	T	12/2	39	9/6	120	0
North Little Rock, AR	565	96	9/18+	17	3/4	68.21	4.46	4/18	T	T	12/19	—	—	127	0
Oklahoma City, OK	1,284	100	8/12	9	3/4	45.34	3.50	5/20-21	4.8	4.5	1/3	49	8/17	95	1
Philadelphia, PA	62	98	7/21	5	1/31	47.43	4.63	6/19-20	13.3	3.0	3/1	52	4/15	146	5
Phoenix, AZ	1,106	115	8/5	30	1/2	5.93	1.19	2/21-22	—	—	—	43	9/1	43	—
Pittsburgh, PA	1,175	90	9/11	-5	1/31+	52.46	3.53	9/1-2	38.6	4.2	2/20	40	1/8	170	15
Portland, ME	72	94	7/21	-2	2/2	52.40	3.77	12/13-14	71.0	9.8	12/30	46	10/17	145	20
Portland, OR	223	98	8/28+	23	2/7+	26.67	1.19	9/17-18	7.0	4.9	2/9	40	1/5	143	1
Providence, RI	53	96	7/21	1	1/21	51.97	2.33	1/24	31.1	5.2	3/4	44	11/1	154	10
Raleigh-Durham, NC	430	100	10/3	17	1/22+	42.97	2.02	4/8-9	T	T	11/12	36	7/11	126	0
Rapid City, SD	3,153	92	9/2	-19	2/7	—	—	—	—	—	—	54	3/14	—	—
Reno, NV	4,407	100	8/15	10	2/11	11.14	1.27	2/13-14	29.0	4.1	2/10	54	2/26	64	10
Richmond, VA	167	100	7/21	13	1/31	42.88	2.60	7/3-4	2.6	1.0	1/12	40	7/3	128	1
St. Louis, MO	710	97	8/19	-6	1/30	53.99	3.30	7/22	23.9	7.8	1/11	43	11/27	135	8
Salt Lake City, UT	4,224	103	7/22	6	1/1	20.10	1.15	3/28-29	44.3	4.5	11/28	43	7/4	105	15
San Antonio, TX	821	103	8/13	27	12/19	22.02	3.20	10/24-25	T	T	2/8	45	6/24	85	0
San Diego, CA	81	94	10/24	41	12/18+	15.28	1.59	11/28-29	—	—	—	38	12/26	62	—
San Francisco, CA	89	100	6/10	38	11/30	23.49	1.71	2/13-14	—	—	—	47	2/14	78	—
San Juan, PR	10	95	9/21	69	1/26	46.92	2.86	9/5-6	0.0	0.0	—	32	4/14	221	0
Sault Ste. Marie, MI	727	88	7/19	-24	1/30	46.16	3.00	9/30	158.0	12.3	1/7	35	2/25	189	46
Savannah, GA	143	102	5/26	29	1/31+	51.36	4.82	6/11-12	0.0	0.0	—	48	4/19	104	0
Scottsbluff, NE	3,949	102	7/18	-16	3/4	19.91	1.59	5/27-28	86.4	12.0	3/13	54	8/20	117	25
Seattle, WA	434	95	6/12	20	2/6+	33.88	3.77	12/19-20	21.0	6.4	2/8	44	1/6	141	6
Spokane, WA	2,384	98	8/7	-1	3/1	15.45	0.90	5/16-17	56.9	7.2	2/11	52	7/23	107	18
Springfield, MO	1,280	97	8/20	3	3/4	54.47	4.29	5/23	5.1	1.2	1/29	41	3/9	129	1
Tampa, FL	40	98	6/25	40	1/21	60.76	3.66	7/9	0.0	0.0	—	36	1/20	129	0
Washington, DC	3	99	7/21	10	1/31	42.34	3.44	7/8	15.9	8.3	1/13	45	3/22	120	3
Wilmington, DE	77	98	10/2	5	1/31	47.97	2.39	6/19-20	17.8	3.9	2/11	52	7/22	131	6
Windsor Locks, CT	165	100	7/21	-7	1/31	52.46	2.45	1/24	83.6	—	2/25	47	2/25	147	16

(+) = Indicates value for extreme also occurred on an earlier date(s). (T) = Trace amount. — = Data not available or unreported. (1) Comprises all forms of frozen precipitation, including hail and sleet. (2) Sustained for at least 2 min., not peak gust.

Record Temperatures by State

Source: National Climatic Data Center, NESDIS, NOAA, U.S. Dept. of Commerce
(as of May 13, 2020)

State	|	LOWEST TEMPERATURE		Approx. elevation (ft)	|	HIGHEST TEMPERATURE		Approx. elevation (ft)
	°F	Date	Station		°F	Date	Station	
Alabama	−27	Jan. 30, 1966	New Market	732	112	Sept. 6, 1925	Centreville	220
Alaska	−80	Jan. 23, 1971	Prospect Creek Camp	955	100	June 27, 1915	Fort Yukon	445
Arizona	−40	Jan. 7, 1971	Hawley Lake	8,180	128	June 29, 1994	Lake Havasu City	449
Arkansas	−29	Feb. 13, 1905	Gravette	1,260	120	Aug. 10, 1936	Ozark	390
California	−45	Jan. 20, 1937	Boca	5,575	134	July 10, 1913	Greenland Ranch	−194
Colorado	−61	Feb. 1, 1985	Maybell	5,944	115	July 20, 2019	John Martin Dam	3,814
Connecticut	−32	Jan. 22, 1961[1]	Coventry	480	106	July 15, 1995[1]	Danbury	405
Delaware	−17	Jan. 17, 1893	Millsboro	20	110	July 21, 1930	Millsboro	20
Florida	−2	Feb. 13, 1899	Tallahassee	192	109	June 29, 1931	Monticello	98
Georgia	−17	Jan. 27, 1940	CCC Fire Camp F-16	1,000	112	Aug. 20, 1983[1]	Greenville	960
Hawaii	12	May 17, 1979	Mauna Kea Observ.	13,773	100	Apr. 27, 1931	Pahala	840
Idaho	−60	Jan. 18, 1943	Island Park	6,290	118	July 28, 1934	Orofino	1,320
Illinois	−38	Jan. 31, 2019	Mount Carroll	640	117	July 14, 1954	East St. Louis	410
Indiana	−36	Jan. 19, 1994	New Whiteland	785	116	July 14, 1936	Collegeville	650
Iowa	−47	Feb. 3, 1996[1]	Elkader	788	118	July 20, 1934	Keokuk	651
Kansas	−40	Feb. 13, 1905	Lebanon	1,841	121	July 24, 1936[1]	Alton	1,685
Kentucky	−37	Jan. 19, 1994	Shelbyville	730	114	July 28, 1930	Greensburg	590
Louisiana	−16	Feb. 13, 1899	Minden	185	114	Aug. 10, 1936	Plain Dealing	251
Maine	−50	Jan. 16, 2009	Big Black River	885	105	July 10, 1911[1]	North Bridgton	449
Maryland	−40	Jan. 13, 1912	Oakland	2,420	109	July 10, 1936[2]	Frederick	380
Massachusetts	−35	Jan. 12, 1981[1]	Chester	640	107	Aug. 2, 1975[3]	Chester	640
Michigan	−51	Feb. 9, 1934	Vanderbilt	905	112	July 13, 1936[3]	Stanwood	830
Minnesota	−60	Feb. 2, 1996	Tower	1,430	115	July 29, 1917[1]	Beardsley	1,089
Mississippi	−19	Jan. 30, 1966	Corinth	385	115	July 29, 1930	Holly Springs	502
Missouri	−40	Feb. 13, 1905	Warsaw	705	118	July 14, 1954[2]	Warsaw	705
Montana	−70	Jan. 20, 1954	Rogers Pass	5,545	117	July 5, 1937[1]	Medicine Lake	1,942
Nebraska	−47	Dec. 22, 1989[1]	Oshkosh	3,390	118	July 24, 1936[1]	Minden	2,160
Nevada	−50	Jan. 8, 1937	San Jacinto	5,203	125	June 29, 1994	Laughlin	605
New Hampshire	−50	Jan. 22, 1885	Mt. Washington	6,271	106	July 4, 1911	Nashua	135
New Jersey	−34	Jan. 5, 1904	River Vale	31	110	July 10, 1936	Runyon	20
New Mexico	−50	Feb. 1, 1951	Gavilan	7,425	122	June 27, 1994	Waste Isolat. Pilot Plant	3,411
New York	−52	Feb. 18, 1979[1]	Old Forge	1,748	108	July 22, 1926	Troy	35
North Carolina	−34	Jan. 21, 1985	Mt. Mitchell	6,240	110	Aug. 21, 1983	Fayetteville	186
North Dakota	−60	Feb. 15, 1936	Parshall	1,950	121	July 6, 1936	Steele	1,853
Ohio	−39	Feb. 10, 1899	Milligan	875	113	July 21, 1934	Gallipolis	569
Oklahoma	−31	Feb. 10, 2011	Nowata	NA	120	Aug. 12, 1936[1]	Altus Irrigation Res. Sta.	1,380
Oregon	−54	Feb. 10, 1933[1]	Seneca	4,659	119	Aug. 10, 1898[1]	Pendleton	1,040
Pennsylvania	−42	Jan. 5, 1904	Smethport	1,469	111	July 10, 1936[1]	Phoenixville	105
Rhode Island	−28	Jan. 11, 1942	Wood River Junction	49	104	Aug. 2, 1975	Providence	60
South Carolina	−19	Jan. 21, 1985	Caesars Head	3,200	113	June 29, 2012	Columbia	242
South Dakota	−58	Feb. 17, 1936	McIntosh	2,179	120	July 15, 2006[1]	Fort Pierre	1,590
Tennessee	−32	Dec. 30, 1917	Mountain City	2,503	113	Aug. 9, 1930[1]	Perryville	371
Texas	−23	Feb. 8, 1933[1]	Seminole	3,336	120	June 28, 1994[1]	Monahans	2,547
Utah	−50	Jan. 5, 1913	East Portal	7,615	117	July 5, 1985	Saint George	2,857
Vermont	−50	Dec. 30, 1933	Bloomfield	1,040	107	July 7, 1912	Vernon	226
Virginia	−30	Jan. 21, 1985	Mountain Lake Bio. Station	3,870	110	July 15, 1954[1]	Balcony Falls	732
Washington	−48	Dec. 30, 1968[3]	Winthrop	1,749	118	Aug. 5, 1961[1]	Ice Harbor Dam	368
West Virginia	−37	Dec. 30, 1917	Lewisburg	2,300	112	July 10, 1936[1]	Martinsburg	534
Wisconsin	−55	Feb. 4, 1996[1]	Couderay	1,300	114	July 13, 1936	Wisconsin Dells	835
Wyoming	−66	Feb. 9, 1933	Riverside Ranger Sta.	6,500	115	July 15, 1988[1]	Diversion Dam	5,590

NA = Not available. (1) Also on earlier dates at the same or other places. (2) Also at other places on the same date and on earlier dates at the same or other places. (3) Also at other places on the same date.

Tropical Cyclone Names in 2021

Source: National Hurricane Center, NOAA, U.S. Dept. of Commerce

NOAA's National Hurricane Center began using name lists in 1953. Presently, six lists, maintained by the World Meteorological Organization, are used in rotation. If there are more than 21 named Atlantic storms in one season, remaining storms take names from the Greek alphabet, starting with Alpha. (This was only necessary in two years: 2005 and 2020.)

Atlantic: Ana, Bill, Claudette, Danny, Elsa, Fred, Grace, Henri, Ida, Julian, Kate, Larry, Mindy, Nicholas, Odette, Peter, Rose, Sam, Teresa, Victor, Wanda.

Eastern North Pacific: Andres, Blanca, Carlos, Dolores, Enrique, Felicia, Guillermo, Hilda, Ignacio, Jimena, Kevin, Linda, Marty, Nora, Olaf, Pamela, Rick, Sandra, Terry, Vivian, Waldo, Xina, York, Zelda.

World Temperature and Precipitation

Source: World Meteorological Organization (WMO)

Average daily maximum and minimum temperatures and annual precipitation based on records for the period 1961-90. Records of extreme temperatures include all available years of data for a given location and are usually for a longer period. Surface elevations are supplied by the WMO and may differ from figures in other sections of *The World Almanac*.

Station	Surface elevation (ft)	Temperature (°F) AVERAGE DAILY January Max.	January Min.	July Max.	July Min.	EXTREME Max.	EXTREME Min.	Avg. annual precipitation (in.)
Algiers, Algeria	82	61.7	42.6	87.1	65.3	NA	NA	27.0
Athens, Greece	49	56.1	44.6	88.9	73.0	NA	NA	14.6
Auckland, New Zealand	20	74.8	61.2	58.5	46.4	NA	NA	49.4
Bangkok, Thailand	66	89.6	69.8	90.9	77.0	104	51	59.0
Beijing, China	177	34.9	15.1	87.4	70.9	105	−17	22.7
Berlin, Germany	190	35.2	26.8	73.6	55.2	107	−4	23.3
Bogotá, Colombia	8,357	67.3	41.7	64.6	45.5	75	21	32.4
Bucharest, Romania	298	34.7	22.1	83.8	60.1	105	−18	23.4
Budapest, Hungary	456	34.2	24.8	79.7	59.7	103	−10	20.3
Buenos Aires, Argentina	82	85.8	67.3	59.7	45.7	104	22	45.2
Cairo, Egypt	243	65.8	48.2	93.9	71.1	118	34	1.0
Cape Town, South Africa	138	79.0	60.3	63.3	44.6	105	28	20.5
Caracas, Venezuela	2,739	79.9	60.8	81.3	66.0	96	45	36.1
Casablanca, Morocco	203	62.8	47.1	77.7	66.7	NA	NA	16.8
Copenhagen, Denmark	16	35.6	28.4	68.9	55.0	NA	NA	NA
Damascus, Syria	2,004	54.3	32.9	97.2	61.9	NA	NA	5.6
Dubai, United Arab Emirates[1]	16	75.2	56.7	105.1	84.0	117	45	3.7
Dublin, Ireland	279	45.7	36.5	66.0	52.5	86	8	28.8
Geneva, Switzerland	1,364	38.3	27.9	76.3	53.2	101	−3	35.6
Havana, Cuba	164	78.4	65.5	88.3	74.8	NA	NA	46.9
Hong Kong, China	203	65.5	56.5	88.7	79.9	97	32	87.2
Istanbul, Turkey	108	47.8	37.2	82.8	65.3	105	7	27.4
Jerusalem, Israel	2,483	53.4	39.4	83.8	63.0	107	26	23.2
Karachi, Pakistan	69	78.4	50.7	91.6	81.3	117	34	8.6
Lagos, Nigeria	125	90.0	72.3	82.8	72.1	NA	NA	59.3
Lima, Peru	43	79.0	66.9	66.4	59.4	NA	NA	0.2
London, England, UK	203	44.1	32.7	71.1	52.3	99	2	29.7
Manila, Philippines	79	85.8	74.8	89.1	76.8	NA	NA	49.6
Mexico City, Mexico	7,570	70.3	43.7	73.8	53.2	NA	NA	33.4
Montreal, Canada	118	21.6	5.2	79.2	59.7	100	−36	37.0
Mumbai (Bombay), India	36	85.3	66.7	86.2	77.5	110	46	85.4
Nairobi, Kenya	5,897	77.9	50.9	71.6	48.6	NA	NA	41.9
New Delhi, India[2]	709	69.8	45.7	94.5	80.2	113	34	31.3
Paris, France	213	42.8	33.6	75.2	55.2	105	−1	25.6
Prague, Czech Republic	1,197	32.7	22.5	73.9	53.2	98	−16	20.7
Reykjavik, Iceland	200	35.4	26.6	55.9	46.9	76	−3	31.5
Riyadh, Saudi Arabia	2,034	68.4	46.8	109.0	81.3	120	28	NA
Rome, Italy	79	53.8	35.4	88.2	62.1	NA	NA	33.0
San Salvador, El Salvador	2,037	86.5	61.3	86.2	66.4	105	45	68.3
São Paulo, Brazil	2,598	81.1	65.7	71.2	53.1	NA	NA	57.4
Seoul, South Korea	285	33.4	19.2	83.3	70.9	NA	NA	NA
Shanghai, China	23	45.9	32.9	88.9	76.6	104	10	43.8
Singapore	52	85.8	73.6	87.4	75.6	NA	NA	84.6
Stockholm, Sweden	171	30.7	23.0	71.4	56.1	97	−26	21.2
Sydney, Australia	10	79.5	65.5	62.4	43.9	114	32	46.4
Tehran, Iran	3,906	45.0	30.0	98.2	75.2	109	−5	9.1
Tokyo, Japan	118	49.1	34.2	83.8	72.1	NA	NA	55.4
Toronto, Canada	567	27.5	12.0	80.2	57.6	105	−26	30.8

NA = Not available. (1) Records are for 1974-91. (2) Records are for 1971-90.

Speed of Winds in the U.S.

Source: National Climatic Data Center, NESDIS, NOAA, U.S. Dept. of Commerce

Based on available records through 2019. Maximum speeds are highest 3-sec. wind speeds.

Station	Avg. mph	Max. mph	Station	Avg. mph	Max. mph	Station	Avg. mph	Max. mph
Albuquerque, NM	8.2	89	Helena, MT	6.8	68	Oklahoma City, OK	11.3	87
Anchorage, AK	6.9	71	Honolulu, HI	10.3	49	Omaha, NE	10.0	96
Atlanta, GA	8.3	71	Houston, TX	7.5	70	Philadelphia, PA	9.3	75
Baltimore, MD	7.2	72	Indianapolis, IN	9.5	85	Phoenix, AZ	6.1	77
Birmingham, AL	6.1	75	Jackson, MS	6.1	72	Pittsburgh, PA	7.8	62
Bismarck, ND	9.4	83	Jacksonville, FL	6.7	86	Portland, ME	7.9	72
Boise, ID	7.6	68	Little Rock, AR	7.0	87	Portland, OR	7.4	67
Boston, MA	11.5	76	Los Angeles, CA	7.5	53	Providence, RI	9.2	66
Buffalo, NY	10.3	75	Louisville, KY	7.8	75	Richmond, VA	7.7	72
Burlington, VT	8.2	63	Miami, FL	8.4	104	St. Louis, MO	9.0	71
Charleston, SC	7.9	69	Milwaukee, WI	10.1	70	Salt Lake City, UT	8.4	75
Chicago, IL	9.9	70	Minneapolis, MN	9.6	71	San Francisco, CA	10.5	71
Cleveland, OH	9.6	68	Mobile, AL	7.4	83	San Juan, PR	7.9	93
Dallas-Ft. Worth, TX	10.5	79	Mount Washington, NH	35.3	231	Seattle, WA	7.9	69
Denver, CO	10.0	80	Nashville, TN	7.0	67	Sioux Falls, SD	10.2	87
Des Moines, IA	9.8	77	New Orleans, LA	8.0	77	Washington, DC	8.9	74
Detroit, MI	9.4	78	New York, NY	6.5	62	Wichita, KS	11.5	101
Fairbanks, AK	4.4	59	Newark, NJ	9.8	78	Wilmington, DE	8.5	78

Wind Chill Temperature

Source: National Weather Service, NOAA, U.S. Dept. of Commerce

Temperature and wind combine to cause heat loss from body surfaces. For example, when the air temperature is 5°F, a 10-mph wind can cause body heat loss equal to that which could occur when the air temperature is –10°F with no wind. In other words, a 10-mph wind can make 5°F feel like –10°F. Wind speeds greater than 45 mph have little additional chilling effect. Direct sunlight can increase the wind chill temperature 10°F to 15°F. When the wind chill temperature falls within the shaded areas, frostbite can occur on exposed skin in the times indicated or less.

Calm	Air temperature (°F)																	
	40	35	30	25	20	15	10	5	0	–5	–10	–15	–20	–25	–30	–35	–40	–45
	Wind chill temperature (°F)																	
5	36	31	25	19	13	7	1	–5	–11	–16	–22	–28	–34	–40	–46	–52	–57	–63
10	34	27	21	15	9	3	–4	–10	–16	–22	–28	–35	–41	–47	–53	–59	–66	–72
15	32	25	19	13	6	0	–7	–13	–19	–26	–32	–39	–45	–51	–58	–64	–71	–77
20	30	24	17	11	4	–2	–9	–15	–22	–29	–35	–42	–48	–55	–61	–68	–74	–81
25	29	23	16	9	3	–4	–11	–17	–24	–31	–37	–44	–51	–58	–64	–71	–78	–84
30	28	22	15	8	1	–5	–12	–19	–26	–33	–39	–46	–53	–60	–67	–73	–80	–87
35	28	21	14	7	0	–7	–14	–21	–27	–34	–41	–48	–55	–62	–69	–76	–82	–89
40	27	20	13	6	–1	–8	–15	–22	–29	–36	–43	–50	–57	–64	–71	–78	–84	–91
45	26	19	12	5	–2	–9	–16	–23	–30	–37	–44	–51	–58	–65	–72	–79	–86	–93

Wind speed (mph)

30 minutes   10 minutes   5 minutes

Heat Index

Source: National Weather Service, NOAA, U.S. Dept. of Commerce

The heat index, or apparent temperature, is a measure of how hot it feels when the relative humidity is factored in with the actual air temperature. For example, when air temperature is 100°F, and relative humidity is 50%, it can feel as if it's 118°F with no humidity. Full sunlight can make one feel even hotter. On the chart, the shaded areas indicate the likelihood of heat disorders with prolonged exposure or strenuous activity.

Relative humidity (%)	Air temperature (°F)																
	80	82	84	86	88	90	92	94	96	98	100	102	104	106	108	110	
	Apparent temperature (°F)																
40	80	81	83	85	88	91	94	97	101	105	109	114	119	124	130	136	
45	80	82	84	87	89	93	96	100	104	109	114	119	124	130	137		
50	81	83	85	88	91	95	99	103	108	113	118	124	131	137			
55	81	84	86	89	93	97	101	106	112	117	124	130	137				
60	82	84	88	91	95	100	105	110	116	123	129	137					
65	82	85	89	93	98	103	108	114	121	128	136						
70	83	86	90	95	100	105	112	119	126	134							
75	84	88	92	97	103	109	116	124	132								
80	84	89	94	100	106	113	121	129									
85	85	90	96	102	110	117	126	135									
90	86	91	98	105	113	122	131										
95	86	93	100	108	117	127											
100	87	95	103	112	121	132											

Caution   Extreme caution   Danger   Extreme danger

Ultraviolet (UV) Index Forecast

Source: National Weather Service (NWS), NOAA, U.S. Dept. of Commerce; U.S. Environmental Protection Agency (EPA); U.S. Food and Drug Administration, U.S. Dept. of Health and Human Services; World Health Organization

The NWS and EPA developed and began offering a UV index in 1994 in response to increasing incidences of skin cancer, cataracts, and other effects from exposure to the sun's harmful rays. In 2004, they adapted their index to the Global Solar UV Index sponsored by the World Health Organization. The UV index is now a regular element of NWS atmospheric forecasts. To see the UV index for a given location, visit www.epa.gov/enviro/uv-index-search. For questions on scientific aspects, visit the NWS Climate Prediction Center online at www.cpc.ncep.noaa.gov.

The UV index, ranging from 0 to 11+, is an indication of the expected intensity of UV radiation reaching the Earth's surface during the solar noon hour (the time of day, dependent on location and time of year, when the sun appears to have reached its highest point in the sky). The lower the UV index value, the less the expected radiation. The UV index forecast is produced daily for 58 cities by the NWS Climate Prediction Center.

UV levels are influenced by the following:

Ozone. Ozone, a form of oxygen, the molecules of which consist of three atoms rather than two, absorbs UV radiation. The more ozone, the lower the UV radiation at the surface.

Sun height. The higher the sun is in the sky, the higher the UV radiation level.

Cloud cover. UV radiation levels are highest under cloudless skies. Even with cloud cover, UV radiation levels can be high due to the scattering of UV radiation by water molecules and fine particles in the atmosphere.

Ground reflection. Reflective surfaces intensify UV exposure. Sand reflects about 15% of UV radiation that reaches it; sea foam, 25%; and snow, as much as 80%.

Altitude. At higher altitudes, a thinner atmosphere filters less UV radiation. For every 1,000 m (3,281 ft) one travels above sea level, UV levels increase by 10%-12%.

Latitude. The closer a location is to the equator, the higher the UV radiation level.

Using the UV Forecast

UV index	Exposure	Protective actions
0-2	Low	Sunglasses on bright days, SPF 30+ sunscreen, cover up if you burn easily
3-5	Moderate	Seek shade during midday hours; hat, sunglasses; sunscreen
6-7	High	Seek shade during midday hours; protective clothing, hat, sunglasses, sunscreen
8-10	Very high	If outside 10 AM-4 PM, seek shade; wear protective clothing, hat, sunglasses, sunscreen; avoid bright surfaces
11+	Extreme	If outside 10 AM-4 PM, seek shade; wear protective clothing, hat, sunglasses, sunscreen; avoid bright surfaces

Lightning

Source: National Weather Service, NOAA, U.S. Dept. of Commerce

Lightning is a powerful electric discharge, or spark, that can occur in the atmosphere when an imbalance of positive and negative charges develops. It can travel within a cloud, between clouds, between a cloud and clear sky, or between a cloud and the ground. Lightning generally accompanies rainstorms, but it can also be seen with snowstorms, volcano eruption clouds, and violent forest fires. In a common form of cloud-to-ground lightning, a negatively charged area in a thunderstorm sends charges down toward positively charged objects. Lightning can travel miles away from the area of a storm.

The transfer of charges in lightning generates a huge amount of heat, sending the temperature in the channel to 50,000°F or more and causing the air within it to expand rapidly. The sound of that expansion is thunder. Sound travels more slowly than light, so lightning is usually observed before thunder is heard.

An estimated 25 mil cloud-to-ground lightning bolts happen in the U.S. each year. They killed an annual average of 41 people in 1990-2019. This is a small number compared to U.S. deaths from fire (3,704 in 2019) and motor vehicle crashes (about 40,000 annually in recent years), but it is still significant. In comparison, tornadoes caused an average of 68 deaths a year and hurricanes an average of 45 over the same 30-year time period. According to the National Weather Service, 20 people were struck and killed by lightning in 2019; 100 more were injured.

Most lightning deaths and injuries occur in summer when people are outdoors. If outdoors, one should run to a safe building or vehicle when thunder is first heard, lightning is seen, or dark threatening clouds are observed developing overhead. Even while indoors, one is advised to stay away from windows and doors and to avoid contact with anything conducting electricity, including corded phones, computers and other electrical equipment, and tubs, showers, and other plumbing. One should stay inside until 30 min. after the last occurrence of lightning or thunder.

More information about lightning can be found online at https://www.weather.gov/safety/lightning

Global Temperature Extremes and Precipitation Records

Source: World Weather & Climate Extremes Archive, World Meteorological Organization (WMO) Commission for Climatology
(records in each category ranked from most to least extreme; as of May 13, 2020)

Highest Temperature Extremes

Continent/area	Highest temp. (°F)	Place	Elevation (ft)	Date
North America	134	Death Valley, CA, U.S. (Greenland Ranch/Furnace Creek)	−179	July 10, 1913
Africa	131[1]	Kebili, Tunisia	125	July 7, 1931
Europe/Middle East/ Greenland	129	Tirat Tsvi, Israel	−722	June 21, 1942
Asia[2]	129.0	Mitribah, Kuwait	398	July 21, 2016
	128.7	Turbat, Pakistan	495	May 28, 2017
Southwest Pacific	123	Oodnadatta, Australia	367	Jan. 2, 1960
South America	120	Rivadavia, Argentina	673	Dec. 11, 1905
Continental Europe	118.4	Athens, Greece (and Elefsina, Greece)	774	July 10, 1977
Antarctica	67.6	Signy Research Station (UK)	23	Jan. 30, 1982

(1) Previous record of 136.4°F set on Sept. 13, 1922, in El Azizia, Libya, was invalidated in 2012; an error had been made in recording the temperature. (2) Record effectively tied due to margin of error in measurement.

Lowest Temperature Extremes

Continent/area	Lowest temp. (°F)	Place	Elevation (ft)	Date
Antarctica	−128.6	Vostok Station (Soviet Union/Russia)	11,220	July 21, 1983
Asia	−90	Verkhoyansk, Russia	350	Feb. 5 and 7, 1892
	−90	Oimekon, Russia	2,625	Feb. 6, 1933
Europe/Middle East/ Greenland	−87	Northice, Greenland	7,680	Jan. 9, 1954
North America	−81.4	Snag, Yukon, Canada	2,120	Feb. 3, 1947
Continental Europe	−72.6	Ust'-Shchugor, Russia	279	Dec. 31, 1978
South America	−27	Sarmiento, Argentina	879	June 1, 1907
Southwest Pacific	−14	Eweburn (now Ranfurly), New Zealand	1,388	July 17, 1903
Africa	−11	Ifrane, Morocco	5,364	Feb. 11, 1935
Australia	−9.4	Charlotte Pass, New South Wales	5,758	June 29, 1994

Highest Measured Average Annual Precipitation Extremes

Continent/area	Highest avg. (in.)[1]	Place	Elevation (ft)	Years in averaging period
Asia	467.4	Mawsynram, India	4,695	38
Southwest Pacific	460.0	Mt. Waialeale, Kauai, HI, U.S.	5,148	30
Africa	405.0	Debundscha, Cameroon	30	32
South America	354.0	Quibdo, Colombia	230	29
Australia	316.3	Bellenden Ker, Queensland	5,102	34
North America	276	Henderson Lake, British Columbia, Canada	12	15
Europe	180.8	Crkvice, Montenegro	3,461	30
Antarctica	>31.5[2]	Along coast of E and W and over the Antarctic Peninsula		3[3]

(1) Official greatest average annual precipitation. The frequently cited record of 523.6 in. in Lloro, Colombia (14 mi SE and at a higher elevation than Quibdo) is an estimate. (2) Water equivalent. (3) July 1996-June 1999.

Lowest Measured Average Annual Precipitation Extremes

Continent/area	Lowest avg. (in.)	Place	Elevation (ft)	Years in averaging period
South America	0.03	Arica, Chile	213	59
Antarctica	0.08	Amundsen-Scott South Pole Station (U.S.)	9,301	10
Africa	<0.1	Wadi Halfa, Sudan	590	39
North America	1.2	Batagues, Mexico	69	14
Asia	1.8	Aden, Yemen	63	50
Southwest Pacific	4.05	Troudaninna, Australia	46	42
Continental Europe	6.4	Astrakhan, Russia	66	25

OCEANOGRAPHY

Tides and Their Causes

Source: National Ocean Service, NOAA, U.S. Dept. of Commerce

The tides are natural phenomena involving the movement of waves in the Earth's large fluid bodies as a result of the gravitational attraction of the sun and moon. These two variable influences combined produce the complex recurrent cycle of the tides. Tides may occur in both oceans and seas; to a limited extent in large lakes and in the atmosphere; and, to a very minute degree, in the Earth itself. The length of time between succeeding tides can vary.

The tide-generating force represents the difference between (1) the centrifugal force produced by Earth's revolution around the common center-of-gravity of the Earth-moon system and (2) the gravitational attraction of the moon acting upon the Earth's overlying waters. The moon is about 390 times closer to Earth than is the sun. So despite its smaller mass, the moon's tide-raising force is two times greater.

The tide-generating forces of the moon and sun acting tangentially to the Earth's surface tend to cause a maximum accumulation of waters at two diametrically opposite points on the Earth's surface and to withdraw compensating amounts of water from all points 90° removed from these tidal bulges. As the Earth rotates beneath the maxima and minima of these tide-generating forces, a sequence of two high tides, separated by two low tides, is produced each lunar day (24 hr. and 50 min., the time it takes for a specific site on the Earth to rotate from an exact point under the moon to the same point under the moon) in what is called a **semidiurnal tide**. Each ocean basin reacts differently to tidal forces.

Twice each month, when the sun, moon, and Earth are directly aligned—the moon between the Earth and sun (at new moon) or on the opposite side of Earth from the sun (at full moon)—the sun and moon exert gravitational forces in a mutual or additive fashion. The highest high tides and lowest low tides, called **spring tides**, are produced at these times. At two positions 90° in between, the moon and sun's gravitational forces—imposed at right angles—counteract each other to the greatest extent, and the range between high and low tides is reduced, resulting in **neap tides**.

The inclination of the moon's monthly orbit and of the sun to the equator during Earth's yearly passage through its orbit produce a difference in the height of succeeding high and low tides, known as the diurnal inequality. In most cases, this produces a so-called **mixed tide**. In extreme cases, these phenomena may result in a **diurnal tide**, with only one high tide and one low tide each day. There are other monthly and yearly variations in the tides because of the elliptical shape of the orbits.

The range of tides in the open ocean is generally less than in the coastal regions, where the incoming tide can be augmented by the continental shelves, as well as by bays and estuaries. The largest tidal ranges in the world occur in the Bay of Fundy, Canada, where the range of tide reaches 53 ft. The highest tides in the U.S. occur near Anchorage, AK, with tidal ranges up to 40 ft.

In every case, actual high or low tide can vary considerably from the average as a result of weather conditions such as strong winds, abrupt barometric pressure changes, or prolonged periods of extreme high or low pressure.

Mean Ranges of Tide

Place	Ft	In.	Place	Ft	In.	Place	Ft	In.
Baltimore, MD.	1	2	Key West, FL	1	3	Provincetown, MA	9	3
Biloxi, MS	1	6	Los Angeles, CA.	3	10	St. Petersburg, FL	1	7
Boston, MA.	9	6	Miami Beach, FL	2	6	San Diego, CA.	4	1
Charleston, SC.	5	3	New London, CT	2	7	San Francisco, CA.	4	1
Eastport, ME.	18	4	New York, NY.	4	6	San Juan, PR.	1	1
Ft. Pulaski, GA	6	11	Newport, RI	3	6	Sandy Hook, NJ.	4	8
Galveston, TX.	1	0	Philadelphia, PA.	6	1	Seattle, WA.	7	8
Honolulu, HI	1	3	Portland, ME.	9	1	Washington, DC.	2	9

Note: Mean range is the difference in height between mean high water and mean low water.

El Niño and La Niña

Source: National Weather Service, NOAA, U.S. Dept. of Commerce

El Niño is a climatically significant disruption of the ocean-atmosphere system characterized by large-scale weakening of trade winds and warming of surface layer waters in the central and eastern equatorial Pacific. The term *El Niño*, Spanish for "the little boy" or "the Christ Child," was originally used by fishing crews to refer to a warm ocean current that appeared around Christmas off the west coast of Ecuador and Peru lasting several months. The term has come to be reserved for exceptionally strong warm currents that bring heavy rains.

El Niño events generally occur at irregular intervals of two to seven years, at an average of once every three to four years. They typically last 12 to 18 months. The intensity of El Niño events varies depending on the area encompassed by the abnormally warm ocean temperatures. Some are strong, such as in 1982-83, 1997-98, and 2015-16. Others are considerably weaker, such as the 2009-10 event. The eastward extent of warmer-than-normal water varies from episode to episode.

El Niño influences weather around the globe, and its impacts are most clearly seen in the winter. During El Niño years, winter temperatures in the continental U.S. tend to be warmer than normal in the northern states and on the West Coast and cooler than normal in the Southeast. Conditions tend to be wetter than normal over central and southern California, the Southwest, and across much of the South, and drier than normal over the northern portions of the Rocky Mountains and in the Ohio Valley. Globally, El Niño brings wetter than normal conditions to Peru and Chile and dry conditions to Australia and Indonesia. It should be noted that El Niño is only one of a number of factors influencing seasonal variations of climate.

La Niña ("the little girl") is characterized by colder than normal sea surface temperatures in the equatorial Pacific. La Niña typically brings wetter, cooler conditions to the Pacific Northwest and drier, warmer conditions to much of the southern U.S. El Niño and La Niña are opposite phases of the El Niño-Southern Oscillation (ENSO) cycle, which involves a shift in tropical sea-level pressure between the Eastern and Western Hemispheres.

NOAA and other agencies monitor these events using satellites, weather balloons, and buoys in the Pacific Ocean. Numerical computer models of the ocean and atmosphere use these data to predict the onset and evolution of El Niño and La Niña. The ENSO-neutral conditions in summer 2020 were expected to be followed by La Niña conditions in the Northern Hemisphere in fall 2020 and continue through winter 2020-21.

DISASTERS

U.S. Weather and Climate Disasters by Type, 1980-2020

Source: National Centers for Environmental Information, National Oceanic and Atmospheric Administration, U.S. Dept. of Commerce
Does not include disasters causing under $1 billion in consumer price index-adjusted losses. The worst year for billion-dollar disasters in this period was 2017, with $321.8 billion in damages, including Hurricanes Harvey, Irma, and Maria, and easily surpassed the previous U.S. annual record of $227.6 billion (CPI-adjusted), established in 2005. As of July 8, 2020.

Disaster type	Number of events	Losses (bil)	Percent of total losses	Average cost (bil)	Deaths
Drought.	27	$252.7	14.1%	$9.4	3,865[1]
Flooding[2]	33	150.4	8.4	4.6	617
Freeze.	9	30.6	1.7	3.4	162
Severe storm	125	268.4	15.0	2.1	1,757
Tropical cyclone	45	954.4	53.3	21.2	6,507
Wildfire	17	85.4	4.8	5.0	347
Winter storm	17	49.6	2.8	2.9	1,048
All disasters[3]	**273**	**1,791.5**	**100.0**	**6.6**	**14,303**

Note: Tropical cyclones include hurricanes, tropical storms, tropical depressions, and associated storm surges and flooding. (1) Drought-associated deaths are the result of heat waves, which do not always occur with droughts. (2) Does not include inland flood damage caused by tropical cyclone events. (3) Cost statistics do not include certain 2020 disasters.

U.S. Weather and Climate Disasters, 2019

Source: National Centers for Environmental Information, National Oceanic and Atmospheric Administration, U.S. Dept. of Commerce
Does not include disasters causing under $1 billion in consumer price index-adjusted losses.

Date	Event and location	Losses (bil)	Deaths
Feb. 23-25	Winter storm, SE, Ohio Valley, Northeast states, incl. MS, AL, TN, IL, IN, OH, CT, MD, MA, NJ, NY, PA, VA, WV	$1.3	2
Mar. 14-31	Flooding, Missouri R. and north-central states, incl. NE, IA, MO, SD, MN, ND, WI, MI.	10.9	3
Mar. 15-July 31	Flooding, Mississippi R., OK, NE, MO, IL, KS, AR, KY, TN, TX, MS, LA, IN, OH.	6.3	4
Mar. 22-24	Hail storm, Dallas-Ft. Worth metroplex, OK	1.6	0
Apr. 13-14	Tornadoes, severe storms, TX, LA, MS, AL, GA, NC, OH, PA	1.3	7
May 7-13	Tornadoes, severe storms, TX, OK, KS, AR, LA, MS, AL, NC	1.5	0
May 16-18	Severe storms, IL, IN, IA, TX	1.0	0
May 20-June 14	Flooding, Arkansas R., AR, OK	3.1	5
May 26-29	Outbreak of 190 tornadoes, severe storms, CO, WY, NE, KS, OK, MO, IA, IL, IN, OH, PA, NJ	4.5	3
June 1-Nov. 30	Wildfires, CA and AK	4.5	3
July 4-5	Hail storms, Denver-Ft. Collins, CO	1.0	0
Aug. 28-Sept. 6	Hurricane Dorian, Bahamas, FL, GA, SC, NC, esp. Outer Banks	1.6	10
Sept. 17-21	Tropical Storm Imelda, 24-36 in. rainfall in SE TX.	5.1	5
Oct. 20	Severe storms, TX, OK, MO, AR, LA, TN.	1.7	2
2019 total	**14 events**	**45.4**	**44**

Note: Compiled using preliminary data, as of July 8, 2020, on damage-related losses and deaths, which are subject to revision.

Some Notable Aircraft Disasters Since 1937

Source: National Transportation Safety Board; World Almanac research
Particularly notable disasters are in bold. Asterisk (*) indicates number of deaths includes people on ground. As of Aug. 2019.

Date	Aircraft	Incident details, site	Deaths
1937, May 6	**German zeppelin Hindenburg**	**Burned at mooring, Lakehurst, NJ**	36*
1944, Aug. 23	U.S. Air Force B-24 Liberator bomber	Hit school, Freckleton, England, UK.	61*
1945, July 28	U.S. Army B-25.	Hit Empire State Building after getting lost in fog, New York, NY.	14*
1952, Dec. 20	U.S. Air Force C-124	Crashed at Moses Lake, WA	87
1953, Mar. 3	**Canadian Pacific DH-106 Comet**	**Crashed on takeoff from Karachi, Pakistan; world's first fatal commercial passenger jet crash**	11
1953, June 18	U.S. Air Force C-124	Crashed, burned near Tokyo, Japan	129
1955, Oct. 6	United Airlines DC-4.	Crashed in Medicine Bow Peak, WY	66
1955, Nov. 1	United Airlines DC-6.	Bomb on board exploded near Longmont, CO.	44[1]
1956, June 20	LAV (Venezuela) Super Constellation	Crashed into Atlantic off Asbury Park, NJ	74
1956, June 30	TWA Super Const., United DC-7	Collided over Grand Canyon, AZ	128
1960, Dec. 16	United DC-8, TWA Super Const.	Collided over New York, NY, killing all 128 on planes, 6 on ground	134*
1962, Mar. 16	Flying Tiger (U.S.) Super Constellation	Vanished in W Pacific en route to Philippines from Guam	107
1962, June 3	Air France Boeing 707	Crashed on takeoff from Paris, France.	130
1962, June 22	Air France Boeing 707	Crashed in storm, Guadeloupe, French W Indies	113
1963, Feb. 1	Lebanese Middle East Airlines Vickers Viscount 754, Turkish Mil. Douglas C-47	Collided over Ankara, Turkey, killing all 17 on planes, 87 on ground.	104*
1963, Nov. 29	Trans-Canada Air Lines DC-8	Crashed after takeoff from Montréal, QC, Canada.	118
1965, May 20	Pakistani Boeing 720	Crashed at airport in Cairo, Egypt.	121
1966, Jan. 24	Air India Boeing 707	Crashed on Mont Blanc, France-Italy.	117
1966, Feb. 4	All-Nippon Boeing 727	Plunged into Tokyo Bay, Japan.	133
1966, Mar. 5	BOAC (British Overseas Airways Corp.) Boeing 707	Crashed into Mt. Fuji, Japan, after encountering severe turbulence	124
1966, Dec. 24	U.S. military-chartered CL-44	Crashed into village in S Vietnam.	129*
1967, Apr. 20	Globe Air Bristol Britannia	Crashed on approach to airport, Nicosia, Cyprus.	126
1967, July 19	Piedmont Boeing 727, Cessna 310	Collided over Hendersonville, NC.	82
1968, Apr. 20	S. African Airways Boeing 707	Crashed on takeoff from Windhoek, Namibia.	122
1968, May 3	Braniff International Electra	Crashed in storm near Dawson, TX.	85
1968, May 12	U.S. Air Force Lockheed C-130B.	Hit by mortar while evacuating Kham Duc Camp, S Vietnam.	155
1969, Mar. 16	VIASA DC-9	Crashed after takeoff from Maracaibo, Venezuela.	155[2]
1970, July 3	British-chartered DH-106 Comet	Crashed near Barcelona, Spain.	112
1970, July 5	Air Canada DC-8	Crashed near Toronto Intl. Airport, ON, Canada.	108
1970, Nov. 14	Southern Airways DC-9	Crashed into mountains near Huntington, WV.	75[3]
1971, July 30	All-Nippon Boeing 727, Japan Air Force F-86 fighter.	Collided over Morioka, Japan.	162[4]
1971, Sept. 4	Alaska Airlines Boeing 727.	Crashed into mountain near Juneau, AK.	111
1972, May 18	Aeroflot Antonov 10A	Wings separated from fuselage; crashed on approach to Kharkov, USSR.	122

Date	Aircraft	Incident details, site	Deaths
1972, June 18	British European Airways Trident-1C	Crashed near Staines after takeoff from London, Eng., UK	118
1972, Aug. 14	East German Ilyushin 62	Crashed on takeoff from East Berlin, E Germany	156
1972, Aug. 31	Aeroflot Ilyushin 18V	Crashed in field near Magnitogorsk, USSR	101
1972, Oct. 1	Aeroflot Ilyushin 18V	Crashed into Black Sea, USSR	109
1972, Oct. 13	Aeroflot Ilyushin 62	Crashed near Moscow, USSR	174
1972, Dec. 3	Spanish-chartered Convair CV-990	Crashed on takeoff from Canary Islands, Spain	155
1972, Dec. 29	Eastern Airlines Lockheed L-1011 TriStar	Crashed on approach to Miami Intl. Airport, FL	99
1973, Jan. 22	Nigerian-chartered Boeing 707	Burst into flames upon landing at Kano Airport, Nigeria	176
1973, Feb. 21	**Libyan Arab Boeing 727**	**Flew off course, shot down by Israeli fighter planes over Sinai Desert**	**108**
1973, Apr. 10	Invicta Airlines (UK) Vickers Vanguard	Crashed during snowstorm on approach to Basel, Switzerland	108
1973, June 3	Soviet Supersonic Tu-144	Crashed near Goussainville, France	14[5]
1973, July 11	Varig Airlines (Brazil) Boeing 707	Crashed on approach to Orly Airport, Paris, France	123
1973, July 31	Delta Airlines DC-9	Crashed while attempting landing in fog, Logan Airport, Boston, MA	89
1973, Sept. 30	Aeroflot Tupolev 104B	Crashed after takeoff from Sverdlovsk, USSR	108
1973, Oct. 13	Aeroflot Tupolev 104B	Crashed on approach to Moscow, USSR	122
1973, Dec. 22	Royal Air Maroc SE 210 Caravelle VIN	Flew into side of a mountain near Tangier, Morocco	106
1974, Mar. 3	Turkish DC-10	Improperly closed cargo door caused crash, Ermenonville, nr. Paris, France	346
1974, Apr. 22	Pan American (U.S.) Boeing 707	Crashed in Bali, Indonesia	107
1974, Apr. 27	Aeroflot Ilyushin 18V	Crashed after takeoff from Leningrad, USSR	109
1974, Dec. 1	TWA Boeing 727	Crashed on approach in storm, Upperville, VA	92
1974, Dec. 4	Dutch-chartered DC-8	Crashed in storm near Colombo, Sri Lanka	191
1975, Apr. 4	U.S. Air Force Galaxy C-5A	Crashed on takeoff nr. Saigon, S Vietnam; carried orphans	155
1975, June 24	Eastern Airlines 727	Crashed in storm, JFK Airport, New York, NY	113
1975, Aug. 3	Alia Royal Jordanian Boeing 707	Hit mountainside in heavy fog near Agadir, Morocco	188
1975, Aug. 20	Czechoslovakian Air Ilyushin 62	Crashed on approach to Damascus, Syria	126
1976, Mar. 6	Aeroflot Ilyushin 18E	Crashed between Moscow, USSR, and Yerevan, Armenia	111
1976, Sept. 10	British Airways Trident, Inex Adria DC-9	Collided near Zagreb, Yugoslavia	176
1976, Sept. 19	Turkish Boeing 727	Hit mountain in southern Turkey	154
1976, Oct. 6	Cubana Airlines DC-8	Bombs set by anti-Castro Cuban exiles detonated mid-flight	73
1976, Oct. 13	Lloyd Aero Boliviano Boeing 707	Crashed into soccer field after takeoff from Santa Cruz, Bolivia	91[6]
1977, Mar. 27	**KLM (Neth.) 747, Pan Am (U.S.) 747**	**Collided on foggy runway, Tenerife, Canary Islands, Spain**	**583**
1977, Nov. 19	TAP Portugal Boeing 727	Crashed in Madeira, Portugal	131
1977, Dec. 4	Malaysian Airlines Boeing 737	Hijacked and forced to fly to Singapore, crashed near Johor Strait	100
1978, Jan. 1	Air India 747	Crashed into sea after takeoff from Bombay, India	213
1978, Sept. 25	Pacific SW Air Boeing 727, Cessna 172	Collided over San Diego, CA	144*
1978, Nov. 15	Indonesian-chartered DC-8	Crashed on approach to airport, Colombo, Sri Lanka	183
1979, May 25	**American Airlines DC-10**	**Crashed after takeoff from O'Hare Airport, Chicago, IL; highest death toll in U.S. aviation history**	**275***
1979, Aug. 11	Aeroflot/Moldova Tu-134, Aeroflot Tu-134	Collided over Ukraine	178
1979, Nov. 26	Pakistani Boeing 707	Crashed near Jidda, Saudi Arabia	156
1979, Nov. 28	Air New Zealand DC-10	Crashed into Mt. Erebus during Antarctica flyover	257
1980, Mar. 14	PLL LOT Ilyushin 62	Crashed making emergency landing, Warsaw, Poland	87[7]
1980, Apr. 25	Dan-Air Services (UK) Boeing 727	Crashed into mountain, Tenerife, Canary Islands, Spain	146
1980, July 8	Aeroflot Tupolev 154B	Crashed after takeoff from Alma-Ata, USSR	166
1980, Aug. 19	Saudi Arabian Lockheed TriStar	Returned to Riyadh airport after fire on board; evacuation delayed	301
1981, Dec. 1	Inex Adria (Yugoslavia) DC-9	Crashed into mountain on island of Corsica, France	180
1982, Jan. 13	Air Florida Boeing 737	Crashed into bridge, Potomac R. after takeoff from Washington, DC	78*
1982, June 8	VASP (Brazil) Boeing 727	Crashed into mountain near Fortaleza, Brazil	137
1982, June 28	Aeroflot Yakovlev 42	Crashed near Mozyr, USSR	132
1982, July 9	Pan Am Boeing 727	Crashed after takeoff from Kenner, LA, near New Orleans	153*
1983, July 11	Ecuadorean Boeing 737	Inexperienced pilot crashed into hill near Cuenca, Ecuador	119
1983, Sept. 1	**S. Korean Boeing 747**	**Shot down after entering restricted Soviet airspace near Sakhalin; plane apparently misidentified**	**269**
1983, Sept. 23	Gulf Air Boeing 737	Bomb exploded in cargo hold over Mina Jebel Ali, UAE	112
1983, Nov. 27	Avianca Boeing 747	Crashed near Barajas Airport, Madrid, Spain	181
1984, Oct. 11	Aeroflot/East Siberia Tu-154	Crashed into vehicles on runway while landing in poor weather, Omsk, Russia	178*
1985, Feb. 19	Spanish Boeing 727	Crashed into Mt. Oiz, Spain	148
1985, June 23	Air India Boeing 747	Crashed into Atlantic off Ireland after bomb detonated on board	329
1985, July 10	Aeroflot Tupolev 154B	Crashed after takeoff from Uzbekistan, USSR	200
1985, Aug. 2	Delta Air Lines Lockheed L-1011 TriStar	Crashed after encountering microburst near Dallas-Ft. Worth Airport, TX	135*
1985, Aug. 12	**Japan Air Lines Boeing 747**	**Crashed into Mt. Ogura, Japan; world's worst single-plane disaster**	**520**
1985, Dec. 12	Arrow Air (U.S.) DC-8	Crashed after takeoff from Gander, NL, Canada	256[8]
1986, Mar. 31	Mexican Boeing 727	Crashed NW of Mexico City, Mexico	167
1986, Aug. 31	Aeromexico DC-9, Piper PA-28	Collided over Cerritos, CA	82*
1987, May 9	Polish IL-62M	Crashed after takeoff from Warsaw, Poland	183
1987, Aug. 16	Northwest Airlines MD-82	Crashed after takeoff from Romulus, MI	156
1987, Nov. 28	S. African Boeing 747	Crashed into Indian Ocean near Mauritius	159
1987, Nov. 29	Korean Air Boeing 707	Bomb planted by 2 N. Korean agents exploded while plane over Andaman Sea off Burma	115
1988, Mar. 17	Colombian Boeing 707	Crashed into mountainside near Venezuela border	143
1988, July 3	**Iran Air Airbus A300**	**Misidentified as hostile aircraft, shot down by U.S. Navy warship *Vincennes* over Persian Gulf**	**290**
1988, Oct. 19	Indian Airlines Boeing 737	Exploded after striking trees near runway, Ahmedabad, India	131
1988, Dec. 21	**Pan Am (U.S.) Boeing 747**	**Libyan agent planted bomb on board; exploded over Lockerbie, Scotland**	**270[9]**
1989, Feb. 8	U.S.-chartered Boeing 707	Crashed into mountain on Azores Isls., off Portugal	144
1989, June 7	Surinam Airways DC-8	Crashed near Paramaribo Airport, Suriname	176
1989, July 19	United Airlines DC-10	Crashed on landing in Sioux City, IA	111
1989, Sept. 3	Cubana Aviacion Ilyushin 62M	Crashed on takeoff from Havana, Cuba	171*
1989, Sept. 19	**UTA (France) DC-10**	**Bomb exploded on board flight from Chad to France while over desert in Niger**	**170**

Date	Aircraft	Incident details, site	Deaths
1989, Oct. 21	TAN-SAHSA (Honduras) Boeing 727....	Crashed into mountain near Tegucigalpa, Honduras............	131
1989, Nov. 27	Avianca (Colombia) Boeing 727........	Bomb exploded on flight from Bogotá, Colombia..............	107
1990, Jan. 25	Avianca (Colombia) Boeing 707.......	Crashed on landing at JFK Airport, New York, NY.........	73
1990, Oct. 2	Xiamen Airlines Boeing 737..........	Hijacked after takeoff fr. Xiamen; collided with China Southern Boeing 757 on runway during emergency landing, Guangzhou, China......................	128
1991, May 26	Lauda Air (Austria) Boeing 767-300.....	Broke up following takeoff from Bangkok, Thailand............	223
1991, July 11	Nigeria Airways DC-8..............	Crashed on landing at Jidda, Saudi Arabia	261
1991, Oct. 5	U.S. Air Force Lockheed C-130 Hercules	Crashed after takeoff from Jakarta, Indonesia...............	135*
1992, July 31	Thai Airbus A300-310................	Crashed into mountain N of Kathmandu, Nepal............	113
1992, Sept. 26	Nigerian Air Force LC-130 Hercules.....	Transport full of military officers crashed near Lagos, Nigeria.....	158
1992, Sept. 28	Pakistan Intl. Air Airbus A300.........	Crashed into hillside near Kathmandu, Nepal	167
1992, Oct. 4	**El Al (Israel) Boeing 747-200F........**	**Crashed into 2 apartment bldgs., Amsterdam, Netherlands ...**	**120***
1992, Nov. 24	China Southern Airlines Boeing 737.....	Crashed on approach to Giulin, China...................	141
1992, Dec. 22	Libyan Arab Air Boeing 727	Collided with Libyan Air Force MiG-23 on approach to Tripoli.....	159
1993, Feb. 8	Iran Air Tu-154, Iranian Air Force jet.....	Collided after military jet took off from Tehran, Iran	131
1993, May 19	SAM Colombia Boeing 727	Crashed into mountain near Medellín, Colombia	132
1993, Nov. 20	Macedonian Yakovlev 42D...........	Crashed into mountain near Skopje, Macedonia	116
1994, Jan. 3	Aeroflot Tu-154....................	Crashed and exploded after takeoff from Irkutsk, Russia.......	125*
1994, Apr. 26	China Airlines Airbus A300...........	Crashed on approach to Nagoya Airport, Japan............	264
1994, June 6	China Northwest Airlines Tu-154	Crashed near Xian, China	160
1994, Sept. 8	USAir Boeing 737-300	Crashed near Pittsburgh Intl. Airport, Aliquippa, PA........	132
1994, Oct. 31	American Eagle ATR-72-210	Crashed in field near Roselawn, IN	68
1995, Dec. 18	Zairean Lockheed L-188C Electra	Overloaded charter crashed in Lunda Norte, Angola	141
1995, Dec. 20	American Airlines Boeing 757	Crashed into mountain N of Cali, Colombia	159
1996, Jan. 8	African Air Antonov-32 cargo plane	Crashed into a market in Kinshasa, Zaire; all deaths on ground ...	237*
1996, Feb. 6	Alas Nacionales (Dom. Rep.) Boeing 757	Crashed into Atlantic off Dominican Republic	189
1996, Feb. 29	Faucett (Peru) Boeing 737...........	Crashed into hillside near Arequipa, Peru	123
1996, Apr. 3	U.S. Air Force Boeing T-43A	Crashed into mountain near Dubrovnik, Croatia	35[10]
1996, May 11	ValuJet DC-9	Crashed into Florida Everglades after improper cargo started fire..	110
1996, July 17	Trans World Airlines Boeing 747	Exploded and crashed into Atlantic off Long Island, NY........	230
1996, Aug. 29	Vnukovo Airlines (Russia) Tu-154	Crashed into mountain on Arctic island of Spitsbergen	141
1996, Nov. 7	ADC Airlines (Nigeria) Boeing 727	Crashed into lagoon SE of Lagos, Nigeria	144
1996, Nov. 12	**Saudi Arabian Boeing 747,** **Kazakh Ilyushin 76 cargo plane.....**	**Collided near New Delhi, India; world's worst midair collision**	**349**
1996, Nov. 23	Ethiopian Airlines Boeing 767........	Hijacked; crashed into Indian O. off the Comoros (fuel ran out)....	127
1997, Aug. 6	Korean Air Boeing 747-300	Crashed into jungle on Guam on approach to airport...........	228
1997, Sept. 26	Indonesian Airbus A300	Crashed near airport, Medan, Indonesia	234
1998, Feb. 16	China Airlines Airbus A300...........	Crashed on approach to airport in Taipei, Taiwan	203*
1998, Sept. 2	Swissair MD-11	Crashed into Atlantic off Nova Scotia, Canada, after onboard fire..	229
1999, Oct. 31	EgyptAir Boeing 767...............	Crashed off Nantucket, MA; result of deliberate actions by copilot, motives unknown	217
2000, Jan. 30	Kenya Airways Airbus A310..........	Crashed into Atlantic after takeoff from Abidjan, Côte d'Ivoire.....	169
2000, Jan. 31	Alaska Airlines MD-83	Crashed into Pacific off coast of Southern CA	88
2000, Apr. 19	Air Philippines Boeing 737-200	Crashed on approach to airport, Davao, Philippines	131
2000, July 25	**Air France Concorde ....**	**Crashed into hotel after takeoff from Paris; world's first Concorde crash ...**	**113***
2000, Aug. 23	Gulf Air Airbus A320................	Crashed into Persian Gulf on approach to airport in Bahrain......	143
2001, July 3	Vladivostokavia Tu-154	Crashed on approach to airport, Irkutsk, Russia	145
2001, Sept. 11	**2 Boeing 767s, 2 Boeing 757s........**	**September 11 terrorist attacks ....**	**265[11]**
2001, Oct. 8	Cessna 525A Citation, Scandinavian Airlines System (SAS) MD-87	Collided in heavy fog on takeoff from Milan, Italy............	118*
2001, Nov. 12	**American Airlines Airbus A300......**	**Crashed after takeoff from JFK Airport, New York, NY ......**	**265***
2002, Feb. 12	Iran Air Tours Tu-154..............	Crashed into mountain on approach to airport, Khorramabad, Iran	119
2002, Apr. 15	Air China Boeing 767	Crashed into mountain in rain and fog on approach to airport, Pusan, S. Korea	129
2002, May 4	EAS Airlines BAC 1-11..............	Crashed shortly after takeoff from Kano, Nigeria	149
2002, May 7	China Northern Airlines MD-82........	Plunged into sea, apparently after a passenger started fire in cabin, NE China	112
2002, May 25	China Airlines Boeing 747	Broke apart in midair, plunged into Taiwan Strait en route to Hong Kong airport	225
2002, July 27	**Ukraine Air Force Sukhoi Su-27 ......**	**Crashed while performing, Lviv, Ukraine; world's worst air-show crash ...**	**77[12]**
2002, Aug. 19	Russian Mi-26 transport helicopter.....	Hit by Chechen missile near Grozny, Chechnya	127
2003, Jan. 8	Turkish Airlines British Aerospace RJ-100	Crashed on approach to airport in Diyarbakir, Turkey	75
2003, Feb. 19	Iranian Revolutionary Guard Ilyushin 76..	Crashed into mountain near Kerman, Iran; passengers were Revolutionary Guard members....................	275
2003, May 26	Ukrain.-Medit. Airlines Yak-42	Crashed into mountain in fog approaching Trabzon, Turkey; passengers incl. Spanish peacekeepers returning from Afghan.	75
2003, July 8	Sudan Airways Boeing 737-200.......	Mechanical problems reported shortly after takeoff; crashed upon return to Port Sudan Airport..................	115
2003, Dec. 25	Union Transp. Africains Boeing 727.....	Overloading caused crash on takeoff from Cotonou, Benin	141
2004, Jan. 3	Flash Airlines Boeing 737-300	Crashed into Red Sea after takeoff from Sharm el Sheikh, Egypt ..	148
2004, Aug. 24	Volga-Aviaexpress Tu-134, Sibir Airlines Tu-154	2 planes that took off from Moscow crashed within minutes of each other; brought down by Chechen suicide bombers	90
2005, Aug. 14	Helios Airways Boeing 737-300	Crashed after air pressure failure on board, near Athens, Greece..	121
2005, Aug. 16	W Caribbean Airways (Colombia) MD-82	Crashed after engine failure, near Machiques, Venezuela.......	160
2005, Sept. 5	Mandala Airlines Boeing 737-200......	Crashed shortly after takeoff from Medan, Sumatra, Indonesia....	145*
2005, Oct. 22	Bellview Airlines Boeing 737-200	Crashed during heavy electrical storm near Lagos, Nigeria......	117

Date	Aircraft	Incident details, site	Deaths
2005, Dec. 6	Islamic Rep. of Iran Air Force Lockheed C-130	Crashed into apartment building after reportedly attempting emergency landing back at airport, Tehran, Iran	116*
2005, Dec. 10	Sosoliso Airlines DC-9-30	Crashed during storm on approach to Port Harcourt, Nigeria	107
2006, May 3	Armavia Airbus A320	Crashed into Black Sea on approach to airport, Sochi, Russia	113
2006, July 9	S7 Airlines Airbus A310	Skidded off runway, crashed into concrete barrier after landing, Irkutsk, Russia	125
2006, Aug. 22	Pulkovo Aviation Tu-154	Crashed after encountering storm, near Donetsk, Ukraine	170
2006, Sept. 29	Gol Airlines Boeing 737	Crashed into Amazon jungle after midair collision with Embraer Legacy jet (which itself landed safely), Brazil	154
2007, May 5	Kenya Airways Boeing 737-800	Crashed shortly after takeoff from Douala, Cameroon	114
2007, July 17	TAM Airlines Airbus 320	Crashed into cargo depot, gas station after skidding off runway, São Paulo, Brazil	199*
2008, Aug. 20	Spanair Boeing-MD-82	Swerved off runway, caught fire on takeoff attempt, Madrid, Spain	154
2009, Feb. 12	Colgan Air Bombardier Dash 8 Q400	Crashed into house after pilot error caused stall near Buffalo, NY	50*
2009, June 1	**Air France Airbus A330**	**Plunged into Atlantic Ocean en route from Rio de Janeiro, Brazil, to Paris, France**	**228**
2009, June 29	Yemenia Airbus A310-300	Fell into Indian Ocean on approach to Moroni, Comoros	152
2009, July 15	Caspian Airlines Tupolev 154	Crashed after takeoff from Tehran, Iran	168
2010, Apr. 10	Polish Air Force Tupolev 154M	Crashed on approach to Smolensk Air Base, killing Polish Pres. Lech Kaczynski, his wife, and several members of parliament	96
2010, May 12	Afriqiyah Airways Airbus A330-200	Crashed short of runway in Tripoli, Libya	103
2010, May 22	Air India Express Boeing 737-800	Overran runway on landing at Mangalore, India	158
2010, July 28	Airblue Airbus 321-231	Crashed into Margalla Hills near Islamabad, Pakistan	152
2012, Apr. 20	Bhoja Airlines Boeing 737-236	Crashed on approach to airport in Islamabad, Pakistan	127
2012, June 3	Dana Air MD-83	Crashed into residential area of Lagos, Nigeria	163*
2014, Mar. 8	Malaysia Airlines Boeing 777	Disappeared over S Indian O. en route fr. Kuala Lumpur to Beijing	239
2014, July 17	Malaysia Airlines Boeing 777	Shot down by Russian missile over disputed eastern Ukraine	298
2014, July 24	Air Algérie Boeing-MD-83	Crashed in desert near Gossi, Mali	116
2014, Dec. 28	Indonesia AirAsia Airbus A320-216	Disappeared over Java Sea between Surabaya and Singapore	162
2015, Mar. 24	Germanwings Airbus A320-211	Copilot deliberately crashed aircraft into French Alps	150
2015, June 30	Indonesian Air Force Lockheed C-130B	Transport plane crashed near Medan Soewondo Air Force Base	139*
2015, Oct. 31	Metrojet Airbus A321-231	Bomb detonated on board after takeoff fr. Sharm el Sheikh, Egypt	224
2016, Nov. 28	LaMia (Bolivia) Avro RJ85	Ran out of fuel and crashed near Medellín, Colombia; passengers incl. Brazilian Chapecoense soccer team	71
2016, Dec. 25	Russian Air Force Tupolev 154B-2	Crashed into Black Sea after takeoff from Sochi, Russia	92
2017, June 7	Myanmar Air Force Shaanxi Y-8-200F	Crashed into Andaman Sea en route to Yangon, Myanmar	122
2018, Apr. 11	Algerian military transport Ilyushin 76	Crashed after takeoff from near Algiers; passengers included Western Sahara separatists, refugees	257
2018, May 18	Cubana de Aviación Boeing 737	Aging aircraft crashed after takeoff from Havana, Cuba	112
2018, Oct. 29	Lion Air Boeing 737 Max 8	Crashed into Java Sea shortly after takeoff from Jakarta, Indonesia	189[13]
2019, Mar. 10	Ethiopian Airlines Boeing 737 Max 8	Crashed minutes after takeoff from Addis Ababa	157[13]
2020, Jan. 8	Ukrainian Airlines Boeing 737-800	Shot down by two Iranian missiles after takeoff from Tehran	176
2020, Jan. 26	Privately-operated Sikorsky S-76B helicopter	Crashed in bad visibility into hillside nr. Calabasas, CA, carrying retired NBA player Kobe Bryant, his daughter, others	9

(1) Bomb planted by Jack G. Graham in insurance plot to kill his mother, Daisie E. King, a passenger. (2) 84 on plane, 71 on ground killed. (3) Incl. 43 Marshall Univ. (WV) football players and coaches. (4) Fighter pilot parachuted to safety. (5) First supersonic plane crash; killed 8 on ground. (6) Crew of 3, 88 on ground killed. (7) Incl. 22 members of U.S. amateur boxing team. (8) Incl. 8 crew and 248 members of U.S. 101st Airborne Division returning from peacekeeping mission in Sinai, Egypt. (9) Incl. 11 on ground. (10) Incl. U.S. Sec. of Commerce Ron Brown. (11) 4 planes were hijacked and crashed, with all on board killed (265, incl. 19 hijackers). American Airlines Flight 11 (Boeing 767-200) with 81 passengers, 11 crew crashed into Tower 1 of World Trade Center (WTC); United Airlines Flight 175 (Boeing 767-200) with 56 passengers, 9 crew crashed into Tower 2 of WTC; American Airlines Flight 77 (Boeing 757-200) with 58 passengers, 6 crew crashed into Pentagon outside Washington, DC; United Airlines Flight 93 (Boeing 757-200), with 37 passengers, 7 crew crashed near Shanksville, PA. The official death toll of 2,997 includes those who died on the ground at the Pentagon and the WTC, and 3 later victims whose deaths the NYC chief medical examiner ruled were caused by exposure to toxic dust created by the disaster. Does not include those with cancers and other medical conditions related to WTC site exposure. (12) The two pilots ejected to safety. All spectator deaths. (13) Two fatal crashes, possibly due to faulty sensors and software, led to worldwide grounding of Boeing 737 Max series.

Some Notable Shipwrecks Since 1854
Does not include most wartime disasters.

Date—vessel(s)	Incident	Est. deaths
1854, Mar. 1—City of Glasgow	British steamer left Liverpool for Philadelphia, never heard from again	480
1854, Sept. 27—Arctic and Vesta	U.S. Collins Line steamer sunk in collision with French steamer nr. Cape Race, Canada	285-351
1856, Jan. 23—Pacific	U.S. Collins Line steamer went missing in N Atlantic	186-286
1857, Sept. 12—Central America	U.S. mail steamship sank off Florida coast with $1.5 mil in gold	427
1858, Sept. 23—Austria	German steamer destroyed by fire in N Atlantic	471
1863, Apr. 27—Anglo-Saxon	British steamer wrecked at Cape Race, Canada	238
1865, Apr. 27—Sultana	Mississippi R. steamer carrying 2,400 released Union prisoners exploded nr. Memphis, TN. Worst maritime disaster in U.S. history	1,800
1869, Feb. 20—Radetzky	Austrian steam frigate exploded in Adriatic Sea	345
1869, Oct. 27—Stonewall	U.S. steamer burned, Mississippi R. below Cairo, IL	200
1872, Nov. 7—Mary Celeste	U.S. half-brig sailing from New York City to Genoa, Italy, with 10 on board found abandoned	Unknown
1873, Jan. 22—Northfleet	British steamer rammed by Spanish steamer Murillo off Dungeness, England, UK	300
1873, Apr. 1—Atlantic	British White Star steamer off Halifax, Nova Scotia, Canada	585
1873, Nov. 23—Ville du Havre and Loch Earn	French steamer sank after collision with British sailing ship	226
1874, Nov. 17—Cospatrick	En route from London to New Zealand, caught fire off Cape of Good Hope	468
1875, May 7—Schiller	German steamer off Isles of Scilly, UK	312
1875, Nov. 4—Pacific	U.S. steamer sank after collision off Cape Flattery, WA	236

Date—vessel(s)	Incident	Est. deaths
1878, Mar. 24—Eurydice	British frigate sank off Isle of Wight, England, UK	398
1878, Sept. 3—Princess Alice	British steamer sank after collision with *Bywell Castle* in Thames R.	700
1878, Dec. 18—Byzantin and Rinaldo	French and British steamers collided in Dardanelles, off Turkey.	210
1883, Jan. 19—Cimbria and Sultan	German steamer sank in collision with British steamer in North Sea.	389
1887, Nov. 15—Wah Yeung	Chinese steamer burned in Canton R., Hong Kong	400
1890, Feb. 17—Duburg.	British steamer wrecked, China Sea.	400
1890, Sept. 16—Ertugrul	Ottoman frigate in typhoon off Japan	587
1891, Mar. 17—Utopia and Anson	British steamer sank in collision with British ironclad off Gibraltar	562
1893, June 22—Victoria	British battleship sank after collision with British warship *Camperdown*, off Syrian coast	358
1895, Jan. 30—Elbe and Craithie	German steamer sank in collision with British steamer in North Sea.	332
1895, Mar. 11—Reina Regenta	Spanish cruiser foundered nr. Gibraltar	400
1898, Feb. 15—USS Maine	Explosion caused battleship to sink in Havana Harbor, Cuba	260
1898, July 4—La Bourgogne and Cromartyshire	French steamer sank in collision with British sailing ship off Nova Scotia, Canada	549
1904, May 15—Yoshino	Japanese cruiser sank after collision with cruiser *Kasuga* in fog off Liao-Tung Peninsula, China	329
1904, June 15—General Slocum	Excursion steamer burned off N. Brother Isl., New York, NY.	1,021
1904, June 28—Norge	Danish steamer wrecked on Rockall Isl., Scotland, UK	620
1906, Aug. 4—Sirio.	Italian steamer wrecked off Cape Palos, Spain.	350
1907, Feb. 11—Larchmont	U.S. steamer sank after collision with U.S. schooner *Harry Knowlton* nr. Block Island, RI	131
1908, Mar. 23—Mutsu Maru	Japanese steamer sank in collision with another steamer nr. Hakodate, Japan	300
1909, July 26—Waratah	British steamer vanished en route from Durban to Cape Town, South Africa	300
1911, Sept. 25—Liberté	French battleship exploded at Toulon	285
1912, Apr. 14-15—Titanic	British White Star steamer hit iceberg in N Atlantic.	1,503
1912, Sept. 28—Kichemaru	Japanese steamer sank off Japan coast	1,000
1914, May 29—Empress of Ireland	Canadian Pacific steamer collided with Norwegian coal transporter *Storstad* in St. Lawrence R., Canada	1,014
1914, Nov. 26—Bulwark	British battleship exploded in Sheerness Harbor, England, UK	788
1915, May 7—Lusitania	British Cunard Line steamer torpedoed and sunk by German submarine off Ireland	1,198
1915, July 24—Eastland.	Steamer capsized, Chicago R., IL	844
1916, Feb. 26—Provence	French cruiser sank in Mediterranean; then-worst disaster in maritime history	3,100
1916, Mar. 5—Principe de Asturias	Spanish steamer wrecked nr. Santos, Brazil.	558
1917, Dec. 6—Mont Blanc and Imo	French ammunition ship and Belgian steamer collided in Halifax Harbor, Canada	1,900+
1918, Apr. 25—Kiang-Kwan	Chinese steamer sank after collision with Chinese gunboat *Chutai* off Hankow, China.	500
1918, July 12—Kawachi	Japanese battleship blew up in Tokayama Bay	500
1918, Oct. 25—Princess Sophia	Canadian-Pacific steamer sank off Vanderbilt Reef, Alaska	398
1919, Jan. 17—Chaonia	French steamer lost in Straits of Messina, Italy	460
1919, Sept. 9—Valbanera.	Spanish steamer lost off FL coast	500
1920, Jan. 11—Afrique	French liner sank nr. La Rochelle, France.	553
1921, Mar. 18—Hong Kong	Chinese steamer wrecked, S China Sea	1,000
1922, Aug. 26—Niitaka	Japanese cruiser sank in storm off Kamchatka, USSR	300
1927, Sept. 20—Gentoku Maru	Japanese steamer capsized in Tsingtao Bay, China	278
1927, Oct. 25—Principessa Mafalda	Italian steamer blew up, sank off Porto Seguro, Brazil	314
1934, Sept. 8—Morro Castle	U.S. steamer en route from Havana to New York, burned off Asbury Park, NJ	134
1940, June 17—Lancastria.	Nazi forces sank Cunard liner evacuating British troops from France	2,500-6,000
1940, July 24—Meknes	French liner torpedoed by Nazis in English Channel	350
1942, Feb. 18—USS Truxtun and USS Pollux	Destroyer and cargo ship ran aground, sank off Newfoundland, Canada	204
1942, Oct. 2—Curacao and Queen Mary	British cruiser sank off Ireland after collision with liner carrying U.S. troops	338
1944, Dec. 17-18—Spence, Monaghan, Hull	3 U.S. destroyers sank during typhoon, Philippine Sea	790
1945, Jan. 30—Wilhelm Gustloff	Liner with German refugees, soldiers sunk by Soviet submarine in Baltic	5,000-9,000
1945, Apr. 16—Goya.	Cargo ship carrying German refugees, soldiers sunk by Soviet submarine in Baltic	6,000-7,000
1945, May 3—Cap Arcona and Thielbeck	German ocean liner and freighter carrying concentration camp inmates sunk by British warplanes in Lubeck Bay, Germany	7,000-8,000
1947, Jan. 19—Himera.	Greek steamer hit mine off Athens, Greece	392
1947, Apr. 16—Grandcamp	Ammonium nitrate explosion aboard French freighter caused fires throughout port, Texas City, TX	576+
1948, Dec. 3—Kiangya.	Chinese refugee ship wrecked in explosion S of Shanghai	1,100+
1954, Sept. 26—Toya Maru	Japanese ferry sank, Tsugaru Strait, Japan.	1,172
1956, July 26—Andrea Doria and Stockholm	Italian liner and Swedish liner collided off Nantucket Isl., MA.	51
1957, July 14—Eshghabad.	Soviet fishing boat ran aground in Caspian Sea.	270
1961, Apr. 8—Dara	British liner exploded in Persian Gulf	236
1961, July 8—Save.	Portuguese ship ran aground off Mozambique.	259
1965, Nov. 13—Yarmouth Castle	Cruise ship burned and sank off Nassau, The Bahamas	89
1970, Dec. 15—Namyong-Ho.	S. Korean ferry sank in Korea Strait	308
1975, Nov. 10—Edmund Fitzgerald	U.S. cargo ship sank during storm on Lake Superior	29
1980, Apr. 22—Don Juan	Sank off Mindoro Isl., Philippines, after colliding with barge	1,000+
1981, Jan. 27—Tamponas II	Indonesian car ferry caught fire and sank in Java Sea.	580
1983, May 25—10th of Ramadan	Nile steamer caught fire and sank in Lake Nasser, Egypt	357
1986, May 25—Shamia	Ferry capsized in storm, Meghna R., Bangladesh	500+

Date—vessel(s)	Incident	Est. deaths
1986, Sept. 1—Admiral Nakhimov and Pyotr Vasev	Soviet cruise ship collided with Soviet freighter in Black Sea	425
1987, Dec. 20—Doña Paz and Victor	Philippine ferry and oil tanker collided in Tablas Strait, Philippines	4,341
1988, Aug. 6	Indian ferry capsized on Ganges R.	400+
1988, Oct. 24—Doña Marilyn	Philippine ferry sank by typhoon near Leyte Isl.	350+
1991, Dec. 14—Salem Express	Ferry rammed coral reef nr. Safaga, Egypt	462
1993, Feb. 17—Neptune	Ferry capsized off Port-au-Prince, Haiti	500+
1993, Oct. 10—Seohae	S. Korean ferry capsized in Yellow Sea during storm	292
1994, Sept. 28—Estonia	Ferry sank in Baltic Sea off Finland	850+
1996, May 21—Bukoba	Overcrowded Tanzanian ferry sank in Lake Victoria	500+
1997, Sept. 8—Pride of la Gonâve	Haitian ferry sank off Montrouis, Haiti	200+
1999, Feb. 6—Harta Rimba	Cargo ship sank off Indonesia	280+
1999, May 1—Miss Majestic	"Duck" boat on tour sank, Lake Hamilton, AR	13
1999, Nov. 24—Dashun	Passenger ferry capsized nr. Yantai, China.	280
2000, June 29—Cahaya Bahari	Overloaded ferry carrying refugees from religious strife capsized in storm off Sulawesi Isl., Indonesia	500+
2001, Oct. 19	Fishing boat overloaded with refugees, mainly from Middle East, sank off Indonesia	350+
2002, May 4—Salahuddin-2	Overloaded Bangladesh ferry sank in Meghna R.	300+
2002, Sept. 26—Joola	Overloaded Senegalese ferry capsized in ocean off The Gambia	1,863
2003, July 8—MV-Nasrin 1	Overcrowded ferry sank nr. Chandpur in Bangladesh R.	400
2003, Oct. 15—Andrew J. Barberi	NYC ferry crashed into dock on approach to Staten Island	11
2004, Feb. 27—Superferry 14	Philippine ferry bombed by Islamic militants; deadliest terrorist attack at sea	116
2006, Feb. 3—Al-Salam Boccaccio 98	Ferry caught fire, sank in Red Sea off Egypt	1,000+
2006, Dec. 30—Senopati Nusantara	High waves capsized ferry en route to Java, Indonesia	400+
2007, Nov. 23—Explorer	Canadian cruise ship hit Antarctic iceberg; first commercial passenger ship to sink in region	0
2008, June 23—Princess of the Stars	Philippine ferry capsized during Typhoon Fengshen nr. Manila	800
2011, Sept. 10—MV Spice Islander	Overloaded ferry sank off coast of Tanzania	240+
2012, Jan. 17—Costa Concordia	Cruise ship ran aground off Italian coast; captain abandoned ship before evacuating passengers	32
2013, Oct. 3	Boat carrying migrants fleeing Eritrea sank near Lampedusa Isl., Italy	360
2014, Apr. 16—Sewol	Ferry carrying 476 people, most students, Korea's SW coast	304
2015, June 1—Dongfangzhixing (Eastern Star)	Chinese cruise ship sank in Yangtze R. during torrential rains	442
2015, Oct. 1—El Faro	Cargo ship en route from FL to Puerto Rico sailed into hurricane	33
2018, June 18—Sinar Bangun	Overloaded ferry sank in bad weather, Lake Toba, Sumatra, Indonesia	167
2018, July 19	"Duck" boat sank in a severe storm, Table Rock Lake, nr. Branson, MO	17
2018, Sept. 20—MV Nyerere	Overloaded Tanzanian ferry capsized in Lake Victoria	227+
2019, Sept. 2—Conception	Dive boat caught fire nr. Santa Cruz Isl., CA, while passengers slept	34

Note: As migration to Europe, mostly from North Africa, began to swell in 2014, deaths of migrants and refugees in shipwrecks and other incidents while crossing the Mediterranean Sea spiked. The UN's Intl. Organization for Migration reported 3,283 deaths in 2014, 4,054 deaths in 2015, 5,143 in 2016, 3,139 in 2017, 2,299 in 2018, 1,283 in 2019, and 558 as of Sept. 8, 2020.

Some Notable Railroad Disasters Since 1925

Date	Location	Deaths	Date	Location	Deaths
1925, June 16	Hackettstown, NJ	50	1987, July 2	Kasumbalesha Shaba, Zaire	125
1933, Dec. 23	Lagny-Pomponne, France	230	1987, Aug. 7	Between Moscow and Rostov, USSR	106
1937, July 16	Near Patna, India	107	1987, Oct. 19	Jakarta, Indonesia	153
1938, Dec. 25	Near Kishinev, Romania	150	1988, June 4	Arzamas, USSR	100
1939, Dec. 22	Genthin, near Magdeburg, Germany	132	1988, July 8	Kerala, India	108
1943, Sept. 6	Frankford Junction, Philadelphia, PA	79	1989, Jan. 15	Maizdi Khan, Bangladesh	135
1943, Dec. 16	Between Rennert and Buie, NC	72	1989, June 4	Ufa, USSR	645
1944, Jan. 16	León Province, Spain	500	1989, Aug. 11	San Rafael R., Sinaloa State, Mexico	112
1944, Mar. 2	Salerno, Italy	521	1990, Jan. 4	Sindh Province, Pakistan	307
1944, Dec. 31	Bagley, UT	50	1991, Mar. 5	Nacala, Mozambique	109
1945, July 16	Munich, Germany	102	1991, June 8	Ghotki, Pakistan	100
1946, Mar. 20	Aracaju, Brazil	185	1991, Sept. 5	Pointe-Noire, Congo Republic	110
1949, Oct. 22	Near Dwor, Poland	200+	1993, Jan. 30	Near Mtito Andei, Kenya	140+
1950, Nov. 22	Richmond Hill, Queens, NY	79	1993, Apr. 25	Near Karachi, Pakistan	150
1951, Feb. 6	Woodbridge, NJ	84	1994, Sept. 22	Lubango, Angola	300
1952, Mar. 4	Near Rio de Janeiro, Brazil	119	1994, Dec. 30	Near Namkham, Myanmar	102
1952, July 9	Rzepin, Poland	160	1995, Jan. 13	Dinajpur, Bangladesh	150
1952, Oct. 8	Harrow, England, UK	112	1995, Aug. 20	Firozabad, India	350
1953, Dec. 24	Tangiwai, New Zealand	151	1995, Nov. 28	Baku, Azerbaijan	337
1953, Dec. 24	Sakvice, Czechoslovakia	103	1997, Mar. 3	Punjab Province, Pakistan	128
1955, Apr. 3	Guadalajara, Mexico	300	1997, May 4	Kisangani, Zaire	100+
1957, Sept. 1	Kendal, Jamaica	178	1998, Feb. 19	Yaounde, Cameroon	120
1957, Sept. 29	Montgomery, W Pakistan	300	1998, June 3	Eschede, Germany	102
1957, Dec. 4	London, England, UK	90	1998, Nov. 26	Khanna, India	108
1958, May 8	Rio de Janeiro, Brazil	128	1999, Aug. 2	Gauhati, India	285
1960, Nov. 14	Pardubice, Czechoslovakia	117	2002, Feb. 20	S of Cairo, Egypt	377
1962, May 3	Tokyo, Japan	163	2002, May 25	Muamba, Mozambique	195
1963, Nov. 9	Yokohama, Japan	162	2002, June 24	Igandu, Tanzania	281
1965, Feb. 27	Near Port Sudan, Sudan	124	2002, Sept. 10	Bihar, India	112
1970, Feb. 1	Buenos Aires, Argentina	236	2004, Feb. 18	Neyshabur, NE Iran	300
1972, June 16	Near Soissons, France	108	2004, Apr. 22	Ryongchon, North Korea	161
1972, Oct. 6	Near Saltillo, Mexico	204	2005, Apr. 25	Near Amagasaki, Japan	107
1974, Aug. 30	Zagreb, Yugoslavia	153	2005, July 13	Ghotki, Pakistan	132
1981, June 6	Near Mansi, India	268	2005, Oct. 29	Andra Pradesh, India	110
1982, Jan. 27	El Asnam, Algeria	120	2007, Aug. 2	Nr. Benaleka, Dem. Rep. of Congo	100
1982, July 11	Tepic, Mexico	120	2010, May 28	W. Bengal, India	148
1983, Feb. 19	Empalme, Mexico	100	2011, July 23	Wenzhou, China	140
1985, Jan. 13	Awash, Ethiopia	392	2016, Nov. 20	Near Kanpur, Uttar Pradesh, India	150
1985, Sept. 12	Viseu, Portugal	118	2019, Oct. 31	Rahim Yar Khan, Pakistan	75
1986, Aug. 6	Bihar, India	202			

Notable Droughts

Source: EM-DAT: The Emergency Events Database, CRED/D. Guha-Sapir, Université catholique de Louvain, Brussels, Belgium, www.emdat.be; World Almanac research

Date	Location	Est. deaths	Date	Location	Est. deaths
1900	Bengal, India	1,250,000	1974-76	Somalia	19,000
1900	Cape Verde islands	11,000	1981-85	Mozambique	100,000
1910-14	Zinder Dept., Niger	85,000	1981-85	Chad	3,000
1920	China	500,000	1983	Swaziland	500
1920	Cape Verde islands	24,000	1983-84	Eritrea, Ethiopia	300,000
1921	S Ukraine, Volga, USSR	1,200,000	1983-85	N Sudan	150,000
1928-30	Shaanxi, Henan, Gansu, China	3,000,000	1987	Somalia, Eritrea, Ethiopia	967
1940-44	Cape Verde islands	20,000	1987	NW India	300
1942	Calcutta, Bengal, India	1,500,000	1988	Central China	1,400
1943	Bangladesh	1,900,000	1991	Jiangxi, Hunan Provinces, China	2,000
1946	Cape Verde islands	30,000	1997	Irian Jaya, Indonesia	672
1965	Ethiopia	2,000	1999-2003	Pakistan	143
1965-67	India	1,500,000	2002	Malawi	500
1966	Lombok, Indonesia	8,000	2006	SW China	134
1973-78	Ethiopia	100,000	2014-17	Tharparkar, Pakistan	166

Some Notable Miscellaneous Disasters Since 1950

Date	Event	Location	Details	Est. deaths
1952, Dec.	Pollution	London, England, UK	Heavy smog blanketed city; impeded breathing	4,000
1959-61	Famine	China	Govt. policies compounded by flooding and drought	15-40 mil
1980, summer	Heat wave	Central, eastern U.S.	Combined direct and indirect deaths est. at 10,000	1,260
1984, Dec. 3	Industrial accident	Bhopal, India	Toxic gas leaked from a Union Carbide factory	16,000
1986, Aug. 21	Gas	Nr. Lake Nyos, Cameroon	Volcanic lake released cloud of carbon dioxide gas	1,700
1990, July 2	Stampede	Mecca, Saudi Arabia	Pilgrims panicked in tunnel leading to the holy city	1,426
1995, June 29	Building collapse	Seoul, South Korea	Improperly built and maintained Sampoong Dept. Store failed with shoppers inside	501
2003, summer	Heat wave	Europe	France suffered most, with 14,800 dead	35,000
2005, Aug. 31	Stampede	Baghdad, Iraq	Rumors of suicide bomber caused panic among religious pilgrims on al-Aimmah Bridge	965
2013, Apr. 24	Building collapse	Savar, Bangladesh	Garment factory found to have substandard foundation	1,100+
2015, Sept. 24	Stampede	Mina, Saudi Arabia	Two groups of pilgrims collided during hajj to Mecca	2,411
2019, July 21-27	Heat wave	France	Record temperatures across Europe	868

Some Notable U.S. Tornadoes Since 1925

Date	Location	Deaths	Date	Location	Deaths
1925, Mar. 18	MO, IL, IN	747	1974, Apr. 3-4	AL; GA; KY; Xenia, OH; other states	315
1927, Apr. 12	Rocksprings, TX	74	1977, Apr. 4	AL, MS, GA	22
1927, May 9	AR; Poplar Bluff, MO	92	1979, Apr. 10	TX, OK	60
1927, Sept. 29	St. Louis, MO	90	1984, Mar. 28	NC, SC	57
1930, May 6	Hill, Navarro, Ellis Cos., TX	41	1985, May 31	NY; PA; OH; Ontario, Can.	75
1932, Mar. 21	Alabama	268	1987, May 22	Saragosa, TX	30
1936, Apr. 5-6	Tupelo, MS; Gainesville, GA	454	1989, Nov. 15	Huntsville, AL	18
1938, Sept. 29	Charleston, SC	32	1990, Aug. 28	Northern IL	25
1942, Mar. 16	Central to NE Mississippi	75	1991, Apr. 26	KS, OK	23
1942, Apr. 27	Rogers and Mayes Cos., OK	52	1992, Nov. 21-23	South, Midwest	26
1944, June 23	OH, PA, WV, MD	150	1994, Mar. 27-28	AL, TN, GA, NC, SC	52
1945, Apr. 12	OK, AR	102	1995, May 6-7	Southern OK, northern TX	23
1947, Apr. 9	TX; Woodward, OK; KS	181	1997, Mar. 1	Central AR	26
1948, Mar. 19	Bunker Hill and Gillespie, IL	33	1997, May 27	Jarrell, TX	27
1949, Jan. 3	LA, AR	58	1998, Feb. 22-23	Central FL	42
1952, Mar. 21-22	AR, MO, TN	208	1998, Apr. 8	AL, GA, MS	39
1953, May 11	Waco, TX	114	1999, May 3	OK, KS	54
1953, June 8	Flint-Beecher, MI; OH	142	2000, Feb. 14	SW Georgia	22+
1953, June 9	Worcester and vicinity, MA	90	2002, Nov. 10-11	AL, MS, TN, IN, OH, PA	36
1953, Dec. 5	Vicksburg, MS	38	2003, May 4-11	TN, MO, KS, IL, OK, WV, AL	48
1955, May 25	Udall, KS; MO; Blackwell, OK; TX	115	2005, Nov. 6	KY, IN	22
1957, May 20	KS, MO	48	2007, Mar. 1	AL, GA, MO, Midwest	20
1958, June 4	NW Wisconsin	30	2008, Feb. 25	TN, AR, KY, AL, MO	57
1959, Feb. 10	St. Louis, MO	21	2008, May 10	MS, OK, GA	23
1960, May 5-6	Southeastern OK, AR	30	2011, Apr. 14-16	Southeast, Midwest, OK to VA	38
1965, Apr. 11	IA, IN, IL, OH, MI, WI	271	2011, Apr. 25-28	362 funnels from TX to NY	321
1966, Mar. 3	Jackson, MS; AL	57	2011, May 22	Joplin, MO	161
1967, Apr. 21	IL, MO, IA, MI	33	2012, Mar. 2-3	Southeast, Ohio Valley (AL, GA, IN, KY, OH, TN)	42
1968, May 15	Midwest	71	2013, May 20	Moore, OK	24
1969, Jan. 23	Mississippi	32	2013, May 31	El Reno, OK	21
1970, May 11	Lubbock, TX	23	2017, Jan. 20-22	AL, FL, GA, LA, MS, SC, TX	24
1971, Feb. 21	Mississippi Delta: MS, LA, AR, TN	110			
1973, May 26-27	South, Midwest	47			

Some Notable Hurricanes, Typhoons, Blizzards, Other Storms

C. = cyclone; H. = hurricane; TS. = tropical storm; T. = typhoon[1].

Date	Location	Est. deaths
1881, Aug. 24-29	H., GA, SC	700
1888, Mar. 11-14	Blizzard, Eastern U.S.	400
1893, Aug. 15-Sept. 2	H., GA, SC	1,000+
1893, Oct. 1	H., LA	1,100+
1900, Sept. 8	H., Galveston, TX	8,000+
1906, Sept. 18	T., Hong Kong	10,000+
1906, Sept. 19-24	H., LA, MS	350
1909, Sept. 20	H., LA	350+
1915, Aug. 16	H., Galveston, TX	275
1915, Sept. 29	H., LA	275
1919, Sept. 6-14	H., Carib., FL Keys, Gulf, TX	600+[2]
1922, July 27	T., Swatow, China	100,000
1926, Sept. 11-22	H., FL, AL, MS	370+
1926, Oct. 20	H., Cuba	600
1928, Sept. 6-20	H., southern FL	2,500+
1930, Sept. 3	H., Dominican Republic	2,000
1935, Aug. 29-Sept. 10	H., Caribbean, SE U.S.	400+
1937, Sept. 2	T., Hong Kong	10,000+
1938, Sept. 21	H., NY, New England	682
1940, Nov. 11-12	NE, Midwest U.S.	154
1942, Oct.	T., W. Sundarbans, Bangladesh	61,000
1942, Oct. 15-16	H., Bengal, India	40,000
1947, Dec. 26	Blizzard, NYC, N Atl. states	55
1952, Oct. 22	T., Philippines	440
1954, Aug. 30	H. Carol, NE U.S.	68
1954, Oct. 5-18	H. Hazel, E Canada, U.S., Haiti	347
1955, Aug. 7-21	H. Diane, Eastern U.S.	400
1955, Sept. 19	H. Hilda, Mexico	200
1956, Feb. 1-29	Blizzard, W Europe	1,000
1957, June 25-30	H. Audrey, TX to AL	390
1958, Feb. 15-16	Blizzard, NE U.S.	171
1959, Sept. 17-19	T. Sarah, Japan, S. Korea	2,000
1959, Sept. 26-27	T. Vera, Honshu, Japan	4,466
1960, Sept. 4-12	H. Donna, Caribbean, E U.S.	148
1961, Oct. 31	H. Hattie, Brit. Honduras	400
1962, Sept. 1	T. Wanda, Hong Kong	130-200
1963, May 28-29	Windstorm, Bangladesh	22,000
1963, Oct. 4-8	H. Flora, Caribbean	6,000
1964, June 30	T. Winnie, N Philippines	107
1964, Sept. 5	T. Ruby, Hong Kong, China	735
1965, May 11-12	Windstorm, Bangladesh	17,000
1965, June 1-2	Windstorm, Bangladesh	30,000
1965, Sept. 7-12	H. Betsy, FL, MS, LA	74
1965, Dec. 15	Windstorm, Bangladesh	10,000
1966, June 4-10	H. Alma, Honduras, SE U.S.	51
1966, Sept. 24-30	H. Inez, Carib., FL, Mexico	293
1967, July 9	T. Billie, SW Japan	347
1967, Sept. 5-23	H. Beulah, Carib., Mex., TX	54
1967, Dec. 12-20	Blizzard, SW U.S.	51
1969, Aug. 17-18	H. Camille, MS, LA	256
1970, Sept. 15	T. Pitang (Georgia), Philippines	300
1970, Oct. 14	T. Sening (Joan), Philippines	583
1970, Oct. 15	T. Titang (Kate), Philippines	526
1970, Nov. 13	C., Bay of Bengal, Bangladesh	300,000-500,000
1971, Aug. 1	T. Rose, Hong Kong	130
1972, June 19-29	H. Agnes, FL to NY	118
1972, Dec. 3	T. Theresa, Philippines	169
1973, June-Aug.	Monsoon rains, India	1,217
1974, July 11	T. Gilda, Japan, S. Korea	108
1974, Sept. 19-20	H. Fifi, Honduras	2,000
1975, Sept. 13-27	H. Eloise, Caribbean, NE U.S.	71
1976, May 20	T. Olga, floods, Philippines	215
1976, Sept. 25-Oct. 2	H. Liza, western Mexico	630
1978, Oct. 27	T. Rita, Philippines	400
1979, Aug. 30-Sept. 7	H. David, Caribbean, E U.S.	1,100
1980, Aug. 4-11	H. Allen, Caribbean, TX	272
1981, Nov. 25	T. Irma, Luzon Isl., Philippines	176
1983, June	Monsoon, India	900
1984, Sept. 2	T. Ike, southern Philippines	1,363
1985, May 25	C., Bangladesh	15,000
1985, Oct. 26-Nov. 6	H. Juan, SE U.S.	97
1987, Nov. 25	T. Nina, Philippines	650
1988, Sept. 10-17	H. Gilbert, Carib., Gulf of Mex.	260
1989, Sept. 16-22	H. Hugo, Caribbean, SE U.S.	86
1990, May 6-11	C. (mult.), SE India	450
1991, Apr. 30	C., Bangladesh	139,000
1991, Nov. 5	TS. Thelma, central Philippines	7,000+
1992, Aug. 24-26	H. Andrew, Southern FL, LA	65
1993, Mar. 12-14	Blizzard, Eastern U.S.	270+
1993, June	Monsoon, Bangladesh	2,000
1994, Nov. 8-18	TS. Gordon, Caribbean, FL	830
1995, Oct. 2-4	H. Opal, S Mexico, FL, AL	59
1995, Nov. 2-3	T. Angela, Philippines	600+
1996, Jan. 7-8	Blizzard, NE U.S.	100
1996, Aug. 22	Blizzard, Himalayas, N India	239
1996, Aug. 29-Sept. 6	H. Fran, Carib., NC, VA, WV	30
1996, Sept. 8	T. Sally, S China	114
1996, Nov. 6	C., Andhra Pradesh, India	1,000+
1996, Dec. 25	TS. Greg, eastern Malaysia	100+
1997, May 19	C., Bangladesh	108
1997, Aug. 18-21	T. Winnie, Taiwan, E China	140+
1997, Oct. 8-10	H. Pauline, SW Mexico	230
1998, June 9	C., Gujarat, India	1,320
1998, Aug.	Monsoon, Bangladesh	326
1998, Sept. 21-23	H. Georges, Carib., FL, U.S. Gulf	600+
1998, Oct. 27-29	H. Mitch, Central America	14,600
1999, Sept. 4-17	H. Floyd, The Bahamas, E U.S.	56
1999, Oct. 29	C., E India	9,392
1999, Dec. 26-29	Gales, France, Switz., Germany	120
2000, Dec. 29	Winter storm, TX, OK, AR	40+
2001, July 30	T. Toraji, Taiwan	200
2001, Nov. 6-12	T. Lingling, S Philip., Vietnam	220+
2002, Aug.-Sept.	T. Rusa, N. and S. Korea	115+
2003, Feb. 16-17	Blizzard, E seaboard U.S.	59
2003, Sept. 7-19	H. Isabel, NC, VA, E seaboard	40+
2003, Sept. 12	T. Maemi, S. Korea	130
2004, Mar. 7-19	C. Gafilo, Madagascar	198
2004, May 19	C., Myanmar	220
2004, Aug. 12-15	T. Rananim, eastern China	164
2004, Aug. 13-14	H. Charley, FL, SC	36
2004, Sept. 5-6	H. Frances, The Bahamas, FL	35
2004, Sept. 7-16	H. Ivan, Barbados, Grenada, U.S. Gulf Coast	115
2004, Sept. 16-26	H. Jeanne, Dom. Rep., Haiti, FL	1,500+
2005, July 7-11	H. Dennis, Jamaica, Haiti, Cuba, FL	50
2005, Aug. 25-29	H. Katrina, LA, MS, FL, AL, GA	1,833+[3]
2005, Aug. 31-Sept. 1	T. Talim, Taiwan, E China	129+
2005, Sept. 21-24	H. Rita, TX, LA	62[4]
2005, Sept. 21-28	T. Damrey, SE Asia; Philippines; Hainan, China	145
2005, Oct. 4	H. Stan, Central Amer., Mex.	1,000+[5]
2006, July 14	TS. Bilis, SE China	612
2006, Aug. 10	T. Saomai, SE China	295
2006, Nov. 30	T. Durian, Philippines	450-1,000+
2007, June 6-7	C. Gonu, Oman, Iran	546[6]
2007, Nov. 15	C. Sidr, southern Bangladesh	3,363
2008, May 2-3	C. Nargis, southern Myanmar	138,366
2008, June 20-25	T. Fengshen, Philippines, China	233
2008, Aug. 26-Sept. 1	H. Gustav, Haiti, Dom. Rep., U.S.	138
2008, Sept. 1-4	TS. Hanna, Haiti	529
2008, Sept. 7-13	H. Ike, Haiti; Cuba; TX	164
2009, May 23-26	C. Alia, India, Bangladesh	260
2009, Aug. 7-9	T. Morakot, mudslides, Taiwan	700+
2009, Sept. 23-30	T. Ketsana, Philippines, Vietnam, Cambodia, Laos	498+
2009, Oct. 3-10	T. Parma, Philippines	375
2009, Oct. 30-Nov. 3	T. Mirinae, Philippines, Vietnam	159+
2010, May 29	TS. Agatha, Guatemala, El Salvador, Honduras	184
2010, July 13-17	T. Conson, Philippines	105+
2011, Oct. 29-30	C., Odisha (Orissa) state, E India	9,893
2011, Dec. 16	TS. Washi, Philippines	1,257
2012, Jan. 24-Feb. 14	Blizzard/cold snap, E Europe	650+
2012, Oct. 22-31	H. Sandy, Cuba, Haiti, Jamaica, Eastern U.S.	245[7]
2012, Dec. 4	T. Bopha, Philippines	1,146
2013, Nov. 8	T. Haiyan, Philippines	7,986
2013, Nov. 10	C., Puntland, Somalia	162
2014, July 15	T. Rammasun, Philippines, China, Vietnam	173
2016, Oct. 4-8	H. Matthew, Haiti, Bahamas, FL, GA, SC, NC	585
2017, Aug. 25-30	H. Harvey, South TX, LA	93+[8]
2017, Aug. 31-Sept. 11	H. Irma, Barbuda, Cuba, FL	134
2017, Sept. 17-28	H. Maria, Dominica, Virgin Isls., Puerto Rico	3,059[9]
2019, Mar. 14-15	C. Idai, Zimbabwe, Mozambique	1,303
2019, May 3-4	C. Fani, Odisha, E India, Bangladesh	81
2019, Aug. 28-Sept. 6	H. Dorian, Bahamas, FL, GA, SC, NC	84
2020, May 16-21	C. Amphan, E India, Bangladesh	98

(1) What hurricanes are called W of Intl. Date Line and N of equator. (2) Incl. about 500 lost at sea. (3) Official toll as of Aug. 2006 was 1,577 in LA, 238 in MS, 14 in FL, and 2 each in AL and GA. (4) Incl. 55 indirect deaths. (5) Incl. deaths from floods and landslides. (6) First documented super cyclone in Arabian Sea. (7) Incl. 87 indirect deaths in the U.S. (8) Downgraded to a tropical storm Aug. 26, Harvey nevertheless caused severe flooding. (9) Puerto Rico's government, Aug. 2018, revised its death toll from 64 to 2,975 in line with a report they commissioned from George Washington Univ. public health experts. A separate Harvard study, in May 2018, estimated the death toll to be at least 4,645.

Some Notable Floods, Tidal Waves

Source: EM-DAT: The Emergency Events Database, CRED/D. Guha-Sapir, Université catholique de Louvain, Brussels, Belgium, www.emdat.be; World Almanac research

Date	Location	Est. deaths	Date	Location	Est. deaths
1703	Awa, Japan	100,000+	1981, July	Sichuan, Hubei Prov., China	1,300
1889, May 31	Johnstown, PA	2,200+	1982, Jan. 23	Near Lima, Peru	600
1903, June 15	Heppner, OR.	325	1982, May 12	Guangdong, China	430
1911	Chang Jiang (Yangtze) R., China	100,000	1982, Sept. 17-21	El Salvador, Guatemala	1,300+
			1984, Aug.-Sept.	South Korea	200+
1913, Mar. 25-27	OH, IN.	732	1987, July 22	Bangladesh	2,055
1915, Aug. 17	Galveston, TX	275	1987, Aug.-Sept.	Northern Bangladesh	1,000+
1927, Jan.-July	Mississippi Valley	246+	1988, June-Sept.	Bangladesh	2,379
1927, Nov. 1	Mostagenem, Algeria	3,000	1988, Sept.	N India	1,000+
1928, Mar. 13	Dam collapse, Saugus, CA.	450	1989, July 14	China	2,000
1928, Sept. 16	Lake Okeechobee, FL	1,770+	1994, May-Oct.	Assam, India.	2,001
1931, Aug.	Huang He R., China	3,700,000	1995, July	NE China	1,200
1933	Shandong, China	18,000	1995, Sept. 1-20	India	1,479
1937, Jan. 22	OH, MS valleys	250	1996, June-July	Guizhou, Hebei, China	2,775
1938, June 9	Huang He R., China	500,000	1997, Oct.-Nov.	Somalia.	2,311
1946, Apr. 1	HI, AK	159	1998, July 17	Papua New Guinea.	3,000
1947, Sept. 20	Honshu Isl., Japan	2,000	1998, July-Aug.	Hunan, Sichuan, China.	3,656
1949, July	China	57,000	1998, July-Sept.	Bangladesh.	1,441
1949, Oct.	Guatemala	40,000	1998, Aug.	India	1,811
1950	Pakistan	2,900	1999, Oct.-Dec.	Central Vietnam	700+
1951, Aug. 28	Manchuria.	4,800	1999, Dec. 15-20	NW Venezuela	30,000
1953, Jan. 31	Storm surge, Zuiderzee, Netherlands	2,000	2000, Feb.-Mar.	Mozambique	700
			2000, Sept. 19-30	India, Bangladesh.	1,000+
1953, June 23	Japan	2,566	2001, Aug. 1-6	Taiwan	100+
1954, Aug.	China	30,000	2001, Nov. 9-10	Northern Algeria	711+
1954, Aug. 17	Farahzad, Iran	2,000	2002, Apr.-Aug.	China	800+
1955, Oct. 7-12	India, Pakistan	1,700	2002, July-Aug.	India, Nepal, Bangladesh	1,100+
1959, Nov. 1	Western Mexico	2,000	2004, May 23-Jun. 1	Dom. Republic, Haiti	2,665
1959, Dec. 2	Frejus, France.	412	2004, June-Sept.	Bangladesh, India, Myanmar, Nepal	2,000+
1960, Oct. 10	Bangladesh.	6,000	2004, June-Sept.	China	500
1960, Oct. 31	Bangladesh.	4,000	2004, Nov.-Dec.	Philippines	1,060+
1961, July	N India	2,000	2004, Dec. 26	Indian Ocean nations	227,898
1962, Sept. 27	Barcelona, Spain	445	2005, July 26-Aug. 5	Western Maharashtra state, India	1,200
1963, Oct. 9	Dam collapse, Vaiont, Italy	1,800			
1967, Jan. 18-24	Eastern Brazil	894	2006, Feb. 17	Leyte Isl., Philippines	1,000
1967, Mar. 19	Rio de Janeiro, Brazil	436	2006, July 17	S of Java, Indonesia	530+
1967, Nov. 26	Lisbon, Portugal	464	2007, July 21-Aug. 3	Bangladesh.	1,110
1968, July	Rajasthan, Gujarat states, India	4,892	2007, July-Sept.	India	1,103
			2008, June-July	India	1,063
1968, Oct. 7	NE India	780	2009, July-Sept.	India	992
1969, Jan. 18-26	Southern CA.	100	2010, May-Aug.	China	1,691
1969, Aug. 20-22	Western VA.	189	2010, June 13-24	Cenxi, China.	377+
1969, Oct. 1-8	Tunisia	500	2010, July-Aug.	Pakistan	1,985
1970, July 22	Himalayas, India.	500	2010, Aug. 1-4	Zhouqu County, China	1,500+
1972, Feb. 26	Buffalo Creek, WV	118	2011, Jan. 11-12	SE Brazil	900
1972, June 9	Rapid City, SD	238	2011, Mar. 11	NE Japan	20,896
1972, Aug. 7	Luzon Isl., Philippines	454	2011, Apr.-May	Northern Colombia	425+
1972, Aug. 19-31	Pakistan	1,500	2011, July-Dec.	Thailand	708+
1974, Mar. 29	Tubaro, Brazil	1,000	2011, July-Dec.	Philippines, Cambodia, Myanmar	2,000+
1974, July	Bangladesh.	28,700			
1974, Aug. 12	Monty-Long, Bangladesh	2,500	2012, July-Oct.	Nigeria	363
1975, Aug. 8	Dam collapse, Henan Prov., China.	171,000	2012, Aug.-Oct.	Pakistan	480
			2012, Sept.-Oct.	Nigeria	431
1976, July 31	Big Thompson Canyon, CO	140	2013, June	Uttarakhand, India	6,054
1978, July	N, NE India	3,800	2015, Nov.-Dec.	S India	500
1979, July 17	Lomblem Isl., Indonesia	539	2018, June-Aug.	Kerala, India	504
1979, Aug. 11	Morbi, India.	10,000	2018, Dec. 22	Sunda Strait, Indonesia	437
1980, June	Sichuan, China.	6,200			
1981, Apr.	N China.	550			

Some Major Earthquakes

Source: Global Volcanism Network, Smithsonian Institution; U.S. Geological Survey, U.S. Dept. of the Interior; World Almanac research

Magnitude of earthquakes (mag.) is a relative measurement of an earthquake's energy. Deaths include those in aftershocks or related events.

Date	Location	Deaths	Mag.	Date	Location	Deaths	Mag.
526, May 20	Antioch, Syria	250,000	NA	1755, Nov. 1	Lisbon, Portugal	60,000	8.75[2]
856	Corinth, Greece	45,000	NA	1783, Feb. 4	Calabria, Italy	30,000	NA
856, Dec. 22	Damghan, Iran	200,000	NA	1797, Feb. 4	Quito, Ecuador	41,000	NA
893, Mar. 23	Ardabil, Iran	150,000	NA	1822, Sept. 5	Asia Minor, Aleppo	22,000	NA
1057	Chihli, China	25,000	NA	1828, Dec. 28	Echigo, Japan.	30,000	NA
1138, Aug. 9	Aleppo, Syria	230,000	NA	1868, Aug. 13-16	Peru, Ecuador.	40,000	NA
1169, Feb. 11	Nr. Mt. Etna, Sicily	15,000	NA[1]	1875, May 16	Venezuela, Colombia	16,000	NA
1268	Silicia, Asia Minor	60,000	NA	1886, May 31	Charleston, SC	60	6.6
1290, Sept. 27	Chihli, China	100,000	NA	1896, June 15	Sanriku, Japan (tsunami)	27,120	8.5
1293, May 20	Kamakura, Japan	30,000	NA	1902, Apr. 19	Quezaltenango and San Marcos, Guatemala	2,000	7.5
1531, Jan. 26	Lisbon, Portugal	30,000	NA				
1556, Jan. 24	Shaanxi, China	830,000	NA	1902, Dec. 16	Uzbekistan, Russia.	4,700	6.4
1667, Nov.	Shemakha, Caucasia (now Azerbaijan)	80,000	NA	1903, Apr. 28	Malazgirt, Turkey.	3,500	7.0
				1905, Apr. 4	Kangra, India	19,000	7.5
1693, Jan. 11	Catania, Italy.	60,000	NA	1906, Jan. 31	Off coast of Esmeraldas, Ecuador	1,000	8.8
1737, Oct. 11	India, Calcutta.	300,000	NA				
1755, June 7	N Persia (current-day Iran)	40,000	NA	1906, Mar. 16	Chia-i, Taiwan.	1,250	6.8

Date	Location	Deaths	Mag.	Date	Location	Deaths	Mag.
1906, Apr. 18-19	San Francisco, CA	3,000+	7.7[3]	1974, May 10	Zhaotong, China	1,540	6.8
1906, Aug. 17	Valparaiso, Chile	3,882	8.6	1974, Dec. 28	Northern Pakistan	5,300	6.2
1907, Oct. 21	Central Asia	12,000	8.1	1975, Feb. 4	Haicheng, China	2,000	7.0
1908, Dec. 28	Messina, Italy	72,000	7.2	1975, Sept. 6	Eastern Turkey	2,300	6.7
1909, Jan. 23	Silakhor, Iran	5,000–		1976, Feb. 4	Guatemala	23,000	7.5
		6,000	7.3	1976, May 6	NE Italy	1,000	6.5
1912, Aug. 9	Murefte, Turkey	2,800	7.4	1976, June 25	Irian Jaya, New Guinea	422	7.1
1914, Oct. 3	Burdur, Turkey	4,000	7.0	1976, July 28	Tangshan, China	242,769	7.5
1915, Jan. 13	Avezzano, Italy	32,610	7.0	1976, Aug. 16	Mindanao, Philippines	8,000	7.9
1917, July 30	Yunnan Prov., China	1,800	7.5	1976, Nov. 24	NW Iran-Turkey border	5,000	7.3
1920, Dec. 16	Gansu, China	200,000	7.8[4]	1977, Mar. 4	Romania	1,500	7.2
1923, Mar. 24	Sichuan, China	3,500	7.3	1978, Sept. 16	NE Iran	15,000	7.8
1923, Mar. 25	Torbat-e Heydariyeh, Iran…	2,200	5.7	1980, Oct. 10	NW Algeria	5,000	7.7
1923, Sept. 1	Yokohama, Japan	142,800	7.9	1980, Nov. 23	Southern Italy	2,735	6.5
1925, Mar. 16	Yunnan Prov., China	5,800	7.0	1981, June 11	Southern Iran	3,000	6.9
1927, Mar. 7	Tango, Japan	3,020	7.6	1981, July 28	Southern Iran	1,500	7.3
1927, May 22	Gansu, China	40,900	7.6	1982, Dec. 13	W Arabian Peninsula	2,800	6.0
1929, May 1	Koppeh Dagh, Iran	3,800	7.2	1983, Oct. 30	Eastern Turkey	1,342	6.9
1930, May 6	Salmas, Iran	2,500	7.2	1985, Sept. 19	Michoacan, Mexico	9,500	8.0
1930, July 23	Irpinia, Italy	1,404	6.5	1986, Oct. 10	El Salvador	1,000+	5.5
1931, Mar. 31	Managua, Nicaragua	2,500	6.0	1987, Mar. 6	Colombia-Ecuador	1,000	7.0
1931, Apr. 27	Armenia-Azerbaijan border	2,800	5.7	1988, Aug. 20	India-Nepal border	1,000	6.8
1931, Aug. 10	Xinjiang, China	10,000	8.0	1988, Dec. 7	Spitak, Armenia	25,000	6.8
1933, Mar. 2	Sanriku, Japan (tsunami)	2,990	8.4	1989, Oct. 17	San Francisco Bay area, CA	63	6.9
1933, Mar. 10	Long Beach, CA	115	6.2	1990, June 20	Western Iran	40,000+	7.4
1933, Aug. 25	Sichuan, China	9,300	7.5	1990, July 16	Luzon, Philippines	1,621	7.7
1934, Jan. 15	Bihar, India-Nepal	10,700	8.1	1991, Feb. 1	Pakistan-Afgh. border	1,200	6.8
1935, Apr. 21	Miao-li, Taiwan	3,270	7.1	1991, Oct. 19	Northern India	2,000	7.0
1935, May 30	Quetta, Pakistan	30,000	7.6	1992, Dec. 12	Flores Isl., Indonesia	2,500	7.5
1939, Jan. 25	Chillan, Chile	28,000	7.8	1993, Sept. 30	Maharashtra, S India	9,748	6.2
1939, Dec. 26	Erzincan, Turkey	32,700	7.8	1994, Jan. 17	Northridge, CA	61	6.7
1943, Sept. 10	Tottori, Japan	1,190	7.4	1994, June 6	Cauca, SW Colombia	1,000	6.8
1943, Nov. 26	Ladik, Turkey	4,000	7.6	1995, Jan. 16	Kobe, Japan	5,502	6.9
1944, Jan. 15	San Juan, Argentina	8,000	7.4	1995, May 27	Sakhalin Isl., Russia	1,989	7.5
1944, Feb. 1	Gerede, Turkey	2,790	7.4	1997, Feb. 28	NW Iran	1,000+	6.1
1945, Jan. 12	Mikawa, Japan	1,961	7.1	1997, May 10	Northern Iran	1,567	7.3
1945, Nov. 27	Makran Coast, Pakistan	4,000	8.0	1998, Feb. 4	Hindu Kush, Afghanistan	2,323	5.9
1946, May 31	Ustukran, Turkey	1,300	5.9	1998, May 30	Afgh.-Tajikistan border	4,000+	6.6
1946, Nov. 10	Ancash, Peru	1,400	7.3	1998, July 17	Papua New Guinea	2,183	7.0
1946, Dec. 20	Honshu, Japan	1,362	8.1	1999, Jan. 25	Armenia, Colombia	1,185+	6.1
1948, June 28	Fukui, Japan	3,769	7.3	1999, Aug. 17	Izmit, western Turkey	17,118+	7.6
1948, Oct. 5	Ashgabat, Turkmenistan	110,000	7.3	1999, Sept. 20	Taichung, Taiwan	2,400	7.6
1949, July 10	Khait, Tajikistan	12,000	7.5	2001, Jan. 26	Gujarat, India	20,085	7.6
1949, Aug. 5	Pelileo, Ecuador	5,050	6.8	2002, Mar. 25-26	Hindu Kush, Afghanistan	1,000+	6.1
1950, Aug. 15	Assam, India	1,526	8.6	2003, May 21	Northern Algeria	2,266	6.8
1954, Sept. 9	Orleansville, Algeria	1,250	6.8	2003, Dec. 26	Bam, SE Iran	31,000	6.6
1956, June 10-17	Northern Afghanistan	2,000	7.7	2004, Dec. 26	Sumatra-Andaman Isls.,		
1957, July 2	Northern Iran	1,200	7.1		Indonesia	227,898	9.1[7]
1960, Feb. 29	Agadir, Morocco	12,000	5.7	2005, Mar. 28	N Sumatra, Indonesia	1,313	8.6
1960, May 21-30	Southern Chile	1,655	9.5[5]	2005, Oct. 8	Kashmir, Pakistan, India	86,000	7.6
1962, Sept. 1	NW Iran	12,255	7.1	2006, May 26	Java, Indonesia	5,749	6.3
1964, Mar. 27	Prince Wm. Sound, AK	131	9.2[6]	2008, May 12	E Sichuan Prov., China	87,857	7.9
1966, Aug. 19	Eastern Turkey	2,529	6.8	2009, Sept. 30	Sumatra, Indonesia	1,117	7.5
1968, Aug. 31	NE Iran	12,000	7.3	2010, Jan. 12	Haiti	316,000[8]	7.0
1969, July 25	Guangdong, China	3,000	5.9	2010, Apr. 13	Southern Qinghai, China	2,698+	6.9
1970, Jan. 5	Yunnan Prov., China	10,000	7.5	2011, Mar. 11	NE Japan	20,896	9.0[9]
1970, May 31	Chimbote, Ancash, Peru	70,000	7.9	2015, Apr. 25	Nepal	8,669+	7.8
1971, Feb. 9	San Fernando Valley, CA	65	6.6	2017, Sept. 19	Mexico City, Mexico	369	7.1
1972, Apr. 10	Southern Iran	5,054	7.1	2017, Nov. 12	NW Iran-Iraq border	530	7.3
1972, Dec. 23	Managua, Nicaragua	5,000	6.2	2018, Sept. 28	Sulawesi, Indonesia	2,220+	7.5

NA = Not available. (1) Once thought to have been a volcanic eruption; evidence indicates a destructive earthquake and tsunami occurred on this date. (2) This earthquake caused the most deadly tsunami to date in the Atlantic Ocean. (3) Incl. deaths from resulting fires; revised estimates of magnitude range from 7.7 to 7.9. (4) Commonly referred to as the Gansu quake; actually located within the Ningxia autonomous region. (5) The largest recorded earthquake; caused a deadly tsunami that spread across the Pacific Ocean as far as Japan. (6) The "Good Friday" earthquake sent a tsunami that hit British Columbia, Canada, and the U.S. Pacific coast. (7) This undersea earthquake triggered devastating Indian Ocean tsunamis. (8) Official govt. death toll announced Jan. 2011; earlier estimate was 230,000. Estimates from other groups vary widely. (9) The most powerful earthquake in Japan's history set off a tsunami that inundated much of the coast and caused a partial meltdown of the Fukushima nuclear power plant.

Some Notable Fires Since 1940

See also Some Notable Explosions Since 1920.

Date	Location	Deaths	Date	Location	Deaths
1940, Apr. 23	Nightclub, Natchez, MS	198	1958, Mar. 19	Garment factory, New York, NY	24
1942, Nov. 28	Cocoanut Grove Nightclub,		1958, Dec. 1	Parochial school, Chicago, IL	95
	Boston, MA	492	1958, Dec. 16	Store, Bogotá, Colombia	83
1942, Dec. 12	Hostel, St. John's, NL, Canada	100	1960, Mar. 12	Chemical plant, Pusan, Korea	68
1943, Sept. 7	Gulf Hotel, Houston, TX	55	1960, July 14	Psychiatric hospital, Guatemala City	225
1944, July 6	Ringling Circus, Hartford, CT	168	1960, Nov. 13	Movie theater, Amude, Syria	152
1946, June 5	LaSalle Hotel, Chicago, IL	61	1960, Dec. 19	USS Constellation, Brooklyn, NY	49
1946, Dec. 7	Winecoff Hotel, Atlanta, GA	119	1961, Jan. 6	Thomas Hotel, San Francisco, CA	20
1946, Dec. 12	Ice plant, tenement, New York, NY	37	1961, Dec. 17	Circus, Niteroi, Brazil	323
1949, Apr. 5	Hospital, Effingham, IL	77	1963, May 4	Theater, Diourbel, Senegal	64
1950, Jan. 7	Mercy Hospital, Davenport, IA	41	1963, Nov. 18	Surfside Hotel, Atlantic City, NJ	25
1953, Mar. 29	Nursing home, Largo, FL	35	1963, Nov. 23	Nursing home, Fitchville, OH	63
1953, Apr. 16	Metalworking plant, Chicago, IL	35	1963, Dec. 29	Roosevelt Hotel, Jacksonville, FL	22
1957, Feb. 17	Home for aged, Warrenton, MO	72	1964, Dec. 18	Nursing home, Fountaintown, IN	20

Date	Location	Deaths	Date	Location	Deaths
1965, Aug. 11-16	Watts riot fires, Los Angeles, CA	30+	1997, June 13	Movie theater, New Delhi, India	60
1966, Dec. 7	Barracks, Erzurum, Turkey	68	1997, July 11	Hotel, Pattaya, Thailand	90
1967, Feb. 7	Restaurant, Montgomery, AL	25	1997, Sept.-Nov.	Drought-fueled fire, Sumatra, Indon.	240
1967, May 22	Dept. store, Brussels, Belgium	322	1998, Apr.-June	Wildfire, Oaxaca, Mexico	50
1967, July 16	State prison, Jay, FL	37	1998, Dec. 3	Orphanage, Manila, Philippines	28
1967, July 29	USS Forrestal, off N Vietnam	134	1999, Mar. 24	Mt. Blanc Tunnel, France, Italy	40
1968, May 11	Wedding hall, Vijayawada, India	58	1999, Oct. 30	Karaoke salon, Inchon, S. Korea	55+
1969, Dec. 2	Nursing home, Notre Dame, QC, Can.	54	2000, Mar. 17	Church, Kanungu, Uganda	530
1970, Jan. 9	Nursing home, Marietta, OH	27	2000, Nov. 11	Cable car, Kaprun, Austria	155
1970, Nov. 1	Dance hall, Grenoble, France	145	2000, Dec. 25	Shopping center, Luoyang, China	309
1970, Dec. 20	Hotel, Tucson, AZ	28	2001, Mar. 26	School, Machakos, Kenya	64
1971, Dec. 25	Hotel, Seoul, S. Korea	162	2001, Aug. 18	Hotel, Quezon City, Philippines	73
1972, May 13	Nightclub, Osaka, Japan	116	2001, Sept. 1	Nightclub, Tokyo, Japan	44
1973, June 24	Bar, New Orleans, LA	32	2001, Dec. 29	Fireworks accident, Lima, Peru	291
1973, Aug. 3	Amusement park, Isle of Man, UK	51	2003, Feb. 18	Subway train, Taegu, S. Korea	198
1973, Nov. 29	Dept. store, Kumamoto, Japan	107	2003, Feb. 20	Nightclub pyrotechnics, Warwick, RI	100
1973, Dec. 2	Theater, Seoul, S. Korea	50	2003, Sept. 15	Prison, Riyadh, Saudi Arabia	94
1974, Feb. 1	Bank building, São Paulo, Brazil	189	2003, Nov. 24	Students' hostel, Moscow, Russia	36
1974, June 30	Discotheque, Port Chester, NY	24	2004, May 17	Prison, San Pedro Sula, Honduras	104
1974, Nov. 3	Hotel, disco, Seoul, S. Korea	88	2004, July 16	Pvt. school, Kumbakonam, India	80+
1975, Dec. 12	Pilgrim camp, Mina, Saudi Arabia	138	2004, Aug. 1	Market, Asunción, Paraguay	400+
1976, Oct. 24	Social club, Bronx, NY	25	2004, Dec. 30	Club, Buenos Aires, Argentina	194
1977, Feb. 25	Rossiya Hotel, Moscow, Russia	45	2005, Feb. 14	Mosque, Tehran, Iran	59
1977, May 28	Nightclub, Southgate, KY	164	2005, Mar. 7	Prison, Higuey, Dom. Republic	159
1977, June 26	Jail, Columbia, TN	42	2005, Sept. 5	Theater, Beni Suef, Egypt	32
1977, Nov. 14	Hotel, Manila, Philippines	47	2006, Dec. 9	Drug treatment center, Moscow, Russ.	45
1978, Aug. 19	Movie theater, Abadan, Iran	425+	2007, Mar. 20	Nursing home, Kamyshevatskaya,	
1979, July 14	Hotel, Saragossa, Spain	80		Russia	62
1979, Dec. 31	Social club, Chapais, QC, Can.	42	2007, Aug. 24-		
1980, May 20	Nursing home, Kingston, Jamaica	157	Sept. 2	Wildfires (arson), Greece	73
1980, Nov. 21	MGM Grand Hotel, Las Vegas, NV	84	2008, Apr. 26	Factory fire, Casablanca, Morocco	55
1980, Dec. 4	Stouffer Inn, Harrison, NY	26	2008, Sept.	Wildfires, Mozambique, S. Africa,	
1981, Jan. 9	Boarding home, Keansburg, NJ	30		Swaziland	89
1981, Feb. 14	Discotheque, Dublin, Ireland	44	2009, Jan. 1	Nightclub fire, Bangkok, Thailand	67
1982, Nov. 8	County jail, Biloxi, MS	29	2009, Jan.-Feb.	Wildfires (arson), Victoria, Australia	173
1983, Feb. 13	Movie theater, Turin, Italy	64	2010, July	Bushfires, Nizhiny Novgorod, Russia	53
1983, Feb. 16	"Ash Wednesday" bushfires,		2010, Dec. 2-5	Grassland fire, Israel	44
	S Australia and Victoria, Australia	75	2012, Feb. 14	Prison fire, Comayagua, Honduras	360+
1983, Dec. 17	Discotheque, Madrid, Spain	83	2012, Nov. 24	Garment factory, Bagladesh	112
1984, May 11	Amusement park, Jackson Twp., NJ	8	2013, Jan. 27	Nightclub, Santa Maria, Brazil	241
1985, Apr. 21	Movie theaters, Tabaco, Philippines	44	2014, May 2	Trade union building, Odessa, Ukraine	40+
1985, Apr. 26	Hospital, Buenos Aires, Argentina	79	2016, Apr. 10	Temple fireworks, Kerala, India	110+
1985, May 11	Soccer stadium, Bradford, Eng., UK	53	2016, Dec. 2	"Ghost Ship" warehouse, Oakland, CA	36
1985, May 13	MOVE headquarters, row houses,		2017, June 14	Grenfell Tower apts., London, Eng., UK	80
	Philadelphia, PA	11	2017, June 17-18	Forest fires, central Portugal	64
1986, Dec. 31	Dupont Plaza Hotel, Puerto Rico	96	2018, July 23	Wildfires, Attica region, Greece	99
1987, May 6-			2018, Nov. 8-25	Camp Fire wildfire, Butte Co., CA	85
June 2	Forest fire, Mohe, China	191	2019, Oct.-2020,		
1987, Nov. 17	Subway, London, England	30	Feb.	Bushfires, Australia	34[1]
1988, Nov. 24	2,000+ buildings, Lashio, Myanmar	134	(1) Research published in Mar. 2020 in Medical Journal of		
1990, Mar. 25	Happy Land social club, Bronx, NY	87	Australia found an additional 417 deaths caused by the fires,		
1991, Mar. 3	Munitions dump, Addis Ababa, Ethiopia	260+	chiefly related to smoke inhalation.		
1991, Aug.-Oct.	Wildfires, Sumatra, Borneo, Indonesia	57			
1991, Sept. 3	Chicken-processing plant, Hamlet, NC	25			
1991, Oct. 20-21	Wildfire, Oakland, Berkeley, CA	24			
1993, Apr. 19	Cult compound, Waco, TX	72			
1993, May 10	Toy factory, Bangkok, Thailand	213			
1993, Nov. 19	Toy factory, Shenzhen, China	87			
1994, Nov. 2	Burning fuel flood, Durunka, Egypt	500			
1994, Nov. 27	Dance hall, Fuxin, China	233			
1994, Dec. 8	Theater, Karamay, China	323			
1995, Oct. 28	Subway train, Baku, Azerbaijan	300			
1995, Dec. 23	School, Mandi Dabwali, India	500+			
1996, Mar. 19	Nightclub, Quezon City, Philippines	150+			
1996, Mar. 28	Shopping mall, Bogor, Indonesia	78			
1996, Nov. 20	Garley Building, Hong Kong	39			
1997, Feb. 23	Worship site, Baripada, India	164			
1997, Apr. 15	Encampment, Mina, Saudi Arabia	343			
1997, June 7	Temple, Thanjavur, India	60+			

U.S. Fires, 2019

Source: National Fire Protection Association

- Public fire departments responded to an estimated 1.3 mil fires in 2019, including 481,500 structure fires (339,500 in homes), 223,000 vehicle fires, and 587,000 fires outside or other fires.

- An estimated 3,704 civilians died in fires in 2019.

- There were an estimated 16,600 civilian fire injuries reported, 12,200 of them in home structure fires.

- Direct property damage from fires amounted to an estimated $14.8 bil. Structure fires accounted for $12.3 bil of property damage, and property loss associated with home fires came to $7.8 bil.

Some Notable Explosions Since 1920

See also Principal U.S. Mine Disasters Since 1867. Some bombings related to political conflicts and terrorism are not included.

Date	Location	Deaths	Date	Location	Deaths
1920, Sept. 16	Wall Street, New York, NY	39	1944, July 17	Munitions ships, depot, Port Chicago,	
1921, Sept. 21	Chem. storage facility, Oppau, Ger.	561		CA	322
1924, Jan. 3	Food plant, Pekin, IL	42	1944, Oct. 20	Liquid natural gas tanks, Cleveland, OH	130
1927, May 18	School bombing, Bath, MI	45	1947, Apr. 16	Freighter, chemical co. plant,	
1928, Apr. 13	Dance hall, West Plains, MO	40		Texas City, TX	576
1937, Mar. 18	School, New London, TX	311	1948, July 28	Farben works, Ludwigshafen, Ger.	184
1940, Sept. 12	Hercules Powder factory, Kenvil, NJ	55	1950, May 19	Munitions barges, S. Amboy, NJ	30
1942, Apr. 26	Honkeiko (Benxihu) colliery, China	1,549	1954, May 26	USS Bennington, off RI	103
1942, June 5	Ordnance plant, Elwood, IL	49	1956, Aug. 7	Dynamite trucks, Cali, Colombia	1,100
1944, Apr. 14	SS Fort Stikine, Bombay docks, India	700	1958, Apr. 18	Sunken munitions ship, Okinawa, Japan	40

Date	Location	Deaths
1959, Apr. 10	WWII bomb, Philippines	38
1959, June 28	Rail tank cars, Meldrim, GA	25
1959, Aug. 7	Truck filled with explosives, Roseburg, OR	14
1959, Nov. 2	Explosives, Jamuri Bazar, India	46
1959, Dec. 13	2 apt. bldgs., Dortmund, Germany	26
1960, Mar. 4	Belgian munitions ship, Havana, Cuba.	100
1962, Oct. 3	New York Telephone Co. office, New York, NY	23
1963, Jan. 2	Packing plant, Terre Haute, IN	17
1963, Mar. 9	Dynamite plant, S. Africa	45
1963, Aug. 13	Explosives dump, Gauhaiti, India	32
1963, Oct. 31	State Fair Coliseum, Indianapolis, IN	73
1963, Nov. 9	Mitsui Miike coal mine, Japan.	458
1964, July 23	Harbor munitions, Bone, Algeria.	100
1965, Aug. 9	Missile silo, Searcy, AR	53
1965, Oct. 21	Bridge, Tila Bund, Pakistan	80
1965, Nov. 24	Armory, Keokuk, IA.	20
1968, Apr. 6	Sports store, Richmond, IN	43
1969, Mar. 31	Coal mine, nr. Barroteran, Mexico	180
1970, Apr. 8	Subway construction, Osaka, Japan	73
1971, June 24	Tunnel under construction, Sylmar, CA	17
1973, Feb. 10	Liquid gas tank, Staten Island, NY	40
1975, Dec. 27	Coal mine, Chasnala, India	431
1976, Apr. 13	Munitions works, Lapua, Finland	40
1977, Nov. 11	Freight train, Iri, S. Korea	57
1977, Dec. 22	Grain elevator, Westwego, LA	35
1978, July 11	Propylene tank truck, Tarragona, Spain	150
1980, Oct. 23	School, Ortuella, Spain.	64
1982, Apr. 25	Antiques exhibition, Todi, Italy	33
1982, Nov. 2	Salang Tunnel, Afghanistan	1,000+
1984, Feb. 25	Oil pipeline, Cubatao, Brazil	508
1984, June 21	Naval supply depot, Severomorsk, USSR	200+
1984, Aug. 19	Gas storage area, NE Mexico City	334
1984, Dec. 3	Chemical plant, Bhopal, India.	3,849
1984, Dec. 5	Coal mine, Taipei, Taiwan	94
1985, June 25	Fireworks factory, Hallett, OK.	21
1988, Apr. 10	Army ammunitions dump nr. Rawalpindi and Islamabad, Pakistan	100
1988, July 6	Oil rig, North Sea off NE Scotland, UK.	167
1989, June 3	Gas pipeline, between Ufa, Asha, USSR	650+
1992, Mar. 3	Coal mine, Kozlu, Turkey	270+
1992, Apr. 22	Gas leak in sewers, Guadalajara, Mexico	200+
1992, May 9	Coal mine, Plymouth, Nova Scotia, Can.	26
1993, Feb. 26	World Trade Center, New York, NY	6
1994, July 18	Jewish community center, Buenos Aires, Argentina	100
1995, Apr. 19	Fed. office building, Oklahoma City, OK	168
1995, Apr. 29	Subway construction, S. Korea	110
1996, Jan. 31	Bank, Colombo, Sri Lanka	53
1996, Mar. 3-4	Jerusalem and Tel Aviv, Israel	33
1996, June 25	U.S. military housing complex, nr. Dhahran, Saudi Arabia	19
1996, July 24	Train, Colombo, Sri Lanka	86
1996, Nov. 16	Military apt., Dagestan region, Russia	68
1996, Nov. 21	Propane gas leak in building, San Juan, Puerto Rico.	33
1996, Nov. 27	Coal mine, Shanxi Prov., China	91+
1996, Dec. 30	Train, Assam, India.	59+
1997, Dec. 2	Coal mine, Novokuznetsk, Russia	68
1998, Feb. 14	2 oil tankers, Yaounde, Cameroon	120
1998, Feb. 14	17 bombs, Coimbatore, India	50
1998, Apr. 4	Coal mine, Donetsk, Ukraine	63
1998, Aug. 7	Bomb, U.S. emb., Nairobi, Kenya.	213
1998, Aug. 7	Bomb, U.S. emb., Dar-es-Salaam, Tanzania	11
1998, Sept. 8	2 buses, São Paulo, Brazil	59
1998, Oct. 17	Oil pipeline, Jesse, Nigeria	700+
1999, May 16	Fuel truck, Punjab Prov., Pakistan	75
1999, Sept. 9	Apartment building, Moscow, Russia	94
1999, Sept. 13	Apartment building, Moscow, Russia	118
1999, Sept. 16	Apartment building, Moscow, Russia	18
1999, Sept. 26	Fireworks factory, Celaya, Mexico	56
2000, Feb. 25	Bombs on 2 buses, Ozamis, Philippines	41
2000, Mar. 11	Coal mine, Krasnodon, Ukraine	80
2000, Apr. 16	Airport hangar, Dem. Rep. of Congo	100+
2000, July 16	Oil pipeline, Warri, Nigeria	30
2000, Sept. 9	Truck explosion, Urumqi, China	60
2000, Oct. 12	USS Cole, Yemen	17
2001, Mar. 6	School, Jianxi Prov., China.	41
2001, Apr. 21	Coal mine, Shaanxi, China	51
2001, June 1	Dance club, Tel Aviv, Israel	21
2001, July 17	Coal mine, Guanxi, China.	76+
2001, Aug. 19	Coal mine, Donetsk region, Ukraine.	52
2001, Sept. 21	Chem. plant, Toulouse, France	29
2002, Jan. 21	Volcanic lava caused gas station blast, Goma, Dem. Rep. of Congo.	50+
2002, Jan. 27	Munitions dump, Lagos, Nigeria	1,000+
2002, May 9	Land mine at parade, Kaspiisk, Russia	34+
2002, June 14	Car bomb outside U.S. consulate, Karachi, Pakistan	12
2002, June 18	Bomb on bus, Jerusalem, Israel	20
2002, July 5	Bomb in market, Larba, Algeria	35+
2002, Aug. 9	Explosion, Jalalabad, Afghanistan	25+
2002, Sept. 5	Car bomb, Kabul, Afghanistan	30
2002, Oct. 12	Nightclub bombings, Bali, Indonesia	202
2003, Aug. 25	Bombs in 2 taxis, Mumbai, India.	52
2003, Dec. 5	Bomb on train, Yessentuki, Russia.	45
2003, Dec. 23	Gas well explosion, Chongqing, China.	233
2004, Jan. 19	Natural gas facility, Skikda, Algeria	27
2004, Feb. 6	Bomb on subway car, Moscow, Russia	39
2004, Mar. 11	Bombs on commuter trains, Madrid, Sp.	191
2005, Feb. 14	Coal mine, NE China	214
2005, Mar. 23	Oil refinery, Texas City, TX.	15
2005, May 2	Arms cache, Baghlan Prov., Afghan.	34+
2005, July 7	Bombs in mass transit, London, Eng., UK	56
2005, Oct. 1	Bombings of restaurants, Bali, Indonesia	26
2005, Nov. 27	Coal mine, NE China	161+
2006, May 12	Oil pipeline, nr. Lagos, Nigeria	200
2006, July 1	Bombings of trains, station, Mumbai, India	207
2007, Mar. 19	Coal mine, Siberia, Russia	108
2007, Mar. 22	Natl. weapons depot, Maputo, Mozamb.	117
2007, June 9	Oil pipeline, Pyongan Prov., N. Korea	110
2007, Nov. 18	Methane gas buildup in coal mine, E Ukraine	90
2008, May 15	Pipeline explosion in Lagos, Nigeria	100+
2008, Sept. 20	Truck bomb outside hotel, Islamabad, Pakistan	40+
2009, Feb. 22	Coal mine, N China	74
2010, May 8-9	Coal mine, Siberia, Russia	91
2010, June 17	Coal mine, Amaga, Colombia.	73
2010, Nov. 19	Coal mine, Ataru, New Zealand	29
2011, Mar. 28	Munitions factory, Abyan, Yemen.	150+
2011, July 13	Bombs in three locations in Mumbai, India	27
2012, Mar. 4	Arms depot, Brazzaville, Congo Rep.	250+
2013, Apr. 17	Fertilizer plant, West, TX.	15
2013, June 3	Poultry plant, Mishzai, China	119+
2013, June 30	Fuel tanker, Kampala, Uganda	30+
2013, July 6	Derailed oil train, Lac-Megantic, QC, Canada	47
2013, Aug. 1	Weapons cache, Homs, Syria	40
2014, May 13	Coal mine, Soma, Turkey	301
2015, Aug. 12	Chemical warehouse, Tianjin, China	173
2017, Oct. 27	Fireworks factory, Tangerang, Indonesia	47+

Global Flu Pandemic

Date: 1918-20. **Fatalities:** 39-50 million.

In 1918, a new influenza nicknamed "Spanish flu" was identified in populations around the world. Initial symptoms included headache and fatigue, followed by a dry cough, loss of appetite, gastrointestinal issues, and sweating. The virus spread in 3-4 waves, the deadliest occurring Sept. 1918-Jan. 1919, with some areas still experiencing illness by 1920. Unlike many viruses, this H1N1 flu strain appeared to hit young populations especially hard, and a disproportionate number of those aged 20-40 died. With medical personnel already in short supply in many areas due to World War I, and no credible available treatments, the virus eventually affected as many as 500 mil—a third of the world's population at the time—and an estimated 675,000 died in the U.S. alone.

Principal U.S. Mine Disasters Since 1867

Source: Bureau of Mines, U.S. Dept. of the Interior; Office of Mine Safety Health Research, Centers for Disease Control
All are bituminous coal mines unless otherwise noted.

Date	Location	Deaths	Date	Location	Deaths	Date	Location	Deaths
1867, Apr. 3	Winterpock, VA	69	1910, May 5	Palos, AL	84	1924, Mar. 8	Castle Gate, UT	172
1869, Sept. 6	Plymouth, PA	110	1910, Nov. 8	Delagua, CO	79	1924, Apr. 28	Benwood, WV	119
1883, Feb. 16	Braidwood, IL	69	1911, Apr. 7	Troop, PA	73	1926, Jan. 13	Wilburton, OK	91
1884, Mar. 13	Pocahontas, VA	112	1911, Apr. 8	Littleton, AL	128	1927, Apr. 30	Everettville, WV	97
1891, Jan. 27	Mt. Pleasant, PA	109	1911, Dec. 9	Briceville, TN	84	1928, May 19	Mather, PA	195
1892, Jan. 7	Krebs, OK	100	1912, Mar. 20	McCurtain, OK	73	1929, Dec. 17	McAlester, OK	61
1895, Mar. 20	Red Canyon, WY	62	1912, Mar. 26	Jed, WV	81	1930, Nov. 5	Millfield, OH	82
1900, May 1	Scofield, UT	200	1913, Apr. 23	Finleyville, PA	98	1940, Jan. 10	Bartley, WV	91
1902, May 19	Coal Creek, TN	184	1913, Oct. 22	Dawson, NM	263	1940, Mar. 16	St. Clairsville, OH	72
1902, July 10	Johnstown, PA	112	1914, Apr. 28	Eccles, WV	181	1940, July 15	Portage, PA	63
1903, June 30	Hanna, WY	169	1915, Mar. 2	Layland, WV	115	1943, Feb. 27	Washoe, MT	74
1904, Jan. 25	Cheswick, PA	179	1917, Apr. 27	Hastings, CO	121	1944, July 5	Powhatan Pt., OH	66
1905, Feb. 20	Virginia City, AL	112	1917, June 8	Butte, MT[1]	163	1947, Mar. 25	Centralia, IL	111
1907, Jan. 29	Stuart, WV	84	1917, Aug. 4	Clay, KY	62	1951, Dec. 21	West Frankfort, IL	119
1907, Dec. 6	Monongah, WV	362	1919, June 5	Wilkes-Barre, PA	92	1968, Nov. 20	Farmington, WV	78
1907, Dec. 19	Van Meter, PA	239	1922, Nov. 6	Spangler, PA	79	1970, Dec. 30	Hyden, KY	38
1908, Nov. 28	Marianna, PA	154	1922, Nov. 22	Dolomite, AL	90	1972, Feb. 26	Saunders, WV	114
1909, Jan. 12	Switchback, WV	67	1923, Feb. 8	Dawson, NM	120	1972, May 2	Kellogg, ID[2]	91
1909, Nov. 13	Cherry, IL	259	1923, Aug. 14	Kemmerer, WY	99	2010, Apr. 5	Montcoal, WV	29
1910, Jan. 31	Primero, CO	75						

Note: The world's worst mine disaster killed 1,549 workers in Manchuria, China, Apr. 26, 1942. (1) Copper mine. (2) Silver mine.

Notable Nuclear Accidents

Sept. 29, 1957: After cooling system failure, nuclear waste at Chelyabinsk-65 in Kyshtym, Russia, exploded. Residents were evacuated but not informed until 1989 about their exposure to radiation.

Oct. 7, 1957: Fire in the Windscale plutonium production reactor N of Liverpool, England, UK, released radioactive material; later blamed for 39 cancer deaths.

Jan. 3, 1961: Reactor explosion at a federal installation near Idaho Falls, ID, killed 3 workers. Radiation contained.

Oct. 5, 1966: Sodium cooling system malfunction caused a partial core meltdown at the Enrico Fermi demonstration breeder reactor, near Detroit, MI. Radiation contained.

Jan. 21, 1969: Coolant malfunction from an experimental underground reactor at Lucens Vad, Switzerland, released radiation into a cavern, which was then sealed.

Mar. 22, 1975: Fire at the Brown's Ferry reactor in Decatur, AL, caused dangerous lowering of cooling water levels.

Mar. 28, 1979: Worst commercial nuclear accident in the U.S. occurred as equipment failures and human mistakes led to a loss of coolant and a partial core meltdown at the Three Mile Island reactor in Middletown, PA.

Feb. 11, 1981: Eight workers were contaminated when 100,000 gallons of radioactive coolant leaked into the containment building of TVA's Sequoyah 1 plant near Chattanooga, TN.

Apr. 25, 1981: Some 100 workers were exposed to radiation during repairs of a nuclear plant at Tsuruga, Japan.

Jan. 6, 1986: Cylinder of nuclear material burst after being improperly heated at a Kerr-McGee plant in Gore, OK. One worker died; 100 were hospitalized.

Apr. 26, 1986: Fires and resulting explosions at the Chernobyl nuclear power plant near Kiev, USSR (now in Ukraine), left at least 31 dead in the immediate aftermath and spread radioactive material over much of Europe. An estimated 135,000 people were evacuated. Tens of thousands of excess cancer deaths (as well as increased birth defects) were expected.

Sept. 1987: Cesium chloride from an improperly discarded hospital irradiation machine contaminated more than 200 people and killed at least 4 in Goiânia, Brazil.

Mar. 11, 2011: A 9.0 magnitude earthquake caused a tsunami that inundated the Fukushima Daiichi nuclear power plant on Japan's NE coast. Three of the plant's reactors suffered partial meltdowns; more than 12,000 tons of radioactive water was released into the sea.

Record Oil Spills

The exact number of barrels in a ton varies with the type of oil, but a general approximation is 7 barrels per ton. By custom, 42 gallons constitute a barrel of crude oil.

Name, location	Date	Cause	Est. tons
BP *Deepwater Horizon* rig, Gulf of Mexico, U.S.	Apr. 20-July 15, 2010	Explosion	700,000[1]
Ixtoc I oil well, S Gulf of Mexico	June 3, 1979	Blowout	600,000
Nowruz oil field, Persian Gulf	Feb. 1983	Blowout	600,000
Atlantic Empress, off Trinidad and Tobago	July 19, 1979	Collision with *Aegean Captain*	276,000
ABT Summer, off Angola	May 28, 1991	Explosion	260,000
Amoco Cadiz, near Portsall, France	Mar. 16, 1978	Grounding	223,000
Castillo de Bellver, off Cape Town, South Africa	Aug. 6, 1983	Fire	150,000-160,000
Haven, off Genoa, Italy	Apr. 11, 1991	Explosion	144,000
Odyssey, off Nova Scotia, Canada	Nov. 10, 1988	Broke apart in storm	132,000
Torrey Canyon, off Land's End, England, UK	Mar. 18, 1967	Grounding	119,000
Sea Star, Gulf of Oman	Dec. 19, 1972	Collision	115,000
Urquiola, La Coruna, Spain	May 12, 1976	Grounding	100,000

(1) The Dept. of Energy estimated the spill at 4.9 mil barrels, or more than 200 mil gallons.

Other Notable Oil Spills

Name, location	Date	Cause	Gallons
Persian Gulf	Jan. 21, 1991	Intentional spillage by Iraq	130,000,000[1]
Braer, off Shetland Islands, UK	Jan. 5, 1993	Grounding	26,000,000
Taylor Energy platform, Gulf of Mexico, U.S.	Sept. 2004-present	Broke apart in storm	Up to 25,000,000
Prestige, off N Spain	Nov. 13-19, 2002	Ship broke in half	22,600,000
Aegean Sea, off N Spain	Dec. 3, 1992	Grounding	21,500,000
Sea Empress, off SW Wales, UK	Feb. 15, 1996	Grounding	18,000,000
Newtown Creek, Greenpoint, Brooklyn, NY	Oct. 5, 1950-present	Industrial explosion[2]	17,000,000
Hawaiian Patriot, off Hawaii in Pacific	Feb. 23-24, 1977	Hull cracked; ship exploded	14,700,000
World Glory, off South Africa	June 13, 1968	Hull failure	13,524,000
Exxon Valdez, Prince William Sound, AK	Mar. 24, 1989	Grounding	10,080,000
Ashland Oil facility, Floreffe, PA; Monongahela R.	Jan. 2, 1988	Storage tank collapse	3,850,000

(1) Est. by Saudi Arabia. Some estimates as low as 25 mil gal. (2) Legacy of refinery operations since mid-1800s and leaking storage tanks. Spill estimated at up to 30 mil gal.

AEROSPACE

Notable Human Spaceflight Missions

Source: National Aeronautics and Space Administration (NASA); Congressional Research Service; World Almanac research

The spaceflights listed are a selection of notable crewed U.S. missions by NASA, unless otherwise noted, plus crewed non-U.S. missions (shown with an asterisk). The non-U.S missions were sponsored by the USSR—later, the Commonwealth of Independent States (CIS) and, from 1997, Russia—or by China. Launch dates are Eastern Standard Time. **EVA** = extravehicular activity. **ASTP** = Apollo-Soyuz Test Project. **STS** = Space Transportation System, NASA's name for the overall shuttle program.

For shuttle flights, mission name is in parentheses following name of orbiter. Duration of flight is listed in hours:minutes for 1961-Apr. 1970; days (d.), hours (hr.), and minutes (min.) thereafter. Number of total flights taken by each crew member is given in parentheses when flight listed is not the person's first.

4/12/1961: *Vostok 1*; 1:48; Yuri A. Gagarin. **1st human orbital flight.**

5/5/1961: *Mercury-Redstone 3*; 0:15; Alan B. Shepard Jr. **1st American in space.**

7/21/1961: *Mercury-Redstone 4*; 0:15; Virgil I. Grissom. Flight successful but spacecraft sank shortly after splashdown; Grissom rescued.

8/6/1961: **Vostok 2*; 25:18; Gherman S. Titov. 1st spaceflight of more than 24 hours.

2/20/1962: *Mercury-Atlas 6*; 4:55; John H. Glenn Jr. **1st American in orbit;** three orbits.

5/24/1962: *Mercury-Atlas 7*; 4:56; M. Scott Carpenter. Manual retrofire error caused 250-mi landing overshoot.

8/11/1962: **Vostok 3*; 94:22; Andrian G. Nikolayev. *Vostok 3* and *4* made 1st group flight.

8/12/1962: **Vostok 4*; 70:57; Pavel R. Popovich. On 1st orbit, it came within 3 mi of *Vostok 3*.

10/3/1962: *Mercury-Atlas 8*; 9:13; Walter M. Schirra Jr. Landed 5 mi from target; six orbits.

5/15/1963: *Mercury-Atlas 9*; 34:19; L. Gordon Cooper. 1st U.S. evaluation of effects of one day in space on a person; 22 orbits.

6/14/1963: **Vostok 5*; 119:06; Valery F. Bykovsky. *Vostok 5* and *6* made 2nd group flight.

6/16/1963: **Vostok 6*; 70:50; Valentina V. Tereshkova. **1st woman in space;** passed within 3 mi of *Vostok 5*.

10/12/1964: **Voskhod 1*; 24:17; Vladimir M. Komarov, Konstantin P. Feoktistov, Boris B. Yegorov. 1st three-person orbital flight; 1st without space suits.

3/18/1965: **Voskhod 2*; 26:02; Pavel I. Belyayev, Aleksei A. Leonov. Leonov made **1st spacewalk** (10 min.).

3/23/1965: *Gemini-Titan 3*; 4:53; Virgil I. Grissom (2), John W. Young. 1st piloted spacecraft to change its orbital path.

6/3/1965: *Gemini-Titan 4*; 97:56; James A. McDivitt, Edward H. White II. White was **1st American to "walk in space"** (23 min.).

8/21/1965: *Gemini-Titan 5*; 190:55; L. Gordon Cooper (2), Charles Conrad Jr. Longest-duration human flight to date.

12/4/1965: *Gemini-Titan 7*; 330:35; Frank Borman, James A. Lovell Jr. Longest-duration *Gemini* flight.

12/15/1965: *Gemini-Titan 6A*; 25:51; Walter M. Schirra Jr. (2), Thomas P. Stafford. Completed 1st U.S. space rendezvous, with *Gemini 7*.

3/16/1966: *Gemini-Titan 8*; 10:41; Neil A. Armstrong, David R. Scott. **1st docking of one space vehicle with another;** mission aborted, control malfunction.

6/3/1966: *Gemini-Titan 9A*; 72:21; Thomas P. Stafford (2), Eugene A. Cernan. Performed simulation of lunar module rendezvous.

7/18/1966: *Gemini-Titan 10*; 70:47; John W. Young (2), Michael Collins. 1st use of Agena target vehicle's propulsion systems; 1st orbital docking.

9/12/1966: *Gemini-Titan 11*; 71:17; Charles Conrad Jr. (2), Richard F. Gordon Jr. 1st tethered flight; highest Earth-orbit altitude (850 mi).

11/11/1966: *Gemini-Titan 12*; 94:34; James A. Lovell Jr. (2), Edwin E. "Buzz" Aldrin Jr. Final *Gemini* mission; 5-hr. EVA.

1/27/1967: *Apollo 1*; Virgil I. Grissom, Edward H. White II, and Roger B. Chaffee died in a fire on the ground at Cape Canaveral, FL.

4/23/1967: **Soyuz 1*; 26:40; Vladimir M. Komarov (2). Crashed on reentry, killing Komarov; **1st space fatality.**

10/11/1968: *Apollo-Saturn 7*; 260:09; Walter M. Schirra Jr. (3), Donn F. Eisele, R. Walter Cunningham. **1st piloted flight of Apollo** spacecraft command-service module only; live TV footage of crew.

12/21/1968: *Apollo-Saturn 8*; 147:00; Frank Borman (2), James A. Lovell Jr. (3), William A. Anders. **1st lunar orbit** and piloted lunar return reentry (command-service module only); views of lunar surface televised to Earth.

1/14/1969: **Soyuz 4*; 71:21; Vladimir A. Shatalov. Docked with *Soyuz 5*.

1/15/1969: **Soyuz 5*; 72:54; Boris V. Volyanov, Aleksei S. Yeliseyev, Yevgeny V. Khrunov. Docked with *Soyuz 4*; Yeliseyev and Khrunov transferred to *Soyuz 4* via a spacewalk.

3/3/1969: *Apollo-Saturn 9*; 241:00; James A. McDivitt (2), David R. Scott (2), Russell L. Schweickart. 1st piloted flight of lunar module.

5/18/1969: *Apollo-Saturn 10*; 192:03; Thomas P. Stafford (3), John W. Young (3), Eugene A. Cernan (2). 1st lunar module orbit of moon, 50,000 ft from moon's surface.

7/16/1969: *Apollo-Saturn 11*; 195:18; Neil A. Armstrong (2), Michael Collins (2), Edwin E. "Buzz" Aldrin Jr. (2). **1st moon landing** made by Armstrong and Aldrin (7/20); collected 47.5 lbs of soil, rock samples; lunar stay time 21:36.

10/11/1969: **Soyuz 6*; 118:43; Georgi S. Shonin, Valery N. Kubasov. 1st welding of metals in space.

10/12/1969: **Soyuz 7*; 118:40; Anatoly V. Flipchenko, Vladislav N. Volkov, Viktor V. Gorbatko. Space lab construction test made; *Soyuz 6, 7,* and *8:* 1st time three spacecraft, seven crew members orbited the Earth at once.

10/13/1969: **Soyuz 8*; 118:51; Vladimir A. Shatalov (2), Aleksei S. Yeliseyev (2). Part of space lab construction team.

11/14/1969: *Apollo-Saturn 12*; 244:36; Charles Conrad Jr. (3), Richard F. Gordon Jr. (2), Alan L. Bean. Conrad and Bean made **2nd moon landing** (11/18); collected 75 lbs of samples; lunar stay time 31:31.

4/11/1970: *Apollo-Saturn 13*; 142:54; James A. Lovell Jr. (4), Fred W. Haise Jr., John L. Swigert Jr. Aborted after service module oxygen tank ruptured; crew returned in lunar module.

6/1/1970: **Soyuz 9*; 17 d., 16 hr., 59 min.; Andrian G. Nikolayev (2), Vitaly I. Sevastyanov. Longest human spaceflight to date.

1/31/1971: *Apollo-Saturn 14*; 9 d., 2 min.; Alan B. Shepard Jr. (2), Stuart A. Roosa, Edgar D. Mitchell. Shepard and Mitchell made **3rd moon landing** (2/5); collected 94 lbs of lunar samples; lunar stay 33:31.

4/19/1971: **Salyut 1*; launched without crew. **1st space station.**

4/22/1971: **Soyuz 10*; 1 d., 23 hr., 46 min.; Vladimir A. Shatalov (3), Aleksei S. Yeliseyev (3), Nikolay N. Rukavishnikov. **1st successful docking with a space station;** failed to enter space station.

6/6/1971: **Soyuz 11*; 23 d., 28 hr., 22 min.; Georgi T. Dobrovolskiy, Vladislav N. Volkov (2), Viktor I. Patsayev. Docked and entered *Salyut 1* space station; **crew died** during reentry from loss of pressurization.

7/26/1971: *Apollo-Saturn 15*; 12 d., 17 hr., 12 min.; David R. Scott (3), James B. Irwin, Alfred M. Worden. Scott and Irwin made **4th moon landing** (7/30). 1st lunar rover use; 1st deep spacewalk; collected 170 lbs of samples; lunar stay 66:55.

4/16/1972: *Apollo-Saturn 16*; 11 d., 1 hr., 51 min.; John W. Young (4), Charles M. Duke Jr., Thomas K. Mattingly II. Young and Duke made 5th moon landing (4/20); collected 209 lbs of lunar samples; lunar stay 71:02.

12/7/1972: *Apollo-Saturn 17*; 12 d., 13 hr., 52 min.; Eugene A. Cernan (3), Ronald E. Evans, Harrison H. Schmitt. Cernan and Schmitt made 6th and **final crewed lunar landing** (12/11); collected 243 lbs of samples; record lunar stay over 75 hr.

5/14/1973: *Skylab 1*; launched without crew. **1st U.S. space station;** fell out of orbit 7/11/1979.

5/25/1973: *Skylab 2*; 28 d., 49 min.; Charles Conrad Jr. (4), Joseph P. Kerwin, Paul J. Weitz. 1st U.S.-piloted orbiting space station; crew repaired damage caused in boost.

7/28/1973: *Skylab 3*; 59 d., 11 hr., 1 min.; Alan L. Bean (2), Owen K. Garriott, Jack R. Lousma. Crew systems and operational tests; scientific activities; three EVAs, 13:44.

11/16/1973: *Skylab 4*; 84 d., 1 hr., 16 min.; Gerald P. Carr, Edward G. Gibson, William R. Pogue. Final *Skylab* mission.

7/15/1975: **Soyuz 19 (ASTP)*; 6 d., 11 hr., 31 min.; Aleksei A. Leonov (2), Valery N. Kubasov (2). U.S.-USSR joint flight; crews linked up in space (7/17), conducted experiments, shared meals, held a joint news conference.

7/15/1975: *Apollo (ASTP)*; 9 d., 7 hr., 28 min.; Vance D. Brand, Thomas P. Stafford (4), Donald K. Slayton. Joint flight with *Soyuz 19*.

12/10/1977: **Soyuz 26*; 96 d., 10 hr.; Yuri V. Romanenko, Georgiy M. Grechko (2). 1st multiple docking at a space station (*Soyuz 26* and *27* docked at *Salyut 6*).

1/10/1978: **Soyuz 27*; 5 d., 22 hr., 59 min.; Vladimir A. Dzhanibekov. See *Soyuz 26*.

3/2/1978: **Soyuz 28*; 7 d., 22 hr., 16 min.; Aleksei A. Gubarev (2), Vladimir Remek. 1st international crew launch; Remek was 1st Czech in space.

4/12/1981: *Columbia (STS-1)*; 2 d., 6 hr., 21 min.; John W. Young (5), Robert L. Crippen. **1st reusable space shuttle** to fly into Earth's orbit.

11/12/1981: *Columbia (STS-2)*; 3 days; Joe H. Engle, Richard H. Truly. 1st scientific payload; 1st reuse of space shuttle.

11/11/1982: *Columbia (STS-5)*; 6 days; Vance D. Brand (2), Robert F. Overmyer, Joseph P. Allen, William B. Lenoir. 1st four-person crew.

6/18/1983: *Challenger (STS-7)*; 7 days; Robert L. Crippen (2), Frederick H. Hauck, John M. Fabian, Sally K. Ride, Norman E. Thagard. Ride was **1st U.S. woman in space**; 1st 5-person crew.

6/27/1983: **Soyuz T-9*; 150 days; Vladimir A. Lyakhov (2), Aleksandr Pavlovich. Docked at *Salyut 7*. 1st construction in space.

8/30/1983: *Challenger (STS-8)*; 7 days; Richard H. Truly (2), Daniel C. Brandenstein, Dale A. Gardner, Guion S. Bluford Jr., William E. Thornton. Bluford was **1st African-American in space; 1st night launch**.

11/28/1983: *Columbia (STS-9)*; 11 days; John W. Young (6), Brewster H. Shaw Jr., Owen K. Garriott (2), Robert A.R. Parker, Byron K. Lichtenberg, Ulf Merbold. 1st six-person crew; 1st Spacelab mission.

2/3/1984: *Challenger (41-B)*; 8 days; Vance Brand (3), Robert L. Gibson, Ronald E. McNair, Bruce McCandless II, Robert L. Stewart. 1st untethered EVA.

2/8/1984: **Soyuz T-10B*; 63 days; Leonid Kizim, Vladimir Solovyov, Oleg Atkov. Docked with *Salyut 7*; crew set space duration record of 237 days (since eclipsed).

4/3/1984: **Soyuz T-11*; 182 days; Yury Malyshev (2), Gennady Strekalov (3), Rakesh Sharma. Docked with *Salyut 7*; Sharma was 1st Indian in space.

4/6/1984: *Challenger (41-C)*; 7 days; Robert L. Crippen (3), Francis R. Scobee, George D. Nelson, Terry J. Hart, James D. van Hoften. 1st in-orbit satellite repair.

8/30/1984: *Discovery (41-D)*; 7 days; Henry W. Hartsfield Jr. (2), Michael L. Coats, Richard M. Mullane, Steven A. Hawley, Judith A. Resnik, Charles D. Walker. 1st flight of non-astronaut (payload specialist Walker).

10/5/1984: *Challenger (41-G)*; 9 days; Robert L. Crippen (4), Jon A. McBride, Kathryn D. Sullivan, Sally K. Ride (2), David C. Leestma, Marc Garneau, Paul D. Scully-Power. 1st seven-person crew.

11/8/1984: *Discovery (51-A)*; 8 days; Frederick H. Hauck (2), David M. Walker, Anna L. Fisher, Dale A. Gardner (2), Joseph P. Allen (2). 1st satellite retrieval/repair.

4/12/1985: *Discovery (51-D)*; 7 days; Karol J. Bobko, Donald E. Williams, Charles D. Walker (2), M. Rhea Seddon, Jeffrey A. Hoffman, S. David Griggs, E. Jake Garn. Garn (R, UT) was **1st U.S. senator in space**.

6/17/1985: *Discovery (51-G)*; 8 days; Daniel C. Brandenstein (2), John O. Creighton, Shannon W. Lucid, John M. Fabian (2), Steven R. Nagel, Prince Sultan Salman al-Saud, Patrick Baudry. Launched three satellites; Salman al-Saud was 1st Arab in space; Baudry was 1st French person on U.S. mission.

10/3/1985: *Atlantis (51-J)*; 5 days; Karol J. Bobko (3), Ronald J. Grabe, David C. Hilmers, Robert L. Stewart (2), William A. Pailes. 1st *Atlantis* flight.

10/30/1985: *Challenger (61-A)*; 8 days; Henry W. Hartsfield Jr. (3), Steven R. Nagel (2), James F. Buchli (2), Guion S. Bluford Jr. (2), Bonnie J. Dunbar, Wubbo J. Ockels, Richard Furrer, Ernst Messerschmid. 1st eight-person crew; 1st German Spacelab mission.

1/12/1986: *Columbia (61-C)*; 7 days; Robert L. Gibson (2), Charles F. Bolden Jr., Franklin R. Chang Díaz, Steven A. Hawley (2), George D. Nelson (2), Robert J. Cenker, Bill Nelson. B. Nelson (D, FL) was **1st U.S. representative in space**.

1/28/1986: *Challenger (51-L)*; 73 seconds; Francis R. Scobee (2), Michael J. Smith, Judith A. Resnik (2), Ellison S. Onizuka (2), Ronald E. McNair, Gregory B. Jarvis, Christa McAuliffe. **Exploded 73 seconds after liftoff; all aboard were killed**, including McAuliffe, a New Hampshire school-teacher who won competition to become 1st private citizen in space.

2/20/1986: **Mir[1]*; launched without crew. Space station with six docking ports launched.

3/13/1986: **Soyuz T-15*; 125 days; Leonid Kizim (3), Vladimir Solovyov (2). Ferry between stations; docked at *Mir*.

9/29/1988: *Discovery (STS-26)*; 4 days; Frederick H. Hauck (3), Richard O. Covey (2), George D. Nelson (3), John M. Lounge (2), David C. Hilmers (2). **1st shuttle flight since *Challenger* explosion** 1/28/1986.

5/4/1989: *Atlantis (STS-30)*; 4 days; David M. Walker (2), Ronald J. Grabe (2), Norman E. Thagard (3), Mary L. Cleave (2), Mark C. Lee. Launched Venus orbiter *Magellan*.

10/18/1989: *Atlantis (STS-34)*; 5 days; Donald E. Williams (2), Michael J. McCulley, Shannon W. Lucid (2), Franklin R. Chang Díaz (2), Ellen S. Baker. Launched Jupiter probe and orbiter *Galileo*.

4/24/1990: *Discovery (STS-31)*; 6 days; Loren J. Shriver (2), Charles F. Bolden Jr. (2), Steven A. Hawley (3), Bruce McCandless (2), Kathryn D. Sullivan (2). **Launched Hubble Space Telescope.**

10/6/1990: *Discovery (STS-41)*; 5 days; Richard N. Richards (2), Robert D. Cabana, Bruce E. Melnick, William M. Shepherd (2), Thomas D. Akers. Launched *Ulysses* spacecraft to investigate interstellar space and the sun.

9/12/1992: *Endeavour (STS-47)*; 8 days; Robert L. Gibson (4), Curtis L. Brown Jr. (2), Mark C. Lee (2), N. Jan Davis (2), Jay Apt (2), Mae Carol Jemison, Mamoru Mohri. Jemison was **1st black woman in space**; Lee and Davis were **1st married couple to travel together in space**; 1st Japanese Spacelab.

6/21/1993: *Endeavour (STS-57)*; 10 days; Ronald J. Grabe (4), Brian J. Duffy (2), G. David Low (3), Nancy J. Sherlock, Janice E. Voss, Peter J. K. Wisoff. Carried Spacelab commercial payload module.

12/2/1993: *Endeavour (STS-61)*; 11 days; Richard O. Covey (3), Kenneth D. Bowersox (2), F. Story Musgrave (5), Kathryn Thornton (2), Claude Nicollier (2), Jeffrey A. Hoffman (4), Thomas D. Akers (3). Hubble Space Telescope repaired; Akers set new U.S. EVA duration record (29 hr., 40 min.).

3/14/1995: **Soyuz TM-21*; 112 days; Norman E. Thagard (5), Vladimir Dezhurov, Gennady Strekalov (4). Docked with *Mir* 3/16. Thagard was 1st American on board Russian spacecraft; Valery Polyakov returned to Earth, 3/22/1995, after record stay in space (439 days).

6/27/1995: *Atlantis (STS-71)*; 10 days; Robert L. Gibson (5), Charles J. Precourt (2), Ellen S. Baker (3), Bonnie J. Dunbar (4), Gregory J. Harbaugh (3), Anatoly Solovyev (4) (to *Mir*), Nikolai M. Budarin (to *Mir*), Norman E. Thagard (5) (from *Mir*), Gennady Strekalov (from *Mir*), Vladimir Dezhurov (from *Mir*). **1st shuttle-*Mir* docking**; exchanged crew members with *Mir*.

11/12/1995: *Atlantis (STS-74)*; 9 days; Kenneth D. Cameron (3), James D. Halsell Jr. (2), Jerry L. Ross (5), William S. McArthur Jr. (2), Chris A. Hadfield. 2nd shuttle-*Mir* docking (11/15-11/18); erected a 15-ft permanent docking tunnel to *Mir* for future use by U.S. orbiters.

9/16/1996: *Atlantis (STS-79)*; 11 days; William F. Readdy (3), Terry W. Wilcutt (2), Thomas D. Akers (4), John E. Blaha (5) (to *Mir*), Jay Apt (4), Carl E. Walz (3), Shannon W. Lucid (5) (from *Mir*). Docked with *Mir* 9/18; exchanged crew members; Lucid set **U.S. and women's duration in space record** (188 days).

11/19/1996: *Columbia (STS-80)*; 18 days; Kenneth D. Cockrell (3), Kent V. Rominger (2), Tamara E. Jernigan (4), Thomas D. Jones (3), F. Story Musgrave (6). Longest-duration shuttle flight; Musgrave, 61, oldest thus far to fly in space; two science satellites deployed, retrieved.

8/5/1997: **Soyuz TM-26*; 198 days; Anatoly Solovyev (5), Pavel Vinogradov. Docked with *Mir* 8/7; repaired damaged space station.

8/7/1997: *Discovery (STS-85)*; 12 days; Curtis L. Brown Jr. (4), Kent V. Rominger (3), N. Jan Davis (3), Robert L. Curbeam Jr., Stephen K. Robinson, Bjarni V. Tryggvason. Deployed and retrieved satellite designed to study Earth's middle atmosphere; demonstrated robotic arm.

4/17/1998: *Columbia (STS-90)*; 16 days; Richard A. Searfoss (3), Scott D. Altman, Richard M. Linnehan (2), Dave R. Williams, Kathryn P. Hire, Jay C. Buckey, James A. Pawelczyk. Studied effects of microgravity on the nervous systems of the crew and more than 2,000 live animals; 1st surgery in space on animals meant to survive.

6/2/1998: *Discovery (STS-91)*; 10 days; Charles J. Precourt (4), Dominic L. Gorie, Wendy B. Lawrence (3), Franklin R. Chang Díaz (6), Janet L. Kavandi, Valery V. Ryumin (4), Andrew S. W. Thomas (2) (from *Mir*). Final docking mission with *Mir*; Thomas from *Mir*, 141 days in space.

10/29/1998: *Discovery (STS-95)*; 10 days; Curtis L. Brown Jr. (5), Steven W. Lindsey (2), Scott E. Parazynski (3), Stephen K. Robinson (2), Pedro Duque, Chiaki Mukai (2), John H. Glenn Jr. (2). The 77-year-old Glenn, one of the original *Mercury* astronauts, and at that point a senator (D, OH), became **oldest person to fly in space**; Duque was 1st Spaniard in space; experiments to study aging performed on Glenn.

12/4/1998: *Endeavour (STS-88)*; 12 days; Robert D. Cabana (4), Frederick W. Sturckow, Nancy J. Currie (3), Jerry L. Ross (6), James H. Newman (3), Sergei K. Krikalev (4). **1st assembly of International Space Station (ISS)**; attached U.S.-built *Unity* connecting module to Russian-built *Zarya* control module; 1st crew to enter ISS.

7/23/1999: *Columbia (STS-93)*; 5 days; Eileen M. Collins (3), Jeffrey S. Ashby, Steven A. Hawley (5), Catherine G. Coleman (2), Michel Tognini (2). Collins was **1st woman space shuttle commander**; deployed Chandra X-ray Observatory telescope.

2/11/2000: *Endeavour (STS-99)*; 12 days; Kevin R. Kregel (4), Dominic L. Gorie (2), Janet L. Kavandi (3), Janice E. Voss (5), Mamoru Mohri (2), Gerhard P.J. Thiele. Used radar to make most complete topographic map of Earth's surface ever produced.

10/31/2000: *Soyuz TM-31*; William M. Shepherd (4), Yuri Gidzenko (2), Sergei Krikalev (5). Established **1st permanent manning of ISS** with three-person crew for a 4-month stay.

7/12/2001: *Atlantis (STS-104)*; 13 days; Steven W. Lindsey (3), Charles O. Hobaugh, Michael L. Gernhardt (4), Janet L. Kavandi (3), James F. Reilly II (2). Installed the Joint Airlock, with nitrogen and oxygen tanks to permit future spacewalks from the ISS; three EVAs.

10/30/2002: *Soyuz TMA-1*[1]; Sergei Zalyotin (2), Frank De Winne (2), Yuri Lonchakov (2). 1st launch of *Soyuz TMA* (crew returned 11/10/2002 on *Soyuz TM-34* already docked at ISS).

1/16/2003: *Columbia (STS 107)*; 16 days; Rick D. Husband (2), William C. McCool, Michael P. Anderson (2), David M. Brown, Kalpana Chawla (2), Laurel B. Clark, Ilan Ramon. **Entire crew lost when Columbia broke apart** upon reentry, 2/1, due to heat shield damage; Ramon was 1st Israeli astronaut.

10/15/2003: *Shenzhou 5*; 21 hr.; Yang Liwei. **1st Chinese manned spacecraft.**

6/21/2004: *SpaceShipOne*[2]; 90 min.; Mike Melvill. **1st privately funded manned spaceflight.**

7/26/2005: *Discovery (STS-114)*; 14 days; Eileen M. Collins (4), James M. Kelly (2), Charles J. Camarda, Wendy B. Lawrence (4), Soichi Noguchi, Stephen K. Robinson (3), Andrew S.W. Thomas (3). **1st space shuttle flight since Columbia disaster**; tested new safety modifications to craft.

6/8/2007: *Atlantis (STS-117)*; 14 days; Frederick W. Sturckow (3), Lee J. Archambault, Patrick G. Forrester (2), John "Danny" Olivas, James F. Reilly (3), Steven R. Swanson, Clayton C. Anderson (to ISS), Sunita L. Williams (from ISS). Delivered truss segments and solar arrays to ISS; set new record for **longest spaceflight by a woman (195 days)**.

8/8/2007: *Endeavour (STS-118)*; 13 days; Scott J. Kelly (2), Charles O. Hobaugh (2), Alvin B. Drew, Barbara R. Morgan, Tracy Caldwell Dyson, Rick A. Mastracchio (2), Dave R. Williams (2). Brought **Teacher in Space** project participant Morgan to ISS; attached new truss.

10/10/2007: *Soyuz TMA-11*[1]; Yuri I. Malenchenko (3), Sheikh Muszaphar Shukor (to ISS), Peggy A. Whitson (2) (from ISS), Yi So-yeon (from ISS). Delivered and installed components of ISS; malfunctioned on return to Earth, landing short of its touchdown area but causing no fatalities.

3/11/2008: *Endeavour (STS-123)*; 16 days; Dominic L. Gorie (4), Gregory H. Johnson, Richard M. Linnehan (4), Robert L. Behnken, Michael J. Foreman, Takao Doi (2), Garrett E. Reisman (to ISS), Léopold Eyharts (from ISS). Delivered components of the Japanese Kibo science laboratory.

4/8/2008: *Soyuz TMA-12*[1]; Oleg Kononenko, Sergei Volkov, Yi So-yeon (to ISS), Richard Garriott (from ISS). Yi became **1st S. Korean in space.**

9/25/2008: *Shenzhou 7*; 68 hr.; Jing Haipeng, Liu Boming, Zhai Zhigang. Zhai completed **1st Chinese spacewalk.**

5/11/2009: *Atlantis (STS-125)*; 13 days; Scott D. Altman (4), Gregory C. Johnson, Andrew J. Feustel, Michael T. Good, John M. Grunsfeld (5), Michael J. Massimino (2), K. Megan McArthur. Final Hubble Space Telescope servicing mission.

6/15/2010: *Soyuz TMA-19*[1]; Fyodor Yurchikhin (3), Shannon Walker (2), Douglas H. Wheelock (2). 100th mission since launching of the International Space Station.

7/8/2011: *Atlantis (STS-135)*; 13 days; Christopher Ferguson (3), Doug Hurley (2), Sandy H. Magnus (3), Rex J. Walheim (3). **Final space shuttle mission.**

5/30/2020: *SpaceX Demo-2*; Robert L. Behnken (3), Douglas G. Hurley (3). **1st commercially operated crewed spaceflight** to carry Americans into orbit.

Note: Four Soviet cosmonauts have died during spaceflight: one person was killed on *Soyuz 1* (1967) when parachute lines tangled during descent; the three-person *Soyuz 11* crew (1971) was asphyxiated. Three Americans died in the *Apollo 1* (1967) fire on the ground at Cape Canaveral, FL; seven Americans died in the *Challenger* (1986) explosion; and six Americans and an Israeli astronaut died aboard *Columbia* (2003). (1) *Soyuz* crew often return from the ISS on spacecraft that launched and were docked at the station before their arrival. (2) Date of first successful flight; later, *SpaceShipOne* flew at least 100 km (62 mi) into space, 9/29/2004, piloted by Mike Melvill, and 10/4/2004, piloted by Brian Binnie, winning the $10-mil Ansari Prize for first private venture to accomplish this feat twice within two weeks.

U.S. Space Shuttles

Source: National Aeronautics and Space Administration (NASA)

After 135 launches, the United States ended its space shuttle program with the safe landing of the *Atlantis* shuttle on July 21, 2011, at Florida's Kennedy Space Center. Two shuttles—*Challenger* in 1986 and *Columbia* in 2003—were destroyed in flight. The surviving shuttles are now on display at museums. *Enterprise* performed atmospheric test flights but never flew in space.

Atlantis: Kennedy Space Center, Titusville, FL; www.kennedyspacecenter.com

Discovery: Udvar-Hazy Center, Smithsonian National Air and Space Museum, Chantilly, VA; discovery.si.edu

Endeavour: California Science Center, Los Angeles, CA; www.californiasciencecenter.org

Enterprise: Intrepid Air, Sea, and Space Museum, New York, NY; www.intrepidmuseum.org/Space_Shuttle_Pavilion

International Space Station

Source: National Aeronautics and Space Administration (NASA)

Construction on the International Space Station (ISS) began in 1998 and was completed in 2011. It has been inhabited continuously since 2000 and visited by more than 240 international crew members from 19 countries.

Cooperating nations: Belgium, Canada, Denmark, France, Germany, Italy, Japan, Netherlands, Norway, Russia, Spain, Sweden, Switzerland, United Kingdom, and U.S. As of Aug. 2020, individuals from all of these countries (except Norway and Switzerland) have flown to the ISS, as have visitors from Brazil, Kazakhstan, Malaysia, South Africa, South Korea, and the United Arab Emirates.

About the ISS
- It has a mass of 924,739 lbs and is about as long as a football field at 357.5 ft.
- It is entirely powered by an acre of solar panels.
- It requires three people to keep it running but has room for up to 10 people to live aboard.
- Astronauts typically spend 4-6 months aboard.

ISS Research
- Effects of long-term exposure to reduced gravity on humans, plants, crystals, cells, and pathogens
- Recording large-scale long-term changes in Earth's environment by observing the planet from orbit
- Testing recycling technologies for human life support

The Future of Human Space Exploration

Source: National Aeronautics and Space Administration (NASA); SpaceX; Boeing; World Almanac research

On May 31, 2020, a SpaceX Crew Dragon capsule safely delivered NASA astronauts Bob Behnken and Doug Hurley to the International Space Station (ISS). It marked the first time a commercial spacecraft took NASA astronauts to the ISS. Since 2011, when NASA ended the space shuttle program, all U.S. astronauts had been transported to the ISS on Russian spacecraft, at a cost of more than $80 mil per seat.

The SpaceX voyage was part of a larger effort by NASA to shift the cost of space exploration to the private sector. In 2019, NASA announced it was opening the ISS to commercial businesses seeking to establish a presence in low-earth orbit. The space station's zero-gravity environment held promise for a variety of commercial aims in manufacturing, production, or research and development. NASA also sought to develop a sustainable low-earth orbit economy.

In Mar. 2020, SpaceX announced that it had partnered with Axiom Space to send three tourists on a 10-day trip to the ISS in late 2021. If successful, it would mark the first human spaceflight to orbit with no government involvement, at a cost of approximately $55 mil per seat. Another space tourism company, Space Adventures, announced it was collaborating with SpaceX to send four private citizens into orbit (but not to the ISS) in late 2021 or 2022. A different (and yet-to-be-built) SpaceX vehicle was expected to fly Japanese billionaire Yusaku Maezawa and several guests around the moon as tourists as early as 2023. NASA was aiming to return humans to the Moon's surface by 2024. In Apr. 2020, it announced partnerships with three private sector companies to develop technology to land the first woman and next man on the moon's surface. The mission, named after Apollo's twin sister Artemis, sought to spend significantly more time on the Moon than did previous lunar landings in pursuit of lessons that could be applied to future human exploration of Mars.

Summary of Worldwide Successful Launches, 1957-2019

Source: National Aeronautics and Space Administration (NASA); Space Launch Report

Year	1957-59	1960-69	1970-79	1980-89	1990-99	2000-09	2010-19	Total
Russia[1]	6	399	1,028	1,132	542	246	240	3,593
U.S.	18	614	247	191	300	206	209	1,785
China	—	—	8	16	33	52	194	303
ESA[2]	—	2	5	14	55	63	71	210
Ukraine	—	—	—	—	59	57	24	140
Japan	—	—	18	26	23	18	36	121
India	—	—	1	9	11	13	42	76
France[2]	—	4	14	5	16	0	0	39
UK[2]	—	1	6	4	7	0	0	18
Germany[2]	—	—	3	7	6	0	0	16
Canada	—	—	4	5	4	0	0	13
New Zealand	—	—	—	—	—	—	7	7
Israel	—	—	—	—	—	3	3	6
Iran	—	—	—	—	—	1	3	4
North Korea	—	—	—	—	—	—	1	1
South Korea	—	—	—	—	—	1	0	1
Total	**24**	**1,020**	**1,334**	**1,409**	**1,056**	**660**	**830**	**6,333**

— = Not applicable. (1) Data for 1957-91 apply to the Soviet Union, for 1992-96 to the Commonwealth of Independent States, after 1996 to Russia. (2) ESA = European Space Agency, which includes France, Germany, and UK after 2009.

Notable Lunar and Planetary Science Missions

Source: National Aeronautics and Space Administration (NASA)

Spacecraft	Launch date[1]	Mission	Mission notes
Mariner 2	Aug. 27, 1962	Venus	Passed within 22,000 mi of Venus 12/14/1962; confirmed high surface temperature on planet; contact lost 1/3/1963 at 54 mil mi.
Ranger 7	July 28, 1964	Moon	Yielded over 4,000 photos of lunar surface.
Mariner 4	Nov. 28, 1964	Mars	1st probe to fly by Mars; passed behind planet 7/14/1965.
Ranger 8	Feb. 17, 1965	Moon	Yielded over 7,000 photos of lunar surface.
Venera 3	Nov. 16, 1965	Venus	Soviet probe; 1st artificial probe to impact on the surface of another planet, 3/1/1966; probe failed to send back data.
Surveyor 3	Apr. 17, 1967	Moon	Scooped and tested lunar soil.
Mariner 5	June 14, 1967	Venus	In solar orbit; closest Venus flyby 10/19/1967; allowed scientists to obtain accurate readings on the composition of the Venusian atmosphere.
Mariner 6	Feb. 24, 1969	Mars	Came within 2,000 mi of Mars 7/31/1969; collected data, photos.
Mariner 7	Mar. 27, 1969	Mars	Came within 2,000 mi of Mars 8/5/1969.
Venera 7	Aug. 17, 1970	Venus	Soviet probe; 1st probe to land safely on the surface of another planet.
Mariner 9	May 30, 1971	Mars	1st craft to orbit Mars 11/13/1971; sent back over 7,000 photos.
Pioneer 10	Mar. 2, 1972	Jupiter	Passed Jupiter 12/4/1973; took readings on Jupiter's composition. Exited planetary system 6/13/1983; last signal received 1/23/2003 from 7.6 bil mi.
Pioneer 11	Apr. 5, 1973	Jupiter, Saturn	Passed Jupiter 12/3/1974, Saturn 9/1/1979; discovered an additional ring and 2 moons around Saturn. Transmission ended 9/30/1995.
Mariner 10	Nov. 3, 1973	Venus, Mercury	Passed Venus 2/5/1974, arrived at Mercury 3/29/1974. 1st time gravity of a planet (Venus) used to whip spacecraft toward another (Mercury); 1st probe to visit 2 planets; took cloud and wind pattern readings in Venusian atmosphere.
Viking 1	Aug. 20, 1975	Mars	Landed on Mars 7/20/1976; 1st probe to land safely on Mars; performed chemical analysis of soil; functioned 6 years.
Viking 2	Sept. 9, 1975	Mars	Sister probe of *Viking 1*; landed on Mars 9/3/1976; functioned 3 years.
Voyager 2	Aug. 20, 1977	Jupiter, Saturn, Uranus, Neptune	Encountered Jupiter 7/9/1979, Saturn 8/25/1981, Uranus 1/24/1986, Neptune 8/25/1989. Confirmed existence of rings around Neptune. As of 8/2020 it was 11.6 bil mi from sun and still returning data to Earth.
Voyager 1	Sept. 5, 1977	Jupiter, Saturn	Encountered Jupiter 3/5/1979; provided evidence of rings around Jupiter; passed near Saturn 11/12/1980; passed *Pioneer 10* to become most distant human-made object 2/17/1998. As of 8/2020 it was 14.0 bil mi from sun and still returning data to Earth.
Pioneer Venus 1	May 20, 1978	Venus	Entered Venus orbit 12/4/1978; studied weather, magnetic field, weather, and surface; fuel ran out; probe was destroyed in atmospheric entry, 8/1992.
Pioneer Venus 2 (multiprobe)	Aug. 8, 1978	Venus	Consisted of a "bus" carrying 1 large and 3 small atmospheric probes. All 4 probes entered the Venus atmosphere 12/9/1978, followed by the bus; took readings of atmosphere; probes impacted surface.

Spacecraft	Launch date[1]	Mission	Mission notes
Magellan	May 4, 1989	Venus	Landed on Venus 8/10/1990; monitored geological activity; mapped more than 99% of planet surface, showed that about 85% is covered by volcanic flows; ceased operating 10/11/1994.
Galileo	Oct. 18, 1989	Jupiter	Used Earth's gravity to propel itself towards Jupiter; encountered Venus 2/10/1990, Jupiter 12/7/1995; encountered moons. Released probe into Jovian atmosphere; intentionally flown into Jupiter 9/21/2003 to prevent accidental contamination of Jupiter's moon Europa.
Mars Global Surveyor	Nov. 7, 1996	Mars	Began orbiting Mars 9/11/1997; began mapping entire surface 3/9/1999; discovered a weak magnetic field on planet; observed Martian moon Phobos; found evidence of liquid water in past 6/22/2000.
Mars Pathfinder	Dec. 4, 1996	Mars	Landed on Mars 7/4/1997; rover *Sojourner* made measurements of climate and soil composition, sent thousands of surface images; ceased operating 9/27/1997.
Cassini-Huygens	Oct. 15, 1997	Saturn	Began orbiting Saturn 6/30/2004; spotted evidence of a subterranean ocean and 300-mi-wide hot spots region on moon Titan; detected an atmosphere on moon Enceladus. Intentionally destroyed 9/15/2017. *Huygens* probe landed on Titan 1/14/2005; found a muddy surface, possible water ice, channels carved by liquid methane springs.
Lunar Prospector	Jan. 6, 1998	Moon	Began orbiting moon 1/11/1998; mapped abundance of 11 elements on moon's surface; discovered evidence of water ice at both lunar poles; crashed into crater near moon's south pole 7/31/1999 to end mission.
Deep Space 1	Oct. 24, 1998	Comet Borrelly	Flew within 1,500 mi of comet; sent back photos showing 6-mi-long nucleus.
Stardust	Feb. 7, 1999	Comet Wild 2	Reached comet 1/2/2004; gathered dust samples, capsule returned to Earth 1/15/2006. Spacecraft, on new mission Stardust-NExT (follow up for Deep Impact), reached comet Tempel 1, 2/14/2011.
2001 Mars Odyssey	Apr. 7, 2001	Mars	Reached Mars 10/24/2001; detected evidence of water ice near south pole; primary mission to study climate and geologic history completed 8/2004; began extended mission, aiming to identify minerals on Mars.
Genesis	Aug. 8, 2001	Sun	Orbited sun, collected particles from solar wind; capsule containing specimens crashed to Earth 9/8/2004; some samples survived.
Mars Express/ Beagle 2 lander	June 3, 2003	Mars	1st European Space Agency probe to another planet; arrived at Mars 12/2003; performed remote sensing including photography in search of subsurface water. *Beagle 2* lander was deployed 12/19/2003, but contact was lost.
Mars Exploration Rovers	June 7 and July 10, 2003	Mars	Rovers *Spirit* and *Opportunity* landed on Mars 1/2004, found further evidence that water existed on surface; *Spirit* took 1st photo of a Martian meteor; survived severe dust storms in 2007. *Opportunity* explored massive Victoria Crater 2007-08, set record for most distance driven off-Earth (25 mi) 7/2014.
MESSENGER	Mar. 2, 2004	Mercury	Began returning images of Mercury during initial flyby 1/14/2008; entered orbit 3/17/2011; delivered 100,000th image 5/3/2012; impacted Mercury 4/30/2015.
Deep Impact	Jan. 12, 2005	Comet Tempel 1	Reached Tempel 1; deployed impact probe that slammed into comet 7/4/2005 with force roughly equivalent to 5 tons of TNT. Flyby spacecraft, on supplemental mission EPOXI, reached comet Hartley 2, 11/4/2010.
Mars Reconnaissance Orbiter	Aug. 12, 2005	Mars	Reached Mars 3/10/2006 and began taking detailed images of Martian surface; in 3/2008, found salt deposits suggesting ancient water supplies; in 6/2008, found largest known impact crater in solar system.
New Horizons (Pluto)	Jan. 19, 2006	Pluto, Charon	Flew past Jupiter 7/2007 on its way to Pluto and its largest moon, Charon. Returned first-ever photographs of Pluto 7/14/2015. Began examining other objects in the Kuiper Belt in 2019.
Phoenix Mars Lander	Aug. 4, 2007	Mars	Landed on Mars 5/25/2008; examined northern polar region, analyzed weather/minerals; water ice verified 7/31/2008; lost contact 11/2/2008.
Dawn	Sept. 27, 2007	Asteroid Belt (bet. Jupiter and Mars)	Will compare evolution of dwarf planet Ceres with Vesta, an asteroid, in an effort to shed light on formation of the solar system. Departed Vesta 8/2012; reached Ceres 3/6/2015.
Kepler/K2	Mar. 9, 2009	Extrasolar planets	Detect potentially habitable Earth-size planets around other Milky Way stars. Kepler confirmed existence of more than 2,600 exoplanets before running out of fuel in Oct. 2018.
Lunar Crater Observation and Sensing Satellite	June 18, 2009	Moon	Impacted the Cabeus crater; detected presence of water ice in moon's surface 10/9/2009. Lunar Reconnaissance Orbiter (LRO), launched with LCROSS, mapped moon's surface.
Juno	Aug. 5, 2011	Jupiter	Entered Jupiter's orbit, 7/4/2016; began returning data and color images that improve understanding of the formation of the planet and solar system. Scheduled to end operations July, 2021.
Mars Science Laboratory	Nov. 26, 2011	Mars	*Curiosity* rover landed on Mars 8/6/2012 and began assessing Mars's past and present ability to support life.
Lunar Atmosphere and Dust Environment Explorer	Sept. 6, 2013	Moon	Studied the fragile lunar atmosphere from orbit for 100 days; impacted with lunar surface 4/17/2014.
Mars Atmosphere and Volatile Evolution (MAVEN)	Nov. 18, 2013	Mars	Entered orbit 9/21/2014; exploring Mars's upper atmosphere to determine how planet's loss of atmospheric gas changed its climate from a warmer, wetter environment to a cold desert.
OSIRIS-REx	Sept. 8, 2016	Bennu (asteroid)	Retrieve a sample by 9/2023 to help understand the source of Earth's organic materials and water and improve understanding of potential asteroid-Earth impacts. Entered into orbit around Bennu 12/31/2018.
Transiting Exoplanet Survey Satellite	Apr. 18, 2018	Extrasolar planets	Survey 200,000 of the brightest nearby stars in search of planets outside our solar system.
InSight	May 5, 2018	Mars	Landed 11/26/2018; began drilling in 2019 beneath surface to investigate how rocky planets form and develop.
Parker Solar Probe	Aug. 12, 2018	Sun	First ever mission to observe and record the sun from within its atmosphere. Will fly within 3.8 mil miles—1/10 Mercury's distance from the sun—of the sun's surface.
ICESat-2	Sept. 15, 2018	Earth	Initiated ultra-precise measurements of Earth's ice sheets and glaciers and how changes are affecting rising sea levels.
Mars Perseverance	July/Aug. 2020	Mars	Rover to investigate potential for human habitation; scheduled to land 2/2021.
James Webb Space Telescope	2021	Universe	Replace Hubble Space Telescope as the world's premier astronomical observatory.
Artemis	2024	Moon	Send the first woman to the Moon. Explore lunar surface in preparation for human flight to Mars.
Europa Clipper	2020s	Europa	Assess if Europa, Jupiter's icy, ocean-bearing moon, is suitable for life.

Note: U.S./NASA missions unless otherwise noted. (1) In Coordinated Universal Time.

General Aviation and Air Taxi Active Aircraft, 2018

Source: Federal Aviation Administration; aircraft not associated with major airlines or the military

Aircraft type	Total active	Personal	Busi-ness	Instruc-tional	Aerial apps.	Aerial obser-vation	Other work	Sight-seeing	Air medical	Other	On-demand operations
Fixed Wing	167,560	111,425	25,028	14,453	3,079	2,521	725	249	239	3,460	6,383
Piston	143,040	107,726	12,936	14,221	820	2,139	377	232	175	2,933	1,482
Turboprop	9,925	1,608	3,175	136	2,126	353	249	3	19	342	1,914
Turbojet	14,596	2,091	8,917	96	133	28	99	13	45	185	2,988
Rotorcraft	9,990	1,271	487	1,363	1,179	2,177	95	270	53	752	2,343
Piston	3,082	938	172	970	372	257	15	213	0	42	104
Turbine	6,907	333	316	393	807	1,920	80	57	53	711	2,238
Other Aircraft	4,114	3,199	71	329	0	5	81	407	0	5	17
Gliders	1,772	1,401	20	297	0	0	32	17	0	4	0
Lighter-than-air	2,343	1,798	51	31	0	5	48	390	0	1	17
Experimental	27,531	25,168	861	517	59	73	82	39	3	714	14
Amateur	21,216	19,760	752	264	0	9	5	28	3	396	0
Exhibition	1,979	1,627	36	63	12	12	44	6	0	179	0
Experimental light-sport	3,580	3,302	5	162	0	24	26	5	0	55	0
Other	755	479	69	28	47	27	7	0	0	84	14
Special Light-sport	2,554	2,115	48	315	0	12	2	9	0	53	0
ALL AIRCRAFT	211,749	143,178	26,496	16,976	4,317	4,787	985	974	295	4,983	8,758

Note: Columns may not add to totals due to rounding. Totals include some categories not shown. **Personal**—Flying for personal reasons; **Business**—Individual or group use for business transportation with or without a professional crew (includes fractional ownership); **Instructional**—Flying under the supervision of a flight instructor; **Aerial applications**—Includes agriculture, forestry, public health, fire fighting, and other applications; **Aerial observation**—Includes aerial mapping/photography, patrol, search and rescue, hunting, traffic advisory, ranching, surveillance, oil and mineral exploration, etc.; **Other work**—Construction work, parachuting, aerial advertising, towing gliders, etc.; **Sightseeing**—Commercial sightseeing; **Air medical services**—Air ambulance services, rescue, human organ transportation, emergency medical services; **Other**—Positioning flights, proficiency flights, training, ferrying, sales demos; **On-demand operations**—On-demand air taxi, air tours, commuter, and air medical services.

Estimated Active Airmen Certificates Held, 2019

Source: Federal Aviation Administration, U.S. Dept. of Transportation

Category	Certificates	Category	Certificates	Category	Certificates
Pilot total	664,565	Rotorcraft (helicopters only)	14,248	**Nonpilot total**	714,201
Student	197,665	Glider (only)	19,143	Mechanic	301,087
Recreational (only)	127	**Flight Instructor**		Repairmen	36,294
Sport (only)	6,467	**Certificates**	113,445	Parachute Rigger	6,800
Airplane[1]		**Instrument**		Ground Instructor	69,991
Private	161,105	**Ratings**	314,168	Dispatcher	22,598
Commercial	100,863	**Remote Pilots**[2]	160,302	Flight Navigator	40
Airline Transport	164,947			Flight Attendant	245,699
				Flight Engineer	31,692

Note: The term airmen includes men and women certified as pilots, mechanics, or other aviation technicians. (1) Includes pilots with an airplane-only certificate as well as those with an airplane and a helicopter and/or glider certificate. (2) Remote pilot certification began in Aug. 2016. These numbers are not included in pilot totals.

World's Most Commonly Flown Aircraft, 2020

Source: Forecast International; World Almanac research

Manufacturer, headquarters, and model	Aircraft type	Number in operation	Avg. age (years)	Manufacturer, headquarters, and model	Aircraft type	Number in operation	Avg. age (years)
Airbus, Netherlands				**Boeing, U.S.**			
A319-100	Jet	1,262	14.9	787-8	Jet	356	5.6
A320-200	Jet	4,241	11.0	787-9 Dreamliner	Jet	538	2.8
A320 neo	Jet	948	1.7	**Bombardier, Canada**			
A321-200	Jet	1,612	8.0	RJ200ER	Jet	363	18.3
A321 neo	Jet	333	1.3	RJ200LR	Jet	131	18.4
A330-200	Jet	512	11.7	RJ700	Jet	324	15.0
A330-300	Jet	710	9.7	RJ900	Jet	440	8.8
A350-900XWB	Jet	317	2.4	**British Aerospace, UK**			
A380-800[1]	Jet	238	6.7	Jetstream 31	TPE	184	31.4
ATR, France				**De Havilland, Canada**			
ATR-42-300	TPE	157	30.0	DHC-6-300	TPE	258	43.3
ATR-72-500	TPE	299	13.9	DHC-8-102	TPE	134	31.7
ATR-72-600	TPE	467	4.5	DHC-8-400Q[2]	TPE	504	9.4
Boeing, U.S.				**Fairchild, US**			
717-200	Jet	136	18.4	SA-227AC	TPE	495	12.1
737 MAX 8	Jet	345	2.1	**Embraer, Brazil**			
737-200 Adv	Jet	141	38.1	ERJ 145LR	Jet	329	18.9
737-300	Jet	373	27.4	Embraer 170LR	Jet	118	13.8
737-400	Jet	290	26.9	Embraer 175	Jet	173	6.5
737-500	Jet	208	25.8	Embraer 175LR	Jet	445	5.0
737-700	Jet	1,001	15.4	Embraer 190AR	Jet	232	11.4
737-800	Jet	4,748	9.3	Embraer 190LR	Jet	203	9.5
737-900ER	Jet	469	6.3	**Fokker, Netherlands**			
747-400[1]	Jet	218	24.5	Fokker 50	TPE	127	29.4
747-400F[1]	Jet	136	20.3	Fokker 100	Jet	169	28.0
757-200	Jet	502	25.7	**Raytheon, U.S.**			
767-300ER	Jet	456	21.6	1900D	TPE	323	23.6
767-300F	Jet	175	10.0	**Saab, Sweden**			
777-200ER	Jet	335	18.3	SF.340B	TPE	192	26.7
777-300ER	Jet	788	7.6	**Sukhoi, Russia**			
777F	Jet	187	5.8	Superjet 100-95	Jet	129	4.7

Note: All aircraft are two-engine planes except where indicated. (1) Four-engine. (2) Manufactured by Bombardier since 1992.

Milestones in Aviation History

Source: National Aeronautics and Space Administration (NASA); Smithsonian National Air and Space Museum; Air Transport Association of America; National Museum of the U.S. Air Force (USAF); National Park Service, U.S. Dept. of the Interior

1903, Dec. 17: Brothers Wilbur and Orville Wright (U.S.) made the first human-carrying, powered flight near Kitty Hawk, NC. Each brother made two flights; the longest, about 852 ft, lasted 59 sec.

1908, May 14: Charles Furnas (U.S.), worker for Wright brothers, became first American airplane passenger.

1911, Feb.: The Burgess Company and Curtiss, Inc. receive authorization to build Wright planes, becoming the first licensed airplane manufacturer in the U.S.

1911, Sept. 23: First transportation of mail by airplane officially approved by the U.S. Postal Service.

1914, Jan. 1: First scheduled passenger airline service began.

1914, June 18: Lawrence Burst Sperry (U.S.) released the controls and stood in his airborne plane, successfully demonstrating his gyrostabilizer, the first autopilot system.

1918, Mar. 6: The Curtiss-Sperry "Flying Bomb" (U.S.) made its first successful flight. The first radio-controlled plane led to the development of cruise missiles.

1918, May 14: First scheduled airmail service began, between New York and Washington, DC, with intermediate stop in Philadelphia. In 1921, scheduled transcontinental airmail service began between New York City and San Francisco.

1919, June 14-15: Capt. John Alcock (UK) and Lt. Arthur W. Brown (U.S.) completed the first nonstop flight across the Atlantic Ocean. They traveled from Newfoundland, Canada, to Ireland in 16 hr., 12 min.

1923, Aug.: Rotating beacons enabled the first U.S. night flights.

1924, Apr. 6-Sept. 28: Two U.S. Army planes landed in Seattle, completing the first circumnavigation of the globe. They completed the 26,000-mi journey in 371 hours of flying time.

1926, May 12-13: Roald Amundsen (Norway), Umberto Nobile (Italy), Lincoln Ellsworth (U.S.), and Oscar Wisting (Norway) made the first flight over the North Pole, in a dirigible that flew between Spitsbergen, Norway, and Teller, AK. Two weeks earlier, Adm. Richard E. Byrd and Floyd Bennett (both U.S.) claimed to have made the first flight over the Pole (May 9, 1926) in a Fokker F-VII. But when Byrd's diary was released to the public in 1996, some historians began to question whether his plane had reached the Pole.

1927, May 20-21: Charles Lindbergh (U.S.) completed the first solo transatlantic flight in the *Spirit of St. Louis*. "Lucky Lindy" traveled 3,610 mi from New York to Paris in 33 hr., 29 min., 30 sec.

1929, Aug. 8-29: Hugo Eckener (Germany) piloted the *Graf Zeppelin* around the world in record time: 20,373 mi in 21 days, 5 hr., 31 min.

1929, Nov. 28: Richard E. Byrd, Harold June, Ashley McKinley (all U.S.) and Bernt Balchen (Norway) became first to fly over the South Pole, in 18 hr., 41 min. round trip from Ross Ice Shelf base.

1930, May 15: Ellen Church (U.S.) became first flight attendant.

1931, June 23-July 1: Wiley Post (U.S.) and Harold Gatty (Austral.-U.S.) broke the speed record for around-the-world flight, traveling 15,474 mi in 8 days, 15 hr., 51 min., in the monoplane *Winnie Mae*.

1931, Oct. 3-5: Clyde Pangborn and Hugh Herndon (both U.S.) completed the first nonstop transpacific flight. They traveled 4,558 mi from Misawa, Japan, to East Wenatchee, WA, in 41 hr., 34 min.

1932, May 20-21: Amelia Earhart (U.S.) completed first solo transoceanic flight by a woman, making the 2,026-mi journey from Newfoundland, Canada, to Ireland in 14 hr., 56 min.

1933, July 15-22: Wiley Post completed the first solo circumnavigation of the globe. His 15,596-mi trip took 7 days, 18 hr., 49 min.

1936, June 25: American Airlines began scheduled passenger service of the first Douglas DC-3 aircraft. The DC-3 was the first aircraft with a kitchen onboard and hence offered the first in-flight hot meal service.

1937, May 6: German *Hindenburg* zeppelin exploded in Lakehurst, NJ, killing 35 of the 97 people aboard (and one on the ground). The airship had made 34 transatlantic flights in 1936.

1938, July 10-13: Howard Hughes (U.S.) and four assistants established a new speed record for circumnavigating the globe: 14,824 mi in 3 days, 9 hr., 17 min.

1939, Aug. 27: The German-made Heinkel He 178 made the first successful flight powered by a jet engine.

1947, Oct. 14: Chuck Yeager (U.S.) broke the sound barrier, reaching Mach 1 in a Bell X-1 rocket-powered aircraft.

1947, Nov. 2: Howard Hughes piloted the *Spruce Goose* on its maiden and only flight. The largest airplane ever built at the time, it could carry 750 troops or two Sherman tanks.

1949, Mar. 2: James Gallagher (U.S.) piloted the first round-the-world flight refueled in midair. The *Lucky Lady* USAF B-50 covered 23,452 mi in 94 hr., 1 min. and refueled four times.

1950, Sept. 22: Col. David Schilling (USAF) made the first nonstop transatlantic jet flight, covering 3,300 mi in 10 hr., 1 min.

1952, Aug. 26: The UK bomber Canberra made the first round-trip transatlantic crossing on the same day, from Northern Ireland to Newfoundland, Canada, and back in 7 hr., 59 min.

1953, May 18: Jacqueline Cochran (U.S.) became the first woman to fly faster than the speed of sound.

1956, Mar. 10: Britain's Fairey FD-2 aircraft set a world speed record of 1,132 mph.

1956, Nov. 11: Convair B-58 (USAF), the first supersonic bomber, was introduced.

1957, Jan. 15-18: Three USAF B-52 Stratofortresses made the first nonstop global flight by jet planes. They were refueled in flight by KC-97 aerial tankers.

1958, Oct. 24: A Mirage III-A achieved Mach 2 (twice the speed of sound) in level flight, first European plane to do so.

1962, Nov. 29: Britain and France signed an agreement to jointly develop the Concorde, a supersonic plane that could fly twice as fast as most U.S. jets.

1969, June 5: The Soviet Tupolev Tu-144 became the first passenger airliner to break the sound barrier.

1970, May 26: The Tupolev Tu-144 became first passenger airline to exceed Mach 2 with a top speed of about 1,335 mph at 53,475 ft.

1976, Aug. 23: The Concorde began the first scheduled supersonic commercial service.

1977, Aug. 23: The *Gossamer Condor*, built by aeronautical engineer Paul MacCready (U.S.), successfully demonstrated human-powered flight through pedaling, completing a figure-8 course of 1.15 mi.

1979, June 12: MacCready's human-powered *Gossamer Albatross* crossed the English Channel in 2 hr., 49 min.

1981, July 7: MacCready-developed *Solar Challenger* became first solar-powered airplane to cross the English Channel.

1995, Aug. 15-16: The Concorde set a new around-the-world speed record of 31 hr., 27 min., 49 sec.

1999, Mar. 1-21: Bertrand Piccard (Switz.) and Brian Jones (UK) completed the first round-the-world flight in a hot-air balloon. Their 29,055-mi journey began in Chateau-d'Oex, Switzerland, and ended 19 days, 21 hr., 55 min. later in the Egyptian desert.

2001, Aug. 13: Solar-powered, propeller-driven plane *Helios* (NASA) reached 96,863 ft, breaking altitude record for non-rocket-powered aircraft.

2002, June 19-July 4: Steve Fossett (U.S.) completed the first nonstop solo circumnavigation of globe in a balloon.

2003, Nov. 26: The Concorde flew its final flight.

2005, Mar. 1-3: Steve Fossett achieved the first nonstop solo circumnavigation in an airplane without refueling.

2006, Feb. 8-11: Steve Fossett flew the longest nonstop, non-refueled solo flight (25,766 mi).

2009, Dec. 15: Boeing's 787 Dreamliner, the company's most fuel-efficient plane and the first to be constructed primarily from composite materials, made its maiden voyage.

2011, Feb. 4: Northrop Grumman and the U.S. Navy reported the first successful flight for the unmanned X-47B fighter jet.

2012, May 22-31: SpaceX became the first private company to successfully launch (and later recover) a spacecraft to the International Space Station.

2016, July 26: *Solar Impulse 2* became first fuel-free plane to circumnavigate the globe. The 17-leg journey began in Mar. 2015.

2019, Apr. 13: *Stratolaunch* aircraft, with world's longest wingspan, made its maiden voyage (and perhaps its last; the company was put up for sale in June 2019). Its design enabled it to launch satellites into space from 35,000 ft, saving rocket fuel.

ASTRONOMY

Edited by Laurence A. Marschall, Prof. Emeritus, Dept. of Physics and Astronomy, Gettysburg College

Celestial Events Summary, 2021

There are four eclipses in 2021: one annular solar eclipse, one total solar eclipse, one total lunar eclipse, and one partial lunar eclipse. The path of totality for the Dec. 4 solar eclipse crosses the Antarctic Ocean and Antarctica, while the path of the annular solar eclipse of June 10 crosses the North Pole. Neither eclipse is easily accessible, though viewers at more temperate latitudes may see partial phases. The total lunar eclipse on May 26 will be visible primarily from the Pacific Ocean and surrounding coasts. The most widely visible lunar eclipse is that of Nov. 18-19, which can be seen by observers in Asia, Australia, and North and South America. Though technically only a partial eclipse, over 97% of the moon will be in shadow at maximum, providing an impressive darkening.

The best meteor shower viewing may be the Perseids in mid-Aug., which occurs in the dark skies of a new moon, and perhaps the Aurigid meteor shower at the end of August. Other meteor showers will be hampered by unfavorably bright moon phases in 2021, though some activity will be visible, especially in stronger showers like the Geminids in Dec. At the start of the year, Venus will be visible in the predawn sky and Mars in the evening sky, where it remains visible until July, when it approaches conjunction with the sun. Venus remains in the morning sky through Mar., then re-emerges in the evening sky by late Mar. as an "evening star" for the rest of the year. Jupiter is a morning object, Mar.-July, becoming visible all night long in Aug. when it reaches opposition, and then as an evening object for the rest of the year. Saturn begins the year too close to the sun to be visible, becoming a predawn object from Apr. to Aug., when it reaches opposition, after which it is visible in the evening for the rest of the year. Mercury, frequently too close to the sun for easy viewing, is first visible in the predawn sky in Mar. It is back in the evening sky in May, and the morning sky in July and Oct. The best opportunities for seeing Mercury in the morning sky are near western elongation Mar. 6, while the best opportunities to see it in the evening sky occur at eastern elongation on May 17.

The crescent moon, with its subdued light, regularly pairs with the two brightest planets, Venus and Jupiter. Waxing crescent pairings are visible in the early evening soon after sunset, while waning crescent pairings are visible in the early morning before sunrise. The waxing crescent moon pairs with Venus in July through Dec., while the waning crescent pairs with Venus in the early morning sky in Jan. The waxing crescent moon pairs with Jupiter in the evening in Dec.; the waning crescent pairs with Jupiter in the predawn sky from Mar. through June. The moon will occult several planets this year: Mercury on Nov. 3, Venus on Nov. 8; and Mars on Apr. 17 and Dec. 31. The most noticeable planetary conjunction of the year occurs when Venus and Mars pass close to each other in the sky on July 12.

Astronomical Positions and Constants

Two celestial bodies are in **conjunction** when they are due north and south of each other, either in **right ascension** (with respect to the north celestial pole) or in **celestial longitude** (with respect to the north ecliptic pole). Celestial bodies in conjunction will rise and set at nearly the same time. For the inner planets—Mercury and Venus—**inferior conjunction** occurs when either planet passes between Earth and the sun, while **superior conjunction** occurs when either Mercury or Venus is on the far side of the sun. Celestial bodies are in **opposition** when their right ascensions differ by exactly 12 hours, or when their celestial longitudes differ by 180°. In this case one of the two objects in opposition will rise while the other is setting. **Quadrature** refers to the arrangement where the coordinates of two bodies differ by exactly 90°. These terms may refer to the relative positions of any two objects as seen from Earth, but one of the bodies is so frequently the sun that mention of the sun is omitted in that case.

When objects are in conjunction, the alignment is not perfect, and one usually passes above or below the other. The geocentric angular separation between the sun and an object is termed **elongation**. Elongation is limited only for Mercury and Venus; the greatest elongation for each of these bodies is approximately the time for longest observation. **Perihelion** is the point in an object's orbit when it is nearest to the sun, and **aphelion** is the point when it is farthest from the sun. **Perigee** is the point in an orbit where an object is nearest Earth, **apogee** the point when it is farthest from Earth. An **occultation** of a planet or a star is an eclipse of it by some other body, usually the moon. A **transit** of the sun occurs when Mercury or Venus passes directly between Earth and the sun, appearing to cross the sun's disk.

The following were adopted as part of the International Astronomical Union System of Astronomical Constants (1976/2009): **Speed of light**, 299,792.458 km per sec., or about 186,282 statute mi per sec.; **solar parallax**, 8".794143; **astronomical unit** (AU or au, mean distance between the Earth and sun), 149,597,870,700 m, or 92,955,807 mi; **constant of nutation**, 9".2025; and **constant of aberration**, 20".49552.

Celestial Events Highlights, 2021

(In Coordinated Universal Time, or UTC, the standard time of the prime meridian.)

January

Mercury, Jupiter, and **Saturn** are too close to the sun for easy visibility.
Venus is low in the SE sky before sunrise.
Mars and **Uranus** are in the evening sky.
Neptune is in the SW in the early evening.

Jan. 1: Beehive star cluster 2.3° S of moon
Jan. 2: Earth at perihelion; Regulus 4.7° S of moon
Jan. 3: Quadrantid meteor shower
Jan. 6: Last quarter moon
Jan. 9: Moon at perigee
Jan. 10: Antares 5.6° S of moon; Mercury 1.6° S of Saturn
Jan. 11: Mercury 1.4° S of Jupiter; Venus 1.5° N of moon
Jan. 13: New moon
Jan. 14: Mercury 2.3° N of moon
Jan. 20: First quarter moon
Jan. 21: Mars 5.1° N of moon; moon at apogee

Jan. 24: Mercury at greatest elongation 18.6° E of sun; Saturn in conjunction with sun; Aldebaran 4.7° S of moon
Jan. 27: Pollux 3.8° N of moon
Jan. 28: Beehive star cluster 2.3° S of moon; full moon
Jan. 29: Jupiter in conjunction with sun; Mercury at perihelion
Jan. 30: Regulus 4.6° S of moon

February

Mercury, Venus, Jupiter, Saturn, and **Neptune** are too close to the sun for easy visibility.
Mars and **Uranus** are in the SW in the early evening.

Feb. 3: Moon at perigee
Feb. 4: Last quarter moon
Feb. 6: Antares 5.5° S of moon
Feb. 8: Mercury at inferior conjunction
Feb. 11: New moon
Feb. 15: Mercury 3.8° W of Jupiter

Feb. 18: Moon at apogee; Mars 3.7° N of moon
Feb. 19: First quarter moon
Feb. 20: Venus at aphelion; Aldebaran 5.0° S of moon
Feb. 23: Mercury 4.0° N of Saturn
Feb. 24: Pollux 3.7° N of moon
Feb. 25: Beehive star cluster 2.4° S of moon
Feb. 26: Regulus 4.6° S of moon
Feb. 27: Full moon

March

Venus, Saturn, and **Neptune** are too close to the sun for easy visibility.
Mercury and **Jupiter** are low in the SE just before sunrise.
Mars and **Uranus** are in the SW in the early evening.

Mar. 2: Moon at perigee
Mar. 3: Mars 2.6° S of Pleiades
Mar. 5: Mercury 0.3° N of Jupiter; Antares 5.2° S of moon
Mar. 6: Last quarter moon; Mercury at greatest elongation 27.3° W of sun
Mar. 9: Saturn 3.7° N of moon
Mar. 10: Jupiter 4.0° N of moon
Mar. 11: Neptune in conjunction with sun; Mercury 3.7° N of moon
Mar. 13: New moon
Mar. 14: Mercury at aphelion
Mar. 18: Moon at apogee
Mar. 19: Mars 1.9° N of moon; Aldebaran 5.2° S of moon
Mar. 20: Vernal equinox 09:37 UTC; Mars 6.9° N of Aldebaran; Venus at greatest elongation 46.6° W of sun
Mar. 21: First quarter moon
Mar. 23: Pollux 3.5° N of moon
Mar. 24: Beehive star cluster 2.6° S of moon
Mar. 26: Regulus 4.7° S of moon; Venus at superior conjunction
Mar. 28: Full moon
Mar. 29: Spica 6.5° S of moon
Mar. 30: Moon at perigee

April

Mercury, Venus, Uranus, and **Neptune** are too close to the sun for easy visibility.
Mars is in the SW in the early evening.
Jupiter and **Saturn** are in the SE just before dawn.

Apr. 1: Antares 4.9° S of moon
Apr. 4: Last quarter moon
Apr. 6: Saturn 4.0° N of moon
Apr. 7: Jupiter 4.4° N of moon
Apr. 12: New moon
Apr. 14: Moon at apogee
Apr. 16: Aldebaran 5.4° S of moon
Apr. 17: Mars 0.1° N of moon; occultation of Mars by the moon
Apr. 19: Mercury at superior conjunction; Pollux 3.2° N of moon
Apr. 20: First quarter moon; Beehive star cluster 2.8° S of moon
Apr. 22: Regulus 4.9° S of moon; Lyrid meteor shower
Apr. 26: Spica 6.5° S of moon
Apr. 27: Mercury at perihelion; full moon; moon at perigee
Apr. 29: Antares 4.8° S of moon
Apr. 30: Uranus in conjunction with sun

May

Venus, Uranus, and **Neptune** are too close to the sun for easy visibility.
Mercury and **Mars** are low in the SW in the early evening.
Jupiter and **Saturn** are in the SE after midnight.

May 3: Saturn 4.2° N of moon; last quarter moon
May 4: Mercury 2.1° S of Pleiades; Jupiter 4.6° N of moon
May 5: Eta-Aquarids meteor shower
May 11: New moon; moon at apogee
May 13: Mercury 2.1° N of moon
May 16: Mars 1.5° S of moon
May 17: Pollux 3.1° N of moon; Mercury at greatest elongation 22.0° E of sun

May 18: Beehive star cluster 2.9° S of moon
May 19: Regulus 5.0° S of moon; first quarter moon
May 23: Spica 6.5° S of moon
May 26: Moon at perigee; full moon; total lunar eclipse; Antares 4.8° S of moon
May 29: Mercury 0.4° S of Venus
May 31: Saturn 4.2° N of moon; Mars 5.2° S of Pollux

June

Mercury and **Uranus** are too close to the sun for easy visibility.
Venus and **Mars** are visible in SW in the early evening.
Jupiter, Saturn, and **Neptune** are visible in the E after midnight.

June 1: Jupiter 4.6° N of moon
June 2: Last quarter moon
June 8: Moon at apogee
June 10: New moon; annular solar eclipse
June 11: Mercury at inferior conjunction
June 12: Venus 1.5° S of moon; Venus at perihelion
June 13: Pollux 3.1° N of moon; Mars 2.8° S of moon
June 14: Beehive star cluster 2.9° S of moon
June 15: Regulus 5.0° S of moon
June 18: First quarter moon
June 21: Summer solstice 03:32 UTC; Venus 5.1° S of Pollux
June 22: Mercury 1.8° N of Aldebaran
June 23: Antares 4.8° S of moon; Mars 0.3° S of Beehive star cluster; moon at perigee
June 24: Full moon
June 27: Saturn 4.0° N of moon
June 28: Jupiter 4.5° N of moon

July

Mars is too close to the sun for easy visibility.
Mercury is low in the SE just before dawn.
Venus is visible in the SW just after sunset.
Jupiter, Saturn, Uranus, and **Neptune** are visible in the morning sky.

July 1: Last quarter moon
July 3: Venus 0.1° N of Beehive star cluster
July 4: Mercury at greatest elongation 21.6° W of sun
July 5: Moon at apogee; Earth at aphelion
July 6: Aldebaran 5.5° S of moon
July 8: Mercury 3.7° S of moon
July 10: New moon
July 12: Venus 3.3° S of moon; Mars 3.8° S of moon
July 13: Mars at aphelion; Regulus 4.9° S of moon
July 17: Spica 6.4° S of moon; first quarter moon
July 20: Antares 4.7° S of moon
July 21: Moon at perigee; Venus 1.0° N of Regulus
July 24: Mercury at perihelion; full moon; Saturn 3.8° N of moon
July 28: Delta Aquarids meteor shower
July 31: Last quarter moon

August

Mercury and **Mars** are too close to the sun for easy visibility.
Venus is visible in the SW just after sunset.
Uranus is visible in the SE after midnight.
Jupiter, Saturn, and **Neptune** rise before midnight and are visible in the SE until dawn.

Aug. 1: Mercury at superior conjunction
Aug. 2: Saturn at opposition; moon at apogee
Aug. 3: Aldebaran 5.7° S of moon
Aug. 6: Pollux 3.1° N of moon
Aug. 8: New moon
Aug. 11: Venus 4.3° S of moon
Aug. 12: Perseid meteor shower
Aug. 13: Spica 6.1° S of moon
Aug. 15: First quarter moon
Aug. 16: Antares 4.5° S of moon

Aug. 17: Moon at perigee
Aug. 19: Mercury 0.1° S of Mars; Jupiter at opposition
Aug. 20: Saturn 3.7° N of moon
Aug. 22: Jupiter 4.0° N of moon; full moon
Aug. 30: Moon at apogee; last quarter moon

September

Mercury and **Mars** are too close to the sun for easy visibility.
Venus, **Jupiter**, and **Saturn** are in the SW in the evening.
Jupiter and **Saturn** are in the SW in the evening.
Uranus and **Neptune** are visible in the SE after midnight.

Sept. 3: Pollux 3.0° N of moon
Sept. 4: Beehive star cluster 2.9° S of moon
Sept. 5: Venus 1.4° N of Spica
Sept. 6: Mercury at aphelion
Sept. 7: New moon
Sept. 9: Spica 5.9° S of moon
Sept. 10: Venus 4.1° S of moon
Sept. 11: Moon at perigee
Sept. 12: Antares 4.2° S of moon
Sept. 13: First quarter moon
Sept. 14: Mercury at greatest elongation 26.8° E of sun; Neptune at opposition
Sept. 17: Saturn 3.8° N of moon
Sept. 18: Jupiter 4.0° N of moon
Sept. 20: Full moon
Sept. 21: Mercury 1.2° S of Spica
Sept. 22: Autumnal equinox 19:21 UTC
Sept. 26: Moon at apogee
Sept. 29: Last quarter moon
Sept. 30: Pollux 2.8° N of moon

October

Mars is too close to the sun for easy visibility.
Mercury is in the SE before dawn.
Venus, **Jupiter**, **Saturn**, and **Neptune** are in the SW in the evening.
Uranus is in the S and SW after midnight.

Oct. 1: Beehive star cluster 3.1° S of moon
Oct. 2: Venus at aphelion
Oct. 3: Regulus 4.9° S of moon
Oct. 6: New moon
Oct. 8: Mars in conjunction with sun; moon at perigee
Oct. 9: Mercury at inferior conjunction; Venus 2.9° S of moon
Oct. 10: Antares 4.0° S of moon
Oct. 13: First quarter moon
Oct. 14: Saturn 3.9° N of moon
Oct. 15: Jupiter 4.1° N of moon
Oct. 16: Venus 1.4° N of Antares
Oct. 20: Mercury at perihelion; full moon
Oct. 21: Orionid meteor shower
Oct. 24: Moon at apogee
Oct. 25: Mercury at greatest elongation 18.4° W of sun
Oct. 27: Pollux 2.6° N of moon

Oct. 28: Last quarter moon; Beehive star cluster 3.3° S of moon
Oct. 29: Venus at greatest elongation 47.0° E of sun
Oct. 30: Regulus 5.1° S of moon

November

Mercury and **Mars** are too close to the sun for easy visibility.
Venus, **Jupiter**, **Saturn**, and **Neptune** are in the SW in the evening.
Uranus is in the SE before dawn.

Nov. 2: Mercury 3.7° N of Spica
Nov. 3: Mercury 1.2° S of moon: occultation of Mercury by the moon
Nov. 4: New moon
Nov. 5: Uranus at opposition; S Taurid meteor shower; moon at perigee
Nov. 6: Antares 3.9° S of moon
Nov. 8: Venus 1.1° S of moon; occultation of Venus by the moon
Nov. 10: Saturn 4.1° N of moon
Nov. 11: First quarter moon; Jupiter 4.4° N of moon
Nov. 12: N Taurid meteor shower
Nov. 17: Leonid meteor shower
Nov. 19: Full moon; partial lunar eclipse
Nov. 21: Moon at apogee
Nov. 24: Pollux 2.5° N of moon
Nov. 25: Beehive star cluster 3.3° S of moon
Nov. 26: Regulus 5.2° S of moon
Nov. 27: Last quarter moon
Nov. 29: Mercury at superior conjunction
Nov. 30: Spica 5.9° S of moon

December

Mercury and **Mars** are too close to the sun for easy visibility.
Venus, **Jupiter**, **Saturn**, **Uranus**, and **Neptune** are in the SW in the early evening.

Dec. 4: New moon; total solar eclipse; moon at perigee
Dec. 7: Venus 1.9° N of moon
Dec. 8: Saturn 4.2° N of moon
Dec. 9: Jupiter 4.5° N of moon
Dec. 11: First quarter moon
Dec. 14: Geminid meteor shower
Dec. 18: Moon at apogee
Dec. 19: Full moon
Dec. 21: Pollux 2.6° N of moon; winter solstice 15:59 UTC
Dec. 22: Beehive star cluster 3.3° S of moon; Ursid meteor shower
Dec. 24: Regulus 5.1° S of moon
Dec. 27: Last quarter moon; Mars 4.4° N of Antares
Dec. 28: Spica 5.8° S of moon
Dec. 29: Mercury 4.2° SE of Venus
Dec. 31: Antares 3.9° S of moon; Mars 1.0° N of moon; occultation of Mars by the moon

Moon Phases, 2021

(In Coordinated Universal Time, or UTC, the standard time of the prime meridian.)

New Moon			Waxing Quarter			Full Moon			Waning Quarter		
Date	Hr.	Min.	Date	Hr.	Min.	Date	Hr.	Min.	Date	Hr.	Min.
Jan. 13	5	00	Jan. 20	21	02	Jan. 28	19	16	Jan. 6	9	37
Feb. 11	19	06	Feb. 19	18	47	Feb. 27	8	17	Feb. 4	17	37
Mar. 13	10	21	Mar. 21	14	40	Mar. 28	18	48	Mar. 6	1	30
Apr. 12	2	31	Apr. 20	6	59	Apr. 27	3	31	Apr. 4	10	02
May 11	19	00	May 19	19	13	May 26	11	14	May 3	19	50
June 10	10	53	June 18	3	54	June 24	18	40	June 2	7	24
July 10	1	17	July 17	10	11	July 24	2	37	July 1	21	11
Aug. 8	13	50	Aug. 15	15	20	Aug. 22	12	02	July 31	13	16
Sept. 7	0	52	Sept. 13	20	39	Sept. 20	23	55	Aug. 30	7	13
Oct. 6	11	05	Oct. 13	3	25	Oct. 20	14	57	Sept. 29	1	57
Nov. 4	21	15	Nov. 11	12	46	Nov. 19	8	58	Oct. 28	20	05
Dec. 4	7	43	Dec. 11	1	36	Dec. 19	4	36	Nov. 27	12	28
									Dec. 27	2	24

Meteorites and Meteor Showers

When a chunk of material, ice or rock, plunges into Earth's atmosphere and burns up in a fiery display, the event is a **meteor**. While the chunk of material is still in space, it is a **meteoroid**. If a portion of the material survives passage through the atmosphere and reaches the ground, the remnant on the ground is a **meteorite**.

Meteorites found on Earth are classified into types, depending on their composition: **irons**, those composed chiefly of iron, a small percentage of nickel, and traces of other metals such as cobalt; **stones**, stony meteors consisting of silicates; and **stony irons**, containing varying proportions of both iron and stone.

Serious study of meteorites as non-Earth objects began in the 20th century. Scientists use sophisticated chemical analysis, X-rays, and mass spectrography in determining their origin and composition. Although most meteorites are now believed to be fragments of asteroids or comets, geochemical studies have shown that a few Antarctic stones came from the moon or from Mars, presumably ejected by the explosive impact of asteroids.

The largest known meteorite, estimated to weigh about 55 metric tons, is the Hoba meteorite near Grootfontein, Namibia. The Manicouagan impact crater in Quebec, Canada, with an estimated diameter of 60 mi, is one of the largest crater structures still visible on the surface of the Earth. Not obvious to the eye because of erosion, larger impact craters identified include the Vredefort crater in South Africa at 185 mi across and the Sudbury crater in Ontario, Canada (125 mi). The Bedout impact site off the NW coast of Australia gained attention in 2004 when scientists identified further evidence in support of the idea that it may be linked to the Permian extinction event 250 mil years ago. A 2019 study of the Chicxulub impact crater (93 mi across) in Yucatán Peninsula and the Gulf of Mexico gave evidence of an associated mass extinction event at the end of the Mesozoic Era (66 mil years ago).

Meteor showers vary in strength, but usually the three most visible meteor showers of the year are the **Perseids**, around Aug. 13, the **Orionids**, around Oct. 21, and the **Geminids**, around Dec. 14. These showers feature meteors at the rate of about 60 per hour. Best observing conditions occur in the absence of moonlight, usually when the moon's phase is between waning crescent and waxing quarter.

For most meteor showers the cometary debris is relatively uniformly scattered along the comet's orbit. However, in the case of the **Leonid** meteor shower, which occurs every year around Nov. 17-18, the debris from Comet Temple-Tuttle seems to be bunched up in one stretch. Hence, the meteor shower produced in most years is relatively weak. However, about every 33 years, Earth encounters the bunched-up debris when it crosses the comet's orbit. Sometimes the expected shower is a disappointment, as in 1899 and 1933; at other times, the dense debris provides a spectacular show, as in 1833 and 1866. The Leonids stormed again more recently, producing rates of 1,000-3,000 meteors per hour in 2001.

Morning and Evening "Stars," 2021

(In Coordinated Universal Time, or UTC, the standard time of the prime meridian.)

	Morning	Evening
Jan.	Venus Jupiter from Jan. 30 Saturn from Jan. 25	Mercury Mars Jupiter to Jan. 29 Saturn to Jan. 24 Uranus Neptune
Feb.	Mercury from Feb. 9 Venus Jupiter Saturn	Mercury to Feb. 8 Mars Uranus Neptune
Mar.	Mercury Venus to Mar. 26 Jupiter Saturn Neptune from Mar. 12	Venus from Mar. 27 Mars Uranus Neptune to Mar. 11
Apr.	Mercury to Apr. 19 Jupiter Saturn Neptune	Mercury from Apr. 20 Venus Mars Uranus to Apr. 30
May	Jupiter Saturn Uranus from May 1 Neptune	Mercury Venus Mars
June	Mercury from June 12 Jupiter Saturn Uranus Neptune	Mercury to June 11 Venus Mars
July	Mercury Jupiter Saturn	Venus Mars

	Morning	Evening
July (cont.)	Uranus Neptune	
Aug.	Mercury to Aug. 1 Jupiter to Aug. 19 Saturn to Aug. 2 Uranus Neptune	Mercury from Aug. 2 Venus Mars Jupiter from Aug. 20 Saturn from Aug. 3
Sept.	Uranus Neptune to Sept. 14	Mercury Venus Mars Jupiter Saturn Neptune from Sept. 15
Oct.	Mercury from Oct. 10 Mars from Oct. 9 Uranus	Mercury to Oct. 9 Venus Mars to Oct. 8 Jupiter Saturn Neptune
Nov.	Mercury to Nov. 29 Mars Uranus to Nov. 5	Mercury from Nov. 30 Venus Jupiter Saturn Uranus from Nov. 6 Neptune
Dec.	Mars	Mercury Venus Jupiter Saturn Uranus Neptune

Greenwich Sidereal Time for 0h UTC, 2021

UTC = Coordinated Universal Time. Add 12 hours to obtain right ascension of mean sun.

Date	Hr.	Min.	Date	Hr.	Min.	Date	Hr.	Min.	Date	Hr.	Min.
Jan. 1	6	43.5	Apr. 1	12	38.3	July 10	19	12.6	Oct. 8	1	7.4
Jan. 11	7	22.9	Apr. 11	13	17.7	July 20	19	52.0	Oct. 18	1	46.8
Jan. 21	8	2.3	Apr. 21	13	57.2	July 30	20	31.4	Oct. 28	2	26.3
Jan. 31	8	41.8									
			May 1	14	36.6	Aug. 9	21	10.8	Nov. 7	3	5.7
Feb. 10	9	21.2	May 11	15	16.0	Aug. 19	21	50.3	Nov. 17	3	45.1
Feb. 20	9	0.6	May 21	15	55.4	Aug. 29	22	29.7	Nov. 27	4	24.5
			May 31	16	34.9						
Mar. 2	10	40.0				Sept. 8	23	9.1	Dec. 7	5	4.0
Mar. 12	11	19.5	June 10	17	14.3	Sept. 18	23	48.5	Dec. 17	5	43.4
Mar. 22	11	58.9	June 20	17	53.7	Sept. 28	0	28.0	Dec. 27	6	22.8
			June 30	18	33.1						

Largest Telescopes

Astronomers indicate the size of telescopes not by length or magnification but by the diameter of the primary light-gathering component, such as the lens or mirror. The larger the diameter of the mirror or lens, the fainter the objects that can be detected. In principle, larger telescopes also have better resolving power—the ability to discern small details—than smaller telescopes. However, the Earth's atmosphere limits the details that can be seen using ground-based telescopes. The Hubble Space Telescope, which orbits the Earth outside of its atmosphere, can achieve higher resolutions with its 2.4-m (7.9-ft) mirror than much larger telescopes on Earth. Adaptive optics systems can compensate for the blurring effects of the Earth's atmosphere, allowing ground-based telescopes to achieve higher levels of detail. Telescopes to detect ultraviolet, X-ray, and gamma radiation must be placed in space or high-altitude balloons because the atmosphere absorbs most of these types of radiation; as a result, such telescopes are generally much smaller than optical, infrared, and radio telescopes.

Refracting (lens) telescopes are currently not made with lens diameters of more than 40 in. Because **reflecting telescopes** can be made less expensively and with more precision than refracting telescopes, all modern large optical telescopes are made with mirrors. **Radio telescopes** are larger than optical telescopes because larger diameters are required to obtain equivalent resolution of radio's longer wavelengths. A technique called interferometry, originally developed for radio telescopes, uses arrays of telescopes to achieve better resolution.

Largest refracting (lens) optical telescope: Yerkes Observatory, 1 m (40 in.), at Williams Bay, WI

Largest reflecting (mirror) optical/infrared telescope: Gran Telescopio Canarias, 10.4 m (34 ft), on La Palma, Canary Islands (segmented mirror)

Largest infrared interferometer: Four 8.2-m (27-ft) telescopes of the Very Large Telescope Interferometer (VLTI) with a 200-m (656-ft) baseline on Cerro Paranal in Chile

Largest fully steerable radio dish: Robert Byrd Green Bank Telescope (GBT), 100 m (328 ft), in Green Bank, WV

Largest single radio dish: Five-hundred-meter Aperture Spherical Telescope (FAST), 500 m (1,640 ft), in Guizhou, China

Largest baseline radio interferometer: 10 25-m (82-ft) diameter telescopes of the Very Long Baseline Array (VLBA), dispersed from Hawaii to the Virgin Islands with a resolution equal to a radio dish of 8,600 km (5,000 mi), making it the highest resolution telescope in the solar system

Largest submillimeter interferometer: 54 12-m (39-ft) and 12 7-m (23-ft) antennas of the Atacama Large Millimeter Array (ALMA), located at a site above 5,000 m (16,400 ft) in the Atacama Desert in Chile. The antennas can be spread out over a 16-km (10-mi) distance to increase the resolving power of the array.

Largest airborne telescope: Stratospheric Observatory for Infrared Astronomy (SOFIA), 2.5-m (8.2-ft) infrared telescope aboard a NASA 747

Constellations

Culturally, constellations are imagined patterns among the stars that, in some cases, have been recognized through millennia. Knowledge of constellations was once necessary in order to function as an astronomer. For today's astronomers, constellations are simply areas of the sky in which objects await observation and interpretation.

Because Western culture has dominated much of modern scientific discourse, constellations and celestial traditions of other cultures are not widely known outside their regions of origin. Even the patterns with which we are most familiar today have undergone considerable change over the centuries. Today, **88 constellations** are officially recognized. Although many have ancient origins, some are modern, devised out of unclaimed stars by astronomers a few centuries ago. Unclaimed stars were those too faint or inconveniently placed to be included in the more prominent constellations. Stars in a constellation are not necessarily near each other; they are just located in the same direction on the celestial sphere.

Common names of stars often referred to parts of the traditional figures they represented, such as Deneb, the tail of the swan, and Betelgeuse, the giant's shoulder. Astronomers may avoid traditional names by labeling stars with Greek letters, generally to denote order of brightness. The "alpha star" would typically be the brightest in a constellation. The "of" implies possession, so the genitive (possessive) form of the constellation name is used, e.g. Alpha Orionis (the first star of Orion) for Betelgeuse. (While Rigel is brighter than Betelgeuse, its designation is Beta Orionis, possibly because Betelgeuse appeared brighter when they were named.)

Asterisms are widely recognized patterns of stars. The so-called Big Dipper is a small part of the constellation Ursa Major, the big bear; the three stars of the Summer Triangle are each in a different constellation, with Vega in Lyra the lyre, Deneb in Cygnus the swan, and Altair in Aquila the eagle. The northeast star of the asterism Great Square of Pegasus is Alpha Andromedae.

Name	Abbr.	Meaning	Name	Abbr.	Meaning	Name	Abbr.	Meaning
Andromeda	And	Chained Maiden	Cygnus	Cyg	Swan	Orion	Ori	Hunter
Antlia	Ant	Air Pump	Delphinus	Del	Dolphin	Pavo	Pav	Peacock
Apus	Aps	Bird of Paradise	Dorado	Dor	Dolphinfish	Pegasus	Peg	Flying Horse
Aquarius	Aqr	Water Bearer	Draco	Dra	Dragon	Perseus	Per	Hero
Aquila	Aql	Eagle	Equuleus	Equ	Little Horse	Phoenix	Phe	Phoenix
Ara	Ara	Altar	Eridanus	Eri	River	Pictor	Pic	Painter
Aries	Ari	Ram	Fornax	For	Furnace	Pisces	Psc	Fishes
Auriga	Aur	Charioteer	Gemini	Gem	Twins	Piscis Austrinus	PsA	Southern Fish
Boötes	Boo	Herder	Grus	Gru	Crane (bird)	Puppis	Pup	Stern (deck)
Caelum	Cae	Chisel	Hercules	Her	Hercules	Pyxis	Pyx	Compass (sea)
Camelopardalis	Cam	Giraffe	Horologium	Hor	Clock	Reticulum	Ret	Reticle
Cancer	Cnc	Crab	Hydra	Hya	Water Snake (female)	Sagitta	Sge	Arrow
Canes Venatici	CVn	Hunting Dogs				Sagittarius	Sgr	Archer
Canis Major	CMa	Greater Dog	Hydrus	Hyi	Water Snake (male)	Scorpius	Sco	Scorpion
Canis Minor	CMi	Littler Dog				Sculptor	Scl	Sculptor
Capricornus	Cap	Sea-Goat	Indus	Ind	Indian	Scutum	Sct	Shield
Carina	Car	Keel	Lacerta	Lac	Lizard	Serpens	Ser	Serpent
Cassiopeia	Cas	Queen	Leo	Leo	Lion	Sextans	Sex	Sextant
Centaurus	Cen	Centaur	Leo Minor	LMi	Littler Lion	Taurus	Tau	Bull
Cepheus	Cep	King	Lepus	Lep	Hare	Telescopium	Tel	Telescope
Cetus	Cet	Whale	Libra	Lib	Balance	Triangulum	Tri	Triangle
Chamaeleon	Cha	Chameleon	Lupus	Lup	Wolf	Triangulum Australe	TrA	Southern Triangle
Circinus	Cir	Compass (drawing)	Lynx	Lyn	Lynx			
			Lyra	Lyr	Lyre	Tucana	Tuc	Toucan
Columba	Col	Dove	Mensa	Men	Table Mountain	Ursa Major	UMa	Greater Bear
Coma Berenices	Com	Berenice's Hair	Microscopium	Mic	Microscope	Ursa Minor	UMi	Littler Bear
Corona Australis	CrA	Southern Crown	Monoceros	Mon	Unicorn	Vela	Vel	Sail
Corona Borealis	CrB	Northern Crown	Musca	Mus	Fly	Virgo	Vir	Maiden
Corvus	Crv	Crow	Norma	Nor	Square (rule)	Volans	Vol	Flying Fish
Crater	Crt	Cup	Octans	Oct	Octant	Vulpecula	Vul	Fox
Crux	Cru	Cross (southern)	Ophiuchus	Oph	Serpent Bearer			

Eclipses, 2021
(In Coordinated Universal Time, or UTC, the standard time of the prime meridian.)

There will be four eclipses in 2021: one annular solar eclipse, one total solar eclipse, one total lunar eclipse, and one partial lunar eclipse, though none occurs under optimal circumstances for viewing. The path of the most prominent solar eclipse, the total solar eclipse of Dec. 4, crosses mostly remote areas of the Antarctic. The path of the other solar eclipse, the annular eclipse of June 10, lies in the far north, its primary distinction being that it passes across the North Pole. The region of visibility for the total lunar eclipse of May 26 lies largely over the Pacific, and though it is also visible in North America and parts of South America, the most profound darkening, during totality, will be relatively short at 14 min. The most observable lunar eclipse, on Nov. 18-19, though widely visible in Asia and the Americas, is only partial, with 97% of the moon in shadow at maximum.

The tables below give the times in UTC of when the moon or sun will reach certain phases of each event. In the case of the lunar eclipses, the times are relevant for any observer who can see the moon. In the case of solar eclipses, the tabulated times refer to when the given event begins or ends from specific points along the eclipse path; as the moon's shadow sweeps quickly across the Earth, the observed duration and degree of eclipse depends on the observer's precise location. Interactive maps are available on the internet to calculate times for specific locations.

I. Total Eclipse of the Moon: May 26

This eclipse will be visible to observers in extreme southeast Asia, Australia, Oceania, Alaska, Canada, the continental U.S., and western South America. Because the moon passes near the north edge of the Earth's shadow, totality is short—only about 14.5 min.

Event	Date	Hr.	Min.
Penumbral eclipse begins. .	May 26	8	48
Partial eclipse begins	May 26	9	45
Total eclipse begins	May 26	11	11
Greatest eclipse	May 26	11	19
Total eclipse ends.	May 26	11	26
Partial eclipse ends	May 26	12	52
Penumbral eclipse ends . . .	May 26	13	50

II. Annular Eclipse of the Sun: June 10

The annular phases of this eclipse are only visible in northeastern Russia, Greenland, and northern Canada; observers in locations further south will see partial phases. The path of annularity passes over the North Pole, the only time this occurs during the 21st century. Times are for an observer at the midpoint of the path, latitude 80° 48.9' N, longitude 66° 48.3' W.

Event	Date	Hr.	Min.
Partial eclipse begins	Dec. 26	9	50
Annular eclipse begins	Dec. 26	10	39
Greatest eclipse	Dec. 26	10	42
Annular eclipse ends	Dec. 26	10	44
Partial eclipse ends	Dec. 26	11	34

III. Partial Eclipse of the Moon: Nov. 18-19

This eclipse will be visible to observers across most of eastern Asia, Australia, and North and South America on Nov. 19, and in Hawaii and parts of southwest Alaska on Nov. 18. Though partial, 97% of the moon will pass through the Earth's umbra, and it should be widely visible in populated regions except in Europe, Africa, and the Middle East.

Event	Date	Hr.	Min.
Penumbral eclipse begins. . .	Nov. 19	6	02
Partial eclipse begins	Nov. 19	7	19
Greatest eclipse	Nov. 19	9	03
Partial eclipse ends	Nov. 19	10	47
Penumbral eclipse ends	Nov. 19	12	04

IV. Total Eclipse of the Sun: Dec. 4

This is a rather short total eclipse, with a maximum duration of 1 min., 54.4 sec., and the path of totality is relatively short, stretching primarily across the Antarctic Ocean, with the only landfalls on Antarctica. Times are for an observer near the coast of Antarctica, latitude 76° 46.7'S, longitude 46° 11.9'W.

Event	Date	Hr.	Min.
Partial eclipse begins	Dec. 4	7	00
Total eclipse begins	Dec. 4	7	32
Greatest eclipse	Dec. 4	7	33
Total eclipse ends.	Dec. 4	7	34
Partial eclipse ends	Dec. 4	8	06

Total Solar Eclipses, 2021-38

Total solar eclipses actually take place nearly as often as total lunar eclipses. But total lunar eclipses are visible over at least half of the Earth, while total solar eclipses can be seen only along a very narrow path up to a few hundred miles wide and a few thousand miles long. Observing a total solar eclipse is thus a rarity for most people.

Solar eclipses can be dangerous to observe. This is not because the sun emits more potent rays, but because the sun is always dangerous to observe directly, and people are particularly likely to stare at it during a solar eclipse.

Date	Duration[1] min.	sec.	Width of path (mi)	Path of totality
2021, Dec. 4	1	54	260	Antarctica
2024, Apr. 8	4	27	122	Mexico, midwestern U.S., E Canada
2026, Aug. 12	2	18	182	Greenland, Iceland, Spain
2027, Aug. 2	6	24	160	Spain, N Africa, Arabian peninsula
2028, July 22	5	10	140	Indian Ocean, Australia, New Zealand
2030, Nov. 25	3	45	105	Namibia, Botswana, South Africa, Indian Ocean, E Australia
2033, Mar. 30	2	37	485	Alaska, E Russia, Arctic
2034, Mar. 20	4	9	100	Central and NE Africa, Arabian Peninsula, Central and E Asia
2035, Sept. 2	2	54	72	China, Korea, Japan, Pacific Ocean
2037, July 13	3	58	125	Australia, New Zealand
2038, Dec. 26	2	18	142	Australia, New Zealand, South Pacific

(1) Length of time at optimal viewing area.

Total Solar Eclipses in the U.S. in the 21st Century

During the 21st century, there are eight total solar eclipses visible somewhere in the continental U.S. The first came after a long gap, in 2017. The last total solar eclipse had been on Feb. 26, 1979, in the northwestern U.S.

Date	Path of totality	Date	Path of totality
Aug. 21, 2017	Oregon to South Carolina	Mar. 30, 2052	Florida to Georgia
Apr. 8, 2024	Mexico to Texas and N through Maine	May 11, 2078	Louisiana to North Carolina
Aug. 23, 2044	Montana to North Dakota	May 1, 2079	New Jersey to the lower edge of New England
Aug. 12, 2045	Northern California to Florida	Sept. 14, 2099	North Dakota to Virginia

Beginnings of the Universe

One of the dominating astronomical discoveries of the 20th century was that the galaxies of the universe all seem to be moving away from Earth. Doppler redshifts were observed for spiral nebulae around 1920 even though they were not yet known to be galaxies. By the early 1930s, Edwin Hubble and M. L. Humason had established that the more distant a galaxy, the faster it was receding. It turned out that they were moving away not just from the Earth but from one another—that is, the **universe is expanding**. Scientists conclude that the universe must once, very long ago, have been extremely compact and dense, and a rapid expansion caused the energy and matter to rapidly expand. The beginning of this expansion is referred to as the **Big Bang**.

On the subatomic level, according to this theory, there were vast changes of energy and matter and the way physical laws operated during the first few minutes after the Big Bang. After those early minutes the percentages of the basic matter of the universe—hydrogen, helium, and lithium—were set. Everything was so compact and hot that radiation dominated the early universe and there were no stable, un-ionized atoms. The universe was opaque, in the sense that any energy emitted was quickly absorbed and then re-emitted. As the universe expanded, density and temperature continued to drop. A few hundred thousand years after the Big Bang, the temperature dropped far enough that electrons and nuclei could combine to form stable atoms as the universe became transparent. Once that occurred, the radiation that had been trapped was free to escape.

In the 1940s, George Gamow and others predicted that remnants of this escaped radiation should be observable. They had started to search for this background radiation when physicists Arno Penzias and Robert Wilson, using a radio telescope, inadvertently found it, for which they won the 1978 Nobel Prize in Physics.

In 2003, NASA's Wilkinson Microwave Anisotropy Probe made measurements of the temperature of this **cosmic microwave background radiation** to within millionths of a degree. From these measurements, scientists were able to deduce that our universe is 13.7 bil years old and that first-generation stars began to form a mere 200 mil years after the Big Bang.

In 2014, scientists operating a telescope in Antarctica claimed to have found direct evidence for cosmic inflation, the rapid expansion of the universe during the 10-32 sec. after the Big Bang that helps explain why variations of the cosmic background radiation are so small. Follow-up observations cast doubt on this, and higher precision measurements are planned.

A related mystery is evidence suggesting hidden matter and hidden energy that cannot be directly observed. The presence of dark matter is indicated by the rotation curves of galaxies and the dynamics of clusters of galaxies. **Dark matter** may be composed of gas; large numbers of cool, compact objects like dead stars; or even subatomic particles. Evidence for **dark energy** is derived from studies of distant Type Ia supernovae indicating that the expansion of the universe is accelerating rather than slowing. Dark energy seems to work on the very fabric of the universe, acting as a force that increases the rate at which space expands. Visible matter seems to constitute only about 4% of the total mass of the universe while the rest of the universe's mass is in the form of dark matter (27%) and dark energy (68%).

Galaxies

By the 20th century, more than 10,000 **nebulae**—cloud-like luminous objects in the sky—had been discovered. Some were correctly identified as star clusters and others as clouds of gas and dust. Those nebulae which were spiral or elliptical in shape were found in regions of the sky far from the glowing band that is our own Milky Way galaxy. Philosopher Immanuel Kant had written in 1775 that some of these fuzzy objects might be **"island universes"** apart from our own. But the idea remained speculative until 1923-24, when Edwin Hubble discovered variable stars—stars whose varying brightness makes their distance from Earth calculable—in some of these nebulae. This provided conclusive evidence that these systems were far enough away to be outside our own island universe, the Milky Way galaxy.

Galaxies range in size from small dwarf elliptical ones, with perhaps 1 mil stars, to spiral galaxies containing 300 bil stars, to giant elliptical galaxies that may be home to more than 10 trillion stars. The diameters of galaxies range from 3,000 light-years in dwarf elliptical galaxies to over 500,000 light-years in giant elliptical galaxies. It is estimated that the Milky Way galaxy is about 100,000 light-years in diameter with about 400 bil stars.

Galaxies also congregate into **clusters**. The smallest are poor clusters of only a few dozen galaxies, while the largest rich clusters may contain thousands. The Milky Way is part of a poor cluster of about three dozen galaxies called the **Local Group**. The largest galaxy of the Local Group is Andromeda, a spiral galaxy visible to the unaided eye in the constellation of Andromeda on a very dark night. The Milky Way is the second largest galaxy in this group; most of the others are small.

The Solar System

The major planets of the solar system, in order of mean distance from the sun, are **Mercury, Venus, Earth, Mars, Jupiter, Saturn, Uranus**, and **Neptune**. The dwarf planets in order of average distance from the sun are **Ceres** (located between Mars and Jupiter), **Pluto, Haumea, Makemake, 2007 OR10**, and **Eris**. All planets orbit counterclockwise around the sun as viewed from above the Earth's North Pole.

Because Mercury and Venus are nearer to the sun than is Earth, their motions about the sun appear from Earth as wide swings first to one side of the sun then to the other, though both planets move around the sun in almost circular orbits. When their passage takes them between Earth and the sun or beyond the sun in relation to Earth, they cannot be seen.

The planets that lie farther from the sun than does Earth may be seen for longer periods. They are invisible only when so located in the sky that they rise and set at about the same time as the sun and are thus overwhelmed by the sun's light.

Mercury and Venus, because they are between Earth and the sun, show phases much as the moon does. The planets farther from the sun are always seen as full, although Mars does occasionally present a slightly gibbous phase, like the moon when it is not quite full.

The planets appear to move rapidly among the stars because they are relatively closer to Earth. The stars are also in motion, some at tremendous speeds, but they are so far away that their motion does not change their apparent positions in the heavens enough to be perceived. The nearest star is about 9,000 times farther away than Neptune. The count for identified **moons** in the solar system orbiting planets and dwarf planets stood at 214 as of mid-2020. Several dwarf planet candidates are also known to have moons.

Planet Superlatives

Largest, most massive planet	Jupiter	Smallest, least massive planet	Mercury
Fastest orbiting planet	Mercury	Slowest orbiting planet	Neptune
Fastest sidereal rotation	Jupiter	Slowest sidereal rotation	Venus
Longest (synodic) day	Mercury	Shortest (synodic) day	Jupiter
Rotational pole closest to ecliptic	Uranus	Hottest planet	Venus
Most moons	Saturn	No moons	Mercury, Venus
Planet with largest moon	Jupiter	Planet with moon with most eccentric orbit	Neptune
Greatest average density	Earth	Lowest average density	Saturn
Tallest mountain	Mars	Deepest oceans	Jupiter
Strongest magnetic fields	Jupiter	Greatest amount of liquid water on surface	Earth
Most circular orbit	Venus		

Selected Characteristics of the Sun and Planets

Object	at unit distance[1] ̈	Radius— at mean least distance[2] ̈	in mi mean radius	Volume[3]	Mass[3]	Density[3]	Sidereal period d.	hr.	min.	sec.	Gravity at surface[3]	Reflect-ing power[4]	Daytime surface temp. (° F)
Sun	959.5	976.0	432,500	1,304,000	333,000	0.26	25	9	7		28.00	—	9,941
Mercury	3.36	6.5	1,516	0.0562	0.0553	0.98	58	15	36		0.38	0.11	845
Venus	8.34	33.0	3,760	0.857	0.815	0.95	243		30R		0.91	0.65	867
Earth	8.78		3,959	1.000	1.000	1.00		23	56	4.2	1.00	0.37	59
Moon	2.40	986.2	1,079	0.0203	0.0123	0.61	27	7	43	40	0.16	0.12	260
Mars	4.67	12.8	2,106	0.151	0.107	0.71		24	37	22	0.38	0.15	−24
Jupiter	96.40	24.5	43,441	1,321.30	317.83	0.24		9	55	30	2.53	0.52	−162
Saturn	80.29	10.05	36,184	763.6	95.16	0.12		10	39	20	1.06	0.47	−218
Uranus	34.97	2.05	15,759	63.1	14.54	0.23		17	14	20R	0.90	0.51	−323
Neptune	33.95	1.2	15,301	57.7	17.15	0.3		16	6	40	1.14	0.41	−330

R = Retrograde rotation. (1) Angular radius, in seconds of arc, if object were seen at a distance of 1 astronomical unit. (2) Angular radius, in seconds of arc, when object is closest to Earth. (3) Earth = 1. (4) A value of 1 would indicate a perfect reflector.

Planets of the Solar System

The International Astronomical Union (IAU) on Aug. 24, 2006, at their General Assembly in Prague, Czech Republic, agreed on a new definition for planet, and in the process effectively removed Pluto's planet status. The ruling came after years of debate as to whether Pluto, discovered in 1930, should still be considered the ninth planet in our solar system because of its size, orbit, and other characteristics. New discoveries of other Pluto-like objects in the solar system, such as the 2003 discovery of Eris, a **Kuiper Belt object** (KBO) comparable in size to Pluto, also contributed to the debate.

Under the IAU's new definition, Mercury, Venus, Earth, Mars, Jupiter, Saturn, Uranus, and Neptune are regarded as "classical" planets. A **planet** is now defined as a celestial body that (a) is in orbit around the sun, (b) has sufficient mass for its self-gravity to overcome rigid body forces so that it assumes a hydrostatic equilibrium (nearly round) shape, and (c) has cleared the neighborhood around its orbit.

Pluto, Eris, Ceres, Makemake, 2007 OR10, and Haumea are regarded as dwarf planets, with the status of Pluto's largest moon, Charon, still to be determined. A **dwarf planet** is a celestial body that (a) is in orbit around the sun, (b) has sufficient mass for its self-gravity to overcome rigid body forces so that it assumes a hydrostatic equilibrium (nearly round) shape, (c) has not cleared the neighborhood around its orbit, and (d) is not a satellite.

The IAU also created a new category, **small solar system bodies**, for all other objects orbiting the sun, including comets, asteroids, KBOs, and other small objects. It has not yet established a process by which other solar system objects will be classified.

Note: AU = astronomical unit (92.96 mil mi, mean distance of Earth from the sun); **d.** = 1 Earth synodic (solar) day (24 hours); **synodic day** = rotation period of a planet measured with respect to the sun (the "true" day, i.e., the time from midday to midday, or from sunrise to sunrise); **sidereal day** = rotation period of a planet with respect to the stars.

Mercury

```
Distance from the sun
  Perihelion . . . . . . . . . . . . . . . . . . . . . . . . .28.6 mil mi
  Semi-major axis (mean distance) . . .36 mil mi (0.387 AU)
  Aphelion . . . . . . . . . . . . . . . . . . . . . . . . . . . 43.4 mil mi
Period of revolution around sun . . . . . . . . . . . . . . .87.97 d.
Orbital eccentricity . . . . . . . . . . . . . . . . . . . . . . . . 0.2056
Orbital inclination . . . . . . . . . . . . . . . . . . . . . . . . . . .7.00°
Synodic day (midday to midday) . . . . . . . . . . . . 175.94 d.
Sidereal day . . . . . . . . . . . . . . . . . . . . . . . . . . . 58.65 d.
Rotational inclination . . . . . . . . . . . . . . . . . . . . . . . 0.01°
Mass (Earth = 1) . . . . . . . . . . . . . . . . . . . . . . . . . 0.0553
Mean radius . . . . . . . . . . . . . . . . . . . . . . . . . . . 1,516 mi
Mean density (Earth = 1) . . . . . . . . . . . . . . . . . . . . 0.984
Natural satellites . . . . . . . . . . . . . . . . . . . . . . . . . . . . 0
Average surface temperature . . . . . . . . . . . . . . . . . 333°F
```

Mercury, named for the Roman gods' messenger, is the closest planet to the sun and the smallest planet in the solar system. Mercury orbits so close to the sun that it can never be observed against a dark sky; it is always seen during morning or evening twilights. In 2008, the *Messenger* spacecraft made the first fly-bys of Mercury since the 1970s. *Messenger* went into orbit about Mercury in Mar. 2011 for a reconnaissance mission; the original one-year science program was extended in 2012. The goals of the mission included mapping, imaging, and measuring the surface composition of Mercury, as well as probing the planet's interior structure and interactions with the sun. Among the discoveries were that at least part of Mercury's metallic core is liquid, that there may be water ice in shadowed craters near the poles, and that the planet's magnetic field is offset from the planet's center.

Orbit and rotation. Mercury moves with great speed around the sun, averaging about 30 mi per second to complete its orbit, which takes about 88 Earth days. Mercury takes nearly 59 days to rotate on its axis. Because its orbital period is only about 50% longer than its sidereal rotation, the time from one sunrise to the next on Mercury is about 176 days—twice as long as a Mercurial year. Oddly, Mercury has a magnetic field, albeit a very weak one. It has been held that both a fluid core and rapid rotation—neither of which Mercury was believed to have—are necessary for the generation of a planetary magnetic field. Mercury may demonstrate the contrary.

Atmosphere. Mercury's atmosphere is almost nonexistent. What very little it has is composed of 42% oxygen, 29% sodium, 22%

hydrogen, 6% helium, 0.5% potassium, and 0.5% other particles. Because of Mercury's lack of atmosphere, the surface during the day may reach a temperature of about 845°F, while the temperature at night may fall as low as −300°F. Earth-based observation has provided evidence of water ice near the poles.

Surface and composition. Mercury's surface is rocky and cratered similar to that of the Earth's moon. The most imposing feature on Mercury, the Caloris Basin, is a huge impact crater more than 800 mi in diameter. Mercury has a huge iron core that extends out to about 75% of the planet's radius; it has a higher percentage of iron than any other planet in the solar system.

Venus

```
Distance from the sun
  Perihelion . . . . . . . . . . . . . . . . . . . . . . . . . 66.8 mil mi
  Semi-major axis (mean distance) . . 67.2 mil mi (0.723 AU)
  Aphelion . . . . . . . . . . . . . . . . . . . . . . . . . . . 67.7 mil mi
Period of revolution around sun . . . . . . . . . . . . . . .224.7 d.
Orbital eccentricity . . . . . . . . . . . . . . . . . . . . . . . .0.0067
Orbital inclination . . . . . . . . . . . . . . . . . . . . . . . . . .3.39°
Synodic day (midday to midday) . . . . . 116.75 d. (retrograde)
Sidereal day . . . . . . . . . . . . . . . . . . . .243.02 d. (retrograde)
Rotational inclination . . . . . . . . . . . . . . . . . . . . . .177.4°
Mass (Earth = 1) . . . . . . . . . . . . . . . . . . . . . . . . . .0.815
Mean radius . . . . . . . . . . . . . . . . . . . . . . . . . . . 3,760 mi
Mean density (Earth = 1) . . . . . . . . . . . . . . . . . . . .0.951
Natural satellites . . . . . . . . . . . . . . . . . . . . . . . . . . . . 0
Average surface temperature . . . . . . . . . . . . . . . . . 867°F
```

Venus, named for the Roman goddess of love, is the second planet out from the sun. Because Venus is almost the same size as Earth, it is believed that the two planets were formed at the same time by the same general process and from the same mixture of chemical elements. Venus can easily be seen from Earth with the naked eye; it is the third-brightest object in the sky, exceeded only by the sun and the moon.

Orbit and rotation. It takes Venus 225 Earth days to complete its orbit around the sun. Its synodic revolution—the amount of time it takes for Venus to return to the same position relative to Earth and the sun, which is a result of the combination of its own motion with that of Earth—is 584 days. Because of this, every 19 months Venus is closer to Earth than to any other planet. The rotation period of Venus appears to be 243 days clockwise. In other words, its rotation is counter to the rotation of the other planets and counter to its own motion around the sun. This rate and sense of rotation make for a solar day (sunrise to sunrise) on Venus of 116.8 Earth days. Night lasts 58 days, and day lasts 58 days. Venus has no detectable magnetic field.

Atmosphere. The Venusian atmosphere is very thick and toxic. It is composed primarily of 96.5% carbon dioxide, 3.5% nitrogen, and trace concentrations of sulfur dioxide, argon, water, carbon monoxide, helium, and neon. In addition, it exerts an atmospheric pressure at the surface more than 90 times Earth's normal sea-level pressure. The planet is covered with a dense, white, cloudy atmosphere that conceals whatever is below. These clouds are believed to contain sulfuric acid, meaning that it rains sulfuric acid on Venus. Due to the thickness of the atmosphere and resulting extreme greenhouse effect, the temperature is essentially the same day and night; the planet has an average surface temperature of about 867°F, making it the hottest planet in the solar system. Winds of about 200 mph in the clouds may account for the consistency in temperature despite the low rotation speed of the planet. However, at the surface, the winds are very slow.

Surface and composition. Radar-produced maps of the planet show large craters, continent-sized highlands, and extensive dry lowlands. No tectonic activity has been found similar to Earth's moving tectonic plates, but a system of global rift zones and numerous broad, low, dome-like structures, called coronae, may have been produced by the upwelling and subsidence of magma from the mantle. Volcanic surface features, such as vast lava plains, fields of small lava domes, and large shield volcanoes, are common. About 1,600 volcanoes and volcanic features appear on the Venusian surface; more than 85% of the surface is covered by volcanic flows. Theia Mons, a huge shield volcano, has a diameter of over 600 mi and a height of over 3.5 mi. (The largest Hawaiian volcano is only about 125 mi in diameter but rises nearly 5.5 mi from the ocean floor.) In recent years, evidence of continuous volcanic activity has been noted by astronomers. Aside from volcanoes, there are highly deformed mountain belts across Venus along with a few meteor-impact craters more than 20 mi wide. Erosion is a very slow process on Venus due to the lack of water. There are indications of some wind movement of dust and sand. The few impact craters on Venus suggest that the surface is generally geologically young—less than 800 mil years old. Despite the fact that probes have landed on Venus, there are very few pictures from the surface because the probes couldn't withstand the high temperature and atmospheric pressure for more than a few hours.

Mars

Distance from the sun	
Perihelion	128.4 mil mi
Semi-major axis (mean distance)	141.6 mil mi (1.524 AU)
Aphelion	154.9 mil mi
Period of revolution around sun	686.98 d. (1.88 yr.)
Orbital eccentricity	0.0935
Orbital inclination	1.85°
Synodic day (midday to midday)	24 hr., 39 min., 35 sec.
Sidereal day	24 hr., 37 min., 22 sec.
Rotational inclination	25.19°
Mass (Earth = 1)	0.107
Mean radius	2,106 mi
Mean density (Earth = 1)	0.713
Natural satellites	2
Average surface temperature	−81°F

Named for the Roman god of war, the Red Planet has some features much like Earth. Mars has climate, seasons, volcanoes, and possibly once had liquid water flowing across its surface. Mars can easily be seen with the naked eye on most clear nights, which is why it was one of the first planets to be studied by ancient astronomers. Later, when telescopes came into use, many observers claimed that canals made by Martians existed on the planet's surface, which led to speculation as to whether there was intelligent life there. Unmanned probes have since put all those theories to rest; the canals turned out to be topographic patterns and dust storms.

Mars is currently being explored by a number of robotic craft, both on the surface and in orbit. The *Curiosity*/Mars Science Laboratory, an SUV-sized robot, landed on the surface in Aug. 2012. Its mission was to understand the history of the Martian geology and climate, search for the presence of organic matter, and assess the planet's past suitability for life. An Indian orbiter is currently using remote sensing to study the Martian surface and atmosphere, while NASA's *MAVEN* spacecraft is studying the upper atmosphere of Mars and its interaction with the solar wind. The European Space Agency *Trace Gas Orbiter* (TGO) began orbiting Mars in Oct. 2016. NASA's *InSight* mission, which landed in 2018, was relaying seismic data that is being used to map the interior of Mars. In 2020, three spacecraft were launched to the red planet, all arriving in 2021: NASA's *Perseverance* lander, equipped with a helicopter named *Ingenuity*, and Mars missions by China and by the United Arab Emirates.

Orbit and rotation. Although Mars's orbital path is nearly circular, it is somewhat more eccentric than that of most other planets. Mars is more than 26 mil mi farther from the sun at its most distant point compared to its closest approach. Its orbit and speed in relation to Earth's bring it fairly close to Earth, at opposition, about every two years. Mars was at opposition on July 27, 2018, and will be close again on Oct. 13, 2020. Every 15-17 years the close approaches are especially favorable for observation. The 2018 opposition was particularly close, and the next such favorable opposition occurs on Sept. 15, 2035.

Mars rotates in 24 hr. and 37 min., almost the same period of time as Earth. Mars's mean distance from the sun is 142 mil mi. Because Mars's axis of rotation is inclined by about 25° from the vertical to the plane of its solar orbit about the sun, the planet has seasons.

Unlike Earth's global magnetic field, the Martian magnetic field is small, weak, and localized and may be the remnant of a stronger field from the planet's past.

Atmosphere. The Martian atmosphere is composed primarily of 95.32% carbon dioxide, 2.7% nitrogen, 1.6% argon, 0.13% oxygen, 0.08% carbon monoxide, and, in very minor quantities, water, hydrogen oxide, and neon. The atmosphere on Mars is very thin. It has an atmospheric pressure between 1% and 2% of Earth's (if Earth's atmosphere were that thin, there would not be enough oxygen to breathe). Because the Martian atmosphere is so thin and because of the planet's weak magnetic field, its surface is bombarded by cosmic radiation about 100 times as intense as on Earth.

Martian weather systems consist mainly of huge dust storms. On the poles, white caps (believed to be both water ice and carbon dioxide ice) grow in winter and shrink in summer. It is mainly the carbon dioxide that comes and goes with the seasons. The water ice is apparently in many layers with dust between them, indicating climatic cycles.

Surface and composition. Mars is an alien world with rust-red sand and pink skies. In the planet's beginning stages when it was much hotter, Mars's surface melted to a sufficient extent to separate into dense and lighter layers. Mars later cooled enough to allow liquid water to possibly flow across its surface. NASA scientists announced in Sept. 2015 the most convincing evidence to date that liquid water flows on the present-day Martian surface. Using imaging and spectroscopy instruments on the Mars Reconnaissance Orbiter, they showed that seasonal flows on Martian slopes contain hydrated minerals that can only form in the presence of liquid water.

Natural satellites. Mars has two small satellites called Phobos and Deimos, each discovered in 1877 by American astronomer Asaph Hall. (Phobos measures about 11 by 17 mi and Deimos about 7 by 9 mi.) Deimos, the outer satellite, revolves around the planet in about 31 hours. Phobos, the inner satellite, whips around Mars in a little more than 7 hours, making three orbits each Martian day. Since it orbits Mars faster than the planet rotates, Phobos rises in the west and sets in the east, opposite to what other bodies appear to do in the Martian sky. Both moons are irregularly shaped and pitted with numerous craters. Their origins are not known; however, some astronomers consider them to be asteroid-like objects that were captured by Mars very early in its history.

Jupiter

Distance from the sun	
Perihelion	460.1 mil mi
Semi-major axis (mean distance)	483.8 mil mi (5.204 AU)
Aphelion	507.4 mil mi
Period of revolution around sun	11.862 yr.
Orbital eccentricity	0.0489
Orbital inclination	1.304°
Synodic day (midday to midday)	9 hr., 55 min., 33 sec.
Sidereal day	9 hr., 55 min., 30 sec.
Rotational inclination	3.13°
Mass (Earth = 1)	317.8
Mean radius	43,441 mi
Mean density (Earth = 1)	0.24
Natural satellites	79
Average temperature*	−162°F

*i.e., temperature where atmospheric pressure equals 1 Earth atmosphere.

Jupiter, named for the Roman ruler of the gods, is the largest planet in the solar system (11 times the diameter of Earth). Its mass is more than twice the mass of all the other planets, moons, and asteroids put together. Visible to the naked eye and known to the ancients, it was a focus of the Italian scientist Galileo Galilei, who viewed the planet and its four largest moons through a homemade telescope.

Orbit and rotation. Jupiter is at an average distance of 484 mil mi from the sun and takes almost 12 Earth years to make a complete revolution. The largest of the planets, Jupiter has an equatorial diameter of 88,846 mi; its polar diameter is more than 5,700 mi shorter. This noticeable oblateness is a result of the liquidity of the planet and its extremely rapid rotation rate—a Jupiter day is less than 10 Earth hours long. A point on Jupiter's equator moves at a speed of 22,000 mph, as compared with 1,000 mph for a point on Earth's equator. Jupiter's magnetic field is by far the strongest of any planet. Electrical activity caused by this field is so strong that it discharges trillions of watts into Jupiter's environment daily. In July 2016, NASA's *Juno* spacecraft entered orbit around the planet to begin a study of Jupiter's composition, magnetic field, and auroras, including close-up view of the poles of the planet. Originally planned for one-year operation, in 2018 the mission was extended until July 2021.

Atmosphere. Jupiter's atmosphere is primarily composed of 90% molecular hydrogen and 10% helium. Minor constituents include methane, ammonia, hydrogen deuteride, ethane, and water. Jupiter has a turbulent atmosphere characterized by thick clouds, high winds, and huge lightning storms many times larger than those on Earth. The atmospheric temperature varies, but the temperature at the tops of clouds may be about –280°F. The Great Red Spot seen prominently on Jupiter is a huge hurricane-like storm that is three times the diameter of Earth. In 2006, the Hubble Space Telescope detected the appearance of a second, smaller red spot.

Surface and composition. Gas giant planets like Jupiter, Saturn, and Neptune do not have a surface like Earth or any of the other rocky planets. The gases become denser with depth, until they may turn into a slush or slurry. Jupiter has a liquid hydrogen ocean more than 35,000 mi deep. It likely has a rocky core about the size of Earth, but 13 times more massive. There is no sharp interface between the gaseous atmosphere and the hydrogen ocean that accounts for most of Jupiter's volume. At lower depths, under enormous pressure, the liquid hydrogen takes on the properties of a metal. It is likely that this liquid metallic hydrogen is the source for both Jupiter's persistent radio noise and for its improbably strong magnetic field.

Natural satellites. Jupiter has 79 known satellites. Four of the moons (in order of distance from Jupiter), Io, Europa, Ganymede, and Callisto—all discovered by Galileo in 1610—are large and bright and are close in diameter to Earth's moon and Mercury. Because they move so rapidly around Jupiter, their change in position from night to night can be seen from Earth using binoculars.

Io is one of the most volcanically active bodies in the solar system. A gaseous, doughnut-shaped ring, or torus, enveloping Io's orbit around Jupiter may have been formed by material ejected from Io's active volcanoes. (This is not to be confused with Jupiter's rings.) These volcanoes, hotter than Earth's volcanoes, erupt mainly molten sulfur and result in a constantly changing surface appearance.

Europa may have a 30-mi-deep salty, liquid ocean beneath its icy crust, perhaps a small metallic core, and a very tenuous atmosphere. Ganymede is the biggest moon in the solar system. With a diameter of 3,120 mi, it is bigger than both Mercury and Pluto. Ganymede also has its own magnetic field produced by a molten core of perhaps iron sulfide. Callisto has the oldest, most heavily cratered surface in the solar system, a very thin atmosphere of carbon dioxide, and possibly a subsurface liquid ocean.

The other known satellites are much smaller, with four closer to Jupiter than Io, five between Ganymede and Callisto, and the rest farther out. Most of Jupiter's moons orbit the planet at high inclinations from the equator, unlike the innermost satellites. These moons may be captured asteroids.

Rings. Jupiter has a diffuse, dark set of rings that were discovered by the *Voyager 1* spacecraft and cannot be seen from Earth without powerful telescopes. They are composed of small dust grains blasted off the four innermost moons by meteoroid impacts.

Saturn

Saturn, named for the Roman ruler of the Titans, is the sixth planet from the sun and most distant of the planets visible to the unaided eye. Saturn is second in size to Jupiter, but its mass is much smaller. Saturn is the only planet less dense than water, meaning that Saturn would float if there were a pool of water gigantic enough to hold it.

Orbit and rotation. Saturn's diameter is almost 74,900 mi at the equator, while its polar diameter is more than 7,300 mi shorter. Like Jupiter, its noticeable oblateness is a result of the liquidity of the planet and its extremely rapid rate of rotation; a day is little more than 10 Earth hours long.

Distance from the sun	
Perihelion . . . . 840.44 mil mi	
Semi-major axis (mean distance) 890.8 mil mi (9.582 AU)	
Aphelion. . . . . 941.07 mil mi	
Period of revolution around sun . . . . 29.458 yr.	
Orbital eccentricity 0.0565	
Orbital inclination . . . . 2.485°	
Synodic day (midday to midday) . . . . 10 hr., 39 min., 23 sec.	
Sidereal day . . . . 10 hr., 39 min., 22 sec.	
Rotational inclination . . . . 26.73°	
Mass (Earth = 1) 95.159	
Mean radius . . . . 36,184 mi	
Mean density (Earth = 1) 0.125	
Natural satellites 82	
Average temperature* . . . . –218°F	
*i.e., temperature where atmospheric pressure equals 1 Earth atmosphere.	

Atmosphere. Saturn's atmosphere is composed primarily of 96.3% hydrogen, 3.3% helium, and traces of methane, ammonia, hydrogen deuteride, ethane, and water. Saturn's atmosphere is much like that of Jupiter, except that the temperature at the top of its cloud layer is at least 50°F colder.

Surface and composition. Saturn's atmosphere resembles Jupiter's; it likely has a small dense center surrounded by a deep ocean of hydrogen.

Natural satellites. Saturn has 82 known natural satellites, 20 of which were discovered in 2019. Saturn's moon Mimas has an impact crater 81 mi across (the moon itself is only 249 mi across). Enceladus has an atmosphere and shows evidence of geysers that spit water ice and vapor. Two tiny moons orbit within the rings, plowing through and making gaps in the rings along their orbits. Pan, the innermost satellite, creates the Encke Gap of Saturn's A-ring. Daphnis creates the Keeler Gap. The most intriguing Saturnian moon is Titan. The second-biggest moon in the solar system, Titan is bigger than Mercury. Its atmosphere is similar to Earth's atmosphere of long ago; it is made up of approximately 95% nitrogen with traces of methane. Titan's atmosphere extends about 360 mi into space whereas most of Earth's atmosphere lies within 37 mi of the surface. Photographs from Titan's surface, taken by the *Huygens* lander in 2005, show a muddy terrain, with possible deposits of water ice, channels carved by liquid methane springs, and an interesting boundary between light and dark material on the surface. In 2006, scientists found sand dunes on Titan's surface. The "sand" is believed to be tiny water ice crystals or organic compounds. Surface phenomena such as sand dunes are signs of erosion and wind. Unlike winds on Earth or Mars, Titan's winds are not the result of uneven solar heating on the moon's surface but rather Saturn's gravitational pull (similar to how the moon acts on the Earth's oceans).

Rings. Saturn's ring system is the planet's most recognizable feature. It begins about 4,000 mi above the visible disk of Saturn lying above its equator and extends about 260,000 mi into space. The diameter of the ring system visible from Earth is about 170,000 mi; the rings are estimated to be about 700 ft thick. The rings are composed of rock and ice and range in size from tiny particles to large chunks of material the size of a bus. There are several divisions in the rings. The 2,920-mi Cassini division, the gap between the A and B rings, is the largest division.

Uranus

Uranus, discovered by Sir William Herschel in 1781, was the first planet discovered using a telescope. It was named for the father of the Titans in Roman mythology.

Orbit and rotation. Uranus has a diameter of over 31,000 mi and spins once in approximately 17.23 hours, according to magnetic data collected by *Voyager 2*. One of the most fascinating features of Uranus is how far over it is tipped. Its north pole is 98° from its orbital plane. Thus, its seasons are extreme. Over its 84-year orbit, when the sun rises at the north pole, it shines there for about 42 Earth years; then it sets, and the north pole is in darkness for 42 Earth years. In addition to its rotational tilt, Uranus's magnetic field axis is tipped 58.6° from its rotational axis and is displaced about 30% of its radius away from the planet's center.

Distance from the sun	
Perihelion	1,703.4 mil mi
Semi-major axis (mean distance)	1,784.8 mil mi
	(19.201 AU)
Aphelion	1,866.4 mil mi
Period of revolution around sun	84.01 yr.
Orbital eccentricity	0.0457
Orbital inclination	0.772°
Synodic day (midday to midday)	17 hr., 14 min., 23 sec.
	(retrograde)
Sidereal day	17 hr., 14 min., 24 sec. (retrograde)
Rotational inclination	97.77°
Mass (Earth = 1)	14.536
Mean radius	15,759 mi
Mean density (Earth = 1)	0.23
Natural satellites	27
Average temperature*	−323°F

*i.e., temperature where atmospheric pressure equals 1 Earth atmosphere.

Atmosphere. The atmosphere is composed primarily of 82.5% hydrogen, 15.2% helium, and 2.3% methane, with small amounts of hydrogen deuteride, ammonia ice, water ice, ammonia hydrosulfide, and methane ice.

Surface and composition. Uranus has no solid surface, and likely no rocky core but rather a mixture of rocks and assorted ices with about 15% hydrogen and some helium.

Natural satellites. Uranus has 27 known moons, which have orbits lying in the plane of the planet's equator. Five moons are relatively large, while 22 are very small and were only discovered with the *Voyager 2* mission or in later observations. Miranda has grooved markings, reminiscent of Jupiter's Ganymede, but often arranged in a chevron pattern. Rifts and channels on Ariel provide evidence of liquid flowing over its surface in the past. Umbriel is extremely dark, prompting some observers to regard its surface as among the oldest in the system. Titania has rifts and fractures but not the evidence of flow found on Ariel. Oberon's main feature is its surface saturated with craters, unrelieved by other formations.

Rings. In the equatorial plane there is also a complex of 11 rings, 9 of which were discovered in 1978 by observers watching Uranus pass before a star.

Neptune

Named for the Roman god of the sea, Neptune was the first planet discovered through mathematical predictions before it was directly observed. Its approximate orbit and position were first calculated independently by British astronomer John Couch Adams and French astronomer Urbain Le Verrier in 1845. In 1846, German astronomer Johann Galle first observed Neptune through a telescope.

Orbit and rotation. Neptune orbits the sun in 164.8 Earth years in a nearly circular orbit. Its magnetic field is considerably asymmetric to the planet's structure, similar to, but not so extreme as, Uranus's magnetic field. Neptune's magnetic field axis is tipped 46.9° from its rotational axis and is displaced more than 55% of its radius away from the planet's center.

Distance from the sun	
Perihelion	2,761.7 mil mi
Semi-major axis (mean distance)	2,793.1 mil mi (30.047 AU)
Aphelion	2,824.5 mil mi
Period of revolution around sun	164.79 yr.
Orbital eccentricity	0.0113
Orbital inclination	1.769°
Synodic day (midday to midday)	16 hr., 6 min., 37 sec.
Sidereal day	16 hr., 6 min., 36 sec.
Rotational inclination	28.32°
Mass (Earth = 1)	17.147
Mean radius	15,301 mi
Mean density (Earth = 1)	0.297
Natural satellites	14
Average temperature*	−330°F

*i.e., temperature where atmospheric pressure equals 1 Earth atmosphere.

Atmosphere. The Neptunian atmosphere is composed primarily of 80% hydrogen, 19% helium, 1.5% methane, and small amounts of hydrogen deuteride, ethane, ammonia ice, water ice, ammonia hydrosulfide, and methane ice. Neptune's atmosphere is quite blue, with quickly changing white clouds often suspended high above an apparent surface. A Great Dark Spot, reminiscent of Jupiter's Great Red Spot, was discovered in 1989 when *Voyager 2* visited the planet. Observations with the Hubble Space Telescope have shown that the Great Dark Spot originally seen by *Voyager* has apparently dissipated, but a new dark spot has since appeared. Lightning and auroras have been found on other giant planets, but only the aurora phenomenon has been seen on Neptune. As with the other giant planets, Neptune emits more energy than it receives from the sun. The excess has been found to be 2.7 times the solar contribution.

Surface and composition. As with the other giant planets, Neptune may have no solid surface or exact diameter. However, a mean value of 30,600 mi may be assigned to a diameter between atmosphere levels where the pressure is about the same as sea level on Earth.

Natural satellites. The largest of Neptune's 14 satellites is Triton. It is the only large moon in a retrograde orbit, which suggests that it was captured rather than having formed along with the planet. Triton's large size, sufficient to raise significant tides on the planet, may one day, billions of years from now, bring Triton close enough to Neptune for Triton to be torn apart. Triton has a tenuous atmosphere of nitrogen with a trace of hydrocarbons and evidence of active geysers injecting material into it. Triton is the coldest object yet measured in the solar system with a surface temperature of −391°F. Only about half of Triton has been observed, but its terrain shows cratering and a strange regional feature described as resembling the skin of a cantaloupe. Nereid has the highest orbital eccentricity (0.75) of any moon. Its long looping orbit suggests that it was also captured. In 2003, two more moons, which orbit farther from their parent planet than any other moons in the solar system, were discovered. In July 2013, archival Hubble Space Telescope images were used to discover the existence of a 14th natural satellite of Neptune. At less than 20 km diameter, it is the smallest of Neptune's known moons. The *Voyager 2* probe in 1989 confirmed the existence of six rings around Neptune composed of very fine particles. There may be some clumps in the rings' structure. It is not known whether Neptune's satellites influence the formation or maintenance of the rings.

Dwarf Planets

Ceres

Distance from the sun	
Perihelion	237 mil mi (2.55 AU)
Semi-major axis (mean distance)	257 mil mi (2.77 AU)
Period of revolution around sun	4.6 yr.
Orbital eccentricity	0.0756
Orbital inclination	10.59°
Sidereal day	9.074 hr.
Mass (Earth = 1)	0.00015
Mean radius	292 mi

Ceres was the first asteroid discovered; Italian astronomer Guiseppe Piazzi first observed it on Jan. 1, 1801. In the 1800s, it was considered a planet but lost that distinction. Ceres is the largest object in the asteroid belt, comprising nearly one third of all the mass of asteroids. In Aug. 2006, it was designated a dwarf planet by the Intl. Astronomical Union (IAU).

After a journey of over seven years, the *Dawn* spacecraft entered into orbit around Ceres in Mar. 2015, making *Dawn* the first spacecraft to visit a dwarf planet. Astronomers are particularly interested in asteroids since they are thought to be rocky protoplanets, examples of the building blocks from which planets formed early in the history of the solar system. *Dawn's* scientific instrumentation consists of cameras for surface imaging, a spectrometer for measuring surface mineralogy, and a neutron detector for measuring elemental composition of Ceres. *Dawn* has produced high-resolution maps of the entire surface and the most accurate measurements of Ceres's size and mass. The images show a heavily cratered surface with features such as extremely reflective spots within a crater—thought to be freshly exposed water ice—and at least one mountain several miles high.

Orbit and rotation. Ceres orbits the sun in the asteroid belt region between Mars and Jupiter.

Surface and composition. Ceres's composition is similar to that of the stony meteorites known as carbonaceous chondrites. These are considered to be the oldest materials in the solar system, with a composition reflecting that of the primitive solar nebula. Extremely dark in color, probably because of their hydrocarbon content, they show evidence of having absorbed water. Thus, unlike the Earth and the moon, they have never melted nor been reheated since they first formed. *Dawn* observations suggest that the surface of Ceres consists largely of water ice, though its interior is mostly rock. Up to 25% of Ceres's mass may be water ice. There is evidence for hydrothermal vents at the surface of Ceres, perhaps indicating that liquid water existed below the surface in the recent past. Further study using *Dawn* will try to confirm observations suggesting that water evaporates from the surface and produces a diffuse atmosphere.

Pluto

Distance from the sun	
Perihelion	2,756.9 mil mi
Semi-major axis (mean distance)	3,670.1 mil mi
	(39.482 AU)
Aphelion	4,583.2 mil mi
Period of revolution around sun	247.74 yr.
Orbital eccentricity	0.2502
Orbital inclination	17.09°
Synodic day (midday to midday)	6 d., 9 hr., 17 min. (retrograde)
Sidereal day	6 d., 9 hr., 18 min. (retrograde)
Rotational inclination	119.59°
Mass (Earth = 1)	0.0022
Mean radius	736.5 mi
Mean density (Earth = 1)	0.339
Natural satellites	5
Average surface temperature	−369°F

Pluto, named for the Roman god of the underworld, is the largest Kuiper Belt object (KBO) by radius, and the second largest by mass. It was first discovered in 1930 by American astronomer Clyde Tombaugh and classified as a planet until 2006, when the IAU changed its designation to dwarf planet. In 2008, Pluto was designated by the IAU as the prototype for a class of objects called plutoids, bodies that (a) have an average distance from the sun greater than Neptune's; (b) are large enough that gravity determines their shape; and (c) have not cleared their orbit of other objects. Haumea, Makemake, and Eris are also plutoids. The *New Horizons* spacecraft, launched on a voyage to Pluto and beyond in 2006, made the first flyby of Pluto on July 14, 2015, and traveled on to a flyby of Kuiper belt object 2014 MU69, nicknamed Ultima Thule, on Jan. 1, 2019.

Orbit and rotation. Pluto's orbit is highly eccentric; although its average distance from the sun is 3.7 bil mi, it may get as close as 2.76 bil mi and as far as 4.58 bil mi. For about 20 years of its 248-year orbit, it is closer to the sun than Neptune. Currently, it is beyond Neptune's orbit.

Atmosphere and surface. Before the *New Horizons* flyby, all observations of Pluto had been made with telescopes nearly 3 bil mi away, so the mission brought new data to light. The mass and density of Pluto suggests that it is composed of a rocky core with an overlying water-ice mantle. Close-up observations of Pluto from *New Horizons* revealed a mixed surface, with some ancient, heavily cratered terrain and other younger, smoother plains with no craters. The smooth terrain, estimated to be no more than 100 mil years old, is much younger than scientists expected and may indicate that geologic processes continue to modify Pluto. Nitrogen ice on the smooth plains appears to be flowing, like glaciers on Earth, onto the more heavily cratered surface. Compositional evidence shows that the smooth areas contain nitrogen, methane, and carbon monoxide ices. Scientists also found several mountain ranges rising more than 2 mi above the smooth plains; they speculated that the mountains are made of water ice thrust up from below Pluto's nitrogen-rich icy surface.

New Horizons also provided the first close-up measurements of Pluto's atmosphere, confirming earlier measurements of methane, nitrogen, and carbon monoxide, the same molecules that form ice on Pluto's surface. Scientists speculate that the atmosphere forms from evaporation of surface ices when the dwarf planet is closer to the sun. The new measurements also revealed hydrocarbon hazes as much as 50 mi above Pluto's surface. The hazes are thought to form when Pluto's tenuous atmosphere is exposed to the sun's ultraviolet rays. Dark regions on Pluto's surface likely result from these hydrocarbons settling. Knowledge of Pluto will continue to improve as more data is analyzed.

Natural satellites. Pluto has five known natural satellites. Charon, the biggest, has a diameter of 750 mi—about half of Pluto's diameter of 1,474 mi. No other planet or dwarf planet has a moon so close to its size. Discovered in 1978, Charon orbits Pluto at a distance of 12,200 mi and takes 6.39 days to move around the dwarf planet. In this same length of time, Pluto and Charon both rotate once on their axes, meaning that the Pluto-Charon system appears to rotate as virtually a rigid body. Both worlds are roughly spherical and have comparable densities. Because of these similarities and their peculiar relationship, there is debate as to whether Charon should one day be designated a dwarf planet. *New Horizons* provided the first detailed look at Charon, revealing a surface with less color and likely dominated by water ice. New evidence suggests Charon may have had a water ocean in the past. Much of Charon's surface is smoother than expected, with few craters, implying that Charon has an active geology capable of resurfacing. The images also reveal fractures extending hundreds of miles and a canyon around 5 mi deep.

Two other moons, discovered in 2005 and 2006, were officially named Nix and Hydra. Two additional moons, discovered in 2011 and 2012, were officially named Kerberos and Styx by the IAU in 2013. In late 2015, NASA released *New Horizons*-sourced images of Nix and Hydra, revealing irregularly shaped objects about 25 and 35 mi across, respectively. Astronomers examining *New Horizons* data have been surprised to find no additional moons, down to the roughly 1-mi-diameter limit of detectability by the spacecraft.

Haumea

Distance from the sun	
Semi-major axis (mean distance)	43.355 AU
Period of revolution around sun	285.48 yr.
Orbital eccentricity	0.189
Orbital inclination	28.20°
Mass (Earth = 1)	0.0007
Mean radius	420 mi
Natural satellites	2

Haumea was discovered in 2004 and was accepted as a dwarf planet by the IAU in 2008.

Orbit and rotation. Haumea has a moderately eccentric orbit and takes about 285 years to go around the sun.

Surface and composition. Spectra of Haumea indicate the presence of almost pure crystalline water ice. The surface reflects about 60% of the sunlight that reaches it. Haumea has a very oblong shape, twice as long as it is wide.

Natural satellites. Haumea has two natural satellites, Hi'iake and Namaka.

Makemake

Distance from the sun	
Semi-major axis (mean distance)	45.715 AU
Period of revolution around sun	309.1 yr.
Orbital eccentricity	0.155
Orbital inclination	28.99°
Mass (Earth = 1)	0.0007
Mean radius	450 mi
Natural satellites	1

Makemake was discovered in 2005 and was accepted as a dwarf planet by the IAU in 2008.

Orbit and rotation. Makemake has a moderately eccentric orbit and takes about 310 years to go around the sun.

Surface and composition. Spectra of Makemake indicate the presence of frozen methane, as well as several organic compounds. The surface is highly reflective and appears similar to that of Pluto.

Natural satellites. Makemake has one natural satellite.

2007 OR10

Distance from the sun	
Semi-major axis (mean distance)	67.143 AU
Period of revolution around sun	550.19 yr.
Orbital eccentricity	0.505
Orbital inclination	30.87°
Mass (Earth = 1)	0.0006
Mean radius	950 mi
Natural satellites	1

2007 OR10 was discovered in 2007 and has not yet received an official name from the IAU.

Orbit and rotation. 2007 OR10 has a highly elliptical orbit and takes about 550 years to go around the sun.

Surface and composition. Spectra of 2007 OR10 indicate the presence of frozen methane and water ice. The surface is highly reflective and appears similar to that of Pluto.

Natural satellites. One natural satellite of 2007 OR10 was discovered by astronomers using the Hubble Space Telescope in 2017.

Eris

Distance from the sun	
Semi-major axis (mean distance)	67.6497 AU
Period of revolution around sun	556.43 yr.
Orbital eccentricity	0.44171
Orbital inclination	44.204°
Mass (Earth = 1)	0.0027
Mean radius	723 mi
Natural satellites	1

Discovered in 2003 by astronomers at the California Institute of Technology, Eris is the largest dwarf planet by mass, about 27% larger than Pluto, although Pluto has a slightly larger radius.

Orbit and rotation. Eris has a highly elliptical orbit and takes about 560 years to go around the sun—more than twice the time it takes Pluto. Its inclination is steep, tilted at 44° to the planetary plane. It also has an extremely eccentric orbit. It will be at its closest to the sun, actually coming inside part of Pluto's orbit, in about 280 years.

Surface and composition. Eris, with a surface covered in frozen methane, may be similar to Pluto and the Neptunian moon Triton. Observations made by the Hubble Space Telescope show that Eris's surface is almost white and uniform, reflecting 86% of the light that hits it. This makes it the most reflective body in the solar system. The dwarf planet's interior is likely a mixture of rock and ice.

Natural satellites. Eris has one moon, Dysnomia.

Small Solar System Bodies

Asteroids

Besides planets and moons, many smaller objects orbit the sun. In 2006, the International Astronomical Union (IAU) officially designated these objects "small solar system bodies." Asteroids or minor planets are found mainly in a belt between the orbits of Mars and Jupiter. Within this belt there may be millions of asteroids of varying sizes. Most asteroids are very small. Ceres, which can be classified both as an asteroid and a dwarf planet, is 588 mi in diameter, about one-quarter the diameter of our moon.

Some of these asteroids are gravitationally locked with Jupiter and the sun so that they have roughly the same orbit as Jupiter but are either 60° ahead or behind the planet. These are the **Trojan asteroids.** Many of the smaller moons of the solar system, especially those in retrograde orbits, may be captured asteroids. Asteroids whose orbits either cross or come close to the Earth's orbit are labeled **Near Earth asteroids,** or NEAs. A handful of asteroids have actually been imaged by the Arecibo and Goldstone radio telescopes and by the NEAR Shoemaker space probe. The *Galileo* spacecraft imaged the asteroids Gaspra and Ida (including Ida's moon Dactyl) on its way to Jupiter. The Japanese *Hayabusa 2*, which is orbiting asteroid Ryugu, is scheduled to return a sample to Earth Dec. 2020; and NASA's OSIRIS-REx mission, currently orbiting asteroid Bennu, is scheduled to return a sample to Earth in Sept. 2023. As of summer 2019, 14 asteroids have been visited by spacecraft.

Comets

Comets are small icy bodies that orbit the sun. When one approaches the sun, the energy from the sun boils off material from the comet's icy nucleus, producing an enlarged head (or **coma**), and in many cases an extended tail. Because of that, comets are brighter when near the sun. For large comets, the head may be 100,000 mi across and the tail more than a million mi long, though both are mainly empty space.

Comets have been known since ancient times. British astronomer Edmund Halley (1656-1742) ultimately realized that a group of historical reports were just repeated visits of the same object. Comets are the only astronomical objects named after their discoverers. In 1986, the European spacecraft *Giotto* took the first close-up images of a comet's nucleus, specifically of Comet Halley, showing it had a peanut-shaped nucleus with a longest dimension of about 10 mi.

In 1995, U.S. observers Alan Hale (1958-) and Thomas Bopp (1949-2018) independently discovered a comet that was then beyond the orbit of Jupiter. It is one of the brightest comets of all time. It also holds the record for length of time visible to the naked eye—19 months—and is the most photographed comet in history. In July 2009, an amateur astronomer discovered a large impact scar in the upper atmosphere of Jupiter, likely the result of another cometary impact. In Mar. 2020, astronomers

using the *NEOWISE* mission of the Wide-field Infrared Survey Explorer (*WISE*) discovered a comet, which in July 2020 was widely visible to the naked eye. Comet *NEOWISE* is the brightest comet since Hale-Bopp. In 2014, the *Rosetta* spacecraft became the first spacecraft to orbit a comet, 67P/Churyumov-Gerasimenko. *Rosetta* also deployed a lander onto the comet surface. As of summer 2020, nine comets have been studied directly by spacecraft

Kuiper Belt

The Kuiper Belt is a doughnut-shaped region that extends to about 50 AU (astronomical units) from the sun and is thought to be the source of short-period comets such as Comets Halley or Swift-Tuttle. It is filled with icy bodies that are in solar orbit. The more than 1,000 objects found in this region in recent years are called Kuiper Belt objects (KBOs). It is estimated that there are more than 70,000 objects 60 mi in diameter or larger within the Kuiper Belt. Dwarf planets Pluto and Eris are considered KBOs. There are at least six KBOs larger than 300 mi in diameter.

On Jan. 1, 2019, *New Horizons* made the first close study of a KBO when it flew by the object 2014 MU 69, nicknamed Ultima Thule (an International Astronomical Union-approved name is yet to be designated). In the first images sent back to Earth, Ultima Thule appears to be a "contact binary," composed of two smaller bodies, 14 mi ("Ultima") and 9 mi ("Thule") across, in close contact with each other. No satellite of Ultima Thule was observed. Data from the flyby transmits across the large distance slowly and will continue to be uploaded through Aug. 2020.

2014 MU 69

Distance from the sun	
Semi-major axis (mean distance)	44.539 AU
Period of revolution around sun	298 yr.
Orbital eccentricity	0.04172
Orbital inclination	2.451°
Mass (Earth = 1)	Unknown
Mean radius	14 mi ("Ultima") and 9 mi ("Thule")

Oort Cloud

The Oort Cloud is a vast spherical region hypothesized to exist around the sun and populated by comets. Dutch astronomer Jan Oort (1900-92) proposed its existence as the origin for long-period comets that enter the inner part of the solar system where the planets orbit. Current technology is not sufficient to detect any members of the Oort Cloud other than observed comets whose orbits may reach out as far as 50,000 AU. Recent examples of such long-period comets are Comets Hale-Bopp and Hyakutake.

The Sun

Distance from Earth, mean	92.96 mil mi (1 AU)
Sidereal day (rotation period)	25.38 d.
Mass (Earth = 1)	332,900
Mean radius	432,200 mi
Mean density (Earth = 1)	0.255
Average surface temperature	9,941°F

The sun is the Earth's primary source of light and heat and its closest star. The biggest object in the solar system, the sun is 332,900 times more massive than Earth and contains 99.86% of the mass of the entire solar system. On the whole, the sun is made up of about 92.1% hydrogen and 7.8% helium, with trace amounts of other elements. It has a mass and luminosity greater than that of 90% of the stars in the Milky Way galaxy. Although most of the stars that can be easily seen on a clear night are bigger and brighter than the sun, its proximity to Earth makes it appear tremendously large and bright. The sun is 400,000 times as bright as the full moon, and it gives Earth 6 mil times as much light as do all the other stars put together. Because of the great distance between the sun and Earth, it takes about 499 sec., or slightly more than 8 min., for light from the sun to reach Earth.

Composition. The sun has six regions. The first three from the inside out are the core, the radiative zone, and the convective zone. Together they form the interior. The others, which comprise the visible surface, are the photosphere, the chromosphere, and the outermost region, the corona.

The sun's heat and energy are produced in its core. Through a series of nuclear fusion reactions, hydrogen nuclei are converted to helium nuclei, releasing energy in the process. Temperatures in the core are theorized to be 28 mil °F. In 2017 astronomers discovered that the core rotates nearly four times faster than the surface, a rapidity left over from the time when the sun was formed. From the core, photons transport the energy outward through the radiative zone. It can take photons several million years to pass through this area. In the convective zone, gases move energy outward at a faster rate. Like a boiling pot, bubbles of gas bring energy to the surface.

The photosphere is the visible surface of the sun, that is, the light that we see as sunlight. When sunlight is analyzed with a spectroscope, it is found to consist of a continuous spectrum composed of all the colors of the rainbow, crossed by many dark lines. The dark "absorption lines" are produced by gaseous materials in the outer layers of the sun. More than 60 of the natural terrestrial elements have been identified in the sun, all in gaseous form because of the sun's intense heat.

Just above the photosphere is the chromosphere, which is visible to the naked eye only in total solar eclipses, during which it appears to be a pinkish-violet layer with occasional great prominences projecting above its general level. With proper instruments, the chromosphere can be seen or photographed whenever the sun is visible. Above the chromosphere

is the corona, also visible to the naked eye only at times of total eclipse or with instruments that permit the brighter portions of the corona to be seen. The corona surges millions of miles from the sun; its atoms are all in a state of extreme excitation and high ionization that indicates temperatures nearly 2 mil °F.

Sunspots. These dark, irregularly shaped regions may reach diameters of thousands of miles. There is an intimate connection between sunspots and the corona. At times of low sunspot activity, the fine streamers of the corona are longer above the sun's equator than over the polar regions of the sun; during periods of high sunspot activity, the corona extends fairly evenly outward from all regions of the sun but to a much greater distance in space. The average life of a sunspot group is two months, but some have lasted for more than a year. Sunspots reach a low point, on average, every 11.3 years, with a peak of activity occurring irregularly between two successive periods of minimal activity. The sun experienced an unusually quiet period in 2008 and 2009; its latest period of maximum activity occurred in 2014, though this was among the weakest maximums ever recorded.

Solar wind and magnetic field. Magnetic arches, called prominences, may extend tens of thousands of miles into the corona and may release enormous amounts of energy heating the corona. Coronal mass ejections are enormous releases of solar energy. Coronal holes are regions where the corona appears dark in X-rays, and are associated with open magnetic field lines, where the magnetic field lines project out into space instead of back toward the sun. It is in these regions where the high-speed solar wind originates.

The solar wind carries the sun's magnetic field, which extends beyond the planets. This is called the interplanetary magnetic field (IMF). Far past Pluto and the Kuiper Belt, the solar wind and the IMF lose their influence. The boundary between them and interstellar space is called the heliopause. In 2013, NASA announced that the *Voyager 1* spacecraft, launched in 1977, seemed at last to have reached the heliopause, at a distance 18 bil km (11 bil mi) from the sun.

Searching for Extrasolar Planets

The sun is a typical star in many respects and—with over 400 bil stars in the Milky Way—it is plausible that many other stars might have planets. Since 1995, astronomers have gathered evidence of thousands of planets orbiting stars other than the sun. Astronomers have not directly observed most of these objects but inferred their existence from observations of their parent stars.

Astronomers have used two main techniques to detect planets. The first, called the radial-velocity method, uses the Doppler effect to detect periodic changes in the motion of a star caused by the gravitational tug of an unseen planet. The magnitude of the star's motion and the time it takes to repeat can be used to infer the planet's mass and distance from its host star. This technique is most sensitive to high-mass planets orbiting close to their stars because that situation produces more noticeable changes in a star's motion.

The second technique, the transit method, relies on the dimming of a star's light as an unseen planet repeatedly passes in front of it. Astronomers are able to infer the diameter of the planet and the distance at which the planet orbits the star. When combined with the mass determined from the radial-velocity method, astronomers can determine the density of the unseen planet and begin to infer its similarity to planets in our solar system.

Astronomers have also used optical gravitational lensing to detect extrasolar planets. This technique, which detects the observed brightening of a distant background star as a planet passes in front of it, has allowed Southern Hemisphere astronomers to find the most distant planet yet detected, about halfway to the center of our own Milky Way galaxy.

The first planets to be discovered outside the solar system tended to be massive "hot Jupiters," orbiting close to their parent stars (closer than Mercury's orbit around the sun) and comparable in mass to the gas giant Jupiter. But as detection instruments and techniques have improved, smaller and more distant planets have been discovered. The planets discovered so far seem to fall into several groups: rocky planets as massive as 1.75 times that of Earth; mini-Neptunes, 2-3.5 times as massive as Earth, with gas surrounding a rocky core; "super Earths" more massive than the mini-Neptunes; and gas giants, as massive or more massive than Jupiter.

In 2005, astronomers obtained the first direct image of an extrasolar planet around a normal star called GQ Lupi, which is like Earth's sun but younger. The planet is about 100 AU (astronomical units) away from the star and estimated to be about twice as massive as Jupiter.

In 2006, astronomers discovered what they call a "super Earth" orbiting a red dwarf 9,000 light-years away. The planet appears to have about 13 times Earth's mass and may be composed of rock and ice, but it is believed not to have liquid on its surface. Such super Earths appear to be common in extrasolar planetary systems. In 2007, astronomers detected water in the atmosphere of an extrasolar planet for the first time.

In 2009, NASA launched Kepler, the first telescope sensitive enough to detect Earth-sized planets around other stars. Kepler's first-released data in 2010 indicated that small planets are more common than large planets. Kepler has now detected a large number of planets with diameters similar to that of Earth. Some of the planets are known to orbit within the host star's habitable zone, meaning that the conditions are such that liquid water could exist on the planetary surface. As of Sept. 2019, astronomers had confirmed over 4,107 planets orbiting more than 3,057 stars; 667 of those stars host more than one planet.

Planets with masses much less than Jupiter's are now regularly discovered. A team of astronomers announced, Aug. 2016, the discovery of a possibly Earth-like planet, Proxima b, in orbit around Proxima Centauri, the star closest to the sun. About 4.2 light-years away, it is the closest known exoplanet. In Feb. 2017, astronomers announced the discovery of at least seven Earth-sized planets orbiting a small star, Trappist-1, located about 40 light-years away. They appear similar in mass and composition to Earth, and three of the planets are in the habitable zone of the star. In June 2017, the Kepler mission announced the discovery of 10 Earth-sized planets, probably rocky in composition, that might support liquid water and could be potentially habitable.

NASA successfully launched the Transiting Exoplanet Survey Satellite (TESS) mission on Apr. 18, 2018, aboard a SpaceX Falcon 9 rocket. This landmark mission was conducting an all-sky survey of extrasolar planets, including those orbiting bright nearby stars, which can be investigated in further detail by large Earth-based and space telescopes. By July 2020, it had finished its primary mission, covering about 75% of space. During this period, TESS found 66 new exoplanets as well as nearly 2,100 candidates needing further detailed observation for confirmation. In Dec. 2019, the European Space Agency launched a complementary mission, Cheops (CHaracterising ExOPlanet Satellite), which is also targeting planets around bright nearby stars.

Earth: Size, Computation of Time, Seasons

Distance from the sun	
Perihelion	91.4 mil mi
Semi-major axis (mean distance) . .	93 mil mi (1.0000 AU)
Aphelion	94.5 mil mi
Period of revolution	365.256 d.
Orbital eccentricity	0.0167
Orbital inclination	0°
Synodic day (midday to midday)	24 hr., 0 min., 0 sec.
Sidereal day (rotation period)	23 hr., 56 min., 4.2 sec.
Rotational inclination	23.45°
Mass (Earth = 1)	1
Mean radius	3,958.8 mi
Mean density (Earth = 1)	1
Natural satellites	1
Average surface temperature	59°F

Earth is the fifth-largest planet and the third from the sun. Its mass is 5.9736 × 10²⁴ kg. Earth's equatorial diameter is 7,926 mi while its polar diameter is only 7,900 mi.

Size and dimensions. Earth is considered a solid mass, yet it has a large, liquid iron, **magnetic core** with a radius of about 2,160 mi. Surprisingly, it has a solid **inner core** that may be a large iron crystal, with a radius of 760 mi. Around the core is a thick shell, or **mantle**, of dense rock. This mantle is composed of materials rich in iron and magnesium. It is somewhat plastic-like, and under slow steady pressure, it can flow like a liquid. The mantle, in turn, is covered by a thin **crust** forming the solid granite and basalt base of the continents and ocean basins. Over broad areas of Earth's surface, the crust has a thin cover of sedimentary rock such as sandstone, shale, and limestone formed by weathering and by deposits of sands, clays, and plant and animal remains.

The temperature inside the Earth increases about 1°F with every 100 to 200 ft in depth, in the upper 100 km (62 mi) of Earth. It reaches nearly 8,000°F-9,000°F at the center. The heat is believed to come from radioactivity in rocks, pressures within Earth, and the original heat of formation.

Atmosphere. Earth's atmosphere is a blanket composed of 78% nitrogen, 21% oxygen, and 1% argon. Present in minute quantities are carbon dioxide, hydrogen, neon, helium, krypton, and xenon. Water vapor displaces other gases and varies from nearly zero to about 4% by volume. The atmosphere rests on Earth's surface with a weight equivalent to a layer of water 34 ft deep. For about 300,000 ft upward, the gases remain in the proportions stated. Gravity holds the gases to Earth. The weight of the air compresses it at the bottom so that the greatest density is at Earth's surface. Pressure and density decrease as height increases.

The lowest layer of the atmosphere extending up from the Earth's surface about 7.5 mi is the **troposphere**, which contains 90% of the air. This is also where most weather phenomena occur. The temperature drops with increasing height through this layer. The **stratosphere** extends about 23 mi above the troposphere; the temperature generally increases with height within this layer. The stratosphere contains **ozone**, which prevents ultraviolet rays from reaching Earth's surface. Since there is very little convection in the stratosphere, jets regularly cruise in the lower parts to provide a smoother ride for passengers.

Above the stratosphere is the **mesosphere**, where the temperature again decreases with height for another 19 mi. Extending above the mesosphere to the outer fringes of the atmosphere is the **thermosphere**, a region where temperature once more increases with height to a value measured in thousands of degrees Fahrenheit. The lower portion of this region, extending from 50 to about 400 mi in altitude, is characterized by high ion density and is thus called the **ionosphere**. Most meteors are in the lower thermosphere or the mesosphere at the time they are observed.

Longitude and latitude. Position on the globe is measured by meridians and parallels. Meridians, which are imaginary lines drawn around Earth through the poles, determine **longitude**. The meridian running through Greenwich, England, is the **prime meridian** of longitude; all others are either E or W. Parallels, which are imaginary circles parallel with the equator, determine **latitude**. The length of a degree of longitude varies as the cosine of the latitude. At the equator a degree of longitude is 69.171 statute mi; this is gradually reduced toward the poles. Value of a longitude degree at the poles is zero.

Latitude is reckoned by the number of degrees N or S of the **equator**, an imaginary circle on Earth's surface everywhere equidistant between the two poles. According to the International Astronomical Union, the length of a degree of latitude is 68.708 statute mi at the equator and varies slightly N and S because of the oblate form of the globe. At the poles, it is 69.403 statute mi.

Definitions of time. Earth rotates on its axis and follows an elliptical orbit around the sun. The rotation makes the sun appear to move across the sky from E to W. This rotation determines day and night, and the complete rotation, in relation to the sun, is called the **apparent or true solar day**. A sundial thus measures **apparent solar time**. This length of time varies, but an average determines a mean solar day of 24 hours.

The mean solar day and **mean solar time** are in universal use for civil purposes. Mean solar time may be obtained from apparent solar time by correcting observations of the sun for the **equation of time**. Mean solar time may be up to 16 min. different from apparent solar time.

Sidereal time is the measure of time defined by the diurnal motion of the vernal equinox and is determined from observation of the meridian transits of stars. One complete rotation of Earth relative to the equinox is called the **sidereal day**. The **mean sidereal day** is 23 hr., 56 min., 4.2 sec. of mean solar time.

The interval required for Earth to make one absolute revolution around the sun is a **sidereal year**; it consisted of 365 days, 6 hr., 9 min., and 9.5 sec. of mean solar time (approximately 24 hr. per day) in 1900 and has been increasing at the rate of 0.0001 second annually.

The **tropical year**, upon which our calendar is based, is the interval between two consecutive returns of the sun to the vernal equinox. The tropical year consisted of 365 days, 5 hr., 48 min., and 46 sec. in 1900. It has been decreasing at the rate of 0.53 sec. per century. The **calendar year** begins at midnight precisely, local clock time, on the night of Dec. 31-Jan. 1. The day and the calendar month also begin at midnight by the clock.

On Jan. 1, 1972, the Bureau International des Poids et Mesures in Paris introduced **International Atomic Time** (TAI) as the most precisely determined time scale for astronomical usage. The fundamental unit of TAI in the international system of units is the second, defined as the duration of 9,192,631,770 periods of the radiation corresponding to the transition between two hyperfine levels of the ground state of the cesium-133 atom. **Coordinated Universal Time** (UTC), which serves as the basis for civil timekeeping and is the standard time of the prime meridian, is officially defined by a formula which relates UTC to mean sidereal time in Greenwich, England. (UTC replaced Greenwich Mean Time as the basis for standard time for the world.)

Zones and seasons. The five zones of Earth's surface are the Torrid, lying between the Tropics of Cancer and Capricorn; the N Temperate, between Cancer and the Arctic Circle; the S Temperate, between Capricorn and the Antarctic Circle; and the two Frigid Zones, between the Polar Circles and the Poles.

The inclination, or tilt, of Earth's axis, 23°45´ away from a perpendicular to Earth's orbit of the sun, determines the seasons. These are commonly marked in the N Temperate Zone, where spring begins at the vernal equinox, summer at the summer solstice, autumn at the autumnal equinox, and winter at the winter solstice. In the S Temperate Zone, the seasons are reversed. Spring begins at the autumnal equinox, summer at the winter solstice, and so on.

The points at which the sun crosses the equator are the **equinoxes**, when day and night are most nearly equal. The points at which the sun is at a maximum distance from the equator are the **solstices**, when days and nights are most unequal. However, at the equator, day and night are equal throughout the year.

In June, the North Pole is tilted 23°27´ toward the sun, and the days in the Northern Hemisphere are longer than the nights, while the days in the Southern Hemisphere are shorter than the nights. In Dec., the North Pole is tilted 23°27´ away from the sun, and the situation is reversed.

Seasons in 2021. In 2021, the four seasons begin in the Northern Hemisphere as shown. (Add 1 hour to Eastern Standard Time for Atlantic Time; subtract 1 hour for Central, 2 for Mountain, 3 for Pacific, 4 for Alaska, 5 for Hawaii-Aleutian. Also shown is Coordinated Universal Time.)

Season	Date	UTC	EST/EDT
Vernal Equinox (spring)	Mar. 20	09:37	05:37 EDT
Northern Solstice (summer)	June 21	03:32	23:32 EDT
			June 20
Autumnal Equinox (fall)	Sept. 22	19:21	15:21 EDT
Southern Solstice (winter)	Dec. 21	15:59	10:59 EST

Poles. The geographic (rotation) poles, or points where Earth's axis of rotation cuts the surface, are not absolutely fixed in the body of Earth. The pole of rotation describes an irregular curve about its mean position.

Two periods have been detected in this motion: (1) an annual period due to seasonal changes in barometric pressure, to load of ice and snow on the surface, and to other seasonal phenomena; (2) a period of about 14 months due to the shape and constitution of Earth. In addition, there are small but as yet unpredictable irregularities. The whole motion is so small that the actual pole at any time remains within a circle of 30 or 40 ft in radius centered at the mean position of the pole.

The pole of rotation for the time being is, of course, the pole having a latitude of 90° and an indeterminate longitude.

Magnetic poles. Although Earth's magnetic field resembles that of an ordinary bar magnet, this magnetic field is probably produced by electric currents in the liquid currents of the Earth's outer core. The **north magnetic pole** of Earth is that region where the magnetic force is downward, and the **south magnetic pole** is that region where the magnetic force is upward. A compass placed at the magnetic poles experiences no directive force in azimuth (i.e., direction).

There are slow changes in the distribution of Earth's magnetic field. This slow temporal change is referred to as the secular change of the main magnetic field, and the magnetic poles shift due to this. The location of the N magnetic pole was first measured in 1831 at Cape Adelaide on the W coast of Boothia Peninsula in Canada's Northwest Territories (about latitude 70° N and longitude 96° W). Since then it has moved over 500 mi. As of 2020 it was estimated to be at latitude 86.50° N, longitude 164.04° E, the Arctic Ocean far north of Siberia. Measurement for several decades by Canadian scientists indicates the motion of the pole has accelerated, now averaging about 34 mi per year.

The direction of the horizontal components of the magnetic field at any point is known as magnetic N at that point, and the angle by which it deviates E or W of true N is known as the magnetic declination.

A compass without error points in the direction of magnetic north. (In general, this is not the direction of the true rotational North Pole.) If you follow the direction indicated by the N end of the compass, you will go along an irregular curve that eventually reaches the north magnetic pole (though not usually by a great-circle route). However, the action of the compass should not be thought of as due to any influence of the distant pole, but simply as an indication of the distribution of Earth's magnetism at the place of observation.

Rotation. The speed of Earth's rotation about its axis is slightly variable. The variations may be classified as:

(A) **Secular.** Tidal friction acts as a brake on the rotation and causes a slow secular increase in the length of the day, about 1 millisecond per century.

(B) **Irregular.** The speed of rotation may increase for a number of years (about 5 to 10) and then start decreasing. The maximum difference from the mean in the length of the day during a century is about 5 milliseconds. The accumulated difference in time has amounted to approximately 44 seconds since 1900. The cause is probably motion in the interior of Earth.

(C) **Periodic.** Seasonal variations exist with periods of 1 year and 6 months. The cumulative effect is such that each year, Earth is late about 30 milliseconds near June 1 and is ahead about 30 milliseconds near Oct. 1. The maximum seasonal variation in the length of the day is about 0.5 millisecond. It is believed that the principal cause of the annual variation is the seasonal change in the wind patterns of the Northern and Southern Hemispheres. The semiannual variation is due chiefly to tidal action of the sun, which distorts the shape of Earth slightly.

The Moon

Distance from Earth	
Perigee	225,744 mi
Semi-major axis (mean distance)	238,855 mi
Apogee	251,966 mi
Period of revolution	27.322 d.
Orbital eccentricity	0.0549
Orbital inclination	5.145°
Synodic orbital period (period of phases)	29.53 d.
Sidereal day (rotation period)	27.322 d.
Rotational inclination	6.68°
Mass (Earth = 1)	0.0123
Mean radius	1,079 mi
Mean density (Earth = 1)	0.607
Average surface temperature	–100°F

The moon is the second-brightest object in the sky (the sun is the first). Earth's only natural satellite, the moon is the force behind the rising and falling of tides, and it helps to regulate Earth's inclination as they orbit the sun. Many probes have been sent to the moon, and between 1969 and 1972, 12 U.S. astronauts walked on its surface. In 2007, Japan and China orbited satellites around the moon, India orbited a spacecraft in fall 2008, and the U.S. sent an orbiter and impactor in 2009. In Sept. 2009, American scientists announced the discovery of a thin layer of water ice near the lunar poles. Since 2009, NASA has been mapping and measuring the surface composition and other properties of the moon using the Lunar Reconnaissance Orbiter. In Sept. 2013, NASA launched *LADEE*, a mission to study the ephemeral lunar atmosphere and lunar dust from a low orbit. In Dec. 2013, China became the third nation to land a spacecraft on the moon when *Chang'e 3* set down on Mare Imbrium. *Chang'e 3* released the *Yutu* rover to study the lunar surface. On July 22, 2019, India successfully launched the *Chandrayaan-2* mission. Scheduled to land a rover near the south pole of the moon on Sept. 7, 2019, mission control lost contact with the lander 1.3 mi from the surface, though an orbiter remained operational.

Orbit and rotation. The moon completes a circuit around Earth in a period that averages 27 days, 7 hr., 43.2 min. This is the moon's sidereal period. Because of the motion of the moon in common with Earth around the sun, the mean duration of the lunar month—the period from one new moon to the next new moon—is 29 days, 12 hr., 44.05 min. This is the moon's synodic period.

The mean distance of the moon from Earth is 238,855 mi, but its orbit about Earth is elliptical, and thus the actual distance varies considerably. The maximum distance from Earth that the moon may reach is 251,966 mi and the least distance is 225,744 mi.

The moon rotates on its axis in a period of time that is exactly equal to its sidereal revolution about Earth—27.322 days. Thus the backside, or farside, of the moon always faces away from Earth. But this does not mean that the backside is always dark. The farside of the moon gets as much direct sunlight as the nearside; at new moon phase, the farside of the moon is fully lit but not visible from Earth.

The moon's revolution about Earth is irregular because of its elliptical orbit. The moon's rotation, however, is regular, and this, together with the irregular revolution, produces what is called libration in longitude, which permits an observer on Earth to see first farther around the eastern side and then farther around the western side of the moon. The moon's variation north or south of the ecliptic permits one to see farther over first one pole of the moon and then the other; this is called libration in latitude. These two libration effects permit observers on Earth to see a total of about 60% of the moon's surface over a period of time.

Atmosphere and surface. The moon, like the planet Mercury, has no real atmosphere to speak of. What little exists is variable and tenuous. With its long day and night, the daytime temperature can reach 260°F. The coldest nighttime temperature is –280°F. This day-to-night contrast is exceeded only by that on Mercury. The lunar surface has not changed much since humans began observing it. The side visible from Earth has large craters and vast dark areas called maria that were once lava. The farside has almost no maria but is pockmarked with craters; it was first photographed in 1959 by the Soviet space probe *Lunik III.*

Recent findings show that up to 300 mil metric tons of water ice may exist in craters at the lunar poles. In its interior, the moon may have a small core, which supports the idea that most of the moon's mass was ripped away from the early Earth when a Mars-sized object collided with Earth.

Harvest moon and hunter's moon. The harvest moon, the full moon nearest the autumnal equinox, ushers in a period of several days when the moon rises soon after sunset. This phenomenon gives farmers in temperate latitudes extra hours of light in which to harvest their crops. The 2020 harvest moon falls on Oct. 1. Harvest moon in the Southern Hemisphere temperate latitudes falls on Apr. 8.

The next full moon after harvest moon is called the hunter's moon; it is accompanied by a similar but less marked phenomenon. In 2020, the hunter's moon occurs on Oct. 31 in the Northern Hemisphere and on Apr. 8 in the Southern Hemisphere.

CALENDAR

Western Calendars

The **Julian calendar**, under which all Western nations measured time until 1582 CE, was authorized by Julius Caesar in 46 BCE. It called for a year of 365¼ days, starting in Jan., with every fourth year being a **leap year** of 366 days. St. Bede, an Anglo-Saxon monk also known as the Venerable Bede, announced in 730 CE that the Julian year was 11 min., 14 sec. too long, a cumulative error of about a day every 128 years, but nothing was done about this for centuries.

By 1582 the accumulated error was estimated at 10 days. In that year, Pope Gregory XIII decreed that the day following Oct. 4, 1582, should be called Oct. 15, thus dropping 10 days and initiating the **Gregorian calendar**.

The Gregorian calendar perpetuated a chronological system devised by the monk Dionysius Exiguus (fl. 6th cent.). His chronology started with the first year following the birth of Jesus Christ, which he inaccurately took to be year 753 in the Roman calendar. Leap years were continued but, to prevent further displacements, centesimal years (years ending in 00) were made common years, not leap years, unless divisible by 400. Under this plan, 1600 and 2000 were leap years; 1700, 1800, and 1900 were not.

The Gregorian calendar was adopted at once by France, Italy, Spain, Portugal, and Luxembourg. Within two years, most German Catholic states, Belgium, and parts of Switzerland and the Netherlands were brought under the new calendar, and Hungary followed in 1587. The rest of the Netherlands, along with Denmark and the German Protestant states, made the change in 1699-1700.

The British government adopted the Gregorian calendar and imposed it on all its possessions, including the American colonies, in 1752, decreeing that the day following Sept. 2, 1752, should be called Sept. 14, a loss of 11 days. All dates preceding were marked OS, for Old Style. In addition, New Year's Day was moved to Jan. 1 from Mar. 25. (Under the old reckoning, for example, Mar. 24, 1700, was followed by Mar. 25, 1701.) Thus George Washington's birth date, which was Feb. 11, 1731, OS, became Feb. 22, 1732, NS (New Style). In 1753, Sweden also went Gregorian.

In 1793, the French revolutionary government adopted a calendar of 12 months of 30 days each with five extra days in Sept. of each common year and six extra days every fourth year. Napoleon reinstated the Gregorian calendar in 1806.

The Gregorian system later spread to non-European regions, replacing traditional calendars at least for official purposes. Japan in 1873, Egypt in 1875, China in 1912, and Turkey in 1925 made the change, usually in conjunction with political upheaval. In China, the republican government began reckoning years from its 1911 founding. After 1949, the People's Republic adopted the Common (or Christian) Era year count, even for the traditional lunar calendar, which it retained. In 1918, the Soviet Union decreed that the day after Jan. 31, 1918, OS, would be Feb. 14, 1918, NS. Greece changed over in 1923. The Russian Orthodox church and some other Christian sects retained the Julian calendar. Saudi Arabia switched to the Gregorian calendar in 2016.

As of 2020, several nations officially used non-Gregorian calendars. Ethiopia used a calendar similar to the Julian system, and Afghanistan and Iran used the traditional Persian, or Solar Hijri, calendar.

To convert from the Julian to the Gregorian calendar, add 10 days to dates Oct. 5, 1582, through Feb. 28, 1700; after that date, add 11 days through Feb. 28, 1800; 12 days through Feb. 28, 1900; and 13 days through Feb. 28, 2100.

A **century** consists of 100 consecutive years. The 1st century CE may be said to have run from the years 1 through 100. The 20th century by this reckoning consisted of the years 1901 through 2000 and ended Dec. 31, 2000, as did the 2nd millennium CE. The 21st century thus technically began on Jan. 1, 2001.

For a **perpetual calendar**, see pages 390-91.

Gregorian Calendar

Choose the desired year from the table below or from the perpetual calendar (for years 1803 to 2080). The number after each year designates which calendar to use for that year, as shown in the perpetual calendar. (The Gregorian calendar was inaugurated Oct. 15, 1582. From that date through Dec. 31, 1582, use calendar 6.)

1583-1802

1583	7	1603	4	1623	1	1643	5	1663	2	1683	6	1703	2	1723	6	1743	3	1763	7	1783	4
1584	8	1604	12	1624	9	1644	13	1664	10	1684	14	1704	10	1724	14	1744	11	1764	8	1784	12
1585	3	1605	7	1625	4	1645	1	1665	5	1685	2	1705	5	1725	2	1745	6	1765	3	1785	7
1586	4	1606	1	1626	5	1646	2	1666	6	1686	3	1706	6	1726	3	1746	7	1766	4	1786	1
1587	5	1607	2	1627	6	1647	3	1667	7	1687	4	1707	7	1727	4	1747	1	1767	5	1787	2
1588	13	1608	10	1628	14	1648	11	1668	8	1688	12	1708	8	1728	12	1748	9	1768	13	1788	10
1589	1	1609	5	1629	2	1649	6	1669	3	1689	7	1709	3	1729	7	1749	4	1769	1	1789	5
1590	2	1610	6	1630	3	1650	7	1670	4	1690	1	1710	4	1730	1	1750	5	1770	2	1790	6
1591	3	1611	7	1631	4	1651	1	1671	5	1691	2	1711	5	1731	2	1751	6	1771	3	1791	7
1592	11	1612	8	1632	12	1652	9	1672	13	1692	10	1712	13	1732	10	1752	14	1772	11	1792	8
1593	6	1613	3	1633	7	1653	4	1673	1	1693	5	1713	1	1733	5	1753	2	1773	6	1793	3
1594	7	1614	4	1634	1	1654	5	1674	2	1694	6	1714	2	1734	6	1754	3	1774	7	1794	4
1595	1	1615	5	1635	2	1655	6	1675	3	1695	7	1715	3	1735	7	1755	4	1775	1	1795	5
1596	9	1616	13	1636	10	1656	14	1676	11	1696	8	1716	11	1736	8	1756	12	1776	9	1796	13
1597	4	1617	1	1637	5	1657	2	1677	6	1697	3	1717	6	1737	3	1757	7	1777	4	1797	1
1598	5	1618	2	1638	6	1658	3	1678	7	1698	4	1718	7	1738	4	1758	1	1778	5	1798	2
1599	6	1619	3	1639	7	1659	4	1679	1	1699	5	1719	1	1739	5	1759	2	1779	6	1799	3
1600	14	1620	11	1640	8	1660	12	1680	9	1700	6	1720	9	1740	13	1760	10	1780	14	1800	4
1601	2	1621	6	1641	3	1661	7	1681	4	1701	7	1721	4	1741	1	1761	5	1781	2	1801	5
1602	3	1622	7	1642	4	1662	1	1682	5	1702	1	1722	5	1742	2	1762	6	1782	3	1802	6

Julian Period

How many days have you lived? To determine this, multiply your age by 365, add the number of days since your last birthday, and account for all leap years. Chances are your calculations will go wrong somewhere. Astronomers, however, find it convenient to express dates and time intervals in days rather than in years, months, and days. This is done by placing events within the Julian period.

The Julian period was devised in 1582 by the French classical scholar Joseph Scaliger (1540-1609). Some sources postulate Scaliger named it after his father, Julius Caesar Scaliger; others cite Scaliger's references to the Julian calendar.

Scaliger began with a zero hour, or starting time, of noon on Jan. 1, 4713 BCE (on the Julian calendar). This was the most recent time that three major chronological cycles began on the same day: (1) the 28-year solar cycle, after which dates in the Julian calendar return to the same days of the week (e.g., Feb. 11 falls on a Monday); (2) the 19-year lunar cycle, after which the phases of the moon return to the same dates of the year; and (3) the 15-year indiction cycle, used in ancient Rome to regulate taxes.

It will take 7,980 years to complete the period, the product of the numbers 28, 19, and 15, which have no common factors.

Noon (Universal Time) of Jan. 1, 2021, will be Julian date (JD) 2,459,216; that many days will have passed since the start of the current Julian period. To find the JD at noon of any date in 2021 may be found by adding to that number the day of the year for that date and subtracting one.

Julian Calendar

To find which of the 14 calendars of the perpetual calendar (pages 390-91) applies to any year under the Julian system, find the century for the desired year in the three leftmost columns below. Locate the desired year from among the four top rows. The number at the intersection of that row and column is the calendar designation for that year. For some years and countries, the Julian new year did not start Jan. 1; to find the correct perpetual calendar for Britain and its possessions, you can generally add one year for dates from Jan. 1 to Mar. 24. For example, to look up Feb. 2, 1705, Old Style, use the year 1706.

Year (last 2 digits of desired year)

		01	02	03	04	05	06	07	08	09	10	11	12	13	14	15	16	17	18	19	20	21	22	23	24	25	26	27	28
		29	30	31	32	33	34	35	36	37	38	39	40	41	42	43	44	45	46	47	48	49	50	51	52	53	54	55	56
		57	58	59	60	61	62	63	64	65	66	67	68	69	70	71	72	73	74	75	76	77	78	79	80	81	82	83	84
Century	00	85	86	87	88	89	90	91	92	93	94	95	96	97	98	99													
0 700 1400	12	7	1	2	10	5	6	7	8	3	4	5	13	1	2	3	11	6	7	1	9	4	5	6	14	2	3	4	12
100 800 1500	11	6	7	1	9	4	5	6	14	2	3	4	12	7	1	2	10	5	6	7	8	3	4	5	13	1	2	3	11
200 900 1600	10	5	6	7	8	3	4	5	13	1	2	3	11	6	7	1	9	4	5	6	14	2	3	4	12	7	1	2	10
300 1000 1700	9	4	5	6	14	2	3	4	12	7	1	2	10	5	6	7	8	3	4	5	13	1	2	3	11	6	7	1	9
400 1100 1800	8	3	4	5	13	1	2	3	11	6	7	1	9	4	5	6	14	2	3	4	12	7	1	2	10	5	6	7	8
500 1200 1900	14	2	3	4	12	7	1	2	10	5	6	7	8	3	4	5	13	1	2	3	11	6	7	1	9	4	5	6	14
600 1300 2000	13	1	2	3	11	6	7	1	9	4	5	6	14	2	3	4	12	7	1	2	10	5	6	7	8	3	4	5	13

Signs of the Zodiac

The zodiac is the apparent yearly path of the sun among the stars as viewed from Earth and was divided by the ancients into 12 equal sections or signs, each named for the constellation situated within its limits in ancient times. Astrologers claim that the temperament and destiny of each individual depend on the zodiac sign under which the person was born and the relationships between the planets at that time and throughout the person's life.

Below are the 12 traditional signs and the traditional range of dates pertaining to each:

♈ **Aries** (Ram), March 21-April 19

♉ **Taurus** (Bull), April 20-May 20

♊ **Gemini** (Twins), May 21-June 21

♋ **Cancer** (Crab), June 22-July 22

♌ **Leo** (Lion), July 23-August 22

♍ **Virgo** (Virgin), August 23-September 22

♎ **Libra** (Scales), September 23-October 23

♏ **Scorpio** (Scorpion), October 24-November 21

♐ **Sagittarius** (Archer), November 22-December 21

♑ **Capricorn** (Goat), December 22-January 19

♒ **Aquarius** (Water Bearer), January 20-February 18

♓ **Pisces** (Fishes), February 19-March 20

Chinese Calendar and Asian Festivals

The Chinese calendar, like the Jewish and Islamic calendars (see the Religion chapter), is a lunisolar calendar. It is divided into 12 months of 29 or 30 days (compensating for the lunar month's mean duration of 29 days, 12 hr., 44.05 min.). This calendar is synchronized with the solar year by the addition of extra months at fixed intervals.

The Chinese calendar runs on a 60-year cycle. The last 36 years of the cycle 1876-1935 along with the cycles 1936-95 and 1996-2055 are shown below grouped by their association with 1 of 12 animals in the Chinese zodiac. Feb. 12, 2021, marks the beginning of the year 4719 in the Chinese calendar and is designated the Year of the Ox.

Both the Western (Gregorian) and traditional lunar calendars are used publicly in China and in North and South Korea, and two New Year's celebrations are held. In Taiwan and Vietnam and in overseas Chinese communities, the lunar calendar is used only to set the dates for traditional festivals, with the Gregorian system in general use.

The 4-day Chinese New Year; the 3-day Vietnamese New Year festival, Tet; and the 3-to-4-day Korean festival, Suhl, begin at the second new moon after the winter solstice. The new moon in East Asia, which is west of the international date line, may be a day later than the new moon in the U.S. The festivals may start, therefore, anywhere between Jan. 21 and Feb. 19 of the Gregorian calendar.

Rat	Ox	Tiger	Hare (Rabbit)	Dragon	Snake	Horse	Sheep (Goat)	Monkey	Rooster	Dog	Pig (Boar)
1900	1901	1902	1903	1904	1905	1906	1907	1908	1909	1910	1911
1912	1913	1914	1915	1916	1917	1918	1919	1920	1921	1922	1923
1924	1925	1926	1927	1928	1929	1930	1931	1932	1933	1934	1935
1936	1937	1938	1939	1940	1941	1942	1943	1944	1945	1946	1947
1948	1949	1950	1951	1952	1953	1954	1955	1956	1957	1958	1959
1960	1961	1962	1963	1964	1965	1966	1967	1968	1969	1970	1971
1972	1973	1974	1975	1976	1977	1978	1979	1980	1981	1982	1983
1984	1985	1986	1987	1988	1989	1990	1991	1992	1993	1994	1995
1996	1997	1998	1999	2000	2001	2002	2003	2004	2005	2006	2007
2008	2009	2010	2011	2012	2013	2014	2015	2016	2017	2018	2019
2020	2021	2022	2023	2024	2025	2026	2027	2028	2029	2030	2031
2032	2033	2034	2035	2036	2037	2038	2039	2040	2041	2042	2043
2044	2045	2046	2047	2048	2049	2050	2051	2052	2053	2054	2055

Note: The first 3-7 weeks of each Western year belong to the previous Chinese year.

Calendar for the Year 2021

January

S	M	T	W	T	F	S
					1	2
3	4	5	6	7	8	9
10	11	12	13	14	15	16
17	18	19	20	21	22	23
24	25	26	27	28	29	30
31						

February

S	M	T	W	T	F	S
	1	2	3	4	5	6
7	8	9	10	11	12	13
14	15	16	17	18	19	20
21	22	23	24	25	26	27
28						

March

S	M	T	W	T	F	S
	1	2	3	4	5	6
7	8	9	10	11	12	13
14	15	16	17	18	19	20
21	22	23	24	25	26	27
28	29	30	31			

April

S	M	T	W	T	F	S
				1	2	3
4	5	6	7	8	9	10
11	12	13	14	15	16	17
18	19	20	21	22	23	24
25	26	27	28	29	30	

May

S	M	T	W	T	F	S
						1
2	3	4	5	6	7	8
9	10	11	12	13	14	15
16	17	18	19	20	21	22
23	24	25	26	27	28	29
30	31					

June

S	M	T	W	T	F	S
		1	2	3	4	5
6	7	8	9	10	11	12
13	14	15	16	17	18	19
20	21	22	23	24	25	26
27	28	29	30			

July

S	M	T	W	T	F	S
				1	2	3
4	5	6	7	8	9	10
11	12	13	14	15	16	17
18	19	20	21	22	23	24
25	26	27	28	29	30	31

August

S	M	T	W	T	F	S
1	2	3	4	5	6	7
8	9	10	11	12	13	14
15	16	17	18	19	20	21
22	23	24	25	26	27	28
29	30	31				

September

S	M	T	W	T	F	S
			1	2	3	4
5	6	7	8	9	10	11
12	13	14	15	16	17	18
19	20	21	22	23	24	25
26	27	28	29	30		

October

S	M	T	W	T	F	S
					1	2
3	4	5	6	7	8	9
10	11	12	13	14	15	16
17	18	19	20	21	22	23
24	25	26	27	28	29	30
31						

November

S	M	T	W	T	F	S
	1	2	3	4	5	6
7	8	9	10	11	12	13
14	15	16	17	18	19	20
21	22	23	24	25	26	27
28	29	30				

December

S	M	T	W	T	F	S
			1	2	3	4
5	6	7	8	9	10	11
12	13	14	15	16	17	18
19	20	21	22	23	24	25
26	27	28	29	30	31	

Federal Holidays and Other Notable Dates, 2021

Some dates may be subject to change, particularly for those events affected by the COVID-19 pandemic.

The dates in bold in the calendar above and named below in italics are U.S. federal holidays, designated by the president or Congress and applicable to federal employees and in the District of Columbia. Most U.S. states also observe these holidays, and many states observe others; practices vary by state. In most states the secretary of state's office can provide details.

January

1 *New Year's Day*; Rose Bowl; Sugar Bowl
2 Orange Bowl
11 College Football Playoff national championship game (Miami Gardens, FL)
18 *Martin Luther King Jr. Day*
18-31 Australian Open tennis tournament
26 Australia Day (observed)
31 NFL Pro Bowl (Las Vegas, NV)

February

2 Groundhog Day
7 Super Bowl LV (Tampa, FL)
12 Chinese New Year; Lincoln's Birthday
12-17 Carnival, Brazil
14 Valentine's Day; NBA All-Star Game (Indianapolis, IN); Daytona 500
15 *Washington's Birthday* (observed), a.k.a. Presidents' Day, or Washington-Lincoln Day (3rd Mon. in Feb.)
15-16 Westminster Dog Show
16 Mardi Gras
17 Ash Wednesday
26 Purim (Feast of Lots) begins previous night

March

6 Iditarod Trail Sled Dog Race begins
14 Daylight saving time begins in U.S.
15 Benito Juárez's Birthday, Mexico
17 St. Patrick's Day
20 First day of spring (Northern Hemisphere)
28 Passover, 1st full day

April

1 April Fools' Day
2 Good Friday
2, 4 NCAA Women's Basketball Final Four (San Antonio, TX)
3, 5 NCAA Men's Basketball Final Four (Indianapolis, IN)
4 Easter
5-11 Masters golf tournament
13 Ramadan (Islamic month of fasting), 1st full day
15 Tax Day (IRS filing deadline)
19 Patriots' Day; Boston Marathon (3rd Mon. in Apr.)
22 Earth Day; Take Our Daughters and Sons to Work Day
25 Academy Awards
30 Arbor Day

May

1 May Day (International Workers' Day); Kentucky Derby
2 Easter (Orthodox)
5 Cinco de Mayo (Battle of Puebla Day), Mexico
9 Mother's Day
15 Armed Forces Day; Preakness Stakes
17-23 PGA Championship (Kiawah Island, SC)
19 Buddha's Birthday, Hong Kong, Korea
23-June 6 French Open tennis tournament
24 Victoria Day, Canada
31 *Memorial Day*, or Decoration Day (last Mon. in May)

June

3-6 U.S. Women's Open golf tournament (San Francisco, CA)
5 Belmont Stakes
14 Flag Day; Dragon Boat Festival, China
17-20 U.S. Open golf tournament (San Diego, CA)
20 Father's Day; First day of summer (Northern Hemisphere)
28-July 11 Wimbledon tennis tournament

July

1 Canada Day
4 *Independence Day*
5 Independence Day (federal holiday observed)
7-14 Running of the Bulls (Pamplona, Spain)
14 Bastille Day, France
15-18 British Open golf tournament (Kent, England, UK)
23-Aug. 8 Summer Olympic Games (Tokyo, Japan; rescheduled from 2020)

August

9 Islamic New Year (Muharram 1) begins previous night

September

6 *Labor Day*, U.S., Canada (1st Mon. in Sept.)
7 Rosh Hashanah (New Year), 1st full day
12 Grandparents' Day, U.S.
16 Independence Day, Mexico (celebration begins previous night); Yom Kippur (Day of Atonement) begins previous night
17 Constitution Day and Citizenship Day, U.S.
22 First day of autumn (Northern Hemisphere)

October

3 German Unity Day, Germany
4 U.S. Supreme Court session begins
11 *Columbus Day* (2nd Mon. in Oct.); Thanksgiving Day, Canada
12 Día de la Raza, Spain, Mexico
31 Halloween

November

1 All Saints' Day
2 Election Day (1st Tues. after 1st Mon. in Nov.)
7 Daylight saving time ends in U.S.; New York City Marathon
11 *Veterans' Day*; Remembrance Day, Canada
14 Remembrance Sunday, UK
25 *Thanksgiving Day*
29-Dec. 6 Hanukkah (Festival of Lights) begins previous night

December

10 Nobel Prizes awarded (winners announced in Oct.)
12 Día de la Virgen de Guadalupe, Mexico
21 First day of winter (Northern Hemisphere)
24 Christmas (federal holiday observed)
25 *Christmas Day*
26 Boxing Day, Australia, Canada, New Zealand, UK
26-Jan. 1 Kwanzaa
31 Cotton Bowl; Orange Bowl

Perpetual Calendar

The number shown for each year indicates which Gregorian calendar to use. For 1583-1802, see "Gregorian Calendar" on page 387. For 1803-20, use numbers for 1983-2000, respectively. The years in the calendar labels are the last and next occurrences of each calendar.

Calendar 1 — 2017/2023: JANUARY, FEBRUARY, MARCH, APRIL, MAY, JUNE, JULY, AUGUST, SEPTEMBER, OCTOBER, NOVEMBER, DECEMBER (columns S M T W T F S)

Calendar 2 — 2018/2029: JANUARY, FEBRUARY, MARCH, APRIL, MAY, JUNE, JULY, AUGUST, SEPTEMBER, OCTOBER, NOVEMBER, DECEMBER (columns S M T W T F S)

Calendar 3 — 2019/2030: JANUARY, FEBRUARY, MARCH, APRIL, MAY, JUNE, JULY, AUGUST, SEPTEMBER, OCTOBER, NOVEMBER, DECEMBER (columns S M T W T F S)

Calendar 4 — 2014/2025: JANUARY, FEBRUARY, MARCH, APRIL, MAY, JUNE, JULY, AUGUST, SEPTEMBER, OCTOBER, NOVEMBER, DECEMBER (columns S M T W T F S)

Calendar 5 — 2015/2026: JANUARY, FEBRUARY, MARCH, APRIL, MAY, JUNE, JULY, AUGUST, SEPTEMBER, OCTOBER, NOVEMBER, DECEMBER (columns S M T W T F S)

Calendar 6 — 2010/2021: JANUARY, FEBRUARY, MARCH, APRIL, MAY, JUNE, JULY, AUGUST, SEPTEMBER, OCTOBER, NOVEMBER, DECEMBER (columns S M T W T F S)

7 2011/2022

JANUARY

S	M	T	W	T	F	S
						1
2	3	4	5	6	7	8
9	10	11	12	13	14	15
16	17	18	19	20	21	22
23	24	25	26	27	28	29
30	31					

FEBRUARY

S	M	T	W	T	F	S
		1	2	3	4	5
6	7	8	9	10	11	12
13	14	15	16	17	18	19
20	21	22	23	24	25	26
27	28					

MARCH

S	M	T	W	T	F	S
		1	2	3	4	5
6	7	8	9	10	11	12
13	14	15	16	17	18	19
20	21	22	23	24	25	26
27	28	29	30	31		

APRIL

S	M	T	W	T	F	S
					1	2
3	4	5	6	7	8	9
10	11	12	13	14	15	16
17	18	19	20	21	22	23
24	25	26	27	28	29	30

MAY

S	M	T	W	T	F	S
1	2	3	4	5	6	7
8	9	10	11	12	13	14
15	16	17	18	19	20	21
22	23	24	25	26	27	28
29	30	31				

JUNE

S	M	T	W	T	F	S
			1	2	3	4
5	6	7	8	9	10	11
12	13	14	15	16	17	18
19	20	21	22	23	24	25
26	27	28	29	30		

JULY

S	M	T	W	T	F	S
					1	2
3	4	5	6	7	8	9
10	11	12	13	14	15	16
17	18	19	20	21	22	23
24	25	26	27	28	29	30
31						

AUGUST

S	M	T	W	T	F	S
	1	2	3	4	5	6
7	8	9	10	11	12	13
14	15	16	17	18	19	20
21	22	23	24	25	26	27
28	29	30	31			

SEPTEMBER

S	M	T	W	T	F	S
				1	2	3
4	5	6	7	8	9	10
11	12	13	14	15	16	17
18	19	20	21	22	23	24
25	26	27	28	29	30	

OCTOBER

S	M	T	W	T	F	S
						1
2	3	4	5	6	7	8
9	10	11	12	13	14	15
16	17	18	19	20	21	22
23	24	25	26	27	28	29
30	31					

NOVEMBER

S	M	T	W	T	F	S
		1	2	3	4	5
6	7	8	9	10	11	12
13	14	15	16	17	18	19
20	21	22	23	24	25	26
27	28	29	30			

DECEMBER

S	M	T	W	T	F	S
				1	2	3
4	5	6	7	8	9	10
11	12	13	14	15	16	17
18	19	20	21	22	23	24
25	26	27	28	29	30	31

8 2012/2040

JANUARY

S	M	T	W	T	F	S
1	2	3	4	5	6	7
8	9	10	11	12	13	14
15	16	17	18	19	20	21
22	23	24	25	26	27	28
29	30	31				

FEBRUARY

S	M	T	W	T	F	S
			1	2	3	4
5	6	7	8	9	10	11
12	13	14	15	16	17	18
19	20	21	22	23	24	25
26	27	28	29			

MARCH

S	M	T	W	T	F	S
				1	2	3
4	5	6	7	8	9	10
11	12	13	14	15	16	17
18	19	20	21	22	23	24
25	26	27	28	29	30	31

APRIL

S	M	T	W	T	F	S
1	2	3	4	5	6	7
8	9	10	11	12	13	14
15	16	17	18	19	20	21
22	23	24	25	26	27	28
29	30					

MAY

S	M	T	W	T	F	S
		1	2	3	4	5
6	7	8	9	10	11	12
13	14	15	16	17	18	19
20	21	22	23	24	25	26
27	28	29	30	31		

JUNE

S	M	T	W	T	F	S
					1	2
3	4	5	6	7	8	9
10	11	12	13	14	15	16
17	18	19	20	21	22	23
24	25	26	27	28	29	30

JULY

S	M	T	W	T	F	S
1	2	3	4	5	6	7
8	9	10	11	12	13	14
15	16	17	18	19	20	21
22	23	24	25	26	27	28
29	30	31				

AUGUST

S	M	T	W	T	F	S
			1	2	3	4
5	6	7	8	9	10	11
12	13	14	15	16	17	18
19	20	21	22	23	24	25
26	27	28	29	30	31	

SEPTEMBER

S	M	T	W	T	F	S
						1
2	3	4	5	6	7	8
9	10	11	12	13	14	15
16	17	18	19	20	21	22
23	24	25	26	27	28	29
30						

OCTOBER

S	M	T	W	T	F	S
	1	2	3	4	5	6
7	8	9	10	11	12	13
14	15	16	17	18	19	20
21	22	23	24	25	26	27
28	29	30	31			

NOVEMBER

S	M	T	W	T	F	S
				1	2	3
4	5	6	7	8	9	10
11	12	13	14	15	16	17
18	19	20	21	22	23	24
25	26	27	28	29	30	

DECEMBER

S	M	T	W	T	F	S
						1
2	3	4	5	6	7	8
9	10	11	12	13	14	15
16	17	18	19	20	21	22
23	24	25	26	27	28	29
30	31					

9 1996/2024

JANUARY

S	M	T	W	T	F	S
	1	2	3	4	5	6
7	8	9	10	11	12	13
14	15	16	17	18	19	20
21	22	23	24	25	26	27
28	29	30	31			

FEBRUARY

S	M	T	W	T	F	S
				1	2	3
4	5	6	7	8	9	10
11	12	13	14	15	16	17
18	19	20	21	22	23	24
25	26	27	28	29		

MARCH

S	M	T	W	T	F	S
					1	2
3	4	5	6	7	8	9
10	11	12	13	14	15	16
17	18	19	20	21	22	23
24	25	26	27	28	29	30
31						

APRIL

S	M	T	W	T	F	S
	1	2	3	4	5	6
7	8	9	10	11	12	13
14	15	16	17	18	19	20
21	22	23	24	25	26	27
28	29	30				

MAY

S	M	T	W	T	F	S
			1	2	3	4
5	6	7	8	9	10	11
12	13	14	15	16	17	18
19	20	21	22	23	24	25
26	27	28	29	30	31	

JUNE

S	M	T	W	T	F	S
						1
2	3	4	5	6	7	8
9	10	11	12	13	14	15
16	17	18	19	20	21	22
23	24	25	26	27	28	29
30						

JULY

S	M	T	W	T	F	S
	1	2	3	4	5	6
7	8	9	10	11	12	13
14	15	16	17	18	19	20
21	22	23	24	25	26	27
28	29	30	31			

AUGUST

S	M	T	W	T	F	S
				1	2	3
4	5	6	7	8	9	10
11	12	13	14	15	16	17
18	19	20	21	22	23	24
25	26	27	28	29	30	31

SEPTEMBER

S	M	T	W	T	F	S
1	2	3	4	5	6	7
8	9	10	11	12	13	14
15	16	17	18	19	20	21
22	23	24	25	26	27	28
29	30					

OCTOBER

S	M	T	W	T	F	S
		1	2	3	4	5
6	7	8	9	10	11	12
13	14	15	16	17	18	19
20	21	22	23	24	25	26
27	28	29	30	31		

NOVEMBER

S	M	T	W	T	F	S
					1	2
3	4	5	6	7	8	9
10	11	12	13	14	15	16
17	18	19	20	21	22	23
24	25	26	27	28	29	30

DECEMBER

S	M	T	W	T	F	S
1	2	3	4	5	6	7
8	9	10	11	12	13	14
15	16	17	18	19	20	21
22	23	24	25	26	27	28
29	30	31				

10 2008/2036

JANUARY

S	M	T	W	T	F	S
		1	2	3	4	5
6	7	8	9	10	11	12
13	14	15	16	17	18	19
20	21	22	23	24	25	26
27	28	29	30	31		

FEBRUARY

S	M	T	W	T	F	S
					1	2
3	4	5	6	7	8	9
10	11	12	13	14	15	16
17	18	19	20	21	22	23
24	25	26	27	28	29	

MARCH

S	M	T	W	T	F	S
						1
2	3	4	5	6	7	8
9	10	11	12	13	14	15
16	17	18	19	20	21	22
23	24	25	26	27	28	29
30	31					

APRIL

S	M	T	W	T	F	S
		1	2	3	4	5
6	7	8	9	10	11	12
13	14	15	16	17	18	19
20	21	22	23	24	25	26
27	28	29	30			

MAY

S	M	T	W	T	F	S
				1	2	3
4	5	6	7	8	9	10
11	12	13	14	15	16	17
18	19	20	21	22	23	24
25	26	27	28	29	30	31

JUNE

S	M	T	W	T	F	S
1	2	3	4	5	6	7
8	9	10	11	12	13	14
15	16	17	18	19	20	21
22	23	24	25	26	27	28
29	30					

JULY

S	M	T	W	T	F	S
		1	2	3	4	5
6	7	8	9	10	11	12
13	14	15	16	17	18	19
20	21	22	23	24	25	26
27	28	29	30	31		

AUGUST

S	M	T	W	T	F	S
					1	2
3	4	5	6	7	8	9
10	11	12	13	14	15	16
17	18	19	20	21	22	23
24	25	26	27	28	29	30
31						

SEPTEMBER

S	M	T	W	T	F	S
	1	2	3	4	5	6
7	8	9	10	11	12	13
14	15	16	17	18	19	20
21	22	23	24	25	26	27
28	29	30				

OCTOBER

S	M	T	W	T	F	S
			1	2	3	4
5	6	7	8	9	10	11
12	13	14	15	16	17	18
19	20	21	22	23	24	25
26	27	28	29	30	31	

NOVEMBER

S	M	T	W	T	F	S
						1
2	3	4	5	6	7	8
9	10	11	12	13	14	15
16	17	18	19	20	21	22
23	24	25	26	27	28	29
30						

DECEMBER

S	M	T	W	T	F	S
	1	2	3	4	5	6
7	8	9	10	11	12	13
14	15	16	17	18	19	20
21	22	23	24	25	26	27
28	29	30	31			

11 2020/2048

JANUARY

S	M	T	W	T	F	S
			1	2	3	4
5	6	7	8	9	10	11
12	13	14	15	16	17	18
19	20	21	22	23	24	25
26	27	28	29	30	31	

FEBRUARY

S	M	T	W	T	F	S
						1
2	3	4	5	6	7	8
9	10	11	12	13	14	15
16	17	18	19	20	21	22
23	24	25	26	27	28	29

MARCH

S	M	T	W	T	F	S
1	2	3	4	5	6	7
8	9	10	11	12	13	14
15	16	17	18	19	20	21
22	23	24	25	26	27	28
29	30	31				

APRIL

S	M	T	W	T	F	S
			1	2	3	4
5	6	7	8	9	10	11
12	13	14	15	16	17	18
19	20	21	22	23	24	25
26	27	28	29	30		

MAY

S	M	T	W	T	F	S
					1	2
3	4	5	6	7	8	9
10	11	12	13	14	15	16
17	18	19	20	21	22	23
24	25	26	27	28	29	30
31						

JUNE

S	M	T	W	T	F	S
	1	2	3	4	5	6
7	8	9	10	11	12	13
14	15	16	17	18	19	20
21	22	23	24	25	26	27
28	29	30				

JULY

S	M	T	W	T	F	S
			1	2	3	4
5	6	7	8	9	10	11
12	13	14	15	16	17	18
19	20	21	22	23	24	25
26	27	28	29	30	31	

AUGUST

S	M	T	W	T	F	S
						1
2	3	4	5	6	7	8
9	10	11	12	13	14	15
16	17	18	19	20	21	22
23	24	25	26	27	28	29
30	31					

SEPTEMBER

S	M	T	W	T	F	S
		1	2	3	4	5
6	7	8	9	10	11	12
13	14	15	16	17	18	19
20	21	22	23	24	25	26
27	28	29	30			

OCTOBER

S	M	T	W	T	F	S
				1	2	3
4	5	6	7	8	9	10
11	12	13	14	15	16	17
18	19	20	21	22	23	24
25	26	27	28	29	30	31

NOVEMBER

S	M	T	W	T	F	S
1	2	3	4	5	6	7
8	9	10	11	12	13	14
15	16	17	18	19	20	21
22	23	24	25	26	27	28
29	30					

DECEMBER

S	M	T	W	T	F	S
		1	2	3	4	5
6	7	8	9	10	11	12
13	14	15	16	17	18	19
20	21	22	23	24	25	26
27	28	29	30	31		

12 2004/2032

JANUARY

S	M	T	W	T	F	S
				1	2	3
4	5	6	7	8	9	10
11	12	13	14	15	16	17
18	19	20	21	22	23	24
25	26	27	28	29	30	31

FEBRUARY

S	M	T	W	T	F	S
1	2	3	4	5	6	7
8	9	10	11	12	13	14
15	16	17	18	19	20	21
22	23	24	25	26	27	28
29						

MARCH

S	M	T	W	T	F	S
	1	2	3	4	5	6
7	8	9	10	11	12	13
14	15	16	17	18	19	20
21	22	23	24	25	26	27
28	29	30	31			

APRIL

S	M	T	W	T	F	S
				1	2	3
4	5	6	7	8	9	10
11	12	13	14	15	16	17
18	19	20	21	22	23	24
25	26	27	28	29	30	

MAY

S	M	T	W	T	F	S
						1
2	3	4	5	6	7	8
9	10	11	12	13	14	15
16	17	18	19	20	21	22
23	24	25	26	27	28	29
30	31					

JUNE

S	M	T	W	T	F	S
		1	2	3	4	5
6	7	8	9	10	11	12
13	14	15	16	17	18	19
20	21	22	23	24	25	26
27	28	29	30			

JULY

S	M	T	W	T	F	S
				1	2	3
4	5	6	7	8	9	10
11	12	13	14	15	16	17
18	19	20	21	22	23	24
25	26	27	28	29	30	31

AUGUST

S	M	T	W	T	F	S
1	2	3	4	5	6	7
8	9	10	11	12	13	14
15	16	17	18	19	20	21
22	23	24	25	26	27	28
29	30	31				

SEPTEMBER

S	M	T	W	T	F	S
			1	2	3	4
5	6	7	8	9	10	11
12	13	14	15	16	17	18
19	20	21	22	23	24	25
26	27	28	29	30		

OCTOBER

S	M	T	W	T	F	S
					1	2
3	4	5	6	7	8	9
10	11	12	13	14	15	16
17	18	19	20	21	22	23
24	25	26	27	28	29	30
31						

NOVEMBER

S	M	T	W	T	F	S
	1	2	3	4	5	6
7	8	9	10	11	12	13
14	15	16	17	18	19	20
21	22	23	24	25	26	27
28	29	30				

DECEMBER

S	M	T	W	T	F	S
			1	2	3	4
5	6	7	8	9	10	11
12	13	14	15	16	17	18
19	20	21	22	23	24	25
26	27	28	29	30	31	

13 2016/2044

JANUARY

S	M	T	W	T	F	S
					1	2
3	4	5	6	7	8	9
10	11	12	13	14	15	16
17	18	19	20	21	22	23
24	25	26	27	28	29	30
31						

FEBRUARY

S	M	T	W	T	F	S
	1	2	3	4	5	6
7	8	9	10	11	12	13
14	15	16	17	18	19	20
21	22	23	24	25	26	27
28	29					

MARCH

S	M	T	W	T	F	S
		1	2	3	4	5
6	7	8	9	10	11	12
13	14	15	16	17	18	19
20	21	22	23	24	25	26
27	28	29	30	31		

APRIL

S	M	T	W	T	F	S
					1	2
3	4	5	6	7	8	9
10	11	12	13	14	15	16
17	18	19	20	21	22	23
24	25	26	27	28	29	30

MAY

S	M	T	W	T	F	S
1	2	3	4	5	6	7
8	9	10	11	12	13	14
15	16	17	18	19	20	21
22	23	24	25	26	27	28
29	30	31				

JUNE

S	M	T	W	T	F	S
			1	2	3	4
5	6	7	8	9	10	11
12	13	14	15	16	17	18
19	20	21	22	23	24	25
26	27	28	29	30		

JULY

S	M	T	W	T	F	S
					1	2
3	4	5	6	7	8	9
10	11	12	13	14	15	16
17	18	19	20	21	22	23
24	25	26	27	28	29	30
31						

AUGUST

S	M	T	W	T	F	S
	1	2	3	4	5	6
7	8	9	10	11	12	13
14	15	16	17	18	19	20
21	22	23	24	25	26	27
28	29	30	31			

SEPTEMBER

S	M	T	W	T	F	S
				1	2	3
4	5	6	7	8	9	10
11	12	13	14	15	16	17
18	19	20	21	22	23	24
25	26	27	28	29	30	

OCTOBER

S	M	T	W	T	F	S
						1
2	3	4	5	6	7	8
9	10	11	12	13	14	15
16	17	18	19	20	21	22
23	24	25	26	27	28	29
30	31					

NOVEMBER

S	M	T	W	T	F	S
		1	2	3	4	5
6	7	8	9	10	11	12
13	14	15	16	17	18	19
20	21	22	23	24	25	26
27	28	29	30			

DECEMBER

S	M	T	W	T	F	S
				1	2	3
4	5	6	7	8	9	10
11	12	13	14	15	16	17
18	19	20	21	22	23	24
25	26	27	28	29	30	31

14 2000/2028

JANUARY

S	M	T	W	T	F	S
						1
2	3	4	5	6	7	8
9	10	11	12	13	14	15
16	17	18	19	20	21	22
23	24	25	26	27	28	29
30	31					

FEBRUARY

S	M	T	W	T	F	S
		1	2	3	4	5
6	7	8	9	10	11	12
13	14	15	16	17	18	19
20	21	22	23	24	25	26
27	28	29				

MARCH

S	M	T	W	T	F	S
			1	2	3	4
5	6	7	8	9	10	11
12	13	14	15	16	17	18
19	20	21	22	23	24	25
26	27	28	29	30	31	

APRIL

S	M	T	W	T	F	S
						1
2	3	4	5	6	7	8
9	10	11	12	13	14	15
16	17	18	19	20	21	22
23	24	25	26	27	28	29
30						

MAY

S	M	T	W	T	F	S
	1	2	3	4	5	6
7	8	9	10	11	12	13
14	15	16	17	18	19	20
21	22	23	24	25	26	27
28	29	30	31			

JUNE

S	M	T	W	T	F	S
				1	2	3
4	5	6	7	8	9	10
11	12	13	14	15	16	17
18	19	20	21	22	23	24
25	26	27	28	29	30	

JULY

S	M	T	W	T	F	S
						1
2	3	4	5	6	7	8
9	10	11	12	13	14	15
16	17	18	19	20	21	22
23	24	25	26	27	28	29
30	31					

AUGUST

S	M	T	W	T	F	S
		1	2	3	4	5
6	7	8	9	10	11	12
13	14	15	16	17	18	19
20	21	22	23	24	25	26
27	28	29	30	31		

SEPTEMBER

S	M	T	W	T	F	S
					1	2
3	4	5	6	7	8	9
10	11	12	13	14	15	16
17	18	19	20	21	22	23
24	25	26	27	28	29	30

OCTOBER

S	M	T	W	T	F	S
1	2	3	4	5	6	7
8	9	10	11	12	13	14
15	16	17	18	19	20	21
22	23	24	25	26	27	28
29	30	31				

NOVEMBER

S	M	T	W	T	F	S
			1	2	3	4
5	6	7	8	9	10	11
12	13	14	15	16	17	18
19	20	21	22	23	24	25
26	27	28	29	30		

DECEMBER

S	M	T	W	T	F	S
					1	2
3	4	5	6	7	8	9
10	11	12	13	14	15	16
17	18	19	20	21	22	23
24	25	26	27	28	29	30
31						

Other Calendars: Year and New Year's Day, 2021

Era	Year	Begins in 2021	Era	Year	Begins in 2021
Byzantine	7530	Sept. 14	Islamic/Muslim (Hijra)	1443	Aug. 9[1]
Chinese (Year of the Ox)	4719	Feb. 12	Japanese[2]	2	Jan. 1
Diocletian	1738	Sept. 11	Jewish	5782	Sept. 7[1]
Grecian (Seleucidae)	2333	Sept. 14 or Oct. 14	Nabonassar (Babylonian)	2770	Apr. 23
Indian (Saka)	1943	Mar. 22	Roman (Ab Urbe Condita)	2774	Jan. 14

(1) Year begins the previous night. (2) Era starts at 0 with new emperor.

Chronological Cycles, 2021

Dominical Letter	C	Roman Indiction	14	Solar Cycle	14
Golden Number (lunar cycle)	VIII	Epact	16	Julian Period (year of)	6734

Special Months

There are many thousands of special months, days, and weeks because of anniversaries, official proclamations, and promotional events, both trivial and serious. Here are a few of the special months:

January: Get Organized Month, National Mentoring Month, National Poverty in America Awareness Month

February: Black History Month, American Heart Month, Library Lovers' Month, Youth Leadership Month

March: Irish-American Heritage Month, National Women's History Month, Red Cross Month, National Frozen Food Month, National Colorectal Cancer Awareness Month

April: National Child Abuse Prevention Month, National Humor Month, Stress Awareness Month, Grange Month, Sexual Assault Awareness and Prevention Month

May: Clean Air Month, Get Caught Reading Month, National Barbecue Month, Asian American and Pacific Islander Heritage Month, National Inventors Month, National Mental Health Month

June: Great Outdoors Month; Lesbian, Gay, Bisexual, and Transgender Pride Month; National Safety Month

July: Cell Phone Courtesy Month, National Hot Dog Month, National Make a Difference to Children Month, Women's Motorcycle Month

August: National Black Business Month, Happiness Happens Month, National Immunization Awareness Month

September: Library Card Sign-Up Month, National Hispanic Heritage Month (Sept. 15-Oct. 15), National Biscuit Month

October: National Domestic Violence Awareness Month, National Breast Cancer Awareness Month, Global Diversity Awareness Month, National Popcorn Poppin' Month

November: National American Indian Heritage Month, National Adoption Month, American Diabetes Month, National Peanut Butter Lovers' Month

December: Safe Toys and Gifts Month, National Impaired Driving Prevention Month, National Tie Month

Standard Time Differences: World Cities

The time indicated in the table is fixed by law and is called the legal time or, more generally, standard time. Use of daylight saving time varies widely. An asterisk (*) indicates morning of the following day. At 12:00 noon, Eastern Standard Time, the standard time (in 24-hour time) in selected cities is as shown.

City	Time		City	Time		City	Time		City	Time	
Abu Dhabi	21	00	Denver	10	00	Lisbon	17	00	St. Petersburg	20	00
Addis Ababa	20	00	Dhaka	23	00	London	17	00	Santiago	13	00
Amsterdam	18	00	Dublin	17	00	Los Angeles	9	00	São Paulo	14	00
Ankara	20	00	Edinburgh	17	00	Madrid	18	00	Sarajevo	18	00
Athens	19	00	Geneva	18	00	Manila	1	00*	Seoul	2	00*
Auckland	5	00*	Helsinki	19	00	Mecca	20	00	Shanghai	1	00*
Baghdad	20	00	Ho Chi Minh City	0	00*	Melbourne	3	00*	Singapore	1	00*
Bangkok	0	00*	Hong Kong	1	00*	Montevideo	14	00	Stockholm	18	00
Beijing	1	00*	Honolulu	7	00	Moscow	20	00	Sydney	3	00*
Belfast	17	00	Houston	11	00	Mumbai (Bombay)	22	30	Taipei	1	00*
Belgrade	18	00	Islamabad	22	00	Munich	18	00	Tashkent	22	00
Berlin	18	00	Istanbul	20	00	Nagasaki	2	00*	Tehran	20	30
Bogotá	12	00	Jakarta	0	00*	Nairobi	20	00	Tel Aviv	19	00
Brussels	18	00	Jerusalem	19	00	New Delhi	22	30	Tokyo	2	00*
Bucharest	19	00	Johannesburg	19	00	New York	12	00	Toronto	12	00
Budapest	18	00	Kabul	21	30	Oslo	18	00	Vancouver	9	00
Buenos Aires	14	00	Karachi	22	00	Paris	18	00	Vienna	18	00
Cairo	19	00	Kathmandu	22	45	Prague	18	00	Vladivostok	3	00*
Cape Town	19	00	Kiev	19	00	Pyongyang	2	00*	Warsaw	18	00
Caracas	13	00	Kinshasa	18	00	Quito	12	00	Wellington	5	00*
Casablanca	17	00	Kolkata (Calcutta)	22	30	Rio de Janeiro	14	00	Yangon (Rangoon)	23	30
Chicago	11	00	Lagos	18	00	Riyadh	20	00	Yokohama	2	00*
Copenhagen	18	00	Lima	12	00	Rome	18	00	Zurich	18	00

Wedding Anniversary Gifts

The traditional names for wedding anniversaries go back many years in social usage and have been used to suggest types of appropriate anniversary gifts. Traditional products for gifts are listed here in capital letters, with allowable revisions in parentheses, followed by common modern gifts for each anniversary.

Anniversary	Gift	Anniversary	Gift	Anniversary	Gift
1st	PAPER, clocks	9th	POTTERY (CHINA), leather goods	25th	SILVER, sterling silver
2nd	COTTON, china			30th	PEARL, diamond
3rd	LEATHER, crystal, glass	10th	TIN, ALUMINUM, diamond	35th	CORAL (JADE), jade
4th	LINEN (SILK), appliances	11th	STEEL, fashion jewelry	40th	RUBY, ruby
5th	WOOD, silverware	12th	SILK, pearls, colored gems	45th	SAPPHIRE, sapphire
6th	IRON, wood objects	13th	LACE, textiles, furs	50th	GOLD, gold
7th	WOOL (COPPER), desk sets	14th	IVORY, gold jewelry	55th	EMERALD, emerald
8th	BRONZE, linens, lace	15th	CRYSTAL, watches	60th	DIAMOND, diamond
		20th	CHINA, platinum		

Birthstones

Source: American Gem Society

Birth month	Ancient[1] birthstone	Modern birthstone	Birth month	Ancient[1] birthstone	Modern birthstone
January	Garnet	Garnet	July	Onyx	Ruby
February	Amethyst	Amethyst	August	Carnelian	Sardonyx or Peridot
March	Jasper	Bloodstone or Aquamarine	September	Chrysolite	Sapphire
April	Sapphire	Diamond	October	Aquamarine	Opal or Tourmaline
May	Agate, Chalcedony, or Carnelian	Emerald	November	Topaz	Topaz
			December	Ruby	Turquoise, Tanzanite, or Zircon
June	Emerald	Pearl, Moonstone, or Alexandrite			

(1) Varied by region and culture. Birthstones listed here are those of ancient Hebrew tradition.

Standard Time and Daylight Saving Time

Source: National Institute of Standards and Technology, U.S. Dept. of Commerce

See also Time Zone map, page 492.

Standard Time

Standard time is reckoned from the prime meridian of longitude in Greenwich, England. The world is divided into 24 zones, each 15 deg of arc, or one hour in time apart. The Greenwich meridian (0 deg) extends through the center of the initial zone. Each zone extends 7.5 deg on either side of its central meridian. Zones to the east are numbered from 1 to 12, with the prefix "minus" indicating the number of hours to be subtracted to obtain Greenwich Time.

Westward zones are similarly numbered, but prefixed "plus," showing the number of hours that must be added to get Greenwich Time. The standard time maintained in many countries does not coincide with zone time. For example, China extends across five time zones, but the entire country is on Greenwich Time plus 8 hours.

The U.S. and possessions are divided into nine standard time zones. All places in each zone use, instead of their local time, the time counted from the transit of the mean sun across the standard time meridian that passes near the middle of that zone. These time zones are designated as Atlantic, Eastern, Central, Mountain, Pacific, Alaska, Hawaii-Aleutian, Samoa, and Chamorro (Guam and Northern Mariana Isls.); the time in these zones is reckoned from the 60th, 75th, 90th, 105th, 120th, 135th, 150th, and 165th meridians west of Greenwich and the 150th meridian east of Greenwich. The time zone line wanders to conform to local geography. The time in the various zones in the U.S. and U.S. territories west of Greenwich is earlier than Greenwich Time by 4, 5, 6, 7, 8, 9, 10, and 11 hours, respectively. However, Chamorro crosses the international date line and is 10 hours later than Greenwich Time.

24-Hour Time

With the 24-hour system, the day begins at midnight, and times are designated 00:00 through 23:59. Twenty-four-hour time is widely used in scientific work throughout the world. In the U.S., it is also used in operations of the armed forces. In Europe, it is frequently used by the transportation networks in preference to the 12-hour AM and PM system.

International Date Line

The date line, approximately coinciding with the 180th meridian, separates the calendar dates. The date must be advanced one day when crossing in a westerly direction and set back one day when crossing in an easterly direction. The date line frequently deviates from the 180th meridian because of decisions by affected nations. The line is deflected eastward through the Bering Strait and westward of the Aleutians to prevent separating the islands by date. The line is deflected eastward of the Tonga and New Zealand islands in the South Pacific. In 1995, Kiribati announced that its islands east of the date line would observe the same date as islands to the west, though most maps do not depict this deviation in the date line. In 2011, Samoa moved west of the date line to ease its relationship with Australia and New Zealand. The line is established by international custom; there is no international authority prescribing its exact course.

Daylight Saving Time

Daylight saving time is achieved by advancing the clock one hour. Since 2007, daylight saving time has begun at 2 AM on the second Sunday in Mar. and has ended at 2 AM on the first Sunday in Nov. **In 2021, daylight saving time begins at 2 AM on Mar. 14 and ends at 2 AM on Nov. 7.** Prior to 2007,

daylight saving time traditionally ran from the first Sunday in Apr. to the last Sunday in Oct.

Daylight saving time was first observed in the U.S. during World War I and again during World War II. In the intervening years, some states and communities observed daylight saving time, using whatever beginning and ending dates they chose. In 1966, Congress passed the Uniform Time Act, which provided that any state or territory choosing to observe daylight saving time must begin and end on the dates established by federal law. Any state could, by law, exempt itself; a 1972 amendment to the act authorized states in more than one time zone to exempt the entire state or one time zone only. Currently, most of Arizona, Hawaii, Puerto Rico, the U.S. Virgin Islands, Guam, American Samoa, and Northern Mariana Isls. do not observe daylight saving time. All of Indiana, which is in two time zones, observed daylight saving time for the first time in 2006.

Congress and the secretary of transportation both have authority to change time zone boundaries, which they have done on a number of occasions since 1966. In 2018, Florida passed legislation that would keep the state on daylight saving time year-round, but either Congress or the Transportation Dept. was required to act before the new law could go into effect. Similar legislation has been proposed in California and other states.

Daylight Saving Time: International Usage

Adjusting clock time so as to gain daylight on summer evenings is common throughout the world.

Canada, which extends over six time zones, generally observes daylight saving time during the same period as the U.S. Most provincial governments observe the four-week extension to daylight saving time that went into effect in 2007. Most of Saskatchewan remains on standard time year-round; communities elsewhere in Canada may also exempt themselves from daylight saving time. Beginning in Mar., the territory Yukon began observing Pacific Daylight Saving Time year-round. Most of Mexico observes daylight saving time, except for the state of Sonora, which shares a border with Arizona.

Member nations of the European Union observe a "summer-time period," a version of daylight saving time, from the last Sunday of Mar. until the last Sunday in Oct. However, the EU Parliament in Mar. 2019 voted to end mandatory DST starting in 2021, and instead allow member countries to follow permanent standard time if they choose.

Turkey stopped observing daylight saving time in 2016; maintaining its "summer hours," it shifted permanently to Greenwich time plus 3 hours. Russia, which uses 11 time zones, moved to permanent standard time in 2014 after a three-year experiment to maintain year-round "summer hours" proved unpopular. From Oct. 2014 on, the country observed "winter hours" year-round. Morocco abandoned daylight saving time in Oct. 2018, with a Ramadan exception. China does not observe daylight saving time. Mongolia discontinued daylight saving time in 2017, two years after it was reintroduced. Japan, which lies within one time zone, also does not modify its legal time during the summer months.

Many countries in the Southern Hemisphere maintain daylight saving time generally from Oct. to Mar. (Brazil, mostly south of the equator, scrapped daylight saving time in 2019.) However, most countries near the equator do not deviate from standard time.

WEIGHTS AND MEASURES

Source: National Institute of Standards and Technology (NIST), U.S. Dept. of Commerce

International System of Units (SI)

Two systems of weights and measures coexist in the U.S. today: the **U.S. Customary System** and the **International System of Units** (SI, for Système International d'Unités). The SI is a more complete, coherent version of the **metric system**. Throughout U.S. history, the customary system—parts of which were inherited but are now different from the British Imperial System—has been generally used. Federal and state legislation gave it, through implication, standing as the primary weights and measures system. The metric system, however, is the only system that Congress has ever specifically sanctioned, dating back to an 1866 law. The U.S. was one of the original 17 countries to sign the International Metric Convention (or Treaty of the Meter) May 20, 1875, which established several intergovernmental organizations to oversee and refine the SI. The U.S. is represented at these organizations by the Natl. Institute of Standards and Technology (NIST).

Since that time, use of the metric system in the U.S. has slowly increased, particularly in the scientific community, the pharmaceutical industry, and the manufacturing sector—the last motivated by the predominant use of the metric system in international commerce.

On Dec. 23, 1975, Pres. Gerald R. Ford signed the Metric Conversion Act of 1975. It defined the "metric system of measurement" as the SI, as established in 1960 by the General Conference on Weights and Measures and interpreted in the U.S. by the secretary of commerce, who delegated that authority to the director of the NIST. The Trade and Competitiveness Act of 1988 declared the metric system the preferred system of weights and measures for U.S. trade and commerce, but explicitly permitted "the continued use of traditional systems of weights and measures in nonbusiness activities." The Code of Federal Regulations made the use of metric units mandatory for federal agencies in 1991. However, the metric system has not yet become the system of choice for most Americans' daily use.

The following are the seven base SI units: **length**—meter; **mass**—kilogram; **time**—second; **electric current**—ampere; **thermodynamic temperature**—kelvin; **amount of substance**—mole; and **luminous intensity**—candela. All seven were redefined as of May 20, 2019, to emphasize the dependence of base unit definitions on physical constants with fixed numerical values and on the other base units.

Frequently Used Conversions

Boldface indicates exact values. For greater accuracy, use the "multiply by" number in parentheses. For weights, avoirdupois (avdp) weight is the system applied to all goods except medicines, precious metals, and precious stones.

U.S. Customary to Metric

	If you have:	Multiply by:		To get:
Length	inches	**25.4**		millimeters
	inches	**2.54**		centimeters
	inches	**0.0254**		meters
	feet	0.3	**(0.3048)**	meters
	yards	0.9	**(0.9144)**	meters
	miles[1]	1.6	**(1.609344)**	kilometers
Area	sq inches	6.5	**(6.4516)**	sq cm
	sq feet	0.09	**(0.09290304)**	sq meters
	sq yards	0.84	**(0.83612736)**	sq meters
	acres	0.4	(0.4046873)	hectares
	sq miles[1]	2.6	(2.58998811)	sq kilometers
Weight	ounces (avdp)	28	(28.34952)	grams
	pounds (avdp)	454	**(453.59237)**	grams
	pounds (avdp)	0.45	**(0.45359237)**	kilograms
	short tons[2]	0.91	**(0.90718474)**	metric tons
	long tons[3]	1	(1.016047)	metric tons
Liquid	ounces	0.03	(0.02957353)	liters
	cups	0.24	(0.23658824)	liters
	pints	0.47	(0.473176473)	liters
	quarts	0.95	(0.946352946)	liters
	gallons	3.79	(3.785412)	liters

Metric to U.S. Customary

	If you have:	Multiply by:		To get:
Length	millimeters	0.04	(0.03937)	inches
	centimeters	0.4	(0.3937)	inches
	meters	39	(39.37)	inches
	meters	3.3	(3.280840)	feet
	meters	1.1	(1.093613)	yards
	kilometers	0.6	(0.621371)	miles[1]
Area	sq cm	0.16	(0.15500)	sq inches
	sq meters	10.8	(10.76391)	sq feet
	sq meters	1.2	(1.195990)	sq yards
	hectares	2.5	(2.471044)	acres
	sq kilometers	0.39	(0.386102)	sq miles[1]
Weight	grams	0.035	(0.03527396)	ounces (avdp)
	grams	0.002	(0.00220462)	pounds (avdp)
	kilograms	2.2	(2.204623)	pounds (avdp)
	metric tons	1.1	(1.102311)	short tons[2]
	metric tons	0.98	(0.9842065)	long tons[3]
Liquid	liters	33.8	(33.81402)	ounces
	liters	4.2	(4.226752)	cups
	liters	2.1	(2.113376)	pints
	liters	1.1	(1.056688)	quarts
	liters	0.26	(0.264172)	gallons

(1) Survey mile. (2) A short ton is 2,000 pounds. (3) A long ton is 2,240 pounds.

Temperature Conversions

The left-hand column below gives a temperature according to the **Celsius** scale, and the right-hand gives the same temperature according to the **Fahrenheit** scale. The lowest number on each scale is equivalent to absolute zero, the theoretical temperature at which all molecular motion would stop.

For temperatures not shown: To convert Fahrenheit to Celsius, subtract 32 degrees and divide by 1.8; to convert Celsius to Fahrenheit, multiply by 1.8 and add 32 degrees.

Celsius	Fahrenheit	Celsius	Fahrenheit	Celsius	Fahrenheit	Celsius	Fahrenheit	Celsius	Fahrenheit
−273.15	−459.67	−45.6	−50	−1.1	30	30	86	65.6	150
−250	−418	**−40**	**−40**	**0**	**32**	32.2	90	70	158
−200	−328	−34.4	−30	4.4	40	35	95	80	176
−184.4	−300	−30	−22	10	50	**37**	**98.6**	90	194
−156.7	−250	−28.9	−20	15.6	60	37.8	100	93.3	200
−150	−238	−23.3	−10	**20**	**68**	40	104	**100**	**212**
−128.9	−200	−20	−4	21.1	70	43.3	110	121.1	250
−101.1	−150	−17.8	0	23.9	75	48.9	120	148.9	300
−100	−148	−12.2	10	25	77	50	122	150	302
−73.3	−100	−10	14	26.7	80	54.4	130	200	392
−50	−58	−6.7	20	29.4	85	60	140	300	572

Note: Although the term *centigrade* is still frequently used, the International Committee on Weights and Measures and the National Institute of Standards and Technology have recommended since 1948 that this scale be called *Celsius*.

Boiling and Freezing Points

Water boils at 212°F (100°C) at sea level. For every 550 feet above sea level, the boiling point of water is lower by about 1°F. Methyl alcohol (wood alcohol) boils at 148.5°F. Average human oral temperature is 98.6°F. Water freezes at 32°F (0°C).

Selected Geometric Formulas

The value of π (the Greek letter pi) is approximately 3.14159265 (equal to the ratio of the circumference of a circle to its diameter). The equivalence is typically rounded further to 3.1416 or 3.14.

Calculating Circumference

Circle: Multiply the diameter by π.

Calculating Area

Circle: Multiply the square of the radius (equal to ½ the diameter) by π.

Rectangle: Multiply the length of the base by the height.

Sphere (surface): Multiply the square of the radius by π and multiply by 4.

Square: Square the length of one side.

Trapezoid: Add the length of the two parallel sides, multiply by the height, and divide by 2.

Triangle: Multiply the base by the height and divide by 2.

Calculating Volume

Cone: Multiply the square of the radius of the base by π, multiply by the height, and divide by 3.

Cube: Cube the length of one edge.

Cylinder: Multiply the square of the radius of the base by π and multiply by the height.

Pyramid: Multiply the area of the base by the height and divide by 3.

Rectangular prism: Multiply the length by the width by the height.

Sphere: Multiply the cube of the radius by π, multiply by 4, and divide by 3.

Playing Cards and Dice Chances

5-Card Poker Hands

Hand	Number possible	Odds against
Royal flush	4	649,739 to 1
Other straight flush	36	72,192 to 1
Four of a kind	624	4,164 to 1
Full house	3,744	693 to 1
Flush	5,108	508 to 1
Straight	10,200	254 to 1
Three of a kind	54,912	46 to 1
Two pairs	123,552	20 to 1
One pair	1,098,240	4 to 3 (1.37 to 1)
Nothing	1,302,540	1 to 1
Total	2,598,960	

Bridge

The odds—against suit distribution in a hand of 4-4-3-2 are about 4 to 1; against 5-4-2-2 about 8 to 1; against 6-4-2-1 about 20 to 1; against 7-4-1-1 about 254 to 1; against 8-4-1-0 about 2,211 to 1; and against 13-0-0-0 about 158,753,389,899 to 1.

Dice
(probabilities on 2 dice)

Total	Odds against (single toss)	Total	Odds against (single toss)
2	35 to 1	8	31 to 5
3	17 to 1	9	8 to 1
4	11 to 1	10	11 to 1
5	8 to 1	11	17 to 1
6	31 to 5	12	35 to 1
7	5 to 1		

Large Numbers

No. of zeros	U.S. term	British[1], French, German	No. of zeros	U.S. term	British[1], French, German
6	million	million	42	tredecillion	septillion
9	billion	milliard	45	quattuordecillion	1,000 septillion
12	trillion	billion	48	quindecillion	octillion
15	quadrillion	1,000 billion	51	sexdecillion	1,000 octillion
18	quintillion	trillion	54	septendecillion	nonillion
21	sextillion	1,000 trillion	57	octodecillion	1,000 nonillion
24	septillion	quadrillion	60	novemdecillion	decillion
27	octillion	1,000 quadrillion	63	vigintillion	1,000 decillion
30	nonillion	quintillion	100	googol	googol
33	decillion	1,000 quintillion	303	centillion	NA
36	undecillion	sextillion	600	NA	centillion
39	duodecillion	1,000 sextillion	googol	googolplex	googolplex

NA = Not available. (1) In recent years, it has become more common in Britain to use U.S. terminology for large numbers.

Prime Numbers to 1,009

A prime number is any positive integer greater than 1 that is divisible only by two positive integers—1 and itself.

	2	3	5	7	11	13	17	19	23
29	31	37	41	43	47	53	59	61	67
71	73	79	83	89	97	101	103	107	109
113	127	131	137	139	149	151	157	163	167
173	179	181	191	193	197	199	211	223	227
229	233	239	241	251	257	263	269	271	277
281	283	293	307	311	313	317	331	337	347
349	353	359	367	373	379	383	389	397	401
409	419	421	431	433	439	443	449	457	461
463	467	479	487	491	499	503	509	521	523
541	547	557	563	569	571	577	587	593	599
601	607	613	617	619	631	641	643	647	653
659	661	673	677	683	691	701	709	719	727
733	739	743	751	757	761	769	773	787	797
809	811	821	823	827	829	839	853	857	859
863	877	881	883	887	907	911	919	929	937
941	947	953	967	971	977	983	991	997	1,009

Common Fractions Converted to Decimals

8ths	16ths	32nds	64ths		8ths	16ths	32nds	64ths		8ths	16ths	32nds	64ths		8ths	16ths	32nds	64ths	
			1	= 0.015625				17	= 0.265625				33	= 0.515625				49	= 0.765625
		1	2	= 0.03125			9	18	= 0.28125			17	34	= 0.53125			25	50	= 0.78125
			3	= 0.046875				19	= 0.296875				35	= 0.546875				51	= 0.796875
	1	2	4	= 0.0625		5	10	20	= 0.3125		9	18	36	= 0.5625		13	26	52	= 0.8125
			5	= 0.078125				21	= 0.328125				37	= 0.578125				53	= 0.828125
		3	6	= 0.09375			11	22	= 0.34375			19	38	= 0.59375			27	54	= 0.84375
			7	= 0.109375				23	= 0.359375				39	= 0.609375				55	= 0.859375
1	2	4	8	= 0.125	3	6	12	24	= 0.375	5	10	20	40	= 0.625	7	14	28	56	= 0.875
			9	= 0.140625				25	= 0.390625				41	= 0.640625				57	= 0.890625
		5	10	= 0.15625			13	26	= 0.40625			21	42	= 0.65625			29	58	= 0.90625
			11	= 0.171875				27	= 0.421875				43	= 0.671875				59	= 0.921875
	3	6	12	= 0.1875		7	14	28	= 0.4375		11	22	44	= 0.6875		15	30	60	= 0.9375
			13	= 0.203125				29	= 0.453125				45	= 0.703125				61	= 0.953125
		7	14	= 0.21875			15	30	= 0.46875			23	46	= 0.71875			31	62	= 0.96875
			15	= 0.234375				31	= 0.484375				47	= 0.734375				63	= 0.984375
2	4	8	16	= 0.25	4	8	16	32	= 0.5	6	12	24	48	= 0.75	8	16	32	64	= 1.0

Roman Numerals

I — 1	IV — 4	VII — 7	X — 10	XX — 20	L — 50	C — 100	D — 500
II — 2	V — 5	VIII — 8	XI — 11	XXX — 30	LX — 60	CC — 200	CM — 900
III — 3	VI — 6	IX — 9	XIX — 19	XL — 40	XC — 90	CD — 400	M — 1,000

Note: The numerals V, X, L, C, D, or M shown with a horizontal line on top denote 1,000 times the original value.

Ancient Measures

Biblical
Cubit	= 21.8 inches
Omer	= 0.45 peck
	= 3.964 liters
Ephah	= 10 omers
Shekel	= 0.497 ounce
	= 14.1 grams

Greek
Cubit	= 18.3 inches
Stadion	= 607.2 or 622 feet
Obolos	= 715.38 milligrams
Drachma	= 4.2923 grams
Mina	= 0.9463 pound
Talent	= 60 mina

Roman
| Cubit | = 17.5 inches |
| Stadium | = 202 yards |
| As, libra, |
| pondus | = 325.971 grams |
| | = 0.71864 pound |

Metric System Prefixes

The following prefixes, in combination with the basic unit names, provide the multiples and submultiples in the metric system. For example, the unit name *meter*, with the prefix *kilo* added, produces *kilometer*, meaning "1,000 meters."

Prefix	Symbol	Multiples	Equivalent	Prefix	Symbol	Multiples	Equivalent
yotta	Y	10^{24}	septillionfold	deci	d	10^{-1}	tenth part
zetta	Z	10^{21}	sextillionfold	centi	c	10^{-2}	hundredth part
exa	E	10^{18}	quintillionfold	milli	m	10^{-3}	thousandth part
peta	P	10^{15}	quadrillionfold	micro	μ	10^{-6}	millionth part
tera	T	10^{12}	trillionfold	nano	n	10^{-9}	billionth part
giga	G	10^{9}	billionfold	pico	p	10^{-12}	trillionth part
mega	M	10^{6}	millionfold	femto	f	10^{-15}	quadrillionth part
kilo	k	10^{3}	thousandfold	atto	a	10^{-18}	quintillionth part
hecto	h	10^{2}	hundredfold	zepto	z	10^{-21}	sextillionth part
deka	da	10^{1}	tenfold	yocto	y	10^{-24}	septillionth part

Weight and Measurement Equivalents

In this table, there is a distinction between the international foot and the survey foot. The international foot, defined in 1959 as exactly equal to 0.3048 meter, is shorter than the survey foot by exactly 2 parts in 1 million. This means that an international mile is about ⅛ inch shorter than the survey mile. The survey foot is still used in the publication of some geodetic surveys within the U.S., but the NIST planned to discourage its use for any purposes after Jan. 1, 2023. In this table, the survey foot is indicated with capital letters, as FEET.

When the name of a unit is enclosed in brackets, e.g., [1 hand], either (1) the unit is not in general current use in the U.S. or (2) the unit is believed to be based on custom and usage rather than on formal definition.

Equivalents involving decimals are, in most instances, rounded to the third decimal place; exact equivalents are so designated.

Lengths

1 angstrom (Å)	= 0.1 nanometer (exactly)
	= 0.0001 micrometer (exactly)
	= 0.0000001 millimeter (exactly)
	= 0.000000004 inch
1 cable's length	= 120 fathoms (exactly)
	= 720 FEET (exactly)
	= 219 meters
1 centimeter (cm)	= 0.3937 inch
1 chain (ch) (engineer's)	= 30.48 meters (exactly)
	= 100 feet
1 chain (Gunter's or surveyor's)	= 66 FEET (exactly)
	= 20.1168 meters
1 decimeter (dm)	= 3.937 inches
1 degree (geographical)	= 364,566.929 feet
	= 69.047 miles (avg.)
	= 111.123 kilometers (avg.)
of latitude	= 68.708 miles at equator
	= 69.403 miles at poles
of longitude	= 69.171 miles at equator
1 dekameter (dam)	= 32.808 feet
1 fathom (fath)	= 6 FEET (exactly)
	= 1.8288 meters
1 foot (ft)	= 12 inches (exactly)
	= 0.3048 meters (exactly)
	= 0.015 chains (surveyor's)
1 furlong (fur)	= 660 FEET (exactly)
	= ⅛ survey mile (exactly)
	= 201.168 meters
[1 hand (height measure for horses, from ground to top of their shoulders)]	= 4 inches
1 inch (in.)	= 2.54 centimeters (exactly)
1 kilometer (km)	= 0.621371 mile
	= 3,280.8 feet
1 league (land)	= 3 survey miles (exactly)
	= 4.828 kilometers
1 link (engineer's)	= 1 foot
	= 0.305 meter
1 link (Gunter's or surveyor's)	= 7.92 inches (exactly)
	= 0.201 meter

1 meter (m). . . . . = 39.37 inches
                            = 1.09361 yards
1 micrometer (μm) . . . . = 0.001 millimeter (exactly)
                            = 0.00003937 inch
1 mil . . . . = 0.001 inch (exactly)
                            = 0.0254 millimeter (exactly)
1 mile (mi) (statute or land). . . . = 5,280 FEET (exactly)
                            = 1.609344 kilometers (exactly)
1 mile (nmi) (international
   nautical) . . . . = 1.852 kilometers (exactly)
                            = 1.151 miles
                            = 6,076.1 feet
1 millimeter (mm) . . . . = 0.03937 inch
1 nanometer (nm). . . . . = 0.001 micrometer (exactly)
                            = 0.00000003937 inch
1 pica (typography). . . . . = 12 points
1 point (pt) (typography). . . . . . = 0.013837 inch (exactly)
                            = 0.351 millimeter
1 rod (rd), pole, or perch. . . . . . = 16½ FEET (exactly)
                            = 5.029 meters
1 yard (yd) . . . . = 3 feet (exactly)
                            = 0.9144 meter (exactly)

Areas or Surfaces

1 acre (A) . . . . = 43,560 square FEET (exactly)
                            = 4,840 square yards
                            = 0.405 hectare
1 are (a) . . . . = 119.599 square yards
                            = 0.025 acre
1 bolt (cloth measure):
   length . . . . = 100 yards
   width. . . . . = 45 or 60 inches
1 hectare (ha). . . . . = 2.471 acres
[1 square (building)] . . . . = 100 square feet
1 square centimeter (cm²) . . . = 0.155 square inch
1 square decimeter (dm²). . . . = 15.500 square inches
1 square foot (ft²) . . . . = 929.030 square centimeters
1 square inch (in.²) . . . . = 6.4516 square centimeters
                            (exactly)
1 square kilometer (km²) . . . . = 247.104 acres
                            = 0.386102 square mile
1 square meter (m²) . . . . = 1.196 square yards
                            = 10.764 square feet
1 square mile (mi²) . . . . = 640 acres (exactly)
                            = 258.999 hectares
1 square millimeter (mm²) . . . = 0.002 square inch
1 square rod (rd²), square
   pole, or square perch . . . . . = 25.293 square meters
1 square yard (yd²). . . . . = 0.836127 square meter

Capacities or Volumes

1 barrel (bbl), liquid. . . . . = 31 to 42 gallons*

*There are a variety of "barrels" established by law or usage. For example, federal taxes on fermented liquors are based on a barrel of 31 gallons. Many state laws fix the "barrel for liquids" as 31½ gallons; one state fixes a 36-gallon barrel for cistern measurement. Federal law recognizes a 40-gallon barrel for "proof spirits." By custom, 42 gallons constitute a barrel of crude oil or petroleum products for statistical purposes, and this equivalent is recognized "for liquids" by some states.

1 barrel (bbl), standard for
   fruits, vegetables, and other
   dry commodities except dry
   cranberries . . . . = 7,056 cubic inches
                            = 105 dry quarts
                            = 3.281 bushels, struck measure
1 barrel, standard, cranberry . . = 86⁴⁵/₆₄ dry quarts
                            = 2.709 bushels, struck measure
                            = 5,826 cubic inches
1 board foot (lumber measure) = a foot-square board 1 inch
                               thick
1 bushel (U.S.) (struck
   measure) . . . . = 2,150.42 cubic inches (exactly)
                            = 35.239 liters
[1 bushel, heaped (U.S.)] . . . . = 2,747.715 cubic inches
                            = 1.278 bushels,
                              struck measure**

**Frequently recognized as 1¼ bushels, struck measure.

[1 bushel (bu) (British Imperial)
   (struck measure)] . . . . = 1.032 U.S. bushels,
                            struck measure
                            = 2,219.36 cubic inches
1 cord (cd) (firewood) . . . . = 128 cubic feet (exactly)

---

1 cubic centimeter (cm³) . . . . = 0.061 cubic inch
1 cubic decimeter (dm³). . . . . . = 61.024 cubic inches
1 cubic foot (ft³) . . . . = 7.481 gallons
                            = 28.317 cubic decimeters
1 cubic inch (in.³) . . . . = 0.554 fluid ounce
                            = 4.433 fluid drams
                            = 16.387 cubic centimeters
1 cubic meter (m³) . . . . = 1.308 cubic yards
1 cubic yard (yd³). . . . . = 0.765 cubic meter
1 cup, measuring . . . . = 8 fluid ounces (exactly)
                            = ½ liquid pint (exactly)
1 dekaliter (daL) . . . . = 2.642 gallons
                            = 1.135 pecks
[1 dram, fluid (fl dr) (British)] . . = 0.961 U.S. fluid dram
                            = 0.217 cubic inch
                            = 3.552 milliliters
1 gallon (gal) (U.S.) . . . . = 4 quarts, liquid (exactly)
                            = 231 cubic inches (exactly)
                            = 3.785 liters
                            = 0.833 British gallon
                            = 128 U.S. fluid ounces (exactly)
[1 gallon (British Imperial)]. . . . = 277.42 cubic inches
                            = 1.201 U.S. gallons
                            = 4.546 liters
                            = 160 British fluid ounces
                              (exactly)
1 gill (gi) . . . . = 7.219 cubic inches
                            = 4 fluid ounces (exactly)
                            = 0.118 liter
1 hectoliter (hL) . . . . = 26.418 gallons
                            = 2.838 bushels
1 liter (L) (1 cubic decimeter
   exactly). . . . . = 1.057 liquid quarts
                            = 0.908 dry quart
                            = 61.024 cubic inches
1 milliliter (mL) (1 cu cm
   exactly). . . . . = 0.271 fluid dram
                            = 16.231 minims
                            = 0.061 cubic inch
1 ounce, liquid (U.S.) . . . . = 1.805 cubic inches
                            = 29.573 milliliters
                            = 1.041 British fluid ounces
[1 ounce, fluid (fl oz) (British)] . = 0.961 U.S. fluid ounce
                            = 1.734 cubic inches
                            = 28.412 milliliters
1 peck (pk) . . . . = 8.810 liters
1 pint (pt), dry. . . . . = 33.600 cubic inches
                            = 0.551 liter
1 pint, liquid . . . . = 28.875 cubic inches (exactly)
                            = 0.473 liter
1 quart (qt), dry (U.S.) . . . . = 67.201 cubic inches
                            = 1.101 liters
                            = 0.969 British quart
1 quart, liquid (U.S.) . . . . = 2 pints, liquid (exactly)
                            = 4 cups (exactly)
                            = 57.75 cubic inches (exactly)
                            = 0.946 liter
                            = 0.833 British quart
[1 quart (British)] . . . . = 69.354 cubic inches
                            = 1.032 U.S. dry quarts
                            = 1.201 U.S. liquid quarts
1 tablespoon (T., Tbs, tbsp.) . . = 3 teaspoons (exactly)
                            = 4 fluid drams
                            = ½ fluid ounce (exactly)
1 teaspoon (t., tsp.) . . . . = ⅓ tablespoon (exactly)
                            = 1⅓ fluid drams***

***The equivalent "1 teaspoon = 1⅓ fluid drams" has been found to correspond more closely with the actual capacities of teaspoons in use than the equivalent "1 teaspoon = 1 fluid dram" given by many dictionaries.

Weights or Masses

1 assay ton* (AT) . . . . = 29.167 grams

*Used in assaying. The assay ton bears the same relation to the milligram that a ton of 2,000 pounds avoirdupois bears to the ounce troy; hence, the weight in milligrams of precious metal obtained from one assay ton of ore gives directly the number of troy ounces to the net ton.

1 carat (c). . . . . = 200 milligrams (exactly)
                            = 3.086 grains
1 dram avoirdupois (dr avdp). . = 27¹¹/₃₂ (= 27.344) grains
                            = 1.772 grams
1 gamma (γ). . . . . = 1 microgram (exactly)
1 grain (gr) . . . . = 64.79891 milligrams (exactly)

1 gram (g)	= 15.432 grains
	= 0.035 ounce, avoirdupois
1 hundredweight, gross (or	
long)** (gross cwt)	= 112 pounds (exactly)
	= 50.802 kilograms

**The gross (or long) ton and hundredweight are used commercially in the U.S. to only a limited extent, usually in restricted industrial fields. These units are the same as the British ton and hundredweight.

1 hundredweight, gross or	
short (cwt or net cwt)	= 100 pounds (exactly)
	= 45.359 kilograms
1 kilogram (kg)	= 2.20462 pounds
1 microgram (μg)	= 0.000001 gram (exactly)
1 milligram (mg)	= 0.015 grain
1 ounce, avoirdupois (oz avdp)	= 437.5 grains (exactly)
	= 0.911 troy ounce
	= 28.3495 grams
1 ounce, troy (oz t)	= 480 grains (exactly)
	= 1.097 avoirdupois ounces
	= 31.103 grams

1 pennyweight (dwt)	= 1.555 grams
1 pound, avoirdupois (lb avdp)	= 7,000 grains (exactly)
	= 1.215 troy pounds
	= 453.59237 grams (exactly)
1 pound, troy (lb t)	= 5,760 grains (exactly)
	= 0.823 avoirdupois pound
	= 373.242 grams
1 stone (st)	= 14 pounds avdp (exactly)
	= 6.350 kilograms
1 ton, gross or long	= 2,240 pounds (exactly)
	= 1.12 net tons (exactly)
	= 1.016 metric tons
1 ton, metric (t)	= 2,204.623 pounds
	= 0.984 gross ton
	= 1.102 net tons
1 ton, net or short (tn)	= 2,000 pounds (exactly)
	= 0.893 gross ton
	= 0.907 metric ton

Electrical Units

The **watt** (W) is the unit of power (electrical, mechanical, thermal). Electrical power is given by the product of the voltage and the current.

Energy is sold by the **joule** (J), but in common practice the billing of electrical energy is expressed in terms of the **kilowatt-hour** (kWh), which is 3,600,000 joules, or 3.6 megajoules.

The **horsepower** (hp) is a nonmetric unit sometimes used in mechanics. It is equal to 746 watts.

The **ohm** (Ω) is the unit of electrical resistance and represents the physical property of a conductor that offers a resistance to the flow of electricity, permitting just 1 ampere to flow at 1 volt of pressure.

Measures of Force and Pressure

Dyne (dyn) = force necessary to accelerate a 1-gram mass
1 centimeter per second squared = 0.000072 poundal

Poundal (pdl) = force necessary to accelerate a 1-pound mass
1 foot per second squared = 13,825.5 dynes = 0.138255 newton

Newton (N) = force needed to accelerate a 1-kilogram mass
1 meter per second squared = 100,000 dynes (exactly)

Pascal (pressure) (Pa) = 1 newton per square meter = 0.020885 pound per square foot

Atmosphere (air pressure at sea level) (atm) = 2,116.217 pounds per square foot = 14.6959 pounds per square inch = 1.0332 kilograms per square centimeter = 101,325 newtons per square meter

Measures of Alcohol

Pony	= 1.0 fluid ounce
Shot	= varies, usu. 1.0-
	1.5 fluid ounces
Jigger	= 1.5 fluid ounces
Pint (pt)	= 16 fluid ounces
	= 0.625 fifth
Fifth	= 25.6 fluid ounces
	= 1.6 pints
	= 0.8 quart
	= 0.757 liter

Quart (qt)	= 32 fluid ounces
	= 1.25 fifths
Wine bottle	
(standard)	= 0.75 liter
	= 25.4 fluid ounces
Magnum	= 1.5 liters

For champagne and brandy:
Jeroboam . . . . = 2 magnums
= 3 liters
= 101 fluid ounces

For champagne:
Rehoboam	= 3 magnums
Methuselah	= 4 magnums
Salmanazar	= 6 magnums
Balthazar	= 8 magnums
Nebuchadnezzar . . .	= 10 magnums

Miscellaneous Measures

Caliber (cal)—the diameter of a gun bore. In the U.S., caliber is traditionally expressed in hundredths of inches, e.g., .22. In Britain, caliber is often expressed in thousandths of inches, e.g., .270. Now it is commonly expressed in millimeters, e.g., the 5.56 mm M16 rifle. The caliber of heavier weapons has long been expressed in millimeters, e.g., the 155 mm howitzer.

Naval guns' caliber refers to the barrel length as a multiple of the bore diameter. For example, a 5-inch, 50-caliber naval gun has a 5-inch bore and a barrel length of 250 inches.

Decibel (dB)—a measure of the relative intensity of sound. The threshold of hearing is given as 0 decibels. A 20-decibel sound is 10 times more intense than a 10-decibel sound; 30 decibels is 100 times more intense. (A 10-decibel increase corresponds generally to the perception of a sound being twice as loud.)

One decibel is the smallest difference between sounds detectable by the human ear. Long or repeated exposure to an 85-decibel-or-higher sound can damage hearing.

10 decibels . . .	breathing
20	rustling leaves
30	whisper
40	refrigerator humming
50	quiet conversation
60	conversation, laughter
70	vacuum cleaner
80	city traffic
90	subway, lawn mower
100	chainsaw

Em—a printer's measure designating the width of any given type size. For example, an em of 10-point type is 10 points. An en is half an em.

Gauge (ga)—the diameter of a shotgun bore. Gauge numbers originally referred to the number of lead balls—of equal diameter as the gun barrel—required to make a pound. Thus, a 16-gauge shotgun's bore was smaller than a 12-gauge shotgun's. Today, an international agreement assigns millimeter measures to each gauge.

Gauge	Bore diameter (mm)	Gauge	Bore diameter (mm)
6	23.34	14	17.60
10	19.67	16	16.81
12	18.52	20	15.90

Horsepower (hp)—the power needed to lift 550 pounds 1 foot in 1 second or to lift 33,000 pounds 1 foot in 1 minute. Equivalent to 746 watts or 2,546 British thermal units per hour.

Karat or carat (k or c)—a measure of fineness for gold equal to $\frac{1}{24}$ part of pure gold in an alloy. 24-karat gold is pure; 18-karat gold is ¼ alloy. The carat is also used as a unit of weight for precious stones; it is equal to 200 milligrams or 3.086 grains.

Knot (kn or kt)—a measure of the speed of ships. A knot equals 1 nautical mile (about 1.151 statute miles) per hour.

Quire (qr)—25 sheets of paper of the same size and quality.

Ream (rm)—500 sheets of paper of the same size and quality.

POSTAL INFORMATION

Administration of the U.S. Postal Service

The Postal Reorganization Act, creating a government-owned postal service under the executive branch and replacing the old executive Post Office Department, was signed into law Aug. 12, 1970. The service officially came into being on July 1, 1971. The U.S. Postal Service is governed by an 11-person board. Nine members are appointed by the president, with Senate approval. These nine choose a postmaster general. The board and the postmaster general choose the 11th member, who serves as deputy postmaster general.

Congress passed the Postal Accountability and Enhancement Act, which overhauled postal service operations for the first time since 1971, on Dec. 8, 2006. New operating provisions included the ability to adjust rates annually, negotiate for contracts, and invest profits in internal improvements. (The Postal Service last received a public service subsidy, i.e., taxpayer dollars, in 1982.)

Historical Postage Rates, 1851-2020

Postage cost for a prepaid, 1-oz. letter (the first-class standard after July 1, 1885).

Effective date	Rate	2020 dollars	Effective date	Rate	2020 dollars	Effective date	Rate	2020 dollars
July 1, 1851	$0.06[1]	$2.08	Dec. 31, 1975	$0.13	$0.60	Jan. 8, 2006	$0.39	$0.50
July 1, 1863	0.06	1.26	May 29, 1978	0.15	0.60	May 14, 2007	0.41	0.51
Oct. 1, 1883	0.04	1.06	Mar. 22, 1981	0.18	0.52	May 12, 2008	0.42	0.50
July 1, 1885	0.02	0.55	Nov. 1, 1981	0.20	0.55	May 11, 2009	0.44	0.53
Nov. 2, 1917	0.03[2]	0.57	Feb. 17, 1985	0.22	0.53	Jan. 22, 2012	0.45	0.51
July 1, 1919	0.02[2]	0.29	Apr. 3, 1988	0.25	0.55	Jan. 27, 2013	0.46	0.51
July 6, 1932	0.03	0.57	Feb. 3, 1991	0.29	0.55	Jan. 26, 2014	0.49[3]	0.54
Aug. 1, 1958	0.04	0.35	Jan. 1, 1995	0.32	0.55	Apr. 10, 2016	0.47	0.50
Jan. 7, 1963	0.05	0.42	Jan. 10, 1999	0.33	0.51	Jan. 22, 2017	0.49	0.52
Jan. 7, 1968	0.06	0.45	Jan. 7, 2001	0.34	0.50	Jan. 21, 2018	0.50	0.52
May 16, 1971	0.08	0.51	June 30, 2002	0.37	0.53	Jan. 27, 2019	0.55	—
Mar. 2, 1974	0.10	0.54						

— = Not applicable. **Note:** 2020 dollars are as of June. (1) For prepaid domestic letters traveling under 3,000 miles. (2) The price increased one cent during World War I; Congress restored its prewar rate in 1919. (3) The Postal Regulatory Commission approved a 6% total price increase: a 1.7% increase for inflation and an additional 4.3% temporary increase to compensate for USPS losses during the 2008-09 recession.

Status of the U.S. Postal Service, 2001-19

Source: *Postal Facts*, U.S. Postal Service

	2001	2005	2010	2013	2014	2015	2016	2017	2018	2019
Total mail items (bil)	207.5	211.7	170.9	158.2	155.5	154.3	154.3	149.5	146.4	142.6
First-class mail items (bil)	103.7	98.1	77.6	65.8	63.8	62.6	61.2	58.7	56.7	54.9
Stamped mail items (bil)	53.6	45.9	28.9	22.6	21.8	20.7	19.7	18.5	17.5	16.5
Marketing mail items (bil)	89.9	100.9	81.8	80.8	80.3	80.0	80.9	78.3	77.3	75.5
Shipping/package volume (bil)	NA	NA	3.1	3.7	4.0	4.5	5.2	5.7	6.2	6.2
Annual revenue (bil)	$65.8	$69.9	$67.1	$67.3	$67.8	$68.8	$71.4	$69.6	$70.6	$71.1
Total retail revenue (bil).	$14.8	$17.3	$17.5	$18.3	$19.0	$19.2	$13.5	$12.9	$12.7	$12.7
Total customer visits (bil)	1.4	1.3	1.1	1.0	0.9	0.9	0.9	0.9	0.8	0.8
Delivery points (mil)	137.7	144.3	150.9	152.9	153.9	155.0	156.1	157.3	158.6	160.0
Total delivery routes	242,600	243,000	230,600	225,152	244,365	226,777	229,104	228,483	231,843	231,807
Total retail offices	38,123	37,142	36,222	35,434	35,649	35,520	35,423	35,005	34,772	34,613
Career employees	775,903	704,716	583,908	491,017	488,300	491,863	508,908	503,103	497,157	496,934

U.S. Domestic Mail Rates

Source: *Price List* (Notice 123), U.S. Postal Service. Effective Oct. 18, 2020. Rates are for retail customers unless noted. Domestic rates apply to the U.S., its territories and possessions, APOs, FPOs, and Freely Associated States.

First-Class Mail

Includes written matter such as letters, postcards, bills, account statements, and any matter sealed or closed against inspection up to 13 oz. In most cases, delivery is within 2-3 business days.

Letters measuring up to 6⅛ by 11½ in. and not more than ¼ in. thick cost 55¢ for the first oz., 15¢ for each additional oz. or fraction thereof, up to 3.5 oz. Square, oversized, or unusually shaped envelope stamps start at 70¢. Postcard postage is 35¢. Large envelopes up to 12 by 15 in. (or letters over 3.5 oz.) cost $1.00 for the first oz. and 20¢ for each additional oz. or fraction thereof. Presort- and automation-compatible mail can qualify for lower rates if certain piece minimums, mailing permits, and other requirements are met.

Forever Stamps. The USPS introduced the nondenominational "Forever" stamp Apr. 12, 2007, at an initial cost of 41¢. The Forever stamp can be purchased at the current First-Class standard rate and will always be valid as First-Class postage on standard envelopes weighing 1 oz. or less, even after rates increase.

Priority Mail

Priority Mail is delivered within 1-3 business days in most cases, with no additional charge for Saturday deliveries. Can be any mailable article up to 70 lbs and not over 108 in. in length and girth combined.

Priority Mail Flat Rate: $7.75, $8.05, $8.40, regardless of weight, if matter fits into designated USPS flat-rate envelopes. $8.30, $15.05, $21.10 if it fits into flat-rate boxes.

Priority Mail Forever Prepaid Flat Rate packaging can be purchased online at the current priority mail flat rate and remains valid for use after future price increases.

Priority Mail Express

Provides guaranteed expedited service for any mailable article up to 70 lbs and not over 108 in. in combined length and girth. Offers next-day delivery to most destinations; $12.50 additional charge for Sunday or holiday delivery. Includes insurance up to $100, mailing receipt, proof of delivery signature record, and tracking.

Priority Mail Express Flat Rate: $26.35, $26.50, $26.95, regardless of weight, if matter fits into designated USPS flat-rate envelopes.

Domestic Mail Services and Fees

Adult signature required: $6.65 per piece; person 21 years of age or older must sign for shipment.

Adult signature restricted delivery: $6.90 per piece; specific addressee or agent 21 years of age or older must sign for shipment.

Certificate of mailing: $1.50 per piece.

Certified mail: $3.55 per piece; provides proof of mailing and electronic verification of delivery or delivery attempt.

Certified mail restricted delivery: $9.00 per piece.

Collect on delivery (COD): $7.85 for amount to be collected/insurance desired up to $50; $9.80 for $50.01-$100; $2.05 for each additional $100.

Domestic money order: $1.25 for money orders $0.01 to $500; $1.75 for $500.01 to $1,000.

Pickup on demand: $24.00 per pickup; available for Priority Mail, Priority Mail Express, and USPS Retail Ground.

Restricted delivery: $5.30 per item when purchased in combination with COD, Insured Mail, or Registered Mail.

Return receipt: If requested at time of mailing, $2.85 for a receipt by mail, $1.70 for email receipt.

Signature confirmation: $2.65 online, $3.15 at post office.

Sunday/holiday delivery: Available for Priority Mail Express only. Fee: $12.50.

Tracking

Formerly known as Delivery Confirmation, tracking can be used with First-Class Mail parcels, Priority Mail, USPS Retail Ground, and Package Services (Bound Printed Matter, Media Mail, and Library Mail). Available free of charge at time of mailing, except for USPS Marketing Mail parcels (electronic option, fee: $0.20).

Change of Address

The USPS will forward mail to another address provided a Change of Address (COA) form has been filed in person or mailed to a post office (free) or submitted online at moversguide.usps.com ($1.05 credit card authentication fee). The form can be picked up at any post office or requested by phone at (800) ASK-USPS.

Special Handling

Provides preferential handling, but not preferential delivery. Available for First-Class Mail, Priority Mail, Priority Mail Express, USPS Retail Ground, Media Mail, and Library Mail for a $11.15 surcharge.

Registered Mail

The most secure service provided by the USPS. Full value of item must be declared at time of registration and mailing. Insurance is included in fee for articles with a declared value of $0.01 up to $50,000. Fee: $12.60 for a declared value of $0, up to $23.75 for articles with a declared value of $4,000.01 to $5,000. For each additional $1,000 or fraction thereof above $5,000, add $1.70.

International Mail Rates

Source: *Price List* (Notice 123), U.S. Postal Service. Effective Oct. 18, 2020. Refer to www.usps.com for USPS price groups not shown here and weight limits by country.

First-Class Mail International

Letter-post items weighing up to 1 oz. and single postcards can be sent airmail for $1.20 to all countries.

Priority Mail International

Delivery is in 6-10 business days in many markets. Items must not be more than 108 in. in length and girth combined; max. weight is 70 lbs, though the limit varies by country.

Priority Mail International Flat Rate: $26.90 to Canada, $33.75-$37.45 to all other countries if matter fits into designated USPS flat-rate envelope (max. weight 4 lbs). Flat-rate boxes are $27.90-$67.05 to Canada, $35.35-$107.05 to all other countries.

Priority Mail Express International

Priority Mail Express International Flat Rate: $45.95 to Canada, $61.65 to Mexico, $66.50-$68.95 to all other countries if matter fits into flat-rate envelope (max. weight 4 lbs).

Global Express Guaranteed

Provides international expedited delivery, in partnership with FedEx, to certain countries. Item to be mailed must not weigh more than 70 lbs nor measure more than 108 in. in combined length and girth. Rate: Starts at $67.80 and $75.50 to Canada and Mexico, respectively, up to $142.95 to countries in price group 4, for items not over 0.5 lb in weight.

International Mail Services and Fees

Business reply: Card: $1.50; envelope (up to 2 oz.): $2.00.

Customs clearance and delivery: $6.50 per piece.

Insurance: Available to many countries for loss of or damage to items. Consult USPS for each country's indemnity limits.

Registered mail: Available for letter-post items only to most countries. Fee: $16.00.

Return receipt: Shows to whom and when item is delivered. Fee: $4.15 per piece (must be purchased at time of mailing).

Postal money order: $10.25 per money order. Only accepted in certain countries.

U.S. Postal Abbreviations

The abbreviations below are approved by the U.S. Postal Service for use in addresses.

Alabama	AL	Illinois	IL	Missouri	MO	Pennsylvania	PA
Alaska	AK	Indiana	IN	Montana	MT	Puerto Rico	PR
American Samoa	AS	Iowa	IA	Nebraska	NE	Rhode Island	RI
Arizona	AZ	Kansas	KS	Nevada	NV	South Carolina	SC
Arkansas	AR	Kentucky	KY	New Hampshire	NH	South Dakota	SD
California	CA	Louisiana	LA	New Jersey	NJ	Tennessee	TN
Colorado	CO	Maine	ME	New Mexico	NM	Texas	TX
Connecticut	CT	Marshall Islands[1]	MH	New York	NY	Utah	UT
Delaware	DE	Maryland	MD	North Carolina	NC	Vermont	VT
District of Columbia	DC	Massachusetts	MA	North Dakota	ND	Virgin Islands	VI
Florida	FL	Michigan	MI	Northern Mariana Isls.	MP	Virginia	VA
Georgia	GA	Micronesia,		Ohio	OH	Washington	WA
Guam	GU	Federated States of[1]	FM	Oklahoma	OK	West Virginia	WV
Hawaii	HI	Minnesota	MN	Oregon	OR	Wisconsin	WI
Idaho	ID	Mississippi	MS	Palau[1]	PW	Wyoming	WY

(1) Although an independent nation, this country is subject to domestic rates and fees.

Canadian Province and Territory Postal Abbreviations

Source: Canada Post

Alberta	AB	Newfoundland and		Nunavut	NU	Quebec	QC
British Columbia	BC	Labrador	NL	Ontario	ON	Saskatchewan	SK
Manitoba	MB	Northwest Territories	NT	Prince Edward Island	PE	Yukon	YT
New Brunswick	NB	Nova Scotia	NS				

Social Security Coverage

Source: Social Security Administration; World Almanac research; provisions shown are as under current law, Aug. 2020

Social Security Benefits

Social Security's **Old-Age, Survivors, and Disability Insurance (OASDI)** program benefits are based on a worker's **primary insurance amount (PIA)**, which is related by law to the average indexed monthly earnings (AIME) on which Social Security contributions have been paid. The full PIA is payable to a worker who retires at full retirement age (FRA), which is 65-67 depending on birth year, and to an entitled disabled worker at any age. Spouses and children of retired or disabled workers and survivors of deceased workers receive set proportions of the PIA subject to a family maximum amount. The PIA is calculated by applying varying percentages to succeeding parts of the AIME. The formula is adjusted annually to reflect changes in average annual wages.

Increases in Social Security benefits are initiated for December of each year, assuming the Consumer Price Index (CPI) for the third calendar quarter of the year increased relative to the base quarter (i.e., the third calendar quarter of the year in which an increase last took effect). The size of the benefit increase is determined by the percentage rise of the CPI between the quarters measured.

The **average monthly benefit** payable to all retired workers amounted to $1,503 in Dec. 2019. The average benefit for disabled workers in that month was $1,258.

Maximum Monthly Retired-Worker Benefits Payable to Individuals Who Retired at Full Retirement Age (FRA)

Retirement year[1]	Maximum benefit— Payable at retirement	Payable effective Dec. 2019
1990	$975	$1,977
1995	1,199	2,048
2000	1,435	2,191
2005	1,939	2,622
2006	2,053	2,667
2007	2,141	2,692
2008	2,185	2,687
2009	2,323	2,700
2010	2,346	2,726
2011	2,366	2,749
2012	2,513	2,819
2013	2,533	2,794
2014	2,642	2,871
2015	2,663	2,846
2016	2,639	2,820
2017	2,687	2,862
2018	2,788	2,912
2019	2,861	2,906
2020	3,011	3,011

(1) Benefits in 2002 and earlier are for retirement at age 65 at beginning of a given year. Benefits in 2003-08 are for starting benefits at exact FRA during the year. Benefits in 2009 and later are for retirement at age 66 at beginning of year.

Amount of Work Required

To qualify for benefits, the worker generally must have worked a certain length of time in covered employment. Just how long depends on when the worker reaches age 62 or, if earlier, when he or she dies or becomes disabled. A person born after 1929 who dies, becomes disabled, or reaches 62 after 1991 must generally have had at least 10 years of work credit to qualify for benefits.

Contribution and Benefit Base

(annual limit on the amount of earnings subject to taxation under OASDI)

Calendar year	OASDI[1]	Calendar year	OASDI[1]	Calendar year	OASDI[1]
1995	$61,200	2004	$87,900	2013	$113,700
1996	62,700	2005	90,000	2014	117,000
1997	65,400	2006	94,200	2015	118,500
1998	68,400	2007	97,500	2016	118,500
1999	72,600	2008	102,000	2017	127,200
2000	76,200	2009	106,800	2018	128,400
2001	80,400	2010	106,800	2019	132,900
2002	84,900	2011	106,800	2020	137,700
2003	87,000	2012	110,100		

(1) Old-Age, Survivors, and Disability Insurance.

A person is **fully insured** when he or she has one quarter of coverage for every year after age 21 is reached (or 1950, if later) up to but not including the year the worker reaches 62, dies, or becomes disabled. In 2020, a person earns one quarter of coverage for each $1,410 of annual earnings in covered employment, up to four quarters per year.

To receive **disability benefits**, the worker, in addition to being fully insured, must generally have credit for 20 quarters of coverage out of the 40 calendar quarters before he or she became

disabled. A disabled blind worker need meet only the fully insured requirement. Persons disabled before age 31 can qualify with a briefer period of coverage. Certain survivor benefits are payable if the deceased worker had 6 quarters of coverage in the 13 quarters preceding death.

Tax Rate Schedule

(percentage of covered earnings)

Year	Total (for employees and employers, each)	OASDI[1]	HI[2]
1979-80	6.13%	5.08%	1.05%
1981	6.65.	5.35.	1.30
1982-83	6.70.	5.40.	1.30
1984	7.00.	5.70.	1.30
1985	7.05.	5.70.	1.35
1986-87	7.15.	5.70.	1.45
1988-89	7.51.	6.06.	1.45
1990 and after[3]	7.65.	6.20.	1.45
Year	**(for self-employed)**		
1979-80	8.10%	7.05%	1.05%
1981	9.30.	8.00.	1.30
1982-83	9.35.	8.05.	1.30
1984	14.00.	11.40.	2.60
1985	14.10.	11.40.	2.70
1986-87	14.30.	11.40.	2.90
1988-89	15.02.	12.12.	2.90
1990 and after[3]	15.30.	12.40.	2.90

(1) Old-Age, Survivors, and Disability Insurance. (2) Hospital Insurance (Medicare). (3) Public Law (PL) 111-147 exempted most employers from paying the employer share of OASDI payroll tax on wages paid Mar. 19-Dec. 31, 2010, to certain qualified individuals hired after Feb. 3, 2010. PL 111-312 reduced the OASDI payroll tax rate for 2011 by 2 percentage points for employees and for self-employed workers. PL 112-96 extended the 2011 rate reduction through 2012. The laws required that the general fund of the Treasury reimbursed the OASI and DI Trust Funds for these temporary reductions.

What Aged Workers Receive

A person may receive monthly old-age benefits when he or she has enough work in covered employment and has reached retirement age—age 62 for reduced benefits or the age below for full benefits.

Full Retirement Age (FRA) by Birth Year

Year of birth	FRA	Year of birth	FRA
1937 or earlier	65	1955	66 and 2 mos.
1938	65 and 2 mos.	1956	66 and 4 mos.
1939	65 and 4 mos.	1957	66 and 6 mos.
1940	65 and 6 mos.	1958	66 and 8 mos.
1941	65 and 8 mos.	1959	66 and 10 mos.
1942	65 and 10 mos.	1960 or later	67
1943-54	66		

Note: If born on Jan. 1, refer to the previous birth year.

In 2000, the retirement earnings test was eliminated beginning with the month when the beneficiary reaches **full retirement age (FRA)**. A person at or above FRA no longer receives reduced benefits because of earnings. However, a person's benefits are reduced $1 for every $3 of earnings above the limit allowed by law ($48,600 for 2020) if he or she retires in the same calendar year but months prior to FRA. For retirees who have not yet attained FRA, the reduction is $1 for every $2 of earnings over the exempt amount ($18,240 for 2020).

For workers who reached age 65 between 1982 and 1989, Social Security benefits are raised by 3% for each year in which the worker did not receive benefits between FRA and 70 (72 before 1984), whether because of earnings from work, because the worker did not apply for benefits, or because the worker declined benefits after entitlement. The **delayed retirement credit** is 1% per year for workers who reached age 65 before 1982. The rate for workers who reached age 65 in 1998-99 is 5.5%; 2000-01, 6.0%; 2002-03, 6.5%; 2004-05, 7.0%; and 2006-07, 7.5%. The delayed retirement credit rose to 8% per year for 2008 and years after.

For workers retiring early, benefits are permanently reduced 5/9 of 1% for each month before the FRA, up to 36 months. If the number of months exceeds 36, then the benefit is further reduced 5/12 of 1% per month.

For example, workers who retire at exactly age 62 have a total of 60 months of reduction if their FRA is 67. The reduction for the first 36 months is 5/9 of 36%, or 20%. The reduction for the remaining 24 months is 5/12 of 24%, or 10%. These workers would see their benefits reduced by 30% by retiring early. The nearer to FRA a person is when he or she begins collecting a benefit, the larger the monthly benefit will be.

Benefits for Worker's Spouse

The spouse of a worker who is getting Social Security retirement or disability payments may become entitled to an insurance benefit of **one-half of the worker's PIA** if claiming benefits at full retirement age. Reduced spouse's benefits are available at age 62 and are permanently reduced 25/36 of 1% for each month before FRA, up to 36 months. If the number of months exceeds 36, then the benefit is further reduced 5/12 of 1% per month. Benefits are also payable to the aged divorced spouse of an insured worker if he or she was married to the worker for at least 10 years. To qualify for divorced spouse benefits, the insured worker does not have to be receiving benefits if the divorce occurred at least two years earlier. Benefits received as a spouse are reduced by the amount of one's PIA.

Benefits for Children of Workers

If a retired or disabled worker has a child under age 18, the **child** will usually get a benefit equal to **one-half of the worker's unreduced benefit**. So will the worker's spouse, regardless of age, if he or she is **caring for an entitled child** of the worker, and the child is under 16 or became disabled before age 22. However, total benefits paid on a worker's earnings record are subject to a family maximum. Total monthly benefits paid to the family of a worker who retired in 2020 at age 66 and always had the maximum earnings creditable under Social Security cannot exceed $5,270.

Entitled children generally stop receiving benefits at age 18, though they can continue receiving benefits until age 19 if they attend elementary or secondary school full-time. A child disabled before age 22 may get a benefit as long as the disability meets the definition in the law.

Benefits may also be paid to a grandchild or step-grandchild of a worker or of his or her spouse, in special circumstances.

OASDI Beneficiaries

Beneficiaries	May 2005	May 2010	May 2019	May 2020
Total (in thous.)[1]	48,068	53,349	63,560	64,697
Age 65 and over, total	33,811	36,914	47,756	49,199
Retired workers. . . .	27,413	30,734	41,584	43,034
Disabled workers. . .	112	339	534	550
Survivors/ dependents	6,286	5,841	5,638	5615
Under age 65, total . . .	14,257	16,435	15,803	15,497
Retired workers. . . .	2,809	3,314	2,772	2,699
Disabled workers. . .	6,239	7,628	7,952	7,781
Survivors/ dependents	5,209	5,492	5,079	5,017
Total monthly benefits (in mil) . . .	**$42,074**	**$56,966**	**$85,758**	**$89,936**

OASDI = Old-Age, Survivors, and Disability Ins. (1) Numbers may not add up to totals due to rounding or incomplete enumeration.

What Disabled Workers Receive

A worker who becomes unable to work may be eligible for a monthly disability benefit. Benefits continue until it is determined that the individual is no longer disabled. When a disabled-worker beneficiary reaches FRA (66 years for workers born 1943-54), the disability benefit becomes a retired-worker benefit.

Benefits—like those for dependents of retired-worker beneficiaries generally—may be paid to dependents of disabled beneficiaries. However, the maximum family benefit in disability cases is generally lower than in retirement cases.

Survivor Benefits

If an insured worker should die, one or more types of benefits may be payable to survivors, again subject to a maximum family benefit described above.

1. If claiming benefits at FRA, the **surviving spouse** will receive a benefit equal to 100% of the deceased worker's benefit. Benefits claimed before FRA are reduced, with a maximum reduction of 28.5% at age 60. However, if the deceased worker claimed benefits before FRA, the surviving spouse's benefits are limited to the amount the worker would be getting if alive, but not less than 82.5% of the worker's PIA. Remarriage after the worker's death ends the surviving spouse's benefit rights. However, if the widow(er) marries,

and the marriage later ends, he or she regains benefit rights. (A marriage after age 60, or age 50 if disabled, is deemed not to have occurred for benefit purposes.) Survivor benefits may also be paid to a divorced spouse if the marriage lasted for at least 10 years.

Disabled widows and widowers may under certain circumstances qualify for benefits after attaining age 50 at the rate of 71.5% of the deceased worker's PIA. The widow or widower must have become totally disabled before or within seven years after the spouse's death or the last month in which he or she received mother's or father's insurance benefits.

2. There is a benefit for each **child under age 18**. The monthly benefit for a child of a deceased worker is 3/4 of the PIA, subject to the family maximum. A child who became disabled before age 22 may also receive benefits. Also, a child can receive benefits until age 19 if he or she is in full-time attendance at an elementary or secondary school.

3. There is a **mother's or father's benefit** for the widow(er) if children of the worker who are under age 16 are in his or her care. The benefit is 75% of the PIA (subject to the family maximum), and it continues until the youngest child reaches age 16, at which time payments stop even if the child's benefit continues. Benefits may continue if the widow(er) has a disabled child beneficiary age 16 or over in his or her care.

4. Dependent parents may be eligible for benefits if they have been receiving at least half their support from the worker before his or her death, have reached age 62, and (except in certain circumstances) have not remarried since the worker's death. Each parent gets 75% of the worker's PIA; if only one parent survives, the benefit is 82% (could be reduced for the family maximum).

5. A **lump sum** cash payment of **$255** is made if the worker was living with a spouse or has a child who is eligible for immediate monthly survivor benefits.

Self-Employed Workers

A self-employed person who has **net earnings of $400 or more** in a year must report such earnings for Social Security tax and credit purposes. Income from real estate, savings, dividends, loans, pensions, or insurance policies are not included unless it is part of a person's business.

A self-employed person receives one quarter of coverage for each $1,410 for 2020, up to a maximum of four quarters per year.

The nonfarm self-employed have the option of reporting their earnings as 2/3 of their gross income from self-employment. This option can be used only if actual net earnings from self-employment income are less than $1,600 and less than 2/3 of their gross income. The option may be used only five times. Also, the self-employed person must have actual net earnings of $400 or more in two of the three taxable years immediately preceding the year in which he or she uses the option.

When a person has both taxable wages and earnings from self-employment, wages are credited for Social Security purposes first; only as much self-employment income as brings total earnings up to the current taxable maximum becomes subject to the self-employment tax.

Farm Owners and Workers

Self-employed farmers whose gross annual earnings from farming are **$7,920** or less may report 2/3 of their gross earnings instead of net earnings for Social Security purposes. Farmers whose gross income is over $7,920 and whose net farm profits were less than $5,717 can report the smaller of 2/3 of gross farm income and $5,280. Cash or crop shares received from a tenant or share farmer count if the owner participated materially in production or management. The self-employed farmer pays contributions at the same rate as other self-employed persons.

Agricultural employees. A worker's earnings from farm work count toward benefits if (1) the employer pays the worker $150 or more in cash during the year or (2) the employer spends $2,500 or more in the year for agricultural labor. Under these rules, a person gets credit for one calendar quarter for each $1,410 in cash pay in 2020.

Foreign farm workers admitted to the U.S. on a temporary basis are not covered.

Household Workers

If an employer pays a household worker (e.g., housekeeper, cook, laundry worker, nurse, babysitter, nanny, gardener) who is age 18 or older **$2,200 or more** in wages in 2020, the wages are covered under Social Security. This includes transportation costs paid for in cash. The job need not be regular or full-time.

The employee should get a Social Security card at the Social Security office and show it to the employer. The employer deducts the amount of the employee's Social Security tax from the worker's pay, adds an identical amount as the employer's Social Security tax, and sends the total amount to the federal government.

Medicare Coverage

Source: Centers for Medicare & Medicaid Services, U.S. Dept. of Health and Human Services

The Medicare health insurance program provides acute-care coverage for Social Security and Railroad Retirement beneficiaries age 65 and over; workers and spouses age 65 and over with sufficient Medicare-only coverage in federal, state, or local government employment; certain persons entitled to receive Social Security or Railroad Retirement disability benefits; certain disabled persons with Medicare-only coverage through government employment; certain persons with end-stage kidney disease; and certain persons in the vicinity of Libby, MT, with asbestos-related conditions. What follows is a basic description that may not cover all circumstances.

The **basic Medicare plan**, available nationwide, is a fee-for-service arrangement where the beneficiary may use any provider accepting Medicare. Some services are not covered, and there are some out-of-pocket costs.

Hospital insurance (Part A). The basic hospital insurance program pays covered services for hospital and post-hospital care, including:
- All necessary inpatient hospital care for the first 60 days of each benefit period, except for a deductible ($1,408 in 2020). For days 61-90, Medicare pays for services over and above the co-insurance ($352 per day in 2020). After 90 days, the beneficiary has 60 lifetime reserve days for which Medicare helps pay. The coinsurance amount for reserve days was $704 in 2020.
- Up to 100 days of care in a skilled-nursing facility in each benefit period. Hospital insurance pays for all covered services for the first 20 days; for days 21-100, the beneficiary pays coinsurance ($176 per day in 2020).
- Part-time home health care provided by nurses or other health workers.
- Limited coverage of hospice care for the terminally ill.

There is a premium for this insurance in certain—but not most—cases.

Medical insurance (Part B). Eligible elderly and disabled persons can receive benefits under this supplementary program only if they sign up and agree to a monthly premium. As of 2007, the monthly premium is tied to annual income. Individuals with an income of $87,000 or less and couples with an income of $174,000 or less pay $144.60 per person if they sign up upon becoming eligible in 2020. Part B covers certain medical services and supplies, including:
- Physicians' and surgeons' services, as well as some services furnished by other medical professionals.
- Services in an emergency room, outpatient clinic, or ambulatory surgical center.
- Home health care not covered under Part A.
- Laboratory tests, X-rays, and other diagnostic radiology services.
- Certain preventative care services and screening tests.
- Most physical and occupational therapy and speech pathology services.
- Comprehensive outpatient rehabilitation facility services and mental health care in a partial hospitalization psychiatric program, if inpatient care would otherwise be required.
- Radiation therapy; renal (kidney) dialysis and transplants; and heart, lung, heart-lung, liver, pancreas, bone marrow, and intestinal transplants.
- Approved durable medical equipment for home use.
- Drugs that are not usually self-administered.
- Certain services for diabetes.
- Ambulance services when other transportation methods are contraindicated.
- Rural health clinic and health center services, including some telemedicine.

Part B services are generally subject to a deductible ($198 in 2020), coinsurance (generally 20% of the remaining allowed charges with certain exceptions), a deductible for blood, and amounts above the allowed charge if a doctor or supplier does not accept the Medicare-approved rate as payment in full. For outpatient hospital services, coinsurance varies by service, usually falling between 20% and 50% of allowed charges. There are no deductibles or coinsurance for certain services, such as lab tests paid under the clinical lab fee schedule, home health agency services (except some durable medical equipment, which is subject to 20% coinsurance), and some preventative care services. Payments for certain physical, speech, and occupational therapy services are subject to certain limits. Dental care, hearing aids, and routine eye care are generally not covered under the basic plan.

To get medical insurance (Part B), persons approaching age 65 may enroll during the seven-month initial enrollment period, which includes the month of their 65th birthday as well as the three months before and after. Persons desiring coverage to begin in the month they reach age 65 must enroll in the three months before their birthday. Persons who enroll after their initial enrollment period may be subject to late-enrollment premiums.

The monthly premium is deducted from the cash benefit for persons receiving Social Security, Railroad Retirement, or Civil Service Retirement benefits. Income from the medical premiums and the federal matching payments are put in a Supplementary Medical Insurance Trust Fund, from which benefits and administrative expenses are paid.

Medicare Advantage (Part C) (formerly Medicare+ Choice). Persons eligible for Medicare may have the option of getting services through a Medicare-certified local coordinated care plan, such as a health maintenance organization (HMO), local preferred provider organization (PPO), provider-sponsored organization (PSO), or other local Medicare-certified **managed care** plan; a regional preferred provider organization (RPPO); a private fee-for-service plan; or, in certain cases, a special-needs plan. Any such plan must provide at least the same benefits as Parts A and B, except for hospice services. They may provide added benefits (such as vision or hearing coverage) or reduce cost sharing or premiums. Enrollees may be required to use the plan's network of participating providers or pay higher out-of-pocket costs to go outside the network.

Prescription Drug Coverage (Part D). Effective Jan. 1, 2006, an optional Medicare prescription drug plan provides insurance coverage for prescription drugs. Medicare recipients pay a monthly premium (averaging about $30 in 2020 for basic coverage, depending on the provider) and a portion of drug costs. As of 2011, the monthly premium was tied to annual income; in 2020, individuals with an income greater than $87,000 and couples with an income greater than $174,000 pay more. The open enrollment period is Oct. 15-Dec. 7. Coverage varies depending on the drug plan selected.

Further details are available on the Internet at www.medicare. gov or by calling 1-800-MEDICARE (1-800-633-4227).

Medicare card. Persons qualifying for hospital insurance under Social Security receive a health insurance card. The card indicates whether the individual has taken out medical insurance protection. It is to be shown to the hospital, skilled-nursing facility, home health agency, doctor, or other provider of covered services.

Payments are generally made only in the 50 states, District of Columbia, Puerto Rico, U.S. Virgin Isls., Guam, American Samoa, and Northern Mariana Isls.

Social Security Financing

Social Security is paid for by a tax on certain earnings (for 2020, on earnings up to $137,700) for **Old-Age, Survivors, and Disability Insurance (OASDI)** and on all earnings (no upper limit) for hospital insurance with the **Medicare** program; the taxable earnings base for OASDI is adjusted annually to reflect changes in average wages. The employed worker and his or her employer share Social Security taxes equally.

Employers remit amounts withheld from employee wages for Social Security and income taxes to the Internal Revenue Service; employer Social Security taxes are also payable at the same time. (Self-employed workers pay Social Security taxes when filing their regular income tax forms.) The Social Security taxes (along with revenues arising from partial taxation of the Social Security benefits of certain high-income people) are transferred to the Social Security Trust Funds; they can be used only to pay benefits, the cost of rehabilitation services, and administrative expenses. By law, money not immediately needed for those purposes is invested in obligations of the federal government, which must pay interest on the money borrowed and must repay the principal when the obligations are redeemed or mature.

On Jan. 1, 1974, the **Supplemental Security Income (SSI)** program, established by the Social Security Amendments of 1972, replaced federal grants to the states to aid the needy aged, blind, and disabled. The program provides for federal payments, based on uniform national standards and eligibility requirements, and for state supplementary payments. The Social Security Administration administers the federal payments—financed by general funds of the Treasury—as well as the state supplement for those states that choose to have it federally administered. States may supplement the federal payment of all recipients and must supplement it for persons otherwise adversely affected by the transition from the former public assistance programs. In May 2020, the number of persons receiving federally administered SSI payments was 8,047,662; the payments totaled about $4.9 bil.

The **maximum monthly federal SSI payment** for individuals without an eligible spouse and with no other countable income, living in their own household, was $783 in 2020. For couples where both members were eligible, the maximum payment was $1,175.

For further information, contact the Social Security Administration toll-free at 1-800-772-1213 or visit its website at www.ssa.gov.

Examples of Monthly Social Security Benefits Available, 2020

Benefit or beneficiary	For low earnings ($24,191)[1]	For med. earnings ($53,757)[1]	For max. earnings ($132,048)[1,2]
Primary insurance amount (worker retiring at 66 years, 0 months)	$1,128.90	$1,861.10	$3,011.50
Maximum family benefit (worker retiring at 66 years, 0 months)	1,693.60	3,395.90	5,270.50
Maximum family disability benefit (worker disabled at 55; in 2020)	1,671.10	2,932.80	4,734.70
Disabled worker (worker disabled at 55):			
Worker alone	1,185.00	1,955.00	3,156.00
Worker, spouse, and 1 child	1,669.00	2,931.00	4,734.00
Retired worker claiming benefits at age 62:			
Worker alone[3]	846.00	1,392.00	2,252.00
Worker with spouse claiming benefits at—			
FRA or over	1,436.00	2,363.00	3,823.00
Age 62[3]	1,239.00	2,039.00	3,299.00
Widow or widower claiming benefits at—			
Age 66 or over[4]	1,128.00	1,861.00	3,011.00
Age 60[4]	807.00	1,330.00	2,153.00
Disabled widow or widower claiming benefits at age 50-59[5]	807.00	1,330.00	2,153.00
1 surviving child[4]	846.00	1,395.00	2,258.00
Widow or widower at FRA or over and 1 child[4]	1,692.00	3,256.00	5,269.00
Widowed mother or father and 1 child[4]	1,692.00	2,790.00	4,516.00
Widowed mother or father and 2 children[4]	1,692.00	3,393.00	5,268.00

FRA = Full retirement age. Note: Effective Jan. 2020. (1) Career average earnings: an average of lifetime earnings indexed to the year prior to entitlement (2019 in this case). (2) Assumes work beginning at age 22. (3) Assumes maximum reduction. (4) Assumes worker lived and worked until FRA without receiving reduced benefits. (5) Effective Jan. 1984, disabled widow(er) claiming a benefit at ages 50-59 receive a benefit equal to 71.5% of the PIA.

Social Security Recipients by Age, Sex, Race, and Hispanic Origin, 2017

Source: Social Security Administration

Characteristic/benefit	Total	White	Black	American Indian, Alaska Native	Asian	Native Hawaiian/ other Pacific Isl.	Hispanic
Social Security beneficiaries (thous.)[1]	51,434	43,626	5,677	883	1,749	133	3,866
Sex							
Male	22,985	19,629	2,436	428	764	64	1,721
Female	28,449	23,996	3,240	455	985	68	2,146
Age							
15-54 years	4,847	3,609	1,041	184	133	18	536
55-64 years	6,438	5,128	1,047	151	185	32	543
65-74 years	22,478	19,294	2,220	341	827	50	1,641
75 years or older	17,671	15,594	1,369	207	604	33	1,146
Supplemental Security Income recipients (thous.)[1]	6,433	4,312	1,689	237	340	24	1,035
Sex							
Male	2,814	1,863	737	120	160	10	443
Female	3,619	2,449	952	117	180	14	593
Age							
15-54 years	3,112	2,140	832	136	94	11	531
55-64 years	1,861	1,267	523	58	38	9	228
65-74 years	884	577	215	30	78	2	166
75 years or older	576	327	119	13	129	2	111
Average annual benefit in 2016 (dollars)							
Social Security	$14,956	$15,219	$13,269	$13,630	$14,085	$14,800	$12,855
Supplemental Security Income	8,024	8,083	7,986	7,531	7,639	NA	8,112

NA = Not available. **Note:** Race categories include people who reported being of that race, alone or in combination with another race. Persons of Hispanic origin may be of any race. The sum of the individual categories may not add up to totals because of rounding and because the totals include persons who reported being of more than one race. (1) Persons 15 or older receiving Social Security benefits or Supplemental Security Income in Mar. 2017.

Old-Age, Survivors, and Disability Insurance Beneficiaries, 2019

Source: Social Security Administration

State or area	Total benefits (thous.)	Total benefi-ciaries	Retirement (old-age) Retired workers	Spouses	Children	Survivors Widow(er)s and parents	Children	Disability Disabled workers	Spouses	Children
Alabama	$1,539,497	1,159,320	731,111	31,033	12,812	78,529	43,128	219,981	2,846	39,880
Alaska	139,300	104,568	75,412	3,147	1,988	5,442	4,654	11,583	158	2,184
Arizona	2,002,298	1,399,403	1,040,894	50,894	15,653	78,367	37,266	149,523	1,990	24,816
Arkansas	905,022	703,896	450,419	16,268	7,489	44,711	25,318	132,680	1,676	25,335
California	8,311,626	6,070,395	4,443,137	305,588	82,492	362,897	154,402	618,003	10,056	93,820
Colorado	1,275,705	897,886	665,194	37,412	8,098	50,543	23,984	96,445	1,037	15,173
Connecticut	1,061,420	689,996	512,703	22,870	7,678	36,513	18,295	78,473	691	12,773
Delaware	333,859	219,490	162,952	6,176	1,734	11,744	6,073	26,574	225	4,012
Dist. of Columbia	112,085	83,899	58,903	2,120	867	3,965	3,157	13,422	26	1,439
Florida	6,621,951	4,747,364	3,514,707	161,937	48,499	268,798	113,458	544,910	7,172	87,883
Georgia	2,536,552	1,871,862	1,288,872	50,158	21,128	113,210	67,795	276,354	3,460	50,885
Hawaii	390,967	277,013	218,219	9,612	3,826	14,570	6,237	20,572	350	3,627
Idaho	490,012	358,633	259,909	12,331	3,978	19,805	10,030	43,495	697	8,388
Illinois	3,219,194	2,267,082	1,627,122	84,413	24,705	144,255	70,089	269,014	3,378	44,106
Indiana	1,957,955	1,370,231	946,375	40,672	13,427	86,843	47,193	198,695	2,466	34,560
Iowa	921,357	657,019	482,117	20,826	6,409	40,268	18,264	76,483	733	11,919
Kansas	803,278	561,634	402,018	18,770	5,973	33,589	17,757	70,426	703	12,398
Kentucky	1,292,021	1,001,700	618,077	32,452	10,094	74,232	38,254	191,326	3,592	33,673
Louisiana	1,159,288	922,223	559,820	41,450	11,034	82,951	42,043	152,643	3,061	29,221
Maine	455,580	349,962	242,442	10,661	3,412	19,192	8,994	54,497	617	10,147
Maryland	1,510,998	1,020,436	742,552	33,177	10,150	56,217	32,929	124,843	826	19,742
Massachusetts	1,838,077	1,287,830	901,679	44,597	14,054	66,711	35,080	188,851	1,434	35,424
Michigan	3,249,744	2,236,852	1,536,620	75,109	23,922	139,023	69,064	329,376	4,852	58,886
Minnesota	1,533,787	1,053,166	784,382	36,935	10,586	55,062	26,344	118,405	962	20,490
Mississippi	858,065	677,464	429,412	15,543	8,871	45,927	30,471	122,113	1,834	23,293
Missouri	1,779,307	1,312,639	897,621	35,736	12,374	80,272	44,782	205,935	2,332	33,587
Montana	319,611	239,410	178,102	7,698	2,544	13,927	6,705	26,058	365	4,011
Nebraska	493,000	352,880	257,481	12,084	3,605	21,072	10,611	40,417	309	7,301
Nevada	764,540	552,219	413,107	15,986	6,102	29,071	14,489	63,167	728	9,569
New Hampshire	462,494	312,043	220,989	9,382	2,585	14,720	7,449	46,341	337	10,240
New Jersey	2,539,495	1,646,792	1,207,715	62,376	19,094	92,329	43,909	186,881	2,214	32,274
New Mexico	578,475	445,742	307,967	16,774	4,526	26,733	15,325	63,154	833	10,430
New York	5,240,721	3,667,022	2,603,254	147,467	46,315	207,475	95,575	477,552	6,118	83,266
North Carolina	2,981,195	2,144,804	1,526,249	50,917	19,870	116,547	64,969	311,730	3,366	51,156
North Dakota	183,880	136,520	99,735	4,833	1,192	9,758	4,540	14,046	114	2,302
Ohio	3,231,289	2,386,362	1,623,359	88,351	20,931	175,757	82,057	338,599	4,453	52,855
Oklahoma	1,071,093	802,326	537,909	24,266	8,664	55,112	29,901	123,472	1,683	21,319
Oregon	1,257,557	891,726	662,320	31,810	9,294	49,521	19,684	102,966	1,400	14,731
Pennsylvania	4,101,737	2,861,155	2,013,791	97,085	25,996	182,826	81,345	390,626	4,556	64,930
Rhode Island	322,326	228,257	160,706	5,743	2,623	11,154	5,868	35,441	257	6,465
South Carolina	1,645,360	1,174,399	828,566	28,705	11,110	67,311	36,863	171,174	1,973	28,697
South Dakota	245,384	182,793	137,577	5,628	1,590	10,859	5,490	18,335	162	3,152
Tennessee	2,005,604	1,478,145	995,471	41,650	14,643	93,854	51,797	237,006	3,157	40,567
Texas	5,816,704	4,338,301	2,954,611	206,031	50,764	315,685	150,771	544,477	9,254	106,708
Utah	594,305	419,037	296,554	21,275	5,450	23,543	16,691	45,483	640	9,401
Vermont	213,972	153,124	109,498	5,021	1,657	7,811	3,727	21,232	176	4,002
Virginia	2,231,955	1,559,858	1,113,220	52,471	15,493	92,892	44,793	203,630	2,510	34,849
Washington	2,017,636	1,376,287	1,005,248	55,307	14,775	75,223	32,173	165,880	1,935	25,746
West Virginia	632,734	478,209	292,653	21,719	5,448	40,741	17,559	83,775	2,329	13,985
Wisconsin	1,803,101	1,257,850	923,461	35,439	12,144	67,451	33,549	156,887	1,442	27,477
Wyoming	165,086	115,406	85,085	3,698	1,062	6,690	3,572	13,173	172	1,954
American Samoa	4,751	6,168	2,588	180	227	591	709	1,312	39	522
Guam	17,471	18,768	12,093	1,083	575	1,591	1,220	1,587	64	555
N. Mariana Isls.	2,266	3,188	1,925	133	178	301	325	258	8	60
Puerto Rico	764,388	828,099	481,024	61,533	10,328	73,153	24,462	148,218	5,179	24,202
U.S. Virgin Isls.	26,726	21,939	16,845	921	432	1,260	668	1,469	35	309
Foreign countries	488,564	682,888	431,883	115,040	11,773	97,759	13,687	9,343	452	2,951
Unknown	1,086	816	590	33	6	95	16	63	1	12
All areas	88,523,452	64,064,496	45,094,245	2,430,526	702,249	3,996,448	1,915,560	8,378,374	113,435	1,433,659

Outcomes of Applications for Disability Benefits, 1999-2017

Source: Social Security Administration

Year of application	Total	Pending final decision	Technical denials[1]	Medical denials Medical	Subsequent nonmedical[2]	Medical allowances Awards	Subsequent denials[2]	Award rate[3]	Allowance rate[4]
1999	1,265,037	0	104,332	445,995	4,056	708,797	1,857	56.0%	61.3%
2000	1,364,323	0	136,054	456,467	3,817	766,047	1,938	56.1	62.6
2005	2,087,733	0	528,760	642,170	6,964	907,877	1,962	43.5	58.4
2006	2,164,394	0	611,199	653,256	7,270	890,752	1,917	41.2	57.5
2007	2,216,565	0	651,753	641,811	7,914	913,269	1,818	41.2	58.5
2008	2,358,629	0	717,133	660,762	9,023	969,935	1,776	41.1	59.2
2009	2,753,012	0	845,213	789,600	10,688	1,105,663	1,848	40.2	58.1
2010	2,981,613	0	978,657	861,857	19,097	1,119,927	2,075	37.6	56.0
2011	2,952,087	5,450	981,943	868,153	20,774	1,073,705	2,062	36.4	54.8
2012	2,955,922	7,618	1,024,501	861,885	23,864	1,035,772	2,282	35.1	54.0
2013	2,790,680	12,103	971,096	820,040	25,035	960,161	2,245	34.6	53.2
2014	2,687,338	23,908	936,915	789,043	27,165	908,021	2,286	34.1	52.7
2015	2,547,661	79,755	904,240	710,383	27,935	823,035	2,313	33.3	52.8
2016	2,422,539	248,982	875,089	589,373	29,145	677,870	2,080	31.2	52.4
2017	2,258,949	320,565	829,717	520,862	28,175	557,804	1,826	28.8	50.5

Note: Data as of July 2018. Applications for more recent years may still be pending; award and allowance rates will change. Does not include Supplemental Security Income-only applications. (1) Application denied for non-medical reason. (2) Denied for non-medical reasons after medical criteria were adjudicated. (3) Percent of all applications, minus pending claims, in which benefits were awarded. (4) Percent of all medical decisions that resulted in an allowance.

OASDI Recipients and Monthly Payments, 1940-2019

Source: Social Security Administration

		Monthly benefits					Monthly benefits		
Year	Total recipients	Total (thous.)	Avg.[1]	Avg. (2019 dollars)[2]	Year	Total recipients	Total (thous.)	Avg.[1]	Avg. (2019 dollars)[2]
1940	222,488	$4,070	$18.29	$323.09	2000	45,414,794	$34,848,920	$767.35	$1,131.73
1945	1,288,107	23,801	18.48	254.44	2005	48,434,445	44,351,772	915.71	1,194.37
1950	3,477,243	126,857	36.48	375.63	2010	54,032,097	58,048,364	1,074.33	1,251.35
1955	7,960,616	411,613	51.71	477.96	2011	55,404,480	62,213,382	1,122.89	1,262.98
1960	14,844,589	936,321	63.07	528.06	2012	56,758,185	65,430,104	1,152.79	1,269.96
1965	20,866,767	1,516,802	72.69	571.04	2013	57,978,610	68,544,382	1,182.24	1,284.82
1970	26,228,629	2,628,326	100.21	639.63	2014	59,007,158	71,693,353	1,214.99	1,300.87
1975	32,085,372	5,727,903	178.52	821.44	2015	59,963,425	73,642,029	1,228.12	1,320.37
1980	35,618,840	10,694,022	300.23	901.82	2016	60,907,307	75,917,962	1,246.45	1,327.10
1985	37,058,353	15,901,643	429.10	999.72	2017	61,903,360	79,732,580	1,288.02	1,342.82
1990	39,832,125	21,686,763	544.45	1,050.95	2018	62,906,222	84,419,840	1,342.00	1,364.31
1995	43,387,259	28,148,078	648.76	1,079.06	2019	64,064,496	88,523,452	1,381.79	1,381.79

OASDI = Old-Age, Survivors, and Disability Insurance. **Note:** Disability insurance payments began in 1957. (1) Avg. monthly benefit does not necessarily reflect individual payments to OASDI recipients. (2) Adjusted for inflation.

Social Security Trust Funds
Source: Social Security Administration

Old-Age and Survivors Insurance (OASI) Trust Fund, 1940-2019
(in millions)

		INCOME				DISBURSEMENTS				
Fiscal year[1]	Total	Net payroll tax contribs.	Income from taxing benefits	General fund reimburse-ments[2]	Net interest[3]	Total	Benefit pymts.[4]	Admin. expenses	Transfers to Railroad Retirement program	Net increase in fund[5]	Year-end balance
1940	$592	$550	—	—	$42	$28	$16	$12	—	$564	$1,745
1950	2,367	2,106	—	$4	257	784	727	57	—	1,583	12,893
1960	10,360	9,843	—	—	517	11,073	10,270	202	$600	−713	20,829
1970	31,746	29,955	—	442	1,350	27,321	26,268	474	579	4,425	32,616
1980	100,051	97,608	—	557	1,886	103,228	100,626	1,160	1,442	−3,177	24,566
1990	278,607	260,069	$2,924	1,471	14,143	223,481	218,948	1,564	2,969	55,126	203,445
1995	326,067	289,525	5,114	11	31,417	294,456	288,607	1,797	4,052	31,611	447,946
2000	484,228	418,219	12,476	1	53,532	353,396	347,868	1,990	3,538	130,832	893,003
2005	599,992	502,998	15,332	—	81,662	436,919	430,439	2,900	3,579	163,073	1,615,623
2010	682,448	552,037	21,068	737	108,606	579,907	572,515	3,462	3,930	102,541	2,398,377
2011	692,510	495,031	21,174	68,886	107,419	599,232	591,477	3,645	4,110	93,278	2,491,654
2012	728,981	500,661	27,150	95,927	105,243	634,700	627,208	3,352	4,139	94,281	2,585,936
2013	739,668	589,976	23,144	26,433	100,115	670,648	663,195	3,410	3,948	69,114	2,655,049
2014	763,295	642,256	24,641	126	96,271	705,645	698,235	3,153	4,257	57,650	2,712,699
2015	795,311	672,246	29,627	211	93,235	741,464	733,711	3,496	4,258	53,855	2,766,554
2016	799,892	679,566	31,121	138	89,067	769,827	762,122	3,417	4,287	30,066	2,796,620
2017	822,442	702,123	35,416	15	84,888	798,961	791,094	3,551	4,316	23,481	2,820,101
2018	822,440	706,127	34,718	11	81,583	841,474	833,034	3,672	4,769	−19,034	2,801,066
2019	900,075	785,576	34,896	15	79,589	896,829	888,068	3,881	4,880	3,246	2,804,312

— = Not applicable. **Note:** Numbers may not add up to totals due to rounding. (1) Fiscal years 1977 and later consist of the 12 months ending on Sept. 30 of each year. Fiscal years prior to 1977 consisted of the 12 months ending on June 30 of each year. (2) Includes reimbursements from the general fund of the Treasury to the OASI Trust Fund for certain legislated measures since 1957. (3) Includes net profits or losses on marketable investments. Beginning in 1967, the trust fund paid administrative expenses on an estimated basis, with a final adjustment including interest made in the following fiscal year. Net interest includes these interest adjustments. Beginning in Oct. 1973, figures include relatively small gifts to the fund. (4) Beginning in 1967, includes payments for vocational rehabilitation services furnished to disabled persons receiving benefits because of their disabilities; beginning in 1983, includes reimbursements paid from the general fund to the trust fund for unnegotiated benefit checks. (5) Net change in assets during fiscal year, including amounts borrowed or repaid by other funds.

Disability Insurance (DI) Trust Fund, 1960-2019
(in millions)

		INCOME				DISBURSEMENTS				
Fiscal year[1]	Total	Net payroll tax contribs.	Income from taxing benefits	General fund reimburse-ments[2]	Net interest[3]	Total	Benefit pymts.[4]	Admin. expenses	Transfers to Railroad Retirement program	Net increase in fund[5]	Year-end balance
1960	$1,034	$987	—	—	$47	$533	$528	$32	−$27	$501	$2,167
1970	4,380	4,141	—	$16	223	2,954	2,795	149	10	1,426	5,104
1980	17,376	16,805	—	118	453	15,320	14,998	334	−12	2,056	7,680
1990	28,215	27,154	$158	138	766	25,124	24,327	717	80	3,091	11,455
1995	70,209	67,986	335	—	1,888	41,374	40,234	1,072	68	28,835	35,206
2000	77,023	70,001	756	—	6,266	56,008	54,244	1,608	159	21,014	113,752
2005	96,765	85,418	1,164	—	10,183	86,360	83,721	2,301	338	10,405	193,298
2010	105,513	93,739	1,745	125	9,904	126,344	122,935	2,947	462	−20,831	186,946
2011	106,225	84,031	1,878	11,745	8,571	131,489	127,990	3,034	465	−25,264	161,682
2012	108,845	85,072	383	16,234	7,156	138,546	135,114	2,920	512	−29,701	131,981
2013	111,262	100,169	1,051	4,504	5,538	142,757	139,446	2,760	551	−31,494	100,486
2014	114,105	109,060	1,022	27	3,997	144,667	141,327	2,897	444	−30,562	69,925
2015	117,965	114,156	1,036	39	2,733	146,234	142,923	2,892	419	−28,269	41,656
2016	150,293	147,577	1,181	23	1,512	146,208	143,053	2,779	376	4,084	45,740
2017	169,480	165,901	1,951	3	1,625	145,776	142,883	2,686	207	23,704	69,444
2018	170,272	167,043	1,000	2	2,227	146,575	143,642	2,759	174	23,698	93,141
2019	150,978	146,848	1,209	2	2,918	147,710	144,893	2,751	66	3,267	96,409

— = Not applicable. **Note:** Numbers may not add up to totals due to rounding. (1) Fiscal years 1977 and later consist of the 12 months ending on Sept. 30 of each year. Fiscal years prior to 1977 consisted of the 12 months ending on June 30 of each year. (2) Includes reimbursements from the general fund of the Treasury to the DI Trust Fund for certain legislated measures since 1957. (3) Includes net profits or losses on marketable investments. Beginning in 1967, the trust fund paid administrative expenses on an estimated basis, with a final adjustment including interest made in the following fiscal year. Net interest includes these interest adjustments. The 1970 report describes the accounting for administrative expenses for years prior to 1967. Beginning in July 1974, figures include relatively small gifts to the fund. (4) Beginning in 1967, includes payments for vocational rehabilitation services furnished to persons receiving benefits because of a disability; beginning in 1983, includes reimbursements paid from the general fund to the trust fund for unnegotiated benefit checks. (5) Net change in assets during fiscal year, including amounts borrowed or repaid by other funds.

Supplementary Medical Insurance Trust Fund (Medicare SMI), 1975-2019

Source: Centers for Medicare & Medicaid Services, U.S. Dept. of Health and Human Services

(in millions)

Fiscal year[1]	Total	INCOME Premium from participants[2]	Govt. contribs.[3]	Transfers from states[4]	Interest and other income[5,6]	DISBURSEMENTS Total	Benefit pymts.[6,7,8]	Admin. expenses	Net change	Year-end balance
1975	$4,322	$1,887	$2,330	—	$106	$4,170	$3,765	$404	$152	$1,424
1980	10,275	2,928	6,932	—	416	10,737	10,144	593	−462	4,532
1990	46,138	11,494	33,210	—	1,434	43,022	41,498	1,524	3,115	14,527
2000	89,239	20,515	65,561	—	3,164	88,992	87,212[9]	1,780	247	45,896
2005	152,505	35,939	115,200	—	1,366	152,735	149,820[10]	2,914	−230	16,885
2008	244,872	54,158[11]	180,434	$7,042	3,238	224,869	221,445[11,12]	3,423	20,003	59,149
2009	262,573	57,709[11]	194,267	7,504	3,093	260,257	256,938[11]	3,318	2,317	61,466
2010	282,734	61,364[11]	213,709	4,493	3,168	272,224	268,710[11]	3,514	10,510	71,976
2011	301,523	64,502[11]	225,178	6,536	5,307	300,672	296,842[11]	3,830	851	72,827
2012	290,864	66,067[11]	210,508	8,324	5,965	291,907	287,777[11]	4,130	−1,043	71,783
2013	313,158	71,300[11]	227,208	8,666	5,985	315,123	311,367[11]	3,756	−1,965	69,818
2014	334,943	75,887[11]	244,351	8,727	5,978	333,438	329,141[11]	4,297	1,504	71,323
2015	357,531	79,399[11]	263,484	8,797	5,851	359,412	355,807[11]	3,606	−1,882	69,441
2016	400,635	86,074[11]	299,491	9,755	5,315	403,888	399,468[11]	4,421	−3,254	66,187
2017	422,445	94,798[11]	309,647	11,072	6,928	414,126	409,265[11]	4,861	8,319	74,506
2018	441,572	106,182[11]	316,746	11,670	6,974	414,095	409,411[11]	4,684	27,477	101,983
2019	463,602	113,540[11]	331,830	12,154	6,077	458,391	453,513[11]	4,878	5,210	107,193

— = Not applicable. **Note:** Numbers may not add up to totals because of rounding. (1) Fiscal year 1975 ended June 30, 1975; fiscal years 1980 and after ended on Sept. 30 of each year. (2) For Part D, premiums include both amounts withheld from Social Security benefits (and certain other federal benefit payments) and amounts paid directly to Part D plans (estimated). (3) For Part B, includes matching payments from the general fund, plus certain interest-adjustment items. For Part D, includes all federal govt. transfers. (4) As of 2006, Medicaid is no longer the primary payer for full-benefit dual eligibles; states paid 90% of estimated costs in 2006, phasing down over a 10-year period to 75% in 2015 and after. (5) Other income includes recoveries of amounts reimbursed from the trust fund that are not trust fund obligations and other miscellaneous income. In 2008, includes an adjustment of $812 mil for interest inadvertently unearned as a result of Hospital Insurance (HI) hospice costs misallocated to, and paid from, the Part B account of the SMI trust fund May 2005-Sept. 2007. (6) Values after 2005 include additional premiums for Medicare Advantage (MA) plans that are deducted from beneficiaries' Social Security benefits, transferred to HI and SMI trust funds, and then transferred to the plans. (7) Includes costs of Peer Review Organizations in 1983-2001 and costs of Quality Review Organizations beginning in 2002. (8) For Part D, includes payments to plans, subsidies to employer-sponsored retiree drug plans, payments to states for low-income eligibility determinations, and Part D drug premiums (the amount collected from beneficiaries and transferred to plans and an estimated amount for premiums paid directly by enrollees to plans). Includes amounts for transitional assistance benefits in 2004-06. (9) Benefit payments less monies transferred from the HI trust fund for home health agency costs. (10) Certain HI hospice costs were misallocated to, and paid from, the Part B account of the SMI trust fund. See also footnote 12. (11) Includes an estimated $2.970 bil (2008), $3.699 bil (2009), $4.221 bil (2010), $4.843 bil (2011), $5.222 bil (2012), $6.306 bil (2013), $7.450 bil (2014), $8.465 bil (2015), $9.095 bil (2016), $10.179 bil (2017), $10.516 bil (2018), and $10.600 bil (2019) for premiums paid directly to Part D plans. (12) Benefit payments were $229.9 bil; amount shown includes transfer of $8.5 bil from the general fund of the Treasury to the Part B account of the SMI trust fund for HI hospice costs that were misallocated to, and paid from, the Part B account from May 2005 to Sept. 2007. (The HI trust fund, in turn, transferred $8.5 bil to the general fund.)

Hospital Insurance Trust Fund (Medicare HI), 1975-2019

Source: Centers for Medicare & Medicaid Services, U.S. Dept. of Health and Human Services

(in millions)

Fiscal year[1]	Total	INCOME Payroll taxes	Taxation of benefits	Transfers from Railroad Retire-ment acct.	Reimb. for uninsured persons	Premiums from voluntary enrollees	Pymts. for military wage credits	Interest and other income[2,3]	DISBURSEMENTS Total	Benefit pymts.[3,4]	Admin. expenses[5]	Net change	Year-end balance
1975	$12,568	$11,291	—	$132	$481	$6	$48	$609	$10,612	$10,353	$259	$1,956	$9,870
1980	25,415	23,244	—	244	697	17	141	1,072	24,288	23,790	497	1,127	14,490
1990	79,563	70,655	—	367	413	113	107	7,908	66,687	65,912	774	12,876	95,631
2000	159,681	137,738	$8,787	465	470	1,392	2	10,827	130,284	127,934[6]	2,350	29,397	168,084
2005	196,921	168,954	8,765	445	286	2,303	0	16,168	184,142	181,292[7]	2,850	12,779	277,723
2008	229,729	197,195	11,733	526	506	2,913	0	16,856	230,240	227,008[8]	3,231	−511	319,000
2009	228,915	194,102	12,376	524	614	2,817	968[9]	17,514	238,001	234,659	3,343	−9,086	309,914
2010	218,004	183,603	13,760	535	−142	3,314	0	16,933	248,978	245,650	3,328	−30,975	278,939
2011	226,486	192,063	15,143	477	275	3,273	0	15,255	259,628	255,717	3,911	−33,142	245,797
2012	241,730	204,752	18,643	511	262	3,400	0	14,162	258,155	254,459	3,696	−16,425	229,372
2013	243,560	212,901	14,310	577	0	3,397	0	12,375	266,546	262,411	4,135	−22,986	206,386
2014	262,753	227,579	18,066	612	432	3,259	0	12,805	266,853	262,520	4,332	−4,100	202,286
2015	272,359	237,697	20,208	595	187	3,277	0	10,396	278,736	273,248	5,488	−6,377	195,909
2016	287,106	250,472	23,022	657	158	3,232	0	9,566	290,648	285,574	5,075	−3,542	192,367
2017	298,524	259,740	24,206	637	147	3,492	0	10,302	293,265	290,279	2,986	5,259	197,626
2018	302,839	264,566	24,192	597	132	3,533	0	9,819	297,168	292,078	5,090	5,671	203,297
2019	319,256	281,441	23,781	570	127	3,823	0	9,513	323,726	318,371	5,355	−4,470	198,826

— = Not applicable. **Note:** Numbers may not add up to totals because of rounding. (1) Fiscal year 1975 ended June 30, 1975; fiscal years 1980 and later ended Sept. 30 of each year. (2) Other income includes recoveries of amounts reimbursed from the trust fund that are not trust fund obligations, receipts from the fraud and abuse control program, and other small amounts of miscellaneous income. In 2008, includes an adjustment of −$853 mil for interest inadvertently earned as a result of HI hospice costs that were misallocated to, and paid from, the Part B account of the Supplementary Medical Insurance (SMI) trust fund from May 2005 to Sept. 2007. (3) Values after 2005 include additional premiums for Medicare Advantage (MA) plans that are deducted from beneficiaries' Social Security benefits, transferred to the HI and SMI trust funds, and then transferred to the plans. (4) Includes costs of Peer Review Organizations from 1983 through 2001 (beginning with implementation of the Prospective Payment System on Oct. 1, 1983), and costs of Quality Improvement Organizations beginning in 2002. (5) Includes costs of experiments and demonstration projects. Beginning in 1997, includes fraud and abuse control expenses. (6) Includes monies transferred to the SMI trust fund for home health agency costs. (7) Certain HI hospice costs were misallocated to, and paid from, the Part B account of the SMI trust fund. (8) Benefit payments were $218.525 bil. Amount shown includes transfer of $8.484 bil to the general fund of the Treasury for HI hospice costs that were misallocated to, and paid from, the Part B account of the SMI trust fund from May 2005 to Sept. 2007. (The general fund, in turn, transferred $8.484 bil to the Part B account of the SMI trust fund.) (9) Includes the lump-sum general revenue adjustment of −$968 mil.

TAXES

Federal Personal Income Tax Return Facts, 2021

Source: George W. Smith IV, CPA, CGMA Partner, Andrews Hooper Pavlik PLC

Deadlines. The deadline for filing a 2020 U.S. individual income tax return (Form 1040) is Apr. 15, 2021.

Extensions. Taxpayers who cannot file a 2020 individual income tax return by the deadline can apply for a six-month extension to Oct. 15, 2021. To qualify for an extension, Form 4868 must be filed no later than Apr. 15, 2021.

E-Filing. The electronic filing program began as a pilot program in 1986; by 2011, 1 bil individual tax returns had been e-filed. As of July 24, 2020, 143.9 mil returns for income tax year 2019 had been e-filed, compared to 131.2 mil as of July 26, 2019.

Penalties. The IRS can levy two potential penalties after the filing due date when there is a balance owed. One penalty is for failing to file a timely tax return; the other is for failure to pay the tax when due. In addition, interest is charged on any unpaid tax balance.

Refunds. As of July 24, 2020, the average refund for the 2020 tax filing season was $2,741, identical to the previous tax year. The IRS refunded $282.0 bil, of which $245.2 bil was refunded with direct deposit.

Statute of limitations. Taxpayers who have not yet filed their 2017 federal tax return have until three years after the deadline to file and claim their refund. After that date, any refunds for 2017 income tax or withholding tax, including the earned income tax credit, will be lost.

Federal Income Tax Rates for Taxable-Income Brackets, 2020

Tax rate	Unmarried individuals	Married filing jointly or surviving spouses	Married filing separately	Head of household other than surviving spouses
10%	$0 to $9,875	$0 to $19,750	$0 to $9,875	$0 to $14,100
12%	$9,876 to $40,125	$19,751 to $80,250	$9,876 to $40,125	$14,101 to $53,700
22%	$40,126 to $85,525	$80,251 to $171,050	$40,126 to $85,525	$53,701 to $85,500
24%	$85,526 to $163,300	$171,051 to $326,600	$85,526 to $163,300	$85,501 to $163,300
32%	$163,301 to $207,350	$326,601 to $414,700	$163,301 to 207,350	$163,301 to $207,350
35%	$207,351 to $518,400	$414,701 to $622,050	$207,351 to $311,025	$207,351 to $518,400
37%	Over $518,400	Over $622,050	Over $311,025	Over $518,400

Standard Deduction, 2020

The standard deduction is a flat amount subtracted from the adjusted gross income of taxpayers who do not itemize deductions.

Single	$12,400
Married filing jointly or qualifying widow(er)	$24,800
Married filing separately	$12,400
Head of household	$18,650

Additional standard deduction. Elderly and/or blind, single or head of household: $1,650. Elderly and/or blind, married or qualifying widow(er): $1,300.

Personal exemption. The deduction for personal exemptions was suspended until Jan. 1, 2026, under the Tax Cuts and Jobs Act of 2017.

FICA and Medicare tax. For Social Security, wages are taxable up to $137,700. For Medicare, all wages are taxable.

Common Income Tax Errors

Periodically, the IRS issues a list of the most commonly made income tax errors.

1. Wrong or missing Social Security numbers.
2. Wrong names.
3. Filing status errors, such as Head of Household instead of Single.
4. Math mistakes, for example, when adding or subtracting items on a form or worksheet.
5. Errors in credits or deductions, like the Earned Income Tax Credit, Child and Dependent Care Credit, and standard deductions.
6. Wrong bank and/or account numbers for direct deposit of any tax refund.
7. Forms not signed or dated. An unsigned tax return is not valid. Both spouses must sign a joint return.
8. E-file PIN errors. E-filed returns can be signed electronically with a personal identification number (PIN). Usually, last year's PIN can be used, but if it is unknown, adjusted gross income information from last year's original return needs to be entered for verification.

Retirement Savings Plans and Income Tax

401(k) plan. The maximum amount that an individual can contribute to a 401(k) plan for 2020 is $19,500. Individuals born before 1971 can put away an additional $6,500, for a total of $26,000.

IRAs. Contributions to IRAs and Roth IRAs were limited to $6,000 in 2020. Anyone born before 1971 can contribute an extra $1,000. Funds may be deposited into a traditional IRA for 2020 until Apr. 15, 2021. Contributions after Apr. 15 will automatically be considered funds deposited for 2021.

Roth IRA. Contributions paid into a Roth IRA are not tax deductible. Distributions of funds including investment earnings held in the account for five years or longer and distributed after age 59½ are free of both income tax and the 10% early-withdrawal penalty. Withdrawals from the account in less than five years can be subject to tax and a 10% withdrawal penalty regardless of age. There are income limitations on contributions.

Distributions. There is a 10% penalty for IRA distributions before age 59½. Distributions paid to a beneficiary due to disability/death of the owner are not subject to this penalty, nor are payments used for certain unreimbursed medical expenses, higher-education expenses, or first-time home buyer acquisition costs (up to $10,000).

The owner of a traditional IRA (or a SIMPLE plan, pension, or profit-sharing plan account) must begin receiving distributions by Apr. 1 of the calendar year following the year in which he or she reaches age 72. Any employee who works beyond 72 and is not a 5% or more owner of the business can continue to defer profit-sharing and pension plan distributions. Required distributions have been waived for 2020.

Tax Credits

A tax deduction reduces a taxpayer's taxable income whereas tax credits reduce the amount of tax owed.

Adoption credit. The adoption credit in 2020 for qualified expenses is $14,300. The credit limit is per child and is adjusted annually for inflation. The credit is not refundable and phases out for taxpayers at higher income levels.

American Opportunity Tax Credit. This education credit provides up to $2,500 per student per year in the first four years of a student's postsecondary education.

Child and dependent care credit. This credit is for expenses for the care of taxpayers' qualifying children under age 13 or care of a disabled spouse or dependent, while the taxpayer works or looks for work.

Child tax credit. The maximum child tax credit is $2,000 for each qualifying child.

Earned Income Credit. Lower-income workers who maintain a household may be eligible for an Earned Income

Credit. This credit is based on total earned income such as wages, commissions, and tips. Military personnel can include tax-free combat pay in income to compute the credit.

Energy credits. There are many energy-related credits—from the purchase of an alternative fuel vehicle and the installation of solar/fuel cell property in a residence, to the production of biodiesel or ethanol.

Alternative Minimum Tax

The Alternative Minimum Tax (AMT) was established in 1969 to prevent individuals with very high incomes from using special tax breaks to pay little or no tax. The AMT 2020 exemption for a single taxpayer is $72,900 and $113,400 for married filing jointly. For married taxpayers filing separate returns, the exemption is $56,700.

Estate and Gift Taxes

Estate tax. The Tax Relief Act of 2010 reinstated the estate tax with a 35% flat rate and increased the exemptions to $5 mil in 2011 and $5.12 mil in 2012. The estate tax rate was increased to 40% for 2013 and subsequent years. The Tax Cuts and Jobs Act of 2017 set the 2020 exemption at $11.6 mil per person, $23.2 mil for married couples.

Gifting. For 2020 U.S. citizens, residents, and non-resident aliens have an annual gift tax exclusion of up to $15,000 per individual to as many individuals as he or she chooses. For married couples the exclusion is $30,000, even if only one spouse does all the gifting.

International property. All property owned worldwide by American citizens is subject to U.S. estate tax rules and regulations.

Resident aliens. Aliens residing in the U.S. are subject to the same rules as American citizens.

Tax Rates for Estates and Trusts

If taxable income is	The tax is
Not over $2,600	10% of the taxable income
Over $2,600 but not over $9,450	$260.00 plus 24% of the excess over $2,600
Over $9,450 but not over $12,950	$1,904.00 plus 35% of the excess over $9,450
Over $12,950	$3,129.00 plus 37% of the excess over $12,950

Taxable Social Security Benefits

Earnings limitations. Social Security recipients who have not reached their full retirement age of 66 in 2020 will lose $1 of their benefits for every $2 of earned income over $18,240. Recipients who reached full retirement age in 2020 will not lose any benefits if they earned $48,600 or less. Recipients will have to pay back some benefits if their income exceeded that amount.

Taxable benefits. Up to 50% of Social Security benefits may be taxable if the person's total income is more than $25,000 but less than $34,000 for a single individual, head of household, qualifying widow(er), or a married person who is filing separately if spouses lived apart all year; or more than $32,000 but less than $44,000 for married individuals filing

jointly. For higher incomes, 85% of Social Security benefits may become taxable.

If the only income received during the year was Social Security, these benefits are not taxable, and the recipient probably does not have to file a tax return.

Retention of Income Tax Records

Federal tax returns generally can be audited for up to three years after filing or six years if the IRS suspects underreported income, so it's wise to keep copies of an income tax return and records for at least seven years after filing a return.

Tax Audits

Audit odds. The IRS audit rate for individual income tax returns in fiscal year 2019 was 0.40%. The odds of an audit generally trend upward with higher taxpayer income, especially on certain types of income. For taxpayers with incomes of $50,000-$75,000, the audit rate was 0.54%. For taxpayers with gross income of $1 mil-$5 mil, the rate was 2.21%. The audit rate was 0.53% for all incomes under $200,000.

The audit selection process is not random. It is based on a set of formulas that are designed to spot questionable returns. If the IRS concludes that a person owes more tax, and he or she disagrees with the findings, the taxpayer can meet with a supervisor.

If the taxpayer still does not agree, he or she can appeal to a separate Appeals Office or take it to the U.S. Tax Court, Federal District Court, or the U.S. Court of Federal Claims.

Tax Court. The U.S. Tax Court is a federal court where taxpayers can dispute tax deficiencies as determined by the Commissioner of Internal Revenue before payment of the disputed amounts. The Tax Court is composed of presidentially appointed members. Many taxpayers choose the Tax Court because they are not required to pay the contested tax up front.

Appeals. For more information about audits, call the IRS at (800) TAX-FORM (829-3676) for its free Publication 556, *Examination of Returns, Appeal Rights, and Claims for Refund* or visit www.irs.gov.

IRS Contact Information

Website: www.irs.gov
Tax questions: (800) 829-1040
Forms/publications: (800) TAX-FORM (829-3676)

Taxpayers can view and download tax forms and publications in Spanish from www.irs.gov/es/spanish/. The IRS site also offers help in Chinese, Korean, Vietnamese, and Russian.

Hearing impaired: (800) 829-4059 (TTY/TDD)

Additional services: The Volunteer Income Tax Assistance (VITA) program offers free tax return preparation help to people who generally make $54,000 or less, persons with disabilities, and taxpayers who speak limited English. Visit www.irs.gov/individuals/free-tax-return-preparation-for-you-by-volunteers or (800) 829-1040.

Report wrongdoing: Report misconduct, waste, fraud, or abuse by an IRS employee to the Treasury Inspector General for Tax Administration at (800) 366-4484 or complaints@tigta.treas.gov.

Working With a Tax Preparer

The following are some suggestions when using a tax preparer:

- **Choose** wisely. Regulations require all paid tax return preparers including attorneys, certified public accountants, and IRS-enrolled agents to have a Preparer Tax Identification Number. Check the preparer's qualifications and history. Ask about service fees in advance.
- **Review** last year's tax return. Make note of any changes since then such as marriage, divorce, number of dependents, retirement, job changes, additional income, or new deductions.
- **Organize** your records with income items first, followed by itemized deductions (medical, taxes, interest, and charitable and other miscellaneous deductions), followed by gains, losses, rentals, or other items.
- **Time** spent with your preparer may affect your bill. If you provide disorganized records and deductions, there may be

an additional cost to have your tax preparer organize your information.
- **Prepare** a list of questions in advance. Ask about any invoices or bills that you are not sure apply.
- **Alert** your preparer if you're waiting to receive additional information. He or she can begin preparing your tax return and include the missing data later to finalize your return. Amending a return after it is completed may incur additional fees.
- **Review** your tax return before signing it. Ask questions about any item you don't understand. Even though your preparer is required to sign the return, you are responsible for its contents.

Total U.S. Tax Collections by Type of Tax, 1960-2019

Source: *Internal Revenue Service Data Book, 2019*, Internal Revenue Service, U.S. Dept. of the Treasury
(as percent of total gross collection or total income taxes)

Fiscal year	Total IRS collections (bil)[1]	Income taxes				Employment taxes[4]	Estate taxes	Gift taxes	Excise taxes[5]
		Total	Business[2]	Individual[3]	Estate and trust[3]				
1960	$92	73.1%	33.0%	67.0%	—	12.2%	1.6%	0.20%	12.9%
1965	114	69.7	32.7	67.3	—	14.9	2.1	0.25	12.9
1970	196	70.9	25.3	74.7	—	19.1	1.7	0.22	8.1
1975	294	68.8	22.6	77.4	—	23.9	1.5	0.13	5.7
1980	519	69.3	20.1	79.9	—	24.7	1.2	0.04	4.7
1985	743	63.8	16.3	83.7	—	30.3	0.8	0.04	5.0
1990	1,056	61.6	16.9	83.1	—	34.8	0.9	0.20	2.6
1995	1,376	61.8	20.5	79.5	—	33.8	1.0	0.13	3.3
2000	2,097	65.5	17.2	82.8	—	30.5	1.2	0.20	2.6
2005	2,269	62.3	21.7	78.3	—	34.0	1.0	0.09	2.5
2010	2,345	62.0	19.1	80.0	0.8%	35.1	0.7	0.12	2.0
2015	3,303	66.1	17.9	80.6	1.5	31.0	0.5	0.06	2.3
2016	3,333	64.8	16.0	82.6	1.4	32.2	0.6	0.07	2.3
2017	3,417	64.6	15.3	83.3	1.3	32.9	0.6	0.06	1.9
2018	3,465	64.5	11.8	86.5	1.7	32.7	0.7	0.03	2.1
2019	3,565	63.4	12.3	86.0	1.7	33.9	0.4	0.04	2.3

— = Not available. **Note:** Numbers may not add up to totals because of rounding. (1) Credits to taxpayer accounts excluded beginning with fiscal year 2009. (2) Incl. taxes on corporation income and unrelated business income from tax-exempt organizations. (3) Income tax reported for estates and trusts is included in individual income tax in FY1960-2007. Estate and trust income tax is reported separately from FY2008 on. (4) Incl. taxes for Old-Age, Survivors, Disability, and Hospital Insurance; federal unemployment insurance; and Railroad Retirement. (5) Excl. excise taxes collected by the U.S. Customs and Border Protection and the Alcohol and Tobacco Tax and Trade Bureau. The IRS collected taxes on alcohol and tobacco until FY1988 and taxes on firearms until FY1991.

Taxes Collected by State Governments, 2019

Source: Annual Survey of State Government Tax Collections, U.S. Census Bureau, U.S. Dept. of Commerce
(as percent of total taxes collected or total sales and gross receipts taxes)

State	Total taxes collected in dollars (mil)[1]	Property taxes	Sales and gross receipts taxes			License taxes[3]	Individual income taxes	Corporation net income taxes	Other taxes[4]
			Total	General	Selective[2]				
Alabama	$11,577	3.6%	48.5%	51.8%	48.2%	4.8%	36.2%	5.9%	0.9%
Alaska	1,781	6.8	15.7	—	100.0	9.0	—	18.7	49.9
Arizona	18,164	6.0	57.5	80.0	20.0	3.2	29.5	2.8	1.0
Arkansas	10,218	11.8	48.2	72.6	27.4	4.0	29.5	5.2	1.4
California	188,235	1.6	32.0	69.0	31.0	5.9	53.2	7.3	0.1
Colorado	15,870	—	37.7	56.4	43.6	4.4	51.5	5.0	1.4
Connecticut	17,994	—	43.3	58.9	41.1	2.3	47.0	5.0	2.4
Delaware	4,596	—	13.1	—	100.0	38.8	37.9	6.3	3.8
Dist. of Columbia	8,679	32.1	24.2	76.1	23.9	2.4	26.5	7.4	7.4
Florida	44,800	—	81.5	76.7	23.3	4.7	—	7.0	6.8
Georgia	24,713	3.5	38.5	65.7	34.3	2.9	49.3	5.1	0.7
Hawaii	8,208	—	61.7	75.2	24.8	3.4	31.3	2.3	1.3
Idaho	4,884	—	51.9	75.3	24.7	7.9	34.2	5.8	0.2
Illinois	42,501	0.1	46.0	61.5	38.5	6.5	38.9	7.3	1.2
Indiana	20,171	0.1	62.4	64.3	35.7	3.8	30.0	3.7	<0.1
Iowa	10,584	0.0	45.9	70.1	29.9	9.4	38.7	5.1	0.9
Kansas	10,030	7.5	45.1	73.7	26.3	4.3	37.7	4.8	0.6
Kentucky	12,896	5.0	48.9	63.1	36.9	4.1	35.9	4.5	1.5
Louisiana	11,749	0.6	54.5	58.4	41.6	3.7	32.6	4.2	4.3
Maine	4,674	0.9	49.8	69.3	30.7	6.2	36.6	5.4	1.1
Maryland	23,606	3.5	41.9	49.4	50.6	3.9	42.6	5.5	2.5
Massachusetts	31,805	0.0	30.1	71.5	28.5	3.8	53.9	9.3	3.0
Michigan	30,270	7.2	47.4	67.0	33.0	6.7	33.5	3.8	1.3
Minnesota	28,176	2.9	39.6	55.6	44.4	5.3	44.0	6.1	2.1
Mississippi	8,289	0.3	63.1	71.3	28.7	6.2	23.7	6.0	0.6
Missouri	13,181	0.3	42.1	67.3	32.7	4.8	50.0	2.8	0.1
Montana	3,169	9.9	20.9	—	100.0	12.3	44.6	5.8	6.5
Nebraska	5,755	0.0	44.8	76.2	23.8	3.2	44.2	7.4	0.4
Nevada	9,745	3.4	80.4	70.2	29.8	7.2	—	—	9.0
New Hampshire	2,969	13.8	33.5	—	100.0	15.7	4.1	28.0	5.0
New Jersey	38,844	0.0	41.3	67.6	32.4	4.4	40.9	10.4	2.9
New Mexico	7,428	1.2	49.6	77.7	22.3	4.5	21.4	2.7	20.6
New York	91,621	—	29.7	56.5	43.5	2.0	59.3	4.7	4.3
North Carolina	29,316	—	43.7	66.1	33.9	7.9	45.2	2.9	0.3
North Dakota	4,970	0.1	31.5	67.4	32.6	4.6	8.4	2.9	52.5
Ohio	30,147	—	61.5	68.5	31.5	7.4	30.9	0.0	0.2
Oklahoma	10,732	—	43.3	66.1	33.9	9.7	33.2	2.8	10.9
Oregon	13,960	0.2	13.4	—	100.0	8.1	70.5	6.5	1.3
Pennsylvania	43,132	0.1	51.3	53.1	46.9	6.4	31.3	6.9	3.9
Rhode Island	3,724	0.1	49.2	61.2	38.8	3.1	37.0	4.7	6.0
South Carolina	11,221	0.4	46.7	66.1	33.9	5.8	42.4	3.5	1.2
South Dakota	1,940	—	83.2	70.9	29.1	14.1	—	2.4	0.3
Tennessee	14,827	—	72.4	73.1	26.9	12.9	1.4	11.4	1.9
Texas	63,330	—	85.1	70.7	29.3	5.8	—	—	9.1
Utah	9,968	—	40.7	69.8	30.2	3.6	49.9	5.2	0.5
Vermont	3,429	32.4	32.8	36.7	63.3	3.7	25.1	4.4	1.7
Virginia	26,286	0.1	32.7	63.5	36.5	3.4	56.6	3.5	3.7
Washington	27,992	12.0	76.4	77.9	22.1	6.2	—	—	5.4
West Virginia	5,938	0.1	49.2	51.2	48.8	4.1	35.3	3.3	8.0
Wisconsin	20,039	0.5	42.1	67.4	32.6	6.3	43.7	6.8	0.5
Wyoming	2,111	13.0	45.2	80.7	19.3	9.9	—	—	32.0
United States	**1,090,242**	**1.6**	**46.3**	**66.4**	**33.6**	**5.4**	**37.8**	**5.3**	**3.1**

— = Tax not collected by state. **Note:** For fiscal year 2019 (July 1, 2018-June 30, 2019) for all states except AL and MI (ends Sept. 30), NY (Mar. 31), and TX (Aug. 31). (1) Incl. taxes not shown separately. (2) Imposed on sales of particular commodities/services, e.g., alcohol and tobacco, motor fuels, public utilities. (3) Related to the exercise of a privilege, such as owning/operating a motor vehicle. (4) Incl. death and gift taxes and severance taxes (on removal of natural resources).

State Government Personal Income Tax Rates, 2020

Source: Reproduced with permission from *CCH State Tax Guide*, published and copyrighted by CCH Inc., a Wolters Kluwer business **Alaska, Florida, Nevada, South Dakota, Texas, Washington,** and **Wyoming** did not have state income taxes and are thus not listed. Tax rates apply in stages—for example, a single person in Connecticut making $60,000 in taxable income would pay 3% on the first $10,000 of income, 5% on the next $40,000, and 5.5% on the last $10,000. For further details on some states, see notes at end of table.

Alabama

Single, Head of household, or Married filing separately
$0 to $500	.2%
$501 to $3,000	.4%
$3,001 and over	.5%

Married filing jointly
$0 to $1,000	.2%
$1,001 to $6,000	.4%
$6,001 and over	.5%

Arizona[1,2,3]

Single or Married filing separately
$0 to $26,500	2.59%
$26,501 to $53,000	3.34%
$53,001 to $159,000	4.17%
$159,001 and over	4.50%

Married filing jointly or Head of household
$0 to $53,000	2.59%
$53,001 to $106,000	3.34%
$106,001 to $318,000	4.17%
$318,001 and over	4.50%

Arkansas[2,3]

For net income less than $22,600:
$0 to $4,599	.0%
$4,600 to $9,099	.2%
$9,100 to $13,699	.3%
$13,700 to $22,599	3.4%

For net income from $22,600 to $80,800:
$0 to $4,599	0.75%
$4,600 to $9,099	2.5%
$9,100 to $13,699	3.5%
$13,700 to $22,599	4.5%
$22,600 to $37,899	.5%
$37,900 and over	.6%

For net income over $80,800:
$0 to $4,599	0.9%
$4,600 to $9,099	2.5%
$9,100 to $13,699	3.5%
$13,700 to $22,599	4.5%
$22,600 to $37,899	.6%
$37,900 and over	6.9%

California[1,2]

Single or Married/registered domestic partner filing separately
$0 to $8,932	.1%
$8,933 to $21,175	.2%
$21,176 to $33,421	.4%
$33,422 to $46,394	.6%
$46,395 to $58,634	.8%
$58,635 to $299,508	9.3%
$299,509 to $359,407	10.3%
$359,408 to $599,012	11.3%
$599,013 and over	12.3%

Head of household
$0 to $17,876	.1%
$17,877 to $42,353	.2%
$42,354 to $54,597	.4%
$54,598 to $67,569	.6%
$67,570 to $79,812	.8%
$79,813 to $407,329	9.3%
$407,330 to $488,796	10.3%
$488,797 to $814,658	11.3%
$814,659 and over	12.3%

Married/registered domestic partner filing jointly or Qualifying widow(er)
$0 to $17,864	.1%
$17,865 to $42,350	.2%
$42,351 to $66,842	.4%
$66,843 to $92,788	.6%
$92,789 to $117,268	.8%
$117,269 to $599,016	9.3%
$599,017 to $718,814	10.3%
$718,815 to $1,198,024	11.3%
$1,198,025 and over	12.3%

Colorado

4.63% of federal taxable income

Connecticut

Single or Married filing separately
$0 to $10,000	.3%
$10,001 to $50,000	.5%
$50,001 to $100,000	5.5%
$100,001 to $200,000	.6%
$200,001 to $250,000	6.5%
$250,001 to $500,000	6.9%
$500,001 and over	6.99%

Head of household
$0 to $16,000	.3%
$16,001 to $80,000	.5%
$80,001 to $160,000	5.5%
$160,001 to $320,000	.6%
$320,001 to $400,000	6.5%
$400,001 to $800,000	6.9%
$800,001 and over	6.99%

Married filing jointly or Qualifying widow(er)
$0 to $20,000	.3%
$20,001 to $100,000	.5%
$100,001 to $200,000	5.5%
$200,001 to $400,000	.6%
$400,001 to $500,000	6.5%
$500,001 to $1,000,000	6.9%
$1,000,001 and over	6.99%

Delaware

$0 to $2,000	.0%
$2,001 to $5,000	2.2%
$5,001 to $10,000	3.9%
$10,001 to $20,000	4.8%
$20,001 to $25,000	5.2%
$25,001 to $60,000	5.55%
$60,001 and over	6.6%

District of Columbia

$0 to $10,000	.4%
$10,001 to $40,000	.6%
$40,001 to $60,000	6.5%
$60,001 to $350,000	8.5%
$350,001 to $1,000,000	8.75%
$1,000,001 and over	8.95%

Georgia

Single
$0 to $750	.1%
$751 to $2,250	.2%
$2,251 to $3,750	.3%
$3,751 to $5,250	.4%
$5,251 to $7,000	.5%
$7,001 and over	5.75%

Head of household, Married filing jointly, or Qualifying widow(er)
$0 to $1,000	.1%
$1,001 to $3,000	.2%
$3,001 to $5,000	.3%
$5,001 to $7,000	.4%
$7,001 to $10,000	.5%
$10,001 and over	5.75%

Married filing separately
$0 to $500	.1%
$501 to $1,500	.2%
$1,501 to $2,500	.3%
$2,501 to $3,500	.4%
$3,501 to $5,000	.5%
$5,001 and over	5.75%

Hawaii

Single or Married filing separately
$0 to $2,400	1.4%
$2,401 to $4,800	3.2%
$4,801 to $9,600	5.5%
$9,601 to $14,400	6.4%
$14,401 to $19,200	6.8%
$19,201 to $24,000	7.2%
$24,001 to $36,000	7.6%
$36,001 to $48,000	7.9%
$48,001 to $150,000	8.25%
$150,001 to $175,000	.9%
$175,001 to $200,000	.10%
$200,001 and over	.11%

Head of household
$0 to $3,600	1.4%
$3,601 to $7,200	3.2%
$7,201 to $14,400	5.5%
$14,401 to $21,600	6.4%
$21,601 to $28,800	6.8%
$28,801 to $36,000	7.2%
$36,001 to $54,000	7.6%
$54,001 to $72,000	7.9%
$72,001 to $225,000	8.25%
$225,001 to $262,500	9%
$262,501 to $300,000	10%
$300,001 and over	11%

Married filing jointly or Surviving spouse
$0 to $4,800	1.4%
$4,801 to $9,600	3.2%
$9,601 to $19,200	5.5%
$19,201 to $28,800	6.4%
$28,801 to $38,400	6.8%
$38,401 to $48,000	7.2%
$48,001 to $72,000	7.6%
$72,001 to $96,000	7.9%
$96,001 to $300,000	8.25%
$300,001 to $350,000	.9%
$350,001 to $400,000	.10%
$400,001 and over	.11%

Idaho[1,2]

Single or Married filing separately
$0 to $1,567	1.125%
$1,568 to $3,135	3.125%
$3,136 to $4,703	3.625%
$4,704 to $6,271	4.625%
$6,272 to $7,839	5.625%
$7,840 to $11,759	6.625%
$11,760 and over	6.925%

Head of household, Married filing jointly, or Surviving spouse
$0 to $3,135	1.125%
$3,136 to $6,271	3.125%
$6,272 to $9,407	3.625%
$9,408 to $12,543	4.625%
$12,544 to $15,679	5.625%
$15,680 to $23,519	6.625%
$23,520 and over	6.925%

Illinois

4.95% of federal AGI

Indiana

3.23% of AGI

Iowa[2]

$0 to $1,666	0.33%
$1,667 to $3,332	0.67%
$3,333 to $6,664	2.25%
$6,665 to $14,994	4.14%
$14,995 to $24,990	5.63%
$24,991 to $33,320	5.96%
$33,321 to $49,980	6.25%
$49,981 to $74,970	7.44%
$74,971 and over	8.53%

Kansas

Single, Head of household, or Married filing separately
$0 to $15,000	3.1%
$15,001 to $30,000	5.25%
$30,001 and over	5.7%

Married filing jointly
$0 to $30,000	3.1%
$30,001 to $60,000	5.25%
$60,001 and over	5.7%

Kentucky

5% of taxable income

Louisiana[1]

Single, Head of household, or Married filing separately
$0 to $12,500	2%
$12,501 to $50,000	4%
$50,001 and over	6%

Married filing jointly

$0 to $25,000	2%
$25,001 to $100,000	4%
$100,001 and over	6%

Maine[2]

Single or Married filing separately
$0 to $22,199	5.8%
$22,200 to $52,599	6.75%
$52,600 and over	7.15%

Head of household
$0 to $33,299	5.8%
$33,300 to $78,899	6.75%
$78,900 and over	7.15%

Married filing jointly or Qualifying widow(er)
$0 to $44,449	5.8%
$44,450 to $105,199	6.75%
$105,200 and over	7.15%

Maryland

Single, Married filing separately, or Dependent taxpayers
$0 to $1,000	2%
$1,001 to $2,000	3%
$2,001 to $3,000	4%
$3,001 to $100,000	4.75%
$100,001 to $125,000	5%
$125,001 to $150,000	5.25%
$150,001 to $250,000	5.5%
$250,001 and over	5.75%

Head of household, Married filing jointly, or Qualifying widow(er)
$0 to $1,000	2%
$1,001 to $2,000	3%
$2,001 to $3,000	4%
$3,001 to $150,000	4.75%
$150,001 to $175,000	5%
$175,001 to $225,000	5.25%
$225,001 to $300,000	5.5%
$300,001 and over	5.75%

Massachusetts

Part A income (short-term capital gains)	12%
Part A income (interest and dividends)	.5%
Part B income	.5%
Part C income	.5%

Michigan

4.25% of taxable income

Minnesota[2]

Single
$0 to $26,960	5.35%
$26,961 to $88,550	6.8%
$88,551 to $164,400	7.85%
$164,401 and over	9.85%

Head of household
$0 to $33,190	5.35%
$33,191 to $133,360	6.8%
$133,361 to $218,540	7.85%
$218,541 and over	9.85%

Married filing jointly
$0 to $39,410	5.35%
$39,411 to $156,570	6.8%
$156,571 to $273,470	7.85%
$273,471 and over	9.85%

Married filing separately
$0 to $19,705	5.35%
$19,706 to $78,285	6.8%
$78,286 to $136,735	7.85%
$136,736 and over	9.85%

Mississippi

$0 to $5,000	3%
$5,001 to $10,000	4%
$10,001 and over	5%

Missouri[2,3]

$0 to $104.	0%
$105 to $1,053	1.5%
$1,054 to $2,106.	2%
$2,107 to $3,159.	2.5%
$3,160 to $4,212.	3%
$4,213 to $5,265.	3.5%
$5,266 to $6,318.	4%
$6,319 to $7,371.	4.5%
$7,372 to $8,424.	5%
$8,425 and over	5.4%

Montana[2]

$0 to $3,100	1%
$3,101 to $5,500.	2%
$5,501 to $8,400.	3%
$8,401 to $11,300.	4%
$11,301 to $14,500.	5%
$14,501 to $18,700.	6%
$18,701 and over	6.9%

Nebraska[2,3]

Single or Married filing separately

$0 to $3,230	2.46%
$3,231 to $19,330.	3.51%
$19,331 to $31,160.	5.01%
$31,161 and over	6.84%

Head of household

$0 to $6,020.	2.46%
$6,021 to $30,940.	3.51%
$30,941 to $46,200. . . .	5.01%
$46,201 and over	6.84%

Married filing jointly or
Surviving spouse

$0 to $6,440	2.46%
$6,441 to $38,680.	3.51%
$38,681 to $62,320. . . .	5.01%
$62,321 and over	6.84%

New Hampshire

5% on interest and dividends only

New Jersey

Single or Married/civil-union
partner filing separately

$0 to $20,000	1.4%
$20,001 to $35,000. . . .	1.75%
$35,001 to $40,000. . . .	3.5%
$40,001 to $75,000. . . .	5.525%
$75,001 to $500,000. . .	6.37%
$100,001 to $1,000,000	8.97%
$1,000,001 and over.	10.750%

Head of household, Married/
civil-union couple filing jointly,
or Qualifying widow(er)/
Surviving civil-union partner

$0 to $20,000	1.4%
$20,001 to $50,000. . . .	1.75%
$50,001 to $70,000. . . .	2.45%
$70,001 to $80,000. . . .	3.5%
$80,001 to $150,000. . .	5.525%
$150,001 to $500,000. .	6.37%
$500,001 to $1,000,000	8.97%
$1,000,001 and over.	10.750%

New Mexico[1]

Single

$0 to $5,500	1.7%
$5,501 to $11,000.	3.2%
$11,001 to $16,000. . . .	4.7%
$16,001 and over	4.9%

Head of household, Married filing
jointly, or Qualifying widow(er)

$0 to $8,000.	1.7%
$8,001 to $16,000.	3.2%
$16,001 to $24,000 . . .	4.7%
$24,001 and over.	4.9%

Married filing separately

$0 to $4,000.	1.7%
$4,001 to $8,000	3.2%
$8,001 to $12,000	4.7%
$12,001 and over.	4.9%

New York

Single or Married filing separately

$0 to $8,500	4%
$8,501 to $11,700.	4.5%
$11,701 to $13,900. . .	5.25%
$13,901 to $21,400. . .	5.9%
$21,401 to $80,650. . .	6.09%
$80,651 to $215,400. .	6.41%
$215,401 to $1,077,550	6.85%
$1,077,551 and over. .	8.82%

Head of household

$0 to $12,800	4%
$12,801 to $17,650. . .	4.5%
$17,651 to $20,900. . .	5.25%
$20,901 to $32,200. . .	5.9%
$32,201 to $107,650. .	6.09%
$107,651 to $269,300.	6.41%
$269,301 to $1,616,450	6.85%
$1,616,451 and over. .	8.82%

Married filing jointly or
Qualifying widow(er)

$0 to $17,150	4%
$17,151 to $23,600. . .	4.5%
$23,601 to $27,900. . .	5.25%
$27,901 to $43,000. . .	5.9%
$43,001 to $161,550. .	6.09%
$161,551 to $323,200.	6.41%
$323,201 to $2,155,350	6.85%
$2,155,351 and over. .	8.82%

North Carolina

5.25% on state taxable income

North Dakota[2]

Single

$0 to $40,125	1.1%
$40,126 to $97,150. . .	2.04%
$97,151 to $202,650. .	2.27%
$202,651 to $440,600.	2.64%
$440,601 and over . . .	2.9%

Head of household

$0 to $53,750	1.1%
$53,751 to $138,800. .	2.04%
$138,801 to $224,700.	2.27%
$224,701 to $440,600.	2.64%
$440,601 and over . . .	2.9%

Married filing jointly or
Surviving spouse

$0 to $67,050	1.1%
$67,051 to $161,950. .	2.04%
$161,951 to $246,700.	2.27%
$246,701 to $440,600.	2.64%
$440,601 and over . . .	2.9%

Married filing separately

$0 to $33,525	1.1%
$33,526 to $80,975. . .	2.04%
$80,976 to $123,350. .	2.27%
$123,351 to $220,300.	2.64%
$220,301 and over . . .	2.9%

Ohio[2]

$22,151 to $44,250. . .	2.85%
$44,251 to $88,450. .	3.326%
$88,451 to $110,650.	3.802%
$110,651 to $221,300	4.413%
$221,301 and over . .	4.797%

Oklahoma

Single or Married filing separately

$0 to $1,000	0.5%
$1,001 to $2,500.	1%
$2,501 to $3,750.	2%
$3,751 to $4,900.	3%
$4,901 to $7,200.	4%
$7,201 and over	5%

Head of household, Married
filing jointly, or Qualifying
widow(er)

$0 to $2,000	0.5%
$2,001 to $5,000.	1%
$5,001 to $7,500.	2%
$7,501 to $9,800.	3%
$9,801 to $12,200. . . .	4%
$12,201 and over	5%

Oregon[2]

Single or Married filing
separately

$0 to $3,600	4.75%
$3,601 to $9,050.	6.75%
$9,051 to $125,000. . .	8.75%
$125,001 and over . . .	9.9%

Married filing jointly,
Head of household, or
Qualifying widow(er)

$0 to $7,200	4.75%
$7,201 to $18,100. . . .	6.75%
$18,101 to $250,000. .	8.75%
$250,001 and over . . .	9.9%

Pennsylvania

3.07% of taxable compensation,
net profits, net gains from the
sale of property, rent, royalties,
patents or copyrights, income
from estates or trusts, dividends,
interest, and winnings

Rhode Island[2]

$0 to $65,250	3.75%
$65,251 to $148,350. .	4.75%
$148,351 and over . . .	5.99%

South Carolina[2]

$0 to $3,069	0%
$3,070 to $6,149.	3%
$6,150 to $9,229.	4%
$9,230 to $12,309. . . .	5%
$12,310 to $15,399. . .	6%
$15,400 and over	7%

Tennessee

1% on interest and dividends

Utah

4.95% on state taxable income

Vermont[2]

Single

$0 to $40,350	3.35%
$40,351 to $97,800. . .	6.6%
$97,801 to $204,000. .	7.6%
$204,001 and over . . .	8.75%

Head of household

$0 to $54,100	3.35%
$54,101 to $139,650. .	6.6%
$139,651 to $226,200.	7.6%
$226,201 and over . . .	8.75%

Married or Civil union filing jointly

$0 to $67,450	3.35%
$67,451 to $163,000. .	6.6%
$163,001 to $248,350.	7.6%
$248,351 and over . . .	8.75%

Married or Civil union
filing separately

$0 to $33,725	3.35%
$33,726 to $81,500. . .	6.6%
$81,501 to $124,175. .	7.6%
$124,176 and over . . .	8.75%

Virginia

$0 to $3,000	2%
$3,001 to $5,000.	3%
$5,001 to $17,000. . . .	5%
$17,001 and over	5.75%

West Virginia

Single, Head of household,
Married filing jointly, or
Widow(er) with dependent child

$0 to $10,000	3%
$10,001 to $25,000. . .	4%
$25,001 to $40,000. . .	4.5%
$40,001 to $60,000. . .	6%
$60,001 and over	6.5%

Married filing separately

$0 to $5,000	3%
$5,001 to $12,500. . . .	4%
$12,501 to $20,000. . .	4.5%
$20,001 to $30,000. . .	6%
$30,001 and over	6.5%

Wisconsin[1,2,3]

Single or Head of household

$0 to $11,760	3.86%
$11,761 to $23,520. . .	5.04%
$23,521 to $258,950. .	6.27%
$258,951 and over . . .	7.65%

Married filing jointly

$0 to $15,680	3.86%
$15,681 to $31,360. . .	5.04%
$31,361 to $345,270. .	6.27%
$345,271 and over . . .	7.65%

Married filing separately

$0 to $7,840	3.86%
$7,841 to $15,680. . . .	5.04%
$15,681 to $172,630. .	6.27%
$172,631 and over . . .	7.65%

AGI = Adjusted gross income; AMT = Alternative minimum tax. (1) Community property state in which, in general, one-half of the community income is taxable to each spouse. (2) Brackets indexed for inflation annually. (3) 2020 adjusted brackets were not available. Bracketed rates listed are for 2019. Other notes, by state: **Arkansas:** For net income from $79,301 to $84,600, deduct bracket adjustment amount as follows: $79,301 to $80,300: deduct $440; $80,301 to $81,300: deduct $340; $81,301 to $82,500: deduct $240; $82,501 to $83,600: deduct $140; $83,601 to $84,600: deduct $40; $84,601 and over: deduct $0. **California:** An additional 1% tax is imposed on taxable income in excess of $1 mil. **Colorado:** Individual taxpayers are subject to an AMT equal to the amount by which 3.47% of their Colorado alternative minimum taxable income exceeds their Colorado normal tax. **Connecticut:** Resident estates and trusts are subject to a 6.99% rate on all income. **Illinois:** Surcharge is imposed on certain types of sales income. **Indiana:** Counties may impose an AGI tax on residents or on nonresidents, or a county option income tax. **Iowa:** An AMT of 6.7% of alternative minimum income is imposed if the minimum tax exceeds the taxpayer's regular income tax liability. **Kansas:** Married filing jointly with taxable income of $5,000 or less, and all other individuals with taxable income of $2,500 or less, have a tax liability of zero. **Massachusetts:** Part A income represents either interest and dividends or short-term capital gains, long-term capital gains from collectibles, and long-term capital gains from pre-1996 installment sales. Part B income represents wages, salaries, tips, pensions, business income, rents, etc. Part C income represents gains from the sale of capital assets held for more than one year. Part A income after exemptions, and Part C income. **Minnesota:** A 6.75% AMT is imposed. **Montana:** Minimum tax, $1. **New Mexico:** Qualified nonresident taxpayers may pay an alternative tax of 0.75% of gross receipts from sales in New Mexico. **New York:** A supplemental tax is imposed to recapture the tax table benefit. **Vermont:** The tax amount is increased by 24% for certain items.

EDUCATION STATISTICS

U.S. Public Schools: Students, Staff, Spending, 1899-2018
Source: National Center for Education Statistics, U.S. Dept. of Education

	1899-1900	1919-20	1939-40	1959-60	1969-70	1979-80	1989-90	1999-2000	2017-18[1]
Population (thous.)									
Total U.S. population[2]	75,995	104,514	131,028	177,830	201,385	225,055	246,819	279,040	325,147
Population 5-17 years of age	21,573	27,571	30,151	43,881	52,386	48,043	44,948	52,811	53,691
Percentage 5-17 years of age	28.4%	26.4%	23.0%	24.7%	26.0%	21.3%	18.2%	18.9%	16.5%
Enrollment (thous.)									
Elementary and secondary[3]	15,503	21,578	25,434	35,182	45,550	41,651	40,543	46,857	50,686
Prekindergarten through grade 8	14,984	19,378	18,832	26,911	32,513	28,034	29,152	33,486	35,496
Grades 9-12	519	2,200	6,601	8,271	13,037	13,616	11,390	13,371	15,190
Percent of pop. ages 5-17 enrolled	71.9%	78.3%	84.4%	80.2%	87.0%	86.7%	90.2%	88.7%	94.4%
Grades 9-12 as percent of all enrolled	3.3%	10.2%	26.0%	23.5%	28.6%	32.7%	28.1%	28.5%	30.0%
High school graduates	62	231	1,143	1,627	2,589	2,748	2,320	2,554	3,320
Instructional staff (thous.)									
Total instructional staff	*	678	912	1,449	2,256	2,406	2,986	3,819	4,340
Teachers, librarians, and other nonsupervisory instructional staff	423	657	875	1,385	2,165	2,300	2,860	3,682	4,151
Revenue and expenditures (mil)									
Total revenue	$220	$970	$2,261	$14,747	$40,267	$96,881	$208,548	$372,944	$705,267
Total expenditures[4]	215	1,036	2,344	15,613	40,683	95,962	212,770	381,838	707,601
Current expenditures[4]	180	861	1,942	12,329	34,218	86,984	188,229	323,889	619,165
Capital outlay	35	154	258	2,662	4,659	6,506	17,781	43,357	61,442
Interest on school debt	*	18	131	490	1,171	1,874	3,776	9,135	18,334
Other programs[5]	*	3	13	133	636	598	2,983	5,457	8,661
Salaries and pupil cost									
Avg. annual salary of instruct. staff[6]	$325	$871	$1,441	$4,995	$8,626	$15,970	$31,367	$41,807	$60,477
Expenditure per capita total pop.	3	10	18	88	202	426	862	1,368	2,176
Current expenditure per pupil ADA[4]	17	53	88	375	816	2,272	4,980	7,394	13,470

* = Data not collected. ADA = Average daily attendance. **Note:** Because of rounding, details may not add up to totals. Prior to 1959-60, data do not include Alaska and Hawaii. (1) Revenues and expenditures are fiscal year 2017 (2016-17 school year) provisional data; high school graduates and expenditure per pupil ADA are projected. (2) Data for 1899-1900 are based on total population from the decennial census. From 1919-20 to 1959-60, total population includes armed forces overseas, as of July 1 preceding the school year. Data for later years are for resident population excluding armed forces overseas. (3) Data for 1899-1960 are school year enrollment; data for later years are fall enrollment. (4) Because of changes in the definition of "current expenditures," data for 1959-60 and later years are not entirely comparable with prior years. (5) Incl. expenditures for community services, adult education, community colleges, private schools, and other progs. not part of public and secondary education. (6) Data prior to 1959-60 include supervisors, principals, teachers, and nonsupervisory instructional staff.

U.S. Public High School Graduation Rates, 2017-18
Source: National Center for Education Statistics, U.S. Dept. of Education

State	Rate[1]	Rank	State	Rate[1]	Rank	State	Rate[1]	Rank	State	Rate[1]	Rank
Alabama	90.0%	5	Illinois	86.5%	24	Montana	86.4%	25	Rhode Island	84.0%	32
Alaska	78.5	49	Indiana	88.1	14	Nebraska	88.7	12	South Carolina	81.0	43
Arizona	78.7	47	Iowa	91.4	1	Nevada	83.2	34	South Dakota	84.1	31
Arkansas	89.2	9	Kansas	87.2	18	New Hampshire	88.8	11	Tennessee	90.0	5
California	83.0	36	Kentucky	90.3	3	New Jersey	90.9	2	Texas	90.0	5
Colorado	80.8	44	Louisiana	81.4	42	New Mexico	73.9	50	Utah	87.0	20
Connecticut	88.4	13	Maine	86.7	22	New York	82.3	37	Vermont	85.1	29
Delaware	86.9	21	Maryland	87.1	19	North Carolina	86.3	26	Virginia	87.5	17
Dist. of Columbia	68.5	51	Massachusetts	87.8	16	North Dakota	88.1	14	Washington	86.7	22
Florida	86.3	26	Michigan	80.6	46	Ohio	82.1	38	West Virginia	90.2	4
Georgia	81.6	41	Minnesota	83.2	34	Oklahoma	81.8	39	Wisconsin	89.7	8
Hawaii	84.5	30	Mississippi	84.0	32	Oregon	78.7	47	Wyoming	81.7	40
Idaho	80.7	45	Missouri	89.2	9	Pennsylvania	85.9	28	**Total U.S.**	**85.3**	—

— Not applicable. (1) The 4-year adjusted cohort graduation rate (ACGR) is the number of students who graduate in 4 years with a regular high school diploma divided by the number of students who form the adjusted cohort for the graduating class. From the beginning of 9th grade (or the earliest high school grade), students who are entering that grade for the first time form a cohort that is "adjusted" by adding any students who subsequently transfer into the cohort and subtracting any students who subsequently transfer out, emigrate to another country, or die.

High School Dropouts by Sex, Race, and Ethnicity, 1960-2018
Source: Current Population Survey, U.S. Census Bureau, U.S. Dept. of Commerce
(data for Oct. of year shown unless otherwise noted)

Year[1]	Total dropout rate				Male dropout rate				Female dropout rate			
	All races[2]	White	Black	Hispanic	All races[2]	White	Black	Hispanic	All races[2]	White	Black	Hispanic
1960[3]	27.2%	NA	NA	NA	27.8%	NA	NA	NA	26.7%	NA	NA	NA
1970[4]	15.0	13.2%	27.9%	NA	14.2	12.2%	29.4%	NA	15.7	14.1%	26.6%	NA
1980	14.1	11.4	19.1	35.2%	15.1	12.3	20.8	37.2%	13.1	10.5	17.7	33.2%
1990	12.1	9.0	13.2	32.4	12.3	9.3	11.9	34.3	11.8	8.7	14.4	30.3
2000	10.9	6.9	13.1	27.8	12.0	7.0	15.3	31.8	9.9	6.9	11.1	23.5
2005	9.4	6.0	10.4	22.4	10.8	6.6	12.0	26.4	8.0	5.3	9.0	18.1
2010	7.4	5.1	8.0	15.1	8.5	5.9	9.5	17.3	6.3	4.2	6.7	12.8
2011	7.1	5.0	7.3	13.6	7.7	5.4	8.3	14.6	6.5	4.6	6.4	12.4
2012	6.6	4.3	7.5	12.7	7.3	4.8	8.1	13.9	5.9	3.8	7.0	11.3
2013	6.8	5.1	7.3	11.7	7.2	5.5	8.2	12.6	6.3	4.7	6.6	10.8
2014	6.5	5.2	7.4	10.6	7.1	5.7	7.1	11.8	5.9	4.8	7.7	9.3
2015	5.9	4.6	6.5	9.2	6.3	5.0	6.4	9.9	5.4	4.1	6.5	8.4
2016	6.1	5.2	6.2	8.6	7.1	5.8	8.2	10.1	5.1	4.6	4.3	7.0
2017	5.8	4.6	5.7	9.5	6.6	5.0	7.0	11.5	5.0	4.3	4.4	7.4
2018	5.7	4.5	5.8	9.0	6.3	5.1	6.0	10.4	5.1	3.8	5.6	7.5

NA = Not available. **Note:** Table shows "status" dropouts, defined as 16- to 24-year-olds who are not enrolled in school and who have not completed a high school program, regardless of when they left school. People who have received GED credentials are not shown. Excludes persons in prison or in the military and other persons not living in households. Race categories exclude persons of Hispanic ethnicity unless otherwise noted. (1) Because of changes in data collection procedures, data for years prior to 1992 may not be comparable to later years. For 2005 and after, white and black data exclude persons identifying themselves as being of two or more races. (2) Includes other racial/ethnic categories not separately shown. (3) Based on the Apr. 1960 decennial census. (4) White and black data include persons of Hispanic ethnicity.

COVID-19 Pandemic Impact on Education by Selected Household Characteristics

Source: 2020 Household Pulse Survey: June 18-23, 2020; U.S. Census Bureau, U.S. Dept. of Commerce

The COVID-19 pandemic led to stay-home orders in most areas of the U.S. for at least some time starting in Mar. 2020. Many public and private schools turned to alternate methods of continuing coursework.

	Classes were moved to a distance-learning format using—		Classes were canceled	Classes changed in another way	No change to classes because schools did not close	Did not report
	Online resources	Paper materials sent home				
Total households (63,519,487)	46,019,802	12,467,956	27,300,693	2,545,079	368,988	1,096,833
Total	72.4%	19.6%	43.0%	4.0%	0.6%	1.7%
Race and Hispanic origin[1]						
White	76.8	21.3	39.0	3.2	0.5	1.0
Black	63.0	22.1	50.1	7.0	0.9	2.7
Asian	77.0	14.2	45.4	2.4	0.7	1.9
Hispanic or Latino	67.4	14.8	46.2	3.9	0.6	2.6
Respondent currently employed						
Yes	76.8	19.4	40.3	3.2	0.7	1.3
No	65.3	19.9	47.1	5.4	0.4	2.4
Household income						
Less than $25,000	57.2	22.7	51.3	5.8	0.6	2.5
$25,000-$34,999	66.5	22.9	54.0	4.3	1.7	0.3
$35,000-$49,999	67.8	18.7	50.9	4.3	0.4	0.7
$50,000-$74,999	71.1	19.4	46.1	3.9	0.2	0.3
$75,000-$99,999	81.1	23.0	38.0	2.8	0.1	0.0
$100,000-$149,999	83.0	20.0	33.9	2.9	0.6	0.1
$150,000-$199,999	86.3	15.2	31.9	4.3	0.3	0.2
$200,000 and above	88.9	11.9	31.1	2.1	0.5	0.0

Note: Totals may not add up to 100 because survey allowed for multiple categories to be marked. (1) Race categories are for one race alone, not in combination with any other race. Hispanic or Latino may be of any race.

Overview of U.S. Public Schools, 2018-19

Source: National Center for Education Statistics, U.S. Dept. of Education; National Education Association (NEA)

State	Local school districts	Elementary schools[1,2]	Secondary schools[2,3]	Classroom teachers	Total enrollment	Pupils per teacher	Teachers' avg. pay	Expend. per pupil
Alabama	139	922	399	46,684	722,212	15.5	$52,009	$9,978
Alaska	54	198	79	7,889	132,554	16.8	70,277	20,306
Arizona	666	1,391	762	63,491	1,122,686	17.7	50,353	8,722
Arkansas	261	689	373	32,051	478,053	14.9	49,438	10,278
California	1,165	7,028	2,488	288,715	6,359,760	22.0	83,059	12,879
Colorado	185	1,337	396	56,855	911,536	16.0	54,935	11,600
Connecticut	205	784	222	41,756	530,612	12.7	76,465	20,126
Delaware	44	165	38	9,600	139,144	14.5	63,662	14,469
Dist. of Columbia	64	177	37	7,067	93,741	13.3	78,477	20,425
Florida	75	2,843	679	142,422	2,846,857	20.0	48,314	9,901
Georgia	214	1,775	457	116,175	1,767,178	15.2	57,095	10,965
Hawaii	1	212	53	11,377	179,698	15.8	63,201	15,061
Idaho	160	466	189	16,572	307,228	18.5	50,757	6,747
Illinois	852	3,086	989	129,178	1,984,519	15.4	67,049	16,659
Indiana	403	1,370	458	61,775	1,053,703	17.1	51,119	10,030
Iowa	330	935	348	37,514	514,824	13.7	57,489	11,510
Kansas	286	917	342	35,278	491,764	13.9	51,082	11,515
Kentucky	173	966	423	39,747	654,275	16.5	53,434	12,064
Louisiana	169	959	281	47,937	719,215	15.0	50,288	11,727
Maine	207	439	145	15,034	189,562	12.6	54,025	13,570
Maryland	24	1,120	240	61,247	896,845	14.6	70,463	15,049
Massachusetts	406	1,413	372	73,878	950,248	12.9	82,042	19,315
Michigan	834	2,272	959	81,944	1,453,135	17.7	62,170	10,626
Minnesota	550	1,379	851	53,836	861,265	16.0	58,221	13,534
Mississippi	155	614	329	31,657	470,668	14.9	45,105	9,258
Missouri	554	1,611	628	75,511	880,267	11.7	50,019	11,434
Montana	401	496	324	10,596	147,785	13.9	50,721	11,664
Nebraska	244	731	305	25,040	325,984	13.0	54,470	12,075
Nevada	21	513	127	21,992	487,018	22.1	55,950	9,847
New Hampshire	165	382	108	16,579	173,433	10.5	59,182	17,399
New Jersey	688	1,952	539	116,826	1,364,714	11.7	74,760	21,326
New Mexico	89	600	229	21,089	329,439	15.6	47,826	11,315
New York	691	3,286	1,121	211,029	2,598,921	12.3	85,889	24,749
North Carolina	115	1,939	553	93,411	1,421,763	15.2	53,940	10,165
North Dakota	175	305	178	8,692	110,842	12.8	53,434	15,239
Ohio	1,043	2,430	989	112,719	1,795,686	15.9	59,713	12,375
Oklahoma	512	1,234	564	42,461	698,586	16.5	52,397	9,214
Oregon	196	890	274	29,946	581,730	19.4	65,125	12,780
Pennsylvania	789	2,102	783	120,834	1,722,461	14.3	68,930	17,260
Rhode Island	63	241	70	10,808	143,436	13.3	67,040	16,801
South Carolina	86	933	282	51,266	781,389	15.2	50,882	10,300
South Dakota	149	442	240	9,709	134,993	13.9	48,204	10,721
Tennessee	146	1,351	351	61,710	999,243	16.2	51,349	9,417
Texas	1,200	6,156	2,076	358,533	5,431,910	15.2	54,121	9,782
Utah	161	688	282	29,944	659,909	22.0	51,858	7,247
Vermont	235	228	65	8,317	87,359	10.5	60,672	17,262
Virginia	132	1,490	436	104,457	1,296,692	12.4	53,267	12,118
Washington	313	1,583	625	62,598	1,091,861	17.4	73,049	15,159
West Virginia	55	544	155	18,777	265,755	14.2	47,681	12,878
Wisconsin	444	1,577	568	55,850	858,833	15.4	58,277	12,697
Wyoming	48	247	101	7,198	93,029	12.9	58,861	16,607
Total U.S.	16,337	67,408	23,882	3,195,571	50,314,320	15.7	62,304	12,978

(1) Includes primary and middle schools (schools with no grade higher than 8th). (2) 2017-18 estimates. (3) Includes schools with no grade lower than 7th.

Revenues for Public Elementary and Secondary Schools by State, 2016-17

Source: National Center for Education Statistics, U.S. Dept. of Education; amounts in thousands

State/territory	Total	Federal Amount	% of tot. rev.	State Amount	% of tot. rev.	Local and intermediate[1] Amount	% of tot. rev.
Alabama	$7,889,120	$863,637	10.9%	$4,350,890	55.2%	$2,674,593	33.9%
Alaska	2,508,281	354,045	14.1	1,600,510	63.8	553,726	22.1
American Samoa	73,876	62,906	85.2	10,738[2]	14.5	232	0.3
Arizona	10,259,496	1,326,469	12.9	4,778,454	46.6	4,154,572	40.5
Arkansas	5,619,332	625,993	11.1	2,950,895	52.5	2,042,443	36.3
California	88,108,864	7,455,046	8.5	50,841,072	57.7	29,812,746	33.8
Colorado	10,600,561	706,162	6.7	4,602,299	43.4	5,292,101	49.9
Connecticut	11,583,918	503,812	4.3	4,494,453	38.8	6,585,653	56.9
Delaware	2,729,986	188,717	6.9	1,323,678	48.5	1,217,591	44.6
District of Columbia	2,526,099	237,820	9.4	NA	NA	2,288,279	90.6
Florida	28,808,723	3,288,570	11.4	11,346,675	39.4	14,173,479	49.2
Georgia	20,443,717	1,925,205	9.4	9,439,804	46.2	9,078,707	44.4
Guam	332,552	60,166	18.1	NA	NA	272,386	81.9
Hawaii	2,844,167	252,145	8.9	2,534,177	89.1	57,844	2.0
Idaho	2,575,178	252,533	9.8	1,706,894	66.3	615,751	23.9
Illinois	35,480,443	2,312,325	6.5	13,710,764	38.6	19,457,354	54.8
Indiana	11,952,546	974,150	8.2	7,087,311	59.3	3,891,085	32.6
Iowa	6,904,458	497,385	7.2	3,732,324	54.1	2,674,750	38.7
Kansas	6,344,151	537,797	8.5	4,031,070	63.5	1,775,284	28.0
Kentucky	7,782,860	912,224	11.7	4,229,780	54.3	2,640,856	33.9
Louisiana	8,949,726	1,168,690	13.1	3,903,101	43.6	3,877,936	43.3
Maine	2,820,246	195,168	6.9	1,093,382	38.8	1,531,696	54.3
Maryland	15,045,717	851,860	5.7	6,625,703	44.0	7,568,154	50.3
Massachusetts	18,423,533	929,798	5.0	6,999,777	38.0	10,493,958	57.0
Michigan	20,163,387	1,734,557	8.6	12,224,090	60.6	6,204,741	30.8
Minnesota	13,242,082	743,953	5.6	8,762,296	66.2	3,735,833	28.2
Mississippi	4,753,225	672,881	14.2	2,415,769	50.8	1,664,576	35.0
Missouri	11,485,402	1,003,289	8.7	3,749,129	32.6	6,732,984	58.6
Montana	1,841,286	225,892	12.3	867,286	47.1	748,107	40.6
Nebraska	4,470,153	349,144	7.8	1,450,774	32.5	2,670,235	59.7
Nevada	4,919,401	444,730	9.0	1,780,380	36.2	2,694,292	54.8
New Hampshire	3,132,306	173,816	5.5	1,007,310	32.2	1,951,180	62.3
New Jersey	30,368,383	1,269,661	4.2	12,920,845	42.5	16,177,878	53.3
New Mexico	4,023,795	589,017	14.6	2,726,305	67.8	708,473	17.6
New York	69,228,226	3,657,578	5.3	28,253,045	40.8	37,317,603	53.9
North Carolina	14,481,275	1,641,260	11.3	9,057,842	62.5	3,782,173	26.1
North Dakota	1,757,100	163,446	9.3	1,014,779	57.8	578,875	32.9
Northern Mariana Islands	87,683	39,503	45.1	47,227[2]	53.9	953	1.1
Ohio	24,762,785	1,949,822	7.9	10,538,278	42.6	12,274,685	49.6
Oklahoma	6,361,194	726,159	11.4	3,007,742	47.3	2,627,292	41.3
Oregon	7,689,411	550,627	7.2	4,018,900	52.3	3,119,884	40.6
Pennsylvania	31,353,132	2,152,130	6.9	12,104,094	38.6	17,096,908	54.5
Puerto Rico	2,819,791	935,887	33.2	1,883,850[2]	66.8	55	0.0
Rhode Island	2,561,477	192,929	7.5	1,087,361	42.5	1,281,187	50.0
South Carolina	9,992,973	913,225	9.1	4,867,687	48.7	4,212,060	42.2
South Dakota	1,580,004	205,299	13.0	540,408	34.2	834,297	52.8
Tennessee	10,077,253	1,161,636	11.5	4,629,304	45.9	4,286,312	42.5
Texas	60,006,975	6,298,581	10.5	23,339,969	38.9	30,368,425	50.6
Utah	5,757,609	459,308	8.0	3,183,265	55.3	2,115,036	36.7
Vermont	1,742,206	113,778	6.5	1,560,743	89.6	67,685	3.9
Virgin Islands (U.S)	193,314	26,259	13.6	NA	NA	167,056	86.4
Virginia	16,611,639	1,131,683	6.8	6,565,661	39.5	8,914,296	53.7
Washington	15,654,623	1,071,035	6.8	9,846,364	62.9	4,737,224	30.3
West Virginia	3,526,416	404,295	11.5	1,917,056	54.4	1,205,066	34.2
Wisconsin	11,591,278	832,985	7.2	5,360,746	46.2	5,397,548	46.6
Wyoming	1,931,277	118,429	6.1	1,141,567	59.1	671,281	34.8
United States[3]	**705,267,398**	**57,310,693**	**8.1**	**331,322,010**	**47.0**	**316,634,696**	**44.9**

NA = Not applicable. **Note:** Percentage totals may not add up to 100 due to rounding. (1) Includes intermediate revenues from education agencies with fundraising capabilities that operate between the state and local government levels. (2) Reported state revenue data are revenues received from the central government of the jurisdiction. (3) U.S. total includes the 50 states and the District of Columbia.

Enrollment in U.S. Public and Private Schools, 1889-2030

Source: National Center for Education Statistics, U.S. Dept. of Education

Of all students enrolled in private schools in fall 2017, 76% attended religious schools and 24% attended nonsectarian schools.

School year[1]	Public school[2]	Private school[2]	% private[3]	School year[1]	Public school[2]	Private school[2]	% private[3]
1889-90	12,723	1,611	11.2%	1969-70	45,550	5,500[4]	10.8%
1899-1900	15,503	1,352	8.0	1979-80	41,651	5,000[4]	10.7
1909-10	17,814	1,558	8.0	1989-90	40,543	5,599	12.1
1919-20	21,578	1,699	7.3	1999-2000	46,857	6,018	11.4
1929-30	25,678	2,651	9.4	2009-10	49,361	5,488	10.0
1939-40	25,434	2,611	9.3	2019-20[5]	50,634	5,716	10.1
1949-50	25,111	3,380	11.9	2020-21[5]	50,654	5,714	10.1
1959-60	35,182	5,675	13.9	2029-30[5]	51,068	5,738	10.1

Note: "Private" includes all nonpublic schools. (1) Fall enrollment. (2) In thousands. Data from fall 1980 onward covers an expanded universe of private schools; comparisons with earlier years should be avoided. (3) Percent of U.S. students enrolled in private schools. (4) Estimated. (5) Projected.

Program for International Student Assessment (PISA) Scores, 2000-18

Source: National Center for Education Statistics, U.S. Dept. of Education
Scores are reported on a scale from 0 to 1,000. The PISA test is administered to 15-year-old students.

Education system	Mathematics 2000	Mathematics 2018	Reading 2000	Reading 2018	Science 2000	Science 2018
Albania	—	437	—	405	—	417
Argentina	—	379	—	402	—	404
Australia*	533	491	528	503	528	503
Austria*	515	499	507	484	519	490
Azerbaijan[1]	—	420	—	389	—	398
Belarus	—	472	—	474	—	471
Belgium*	520	508	507	493	496	499
Bosnia and Herzegovina	—	406	—	403	—	398
Brazil[2]	334	384	396	413	375	404
Brunei	—	430	—	408	—	431
Bulgaria[2]	—	436	—	420	—	424
Canada*	533	512	534	520	529	518
Chile*	—	417	—	452	—	444
China[3]	—	591	—	555	—	590
Colombia[2]*	—	391	—	412	—	413
Costa Rica[2]	—	402	—	426	—	416
Croatia	—	464	—	479	—	472
Cyprus	—	451	—	424	—	439
Czechia*	498	499	492	490	511	497
Denmark*	514	509	497	501	481	493
Dom. Rep.[2]	—	325	—	342	—	336
Estonia*	—	523	—	523	—	530
Finland*	536	507	546	520	538	522
France*	517	495	505	493	500	493
Georgia	—	398	—	380	—	383
Germany*	490	500	484	498	487	503
Greece*	447	451	474	457	461	452
Hong Kong	—	551	—	524	—	517
Hungary*	488	481	480	476	496	481
Iceland*	514	495	507	474	496	475
Indonesia	—	379	—	371	—	396
Ireland*	503	500	527	518	513	496
Israel*	—	463	—	470	—	462
Italy*	457	487	487	476	478	468
Japan*	557	527	522	504	550	529
Jordan[2]	—	400	—	419	—	429
Kazakhstan	—	423	—	387	—	397
Korea, South*	547	526	525	514	552	519
Kosovo	—	366	—	353	—	365
Latvia*	463	496	458	479	460	487
Lebanon	—	393	—	353	—	384
Lithuania*	—	481	—	476	—	482
Luxembourg*	446	483	441	470	443	477
Macau	—	558	—	525	—	544
Malaysia[2]	—	440	—	415	—	438
Malta	—	472	—	448	—	457
Mexico[2]*	387	409	422	420	422	419
Moldova	—	421	—	424	—	428
Montenegro	—	430	—	421	—	415
Morocco[2]	—	368	—	359	—	377
Netherlands*	—	519	—	485	—	503
New Zealand*	537	494	529	506	528	508
N. Macedonia	—	394	—	393	—	413
Norway*	499	501	505	499	500	490
Panama[2]	—	353	—	377	—	365
Peru[2]	—	400	—	401	—	404
Philippines[2]	—	353	—	340	—	357
Poland*	470	516	479	512	483	511
Portugal*	454	492	470	492	459	492
Qatar	—	414	—	407	—	419
Romania[2]	—	430	—	428	—	426
Russia	—	488	462	479	460	478
Saudi Arabia	—	373	—	399	—	386
Serbia	—	448	—	439	—	440
Singapore	—	569	—	549	—	551
Slovakia*	—	486	—	458	—	464
Slovenia*	—	509	—	495	—	507
Spain*	476	481	493	—	491	483
Sweden*	510	502	516	506	512	499
Switzerland*	529	515	494	484	496	495
Taiwan	—	531	—	503	—	516
Thailand[2]	—	419	—	393	—	426
Turkey[2]*	—	454	—	466	—	468
U.S.*	493	478	504	505	499	502
UK*	529	502	523	504	532	505
Ukraine	—	453	—	466	—	469
UAE	—	435	—	432	—	434
Uruguay	—	418	—	427	—	426
OECD average[4]	500	489	500	487	500	489

— = Not available. * = Organization for Economic Cooperation and Development (OECD) nation as of 2018. (1) Less than 50% of the 15-year-old population is covered by the PISA sample. (2) 50-75% of the 15-year-old population is covered by the PISA sample. (3) Scores for China only include Beijing, Shanghai, Jiangsu, and Zhejiang provinces. (4) The average of the national averages of the OECD member countries, with each country weighted equally.

Mathematics, Reading, and Science Achievement of U.S. Students, 1998-2019

Source: National Assessment of Educational Progress, National Center for Education Statistics, U.S. Dept. of Education

Percent of public school students in a grade who scored at or above basic levels in national tests. Basic level denotes a partial mastery of prerequisite knowledge and skills fundamental for proficient work at each grade.

State	4th grade Math 2000	4th grade Math 2019	4th grade Reading 1998	4th grade Reading 2019	8th grade Math 2000	8th grade Math 2019	8th grade Reading 1998	8th grade Reading 2019	8th grade Science 2000	8th grade Science 2015
AL	55	71	56	58	53	57	67	64	53	54
AK	—	73	—	63	—	63	—	—	—	—
AZ	57	77	51	61	60	68	72	70	55	61
AR	55	75	54	62	49	63	68	68	53	62
CA	50	75	48	63	50	61	63	68	38	56
CO	—	80	67	71	—	73	77	77	—	—
CT	76	82	76	70	70	72	81	78	64	70
DE	—	79	53	62	—	65	64	69	—	62
DC	24	73	27	57	23	55	44	58	—	—
FL	—	87	53	70	—	66	67	72	—	66
GA	57	77	54	63	54	67	68	72	52	65
HI	55	78	45	63	51	65	59	68	40	58
ID	68	82	—	69	70	74	—	77	71	76
IL	63	77	—	64	67	69	—	74	59	63
IN	77	84	—	67	74	73	—	75	66	70
IA	75	81	67	68	—	72	—	73	—	75
KS	76	79	70	66	76	71	81	74	—	71
KY	59	81	62	67	60	67	74	73	60	73
LA	57	73	44	55	47	61	63	68	44	—
ME	73	81	72	67	73	71	83	75	72	77
MD	60	76	58	64	62	65	70	73	57	67
MA	77	85	70	76	70	78	79	81	70	75
MI	71	76	62	64	68	68	—	73	68	69
MN	76	85	67	69	80	77	78	74	72	76
MS	45	84	47	65	42	62	62	67	41	51
MO	71	80	61	64	64	70	75	74	66	75
MT	72	82	72	69	79	73	83	76	79	78
NE	65	84	—	69	73	74	—	74	71	75
NV	60	77	51	64	55	62	70	69	52	62
NH	—	86	74	71	—	77	—	78	—	81
NJ	—	85	—	72	—	76	—	77	—	71
NM	50	72	51	53	48	56	71	61	48	55
NY	66	76	62	66	63	66	76	70	58	63
NC	73	82	58	67	67	71	74	72	54	64
ND	73	84	—	69	76	75	—	75	72	79
OH	73	82	—	68	73	73	—	75	72	72
OK	67	80	66	63	62	66	80	71	60	66
OR	65	75	58	64	71	67	78	73	68	72
PA	—	81	—	68	—	70	—	73	—	—
RI	65	81	64	66	59	64	76	71	58	64
SC	59	77	53	61	53	64	66	69	48	65
SD	—	83	—	69	—	76	—	74	—	77
TN	59	79	57	66	52	68	71	73	55	71
TX	76	84	59	61	67	68	74	67	52	70
UT	69	82	62	72	66	72	77	77	67	82
VT	73	81	—	68	73	75	—	77	71	79
VA	71	87	62	69	65	75	78	71	61	74
WA	—	79	64	65	—	72	76	74	—	70
WV	65	74	60	60	58	62	75	67	57	63
WI	—	80	69	66	—	76	78	76	—	75
WY	71	87	64	73	69	76	76	75	69	79
U.S.	64	80	58	65	62	68	71	72	57	67

— = Not available.

Fighting, Bullying, and Safety Concerns of High School Students, 2019

Source: *Youth Risk Behavior Surveillance–United States, 2019*, Centers for Disease Control and Prevention

	In a physical fight on school property[1]			Bullied on school property[2]			Electronically bullied[2,3]			Did not go to school because of safety concerns[4]		
	Female	Male	Total	Female	Male	Total	Female	Male	Total	Female	Male	Total
Race/ethnicity												
White, non-Hispanic ...	2.2%	10.2%	6.4%	28.3%	18.0%	23.1%	25.3%	12.0%	18.6%	8.1%	5.2%	6.7%
Black, non-Hispanic ...	11.7	18.8	15.5	17.2	13.3	15.1	11.1	6.1	8.6	10.8	12.2	11.5
Hispanic, any race.....	5.6	10.2	7.8	18.6	10.9	14.8	15.9	9.3	12.7	11.8	9.9	10.9
Grade												
9	5.6	15.8	11.0	27.0	18.0	22.4	21.3	11.9	16.5	10.0	7.6	8.8
10	5.1	11.4	8.3	25.3	17.4	21.3	21.1	11.0	16.0	9.2	7.1	8.1
11	3.5	9.2	6.4	21.2	12.4	16.9	20.3	8.6	14.4	10.7	8.1	9.5
12	2.8	8.5	5.8	20.5	12.8	16.7	18.6	11.9	15.4	8.8	7.0	8.1
Sexual identity												
Heterosexual (straight)	3.8	11.0	7.8	20.8	14.0	17.1	19.1	9.9	14.1	8.9	6.4	7.5
Gay, lesbian, or bisexual.........	6.3	13.5	8.2	32.0	31.7	32.0	27.1	25.5	26.6	11.5	18.3	13.5
Not sure	4.0	16.8	9.6	28.0	23.7	26.9	20.1	16.8	19.4	15.4	15.1	15.5
Total...............	4.4	11.4	8.0	23.6	15.4	19.5	20.4	10.9	15.7	9.8	7.5	8.7

(1) One or more times during the 12 months before the survey. (2) During the 12 months before the survey. (3) Including being bullied through texting, Instagram, Facebook, or other social media. (4) On at least one day during the 30 days before the survey.

Characteristics of Public Charter Schools and Students, 1999-2018

Source: National Center for Education Statistics, U.S. Dept. of Education

	1999-2000	2003-04	2005-06	2007-08	2009-10	2011-12	2013-14	2017-18
Number of charter school students..................	339,678	789,479	1,012,906	1,276,731	1,610,285	2,057,599	2,519,065	3,143,269
			Percentage of charter school students who were—					
Sex								
Male	51.0%	50.3%	49.9%	49.5%	49.5%	49.6%	49.6%	49.6%
Female	49.0	49.7	50.1	50.5	50.5	50.4	50.4	50.4
Race/ethnicity								
White.......................	42.5	41.8	40.5	38.8	37.3	35.6	34.9	32.1
Black.......................	33.5	31.9	32.1	31.8	30.3	28.7	27.1	25.8
Asian/Pacific Islander	2.8	3.2	3.6	3.8	3.9	4.0	4.1	4.4
Amer. Ind./Alaska Native......	1.5	1.5	1.4	1.2	1.0	0.9	0.8	0.7
Two or more races............	NA	NA	NA	NA	1.4	2.8	3.0	3.9
Hispanic	19.6	21.5	22.4	24.5	26.0	28.0	30.0	33.1
Number of charter schools	1,524	2,977	3,780	4,388	4,952	5,696	6,465	7,193
			Percentage of charter schools that were—					
School level								
Elementary	54.6%	52.0%	52.1%	53.3%	54.1%	54.9%	56.2%	56.5%
Secondary..................	25.9	26.2	28.0	27.8	26.8	24.9	23.5	23.2
Combined...................	18.6	21.0	18.6	18.3	18.8	19.5	19.6	20.3
Enrollment size								
Under 300..................	77.1	71.1	69.6	65.6	61.5	55.8	51.7	44.8
300-499....................	12.0	15.6	16.5	19.3	20.8	23.1	24.3	25.5
500-999....................	8.6	10.1	10.9	12.0	14.0	17.0	19.0	23.3
1,000 or more	2.4	3.2	3.0	3.1	3.7	4.2	4.9	6.3
Locale								
City	NA	52.7	52.5	54.3	54.8	55.4	56.5	56.1
Suburban	NA	22.0	22.2	22.0	21.1	21.2	26.1	26.3
Town	NA	9.6	9.4	8.5	8.0	7.4	7.0	6.1
Rural......................	NA	15.8	16.0	15.2	16.1	16.0	10.4	11.5

NA = Not available. **Note:** Race categories exclude persons of Hispanic ethnicity, who may be of any race.

Homeschooled Students, 2015-16

Source: National Center for Education Statistics, U.S. Dept. of Education

A total of 1,689,726 U.S. students in grades K-12 were homeschooled in 2015-16, down from 1,772,987 in 2012 and up from 1,520,140 in 2007 and 850,171 in 1999. In a 2016 U.S. Dept. of Education survey of parents who homeschool their children, the reason they gave as most important in their decision to homeschool was concern over the school environment, with such factors as safety, drugs, or negative peer pressure (34%); dissatisfaction with academic instruction in schools (17%); desire to provide religious instruction (16%); desire to provide a nontraditional approach to education (6%); the child has other special needs (6%); the child has a physical or mental health problem (6%); and desire to provide moral instruction (5%). In all, 80% cited concern over school environment as one of their reasons, 67% cited moral instruction, 61% cited dissatisfaction with academic instruction, and 51% cited religious instruction.

Characteristic	No. of students (thous.)	% distrib.	Home-schooling rate[1]	Characteristic	No. of students (thous.)	% distrib.	Home-schooling rate[1]
Household locale				**Parents' education**			
City.................	493	29%	3.0%	High school diploma or less...............	510	30%	3.3%
Suburban	651	39	2.9	Vocational/technical, assoc. degree, or			
Town................	177	10	4.3	some college........	418	25	3.1
Rural...............	368	22	4.4	Bachelor's degree/some			
Race/ethnicity[2]				graduate school	501	30	3.6
White	998	59	3.8	Graduate/professional			
Black...............	132	8	1.9	degree..............	260	15	3.0
Asian/Pacific Islander ...	44	3	1.4	Total...............	1,690	NA	3.3
Other[3]	69	4	2.7				
Hispanic	444	26	3.5				

NA = Not applicable. **Note:** Numbers may not add up to totals because of rounding. Homeschooled students are school-age children in a grade equivalent to K-12 who receive instruction at home all or most of the time. Excludes students enrolled in public or private school more than 25 hours per week or homeschooled because of temporary illness only. (1) Percentage of total subgroup (e.g., all "City" students) that is homeschooled. (2) Race categories exclude persons of Hispanic ethnicity, who may be of any race. (3) Includes two or more races and race ethnicity not reported.

Students With Disabilities Receiving Educational Services, 1976-2019

Source: Office of Special Education and Rehabilitative Services, U.S. Dept. of Education

Students served by federally funded educational programs for disabled students include children and young adults 3-21 years old.
(numbers served in thousands)

Type of disability	1976 -77	1980 -81	1990 -91	2000 -01	2010 -11	2012 -13	2013 -14	2014 -15	2015 -16	2016- 17[1,2]	2017 -18[1,3]	2018 -19[1]
Autism................	—	—	—	93	417	498	538	576	617	661	710	762
Deaf-blindness.......	—	3	1	1	2	1	1	1	1	1	1	2
Developmental delay	—	—	—	213	382	402	410	419	434	446	461	479
Emotional disturbance	283	347	389	480	390	362	354	349	347	348	353	358
Hearing impairment......	88	79	58	77	78	77	77	76	75	75	75	74
Intellectual disability	961	830	534	624	448	430	425	423	425	431	436	439
Multiple disabilities......	—	68	96	131	130	133	132	132	131	132	132	133
Orthopedic impairment....	87	58	49	82	63	59	56	52	47	42	41	39
Other health impairment[4]....	141	98	55	303	716	779	817	862	909	955	1,002	1,049
Specific learning disability ..	796	1,462	2,129	2,860	2,361	2,277	2,264	2,278	2,298	2,318	2,342	2,368
Speech or language impairment...........	1,302	1,168	985	1,388	1,396	1,356	1,334	1,332	1,337	1,337	1,357	1,378
Traumatic brain injury.....	—	—	—	16	26	26	26	26	27	27	27	27
Visual impairment........	38	31	23	29	28	28	28	28	27	27	27	27
All disabilities...........	3,694	4,144	4,710[5]	6,296	6,436	6,429	6,464	6,555	6,677	6,802	6,964	7,134

— = Not available. **Note:** Details may not add up to totals because of rounding and/or incomplete enumeration. (1) Includes Wisconsin's 2015-16 student data (2016-17, 2017-18, and 2018-19 data were not available). (2) Includes Nebraska's 2015-16 data for 3-to-5-year-old students (2016-17 data were not available). (3) Includes 2016-17 data for 3-to-5-year-old students in Minnesota and 6-to-21-year-old students in Maine and Vermont because 2017-18 data were not available. (4) Includes limited strength, vitality, or alertness due to chronic or acute health problems such as a heart condition, tuberculosis, rheumatic fever, nephritis, asthma, sickle cell anemia, hemophilia, epilepsy, lead poisoning, leukemia, or diabetes. (5) Total includes 390 preschool disabled students. For all other years, preschool children were included in the counts by disability condition.

Population With Upper Secondary Education in Selected Countries, 2019

Source: Organization for Economic Cooperation and Development

Sorted by percentage of the population ages 25-64 that have received at least an upper secondary (senior high school) education.

Country	%	Country	%	Country	%	Country	%	Country	%
Japan	100%	Switzerland......	89%	Australia	83%	Luxembourg	75%	Colombia	57%
Russia[1]	95	Slovenia	89	Norway	83	South Africa[1].....	74	Brazil[1]..........	53
Czechia.........	94	South Korea	89	Denmark	82	Greece	74	Portugal	52
Lithuania........	93	Latvia	88	New Zealand	81	United Kingdom ..	68	Costa Rica	43
Poland	93	Israel...........	87	France...........	80	Chile[2]	67	Turkey..........	42
Canada	92	Germany........	87	Ireland..........	80	Argentina[1].......	64	Mexico	40
Slovakia	91	Austria	86	Netherlands	80	Italy	62	Indonesia[2].......	38
United States ...	91	Hungary........	85	Belgium.........	79	Spain	61	India[4]..........	29
Finland	90	Sweden.........	84	Iceland	79	Saudi Arabia[3]....	57	China[5]..........	24
Estonia	90								

(1) 2018. (2) 2017. (3) 2016. (4) 2011. (5) 2010.

Financial Aid to U.S. Undergraduate Students, 2000-18

Source: National Center for Education Statistics, U.S. Dept. of Education

Type of institution/ year	Number enrolled	Number receiving financial aid	Percent receiving aid	Percent of enrolled students in student aid programs				Average award[1]			
				Federal grants	State/ local grants	Institu- tional grants	Student loans[2]	Federal grants	State/ local grants	Institu- tional grants	Student loans[2]
All institutions											
2000-01	1,976,600	1,390,527	70.3%	31.6%	31.2%	31.1%	40.1%	$3,597	$2,949	$6,856	$5,445
2017-18	2,463,084	2,057,247	83.5	42.6	33.6	46.6	44.4	5,028	3,760	11,469	7,228
Public											
2000-01	1,333,236	872,109	65.4	30.0	33.5	22.7	30.7	3,483	2,469	3,290	4,412
2017-18	1,766,003	1,438,174	81.4	42.8	38.9	38.9	37.2	5,008	3,632	5,665	6,617
4-year											
2000-01	804,793	573,430	71.3	26.6	36.5	29.6	40.7	3,716	2,991	3,784	4,646
2017-18	1,183,447	994,201	84.0	37.9	38.3	50.3	46.0	5,060	4,338	6,218	7,004
2-year											
2000-01	528,443	298,679	56.5	35.2	28.8	12.1	15.3	3,215	1,460	1,452	3,465
2017-18	582,556	443,973	76.2	53.0	40.0	15.9	19.4	4,932	2,257	2,107	4,753
Private nonprofit											
2000-01	439,369	363,044	82.6	28.4	31.8	68.1	57.7	4,164	4,336	10,657	5,814
2017-18	550,431	496,948	90.3	35.8	23.8	79.2	60.6	5,323	4,460	21,053	8,268
4-year											
2000-01	419,499	347,638	82.9	27.4	32.2	70.1	58.1	4,239	4,342	10,788	5,786
2017-18	516,571	464,446	89.9	32.6	24.9	83.0	58.8	5,253	4,464	21,318	8,357
2-year											
2000-01	19,870	15,406	77.5	49.2	23.9	25.7	49.5	3,283	4,183	3,135	6,522
2017-18	33,860	32,502	96.0	84.1	6.3	20.0	88.5	5,740	4,215	4,323	7,369
Private for-profit											
2000-01	203,995	155,374	76.2	49.3	15.2	6.2	63.5	3,345	3,607	2,227	7,981
2017-18	146,650	122,125	83.3	65.4	7.2	17.0	69.1	4,577	3,402	3,997	7,771
4-year											
2000-01	81,075	51,739	63.8	36.1	11.9	8.3	57.7	3,320	4,178	2,337	8,315
2017-18	52,371	43,342	82.8	62.2	9.1	30.6	65.1	4,989	3,901	4,981	8,502
2-year											
2000-01	122,920	103,635	84.3	58.0	17.3	4.8	67.3	3,355	3,347	2,101	7,792
2017-18	94,279	78,783	83.6	67.2	6.1	9.5	71.3	4,365	2,991	2,232	7,401

Note: Data for full-time, first-time, degree-seeking undergraduate students. (1) Average amounts for students participating in indicated programs, in constant 2018-19 dollars. (2) Includes only loans made directly to students. Does not include Parent Loans for Undergraduate Students (PLUS) and other loans made directly to parents.

Charges at U.S. Institutions of Higher Education, 1969-2019

Source: National Center for Education Statistics, U.S. Dept. of Education

Data are for the entire academic year and are average charges, in current dollars, for full-time students at degree-granting postsecondary institutions. Room and board based on full-time students. For 1989-90 on, board is based on 20 meals per week.

	Tuition and fees			Board rates			Dormitory charges		
Public (in-state)	All institutions	2-yr	4-yr	All institutions	2-yr	4-yr	All institutions	2-yr	4-yr
1969-70	$323	$178	$358	$508	$465	$510	$366	$308	$369
1979-80	583	355	738	867	893	865	715	574	725
1989-90	1,356	756	1,780	1,635	1,581	1,638	1,513	962	1,557
1999-2000	2,504	1,348	3,349	2,364	1,834	2,406	2,440	1,549	2,519
2005-06	3,874	1,935	5,351	3,035	2,306	3,093	3,545	2,251	3,664
2006-07	4,102	2,017	5,666	3,192	2,390	3,255	3,757	2,408	3,878
2007-08	4,288	2,058	5,943	3,332	2,414	3,404	3,951	2,505	4,082
2008-09	4,512	2,136	6,312	3,507	2,749	3,569	4,190	2,664	4,331
2009-10	4,763	2,283	6,717	3,655	2,571	3,755	4,401	2,854	4,564
2010-11	5,075	2,441	7,132	3,845	2,683	3,956	4,646	2,955	4,832
2011-12	5,563	2,651	7,713	3,946	2,866	4,042	4,849	3,100	5,031
2012-13	5,899	2,792	8,070	4,061	2,888	4,163	5,062	3,247	5,241
2013-14	6,120	2,881	8,312	4,205	2,955	4,308	5,304	3,448	5,479
2014-15	6,370	2,955	8,543	4,313	3,072	4,412	5,504	3,559	5,677
2015-16	6,612	3,038	8,778	4,469	3,118	4,576	5,686	3,759	5,850
2016-17	6,818	3,156	8,804	4,562	3,111	4,666	5,859	3,823	6,018
2017-18	7,051	3,242	9,036	4,682	3,204	4,785	6,060	3,834	6,227
2018-19	7,250	3,313	9,212	4,843	3,581	4,927	6,290	4,055	6,459
Private (nonprofit and for-profit)									
1969-70	$1,533	$1,034	$1,562	$560	$546	$561	$434	$413	$436
1979-80	3,130	2,062	3,225	955	923	957	827	766	831
1989-90	8,147	5,196	8,396	1,948	1,811	1,953	1,923	1,663	1,935
1999-2000	14,100	8,225	14,616	2,877	2,753	2,879	3,236	3,067	3,242
2005-06	18,862	12,450	19,292	3,645	4,781	3,637	4,400	4,173	4,404
2006-07	20,047	12,708	20,517	3,787	3,430	3,790	4,606	4,147	4,613
2007-08	20,972	13,128	21,427	3,992	4,074	3,992	4,803	4,484	4,808
2008-09	21,575	13,567	22,040	4,164	4,603	4,161	5,025	4,553	5,031
2009-10	21,764	14,862	22,269	4,329	4,390	4,329	5,248	5,211	5,248
2010-11	22,042	13,687	22,677	4,430	4,475	4,430	5,403	4,939	5,410
2011-12	22,850	13,961	23,464	4,586	4,475	4,586	5,622	5,169	5,627
2012-13	23,943	14,149	24,523	4,709	3,977	4,712	5,831	5,228	5,837
2013-14	25,110	14,170	25,707	4,864	4,211	4,866	6,021	5,489	6,026
2014-15	26,182	14,261	26,739	5,019	4,560	5,021	6,221	5,506	6,228
2015-16	27,436	14,528	27,942	5,123	4,181	5,128	6,457	5,666	6,464
2016-17	28,945	14,589	29,476	5,268	4,350	5,273	6,710	5,949	6,717
2017-18	30,274	14,894	30,723	5,437	4,645	5,440	6,961	6,057	6,968
2018-19	31,519	15,727	31,875	5,616	6,933	5,608	7,171	5,967	7,179

U.S. Student Loan Balances by Age, 2004-17

Source: *2018 Student Loan Update*, Federal Reserve Bank of New York; Equifax

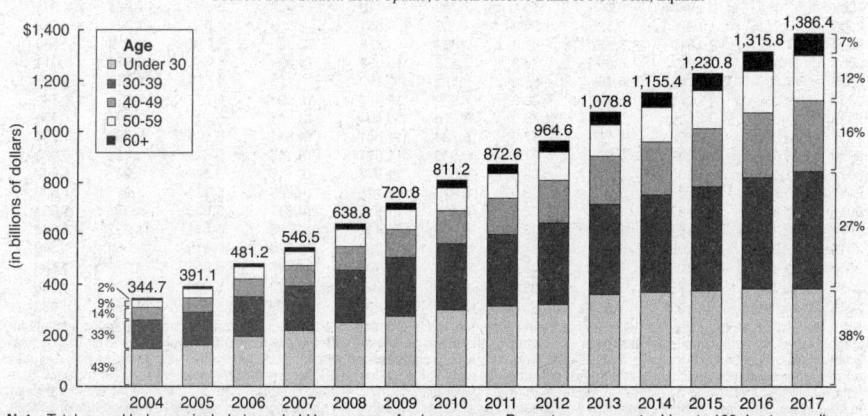

Note: Total annual balances include loans held by persons of unknown ages. Percentages may not add up to 100 due to rounding.

Student Loan Debt by State, 2004-18

Source: *Student Debt and the Class of 2018*, Project on Student Debt, Institute for College Access & Success

State[1]	Average debt 2004	Average debt 2014	Average debt 2018	% with debt 2004	% with debt 2018	State[1]	Average debt 2004	Average debt 2014	Average debt 2018	% with debt 2004	% with debt 2018
Alabama	$18,042	$29,425	$29,469	57%	51%	Missouri	$15,511	$25,844	$29,224	59%	58%
Alaska	15,648	26,742	—	48	—	Montana	18,019	26,946	28,032	68	57
Arizona	18,147	22,609	—	48	—	Nebraska	17,384	26,278	26,422	62	55
Arkansas	16,210	25,344	26,579	59	53	Nevada	14,144	20,211	22,600	46	51
California	16,071	21,382	22,585	49	49	New Hampshire	21,441	33,410	36,776	65	76
Colorado	16,352	25,064	24,888	53	52	New Jersey	16,223	28,318	34,387	58	64
Connecticut	18,906	29,750	38,669	57	59	New Mexico	—	18,969	21,858	—	49
Delaware	14,780	33,808	34,144	45	62	New York	18,857	27,822	31,127	62	59
District of Columbia	19,357	—	34,046	58	51	North Carolina	16,863	25,218	26,683	51	56
Florida	18,857	24,947	24,428	51	44	North Dakota	22,409	—	—	73	—
Georgia	15,354	26,518	28,824	53	57	Ohio	19,182	29,353	30,323	62	60
Hawaii	13,509	24,554	24,162	29	47	Oklahoma	16,942	23,430	25,221	55	47
Idaho	22,273	26,091	27,682	68	62	Oregon	17,267	26,106	28,628	63	55
Illinois	15,650	28,984	29,855	56	66	Pennsylvania	19,556	33,264	37,061	69	65
Indiana	19,425	29,222	29,064	54	57	Rhode Island	19,328	31,841	36,036	68	63
Iowa	24,204	29,732	30,045	76	63	South Carolina	16,775	29,163	30,838	55	58
Kansas	16,266	25,521	26,764	57	58	South Dakota	19,023	26,023	31,895	82	72
Kentucky	14,250	25,939	28,435	52	64	Tennessee	16,905	25,510	26,838	41	55
Louisiana	18,993	23,025	27,151	61	49	Texas	17,170	26,250	27,293	51	56
Maine	19,410	30,908	32,676	64	61	Utah	12,362	18,921	19,728	43	36
Maryland	12,597	27,457	29,178	52	55	Vermont	20,706	29,060	31,431	56	63
Massachusetts	17,021	29,391	31,882	60	57	Virginia	15,831	26,432	30,363	57	57
Michigan	18,754	29,450	32,158	58	59	Washington	17,415	24,804	23,524	56	48
Minnesota	19,580	31,579	32,317	72	68	West Virginia	18,246	26,854	30,014	69	65
Mississippi	15,503	26,177	30,117	60	58	Wisconsin	16,560	28,810	31,705	60	64
						Wyoming	15,352	23,708	24,474	44	46
						U.S.	**18,550**	**28,950**	**29,200**	**65**	**65**

— = Usable cases covered less than 30% of bachelor's degree recipients, or underlying data showed a state-level change of 30% or more in average debt from previous year. (1) Location of surveyed colleges (not necessarily location of degree recipient).

College Enrollment by Selected Characteristics, 1947-2018

Source: National Center for Education Statistics, U.S. Dept. of Education
(numbers in thousands)

Year	Total enrollment[1]	Attendance status Full-time	Attendance status Part-time	Attendance status % part-time	Sex of student Male	Sex of student Female	Control of institution Public	Control of institution Total	Control of institution Private Nonprofit	Control of institution For-profit
1947[2]	2,338	NA	NA	NA	1,659	679	1,152	1,186	NA	NA
1950[2]	2,281	NA	NA	NA	1,560	721	1,140	1,142	NA	NA
1955[2]	2,653	NA	NA	NA	1,733	920	1,476	1,177	NA	NA
1965	5,921	4,096	1,825[3]	30.8%	3,630	2,291	3,970	1,951	NA	NA
1970	8,581	5,816	2,765	32.2	5,044	3,537	6,428	2,153	2,134	18
1975	11,185	6,841	4,344	38.8	6,149	5,036	8,835	2,350	2,311	39
1980	12,097	7,098	4,999	41.3	5,874	6,223	9,457	2,640	2,528	112[4]
1985	12,247	7,075	5,172	42.2	5,818	6,429	9,479	2,768	2,572	196
1990	13,819	7,821	5,998	43.4	6,284	7,535	10,845	2,974	2,760	214
1995	14,262	8,129	6,133	43.0	6,343	7,919	11,092	3,169	2,929	240
2000	15,312	9,010	6,303	41.2	6,722	8,591	11,753	3,560	3,109	450
2002	16,612	9,946	6,665	40.1	7,202	9,410	12,752	3,860	3,265	594
2003	16,911	10,326	6,585	38.9	7,260	9,651	12,859	4,053	3,341	712
2004	17,272	10,610	6,662	38.6	7,387	9,885	12,980	4,292	3,412	880
2005	17,487	10,797	6,690	38.3	7,456	10,032	13,022	4,466	3,455	1,011
2006	17,754	10,958	6,797	38.3	7,572	10,182	13,175	4,579	3,513	1,066
2007	18,258	11,271	6,987	38.3	7,820	10,438	13,501	4,757	3,571	1,186
2008	19,082	11,735	7,347	38.5	8,178	10,904	13,971	5,111	3,661	1,450
2009	20,314	12,605	7,708	37.9	8,733	11,581	14,811	5,503	3,768	1,735
2010	21,019	13,087	7,932	37.7	9,046	11,974	15,142	5,877	3,854	2,023
2011	21,011	13,003	8,008	38.1	9,034	11,976	15,116	5,894	3,927	1,967
2012	20,644	12,734	7,910	38.3	8,919	11,725	14,885	5,760	3,951	1,808
2013	20,377	12,597	7,780	38.2	8,861	11,515	14,747	5,630	3,971	1,658
2014	20,209	12,454	7,755	38.4	8,798	11,412	14,655	5,554	3,997	1,557
2015	19,988	12,288	7,701	38.5	8,724	11,264	14,573	5,415	4,066	1,349
2016	19,847	12,125	7,722	38.9	8,638	11,208	14,586	5,261	4,079	1,182
2017	19,778	12,076	7,702	38.9	8,571	11,207	14,572	5,206	4,108	1,098
2018	19,646	11,992	7,654	39.0	8,443	11,203	14,529	5,117	4,134	982

NA = Not available. **Note:** Data for 1947-95 are for institutions of higher education, while later data are for degree-granting institutions. Degree-granting institutions grant associate's or higher degrees and participate in Title IV federal financial aid programs. The degree-granting classification is very similar to the earlier higher education classification, but it includes more two-year colleges and excludes a few higher education institutions that do not grant degrees. (1) Fall enrollment. (2) Degree-credit enrollment only. (3) Includes part-time resident students and all extension students (students attending courses at sites separate from the primary reporting campus). In later years, part-time student enrollment was collected as a distinct category. (4) Large increases are due to the addition of schools accredited by the Accrediting Commission of Career Schools and Colleges of Technology.

U.S. Bachelor's Degrees Conferred, 1899-2030

Source: National Center for Education Statistics, U.S. Dept. of Education
(*) figures are projected.

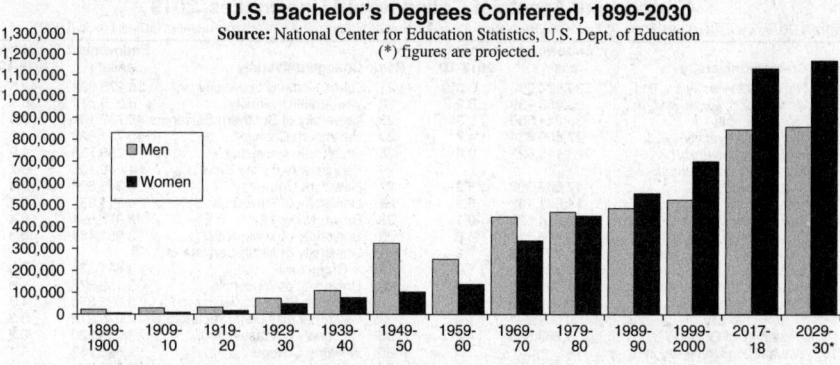

Financial Aid for College and Other Postsecondary Education

Reviewed by National Association of Student Financial Aid Administrators; as of June 2020

The cost of postsecondary education in the U.S. continues to increase, but financial aid—in the form of **grants** (no repayment needed), **loans**, and/or **work-study** programs—is widely available to help families meet these expenses. Most federal aid is limited to families that demonstrate financial need as determined by standard formulas and is designed to help students attend the college of their choice regardless of their ability to pay. Financial aid personnel at each school can provide information about all aid programs (federal, state, institutional, and private) available to students, how to apply, and deadlines.

All applicants for federal aid must file a Free Application for Federal Student Aid (**FAFSA**), generally as soon as possible after Oct. 1 for the academic year starting the following Aug. or Sept. This change from Jan. in prior years allows students to apply for aid earlier. Applicants can file a FAFSA form online at fafsa.gov, on the myStudentAid mobile app, or by completing a printed-out form and mailing it.

Figures provided should match federal income tax forms filed for the previous year. (The use of tax data that has already been filed ensures timely processing.) Thus, the application for the 2020-21 academic year, available Oct. 1, 2019, should be filed with 2018 tax information. This is made easier by the availability of the IRS Data Retrieval Tool, which allows online applicants to access and transfer IRS tax return information directly into their FAFSA. Many other sources of aid—state governments, employers and unions, civic organizations, and the institutions themselves—also use the FAFSA to determine eligibility for aid. Some federal programs pay for postsecondary education in return for service: AmeriCorps, Reserve Officers' Training Corps (Army, Navy, and Air Force), the G.I. Bill, and the National Health Service Corps. A student must reapply for aid annually.

Students, parents, and borrowers are required to use an **FSA ID**, made up of a username and password, to access certain U.S. Dept. of Education websites. An FSA ID is used to confirm identity when accessing financial aid information and electronically signing federal student aid documents.

A **federal formula**, based on information provided on the FAFSA, takes into account such factors as family income in the preceding calendar year, parental and student assets (excluding the parents' home, farm, or certain small businesses), and length of time to parents' retirement. Financial aid personnel have the authority to consider unusual expenses, such as very high medical expenses, which are not reported on the FAFSA. Outside scholarships are also taken into account in determining eligibility for federal, institutional, and state financial aid programs.

The formula determines a family's **expected family contribution** (EFC), which is divided among the number of family members—excluding parents—in college. The EFC is subtracted from the total cost of attending college for each person. The difference determines financial need and the maximum federal aid for which the family may be eligible. (Some institutions use a separate formula for need-based institutional aid.) Some schools guarantee they will meet the full financial need of each admitted student. Schools might try to cover a student's financial need using a combination of tools but be unable to because of a lack of funds.

The **aid package** offered by each school may include one or more of the following: Federal Pell Grants, for those who demonstrate sufficient financial need; Federal Supplemental Educational Opportunity Grants, for those who still have significant need after receiving Federal Pell Grants; grants from the school; Federal Work-Study or other work programs; and federal Direct Subsidized and Unsubsidized Loans (often referred to as Direct Loans). Parents of undergraduates and students in graduate or professional school may apply for a PLUS Loan. Direct Unsubsidized Loans and Direct PLUS Loans are available regardless of financial need, but students and parents must still complete the FAFSA to get these loans. Professional judgment, which allows an institution to take into account current financial circumstances not reflected in the FAFSA, is also available. Students and families that have incurred a loss of income or job elimination can work directly with the financial aid office of their chosen institution to ensure an accurate reflection of their current financial situation.

Loans have varying interest rates and other requirements. Repayment of Direct Subsidized Loans and Direct Unsubsidized Loans generally does not begin until after graduation; deferments, income-based repayment plans, and loan forgiveness are available on federal loans for students who meet certain requirements. For PLUS Loans, parents and graduate-level students must pass a credit check and may need to begin repayment of both principal and interest while the student is still in school.

Terms may vary, but federal student loans must be repaid, even if financial circumstances change, education is incomplete or not as expected, or post-graduation income is less than expected. The loan servicer or lender is required to provide a loan repayment schedule that states the first payment due date, the number and frequency of payments, and the amount due. Some loans have a grace period, a set period of time (in most cases six months) after graduation before repayment begins. Direct loans have a number of repayment plan options—including graduated repayments, extended repayment, income-based repayment—or offer loan consolidation. In most cases, student loan debt cannot be discharged in bankruptcy. Certain federal income **tax credits and refunds** are available to families who meet requirements.

Rules for financial aid are complex and changeable. Comprehensive resources on financial aid from the U.S. Dept. of Education, including fact sheets, videos, worksheets, and other tools, are available online at studentaid.ed.gov/sa/resources/.

Further information available from the Federal Student Aid Information Center: 1-800-4-FED-AID, Mon.-Fri., 8 AM-11 PM ET; Sat.-Sun., 11 AM-5 PM ET; studentaid.gov; web chat also available.

Endowment Assets of Colleges and Universities, 2019

Source: *2019 NACUBO-TIAA Study of Endowments*, National Association of College and University Business Officers (NACUBO)

Rank	College/university	Endowment assets[1]	% change, 2018-19	Rank	College/university	Endowment assets[1]	% change, 2018-19
1.	Harvard University	$39,427,896	3.0%	21.	Johns Hopkins University	$6,275,939	49.8%
2.	University of Texas System	30,958,239	0.2	22.	Vanderbilt University	6,270,877	36.1
3.	Yale University	30,314,800	3.3	23.	University of Southern California	5,732,101	3.3
4.	Stanford University	27,699,834	4.7	24.	Dartmouth College	5,731,322	4.3
5.	Princeton University	26,116,022	0.8	25.	Ohio State University	5,256,759	0.9
6.	Massachusetts Institute of Technology	17,569,328	6.3	26.	Pennsylvania State University	4,546,105	6.2
7.	University of Pennsylvania	14,649,762	6.3	27.	New York University	4,345,608	2.0
8.	Texas A&M University System	13,514,528	−0.1	28.	University of Pittsburgh	4,311,387	2.7
9.	University of Michigan	12,448,817	4.6	29.	Brown University	3,976,694	10.4
10.	University of California	11,797,543	7.2	30.	University of Minnesota	3,951,464	6.3
11.	University of Notre Dame	11,268,365	5.0	31.	University of North Carolina at Chapel Hill	3,671,351	7.0
12.	Northwestern University	11,091,516	0.0	32.	University of Wisconsin	3,152,578	5.6
13.	Columbia University	10,950,738	0.8	33.	Michigan State University	3,033,279	4.3
14.	Duke University	8,609,004	1.0	34.	California Institute of Technology	2,975,376	3.3
15.	University of Chicago	8,263,868	4.2	35.	University of Washington	2,935,220	6.2
16.	Washington University in St. Louis	7,953,986	4.7	36.	Williams College	2,888,962	5.1
17.	Emory University	7,872,381	8.0	37.	UCLA	2,746,930	8.9
18.	Cornell University	7,328,241	1.4	38.	Purdue University	2,625,278	4.0
19.	University of Virginia	7,058,235	3.0	39.	Carnegie Mellon University	2,542,650	6.6
20.	Rice University	6,481,102	3.2	40.	Boston College	2,523,300	1.8

Note: Market value of endowment assets in the fiscal year. (1) In thousands.

Average ACT Scores and Characteristics of College-Bound Students, 1990-2019

Source: ACT, Inc. (formerly American College Testing)

SCORES	Unit	1990	1995	2000	2005	2010	2013	2014	2015	2016	2017	2018	2019
Composite score	Points	20.6	20.8	21.0	20.9	21.0	20.9	21.0	21.0	20.8	21.0	20.8	20.7
Male	Points	21.0	21.0	21.2	21.1	21.2	20.9	21.1	21.1	20.9	21.0	20.8	20.6
Female	Points	20.3	20.7	20.9	20.9	20.9	20.9	20.9	21.0	20.9	21.1	20.9	20.8
English score	Points	20.5	20.2	20.5	20.4	20.5	20.2	20.3	20.4	20.1	20.3	20.2	20.1
Male	Points	20.1	19.8	20.0	20.0	20.1	19.8	20.0	20.0	19.8	19.9	19.7	19.6
Female	Points	20.9	20.6	20.9	20.8	20.8	20.6	20.7	20.8	20.6	20.8	20.7	20.6
Math score	Points	19.9	20.2	20.7	20.7	21.0	20.9	20.9	20.8	20.6	20.7	20.5	20.4
Male	Points	20.7	20.9	21.4	21.3	21.6	21.4	21.4	21.3	21.0	21.2	20.9	20.8
Female	Points	19.3	19.7	20.2	20.2	20.5	20.5	20.5	20.4	20.3	20.4	20.2	20.0
PARTICIPANTS													
Total number	(Thous.)	817	945	1,065	1,186	1,569	1,799	1,846	1,924	2,090	2,030	1,915	1,783
Male	Percent	46%	44%	43%	44%	45%	46%	46%	47%	46%	46%	47%	46%
White	Percent	79	80	72	66	62	58	56	55	54	52	52	52
Black	Percent	9	9	10	12	14	13	13	13	13	13	13	12
Hispanic[1]	Percent	4	5	5	7	10	14	15	16	16	17	16	16
Composite score													
27 or above	Percent	12	13	14	14	16	13	17	18	17	18	18	18
18 or below	Percent	35	34	32	34	35	36	36	37	39	38	40	41

Note: Minimum score, 1; maximum score, 36. Test scores and characteristics of college-bound students are based on the performance of all ACT-tested students who graduated in the spring of a given school year and took the ACT assessment during junior or senior year of high school. (1) Persons of Hispanic origin may be of any race.

Average ACT Composite Scores by State, 2019

Source: ACT, Inc. (formerly American College Testing)

State	Avg. comp. score	% grads taking ACT	State	Avg. comp. score	% grads taking ACT	State	Avg. comp. score	% grads taking ACT
Alabama	18.9	100%	Louisiana	18.8	100%	Ohio	20.0	100%
Alaska	20.1	38	Maine	24.3	6	Oklahoma	18.9	100
Arizona	19.0	73	Maryland	22.3	28	Oregon	21.1	42
Arkansas	19.3	100	Massachusetts	25.5	21	Pennsylvania	23.6	17
California	22.6	23	Michigan	24.4	19	Rhode Island	24.7	12
Colorado	23.8	27	Minnesota	21.4	95	South Carolina	18.8	78
Connecticut	25.5	22	Mississippi	18.4	100	South Dakota	21.6	75
Delaware	24.0	13	Missouri	20.8	82	Tennessee	19.4	100
District of Columbia	23.5	32	Montana	19.8	100	Texas	20.5	39
Florida	20.1	54	Nebraska	20.0	100	Utah	20.3	100
Georgia	21.4	49	Nevada	17.9	100	Vermont	24.1	20
Hawaii	19.0	80	New Hampshire	25.0	14	Virginia	24.0	21
Idaho	22.5	31	New Jersey	24.2	25	Washington	22.1	24
Illinois	24.3	35	New Mexico	19.3	63	West Virginia	20.8	49
Indiana	22.5	29	New York	24.5	22	Wisconsin	20.3	100
Iowa	21.6	66	North Carolina	19.0	100	Wyoming	19.8	100
Kansas	21.2	72	North Dakota	19.9	96	**U.S.**	**20.7**	**52**
Kentucky	19.8	100						

Mean SAT Scores of College-Bound Seniors, 1975-2020
Source: The College Board
(for school year ending in year shown)

	1975	1980	1985	1990	1995	2000	2005	2010	2014	2015	2016[2,3]	2017[3]	2018[3]	2019[3]	2020[3]
Reading and writing[1]	512	502	509	500	504	505	508	500	497	495	494	533	536	531	528
Male	515	506	514	505	505	507	513	502	499	497	495	532	534	529	523
Female	509	498	503	496	502	504	505	498	495	493	493	534	539	534	532
Math score	498	492	500	501	506	514	520	515	513	511	508	527	531	528	523
Male	518	515	522	521	525	533	538	533	530	527	524	538	542	537	531
Female	479	473	480	483	490	498	504	499	499	496	494	516	522	519	516
Writing score	NA	NA	NA	NA	NA	NA	NA	491	487	484	482	NA	NA	NA	NA
Male	NA	NA	NA	NA	NA	NA	NA	485	481	478	475	NA	NA	NA	NA
Female	NA	NA	NA	NA	NA	NA	NA	497	492	490	487	NA	NA	NA	NA

NA = Not applicable. **Note:** In 1995, the College Board recentered the scoring scale for the SAT. Earlier scores have been adjusted to account for this recentering. (1) Verbal section, 1975-2005; critical reading, 2006-16. (2) Through Jan. 2016. (3) Beginning in Mar. 2016, students took a redesigned SAT. The College Board advised against comparing 2016-20 SAT results with earlier data.

Mean SAT Scores by State, 1990-2020
Source: The College Board; National Center for Education Statistics, U.S. Dept. of Education
(for school year ending in year shown; V = Verbal, M = Math, CR = Critical reading, W = Writing, ERW = Evidence-based reading and writing)

	1990		2000		2010			2015			2020[1]		% grads
State	V	M	V	M	CR	M	W	CR	M	W	ERW	M	taking SAT[2]
Alabama	545	534	559	555	556	550	544	545	538	533	576	551	7%
Alaska	514	501	519	515	518	515	491	509	503	482	555	543	37
Arizona	521	520	521	523	519	525	500	523	527	502	571	568	29
Arkansas	545	532	563	554	566	566	552	568	569	551	590	567	4
California	494	508	497	518	501	516	500	495	506	491	527	522	67
Colorado	533	534	534	537	568	572	555	582	587	567	511	501	100
Connecticut	506	496	508	509	509	514	513	504	506	504	527	512	100
Delaware	510	496	502	496	493	495	481	462	461	445	497	481	100
District of Columbia	483	467	494	486	474	464	466	441	440	432	498	482	100
Florida	495	493	498	500	496	498	479	486	480	468	512	479	100
Georgia	478	473	488	486	488	490	475	490	485	475	537	516	68
Hawaii	480	505	488	519	483	505	470	487	508	477	549	546	51
Idaho	542	524	540	541	543	541	517	467	463	442	500	484	100
Illinois	542	547	568	586	585	600	577	599	616	587	504	503	98
Indiana	486	486	498	501	494	505	477	496	499	478	540	534	64
Iowa	584	588	589	600	603	613	580	589	600	566	611	609	3
Kansas	566	563	574	580	590	595	567	588	592	568	617	620	4
Kentucky	548	541	548	550	575	575	563	588	587	574	609	598	4
Louisiana	551	537	562	558	555	550	547	563	559	553	597	573	5
Maine	501	490	504	504	468	467	454	468	473	451	504	491	98
Maryland	506	502	507	509	501	506	495	491	493	478	522	507	88
Massachusetts	503	498	511	513	512	526	509	516	529	507	560	559	80
Michigan	529	534	557	569	585	605	576	594	609	585	503	495	100
Minnesota	552	558	581	594	594	607	580	595	607	576	624	633	4
Mississippi	552	538	562	549	566	548	552	580	563	570	610	593	3
Missouri	548	541	572	577	593	595	580	596	599	582	610	603	4
Montana	540	542	543	546	538	538	517	561	556	538	598	587	10
Nebraska	559	562	560	571	585	593	568	589	590	576	615	614	3
Nevada	511	511	510	517	496	501	473	494	494	470	579	571	17
New Hampshire	518	510	520	519	520	524	510	525	530	511	531	524	93
New Jersey	495	498	498	513	495	514	497	500	521	499	541	540	82
New Mexico	554	546	549	543	553	549	534	551	544	528	533	522	19
New York	489	496	494	506	484	499	478	489	502	478	528	530	79
North Carolina	478	470	492	496	497	511	477	498	504	476	553	544	48
North Dakota	579	578	588	609	580	594	559	597	608	586	615	617	2
Ohio	526	522	533	539	538	548	522	557	563	537	536	534	21
Oklahoma	553	542	563	560	569	568	547	576	569	548	490	481	20
Oregon	515	509	527	527	523	524	499	523	521	502	557	547	51
Pennsylvania	497	490	498	497	492	501	480	499	504	482	543	534	67
Rhode Island	498	488	505	500	494	495	488	494	494	484	501	489	100
South Carolina	475	467	484	482	484	495	468	488	487	467	524	503	68
South Dakota	580	570	587	588	592	603	571	592	597	564	609	610	3
Tennessee	558	544	563	553	576	571	565	581	574	568	601	585	7
Texas	490	489	493	500	484	505	473	470	486	454	510	500	73
Utah	566	555	570	569	568	559	547	579	575	554	601	603	3
Vermont	507	493	513	508	519	521	506	523	524	507	559	545	63
Virginia	501	496	509	500	512	512	497	518	516	499	567	549	65
Washington	513	511	526	528	524	532	508	502	510	484	539	534	69
West Virginia	520	514	526	511	515	507	500	509	497	495	480	456	98
Wisconsin	552	559	584	597	595	604	579	591	605	575	615	628	3
Wyoming	534	538	545	545	570	567	546	589	586	562	614	606	2
National average	500	501	505	514	501	516	492	495	511	484	528	523	NA

NA = Not available. **Note:** In 1995, the College Board recentered the scoring scale for the SAT. In 2005, the Verbal portion became Critical reading, and a writing test was added. In 2016, this portion became Evidence-based reading and writing. (1) Beginning in Mar. 2016, students took a redesigned SAT test. The College Board advised against comparing 2020 SAT results with earlier data. (2) Percentage of students from the class of 2020 who took the SAT during high school.

Four-Year Colleges and Universities

Note: These listings include only accredited degree-granting institutions in the U.S. and U.S. territories with a total enrollment of 1,200 or more. Only four-year colleges and universities that award a bachelor's degree as their highest undergraduate degree are included. Data reported for institutions that provided updated information on Peterson's Annual Survey of Undergraduate Institutions for the 2019-20 academic year, with some exceptions where the previous academic year was the most recent available.

All institutions are coeducational except those where the ZIP code is followed directly by a number in parentheses: (1) = men only; (2) = primarily men; (3) = women only; (4) = primarily women; (5) undergraduate: men only, graduate: coed; (6) undergraduate: women only, graduate: coed.

The **Tuition & fees** column shows the annual tuition and required fees for full-time students or, where indicated, the tuition and standard fees per unit for part-time students. Where tuition varies according to residence, the figure is given for the most local resident and is coded as follows: (A) = area residents; (S) = state residents; all other figures apply to all students regardless of residence. Where annual expenses are expressed as a lump sum (including full-time tuition, mandatory fees, and room and board), the figure is entered under Tuition & fees and coded (C) = comprehensive fee. **Room & board** is the typical cost for one academic year.

Control: (1) independent (nonprofit); (2) independent-religious; (3) proprietary (profit-making); (4) federal; (5) state; (6) commonwealth (Puerto Rico); (7) territory (U.S. territories); (8) county; (9) district; (10) city; (11) state and local; (12) state-related; (13) private—unspecified; (14) public—unspecified. **Degree** means the highest degree offered: B = bachelor's, M = master's, D = doctorate.

Enrollment is the total number of matriculated undergraduate and (if applicable) graduate students.

Faculty is the total number of full-time and part-time faculty members teaching courses.

Grad. rate is the percentage of full-time, first-time bachelor's (or equivalent) degree-seeking undergraduate students entering school in 2013 (or most recent available year prior) who obtained their degrees within six years.

NA indicates category is inapplicable, or data is not available from a consistent source.

Name, address	Year founded	Tuition & fees	Room & board	Control, degree	Enroll-ment	Faculty	Grad. rate
Abilene Christian Univ., Abilene, TX 79699	1906	$37,800	$11,350	2-D	5,292	492	61.5%
Abraham Baldwin Agr Coll., Tifton, GA 31793	1933	$4,128 (S)	NA	5-B	3,327	162	NA
Acad. of Art Univ., San Francisco, CA 94105-3410.	1929	$30,630	$18,386	3-M	9,826	1,059	40.8
Adams State Univ., Alamosa, CO 81101	1921	$9,440 (A)	$8,760	5-D	3,101	187	40.0
Adelphi Univ., Garden City, NY 11530-0701.	1896	$38,660	$16,030	1-D	8,149	1,060	67.5
Adrian Coll., Adrian, MI 49221-2575.	1859	NA	NA	2-M	1,656	195	54.0
Adventist Univ. of Health Scis., Orlando, FL 32803	1992	$16,350	$4,200	1-D	1,688	246	NA
Alabama A&M Univ., Huntsville, AL 35811.	1875	$10,024 (S)	$7,522	5-D	5,814	290	100.0
Alabama State Univ., Montgomery, AL 36101-0271	1867	$11,068 (A)	$6,050	5-D	4,190	360	33.0
Albany Coll. of Pharm & Health Scis., Albany, NY 12208	1881	NA	NA	1-D	1,559	132	77.0
Albany State Univ., Albany, GA 31705-2717	1903	$6,726 (S)	$8,476	5-M	6,615	398	33.7
Albertus Magnus Coll., New Haven, CT 06511-1189.	1925	$32,060	$13,200	2-M	1,419	174	61.0
Albion Coll., Albion, MI 49224-1831.	1835	$50,590	$12,380	2-B	1,475	156	70.2
Albright Coll., Reading, PA 1856.	1856	$25,642	$12,480	2-M	1,934	148	53.0
Alcorn State Univ., Lorman, MS 39096-7500.	1871	$7,290 (S)	$10,788	5-D	3,523	221	40.0
Alfred Univ., Alfred, NY 14802-1205.	1836	$36,276	$12,924	1-D	2,382	201	57.0
Allegheny Coll., Meadville, PA 16335.	1815	$50,980	$13,080	1-B	1,775	198	73.7
Alliant Intl. Univ.–San Diego, San Diego, CA 92131	1952	NA	NA	1-D	3,046	520	NA
Alma Coll., Alma, MI 48801-1599.	1886	$41,398	$11,384	2-B	1,426	158	67.6
Alvernia Univ., Reading, PA 19607-1799.	1958	NA	NA	2-D	2,872	319	53.0
Alverno Coll., Milwaukee, WI 53234-3922 (6)	1887	$29,456	$8,800	2-D	1,743	238	49.0
Amberton Univ., Garland, TX 75041-5595.	1971	$13,020	NA	2-M	1,379	40	NA
Amer. InterContinental Univ. Online, Schaumburg, IL 60173.	1970	NA	NA	3-M	22,424	396	NA
Amer. Intl. Coll., Springfield, MA 01109-3189	1885	$35,680	$14,100	1-D	3,283	320	41.0
Amer. Musical & Dramatic Acad., Los Angeles, Los Angeles, CA 90028	1964	NA	NA	3-B	1,495	NA	NA
Amer. Publ Univ. System, Charles Town, WV 25414.	1991	$6,880	NA	3-D	45,249	NA	NA
Amer. Univ. of Puerto Rico, Bayamon, PR 00960-2037.	1963	NA	NA	1-M	2,468	162	NA
Amer. Univ., Washington, DC 20016-8001	1893	$51,361	$14,980	2-D	14,318	1,566	79.0
Amherst Coll., Amherst, MA 01002-5000.	1821	$60,890	$15,910	1-B	1,839	292	95.0
Anderson Univ., Anderson, IN 46012.	1917	$31,200	$10,040	2-D	1,567	NA	60.0
Anderson Univ., Anderson, SC 29621.	1911	$29,980	$10,640	2-D	3,497	341	NA
Andrews Univ., Berrien Springs, MI 49104.	1874	$31,008	$9,540	2-D	3,412	317	59.3
Angelo State Univ., San Angelo, TX 76909	1928	$9,011 (A)	$9,630	5-D	10,568	376	40.0
Anna Maria Coll., Paxton, MA 01612	1946	$37,860	$14,230	2-D	1,445	40	0.4
Appalachian State Univ., Boone, NC 28608.	1899	$7,410 (A)	$8,568	5-D	19,280	1,434	0.7
Aquinas Coll., Grand Rapids, MI 49506.	1886	$35,086	$9,976	2-M	1,600	200	61.0
Arcadia Univ., Glenside, PA 19038-3295.	1853	$44,440	$13,900	2-D	3,465	377	66.2
Arizona State Univ. at the Downtown Phoenix campus, Phoenix, AZ 85004	2006	$11,338 (S)	$14,924	5-D	11,420	1,138	70.1
Arizona State Univ. at the Polytechnic campus, Mesa, AZ 85212	1996	$10,803 (S)	$12,728	5-D	5,243	313	61.0
Arizona State Univ. at the Tempe campus, Tempe, AZ 85287	1885	$11,338 (S)	$13,164	5-D	53,286	2,897	70.7
Arizona State Univ. at the West campus, Glendale, AZ 85306	1984	$10,803 (S)	$11,914	5-D	4,929	NA	70.4
Arkansas State Univ., State University, AR 72467.	1909	NA	NA	5-D	13,930	729	46.0
Arkansas Tech Univ., Russellville, AR 72801	1909	$320/cr. hr. (S)	NA	5-D	11,829	582	41.0
Armstrong State Univ., Savannah, GA 31419-1997.	1935	$6,384 (S)	$10,630	5-D	7,041	478	32.0
Art Ctr. Coll. of Design, Pasadena, CA 91103	1930	$43,416	NA	1-M	2,251	NA	68.0
Asbury Univ., Wilmore, KY 40390-1198.	1890	$1,179/cr. hr.	NA	2-M	1,973	204	68.8
Ashford Univ., San Diego, CA 92123.	1918	NA	NA	3-M	10,568	748	20.0
Ashland Univ., Ashland, OH 44805-3702.	1878	$21,980	$10,190	2-D	6,579	518	62.0
Ashworth Coll., Norcross, GA 30092	1987	NA	NA	3-M	57,650	NA	NA
Aspen Univ., Denver, CO 80246-1930.	1987	NA	NA	1-D	5,434	190	20.0
Assumption Coll., Worcester, MA 01609-1296.	1904	$42,316	$13,128	2-M	2,376	222	69.9
Athens State Univ., Athens, AL 35611.	1822	$7,710 (S)	NA	5-M	2,945	189	NA
Atlantic Univ. Coll., Guaynabo, PR 00970	1983	NA	NA	1-M	1,236	NA	NA
Auburn Univ. at Montgomery, Montgomery, AL 36124-4023.	1967	$8,860 (S)	$7,268	5-D	5,188	343	34.0
Auburn Univ., Auburn University, AL 36849	1856	$11,492 (A)	$13,600	5-D	30,460	1,644	78.8
Augsburg Coll., Minneapolis, MN 55454-1351.	1869	$41,086	$10,885	2-D	3,425	399	57.5
Augusta Univ., Augusta, GA 30912	1828	$8,644 (S)	$5,800	5-D	7,938	1,482	31.4
Augustana Coll., Rock Island, IL 61201-2296	1860	$45,136	$11,216	2-B	2,546	260	0.7
Augustana Univ., Sioux Falls, SD 57197	1860	$35,884	$8,616	2-M	2,113	191	58.1
Aurora Univ., Aurora, IL 60506-4892	1893	$25,960	$12,020	1-D	6,246	521	54.3

Name, address	Year founded	Tuition & fees	Room & board	Control, degree	Enroll- ment	Faculty	Grad. rate
Austin Coll., Sherman, TX 75090-4400	1849	$41,155	$12,752	2-M	1,314	116	72.0%
Austin Peay State Univ., Clarksville, TN 37044	1927	$8,303 (S)	$11,114	5-D	11,048	704	41.0
Avila Univ., Kansas City, MO 64145-1698	1916	$21,115	$7,340	2-M	1,529	238	55.0
Azusa Pacific Univ., Azusa, CA 91702-7000	1899	$41,410	$10,076	2-D	10,095	1,235	70.0
Babson Coll., Babson Park, MA 02457-0310	1919	$54,144	$17,666	1-M	3,273	267	93.0
Baker Coll., Flint, MI 48507	1911	$10,990	$5,900	1-D	24,677	NA	NA
Baker Univ., Baldwin City, KS 66006-0065	1858	$29,880	$8,350	2-D	1,214	NA	NA
Baldwin Wallace Univ., Berea, OH 44017-2088	1845	$34,504	$11,946	2-M	3,504	426	65.2
Ball State Univ., Muncie, IN 47306	1918	$10,020 (A)	$10,870	5-D	22,510	1,766	65.6
Bard Coll., Annandale-on-Hudson, NY 12504	1860	$56,036	$15,876	1-D	2,285	267	76.9
Barnard Coll., New York, NY 10027-6598 (3)	1889	$57,668	$17,856	1-B	2,631	357	92.0
Barry Univ., Miami Shores, FL 33161-6695	1940	$29,850	$11,224	2-D	7,401	1,083	35.0
Baruch Coll. of the City Univ. of New York, New York, NY 10010-5585.	1919	$7,461 (S)	NA	11-M	18,679	1,089	69.9
Bastyr Univ., Kenmore, WA 98028-4966	1978	$26,091	NA	1-D	1,266	299	NA
Bates Coll., Lewiston, ME 04240-6028	1855	$55,683	$15,705	1-B	1,820	199	91.0
Bay Path Univ., Longmeadow, MA 01106-2292 (6)	1897	NA	NA	1-D	3,298	478	58.1
Bayamón Central Univ., Bayamón, PR 00960-1725	1970	$5,847	$5,724	2-M	2,221	145	29.0
Baylor Univ., Waco, TX 76798	1845	$49,246	$13,274	2-D	18,033	1,431	78.1
Becker Coll., Worcester, MA 01609	1784	$40,150	$13,800	1-M	1,698	247	45.0
Belhaven Univ., Jackson, MS 39202-1789.	1883	$27,025	$8,800	2-D	4,560	429	NA
Bellarmine Univ., Louisville, KY 40205.	1950	$44,620	$9,030	2-D	3,331	416	66.0
Bellevue Univ., Bellevue, NE 68005-3098	1965	$9,390	NA	1-D	10,304	411	37.0
Belmont Abbey Coll., Belmont, NC 28012-1802	1876	$18,500	$10,390	2-B	1,507	124	45.0
Belmont Univ., Nashville, TN 37212.	1951	$35,650	$12,520	2-D	8,428	894	72.0
Bemidji State Univ., Bemidji, MN 56601-2699	1919	$4,299 (A)	$8,660	5-M	4,868	246	45.0
Benedict Coll., Columbia, SC 29204	1870	NA	NA	2-B	2,641	NA	NA
Benedictine Coll., Atchison, KS 66002-1499	1859	$30,530	$10,450	2-M	2,157	180	64.0
Benedictine Univ., Lisle, IL 60532	1887	$34,290	$4,960	2-D	4,401	401	45.7
Bentley Univ., Waltham, MA 02452-4705.	1917	$51,830	$16,960	1-D	5,314	513	90.0
Berea Coll., Berea, KY 40404	1855	NA	NA	1-B	1,688	189	68.0
Berkeley Coll.–New York City campus, New York, NY 10017	1936	$27,000	NA	3-B	2,623	162	31.0
Berkeley Coll.–Woodland Park campus, Woodland Park, NJ 07424	1931	$27,000	NA	3-M	2,858	293	33.0
Berklee Coll. of Mus, Boston, MA 02215-3693	1945	$47,230	$18,830	1-M	6,999	986	65.0
Berry Coll., Mount Berry, GA 30149.	1902	$37,246	$13,070	2-M	2,034	227	69.0
Beth Medrash Govoha, Lakewood, NJ 08701-2797 (1)	1943	NA	NA	2-M	5,788	NA	NA
Bethel Coll., Mishawaka, IN 46545-5591	1947	$29,790	$9,310	2-M	1,450	193	67.0
Bethel Univ., McKenzie, TN 38201.	1842	$17,010	$9,198	2-M	4,339	469	75.1
Bethel Univ., St. Paul, MN 55112-6999	1871	$39,030	$10,960	2-D	4,339	291	73.3
Bethune-Cookman Univ., Daytona Beach, FL 32114-3099	1904	$14,814	$9,462	2-M	2,901	236	33.0
Binghamton Univ., State Univ. of New York, Binghamton, NY 13902-6000.	1946	$10,494 (A)	$16,549	5-D	18,124	1,074	81.0
Biola Univ., La Mirada, CA 90639-0001	1908	$53,490	$11,514	2-D	6,103	525	73.5
Birmingham-Southern Coll., Birmingham, AL 35254	1856	$17,650	$12,300	2-B	1,209	133	65.0
Black Hills State Univ., Spearfish, SD 57799	1883	$9,009 (S)	$7,142	5-M	4,035	NA	39.0
Bloomfield Coll., Bloomfield, NJ 07003-9981	1868	$29,950	$11,950	2-M	2,000	230	31.7
Bloomsburg Univ. of Pennsylvania, Bloomsburg, PA 17815-1301.	1839	$10,958 (S)	$9,686	5-D	8,683	521	59.9
Bluefield State Coll., Bluefield, WV 24701-2198	1895	$7,056 (S)	NA	5-B	2,758	124	24.7
Bob Jones Univ., Greenville, SC 29614.	1927	$18,150	$6,976	2-D	2,936	217	68.0
Boise State Univ., Boise, ID 83725-0399	1932	$8,068 (S)	$9,760	5-D	26,272	NA	50.3
Boston Coll., Chestnut Hill, MA 02467-3800	1863	$56,780	$14,826	2-D	14,171	1,386	91.9
Boston Univ., Boston, MA 02215	1839	$58,072	$16,640	1-D	33,720	2,685	88.0
Bowdoin Coll., Brunswick, ME 04011.	1794	$56,350	$15,360	1-B	1,835	229	95.0
Bowie State Univ., Bowie, MD 20715-9465	1865	$8,445 (S)	$9,916	5-D	6,436	408	39.0
Bowling Green State Univ., Bowling Green, OH 43403	1910	$11,317 (S)	$10,396	5-D	17,733	1,176	59.6
Bradley Univ., Peoria, IL 61625-0002.	1897	$35,480	$11,280	1-D	5,882	NA	72.2
Brandeis Univ., Waltham, MA 02454-9110	1948	$59,635	$16,380	1-D	5,825	550	87.0
Brenau Univ., Gainesville, GA 30501 (4)	1878	$31,720	$12,500	1-D	2,817	108	47.2
Brescia Univ., Owensboro, KY 42301-3023.	1950	$22,100	$9,350	2-M	1,338	124	39.0
Briar Cliff Univ., Sioux City, IA 51104-0100	1930	NA	NA	2-D	1,316	122	44.0
Bridgewater Coll., Bridgewater, VA 22812-1599	1880	$37,720	$13,360	2-M	1,754	165	59.0
Bridgewater State Univ., Bridgewater, MA 02325	1840	$38/cr. hr. (S)	NA	5-M	10,990	NA	58.7
Brigham Young Univ., Provo, UT 84602-1001.	1875	$5,970	$7,808	2-D	34,395	1,851	78.0
Brigham Young Univ.–Hawaii, Laie, HI 96762-1294	1955	NA	NA	2-B	2,555	228	52.0
Brigham Young Univ.–Idaho, Rexburg, ID 83460	1888	NA	NA	2-B	32,458	792	44.0
Brookline Coll., Phoenix, AZ 85021	1979	NA	NA	3-M	1,468	43	NA
Brooklyn Coll. of the City Univ. of New York, Brooklyn, NY 11210-2889.	1930	$7,240 (S)	NA	11-M	17,580	1,586	51.0
Brown Univ., Providence, RI 02912	1764	$60,596	$15,908	1-D	10,333	947	95.6
Bryan Coll., Dayton, TN 37321.	1930	$16,900	$7,800	2-M	1,489	117	46.0
Bryant & Stratton Coll.–Wauwatosa campus, Wauwatosa, WI 53226		NA	NA	3-B	1,264	NA	NA
Bryant Univ., Smithfield, RI 02917	1863	$46,863	$16,204	1-M	3,640	330	80.9
Bryn Mawr Coll., Bryn Mawr, PA 19010-2899 (6).	1885	$56,610	$17,720	1-D	1,719	200	84.1
Bucknell Univ., Lewisburg, PA 17837.	1846	$58,202	$14,670	1-M	3,697	435	90.0
Buffalo State Coll., State Univ. of New York, Buffalo, NY 14222-1095.	1867	$8,672 (A)	$14,506	5-M	9,118	826	46.0
Butler Univ., Indianapolis, IN 46208-3485	1855	$43,400	$14,380	1-D	5,515	645	82.0
Cabrini Univ., Radnor, PA 19087	1957	$33,845	$12,965	2-D	2,075	NA	0.0
Caldwell Univ., Caldwell, NJ 07006-6195.	1939	$36,900	$12,760	2-D	2,200	308	69.0
California Baptist Univ., Riverside, CA 92504-3206	1950	$36,340	$12,600	2-D	11,045	857	63.0
California Coll. of the Arts, San Francisco, CA 94107	1907	$49,148	$10,136	1-M	1,983	485	58.0
California Inst. of Integral Stds., San Francisco, CA 94103	1968	$20,980	NA	1-D	1,557	201	NA
California Inst. of Tech, Pasadena, CA 91125-0001	1891	$56,862	$17,337	1-D	2,237	369	93.6
California Inst. of the Arts, Valencia, CA 91355-2340.	1961	$53,466	$12,135	1-D	1,520	400	61.4
California Lutheran Univ., Thousand Oaks, CA 91360-2787	1959	$45,982	$14,595	2-D	4,303	480	68.0
California Polytechnic State Univ., San Luis Obispo, San Luis Obispo, CA 93407	1901	$9,943 (S)	$14,208	5-M	21,242	1,487	83.0
California State Polytechnic Univ., Pomona, Pomona, CA 91768-2557.	1938	$7,396 (A)	$15,791	5-D	27,915	1,452	69.0
California State Univ., Bakersfield, Bakersfield, CA 93311	1970	NA	NA	5-D	10,999	777	NA
California State Univ., Chico, Chico, CA 95929-0722	1887	$7,806 (A)	$11,360	5-M	17,014	925	NA
California State Univ., Dominguez Hills, Carson, CA 90747-0001	1960	$8,140 (S)	$13,984	5-D	17,977	1,086	44.5

Name, address	Year founded	Tuition & fees	Room & board	Control, degree	Enroll-ment	Faculty	Grad. rate
California State Univ., East Bay, Hayward, CA 94542-3000	1957	$6,939 (S)	$13,980	5-D	15,435	882	42.2%
California State Univ., Fresno, Fresno, CA 93740-8027	1911	NA	NA	5-D	24,139	1,377	NA
California State Univ., Fullerton, Fullerton, CA 92831-3599	1957	$8,108 (A)	NA	5-D	40,445	2,115	69.8
California State Univ., Long Beach, Long Beach, CA 90840	1949	$6,846 (A)	$13,070	5-D	38,075	2,372	73.5
California State Univ., Los Angeles, Los Angeles, CA 90032-8530	1947	$6,768 (A)	$15,992	5-D	26,360	1,745	52.0
California State Univ., Monterey Bay, Seaside, CA 93955-8001	1994	$7,143 (A)	$13,711	5-M	7,616	516	63.0
California State Univ., Northridge, Northridge, CA 91330	1958	$8,554 (S)	$16,188	5-D	38,391	2,093	55.2
California State Univ., Sacramento, Sacramento, CA 95819	1947	$7,368 (A)	$15,224	5-D	31,156	1,725	55.0
California State Univ., San Bernardino, San Bernardino, CA 92407	1965	$6,956 (A)	$13,435	5-D	20,311	1,021	55.0
California State Univ., San Marcos, San Marcos, CA 92096-0001	1990	$13,454 (S)	$13,150	5-M	14,519	900	53.9
California State Univ., Stanislaus, Turlock, CA 95382	1957	$7,584 (A)	$10,950	5-D	10,974	694	58.7
California State Univ. Channel Islands, Camarillo, CA 93012	2002	NA	NA	5-D	3,599	294	NA
California Univ. of Pennsylvania, California, PA 15419-1394	1852	$10,902 (S)	$10,186	5-D	7,312	NA	NA
Calvin Coll., Grand Rapids, MI 49546-4388	1876	$37,806	$10,800	2-D	3,570	332	72.0
Cambridge Coll., Boston, MA 02129	1971	NA	NA	1-D	2,356	320	NA
Cameron Univ., Lawton, OK 73505-6377	1908	$6,450 (S)	$5,452	5-M	4,142	242	26.0
Campbell Univ., Buies Creek, NC 27506	1887	$32,500	$11,210	2-D	6,185	573	55.0
Campbellsville Univ., Campbellsville, KY 42718-2799	1906	$25,400	$8,000	2-D	13,744	588	36.7
Canisius Coll., Buffalo, NY 14208-1098	1870	$30,230	$11,758	2-M	3,102	372	73.0
Capella Univ., Minneapolis, MN 55402	1993	NA	NA	3-D	36,375	NA	NA
Capital Univ., Columbus, OH 43209-2394	1830	$38,298	$11,602	2-D	3,226	398	61.9
Cardinal Stritch Univ., Milwaukee, WI 53217-3985	1937	$33,770	$9,488	2-D	1,796	198	50.0
Caribbean Univ., Bayamón, PR 00960-0493	1969	NA	NA	1-D	3,547	361	20.0
Carleton Coll., Northfield, MN 55057-4001	1866	$57,111	$14,658	1-B	2,097	NA	NA
Carlow Univ., Pittsburgh, PA 15213-3165 (4)	1929	$30,528	$11,902	2-D	2,022	245	57.0
Carnegie Mellon Univ., Pittsburgh, PA 15213-3891	1900	$58,924	$15,550	1-D	14,799	1,183	90.5
Carroll Coll., Helena, MT 59625-0002	1909	$35,486	$9,980	2-B	1,330	145	69.0
Carroll Univ., Waukesha, WI 53186-5593	1846	$31,918	$9,896	2-D	3,451	401	66.0
Carson-Newman Univ., Jefferson City, TN 37760	1851	$29,500	$8,150	2-D	2,560	NA	45.0
Carthage Coll., Kenosha, WI 53140	1847	$63,000	$12,400	2-M	2,758	313	60.0
Case Western Reserve Univ., Cleveland, OH 44106	1826	$52,948	$16,080	1-D	11,874	999	84.4
Castleton Univ., Castleton, VT 05735	1787	NA	NA	5-M	2,343	228	50.0
Catawba Coll., Salisbury, NC 28144-2488	1851	$78,510	$10,804	2-M	1,331	147	1.0
Cedar Crest Coll., Allentown, PA 18104-6196 (4)	1867	$41,567	$12,322	2-D	1,526	222	51.0
Cedarville Univ., Cedarville, OH 45314	1887	$32,564	$7,922	2-D	4,302	341	75.1
Centenary Univ., Hackettstown, NJ 07840-2100	1867	$32,998	$11,444	2-D	2,203	NA	58.0
Central Coll., Pella, IA 50219	1853	$18,600	$10,280	2-B	1,274	NA	67.0
Central Connecticut State Univ., New Britain, CT 06050-4010	1849	$11,068 (A)	$12,528	5-D	11,154	981	57.0
Central Michigan Univ., Mount Pleasant, MI 48859	1892	$13,260 (S)	$10,328	5-D	19,431	1,134	61.1
Central Penn Coll., Summerdale, PA 17093-0309	1881	$18,714	$7,416	3-M	1,224	102	34.0
Central State Univ., Wilberforce, OH 45384	1887	$6,726 (A)	$10,480	5-B	2,033	217	28.0
Central Washington Univ., Ellensburg, WA 98926	1891	$7,562 (A)	$12,637	5-M	11,768	641	58.0
Centre Coll., Danville, KY 40422-1394	1819	$43,000	$10,740	2-B	1,411	150	84.0
Chadron State Coll., Chadron, NE 69337	1911	NA	NA	5-M	2,649	NA	NA
Chamberlain Coll. of Nurs., Addison, IL 60101	NA	NA	NA	3-D	23,964	1,055	NA
Chaminade Univ. of Honolulu, Honolulu, HI 96816-1578	1955	$26,914	$14,610	2-D	1,675	130	59.0
Champlain Coll., Burlington, VT 05402-0670	1878	$41,828	$15,766	1-M	2,715	273	64.9
Chapman Univ., Orange, CA 92866	1861	$57,214	$16,138	2-D	1,378	1,128	81.0
Charleston Southern Univ., Charleston, SC 29423-8087	1964	$26,060	$10,400	2-M	3,493	315	35.0
Charter Oak State Coll., New Britain, CT 06053-2142	1973	$10,243 (S)	NA	5-M	1,611	182	NA
Chatham Univ., Pittsburgh, PA 15232-2826 (4)	1869	$39,902	$12,853	1-D	2,437	344	70.0
Chestnut Hill Coll., Philadelphia, PA 19118-2693	1924	$37,200	$11,000	2-D	1,846	NA	NA
Chicago State Univ., Chicago, IL 60628	1867	NA	NA	5-D	5,211	366	19.0
Chowan Univ., Murfreesboro, NC 27855	1848	$24,980	$9,400	2-M	1,503	132	23.0
Christian Brothers Univ., Memphis, TN 38104-5581	1871	$34,820	$7,950	2-M	1,968	211	56.0
Christopher Newport Univ., Newport News, VA 23606-3072	1960	$14,924 (A)	$11,760	5-M	4,919	476	78.0
City Coll. of the City Univ. of New York, New York, NY 10031-9198	1847	$14,500 (A)	$12,123	11-D	15,682	1,755	48.3
City Univ. of Seattle, Seattle, WA 98121	1973	NA	NA	1-D	2,065	332	29.0
Claflin Univ., Orangeburg, SC 29115	1869	$16,672	$9,294	2-M	1,886	NA	44.0
Claremont McKenna Coll., Claremont, CA 91711	1946	$56,475	$17,300	1-M	1,346	171	91.1
Clarion Univ. of Pennsylvania, Clarion, PA 16214	1867	$7,716 (S)	NA	5-D	4,703	289	54.0
Clark Atlanta Univ., Atlanta, GA 30314	1865	$24,907	$11,506	2-D	3,920	305	44.0
Clark Univ., Worcester, MA 01610-1477	1887	$47,200	$9,480	1-D	3,122	NA	82.0
Clarkson Univ., Potsdam, NY 13699	1896	$52,724	$15,786	1-D	4,301	359	80.8
Clayton State Univ., Morrow, GA 30260-0285	1969	$6,554 (A)	$10,397	5-M	6,879	328	31.0
Clemson Univ., Clemson, SC 29634	1889	$14,970 (S)	$6,812	5-D	25,822	1,763	84.0
Cleveland State Univ., Cleveland, OH 44115	1964	$9,874 (A)	$14,348	5-D	16,943	1,188	40.0
Coastal Carolina Univ., Conway, SC 29528-6054	1954	$11,640 (S)	$9,290	5-D	10,484	775	46.9
Coe Coll., Cedar Rapids, IA 52402-5092	1851	$47,220	$10,134	2-B	1,428	158	65.2
Colby Coll., Waterville, ME 04901-8840	1813	$57,280	$14,720	1-B	2,003	223	89.0
Colgate Univ., Hamilton, NY 13346-1386	1819	$60,015	$15,035	1-M	2,992	360	91.0
Coll. for Creative Stds, Detroit, MI 48202-4034	1926	NA	NA	1-M	1,459	289	62.0
Coll. of Charleston, Charleston, SC 29424-0001	1770	$12,978 (S)	$12,123	5-M	10,545	944	66.0
Coll. of Coastal Georgia, Brunswick, GA 31520	1961	$3,204 (S)	$10,328	5-B	3,535	170	27.0
Coll. of Mount St. Vincent, Riverdale, NY 10471-1093	1911	$40,980	$12,000	1-M	2,060	220	54.0
Coll. of St. Benedict, Saint Joseph, MN 56374 (3)	1913	$48,442	$11,346	2-B	1,748	169	80.0
Coll. of St. Elizabeth, Morristown, NJ 07960-6989	1899	$34,956	$12,744	2-D	1,281	199	53.0
Coll. of Staten Island of the City Univ. of New York, Staten Island, NY 10314-6600	1955	$7,489 (S)	$14,745	11-D	12,782	1,134	NA
Coll. of the Holy Cross, Worcester, MA 01610-2395	1843	$56,520	$15,560	2-B	3,174	336	90.0
Coll. of the Ozarks, Point Lookout, MO 65726	1906	$310/cr. hr.	NA	2-B	1,546	142	71.0
Colorado Christian Univ., Lakewood, CO 80226	1914	$30,370	$10,516	2-M	1,343	NA	NA
Colorado Mesa Univ., Grand Junction, CO 81501-3122	1925	$9,306 (S)	$11,168	5-D	9,492	590	39.1
Colorado Mountain Coll., Glenwood Springs, CO 81601	1965	$2,700 (A)	$9,685	9-B	4,904	NA	NA
Colorado Mountain Coll., Leadville, CO 80461	1965	NA	NA	9-B	1,209	NA	NA
Colorado Mountain Coll., Steamboat Springs, CO 80487	1965	$2,400 (A)	$10,322	9-B	2,606	NA	NA
Colorado Sch. of Mines, Golden, CO 80401-1887	1874	$19,062 (S)	$14,211	5-D	6,605	594	83.1
Colorado State Univ., Fort Collins, CO 80523	1870	$11,831 (S)	$11,964	5-D	33,996	2,060	69.7
Colorado State Univ.-Global campus, Greenwood Village, CO 80111		$10,500 (A)	NA	5-M	12,670	572	NA
Colorado State Univ.-Pueblo, Pueblo, CO 81001-4901	1933	$10,445 (A)	$10,740	5-D	6,736	NA	NA
Colorado Tech Univ. Colorado Springs, Colorado Springs, CO 80907	1965	NA	NA	3-D	2,359	343	NA

Name, address	Year founded	Tuition & fees	Room & board	Control/degree	Enrollment	Faculty	Grad. rate
Colorado Tech Univ. Online, Colorado Springs, CO 80907	NA	NA	NA	3-M	25,797	613	NA
Columbia Coll., Columbia, SC 29203-5998 (4)	1854	$19,890	$8,295	2-M	1,243	162	60.0%
Columbia Coll. Chicago, Chicago, IL 60605-1996	1890	$28,318	$16,456	1-M	6,947	856	50.0
Columbia Intl. Univ., Columbia, SC 29203	1923	$24,650	$8,950	2-D	1,460	125	50.0
Columbia Southern Univ., Orange Beach, AL 36561	1993	$5,775	NA	3-D	20,034	564	NA
Columbia Univ., New York, NY 10027	1754	$61,850	$14,490	1-D	6,298	1,823	96.0
Columbia Univ., Sch. of General Studies, New York, NY 10027-6939	1754	$59,462	$14,352	1-B	2,068	NA	NA
Columbus State Univ., Columbus, GA 31907-5645	1958	$7,200 (A)	$9,380	5-D	8,076	524	38.3
Concord Univ., Athens, WV 24712-1000	1872	$8,385 (S)	$9,762	5-M	1,886	160	40.0
Concordia Coll., Moorhead, MN 56562	1891	$41,566	$8,610	2-M	2,042	210	0.7
Concordia Coll.–New York, Bronxville, NY 10708-1998.	1881	$32,900	$12,690	2-M	1,597	148	44.0
Concordia Univ., St. Paul, St. Paul, MN 55104-5494	1893	$23,400	$9,600	2-D	5,139	439	52.0
Concordia Univ. Chicago, River Forest, IL 60305-1499	1864	$33,636	$10,226	2-D	6,132	492	47.0
Concordia Univ. Irvine, Irvine, CA 92612-3299	1972	$38,000	$12,270	2-D	3,911	380	63.0
Concordia Univ. Texas, Austin, TX 78726	1926	NA	NA	2-M	2,504	302	35.0
Concordia Univ. Wisconsin, Mequon, WI 53097-2402	1881	$31,182	$11,470	2-D	5,776	414	63.8
Concordia Univ., Nebraska, Seward, NE 68434	1894	$32,220	$8,470	2-M	2,520	253	67.0
Connecticut Coll., New London, CT 06320	1911	$56,890	$15,700	1-B	1,844	233	85.0
Converse Coll., Spartanburg, SC 29302 (6)	1889	$18,690	$10,930	1-M	1,319	84	55.0
Coppin State Univ., Baltimore, MD 21216-3698.	1900	$6,625 (S)	$10,396	5-M	2,738	312	15.0
Cornell Coll., Mount Vernon, IA 52314-1098	1853	$44,096	$9,760	2-M	NA	NA	NA
Cornell Univ., Ithaca, NY 14853	1865	$59,316	$15,846	1-D	24,027	2,216	95.0
Cornerstone Univ., Grand Rapids, MI 49525-5897	1941	$24,500	$9,300	2-D	2,361	374	53.0
Creighton Univ., Omaha, NE 68178-0001	1878	$43,018	$11,600	2-D	8,821	1,028	81.0
Crown Coll., St. Bonifacius, MN 55375-9001	1916	NA	NA	2-M	1,269	160	50.0
Cumberland Univ., Lebanon, TN 37087	1842	$22,891	$8,600	1-M	1,481	159	37.0
Curry Coll., Milton, MA 02186-9984	1879	$40,870	$16,340	1-M	2,799	361	48.0
Daemen Coll., Amherst, NY 14226-3592	1947	$28,580	$12,915	1-D	2,636	304	55.3
Dakota State Univ., Madison, SD 57042-1799.	1881	$9,535 (S)	$7,033	5-D	3,268	148	43.5
Dallas Baptist Univ., Dallas, TX 75211-9299	1965	$31,940	$8,568	2-D	4,487	610	58.3
Dalton State Coll., Dalton, GA 30720	1963	$4,246 (S)	NA	5-B	5,188	271	38.0
Dartmouth Coll., Hanover, NH 03755.	1769	$57,204	$16,374	1-D	6,608	791	95.0
Davenport Univ., Grand Rapids, MI 49512	1866	$24,150	NA	1-M	6,429	610	56.0
Davidson Coll., Davidson, NC 28035	1837	$55,060	$15,225	2-B	1,837	220	91.0
Dean Coll., Franklin, MA 02038-1994	1865	$41,318	$17,648	1-B	1,320	150	45.0
Delaware State Univ., Dover, DE 19901-2277	1891	NA	NA	5-D	4,353	NA	37.0
Delaware Technical Community College, Dover, DE 19904	NA	NA	NA	5-B	14,029	NA	NA
Delaware Valley Univ., Doylestown, PA 18901-2697.	1896	$40,620	$14,620	1-D	2,369	282	60.7
Delta State Univ., Cleveland, MS 38733-0001	1924	$8,121 (A)	$7,985	5-D	3,751	264	39.0
Denison Univ., Granville, OH 43023	1831	$56,680	$13,720	1-B	2,293	285	84.7
DePaul Univ., Chicago, IL 60604-2287	1898	$41,202	$14,736	2-D	22,064	1,832	74.0
DePauw Univ., Greencastle, IN 46135	1837	$52,710	$13,788	2-B	1,972	255	84.0
DeSales Univ., Center Valley, PA 18034-9568	1964	$38,700	$13,000	2-D	3,460	405	68.8
DeVry Coll. of New York–Midtown Manhattan campus, New York, NY 10016	1998	NA	NA	3-M	1,495	87	NA
DeVry Univ. Online, Addison, IL 60101	2000	NA	NA	3-M	15,551	1,513	NA
Dickinson Coll., Carlisle, PA 17013-2896.	1773	$58,680	$14,672	1-B	2,133	271	82.9
Dickinson State Univ., Dickinson, ND 58601-4896	1918	$7,784 (A)	$7,686	5-M	1,350	128	41.1
Dillard Univ., New Orleans, LA 70122-3097	1869	$19,281	$6,156	2-B	1,235	125	50.7
Dixie State Univ., St. George, UT 84770-3876.	1911	$5,496 (A)	$6,974	5-M	11,193	535	21.8
Dominican Coll., Orangeburg, NY 10962-1210	1952	$29,844	$13,414	1-D	1,868	211	47.0
Dominican Univ. of California, San Rafael, CA 94901-2298	1890	$47,910	$15,634	2-D	1,879	348	70.0
Dominican Univ., River Forest, IL 60305-1099.	1901	$35,420	$10,865	2-D	3,029	428	62.0
Dordt Coll., Sioux Center, IA 51250-1697	1955	$32,820	$10,470	2-M	1,737	115	75.0
Drake Univ., Des Moines, IA 50311-4516	1881	$44,334	$11,152	1-D	4,884	474	82.0
Drew Univ., Madison, NJ 07940-1493	1867	$40,660	$14,672	2-D	2,319	265	69.0
Drexel Univ., Philadelphia, PA 19104-2875	1891	$54,516	$14,241	1-D	24,205	1,984	69.0
Drury Univ., Springfield, MO 65802	1873	$30,915	$9,172	1-M	1,743	140	57.4
Duke Univ., Durham, NC 27708	1838	$57,931	$15,588	2-D	10,532	1,563	1.0
Duquesne Univ., Pittsburgh, PA 15282-0001	1878	$39,992	$13,088	2-D	9,274	990	79.1
D'Youville Coll., Buffalo, NY 14201-1084	1908	$874/cr. hr.	$9,500	1-D	3,048	379	62.0
East Carolina Univ., Greenville, NC 27858-4353	1907	$7,239 (S)	$9,712	5-D	28,651	1,519	0.7
East Central Univ., Ada, OK 74820	1909	$7,052 (A)	$7,072	5-M	3,613	232	37.0
East Stroudsburg Univ. of Pennsylvania, East Stroudsburg, PA 18301-2999	1893	$10,688 (S)	$11,760	5-D	6,214	335	52.0
East Tennessee State Univ., Johnson City, TN 37614	1911	NA	NA	5-D	14,317	1,023	41.0
East Texas Baptist Univ., Marshall, TX 75670-1498	1912	$27,210	$9,328	2-M	1,593	148	44.0
Eastern Connecticut State Univ., Willimantic, CT 06226-2295	1889	$5,678 (S)	$13,520	5-M	5,261	499	56.0
Eastern Illinois Univ., Charleston, IL 61920	1895	$11,989 (S)	$10,030	5-M	7,806	493	52.6
Eastern Kentucky Univ., Richmond, KY 40475-3102	1906	$9,806 (A)	$10,173	5-D	14,980	1,054	50.2
Eastern Mennonite Univ., Harrisonburg, VA 22802-2462	1917	$39,220	$11,730	2-D	1,360	204	58.0
Eastern Michigan Univ., Ypsilanti, MI 48197	1849	$11,128 (A)	$10,248	5-D	18,833	1,261	45.0
Eastern New Mexico Univ., Portales, NM 88130	1934	$6,528 (S)	$7,526	5-M	5,694	241	0.3
Eastern Oregon Univ., La Grande, OR 97850-2899	1929	NA	NA	5-M	3,067	182	27.1
Eastern Univ., St. Davids, PA 19087-3696.	1952	$34,706	$11,824	2-D	3,100	421	62.0
Eastern Washington Univ., Cheney, WA 99004-2431	1882	$7,461 (A)	$12,708	5-D	12,325	694	53.4
Eckerd Coll., St. Petersburg, FL 33711	1958	$46,096	$13,026	2-B	2,007	189	66.0
ECPI Univ., Virginia Beach, VA 23462	1966	$16,584	NA	3-M	24,881	1,164	48.0
Edgewood Coll., Madison, WI 53711-1997	1927	$31,700	$11,700	2-D	2,038	256	64.4
Edinboro Univ. of Pennsylvania, Edinboro, PA 16444	1857	$10,543 (S)	$9,800	5-D	4,646	311	49.0
EDP Univ. of Puerto Rico, Hato Rey, PR 00918	1968	$6,200	NA	1-M	1,782	198	55.0
Elizabeth City State Univ., Elizabeth City, NC 27909-7806	1891	$3,327 (S)	$10,302	5-M	1,769	138	NA
Elizabethtown Coll., Elizabethtown, PA 17022-2298	1899	$32,960	$12,060	2-D	1,844	195	69.4
Elmhurst Coll., Elmhurst, IL 60126-3296	1871	$37,754	$10,710	2-M	3,483	381	64.0
Elms Coll., Chicopee, MA 01013-2839.	1928	$38,391	$14,010	2-D	1,495	200	73.0
Elon Univ., Elon, NC 27244-2010.	1889	$37,921	$13,131	2-D	7,088	605	85.0
Embry-Riddle Aeron Univ.–Daytona, Daytona Beach, FL 32114-3900	1926	$37,964	$12,410	1-D	7,056	NA	62.0
Embry-Riddle Aeron Univ.–Prescott, Prescott, AZ 86301-3720.	1978	$37,864	$12,174	1-M	2,946	NA	NA
Emerson Coll., Boston, MA 02116-4624	1880	$48,728	$18,400	1-D	4,582	459	81.0
Emmanuel Coll., Boston, MA 02115	1919	$42,516	$15,846	2-M	2,222	205	66.0

Name, address	Year founded	Tuition & fees	Room & board	Control, degree	Enrollment	Faculty	Grad. rate
Emory & Henry Coll., Emory, VA 24327-0947	1836	$35,300	$13,125	2-D	1,292	181	53.8%
Emory Univ., Atlanta, GA 30322-1100	1836	$55,998	$15,572	2-D	14,417	1,247	90.0
Emporia State Univ., Emporia, KS 66801-5415	1863	$6,960 (S)	$9,408	5-D	5,877	282	49.6
Endicott Coll., Beverly, MA 01915-2096	1939	$35,320	$16,130	1-D	5,082	590	74.0
Eugene Lang Coll. of Lib Arts, New York, NY 10011-8601	1975	NA	NA	1-B	1,885	265	56.0
Evangel Univ., Springfield, MO 65802	1955	$24,327	$8,522	2-D	2,300	NA	NA
Everglades Univ., Boca Raton, FL 33431	1989	NA	NA	1-M	1,451	229	51.0
Everglades Univ., Maitland, FL 32751	NA	$18,320	NA	1-M	1,451	229	51.0
Everglades Univ., Sarasota, FL 34240	2003	NA	NA	1-M	1,451	229	51.0
Excelsior Coll., Albany, NY 12203-5159	1970	$530/credit	NA	1-M	23,501	1,301	NA
Fairfield Univ., Fairfield, CT 06824	1942	$51,325	$15,610	2-D	5,349	643	83.0
Fairleigh Dickinson Univ., Coll. at Florham, Madison, NJ 07940-1099	1942	$44,720	$13,716	1-D	3,512	453	54.7
Fairleigh Dickinson Univ., Metropolitan campus, Teaneck, NJ 07666-1914	1942	$42,218	$13,670	1-D	7,846	682	48.1
Fairleigh Dickinson University, Teaneck, NJ 07666	1942	$43,468	$13,661	1-D	11,479	1,222	NA
Fairmont State Univ., Fairmont, WV 26554	1865	$7,514 (S)	$9,004	5-M	3,972	309	0.4
Farmingdale State Coll., Farmingdale, NY 11735	1912	$8,538 (S)	$13,318	5-M	9,996	787	56.6
Fashion Inst. of Tech, New York, NY 10001-5992 (4)	1944	$6,110 (S)	$14,556	11-M	8,726	1,011	80.0
Faulkner Univ., Montgomery, AL 36109-3398	1942	$21,690	$7,550	2-D	3,350	280	37.6
Fayetteville State Univ., Fayetteville, NC 28301-4298	1867	$4,975 (S)	$8,616	5-D	6,551	342	34.0
Felician Univ., Lodi, NJ 07644-2117	1942	$35,000	$13,140	2-D	2,262	236	47.0
Ferris State Univ., Big Rapids, MI 49307	1884	$12,930 (S)	$10,044	5-D	12,472	876	53.0
FIDM/Fashion Inst. of Design & Merchandising, Los Angeles campus, Los Angeles, CA 90015-1421	1969	$32,310	NA	3-M	2,159	NA	70.9
Fisher Coll., Boston, MA 02116-1500	1903	$32,700	$16,569	1-M	1,628	141	34.0
Fitchburg State Univ., Fitchburg, MA 01420-2697	1894	$10,505 (S)	$11,261	5-M	7,252	336	58.0
Flagler Coll., St. Augustine, FL 32085-1027	1968	$682/cr. hr.	NA	1-M	2,902	317	53.1
Flagler Coll.–Tallahassee, Tallahassee, FL 32304	2000	NA	NA	1-B	2,689	249	54.8
Florida A&M Univ., Tallahassee, FL 32307-3200	1887	$5,785 (A)	$10,986	5-D	9,626	704	53.0
Florida Atlantic Univ., Boca Raton, FL 33431-0991	1961	$6,099 (S)	$12,030	5-D	30,061	1,483	50.0
Florida Gulf Coast Univ., Fort Myers, FL 33965-6565	1991	$6,170 (A)	$8,580	5-D	15,026	799	50.0
Florida Inst. of Tech, Melbourne, FL 32901-6975	1958	$42,470	$12,880	1-D	6,078	476	59.0
Florida Intl. Univ., Miami, FL 33199	1965	$6,566 (A)	$11,136	5-D	58,827	2,119	61.0
Florida Memorial Univ., Miami-Dade, FL 33054	1879	NA	NA	2-M	1,750	173	33.0
Florida Natl. Univ., Hialeah, FL 33012	1982	$13,688	NA	3-M	3,981	190	91.0
Florida Polytechnic University, Lakeland, FL 33805	NA	$4,940 (S)	$11,430	5-M	1,336	90	NA
Florida Southern Coll., Lakeland, FL 33801-5698	1885	$37,640	$11,880	2-D	3,305	335	68.0
Florida State Univ., Tallahassee, FL 32306	1851	$6,517 (A)	$10,780	5-D	42,218	1,928	83.1
Fordham Univ., New York, NY 10458	1841	$55,788	$19,066	2-D	16,972	1,889	82.7
Fort Hays State Univ., Hays, KS 67601-4099	1902	NA	NA	5-D	15,908	732	44.0
Fort Lewis Coll., Durango, CO 81301-3999	1911	$8,881 (S)	$9,878	5-M	3,308	253	41.0
Fort Valley State Univ., Fort Valley, GA 31030	1895	$6,664 (S)	$8,084	5-M	2,776	118	28.0
Framingham State Univ., Framingham, MA 01701-9101	1839	$11,100 (S)	$12,604	5-M	5,456	325	61.0
Francis Marion Univ., Florence, SC 29502-0547	1970	$11,160 (A)	$8,230	5-D	4,240	303	43.0
Franciscan Univ. of Steubenville, Steubenville, OH 43952-1763	1946	$30,180	$8,870	2-M	3,039	265	76.8
Franklin & Marshall Coll., Lancaster, PA 17604-3003	1787	$58,800	$14,450	1-B	2,269	273	85.4
Franklin Pierce Univ., Henderson, NH 03461-0060	1962	$40,680	$14,454	1-D	2,053	319	49.5
Franklin Univ., Columbus, OH 43215-5399	1902	$15,780	NA	1-M	5,734	814	13.0
Freed-Hardeman Univ., Henderson, TN 38340-2399	1869	$22,950	$7,950	2-D	2,117	178	57.8
Fresno Pacific Univ., Fresno, CA 93702-4709	1944	$32,458	$8,950	2-M	3,596	479	64.0
Friends Univ., Wichita, KS 67213	1898	$30,120	$8,350	2-M	1,818	190	48.0
Frostburg State Univ., Frostburg, MD 21532-1099	1898	$9,410 (A)	$5,274	5-D	5,294	368	54.0
Full Sail Univ., Winter Park, FL 32792-7437 (2)	1979	NA	NA	3-M	8,921	702	NA
Furman Univ., Greenville, SC 29613	1826	$52,092	$13,362	1-M	2,728	338	82.5
Gallaudet Univ., Washington, DC 20002-3625	1864	$17,038	$8,000	1-D	1,485	260	0.0
Gannon Univ., Erie, PA 16541-0001	1925	NA	NA	2-D	4,444	373	67.2
Gardner-Webb Univ., Boiling Springs, NC 28017	1905	$31,640	$10,390	2-D	3,818	300	44.0
Geneva Coll., Beaver Falls, PA 15010-3599	1848	$29,040	$10,850	2-M	1,432	213	72.0
George Fox Univ., Newberg, OR 97132-2697	1891	$37,130	$11,650	2-D	3,899	NA	NA
George Mason Univ., Fairfax, VA 22030	1972	$12,564 (S)	$11,755	5-D	37,863	2,860	71.0
Georgetown Coll., Georgetown, KY 40324-1696	1829	$40,800	$10,670	2-M	1,484	156	54.0
Georgetown Univ., Washington, DC 20057	1789	$55,794	$11,404	2-D	19,204	2,322	94.0
Georgia Coll. & State Univ., Milledgeville, GA 31061	1889	$9,524 (S)	NA	5-D	7,031	416	63.6
Georgia Gwinnett Coll., Lawrenceville, GA 30043	NA	$5,752 (A)	NA	5-B	12,831	769	21.4
Georgia Inst. of Tech, Atlanta, GA 30332-0001	1885	$12,682 (S)	$14,830	5-D	36,490	1,222	89.9
Georgia Southern Univ., Statesboro, GA 30458	1906	$7,556 (A)	$10,070	5-D	26,054	1,298	49.0
Georgia Southwestern State Univ., Americus, GA 31709-4693	1906	$6,336 (S)	$8,120	5-M	2,950	165	38.1
Georgia State Univ., Atlanta, GA 30302-3083	1913	$8,948 (A)	$14,958	5-D	35,059	1,608	55.0
Georgian Court Univ., Lakewood, NJ 08701-2697	1908	$33,768	$11,424	2-D	2,411	280	54.0
Gettysburg Coll., Gettysburg, PA 17325-1483	1832	$58,390	$13,460	2-B	2,371	316	81.0
Glenville State Coll., Glenville, WV 26351-1200	1872	$7,308 (S)	$9,942	5-B	1,577	120	47.0
Global Univ., Springfield, MO 65804	1948	NA	NA	2-D	4,551	633	NA
Golden Gate Univ., San Francisco, CA 94105-2968	1901	NA	NA	1-D	2,685	489	NA
Goldey-Beacom Coll., Wilmington, DE 19808-1999	1886	NA	NA	1-M	1,352	56	49.0
Gonzaga Univ., Spokane, WA 99258	1887	$46,920	$12,951	2-D	7,548	844	85.0
Gordon Coll., Wenham, MA 01984-1899	1889	$39,230	$11,420	2-M	1,857	251	70.0
Goucher Coll., Baltimore, MD 21204-2794	1885	$47,300	$13,882	1-M	2,168	175	65.8
Governors State Univ., University Park, IL 60484	1969	$12,616 (S)	$8,102	5-D	4,854	520	NA
Grace Coll., Winona Lake, IN 46590-1294	1948	$24,768	$9,134	2-D	2,333	184	60.0
Graceland Univ., Lamoni, IA 50140	1895	$31,320	$9,440	2-D	1,739	158	45.0
Grambling State Univ., Grambling, LA 71245	1901	$16,706 (A)	$5,572	5-M	5,232	188	NA
Grand Canyon Univ., Phoenix, AZ 85017-1097	1949	NA	NA	2-D	NA	NA	NA
Grand Valley State Univ., Allendale, MI 49401-9403	1960	$12,860 (S)	$8,820	5-D	24,033	1,774	66.1
Grand View Univ., Des Moines, IA 50316-1599	1896	$29,960	$9,614	2-M	1,889	224	55.0
Granite State Coll., Concord, NH 03301	1972	$7,761 (A)	NA	11-M	2,005	182	46.0
Grantham Univ., Lenexa, KS 66219	1951	NA	NA	3-M	9,463	10	NA
Grinnell Coll., Grinnell, IA 50112-1690	1846	$56,680	$13,864	1-B	1,733	218	89.0
Grove City Coll., Grove City, PA 16127-2104	1876	$18,470	$10,060	2-B	2,272	205	85.1
Guilford Coll., Greensboro, NC 27410-4173	1837	$40,120	$12,200	2-D	1,541	176	56.0
Gustavus Adolphus Coll., St. Peter, MN 56082-1498	1862	$48,460	$10,430	2-B	2,235	213	78.0
Gwynedd Mercy Univ., Gwynedd Valley, PA 19437-0901	1948	$35,600	$12,680	2-D	2,990	325	61.6

Name, address	Year founded	Tuition & fees	Room & board	Control, degree	Enroll- ment	Faculty	Grad. rate
Hamilton Coll., Clinton, NY 13323-1296.	1812	$58,510	$14,860	1-B	1,924	235	93.3%
Hamline Univ., St. Paul, MN 55104-1284.	1854	$44,230	$10,810	2-D	3,404	272	70.0
Hampton Univ., Hampton, VA 23668	1868	$29,412	$12,986	1-D	4,619	311	54.4
Harding Univ., Searcy, AR 72149-0001	1924	$21,540	$7,438	2-D	5,121	403	67.0
Hardin-Simmons Univ., Abilene, TX 79698-0001.	1891	$31,366	$9,740	2-D	2,324	237	51.0
Harrisburg Univ. of Sci & Tech, Harrisburg, PA 17101. . ,.	2005	$23,900	$6,800	1-D	4,071	NA	NA
Harris-Stowe State Univ., St. Louis, MO 63103-2136	1857	$5,484 (A)	$9,491	5-B	1,630	180	17.0
Harvard Univ., Cambridge, MA 02138	1636	$51,925	$17,682	1-D	11,453	1,153	97.0
Hastings Coll., Hastings, NE 68901	1882	$30,050	$9,700	2-M	1,212	119	58.0
Haverford Coll., Haverford, PA 19041-1392.	1833	$58,900	$17,066	1-B	1,317	161	90.0
Hawai'i Pacific Univ., Honolulu, HI 96813	1965	$27,850	$19,200	1-D	4,146	359	44.0
Heidelberg Univ., Tiffin, OH 44883-2462	1850	$31,000	$10,400	2-M	1,209	124	49.0
Henderson State Univ., Arkadelphia, AR 71999-0001	1890	NA	NA	5-M	3,565	257	34.0
Heritage Univ., Toppenish, WA 98948-9599	1982	$18,188	NA	1-M	1,241	185	16.0
High Point Univ., High Point, NC 27268.	1924	$36,268	$14,702	2-D	5,330	460	65.0
Hillsdale Coll., Hillsdale, MI 49242-1298	1844	$29,482	$11,910	1-D	1,526	211	86.0
Hiram Coll., Hiram, OH 44234	1850	$24,500	$10,290	1-M	1,284	123	54.0
Hobart & William Smith Colls, Geneva, NY 14456.	1822	$58,650	$15,090	1-M	2,070	220	77.0
Hodges Univ., Naples, FL 34119	1990	$14,180	NA	1-M	1,724	119	NA
Hofstra Univ., Hempstead, NY 11549	1935	$47,510	$16,428	1-D	10,804	1,245	65.0
Holy Family Univ., Philadelphia, PA 19114	1954	$30,346	$13,576	2-D	3,081	310	54.8
Hood Coll., Frederick, MD 21701-8575	1893	$41,060	$12,880	1-D	2,052	240	61.0
Hope Coll., Holland, MI 49422-9000	1866	$35,330	$10,630	2-B	3,056	328	81.0
Houston Baptist Univ., Houston, TX 77074-3298.	1960	$34,500	$9,130	2-D	3,741	303	44.1
Howard Univ., Washington, DC 20059-0002	1867	$28,440	$12,380	1-D	9,399	1,114	65.0
Humboldt State Univ., Arcata, CA 95521-8299.	1913	$7,858 (S)	$15,610	5-M	6,983	534	49.0
Hunter Coll. of the City Univ. of New York, New York, NY 10065-5085.	1870	$7,180 (S)	$4,857	11-D	23,202	2,110	53.0
Huntington Univ., Huntington, IN 46750-1299	1897	$26,180	$8,668	2-D	1,295	112	65.0
Husson Univ., Bangor, ME 04401-2999.	1898	$19,772	$10,632	1-D	3,729	435	58.0
Idaho State Univ., Pocatello, ID 83209.	1901	NA	NA	5-D	12,445	826	31.0
Illinois Inst. of Tech, Chicago, IL 60616	1890	$47,296	$12,762	1-D	6,515	347	70.0
Illinois State Univ., Normal, IL 61790	1857	$14,832 (S)	$9,850	5-D	20,878	1,372	69.5
Illinois Wesleyan Univ., Bloomington, IL 61702-2900.	1850	$51,336	$11,840	1-B	1,629	189	77.0
Immaculata Univ., Immaculata, PA 19345	1920	$27,750	$12,620	2-D	2,497	311	67.0
Indian River State Coll., Fort Pierce, FL 34981-5596.	1960	NA	NA	5-B	17,665	859	NA
Indiana State Univ., Terre Haute, IN 47809	1865	$9,466 (A)	$11,016	5-D	12,146	692	41.0
Indiana Tech, Fort Wayne, IN 46803-1297	1930	$28,000	$13,236	1-D	2,136	133	39.0
Indiana Univ. Bloomington, Bloomington, IN 47405-7000	1820	$10,947 (A)	$10,830	5-D	43,503	2,495	78.9
Indiana Univ. East, Richmond, IN 47374-1289	1971	$7,527 (S)	NA	5-M	3,766	287	39.8
Indiana Univ. Kokomo, Kokomo, IN 46902-9003	1945	$7,527 (S)	NA	5-M	3,123	NA	NA
Indiana Univ. Northwest, Gary, IN 46408-1197	1959	$7,527 (S)	NA	5-M	3,959	NA	NA
Indiana Univ. of Pennsylvania, Indiana, PA 15705.	1875	$13,144 (S)	$12,744	5-D	10,302	556	0.6
Indiana Univ. South Bend, South Bend, IN 46615	1922	$7,527 (S)	$7,346	5-M	5,214	NA	NA
Indiana Univ. Southeast, New Albany, IN 47150-6405	1941	$6,922 (S)	$6,290	5-M	4,946	440	35.6
Indiana Univ.-Purdue Univ. Fort Wayne, Fort Wayne, IN 46805-1499	1917	$9,708 (S)	$9,620	5-M	10,208	733	37.4
Indiana Univ.-Purdue Univ. Indianapolis, Indianapolis, IN 46202 . .	1969	$9,701 (S)	$10,000	5-D	29,579	NA	NA
Indiana Wesleyan Univ., Marion, IN 46953-4974.	1920	$25,980	$8,312	2-D	3,071	267	65.0
Inter Amer. Univ. of Puerto Rico, Aguadilla campus, Aguadilla, PR 00605	1957	$5,254	NA	1-M	3,903	228	30.0
Inter Amer. Univ. of Puerto Rico, Arecibo campus, Arecibo, PR 00614-4050.	1957	NA	NA	1-M	4,878	298	NA
Inter Amer. Univ. of Puerto Rico, Barranquitas campus, Barranquitas, PR 00794	1957	$6,432	NA	1-D	1,673	134	55.0
Inter Amer. Univ. of Puerto Rico, Bayamón campus, Bayamón, PR 00957	1912	$6,012	$8,531	1-M	4,500	248	29.0
Inter Amer. Univ. of Puerto Rico, Fajardo campus, Fajardo, PR 00738-7003.	1965	$8,976	$8,123	1-M	1,937	114	61.0
Inter Amer. Univ. of Puerto Rico, Guayama campus, Guayama, PR 00785	1958	NA	NA	1-M	1,927	164	35.0
Inter Amer. Univ. of Puerto Rico, Metropolitan campus, San Juan, PR 00919-1293	1960	$8,796	NA	1-D	7,791	466	NA
Inter Amer. Univ. of Puerto Rico, Ponce campus, Mercedita, PR 00715-1602.	1962	NA	NA	1-M	5,288	284	30.0
Inter Amer. Univ. of Puerto Rico, San Germán campus, San Germán, PR 00683-5008.	1912	$6,432	$4,464	1-D	4,404	296	44.0
Iona Coll., New Rochelle, NY 10801-1890.	1940	$41,580	$16,208	2-M	3,613	319	64.0
Iowa State Univ. of Sci & Tech, Ames, IA 50011.	1858	$9,320 (S)	$9,149	5-D	34,992	1,892	73.0
Ithaca Coll., Ithaca, NY 14850	1892	$46,610	$15,844	1-D	6,266	753	74.5
Jackson State Univ., Jackson, MS 39217	1877	$7,946 (S)	$9,552	5-D	1,919	527	NA
Jacksonville State Univ., Jacksonville, AL 36265-1602	1883	$11,120 (A)	$8,000	5-D	9,021	495	41.3
Jacksonville Univ., Jacksonville, FL 32211	1934	$39,900	$14,810	1-D	4,164	429	52.0
James Madison Univ., Harrisonburg, VA 22807	1908	$11,576 (S)	$10,582	5-D	21,820	1,592	84.2
John Brown Univ., Siloam Springs, AR 72761-2121	1919	$27,668	$9,456	2-M	2,150	181	72.0
John Carroll Univ., University Heights, OH 44118	1886	$44,405	$12,560	2-M	3,506	378	76.0
John F. Kennedy Univ., Pleasant Hill, CA 94523-4817 (4).	1964	NA	NA	1-D	1,580	237	NA
John Jay Coll. of Criminal Justice of the City Univ. of New York, New York, NY 10019	1964	$7,270 (S)	NA	11-M	15,880	NA	52.0
Johns Hopkins Univ., Baltimore, MD 21218.	1876	$57,510	$16,800	1-D	8,176	757	94.1
Johnson & Wales Univ., Charlotte, NC 28202	2004	NA	NA	1-B	2,255	120	49.0
Johnson & Wales Univ., Denver, CO 80220	1993	NA	NA	1-M	1,388	127	53.0
Johnson & Wales Univ., North Miami, FL 33181	1992	NA	NA	1-B	1,752	79	41.0
Johnson & Wales Univ., Providence, RI 02903-3703.	1914	NA	NA	1-D	9,454	617	55.0
Johnson C. Smith Univ., Charlotte, NC 28216-5398.	1867	$18,784	$7,100	1-M	1,494	174	NA
Johnson State Coll., Johnson, VT 05656	2018	$13,204 (S)	$11,598	5-M	1,662	179	35.0
Judson Univ., Elgin, IL 60123-1498	1963	$29,870	$10,790	2-D	1,233	186	57.0
Juniata Coll., Huntingdon, PA 16652-2119	1876	$49,175	$13,050	2-M	1,449	158	80.0
Kalamazoo Coll., Kalamazoo, MI 49006-3295.	1833	$52,530	$10,530	2-B	1,286	141	85.6
Kansas State Univ., Manhattan, KS 66506	1863	$10,383 (S)	$9,680	5-D	21,719	1,138	65.3
Kean Univ., Union, NJ 07083	1855	$12,595 (S)	$14,802	5-D	14,309	1,391	47.0
Keene State Coll., Keene, NH 03435.	1909	$14,568 (S)	$11,560	5-M	3,569	NA	60.0

Name, address	Year founded	Tuition & fees	Room & board	Control, degree	Enrollment	Faculty	Grad. rate
Keiser Univ., Fort Lauderdale, FL 33309	1977	$32,868	$14,086	1-D	19,605	1,802	NA
Kendall Coll., Chicago, IL 60642	1934	NA	NA	1-B	1,200	279	17.0%
Kennesaw State Univ., Kennesaw, GA 30144	1963	$7,432 (S)	$11,467	5-D	37,807	1,942	46.2
Kent State Univ. at Geauga, Burton, OH 44021-9500	1964	$258/cr. hr. (S)	NA	5-M	2,179	130	32.0
Kent State Univ. at Stark, Canton, OH 44720-7599	1946	$258/cr. hr. (S)	NA	5-M	4,771	249	28.8
Kent State Univ., Kent, OH 44242-0001	1910	$10,012 (S)	$11,362	5-D	28,972	1,846	57.0
Kentucky State Univ., Frankfort, KY 40601	1886	$9,190 (A)	$6,690	12-D	2,171	135	NA
Kenyon Coll., Gambier, OH 43022	1824	$61,100	$12,830	1-B	1,734	196	89.0
Kettering Univ., Flint, MI 48504	1919	$44,380	$8,400	1-M	2,221	152	51.0
Keuka Coll., Keuka Park, NY 14478	1890	$34,032	$12,144	2-M	1,777	200	55.4
Keystone Coll., La Plume, PA 18440	1868	$17,000	$11,900	1-M	1,364	168	46.0
King Univ., Bristol, TN 37620-2699	1867	$31,840	$9,386	2-D	1,974	264	58.2
King's Coll., Wilkes-Barre, PA 18711-0801	1946	$40,080	$14,008	2-M	2,519	227	63.6
Knox Coll., Galesburg, IL 61401	1837	$49,974	$10,170	1-B	1,258	144	73.9
Kutztown Univ. of Pennsylvania, Kutztown, PA 19530-0730	1866	$10,950 (S)	$10,434	5-D	8,199	440	54.0
La Roche Coll., Pittsburgh, PA 15237-5898	1963	$30,320	$12,270	2-D	1,401	188	55.0
La Salle Univ., Philadelphia, PA 19141-1199	1863	$31,650	$15,150	2-D	5,191	512	67.0
La Sierra Univ., Riverside, CA 92505	1922	$35,208	$13,245	2-D	2,356	118	85.0
Lafayette Coll., Easton, PA 18042	1826	$57,052	$16,874	2-B	2,662	296	88.0
Lake Forest Coll., Lake Forest, IL 60045	1857	$49,822	$10,954	1-M	1,512	178	70.0
Lake Superior State Univ., Sault Sainte Marie, MI 49783	1946	$12,661 (A)	$10,472	5-B	1,984	151	49.0
Lakeland Univ., Plymouth, WI 53073	1862	NA	NA	2-M	3,749	216	48.0
Lamar Univ., Beaumont, TX 77710	1923	$10,342 (S)	$9,158	5-D	15,460	597	34.0
Lancaster Bible Coll., Lancaster, PA 17601	1933	$26,070	$9,000	2-D	2,122	86	53.0
Lander Univ., Greenwood, SC 29649-2099	1872	NA	NA	5-M	3,049	249	40.0
Lane Coll., Jackson, TN 38301-4598	1882	NA	NA	2-B	1,427	75	24.0
Langston Univ., Langston, OK 73050	1897	NA	NA	5-D	2,222	147	50.0
Lasell Coll., Newton, MA 02466-2709	1851	$39,000	$16,000	1-M	2,090	288	59.0
Lawrence Tech. Univ., Southfield, MI 48075-1058	1932	$36,630	$10,900	1-D	2,848	337	57.9
Lawrence Univ., Appleton, WI 54911	1847	$49,122	$10,719	1-B	1,445	197	79.0
Le Moyne Coll., Syracuse, NY 13214	1946	$35,910	$14,470	2-D	3,326	360	74.4
Lebanon Valley Coll., Annville, PA 17003-1400	1866	$46,030	$12,500	2-D	1,915	235	77.5
Lee Univ., Cleveland, TN 37320-3450	1918	$19,540	$8,260	2-D	5,189	465	59.0
Lehigh Univ., Bethlehem, PA 18015	1865	$57,450	$14,740	1-D	6,953	715	89.8
Lehman Coll. of the City Univ. of New York, Bronx, NY 10468-1589	1931	$7,410 (S)	NA	11-M	15,143	1,020	45.5
Lenoir-Rhyne Univ., Hickory, NC 28601	1891	$1,600/cr. hr.	NA	2-D	2,742	285	52.0
Lesley Univ., Cambridge, MA 02138-2790 (4)	1909	$29,450	$17,630	1-D	4,510	571	60.0
LeTourneau Univ., Longview, TX 75607-7001	1946	$32,490	$10,070	2-M	3,150	267	61.0
Lewis & Clark Coll., Portland, OR 97219-7899	1867	$52,780	$13,008	1-D	3,250	438	77.0
Lewis Univ., Romeoville, IL 60446	1932	$34,478	$11,050	2-D	6,359	642	67.0
Lewis-Clark State Coll., Lewiston, ID 83501-2698	1893	$10,552 (A)	$6,650	5-B	3,684	267	39.6
Liberty Univ., Lynchburg, VA 24515	1971	$24,910	$10,462	2-D	14,929	NA	59.0
Life Univ., Marietta, GA 30060-2903	1974	$13,101	$14,400	1-D	2,728	94	28.0
LIM Coll., New York, NY 10022-5268 (4)	1939	$28,756	$21,346	3-M	1,732	221	53.0
Limestone Coll., Gaffney, SC 29340-3799	1845	$26,300	$9,900	1-M	2,219	298	42.0
Lincoln Memorial Univ., Harrogate, TN 37752-1901	1897	$25,038	$10,638	1-D	4,867	323	55.7
Lincoln Univ., Jefferson City, MO 65101	1866	$7,910 (S)	$7,282	5-M	2,436	160	26.0
Lincoln Univ., Lincoln University, PA 19352	1854	$11,266 (S)	$9,828	12-M	2,241	208	47.0
Lindenwood Univ., St. Charles, MO 63301-1695	1827	$18,600	$9,300	2-D	8,406	1,174	50.0
Lindsey Wilson Coll., Columbia, KY 42728	1903	$24,850	$9,385	2-M	2,565	239	33.0
Linfield Coll., McMinnville, OR 97128-6894	1858	$45,062	$12,930	2-M	1,414	158	74.0
Lipscomb Univ., Nashville, TN 37204-3951	1891	$34,744	$13,804	2-D	4,595	608	67.7
Lock Haven Univ. of Pennsylvania, Lock Haven, PA 17745-2390	1870	$10,878 (S)	$10,368	5-M	3,158	216	54.0
Logan Univ., Chesterfield, MO 63017	1935	$8,300	NA	1-D	1,371	114	NA
Loma Linda Univ., Loma Linda, CA 92350	1905	NA	NA	2-D	4,270	840	NA
Long Island Univ.–LIU Brooklyn, Brooklyn, NY 11201-8423	1926	$37,763	$14,020	1-D	6,982	729	32.0
Long Island Univ.–LIU Post, Brookville, NY 11548-1300	1954	$37,763	$14,020	1-D	8,499	650	48.0
Longwood Univ., Farmville, VA 23909	1839	$13,520 (S)	$11,668	5-M	4,468	355	65.6
Loras Coll., Dubuque, IA 52004-0178	1839	$35,218	$8,600	2-M	1,400	143	66.1
Los Angeles Film Sch., Hollywood, CA 90028	1999	NA	NA	3-B	4,500	171	NA
Louisiana Coll., Pineville, LA 71359-0001	1906	$17,500	$5,646	2-M	1,229	127	37.0
Louisiana State Univ. & A&M Coll., Baton Rouge, LA 70803	1860	$11,962 (S)	$12,276	5-D	30,985	NA	NA
Louisiana State Univ. at Alexandria, Alexandria, LA 71302-9121	1960	NA	NA	5-B	3,277	172	33.0
Louisiana State Univ. Health Scis. Ctr., New Orleans, LA 70112-2223	1931	$8,308 (S)	$5,598	5-D	2,804	897	NA
Louisiana State Univ. in Shreveport, Shreveport, LA 71115-2399	1965	NA	NA	5-D	8,579	246	31.0
Louisiana Tech Univ., Ruston, LA 71272	1894	$9,645 (S)	NA	5-D	23,306	NA	NA
Lourdes Univ., Sylvania, OH 43560-2898	1958	$22,480	$10,100	2-M	1,426	185	28.0
Loyola Marymount Univ., Los Angeles, CA 90045	1911	$50,283	$15,610	2-D	9,822	NA	79.9
Loyola Univ. Chicago, Chicago, IL 60660	1870	$46,898	$15,020	2-D	17,159	1,660	74.2
Loyola Univ. Maryland, Baltimore, MD 21210-2699	1852	$800/credit	$16,490	2-D	5,473	476	83.0
Loyola Univ. New Orleans, New Orleans, LA 70118-6195	1912	$42,030	$13,606	2-D	4,384	447	62.3
Lubbock Christian Univ., Lubbock, TX 79407-2099	1957	$23,330	$7,940	2-M	1,770	172	49.8
Luther Coll., Decorah, IA 52101	1861	$44,070	$4,560	2-B	2,005	207	79.3
Lynchburg Coll., Lynchburg, VA 24501-3199	1903	$41,880	$12,138	2-D	2,956	293	58.0
Lynn Univ., Boca Raton, FL 33431-5598	1962	$39,850	$12,470	1-D	3,247	222	51.0
Macalester Coll., St. Paul, MN 55105-1899	1874	$58,478	$13,084	1-B	2,098	250	90.8
Madonna Univ., Livonia, MI 48150-1173	1947	$23,100	$11,450	2-D	3,044	NA	NA
Maharishi Univ. of Mgmt, Fairfield, IA 52557	1971	$16,530	$7,400	1-D	1,599	156	64.0
Malone Univ., Canton, OH 44709	1892	$32,416	$9,900	2-M	1,561	163	53.5
Manchester Univ., North Manchester, IN 46962-1225	1889	$33,624	$10,050	2-D	1,530	140	57.0
Manhattan Coll., Riverdale, NY 10471	1853	$44,564	$16,870	2-M	4,058	433	71.0
Manhattanville Coll., Purchase, NY 10577-2132	1841	$40,330	$14,810	1-D	2,535	360	60.4
Mansfield Univ. of Pennsylvania, Mansfield, PA 16933	1857	$10,596 (A)	$10,147	5-M	1,663	132	53.8
Marian Univ., Fond du Lac, WI 54935-4699	1936	$27,400	$7,222	2-D	1,971	233	NA
Marian Univ., Indianapolis, IN 46222-1997	1851	$36,000	$11,320	2-D	3,519	326	62.3
Marist Coll., Poughkeepsie, NY 12601-1387	1929	$40,525	$17,920	1-M	6,624	595	83.0
Marquette Univ., Milwaukee, WI 53201-1881	1881	$45,666	$13,656	2-D	11,819	1,244	81.8
Mars Hill Univ., Mars Hill, NC 28754	1856	$32,968	$9,592	2-M	1,410	147	34.0
Marshall Univ., Huntington, WV 25755	1837	$8,532 (A)	$10,644	5-D	12,852	739	38.8
Martin Univ., Indianapolis, IN 46218-3867	1977	NA	NA	1-M	1,236	43	13.0
Mary Baldwin Univ., Staunton, VA 24401-3610 (4)	1842	$31,085	$9,410	1-D	1,654	235	45.0

Name, address	Year founded	Tuition & fees	Room & board	Control, degree	Enroll- ment	Faculty	Grad. rate
Maryland Inst. Coll. of Art, Baltimore, MD 21217	1826	$48,630	$13,280	1-M	2,110	352	72.0%
Marymount Manhattan Coll., New York, NY 10021-4597	1936	$37,410	$18,434	1-B	1,892	376	53.0
Marymount Univ., Arlington, VA 22207-4299	1950	$33,950	$14,400	2-D	3,363	347	58.0
Maryville Univ. of St. Louis, St. Louis, MO 63141-7299	1872	$28,470	$10,300	1-D	10,013	953	71.0
Marywood Univ., Scranton, PA 18509-1598	1915	$36,928	$14,338	2-D	2,679	372	67.0
Massachusetts Coll. of Art & Design, Boston, MA 02115-5882	1873	$13,700 (S)	NA	5-M	2,065	NA	NA
Massachusetts Coll. of Lib Arts, North Adams, MA 01247-4100	1894	$10,930 (S)	$11,430	5-M	1,452	172	54.0
Massachusetts Inst. of Tech, Cambridge, MA 02139-4307	1861	$55,818	$17,320	1-D	11,520	1,651	95.0
Massachusetts Maritime Acad., Buzzards Bay, MA 02532-1803	1891	$10,314 (S)	$13,352	5-M	1,792	149	76.0
Mayville State Univ., Mayville, ND 58257-1299	1889	$6,667 (S)	$7,240	5-M	1,212	115	45.0
McDaniel Coll., Westminster, MD 21157-4390	1867	$44,540	$11,772	1-M	2,888	583	67.6
McKendree Univ., Lebanon, IL 62254-1299	1828	$31,640	$9,920	2-D	2,292	219	60.0
McNeese State Univ., Lake Charles, LA 70609	1939	$8,102 (S)	$8,624	5-M	7,649	427	NA
MCPHS Univ., Boston, MA 02115-5896	1823	$32,705	$16,400	1-D	7,064	826	78.0
Med. Univ. of South Carolina, Charleston, SC 29425	1824	NA	NA	5-D	2,775	223	NA
Medaille Coll., Buffalo, NY 14214-2695	1875	NA	NA	1-D	2,383	411	37.0
Medgar Evers Coll. of the City Univ. of New York, Brooklyn, NY 11225-2298	1969	$6,650 (S)	NA	11-B	6,652	534	54
Mercer Univ., Macon, GA 31207	1833	$36,894	$12,522	2-D	7,276	782	66.0
Mercy Coll. of Ohio, Toledo, OH 43604 (4)	1993	$18,850	NA	2-M	1,560	204	NA
Mercy Coll., Dobbs Ferry, NY 10522-1189	1951	$19,594	$14,400	2-D	10,557	1,028	43.6
Mercyhurst Univ., Erie, PA 16546	1926	$38,070	$12,880	2-M	2,777	NA	67.0
Meredith Coll., Raleigh, NC 27607-5298 (6)	1891	$37,176	$10,930	1-M	1,810	217	65.8
Merrimack Coll., North Andover, MA 01845-5800	1947	$41,700	$16,450	2-M	4,971	492	75.0
Messiah Coll., Mechanicsburg, PA 17055	1909	$37,180	$10,900	2-D	3,374	364	81.0
Methodist Univ., Fayetteville, NC 28311-1498	1956	$33,846	$12,665	2-M	2,416	213	44.0
Metropolitan State Univ. of Denver, Denver, CO 80204	1963	$7,666 (S)	NA	5-M	19,694	1,492	28.2
Metropolitan State Univ., St. Paul, MN 55106-5000	1971	$8,114 (S)	NA	5-D	8,354	NA	NA
Miami Univ. Hamilton, Hamilton, OH 45011-3399	1968	$6,475 (A)	NA	5-M	2,540	234	33.0
Miami Univ. Middletown, Middletown, OH 45042-3497	1966	$6,475 (A)	NA	5-M	1,842	171	32.0
Miami Univ., Oxford, OH 45056	1809	$15,232 (A)	$13,397	12-D	19,716	1,280	81.9
Michigan State Univ., East Lansing, MI 48824	1855	$14,460 (S)	$10,522	5-D	49,809	2,900	81.0
Michigan Tech Univ., Houghton, MI 49931	1885	$15,960 (S)	$11,004	5-D	7,041	438	69.5
Mid-America Christian Univ., Oklahoma City, OK 73170-4504	1953	$18,838	$8,391	2-M	1,768	NA	NA
MidAmerica Nazarene Univ., Olathe, KS 66062-1899	1966	$32,872	$9,282	2-M	1,909	230	42.9
Middle Georgia State Univ., Macon, GA 31206	2015	$4,039 (S)	$8,260	5-M	7,341	387	24.0
Middle Tennessee State Univ., Murfreesboro, TN 37132	1911	$11,176 (S)	$8,976	5-D	21,721	1,264	46.8
Middlebury Coll., Middlebury, VT 05753-6002	1800	$56,216	$16,032	1-D	2,674	357	95.0
Midland Coll., Midland, TX 79705-6329	1969	$4,590 (A)	$5,000	11-B	5,512	NA	NA
Midway Univ., Midway, KY 40347-1120	1847	$24,850	$8,600	2-M	1,702	129	37.0
Midwestern State Univ., Wichita Falls, TX 76308	1922	NA	NA	5-B	5,969	366	45.6
Miles Coll., Fairfield, AL 35064	1905	NA	NA	2-B	1,738	147	NA
Millersville Univ. of Pennsylvania, Millersville, PA 17551-0302	1855	$12,250 (S)	$12,980	5-D	7,802	474	56.5
Milligan Coll., Milligan College, TN 37682	1866	$35,600	$7,400	2-D	1,310	178	63.0
Millikin Univ., Decatur, IL 62522-2084	1901	$39,592	$11,450	2-D	2,083	287	59.0
Mills Coll., Oakland, CA 94613-1000 (6)	1852	$30,257	$13,448	1-D	1,309	174	64.0
Milwaukee Sch. of Engineering, Milwaukee, WI 53202-3109 (2)	1903	$43,575	$6,339	1-M	2,746	270	65.0
Minnesota State Univ. Mankato, Mankato, MN 56001	1868	$289/cr. hr. (A)	NA	5-D	1,847	NA	50.0
Minnesota State Univ. Moorhead, Moorhead, MN 56563	1885	$8,572 (S)	$9,280	5-D	5,860	309	46.0
Minot State Univ., Minot, ND 58707-0002	1913	$7,590 (S)	$7,315	5-D	3,121	312	45.0
Misericordia Univ., Dallas, PA 18612-1098	1924	$34,560	$14,220	2-D	2,544	298	68.0
Mississippi Coll., Clinton, MS 39058	1826	$18,610	$10,610	2-D	5,059	437	59.0
Mississippi State Univ., Mississippi State, MS 39762	1878	$8,910 (S)	$10,436	5-D	22,226	1,365	61.5
Mississippi Univ. for Women, Columbus, MS 39701-9998	1884	NA	NA	5-D	2,673	215	48.0
Mississippi Valley State Univ., Itta Bena, MS 38941-1400	1946	$6,550 (S)	$7,764	5-M	2,455	172	31.0
Missouri Baptist Univ., St. Louis, MO 63141-8660	1964	$28,220	$9,070	2-D	5,313	528	38.0
Missouri Southern State Univ., Joplin, MO 64801-1595	1937	NA	NA	5-M	5,604	NA	33.0
Missouri State Univ., Springfield, MO 65897	1905	$7,588 (S)	$9,128	5-D	23,453	1,142	55.9
Missouri Univ. of Sci & Tech, Rolla, MO 65409	1870	$10,653 (A)	$10,402	5-D	8,096	430	77.0
Missouri Valley Coll., Marshall, MO 65340-3197	1889	$21,100	$9,400	2-M	1,768	153	26.9
Missouri Western State Univ., St. Joseph, MO 64507-2294	1915	$6,909 (S)	$8,348	5-M	5,533	343	34.0
Molloy Coll., Rockville Centre, NY 11571-5002	1955	$32,600	$15,560	1-D	5,113	725	74.0
Monmouth Univ., West Long Branch, NJ 07764-1898	1933	$40,680	$15,260	1-D	6,371	695	70.0
Monroe Coll., Bronx, NY 10468	1933	$15,428	$10,850	3-M	6,862	471	68.0
Montana State Univ. Billings, Billings, MT 59101	1927	$5,921 (S)	$8,186	5-M	4,315	325	0.3
Montana State Univ., Bozeman, MT 59717	1893	$7,472 (A)	$10,300	5-D	16,766	1,146	56.0
Montana State Univ.–Northern, Havre, MT 59501-7751	1929	$5,954 (S)	NA	5-M	1,273	96	30.0
Montana Tech of The Univ. of Montana, Butte, MT 59701-8997	1895	$7,397 (S)	$10,170	5-D	2,421	185	52.0
Montclair State Univ., Montclair, NJ 07043-1624	1908	$13,073 (S)	$15,674	5-D	21,115	1,855	65.2
Moody Bible Inst., Chicago, IL 60610-3284	1886	NA	NA	2-M	3,349	211	68.0
Moravian Coll., Bethlehem, PA 18018-6650	1742	$47,367	$14,471	2-D	2,595	339	69.0
Morehead State Univ., Morehead, KY 40351	1922	$9,290 (S)	$9,490	5-D	9,660	416	45.9
Morehouse Coll., Atlanta, GA 30314 (1)	1867	$54,346	$14,272	1-B	2,238	214	54.0
Morgan State Univ., Baltimore, MD 21251	1867	$7,899 (S)	$10,862	5-D	7,005	690	43.0
Morningside Coll., Sioux City, IA 51106	1894	$32,720	$9,840	2-M	2,684	240	56.0
Morrisville State Coll., Morrisville, NY 13408	1908	$8,481 (S)	$13,550	5-B	3,003	253	30.0
Mount Aloysius Coll., Cresson, PA 16630-1999	1939	$23,110	$10,648	2-M	1,834	154	NA
Mount Holyoke Coll., South Hadley, MA 01075 (3)	1837	$52,258	$15,320	1-M	2,335	NA	NA
Mount Mary Univ., Milwaukee, WI 53222-4597 (6)	1913	$32,120	$9,180	2-D	1,358	190	64.9
Mount Mercy Univ., Cedar Rapids, IA 52402-4797	1928	$35,574	$10,112	2-D	1,808	176	64.0
Mount St. Joseph Univ., Cincinnati, OH 45233-1670	1920	$31,200	$9,830	2-D	2,168	220	60.7
Mount St. Mary Coll., Newburgh, NY 12550-3494	1960	$34,412	$16,658	1-M	2,236	251	63.0
Mount St. Mary's Univ., Emmitsburg, MD 21727-7799	1808	$43,650	$6,940	2-M	2,362	256	68.8
Mount St. Mary's Univ., Los Angeles, CA 90049 (4)	1925	$42,792	$12,455	2-D	3,280	NA	NA
Mount Vernon Nazarene Univ., Mount Vernon, OH 43050-9500	1968	$31,610	$8,890	2-M	2,205	257	204.0
Muhlenberg Coll., Allentown, PA 18104-5586	1848	$54,600	$12,165	2-B	2,251	328	84.6
Murray State Univ., Murray, KY 42071	1922	$9,084 (S)	$9,190	5-D	9,569	578	49.0
Musicians Inst., Hollywood, CA 90028	1976	NA	NA	3-B	1,337	204	NA
Muskingum Univ., New Concord, OH 43762	1837	$29,740	$12,032	2-M	2,369	107	52.7
Natl. Louis Univ., Chicago, IL 60603	1886	NA	NA	1-D	4,918	290	50.0
Natl. Univ., La Jolla, CA 92037-1011	1971	$13,320	NA	1-D	16,930	1,390	42.0
Navajo Tech Univ., Crownpoint, NM 87313	1979	NA	NA	1-M	1,600	136	14.0

Name, address	Year founded	Tuition & fees	Room & board	Control, degree	Enroll- ment	Faculty	Grad. rate
Nazareth Coll. of Rochester, Rochester, NY 14618.	1924	$35,416	$14,230	1-D	2,979	513	67.0%
Nebraska Wesleyan Univ., Lincoln, NE 68504-2796	1887	$35,564	$10,172	2-M	2,044	280	64.6
Neumann Univ., Aston, PA 19014-1298.	1965	$31,400	$13,020	2-D	2,391	258	52.0
Nevada State Coll., Henderson, NV 89002	2002	$5,138 (S)	NA	5-B	3,747	267	15.0
New England Coll., Henniker, NH 03242-3293	1946	$37,490	$14,170	1-D	3,538	328	39.0
New England Inst. of Tech, East Greenwich, RI 02818	1940	$31,545	$14,505	1-D	2,498	279	NA
New Jersey City Univ., Jersey City, NJ 07305-1597	1927	$12,414 (S)	$14,574	5-D	7,949	804	41.0
New Jersey Inst. of Tech, Newark, NJ 07102	1881	$17,674 (S)	$13,900	5-D	11,518	879	67.0
New Mexico Highlands Univ., Las Vegas, NM 87701	1893	$6,278 (A)	$8,126	5-M	2,902	237	22.1
New Mexico Inst. of Mining & Tech, Socorro, NM 87801	1889	$8,156 (S)	$8,624	5-D	1,832	162	NA
New Mexico State Univ., Las Cruces, NM 88003-8001	1888	$7,087 (S)	$9,538	5-D	14,432	976	46.0
New Orleans Baptist Theol. Sem., New Orleans, LA 70126-4858 (2)	1917	NA	NA	2-D	2,036	NA	NA
New York City Coll. of Tech of the City Univ. of New York, Brooklyn, NY 11201-2983.	1946	$7,320 (A)	NA	11-B	17,036	1,716	31.0
New York Inst. of Tech, Old Westbury, NY 11568-8000	1955	$39,760	$14,290	1-D	7,230	1,016	53.0
New York Univ., New York, NY 10012-1019	1831	$53,308	$18,684	1-D	52,885	6,646	85.0
Newberry Coll., Newberry, SC 29108-2197	1856	$26,424	$10,666	2-B	1,271	142	53.0
Newman Univ., Wichita, KS 67213-2097.	1933	$30,564	$8,406	2-M	3,205	162	59.0
Niagara Univ., Niagara University, NY 14109	1856	$35,240	$11,850	2-D	3,727	411	73.0
Nicholls State Univ., Thibodaux, LA 70310.	1948	$7,898 (A)	$9,818	5-M	10,471	329	44.0
Nichols Coll., Dudley, MA 01571-5000.	1815	$36,540	$13,950	1-M	1,553	140	59.0
Norfolk State Univ., Norfolk, VA 23504	1935	$9,490 (S)	$10,360	5-D	4,660	NA	34.0
North Carolina Agr & Tech State Univ., Greensboro, NC 27411	1891	$6,567 (A)	$7,930	5-D	12,142	759	53.0
North Carolina Central Univ., Durham, NC 27707-3129	1910	$6,534 (A)	$10,227	5-D	8,207	564	42.0
North Carolina State Univ., Raleigh, NC 27695	1887	$9,101 (S)	$11,359	5-D	35,479	NA	NA
North Carolina Wesleyan Coll., Rocky Mount, NC 27804-8677	1956	$30,150	$10,050	2-B	2,093	313	31.0
North Central Coll., Naperville, IL 60566-7063.	1861	$41,180	$11,792	2-M	2,888	314	69.1
North Dakota State Univ., Fargo, ND 58102	1890	$9,619 (S)	$8,878	5-D	13,796	782	57.6
North Greenville Univ., Tigerville, SC 29688-1892.	1892	$22,050	$10,450	2-D	2,428	266	59.0
North Park Univ., Chicago, IL 60625-4895.	1891	NA	NA	2-D	3,138	305	56.0
Northcentral Univ., San Diego, CA 92106	1996	NA	NA	3-D	10,698	NA	NA
Northeastern Illinois Univ., Chicago, IL 60625-4699	1961	$13,998 (A)	$8,426	5-M	7,423	563	21.5
Northeastern State Univ., Tahlequah, OK 74464-2399	1846	$6,915 (A)	$7,340	5-D	7,496	422	31.6
Northeastern Univ., Boston, MA 02115-5096.	1898	$53,506	$16,930	1-D	27,391	1,844	89.1
Northern Arizona Univ., Flagstaff, AZ 86011	1899	$11,896 (A)	$10,780	5-D	30,736	1,758	56.7
Northern Illinois Univ., De Kalb, IL 60115-2854	1895	$12,261 (A)	$10,880	5-D	16,609	1,055	49.0
Northern Kentucky Univ., Highland Heights, KY 41099	1968	$10,032 (S)	$10,022	5-D	15,678	1,082	47.7
Northern Michigan Univ., Marquette, MI 49855-5301.	1899	$11,255 (A)	$10,774	5-D	7,732	402	53.2
Northern New Mexico Coll., Española, NM 87532.	1909	NA	NA	5-B	2,272	253	NA
Northern State Univ., Aberdeen, SD 57401-7198	1901	$8,750 (S)	$8,925	5-M	3,427	134	52.0
Northwest Missouri State Univ., Maryville, MO 64468-6001	1905	$10,297 (S)	$10,106	5-M	7,104	NA	51.0
Northwest Nazarene Univ., Nampa, ID 83686-5897	1913	$32,630	$8,800	2-D	1,854	112	63.0
Northwest Univ., Kirkland, WA 98033	1934	$33,980	$9,420	2-D	2,583	252	58.9
Northwestern Coll., Orange City, IA 51041-1996.	1882	$56,691	$17,019	2-M	1,412	NA	NA
Northwestern Oklahoma State Univ., Alva, OK 73717-2799	1897	$7,244 (S)	$4,680	5-D	1,992	159	27.0
Northwestern State Univ. of Louisiana, Natchitoches, LA 71497	1884	$8,768 (S)	$9,244	5-D	10,900	563	44.7
Northwestern Univ., Evanston, IL 60208	1851	$56,691	$17,019	1-D	21,946	1,753	93.8
Northwood Univ., Michigan Campus, Midland, MI 48640-2398	1959	$29,480	$11,110	1-M	1,522	168	68.0
Norwich Univ., Northfield, VT 05663	1819	$41,496	$14,352	1-M	3,672	332	57.0
Notre Dame Coll., South Euclid, OH 44121-4293	1922	$30,750	$10,250	2-M	1,393	192	0.4
Notre Dame of Maryland Univ., Baltimore, MD 21210-2476 (4).	1873	NA	NA	2-D	2,764	136	56.0
Nova Southeastern Univ., Fort Lauderdale, FL 33314-7796	1964	$33,430	$13,656	1-D	20,576	1,521	57.0
Nyack Coll., New York, NY 10004	1882	$25,500	$10,000	2-D	1,981	221	38.4
Oakland City Univ., Oakland City, IN 47660-1099	1885	$24,990	$10,400	2-D	1,419	155	49.0
Oakland Univ., Rochester, MI 48309-4401	1957	$13,346 (A)	$10,430	5-D	19,013	1,236	56.8
Oakwood Univ., Huntsville, AL 35896	1896	NA	NA	2-M	1,824	171	46.0
Oberlin Coll., Oberlin, OH 44074	1833	$56,868	$16,826	1-M	2,812	381	86.0
Occidental Coll., Los Angeles, CA 90041-3314	1887	$56,576	$16,034	1-M	1,985	260	86.0
Oglala Lakota Coll., Kyle, SD 57752-0490.	1970	NA	NA	11-M	1,300	119	11.0
Oglethorpe Univ., Atlanta, GA 30319-2797	1835	$41,410	$13,800	1-B	1,264	115	48.0
Ohio Christian Univ., Circleville, OH 43113	1948	$20,790	$8,320	2-M	2,843	419	41.0
Ohio Dominican Univ., Columbus, OH 43219-2099.	1911	$32,880	$11,340	2-M	1,641	161	46.4
Ohio Northern Univ., Ada, OH 45810-1599	1871	$34,440	$12,400	2-D	2,958	284	70.9
Ohio Univ., Athens, OH 45701-2979	1804	$12,612 (S)	$12,172	5-D	27,022	1,330	65.0
Ohio Univ.–Chillicothe, Chillicothe, OH 45601	1946	$5,674 (S)	NA	5-M	1,479	127	14.0
Ohio Univ.–Lancaster, Lancaster, OH 43130-1097	1968	$5,674 (S)	NA	5-M	1,514	122	25.0
Ohio Wesleyan Univ., Delaware, OH 43015	1842	$47,130	$13,330	2-B	1,494	193	65.0
Oklahoma Baptist Univ., Shawnee, OK 74804.	1910	$31,352	$7,720	2-M	1,856	153	56.5
Oklahoma Christian Univ., Oklahoma City, OK 73136-1100	1950	$23,750	$8,550	2-M	2,248	219	56.0
Oklahoma City Univ., Oklahoma City, OK 73106-1402	1904	$32,594	$9,236	2-D	2,821	268	63.0
Oklahoma Panhandle State Univ., Goodwell, OK 73939-0430	1909	$6,364 (A)	$5,810	5-B	1,387	91	24.0
Oklahoma State Univ., Stillwater, OK 74078	1890	$9,018 (S)	$9,106	5-D	24,041	1,337	64.7
Oklahoma Wesleyan Univ., Bartlesville, OK 74006-6299	1909	$26,956	$8,344	2-M	1,527	111	45.0
Old Dominion Univ., Norfolk, VA 23529	1930	$11,020 (S)	$12,836	5-D	23,675	1,551	52.8
Olivet Nazarene Univ., Bourbonnais, IL 60914	1907	$36,950	$8,990	2-D	4,317	NA	64.0
O'More Coll. of Design, Nashville, TN 37212.	1970	$35,650	$12,520	1-B	8,250	915	73.0
Oral Roberts Univ., Tulsa, OK 74171.	1963	$30,930	$8,650	2-D	4,042	349	51.0
Oregon Health & Sci Univ., Portland, OR 97239-3098.	1974	$20,365 (S)	NA	12-D	2,895	110	NA
Oregon Inst. of Tech, Klamath Falls, OR 97601-8801	1947	$10,485 (S)	$9,133	5-M	5,490	305	44.3
Oregon State Univ., Corvallis, OR 97331.	1868	$11,166 (S)	$12,855	5-D	30,896	1,697	65.3
Ottawa Univ., Ottawa, KS 66067-3399.	1865	$31,580	$11,200	2-M	3,595	68	73.0
Otterbein Univ., Westerville, OH 43081	1847	$33,074	$11,768	2-D	2,853	312	65.7
Ouachita Baptist Univ., Arkadelphia, AR 71998-0001	1886	$27,900	$8,000	2-B	1,660	170	64.0
Our Lady of the Lake Coll., Baton Rouge, LA 70808	1990	$13,287	NA	2-D	1,362	NA	50.0
Our Lady of the Lake Univ., San Antonio, TX 78207-4689	1895	$30,196	$7,990	2-D	3,212	299	42.4
Pace Univ., New York, NY 10038	1906	$45,280	$18,529	1-D	13,609	1,369	50.5
Pace Univ., Pleasantville campus, Pleasantville, NY 10570	1906	$45,280	$16,600	1-D	3,710	467	60.1
Pacific Lutheran Univ., Tacoma, WA 98447.	1890	$46,200 ·	$11,150	2-D	3,062	308	69.2
Pacific Univ., Forest Grove, OR 97116-1797.	1849	$48,260	$13,420	1-D	3,832	NA	69.0
Palm Beach Atlantic Univ., West Palm Beach, FL 33416-4708	1968	$33,475	$5,696	2-D	3,691	371	59.0
Palm Beach State Coll., Lake Worth, FL 33461-4796	1933	$3,070 (S)	NA	5-B	30,052	1,170	NA
Park Univ., Parkville, MO 64152-3795	1875	NA	NA	1-M	9,800	174	42.0

Name, address	Year founded	Tuition & fees	Room & board	Control, degree	Enroll-ment	Faculty	Grad. rate
Parsons Sch. of Design, New York, NY 10011	1896	NA	NA	1-M	5,339	1,212	78.0%
Penn State Abington, Abington, PA 19001	1950	$15,524 (A)	$8,420	12-B	3,746	334	54.1
Penn State Altoona, Altoona, PA 16601	1939	$15,206 (A)	$11,884	12-B	3,070	312	61.8
Penn State Berks, Reading, PA 19610	1924	$15,206 (A)	$13,080	12-B	2,482	244	58.4
Penn State Brandywine, Media, PA 19063	1966	$14,476 (A)	$12,586	12-B	1,332	165	46.6
Penn State Erie, The Behrend Coll., Erie, PA 16563	1948	$15,206 (A)	$11,884	12-M	4,108	372	66.7
Penn State Harrisburg, Middletown, PA 17057	1966	$15,206 (A)	$13,750	12-D	4,898	487	63.7
Penn State Univ. Park, University Park, PA 16802	1855	$18,450 (A)	$11,884	12-D	47,223	3,511	85.9
Pennsylvania Coll. of Health Scis., Lancaster, PA 17601	1903	NA	NA	1-D	1,793	213	64.0
Pennsylvania Coll. of Tech, Williamsport, PA 17701-5778	1965	$17,160 (S)	$11,715	12-M	4,983	448	62.1
Pepperdine Univ., Malibu, CA 90263	1937	$58,002	$16,160	2-D	8,824	802	80.0
Peru State Coll., Peru, NE 68421	1867	$7,601 (S)	$9,060	5-M	2,358	109	NA
Pfeiffer Univ., Misenheimer, NC 28109-0960	1885	$31,790	$11,950	2-M	1,277	NA	44.0
Piedmont Coll., Demorest, GA 30535	1897	$27,500	$10,850	2-D	2,510	271	45.0
Pittsburg State Univ., Pittsburg, KS 66762	1903	$7,298 (S)	$7,700	5-D	6,645	432	NA
Plymouth State Univ., Plymouth, NH 03264-1595	1871	$14,099 (S)	$11,100	5-D	4,667	419	54.0
Point Loma Nazarene Univ., San Diego, CA 92106-2899	1902	$36,950	$10,650	2-D	4,567	474	74.7
Point Park Univ., Pittsburgh, PA 15222-1984	1960	$32,750	$12,440	1-D	4,224	519	0.6
Point Univ., West Point, GA 31833	1937	$21,285	$8,000	2-M	2,389	NA	28.0
Polk State Coll., Winter Haven, FL 33881-4299	1964	$3,367 (S)	$8,080	5-B	10,827	368	NA
Polytechnic Univ. of Puerto Rico, Hato Rey, PR 00918	1966	$8,640	$11,928	1-D	4,360	221	0.2
Pomona Coll., Claremont, CA 91711	1887	$54,762	$17,218	1-B	1,717	250	93.0
Pontifical Catholic Univ. of Puerto Rico, Ponce, PR 00717-0777	1948	NA	NA	2-D	7,682	385	39.0
Portland State Univ., Portland, OR 97207-0751	1946	$9,578 (S)	$11,172	5-D	26,021	1,535	46.5
Post Univ., Waterbury, CT 06723-2540	1890	$15,458	$11,600	1-M	8,540	NA	NA
Prairie View A&M Univ., Prairie View, TX 77446	1878	$10,786 (A)	$9,076	5-D	9,516	NA	NA
Pratt Inst., Brooklyn, NY 11205-3899	1887	$55,630	$13,988	1-M	4,875	1,202	70.4
Presbyterian Coll., Clinton, SC 29325	1880	$39,460	$10,680	2-D	1,353	121	71.0
Princeton Univ., Princeton, NJ 08544-1019	1746	$50,340	$16,360	1-D	8,419	1,263	97.9
Providence Coll., Providence, RI 02918	1917	$54,388	$15,590	2-M	4,890	530	87.0
Purchase Coll., State Univ. of New York, Purchase, NY 10577-1400	1967	$8,953 (S)	$14,548	5-M	4,187	469	61.0
Purdue Univ. Northwest, Hammond, IN 46323-2094	2016	$7,942 (S)	$7,821	5-D	8,617	692	38.0
Purdue Univ., West Lafayette, IN 47907	1869	$9,992 (A)	$10,030	5-D	44,551	2,739	82.0
Queens Coll. of the City Univ. of New York, Queens, NY 11367-1597	1937	$514/credit (S)	$12,752	11-M	3,057	1,633	62.0
Queens Univ. of Charlotte, Charlotte, NC 28274-0002	1857	$37,332	$12,902	2-M	2,463	312	59.2
Quinnipiac Univ., Hamden, CT 06518-1940	1929	$47,960	$14,990	1-D	10,200	1,084	75.0
Radford Univ., Radford, VA 24142	1910	$11,350 (S)	$9,637	5-D	11,870	873	55.4
Ramapo Coll. of New Jersey, Mahwah, NJ 07430-1680	1969	$14,678 (S)	$12,840	5-M	6,142	522	71.9
Randolph-Macon Coll., Ashland, VA 23005-5505	1830	$43,940	$12,680	2-B	1,543	180	68.0
Rasmussen Coll. Bloomington, Bloomington, MN 55435	1904	NA	NA	3-B	1,255	NA	NA
Rasmussen Coll. Ocala, Ocala, FL 34474	1984	NA	NA	3-B	1,482	NA	NA
Reed Coll., Portland, OR 97202-8199	1908	$58,440	$14,620	1-M	1,503	153	81.0
Regent Univ., Virginia Beach, VA 23464-9800	1977	$20,120	$7,220	2-D	10,409	785	58.0
Regis Coll., Weston, MA 02493	1927	$42,650	$15,790	2-D	3,194	401	71.0
Regis Univ., Denver, CO 80221-1099	1877	$36,810	$11,560	2-D	7,907	704	71.0
Reinhardt Univ., Waleska, GA 30183-2981	1883	$24,300	$10,500	2-M	1,524	NA	41.0
Rensselaer Polytechnic Inst., Troy, NY 12180-3590	1824	$55,375	$15,580	1-D	7,617	541	85.0
Rhode Island Coll., Providence, RI 02908-1991	1854	$8,929 (S)	$12,978	5-D	7,523	742	49.0
Rhode Island Sch. of Design, Providence, RI 02903-2784	1877	$54,890	$14,430	1-M	2,500	459	89.0
Rhodes Coll., Memphis, TN 38112-1690	1848	$2,045/cr. hr.	$11,631	1-M	2,010	223	83.0
Rice Univ., Houston, TX 77251-1892	1912	$49,112	$14,140	1-M	7,282	887	92.6
Rider Univ., Lawrenceville, NJ 08648-3001	1865	$42,860	$15,280	1-D	4,677	551	NA
Ringling Coll. of Art & Design, Sarasota, FL 34234-5895	1931	$47,970	$15,580	1-B	1,658	181	NA
Rivier Univ., Nashua, NH 03060	1933	NA	NA	2-D	2,157	209	49.0
Roanoke Coll., Salem, VA 24153-3794	1842	$46,870	$14,580	2-B	2,005	210	69.7
Robert Morris Univ. Illinois, Chicago, IL 60605	1913	$28,530	$14,808	1-M	2,307	184	76.0
Robert Morris Univ., Moon Township, PA 15108-1189	1921	$32,130	$12,070	1-D	4,608	400	64.7
Roberts Wesleyan Coll., Rochester, NY 14624-1997	1866	$32,494	$10,898	2-D	1,780	104	62.6
Rochester Inst. of Tech, Rochester, NY 14623-5603	1829	$51,240	$13,976	1-D	16,254	1,459	69.0
Rockford Univ., Rockford, IL 61108-2393	1847	$30,930	$8,660	1-M	1,211	156	41.0
Rockhurst Univ., Kansas City, MO 64110-2561	1910	$37,590	$9,570	2-D	3,043	239	75.0
Roger Williams Univ., Bristol, RI 02809	1956	$35,169	$15,390	1-D	4,838	523	67.0
Rogers State Univ., Claremore, OK 74017-3252	1909	$7,470 (S)	$8,975	5-M	3,614	228	34.0
Rollins Coll., Winter Park, FL 32789-4499	1885	$53,716	$15,200	1-D	2,662	225	73.9
Roosevelt Univ., Chicago, IL 60605	1945	$31,493	$12,000	1-D	4,071	578	41.0
Rose-Hulman Inst. of Tech, Terre Haute, IN 47803-3999 (2)	1874	$49,527	$15,414	1-M	2,038	196	84.9
Rowan Univ., Glassboro, NJ 08028-1701	1923	$387/cr. hr. (A)	NA	5-D	19,618	1,640	0.7
Rush Univ., Chicago, IL 60612-3832	1969	NA	NA	1-D	1,566	796	NA
Rutgers Univ.–Camden, Camden, NJ 08102-1401	1926	$15,264 (S)	$12,691	5-D	7,233	700	64.6
Rutgers Univ.–New Brunswick, Piscataway, NJ 08854-8097	1766	$15,407 (S)	$13,075	5-D	50,173	4,309	83.7
Rutgers Univ.–Newark, Newark, NJ 07102	1908	$14,826 (S)	$13,929	5-D	13,605	1,031	69.0
Sacred Heart Univ., Fairfield, CT 06825	1963	$43,070	$15,960	2-D	9,156	970	73.0
Saginaw Valley State Univ., University Center, MI 48710	1963	$10,814 (S)	$10,440	5-D	8,265	NA	44.0
St. Ambrose Univ., Davenport, IA 52803-2898	1882	$32,758	$11,354	2-D	2,968	342	62.0
St. Anselm Coll., Manchester, NH 03102-1310	1889	$42,840	$15,120	2-B	2,043	234	78.0
St. Augustine Univ., Chicago, IL 60640-3501	1980	$11,400	NA	1-B	1,430	154	NA
St. Bonaventure Univ., St. Bonaventure, NY 14778-2284	1858	$36,515	$13,620	2-M	2,422	204	74.0
St. Catherine Univ., St. Paul, MN 55105 (6)	1905	$42,263	$9,260	2-D	4,401	509	63.3
St. Cloud State Univ., St. Cloud, MN 56301-4498	1869	$8,260 (S)	$8,900	5-D	12,608	656	47.0
St. Edward's Univ., Austin, TX 78704	1885	$47,190	NA	2-M	4,601	481	64.0
St. Francis Coll., Brooklyn Heights, NY 11201-4398	1884	NA	NA	2-M	2,672	300	52.0
St. Francis Univ., Loretto, PA 15940-0600	1847	$39,378	$12,472	2-D	2,619	212	2.4
St. John Fisher Coll., Rochester, NY 14618-3597	1948	$35,150	$12,650	2-D	3,719	449	71.0
St. John's Univ., Collegeville, MN 56321 (5)	1857	$49,000	$11,362	2-M	1,723	165	75.0
St. John's Univ., Queens, NY 11439	1870	$44,510	$18,312	2-D	21,721	1,543	63.0
St. Joseph's Coll. of Maine, Standish, ME 04084	1912	$36,720	$14,090	2-M	3,355	126	50.0
St. Joseph's Coll., Long Island campus, Patchogue, NY 11772-2399	1916	$29,200	NA	1-M	3,959	425	72.0
St. Joseph's Univ., Philadelphia, PA 19131-1395	1851	$47,940	$14,840	2-D	7,361	681	81.2
St. Lawrence Univ., Canton, NY 13617	1856	$56,766	$14,628	1-M	2,434	219	84.0
St. Leo Univ., Saint Leo, FL 33574-6665	1889	$24,640	$13,500	2-D	5,351	168	46.9
St. Louis Coll. of Pharm., St. Louis, MO 63110-1088	1864	$29,596	$12,256	1-D	1,309	171	71.0

Name, address	Year founded	Tuition & fees	Room & board	Control, degree	Enroll-ment	Faculty	Grad. rate
St. Louis Univ., St. Louis, MO 63103	1818	$45,424	$12,600	2-D	11,684	1,094	79.0%
St. Martin's Univ., Lacey, WA 98503	1895	$38,560	$12,000	2-M	1,609	NA	NA
St. Mary's Coll. of California, Moraga, CA 94575	1863	$50,660	$15,706	2-D	3,692	373	76.0
St. Mary's Coll. of Maryland, St. Mary's City, MD 20686-3001	1840	$14,496 (S)	$12,816	5-M	1,513	210	77.0
St. Mary's Coll., Notre Dame, IN 46556 (3)	1844	$45,720	$13,470	2-D	1,580	213	79.1
St. Mary's Univ. of Minnesota, Winona, MN 55987-1399	1912	$38,280	$9,630	2-D	5,548	528	64.0
St. Mary's Univ., San Antonio, TX 78228	1852	$34,740	$10,980	2-D	3,514	384	60.0
St. Michael's Coll., Colchester, VT 05439	1904	$48,175	$13,600	2-M	1,878	NA	83.0
St. Norbert Coll., De Pere, WI 54115-2099	1898	$40,885	$10,885	2-M	2,081	200	74.0
St. Olaf Coll., Northfield, MN 55057-1098	1874	$51,450	$11,660	2-B	3,072	326	86.3
St. Peter's Univ., Jersey City, NJ 07306-5997	1872	$38,760	$15,950	2-D	3,233	352	60.0
St. Petersburg Coll., St. Petersburg, FL 33733-3489	1927	NA	NA	11-B	28,853	1,475	33.0
St. Thomas Aquinas Coll., Sparkill, NY 10976	1952	$33,050	$13,650	1-M	1,937	160	58.1
St. Thomas Univ., Miami Gardens, FL 33054-6459	1961	$34,080	$11,320	2-D	4,824	145	42.8
St. Vincent Coll., Latrobe, PA 15650-2690	1846	$36,904	$12,161	2-D	1,739	224	69.0
St. Xavier Univ., Chicago, IL 60655-3105	1847	NA	NA	2-M	4,709	360	52.0
Salem State Univ., Salem, MA 01970-5353	1854	$10,884 (S)	$12,896	5-M	7,706	757	57.0
Salisbury Univ., Salisbury, MD 21801-6837	1925	$10,044 (S)	$12,360	5-D	8,617	670	70.3
Salve Regina Univ., Newport, RI 02840-4192	1934	$42,920	$15,400	2-D	2,771	295	78.0
Sam Houston State Univ., Huntsville, TX 77341	1879	$10,183 (S)	$9,180	5-D	21,363	988	55.0
Samford Univ., Birmingham, AL 35229	1841	$32,850	$10,980	2-D	5,692	559	76.0
Samuel Merritt Univ., Oakland, CA 94609-3108 (4)	1909	NA	NA	1-D	2,141	392	NA
San Diego State Univ., San Diego, CA 92182	1897	$7,510 (A)	$17,752	5-D	35,081	1,910	74.0
San Francisco State Univ., San Francisco, CA 94132-1722	1899	$7,266 (A)	$14,384	5-D	28,880	1,824	57.0
San Jose State Univ., San Jose, CA 95192-0001	1857	$7,852 (A)	$16,248	5-D	32,926	1,858	0.6
Santa Clara Univ., Santa Clara, CA 95053	1851	$55,629	$15,972	2-D	8,669	916	91.2
Santa Fe Coll., Gainesville, FL 32606	1966	NA	NA	11-B	15,745	829	NA
Sarah Lawrence Coll., Bronxville, NY 10708-5999	1926	$57,520	$15,820	1-M	1,670	305	78.0
Savannah Coll. of Art & Design, Savannah, GA 31402-3146	1978	$37,575	$14,979	1-M	15,568	774	69.0
Savannah State Univ., Savannah, GA 31404	1890	$6,918 (A)	$10,616	5-M	4,077	220	27.0
Sch. of the Art Inst. of Chicago, Chicago, IL 60603-3103	1866	$53,160	$16,700	1-M	3,570	781	70.0
Sch. of Visual Arts, New York, NY 10010-3994	1947	$43,400	$18,800	3-M	4,557	1,102	67.0
Schreiner Univ., Kerrville, TX 78028-5697	1923	$31,938	$10,579	2-M	1,342	123	45.0
Seattle Pacific Univ., Seattle, WA 98119-1997	1891	$47,244	$12,687	2-D	3,529	373	68.0
Seattle Univ., Seattle, WA 98122-1090	1891	$48,390	$12,780	2-D	7,199	760	73.0
Seton Hall Univ., South Orange, NJ 07079-2697	1856	$42,170	$15,784	2-D	9,903	952	64.0
Seton Hill Univ., Greensburg, PA 15601	1883	$37,946	$12,516	2-M	2,079	215	65.0
Sewanee: The Univ. of the South, Sewanee, TN 37383-1000	1857	$47,980	$13,700	2-D	1,768	232	79.1
Shaw Univ., Raleigh, NC 27601-2399	1865	$16,480	$8,158	2-M	1,291	117	19.0
Shawnee State Univ., Portsmouth, OH 45662	1986	$8,556 (S)	$10,864	5-M	3,582	314	27.9
Shenandoah Univ., Winchester, VA 22601-5195	1875	$33,830	$10,810	2-D	3,791	507	60.0
Shepherd Univ., Shepherdstown, WV 25443	1871	$7,784 (S)	$10,654	5-D	3,554	321	48.6
Shippensburg Univ. of Pennsylvania, Shippensburg, PA 17257-2299	1871	$12,718 (S)	$12,268	5-D	6,084	359	58.0
Siena Coll., Loudonville, NY 12211-1462	1937	$39,500	$15,915	2-M	3,299	346	79.7
Siena Heights Univ., Adrian, MI 49221-1796	1919	$27,152	$10,990	2-M	2,364	220	47.0
Simmons Coll., Boston, MA 02115 (6)	1899	$43,330	$15,660	1-D	6,635	970	81.0
Simpson Coll., Indianola, IA 50125-1297	1860	$42,246	$9,282	2-M	1,359	185	71.5
Skidmore Coll., Saratoga Springs, NY 12866	1903	$56,172	$15,000	1-B	2,663	399	89.0
Slippery Rock Univ. of Pennsylvania, Slippery Rock, PA 16057-1383	1889	$10,517 (S)	$10,446	5-D	8,824	NA	NA
Smith Coll., Northampton, MA 01063 (6)	1871	$56,114	$18,760	1-D	2,894	307	88.8
Sonoma State Univ., Rohnert Park, CA 94928-3609	1960	NA	NA	5-M	9,201	597	58.0
South Carolina State Univ., Orangeburg, SC 29117-0001	1896	$11,060 (S)	$9,890	5-D	2,479	198	35.0
South Dakota Sch. of Mines & Tech, Rapid City, SD 57701-3995	1885	$10,560 (S)	$8,440	5-D	2,859	177	47.2
South Dakota State Univ., Brookings, SD 57007	1881	$9,200 (S)	$8,307	5-D	11,518	648	56.0
Southeast Missouri State Univ., Cape Girardeau, MO 63701-4799	1873	$7,800 (S)	$9,279	5-M	10,637	576	49.8
Southeastern Baptist Theol. Sem., Wake Forest, NC 27587	1950	NA	NA	2-D	3,164	123	60.0
Southeastern Louisiana Univ., Hammond, LA 70402	1925	$8,329 (S)	$8,600	5-D	14,260	624	NA
Southeastern Oklahoma State Univ., Durant, OK 74701-0609	1909	NA	NA	5-M	4,824	213	34.8
Southeastern Univ., Lakeland, FL 33801-6099	1935	$26,620	$10,030	2-D	8,759	NA	NA
Southern Adventist Univ., Collegedale, TN 37315-0370	1892	$21,950	$6,940	2-D	2,834	172	NA
Southern Arkansas Univ.–Magnolia, Magnolia, AR 71753	1909	$8,980 (S)	$6,520	5-M	4,474	301	42.0
Southern Connecticut State Univ., New Haven, CT 06515-1355	1893	$10,954 (S)	$12,860	5-D	10,320	964	51.0
Southern Illinois Univ. Carbondale, Carbondale, IL 62901-4701	1869	$14,864 (S)	$10,622	5-D	11,695	928	47.6
Southern Illinois Univ. Edwardsville, Edwardsville, IL 62026	1957	$12,219 (S)	$10,701	5-D	13,061	881	49.0
Southern Methodist Univ., Dallas, TX 75275	1911	$58,540	$17,110	2-D	11,824	1,151	81.0
Southern Nazarene Univ., Bethany, OK 73008	1899	NA	NA	2-M	3,906	NA	60.0
Southern New Hampshire Univ., Manchester, NH 03106-1045	1932	$9,980	$12,800	1-D	3,305	449	68.0
Southern Oregon Univ., Ashland, OR 97520	1926	$9,615 (S)	$12,255	5-M	6,005	319	46.0
Southern Tech Coll., Fort Myers, FL 33907	1940	NA	NA	3-B	1,259	160	20.0
Southern Univ. & A&M Coll., Baton Rouge, LA 70813	1880	NA	NA	5-D	6,693	423	29.0
Southern Univ. at New Orleans, New Orleans, LA 70126-1009 (4)	1959	NA	NA	5-M	3,141	102	5.2
Southern Utah Univ., Cedar City, UT 84720-2498	1897	$6,770 (A)	$7,520	5-M	11,224	621	44.1
Southern Wesleyan Univ., Central, SC 29630-1020	1906	NA	NA	2-M	1,883	193	39.0
Southwest Baptist Univ., Bolivar, MO 65613-2597	1878	$25,440	$8,040	2-D	3,281	337	47.0
Southwest Minnesota State Univ., Marshall, MN 56258	1963	NA	NA	5-M	6,896	227	43.0
Southwestern Assemblies of God Univ., Waxahachie, TX 75165-5735	1927	$20,952	$7,500	2-M	2,162	148	NA
Southwestern Coll., Winfield, KS 67156-2499	1885	$33,250	$8,500	2-M	1,513	207	42.0
Southwestern Oklahoma State Univ., Weatherford, OK 73096-3098	1901	$7,695 (A)	$6,030	5-D	4,932	295	36.0
Southwestern Univ., Georgetown, TX 78626	1840	$45,120	$12,450	2-B	1,507	154	69.0
Spalding Univ., Louisville, KY 40203-2188	1814	$24,500	$7,400	2-D	2,322	170	47.0
Spelman Coll., Atlanta, GA 30314-4399 (3)	1881	$29,064	$13,865	1-B	2,171	251	75.0
Spring Arbor Univ., Spring Arbor, MI 49283-9799	1873	$28,810	$10,010	2-M	3,333	116	52.0
Spring Hill Coll., Mobile, AL 36608-1791	1830	$40,648	$13,652	2-M	1,317	126	55.7
Springfield Coll., Springfield, MA 01109-3797	1885	$38,565	$12,930	1-D	3,119	398	73.5
Stanford Univ., Stanford, CA 94305-2004	1891	$56,169	$17,255	1-D	17,249	2,517	94.4
State Coll. of Florida Manatee-Sarasota, Bradenton, FL 34206-7046	1957	NA	NA	5-B	9,073	444	NA
State Univ. of New York at Fredonia, Fredonia, NY 14063-1136	1826	$8,717 (S)	$12,830	5-M	4,463	433	64.0
State Univ. of New York at New Paltz, New Paltz, NY 12561	1828	$8,502 (S)	$13,928	5-M	7,757	667	76.0
State Univ. of New York at Oswego, Oswego, NY 13126	1861	$8,717 (S)	$14,603	5-M	7,830	572	67.0

Name, address	Year founded	Tuition & fees	Room & board	Control, degree	Enroll-ment	Faculty	Grad. rate
State Univ. of New York at Plattsburgh, Plattsburgh, NY 12901-2681	1889	$9,144 (S)	$14,225	5-M	5,258	426	68.0%
State Univ. of New York Coll. at Cortland, Cortland, NY 13045	1868	$8,806 (S)	$13,100	5-M	6,834	662	70.7
State Univ. of New York Coll. at Geneseo, Geneseo, NY 14454-1401	1871	$8,927 (S)	$14,018	5-M	5,344	400	79.9
State Univ. of New York Coll. at Old Westbury, Old Westbury, NY 11568-0210.	1965	$8,368 (S)	$11,530	5-M	4,461	351	43.0
State Univ. of New York Coll. at Oneonta, Oneonta, NY 13820-4015	1889	$8,922 (A)	NA	5-M	6,528	479	75.3
State Univ. of New York Coll. at Potsdam, Potsdam, NY 13676	1816	$8,711 (S)	$13,900	5-M	3,339	354	60.5
State Univ. of New York Coll. of Agr & Tech at Cobleskill, Cobleskill, NY 12043	1916	$8,634 (A)	$13,700	5-B	2,208	203	54.0
State Univ. of New York Coll. of Enviral Sci & Tech at Syracuse, NY 13210-2779.	1911	$9,115 (S)	$16,270	5-D	2,256	172	78.0
State Univ. of New York Coll. of Tech at Canton, Canton, NY 13617	1906	$8,660 (S)	$13,200	5-B	3,228	232	53.0
State Univ. of New York Coll. of Tech at Delhi, Delhi, NY 13753.	1913	$8,920 (S)	$12,900	5-M	3,086	223	57.0
State Univ. of New York Downstate Med. Ctr., Brooklyn, NY 11203-2098.	1858	NA	NA	5-D	1,694	981	NA
State Univ. of New York Empire State Coll., Saratoga Springs, NY 12866-4391.	1971	$7,605 (A)	NA	5-M	10,440	795	NA
State Univ. of New York Maritime Coll., Throggs Neck, NY 10465-4198.	1874	$8,508 (S)	$13,256	5-M	1,734	146	62.6
State Univ. of New York Polytechnic Inst., Utica, NY 13502	1966	$8,561 (S)	$14,025	5-D	2,933	274	52.0
State Univ. of New York Upstate Med. Univ., Syracuse, NY 13210.	1950	NA	NA	5-D	1,787	54	NA
Stephen F. Austin State Univ., Nacogdoches, TX 75962.	1923	$7,620 (S)	$9,012	5-D	12,969	758	52.1
Stetson Univ., DeLand, FL 32723	1883	$49,500	$14,540	1-D	4,429	432	65.0
Stevens Inst. of Tech, Hoboken, NJ 07030	1870	$55,952	$16,244	1-D	7,283	391	84.7
Stevenson Univ., Stevenson, MD 21153	1952	$37,142	$13,624	1-M	3,579	380	60.2
Stockton Univ., Galloway, NJ 08205-9441.	1969	$14,048 (S)	$12,496	5-D	9,934	721	77.4
Stonehill Coll., Easton, MA 02357	1948	$44,420	$16,620	2-M	2,542	300	82.0
Stony Brook Univ., State Univ. of New York, Stony Brook, NY 11794	1957	$10,175 (S)	$14,278	5-D	26,814	1,600	76.0
Suffolk Univ., Boston, MA 02108-2770.	1906	$41,908	$18,134	1-D	7,288	650	57.7
Sul Ross State Univ., Alpine, TX 79832.	1920	$8,251 (S)	$9,326	5-M	2,406	180	25.0
Sullivan Univ., Louisville, KY 40205.	1962	NA	NA	3-D	3,323	213	NA
Susquehanna Univ., Selinsgrove, PA 17870	1858	$51,140	$13,680	2-M	2,315	227	71.8
Swarthmore Coll., Swarthmore, PA 19081-1397	1864	$57,256	$16,654	1-B	1,667	224	94.1
Syracuse Univ., Syracuse, NY 13244	1870	$55,926	$16,356	1-D	22,850	1,733	83.0
Tarleton State Univ., Stephenville, TX 76402.	1899	$9,138 (S)	$10,712	5-D	13,176	703	49.1
Taylor Univ., Upland, IN 46989-1001.	1846	$35,305	$9,950	2-M	2,174	207	0.8
Temple Univ., Philadelphia, PA 19122-6096	1884	$19,748 (S)	$12,188	12-D	38,822	2,942	74.0
Tennessee State Univ., Nashville, TN 37209-1561	1912	$7,684 (S)	$7,806	5-D	8,753	658	NA
Tennessee Tech Univ., Cookeville, TN 38505	1915	$8,731 (S)	$9,736	5-D	10,186	645	49.0
Texas A&M Intl. Univ., Laredo, TX 78041	1969	$9,254 (S)	$8,809	5-D	8,305	400	47.0
Texas A&M Univ., College Station, TX 77843	1876	$12,445 (A)	$11,400	5-D	68,390	3,706	81.9
Texas A&M Univ.–Central Texas, Killeen, TX 76549.	2009	$8,696 (S)	$9,136	5-M	2,430	189	NA
Texas A&M Univ.–Comm, Commerce, TX 75429	1889	$8,958 (S)	$8,868	5-D	11,725	660	48.0
Texas A&M Univ.–Corpus Christi, Corpus Christi, TX 78412.	1947	$4,992 (S)	$10,220	5-D	11,452	662	0.4
Texas A&M Univ.–Kingsville, Kingsville, TX 78363	1925	$9,136 (A)	$8,848	5-D	7,479	440	39.0
Texas A&M Univ.–Texarkana, Texarkana, TX 75503	1971	$8,070 (S)	$8,732	5-D	2,066	NA	30.0
Texas Christian Univ., Fort Worth, TX 76129-0002	1873	$51,660	$14,040	2-D	11,024	1,087	83.0
Texas Lutheran Univ., Seguin, TX 78155-5999	1891	$30,860	$10,440	2-M	1,476	135	56.0
Texas Southern Univ., Houston, TX 77004-4584.	1947	NA	NA	5-D	9,034	709	NA
Texas State Univ., San Marcos, TX 78666	1899	$11,550 (S)	$11,336	5-D	38,187	2,077	54.3
Texas Tech Univ., Lubbock, TX 79409	1923	$11,320 (S)	$9,772	5-D	38,742	1,802	59.0
Texas Wesleyan Univ., Fort Worth, TX 76105.	1890	$30,300	$10,559	2-D	2,619	234	30.0
Texas Woman's Univ., Denton, TX 76204 (4)	1901	$9,748 (A)	$9,050	5-D	15,826	912	43.0
The Catholic Univ. of America, Washington, DC 20064.	1887	$49,416	$15,820	2-D	5,771	702	71.0
The Citadel, The Military Coll. of South Carolina, Charleston, SC 29409 (2)	1842	$14,483 (A)	$7,957	5-M	3,767	327	72.0
The Coll. at Brockport, State Univ. of New York, Brockport, NY 14420-2997.	1867	$8,926 (A)	$14,160	5-M	7,924	645	63.9
The Coll. of New Jersey, Ewing, NJ 08628	1855	$16,923 (S)	$14,048	5-M	7,686	853	86.0
The Coll. of New Rochelle, New Rochelle, NY 10805-2308.	1904	$37,760	$14,562	1-M	2,023	365	35.0
The Coll. of St. Rose, Albany, NY 12203-1419	1920	$34,354	$13,158	1-M	4,004	341	61.3
The Coll. of St. Scholastica, Duluth, MN 55811-4199	1912	$39,410	$10,340	2-D	3,906	403	69.0
The Coll. of William & Mary, Williamsburg, VA 23187-8795.	1693	$23,628 (S)	$12,926	5-D	8,773	NA	NA
The Coll. of Wooster, Wooster, OH 44691-2363	1866	$50,250	$11,850	2-B	1,947	217	77.0
The Colorado Coll., Colorado Springs, CO 80903-3294	1874	$60,864	$13,392	1-M	2,124	246	83.1
The Culinary Inst. of America, Hyde Park, NY 12538-1499	1946	$33,690	$11,880	1-M	3,094	211	NA
The Evergreen State Coll., Olympia, WA 98505	1967	$7,674 (S)	$11,346	5-M	2,854	190	NA
The George Washington Univ., Washington, DC 20052	1821	$56,935	$14,300	1-D	27,814	2,658	82.0
The Master's Univ., Santa Clarita, CA 91321-1200	1927	$25,390	$11,200	2-D	1,908	212	50.0
The New School for Public Engagement, New York, NY 10011	1919	NA	NA	1-D	1,448	356	NA
The Ohio State Univ., Columbus, OH 43210	1870	$11,084 (S)	$12,708	5-D	61,391	5,911	85.8
The Ohio State Univ. at Marion, Marion, OH 43302-5695	1958	$7,912 (S)	NA	5-B	1,274	103	7.7
The Ohio State Univ.–Newark campus, Newark, OH 43055-1797.	1957	$7,912 (S)	$10,860	5-M	2,943	174	5.3
The Sage Colls, Troy, NY 12180	1916	$31,883	$13,058	1-D	2,471	279	71.0
The Southern Baptist Theol. Sem., Louisville, KY 40280-0004	1858	NA	NA	2-D	3,190	NA	NA
The Univ. of Akron, Akron, OH 44325	1870	$10,270 (S)	$12,296	5-D	17,599	1,269	45.0
The Univ. of Alabama at Birmingham, Birmingham, AL 35294	1969	$10,710 (S)	$10,910	5-D	22,080	1,180	63.3
The Univ. of Alabama in Huntsville, Huntsville, AL 35899	1950	$11,122 (S)	$10,632	5-D	9,988	619	57.6
The Univ. of Alabama, Tuscaloosa, AL 35487.	1831	$10,780 (S)	$10,836	5-M	38,100	1,955	71.1
The Univ. of Arizona, Tucson, AZ 85721.	1885	$12,379 (A)	$13,050	5-D	45,918	2,488	64.7
The Univ. of Findlay, Findlay, OH 45840-3653	1882	$35,410	$10,200	2-D	4,714	393	64.9
The Univ. of Iowa, Iowa City, IA 52242-1316.	1847	$9,492 (S)	$11,172	5-D	31,240	1,668	72.2
The Univ. of Kansas, Lawrence, KS 66045	1866	$11,166 (S)	$10,350	5-D	27,552	1,632	66.0
The Univ. of Montana Western, Dillon, MT 59725-3598	1893	$5,725 (A)	$8,044	5-B	1,358	91	45.0
The Univ. of North Carolina at Chapel Hill, Chapel Hill, NC 27599	1789	$9,232 (S)	$11,740	5-D	30,151	2,314	90.9
The Univ. of North Carolina at Charlotte, Charlotte, NC 28223-0001	1946	$7,096 (S)	$11,060	5-D	29,615	1,637	64.2
The Univ. of North Carolina at Greensboro, Greensboro, NC 27412-5001	1891	$7,403 (S)	$9,264	5-D	20,196	1,146	58.6
The Univ. of North Carolina at Pembroke, Pembroke, NC 28372-1510	1887	$3,490 (A)	$8,924	5-M	7,698	416	41.0
The Univ. of North Carolina Wilmington, Wilmington, NC 28403-3297	1947	$7,181 (S)	$10,897	5-D	17,499	1,110	71.6
The Univ. of Scranton, Scranton, PA 18510.	1888	$45,790	$15,310	2-D	5,253	465	83.0
The Univ. of South Dakota, Vermillion, SD 57069	1862	$9,332 (A)	$8,410	5-D	9,920	723	58.9
The Univ. of Tampa, Tampa, FL 33606-1490	1931	$30,884	$11,526	1-D	9,628	815	58.0

Name, address	Year founded	Tuition & fees	Room & board	Control, degree	Enrollment	Faculty	Grad. rate
The Univ. of Tennessee at Chattanooga, Chattanooga, TN 37403-2598	1886	$9,656 (S)	$10,159	5-D	11,650	717	48.5%
The Univ. of Tennessee at Martin, Martin, TN 38238	1900	$9,748 (S)	$6,396	5-M	7,296	494	47.2
The Univ. of Tennessee, Knoxville, TN 37996	1794	$13,264 (S)	$11,482	5-D	29,460	1,829	72.2
The Univ. of Texas at Arlington, Arlington, TX 76019	1895	$10,250 (S)	$10,302	5-D	39,740	NA	42.0
The Univ. of Texas at Austin, Austin, TX 78712-1111	1883	$10,824 (S)	$11,812	5-D	51,090	3,104	85.6
The Univ. of Texas at Dallas, Richardson, TX 75080	1969	$13,442 (S)	$11,532	5-D	29,543	1,361	71.4
The Univ. of Texas at El Paso, El Paso, TX 79968-0001	1913	$8,961 (A)	$9,496	5-D	25,177	1,354	37.0
The Univ. of Texas at San Antonio, San Antonio, TX 78249-0617	1969	$9,723 (A)	$7,590	5-D	32,594	1,301	42.0
The Univ. of Texas at Tyler, TX 75799-0001	1971	$8,742 (A)	$9,502	5-D	10,206	529	45.2
The Univ. of Texas Health Sci Ctr. at Houston, Houston, TX 77225-0036	1972	NA	NA	5-D	4,811	128	95.0
The Univ. of Texas Health Sci Ctr. at San Antonio, San Antonio, TX 78229-3900	1976	NA	NA	5-D	3,093	NA	NA
The Univ. of Texas Med. Branch, Galveston, TX 77555	1891	NA	NA	5-D	2,430	NA	NA
The Univ. of Texas of the Permian Basin, Odessa, TX 79762-0001	1969	$9,940 (A)	$9,846	5-M	5,283	280	40.0
The Univ. of Texas Rio Grande Valley, Edinburg, TX 78539	1927	$8,916 (A)	$8,342	5-D	29,113	1,433	0.0
The Univ. of the Arts, Philadelphia, PA 19102-4944	1876	$44,780	$16,322	1-M	1,914	467	62.0
The Univ. of Toledo, Toledo, OH 43606-3390	1872	$10,539 (A)	$12,285	5-D	19,782	1,119	51.2
The Univ. of Tulsa, Tulsa, OK 74104-3189	1894	$43,500	$12,062	1-D	4,387	447	72.3
The Univ. of Virginia's Coll. at Wise, Wise, VA 24293	1954	$10,252 (A)	$10,751	5-B	2,002	183	41.3
The Univ. of West Alabama, Livingston, AL 35470	1835	$10,990 (S)	$7,510	5-D	5,653	314	34.0
Thomas Coll., Waterville, ME 04901-5097	1894	$26,900	$10,850	1-M	1,367	87	45.0
Thomas Edison State Univ., Trenton, NJ 08608	1972	$7,519 (S)	NA	5-D	16,233	NA	NA
Thomas Jefferson Univ., Philadelphia, PA 19107	1824	$43,366	$14,287	1-D	8,105	1,389	69.7
Thomas More Coll., Crestview Hills, KY 41017-3495	1921	$31,200	$8,650	2-M	2,254	139	48.0
Thomas Univ., Thomasville, GA 31792-7499	1950	$16,940	$7,040	1-M	1,596	53	NA
Tiffin Univ., Tiffin, OH 44883-2161	1888	$27,610	$11,700	1-D	3,013	279	39.0
Toccoa Falls Coll., Toccoa Falls, GA 30598	1907	$21,120	$8,500	2-B	1,833	139	45.0
Touro Coll., New York, NY 10010	1971	$20,750	$12,486	1-D	11,631	1,343	62.4
Touro Univ. Worldwide, Los Alamitos, CA 90720	NA	$10,800	NA	1-D	1,304	119	NA
Towson Univ., Towson, MD 21252-0001	1866	$10,198 (S)	$13,446	5-D	22,709	1,764	71.0
Trevecca Nazarene Univ., Nashville, TN 37210-2877	1901	$26,898	$9,100	2-D	4,124	287	54.1
Trine Univ., Angola, IN 46703-1764	1884	$33,490	$6,700	1-D	3,970	124	65.0
Trinity Coll., Hartford, CT 06106-3100	1823	$59,050	$15,300	1-M	2,235	298	84.0
Trinity Intl. Univ., Deerfield, IL 60015-1284	1897	NA	NA	2-D	2,671	82	52.0
Trinity Univ., San Antonio, TX 78212-7200	1869	$46,456	$13,740	2-M	2,692	354	76.0
Trinity Washington Univ., Washington, DC 20017-1094 (3)	1897	NA	NA	2-M	1,630	NA	NA
Troy Univ., Troy, AL 36082	1887	$12,460 (S)	$8,185	5-D	16,436	1,118	48.3
Truett McConnell Univ., Cleveland, GA 30528	1946	$21,938	$8,160	2-M	3,055	NA	NA
Truman State Univ., Kirksville, MO 63501-4221	1867	$8,120 (S)	$9,012	5-M	5,231	344	75.4
Tufts Univ., Medford, MA 02155	1852	$58,578	$15,086	1-D	11,546	1,077	93.0
Tulane Univ., New Orleans, LA 70118-5669	1834	$56,800	$15,774	1-D	11,913	1,269	86.2
Tusculum Coll., Greeneville, TN 37743-9997	1794	$24,860	$9,190	2-M	1,767	110	33.0
Tuskegee Univ., Tuskegee, AL 36088	1881	NA	NA	1-D	2,995	244	46.0
Union Coll., Schenectady, NY 12308-2311	1795	$59,427	$14,583	1-B	2,189	242	82.3
Union Univ., Jackson, TN 38305-3697	1823	$34,780	$10,880	2-D	3,172	223	68.2
United States Air Force Acad., USAF Academy, CO 80840-5025	1954	$0 (C)	NA	4-B	4,336	631	82.0
United States Military Acad., West Point, NY 10996	1802	NA	NA	4-B	4,457	607	85.0
United States Naval Acad., Annapolis, MD 21402-5000	1845	$0 (A)	NA	4-B	4,525	344	91.0
United Talmudical Sem., Brooklyn, NY 11211 (1)	1949	NA	NA	2-M	1,500	NA	NA
Univ. at Albany, State Univ. of New York, Albany, NY 12222-0001	1844	$9,956 (A)	$13,864	5-D	17,944	1,210	65.1
Univ. at Buffalo, the State Univ. of New York, Buffalo, NY 14260	1846	$10,524 (S)	$14,631	5-D	31,923	1,834	75.2
Univ. of Alaska Anchorage, Anchorage, AK 99508	1954	$7,688 (S)	$12,200	5-D	12,821	1,052	NA
Univ. of Alaska Fairbanks, Fairbanks, AK 99775-7520	1917	$10,308 (A)	$10,440	5-D	7,260	855	41.7
Univ. of Alaska Southeast, Juneau, AK 99801	1972	$7,560 (A)	$8,900	5-M	2,150	169	31.6
Univ. of Arkansas, Fayetteville, AR 72701	1871	$9,384 (S)	$11,330	5-D	27,559	1,443	66.2
Univ. of Arkansas at Little Rock, Little Rock, AR 72204-1099	1927	NA	NA	5-D	9,581	NA	40.0
Univ. of Arkansas at Monticello, Monticello, AR 71656	1909	NA	NA	5-M	3,920	234	24.0
Univ. of Arkansas at Pine Bluff, Pine Bluff, AR 71601-2799	1873	NA	NA	5-D	2,658	199	26.0
Univ. of Arkansas for Med. Scis., Little Rock, AR 72205-7199	1879	NA	NA	5-D	2,768	NA	NA
Univ. of Arkansas—Fort Smith, Fort Smith, AR 72913-3649	1928	$7,127 (S)	$8,226	11-M	6,823	412	27.0
Univ. of Baltimore, Baltimore, MD 21201-5779	1925	NA	NA	5-D	3,526	405	NA
Univ. of Bridgeport, Bridgeport, CT 06604	1927	$32,860	NA	1-D	5,434	559	42.0
Univ. of California, Berkeley, Berkeley, CA 94720	1868	$14,253 (S)	$17,220	5-D	43,695	2,525	93.0
Univ. of California, Davis, Davis, CA 95616	1908	$14,653 (S)	$16,100	5-D	38,634	2,089	86.7
Univ. of California, Irvine, Irvine, CA 92697	1965	$13,727 (S)	$16,135	5-D	36,908	1,720	85.0
Univ. of California, Los Angeles, Los Angeles, CA 90095	1919	$13,564 (S)	$16,625	5-D	45,742	3,343	91.4
Univ. of California, Merced, Merced, CA 95343	2005	$13,538 (S)	$17,046	5-D	8,847	420	69.0
Univ. of California, Riverside, Riverside, CA 92521-0102	1954	$15,626 (S)	$17,350	5-D	25,548	1,196	76.0
Univ. of California, San Diego, La Jolla, CA 92093	1959	$14,480 (S)	$14,295	5-D	38,396	1,465	84.0
Univ. of California, Santa Barbara, Santa Barbara, CA 93106-2014	1909	$14,391 (S)	$15,389	5-D	26,314	1,208	88.4
Univ. of California, Santa Cruz, Santa Cruz, CA 95064	1965	$14,054 (S)	$16,916	5-D	19,494	866	75.0
Univ. of Central Arkansas, Conway, AR 72035-0001	1907	$9,188 (S)	$7,198	5-D	11,177	NA	NA
Univ. of Central Florida, Orlando, FL 32816	1963	$6,368 (A)	$9,580	5-D	69,525	2,159	72.0
Univ. of Central Missouri, Warrensburg, MO 64093	1871	$8,043 (S)	$8,962	5-M	11,229	625	51.0
Univ. of Central Oklahoma, Edmond, OK 73034-5209	1890	$7,487 (S)	$8,050	5-M	15,973	1,030	37.4
Univ. of Charleston, Charleston, WV 25304-1099	1888	$30,900	$9,180	1-D	2,718	NA	38.1
Univ. of Chicago, Chicago, IL 60637-1513	1890	$59,298	$17,004	1-D	14,739	1,759	95.0
Univ. of Cincinnati, Cincinnati, OH 45221	1819	$11,010 (S)	$11,530	5-D	39,263	3,708	71.3
Univ. of Colorado Boulder, Boulder, CO 80309	1876	$12,500 (S)	$14,778	5-D	37,650	2,330	69.0
Univ. of Colorado Colorado Springs, Colorado Springs, CO 80918	1965	$10,463 (S)	$10,798	5-D	12,180	792	45.2
Univ. of Colorado Denver, Denver, CO 80217-3364	1912	$11,447 (S)	$12,620	5-D	25,645	NA	45.0
Univ. of Connecticut, Storrs, CT 06269	1881	$17,226 (A)	$13,258	5-D	27,412	1,515	85.0
Univ. of Dallas, Irving, TX 75062-4736	1955	$44,810	$13,080	2-D	2,481	231	71.0
Univ. of Dayton, Dayton, OH 45469	1850	$44,100	$14,050	2-D	11,473	1,015	81.6
Univ. of Delaware, Newark, DE 19716	1743	$14,280 (A)	$13,208	12-D	23,245	1,845	80.8
Univ. of Denver, Denver, CO 80208	1864	$53,775	$14,178	1-D	12,931	1,426	77.0
Univ. of Detroit Mercy, Detroit, MI 48221	1877	$29,416	$10,190	2-D	5,080	770	NA
Univ. of Dubuque, Dubuque, IA 52001-5099	1852	$36,610	$10,500	2-D	2,303	403	42.0
Univ. of Evansville, Evansville, IN 47722	1854	$36,416	$12,460	2-D	2,516	262	73.0
Univ. of Florida, Gainesville, FL 32611	1853	$6,381 (A)	$10,590	5-D	52,218	NA	NA
Univ. of Georgia, Athens, GA 30602	1785	$12,080 (S)	$10,314	5-D	38,920	2,409	87.1
Univ. of Guam, Mangilao, GU 96923	1952	$5,804 (A)	$3,850	7-M	3,563	287	37.9

Name, address	Year founded	Tuition & fees	Room & board	Control, degree	Enroll- ment	Faculty	Grad. rate
Univ. of Hartford, West Hartford, CT 06117-1599	1877	$43,560	$13,200	1-D	6,773	816	61.0%
Univ. of Hawaii at Hilo, Hilo, HI 96720-4091	1970	NA	NA	5-D	3,924	338	38.0
Univ. of Hawaii at Manoa, Honolulu, HI 96822	1907	$12,186 (A)	$13,366	5-D	17,490	1,413	60.5
Univ. of Hawaii–West Oahu, Kapolei, HI 96707	1976	$7,584 (A)	NA	5-B	3,049	NA	28.0
Univ. of Holy Cross, New Orleans, LA 70131-7399	1916	$14,180	NA	2-M	1,298	NA	NA
Univ. of Houston, Houston, TX 77204	1927	$11,276 (S)	$9,368	5-D	46,148	2,406	61.3
Univ. of Houston–Clear Lake, Houston, TX 77058-1002	1971	$7,961 (S)	$5,109	5-D	9,082	494	NA
Univ. of Houston–Downtown, Houston, TX 77002	1974	$8,664 (A)	NA	5-M	14,640	730	28.5
Univ. of Houston–Victoria, Victoria, TX 77901-4450	1973	$307/cr. hr. (A)	NA	5-M	4,407	239	NA
Univ. of Idaho, Moscow, ID 83844-2282	1889	$8,304 (S)	$9,080	5-D	11,926	684	56.0
Univ. of Illinois at Chicago, Chicago, IL 60607-7128	1946	$13,874 (A)	$12,479	5-D	33,390	1,742	61.0
Univ. of Illinois at Springfield, Springfield, IL 62703-5407	1969	$11,813 (S)	$11,660	5-D	4,275	344	54.0
Univ. of Illinois at Urbana–Champaign, Champaign, IL 61820.	1867	$16,210 (A)	$11,672	5-D	49,702	2,464	84.0
Univ. of Indianapolis, Indianapolis, IN 46227-3697	1902	$29,688	$10,288	2-D	5,711	NA	55.0
Univ. of Kentucky, Lexington, KY 40506-0032	1865	$12,360 (S)	$13,210	5-D	29,402	2,033	66.1
Univ. of La Verne, La Verne, CA 91750-4443	1891	$44,550	$13,800	1-D	4,484	534	73.2
Univ. of Louisiana at Lafayette, Lafayette, LA 70504	1898	$10,382 (A)	$10,708	5-D	16,933	848	51.0
Univ. of Louisiana at Monroe, Monroe, LA 71209-0001	1931	$8,734 (S)	$7,868	5-D	8,489	441	47.0
Univ. of Louisville, Louisville, KY 40292-0001	1798	$11,928 (S)	$9,452	5-D	21,670	1,634	58.6
Univ. of Maine at Augusta, Augusta, ME 04330-9410	1965	$8,168 (S)	NA	5-B	4,683	238	26.0
Univ. of Maine at Farmington, Farmington, ME 04938	1863	$9,572 (S)	$10,096	5-M	1,930	199	58.0
Univ. of Maine at Fort Kent, Fort Kent, ME 04743-1292	1878	$8,115 (S)	$8,220	5-B	1,589	86	36.0
Univ. of Maine at Presque Isle, Presque Isle, ME 04769-2888	1903	$8,574 (S)	$8,738	5-B	1,554	95	37.0
Univ. of Maine, Orono, ME 04469	1865	$11,438 (A)	$10,966	5-D	11,561	866	58.0
Univ. of Mary, Bismarck, ND 58504-9652	1959	$20,154	$7,840	2-D	3,779	285	54.0
Univ. of Mary Hardin-Baylor, Belton, TX 76513	1845	$29,800	$8,782	2-D	3,846	281	51.2
Univ. of Mary Washington, Fredericksburg, VA 22401-5358	1908	$13,270 (A)	$11,500	5-M	4,488	395	64.0
Univ. of Maryland Eastern Shore, Princess Anne, MD 21853	1886	$8,740 (A)	$10,280	5-D	2,888	295	41.0
Univ. of Maryland Univ. Coll., Adelphi, MD 20783	1947	$7,560 (S)	NA	5-D	58,281	3,745	NA
Univ. of Maryland, Baltimore Cty, Baltimore, MD 21250	1963	$12,028 (S)	$12,000	5-D	13,602	931	0.7
Univ. of Maryland, Coll. Park, College Park, MD 20742	1856	$10,779 (S)	$12,935	5-D	40,743	2,615	87.1
Univ. of Massachusetts Amherst, Amherst, MA 01003	1863	$16,389 (S)	$13,598	5-D	31,350	1,787	77.0
Univ. of Massachusetts Boston, Boston, MA 02125-3393	1964	$14,613 (S)	$16,902	5-D	15,989	1,135	49.0
Univ. of Massachusetts Dartmouth, North Dartmouth, MA 02747-2300	1895	$14,358 (S)	$14,064	5-D	8,154	599	59.3
Univ. of Massachusetts Lowell, Lowell, MA 01854.	1894	$15,180 (S)	$12,748	5-D	18,355	1,136	66.0
Univ. of Memphis, Memphis, TN 38152	1912	$9,912 (S)	$10,175	5-D	21,685	1,500	53.0
Univ. of Miami, Coral Gables, FL 33124.	1925	$53,682	$15,470	1-D	17,811	1,694	83.0
Univ. of Michigan, Ann Arbor, MI 48109.	1817	$15,558 (S)	$11,996	5-D	48,090	3,562	93.0
Univ. of Michigan–Dearborn, Dearborn, MI 48128	1959	$14,236 (S)	$2,262	5-D	9,195	549	1.0
Univ. of Michigan–Flint, Flint, MI 48502-1950	1956	$12,406 (S)	$9,116	5-D	7,297	550	40.0
Univ. of Minnesota, Crookston, Crookston, MN 56716-5001	1966	$12,116 (A)	$9,020	5-B	2,790	124	50.0
Univ. of Minnesota, Duluth, Duluth, MN 55812-2496	1947	$13,681 (S)	$8,374	5-D	10,858	592	62.0
Univ. of Minnesota, Morris, Morris, MN 56267-2134	1959	$13,578 (S)	$8,632	5-B	1,499	155	58.3
Univ. of Minnesota, Twin Cities campus, Minneapolis, MN 55455-0213	1851	$15,027 (S)	$10,768	5-D	51,327	3,828	83.0
Univ. of Mississippi, University, MS 38677	1844	$8,828 (S)	$10,734	5-D	21,617	1,385	65.8
Univ. of Mississippi Med. Ctr., Jackson, MS 39216-4505	1955	NA	NA	5-D	2,092	836	NA
Univ. of Missouri, Columbia, MO 65211	1839	$10,477 (S)	$10,310	5-D	30,046	1,329	71.0
Univ. of Missouri–Kansas City, Kansas City, MO 64110-2499.	1929	$9,884 (S)	NA	5-D	16,405	1,218	50.0
Univ. of Missouri–St. Louis, St. Louis, MO 63121	1963	$11,079 (S)	$9,550	5-D	16,007	743	52.0
Univ. of Mobile, Mobile, AL 36613	1961	$23,860	$9,700	2-M	1,989	172	45.0
Univ. of Montana, Missoula, MT 59812	1893	$7,354 (S)	$9,966	5-D	11,865	728	48.0
Univ. of Montevallo, Montevallo, AL 35115	1896	$13,710 (A)	$9,810	5-M	2,559	230	55.0
Univ. of Mount Olive, Mount Olive, NC 28365	1951	$20,600	$8,550	2-M	3,371	276	44.0
Univ. of Mount Union, Alliance, OH 44601-3993	1846	$31,700	$10,500	2-D	2,309	253	62.0
Univ. of Nebraska at Kearney, Kearney, NE 68849-0001	1903	$7,701 (S)	$9,942	5-M	6,279	454	59.8
Univ. of Nebraska at Omaha, Omaha, NE 68182	1908	$7,980 (S)	$9,920	5-D	15,153	1,139	53.6
Univ. of Nebraska Med. Ctr., Omaha, NE 68198	1869	NA	NA	5-D	3,625	1,232	NA
Univ. of Nebraska–Lincoln, Lincoln, NE 68588	1869	$9,366 (S)	$11,830	5-D	25,390	1,405	63.0
Univ. of Nevada, Las Vegas, Las Vegas, NV 89154	1957	$7,986 (S)	$10,924	5-D	30,457	1,820	42.0
Univ. of Nevada, Reno, Reno, NV 89557	1874	$8,452 (S)	$10,686	5-D	21,003	1,318	61.0
Univ. of New England, Biddeford, ME 04005-9526	1831	$38,750	$14,410	1-D	7,483	528	67.5
Univ. of New Hampshire, Durham, NH 03824	1866	$18,938 (A)	$12,242	5-D	14,784	997	77.0
Univ. of New Haven, West Haven, CT 06516	1920	$40,440	$16,360	1-D	6,793	652	61.0
Univ. of New Mexico, Albuquerque, NM 87131-2039.	1889	$7,875 (S)	$9,390	5-D	22,793	1,406	53.5
Univ. of New Orleans, New Orleans, LA 70148	1958	$8,772 (S)	$10,712	5-D	7,964	387	32.0
Univ. of North Alabama, Florence, AL 35632-0001	1830	$10,800 (S)	$7,966	5-M	8,046	462	48.6
Univ. of North Carolina at Asheville, Asheville, NC 28804-3299	1927	$7,466 (S)	$9,950	5-M	3,600	323	59.2
Univ. of North Dakota, Grand Forks, ND 58202	1883	$9,737 (S)	$9,544	5-D	13,581	760	0.6
Univ. of North Florida, Jacksonville, FL 32224	1965	$6,389 (S)	$9,921	5-D	17,117	995	61.0
Univ. of North Georgia, Dahlonega, GA 30597	1873	$7,566 (A)	$11,510	5-D	19,748	1,019	58.3
Univ. of North Texas at Dallas, Dallas, TX 75241	2001	$8,140 (A)	$8,948	5-D	4,209	285	NA
Univ. of North Texas, Denton, TX 76203	1890	$303/cr. hr. (A)	NA	5-D	39,192	1,715	57.4
Univ. of Northern Colorado, Greeley, CO 80639	1890	$10,188 (A)	$11,204	5-D	12,862	NA	47.7
Univ. of Northern Iowa, Cedar Falls, IA 50614	1876	$8,938 (S)	$9,160	5-D	10,497	639	67.3
Univ. of Northwestern Ohio, Lima, OH 45805-1498	1920	NA	NA	1-M	3,848	127	57.0
Univ. of Northwestern–St. Paul, St. Paul, MN 55113-1598	1902	$33,200	$10,000	2-M	3,525	292	68.0
Univ. of Notre Dame, Notre Dame, IN 46556	1842	$57,699	$15,984	2-D	12,681	1,396	96.0
Univ. of Oklahoma, Norman, OK 73019-0390	1890	$9,062 (S)	$10,994	5-D	31,207	1,935	70.3
Univ. of Oregon, Eugene, OR 97403	1876	$10,755 (S)	$12,783	5-D	22,644	NA	NA
Univ. of Pennsylvania, Philadelphia, PA 19104	1740	$60,042	$16,784	1-D	22,432	1,960	96.0
Univ. of Phoenix–Bay Area campus, San Jose, CA 95134-1805.	NA	NA	NA	3-M	2,240	318	NA
Univ. of Phoenix–Central Valley campus, Fresno, CA 93720-1552.	2004	NA	NA	3-M	2,235	272	NA
Univ. of Phoenix–Dallas campus, Dallas, TX 75251	2001	NA	NA	3-M	1,371	181	NA
Univ. of Phoenix–Houston campus, Houston, TX 77079-2004	2001	NA	NA	3-M	2,748	325	NA
Univ. of Phoenix–Las Vegas campus, Las Vegas, NV 89135	1994	NA	NA	3-M	3,162	279	NA
Univ. of Phoenix–Online campus, Phoenix, AZ 85034-7209	1989	NA	NA	3-D	292,797	11,477	NA
Univ. of Phoenix–Phoenix campus, Tempe, AZ 85282-2371.	1976	NA	NA	3-M	5,379	985	NA
Univ. of Phoenix–Sacramento Valley campus, Sacramento, CA 95833-4334.	1993	NA	NA	3-M	3,842	518	NA
Univ. of Phoenix–San Diego campus, San Diego, CA 92123	1988	NA	NA	3-M	3,212	399	NA
Univ. of Pikeville, Pikeville, KY 41501	1889	$22,050	$8,050	2-D	2,262	100	28.0
Univ. of Pittsburgh at Bradford, Bradford, PA 16701-2812.	1963	$14,158 (A)	$10,532	12-B	1,326	149	43.2

Name, address	Year founded	Tuition & fees	Room & board	Control, degree	Enroll-ment	Faculty	Grad. rate
Univ. of Pittsburgh at Greensburg, Greensburg, PA 15601-5860	1963	$14,148 (A)	$10,870	12-B	1,439	NA	33.9%
Univ. of Pittsburgh at Johnstown, Johnstown, PA 15904-2990	1927	$14,156 (A)	$10,060	12-B	2,462	149	57.0
Univ. of Pittsburgh, Pittsburgh, PA 15260	1787	$19,718 (A)	$11,250	12-D	28,391	2,388	82.9
Univ. of Portland, Portland, OR 97203-5798	1901	$47,818	$13,968	2-D	4,251	480	82.2
Univ. of Puerto Rico in Aguadilla, Aguadilla, PR 00604	1972	NA	NA	6-B	3,139	155	46.0
Univ. of Puerto Rico in Arecibo, Arecibo, PR 00614	1967	NA	NA	6-B	3,638	231	46.0
Univ. of Puerto Rico in Bayamón, Bayamón, PR 00959	1971	$4,084 (S)	NA	6-B	4,189	227	34.0
Univ. of Puerto Rico in Carolina, Carolina, PR 00984-4800	1974	NA	NA	6-B	3,392	222	48.0
Univ. of Puerto Rico in Cayey, Cayey, PR 00736	1967	NA	NA	6-B	3,830	123	48.0
Univ. of Puerto Rico in Humacao, Humacao, PR 00792	1962	NA	NA	6-B	3,723	250	51.0
Univ. of Puerto Rico in Ponce, Ponce, PR 00732-7186	1970	NA	NA	6-B	2,540	164	44.0
Univ. of Puerto Rico in Utuado, Utuado, PR 00641-2500	1979	NA	NA	6-B	1,623	58	18.0
Univ. of Puerto Rico, Mayagüez campus, Mayagüez, PR 00681-9000	1911	NA	NA	6-D	13,224	501	47.0
Univ. of Puerto Rico, Med. Scis. campus, San Juan, PR 00936-5067 (4)	1950	NA	NA	6-D	2,253	1,147	NA
Univ. of Puerto Rico, Río Piedras campus, San Juan, PR 00931-3300	1903	NA	NA	6-D	14,932	1,271	57.0
Univ. of Puget Sound, Tacoma, WA 98416	1888	$53,800	$13,480	1-D	2,608	291	76.2
Univ. of Redlands, Redlands, CA 92373-0999	1907	$50,980	$14,670	1-D	5,215	NA	72.0
Univ. of Rhode Island, Kingston, RI 02881	1892	$14,566 (S)	$8,010	5-D	18,098	NA	NA
Univ. of Richmond, University of Richmond, VA 23173	1830	$56,860	$13,430	1-D	3,914	600	89.0
Univ. of Rio Grande, Rio Grande, OH 45674	1876	NA	NA	1-M	2,161	175	43.0
Univ. of Rochester, Rochester, NY 14627	1850	$53,825	$15,860	1-D	11,817	940	86.2
Univ. of St. Francis, Fort Wayne, IN 46808-3994	1890	$32,420	$10,490	2-D	2,249	298	52.5
Univ. of St. Francis, Joliet, IL 60435-6169	1920	$35,000	$10,210	2-D	3,079	303	62.0
Univ. of St. Joseph, WeSt. Hartford, CT 06117-2700 (4)	1932	$709/cr. hr.	$3,448	2-D	2,398	301	68.0
Univ. of St. Mary, Leavenworth, KS 66048-5082	1923	$29,930	$8,140	2-D	1,240	159	44.1
Univ. of St. Thomas, Houston, TX 77006-4696	1947	$31,560	$9,470	2-D	3,517	356	67.8
Univ. of St. Thomas, St. Paul, MN 55105-1096	1885	$45,780	$11,162	2-D	9,871	819	76.1
Univ. of San Diego, San Diego, CA 92110-2492	1949	$52,864	$15,156	2-D	9,181	967	81.0
Univ. of San Francisco, San Francisco, CA 94117	1855	$52,482	$15,990	2-D	10,636	1,139	75.0
Univ. of Sioux Falls, Sioux Falls, SD 57105-1699	1883	$19,520	$7,770	2-M	1,675	139	61.6
Univ. of South Alabama, Mobile, AL 36688-0002	1963	$10,070 (A)	$7,800	5-D	14,397	1,060	46.0
Univ. of South Carolina Aiken, Aiken, SC 29801	1961	$10,760 (S)	$7,946	5-M	3,720	302	39.0
Univ. of South Carolina Beaufort, Bluffton, SC 29909	1959	$10,780 (S)	$7,120	5-M	2,119	NA	30.0
Univ. of South Carolina Upstate, Spartanburg, SC 29303-4999	1967	$11,688 (S)	$9,480	5-M	6,306	484	52.0
Univ. of South Carolina, Columbia, SC 29208	1801	$12,688 (S)	$10,670	5-D	35,364	2,235	77.0
Univ. of South Florida Sarasota-Manatee, Sarasota, FL 34243	1956	$5,587 (S)	NA	5-M	2,069	160	NA
Univ. of South Florida, St. Petersburg, St. Petersburg, FL 33701	1965	$5,821 (A)	$11,836	5-M	4,980	NA	37.0
Univ. of South Florida, Tampa, FL 33620-9951	1956	$6,410 (A)	$11,836	5-D	44,231	1,946	75.0
Univ. of Southern California, Los Angeles, CA 90089	1880	$58,195	$15,916	1-D	47,310	3,628	92.0
Univ. of Southern Indiana, Evansville, IN 47712-3590	1965	NA	NA	5-D	8,631	650	49.8
Univ. of Southern Maine, Portland, ME 04103	1878	$9,850 (S)	$9,826	5-D	8,429	824	40.2
Univ. of Southern Mississippi, Hattiesburg, MS 39406-0001	1910	$8,108 (S)	$10,638	5-D	14,133	871	48.9
Univ. of the Cumberlands, Williamsburg, KY 40769-1372	1889	$23,000	$9,000	2-D	7,693	378	37.0
Univ. of the District of Columbia, Washington, DC 20008-1175	1976	$8,252 (S)	NA	9-D	4,803	576	14.0
Univ. of the Incarnate Word, San Antonio, TX 78209-6397	1881	$32,286	$13,014	2-D	8,175	770	52.0
Univ. of the Pacific, Stockton, CA 95211-0197	1851	$49,588	$13,740	1-D	6,447	894	67.0
Univ. of the Sacred Heart, San Juan, PR 00914-0383	1935	NA	NA	2-M	5,666	367	35.3
Univ. of the Scis., Philadelphia, PA 19104-4495	1821	$25,000	NA	1-D	2,664	419	72.0
Univ. of the Virgin Islands, St. Thomas, VI 00802	1962	$5,235 (S)	$9,900	7-D	2,088	195	32.0
Univ. of Utah, Salt Lake City, UT 84112-1107	1850	$9,498 (A)	$10,201	5-D	32,818	2,167	70.0
Univ. of Vermont, Burlington, VT 05405	1791	$19,062 (S)	$13,354	5-D	13,548	804	0.8
Univ. of Virginia, Charlottesville, VA 22903	1819	$18,878 (A)	$12,350	5-D	25,018	1,601	94.6
Univ. of Washington, Bothell, Bothell, WA 98011	1990	$11,390 (S)	$12,636	5-M	5,922	336	69.0
Univ. of Washington, Seattle, WA 98195	1861	$11,465 (S)	$13,296	5-D	47,554	2,445	84.0
Univ. of Washington, Tacoma, Tacoma, WA 98402-3100	1990	$11,639 (S)	$12,636	5-D	5,330	348	56.0
Univ. of West Florida, Pensacola, FL 32514-5750	1963	$6,360 (A)	$10,248	5-D	12,582	620	46.4
Univ. of West Georgia, Carrollton, GA 30118	1933	$7,488 (S)	$10,340	5-D	13,238	723	42.3
Univ. of Wisconsin–Eau Claire, Eau Claire, WI 54702-4004	1916	$8,840 (S)	$8,216	5-D	10,732	611	67.2
Univ. of Wisconsin–Green Bay, Green Bay, WI 54311-7001	1968	$7,878 (A)	$6,790	5-D	9,041	358	50.0
Univ. of Wisconsin–La Crosse, La Crosse, WI 54601-3742	1909	$8,953 (S)	$6,465	5-D	10,558	647	69.0
Univ. of Wisconsin–Madison, Madison, WI 53706-1380	1848	$10,725 (S)	$11,558	5-D	44,411	3,012	87.3
Univ. of Wisconsin–Milwaukee, Milwaukee, WI 53201-0413	1956	$9,588 (A)	$10,792	5-D	26,139	1,646	44.0
Univ. of Wisconsin–Oshkosh, Oshkosh, WI 54901	1871	$7,622 (S)	$7,690	5-D	14,087	578	54.0
Univ. of Wisconsin–Parkside, Kenosha, WI 53141-2000	1968	$7,421 (S)	$8,200	5-M	4,420	282	44.5
Univ. of Wisconsin–Platteville, Platteville, WI 53818-3099	1866	$7,846 (A)	$7,770	5-M	8,240	494	56.1
Univ. of Wisconsin–River Falls, River Falls, WI 54022	1874	NA	NA	5-M	6,012	354	57.5
Univ. of Wisconsin–Stevens Point, Stevens Point, WI 54481-3897	1894	$8,290 (A)	$7,428	5-D	8,247	423	60.0
Univ. of Wisconsin–Stout, Menomonie, WI 54751	1891	$9,463 (A)	$6,944	5-D	8,393	463	58.2
Univ. of Wisconsin–Superior, Superior, WI 54880-4500	1893	$8,132 (S)	$7,280	5-M	2,608	224	48.0
Univ. of Wisconsin–Whitewater, Whitewater, WI 53190-1790	1868	$7,695 (S)	$6,878	5-D	12,448	680	62.5
Univ. of Wyoming, Laramie, WY 82071	1886	$5,791 (A)	$10,615	5-D	12,249	731	59.8
Universidad Adventista de las Antillas, Mayagüez, PR 00681-0118	1957	$6,295	$5,600	2-M	1,214	107	39.0
Universidad del Este, Carolina, PR 00984	1949	NA	NA	1-M	13,058	NA	25.0
Universidad del Turabo, Gurabo, PR 00778-3030	1972	NA	NA	1-D	17,509	1,171	19.0
Universidad Metropolitana, San Juan, PR 00928-1150	1980	NA	NA	1-D	13,919	1,250	26.0
Upper Iowa Univ., Fayette, IA 52142-1857	1857	$30,450	$8,460	1-M	4,279	NA	47.0
Urbana Univ., Urbana, OH 43078-2091	1850	NA	NA	1-M	1,551	120	NA
Ursinus Coll., Collegeville, PA 19426	1869	$53,610	$13,120	1-B	1,435	171	76.8
Utah State Univ., Logan, UT 84322	1888	$7,860 (S)	$5,960	5-D	27,810	1,282	54.0
Utah Valley Univ., Orem, UT 84058-5999	1941	$5,726 (S)	NA	5-M	41,728	1,914	29.0
Utica Coll., Utica, NY 13502-4892	1946	$22,110	$11,670	1-D	4,947	477	54.0
Valdosta State Univ., Valdosta, GA 31698	1906	$6,583 (A)	$8,332	5-D	11,270	565	39.9
Valencia Coll., Orlando, FL 32802-3028	1967	$2,473 (S)	NA	5-B	47,940	NA	NA
Valley City State Univ., Valley City, ND 58072	1890	$7,707 (S)	$6,610	5-M	1,665	122	50.0
Valparaiso Univ., Valparaiso, IN 46383	1859	$43,286	$12,620	2-D	3,519	396	71.3
Vanderbilt Univ., Nashville, TN 37240-1001	1873	$55,032	$17,670	1-D	13,131	1,233	93.0
Vanguard Univ. of Southern California, Costa Mesa, CA 92626	1920	$36,550	$12,222	2-M	2,169	240	61.0
Vassar Coll., Poughkeepsie, NY 12604	1861	$58,770	$14,220	1-M	2,441	355	91.0
Vaughn Coll. of Aeronautics & Tech, Flushing, NY 11369 (2)	1932	$26,640	$14,724	1-M	1,545	184	52.0
Vermont Tech Coll., Randolph Center, VT 05061-0500	1866	$16,471 (S)	$11,694	5-M	1,679	214	0.5
Villanova Univ., Villanova, PA 19085-1699	1842	$55,280	$14,444	2-D	10,848	1,066	89.8

Name, address	Year founded	Tuition & fees	Room & board	Control, degree	Enroll-ment	Faculty	Grad. rate
Virginia Commonwealth Univ., Richmond, VA 23284-9005	1838	$14,490 (S)	$10,428	5-D	30,103	2,133	67.0%
Virginia Military Inst., Lexington, VA 24450	1839	$18,862 (A)	$9,482	5-B	1,685	211	77.9
Virginia Polytechnic Inst. & State Univ., Blacksburg, VA 24061	1872	$14,079 (S)	$9,556	5-D	36,383	2,268	86.0
Virginia State Univ., Petersburg, VA 23806-0001	1882	$9,154 (S)	$11,544	5-D	4,584	355	44.0
Virginia Union Univ., Richmond, VA 23220-1170.	1865	$17,448	$8,598	2-D	1,922	138	32.0
Virginia Wesleyan Univ., Virginia Beach, VA 23455.	1961	$36,910	$10,338	2-M	1,487	131	46.8
Viterbo Univ., La Crosse, WI 54601-4797	1890	$29,350	$9,670	2-D	2,592	296	54.0
Wagner Coll., Staten Island, NY 10301-4495.	1883	$49,010	$14,800	1-D	2,160	302	73.0
Wake Forest Univ., Winston-Salem, NC 27109	1834	$57,760	$9,848	1-D	8,495	824	88.3
Walden Univ., Minneapolis, MN 55401	1970	NA	NA	3-D	52,799	2,754	NA
Waldorf Univ., Forest City, IA 50436	1903	$22,076	$7,524	2-M	2,487	171	30.0
Walla Walla Univ., College Place, WA 99324	1892	$29,931	$8,376	2-M	1,864	189	59.3
Walsh Coll. of Accountancy & Bus Admin, Troy, MI 48083	1922	$18,309	NA	1-D	1,811	156	NA
Walsh Univ., North Canton, OH 44720-3396	1958	$29,980	$10,680	2-D	2,694	280	62.0
Wartburg Coll., Waverly, IA 50677-0903	1852	$45,680	$9,592	2-M	1,505	155	62.4
Washburn Univ., Topeka, KS 66621	1865	$8,870 (S)	$9,144	10-D	6,285	469	28.3
Washington Adventist Univ., Takoma Park, MD 20912	1904	NA	NA	2-M	1,493	134	26.0
Washington & Jefferson Coll., Washington, PA 15301	1781	$49,338	$13,044	1-M	1,357	NA	NA
Washington & Lee Univ., Lexington, VA 24450	1749	$2,006/sem. hr.	$15,810	1-D	2,264	321	94.0
Washington Coll., Chestertown, MD 21620-1197	1782	$49,768	$12,722	1-B	1,288	158	73.4
Washington State Univ., Pullman, WA 99164	1890	$11,841 (S)	$11,648	5-D	21,259	1,830	61.0
Washington State Univ.–Global campus, Pullman, WA 99164-5220	NA	NA	NA	5-M	3,007	NA	NA
Washington State Univ.–Spokane, Spokane, WA 99210-1495	1989	$10,719 (S)	NA	5-D	1,685	NA	94.0
Washington State Univ.–Tri-Cities, Richland, WA 99354	1989	$10,765 (S)	$11,648	5-D	1,813	NA	50.0
Washington State Univ.–Vancouver, Vancouver, WA 98686	1989	$10,552 (S)	NA	5-D	3,585	NA	63.0
Washington Univ. in St. Louis, St. Louis, MO 63130-4899	1853	$57,386	$17,402	1-D	16,191	1,510	95.0
Wayland Baptist Univ., Plainview, TX 79072-6998	1908	$23,298	$7,722	2-D	4,827	537	19.5
Wayne State Coll., Wayne, NE 68787	1910	$6,989 (S)	$7,668	5-M	3,890	215	51.0
Wayne State Univ., Detroit, MI 48202	1868	NA	NA	5-D	26,844	1,763	47.6
Waynesburg Univ., Waynesburg, PA 15370-1222	1849	$26,640	$10,890	2-D	1,628	219	66.0
Weber State Univ., Ogden, UT 84408-1001	1889	$5,967 (S)	$8,400	5-D	29,843	1,539	31.3
Webster Univ., St. Louis, MO 63119-3194	1915	$28,600	$11,380	1-D	9,717	520	58.0
Wellesley Coll., Wellesley, MA 02481 (3)	1870	$58,448	$17,772	1-B	2,519	346	91.0
Wentworth Inst. of Tech, Boston, MA 02115-5998	1904	$34,970	$14,190	1-M	4,453	381	66.0
Wesley Coll., Dover, DE 19901-3875.	1873	NA	NA	2-M	1,770	177	32.0
Wesleyan Univ., Middletown, CT 06459.	1831	$57,004	$15,724	1-D	3,230	430	92.0
West Chester Univ. of Pennsylvania, West Chester, PA 19383.	1871	$10,421 (S)	$9,326	5-D	17,669	995	76.6
West Coast Univ., North Hollywood, CA 91606	1909	NA	NA	3-M	1,792	NA	NA
West Liberty Univ., West Liberty, WV 26074	1837	$7,990 (A)	$9,614	5-M	2,496	NA	NA
West Texas A&M Univ., Canyon, TX 79015	1909	$8,688 (A)	$7,196	5-D	10,029	483	54.0
West Virginia State Univ., Institute, WV 25112-1000	1891	$8,750 (S)	$12,486	5-B	3,692	193	26.3
West Virginia Univ. Inst. of Tech, Beckley, WV 25801	1895	$7,560 (S)	$11,628	5-B	1,755	124	21.5
West Virginia Univ., Morgantown, WV 26506.	1867	$8,972 (S)	$11,062	5-D	26,839	NA	NA
West Virginia Wesleyan Coll., Buckhannon, WV 26201.	1890	$31,640	$8,856	2-M	1,449	150	49.6
Westcliff University, Irvine, CA 92606	1993	$54,085	$9,500	3-D	2,608	147	NA
Western Carolina Univ., Cullowhee, NC 28723	1889	$1,000 (S)	NA	5-D	12,167	772	57.6
Western Connecticut State Univ., Danbury, CT 06810-6885	1903	$11,781 (S)	$13,921	5-D	5,631	650	52.4
Western Governors Univ., Salt Lake City, UT 84107	1998	NA	NA	1-M	57,821	1,654	NA
Western Illinois Univ., Macomb, IL 61455-1390	1899	$11,666 (S)	$9,800	5-D	8,294	587	50.4
Western Kentucky Univ., Bowling Green, KY 42101	1906	$10,802 (A)	$8,432	5-D	18,171	1,044	51.6
Western Michigan Univ., Kalamazoo, MI 49008.	1903	$13,017 (S)	$10,567	5-D	22,562	1,463	52.6
Western New England Univ., Springfield, MA 01119	1919	$39,226	$14,244	1-D	3,833	338	64.9
Western New Mexico Univ., Silver City, NM 88062-0680	1893	$8,609 (S)	$11,390	5-M	3,193	225	NA
Western Oregon Univ., Monmouth, OR 97361	1856	$9,540 (S)	$10,415	5-M	4,929	379	41.3
Western State Colorado Univ., Gunnison, CO 81231	1901	$10,437 (S)	$9,704	5-M	3,493	187	51.0
Western Washington Univ., Bellingham, WA 98225-5996	1893	$8,341 (S)	$12,037	5-D	16,142	984	68.0
Westfield State Univ., Westfield, MA 01086	1839	$10,849 (S)	$11,453	5-M	5,810	528	61.1
Westminster Coll., New Wilmington, PA 16172-0001	1852	$36,806	$11,130	2-M	1,254	144	69.5
Westminster Coll., Salt Lake City, UT 84105-3697	1875	$37,960	$11,097	1-D	2,215	384	58.0
Westmont Coll., Santa Barbara, CA 93108-1099.	1937	$46,594	$14,646	2-B	1,277	154	78.0
Wheaton Coll., Norton, MA 02766	1834	$56,366	$14,378	1-B	1,774	187	75.0
Wheaton Coll., Wheaton, IL 60187-5593	1860	$39,100	$10,990	2-D	3,004	343	88.8
Wheeling Jesuit Univ., Wheeling, WV 26003-6295	1954	$29,290	$9,900	2-D	1,289	142	58.0
Whitman Coll., Walla Walla, WA 99362-2083	1859	$53,820	$13,512	1-B	1,475	209	87.4
Whittier Coll., Whittier, CA 90608-0634	1887	$49,314	NA	1-D	1,833	165	72.0
Whitworth Univ., Spokane, WA 99251-0001	1890	$46,250	$12,150	2-M	2,776	NA	75.0
Wichita State Univ., Wichita, KS 67260	1895	$8,299 (S)	$12,620	5-D	16,052	826	50.0
Widener Univ., Chester, PA 19013-5792	1821	$48,740	$14,812	1-D	6,601	NA	57.0
Wilkes Univ., Wilkes-Barre, PA 18766-0002	1933	$37,622	$15,108	1-D	4,680	448	63.0
Willamette Univ., Salem, OR 97301-3931	1842	$53,624	$13,328	2-D	2,265	255	70.0
William Carey Univ., Hattiesburg, MS 39401	1906	NA	NA	2-M	3,248	NA	NA
William Paterson Univ. of New Jersey, Wayne, NJ 07470-8420	1855	$13,370 (A)	$11,900	5-D	10,105	1,055	55.0
William Penn Univ., Oskaloosa, IA 52577-1799.	1873	$26,600	$7,176	2-M	1,261	153	34.0
William Woods Univ., Fulton, MO 65251-1098.	1870	$24,185	$9,700	2-D	2,281	240	59.0
Williams Coll., Williamstown, MA 01267.	1793	$59,660	$15,000	1-M	2,134	363	95.0
Wilmington Coll., Wilmington, OH 45177	1870	$500/cr. hr.	NA	2-M	1,231	101	55.0
Wilmington Univ., New Castle, DE 19720-6491	1967	$8,978	NA	1-D	14,118	2,466	28.0
Wingate Univ., Wingate, NC 28174	1896	$38,896	$9,910	2-D	6,445	366	54.0
Winona State Univ., Winona, MN 55987	1858	$9,666 (S)	$9,086	5-D	7,596	463	59.3
Winston-Salem State Univ., Winston-Salem, NC 27110-0003.	1892	$8,490 (S)	$9,586	5-M	6,427	425	48.0
Winthrop Univ., Rock Hill, SC 29733	1886	$15,666 (S)	$9,340	5-M	5,813	563	56.3
Wittenberg Univ., Springfield, OH 45501-0720	1845	$41,476	$10,830	2-M	1,619	189	62.0
Wofford Coll., Spartanburg, SC 29303-3663	1854	$47,650	$13,790	2-B	1,667	166	84.6
Woodbury Univ., Burbank, CA 91504-1052	1884	$42,596	$13,331	1-M	1,236	214	54.2
Worcester Polytechnic Inst., Worcester, MA 01609-2280	1865	$54,146	$15,838	1-D	6,894	502	89.0
Worcester State Univ., Worcester, MA 01602-2597.	1874	$10,161 (S)	$12,360	5-M	6,204	444	57.6
Wright State Univ., Dayton, OH 45435.	1964	$9,578 (S)	$12,084	5-D	12,618	NA	44.0
Xavier Univ. of Louisiana, New Orleans, LA 70125	1925	$25,185	$10,000	2-D	3,325	272	51.3
Xavier Univ., Cincinnati, OH 45207	1831	$42,460	$13,310	2-D	6,993	824	73.0
Yale Univ., New Haven, CT 06520.	1701	$57,700	$17,200	1-D	13,609	1,871	97.0
Yeshiva Univ., New York, NY 10033-3201	1886	$44,900	$12,500	1-D	5,213	674	82.0
York Coll. of Pennsylvania, York, PA 17403-3651	1787	$21,790	$11,890	1-D	4,305	443	63.0
York Coll. of the City Univ. of New York, Jamaica, NY 11451	1967	$7,157 (S)	NA	11-M	8,360	NA	30.0
Youngstown State Univ., Youngstown, OH 44555-0001	1908	$9,279 (S)	$9,700	5-D	12,150	989	41.4

DIRECTORY

Associations and Organizations

Source: World Almanac research

Selected list, generally by category and first distinctive key word in each title. Listed by acronym when that is the official name. Year established is in parentheses. Entries for religious organizations include addresses and leadership information for 2020.

Academic and Educational

Academies, Natl. (1863): (202) 334-2000; www.nationalacademies.org

African American Life and History, Assn. for the Study of (1915): (202) 238-5910; www.asalh.org

Alpha Delta Kappa (1947): (816) 363-5525; www.alphadeltakappa.org

AMIDEAST (America-Mideast Educational and Training Services, Inc.) (1951): (202) 776-9600; www.amideast.org

Anthropological Assn., American (1902): (703) 528-1902; www.americananthro.org

Archaeological Institute of America (1879): (857)-305-9350; www.archaeological.org

Arts, Americans for the (1960): (202) 371-2830; www.americansforthearts.org

Arts and Sciences, American Academy of (1780): (617) 576-5000; www.amacad.org

Beta Gamma Sigma Inc. (1913): (314) 432-5650; www.betagammasigma.org

Beta Sigma Phi Intl. (1931): (816) 444-6800; bspinternational.org

Biological Sciences, American Institute of (1947): (703) 674-2500; www.aibs.org

Classical Studies, Society for (fmr. American Philological Assn.) (1869): (212) 992-7828; www.classicalstudies.org

College Board (1900): (212) 713-8000; www.collegeboard.org

Colleges and Universities, Assn. of American (1915): (202) 387-3760; www.aacu.org

Community Colleges, American Assn. of (1920): (202) 728-0200; www.aacc.nche.edu

Consumer Interests, American Council on (1953): (727) 493-2131; www.consumerinterests.org

Delta Kappa Gamma Society Intl. (1929): (512) 478-5748; www.dkg.org

Education, American Council on (1918): (202) 939-9300; www.acenet.edu

Education, Council for Advancement and Support of (1974): (202) 328-2273; www.case.org

Education of Young Children, Natl. Assn. for the (1926): (202) 232-8777; www.naeyc.org

Educators for World Peace, Intl. Assn. of (1973): (256) 534-5501

English-Speaking Union of the U.S. (1920): (212) 818-1200; www.esuus.org

Entomological Society of America (1889): (301) 731-4535; www.entsoc.org

Family Relations, Natl. Council on (1938): (888) 781-9331; www.ncfr.org

Foreign Study, American Institute for (1964): (866) 906-2437; www.aifs.com

Freedom of Information Coalition, Natl. (1958): (352) 294-7082; www.nfoic.org

French Institute/Alliance Française (1971): (212) 355-6100; www.fiaf.org

Genealogical Society, Natl. (1903): (703) 525-0050; www.ngsgenealogy.org

Genetic Assn., American (1914): (541) 264-5612; www.theaga.org

Geological Society of America (1888): (303) 357-1000; www.geosociety.org

Hemispheric Affairs, Council on (1975): (202) 223-4975; www.coha.org

Industrial and Applied Mathematics, Society for (1952): (215) 382-9800; www.siam.org

Intl. Education, Institute of (1919): (212) 883-8200; www.iie.org

Intl. Educational Exchange, Council on (1947): (207) 553-4000; www.ciee.org

Intl. Law, American Society of (1906): (202) 939-6000; www.asil.org

Irish American Cultural Inst. (1962): (973) 605-1991; www.iaci-usa.org

IRTS Foundation (fmr. Intl. Radio and TV Society Foundation) (1939): (212) 867-6650; www.irts.org

Law Libraries, American Assn. of (1906): (312) 939-4764; www.aallnet.org

Learned Societies, American Council of (1919): (212) 697-1505; www.acls.org

Libraries Assn., Special (1909): (703) 647-4900; www.sla.org

Linguistic Society of America (1924): (202) 835-1714; www.linguisticsociety.org

Literacy Assn., Intl. (fmr. Intl. Reading Assn.) (1956): (302) 731-1600; www.literacyworldwide.org

Mathematical Society, American (1888): (401) 455-4000; www.ams.org

Mensa, Ltd., American (1960): (817) 607-0060; www.us.mensa.org

Meteorological Society, American (1919): (617) 227-2425; www.ametsoc.org

Metric Assn., Inc., U.S. (1916): www.us-metric.org

Microbiology, American Society for (1899): (202) 737-3600; www.asm.org

Modern Language Assn. of America (1883): (646) 576-5000; www.mla.org

Museums, American Alliance of (1906): (202) 289-1818; www.aam-us.org

Music Education, Natl. Assn. for (fmr. Music Educators Natl. Conference) (1907): (703) 860-4000; www.nafme.org

Musicological Society, American (1934): (877) 679-7648; www.amsmusicology.org

Negro College Fund, United (1944): (800) 331-2244; www.uncf.org

Oriental Society, American (1842): (734) 647-4760; www.americanorientalsociety.org

ORT America (1922): (212) 505-7700; www.ortamerica.org

PEN American Center (1922): (212) 334-1660; www.pen.org

Phi Beta Kappa Society (1776): (202) 265-3808; www.pbk.org

Phi Theta Kappa Honor Society (1918): (800) 946-9995; www.ptk.org

Philosophical Assn., American (1900): (302) 831-1112; www.apaonline.org

Physics, American Inst. of (1931): (301) 209-3100; www.aip.org

Physiological Society, American (1887): (301) 634-7164; www.the-aps.org

Poetry Society of America (1910): (212) 254-9628; www.poetrysociety.org

Poets, Academy of American (1934): (212) 274-0343; www.poets.org

Political Science, Academy of (1880): (212) 870-2500; www.psqonline.org

Religion, American Academy of (1909): (404) 727-3049; www.aarweb.org

Science, American Assn. for the Advancement of (1848): (202) 326-6400; www.aaas.org

Science Fiction Society, World (1939): www.wsfs.org

Sciences, Natl. Academy of (1863): (202) 334-2000; www.nasonline.org

Sigma Beta Delta (1994): (314) 516-4723; www.sigmabetadelta.org

Sociological Assn., American (1905): (202) 383-9005; www.asanet.org

Tau Beta Pi Assn. (1885): (865) 546-4578; www.tbp.org

Teach For America (1990): (212) 279-2080; www.teachforamerica.org

Theological Schools in the U.S. and Canada, Assn. of (1918): (412) 788-6505; www.ats.edu

Theosophical Society in America (1875): (630) 668-1571; www.theosophical.org

Universities, Assn. of American (1900): (202) 408-7500; www.aau.edu

World Learning (1932): (802) 257-7751; www.worldlearning.org

Animal Welfare and Environment

Animal Welfare Institute (1951): (202)337-2332; www.awionline.org

Animals, American Society for the Prevention of Cruelty to (ASPCA) (1866): (212) 876-7700; www.aspca.org

Animals, People for the Ethical Treatment of (PETA) (1980): (757) 622-7382; www.peta.org

Appalachian Trail Conservancy (1925): (304) 535-6331; www.appalachiantrail.org

Audubon Society, Natl. (1905): (212) 979-3000; www.audubon.org

Cat Fanciers' Assn., Inc., The (1906): (330) 680-4070; www.cfa.org

Conservation Intl. (1987): (703) 341-2400; www.conservation.org

Defenders of Wildlife (1947): (800) 385-9712; www.defenders.org

Ducks Unlimited (1937): (901) 758-3825; www.ducks.org

Forest History Society (1946): (919) 682-9319; www.foresthistory.org

Foresters, Society of American (1900): (301) 897-8720; www.eforester.org

Friends of the Earth (1969): (202) 783-7400; www.foe.org

Garden Club of America (1913): (212) 753-8287; www.gcamerica.org

Garden Clubs, Inc., Natl. (1929): (314) 776-7574; www.gardenclub.org

Geographic Society, Natl. (1888): (202) 857-7000; www.nationalgeographic.org

Green Mountain Club (1910): (802) 244-7037; www.greenmountainclub.org

Greenpeace (1971): (202) 462-1177; www.greenpeace.org

Hiking Society, American (1976): (301) 565-6704; www.americanhiking.org

Horse Council, American (1969): (202) 296-4031; www.horsecouncil.org

Humane Society of the U.S., The (1954): (202) 452-1100; www.humanesociety.org

Natural Resources Defense Council (1970): (212) 727-2700; www.nrdc.org

Nature Conservancy, The (1951): (703) 841-5300; www.nature.org

Ocean Conservancy (1972): (202) 429-5609; www.oceanconservancy.org

Ornithological Society, American (fmr. Amer. Ornithologists' Union) (1883): (312) 665-7936; www.americanornithology.org

Recreation and Park Assn., Natl. (1965): (800) 626-6772; www.nrpa.org

Recycling Coalition, Inc., Natl. (1978): (202) 618-2107; www.nrcrecycles.org

Rose Society, American (1892): (318) 938-5402; www.rose.org

Save the Redwoods League (1918): (415) 362-2352; www.savetheredwoods.org

Sierra Club (1892): (415) 977-5500; www.sierraclub.org

Water Environment Federation (1928): (800) 666-0206; www.wef.org

Wildflower Center, Lady Bird Johnson (1982): (512) 232-0100; www.wildflower.org

Wildlife Federation, Natl. (1936): (800) 822-9919; www.nwf.org

World Wildlife Fund (1961): (202) 293-4800; www.worldwildlife.org

Children and Social Services

Big Brothers Big Sisters of America (1904): (813) 720-8778; www.bbbs.org

Boy Scouts of America: see Scouts BSA

Boys & Girls Clubs of America (1906): (404) 487-5700; www.bgca.org

Camp Fire (fmr. Camp Fire Boys & Girls) (1910): (816) 285-2010; www.campfire.org

Child Welfare League of America (1920): (202) 688-4200; www.cwla.org

Children's Book Council, The (1945): (212) 966-1990; www.cbcbooks.org

Feeding America (fmr. America's Second Harvest) (1976): (800) 771-2303; www.feedingamerica.org

4-H Council, Natl. (1914): (301) 961-2800; www.4-h.org

Future Business Leaders of America-Phi Beta Lambda, Inc. (1942): (800) 325-2946; www.fbla-pbl.org

Future Farmers of America Org., Natl. (1928): (317) 802-6060; www.ffa.org

Gifted Children, Natl. Assn. for the (1954): (202) 785-4268; www.nagc.org

Girl Scouts of the USA (1912): (212) 852-8000; www.girlscouts.org

Honor Society, Natl. (1921): (703) 860-0200; www.nhs.us

Junior Achievement USA® (1919): (719) 540-8000; www.juniorachievement.org

Junior Auxiliaries, Inc., Natl. Assn. of (1941): (662) 332-3000; www.najanet.org
Junior Chamber Intl. USA (1914): (636) 778-3010; www.jciusa.org
Junior Honor Society, Natl. (1929): (703) 860-0200; www.njhs.us
Missing and Exploited Children, Natl. Center for (1984): (703) 224-2150; www.missingkids.org
Pilot Intl. (1921): (478) 477-1208; www.pilotinternational.org
Scouts BSA (fmr. Boy Scouts of America, as of Feb. 2019) (1910), (972) 580-2000; www.scouting.org
Student Council, Natl. (1931): (703) 860-0200; www.natstuco.org

Fraternal

Eagles, Fraternal Order of (1898): (614) 883-2200; www.foe.com
Eastern Star, General Grand Chapter, Order of the (1876): (202) 667-4737; www.easternstar.org
Elks of the USA, Benevolent and Protective Order of (1868): (773) 755-4700; www.elks.org
Freemasonry, Scottish Rite of, Supreme Council, 33° Northern Masonic Jurisdiction (1813): (781) 862-4410; www.scottishritenmj.org
Freemasonry, Scottish Rite of, Supreme Council, 33° Southern Jurisdiction (1802): (202) 232-3579; scottishrite.org
Kiwanis Intl. (1915): (317) 875-8755; www.kiwanis.org
Knights of Columbus (1882): (203) 752-4000; www.kofc.org
Knights of Pythias, Order of (1864): (781) 341-2422; www.pythias.org
Lions Clubs Intl. (1917): (630) 571-5466; www.lionsclubs.org
Moose Intl., Inc. (1888): (630) 859-2000; www.mooseintl.org
Odd Fellows, Independent Order of (1819): (336) 725-5955; www.ioof.org
Rotary Intl. (1905): (847) 866-3000; www.rotary.org
Shriners Intl. (1872): (813) 281-0300; www.shrinersinternational.org
Sons and Daughters of Italy in America, Order (1905): (202) 547-2900; www.osia.org
Sons of Norway (1895): (612) 827-3611; www.sofn.com
Woodmen of America, Modern (1883): (800) 447-9811; www.modernwoodmen.org

Historical

American Battlefield Trust (1987): (202) 367-1861; www.battlefields.org
Colonial Dames XVII Century, Natl. Soc. (1915): (202) 293-1700; www.colonialdames17c.org
Daughters of the American Revolution (1890): (202) 628-1776; www.dar.org
Daughters of the Confederacy, United (1894): (804) 355-1636; www.hqudc.org
Historic Preservation, Natl. Trust for (1949): (202) 588-6000; www.saving places.org
Historical Assn., American (1884): (202) 544-2422; www.historians.org
Lewis and Clark Trail Heritage Foundation (1969): (406) 454-1234; lewisandclark.org
Mayflower Descendants, General Soc. of (1897): (508) 746-3188; www.themayflowersociety.org
Pilgrims, Natl. Soc. Sons and Daughters of the (1908): www.nationalsddp.org
Railway Historical Society, Natl. (1935): (215) 557-6606; www.nrhs.com
Sons of the American Revolution (1889): (502) 589-1776; www.sar.org
Sons of Confederate Veterans (1896): (800) 380-1896; www.scv.org
State and Local History, American Assn. for (1940): (615) 320-3203; www.aaslh.org
Supreme Court Historical Society (1974): (202) 543-0400; www.supremecourthistory.org
Theodore Roosevelt Assn. (1920): (516) 921-6319; www.theodoreroosevelt.org
Thoreau Society (1941): (978) 369-5310; www.thoreausociety.org
Titanic Historical Society, Inc. (1963): (413) 543-4770; www.titanichistoricalsociety.org

Victorian Society in America (1966): (215) 636-9872; www.victoriansociety.org

Industrial and Trade

Aerospace Industries Assn. (1919): (703) 358-1000; www.aia-aerospace.org
Better Business Bureaus, Council of (1912): (508) 652-4800; www.bbb.org
Chamber of Commerce, U.S. (1912): (202) 659-6000; www.uschamber.com
Chemistry Council, American (1872): (202) 249-7000; www.americanchemistry.com
Construction Specifications Institute (1948): (800) 689-2900; www.csiresources.org
CropLife America (1933): (202) 296-1585; www.croplifeamerica.org
Electrical Manufacturers Assn., Natl. (1926): (703) 841-3200; www.nema.org
Fire Protection Assn., Natl. (NFPA) (1896): (617) 770-3000; www.nfpa.org
Fisheries Soc., American (1870): (301) 897-8616; www.fisheries.org
Foreign Trade Council, Natl. (1914): (202) 887-0278; www.nftc.org
Funeral Consumers Alliance (1963): (802) 865-8300; www.funerals.org
Hotel & Lodging Assn., American (1910): (202) 289-3100; www.ahla.com
Insurance Assn., American Property Casualty (1866): (847) 297-7800; www.pciaa.net
Magazine Media, Assn. of (1919): (212) 872-3700; www.magazine.org
Manufacturers, Natl. Assn. of (1895): (202) 637-3000; www.nam.org
News Media Alliance (fmr. Newspaper Assn. of America) (1992): (571) 366-1000; www.newsmediaalliance.org
Nuclear Society, American (1954): (708) 352-6611; www.ans.org
Orchestras, League of American (1942): (212) 262-5161; www.americanorchestras.org
Petroleum Institute, American (1919): (202) 682-8000; www.api.org
Printing Industries of America, Inc. (1887): (412) 741-6860; www.printing.org
Publishers, Assn. of American (1970): (202) 347-3375; www.publishers.org
Retail Federation, Natl. (1908): (202) 783-7971; www.nrf.com
Safety Council, Natl. (1913): (630) 285-1121; www.nsc.org
Shipbuilders Council of America (1920): (202) 737-3234; www.shipbuilders.org
Small Business Assn., Natl. (1937): (800) 345-6728; www.nsba.biz
Software & Information Industry Assn. (1999): (202) 289-7442; www.siia.net
Tall Buildings and Urban Habitat, Council on (1969): (312) 283-5645; www.ctbuh.org
Toy Assn., Inc. (1916): (212) 675-1141; www.toyassociation.org
Water Works Assn., American (1881): (303) 794-7711; www.awwa.org
Zoos & Aquariums, Assn. of (1924): (301) 562-0777; www.aza.org

Lifestyle and Travel

AAA (American Automobile Assn.) (1902): (407) 444-7000; www.aaa.com
AARP (fmr. American Assn. of Retired Persons) (1958): (888) 687-2277; www.aarp.org
AFS Intercultural Programs USA (1947): (800) 237-4636; www.afsusa.org
Aircraft Owners and Pilots Assn. (1939): (800) 872-2672; www.aopa.org
Appalachian Mountain Club (1876): (617) 523-0636; www.outdoors.org
Boat Owners Assn. of the U.S. (1966): (800) 395-2628; www.boatus.com
Camp Assn., American (1910): (765) 342-8456; www.acacamps.org
Consumer Federation of America (1968): (202) 387-6121; www.consumerfed.org
Consumers Union (1936): (914) 378-2000; www.consumersunion.org
Green America (fmr. Co-op America) (1982): (800) 584-7336; www.green america.org
Hostelling Intl. USA (1934): (240) 650-2100; www.hiusa.org

Jewish Community Centers Assn. of North America (1917): (212) 532-4949; www.jcca.org
Motorcyclist Assn., American (1924): (614) 856-1900; www.americanmotorcyclist.com
Planetary Society (1980): (626) 793-5100; www.planetary.org
SCRABBLE® Players Assn., N. American (2009): www.scrabbleplayers.org
Sports Car Club of America (1944): (785) 357-7222; www.scca.com
Toastmasters Intl. (1924): (720) 439-5050; www.toastmasters.org
Vertical Flight Society (fmr. American Helicopter Society Intl.) (1943): (703) 684-6777; www.vtol.org
YMCA (Young Men's Christian Assn.) of the USA (1851): (800) 872-9622; www.ymca.net
YWCA (Young Women's Christian Assn.) USA (1858): (202) 467-0801; www.ywca.org

Military and Veterans

Air Force Assn. (1946): (703) 247-5800; www.afa.org
American Legion (1919): (317) 630-1200; www.legion.org
American Legion Auxiliary (1919): (317) 569-4500; www.alaforveterans.org
AMVETS (American Veterans) (1944): (877) 726-8387; www.amvets.org
Army, Assn. of the United States (1950): (703) 841-4300; www.ausa.org
Blinded Veterans Assn. (1958): (800) 669-7079; www.bva.org
Civil Air Patrol (1941): (877) 227-9142; www.gocivilairpatrol.com
Coast Guard Combat Veterans Assn. (1985): (410) 600-4000; www.coastguardcombatvets.org
Disabled American Veterans (1920): (877) 426-2838; www.dav.org
82nd Airborne Division Assn., Inc. (1944): (910) 223-1182; www.82ndairborneassociation.org
Ex-Prisoners of War, American (1942): (817) 649-2979; www.axpow.org
Fleet Reserve Assn. (1924): (703) 683-1400; www.fra.org
Iraq and Afghanistan Veterans of America (2004): (212) 982-9699; www.iava.org
Jewish War Veterans of the U.S.A. (1896): (202) 265-6280; www.jwv.org
Legion of Valor Museum (1991): (559) 498-0510; www.fresnovetsmuseum.com
Marine Corps League (1937): (703) 207-9588; www.mclnational.org
Military Officers Assn. of America (1929): (703) 549-2311; www.moaa.org
Military Order of the World Wars (1919): (703) 683-4911; www.moww.org
National Guard Assn. of the U.S. (1878): (202) 789-0031; www.ngaus.org
Naval Institute, U.S. (1873): (410) 268-6110; www.usni.org
Navy League of the United States (1902): (703) 528-1775; www.navyleague.org
Ninety-Nines, Inc. (Intl. Org. of Women Pilots) (1929): (405) 685-7969; www.ninety-nines.org
Non Commissioned Officers Assn. (1960): (210) 653-6161; www.ncoausa.org
Paralyzed Veterans of America (1946): (800) 424-8200; www.pva.org
POW/MIA Families, Natl. League of (1970): (703) 465-7432; www.pow-miafamilies.org
Purple Heart, Military Order of the (1932): (703) 642-5360; www.purpleheart.org
Reserve Officers Assn. of the U.S. (1922): (202) 479-2200; www.roa.org
Sons of the American Legion (1932): (317) 630-1200; www.legion.org/sons
Tin Can Sailors (Natl. Assn. of Destroyer Veterans) (1976): (800) 223-5535; www.destroyers.org
Uniformed Services Assn. (2018): www.uniformedservicesassociation.org
USO, Inc. (United Service Org.) (1941): (888) 484-3876; www.uso.org
USS Missouri Memorial Assn., Inc. (1998): (808) 455-1600; www.ussmissouri.org
Veterans of Foreign Wars (1899): (816) 756-3390; www.vfw.org
Veterans of Foreign Wars Auxiliary (1914): (816) 561-8655; vfwauxiliary.org
Vietnam Veterans of America (1978): (301) 585-4000; www.vva.org

Women's Army Corps Veterans' Assn. (1946): (256) 820-6824; www.armywomen.org

Wounded Warrior Project (2002): (877) 832-6997; www.woundedwarriorproject.org

Political

Abortion Federation, Natl. (1977): (202) 667-5881; www.prochoice.org

Action Network, American (2010): (202) 559-6420; americanactionnetwork.org

Advancement and Support of Education, Council for (1974): (202) 328-2273; www.case.org

American Indians, Natl. Congress of (1944): (202) 466-7767; www.ncai.org

American-Islamic Relations, Council on (1994): (202) 488-8787; www.cair.com

Black Lives Matter (2012): www.blacklivesmatter.com

Brady Campaign to Prevent Gun Violence (1974): (202) 370-8100; www.bradycampaign.org

Center for Responsive Politics (1983): (202) 857-0044; www.opensecrets.org

Cities, Natl. League of (1924): (202) 626-3100; www.nlc.org

Civil Liberties Union, American (ACLU) (1920): (212) 549-2500; www.aclu.org

Coalition to Stop Gun Violence (1974): (202) 408-0061; www.csgv.org

Common Cause (1970): (202) 833-1200; www.commoncause.org

Concerned Women for America (1979): (202) 488-7000; www.concernedwomen.org

Congress of Racial Equality (CORE) (1942): (212) 598-4000; www.core-online.org

Conservation Voters, League of (1969): (202) 785-8683; www.lcv.org

Constitution Party (1992): (717) 390-1993; www.constitutionparty.org

Counties, Natl. Assn. of (1935): (202) 393-6226; www.naco.org

Crime and Delinquency, Natl. Council on (1907): (800) 306-6223; www.nccdglobal.org

Crossroads GPS (Grassroots Political Strategies) (2010): (202) 706-7051; www.crossroadsgps.org

Democratic Natl. Committee (1848): (202) 863-8000; www.democrats.org

Democratic Socialists of America (1982): (212) 727-8610; www.dsausa.org

Everytown for Gun Safety (2013): (646) 324-8250; www.everytown.org

Feminists for Life of America (1972): (703) 836-3354; www.feministsforlife.org

Future Fund, Amer. (2007): (515) 661-4233; www.americanfuturefund.com

Gay & Lesbian Alliance Against Defamation (GLAAD) (1985): (212) 629-3322; www.glaad.org

Governors Assn., Natl. (1908): (202) 624-5300; www.nga.org

Grange of the Order of Patrons of Husbandry, Natl. (1867): (202) 628-3507; www.nationalgrange.org

Gray Panthers (1970): (202) 737-6637

Green Party of the USA (1984): (202) 319-7191; www.gp.org

Hispanic Leadership Agenda, Natl. (1991): (202) 637-5120; www.nationalhispanic leadership.org

Homeless, Natl. Coalition for the (1984): (202) 462-4822; www.nationalhomeless.org

Human Rights Campaign (1980): (202) 628-4160; www.hrc.org

Immigration Equality (1994): (212) 714-2904; immigrationequality.org

Immigration Reform, Federation for American (FAIR) (1979): (202) 328-7004; www.fairus.org

Japanese American Citizens League (1929): (202) 223-1240; www.jacl.org

Jewish Committee, American (1906): (212) 751-4000; www.ajc.org

John Birch Society (1958): (920) 749-3780; www.jbs.org

LGBTQ Task Force, Natl. (fmr. Natl. Gay and Lesbian Task Force) (1973): (202) 393-5177; www.thetaskforce.org

Libertarian Party (1971): (202) 333-0008; www.lp.org

Mayors, U.S. Conference of (1932): (202) 293-7330; www.usmayors.org

Men, Natl. Coalition for (1977): (888) 223-1280; www.ncfm.org

NAACP (Natl. Assn. for the Advancement of Colored People) (1909): (410) 580-5777; www.naacp.org

NRA (National Rifle Assn.) (1871): (800) 672-3888; www.nra.org

Parliamentarians, Natl. Assn. of (1930): (816) 833-3892; www.parliamentarians.org

Patriot Majority (2005): www.patriot majority.org

National Popular Vote (2006): (650) 472-1587; www.nationalpopularvote.com

Progress, Center for American (2003): (202) 682-1611; www.americanprogress.org

Reform Party Natl. Committee (1995): (972) 275-9297; www.reformparty.org

Republican Natl. Committee (1856): (202) 863-8500; www.gop.com

Southern Christian Leadership Conference (1957): (404) 522-1420; nationalsclc.org

Southern Poverty Law Center (1971): (334) 956-8200; www.splcenter.org

State Governments, Council of (1933): (859) 244-8000; www.csg.org

Tax Foundation (1937): (202) 464-6200; www.taxfoundation.org

Tax Reform, Americans for (1985): (202) 785-0266; www.atr.org

Taxpayers Union, Natl. (1969): (703) 683-5700; www.ntu.org

Tea Party Patriots (2009): www.teapartypatriots.org

Term Limits, U.S. (1992): (202) 261-3532; www.termlimits.org

Urban League, Natl. (1910): (212) 558-5300; www.nul.org

Women, Natl. Organization for (NOW) (1966): (202) 628-8669; www.now.org

Women and Families, Natl. Partnership for (1971): (202) 986-2600; www.nationalpartnership.org

Women Voters, League of (1920): (202) 429-1965; www.lwv.org

Woman's Christian Temperance Union (1874): (847) 864-1397; www.wctu.org

Zionist Organization of America (1897): (212) 481-1500; www.zoa.org

Religious

African Methodist Episcopal Church (1787): 500 8th Ave. S., Nashville, TN 37203; (615) 254-0911; www.ame-church.com; Gen. Sec., Dr. Jeffery Cooper

African Methodist Episcopal Zion Church (1796): 3225 Sugar Creek Rd., Charlotte, NC 28269; (704) 599-4630; www.amez.org; Senior Bishop, George E. Battle Jr.

American Baptist Churches USA (1907): P.O. Box 851, Valley Forge, PA 19482; (610) 768-2000; www.abc-usa.org; Gen. Sec., Rev. Dr. Lee B. Spitzer

Antiochian Orthodox Christian Archdiocese of North America (1895): P.O. Box 5238, Englewood, NJ 07631; (201) 871-1355; www.antiochian.org; Primate, Archbishop Metropolitan Joseph

Armenian Apostolic Church of America: *Eastern Prelacy* (1958): 138 E. 39th St., NY, NY 10016; (212) 689-7810; www.armenianprelacy.org; Prelate, Archbishop Anoushavan Tanielian; *Western Prelacy* (1973): 6252 Honolulu Ave., La Crescenta, CA 91214; (818) 248-7737; www.western prelacy.org; Prelate, Archbishop Moushegh Mardirossian

Assemblies of God USA (1914): 1445 N. Boonville Ave., Springfield, MO 65802; (417) 862-2781; www.ag.org; Gen. Supt., Doug Clay

Atheists, American (1963): 225 Cristiani St., Cranford, NJ 07016; (908) 276-7300; www.atheists.org; Board Chair, Neal Cary

Bahá'ís of the U.S., Natl. Spiritual Assembly of the (1909): 1233 Central St., Evanston, IL 60201; (847) 733-3400; www.bahai.us; Sec., Kenneth E. Bowers

Baptist Bible Fellowship Intl. (1950): 720 E. Kearney St., Springfield, MO 65803; (417) 862-5001; www.bbfi.org; Pres., Tim Adrian

Baptist Convention, Southern (1845): 901 Commerce St., Nashville, TN 37203; (615) 244-2355; www.sbc.net; Pres., J.D. Greear

Baptist Convention, USA, Inc., Natl. (1886): 1700 Baptist World Center Dr., Nashville, TN 37207; (615) 228-6292; www.national baptist.com; Pres., Dr. Jerry Young

Baptist Convention of America Intl., Inc., Natl. (1880): 1000 S. 4th St., Louisville, KY 40203; (844) 610-6222; www.nbcainc.com; Pres., Rev. Samuel C. Tolbert Jr.

Baptist Convention of America, Natl. Missionary (1880): 6925 Wofford Dr., Dallas, TX 75227; (877) 886-6222; www.nmbca.org; Pres., Dr. Anthony E. Sharp

Bible Society, American (1816): 101 N. Independence Mall East FL8, Philadelphia, PA 19106; (215) 309-0900; www.americanbible.org; Pres., Robert Briggs

Biblical Literature, Society of (1880): 825 Houston Mill Rd., Atlanta, GA 30329; (404) 727-3100; www.sbl-site.org; Exec. Dir., Dr. John F. Kutsko

B'nai B'rith Intl. (1843): 1120 20th St. NW, Ste. 300 N, Washington, DC 20036; (202) 857-6600; www.bnaibrith.org; Pres., Charles O. Kaufman

Brethren in Christ Church (c. 1778): 431 Grantham Rd., Mechanicsburg, PA 17055; (717) 697-2634; www.bicus.org; Natl. Dir., Dr. Alan Robinson

Buddhist Churches of America (1899): 1710 Octavia St., San Francisco, CA 94109; (415) 776-5600; www.buddhistchurchesofamerica.org; Pres., Dr. Kent Matsuda

Catholic Bishops, U.S. Conference of (2001): 3211 4th St. NE, Washington, DC 20017; (202) 541-3000; www.usccb.org; Gen. Sec., Msgr. J. Brian Bransfield

Christian Church (Disciples of Christ) (1832): Disciples Center, P.O. Box 1986, Indianapolis, IN 46206; (317) 635-3100; www.disciples.org; Gen. Min. and Pres., Rev. Teresa Hord Owens

Christian Methodist Episcopal Church (1870): 4466 Elvis Presley Blvd., Memphis, TN 38116; (901) 345-0580; www.thecmechurch.org; Senior Bishop, Lawrence L. Reddick III

Church of the Brethren (1708): General Offices, 1451 Dundee Ave., Elgin, IL 60120; (847) 742-5100; www.brethren.org; Gen. Sec., David A. Steele

Church of Christ (1830): P.O. Box 472, Independence, MO 64051; (816) 206-0147; www.churchofchrist1830.org; Sec., Council of Apostles, Duane L. Ely

Church of God (Anderson, IN) (1881): Box 2420, Anderson, IN 46018; (765) 642-0256; www.jesusisthesubject.org; Gen. Dir., Jim Lyon

Church of God (Cleveland, TN) (1886): 2490 Keith St. NW, Cleveland, TN 37311; (423) 472-3361; www.churchofgod.org; Gen. Overseer, Tim Hill

Church of God in Christ (1897): Mason Temple, 930 Mason St., Memphis, TN 38126; (901) 947-9300; www.cogic.org; Presiding Bishop, Bishop Charles E. Blake Sr.

Church of Jesus Christ (1862): World Operations Ctr., 110 Walton Tea Room Rd., Greensburg, PA 15601; (724) 837-4425; www.thechurchofjesuschrist.org; Pres., Brother Joel Gehly

Church of the Nazarene (1908): Global Ministry Center, 17001 Prairie Star Pkwy., Lenexa, KS 66220; (913) 577-0500; www.nazarene.org; Gen. Sec., Gary Hartke

Community of Christ (reorganized Church of Jesus Christ of Latter-day Saints) (1830): Intl. Headquarters, 1001 W. Walnut, Independence, MO 64050; (816) 833-1000; www.cofchrist.org; Pres., Stephen M. Veazey

Community Churches, International Council of (1950): 21116 Washington Pkwy., Frankfort, IL 60423; (815) 464-5690; www.icccnow.org; Exec. Dir., Rev. Phil Tom

Conservative Judaism, United Synagogue of (1913): 120 Broadway, Ste. 1540, NY, NY 10271; (212) 533-7800; www.uscj.org; Interim CEO, Leslie Lichter

Converge Worldwide (fmr. Baptist General Conference) (1852): 2002 S. Arlington Heights Rd., Arlington Heights, IL 60005; (800) 323-4215; www.converge.org; Pres., Scott Ridout

Cumberland Presbyterian Church (1810): 8207 Traditional Pl., Cordova, TN 38016; (901) 276-4572; www.cumberland.org

Episcopal Church (1789): 815 Second Ave., NY, NY 10017; (212) 716-6000; www.episcopalchurch.org; Presiding Bishop and Primate, Most Rev. Michael B. Curry

Evangelical Lutheran Church in America (1988): 8765 W. Higgins Rd., Chicago, IL 60631; (773) 380-2700; www.elca.org; Presiding Bishop, Rev. Elizabeth A. Eaton

First Church of Christ, Scientist, The (1879): 210 Massachusetts Ave., Boston, MA 02115; (617) 450-2000; www.chris tianscience.com; Pres., Anne-Françoise Bouffé, C.S.B.

Free Methodist Church USA (1860): 770 N. High School Rd., Indianapolis, IN 46214; (317) 244-3660; www.fmcusa.org; Chief Operating Officer, Mark Dowley

Freedom From Religion Foundation (1978): P.O. Box 750, Madison, WI 53701; (608) 256-8900; www.ffrf.org; Pres., Annie Laurie Gaylor and Dan Barker

Friends General Conference (1900): 1216 Arch St., #2B, Philadelphia, PA 19107; (215) 561-1700; www.fgcquaker.org; Gen. Sec., Barry Crossno

Gideons Intl., The (1899): P.O. Box 140800, Nashville, TN 37214; (615) 564-5000; www.gideons.org; Exec. Dir., Dan Heighway

Greek Orthodox Archdiocese of America (1922): 8 E. 79th St., NY, NY 10075; (212) 570-3500; www.goarch.org; Primate, Archbishop Elpidophoros

Hadassah, the Women's Zionist Organization of America, Inc. (1912): 40 Wall St., NY, NY 10005; (800) 664-5646; www.hadassah.org; Exec. Dir. and CEO, Janice Weinman

Interfaith Alliance (1994): 2101 L St. NW, Ste. 400, Washington, DC 20037; (202) 466-0567; www.interfaithalliance.org; Pres., Rabbi Jack Moline

Islamic Society of North America: 6555 S. County Rd. 750 East, Plainfield, IN 46168; (317) 839-8157; www.isna.net; Pres., Sayyid M. Syeed

Jehovah's Witnesses (1931): 900 Red Mills Rd., Wallkill, NY 12589; (845) 744-6000; www.jw.org

Jewish Congress, American (1918): 745 Fifth Ave., 30th Fl., NY, NY 10151; (212) 879-4500; www.ajcongress.org; Pres., Jack Rosen

Jewish Reconstructionist Communities (2012): 1299 Church Rd., Wyncote, PA 19095; (215) 576-0800; www.reconstructingjudaism.org; Pres., Rabbi Deborah Waxman

Jewish Women, Natl. Council of (1893): 2055 L St. NW, Ste. 650, Washington, D.C. 20036; (202) 296-2588; www.ncjw.org; Pres., Beatrice Kahn

Latter-day Saints, The Church of Jesus Christ of (Mormons) (1830): 50 W. North Temple St., Salt Lake City, UT 84150; (801) 240-2640; www.lds.org; Pres., Russell M. Nelson

Lutheran Church—Missouri Synod (1847): 1333 S. Kirkwood Rd., St. Louis, MO 63122; (800) 248-1930; www.lcms.org; Pres., Rev. Dr. Matthew C. Harrison

Mennonite Church USA (2001): 718 N. Main St., Newton, KS 67114; (316) 283-5100; www.mennoniteusa.org; Exec. Dir., Glen Guyton

Moravian Church in North America (1735): www.moravian.org; *Northern Prov.*: 1021 Center St., P.O. Box 1245, Bethlehem, PA 18016; (610) 867-7566; Pres., Rev. Dr. Betsy Miller; *Southern Prov.*: 459 S. Church St., Winston-Salem, NC 27101; (336) 725-5811; Pres., Rev. David Guthrie

North American Shia Ithna-asheri Muslim Communities, Org. of (1986): P.O. Box 29691, Minneapolis, MN 55429; (905) 763-7512; nasimco.org; Pres., Br. Arif Jacksi

Orthodox Union (1898): 11 Broadway, NY, NY 10004; (212) 563-4000; www.ou.org; Pres., Mark Bane

Pentecostal Assemblies of the World, Inc. (1906): 3939 N. Meadows Dr., Indianapolis, IN 46205; (317) 547-9541; www.pawinc.org; Presiding Bishop, Theodore L. Brooks, Sr.

Presbyterian Church (U.S.A.) (1983): 100 Witherspoon St., Louisville, KY 40202;

(800) 728-7228; www.pcusa.org; Pres., Kathy Lueckert

Progressive Natl. Baptist Convention, Inc. (1961): 601 50th St. NE, Washington, DC 20019; (202) 396-0558; www.pnbc.org; Pres., Dr. Timothy Stewart

Rabbis, Central Conference of American (1889): 355 Lexington Ave., NY, NY 10017; (212) 972-3636; www.ccarnet.org; Chief Exec., Rabbi Hara Person

Reform Judaism, Union for (1873): 633 3rd Ave., NY, NY 10017; (212) 650-4000; www.urj.org; Pres., Rabbi Rick Jacobs

Secular Humanism, Council for (1980): P.O. Box 664, Amherst, NY 14226; (716) 636-7571; www.secularhumanism.org; Pres., Robyn A. Blumner

Separation of Church and State, Americans United for (1947): 1310 L St. NW, Ste. 200, Washington, DC 20005; (202) 466-3234; www.au.org; Pres. and CEO, Rachel Laser

Seventh-day Adventist Church (1863): 12501 Old Columbia Pike, Silver Spring, MD 20904; (301) 680-6000; www.adventist.org; Pres., Ted N. C. Wilson

Seventh Day Baptist (1802): P.O. Box 1678, Janesville, WI 53547; (608) 752-5055; www.seventhdaybaptist.org; Gen. Sec., Rev. Andrew Samuels

Unitarian Universalist Assn. of Congregations (1961): 24 Farnsworth St., Boston, MA 02210; (617) 742-2100; www.uua.org; Pres., Rev. Susan Frederick-Gray

United Church of Christ (1957): 700 Prospect Ave., Cleveland, OH 44115; (216) 736-2100; www.ucc.org; Pres., Rev. John C. Dorhauer

United Methodist Church (1968): 100 Maryland Ave. NE, Washington, DC 20002; (202) 488-5600; www.umc.org; Council of Bishops Pres., Cynthia Fierro Harvey

United Pentecostal Church Intl. (1945): 36 Research Park Court, Weldon Spring, MO 63304; (636) 229-7900; www.upci.org; Gen. Supt., David K. Bernard

Wesleyan Church, The (1843): 13300 Olio Rd., Fishers, IN 46037; (317) 774-7900; www.wesleyan.org; Gen. Supt., Rev. Dr. Wayne Schmidt

Businesses and Corporations

Source: World Almanac research

Listed below are major corporations offering products and services to U.S. consumers, as of July 2020. Alphabetization is by first key word. Listings generally include examples of products offered.

Company name (NYSE/Nasdaq symbol, if traded on those markets): Address; Telephone number; Website; Top executive; Business, products, or services.

Abbott Laboratories (ABT): 100 Abbott Park Rd., Abbott Park, IL 60064; (224) 667-6100; www.abbott.com; Robert B. Ford; develops, mfr. pharmaceutical, nutritional, diagnostic prods.

AbbVie Inc. (ABBV): 1 N. Waukegan Rd., N. Chicago, IL 60064; (847) 932-7900; www.abbvie.com; Richard A. Gonzalez; pharmaceuticals. Acquired Irish Botox-mfr. Allergan, 5/8/2020.

ABC: see Walt Disney Co.

Accenture Inc. (ACN): 161 N. Clark St., Chicago, IL 60601; (312) 737-8842; www.accenture.com; Julie Sweet; management consulting.

Activision Blizzard Inc. (ATVI): 3100 Ocean Park Blvd., Santa Monica, CA 90405; (310) 255-2000; www.activisionblizzard.com; Bobby Kotick; video game publisher (*World of Warcraft, Call of Duty, Candy Crush Saga*).

adidas Group: Adi-Dassler-Strasse 1, D-91074 Herzogenaurach, Germany; +49 (0) 9132-84-0; www.adidas-group.com; Kasper Rorsted; apparel and accessories mfr. (Reebok).

Advance Publications, Inc.: 950 W. Fingerboard Rd., Staten Island, NY 10305; (718) 981-1234; www.advance.com; Steven Newhouse; communications, newspaper and magazine publisher (Condé Nast subsids.: *New Yorker, Vanity Fair, Vogue*). Agreed to acquire The IRONMAN Group sports participation platform, 3/26/2020.

Aetna, Inc.: see CVS Health

Aflac, Inc. (AFL): 1932 Wynnton Rd., Columbus, GA 31999; (706) 596-3272; www.aflac.com; Daniel P. Amos; supplemental health and life insurance.

Airbnb: 888 Brannan St., 4th Fl., San Francisco, CA 94117; (415) 800-5959; www.airbnb.com; Brian Chesky; online marketplace for short-term global accommodations.

Alaska Air Group, Inc. (ALK): 19300 International Blvd., Seattle, WA 98188; (206) 433-3200; www.alaskaair.com; Bradley D. Tilden; airline carriers (Alaska Airlines, Horizon Air).

Albertsons Companies, Inc. (ACI): 250 E. Parkcenter Blvd., Boise, ID 83706; (208) 395-6200; www.albertsonscompanies.com; Vivek Sankaran; grocery and drug retail operation (Albertsons, Jewel-Osco, Safeway, Shaw's, Vons).

Alcoa Inc. (AA): 201 Isabella St., Ste. 500, Pittsburgh, PA 15212; (412) 553-4545; www.alcoa.com; Roy Harvey; prod., mfr. of aluminum, aluminum prods. (aerospace, automotive, industrial materials and components).

Alibaba Group (BABA): 969 West Wen Yi Rd., Yu Hang District, Hangzhou 311121, China; +86 571-8502-2088; www.alibaba.com; Daniel Zhang; online shopping, logistics, marketing; data mgmt.; financial serv. Record-high U.S. IPO, 9/19/2014. Acquired Pakistani online retailer Daraz Group, 5/8/2018.

Allstate Corp. (ALL): 2775 Sanders Rd., Northbrook, IL 60062; (847) 402-5000; www.allstate.com; Thomas J. Wilson; personal property and casualty insurance; financial services.

Alphabet Inc. (GOOG): 1600 Amphitheatre Pkwy., Mountain View, CA 94043; (650) 253-0000; www.abc.xyz; Sundar Pichai; Google and other internet-related prods. and services (leading search engine, ad sales; YouTube). Reorganized corp. as Alphabet, 10/2/2015. Agreed to acquire Israeli cloud migration startups Velostrata, 2018, Alooma, 2019. Agreed to acquire Fitbit, 11/1/2019.

Altice USA (ATUS): 1111 Stewart Ave., Bethpage, NY 11714; (516) 803-2300; www.alticeusa.com; Dexter Goei; telecom, internet, cable provider.

Altria Group, Inc. (MO): 6601 W. Broad St., Richmond, VA 23230; (804) 484-8897; www.altria.com; Howard A. Willard III; tobacco co. (Marlboro, Merit, Parliament, Virginia Slims). (Altria spun off Philip Morris's intl. operations in 2008 but owns Philip Morris brands in U.S.)

Amazon.com, Inc. (AMZN): 410 Terry Ave. N., Seattle, WA 98109; (206) 266-1000; www.amazon.com; Jeffrey P. Bezos; online retailer and e-commerce platform; cloud computing (AWS); media streaming/production (Audible, Prime Video, Twitch). Acquired grocer Whole Foods, 8/28/2017.

American Airlines Group, Inc. (AAL): 4333 Amon Carter Blvd., Ft. Worth, TX

76155; (817) 963-1234; www.aa.com; Doug Parker; airlines (American Airlines, American Eagle).

American Electric Power Co., Inc. (AEP): 1 Riverside Plz., Columbus, OH 43215; (614) 716-1000; www.aep.com; Nicholas K. Akins; public utilities.

American Express Co. (AXP): World Financial Ctr., 200 Vesey St., 50th Fl., NY, NY 10285; (212) 640-2000; www.american express.com; Stephen J. Squeri; charge and credit cards, travel-related services.

American Greetings Corp.: 1 American Blvd., Cleveland, OH 44145; (216) 252-7300; www.americangreetings.com; Joe Arcuri; greeting cards, stationery, party goods, gift items.

American Intl. Group, Inc. (AIG): 175 Water St., 15th Fl., NY, NY 10038; (212) 770-7000; www.aigcorporate.com; Brian Duperreault; insurance, financial services. AIG received $182 bil in govt. bailouts, 2008.

AmerisourceBergen (ABC): 1300 Morris Dr., Chesterbrook, PA, 19087; (610) 727-7000; www.amerisourcebergen.com; Steven H. Collis; distrib. of generic and brand-name pharmaceuticals.

Amgen, Inc. (AMGN): 1 Amgen Center Dr., Thousand Oaks, CA 91320; (805) 447-1000; www.amgen.com; Robert A. Bradway; biopharmaceuticals.

Anheuser-Busch InBev (BUD): Brouwerijplein 1, 3000 Leuven, Belgium; +32 (16) 276111; www.ab-inbev.com; Carlos Brito; brewer (Budweiser, Bud Light, Michelob, Corona, Foster's, Stella Artois), soft drinks. Acquired brewing competitor SABMiller for $100 bil+, 10/10/2016.

Anthem, Inc. (ANTM): 220 Virginia Ave., Indianapolis, IN 46204; (317) 488-6000; www.anthem.com; Gail K. Boudreaux; health insurance co.

Apple Inc. (AAPL): 1 Apple Park Way, Cupertino, CA 95014; (408) 996-1010; www.apple.com; Tim Cook; mfr. of computers (Mac), digital media devices (iPod, iPhone, iPad) and distrib. (iTunes store, Apple Music). Acquired music ID app Shazam, 9/24/2018; became world's first-ever publicly traded co. worth $1 tril., 8/1/2018.

ARAMARK Corp. (ARMK): 2400 Market St., Philadelphia, PA 19103; (215) 238-3000; www.aramark.com; John Zillmer; food/support services to institutions and facilities, uniforms and career apparel.

ArcelorMittal USA, Inc.: 1 South Dearborn, Chicago, IL 60603; (312) 346-0300; www.usa.arcelormittal.com; John L. Brett; steel; U.S. subsidiary of Arcelor Mittal, based in Luxembourg.

Archer Daniels Midland Co. (ADM): 77 W. Wacker Dr., Ste. 4600, Chicago, IL 60601; (312) 634-8100; www.adm.com; Juan R. Luciano; agricultural commodities and prods.

Armstrong World Industries, Inc. (AWI): 2500 Columbia Ave., P.O. Box 3001, Lancaster, PA 17604; (717) 672-9611; www.armstrong.com; Victor D. Grizzle; mfr. of flooring, ceiling prods., cabinets.

AT&T Inc. (T): 208 S. Akard St., Dallas, TX 75202; (210) 821-4105; www.att.com; Randall L. Stephenson; telecommunications, global information mgmt., mass media prod., distrib. (WarnerMedia, incl. CNN, HBO; DirecTV).

Automatic Data Processing, Inc. (ADP): 1 ADP Blvd., Roseland, NJ 07068; (973) 974-5000; www.adp.com; Carlos A. Rodriguez; payroll and tax processing serv.

AutoNation, Inc. (AN): 200 SW 1st Ave., Ste. 1600, Ft. Lauderdale, FL 33301; (954) 769-6000; www.autonation.com; Mike Jackson; auto retailer; new and used vehicles; auto parts, maintenance, and repair; auto finance and insurance.

Bank of America Corp. (BAC): 100 N. Tryon St., Charlotte, NC 28255; (704) 386-5681; www.bankofamerica.com; Brian T. Moynihan; banking and financial services.

Barnes & Noble, Inc.: 122 Fifth Ave., NY, NY 10011; (212) 633-3300; www.barnesandnobleinc.com; James Daunt;

bookseller, publisher (Sterling Pub. Co.). Acquired by investment firm Elliott Management Corp., 8/7/2019.

Bayer AG: Kaiser-Wilhelm-Allee, D-51368 Leverkusen, Germany; +49 214-30-40126, www.bayer.com; Werner Baumann; pharmaceuticals, health care and biotech prods.; acquired Monsanto for $63 bil, 6/7/2018.

Baxter International Inc. (BAX): 1 Baxter Pkwy., Deerfield, IL 60015; (224) 948-2000; www.baxter.com; José Almeida; mfr. of health care prods.

Bear Stearns Cos. Inc.: see JPMorgan Chase & Co.

Becton, Dickinson & Co. (BDX): 1 Becton Dr., Franklin Lakes, NJ 07417; (201) 847-6800; www.bd.com; Tom Polen; medical, laboratory, diagnostic prods. Acquired medical tech co. C.R. Bard Inc., 12/29/2017.

Bed Bath & Beyond Inc. (BBBY): 650 Liberty Ave., Union, NJ 07083; (908) 688-0888; www.bedbathandbeyond.com; Mark J. Tritton; home goods retailer.

Berkshire Hathaway Inc. (BRK.A): 3555 Farnam St., Ste. 1440, Omaha, NE 68131; (402) 346-1400; www.berkshirehathaway.com; Warren E. Buffett; diversified holdings incl. insurance (GEICO), building materials (Benjamin Moore & Co., Shaw), apparel (Fruit of the Loom), food (Dairy Queen), Precision Castparts, Duracell.

Bertelsmann AG: Carl-Bertelsmann-Str. 270, 33311 Gütersloh, Germany; +49 (0) 5241-80-62321; www.bertelsmann.de; Thomas Rabe; intl. media corp., trade book publisher (Penguin Random House: Knopf, Doubleday).

Best Buy Co., Inc. (BBY): 7601 Penn Ave. S., Richfield, MN 55423; (612) 291-1000; www.bestbuy.com; Corie Barry; retailer of software, appliances, consumer electronics.

Blackstone Group LP, The (BX): 345 Park Ave., NY, NY 10154; (212) 583-5000; www.blackstone.com; Stephen A. Schwarzman; asset mgmt., financial services. Acquired majority stake in tech co. HealthEdge, 4/9/2020.

Boeing Co. (BA): 100 N. Riverside, Chicago, IL 60606; (312) 544-2000; boeing.com; David L. Calhoun; world's leading aerospace co., mfr. of commercial jet and military aircraft; one of the largest U.S. defense contractors. Suspended production of 737 MAX aircraft starting Jan. 2020 following two fatal crashes in 2018 and 2019.

Booking Holdings Inc. (BKNG) (fmr. The Priceline Group): 800 Connecticut Ave., Norwalk, CT 06854; (203) 299-8000; www.bookingholdings.com; Glenn D. Fogel; online travel/hospitality services (Priceline, booking.com, Kayak, Open Table).

Brighthouse Financial, Inc. (BHF): 11225 N. Community House Rd., Charlotte, NC 28277; (800) 638-5000; www.brighthousefinancial.com; Eric Steigerwalt; life insurance, annuities.

Brink's Co., The (BCO): 1801 Bayberry Ct., P.O. Box 18100, Richmond, VA 23226; (804) 289-9600; www.brinkscompany.com; Doug A. Pertz; security (armored transport, money processing, trans. of valuables).

Bristol-Myers Squibb Co. (BMY): 430 E. 29th St., 14th Fl., NY, NY 10016; (212) 546-4000; www.bms.com; Giovanni Caforio; development, mfr., and sale of pharmaceuticals (Plavix, Eliquis, Atripla). Acquired Celgene in $74-bil deal, 11/20/2019.

Brown-Forman Corp. (BF.B): 850 Dixie Hwy., Louisville, KY 40210; (502) 585-1100; www.brown-forman.com; Lawson E. Whiting; distilled spirits (Jack Daniel's, Finlandia), wine and champagne (Sonoma-Cutrer, Korbel).

Brunswick Corp. (BC): 26125 N. Riverwoods Blvd., Ste. 500, Mettawa, IL 60045; (847) 735-4700; www.brunswick.com; David M. Foulkes; leisure and recreation

prods., incl. marine engines and boats; fitness equip.

Burger King: see Restaurant Brands Intl.

Caesars Entertainment Inc. (CZR): One Caesars Palace Dr., Las Vegas, NV 89109; (702) 407-6000; www.caesars.com; Tom Reeg; casinos; gambling services (Caesars, Harrah's, Horseshoe, World Series of Poker). Acquired by Eldorado Resorts, 7/20/2020.

Campbell Soup Co. (CPB): One Campbell Pl., Camden, NJ 08103; (856) 342-4800; www.campbellsoupcompany.com; Mark Clouse; soup mfr.; sauces (Pace, Prego), V8 juice, Pepperidge Farm prods. Acquired Snyder's-Lance (Pop Secret, Cape Cod/Kettle chips), 3/26/2018. Agreed to sell Garden Fresh Gourmet, 2/26/2019, sold Bolthouse Farms, 6/17/2019.

Capital One Financial Corporation (COF): 1680 Capital One Dr., McLean, VA 22102; (703) 720-1000; www.capitalone.com; Richard D. Fairbank; financial services.

Cardinal Health, Inc. (CAH): 7000 Cardinal Pl., Dublin, OH 43017; (614) 757-5000; www.cardinalhealth.com; Mike Kaufmann; pharmaceutical and med. equip. dist. co.

Carlyle Group, The (CG): 1001 Pennsylvania Ave. NW, Washington, DC 20004; (202) 729-5626; www.carlyle.com; Kewsong Lee; private equity group.

Caterpillar Inc. (CAT): 501 SW Jefferson Ave., Peoria, IL 61630; (309) 675-2337; www.caterpillar.com; Jim Umpleby; mfr. of construction and mining equip.

CBRE Group, Inc. (CBRE): 400 S. Hope St., 25th Fl., Los Angeles, CA 90071; (213) 613-3333; www.cbre.us; Bob Sulentic; commercial real estate.

CBS Corp.: see ViacomCBS

CenturyLink, Inc. (CTL): 100 CenturyLink Dr., Monroe, LA 71203; (318) 388-9000; www.centurylink.com; Jeff Storey; telecommunications provider.

Charter Communications, Inc. (CHTR): 400 Atlantic St., Stamford, CT 06901; (203) 905-7801; www.charter.com; Tom Rutledge; internet, cable TV, telecom provider (Spectrum).

Chevron Corp. (CVX): 6001 Bollinger Canyon Rd., San Ramon, CA 94583; (925) 842-1000; www.chevron.com; Michael K. Wirth; integrated energy co.

Chiquita Brands Intl., Inc.: 1855 Griffin Rd., Ste. C-436, Ft. Lauderdale, FL, 33004; (954) 924-5700; www.chiquita.com; Carlos Lopez Flores; fruits and vegetables. Acquired by Cutrale-Safra, 1/6/2015.

CHS Inc. (CHSCP): 5500 Cenex Dr., Inver Grove Heights, MN 55077; (651) 355-6000; www.chsinc.com; Jay Debertin; grain marketing, oil refining, and pipeline operations.

Chubb Ltd. (CB): 15 Mountain View Rd., Warren, NJ 07059; (908) 903-2000; www.chubb.com; Evan Greenberg; property/casualty insurance. ACE Limited acquired The Chubb Corporation, 1/14/16.

Church & Dwight Co., Inc. (CHD): Princeton South Corporate Center, 500 Charles Ewing Blvd., Ewing, NJ 08628; (609) 806-1200; www.churchdwight.com; Matthew T. Farrell; ARM & HAMMER baking soda; household and personal care prods. (Oxi-Clean, Arrid, Trojan, First Response).

Cigna Corp. (CI): 900 Cottage Grove Rd., Bloomfield, CT 06002; (860) 226-6000; www.cigna.com; David M. Cordani; insurance provider. Acquired pharmacy benefit manager Express Scripts for $54 bil, 12/20/2018.

Cintas Corp. (CTAS): 6800 Cintas Blvd., Cincinnati, OH 45262; (513) 459-1200; www.cintas.com; Scott D. Farmer; uniform supplier.

Cisco Systems, Inc. (CSCO): 170 W. Tasman Dr., San Jose, CA 95134; (408) 526-4000; www.cisco.com; Chuck Robbins; networking and communication prods. Bought comm. services co. BroadSoft, 2/2/2018. Acquired cloud-based authentication provider Duo Security, 10/1/2018.

Citigroup, Inc. (C): 388 Greenwich St., NY, NY 10013; (212) 559-1000; www.citigroup.com;

Michael L. Corbat; diversified financial services.

Clorox Co. (CLX): 1221 Broadway, Oakland, CA 94612; (510) 271-7000; www. clorox.com; Benno Dorer; consumer prods. (Clorox, Formula 409, Pine-Sol, S.O.S., Tilex, Scoop Away, Fresh Step, Kingsford, Hidden Valley, Glad, Brita, Burt's Bees).

Coach, Inc.: see Tapestry.

Coca-Cola Co. (KO): 1 Coca-Cola Plz. NW, Atlanta, GA 30313; (404) 676-2121; www. coca-cola.com; James Quincey; beverages (Coca-Cola, Sprite, Dasani, Fanta, Minute Maid, Vitaminwater). Acquired coffee mfr. Costa Ltd., 1/3/2019.

Colgate-Palmolive Co. (CL): 300 Park Ave., NY, NY 10022; (212) 310-2000; www.colgate.com; Noel Wallace; soap (Irish Spring), detergent (Palmolive), household cleansers (Ajax), toothpaste (Colgate, Tom's of Maine), pet food (Hill's Science Diet).

Comcast Corp. (CMCSA): 1701 JFK Blvd., Philadelphia, PA 19103; (215) 286-1700; www.comcast.com; Brian L. Roberts; cable provider; broadband media services; programming (E!, NBC, Bravo, USA, Telemundo). Acquired DreamWorks Animation, 8/22/2016; majority of UK pay-TV giant SKY, 10/9/2018.

Conagra Brands, Inc. (CAG): 222 W. Merchandise Mart Plaza, Ste. 1300, Chicago, IL 60654; (312) 549-5000; www.conagra foods.com; Sean Connolly; food processor (Chef Boyardee, Healthy Choice frozen dinners, Egg Beaters, Reddi-wip); food service supplier. Acquired Pinnacle Foods, 10/26/2018.

ConocoPhillips Co. (COP): 925 N. Eldridge Pkwy., Houston, TX 77079; (281) 293-1000; www.conocophillips.com; Ryan M. Lance; oil and gas exploration and prod. co.

Consolidated Edison, Inc. (ED): 4 Irving Plc., NY, NY 10003; (212) 460-4600; www.conedison.com; John McAvoy; electric, natural gas utilities.

Continental Airlines, Inc.: see United Continental Holdings, Inc.

Corning Inc. (GLW): 1 Riverfront Plz., Corning, NY 14831; (607) 974-9000; www.corning.com; Wendell P. Weeks; mfr. of telecommunications, specialty equip., fiber optics.

Corteva, Inc. (CTVA): CRP 705/L1S11, Wilmington, DE 19880; (302) 485-3400; www.corteva.com; James C. Collins Jr.; agricultural chem. dev./mfr. Separated 6/1/2019 from now-dissolved DowDuPont (6/1/2019); see Dow or Dupont.

Costco Wholesale Corp. (COST): 999 Lake Dr., Issaquah, WA 98027; (425) 313-8100; www.costco.com; W. Craig Jelinek; wholesale warehouse stores.

Countrywide Financial: see Bank of America Corp.

Crown Holdings, Inc. (CCK): 770 Township Line Rd. Yardley, PA 19067; (215) 698-5100; www.crowncork.com; Timothy J. Donahue; producer of packaging prods.

CSX Corp. (CSX): 500 Water St., 15th Fl., Jacksonville, FL 32202; (904) 359-3200; www.csx.com; James M. Foote; rail freight transport.

CVS Health (CVS): 1 CVS Dr., Woonsocket, RI 02895; (401) 765-1500; www. cvs.com; Larry J. Merlo; retail drugstores. Acquired health insurer Aetna for $78 bil, 11/28/2018.

Dana Holding Corp. (DAN): 3939 Technology Dr., Maumee, OH 43537; (419) 887-3000; www.dana.com; James Kamsickas; truck and auto parts, supplies.

Darden Restaurants, Inc. (DRI): 1000 Darden Center Dr., Orlando, FL 32837; (407) 245-4000; www.darden.com; Eugene Lee Jr.; casual-dining restaurants (Olive Garden, LongHorn Steakhouse).

Dean Foods Co.: 2711 N. Haskell Ave., Ste. 3400, Dallas, TX 75204; (214) 303-3400; www.deanfoods.com; Eric Beringause; milk and specialty dairy prods. (Land O'Lakes); ice cream prods. (Friendly's). Acquired by Dairy Farmers of America subsidiaries, 5/1/2020.

Deere & Co. (DE): One John Deere Pl., Moline, IL 61265; (309) 765-8000; www.deere.com; John C. May; mfr. of farm equip., industrial equip., lawn and garden tractors.

Dell Inc. (DELL): 1 Dell Way, Round Rock, TX 78682; (512) 338-4400; www.dell.com; Michael S. Dell; laptop and desktop computers, network accessories, peripherals, tablets, smartphones.

Delta Air Lines, Inc. (DAL): 1030 Delta Blvd., Atlanta, GA 30354; (404) 715-2600; www.delta.com; Ed Bastian; air transportation.

Dillard's, Inc. (DDS): 1600 Cantrell Rd., Little Rock, AR 72201; (501) 376-5200; www.dillards.com; William Dillard II; dept. store chain.

Dish Network Corp. (DISH): 9601 S. Meridian Blvd., Englewood, CO 80112; (303) 723-1000; www.dish.com; W. Erik Carlson; satellite media services.

Walt Disney Co., The (DIS): 500 S. Buena Vista St., Burbank, CA 91521; (818) 560-1000; disney.com; Bob Chapek; motion pictures (Lucasfilm, Touchstone, Pixar); TV (ABC, ESPN, National Geographic); media streaming (Hulu); radio; publishing; theme parks and resorts. Acquired 21st Century Fox's entertainment assets for $71.3 bil, 3/20/2019.

Doctor's Associates Inc.: 325 Sub Way, Milford, CT 06461; (203) 877-4281; www.subway.com; John Chidsey; restaurants (Subway).

Dole Food Co., Inc.: One Dole Dr., Westlake Village, CA 91362; (818) 879-6600; www.dole.com; Johan Linden; food prods., fresh fruits, vegetables.

Dollar Tree (DLTR): 500 Volvo Pkwy., Chesapeake, VA 23320; (757) 321-5000; www. dollartree.com; Gary M. Philbin; discount retailer. Acquired Family Dollar, 7/6/2015.

R. R. Donnelley & Sons Co. (RRD): 35 W. Wacker Dr., Chicago, IL 60601; (312) 326-8000; www.rrdonnelley.com; Daniel L. Knotts; commercial printing; marketing.

Dow Inc. (DOW): 2111 H.H. Dow Way, Midland, MI 48674; (989) 636-1000; www.dow. com; Jim Fitterling; commodity chemical prod. Spun off 4/1/2019 from DowDuPont, which formed from merger of Dow and DuPont, 8/31/2017; see Corteva and DuPont.

Dow Jones & Co., Inc.: see News Corp.

Dr Pepper Snapple Group, Inc.: see Keurig Dr Pepper.

Duke Energy Corp. (DUK): 550 S. Tryon St., Charlotte, NC 28202; (980) 373-8649; www.duke-energy.com; Lynn J. Good; utilities, fiber optic networks.

Dun & Bradstreet Corp. (DNB): 103 JFK Pkwy., Short Hills, NJ 07078; (973) 921-5500; www.dnb.com; Anthony Jabbour; business information, research.

DuPont de Nemours, Inc. (DD): 974 Centre Rd., Chestnut Run Plaza, Bldg. 702, Wilmington, DE 19805; (302) 774-1000; www.dupont.com; Edward Breen; specialty chemical mfr. Separated 6/3/2019 from DowDuPont, which formed from merger between Dow and DuPont, 8/31/2017; see Corteva and Dow.

DXC Technology (DXC): 1775 Tysons Blvd., Tysons, VA 22102; (703) 245-9700; www. dxc.technology; Mike Salvino; information tech. serv. Formed through merger of Computer Sciences Corp and Hewlett Packard Enterprise's enterprise serv. unit, 4/3/2017.

Eastman Kodak Co. (KODK): 343 State St., Rochester, NY 14650; (585) 724-4000; www.kodak.com; Jim Continenza; imaging technology and services.

Eaton Corp. (ETN): 1000 Eaton Blvd., Cleveland, OH 44122; (440) 523-5000; www.eaton.com; Craig Arnold; mfr. vehicle components, controls.

eBay Inc. (EBAY): 2065 Hamilton Ave., San Jose, CA 95125; (408) 376-7400; www. ebay.com; Jamie Iannone; e-commerce (StubHub). Spun off PayPal, 7/17/2015.

Edison Intl. (EIX): 2244 Walnut Grove Ave., Rosemead, CA 91770; (626) 302-2222;

www.edison.com; Pedro Pizarro; electric utilities.

Electronic Arts Inc. (EA): 209 Redwood Shores Pkwy., Redwood City, CA 94065; (650) 628-1500; www.ea.com; Andrew Wilson; video game publisher (Madden NFL, Battlefield, The Sims, UFC).

Electronic Data Systems: see Hewlett Packard Enterprise.

Eli Lilly and Co. (LLY): Lilly Corporate Center, Indianapolis, IN 46285; (317) 276-2000; www.lilly.com; David A. Ricks; pharmaceutical research, development, and manufacturing (Prozac, Strattera, Cialis).

EMC Corp.: see Dell Inc.

Emerson Electric Co. (EMR): 8000 W. Florissant Ave., St. Louis, MO 63136; (314) 553-2000; www.emerson.com; David N. Farr; electrical, electronics prods. and systems.

Energizer Holdings, Inc. (ENR): 533 Maryville Univ. Dr., St. Louis, MO 63141; (314) 985-2000; www.energizer.com; Alan Hoskins; batteries, flashlights, personal care prods.

Enterprise Products Partners L.P. (EPD): 1100 Louisiana St., 10th Fl., Houston, TX 77002; (713) 381-6500; www.enterprise products.com; W. Randall Fowler; oil processing/transport and waterborne freight.

Estée Lauder Cos. Inc. (EL): 767 Fifth Ave., NY, NY 10153; (212) 572-4200; www. elcompanies.com; Fabrizio Freda; cosmetics (Clinique, Bobbi Brown), fragrance, skin care prods. (GLAMGLOW).

Exelon Corp. (EXC): 10 S. Dearborn St., 48th Fl., Chicago, IL 60680; (800) 483-3220; www.exeloncorp.com; Christopher M. Crane; electricity generation/distrib.; natural gas.

Express Scripts Holding Co.: 1 Express Way, St. Louis, MO 63121; (314) 996-0900; www.express-scripts.com; Tim Wentworth; U.S. pharmacy benefits mgmt. co. Acquired by health insurance co. Cigna for $54 bil, 12/20/2018.

ExxonMobil Corp. (XOM): 5959 Las Colinas Blvd., Irving, TX 75039; (972) 444-1000; www.exxonmobil.com; Darren W. Woods; integrated energy, oil co.

Facebook, Inc. (FB): 1 Hacker Way, Menlo Park, CA 94025; (650) 308-7300; www. facebook.com; Mark Zuckerberg; social networking/messaging platforms, services (Facebook, WhatsApp).

Federal Home Loan Mortgage Corp. (Freddie Mac): 8200 Jones Branch Dr., McLean, VA 22102; (703) 903-2000; www. freddiemac.com; David Brickman; residential mortgage provider. Under U.S. govt. mgmt. since 9/7/2008.

Federal Natl. Mortgage Assn. (Fannie Mae): 3900 Wisconsin Ave. NW, Washington, DC 20016; (202) 752-7000; www.fanniemae.com; Hugh R. Frater; provider of residential mortgage funds. Under U.S. govt. mgmt. since 9/7/2008.

FedEx Corp. (FDX): 942 S. Shady Grove Rd., Memphis, TN 38120; (901) 818-7500; www.fedex.com; Frederick W. Smith; delivery services.

First Data Corp.: see Fiserv

FirstEnergy Corp. (FE): 76 S. Main St., Akron, OH 44308; (800) 736-3402; www. firstenergycorp.com; Charles E. Jones; public electricity supplier.

Fiserv, Inc. (FISV): 255 Fiserv Dr., Brookfield, WI 53045; (800) 872-7882; www. fiserv.com; Jeffrey W. Yabuki; financial serv. tech. (First Data; Clover).

Fluor Corp. (FLR): 6700 Las Colinas Blvd., Irving, TX 75039; (469) 398-7000; www. fluor.com; Carlos M. Hernandez; international engineering and construction co.

Foot Locker, Inc. (FL): 330 W. 34th St., NY, NY 10001; (212) 720-3700; www.foot locker-inc.com; Richard A. Johnson; retail athletic stores (Footaction, Foot Locker, Champs Sports).

Ford Motor Co. (F): 1 American Rd., Dearborn, MI 48126; (313) 322-3000; www. ford.com; William C. Ford Jr.; auto mfr.; motor vehicle sales (Ford, Lincoln); auto financing (Ford Motor Credit).

Fox Corp. (FOXA): 1211 Ave. of the Americas, NY, NY 10036; (212) 852-7000; www.foxcorporation.com; Lachlan Murdoch; TV broadcasting (FOX, Fox News). Formed after 3/20/2019 acquisition of most of 21st Century Fox by Walt Disney Co.; see also Disney, News Corp.

Gannett Co., Inc. (GCI): 7950 Jones Branch Dr., McLean, VA 22107; (703) 854-6000; www.gannett.com; Mike Reed; newspaper publisher (*USA Today*).

Gap Inc. (GPS): 2 Folsom St., San Francisco, CA 94105; (650) 952-4400; www.gapinc.com; Sonia Syngal; casual apparel retailer (Athleta, Banana Republic, Old Navy).

Garrett Motion (GTX): Z.A. La Pièce 16, 1180 Rolle, Switzerland; (973) 867-7014; www.garrettmotion.com; Olivier Rabiller; transport systems and tech; spun off from Honeywell, 10/1/2018.

General Dynamics Corp. (GD): 2941 Fairview Park Dr., Ste. 100, Falls Church, VA 22042; (703) 876-3000; www.generaldynamics.com; Phebe N. Novakovic; defense contractor: aerospace, combat systems, marine systems, computing devices.

General Electric Co. (GE): 41 Farnsworth St., Boston, MA 02210; (617) 443-3000; www.ge.com; H. Lawrence Culp Jr.; electrical, electronic equip., financial services, radio and TV broadcasting, aircraft engines, power generation.

General Mills, Inc. (GIS): One General Mills Blvd., Minneapolis, MN 55426; (763) 764-7600; www.generalmills.com; Jeff Harmening; food mfr. (Annie's Homegrown, Betty Crocker, Bisquick, Cheerios, Chex, Häagen-Dazs, Pillsbury, Progresso, Total, Wheaties, Yoplait). Acquired Blue Buffalo Pet Prods., 4/24/2018.

General Motors Co. (GM): 300 Renaissance Ctr., Detroit, MI 48265; (313) 556-5000; www.gm.com; Mary T. Barra; auto mfr. (Chevrolet, Cadillac, Buick, GMC); auto financing (GM Financial); vehicle security (OnStar). General Motors Corp. filed for Ch. 11 reorganization, 6/1/2009; sold profitable components to a new, smaller co. called General Motors Co., 7/10/2009. Sold European brands to France's Peugeot, 7/31/2018.

Genuine Parts Co. (GPC): 2999 Wildwood Pkwy., Atlanta, GA 30339; (678) 934-5000; www.genpt.com; Paul D. Donahue; distrib. auto (NAPA), industrial replacement parts.

Gilead Sciences, Inc. (GILD): 333 Lakeside Dr., Foster City, CA 94404; (650) 574-3000; www.gilead.com; Daniel O'Day; PhD; biopharmaceuticals.

Goldman Sachs Group, Inc. (GS): 200 West St., 29th Fl., NY, NY 10282; (212) 902-1000; www.goldmansachs.com; David Solomon; investment banking, asset mgmt., securities services.

Goodyear Tire & Rubber Co. (GT): 200 Innovation Way, Akron, OH 44316; (330) 796-2121; www.goodyear.com; Richard J. Kramer; tires and other auto prods.

Google, Inc.: see Alphabet Inc.

Graham Holdings Co. (GHC): 1300 N. 17th St., 17th Fl., Arlington, VA 22209; (703) 345-6300; www.ghco.com; Timothy O'Shaughnessy; media (newspapers, Slate.com, TV), education (Kaplan), home health care. Fmr. Washington Post Co.; renamed after 2013 sale of newspaper to Nash Holdings LLC.

Halliburton Co. (HAL): 3000 N. Sam Houston Pkwy. E., Houston, TX 77032; (281) 871-4000; www.halliburton.com; Jeff Miller; oil field mgmt., energy services.

Hanesbrands Inc. (HBI): 1000 E. Hanes Mill Rd., Winston-Salem, NC 27105; (336) 519-8080; www.hanesbrands.com; Gerald W. Evans Jr.; apparel mfr. (Hanes, Barely There, Bali, Champion, Gear for Sports, Just My Size, L'eggs, Maidenform, Playtex, Wonderbra).

Harley-Davidson, Inc. (HOG): 3700 W. Juneau Ave., Milwaukee, WI 53208; (414) 342-4680; www.harley-davidson.com; Jochen Zeitz; mfr. motorcycles, parts, accessories.

Hartford Financial Services Group, Inc. (HIG): One Hartford Plz., Hartford, CT 06155; (860) 547-5000; www.thehartford.com; Christopher J. Swift; insurance, financial services.

Hasbro, Inc. (HAS): 1027 Newport Ave., Pawtucket, RI 02862; (401) 431-8697; www.hasbro.com; Brian Goldner; toy and game mfr. (Playskool, G.I. Joe, Nerf, Play-Doh).

HCA Healthcare, Inc. (HCA): 1 Park Plz., Nashville, TN 37203; (615) 344-9551; www.hcahealthcare.com; Samuel N. Hazen; owns and operates hospitals; other diagnostic, surgical, health treatment centers.

H. J. Heinz Co.: see Kraft Heinz Co.

Henkel Corp.: 200 Elm St., Stamford, CT 06902; (475) 210-0230; www.henkelna.com; Mike Olosky; consumer prods. (Dial soap, Purex detergent, Right Guard antiperspirant, Renuzit air fresheners); U.S. subsidiary of Germany's Henkel co.

Hershey Co., The (HSY): 100 Crystal A Dr., Hershey, PA 17033; (717) 534-4200; www.thehersheycompany.com; Michele Buck; chocolate prods. mfr. (Almond Joy, Brookside, Jolly Rancher, Kit Kat, Milk Duds, Reese's, Twizzlers, York). Acquired Amplify Snack Brands, 1/31/2018.

Hertz Global Holdings, Inc. (HTZ): 225 Brae Blvd., Park Ridge, NJ 07656; (201) 307-2000; www.hertz.com; Paul Stone; car rentals. Filed for Ch. 11 bankruptcy amid the coronavirus pandemic, 5/22/2020.

Hess Corp. (HES): 1185 Ave. of the Americas, 40th Fl., NY, NY 10036; (212) 997-8500; www.hess.com; John B. Hess; integrated oil and gas co.

Hewlett Packard Enterprise (HPE): 6280 America Center Dr., San Jose, CA 95002; (650) 687-5817; www.hpe.com; Antonio Neri; computer prods. (software, servers, storage), consulting, support. Spun off from Hewlett-Packard Co., now HP Inc., 11/2/2015. Spun off and merged enterprise serv. unit with Computer Sciences Corp. to form DXC Technology, 4/3/2017; sold non-core software unit to UK's Micro Focus Intl., 9/1/2017.

Hillshire Brands Co.: see Tyson Foods, Inc.

Hilton Worldwide (HLT): 7930 Jones Branch Dr., Ste. 1100, McLean, VA 22102; (703) 883-1000; www.hiltonworldwide.com; Christopher J. Nassetta; hotels and resorts (Doubletree, Embassy, Hampton). Sold landmark Waldorf Astoria, 2/11/2015.

Home Depot, Inc. (HD): 2455 Paces Ferry Rd. NW, Atlanta, GA 30339; (770) 433-8211; www.homedepot.com; Craig Menear; home improvement store.

Honeywell Intl. Inc. (HON): 115 Tabor Rd., Morris Plains, NJ 07962; (973) 455-2000; www.honeywell.com; Darius Adamczyk; aerospace systems; performance/building tech. Spun off transport systems businesses into Garrett Motion (GTX), 10/1/2018, home security and ADI global dist. businesses into Resideo (REZI), 10/29/2018.

Hormel Foods, Inc. (HRL): 1 Hormel Pl., Austin, MN 55912; (507) 437-5611; www.hormelfoods.com; Jim Snee; food processor, primarily meat (SPAM, Dinty Moore, Jennie-O, Skippy, Applegate Farms). Sold Muscle Milk to PepsiCo, 3/16/2019.

Hostess Brands (TWNK): 1 E. Armour Blvd., Kansas City, MO 64111; (816) 701-4600; www.hostessbrands.com; Andrew P. Callahan; baked goods wholesaler, distrib.

Houghton Mifflin Harcourt Co. (HMHC): 125 High St., Boston, MA 02110; (617) 351-5000; www.hmhco.com; John J. Lynch Jr.; publisher of textbooks and other educational prods. (Holt McDougal, Clarion), trade and reference books. Acquired Scholastic's educational tech. business, 5/29/2015.

HP Inc. (HPQ): 1501 Page Mill Rd., Palo Alto, CA 94304; (650) 857-1501; www8.hp.com; Enrique Lores; computers, electronic prods. and systems.

H&R Block, Inc. (HRB): 1301 Main St., Kansas City, MO 64105; (816) 854-3000;

www.hrblock.com; Jeffrey J. Jones II; tax return preparation; business and consulting services.

Humana Inc. (HUM): 500 W. Main St., Louisville, KY 40202; (502) 580-1000; www.humana.com; Bruce D. Broussard; managed health care service provider, related specialty prods.

IAC/InterActiveCorp (IAC): 555 W. 18th St., NY, NY 10011; (212) 314-7300; www.iac.com; Barry Diller; internet conglomerate (Ask.com, Match.com, Citysearch, The Daily Beast, HomeAdvisor, Vimeo).

iHeartMedia, Inc. (IHRT) (fmr. Clear Channel Communications): 200 E. Basse Rd., Ste. 100, San Antonio, TX 78209; (210) 822-2828; www.iheartmedia.com; Robert Pittman; radio stations. Emerged from bankruptcy, spun off of outdoor ad business, Clear Channel Outdoor Holdings, Inc., 5/1/2019.

Illinois Tool Works Inc. (ITW): 155 Harlem Ave., Glenview, IL 60025; (224) 661-8870; www.itw.com; E. Scott Santi; consumer, industrial tools; food equip. (Hobart), packaging (Zip-Pak).

Ingersoll-Rand plc (IR): 170/175 Lakeview Dr., Airside Business Park, Swords, Dublin, Ireland; 353-1-870-7400; company.ingersollrand.com; Vicente Reynal; low-speed vehicles (Club Car); refrigeration equip. (Thermo King); industrial equip.; air conditioning systems (Trane, American Standard).

Intel Corp. (INTC): 2200 Mission College Blvd., Santa Clara, CA 95054; (408) 765-8080; www.intel.com; Robert Swan; mfr. semiconductors, microprocessors (Core, Centrino).

International Business Machines Corp. (IBM): One New Orchard Rd., Armonk, NY 10504; (914) 499-1900; www.ibm.com; Arvind Krishna; advanced information processing technology equip., services. Acquired cloud software co. Red Hat, 7/9/2019.

International Paper Co. (IP): 6400 Poplar Ave., Memphis, TN 38197; (901) 419-9000; www.internationalpaper.com; Mark Sutton; paper/forest prods.

INTL FCStone Inc. (INTL): 155 East 44th St., Ste. 900, NY, NY 10017; (212) 485-3500; www.intlfcstone.com; Sean O'Connor; securities and commodities advising.

J.C. Penney Co., Inc.: 6501 Legacy Dr., Plano, TX 75024; (972) 431-1000; www.jcpenney.com; Jill Soltau; dept. store retailer, general merchandise catalog sales. Filed for Ch. 11 bankruptcy amid the coronavirus pandemic, 5/15/2020; delisted from NYSE, 5/20/2020.

J.Crew Group, Inc.: 225 Liberty St., NY, NY 10281; (212) 209-2500; www.jcrew.com; Jan Singer; retail and mail order apparel and accessories. Filed for Ch. 11 bankruptcy amid the coronavirus pandemic, 5/4/2020.

JetBlue Airways Corp. (JBLU): 27-01 Queens Plz. N., Long Island City, NY 11101; (718) 286-7900; www.jetblue.com; Robin Hayes; air transportation.

Jo-Ann Stores, Inc.: 5555 Darrow Rd., Hudson, OH 44236; (330) 656-2600; www.joann.com; Wade Miquelon; specialty fabric and craft stores.

Johnson Controls Intl. (JCI): 5757 N. Green Bay Ave., Milwaukee, WI 53209; (414) 524-1200; www.johnsoncontrols.com; George R. Oliver; equip. and controls for heating, ventilating, AC, refrigeration, and building security; auto interiors, batteries.

Johnson & Johnson (JNJ): 1 Johnson & Johnson Plz., New Brunswick, NJ 08933; (732) 524-0400; www.jnj.com; Alex Gorsky; health care prods. (Band-Aid, Neosporin), pharmaceuticals (Tylenol, Motrin, Sudafed), toiletries (Neutrogena, Aveeno, Vogue Intl.).

S. C. Johnson & Son, Inc.: 1525 Howe St., Racine, WI 53403; (262) 260-2000; www.scjohnson.com; H. Fisk Johnson; cleaning and other household prods. (Windex,

Pledge, Fantastik, Raid, OFF!, Shout, Glade, Scrubbing Bubbles, Ziploc).

JPMorgan Chase & Co. (JPM): 383 Madison Ave, NY, NY 10017; (212) 270-6000; www.jpmorganchase.com; James Dimon; financial services.

Kate Spade & Co.: see Tapestry, Inc.

KBR, Inc. (KBR): 601 Jefferson St., Ste. 3400, Houston, TX 77002; (713) 753-2000; www.kbr.com; Stuart Bradie; engineering; construction mgmt. services.

Kellogg Co. (K): One Kellogg Sq., Battle Creek, MI 49016; (269) 961-2000; www.kelloggcompany.com; Steven A. Cahillane; mfr. of ready-to-eat cereals, other food prods. (Frosted Flakes, Rice Krispies, Pop-Tarts, Nutri-Grain, Keebler, Eggo, Pringles, Gardenburger).

Kelly Services, Inc. (KELYA): 999 W. Big Beaver Rd., Troy, MI 48084; (248) 362-4444; www.kellyservices.com; Peter Quigley; temporary staffing services.

Keurig Dr Pepper (KDP): 53 South Ave., Burlington, MA 01803; (877) 208-9991; www.keurigdrpepper.com; Robert Gamgort; coffee, tea, and nonalcoholic beverages (Green Mountain Coffee, Caribou Coffee, Straight Up Tea, Dr Pepper, 7UP, Snapple, Mott's).

Kimberly-Clark Corp. (KMB): 351 Phelps Dr., Irving, TX 75038; (972) 281-1200; www.kimberly-clark.com; Michael D. Hsu; personal care prods. (Kleenex, Scott, Cottonelle, Huggies, Kotex).

Kinder Morgan, Inc. (KMI): 1001 Louisiana St., Ste. 1000, Houston, TX 77002; (713) 369-9000; www.kindermorgan.com; Richard D. Kinder; energy trans. and storage.

Kmart Corp.: see Transformco

Koch Industries, Inc.: P.O. Box 2256, Wichita, KS 67201; (316) 828-5500; www.kochind.com; Charles G. Koch; forest prod. mfr.; oil refineries/pipeline; chemicals; pollution-control equip.; ranching.

Kraft Heinz Co. (KHC): 1 PPG Pl., Ste. 3100, Pittsburgh, PA 15222; (412) 456-5700; www.kraftheinzcompany.com; Miguel Patricio; food and beverage mfr. (Ore-Ida, 57 Varieties ketchup, Velveeta, Crystal Light, Maxwell House, Kool-Aid, Lunchables, Jell-O, Oscar Mayer). Formed from merger of Kraft Foods Group with H.J. Heinz Co., 7/2/2015.

Kroger Co. (KR): 1014 Vine St., Cincinnati, OH 45202; (513) 762-4000; www.thekrogerco.com; W. Rodney McMullen; grocery, convenience, and mall jewelry stores.

L Brands, Inc. (LB) (fmr. Limited Brands): 3 Limited Pkwy., Columbus, OH 43230; (614) 415-7000; www.lb.com; Andrew Meslow; apparel stores (Victoria's Secret, PINK), home decor, personal care (Bath & Body Works).

Las Vegas Sands Corp. (LVS): 3355 Las Vegas Blvd. S., Las Vegas, NV 89109; (702) 414-1000; www.sands.com; Sheldon G. Adelson; casino-resort operator (Venetian, Palazzo, Sands Macao).

La-Z-Boy Inc. (LZB): One La-Z-Boy Dr., Monroe, MI 48162; (855) 802-6636; www.la-z-boy.com; Kurt L. Darrow; reclining chairs, other furniture.

Levi Strauss & Co. (LEVI): 1155 Battery St., San Francisco, CA 94111; (415) 501-6000; www.levistrauss.com; Charles Bergh; blue jeans, casual sportswear (Dockers).

Liberty Mutual Holding Co. Inc.: 175 Berkeley St., Boston, MA 02116; (617) 357-9500; www.libertymutual.com; David H. Long; insurance prods. and services.

LinkedIn Corp.: see Microsoft

Liz Claiborne, Inc.: see J.C. Penney Co., Inc.

L.L.Bean, Inc.: 15 Casco St., Freeport, ME 04033; (207) 552-2000; www.llbean.com; Stephen Smith; catalog and retail outdoor apparel, footwear, gear.

Lockheed Martin Corp. (LMT): 6801 Rockledge Dr., Bethesda, MD 20817; (301) 897-6000; www.lockheedmartin.com; Jim Taiclet; leading U.S. defense contractor; aircraft, electronics, missiles, information tech., and communications. Bought

Sikorsky Aircraft from United Technologies, 11/6/2015.

Loews Corp. (L): 667 Madison Ave., NY, NY 10065; (212) 521-2000; www.loews.com; James S. Tisch; hotels, insurance (CNA Financial), offshore drilling (Diamond).

Lorillard, Inc.: see Reynolds American Inc.

Lowe's Cos., Inc. (LOW): 1000 Lowe's Blvd., Mooresville, NC 28117; (704) 758-1000; www.lowes.com; Marvin R. Ellison; building material and home improvement superstores.

LSC Communications: 191 N. Wacker Dr., Ste. 1400, Chicago, IL 60606; (773) 272-9200; www.lsccom.com; Thomas J. Quinlan III; printing services, supply chain mgmt.

Macy's, Inc. (M): 7 W. 7th St., Cincinnati, OH 45202; (513) 579-7000; www.macysinc.com; Jeff Gennette; retailer (Macy's, Bloomingdale's, Bluemercury). Announced closure of approx. 125 stores over next 3 years, 2/5/2020.

ManpowerGroup (MAN): 100 Manpower Pl., Milwaukee, WI 53212; (414) 961-1000; www.manpowergroup.com; Jonas Prising; employment services.

Marathon Oil Corp. (MRO): 5555 San Felipe St., Houston, TX 77056; (713) 629-6600; www.marathonoil.com; Lee M. Tillman; integrated oil co. Acquired Andeavor for $23.3 bil, 10/1/2018.

Marriott International, Inc. (MAR): 10400 Fernwood Rd., Bethesda, MD 20817; (301) 380-3000; www.marriott.com; Arne M. Sorenson; hotels (Renaissance, Courtyard, Fairfield Inn, Ritz-Carlton).

Mars, Inc.: 6885 Elm St., McLean, VA 22101; (703) 821-4900; www.mars.com; Grant F. Reid; food mfr., including of chocolate (M&M's, Snickers, Dove), food (Uncle Ben's), pet food (Pedigree, Whiskas, Iams, Eukanuba, Sheba) and services.

Massachusetts Mutual Life Insurance Co. (MassMutual Financial Group): 1295 State St., Springfield, MA 01111; (413) 744-1000; www.massmutual.com; Roger W. Crandall; financial planning and investment, life insurance.

MasterCard Inc. (MA): 2000 Purchase St., Purchase, NY 10577; (914) 249-2000; www.mastercard.com; Ajay Banga; financial services.

Mattel, Inc. (MAT): 333 Continental Blvd., El Segundo, CA 90245; (310) 252-2000; www.mattel.com; Ynon Kreiz; toymaker (Barbie, Fisher-Price, Hot Wheels, Matchbox, American Girls).

McClatchy Co. (MNIQQ): 2100 Q St., Sacramento, CA 95816; (916) 321-1855; www.mcclatchy.com; Craig I. Forman; newspaper publisher. Filed for Ch. 11 bankruptcy, 2/13/2020.

McDonald's Corp. (MCD): 2111 McDonald's Plz., Oak Brook, IL 60523; (630) 623-3000; www.mcdonalds.com; Chris Kempczinski; fast food.

McGraw-Hill Financial: see S&P Global, Inc.

McKesson Corp. (MCK): 1 Post St., San Francisco, CA 94104; (415) 983-8300; www.mckesson.com; Brian Tyler; distrib. of drugs and toiletries; provides mgmt. software and services.

Medco Health Solutions, Inc.: see Express Scripts Holding Co.

Merck & Co., Inc. (MRK): 2000 Galloping Hill Rd., Kenilworth, NJ 07033; (908) 740-4000; www.merck.com; Kenneth C. Frazier; pharmaceuticals (Gardasil, Keytruda, Propecia, Singulair, Vytorin, Zocor). Acquired cancer drug prod. Peloton Therapeutics, 7/2019.

Meredith Corp. (MDP): 1716 Locust St., Des Moines, IA 50309; (515) 284-3000; www.meredith.com; Tom Harty; magazine publishing (Better Homes and Gardens, Eating Well, Parents, Family Circle, Every Day With Rachael Ray, FamilyFun), book publishing, broadcasting, online media (allrecipes.com). Acquired publisher Time Inc. (Entertainment Weekly, People), 1/31/2018; sold Time, 11/1/2018; sold Sports Illustrated brand, 5/27/2019.

Merrill Lynch & Co., Inc.: see Bank of America Corp.

MetLife, Inc. (MET): 200 Park Ave., NY, NY 10166; (212) 578-2211; www.metlife.com; Michel A. Khalaf; insurance, financial services.

MGM Resorts Intl. (MGM): 3600 S. Las Vegas Blvd., Las Vegas, NV 89109; (702) 693-7120; www.mgmresorts.com; Bill Hornbuckle; hotel-casino operator (Mirage, New York-New York, Luxor, Bellagio, Circus Circus, Monte Carlo).

Microsoft Corp. (MSFT): One Microsoft Way, Redmond, WA 98052; (425) 882-8080; www.microsoft.com; Satya Nadella; software (Windows, Word, Excel); video games (Minecraft, Xbox); networking site LinkedIn. Acquired AI start-up Bonsai, 7/2018; code repository GitHub, 10/26/2018.

Molson Coors Brewing Co. (TAP): 1801 California St., Ste. 4600, Denver, CO 80202; (303) 927-2337; www.molsoncoors.com; Gavin Hattersley; brewer. Acquired SABMiller's global Miller brands and majority stake in joint venture, MillerCoors, following Anheuser-Busch InBev's buyout of SABMiller, 10/11/2016.

Mondelez International, Inc. (MDLZ): 100 Deforest Ave., East Hanover, NJ 07936; (855) 535-5648; www.mondelezinternational.com; Dirk Van de Put; global food mfr., including Nabisco (Oreo), Cadbury, Tang, Trident.

Monsanto Co.: see Bayer AG

Morgan Stanley (MS): 1585 Broadway, NY, NY 10036; (212) 761-4000; www.morganstanley.com; James P. Gorman; diversified financial services. Agreed to acquire online trading firm E-Trade for approx. $13 bil, 2/20/2020.

Motorola Solutions, Inc. (MSI): 500 W Monroe St., Ste. 4400, Chicago, IL 60661; (847) 576-5000; www.motorolasolutions.com; Gregory Q. Brown; electronic equip. and components; communication devices.

Nationwide Mutual Insurance Co.: One Nationwide Plz., Columbus, OH 43215; (614) 249-7111; www.nationwide.com; Kirt Walker; property/casualty, life insurance; financial services.

Navistar Intl. Corp. (NAV): 2701 Navistar Dr., Lisle, IL 60532; (331) 332-5000; www.navistar.com; Troy Clarke; mfr. heavy-duty trucks, parts, school buses.

NBCUniversal: 30 Rockefeller Plz., NY, NY 10112; (212) 664-4444; www.nbcuni.com; Jeff Shell; news/entertainment producer; TV and CATV (NBC, Bravo, USA, Telemundo); film production. Owned by Comcast and General Electric.

NCR Corp. (NCR): 864 Spring St. NW, Atlanta, GA 30308; (937) 445-1936; www.ncr.com; Michael Hayford; mfr. ATMs, retail technology, hardware and software; computer services and supplies.

Nestlé USA, Inc.: 800 N. Brand Blvd., Glendale, CA 91203; (818) 549-6000; www.nestleusa.com; Steve Presley; beverages (Nestea, Ovaltine), food (Buitoni, Coffee-Mate), frozen foods (Stouffer's, Häagen-Dazs, Lean Cuisine), pet foods (Purina, Alpo, Friskies). Subsidiary of Nestlé SA in Switzerland; sold U.S. candy business to Italy's Ferrero, 3/31/2018.

Netflix, Inc. (NFLX): 100 Winchester Cir., Los Gatos, CA 95032; (408) 540-3700; www.netflix.com; Reed Hastings; online DVD rentals; streaming video.

New York Life Insurance Co.: 51 Madison Ave., NY, NY 10010; (212) 576-7000; www.newyorklife.com; Theodore A. Mathas; life insurance, annuities, mutual funds.

New York Times Co. (NYT): 620 8th Ave., NY, NY 10018; (212) 556-1234; www.nytco.com; A. G. Sulzberger; newspapers.

Newell Brands (NWL): 6655 Peachtree Dunwoody Rd., Atlanta, GA 30328; (770) 418-7000; www.newellbrands.com; Ravi Saligram; housewares (Rubbermaid, Calphalon); writing utensils (Parker, Sharpie, Paper Mate); juvenile prods. (Graco). Sold Goody, 8/13/2018.

News Corp. (NWS): 1211 Ave. of the Americas, NY, NY 10036; (212) 416-3400; www.newscorp.com; K. Rupert Murdoch; publisher (HarperCollins), *Wall Street Journal*, *Barron's*); digital media (MarketWatch).

NextEra Energy, Inc. (NEE): 700 Universe Blvd., Juno Beach, FL 33408; (561) 694-4000; www.nexteraenergy.com; James L. Robo; electricity generation/distrib.

NIKE, Inc. (NKE): 1 Bowerman Dr., Beaverton, OR 97005; (503) 671-6453; www.nike.com; John Donahoe; athletic footwear and apparel mfr.

Nokia (NOK): Karaportti 3, Espoo 02610, Finland; +358 (0) 10 44 88 000; www.nokia.com; Pekka Lundmark; telecom. equip., computer software.

Nordstrom, Inc. (JWN): 1600 7th Ave., Ste. 2600, Seattle, WA 98101; (206) 628-2111; www.nordstrom.com; Erik B. Nordstrom; upscale dept. store chain.

Norfolk Southern Corp. (NSC): Three Commercial Pl., Norfolk, VA 23510; (855) 667-3655; www.nscorp.com; James A. Squires; railway operator; freight carrier.

Northrop Grumman Corp. (NOC): 2980 Fairview Park Dr., Falls Church, VA 22042; (703) 280-2900; www.northropgrumman.com; Kathy J. Warden; defense contractor: aircraft, electronics, data systems, information systems, missiles.

Northwest Airlines Corp.: see Delta Air Lines, Inc.

Northwestern Mutual Life Insurance Co.: 720 E. Wisconsin Ave., Milwaukee, WI 53202; (414) 271-1444; www.northwesternmutual.com; John E. Schlifske; life insurance, investment prods. and services, annuities.

Oath Inc.: see Verizon Communications Inc.

Occidental Petroleum Corp. (OXY): Five Greenway Plz., Ste. 110, Houston, TX 77046; (713) 215-7000; www.oxy.com; Vicki A. Hollub; oil, natural gas, chemicals, plastics. Bought Anadarko Petroleum Corp. for $55 bil, 8/8/2019.

Office Depot, Inc. (ODP): 6600 N. Military Trl., Boca Raton, FL 33496; (561) 438-4800; www.officedepot.com; Gerry P. Smith; office supply retail stores.

Omnicom Group Inc. (OMC): 437 Madison Ave., NY, NY 10022; (212) 415-3600; www.omnicomgroup.com; John D. Wren; advertising, marketing, interactive/digital media.

Oracle Corp. (ORCL): 500 Oracle Pkwy., Redwood Shores, CA 94065; (650) 506-7000; www.oracle.com; Lawrence J. Ellison; database and file mgmt. software. Acquired DataScience.com, 6/6/2018.

Payless ShoeSource, Inc.: 3231 SE 6th Ave., Topeka, KS 66607; (785) 233-5171; www.collectivebrands.com; Jared Margolis; shoe mfr./retailer. Filed for Ch. 11 bankruptcy after announcing upcoming closure of 2,300+ U.S./Canadian stores, 2/18/2019. Emerged from bankruptcy, 1/16/2020.

PepsiCo, Inc. (PEP): 700 Anderson Hill Rd., Purchase, NY 10577; (914) 253-2000; www.pepsico.com; Ramon Laguarta; soft drinks and other beverages (Pepsi-Cola, Mountain Dew, Gatorade, Tropicana), snacks and cereals (Fritos, Lay's, Ruffles, Quaker). Acquired SodaStream, 12/5/2018; Muscle Milk, 4/16/2019.

Pfizer, Inc. (PFE): 235 E. 42nd St., NY, NY 10017; (212) 733-2323; www.pfizer.com; Albert Bourla; biopharmaceuticals (Celebrex, Hospira, Lipitor, Viagra, Zoloft); human and animal health care prods. Acquired oncology-focused Array BioPharma, 7/30/2019. Merged consumer healthcare division with GlaxoSmithKline, 8/1/2019.

PG&E Corp. (PCG): 77 Beale St., 24th Fl., San Francisco, CA 94105; (415) 973-8200; www.pgecorp.com; William D. Johnson; operates Pacific Gas and Electric public utility. Filed for Ch. 11 bankruptcy amid California lawsuits, 1/29/2019. Emerged from bankruptcy, 7/1/2020. Pleaded guilty to manslaughter for causing 2018 Camp Fire, 6/16/2020.

Philip Morris Intl. Inc. (PM): 120 Park Ave., 7th Fl., NY, NY 10017; (917) 663-2000; www.pmi.com; André Calantzopoulos; intl. mfr. and distrib. of tobacco. (Altria spun off intl. Philip Morris operations in 2008 but owns Philip Morris brands in U.S.)

Phillips 66 Co. (PSX): P.O. Box 421959, Houston, TX 77242; (281) 293-6600; www.phillips66.com; Greg C. Garland; oil, gas refining and marketing.

Pitney Bowes Inc. (PBI): 3001 Summer St., Stamford, CT 06926; (203) 356-5000; www.pb.com; Marc B. Lautenbach; postage meters and mailing equip.

Post Holdings, Inc. (POST): 2503 S. Hanley Rd., St. Louis, MO 63144; (314) 644-7600; www.postfoods.com; Robert V. Vitale; ready-to-eat cereals.

PPG Industries, Inc. (PPG): 1 PPG Pl., Pittsburgh, PA 15272; (412) 434-3131; www.ppg.com; Michael H. McGarry; glass prods., silicas, fiberglass, chemicals, sealants.

Priceline Group Inc.: see Booking Holdings.

Procter & Gamble Co. (PG): 1 Procter & Gamble Plz., Cincinnati, OH 45202; (513) 983-1100; www.pg.com; David S. Taylor; soaps and detergents (Ivory, Cheer, Tide, Mr. Clean); toiletries (Crest, Scope, Head & Shoulders, Old Spice); pharmaceuticals (Pepto-Bismol, Vicks cough medicines); paper prods. (Charmin toilet tissues, Bounty towels), Tampax tampons; disposable diapers (Pampers, Luvs); Gillette razors.

Prudential Financial, Inc. (PRU): 751 Broad St., Newark, NJ 07102; (973) 802-6000; www.prudential.com; Charles F. Lowrey; insurance, financial services.

Publix Super Markets Inc.: 3300 Publix Corporate Pkwy., Lakeland, FL 33811; (863) 688-1188; www.publix.com; Todd Jones; supermarket chain.

PVH Corp. (PVH): 200 Madison Ave., NY, NY 10016; (212) 381-3500; www.pvh.com; Emanuel Chirico; apparel mfr., including licensed brands (Calvin Klein, IZOD, Tommy Hilfiger).

Qualcomm, Inc. (QCOM): 5775 Morehouse Dr., San Diego, CA 92121; (858) 587-1121; www.qualcomm.com; Steve Mollenkopf; semiconductor, telecommunications equip design. Merger with Singapore-based Broadcom blocked by White House over natl. security, 3/12/2018.

Quest Diagnostics Inc. (DGX): 500 Plaza Dr., Secaucus, NJ 07094; (973) 520-2700; www.questdiagnostics.com; Stephen Rusckowski; leading clinical laboratory. Agreed to acquire U.S. lab services business of UK-based Oxford Immunotec, 9/25/2018.

Ralcorp Holdings, Inc.: see ConAgra Foods, Inc.

Ralph Lauren Corp. (RL): 650 Madison Ave., NY, NY 10022; (212) 318-7000; www.ralphlauren.com; Patrice Louvet; men's and women's apparel, home furnishings, fragrances.

Raytheon Technologies Corp. (RTX): 870 Winter St., Waltham, MA 02451; (781) 522-3000; www.rtx.com; Gregory J. Hayes; aerospace, defense, communications systems. Formed through merger of Raytheon Corp. with United Technologies Corp.; spun off Carrier and Otis, 4/3/2020.

Reader's Digest Assn., Inc.: see Trusted Media Brands, Inc.

Republic Services, Inc. (RSG): 18500 N. Allied Way, Phoenix, AZ 85054; (480) 627-2700; www.republicservices.com; Donald W. Slager; waste mgmt. co.

Resideo Technologies, Inc. (REZI): 901 E. Sixth St., Austin, TX 78702; www.resideo.com; Jay Geldmacher; spin-off of home control systems, ADI global dist. businesses from Honeywell, 10/29/2018.

Restaurant Brands Intl. (QSR): 226 Wyecroft Rd., Oakville, ON L6K 3X7, Canada; (905) 845-6511; www.rbi.com; José Cil; fast food restaurants (Burger King, Popeyes, Tim Hortons).

Revlon, Inc. (REV): One New York Plaza, NY, NY 10004; (212) 527-4000; www.revlon.com; Debra G. Perelman; cosmetics, skin care.

Reynolds American Inc.: 401 N. Main St., Winston-Salem, NC 27101; (336) 741-2000; www.reynoldsamerican.com; Ricardo Oberlander; cigarettes (Camel, Pall Mall, Doral, Newport), smokeless tobacco (Grizzly, Kodiak), e-cigarettes (VUSE). Subsidiary of British American Tobacco, world's largest tobacco co.

Rite Aid Corp. (RAD): 30 Hunter Ln., Camp Hill, PA 17011; (717) 761-2633; www.riteaid.com; Heyward Donigan; retail drugstores. Sold 1,932 stores and related assets to Walgreens Boots Alliance, 3/27/2018.

Rockwell Automation, Inc. (ROK): 1201 S. 2nd St., Milwaukee, WI 53204; (414) 382-2000; www.rockwellautomation.com; Blake Moret; industrial automation co.

Ryder System, Inc. (R): 11690 NW 105th St., Miami, FL 33178; (305) 500-3726; www.ryder.com; Robert E. Sanchez; truck-leasing service.

SABMiller plc: see Anheuser-Busch InBev.

Safeway Inc.: see Albertsons Companies, LLC.

S&P Global, Inc. (SPGI): 55 Water St., NY, NY 10041; (212) 438-1000; www.spglobal.com; Douglas L. Peterson; financial information, services (Standard & Poor's). Formerly McGraw-Hill Financial; renamed 4/27/16.

Schering-Plough Corp.: see Merck & Co., Inc.

Schlumberger Limited Co. (SLB): 3600 Briarpark Dr., Houston, TX 77042; (713) 375-3400; www.slb.com; Paal Kibsgaard; oil equip. and services.

Sears Holdings Corp.: see Transformco

Shell Oil Co.: 1000 Main St., Ste. 1700, Houston, TX 77002; (713) 767-5300; www.shell.us; Gretchen Watkins; integrated oil co.; subsidiary of Royal Dutch Shell.

Sherwin-Williams Co. (SHW): 101 W. Prospect Ave., Cleveland, OH 44115; (216) 566-2000; www.sherwin-williams.com; John G. Morikis; paint and varnish producer (Dutch Boy, Krylon, Minwax, Valspar).

Simon Property Group, Inc. (SPG): 225 W. Washington St., Indianapolis, IN 46204; (317) 636-1600; www.simon.com; David E. Simon; global real estate.

Sinclair Broadcast Group, Inc. (SBGI): 10706 Beaver Dam Rd., Hunt Valley, MD 21030; (410) 568-1500; www.sbgi.net; Christopher S. Ripley; TV broadcasting (192 stations); local news producer. Acquired 21 regional sports networks from Walt Disney Co., 8/23/2019.

Sirius XM Holdings Inc. (SIRI): 1221 Ave. of the Americas, 36th Fl., NY, NY 10020; (212) 584-5100; www.siriusxm.com; James E. Meyer; satellite radio.

Smithfield Foods, Inc.: 200 Commerce St., Smithfield, VA 23430; (757) 365-3000; www.smithfieldfoods.com; Kenneth M. Sullivan; pork producer and processor. Subsidiary of China-based WH Group since 9/26/2013.

J. M. Smucker Co. (SJM): One Strawberry Ln., Orrville, OH 44667; (330) 682-3000; www.smuckers.com; Mark T. Smucker; leading producer of fruit spreads, peanut butter (Jif), oils (Crisco), coffee (Folgers), baking prods. (Pillsbury), pet foods (Milk-Bone, Kibbles 'n Bits).

Snap Inc. (SNAP): 2772 Donald Douglas Loop N., Santa Monica, CA 90405; (310) 399-3339; www.snap.com; Evan Spiegel; social media and tech co. (Bitmoji, Snapchat, Spectacles).

Sony Corp. of America: 25 Madison Ave., NY, NY 10016; (212) 833-6800; www.sony.com; Kenichiro Yoshida; U.S. subsidiary of Japan-based Sony Corp.; electronics, movies, music.

Southwest Airlines Co. (LUV): 2702 Love Field Dr., Dallas, TX 75235; (214) 792-4000; www.southwest.com; Gary C. Kelly; air transportation.

Sprint Corp.: 6200 Sprint Pkwy., Overland Park, KS 66251; (703) 433-4000; www.sprint.com; Michel Combes; wireless and long-distance telecommunications. Acquired by T-Mobile, 4/1/2020.

Stanley Black & Decker, Inc. (SWK): 1000 Stanley Dr., New Britain, CT 06053; (860) 225-5111; www.stanleyblackanddecker.com; James M. Loree; hand and power tools (DeWalt, Bostitch, Irwin, Lenox), fastening prods. (Gripco, Masterfix).

Staples, Inc.: 500 Staples Dr., Framingham, MA 01702; (508) 253-5000; www.staples.com; J. Alexander Douglas; office-supply retailer.

Starbucks Corp. (SBUX): 2401 Utah Ave. S., Seattle, WA 98134; (206) 447-1575; www.starbucks.com; Kevin Johnson; coffee producer; world's leading specialty coffee retailer.

Starwood Hotels & Resorts Worldwide, Inc.: see Marriott International, Inc.

State Farm Mutual Automobile Ins. Co.: 1 State Farm Plz., Bloomington, IL 61710; (309) 766-2311; www.statefarm.com; Michael L. Tipsord; auto/homeowners insurance.

Sun Microsystems, Inc.: see Oracle Corp.

SuperValu Inc.: East View Innovation Ctr., 11840 Valley View Rd., Eden Prairie, MN 55344; (952) 828-4000; www.supervalu.com; Steven L. Spinner; food retailer, wholesale distrib. (Cub Foods, Shoppers). Acquired by rival food wholesaler United Natural Foods Inc. (UNFI), 10/22/2018.

Sysco Corp. (SYY): 1390 Enclave Pkwy., Houston, TX 77077; (281) 584-1390; www.sysco.com; Kevin Hourican; foodservice distrib.

Tapestry, Inc. (TPR) (fmr. Coach Inc.): 10 Hudson Yards, NY, NY 10001; (212) 594-1850; www.tapestry.com; Joanne Crevoiseart; luxury fashion brands (Coach, Kate Spade, Stuart Weitzman).

Target Corp. (TGT): 1000 Nicollet Mall, Minneapolis, MN 55403; (612) 304-6073; www.target.com; Brian Cornell; discount retailer.

TEGNA, Inc. (TGNA): 8350 Broad St., Ste. 2000, Tysons, VA 22102; (703) 873-6600; www.tegna.com; Dave Lougee; network and cable TV, digital marketing, websites.

Tenneco Inc. (TEN): 500 N. Field Dr., Lake Forest, IL 60045; (847) 482-5000; www.tenneco.com; Brian Kesseler; automotive parts (Monroe, Walker).

Tesla Motors, Inc. (TSLA): 3500 Deer Creek Rd., Palo Alto, CA 94304; (650) 681-5000; www.teslamotors.com; Elon Musk; electric vehicles and batteries.

Texas Instruments (TXN): 12500 TI Blvd., Dallas, TX 75243; (972) 995-2011; www.ti.com; Richard K. Templeton; processors, semiconductors, software, handheld calculators.

Textron Inc. (TXT): 40 Westminster St., Providence, RI 02903; (401) 421-2800; www.textron.com; Scott C. Donnelly; aircraft (Cessna, Bell, Beechcraft); pilot training; industrial, auto prods.; financial services.

3M Co. (MMM): 3M Center, St. Paul, MN 55144; (651) 733-1110; www.3m.com; Michael F. Roman; abrasives, adhesives, electrical, health care, printing, consumer prods. (Post-it, Scotch-Brite, Scotch Tape, Scotchgard).

TIAA: 730 Third Ave., NY, NY 10017; (401) 490-9000; www.tiaa.org; Roger W. Ferguson Jr.; financial services provider.

Time Inc.: see Meredith Corp.

TJX Cos., Inc. (TJX): 770 Cochituate Rd., Framingham, MA 01701; (508) 390-1000; www.tjx.com; Ernie Herrman; off-price apparel retailer (T.J. Maxx, Marshalls); home furnishing retailer (HomeGoods).

T-Mobile US, Inc. (TMUS): 12920 SE 38th St., Bellevue, WA 98006; (425) 378-4000; www.t-mobile.com; Michael Sievert; wireless telecommunications. Acquired Sprint, 4/1/2020.

Toro Co. (TTC): 8111 Lyndale Ave. S, Bloomington, MN 55420; (952) 888-8801; www.thetorocompany.com; Richard M. Olson; lawn and turf maintenance prods.

(Lawn-Boy), snow removal equip.; irrigation systems.

Transformco: 3333 Beverly Rd., Hoffman Estates, IL 60179; (847) 286-2500; www.transformco.com; Eddie S. Lampert; retail department stores. Formed in 2019 after Sears Holding Corp. (Kmart, Sears) filed for Ch. 11 bankruptcy in 2018. Lampert won auction to keep open about 400 U.S. stores.

The Travelers Companies, Inc. (TRV): 485 Lexington Ave., NY, NY 10017; (917) 778-6000; www.travelers.com; Alan D. Schnitzer; insurance.

Tribune Media Co.: 435 N. Michigan Ave., Chicago, IL 60611; (312) 222-9100; www.tribunemedia.com; Peter M. Kern; broadcasting (incl. WGN and 41 other owned/operated television stations, radio), Tribune Studios.

Tribune Publishing Co. (TPCO): 435 N. Michigan Ave., Chicago, IL 60611; (312) 222-9100; www.tribpub.com; Terry Jimenez; newspaper publisher (*Chicago Tribune, NY Daily News*). Sold *L.A. Times*, 6/18/2018.

Trusted Media Brands, Inc. (fmr. Reader's Digest Assn.): 750 Third Ave., 3rd Fl., NY, NY 10017; (914) 238-1000; www.tmbi.com; Bonnie Kintzer; publisher (*Taste of Home*, *Reader's Digest*, *Birds & Blooms*); marketer of books, music, video prods.

21st Century Fox, Inc.: see Disney, Fox Corp.

Twitter, Inc. (TWTR): 1355 Market St., Ste. 900, San Francisco, CA, 94103; (415) 222-9670; twitter.com; Jack Dorsey; microblogging/social networking services.

Tyco Intl. Ltd.: see Johnson Controls Intl.

Tyson Foods, Inc. (TSN): 2200 W. Don Tyson Pkwy., Springdale, AR 72762; (479) 290-4000; www.tysonfoods.com; Noel White; fresh and processed poultry; beef and pork prods. (Ball Park, Hillshire Farm, Jimmy Dean); Sara Lee prods.

Uber (UBER): 1455 Market St., 4th Fl., San Francisco, CA, 94103; (415) 986-2715; www.uber.com; Dara Khosrowshahi; mobile app-based taxi and food delivery services. IPO and largest first-day dollar loss in U.S. history, 5/10/2019; acquired Middle Eastern rival Careem, 1/2/2020.

UBS Financial Services Inc.: 1285 Ave. of the Americas, NY, NY 10019; (212) 713-2000; www.ubs.com; Sergio P. Ermotti; financial services; subsidiary of Switzerland's UBS AG.

Unilever USA (UN/UL): 800 Sylvan Ave., Englewood Cliffs, NJ 07632; (201) 894-4000; www.unileverusa.com; Alan Jope; food (Hellmann's, Knorr, Lipton, Klondike), hygiene prods. (Dove, Q-tips, Vaseline, Dermalogica, Murad). Subsidiary of Unilever NV (Neth.) and Unilever plc (UK).

Union Pacific Corp. (UNP): 1400 Douglas St., Omaha, NE, 68179; (402) 544-5000; www.up.com; Lance M. Fritz; one of the largest railroad freight cos. in U.S.

Unisys Corp. (UIS): 801 Lakeview Dr., Ste. 100, Blue Bell, PA 19422; (215) 986-4011; www.unisys.com; Peter A. Altabef; designs, manuf. IT systems; IT consulting.

United Airlines Holdings, Inc. (UAL): 233 S. Wacker Dr., Chicago IL 60606; (312) 997-8000; www.united.com; Scott Kirby; air transportation (United Airlines).

United Parcel Service, Inc. (UPS): 55 Glenlake Pkwy. NE, Atlanta, GA 30328; (404) 828-6000; www.ups.com; Carol Tomé; shipping, logistics.

United States Steel Corp. (X): 600 Grant St., Pittsburgh, PA 15219; (412) 433-1121; www.ussteel.com; David B. Burritt; steel, tin prods., resource mgmt.

United Technologies Corp.: see Raytheon Technologies Corp.

UnitedHealth Group Inc. (UNH): UHG Center, 9900 Bren Rd. E., Minnetonka, MN 55343; (952) 936-1300; www.unitedhealthgroup.com; David S. Wichmann; health insurance.

U.S. Bancorp (USB): 800 Nicollet Mall, Minneapolis, MN, 55402; (651) 466-3000;

www.usbank.com; Andrew Cecere; financial services.

Valero Energy Corp. (VLO): One Valero Way, San Antonio, TX 78249; (210) 345-2000; www.valero.com; Joe Gorder; fuel mfg. and marketing.

Verizon Communications Inc. (VZ): 1 Verizon Way, Basking Ridge, NJ 07920; (908) 559-5490; www.verizon.com; Hans Vestberg; telecom services; digital media. Subsidiary Verizon Media (fmr. Oath, Inc.) formed through acquisition of Yahoo's core internet business and AOL. Agreed to sell social networking site Tumblr to WordPress owner Automattic, 8/12/2019.

VF Corp. (VFC): 8505 East Orchard Rd., Greenwood Village, CO 80111; (336) 424-6000; www.vfc.com; Steve Rendle; apparel (North Face, Timberland), backpacks (JanSport), shoes (Vans). Spun off VF Outlet and jeans business (including Lee, Rock & Republic and Wrangler) into separate co. Kontoor Brands, Inc., 5/23/2019.

ViacomCBS Inc. (VIAC/VIACA): 1515 Broadway, NY, NY 10036; (212) 258-6000; www.viacomcbs.com; Robert Bakish; TV networks (CBS), and CATV (BET, Comedy Central, MTV, VH1, Nickelodeon); movies (Paramount); radio stations; book publishing (Simon & Schuster). Subsidiary of National Amusements.

Visa Inc. (V): 900 Metro Center Blvd., Foster City, CA 94404; (650) 432-3200; www.visa.com; Alfred F. Kelly Jr.; financial services.

Visteon Corp. (VC): One Village Center Dr., Van Buren Twp., MI 48111; (734) 710-5000; www.visteon.com; Sachin Lawande; automotive parts mfr.

Walgreens Boots Alliance, Inc. (WBA): 108 Wilmot Rd., Deerfield, IL 60015; (847) 315-3700; www.walgreensbootsalliance.com; Stefano Pessina; retail drugstores, pharmaceutical wholesale/distrib. (Alliance Healthcare). Acquired 1,932 RiteAid stores and related assets, 3/27/2018.

Walmart Inc. (WMT): 702 SW 8th St., Bentonville, AR 72716; (479) 273-4000; www.walmartstores.com; Doug McMillon; discount stores, warehouse clubs (Sam's Club). Announced imminent closure of 63 Sam's Club stores, 1/11/2018. Acquired 77% stake in Indian retail giant Flipkart, 8/18/2018.

WarnerMedia Inc. (fmr. Time Warner): 30 Hudson Yards, NY, NY 10001; (212) 484-8000; www.warnermediagroup.com; Jason Kilar; TV and CATV (Cartoon Network, HBO, CNN, TBS, TNT), motion pictures (Warner Bros.), recordings. AOL and Time Warner completed the largest corporate merger in history in 2001; spun off AOL, 12/9/2009. Acquired by AT&T in $85.4-bil buyout, 6/14/2018.

Washington Post Co.: see Graham Holdings Co.

Waste Management, Inc. (WM): 1001 Fannin St., Ste. 4000, Houston, TX 77002; (713) 512-6200; www.wm.com; James C. Fish Jr.; waste, recycling.

WellPoint, Inc.: see Anthem, Inc.

Wells Fargo & Co. (WFC): 420 Montgomery St., San Francisco, CA 94104; (866) 249-3302; www.wellsfargo.com; Timothy J. Sloan; financial services.

Wendy's Co. (WEN): 1 Dave Thomas Blvd., Dublin, OH 43017; (614) 764-3100; www.aboutwendys.com; Todd A. Penegor; fast food restaurants.

Western Union Co. (WU): 12500 E. Belford Ave., Englewood, CO 80112; (720) 332-1000; www.westernunion.com; Hikmet Ersek; money transfers, payment services.

WestRock Co. (WRK): 1000 Abernathy Rd. NE, Atlanta, GA 30328; (770) 448-2193; www.westrock.com; Steven C. Vorhees; packaging, shipping containers; chemicals.

Weyerhaeuser Co. (WY): 220 Occidental Ave. S., Seattle, WA 98104; (206) 539-3000; www.weyerhaeuser.com; Devin W. Stockfish; produces, distributes wood prods.; real estate development.

Whirlpool Corp. (WHR): 2000 N. M-63, Benton Harbor, MI 49022; (269) 923-5000; www.whirlpoolcorp.com; Marc Bitzer; mfr. of major home appliances (KitchenAid, Amana, Maytag).

Whole Foods Market, Inc.: see Amazon

Winnebago Industries, Inc. (WGO): 605 W. Crystal Lake Rd., Forest City, IA 50436; (641) 585-3535; www.winnebagoind.com;

Michael J. Happe; mfr. of motor homes, recreational vehicles (RVs).

Wm. Wrigley Jr. Co.: see Mars, Inc.

World Fuel Services Corp. (INT): 9800 NW 41st St., Ste. 400, Miami, FL 33178; (305) 428-8000; www.wfscorp.com; Michael J. Kasbar; marketer and financer of fuel to large-scale aviation and marine-related firms.

Xerox Corp. (XRX): 201 Merritt 7, Norwalk, CT 06851; (203) 968-3000; www.xerox. com; John Visentin; printers, multifunction devices, document publishing technology and support.

Yum! Brands, Inc. (YUM): 1441 Gardiner Ln., Louisville, KY 40213; (502) 874-8300; www.yum.com; Greg Creed; fast food restaurants (Pizza Hut, KFC, Taco Bell).

Labor Unions and Professional Organizations

Source: Bureau of Labor Statistics, U.S. Dept. of Labor; AFL-CIO; World Almanac research

= Member of Change to Win Federation, formed in 2005 by unions disaffiliated from AFL-CIO. * = Independent union or one not otherwise affiliated with Change to Win or AFL-CIO. All other unions listed are affiliated with AFL-CIO as of 2020. Year established is in parentheses.

Labor Unions

Air Line Pilots Assn. (ALPA) (1931): 63,007 members, 34 U.S. and Canadian airlines; (703) 689-2270; www.alpa.org

American Federation of Labor and Congress of Industrial Organizations (AFL-CIO) (1955): federation of 55 unions, 12,441,501 members; (202) 637-5000; www.aflcio.org

Automobile, Aerospace & Agricultural Implement Workers of America, International Union, United (UAW) (1935): 395,703 members, 600+ locals; (313) 926-5000; www.uaw.org

Bakery, Confectionery, Tobacco Workers, and Grain Millers International Union (BCTGM) (1886): 63,913 members, 136 locals; (301) 933-8600; www.bctgm.org

Bricklayers and Allied Craftworkers, International Union of (BAC) (1865): 72,804 members, 40+ locals; (202) 783-3788; www.bacweb.org

*****Carpenters and Joiners of America, United Brotherhood of (UBC)** (1881): 437,634 members, 600+ locals; (202) 546-6206; www.carpenters.org

#**Change to Win Federation** (2005): 3 unions, ex-affiliates of AFL-CIO, 2,516,274 members; (202) 721-0660; www.changetowin.org

Communications Workers of America (CWA) (1938): 661,604 members, 1,200 locals; (202) 434-1100; www.cwa-union.org

*****Education Assn., Natl. (NEA)** (1857): 2,975,933 members, 14,000+ affiliates; (202) 833-4000; www.nea.org

Electrical Workers, International Brotherhood of (IBEW) (1891): 677,748 members, 900 locals; (202) 833-7000; www.ibew.org

Engineers, International Union of Operating (IUOE) (1896): 401,999 members, 123 locals; (202) 429-9100; www.iuoe.org

#**Farm Workers of America, United (UFW)** (1962): 7,483 members; (661) 823-6151; www.ufw.org

Federal Employees, Natl. Federation of (NFFE; affiliated with IAM) (1917): 110,000 members, about 200 locals; (202) 216-4420; www.nffe.org

Fire Fighters, International Assn. of (IAFF) (1918): 318,684 members, 3,500+ locals; (202) 737-8484; www.iaff.org

Flight Attendants, Assn. of (AFA-CWA) (1945): 43,178 members, 20 airlines; merged with Communications Workers of America in 2004; (202) 434-1300; www.afanet.org

Food and Commercial Workers International Union, United (UFCW) (1979): 1,230,309 members, 1,000+ locals; (202) 223-3111; www.ufcw.org

Glass, Molders, Pottery, Plastics and Allied Workers Intl. Union (GMP) (1842): 22,290 members, 250+ locals; (610) 565-5051; www.gmpiu.org

Government Employees, American Federation of (AFGE) (1932): 323,285 members, 980+ locals; (202) 737-8700; www.afge.org

#**Graphic Communications Conference (GCC/IBT)** (1983): 59,112 members; merged with Teamsters in 2005; (202) 462-1400; www.gciu.org

Iron Workers, Intl. Assn. of Bridge, Structural, Ornamental, and Reinforcing (1896): 129,876 members, 200+ locals; (202) 383-4800; www.ironworkers.org

Laborers' International Union of North America (LiUNA) (1903): 584,757 members, 400 locals; (202) 737-8320; www.liuna.org

Letter Carriers, Natl. Assn. of (NALC) (1889): 290,315 members, 2,000+ locals; (202) 393-4695; www.nalc.org

#**Locomotive Engineers and Trainmen, Brotherhood of (BLET)** (1863): 57,946 members, 500+ locals; (216) 241-2630; www.ble-t.org

Longshoremen's Assn., Intl. (ILA) (1892): 32,921 members, approx. 200 locals; (212) 425-1200; www.ilaunion.org

Machinists and Aerospace Workers, International Assn. of (IAM) (1888): 579,639 members; affiliated with TCU in 2005; (301) 967-4500; www.goiam.org

#**Maintenance of Way Employes, Division of the Intl. Brotherhood of Teamsters; Brotherhood of (BMWED)** (1887): 33,418 members, 770 locals; merged with Teamsters in 2004; (248) 662-2660; www.bmwe.org (Note: In honor of tradition, the union maintains the variant spelling of "employes" in its logo.)

Mine Workers of America, United (UMWA) (1890): 59,214 members, 600 locals; (703) 291-2400; www.umwa.org

Musicians of the United States and Canada, American Federation of (AFM) (1896): 73,071 members, 240+ locals; (212) 869-1330; www.afm.org

NewsGuild—Communications Workers of America, The (TNG-CWA) (1933): 25,000 members, 90 locals; (202) 434-7177; www.newsguild.org

*****Nurses Assn., American (ANA)** (1911): 195,884 members, 54 constituent state and territorial assns.; (301) 628-5000; www.nursingworld.org

Office and Professional Employees Intl. Union (OPEIU) (1945): 87,090 members, 200 locals; (800) 346-7348; www.opeiu.org

Painters and Allied Trades, International Union of (IUPAT) (1887): 112,838 members, 425 locals; (410) 564-5900; www.iupat.org

Plumbing and Pipe Fitting Industry of the U.S. and Canada, United Assn. of Journeymen and Apprentices of the (UA) (1889): 335,000 members, 300+ locals; (410) 269-2000; www.ua.org

*****Police, Fraternal Order of** (1915): 350,175 members, 2,200+ affiliates; (615) 399-0900; www.fop.net

Police Assns., International Union of (IUPA) (1979): 100,000+ members; (941) 487-2560; www.iupa.org

Postal Workers Union, American (APWU) (1971): 223,912 members, 900+ locals; (202) 842-4200; www.apwu.org

Roofers, Waterproofers and Allied Workers, United Union of (1906): 22,540 members; (202) 463-7663; www.unionroofers.com

*****Rural Letter Carriers' Assn., Natl.** (1903): 116,910 members, 50 state orgs.; (703) 684-5545; www.nrlca.org

*****Security, Police, Fire Professionals of America, Intl. Union, (SPFPA)** (1948):

17,900 members, 200 locals; (586) 772-7250; www.spfpa.org

#**Service Employees International Union (SEIU)** (1921): 1,962,922 members, 150+ locals; (202) 730-7000; www.seiu.org

Sheet Metal, Air, Rail, and Transportation Workers, Int. Assn. of (SMART) (2008, from merger of Sheet Metal Workers' Intl. Assn. and United Transportation Union): 206,647 members, 700 locals; (202) 662-0800; www.smart-union.org

State, County, and Municipal Employees, American Federation of (AFSCME) (1932): 1,339,779 members, 3,400 locals; (202) 429-1000; www.afscme.org

Steel, Paper and Forestry, Rubber, Manufacturing, Energy, Allied Industrial and Service Workers International Union, United (USW) (2005): 575,192 members, 1,800+ locals; formed from merger of United Steelworkers of America (USWA) (1936) and Paper, Allied-Industrial, Chemical and Energy Workers (PACE) (1999); (412) 562-2400; www.usw.org

Teachers, American Federation of (AFT) (1916): 1,684,544 members, 3,000+ locals; (202) 879-4400; www.aft.org

#**Teamsters, International Brotherhood of (IBT)** (1903): 1,324,501 members, 475 locals; (202) 624-6800; www.teamster.org

Theatrical Stage Employees, Moving Picture Technicians, Artists and Allied Crafts of the U.S., Its Territories, and Canada, Intl. Alliance of (IATSE) (1893): 145,525 members, 375+ locals; (212) 730-1770; www.iatse.net

Transit Union, Amalgamated (ATU) (1892): 201,645 members, 270 locals; (301) 431-7100; www.atu.org

Transport Workers Union of America (TWU) (1934): 140,352 members, 100 locals; (202) 719-3900; www.twu.org

Transportation Communications Intl. Union (TCU) (1899): affiliated with IAM in 2005; see Machinists and Aerospace Workers.

*****Treasury Employees Union, Natl. (NTEU)** (1938): 80,059 members, 200+ chapters; (202) 572-5500; www.nteu.org

UNITE HERE (UNITE, 1900; HERE, 1891; merged 2004): 307,890 members, 131 locals; (212) 265-7000; www.unitehere.org

#**Workers United** (affiliated with SEIU) (2009): 80,710 members

*****Writers Guild of America, East** (1954): 5,116 members; (212) 767-7800; www.wgaeast.org

*****Writers Guild of America, West** (1933): 24,440 members; (323) 951-4000; www.wga.org

Professional Organizations and Societies

Accountants, American Institute of Certified Public (1887): 431,000+ members; (888) 777-7077; www.aicpa.org

ACMP—Associated Chamber Music Players (1947): 2,500+ members; (212) 645-7424; www.acmp.net

Actuaries, Soc. of (1949): 31,300+ members; (847) 706-3500; www.soa.org

Administrative Professionals, Intl. Assn. of (1942): 24,000 members; (816) 891-6600; www.iaap-hq.org

Agricultural and Biological Engineers, American Soc. of (1907): 7,000+ members; (269) 429-0300; www.asabe.org

AIGA (fmr. American Institute of Graphic Arts) (1914): 18,000+ members; (212) 807-1990; www.aiga.org

Air & Waste Management Assn. (1907): 5,000+ members; (412) 232-3444; www.awma.org

AMSUS—The Society of Federal Health Professionals (1891): nearly 8,000 members; (301) 897-8800; www.amsus.org

APICS—The Assn. for Supply Chain Management (1957): 45,000+ members; (773) 867-1777; www.apics.org

Architects, American Institute of (1857): 95,000+ members; (202) 626-7300; www.aia.org

ASIS Intl. (fmr. Amer. Soc. for Industrial Security) (1955): 34,000 members; (703) 519-6200; www.asisonline.org

Astrologers, Inc., American Federation of (1938): 4,000 members; (480) 838-1751; www.astrologers.com

Astronomical Society, American (1899): 7,700 members; (202) 328-2010; www.aas.org

Authors Guild, The (1912): 11,300+ members; (212) 563-5904; www.authorsguild.org

Bankers of America, Independent Community (1930): nearly 5,700 banks; (202) 659-8111; www.icba.org

Bar Assn., American (1878): 356,000+ members; (312) 988-5000; www.abanet.org

Bar Assn., Federal (1920): 19,000+ members; (571) 481-9100; www.fedbar.org

Biochemistry and Molecular Biology, American Society for (1906): 12,000+ members; (240) 283-6600; www.asbmb.org

Broadcasters, Natl. Assn. of (1923): 8,300 members; (202) 429-5300; www.nab.org

Business Women's Assn., American (1949): 40,000 members; (800) 228-0007; www.abwa.org

Cartoonists Society, Natl. (1946): 500+ members; (407) 994-6703; www.reuben.org

Ceramic Society, American (1898): 11,000+ members; (614) 890-4700; www.ceramics.org

Chemical Society, American (1876): 152,000+ members; (202) 872-4600; www.acs.org

Chiefs of Police, Intl. Assn. of (1893): 31,000+ members; (703) 836-6767; www.theiacp.org

Chiropractic Assn., American (1963): 15,000+ members; (703) 276-8800; www.acatoday.org

Civil Engineers, American Soc. of (1852): 150,000+ members; (703) 295-6300; www.asce.org

College Admission Counseling, Natl. Assn. for (1937): more than 15,000 members; (703) 836-2222; www.nacacnet.org

Communication Assn., Natl. (1914): 8,000+ members; (202) 464-4622; www.natcom.org

Composers, Authors & Publishers, American Soc. of (ASCAP) (1914): 750,000 members; (212) 621-6000; www.ascap.com

Computing Machinery, Assn. for (1947): nearly 100,000 members; (212) 626-0500; www.acm.org

Computing Professionals, Institute for the Certification of (1973): nearly 55,000 members; (847) 299-4227; www.iccp.org

Counseling Assn., American (1952): 50,000+ members; (800) 347-6647; www.counseling.org

Country Music Assn. (1958): 7,500+ members; (615) 244-2840; www.cmaworld.com

Dental Assn., American (1859): 163,000+ members; (312) 440-2500; www.ada.org

Directors Guild of America (1936): 18,000+ members; (310) 289-2000; www.dga.org

Electrical and Electronics Engineers, Institute of (1963): 420,000+ members; (732) 562-5501; www.ieee.org

Electronics Technicians, Intl. Soc. of Certified (1980): 50,000+ members; (817) 921-9101; www.iscet.org

Emergency Medical Technicians, Natl. Assn. of (1975): 72,000+ members; (601) 924-7744; www.naemt.org

Energy Engineers, Assn. of (1977): 18,000+ members; (770) 447-5083; www.aeecenter.org

Engineers, Natl. Society of Professional (1934): 26,000+ members; (703) 684-2800; www.nspe.org

Environmental Assessment Assn. (1972): 3,500 members; (877) 743-6806; www.eaa-assoc.org

Environmental Health Assn., Natl. (1937): 6,000 members; (303) 756-9090; www.neha.org

Family Physicians, American Academy of (1947): 136,700 members; (913) 906-6000; www.aafp.org

Farm Bureau Federation, American (1919): 6.2 mil+ members; (202) 406-3600; www.fb.org

Farmers Union, Natl. (1902): nearly 200,000 families; (202) 554-1600; www.nfu.org

Financial Professionals, Assn. for (1979): 16,000+ members; (301) 907-2862; www.afponline.org

Financial Service Professionals, Soc. of (1928): 11,000 members; (610) 526-2500; www.societyoffsp.org

Fire Chiefs, Intl. Assn. of (1873): nearly 12,000 members; (703) 273-0911; www.iafc.org

Fire Protection Engineers, Soc. of (1950): 4,600+ members; (301) 718-2910; www.sfpe.org

Food Technologists, Institute of (1939): 15,000+ members; (312) 782-8424; www.ift.org

Forensic Sciences, American Academy of (1948): 6,600+ members; (719) 636-1100; www.aafs.org

Funeral Directors Assn., Natl. (1882): 20,000+ members; (262) 789-1880; www.nfda.org

General Contractors of America, Associated (1918): 27,000+ cos.; (703) 548-3118; www.agc.org

Geographers, American Assn. of (1904): 10,000 members; (202) 234-1450; www.aag.org

Ground Water Assn., Natl. (1948): 12,000+ members; (614) 898-7791; www.ngwa.org

Heating, Refrigerating and Air-Conditioning Engineers, Inc., American Soc. of (1894): 57,000+ members; (404) 636-8400; www.ashrae.org

Home Builders, Natl. Assn. of (1942): 140,000+ members; (202) 266-8200; www.nahb.org

Human Resource Management, Soc. for (SHRM) (1948): 300,000+ members; (703) 548-3440; www.shrm.org

Illustrators, Society of (1901): 1,000 members; (212) 838-2560; www.societyillustrators.org

Industrial Designers Society of America (1965): 3,200+ members; (703) 707-6000; www.idsa.org

Intelligence Officers, Assn. of Former (1975): 24 chap., 5,000+ members; (703) 790-0320; www.afio.com

Interior Designers, American Soc. of (1975): 19,000 members; (202) 546-3480; www.asid.org

Jail Assn., American (1981): 3,500 members; (301) 790-3930; www.aja.org

Journalists, Society of Professional (1909): 6,000 members; (317) 927-8000; www.spj.org

Landscape Architects, American Society of (1899): 15,000+ members; (202) 898-2444; www.asla.org

Legal Administrators, Assn. of (1971): 9,000 members; (847) 267-1252; www.alanet.org

Library Assn., American (1876): nearly 58,000 members; (800) 545-2433; www.ala.org

Lifesaving Assn., U.S. (1964): 112 chap., 12,600+ members; (866) 367-8752; www.usla.org

Logistics, Intl. Society of (SOLE) (1966): 90+ chap., 3,000+ members; (301) 459-8446; www.sole.org

Magicians, Intl. Brotherhood of (1922): 10,000 members; (636) 724-2400; www.magician.org

Management Accountants, Inst. of (1919): 125,000+ members; (201) 573-9000; www.imanet.org

Management Assn., American (1923): 4,100 cos., 38,000 ind.; (877) 566-9441; www.amanet.org

Marketing Assn., American (1937): 30,000+ members; (312) 542-9000; www.ama.org

Master Brewers Assn. of the Americas (1887): 4,000+ members; (651) 454-7250; www.mbaa.com

Material and Process Engineering, Soc. for the Advancement of (1944): 5,000+ members; (626) 331-0616; www.sampe.org

Mechanical Engineers, American Soc. of (1880): 100,000+ members; (973) 882-1170; www.asme.org

Medical Assn., American (1847): 250,000 members; (800) 621-8335; www.ama-assn.org

Medical Library Assn. (1898): 3,000+ members, 400+ institutions; (312) 419-9094; www.mlanet.org

Motion Picture Arts & Sciences, Academy of (1927): 8,000+ members; (310) 247-3000; www.oscars.org

Motion Picture and Television Engineers, Soc. of (1916): 7,000+ members; (914) 761-1100; www.smpte.org

Mystery Writers of America (1945): 3,000+ members; (212) 888-8171; www.mystery writers.org

NALS...the association for legal professionals (fmr. Natl. Assn. of Legal Secretaries) (1929): 6,000 members; (918) 582-5188; www.nals.org

Notaries, American Society of (1965): approx. 20,000 members; (850) 671-5164; www.notaries.org

Nursing, Natl. League for (1893): 40,000 members, 1,200 institutions; (800) 669-1656; www.nln.org

Operations Management, Assn. for (APICS) (1957): 45,000+ members, 300+ intl. partners; (773) 867-1777; www.apics.org

Optometric Assn., American (1898): 40,000+ members; (800) 365-2219; www.aoa.org

Organists, American Guild of (1896): 14,700 members; (212) 870-2310; www.agohq.org

Pharmacists Assn., American (1852): 60,000+ members; (202) 628-4410; www.pharmacist.com

Physical Therapy Assn., American (1921): 100,000+ members; (703) 684-2782; www.apta.org

Plastics Engineers, Society of (1942): 22,500+ members; (203) 775-0471; www.4spe.org

Police Assn.—United States Section, Intl. (1962): 10,000 members; (855) 241-9998; www.ipa-usa.org

Population Assn. of America (1930): 3,000 members; (301) 565-6710; www.populationassociation.org

Postmasters and Managers of America, United (2015): (703) 683-9027; www.unitedpma.org

Press Club, Natl. (1908): 3,500+ members; (202) 662-7500; www.press.org

Professional Ball Players of America, Assn. of (1924): 101,500+ members; (480) 404-9339; www.apbpa.org

Professional Beauty Assn. (1904): 7,000+ indiv. members, 1,900+ cos.; (480) 281-0424; www.probeauty.org

Psychiatric Assn., American (1844): 38,800 members; (202) 559-3900; www.psychiatry.org

Psychological Assn., American (1892): nearly 121,000+ members; (202) 336-5500; www.apa.org

Public Administration, American Soc. for (1939): 8,000 members; (202) 393-7878; www.aspanet.org

Public Health Assn., American (1872): 25,000+ members; (202) 777-2742; www.apha.org

Public Relations Soc. of America (1947): 30,000+ members; (212) 460-1400; www.prsa.org

Range Management, Society for (1948): 4,000+ members; (303) 986-3309; www.rangelands.org

Real Estate Appraisers, Natl. Assn. of (1966): 10,000+ members; (877) 743-6806; www.narea-assoc.org

Rehabilitation Assn., Natl. (1923): 5,600 members; (703) 836-0850; www.nationalrehab.org

Road & Transportation Builders Assn., American (1902): 6,000+ members; (202) 289-4434; www.artba.org

Safety Professionals, American Soc. of (1911): nearly 40,000 members; (847) 699-2929; www.asse.org

School Administrators, American Assn. of (1865): 13,000+ members; (703) 528-0700; www.aasa.org

Science Teachers Assn., Natl. (1944): 50,000 members; (703) 243-7100; www.nsta.org

Screen Actors Guild—American Federation of Television and Radio Artists (2012): 160,000 members; (855) 724-2387; www.sagaftra.org

Songwriters Guild of America (1931): 5,000+ members; (615) 742-9945; www.songwritersguild.com

Sportscasters Assn., American (1979): 500+ members; (212) 227-8080; www.americansportscastersonline.com

Surgeons, American College of (1913): 82,000+ members; (312) 202-5000; www.facs.org

Tax Administrators, Federation of (1937): (202) 624-5890; www.taxadmin.org

Teachers of English, Natl. Council of (1911): 25,000+ members; (217) 328-3870; www.ncte.org

Teachers of English to Speakers of Other Languages, Inc. (1966): 12,000+ members; (703) 836-0774; www.tesol.org

Teachers of French, American Assn. of (1927): 9,000 members; (815) 310-0490; www.frenchteachers.org

Teachers of German, American Assn. of (1926): nearly 3,500 members; (856) 795-5553; www.aatg.org

Teachers of Mathematics, Natl. Council of (1920): 60,000 members; (703) 620-9840; www.nctm.org

Teachers of Spanish and Portuguese, American Assn. of (1917): 10,000+ members; (205) 506-0600; www.aatsp.org

Television Arts and Sciences, Natl. Academy of (1955): (212) 586-8424; www.emmyonline.org

Theological Library Assn., American (1946): 800+ members; (312) 454-5100; www.atla.com

Transportation Engineers, Inst. of (1930): 15,000+ members; (202) 785-0060; www.ite.org

Travel Agents, American Soc. of (1931): 12,000 members; (703) 739-2782; www.asta.org

Underwriters, Soc. of Chartered Property and Casualty (1917): nearly 20,000 members; (800) 932-2728; www.cpcusociety.org

University Women, American Assn. of (1881): 100,000+ members; (202) 785-7700; www.aauw.org

Veterinary Medical Assn., American (1863): 95,000+ members; (800) 248-2862; www.avma.org

Women in Communications, The Assn. for (1909): 1,100+ members; (417) 886-8606; www.womcom.org

Women Engineers, Society of (1950): 42,000 members; (877) 793-4636; swe.org

Women in Media, Alliance for (1951): nearly 10,000 members; (202) 750-3664; www.allwomeninmedia.org

Professional Sports Organizations

Source: World Almanac research

Major League Baseball

Office of the Commissioner, 1271 Avenue of the Americas, NY, NY 10020; (212) 931-7800; www.mlb.com

American League

Baltimore Orioles (1953): 333 W. Camden St., Baltimore, MD 21201; (410) 685-9800; www.orioles.com

Boston Red Sox (1901): 4 Jersey St., Boston, MA 02215; (617) 267-9440; www.redsox.com

Chicago White Sox (1900, as Chicago White Stockings): 333 W. 35th St., Chicago, IL 60616; (312) 674-1000; www.whitesox.com

Cleveland Indians (1901, as Cleveland Blues): 2401 Ontario St., Cleveland, OH 44115; (216) 420-4200; www.indians.com

Detroit Tigers (1901): 2100 Woodward Ave., Detroit, MI 48201; (313) 471-2000; www.tigers.com

Houston Astros (1962, as Houston Colt 45s): 501 Crawford St., Houston, TX 77002; (713) 259-8000; www.astros.com (National League, 1962-2012; AL West, 2013-present.)

Kansas City Royals (1969): One Royal Way, Kansas City, MO 64129; (816) 921-8000; www.royals.com

Los Angeles Angels of Anaheim (1961): 2000 Gene Autry Way, Anaheim, CA 92806; (714) 940-2000; www.angels.com

Minnesota Twins (1960): 1 Twins Way, Minneapolis, MN 55403; (612) 659-3400; www.twinsbaseball.com

New York Yankees (1903): One E. 161st St., Bronx, NY 10451; (718) 293-4300; www.yankees.com

Oakland Athletics (1901, as Philadelphia Athletics): 7000 Coliseum Way, Oakland, CA 94621; (510) 638-4900; www.athletics.com

Seattle Mariners (1977): P.O. Box 4100, Seattle, WA 98104; (206) 346-4000; www.mariners.com

Tampa Bay Rays (1995, as Tampa Bay Devil Rays): 1 Tropicana Field Dr., St. Petersburg, FL 33705; (727) 825-3137; www.raysbaseball.com

Texas Rangers (1960, as Washington Senators): 1000 Ballpark Way, Arlington, TX 76011; (817) 273-5222; www.texas rangers.com

Toronto Blue Jays (1976): One Blue Jays Way, Ste. 3200, Toronto, ON M5V 1J1, Canada; (416) 341-1000; www.bluejays.com

National League

Arizona Diamondbacks (1998): 401 E. Jefferson St., Phoenix, AZ 85004; (602) 462-6500; www.dbacks.com

Atlanta Braves (1876, as Boston Red Stockings): 755 Battery Ave., Atlanta, GA 30339; (404) 522-7630; www.braves.com

Chicago Cubs (1876, as Chicago White Stockings): 1060 W. Addison, Chicago, IL 60613; (773) 404-2827; www.cubs.com

Cincinnati Reds (1869, as Cincinnati Red Stockings): 100 Main St., Cincinnati, OH 45202; (513) 765-7000; www.reds.com

Colorado Rockies (1991): 2001 Blake St., Denver, CO 80205; (303) 292-0200; www.rockies.com

Los Angeles Dodgers (1890): 1000 Elysian Park Ave., Los Angeles, CA 90012; (323) 224-1500; www.dodgers.com

Miami Marlins (1991, as Florida Marlins): 501 Marlins Way, Miami, FL 33125; (305) 480-1300; www.marlins.com

Milwaukee Brewers (1970): One Brewers Way, Milwaukee, WI 53214; (414) 902-4400; www.brewers.com

New York Mets (1961): Citi Field, 41 Seaver Way, Flushing, NY 11368; (718) 507-6387; www.mets.com

Philadelphia Phillies (1883): One Citizens Bank Way, Philadelphia, PA 19148; (215) 463-6000; www.phillies.com

Pittsburgh Pirates (1887, as Pittsburgh Alleghenies): 115 Federal St., Pittsburgh, PA 15212; (412) 323-5000; www.pirates.com

St. Louis Cardinals (1892, as St. Louis Browns): 700 Clark St., St. Louis, MO 63102; (314) 345-9600; www.cardinals.com

San Diego Padres (1969): 100 Park Blvd., San Diego, CA 92101; (619) 795-5000; www.padres.com

San Francisco Giants (1883, as New York Gothams): 24 Willie Mays Plz., San Francisco, CA 94107; (415) 972-2000; www.sfgiants.com

Washington Nationals (1969, as Montréal Expos): 1500 South Capitol St., SE, Washington, DC 20003; (202) 675-6287; www.nationals.com

National Basketball Association

League Office, 645 Fifth Ave., NY, NY 10022; (212) 407-8000; www.nba.com

Atlanta Hawks (1949, as Tri-Cities Blackhawks): 101 Marietta St. NW, Ste. 1900, Atlanta, GA 30303; (866) 715-1500; www.nba.com/hawks

Boston Celtics (1946): 226 Causeway St., 4th Fl., Boston, MA 02114; (866) 423-5849; www.nba.com/celtics

Brooklyn Nets (1967, as New Jersey Americans): 15 MetroTech Ctr., 11th Fl., Brooklyn, NY 11201; (718) 933-3000; www.nba.com/nets

Charlotte Hornets (2004, as Charlotte Bobcats): 333 E. Trade St., Charlotte, NC 28202; (704) 688-8600; www.nba.com/hornets

Chicago Bulls (1966): 1901 W. Madison St., Chicago, IL 60612; (312) 455-4000; www.nba.com/bulls

Cleveland Cavaliers (1970): One Center Ct., Cleveland, OH 44115; (216) 420-2000; www.nba.com/cavaliers

Dallas Mavericks (1980): 2909 Taylor St., Dallas, TX 75226; (214) 747-6287; www.nba.com/mavericks

Denver Nuggets (1967, as Denver Rockets): 1000 Chopper Cir., Denver, CO 80204; (303) 405-1100; www.nba.com/nuggets

Detroit Pistons (1957): 66 Sibley St., Detroit, MI 48201; (248) 377-0100; www.nba.com/pistons

Golden State Warriors (1946, as Philadelphia Warriors): 1011 Broadway, Oakland, CA 94607; (510) 986-2200; www.nba.com/warriors

Houston Rockets (1967, as San Diego Rockets): 1510 Polk St., Houston, TX 77002; (713) 627-3865; www.nba.com/rockets

Indiana Pacers (1967): 125 S. Pennsylvania St., Indianapolis, IN 46204; (317) 917-2500; www.nba.com/pacers

Los Angeles Clippers (1970, as Buffalo Braves): 1111 S. Figueroa St., Ste. 1100,

Los Angeles, CA 90015; (213) 742-7500; www.nba.com/clippers

Los Angeles Lakers (1947, as Minneapolis Lakers): 555 N. Nash St., El Segundo, CA 90245; (310) 426-6000; www.nba.com/lakers

Memphis Grizzlies (1995, as Vancouver Grizzlies): 191 Beale St., Memphis, TN 38103; (901) 888-4667; www.nba.com/grizzlies

Miami Heat (1988): 601 Biscayne Blvd., Miami, FL 33132; (786) 777-1000; www.nba.com/heat

Milwaukee Bucks (1968): 1111 Vel R. Phillips Ave., Milwaukee, WI 53203; (414) 227-0599; www.nba.com/bucks

Minnesota Timberwolves (1989): 600 Hennepin Ave., Ste. 300, Minneapolis, MN 55403; (612) 673-1600; www.nba.com/timberwolves

New Orleans Pelicans (1988, as Charlotte Hornets): 5800 Airline Dr., Metairie, LA 70003; (504) 593-4700; www.nba.com/pelicans

New York Knickerbockers (1946): Two Pennsylvania Plz., NY, NY 10121; (212) 465-6471; www.nba.com/knicks

Oklahoma City Thunder (1967, as Seattle SuperSonics): 208 Thunder Dr., Oklahoma City, OK 73102; (405) 208-4800; www.nba.com/thunder

Orlando Magic (1989): 8701 Maitland Summit Blvd., Orlando, FL 32810; (407) 916-2400; www.nba.com/magic

Philadelphia 76ers (1937, as Syracuse Nationals): 3601 S. Broad St., Philadelphia, PA 19148; (215) 339-7676; www.nba.com/sixers

Phoenix Suns (1968): 201 E. Jefferson St., Phoenix, AZ 85004; (602) 379-7900; www.nba.com/suns

Portland Trail Blazers (1970): One Center Ct., Ste. 200, Portland, OR 97227; (503) 234-9291; www.nba.com/blazers

Sacramento Kings (1945, as Rochester Royals): 500 David J. Stern Walk, Sacramento, CA 95814; (916) 928-0000; www.nba.com/kings

San Antonio Spurs (1967, as Dallas Chaparrals): One AT&T Center, San Antonio, TX 78219; (210) 444-5000; www.nba.com/spurs

Toronto Raptors (1995): 40 Bay St., Toronto, ON M5J 2X2, Canada; (416) 366-3865; www.nba.com/raptors

Utah Jazz (1974, as New Orleans Jazz): 301 W. South Temple, Salt Lake City, UT 84101; (801) 325-2500; www.nba.com/jazz

Washington Wizards (1961, as Chicago Packers): 601 F St. NW, Washington, DC 20004; (202) 661-5000; www.nba.com/wizards

National Hockey League

NHL Headquarters, 1185 Ave. of the Americas, 15th Fl., NY, NY 10036; (212) 789-2000; www.nhl.com

Anaheim Ducks (1993): 2695 E. Katella Ave., Anaheim, CA 92806; (877) 945-3946; ducks.nhl.com

Arizona Coyotes (1979, as Winnipeg Jets): 9400 W. Maryland Ave., Glendale, AZ 85305; (623) 772-3200; coyotes.nhl.com

Boston Bruins (1924): 100 Legends Way, Boston, MA 02114; (617) 624-1900; bruins.nhl.com

Buffalo Sabres (1970): One Seymour H. Knox III Plz., Buffalo, NY 14203; (716) 855-4100; sabres.nhl.com

Calgary Flames (1980): P.O. Box 1540, Station M, Calgary, AB T2P 3B9, Canada; (403) 777-2177; flames.nhl.com

Carolina Hurricanes (1972, as New England Whalers): 1400 Edwards Mill Rd., Raleigh, NC 27607; (919) 467-7825; hurricanes.nhl.com

Chicago Blackhawks (1926): 1901 W. Madison St., Chicago, IL 60612; (312) 455-7000; blackhawks.nhl.com

Colorado Avalanche (1972, as Quebec Nordiques): 1000 Chopper Cir., Denver, CO 80204; (303) 405-1100; avalanche.nhl.com

Columbus Blue Jackets (2000): 200 W. Nationwide Blvd., Suite Level, Columbus, OH 43215; (614) 246-4625; bluejackets.nhl.com

Dallas Stars (1967, as Minnesota North Stars): 2601 Ave. of the Stars, Frisco, TX 75034; (214) 387-5500; stars.nhl.com

Detroit Red Wings (1926, as Detroit Cougars): 66 Sibley St., Detroit, MI 48201; (313) 471-7444; redwings.nhl.com

Edmonton Oilers (1972, as Alberta Oilers): 300, 10214 104 Ave. NW, Edmonton, AB T5G 0H6, Canada; (780) 414-4000; oilers.nhl.com

Florida Panthers (1993): One Panther Pkwy., Sunrise, FL 33323; (954) 835-7000; panthers.nhl.com

Los Angeles Kings (1967): 1111 S. Figueroa St., Ste. 3100, Los Angeles, CA 90015; (213) 742-7100; kings.nhl.com

Minnesota Wild (2000): 317 Washington St., St. Paul, MN 55102; (651) 602-6000; wild.nhl.com

Montréal Canadiens (1917): 1909, avenue des Canadiens-de- Montréal, Montréal, QC H4B 5G0, Canada; (514) 932-2582; canadiens.nhl.com

Nashville Predators (1998): 501 Broadway, Nashville, TN 37203; (615) 770-2355; predators.nhl.com

New Jersey Devils (1974, as Kansas City Scouts): Prudential Center, 25 Lafayette St., Newark, NJ 07102; (973) 757-6100; devils.nhl.com

New York Islanders (1972): 168 39th St., 7th Fl., Brooklyn, NY 11231; (917) 618-6700; islanders.nhl.com

New York Rangers (1926): Two Pennsylvania Plz., NY, NY 10121; (212) 465-6000; rangers.nhl.com

Ottawa Senators (1992): 1000 Palladium Dr., Ottawa, ON K2V 1A5, Canada; (613) 599-0250; senators.nhl.com

Philadelphia Flyers (1967): 3601 S. Broad St., Philadelphia, PA 19148; (215) 336-3600; flyers.nhl.com

Pittsburgh Penguins (1967): 1001 5th Ave., Pittsburgh, PA 15219; (412) 642-1800; penguins.nhl.com

St. Louis Blues (1967): 1401 Clark Ave. at Brett Hull Way, St. Louis, MO 63103; (314) 622-2500; blues.nhl.com

San Jose Sharks (1991): 525 W. Santa Clara St., San Jose, CA 95113; (408) 287-7070; sharks.nhl.com

Tampa Bay Lightning (1992): 401 Channelside Dr., Tampa, FL 33602; (813) 301-6500; lightning.nhl.com

Toronto Maple Leafs (1919, as Toronto St. Pats): 40 Bay St., Ste. 400, Toronto, ON M5J 2X2, Canada; (416) 815-5700; maple leafs.nhl.com

Vancouver Canucks (1946, joined NHL in 1970): 800 Griffiths Way, Vancouver, BC V6B 6G1, Canada; (604) 899-7400; canucks.nhl.com

Vegas Golden Knights (2017): 3780 S. Las Vegas Blvd., Las Vegas, NV 89158; (702) 645-4259; goldenknights.nhl.com

Washington Capitals (1974): 627 N. Glebe Rd., Ste. 850, Arlington, VA 22203; (202) 266-2200; capitals.nhl.com

Winnipeg Jets (1999, as Atlanta Thrashers): 345 Graham Ave., Winnipeg, MB R3C 5S6, Canada; (204) 987-7825; jets.nhl.com

National Football League

League Office, 345 Park Ave., NY, NY 10154; (212) 450-2000; www.nfl.com

Arizona Cardinals (1898, as Morgan Athletic Club): P.O. Box 888, Phoenix, AZ 85001; (602) 379-0101; www.azcardinals.com

Atlanta Falcons (1966): 4400 Falcon Pkwy., Flowery Branch, GA 30542; (770) 965-3115; www.atlantafalcons.com

Baltimore Ravens (1996): 1101 Russell St., Baltimore, MD 21230; (410) 261-7283; www.baltimoreravens.com

Buffalo Bills (1960): One Bills Dr., Orchard Park, NY 14127; (716) 648-1800; www.buffalobills.com

Carolina Panthers (1995): 800 S. Mint St., Charlotte, NC 28202; (704) 358-7000; www.panthers.com

Chicago Bears (1920, as Decatur Staleys): 1920 Football Dr., Lake Forest, IL 60045; (847) 615-2327; www.chicagobears.com

Cincinnati Bengals (1968): One Paul Brown Stadium, Cincinnati, OH 45202; (513) 621-3550; www.bengals.com

Cleveland Browns (1946): 76 Lou Groza Blvd., Berea, OH 44017; (440) 824-3434; www.clevelandbrowns.com

Dallas Cowboys (1960): One AT&T Way, Arlington, TX 76011; (817) 892-4000; www.dallascowboys.com

Denver Broncos (1960): 13655 Broncos Pkwy., Englewood, CO 80112; (303) 649-9000; www.denverbroncos.com

Detroit Lions (1930, as Portsmouth Spartans): 222 Republic Dr., Allen Park, MI 48101; (313) 262-2000; www.detroitlions.com

Green Bay Packers (1919): 1265 Lombardi Ave., Green Bay, WI 54304; (920) 569-7500; www.packers.com

Houston Texans (2002): Two NRG Park, Houston, TX 77054; (832) 667-2002; www.houstontexans.com

Indianapolis Colts (1953, as Baltimore Colts): 7001 W. 56th St., Indianapolis, IN 46254; (317) 297-2658; www.colts.com

Jacksonville Jaguars (1995): One EverBank Field Dr., Jacksonville, FL 32202; (904) 633-2000; www.jaguars.com

Kansas City Chiefs (1960, as Dallas Texans): One Arrowhead Dr., Kansas City, MO 64129; (816) 920-9300; www.chiefs.com

Las Vegas Raiders (1960, as Oakland Raiders): 1475 Raiders Way, Henderson, NV 89052; (510) 864-5000; www.raiders.com

Los Angeles Chargers (1960): 18400 Avalon Blvd., Carson, CA 92626; (714) 540-7100; www.chargers.com

Los Angeles Rams (1937, as Cleveland Rams): 29899 Agoura Rd., Agoura Hills, CA 91301; (310) 277-4700; www.therams.com

Miami Dolphins (1966): 347 Don Shula Dr., Miami Gardens, FL 33056; (305) 943-8000; www.miamidolphins.com

Minnesota Vikings (1961): 9520 Viking Dr., Eden Prairie, MN 55344; (952) 828-6500; www.vikings.com

New England Patriots (1960): One Patriot Pl., Foxboro, MA 02035; (508) 543-8200; www.patriots.com

New Orleans Saints (1967): 5800 Airline Dr., Metairie, LA 70003; (504) 733-0255; www.neworleanssaints.com

New York Giants (1925): 1925 Giants Dr., E. Rutherford, NJ 07073; (201) 935-8111; www.giants.com

New York Jets (1960, as New York Titans): One Jets Dr., Florham Park, NJ 07932; (800) 469-5387; www.newyorkjets.com

Philadelphia Eagles (1933): One NovaCare Way, Philadelphia, PA 19145; (215) 463-2500; www.philadelphiaeagles.com

Pittsburgh Steelers (1933): 3400 S. Water St., Pittsburgh, PA 15203; (412) 432-7800; www.steelers.com

San Francisco 49ers (1946): 4949 Centennial Blvd., Santa Clara, CA 95054; (408) 562-4949; www.49ers.com

Seattle Seahawks (1976): 12 Seahawks Way, Renton, WA 98056; (888) 635-4295; www.seahawks.com

Tampa Bay Buccaneers (1976): One Buccaneer Pl., Tampa, FL 33607; (813) 870-2700; www.buccaneers.com

Tennessee Titans (1960, as Houston Oilers): 460 Great Circle Rd., Nashville, TN 37228; (615) 565-4000; www.titansonline.com

Washington Redskins (1932, as Boston Braves): 21300 Redskin Park Dr., Ashburn, VA 20147; (703) 726-7000; www.redskins.com

Health Organizations

Source: World Almanac research

Entries are roughly alphabetized by the basic condition addressed or organization name. Year established is in parentheses. Always check with a physician before any new health-related undertaking.

Al-Anon Family Groups (1951): (757) 563-1600; al-anon.org

Alcoholics Anonymous (1935): (212) 870-3400; www.aa.org

Aging, Natl. Institute on (1974): (800) 222-2225; www.nia.nih.gov

Aging's Eldercare Locator, Admin. on (1991): (800) 677-1116; www.eldercare.gov

AIDSinfo: (800) 448-0440; www.aidsinfo.nih.gov

Allergy, Asthma and Immunology, American Academy of (1943): (414) 272-6071; www.aaaai.org

ALS Assn. [Lou Gehrig's disease] (1985): (202) 407-8580; www.alsa.org

Alzheimer's Assn. (1979): (800) 272-3900; www.alz.org

Anorexia Nervosa and Associated Disorders, Natl. Assn. of (1976): (630) 577-1333; www.anad.org

Arc of the United States, The [intellectual/developmental disabilities] (1950): (800) 433-5255; www.thearc.org

Arthritis Foundation (1948): (800) 283-7800; www.arthritis.org

Arthritis and Musculoskeletal and Skin Diseases, Natl. Institute of (1986): (877) 226-4267; www.niams.nih.gov

Asthma and Allergy Foundation of America (1953): (800) 727-8462; www.aafa.org

Autism Society (1965): (800) 328-8476; www.autism-society.org

Blind, American Council of the (1961): (202) 467-5081; (800) 424-8666; www.acb.org

Blind, Natl. Federation of the (1940): (410) 659-9314; www.nfb.org

Blindness, Foundation Fighting (1971): (800) 683-5555; www.blindness.org

Blindness, Prevent (1908): (800) 331-2020; www.preventblindness.org

Brain Tumor Society, Natl. (2008): (617) 924-9997; www.braintumor.org

Breast Cancer Diagnosis, After (ABCD) (1999): (414) 977-1780; (800) 977-4121; www.abcdbreastcancersupport.org

Cancer Institute's Cancer Information Service, Natl. (1975): (800) 422-6237; www.cancer.gov

Cancer Society, American (1913): (800) 227-2345; www.cancer.org

Centers for Disease Control and Prevention (CDC) (1946): (800) 232-4636; www.cdc.gov

Cerebral Palsy, United (1949): (202) 776-0406; (800) 872-5827; www.ucp.org

Child Abuse and Family Violence, Natl. Council on (1984): (202) 429-6695; www.nccafv.org

Childhelp Natl. Child Abuse Hotline (1959): (800) 422-4453; www.childhelp.org

Children, Natl. Center for Missing and Exploited (1984): (703) 224-2150; (800) 843-5678; www.missingkids.com

Children's Tumor Foundation (1978): (212) 344-6633; (800) 323-7938; www.ctf.org

Chronic Pain Assn., American (1980): (800) 533-3231; www.theacpa.org

Continence, Natl. Assn. for (1982): (843) 419-5307; (800) 252-3337; www.nafc.org

Cooley's Anemia Foundation (1954): (800) 522-7222; www.thalassemia.org

Crohn's and Colitis Foundation of America (1967): (800) 932-2423; www.ccfa.org

Cystic Fibrosis Foundation (1955): (800) 344-4823 or (301) 951-4422; www.cff.org

Deaf, Natl. Assn. of the (1880): (301) 587-1788, TTY (301) 587-1789; www.nad.org

Depression and Bipolar Support Alliance (1985): (800) 826-3632; www.dbsalliance.org

Diabetes Assn., American (1940): (800) 342-2383; www.diabetes.org

Diabetes and Digestive and Kidney Diseases, Natl. Institute of (1950): (301) 496-3583; www.kidney.niddk.nih.gov

Dial-A-Hearing Screening Test: (800) 222-EARS (222-3277)

Domestic Violence Hotline, Natl. (1996): (800) 799-7233, TTY (800) 787-3224; www.thehotline.org

Down Syndrome Congress, Natl. (1973): (800) 232-6372; www.ndsccenter.org

Down Syndrome Society, Natl. (1979): (800) 221-4602; www.ndss.org

Dyslexia Assn., Intl. (1949): (410) 296-0232; dyslexiaida.org

Easterseals [special needs] (1919): (800) 221-6827; www.easterseals.com

Eating Disorders Assn., National (2001): (800) 931-2237; www.nationaleatingdisorders.org

Endometriosis Assn. (1980): (414) 355-2200; www.endometriosisassn.org

Epilepsy Foundation (1967): (800) 332-1000; www.epilepsy.com

Fat Acceptance, Natl. Assn. to Advance (1969): (916) 558-6880; www.naafa.org

First Candle [sudden infant death syndrome] (1987): (800) 221-7437; www.firstcandle.org

FoodSafety.gov: Food: (888) 723-3366; Meat, poultry, eggs: (888) 674-6854; Illness or food poisoning: (800) 232-4636 (CDC)

Gamblers Anonymous (1957): (626) 960-3500; www.gamblersanonymous.org

Geriatrics Society, American (1942): (212) 308-1414; www.americangeriatrics.org

Headache Foundation, Natl. (1970): (888) 643-5552; www.headaches.org

HealthyWomen (1988): (877) 986-9472; www.healthywomen.org

Hearing Society, Intl. (1951): (734) 522-7200; www.ihsinfo.org

Heart Assn., American (1924): (800) 242-8721; www.heart.org

Hearts, Inc., Mended (1951): (888) 432-7899; www.mendedhearts.org

Hospice Foundation of America (1982): (800) 854-3402; www.hospicefoundation.org

Hospice Intl., Children's (1983): (703) 684-0330; www.chionline.org

Hospital Assn., American (1899): (312) 422-3000; (800) 424-4301; www.aha.org

Huntington's Disease Society of America (1967): (800) 345-4372; www.hdsa.org

JDRF [fmr. Juvenile Diabetes Research Foundation] (1970): (800) 533-2873; www.jdrf.org

Kidney Foundation, Natl. (1950): (800) 622-9010; www.kidney.org

Kidney Fund, American (1971): (866) 300-2900; www.kidneyfund.org

La Leche League Intl. [breastfeeding] (1957): (800) 525-3243; www.llli.org

Leukemia and Lymphoma Society (1949): (800) 955-4572; www.lls.org

Lighthouse Guild [visual impairments] (1914): (800) 284-4422; www.lighthouseguild.org

Liver Foundation, American (1976): (800) 465-4837; www.liverfoundation.org

Living Bank [organ donation] (1968): (713) 961-9431; (800) 528-2971; www.livingbank.org

Lung Assn., American (1904): (800) 586-4872; www.lung.org

Lung Line (1983): (800) 222-5864; www.nationaljewish.org/about/contact/lung-line/

Lupus Foundation of America, Inc. (1977): (202) 349-1155; (800) 558-0121; www.lupus.org

March of Dimes [babies' health] (1938): (914) 997-4488; www.marchofdimes.org

Marfan Foundation. (1981): (800) 8-MARFAN (862-7326); www.marfan.org

Mayo Clinic (1889): (507) 284-2511; www.mayoclinic.org

ME/CFS Initiative, Solve [myalgic encephalomyelitis/chronic fatigue syndrome] (1987): (704) 364-0016; solvecfs.org

Mental Health, Natl. Institute of (1946): (866) 615-6464; www.nimh.nih.gov

Mental Health America (1909): (703) 684-7722; (800) 969-6642; www.mentalhealthamerica.net

Mental Illness, Natl. Alliance on (1979): (800) 950-6264; www.nami.org

Multiple Sclerosis Society, Natl. (1946): (800) 344-4867; www.nationalmssociety.org

Muscular Dystrophy Assn. (1950): (800) 572-1717; www.mda.org

Myeloma Foundation, Intl. (1990): (800) 452-2873; www.myeloma.org

Narcotics Anonymous (1953): (818) 773-9999; www.na.org

Natl. Health Council (1920): (202) 785-3910; www.nationalhealthcouncil.org

Natl. Health Information Center (1979): (240) 453-8280; www.health.gov/NHIC/

Natl. Institutes of Health (NIH) (1887): (301) 496-4000; www.nih.gov

Neurological Disorders and Stroke, Natl. Institute of (1950): (301) 496-5751; (800) 352-9424; www.ninds.nih.gov

Organ Sharing, United Network for (1984): (804) 782-4800; (888) 894-6361; www.unos.org

Osteoporosis Foundation, Natl. (1984): (800) 231-4222; www.nof.org

Overeaters Anonymous (1960): (505) 891-2664; www.oa.org

Parkinson's Foundation (1957): (800) 473-4636; www.parkinson.org

Pediatrics, American Academy of (1930): (800) 433-9016; www.aap.org

Phoenix House [substance abuse] (1967): (888) 671-9392; www.phoenixhouse.org

Planned Parenthood Federation of America, Inc. (1916): (800) 230-7526; www.plannedparenthood.org

Plastic Surgeons, American Society of (1931): (800) 514-5058; www.plasticsurgery.org

Post-Polio Health Intl. (1960): (314) 534-0475; www.post-polio.org

Psoriasis Foundation, Natl. (1966): (800) 723-9166; www.psoriasis.org

RAINN (Rape, Abuse, & Incest Natl. Network) (1994): (800) 656-4673; www.rainn.org

Rare Disorders, Natl. Org. for (1983): (203) 744-0100; www.rarediseases.org

Rehabilitation Information Center, Natl. (1977): (800) 346-2742, TTY (301) 459-5984; www.naric.com

Reye's Syndrome Foundation, Natl. (1974): (800) 233-7393; www.reyessyndrome.org

Runaway Safeline, Natl. (1971): (800) 786-2929; www.1800runaway.org

Scleroderma Foundation (1989): (978) 463-5843; (800) 722-4673; www.scleroderma.org

Sexual Health Assn., American (1914): (919) 361-8400; www.ashasexualhealth.org

Sickle Cell Disease Assn. of America (1971): (410) 528-1555; (800) 421-8453; www.sicklecelldisease.org

Sjögren's Syndrome Foundation (1983): (800) 475-6473; www.sjogrens.org

Speech-Language-Hearing Assn., American (1925): (800) 638-8255; TTY (301) 296-5650; www.asha.org

Spinal Assn., United (1946): (718) 803-3782; www.unitedspinal.org

Stroke Assn., American (1984): (800) 787-6537; www.stroke.org

Stuttering Assn., Natl. (1977): (212) 944-4050; (800) 937-8888; www.westutter.org

Stuttering Foundation of America (1947): (800) 992-9392; www.stutteringhelp.org

Substance Abuse and Mental Health Services Admin.: (877) 726-4727; www.samhsa.gov

Sudden Infant Death Syndrome Institute, Amer. (1983): (239) 431-5425; www.sids.org

Suicide Prevention Lifeline, Natl. (2004): (800) 273-TALK (8255); www.suicidepreventionlifeline.org

Therapy Dogs Intl. (1976): (973) 252-9800; www.tdi-dog.org

Tourette Assn. of America (fmr. Tourette Syndrome Assn.) (1972): (718) 224-2999; www.tourette.org

Tuberous Sclerosis Alliance (1974): (301) 562-9890; (800) 225-6872; www.tsalliance.org

Urological Assn., American (1902): (866) 746-4282; www.auanet.org

Women's Health Network, Natl. (1975): (202) 682-2640; www.nwhn.org

UNITED STATES FACTS

Superlative U.S. Statistics

Source: U.S. Geological Survey, U.S. Dept. of the Interior; U.S. Census Bureau, U.S. Dept. of Commerce; World Almanac research

Superlative Statistics for the 50 States

Total area for 50 states and Washington, DC		3,796,742 sq mi
Land area for 50 states and Washington, DC		3,531,905 sq mi
Water area for 50 states and Washington, DC		264,837 sq mi
Largest state	Alaska	665,384 sq mi
Smallest state	Rhode Island	1,545 sq mi
Largest county (excluding Alaska)	San Bernardino County, CA	20,105 sq mi
Smallest county	Arlington County, VA[1]	26 sq mi
Largest incorporated city (by area, pop. 1,000+)	Sitka, AK	4,815 sq mi
Northernmost city	Utqiagvik (formerly Barrow), AK	71°17′ N
Northernmost point	Point Barrow, AK	71°23′ N
Southernmost city	Honolulu, HI	21°18′ N[2]
Southernmost settlement	Discovery Harbor, HI	19°02′ N
Southernmost point	Ka Lae (South Cape), island of Hawaii	18°54′ N (155°41′ W)
Easternmost city	Eastport, ME	66°59′24″ W
Easternmost incorporated place	Lubec, ME	66°59′ W
Easternmost point[3]	Pochnoi Point, Semisopochnoi Island, AK	179°46′ E
Westernmost city	Adak (formerly Adak Station), AK	176°39′ W
Westernmost incorporated place	Adak (formerly Adak Station), AK	176°39′ W
Westernmost point	Amatignak Island, AK	179°06′ W
Highest incorporated city	Leadville, CO	10,158 ft
Lowest settlement	Bombay Beach, CA	−208 ft
Highest point on Atlantic coast	Cadillac Mountain, Mount Desert Island, ME	1,530 ft
Oldest national park	Yellowstone National Park (1872), WY-MT-ID	2,219,791 acres
Largest national park	Wrangell-St. Elias, AK	8,323,146 acres
Longest river system	Mississippi-Missouri-Red Rock	3,710 mi
Highest mountain	Denali (formerly Mt. McKinley), AK	20,310 ft
Lowest point	Death Valley, CA	−282 ft
Deepest lake	Crater Lake, OR	1,949 ft
Rainiest spot	Mount Waialeale, Kauai, HI	annual avg. rainfall 460 in. (30-yr period)
Largest gorge	Grand Canyon, Colorado River, AZ	277 mi long, 600 ft to 18 mi wide, 1 mi deep
Deepest gorge	Hells Canyon, Snake River, OR-ID	7,913 ft
Largest dam	New Cornelia Tailings, Ten Mile Wash, AZ[4]	7.4 bil cu ft material used
Tallest building	One World Trade Center, New York, NY	1,782 ft
Largest building	Boeing Everett Production Facility, Everett, WA	472,000,000 cu ft; covers 98.3 acres
Largest office building	Pentagon, Arlington, VA	77,015,000 cu ft; covers 29 acres
Tallest supported structure	KVLY-TV Tower, Blanchard, ND	2,063 ft
Tallest freestanding tower	Stratosphere Tower, Las Vegas, NV	1,149 ft
Longest bridge span	Verrazano-Narrows Bridge, New York, NY	4,260 ft
Highest bridge	Royal Gorge Bridge, Cañon City, CO	bridge deck 955 ft above water
Deepest well (onshore)	Bertha Rogers No. 1 (inactive gas well), Washita County, OK	31,441 ft

Superlative Statistics for the 48 Contiguous States

Total area for 48 states and Washington, DC		3,120,426 sq mi
Land area for 48 states and Washington, DC		2,954,841 sq mi
Water area for 48 states and Washington, DC		165,585 sq mi
Largest state	Texas	268,596 sq mi
Northernmost incorporated place	Sumas, WA	49°00′ N
Northernmost settlement	Caribou, MN	48°59′ N
Northernmost point	Northwest Angle, MN	49°21′ N
Southernmost city	Key West, FL	24°33′ N
Southernmost mainland city	Florida City, FL	25°27′ N
Southernmost point	Coalbin Rock, FL	24°27′ N
Easternmost incorporated place	Lubec, ME	66°59′ W
Easternmost point	Sail Rock, ME	66°57′ W
Westernmost city	Port Orford, OR	124°30′ W
Westernmost point	Bodelteh Islands, WA	124°45′ W
Highest mountain	Mount Whitney, CA	14,505 ft

(1) Smallest total area. Smallest county by land area is Kalawao County, Hawaii, at 12 sq mi; its total area (including water) is 53 sq mi.
(2) Latitude is for Urban Honolulu census designated place. (3) As measured if the prime meridian and 180° longitude are considered east-west boundaries. (4) Privately owned industrial dam composed of tailings, remnants of a mining process.

Highest and Lowest Elevations in U.S. States and Territories

Source: U.S. Geological Survey, U.S. Dept. of the Interior
(negative sign indicates below sea level)

State/territory	Highest point Name	County	Elev. (ft)	Lowest point Name	County	Elev. (ft)
Alabama	Cheaha Mountain	Cleburne	2,413	Gulf of Mexico		Sea level
Alaska	Denali (fmr. Mt. McKinley)	Denali	20,310	Pacific Ocean		Sea level
American Samoa	Lata Mountain	Tau Island	3,160	Pacific Ocean		Sea level
Arizona	Humphreys Peak	Coconino	12,637	Colorado R.	Yuma	70
Arkansas	Magazine Mountain	Logan	2,753	Ouachita R.	Ashley-Union	55
California	Mount Whitney	Inyo-Tulare	14,505	Death Valley	Inyo	−282
Colorado	Mount Elbert	Lake	14,440	Arikaree R.	Yuma	3,315
Connecticut	S. slope of Mt. Frissell (peak in MA)	Litchfield	2,380	Long Island Sound		Sea level
Delaware	Nr. Ebright Azimuth	New Castle	450	Atlantic Ocean		Sea level
Dist. of Columbia	Fort Reno Park	NW quadrant	409	Potomac R.		1
Florida	Britton Hill	Walton	345	Atlantic Ocean		Sea level
Georgia	Brasstown Bald	Towns-Union	4,840	Atlantic Ocean		Sea level
Guam	Mount Lamlam	Agat District	1,332	Pacific Ocean		Sea level
Hawaii	Pu'u Wekiu, Mauna Kea	Hawaii	13,796	Pacific Ocean		Sea level
Idaho	Borah Peak	Custer	12,668	Snake R.	Nez Perce	710
Illinois	Charles Mound	Jo Daviess	1,235	Mississippi R.	Alexander	279
Indiana	Hoosier Hill	Wayne	1,257	Ohio R.	Posey	320
Iowa	Hawkeye Point	Osceola	1,670	Mississippi R.	Lee	480
Kansas	Mount Sunflower	Wallace	4,039	Verdigris R.	Montgomery	679
Kentucky	Black Mountain	Harlan	4,139	Mississippi R.	Fulton	257
Louisiana	Driskill Mountain	Bienville	535	New Orleans	Orleans	−8
Maine	Mount Katahdin	Piscataquis	5,269	Atlantic Ocean		Sea level
Maryland	Hoye Crest	Garrett	3,360	Bloody Point Hole, Chesapeake Bay	Queen Anne	−174
Massachusetts	Mount Greylock	Berkshire	3,491	Atlantic Ocean		Sea level
Michigan	Mount Arvon	Baraga	1,979	Lake Erie		571
Minnesota	Eagle Mountain	Cook	2,301	Lake Superior		601
Mississippi	Woodall Mountain	Tishomingo	806	Gulf of Mexico		Sea level
Missouri	Taum Sauk Mountain	Iron	1,772	St. Francis R.	Dunklin	230
Montana	Granite Peak	Park	12,807	Kootenai R.	Lincoln	1,800
Nebraska	Panorama Point	Kimball	5,424	Missouri R.	Richardson	840
Nevada	Boundary Peak	Esmeralda	13,146	Colorado R.	Clark	479
New Hampshire	Mount Washington	Coos	6,289	Atlantic Ocean		Sea level
New Jersey	High Point	Sussex	1,803	Atlantic Ocean		Sea level
New Mexico	Wheeler Peak	Taos	13,167	Red Bluff Reservoir	Eddy	2,842
New York	Mount Marcy	Essex	5,343	Atlantic Ocean		Sea level
North Carolina	Mount Mitchell	Yancey	6,683	Atlantic Ocean		Sea level
North Dakota	White Butte	Slope	3,506	Red R. of the North	Pembina	750
Northern Mariana Isls.	Mount Agrihan	Agrihan Island	3,166	Pacific Ocean		Sea level
Ohio	Campbell Hill	Logan	1,550	Ohio R.	Hamilton	455
Oklahoma	Black Mesa	Cimarron	4,973	Little R.	McCurtain	289
Oregon	Mount Hood	Clackamas-Hood R.	11,247	Pacific Ocean		Sea level
Pennsylvania	Mount Davis	Somerset	3,213	Delaware R.	Delaware	Sea level
Puerto Rico	Cerro de Punta	Ponce District	4,390	Atlantic Ocean		Sea level
Rhode Island	Jerimoth Hill	Providence	812	Atlantic Ocean		Sea level
South Carolina	Sassafras Mountain	Pickens	3,560	Atlantic Ocean		Sea level
South Dakota	Harney Peak	Pennington	7,244	Big Stone Lake	Roberts	966
Tennessee	Clingmans Dome	Sevier	6,644	Mississippi R.	Shelby	178
Texas	Guadalupe Peak	Culberson	8,751	Gulf of Mexico		Sea level
Utah	Kings Peak	Duchesne	13,518	Beaver Dam Wash	Washington	2,000
Vermont	Mount Mansfield	Chittenden	4,395	Lake Champlain		95
Virgin Islands	Crown Mountain	St. Thomas Island	1,556	Atlantic Ocean		Sea level
Virginia	Mount Rogers	Grayson-Smyth	5,729	Atlantic Ocean		Sea level
Washington	Mount Rainier	Pierce	14,410	Pacific Ocean		Sea level
West Virginia	Spruce Knob	Pendleton	4,863	Potomac R.	Jefferson	240
Wisconsin	Timms Hill	Price	1,951	Lake Michigan		579
Wyoming	Gannett Peak	Fremont	13,810	Belle Fourche R.	Crook	3,099

U.S. Coastline by State

Source: National Oceanic and Atmospheric Administration (NOAA), U.S. Dept. of Commerce
(in statute miles; only states with coastline or shoreline are shown)

	Coastline[1]	Shoreline[2]		Coastline[1]	Shoreline[2]
Atlantic Coast	2,069	28,673	**Gulf Coast**	1,631	17,141
Connecticut	0	618	Alabama	53	607
Delaware	28	381	Florida	770	5,095
Florida	580	3,331	Louisiana	397	7,721
Georgia	100	2,344	Mississippi	44	359
Maine	228	3,478	Texas	367	3,359
Maryland	31	3,190			
Massachusetts	192	1,519	**Pacific Coast**	7,623	40,298
New Hampshire	13	131	Alaska	5,580	31,383
New Jersey	130	1,792	California	840	3,427
New York	127	1,850	Hawaii	750	1,052
North Carolina	301	3,375	Oregon	296	1,410
Pennsylvania	0	89	Washington	157	3,026
Rhode Island	40	384			
South Carolina	187	2,876	**Arctic Coast**	1,060	2,521
Virginia	112	3,315	**United States**	12,383	88,633[3]

(1) Length of general outline of seacoast. Measurements were made in 1948 with a unit measure of 30 minutes of latitude on charts as near the scale of 1:1,200,000 as possible. Includes coastlines of large sounds and bays. (2) Shoreline of outer coast, offshore islands, sounds, bays, rivers, and creeks to the head of tidewater or to a point where tidal waters narrow to a width of 100 ft. Figures obtained in 1939-40 with a recording instrument on the largest-scale charts and maps then available. (3) Total length of U.S. tidal shoreline is 95,471 statute miles, which incl. measurements of outlying U.S. territories and possessions.

States: Capitals, Key Dates, Geographic Data

Source: *Statistical Abstract of the United States*, U.S. Census Bureau, U.S. Dept. of Commerce

The 13 colonies that declared independence from Great Britain and fought the War of Independence (American Revolution) became the 13 original states. They were, in the order in which they ratified the Constitution: Delaware, Pennsylvania, New Jersey, Georgia, Connecticut, Massachusetts, Maryland, South Carolina, New Hampshire, Virginia, New York, North Carolina, and Rhode Island.

			Entered Union		Extent (mi) Length Width (approx. mean)		Area (sq mi)			Rank by tot.
State	Settled[1]	Capital	Date	Order	Length	Width	Land	Water	Total	area
AL	1702	Montgomery	Dec. 14, 1819	22	330	190	50,645	1,775	52,420	30
AK	1784	Juneau	Jan. 3, 1959	49	1,480[2]	810	570,641	94,743	665,384	1
AZ	1776	Phoenix	Feb. 14, 1912	48	400	310	113,594	396	113,990	6
AR	1686	Little Rock	June 15, 1836	25	260	240	52,035	1,143	53,179	29
CA	1769	Sacramento	Sept. 9, 1850	31	770	250	155,779	7,916	163,695	3
CO	1858	Denver	Aug. 1, 1876	38	380	280	103,642	452	104,094	8
CT	1634	Hartford	Jan. 9, 1788	5	110	70	4,842	701	5,543	48
DE	1638	Dover	Dec. 7, 1787	1	96	30	1,949	540	2,489	49
DC	NA	NA	NA	NA	NA	NA	61	7	68	51
FL	1565	Tallahassee	Mar. 3, 1845	27	447	361	53,625	12,133	65,758	22
GA	1733	Atlanta	Jan. 2, 1788	4	300	230	57,513	1,912	59,425	24
HI	1820	Honolulu	Aug. 21, 1959	50	NA	NA	6,423	4,509	10,932	43
ID	1842	Boise	July 3, 1890	43	479	305	82,643	926	83,569	14
IL	1720	Springfield	Dec. 3, 1818	21	390	210	55,519	2,395	57,914	25
IN	1733	Indianapolis	Dec. 11, 1816	19	270	140	35,826	593	36,420	38
IA	1788	Des Moines	Dec. 28, 1846	29	310	200	55,857	416	56,273	26
KS	1727	Topeka	Jan. 29, 1861	34	400	210	81,759	520	82,278	15
KY	1774	Frankfort	June 1, 1792	15	380	140	39,486	921	40,408	37
LA	1699	Baton Rouge	Apr. 30, 1812	18	380	130	43,204	9,174	52,378	31
ME	1624	Augusta	Mar. 15, 1820	23	320	190	30,843	4,537	35,380	39
MD	1634	Annapolis	Apr. 28, 1788	7	250	90	9,707	2,699	12,406	42
MA	1620	Boston	Feb. 6, 1788	6	190	50	7,800	2,754	10,554	44
MI	1668	Lansing	Jan. 26, 1837	26	490	240	56,539	40,175	96,714	11
MN	1805	St. Paul	May 11, 1858	32	400	250	79,627	7,309	86,936	12
MS	1699	Jackson	Dec. 10, 1817	20	340	170	46,923	1,509	48,432	32
MO	1735	Jefferson City	Aug. 10, 1821	24	300	240	68,742	965	69,707	21
MT	1809	Helena	Nov. 8, 1889	41	630	280	145,546	1,494	147,040	4
NE	1823	Lincoln	Mar. 1, 1867	37	430	210	76,824	524	77,348	16
NV	1849	Carson City	Oct. 31, 1864	36	490	320	109,781	791	110,572	7
NH	1623	Concord	June 21, 1788	9	190	70	8,953	397	9,349	46
NJ	1660	Trenton	Dec. 18, 1787	3	150	70	7,354	1,368	8,723	47
NM	1610	Santa Fe	Jan. 6, 1912	47	370	343	121,298	292	121,590	5
NY	1614	Albany	July 26, 1788	11	330	283	47,126	7,429	54,555	27
NC	1660	Raleigh	Nov. 21, 1789	12	500	150	48,618	5,201	53,819	28
ND	1812	Bismarck	Nov. 2, 1889	39	340	211	69,001	1,698	70,698	19
OH	1788	Columbus	Mar. 1, 1803	17	220	220	40,861	3,965	44,826	34
OK	1889	Oklahoma City	Nov. 16, 1907	46	400	220	68,595	1,304	69,899	20
OR	1811	Salem	Feb. 14, 1859	33	360	261	95,988	2,391	98,379	9
PA	1682	Harrisburg	Dec. 12, 1787	2	283	160	44,743	1,312	46,054	33
RI	1636	Providence	May 29, 1790	13	40	30	1,034	511	1,545	50
SC	1670	Columbia	May 23, 1788	8	260	200	30,061	1,960	32,020	40
SD	1859	Pierre	Nov. 2, 1889	40	370	210	75,811	1,305	77,116	17
TN	1769	Nashville	June 1, 1796	16	491	115	41,235	909	42,144	36
TX	1682	Austin	Dec. 29, 1845	28	790	660	261,232	7,365	268,596	2
UT	1847	Salt Lake City	Jan. 4, 1896	45	350	270	82,170	2,727	84,897	13
VT	1724	Montpelier	Mar. 4, 1791	14	160	80	9,217	400	9,616	45
VA	1607	Richmond	June 25, 1788	10	430	200	39,490	3,285	42,775	35
WA	1811	Olympia	Nov. 11, 1889	42	360	240	66,456	4,842	71,298	18
WV	1727	Charleston	June 20, 1863	35	240	130	24,038	192	24,230	41
WI	1766	Madison	May 29, 1848	30	310	260	54,158	11,339	65,496	23
WY	1834	Cheyenne	July 10, 1890	44	360	280	97,093	720	97,813	10

NA = Not applicable. **Note:** Land and water areas, which are as of Jan. 1, 2010, may not add up to totals because of rounding. (1) First permanent settlement by Europeans. (2) Does not include Aleutian Islands or Alexander Archipelago.

Continental Divide of the U.S.

The Continental Divide of the U.S., also known as the Great Divide, is located at the watershed created by the mountain ranges, or tablelands, of the Rocky Mountains. This watershed separates the waters that ultimately drain into the Atlantic Ocean and its marginal seas from those waters that drain into the Pacific Ocean. The majority of water flowing E in the U.S. drains into the Gulf of Mexico and then the Atlantic. The majority of water flowing W drains through the Columbia River or Colorado River, which flows into the Gulf of California before reaching the Pacific.

The location and route of the Continental Divide across the U.S. can be described as follows:

Beginning at the U.S.-Mexico border, near longitude 108°45′ W, the Divide, in a northerly direction, crosses New Mexico along the western edge of the Rio Grande drainage basin, entering Colorado near longitude 106°41′ W. From there by an irregular route N across Colorado along the western summits of the Rio Grande and Arkansas, South Platte,

and North Platte river basins, and across Rocky Mountain National Park, entering Wyoming near longitude 106°52′ W.

From there in a northwesterly direction, forming the western rims of the North Platte, Big Horn, and Yellowstone river basins, crossing the SW portion of Yellowstone National Park. From there in a westerly and then northerly direction forming the boundary between Idaho and Montana, to a point on the boundary near longitude 114°00′ W. From there northeasterly and northwesterly through Montana and Glacier National Park, entering Canada near longitude 114°04′ W.

Depending on how a "divide" is defined, the U.S. can also be characterized as having a Northern (or Laurentian) Divide, Eastern Divide, and St. Lawrence Seaway Divide. Some of the waters at the Northern Divide drain into Hudson Bay and the Arctic Ocean. The Appalachian Mountains mark the Eastern Divide, with waters joining the Atlantic or Gulf of Mexico. The waters at the St. Lawrence Seaway Divide, near Chicago, flow into the Gulf of St. Lawrence or Gulf of Mexico.

Chronological List of Territories, With State Admissions to Union

Source: U.S. National Archives and Records Administration

Territory	Date of act creating territory	When act took effect	Date of admission as state	Years as terr.
Northwest Territory[1]	July 13, 1787	No fixed date	Mar. 1, 1803[2]	16
Territory South of Ohio River (Southwest Territory)	May 26, 1790	No fixed date	June 1, 1796[3]	6
Mississippi	Apr. 7, 1798	When president acted	Dec. 10, 1817	19
Indiana	May 7, 1800	July 4, 1800	Dec. 11, 1816	16
Orleans	Mar. 26, 1804	Oct. 1, 1804	Apr. 30, 1812[4]	7
Michigan	Jan. 11, 1805	June 30, 1805	Jan. 26, 1837	31
Louisiana-Missouri[5]	Mar. 3, 1805	July 4, 1805	Aug. 10, 1821	16
Illinois	Feb. 3, 1809	Mar. 1, 1809	Dec. 3, 1818	9
Alabama	Mar. 3, 1817	When MS formed state govt.	Dec. 14, 1819	2
Arkansas	Mar. 2, 1819	July 4, 1819	June 15, 1836	17
Florida	Mar. 30, 1822	No fixed date	Mar. 3, 1845	23
Wisconsin	Apr. 20, 1836	July 3, 1836	May 29, 1848	12
Iowa	June 12, 1838	July 3, 1838	Dec. 28, 1846	8
Oregon	Aug. 14, 1848	Date of act	Feb. 14, 1859	10
Minnesota	Mar. 3, 1849	Date of act	May 11, 1858	9
New Mexico	Sept. 9, 1850	On president's proclamation	Jan. 6, 1912	61
Utah	Sept. 9, 1850	Date of act	Jan. 4, 1896	46
Washington	Mar. 2, 1853	Date of act	Nov. 11, 1889	36
Kansas	May 30, 1854	Date of act	Jan. 29, 1861	6
Nebraska	May 30, 1854	Date of act	Mar. 1, 1867	12
Colorado	Feb. 28, 1861	Date of act	Aug. 1, 1876	15
Dakota	Mar. 2, 1861	Date of act	Nov. 2, 1889	28
Nevada	Mar. 2, 1861	Date of act	Oct. 31, 1864	3
Arizona	Feb. 24, 1863	Date of act	Feb. 14, 1912	49
Idaho	Mar. 3, 1863	Date of act	July 3, 1890	27
Montana	May 26, 1864	Date of act	Nov. 8, 1889	25
Wyoming	July 25, 1868	When officers were qualified	July 10, 1890	22
Alaska	May 17, 1884[6]	No fixed date	Jan. 3, 1959	75
Oklahoma	May 2, 1890	Date of act	Nov. 16, 1907	17
Hawaii	Apr. 30, 1900	June 14, 1900	Aug. 21, 1959	59

Note: California was never organized as a territory. It was administered by the military after its acquisition from Mexico (1848) until its admission as a state (1850). (1) Included what is now Ohio, Indiana, Illinois, Michigan, Wisconsin, and E Minnesota. (2) Date of admission for Ohio, the first state created out of territory, based on the date its General Assembly first met. Congress approved Ohio's entry into the Union on Feb. 19, 1803. (3) Admitted as the state of Tennessee. (4) Admitted as the state of Louisiana. (5) The act renaming Louisiana Territory as Missouri Territory (June 4, 1812) became effective Dec. 7, 1812. (6) Act constituted Alaska as a district, though it was often referred to and administered as a territory. The Territory of Alaska was formally organized by an act of Aug. 24, 1912.

U.S. Geographic Centers

Source: U.S. Geological Survey, U.S. Dept. of the Interior

There is no generally accepted definition of a geographic center and no uniform method for determining it. Geographic center is defined here as the center of gravity of the surface of an area, or that point on which an area would balance if it were a plane of uniform thickness.

No government agency has officially established any points marking the geographic center of the U.S., the conterminous U.S. (48 states), or the North American continent. In 1941, private citizens erected a monument in Lebanon, KS, marking it as the geographic center of the then U.S. (conterminous). Residents of Rugby, ND, installed a cairn after the U.S. Geologic Survey, in 1931, determined it to be the center of the North American continent. In 2017, a Univ. at Buffalo geography professor announced that Center, ND, was the continental center according to a mathematical method he developed. The geographic centers in the following list are approximate. They are indicated by county then city unless otherwise noted.

U.S. (50 states): W of Castle Rock, Butte County, South Dakota; 44°58′ N, 103°46′ W
Conterminous U.S. (48 states): nr. Lebanon, Smith County, Kansas; 39°50′ N, 98°35′ W
North American continent: 6 mi W of Balta, Pierce County, North Dakota; 48°10′ N, 100°10′ W
Alabama: Chilton, 12 mi SW of Clanton
Alaska: 63°50′ N, 152° W, approx. 60 mi NW of Denali
Arizona: Yavapai, 55 mi E-SE of Prescott
Arkansas: Pulaski, 12 mi NW of Little Rock
California: Madera, 38 mi E of Madera
Colorado: Park, 30 mi NW of Pikes Peak
Connecticut: Hartford, at East Berlin
Delaware: Kent, 11 mi S of Dover
District of Columbia: near 4th and L Sts. NW
Florida: Hernando, 12 mi N-NW of Brooksville
Georgia: Twiggs, 18 mi SE of Macon
Hawaii: Hawaii; 20°15′ N, 156°20′ W, off Maui Island
Idaho: Custer, SW of Challis
Illinois: Logan, 28 mi NE of Springfield
Indiana: Boone, 14 mi N-NW of Indianapolis
Iowa: Story, 5 mi NE of Ames
Kansas: Barton, 15 mi NE of Great Bend
Kentucky: Marion, 3 mi N-NW of Lebanon
Louisiana: Avoyelles, 3 mi SE of Marksville
Maine: Piscataquis, 18 mi N of Dover
Maryland: Prince George's, 4.5 mi NW of Davidsonville
Massachusetts: Worcester, N part of city of Worcester
Michigan: Wexford, 5 mi N-NW of Cadillac

Minnesota: Crow Wing, 10 mi SW of Brainerd
Mississippi: Leake, 9 mi W-NW of Carthage
Missouri: Miller, 20 mi SW of Jefferson City
Montana: Fergus, 11 mi W of Lewistown
Nebraska: Custer, 10 mi NW of Broken Bow
Nevada: Lander, 26 mi SE of Austin
New Hampshire: Belknap, 3 mi E of Ashland
New Jersey: Mercer, 5 mi SE of Trenton
New Mexico: Torrance, 12 mi S-SW of Willard
New York: Madison, 12 mi S of Oneida and 26 mi SW of Utica
North Carolina: Chatham, 10 mi NW of Sanford
North Dakota: Sheridan, 5 mi SW of McClusky
Ohio: Delaware, 25 mi N-NE of Columbus
Oklahoma: Oklahoma, 8 mi N of Oklahoma City
Oregon: Crook, 25 mi S-SE of Prineville
Pennsylvania: Centre, 2.5 mi SW of Bellefonte
Rhode Island: Kent, 1 mi S-SW of Crompton
South Carolina: Richland, 13 mi SE of Columbia
South Dakota: Hughes, 8 mi NE of Pierre
Tennessee: Rutherford, 5 mi NE of Murfreesboro
Texas: McCulloch, 15 mi NE of Brady
Utah: Sanpete, 3 mi N of Manti
Vermont: Washington, 3 mi E of Roxbury
Virginia: Buckingham, 5 mi SW of Buckingham
Washington: Chelan, 10 mi W-SW of Wenatchee
West Virginia: Braxton, 4 mi E of Sutton
Wisconsin: Wood, 9 mi SE of Marshfield
Wyoming: Fremont, 58 mi E-NE of Lander

Lengths of U.S. Boundaries

The length of the boundary between the U.S. and Canada is 5,525 mi—3,987 mi between the conterminous U.S. and Canada and 1,538 mi between Alaska and Canada. A 1925 treaty established a permanent International Boundary Commission to maintain the boundary. The U.S.-Mexican border was established by multiple treaties (1848, 1853, 1970) at 1,954-miles long. (The U.S. Census Bureau has put the border at 1,933-miles long.) It largely follows the Rio Grande and Colorado River, from the Gulf of Mexico to the Pacific Ocean. It is overseen by the International Boundary and Water Commission.

Origins of the Names of U.S. States and Territories

Source: State officials; Smithsonian Institution; Topographic Division, U.S. Geological Survey, U.S. Dept. of the Interior

Alabama: Choctaw word for a Chickasaw tribe. First noted in accounts of Hernando de Soto expedition.

Alaska: Russian version of Aleutian (Eskimo) word *alakshak* for "peninsula," "great lands," or "land that is not an island."

American Samoa: Etymology varies.

Arizona: Spanish version of Pima Indian word for "little spring place" or Aztec *arizuma*, meaning "silver-bearing."

Arkansas: Algonquin name for Quapaw Indians, meaning "south wind."

California: Bestowed by Spanish conquistadors (possibly Hernán Cortés). It was the name of an imaginary island in the 1510 Spanish novel *Las Sergas de Esplandián* (The Exploits of Esplandián), by Garci Rodríguez de Montalvo. The Spanish first visited *Baja* (Lower) *California* in 1533. The present-day U.S. state was called *Alta* (Upper) *California*.

Colorado: From Spanish for "red," first applied to Colorado River.

Connecticut: From Mohican and other Algonquin words meaning "long river place."

Delaware: Named for Lord De La Warr, early governor of Virginia; first applied to river, then to Indian tribe (Lenni-Lenape).

District of Columbia: For Christopher Columbus, 1791.

Florida: Named by Juan Ponce de León *Pascua Florida*, "Flowery Easter," on Easter Sunday, 1513.

Georgia: Named by colonial administrator James Oglethorpe for King George II of England in 1732.

Guam: From Chamorro name, *Guahan*, meaning "we have."

Hawaii: Possibly derived from *Hawaiki* or *Owhyhee*, Polynesian word for "homeland."

Idaho: Said to be a coined name with the invented meaning "gem of the mountains;" suggested for the Pikes Peak mining territory (Colorado), then applied to the new mining territory of the Pacific Northwest. Another theory suggests *Idaho* may be Kiowa Apache term for the Comanche.

Illinois: French for *Illini* or "land of *Illini*," Algonquin word meaning "men" or "warriors."

Indiana: Means "land of the Indians."

Iowa: Indian word variously translated as "here I rest" or "beautiful land." Named for the Iowa River, which was named for the Iowa Indians.

Kansas: Sioux word for "south wind people."

Kentucky: Indian word variously translated as "dark and bloody ground," "meadowland," and "land of tomorrow."

Louisiana: Part of territory called Louisiana by René-Robert Cavelier Sieur de La Salle for French King Louis XIV.

Maine: From Maine, historic French province. Also descriptive, referring to the mainland as distinct from coastal islands.

Maryland: For Queen Henrietta Maria, wife of Charles I of England.

Massachusetts: From Indian tribe whose name meant "at or about the Great Hill" in Blue Hills region south of Boston.

Michigan: From Chippewa *mici gama*, meaning "great water," after lake of the same name.

Minnesota: From Dakota Sioux word meaning "cloudy water" or "sky-tinted water" of the Minnesota River.

Mississippi: Probably Chippewa *mici zibi*, meaning "great river" or "gathering-in of all the waters." Also Algonquin word *messipi*.

Missouri: Algonquin Indian term meaning "river of the big canoes."

Montana: Latin or Spanish for "mountainous."

Nebraska: From Omaha or Otos Indian word meaning "broad water" or "flat river," describing the Platte River.

Nevada: Spanish, meaning "snow-clad."

New Hampshire: Named by Capt. John Mason of Plymouth Council, in 1629, for his home county in England.

New Jersey: The Duke of York, in 1664, gave a patent to Lord John Berkeley and Sir George Carteret for *Nova Caesaria*, or New Jersey, after England's Isle of Jersey.

New Mexico: Spaniards in Mexico applied term to land north and west of Rio Grande in the 16th century.

New York: For James, Duke of York and Albany, who received patent for New Netherland from his brother Charles II and sent an expedition to capture it, 1664.

North Carolina: In 1619, Charles I gave patent to Sir Robert Heath for Province of Carolana, from *Carolus*, Latin name for Charles. Charles II granted a new patent to Earl of Clarendon and others. Divided into North and South Carolina, 1710.

North Dakota: Sioux word *Dakota*, meaning "friend" or "ally."

Northern Mariana Isls.: For Mariana of Austria, queen regent of Spain.

Ohio: Iroquois word for "fine or good river."

Oklahoma: Choctaw word meaning "red man," proposed by Rev. Allen Wright, Choctaw-speaking Indian.

Oregon: Origin unknown. One theory is that the name derives from *wauregan*, meaning "beautiful," term used by Indians in New England.

Pennsylvania: William Penn, Quaker who was made full proprietor of area by King Charles II in 1681, suggested "Sylvania," or "woodland," for his tract. The king's government owed 16,000 pounds to Penn's father, Adm. William Penn, and the land was granted as partial settlement. Charles II added "Penn" to "Sylvania," against the modest proprietor's desires, in honor of the admiral.

Puerto Rico: Spanish for "rich port."

Rhode Island: Origin unknown. One theory notes that Giovanni de Verrazzano recorded observing an island about the size of the Greek island of Rhodes in 1524. Another theory is that Dutch explorer Adriaen Block named the state *Roode Eylandt* for its red clay.

South Carolina: See North Carolina.

South Dakota: See North Dakota.

Tennessee: *Tanasi* was the name of Cherokee villages on the Little Tennessee River. From 1784 to 1788, this was the State of Franklin, or Frankland.

Texas: Variant of word used by Caddo and other Indians meaning "friends" or "allies" and applied to them by the Spanish in eastern Texas. Also written *Texias, Tejas, Teysas*.

Utah: From a Navajo word meaning "upper," or "higher up," as applied to Shoshone tribe called Ute. Proposed name *Deseret*, "land of honeybees," from Book of Mormon, was rejected by Congress.

Vermont: From French words *vert* (green) and *mont* (mountain). The Green Mountains were said to have been named by Samuel de Champlain. When the state was formed in 1777, Dr. Thomas Young suggested combining *vert* and *mont*.

Virgin Islands, U.S.: From Spanish name *Las Once Mil Virgenes* (11,000 Virgins), which Christopher Columbus gave to island group.

Virginia: Named by Sir Walter Raleigh, who outfitted an expedition in 1584, in honor of England's Queen Elizabeth, the Virgin Queen.

Washington: Named after George Washington. When the bill creating the Territory of Columbia was introduced in the 32nd Congress, its name was changed to Washington because of the existence of the District of Columbia.

West Virginia: So named when western counties of Virginia refused to secede from the U.S. in 1863.

Wisconsin: Indian name, spelled *Ouisconsin* or *Mesconsing* by early chroniclers, believed to mean "grassy place" in Chippewa. Congress made it *Wisconsin*.

Wyoming: From Algonquin words for "large prairie place," "at the big plains," or "on the great plain."

Territorial Sea of the U.S.

According to a Dec. 27, 1988, proclamation by Pres. Ronald Reagan, "The territorial sea of the United States henceforth extends to 12 nautical miles from the baselines of the United States determined in accordance with international law. In accordance with international law, as reflected in the applicable provisions of the 1982 United Nations Convention on the Law of the Sea, within the territorial sea of the United States, the ships of all countries enjoy the right of innocent passage and the ships and aircraft of all countries enjoy the right of transit passage through international straits."

Major Accessions of Territory by the U.S.

Source: U.S. Dept. of the Interior; U.S. Census Bureau, U.S. Dept. of Commerce

Not including territories such as the Panama Canal Zone and the Philippines, which are no longer under U.S. jurisdiction.

Accession	Date	Area (sq mi)	Accession	Date	Area (sq mi)	Accession	Date	Area (sq mi)
Territory in 1790[1]	NA	888,685	Mexican Cession	1848	529,017	Guam[3]	1899	212
Louisiana Purchase	1803	827,192	Gadsden Purchase	1853	29,640	American Samoa[4]	1900	76
Treaty of Florida	1819	72,003	Alaska	1867	586,412	U.S. Virgin Islands	1917	133
Texas	1845	390,143	Hawaii	1898	6,450	Northern Marianas[5]	1986	179
Oregon Territory	1846	285,680	Puerto Rico[2]	1899	3,435			

NA = Not applicable. (1) Includes that part of a drainage basin of Red River of the North, south of 49th parallel, sometimes considered part of Louisiana Purchase. (2) Ceded by Spain in 1898, ratified in 1899, and became the Commonwealth of Puerto Rico by Act of Congress on July 25, 1952. (3) Acquired in 1898; ratified 1899. (4) Acquired in 1899; ratified 1900. (5) Part of the UN Trust Territory of the Pacific Islands, which U.S. began administering in 1947; became U.S. commonwealth Nov. 3, 1986.

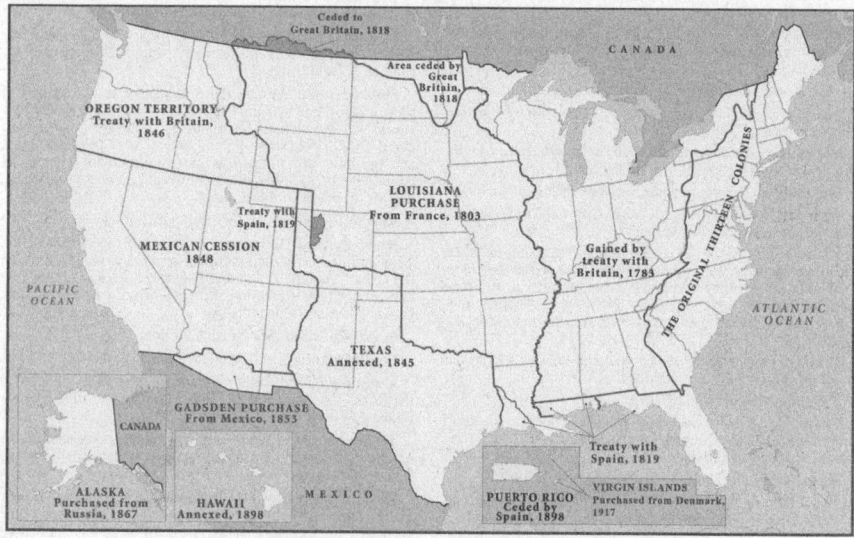

National Park System Recreation Visits, 1904-2019

Source: National Park Service (NPS), U.S. Dept. of the Interior

An NPS-administered site, regardless of its designation (as a park, monument, or preserve, etc.), is generally referred to as a unit. Not all units report public use statistics.

Year	Units reporting visits	Recreation visits	Year	Units reporting visits	Recreation visits
1904	6	120,690	2000	344	285,891,275
1905	6	140,954	2001	345	279,873,926
1910	9	173,416	2002	349	277,299,880
1915	12	314,299	2003	353	266,230,290
1920	26	1,022,091	2004	356	276,908,337
1925	39	1,900,499	2005	356	273,488,751
1930	45	3,038,935	2006	359	272,623,980
1935	85	7,435,659	2007	360	275,581,547
1940	113	16,410,148	2008	360	274,852,949
1945	143	10,855,548	2009	360	285,579,941
1950	139	32,706,172	2010	363	281,303,769
1955	150	48,891,000	2011	367	278,939,216
1960	166	71,586,000	2012	367	282,765,682
1965	182	118,662,500	2013	370	273,630,895
1970	217	168,135,100	2014	376	292,800,082
1975	251	188,085,700	2015	378	307,247,252
1980	275	220,463,211	2016	382	330,971,689
1985	303	263,441,808	2017	385	330,882,751
1990	316	255,581,467	2018	385	318,211,833
1995	328	269,564,307	2019	385	327,516,619

Most-Visited Sites in the National Park System, 2019

Source: National Park Service (NPS), U.S. Dept. of the Interior

Attendance at 385 of 419 NPS-administered sites totaled 327,516,619 recreation visits in 2019. (Not all units report public use statistics.)

Rank	Site (location)	Rec. visits
1.	Golden Gate Natl. Recreation Area (CA)	15,002,227
2.	Blue Ridge Parkway (NC-VA)	14,976,085
3.	Great Smoky Mountains Natl. Park (NC-TN)	12,547,743
4.	Gateway Natl. Recreation Area (NJ-NY)	9,405,622
5.	Lincoln Memorial (DC)	7,808,182
6.	Lake Mead Natl. Recreation Area (AZ-NV)	7,499,049
7.	George Washington Memorial Parkway (DC-MD-VA)	7,487,265
8.	Natchez Trace Parkway (AL-MS-TN)	6,296,041
9.	Grand Canyon Natl. Park (AZ)	5,974,411
10.	Gulf Islands Natl. Seashore (FL-MS)	5,600,240
11.	Chesapeake & Ohio Canal Natl. Historical Park (DC-MD-WV)	5,116,787
12.	World War II Memorial (DC)	4,831,327
13.	Rocky Mountain Natl. Park (CO)	4,670,053
14.	Vietnam Veterans Memorial (DC)	4,580,587
15.	Independence Natl. Historical Park (PA)	4,532,459
16.	Zion Natl. Park (UT)	4,488,268
17.	Yosemite Natl. Park (CA)	4,422,861
18.	Castle Clinton Natl. Monument (NY)	4,361,034
19.	Glen Canyon Natl. Recreation Area (AZ-UT)	4,330,563
20.	Statue of Liberty Natl. Monument (NY)	4,240,461
21.	Cape Cod Natl. Seashore (MA)	4,096,104
22.	Yellowstone Natl. Park (ID-MT-WY)	4,020,288
23.	San Francisco Maritime Natl. Historical Park (CA)	4,016,598
24.	Korean War Veterans Memorial (DC)	3,841,633
25.	Martin Luther King, Jr. Memorial (DC)	3,667,562

Rank	Site (location)	Rec. visits
26.	Acadia Natl. Park (ME)	3,437,286
27.	Grand Teton Natl. Park (WY)	3,405,614
28.	Chattahoochee River Natl. Recreation Area (GA)	3,393,133
29.	Delaware Water Gap Natl. Recreation Area (NJ-PA)	3,374,865
30.	Colonial Natl. Historical Park (VA)	3,327,268
31.	Franklin Delano Roosevelt Memorial (DC)	3,303,573
32.	Olympic Natl. Park (WA)	3,245,806
33.	Boston Natl. Historical Park (MA)	3,201,834
34.	Thomas Jefferson Memorial (DC)	3,096,895
35.	Glacier Natl. Park (MT)	3,049,839
36.	Joshua Tree Natl. Park (CA)	2,988,547
37.	Kennesaw Mountain Natl. Battlefield Park (GA)	2,621,050
38.	Cape Hatteras Natl. Seashore (NC)	2,606,632
39.	Bryce Canyon Natl. Park (UT)	2,594,904
40.	Rock Creek Park (DC)	2,416,232
41.	Assateague Island Natl. Seashore (MD-VA)	2,344,536
42.	Point Reyes Natl. Seashore (CA)	2,265,301
43.	Valley Forge Natl. Historical Park (PA)	2,259,944
44.	Cuyahoga Valley Natl. Park (OH)	2,237,997
45.	Indiana Dunes Natl. Park (IN)	2,134,285
46.	Stonewall Natl. Monument (NY)	2,088,929
47.	Gateway Arch Natl. Park (MO)	2,055,309
48.	Mount Rushmore Natl. Memorial (SD)	1,963,540
49.	Canaveral Natl. Seashore (FL)	1,884,122
50.	National Capital Parks Central (DC)	1,770,794

(1) Incl. recreation visits to Constitution Gardens.

National Parks and Other Areas Administered by National Park Service

As of Dec. 31, 2019, the National Park Service (NPS) administered about 85,103,543 acres of federal and non-federal land across 419 sites. Date when area was authorized or established by Congress or by presidential proclamation is given in parentheses; any date that follows indicates when a site received its current designation or was transferred to the NPS. Figure after the date is gross area acres as of Dec. 31, 2019. Listings do not include parks administered by other agencies, such as the Forest Service or Bureau of Land Management. NA = not available.

The following units have been authorized but are not yet established: Adams Mem. (DC, authorized 2001), Dwight D. Eisenhower Mem. (DC, 2002), Ronald Reagan Boyhood Home Natl. Historic Site (IL, 2002), Coltsville Natl. Historical Park (CT, 2014), Desert Storm/Desert Shield Mem. (DC, 2014), Global War on Terrorism Mem. (DC, 2017), Ste. Genevieve Natl. Historical Park (MO, 2018), Medgar and Myrlie Evers Home Natl. Monument (MS, 2019), and Mill Springs Battlefield Natl. Monument (KY, 2019).

National Parks

Acadia, ME (1916/1919): 49,077. Incl. Mount Desert Isl., half of Isle au Haut, Schoodic Peninsula on mainland. Highest elevation on Eastern seaboard.

American Samoa, AS (1988): 8,257. Paleotropical rain forest, coral reef.

Arches, UT (1929/1971): 76,679. Contains giant red sandstone arches and other products of erosion.

Badlands, SD (1939/1978): 242,756. Reformations and native prairie; animal fossils 25-37 mil years old.

Big Bend, TX (1935): 801,163. Rio Grande, Chisos Mtns.

Biscayne, FL (1968/1980): 172,971. Aquatic park encompassing chain of islands south of Miami.

Black Canyon of the Gunnison, CO (1933/1999): 30,780. Has canyon 2,900 ft deep and 40 ft wide at narrowest part.

Bryce Canyon, UT (1923/1928): 35,835. Colorful display of erosion effects.

Canyonlands, UT (1964): 337,598. At junction of Colorado and Green Rivers; extensive evidence of prehistoric peoples.

Capitol Reef, UT (1937/1971): 241,905. nearly 100-mi-long uplift of sandstone cliffs (Waterpocket Fold) dissected by gorges.

Carlsbad Caverns, NM (1923/1930): 46,766. More than 119 limestone caves, incl. Carlsbad Cavern; Chihuahuan Desert.

Channel Islands, CA (1938/1980): 249,561. Sea lion breeding place, nesting seabirds, unique plants.

Congaree, SC (1976/2003): 26,476. Largest intact tract of old-growth bottomland hardwood forest in U.S.

Crater Lake, OR (1902): 183,224. Deepest U.S. lake, in crater of Mt. Mazama, volcano that erupted about 7,700 years ago.

Cuyahoga Valley, OH (1974/2000): 32,572. Along Ohio and Erie Canal system between Akron and Cleveland.

Death Valley, CA-NV (1933/1994): 3,408,407. Large desert. Incl. lowest point in North America and Scotty's Castle (closed until 2020 due to flood damage).

Denali, AK (1917/1980): 4,740,911. Formerly known as Mt. McKinley; highest mountain in U.S.

Dry Tortugas, FL (1935/1992): 64,701. Ft. Jefferson and seven coral reef and sand islands near Key West.

Everglades, FL (1934): 1,508,939. Largest remaining subtropical wilderness in continental U.S; incl. East Everglades Expansion Area acreage added in 1989.

Gates of the Arctic, AK (1978/1980): 7,523,897. Vast wilderness in north central region. Limited federal facilities.

Gateway Arch National Park, St. Louis, MO (1935/2018): 193. Former Jefferson Natl. Expansion Natl. Memorial commemorates 19th cent. westward expansion; incl. Gateway Arch (authorized 1954).

Glacier, MT (1910): 1,013,126. Rocky Mt. scenery; numerous glaciers and glacial lakes. Part of Waterton-Glacier Intl. Peace Park established by U.S. and Canada in 1932.

Glacier Bay, AK (1925/1980): 3,223,383. Tidewater glaciers that move down mountainsides and break up into sea.

Grand Canyon, AZ (1919/1919): 1,201,647. Carved by Colorado River.

Grand Teton, WY (1929): 310,044. Incl. highest peaks of Teton Mtns.; summer feeding ground of largest American elk herd.

Great Basin, NV (1922/1986): 77,180. Incl. Wheeler Peak, Lexington Arch, Lehman Caves.

Great Sand Dunes, CO (1932/2004): 107,342. North America's tallest dunes.

Great Smoky Mountains, NC-TN (1926/1934): 522,427. Most biologically diverse NPS unit, with 19,000+ documented species.

Guadalupe Mountains, TX (1966): 86,367. Extensive Permian limestone fossil reef; tremendous earth fault.

Haleakalā, HI (1916/1960): 33,265. Dormant volcano on island of Maui with large craters.

Hawai'i Volcanoes, HI (1916/1961): 325,605. Contains Kīlauea and Mauna Loa, active volcanoes.

Hot Springs, AR (1832/1921): 5,554. Waters from park's 47 hot springs used for bathing and drinking.

Indiana Dunes, IN (1966/2019): 15,349. Stretches 15 mi along Lake Michigan.

Isle Royale, MI (1931): 571,790. Largest island in Lake Superior.

Joshua Tree, CA (1936/1994): 795,156. Desert region incl. Joshua trees, other plant and animal life.

Katmai, AK (1918/1980): 3,674,529. "Valley of Ten Thousand Smokes," scene of 1912 volcanic eruption.

Kenai Fjords, AK (1978/1980): 669,650. Marine mammals, birdlife; over 30 glaciers flow from Harding Icefield.

Kings Canyon, CA (1890/1940): 461,901. Mountain wilderness, dominated by Kings River Canyons and High Sierra; giant sequoias.

Kobuk Valley, AK (1978/1980): 1,750,716. Geological and recreational sites. Limited federal facilities.

Lake Clark, AK (1978/1980): 2,619,816. Across Cook Inlet from Anchorage; scenic wilderness, fish and wildlife. Limited federal facilities.

Lassen Volcanic, CA (1907/1916): 106,589. Contains Lassen Peak, recently active volcano; other volcanic phenomena.

Mammoth Cave, KY (1926/1941): 54,012. Longest known cave system in world (more than 405 mi currently surveyed), river 300 ft below surface.

Mesa Verde, CO (1906): 52,485. Most notable and best preserved prehistoric cliff dwellings in U.S.

Mount Rainier, WA (1899): 236,382. Most glaciated peak in contiguous U.S.

North Cascades, WA (1968): 504,781. Mountainous region with many glaciers, lakes.

Olympic, WA (1909/1938): 922,649. Wilderness containing glacier-capped mountains, remnant of temperate rain forest, shoreline, endemic animal species.

Petrified Forest, AZ (1906/1962): 221,390. Extensive petrified wood and Indian artifacts. Contains part of Painted Desert.

Pinnacles, CA (1908/2013): 26,686. A release site for captive-bred California condors; talus caves.

Redwood, CA (1968): 138,999. 40 mi of Pacific coastline, groves of ancient redwoods, the world's tallest trees.

Rocky Mountain, CO (1915): 265,807. On Continental Divide; incl. peaks over 14,000 ft.

Saguaro, AZ (1933/1994): 91,716. Part of Sonoran Desert; incl. giant saguaro cacti, unique to region.

Sequoia, CA (1890): 404,063. Giant sequoia groves; world's largest tree (by volume). Mt. Whitney, highest mountain in conterminous U.S.

Shenandoah, VA (1926): 199,224. Portion of Blue Ridge Mtns. Overlooks Shenandoah Valley; Skyline Drive.

Theodore Roosevelt, ND (1947/1978): 70,447. Contains part of Roosevelt's ranch and scenic badlands.

Virgin Islands, VI (1956): 15,052. Covers more than half of St. John Isl. and nearly all of Hassel Isl.; beaches, Carib Indian petroglyphs, evidence of colonial Danes.

Voyageurs, MN (1971): 218,222. Abundant lakes, forests, wildlife.

White Sands, NM (1933/2019): 146,344. World's largest gypsum dunefield.

Wind Cave, SD (1903): 33,971. Limestone caverns in Black Hills; extensive wildlife incl. bison herd.

Wrangell-St. Elias, AK (1978/1980): 8,323,146. Largest area in park system; most peaks over 16,000 ft.

Yellowstone, ID-MT-WY (1872): 2,219,791. World's first national park. More than 10,000 thermal features (geysers, hot springs); Yellowstone River falls and canyons; largest bison herd on U.S. public land.

Yosemite, CA (1890): 761,748. Yosemite Valley, country's highest waterfall, grove of sequoias, mountains.

Zion, UT (1909/1919): 147,243. Unusual shapes, landscapes resulting from erosion, faulting; evidence of past volcanic activity.

National Historical Parks

Abraham Lincoln Birthplace, Hodgenville, KY (1916/2009): 345. Memorial building, sinking spring.

Adams, Quincy, MA (1946/1998): 24. Home of Pres. John Adams, John Quincy Adams, and descendants.

Appomattox Court House, VA (1930/1954): 1,775. Where Confederate Gen. Lee surrendered to Gen. Grant, signaling Civil War's end.

Blackstone River Valley, MA-RI (2014): 1,489. Preserves the valley's industrial heritage.

Boston, MA (1974): 44. Incl. Faneuil Hall, Old North Church, Bunker Hill, Paul Revere House.

Cane River Creole, LA (1994): 206. Preserves Creole culture as it developed along the Cane River.

Cedar Creek and Belle Grove, VA (2002): 3,707. Civil War battle site and an antebellum plantation in Shenandoah Valley.

Chaco Culture, NM (1907/1980): 33,960. Ruins of pueblos built by prehistoric peoples incl. Pueblo, Hopi, and Navajo.

Chesapeake & Ohio Canal, MD-DC-WV (1938/1971): 19,612. 184.5-mi historic canal; DC to Cumberland, MD.

Colonial, VA (1930/1936): 8,675. Incl. most of Jamestown Isl., site of first successful English colony; Yorktown, site of Cornwallis's surrender to George Washington.

Cumberland Gap, KY-TN-VA (1940): 24,547. Mountain pass of Wilderness Road, which carried first great migration of pioneers into America's interior.

Dayton Aviation Heritage, OH (1992): 111. Commemorates area's involvement in aviation.

First State, DE-PA (2013/2014): 1,155. Locations date from colonial past of DE, first state to ratify Constitution.

Fort Sumter and Fort Moultrie, SC (1948/2019): 235. Charleston Harbor sites, where Confederate forces fired the first shots of the Civil War.

George Rogers Clark, Vincennes, IN (1966): 26. Commemorates American defeat of British in West during Revolution.

Golden Spike, UT (1957/2019): 2,735. Commemorates completion of first transcontinental railroad in 1869.

Harpers Ferry, MD-VA-WV (1944/1963): 3,669. At confluence of Shenandoah and Potomac Rivers, the site of John Brown's 1859 raid on the Army arsenal.

Harriet Tubman, NY (2017): 32. Buildings incl. her home, a church, Tubman Home for the Aged.

Harriet Tubman Underground Railroad, MD (2013/2014): 480. Protects landscapes on the Eastern Shore, where Tubman was born and guided other slaves to freedom.

Hopewell Culture, OH (1923/1992): 1,776. Remains of ceremonial mounds built in the Ohio River Valley, 200 BCE-500 CE.

Independence, Philadelphia, PA (1948): 45. Several properties associated with American Revolution and founding of U.S., incl. Independence Hall, Liberty Bell Center.

Jean Lafitte (and Preserve), LA (1907/1978): 25,876. Incl. Chalmette, site of 1815 Battle of New Orleans; French Quarter.

Kalaupapa, HI (1980): 10,779. Former colony on Molokai Isl. for those with Hansen's disease (leprosy).

Kaloko-Honokōhau, HI (1978): 1,163. Preserves native culture of Hawaii.

Keweenaw, MI (1992): 1,870. Site of first significant copper mine in U.S.

Klondike Gold Rush, AK-WA (1976): 12,996. Preserves Chilkoot Trail used in 1898 Gold Rush. Museum in Seattle.

Lewis and Clark, OR-WA (1958/2004): 3,410. Lewis and Clark encampment, 1805-06. Incorporates former Fort Clatsop Natl. Mem. Park.

Lowell, MA (1978): 142. Textile mills, canal, 19th-cent. structures; park shows planned city of Industrial Revolution.

Lyndon B. Johnson, TX (1969/1980): 1,572. 36th president's birthplace, boyhood home, ranch.

Manhattan Project, NM-TN-WA (2015): 114. Jointly operated with Dept. of Energy, consists of three sites (Los Alamos, NM; Oak Ridge, TN; Hanford, WA) where U.S. developed world's first atomic weapons.

Marsh-Billings-Rockefeller, VT (1992): 643. Boyhood home of conservationist George Perkins Marsh.

Martin Luther King Jr., Atlanta, GA (1980/2018): 39. Birthplace, grave, church of the civil rights leader.

Minute Man, MA (1959): 1,028. Where Minute Men battled British, Apr. 19, 1775. Also includes The Wayside, home to authors Louisa May Alcott and Nathaniel Hawthorne.

Morristown, NJ (1933): 1,711. Site of important military encampments during the American Revolution; Washington's headquarters, 1779-80.

Natchez, MS (1988): 108. Antebellum estate, other preserved properties related to history of Natchez as a Cotton Belt city.

New Bedford Whaling, MA (1996): 34. Preserves structures and relics associated with the city's 19th-cent. whaling industry.

New Orleans Jazz, LA (1994): 5. Preserves, educates, and interprets jazz as it has evolved in New Orleans.

Nez Perce, ID-MT-OR-WA (1965): 4,565. Illustrates history and culture of Nez Perce, or Nimiipuu, homeland (38 sites).

Ocmulgee Mounds, GA (1934/2019): 3,336. First inhabited by Paleo Indians by c. 15,000 BCE. Ancestral land of the Muscogee (Creek), who were forcibly moved to OK in 1830s.

Palo Alto Battlefield, TX (1978/2009): 3,442. Scene of first battle of the Mexican War.

Paterson Great Falls, NJ (2011): 51. Falls helped make city one of U.S.'s earliest industrial centers.

Pecos, NM (1965/1990): 6,693. Ruins of ancient Pueblo of Pecos, archaeological sites, and two associated Spanish colonial missions from 17th and 18th centuries.

Pu'uhonua o Hōnaunau, HI (1955/1978): 420. Until 1819, a sanctuary for Hawaiians vanquished in battle and for those guilty of crimes or breaking taboos.

Reconstruction Era, SC (2017/2019): 16. Beaufort Co. sites that tell the story of how formerly enslaved people were integrated into free society.

Rosie the Riveter/WWII Home Front, Richmond, CA (2000): 145. Site of shipyard that employed thousands of women during WWII; commemorates women who worked in wartime industries.

Saint-Gaudens, Cornish, NH (1964/2019): 191. Home, studio, and gardens of sculptor Augustus Saint-Gaudens.

Salt River Bay (and Ecological Preserve), St. Croix, VI (1992): 989. Only known site where, in 1493, members of a Columbus party landed on what is now U.S. territory.

San Antonio Missions, TX (1978): 948. Four Spanish missions, 18th-cent. irrigation system.

San Francisco Maritime, CA (1988): 50. Artifacts, photographs, and historic vessels related to development of the Pacific Coast.

San Juan Island, WA (1966): 2,146. Commemorates peaceful relations between U.S., Canada, and Great Britain since the 1872 boundary disputes.

Saratoga, NY (1938): 3,579. Scene of a major 1777 battle that became a turning point in the American Revolution.

Sitka, AK (1910/1972): 116. Scene of Tlingit Indians' last major resistance to Russian colonizers, 1804.

Thomas Edison, West Orange, NJ (1955/2009): 21. Inventor's home and laboratory.

Tumacacori, AZ (1908/1990): 360. Historic Spanish mission building near site first visited by Father Kino in 1691.

Valley Forge, PA (1976): 3,469. Continental Army campsite in 1777-78 winter.

War in the Pacific, GU (1978): 2,031. Seven units illustrating the Pacific theater of WWII.

Women's Rights, NY (1980): 7. Where Lucretia Mott, Elizabeth Cady Stanton, and others organized movement in 1848.

National Battlefields/Parks/Sites

Antietam, MD (1890/1978): 3,229. Battle here ended first Confederate invasion of North, Sept. 17, 1862.

Big Hole, MT (1910/1963): 976. Site of major battle with Nez Perce Indians, Aug. 9-10, 1877.

Brices Cross Roads, Baldwyn, MS (1929): 1. Site of Confederate victory, June 10, 1864.

Cowpens, SC (1929/1972): 842. American Revolution battlefield, Jan. 17, 1781.

Fort Donelson, TN-KY (1928/1985): 1,319. Site of first major Union victory, Feb. 16, 1862.

Fort Necessity, PA (1931/1961): 903. Site of first battle of French and Indian War, July 3, 1754.

Kennesaw Mountain, GA (1917/1935): 2,914. Site of major battle of Atlanta campaign in Civil War.

Manassas, VA (1940): 5,073. Scene of two Civil War battles.

Monocacy, MD (1934/1976): 1,627. Civil War battle in defense of Washington, DC, fought here, July 9, 1864.

Moores Creek, Currie, NC (1926/1980): 88. Commemorates Feb. 27, 1776, battle between Patriots and Loyalists.

Petersburg, VA (1926/1962): 9,368. Scene of Union campaigns, 1864-65.

Richmond, VA (1936): 8,171. Site of battles defending Confederate capital.

River Raisin, Monroe, MI (2010): 42. Site of major battles of War of 1812.

Stones River, TN (1927/1960): 709. Scene of federal offensive to trisect Confederacy, Dec. 31, 1862-Jan. 2, 1863.

Tupelo, MS (1929/1961): 1. Site of crucial battle over Union Gen. Sherman's supply line, July 14-15, 1865.

Wilson's Creek, MO (1960/1970): 2,408. Site of second major Civil War battle, Aug. 10, 1861, for control of Missouri.

National Military Parks

Chickamauga and Chattanooga, GA-TN (1890): 9,523. Where Gen. Sherman and Union armies gained control of TN, 1863.

Fredericksburg and Spotsylvania, VA (1927/1933): 8,405. Sites of several major Civil War battles and campaigns.

Gettysburg, PA (1895/1933): 6,032. Site of decisive Confederate defeat in North, July 1863, and of Gettysburg Address.

Guilford Courthouse, NC (1917/1933): 254. American Revolution battle site.

Horseshoe Bend, AL (1956): 2,040. On Tallapoosa River, where Gen. Andrew Jackson broke power of Upper Creek Indian Confederacy on Mar. 27, 1814.

Kings Mountain, SC (1931/1933): 3,945. Site of American Revolution battle fought on Oct. 7, 1780.

Pea Ridge, AR (1956): 4,300. Civil War battle, Mar. 7-8, 1862.

Shiloh, TN-MS (1894/1933): 9,361. Major Civil War battle site, Apr. 6-7, 1862; incl. Shiloh Indian burial mounds.

Vicksburg, MS-LA (1899/1933): 2,524. Union victory gave North control of Mississippi and split Confederate forces.

National Memorials

Arkansas Post, AR (1960): 758. First permanent French settlement in lower Mississippi River valley.

Arlington House, The Robert E. Lee Memorial, VA (1925/1972): 28. Lee's home overlooking the Potomac River.

Chamizal, El Paso, TX (1966/1974): 55. Commemorates 1963 settlement of 99-year border dispute with Mexico.

Coronado, AZ (1941/1952): 4,830. Commemorates first European exploration of the Southwest.

De Soto, Bradenton, FL (1948): 30. Commemorates 16th-cent. Spanish explorations.

Federal Hall, New York, NY (1939/1955): 0.45. First seat of U.S. government under the Constitution.

Flight 93, Shanksville, PA (2002): 2,319. Commemorates passengers and crew of Flight 93, who died thwarting an attack on Sept. 11, 2001.

Fort Caroline, Jacksonville, FL (1950): 138. On St. Johns River, site of first attempt by France, in 16th cent., at permanent North American settlement.

Franklin Delano Roosevelt Memorial, DC (1982): 8. Statues of Pres. Franklin Roosevelt and Eleanor Roosevelt; waterfalls and gardens.

General Grant, New York, NY (1958): 0.76. Tomb of Ulysses Grant and wife; largest mausoleum in U.S.

Hamilton Grange, New York, NY (1962): 1.75. Home of Alexander Hamilton.

Johnstown Flood, PA (1964): 178. Commemorates 1889 flood.

Korean War Veterans Memorial, DC (1986/1995): 1.56. Honors those who served in the Korean War.

Lincoln Boyhood, Lincoln City, IN (1962): 200. Site of Abraham Lincoln's boyhood home and grave site of his mother.

Lincoln Memorial, DC (1911/1933): 7. Marble statue of 16th president.

Lyndon Baines Johnson Memorial Grove on the Potomac, DC (1973): 17. Overlooks Potomac River; vista of the Capitol.

Martin Luther King Jr., DC (1996): 2.74. Granite statue of Dr. King close to where he delivered "I Have a Dream" speech.

Mount Rushmore, SD (1925): 1,278. Heads of presidents Washington, Jefferson, Lincoln, T. Roosevelt sculpted into mountain.

Pearl Harbor, HI (2019): 22. Site of Dec. 7, 1941, Japanese attack.

Perry's Victory and International Peace Memorial, Put-in-Bay, OH (1936/1972): 25. World's most massive Doric column promotes pursuit of peace through arbitration and disarmament.

Port Chicago Naval Magazine, Danville, CA (2009): 5. Where 1944 munitions ship explosion killed 320 men.

Roger Williams, Providence, RI (1965): 4.56. Memorial to founder of Rhode Island.

Thaddeus Kosciuszko, Philadelphia, PA (1972): 0.02. Memorial to Polish hero of American Revolution.

Theodore Roosevelt Island, DC (1932/1933): 89. Statue of Roosevelt in wooded island sanctuary.

Thomas Jefferson Memorial, DC (1934/1943): 18. Statue of Jefferson in an inscribed circular, colonnaded structure.

Vietnam Veterans Memorial, DC (1980): 2.18. Black granite wall with names of those missing or killed in action in Vietnam War.

Washington Monument, DC (1876/1933): 106. Obelisk honoring first U.S. president. Construction began in 1848 with private funding.

World War I Memorial, DC (1981/2014): 1.39. Formerly Pershing Park, dedicated to Gen. John J. Pershing.

World War II Memorial, DC (1993/2004): 8. Oval plaza with central pool commemorating those who fought and died.

Wright Brothers, Kill Devil Hills, NC (1927/1953): 428. Site of first powered flight, by Orville and Wilbur Wright.

National Historic Sites

Allegheny Portage Railroad, PA (1964): 1,284. Linked Pennsylvania Canal system and the West.

Andersonville, GA (1970): 516. Civil War POW camp.

Andrew Johnson, Greeneville, TN (1935/1963): 17. Two homes, his tailor shop, and cemetery where 17th U.S. president is buried.

Bent's Old Fort, CO (1960): 799. Replica of fort on Sante Fe Trail.

Boston African-American, MA (1980): 0.59. Pre-Civil War black-owned structures.

Brown v. Board of Education, Topeka, KS (1992): 1.85. Commemorates landmark 1954 U.S. Supreme Court decision, which ended legal segregation in schools.

Carl Sandburg Home, Flat Rock, NC (1968): 268. Home of Pulitzer Prize-winning poet and biographer.

Carter G. Woodson Home, DC (1976/2006): 0.15. Home of "Father of Black History."

Charles Pinckney, Mt. Pleasant, SC (1988): 28. Farm of a principal author and signer of the Constitution.

Christiansted, St. Croix, VI (1952/1961): 27. Preserves historic structures from time of Danish colony.

Clara Barton, Glen Echo, MD (1974): 9. Home of American Red Cross founder.

Edgar Allan Poe, Philadelphia, PA (1978/1980): 0.52. Writer's home.

Eisenhower, Gettysburg, PA (1967): 690. Home of 34th pres.

Eleanor Roosevelt, Hyde Park, NY (1977): 181. Former first lady's personal retreat.

Eugene O'Neill, Danville, CA (1976): 13. Home where playwright wrote his final plays, incl. *The Iceman Cometh.*

First Ladies, Canton, OH (2000): 0.46. Home of first lady Ida Sexton McKinley. Library now devoted to U.S. first ladies.

Ford's Theatre, DC (1866/1970): 0.3. Incl. theater where Lincoln was assassinated, house where he died, and Lincoln Museum.

Fort Bowie, AZ (1964): 999. Focal point of operations against Geronimo and Apaches.

Fort Davis, TX (1961): 523. Frontier outpost in West Texas; established to guard the San Antonio-El Paso Road.

Fort Laramie, WY (1938/1960): 873. Military post on Oregon Trail.

Fort Larned, KS (1964/1966): 718. Military post on Santa Fe Trail.

Fort Point, CA (1970): 29. West Coast fortification; protected San Francisco during and after Civil War.

Fort Raleigh, NC (1941): 513. First attempted English settlement in North America.

Fort Scott, KS (1965/1978): 20. Commemorates U.S. frontier. Focal point of black troop activity, training during Civil War.

Fort Smith, AR-OK (1961): 75. One of the earliest U.S. posts in Missouri Territory, active 1817-96.

Fort Union Trading Post, MT-ND (1966): 440. Principal fur-trading post on upper Missouri, 1829-67.

Fort Vancouver, WA-OR (1948/1961): 207. Headquarters for Hudson's Bay Company.

Frederick Douglass, DC (1962/1988): 9. Home of black abolitionist, writer, orator.

Frederick Law Olmsted, Brookline, MA (1979): 7. Home of city planner, famous for designing Central Park in NYC.

Friendship Hill, PA (1978): 675. Home of Albert Gallatin, Jefferson's and Madison's secretary of treasury.

Grant-Kohrs Ranch, MT (1972): 1,618. Ranch house owned by John Grant, 19th-cent. range-cattle industry pioneer.

Hampton, Towson, MD (1948): 62. 18th-cent. Georgian mansion, which in 1790 was largest house in U.S.

Harry S Truman, Independence, MO (1982/1983): 13. House of 33rd pres. from 1919 on and farm where he worked as young man.

Herbert Hoover, West Branch, IA (1965): 187. Birthplace and boyhood home of 31st president.

Home of Franklin D. Roosevelt, Hyde Park, NY (1944): 838. FDR's birthplace, home, and "summer White House."

Honouliuli, HI (2015/2019): 154. Camp where POWs and civilians suspected of disloyalty—mostly Americans of Japanese ancestry—were imprisoned during WWII.

Hopewell Furnace, PA (1938/1985): 848. 19th-cent. iron-making village.

Hubbell Trading Post, AZ (1965): 160. Oldest continuously operating trading post in SW; founded in 1878 on Navajo Nation.

James A. Garfield, Mentor, OH (1980): 8. Home of 20th president; site of his front-porch campaign.

Jimmy Carter, Plains, GA (1987): 72. Birthplace and home of 39th president.

John Fitzgerald Kennedy, Brookline, MA (1967): 0.09. Birthplace and childhood home of 35th president.

John Muir, Martinez, CA (1964): 344. Home of Sierra Club co-founder and "Father of the National Park Service."

Knife River Indian Villages, ND (1974): 1,749. Remnants of villages last occupied by Hidatsa and Mandan Indians.

Lincoln Home, Springfield, IL (1971): 12. Lincoln's residence when he was elected 16th president, 1860.

Little Rock Central High School, AR (1998): 28. Commemorates 1957 desegregation during which federal troops were called in to protect nine black students.

Longfellow House—Washington's Headquarters, Cambridge, MA (1972/2010): 1.98. Poet's home, 1837-82; Washington's headquarters during Boston siege, 1775-76.

Maggie L. Walker, Richmond, VA (1978): 1.29. Home of black leader and first female bank president, daughter of former slave.

Manzanar, Lone Pine, CA (1992): 814. Manzanar War Relocation Ctr., a WWII Japanese-American internment camp.

Martin Van Buren, Kinderhook, NY (1974): 285. Lindenwald, home of 8th president.

Mary McLeod Bethune Council House, DC (1982/1991): 0.07. Commemorates Bethune's leadership in the black women's movement.

Minidoka, ID (2001/2008): 396. WWII Japanese internment ctr.

Minuteman Missile, SD (1999): 44. Missile launch facilities dating to Cold War era.

Nicodemus, KS (1996): 4.59. Only remaining Western town established by African Americans during Reconstruction.

Ninety Six, SC (1976): 1,022. Colonial trading village and site of Gen. Nathanael Greene's siege on Loyalist-held fort in 1781.

Pennsylvania Avenue, DC (1965/1996): 18. Incl. area between Capitol and White House, encompassing U.S. Navy Memorial, Freedom Plaza, Old Post Office Pavilion, other sites.

President William Jefferson Clinton Birthplace Home, Hope, AR (2010): 0.68. Birthplace and early home of 42nd pres.

Pu'ukoholā Heiau, Kawaihae, HI (1972): 86. Ruins of temple built by King Kamehameha, first king of united Hawaiian islands.

Sagamore Hill, Oyster Bay, NY (1962): 83. Home of Pres. Theodore Roosevelt from 1885 until his death in 1919.

Saint Paul's Church, Mount Vernon, NY (1943/1978): 6. One of the oldest parishes (1665-1980) in New York State.

Salem Maritime, MA (1938): 9. Major fishing and whaling port famous for 1692 witchcraft trials.

San Juan, PR (1949): 75. 16th-cent. Spanish fortifications.

Sand Creek Massacre, CO (2000): 12,583. Site where around 230 Cheyenne and Arapaho Indians—mostly women, children, and elderly—were killed by U.S. soldiers in 1864.

Saugus Iron Works, MA (1974): 9. Reconstructed 17th-cent. colonial ironworks.

Springfield Armory, MA (1974): 55. Small-arms manufacturing center for nearly 200 years.

Steamtown, Scranton, PA (1986): 62. Rail yard, roadhouse, repair shops of former Delaware, Lackawanna & Western Railroad.

Theodore Roosevelt Birthplace, New York, NY (1962): 0.11. Reconstructed brownstone where 26th president was born.

Theodore Roosevelt Inaugural, Buffalo, NY (1966): 1.18. Wilcox House, where 26th president took oath of office, 1901.

Thomas Stone, Port Tobacco, MD (1978): 328. Haberdeventure, home of signer of Declaration of Independence.

Tuskegee Airmen, AL (1998): 90. Airfield where pilots of all-black WWII air corps unit received flight training.

Tuskegee Institute, AL (1974): 58. College founded by Booker T. Washington in 1881 for blacks.

Ulysses S. Grant, St. Louis, MO (1989): 10. Home of Grant during pre-Civil War years.

Vanderbilt Mansion, Hyde Park, NY (1940): 212. Mansion of 19th-cent. financier.

Washita Battlefield, OK (1996): 315. Scene of Nov. 27, 1868, battle between Plains tribes and U.S. army.

Weir Farm, Wilton, CT (1990): 74. Home and studio of American impressionist painter J. Alden Weir.

Whitman Mission, Walla Walla, WA (1936/1963): 139. Site of Protestant missionaries to Cayuse Indians beginning in 1830s.

William Howard Taft, Cincinnati, OH (1969): 3.64. Birthplace and early home of 27th president.

Name	Location	Year[1]	Acreage
National Lakeshores			
Apostle Islands	WI	1970	69,377
Pictured Rocks	MI	1966	73,236
Sleeping Bear Dunes	MI	1970	71,252
National Monuments			
African Burial Ground	NY	2006	0.35
Agate Fossil Beds	NE	1965	3,058
Alibates Flint Quarries	TX	1965	1,371
Aniakchak[2]	AK	1980	137,176
Aztec Ruins	NM	1923	318
Bandelier	NM	1916	33,677
Belmont-Paul Women's Equality	DC	2016	0.34
Birmingham Civil Rights	AL	2017	0.88
Booker T. Washington	VA	1956	239
Buck Island Reef	VI	1961	19,015
Cabrillo	CA	1913	160
Camp Nelson	KY	2018	380
Canyon de Chelly	AZ	1931	83,840
Cape Krusenstern	AK	1978	649,096
Capulin Volcano	NM	1916	793
Casa Grande Ruins	AZ	1918	473
Castillo de San Marcos	FL	1924	19
Castle Clinton	NY	1946	1
Castle Mountains	CA	2016	21,026
Cedar Breaks	UT	1933	6,155
César E. Chávez	CA	2012	117
Charles Young Buffalo Soldiers	OH	2013	60
Chiricahua	AZ	1924	12,025
Colorado	CO	1911	20,536
Craters of the Moon	ID	1924	53,438
Devils Postpile	CA	1911	800
Devils Tower	WY	1906	1,347
Dinosaur	CO-UT	1915	210,282
Effigy Mounds	IA	1949	2,526
El Malpais	NM	1987	114,347

Name	Location	Year[1]	Acreage
El Morro	NM	1906	1,279
Florissant Fossil Beds	CO	1969	6,278
Fort Frederica	GA	1936	305
Fort Matanzas	FL	1924	300
Fort McHenry (and Historic Shrine)	MD	1939	43
Fort Monroe	VA	2011	367
Fort Pulaski	GA	1924	5,623
Fort Stanwix	NY	1935	16
Fort Union	NM	1954	721
Fossil Butte	WY	1972	8,198
Freedom Riders	AL	2017	6
George Washington Birthplace	VA	1930	653
George Washington Carver	MO	1943	240
Gila Cliff Dwellings	NM	1907	533
Governors Island	NY	2001	23
Grand Portage	MN	1958	710
Hagerman Fossil Beds	ID	1988	4,351
Hohokam Pima[3]	AZ	1972	1,690
Homestead NM of America	NE	1936	210
Hovenweep	CO-UT	1923	785
Jewel Cave	SD	1908	1,274
John Day Fossil Beds	OR	1974	14,062
Katahdin Woods and Waters	ME	2016	87,564
Lava Beds	CA	1925	46,692
Little Bighorn Battlefield	MT	1946	765
Montezuma Castle	AZ	1906	1,016
Muir Woods	CA	1908	554
Natural Bridges	UT	1908	7,636
Navajo	AZ	1909	360
Oregon Caves (and Preserve)	OR	1909	4,554
Organ Pipe Cactus	AZ	1937	330,689
Petroglyph	NM	1990	7,209
Pipe Spring	AZ	1923	40
Pipestone	MN	1937	282
Poverty Point[2]	LA	1988	911

Name	Location	Year[1]	Acreage
Pullman.	IL	2015	0.40
Rainbow Bridge.	UT	1910	160
Russell Cave.	AL	1961	310
Salinas Pueblo Missions	NM	1909	1,071
Scotts Bluff	NE	1919	3,005
Statue of Liberty	NJ-NY	1924	58
Stonewall	NY	2016	8
Sunset Crater Volcano	AZ	1930	3,040
Timpanogos Cave.	UT	1922	250
Tonto	AZ	1907	1,120
Tule Lake	CA	2019	37
Tule Springs Fossil Beds	NV	2014	22,650
Tuzigoot	AZ	1939	812
Virgin Islands Coral Reef	VI	2001	12,708
Waco Mammoth	TX	2015	107
Walnut Canyon	AZ	1915	3,201
Wupatki.	AZ	1924	35,402
Yucca House[2].	CO	1919	34

National Parkways

Name	Location	Year[1]	Acreage
Blue Ridge	NC-VA	1933	99,386
George Washington Memorial	MD-DC-VA	1930	6,820
John D. Rockefeller, Jr. Memorial	WY	1972	23,777
Natchez Trace	MS-TN-AL	1938	52,302

National Preserves

Name	Location	Year[1]	Acreage
Aniakchak[2]	AK	1980	464,118
Bering Land Bridge	AK	1980	2,697,391
Big Cypress[4]	FL	1974	720,564
Big Thicket	TX	1974	113,122
Craters of the Moon	ID	2002	698,940
Denali	AK	1980	1,334,118
Gates of the Arctic	AK	1980	948,608
Glacier Bay	AK	1980	58,406
Great Sand Dunes	CO	2004	41,686
Katmai.	AK	1980	418,699
Lake Clark.	AK	1980	1,410,294
Little River Canyon	AL	1992	15,292
Mojave	CA	1994	1,545,709
Noatak	AK	1980	6,587,071
Tallgrass Prairie	KS	1996	10,883
Timucuan Ecological and Historic	FL	1988	46,263
Valles Caldera	NM	2014	89,766
Wrangell-St. Elias	AK	1980	4,852,645
Yukon-Charley Rivers	AK	1980	2,526,512

National Recreation Areas

Name	Location	Year[1]	Acreage
Amistad.	TX	1990	62,945
Bighorn Canyon	MT-WY	1966	120,296
Boston Harbor Islands	MA	1996	1,482
Chattahoochee River	GA	1978	11,272
Chickasaw	OK	1976	9,899
Curecanti	CO	1965	43,591
Delaware Water Gap	NJ-PA	1965	68,664
Gateway	NJ-NY	1972	26,607
Gauley River.	WV	1988	11,566
Glen Canyon.	AZ-UT	1972	1,254,117
Golden Gate	CA	1972	82,116
Lake Chelan	WA	1968	61,939
Lake Mead	AZ-NV	1964	1,495,816
Lake Meredith	TX	1990	44,978
Lake Roosevelt (fmr. Coulee Dam)	WA	1946	100,390
Ross Lake.	WA	1968	117,575
Santa Monica Mountains.	CA	1978	156,633
Whiskeytown-Shasta-Trinity[5]	CA	1972	42,503

National Reserves

Name	Location	Year[1]	Acreage
City of Rocks.	ID	1988	14,407
Ebey's Landing Historical	WA	1978	19,334

National Rivers

Name	Location	Year[1]	Acreage
Big South Fork (and Rec. Area)	KY-TN	1991	123,693
Buffalo	AR	1972	94,293
Mississippi (and Rec. Area)	MN	1988	53,775
New River Gorge	WV	1978	72,186
Ozark Scenic Riverways	MO	1972	80,784

National Seashores

Name	Location	Year[1]	Acreage
Assateague Island[6]	MD-VA	1965	41,347
Canaveral	FL	1975	57,662
Cape Cod	MA	1966	43,608
Cape Hatteras.	NC	1953	30,351
Cape Lookout	NC	1966	28,243

Name	Location	Year[1]	Acreage
Cumberland Island	GA	1972	36,347
Fire Island.	NY	1964	19,581
Gulf Islands.	FL-MS	1971	138,306
Padre Island	TX	1968	130,434
Point Reyes	CA	1972	71,053

International Historic Site

Name	Location	Year[1]	Acreage
Saint Croix Island	ME	1984	7

Other Designations

Name	Location	Year[1]	Acreage
Catoctin Mountain Park.	MD	1954	5,891
Constitution Gardens	DC	1974	39
Fort Washington Park	MD	1940	341
Greenbelt Park	MD	1950	1,175
National Capital Parks-East	DC-MD	1933	8,707
National Mall and Memorial Parks	DC	1933	156
Piscataway Park	MD	1961	4,616
Prince William Forest Park	VA	1948	16,081
Rock Creek Park.	DC	1933	1,755
White House.	DC	1933	18
Wolf Trap National Park for the Performing Arts	VA	2002	130

National Wild and Scenic Rivers

Rivers in this system are designated by Congress or the Secretary of the Interior. As of Mar. 2019 (the last designation), the system included 13,413 miles of 226 rivers in 41 states and Puerto Rico. Not all of the rivers that the NPS administers are official units of the park system. Only official NPS units are listed here.

Name	Location	Year[1]	Acreage
Alagnak Wild[2]	AK	1980	30,665
Bluestone Scenic	WV	1988	4,310
Delaware Scenic[7]	NJ-PA	1978	1,973
Great Egg Harbor Scenic and Rec.	NJ	1992	43,311
Missouri Recreational	NE-SD	1991	48,457
Niobrara Scenic	NE	1991	29,101
Obed	TN	1976	5,490
Rio Grande	TX	1978	13,123
Saint Croix Scenic Riverway[8]	MN-WI	1968	92,743
Upper Delaware Scenic and Rec.	NY-PA	1978	75,000

Affiliated Areas

Affiliated areas are administered in connection with the NPS but are not owned by that agency.

Name	Location	Year[1]	Acreage
Aleutian World War II Natl. Historic Area	AK	1996	135
American Memorial Park.	MP	1978	133
Benjamin Franklin Natl. Memorial (NMEM)	PA	1972	NA
Chicago Portage Natl. Historic Site (NHS)	IL	1952	91
Chimney Rock NHS	NE	1956	83
Fallen Timbers Battlefield and Fort Miamis NHS	OH	1999	185
Father Marquette NMEM	MI	1975	52
Gloria Dei (Old Swedes') Church NHS.	PA	1942	3.71
Green Springs Natl. Historic Landmark District.	VA	1974	15,645
Historic Camden Revolutionary War Site.	SC	1982	107
Ice Age Natl. Scientific Reserve	WI	1964	32,500
International Peace Garden	ND-MB	1949	2,330
Iñupiat Heritage Center.	AK	1999	0
Jamestown NHS.	VA	1940	22
Kate Mullany NHS.	NY	2004	0.06
Lower East Side Tenement NHS	NY	1998	1.2
Natural Bridge State Park.	VA	2016	NA
Oklahoma City NMEM	OK	2004	6
Parkers Crossroads Battlefield	TN	2019	NA
Pinelands Natl. Reserve	NJ	1978	1,164,025
Red Hill Patrick Henry NMEM	VA	1986	NA
Roosevelt Campobello Intl. Park	NB	1964	2,722
Thomas Cole NHS	NY	1999	3.4
Touro Synagogue NHS.	RI	1946	0.23
Wing Luke Museum of the Asian Pacific American Experience.	WA	2013	NA

NA = Not available. (1) Year established or current designation received. (2) No federal facilities; state services may be available at certain sites. (3) Located on Gila River Indian Reservation; not open to the public. (4) Incl. acreage added in 1988 expansion. (5) Shasta and Trinity units are administered by the Forest Service. Figure given is NPS acreage only. (6) Figure given includes acreage administered by U.S. Fish and Wildlife Service. (7) Comprises the Lower Delaware Wild and Scenic (2000) and Middle Delaware Scenic, whose year and acreage are given in table. (8) Incl. Lower Saint Croix acreage added in 1972.

National Trails System

Source: National Park Service and Bureau of Land Management, U.S. Dept. of the Interior; U.S. Forest Service, USDA

As of mid-2020, the National Trails System included 11 national scenic trails, 19 national historic trails, almost 1,300 national recreation trails, and 7 connecting and side trails. National scenic trails and national historic trails are established by Congress and administered by the NPS, Forest Service, or BLM. Official NPS units are indicated by an asterisk.

Name	Location	Year[1]	Length (mi)[2]
National Scenic Trails			
*Appalachian	ME to GA	1968	2,180+
Arizona	AZ	2009	800
Continental Divide	MT, ID, WY, CO, NM	1978	3,100
Florida	FL	1983	1,300
Ice Age	WI	1980	1,200
*Natchez Trace	MS-AL-TN	1983	65
New England	MA-CT	2009	215
North Country	NY to ND	1980	4,600
Pacific Crest	CA-OR-WA	1968	2,650
Pacific Northwest	MT-ID-WA	2009	1,200
*Potomac Heritage	VA to PA	1983	924
National Historic Trails[3]			
Ala Kahakai	HI	2000	175
California	MO, NE to CA, OR	1992	5,665
Capt. John Smith Chesapeake..	NY to VA	2006	3,000
El Camino Real de los Tejas....	TX-LA	2004	2,580
El Camino Real de Tierra Adentro	NM-TX	2000	404
Iditarod	AK	1978	2,300
Juan Bautista de Anza	AZ-CA	1990	1,200
Lewis and Clark	PA to Pacific	1978	4,900
Mormon Pioneer	IL to UT	1978	1,300
Nez Perce (Nee-Me-Poo)	OR to MT	1986	1,170
Old Spanish	NM to CA	2002	2,700
Oregon	MO to OR	1978	2,170
Overmountain Victory	NC, SC, TN, VA	1980	330
Pony Express	MO to CA	1992	2,000
Santa Fe	MO, KS, OK, CO, NM	1987	1,203
Selma to Montgomery	AL	1996	54
Star-Spangled Banner	VA-DC-MD	2008	560
Trail of Tears	GA, NC to OK	1987	5,043
Washington-Rochambeau Revolutionary Route	MA to VA	2009	680+

(1) Year designation was received. (2) Authorized or currently completed length. (3) Trails may include both overland and water routes.

U.S. Forest Service Special Designated Areas

Source: U.S. Forest Service, U.S. Dept. of Agriculture; as of Sept. 30, 2019

These areas within the National Forest System have been specially designated by presidential proclamation or act of Congress. Size does not include acreage within National Forest boundaries not federally owned or administered by the Forest Service.

NGR = Natl. Game Refuge; NM = Natl. Monument; NRA = Natl. Recreation Area; NS(A) = Natl. Scenic (Area); NVM = Natl. Volcanic Monument; SMA = Special Management Area.

Area	Location	Estab.	Acreage
Admiralty Island NM	AK	1980	1,003,301
Allegheny NRA	PA	1984	23,790
Ancient Bristlecone Pine Forest	CA	2009	31,799
Arapaho NRA	CO	1978	31,162
Ashley Karst NRA & Geologic Area	UT	2019	173,453
Barkshead (Ozark #2) NGR	AR	1926	5,851
Bear Creek NSA	VA	2009	5,122
Bears Ears NM	UT	2016	32,547
Beech Creek NSA & Botanical Area			
Beech Creek NSA	OK	1988	8,042
Beech Creek Natl. Botanical Area	OK	1988	538
Berryessa Snow Mountain NM	CA	2015	197,360
Big Levels NGR	VA	1935	12,147
Black Mountain (Ozark #5) NGR	AR	1926	18,929
Bowen Gulch Protection Area	CO	1993	10,862
Bridgeport Winter Recreation Area.	CA	2009	7,250
Browns Canyon NM	CO	2015	11,819
Caney Creek (Ouachita #4) NGR..	AR	1935	8,038
Cascade Head NS Research Area	OR	1974	7,162
Catahoula Wildlife Mgmt. Preserve	LA	1941	37,629
Cherokee Game Refuge #1	TN	1924	9,862
Chimney Rock NM	CO	2012	4,724
Columbia River Gorge NSA	OR-WA	1986	83,063
Burdoin Mountain SMA	WA	1986	7,248
Gates of Columbia R. Gorge SMA	OR-WA	1986	53,291
Rowena SMA	OR-WA	1986	3,606
Wind Mountain SMA	WA	1986	14,803
Coosa Bald NSA	GA	1991	7,044
Cradle of Forestry in America			
Natl. Historic Area	NC	1968	7,793
Crystal Springs Watershed	OR	2009	2,094
Cultus Creek	OR	2009	278
Ed Jenkins NRA	GA	1991	23,540
Flaming Gorge NRA	UT-WY	1968	187,162
Fossil Ridge Rec. Mgmt. Area	CO	1993	43,383
Frank and Jeanne Moore Wild Steelhead SMA	OR	2019	102,761
Francis Marion Natl. Wildlife Pres...	SC	1948	53,199
Frank Church-River of No Return Special Mining Mgmt. Zone-Clear Creek	ID	1980	40,555
Giant Sequoia NM	CA	2000	328,361
Grand Canyon Natl. Game Preserve	AZ	1906	622,273
Grand Island NRA	MI	1990	13,335
Grey Towers Natl. Historic Site	PA	2004	95
Haw Creek (Ozark #4) NGR	AR	1926	3,783
Hells Canyon NRA	OR-ID	1975	634,706
Hermosa Creek SMA	CO	2014	70,394
Indian Nations Scenic Wildlife Area	OK	1988	44,519
James Peak Protection Area	CO	2002	17,511
Jemez NRA	NM	1993	48,871
Jewel Cave NM	SD	1908	2,540
Kelly Butte SMA	WA	1998	5,669
Kings River SMA	CA	1987	50,888
Land Between the Lakes NRA	KY-TN	1998	171,242
Livingston (Ozark #1) NGR	AR	1926	8,755
Misty Fiords NM	AK	1980	2,293,162
Moccasin (Ozark #3) NGR	AR	1926	4,048
Mono Basin NSA	CA	1984	51,320
Moosalamoo NRA	VT	2006	15,913
Mount Baker NRA	WA	1984	8,789
Mount Hood NRA	OR	2009	34,465
Mount Pleasant NSA	VA	1994	6,864
Mount Rogers NRA	VA	1966	115,001
Mount St. Helens NVM	WA	1982	112,864
Newberry NVM	OR	1990	56,563
Noontooly NGR	GA	1938	24,655
Norbeck Wildlife Preserve	SD	1920	32,079
North Cascades NSA	WA	1984	88,049
Oak Mountain (Ouachita #2) NGR	AR	1935	8,872
Ocala NGR	FL	1930	68,241
Opal Creek Scenic Recreation Area	OR	1996	13,666
Oregon Dunes NRA	OR	1972	30,238
Ouachita Natl. Wildlife Preserve...	AR	1935	137,958
Quinault SMA	WA	1988	5,499
Piedra SMA	CO	1993	60,514
Pigeon Creek (Ouachita #1) NGR	AR	1935	8,107
Pine Ridge NRA	NE	1986	6,636
Pisgah Natl. Game Refuge	NC	1916	71,899
Rattlesnake NRA	MT	1980	60,081
Red Dirt Natl. Wildlife Mgmt. Pres.	LA	1941	40,213
Robert S. Kerr Botanical Area	OK	1988	7,971
Robert T. Stafford White Rocks NRA	VT	1984	36,563
Roubideau SMA	CO	1993	18,837
Saint Francis Dam NM	CA	2019	353
San Gabriel Mountains NM	CA	2014	336,876
Sand to Snow NM	CA	2016	70,942
Santa Rosa/San Jacinto Mtns. NM...	CA	2000	70,056
Sawtooth NRA	ID	1972	732,177
Seng Mountain NSA	VA	2009	5,195
Sheep Mountain Game Refuge	WY	1924	21,569
Smith River NRA	CA	1990	323,051
Spring Mountains NRA	NV	1993	316,697
Spruce Knob-Seneca Rocks NRA	WV	1965	57,511
Tabeguache SMA	CO	1993	8,945
Tahquitz Natl. Game Preserve	CA	1926	18,813
Upper Big Branch NRA	OR	2009	1,581
Whiskeytown-Shasta-Trinity NRA	CA	1965	173,065
Winding Stair Mountain NRA	OK	1988	26,617

National Heritage Areas

Source: National Park Service (NPS), U.S. Dept. of the Interior; Alliance of National Heritage Areas

National Heritage Areas (NHAs) are designated by Congress for their national importance. NHAs are not units of the National Park system, though the NPS advises and provides limited financial assistance. NHC = Natl. Heritage Corridor. As of mid-2020.

Name	Location	Year[1]	Size (sq mi)	Name	Location	Year[1]	Size (sq mi)
Abraham Lincoln	IL	2008	25,975	Mississippi Delta	MS	2009	10,976
Appalachian Forest	MD-WV	2019	NA[2]	Mississippi Gulf Coast	MS	2004	4,289
Arabia Mountain	GA	2006	64	Mississippi Hills	MS	2009	NA[5]
Atchafalaya	LA	2006	10,400	Mormon Pioneer	UT	2006	16,070
Augusta Canal	GA	1996	3+	MotorCities	MI	1998	10,000+
Baltimore	MD	2009	18	Mountains to Sound Greenway	WA	2019	2,344
Blue Ridge	NC	2003	10,515	Muscle Shoals	AL	2009	3,913
Cache La Poudre River[3]	CO	2009	45	National Aviation Heritage Area	OH	2004	NA[6]
Cane River	LA	1994	181	National Coal Heritage Area	WV	1996	5,300
Champlain Valley Natl. Heritage Partnership	NY-VT	2006	NA[4]	Niagara Falls[3]	NY	2008	13
Crossroads of the American Revolution	NJ	2006	2,155	Northern Plains	ND	2009	800
				Northern Rio Grande	NM	2006	10,000
Delaware & Lehigh NHC[3]	PA	1988	165	Ohio & Erie Canalway[3]	OH	1996	110
Erie Canalway NHC	NY	2000	4,834	Oil Region	PA	2004	708
Essex	MA	1996	500	Path of Progress Natl. Heritage Tour Route[3]	PA	1988	500
Freedom's Frontier	KS-MO	2006	31,021	Rivers of Steel	PA	1996	5,000+
Freedom's Way	MA-NH	2009	994	Sacramento-San Joaquin Delta	CA	2019	NA
Great Basin Natl. Heritage Route	NV-UT	2006	15,704	Sangre de Cristo	CO	2009	3,000+
Gullah Geechee Cultural Heritage Corridor	NC, SC, GA, FL	2006	12,818	Santa Cruz Valley	AZ	2019	3,325
				Schuylkill River Greenways	PA	2000	1,750
Illinois & Michigan Canal NHC	IL	1984	862	Shenandoah Valley Battlefields Natl. Historic District	VA	1996	3,939
John H. Chafee Blackstone River Valley NHC	MA-RI	1986	720+	Silos & Smokestacks	IA	1996	20,000+
Journey Through Hallowed Ground[3]	PA, MD, WV, VA	2008	180	South Carolina NHC	SC	1996	NA[7]
				South Park	CO	2009	1,800
Kenai Mountains-Turnagain Arm	AK	2009	650	Susquehanna	PA	2019	NA
Lackawanna Heritage Valley	PA	2000	350	Tennessee Civil War[8]	TN	1996	42,144
The Last Green Valley NHC	CT-MA	1994	1,105	Upper Housatonic Valley	MA-CT	2006	964
Maritime Washington[3]	WA	2019	3,000	Wheeling	WV	2000	12
Maurice D. Hinchey Hudson River Valley	NY	1996	6,250	Yuma Crossing	AZ	2000	21

NA = Not available. (1) Year designation was received. (2) Covers 18 counties in both states. (3) Figure given is length of area. (4) 11 counties in both states. (5) Parts of 30 counties. (6) 8 counties. (7) 17 counties. (8) Spans entire state of Tennessee.

Attractions in and Around Washington, DC

Most attractions are free. Hours are subject to change, especially on holidays, when some attractions may be closed. For a free official visitors guide and map, visit washington.org or call Destination DC at 1-800-422-8644. **Note:** As of Sept. 2020, attractions were either closed or had specific safety guidelines due to COVID-19. The visitation information given below is for normal circumstances. Visit the website for updated visitor information on each individual attraction.

Arlington

Arlington National Cemetery, on the former Custis-Lee estate in Arlington, VA, was first used as a burial site during the Civil War. It is the final resting place of Pres. William Howard Taft and Pres. John F. Kennedy and his wife, Jacqueline Bouvier Kennedy Onassis. More than 400,000 U.S. military personnel from every major war are buried at Arlington. The **Tomb of the Unknown Soldier,** dedicated in 1921, is guarded by soldiers 24 hrs. a day. Unknowns from World War I, World War II, and Korea are interred in the plaza. (Vietnam Unknown was exhumed in 1998 and identified through DNA testing.)

A number of monuments and memorials are located throughout the 624-acre cemetery. They include the **Women in Military Service for America Memorial** (dedicated 1997), which honors the nearly 3 mil women who have served or currently serve in the U.S. military.

Open daily 8 AM-5 PM (8 AM-7 PM, Apr.-Sept.). Arlington, VA; (877) 907-8585. **Website:** www.arlingtoncemetery.mil

The **U.S. Marine Corps War Memorial** stands north of Arlington National Cemetery. A bronze statue depicts the raising of the U.S. flag on Mt. Suribachi, Feb. 23, 1945, during the WWII battle of Iwo Jima. The memorial grounds are open daily 6 AM-midnight; (703) 235-1530. **Website:** www.nps.gov/gwmp/planyourvisit/usmc_memorial.htm

Bureau of Engraving and Printing

The Bureau of Engraving and Printing of the U.S. Treasury Dept. is the headquarters for the making of U.S. paper money. Free public tours are offered Mon.-Fri., 9 AM-6 PM (same-day tickets required Mar.-early Sept.). 14th and C Sts. SW; (866) 874-2330. **Website:** www.moneyfactory.gov

The Capitol

The United States Capitol was originally designed by Dr. William Thornton, an amateur architect, whose submission in 1793 won him $500 and a city lot. Three other architects designed or supervised construction of the Capitol before its completion.

The present cast-iron dome at its greatest exterior height measures 135 ft, 5 in. and is topped by the bronze Statue of Freedom, which stands 19½ ft and weighs 15,000 lbs. On its base are the words *E Pluribus Unum* (out of many, one).

The Capitol Visitor Center is open to the public Mon.-Sat., 8:30 AM-4:30 PM. Free guided tours are available by pass 8:40 AM to 3:20 PM. The Senate and House galleries are not part of the tour. To enter either gallery or to observe Congress in session, those living in the U.S. may obtain tickets from their U.S. representative or senators. Visitors from other countries may inquire at the House and Senate appointment desks. Between Constitution and Independence Aves., bounded by First St.; (202) 226-8000. **Website:** www.visitthecapitol.gov

Federal Bureau of Investigation

The Federal Bureau of Investigation discontinued tours of its headquarters following the Sept. 11, 2001, terrorist attacks. A self-guided tour called the FBI Experience opened in 2017. Open 9 AM-4:30 PM Mon.-Fri.; visits must be arranged at least four weeks in advance through the office of one's congressional delegate. J. Edgar Hoover Bldg., Pennsylvania Ave., between 9th and 10th Sts. NW; (202) 324-3000. **Website:** www.fbi.gov

Folger Shakespeare Library

The Folger Shakespeare Library, on Capitol Hill, is a research institution with the world's largest collection of Shakespearean materials and other rare books and manuscripts of the Renaissance period. Beginning in 2020, the building was closed to visitors for renovations. 201 E. Capitol St. SE; (202) 544-4600. **Website:** www.folger.edu

Holocaust Memorial Museum

The U.S. Holocaust Memorial Museum (opened 1993) documents the Holocaust through artifacts and interactive videos and educates the public on other genocides. The permanent exhibition is recommended for visitors age 11 and up.

The museum is open daily, 10 AM-5:30 PM. Entry into the permanent exhibition is timed, Mar. through Aug. Timed passes are available at the door each day on a first-come, first-served basis; advance passes can be ordered online for a fee. 100 Raoul Wallenberg Pl. SW; (202) 488-0400. **Website:** www.ushmm.org

Jefferson Memorial

Dedicated Apr. 13, 1943, the Thomas Jefferson Memorial stands on the south shore of the Tidal Basin in West Potomac Park. The circular stone structure combines architectural elements of the dome of the Pantheon in Rome and the rotunda designed by Jefferson for the Univ. of Virginia.

The memorial is open 24 hrs. a day and staffed 9:30 AM-10 PM. Ohio and E. Basin Drs. SW; (202) 426-6841. **Website:** www.nps.gov/thje/

Kennedy Center

The John F. Kennedy Center for the Performing Arts opened in 1971. Designed by Edward Durell Stone, it includes an opera house, concert hall, theaters, restaurants, and a library. Free tours available Mon.-Fri., 10 AM-5 PM, and Sat.-Sun., 10 AM-1 PM. 2700 F St. NW; (800) 444-1324. **Website:** www.kennedy-center.org

Martin Luther King Jr. Memorial

The MLK, Jr. Memorial (dedicated 2011) features a 30-ft figure of Dr. King, sculpted by artist Lei Yixin, emerging from a block of granite. The memorial is located on the Tidal Basin, between the Lincoln and Jefferson Memorials.

The memorial is open 24 hrs. a day and staffed 9:30 AM-10 PM. Independence Ave. SW and West Basin Dr. SW; (202) 426-6841. **Website:** www.nps.gov/mlkm/

Korean War Veterans Memorial

The Korean War Veterans Memorial, dedicated 1995 at the Mall's west end, features a multiservice formation of 19 combat-ready soldiers in ponchos. A granite wall, with images of service members, juts into the Pool of Remembrance.

The memorial is open 24 hrs. a day and staffed 9:30 AM-10 PM. Independence Ave. SW and French Dr. SW; (202) 426-6841. **Website:** www.nps.gov/kowa/

Library of Congress

Established by and for Congress in 1800, the Library of Congress extends its services to other government agencies and libraries, scholars, and the public. It contains more than 170 mil items in 470 languages, making it the world's largest library collection.

The Thomas Jefferson Building (Main Reading Room and exhibition galleries) is open Mon.-Sat., 8:30 AM-4:30 PM. The James Madison Building and John Adams Building have longer hours. First St. SE between Independence Ave. SE and East Capitol St.; (202) 707-8000. **Website:** www.loc.gov

Lincoln Memorial

Designed by Henry Bacon and dedicated in 1922, the Lincoln Memorial in West Potomac Park is a large marble hall enclosing a statue, designed by Daniel Chester French, of Abraham Lincoln seated in an armchair. The text of the Gettysburg Address is engraved in the south chamber, that of Lincoln's second inaugural speech in the north chamber.

The memorial is open 24 hrs. a day and staffed 9:30 AM-10 PM. Independence Ave. and French Dr. SW; (202) 426-6841. **Website:** www.nps.gov/linc/

Mount Vernon

Mount Vernon, George Washington's estate, is about 15 mi from Washington, DC, in northern Virginia. A one-and-a-half story house was first built on the site by Washington's father, Augustine Washington, in 1734. In 1754, George Washington began running and expanding the estate, named after Adm. Edward Vernon by Washington's half-brother Lawrence. The estate has been restored to its 18th-cent. appearance. Washington and his wife, Martha, are buried on the grounds.

Open all year; hours vary seasonally. Mount Vernon, VA; (703) 780-2000. Admission: adults $20, youth (6-11) $12, ages 5 and under free. **Website:** www.mountvernon.org

National Archives and Records

Original copies of the Declaration of Independence, the Constitution, and the Bill of Rights are on display at the National Archives Museum. The National Archives also holds other U.S. government records, historic maps, photographs, and manuscripts.

The museum is open daily 10 AM-5:30 PM. Constitution Ave. bet. 7th and 9th Sts. NW; (866) 272-6272. **Website:** www.archives.gov

National Gallery of Art

The National Gallery of Art, established by Congress, opened in 1941. The original West Building was designed by John Russell Pope. The East Building, opened in 1978, was designed by I. M. Pei. Galleries are open Mon.-Sat., 10 AM-5 PM, and Sun., 11 AM-6 PM. Constitution Ave NW between 3rd and 9th Sts.; (202) 737-4215. **Website:** www.nga.gov

National World War II Memorial

The National WWII Memorial, opened in 2004, is dedicated to the approx. 16 mil veterans who served and the more than

400,000 who died in the war. The 8.25-acre site is at the east end of the Lincoln Memorial Reflecting Pool.

The 43-ft archways at the north and south entrances represent the Atlantic and Pacific theaters. A wall of 4,048 gold stars, each representing 100 American deaths, stands in an oval plaza surrounded by 56 pillars standing for the states, territories, and the Dist. of Columbia.

The memorial is open 24 hrs. a day and staffed 9:30 AM-10 PM. 17th St. and Independence Ave. SW; (202) 426-6841. **Website:** www.nps.gov/wwii/

The Pentagon

The Pentagon, headquarters of the Dept. of Defense, is the largest low-rise office building in the U.S. It houses some 26,000 employees in offices occupying 3,705,793 sq ft. The building was severely damaged when struck by a plane on Sept. 11, 2001.

Tours are free and available by reservation only, which must be made online 14-90 days in advance. Visitors age 18 and older must present a current valid photo ID. Arlington, VA; (703) 697-1776. **Website:** pentagontours.osd.mil/Tours/

Franklin Delano Roosevelt Memorial

Opened in 1997, the FDR Memorial features four spaces with bronze statues and panels depicting FDR through his four terms in office. The 8.14-acre memorial is on the Tidal Basin.

Open daily with staff on grounds 9:30 AM-10 PM. Ohio and W. Basin Drs. SW; (202) 426-6841. **Website:** www.nps.gov/frde/

Smithsonian Institution

The Smithsonian Institution, established in 1846, is the world's largest museum and research complex. It holds some 155.5 mil artifacts and specimens in its trust. Seventeen of its 19 museums and the **National Zoo** are in the DC area. The **Smithsonian Institution Building** (or The Castle) houses the Smithsonian Visitor Center. Also on the National Mall are the **National Museum of African American History and Culture,** the **National Museum of African Art,** the **National Air and Space Museum, National Museum of American History,** the **National Museum of the American Indian,** the **Arts and Industries Building** (a special-events space), the **Freer Gallery of Art,** the **Hirshhorn Museum and Sculpture Garden,** the **National Museum of Natural History,** and the **Arthur M. Sackler Gallery.** Located nearby are the **National Postal Museum,** the **Smithsonian American Art Museum,** the **National Portrait Gallery,** and the **Renwick Gallery.** The **Anacostia Community Museum** is in SE DC. The Air and Space Museum's **Udvar-Hazy Center** is near Dulles Airport in Virginia.

Most museums are open daily, 10 AM-5:30 PM (later in summer); (202) 633-1000. **Website:** www.si.edu

Vietnam Veterans Memorial

Originally dedicated in 1982, the Vietnam Veterans Memorial recognizes those who served in the Vietnam War. The names of more than 58,000 Americans who lost their lives or remain missing are inscribed on polished black-granite walls arranged to form a V, designed by Maya Ying Lin.

Two additions have been made to Lin's design, the Frederick Hart sculpture *Three Servicemen* (1984), and the Vietnam Women's Memorial (1993), sculpted by Glenna Goodacre, honoring the approx. 11,000 women who served in Vietnam.

The memorial is open 24 hrs. a day and staffed 9:30 AM-10 PM. Constitution Ave. and Bacon Dr. NW; (202) 426-6841. **Website:** www.nps.gov/vive/

Washington Monument

The Washington Monument (dedicated 1885) is a tapering shaft, or obelisk, of white marble, 555 ft, 5⅛ in. in height and 55 ft, 1½ in. square at the base. Eight small windows, two on each side, are located on the observation deck at the 500-ft level.

The monument is open daily 9 AM-5 PM. 15th St. and Constitution Ave. NW; (202) 426-6841. **Website:** www.nps.gov/wamo/

White House

The White House, the president's residence, stands on 18 acres on the south side of Pennsylvania Ave., between the Treasury and the old Executive Office Building. The sandstone walls, quarried at Aquia Creek, VA, were first made white with lime-based whitewash in 1798, though the name did not become official until 1901.

Free self-guided tours of the residence's public areas are available Tues.-Thurs., 7:30-11:30 AM, and Fri. and Sat., 7:30 AM-1:30 PM. Tour requests must be made at least 21 days in advance through one's member of Congress. Foreign visitors may make requests through their embassy. Tours are scheduled on a first-come, first-served basis. 1600 Pennsylvania Ave. NW; (202) 456-7041. **Website:** www.whitehouse.gov

The White House Visitor Center at 1450 Pennsylvania Ave. NW is open daily 7:30 AM-4 PM; (202) 208-1631. **Website:** www.nps.gov/whho/

U.S. HISTORY: CHRONOLOGY OF EVENTS

1492 Christopher Columbus and crew sighted land Oct. 12 in what is now the Bahamas.

1513 Juan Ponce de León explored Florida coast.

1524 Giovanni da Verrazzano led French expedition along coast from Carolina north to Nova Scotia; entered New York Harbor.

1526 San Miguel de Guadalupe, **first European settlement** in what became U.S. territory, was established in the summer off South Carolina coast; abandoned in Oct.

1539 Hernando de Soto landed in Florida May 28; crossed Mississippi River, 1541.

1540 Francisco Vásquez de Coronado explored Southwest north of Rio Grande. **Hernando de Alarcón** reached Colorado River; **García López de Cárdenas** reached Grand Canyon. Others explored California coast.

1562 First French colony in what became U.S. territory founded on Parris Island off South Carolina coast; abandoned, 1564.

1565 St. Augustine, FL, oldest continuously occupied European settlement in U.S., founded Sept. 8 by Pedro Menéndez de Avilés. Spain ceded settlement to U.S. in 1821.

1579 Sir Francis Drake entered San Francisco Bay and claimed region for Britain.

1585 First English colony in America, sponsored by Sir Walter Raleigh, founded on **Roanoke Island**, off North Carolina coast; colony failed.

1587 Second colony attempted on Roanoke Island. Virginia Dare of colony became **first English infant born** in the New World. Settlers of second colony found to have vanished, 1590.

1607 Capt. **John Smith** and 105 cavaliers in three ships landed on Virginia coast and started Jamestown, **first permanent English settlement** in New World.

1609 Henry Hudson, English explorer of Northwest Passage, employed by Dutch, sailed into New York Harbor in Sept. and up Hudson to Albany. **Samuel de Champlain** explored Lake Champlain, to the north. Spaniards settled **Santa Fe, NM.**

1619 House of Burgesses, **first representative assembly** in New World, elected July 30 at Jamestown, VA. **Introduction of slavery:** first Black laborers in English North American colonies, brought to Jamestown in Aug. Chattel slavery laws passed in Massachusetts, 1641, and Virginia, 1661.

1620 Pilgrims, Puritan separatists, left Plymouth, England, Sept. 16 on *Mayflower;* reached Cape Cod Nov. 19; 103 passengers landed at Plymouth, Dec. 26. **Mayflower Compact,** signed Nov. 11, was agreement to form a self-government. Half of colony died during harsh winter.

1624 Dutch settled in Albany and along Hudson River, establishing the colony of **New Netherland** in May.

1626 Peter Minuit bought **Manhattan** for Dutch West India Co. from Manahatta Indians during summer for goods valued at $24; named island **New Amsterdam.**

1630 Settlement of **Boston** established by Massachusetts colonists led by John Winthrop; Winthrop began *The History of New England.* **William Bradford,** a governor of Plymouth Colony, began his chronicle *History of Plymouth Plantation (1620-1647),* first published in entirety in 1856.

1634 Maryland founded as Catholic colony under charter to Lord Baltimore. Act of Toleration passed 1649 provided for religious tolerance.

1635 Boston Latin School, **oldest public school** in continuous existence in U.S., founded Apr. 23.

1636 Roger Williams founded **Providence, RI,** in June, as a democratically ruled colony with separation of church and state. Charter granted, 1644. **Harvard College** founded; oldest institution of higher learning in U.S.

1640 First book printed in America, the so-called *Bay Psalm Book.*

1647 Liberal constitution drafted in Rhode Island. First law in America providing for **free compulsory basic education** enacted in Massachusetts.

1660 British Parliament passed first **Navigation Act** Dec. 1, regulating colonial commerce to suit English needs.

1661 Missionary John Eliot's translation of the New Testament into Algonquian became the **first Bible printed** in North America.

1664 British troops Sept. 8 seized New Netherland from Dutch. Charles II granted New Netherland and city of New Amsterdam to brother, Duke of York; both renamed **New York.** Dutch recaptured colony 1673 but ceded it to Britain Nov. 10, 1674.

1670 Charles Town, SC, founded by English colonists in Apr.

1673 Regular mail service on horseback instituted Jan. 1 between New York and Boston. **Jacques Marquette** and **Louis Jolliet** reached the upper Mississippi and traveled down it.

1674 Future **Salem witch trial** judge Samuel Sewall began renowned diary covering events through 1729.

1676 Bloody **Indian war** in New England ended Aug. 12. King Philip, Wampanoag chief, and Narragansett Indians killed. **Nathaniel Bacon** led planters against autocratic British Gov. Sir William Berkeley, burned Jamestown, VA, Sept. 19. Rebellion collapsed when Bacon died; 23 followers executed.

1678 A book of poetry by **Anne Bradstreet** (first published in Britain) revised and expanded for posthumous publication in Massachusetts. Considered first female poet in American colonies.

1679 Fire destroyed 150 houses in Boston. City imported **first fire engines** from England.

1681 John Bunyan's *The Pilgrim's Progress* published in America; became best seller.

1682 René-Robert Cavelier, Sieur de La Salle, claimed lower Mississippi River country for France and called it Louisiana Apr. 9. Had French outposts built in Illinois and Texas, 1684. Killed during mutiny, 1687. Spanish colonists became the **first Europeans to settle Texas,** at site of present-day El Paso.

1683 William Penn signed treaty with Delaware Indians Apr. 23 and made payment for **Pennsylvania** lands. The **first German colonists** in America settled near Philadelphia.

1689 New York's English colonial governor, **Sir Edmund Andros,** resigned after armed uprising in Boston on Apr. 18.

1690 First colonial newspaper, *Publick Occurrences,* published by Benjamin Harris but shut down after one issue for lack of official permission. Harris also published *New England Primer* for use as elementary school textbook. Large-scale **whaling** operations began in Nantucket, MA.

1692 Hysteria over **witchcraft** began in Salem Village (now Danvers), MA; 14 women and 6 men were executed by special court.

1697 *The Essays* of **Sir Francis Bacon,** first published in England in 1597, was published in America; it became a best seller.

1699 Former privateer Capt. **William Kidd** arrested and sent to England; hanged for piracy, 1701. French settlements made in Mississippi, Louisiana.

1702 Legislation enacted making **Church of England** the established church in Maryland.

1704 Indians and French allies attacked **Deerfield,** MA, Feb. 29; killed 40, captured and marched off 100. *Boston News Letter,* **first regular newspaper,** started by postmaster John Campbell.

1710 British-colonial troops captured French fort, Port Royal, Nova Scotia, in **Queen Anne's War,** 1702-13. France yielded Nova Scotia by treaty, 1713.

1712 Enslaved Black laborers rebelled against white colonists in New York City Apr. 6 and 9 whites were killed; 40 rebels put on trial and around 20 executed, with 6 committing suicide.

1716 First theater in colonies opened in Williamsburg, VA.

1620: Pilgrims and other colonists sign the Mayflower Compact to form a "civil body politic."

1770: British troops fired into a threatening Boston mob, killing five in "Boston Massacre"; the incident was cited by those seeking to unite colonists against British rule.

1726 **Great Awakening**, general revival of evangelical religion, began in colonies.

1731 America's **first subscription library** (paying members could freely borrow books) cofounded in Philadelphia by Benjamin Franklin.

1732 Benjamin Franklin published the **first** *Poor Richard's Almanack*; published annually until 1757. Georgia, last of 13 colonies, chartered.

1733 **Influenza epidemic** swept through New York City and Philadelphia.

1735 Editor **John Peter Zenger** was acquitted of libel Aug. 5 in New York City after criticizing the British governor's conduct in office.

1739 A series of **slave uprisings** put down in South Carolina.

1741 Famous sermon "Sinners in the Hands of an Angry God," delivered July 8 at Enfield, MA, by Jonathan Edwards, one of the most important preachers in the **Great Awakening** religious revival. Danish navigator **Vitus Bering**, commanding Russian expedition, reached Alaska.

1744 **King George's War** pitted British and colonials versus French. Colonials captured Louisbourg, Cape Breton Isl., Nova Scotia, June 17, 1745. Returned to France 1748 by Treaty of Aix-la-Chapelle.

1752 According to legend, **Benjamin Franklin**, flying kite in thunderstorm, proved lightning is electricity, June 15; invented lightning rod. **Liberty Bell**, cast in England, was delivered to Pennsylvania.

1754 **French and Indian War** began with Ft. Necessity campaign in Pennsylvania. Skirmish May 28, battle at fort July 3-4. British moved Acadian French from Nova Scotia to Louisiana Oct. 8, 1755. British captured Québec Sept. 18, 1759, in battles in which French Gen. Joseph de Montcalm and British Gen. James Wolfe were killed. Peace pact signed Feb. 10, 1763. French lost Canada and Midwest. Delegates from seven colonies to New York for **Albany Congress**, July 19, approved plan of union by Benjamin Franklin; plan rejected by the colonies.

1757 **First streetlights** appeared in Philadelphia.

1764 **Sugar Act**, Apr. 5, placed duties on lumber, foodstuffs in colonies. First law passed by Parliament to specifically raise revenue from colonies, alleviate French and Indian War debts. British enforced this act, unlike with **Molasses Act** of 1733.

1765 **Stamp Act**, enacted by Parliament Mar. 22, required revenue stamps to help fund royal troops. Nine colonies, at Stamp Act Congress in New York Oct. 7-25, adopted Declaration of Rights. Stamp Act repealed Mar. 17, 1766. **Quartering Act**, requiring colonists to house British troops, went into effect Mar. 24.

1767 **Townshend Acts** levied taxes on glass, lead, paper, paint, and tea. In 1770 all duties except on tea were repealed.

1770 British troops fired Mar. 5 into Boston mob, killed five including **Crispus Attucks**, a Black man, reportedly leader of group; later called **Boston Massacre**.

1773 East India Co. tea ships turned back at Boston, New York, and Philadelphia in May. Cargo ship burned at Annapolis, Oct. 14; cargo thrown overboard at **Boston Tea Party**, Dec. 16, to protest the tea tax. **First museum** in the colonies was officially established in Charleston, SC; later named the Charleston Museum.

1774 **"Intolerable Acts"** of Parliament curtailed Massachusetts self-rule; barred use of Boston Harbor until dumped tea was paid for. **First Continental Congress** held in Philadelphia Sept. 5-Oct. 26; called for civil disobedience against British. Rhode Island **abolished slavery**.

1775 **Patrick Henry** addressed Virginia convention, Mar. 23, said, "Give me liberty, or give me death!" **Paul Revere**, **William Dawes**, and Dr. **Samuel Prescott**, Apr. 18, rode to alert patriots that British were on their way to Concord, MA, to destroy arms. At **Lexington**, MA, Apr. 19, Minutemen lost eight men. On return from **Concord**, British suffered 273 casualties. Col. Ethan Allen (joined by Col. Benedict Arnold) captured **Ft. Ticonderoga** in New York, May 10, also Crown Point. Colonials headed for **Bunker Hill** and fortified nearby Breed's Hill, Charlestown, MA. Repulsed British under Gen. William Howe twice before retreating, June 17. Continental Congress June 15 named **George Washington** commander in chief; established a postal system, July 26. Benjamin Franklin became the **first postmaster general**.

1776 **Thomas Paine's** *Common Sense*, famous pro-independence pamphlet, published Jan. 10; quickly sold some 100,000 copies. France and Spain agreed May 2 to provide arms to U.S. In Continental Congress June 7, Richard Henry Lee (VA) moved "that these United Colonies are, and of right ought to be, free and independent states." Resolution adopted July 2. **Declaration of Independence** approved July 4, signed Aug. 2. Col. William Moultrie's batteries at **Charleston, SC**, repulsed British sea attack June 28. Washington lost **Battle of Long Island** Aug. 27; evacuated New York. **Nathan Hale** executed as spy by British Sept. 22. Brig. Gen. Arnold's Lake Champlain fleet was defeated in **Battle of Valcour Island** Oct. 11, but British returned to Canada. Howe failed to destroy Washington's army at White Plains, NY, Oct. 28. Hessians captured Ft. Washington, Manhattan, and 3,000 men, Nov. 16; captured Ft. Lee, NJ, Nov. 20. Washington, in Pennsylvania, recrossed **Delaware River** Dec. 25-26, defeated Hessians at **Battle of Trenton**, NJ, Dec. 26.

1777 Washington defeated Lord Charles Cornwallis at **Princeton**, NJ, Jan. 3. Continental Congress, June 14, authorized an **American flag**, the Stars and Stripes. Maj. Gen. John Burgoyne's force of 8,000 from Canada captured **Ft. Ticonderoga**, NY, July 6. Americans beat back Burgoyne at Bemis Heights, Oct. 7, cut off British escape route. Burgoyne surrendered 5,000 men at Saratoga, NY, Oct. 17. **Articles of Confederation** adopted by Continental Congress, Nov. 15; took effect Mar. 1, 1781.

1778 **France signed treaty** of aid with U.S. Feb. 6; sent fleet. British evacuated Philadelphia, June 18.

1779 **George Rogers Clark** took Ft. Vincennes in what is now Indiana in Feb. **John Paul Jones** on the *Bonhomme Richard* defeated *Serapis* in British North Sea waters, Sept. 23.

1780 Charleston, SC, fell to the British May 12, but Loyalists were defeated in battle of **Kings Mountain**, NC, Oct. 7 in what Thomas Jefferson called "the turn of the tide of success." **Benedict Arnold** found to be a traitor Sept. 23. Arnold escaped, made brigadier general in British army.

1781 Bank of North America, **first commercial bank**, incorporated May 26. Cornwallis retired to **Yorktown, VA**. French fleet under Adm. François-Joseph-Paul, count de Grasse gained control of harbor; Washington's troops and French force led by Jean Baptiste de Rochambeau arrived near Yorktown, Sept. 28. After long siege, **Cornwallis surrendered** Oct. 19.

1782 New British cabinet agreed in Mar. to **recognize U.S. independence**. Preliminary agreement signed in Paris, Nov. 30. Use of **scarlet letter A**, sewn on clothing or branded on skin of adulterers, discontinued in New England.

1783 Massachusetts Supreme Court decision in final Quock Walker trial **declared slavery illegal**. Newspapers typically published weekly; **first regular daily newspaper**, *Pennsylvania Evening Post*, went on sale in Philadelphia, May 30. Britain, U.S. signed **Paris peace treaty**, Sept. 3, recognizing American independence; Congress ratified it Jan. 14, 1784. Washington ordered army disbanded Nov. 3, bade farewell to his officers at Fraunces Tavern, New York City, Dec. 4.

1784 Thomas Jefferson's proposal to **ban slavery in new territories** after 1802 was narrowly defeated, Mar. 1.

1785 Regular **stagecoach routes** established between Albany, NY; New York City; and Philadelphia.

1786 Delegates from five states at Annapolis, MD, Sept. 11-14 asked Congress to call a **constitutional convention**.

1787 **Shays's Rebellion** of debt-ridden farmers in Massachusetts failed, Jan. 25. **Constitutional convention** opened in Philadelphia, May 25, with Washington presiding. Constitution accepted by delegates, Sept. 17. Delaware was first state to ratify it, Dec. 7; Pennsylvania and New Jersey followed. **Northwest Ordinance** adopted July 13 by Continental Congress for Northwest Territory, north of Ohio River, west of New York; made rules for statehood and guaranteed freedom of religion, support for schools, no slavery. *Federalist Papers* first appeared in *NY Independent Journal*.

1788 A large fire in **New Orleans**, then a Spanish territory, destroyed much of the city, Mar. 21. **Constitution adopted** June 21 after being ratified by the requisite ninth state (New Hampshire); also ratified by Georgia, Connecticut, Massachusetts, Maryland, South Carolina, Virginia, and New York throughout the year. **First U.S. senators elected** Sept. 30, from Pennsylvania.

1789 **George Washington** chosen president by all electors voting (73 eligible, 69 voting, 4 absent); **John Adams**, vice president, got 34 votes. **First Congress** met at Federal Hall, New York City, and declared Constitution in effect, Mar. 4; Washington inaugurated there Apr. 30; **first inaugural ball** held May 7. U.S. **State Dept.** established by Congress July 27. (Thomas Jefferson installed as first secretary of state Feb. 1790.) **War Dept.** created Aug. 7, with Henry Knox as secretary; **Treasury Dept.** created Sept. 2, with Alexander Hamilton to be secretary. **Supreme Court** created by Federal Judiciary Act, Sept. 24; **John Jay** confirmed by Congress as first Supreme Court chief justice, Sept. 26.

1790 **First Supreme Court session** held Feb. 2 in New York City. Congress, Mar. 1, authorized decennial **U.S. census**. Collection of data took 18 months. **Naturalization Act** (two-year residency) passed Mar. 26. John Carroll consecrated as **first American Catholic bishop**, Aug. 15. Congress met in **Philadelphia**, new temporary capital, Dec. 6.

1791 **Bill of Rights**, submitted to states, Sept. 25, 1789, went into effect Dec. 15. First Bank of the United States, **first bank chartered by federal government**, established in Philadelphia.

1792 Coinage Act established **U.S. Mint** in Philadelphia, Apr. 2. Gen. **"Mad" Anthony Wayne** made commander in Ohio-Indiana area, trained American Legion, established string of forts. Routed Indians at Fallen Timbers on Maumee River, Aug. 20, 1794; checked British at Fort Miami, OH, same year. **White House** cornerstone laid Oct. 13.

1793 **Washington** inaugurated for second term, Mar. 4, having received 132 electoral votes; **John Adams** again became vice president, having received second highest total, 77. Washington declared **U.S. neutrality**, Apr. 22, in war between Britain and France. Eli Whitney invented **cotton gin** (patented 1794), reviving Southern slavery.

1794 **Whiskey Rebellion**, western Pennsylvania farmers protesting liquor tax of 1791, suppressed by federal militia in Sept. **Jay's Treaty**, controversial treaty with Britain negotiated by John Jay, signed Nov. 19, ratified June 24, 1795. This treaty intended to settle long-standing differences between U.S. and Britain.

1795 U.S. bought peace from **Algerian pirates** by paying $1 mil ransom for 115 seamen Sept. 5, followed by annual tributes. Gen. Wayne signed **Treaty of Greenville** with Indians, opening Northwest Territory to settlers. Univ. of North Carolina became **first operating state university**.

1796 **Washington's farewell address** as president delivered Sept. 17. Warned against permanent alliances with foreign powers, big public debt, large military establishment, and devices of "small, artful, enterprising minority."

1797 **John Adams** inaugurated as second president Mar. 4, having received 71 electoral votes; **Thomas Jefferson** became vice president, having received 68. U.S. frigate *United States* launched at Philadelphia, May 10; *Constellation* at Baltimore, Sept. 7; *Constitution* (Old Ironsides) at Boston, Oct. 21.

1798 **Alien and Sedition Acts** passed by Federalists June-July; intended to silence political opposition. **War with France threatened** over French raids on U.S. shipping and rejection of U.S. diplomats. Navy (45 ships) and 365 privateers captured 84 French ships. USS *Constellation* took

1787: Fifty-five delegates representing 12 states meet in Philadelphia, PA, beginning May 25, and draft a new U.S. Constitution.

French warship *Insurgente*, 1799. Napoleon stopped French raids after becoming first consul.

1800 Federal government moved to **Washington, DC**.

1801 **John Marshall** named Supreme Court chief justice, Jan. 20. **Thomas Jefferson**, who had received same number of electoral votes as Aaron Burr in 1800 election, won out over Burr in House vote Feb. 17; Burr named vice president. **Tripoli declared war** June 10 against U.S., which refused added tribute to commerce-raiding Arab corsairs. Land and naval campaigns forced Tripoli to negotiate peace, June 4, 1805. **Oldest U.S. art institution**, Pennsylvania Academy of Fine Arts, founded in Philadelphia.

1802 Congress established U.S. Military Academy at **West Point**, NY.

1803 Supreme Court, in *Marbury v. Madison*, overturned U.S. law for first time, Feb. 24. Napoleon sold all of Louisiana, stretching to Canadian border, to U.S. for $11.25 mil in bonds, plus $3.75 mil indemnities to American citizens with claims against France. U.S. took title Dec. 20. **Louisiana Purchase** doubled U.S. area.

1804 **Meriwether Lewis** and **William Clark** expedition ordered by Pres. Thomas Jefferson to explore what is now Northwest U.S. Started from St. Louis May 14; ended Sept. 23, 1806, back in St. Louis. Vice Pres. **Aaron Burr** shot Alexander Hamilton in duel July 11 in Weehawken, NJ; Hamilton died next day.

1805 U.S. Marines aided by Arab mercenaries, Apr. 27, captured Tripolitan port of Derna. Major victory in war against **Barbary pirates**; inspiration for "to the shores of Tripoli" in Marines Corps hymn.

1807 Robert Fulton made **first practical steamboat trip**; left New York City Aug. 17 and reached Albany, NY, 150 mi away, in 32 hr. **Embargo Act** banned all trade with foreign countries, forbidding ships to set sail for foreign ports Dec. 22.

1808 Legislation **outlawing slave imports** goes into effect. Some 250,000 people were illegally imported as slaves, 1808-60.

1810 **Third U.S. Census** found population of 7,239,881. The enslaved population was put at 1,191,364 and the population of all other non-white free persons at 186,446.

1811 Indiana Territory governor William Henry Harrison defeated Indians led by Tenskwatawa, called the Prophet, in **Battle of Tippecanoe**, Nov. 7. Construction began on **Cumberland Road** in Cumberland, MD; road became important route to West. About 400 **slaves revolted** in Louisiana and marched on New Orleans. The insurrection was suppressed; two whites, some 75 slaves killed.

1812 **War of 1812** had three main causes: Britain seized U.S. ships trading with France; Britain had seized 4,000 naturalized U.S. sailors by 1810; Britain armed Indians, who raided Western border. U.S. stopped trade with Europe 1807 and 1809. Trade with Britain only was stopped 1810. Unaware that Britain had raised blockade against France two days before, **Congress declared war** June 18. British took **Detroit** Aug. 16.

1813 Oliver H. Perry defeated British fleet at **Battle of Lake Erie**, Sept. 10. U.S. won **Battle of the Thames**, Ontario, Oct. 5, but failed in Canadian invasion attempts. York (Toronto) and Buffalo, NY, were burned.

1814 Troops under Andrew Jackson defeated Creek Indians led by Chief Weatherford at Battle of Horseshoe Bend in

Alabama, Mar. 29, ending **Creek Indian War**, begun a year earlier. British landed in Maryland in Aug., defeated U.S. force Aug. 24, **burned Capitol and White House**. Maryland militia stopped British advance, Sept. 12. British bombardment of Ft. McHenry, Baltimore, for 25 hr., Sept. 13-14, failed, inspiring **Francis Scott Key** to write the words to **"The Star-Spangled Banner."** U.S. won naval **Battle of Lake Champlain** Sept. 11. Peace treaty with Great Britain signed at Ghent, Belgium, Dec. 24.

1815 Some 5,300 British, unaware of peace treaty, attacked U.S. entrenchments near **New Orleans**, Jan. 8. British had more than 2,000 casualties; Americans lost 71. U.S. flotilla finally ended attacks by **pirates** from Ottoman states of Algiers, Tunis, Tripoli.

1816 **Second Bank of the U.S.** chartered Apr. 10. The **American Colonization Society**, which sought to address slavery issue by encouraging Black people to migrate to Africa, formed in Washington, DC, Dec. 1816-Jan. 1817.

1817 Thomas Hopkins Gallaudet established the **first free public school for the deaf** in Hartford, CT.

1818 Connecticut expanded **suffrage** among white male voters. Massachusetts followed suit in 1820, and New York in 1821, reducing or eliminating property qualifications.

1819 Spain ceded **Florida** to U.S. Feb. 22. American steamship *Savannah* made first part-steam-powered, part-sail-powered **crossing of Atlantic**, traveling from Savannah, GA, to Liverpool, England, in 29 days. **Washington Irving**'s *Sketch Book* became best seller.

1820 First organized immigration of Black people from **U.S. to Africa** began with a group of 86 sailing to Sierra Leone in Feb. Henry Clay's **Missouri Compromise** bill passed by Congress, Mar. 3. Slavery was allowed in Missouri but not west of the Mississippi River, north of 36° 30′ (the southern line of Missouri). Compromise repealed 1854.

1821 Emma Willard founded Troy Female Seminary, **first U.S. women's college**. Stephen Austin established **first American community in Texas**, San Felipe de Austin. **James Fenimore Cooper**'s *The Spy*, novel set during American Revolution, published and became a best seller.

1822 Tension between sports and academics surfaced when Yale College Pres. Timothy Dwight banned a **primitive form of football**, setting fines for violators.

1823 **Monroe Doctrine**, opposing European intervention in the Americas, enunciated by Pres. James Monroe Dec. 2. The **Hudson River School**, painters who focused on the beauties of nature, began to receive public attention.

1824 Pawtucket, RI, **weavers strike** is first organized factory strike in U.S. and one of earliest known involving women workers. **Slavery abolished** in state of Illinois Aug. 2.

1825 After a deadlocked election, **John Quincy Adams** was elected president by the House, Feb. 9. **Erie Canal** opened; first boat left Buffalo, NY, Oct. 26, reached New York City Nov. 4. John Stevens, of Hoboken, NJ, built and operated **first experimental steam locomotive** in U.S.

1826 **Thomas Jefferson** and **John Adams** both died July 4. **James Fenimore Cooper**'s *The Last of the Mohicans* published.

1827 Massachusetts became first state to pass a law providing for tax-supported **public high schools**.

1828 Baltimore & Ohio, the **first U.S. passenger railroad**, began operations July 4. South Carolina Dec. 19 declared right of **state nullification of federal laws**, opposing the "Tariff of Abominations." **Noah Webster** published his *American Dictionary of the English Language*.

1829 **Andrew Jackson** inaugurated as president, Mar. 4.

1830 Famous **debate** culminating Jan. 27 between Sen. **Daniel Webster** (MA) and Robert Hayne (SC), on state right to nullify federal law. **Mormon church** organized by Joseph Smith in Fayette, NY, Apr. 6. Pres. Jackson, May 28, signed **Indian Removal Act**, granting president authority to negotiate treaties whereby Indians living east of Mississippi R. give up lands in exchange for lands in West.

1831 William Lloyd Garrison began **abolitionist newspaper** *The Liberator* Jan. 1. **Nat Turner**, an enslaved man in Virginia, led local rebellion, starting Aug. 21; 57 whites killed. Troops called in, 100 rebellion participants killed. Turner captured, tried, and hanged Nov. 11.

1832 **Black Hawk War** in Illinois and Wisconsin Apr.-Sept. pushed Sauk and Fox Indians west across Mississippi.

1833 **American Anti-Slavery Society** founded in Philadelphia, Dec. 4. **Oberlin College** became first to adopt coeducation in U.S.

1835 According to tradition, the **Liberty Bell** cracked July 8 while tolling death of Chief Justice John Marshall. **Seminole Indians** in Florida under Osceola began attacks Nov. 1, protesting forced removal. The unpopular war ended Aug. 14, 1842; most of the Indians sent to Oklahoma. **Texas** proclaimed right to secede from Mexico; **Sam Houston** put in command of Texas army, Nov. 2-4. **Gold** discovered on Cherokee land in Georgia. Indians forced to cede lands, Dec. 20, and to cross Mississippi.

1836 Texans besieged at **Alamo** in San Antonio by Mexicans under Antonio López de Santa Anna, Feb. 23-Mar. 6; entire garrison killed. Texas independence had been declared, Mar. 2. At San Jacinto Apr. 21, Sam Houston and Texans defeated Mexicans. Ralph Waldo Emerson published his first work, *Nature*, espousing his philosophy of **transcendentalism**. Marcus Whitman, H. H. Spaulding, and wives reached Fort Walla Walla on Columbia River, OR, **first white women to cross the Continental Divide**, in the Rocky Mountains.

1838 Cherokee Indians forced to walk **"Trail of Tears"** from southeast U.S. to area in present-day Oklahoma. At least 4,000—nearly one-fifth of Cherokee population—are estimated to have died.

1841 First emigrant wagon train bound for California, 47 people, left Independence, MO, May 1; reached California Nov. 4. Edgar Allan Poe published one of the **first American detective stories**, *The Murders in the Rue Morgue*.

1842 **Webster-Ashburton Treaty** signed Aug. 9, fixing U.S.-Canada border in Maine and Minnesota. **First use of anesthetic** (sulfuric ether gas) in an operation performed by Georgia doctor Crawford Long.

1843 More than 1,000 settlers left Independence, MO, for Oregon May 22, arriving in Oct. via **Oregon Trail**.

1844 **First message over first telegraph line** sent May 24 by inventor Samuel F. B. Morse from Washington to Baltimore: "What hath God wrought?"

1845 Congress **overrode a presidential veto for the first time**, Mar. 3, after Pres. John Tyler vetoed a tariff bill. Congress of **Texas** voted for annexation by U.S., July 4; Texas admitted to Union, Dec. 29. **Edgar Allan Poe**'s poem "The Raven" published.

1846 **Mexican War** began after Pres. James K. Polk ordered Gen. Zachary Taylor to seize disputed Texan land settled by Mexicans. After border clash, U.S. declared war May 13; Mexico declared war May 23. About 12,000 U.S. troops took Vera Cruz Mar. 27, 1847, and Mexico City Sept. 14, 1847. Treaty signed Feb. 2, 1848, ended war, and Mexico ceded claims to Texas, California, and other territory. Bear flag of **Republic of California** raised by American settlers at Sonoma, June 14. Treaty with Britain June 15 set **Oregon territory** boundary at 49th parallel (extension of existing line). Expansionists had used slogan "54°40′ or fight." The term **"manifest destiny,"** coined by journalist in 1845, also came into play. **Mormons**, after violent clashes with settlers over polygamy, left Nauvoo, IL, for West under Brigham Young. They settled July 1847 at Salt Lake City, UT. Elias Howe invented **sewing machine**.

1848: The Seneca Falls Convention, July 19-20, launched the cause of women's rights as an organized movement in the U.S., but a resolution demanding the right to vote only narrowly passed there.

1865: Confederate Gen. Robert E. Lee surrenders to Union Gen. Ulysses S. Grant at Appomattox Court House, VA.

1847 First adhesive U.S. postage stamps—Benjamin Franklin 5¢, Washington 10¢—sold July 1. **Henry Wadsworth Longfellow**'s *Evangeline* published.

1848 **Gold** discovered Jan. 24 in California; 80,000 prospectors emigrated in 1849. Lucretia Mott and Elizabeth Cady Stanton held Seneca Falls, NY, **Women's Rights Convention** July 19-20.

1850 Sen. Henry Clay's **Compromise of 1850** admitted California as 31st state Sept. 9, with slavery forbidden; made Utah and New Mexico territories; made **Fugitive Slave Law** harsher; and ended District of Columbia slave trade. **Nathaniel Hawthorne**'s *The Scarlet Letter* published.

1851 **Herman Melville**'s *Moby-Dick* published.

1852 **Harriet Beecher Stowe**'s *Uncle Tom's Cabin* published.

1853 Japan receives Comm. Matthew C. Perry, July 14. He negotiated treaty to **open Japan** to U.S. ships. New York City hosted **first World's Fair** in the U.S., beginning July 14. **Stephen Foster** published "My Old Kentucky Home."

1854 **Republican Party** formed at Ripon, WI, Feb. 28. Opposed Kansas-Nebraska Act, which left issue of slavery to vote of settlers. Act became law May 30. Treaty ratified with Mexico Apr. 25, providing for **Gadsden Purchase** of a strip of land. **Henry David Thoreau**'s *Walden* published.

1855 First railroad train crossed **Mississippi River** on river's first bridge, between Rock Island, IL, and Davenport, IA, Apr. 21. **Walt Whitman**'s *Leaves of Grass* published.

1856 Proslavery group sacked **Lawrence, KS**, May 21; abolitionist John Brown led antislavery contingent against Missourians at Osawatomie, KS, Aug. 30. Antislavery Republican Party's **first presidential nominee**, John C. Frémont, defeated by James Buchanan. Abraham Lincoln made 50 speeches for Frémont. **First U.S. kindergarten** opened in Watertown, WI.

1857 In **Dred Scott** case, which involved determination of constitutionality of already-repealed Missouri Compromise, Supreme Court decided Mar. 6 that enslaved individuals did not become free in a free state, and Black persons were not and could not be citizens. **Currier & Ives**, firm of American lithographers, issued their first print.

1858 First Atlantic cable completed by Cyrus W. Field Aug. 5. **Lincoln-Douglas debates** in Illinois, Aug. 21-Oct. 15.

1859 Edwin L. Drake drilled the **first commercially productive oil well** near Titusville, PA, Aug. 27. Abolitionist John Brown, with 21 men, seized U.S. armory at **Harpers Ferry**, WV, Oct. 16. U.S. Marines captured raiders, killing several. Brown was hanged for treason Dec. 2.

1860 Shoeworkers in Lynn, MA, went on strike Feb. 22. Within a week, strike spread to include 20,000 shoeworkers throughout New England in country's **largest strike to date**. **First Pony Express** between Sacramento, CA, and St. Joseph, MO, started Apr. 3. Republican **Abraham Lincoln** elected president Nov. 6 in four-way race.

1861 Seven southern states set up **Confederate States of America** Feb. 8, with **Jefferson Davis** as president. Civil War began as Confederates fired on **Ft. Sumter** in Charleston, SC, Apr. 12; they captured it Apr. 14. Pres. Lincoln called for 75,000 volunteers Apr. 15. Lincoln blockaded Southern ports Apr. 19, cutting off vital exports and aid. By May, 11 states had seceded. Confederates repelled Union forces at first **Battle of Bull Run**, July 21. **First transcontinental telegraph line** put in operation.

1862 Union forces were victorious in Western campaigns, took New Orleans May 1. Battles in East were largely inconclusive despite heavy casualties. The **Battle of Antietam**, in western Maryland Sept. 17, was bloodiest one-day battle of war; each side lost more than 2,000 men. **Homestead Act**, which granted free farms to settlers, approved May 20. **Land Grant Act**, which provided for public land sale to benefit agricultural education, approved July 7. It eventually led to establishment of state university systems.

1863 Pres. Lincoln issued **Emancipation Proclamation** Jan. 1, freeing "all slaves in areas still in rebellion." Union forces won major victory at Gettysburg, PA, July 1-3. Confederate forces under siege surrendered **Vicksburg, MS**, to Union forces under Gen. Ulysses S. Grant, July 4; control of Mississippi River in Union hands. About 1,000 were killed or wounded in **draft riots** in New York City; white mobs attacked and hanged Black individuals July 13-16. Pres. Lincoln gave his **Gettysburg Address** Nov. 19. Lincoln declared **Thanksgiving** a national holiday.

1864 Gen. **William Tecumseh Sherman** marched through Georgia, taking Atlanta Sept. 1 and Savannah Dec. 22. **Sand Creek massacre** of Cheyenne and Arapaho Indians Nov. 29. Soldiers drove Indians out of village; about 150 killed.

1865 Gen. **Robert E. Lee surrendered** 27,800 Confederate troops to Gen. Grant at Appomattox Court House in VA, Apr. 9. J. E. Johnston surrendered 31,200 to Sherman at Durham Station, NC, Apr. 18. Last rebel troops surrendered May 26. Pres. Lincoln shot Apr. 14 by **John Wilkes Booth** in Ford's Theater, Washington, DC; died the following morning. Vice Pres. **Andrew Johnson** was sworn in as president. Booth was tracked down and fatally wounded, perhaps by his own hand, Apr. 26. Four co-conspirators were hanged July 7. **13th Amendment**, abolishing slavery except as a punishment for crime, ratified Dec. 6.

1866 Congress took control of Southern **Reconstruction**, backed freedmen's rights in legislation vetoed by Pres. Andrew Johnson; veto overridden by Congress, Apr. 9. **Ku Klux Klan** formed secretly in South to terrorize Black residents who voted. Disbanded 1869-71.

1867 **Alaska** sold to U.S. by Russia for $7.2 mil Mar. 30, through efforts of Sec. of State William H. Seward. Fraternal society the **Grange** was organized Dec. 4 to protect farmer interests. **Horatio Alger**'s *Ragged Dick* published.

1868 Pres. Andrew Johnson dismissed Sec. of War Edwin M. Stanton without Senate approval. **Johnson impeached** by the House Feb. 24 for violation of Tenure of Office Act, though charges were actually made in response to his opposition to congressional Reconstruction. He was acquitted by the Senate Mar.-May. **14th Amendment**, providing for citizenship of all persons born or naturalized in U.S. and subject to the jurisdiction thereof, ratified July 9. **Louisa May Alcott**'s *Little Women* published. *The World Almanac*, a publication of the *New York World* newspaper, appeared for first time.

1869 First **Transcontinental railroad** completed; golden spike driven at Promontory Summit, UT, May 10, marking junction of Central Pacific and Union Pacific lines. Attempt to "corner" gold led to financial **"Black Friday"** in New York Sept. 24. **Woman suffrage law** passed in Wyoming Territory Dec. 10. **Knights of Labor** labor union formed in Philadelphia. By 1886, it had 700,000 members nationally.

1870 **15th Amendment**, making race no bar to voting rights, ratified Feb. 8. **First U.S. boardwalk** completed, in Atlantic City, NJ. **U.S. Weather Bureau** founded.

1871 **Great Chicago fire** destroyed city Oct. 8-11. **National Rifle Association (NRA)** founded.

1872 **Amnesty Act** May 22 restored civil rights to citizens of the South, except for 500 Confederate leaders. Congress established Yellowstone, **first national park**. James McNeill Whistler painted famous portrait known informally as **"Whistler's Mother."**

1873 First U.S. postal card issued May 1. **Jesse James** and his gang robbed their first passenger train July 21. Banks failed, panic began in Sept. **Depression** lasted five years. **"Boss" William Tweed** of New York City was convicted Nov. 19 of stealing public funds; he died in jail in 1878. New York's Bellevue Hospital started **first nursing school.**

1874 **Women's Christian Temperance Union** established in Cleveland. **First public zoo** in U.S. established in Philadelphia.

1875 Congress passed **Civil Rights Act** Mar. 1, giving equal rights to Black people in public accommodations and jury duty. Supreme Court invalidated act in 1883. First **Kentucky Derby** held May 17. First **Jim Crow segregation law** enacted, in Tennessee.

1876 Alexander Graham Bell patented the telephone Mar. 7. Col. **George A. Custer** and 264 soldiers of the 7th Cavalry were killed June 25 in "last stand," **Battle of the Little Bighorn**, MT, in Sioux Indian War. Democrat **Samuel J. Tilden** received majority of popular votes for president over Republican **Rutherford B. Hayes**, Nov. 7, but 22 electoral votes were in dispute. Congress agreed to certify Hayes as winner in Feb. 1877 after Republicans agreed to end federal Reconstruction of South.

1877 Molly Maguires—Irish terrorist society in mining areas of Scranton, PA—was broken up by hanging, June 21, of 11 leaders for murders of mine officials and police. Pres. Hayes sent federal troops to control violent national **railroad strike**, which began in July.

1878 First **commercial telephone exchange** opened, New Haven, CT, Jan. 28. **Thomas A. Edison** founded Edison Electric Light Co. on Oct. 15.

1879 F. W. Woolworth opened his first five-and-ten store, in Utica, NY, Feb. 22. French actress **Sarah Bernhardt** made her U.S. debut Nov. 8 at New York City's Booth Theater. Economist and social philosopher **Henry George** published *Progress & Poverty*, advocating single tax on land.

1881 Clara Barton founded **American Red Cross** May 21. Pres. **James A. Garfield** shot in Washington, DC, July 2, by mentally disturbed office seeker; died Sept. 19. Famous gun battle between the Earp brothers and outlaw rustlers Oct. 26 near the **OK Corral**, Tombstone, AZ. **Booker T. Washington** founded Tuskegee Institute for Black students. **Helen Hunt Jackson**'s *A Century of Dishonor*, about mistreatment of American Indians, published.

1882 Chinese Exclusion Act, barring immigration of Chinese laborers for 10 years, later made permanent, passed by Congress May 6; first significant law to restrict immigration to U.S.

1883 Civil Service Act, or **Pendleton Act**, passed Jan. 16, created foundations of American civil service system. The **Brooklyn Bridge** opened May 24 as world's longest suspension bridge. Transcontinental **Northern Pacific Railroad** was completed Sept. 8. **Buffalo Bill Cody**'s Wild West Show began its 30-year touring run.

1884 Switchback Railway—**first U.S. roller coaster** built as amusement park ride—opened at Coney Island in New York City. **Mark Twain**'s *The Adventures of Huckleberry Finn* published.

1885 Washington Monument dedicated Feb. 21.

1886 Haymarket riot and bombing, May 4, followed labor battles for 8-hr. work day in Chicago; seven police and four workers died. Eight anarchists found guilty Aug. 20; four hanged Nov. 11. **Coca-Cola** first sold, May 8, at Jacob's Pharmacy in Atlanta. Apache Indian **Geronimo** surrendered Sept. 4, ending last major Indian war. **Statue of Liberty**

dedicated Oct. 28. **American Federation of Labor** (AFL) formed Dec. 8 by 25 craft unions.

1887 Interstate Commerce Act enacted Feb. 4, created Interstate Commerce Commission.

1888 Great blizzard struck Eastern U.S. Mar. 11-14, causing about 400 deaths. Ernest Thayer's poem **"Casey at the Bat"** recited for first time in public at New York City theater in May.

1889 U.S. opened 2-mil acre **Oklahoma District** to settlement Apr. 22, initiating land run; "sooner" settlers illegally entered the territory before that date to stake favorable claims. More than 2,200 lives lost in **Johnstown flood** (PA) May 31. **Electric lights** installed at White House.

1890 Sherman Antitrust Act passed July 2, began federal effort to curb monopolies. After decades of broken treaties and diminished reservations, U.S. Army massacre at **Wounded Knee**, SD, Dec. 29, kills about 250 Lakota Sioux men, women, and children; at least 25 soldiers were killed. **Jacob Riis**'s *How the Other Half Lives*, about city slums, published, instigating reform legislation in New York City. **Emily Dickinson**'s poems published, four years after her death.

1891 Forest Reserve Act, Mar. 3, let president close public forest land to settlement for establishment of national parks. **Carnegie Hall**, in New York City, opened May 5.

1892 Ellis Island, in New York Bay, opened Jan. 1 to receive immigrants; closed 1954. **Homestead strike** (PA) at Carnegie steel mills; 7 guards and 11 strikers and spectators shot to death July 6. James J. Corbett defeated John L. Sullivan Sept. 7 to become **first world heavyweight champion** under Marquess of Queensbury rules.

1893 Columbian Exposition world's fair held May-Oct. in Chicago. Financial panic led to four-year **depression**. **Mormon Temple** dedicated in Salt Lake City, UT.

1894 Thomas A. Edison's **kinetoscope**, for motion pictures (invented 1887), given first public showing Apr. 14. **Jacob S. Coxey** led army of unemployed from the Midwest, reaching Washington, DC, Apr. 30. Coxey arrested May 1 for trespassing on Capitol grounds; his army disbanded. **Pullman strike** began May 11 at railroad car plant in Chicago. Milton Hershey founded **Hershey Chocolate Company**.

1895 "America, the Beautiful" appeared for first time, in church publication, July 4. **Stephen Crane**'s *The Red Badge of Courage* published.

1896 Supreme Court, in *Plessy v. Ferguson*, May 18, approved racial segregation under the **"separate but equal"** doctrine. **William Jennings Bryan** delivered 'Cross of Gold' speech July 9; won Democratic Party nomination. **John Philip Sousa** composed "Stars and Stripes Forever" on Dec. 25.

1897 Olney-Pauncefote Treaty with Britain, Jan. 11, gave wide scope to arbitration in settling disputes; never ratified by U.S. John J. McDermott won **first Boston Marathon** Apr. 19. First Klondike gold arrived in San Francisco July 14, helping set off **Klondike gold rush**. **First subway service** in country opens to public in Boston, Sept. 1.

1898 U.S. battleship *Maine* exploded Feb. 15 in Havana, Cuba; 260 killed. U.S. blockaded Cuba Apr. 22 in aid of independence forces. U.S. declared **war on Spain** Apr. 24; destroyed Spanish fleet in Philippines May 1; took Guam June 20. U.S. took **Puerto Rico** July 25-Aug. 12. Spain agreed Dec. 10 to cede Philippines, Puerto Rico, and Guam, and approved independence for Cuba. Annexation of **Hawaii** signed by Pres. William McKinley, July 7.

1899 Filipino insurgents, unable to get recognition of independence from U.S., started guerrilla war Feb. 4. Their leader, Emilio Aguinaldo, captured May 23, 1901. **Philippine insurrection** ended 1902. Some 200,000 civilians and 20,000 Filipino troops died, mostly from disease and starvation. Pres. McKinley signed treaty officially ending **Spanish-American War**, Feb. 10. U.S. declared **Open Door Policy** Sept. 6, to make China an open international market. Philosopher **John Dewey**'s *School and Society*, advocating progressive education ("learn by doing"), published. Pianist Scott Joplin's "Maple Leaf Rag" published, popularizing **ragtime music**.

1900 International Ladies' Garment Workers Union founded in New York City June 3. Fought sweatshop working conditions. **Carry Nation**, Kansas temperance leader, began raiding saloons with a hatchet. U.S. helped suppress **Boxer Rebellion** in Beijing, China. Eastman Kodak Co. introduced the **Brownie camera**, popularizing picture-taking.

1891: Survivors of the Wounded Knee massacre—in which a U.S. Army cavalry regiment near Wounded Knee Creek, SD, killed 250-300 Lakota Sioux men, women, and children—are moved to the Pine Ridge Reservation.

1901 Texas had first significant oil strike at **Spindletop** well near Beaumont, Jan. 10. U.S. withdrew troops from **Cuba** May 20, and Cuba became independent. Pres. **McKinley** shot Sept. 6 in Buffalo, NY, by anarchist Leon Czolgosz; died Sept. 14. Vice Pres. **Theodore Roosevelt** sworn in as youngest-ever president, at age 42 years, 11 months. **Booker T. Washington**'s *Up From Slavery* published.

1902 Permanent **Bureau of the Census** established Mar. 6. **Helen Keller** autobiography appeared in serial form.

1903 Treaty between U.S. and Colombia to have U.S. dig **Panama Canal** signed Jan. 22, but rejected by Colombia's Congress. Panama declared independence from Colombia with U.S. support Nov. 3; recognized by Pres. Roosevelt Nov. 6. U.S., Panama signed canal treaty Nov. 18. Wisconsin set first plural **direct primary voting system**, May 23. **Henry Ford** founded Ford Motor Co., June 16. Boston defeated Pittsburgh, 5 games to 3, Oct. 13 in **first modern World Series**. **First successful flight** in heavier-than-air mechanically propelled airplane by **Orville Wright** Dec. 17 near Kitty Hawk, NC, 120 ft in 12 sec. Later flight same day by **Wilbur Wright**, 852 ft in 59 sec. Improved plane patented, 1906. **Iroquois Theater fire** in Chicago killed about 600 out of 1,900 in audience, Dec. 30. Pioneering film *Great Train Robbery* produced.

1904 St. Louis hosted **first Olympics in U.S.**, July 1-Nov. 23. First section of **New York City subway** system opened, Oct. 27. **Ida Tarbell** published muckraking *The History of the Standard Oil Company*. **Henry James**'s last major novel, *The Golden Bowl*, published.

1905 **Industrial Workers of the World**, which advocated Marxian theory of class struggle between workers and capitalists, founded in Chicago, June 27. **Rotary**, oldest service club organization in U.S., founded in Chicago.

1906 **San Francisco earthquake** and fire, Apr. 18-19, caused more than 3,000 deaths and $400 mil in damages. **Upton Sinclair**'s *The Jungle*, which exposed working conditions in meat-packing industry, published. Helped spur passage of the **Pure Food and Drug Act** and **Meat Inspection Act** June 30.

1907 Financial panic and **depression** started Mar. 13. Pres. Roosevelt sent **"Great White Fleet"** of 16 U.S. battleships around the world in show of power.

1908 Springfield, IL, torn by **anti-Black rioting**, Aug. 14-15. Henry Ford introduced **Model T** car, priced at $850, Oct. 1.

1909 Adm. Robert E. Peary claimed to have reached **North Pole** Apr. 6 on sixth attempt, accompanied by Black explorer Matthew Henson and four Inuit men; may have fallen short. National Conference on the Negro convened May 30, leading to founding of **National Association for the Advancement of Colored People** (NAACP).

1910 Boy Scouts of America founded Feb. 8. Former Pres. Roosevelt called for **"new nationalism"** in famous speech in Kansas, Aug. 10.

1911 Building with New York City's **Triangle Shirtwaist Co.** factory caught fire Mar. 25; 146 died. Supreme Court ruled May 15 that **Standard Oil Co.** must be dissolved because it unreasonably restrained trade. **First transcontinental airplane flight** (with numerous stops) by C. P. Rodgers,

from New York, NY, to Pasadena, CA, Sept. 17-Nov. 5; time in air 82 hr., 4 min.

1912 American Girl Guides founded Mar. 12; name changed in 1913 to **Girl Scouts**. U.S. Marines, Aug. 14, sent to **Nicaragua**, which was in default of loans to U.S. and Europe.

1913 **16th Amendment**, authorizing federal income tax, ratified Feb. 3. The **Armory Show** in New York City brought modern art to U.S. for first time, Feb. 17. **17th Amendment**, providing for direct popular election of U.S. senators (originally elected by state legislatures), ratified Apr. 8. **Federal Reserve System** authorized Dec. 23, in major reform of U.S. banking and finance.

1914 **Ford Motor Co.** raised basic wage rates from $2.40 for 9-hr. day to $5 for 8-hr. day, Jan. 5, increasing stability in labor force. When U.S. sailors were arrested in Tampico, Mexico, Apr. 9, Atlantic fleet was sent to **Veracruz**, occupied city. Pres. Woodrow Wilson proclaimed **U.S. neutrality** in the European war, Aug. 4. The **Panama Canal** officially opened Aug. 15. The **Clayton Antitrust Act** passed Oct. 15, strengthening federal antimonopoly powers.

1915 **First transcontinental telephone call**, New York to San Francisco, completed Jan. 25 by Alexander Graham Bell and Thomas A. Watson. British ship *Lusitania* sunk May 7 by German submarine; 1,198 passengers died, including 128 Americans. (In notice in morning newspapers the day *Lusitania* set sail, Germany had warned Americans against taking passage on British vessels.) As result of U.S. campaign, Germany issued apology and promise of payments, Oct. 5. U.S. troops landed in **Haiti**, July 28. Haiti became virtual U.S. protectorate under Sept. 16 treaty. Pres. Wilson asked for a military fund increase, Dec. 7. D. W. Griffith's film *The Birth of a Nation* released. William J. Simmons partly inspired by film to revive **Ku Klux Klan**, which peaks in 1920s.

1916 Gen. **John J. Pershing** entered Mexico in Mar. to pursue **Francisco (Pancho) Villa**, who had raided U.S. border areas. Forces withdrew Feb. 5, 1917. **Rural Credits Acts** passed July 17, followed by **Warehouse Act** Aug. 11; both provided financial aid to farmers. Bomb exploded during **San Francisco Preparedness Day parade** July 22, killed 10. Thomas J. Mooney, labor organizer, and Warren K. Billings, shoeworker, convicted 1917; both later pardoned. U.S. bought **Virgin Islands** from Denmark Aug. 4. U.S. established military government in the **Dominican Republic** Nov. 29. Jeannette Rankin (R, MT) elected to House of Representatives, **first woman to be a member of Congress.**

1917 Germany, suffering from British blockade, declared almost unrestricted **submarine warfare** Jan. 31. U.S. cut diplomatic ties with Germany Feb. 3 and formally **declared war** Apr. 6. Jones Act, passed Mar. 2, made **Puerto Rico** a U.S. territory, its inhabitants U.S. citizens. **Conscription law** passed May 18. First U.S. troops arrived in Europe June 26.

1918 Pres. Wilson set out his **14 Points** as basis for peace, Jan. 8. More than 1 mil American troops were in Europe by July. Allied counteroffensive launched at Château-Thierry July 18. War ended with signing of **armistice** Nov. 11. **Influenza pandemic** killed an estimated 50-100 mil worldwide, 675,000 in U.S.

1919 **18th Amendment**, providing for prohibition of manufacture, sale, or transportation of alcoholic beverages, ratified Jan. 16, to take effect on Jan. 16, 1920. **First transatlantic flight**, by U.S. Navy seaplane, left Rockaway, NY, May 8; stopped at Newfoundland, Azores, Lisbon May 27. **Boston police strike** Sept. 9, earliest strike conducted by government employees. About 250 **foreign-born radicals** deported Dec. 21 to Soviet Union.

1920 In national **Red Scare**, some 2,700 Communists, anarchists, and other radicals were arrested Jan.-May. **League of Women Voters** founded Feb. 14. Senate refused Mar. 19 to ratify **League of Nations Covenant**. Nicola Sacco and Bartolomeo Vanzetti accused of killing two men in Massachusetts payroll holdup Apr. 15; found guilty 1921. A sevenyear campaign for their release failed; both executed Aug. 23, 1927. Verdict repudiated 1977 by proclamation of Massachusetts Gov. Michael Dukakis. **19th Amendment** ratified Aug. 18, giving women the vote. **First regular licensed radio broadcasting** began Aug. 20. **Wall St. bombing** in New York City killed 39, injured 200-300, did $2 mil damage, Sept. 16. **Sinclair Lewis**'s *Main Street* published.

1903: Henry Ford incorporates Ford Motor Co. in Dearborn, MI, June 16, and sells the first Model A on July 23.

1920: Women are given the right to vote with the ratification of the 19th amendment, though other laws made voting rights difficult or impossible for many Americans to exercise.

1921 Congress sharply curbed immigration, set **national quota system** May 19. **"Black Wall Street"** in Tulsa, OK, looted and burned by white rioters, May 31-June 1. Joint congressional resolution declaring **peace with Germany, Austria, and Hungary** signed July 2 by Pres. Warren G. Harding; treaties were signed in Aug. In so-called **Black Sox scandal**, eight Chicago White Sox players were banned from baseball Aug. 4 for conspiring with gamblers to throw the 1919 World Series. Limitation of Armaments Conference met in Washington, DC, Nov. 12-Feb. 6, 1922. Major powers agreed to curtail naval construction, outlaw poison gas, restrict submarine attacks on merchant vessels, and respect China's integrity.

1922 During nationwide coal strike, union miners killed some 21 strikebreakers at Herrin, IL, June 21-22, in incident referred to as the **Herrin Massacre. T. S. Eliot**'s *The Waste Land* published.

1923 **First sound-on-film motion picture**, *Phonofilm*, shown at Rivoli Theater, New York City, beginning in Apr. Pres. Calvin Coolidge addressed Congress, Dec. 6; **first radio broadcast of president's annual speech.**

1924 Law approved by Congress June 15 made all **Native Americans U.S. citizens. Immigration law** enacted May 26 established permanent national quotas favoring N and W Europeans. **Nellie Tayloe Ross** elected governor of Wyoming, and **Miriam (Ma) Ferguson** elected governor of Texas Nov. 9. Ross inaugurated as nation's **first female governor** Jan. 5, 1925. Ferguson installed Jan. 20, 1925. **George Gershwin** wrote "Rhapsody in Blue."

1925 In so-called "Monkey Trial," John T. Scopes found guilty of having taught **evolution** in Dayton, TN, high school and fined, July 24. **F. Scott Fitzgerald**'s *The Great Gatsby* published.

1926 Dr. Robert H. Goddard, Mar. 16, demonstrated **first liquid-fuel rocket.** Congress established **Army Air Corps** July 2. **Air Commerce Act** passed Nov. 2, established government agencies for development of airports, radio navigation, and other services. **Ernest Hemingway**'s *The Sun Also Rises* published.

1927 Capt. **Charles A. Lindbergh** left Roosevelt Field, NY, May 20 alone in *Spirit of St. Louis* on first New York-Paris nonstop flight. Reached Le Bourget airfield May 21, 3,610 mi in 33½ hr. *The Jazz Singer*, **first feature-length film** in which **spoken dialogue was part of narrative action**, released Oct. 6. The musical *Show Boat* opened in New York City Dec. 27.

1928 **Amelia Earhart** became first woman to fly across the Atlantic, June 17. **Herbert Hoover** elected president Nov. 6, defeating New York Gov. Alfred E. Smith, a Catholic.

1929 Gangsters killed seven rivals in Chicago **St. Valentine's Day massacre** Feb. 14, which won Al Capone control of Chicago's underworld. Stock market crash Oct. 29 marked end of past prosperity as stock prices plummeted. Stock losses for 1929-31 estimated at $50 bil; beginning of **Great Depression.** Albert B. Fall, former interior sec., was convicted of accepting $10,000 bribe in leasing of the **Elk Hills (Teapot Dome)** naval oil reserve; sentenced Nov. 1 to a year in prison and fined. **William Faulkner**'s *The Sound and the Fury* published.

1930 London **Naval Reduction Treaty** signed by U.S., Britain, Italy, France, and Japan Apr. 22; in effect Jan. 1,

1931; expired Dec. 31, 1936. **Hawley-Smoot Tariff** signed; rate hikes slash world trade. **Sinclair Lewis** became first American to win a Nobel Prize in literature. **Dashiell Hammett**'s *The Maltese Falcon* published.

1931 **Empire State Building** opened in New York City May 1, displacing NYC's Chrysler Building as world's tallest. **Al Capone** convicted of tax evasion Oct. 17. **Charlie Chaplin** film *City Lights* released.

1932 **Reconstruction Finance Corp.** established Jan. 22 to stimulate banking and business. Unemployment at 12 mil. Twenty-month-old **Charles Lindbergh Jr.** kidnapped Mar. 1; found dead May 12. Bruno Hauptmann found guilty Feb. 1935; executed Apr. 3, 1936. Unemployed World War I veterans demanding Congress pay promised bonus early launched **Bonus March** on Washington, DC, May 29. **Franklin D. Roosevelt** elected president for first time in Democratic landslide, Nov. 8. Chicago Bears won **first NFL title game** Dec. 18, defeating the Portsmouth (OH) Spartans, 9-0.

1933 Pres. Roosevelt named **Frances Perkins** U.S. sec. of labor; **first woman in U.S. cabinet.** Pres. Roosevelt ordered **all U.S. banks closed** Mar. 6. In a "100 days" special session, Mar. 9-June 16, Congress passed **New Deal**, including measures to regulate banks, distribute funds to the jobless, create jobs, raise agricultural prices, and set wage and production standards for industry. **Gold standard** dropped by U.S. in favor of "modified gold bullion standard"; announced by Pres. Roosevelt Apr. 19, ratified by Congress June 5. **Tennessee Valley Authority (TVA)** created by act of Congress, May 18. **Prohibition** ended in the U.S. as 36th state ratified **21st Amendment** Dec. 5. Pres. Roosevelt foreswore armed intervention in **Western Hemisphere** nations, Dec. 26.

1934 Pres. Roosevelt signed law creating **Securities and Exchange Commission**, June 6. U.S. troops pulled out of **Haiti**, Aug. 6.

1935 **Works Progress Administration (WPA)** instituted May 6. Rural Electrification Administration created May 11. National Industrial Recovery Act struck down by Supreme Court May 27. **Boulder Dam** (later renamed **Hoover Dam**) completed, May 29. **Social Security Act** passed by Congress Aug. 8-9. Comedian **Will Rogers** and aviator Wiley Post killed Aug. 15 in Alaska plane crash. Sen. **Huey Long**, former Louisiana governor, shot Sept. 8 by a political rival's son-in-law; died Sept. 10. George Gershwin's jazz opera *Porgy and Bess* opened Oct. 10 in New York. **Committee for Industrial Organization** (later Congress of Industrial Organizations) formed to expand industrial unionism Nov. 9.

1936 **Jesse Owens** won four gold medals at the **Berlin Olympics** in Aug. **Baseball Hall of Fame** founded in Cooperstown, NY. **Margaret Mitchell**'s *Gone With the Wind* published.

1937 Airship *Hindenburg* caught fire May 6 as it was landing in Lakehurst, NJ; 36 killed. **Golden Gate Bridge** in San Francisco opened May 27. **Joe Louis** knocked out James J. Braddock to become world heavyweight champ June 22. Aviator **Amelia Earhart** and copilot Fred Noonan disappeared July 2 near Howland Isl., in the Pacific. Pres. Roosevelt proposed judicial reforms that would allow him to appoint additional Supreme Court justices; his **"court-packing"** plan defeated. Auto, steel labor unions won first big contracts.

1938 **National minimum wage** enacted June 25. Orson Welles's radio dramatization of H. G. Wells's *War of the Worlds*, Oct. 30, caused Martian invasion scare among some who had missed the introduction. **Seabiscuit** beat War Admiral in match race of the century, at Pimlico track, MD, Nov. 1. The work of folk artist Anna Mary Robertson Moses, **"Grandma Moses,"** discovered. **Thornton Wilder**'s *Our Town* produced on Broadway.

1939 Opera singer **Marian Anderson** performed for integrated crowd of 75,000 at Lincoln Memorial Apr. 9 after Daughters of the American Revolution refused to let Anderson sing in DC's Constitution Hall. **New York World's Fair**—theme: "The World of Tomorrow"—opened Apr. 30, closed Oct. 31. Reopened for second season May 11-Oct. 27, 1940. **Lou Gehrig**, seriously ill with disease that would come to bear his name, said farewell to fans at Yankee Stadium, July 4. Albert Einstein alerted Pres. Roosevelt to **A-bomb possibilities** in Aug. 2 letter. **U.S. declared its neutrality** in European war Sept. 5. Pres. Roosevelt proclaimed limited **national emergency** Sept. 8, unlimited emergency May 27, 1941. Both ended by Pres. Harry Truman, Apr. 28, 1952.

1942: Pres. Franklin D. Roosevelt orders the relocation of 117,000 Japanese-Americans to detention camps for the duration of the war.

Pocket Books, **first paperback publisher** in U.S., established. **John Steinbeck**'s *The Grapes of Wrath* published. *The Wizard of Oz* and *Gone With the Wind* released, the latter to become highest-grossing film of all time (inflation-adjusted).

1940 U.S. OK'd sale of **surplus war material** to Britain June 3; announced transfer of 50 overaged destroyers Sept. 3. **First peacetime military draft** in U.S. history approved, Sept. 14. **Forty-hour work week** went into effect, Oct. 24. Pres. **Roosevelt** elected Nov. 5 to third presidential term. **Richard Wright**'s *Native Son* published.

1941 **Four Freedoms**—freedom of speech and religion, freedom from want and fear—termed essential by Pres. Roosevelt in speech to Congress Jan. 6. **Lend-Lease Act** signed Mar. 11 provided $7 bil in military credits for Britain. Lend-lease for USSR approved in Nov. Pres. Roosevelt signed executive order June 25 barring federal government and war contractors from **racial discrimination**. Order also established Fair Employment Practice Committee. The **Atlantic Charter**, 8-point declaration of principles, issued by Pres. Roosevelt and British Prime Min. Winston Churchill, Aug. 14. Japan attacked **Pearl Harbor**, Hawaii, 7:55 AM Hawaiian time, Dec. 7; 19 ships sunk or damaged, 2,403 dead. Pres. Roosevelt called it "a date which will live in infamy." U.S. declared war on Japan Dec. 8. Germany and Italy declared war on U.S. Dec. 11. U.S. responded with declaration of war later on same day. Japanese invaded **Philippines**, Dec. 22; Wake Island fell, Dec. 23. *Citizen Kane*, directed by Orson Welles, released.

1942 Pres. Roosevelt issued executive order Feb. 19 authorizing relocation of Japanese-Americans. Federal government began forcibly moving 117,000 Japanese-Americans from West Coast to **detention camps**; exclusion lasted three years. Japanese troops took **Bataan** peninsula Apr. 8 and **Corregidor** May 6. **Battle of Midway** June 4-7 was Japan's first major defeat. Marines landed on **Guadalcanal** Aug. 7; last Japanese not expelled until Feb. 9, 1943. U.S., Britain invaded **North Africa** Nov. 8. **First nuclear chain reaction** (fission of uranium isotope U-235) produced at Univ. of Chicago under physicists Arthur Compton, Enrico Fermi, others, Dec. 2. The movie *Casablanca*, starring Humphrey Bogart and Ingrid Bergman, released.

1943 *Oklahoma!* opened Mar. 31 on Broadway. Pres. Roosevelt signed June 10 pay-as-you-go income tax bill. Starting July 1, wage and salary earners were subject to **paycheck withholding tax**. Detroit race riot June 21 left 34 dead, 700 injured. Six killed in riot in New York City's **Harlem** section Aug. 2. U.S., Britain invaded **Sicily** July 9, Italian mainland Sept. 3. Marines in Nov. recaptured the **Gilbert Islands**, captured by Japan in 1941 and 1942.

1944 U.S., Allied forces invaded Europe at Normandy, France, on **"D-Day,"** June 6, in massive amphibious operation. **GI Bill of Rights**, providing benefits to veterans, signed by Pres. Roosevelt June 22. Representatives of the U.S. and other major powers met at **Dumbarton Oaks**, Washington, DC, Aug. 21-Oct. 7, to work out formation of postwar world organization that would become the **United Nations**. U.S. forces

landed on **Leyte**, Philippines, Oct. 20. Pres. **Roosevelt** elected to fourth term as president Nov. 7. **Battle of the Bulge**, failed Nazi counteroffensive, waged Dec. 16 to Jan. 28, 1945.

1945 **Yalta Conference** met in the Crimea, USSR, Feb. 4-11. Pres. Roosevelt, Prime Min. Churchill, and Soviet leader Joseph Stalin agreed that their countries, plus France, would occupy Germany and that the Soviet Union would enter war against Japan. Marines landed on **Iwo Jima** Feb. 19, declared victory Mar. 26 after heavy casualties. U.S. forces invaded **Okinawa** Apr. 1, captured it June 21. Pres. **Roosevelt** died in Warm Springs, GA, Apr. 12; Vice Pres. **Harry S. Truman** became president. Germany surrendered May 7; May 8 proclaimed **V-E Day**. **First atomic bomb**, produced at Los Alamos, NM, exploded at Alamogordo, NM, July 16. Bomb dropped on **Hiroshima**, Japan, Aug. 6, killing about 75,000; bomb dropped on **Nagasaki**, Japan, Aug. 9, killing about 40,000. Japan agreed to surrender Aug. 14; formally surrendered Sept. 2. At **Potsdam Conference**, July 17-Aug. 2, leaders of U.S., USSR, and Britain agreed on disarmament of Germany, occupation zones, war crimes trials. **Empire State Building** struck accidentally by Army B-25 bomber, July 28, killing 14. U.S. forces entered **Korea** south of 38th parallel to displace Japanese Sept. 8. Gen. **Douglas MacArthur** took over supervision of Japan Sept. 9.

1946 **Steel strike** by 750,000 started Jan. 21, settled in four weeks. Strike by 400,000 **mine workers** began Apr. 1 (settled May 29); other industries (including rail, maritime) followed. Former Prime Min. Winston Churchill employed the phrase **"Iron Curtain"** in Mar. 5 speech at Westminster College in Fulton, MO. Atomic bomb tested off **Bikini Atoll** in Pacific, July 1. In all, U.S. conducted 23 nuclear tests between 1946 and 1958. **Philippines** given independence by U.S. July 4. Mother Frances Xavier Cabrini **first American to be canonized**, July 7. Dr. Benjamin Spock's *Baby and Child Care* published as **baby boom** began.

1947 Pres. Truman asked Congress for financial and military aid for Greece and Turkey to help combat Communist subversion, Mar. 12; **Truman Doctrine** approved May 15. UN Security Council voted Apr. 2 to place under U.S. trusteeship the **Pacific islands** formerly mandated to Japan. **Jackie Robinson** joined Brooklyn Dodgers Apr. 11, breaking color barrier in major league baseball. The **Marshall Plan** for U.S. aid to European countries proposed by Sec. of State George C. Marshall June 5. Congress authorized some $12 bil in next four years. **Taft-Hartley Labor Act** restricting labor union power vetoed by Pres. Truman June 20; Congress overrode veto. Air Force Capt. **Chuck Yeager** broke sound barrier, Oct. 14, in X-1 rocket plane. First families moved to new suburban Levittown, NY, development Oct. 1 (original construction ended 1951).

1948 **Organization of American States** (OAS) founded Apr. 30 by 21 countries. USSR halted all surface traffic into **West Berlin** June 24; in response, U.S. and British troops launched an **airlift**. Soviet blockade halted May 12, 1949; airlift ended Sept. 30. Pres. **Truman** elected Nov. 2, defeating NY Gov. Thomas E. Dewey in historic upset. Former State Dept. official **Alger Hiss** indicted Dec. 15 for perjury, after denying he had passed government documents to Whittaker Chambers to go to a Communist spy ring; convicted Jan. 21, 1950. **Kinsey Report** on sexuality in the human male published.

1949 North Atlantic Treaty Organization (**NATO**) established Aug. 24 by U.S., Canada, and 10 Western European nations, agreeing that an armed attack against one would be considered an attack against all. Eleven leaders of U.S. **Communist Party** convicted Oct. 14 of advocating violent overthrow of U.S. government; sentenced to prison. Supreme Court upheld convictions, 1951. Pres. Truman, Oct. 26, signed legislation raising **federal minimum wage** from 40¢ an hour to 75¢. **Arthur Miller**'s *Death of a Salesman* opened on Broadway.

1950 Masked bandits robbed **Brink's, Inc.**, Boston express office, Jan. 17, of $2.8 mil. Case solved 1956; eight sentenced to life. Pres. Truman authorized production of **H-bomb** Jan. 31. Special Senate committee to investigate organized crime established May 3, chaired by Sen. **Estes Kefauver** (D, TN).

North Korean forces **invaded South Korea** June 25. UN asked for troops to restore peace. Pres. Truman ordered Air Force and Navy to Korea June 27. Truman approved ground forces, airstrikes against North Korea June 30. U.S. sent

35 military advisers to **South Vietnam** June 27 and agreed to aid anti-Communist government. U.S. forces landed at **Inchon**, South Korea, Sept. 15. UN forces took Pyongyang Oct. 20, reached China border Nov. 20. China sent troops across border Nov. 26. U.S. banned shipments Dec. 8 to **Communist China** and to Asiatic ports trading with it.

Army **seized all U.S. railroads** Aug. 27 on Truman's order to prevent general strike; returned to owners in 1952. Two members of **Puerto Rican nationalist movement** tried to kill Pres. Truman Nov. 1.

Peanuts comic strip appeared in newspapers. Variety show *Your Show of Shows* debuted on TV. David Riesman's *The Lonely Crowd* published.

1951 **22nd Amendment**, limiting presidential term of office, ratified Feb. 27. **Julius Rosenberg**; his wife, **Ethel Rosenberg**; and **Morton Sobell** found guilty Mar. 29 of conspiracy to commit wartime espionage. Rosenbergs received death penalty. Sobell sentenced to 30 years; released 1969.

Pres. Truman removed Gen. **Douglas MacArthur** from Korea command Apr. 11 for unauthorized policy statements. **Korea cease-fire** talks began in July; lasted two years. Fighting ended July 27, 1953.

Transcontinental TV began Sept. 4 with Pres. Truman's address at Japanese Peace Treaty Conference in San Francisco. **Japanese peace treaty** signed in San Francisco Sept. 8 by U.S., Japan, and 47 other nations. **J. D. Salinger**'s *Catcher in the Rye* published. *I Love Lucy* sitcom premiered on TV.

1952 Pres. Truman ordered seizure of nation's **steel mills** Apr. 8 to avert strike; ruled illegal by Supreme Court June 2. **Peace contract** between West Germany, U.S., Great Britain, and France signed May 26. **Immigration** measure, passed over veto June 26-27, barred those deemed subversive and removed some barriers to Asian immigration, though quotas remained for nationalities and regions. **Puerto Rico** proclaimed commonwealth July 25, after referendum Mar. 3. Richard Nixon, as vice-pres. candidate, gave **"Checkers" speech**, so called because of sentimental reference to his dog Checkers, Sept. 23. **First hydrogen device explosion** Nov. 1 in Pacific. **Ralph Ellison**'s *Invisible Man* published.

1953 Federal jury in New York convicted 13 **Communist** leaders on conspiracy charges, Jan. 20. **Julius and Ethel Rosenberg** executed in electric chair, June 19, for relaying nuclear secrets to Soviet Union. **Korean War armistice** signed July 27. California Gov. **Earl Warren** sworn in Oct. 5 as 14th chief justice of U.S. Supreme Court.

1954 *Nautilus*, **first atomic-powered submarine**, launched at Groton, CT, Jan. 21. Five members of Congress were wounded in the House Mar. 1 by four **Puerto Rican independence supporters** who fired at random from a spectators' gallery.

At televised hearings, Apr. 22-June 17, before a Senate subcommittee, Army officials accused Sen. **Joseph McCarthy** (R, WI) of seeking preferential treatment for a draftee, and McCarthy accused Army of hindering probe of Communist infiltration. McCarthy was cleared in the hearings, but the Senate later voted to condemn him, 67-22, for abuse of the Senate during hearings and debates.

Supreme Court ruled unanimously May 17 that racial segregation in public schools was unconstitutional, in *Brown v.*

Board of Education of Topeka. **Ernest Hemingway** won Nobel Prize in literature.

1955 U.S. agreed Feb. 12 to help train **South Vietnamese army**. Supreme Court ordered "all deliberate speed" in **integration** of public schools, May 31. A summit meeting of leaders of **Big 4**—U.S., Britain, France, and USSR—took place July 18-23 in Geneva, Switzerland.

Rosa Parks refused Dec. 1 to give her seat to white man on bus in Montgomery, AL. Her arrest, detention, and conviction provided catalyst for Black community's planned boycott, fronted by Rev. **Martin Luther King Jr.**, of Montgomery's bus system, Dec. 5, 1955-Dec. 20, 1956. Bus segregation ordinance declared unconstitutional by federal court in 1956.

America's two largest labor organizations merged Dec. 5, creating **AFL-CIO**. Russian-born U.S. citizen **Vladimir Nabokov**'s *Lolita* published.

1956 Massive resistance to Supreme Court **desegregation rulings** was called for Mar. 12 by 101 Southern congressmen. U.S. Supreme Court, Apr. 23, unanimously ruled against **racial segregation** on intrastate buses.

Federal-Aid Highway Act signed June 29, creating **interstate highway system**. **First transatlantic telephone cable** activated Sept. 25. In Game 5, Oct. 8, Yankee right-hander Don Larsen pitched **only perfect World Series game**. **Eugene O'Neill**'s *Long Day's Journey Into Night* opened Nov. 7 on Broadway.

1957 Congress approved **Civil Rights Act of 1957**, Apr. 29, first such bill since Reconstruction to protect voting rights. Pres. **Dwight D. Eisenhower** signed act into law Sept. 9; provided for creation of Civil Rights Commission. The U.S. surgeon general July 12 said studies showed "direct link" between cigarette **smoking and lung cancer**.

Arkansas Gov. Orval Faubus (D) called National Guard Sept. 4 to bar nine Black students from entering all-white high school in **Little Rock**. Faubus complied Sept. 21 with federal court order to remove Guard, but local authorities ordered Black students to withdraw. Pres. Eisenhower sent troops Sept. 24 to enforce court order.

Jack Kerouac's *On the Road* published.

1958 Army launched **first U.S. Earth-orbiting satellite**, *Explorer I*, Jan. 31 from Cape Canaveral, FL; discovered Van Allen radiation belt. U.S. Marines sent to **Lebanon** to protect elected government from threatened overthrow July-Oct. Nuclear sub *Nautilus* made **first undersea crossing of North Pole** Aug. 5. Presidential aide **Sherman Adams** resigned Sept. 22 over scandal involving alleged improper gifts. **First domestic jet airline passenger service** in U.S. opened by National Airlines Dec. 10 between New York and Miami.

1959 Alaska admitted as 49th state, Jan. 3; Hawaii admitted as 50th, Aug. 21. **St. Lawrence Seaway** linking Atlantic Ocean and Great Lakes opened to traffic, Apr. 25.

Vice Pres. Richard Nixon, on tour of USSR, held **"kitchen debate,"** July 24, with Soviet Prem. Nikita Khrushchev at U.S. exhibit in Moscow. Prem. **Khrushchev** paid unprecedented visit to U.S. Sept. 15-27; made transcontinental tour.

Pres. Eisenhower issued injunction Oct. 12, upheld and made effective by Supreme Court Nov. 7, ending record **116-day steel strike**. In quiz show scandal, Columbia Univ. Prof. Charles Van Doren admitted to U.S. House subcommittee Nov. 2 that he had been coached before appearances on NBC-TV's *21* in 1956; he had won $129,000. William Wyler's *Ben-Hur* released; the movie won a record 11 Academy Awards the following year.

1960 **Sit-ins** began Feb. 1 when four Black college students in Greensboro, NC, refused to move from a Woolworth lunch counter after being denied service. By Sept. 1961, more than 70,000 students had participated in sit-ins. Pres. Eisenhower signed **Civil Rights Act** May 6.

A U.S. **U-2 reconnaissance plane** was shot down in the Soviet Union May 1; pilot Gary Powers captured. The incident led to cancellation of Paris summit conference; Powers traded for Soviet spy, 1962. A **birth control pill** approved as safe for first time by Food and Drug Administration May 9. Vice Pres. **Richard Nixon** and Sen. **John F. Kennedy** faced each other Sept. 26 in first in series of televised debates. Kennedy defeated Nixon to win presidency, Nov. 8. U.S. announced Dec. 15 its backing of rightist group in **Laos**, which took power the next day.

Alfred Hitchcock film *Psycho* released.

1951: Construction is completed on the original Levittown development, creating a new template for mass produced, single-family suburban homes.

1960: Student-led sit-in actions against racial segregation at lunch counters gain traction as nonviolent displays of protest.

1961 U.S. severed diplomatic and consular relations with Cuba Jan. 3, after disputes over nationalizations of U.S. firms, U.S. military presence at Guantánamo base. U.S.-directed invasion of Cuba's **Bay of Pigs** Apr. 17 by Cuban exiles unsuccessfully attempted to overthrow the regime of Prem. Fidel Castro.

Peace Corps created by executive order, Mar. 1. **23rd Amendment**, giving DC citizens the right to vote in presidential elections, ratified Mar. 29. Alan B. Shepard Jr. rocketed from Cape Canaveral, FL, in a Mercury capsule May 5, in **first U.S.-crewed suborbital space flight.**

"Freedom Rides" from Washington, DC, across Deep South were launched May 20 to protest segregation in interstate transportation.

Joseph Heller's *Catch-22* published.

1962 Pres. Kennedy said Feb. 14 that U.S. military advisers in **Vietnam** would fire if fired upon. Lt. Col. John H. Glenn Jr. became **first American in orbit** Feb. 20 when he circled the Earth three times in the Mercury capsule *Friendship 7*.

In *Baker v. Carr*, Mar. 26, U.S. Supreme Court ruled that constitutional challenges to unequal distribution of voters among legislative districts could be resolved by federal courts. **James Meredith** became first Black student at Univ. of Mississippi Oct. 1 after 3,000 federal troops put down riots.

A Soviet **offensive missile buildup** in Cuba was revealed Oct. 22 by Pres. Kennedy, who ordered naval and air quarantine on shipment of offensive military equipment to the island. He and Soviet Prem. Khrushchev agreed Oct. 28 on formula to end crisis. Kennedy announced Nov. 2 that missile bases in Cuba were being dismantled. **Rachel Carson**'s *Silent Spring* launched environmentalist movement.

1963 In *Gideon v. Wainwright*, Mar. 18, Supreme Court ruled that all criminal defendants have a right to counsel.

March for civil rights began May 2 in Birmingham, AL; led to desegregation accord, which in turn sparked rioting and violence. Univ. of Alabama **desegregated** after Gov. George Wallace stepped aside when confronted by federally deployed National Guard troops June 11. Civil rights leader **Medgar Evers** assassinated June 12. On Aug. 28, 200,000 joined in **March on Washington** in support of Black demands for equal rights led by **Rev. Martin Luther King Jr.**; highlight was King's **"I Have a Dream" speech**.

Supreme Court ruled June 17 that laws requiring **recitation of Lord's Prayer or Bible verses** in public schools were unconstitutional. Pres. Kennedy, on Europe trip, addressed huge crowd in **West Berlin**, June 23. **Limited nuclear test-ban treaty** agreed upon July 25 by the U.S., the Soviet Union, and Britain. Four Black girls killed in bombing of **16th St. Baptist Church** in Birmingham, AL, Sept. 15.

South Vietnam Pres. **Ngo Dinh Diem** assassinated Nov. 2; U.S. had earlier withdrawn support. Pres. **Kennedy** shot and fatally wounded Nov. 22 as he rode in motorcade through downtown Dallas, TX. Vice Pres. **Lyndon B. Johnson** sworn in as president. **Lee Harvey Oswald** arrested and charged with murder but was himself shot and fatally wounded Nov. 24. Nightclub owner **Jack Ruby** convicted of Oswald's murder; Ruby died in 1967 while awaiting retrial following reversal of his conviction. **Betty Friedan**'s feminist work *The Feminine Mystique* published.

1964 **Panama** suspended relations with U.S. Jan. 9 after riots. U.S. offered Dec. 18 to negotiate new canal treaty. **The Beatles** appeared Feb. 9 on *The Ed Sullivan Show*. Supreme Court ruled Feb. 17 that **congressional districts** as near as practicable be equal in population. U.S. reported May 27 it was sending military planes to **Laos**.

Three **civil rights workers** reported missing in Mississippi June 22; bodies found Aug. 4. Eighteen white men tried. On Oct. 20, 1967, an all-white federal jury convicted seven of conspiracy in the slayings. Omnibus **civil rights bill** signed by Pres. Johnson July 2, banning discrimination in voting, jobs, public accommodations.

Congress Aug. 7 passed **Tonkin Gulf Resolution**, authorizing presidential action in Vietnam, after North Vietnamese boats reportedly attacked U.S. destroyers Aug. 2. (Resolution repealed, 1971.) Congress approved War on Poverty bill Aug. 11, providing for a domestic Peace Corps (**VISTA**), **Job Corps**, and antipoverty funding. The **Warren Commission** released a report Sept. 27 concluding that Lee Harvey Oswald was solely responsible for the Kennedy assassination. Pres. **Johnson** elected to full term, Nov. 3, defeating Sen. **Barry Goldwater** (R, AZ) in landslide. **Verrazzano-Narrows Bridge** opened in New York City, Nov. 21, with world's then-longest suspension span.

1965 In State of the Union address Jan. 4, Pres. Johnson outlined plans for **"Great Society,"** program of civil rights, antipoverty, and health-care legislation. Johnson in Feb. ordered continuous bombing of **North Vietnam** below 20th parallel.

Malcolm X assassinated by Nation of Islam members Feb. 21 at New York City rally. March from **Selma to Montgomery**, AL, Mar. 21-25, by Rev. Martin Luther King Jr. to demand federal protection of voting rights for Black citizens. Some 14,000 U.S. troops sent to **Dominican Republic** during civil war Apr. 28. All troops withdrawn by next year. Bill establishing **Medicare**, government health insurance program for elderly, signed by Pres. Johnson July 30.

New **Voting Rights Act**, which banned literacy tests and other voter qualification tests, signed Aug. 6. Arrest of Black motorist by white police officers precipitated **Watts riot** in predominantly Black Los Angeles neighborhood Aug. 11-16. Riots resulted in 34 deaths and $200 mil in property damage.

Major **immigration law**, signed Oct. 3, replaced national quota system with emphasis on immigrants' skills and family unification. **Electric power failure** blacked out most of northeastern U.S., parts of two Canadian provinces the night of Nov. 9-10.

1966 U.S. forces began firing into **Cambodia** May 1. Bombing of **Hanoi** area of North Vietnam by U.S. planes began June 29. By Dec. 31, 385,300 U.S. troops were stationed in South Vietnam, plus 60,000 offshore and 33,000 in Thailand.

Supreme Court ruled June 13, in *Miranda v. Arizona*, that suspects must be read their rights before police questioning. Medicare began July 1. In **Univ. of Texas shooting** rampage, 25-year-old student Charles Whitman killed 15 and wounded 31 from tower observation deck on Austin campus, Aug. 1; shot dead by police.

Dept. of Transportation created, Oct. 15. Edward Brooke (R, MA) elected Nov. 8 as first Black U.S. senator in 85 years. Robert C. Weaver named secretary of newly created Dept. of Housing and Urban Development, becoming **first Black cabinet member**.

1967 Green Bay Packers beat Kansas City Chiefs, 35-10, in **first Super Bowl**, Jan. 15, in Los Angeles. Three astronauts died Jan. 27 in *Apollo 1* fire on ground at Cape Canaveral, FL. **25th Amendment**, providing for presidential succession, ratified Feb. 10. Pres. Johnson and Soviet Prem. **Aleksei Kosygin** met June 23 and 25 at Glassboro State College in New Jersey; agreed not to let any crisis push them into war.

Riots erupted among residents of predominantly Black **Newark**, NJ, July 12-17; 26 killed, 1,500 injured, more than 1,000 arrested. In **Detroit**, MI, July 23-30, 43 died, 2,000 injured; 5,000 left homeless by rioting, looting, and burning in city's Black neighborhoods. **Thurgood Marshall** sworn in Oct. 2 as first Black U.S. Supreme Court justice. **Antiwar march** on Washington, DC, Oct. 21-22, drew at least 70,000 participants. Carl B. Stokes (D, Cleveland) and Richard G. Hatcher (D, Gary, IN) elected **first Black mayors** of major U.S. cities Nov. 7.

1968 In **"Tet offensive,"** Communist troops attacked several provincial capitals and other major cities, including Saigon, Jan. 30, but suffered heavy casualties. Pres. Johnson **curbed bombing** of North Vietnam Mar. 31. Peace talks began in Paris May 10. All bombing of North halted Oct. 31.

Rev. **Martin Luther King Jr.** assassinated Apr. 4 in Memphis, TN. **James Earl Ray**, an escaped convict, pleaded guilty to slaying, was sentenced to 99 years. Students at **Columbia Univ.**, Apr. 23-24, seized school buildings in protest against school's involvement in military research, among other issues. Sen. **Robert F. Kennedy** (D, NY) shot June 5 in Los Angeles after celebrating presidential primary victories, died June 6. **Sirhan Sirhan** convicted of murder, 1969; death sentence commuted to life in prison, 1972.

Vice Pres. Hubert Humphrey nominated for president at **Democratic National Convention** in Chicago, marked by clash between police and antiwar protesters, Aug. 26-29. Republican nominee **Richard Nixon** won presidency, defeating Humphrey in close race Nov. 5.

Apollo 8 **orbited moon** in five-day mission, Dec. 21-27. North Korea released 82-man crew of the USS *Pueblo* Dec. 22, 11 months after seizing the ship in Sea of Japan; one crew member had been killed in battle.

1969 Expanded four-party **Vietnam peace talks** began Jan. 18. U.S. force peaked at 543,400 in Apr.; withdrawal started July 8. Pres. Nixon set Vietnamization policy of expanding role of South Vietnamese forces Nov. 3. Earl Warren retired upon swearing in **Warren Burger**, June 23, as Supreme Court chief justice. In incident that marked birth of **gay rights** movement, police clashed with patrons of gay bar, the **Stonewall Inn**, in New York City June 28.

U.S. astronaut **Neil Armstrong**, commander of the *Apollo 11* mission, became the **first person to set foot on the moon**, July 20, followed by astronaut **Edwin "Buzz" Aldrin**. Astronaut **Michael Collins** remained aboard command module.

Woodstock rock music festival near Bethel, NY, drew 400,000 people, Aug. 15-18. **Anti-Vietnam War demonstrations** held in cities across the U.S., marking Vietnam Moratorium day, Oct. 15; on Nov. 12, some 250,000 marched in Washington, DC. Massacre of hundreds of civilians by U.S. troops at **My Lai**, South Vietnam, in 1968 reported Nov. 16. **Kurt Vonnegut**'s *Slaughterhouse Five* published. *Sesame Street* launched on public TV.

1970 A federal jury Feb. 18 found the **"Chicago 7"** antiwar activists not guilty of conspiring to incite riots during 1968 Democratic National Convention. However, five were convicted of crossing state lines with intent to incite riots.

Three astronauts safely returned to Earth Apr. 17 after oxygen tank on *Apollo 13* ruptured. Lunar landing had been canceled. Millions of Americans participated in antipollution demonstrations Apr. 22 to mark **first Earth Day**.

U.S. and South Vietnamese forces crossed **Cambodian** borders Apr. 30 to get at enemy bases. Four students killed May 4 at **Kent State Univ.** in Ohio by National Guardsmen during war protest. In protest at **Jackson State Univ.** in Mississippi, two killed when police fired on protesters.

First female U.S. generals appointed June 11. **Postal reform** measure signed Aug. 12 created an independent U.S. Postal Service. Pres. Nixon, Dec. 31, signed **clean air bill** calling for development of cleaner auto engine and national air quality standards for 10 major pollutants. Garry Trudeau's *Doonesbury* comic strip launched in 30 papers.

1971 **Charles Manson** and three of his cult followers found guilty Jan. 25 of first-degree murder in 1969 slaying of actress Sharon Tate and six others. A court-martial jury Mar. 29 convicted Lt. **William Calley** in murder of 22 South Vietnamese at **My Lai** on Mar. 16, 1968. He was sentenced to life in prison Mar. 31, later reduced to 20 years.

Pres. Nixon, Apr. 14, relaxed 20-year **trade embargo with China**. *New York Times* began publishing June 13 classified **Pentagon Papers**, a secret Pentagon study on U.S. involvement in Vietnam leaked by Daniel Ellsberg, military analyst consulting for government. Supreme Court June 30 upheld, 6-3, right to publish the documents. **26th Amendment**, lowering the minimum voting age to 18, ratified June 30. Pres. Nixon, Aug. 15, instituted 90-day **wage and price freeze**.

1969: *Apollo 11* **lands on the lunar surface; Neil Armstrong and Edwin "Buzz" Aldrin are first humans to walk on the moon.**

U.S. bombers initiated massive five-day strike Dec. 26 in North Vietnam in retaliation for alleged violations of agreements reached prior to 1968 bombing halt.

1972 Pres. Nixon arrived in **Beijing** Feb. 21 for eight-day visit to China, in "journey for peace." Joint communiqué released Feb. 27 called for increased Sino-U.S. contacts. Senate, Mar. 22, approved **Equal Rights Amendment** banning discrimination on basis of sex; sent measure to states for ratification.

North Vietnamese forces launched biggest attacks in four years across the demilitarized zone Mar. 30. The U.S. responded Apr. 15 with **resumption of bombing** of Hanoi and Haiphong. Pres. Nixon announced May 8 the mining of North Vietnam ports.

Gov. **George C. Wallace** (D, AL), campaigning for president at Laurel, MD, shopping center May 15, shot and seriously wounded. **Arthur Bremer** convicted Aug. 4, sentenced to 63 years for shooting Wallace and three others. In **first visit of U.S. president to Moscow**, Pres. Nixon arrived May 22 for summit talks with Kremlin leaders that culminated in landmark strategic arms pact (**SALT I**). Five men arrested June 17 for breaking into Democratic National Committee offices in **Watergate** office complex in Washington, DC. U.S. Supreme Court in *Furman v. Georgia* June 29 ruled **capital punishment** as practiced was unconstitutional.

Mark Spitz won seven gold medals in world record times at the Munich Olympics in Aug.-Sept.

Last U.S. combat troops left Vietnam Aug. 11. Pres. **Nixon** reelected Nov. 7 in landslide, carrying 49 states to defeat Sen. George McGovern (D, SD). Three astronauts, part of *Apollo 17*, made 6th and last lunar landing on Dec. 11. Full-scale **bombing of North Vietnam** resumed after Paris peace negotiations reached impasse Dec. 18.

The Godfather, directed by Francis Ford Coppola, is released.

1973 In *Roe v. Wade*, Supreme Court ruled, 7-2, Jan. 22, fetus not a person with constitutional rights and that right to privacy protected woman's decision to have abortion; states may not ban abortions during first three months of pregnancy but may regulate, not ban, abortions during second trimester.

Four-party **Vietnam peace pacts** signed in Paris Jan. 27. **End of military draft** announced on same day. Last U.S. troops left Vietnam Mar. 29. North Vietnam released some 590 U.S. prisoners by Apr. 1. Pres. Nixon announced, Apr. 30, resignation of top Nixon aides H. R. Haldeman and John Ehrlichman and firing of White House Counsel **John Dean** as a consequence of the widening **Watergate** scandal. Dean told Senate hearings June 25 that Nixon, his aides, and Justice Dept. had conspired to cover up Watergate facts. The U.S.

officially ceased bombing in **Cambodia** at midnight Aug. 14 in accord with June congressional action.

Vice Pres. **Spiro Agnew**, Oct. 10, resigned and pleaded no contest to charge of tax evasion while Maryland governor. **Gerald R. Ford**, Oct. 12, became **first appointed vice president** under 25th Amendment; sworn in Dec. 6. The **"Saturday Night Massacre"** occurred Oct. 20, when Pres. Nixon ordered Atty. Gen. Elliot Richardson to fire Watergate special prosecutor **Archibald Cox**, who had sought handover of Nixon's subpoenaed **White House tapes**. Richardson refused to comply and resigned; Dep. Atty. Gen. William Ruckelshaus refused and was fired. Solicitor Gen. Robert Bork, as acting atty. gen., then fired Cox. Nixon administration named **Leon Jaworski**, Nov. 1, to succeed Cox.

Skylab, **first U.S. space station**, launched May 14. **Secretariat** became first Triple Crown winner since Citation in 1948 by winning Belmont Stakes June 9 in record time. **Billie Jean King** defeated Bobby Riggs in three straight sets in tennis's nationally televised "Battle of the Sexes," Sept. 20. Total **ban on oil exports** to U.S. imposed by Arab oil-producing nations Oct. 19-21 after outbreak of an Arab-Israeli war; lifted Mar. 1974. Congress overrode Nov. 7 Pres. Nixon's veto of **war powers bill** curbing president's power to commit forces to hostilities abroad without congressional approval.

1974 On Apr. 8, **Hank Aaron** of the Atlanta Braves hit his 715th career home run to break Babe Ruth's record.

House Judiciary Committee opened **impeachment** hearings May 9 against Pres. Nixon. John Ehrlichman and three **White House "plumbers"** found guilty July 12 of conspiring to violate the civil rights of the psychiatrist of **Pentagon Papers** leaker Daniel Ellsberg by breaking into psychiatrist's office. Supreme Court ruled, 8-0, July 24 that Pres. Nixon had to turn over 64 **audio tapes of White House conversations**. House Judiciary Committee, in televised hearings July 24-30, recommended **articles of impeachment** against Pres. Nixon, involving conspiracy to obstruct justice in Watergate cover-up, abuses of power, and defiance of committee subpoenas.

Pres. **Nixon** announced his **resignation**, Aug. 8, and stepped down the next day. His support in Congress had begun to collapse Aug. 5 after release of tapes appearing to implicate him in Watergate cover-up. Vice Pres. **Ford** sworn in Aug. 9 as 38th U.S. president. Pres. Ford, Aug. 20, nominated **Nelson Rockefeller** to be vice president; Rockefeller sworn in Dec. 10. Citing need to move on, Pres. Ford, Sept. 8, issued

1974: Pres. Richard Nixon resigns from office and departs the White House.

pardon to Nixon for any federal crimes he committed while president.

New York Times published article Dec. 22 on CIA engagement in illegal domestic surveillance. Reports of other apparently illegal CIA activities, recorded in **"family jewels"** file kept by the CIA, leaked out over the years.

1975 Former Atty. Gen. John Mitchell and ex-presidential advisers H. R. Haldeman and John Ehrlichman found guilty Jan. 1 of **Watergate cover-up** charges. Mitchell released 1979, last of 25 jailed over scandal to leave prison.

Bill Gates and Paul Allen founded Microsoft, Apr. 4. U.S. launched **evacuation from Saigon** of Americans and some South Vietnamese Apr. 29 as Communist forces completed takeover of South Vietnam; **South Vietnamese** government officially surrendered Apr. 30. U.S. merchant ship *Mayaguez* and its crew of 39 seized by Cambodian forces in Gulf of Siam May 12. In rescue operation, U.S. Marines attacked Koh Tang Island, recovered ship and crew but inadvertently left three Marines behind. Congress voted $405 mil for **South Vietnam refugees** May 16; 140,000 flown to U.S.

Publishing heiress **Patricia (Patty) Hearst**, kidnapped Feb. 5, 1974, by Symbionese Liberation Army (SLA), captured in San Francisco Sept. 18 with other militants. She was convicted Mar. 20, 1976, of bank robbery.

1976 In **right-to-die** case, New Jersey Supreme Court, Mar. 31, allowed comatose Karen Ann Quinlan to be removed from respirator; she survived until 1985. U.S. Supreme Court reinstated **death penalty**, July 2, subject to conditions.

U.S. celebrated **200th anniversary of independence** July 4 with festivals, parades, and New York City's Operation Sail, gathering of tall ships from around the world. **"Legionnaire's disease"** killed 29 people who attended American Legion convention July 21-24 in Philadelphia.

Viking 1 made successful landing on Mars, July 20. Two U.S. officers on routine mission near DMZ slain by **North Korean soldiers** Aug. 18; North Korea stated "regret."

1977 Convicted murderer Gary Gilmore executed by Utah firing squad Jan. 17; **first use of capital punishment** in U.S. since 1967. Pres. Jimmy Carter Jan. 21 pardoned most Vietnam War **draft evaders**.

Natural gas shortage caused by severe winter weather led Congress Feb. 2 to approve emergency gas bill temporarily authorizing reallocation from surplus areas. Pres. Carter signed act Aug. 4 creating new cabinet-level **Energy Dept.** FBI Dec. 7 released 40,000 pages of previously secret files relating to **Kennedy assassination**.

George Lucas's first *Star Wars* film released.

1978 Senate voted Apr. 18 to turn over **Panama Canal** to Panama on Dec. 31, 1999; Mar. 16 vote had given approval to treaty guaranteeing area's neutrality after the year 2000. Californians, June 6, approved **Proposition 13**, state constitutional amendment slashing property taxes.

Supreme Court, June 28, ruled that while race could be a factor in admission to institutions of higher education, **numerical quotas** could not be used.

Egyptian Pres. **Anwar al-Sadat** and Israeli Prem. **Menachem Begin** reached accord on "framework for peace," Sept. 17, after Pres. Carter-mediated talks at **Camp David**. A mass murder-suicide, mostly by poisoning, kills more than 900 American members of the **Peoples Temple** cult led by Jim Jones in Guyana Nov. 18, 1978.

1979 Partial meltdown released radioactive material Mar. 28 at nuclear reactor on **Three Mile Island** near Middletown, PA. American Airlines DC-10 **jetliner crashed** May 25 after losing an engine following takeoff from Chicago, killing 275 people.

In speech July 15, Pres. Carter spoke of national "crisis of confidence" and outlined proposed 10-year, $140-bil program to reduce **dependence on foreign oil**. Militant followers of **Ayatollah Khomeini** took hostage some 90 people, including 66 Americans, Nov. 4 at **American embassy in Tehran**, Iran. Khomeini demanded return of ailing former Shah Muhammad Reza Pahlavi to stand trial.

1980 Pres. Carter announced, Jan. 4, economic **sanctions against USSR** in retaliation for Soviet invasion of Afghanistan. At his request, U.S. Olympic Committee voted, Apr. 12, against U.S. participation in **Moscow Summer Olympics**. At **Winter Olympics** in Lake Placid, NY, U.S. hockey team

1981: Minutes after Pres. Ronald Reagan's inauguration, 52 American hostages held for 14.5 months in Iran arrive back in the U.S.

defeated Russian team Feb. 22, en route to gold medal in **"miracle on ice."**

Eight Americans were killed, Apr. 24, in **attempt to rescue hostages** held by Iranian militants. **Mt. St. Helens**, in Washington state, erupted May 18; the blast and later ones left 57 dead.

In sweeping victory, Nov. 4, **Ronald Reagan (R)** was elected president, defeating incumbent Pres. Carter. Former Beatle **John Lennon** was shot and killed by Mark David Chapman, Dec. 8, in New York City.

1981 Minutes after Reagan's inauguration Jan. 20, 52 **American hostages in Iran** were freed, after being held 444 days. Pres. **Reagan** was shot and seriously wounded, Mar. 30, in Washington, DC, along with a Secret Service agent, a police officer, and Press Sec. **James Brady**. John W. Hinckley Jr. was arrested, found not guilty by reason of insanity, and committed (released in 2016).

World's **first reusable spacecraft**, space shuttle *Columbia*, sent into space, Apr. 12. U.S. Centers for Disease Control, June 5, reported first cases of what became known as **AIDS**. **Air controllers** went on strike Aug. 3; most were fired by Reagan after defying back-to-work order. Reagan, Aug. 13, signed **tax-cut legislation** expected to save taxpayers $750 bil over five years. The Senate, Sept. 21, confirmed **Sandra Day O'Connor**, 99-0, as **first female Supreme Court justice**.

1982 **Equal Rights Amendment** was defeated when ratification deadline passed June 30 with support from only 35 of the 38 states needed. The economy showed signs of recovery from a **recession** that began in mid-1981, as the Dow Jones industrial average, Oct. 13, hit highest level in 18 months.

NFL strike ended Nov. 16 after 57 days, with $1.6-bil pact. **Michael Jackson's** album *Thriller* was released Nov. 30. **Dr. Barney Clark** became **first permanent artificial heart recipient**, Dec. 2.

1983 Pres. Reagan, Jan. 3, declared **Times Beach**, MO, a federal disaster area because of toxic **dioxin** in soil, prompting town's closure. **Harold Washington** (D) was elected Apr. 12 as **first Black mayor of Chicago**. On Apr. 20, Reagan signed bipartisan bill designed to save **Social Security** from bankruptcy.

Sally Ride became **first American woman to travel in space**, with launch June 18 of space shuttle *Challenger*. On Sept. 1, a **South Korean passenger jet** in Soviet air space was apparently misidentified and shot down; 269 people, including 61 Americans, killed. On Oct. 23, 241 U.S. service members were killed when a **suicide truck bomb** blew up Marine barracks in **Lebanon**. U.S. troops, with small force from six Caribbean nations, invaded **Grenada** Oct. 25; deposed Marxist regime.

1984 Seven regional companies took over local telephone service from **AT&T**, Jan. 1. On May 7, Vietnam War veterans reached $180-mil settlement with chemical companies in suit over the herbicide **Agent Orange**.

Former Vice Pres. **Walter Mondale** won Democratic presidential nomination, June 6. He chose Rep. **Geraldine Ferraro**

(D, NY) as vice presidential candidate; first woman nominated to that post by a major party. Pres. Reagan signed bill July 17 cutting federal transportation aid to states that keep their **drinking age** under 21. **Reagan** was reelected Nov. 6 in Republican landslide, carrying 49 states for record 525 electoral votes.

1985 First international **AIDS conference** met in Atlanta, GA, Apr. 15-17. Philadelphia police bombed row house occupied by **MOVE radical group**, May 13; 11 killed, some 60 homes destroyed. On June 14, **terrorists seized TWA jet** after take-off from Athens, Greece, with 153 aboard; 39 Americans held hostage for 17 days; one U.S. service member killed.

Reversing a highly unpopular decision, **Coca-Cola** said, July 10, it would resume marketing soda made under its original "Classic" formula. **Live Aid** rock concert, broadcast around the world July 13, raised $70 mil for **famine relief** in Ethiopia. On Oct. 7, four **Palestinian hijackers** seized Italian cruise ship *Achille Lauro* in the Mediterranean for two days; one American was killed. U.S. and Soviet leaders met at **summit in Geneva**, Nov. 19-20. **General Electric** agreed Dec. 11 to buy RCA Corp.

1986 U.S. officially observed **Martin Luther King Jr. Day** for first time, Jan. 20. Space shuttle *Challenger* exploded 73 seconds after liftoff, Jan. 28, killing six astronauts and teacher **Christa McAuliffe**. **Robert Penn Warren** named America's **first poet laureate**, Feb . 26.

The Senate, Sept. 17, confirmed **William Rehnquist** as Supreme Court chief justice (65-33) and **Antonin Scalia** as associate justice (98-0). Congress completed action Oct. 2 to override a Reagan veto and place economic sanctions on **South Africa**. On Nov. 3, news broke of the **Iran-Contra scandal**, involving secret U.S. sale of arms to Iran and diversion of proceeds to support anti-Communist "Contra" insurgents in Nicaragua.

Pres. Reagan, Nov. 7, signed measure giving legal status to some 2.7 mil **undocumented immigrants** who had applied for amnesty. In plea deal, financier **Ivan Boesky**, Nov. 14, agreed to pay $100 mil and serve time in prison for **insider trading**.

1987 Pres. Reagan produced nation's **first trillion-dollar budget**, Jan. 5. FDA, Mar. 20, approved AZT—first drug shown to be effective in fight against **AIDS**.

Senate and House committees held joint televised hearings, May 5-Aug. 3, investigating **Iran-Contra affair**; Pres. Reagan in speech to nation, Aug. 12, denied knowing of diversion of funds to Contras. An **Iraqi missile** killed 37 sailors on the **USS Stark** in the Persian Gulf, May 17; Iraq called it an accident.

Dow industrial average fell 508 points Oct. 19, ending bull market that began mid-1982. Pres. Reagan and Soviet leader **Mikhail Gorbachev**, Dec. 8, signed pact to dismantle all 1,752 U.S. and 859 Soviet intermediate- and shorter-range missiles.

1988 *Phantom of the Opera* opened Jan. 26; became longest-running Broadway show ever. In report issued May 16, Surgeon Gen. **C. Everett Koop** declared cigarettes addictive. U.S. missile fired from Navy warship *Vincennes* in the Persian Gulf mistakenly struck a commercial **Iranian airliner**, July 3, killing all 290 aboard.

George H. W. Bush (R) was elected president, Nov. 8, decisively defeating Massachusetts Gov. **Michael Dukakis** (D). **Pan Am Flight 103** exploded over **Lockerbie**, Scotland, due to terrorist bomb, Dec. 21; 270 killed, including 11 on the ground. Investment firm **Drexel Burnham Lambert** agreed, Dec. 21, to plead guilty to **insider trading** and other violations, and pay penalties of $650 mil.

U.S. suffered widespread **drought** conditions, the worst in over 50 years.

1989 Major oil spill occurred when *Exxon Valdez* struck Bligh Reef in Alaska's Prince William Sound, Mar. 24. Former National Security Council staffer **Oliver North** was convicted, May 4, on charges related to **Iran-Contra scandal** (overturned in 1991). TV sitcom *Seinfeld* premiered July 5 on NBC.

Pres. Bush signed $125 bil bailout measure, Aug. 9, to rescue **savings and loan industry**. Baseball legend Pete Rose **banned** from game for life Aug. 24 for involvement with gamblers. **Hurricane Hugo** swept through the Caribbean and SE U.S. in Sept.; caused at least 86 deaths and billions

1989: The **Exxon Valdez** oil spill causes environmental devastation in Alaska's Prince William Sound.

in property damages. Army Gen. **Colin Powell**, Oct. 1, became first Black chairman of **Joint Chiefs of Staff**. An earthquake struck **San Francisco Bay** area just before a World Series game, Oct. 17, causing 63 deaths.

U.S. troops invaded **Panama**, Dec. 20, overthrowing government of **Manuel Noriega**. Noriega surrendered to U.S. authorities; convicted and imprisoned for drug trafficking. **L. Douglas Wilder** (D) declared governor of Virginia Dec. 22, after recount; first elected Black governor in U.S.

1990 Junk bond financier **Michael Milken** pleaded guilty to fraud-related charges, Apr. 14; agreed to pay $500 mil in restitution and sentenced to 10 years in prison. U.S. fell into **recession** (July 1990-Mar. 1991). Pres. Bush signed **Americans With Disabilities Act** barring discrimination against and requiring accommodations for the disabled, July 26.

Operation Desert Shield forces left for Saudi Arabia Aug. 7, following invasion of **Kuwait** by Iraq. **David Souter** was confirmed Oct. 2 (90-9) to serve on **Supreme Court**. Bush Nov. 15 signed new **Clean Air Act**, focused on limiting urban pollution, cancer-causing emissions from industrial sources.

1991 After **Iraq** rebuffed UN resolution to withdraw from **Kuwait**, U.S., with allies, launched massive air attacks against Iraq, Jan. 16, followed by ground war; with Kuwait liberated and Iraqi resistance marked by allegations Feb. 27, declared cease-fire. About 300 coalition troops and many thousands of Iraqi troops died.

U.S. Senate, voting 52-48 on Oct. 15, confirmed nomination of **Clarence Thomas** to replace retiring Justice Thurgood Marshall, after confirmation hearings marked by allegations that Thomas had sexually harassed former aide **Anita Hill**.

1992 Trans World Airlines (**TWA**) filed for bankruptcy, Jan. 31. **Riots** swept South Central **Los Angeles** Apr. 29 after jury acquitted four white police officers on all but one count in the 1991 videotaped beating of Black motorist **Rodney King**. Death toll in L.A. violence was put at 53; two officers convicted Apr. 1993, in federal trial. **27th Amendment**, regarding congressional pay raises, ratified May 7.

Hurricane Andrew ravaged South Florida and Louisiana Aug. 24-26, causing 65 deaths. White supremacist and fugitive **Randall Weaver** surrendered Aug. 31 after 11-day FBI siege at his **Ruby Ridge**, ID, cabin, during which his wife, son, and a deputy sheriff were killed.

Bill Clinton (D) elected president, Nov. 3, defeating Pres. **Bush** and independent **Ross Perot**. A UN-sanctioned military force, led by U.S. troops, arrived in **Somalia** Dec. 9. Presidents of U.S., Canada, and Mexico Dec. 17 signed North American Free Trade Agreement (**NAFTA**), which took effect Jan. 1, 1994.

1993 A bomb exploded in garage beneath the **World Trade Center** in New York City, Feb. 26, killing six; four men found guilty of involvement (Mar. 1994, Nov. 1997). Four federal agents were killed, Feb. 28, during raid on **Branch Davidian** compound near **Waco**, TX; siege by agents ended Apr. 19 when the compound burned down, leaving over 70 cult members dead. Eleven members acquitted, Feb. 1994, in deaths of federal agents.

Janet Reno became first female U.S. attorney general, Mar. 12. **"Motor-voter"** bill was signed by Pres. Clinton,

May 20. **"Great Flood of 1993"** inundated parts of nine Midwestern states in summer, leaving about 50 dead and $15 bil in damages.

Pres. Clinton, July 2, approved closing 33 major military bases. On July 19 he announced **"don't ask, don't tell, don't pursue"** policy for homosexuals in the military (rescinded 2010). Senate, voting 96-3 on Aug. 3, confirmed nomination of **Ruth Bader Ginsburg** to Supreme Court. Clinton, Aug. 10, signed measure to reduce **federal budget deficits** by $496 bil over five years, through spending cuts and new taxes. **Brady Bill**, a major gun-control measure, signed into law Nov. 30.

1994 Predawn **earthquake** in Los Angeles area, Jan. 17, claimed 61 lives. Pres. Clinton Feb. 3 lifted 19-year ban on U.S. trade with **Vietnam**. Byron De La Beckwith was convicted Feb. 5 of 1963 murder of civil rights leader **Medgar Evers**. Longtime CIA officer **Aldrich Ames** pleaded guilty, Apr. 28, to spying for Russians; received life in prison.

U.S. troops, Mar. 25, ended aid and peacekeeping mission in **Somalia**, begun in 1992. **Kenneth Starr** was named Aug. 5 as independent counsel to probe **Whitewater** affair. MLB players went on strike following Aug. 11 games. World Series canceled; strike ended Apr. 25, 1995. Senate Majority Leader **George Mitchell** (D, ME), Sept. 26, dropped efforts to pass Pres. Clinton's **health-care reform** package.

Republicans gained control of Congress in Nov. 8 elections, after many years of Democratic control.

1995 **Newt Gingrich** (R, GA) elected U.S. House speaker. A bill to end Congress's exemption from federal labor laws, first in series of measures in Republicans' **"Contract With America,"** cleared Congress Jan. 17; signed into law Jan. 23. Pres. Clinton, Jan. 31, authorized $20-bil loan to **Mexico**. Last UN peacekeeping troops withdrew from **Somalia** Feb. 28-Mar. 3, with aid of U.S. Marines. In **Haiti**, peacekeeping responsibilities were transferred from U.S. to UN forces Mar. 31, with U.S. providing 2,400 soldiers.

Truck bomb exploded outside **Oklahoma City** federal office building Apr. 19, killing 168 people. Antigovernment extremist Timothy McVeigh was convicted as bomber;

1995: The Murrah Federal Building in Oklahoma City is targeted in the deadliest act of domestic terrorism in U.S. history.

executed June 2011; a co-conspirator convicted on related charges was sentenced to life. U.S. space shuttle *Atlantis* docked for first time with Russian space station *Mir*, June 29-July 4. The U.S. announced July 11 it was reestablishing **relations with Vietnam**.

Ten **Muslim militants** were convicted, Oct. 1, in failed plot to blow up **UN Headquarters** and assassinate political leaders. Former football star **O.J. Simpson** found not guilty Oct. 3 of June 1994 murders of his former wife and her friend. Hundreds of thousands of Black men participated in **Million Man March** in Washington, DC, Oct. 16, organized by **Louis Farrakhan**. Cumulative number of **AIDS** cases reported in the U.S. passed 500,000 by Oct. 31, with more than 310,000 deaths.

Five Americans were known killed, Nov. 13, in bombing of U.S. military post in **Riyadh, Saudi Arabia**. Budget impasse between Congress and Pres. Clinton led to partial **government shutdown** Nov. 14; operations resumed Nov. 20 under continuing resolutions. After talks outside Dayton, OH, warring parties in **Bosnia and Herzegovina** reached agreement Nov. 21 to end their conflict; U.S. sent troops to join peacekeeping force.

A 1973 federal law imposing **55-mph speed limit** was repealed Nov. 28.

1996 U.S. Senate, Jan. 26, approved, 87-4, Second Strategic Arms Reduction Treaty (**START II**) with Russia. Congress, Mar. 27-28, approved **line item veto**; struck down by Supreme Court, June 1998.

Arkansas Gov. **Jim Guy Tucker** (D) and two other Clinton associates were convicted May 28 of fraud and conspiracy in **Whitewater** case. The antitax **Freemen** surrendered to federal authorities June 13 after 81-day standoff near Jordan, MT; four were convicted, July 1998, of conspiring to defraud banks. Bomb exploded at **Khobar Towers** military complex in Saudi Arabia, June 25, killing 19 U.S. service personnel. **Pipe bomb** exploded July 27 in **Atlanta, GA**, park during **Summer Olympics**; one person killed.

Major **welfare reform** bill signed into law, Aug. 22. Defense of Marriage Act (**DOMA**), passed by wide margins and signed Sept. 21, barred federal recognition of same-sex marriages. U.S. signed **Comprehensive Test Ban Treaty**, Sept. 24, which banned all nuclear weapons tests; Senate failed to ratify treaty. Pres. **Clinton reelected**, Nov. 5, over Sen. Bob Dole (R, KS).

1997 Madeleine Albright sworn in as first woman sec. of state Jan. 23. Former CIA official Harold Nicholson pleaded guilty, Mar. 3, to **spying for Russia**. Thirty-nine members of **Heaven's Gate** religious cult found dead in Rancho Santa Fe, CA, house Mar. 26, in apparent mass suicide.

The film *Titanic* was released Dec. 14; went on to win 11 Oscars.

1998 Media outlets Jan. 21 reported evidence of sexual relationship between Pres. Clinton and former White House intern **Monica Lewinsky**. Clinton initially denied affair, but in address to the nation, Aug. 17, acknowledged relationship that was "not appropriate." On Sept. 9, independent counsel **Kenneth Starr** sent findings to House, which, Dec. 19, approved two articles of **impeachment**.

"**Unabomber**" Theodore Kaczynski, arrested in Montana in 1993, pleaded guilty Jan. 22 to bombings that killed three people; sentenced to four life terms plus 30 years. **Bombs at U.S. embassies** in Kenya and Tanzania killed at least 257, Aug. 7; U.S. launched retaliatory strikes. On Sept. 30, Pres. Clinton announced federal **budget surplus** of $70 bil for fiscal 1998, first since 1969.

Pres. Clinton, Nov. 13, agreed to pay $850,000 to **Paula Jones,** settling suit for an alleged unwanted sexual advance. Biggest U.S. **tobacco companies**, Nov. 23, agreed to pay states and territories $206 bil over 25 years to cover public health costs.

1999 *The Sopranos* TV drama debuted, Jan. 10. Pres. Clinton was acquitted, Feb. 12, in **impeachment trial**. Perjury article drew 45 votes; obstruction of justice article drew 50-50 vote, short of the needed two-thirds.

Dr. **Jack Kevorkian** convicted of second-degree murder Mar. 26 in death of terminally ill man. One man pleaded guilty Apr. 5, another convicted Nov. 4, in 1998 kidnapping and beating death of **Matthew Shepard**, an openly gay student at Univ. of Wyoming. Two teenagers killed 12 fellow students and a teacher Apr. 20 at **Columbine High School** in

Littleton, CO, then committed suicide. **John F. Kennedy Jr.** died in crash of private plane July 16.

2000 Midnight celebrations marked changeover to year 2000; feared **Y2K** computer glitch caused few problems. The first state law recognizing **same-sex civil union** was enacted in Vermont, Apr. 26. U.S. and British scientists, June 26, announced they had determined structure of the **human genome**. Six-year-old **Elián González** was returned to his father in Cuba June 28, after rescue from a refugee boat wreck in which his mother drowned.

Tiger Woods, at 24, became youngest player to win all four golf majors, July 23. FDA announced, Sept. 28, approval of **RU-486**, a pill that induces **abortion** Seventeen U.S. sailors died Oct. 12 in terrorist bombing of USS *Cole*, in Aden, Yemen.

With contested Nov. 7 **presidential election** result showing Texas Gov. **George W. Bush** (R) barely ahead of Vice Pres. **Al Gore** (D) in Florida, state's Supreme Court, Dec. 8, ordered partial manual recounts. U.S. Supreme Court reversed order, Dec. 12, leaving Bush as winner.

2001 AOL-Time Warner megamerger completed Jan. 11. **U.S. Navy spy plane** collided with **Chinese fighter plane** over South China Sea Apr. 1, killing fighter pilot; 24 U.S. crew members detained in Hainan until U.S. apology, Apr. 12. Pres. Bush signed, June 7, $1.35-tril **tax-cut** package. On Aug. 9 he announced he would allow federal funding of limited research on existing **stem-cell** lines from human embryos.

In worst-ever **terrorist attack** on U.S., **Sept. 11**, two hijacked airliners struck **World Trade Center twin towers** in New York City. A third plane destroyed part of the **Pentagon**; a fourth crashed in a field near **Shanksville, PA**. Some 3,000 people were killed, including about 2,750 at World Trade Center. U.S. and Britain, Oct. 7, launched airstrikes against Afghan-based terrorist organization **al-Qaeda** and Afghanistan's ruling **Taliban** militia. Bush Oct. 26 signed USA **Patriot Act**, with wide-ranging provisions aimed at preventing terrorism. **Taliban** surrendered Kabul, Nov. 13, and fled from Kandahar, their stronghold, Dec. 7. U.S. government, Dec. 11, indicted al-Qaeda operative **Zacarias Moussaoui** as **Sept. 11 co-conspirator**; sentenced in 2006 to life in prison. Five people died and 14 became ill from exposure to **anthrax** through U.S. postal system, Oct. 4-Nov. 21.

Energy-trading company **Enron** filed for bankruptcy, Dec. 2. Bush announced, Dec. 13, U.S. withdrawal from 1972 **Antiballistic Missile Treaty** with Russians.

2002 Taliban and al-Qaeda fighters captured in Afghanistan sent to U.S. naval base at **Guantánamo Bay** in Cuba, starting Jan. 11. In State of the Union address, Jan. 29, Pres. Bush called Iran, Iraq, and North Korea part of **"axis of evil."** By Mar. 6, 1,200 U.S. troops were involved in **Operation Anaconda** against al-Qaeda and Taliban forces in **Afghanistan**.

Independent prosecutor's report, Mar. 20, found **insufficient evidence** that Pres. Clinton or Hillary Clinton committed a crime in connection with **Whitewater**. Pres. Bush, Mar. 27, signed McCain-Feingold **campaign-finance reform bill** banning unregulated, unrestricted "soft money" donations (part of bill struck down by Supreme Court, June 2007). **"Shoe-Bomber"** pleaded guilty Oct. 4 in Dec. 2001 attempted attack aboard airliner; sentenced 2003 to life. On Oct. 10-11 the House, 296-133, and Senate, 77-23, gave Bush backing to use military

2001: The attacks of Sept. 11, 2001, kill more than 2,750 people in New York City, including 343 firefighters.

force against **Iraq**. Bush administration revealed Oct. 16 that **North Korea** had acknowledged developing **nuclear arms** in violation of a 1994 agreement. Bush signed measure, Nov. 25, creating cabinet **Dept. of Homeland Security**.

U.S. **Catholic bishops**, Nov. 13, tightened policies for dealing with priests who **sexually abuse** minors. **Trent Lott** (R, MS) bowed out as Senate majority leader Dec. 20 after remarks that appeared to support segregation.

2003 Space shuttle *Columbia* broke apart Feb. 1 during descent; all seven crew members killed. Senate, Mar. 6, approved **Strategic Offensive Reductions Treaty** (SORT) for reducing nuclear stockpiles. U.S.-led military offensive aimed at ousting Iraqi dictator **Saddam Hussein** began Mar. 19, as cruise missiles hit targets in Baghdad; U.S. forces controlled much of the capital by Apr. 9. Pres. Bush, speaking from aircraft carrier May 1, declared **end of major combat operations**, though insurgent attacks continued.

Pres. Bush signed measure May 27 providing $15 bil to fight **AIDS** especially in **Africa**. He signed bill May 28 providing $330 bil in **tax cuts** over several years. A power failure caused **blackouts** affecting some 50 mil people, mostly in NE U.S. and Canada, Aug. 14.

The **archdiocese of Boston** agreed to pay up to $85 mil, in **sex abuse settlement** announced Sept. 9. Californians, Oct. 7, voted to recall Gov. **Gray Davis** (D) and replace him with actor-turned-politician **Arnold Schwarzenegger** (R). Rev. **Gene Robinson** consecrated Nov. 2 as Episcopal Church's first openly gay bishop. Virginia jury, Nov. 17, found **"Beltway sniper"** guilty in 2002 Washington, DC, area attacks that killed 10; executed Nov. 2009; his teen accomplice was convicted and sentenced to life in prison.

Pres. Bush signed bill Dec. 8 to overhaul **Medicare**, adding prescription drug benefit. **Saddam Hussein captured** by U.S. forces Dec. 13, in underground hideout; later tried and executed (2006) by Iraqi authorities.

2004 *The Lord of the Rings: The Return of the King* won a record-tying 11 Oscars, Feb. 29.

Photos showing **abuse** of **Abu Ghraib** prison inmates in Iraq by American soldiers emerged Apr. 3; two soldiers found guilty (2005) and sentenced to prison. U.S.-led coalition **transferred power** to interim Iraqi government, June 28. **9/11 Commission Report**, released July 22, called for restructuring U.S. intelligence operations.

On May 17, pursuant to a 2003 court decision, **Massachusetts** became first state to legalize **same-sex marriage**. **Boston Red Sox** won **World Series** Oct. 27, for first time since 1918.

Pres. **Bush reelected** Nov. 2, defeating Sen. **John Kerry** (D, MA). Bush signed **intelligence reform bill** Dec. 17, creating a director of national intelligence.

2005 **Condoleezza Rice** became first Black woman sec. of state, Jan. 26. **Terri Schiavo**, in vegetative state since 1990, died Mar. 31, after feeding tube was removed following legal battle.

Hurricane Katrina hit Gulf coast, Aug. 29, causing widespread devastation. **John G. Roberts Jr.** was confirmed by Senate, Sept. 29, 78-22, to replace Chief Justice **William H. Rehnquist**, who died Sept. 3.

NY Times, Dec. 16, reported that Pres. Bush in 2002 had secretly authorized NSA to **eavesdrop without court warrant** on people in U.S. suspected of terrorist activities. Bush, Dec. 30, signed **anti-torture legislation**.

2006 Former GOP lobbyist **Jack Abramoff** pleaded guilty Jan. 3 to bribery and other charges; sentenced to prison. **Samuel Alito Jr.** confirmed to Supreme Court, Jan. 31, 58-42. The Court ruled June 29 that system for trying terrorism detainees at **Guantánamo Bay** was unauthorized. Bush, July 19, issued his **first veto**, on bill to end funding constraints on human embryonic **stem cell research**. On Sept. 6 he confirmed existence of **secret overseas prisons**, run by CIA, for terrorism suspects.

Democrats won control of House and Senate in **midterm elections** Nov. 7. Bush announced Nov. 8 that Defense sec. **Donald Rumsfeld**, a focus of criticism over Iraq war, had resigned.

2007 Rep. **Nancy Pelosi** (D, CA) chosen Jan. 4 as **first woman Speaker** of the House. On Jan. 10, Pres. Bush announced troop **"surge"** in Iraq. Reports of substandard conditions at **Walter Reed** Army Medical Center led to ousters of officials, Mar. 1-2. A **Virginia Tech** student fatally shot 32 people on campus, Apr. 16, before killing himself. On Apr. 18, Supreme Court upheld, 5-4, a 2003 federal law banning so-called

partial-birth abortions. Congress May 24 approved Iraq and Afghanistan war funding, with benchmarks for withdrawal of troops from Iraq; same bill raised federal hourly **minimum wage** from $5.15 to $7.25 over two years. Pres. Bush July 20 banned **"cruel, inhuman, or degrading"** treatment of imprisoned terror suspects.

Harry Potter and the Deathly Hallows, final novel in J. K. Rowling's blockbuster series, released July 21. Congress, Aug. 4, cleared bill allowing **NSA** to monitor communications without warrants if believed related to terrorism. **Barry Bonds** tied Hank Aaron's all-time career **home-run record** at 755 on Aug. 4 and hit No. 756 on Aug. 7.

Report by former U.S. Sen. **George Mitchell** (D, ME), released Dec. 13, presented evidence of **performance-enhancing drug use** by 86 **MLB** players. Bush, Dec. 19, signed energy bill increasing automobile **fuel-economy** standards.

2008 The Fed cut key interest rates, Jan. 22 and 30, to aid economy; $168-bil **economic stimulus** package, signed Feb. 13 by Pres. Bush, provided tax rebates. **Oil prices spiked** above $140 per barrel. With financial system in crisis, federal government Sept. 7 took control of mortgage finance companies **Fannie Mae** and **Freddie Mac; Lehman Brothers** declared bankruptcy Sept. 15. U.S., Sept. 16, took over insurance giant **AIG** in $85-bil bailout. On Sept. 20, a Treasury Dept. plan was introduced to purchase up to $700 bil of **"toxic" mortgage-backed securities**. Revised Troubled Asset Relief Program (**TARP**) cleared Congress Oct. 3; gave Treasury immediate access to half of $700 bil in TARP funds. On Oct. 21 Fed pledged $540 bil as a backup to protect money market funds.

After defeating Sen. **Hillary Clinton** (NY) for the Democratic nomination, Sen. **Barack Obama** (IL) was elected, Nov. 4, as **first Black president** in U.S. history, defeating Sen. **John McCain** (R, AZ). California voters approved **Proposition 8**, banning same-sex marriage.

U.S. government Nov. 23 announced massive **bailout** to protect **Citigroup** from mortgage losses. Dow Jones industrial average dropped 7.7% Dec. 1 after report that the economy was in **recession** that began Dec. 2007; Dow closed the year down 33.8%, its worst since 1931. Fed, Dec. 16, cut **benchmark interest rate** to near zero. Pres. Bush, Dec. 19, announced that $17 bil in TARP funds would be used to help keep **General Motors** and **Chrysler** afloat.

Obama named **Hillary Clinton**, Dec. 1, to be **sec. of state**.

2009 Pres. **Obama** issued executive orders Jan. 22 restricting CIA interrogation practices and calling for U.S. military prison at **Guantánamo Bay**, Cuba, to close (closing blocked by Congress). Illinois Gov. **Rod Blagojevich** (D) was convicted of corruption and removed from office, Jan. 29 (sentence commuted by Trump, 2020). Treasury Sec. **Timothy Geithner**, Feb. 10, outlined $2-tril program to stabilize banking and ease credit markets with **stress tests** for banks. Pres. Obama signed **stimulus** bill Feb. 17, with $212 bil in tax cuts and $575 bil in new spending; introduced $275-bil program Feb. 18 to aid homeowners. Geithner, Mar. 23, introduced incentives to encourage purchases of **"toxic assets."**

After outbreak of **swine flu**, U.S. officials declared public health emergency Apr. 26. **Chrysler** filed for bankruptcy, Apr. 30. Obama, May 19, tightened vehicle **fuel efficiency** standards. **General Motors** filed for bankruptcy June 1, under plan providing new federal funds. On June 9, 10 financial

2005: Hurricane Katrina and subsequent failure of levees cause unprecedented destruction in New Orleans and along the Gulf Coast.

2008: Sen. Barack Obama is elected the first Black president of the United States.

firms received go-ahead from U.S. Treasury to **return** some $68 bil in **TARP funds**.

George Tiller, Kansas doctor and abortion provider, was murdered May 31; anti-abortion extremist later convicted. Speaking June 4 in Egypt, Pres. Obama called for "**new beginning**" in relations with **Muslim world**. Financier **Bernard Madoff** sentenced June 29 to 150 years, after pleading guilty in massive **Ponzi scheme**. **Sonia Sotomayor** confirmed Aug. 6, as Supreme Court's **first Hispanic justice**.

Government reported Oct. 29 that GDP grew at 3.5% annual rate July-Sept., signaling technical **end of recession**. Obama announced Oct. 30 end to travel and immigration restrictions on people with **AIDS**. On Nov. 5, 13 were killed in shooting at **Ft. Hood**, TX; an Army major was convicted in the murders.

Obama, Nov. 6, signed measure to extend unemployment benefits and give $8,000 tax credit to first-time homebuyers. A surge of 30,000 troops to **Afghanistan** was announced Dec. 1. Obama received **Nobel Peace Prize**, Dec. 10, and brokered multination **greenhouse-gas accord**, reached Dec. 18 in Copenhagen. Detroit-bound air passengers, Dec. 25, thwarted attempt by Nigerian radical to ignite **explosives in his underwear**.

2010 In *Citizens United v. FEC*, U.S. Supreme Court Jan. 21 held that corporations and unions could spend unlimited funds on advertising to influence election outcomes. Obama, Mar. 18, signed $18-bil **job-stimulus** measure. On Mar. 21, the House, with no GOP support, gave final approval to "**Obamacare**" health-care reform bill. Pres. Obama and Russian Pres. **Dmitri Medvedev**, Apr. 8, signed New Strategic Arms Reduction Treaty, or **New START**.

On Apr. 20, *Deepwater Horizon* drilling platform exploded in Gulf of Mexico, killing 11 and creating huge oil spill; $20-bil settlement against energy giant **BP** approved in 2016. **Elena Kagan** was confirmed as **Supreme Court** justice, 63-37, Aug. 5. Obama signed **financial reform** bill, July 21. Over 75,000 Afghanistan documents, many of them classified, were published July 25 on **WikiLeaks** website. Last **U.S. combat unit left Iraq** Aug. 19 and Obama, Aug. 31, declared U.S. combat mission in Iraq ended; 50,000 troops remained in noncombat units.

The **Fed** Nov. 3 announced plan to buy $600 bil in **Treasury securities** to stimulate economy. Bipartisan **Simpson-Bowles** commission, Dec. 1, called for deep spending cuts to stabilize national debt. Obama, Dec. 17, signed $858-bil compromise measure temporarily extending G. W. **Bush-era tax cuts** and unemployment insurance benefits.

2011 Gunman in **Tucson**, AZ, Jan. 8, killed 6 people and injured 13, including Rep. **Gabrielle Giffords** (D, AZ).

On May 2, in Abbottabad, Pakistan, Navy **SEALs** killed al-Qaeda leader **Osama bin Laden**. On May 26 Obama signed measure extending key provisions of **USA Patriot Act**.

Tornado hit **Joplin**, MO, May 22, claiming about 160 lives. NASA's **space shuttle** program ended with landing of *Atlantis*, July 21. **Budget control act**, Aug. 1-2, raised **debt ceiling** and cut some $900 bil in spending, with another $1.5 tril in cuts to be worked out by **supercommittee**. A left-wing protest movement began Sept. 17 as **Occupy Wall Street** expanded across the U.S. and abroad.

Anwar al-Awlaki, a Muslim cleric linked to terrorist attacks in U.S., was killed Sept. 30 in U.S. drone attack in **Yemen**.

U.S. military mission in **Iraq** formally ended Dec. 15; last troop convoy left Dec. 18.

2012 Pres. Obama Feb. 10 announced compromise **health insurance** mandate that avoided requiring religiously affiliated employers to directly provide **contraceptive coverage**. On June 15 he announced Deferred Action for Childhood Arrivals (**DACA**) program, shielding from deportation certain **undocumented immigrants** who entered as minors.

Jerry Sandusky, former assistant football coach at **Penn State**, was convicted June 22 in sexual abuse of ten boys. Twelve people were killed July 20, in **movie-theater shooting** in Aurora, CO; shooter convicted in 2015.

A gunman opened fire Aug. 5 at a **Sikh temple** in Oak Creek, WI, leaving six dead, before killing himself. NASA rover *Curiosity* landed on **Mars** Aug. 6.

Islamist terrorists attacked U.S. facility in **Benghazi**, Libya, Sept. 11-12, killing U.S. **ambassador** and three other Americans; later report blamed State Dept. for "grossly inadequate" security. Inspector general's report, Sept. 19, cited flaws in Justice Dept. gun-buying **Operation Fast and Furious**. **Hurricane Sandy** made landfall in the U.S. Oct. 29, devastating mid-Atlantic coastal areas and leaving over 200 dead.

Pres. **Obama reelected** Nov. 6, defeating former Massachusetts Gov. **Mitt Romney** (R). Colorado and Washington became first states to vote to decriminalize recreational **marijuana**. A gunman killed 20 young children and 6 adults before killing himself, Dec. 14, at **Sandy Hook** Elementary School in **Newtown**, CT.

2013 Averting "**fiscal cliff**," Senate passed compromise Jan. 1, making **Bush-era tax** cuts permanent up to certain ceilings, while deferring automatic spending cuts (**sequestration**). Sequestration took effect Mar. 1, triggering $1.2 tril in spending cuts to both defense and domestic programs over ten years. Sen. **John Kerry** confirmed as sec. of state, Jan. 29.

Bombs at the Boston Marathon, Apr. 15, killed three spectators and injured 264. Two Chechen-born brothers were implicated; one died in battle with police; the other was convicted and sentenced to death in 2015. **Boy Scouts** leadership voted May 23 to let openly gay youths be members.

The *Guardian*, June 5, disclosed details of classified **NSA electronic surveillance** program; NSA contractor **Edward Snowden** claimed responsibility for leaks, after having fled the country. Supreme Court, June 25, overturned key provision of the 1965 **Voting Rights Act**, and June 26, struck down part of 1996 Defense of Marriage Act (**DOMA**) that denied federal benefits to same-sex couples.

A jury, July 13, found George Zimmerman not guilty of murder in shooting, Feb. 2012, of **Trayvon Martin**, an unarmed Black teenager, in Sanford, FL. **Detroit** filed for **bankruptcy**, July 18. Army Pfc. **Chelsea Manning** was sentenced Aug. 21 to 35 years for releasing military and diplomatic documents to **WikiLeaks** (Obama commuted sentence, 2017). Army Staff Sgt. **Robert Bales** pleaded guilty to killing 16 Afghan civilians; sentenced to life, Aug. 23. A gunman killed 12 people at the **Navy Yard** in Washington, DC, Sept. 16; he was killed by responding police.

Health insurance exchanges opened Oct. 1 in **Obamacare** rollout plagued by technical glitches. U.S. **government partially shut down** Oct. 1 over budget impasse; resolved by Congress Oct. 16. JPMorgan Chase agreed, Nov. 19, to $13-bil settlement on charges of deceptive mortgage-sale practices. Dow up 26.5% in 2013, biggest yearly gain since 1995.

2014 **Janet Yellen** was confirmed Jan. 6 as first woman **Federal Reserve** chair. General Motors, Feb. 7, began recall of vehicles with defects ultimately linked to over 120 deaths. **Toyota** agreed Mar. 20 to $1.2-bil fine on charges it concealed information about defective parts.

Gunman killed 6 people and injured 13 before killing himself, May 23, near **Univ. of California-Santa Barbara**. U.S. Army Sgt. **Bowe Bergdahl**, captured by Taliban in 2009 after leaving his post in Afghanistan, was freed May 31 in exchange for U.S. release of five Taliban captives. Veterans Affairs Sec. **Eric Shinseki** resigned May 30 after revelations that **VA hospitals** had hidden long waiting times.

The Sunni extremist Islamic State of Iraq and Syria (**ISIS**) expanded its territory, declaring a "**caliphate**" June 29. Pres. Obama announced June 19 that the U.S. would send **military advisers to Iraq**; he authorized airstrikes there, Aug. 7. ISIS released videos in Aug.-Nov. showing **beheadings** of three Americans.

A white police officer fatally shot unarmed Black 18-year-old **Michael Brown**, Aug. 9, in **Ferguson**, MO, precipitating sometimes violent **protests**; grand jury declined to indict the officer. **Bank of America** agreed Aug. 21 to $16.65-bil settlement on charges it misled investors. U.S. announced Sept. 16 it was sending military personnel to West Africa in response to **Ebola** epidemic.

Afghan and U.S. officials signed agreement Sept. 30 providing for 9,800 American and at least 2,000 NATO troops to remain in **Afghanistan** after end of combat mission in Dec. 2014. U.S. jury Oct. 22 convicted four former contract security guards in 2007 shootings that killed 17 **Iraqi civilians**. New York City's **One World Trade Center** welcomed first tenants Nov. 3.

GOP gained control of Senate in **midterm elections** Nov. 4. Pres. Obama Nov. 7 approved increase of U.S. noncombat military personnel in Iraq, to about 3,000. **Tamir Rice**, a Black 12-year-old holding a pellet gun, was fatally shot by a white police officer, Nov. 22, in **Cleveland**, OH; grand jury declined to indict. A grand jury decided Dec. 3 not to indict a **New York City** police officer for allegedly using a nonregulation **chokehold** to detain **Eric Garner**, a Black man who died July 17 in custody. A Black man shot and killed two **New York City police** officers in their patrol car, Dec. 20, then killed himself.

Hackers accessed Sony Pictures Entertainment data and, Dec. 16, threatened violence against U.S. theaters showing comedy about plot to assassinate North Korean dictator **Kim Jong Un**. U.S.-led NATO mission in **Afghanistan** ended combat operations Dec. 28, after over 13 years.

2015 **Standard & Poor's** agreed Feb. 3 to pay $1.4 bil to settle suits over alleged inflated ratings for subprime mortgage bonds. **Morgan Stanley**, Feb. 15, agreed to pay $2.6 bil to resolve claims of deception over mortgage-backed securities. Justice Dept. Mar. 4 released report exposing widespread mistreatment of Black individuals by **Ferguson**, MO, police and court system.

A New York court Mar. 5 approved $8.5-bil settlement between **Bank of America** and investors in mortgage securities issued by **Countrywide Financial Corp**. Federal judge, Mar. 20, approved settlement in which **AIG** paid $970.5 mil to shareholders claiming they were misled over high-risk mortgage loans. Facing a fourth year of severe drought, **California** Gov. **Jerry Brown** (D) issued mandatory **water restrictions** Apr. 1.

By July, 17 Republicans announced they would seek the party's 2016 presidential nomination, including real estate mogul **Donald Trump**. Former Sec. of State **Hillary Clinton** (D) launched presidential campaign Apr. 12, followed by main challenger for Democratic nomination Sen. **Bernie Sanders** (VT).

In foreign relations milestone Apr. 11, Pres. Obama met in Panama with Cuban Pres. **Raúl Castro**. The Apr. 19 death of a Black man, **Freddie Gray**, from injury in a **Baltimore** police van, spurred riots and led to indictment of six officers; no convictions resulted. Obama June 2 signed a bill to end **NSA's bulk collection** of phone data, with telecom companies to hold custody of data instead. **American Pharoah**, June 6, became first in 37 years to take horse racing's **Triple Crown**.

A **white supremacist** fatally shot nine Black bible study attendees, June 17, at a historic **Black church** in **Charleston**, SC; shooter sentenced to death, 2017. On June 26, the Supreme Court ruled that **same-sex couples** had constitutional right to marry.

Iran and six world powers led by the U.S. formally agreed July 14 on deal to limit **Iranian nuclear capability** in return for lifting economic sanction. NASA's *New Horizons* spacecraft, July 14, carried out first-ever flyby of **Pluto**. **U.S.** and **Cuba** reopened embassies in their countries July 20, reestablishing relations. Pres. Obama Aug. 3 unveiled a final EPA **Clean Power Plan** for imposing limits on carbon dioxide emissions from power plants (enforcement suspended pending litigation).

General Motors agreed Sept. 17 to pay $900 mil for failure to issue recall for a defect that led to over 120 deaths. **Pope Francis** visited the U.S. Sept. 22-27, and addressed joint session of Congress. A student shooter at a community college, Oct. 1, in **Roseburg**, OR, killed nine; he was wounded by police and killed himself. A U.S. airstrike hit an **Afghanistan hospital** Oct. 3, killing more than 40; military report blamed human error.

U.S. and 11 other nations completed negotiations, Oct. 5, on **Trans-Pacific Partnership** trade agreement. Rep. **Paul Ryan** (R, WI) was elected Speaker of the House, Oct. 29, replacing **John Boehner** (R, OH). An Oct. 22 U.S.-Iraqi mission freed about 70 hostages held by **ISIS** in Iraq; one U.S. soldier was killed. On Oct. 30, Obama announced he would deploy special operations forces to fight ISIS in **Syria**.

After years of delay, Pres. Obama Nov. 6 announced decision against approving **Keystone XL** oil pipeline. Three people were killed Nov. 27 at **Planned Parenthood** clinic in Colorado Springs, CO; alleged shooter found incompetent to stand trial. A married couple said by the FBI to be **Muslim extremists** fatally shot 14 people at a Dec. 2 office party in **San Bernardino**, CA; both died in shootout with police.

Defense Dept., Dec. 3, announced that all military combat positions would be opened to women. U.S. and 194 other parties reached agreement in Paris, Dec. 12, on plan to reduce greenhouse gases linked to **climate change**. The Fed, Dec. 16, raised key interest rates from near-zero levels. Obama signed $1.8-tril **spending and tax relief package** Dec. 18.

2016 Armed protesters, Jan. 2, began 41-day occupation of Oregon's **Malheur National Wildlife Refuge**, in land dispute; one fatally shot, Jan. 26, in confrontation with law enforcement. Obama declared federal state of emergency in **Flint**, MI, Jan. 16, because of **lead-contaminated drinking water**. Following the death in Feb. of conservative Supreme Court Justice **Antonin Scalia**, Obama Mar. 16 nominated appellate court judge **Merrick Garland** to his seat, but Senate Republicans refused to schedule confirmation hearings. Obama made historic visit to **Cuba**, Mar. 20-22.

North Carolina Gov. **Pat McCrory** (R) Mar. 23 signed **"bathroom bill"** requiring that persons use state facilities corresponding to birth-certificate gender; boycotts followed. (Measure partly repealed, 2017.) Justice Dept. announced Apr. 11 that **Goldman Sachs** would pay $5.1 bil to settle charges of selling faulty mortgage-backed securities.

U.S. **drone strike** killed Afghan Taliban leader **Akhtar Muhammad Mansour** May 21. On trip to East Asia, May 21-28, Obama visited **Hiroshima**, and declared, in Hanoi, that the U.S. would end arms embargo against **Vietnam**. A gunman who declared allegiance to **ISIS** killed 49 mostly Hispanic people June 12 at a **gay nightclub** in Orlando, FL. The musical *Hamilton* won 11 Tony Awards June 12.

Iraqi troops and Shiite-dominated militias, aided by U.S. airstrikes, gained control of **Fallujah** June 26. A House Select Committee, June 28, released final report on 2012 attack in **Benghazi**, Libya, showing no evidence of wrongdoing by Sec. of State Clinton.

In settlement announced June 28, **Volkswagen** agreed to pay some $15 bil for cheating in emissions tests. Defense Dept. announced, June 30, that **transgender individuals** could openly serve in the military. Protests followed two **fatal police shootings** of a Black man in **Baton Rouge**, LA, July 5, and in a **St. Paul**, MN, suburb, July 6. Five police officers were killed by a sniper, July 7 in **Dallas**, TX, and three in an ambush, July 17 in **Baton Rouge**, LA.

After investigating Hillary Clinton's use of a **private email server** as sec. of state, FBI Dir. **James Comey**, July 5, said she did not show intent to violate the law but had been "extremely careless." Meeting July 18-21 in Cleveland, OH, **Republicans nominated Donald Trump** for president and Gov. **Mike Pence** (IN) for vice president. **WikiLeaks** July 22 published Democratic National Committee emails perceived as showing party bias against Sanders; DNC chair **Debbie Wasserman Schultz** resigned. Meeting July 25-28 in Philadelphia, **Democrats nominated Hillary Clinton** for president and Sen. **Tim Kaine** (VA) for vice president. Fox News Channel

2014: The fatal police shooting of unarmed Black 18-year-old Michael Brown in Ferguson, MO, draws attention to racial disparities in law enforcement.

chair and CEO **Roger Ailes** resigned July 21 amid **sexual harassment** charges.

A Justice Dept. report released Aug. 10 concluded that **Baltimore police** routinely used **excessive force** against Black residents. Riots broke out in **Milwaukee**, WI, Aug. 13-15, following **police shooting** of an armed Black man fleeing a traffic stop. Regulators fined **Wells Fargo** $185 mil Sept. 8 for illicit revenue scheme. Following protests by **Standing Rock** Sioux Tribe, the Obama administration Sept. 9 temporarily blocked construction on the **Dakota Access** oil pipeline (later resumed; pipeline opened June 2017).

The *Washington Post* Oct. 7 made public 2005 video footage that showed **Trump** bragging about **groping women**; a number of women subsequently alleged that he had sexually harassed them. **WikiLeaks** Oct. 7 began releasing apparently hacked emails from Clinton campaign chair **John Podesta**. FBI Dir. **Comey** informed Congress Oct. 28 that the agency had discovered more Clinton emails but, Nov. 6, said its review found no basis for charges.

AT&T agreed Oct. 22 to acquire **Time Warner** for about $85 bil. Two **Des Moines**-area police officers were killed in ambushes by gunman, Nov. 2. **Chicago Cubs** won World Series Nov. 2, for first time since 1908.

In Nov. 8 presidential election, **Donald Trump** (R) defeated **Hillary Clinton** (D), with 304 electoral votes out of 538, though losing popular vote by about 2.9 mil. On Nov. 13, Trump named Republican National Committee chair **Reince Priebus** as chief of staff and right-wing media executive **Steve Bannon** as chief strategist and senior counselor. Retired Lt. Gen. **Michael Flynn** signed on, Nov. 18, as national security adviser. On Nov. 18, Trump agreed to pay $25 mil to settle fraud suits against **Trump University** real estate training program. Trump named Exxon Mobil CEO **Rex Tillerson**, Dec. 13, as sec. of state.

Tech pioneer **Yahoo** Dec. 14 revealed an Aug. 2013 hack, affecting some 3 bil user accounts. Following evidence of **Russian hacking**, Obama Dec. 29 expelled 35 Russian diplomats.

2017 Pres. Donald **Trump** inaugurated Jan. 20. **Women's Marches**, Jan. 21, in Washington, DC, and dozens of other cities drew millions of protesters. On Jan. 23, Pres. Trump withdrew U.S. from the unratified **Trans-Pacific Partnership** trade agreement and reinstated ban on federal funding for foreign health care organizations providing abortions. He signed an order, Jan. 25, to build a Mexican **border wall** and issued a controversial executive order, Jan. 27, banning admission of travelers from certain **Muslim-majority nations**; in revised form, which included some non-Muslim nations, the ban was upheld, 5-4, June 2018, by the U.S. Supreme Court.

After a suspected **chemical attack** in Syria that killed over 80 civilians Apr. 4, Pres. Trump authorized a **cruise-missile strike** against a government airfield. The U.S. military, Apr. 13, bombed a complex of caves and tunnels in **Afghanistan**; 94 militants reportedly killed.

After Republicans used the so-called **nuclear option** to end a Democratic filibuster, the Senate voted, 54-45, Apr. 7, to confirm nomination of **Neil Gorsuch** to Supreme Court. **Fox News** separated from longtime host **Bill O'Reilly** Apr. 19, following reports of sexual harassment.

Congress Apr. 28 passed stopgap measure that included money for Obamacare subsidies; an **omnibus spending bill**

2017: A gunman shooting from a high-rise hotel window in Las Vegas kills 58 people and injures hundreds more attending an outdoor country music festival Oct. 1.

the next day included increases for defense and border security, but no money for a border wall. **Puerto Rico** filed for a form of bankruptcy, May 3.

Pres. Trump fired FBI Dir. **James Comey** May 9, prompting charges that it was an attempt to stifle inquiry; Justice Dept., May 17, appointed former FBI Dir. **Robert Mueller III** as special counsel to head investigation into Russian election meddling.

New Orleans, May 19, took down statue of Confederate Gen. **Robert E. Lee**. Financially ailing Ringling Brothers and Barnum & Bailey Circus held final **"Greatest Show on Earth,"** May 21 in Uniondale, NY.

On June 1 Trump announced intention to pull the U.S. out of the 2015 **Paris climate change agreement**, launching a four-year exit process. A gunman targeting Republicans June 14 at a practice for the bipartisan **Congressional Baseball Game** critically injured House majority whip **Steve Scalise** (R, LA) and wounded four others.

Iraqi Prime Min. **Haider al-Abadi** announced July 9 that Iraqi security forces, supported by U.S.-backed coalition, had recaptured **Mosul**, ISIS's last major stronghold in Iraq; after further advances, he declared victory over ISIS, Dec. 9. American college student **Otto Warmbier** returned to U.S., June 13, in a comatose state after 17-month imprisonment and alleged torture in **North Korea**; he died six days later.

A White House shake-up led to the resignation, July 27, of **Reince Priebus** as chief of staff; he was replaced by Homeland Security Sec. **John Kelly**. Pres. Trump Aug. 2 signed bipartisan bill imposing new economic sanctions against **Russia** as well as Iran and **North Korea**, which July 4 had launched what was thought to be an intercontinental-capable **ballistic missile**.

A **white nationalist rally** in **Charlottesville**, VA, Aug. 12, erupted in clashes with counterdemonstrators. A white nationalist who drove a car into the crowd, killing a counterprotester and injuring 19 others was arrested fleeing the scene. In a widely denounced statement Trump condemned bigotry and violence "on many sides." Trump chief strategist **Steve Bannon** left the administration Aug. 18.

On Aug. 21, millions viewed the first coast-to-coast total **solar eclipse** visible from U.S. since 1918. **Hurricane Harvey** hit Texas, Aug. 25, causing 89 deaths; costliest U.S. storm since Katrina. **North Korea** Sept. 3 conducted its sixth nuclear weapons test, claiming it was a hydrogen bomb; the UN and U.S. imposed economic sanctions. Trump administration, Sept. 5, announced plan to phase out the Deferred Action for Childhood Arrivals (**DACA**) program (implementation stalled by legal challenges). Credit reporting firm **Equifax** revealed Sept. 7 that hackers had gained access to personal information on some 143 mil Americans and agreed, July 2019, to pay up to $700 mil to resolve claims. **Hurricane Maria** hit **Puerto Rico**, Sept. 20, causing widespread devastation and nearly 3,000 deaths. NASA retired the unmanned Saturn probe *Cassini*, after an almost 20-year mission. **Toys R Us** filed for bankruptcy, Sept. 18. A gunman firing from a hotel balcony killed 58 people and injured hundreds at an outdoor country music concert, Oct. 1, in **Las Vegas**.

An Oct. 5 *NY Times* report detailing multiple accusations of sexual assault or harassment against movie producer **Harvey Weinstein** set off a wave of **"Me Too"** allegations. Among those accused of misconduct by year's end were actor **Kevin Spacey** and broadcast journalists **Matt Lauer** and **Charlie Rose**.

U.S.-backed militias in Syria reported, Oct. 20, capture of **Raqqa**, de facto capital of ISIS's self-proclaimed caliphate. Trump, Oct. 26, declared the **opioid addiction epidemic** a public health emergency. Former Trump adviser **Michael Flynn** pleaded guilty Nov. 30 to lying to the FBI about conversations with Russia's U.S. ambassador.

Eight people were rammed and killed by a truck driven along a **bike path** in **New York City**, Oct. 31; an Uzbek immigrant was arrested. A white gunman killed 26 people and wounded 20, Nov. 5, at a **Baptist church** in Sutherland Springs, TX; shooter fled and died by suicide. U.S. Navy report, Nov. 1, blamed multiple personnel errors for collisions involving the USS *Fitzgerald* (June 17; 7 sailors killed) and USS *John S. McCain* (Aug. 21; 10 sailors killed).

Pres. Trump, Dec. 4, announced that two **national monuments** in Utah would be slashed in acreage. Trump, Dec. 6, recognized **Jerusalem** as Israel's capital. FCC voted 3-2, Dec. 14, to scrap **net neutrality** rules.

AFGHANISTAN	ALBANIA	ALGERIA	ANDORRA	ANGOLA
ANTIGUA AND BARBUDA	ARGENTINA	ARMENIA	AUSTRALIA	AUSTRIA
AZERBAIJAN	THE BAHAMAS	BAHRAIN	BANGLADESH	BARBADOS
BELARUS	BELGIUM	BELIZE	BENIN	BHUTAN
BOLIVIA	BOSNIA AND HERZEGOVINA	BOTSWANA	BRAZIL	BRUNEI
BULGARIA	BURKINA FASO	BURUNDI	CABO VERDE	CAMBODIA
CAMEROON	CANADA	CENTRAL AFRICAN REPUBLIC	CHAD	CHILE
CHINA	COLOMBIA	COMOROS	CONGO, DEM. REP. OF THE	CONGO REPUBLIC
COSTA RICA	CÔTE D'IVOIRE	CROATIA	CUBA	CYPRUS
CZECHIA (CZECH REPUBLIC)	DENMARK	DJIBOUTI	DOMINICA	DOMINICAN REPUBLIC
ECUADOR	EGYPT	EL SALVADOR	EQUATORIAL GUINEA	ERITREA

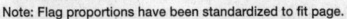

Note: Flag proportions have been standardized to fit page.

490

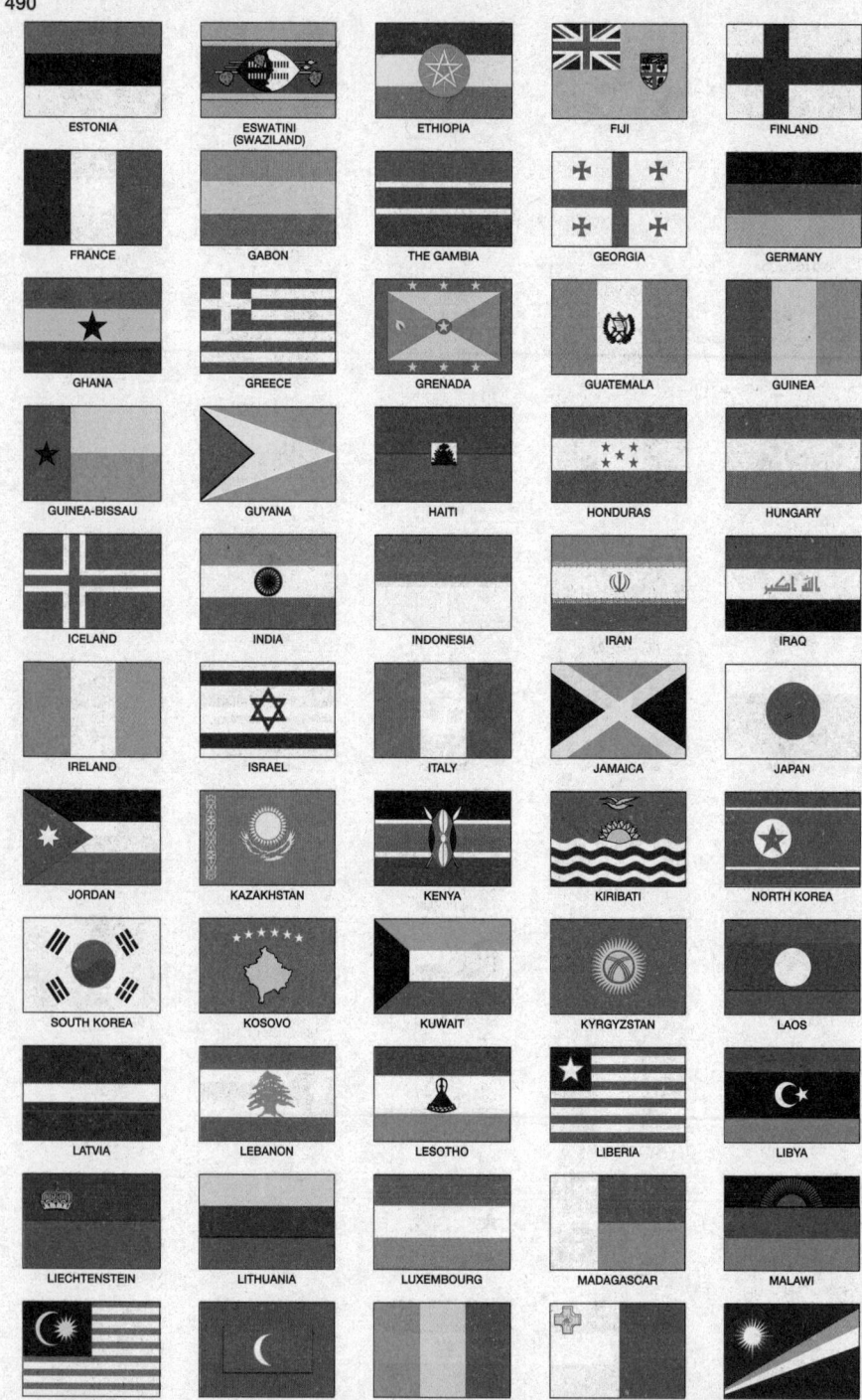

ESTONIA

ESWATINI (SWAZILAND)

ETHIOPIA

FIJI

FINLAND

FRANCE

GABON

THE GAMBIA

GEORGIA

GERMANY

GHANA

GREECE

GRENADA

GUATEMALA

GUINEA

GUINEA-BISSAU

GUYANA

HAITI

HONDURAS

HUNGARY

ICELAND

INDIA

INDONESIA

IRAN

IRAQ

IRELAND

ISRAEL

ITALY

JAMAICA

JAPAN

JORDAN

KAZAKHSTAN

KENYA

KIRIBATI

NORTH KOREA

SOUTH KOREA

KOSOVO

KUWAIT

KYRGYZSTAN

LAOS

LATVIA

LEBANON

LESOTHO

LIBERIA

LIBYA

LIECHTENSTEIN

LITHUANIA

LUXEMBOURG

MADAGASCAR

MALAWI

MALAYSIA

MALDIVES

MALI

MALTA

MARSHALL ISLANDS

Note: Flag proportions have been standardized to fit page.

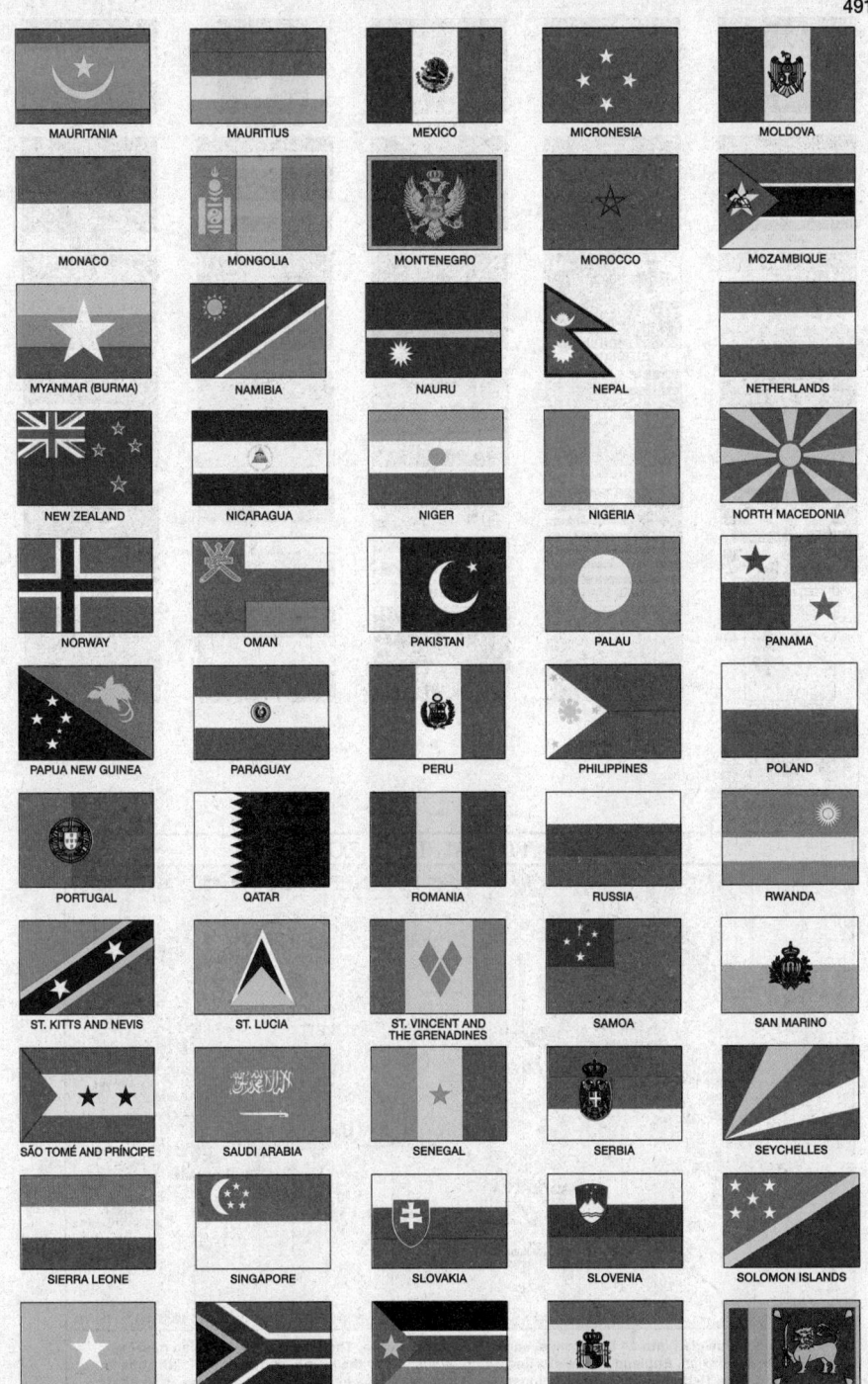

MAURITANIA

MAURITIUS

MEXICO

MICRONESIA

MOLDOVA

MONACO

MONGOLIA

MONTENEGRO

MOROCCO

MOZAMBIQUE

MYANMAR (BURMA)

NAMIBIA

NAURU

NEPAL

NETHERLANDS

NEW ZEALAND

NICARAGUA

NIGER

NIGERIA

NORTH MACEDONIA

NORWAY

OMAN

PAKISTAN

PALAU

PANAMA

PAPUA NEW GUINEA

PARAGUAY

PERU

PHILIPPINES

POLAND

PORTUGAL

QATAR

ROMANIA

RUSSIA

RWANDA

ST. KITTS AND NEVIS

ST. LUCIA

ST. VINCENT AND
THE GRENADINES

SAMOA

SAN MARINO

SÃO TOMÉ AND PRÍNCIPE

SAUDI ARABIA

SENEGAL

SERBIA

SEYCHELLES

SIERRA LEONE

SINGAPORE

SLOVAKIA

SLOVENIA

SOLOMON ISLANDS

SOMALIA

SOUTH AFRICA

SOUTH SUDAN

SPAIN

SRI LANKA

Note: Flag proportions have been standardized to fit page.

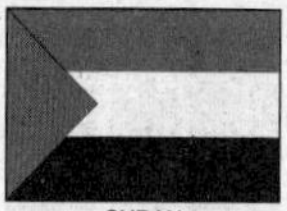

SUDAN

SURINAME

SWEDEN

SWITZERLAND

SYRIA

TAIWAN

TAJIKISTAN

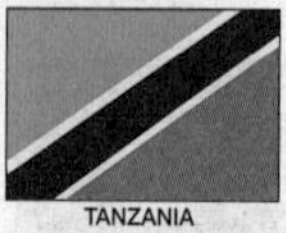

TANZANIA

THAILAND

TIMOR-LESTE
(EAST TIMOR)

TOGO

TONGA

TRINIDAD AND TOBAGO

TUNISIA

TURKEY

TURKMENISTAN

TUVALU

UGANDA

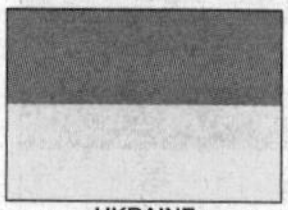

UKRAINE

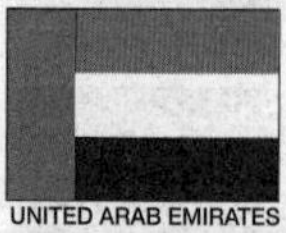

UNITED ARAB EMIRATES

UNITED KINGDOM

UNITED STATES

URUGUAY

UZBEKISTAN

VANUATU

VATICAN CITY

VENEZUELA

VIETNAM

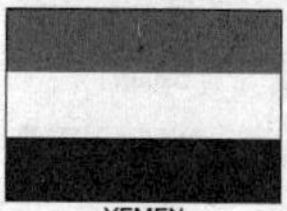

YEMEN

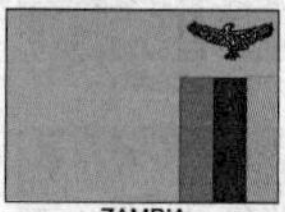

ZAMBIA

ZIMBABWE

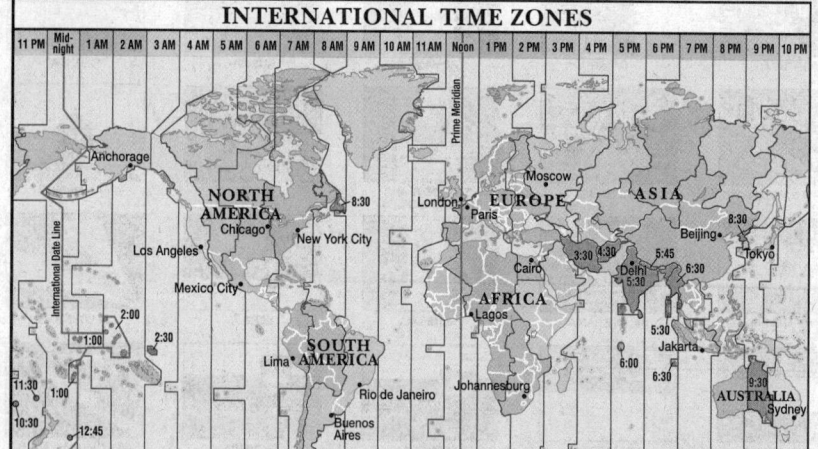

INTERNATIONAL TIME ZONES

The world is divided into 24 time zones, each 15° longitude wide. The longitudinal meridian passing through Greenwich, England, is the starting point, and is called the *prime meridian*. The 12th zone is divided by the 180th meridian (International Date Line). When the line is crossed going west, the date is advanced one day; when crossed going east, the date becomes a day earlier.

Note: Flag proportions have been standardized to fit page.

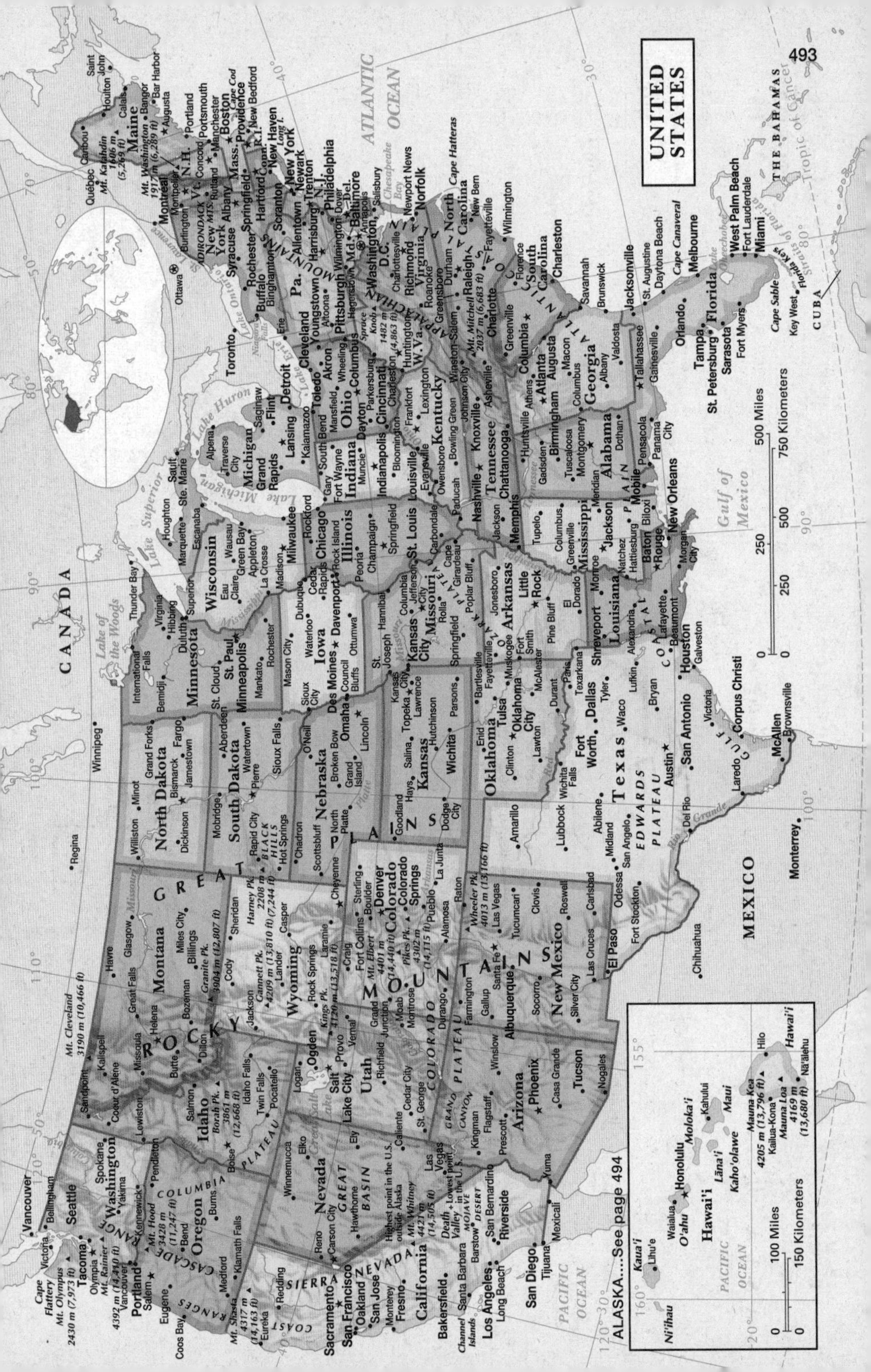
UNITED STATES
CANADA
MEXICO
ATLANTIC OCEAN
PACIFIC OCEAN
Gulf of Mexico
THE BAHAMAS
CUBA
Tropic of Cancer
Straits of Florida
Lake Superior
Lake Michigan
Lake Huron
Lake Erie
Lake Ontario
Lake of the Woods
GREAT PLAINS
ROCKY MOUNTAINS
APPALACHIAN MOUNTAINS
CASCADE RANGE
COAST RANGES
SIERRA NEVADA
GREAT BASIN
COLORADO PLATEAU
COLUMBIA PLATEAU
EDWARDS PLATEAU
OZARK PLATEAU
GULF COASTAL PLAIN
ATLANTIC COASTAL PLAIN
MOJAVE DESERT
GRAND CANYON
BLACK HILLS
Mt. Cleveland 3190 m (10,466 ft)
Mt. Olympus 2430 m (7,973 ft)
Mt. Rainier 4392 m (14,410 ft)
Mt. Hood 3428 m (11,247 ft)
Mt. Shasta 4317 m (14,163 ft)
Mt. Whitney 4421 m (14,505 ft)
Highest point in the U.S. outside Alaska
Death Valley Lowest point in the U.S.
Borah Pk. 3861 m (12,668 ft)
Granite Pk. 3904 m (12,807 ft)
Gannett Pk. 4209 m (13,810 ft)
Harney Pk. 2208 m (7,244 ft)
Kings Pk. 4120 m (13,518 ft)
Mt. Elbert 4401 m (14,440 ft)
Pikes Pk. 4302 m (14,115 ft)
Wheeler Pk. 4013 m (13,166 ft)
Mt. Mitchell 2037 m (6,683 ft)
Spruce Knob 1482 m (4,863 ft)
Mt. Washington 1917 m (6,289 ft)
Mt. Katahdin 1606 m (5,269 ft)
Cape Flattery
Cape Hatteras
Cape Cod
Cape Canaveral
Cape Sable
Florida Keys
Channel Islands
Washington
Oregon
California
Nevada
Idaho
Montana
Wyoming
Utah
Arizona
Colorado
New Mexico
North Dakota
South Dakota
Nebraska
Kansas
Oklahoma
Texas
Minnesota
Iowa
Missouri
Arkansas
Louisiana
Wisconsin
Illinois
Michigan
Indiana
Ohio
Kentucky
Tennessee
Mississippi
Alabama
Georgia
Florida
South Carolina
North Carolina
Virginia
W. Va.
Pa.
New York
Vt.
N.H.
Maine
Mass.
R.I.
Conn.
N.J.
Del.
Md.
Washington D.C.
Seattle
Tacoma
Olympia
Spokane
Portland
Salem
Eugene
San Francisco
Oakland
San Jose
Sacramento
Fresno
Los Angeles
Long Beach
San Diego
Las Vegas
Reno
Carson City
Salt Lake City
Ogden
Boise
Helena
Billings
Cheyenne
Denver
Colorado Springs
Albuquerque
Santa Fe
Phoenix
Tucson
El Paso
Bismarck
Fargo
Pierre
Sioux Falls
Lincoln
Omaha
Topeka
Wichita
Kansas City
Oklahoma City
Tulsa
Dallas
Fort Worth
Austin
San Antonio
Houston
Corpus Christi
Minneapolis
St. Paul
Des Moines
St. Louis
Little Rock
Baton Rouge
New Orleans
Jackson
Memphis
Nashville
Milwaukee
Chicago
Springfield
Indianapolis
Detroit
Lansing
Columbus
Cleveland
Cincinnati
Louisville
Frankfort
Atlanta
Birmingham
Montgomery
Mobile
Tallahassee
Jacksonville
Tampa
St. Petersburg
Orlando
Miami
Columbia
Charleston
Charlotte
Raleigh
Richmond
Norfolk
Pittsburgh
Harrisburg
Philadelphia
Baltimore
Annapolis
Dover
Trenton
Newark
New York
Albany
Hartford
Providence
Boston
Concord
Montpelier
Augusta
Vancouver
Winnipeg
Regina
Toronto
Ottawa
Montreal
Québec
Monterrey
Chihuahua
Tijuana
Mexicali
ALASKA....See page 494
Hawai'i
Kaua'i
Ni'ihau
O'ahu
Honolulu
Moloka'i
Lāna'i
Maui
Kaho'olawe
Mauna Kea 4205 m (13,796 ft)
Mauna Loa 4169 m (13,680 ft)
Hilo
0 250 500 Miles
0 250 500 750 Kilometers
0 100 Miles
0 150 Kilometers

NORTH AMERICA AND THE CARIBBEAN

ATLANTIC

OCEAN

Natal
João Pessoa
Recife
Maceió
Fortaleza
Mossoró
Juàzeiro do Norte
Campina Grande
Aracaju
Alagoinhas
Salvador
Juàzeiro
Petrolina
Feira de Santana
Jequié
Ilhéus
Itabuna
Vitória da Conquista
Teófilo Otoni
Governador Valadares
Vitória

São Luís
Teresina
Caxias
Floriano
Montes Claros
Juiz de Fora
Niterói
Rio de Janeiro

Belém
Imperatriz
Araguaína
Marabá
Guápi
Brasília
Goiânia
Uberlândia
Anápolis
Belo Horizonte
Ribeirão Preto
Jundiaí
Campinas
Volta Redonda
Santos

BRAZILIAN HIGHLANDS
Pico da Bandeira 2890 m (9,482 ft)

Macapá
Altamira
Santarém
Itaituba

MATO GROSSO PLATEAU
Rondonópolis
São José do Rio Preto
Presidente Prudente
Bauru
Londrina
Sorocaba
São Paulo

Marajó Island
Kourou
Cayenne
French Guiana (Fr.)

BRAZIL

Corumbá
Campo Grande
Dourados
Concepción
PARAGUAY
CHACO

Manaus
Porto Velho
Guajará-Mirim
Ji-Paraná
Trinidad
BOLIVIA
Santa Cruz
Cochabamba
Sucre
Potosí
Camiri
Tarija
San Salvador de Jujuy

New Amsterdam
Paramaribo
SURINAME
GUYANA
Georgetown

AMAZON
SELVAS
BASIN

Pico do Neblina 2994 m (9,823 ft)

Boa Vista

Ciudad Guayana
Ciudad Bolívar
San Fernando de Apure
Puerto Ayacucho

VENEZUELA

Maturín
El Tigre
Barcelona
Caracas
Valencia
Barquisimeto
Valera

GUIANA HIGHLANDS

Maracaibo
Coro
Cabimas
Mérida
San Cristóbal

Leticia
Benjamin Constant
Crozeiro do Sul

Rio Branco
Riberalta
Cobija

La Paz
Oruro
Illimani 6462 m (21,201 ft)
Nev. Sajama 6542 m (21,463 ft)
Puerto Maldonado
Cuzco
ALTIPLANO
Calama

Puerto Maldonado

Margarita I.
Cumaná

Bonaire (Neth.)
Curaçao (Neth.)
Aruba (Neth.)

TRINIDAD AND TOBAGO
Port of Spain

ST. VINCENT AND THE GRENADINES
BARBADOS
GRENADA

Caribbean Sea

Pico Cristóbal Colón 5775 m (18,947 ft)
Santa Marta
Barranquilla
Cartagena
Valledupar
Sincelejo
Montería
Cúcuta
Bucaramanga
Barrancabermeja
Medellín
Manizales
Pereira
Armenia
Ibagué
Cali
Palmira
Buenaventura
Popayán
Pasto
Florencia
Neiva
Tunja
Bogotá
Villavicencio

COLOMBIA
Nevado del Huila 5364 m (17,598 ft)

LLANOS

Tumaco
Esmeraldas
Quito
Ambato
Riobamba
Latacunga
Cotopaxi 5911 m (19,393 ft)
Chimborazo 6268 m (20,564 ft)
Portoviejo
Manta
Guayaquil
Cuenca
Loja
Machala
Tumbes
Talara
Sullana
Piura
Chiclayo
Trujillo
Chimbote
Nev. Huascarán 6768 m (22,205 ft)
Nev. Yerupajá 6634 m (21,765 ft)

ECUADOR

ANDES

PERU

LA MONTAÑA

Iquitos
Yurimaguas
Pucallpa
Cajamarca
Cerro de Pasco
Huánuco
Lima
Callao
Ica
Ayacucho
Huancayo
Ayaviri
Juliaca
Puno
Arequipa
Tacna
Arica
Iquique
Antofagasta

ATACAMA DESERT

ANDES

Panama City
PANAMA
COSTA RICA
San José
Managua
NICARAGUA
Tegucigalpa
HONDURAS
San Salvador
EL SALVADOR
CENTRAL AMERICA

Agujá Point

Galápagos Islands (Ecuador)

Equator

PACIFIC OCEAN

PACIFIC OCEAN

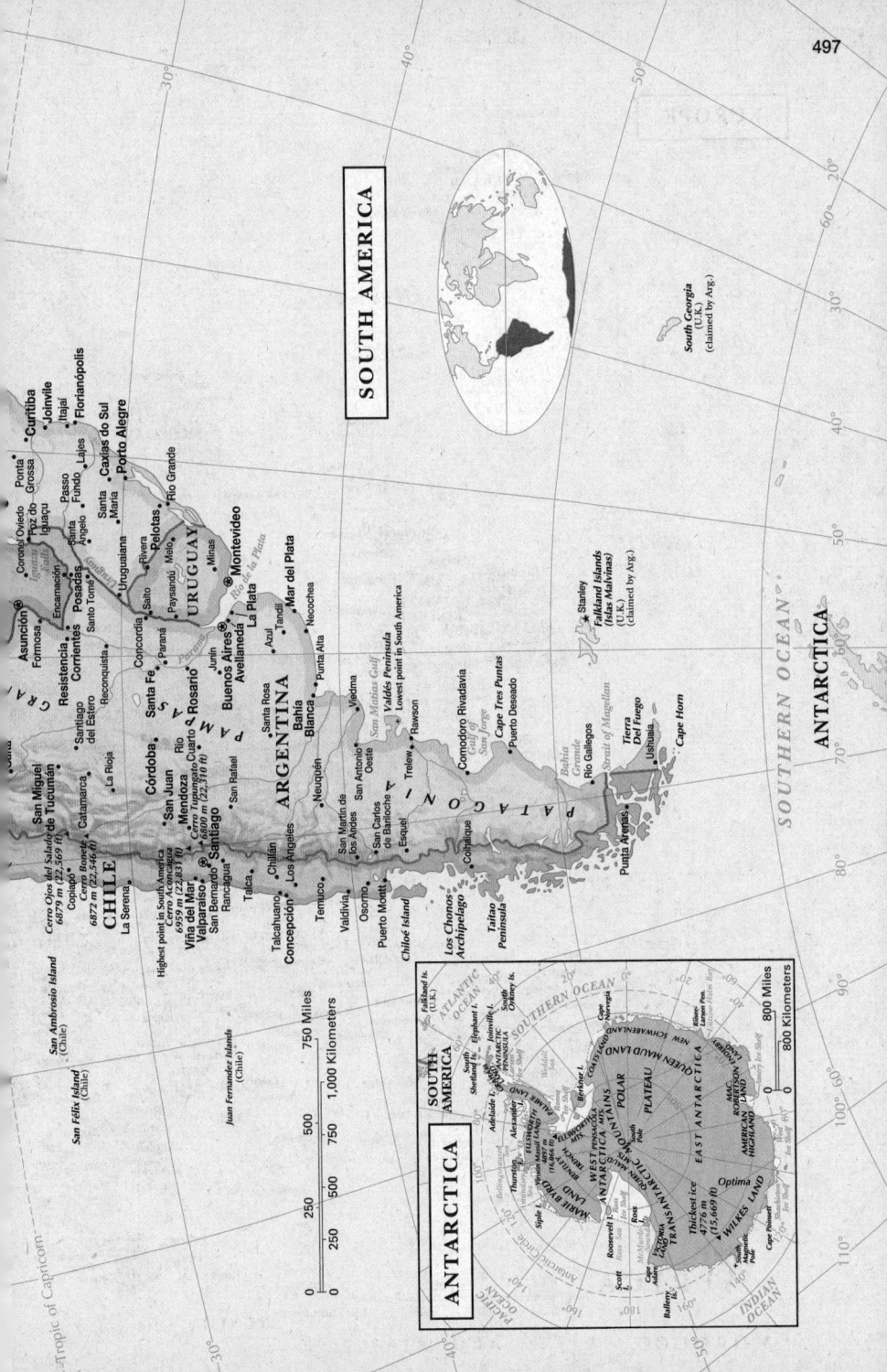

ATLANTIC
OCEAN

ARCTIC OCEAN

Arctic Circle

IRELAND

UNITED
KINGDOM

Madrid
SPAIN
PORT.
Paris
FRANCE
BEL. NETH.
London

NORWAY
Oslo
SWEDEN
DEN.
Copenhagen
Stockholm
FINLAND
Helsinki

GERMANY
Berlin
SWITZ.
CZECHA
(CZECH
REP.)
POLAND
Warsaw

Severnaya
Zemlya

Dickson

Noril'sk

CEN
SIBE
Tura

ITALY
SLOV.
Rome
AUS.
SLVK.
HUNG.
CRO.
BOS. &
HERZ.
MONT. SERB.
ALB.
N. MAC.
LITH. LAT.
EST.
BELARUS

EUROPE

ROMANIA MOL.
Kyiv
(Kiev)
Bucharest
UKRAINE
BUL.

Moscow

RUSSIA
WEST
SIBERIAN
PLAIN
PLA

Vorkuta
Salekhard
Novyy
Urengoy
Surgut

URAL MOUNTAINS

Serov
Nizhniy Tagil
Yekaterinburg
Chelyabinsk
Magnitogorsk
Kurgan
Tyumen
Tobol'sk
Petropavlovsk
Omsk

Nizhnevartovsk
Kolpashevo
Tomsk
Achinsk
Krasnoyarsk
Kemerovo
Novokuznetsk
SAYAN MTS.

Semey (Semipalatinsk)
Öskemen
ALTAY MTS.
Dund-Us

GREECE
Athens

İzmir Bursa
Ankara
TURKEY
Samsun
Trabzon
Erzurum
Adana
5137 m (16,854 ft)
Mt. Ararat
GEORGIA
Tbilisi

CAUCASUS MTS.

Black Sea

LIBYA

Mediterranean Sea

CYPRUS
Nicosia
LEBANON
Latakia
Beirut
SYRIA
Damascus

Cairo
Tel Aviv-Yafo
Jerusalem
ISRAEL
Al Aqabah JORDAN
Amman

EGYPT

AFRICA

Diyarbakir
Yerevan
ARMENIA
AZERBAIJAN
Ganca
Baku
Tabriz
Mosul
Kirkuk
Erbil
IRAQ
Baghdad
Al Hillah
Tehran
Kermanshah
Basht
Qom
Esfahan
Kuwait
City
KUWAIT
Shiraz

ZAGROS MOUNTAINS

KAZAKHSTAN

Oral
Atyrau
Aral
Sea
Aqtaū

USTYURT
PLATEAU

Caspian Sea

Turkmenbashy

Qaraghandy
(Karaganda)
KAZAKH
UPLAND
Ayagoz

Pavlodar
Nur-Sultan
Barnaul
Tashtagol
Yining

TIEN SHAN
Jengish Chokusu
7439 m (24,406 ft)
Urümqi
Turpan
Depression

Semey

Zhezkazgan
Qyzylorda
UZBEKISTAN
Nukus
Urganch
KYZYL KUM
DESERT
Taraz
Balqash
Lake
Balkhash
Taldykorgan
Almaty

Bishkek
KYRGYZSTAN
Kashi
Shache
K2
8611 m (28,250 ft)

TAKLIMAKAN
DESERT

KUNLUN MTS.

Turkmenbashy
TURKMENISTAN
Ashgabat
Mt. Damavand
5610 m
(18,406 ft)
Gorgan
DASHT-E
KAVIR
Mashhad
DASHT-E LUT
Birjand
IRAN
Yazd
Kerman
Zahedan

Tashkent
Dushanbe
TAJIKISTAN
PAMIRS
Lenin Peak 7134 m (23,406 ft)
7495 m (24,590 ft)
Ismail Samani Pk.
Mazar-e Sharif
Herat
AFGHANISTAN
Kabul
Kandahar
Peshawar
Farah
Islamabad
Rawalpindi
Srinagar

HINDU KUSH
PLATEAU OF TIBET

Helmand

SUDAN
Khartoum
ERITREA
Asmara

Red Sea

Jeddah
Mecca
At Taif
SAUDI
ARABIA
RIYADH
Riyadh

Tabuk
Hail
Buraydah
Al Basrah
BAHRAIN
Manama
QATAR
Doha
UNITED ARAB
EMIRATES
Abu Dhabi
Persian
Gulf
Bandar-e Abbas
Gulf of Oman

Muscat
OMAN
Sur
Ras al Hadd

Quetta
PAKISTAN
Sukkur
Multan
Faisalabad
Lahore
Chandigarh

Turbat

THAR
DESERT
Hyderabad
Karachi

Delhi
New
Delhi
Agra
Jodhpur
Jaipur

Mt. Everest
8850 m
(29,035 ft)
Highest point
in Asia
HIMALAYA

Lhasa

NEPAL
BHUTAN
Kathmandu
Thimphu
Lucknow
Kanpur
Varanasi
Patna
Imphal
BANGLADESH
Dhaka
Ranchi
Asansol
Khulna
Chittagong
Akyab

Brahmaputra

Ganges

Ahmadabad
Jodhpur
Allahabad

INSET AREA IN NAFUD

Mumbai
(Bombay)
Pune
DECCAN
Nagpur
PLATEAU
Hyderabad
INDIA
Raipur
Cuttack
Kolkata
(Calcutta)

YEMEN
Sanaa
Aden
Al Mukalla
Salalah

Gulf of Aden

Socotra
(Yemen)

Arabian
Sea

RU AL KHALI

SOMALIA

ADDIS
Ababa
ETHIOPIA
DJI.

WESTERN GHATS

Panaji
Hubballi
(Hubli)
Bengaluru (Bangalore)
Laccadive Is.
(India)
Mysuru
(Mysore)
Coimbatore
Kochi
Thiruvananthapuram
Cape Comorin

Solapur

EASTERN GHATS

Visakhapatnam
Vijayawada
Chennai
(Madras)
Madurai
Trincomalee
SRI LANKA
Colombo
Sri Jayewardenepura Kotte
Galle
Male

Bay of
Bengal

Andaman
Is.
(India)

Nicobar
Is.
(India)

MYANMAR
(BURMA)
Pathein

MALDIVES

Equator

INDIAN
OCEAN

Inset map:

TURKEY
Adana
Mersin
Antalya
Şanlıurfa
Al Hasakah
Mosul
Antakya
Latakia
CYPRUS
Nicosia
Limassol
Aleppo
Ar Raqqah
Hamah
Abu
Kamal
Homs
Tadmur
Bayji

Mediterranean
Sea
LEBANON
Beirut
Haifa
ISRAEL
Tel Aviv-Yafo
Port Jerusalem
Said
GAZA
STRIP
Cairo
Giza
EGYPT
Suez
Tanta

SYRIA
Damascus
The West Bank
currently occupied
by Israel. Permanent
status to be determined.
WEST
BANK
Jericho
Amman
JORDAN
Ma'an
Elat
Al Aqabah
Tabuk
SINAI

Ar Ramadi
IRAQ
SYRIAN
DESERT

SAUDI
ARABIA
AN NAFUD

0   250 Miles
0   250 Kilometers

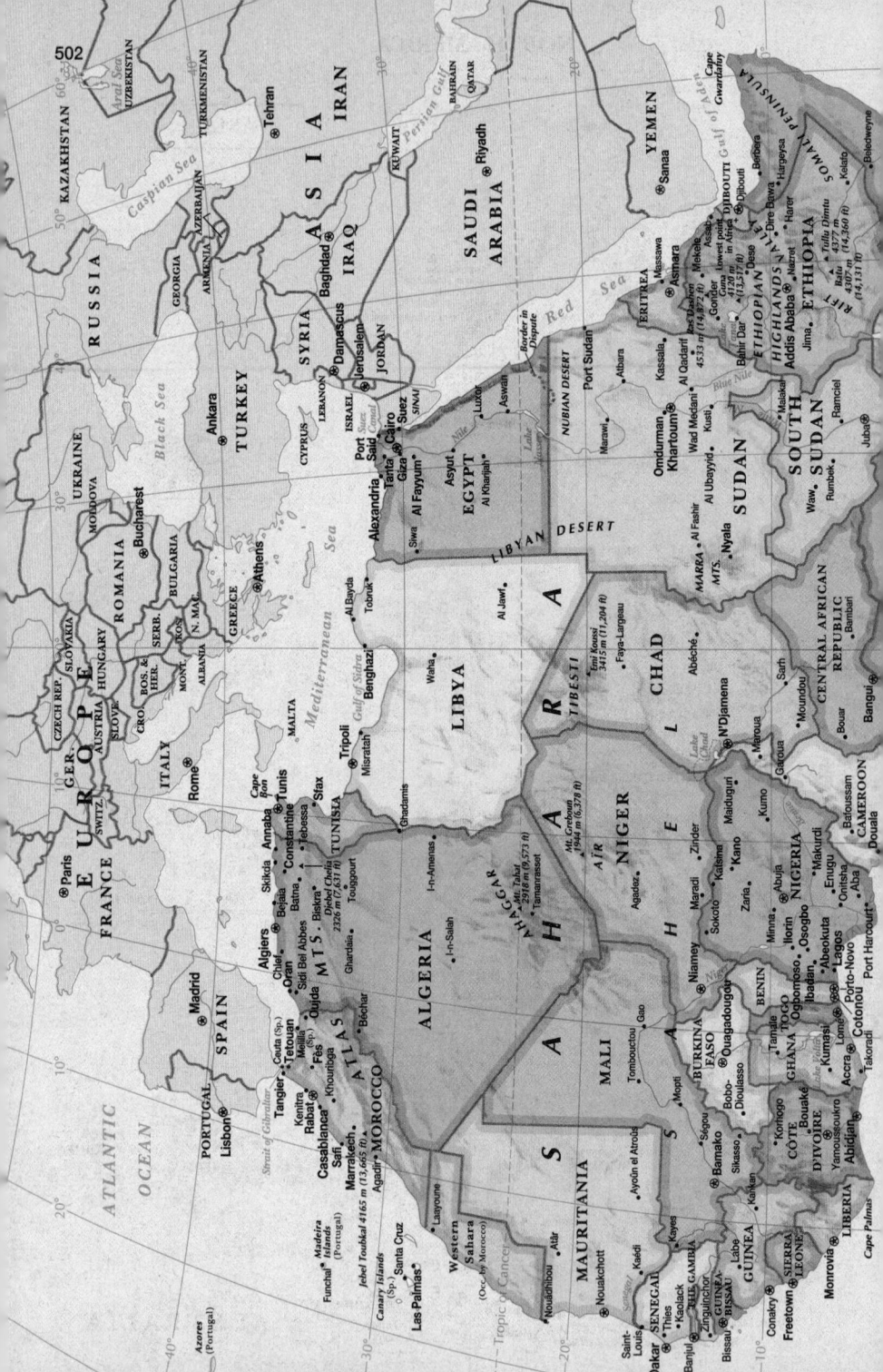

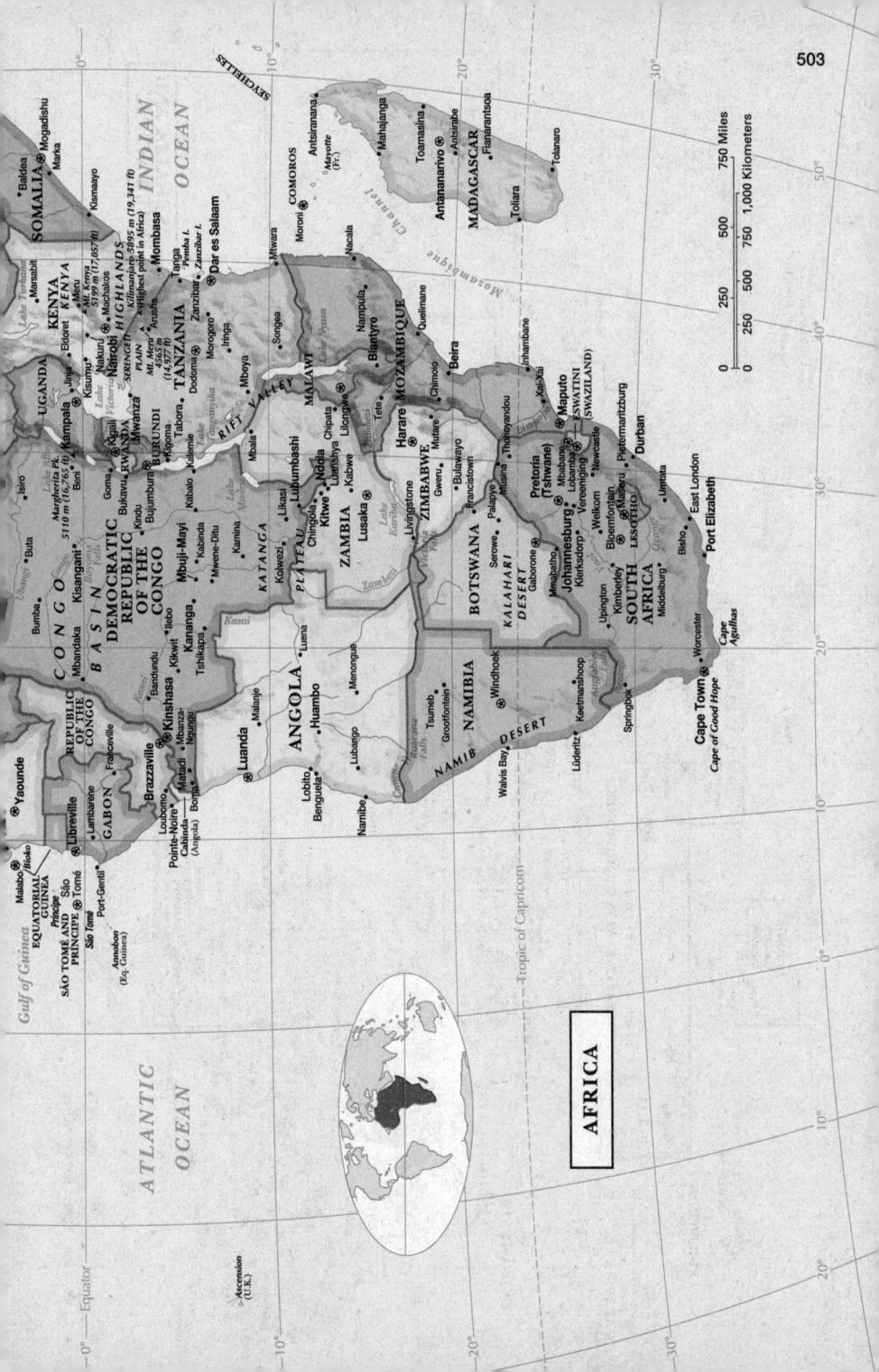

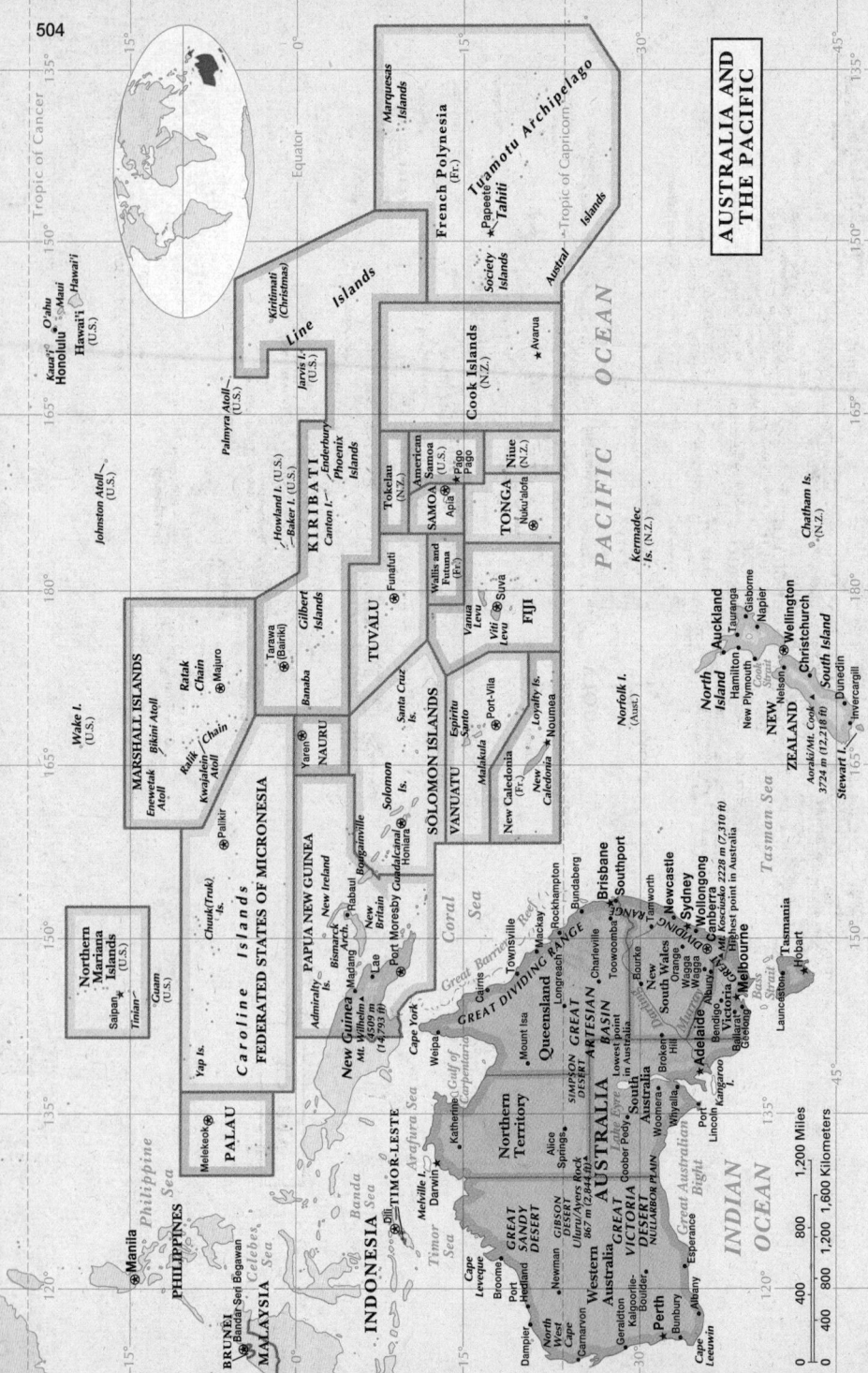

AUSTRALIA AND THE PACIFIC